Periodical Title
Abbreviations:
By Abbreviation

Gale's publications in the acronyms and abbreviations field include:

Periodical Title Abbreviations series:

Periodical Title Abbreviations: By Abbreviation (Volume 1). A guide to abbreviations commonly used for periodical titles, arranged alphabetically by abbreviation.

Periodical Title Abbreviations: By Title (Volume 2). A guide to abbreviations commonly used for periodical titles, arranged alphabetically by title.

New Periodical Title Abbreviations (Volume 3). An interedition supplement in which terms are arranged alphabetically both by abbreviation and by title.

Acronyms, Initialisms & Abbreviations Dictionary series:

Acronyms, Initialisms & Abbreviations Dictionary (Volume 1). A guide to acronyms, initialisms, abbreviations, and similar contractions, arranged alphabetically by abbreviation.

New Acronyms, Initialisms & Abbreviations (Volume 2). An interedition supplement in which terms are arranged alphabetically both by abbreviation and by meaning.

Reverse Acronyms, Initialisms & Abbreviations Dictionary (Volume 3). A companion to Volume 1 in which terms are arranged alphabetically by meaning of the acronym, initialism, or abbreviation.

Acronyms, Initialisms & Abbreviations Dictionary Subject Guide series:

Computer & Telecommunications Acronyms (Volume 1). A guide to acronyms, initialisms, abbreviations, and similar contractions used in the field of computers and telecommunications in which terms are arranged alphabetically both by abbreviation and by meaning.

Future Subject Guide topics will include business and trade, health and medicine, military and government, and associations and institutions.

International Acronyms, Initialisms & Abbreviations Dictionary series:

International Acronyms, Initialisms & Abbreviations Dictionary (Volume 1). A guide to foreign and international acronyms, initialisms, abbreviations, and similar contractions, arranged alphabetically by abbreviation.

New International Acronyms, Initialisms & Abbreviations (Volume 2). An interedition supplement in which terms are arranged alphabetically both by abbreviation and by meaning.

Reverse International Acronyms, Initialisms & Abbreviations Dictionary (Volume 3). A companion to Volume 1 in which terms are arranged alphabetically by meaning of the acronym, initialism, or abbreviation.

ISSN 0737-7843

Periodical Title Abbreviations: By Abbreviation

Covering: Periodical Title Abbreviations and
Selected Monograph Abbreviations in Science, the
Social Sciences, the Humanities, Law, Medicine, Religion,
Library Science, Engineering, Education, Business, Art,
and Many Other Fields

SIXTH EDITION

Volume 1

compiled and edited by
Leland G. Alkire, Jr.
Eastern Washington University

GALE RESEARCH COMPANY • BOOK TOWER • DETROIT, MICHIGAN 48226

Editor: **Leland G. Alkire, Jr.**

Editorial Assistants: Karen A. Schatz, Cheryl Westerman-Alkire

Gale Research Company Staff

Project Coordinator: Prindle LaBarge
Consulting Editors: Helen E. Sheppard, Julie E. Towell
Senior Assistant Editor: Anthony J. Scolaro
Assistant Editors: Barbara Cumming Cameron, Pamela Dear,
Claire A. Selestow
Editorial Assistants: Ellen Ankenbrandt, Valerie Lockhart

Production Manager: Mary Beth Trimper
Production Associate: Darlene K. Maxey
Art Director: Arthur Chartow

Editorial Data Systems Director: Dennis LaBeau
Supervisor of Systems and Programming: Diane H. Belickas
Program Design: Barry M. Trute

Editorial Data Entry Supervisor: Doris D. Goulart
Editorial Data Entry Associate: Jean Hinman Portfolio
Senior Data Entry Assistant: Joyce M. Stone

Chairman: Frederick G. Ruffner
President: Thomas A. Paul
Publisher: Dedria Bryfonski
Associate Editorial Director: Ellen T. Crowley
Director, Indexes and Dictionaries Division: Ann Evory
Senior Editor, Dictionaries: Donna Wood

Computerized photocomposition by
Computer Composition Corporation
Madison Heights, Michigan

Printed in the United States of America

Contents

5

Acknowledgments

A hearty thanks to the many individuals attached to Eastern Washington University for their aid and encouragement. Among these are:

Don Lake, Head of Reference
Suzanne Schenk, Interlibrary Loans
William Kidd, Associate Provost
Dr. Wayne Kraft, Department of Modern Languages and Literatures
Dr. Edmund Yarwood, Chairman, Department of Modern Languages and Literatures

A special acknowledgment to David J. Jones for contribution of terms from his book, *Australian Periodical Title Abbreviations*.

Finally, a salute to the Acronyms Department of Gale Research Company for their unstinting tact, patience, and understanding as well as for their considerable editorial efforts in bringing this volume into print.

Introduction

Purpose and Scope

Periodical Title Abbreviations: By Abbreviation (PTA-A) translates magazine, journal, and newspaper title abbreviations into full titles. It does so in response to what has generally been recognized as a major bibliographic obstacle. In spite of attempts by organizations and individuals to prescribe standard periodical abbreviations or rules for constructing periodical abbreviations, the uniform abbreviated citation has remained an admirable but elusive ideal. Many indexing and abstracting services use homegrown abbreviation systems which, more often than not, disregard the efforts of such bodies as the National Clearinghouse for Periodical Title Word Abbreviations—or such documents as the *American Standard for Periodical Title Abbreviations.* As a consequence, the present edition of *PTA-A* is intended to be used neither as an authority file nor as a standard for periodical abbreviations, but merely as a record of the myriad ways in which commonly used indexing and abstracting services abbreviate periodical titles. While it may be vexing to the user of this dictionary that the same title is abbreviated several different ways, and disconcerting that a single abbreviation can stand for more than one title, *Periodical Title Abbreviations: By Abbreviation* is nonetheless intended only as a record of things as they are, *not* as they "should" be. At the very least, however, it may be hoped that this volume will serve to prevent the creation of additional abbreviations where none are needed.

In those occasional instances where the same abbreviation is used for two or more periodical titles, the user should consult such standard serial sources as the *Union List of Serials, New Serial Titles, Ulrich's International Periodicals Directory,* or *The British Union Catalogue of Periodicals* for the publishing history of the periodical one suspects the abbreviation represents. Normally, when this information is compared with the year and volume of the citation in question, satisfactory identification is possible.

For discussions of the full range of difficulties associated with periodical abbreviations, the reader is directed to the following publications:

> Kinney, Mary R., *The Abbreviated Citation—A Bibliographical Problem,* Association of College and Research Libraries Monographs, Number 28, Chicago, American Library Association, 1967.

> Alkire, Leland G., "The Initial Problem," *Serials Librarian,* vol. 2, summer 1978: 401-404.

(Excerpts from "The Initial Problem" follow this introduction.)

Expansion of Coverage

With this edition, the contents of *Periodical Title Abbreviations: By Abbreviation* have been expanded to a total of over 103,000 entries. This represents a 20 percent increase over the previous edition. The current edition includes over 1,500 new legal abbreviations as well as over 2,000 new CODEN entries. Abbreviations in all fields have been updated and expanded.

Although some abbreviations from *Chemical Abstracts* appear in *PTA,* many have not been included because of the large number of complicated serial and monographic entries contained in that source. Thus, users will still need to use *Chemical Abstracts Service Source Index* in conjunction with *Periodical Title Abbreviations: By Abbreviation.*

Arrangement, Format, and Other Editorial Policies

The abbreviations in this volume are arranged in strict letter-by-letter sequence, regardless of spacing, punctuation, or capitalization. Neither ampersands, articles, conjunctions, nor prepositions are considered in the alphabetizing. If the same abbreviation has more than one meaning, the various *translations* are then arranged alphabetically. Because of font limitations, many diacritical marks have been eliminated or altered according to accepted standards. Thus, the German word *für* becomes *fuer*.

In all decisions, the principle of simplicity of use has been kept foremost. In certain indexing services, periodical abbreviations were found to change from one year to the next. While this accounts for the seemingly elegant variation of some abbreviations found in this dictionary, the user should also be aware that several thousand nearly repetitive entries have been eliminated after having been judged to add nothing to the identification process. With these exceptions, and with minor alterations in the interest of uniform format and corrections of typographical errors found in the source materials, the abbreviations and periodical titles reproduced in this dictionary conform to the information found in the source materials.

Like sailors long at sea, who derive great satisfaction from a curious cloud formation or the sight of a bird, those who labor over abbreviation dictionaries look for and celebrate anything which serves to break the monotony. In this work, typographical errors provided occasional diversions; some repeatable and several not. My lightest moment came with the permutation of the *Yen Ching Journal* into the *Wenching Journal*. Many such errors have been eliminated, but no doubt some will remain. Though no work of this sort is ever completely error-proof, those which abide must be laid at my door. I ask only the user's understanding of the difficulties involved in dealing with a dozen or more languages simultaneously, and the problems posed by error-sprinkled source materials.

Suggestions for New Material

As in the past, the users of the *Periodical Title Abbreviations* series remain a valuable source in the identification of abbreviations not yet included in the *PTA* system. Users wishing to suggest new entries may do so by mailing a photocopy of the source of the suggested entries (i.e., the key to abbreviations in an index, abstract, or book), along with a complete bibliographic citation of the publication from which the pages were copied, to:

Leland G. Alkire
Kennedy Library
Eastern Washington University
Cheney, WA 99004

Excerpts from "The Initial Problem"*

In a July 1960 letter to *Science* magazine, a somewhat mournful plea was raised by one J. B. Sykes, in favor of "more sparing use of abbreviations when citing references to periodicals." He rightly saw that abbreviated titles often create some difficulty for the user.

In the years since Sykes' complaint, abbreviated periodical citations have proliferated in a way that has exceeded the expectations of even the most pessimistic of observers. Despite organized and sustained efforts, both before and after 1960, either to abandon outright the use of abbreviated citations or, failing this, to adopt a standardized system of abbreviating periodical titles, we are presently faced with a greater diversity than ever before.

Observers of language, such as George Orwell, Jacques Barzun, and Stephen Leacock, have variously lamented, railed, and poked fun at abbreviated forms. But the battle has been a losing one. In government, business, and academe, an element of gamesmanship has long dictated that those "in-the-know" should speak in direct, if sometimes barbaric sounding terms, such as NASA, NATO, and ICSU. Further, in a kind of variant of punning, we are surrounded by a buzzing swarm of acronyms which not only identifies their users as the cognoscenti, but which also implies an element of one-upmanship. Some, like CORE and NOW, are clever and apt, but what was once bright and chic begins to wear thin through overuse. Yet in spite of what, in some quarters, has become a cautionary approach to the short-form phenomenon, it must be admitted that both the acronym and the abbreviation serve as time and space savers in these information-heavy times.

The real trouble with short-form usage lies in the tendency of abbreviated forms to duplicate one another. When we encounter a reference to an organization called AID, we must ask: Does it refer to the Agency for International Development or the Americans of Italian Descent? When such multimeaning abbreviations are used without accompanying definitions or in contexts that leave one in doubt, the result is often a breakdown in basic communication.

Small specialized professional groups are perhaps the greatest purveyors of this sort of noncommunication. Imagine, for a moment, a nonlibrarian, or even a librarian who has been away from the profession for a time, picking up a recent library publication and attempting to negotiate the foaming rapids of OCLC, CONSER, MULS, ISSN, and AACR. They will scarcely find themselves paddling in familiar waters. Indeed, some would ask if we are not entering a time when professional subspecialists will be decreasingly able to decipher one another's abb pro jarg (abbreviated professional jargon).

Whatever future may await us as librarians, as researchers, and as users of the English language, one thing is clear: The concern of J. B. Sykes in 1960 regarding the problem of abbreviated periodical titles haunts us in ways that are increasingly troublesome. When a reference, periodicals, or interlibrary loan librarian encounters a citation in which the title has been reduced to an abbreviation, AM for example, where does he or she turn? Acta Musicologia, Atlantic Monthly, Americas, or any one of the eleven journals to which this abbreviation is commonly applied, all represent logical choices. To use another even more disconcerting example, the abbreviation MHM can mean either Maryland History Magazine or Michigan History Magazine, depending on the source of the citation. The list of such competitors could be extended indefinitely since tens of thousands of periodical abbreviations are currently employed by indexing and abstracting services, as well as by scholarly journals and bibliographies. Many of these publications, as must be obvious by now, employ periodical title abbreviations without regard to how such forms are used elsewhere.

This disorderly situation is further compounded by the assumption of scholars, students, and other users that a given abbreviation is not only unique, but that it is part of a generally acknowledged language, which others, particularly librarians, will immediately recognize. Often, because of experience, intuition, and the subject of the article in question, a little detective work will reveal the full title. Yet this work takes time, and inevitably, after a number of such requests, the librarian will draw a blank, particularly when the patron is uncertain as to the origin of the citation.

Attempts to bring order to this disarray have been numerous, if only partially successful, but one can hope, if orderly access to periodical information is seen as a desirable end, that the current proliferation of systems of abbreviation will one day be rationalized and reduced to a single, understandable system.

In the meantime, a few of us continue to recall that moment in the Apollo 12 Moon Mission when Ground Control discovered that a minor equipment failure was caused by something called the Digital Uplink Assembly. When the controllers radioed up that the fault lay with the DUA, the response from the crew of the Apollo 12 was: "What's a DUA?"

---

*Excerpted by permission of Haworth Press, *Serials Librarian,* vol. 2, summer 1978: 401-404.

Major Sources of Abbreviations Contained in Periodical Title Abbreviations Series

Abstract Bulletin of the Institute of Paper Chemistry
ACTFL (American Council on the Teaching of Foreign Languages) Annual Bibliography of Books and Articles on Pedagogy in Foreign Languages
Alternative Press Index
American Journal of Archaeology
American-German Review
American Literature Abstracts
Annee-Philologique
Annual Bibliography of English Language and Literature
Applied Science and Technology Index
Art Index
Arts and Humanities Citation Index
Bibliographic Index
Bibliography of Asian Studies
Bibliography of Corn
Bibliography and Index of Geology
Bibliography of North American Geology
Bibliography of Wheat
Biography Index
Biological and Agricultural Index
Serial Sources for the BIOSIS Data Base
Book Review Digest
Book Review Index
British Education Index
British Technology Index
Business Education Index
Business Periodicals Index
Canadian Periodicals Index
Catholic Periodical Index
Chicorel Index to Mental Health Book Reviews
Christian Periodicals Index
Classified Shakespeare Bibliography
Combined Retrospective Index to Book Reviews in Scholarly Journals
Cumulated Index Medicus
Cumulative Index to Nursing and Allied Health Literature
Current Book Review Citations
Current Index to Statistics
DSH (Deafness, Speech, and Hearing) Abstracts
Education Index
Elsevier Book Series Abbreviations
Engineering Index
English Language Notes
ELH (English Literary History)
Film Literature Index
Forestry Abstracts

French Periodical Index
Geological Literature of North America, 1785-1918
Germanic Review
Harvard Guide to American History
Hospital Literature Index
Humanities Index
IMM (Institution of Mining and Metallurgy) Abstracts
Index of American Periodical Verse
Index Catalogue of Medical and Veterinary Zoology
Index Chemicus
Index of Economic Articles
Index to Legal Periodicals
Index to Little Magazines
Index to Periodicals by and about Negroes
Index to Religious Periodical Literature
Index to Science Fiction Magazines
Industrial Arts Index
INIS (International Nuclear Information System) Authority List for Journal Titles
INSPEC (Information Service for Physics, Electrotechnology, and Control)
Insurance Periodicals Index
International Bibliography of the History of Religions
International Bibliography of Social Sciences: Anthropology
International Bibliography of Social Sciences: Political Science
International Bibliography of Social Sciences: Sociology
International Index
International Nursing Index
Journal of Aesthetics and Art Criticism
Journal of American Folklore
Journal of English and Germanic Philology
Keats-Shelley Journal
Library and Information Science Abstracts
Library Literature
Mathematical Reviews
Metals Abstracts. Annual Index
Modern Humanities Research Association. Annual Bibliography of English Language and Literature
Modern Language Quarterly
Modern Philology
Music Index
Music Therapy Index
New Grove Dictionary of Music and Musicians
New Periodicals Index
Nineteenth Century Reader's Guide

Philological Quarterly
Philosopher's Index
Physikalische Berichte
PMLA (Publications of the Modern Language Association of America) Bibliography
Poetry Explication
Poole's Index to Periodical Literature
Popular Periodical Index
Predicasts. Source Directory
Progress of Medieval and Renaissance Studies in the United States and Canada
Quarterly Journal of Speech
Reader's Guide to Periodicals
Revue d'Histoire Ecclesiastique
Romanic Review
Scandinavian Studies
Science Citation Index
Science Fiction Book Review Index

Selective Bibliography of Shakespeare (McManaway and Roberts)
Shakespeare Quarterly
Social Science Citation Index
Social Sciences Index
Soils and Fertilizers
Southern Folklore Quarterly
Speech Monographs
Studies in Philology
Surface and Vacuum Physics Index
Topicator
Ulrich's International Periodicals Directory
Victorian Studies
Writings on American History
Yearbook of Comparative and General Literature
Year's Work in English Studies
Year's Work in Modern Language Studies

Periodical Title Abbreviations: By Abbreviation

A

A — Admap
A — America
A — Archiv fuer das Studium der Neueren Sprachen
A — Arthuriana
A — Aufbau
A — [*The*] Australian
AA — Abstracts in Anthropology
AA — Advertising Age
AA — Aegyptologische Abhandlungen
AA — African Affairs
A & A — Afrique et l'Asie
AA — Al Ahram [*Cairo*]
AA — Alttestamentliche Abhandlungen
AA — Amazing Stories. Annual
AA — American Anthropologist
AA — American Archivist
AA — Anglo-American Magazine
A & A — Antike und Abendland
AA — Antwerpsch Archievenblad
AA — Apicultural Abstracts
AA — Archaeologischer Anzeiger
A & A — Art and Archaeology
AA — Art and Architecture
A & A — Arta si Arheologia
AA — Artibus Asiae
A & A — Arts and Architecture
AA — Asian Affairs
A & A — Astronautics and Aeronautics
AA — Aut Aut
AAA — Acta Academiae Aboensis
AAA — Acta Apostolorum Apocrypha
AAA — Aerosol Age
AAA — American Arab Affairs
AAA — Annals. American Academy of Political and Social Science
AAA — Annals of Archaeology and Anthropology [*Liverpool*]
AAA — Archivio. Alto Adige
AAA — Athens Annals of Archaeology
AAAA — Activities, Adaptation, and Aging
AAAB — Annales. Academie Royale d'Archeologie de Belgique
AAABC — Astronomy and Astrophysics. Abstracts
AAAC — About Arts and Crafts. Department of Indian and Northern Affairs
AAAd — Antichita Altoadriatiche
AAAd — Archivio. Alto Adige
AAAG — Annals. Association of American Geographers
AAAH — Acta Academiae Aboensis. Humaniora
AAAH — Acta ad Archaeologiam et Artium Historiam Pertinentia
AAA Hum — Acta Academiae Aboensis. Humaniora
AAAN — Alaska Anthropological Association. Newsletter
AAAPSS — Annals. American Academy of Political and Social Science
AAAr — Atti. Accademia degli Arcadi
AAASAH — Acta Academiae Aboensis. Series A. Humaniora
AAASH — Acta Antiqua. Academiae Scientiarum Hungaricae
AAAS Publication — American Association for the Advancement of Science. Publication

AAAS Selected Symposia Series — American Association for the Advancement of Science. Selected Symposia Series
AAAS Sel Sympos Ser — American Association for the Advancement of Science. Selected Symposia Series
AAAZ — Archaeologischer Anzeiger zur Archaeologischen Zeitung
AAB — Abhandlungen der Deutschen
AABAn — Annales. Academie Royale d'Archeologie de Belgique
AABCAD — Anais. Academia Brasileira de Ciencias
AAC — Airworthiness Advisory Circular
AACC News — Affirmative Action Coordinating Center. Newsletter
AACE (Am Assoc Cost Eng) Bull — AACE (American Association of Cost Engineers) Bulletin
AACE Bull — American Association of Cost Engineers. Bulletin
Aachen Kuntsbl — Aachener Kuntsblaetter
A A Chron — Arthur Andersen Chronicle
AACMP — Anales. Academia de Ciencias Morales y Politicas
AACN — Arts and Culture of the North
AACOB — Applied Acoustics
AACR — Anglo-American Cataloguing Rules
AACRA — Anesthesia and Analgesia (Cleveland)
AAD — Army Aviation Digest
AADE J — AADE [*American Association of Dental Editors*] Journal
AAE — Advertising Age Europe
AAe — Analecta Aegyptiaca
AAEC — Annuario. Accademia Etrusca di Cortona
AAEC Nucl News — AAEC [*Australian Atomic Energy Commission*] Nuclear News
AAEC Nucl News (AU) — AAEC [*Australian Atomic Energy Commission*] Nuclear News (Australia)
AAED — Alcoholism and Alcohol Education
AAEPC — Anales. Asociacion Espanola para el Progreso de las Ciencias
AAERA5 — Alabama. Agricultural Experiment Station. Progress Report Series (Auburn University)
AAES — American Archaeological Expedition to Syria. Publication
AAESDA Bul — AAESDA [*Association of Architects, Engineers, Surveyors, and Draughtsmen of Australia*] Bulletin
AAF — Anglo-American Forum
AAF — Atti. Accademia Fiorentina
AAFBA — Annales Academiae Scientiarum Fennicae. Series A-IV. Biologica
AAFPA — Annales Academiae Scientiarum Fennicae. Series A-VI. Physica
A Afr — Annales Africaines
AAFRA — Arcispedale S. Anna di Ferrara
AAFV — Anuario. Asociacion Francisco de Vitoria
AAG — Abhandlungen. Akademie der Wissenschaften in Goettingen
AAg — Afrique Agriculture
AAG — Annals of American Geographers
AAg — Archivo Agustiniano
AAGCA4 — Atti. Accademia Gioenia di Scienze Naturali in Catania
AAGEA — Arkhiv Anatomii, Gistologii, i Embriologii
AAGNA — Atti. Associazione Genetica Italiana
AAGNA3 — Atti. Associazione Genetica Italiana
AAGRCH — Australia. Commonwealth Scientific and Industrial Research Organisation. Division of Applied Geomechanics. Technical Report
AAGTCN — Australia. Commonwealth Scientific and Industrial Research Organisation. Division of Applied Geomechanics. Technical Paper

AAH — Acta Antiqua. Academiae Scientiarum Hungaricae
AAHAA3 — Australia. Commonwealth Scientific and Industrial Research Organisation. Division of Animal Health. Annual Report
AAHG — Anzeiger fuer die Altertumswissenschaft. Herausgegeben von der Oesterreichischen Humanistischen Gesellschaft
AAHPAE — Australia. Commonwealth Scientific and Industrial Research Organisation. Division of Animal Health and Production. Technical Paper
AAHRAK — Arizona. Commission of Agriculture and Horticulture. Annual Report
AAJ — Australian Anthropological Journal
AAJBDJ — Al-Khalij Al-Arabi
AAJDAI — Archaeologischer Anzeiger. Beiblatt zum Jahrbuch des Kaiserlich Deutschen Archaeologischen Instituts
AAJID — AJRI. American Journal of Reproductive Immunology
AAJID6 — AJRI. American Journal of Reproductive Immunology
AAJNDL — AJNR. American Journal of Neuroradiology
AAJRD — AJR. American Journal of Roentgenology
AAL — Annals of Archaeology. University of Liverpool
AAL — Asien, Afrika, Lateinamerika
AAL — Atti. Accademia dei Lincei
AALBAQ — Atti. Accademia Nazionale dei Lincei. Memorie. Classe di Scienze Fisiche, Matematiche, e Naturali. Sezione 3a
AALGA7 — Atti. Accademia Ligure di Scienze e Lettere
AALIAM — Arcadia, Accademia Letteraria Italiana. Atti e Memorie
AALM — Atti. Reale Accademia dei Lincei. Memorie. Classe di Scienze Morali, Storiche, e Filologiche [Rome]
AALN — Atti. Reale Accademia dei Lincei. Notizie degli Scavi di Antichita. Classe di Scienze Morali, Storiche, e Filologiche [Rome]
AALR — Anglo-American Law Review
AALR — Australian Argus Law Reports
AALS News — Association of American Library Schools. Newsletter
AALS Proc — Association of American Law Schools. Proceedings
AAM — Arte Antica e Moderna
AAM — Atti e Memorie. Accademia di Scienze, Lettere, ed Arti di Modena
AAM — Atti e Memorie. Reale Accademia Virgiliana di Scienze, Lettere, ed Arti di Montova
A Amer Acad Polit Soc Sci — Annals. American Academy of Political and Social Science
AAMFA — Atti. Accademia dei Fisiocritici in Siena. Sezione Medico-Fisica
AAMFA9 — Atti. Accademia dei Fisiocritici in Siena. Sezione Medico-Fisica
AAMLAR — Atti. Accademia Medica Lombarda
AAMod — Atti e Memorie. Accademia di Scienze, Lettere, ed Arti di Modena
AAMSC — Annals. Academy of Medicine (Singapore)
AAMZ — Abhandlungen. Akademie der Wissenschaften und der Literatur in Mainz [Wiesbaden]
AAN — Aanwinsten van de Centrale Bibliotheek [Brussels]
AAn — Acta Antiqua [Budapest]
AAn — American Anthropologist
AAN — Annuaire de l'Afrique du Nord
AAn — Archiv fuer Anthropologie
AAN — Atti. Accademia di Scienze Morali e Politiche della Societa Nazionale di Scienze, Lettere, ed Arti di Napoli
AAN — Atti. Reale Accademia di Archeologia, Lettere, e Belle Arti di Napoli
AANA J — AANA [American Association of Nurse Anesthetists] Journal
AANDD — Aparatura Naukowa i Dydaktyczna
AANFA — Annales de l'Anesthesiologie Francaise
AANL — Atti. Accademia Nazionale dei Lincei
AANLAW — Atti. Accademia Nazionale dei Lincei. Rendiconti. Classe di Scienze Fisiche, Matematiche, e Naturali
AANLR — Atti. Accademia Nazionale dei Lincei. Rendiconti. Classe di Scienze Morali, Storiche, e Filologiche
AANNT — AANNT [American Association of Nephrology Nurses and Technicians] Journal
AaNo — Aarboeger foer Nordisk Oldkyndighed og Historie
AAnt — Acta Antiqua. Academiae Scientiarum Hungaricae
AANT — Arctic Anthropology
AANTA — American Antiquity
A ANTH — American Anthropologist
AAnthr — American Anthropologist
AAntHung — Acta Antiqua. Academiae Scientiarum Hungaricae
A Antiqua Acad Sci Hung — Acta Antiqua. Academiae Scientiarum Hungaricae
A Antropol — Anales de Antropologia
AANZ — Archaeologischer Anzeiger zur Archaeologischen Zeitung
AAOJ — American Antiquarian and Oriental Journal
AAP — Atti. Accademia di Palermo
AAP — Atti. Accademia Pontaniana [Naples]
AAP — Atti e Memorie. Accademia di Padova
AAP — Atti e Memorie. Reale Accademia di Scienze, Lettere, ed Arti in Padova
AAPad — Atti e Memorie. Accademia di Padova
AAPal — Atti. Accademia di Palermo
AAPal — Atti. Accademia di Scienze, Lettere, ed Arti di Palermo
AAPA Newsl — AAPA [Australian Asphalt Pavement Association] Newsletter

AAPat — Atti e Memorie. Accademia Patavina
AAPB — [An] Australian Prayer Book
AAPF — Arctos: Acta Philologica Fennica
AAPG — American Association of Petroleum Geologists. Bulletin
AAPGB — American Association of Petroleum Geologists. Bulletin
AAPG Bull — AAPG [American Association of Petroleum Geologists] Bulletin
AAPG Continuing Education — American Association of Petroleum Geologists. Continuing Education
AAPG Explorer — American Association of Petroleum Geologists. Explorer
AAPG Mem — AAPG [American Association of Petroleum Geologists] Memoir
AAPG Memoir — American Association of Petroleum Geologists. Memoir
AAPG Stud Geol — AAPG [American Association of Petroleum Geologists] Studies in Geology
AAPJ — Acta Academiae Paedagogicae Jyvaskylaensis
AAPLA — Annales de l'Amelioration des Plantes
AAPN — Atti. Accademia Pontaniana (Naples)
AAPont — Atti. Accademia Pontaniana [Naples]
AAPP Abstr — Amino Acids, Peptides, and Proteins. Abstracts
AAPS — Annals. American Academy of Political and Social Science
AAPS Newsletter — Association of American Physicians and Surgeons. Newsletter
AAPSSA — American Academy of Political and Social Science. Annals
AAPSS Mg — American Academy of Political and Social Science. Monographs
AAPTCY — Australia. Commonwealth Scientific and Industrial Research Organisation. Division of Atmospheric Physics. Technical Paper
AAPVA4 — Archives des Recherches Agronomiques et Pastorales au Vietnam
AAQ — Architectural Association. Quarterly
AAR — Affirmative Action Register
AAR — Ann Arbor Review
AAR — Annales. Academie des Sciences de Russie
AAR — Atti. Reale Accademia d'Italia (Roma). Memorie. Classe di Scienze Morali e Storiche
AARA — Atti. Accademia Roveretana degli Agiati
AARAB — Annales. Academie Royale d'Archeologie de Belgique
AARB — Annuaire. Academie Royale de Belgique
Aarbok Univ Bergen Mat-Naturvitensk Ser — Aarbok foer Universitetet i Bergen. Matematisk-Naturvitenskapelig Serie
AArch — Acta Archaeologica
A Arch — American Archivist
A Arch Acad Sci Hung — Acta Archaeologica. Academiae Scientiarum Hungaricae
AArchAnthr — Annals of Archaeology and Anthropology
A Arch Carpathica — Acta Archaeologica Carpathica [Crakow]
AArchHung — Acta Archaeologica. Academiae Scientiarum Hungaricae
A Arch Lodziensia — Acta Archaeologica Lodziensia
AArchSlov — Acta Archaeologica/Arheoloski Vestnik. Slovenska Akademija
AArchSyr — Annales Archeologiques de Syrie
AARDS — Australian Advertising Rate and Data Service
AAREA — Anesthesie, Analgesie, Reanimation [Paris]
Aarhus Univ Lab Fys Geogr Skr — Aarhus Universitet. Laboratoriet foer Fysisk Geografi Skrifter
AARL — Australian Academic and Research Libraries
AArmL — Annual of Armenian Linguistics
AARN Newsl — AARN [Alberta Association of Registered Nurses] Newsletter
AARN News Lett — AARN [Alberta Association of Registered Nurses] News Letter
AARP — Art and Archaeology. Research Papers
AARS — Annals of Regional Science
Aarsberet Inst Sterilitetsforsk K Vet Landbohoejsk — Aarsberetning Institut foer Sterilitetsforskning Kongelige Veterinaer og Landbohoejskole
Aarsskr K Vet Landbohoejsk (DK) — Aarsskrift den Kongelige Veterinaer og Landbohoejskole (Denmark)
Aarsskr Yearb Annu Jahrb Copenh Vet Landbohojsk — Aarsskrift/Yearbook/Annuaire/Jahrbuch. Copenhagen Veterinaer og Landbohoejskole
AArt — American Artist
AARV-A — Architectural Review
AAS — Acta Apostolicae Sedis [Cittal del Vaticano]
AAS — American Antiquarian Society. Proceedings
AAS — Annales Archeologiques de Syrie [Damascus]
AAS — Annual Abstracts of Statistics [Baghdad]
AAS — Asian and African Studies
AASB — Atti. Accademia delle Scienze. Istituto di Bologna
AASBA — American Astronomical Society. Bulletin
AASC — Acta Agriculturae Scandinavica
AASF — Annales Academiae Scientiarum Fennicae
A/asian Irrigator — Australasian Irrigator and Pasture Improver
A/asian J Philos — Australasian Journal of Philosophy
AASLA — Atti. Accademia di Scienze, Lettere, ed Arti di Palermo
AASLAN — Atti. Accademia di Scienze, Lettere, ed Arti di Palermo. Parte Prima. Scienze
AASL SLMQ — AASL [American Association of School Librarians] School Library Media Quarterly
AASN — Atti. Accademia di Scienze Morali e Politiche di Napoli

AASOR — Annual. American Schools of Oriental Research
AAS Photo-Bull — AAS [*American Astronomical Society*] Photo-Bulletin
AASRA7 — Atti. Accademia delle Scienze di Ferrara
AASRC Newsl — AASRC [*American Association of Small Research Companies*] Newsletter
AAS Sci Technol Ser — AAS [*American Astronautical Society*] Science and Technology Series
A Assoc Amer Geogr — Annals. Association of American Geographers
AAST — Atti. Reale Accademia delle Scienze di Torino. Classe di Scienze Morali, Storiche, e Filologiche
AASTD — ASSET. Abstracts of Selected Solar Energy Technology
AASYA — Arkiv foer Astronomi
AAT — Atti. Accademia delle Scienze di Torino
AATA — Art and Archaeology. Technical Abstracts
AATB — Afro-Asian Theatre Bulletin
AATC — Atti e Memorie. Accademia Toscana la Colombaria
AATFAA — Atti. Accademia delle Scienze di Torino. I. Classe di Scienze Fisiche, Matematiche, e Naturali
AATFNB — American Association of Teachers of French. National Bulletin
AATMA — Archiwum Automatyki i Telemechaniki
AATSEEL — American Association of Teachers of Slavic and East European Languages. Bulletin
AATSEEL Bull — American Association of Teachers of Slavic and East European Languages. Bulletin
AATSEEL Jour — American Association of Teachers of Slavic and East European Languages. Journal
AAU — Americas
AAU — Atti. Accademia di Scienze, Lettere, ed Arti di Udine
AAug — Analecta Augustiniana
AAUPB — American Association of University Professors. Bulletin
AAUPB — Proceedings. Astronomical Society of Australia
AAUP Bul — American Association of University Professors. Bulletin
AAUP Bull — American Association of University Professors. Bulletin
AAV — Acta Academiae Velehradensis
AAV — Atti. Accademia di Agricoltura, Scienze, e Lettere di Verona
AAV — Aus Aachens Vorzeit
AAVN — Australian Audio-Visual News
AAVPC — Annuarium van de Apologetische Vereeniging (Petrus Canisius)
AAW — Afro-Asian Writings
AAW — Annales. Cercle Archeologique du Pays de Waes
AAW — Anzeiger. Akademie der Wissenschaften [*Vienna*]
AAW — Anzeiger fuer die Altertumswissenschaft [*Innsbruck*]
AAWA — Afro-Asian and World Affairs
AAWG — Abhandlungen. Akademie der Wissenschaften in Goettingen
AAWGPh — Abhandlungen. Akademie der Wissenschaften in Goettingen. Philologisch-Historische Klasse
AAWL — Abhandlungen. Akademie der Wissenschaften und der Literatur in Mainz. Geistes- und Sozialwissenschaftliche Klasse
AAWM — Abhandlungen. Akademie der Wissenschaften in Mainz. Geistes- und Sozialwissenschaftliche Klasse
AAWW — Anzeiger. Akademie der Wissenschaften (Wien)
AAWW — Anzeiger. Oesterreichische Akademie der Wissenschaften (Wien). Philosophisch-Historische Klasse
AAYPA — Annals. American Academy of Political and Social Science
AB — AB Bookman's Weekly
Ab — Abruzzo
AB — Acta Baltica
AB — Africana Bulletin [*Warsaw*]
AB — American Association of Teachers of Slavic and East European Languages. Bulletin
AB — American Bookman
AB — Analecta Biblica [*Rome*]
AB — Analecta Bollandiana
AB — Antiquarian Bookman
AB — Art Bulletin
Ab — Artbibliographies Modern
AB — Augustana Bulletin
AB — Australian Business
A 1888 B — Australia 1888 Bulletin
A 1938-1988 B — Australia 1938-1988 Bicentennial History Project. Bulletin
Aba — Abaco
ABA — Abhandlungen. Bayerische Akademie der Wissenschaften [*Munich*]
ABa — Annee Balzacienne
ABA Antitrust L J — American Bar Association. Antitrust Law Journal
ABABA — Annales de Biologie Animale, Biochimie, et Biophysique
ABA Banking J — ABA [*American Bankers Association*] Banking Journal
ABA Bank J — ABA [*American Bankers Association*] Banking Journal
ABAG — Amsterdamer Beitraege zur Aelteren Germanistik
ABA J — American Bar Association. Journal
ABA Jo — American Bar Association. Journal
ABA Jour — American Bar Association. Journal
Abak Artikulaere Periartikulaere Entzuendungen — Abakterielle, Artikulaere, und Periartikulaere Entzuendungen
ABalt-Slav — Acta Baltico-Slavica
A Balzac — Annee Balzacienne
AbAn — Abstracts in Anthropology

ABAP — Anais. Bibliotecas e Arquivos de Portugal
ABA Sect Antitrust L — American Bar Association. Section of Antitrust Law
ABA Sect Crim L — American Bar Association. Section of Criminal Law
ABA Sect Ins N & CL — American Bar Association. Section of Insurance, Negligence, and Compensation Law
ABA Sect Int & Comp L — American Bar Association. Section of International and Comparative Law
ABA Sect Int & Comp L Bull — American Bar Association. Section of International and Comparative Law. Bulletin
ABA Sect Lab Rel L — American Bar Association. Section of Labor Relations Law
ABA Sect M & NRL — American Bar Association. Section of Mineral and Natural Resources Law
ABA Sect Real Prop L — American Bar Association. Section of Real Property, Probate, and Trust Law. Proceedings
Ab Atomenergi Stockholm Rapp — Aktiebolaget Atomenergi Stockholm Rapport
ABAW — Abhandlungen. Bayerische Akademie der Wissenschaften. Philosophisch-Historische Klasse
ABB — Absatzwirtschaft; Zeitschrift fuer Marketing
ABB — Applied Biochemistry and Biotechnology
ABB — Archives et Bibliotheques de Belgique
ABB — Australian Bankruptcy Bulletin
ABBGB — Animal Blood Groups and Biochemical Genetics
AB Bkman's W — AB Bookman's Weekly
ABC — Abstracts in Biocommerce [*Biocommerce Data Ltd.*] [*England*]
ABC — American Book Collector
ABC — Australian Bankruptcy Cases
ABC — Australian Business Computer
ABCAA — Arquivos Brasileiros de Cardiologia
ABCA Bul — ABCA [*American Business Communication Association*] Bulletin
ABCD — Archives, Bibliotheques, Collections, Documentation
ABCLA — Annales de Biologie Clinique
ABC Pol Sci — Advance Bibliography of Contents: Political Science and Government
ABCXA — Annales Biologiques
ABDEB3 — Anais Brasileiros de Dermatologia
Abdom Surg — Abdominal Surgery
ABDSAA — Anais Brasileiros de Dermatologia e Sifilografia
ABE — Akron Business and Economic Review
ABEBA — Annales Universitatis Scientiarum Budapestensis de Rolando Eoetvoes Nominatae. Sectio Biologica
A'Beckett — A'Beckett's Reserved Judgements [*Port Phillip*]
A'Beck Judg (VIC) — A'Beckett's Reserved Judgements (Victoria)
A'Beck Judg (Vict) — A'Beckett's Reserved Judgments (Victoria)
A'Beck Res Judgm — A'Beckett's Reserved Judgements
A'Beck RJ (NSW) — A'Beckett's Reserved Judgements (New South Wales)
A'Beck RJ (PP) — A'Beckett's Reserved Judgements (Port Phillip)
ABEEA — Annual Bulletin of the Electric Statistics for Europe
ABEGB — Advances in Biomedical Engineering
Abeille Fr — Abeille de France [*Later, Abeille de France et l'Apiculteur*]
Abeille Fr Apic — Abeille de France et l'Apiculteur
Abeille Med (Paris) — Abeille Medicale (Paris)
Abeill Fr Apicul — Abeille de France et l'Apiculteur
ABelges — Archives Belges
ABELL — Annual Bibliography of English Language and Literature
ABENA — Arquivos Brasileiros de Endocrinologia e Metabologia
ABE News — Action for Better Education Newsletter
A Ben R — American Benedictine Review
AbEnSt — Abstracts of English Studies
Aberdeen Univ Rev — Aberdeen University. Review
Aberdeen Univ Stu — Aberdeen University. Studies
ABFE — Acta Botanica Fennica
AbFolkSt — Abstracts of Folklore Studies
ABF Research J — American Bar Foundation. Research Journal
ABF Res J — American Bar Foundation. Research Journal
AbFS — Abstracts of Folklore Studies
ABFZA — Analele. Universitatii Bucuresti. Fizica
ABG — Archiv fuer Begriffsgeschichte
ABGE — Albertan Geographer [*Canada*]
ABGLA — Analele. Universitatii Bucuresti. Seria: Geologie
Ab G R — Above the Ground Review
Abh Akad Wiss DDR Abt Math Naturwiss Tech 1978 — Abhandlungen. Akademie der Wissenschaften der DDR. Abteilung Mathematik, Naturwissenschaften, Technik. 1978 [*Berlin*]
Abh Akad Wiss DDR Abt Math Naturwiss Tech 1979 — Abhandlungen. Akademie der Wissenschaften der DDR. Abteilung Mathematik, Naturwissenschaften, Technik. 1979 [*Goettingen*]
Abh Akad Wiss DDR Abt Math Naturwiss Tech 1981 — Abhandlungen. Akademie der Wissenschaften der DDR. Abteilung Mathematik, Naturwissenschaften, Technik. 1981
Abh Akad Wiss Goettingen Math-Physik Kl — Abhandlungen. Akademie der Wissenschaften in Goettingen. Mathematisch-Physikalische Klasse [*West Germany*]

Abh Akad Wiss Goettingen Math-Phys Kl — Abhandlungen. Akademie der Wissenschaften in Goettingen. Mathematisch-Physikalische Klasse

AbhAkWiss Berlin — Abhandlungen. Deutsche Akademie der Wissenschaften zu Berlin

A Bhandarkar Or Res Inst — Annals. Bhandarkar Oriental Research Institute

Abh Arbgem Tier- u Pflageogr — Abhandlungen. Arbeitsgemeinschaft fuer Tier- und Pflanzengeographische Heimatforschung im Saarland

AbhBAW — Abhandlungen. Bayerische Akademie der Wissenschaften

Abh Bayer Akad Wiss Math-Naturwiss Kl — Abhandlungen. Bayerische Akademie der Wissenschaften. Mathematisch-Naturwissenschaftliche Klasse

Abh Ber Dtsch Mus — Abhandlungen und Berichte. Deutsches Museum [*West Germany*]

Abh (Berlin) — Abhandlungen (Berlin)

Abh Ber Naturkundemus Goerlitz — Abhandlungen und Berichte. Naturkundemuseums Goerlitz [*East Germany*]

Abh Ber Staat Mus Volk Dres — Abhandlungen und Berichte. Staatlichen Museums fuer Voelkerkunde Dresden [*Forschungsstelle*]

Abh Braunschweig Wiss Gesellsch — Abhandlungen. Braunschweigische Wissenschaftliche Gesellschaft

Abh Braunschw Wiss Ges — Abhandlungen. Braunschweigische Wissenschaftliche Gesellschaft

Abh Deut Akad Wiss Berlin Kl Math — Abhandlungen. Deutsche Akademie der Wissenschaften zu Berlin. Klasse fuer Mathematik, Physik, und Technik

Abh Deutsch Akad Wiss Berlin Kl Math Phys Tech — Abhandlungen. Deutsche Akademie der Wissenschaften zu Berlin. Klasse fuer Mathematik, Physik, und Technik

Abh Dtsch Akad Wiss Berlin Kl Bergbau Huettenwes Montangeol — Abhandlungen. Deutsche Akademie der Wissenschaften zu Berlin. Klasse fuer Bergbau, Huettenwesen, und Montangeologie

Abh Dtsch Akad Wiss Berlin Kl Chem Geol Biol — Abhandlungen. Deutsche Akademie der Wissenschaften zu Berlin. Klasse fuer Chemie, Geologie, und Biologie

Abh Dtsch Akad Wiss Berlin Kl Math Allg Naturwiss — Abhandlungen. Deutsche Akademie der Wissenschaften zu Berlin. Klasse fuer Mathematik und Allgemeine Naturwissenschaften

Abh Dtsch Akad Wiss Berlin Kl Math Phys Tech — Abhandlungen. Deutsche Akademie der Wissenschaften zu Berlin. Klasse fuer Mathematik, Physik, und Technik [*East Germany*]

Abh Dtsch Akad Wiss Berlin Kl Med — Abhandlungen. Deutsche Akademie der Wissenschaften zu Berlin. Klasse fuer Medizin

Abh Dtsch Akad Wiss Berlin Math-Naturwiss Kl — Abhandlungen. Deutsche Akademie der Wissenschaften zu Berlin. Mathematisch-Naturwissenschaftliche Klasse

Abh Dtsch Akad Wiss Berl Kl Chem Geol Biol — Abhandlungen. Deutsche Akademie der Wissenschaften zu Berlin. Klasse fuer Chemie, Geologie, und Biologie

Abh Dtsch Akad Wiss Berl Kl Med — Abhandlungen. Deutsche Akademie der Wissenschaften zu Berlin. Klasse fuer Medizin

Abh Dtsch Kaeltetech Ver — Abhandlungen. Deutscher Kaeltetechnische Verein

Abh Geb Hirnforsch Verhaltenphysiol — Abhandlungen. Gebiet der Hirnforschung und Verhaltensphysiologie

Abh Geol Dienstes (Berl) — Abhandlungen. Geologischer Dienst (Berlin)

Abh Geol Landesamtes Baden Wuerttemb — Abhandlungen. Geologisches Landesamt in Baden Wuerttemberg

Abh Gesamtgeb Hyg — Abhandlungen aus dem Gesamtgebiete der Hygiene

AbhGWG — Abhandlungen. Gesellschaft der Wissenschaften zu Goettingen

Abh Inst Hochspannungstech Elektr Anlagen — Abhandlungen. Institut fuer Hochspannungstechnik und Elektrische Anlagen [*West Germany*]

Abh Inst Hochspannungstechnik Elektr Anlagen — Abhandlungen. Institut fuer Hochspannungstechnik und Elektrische Anlagen

Abh Inst Metallhuettenwes Elektrometall Tech Hochsch Aachen — Abhandlungen. Institut fuer Metallhuettenwesen und Elektrometallurgie der Technischen Hochschule (Aachen)

Abh Kinderheilkd Ihren Grenzgeb — Abhandlungen aus der Kinderheilkunde und Ihren Grenzgebieten

AbhKM — Abhandlungen fuer die Kunde des Morgenlandes

Abh Kunde Morgenl — Abhandlungen fuer die Kunde des Morgenlandes

Abh Landesmus Naturkd Muenster Westfalen — Abhandlungen. Landesmuseum fuer Naturkunde zu Muenster in Westfalen

Abh Landes Prov Westfalen Mus Naturkd — Abhandlungen. Landesmuseum der Provinz Westfalen Museum fuer Naturkunde

Abh Math-Phys Kl Saechs Akad Wiss — Abhandlungen. Mathematisch-Physischen Klasse der Saechsischen Akademie der Wissenschaften

Abh Math Sem Univ (Hamburg) — Abhandlungen aus dem Mathematischen Seminar der Universitaet (Hamburg)

Abh Meteorol Dienstes DDR — Abhandlungen. Meteorologischer Dienst der Deutschen Demokratischen Republik

Abh Naturwiss Ver Bremen — Abhandlungen. Naturwissenschaftlicher Verein zu Bremen

Abh Naturw Ver Bremen — Abhandlungen. Naturwissenschaftlicher Verein zu Bremen

Abh Pathophysiol Regul — Abhandlungen ueber die Pathophysiologie der Regulationen

Abh Philos Ges — Abhandlungen zur Philosophie und Ihrer Geschichte

Abh Preuss Akad Wiss Math Naturwiss Kl — Abhandlungen. Preussische Akademie der Wissenschaften. Mathematisch-Naturwissenschaftliche Klasse

Abh Preuss Akad Wiss Phys Math Kl — Abhandlungen. Preussische Akademie der Wissenschaften. Physikalisch-Mathematische Klasse

ABHRAR — Anais Botanicos. Herbario "Barbosa Rodrigues"

Abh Rheinisch-Westfael Akad Wiss — Abhandlungen. Rheinisch-Westfaelische Akademie der Wissenschaften

ABHSA — American Behavioral Scientist

Abh Saechs Akad Wiss Leipzig Math-Natur Kl — Abhandlungen. Saechsische Akademie der Wissenschaften zu Leipzig. Mathematisch-Naturwissenschaftliche Klasse

Abh Saechs Akad Wiss Leipzig Math Naturwiss Kl — Abhandlungen. Saechsische Akademie der Wissenschaften zu Leipzig. Mathematisch-Naturwissenschaftliche Klasse

Abh Senckenb Naturforsch Ges — Abhandlungen. Senckenbergischen Naturforschenden Gesellschaft

Abh Staatl Mus Mineral Geol Dresden — Abhandlungen. Staatliches Museum fuer Mineralogie und Geologie zu Dresden

AbhTANT — Abhandlungen zur Theologie des Alten und Neuen Testaments

Abh Verh Naturwiss Ver Hamb — Abhandlungen und Verhandlungen. Naturwissenschaftlicher Verein in Hamburg

Abh Verh Naturwiss Ver Hamburg — Abhandlungen und Verhandlungen. Naturwissenschaftlicher Verein in Hamburg

ABI — Accademia e Biblioteche d'Italia

ABI — Australian Business Index

ABIA SAPRO Bol Inf — ABIA [*Associacao Brasileira das Industrias de Alimentacao*] SAPRO [*Setor de Alimentos Calorico-Proteicos*] Boletim Informativo

ABIBD — Applied Biochemistry and Biotechnology

ABIBUZ — Acta Botanica. Instituti Botanici. Universitatis Zagrebensis

Abidjan Univ Ann Sci — Abidjan Universite. Annales. Sciences

ABIM — Abridged Index Medicus

A Biol Colloq Ore St Coll — Annual Biology Colloquium. Oregon State College

ABIP — Australian Books in Print

ABIPB — Proceedings. Australian Biochemical Society

ABIPC — Abstract Bulletin. Institute of Paper Chemistry

ABIRBD — Australia. Commonwealth Scientific and Industrial Research Organisation. Division of Irrigation Research. Report

ABIS — Acta Botanica Islandica

ABITA — American Biology Teacher

ABJOA — American Bee Journal

ABK — Aachener Beitraege zur Komparatistik

ABK — Ajia Bunka [*Asian Culture*]

ABKK — Amtliche Berichte. Koenigliche Kunstsammlungen [*Berlin*]

AbKM — Abhandlungen fuer die Kunde des Morgenlandes

AbKSGW — Abhandlungen. Koenigliche Saechsische Gesellschaft der Wissenschaften

ABL — American Business Law Journal

ABL — Business Law Cases for Australia [*Commerce Clearing House*]

Ablauf-Planungsforsch — Ablauf- und Planungsforschung

ABM — Academie Royale de Belgique

ABM — Art Bibliographies Modern

ABMB — Archives, Bibliotheques, et Musees de Belgique [*Later, Archives et Bibliotheques de Belgique*]

ABMEC — Annals of Biomedical Engineering

ABMGA — Acta Biologica et Medica Germanica

AbMilt — Abstracts of Military Bibliography

ABMK — Archiwa, Biblioteki, i Muzea Koscielne

ABMMC — Analele. Universitatii Bucuresti. Matematica-Mecanica

ABMR — ABM [*Australian Board of Missions*] Review

ABMR — Antiquarian Book Monthly Review

ABM Rev — ABM [*Australian Board of Missions*] Review

ABMXA — Archivos de Biologia y Medicina Experimentales [*Chile*]

ABN — Anais. Biblioteca Nacional [*Rio De Janeiro*]

ABN — Arhiv Bioloskih Nauka

ABN — Arnold Bennett Newsletter

ABNG — Amsterdamer Beitraege zur Neueren Germanistik

ABNN — Alberta Native News

ABN Review — ABN [*Algemene Bank Nederland*] Economic Review

ABOA — Acta Borealia. B. Humaniora

ABOA — Australian Bibliography of Agriculture

ABOBAE — Anais. Congresso Nacional. Sociedade Botanica do Brasil

ABOD — Arbeiten zur Bayerisch-Oesterreichischen Dialektgeografie

ABOF — Annales Botanici Fennici

ABOFA — Annales Botanici Fennici

A Bohuslaens Hembygds — Arsskrift. Bohuslaens Hembygdsfoerbund

ABOIB — Acta Botanica Indica

ABORI — Annals. Bhandarkar Oriental Research Institute

Aborig Aff Info Paper — Aboriginal Affairs Information Paper

Aborig Child Sch — Aboriginal Child at School

Aboriginal Q — Aboriginal Quarterly
Aborig LB — Aboriginal Law Bulletin
Abor N — Aboriginal News
ABoT — Ankara Arkeoloji Muzesinde Bulunan Bogazkoy Tableteri [*Istanbul*]
ABourg — Annales de Bourgogne
ABP — Arquivo de Bibliografia Portuguesa
AB & P — Australian Bookseller and Publisher
ABP — Centraal Planbureau. Bibliotheek. Aanwinsten [*'S-Gravenhage*]
ABPBBK — Annual Review of Biophysics and Bioengineering
ABPCA — Abstract Bulletin. Institute of Paper Chemistry
AbPhoto — Abstracts of Photographic Science and Engineering Literature
ABPK — Amtliche Berichte. Preussische Kunstsammlunge [*Berlin*]
ABPR — African Book Publishing Record
ABQ — Erasmusuniversiteit Rotterdam. Universiteitsbibliotheek. Aanwinstenlijst
ABR — Accounting and Business Research
ABr — Altbabylonische Briefe
ABR — American Benedictine Review
ABR — American Book Review
ABr — Annales de Bretagne et des Pays de l'Ouest
ABR — Australian Biblical Review
ABR — Australian Book Review
ABRA — Abracadabra. Association of British Columbia Drama Educators
Abrasive Clean Methods — Abrasive and Cleaning Methods
Abrasive Eng — Abrasive Engineering
Abrasive Eng Soc Mag — Abrasive Engineering Society. Magazine
Abrasiv Eng — Abrasive Engineering
A'B Res Judgm — A'Beckett's Reserved Judgements [*Port Phillip*]
ABret — Annales de Bretagne [*Later, Annales de Bretagne et des Pays de l'Ouest*]
Abridg Wkly Weath Rep Canb — Abridged Weekly Weather Report for Canberra
AbrIMed — Abridged Index Medicus
A'B RJ (NSW) — A'Beckett's Reserved and Equity Judgements (New South Wales)
A'B RJPP — A'Beckett's Reserved Judgments (Port Philip)
Abr RG — Abridged Reader's Guide to Periodical Literature
A Br Sch Archeol Athens — Annual. British School of Archaeology at Athens
Abr Sci Publ Kodak Res Lab — Abridged Scientific Publications from the Kodak Research Laboratories
Abr Sci Pubs — Abridged Scientific Publications
ABs — Abside
ABS — Acta Baltico-Slavica
ABS — American Behavioral Scientist
ABS — Australian Building Specification
ABSA — Annual. British School at Athens
Abs Bull Inst Paper Chem — Abstract Bulletin. Institute of Paper Chemistry
Abs Crim Pen — Abstracts on Criminology and Penology
ABSHF — Annuaire-Bulletin. Societe de l'Histoire de France
ABSLAU — Danish Pest Infestation Laboratory. Annual Report
AbSocWk — Abstracts for Social Workers
Absorpt Spectra Ultraviolet Visible Reg — Absorption Spectra in the Ultraviolet and Visible Region
Abs Pap ACS — Abstracts of Papers. American Chemical Society
Abstracts Amer Math Soc — Abstracts of Papers Presented to the American Mathematical Society
Abstracts Bulgar Sci Lit Math Phys Sci — Abstracts of Bulgarian Scientific Literature. Mathematical and Physical Sciences
Abstr Annu Meet Am Soc Microbiol — Abstracts of the Annual Meeting. American Society for Microbiology
Abstr Anthropol — Abstracts in Anthropology
Abstr Bacteriol — Abstracts of Bacteriology
Abstr Bulg Scient Lit — Abstracts of Bulgarian Scientific Literature
Abstr Bulg Sci Lit Agric For Vet Med — Abstracts of Bulgarian Scientific Literature. Agriculture and Forestry, Veterinary Medicine
Abstr Bulg Sci Lit Biol Biochem — Abstracts of Bulgarian Scientific Literature. Biology and Biochemistry
Abstr Bulg Sci Lit Biol Med — Abstracts of Bulgarian Scientific Literature. Biology and Medicine
Abstr Bulg Sci Lit Chem — Abstracts of Bulgarian Scientific Literature. Chemistry
Abstr Bulg Sci Lit Chem Chem Technol — Abstracts of Bulgarian Scientific Literature. Chemistry and Chemical Technology
Abstr Bulg Sci Lit Geol Geogr — Abstracts of Bulgarian Scientific Literature. Geology and Geography
Abstr Bulg Sci Lit Math Phys Astron Geophys Geod — Abstracts of Bulgarian Scientific Literature. Mathematics, Physics, Astronomy, Geophysics, Geodesy
Abstr Bulg Sci Lit Ser A Plant Breed For Econ — Abstracts of Bulgarian Scientific Literature. Series A. Plant Breeding and Forest Economy
Abstr Bulg Sci Med Lit — Abstracts of Bulgarian Scientific Medical Literature
Abstr Bull — Monthly Abstract Bulletin
Abstr Bull Geol Surv S Aust — Abstracts Bulletin. Geological Survey of South Australia
Abstr Bull Inst Pap Chem — Abstract Bulletin. Institute of Paper Chemistry
Abstr Comput Lit — Abstracts of Computer Literature

Abstr Congr Pol Phthisiopneumonol Soc — Abstracts. Congress of the Polish Phthisiopneumonological Society
Abstr Crim & Pen — Abstracts on Criminology and Penology
Abstr Doct Diss Ohio St Univ — Abstracts of Doctoral Dissertations. Ohio State University
Abstr Engl Stud — Abstracts of English Studies
Abstr Entomol — Abstracts of Entomology
Abstr Folk Stud — Abstracts of Folklore Studies
Abstr Geochronology Isot Geol — Abstracts of Geochronology and Isotope Geology
Abstr Health Care Manage Stud — Abstracts of Health Care Management Studies
Abstr Health Eff Environ Pollut — Abstracts on Health Effects of Environmental Pollutants
Abstr Hosp Manage Stud — Abstracts of Hospital Management Studies
Abstr Hyg — Abstracts on Hygiene
Abstr Jap Lit Forest Genet — Abstracts of Japanese Literature in Forest Genetics and Related Fields
Abstr J Earthq Eng — Abstract Journal in Earthquake Engineering
Abstr J Inf (Moscow) — Abstract Journal Informations (Moscow)
Abstr Jpn Med — Abstracts of Japanese Medicine
Abstr Meet Weed Soc Am — Abstracts. Meeting of the Weed Society of America
Abstr Mil Bibl — Abstracts of Military Bibliography
Abstr Mtg ACS — Abstracts of Papers. Meeting of the American Chemical Society
Abstr Mtg Weed Soc Amer — Abstracts. Meeting of the Weed Society of America
Abstr Mycol — Abstracts of Mycology
Abstr N Amer Geol — Abstracts of North American Geology
Abstr Pap Aust Workshop Coal Hydrogenation — Australian Workshop on Coal Hydrogenation. Abstract and Papers
Abstr Pap Commun R Soc (London) — Abstracts of the Papers Communicated to the Royal Society (London)
Abstr Pap J Jpn Soc Intern Med — Abstracts of Papers. Journal of the Japanese Society of Internal Medicine
Abstr Pap Pac Sci Congr — Abstracts of the Papers. Pacific Science Congress
Abstr Pap Presented Ann Meet Am Soc Range Mange — Abstracts of Papers Presented at the Annual Meeting. American Society of Range Management
Abstr Pap Presented Annu Meet Korean Surg Soc — Abstracts of Papers Presented at the Annual Meeting. Korean Surgical Society
Abstr Pap Printed Philos Trans R Soc (London) — Abstracts of the Papers Printed in the Philosophical Transactions of the Royal Society (London)
Abstr Pap Soc Amer For — Abstracts of Papers. Society of American Foresters Meeting
Abstr Photogr Sci Eng Lit — Abstracts of Photographic Science and Engineering Literature
Abstr Pop Cult — Abstracts of Popular Culture
Abstr Proc Linn Soc NSW — Abstracts of the Proceedings. Linnean Society of New South Wales
Abstr Proc Soc NSW — Abstracts of Proceedings. Royal Society of New South Wales
Abstr Publ Pap List Transl CSIRO (Aust) — Abstracts of Published Papers and List of Translations. Commonwealth Scientific and Industrial Research Organisation (Australia)
Abstr Refin Lit — Abstracts of Refining Literature
Abstr Rep Geol Surv West Austr — Abstracts. Reports of the Geological Survey of Western Australia
Abstr Res Tob Salt Camphor — Abstracts of Researches. Tobacco, Salt, Camphor
Abstr Rom Sci Tech Lit — Abstracts of Romanian Scientific and Technical Literature
Abstr Rom Tech Lit — Abstracts of Romanian Technical Literature
Abstr Sov Med — Abstracts of Soviet Medicine
Abstr Sov Med Part A — Abstracts of Soviet Medicine. Part A. Basic Medical Sciences
Abstr Sov Med Part B — Abstracts of Soviet Medicine. Part B. Clinical Medicine
Abstr Tech Pap Water Pollut Control Fed — Abstracts of Technical Papers. Water Pollution Control Federation
Abstr Trop Agri — Abstracts on Tropical Agriculture
Abstr Uppsala Diss Med — Abstracts of Uppsala Dissertations in Medicine
Abstr Uppsala Diss Sci — Abstracts of Uppsala Dissertations in Science
Abstr Wld Med — Abstracts of World Medicine
Abstr World Med — Abstracts of World Medicine
Absts Soc Workers — Abstracts for Social Workers
ABSUD — Amtsblatt. Bayerisches Staatsministerium fuer Landesentwicklung und Umweltfragen
ABUC — Archivio Bibliographico. Bibliotheca da Universidade de Coimbra
ABul — Art Bulletin
ABull — Art Bulletin
A Bus L Rev — Australian Business Law Review
ABU Tech Rev — ABU [*Asian Broadcasting Union*] Technical Review
ABV — Attic Black-Figure Vase Painters

AbVoc — Abstracts of Research and Related Materials in Vocational and Technical Education
ABVSD — Annales. Association Belge de Radioprotection
ABWADK — Australian Birdwatcher
ABWGA — Abhandlungen. Braunschweigische Wissenschaftliche Gesellschaft
AC — AC [*Asbestos and Cement*]. The Fibrecement Review
AC — Accent on Worship, Music, and the Arts
AC — Achimoowin. James Smith Reserve [*Saskatchewan, Canada*]
AC — Advance California Reports
AC — Albia Christiana
AC — American City
AC — Analecta Cisterciensia
AC — Anales Cervantinos
AC — Annales-Conferencia
AC — Antiquite Classique
AC — Archaeologia Cambrensis
AC — Archaeologia Classica
AC — Archivos del Folklore Chileno
ACA — Advance California Appellate Reports
ACA — American Composers Alliance. Bulletin
ACA — Australian Corporate Affairs Reporter
ACAAB — Annales de Cardiologie et d'Angeiologie
ACACA — Analytica Chimica Acta
ACACB — Acta Crystallographica. Section A. Crystal Physics, Diffraction, Theoretical and General Crystallography
ACACS — Annales. Cercle Archeologique du Canton de Soignies
Acad — [*The*] Academy
Acad Ag France Comptes Rendus — Academie d'Agriculture de France. Comptes Rendus des Seances
Acad Ag France Compt Rend — Academie d'Agriculture de France. Comptes Rendus des Seances
Acad Brasileira Cienc Anais — Academia Brasileira de Ciencias. Anais
Acad Bul — Academy of Motion Picture Arts and Sciences. Bulletin
Acad Cienc Artes Barc — Academia de Ciencias y Artes de Barcelona. Memorias
Acad Cienc Cuba Inst Geol Actas — Academia de Ciencias de Cuba. Instituto de Geologia. Actas
Acad Cienc Cuba Inst Geol Paleontol Publ Espec — Academia de Ciencias de Cuba. Instituto de Geologia y Paleontologia. Publicacion Especial
Acad Cienc Cuba Inst Geol Ser Geol — Academia de Ciencias de Cuba. Instituto de Geologia. Serie Geologica
Acad Cienc Cuba Ser Biol — Academia de Ciencias de Cuba. Serie Biologica
Acad Cienc Med Fis y Naturales Habana Anales — Academia de Ciencias Medicas, Fisicas, y Naturales de la Habana. Anales
Academy of Mgmt Jrnl — Academy of Management. Journal
Academy of Mgmt Review — Academy of Management. Review
Acad Esp Bol — Real Academia Espanola. Boletin
Acad d Inscrip Memoires — Academie des Inscriptions et Belles-Lettres. Memoires [*Paris*]
Acad d Inscr Mon et Mem — Academie des Inscriptions et Belles-Lettres. Monuments et Memoires [*Paris*]
Acad d Inscr (Paris) Mem — Academie des Inscriptions et Belles-Lettres. Memoires (Paris)
Acad Inscr (Paris) Mem Div Savants — Academie des Inscriptions et Belles-Lettres. Memoires Presentes par Divers Savants (Paris)
Acad d Inscr (Paris) Mon et Mem — Academie des Inscriptions et Belles-Lettres. Monuments et Memoires (Paris)
Acad Inscr (Paris) Mon et Mem — Institut de France (Paris). Academie des Inscriptions et Belles-Lettres. Monuments et Memoires
Acad L Rev — Academy Law Review [*Kerala, India*]
Acad Manage J — Academy of Management. Journal
Acad Manage Rev — Academy of Management. Review
Acad Marketing Science J — Academy of Marketing Science. Journal
Acad Med NJ Bull — Academy of Medicine of New Jersey. Bulletin
Acad Mgt J — Academy of Management. Journal
Acad Mgt R — Academy of Management. Review
Acad Nac Cienc Mem Rev — Academia Nacional de Ciencias. Memorias y Revista
Acad Nac Cienc Misc (Cordoba) — Academia Nacional de Ciencias. Miscelanea (Cordoba)
Acad of Nat Sci Jour — Academy of Natural Sciences. Journal
Acad Nat Sci Philadelphia Spec Pub — Academy of Natural Sciences of Philadelphia. Special Publication
Acad Natur Sci Phila Proc — Academy of Natural Sciences of Philadelphia. Proceedings
Acad Pap — Academy Papers. American Academy of Physical Education
Acad Pol Sci — Academy of Political Science
Acad Pol Sci Bull Ser Sci Terre — Academie Polonaise des Sciences. Bulletin. Serie des Sciences de la Terre
Acad Pol Sci Proc — Academy of Political Science. Proceedings
Acad R Belg Annu — Academie Royale de Belgique. Annuaire
Acad R Belg Cl Sci Collect Octavo Mem — Academie Royale de Belgique. Classe des Sciences. Collection in Octavo. Memoires
Acad R Belg Cl Sci Collect Quarto Mem — Academie Royale de Belgique. Classe des Sciences. Collection in Quarto. Memoires

Acad R Belg Cl Sci Mem — Academie Royale de Belgique. Classe des Sciences. Memoires
Acad R Belg Mem Cl Sci Collect Octavo — Academie Royale de Belgique. Memoires. Classe des Sciences. Collection in Octavo
Acad R Belg Mem Cl Sci Collect Quarto — Academie Royale de Belgique. Memoires. Classe des Sciences. Collection in Quarto
Acad Repub Pop Rom Bul Stiint A — Academia Republicii Populare Romine. Buletin Stiintific. Seria A [*Romania*]
Acad Repub Pop Rom Bul Stiint Sect Biol Stiinte Agric — Academia Republicii Populare Romine. Buletin Stiintific. Sectia de Biologie si Stiinte Agricole
Acad Repub Pop Rom Fil (Cluj) Stud Cercet Agron — Academia Republicii Populare Romine Filiala (Cluj). Studii si Cercetari de Agronomie
Acad Repub Pop Rom Fil (Cluj) Stud Cercet Biol — Academia Republicii Populare Romine Filiala (Cluj). Studii si Cercetari de Biologie
Acad Repub Pop Rom Fil (Cluj) Stud Cercet Stiint — Academia Republicii Populare Romine Filiala (Cluj). Studii si Cercetari Stiintifice
Acad Repub Pop Rom Fil (Cluj) Stud Cercet Stiint Ser 2 — Academia Republicii Populare Romine Filiala (Cluj). Studii si Cercetari Stiintifice. Seria 2. Stiinte Biologice, Agricole, si Medicale
Acad Repub Pop Rom Stud Cercet Biochim — Academia Republicii Populare Romine. Institutul de Biochimie. Studii si Cercetari de Biochimie [*Romania*]
Acad Repub Pop Rom Stud Cercet Biol Ser Biol Anim — Academia Republicii Populare Romine. Studii si Cercetari de Biologie. Seria Biologie Animala
Acad Repub Pop Rom Stud Cercet Biol Ser Biol Veg — Academia Republicii Populare Romine. Studii si Cercetari de Biologie. Seria Biologie Vegetala
Acad Repub Pop Rom Stud Cercet Chim — Academia Republicii Populare Romine. Studii si Cercetari de Chimice
Acad Repub Pop Rom Stud Cercet Fiz — Academia Republicii Populare Romine. Institutul de Fizica Atomica si Institutul de Fizica. Studii si Cercetari de Fizica [*Romania*]
Acad Repub Pop Rom Stud Cercet Fiziol — Academia Republicii Populare Romine. Institutul de Fiziologie Normala si Patologica Dr. D. Danielolpolu. Studii si Cercetari de Fiziologie [*Romania*]
Acad Repub Pop Rom Stud Cercet Geol — Academia Republicii Populare Romine. Studii si Cercetari de Geologie
Acad Repub Pop Rom Stud Cercet Stiint Ser Stiint Med — Academia Republicii Populare Romine. Studii si Cercetari Stiintifice. Seria Stiinte Medicina
Acad Rev — Academy Review
Acad Roy Belg Bull Cl Sci — Academie Royale de Belgique. Bulletin. Classe des Sciences
Acad Roy Belg Cl Sci Mem Coll in-8 — Academie Royale de Belgique. Classe des Sciences. Memoires. Collection in Octavo
Acad Roy Sci O-Mer B — Academie Royale des Sciences d'Outre-Mer. Bulletin des Seances
Acad Roy Sci Outre-Mer Bul Seances — Academie Royale des Sciences d'Outre-Mer. Bulletin des Seances
Acad R Sci Colon (Brussels) Bull Seances — Academie Royale des Sciences Coloniales (Brussels). Bulletin des Seances [*Belgium*]
Acad R Sci Colon (Brussels) Cl Sci Nat Med Mem Collect — Academie Royale des Sciences Coloniales (Brussels). Classe des Sciences Naturelles et Medicales. Memoires. Collection in Octavo
Acad R Sci Lett B-Arts Belg Cl Sci Bull — Academie Royale des Sciences, des Lettres, et des Beaux-Arts de Belgique. Classe des Sciences. Bulletin
Acad R Sci Outre-Mer (Brussels) Bull Seances — Academie Royale des Sciences d'Outre-Mer (Brussels). Bulletin des Seances
Acad R Sci Outre-Mer Bull — Academie Royale des Sciences d'Outre-Mer. Bulletin des Seances
Acad Sci Belg Bul Cl Beaux-Arts — Academie Royale de Belgique. Bulletin. Classe des Beaux-Arts
Acad Sci Belg Bul Cl Lett — Academie Royale de Belgique. Bulletin. Classe des Lettres et des Sciences Morales et Politiques
Acad Sci Belg Bul Cl Sci — Academie Royale de Belgique. Bulletin. Classe des Sciences
Acad d Sci d Belgique Mem 4 Cl d Lett — Academie Royale des Sciences, des Lettres, et des Beaux-Arts de Belgique. Memoires 4. Classe des Lettres
Acad d Sci d Belgique Mem 8 Cl d Lett — Academie Royale des Sciences, des Lettres, et des Beaux-Arts de Belgique. Memoires 8. Classe des Lettres
Acad d Sci d Belgique Mem 4 Cl d Sci — Academie Royale des Sciences, des Lettres, et des Beaux-Arts de Belgique. Memoires 4. Classe des Sciences
Acad d Sci d Belgique Mem 8 Cl d Sci — Academie Royale des Sciences, des Lettres, et des Beaux-Arts de Belgique. Memoires 8. Classe des Sciences
Acad Sci Belg Mem 8 Cl Lett — Academie Royale de Belgique. Memoires. Classe des Lettres et des Sciences Morales et Politiques. Collection in Octavo
Acad Sci Belg Mem 8 Cl Sci — Academie Royale de Belgique. Memoires. Classe des Sciences. Collection in Octavo
Acad Sci Fenn Ann Ser A-III Geol-Geogr — Academia Scientiarum Fennicae. Annales. Series A-III (Geologica-Geographica)
Acad d Sci Mor et Pol (Paris) Mem — Academie des Sciences Morales et Politiques (Paris). Memoires

Acad Sci (Paris) CR Ser B — Academie des Sciences (Paris). Comptes Rendus Hebdomadaires des Seances. Serie B. Sciences Physiques

Acad Sci (Paris) CR Ser C — Academie des Sciences (Paris). Comptes Rendus Hebdomadaires des Seances. Serie C. Sciences Chimiques

Acad Sci (Paris) CR Ser D — Academie des Sciences (Paris). Comptes Rendus Hebdomadaires des Seances. Serie D. Sciences Naturelles

Acad Sci (Paris) Mem — Academie des Sciences (Paris). Memoires

Acad d Sci (Paris) Mem — Academie des Sciences (Paris). Memoires

Acad d Sci (Paris) Mem Div Savants — Academie des Sciences (Paris). Memoires Presentes par Divers Savants

Acad Sci St Louis Trans — Academy of Science of St. Louis. Transactions

Acad of Sci of St Louis Trans — Academy of Science of St. Louis. Transactions

Acad Sci Toulouse Mem — Academie des Sciences, Inscriptions, et Belles-Lettres de Toulouse. Memoires

Acad Sci USSR Dokl Earth Sci Sec — Doklady Academy of Sciences of the USSR. Earth Science Sections

Acad Serb Sci Arts Classe Sci Math Nat (Glas) — Academie Serbe des Sciences et des Arts. Classe des Sciences Mathematiques et Naturelles (Glas)

Acad Sin Inst Bot Annu Rep — Academia Sinica. Institute of Botany. Annual Report

Acad Sin Inst Vertebr Palaeontol Palaeoanthropol Mem — Academia Sinica. Institute of Vertebrate Palaeontology and Palaeoanthropology. Memoir

Acad Sin Inst Zool Monogr Ser — Academia Sinica. Institute of Zoology. Monograph Series

Acad Sin Mem Inst Chem — Academia Sinica. Memoirs. Institute of Chemistry

Acad Sin Nanjing Inst Geol Palaeontol Mem — Academia Sinica. Nanjing Institute of Geology and Palaeontology. Memoirs

Acad (Syr) — Academy (Syracuse)

Acad Tcheque Sci Bull Int Cl Sci Math Nat Med — Academie Tcheque des Sciences. Bulletin International. Classe des Sciences Mathematiques et Naturelles, et de la Medecine

Acad Ther — Academic Therapy

Acad Therapy — Academic Therapy

ACAE — Actes. Congres International des Sciences Anthropologiques et Ethnologiques

ACAE — Annales. Cercle Archeologique d'Enghien

ACAEA — Acta Anaesthesiologica

ACAHA — Acta Chirurgica. Academiae Scientiarum Hungaricae

ACAM — Annales. Cercle Archeologique de Mons

AcAn — Acta Antiqua. Academiae Scientiarum Hungaricae [*Budapest*]

ACAO — Alaska Construction and Oil

ACAPW — Annales. Cercle Archeologique du Pays de Waes

Ac Ar — Acta Archaeologica

ACAR — Acta Arctica

A Car — Analecta Cartusiana

Ac Arch (Ljub) — Acta Archaeologica (Ljubljana)

A Card — Acta Cardiologica

Acarol — Acarologia

Ac As — Acta Asiatica

ACAS — Chinese Art Society of America. Archives

ACASA — Chinese Art Society of America. Archives

A Catedra F Suarez — Anales. Catedra Francisco Suarez

ACB — Australian Computer Bulletin

ACBCA — Acta Crystallographica. Section B. Structural Crystallography and Crystal Chemistry

Ac Belg B — Academie Royale de Belgique. Bulletin

ACBLF Bul — Association Canadienne des Bibliothecaires de Langue Francaise. Bulletin

ACC — Accent

ACC — Accountant [*London*]

ACC — Alcuin Club. Collections

ACC — Australian Company Law Cases

ACCAA — Acta Cardiologica [*Bruxelles*]

Accad Bibliot d'Italia — Accademia e Biblioteche d'Italia

Accad e Bibl Italia — Accademia e Biblioteche d'Italia

Accad Med — Accademia Medica

Accad Naz Lincei Atti Cl Sci Fis Mat Nat Rend — Accademia Nazionale dei Lincei. Atti. Classe di Scienze Fisiche, Matematiche, e Naturali. Rendiconti

Accad Naz Lincei Atti Cl Sci Fis Mat e Nat Rend — Atti. Accademia Nazionale dei Lincei. Rendiconti. Classe di Scienze Fisiche, Matematiche, e Naturali

Accad Naz Sci Lett Arti (Modena) Atti Mem — Accademia Nazionale di Scienze, Lettere, ed Arti (Modena). Atti e Memorie

Accad Pugliese Sci Att Relaz Parte 2 — Accademia Pugliese delle Scienze. Atti e Relazioni. Parte 2. Classe di Scienze Fisiche, Mediche, e Naturali

Accad Sci Fis e Mat Rend — Accademia delle Scienze Fisiche e Matematiche. Rendiconto

ACCB — Australian Copyright Council. Bulletin

Acc Bus Res — Accounting and Business Research

ACCCA — Acta Cientifica Compostelana

Acc Chem Re — Accounts of Chemical Research

Acc Chem Res — Accounts of Chemical Research

Acc Cient Int — Accion Cientifica International

ACCEL — American College of Cardiology. Extended Learning

ACCFC — Ag Chem and Commercial Fertilizer [*Later, Farm Chemicals*]

Acc Gar Equip — Accessory and Garage Equipment

Acciaio Inossid — Acciaio Inossidabile

Accid Anal Prev — Accident Analysis and Prevention

Accid Anal Prev (Elmsford NY) — Accident Analysis and Prevention (Elmsford, New York)

Accident Anal Prev — Accident Analysis and Prevention

Accident Prevention Bul — Accident Prevention Bulletin

Ac Cienc Med Habana An — Academia de Ciencias Medicas, Fisicas, y Naturales de la Habana. Annales

Accion Farm — Accion Farmaceutica

Acc Med (A) — Accion Medica (Argentina)

Acc Med (B) — Accion Medica (Bolivia)

Acc Med (M) — Accion Medica (Mexico)

Accountants and Secretaries' Educ J — Accountants and Secretaries' Educational Journal

Accounting R — Accounting Review

Account Mag — Accountants Magazine

Account R — Accounting Review

Account Res — Accounting Research

ACCP — Arquivos. Centro Cultural Portugues

Acc Res — Accounting Research

Acc Review — Accounting Review

Acct & Bus Res — Accounting and Business Research

Acct Chem Res — Accounts of Chemical Research

Acctg Rev — Accounting Review

Acct R — Accounting Review

Accts Sec Educ J — Accountants and Secretaries' Educational Journal

ACCV — Anales. Centro de Cultura Valenciana

ACD — Acta Classica. Universitatis Scientiarum Debreceniensis

ACDACX — Australia. Commonwealth Scientific and Industrial Research Organisation. Division of Applied Chemistry. Annual Report

ACDLAU — Australia. Commonwealth Scientific and Industrial Research Organisation. Division of Land Use Research. Technical Paper

ACE — Annals of Public and Cooperative Economy [*Formerly, Annals of Collective Economy*]

ACEA Bull — ACEA [*Australian Council for Educational Administration*] Bulletin

Ac Ec — Acta Ecclesiastica

ACEC — Actes. Congres de la Federation International des Associations d'Etudes Classiques

ACEC Rev — ACEC [*Ateliers de Constructions Electriques de Charleroi*] Reviews

ACEF — Acta Entomologica Fennica

ACELB — Actas. Coloquio Internacional de Estudos Luso-Brasileiros

Ac Energ — Acero y Energia

ACE News — ACE [*Agricultural Communication in Education*] Newsletter

ACEPC — Preprints of Papers Presented at National Meeting. Division of Environmental Chemistry. American Chemical Society

ACer — Anales Cervantinos

ACER — Annales. Centre d'Etude des Religions

ACERB — Allis-Chalmers Engineering Review

ACER Bull — Australian Council for Educational Research. Bulletin

Acero Energ Numero Espec — Acero y Energia. Numero Especial

ACER Test News — Australian Council for Educational Research. Test News

ACES Rev — ACES [*Australian Council for Educational Standards*] Review

Acet — Acetylene

Acet J — Acetylene Journal

Acet Light Weld J — Acetylene Lighting and Welding Journal

Acet Weld — Acetylene Welding

ACF — Annali di Ca' Foscari

ACF — Annuaire. College de France

ACFBAA — Anales. Academia Nacional de Ciencias Exactas, Fisicas, y Naturales de Buenos Aires

ACFCBE — Australia. Commonwealth Scientific and Industrial Research Organisation. Division of Fisheries and Oceanography. Circular

ACFF — Annales. Comite Flamand de France

ACFRBP — Australia. Commonwealth Scientific and Industrial Research Organisation. Division of Food Research. Report of Research

ACFW — Australian Child and Family Welfare

Ac Gioenia Sc Nat Catania B — Accademia Gioenia de Scienze Naturali in Catania. Bollettino delle Sedute

ACGKH — Aichi Gakugei Daigaku Kenkyu Hokoku [*Bulletin of the Aichi Gakugei University: Cultural Sciences*]

ACGSA — Annales Chirurgiae et Gynaecologiae Fenniae. Supplementum

ACGYA — Annales Chirurgiae et Gynaecologiae Fenniae

A Ch — Annales de Chimie

A Ch — Annales Chopin

Achats et Entretien Mater Ind — Achats et Entretien du Materiel Industriel

Achats Entret Mater Ind — Achats et Entretien du Materiel Industriel [*France*]

A Chem Scand — Acta Chemica Scandinavica

A Chir Belg — Acta Chirurgica Belgica

A Chir It — Acta Chirurgica Italica

A Chir Jug — Acta Chirurgica Jugoslavica

A Chir Plast — Acta Chirurgiae Plasticae

A Chir Scand — Acta Chirurgica Scandinavica

A Ch J — American Chemical Journal
ACHR — American Catholic Historical Researches
ACHS — American Catholic Historical Society. Records
ACHSB — Annales. Cercle Hutois des Sciences et Beaux-Arts
ACHVA — Air Conditioning, Heating, and Ventilating
ACIAm — Actas. Congreso Internacional de Americanistas
ACIBAP — Australia. Commonwealth Scientific and Industrial Research Organisation. Bulletin
ACIDB — Acta Ciencia Indica
Acid Open Hearth Res Assoc Bull — Acid Open Hearth Research Association. Bulletin
Aciers Spec — Aciers Speciaux
Aciers Spec Met Alliages — Aciers Speciaux, Metaux, et Alliages
ACIFA — Analele Stiintifice. Universitatii Al. I. Cuza din Iasi. Sectiunea 1. Matematica, Fizica, Chimie
Ac Imp Lyon Cl Sc Mem — Academie Imperiale des Sciences, Belles-Lettres, et Arts de Lyon. Classe des Sciences. Memoires
ACISE — Atti. Convegno Internazionale di Studie Etiopici
ACIS Newsletter — American Committee for Irish Studies. Newsletter
ACISR — Atti. Congresso Internazionale di Studi Romanzi
ACist — Analecta Cisterciensia
ACJ — Alternative Criminology Journal
ACJ — Australian Commercial Journal
ACK — Archiv fuer Christliche Kunst
AcL — Acta Linguistica
ACl — Antiquite Classique
ACL — Australian Chess Lore
ACL — Australian College Libraries
ACL — Australian Current Law
ACLAN — American Comparative Literature Association. Newsletter
AClass — Acta Classica. Verhandelinge van die Klassieke Vereniging van Suid-Afrika
ACL Bull — Australian Current Law Bulletin
ACLC — Australian Company Law Cases
ACLD — Australian Current Law Digest
AcLLB — Academie Royale de Langue et de Litterature Francaise de Belgique. Bulletin
ACLR — Australian Company Law Reports
ACLR — Australian Construction Law Reporter
ACLR — Australian Current Law Review
ACL Rev — Australian Current Law Review
ACLSC — Annals of Clinical and Laboratory Science
ACLSN — American Council of Learned Societies. Newsletter
ACLZAA — Anais. Congresso Latino-Americano de Zoologia
Ac M — Acta Musicologica
ACM — Anuarul Comisiunii Monumentelor Istorice. Sectia pentru Transilvania
Ac Mex Cienc An — Academia Mexicana de Ciencias Exactas, Fisicas, y Naturales. Anuario
ACMIC — Application of Computer Methods in the Mineral Industry. Proceedings of the International Symposium
ACMPD — Annual Conference on Materials for Coal Conversion and Utilization. Proceedings
ACM Proc — ACM [*Association for Computing Machinery*] National Conference Proceedings
ACMTBW — Museo "Felipe Poey." Academia de Ciencias de Cuba. Trabajos de Divulgacion
ACM Trans Database Syst — ACM [*Association for Computing Machinery*] Transactions on Database Systems
ACM Trans Database Systems — ACM [*Association for Computing Machinery*] Transactions on Database Systems
ACM Trans Math Softw — ACM [*Association for Computing Machinery*] Transactions on Mathematical Software
ACM Trans Math Software — ACM [*Association for Computing Machinery*] Transactions on Mathematical Software
ACM Trans Off Inf Syst — ACM [*Association for Computing Machinery*] Transactions on Office Information Systems
ACNAAD — Anales. Academia Chilena de Ciencias Naturales
ACNI — Acta Naturalia Islandica
ACNRA — Archivum Chirurgicum Neerlandicum
ACNSA — Activitas Nervosa Superior [*Praha*]
Ac N Sc Phila J — Academy of Natural Sciences of Philadelphia. Journal
Ac N Sc Phila Min G Sec Pr — Academy of Natural Sciences of Philadelphia. Mineralogical and Geological Section. Proceedings
Ac N Sc Phila Pr — Academy of Natural Sciences of Philadelphia. Proceedings
ACo — Acta Comeniana
ACO — Acta Oeconomica [*Budapest*]
ACO — Actes. Congres International des Orientalistes
ACOED — Actualite, Combustibles, Energie
ACOFAR — Agrupacion de Cooperativas Farmaceuticas
ACOID — Alaska Construction and Oil
ACom — Acta Comeniana
ACOMD — Ars Combinatoria
ACOME — Archivum Combustionis
ACOPD — ASEE [*American Society for Engineering Education*] Annual Conference Proceedings

Acor — Acoreana
AcOr — Acta Orientalia
AcOr(B) — Acta Orientalia. Academiae Scientiarum Hungaricae [*Budapest*]
AcOr(K) — Acta Orientalia (Copenhagen)
AcOr(L) — Acta Orientalia (Leiden)
ACOSS Q — ACOSS [*Australian Council of Social Service*] Quarterly
Acoust Abstr — Acoustics Abstracts
Acoust Bull — Acoustics Bulletin
Acoust Hologr — Acoustical Holography
Acoustical Soc Am — Acoustical Society of America. Journal
Acoustics Abs — Acoustics Abstracts
Acoust Imaging — Acoustical Imaging
Acoust and Noise Control Can — Acoustics and Noise Control in Canada
Acoust Soc Am J — Acoustical Society of America. Journal
ACPCD — Annual Reports on the Progress of Chemistry. Section C. Physical Chemistry
ACPCDW — Annual Reports on the Progress of Chemistry. Section C. Physical Chemistry
ACPDA — Acta Paedopsychiatrica
ACPE — Australian Chemical Processing and Engineering
ACPFM — Amitie Charles Peguy. Feuillets Mensuels
ACPMA — Actualites Pharmacologiques
ACPR — American Clinical Products Review
ACQ — American Catholic Quarterly
ACQR — American Catholic Quarterly Review
Acqua Ind — Acqua Industriale [*Italy*]
Acqua Ind Inquinamento — Acqua Industriale. Inquinamento
Acquis Med Recent — Acquisitions Medicales Recentes
ACR — Accounting Review
Acr — Acropole. Revue du Monde Hellenique
ACR — American Choral Review
ACR — American Classical Review
ACR — Australian Coin Review
ACR — Australian Criminal Reports
ACRDA — Acta Radiologica. Diagnosis
A Crim R — Australian Criminal Reports
ACRL C & RL — ACRL [*Association of College and Research Libraries*] College and Research Libraries
Across the Bd — Across the Board
Across Board (NY) — Across the Board. Conference Board (New York)
A & CS — Area and Culture Studies [*Tokyo*]
ACSB — Appraisal. Children's Science Books
ACSBA — American Ceramic Society. Bulletin
Ac Sc Kansas City Tr — Academy of Science of Kansas City. Transactions
Ac Sc (Paris) C R — Academie des Sciences (Paris). Comptes Rendus
Ac Sc Sioux City Pr — Academy of Science and Letters of Sioux City, Iowa. Proceedings
Ac Sc St L Tr — Academy of Science of St. Louis. Transactions
ACS Div Environ Chem Prepr — American Chemical Society. Division of Environmental Chemistry. Preprints
ACS Div Fuel Chem Prepr — American Chemical Society. Division of Fuel Chemistry. Preprints
ACS Div Pet Chem Prepr — American Chemical Society. Division of Petroleum Chemistry. Preprints
AC & SJ — Australian Conveyancer and Solicitors' Journal
ACSMA6 — Archivio Stomatologico
ACS Monogr — ACS [*American Chemical Society*] Monograph
ACS Natl Meet Abstr Pap — American Chemical Society. National Meeting. Abstracts of Papers
ACSPD — Aciers Speciaux
ACSR — American Catholic Sociological Review
ACSS — Analytical Chemistry Symposia Series [*Elsevier Book Series*]
ACSSCQ — AIChE [*American Institute of Chemical Engineers*] Symposium Series
ACS Symp S — ACS [*American Chemical Society*] Symposium Series
ACS Symp Ser — ACS [*American Chemical Society*] Symposium Series
ACSTN — ACST [*Alaska Council on Science and Technology*] Notes
ACSU — Atti. Colloquio Slavistico di Uppsala
ACSUB — Annals of Clinical Research. Supplement
ACSVAX — Anales. Casa de Salud Valdecilla (Santander)
ACT — Accountant
Act — Action [*Tunis*]
ACT — Atlantic Canada Teacher
Acta A — Acta Archaeologica
ActaA — Acta Asiatica
Acta Acad Aboensis — Acta Academiae Aboensis
Acta Acad Abo Ser B — Acta Academiae Aboensis. Series B. Mathematica et Physica
Acta Acad Abo Ser B Math Phys Mat Naturvetensk Tek — Acta Academiae Aboensis. Series B. Mathematica et Physica. Matematik Naturvetenskaper Teknik
Acta Acad Int Hist Med — Acta Academiae Internationalis Historiae Medicinae
Acta Acad Paedagog Civitate Pecs Ser 6 Math-Phys-Chem-Tech — Acta Academiae Paedagogicae in Civitate Pecs. Seria 6. Mathematica-Physica-Chemica-Technica

Acta Acad Polytech Pollack Mihaly Pecs — Acta Academiae Polytechnicae Pollack Mihaly Pecs
Acta Acad Reeks B — Acta Academica. Reeks B
Acta Acad Regiae Sci Ups — Acta Academiae Regiae Scientiarum Upsaliensis
Acta Acust — Acta Acustica
Acta Adriat — Acta Adriatica
Acta Agrar Silvestria — Acta Agraria et Silvestria
Acta Agrar Silvestria Ser Agrar — Acta Agraria et Silvestria. Series Agraria
Acta Agrar Silvestria Ser Zootech — Acta Agraria et Silvestria. Series Zootechnia
Acta Agrar Silv Ser Agrar — Acta Agraria et Silvestria. Series Agraria
Acta Agrar Silv Ser Silv — Acta Agraria et Silvestria. Series Silvestris
Acta Agric Scand — Acta Agriculturae Scandinavica
Acta Agric Scand Suppl — Acta Agriculturae Scandinavica. Supplementum
Acta Agric Sin — Acta Agriculturae Sinica
Acta Agric Suec — Acta Agriculturae Suecana
Acta Agric Suecana — Acta Agriculturae Suecana
Acta Agric Univ Pekinensis — Acta Agriculturae Universitatis Pekinensis
Acta Agrobot — Acta Agrobotanica
Acta Agron — Acta Agronomica
Acta Agron Acad Sci Hung — Acta Agronomica. Academiae Scientiarum Hungaricae [*Budapest*]
Acta Agron (Budapest) — Acta Agronomica. Academiae Scientiarum Hungaricae (Budapest)
Acta Agron Hung — Acta Agronomica. Academiae Scientiarum Hungaricae [*Budapest*]
Acta Agron (Palmira) — Acta Agronomica (Palmira)
Acta Agr Scand — Acta Agriculturae Scandinavica
Acta Agr Silv Ser Roln — Acta Agraria et Silvestria. Series Rolnictwo
Acta Agr Sinica — Acta Agriculturae Sinica
Acta Albert — Acta Albertina
Acta Aliment Acad Sci Hung — Acta Alimentaria. Academiae Scientiarum Hungaricae
Acta Aliment Pol — Acta Alimentaria Polonica
Acta Allergol — Acta Allergologica
Acta Allergol Suppl — Acta Allergologica. Supplementum
Acta Am — Acta Americana
Acta Anaesthesiol — Acta Anaesthesiologica
Acta Anaesthesiol Belg — Acta Anaesthesiologica Belgica
Acta Anaesthesiol Ital — Acta Anaesthesiologica Italica
Acta Anaesthesiol (Padova) — Acta Anaesthesiologica (Padova)
Acta Anaesthesiol Scand — Acta Anaesthesiologica Scandinavica
Acta Anaesthesiol Scand Suppl — Acta Anaesthesiologica Scandinavica. Supplementum
Acta Anaesthes Scand — Acta Anaesthesiologica Scandinavica
Acta Anat — Acta Anatomica
Acta Anat (Basel) — Acta Anatomica (Basel)
Acta Anat Nippon — Acta Anatomica Nipponica
Acta Anat Sin — Acta Anatomica Sinica
Acta Anat Suppl — Acta Anatomica. Supplementum
Acta Ant H — Acta Antiqua. Academiae Scientiarum Hungaricae
Acta Anthr Biol — Acta Anthropobiologica
Acta Anthr (Mex) — Acta Anthropologica (Mexico)
Acta Anthropogenet — Acta Anthropogenetica
Acta Arachnol — Acta Arachnologica
Acta Arch — Acta Archaeologica
Acta Archaeol Acad Sci Hung — Acta Archaeologica. Academiae Scientiarum Hungaricae
Acta Archaeol (Budapest) — Acta Archaeologica (Budapest)
Acta Archaeol (Kobenhavn) — Acta Archaeologica (Kobenhavn)
Acta Arch Carp — Acta Archaeologica Carpathica
Acta Arch Lund — Acta Archaeologica Lundensia
Acta Arct — Acta Arctica
Acta Argent Fisiol Fisiopatol — Acta Argentina de Fisiologia y Fisiopatologia
Acta Arith — Acta Arithmetica
Acta Asiat — Acta Asiatica
Acta Astron — Acta Astronomica
Acta Astronaut — Acta Astronautica
Acta Astronom Sinica — Acta Astronomica Sinica
Acta Astron Sin — Acta Astronomica Sinica
Acta Astron Sinica — Acta Astronomica Sinica [*People's Republic of China*]
Acta Astrophys Sinica — Acta Astrophysica Sinica
Acta Audiol Foniat Hispano-Amer — Acta Audiologica y Foniatrica Hispano-Americana
Acta Automat Sinica — Acta Automatica Sinica [*People's Republic of China*]
Acta Belg Arte Med Pharm Mil — Acta Belgica de Arte Medicinali et Pharmaceutica Militari
Acta Biochim — Acta Biochimica
Acta Biochim Biophys Acad Sci Hung — Acta Biochimica et Biophysica. Academiae Scientiarum Hungaricae
Acta Biochim Biophys Sin — Acta Biochimica et Biophysica Sinica
Acta Biochim Biophys Sinica — Acta Biochimica et Biophysica Sinica
Acta Biochim Iran — Acta Biochimica Iranica
Acta Biochim Pol — Acta Biochimica Polonica
Acta Biochim Polon — Acta Biochimica Polonica
Acta Biochim Pol (Trans) — Acta Biochimica Polonica (Translation)

Acta Biochim Sin — Acta Biochimica Sinica
Acta Biol — Acta Biologica
Acta Biol Acad Sci Hung — Acta Biologica. Academiae Scientiarum Hungaricae
Acta Biol Acad Sci Hung Suppl — Acta Biologica. Academiae Scientiarum Hungaricae. Supplementum
Acta Biol (Budapest) — Acta Biologica. Academiae Scientiarum Hungaricae (Budapest)
Acta Biol Cracov Ser Bot — Acta Biologica Cracoviensia. Series Botanica
Acta Biol Cracov Ser Zool — Acta Biologica Cracoviensia. Series Zoologia
Acta Biol Debrecina — Acta Biologica Debrecina
Acta Biol Exper Sinica — Acta Biologiae Experimentalis Sinica
Acta Biol Exp Pol Acad Sci — Acta Biologiae Experimentalis. Polish Academy of Sciences
Acta Biol Exp Sin — Acta Biologiae Experimentalis Sinica
Acta Biol Exp (Warsaw) — Acta Biologiae Experimentalis (Warsaw)
Acta Biol Hung — Acta Biologica. Academiae Scientiarum Hungaricae
Acta Biol Iugosl Ser B Mikrobiol — Acta Biologica Iugoslavica. Serija B. Mikrobiologija
Acta Biol Iugosl Ser C Iugosl Physiol Pharmacol Acta — Acta Biologica Iugoslavica. Serija C. Iugoslavica Physiologica et Pharmacologica Acta
Acta Biol Iugosl Ser E Ichthyol — Acta Biologica Iugoslavica. Serija E. Ichthyologia
Acta Biol Katowice — Acta Biologica Katowice
Acta Biol Latv — Acta Biologica Latvica
Acta Biol Med (Gdansk) — Acta Biologica et Medica (Gdansk)
Acta Biol Med Ger — Acta Biologica et Medica Germanica
Acta Biol Parana — Acta Biologica Paranaense
Acta Biol Venez — Acta Biologica Venezuelica
Acta Biotheor — Acta Biotheoretica [*Leiden*]
Acta Biotheor (Leiden) — Acta Biotheoretica (Leiden)
Acta Borealia A Sci — Acta Borealia. A. Scientia
Acta Bot — Acta Botanica
Acta Bot Acad Sci Hung — Acta Botanica. Academiae Scientiarum Hungaricae
Acta Bot (Budapest) — Acta Botanica. Academiae Scientiarum Hungaricae (Budapest)
Acta Bot Colomb — Acta Botanica Colombiana
Acta Bot Croat — Acta Botanica Croatica
Acta Bot Fenn — Acta Botanica Fennica
Acta Bot Horti Bucur — Acta Botanica Horti Bucurestiensis
Acta Bot Hung — Acta Botanica. Academiae Scientiarum Hungaricae
Acta Bot Hung — Acta Botanica Hungarica
Acta Bot Indica — Acta Botanica Indica
Acta Bot Indica (IN) — Acta Botanica Indica (India)
Acta Bot Inst Bot Univ Zagreb — Acta Botanica. Instituti Botanici. Universitatis Zagrebensis
Acta Bot Isl — Acta Botanica Islandica
Acta Bot Neerl — Acta Botanica Neerlandica
Acta Bot Neerland — Acta Botanica Neerlandica
Acta Bot Sin — Acta Botanica Sinica
Acta Bot Sinica — Acta Botanica Sinica
Acta Bot Taiwan — Acta Botanica Taiwanica
Acta Bot Venez — Acta Botanica Venezuelica
Acta Brev Neerl Physiol — Acta Brevia Neerlandica de Physiologia, Pharmacologia, Microbiologia
Acta Brev Sin — Acta Brevia Sinensia
Acta Cancerol — Acta Cancerologica
Acta Cardiol (Brux) — Acta Cardiologica (Bruxelles)
Acta Cardiol Suppl — Acta Cardiologica. Supplementum [*Bruxelles*]
Acta Chem Fenn — Acta Chemica Fennica [*Finland*]
Acta Chem Mineralog Phys — Acta Chemica, Mineralogica, et Physica
Acta Chem Mineral Phys — Acta Chemica, Mineralogica, et Physica
Acta Chem Scand — Acta Chemica Scandinavica
Acta Chem Scand (B) — Acta Chemica Scandinavica. Series B. Organic Chemistry and Biochemistry
Acta Chem Scand (DK) — Acta Chemica Scandinavica (Denmark)
Acta Chem Scand Ser A — Acta Chemica Scandinavica. Series A. Physical and Inorganic Chemistry
Acta Chem Scand Ser B — Acta Chemica Scandinavica. Series B. Organic Chemistry and Biochemistry
Acta Chem Scand Ser B Org Chem Biochem — Acta Chemica Scandinavica. Series B. Organic Chemistry and Biochemistry
Acta Chim Acad Sci Hung — Acta Chimica. Academiae Scientiarum Hungaricae
Acta Chim Hung — Acta Chimica Hungarica
Acta Chir Acad Sci Hung — Acta Chirurgica. Academiae Scientiarum Hungaricae
Acta Chir Austriaca — Acta Chirurgica Austriaca
Acta Chir Austriaca Suppl — Acta Chirurgica Austriaca. Supplement
Acta Chir Belg — Acta Chirurgica Belgica
Acta Chir Belg Suppl — Acta Chirurgica Belgica. Supplement
Acta Chir Hell — Acta Chirurgica Hellenica
Acta Chir Ital — Acta Chirurgica Italica
Acta Chir Iugosl — Acta Chirurgica Iugoslavica

Acta Chir Orthop Traumatol Cech — Acta Chirurgiae, Orthopaedicae, et Traumatologiae Cechoslovaca
Acta Chir Plast — Acta Chirurgiae Plasticae [*Czechoslovakia*]
Acta Chir Plast (Prague) — Acta Chirurgiae Plasticae (Prague)
Acta Chir Scand — Acta Chirurgica Scandinavica
Acta Chir Scand Suppl — Acta Chirurgica Scandinavica. Supplementum
Acta Ci Compostelana — Acta Cientifica Compostelana
Acta Cienc Indica — Acta Ciencia Indica
Acta Cienc Indica (IN) — Acta Ciencia Indica (India)
Acta Cienc Indica Math — Acta Ciencia Indica. Mathematics
Acta Cienc Indica Physica — Acta Ciencia Indica. Physica
Acta Cienc Indica Ser Chem — Acta Ciencia Indica. Series Chemistry [*India*]
Acta Cienc Indica Ser Math — Acta Ciencia Indica. Series Mathematics [*India*]
Acta Cient — Acta Cientifica
Acta Cient Compostelana — Acta Cientifica Compostelana
Acta Cient Potosina — Acta Cientifica Potosina
Acta Cient Venez — Acta Cientifica Venezolana
Acta Cient Venezolana — Acta Cientifica Venezolana. Asociacion Venezolana para el Avance de la Ciencia
Acta Cient Venez Supl — Acta Cientifica Venezolana. Suplemento [*Venezuela*]
Acta Ci Indica — Acta Ciencia Indica
Acta Cl — Acta Classica
Acta Clin Belg — Acta Clinica Belgica
Acta Clin Belg Suppl — Acta Clinica Belgica. Supplementum
Acta Comment Univ Dorp — Acta et Commentationes Universitatis Dorpatensis
Acta Criminol Med Leg Jpn — Acta Criminologiae Medicinae Legalis Japonica
Acta Cryst — Acta Crystallographica
Acta Crystallogr — Acta Crystallographica
Acta Crystallogr A — Acta Crystallographica. Section A
Acta Crystallogr B — Acta Crystallographica. Section B
Acta Crystallogr Sect A — Acta Crystallographica. Section A. Crystal Physics, Diffraction, Theoretical and General Crystallography [*Denmark*]
Acta Crystallogr Sect B — Acta Crystallographica. Section B. Structural Crystallography and Crystal Chemistry [*Denmark*]
Acta Crystallogr Sect B Struct Crystallogr Cryst Chem — Acta Crystallographica. Section B. Structural Crystallography and Crystal Chemistry
Acta Cryst Sect A — Acta Crystallographica. Section A. Crystal Physics, Diffraction, Theoretical and General Crystallography
Acta Cuyana Ing — Acta Cuyana de Ingenieria
Acta Cybernet — Acta Cybernetica
Acta Cytol — Acta Cytologica
Acta Cytol (Baltimore) — Acta Cytologica (Baltimore)
Acta Davos — Acta Davosiana
Acta Dermatol — Acta Dermatologica [*Japan*]
Acta Dermatol (Kyoto) (Engl Ed) — Acta Dermatologica (Kyoto) (English Edition)
Acta Dermat Vener — Acta Dermato-Venereologica
Acta Derm-Venereol — Acta Dermato-Venereologica
Acta Derm-Venereol (Stockh) — Acta Dermato-Venereologica (Stockholm)
Acta Derm-Venereol Suppl — Acta Dermato-Venereologica. Supplementum [*Stockholm*]
Acta Derm-Venereol Suppl (Stockh) — Acta Dermato-Venereologica. Supplementum (Stockholm)
Acta Diabetol Lat — Acta Diabetologica Latina
Acta Eccl — Acta Ecclesiastica
Acta Electron — Acta Electronica
Acta Embryol Exp — Acta Embryologiae Experimentalis [*Later, Acta Embryologiae et Morphologiae Experimentalis*] [*Palermo*]
Acta Embryol Exp (Palermo) — Acta Embryologiae Experimentalis [*Later, Acta Embryologiae et Morphologiae Experimentalis*] (Palermo)
Acta Embryol Morphol Exp — Acta Embryologiae et Morphologiae Experimentalis
Acta Endocrinol — Acta Endocrinologica
Acta Endocrinol (Copenh) — Acta Endocrinologica (Copenhagen)
Acta Endocrinol Cubana — Acta Endocrinologica Cubana
Acta Endocrinol Panam — Acta Endocrinologica Panamericana
Acta Endocrinol Suppl — Acta Endocrinologica. Supplementum [*Copenhagen*]
Acta Endocrinol Suppl (Copenh) — Acta Endocrinologica. Supplementum (Copenhagen)
Acta Energ Solaris Sin — Acta Energiae Solaris Sinica [*People's Republic of China*]
Acta Ent — Acta Entomologica
Acta Ent Bohemoslov — Acta Entomologica Bohemoslovaca
Acta Ent Fenn — Acta Entomologica Fennica
Acta Ent Jugosl — Acta Entomologica Jugoslavica
Acta Ent Litu — Acta Entomologica Lituanica
Acta Ent Mus Natn (Prague) — Acta Entomologica. Musei Nationalis (Prague)
Acta Entomol Bohemoslov — Acta Entomologica Bohemoslovaca
Acta Entomol Fenn — Acta Entomologica Fennica
Acta Entomol Jugosl — Acta Entomologica Jugoslavica
Acta Entomol Litu — Acta Entomologica Lituanica
Acta Entomol Sin — Acta Entomologica Sinica

Acta Entomol Sinica — Acta Entomologica Sinica
Acta Ent (Prag) — Acta Entomologica. Musei Nationalis (Prague)
Acta Erudit — Acta Eruditorum
Acta Ethn — Acta Ethnologica
Acta Ethnog Hung — Acta Ethnographica. Academiae Scientiarum Hungaricae
Acta Ethnogr Acad Sci Hung — Acta Ethnographica. Academiae Scientiarum Hungaricae
Acta Ethnogr (Budapest) — Acta Ethnographica (Budapest)
Acta Eur Fertil — Acta Europaea Fertilitatis
Acta Fac Med Fluminensis — Acta Facultatis Medicae Fluminensis
Acta Fac Med Univ Brun — Acta Facultatis Medicae Universitatis Brunensis
Acta Fac Pharm Bohemoslov — Acta Facultatis Pharmaceuticae Bohemoslovenicae
Acta Fac Pharm Univ Comenianae — Acta Facultatis Pharmaceuticae Universitatis Comenianae
Acta Fac Rerum Nat Univ Comenianae Anthropol — Acta Facultatis Rerum Naturalium Universitatis Comenianae. Anthropologica
Acta Fac Rerum Nat Univ Comenianae Bot — Acta Facultatis Rerum Naturalium Universitatis Comenianae. Botanica
Acta Fac Rerum Nat Univ Comenianae Chim — Acta Facultatis Rerum Naturalium Universitatis Comenianae. Chimia
Acta Fac Rerum Nat Univ Comenianae Form Prot Nat (CS) — Acta Facultatis Rerum Naturalium Universitatis Comenianae. Formatio et Protectio Naturae (Czechoslovakia)
Acta Fac Rerum Nat Univ Comenianae Genet — Acta Facultatis Rerum Naturalium Universitatis Comenianae. Genetica
Acta Fac Rerum Nat Univ Comenianae Microbiol — Acta Facultatis Rerum Naturalium Universitatis Comenianae. Microbiologia
Acta Fac Rerum Nat Univ Comenianae Phys — Acta Facultatis Rerum Naturalium Universitatis Comenianae. Physica
Acta Fac Rerum Nat Univ Comenianae Physiol Plant — Acta Facultatis Rerum Naturalium Universitatis Comenianae. Physiologia Plantarum
Acta Fac Rerum Nat Univ Comenianae Zool — Acta Facultatis Rerum Naturalium Universitatis Comenianae. Zoologia
Acta Fac Rerum Natur Univ Comenian Math — Acta Facultatis Rerum Naturalium Universitatis Comenianae. Mathematica
Acta Faun Entomol Mus Natl Pragae — Acta Faunistica Entomologica. Musei Nationalis Pragae
Acta For Fenn — Acta Forestalia Fennica
Acta Fytotech — Acta Fytotechnica
ActaG — Acta Germanica [*Capetown*]
Acta Gastro-Enterol Belg — Acta Gastro-Enterologica Belgica
Acta Gastroenterol Latinoam — Acta Gastroenterologica Latinoamericana
Acta Genet Med Gemellol — Acta Geneticae, Medicae, et Gemellologiae
Acta Genet Sin — Acta Genetica Sinica
Acta Genet Stat Med — Acta Genetica et Statistica Medica
Acta Geobot Barc — Acta Geobotanica Barcinonensia
Acta Geod Geophys Montan — Acta Geodaetica, Geophysica, et Montanistica
Acta Geod Geophys Montanistica — Acta Geodaetica, Geophysica, et Montanistica [*Hungary*]
Acta Geogr — Acta Geographica
Acta Geogr Lodz — Acta Geographica Lodziensia
Acta Geogr Sinica — Acta Geographica Sinica
Acta Geol Acad Sci Hung — Acta Geologica. Academiae Scientiarum Hungaricae
Acta Geol Geogr Univ Comenianae Geol — Acta Geologica et Geographica. Universitatis Comenianae. Geologica
Acta Geol Hisp — Acta Geologica Hispanica
Acta Geol Hung — Acta Geologica. Academiae Scientiarum Hungaricae
Acta Geol Lilloana — Acta Geologica Lilloana
Acta Geol Pol — Acta Geologica Polonica
Acta Geol Sin — Acta Geologica Sinica
Acta Geol Sin (Engl Transl) — Acta Geologica Sinica (English Translation)
Acta Geol Sinica — Acta Geologica Sinica
Acta Geol Taiwan — Acta Geologica Taiwanica
Acta Geol Taiwanica — Acta Geologica Taiwanica
Acta Geophys Pol — Acta Geophysica Polonica
Acta Geophys Polonica — Acta Geophysica Polonica
Acta Geophys Sin — Acta Geophysica Sinica
Acta Gerontol — Acta Gerontologica
Acta Gerontol Geriatr Belg — Acta Gerontologica et Geriatrica Belgica
Acta Gerontol Jpn — Acta Gerontologica Japonica
Act Agron H — Acta Agronomica. Academiae Scientiarum Hungaricae [*Budapest*]
Acta Gynaecol Obstet Hispano Lusitana — Acta Gynaecologica et Obstetrica. Hispano Lusitana [*Portugal*]
Acta Haematol — Acta Haematologica
Acta Haematol (Basel) — Acta Haematologica (Basel)
Acta Haematol Jpn — Acta Haematologica Japonica
Acta Haematol Pol — Acta Haematologica Polonica
Acta Helvet — Acta Helvetica Physico-Mathematico-Botanico-Medica
Acta Hepato-Gastroenterol — Acta Hepato-Gastroenterologica [*Stuttgart/New York*]
Acta Hepato-Gastroenterol (Stuttg) — Acta Hepato-Gastroenterologica (Stuttgart/New York)

Acta Hepato-Splenol — Acta Hepato-Splenologica [*West Germany*]
Acta Herpetol Jpn — Acta Herpetologica Japonica
Acta Hist Art — Magyar Tudomanyos Akademia. Acta Historiae Artium
Acta Hist Leopold — Acta Historica Leopoldina
Acta Histochem — Acta Histochemica
Acta Histochem Cytochem — Acta Histochemica et Cytochemica
Acta Histochem (Jena) — Acta Histochemica (Jena)
Acta Histochem Supplementb — Acta Histochemica. Supplementband [*Jena*]
Acta Histochem Suppl (Jena) — Acta Histochemica. Supplementband (Jena)
Acta Hist Rerum Natur Nec Non Tech — Acta Historiae Rerum Naturalium Nec Non Technicarum
Acta Hist Sci Nat Med — Acta Historica Scientiarum, Naturalium, et Medicinalium [*Odense*]
Acta Hist Sci Nat Med (Odense) — Acta Historica Scientiarum, Naturalium, et Medicinalium (Odense)
Acta Hort — Acta Horticulturalia [*Peking*]
Acta Hortic (Peking) — Acta Horticulturalia (Peking)
Acta Hortic (The Hague) — Acta Horticulturae (The Hague)
Acta Horti Gotob — Acta Horti Gotoburgensis
Acta Horti Gotoburg — Acta Horti Gotoburgensis
Acta Hosp — Acta Hospitalia
Acta Human Sci Univ Sangio Kyotien Natur Sci Ser — Acta Humanistica et Scientifica. Universitatis Sangio Kyotiensis. Natural Science Series
Acta Humboldtiana Ser Geog et Ethnograph — Acta Humboldtiana. Series Geographica et Ethnographica
Acta Hydrobiol — Acta Hydrobiologica
Acta Hydrobiol Sin — Acta Hydrobiologica Sinica [*People's Republic of China*]
Acta Hydrochim Hydrobiol — Acta Hydrochimica et Hydrobiologica [*East Germany*]
Acta Hydrophys — Acta Hydrophysica [*East Germany*]
Acta Hydrophys (Berl) — Acta Hydrophysica (Deutsche Akademie der Wissenschaften zu Berlin. Zentralinstitut Physik der Erde. Selbstaendige Abteilung Physikalische Hydrographie)
Acta Hymenopt (Tokyo) — Acta Hymenopterologica (Tokyo)
Acta Iber Radiol-Cancerol — Acta Iberica Radiologia-Cancerologica
Acta Ichthyol Piscatoria — Acta Ichthyologica et Piscatoria
Acta Inf — Acta Informatica
Acta Inform — Acta Informatica
Acta Informat — Acta Informatica
Acta Inst Anesthesiol — Acta. Institut d'Anesthesiologie
Acta Inst For Zvolenensis — Acta Instituti Forestalis Zvolenensis
Acta Inst For Zvolenensis Vysk Ustav Lesn Hospod — Acta Instituti Forestalis Zvolenensis. Vyskumny Ustav Lesneho Hospodarstva
Acta Inst Psychol Univ Zagrabiensis — Acta Instituti Psychologici Universitatis Zagrabiensis
Acta Isot — Acta Isotopica
Acta Jur Acad Sci Hung — Acta Juridica. Academiae Scientiarum Hungaricae
Acta Jur (Budapest) — Acta Juridica (Budapest)
Acta Jur (Cape Town) — Acta Juridica (Cape Town)
Acta Juridica — Acta Juridica. Academiae Scientiarum Hungaricae
Acta Juridica Acad Sci Hungaricae — Acta Juridica. Academiae Scientiarum Hungaricae
Acta Krausi Cuad Inst Nac Microbiol (B Aires) — Acta Krausi. Cuaderno del Instituto Nacional de Microbiologia (Buenos Aires)
Acta Krausi Cuad Inst Nac Microbiol (Buenos Aires) — Acta Krausi. Cuaderno del Instituto Nacional de Microbiologia (Buenos Aires)
ActaL — Acta Latgalica
Acta Leiden — Acta Leidensia
Acta Leiden Inst Trop Geneeskd — Acta Leidensia. Instituut voor Tropische Geneeskunde
Acta Leprol (Geneve) — Acta Leprologica (Geneve)
Acta Limnol Indica — Acta Limnologica Indica
Acta Linguist — Acta Linguistica
Acta Linguist Hung — Acta Linguistica. Academiae Scientiarum Hungaricae
Acta Lit Hung — Acta Litteraria. Academiae Scientiarum Hungaricae
Act Allerg — Acta Allergologica
Acta Lund — Acta Universitatis Lundensis
ACTA Mag — ACTA [*Art Craft Teachers Association*] Magazine
Acta Manilana A — Acta Manilana. Series A. Natural and Applied Sciences
Acta Manilana Ser A — Acta Manilana. Series A
Acta Manilana Ser A Nat Appl Sci — Acta Manilana. Series A. Natural and Applied Sciences
Acta Marx-Lenin — Acta Marxistica-Leninistica
Acta Math — Acta Mathematica
Acta Math Acad Sci Hungar — Acta Mathematica. Academiae Scientiarum Hungaricae
Acta Math Appl Sin — Acta Mathematicae Applicatae Sinica
Acta Math Appl Sinica — Acta Mathematicae Applicatae Sinica
Acta Math Sci — Acta Mathematica Scientia
Acta Math Sin — Acta Mathematica Sinica
Acta Math Sinica — Acta Mathematica Sinica
Acta Math Univ Comenian — Acta Mathematica. Universitatis Comenianae
Acta Math Vietnam — Acta Mathematica Vietnamica
Acta Mech — Acta Mechanica
Acta Mech Sin — Acta Mechanica Sinica [*People's Republic of China*]

Acta Mech Sinica — Acta Mechanica Sinica
Acta Mech Solida Sin — Acta Mechanica Solida Sinica
Acta Med Acad Sci Hung — Acta Medica. Academiae Scientiarum Hungaricae
Acta Med Austriaca — Acta Medica Austriaca
Acta Med Austriaca Suppl — Acta Medica Austriaca. Supplement
Acta Med Biol — Acta Medica et Biologica
Acta Med Bulg — Acta Medica Bulgarica. Medicina i Fizkultura
Acta Med Costarric — Acta Medica Costarricense
Acta Med (Fukuoka) — Acta Medica (Fukuoka)
Acta Med Hidalg — Acta Medica Hidalguense
Acta Med Hist Patav — Acta Medicae Historiae Patavina
Acta Med Hondur — Acta Medica Hondurena
Acta Medicotech — Acta Medicotechnica
Acta Med Iran — Acta Medica Iranica
Acta Med Iugosl — Acta Medica Iugoslavica
Acta Med Iugosl (Eng Transl) — Acta Medica Iugoslavica (English Translation)
Acta Med Keijo — Acta Medicinalia in Keijo
Acta Med Leg Soc — Acta Medicinae Legalis et Socialis [*Liege*]
Acta Med Leg Soc (Liege) — Acta Medicinae Legalis et Socialis (Liege)
Acta Med Medianae — Acta Medica Medianae
Acta Med (Mex) — Acta Medica (Mexico)
Acta Med Nagasaki — Acta Medica Nagasakiensia
Acta Med Okayama — Acta Medica Okayama
Acta Med Orient — Acta Medica Orientalia
Acta Med Pat — Acta Medica Patavina
Acta Med Pata — Acta Medica Patavina
Acta Med Peru — Acta Medica Peruana
Acta Med Philipp — Acta Medica Philippina
Acta Med Pol — Acta Medica Polona
Acta Med (Rio De Janeiro) — Acta Medica (Rio De Janeiro)
Acta Med Roman — Acta Medica Romana
Acta Med Romana — Acta Medica Romana
Acta Med Scand — Acta Medica Scandinavica
Acta Med Scand Suppl — Acta Medica Scandinavica. Supplementum
Acta Med Tenerife — Acta Medica de Tenerife
Acta Med Turc — Acta Medica Turcica
Acta Med Turc Suppl — Acta Medica Turcica. Supplementum
Acta Med Univ Kagoshima — Acta Medica Universitatis Kagoshimaensis
Acta Med Venez — Acta Medica Venezolana
Acta Med Vet — Acta Medica Veterinaria
Acta Med Vet (Madr) — Acta Medica Veterinaria (Madrid)
Acta Med Vietnam — Acta Medica Vietnamica
Acta Metall — Acta Metallurgica
Acta Metall Sin — Acta Metallurgica Sinica
Acta Meteorol Sin — Acta Meteorologica Sinica
Acta Met Sin — Acta Metallurgica Sinica
Acta Mex Cienc y Tecnol — Acta Mexicana de Ciencia y Tecnologia
Acta Mexicana Cienc Tecn — Acta Mexicana de Ciencia y Tecnologia. Instituto Politecnico Nacional
Acta Mexicana Ci Tecn — Acta Mexicana de Ciencia y Tecnologia
Acta Microbiol — Acta Microbiologica
Acta Microbiol Acad Sci Hung — Acta Microbiologica. Academiae Scientiarum Hungaricae
Acta Microbiol Bulg — Acta Microbiologica Bulgarica
Acta Microbiol Hell — Acta Microbiologica Hellenica
Acta Microbiol Hung — Acta Microbiologica Hungarica
Acta Microbiol Pol — Acta Microbiologica Polonica
Acta Microbiol Polon — Acta Microbiologica Polonica
Acta Microbiol Pol Ser A — Acta Microbiologica Polonica. Series A. Microbiologia Generalis
Acta Microbiol Pol Ser A Microbiol Gen — Acta Microbiologica Polonica. Series A. Microbiologia Generalis
Acta Microbiol Pol Ser B — Acta Microbiologica Polonica. Series B. Microbiologia Applicata
Acta Microbiol Pol Ser B Microbiol Appl — Acta Microbiologica Polonica. Series B. Microbiologia Applicata
Acta Microbiol Sin — Acta Microbiologica Sinica
Acta Microbiol Sinica — Acta Microbiologica Sinica
Acta Microbiol Virol Immunol — Acta Microbiologica, Virologica, et Immunologica
Acta Microbiol Virol Immunol (Sofiia) — Acta Microbiologica, Virologica, et Immunologica (Sofiia)
Acta Mineral-Petrogr — Acta Mineralogica-Petrographica
Acta Mineral-Petrogr (Szeged) — Acta Mineralogica-Petrographica (Acta Universitatis Szegediensis)
Acta Mont — Acta Montana
Acta Moravs Muz — Acta Moravske Muzeum
Acta Morphol Acad Sci Hung — Acta Morphologica. Academiae Scientiarum Hungaricae
Acta Morphol Acad Sci Hung Suppl — Acta Morphologica. Academiae Scientiarum Hungaricae. Supplementum
Acta Morphol Neerl-Scand — Acta Morphologica Neerlando-Scandinavica
Acta Mus — Acta Musicologica
Acta Mus Hist Nat — Acta Musei Historiae Naturalis

Acta Mus Horti Bot Bohemiae Borealis Hist Nat — Acta Musei et Horti Botanici Bohemiae Borealis. Historia Naturalis
Acta Music — Acta Musicologica
Acta Mus Macedonici Sci Nat — Acta Musei Macedonici. Scientiarum Naturalium
Acta Mus Maced Sci Nat — Acta Musei Macedonici. Scientiarum Naturalium
Acta Mus Morav — Acta Musei Moraviae
Acta Mus Morav Sci Natur — Acta Musei Moraviae. Scientiae Naturales
Acta Mus Morav Sci Soc — Acta Musei Moraviae. Scientiae Sociales
Acta Mus Nap — Acta Musei Napocensis
Acta Mus Napocensis — Acta Musei Napocensis
Acta Mus Natl Pragae Ser B Hist Nat — Acta Musei Nationalis Pragae. Series B. Historia Naturalis
Acta Mus Silesiae Ser A Sci Nat — Acta Musei Silesiae. Series A. Scientiae Naturales
Acta Mycol — Acta Mycologica
Act Anae Sc — Acta Anaesthesiologica Scandinavica
Acta Nat Isl — Acta Naturalia Islandica
Act Anatom — Acta Anatomica
Acta Neerl Morphol Norm Pathol — Acta Neerlandica Morphologiae Normalis et Pathologicae
Acta Neurobiol Exp — Acta Neurobiologiae Experimentalis
Acta Neurobiol Exp Suppl — Acta Neurobiologiae Experimentalis. Supplementum
Acta Neurobiol Exp (Warsaw) — Acta Neurobiologiae Experimentalis (Warsaw)
Acta Neurobiol Exp (Warsz) — Acta Neurobiologiae Experimentalis (Warszawa)
Acta Neurochir — Acta Neurochirurgica
Acta Neurochir Suppl — Acta Neurochirurgica. Supplementum [*Wien*]
Acta Neurochir Suppl (Wien) — Acta Neurochirurgica. Supplementum (Wien)
Acta Neurochir (Wien) — Acta Neurochirurgica (Wien)
Acta Neurol — Acta Neurologica
Acta Neurol Belg — Acta Neurologica Belgica
Acta Neurol Latinoam — Acta Neurologica Latinoamericana
Acta Neurol Latinoamer — Acta Neurologica Latinoamericana
Acta Neurol (Naples) — Acta Neurologica (Naples)
Acta Neurol (Napoli) — Acta Neurologica (Napoli)
Acta Neurol Psychiatr Belg — Acta Neurologica et Psychiatrica Belgica
Acta Neurol Quad — Acta Neurologica. Quaderni
Acta Neurol Scand — Acta Neurologica Scandinavica
Acta Neurol Scand Suppl — Acta Neurologica Scandinavica. Supplementum
Acta Neuropathol — Acta Neuropathologica
Acta Neuropathol (Berl) — Acta Neuropathologica (Berlin)
Acta Neuropathol Suppl — Acta Neuropathologica. Supplement [*Berlin*]
Acta Neuropathol Suppl (Berl) — Acta Neuropathologica. Supplement (Berlin)
Acta Neuropsiquiat Argent — Acta Neuropsiquiatrica Argentina
Acta Neuroveg — Acta Neurovegetativa
Acta Neuroveg Suppl — Acta Neurovegetativa. Supplementum
Acta Nipp Med Trop — Acta Nipponica Medicinae Tropicalis
Acta Nippon Med Trop — Acta Nipponica Medicinae Tropicalis
Act An-Path — Actualites Anatomo-Pathologiques
ActAntHung — Acta Antiqua Hungarica
Act Antiq H — Acta Antiqua. Academiae Scientiarum Hungaricae
Acta Num — Acta Numismatica
Acta Nutr Sin — Acta Nutrimenta Sinica
Acta O — Acta Orientalia
Acta Obstet Ginecol Hisp-Lusit — Acta Obstetrica y Ginecologica Hispano-Lusitana
Acta Obstet Ginecol Hisp-Lusit Supl — Acta Obstetrica y Ginecologica Hispano-Lusitana. Suplemento
Acta Obstet Gynaecol Jpn — Acta Obstetrica et Gynaecologica Japonica
Acta Obstet Gynaecol Jpn (Engl Ed) — Acta Obstetrica et Gynaecologica Japonica (English Edition)
Acta Obstet Gynecol Scand — Acta Obstetricia et Gynecologica Scandinavica
Acta Obstet Gynecol Scand Suppl — Acta Obstetricia et Gynecologica Scandinavica. Supplement
Acta Oceanogr Taiwan — Acta Oceanographica Taiwanica
Acta Odont — Acta Odontologica
Acta Odontol Scand — Acta Odontologica Scandinavica
Acta Odontol Scand Suppl — Acta Odontologica Scandinavica. Supplementum
Acta Odontol Venez — Acta Odontologica Venezolana
Acta Oecol-Oecol Plant — Acta Oecologica-Oecologica Plantarum
Acta Oecon — Acta Oeconomica [*Budapest*]
Acta Oeconomica — Acta Oeconomica. Academiae Scientiarum Hungaricae
Acta Oncol — Acta Oncologica [*Madrid*]
Acta Oncol Bras — Acta Oncologica Brasileira
Acta Oncol (Madr) — Acta Oncologica (Madrid)
Acta Oper-Oecon — Acta Operativo-Oeconomica
Acta Ophthalmol — Acta Ophthalmologica
Acta Ophthalmol (Copenh) — Acta Ophthalmologica (Copenhagen)
Acta Ophthalmol Iugosl — Acta Ophthalmologica Iugoslavica
Acta Ophthalmol Suppl — Acta Ophthalmologica. Supplementum [*Kobenhavn*]
Acta Ophthalmol Suppl (Copenh) — Acta Ophthalmologica. Supplementum (Copenhagen)

Acta Or — Acta Orientalia
Acta Or (B) — Acta Orientalia. Academiae Scientiarum Hungaricae (Budapest)
Acta Orient — Acta Orientalia
Acta ORL Belg — Acta Oto-Rhino-Laryngologica Belgica
Acta ORL Espan — Acta Otorinolaringologica Espanola
Acta Ornith — Acta Ornithologica
Acta Ornithol (Engl Transl) — Acta Ornithologica (English Translation)
Acta Ornithol (Warsaw) — Acta Ornithologica (Warsaw)
Acta Orthop Belg — Acta Orthopaedica Belgica
Acta Orthop Scand — Acta Orthopaedica Scandinavica
Acta Orthop Scand Suppl — Acta Orthopaedica Scandinavica. Supplementum
Acta Oto-Laryngol — Acta Oto-Laryngologica
Acta Otolaryngol (Stockh) — Acta Otolaryngologica (Stockholm)
Acta Oto-Laryngol Suppl — Acta Oto-Laryngologica. Supplementum
Acta Otolaryngol Suppl (Stockh) — Acta Otolaryngologica. Supplement (Stockholm)
Acta Oto-Rhino-Lar Belg — Acta Oto-Rhino-Laryngologica Belgica
Acta Oto-Rhino-Laryngol Belg — Acta Oto-Rhino-Laryngologica Belgica
Acta Oto-Rino-Laringol Esp — Acta Oto-Rino-Laringologica Espanola
Acta Oto-Rino-Laringol Ibero-Am — Acta Oto-Rino-Laringologica Ibero-Americana
Acta Paed Hung — Acta Paediatrica. Academiae Scientiarum Hungaricae
Acta Paediatr — Acta Paediatrica
Acta Paediatr Acad Sci Hung — Acta Paediatrica. Academiae Scientiarum Hungaricae
Acta Paediatr Belg — Acta Paediatrica Belgica
Acta Paediatr Jpn (Overseas Ed) — Acta Paediatrica Japonica (Overseas Edition)
Acta Paediatr Lat — Acta Paediatrica Latina
Acta Paediatr Scand — Acta Paediatrica Scandinavica
Acta Paediatr Scand Suppl — Acta Paediatrica Scandinavica. Supplementum
Acta Paediatr Sin — Acta Paediatrica Sinica
Acta Paediatr (Stockholm) — Acta Paediatrica (Stockholm)
Acta Paediatr Suppl — Acta Paediatrica. Supplement
Acta Paediat (Uppsala) — Acta Paediatrica (Uppsala)
Acta Paed Lat — Acta Paediatrica Latina
Acta Paedopsychiat — Acta Paedopsychiatrica
Acta Paedopsychiatr — Acta Paedopsychiatrica
Acta Paedopsychiatr (Basel) — Acta Paedopsychiatrica (Basel)
Acta Palaeobot — Acta Palaeobotanica
Acta Palaeontol Pol — Acta Palaeontologica Polonica
Acta Palaeontol Sin — Acta Palaeontologica Sinica
Acta Paracels — Acta Paracelsica
Acta Parasitol Iugosl — Acta Parasitologica Iugoslavica
Acta Parasitol Lith — Acta Parasitologica Lithuanica
Acta Parasitol Pol — Acta Parasitologica Polonica
Acta Pathol Jpn — Acta Pathologica Japonica
Acta Pathol Microbiol Immunol Scand Sect A — Acta Pathologica, Microbiologica, et Immunologica Scandinavica. Section A
Acta Pathol Microbiol Immunol Scand Sect A Suppl — Acta Pathologica, Microbiologica, et Immunologica Scandinavica. Section A. Supplement
Acta Pathol Microbiol Immunol Scand Sect B Microbiol — Acta Pathologica, Microbiologica, et Immunologica Scandinavica. Section B. Microbiology
Acta Pathol Microbiol Immunol Scand Sect C Immunol — Acta Pathologica, Microbiologica, et Immunologica Scandinavica. Section C. Immunology
Acta Pathol Microbiol Scand — Acta Pathologica et Microbiologica Scandinavica
Acta Pathol Microbiol Scand (A) — Acta Pathologica et Microbiologica Scandinavica. Section A
Acta Pathol Microbiol Scand (B) — Acta Pathologica et Microbiologica Scandinavica. Section B
Acta Pathol Microbiol Scand (C) — Acta Pathologica et Microbiologica Scandinavica. Section C
Acta Pathol Microbiol Scand Sect A — Acta Pathologica et Microbiologica Scandinavica. Section A
Acta Pathol Microbiol Scand Sect A Pathol — Acta Pathologica et Microbiologica Scandinavica. Section A. Pathology
Acta Pathol Microbiol Scand Sect A Suppl — Acta Pathologica et Microbiologica Scandinavica. Section A. Supplement
Acta Pathol Microbiol Scand Sect B — Acta Pathologica et Microbiologica Scandinavica. Section B
Acta Pathol Microbiol Scand Sect B Microbiol — Acta Pathologica et Microbiologica Scandinavica. Section B. Microbiology
Acta Pathol Microbiol Scand Sect B Microbiol Immunol — Acta Pathologica et Microbiologica Scandinavica. Section B. Microbiology and Immunology
Acta Pathol Microbiol Scand Sect B Suppl — Acta Pathologica et Microbiologica Scandinavica. Section B. Supplement
Acta Pathol Microbiol Scand Sect C — Acta Pathologica et Microbiologica Scandinavica. Section C
Acta Pathol Microbiol Scand Sect C Immunol — Acta Pathologica et Microbiologica Scandinavica. Section C. Immunology
Acta Pathol Microbiol Scand Suppl — Acta Pathologica et Microbiologica Scandinavica. Supplementum

Acta Pathol Microbiol Sect A — Acta Pathologica et Microbiologica Scandinavica. Section A. Pathology
Acta Ped Esp — Acta Pediatrica Espanola
Acta Pediatr Esp — Acta Pediatrica Espanola
Acta Pedol Sin — Acta Pedologica Sinica
Acta Pedol Sinica — Acta Pedologica Sinica
Acta Pet Sin — Acta Petrolei Sinica
Acta Phaenol — Acta Phaenologica
Acta Pharm — Acta Pharmaceutica
Acta Pharmaceut Jugoslav — Acta Pharmaceutica Jugoslavica
Acta Pharmacol Sin — Acta Pharmacologica Sinica
Acta Pharmacol Toxicol — Acta Pharmacologica et Toxicologica
Acta Pharmacol Toxicol (Copenh) — Acta Pharmacologica et Toxicologica (Copenhagen)
Acta Pharmacol Toxicol Suppl — Acta Pharmacologica et Toxicologica. Supplementum
Acta Pharmac Tox — Acta Pharmacologica et Toxicologica
Acta Pharm Hung — Acta Pharmaceutica Hungarica
Acta Pharm Int — Acta Pharmaceutica Internationalia
Acta Pharm Iugosl — Acta Pharmaceutica Iugoslavica
Acta Pharm Jugosl — Acta Pharmaceutica Jugoslavica
Acta Pharm Sin — Acta Pharmaceutica Sinica
Acta Pharm Sinica — Acta Pharmaceutica Sinica [*People's Republic of China*]
Acta Pharm Suec — Acta Pharmaceutica Suecica
Acta Pharm Tox — Acta Pharmacologica et Toxicologica
Acta Phil Fennica — Acta Philosophica Fennica
Acta Philol Scand — Acta Philologica Scandinavica
Acta Philos Fenn — Acta Philosophica Fennica
Acta Phys Acad Sci Hung — Acta Physica. Academiae Scientiarum Hungaricae
Acta Phys Austriaca — Acta Physica Austriaca
Acta Phys Austriaca Suppl — Acta Physica Austriaca. Supplementum
Acta Phys Chem — Acta Physica et Chemica
Acta Phys Chem Univ Szeged — Acta Physica et Chemica. Nova Series. Acta Universitatis Szegediensis
Acta Phys Chim (Debrecina) — Acta Physica et Chimica (Debrecina) [*Hungary*]
Acta Phys Hung — Acta Physica Hungarica
Acta Phy Sin Abstr — Acta Physica Sinica. Abstracts
Acta Physiochim — Acta Physiochimica
Acta Physiol Acad Sci Hung — Acta Physiologica. Academiae Scientiarum Hungaricae
Acta Physiol Hung — Acta Physiologica. Academiae Scientiarum Hungaricae
Acta Physiol Hung — Acta Physiologica Hungarica
Acta Physiol Lat Am — Acta Physiologica Latino Americana
Acta Physiol Lat Am (Supl) — Acta Physiologica Latino Americana. Suplemento
Acta Physiol Latinoam — Acta Physiologica Latinoamericana [*Argentina*]
Acta Physiol Pharmacol Bulg — Acta Physiologica et Pharmacologica Bulgarica
Acta Physiol Pharmacol Latinoam — Acta Physiologica et Pharmacologica Latinoamericana
Acta Physiol Pharmacol Neerl — Acta Physiologica et Pharmacologica Neerlandica
Acta Physiol Pol — Acta Physiologica Polonica
Acta Physiol Pol (Engl Transl) — Acta Physiologica Polonica (English Translation)
Acta Physiol Pol Supl — Acta Physiologica Polonica. Suplement [*Poland*]
Acta Physiol Pol (Transl) — Acta Physiologica Polonica (Translation)
Acta Physiol Scand — Acta Physiologica Scandinavica
Acta Physiol Scand Suppl — Acta Physiologica Scandinavica. Supplementum
Acta Physiol Sin — Acta Physiologica Sinica
Acta Phys Pol — Acta Physica Polonica
Acta Phys Pol A — Acta Physica Polonica. Series A
Acta Phys Pol B — Acta Physica Polonica. Series B
Acta Phys Polon A — Acta Physica Polonica. Series A [*Warsaw*]
Acta Phys Polon B — Acta Physica Polonica. Series B
Acta Phys Sin — Acta Physica Sinica
Acta Phys Sinica — Acta Physica Sinica
Acta Phys Slov — Acta Physica Slovaca
Acta Phys Slovaca — Acta Physica Slovaca
Acta Phys Univ Comenianae — Acta Physica Universitatis Comenianae
Acta Phytochim — Acta Phytochimica
Acta Phytogeogr Suec — Acta Phytogeographica Suecica
Acta Phytomed — Acta Phytomedica
Acta Phytopathol — Acta Phytopathologica
Acta Phytopathol Acad Sci Hung — Acta Phytopathologica. Academiae Scientiarum Hungaricae
Acta Phytopathol (Budapest) — Acta Phytopathologica (Budapest)
Acta Phytopathol Sinica — Acta Phytopathologica Sinica
Acta Phytophylacica Sin — Acta Phytophylacica Sinica
Acta Phytophyl Sinica — Acta Phytophylacica Sinica
Acta Phytophysiol Sinica — Acta Phytophysiologica Sinica
Acta Phytotaxon Barc — Acta Phytotaxonomica Barcinonensia
Acta Phytotaxon Geobot — Acta Phytotaxonomica et Geobotanica
Acta Phytotaxon Sin — Acta Phytotaxonomica Sinica

Acta Phytother — Acta Phytotherapeutica
Acta Polit — Acta Politica
Acta Politec Mex — Acta Politecnica Mexicana
Acta Pol Mar — Acta Poloniae Maritima
Acta Pol Pharm — Acta Poloniae Pharmaceutica
Acta Pol Pharm (Engl Transl) — Acta Poloniae Pharmaceutica (English Translation)
Acta Pol Pharm (Transl) — Acta Poloniae Pharmaceutica (English Translation)
Acta Polym — Acta Polymerica [*East Germany*]
Acta Polytech Chem Incl Metall Ser — Acta Polytechnica. Chemistry Including Metallurgy Series [*Sweden*]
Acta Polytech III — Acta Polytechnica. Series III
Acta Polytech IV (Prague) — Acta Polytechnica. Rada IV. Technicko-Teoreticka (Prague)
Acta Polytech Prace CVUT — Acta Polytechnica. Prace CVUT v Praze
Acta Polytech Rada IV Tech-Teor — Acta Polytechnica. Rada IV. Technicko-Teoreticka
Acta Polytech Scand — Acta Polytechnica Scandinavica
Acta Polytech Scand Appl Phys Ser — Acta Polytechnica Scandinavica. Applied Physics Series [*Finland*]
Acta Polytech Scand Chem Incl Metall Ser — Acta Polytechnica Scandinavica. Chemistry Including Metallurgy Series
Acta Polytech Scand Chem Technol Metall Ser — Acta Polytechnica Scandinavica. Chemical Technology and Metallurgy Series
Acta Polytech Scand Civ Eng Build Constr Ser — Acta Polytechnica Scandinavica. Civil Engineering and Building Construction Series [*Sweden*]
Acta Polytech Scand Civ Eng Build Constru Ser — Acta Polytechnica Scandinavica. Civil Engineering and Building Construction Series
Acta Polytech Scand Elec Eng Ser — Acta Polytechnica Scandinavica. Electrical Engineering Series
Acta Polytech Scand Electr Ser — Acta Polytechnica Scandinavica. Electrical Series
Acta Polytech Scand Math Comput Mach Ser — Acta Polytechnica Scandinavica. Mathematics and Computing Machinery Series [*Finland*]
Acta Polytech Scand Math and Comput Mach Ser — Acta Polytechnica Scandinavica. Mathematics and Computing Machinery Series
Acta Polytech Scand Math Comput Sci Ser — Acta Polytechnica Scandinavica. Mathematics and Computer Science Series
Acta Polytech Scand Mech Eng Ser — Acta Polytechnica Scandinavica. Mechanical Engineering Series
Acta Polytech Scand Phys Incl Nucleon Ser — Acta Polytechnica Scandinavica. Physics Including Nucleonics Series [*Finland*]
Acta Polytech Scand Phys Incl Nucl Ser — Acta Polytechnica Scandinavica. Physics Including Nucleonics Series
Acta Polytech Scand Phys Nucl Ser — Acta Polytechnica Scandinavica. Physics Including Nucleonics Series
Acta Pont Inst Bibl — Acta Pontificii Instituti Biblici
Acta Praehist — Acta Praehistorica
Acta Praehist et Archaeol — Acta Praehistorica et Archaeologica
Acta Protozool — Acta Protozoologica
Acta Psiquiatr Psicol Am Lat — Acta Psiquiatrica y Psicologica de America Latina
Acta Psiquiatr Psicol (Argent) — Acta Psiquiatrica y Psicologica (Argentina)
Acta Psychiat Belg — Acta Psychiatrica Belgica
Acta Psychiatr Belg — Acta Psychiatrica Belgica
Acta Psychiatr Neurol Scand — Acta Psychiatrica et Neurologica Scandinavica
Acta Psychiatr Neurol Scand Suppl — Acta Psychiatrica et Neurologica Scandinavica. Supplementum
Acta Psychiatr Scand — Acta Psychiatrica Scandinavica
Acta Psychiatr Scand Suppl — Acta Psychiatrica Scandinavica. Supplementum
Acta Psychiat Scand — Acta Psychiatrica et Neurologica Scandinavica
Acta Psychiat Scand — Acta Psychiatrica Scandinavica [*Denmark*]
Acta Psychiat Scand Suppl — Acta Psychiatrica Scandinavica. Supplementum [*Denmark*]
Acta Psychol — Acta Psychologica [*Amsterdam*]
Acta Psychol (Amst) — Acta Psychologica (Amsterdam)
Acta Psychol Fenn — Acta Psychologica Fennica
Acta Psychol Taiwan — Acta Psychologica Taiwanica
Acta Psychother Psychosom — Acta Psychotherapeutica et Psychosomatica
Acta Psychother Psychosom Orthopaedagog — Acta Psychotherapeutica, Psychosomatica, et Orthopaedagogica
Acta Psych Scand — Acta Psychiatrica Scandinavica
Acta Radiobot Genet — Acta Radiobotanica et Genetica [*Japan*]
Acta Radiol — Acta Radiologica
Acta Radiol Diagn — Acta Radiologica. Series One. Diagnosis [*Stockholm*]
Acta Radiol Diagn (Stockh) — Acta Radiologica. Series One. Diagnosis (Stockholm)
Acta Radiol Interam — Acta Radiologica Interamericana
Acta Radiol Oncol Radiat Phys Biol — Acta Radiologica. Series Two. Oncology, Radiation, Physics, and Biology [*Stockholm*]
Acta Radiol Oncol Radiat Therapy Phys and Biol — Acta Radiologica. Oncology, Radiation Therapy, Physics, and Biology
Acta Radiol Oncol Radiat Ther Phys Biol — Acta Radiologica. Oncology, Radiation Therapy, Physics, and Biology [*Stockholm*]

Acta Radiol (Stockh) — Acta Radiologica (Stockholm)
Acta Radiol Suppl — Acta Radiologica. Supplementum [*Stockholm*]
Acta Radiol Suppl (Stockh) — Acta Radiologica. Supplementum (Stockholm)
Acta Radiol Ther Phys Biol — Acta Radiologica. Therapy, Physics, Biology [*Later, Acta Radiologica. Series Two. Oncology, Radiation, Physics, and Biology*] [*Stockholm*]
Acta Radiol Ther (Stockh) — Acta Radiologica. Therapy, Physics, Biology (Stockholm) [*Later, Acta Radiologica. Series Two. Oncology, Radiation, Physics, and Biology (Stockholm)*]
Act Archaeo — Acta Archaeologica
Acta Regiae Soc Sci Litt Gothob Zool — Acta Regiae Societatis Scientiarum et Litterarum Gothoburgensis. Zoologica
Acta Rerum Nat Mus Nat Slov Bratisl — Acta Rerum Naturalium Musei Nationalis Slovaci Bratislava
Acta Rheumatol Scand — Acta Rheumatologica Scandinavica
Acta Rheumatol Scand Suppl — Acta Rheumatologica Scandinavica. Supplementum
Acta Rheumat Scand — Acta Rheumatologica Scandinavica
Acta Rhumatol — Acta Rhumatologica
Acta Rhumatol Belg — Acta Rhumatologica Belgica
Acta Sag — Acta Sagittariana
Acta Salmant Cien — Acta Salmanticensia. Serie de Ciencias
Acta Salmanticensia Ser Cienc — Acta Salmanticensia. Serie de Ciencias
Acta Salmanticensia Ser Filos Letra — Acta Salmanticensia. Serie Filosofia y Letras
Acta Salmanticensia Ser Med — Acta Salmanticensia. Serie de Medicina
Acta Scaenograph — Acta Scaenographica
Acta Sch Med Gifu — Acta Scholae Medicinalis Universitatis in Gifu [*Japan*]
Acta Sch Med Univ Gifu — Acta Scholae Medicinalis Universitatis in Gifu
Acta Sch Med Univ Imp (Kioto) — Acta Scholae Medicinalis Universitatis Imperialis (Kioto)
Acta Sch Med Univ Kioto — Acta Scholae Medicinalis Universitatis in Kioto
Acta Sci Math (Szeged) — Acta Scientiarum Mathematicarum (Szeged)
Acta Sci Nat Acad Sci Bohemoslov (Brno) — Acta Scientiarum Naturalium. Academiae Scientiarum Bohemoslovacae (Brno)
Acta Sci Nat Univ Pekin — Acta Scientiarum Naturalium. Universitatis Pekinensis [*People's Republic of China*]
Acta Sci Nat Univ Sunyatseni (Zhongshandaxue Xuebao) — Acta Scientiarum Naturalium. Universitatis Sunyatseni (Zhongshandaxue Xuebao)
Acta Sci Nat Univ Szechuan — Acta Scientiarum Naturalium. Universitatis Szechuanensis [*People's Republic of China*]
Acta Sci Natur Univ Pekinensis — Acta Scientiarum Naturalium. Universitatis Pekinensis
Acta Sci Sin — Acta Scientia Sinica
Acta Sci Vietnam — Acta Scientiarum Vietnamicarum
Actas Congr Uniao Fitopatol Mediterr — Actas. Congresso da Uniao Fitopatologica Mediterranea
Actas Dermosifiliogr — Actas Dermosifiliograficas
Acta Seismol Sin — Acta Seismologica Sinica [*People's Republic of China*]
Actas Jornadas For — Actas Jornadas Forestales
Actas Luso-Esp Neurol Psiquiatr — Actas Luso-Espanolas de Neurologia, Psiquiatria, y Ciencias Afines
Actas-Luso Esp Neurol Psiquiatr Cienc Afines — Actas Luso-Espanolas de Neurologia, Psiquiatria, y Ciencias Afines
Actas Mem Congr Nat Esp — Actas y Memorias. Congreso de Naturalistas Espanoles
Acta Soc — Acta Sociologica
Acta Soc Bot Pol — Acta Societatis Botanicorum Poloniae
Acta Soc Bot Polon — Acta Societatis Botanicorum Poloniae
Acta Soc Ent Jugosl — Acta Societatis Entomologicae Jugoslavensis
Acta Soc Entomol Cech — Acta Societatis Entomologicae Cechosloveniae
Acta Soc Ent Serbo Cro Slov — Acta Societatis Entomologicae Serbo-Croato-Slovenae
Acta Soc Fauna Flora Fenn — Acta Societatis pro Fauna et Flora Fennica
Acta Sociol — Acta Sociologica
Acta Soc Med Ups — Acta Societatis Medicorum Upsaliensis
Acta Soc Med Upsal — Acta Societatis Medicorum Upsaliensis
Acta Soc Ophthalmol Jpn — Acta Societatis Ophthalmologicae Japonicae
Acta Soc Paed Hell — Acta Societatis Paediatricae Hellenicae
Acta Soc Path Jap — Acta Societatis Pathologicae Japonicae
Acta Soc Phil Lips — Acta Societatis Philologae Lipsiensis
Acta Soc Sci Fenn Ser B — Acta Societatis Scientiarum Fennicae. Series B
Acta Soc Zool Cechosl — Acta Societatis Zoologicae Cechoslovenicae
Actas Reun Argent Cienc Suelo — Actas. Reunion Argentina de la Ciencia del Suelo
Acta Stomatol Belg — Acta Stomatologica Belgica
Acta Stomatol Croat — Acta Stomatologica Croatica
Acta Stom Pat — Acta Stomatologica Patavina
Act Astron — Acta Astronautica
Actas Urol Esp — Actas Urologicas Espanolas
Acta Symp Evolut Insect — Acta Symposii de Evolutione Insectorum
Acta Tech Acad Sci Hung — Acta Technica. Academiae Scientiarum Hungaricae
Acta Tech Agric — Acta Technologica Agriculturae [*Brno*]. A. Facultas Agronomica
Acta Tech (Budap) — Acta Technica (Budapest)

Acta Tech CSAV — Acta Technica. CSAV [*Ceskoslovenska Akademie Ved*]
Acta Tech Hung — Acta Technica Hungarica
Acta Techn Gedan — Acta Technica Gedanensia
Acta Techn Hung — Acta Technica Hungarica
Acta Tech (Prague) — Acta Technica (Prague)
Acta Teilhard — Acta Teilhardiana
Acta Theriol — Acta Theriologica
Acta Trop — Acta Tropica
Acta Trop (Basel) — Acta Tropica (Basel)
Acta Trop Suppl — Acta Tropica. Supplementum
Acta Tuberc Belg — Acta Tuberculosea Belgica
Acta Tuberc Jpn — Acta Tuberculosea Japonica
Acta Tuberc Pneumol Belg — Acta Tuberculosea et Pneumologica Belgica
Acta Tuberc Pneumol Scand — Acta Tuberculosea et Pneumologica Scandinavica
Acta Tuberc Pneumol Scand Suppl — Acta Tuberculosea et Pneumologica Scandinavica. Supplementum
Acta Tuberc Scand — Acta Tuberculosea Scandinavica
Acta Tuberc Scand Suppl — Acta Tuberculosea Scandinavica. Supplementum
Acta Unio Int Contra Cancrum — Acta Unio Internationalis Contra Cancrum
Acta Univ Agr (Brno) — Acta Universitatis Agriculturae (Brno). Facultas Silviculturae. Section C
Acta Univ Agric (Brno) Fac Agron — Acta Universitatis Agriculturae (Brno). Facultas Agronomica
Acta Univ Agric (Brno) Fac Silvic — Acta Universitatis Agriculturae (Brno). Facultas Silviculturae
Acta Univ Agric (Brno) Fac Vet — Acta Universitatis Agriculturae (Brno). Facultas Veterinaria
Acta Univ Agric Fac Agron — Acta Universitatis Agriculturae. Facultas Agronomica
Acta Univ Agric Fac Silvic — Acta Universitatis Agriculturae. Facultas Silviculturae
Acta Univ Agric Fac Vet — Acta Universitatis Agriculturae. Facultas Veterinaria
Acta Univ Agric Ser C (Brno) — Acta Universitatis Agriculturae (Brno). Facultas Silviculturae. Series C
Acta Univ Carol Biol — Acta Universitatis Carolinae: Biologica
Acta Univ Carol Geogr — Acta Universitatis Carolinae: Geographica
Acta Univ Carol Geol — Acta Universitatis Carolinae: Geologica
Acta Univ Carol Geol Monogr — Acta Universitatis Carolinae: Geologica. Monographia
Acta Univ Carol Hist — Acta Universitatis Carolinae: Historia
Acta Univ Carolinae Geol — Acta Universitatis Carolinae: Geologica
Acta Univ Carolinae Math et Phys — Acta Universitatis Carolinae: Mathematica et Physica
Acta Univ Carolin Math Phys — Acta Universitatis Carolinae: Mathematica et Physica
Acta Univ Carol Math Phys — Acta Universitatis Carolinae: Mathematica et Physica
Acta Univ Carol Med — Acta Universitatis Carolinae: Medica
Acta Univ Carol Med Monogr — Acta Universitatis Carolinae: Medica. Monographia
Acta Univ Carol Med Monogr (Praha) — Acta Universitatis Carolinae: Medica. Monographia (Praha)
Acta Univ Carol Med (Praha) — Acta Universitatis Carolinae: Medica (Praha)
Acta Univ Carol Med Suppl — Acta Universitatis Carolinae: Medica. Supplementum [*Czechoslovakia*]
Acta Univ Debrecen Ludovico Kossuth Nominatae — Acta Universitatis Debreceniensis de Ludovico Kossuth Nominatae
Acta Univ Debrecen Ludovico Kossuth Nominatae Ser Biol — Acta Universitatis Debreceniensis de Ludovico Kossuth Nominatae. Series Biologica
Acta Univ Debrecen Ludovico Kossuth Nominatae Ser Phys Chim — Acta Universitatis Debreceniensis de Ludovico Kossuth Nominatae. Series Physica et Chimica
Acta Univ Lodz — Acta Universitatis Lodziensis
Acta Univ Lund Sect II Med Math Sci Rerum Nat — Acta Universitatis Lundensis. Sectio II. Scientiae Rerum Naturalium Medica, Mathematica
Acta Univ Nicolai Copernici Biol — Acta Universitatis Nicolai Copernici. Biologia
Acta Univ Nicolai Copernici Geogr — Acta Universitatis Nicolai Copernici. Geografia
Acta Univ Nicolai Copernici Pr Limnol — Acta Universitatis Nicolai Copernici. Prace Limnologiczne
Acta Univ Ouluensis Ser A — Acta Universitatis Ouluensis. Series A. Scientiae Rerum Naturalium. Geologica
Acta Univ Ouluensis Ser C — Acta Universitatis Ouluensis. Series C. Technica
Acta Univ Oulu Ser A Sci Rerum Natur Math — Acta Universitatis Ouluensis. Series A. Scientiae Rerum Naturalium. Mathematica
Acta Univ Palacki Olomuc — Acta Universitatis Palackianae Olomucensis
Acta Univ Palacki Olomuc Fac Med — Acta Universitatis Palackianae Olomucensis. Facultatis Medicae
Acta Univ Palacki Olomuc Fac Med Suppl — Acta Universitatis Palackianae Olomucensis. Facultatis Medicae. Supplementum

Acta Univ Palacki Olomuc Fac Rerum Nat — Acta Universitatis Palackianae Olomucensis. Facultas Rerum Naturalium
Acta Univ Palacki Olomuc Fac Rerum Nat Biol — Acta Universitatis Palackianae Olomucensis. Facultas Rerum Naturalium. Biologica
Acta Univ Palacki Olomuc Fac Rerum Nat Chem — Acta Universitatis Palackianae Olomucensis. Facultas Rerum Naturalium. Chemica
Acta Univ Palacki Olomuc Fac Rerum Nat Math — Acta Universitatis Palackianae Olomucensis. Facultas Rerum Naturalium. Mathematica
Acta Univ Palacki Olomuc Fac Rerum Nat Phys — Acta Universitatis Palackianae Olomucensis. Facultas Rerum Naturalium. Physica
Acta Univ Szeged Acta Biol — Acta Universitatis Szegediensis. Acta Biologica
Acta Univ Szeged Acta Phys et Chem — Acta Universitatis Szegediensis. Acta Physica et Chemica
Acta Univ Tamper Ser A — Acta Universitatis Tamperensis. Series A
Acta Univ Tsinghuan — Acta Universitatis Tsinghuanensis
Acta Univ Ups — Acta Universitatis Upsaliensis
Acta Univ Ups Abstr Upps Diss Med — Acta Universitatis Upsaliensis. Abstracts of Uppsala Dissertations in Medicine [*Sweden*]
Acta Univ Ups Abstr Upps Diss Sci — Acta Universitatis Upsaliensis. Abstracts of Uppsala Dissertations in Science
Acta Univ Upsal Abstr Uppsala Diss Fac Sci — Acta Universitatis Upsaliensis. Abstracts of Uppsala Dissertations. Faculty of Science
Acta Univ Upsal Abstr Upps Diss Fac Sci — Acta Universitatis Upsaliensis. Abstracts of Uppsala Dissertations. Faculty of Science
Acta Univ Ups Nova Acta Regiae Soc Sci Up Ser VC — Acta Universitatis Upsaliensis. Nova Acta Regiae Societatis Scientiarum Upsaliensis. Series VC
Acta Univ Ups Nova Acta Regiae Soc Sci Ups Ser VC — Acta Universitatis Upsaliensis. Nova Acta Regiae Societatis Scientiarum Upsaliensis. Series VC
Acta Univ Wratislav — Acta Universitatis Wratislaviensis
Acta Univ Wratislaviensis — Acta Universitatis Wratislaviensis [*Poland*]
Acta Univ Wratislav Mat Fiz Astron — Acta Universitatis Wratislaviensis. Matematyka, Fizyka, Astronomia
Acta Univ Wratislav Pr Geol Mineral — Acta Universitatis Wratislaviensis. Prace Geologiczno-Mineralogiczne
Acta Univ Wratislav Pr Zool — Acta Universitatis Wratislaviensis. Prace Zoologiczne [*Poland*]
Acta Urol Belg — Acta Urologica Belgica
Acta Urol Jpn — Acta Urologica Japonica
Acta Vertebr — Acta Vertebratica
Acta Vet Acad Sci Hung — Acta Veterinaria. Academiae Scientiarum Hungaricae
Acta Vet (Belgr) — Acta Veterinaria (Belgrade)
Acta Vet (Beogr) — Acta Veterinaria (Beograd) [*Yugoslavia*]
Acta Vet (Brno) — Acta Veterinaria (Brno)
Acta Vet (Brno) Suppl — Acta Veterinaria (Brno). Supplementum
Acta Vet Hung — Acta Veterinaria Hungarica
Acta Vet Scand — Acta Veterinaria Scandinavica
Acta Vet Scand Suppl — Acta Veterinaria Scandinavica. Supplementum
Acta Vet Zootech Sin — Acta Veterinaria et Zootechnica Sinica
Acta Virol (Engl Ed) — Acta Virologica (English Edition)
Acta Virol (Prague) — Acta Virologica (Prague)
Acta Virol (Prague) (Engl Ed) — Acta Virologica (Prague) (English Edition)
Acta Virol (Praha) — Acta Virologica (Praha)
Acta Vitaminol — Acta Vitaminologica [*Later, Acta Vitaminologica et Enzymologica*]
Acta Vitaminol Enzymol — Acta Vitaminologica et Enzymologica [*Milano*]
Acta Vitaminol Enzymol (Milano) — Acta Vitaminologica et Enzymologica (Milano)
Acta Zool — Acta Zoologica
Acta Zool Acad Sci Hung — Acta Zoologica. Academiae Scientiarum Hungaricae
Acta Zool Bulg — Acta Zoologica Bulgarica
Acta Zool Colomb — Acta Zoologica Colombiana
Acta Zool Cracov — Acta Zoologica Cracoviensia
Acta Zool Cracov (Engl Transl) — Acta Zoologica Cracoviensia (English Translation)
Acta Zool Fenn — Acta Zoologica Fennica
Acta Zool Hung — Acta Zoologica. Academiae Scientiarum Hungaricae
Acta Zool Lilloana — Acta Zoologica Lilloana
Acta Zool Mex — Acta Zoologica Mexicana
Acta Zool Oecol Univ Lodz — Acta Zoologica et Oecologica. Universitatis Lodziensis
Acta Zool Pathol Antverp — Acta Zoologica et Pathologica Antverpiensia
Acta Zool Pathol Antverpiensia — Acta Zoologica et Pathologica Antverpiensia
Acta Zool Sin — Acta Zoologica Sinica
Acta Zool (Stockh) — Acta Zoologica (Stockholm)
Acta Zool Taiw — Acta Zoologica Taiwanica
Acta Zootech Univ Agric (Nitra) — Acta Zootechnica. Universitatis Agriculturae (Nitra)
Act Bio C B — Acta Biologica Cracoviensia. Series Botanica
Act Bioch H — Acta Biochimica et Biophysica. Academiae Scientiarum Hungaricae
Act Biochim — Actualites Biochimiques
Act Bioch P — Acta Biochimica Polonica

Act Bio C Z — Acta Biologica Cracoviensia. Series Zoologia
Act Bio Ira — Acta Biochimica Iranica
Act Biol H — Acta Biologica. Academiae Scientiarum Hungaricae
Act Bio Med — Acta Biologica et Medica Germanica
Act Bot Nee — Acta Botanica Neerlandica
Act Card — Actualites Cardiologiques et Angeiologiques Internationales
Act Chem A — Acta Chemica Scandinavica. Series A. Physical and Inorganic Chemistry
Act Chem B — Acta Chemica Scandinavica. Series B. Organic Chemistry and Biochemistry
Act Chim H — Acta Chimica. Academiae Scientiarum Hungaricae
Act Chir B — Acta Chirurgica Belgica
Act Chir H — Acta Chirurgica. Academiae Scientiarum Hungaricae
Act Chir Sc — Acta Chirurgica Scandinavica
Act Ci — Actas Ciba
Act Cient V — Acta Cientifica Venezolana
Act Clin B — Acta Clinica Belgica
Act Clin Ther — Actualites de Clinique Therapeutique
Act Coll — Actes et Colloques
Act Cryst A — Acta Crystallographica. Section A
Act Cryst B — Acta Crystallographica. Section B
Act Cult Vet — Actualites et Culture Veterinaires
Act Cytol — Acta Cytologica
Act Dent — Actualite Dentaire
Act Der-Ven — Acta Dermato-Venereologica
Act Diabet — Acta Diabetologica Latina
Act Ec — Actualite Economique
Act Endocr — Acta Endocrinologica
Act Ent Boh — Acta Entomologica Bohemoslovaca
Actes Colloq Int — Actes. Colloque International
Actes Congr Int Hist Sci — Actes. Congres International d'Histoire des Sciences
Actes Rech Sci Soc — Actes de la Recherche en Sciences Sociales
Actes Soc Helv Sci Nat Parte Sci — Actes. Societe Helvetique des Sciences Naturelles. Parte Scientifique
Act Ethnogr — Acta Ethnographica
Act Gastr B — Acta Gastro-Enterologica Belgica
Act Genet M — Acta Geneticae, Medicae, et Gemellologiae
Act Geogr — Acta Geographica [*France*]
Act Gyn — Actualites Gynecologiques
Act Haemat — Acta Haematologica
Act Hem — Actualites Hematologiques
Act Hep-Gas — Acta Hepato-Gastroenterologica [*Stuttgart/New York*]
Act Hist Cy — Acta Histochemica et Cytochemica
Act Histoch — Acta Histochimica
ACTIE3 — Anales. Catedra de Tisioneumologia
Actinides Lanthanides Rev — Actinides and Lanthanides. Reviews
Actinides Rev — Actinides Reviews
Action — United Evangelical Action
Activity Bul — Activity Bulletin for Teachers in Secondary Schools
Activ Nerv — Activitas Nervosa Superior [*Praha*]
Activ Nerv Super — Activitas Nervosa Superior [*Czechoslovakia*]
Activ Petrol — Actividades Petroleras
Act Jur — Actualite Juridique
ActLingH — Acta Linguistica. Academiae Scientiarum Hungaricae
ActLitH — Acta Litteraria. Academiae Scientiarum Hungaricae
Act Math — Acta Mathematica
Act Math H — Acta Mathematica. Academiae Scientiarum Hungaricae
Act Mechan — Acta Mechanica
Act Med — Actualidad Medica
Act Med H — Acta Medica. Academiae Scientiarum Hungaricae
Act Med Oka — Acta Medicinae Okayama
Act Med Per — Actualidad Medica Peruana
Act Med Sc — Acta Medica Scandinavica
Act Metall — Acta Metallurgica
Act Mic P A — Acta Microbiologica Polonica. Series A. Microbiologia Generalis
Act Mic P B — Acta Microbiologica Polonica. Series B. Microbiologia Applicata
Act Micro H — Acta Microbiologica. Academiae Scientiarum Hungaricae
Act Morph H — Acta Morphologica. Academiae Scientiarum Hungaricae
Act Morph N — Acta Morphologica Neerlando-Scandinavica
Act Mozart — Acta Mozartiana
Act Music — Acta Musicologica
ActN — Action Nationale
Act Nat — Action Nationale
Act Nerv Super — Activitas Nervosa Superior [*Praha*]
Act Nerv Super (Praha) — Activitas Nervosa Superior (Praha)
Act Neurob — Acta Neurobiologiae Experimentalis
Act Neuroch — Acta Neurochirurgica
Act Neurop — Acta Neuropathologica
Act Neuro-phys — Actualites Neurophysiologiques
Act Neur Sc — Acta Neurologica Scandinavica
Act Obst Sc — Acta Obstetricia et Gynecologica Scandinavica
Act Odon Sc — Acta Odontologica Scandinavica
Act Oecon — Acta Oeconomica [*Budapest*]

Act O-Mer — Actualites d'Outre-Mer
Act Ophth (K) — Acta Ophthalmologica (Kobenhavn)
ActOr — Acta Orientalia [*Copenhagen*]
ActOrHung — Acta Orientalia. Academiae Scientiarum Hungaricae
      [*Budapest*]
Act Orth Sc — Acta Orthopaedica Scandinavica
Act Oto-Lar — Acta Oto-Laryngologica
Act Paed H — Acta Paediatrica. Academiae Scientiarum Hungaricae
Act Paedops — Acta Paedopsychiatrica
Act Paed Sc — Acta Paediatrica Scandinavica
ACT Pap Educ — ACT [*Australian Capital Territory*] Papers on Education
Act Pat Jap — Acta Pathologica Japonica
Act Pat S A — Acta Pathologica et Microbiologica Scandinavica. Section A
Act Pat S B — Acta Pathologica et Microbiologica Scandinavica. Section B
Act Pat S C — Acta Pathologica et Microbiologica Scandinavica. Section C
ACTPCM — Australia. Commonwealth Scientific and Industrial Research
      Organisation. Division of Food Research. Technical Paper
Act Ped — Actualidad Pediatrica
Act Pharm — Action Pharmaceutique
Act Pharm S — Acta Pharmaceutica Suecica
Act Pharm T — Acta Pharmacologica et Toxicologica
Act Phy P A — Acta Physica Polonica. Series A
Act Phy P B — Acta Physica Polonica. Series B
Act Phys Au — Acta Physica Austriaca
Act Phys Ch — Acta Physica et Chemica
Act Phys H — Acta Physica. Academiae Scientiarum Hungaricae
Act Physl H — Acta Physiologica. Academiae Scientiarum Hungaricae
Act Physl L — Acta Physiologica Latino Americana
Act Physl P — Acta Physiologica Polonica
Act Physl S — Acta Physiologica Scandinavica
Act Pol Ph — Acta Poloniae Pharmaceutica
Act Poly Ch — Acta Polytechnica Scandinavica. Chemistry Series
Act Poly Ci — Acta Polytechnica Scandinavica. Civil Engineering and Building
      Construction Series
Act Poly El — Acta Polytechnica Scandinavica. Electrical Engineering Series
Act Poly Ma — Acta Polytechnica Scandinavica. Mathematics and Computing
      Machinery Series
Act Poly Me — Acta Polytechnica Scandinavica. Mechanical Engineering
      Series
Act Poly Ph — Acta Polytechnica Scandinavica. Physics Including Nucleonics
      Series
Act Psiq Ps — Acta Psiquiatrica y Psicologica de America Latina
Act Psychol — Acta Psychologica [*Amsterdam*]
Act Psych T — Acta Psychologica Taiwanica
Act Psyc Sc — Acta Psychiatrica Scandinavica
ACTR — Australian Capital Territory. Reports
Act Rad Dgn — Acta Radiologica. Series One. Diagnosis [*Stockholm*]
Act Rad TPB — Acta Radiologica. Therapy, Physics, Biology [*Later, Acta*
      Radiologica. Series Two. Oncology, Radiation, Physics, and Biology]
      [*Stockholm*]
Act Reg — Acta Regia; An Abstract of Rymer's Foedera
Act Rep Res Dev Assoc Mil Food Packag Syst — Activities Report. Research
      and Development Associates for Military Food and Packaging Systems
Act Rep Res Dev Assoc Mil Food Packag Syst Inc — Activities Report.
      Research and Development Associates for Military Food and Packaging
      Systems, Incorporated
ACT Res Rep — American College Testing. Research Reports
Act Sci Mat — Acta Scientiarum Mathematicarum
Act Sludge Process Control Ser — Activated Sludge Process Control Series
Act Sociol — Acta Sociologica
Act Soc Linn Bordeaux — Actes. Societe Linneenne de Bordeaux
Act Syst (GB) — Active Systems (Great Britain)
ACT Teach — ACT [*Australian Capital Territory*] Teachers Federation.
      Teacher
Act Techn H — Acta Technica. Academiae Scientiarum Hungaricae
Actual Agron — Actualites Agronomiques
Actual Auto — Actualite Automobile
Actual Biochim — Actualites Biochimiques
Actual Biol — Actualidades Biologicas
Actual Biol (Paris) — Actualites Biologiques (Paris)
Actual Chim — Actualite Chimique
Actual Chim Ind — Actualite Chimique et Industrielle
Actual Chine Popul — Actualite en Chine Populaire
Actual Combust Energ — Actualite, Combustibles, Energie [*France*]
Actual Endocrinol (Paris) — Actualites Endocrinologiques (Paris)
Actual Formation Perm — Actualite de la Formation Permanente
Actual Hemat — Actualites Hematologiques
Actual Hepato-Gastro-Enterol Hotel-Dieu — Actualites Hepato-Gastro-
      Enterologiques de l'Hotel-Dieu [*France*]
Actual Hotel-Dieu — Actualites de l'Hotel-Dieu
Actual Industr Lorraines — Actualites Industrielles Lorraines
Actualites Sci Indust — Actualites Scientifiques et Industrielles
Actual Jur — Actualite Juridique
Actual Mar — Actualites Marines
Actual Med — Actualidades Medicas
Actual Med-Chir (Mars) — Actualites Medico-Chirurgicales (Marseille)

Actual Neurophysiol — Actualites Neurophysiologiques [*Paris*]
Actual Neurophysiol (Paris) — Actualites Neurophysiologiques (Paris)
Actual Odontostomatol — Actualites Odontostomatologiques [*Paris*]
Actual Pharm — Actualites Pharmacologiques
Actual Pharmacol — Actualites Pharmacologiques
Actual Pharmacol (Paris) — Actualites Pharmacologiques (Paris)
Actual Rel Mo — Actualite Religieuse dans le Monde
Actual Sci Techn — Actualites Scientifiques et Techniques
Actual Specif Eng — Actual Specifying Engineer
Actual Ther — Actualite Therapeutique
Actuar Note — Actuarial Note
ACTU Bul — ACTU [*Australian Council of Trade Unions*] Bulletin
Actu Econ — Actualite Economique
Actuel Develop — Actuel Developpement
Actuelle Gerontol — Actuelle Gerontologie
Act Univ La Plata — Actos Universitarios. Universidad Nacional de La Plata
Act Vet H — Acta Veterinaria. Academiae Scientiarum Hungaricae
Act Vet Sc — Acta Veterinaria Scandinavica
Act Virolog — Acta Virologica [*English Edition*]
Act Vit Enz — Acta Vitaminologica et Enzymologica [*Milano*]
Act Zool H — Acta Zoologica. Academiae Scientiarum Hungaricae
ACUM — Annales. Centre Universitaire Mediterraneen de Nice
ACUN — Annales. Centre Universitaire de Nice
ACUNSOP — Association of Canadian Universities for Northern Studies.
      Occasional Publications
Acupunct Electro-Ther Res — Acupuncture and Electro-Therapeutics Research
ACUR-A — Architectural Record
ACUSA — Acustica
ACUSD — Acta Classica. Universitatis Scientiarum Debreceniensis
Acust — Acustica
Ac UU — Acta Universitatis Upsaliensis
ACUU — Acta Universitatis Upsaliensis. Abstracts of Uppsala Dissertations.
      Faculty of Science
ACV — Australian and New Zealand Conveyancing Report
ACVNAO — Atti. Museo Civico di Storia Naturale di Trieste
ACVSA — Acta Cientifica Venezolana. Suplemento
ACVTA — Acta Veterinaria
ACW — Ancient Christian Writers [*Westminster, MD*]
ACWR — Alaska Cooperative Wildlife Research Unit
ACYTA — Acta Cytologica
ACZ — Prosi Bulletin Mensuel
ACZBA8 — Centro de Estudos Zoologicos. Universidade do Brasil. Avulso
ACZMN — Arctic Coastal Zone Management. Newsletter
Ad — Adelphi
AD — Africa Diary
AD — Amazing Detective Tales
AD — American Documentation
AD — Aptechnoe Delo
AD — Architectural Design
AD — Architectural Digest
AD — Archiv fuer Diplomatik
AD — Army Digest
AD — Art Digest
AD — Australian Digest
ADA — Anzeiger fuer Deutsches Altertum und Deutsche Literatur
ADA — Arquivo do Distrito de Aveiro
Ad Age Eur — Advertising Age Europe
ADAI — Abhandlungen. Deutsches Archaeologisches Institut [*Cairo*]
ADAJ — Annual. Department of Antiquities of Jordan
ADAM Int R — ADAM [*Arts, Drama, Architecture, Music*] International
      Review
Adapt Sistemy Avtomat Upravlenija — Adaptivnye Sistemy Avtomaticeskogo
      Upravlenija
Adapt Sistemy Avtomat Upravleniya — Kievskii Politekhnicheskii Institut
      Adaptivnye Sistemy Avtomaticheskogo Upravleniya
ADARA — American Dairy Review
ADAS Q Rev — ADAS [*Agricultural Development and Advisory Service*]
      Quarterly Review
ADAS Q Rev (GB) — ADAS [*Agricultural Development and Advisory Service*]
      Quarterly Review (Great Britain)
ADAW — Abhandlungen. Deutsche Akademie der Wissenschaften zu Berlin.
      Klasse fuer Sprachen, Literatur, und Kunst
ADB — Algemeen Dagblad
ADB — Australian Dictionary of Biography
ADB — Australian Digest Bulletin
ADBRDE — Australia. Commonwealth Scientific and Industrial Research
      Organisation. Division of Building Research. Annual Report
Addict Behav — Addictive Behaviors
Addict Dis — Addictive Diseases
Addison-Wesley Ser Comput Sci Inform Process — Addison-Wesley Series in
      Computer Science and Information Processing
Address Proc Ontario Soil Crop Impr Ass — Addresses and Proceedings.
      Ontario Soil and Crop Improvement Association
Address Proc Saskatchewan Univ Farm Home Week — Addresses and
      Proceedings. Saskatchewan University Farm and Home Week
ADE — Archivio di Diritto Ecclesiastico

ADEB — Association of Departments of English. Bulletin
ADEGB — Automotive Design Engineering
ADEJB — Arizona Dental Journal
Adel — Adelphi
Adel — New Adelphi
Adelaide Children's Hosp Records — Adelaide Children's Hospital. Records
Adelaide Law Rev — Adelaide Law Review
Adelaide LR — Adelaide Law Review
Adelaide L Rev — Adelaide Law Review
Adel Law R — Adelaide Law Review
Adel Law Rev — Adelaide Law Review
Adel LR — Adelaide Law Review
Adel L Rev — Adelaide Law Review
Adel Stock and Station J — Adelaide Stock and Station Journal
A Delt — Archaiologikon Deltion
Adel Univ Grad Gaz — Adelaide University Graduates Union. Gazette
Adel Univ Grad Union Gaz — Adelaide University Graduates Union. Monthly Newsletter and Gazette
Adel Univ Mag — Adelaide University. Magazine
ADESAT — Anales del Desarrollo
ADETBX — Australia. Commonwealth Scientific and Industrial Research Organisation. Division of Entomology. Annual Report
ADEVD — Area Development
ADF — Ad Forum
ADFCA — Advances in Fluorine Chemistry
ADFLB — Association of Departments of Foreign Languages. Bulletin
ADFOAM — Australia. Commonwealth Scientific and Industrial Research Organisation. Division of Fisheries and Oceanography. Report
ADFPBQ — Australia. Commonwealth Scientific and Industrial Research Organisation. Division of Food Preservation. Report of Research
ADFRAV — Alaska. Department of Fisheries. Research Report
ADGB — Archiv fuer Geschichte des Buchwesens
ADGEA — Advances in Genetics
ADGOA — Advances in Geophysics
ADH — Adherent
Adhaes — Adhaesion
Adhes Adhes — Adhesion and Adhesives [*Japan*]
Adhes Age — Adhesives Age
Adhesives — Adhesives Age
Adhes Resins — Adhesives and Resins
ADHGA — Advances in Human Genetics
ADHS — Armidale and District Historical Society. Journal
ADHYA — Advances in Hydroscience
AdI — Annali. Istituto di Corrispondenza Archeologica
ADI — Anuario. Departamento de Ingles [*Barcelona*]
ADIHDJ — Annual Research Reviews. Anti-Diuretic Hormone
ADIMA — Advances in Immunology
ADIOA — Journal. Audio Engineering Society
ADIRBD — Australia. Commonwealth Scientific and Industrial Research Organisation. Division of Irrigation Research. Annual Report
AdL — Amor di Libro
AdL — Anuario de Letras
Ad Law Rev — Administrative Law Review
AdLB — Adyar Library Bulletin
Adler Mus Bull — Adler Museum Bulletin
ADL-Nachr — ADL-Nachrichten
Ad L R — Adelaide Law Reports
Ad LR — Administrative Law Review
Ad L Rev — Administrative Law Review
ADM — Annals of Discrete Mathematics [*Elsevier Book Series*]
ADM — Office Administration and Automation
Adm Bull — Administrators' Bulletin
Adm Change — Administrative Change
Adm y Desarr — Administracion y Desarrollo
ADMIA — Advances in Microwaves
ADMIG Bulletin — Australian Drug and Medical Information Group. Bulletin
Admin — Administration
Admin Man — Administrator. Manitoba Association of Principals
Admin Manage — Administrative Management
Admin Ment Hlth — Administration in Mental Health
Admin Mgmt — Administrative Management
Admin Science Q — Administrative Science Quarterly
Admin Sci Q — Administrative Science Quarterly
Admin Sci R — Administrative Science Review
Admin and Society — Administration and Society
ADML — Automatic Documentation and Mathematical Linguistics
Adm Law R — Administrative Law Review
Adm L Rev — Administrative Law Review
Adm Manage — Administrative Management
Adm Ment He — Administration in Mental Health
Adm Ment Health — Administration in Mental Health
Adm Mgmt — Administrative Management
Adm Mgt — Administrative Management
Adm Notebk — Administrator's Notebook
ADMO — Australian Directory of Music Organisations
ADMOA — Advances in Morphogenesis

ADMPAQ — Australia. Commonwealth Scientific and Industrial Research Organisation. Division of Mathematical Statistics. Technical Paper
ADMR — Australian Directory of Music Research
ADMRB — Advances in Materials Research
ADM Rev — ADM [*Asociacion Dental Mexicana*] Revista [*Mexico*]
ADM (Rev Asoc Dent Mex) — ADM (Revista de la Asociacion Dental Mexicana)
Adm Sci — Administrative Science Quarterly
Adm Sci Q — Administrative Science Quarterly
Adm Sci Qua — Administrative Science Quarterly
Adm and Soc — Administration and Society
Adm Socie — Administration and Society
Adm Soc Work — Administration in Social Work
Adm Tss — Administrativ Tidsskrift
ADN — Alcohol and Drug News
ADNDA — Atomic Data and Nuclear Data Tables
ADOCA — Advances in Organic Chemistry
ADOG — Abhandlungen. Deutsche Orient-Gesellschaft
ADOL — Adolescence
ADOLA — Adolescence
Adoles — Adolescence
Adolesc Psychiatry — Adolescent Psychiatry
ADORB — Advances in Oto-Rhino-Laryngology
ADP — Archivo de Derecho Publico
ADPA — Accounting and Data Processing Abstracts
ADPCA — Advances in Photochemistry
ADPEA — Advances in Pediatrics
ADPh — Arbeiten zur Deutschen Philologie
ADPPB — Advances in Particle Physics
ADPRA — Advances in Parasitology
ADPV — Abhandlungen. Deutscher Palaestina-Verein
ADQ — Australia Newsletter
ADQEA — Advances in Quantum Electronics
A Dr — Annales de Droit
ADREA — American Dyestuff Reporter
ADRED — Archives for Dermatological Research
A Dr Marit Aer — Annuaire de Droit Maritime et Aerien
ADRPB — Advances in Reproductive Physiology
ADRRCP — Australia. Commonwealth Scientific and Industrial Research Organisation. Division of Dairy Research. Annual Report
ADRS — Archivio. R. Deputazione Romana di Storia Patria
ADRSP — Archivio. R. Deputazione Romana di Storia Patria
Ad Serv Leafl Timb Res Developm Ass — Advisory Service Leaflet. Timber Research and Development Association
ADSPA — Annales de Dermatologie et de Syphiligraphie [*Later, Annales de Dermatologie et de Venereologie*]
ADSPM — Atti e Memorie. Deputazione di Storia Patria per le Antiche Provincie Modenesi
ADSPR — Atti e Memorie. Deputazione di Storia Patria per le Provincie di Romagna
ADSUA — Advances in Surgery
ADT — Adformatie. Weekblad voor Reclame en Marketing
ADT — Amazing Detective Tales
AdTb — Altdeutsche Textbibliothek
Adult Dis — Adult Diseases [*Japan*]
Adult Ed — Adult Education
Adult Ed Bul — Adult Education Bulletin
Adult Ed J — Adult Education Journal
Adult Ed and Lib — Adult Education and the Library
Adult Educ — Adult Education
Adult Ed-W — Adult Education-Washington
Adult Lead — Adult Leadership
ADV — Arbeitsgemeinschaft Deutscher Verfolgten-Organisationen
Adv Abstr Contrib Fish Aquat Sci India — Advance Abstracts of Contributions on Fisheries and Aquatic Sciences in India
Adv Acarol — Advances in Acarology
Adv Act Anal — Advances in Activation Analysis
Adv Aerosol Phys — Advances in Aerosol Physics
Adv Age — Advertising Age
Adv Agency Mag — Advertising Agency Magazine
Adv Agron — Advances in Agronomy
Adv Agron Crop Sci — Advances in Agronomy and Crop Science
Advan Agron — Advances in Agronomy
Adv Anal Chem Instrum — Advances in Analytical Chemistry and Instrumentation
Advan Appl Mech — Advances in Applied Mechanics
Advan Appl Probab — Advances in Applied Probability
Advan Astronaut Sci — Advances in the Astronautical Sciences
Adv Anat Embryol Cell Biol — Advances in Anatomy, Embryology, and Cell Biology
Advanced Mgt — Advanced Management Journal
Advanced Mgt J — Advanced Management Journal
Advanced Mgt-Office Exec — Advanced Management-Office Executive
Advancement Sci — Advancement of Science
Advances in Appl Mech — Advances in Applied Mechanics
Advances in Chem Ser — Advances in Chemistry Series

Advances in Math Suppl Studies — Advances in Mathematics. Supplementary Studies
Advan Chem Eng — Advances in Chemical Engineering
Advan Chem Ser — Advances in Chemistry Series
Advan Clin Chem — Advances in Clinical Chemistry
Advan Cryog Eng — Advances in Cryogenic Engineering
Advan Electron and Electron Phys — Advances in Electronics and Electron Physics
Advan Front Plant Sci — Advancing Frontiers of Plant Sciences
Advan Genet — Advances in Genetics
Advan Geophys — Advances in Geophysics
Adv Anim Physiol Anim Nutr — Advances in Animal Physiology and Animal Nutrition
Advan Manage J — Advanced Management Journal
Advan Mol Relaxation Processes — Advances in Molecular Relaxation Processes [*Later, Advances in Molecular Relaxation and Interaction Processes*]
Advan Phys — Advances in Physics
Advan Polymer Sci Fortschr Hochpolym-Forsch — Advances in Polymer Science/Fortschritte der Hochpolymeren-Forschung
Advan Thanatol — Advances in Thanatology
Adv Antimicrob Antineoplast Chemother — Advances in Antimicrobial and Antineoplastic Chemotherapy
Advan Virus Res — Advances in Virus Research
Adv Appl Math — Advances in Applied Mathematics
Adv Appl Mech — Advances in Applied Mechanics
Adv Appl Microbiol — Advances in Applied Microbiology
Adv Appl P — Advances in Applied Probability
Adv Appl Prob — Advances in Applied Probability [*England*]
Adv Appl Probab — Advances in Applied Probability
Adv Ap Pr — Advances in Applied Probability
Adv Aquat Microbiol — Advances in Aquatic Microbiology
Adv Astron Astrophys — Advances in Astronomy and Astrophysics
Adv Astronaut Sci — Advances in the Astronautical Sciences
Adv At Mol Phys — Advances in Atomic and Molecular Physics
Adv Behav Biol — Advances in Behavioral Biology
Adv Biochem Biophys — Advances in Biochemistry and Biophysics [*People's Republic of China*]
Adv Biochem Eng — Advances in Biochemical Engineering
Adv Biochem Psychopharmacol — Advances in Biochemical Psychopharmacology
Adv Bioeng — Advances in Bioengineering
Adv Bioeng Instrum — Advances in Bioengineering and Instrumentation
Adv Biol Med Phys — Advances in Biological and Medical Physics
Adv Biol Skin — Advances in Biology of the Skin
Adv Biomed Eng — Advances in Biomedical Engineering
Adv Biomed Eng Med Phys — Advances in Biomedical Engineering and Medical Physics
Adv Biophys — Advances in Biophysics [*Tokyo*]
Adv Biosci — Advances in the Biosciences
Adv Blood Grouping — Advances in Blood Grouping
Adv Bot Res — Advances in Botanical Research
Adv Cancer Res — Advances in Cancer Research
Adv Carbohyd Chem — Advances in Carbohydrate Chemistry and Biochemistry
Adv Carbohydr Chem — Advances in Carbohydrate Chemistry [*Later, Advances in Carbohydrate Chemistry and Biochemistry*]
Adv Carbohydr Chem Biochem — Advances in Carbohydrate Chemistry and Biochemistry
Adv Cardiol — Advances in Cardiology
Adv Catal — Advances in Catalysis and Related Subjects
Adv Cell Biol — Advances in Cell Biology
Adv Cell Mol Biol — Advances in Cell and Molecular Biology
Adv Cereal Sci Technol — Advances in Cereal Science and Technology
Adv Chem — Advances in Chemistry
Adv Chem Eng — Advances in Chemical Engineering
Adv Chemoreception — Advances in Chemoreception
Adv Chemother — Advances in Chemotherapy
Adv Chem Phys — Advances in Chemical Physics
Adv Chem Se — Advances in Chemistry Series
Adv Chem Ser — Advances in Chemistry Series
Adv Child Dev Behav — Advances in Child Development and Behavior
Adv Chromatogr — Advances in Chromatography
Adv Clin Chem — Advances in Clinical Chemistry
Adv Clin Pharmacol — Advances in Clinical Pharmacology
Adv Coll In — Advances in Colloid and Interface Science
Adv Coll Inter Sci — Advances in Colloid and Interface Science
Adv Colloid and Interface Sci — Advances in Colloid and Interface Science
Adv Colloid Interface Sci — Advances in Colloid and Interface Science
Adv Colloid Sci — Advances in Colloid Science
Adv Comp — Advances in Computers
Adv Comp Physiol Biochem — Advances in Comparative Physiology and Biochemistry
Adv Control Syst — Advances in Control Systems
Adv Corros Sci Technol — Advances in Corrosion Science and Technology
Adv Cryog Eng — Advances in Cryogenic Engineering

Adv Cyclic Nucleotide Res — Advances in Cyclic Nucleotide Research
Adv Cytopharmacol — Advances in Cytopharmacology
Adv Desert Arid Land Technol Dev — Advances in Desert and Arid Land Technology and Development
Adv Drug Res — Advances in Drug Research
Adv Earth Oriented Appl Space Technol — Advances in Earth-Oriented Applications of Space Technology [*Later, Earth-Oriented Applications of Space Technology*]
Adv Earth and Planet Sci — Advances in Earth and Planetary Sciences
Adv Earth Planet Sci — Advances in Earth and Planetary Sciences
Adv Ecol Res — Advances in Ecological Research
Adv Electrochem Electrochem Eng — Advances in Electrochemistry and Electrochemical Engineering
Adv Electron — Advances in Electronics
Adv Electron Circuit Packag — Advances in Electronic Circuit Packaging
Adv Electron Electron Phys — Advances in Electronics and Electron Physics
Adv Electron Electron Phys Suppl — Advances in Electronics and Electron Physics. Supplement
Adv Electron Tube Tech — Advances in Electron Tube Techniques
Adv Energy Convers — Advanced Energy Conversion [*England*]
Adv Energy Syst Technol — Advances in Energy Systems and Technology
Adv Engng Software — Advances in Engineering Software
Adv Eng Software — Advances in Engineering Software
Adventures Exp Phys — Adventures in Experimental Physics
Adv Environ Sci — Advances in Environmental Sciences
Adv Environ Sci Technol — Advances in Environmental Science and Technology
Adv Envir Sci — Advances in Environmental Sciences
Adv Enzym — Advances in Enzymology
Adv Enzyme Regul — Advances in Enzyme Regulation
Adv Enzymol — Advances in Enzymology
Adv Enzymol Relat Areas Mol Biol — Advances in Enzymology and Related Areas of Molecular Biology
Adv Enzymol Relat Subj Biochem — Advances in Enzymology and Related Subjects of Biochemistry [*Later, Advances in Enzymology and Related Areas of Molecular Biology*]
Adverse Drug React Bull — Adverse Drug Reaction Bulletin
Advert Age — Advertising Age
Advert Bus — Advertising Business
Advert Q — Advertising Quarterly
Advert World — Advertising World
Adv Ethol — Advances in Ethology
Adv Exp Med Biol — Advances in Experimental Medicine and Biology
Adv Exp Soc Psychol — Advances in Experimental Social Psychology
Adv Fire Retardants — Advances in Fire Retardants
Adv Fluorine Chem — Advances in Fluorine Chemistry
Adv Fluorine Res Dent Caries Prev — Advances in Fluorine Research and Dental Caries Prevention
Adv Food Res — Advances in Food Research
Adv Food Res Suppl — Advances in Food Research. Supplement
Adv Free Radical Chem — Advances in Free Radical Chemistry
Adv Frontiers Plant Sci — Advancing Frontiers of Plant Sciences
Adv Front Pl Sci — Advancing Frontiers of Plant Sciences
Adv Genet — Advances in Genetics
Adv Genetic — Advances in Genetics
Adv Geophys — Advances in Geophysics
Adv Gerontol Res — Advances in Gerontological Research
Advg Front Pl Sci — Advancing Frontiers of Plant Sciences
Adv Heat Transfer — Advances in Heat Transfer
Adv Heterocycl Chem — Advances in Heterocyclic Chemistry
Adv High Pressure Res — Advances in High Pressure Research [*England*]
Adv High Temp Chem — Advances in High Temperature Chemistry
Adv Hologr — Advances in Holography
Adv Hum Fertil Reprod Endocrinol — Advances in Human Fertility and Reproductive Endocrinology
Adv Hum Gen — Advances in Human Genetics
Adv Hum Genet — Advances in Human Genetics
Adv Hydrosci — Advances in Hydroscience
Adv Image Pickup Disp — Advances in Image Pickup and Display
Adv Immunol — Advances in Immunology
Adv Infrared Raman Spectrosc — Advances in Infrared and Raman Spectroscopy
Adv Inf Syst Sci — Advances in Information Systems Science
Adv Inorg Chem Radiochem — Advances in Inorganic Chemistry and Radiochemistry
Adv Insect Physiol — Advances in Insect Physiology
Adv Instrum — Advances in Instrumentation
Adv Intern Med — Advances in Internal Medicine
Advis Leafl Br Beekprs Ass — Advisory Leaflet. British Beekeepers Association
Advis Leafl Dep For Queensl — Advisory Leaflet. Queensland Department of Forestry
Advis Leafl QD Dep Agric — Advisory Leaflet. Queensland Department of Agriculture
Advis Leafl W Scotl Agric Coll — Advisory Leaflet. West of Scotland Agricultural College

Adv Leafl Dep For QD — Advisory Leaflet. Queensland Department of Forestry

Adv Leafl Min Agr Fish Food (Gt Brit) — Advisory Leaflet. Ministry of Agriculture, Fisheries, and Food (Great Britain)

Adv Leafl Queensland Dept Agr Stock Div Plant Ind — Advisory Leaflet. Queensland Department of Agriculture and Stock. Division of Plant Industry

Adv Leafl W Scot Agr Coll — Advisory Leaflet. West of Scotland Agricultural College

Adv Lipid Res — Advances in Lipid Research

Adv Liq Cryst — Advances in Liquid Crystals

Adv Macromol Chem — Advances in Macromolecular Chemistry

Adv Magn Reson — Advances in Magnetic Resonance

Adv Manag — Advanced Management

Adv Manage J — Advanced Management Journal

Adv Mar Bio — Advances in Marine Biology

Adv Mass Spectrom — Advances in Mass Spectrometry

Adv Mater Res — Advances in Materials Research

Adv Math — Advances in Mathematics

Adv Metab Disord — Advances in Metabolic Disorders

Adv Metab Disord Suppl — Advances in Metabolic Disorders. Supplement

Adv Mgmt — Advanced Management

Adv Mgmt J — Advanced Management Journal

Adv Microb Ecol — Advances in Microbial Ecology

Adv Microbial Physiol — Advances in Microbial Physiology [*England*]

Adv Microbiol Sea — Advances in Microbiology of the Sea

Adv Microb Physiol — Advances in Microbial Physiology

Adv Microcirc — Advances in Microcirculation

Adv Microwaves — Advances in Microwaves

Adv Mod Biol — Advances in Modern Biology

Adv Mod Gen — Advances in Modern Genetics

Adv Mod Nutr — Advances in Modern Nutrition

Adv Mol Rel — Advances in Molecular Relaxation Processes [*Later, Advances in Molecular Relaxation and Interaction Processes*]

Adv Mol Relaxation and Interaction Processes — Advances in Molecular Relaxation and Interaction Processes

Adv Mol Relaxation Interact Processes — Advances in Molecular Relaxation and Interaction Processes [*Netherlands*]

Adv Mol Relaxation Processes — Advances in Molecular Relaxation Processes [*Later, Advances in Molecular Relaxation and Interaction Processes*]

Adv Mol Relax Interact Processes — Advances in Molecular Relaxation and Interaction Processes

Adv Molten Salt Chem — Advances in Molten Salt Chemistry

Adv Morphog — Advances in Morphogenesis

Advmt Sci — Advancement of Science

Advmt Sci (Lond) — Advancement of Science (London)

Adv Myocardiol — Advances in Myocardiology

Adv Nephrol — Advances in Nephrology

Adv Nephrol Necker Hosp — Advances in Nephrology. Necker Hospital

Adv Neurochem — Advances in Neurochemistry

Adv Neurol — Advances in Neurology

Adv Neurol Sci — Advances in Neurological Sciences

Adv Neurosurg — Advances in Neurosurgery

Adv Nucl Phys — Advances in Nuclear Physics

Adv Nucl Quadrupole Reson — Advances in Nuclear Quadrupole Resonance [*England*]

Adv Nucl Sci Technol — Advances in Nuclear Science and Technology

Adv Nurs Sci — Advances in Nursing Science

Adv Nutr Res — Advances in Nutritional Research

Adv Obstet — Advances in Obstetrics and Gynecology

Adv Obstet Gynecol (Baltimore) — Advances in Obstetrics and Gynecology (Baltimore)

Adv Obstet Gynecol (Osaka) — Advances in Obstetrics and Gynecology (Osaka) [*Japan*]

Advocates Q — Advocates Quarterly

Adv Ophthal — Advances in Ophthalmology

Adv Ophthalmol — Advances in Ophthalmology [*Netherlands*]

Adv Opt Electron Microsc — Advances in Optical and Electron Microscopy

Adv Oral Biol — Advances in Oral Biology

Adv Organometal Chem — Advances in Organometallic Chemistry

Adv Org Chem — Advances in Organic Chemistry. Methods and Results

Adv Org Chem Methods Results — Advances in Organic Chemistry. Methods and Results

Adv Oto-Rhino-Laryngol — Advances in Oto-Rhino-Laryngology

Adv Pain Res Ther — Advances in Pain Research and Therapy

Adv Parasitol — Advances in Parasitology

Adv Particle Phys — Advances in Particle Physics

Adv Part Phys — Advances in Particle Physics

Adv Pathobiol — Advances in Pathobiology

Adv Pediatr — Advances in Pediatrics

Adv Pest Control Res — Advances in Pest Control Research

Adv Pet Chem Refin — Advances in Petroleum Chemistry and Refining

Adv Petrol Chem Refin — Advances in Petroleum Chemistry and Refining

Adv Pharmacol — Advances in Pharmacology [*Later, Advances in Pharmacology and Chemotherapy*]

Adv Pharmacol Chemother — Advances in Pharmacology and Chemotherapy

Adv Pharm Sci — Advances in Pharmaceutical Sciences

Adv Photochem — Advances in Photochemistry

Adv Phys — Advances in Physics

Adv in Phys — Advances in Physics

Adv Phy Sci — Advances in Physical Sciences

Adv Physics — Advances in Physics

Adv Phys Org Chem — Advances in Physical Organic Chemistry

Adv Phys Sci (USSR) — Advances in Physical Sciences (USSR)

Adv Planned Parent — Advances in Planned Parenthood

Adv Plann Parent — Advances in Planned Parenthood

Adv Plasma Phys — Advances in Plasma Physics

Adv Pollen-Spore Res — Advances in Pollen-Spore Research

Adv Polymer Sci — Advances in Polymer Science

Adv Polym Sci — Advances in Polymer Science

Adv Polym Technol — Advances in Polymer Technology

Adv Printing Sci — Advances in Printing Science and Technology

Adv Proc Fluid Power Test Symp — Advance Proceedings. Fluid Power Testing Symposium

Adv Prostaglandin Thromboxane Res — Advances in Prostaglandin and Thromboxane Research

Adv Protein Chem — Advances in Protein Chemistry

Adv Psychobiol — Advances in Psychobiology

Adv Psychosom Med — Advances in Psychosomatic Medicine

Adv Psy Med — Advances in Psychosomatic Medicine

Adv Quantum Chem — Advances in Quantum Chemistry

Adv Quantum Electron — Advances in Quantum Electronics

Adv Radiat Biol — Advances in Radiation Biology

Adv Radiat Chem — Advances in Radiation Chemistry

Adv Raman Spectrosc — Advances in Raman Spectroscopy

Adv Rel St — Advanced Religious Studies

Adv Reprod Physiol — Advances in Reproductive Physiology

Adv R Physl — Advances in Reproductive Physiology

ADVSA — Advances in Veterinary Science [*Later, Advances in Veterinary Science and Comparative Medicine*]

Adv Sci — Advancement of Science

Adv of Science — Advancement of Science

Adv & Sell — Advertising and Selling

Adv Ser Agric Sci — Advanced Series in Agricultural Sciences

Adv Sex Horm Res — Advances in Sex Hormone Research

Adv Shock Res — Advances in Shock Research

Adv Sleep Res — Advances in Sleep Research

Adv Small Anim Pract — Advances in Small Animal Practice

Adv Space Sci — Advances in Space Science

Adv Space Sci Technol — Advances in Space Science and Technology

Adv Spa Sci — Advances in Space Science and Technology

Adv Spectros — Advances in Spectroscopy

Adv Spectrosc — Advances in Spectroscopy

Adv Stereoencephalotomy — Advances in Stereoencephalotomy

Adv Steroid Biochem — Advances in Steroid Biochemistry and Pharmacology

Adv Steroid Biochem Pharmacol — Advances in Steroid Biochemistry and Pharmacology

Adv Struct Res Diffr Methods — Advances in Structure Research by Diffraction Methods

Adv Study Behav — Advances in the Study of Behavior

Adv Study Birth Defects — Advances in the Study of Birth Defects

Adv Surf Coat Technol — Advances in Surface Coating Technology [*England*]

Adv Surg — Advances in Surgery

Adv Tech Lib — Advanced Technology Libraries

Adv Technol Libr — Advanced Technology Libraries

Adv Teratol — Advances in Teratology

Adv Textile Process — Advances in Textile Processing

Adv Theor Phys — Advances in Theoretical Physics

Adv Ther — Advanced Therapeutics

Adv Tracer Methodol — Advances in Tracer Methodology

Adv Tuberc Res — Advances in Tuberculosis Research

Adv Urethane Sci Technol — Advances in Urethane Science and Technology

Adv Vehicle News — Advanced Vehicle News

Adv Vet Med (Berl) — Advances in Veterinary Medicine (Berlin)

Adv Vet Sci — Advances in Veterinary Science [*Later, Advances in Veterinary Science and Comparative Medicine*]

Adv Vet Sci Comp Med — Advances in Veterinary Science and Comparative Medicine

Adv Virus Res — Advances in Virus Research

Adv Waste Treat Res — Advances in Waste Treatment Research

Adv Waste Treat Res Publ — Advanced Waste Treatment Research Publication

Adv Water Resour — Advances in Water Resources [*England*]

Adv X-Ray Anal — Advances in X-Ray Analysis

ADWMA — Abhandlungen. Deutsche Akademie der Wissenschaften zu Berlin. Klasse fuer Medizin

Ad World — Advertising World

ADz — Akademiska Dzive

AE — Acta Ethnographica

AE — Adult Education

Ae — Aegyptus

AE — Aesthetics

Ae — Aevum
AE — Alaska Economic Report
AE — American Ensemble
AE — Ancient Egypt
AE — Annales de l'Est
AE — Annales d'Ethiopie
AE — Annee Epigraphique
AE — Annuaire Europeen
AE — Arab Economist
AE — Archaiologike Ephemeris
AE — Arheologija un Etnografija
AE — Arkheograficheskii Ezhegodnik
AE — Australian Encyclopaedia
AE — Automotive Engineer
AE — Internationales Archiv fuer Ethnographie
AeA — Aegyptologische Abhandlungen [*Wiesbaden*]
AEA — Agro-Ecological Atlas of Cereal Growing in Europe [*Elsevier Book Series*]
AEA — America. Revista de la Asociacion de Escritores y Artistas Americanos
AEA — Anuario de Estudios Atlanticos
AEA — Archivo Espanol de Arqueologia
AEA — Archivo Espanol de Arte
AEAA — Archivo Espanol de Arte y Arqueologia
AeAb — Aegyptologische Abhandlungen [*Wiesbaden*]
AEArq — Archivo Espanol de Arqueologia
AEAls — Archives de l'Eglise d'Alsace
AEASH — Acta Ethnographica. Academiae Scientiarum Hungaricae
AEB — Analytical and Enumerative Bibliography
AEB — Annual Egyptological Bibliography
Aeb — Archives et Bibliotheques
AEBA — Agricultural Economics Bulletin for Africa
AEC — American Economist
AEC — Arab Economist
Ae Ch Salz — Aevum Christianum. Salzburger Beitraege zur Religions- und Geistesgeschichte des Abendlandes
AE Clemson Agr Exp Sta — AE. Clemson Agricultural Experiment Station
AECL Res & Dev Eng — AECL [*Atomic Energy of Canada Limited*] Research and Development in Engineering
AECO — Archivum Europae Centro-Orientalis
AECODH — Agro-Ecosystems
A Econ — Actualite Economique
A Econ (Clermont) — Annales Economiques (Clermont)
A Econ Polit — Annales d'Economie Politique
A Econ Publ Soc Coop — Annales de l'Economie Publique, Sociale, et Cooperative
A Econ Soc Measurement — Annals of Economic and Social Measurement
A Ec R — American Ecclesiastical Review
AEC Symp Ser — AEC [*US Atomic Energy Commission*] Symposium Series
AECTC — Archives of Environmental Contamination and Toxicology [*West Germany*]
AED — Africa Economic Digest. AED. Weekly Business News, Analysis, and Forecast
A Ed — American Education
AEDAAB — Anales de Edafologia y Agrobiologia
AE Del Agr Exp Stat Dept Agr Econ — AE. Delaware Agricultural Experiment Station. Department of Agricultural Economics
AEDS J — AEDS [*Association for Educational Data Systems*] Journal
AEDS Jrnl — AEDS [*Association for Educational Data Systems*] Journal
AEDS Mon — AEDS [*Association for Educational Data Systems*] Monitor
AEDS Monit — AEDS [*Association for Educational Data Systems*] Monitor
AEE — Ancient Egypt and the East
AEECAM — Anales. Estacion Experimental de Aula Dei [*Zaragoza*]
AEEEA — Advances in Electrochemistry and Electrochemical Engineering
AeF — Aegyptologische Forschungen [*Glueckstadt*]
AEF — Anejos de Estudios Filologicos
AEFDAU — Alabama. Agricultural Experiment Station. Auburn University. Forestry Departmental Series
AEFVAG — Anales de Edafologia y Fisiologia Vegetal
Aeg — Aegyptus: Rivista Italiana di Egittologia e di Papirologia
AEG — Australian Estate and Gift Duty Reporter
Aeg Christ — Aegyptica Christiana
Aegean Earth Sci — Aegean Earth Sciences
Aeg Forsch — Aegyptologische Forschungen
AEG Kernreakt — AEG [*Allgemeine Elektrizitaets-Gesellschaft*] Kernreaktoren
AEG Prog — AEG [*Allgemeine Elektrizitaets-Gesellschaft*] Progress [*West Germany*]
AEGR — Australian Estate and Gift Duty Reporter
AEG Telefunken Prog — AEG [*Allgemeine Elektrizitaets-Gesellschaft*] - Telefunken Progress
AEG-Telefunken Progr — AEG [*Allgemeine Elektrizitaets-Gesellschaft*] - Telefunken Progress
AEH — Acta Ethnographica. Academiae Scientiarum Hungaricae
AEHEG — Annales. Ecole des Hautes-Etudes de Gand
AEHLA — Archives of Environmental Health
AEHR — Australian Economic History Review

Aehrodin Razrezh Gazov — Aehrodinamika Razrezhennykh Gazov
AEICA8 — Contributions. American Entomological Institute [*Ann Arbor*]
AEI Econom — AEI [*American Enterprise Institute*] Economist
AEI Eng — AEI [*Associated Electrical Industries*] Engineering [*England*]
AEI Eng Rev — AEI [*Associated Electrical Industries*] Engineering Review
AE Inform Ser Univ NC State Coll Agr Eng Dept Agr Econ — AE Information Series. University of North Carolina. State College of Agriculture and Engineering. Department of Agricultural Economics
AEJ — Adult Education Journal
AEKG — Archiv fuer Elsaessische Kirchengeschichte
AEL — Acta Ethnologica et Linguistica
AEL — Atomic Energy Levels and Grotrian Diagrams [*Elsevier Book Series*]
A Electr — Acta Electronica
AELK — Allgemeine Evangelisch-Lutherische Kirchenzeitung [*Luthardt*]
AELKZ — Allgemeine Evangelisch-Lutherische Kirchenzeitung [*Luthardt*]
AELR — All England Law Reports
AEM — Anuario de Estudios Medievales
AEM — Archaeologisch-Epigraphische Mitteilungen aus Oesterreich [*Ungarn*]
AEM — Archeion Euboikon Meleton
AEMBA — Advances in Experimental Medicine and Biology
AEMBB — Bulletin. Association des Anciens Eleves de l'Ecole Francaise de Meunerie
A Embr Morph Exp — Acta Embryologiae et Morphologiae Experimentalis
AE Mich State Univ Agr Appl Sci Ext Div Agr Econ Dept — AE. Michigan State University of Agriculture and Applied Science. Extension Division. Agricultural Economics Department
AEMXA — Acta Embryologiae et Morphologiae Experimentalis
AEN — Annales de l'Est et du Nord
AENBAU — Anales. Escuela Nacional de Ciencias Biologicas [*Mexico*]
A End Gyn — Acta Endocrinologica et Gynaecologica Hispanolusitana
A End Ib — Acta Endocrinologica Iberica
AENF — Annales Entomologici Fennici
AEOA — Annales de l'Extreme Orient et de l'Afrique
AEODA7 — Anales Espanoles de Odontoestomatologia
AEOTD — Advances in Earth-Oriented Applications of Space Technology [*Later, Earth-Oriented Applications of Space Technology*]
AeP — Anima e Pensiero
AEP — Australian Economic Papers
AEpigr — Annee Epigraphique
Aeq — Aequatoria
AEQBDE — Anales. Escuela de Quimica y Farmacia y Bioquimica. Universidad de Concepcion
AEQUA — Aequatoria
Aequ Math — Aequationes Mathematicae
AER — American Ecclesiastical Review
AER — American Economic Review
AeR — Atene e Roma
AER — Australian Economic Review
AERAA — Advances in Enzymology and Related Areas of Molecular Biology
AE Res NY State Coll Agr Dept Agr Econ — AE Research. New York State College of Agriculture. Department of Agricultural Economics
AERGB — Applied Ergonomics
AERJ — American Educational Research Journal
AERNA — American Economic Review
Aero Dig — Aero Digest
Aerodin Razrezh Gazov — Aerodinamika Razrezhennykh Gazov [*USSR*]
Aerodyn Note — Aerodynamics Note
Aerodyn Techn Mem — Aerodynamics Technical Memorandum
Aero Eng R — Aeronautical Engineering Review
Aero J — Aeronautical Journal
Aeromed Acta — Aeromedica Acta
Aeromed Rev — Aeromedical Reviews
Aeronaut Astronaut — Aeronautique et l'Astronautique
Aeronaut Eng Rev — Aeronautical Engineering Review
Aeronaut J — Aeronautical Journal
Aeronaut Q — Aeronautical Quarterly
Aeronaut Res Lab Dep Def Aust Rep — Aeronautical Research Laboratories. Department of Defence. Australia. Reports
Aeron J — Aeronautical Journal
Aeron Q — Aeronautical Quarterly
Aeron Res Rep — Aeronautical Research Report
Aero Quart — Aeronautical Quarterly [*London*]
Aero Res Tech Notes — Aero Research Technical Notes
Aero Safe — Aerospace Safety
Aerosl Age — Aerosol Age
Aerosol Rep — Aerosol Report
Aerosol Sci — Aerosol Science [*England*]
Aero/Space Eng — Aero/Space Engineering
Aerospace Hist — Aerospace Historian
Aerospace Med — Aerospace Medicine
Aerospace Tech — Aerospace Technology
Aerosp Eng — Aerospace Engineering
Aerosp Med — Aerospace Medicine
Aerosp Technol — Aerospace Technology

AERO Sun-T — AERO [*Alternative Energy Resources Organization*] Sun-Times

Aerotec Missili Spazio — Aerotechnica Missili e Spazio

Aerotec Missili & Spazio — Aerotechnica Missili e Spazio

AE RS PA State Univ Agr Sta Dept Agr Econ Rural Sociol — AE and RS. Pennsylvania State University. Agricultural Experiment Station. Department of Agricultural Economics and Rural Sociology

AErt — Archaeologiai Ertesito

AERTJ — Association of Education by Radio-Television. Journal

Aerztebl Baden-Wuerttemb — Aerzteblatt fuer Baden-Wuerttemberg

Aerztl Forsch — Aerztliche Forschung

Aerztl Fortbildungskurse Zuercher Kanton Liga Tuberk Arosa — Aerztliche Fortbildungskurse der Zuercher Kantonalen Liga Gegen die Tuberkulose in Arosa

Aerztl Jugendkd — Aerztliche Jugendkunde

Aerztl Lab — Aerztliche Laboratorium

Aerztl Monatsh Berufliche Fortbild — Aerztliche Monatshefte fuer Berufliche Fortbildung

Aerztl Praxis — Aerztliche Praxis

Aerztl Wochenschr — Aerztliche Wochenschrift

AeS — Aegyptologische Studien [*Berlin*]

AES — Archives Europeennes de Sociologie

AESAA — Annals. Entomological Society of America

AESC — Annales: Economies, Societes, Civilisations

AESIS Quarterly — Australian Earth Sciences Information System. Quarterly

AEsp — Archivo Espanol de Arqueologia

AESQAW — Anais. Escola Superior de Agricultura "Luiz De Queiroz." Universidade de Sao Paulo

AESTC — Advances in Environmental Science and Technology

AESTD — Atomnye Elektricheskie Stantsii

Aesthet Med — Aesthetische Medizin [*West Germany*]

AESUAB — Agricultural Experiment Station. University of Alaska. Bulletin

AESUATB — Agricultural Experiment Station. University of Alaska. Technical Bulletin

AETEB — Aerospace Technology

AETh — Abhandlungen zur Evangelischen Theologie [*Bonn*]

Aetherische Oele Riechst Parfuem Essenzen Aromen — Aetherische Oele, Riechstoffe, Parfuemerien, Essenzen, und Aromen

A Et Int — Annales d'Etudes Internationales

AETJA — Automatic Electric Technical Journal

AETQA — Annales. Societe Entomologique du Quebec

AEU — Archiv fuer Elektronik und Uebertragungstechnik

AEU — Asia Electronics Union. Journal

AEU-Arch El — AEU-Archiv fuer Elektronik und Uebertragungstechnik

AEU-Arch Elektron Uebertragungstech — AEU-Archiv fuer Elektronik und Uebertragungstechnik

AEUMJ — Amalgamated Engineering Union. Monthly Journal

AEU Mon J — Amalgamated Engineering Union. Monthly Journal

AEUNA — AEU. Asia Electronics United

AE Univ Ill Coll Agr Exp Sta Coop Ext Serv — AE. University of Illinois. College of Agriculture. Experiment Station. Cooperative Extension Service

Aev — Aevum

AEX — Export

AeZ — Aegyptische Zeitschrift

AEZRA — Advances in Enzyme Regulation

AF — American Fabrics

AF — American Forests

AF — Amerique Francaise

AF — Anglistische Forschungen

AF — Architectural Forum

AF — Archivio di Filosofia

AF — Arte Figurative

AF — Asiatische Forschungen

AF — Ausgrabungen und Funde. Nachrichtenblatt fuer Vor- und Fruehgeschichte

Af A — Afrique et l'Asie [*Later, Afrique et l'Asie Modernes*]

AFA — Archiv fuer Anthropologie

AFA — Archivo de Filologia Aragonesa

AFA — Asociacion Folklorica Argentina. Anales

AFAA Rept — AFA [*Aborigines' Friends' Association*] Annual Report

A Fac Agrar (Bari) — Annali. Facolta di Agraria (Bari)

A Fac Agrar (Milano) — Annali. Facolta di Agraria (Milano)

A Fac Dr Liege — Annales. Faculte de Droit de Liege

A Fac Dr Lyon — Annales. Faculte de Droit de Lyon

A Fac Dr Sci Polit (Clermont) — Annales. Faculte de Droit et de Science Politique (Clermont)

A Fac Econ Com (Palermo) — Annali. Facolta di Economia e Commercio (Palermo)

A Fac Sci Polit (Genova) — Annali. Facolta di Scienza Politica (Genova)

AFAMA5 — Anais. Faculdade de Medicina de Porto Alegre

A Family Stud — Annals of Family Studies

AFAR — Australian Foreign Affairs Record

AFAS — Afrique et l'Asie. Revue Politique, Sociale, et Economique et Bulletin des Anciens du CHEAM

AfB — Africana Bulletin [*Warsaw*]

AFBMAA — Anales. Facultad de Farmacia y Bioquimica. Universidad Nacional Mayor de San Marcos de Lima

AFBRB — American Foundation for the Blind. Research Bulletin

AFB Res Bull — American Foundation for the Blind. Research Bulletin

AFBU — Agriculture and Forestry Bulletin. University of Alberta

AFC — Anales de Filologia Clasica

AFCCDM — Anales. Facultad de Ciencias Quimicas y Farmacologicas. Universidad de Chile

AFCE — Air Force Civil Engineer

AFCU — Archivos del Folklore Chileno. Universidad de Chile

AFD — African Development

AfD — Archiv fuer Diplomatik

AFDI — Annuaire Francais de Droit International

AFDM — Air Force Driver Magazine

Afd Math Beslisk — Afdeling Mathematische Besliskunde [*Amsterdam*]

Afd Math Statist — Afdeling Mathematische Statistiek [*Amsterdam*]

Afd Numer Wisk — Afdeling Numerieke Wiskunde

Afd Toegepaste Wisk — Afdeling Toegepaste Wiskunde

Afd Zuiv Wisk — Afdeling Zuivere Wiskunde

AFEQD — Air Force Engineering and Services Quarterly

AFER — African Ecclesial Review

AFF — Anali Filoloskog Fakulteta [*Belgrade*]

Affarsvarld — Affarsvarlden

Aff Est — Affari Esteri

AFFPA5 — Anais. Faculdade de Farmacia do Porto

AFFSAE — Anais. Faculdade de Farmacia e Odontologia. Universidade de Sao Paulo

Aff Soc Int — Affari Sociali Internazionali

AFG — Auslandsanfragen. Waren Vertretungen Kooperationen

AFGIL — Alaska. Department of Fish and Game. Information Leaflet

AFGK — Archiv fuer Frankfurts Geschichte und Kunst

AFGPRB — Alaska. Department of Fish and Game. Project Progress Reports on Bears

AFGPRC — Alaska. Department of Fish and Game. Project Progress Reports on Caribou

AFGPRD — Alaska. Department of Fish and Game. Project Progress Reports on Deer

AFGPRG — Alaska. Department of Fish and Game. Project Progress Reports on Mountain Goats

AFGPRM — Alaska. Department of Fish and Game. Project Progress Reports on Moose

AFGPRS — Alaska. Department of Fish and Game. Project Progress Reports on Sheep

AFGPRWQ — Alaska. Department of Fish and Game. Project Progress Reports on Wildlife

AFGRR — Alaska. Department of Fish and Game. Research Reports

AFGSDTP — Alaska. Department of Fish and Game. Subsistence Division. Technical Paper

AFGT — Alaska Fish Tales and Game Trails

AFGWTB — Alaska. Department of Fish and Game. Wildlife Technical Bulletin

AFH — Afrika Heute

AFH — Archivum Franciscanum Historicum [*Firenze*]

Afh Fys Kemi Mineral — Afhandlingar i Fysik, Kemi, och Mineralogi

AFHL — Annuaire. Federation Historique de Lorraine

AFI — Amities France-Israel

AFI Ed News — AFI [*American Film Institute*] Education Newsletter

AFig — Arti Figurative. Rivista d'Arte Antica e Moderna

A Filos — Archivio di Filosofia

AFIPS Conf Proc — AFIPS [*American Federation of Information Processing Societies*] Conference Proceedings

AFIPS Conf Proc Fall Jt Comput Conf — American Federation of Information Processing Societies. Conference Proceedings. Fall Joint Computer Conference

AFIPS Conf Proc Fall Spring Jt Comput Conf — American Federation of Information Processing Societies. Conference Proceedings. Fall and Spring Joint Computer Conferences

AFIPS Conf Proc Spring Jt Comput Conf — American Federation of Information Processing Societies. Conference Proceedings. Spring Joint Computer Conference

AFIPS Nat Comput Conf Expo Conf Proc — AFIPS [*American Federation of Information Processing Societies*] National Computer Conference and Exposition. Conference Proceedings

AFIPS Natl Comp Conf Expo Conf Proc — American Federation of Information Processing Societies. National Computer Conference and Exposition. Conference Proceedings

AFIPS Washington Rep — AFIPS [*American Federation of Information Processing Societies*] Washington Report

AFISAT — Atti. Accademia delle Scienze di Siena. Detta de Fisiocritici

AFJ — Armed Forces Journal

AF JAG L Rev — Air Force JAG [*Judge Advocate General*] Law Review [*Later, Air Force Law Review*]

AFJZA — Allgemeine Forst- und Jagdzeitung

AfK — Archiv fuer Keilschriftforschung

AfK — Archiv fuer Kulturgeschichte [*Cologne/Graz*]

AFK — New African

Af L — Afroasiatic Linguistics
AFL — Australian Family Law and Practice
AFLA — Annales. Faculte des Lettres d'Aix
AFLB — Annali. Facolta di Lettere e Filosofia. Universita di Bari
AFLC — Annali. Facolta di Lettere, Filosofia, e Magistero. Universita di Cagliari
AFL-CIO Am Fed — AFL-CIO American Federationist
AFLD — Annales. Faculte des Lettres et Sciences Humaines de l'Universite de Dakar
AFLFB — Annali. Facolta di Lettere e Filosofia. Universita di Bari
AFLFP — Annali. Facolta di Lettere e Filosofia. Universita di Perugia
AFLFUM — Annali. Facolta di Lettere e Filosofia. Universita di Macerata
AFLL — Annali. Facolta di Lettere di Lecce
AFLN — Annali. Facolta di Lettere e Filosofia. Universita di Napoli
AFLNice — Annales. Faculte des Lettres et Sciences Humaines de Nice
AFLNW — Arbeitsgemeinschaft fuer Forschung des Landes Nordrhein-Westfalen. Geisteswissenschaften
AFLNW/G — Veroeffentlichungen. Arbeitsgemeinschaft fuer Forschung des Landes Nordrhein/Westfalen/Geisteswissenschaften [*Cologne/Opladen*]
AFLPer — Annali. Facolta di Lettere e Filosofia (Perugia)
AFLQ — Archives de Folklore. Universite Laval (Quebec)
AF L R — Air Force Law Review
AFL Rev — Air Force Law Review
AFLSHY — Annales. Faculte des Lettres et Sciences Humaines de Yaounde
AFLT — African Literature Today
AFLT — Annales Publiees par la Faculte des Lettres de Toulouse
AFLT Forum — Arizona Foreign Language Teachers Forum
AFLToul — Annales Publiees par la Faculte des Lettres et Sciences Humaines de Toulouse [*Via Domitia*]
AFM — Annales Fonds Maeterlinck
AfM — Archiv fuer Musikwissenschaft
AFMAA — Annales Academiae Scientiarum Fennicae. Series A-V. Medica
AFMag — Annali. Facolta di Magistero. Universita di Palermo
AFML — Annali. Facolta di Magistero. Universita di Lecce
AFMMAV — Anais. Faculdade de Medicina. Universidade Federal de Minas Gerais [*Belo Horizonte*]
Af Mo — African Monthly [*Grahamstown*]
AFMUB — Annali. Facolta di Magistero. Universita di Bari
Af Mus — African Music
AFMVB — Annali. Facolta di Medicina Veterinaria. Universita di Pisa
AFNG — Arbeitsgemeinschaft fuer Forschung des Landes Nordrhein-Westfalen. Geisteswissenschaften
AFO — AEI [*American Enterprise Institute*] Economist
AFO — Archiv fuer Orientforschung
AFOAA5 — Agricultural Research Council. Food Research Institute [*Norwich*]. Annual Report
AFOAB6 — Australia. Commonwealth Scientific and Industrial Research Organisation. Division of Fisheries and Oceanography. Annual Report
AFOCEL — Association Foret-Cellulose
AfOF — Archiv fuer Orientforschung [*Berlin*]
A Folk — Archives de Folklore
AFONA — Arizona Forestry Notes
AFONAA — Arizona Forestry Notes
A Fond G Feltrinelli — Annali. Fondazione Giangiacomo Feltrinelli
A Fond L Einaudi — Annali. Fondazione Luigi Einaudi
AFOPAG — Australia. Commonwealth Scientific and Industrial Research Organisation. Division of Fisheries and Oceanography. Technical Paper
A Forum — African Forum: A Quarterly Journal of Contemporary Affairs
AFOSAP — Annual Report. Institute for Fermentation (Osaka)
AFP — African Construction, Building, Civil Engineering, Land Development
AfP — Archiv fuer Papyrusforschung [*Leipzig*]
AFP — Archivum Fratrum Praedicatorum [*Roma*]
AFPOAI — Anais. Faculdade de Ciencias. Universidade do Porto
AFPPAL — Australia. Commonwealth Scientific and Industrial Research Organisation. Division of Forest Products. Technological Paper
AFPYA — American Family Physician
AFPYB — American Family Physician
AFQ — Alberta Folklore Quarterly
AFR — Africa Confidential
AFR — Africa. Revista Espanola de Colonizacion
AFR — Alaska. Department of Fish and Game. Sport Fish Division. Federal Aid in Fish Restoration Studies
AFR — Anglo-French Review
AFR — Archiv fuer Reformationsgeschichte. Texte und Untersuchungen
AFR — Australian Financial Review
AFR — Avon Fantasy Reader
AfrA — African Arts [*Los Angeles*]
AfrAb — African Abstracts
AfrAf — African Affairs
Afr Aff — African Affairs
Afr Affairs — African Affairs
Afr Agric — Afrique Agriculture
AfrAm S — Afro-American Studies
Afr-Am Stud — Afro-American Studies
Afr Art — African Arts

Afr Arts — African Arts [*Los Angeles*]
Afr Asie — Afrique et l'Asie Modernes [*Formerly, Afrique et l'Asie*]
Afr et Asie Mod — Afrique et l'Asie Modernes [*Formerly, Afrique et l'Asie*]
Afr Asie Mod — Afrique et l'Asie Modernes [*Formerly, Afrique et l'Asie*]
Afr Beekeep — African Beekeeping
AFRCA — Acta Facultatis Rerum Naturalium Universitatis Comenianae. Chimia
Afr Communist — African Communist
Afr Contemp — Afrique Contemporaine
Afr Contemporaine — Afrique Contemporaine
Afr Develop — African Development
Afr Dig — Africa Digest
AFRE — African Environment
AFREA — Advances in Food Research
Afr Econ H — African Economic History
Afr Fr Chir — Afrique Francaise Chirurgicale
Afr Heute — Afrika Heute
Afr Hist Stud — African Historical Studies
Africa — Africa Fouilles. Monuments et Collections Archeologiques en Tunisie
Afric Affairs — African Affairs
Africa IAI — Africa. International African Institute
AfricaL — Africa (London)
Africana — Africana Bulletin [*Warsaw*]
African Admin Studies — African Administrative Studies
Africana J — Africana Journal
Africana Lib J — Africana Library Journal
Africana Marburg — Africana Marburgensia
Africana Res B — Africana Research Bulletin
African Bus — African Business
African Econ Hist — African Economic History
African J Ednl Research — African Journal of Educational Research
African LS — African Law Studies
African Stud — African Studies
African Stud Bul — African Studies Bulletin
African Studies R — African Studies Review
African Stud R — African Studies Review
Africa R — Africa Report
Africa Rep — Africa Report
Africa Rept — Africa Report
Africa T — Africa Today
Afric Lit Today — African Literature Today
Afric Stud — African Studies
Afric Stud R — African Studies Review
Afri Econ — Review of African Political Economy
Afrika Mat — Afrika Matematika. The First Pan-African Mathematical Journal
Afr Industr Infrastruct — Afrique Industrie Infrastructures
Afr Inst B — Africa Institute. Bulletin
Afr Inst Bull — Africa Institute. Bulletin
AfrIt — Africa Italiana
Afr J Med Med Sci — African Journal of Medicine and Medical Sciences
Afr J Med Sci — African Journal of Medical Sciences [*Later, African Journal of Medicine and Medical Sciences*]
Afr J Psychiatr — African Journal of Psychiatry
Afr J Trop Hydrobiol Fish — African Journal of Tropical Hydrobiology and Fisheries
Afr J Trop Hydrobiol Fish Spec Issue — African Journal of Tropical Hydrobiology and Fisheries. Special Issue
AfrL — Africana Linguistica [*Tervuren*]
Afr Lang Stud — African Language Studies
Afr Law Stud — African Law Studies
Afr L Digest — African Law Digest
Afr Litter et Artist — Afrique Litteraire et Artistique
Afr Lit Tod — African Literature Today
AfrLJ — Africana Library Journal
AfrLRev — African Language Review
AfrLS — African Language Studies
Afr L Stud — African Law Studies
AfrM — Africana Marburgensia
Afr Med — Afrique Medicale
AfrN — African Notes [*Ibadan*]
AFRNA — Acta Facultatis Rerum Naturalium Universitatis Comenianae. Physica
Afroasiatic Ling — Afroasiatic Linguistics
AFrP — Athlone French Poets
Afr Perspect — Africa Perspective
Afr Post — Afrika Post
Afr Q — Africa Quarterly
Afr R — African Review
Afr Relig Res — African Religious Research
Afr Rep — Africa Report
Afr Report — Africa Report
Afr Res Bull — Africa Research Bulletin Series
Afr Res Doc — African Research and Documentation
AfrS — African Studies [*Johannesburg*]
AfrSch — African Scholar

Afr Soc Res — African Social Research
Afr Soc Secur Ser — African Social Security Series
Afr Soils — African Soils
Afr Spectrum — Afrika Spectrum
AfrSR — African Studies Review
Afr Stud — African Studies
Afr Stud R — African Studies Review
Afr-T — Africa-Tervuren
Afr Today — Africa Today
Afr Uebersee — Afrika und Uebersee
Afr Wildl — African Wildlife
Afr-Wirtsch — Afrika-Wirtschaft
Afr WS — African Writers Series
AFS — African Studies [*Johannesburg*]
AFS — Alaska. Department of Fish and Game. Sport Fish Division. Anadromous Fish Studies
AFS — Asian Folklore Studies
AFS Cast Met Res J — AFS [*American Foundrymen's Society*] Cast Metals Research Journal
AF/SD — Air Force and Space Digest
AFS Int Cast Met J — AFS [*American Foundrymen's Society*] International Cast Metals Journal
AFSM — Air Force Screen Magazine
AFSPEC — Afrika Spectrum
AFSWP-TP — Armed Forces Special Weapons Project [*later, DASA*]. Technical Publications
AFT — Australian Federal Tax Reporter
AFTU — Archiv fuer Reformationsgeschichte. Texte und Untersuchungen
AFUW Bul — Australian Federation of University Women. Bulletin
AFZSA — Allgemeine Forstzeitschrift
AFZTA — Allgemeine Forstzeitung
AG — Advance Guard
AG — Anales Galdosianos
AG — Anglica Germanica
AG — Annales de Geographie
AG — Annales Geophysicae
AG — Archivo Giuridico
AG — Australian Geographer
AGA — Aerodrome and Ground Aids
AGA — American Gas Association. Monthly
Ag Abh — Aegyptologische Abhandlungen
AGAJU — Arbeiten zur Geschichte des Antiken Judentums und des Urchristentums
Ag Am — Agriculture in the Americas
AGAMA — American Gas Association. Monthly
AGARD Advis Rep — AGARD [*Advisory Group for Aerospace Research and Development*] Advisory Report
AGARD Adv Rep — AGARD [*Advisory Group for Aerospace Research and Development*] Advisory Report
AGARD Agardogr — AGARD [*Advisory Group for Aerospace Research and Development*] Agardograph
AGARD Conf Proc — AGARD [*Advisory Group for Aerospace Research and Development*] Conference Proceedings
AGARD CP — AGARD [*Advisory Group for Aerospace Research and Development*] Conference Proceedings
AGARD Lect Ser — AGARD [*Advisory Group for Aerospace Research and Development*] Lecture Series
AGARD (NATO) — AGARD [*Advisory Group for Aerospace Research and Development*] (North Atlantic Treaty Organization)
AGARD Rep — AGARD [*Advisory Group for Aerospace Research and Development*] Report
AGARD Specif — AGARD [*Advisory Group for Aerospace Research and Development*] Specification
AGAU — Archief voor de Geschedenis van het Aartsbisdom Utrecht
AGB — Anhaltische Geschichtsblaetter
AGB — Archiv fuer Geschichte des Buchwesens
AGB — Association Guillaume Bude. Bulletin
AGBA — Agriculture Bulletin. University of Alberta [*Later, Agriculture and Forestry Bulletin*]
AGBO — Agroborealis
AGBOBO — Agroborealis
AGC — African Business
AGCACM — Agrichemical Age
AGCCBR — Agrociencia
Ag Chem — Agricultural Chemicals
Ag Chem Commer Fert — Ag Chem and Commercial Fertilizer [*Later, Farm Chemicals*]
Ag Chemicals — Agricultural Chemicals
AGCNCR — Agrociencia. Serie A
AGCODV — Agronomia Costarricense
AGCPA — AGARD [*Advisory Group for Aerospace Research and Development*] Conference Proceedings
AGD — Australian Government Digest
Ag Digest — Agricultural Digest
AGDSAB — Aichi-Gakuin Daigaku Shigakkai-Shi

Age & Ageing — Age and Ageing Science. Annuals
Age Ageing Suppl — Age and Ageing. Supplement
Ag Econ Res — Agricultural Economics Research
Ag Ed — Agricultural Education Magazine
Aged Care Serv Rev — Aged Care and Services Review
AGEFAB — Archives of Poultry Science
AGEFAB — Archives de Science Avicole
Age Lit Supp — Age Literary Supplement
Ag Eng — Agricultural Engineering [*St. Joseph, MI*]
Agent Actio — Agents and Actions
Agents Actions Suppl — Agents and Actions. Supplement
Age Nucl — Age Nucleaire
A Geogr — Annales de Geographie
AGEPA — Annales de Geophysique
AGEPB — Archiv fuer die Gesamte Psychologie
AGER — Agricultural Economics Research
Ag Europe — Agra Europe
Agfa Kinetech Mitt — Agfa Kinetechnische Mitteilungen
AGFB — Association de Geographes Francais. Bulletin
AGF Mitt — AGF [*Arbeitsgemeinschaft der Grossforschungseinrichtungen*] Mitteilungen
AgFo — Aegyptologische Forschungen [*Glueckstadt*]
Ag Food Jl — Agriculture and Food Chemistry. Journal
AGFYA — Arkiv foer Geofysik
AGG — Abhandlungen. Gesellschaft der Wissenschaften zu Goettingen. Philosophisch-Historische Klasse
Ag Gaz of Canada — Agricultural Gazette of Canada
Ag Gaz of New South Wales — Agricultural Gazette of New South Wales
Ag Gaz NSW — Agricultural Gazette of New South Wales
AGGCA — Acta Geologica et Geographica. Universitatis Comenianae. Geologica
Aggiorn Mal Infez — Aggiornamenti sulle Malattie da Infezione [*Italy*]
Aggiorn Pediatr — Aggiornamento Pediatrico
Aggiorn Soc — Aggiornamenti Sociali
AGGLA5 — Agronomski Glasnik
AGGRBO — Ahrokhimia i Hruntoznavstvo Respublikanskii Mizhvidomchyi Tematichnyi Zbirnyk
Aggressive Behav — Aggressive Behavior
AGHA — Archiv fuer Geschichte des Hochstifts Augsburg
AGHDAK — International Journal of Aging and Human Development
Ag Hist — Agricultural History
Ag Hist R — Agricultural History Review
AGHJA4 — Agrohemija
AGHPB — Annales de Gastroenterologie et d'Hepatologie
AGHVA6 — Brain and Behavior Research Monograph Series
AGI — Archivio Glottologico Italiano [*Torino*]
AGIAA — Associazione Geofisica Italiana. Atti del Convegno Annuale
Aging Hum Dev — Aging and Human Development
Aging Leis Living — Aging and Leisure Living
Ag Inst R — Agriculture Institute Review
AGIPA — Agricoltura Italiana (Pisa)
AGIS — Attorney General's Information Service
Ag J of British Columbia — Agricultural Journal of British Columbia
Ag J of Egypt — Agricultural Journal of Egypt
Ag J of India — Agricultural Journal of India
AGJOAT — Agronomy Journal
AGJU — Arbeiten zur Geschichte des Antiken Judentums und des Urchristentums
AGKBZH — Archiwum Glownej Komisji Badania Zbrodni Hitlerowskich
AGKKN — Archief voor de Geschiedenis van de Katholieke Kerk in Nederland
AGKYAU — Agrokhimiya
AGLAAV — Agricultura (Lisboa)
AGLABW — Agricultural Research Council. Meat Research Institute [*Bristol*]. Annual Report
AglGr — Anglo-German Review
Ag & Livestock India — Agriculture and Livestock in India
AGLOA — Angeiologie
AGLRA — American Glass Review
AGLUAN — Agronomia Lusitana
AGM — Sudhoffs Archiv fuer Geschichte der Medizin und der Naturwissenschaften
AGMA News Bul — Art Galleries and Museums Association of Australia and New Zealand. News Bulletin
AGMOAA — Agronomia [*Monterrey, Mexico*]
AgN — Age Nouveau
AGN — Anzeiger. Germanisches Nationalmuseum
Ag NL — Agricultural Newsletter
AGNM — Anzeiger. Germanisches Nationalmuseum
AGNMBA — Agronomia [*Caracas*]
AGNNAC — Agricultural Research News Notes [*Lima*]
AGNO — Agriculture North [*Canada*]
AGO — American Guild of Organists. Quarterly
AGORA — Archiwum Gornictwa
Agora Inf Changing World — Agora. Informatics in a Changing World
Agora Math — Agora Mathematica [*Paris*]
Ag Outlook — Agricultural Outlook

AGP — Archiv fuer Geschichte der Philosophie
AGP — Arctic Gas Profile
AGP — Australian Government Publications
AGPAAH — Agriculture (Paris)
AGPh — Archiv fuer Geschichte der Philosophie
AGPLAG — Agroplantae
AGPYAL — Agrochemophysica
AGR — Agrarwirtschaft
Agr — Agricultura
Ag R — Agricultural Review
AGR — American-German Review
Agr Abroad — Agriculture Abroad
A Graefe's A — Albrecht Von Graefe's Archiv fuer Klinische und
    Experimentelle Ophthalmologie
Agr Alger — Agriculture Algerienne
Agr Amer — Agricultura de las Americas
Agr Ammonia News — Agricultural Ammonia News
Agr Anim Husb — Agriculture and Animal Husbandry
Agrarpolit Rev — Agrarpolitische Revue
Agrar Rundsch — Agrarische Rundschau
Agrartoert Szle — Agrartoerteneti Szemle
Agrartort Szemle — Agrartoerteneti Szemle
Agrartud — Agrartudomany
Agrartud Egy Agrarkozgazd Kar Kiad — Agrartudomanyi Egyetem
    Agrarkozgazdasagi Karanak Kiadvanyai
Agrartud Egy Agron Kar Kiad — Agrartudomanyi Egyetem Agronomiai
    Karanak Kiadvanyai
Agrartud Egy Allattenyesz Karanak Kozl (Godollo) — Agrartudomanyi
    Egyetem Allattenyesztesi Karanak Koezlemenyei (Goedoelloe)
Agrartud Egyetem Memoegazdasagtud Kar Koezlem (Goedoelloe) —
    Agrartudomanyi Egyetem Memoegazdasagtudomanyi Karanak
    Koezlemenyei (Goedoelloe)
Agrartud Egyetem Tud Tajekoz (Goedoelloe) — Agrartudomanyi Egyetem
    Tudomanyos Tajekoztatoja (Goedoelloe)
Agrartud Egyet Mezoegtud Kar Koezl (Goedoelloe) — Agrartudomanyi
    Egyetem Mezoegazdasagtudomanyi Karanak Koezlemenyei
    (Goedoelloe)
Agrartud Egy Kert Szologazdasagtud Karanak Evk — Agrartudomanyi
    Egyetem Kert-es Szologazdasagtudomanyi Karanak Evkonyve
Agrartud Egy Kert Szologazdasagtud Karanak Kozl — Agrartudomanyi
    Egyetem Kert-es Szologazdasagtudomanyi Karanak Koezlemenyei
Agrartud Egy Kozl (Godollo) — Agrartudomanyi Egyetem Koezlemenyei
    (Goedoelloe)
Agrartud Egy Mezogazdasagtud Karanak Kozl — Agrartudomanyi Egyetem
    Mezoegazdasagtudomanyi Karanak Koezlemenyei [*Hungary*]
Agrartud Egy Mezogazd Gepeszmern Karanak Kozl — Agrartudomanyi
    Egyetem Mezoegazdasagi Gepeszmernoki Karanak Koezlemenyei
Agrartud Egy Mezogazd Karanak Evk — Agrartudomanyi Egyetem
    Mezoegazdasagi Karanak Evkonyve
Agrartud Egy Tud Tajek — Agrartudomanyi Egyetem Tudomanyos
    Tajekoztatoja [*Hungary*]
Agrartud Foisk Tud Koezlem (Debrecen) — Agrartudomanyi Foiskola
    Tudomanyos Koezlemenyei (Debrecen)
Agrartud Foisk Tud Ulesszakanak Eloadasai Debreceni — Agrartudomanyi
    Foiskola Tudomanyos Ulesszakanak Eloadasai Debreceni
Agrartud Kozl — Agrartudomanyi Koezlemenyek
Agrartud Sz — Agrartudomanyi Szemle
Agrarwirt — Agrarwirtschaft
Agr Asia — Agriculture Asia
Agra Univ J Res — Agra University. Journal of Research [*India*]
Agra Univ J Res Sci — Agra University. Journal of Research Science
Agr Aviation — Agricultural Aviation
Agrawirts — Agrarwirtschaft
Agr Banking Finan — Agricultural Banking and Finance
AGRBAU — Agrobiologiya
Agr Biol Ch — Agricultural and Biological Chemistry [*Tokyo*]
Agr Biol Chem — Agricultural and Biological Chemistry [*Tokyo*]
Agr Bresciano — Agricoltore Bresciano
Agr Bull Canterbury Chamber Commer — Agricultural Bulletin. Canterbury
    Chamber of Commerce
Agr Bull Oreg Dept Agr — Agricultural Bulletin. Oregon Department of
    Agriculture
Agr Bull Saga Univ — Agricultural Bulletin. Saga University
AGRCAX — Agrochimica
AGRCCZ — Agrociencia. Serie C
Agr Chem — Agricultural Chemicals
Agr Econ Inform Ser Univ MD Coop Ext Serv — Agricultural Economics
    Information Series. University of Maryland. Cooperative Extension
    Service
Agr Econ Mimeo Mich State Univ Agr Appl Sci Coop Ext Serv — Agricultural
    Economics Mimeo. Michigan State University of Agriculture and
    Applied Science. Cooperative Extension Service
Agr Econ Mimeo Rep Fla Agr Exp Sta — Agricultural Economics Mimeo
    Report. Florida Agricultural Experiment Station
Agr Econ Pam S Dak Agr Exp Sta — Agricultural Economics Pamphlet. South
    Dakota Agricultural Experiment Station

Agr Econ Re — Agricultural Economics Research
Agr Econ Rep Kans Agr Exp Sta — Agricultural Economics Report. Kansas
    Agricultural Experiment Station
Agr Econ Rep Mich State Univ Agr Appl Sci Coop Ext Serv — Agricultural
    Economics Report. Michigan State University of Agriculture and
    Applied Science. Cooperative Extension Service
Agr Econ Rep N Dak Agr Exp Sta — Agricultural Economics Report. North
    Dakota Agricultural Experiment Station
Agr Econ Res — Agricultural Economics Research
Agr Educ Ma — Agricultural Education Magazine
Agr Eng — Agricultural Engineering [*St. Joseph, MI*]
Agr Eng Ext Bull NY State Coll Agr Dept Agr Eng — Agricultural Engineering
    Extension Bulletin. New York State College of Agriculture. Department
    of Agricultural Engineering
Ag Res — Agricultural Research
Agressolog — Agressologie
Agr Ferrarese — Agricoltore Ferrarese
Agr Ganad — Agricultura y Ganaderia
Agr Gaz NSW — Agricultural Gazette of New South Wales
Agr (Gt Brit) — Agriculture (Great Britain). Ministry of Agriculture, Fisheries,
    and Food
Agr Hist — Agricultural History
Agr Hist Rev — Agricultural History Review
Agr Hor Gen — Agri Hortique Genetica
Agr Hort — Agriculture and Horticulture
AGRIAH — Agricultura (Heverlee)
Agribus Decis — Agribusiness Decision
Agric Adm — Agricultural Administration
Agric Alger — Agriculture Algerienne [*Algeria*]
Agric Am — Agricultura de las Americas
Agric Anim Hub — Agriculture and Animal Husbandry
Agric Biol Chem — Agricultural and Biological Chemistry [*Tokyo*]
Agric & Biol Chem — Agricultural and Biological Chemistry [*Tokyo*]
Agric Bull Fed Malay States — Agricultural Bulletin. Federated Malay States
Agric Bull Saga Univ — Agricultural Bulletin. Saga University
Agric Bur NSW State Congr — Agricultural Bureau of New South Wales.
    State Congress
Agric Can Monogr — Agriculture Canada. Monograph
Agric Can Res Branch Rep — Agriculture Canada. Research Branch Report
Agric Chem — Agricultural Chemicals
Agric Circ US Dep Agric — Agriculture Circular. United States Department of
    Agriculture
Agric Colon — Agricoltura Coloniale
Agric Econ — Agricultural Economist
Agric Econ B Afr — Agricultural Economics Bulletin for Africa
Agric Econ Ext Ser Univ KY Coop Ext Serv — Agricultural Economics
    Extension Series. University of Kentucky. Cooperative Extension
    Service
Agric Econ Fm Mgmt Occ Pap Dep Agric QD Univ — Agricultural Economics
    and Farm Management Occasional Paper. Department of Agriculture.
    University of Queensland
Agric Econ Rep Dep Agric Econ Mich State Univ — Agricultural Economics
    Report. Department of Agricultural Economics. Michigan State
    University
Agric Econ Res — Agricultural Economics Research
Agric Econ Research — Agricultural Economics Research
Agric Econ Res Rep Miss Agric For Exp Sta — Agricultural Economics
    Research Report. Mississippi Agricultural and Forestry Experiment
    Station
Agric Educ — Agricultural Education
Agric Educ Mag — Agricultural Education Magazine
Agric Electr Inst Rep — Agricultural Electricity Institute. Report
Agric El Salvador — Agricultura en El Salvador
Agric-Energy Transp Dig — Agricultural-Energy Transportation Digest
Agric Eng — Agricultural Engineering
Agric Eng (Aust) — Agricultural Engineering (Australia)
Agric Engin — Agricultural Engineering [*St. Joseph, MI*]
Agric Eng J — Agricultural Engineering Journal
Agric Engng (Aust) — Agricultural Engineering (Australia)
Agric Eng (S Afr) — Agricultural Engineering (South Africa)
Agric Eng (St Joseph Mich) — Agricultural Engineering (St. Joseph, MI)
Agric Environ — Agriculture and Environment
Agric Exp — Agricultura Experimental
Agric Exp Stn Univ VT Bull — Agricultural Experiment Station. University of
    Vermont. Bulletin
Agric Fact Sh US Dep Agric — Agriculture Fact Sheet. US Department of
    Agriculture
Agric Fd Chemy — Agricultural and Food Chemistry
Agric Fin R — Agricultural Finance Review
Agric Fin Rev — Agricultural Finance Review
Agric Ganad — Agricultura y Ganaderia
Agric Gaz Can — Agricultural Gazette of Canada
Agric Gaz NSW — Agricultural Gazette of New South Wales
Agric Gaz Tasm — Agricultural Gazette of Tasmania
Agric Handb US Dep Agric — Agriculture Handbook. United States
    Department of Agriculture

Agric Handb US Dep Agric Agric Res Serv — Agriculture Handbook. United States Department of Agriculture. Agricultural Research Service

Agrichem W — Agrichemical West

Agric Hist — Agricultural History

Agric Hist R — Agricultural History Review

Agric Hokkaido — Agriculture in Hokkaido [*Japan*]

Agric Hort — Agriculture and Horticulture [*Japan*]

Agric Hort Engng Abstr — Agricultural and Horticultural Engineering Abstracts

Agric Inf Bull US Dep Agric — Agriculture Information Bulletin. United States Department of Agriculture

Agric Inform Bull US Dep Agric — Agriculture Information Bulletin. United States Department of Agriculture

Agric Inst Rev — Agricultural Institute Review

Agric Ital (Pisa) — Agricoltura Italiana (Pisa)

Agric Ital (Rome) — Agricoltura Italiana (Rome)

Agric J Br Guiana — Agricultural Journal of British Guiana

Agric J (Bridgetown Barbados) — Agricultural Journal (Bridgetown, Barbados)

Agric J Cape GH — Agricultural Journal of the Cape Of Good Hope

Agric J (Cape Town) — Agricultural Journal (Cape Town)

Agric J Dep Agric Fiji Isl — Agricultural Journal. Department of Agriculture. Fiji Islands

Agric J Dept Agric (Victoria BC) — Agricultural Journal. Department of Agriculture (Victoria, British Columbia)

Agric J Egypt — Agricultural Journal of Egypt

Agric J India — Agricultural Journal of India

Agric J & Mining Rec Maritzburg — Agricultural Journal and Mining Record. Maritzburg

Agric J S Afr — Agricultural Journal of South Africa

Agric J Union S Afr — Agricultural Journal of the Union of South Africa

Agric Lit Czech — Agricultural Literature of Czechoslovakia

Agric Livestock India — Agriculture and Livestock in India

Agric Mach J — Agricultural Machinery Journal

Agric Mark (Washington) — Agricultural Marketing (Washington, DC)

Agric Mech Asia — Agricultural Mechanization in Asia [*Japan*]

Agric Met — Agricultural Meteorology

Agric Meteorol — Agricultural Meteorology

Agric Mexicano — Agricultor Mexicano y Hogar

Agric News (Barbados) — Agricultural News (Barbados)

Agric News Lett E I Du Pont De Nemours Co — Agricultural News Letter. E. I. Du Pont De Nemours and Company

Agric Newsl (Manila) — Agricultural Newsletter (Manila)

Agric Nuova — Agricoltura Nuova

Agricoltura Ital (Pisa) — Agricoltura Italiana (Pisa)

Agric Outl — Agricultural Outlook

Agric Outlook — Agricultural Outlook

Agric (Pak) — Agriculture (Pakistan)

Agric Pakistan — Agriculture Pakistan

Agric Prat — Agriculture Pratique [*France*]

Agric Prog — Agricultural Progress

Agric Pugliese — Agricoltura Pugliese

Agric Rec — Agricultural Record

Agric Rec (S Aust) — Agricultural Record (South Australia)

Agric Rec South Aust Dep Agric — Agricultural Record. South Australia. Department of Agriculture

Agric Res — Agricultural Research

Agric Res Corp (Gezira) Tech Bull — Agricultural Research Corporation (Gezira). Technical Bulletin

Agric Res Counc Food Res Inst (Norwich) Annu Rep — Agricultural Research Council. Food Research Institute (Norwich). Annual Report

Agric Res Counc (GB) Letcombe Lab Annu Rep — Agricultural Research Council (Great Britain). Letcombe Laboratory. Annual Report

Agric Res Counc (GB) Radiobiol Lab — Agricultural Research Council (Great Britain). Radiobiological Laboratory

Agric Res Counc (GB) Radiobiol Lab ARCRL — Agricultural Research Council (Great Britain). Radiobiological Laboratory. ARCRL

Agric Res Counc Meat Res Inst (Bristol) Annu Rep — Agricultural Research Council. Meat Research Institute (Bristol). Annual Report

Agric Res Counc Meat Res Inst (Bristol) Memo — Agricultural Research Council. Meat Research Institute (Bristol). Memorandum

Agric Res Counc Rep — Agricultural Research Council. Report

Agric Res Guyana — Agricultural Research Guyana

Agric Res Inst Ukiriguru Prog Rep — Agricultural Research Institute Ukiriguru. Progress Report

Agric Res J Kerala — Agricultural Research Journal of Kerala

Agric Res (Kurashiki) — Agricultural Research (Kurashiki)

Agric Res Man US Dep Agric Sci Educ Adm — Agricultural Research Manual. US Department of Agriculture. Science and Education Administration

Agric Res (New Delhi) — Agricultural Research (New Delhi)

Agric Res News Notes (Lima) — Agricultural Research News Notes (Lima)

Agric Res Organ Div For Ilanot Leafl — Agricultural Research Organization. Division of Forestry. Ilanot Leaflet

Agric Res Organ Volcani Cent Spec Publ — Agricultural Research Organization. Volcani Center. Special Publication

Agric Res Rep (Wageningen) — Agricultural Research Reports (Wageningen)

Agric Res Rep (Wageningen) (Versl Landbouwk Onderz) — Agricultural Research Reports (Wageningen) (Verslagen van Landbouwkundige Onderzoekingen)

Agric Res Rev — Agricultural Research Review

Agric Res Rev (Cairo) — Agricultural Research Review (Cairo)

Agric Res US Dep Agric Res Serv — Agricultural Research. United States Department of Agriculture. Research Service

Agric Res (Wash DC) — Agricultural Research (Washington, DC)

Agric Romande — Agriculture Romande

Agric Sao Paulo — Agricultura em Sao Paulo

Agric Sci (Jogjakarta) — Agricultural Science (Jogjakarta)

Agric Sci R — Agricultural Science Review

Agric Sci Rev Coop State Res Serv US Dep Agric — Agricultural Science Review. Cooperative State Research Service. US Department of Agriculture

Agric Sci (Sofia) — Agricultural Science (Sofia)

Agric Serv Bull FAO — Agricultural Services Bulletin. Food and Agriculture Organization of the United Nations

Agric Situa — Agricultural Situation [*Later, Farmline Magazine*]

Agric Situation India — Agricultural Situation in India

Agric Tec Mex — Agricultura Tecnica en Mexico

Agric Tec (Santiago) — Agricultura Tecnica (Santiago)

Agric Trop — Agricultura Tropical

Agricultura Am — Agricultura de las Americas

Agricultura Tec — Agricultura Tecnica

Agricultura Tec Mex — Agricultura Tecnica en Mexico

Agricultura Trop — Agricultura Tropical

Agriculture in Ire — Agriculture in Northern Ireland

Agriculture (Pakist) — Agriculture (Pakistan)

Agric Venez — Agricultura Venezolana

Agric Venezie — Agricoltura delle Venezie [*Italy*]

Agric Vet Chem — Agricultural and Veterinary Chemicals

Agric Wastes — Agricultural Wastes [*England*]

Agric Water Manage — Agricultural Water Management

Agri Dec — Agriculture Decisions

Agri Hort Genet — Agri Hortique Genetica

Agri Ind — Agriculture Index

Agr Inform Bull USDA — Agriculture Information Bulletin. United States Department of Agriculture

Agr Inst Rev — Agricultural Institute Review

Agriscene (Aust) — Agriscene (Australia)

Agr Israel — Agriculture in Israel

Agr Ital — Agricoltura d'Italia [*Rome*]

AGRJAK — Agronomia [*Rio De Janeiro*]

AGRLAQ — Agriculture (London)

Agr Leaders Dig — Agricultural Leaders Digest

Agr (Lisboa) — Agricultura (Lisboa)

Agr Livestock India — Agriculture and Livestock in India

Agr Market (Nagpur) — Agricultural Marketing (Nagpur)

Agr Market (Washington DC) — Agricultural Marketing (Washington, DC)

AGRMBU — Agronomia [*Manizales*]

Agr Mech — Agricultural Mechanization

Agr Merchant — Agricultural Merchant

Agr Meteor — Agricultural Meteorology

Agr Meteorol — Agricultural Meteorology

Agr Milanese — Agricoltura Milanese

Agr (Montreal) — Agriculture (Montreal)

Agr Napoletana — Agricoltura Napoletana

AGRNAW — Agronomico [*Campinas*]

AGRNDZ — Agronomie [*Paris*]

Agr Newslett — Agricultural Newsletter

Agr N Ireland — Agriculture in Northern Ireland

AGROB2 — Agrochemia (Bratislava)

Agrobiol — Agrobiologiya

Agrobot — Agrobotanika

Agrochem — Agrochemia [*Bratislava*]

Agrochem Cour — Agrochem Courier

Agrochim — Agrochimica

Agrocienc Ser A — Agrociencia. Serie A

Agrocienc Ser C — Agrociencia. Serie C

Agro-Ecosyst — Agro-Ecosystems

Agrokem Talajtan — Agrokemia es Talajtan

Agrokem Talajtan Suppl — Agrokemia es Talajtan. Supplement

Agrokhim — Agrokhimiya

Agrokhim Gruntoznst — Agrokhimiya i Gruntoznaustvo

Agron — Agronomy

Agron Abstr — Agronomy Abstracts

Agron Angol — Agronomia Angolana

Agron Angolana — Agronomia Angolana

Agron Branch Rep (South Aust Dep Agric Fish) — Agronomy Branch Report (South Australia Department of Agriculture and Fisheries)

Agron Costarric — Agronomia Costarricense

Agron Dept Ser Ohio Agr Exp Sta — Agronomy Department Series. Ohio Agricultural Experiment Station

Agron Glas — Agronomski Glasnik

Agron Glasn — Agronomski Glasnik

Agron J — Agronomy Journal
Agron (Lima) — Agronomia (Lima)
Agron Lusit — Agronomia Lusitana
Agron Lusitana — Agronomia Lusitana [*Portugal*]
Agron (Manizales) — Agronomia (Manizales)
Agron (Mexico) — Agronomia (Monterrey, Mexico)
Agron Mimeogr Circ N Dak Agr Exp Sta — Agronomy. Mimeograph Circular.
    North Dakota Agricultural Experiment Station
Agron Mocambicana — Agronomia Mocambicana
Agronomia Angol — Agronomia Angolana
Agronomia Lusit — Agronomia Lusitana
Agronomia Trop — Agronomia Tropical. Revista del Instituto Nacional de
    Agricultura
Agron Pam S Dak Agr Exp Sta — Agronomy Pamphlet. South Dakota
    Agricultural Experiment Station
Agron Soils Res Ser Clemson Agr Exp Sta — Agronomy and Soils Research
    Series. Clemson Agricultural Experiment Station
Agron Sulriogr — Agronomia Sulriograndense
Agron Sulriograndense — Agronomia Sulriograndense
Agron Trop — Agronomia Tropical [*Maracay, Venezuela*]
Agron Trop Agron Gen Etude Tech — Agronomie Tropicale. Agronomie
    Generale. Etudes Techniques [*Paris*]
Agron Trop Agron Gen Etud Sci — Agronomie Tropicale. Agronomie Generale.
    Etudes Scientifiques [*Paris*]
Agron Trop (Maracay) — Agronomia Tropical (Maracay, Venezuela)
Agron Trop (Paris) — Agronomie Tropicale (Paris)
Agron Trop Riz Rizic Cult Vivrieres Trop — Agronomie Tropicale. Serie Riz et
    Riziculture et Cultures Vivrieres Tropicales
Agron Trop Ser Agron Gen Etud Sci — Agronomie Tropicale. Serie Agronomie
    Generale. Etudes Scientifiques
Agron Trop Ser Agron Gen Etud Tech — Agronomie Tropicale. Serie
    Agronomie Generale. Etudes Techniques
Agron Trop Ser Riz Rizic Cult Vivrieres Trop — Agronomie Tropicale. Serie
    Riz et Riziculture et Cultures Vivrieres Tropicales
Agron Vet — Agronomia y Veterinaria
Agron Views Univ Nebr Coll Agr Home Econ Ext Serv — Agronomy Views.
    University of Nebraska. College of Agriculture and Home Economics.
    Extension Service
Agros (Lisb) — Agros (Lisboa)
Agrotec (Madrid) — Agrotecnia (Madrid)
Agrotekh Provid Kul'tur — Agrotekhnika Providnikh Kul'tur
Agr Pakistan — Agriculture Pakistan
Agr (Paris) — Agriculture (Paris)
Agr Policy Rev — Agricultural Policy Review
Agr Prat — Agriculture Pratique
Agr Progr — Agricultural Progress
AGRRA — Agricultural Research Review
AGRRAA — Agricultural Research Review [*Cairo*]
Agr Res — Agricultural Research
Agr Res (India) — Agricultural Research (India)
Agr Res J Kerala — Agricultural Research Journal of Kerala
Agr Res (Pretoria) — Agricultural Research (Pretoria)
Agr Res Rev — Agricultural Research Review [*Cairo*]
Agr Res (Washington DC) — Agricultural Research (Washington, DC)
Agr Romande — Agriculture Romande
Agr (Santo Domingo) — Agricultura (Santo Domingo)
Agr Sao Paulo — Agricultura em Sao Paulo
Agr Sci Rev — Agricultural Science Review
Agr Sit Ind — Agricultural Situation in India
Agr Situation — Agricultural Situation [*Later, Farmline Magazine*]
Agr Situation India — Agricultural Situation in India
Agr Spezia — Agricoltura della Spezia
Agr Statist N Dak Crop Livestock Rep Serv — Agricultural Statistics. North
    Dakota Crop and Livestock Reporting Service
Agr Tec — Agricultura Tecnica
Agr Tec Mex — Agricultura Tecnica en Mexico
Agr Trop — Agricultura Tropical
AGR Univ KY Coop Ext Serv — AGR. University of Kentucky. Cooperative
    Extension Service
Agr Venezie — Agricoltura delle Venezie
Agr Vet Chem — Agricultural and Veterinary Chemicals
AGRYAV — Agronomy
AGS — Agency Sales
Ag Sci J — Agricultural Science Journal
Ag Sci R — Agricultural Science Review
AGSD — Acta Germanica zur Sprache und Dichtung Deutschlands
Ag Situation — Agricultural Situation [*Later, Farmline Magazine*]
AGSLAV — Agronomia Sulriograndense
AGSOA — Agressologie
Ag Sply Ind — Agricultural Supply Industry
AGSU — Arbeiten zur Geschichte des Spaetjudentums und Urchristentums
AGSYD5 — Agricultural Systems
AGT — Australian Grade Teacher
AGTBA6 — Agricultura Tropical
AGTCA9 — Agricultura Tecnica [*Santiago*]
AGTG — Agenutemagen. Indians of New Brunswick [*Canada*]

AGTOAB — Agronomie Tropicale. Agronomie Generale. Etudes Techniques
AGTQA — Annales de Genetique
AGTSAN — Agrokemia es Talajtan. Supplement
Agua Energ — Agua y Energia
AGUSD — Gas + Architecture
AGVEAP — Agricultura Venezolana
AGVO — Arbeitsgemeinschaft Vorderer Orient
AGW — Abhandlungen. Gesellschaft der Wissenschaften zu Goettingen
Agway Coop — Agway Cooperator
AGWD — Australian Government Weekly Digest
AGWG — Abhandlungen. Gesellschaft der Wissenschaften zu Goettingen
AGYRA — Agricultural Research
AGZPAA — Agrikultura (Nitre)
AH — Aboriginal History
AH — Agricultural History
AH — American Heritage
AH — American Historical Review
AH — Anjou Historique
AH — Archivium Hibernicum
AH — Archivo Hispalense
AH — Art for Humanity
AHA — Hitotsubashi Academy. Annals
AHA — Hitotsubashi Journal of Economics
AHAB — Australian Historical Association. Bulletin
AHAG — Annales. Societe d'Histoire et d'Archeologie de Gand
AHAM — Anales de Historea Antigua y Medieval
AHAM — Association of Home Appliance Manufacturers. Trends and
    Forecasts
AHA Newsletter — American Historical Association. Newsletter
AHAW — Abhandlungen. Heidelberger Akademie der Wissenschaften
AHAWPK — Abhandlungen. Heidelberger Akademie der Wissenschaften.
    Philosophisch-Historische Klasse
AHB — Archaeologisch-Historische Bijdragen
AHB — [*The*] Australian Hymn Book
AHC — Annuarium Historiae Conciliorum
AHCCAX — Aichi Cancer Center Research Institute. Annual Report
AHCE — Asociacion para la Historia de la Ciencia Espanola
AHCI — Arts and Humanities Citation Index
AHCP — Arquivos de Historia de Cultura Portuguesa
AHD — Archives d'Histoire Dominicaine
AHDE — Anuario de la Historia del Derecho Espanol
AHDL — Archives d'Histoire Doctrinale et Litteraire [*Paris*]
AHDLMA — Archives d'Histoire Doctrinale et Litteraire du Moyen-Age
AHDO — Archives d'Histoire du Droit Oriental
AHDRA — Archiwum Hydrotechniki
AHE — Annales d'Histoire Economique
AHEAD — Australian Health Education Advisory Digest
AHEB — Analectes pour Servir a l'Histoire Ecclesiastique de la Belgique
AHEMA — Anatomia, Histologia, Embryologia
AHES — Annales d'Histoire Economique et Sociale
AHF — Abba Hushi Files [*Haifa*]
AHF — Archivum Historii, Filozofii, i Mysli Spolecznej
AHF — Australian High Court and Federal Court Practice
AHG — Archives Historique de la Gironde
AHGAK — Archiv fuer Hessische Geschichte und Altertumskunde
AHHI — Alon Hahevra Hanumismatit le'Israel
AHIL Q — Association of Hospital and Institution Libraries. Quarterly
A HistHung — Acta Historica. Academiae Scientiarum Hungaricae
AHJOA — American Heart Journal
AHL — Abstracts of Hungarian Economic Literature
AHL — Annuaire d'Histoire Liegeoise
AHMA — Archives d'Histoire Doctrinale et Litteraire du Moyen-Age
AHN — Acta Historiae Neerlandica
AHNRH — Annalen des Historischen Vereins fuer den Niederrhein
AHO — Technische Hogeschool Delft. Bibliotheek. Aanwinsten
AHORA — Acta Horticulturae
AHP — Archivum Historiae Pontificiae
AHPAA — Annales. Institut Henri Poincare. Section A (Physique Theorique)
AHPBA — Annales. Institut Henri Poincare. Section B (Calcul des
    Probabilites et Statistique)
AHPRB — Advances in High Pressure Research [*England*]
AHQ — Arkansas Historical Quarterly
AHR — American Historical Review
AHR — Australasian Home Reader
AHRF — Annales Historiques de la Revolution Francaise
Ahrokhim Hruntozn Resp Mizhvid Temat Zb — Ahrokhimia i Hruntoznavstvo
    Respublikanskii Mizhvidomchyi Tematichnyi Zbirnyk
AHRRBI — Australia. Commonwealth Scientific and Industrial Research
    Organization. Division of Horticulture. Research Report
AHRTA — Arhiv za Higijenu Rada i Toksikologiju
AHRTAN — Arhiv za Higijenu Rada i Toksikologiju
AHRW — Alcohol Health and Research World
AHS — Annales d'Histoire Sociale
AHS — Archives Heraldiques Suisses
AHSI — Archivum Historicum Societatis Iesu
AHSM — Antiquarian Horological Society. Monograph

AHSoc — Annales d'Histoire Sociale
AHSSOP — Alberta. Historic Sites Service. Occasional Papers [*Canada*]
AHSUA — Acta Histochemica. Supplementband
AHTCB — Advances in High Temperature Chemistry
AHTJA — Archivum Histologicum Japonicum
AHTRA — Advances in Heat Transfer
A Humor — American Humor
AHUNA — Archivos de Hospitales Universitarios
AHUTA — Archiwum Hutnictwa
AHVMF — Archiv des Historischen Vereins von Mainfranken
AHVNR — Annalen des Historischen Vereins fuer den Niederrhein
AHVNRh — Annalen des Historischen Vereins fuer den Niederrhein
AHVsLund — Kungliga Humanistiska Vetenskapssamfundet i Lund. Arsberattelse
AHVsUppsala — Kungliga Humanistiska Vetenskapssamfundet i Uppsala. Arsbok
AHVUA — Archiv des Historischen Vereins von Unterfranken und Aschaffenburg
AHW — Altona, Hamburg, Wandsbek
AHZ — Allgemeine Homoeopathische Zeitung
AI — Acta Iranica
AI — Africa Italiana
AI — Afrique Industrie
AI — America Indigena
AI — American Imago
AI — Ancient India
AI — Annals of Iowa
AI — Archives Israelites de France [*Paris*]
AI — Ars Islamica
AI — Art International
AI — Artificial Intelligence [*Elsevier Book Series*]
AI — Aslib Information
AI — L'Avenir Illustre [*Casablanca*]
AIa — Annals of Iowa
AIA — Archivo Ibero-Americano [*Madrid*]
AIA — Art in America
AIAA Bull — AIAA [*American Institute of Aeronautics and Astronautics*] Bulletin
AIAA J — AIAA [*American Institute of Aeronautics and Astronautics*] Journal
AIAA Journal — American Institute of Aeronautics and Astronautics. Journal
AIAA Monogr — AIAA [*American Institute of Aeronautics and Astronautics*] Monographs
AIAA Pap — AIAA [*American Institute of Aeronautics and Astronautics*] Paper
AIAA Stud J — AIAA [*American Institute of Aeronautics and Astronautics*] Student Journal
AIA J — AIA [*American Institute of Architects*] Journal
AIA Jnl — AIA [*American Institute of Architects*] Journal
AIAK — Akten des Internationalen Amerikanisten-Kongresses
AIAL — Annales. Institut Archeologique du Luxembourg
AIA Lux — Annales. Institut Archeologique du Luxembourg
AIANAT — Arctic Institute of North America. Annual Report
AIARA — Archives of Interamerican Rheumatology
AIASAA — Arctic Institute of North America. Special Publication
AIAS News — Australian Institute of Aboriginal Studies. Newsletter
AIAS Newslett — AIAS [*Australian Institute of Aboriginal Studies*] Newsletter
AIATAD — Arctic Institute of North America. Technical Paper
AIB — Academie des Inscriptions et Belles-Lettres. Memoires Presentes par Divers Savants
AIB — Advances in Inorganic Biochemistry [*Elsevier Book Series*]
AIB — Arkheologiia i Istoriia Bospora. Sbornik Statei
AIB — Augustana Institute Bulletin
AIB Boll — Associazione Italiana Biblioteche. Bollettino d'Informazioni
AIBL — Academie des Inscriptions et Belles-Lettres. Comptes Rendus des Seances
AIBLA — Archives Italiennes de Biologie
AIBLCr — Academie des Inscriptions et Belles-Lettres. Comptes Rendus des Seances
AIBPD — Annales. Institut du Petrole (Belgium)
AIBR — Australian Insurance and Banking Record
AIBS Bull — AIBS [*American Institute of Biological Sciences*] Bulletin
AIBS Newsl — AIBS [*American Institute of Biological Sciences*] Newsletter
AIC — Advances in Consumer Research Proceedings
AIC — Aeronautical Information Circular
AICA Bull — AICA [*Australasian Institute of Cost Accountants*] Bulletin
AICC — American Indian Crafts and Culture
AICCER — All India Congress Committee. Economic Review
AIChE Annu Meet Prepr — AIChE [*American Institute of Chemical Engineers*] Annual Meeting. Preprints
AIChE Annu Meet Program Abstr — AIChE [*American Institute of Chemical Engineers*] Annual Meeting. Program Abstracts
AIChEJ — AIChE [*American Institute of Chemical Engineers*] Journal
AIChE Monogr Ser — AIChE [*American Institute of Chemical Engineers*] Monograph Series

AIChE Natl (or Annu) Meet Prepr — AIChE [*American Institute of Chemical Engineers*] National (or Annual) Meeting. Preprints
AIChE Pap — AIChE [*American Institute of Chemical Engineers*] Papers
AIChE Symp Ser — AIChE [*American Institute of Chemical Engineers*] Symposium Series
Aichi Cancer Cent Res Inst Annu Rep — Aichi Cancer Center Research Institute. Annual Report
Aichi-Gakuin J Dent Sci — Aichi-Gakuin Journal of Dental Science
Aichi J Exp Med — Aichi Journal of Experimental Medicine
Aichi Univ Educ Res Rep Nat Sci — Aichi University of Education. Research Report. Natural Sciences [*Japan*]
AICIA — Archivio Italiano di Chirurgia
AICP — Anthropological Index to Current Periodicals in the Library of the Royal Anthropological Institute
AICRA — Advances in Inorganic Chemistry and Radiochemistry
AICS — Anuarul. Institutul de Studii Clasice
AID — Aerospace Information Digest
AID — Australian Industries Development Association. Bulletin
Ai Daig Bung R — Aichi Daigaku Bungaku Ronso
AIDC (Am Ind Development Council) J — AIDC (American Industrial Development Council) Journal
AIDI — Annuaire. Institut de Droit International
AIDP — Advances in Disease Prevention
AIDPA — American Institute of Industrial Engineers. Detroit Chapter. Proceedings of the Annual Conference
AID Res Dev Abstr — AID [*Agency for International Development*] Research and Development Abstracts
AIEA — Archivos. Instituto de Estudios Africanos
AIEC — Anales. Instituto de Etnografia Americana. Universidad Nacional de Cuyo
AIEC — Anuario. Institut de'Estudios Catalans
AIEE Proc — American Institute of Electrical Engineers. Proceedings
AIEE Trans — Transactions. American Institute of Electrical Engineers
AIEG — Anales. Instituto de Estudios Gerundenses
AIEM — Anales. Instituto de Estudios Madrilenos
AIEN — Anales. Instituto Etnico Nacional, Argentina
AIEO — Annales. Institut d'Etudes Occitanes
AIEO — Annales. Institut d'Etudes Orientales [*Alger*]
AIF — Annales. Institut Francais de Zagreb
AIF — Anzeiger fuer Indogermanische Sprach- und Altertumskunde
AIFEA — Archivos. Instituto de Farmacologia Experimental [*Madrid*]
AIF News — Agricultural, Insecticide, and Fungicide Association. News
AIFUA — Annales. Institut Fourier. Universite de Grenoble
AIGC — Annuario. Istituto Giapponese di Cultura in Roma
AIGMA — Anales. Instituto de Geofisica. Universidad Nacional Autonoma de Mexico
AIGPAV — Atti. Istituto Geologico. Universita di Pavia
AIGR — Anuarul. Institutului Geologic al Romaniei
AIH — Aussenhandelsdienst der Industriekammern und Handelskammern und Wirtschaftsverbande [*Frankfurt Am Main*]
AIHAA — American Industrial Hygiene Association. Journal
AIHAAP — American Industrial Hygiene Association. Journal
AIHI — Archives Internationales d'Histoire des Idees
AIHM — Archivos Iberoamericanos de Historia de la Medicina
AIHS — Archives Internationales d'Histoire des Sciences
AIIE — Anales. Instituto de Investigaciones Esteticas
AIIE Ind Engng — American Institute of Industrial Engineers. Industrial Engineering
AIIE Trans — AIIE [*American Institute of Industrial Engineers*] Transactions
AIIJD — Journal. American Intraocular Implant Society
AIIN — Annali. Istituto Italiano di Numismatica
AIIN — Atti e Memorie. Istituto Italiano di Numismatica
AIIS — Annali. Istituto Italiano per gli Studi Storici
AIK — Aviacija i Kosmonavtika
AIL — Anales. Instituto de Linguistica. Universidad Nacional de Cuyo
AIL — Australian Industrial Law Review
AILC — Anales. Instituto de Linguistica. Universidad Nacional de Cuyo
AILC — Anales. Instituto de Literaturas Clasicas
AILM — Anales. Istituto di Linguistica di Mendoza
AILR — Australian Industrial Law Review
AIM — Aboriginal-Islander-Message
AIM — Abridged Index Medicus
AIM — Abstracts of Instructional Materials in Vocational and Technical Education [*ERIC*]
AIM — American Inkmaker
AIM — Annali dell'Isturzione Media
AIMAA — Archivio Italiano delle Malattie dell'Apparato Digerente
AIMEA — Annals of Internal Medicine
AIME Proc Annu Miner Symp — American Institute of Mining, Metallurgical, and Petroleum Engineers. Proceedings. Annual Minerals Symposium
AIME Trans — American Institute of Mining, Metallurgical, and Petroleum Engineers. Transactions
AIMJA9 — Ain Shams Medical Journal
AIMK — Akademija Istorii Material'noj Kul'tury
AIMNA — Advances in Internal Medicine
AIN — Atti e Memorie. Istituto Italiano di Numismatica

AINAH — Anales. Instituto Nacional de Antropologia e Historia
AINARP — Arctic Institute of North America. Research Paper
AINCAR — India. Coffee Board. Research Department. Annual Report
AInd — Art Index
Ain Shams Med J — Ain Shams Medical Journal
Ain Shams Sci Bull — Ain Shams Science Bulletin
Ain Shams Univ Fac Agric Bull — Ain Shams University. Faculty of Agriculture. Bulletin
AInst — Annales Institutorum Quae in Urbe Erecta Sunt
A Inst Anat Univ Hels — Acta Instituti Anatomici Universitatis Helsinkiensis
A Inst Anesth — Acta. Institut d'Anesthesiologie
A Inst Comp Stud Cult — Annals. Institute of Comparative Studies of Culture
A Inst Et Trav Secur Soc — Annales. Institut d'Etudes du Travail et de la Securite Sociale
A Int Criminol — Annales Internationales de Criminologie
AIOK — Akten des Internationalen Orientalisten-Kongresses
AiolikaG — Aiolika Grammata
AION — Annali. Istituto Universitario Orientale (Napoli)
AION-G — Annali. Istituto Universitario Orientale. Sezione Germanica (Napoli)
AION-L — Annali. Istituto Universitario Orientale. Sezione Linguistica (Napoli)
AION Ling — Annali. Istituto Universitario Orientale. Sezione Linguistica [Napoli]
AION-O — Annali. Istituto Universitario Orientale. Sezione Orientale (Napoli)
AION-R — Annali. Istituto Universitario Orientale. Sezione Romanza (Napoli)
AION-S — Annali. Istituto Universitario Orientale. Sezione Slava (Napoli)
AION-SG — Annali. Istituto Universitario Orientale. Sezione Germanica (Napoli)
AION-SL — Annali. Istituto Universitario Orientale. Sezione Linguistica (Napoli)
AION-SO — Annali. Istituto Universitario Orientale. Sezione Orientale (Napoli)
AION-SR — Annali. Istituto Universitario Orientale. Sezione Romanza (Napoli)
AION-SS — Annali. Istituto Universitario Orientale. Sezione Slava (Napoli)
AIORA — Archivio Italiano di Otologia, Rinologia, e Laringologia
AIOUAlger — Annales. Institut Oriental. Universite d'Alger
AIP — Aeronautical Information Publication [FAA]
AIPAA — Annales. Institut Pasteur [Paris]
AIP Conference Proceedings — American Institute of Physics. Conference Proceedings
AIP Conf Proc — AIP [American Institute of Physics] Conference Proceedings
AIP Conf Proc Part Fields Subser — AIP [American Institute of Physics] Conference Proceedings. Particles and Fields Subseries
AIPE Newsl — AIPE [American Institute of Plant Engineers] Newsletter
AIPhO — Annuaire. Institut de Philologie et d'Histoire Orientales [Bruxelles]
AIPhOS — Annuaire. Institut de Philologie et d'Histoire Orientales et Slaves [Bruxelles]
AIPJA — Journal. American Institute of Planners
AIPLA — Annales. Institut Pasteur de Lille
AIPS — Annuaire. Institut de Philologie et d'Histoire Orientales et Slaves [Bruxelles]
AIPUA — Archivio Italiano di Patologia e Clinica dei Tumori
AIQ — American Indian Quarterly
AIQSA — Annals of the IQSY [International Quiet Sun Year]
AIR — ADAM [Arts, Drama, Architecture, Music] International Review
AIR — Air et Cosmos. Hebdomadaire de l'Actualite Aerospatiale et des Techniques Avancees
Airc Engng — Aircraft Engineering
Air Clean — Air Cleaning [Japan]
Air Commerce Bul — Air Commerce Bulletin
Air Cond Heat & Refrig N — Air Conditioning, Heating, and Refrigeration News
Air Cond Heat Refrig News — Air Conditioning, Heating, and Refrigeration News
Air Cond Heat & Ven — Air Conditioning, Heating, and Ventilating
Air Cond Heat Vent — Air Conditioning, Heating, and Ventilating
Air Cond Oil Heat — Air Conditioning and Oil Heat
Aircond Refrig Bus — Airconditioning and Refrigeration Business
Air Cond & Refrig N — Air Conditioning and Refrigeration News
Aircr Eng — Aircraft Engineering
Aircr Prod — Aircraft Production
AIRD — Australian Industrial Research Directory
AIREEN — AIDS Research
Air Eng — Air Engineering
Air-Espace Tech — Air-Espace Techniques
Air F Civ Eng — Air Force Civil Engineer
Air F Comp — Air Force Comptroller
Air Force Civil Eng — Air Force Civil Engineer
Air Force Eng Serv Q — Air Force Engineering and Services Quarterly [United States]
Air Ind — Air Industriel
AirPolAb — Air Pollution Abstracts

Air Poll Cont Assn J — Air Pollution Control Association. Journal
Air Poll Control Assn J — Air Pollution Control Association. Journal
Air Pollut — Air Pollution
Air Pollut Assoc J — Air Pollution Control Association. Journal
Air Pollut Control — Air Pollution Control
Air Pollut Control Assoc Annu Meet Pap — Air Pollution Control Association. Annual Meeting. Papers
Air Pollut Control Dist Cty Los Angeles Annu Rep — Air Pollution Control District. County of Los Angeles. Annual Report
Air Pollut Found Rep — Air Pollution Foundation. Report
Air Pollut News — Air Pollution News [Japan]
Airports Int — Airports International
Air Qual Instrum — Air Quality Instrumentation
Air Qual Monogr — Air Quality Monographs
AIRR — Air Reservist
Air Reserv — Air Reservist
Air Transp World — Air Transport World
Air Univ R — Air University. Review
Air Univ Rev — Air University. Review
AirUnLibI — Air University. Library Index to Military Periodicals
Air/Water Poll Rept — Air/Water Pollution Report
Air Water Pollut — Air and Water Pollution
AISD — Annali. Istituto di Studi Danteschi
AISIN — Alon. Internal Quarterly of the Israel Numismatic Society
AISI Steel Prod Man — American Iron and Steel Institute. Steel Products Manual
AISJB — Journal. American Society for Information Science
AISLN — Annali. Istituto Superiore di Scienze e Lettere di Santa Chiera (Napoli)
AISNC — ASIS [American Society for Information Science] Newsletter
AISP — Annales. Institut Superieur de Philosophie
AIS Technical Soc Bul — AIS [Australian Iron and Steel] Technical Society. Bulletin
AITBA — Annales. Institut Technique du Batiment et des Travaux Publics
AITEA — Archivum Immunologiae et Therapiae Experimentalis
AITL & P — Australian Income Tax Law and Practice
AITR — Australian Income Tax Reports
AITR — Australian and New Zealand Income Tax Reports
AIUO — Annali. Istituto Universitario Orientale. Sezione Germanica [Napoli]
AI(U)ON — Annali. Istituto Universitario Orientale (Napoli)
AIV — Atti. Reale Istituto Veneto di Scienze, Lettere, ed Arti. Classe di Scienze Morali e Lettere
AIVLAQ — Atti. Istituto Veneto di Scienze, Lettere, ed Arti. Classe di Scienze Matematiche e Naturali
AIVMB — Archivos de Investigacion Medica
AIVNDZ — Atti. Istituto Veneto di Scienze, Lettere, ed Arti [Venezia]. Classe di Scienze Fisiche, Matematiche, e Naturali
AIVSML — Atti. Reale Istituto Veneto di Scienze, Lettere, ed Arti. Classe di Scienze Morali e Lettere
AIWR — Arctic International Wildlife Range Society. Newsletter
AIZLA — Archiwum Inzynierii Ladowej
AJ — Alaska Journal of Commerce and Pacific Rim Reporter
AJ — Alliance Journal
AJ — Antiquaries Journal [London]
AJ — Archaeological Journal
AJ — Architects' Journal
AJ — Art Journal
AJ — Asiatisches Jahrbuch
AJ — Australian Journal
AJA — American Jewish Archives
AJA — American Journal of Archaeology
AJA — Anglo-Jewish Archives
AJADD — Australian Journal of Alcoholism and Drug Dependence
AJAE — American Journal of Agricultural Economics
AJAEB — American Journal of Agricultural Economics
AJANA — American Journal of Anatomy
AJANA2 — American Journal of Anatomy
AJAPB9 — American Journal of Acupuncture
AJAr — American Journal of Archaeology
AJ Archaeol — American Journal of Archaeology
AJAS — AJAS: Australasian Journal of American Studies
AJAS — Australian Journal of Applied Science
AJATA — American Journal of Art Therapy
AJB — Australian Journal of Botany
AJBA — Australian Journal of Biblical Archaeology
AJBI — Annual. Japanese Biblical Institute
AJBOA — American Journal of Botany
AJBOAA — American Journal of Botany
AJBTA — Australian Journal of Botany
AJCBDD — American Journal of Clinical Biofeedback
AJCDA — American Journal of Cardiology
AJCDAG — American Journal of Cardiology
AJCL — American Journal of Comparative Law
AJCMBA — American Journal of Chinese Medicine
AJCNA — American Journal of Clinical Nutrition
AJCNAC — American Journal of Clinical Nutrition

AJCOD — American Journal of Clinical Oncology
AJCODI — American Journal of Clinical Oncology
AJCP — Australian Joint Copying Project
AJCPA — American Journal of Clinical Pathology
AJCPAI — American Journal of Clinical Pathology
AJCPD — American Journal of Physiology. Cell Physiology
AJDA — Actualite Juridique. Droit Administratif. Revue Mensuelle
AJDABD — American Journal of Drug and Alcohol Abuse
AJDC — American Journal of Diseases of Children
AJDCA — American Journal of Diseases of Children
AJDCAI — American Journal of Diseases of Children
AJDDA — American Journal of Digestive Diseases [*Later, Digestive Diseases and Sciences*]
AJDDAL — American Journal of Digestive Diseases [*Later, Digestive Diseases and Sciences*]
AJE — American Journal of Economics and Sociology [*New York*]
AJEED — Abstract Journal in Earthquake Engineering
AJEPA — American Journal of Epidemiology
AJEPAS — American Journal of Epidemiology
AJER — Alberta Journal of Educational Research
AJES — Aligarh Journal of English Studies
AJES — American Journal of Economics and Sociology [*New York*]
AJESA — American Journal of Economics and Sociology [*New York*]
AJETA6 — American Journal of EEG Technology
AJEVAC — American Journal of Enology and Viticulture
AJFE — Alternatives. Journal of the Friends of the Earth [*Canada*]
AJFS — Australian Journal of Forensic Sciences
AJFS — Australian Journal of French Studies
AJGAA — American Journal of Gastroenterology
AJGAAR — American Journal of Gastroenterology
AJGV — Akademischer Verein fuer Juedische Geschichte und Literatur
AJHEA — American Journal of Public Health
AJHEAA — American Journal of Public Health
AJHED — American Journal of Hematology
AJHEDD — American Journal of Hematology
AJHGA — American Journal of Human Genetics
AJHGAG — American Journal of Human Genetics
AJHNA3 — American Journal of Clinical Hypnosis
AJHPA — American Journal of Hospital Pharmacy
AJHPA9 — American Journal of Hospital Pharmacy
AJHQ — American Jewish Historical Quarterly
AJHS — American Jewish Historical Society. Publications
AJHS J — Australian Jewish Historical Society. Journal
AJHYA2 — American Journal of Hygiene
Ajia Keizai — Ajia Keizai. Journal of the Institute of Developing Economics
AJICDC — American Journal of Infection Control
A J I Law — American Journal of International Law
AJIMD8 — American Journal of Industrial Medicine
AJINB — American Journal of International Law
AJJ — American Chamber of Commerce in Japan. Journal
AJJR — Annales. Societe Jean-Jacques Rousseau
AJKDD — American Journal of Kidney Diseases
AJLMDN — American Journal of Law and Medicine
AJLS — Australian Journal of Law and Society
AJM — Archivo Jose Marti [*Cuba*]
AJM — Australian Journal of Management
AJMAA — American Journal of Mathematics
AJMD — American Journal of Mental Deficiency
AJMDA — American Journal of Mental Deficiency
AJMDAW — American Journal of Mental Deficiency
AJME — Australian Journal of Music Education
AJMEA — American Journal of Medicine
AJMEA — Australian Journal of Music Education
AJMEAZ — American Journal of Medicine
AJMFA — Australian Journal of Marine and Freshwater Research
AJMGDA — American Journal of Medical Genetics
AJMNA — Australian Journal of Mental Retardation
AJMSA — American Journal of the Medical Sciences
AJMSA9 — American Journal of the Medical Sciences
AJMTA — American Journal of Medical Technology
AJMTAC — American Journal of Medical Technology
AJN — American Journal of Numismatics
AJN — Australian Jewish News
AJNAD — Arab Journal of Nuclear Sciences and Applications
AJNED9 — American Journal of Nephrology
AJNR — AJNR. American Journal of Neuroradiology
AJNR Am J Neuroradiol — AJNR. American Journal of Neuroradiology
AJNT — Ajurnarmat. Inuit Cultural Institute
AJNUA — American Journal of Nursing
AJNum — American Journal of Numismatics
AJOAAX — American Journal of Optometry and Archives of American Academy of Optometry [*Later, American Journal of Optometry and Physiological Optics*]
AJOGA — American Journal of Obstetrics and Gynecology
AJOGAH — American Journal of Obstetrics and Gynecology
AJOHA — American Journal of Orthodontics

AJOHAK — American Journal of Orthodontics
AJOMA — Alabama Journal of Medical Sciences
AJOMAZ — Alabama Journal of Medical Sciences
AJOOA7 — American Journal of Orthodontics and Oral Surgery [*Later, American Journal of Orthodontics*]
AJOPA — American Journal of Ophthalmology
AJOPAA — American Journal of Ophthalmology
AJOPs — American Journal of Orthopsychiatry
AJORA — American Journal of Orthopsychiatry
AJORAG — American Journal of Orthopsychiatry
AJOT — American Journal of Occupational Therapy
AJOTA — American Journal of Occupational Therapy
AJOTAM — American Journal of Occupational Therapy
AJOTBN — American Journal of Otology
Ajour Ind-Tek — Ajour Industril-Teknikk [*Norway*]
AJOYA — American Journal of Optometry
AJP — American Journal of Pharmacy
AJP — American Journal of Philology
AJP — American Journal of Psychoanalysis
AJPA — American Journal of Physical Anthropology
AJPA — Australian Journal of Public Administration
AJPAA — American Journal of Pathology
AJPAA4 — American Journal of Pathology
AJPBA — American Journal of Physical Medicine
AJPBA7 — American Journal of Physical Medicine
AJPCA — American Journal of Psychology
AJPCAA — American Journal of Psychology
AJPDA — American Journal of Pharmaceutical Education
AJPDAD — American Journal of Pharmaceutical Education
AJPEA — American Journal of Public Health and the Nation's Health [*Later, American Journal of Public Health*]
AJPED — American Journal of Physiology. Endocrinology, Metabolism, and Gastrointestinal Physiology
AJPEEK — American Journal of Perinatology
AJPh — American Journal of Philology
AJPH — American Journal of Public Health
AJPH — Australian Journal of Politics and History
AJPHA — American Journal of Physiology
AJPHAP — American Journal of Physiology
AJPhil — American Journal of Philology
AJPIA — American Journal of Physics
AJPMEA — American Journal of Preventive Medicine
AJPNA — American Journal of Physical Anthropology
AJPNA9 — American Journal of Physical Anthropology
AJPOA — American Journal of Proctology [*Later, American Journal of Proctology, Gastroenterology, and Colon and Rectal Surgery*]
AJPOAC — American Journal of Proctology [*Later, American Journal of Proctology, Gastroenterology, and Colon and Rectal Surgery*]
AJ Pol & Hist — Australian Journal of Politics and History
AJPPD — American Journal of Physiology. Heart and Circulatory Physiology
AJPRA — American Journal of Pharmacy and the Sciences Supporting Public Health [*Later, American Journal of Pharmacy*]
AJPRAL — American Journal of Pharmacy and the Sciences Supporting Public Health [*Later, American Journal of Pharmacy*]
AJPs — American Journal of Psychology
AJPSA — American Journal of Psychiatry
AJPSAO — American Journal of Psychiatry
AJPst — American Journal of Psychotherapy
AJPsy — American Journal of Psychiatry
A J Psy — American Journal of Psychology
AJPsych — American Journal of Psychology
AJ Psychol — American Journal of Psychology
AJPTAR — American Journal of Psychotherapy
AJPTDU — American Journal of Primatology
AJPXA — Australasian Journal of Pharmacy. Science Supplement
AJPYA8 — American Journal of Psychoanalysis
AJQ — Australian Jazz Quarterly
AJR — AJR. American Journal of Roentgenology
AJR — Australian Journal of Reading
AJR — Australian Jurist Reports
A (Jr A) — Arizoniana (Journal of Arizona History)
AJR Am J Roentgenol — AJR. American Journal of Roentgenology
AJRFD — American Journal of Physiology. Renal, Fluid, and Electrolyte Physiology
AJRI — American Journal of Reproductive Immunology
AJRMEK — AJRIM. American Journal of Reproductive Immunology and Microbiology
AJR (NC) — Australian Jurist Reports (Notes of Cases)
AJROA — American Journal of Roentgenology
AJROAM — AJR. American Journal of Roentgenology
AJRRA — American Journal of Roentgenology, Radium Therapy, and Nuclear Medicine [*Later, American Journal of Roentgenology*]
AJRRAV — American Journal of Roentgenology, Radium Therapy, and Nuclear Medicine [*Later, American Journal of Roentgenology*]
AJRTA — American Journal of Roentgenology and Radium Therapy [*Later, American Journal of Roentgenology*]

AJS — Actes Juridiques Susiens
AJS — American Journal of Science
AJS — American Journal of Sociology
AJSBD — American Journal of Small Business
AJSCA — American Journal of Science
AJSCAP — American Journal of Science
AJSci — American Journal of Science
AJSemL — American Journal of Semitic Languages and Literatures
AJSL — American Journal of Semitic Languages and Literatures
AJSLL — American Journal of Semitic Languages and Literatures [*Chicago, IL*]
AJSMD — American Journal of Sports Medicine
AJSOA — American Journal of Sociology
AJ Soc — American Journal of Sociology
AJ Soc Iss — Australian Journal of Social Issues
AJSPDX — American Journal of Surgical Pathology
AJSR — Australian Journal of Scientific Research
AJSUA — American Journal of Surgery
AJSUAB — American Journal of Surgery
AJT — American Journal of Theology
AJTh — American Journal of Theology
AJTHA — American Journal of Tropical Medicine and Hygiene
AJTHAB — American Journal of Tropical Medicine and Hygiene
AJTRDA — American Journal of Therapeutics and Clinical Reports
AJu — Archives Juives
A Jur Rep — Australian Jurist Reports
AJUS — Antarctic Journal of the United States
AJVRA — American Journal of Veterinary Research
AJVRAH — American Journal of Veterinary Research
AJY — American Jewish Yearbook
AJZOA — Australian Journal of Zoology
AK — Alaska Music Educator
AK — Antike Kunst
AK — Archiv fuer Kulturgeschichte
AK — Ateneum Kaplanskie
AKABA7 — Arkansas. Agricultural Experiment Station. Bulletin
Akad Nauk Armjan SSR Dokl — Akademija Nauk Armjanskoi SSR. Doklady
Akad Nauk Arm SSR Dokl — Akademiya Nauk Armyanskoy SSR. Doklady
Akad Nauka Umjet Bosne Hercegov Rad Odjelj Prirod Mat Nauka — Akademija Nauka i Umjetnosti Bosne i Hercegovine. Radovi Odjeljenje Prirodnih i Matematickih Nauka
Akad Nauka i Umjet Bosne i Hercegov Rad Odjelj Tehn Nauka — Akademija Nauka i Umjetnosti Bosne i Hercegovine. Radovi Odjeljenje Tehnickih Nauka
Akad Nauk Azerbaidzan SSR Dokl — Akademija Nauk Azerbaidzanskoi SSR. Doklady
Akad Nauk Azerb SSR Dokl — Akademiya Nauk Azerbaydzhanskoy SSR. Doklady
Akad Nauk BSSR Dokl — Akademiya Nauk BSSR. Doklady
Akad Nauk Gruzin SSR Trudy Tbiliss Mat Inst Razmadze — Akademija Nauk Gruzinskoi SSR. Trudy Tbilisskogo Matematiceskogo Instituta Imeni A. M. Razmadze
Akad Nauk Gruz SSR Geol Inst Tr — Akademiya Nauk Gruzinskoy SSR. Geologicheskiy Institut. Trudy
Akad Nauk Gruz SSR Soobshch — Akademiya Nauk Gruzinskoy SSR. Soobshcheniya
Akad Nauk Kazah SSR Trudy Astrofiz Inst — Akademija Nauk Kazahskoi SSR. Trudy Astrofiziceskogo Instituta
Akad Nauk Kazah SSR Trudy Inst Mat i Meh — Akademija Nauk Kazahskoi SSR. Trudy Instituta Matematiki i Mehaniki
Akad Nauk Kaz SSR Inst Geol Nauk Tr — Akademiya Nauk Kazakhskoy SSR. Institut Geologicheskikh Nauk. Trudy
Akad Nauk Kaz SSR Izv Ser Geol — Akademiya Nauk Kazakhskoy SSR. Izvestiya. Seriya Geologicheskaya
Akad Nauk SSSR Dokl — Akademiya Nauk SSSR. Doklady
Akad Nauk SSSR Doklady Izvestiia Ser Geol — Akademiia Nauk SSSR. Doklady. Izvestiia. Seriia Geologicheskaia
Akad Nauk SSSR Geol Inst Tr — Akademiya Nauk SSSR. Geologicheskiy Institut. Trudy
Akad Nauk SSSR Geol Inst Trudy — Akademiya Nauk SSSR. Geologicheskiy Institut. Trudy
Akad Nauk SSSR Geomorfol Kom Plenum Mater — Akademiya Nauk SSSR. Geomorfologicheskaya Komissiya. Plenum. Materialy
Akad Nauk SSSR Izv Ser Fiz — Akademiya Nauk SSSR. Izvestiya. Seriya Fizicheskaya
Akad Nauk SSSR Izv Ser Geogr — Akademiya Nauk SSSR. Izvestiya. Seriya Geograficheskaya
Akad Nauk SSSR Izv Ser Geol — Akademiya Nauk SSSR. Izvestiya. Seriya Geologicheskaya
Akad Nauk SSSR Komi Fil Inst Geol Tr — Akademiya Nauk SSSR. Komi Filial. Institut Geologii. Trudy
Akad Nauk SSSR Kom Izuch Chetvertich Perioda Byull — Akademiya Nauk SSSR. Komissiya po Izucheniyu Chetvertichnogo Perioda. Byulleten
Akad Nauk SSSR Kom Opred Absol Vozrasta Geol Form Tr — Akademiya Nauk SSSR. Kommissiya po Opredeleniyu Absolyutnogo Vozrasta Geologicheskikh Formatsiy. Trudy

Akad Nauk SSSR Metallofizka — Akademiya Nauk SSSR. Metallofizika
Akad Nauk SSSR Mezhduvedomstv Geofiz Kom Geofiz Byull — Akademiya Nauk SSSR. Mezhduvedomstvennoy Geofizicheskiy Komitet pri Presidiume Geofizicheskiy Byulleten
Akad Nauk SSSR Paleontol Inst Tr — Akademiya Nauk SSSR. Paleontologicheskiy Institut Trudy
Akad Nauk SSSR Sibirsk Otdel Vychisl Tsentr Preprint — Akademiya Nauk SSSR. Sibirskoe Otdelenie Vychislitelnyi Tsentr. Preprint
Akad Nauk SSSR Sibirsk Otdel Vycisl Centr Preprint — Akademija Nauk SSSR. Sibirskoe Otdelenie. Vycislitelnyi Centr. Preprint [*Novosibirsk*]
Akad Nauk SSSR Sib Otd Inst Geol Geofiz Tr — Akademiya Nauk SSSR. Sibirskoye Otdeleniye. Institut Geologii i Geofiziki. Trudy
Akad Nauk SSSR Trudy Jakutsk Filial Ser Fiz — Akademiya Nauk SSSR. Trudy Jakutskogo Filiala. Serija Fiziceskaja
Akad Nauk SSSR Ural Fil Tr Inst Khim — Akademiya Nauk SSSR. Ural'skii Filial. Trudy Instituta Khimii
Akad Nauk SSSR Ural Nauchn Tsentr Inst Geol Geokhim Tr — Akademiya Nauk SSSR. Ural'skiy Nauchnyi Tsentr. Institut Geologii i Geokhimii. Trudy
Akad Nauk SSSR Vestn — Akademiya Nauk SSSR. Vestnik
Akad Nauk Tadzh SSR Dokl — Akademiya Nauk Tadzhikskoy SSR. Doklady
Akad Nauk Tadzh SSR Otd Fiz-Mat Geol-Khim Nauk Izv — Akademiya Nauk Tadzhikskoy SSR. Otdeleniye Fiziko-Matematicheskikh i Geologo-Khimicheskikh Nauk. Izvestiya
Akad Nauk Turkm SSR Izv Ser Fiz-Tekh Khim Geol Nauk — Akademiya Nauk Turkmenskoy SSR. Izvestiya. Seriya Fiziko-Tekhnicheskikh. Khimicheskikh i Geologicheskikh Nauk
Akad Nauk Ukrain SSR Inst Mat Preprint — Akademiya Nauk Ukrainskoi SSR. Institut Matematiki. Preprint
Akad Nauk Ukr RSR Dopov Ser B — Akademiya Nauk Ukrainskoy RSR. Dopovidi. Seriya B. Geologiya, Geofizika, Khimiya, ta Biologiya
Akad Nauk Ukr RSR Inst Teploenerg Zb Pr — Akademia Nauk Ukrainskoi RSR. Institut Teploenergetiki. Zbirnik Prats [*Ukrainian SSR*]
Akad Nauk Ukr SSR Metallofiz — Akademiya Nauk Ukrainskoi SSR. Metallofizika
Akad Nauk Ukr SSR Ser Metallofiz — Akademiya Nauk Ukrainskoi SSR. Seriya Metallofizika [*Ukrainian SSR*]
Akad Wiss DDR Zentralinst Phys Erde Veroeff — Akademie der Wissenschaften der DDR. Zentralinstitut fuer Physik der Erde. Veroeffentlichungen
Akad d Wiss Denksch Philos-Hist Kl — Akademie der Wissenschaften in Wien. Philosophisch-Historische Klasse. Denkschriften
Akad Wiss Goettingen Math Phys Kl Abh Folge 3 — Akademie der Wissenschaften in Goettingen. Mathematisch-Physikalische Klasse. Abhandlungen. Folge 3
Akad Wiss Gottingen Nachr Math-Physikal Kl — Akademie der Wissenschaften in Goettingen. Nachrichten. Mathematisch-Physikalische Klasse
Akad Wiss Lit Abh Math-Naturwiss Kl (Mainz) — Akademie der Wissenschaften und der Literatur in Mainz. Abhandlungen der Mathematisch-Naturwissenschaftlichen Klasse
Akad Wiss Lit Mainz Abh Math-Natur Kl — Akademie der Wissenschaften und der Literatur in Mainz. Abhandlungen der Mathematisch-Naturwissenschaftlichen Klasse
Akad Wiss Lit Mainz Abh Math-Naturwiss Kl — Akademie der Wissenschaften und der Literatur in Mainz. Abhandlungen der Mathematisch-Naturwissenschaftlichen Klasse
Akad Wiss Lit Mainz Jahrb — Akademie der Wissenschaften und der Literatur in Mainz. Jahrbuch (Wiesbaden)
Akad Wiss Lit Mainz Math-Naturwiss Kl Abh — Akademie der Wissenschaften und der Literatur in Mainz. Abhandlungen der Mathematisch-Naturwissenschaftlichen Klasse. (Wiesbaden)
Akad d Wiss Sitzungsb Philos-Hist Kl — Akademie der Wissenschaften in Wien. Philosophisch-Historische Klasse. Sitzungsberichte
AKAJAV — Journal. American Killifish Association
AKAMA6 — Arkansas. Agricultural Experiment Station. Mimeograph Series
AKARAL — Arkansas. Agricultural Experiment Station. Report Series
AKASAO — Arkansas Academy of Science. Proceedings
AKAW — Abhandlungen. Koenigliche Preussische Akademie der Wissenschaften zu Berlin
AKAW — Anzeiger. Kaiserliche Akademie der Wissenschaften [*Wien*]
AKB — Internationales Afrikaforum
AKCBA — Akita-Kenritsu Chuo Byoin Igaku Zasshi
AKCBAH — Akita Central Hospital. Medical Journal
AKCBAH — Akita-Kenkritsu Chuo Byoin Igaku Zasshi
AKCVA — Archiv fuer Klinische Chirurgie. Langenbecks
AKDDA — Bulletin. Akron Dental Society [*Ohio*]
AKDEDY — Aktuelle Dermatologie
AKDJA — Arkansas Dental Journal
AKDV — Anzeiger fuer Kunde der Deutschen Vorzeit
AKG — Arbeiten zur Kirchengeschichte
AKG — Archiv fuer Kulturgeschichte
AKG — Kerngetallen van Nederlandse Effecten (Amsterdam)

AKGIA — Akusherstvo i Ginekologiya

AKGIAO — Akusherstvo i Ginekologiya [*Moscow*]

AKGRAH — Aktuelle Gerontologie

Akita Cent Hosp Med J — Akita Central Hospital. Medical Journal

AKK — Archiv fuer Katholisches Kirchenrecht

AKKR — Archiv fuer Katholisches Kirchenrecht

AKM — Abhandlungen fuer die Kunde des Morgenlandes

AKMDA — Arkhimedes

AKML — Abhandlungen zur Kunst, Musik, und Literaturwissenschaft

AKMTA — Arkiv foer Matematik

AKNKDY — Akita-Kenkritsu Nogyo Tanki Daigaku Kenkyu Hokoku

AKNUAR — Aktuelle Neurologie

AKOGAO — Albrecht Von Graefe's Archive for Clinical and Experimental Ophthalmology

AKONA — Archiv fuer Klinische und Experimentelle Ohren-, Nasen-, und Kehlkopfheilkunde

AKPOD — Avtomatizatsiya i Kontrol'no-Izmeritel'nye Pribory v Nefteptererabatyvayushchei i Neftekhimicheskoi Promyshlennosti

AKRHDB — Aktuelle Rheumatologie

Akron Bus & Econ R — Akron Business and Economic Review

Akron L Rev — Akron Law Review

Ak St — Auckland Star

AKTLAU — Agrokemia es Talajtan

Akt Probl Inf Dokum — Aktualne Problemy Informacji i Dokumentacji

AKTRAE — Aktuelle Traumatologie

Aktual Probl Inf & Dok — Aktualne Problemy Informacji i Dokumentacji

Aktual Probl Inf Dok — Aktualne Problemy Informacji i Dokumentacji

Aktual Probl Onkol Med Radiol — Aktual'nye Problemy Onkologii i Meditsinskoi Radiologii [*Belorussian SSR*]

Aktual Probl Prof Patol Resp Mezhved Sb — Aktualnye Problemy Professional'noi Patologii Respublikanskoi Mezhvedomstvennyi Sbornik

Aktual Vopr Dermatol Venerol — Aktual'nye Voprosy Dermatologii i Venerologii

Aktual Vopr Epidemiol — Aktualnye Voprosy Epidemiologii

Aktual Vopr Farm — Aktualnye Voprosy Farmatsii

Aktual Vopr Ginekol — Aktualnye Voprosy Ginekologii

Aktual Vopr Oftal — Aktualnye Voprosy Oftal'mologii

Aktual Vopr Oftal'mol — Aktualnye Voprosy Oftal'mologii

Aktual Vopr Patol Pecheni — Aktual'nye Voprosy Patologii Pecheni

Aktual Vopr Sovrem Biokhim — Aktual'nye Voprosy Sovremennoi Biokhimii

Aktual Vopr Sovrem Onkol — Aktual'nye Voprosy Sovremennoi Onkologii

Aktuel Fragen Psychiat Neurol — Aktuelle Fragen der Psychiatrie und Neurologie [*Switzerland*]

Aktuel Fragen Psychiatr Neurol — Aktuelle Fragen der Psychiatrie und Neurologie

Aktuel Fragen Psychother — Aktuelle Fragen der Psychotherapie

Aktuel Gerontol — Aktuelle Gerontologie

Aktuellt Lantbrukshogs — Aktuellt fran Lantbrukshogskolan

Aktuel Neurol — Aktuelle Neurologie

Aktuel Otorhinolaryngol — Aktuelle Otorhinolaryngologie

Aktuel Probl Chir — Aktuelle Probleme in der Chirurgie [*Later, Aktuelle Probleme in Chirurgie und Orthopaedie*]

Aktuel Probl Chir Orthop — Aktuelle Probleme in Chirurgie und Orthopaedie

Aktuel Probl Phoniatr Logop — Aktuelle Probleme der Phoniatrie und Logopaedie

Aktuel Probl Polym-Phys — Aktuelle Probleme der Polymer-Physik

Aktuel Rheumatol — Aktuelle Rheumatologie [*West Germany*]

Aktuel Traumatol — Aktuelle Traumatologie

Aktuel Urol — Aktuelle Urologie

AKultG — Archiv fuer Kulturgeschichte [*Weimar*]

Akush Ginekol (Mosc) — Akusherstvo i Ginekologiya (Moscow)

Akush Ginekol (Moscow) — Akusherstvo i Ginekologiya (Moscow)

Akush Ginekol (Sofia) — Akusherstvo i Ginekologiya (Sofia) [*Bulgaria*]

Akust Beih — Akustische Beihefte [*Switzerland*]

Akust Ul'trazvuk Tekh — Akustika i Ul'trazvukovaya Tekhnika

Akust Zh — Akusticheskii Zhurnal

AKVBAA — Arkiv foer Botanik

Ak Waik Hist J — Auckland-Waikato Historical Journal

Akw Notes — Akwesasne Notes

AKWS — Akwesasne Notes

Akz — Akzente

AKZHA — Akusticheskii Zhurnal

AKZMA — ATOMKI [*Atommag Kutato Intezet*] Koezlemenyek. Supplement

AL — Acta Linguistica

AL — Ala Breve

AL — Alighieri

AL — American Literature

AL — Annali Lateranensi

ALA — Afrique Litteraire et Artistique

ALA — Annales. Faculte des Lettres d'Aix-en-Provence

Ala Acad Sci Jour — Alabama Academy of Science. Journal

Ala Ag Exp — Alabama. Agricultural Experiment Station. Publications

Ala Agribus — Alabama Agribusiness

Ala Agric Exp Stn Annu Rep — Alabama. Agricultural Experiment Station. Annual Report

Ala Agric Exp Stn Auburn Univ Agron Soils Dep Ser — Alabama. Agricultural Experiment Station. Auburn University. Agronomy and Soils Departmental Series

Ala Agric Exp Stn Auburn Univ For Dep Ser — Alabama. Agricultural Experiment Station. Auburn University. Forestry Departmental Series

Ala Agric Exp Stn Bull — Alabama. Agricultural Experiment Station. Bulletin

Ala Agric Exp Stn Bull (Auburn Univ) — Alabama. Agricultural Experiment Station. Bulletin (Auburn University)

Ala Agric Exp Stn Cir — Alabama. Agricultural Experiment Station. Circular

Ala Agric Exp Stn Leafl — Alabama. Agricultural Experiment Station. Leaflet

Ala Agric Exp Stn Leafl (Auburn Univ) — Alabama. Agricultural Experiment Station. Leaflet (Auburn University)

Ala Agric Exp Stn Prog Rep Ser — Alabama. Agricultural Experiment Station. Progress Report Series

Ala Agric Exp Stn Prog Rep Ser (Auburn Univ) — Alabama. Agricultural Experiment Station. Progress Report Series (Auburn University)

Alabama Geol Soc Bull — Alabama. Geological Society. Bulletin

Alabama Geol Survey Inf Ser — Alabama. Geological Survey. Information Series

Alabama Geol Survey Map — Alabama. Geological Survey. Map

Alabama L Rev — Alabama Law Review

ALA Bul — American Library Association. Bulletin

Ala Bus — Alabama Business

Ala Bus and Econ Repts — Alabama Business and Economic Reports

Ala Conserv — Alabama Conservation

Ala Corn Variety Rep — Alabama Corn Variety Report

Ala Geol Surv Atlas Ser — Alabama. Geological Survey. Atlas Series

Ala Geol Surv Bull — Alabama. Geological Survey. Bulletin

Ala Geol Surv Circ — Alabama. Geological Survey. Circular

Ala Geol Surv Cty Rep — Alabama. Geological Survey. County Report

Ala Geol Survey and State Oil and Gas Board Ann Repts — Alabama. Geological Survey and State Oil and Gas Board. Annual Reports

Ala Geol Surv Geo-Petro Notes — Alabama. Geological Survey. Geo-Petro Notes

Ala Geol Surv Inf Ser — Alabama. Geological Survey. Information Series

Ala Geol Surv Map — Alabama. Geological Survey. Map

Ala G S — Alabama. Geological Survey

Ala His S — Alabama Historical Society. Transactions

ALA Hosp Bk Guide — American Library Association. Association of Hospital and Institution Libraries. Book Guide

AlaHQ — Alabama Historical Quarterly

Ala Ind Sc Soc Pr — Alabama Industrial and Scientific Society. Proceedings

ALA Intellectual Freedom Newsl — American Library Association. Intellectual Freedom Committee. Newsletter

ALAJ — Alaska Journal

Ala J Med Sci — Alabama Journal of Medical Sciences

Ala Law — Alabama Lawyer

Ala Libn — Alabama Librarian

ALA Lib Period Round Table Newsl — American Library Association. Library Periodicals Round Table. Newsletter

ALA Lib Serv to Labor News — American Library Association. Adult Services Division. Joint Committee on Library Service to Labor Groups. Library Service to Labor Newsletter

Ala L Rev — Alabama Law Review

Ala Mar Resour Bull — Alabama Marine Resources. Bulletin

Al-An — Al-Andalus

Ala Nurse — Alabama Nurse

ALAPDP — Arizona Land and People

Ala R — Alabama Review

ALA Ref Serv Div — American Library Association. Reference Services Division. Reference Quarterly

Ala Rev — Alabama Review

ALARM — Australian Library Annual Reports on Microfiche

ALAS — Alaska

ALASA — Allergie und Asthma

ALASH — Acta Linguistica. Academiae Scientiarum Hungaricae

Alaska Ag Exp — Alaska. Agricultural Experiment Station. Publications

Alaska Agric Exp Stn Bull — Alaska. Agricultural Experiment Station. Bulletin

Alaska Agric Exp Stn Circ — Alaska. Agricultural Experiment Station. Circular

Alaska BB — Alaska Bar Brief

Alaska Constr Oil — Alaska Construction and Oil

Alaska Dep Fish Res Rep — Alaska. Department of Fisheries. Research Report

Alaska Dept Mines Rept Commissioner Mines Bienn — Alaska. Department of Mines. Report of the Commissioner of Mines. Biennium

Alaska Div Geol Geophys Surv Geochem Rep — Alaska. Division of Geological and Geophysical Surveys. Geochemical Report

Alaska Div Geol Geophys Surv Geol Rep — Alaska. Division of Geological and Geophysical Surveys. Geologic Report

Alaska Div Geol Surv Geochem Rep — Alaska. Division of Geological Survey. Geochemical Report

Alaska Div Mines Geol Geochem Rep — Alaska. Division of Mines and Geology. Geochemical Report

Alaska Div Mines Geol Geol Rep — Alaska. Division of Mines and Geology. Geologic Report

Alaska Div Mines and Geology Geochem Rept — Alaska. Department of Natural Resources. Division of Mines and Geology. Geochemical Report
Alaska Div Mines and Geology Geol Rept — Alaska. Department of Natural Resources. Division of Mines and Geology. Geologic Report
Alaska Div Mines and Minerals Inf Circ Rept — Alaska. Division of Mines and Minerals. Information Circular. Report
Alaska Div Mines Miner Rep — Alaska. Division of Mines and Minerals. Report
Alaska Ind — Alaska Industry
Alaska Med — Alaska Medicine
Alaska Rev Bus Econ Cond — Alaska Review of Business and Economic Conditions
Alaska Sci Conf Proc — Alaska Science Conference. Proceedings
Alaska Univ Anthrop Pa — Alaska University. Anthropological Papers
Alaska Univ Geophys Inst Rep — Alaska University. Geophysical Institute. Report
Alaska Univ Mineral Industry Research Lab Rept — Alaska University. Mineral Industry Research Laboratory. Report
Alaska Univ Mineral Industry Research Lab Rept — University of Alaska. Mineral Industry Research Laboratory. Report
Alaska Univ School Mines Pub Bull — Alaska University. School of Mines Publication. Bulletin
ALAT — Alaska Today
Alauda Rev Int Ornithol — Alauda. Revue Internationale d'Ornithologie
ALA Wash Newsl — American Library Association. Washington Newsletter
ALAZ — ALA [*American Latvian Association*] Zurnals
ALB — Aboriginal Law Bulletin
ALB — Adyar Library Bulletin
Alb — Albania
ALB — Allgemeines Literaturblatt
ALB — Almanacco Letterario Bompiani
ALB — Annales. Faculte des Lettres de Besancon
Albany Felt Guide — Albany Felt Guidelines
Albany Inst Pr — Albany Institute. Proceedings
Albany Inst Tr — Albany Institute. Transactions
Albany L R — Albany Law Review
Albany L Rev — Albany Law Review
Albany News Dig — Albany International Weekly News Digest
Alber J Edu — Alberta Journal of Educational Research
Alberta Dep Lands For Annu Rep — Alberta. Department of Lands and Forests. Annual Report
Alberta Dept Mines and Minerals Mines Div Ann Rept — Alberta. Department of Mines and Minerals. Mines Division. Annual Report
Alberta Gaz — Alberta Gazette
Alberta His — Alberta History
Alberta J Educ Res — Alberta Journal of Educational Research
Alberta Lands For Annu Rep — Alberta Lands and Forests. Annual Report
Alberta L (Can) — Alberta Law Reports (Canada)
Alberta L R — Alberta Law Review
Alberta L Rev — Alberta Law Review
Alberta Med Bull — Alberta Medical Bulletin
Alberta M L J — Alberta Modern Language Journal
Alberta Res Annu Rep — Alberta Research. Annual Report
Alberta Res Counc Bull — Alberta Research Council. Bulletin
Alberta Res Counc Inf Ser — Alberta Research Council. Information Series
Alberta Res Counc Rep — Alberta Research Council. Report
Alberta Research Council Bull — Alberta Research Council. Bulletin
Alberta Research Council Inf Ser — Alberta Research Council. Information Series
Alberta Research Council Mem — Alberta Research Council. Memoir
Alberta Research Council Mimeo Circ — Alberta Research Council. Mimeographed Circular
Alberta Research Council Prelim Rept — Alberta Research Council. Preliminary Report
Alberta Research Council Prelim Soil Survey Rept — Alberta Research Council. Preliminary Soil Survey Report
Alberta Research Council Rept — Alberta Research Council. Report
Alberta Res Econ Geol Rep — Alberta Research. Economic Geology Report
Alberta Res Inf Ser — Alberta Research. Information Series
Alberta Res Rep — Alberta Research. Report
Alberta Soc Pet Geol Annu Field Conf Guideb — Alberta Society of Petroleum Geologists. Annual Field Conference. Guidebook
Alberta Soc Petroleum Geologists Jour News Bull — Alberta Society of Petroleum Geologists. Journal. News Bulletin
Alberta Univ Dept Civil Eng Struct Eng Rep — Alberta University. Department of Civil Engineering. Structural Engineering Reports
ALBI — Alaska Business and Industry [*Supersedes Alaska Industry*]
ALBJ — Alberta Business Journal
ALBLB — American Lung Association. Bulletin
Alb LR — Alberta Law Reports
Alb L Rev — Albany Law Review
ALBN — Alberta Naturalist
ALBr — Anuario da Literatura Brasileira
Albrecht Thaer Arch — Albrecht-Thaer-Archiv
Albrecht V Graefe's Arch Ophthal — Albrecht Von Graefe's Archiv fuer Ophthalmologie

Albrecht Von Graefe's Arch Clin Exp Ophthalmol — Albrecht Von Graefe's Archive for Clinical and Experimental Ophthalmology
Albrecht Von Graefe's Arch Klin Exp Ophthalmol — Albrecht Von Graefe's Archiv fuer Klinische und Experimentelle Ophthalmologie [*West Germany*]
Albrecht Von Graefe's Arch Ophthalmol — Albrecht Von Graefe's Archiv fuer Ophthalmologie
Alb Stud — Albertina Studien
ALBVA — Animal Learning and Behavior
ALBYBL — American Laboratory [*Fairfield, Connecticut*]
Alby LR — Albany Law Review
Alc — Alcantara
ALCGP — Annali del Liceo Classico Garibaldi di Palermo
Alcheringa (Assoc Australas Palaeontol) — Alcheringa (Association of Australasian Palaeontologists)
ALCNAQ — Alabama Conservation
ALCO — Alberta Conservationist
ALCOA Res Lab Tech Pap — ALCOA [*Aluminum Company of America*] Research Laboratories. Technical Paper
Alcoh Health & Res W — Alcohol Health and Research World
Alcohol Health Res World — Alcohol Health and Research World
Alco Prod Rev — Alco Products Review
ALCR — Alaska Conservation Review
Al Culukidzis Sahelob Khutnaisi Sahelmc Ped Inst Srom — Al. Culukidzis Sahelobis Khutnaisis Sahelmcipho Pedagogiuri Institutis Sromebi
ALD — Administrative Law Decisions. Australian
ALD — African Law Digest
ALD — Fortschrittliche Betriebsfuehrung und Industrial Engineering
ALDGA — Alloy Digest
ALDJA — Journal. Alabama Dental Association
ALE — Antitrust Law and Economics Review
A Lead — Adult Leadership
ALEC — Anales de la Literatura Espanola Contemporanea
ALED — Alaska Education News
ALELWLE — American Literature, English Literature, and World Literature in English
ALEN — Alaska Education News
ALES — Alaska Earthlines/Tidelines. Alaska Geographic Society
ALET — Alaska Economic Trends
ALet — Armas y Letras
ALet — Aspetti Letterari
Alexander Blain Hosp Bull — Alexander Blain Hospital. Bulletin
Alexandria J Agric Res — Alexandria Journal of Agricultural Research
Alexandria J Agr Res — Alexandria Journal of Agricultural Research
Alexandria Med J — Alexandria Medical Journal
Alexanor Rev Lepid Fr — Alexanor; Revue des Lepidopteristes Francais
Alex Dent J — Alexandria Dental Journal
Alex J Agric Res — Alexandria Journal of Agricultural Research
Alfaatih Univ Bull Fac Eng — Alfaatih University. Bulletin of the Faculty of Engineering
ALFE — Acta Lapponica Fenniae
ALFM — Alaska Farm Magazine [*Superseded by Alaska Farm and Garden*]
ALFOAA — Alberta Lands and Forests. Annual Report
Alfold — Alfoeld: Irodalmi es Muvelodesi Folyoirat
ALFRA — Alta Frequenza
Alfred P Sloan Found Rep — Alfred P. Sloan Foundation. Report
Alfred Univ NY State Coll Ceram Mon Rep — Alfred University. New York State. College of Ceramics. Monthly Report
Alfr Hosp Clin Rep — Alfred Hospital. Clinical Reports
ALG — Africa. An International Business, Economic, and Political Monthly
ALG — Algol
ALGAB — Alberta Gazette
ALGE — Alaska Geographic
ALGED — Alaska Geographic
Algerie Med — Algerie Medicale [*Algeria*]
Alger Med — Algerie Medicale
Alger Serv Geol Bull — Algeria. Service Geologique. Bulletin
ALGGM — Annuario. Liceo Ginnasio G. Mameli
ALGHJ — Arbeiten zur Literatur und Geschichte des Hellenistischen Judentums
Alg Log — Algebra and Logic
Algodon Bol Cam Algodonera Peru — Algodon Boletin de la Camara Algodonera del Peru
Algol Stud — Algological Studies
Algoritmi i Algoritm Jazyki — Algoritmy i Algoritmiceskie Jazyki
Algot Holmbergs Arsb — Algot Holmbergs Arsbok
ALGP — Annuario. Liceo Ginnasio Statale G. Palmieri
Alg Pap-Rund — Allgemeine Papier-Rundschau
Alg Proefstn Alg Ver Rubberplant Oostkust Sumatra Vlugschr — Algemeen Proefstation der Algemeene Vereniging van Rubberplanters ter Oostkust van Sumatra. Vlugschrift
Alg Zuivelbl — Algemeen Zuivelblad
Alg Zuivel Melkhyg Weekbl — Algemeen-Zuivel-en Melkhygienisch Weekblad
ALH — Acta Linguistica. Academiae Scientiarum Hungaricae
ALH — Acta Linguistica Hafniensia
ALHa — Acta Linguistica Hafniensia

ALHN — Alaska History News
ALi — Amor de Libro
A Lib — American Libraries [*Chicago*]
Alicyclic Chem — Alicyclic Chemistry
ALIDA — Alliance Industrielle
ALIE — America Latina Informe Economico
Aligarh Bull Math — Aligarh Bulletin of Mathematics
Aligarh Muslim Univ Publ Zool Ser — Aligarh Muslim University Publications. Zoological Series
ALIL — Anuar de Lingvistica si Istorie Literara
ALIM — America Latina Informe de Mercados
ALIMC — Allergie und Immunologie
Aliment Anim — Alimentazione Animale
Aliment Ital — Alimentazione Italiana
Aliment Nutr Anim — Alimentos y Nutricion Animal
Aliment Vie — Alimentation et la Vie
ALIN — Alaska Industry
ALing — Archivum Linguisticum
ALingHung — Acta Linguistica. Academiae Scientiarum Hungaricae
ALIP — Alaska in Perspective
ALIP — America Latina Informe Politico
Aliphatic Alicyclic Saturated Heterocycl Chem — Aliphatic, Alicyclic, and Saturated Heterocyclic Chemistry
Aliphatic Relat Nat Prod Chem — Aliphatic and Related Natural Product Chemistry
ALI Proc — American Law Institute. Proceedings
ALIR — Australian Library and Information Research
ALitASH — Acta Litteraria. Academiae Scientiarum Hungaricae
ALitH — Acta Litteraria. Academiae Scientiarum Hungaricae
ALJ — Alemannisches Jahrbuch
ALJ — Allahabad Law Journal
ALJ — Australian Law Journal
ALJ — Australian Library Journal
ALJOD — Australian Law Journal
ALJR — Australian Law Journal. Reports
Alkalmaz Mat Lapok — Alkalmazott Matematikai Lapok
Alkaloidal Clin — Alkaloidal Clinic
Alkaloids Chem Physiol — Alkaloids Chemistry and Physiology
ALKM — Archiv fuer Literatur und Kirchengeschichte des Mittelalters
Alkohol Ind — Alkohol Industrie
Alkohol Ind Wiss Tech Brennereibeil — Alkohol Industrie. Wissenschaftliche Technische Brennereibeilage
AlL — Almanach des Lettres
ALL — Archiv fuer Lateinische Lexikographie und Grammatik [*Munich/Leipzig*]
ALL — Australian Labour Law Reporter
AL/LA — African Languages/Langues Africaines
AllaB — Alla Bottega
Allahabad Fmr — Allahabad Farmer
Allahabad LJ — Allahabad Law Journal
Allahabad Univ Studies — Allahabad University Studies
Alla LJ — Allahabad Law Journal
Allam- es Jogtud — Allam- es Jogtudomany
Allan Hancock Found Publ Occas Pap — Allan Hancock Foundation. Publications. Occasional Paper
Allan Hancock Monogr Mar Biol — Allan Hancock Monographs in Marine Biology
Allatgyogy Oltoanyagellenorzo Intez Evk — Allatgyogyaszati Oltoanyagellenorzo Intezet Evkonyve
Allat Lapok — Allatorvosi Lapok
Allatorv Lapok — Allatorvosi Lapok
Allattani Kozl — Allattani Kozlemenyek
Allatteny — Allattenyesztestani Tanszek
ALLCB — ALLC [*Association for Literary and Linguistic Computing*] Bulletin
ALLC J — ALLC [*Association for Literary and Linguistic Computing*] Journal
Allegheny Ludlum Horiz — Allegheny Ludlum Horizons
Allem Aujourd — Allemagnes d'Aujourd'hui
All Eng — All England Law Reports
All ER — All England Law Reports
Allerg Abstr — Allergy Abstracts
Allerg Asthma — Allergie und Asthma
Allerg Asthmaforsch — Allergie und Asthmaforschung
Allerg Immunol — Allergie und Immunologie
Allerg Immunol (Leipz) — Allergie und Immunologie (Leipzig)
Allergol Immunopathol — Allergologia et Immunopathologia [*Madrid*]
Allevamenti Vet — Allevamenti e Veterinaria
Alley Mus — Alley Music
ALLG — Archiv fuer Lateinische Lexikographie und Grammatik
All Gazdasag — Allami Gazdasag
Allg Brau Hopfenztg — Allgemeine Brauer- und Hopfenzeitung
Allg Deutsche Naturh Ztg — Allgemeine Deutsche Naturhistorische Zeitung
Allg Dt Imkerztg — Allgemeine Deutsche Imkerzeitung
Allg Dtsch Imkerztg — Allgemeine Deutsche Imkerzeitung

Allgem Berg- u Huettenm Ztg — Allgemeine Berg- und Huettenmaennische Zeitung
Allgemein Statist Arch — Allgemeines Statistisches Archiv
Allg Fischwirtschaftsztg — Allgemeine Fischwirtschaftszeitung
Allg Fisch-Ztg — Allgemeine Fischerei-Zeitung
Allg Forst Holzwirtsch Zeit — Allgemeine Forst- und Holzwirtschaftliche Zeitung
Allg Forst Holzwirtsch Ztg — Allgemeine Forst- und Holzwirtschaftliche Zeitung
Allg Forst Jagdztg — Allgemeine Forst- und Jagdzeitung
Allg Forst- u Jagdztg — Allgemeine Forst- und Jagdzeitung
Allg Forstz — Allgemeine Forstzeitschrift
Allg Forstzeitschr — Allgemeine Forstzeitschrift
Allg Forstztg — Allgemeine Forstzeitung
Allg Gerber Ztg — Allgemeine Gerber Zeitung
Allg Imkerkal — Allgemeine Imkerkalender
Allg Lederind Ztg — Allgemeine Lederindustrie Zeitung
ALLG Newsletter — Australian Law Librarians' Group. Newsletter
Allg Oel-Fett-Ztg — Allgemeine Oel- und Fett-Zeitung [*West Germany*]
Allg Oesterr Chem Tech-Ztg — Allgemeine Oesterreichische Chemiker und Techniker-Zeitung [*Austria*]
Allg Papier-Rundschau — Allgemeine Papier-Rundschau
Allg Pap Rundsch — Allgemeine Papier-Rundschau
Allg Prakt Chem — Allgemeine und Praktische Chemie
Allg Stat Arch — Allgemeines Statistisches Archiv
Allg Statis Arch — Allgemeines Statistisches Archiv
Allg Text Z — Allgemeine Textil-Zeitschrift
Allg Tonind Ztg — Allgemeine Tonindustrie Zeitung
Allg Waermetech — Allgemeine Waermetechnik [*West Germany*]
Allg Wien Med Ztg — Allgemeine Wiener Medizinische Zeitung
Allg Z Bierbrau Malzfabr — Allgemeine Zeitschrift fuer Bierbrauerei und Malzfabrikation
Allg Zellforsch Mikrosk Anat — Allgemeine Zellforschung und Mikroskopische Anatomie
Allg Z Ent — Allgemeine Zeitschrift fuer Entomologie
Allg Z Psychiatr Ihre Grenzgeb — Allgemeine Zeitschrift fuer Psychiatrie und Ihre Grenzgebiete
Allg Ztschr Psychiat — Allgemeine Zeitschrift fuer Psychiatrie und Psychisch-Gerichtliche Medizin
ALLI — Alliance/l'Alliance. Voice of Metis and Non-Status Indians of Quebec [*Canada*]
Alliance Ind — Alliance Industrielle
Alliance Recd — Alliance Record
Allianz Ber Betriebstech Schadenverhuetung — Allianz Berichte fuer Betriebstechnik und Schadenverhuetung
Allied Health & Behav Sci — Allied Health and Behavioral Sciences
Allied Ind Wkr — Allied Industrial Worker
Allied Irish Bank R — Allied Irish Bank Review
Allied Vet — Allied Veterinarian
All India Rptr — All India Reporter
All Ind Rep — All India Reporter
Allis-Chalmers Electr Rev — Allis-Chalmers Electrical Review
Allis-Chalmers Eng Rev — Allis-Chalmers Engineering Review
Allison Res Eng — Allison Research and Engineering
Allmaenna Svenska Utsaedesaktiebol Svaloef — Allmaenna Svenska Utsaedesaktiebolaget Svaloef
Allm Sven Laekartidn — Allmaenna Svenska Laekartidningen
Alloy Cast Bull — Alloy Casting Bulletin
Alloy Dig — Alloy Digest
Alloy Met Rev — Alloy Metals Review
All Pak Legal Dec — All Pakistan Legal Decisions
All Pak Leg Dec — All Pakistan Legal Decisions
ALLR — Australian Labour Law Reporter
Allum Nuova Met — Alluminio e Nuova Metallurgia
Allum Nuova Metall — Alluminio e Nuova Metallurgia [*Italy*]
All the Year — All the Year Round
ALM — Al Markazi. Central Bank of Oman
ALM — Archives des Lettres Modernes
ALMA — Archivum Latinitatis Medii Aevi
Alma-Atin Gos Ped Inst Ucen Zap — Alma-Atinskii Gosudarstvennyi Pedagogiceskii Institut Imeni Abaja. Ucenye Zapiski
Almanak Agric Brasil — Almanak Agricola Brasileiro
ALMArv — Annales Latini Montium Arvernorum. Bulletin du Groupe d'Etudes Latines. Universite de Clermont
ALMD — Alaska Medicine
ALMD — Australian Legal Monthly Digest
ALMDB — Alaska Medicine
ALMG — Alaska Mines and Geology
AlmOAW — Almanach. Oesterreichische Akademie der Wissenschaften
ALMPB — Annals. Medical Section. Polish Academy of Sciences
ALMRB — Memorias. Academia das Ciencias de Lisboa. Classe de Ciencias
ALMTB — Alimenta
ALN — Administrative Law Decisions. Notes
ALN — Australian Law News
ALN — Australian Library News
ALNN — Alaska Native News

ALNU — Alaska Nurse
ALOF — Alaska Offshore
ALOG — Army Logistician
ALOR — Alter Orient
ALOS — Annual. Leeds University Oriental Society
ALPD — Australian Legal Profession Digest
ALPDA — Advances in Lipid Research
Alpenlaend Bienenztg — Alpenlaendische Bienenzeitung
ALPH — Alaskan Philatelist
Alpine J — Alpine Journal
ALPS — Alabama Linguistic and Philological Series
ALPS — Arts, Letters, Printers and Publishers, and Systems
ALPVB — Analyse et Prevision
ALQ — Abraham Lincoln Quarterly
ALQ — Annales du Marche Commun; Revue Bimestrielle pour l'Information et l'Harmonisation du Commerce et de l'Industrie
ALR — Adelaide Law Review
ALR — African Language Review
ALR — Afrika Spectrum
ALR — Alberta Law Reports
ALR — American Literary Realism, 1870-1910
ALR — Argus Law Reports
ALR — Australian Argus Law Reports
ALR — Australian Law Reports
ALR — Australian Left Review
ALRAC — Australian Law Reform Agencies Conference
ALRC DP — Australian Law Reform Commission. Discussion Paper
ALR (CN) — Argus Law Reports (Current Notes)
ALRED — Arizona Law Review
AL Rev — American Law Review
ALRIAI — Arid Lands Resource Information Paper
ALS — African Language Studies
ALS — Australian Literary Studies
ALSAA — Allgemeines Statistisches Archiv
ALSC — Alaska Seas and Coast
ALSIB — Alaska Industry
ALSK — Alaskana
ALSPAA — American Littoral Society. Special Publication
ALSSDM — Annual Reviews of Plant Sciences
ALT — African Literature Today
ALT — Annales. Faculte des Lettres de Toulouse
ALT — Australian Law Times
ALT — Rohstoff-Rundschau; Fachblatt des Gesamten Handels mit Altstoffen und Abfallstoffen, mit Ausfuehrlichen Berichten ueber die Internationalen Rohstoffmarkte und Altstoffmarkte
Alta — Alberta Law Reports
Alta Couns — Alberta Counsellor
Alta Counslttr — Alberta Counselletter
Alta Dir — Alta Direccion
Alta Engl — Alberta English
Alta Freq — Alta Frequenza
Alta Freq Suppl — Alta Frequenza. Supplemento
Alta Hist — Alberta History
Alta Hist R — Alberta Historical Review
Alta LR — Alberta Law Reports
Alta LR (2d) — Alberta Law Reports, Second Series
Alta L Rev — Alberta Law Review
Alte Mod Kunst — Alte und Moderne Kunst. Oesterreichische Fachzeitschrift des Marktes fuer Antiquitaeten, Bilder, Kunstgegenstaende Alter, und Moderner Kunst
Alt Energy — Alternative Energy Trends and Forecasts
Alt Energy — Alternative Sources of Energy
Alternate Energy Mag — Alternate Energy Magazine
Alternat Non-Violentes — Alternatives Non-Violentes
Alternatv — Alternatives
Altern Energy Sources — Alternative Energy Sources
Altes Haus-Mod — Altes Haus - Modern [*West Germany*]
Althaus Mod — Althaus Modernisierung [*West Germany*]
ALTL — Alaska Tidelines
Alt-Neuindische Stud — Alt- und Neuindische Studien [*Wiesbaden*]
Alt O — Der Alte Orient
Alt Press Ind — Alternative Press Index
ALTRD — Alternatives
ALTREU — Allgemeine Treuhandstelle fuer die Juedische Auswanderung
Alum — Aluminium
ALUMA — Aluminium
Alumin Cour — Aluminium Courier
Alumin Wld — Aluminium World
Alum Magnesium — Aluminum and Magnesium
Alum News Lett — Aluminum News Letter
Alumni Bull Sch Dent Indiana Univ — Alumni Bulletin. School of Dentistry. Indiana University
Alumni Bull Univ Mich Sch Dent — Alumni Bulletin. University of Michigan. School of Dentistry
Alum Non Ferrous Rev — Aluminum and The Non-Ferrous Review
Alum Rev — Aluminum Review

Alum Wld — Aluminium World
ALUOS — Leeds University Oriental Society. Annual
ALV — Archiv fuer Literatur und Volksdichtung
ALW — Archiv fuer Liturgiewissenschaft
ALWG Newsletter — Australian Legal Workers Group. Newsletter
Alyum Splavy Sb Statei — Alyuminievye Splavy. Sbornik Statei [*USSR*]
Alza Conf Ser — Alza Conference Series
AM — Acta Musicologica
A/M — Administrative Management
AM — Alma Mater
AM — America
AM — American Machinist
AM — American Mercury
Am — Americana
AM — [*The*] Americas: A Quarterly Review of Inter-American Cultural History
A d M — Annales du Midi; Revue de la France Meridionale
AM — Annales du Midi; Revue de la France Meridionale [*Toulouse*]
AM — Annali Manzoniani
A & M — Archives and Manuscripts
AM — Archivio Muratoriano
AM — Asia Major
AM — Athenische Mitteilungen
AM — Atlantic Monthly
AM — Australian Magazine
AM — Australian Monthly
AMA — Academy of Management. Journal
AMA — Agricultural Mechanization in Asia [*Japan*]
AMA — Amazing Stories. Annual
AmA — American Annual
AmA — American Anthropologist
AMA — Atti e Memorie dell'Arcadia
AMAAA — Atti e Memorie. Accademia di Storia dell'Arte Sanitaria
AMAABJ — Argentina. Instituto Nacional de Tecnologia. Agropecuaria Manual. Agropecuario
AMAABJ — INTA [*Instituto Nacional de Tecnologia Agropecuaria*]. Manual Agropecuario
AMA Arch Ind Health — AMA [*American Medical Association*] Archives of Industrial Health
Am Acad Arts & Sci Mem — American Academy of Arts and Sciences. Memoirs
Am Acad Arts & Sci Proc — American Academy of Arts and Sciences. Proceedings
Am Acad Optom Ser — American Academy of Optometry Series
Am Acad Pol & Soc Sci Ann — American Academy of Political and Social Science. Annals
Am Acad Relig J — American Academy of Religion. Journal
Am Acad Rome Mem — American Academy in Rome. Memoirs
AMACC — Antimicrobial Agents and Chemotherapy
AMAJ — American Alpine Journal
Amal Engr Union MJ — Amalgamated Engineering Union. Monthly Journal
Am Alma — American Almanac
Am Alpine Jour — American Alpine Journal
AMAM — Atti e Memorie. Accademia di Scienze, Lettere, ed Arti di Modena
AMan — Accademia di Mantova. Atti e Memorie
Am Ann — Americana Annual
Am Ann Deaf — American Annals of the Deaf
Am Ant — American Anthropologist
Am Ant — American Antiquity
Am Anth — American Anthropologist
Am Anthro — American Anthropologist
Am Anthrop — American Anthropologist
Am Anthropol — American Anthropologist
Am Antiq — American Antiquarian
Am Antiq — American Antiquity
Am Antiq Soc Proc — American Antiquarian Society. Proceedings
Am Antiquit — American Antiquity
AMAP — Atti e Memorie. Accademia Patavina di Scienze, Lettere, ed Arti
AMAPe — Atti e Memorie. Accademia Petrarca
Am Arch — American Architect
Am Arch — American Architect and Building News
Am Archiv — American Archivist
Am Archivis — American Archivist
Am Archivist — American Archivist
Am Arch Rehabil Ther — American Archives of Rehabilitation Therapy
Am Artist — American Artist
Am Art J — American Art Journal
Am Art Rev — American Art Review
Am As Museums Pr — American Association of Museums. Proceedings
Am As Petroleum G B — American Association of Petroleum Geologists. Bulletin
Am As Pr Mem — American Association for the Advancement of Science. Proceedings. Memoirs
Am Assn Coll Reg J — American Association of Collegiate Registrars. Journal
Am Assn Col Teach Educ Yrbk — American Association of Colleges for Teacher Education. Yearbook

Am Assn Pet Geol Bul — American Association of Petroleum Geologists. Bulletin
Am Assn Pet Geologists Bull — American Association of Petroleum Geologists. Bulletin
Am Assn Sch Adm Off Rep — American Association of School Administrators. Official Report
Am Assn Univ Prof B — American Association of University Professors. Bulletin
Am Assn Univ Women J — American Association of University Women. Journal
Am Assoc Adv Sci Comm Desert Arid Zones Res Contrib — American Association for the Advancement of Science. Committee on Desert and Arid Zones Research. Contribution
Am Assoc Adv Sci Publ — American Association for the Advancement of Science. Publication
Am Assoc Adv Sci Symp — American Association for the Advancement of Science. Symposium
Am Assoc Pet Geol Bull — American Association of Petroleum Geologists. Bulletin
Am Assoc Pet Geol Mem — American Association of Petroleum Geologists. Memoir
Am Assoc Pet Geol Repr Ser — American Association of Petroleum Geologists. Reprint Series
Am Assoc Petroleum Geologists Mem — American Association of Petroleum Geologists. Memoir
Am Assoc Petroleum Geologists Pacific Sec Correlation Sec — American Association of Petroleum Geologists. Pacific Section. Correlation Section
Am Assoc State Local Hist Bull — American Association for State and Local History. Bulletin
Am Assoc Univ Prof Bull — American Association of University Professors. Bulletin
Am Assoc Zoo Vet Annu Proc — American Association of Zoo Veterinarians. Annual Proceedings
Am Astronaut Soc Publ Sci Technol — American Astronautical Society. Publications. Science and Technology
Am Astron Soc Bull — American Astronomical Society. Bulletin
AMAT — Atti e Memorie. Accademia Toscana la Colombaria
Amat Build Man — Amateur Builder's Manual
Amat Cine World — Amateur Cine World
Amat Ent — Amateur Entomologist
Amat Geol — Amateur Geologist
Amat Photogr — Amateur Photographer
Am Aviation — American Aviation
AMAZAP — Amazoniana
AMB — Abstracts of Military Bibliography
AMB — AMB. Revista da Associacao Medica Brasileira
Am Baby — American Baby for Expectant and New Parents
Am Baby Expectant New Parents — American Baby for Expectant and New Parents
Am Bank — American Banker
Am Bankr L J — American Bankruptcy Law Journal
Am Bankrupt — American Bankruptcy Law Journal
Am Bar A J — American Bar Association. Journal
Am Bar Ass J — American Bar Association. Journal
Am Bar Assn J — American Bar Association. Journal
Am Bar Assoc J — American Bar Association. Journal
Am Bar Asso Jour — American Bar Association. Journal
Am Bar Found Res J — American Bar Foundation. Research Journal
AMBBB — Acta Microbiologica Polonica. Series B. Microbiologia Applicata
Am Bee J — American Bee Journal
Am Beekeep Fed Newsl — American Beekeeping Federation. Newsletter
Am Behavioral Sci — American Behavioral Scientist
Am Behav Sci — American Behavioral Scientist
Am Benedictine Rev — American Benedictine Review
AmBenR — American Benedictine Review [St. Paul, MN]
Am B Found Res J — American Bar Foundation. Research Journal
AMBIB — Abhandlungen. Akademie der Wissenschaften in Goettingen. Mathematisch-Physikalische Klasse. Beitraege zum Internationalen Geophysikalischen Jahr
Am Bibliop — American Bibliopolist
Am Bib Repos — American Biblical Repository
Am Biol Tea — American Biology Teacher
Am Biol Teach — American Biology Teacher
Ambio Spec Rep — Ambio. Special Report
Am Biotechnol Lab — American Biotechnology Laboratory
Am Birds — American Birds
Am Bk Collec — American Book Collector
Am Bk Collector — American Book Collector
Am Bld — American Builder
AMBNA — Acta Medica et Biologica (Niigata)
Am Book Publ Recd — American Book Publishing Record
Am Book Rev — American Book Review
Am Bottler — American Bottler
Am B Q — American Baptist Quarterly
Am Brew — American Brewer

Am Brew Rev — American Brewer's Review
Am Bsns — American Business
Am Bsns Ed — American Business Education
Am Bsns Ed Yrbk — American Business Education Yearbook
AMBT — American Biology Teacher
AMBUEJ — American Malacological Bulletin
Ambulance J — Ambulance Journal
Am Bur Geog B — American Bureau of Geography. Bulletin
Am Business — American Business
Am Bus Law — American Business Law Journal
Am Bus Law J — American Business Law Journal
Am Bus L J — American Business Law Journal
Am Butter R — American Butter and Cheese Review
Am Cath His Rec — American Catholic Historical Society. Records
Am Cath His S — American Catholic Historical Society. Records [Philadelphia]
AmCathHS — American Catholic Historical Society. Records
Am Cath Q — American Catholic Quarterly Review
Am Cattle Prod — American Cattle Producer
Am Ceramic Soc Jour — American Ceramic Society. Journal
Am Ceram S — American Ceramic Society. Bulletin
Am Ceram Soc Bull — American Ceramic Society. Bulletin
Am Cer Soc Bul — American Ceramic Society. Bulletin
Am Cer Soc J — American Ceramic Society. Journal
Am Chem J — American Chemical Journal
Am Chem Soc Div Environ Chem Prepr — American Chemical Society. Division of Environmental Chemistry. Preprints
Am Chem Soc Div Fuel Chem Prepr — American Chemical Society. Division of Fuel Chemistry. Preprints
Am Chem Soc Div Fuel Chem Prepr Pap — American Chemical Society. Division of Fuel Chemistry. Preprints of Papers
Am Chem Soc Div Fuel Prepr — American Chemical Society. Division of Fuel Chemistry. Preprints
Am Chem Soc Div Gas Fuel Chem Prepr — American Chemical Society. Division of Gas and Fuel Chemistry. Preprints
Am Chem Soc Div Org Coat Plast Chem Pap — American Chemical Society. Division of Organic Coatings and Plastics Chemistry. Papers
Am Chem Soc Div Pet Chem Gen Pap Prepr — American Chemical Society. Division of Petroleum Chemistry. General Papers. Preprints
Am Chem Soc Div Pet Chem Prepr — American Chemical Society. Division of Petroleum Chemistry. Preprints
Am Chem Soc Div Pet Chem Symp — American Chemical Society. Division of Petroleum Chemistry. Symposia
Am Chem Soc Div Petr Chem Prepr — American Chemical Society. Division of Petroleum Chemistry. Preprints
Am Chem Soc Div Polym Chem Prepr — American Chemical Society. Division of Polymer Chemistry. Preprints
Am Chem Soc Div Water Air Waste Chem Gen Pap — American Chemical Society. Division of Water, Air, and Waste Chemistry. General Papers
Am Chem Soc J — American Chemical Society. Journal
Am Chem Soc Mon — American Chemical Society. Monograph
Am Chem Soc Rubber Div Symp — American Chemical Society. Rubber Division. Symposia
Am Child — American Child
Am Childh — American Childhood
Am Chiro — American Chiropractor
Am Choral R — American Choral Review
AmChQ — American Church Quarterly [New York]
Am Christmas Tree J — American Christmas Tree Journal
Am Church Mo — American Church Monthly
Am Church R — American Church Review
AMCIA — American City
AMCILR — Actas y Memorias. Congreso Internacional de Linguistica Romanica
AMCIM — Actes et Memoires. Congres International de Langue et Litterature du Midi de la France
Am Cin — American Cinematographer
Am Cinem — American Cinematographer
Am Cinematog — American Cinematographer
AMCISO — Actes et Memoires. Congres International des Sciences Onomastiques
AMCIT — Actes et Memoires. Congres International de Toponymie
Am City — American City
Am City (C ed) — American City (City Edition)
Am City Cty — American City and County
Am City (T & C ed) — American City (Town and Country Edition)
Am Coll — American Collector
Am Coll Physicians Bull — American College of Physicians. Bulletin
Am Concrete Inst J — American Concrete Institute. Journal
Am Concr Inst J — American Concrete Institute. Journal
Am Concr Inst Monogr — American Concrete Institute. Monograph
Am Co-Op J — American Co-Operative Journal
Am Correct Ther J — American Corrective Therapy Journal
Am Craft — American Craft
Am Creamery — American Creamery and Poultry Produce Review
Am Crim Law — American Criminal Law Review

Am Crim L Q — American Criminal Law Quarterly
Am Crim L Rev — American Criminal Law Review
Am Cryst Assoc Trans — American Crystallographic Association. Polycrystal Book Service. Transactions
Am Cyanamid Co Miner Dressing Notes — American Cyanamid Company. Mineral Dressing Notes
Am Cyanamid Co Tech Bull — American Cyanamid Company. Technical Bulletin
AmD — American Dialog
AMD — Scheppend Ambacht. Tweemaandelijks Tijdschrift voor Toegepaste Kunst
Am Daffodil Yearb — American Daffodil Yearbook
Am Dairy Prod R — American Dairy Products Review
Am Dairy R — American Dairy Review
Am Dairy Rev — American Dairy Review
AMDEL Bul — AMDEL [*Australian Mineral Development Laboratories*] Bulletin
AMDEL Bull — AMDEL [*Australian Mineral Development Laboratories*] Bulletin
Am Demogr — American Demographics
AMDIB — Annales de Medecine Interne
Am Dietet Assn J — American Dietetic Association. Journal
AMDM — Atti e Memorie. Deputazione di Storia Patria per le Antiche Provincie Modenesi
Am Doc — American Documentation
Am Drop Forger — American Drop Forger
Am Drug — American Druggist
Am Druggist — American Druggist
Am Druggist Merch — American Druggist Merchandising
Am Drug Pharm Rec — American Druggist and Pharmaceutical Record
Am Drycleaner — American Drycleaner
AMDSPAM — Atti e Memorie. Deputazione di Storia Patria per le Antiche Provincie Modenesi
AMDSPPM — Atti e Memorie. Deputazione di Storia Patria per le Provincie delle Marche
AMD Symp Ser (Am Soc Mech Eng) — AMD Symposia Series (American Society of Mechanical Engineers)
Am Dye Rep — American Dyestuff Reporter
Am Dyest Rep — American Dyestuff Reporter
Am Dyestuff Reptr — American Dyestuff Reporter
AME — Automatenmarkt
AMEAB5 — Australia. Commonwealth Scientific and Industrial Research Organisation. Division of Mechanical Engineering. Annual Report
AMEBA — Annales Medicinae Experimentalis et Biologiae Fenniae
Am Eccles Rev — American Ecclesiastical Review
Am Ecl — American Eclectic
Am Econ — American Economist
Am Econ Assn Bul — American Economic Association. Bulletin
Am Econ Assoc — American Economic Association. Publications
Am Econ Assoc Publ — American Economic Association. Publications
Am Economist — American Economist
Am Econ R — American Economic Review
Am Econ Rev — American Economic Review
Am Econ R Pa & Proc — American Economic Review. Papers and Proceedings
Am Ec Rev — American Economic Review
AMED — American Education
Am Ed Res J — American Educational Research Journal
Am Educ — American Education
Am Educ Res — American Educational Research Journal
A Meet Ent Soc Am — Annual Meeting. Entomological Society of America
A Meet Kans St Hort Soc — Annual Meeting. Kansas State Horticultural Society
Am Egg & Poultry R — American Egg and Poultry Review
AMELA3 — American Journal of Medical Electronics
Am Electrochem Soc Trans — American Electrochemical Society. Transactions
Am Electroplat Soc Ann Tech Conf — American Electroplaters' Society. Annual Technical Conference
AMEMA — Anales de Mecanica y Electricidad
Amenage Territ Droit Foncier — Amenagement du Territoire et Droit Foncier
Amenag et Nature — Amenagement et Nature
Amenag Territ Develop Region — Amenagement du Territoire et Developpement Regional
Am Enameler — American Enameler
Am Eng — American Engineer
Am Ens — American Ensemble
Am Enterp Inst Public Policy Res Natl Energy Study — American Enterprise Institute for Public Policy Research. National Energy Study
Amer — American
AmER — American Ecclesiastical Review [*Washington, DC*]
Amer Acad of Arts and Sciences Proc — American Academy of Arts and Sciences. Proceedings
Amer Acad Arts & Sci Mem — American Academy of Arts and Sciences. Memoirs
Amer Anthropol — American Anthropologist
Amer Antiq — American Antiquity

Amer Antiq Soc Proc — American Antiquarian Society. Proceedings
Amer Arch Rehab Ther — American Archives of Rehabilitation Therapy
Amerasia J — Amerasia Journal
Amer Assoc Pet Geol Bull — American Association of Petroleum Geologists. Bulletin
Amer Baker — American Baker
Amer Bee J — American Bee Journal
Amer Behav Scientist — American Behavioral Scientist
Amer Bookman — Bookman [*Published in US*]
Amer Brewer — American Brewer
Amer Cattle Prod — American Cattle Producer
Amer Ceram Soc Bull — American Ceramic Society. Bulletin
Amer Chem Soc Div Fuel Chem Prepr — American Chemical Society. Division of Fuel Chemistry. Preprints
Amer Chem Soc Div Org Coatings Plast Chem Prepr — American Chemical Society. Division of Organic Coatings and Plastics Chemistry. Preprints
Amer Chem Soc Div Petrol Chem Prepr — American Chemical Society. Division of Petroleum Chemistry. Preprints
Amer Chem Soc Div Water Air Waste Chem Gen Pap — American Chemical Society. Division of Water, Air, and Waste Chemistry. General Papers
Amer Chem Soc Petrol Chem Div Preprints — American Chemical Society. Petroleum Chemistry Division. Preprints
Amer Choral R — American Choral Review
Amer Cinematogr — American Cinematographer
Amer City — American City
Amer Classic Screen — American Classic Screen
Amer Concr Inst Monogr — American Concrete Institute. Monograph
Amer Concr Inst Stand — American Concrete Institute. Standards
Amer Corp — American Corporation
Amer Correct Ther J — American Corrective Therapy Journal
Amer Dairy Rev — American Dairy Review
Amer Doc — American Documentation
Amer Drug — American Druggist
Amer Dyestuff Rep — American Dyestuff Reporter
Amer Dyestuff Reporter — American Dyestuff Reporter
Amer Economist — American Economist
Amer Econ R — American Economic Review
Amer Econ Rev — American Economic Review
Amer Eng — American Engineer
Amer Ethnol — American Ethnologist
Amer F — American Film
Amer Feder — American Federationist
Amer Gas Ass Mon — American Gas Association. Monthly
Amer Gas Ass Oper Sect Proc — American Gas Association. Operating Section. Proceedings
Amer Gas J — American Gas Journal
Amer Gear Mfr Ass Stand — American Gear Manufacturers Association. Standards
AmerH — America: History and Life
Amer Highways — American Highways
American Assoc Arch Bib — American Association of Architectural Bibliographers. Papers
American Business Law Jrnl — American Business Law Journal
American Church R — American Church Review
American F — American Film
Amer Imago — American Imago
Amer Indig — America Indigena
Amer Industr Hyg Assoc J — American Industrial Hygiene Association. Journal
Amer Iron Steel Inst Contrib Met Steel — American Iron and Steel Institute. Contributions to the Metallurgy of Steel
Amer Iron Steel Inst Reg Tech Meetings Addresses — American Iron and Steel Institute. Regional Technical Meetings. Addresses
Amer Iron Steel Steel Res Constr Bull — American Iron and Steel Institute. Steel Research for Construction. Bulletin
Amer J Agr Econ — American Journal of Agricultural Economics
Amer J Agric Econ — American Journal of Agricultural Economics
Amer J Archaeol — American Journal of Archaeology
Amer J Art Ther — American Journal of Art Therapy
Amer J Bot — American Journal of Botany
Amer J Chinese Medicine — American Journal of Chinese Medicine
Amer J Clin Hypnosis — American Journal of Clinical Hypnosis
Amer J Clin Nutr — American Journal of Clinical Nutrition
Amer J Clin Pathol — American Journal of Clinical Pathology
Amer J Comp L — American Journal of Comparative Law
Amer J Comp Law — American Journal of Comparative Law
Amer J Digest Dis — American Journal of Digestive Diseases [*Later, Digestive Diseases and Sciences*]
Amer J Dis Child — American Journal of Diseases of Children
Amer J Econ & Soc — American Journal of Economics and Sociology [*New York*]
Amer J Econ Sociol — American Journal of Economics and Sociology [*New York*]
Amer J Hum Genetics — American Journal of Human Genetics
Amer J Hyg — American Journal of Hygiene
Amer J Int Law — American Journal of International Law

Amer J Int'l L — American Journal of International Law
Amer J Juris — American Journal of Jurisprudence
Amer J Ment Defic — American Journal of Mental Deficiency
Amer J Orthopsychiat — American Journal of Orthopsychiatry
Amer Jour Psych — American Journal of Psychology
Amer J Pathol — American Journal of Pathology
Amer J Philo — American Journal of Philology
Amer J Phys — American Journal of Physics
Amer J of Phys — American Journal of Physics
Amer J Phys Anthropol — American Journal of Physical Anthropology
Amer J Physiol — American Journal of Physiology
Amer J Phys Med — American Journal of Physical Medicine
Amer J Polit Sci — American Journal of Political Science
Amer J Psychiatry — American Journal of Psychiatry
Amer J Psychoanal — American Journal of Psychoanalysis
Amer J Psychol — American Journal of Psychology
Amer J Psychother — American Journal of Psychotherapy
Amer J Sci — American Journal of Science
Amer J Sci Radiocarbon Suppl — American Journal of Science. Radiocarbon Supplement
Amer J Sociol — American Journal of Sociology
Amer J Theol Phil — American Journal of Theology and Philosophy
Amer J Vet Res — American Journal of Veterinary Research
Amer Kenkyu — America Kenkyu
Amer Lat — America Latina
Amer Law — American Lawyer
Amer Law Rev — American Law Review
Amer Lawy — American Lawyer
AmerLitAb — American Literature Abstracts
Amer Livestock J — American Livestock Journal
Amer Mach — American Machinist
Amer Manage Ass Res Stud — American Management Associations. Research Study
Amer Math Soc Colloq Publ — American Mathematical Society. Colloquium Publications
Amer Math Soc Transl — American Mathematical Society. Translations
Amer Midl Nat — American Midland Naturalist
Amer Miller Process — American Miller and Processor
Amer Mineral — American Mineralogist
Amer Nat — American Naturalist
Amer Natur — American Naturalist
Amer Nurserym — American Nurseryman
Amer O — American Opinion
Amer Oil Gas Reporter — American Oil and Gas Reporter
Amer Oriental Soc Jour — American Oriental Society. Journal
Amer Pap Ind — American Paper Industry
Amer Petrol Inst Div Prod Drilling Prod Pract Pap — American Petroleum Institute. Division of Production, Drilling, and Production Practice. Papers
Amer Petrol Inst Stand — American Petroleum Institute. Standards
Amer Philos Soc Proc — American Philosophical Society. Proceedings
Amer Philos Soc Trans — American Philosophical Society. Transactions
Amer Phil Quart — American Philosophical Quarterly
Amer Photogr — American Photographer
Amer Polit Quart — American Politics Quarterly
Amer Polit Sci R — American Political Science Review
Amer Po R — American Poetry Review
Amer Prem — American Premiere
Amer Psychol — American Psychologist
Amer Recorder — American Recorder
Amer Rehab — American Rehabilitation
AmerS — American Studies
Amer Scholar — American Scholar
Amer Sci — American Scientist
Amer Sci Press Ser Math Management Sci — American Sciences Press Series in Mathematical and Management Sciences
Amer Soc Abrasive Method Nat Tech Conf Proc — American Society for Abrasive Methods. National Technical Conference. Proceedings
Amer Sociologist — American Sociologist
Amer Sociol R — American Sociological Review
Amer Soc Quality Contr Tech Conf Trans — American Society for Quality Control. Annual Technical Conference. Transactions
Amer Sp — American Speech
Amer Stat — American Statistician
Amer Stat Ind — American Statistics Index
Amer Statist — American Statistician
Amer Univ L Rev — American University Law Review
Amer Veg Grower — American Vegetable Grower
Amer Welding Soc Stand — American Welding Society. Standards
Amer Woods US For Serv — American Woods. United States Forest Service
Amer Zool — American Zoologist
AMESA — Archiwum Mechaniki Stosowanej [*Archives of Mechanics*]
Ames Lab Bull Ser — Ames Laboratory. Bulletin Series
Am Ethnol — American Ethnologist
Am Ex — American Examiner
AMEX — AMEX-Canada

Am Exporter — American Exporter
A Mezzogiorno — Annali del Mezzogiorno
AMF — A. Merritt's Fantasy Magazine
AmF — [*The*] Americas: A Quarterly Review of Inter-American Cultural History
A Mf — Archiv fuer Musikforschung
Am Fabrics — American Fabrics
Am Fam Phys — American Family Physician
Am Fam Physician — American Family Physician
Am Fam Physician GP — American Family Physician - GP
Am Farm Bur N L — American Farm Bureau Federation. Weekly News Letter
Am Fed — American Federationist
Am Federationist — American Federationist
Am Feed Manuf Assoc Proc Meet Nutr Counc — American Feed Manufacturers Association. Proceedings. Meeting of the Nutrition Council
Am Fencing — American Fencing
Am Fern J — American Fern Journal
Am Fert — American Fertilizer and Allied Chemicals
Am Fert Allied Chem — American Fertilizer and Allied Chemicals
Am Film — American Film
Am Fisheries Soc Trans — American Fisheries Society. Transactions
Am Fish Soc Monogr — American Fisheries Society. Monograph
Am Fish Soc Spec Publ — American Fisheries Society. Special Publication
Am Fish Soc Trans — American Fisheries Society. Transactions
Am Flint — American Flint
Am Flor — American Florist
AMFO — American Forests
AMFOA — American Forests
Am For — American Forests
Am Forests — American Forests
Am For Serv Jour — American Foreign Service Journal
Am Found Blind Res Bull — American Foundation for the Blind. Research Bulletin
Am Found Blind Res Ser — American Foundation for the Blind. Research Series
Am Foundryman — American Foundryman
Am Fox and Fur Farmer — American Fox and Fur Farmer
Am Fruit Grower — American Fruit Grower
Am Fruit Grow Mag — American Fruit Grower Magazine
Am G — American Geologist
AMG — Association Management
Am Game Bull Am Game Protect Ass — American Game Bulletin. American Game Protective Association
Am Gas As M — American Gas Association. Monthly
Am Gas Assoc Annu Rep — American Gas Association. Annual Report
Am Gas Assoc Bull Abstr — American Gas Association. Bulletin of Abstracts
Am Gas Assoc Mon — American Gas Association. Monthly
Am Gas Assoc Oper Sect Proc — American Gas Association. Operating Section. Proceedings
Am Gas Assoc Prepr — American Gas Association. Preprints
Am Gas Assoc Proc — American Gas Association. Proceedings
Am G As B — American Geological Association. Bulletin
Am Gas Inst Abstr — American Gas Institute. Abstracts
Am Gas J — American Gas Journal
AMGBA — Archiv fuer Meteorologie, Geophysik, und Bioklimatologie. Serie B
Am Geneal — American Genealogist
Am Geog Soc B J — American Geographical Society. Bulletin. Journal
Am Geog Soc Bul — American Geographical Society. Bulletin
Am Geog Soc Jour — American Geographical Society. Journal
Am Geog Soc Special Pub — American Geographical Society. Special Publication
Am Geog Stat Soc J — American Geographical and Statistical Society. Journal
Am Geol — American Geologist
Am Geol Inst Repr Ser — American Geological Institute. Reprint Series
Am Geol Inst Rept — American Geological Institute. Report
Am Geophys Union Trans — American Geophysical Union. Transactions
AMGGA — Archiv fuer Meteorologie, Geophysik, und Bioklimatologie. Serie A
AMGHB2 — Ameghiniana
Am Glass Rev — American Glass Review
Am Gynecol Soc Trans — American Gynecological Society. Transactions
Am Harp J — American Harp Journal
AMHCB — Applied Mathematics and Computation
AMHE — American Health
Am Health — American Health
Am Health Care Assoc J — American Health Care Association. Journal
Am Heart Assoc Monogr — American Heart Association. Monograph
Am Heart J — American Heart Journal
Am Her — American Heritage
Am Heritage — American Heritage
Am Highw — American Highways
Am His R — American Historical Review
Am Hist Assn Ann Rep — American Historical Association. Annual Report
Am Hist Assn Rept — American Historical Association. Reports
Am Hist Ill — American History Illustrated

Am Hist Illus — American History Illustrated
Am Hist M — American Historical Magazine [*New York*]
Am Hist R — American Historical Review
Am Hist Rec — American Historical Record
Am Hist Reg — American Historical Register
Am Hist Rev — American Historical Review
Am Home — American Home
Am Homes — American Homes and Gardens
Am Horol Jeweler — American Horologist and Jeweler
Am Hort — American Horticulturist
Am Hort Mag — American Horticultural Magazine
AMHR — Annuaire. Musee d'Histoire de la Religion et de l'Atheisme
AMHSJ — AMHS [*American Material Handling Society*] Journal
AMI — Archaeologische Mitteilungen aus Iran
AMI — Journal of American Insurance
AMIAA — American Imago
AMIB — American Indian Basketry Magazine
AMICD — Annual Meeting. International Water Conference
A Micr Acad Sci Hung — Acta Microbiologica. Academiae Scientiarum Hungaricae
AMid — Annales du Midi; Revue de la France Meridionale [*Toulouse*]
AMIGB — Acta Microbiologica Polonica. Series A. Microbiologia Generalis
AMIHA — AMA [*American Medical Association*] Archives of Industrial Health
AMIKA — American Inkmaker
Am Ill — Americana Illustrated
Am Im — American Imago
Am Imago — American Imago
Am I M Eng Tr B — American Institute of Mining Engineers. Transactions. Bulletin
Am Import/Export Bull — American Import/Export Bulletin
Am Import/Export Manage — American Import/Export Management
Am Import/Export Mgt — American Import/Export Management
AMIN — Amerindian
AMINCO Lab News — AMINCO [*American Instrument Company*] Laboratory News
Am Ind — America Indigena
Am Ind — American Industries
Am Ind Hyg — American Industrial Hygiene Association. Journal
Am Ind Hyg Ass J — American Industrial Hygiene Association. Journal
Am Ind Hyg Assn J — American Industrial Hygiene Association. Journal
Am Ind Hyg Assoc J — American Industrial Hygiene Association. Journal
Am Ind Hyg Assoc Q — American Industrial Hygiene Association. Quarterly
Am Ind Hygiene Assn J — American Industrial Hygiene Association. Journal
Am Indian J — American Indian Journal
Am Indian L Rev — American Indian Law Review
Am Indigena — America Indigena
Am Ind LR — American Indian Law Review
A Mines Belg — Annales des Mines de Belgique
Am Ink — American Inkmaker
Am Inkmaker — American Inkmaker
Amino Acid Nucleic Acid — Amino Acid and Nucleic Acid
Amino Acids Pept Proteins — Amino Acids, Peptides, and Proteins
Am Inst Aeronaut Astronaut Monogr — American Institute of Aeronautics and Astronautics. Monographs
Am Inst Archit J — American Institute of Architects. Journal
Am Inst Archit Q Bull — American Institute of Architects. Quarterly Bulletin
Am Inst Arch J — American Institute of Architects. Journal
Am Inst Bank Bul — American Institute of Banking. Bulletin
Am Inst Biol Sci Publ — American Institute of Biological Sciences. Publications
Am Inst Biol Sci Symp — American Institute of Biological Sciences. Symposia
Am Inst Ind Eng Detroit Chapter Proc Annu Conf — American Institute of Industrial Engineers. Detroit Chapter. Proceedings of the Annual Conference
Am Inst of Instruc — American Institute of Instruction
Am Instit Crim Law and Criminol Jour — American Institute of Criminal Law and Criminology. Journal
Am Inst Min Metall Eng Tech Publ — American Institute of Mining and Metallurgical Engineers. Technical Publications
Am Inst Oral Biol Annu Meet — American Institute of Oral Biology. Annual Meeting
Am Inst Phys Conf Proc — American Institute of Physics. Conference Proceedings
Am Inst Plan — American Institute of Planners. Journal
Am Inst Plan J — American Institute of Planners. Journal
Am Inst Plann J — American Institute of Planners. Journal
Am Inst Plann Pap — American Institute of Planners. Papers
Am Inst Plant Eng J — American Institute of Plant Engineers. Journal
Am Inst Prof Geol Calif Sect Annu Meet Proc — American Institute of Professional Geologists. California Section. Annual Meeting. Proceedings
Am Inst Refrig Proc — American Institute of Refrigeration. Proceedings
AMIran — Archaeologische Mitteilungen aus Iran
Am Irish His S J — American Irish Historical Society. Journal
AMIS — Amis du Film et de la Television

AMISEE — Israel. Geological Society. Annual Meeting
AMIS J — American Musical Instrument Society. Journal
AMIS N — American Musical Instrument Society. Newsletter
AMIUA — Acta Medica Iugoslavica
AMJ — Advanced Management Journal
Am J Acupunct — American Journal of Acupuncture
Am J Ag Econ — American Journal of Agricultural Economics
Am J Agr — American Journal of Agriculture and Science
Am J Agr Ec — American Journal of Agricultural Economics
Am J Agr Econ — American Journal of Agricultural Economics
Am J Agric Econ — American Journal of Agricultural Economics
Am J Anat — American Journal of Anatomy
Am J Arab St — American Journal of Arabic Studies
Am J Archae — American Journal of Archaeology
Am J Archaeol — American Journal of Archaeology
Am J Art Th — American Journal of Art Therapy
Am J Art Ther — American Journal of Art Therapy
Am J Bot — American Journal of Botany
Am J Canc — American Journal of Cancer
Am J Cancer — American Journal of Cancer
Am J Card — American Journal of Cardiology
Am J Cardiol — American Journal of Cardiology
Am J Chinese Med — American Journal of Chinese Medicine
Am J Chin Med — American Journal of Chinese Medicine
Am J Clin Hypn — American Journal of Clinical Hypnosis
Am J Clin Hypnosis — American Journal of Clinical Hypnosis
Am J Clin Med — American Journal of Clinical Medicine
Am J Clin N — American Journal of Clinical Nutrition
Am J Clin Nutr — American Journal of Clinical Nutrition
Am J Clin Nutrition — American Journal of Clinical Nutrition
Am J Clin P — American Journal of Clinical Pathology
Am J Clin Path — American Journal of Clinical Pathology
Am J Clin Pathol — American Journal of Clinical Pathology
Am J Community Psychol — American Journal of Community Psychology
Am J Compar Law — American Journal of Comparative Law
Am J Comp L — American Journal of Comparative Law
Am J Comp Law — American Journal of Comparative Law
Am J Conch — American Journal of Conchology
Am J Corr — American Journal of Correction
Am J Correction — American Journal of Correction
Am J Crim L — American Journal of Criminal Law
Am J Dent Sci — American Journal of Dental Science
Am J Dermatopathol — American Journal of Dermatopathology
Am J Dig Di — American Journal of Digestive Diseases [*Later, Digestive Diseases and Sciences*]
Am J Dig Dis — American Journal of Digestive Diseases [*Later, Digestive Diseases and Sciences*]
Am J Dig Dis Nutr — American Journal of Digestive Diseases and Nutrition
Am J Dis Ch — American Journal of Diseases of Children
Am J Dis Child — American Journal of Diseases of Children
Am J Drug Alcohol Abuse — American Journal of Drug and Alcohol Abuse
Am J Econ — American Journal of Economics and Sociology [*New York*]
Am J Econ S — American Journal of Economics and Sociology [*New York*]
Am J Econ & Soc — American Journal of Economics and Sociology [*New York*]
Am J Econ Soc — American Journal of Economics and Sociology
Am J Econ & Sociol — American Journal of Economics and Sociology [*New York*]
Am J Econ Sociol — American Journal of Economics and Sociology [*New York*]
Am J Econ Sociol (New York) — American Journal of Economics and Sociology (New York)
Am J Educ — American Journal of Education
Am J EEG Technol — American Journal of EEG Technology
Am J Enol V — American Journal of Enology and Viticulture
Am J Enol Viti — American Journal of Enology and Viticulture
Am J Enol Vitic — American Journal of Enology and Viticulture
Am J Epidem — American Journal of Epidemiology
Am J Epidemiol — American Journal of Epidemiology
Am Jew Arch — American Jewish Archives
Am Jew His — American Jewish Historical Society. Publications
Am Jew Hist Q — American Jewish Historical Quarterly
Am Jew Hist Soc Publ — American Jewish Historical Society. Publications
Am Jewish A — American Jewish Archives
Am Jewish H — American Jewish Historical Quarterly
Am Jew Yb — American Jewish Yearbook
Am Jew Yr Bk — American Jewish Year Book
Am J Forensic Med Pathol — American Journal of Forensic Medicine and Pathology
Am J Gastro — American Journal of Gastroenterology
Am J Gastroenterol — American Journal of Gastroenterology
Am J Health Plann — American Journal of Health Planning
Am J Hematol — American Journal of Hematology
Am J Hosp P — American Journal of Hospital Pharmacy
Am J Hosp Pharm — American Journal of Hospital Pharmacy
Am J Hu Gen — American Journal of Human Genetics

Am J Human Genet — American Journal of Human Genetics
Am J Hum Genet — American Journal of Human Genetics
Am J Hyg — American Journal of Hygiene
Am J Hyg Monogr Ser — American Journal of Hygiene. Monographic Series
Am J Ind Med — American Journal of Industrial Medicine
Am J Ind Psych — American Journal of Individual Psychology
Am J Inf Con — American Journal of Infection Control
Am J Infect Control — American Journal of Infection Control
Am J Int L — American Journal of International Law
Am J Int Law — American Journal of International Law
Am J Int Law Proc — American Journal of International Law. Proceedings
Am J Int'l L — American Journal of International Law
Am J Int L Supp — American Journal of International Law. Supplement
Am J IV Clin Nutr — American Journal of Intravenous Therapy and Clinical Nutrition
Am J IV Ther — American Journal of Intravenous Therapy [*Later, American Journal of Intravenous Therapy and Clinical Nutrition*]
Am J IV Therapy — American Journal of Intravenous Therapy [*Later, American Journal of Intravenous Therapy and Clinical Nutrition*]
Am J IV Ther Clin Nutr — American Journal of Intravenous Therapy and Clinical Nutrition
Am J Juris — American Journal of Jurisprudence
Am J Jurispr — American Journal of Jurisprudence
Am J Jurisprud — American Journal of Jurisprudence
Am J Kidney Dis — American Journal of Kidney Diseases
Am J Law Med — American Journal of Law and Medicine
Am J Law & Med — American Journal of Law and Medicine
Am J Legal Hist — American Journal of Legal History
Am J Leg Hist — American Journal of Legal History
Am JL & Med — American Journal of Law and Medicine
Am Jl Ph — American Journal of Pharmacy
Am J Math — American Journal of Mathematics
Am J Math Manage Sci — American Journal of Mathematical and Management Sciences
Am J Med — American Journal of Medicine
Am J Med Electron — American Journal of Medical Electronics
Am J Med Genet — American Journal of Medical Genetics
Am J Med Jurispr — American Journal of Medical Jurisprudence
Am J Med Sc — American Journal of the Medical Sciences
Am J Med Sci — American Journal of the Medical Sciences
Am J Med Te — American Journal of Medical Technology
Am J Med Technol — American Journal of Medical Technology
Am J Men Deficiency — American Journal of Mental Deficiency
Am J Mental Deficiency — American Journal of Mental Deficiency
Am J Ment D — American Journal of Mental Deficiency
Am J Ment Defic — American Journal of Mental Deficiency
Am J Ment Dis — American Journal of Mental Diseases
Am J Micr (NY) — American Journal of Microscopy and Popular Science (New York)
Am JM Sc — American Journal of the Medical Sciences
AMJN — American Journal of Nursing
Am J Neurop — American Journal of Neuropathy
Am Jnl Archae — American Journal of Archaeology
Am Jnl Econ & Soc — American Journal of Economics and Sociology [*New York*]
Am Jnl Philol — American Journal of Philology
Am Jnl Soc — American Journal of Sociology
Am J Nurs — American Journal of Nursing
Am J Nursing — American Journal of Nursing
Am J Obstet Gynecol — American Journal of Obstetrics and Gynecology
Am J Obst G — American Journal of Obstetrics and Gynecology
Am J Occup Ther — American Journal of Occupational Therapy
Am J Occu T — American Journal of Occupational Therapy
Am J Ophth — American Journal of Ophthalmology
Am J Ophthalmol — American Journal of Ophthalmology
Am J Optom — American Journal of Optometry and Physiological Optics
Am J Optom Arch Am Acad Optom — American Journal of Optometry and Archives of American Academy of Optometry [*Later, American Journal of Optometry and Physiological Optics*]
Am J Optom and Arch Am Acad Optom — American Journal of Optometry and Archives of American Academy of Optometry [*Later, American Journal of Optometry and Physiological Optics*]
Am J Optom Physiol Opt — American Journal of Optometry and Physiological Optics
Am J Optom & Physiol Opt — American Journal of Optometry and Physiological Optics
Am J Orth — American Journal of Orthopedics
Am J Orthod — American Journal of Orthodontics
Am J Orthod Oral Surg — American Journal of Orthodontics and Oral Surgery [*Later, American Journal of Orthodontics*]
Am J Orthod Oral Surg Oral Surg — American Journal of Orthodontics and Oral Surgery [*later, American Journal of Orthodontics*]. Oral Surgery
Am J Orthop — American Journal of Orthopsychiatry
Am J Orthopsych — American Journal of Orthopsychiatry
Am J Orthopsychiat — American Journal of Orthopsychiatry
Am J Orthopsychiatr — American Journal of Orthopsychiatry

Am J Orthopsychiatry — American Journal of Orthopsychiatry
Am J Orth Surg — American Journal of Orthopedic Surgery
Am J Otol — American Journal of Otology
Am J Otolaryngol — American Journal of Otolaryngology
Am Jour Econ Sociol — American Journal of Economics and Sociology [*New York*]
Am Jour Internatl Law — American Journal of International Law
Am Jour Legal Hist — American Journal of Legal History
Am Journ Phil — American Journal of Philology
Am Jour Phys Anthropol — American Journal of Physical Anthropology
Am Jour Pol — American Journal of Politics
Am Jour Psychiatry — American Journal of Psychiatry
Am Jour Sociol — American Journal of Sociology
Am JPA — American Journal of Physical Anthropology
Am J P Anth — American Journal of Physical Anthropology
Am J Path — American Journal of Pathology
Am J Pathol — American Journal of Pathology
Am J Pediatr Hematol Oncol — American Journal of Pediatric Hematology/ Oncology
AmJPh — American Journal of Philology [*Baltimore*]
Am J Phar E — American Journal of Pharmaceutical Education
Am J Pharm — American Journal of Pharmacy and the Sciences Supporting Public Health [*Later, American Journal of Pharmacy*]
Am J Pharm Educ — American Journal of Pharmaceutical Education
Am J Pharm Sci Supporting Public Health — American Journal of Pharmacy and the Sciences Supporting Public Health [*Later, American Journal of Pharmacy*]
Am J Phil — American Journal of Philology
Am J Philol — American Journal of Philology
Am J Photogr — American Journal of Photography
Am J Phys — American Journal of Physics
Am J Phys Anthro — American Journal of Physical Anthropology
Am J Phys Anthrop — American Journal of Physical Anthropology
Am J Phys Anthrop ns — American Journal of Physical Anthropology. New Series
Am J Phys Anthropol — American Journal of Physical Anthropology
Am J Physics — American Journal of Physics
Am J Physiol — American Journal of Physiology
Am J Physiol Cell Physiol — American Journal of Physiology. Cell Physiology
Am J Physiol Endocrinol Metab Gastrointest Physiol — American Journal of Physiology. Endocrinology, Metabolism, and Gastrointestinal Physiology
Am J Physiol Heart Circ Physiol — American Journal of Physiology. Heart and Circulatory Physiology
Am J Physiol Renal Fluid Electrolyte Physiol — American Journal of Physiology. Renal, Fluid, and Electrolyte Physiology
Am J Physl — American Journal of Physiology
Am J Phys M — American Journal of Physical Medicine
Am J Phys Med — American Journal of Physical Medicine
Am J Pol — American Journal of Politics
Am J Pol Sc — American Journal of Political Science
Am J Pol Sci — American Journal of Political Science
Am J Proctol — American Journal of Proctology [*Later, American Journal of Proctology, Gastroenterology, and Colon and Rectal Surgery*]
Am J Proctol Gastroenterol Colon Rectal Surg — American Journal of Proctology, Gastroenterology, and Colon and Rectal Surgery
Am J Proctol Gastroenterol Colon Rectal Surg (Georgetown) — American Journal of Proctology, Gastroenterology, and Colon and Rectal Surgery (Georgetown)
Am J Progr Ther — American Journal of Progressive Therapeutics
Am J Psych — American Journal of Psychiatry
Am J Psycha — American Journal of Psychoanalysis
Am J Psychi — American Journal of Psychiatry
Am J Psychiat — American Journal of Psychiatry
Am J Psychiatry — American Journal of Psychiatry
Am J Psycho — American Journal of Psychology
Am J Psychoanal — American Journal of Psychoanalysis
Am J Psychol — American Journal of Psychology
Am J Psychoth — American Journal of Psychotherapy
Am J Psychother — American Journal of Psychotherapy
Am J Psycht — American Journal of Psychotherapy
Am J Pub He — American Journal of Public Health
Am J Pub Health — American Journal of Public Health
Am J Public Health — American Journal of Public Health
Am J Public Health Nation's Health — American Journal of Public Health and the Nation's Health [*Later, American Journal of Public Health*]
Am J Public Health Suppl — American Journal of Public Health. Supplement
Am J Roentg — American Journal of Roentgenology
Am J Roentgenol — American Journal of Roentgenology
Am J Roentgenol Radium Ther — American Journal of Roentgenology and Radium Therapy [*Later, American Journal of Roentgenology*]
Am J Roentgenol Radium Ther Nucl Med — American Journal of Roentgenology, Radium Therapy, and Nuclear Medicine [*Later, American Journal of Roentgenology*]
Am J S — American Journal of Sociology
Am J Sc and Arts — American Journal of Science and Arts

Am J School Hygiene — American Journal of School Hygiene
Am J Sci — American Journal of Science
Am J Sci Arts — American Journal of Science and Arts
Am J Sem Lang — American Journal of Semitic Languages and Literatures
Am J Small Bus — American Journal of Small Business
Am J Soc — American Journal of Sociology
Am J Socio — American Journal of Sociology
Am J Sociol — American Journal of Sociology
Am J Soc Sci — American Journal of Social Science
Am J Sports Med — American Journal of Sports Medicine
Am J Stomat — American Journal of Stomatology
Am J Surg — American Journal of Surgery
Am J Surg Pathol — American Journal of Surgical Pathology
Am J Syph Gonorrhea Vener Dis — American Journal of Syphilis, Gonorrhea, and Venereal Diseases
AmJTh — American Journal of Theology
Am J Theol — American Journal of Theology
Am J Ther Clin Rep — American Journal of Therapeutics and Clinical Reports
Am J Trop Dis (New Orleans) — American Journal of Tropical Diseases and Preventive Medicine (New Orleans)
Am J Trop M — American Journal of Tropical Medicine and Hygiene
Am J Trop Med — American Journal of Tropical Medicine [*Later, American Journal of Tropical Medicine and Hygiene*]
Am J Trop Med Hyg — American Journal of Tropical Medicine and Hygiene
Am Jud Soc — American Judicature Society. Journal
Am Jud Soc'y — Journal. American Judicature Society
Am J Vet Med — American Journal of Veterinary Medicine
Am J Vet Re — American Journal of Veterinary Research
Am J Vet Res — American Journal of Veterinary Research
AmL — Amor de Libro
Am Lab — American Laboratory
Am Lab (Boston) — American Laboratory (Boston)
Am Lab (Fairfield Conn) — American Laboratory (Fairfield, Connecticut)
Am Lab Leg Rev — American Labor Legislation Review
Am Labor Legis Rev — American Labor Legislation Review
Am Labor Leg R — American Labor Legislation Review
Am Landrace — American Landrace
Am Laund Dig — American Laundry Digest
Am Laundry Dig — American Laundry Digest
Am Law — American Lawyer
Am Law R — American Law Review
Am Law Rev — American Law Review
Am Lawy — American Lawyer
Am Lect Ser — American Lecture Series
Am Legion M — American Legion Magazine
Am Li — Amor de Libro
Am Lib — American Libraries [*Chicago*]
Am Lib Assn Bul — American Library Association. Bulletin
Am Libr — American Libraries [*Chicago*]
Am Libr (Chicago) — American Libraries (Chicago)
Am Libs — American Libraries [*Chicago*]
AmLit — American Literature
Am Lit M — American Literary Magazine
Am Lit Real — American Literary Realism, 1870-1910
Am Lit Realism — American Literary Realism, 1870-1910
Am Littoral Soc Spec Publ — American Littoral Society. Special Publication
Am Livestock J — American Livestock Journal
Am Logger Lumberman — American Logger and Lumberman
Am L Rev — American Law Review
Am L S — American Library Scholarship
AMLSBQ — American Lecture Series
Am Lumberman — American Lumberman
Am Lung Assoc Bull — American Lung Association. Bulletin
Am Luth — American Lutheran
Am M — American Magazine
AmM — American Mercury
AMM — Annuaire du Monde Musulman
Am Mach — American Machinist
Am Machin — American Machinist
Am Mach/Metalwork Manuf — American Machinist/Metalworking Manufacturing
Am Mag — American Magazine
Am Mag Art — American Magazine of Art
Am Malacolog Union Ann Rept — American Malacological Union. Annual Report
Am Malacol Union Bull — American Malacological Union. Bulletin [*Later, American Malacological Bulletin*]
Am Malacol Union Inc Annu Rep — American Malacological Union, Incorporated. Annual Report
Am Malacol Union Inc Bull — American Malacological Union, Incorporated. Bulletin [*Later, American Malacological Bulletin*]
Am Management R — American Management Review
Am Manuf — American Manufacturer
Am Mar Cas — American Maritime Cases
Am Marine Engineer — American Marine Engineer
Am M Art — American Magazine of Art

Am Math M — American Mathematical Monthly
Am Math Mo — American Mathematical Monthly
Am Math Mon — American Mathematical Monthly
Am Math Soc Bul — American Mathematical Society. Bulletin
Am Math Soc Mem — American Mathematical Society. Memoirs
Am Math Soc Memoirs — American Mathematical Society. Memoirs
Am M Civics — American Magazine of Civics
Am M Cong — American Mining Congress
Am Meat Inst Found Bull — American Meat Institute. Foundation Bulletin
Am Meat Inst Found Circ — American Meat Institute. Foundation Circular
Am Med — American Medicine
Am Med Assn J — American Medical Association. Journal
Am Med News — American Medical News
Am Med News Impact — American Medical News Impact
AmMerc — American Mercury
Am Mercury — American Mercury
Am Meteorological J — American Meteorological Journal
Am Meteorol Soc Bull — American Meteorological Society. Bulletin
Am Meth M — American Methodist Magazine
Am Met Mark — American Metal Market
Am Met Mark Metalwork News Ed — American Metal Market. Metalworking News Edition
Am Met Soc Bull — American Meteorological Society. Bulletin
AMMIA — American Mineralogist
Am Micro Soc Pr — American Microscopical Society. Proceedings
Am Micros Soc Trans — American Microscopical Society. Transactions
Am Midland Natural — American Midland Naturalist
Am Midl Nat — American Midland Naturalist
Am Midl Natur — American Midland Naturalist
Am Milk R — American Milk Review
Am Miller Process — American Miller and Processor
Am Min — American Mineralogist
Am Miner — American Mineralogist
Am Mineral — American Mineralogist
Am Mineralogist — American Mineralogist
Am Miner J — American Mineralogical Journal
AMMKA — American Metal Market
AMMO — Australian Mining, Minerals, and Oil
AMMOHOUSE Bull — AMMOHOUSE [*Ammunition House*] Bulletin
Am Mo M — American Monthly Magazine
Ammonia Plant Saf — Ammonia Plant Safety and Related Facilities
Am Mo R — American Monthly Review
Am Mosq Control Assoc Bull — American Mosquito Control Association. Bulletin
AMMSN — Acta Musei Macedonici. Scientiarum Naturalium
Am Mtl Mkt — American Metal Market
Am Mus Dgt — American Musical Digest
Am Musicol Soc J — American Musicological Society. Journal
Am Mus J — American Museum Journal
Am Mus Nat History Bull — American Museum of Natural History. Bulletin
Am Mus Nat History Bull Sci Guide Special Pub — American Museum of Natural History. Bulletin. Science Guide. Special Publication
Am Mus N H B Mem — American Museum of Natural History. Bulletin. Memoirs
Am Mus Novit — American Museum Novitates
Am Mus Novitates — American Museum Novitates
Am Mus Tcr — American Music Teacher
Am Mus Teach — American Music Teacher
AMMYA — American Mathematical Monthly
AMMYAE — American Mathematical Monthly
AMN — Amazing Stories. Science Fiction Novels
AMN — Analecta Mediaevalia Namurcensia
AMN — Arizona Music News
AMN — SAM [*Society for Advancement of Management*] Advanced Management Journal
AMNAA — American Midland Naturalist
AMNAAF — American Midland Naturalist
Am Nat — American Naturalist
Am Natl Red Cross Annu Sci Symp — American National Red Cross. Annual Scientific Symposium
Am Natl Stand Inst Stand — American National Standards Institute. Standards
Am Natural — American Naturalist
AMNDS — Annales de la Mission de N.-D. de Sion en Terre Sainte (1877-1912)
Am Neptune — American Neptune
AMNGA — Arkiv foer Mineralogi och Geologi
AMNGAX — Arkiv foer Mineralogi och Geologi
AMNIB — Acta Manilana. Series A. Natural and Applied Sciences
Am Note Que — American Notes and Queries
Am Notes & Queries — American Notes and Queries
AMNP — Annuaire. Musee National Archeologique (Plovdiv)
Am N & Q — American Notes and Queries
AMNTA — American Naturalist
AMNTA4 — American Naturalist
Am Num Soc Mus Notes — American Numismatic Society. Museum Notes

Am Nurse — American Nurse
Am Nurserman — American Nurseryman
Am Nurseryman — American Nurseryman
Am Nut J — American Nut Journal
AMO — Acta Medica Orientalia
AMo — Atlantic Monthly
AMOBAN — AMMOHOUSE [*Ammunition House*] Bulletin
AMOCBR — Agronomia Mocambicana
Am Oil Chemists Soc J — American Oil Chemists' Society. Journal
Am Oil Chem Soc J — American Oil Chemists' Society. Journal
AMOMB — Applied Mathematics and Optimization
AMon — Analecta Monastica
AMontserr — Analecta Montserratensia
Am Opinion — American Opinion
Am Orchid Soc Bull — American Orchid Society. Bulletin
Am Orch Soc B — American Orchid Society. Bulletin
Am Orch Soc Yb — American Orchid Society. Yearbook
Am Org — American Organist
Am Orient Soc J — American Oriental Society. Journal
Am Orn — American Ornithology
Am Orth J — American Orthoptic Journal
Am Orthopt J — American Orthoptic Journal
AmOx — American Oxonian
AMP — Acta Medica Polona
Am P — American Psychologist
Amp — Ampurias
AMP — Audiovisual Market Place
Am P Advocate — American Poultry Advocate
Am Paint — American Paint and Coatings Journal
Am Paint Coat J — American Paint and Coatings Journal
Am Paint Contract — American Painting Contractor
Am Painter Decor — American Painter and Decorator
Am Paint J — American Paint Journal [*Later, American Paint and Coatings Journal*]
Am Paper Ind — American Paper Industry
Am Paper Merch — American Paper Merchant
Am Pap Ind — American Paper Industry
AMPCA — Archivio "E. Maragliano" di Patologia e Clinica
AMPCB — American Psychological Association. Proceedings of the Annual Convention
AMPDA — Australian Machinery and Production Engineering
AMPEA3 — American Miller and Processor
Am Perfum Cosmet — American Perfumer and Cosmetics
Am Perfum Cosmet Toilet Prep — American Perfumer, Cosmetics, Toilet Preparations
Am Perfumer — American Perfumer and Cosmetics
Am Perfumer Arom — American Perfumer and Aromatics
Am Perfumer & Aromatics — American Perfumer and Aromatics
Am Pet Inst Bul — American Petroleum Institute. Bulletin
Am Pet Inst Proc — American Petroleum Institute. Proceedings
Am Pet Inst Publ — American Petroleum Institute. Publication
Am Petr Inst Quart — American Petroleum Institute. Quarterly
Am Petroleum Inst Drilling and Production Practice — American Petroleum Institute. Drilling and Production Practice
AMPH — American Pharmacy
Am Pharm — American Pharmacy
AMPHDF — American Pharmacy
Am Philos Q — American Philosophical Quarterly
Am Philos Soc Lib Bull — American Philosophical Society. Library Bulletin
Am Philos Soc Proc — American Philosophical Society. Proceedings
Am Philos Soc Trans — American Philosophical Society. Transactions
Am Philos Soc YB — American Philosophical Society. Yearbook
Am Philos Soc Yearbook — American Philosophical Society. Yearbook
Am Phot — American Photography
Am Photo Engraver — American Photo Engraver
Am Photog — American Photography
Am Photogr — American Photography
Am Phys Ed Assn Res Q — American Physical Education Association. Research Quarterly
Am Phys Educ R — American Physical Education Review
Am Phys Teach — American Physics Teacher
Am Phytopathol Soc Monogr — American Phytopathological Society. Monograph
AMPI (Assoc Med Phys India) Med Phys Bull — AMPI (Association of Medical Physicists of India) Medical Physics Bulletin
AMPIB — Advances in Microbial Physiology
Am P J — American Poultry Journal
Am Plan Assn J — American Planning Association. Journal
Am Plann Assoc J — American Planning Association. Journal
Am Planning — American Planning and Civic Planning
AMPLJ — Australian Mining and Petroleum Law Journal
AMPM — Institut de France. Academie des Sciences Morales et Politiques. Memoires
AMPMA — Archives des Maladies Professionnelles de Medecine du Travail et de Securite Sociale
AMP News — AMP [*Australian Mutual Provident Society*] News and Views

Am Poet Rev — American Poetry Review
Am Poetry — American Poetry Review
Am Poli Sci — American Political Science Review
Am Politics Q — American Politics Quarterly
Am Polit Q — American Politics Quarterly
Am Polit Sci R — American Political Science Review
Am Pol Q — American Politics Quarterly
Am Pol Sci — American Political Science Review [*Baltimore*]
Am Pol Science R — American Political Science Review
Am Pol Science Rev — American Political Science Review
Am Pol Sci R — American Political Science Review
Am Pol Sci Rev — American Political Science Review
Am Pol Sc Rev — American Political Science Review
Am Pom Soc Pro — American Pomological Society. Proceedings
Am Postal Wkr — American Postal Worker
Am Potato J — American Potato Journal
Am Pot J — American Potato Journal
Am Poultry J — American Poultry Journal
Am Pract — American Practitioner
Am Pract Dig Treat — American Practitioner and Digest of Treatment
Am Prefs — American Prefaces
Am Presb R — American Presbyterian Review
Am Pressman — American Pressman
Am Pressman Rept — American Pressman Reports
Am Print — American Printer
Am Prod R — American Produce Review
Am Prof Pharm — American Professional Pharmacist
AM-Ps — Annales Medico-Psychologiques
AMPSA — American Psychologist
AMPSAB — American Psychologist
Am Psychoana Assn J — American Psychoanalytic Association. Journal
Am Psychoanal Assn J — American Psychoanalytic Association. Journal
Am Psychoanal Assoc J Monogr Ser — American Psychoanalytic Association. Journal. Monograph Series
Am Psychol — American Psychologist
Am Ptr & Lith — American Printer and Lithographer [*Later, American Printer*]
Am Pub Health Ass Rep — American Public Health Association. Reports
AMPYA — Annales Medico-Psychologiques
AMQ — Amazing Stories. Quarterly
Am Q — American Quarterly
Am Q — American Quarterly Review [*1827-1837*]
Am Q J Agr — American Quarterly Journal of Agriculture and Science
Am Q Micro J — American Quarterly Microscopical Journal
Am Q Obs — American Quarterly Observer
Am Q Reg — American Quarterly Register
Am Quar — American Quarterly
Am Quart — American Quarterly
AMR — Academy of Management. Review
AMR — Amazing Stories. Quarterly Reissue
AMR — Ambtenaar
AMR — American Book Review
Am R — American Review [*Formerly, New American Review*]
AMR — Applied Mechanics Reviews
AMR — Australian Marketing Researcher
Am Rabbit J — American Rabbit Journal
AMRAC — Annales. Musee Royal de l'Afrique Centrale
Am Railw Eng Assoc Bull — American Railway Engineering Association. Bulletin
Am Railw Eng Assoc Proc — American Railway Engineering Association. Proceedings
AMRBB5 — Alabama Marine Resources. Bulletin
AMRC Rev — AMRC [*Australian Meat Research Committee*] Review
Am Real Estate & Urb Econ Assn J — American Real Estate and Urban Economics Association. Journal
Am Rec G — American Record Guide
Am Rec Guide — American Record Guide
Am Recorder — American Recorder
Am Record Gd — American Record Guide
Am Red Angus — American Red Angus
AMREEH — Amphibia-Reptilia
Am Ref Bk Ann — American Reference Books Annual
Am Refract Inst Inf Circ — American Refractories Institute. Information Circular
Am Refract Inst Tech Bull — American Refractories Institute. Technical Bulletin
Am Rehabil — American Rehabilitation
Am Rev — American Review [*Formerly, New American Review*]
Am Rev Resp Dis — American Review of Respiratory Disease
Am Rev Respir Dis — American Review of Respiratory Disease
Am Rev Sov Med — American Review of Soviet Medicine
Am Rev Sov Union — American Review on the Soviet Union
Am Rev Tub — American Review of Tuberculosis and Pulmonary Diseases
Am Rev Tuberc — American Review of Tuberculosis
Am Rev Tuberc Pulm Dis — American Review of Tuberculosis and Pulmonary Diseases

AMrhKG — Archiv fuer Mittelrheinische Kirchengeschichte
AMRIA — Americas
AMRIB — America
AMRM — Australasian Model Railroad Magazine
AMRMC5 — Agricultural Research Council. Meat Research Institute [*Bristol*]. Memorandum
Am Rocket Soc Pap — American Rocket Society. Paper
Am Rose Annu — American Rose Annual
Am R Public Admin — American Review of Public Administration
AMRR — Arctic Medical Research Report. Nordic Council
Am R Resp D — American Review of Respiratory Disease
AMRWA — Anglo-German Medical Review
AMS — Academy of Marketing Science. Journal
AMS — Acta Martyrum et Sanctorum
AMS — Advances in Management Studies
AMS — American Musicological Society. Journal
AmS — American Speech
AmS — American Studies
Ams — Americas
AMS — [*The*] Americas: A Quarterly Review of Inter-American Cultural History
AMS — Joseph Quincy Adams Memorial Studies
AMSAC — AMSAC [*American Society of African Culture*] Newsletter
AMSAPM — Atti e Memorie. Deputazione di Storia Patria per le Antiche Provincie Modenesi
AMSC — Advances in Molten Salt Chemistry [*Elsevier Book Series*]
AMSCA — American Scientist
AMSCAC — American Scientist
Am Scand R — American-Scandinavian Review
AMSCC — Advances in Molten Salt Chemistry
Am Scenic and Historic Preservation Soc An Rp — American Scenic and Historic Preservation Society. Annual Report
Am Sch — American Scholar
Am Sch Bd J — American School Board Journal
Am Sch Board J — American School Board Journal
Am Sch Brd J — American School Board Journal
Am Schol — American Scholar
Am Scholar — American Scholar
Am School Bd J — American School Board Journal
Am Sch Orient Res Bul — American Schools of Oriental Research. Bulletin
Am Sch & Univ — American School and University
Am Sci — American Scientist
Am Scient — American Scientist
Am Scientist — American Scientist
AMSDSP — Atti e Memorie. Societa Dalmata di Storia
Am Sec Educ — American Secondary Education
Am Seph — American Sephardi
AMSER — Atti e Memorie. Reale Deputazione di Storia Patria per l'Emilia et la Romagna
Am Sheep B & W — American Sheep Breeder and Wool Grower
AMSI — Atti e Memorie. Societa Istriana di Archeologia e Storia Patria
AMSIstriana — Atti e Memorie. Societa Istriana di Archeologia e Storia Patria
AMSJ — American Musicological Society. Journal
AMSJAX — Journal. Aero Medical Society of India
AMS Jl — American Musicological Society. Journal
Am Sl — American Slavic and East European Review
Am Slavic R — American Slavic and East European Review
AMSM — Atti e Memorie. Reale Deputazione di Storia Patria per le Marche
Am Soc — American Sociologist
Am Soc Abrasive Methods Natl Tech Conf Proc — American Society for Abrasive Methods. National Technical Conference. Proceedings
Am Soc Ag Eng — American Society of Agricultural Engineers. Transactions
Am Soc Agron J — American Society of Agronomy. Journal
Am Soc Anim Prod Rec Proc Annu Meet — American Society of Animal Production. Record of Proceedings. Annual Meeting
Am Soc Brew Chem Proc — American Society of Brewing Chemists. Proceedings
Am Soc C E Proc — American Society of Civil Engineers. Proceedings
Am Soc Church Hist Papers — American Society of Church History. Papers
Am Soc Civ E J Struct Div — American Society of Civil Engineers. Journal. Structural Division
Am Soc Civ E J Waterway Port Div — American Society of Civil Engineers. Waterway, Port, Coastal, and Ocean Division
Am Soc Civ Eng Hydraul Div Annu Spec Conf Proc — American Society of Civil Engineers. Hydraulics Division. Annual Specialty Conference. Proceedings
Am Soc Civ Eng Proc Eng Issues J Prof Act — American Society of Civil Engineers. Proceedings. Engineering Issues. Journal of Professional Activities
Am Soc Civ Eng Proc J Hydraul Div — American Society of Civil Engineers. Proceedings. Journal. Hydraulics Division
Am Soc Civ Eng Proc J Irrig Drain Div — American Society of Civil Engineers. Proceedings. Journal. Irrigation and Drainage Division
Am Soc Civ Eng Proc Transp Eng J — American Society of Civil Engineers. Proceedings. Transportation Engineering Journal

Am Soc Civ Eng Trans — American Society of Civil Engineers. Transactions
Am Soc Civ E Transp Eng J — American Society of Civil Engineers. Transportation Engineering Journal
Am Soc Civil Engineers Proc Jour Hydraulics Div — American Society of Civil Engineers. Proceedings. Journal. Hydraulics Division
Am Soc Civil Engineers Proc Jour Sanitary Eng Div — American Society of Civil Engineers. Proceedings. Journal. Sanitary Engineering Division
Am Soc Civil Engineers Proc Jour Structural Div — American Society of Civil Engineers. Proceedings. Journal. Structural Division
Am Soc Civil Engineers Proc Jour Surveying and Mapping Div — American Society of Civil Engineers. Proceedings. Journal. Surveying and Mapping Division
Am Soc Civil Engineers Trans — American Society of Civil Engineers. Transactions
Am Soc Civil Eng Proc — American Society of Civil Engineers. Proceedings
Am Soc Civil Eng Proc J Geotech Eng Div — American Society of Civil Engineers. Proceedings. Journal. Geotechnical Engineering Division
Am Soc Civil Engrs Constr — American Society of Civil Engineers. Proceedings. Journal. Construction Division
Am Soc Civil Engrs Geotech — American Society of Civil Engineers. Proceedings. Journal. Geotechnical Division
Am Soc Civil Engrs Struct — American Society of Civil Engineers. Proceedings. Journal. Structural Division
Am Soc Civil Engrs Urb Plann — American Society of Civil Engineers. Journal of Urban Planning
Am Soc Eng Educ COED Trans — American Society for Engineering Education. Computers in Education Division. Transactions
Am Soc Eng Educ Comput Educ Div Trans — American Society for Engineering Education. Computers in Education Division. Transactions
Am Soc Heat Vent Eng Guide — American Society of Heating and Ventilating Engineers. Guide
Am Soc Hort Sci J — American Society for Horticultural Science. Journal
Am Soc Info Science Bul — Bulletin. American Society for Information Science
Am Soc Inf Sci J — American Society for Information Science. Journal
Am Soc Int Law Proc — American Society of International Law. Proceedings
Am Soc Int'l L Proc — American Society of International Law. Proceedings
Am Soc Int L Proc — American Society of International Law. Proceedings
Am Sociol — American Sociologist
Am Sociol R — American Sociological Review
Am Sociol Rev — American Sociological Review
Am Sociol S — American Sociological Society. Publications
Am Socio Rev — American Sociological Review
Am Soc Limnol Oceangr Spec Symp — American Society of Limnology and Oceanography. Special Symposium
Am Soc Mechanical Engineers Trans — American Society of Mechanical Engineers. Transactions
Am Soc Mech Eng Appl Mech Div Appl Mech Symp Ser — American Society of Mechanical Engineers. Applied Mechanics Division. Applied Mechanics Symposia Series
Am Soc Mech Eng Heat Transfer Div Publ HTD — American Society of Mechanical Engineers. Heat Transfer Division. Publication HTD
Am Soc Mech Eng Pap — American Society of Mechanical Engineers. Papers
Am Soc Mech Eng Pressure Vessels Piping Div PVP — American Society of Mechanical Engineers. Pressure Vessels and Piping Division. PVP
Am Soc Munic Eng Off Proc — American Society of Municipal Engineers. Official Proceedings
Am Soc Munic Imp — American Society for Municipal Improvements. Proceedings
Am Soc Naval Eng J — American Society of Naval Engineers. Journal
Am Soc Photogramm Annu Meet Proc — American Society of Photogrammetry. Annual Meeting. Proceedings
Am Soc Photogramm Fall Conv Proc — American Society of Photogrammetry. Fall Convention. Proceedings
Am Soc Psychical Res J — American Society for Psychical Research. Journal
Am Soc Psych Res J — American Society for Psychical Research. Journal
Am Soc R — American Sociological Review
Am Soc Rev — American Sociological Review
Am Soc Safety Eng J — American Society of Safety Engineers. Journal
Am Soc Sci J — American Journal of Social Science
Am Soc Testing Materials Special Tech Pub — American Society for Testing and Materials. Special Technical Publication
Am Soc Testing and Materials Spec Tech Pub — American Society for Testing and Materials. Special Technical Publication
Am Soc Test Mater Annu Book ASTM Stand — American Society for Testing and Materials. Annual Book of ASTM Standards
Am Soc Test Mater Spec Tech Publ — American Society for Testing and Materials. Special Technical Publication
Am Soc Trop Med Papers — American Society of Tropical Medicine. Papers
Am Sp — American Speech
AMSPA — Advances in Mass Spectrometry
Am Spect — American Spectator
Am Spectator — American Spectator
Am Speech — American Speech
AMSPR — Atti e Memorie. Deputazione di Storia Patria per le Provincie di Romagna
AMSR — Amer-Scandinavian Review

Amst — Amerikastudien [*American Studies*]
Am Stat — American Statistician
Am Stat Assn J — American Statistical Association. Journal
Am Stat Assoc Quar Publ — American Statistical Association. Quarterly
   Publications
Am Statis Assn — American Statistical Association. Quarterly Publications
Am Statistician — American Statistician
Am Statistn — American Statistician
Amstel — Amstelodamum
Amsterdams Sociol Tijds — Amsterdams Sociologisch Tijdschrift
Am Stockman — American Stockman
Am Stomat — American Stomatologist
Amst St IV — Amsterdam Studies in the Theory and History of Linguistic
   Science. Series IV. Current Issues in Linguistic Theory
Am Stud — American Studies
Am Stud Int — American Studies International
Am Stud Sc — American Studies in Scandinavia
AMSUA — American Surgeon
AMSUAW — American Surgeon
Am Sugar Ind — American Sugar Industry
Am Surg — American Surgeon
AMT — American Music Teacher Magazine
AMt — Analecta Montserratensia
Am Tcr — American Teacher
AMTDA — Advances in Metabolic Disorders
Am Teach — American Teacher
Am Teleph J — American Telephone Journal
Am Theol Lib Assn Newsl — American Theological Library Association.
   Newsletter
Am Thresherman — American Thresherman
AMTIC — Archivio Monaldi per la Tisiologia e le Malattie dell'Apparato
   Respiratorio
Amtl Ber — Amtliche Berichte. Koenigliche Kunstsammlungen
Amtl Ztg Deutsch Fleischer-Verbandes — Amtliche Zeitung. Deutscher
   Fleischer-Verband
Am Tom Yb — American Tomato Yearbook
Am Transcen — American Transcendental Quarterly
Am Trust Rev Pacific — American Trust Review of the Pacific
Amtsbl Bayer Staatsminist Landesentwickl Umweltfragen — Amtsblatt.
   Bayerisches Staatsministerium fuer Landesentwicklung und
   Umweltfragen
Amtsbl Eur Gem — Amtsblatt. Europaeische Gemeinschaften
Amts- Mitteilungsbl Bundesanst Materialpruef — Amts- und Mitteilungsblatt.
   Bundesanstalt fuer Materialpruefung
Am Tung News — American Tung News
Am Tung Oil Top — American Tung Oil Topics
AMu — Annales Musicologiques
AMUBBK — American Malacological Union, Incorporated. Bulletin [*Later,
   American Malacological Bulletin*]
AMUGS — Antike Muenzen und Geschnittene Steine
Am ULR — American University Law Review
Am U L Rev — American University Law Review
AMUNAL — American Museum Novitates
Am Univ Beirut Fac Agric Sci Publ — American University of Beirut. Faculty
   of Agricultural Sciences. Publication
Am Univ L Rev — American University Law Review
AMur — Archivio Muratoriano
A Mus — Acta Musicologica
AMus — Asian Music
A Mus Napocensis — Acta Musei Napocensis
A Mus Porol — Acta Musei Porolissensis
AMUTA — American Music Teacher
AMV — Archiv fuer Mathematische Versicherungswissenschaft
Am Veg Grow — American Vegetable Grower
Am Veg Grower — American Vegetable Grower
Am Veg Grow Greenhouse Grow — American Vegetable Grower and
   Greenhouse Grower
Am Vet Med Assn J — American Veterinary Medical Association. Journal
Am Vet Med Assn Proc — American Veterinary Medical Association.
   Proceedings
Am Vet Med Assoc Sci Proc Annu Meet — American Veterinary Medical
   Association. Scientific Proceedings of the Annual Meeting
Am Vet Rev — American Veterinary Review
Am Voc J — American Vocational Journal
AMVRA — Annales de Medecine Veterinaire
AMVTA — Annali. Facolta di Medicina Veterinaria di Torino
AMW — Archiv fuer Musikwissenschaft
Am Water Resour Assoc Symp Proc — American Water Resources
   Association. Symposium. Proceedings
Am Water Works Assn J — American Water Works Association. Journal
Am Water Works Assoc J — American Water Works Association. Journal
Am Water Works Assoc Jour Southeastern Sec — American Water Works
   Association. Journal. Southeastern Section
Am Weld Soc J — American Welding Society. Journal
Am West — American West
Am Whig R — American Whig Review

AMXCB — Acta Mexicana de Ciencia y Tecnologia
AMZ — Allgemeine Musikalische Zeitung
AMZ — Amazing Stories
Am Zinc Inst J — American Zinc Institute. Journal
AMZOA — American Zoologist
AMZOAF — American Zoologist
Am Zool — American Zoologist
Am Zoolog — American Zoologist
AN — Acta Neophilologica
AN — Advertising News
AN — African Notes [*Ibadan*]
AN — Age Nouveau
AN — Americana Norvegica
An — Annales. Revue Mensuelle de Lettres Francaises
An — Anthropos
An — Antonianum
AN — Aquileia Nostra
AN — Art News
An A — Anatomischer Anzeiger
AnAB — Annales. Societe d'Archeologie de Bruxelles
ANABA — Asociacion Nacional de Bibliotecarios, Arquiveros, y Arqueologos
   [*Madrid*]
An Acad Bras Cienc — Anais. Academia Brasileira de Ciencias
An Acad Bras Cienc Supl — Anais. Academia Brasileira de Ciencias.
   Suplemento
An Acad Chil Cienc Nat — Anales. Academia Chilena de Ciencias Naturales
An Acad Cienc Med Fis Nat Habana — Anales. Academia de Ciencias
   Medicas, Fisicas, y Naturales de La Habana
An Acad Nac Cienc Exactas Fis Nat B Aires — Anales. Academia Nacional de
   Ciencias Exactas, Fisicas, y Naturales de Buenos Aires
An Acad Nac Cienc Exactas Fis Nat Buenos Aires — Anales. Academia
   Nacional de Ciencias Exactas, Fisicas, y Naturales de Buenos Aires
An Acad Nac Farm — Anales. Academia Nacional de Farmacia
An Acad Port Hist — Anais. Academia Portuguesa da Historia
An Acad Repub Soc Rom — Analele. Academiei Republicii Socialiste Romania
An Acad Rom — Analele. Academiei Romane
An Ac Brasi — Anais. Academia Brasileira de Ciencias
ANA Clin Conf — ANA [*American Nurses' Association*] Clinical Conferences
ANA Clin Sess — ANA [*American Nurses' Association*] Clinical Session
An Ac R — Analele. Academiei Romane
An Adm Nac Bosques Minist Agric Ganad (Repub Argent) — Anales.
   Administracion Nacional de Bosques. Ministerio de Agricultura y
   Ganaderia (Republica Argentina)
AnAeg — Analecta Aegyptiaca [*Copenhagen*]
Anaesth — Anaesthesia
Anaesth — Anaesthesist
Anaesthesiol Intensivmed Prax — Anaesthesiologische und
   Intensivmedizinische Praxis
Anaesthesiol Resuscitation — Anaesthesiology and Resuscitation
Anaesthesiol Wiederbeleb — Anaesthesiologie und Wiederbelebung
Anaesthesiol Wiederbelebung — Anaesthesiologie und Wiederbelebung
Anaesth Intensivther Notfallmed — Anaesthesie, Intensivtherapie,
   Notfallmedizin
Anaesth Resusc Intensive Ther — Anaesthesia, Resuscitation, and Intensive
   Therapy
ANAFJ — Army-Navy-Air Force Journal
ANAGA — Annales Agronomiques
An Agron — Anales Agronomicos
AnAI — Annuaire des Archives Israelites
ANAIA — Annales de la Nutrition et de l'Alimentation
Anais Acad Bras Cienc — Anais. Academia Brasileira de Ciencias
Anais Esc Sup Agric "Luiz Queiroz" — Anais. Escola Superior de Agricultura
   "Luiz De Queiroz"
Anais Fac Cienc Porto — Anais. Faculdade de Ciencias. Universidade do Porto
Anais II Congr Latin-Amer Zool — Anais. II Congresso Latino-Americano de
   Zoologia
Anais Inst Sup Agron Lisboa — Anais. Instituto Superior de Agronomia.
   Universidade Tecnica de Lisboa
Anais Inst Sup Agron Univ Tec Lisb — Anais. Instituto Superior de Agronomia.
   Universidade Tecnica de Lisboa
Anais Soc Ent Brasil — Anais. Sociedade Entomologica do Brasil
Anal — Analyst
ANALA — Analyst (London)
Anal Abstr — Analytical Abstracts
Anal Acad Nac Cienc Exactas Fis Nat — Anales. Academia Nacional de
   Ciencias Exactas, Fisicas, y Naturales
Anal Acad Rom — Analele. Academiei Romane
Anal Adv — Analytical Advances
Anal Aug — Analecta Augustiniana
ANALB — Analytical Letters
Anal Ber Gesellschaftswiss — Analysen und Berichte aus
   Gesellschaftswissenschaften [*West Germany*]
Anal Biochem — Analytical Biochemistry
Anal Boll — Analecta Bollandiana
Anal Bolland — Analecta Bollandiana
Anal Calorim — Analytical Calorimetry

Anal Charact Oils Fats Fat Prod — Analysis and Characterization of Oils, Fats, and Fat Products
Anal Chem — Analytical Chemistry
Anal Chim Ac — Analytica Chimica Acta
Anal Chim Acta — Analytica Chimica Acta
Anal Chimica Acta — Analytica Chimica Acta
Anal Cist — Analecta Cisterciensia
Anal Drugs Metab Gas Chromatogr Mass Spectrom — Analysis of Drugs and Metabolites by Gas Chromatography. Mass Spectrometry
Analecta Farm Gerund — Analecta Farmacia Gerundense
Analecta Geol — Analecta Geologica
Analecta Vet — Analecta Veterinaria
Anale Stat Cent Apic Seri — Anale. Statiunea Centrala de Apicultura si Sericultura
Anal Financ — Analyse Financiere
Anal Fran — Analecta Franciscana
Anal Greg — Analecta Gregoriana
Anal Hus Yb — Analecta Husserliana. Yearbook of Phenomenological Research
Anali Accad Agric (Torino) — Annali. Accademia di Agricoltura (Torino)
AnaliFF — Anali Filoloskog Fakulteta Beogradskog Univerziteta
Anal Inst Cent Cerc Agric Sect Pedol — Anale. Institutul Central de Cercetari Agricole. Sectiei de Pedologie
Anal Inst Cerc Agron — Analele. Institutului de Cercetari Agronomice. Academia Republicii Populare Romine
Anal Inst Cerc pentru Cereale Pl Tehn-Fundulea — Analele. Institutului de Cercetari pentru Cereale si Plante Tehnice-Fundulea
Anal Inst Cerc Prot Plantelor — Analele. Institutului de Cercetari pentru Protectia Plantelor
Anal Inst Cerc Zooteh — Analele. Institutului de Cercetari. Zootehnice
Anal Instrum — Analysis Instrumentation
Analise Conjunctural Econ Nordestina — Analise Conjuntural da Economia Nordestina
Anal Khim Neorg Soedin — Analiticheskaya Khimiya Neorganicheskikh Soedinenij
Anal Kontrol Proizvod Azotn Promsti — Analiticheskii Kontrol Proizvodstva v Azotnoi Promyshlennosti
Anal Lett — Analytical Letters
Anal Letter — Analytical Letters
Anal Letters — Analytical Letters
Anal Ling — Analecta Linguistica
Anal M — Analectic Magazine
Anal Math — Analysis Mathematica
Anal Methods Pestic Plant Growth Regul — Analytical Methods for Pesticides and Plant Growth Regulators
Anal Methods Pestic Plant Growth Regul Food Addit — Analytical Methods for Pesticides, Plant Growth Regulators, and Food Additives
Anal Mon — Analecta Monastica
Anal Mont — Analecta Montserratensia
Anal Numer Theor Approx — L'Analyse Numerique et la Theorie de l'Approximation
Anal O — Analecta Orientalia
Anal Or — Analecta Orientalia
Anal Praem — Analecta Praemonstratensia
Anal et Previs — Analyse et Prevision
Anal Previs — Analyse et Prevision
Anal Prichin Avarii Povrezhdenii Stroit Konstr — Analiz Prichin Avarii i Povrezhdenii Stroitel'nykh Konstruktsii
Anal Proc — Analytical Proceedings
Anal Proc R Soc Chem — Analytical Proceedings. Royal Society of Chemistry [*United Kingdom*]
Anal Profiles Drug Subst — Analytical Profiles of Drug Substances
Anal Progn — Analysen und Prognosen ueber die Welt von Morgen
Anal Progn Welt Morgen — Analysen und Prognosen ueber die Welt von Morgen [*West Germany*]
Anal Pyrolysis — Analytical Pyrolysis
Anal Quant Cytol — Analytical and Quantitative Cytology
Anal Rev Tech Merlin Gerin — Analyses. Revue Technique Merlin Gerin
Anal Soc — Analise Social
Anal Spectrosc Ser — Analytical Spectroscopy Series
Anal Stiint Univ Cuza Iasi Chim — Analele Stiintifice. Universitatii Al. I. Cuza din Iasi. Sectiunea 1C. Chimie
Anal Univ Buc Biol Anim — Analele. Universitatii Bucuresti. Biologie Animala
Anal Univ Buc Ser Stiint Nat Biol — Analele. Universitatii Bucuresti. Seria Stiintele Naturii. Biologie
Anal Univ Bucuresti — Analele. Universitatii Bucuresti. Stiinte Sociale. Seria Istorie
Analysts J — Analysts Journal
Analyt Abstr — Analytical Abstracts
Analyt Bioc — Analytical Biochemistry
Analyt Biochem — Analytical Biochemistry
Analyt Chem — Analytical Chemistry
Analyt Chim — Analytica Chimica Acta
Analyt Lett — Analytical Letters
Analyt Tables For Trade Sect D — Analytical Tables of Foreign Trade. Section D

An Am Acad Pol Soc Sci — Annals. American Academy of Political and Social Science
ANAMD — Archiwum Nauki o Materialach
ANANA — Anatomischer Anzeiger; Zentralblatt fuer die Gesamte Wissenschaftliche Anatomie
An Anat — Anales de Anatomia
ANA Nurs Res Conf — American Nurses' Association. Nursing Research Conferences
ANAPA — Annales d'Anatomie Pathologique
ANA Publ — American Nurses' Association. Publications
AnAr — Anadolu Arastirmalari
Anarch — Anarchism
AnArchSyr — Annales Archeologiques de Syrie [*Damascus*]
ANARE Data Rep — ANARE [*Australian National Antarctic Research Expeditions*] Data Reports
ANARE Data Rep Ser B — ANARE [*Australian National Antarctic Research Expeditions*] Data Reports. Series B
ANARE Data Rep Ser C — ANARE [*Australian National Antarctic Research Expeditions*] Data Reports. Series C
ANARE Interim Rep — ANARE [*Australian National Antarctic Research Expeditions*] Interim Reports
ANARE Interim Rep Ser A — ANARE [*Australian National Antarctic Research Expeditions*] Interim Reports. Series A
ANAREN — ANARE [*Australian National Antarctic Research Expeditions*] News
ANARE Rep — ANARE [*Australian National Antarctic Research Expeditions*] Report
ANARE Rep Ser B — ANARE [*Australian National Antarctic Research Expeditions*] Reports. Series B
ANARE Rep Ser C — ANARE [*Australian National Antarctic Research Expeditions*] Reports. Series C
ANARE Sci Rep — ANARE [*Australian National Antarctic Research Expeditions*] Scientific Reports
ANARE Sci Rep Ser A-IV Publ — ANARE [*Australian National Antarctic Research Expeditions*] Scientific Reports. Series A-IV. Publications
ANARE Sci Rep Ser B IV Med Sci — ANARE [*Australian National Antarctic Research Expeditions*] Scientific Reports. Series B-IV. Medical Science
ANARE Sci Rep Ser B I Zool — ANARE [*Australian National Antarctic Research Expeditions*] Scientific Reports. Series B-I. Zoology
An Arqueol Etnol — Anales de Arqueologia y Etnologia
ANASA — Anaesthesia
An Asoc Quim (Argent) — Anales. Asociacion Quimica (Argentina)
An Asoc Quim Farm Urug — Anales. Asociacion de Quimica y Farmacia del Uruguay
An As Quim — Anales. Asociacion Quimica [*Argentina*]
An As Quim Farm Urug — Anales. Asociacion de Quimica y Farmacia del Uruguay
An Assoc Bras Quim — Anais. Associacao Brasileira de Quimica
An Assoc Quim Bras — Anais. Associacao Quimica do Brasil
Anasth Intensivther Notfallmed — Anaesthesie, Intensivtherapie, Notfallmedizin
ANATA — Der Anaesthesist
Anat Anz — Anatomischer Anzeiger; Zentralblatt fuer die Gesamte Wissenschaftliche Anatomie
Anat Chir — Anatomia e Chirurgia
Anat Embryo — Anatomy and Embryology
Anat Embryol — Anatomy and Embryology [*West Germany*]
Anat Entw Gesch Monogr — Anatomische und Entwicklungsgeschichtliche Monographien
Anat His Em — Anatomia, Histologia, Embryologia. Zentralblatt fuer Veterinaermedizin, Reihe C
Anat Histol Embryol — Anatomia, Histologia, Embryologia
Anat Rec — Anatomical Record
AnatS — Anatolian Studies
Anat Skr — Anatomiske Skrifter
AnatSt — Anatolian Studies [*London*]
Anat Stud — Anatolian Studies
ANAZAW — Anais Azevedos
An Azevedos — Anais Azevedos
ANB — Andover Newton Bulletin
AnB — Animal Behaviour
AnB — Annales de Bourgogne
ANB — Australian National Bibliography
Anbar Abs (Account Data) — Anbar Abstracts (Accounting and Data)
Anbar Abs (Mktng Distr) — Anbar Abstracts (Marketing and Distribution)
Anbar Abs (Personn Trng) — Anbar Abstracts (Personnel and Training)
Anbar Abs (Top Mgmt) — Anbar Abstracts (Top Management)
Anbar Abs (Wk Study) — Anbar Abstracts (Work Study)
Anbar Mgmt Serv — Anbar Management Services Joint Index
ANBCA — Analytical Biochemistry
ANBEA — Animal Behaviour
An Bhand Or Res Inst — Annals. Bhandarkar Oriental Research Institute
An Bi — Analecta Biblica
ANBI — Annales Biologiques

AnBibl — Analecta Biblica. Investigationes Scientificae in Res Biblicas [*Rome*]
ANBOA — Annals of Botany
AnBol — Analecta Bollandiana
AnBoll — Analecta Bollandiana [*Brussels*]
An Bot Herb "Barbosa Rodrigues" — Anais Botanicos. Herbario "Barbosa Rodrigues"
AnBr — Annales de Bretagne [*Later, Annales de Bretagne et des Pays de l'Ouest*]
ANBRAD — Anales de Bromatologia
An Bras Dermatol — Anais Brasileiros de Dermatologia
An Bras Dermatol Sifilogr — Anais Brasileiros de Dermatologia e Sifilografia
An Bras Gin — Anais Brasileiros de Ginecologia
An Bras Ginecol — Anais Brasileiros de Ginecologia [*Brazil*]
AnBret — Annales de Bretagne [*Later, Annales de Bretagne et des Pays de l'Ouest*]
An Brom — Annales de Bromatologia
An Bromat — Anales de Bromatologia
An Bromatol — Anales de Bromatologia
ANC — Asia Research Bulletin
An Casa Salud Valdecilla — Anales. Casa de Salud Valdecilla
An Casa Salud Valdecilla (Santander) — Anales. Casa de Salud Valdecilla (Santander)
An Catedra de Patol Clin Tuberc Univ B Aires — Anales. Catedra de Patologia y Clinica de la Tuberculosis. Universidad de Buenos Aires
An Cated Suarez — Anales. Catedra Francisco Suarez
AncEg — Ancient Egypt
An Cent Invest Tisiol — Anales. Centro de Investigaciones Tisiologicas
AnCEtRel — Annales. Centre d'Etude des Religions [*Brussels*]
ANCHA — Analytical Chemistry
ANCHB — Annales de Chirurgie
An Chem — Analytical Chemistry
An Chopin — Annales Chopin
Anchor Rev — Anchor Review
ANCIAP — Anales de Cirugia [*Rosario*]
An Cient — Anales Cientificos
An Cient (La Molina) — Anales Cientificos (La Molina)
An Cient (Lima) — Anales Cientificos (Lima)
Ancient Monuments Soc Trans — Ancient Monuments Society. Transactions
Anc Ind — Ancient India
An Circ Med Argent — Anales. Circa Medico Argentino
An Cir (Rosario) — Anales de Cirugia (Rosario)
An Cist — Analecta Cisterciensia
An Cl — Antiquite Classique
An Clim — Anales Climatologicos. Servicio Meteorologico Nacional [*Argentina*]
An Clim Port — Anuario Climatologico de Portugal
ANCOLD Bull — ANCOLD [*Australian National Committee on Large Dams*] Bulletin
An Com Invest Cient Prov Buenos Aires — Anales. Comision de Investigaciones Cientificas. Provincia de Buenos Aires
An Cong Lat-Am Zool — Anais. Congresso Latino-Americano de Zoologia
An Cong Nac Soc Bot Bras — Anais. Congresso Nacional. Sociedade Botanica do Brasil
An Congr Nac Med Vet Zootec — Anales. Congreso Nacional de Medicina Veterinaria y Zootecnia
ANCPA — Annales de Chimie (Paris)
AnCracov — Analecta Cracoviana [*Cracow*]
ANCS — ANCSA News. Alaska Native Claims Settlement Act. Bureau of Land Management
Anc Soc — Ancient Society
Anc World — Ancient World
And — Anderseniana
AND — Australian News Digest
Andean Rpt — Andean Report
An Desarrollo — Anales del Desarrollo
ANDFA — American Annals of the Deaf
Andhra Agric J — Andhra Agricultural Journal
Andhra Agr J — Andhra Agricultural Journal
Andhra Pradesh Ground Water Dep Dist Ser — Andhra Pradesh Ground Water Department. District Series
Andhra Pradesh Ground Water Dep Res Ser — Andhra Pradesh Ground Water Department. Research Series
Andhra WR — Andhra Weekly Reporter [*India*]
Andh WR — Andhra Weekly Reporter [*India*]
An Dir Gen Of Quim Nac (Argentina) — Anales. Direccion General de Oficinas Quimica Nacionales (Argentina)
An Dir Nac Quim (Argentina) — Anales. Direccion Nacional de Quimica (Argentina)
An Dispensario Publico Nac Enferm Apar Dig (Argentina) — Anales. Dispensario Publico Nacional para Enfermedades del Aparato Digestivo (Argentina)
ANDLA — Andrologie
AndNewQ — Andover Newton Quarterly
AndNewtQ — Andover Newton Quarterly [*Newton, MA*]
And R — Andover Review

AndrUnSS — Andrews University. Seminary Studies
And WR — Andhra Weekly Reporter [*India*]
AnE — Annales de l'Est et du Nord
An Edafol Agrobiol — Anales de Edafologia y Agrobiologia
An Edafol Fisiol Veg — Anales de Edafologia y Fisiologia Vegetal
AnEgB — Annual Egyptological Bibliography [*Leiden*]
ANEMD — Anatomy and Embryology
AnEN — Annales de l'Est et du Nord
ANESA — Anesthesiology
An Esc Farm Fac Cienc Med Univ Nac Mayor San Marcos — Anales. Escuela de Farmacia. Facultad de Ciencias Medicas. Universidad Nacional Mayor de San Marcos
An Esc Nac Cienc Biol (Mex) — Anales. Escuela Nacional de Ciencias Biologicas (Mexico)
An Esc Nac Saude Publica Med Trop — Anais. Escola Nacional de Saude Publica e de Medicina Tropical
An Esc Quim Farm Bioquim Univ Concepcion — Anales. Escuela de Quimica y Farmacia y Bioquimica. Universidad de Concepcion
An Esc Super Agric "Luiz De Queiroz" Univ Sao Paulo — Anais. Escola Superior de Agricultura "Luiz De Queiroz." Universidade de Sao Paulo
An Esc Super Agr "Luiz De Queiroz" — Anais. Escola Superior de Agricultura "Luiz De Queiroz"
An Esc Super Med Vet (Lisb) — Anais. Escola Superior de Medicina Veterinaria (Lisbon)
An Esp Odontoestomatol — Anales Espanoles de Odontoestomatologia
An Esp Pediatr — Anales Espanoles de Pediatria
An Estac Exp Aula Dei — Anales. Estacion Experimental de Aula Dei
An Estac Exp Aula Dei Cons Super Invest Cient — Anales. Estacion Experimental de Aula Dei. Consejo Superior de Investigaciones Cientificas
An Estac Exp Aula Dei (Zaragoza) — Anales. Estacion Experimental de Aula Dei (Zaragoza)
Anesteziol Reanimatol — Anesteziologiya i Reanimatologiya
Anesth Abstr — Anesthesia Abstracts
Anesth Anal — Anesthesia and Analgesia [*Cleveland*]
Anesth Analg (Cleve) — Anesthesia and Analgesia (Cleveland)
Anesth Analg (Paris) — Anesthesie, Analgesie, Reanimation (Paris)
Anesth Analg Reanim — Anesthesie, Analgesie, Reanimation [*Paris*]
Anesth An R — Anesthesie, Analgesie, Reanimation [*Paris*]
Anesthesiol — Anesthesiology
Anesthesiol Clin — International Anesthesiology Clinics
Anesthesiol Reanim — Anesthesiologie et Reanimation
Anesth Intensive Care — Anaesthesia and Intensive Care
Anesth Prog — Anesthesia Progress
Anest Reanim — Anestezja i Reanimacja
AnEth — Annales d'Ethiopie [*Paris/Addis-Ababa*]
ANEXA — Acta Neurobiologiae Experimentalis
ANF — Arkiv foer Nordisk Filologi
An Fac Cienc Fis Mat Univ Concepcion — Anales. Facultad de Ciencias Fisicas y Matematicas. Universidad de Concepcion
An Fac Cienc Univ Porto — Anais. Faculdade de Ciencias. Universidade do Porto
An Fac Ci Univ Porto — Anais. Faculdade de Ciencias. Universidade do Porto
An Fac Farm Bioquim Univ Nac Mayor San Marcos — Anales. Facultad de Farmacia y Bioquimica. Universidad Nacional Mayor de San Marcos
An Fac Farm Bioquim Univ Nac Mayor San Marcos Lima — Anales. Facultad de Farmacia y Bioquimica. Universidad Nacional Mayor de San Marcos de Lima
An Fac Farm Odontol Univ Sao Paulo — Anais. Faculdade de Farmacia e Odontologia. Universidade de Sao Paulo
An Fac Farm Porto — Anais. Faculdade de Farmacia do Porto
An Fac Ing Univ Concepcion — Anales. Facultad de Ingenieria. Universidad de Concepcion
An Fac Med Lima — Anales. Facultad de Medicina de Lima
An Fac Med (Montevideo) — Anales. Facultad de Medicina. Universidad de la Republica (Montevideo)
An Fac Med Porto Alegre — Anais. Faculdade de Medicina de Porto Alegre
An Fac Med Univ Fed Minas Gerais (Belo Horizonte) — Anais. Faculdade de Medicina. Universidade Federal de Minas Gerais (Belo Horizonte)
An Fac Med Univ Fed Pernambuco — Anais. Faculdade de Medicina. Universidade Federal de Pernambuco
An Fac Med Univ Nac Mayor San Marcos Lima — Anales. Facultad de Medicina. Universidad Nacional Mayor de San Marcos de Lima
An Fac Med Univ Nac Mayor San Marcos Lima (Peru) — Anales. Facultad de Medicina. Universidad Nacional Mayor de San Marcos de Lima (Peru)
An Fac Med Univ Parana (Curitiba) — Anais. Faculdade de Medicina. Universidade do Parana (Curitiba)
An Fac Med Univ Recife — Anais. Faculdade de Medicina. Universidade do Recife
An Fac Med Univ Repub (Montev) — Anales. Facultad de Medicina. Universidade de la Republica (Montevideo)
An Fac Med Univ Sao Paulo — Anais. Faculdade de Medicina. Universidade de Sao Paulo
An Fac Odontol Univ Fed Rio De J — Anais. Faculdade de Odontologia. Universidade Federal do Rio De Janeiro

An Fac Odontol (Univ Repub Urug) — Anales. Facultad de Odontologia (Universidad de la Republica, Uruguay)
An Fac Quim Farm (Santiago) — Anales. Facultad de Quimica y Farmacia. Universidad de Chile (Santiago)
An Fac Quim Farm Univ Chile — Anales. Facultad de Quimica y Farmacia. Universidad de Chile [*Santiago*]
An Fac Quim Farm Univ Concepcion — Anales. Facultad de Quimica y Farmacia. Universidad de Concepcion
An Fac Quim Univ Repub Orient Urug — Anales. Facultad de Quimica. Universidad de la Republica Oriental del Uruguay
An Fac Vet Leon — Anales. Facultad de Veterinaria de Leon
An Fac Vet Univ Madrid Inst Invest Vet — Anales. Facultad de Veterinaria. Universidad de Madrid. Instituto de Investigaciones Veterinarias
An Fac Vet Urug — Anales. Facultad de Veterinaria del Uruguay
An Farm Bioquim (Buenos Aires) — Anales de Farmacia y Bioquimica (Buenos Aires)
An Farm Hosp — Anales de Farmacia Hospitalaria
An Farm Quim Sao Paulo — Anais da Farmacia e Quimica de Sao Paulo
An Fis — Anales de Fisica
An Fisica — Anales de Fisica
An Fis Ser A — Anales de Fisica. Serie A
An Fis Ser B — Anales de Fisica. Serie B
AnFP — Analecta Sacri Ordinis Fratrum Praedicatorum
ANFRIDI — Annuaire Francais de Droit International
Ang — Angelicum [*Rome*]
Ang — Anglia
Ang Bbl — Anglia Beiblatt
ANGED — Annales Geophysicae
An Geog — Annales de Geographie
Angew Bot — Angewandte Botanik
Angew Chem — Angewandte Chemie
Angew Chem Int Ed Engl — Angewandte Chemie. International Edition in English
Angew Chem Intern Ed — Angewandte Chemie. International Edition in English
Angew Elektron — Angewandte Elektronik
Angew Elektron Mess & Regeltech — Angewandte Elektronik. Mess und Regeltechnik
Angew Inf — Angewandte Informatik/Applied Informatics
Angew Inf Appl Inf — Angewandte Informatik/Applied Informatics
Angew Infor — Angewandte Informatik/Applied Informatics
Angew Makro — Angewandte Makromolekulare Chemie
Angew Makromol Chem — Angewandte Makromolekulare Chemie
Angew Met — Angewandte Meteorologie
Angew Ornithol — Angewandte Ornithologie
Angew Parasitol — Angewandte Parasitologie
Angew Pflanzensoziol — Angewandte Pflanzensoziologie
Angew Systemanal — Angewandte Systemanalyse [*West Germany*]
ANGIA — Angiology
ANGL — Annals of Glaciology
ANGLA — Angiologica
AnglB — Anglia Beiblatt
Angl Bei — Anglia Beiblatt
Angle Orthod — Angle Orthodontist
Anglican R — Anglican Review
Anglo-Am LR — Anglo-American Law Review
Anglo-Am L Rev — Anglo-American Law Review
Anglo-Ger Med Rev — Anglo-German Medical Review
Angl Orthod — Angle Orthodontist
Anglosax En — Anglosaxon England
Anglo-Welsh — Anglo-Welsh Review
Angl Th R — Anglican Theological Review
AnglTR — Anglican Theological Review [*Evanston, IL/Sewanee, TN*]
ANGOA — Angiologia
Angola Serv Geol Minas Bol — Angola. Servicos de Geologia e Minas. Boletim
Angora Goat Mohair J — Angora Goat and Mohair Journal
An G Paleont — Annales de Geologie et de Paleontologie
Ang Theol Rev — Anglican Theological Review
An Hist — Anais de Historia
An Hosp Mil Cent (Lima Peru) — Anales. Hospital Militar Central (Lima, Peru)
An Hosp St Cruz San Pablo — Anales. Hospital de la Santa Cruz y San Pablo
ANIFA — Annales de Chirurgie Infantile
Anilinokras Promst — Anilinokrasochnaya Promyshlennost
An Ilus Col Of Med Prov Lerida — Anales Ilustrados. Colegio Oficial de Medicina. Provincia de Lerida
Animal Behav — Animal Behaviour
Animal Prod — Animal Production
Anim Behav — Animal Behaviour
Anim Behav Monogr — Animal Behaviour. Monographs
Anim Blood Groups Biochem Genet — Animal Blood Groups and Biochemical Genetics
Anim Blood Groups Biochem Genet (Suppl) — Animal Blood Groups and Biochemical Genetics (Supplement)
Anim Breed — Animal Breeding
Anim Breed Abstr — Animal Breeding Abstracts

ANIMC — Annales d'Immunologie
Anim Feed Sci Technol — Animal Feed Science and Technology [*Netherlands*]
Anim Health — Animal Health
Anim Hlth Yb — Animal Health Yearbook
Anim Husb — Animal Husbandry
Anim Husb Agric J — Animal Husbandry and Agricultural Journal
Anim Husb Mimeogr Ser Fla Agr Exp Sta — Animal Husbandry Mimeograph Series. Florida Agricultural Experiment Station
Anim Husb (Tokyo) — Animal Husbandry (Tokyo)
Anim Kingdom — Animal Kingdom
Anim Lear B — Animal Learning and Behavior
Anim Learn Behav — Animal Learning and Behavior
Anim Nutr Health — Animal Nutrition and Health
Anim Nutr Res Counc Proc Annu Meet — Animal Nutrition Research Council. Proceedings of the Annual Meeting
Anim Prod — Animal Production
Anim Produc — Animal Production
Anim Quar — Animal Quarantine
Anim Res Lab Tech Pap Aust CSIRO — Animal Research Laboratories Technical Paper. Australia Commonwealth Scientific and Industrial Research Organisation
Anim Sci J Pak — Animal Science Journal of Pakistan
Anim Sci Mimeogr Rep Fla Agr Exp Sta — Animal Science Mimeograph Report. Florida Agricultural Experiment Station
Anim Sci Mimeogr Ser Ohio State Agr Exp Sta — Animal Science Mimeograph Series. Ohio State Agricultural Experiment Station
Anim Sci (Sofia) — Animal Science (Sofia)
AnINA — Anales. Instituto Nacional de Antropologia e Historia
An Ing — Anales de Ingenieria
An Inst Agron (Lisboa) — Anais. Instituto Superior de Agronomia (Lisboa)
An Inst Biol (Mexico) — Anales. Instituto de Biologia. Universidad Nacional Autonoma de Mexico
An Inst Biol Univ Mex — Anales. Instituto de Biologia. Universidad Nacional Autonoma de Mexico
An Inst Biol Univ Nac Auton Mex — Anales. Instituto de Biologia. Universidad Nacional Autonoma de Mexico
An Inst Biol Univ Nac Auton Mex Ser Biol Exp — Anales. Instituto de Biologia. Universidad Nacional Autonoma de Mexico. Serie Biologia Experimental
An Inst Biol Univ Nac Auton Mex Ser Bot — Anales. Instituto de Biologia. Universidad Nacional Autonoma de Mexico. Serie Botanica
An Inst Biol Univ Nac Auton Mex Ser Cienc Mar Limnol — Anales. Instituto de Biologia. Universidad Nacional Autonoma de Mexico. Serie Ciencias del Mar y Limnologia
An Inst Biol Univ Nac Auton Mex Ser Zool — Anales. Instituto de Biologia. Universidad Nacional Autonoma de Mexico. Serie Zoologia
An Inst Bot A J Cavanilles — Anales. Instituto Botanico A. J. Cavanilles
An Inst Bot A J Cavanilles (Madrid) — Anales. Instituto Botanico A. J. Cavanilles (Madrid)
An Inst Cent Cercet Agric Sect Pedol — Analele. Institutul Central de Cercetari Agricole. Sectiei de Pedologie
An Inst Cent Cercet Agr Sect Econ Agr (Bucharest) — Anale. Institutul Central de Cercetari Agricole. Sectiei de Economice Agricole (Bucharest)
An Inst Cent Cercet Agr Sect Econ Agr (Bucharest) — Analele. Institutul Central de Cercetari Agricole. Sectiei de Economice Agricole (Bucharest)
An Inst Cent Cercet Agr Sect Prot Plant — Anale. Institutul Central de Cercetari Agricole. Sectiei de Protectia Plantelor
An Inst Cent Cercet Agr Ser A (Bucharest) — Anale. Institutul Central de Cercetari Agricole. Series A (Bucharest)
An Inst Cent Cercet Agr Ser B (Bucharest) — Anale. Institutul Central de Cercetari Agricole. Series B (Bucharest)
An Inst Cent Cercet Agr Ser C (Bucharest) — Anale. Institutul Central de Cercetari Agricole. Series C (Bucharest)
An Inst Cercet pentru Cereale Plante Teh-Fundulea — Analele. Institutului de Cercetari pentru Cereale si Plante Tehnice-Fundulea [*Romania*]
An Inst Cercet Cereale Plante Teh-Fundulea — Analele. Institutului de Cercetari pentru Cereale si Plante Tehnice-Fundulea
An Inst Cercet pentru Cereale Plante Teh-Fundulea Ser A — Analele. Institutului de Cercetari pentru Cereale si Plante Tehnice-Fundulea. Seria A
An Inst Cercet pentru Cereale Plante Teh-Fundulea Ser B — Analele. Institutului de Cercetari pentru Cereale si Plante Tehnice-Fundulea. Seria B
An Inst Cercet pentru Cereale Plante Teh-Fundulea Ser C — Analele. Institutului de Cercetari pentru Cereale si Plante Tehnice-Fundulea. Seria C
An Inst Cercet Cul Cartofului Sfeclei Zahar (Brasov) Cartofu — Anale. Institutul de Cercetari pentru Cultura Cartofului si Sfeclei de Zahar (Brasov). Cartoful
An Inst Cercet Imbunatatiri Funciare Pedol Ser Hidroteh — Analele. Institutului de Cercetari pentru Imbunatatiri Funciare si Pedologie. Seria Hidrotehnica
An Inst Cercet Imbunatatiri Funciare Pedol Ser Pedol — Analele. Institutului de Cercetari pentru Imbunatatiri Funciare si Pedologie. Seria Pedologie

An Inst Cercet Pedol Agrochim — Analele. Institutului de Cercetari pentru Pedologie si Agrochimie
An Inst Cercet Prot Plant — Analele. Institutului de Cercetari pentru Protectia Plantelor
An Inst Cercet Prot Plant Acad Stiinte Agric Silvice — Analele. Institutului de Cercetari pentru Protectia Plantelor. Academia de Stiinte. Agricole si Silvice
An Inst Cercet Prot Plant Inst Cent Cercet Agric (Bucharest) — Analele. Institutului de Cercetari pentru Protectia Plantelor. Institutul Central de Cercetari Agricole (Bucharest)
An Inst Cercet Zooteh (Bucharest) — Analele. Institutului de Cercetari. Zootehnice (Bucharest)
An Inst Corachan — Anales. Instituto Corachan [*Spain*]
An Inst Esp Edafol Ecol Fisiol Veg — Anales. Instituto Espanol de Edafologia, Ecologia, y Fisiologia Vegetal
An Inst Estud Madrilenos — Anales. Instituto de Estudios Madrilenos
An Inst Farmacol Esp — Anales. Instituto de Farmacologia Espanola
An Inst For Invest Exper (Madr) — Anales. Instituto Forestal de Investigaciones y Experiencias (Madrid)
An Inst Geofis UNAM — Anales. Instituto de Geofisica. Universidad Nacional Autonoma de Mexico
An Inst Geofis Univ Nac Auton Mex — Anales. Instituto de Geofisica. Universidad Nacional Autonoma de Mexico
An Inst Hig Med Trop [*Lisbon*] — Anais. Instituto de Higiene e Medicina Tropical [*Lisbon*]
An Inst Hig Med Trop (Lisb) — Anais. Instituto de Higiene e Medicina Tropical (Lisbon)
An Insti Nac Invest Agrar (Spain) Ser Prot Veg — Anales. Instituto Nacional de Investigaciones Agrarias (Spain). Serie Proteccion Vegetal
An Inst Invest Cient Tecnol Univ Nac Litoral — Anales. Instituto de Investigaciones Cientificas y Tecnologicas. Universidad Nacional del Litoral
An Inst Invest Cient Univ Nuevo Leon — Anales. Instituto de Investigaciones Cientificas. Universidad de Nuevo Leon
An Inst Invest Vet — Anales. Instituto de Investigaciones Veterinarias
An Inst Invest Vet (Madrid) — Anales. Instituto de Investigaciones Veterinarias (Madrid)
An Inst Ist Arh (Cluj) — Anuarul. Institutului de Istorie si Arheologie (Cluj-Napoca)
An In St Ma — Annals. Institute of Statistical Mathematics
An Inst Mat Univ Nac Autonoma Mexico — Anales. Instituto de Matematicas. Universidad Nacional Autonoma de Mexico
An Inst Med Nac (Mexico) — Anales. Instituto Medico Nacional (Mexico)
An Inst Med Reg — Anales. Instituto de Medicina Regional
An Inst Med Trop — Anais. Instituto de Medicina Tropical [*Lisbon*]
An Inst Med Trop (Lisb) — Anais. Instituto de Medicina Tropical (Lisbon)
An Inst Mun Hig Zaragoza — Anales. Instituto Municipal de Higiene de Zaragoza
An Inst Nac Antropol Hist — Anales. Instituto Nacional de Antropologia e Historia
An Inst Nac Invest Agrar Ser Gen — Anales. Instituto Nacional de Investigaciones Agrarias. Serie General
An Inst Nac Invest Agrar Ser Hig Sanid Anim — Anales. Instituto Nacional de Investigaciones Agrarias. Serie Higiene y Sanidad Animal
An Inst Nac Invest Agrar Ser Prod Anim — Anales. Instituto Nacional de Investigaciones Agrarias. Serie Produccion Animal
An Inst Nac Invest Agrar Ser Prod Veg — Anales. Instituto Nacional de Investigaciones Agrarias. Serie Produccion Vegetal
An Inst Nac Invest Agrar Ser Prot Veg — Anales. Instituto Nacional de Investigaciones Agrarias. Serie Proteccion Vegetal
An Inst Nac Invest Agrar Ser Recur Nat — Anales. Instituto Nacional de Investigaciones Agrarias. Serie Recursos Naturales
An Inst Nac Invest Agrar Ser Tecnol Agrar — Anales. Instituto Nacional de Investigaciones Agrarias. Serie Tecnologia Agraria
An Inst Nac Invest Agrar (Spain) Ser Prod Anim — Anales. Instituto Nacional de Investigaciones Agrarias (Spain). Serie Produccion Animal
An Inst Nac Invest Agrar (Spain) Ser Prod Veg — Anales. Instituto Nacional de Investigaciones Agrarias (Spain). Serie Produccion Vegetal
An Inst Nac Invest Agron (Madr) — Anales. Instituto Nacional de Investigaciones Agronomicas (Madrid)
An Inst Nac Microbiol (B Aires) — Anales. Instituto Nacional de Microbiologia (Buenos Aires)
An Inst Oncol Angel H Roffo — Anales. Instituto de Oncologia "Angel H. Roffo"
An Inst Oncol "Angel H Roffo" (B Aires) — Anales. Instituto de Oncologia "Angel H. Roffo" (Buenos Aires)
An Inst Patagonia — Anales. Instituto de la Patagonia
An Inst Pinheiros — Anais. Instituto Pinheiros
An Inst Radio Quir Guipuzcoa — Anales. Instituto Radio Quirurgico de Guipuzcoa
An Inst Stud Cercet Pedol — Analele. Institutului de Studii si Cercetari Pedologice
An Inst Super Agron (Lisboa) — Anais. Instituto Superior de Agronomia (Lisboa)
An Inst Super Agron Univ Tec Lisb — Anais. Instituto Superior de Agronomia. Universidade Tecnica de Lisboa

An Inst Vinho Porto — Anais. Instituto do Vinho do Porto
An Invest Text — Anales de Investigacion Textil
AnIowa — Annals of Iowa
ANIPA — Animal Production
Ani Sci — Animal Science
ANJ — Australian Numismatic Journal
An Junta Invest Ultramar — Anais. Junta de Investigacoes do Ultramar
ANK — Consommation
Ankara Univ Tip Fak Mecm — Ankara Universitesi. Tip Fakultesi. Mecmuasi
Ankara Univ Tip Fak Mecm Suppl — Ankara Universitesi. Tip Fakultesi. Mecmuasi. Supplementum
Ankara Univ Vet Fak Derg — Ankara Universitesi. Veteriner Fakultesi. Dergisi
Ankara Univ Ziraat Fak Yayin — Ankara Universitesi. Ziraat Fakultesi. Yayinlari
An Klin Boln Dr M Stojanovic — Anali Klinicke Bolnice Dr. M. Stojanovic
An Klin Boln Dr M Stojanovic Supl — Anali Klinicke Bolnice Dr. M. Stojanovic. Suplement
AnkUDerg — Ankara Universitesi Dil ve Tarih-Cografya Fakultesi. Dergisi
ANL — Accademia Nazionale dei Lincei [*Rome*]
AnL — Anthropological Linguistics
ANL — Atti. Reale Accademia Nazionale dei Lincei. Classe di Scienze Morali, Storiche, e Filologiche [*Rome*]
ANLA — Atti. Reale Accademia Nazionale dei Lincei. Classe di Scienze Morali, Storiche, e Filologiche [*Rome*]
An Lactol Quim Agric (Zaragoza) — Anales de Lactologia y Quimica Agricola (Zaragoza)
ANLADF — Auris Nasus Larynx
ANLBA — Bulletin. Australian Mathematical Society
AnLeeds — Annual. Leeds University Oriental Society [*Leiden*]
An Leeds UOS — Annual. Leeds University Oriental Society [*Leiden*]
Anleit Bienenzuechter — Anleitungen Bienenzuechter
ANLIB — Annales de Limnologie
ANLKB — Archiv fuer die Naturkunde Liv-, Est-, und Kurlands
ANLMSF — Accademia Nazionale dei Lincei. Rendiconti. Classe di Scienze Morali, Storiche, e Filologiche
AnLov — Analecta Lovanensia
ANLSD — Argonne National Laboratory. Energy and Environmental Systems Division. Report ANL/CNSV
Anls Prob — Annals of Probability
Anls Stat — Annals of Statistics
AnM — Annales du Midi; Revue de la France Meridionale [*Toulouse*]
AnM — Annuale Mediaevale
An M — Anuario Musical
An Mag N H — Annals and Magazine of Natural History
ANMBC — Annales de Microbiologie
An M Belgique — Annales des Mines de Belgique
ANMCB — Angewandte Makromolekulare Chemie
An Mec Elect — Anales de Mecanica y Electricidad
An Mec & Electr — Anales de Mecanica y Electricidad
An Mec Electr — Anales de Mecanica y Electricidad [*Spain*]
An Med — Anales de Medicina
An Med Acad Cienc Med Cataluna Baleares — Anales de Medicina. Academia de Ciencias Medicas de Cataluna y Baleares
An Med Assoc Med Hosp Am Br Cowdray — Anales Medicos. Asociacion Medica. Hospital Americano-Britanico Cowdray
An Med Cir — Anales de Medicina. Cirugia
An Med Espec — Anales de Medicina. Especialidades
An Med (Lima) — Anales de Medicina (Lima)
An Med Sec Med — Anales de Medicina. Seccion de Medicina [*Spain*]
An Med (Sevilla) — Anales de Medicina (Sevilla)
An Mex Cienc — Anales Mexicanos de Ciencias
An Microbiol (Rio De J) — Anais de Microbiologia (Rio De Janeiro)
An Minelor Rom — Analele Minelor din Romania
An Mines — Annales des Mines [*Paris*]
ANMR — Alaska Native Management Report
An Mus Argent Cienc Nat Bernardino Rivadavia — Anales. Museo Argentino de Ciencias Naturales Bernardino Rivadavia
An Mus Hist Nat Valparaiso — Anales. Museo de Historia Natural de Valparaiso
An Mus Nac David J Guzman — Anales. Museo Nacional David J. Guzman
An Mus Nac Hist Nat Montev — Anales. Museo Nacional de Historia Natural de Montevideo
AnN — Annales de Normandie
AnnAB — Annuaire. Academie Royale de Belgique
Ann Abeille — Annales de l'Abeille
Ann Acad Med Gedanensis — Annales Academiae Medicae Gedanensis
Ann Acad Med Lodz — Annales Academiae Medicae Lodzensis
Ann Acad Med Lodz Supl — Annales Academiae Medicae Lodzensis. Suplement
Ann Acad Med (Singapore) — Annals. Academy of Medicine (Singapore)
Ann Acad Med Stetin — Annales Academiae Medicae Stetinensis
Ann Acad Med Stetin Supl — Annales Academiae Medicae Stetinensis. Suplement
Ann Acad Regiae Sci Ups — Annales Academiae Regiae Scientiarum Upsaliensis

Ann Acad Sci Fenn A I — Annales Academiae Scientiarum Fennicae. Series A-I (Mathematica)
Ann Acad Sci Fenn A II — Annales Academiae Scientiarum Fennicae. Series A-II (Chemica)
Ann Acad Sci Fenn A VI — Annales Academiae Scientiarum Fennicae. Series A-VI (Physica)
Ann Acad Sci Fenn (Biol) — Annales Academiae Scientiarum Fennicae. Series A-IV (Biologia)
Ann Acad Sci Fenn (Med) — Annales Academiae Scientiarum Fennicae. Series A-V (Medica)
Ann Acad Sci Fenn Ser A I — Annales Academiae Scientiarum Fennicae. Series A-I (Mathematica)
Ann Acad Sci Fenn Ser A II — Annales Academiae Scientiarum Fennicae. Series A-II (Chemica)
Ann Acad Sci Fenn Ser A II (Chem) — Annales Academiae Scientiarum Fennicae. Series A-II (Chemica)
Ann Acad Sci Fenn Ser A III — Annales Academiae Scientiarum Fennicae. Series A-III (Geologica-Geographica)
Ann Acad Sci Fenn Ser A I (Math) — Annales Academiae Scientiarum Fennicae. Series A-I (Mathematica)
Ann Acad Sci Fenn Ser AI (Math) Dissertationes — Annales Academiae Scientiarum Fennicae. Series A-I (Mathematica). Dissertatione s
Ann Acad Sci Fenn Ser AI (Math Phy) — Annales Academiae Scientiarum Fennicae. Series A-I (Mathematica-Physica)
Ann Acad Sci Fenn Ser A IV — Annales Academiae Scientiarum Fennicae. Series A-IV (Biologia)
Ann Acad Sci Fenn Ser A IV (Biol) — Annales Academiae Scientiarum Fennicae. Series A-IV (Biologia)
Ann Acad Sci Fenn Ser A V — Annales Academiae Scientiarum Fennicae. Series A-V (Medica)
Ann Acad Sci Fenn Ser A VI — Annales Academiae Scientiarum Fennicae. Series A-VI (Physica)
Ann Acad Sci Fenn Ser A VI (Phys) — Annales Academiae Scientiarum Fennicae. Series A-VI (Physica)
Ann Acad Sci Fenn Ser A V (Med) — Annales Academiae Scientiarum Fennicae. Series A-V (Medica)
Ann Acad Sci Fenn Ser A-V (Med-Anthropol) — Annales Academiae Scientiarum Fennicae. Series A-V (Medica-Anthropologica)
Ann Accad Agric (Torino) — Annali. Accademia de Agricoltura (Torino)
Ann Accad Ital Sci For — Annali. Accademia Italiana di Scienze Forestali
Ann ACFAS — Annales. ACFAS [*Association Canadienne Francaise pour l'Avancement des Sciences*]
Ann Ac Fenn — Annales Academiae Scientiarum Fennicae
Ann Agr Fenn — Annales Agriculturae Fenniae
Ann Agric Exp Stn Gov Gen Chosen — Annals. Agricultural Experiment Station. Government General of Chosen
Ann Agric Fenn — Annales Agriculturae Fenniae
Ann Agric Fenn Ser Agrogeol -Chim -Phys — Annales Agriculturae Fenniae. Seria Agrogeologia, -Chimica, et -Physica [*Finland*]
Ann Agric Fenn Suppl — Annales Agriculturae Fenniae. Supplementum
Ann Agric Sci (Cairo) — Annals of Agricultural Science (Cairo)
Ann Agric Sci (Moshtohor) — Annals of Agricultural Science (Moshtohor)
Ann Agric Sci Univ A'in Shams — Annals of Agricultural Science. University of A'in Shams
Ann Agri Sci — Annals of Agriculture Science
Ann Agron — Annales Agronomiques
Ann Agron Hors-Ser — Annales Agronomiques. Hors-Serie [*France*]
Ann Agron (Paris) — Annales Agronomiques (Paris)
An-Nahar Arab Rept and Memo — An-Nahar Arab Report and Memo
AnnAIF — Annuaire. Archives Israelites (de France)
ANNA J — ANNA [*American Nephrology Nurses Association*] Journal
Annales-ESC — Annales: Economies, Societes, Civilisations
Annales Int'l de Crimin — Annales Internationales de Criminologie
Ann Alger Chir — Annales Algeriennes de Chirurgie
Annali Accad Naz Agric (Bologna) — Annali. Accademia Nazionale di Agricoltura (Bologna)
Annali Chim Appl — Annali di Chimica Applicata
Annali Fac Agr Portici — Annali. Facolta di Agraria di Portici della Reale Universita di Napoli
Annali Fac Agr Univ Bari — Annali. Facolta di Agraria. Universita di Bari
Annali Fac Agr Univ Milano — Annali. Facolta di Agraria. Universita di Milano
Annali Fac Agr Univ Perugia — Annali. Facolta di Agraria. Universita degli Studi di Perugia
Annali Fac Sci Agr Univ Napoli — Annali. Facolta di Scienze Agrarie. Universita degli Studi di Napoli
Annali Fac Sci Agr Univ Torino — Annali. Facolta di Scienze Agrarie. Universita degli Studi di Torino
Annali Geofisica — Annali di Geofisica
Annali Idrol — Annali Idrologici
Annali Ig Sper — Annali d'Igiene. Sperimentali
Annali Microbiol — Annali di Microbiologia. Ed. Enzimologia
Annali Sper Agr — Annali della Sperimentazione Agraria
Annali Staz Chim-Agr Sper Roma — Annali. Reale Stazione Chimico-Agraria Sperimentale di Roma

Annali Staz Sper Risicolt Vercelli — Annali. Stazione Sperimentale di Risicoltura e delle Colture Irrigue. Vercelli
Ann Allergy — Annals of Allergy
Annals — Annals. American Academy of Political and Social Science
Annals Air and Space — Annals of Air and Space Law
Annals Air and Space L — Annals of Air and Space Law
Annals Am Acad — Annals. American Academy of Political and Social Science
Annals General Prac — Annals of General Practice
Annals of Gen Prac — Annals of General Practice
Annals Gen Pract — Annals of General Practice
Annals Internat Studies — Annals of International Studies
Annals KY Nat History — Annals of Kentucky Natural History
Annals Lib Sci — Annals of Library Science
Annals and Mag Nat History — Annals and Magazine of Natural History
Annals Math Log — Annals of Mathematical Logic
Annals Occup Hyg — Annals of Occupational Hygiene
Annals Public and Coop Economy — Annals of Public and Cooperative Economy [*Formerly, Annals of Collective Economy*]
Ann Am Acad — Annals. American Academy of Political and Social Science
Ann Am Acad Poli Soc Sci — Annals. American Academy of Political and Social Science
Ann Am Acad Pol Sci — Annals. American Academy of Political and Social Science
Ann Am Acad Pol Soc Sci (Philadelphia) — Annals. American Academy of Political and Social Science (Philadelphia)
Annamalai Univ Agric Res Annu — Annamalai University. Agricultural Research Annual
Ann Amelior Plantes — Annales de l'Amelioration des Plantes [*Paris*]
Ann Amelior Plantes Inst Nat Rech Agron Ser B — Annales de l'Amelioration des Plantes. Institut National de la Recherche Agronomique. Serie B
Ann Amelior Plant (Paris) — Annales de l'Amelioration des Plantes (Paris)
Ann Amer Acad Polit Soc Sci — Annals. American Academy of Political and Social Science
Ann Am Poli — Annals. American Academy of Political and Social Science
Ann Anat Pathol — Annales d'Anatomie Pathologique [*Paris*]
Ann Anat Pathol Anat Norm Med Chir — Annales d'Anatomie Pathologique et d'Anatomie Normale. Medico Chirurgicale
Ann Anat Pathol (Paris) — Annales d'Anatomie Pathologique (Paris)
Ann Anesthesiol Fr — Annales de l'Anesthesiologie Francaise
Ann Anim Ps — Annual of Animal Psychology
Ann Ap Biol — Annals of Applied Biology
Ann A Plant — Annales de l'Amelioration des Plantes [*Paris*]
Ann App Biol — Annals of Applied Biology
Ann Appl Biol — Annals of Applied Biology
Ann Arch — Annales Archeologiques
Ann Archeol Syrie — Annales Archeologiques de Syrie
Ann Arid Zone — Annals of Arid Zone
Ann As Am G — Annals. Association of American Geographers
Ann Ass Amer Geogr — Annals. Association of American Geographers
Ann Ass Int Calcul Analogique — Annales. Association Internationale pour le Calcul Analogique
Ann Assn Am Geog — Annals. Association of American Geographers
Ann Assoc Belge Radioprot — Annales. Association Belge de Radioprotection [*Belgium*]
Ann Assoc Int Calcul Analogique — Annales. Association Internationale pour le Calcul Analogique
Ann Assur Sci Proc Reliab Maint Conf — Annals of Assurance Sciences. Proceedings of Reliability and Maintainability Conference
Ann Astrophys — Annales d'Astrophysique [*France*]
Ann Astrophys Suppl — Annales d'Astrophysique. Supplement
Ann Bar-Il — Annual. Bar-Ilan University Studies in Judaica and Humanities
Ann Belg Med Mil — Annales Belges de Medecine Militaire
Ann Belg Ver Hosp — Annalen Belg Vereniging voor Hospitaalgeschiedenis
Ann Belg Ver Trop Geneeskd — Annales. Belgische Vereniging voor Tropische Geneeskunde
Ann Belg Ver Trop Geneeskd Parasitol Mensel Dierl Mycol — Annales. Belgische Verenigingen voor Tropische Geneeskunde voor Parasitologie en voor Menselijke en Dierlijke Mycologie
AnnBhl — Annals. Bhandarkar Oriental Research Institute
Ann Biochem Exp Med — Annals of Biochemistry and Experimental Medicine [*Calcutta and New Delhi*]
Ann Biochem Exp Med (Calcutta) — Annals of Biochemistry and Experimental Medicine (Calcutta and New Delhi)
Ann Biol — Annales Biologiques
Ann Biol An — Annales de Biologie Animale, Biochimie, et Biophysique
Ann Biol Anim Biochim Biophys — Annales de Biologie Animale, Biochimie, et Biophysique
Ann Biol Cl — Annales de Biologie Clinique [*Paris*]
Ann Biol Clin (Paris) — Annales de Biologie Clinique (Paris)
Ann Biol Norm Pathol — Annali Biologia Normale e Pathologica
Ann Biomed — Annals of Biomedical Engineering
Ann Biomed Eng — Annals of Biomedical Engineering
Ann Bogor — Annales Bogoriensis
Ann Bot — Annals of Botany

Ann Bot Fenn — Annales Botanici Fennici
Ann Bot (London) — Annals of Botany (London)
Ann Bot (Rome) — Annali di Botanica (Rome)
Ann Bot Soc Zool Bot Fenn "Vanamo" — Annales Botanici Societatis Zoologicae Botanicae Fennicae "Vanamo"
AnnBourg — Annales de Bourgogne
Ann Bourgogne — Annales de Bourgogne
Ann Brass Distill — Annales de la Brasserie et de la Distillerie
AnnBret — Annales de Bretagne [*Later, Annales de Bretagne et des Pays de l'Ouest*]
Ann de Bret — Annales de Bretagne [*Later, Annales de Bretagne et des Pays de l'Ouest*]
Ann Bretagne — Annales de Bretagne et des Pays de l'Ouest
Ann Brux I — Annales. Societe Scientifique de Bruxelles. Serie I
Ann B S Arch Ath — Annual. British School of Archaeology at Athens
Ann Bull Soc R Med Gand — Annales et Bulletin. Societe Royale de Medecine de Gand
Ann Bull Soc R Sci Med Nat Bruxelles — Annales et Bulletin. Societe Royale des Sciences Medicales et Naturelles de Bruxelles
Ann Cape Prov Mus — Annals. Cape Provincial Museums
Ann Cape Prov Mus Hum Sci — Annals. Cape Provincial Museums. Human Sciences
Ann Cape Prov Mus Nat Hist — Annals. Cape Provincial Museums. Natural History
Ann Card An — Annales de Cardiologie et d'Angeiologie
Ann Cardiol Angeiol — Annales de Cardiologie et d'Angeiologie
Ann Carnegie Mus — Annals. Carnegie Museum
Ann Cent Enseign Super Brazzaville — Annales. Centre d'Enseignement Superieur de Brazzaville
Ann Cerc Archeol Canton Soignies — Annales. Cercle Archeologique du Canton de Soignies
Ann Cerc Archeol Enghien — Annales. Cercle Archeologique d'Enghien
Ann Chem — Annalen der Chemie [*Justus Liebigs*]
Ann Chem (Justus Liebigs) — Annalen der Chemie (Justus Liebigs)
Ann Chim — Annali di Chimica
Ann Chim Anal — Annales de Chimie Analytique
Ann Chim Anal Chim Appl — Annales de Chimie Analytique et de Chimie Applique et Revue de Chimie Analytique Reunies
Ann Chim Anal Rev Chim Anal Reunies — Annales de Chimie Analytique et Revue de Chimie Analytique Reunies
Ann Chim Appl — Annali di Chimica Applicata [*Italy*]
Ann Chim (Fr) — Annales de Chimie (Paris, France)
Ann Chim (Paris) — Annales de Chimie (Paris, France)
Ann Chim (Rome) — Annali di Chimica (Rome)
Ann Chir — Annales de Chirurgie
Ann Chir Gy — Annales Chirurgiae et Gynaecologiae Fenniae [*Helsinki*]
Ann Chir Gynaecol — Annales Chirurgiae et Gynaecologiae Fenniae [*Helsinki*]
Ann Chir Gynaecol Fenn — Annales Chirurgiae et Gynaecologiae Fenniae [*Helsinki*]
Ann Chir Gynaecol Fenn Suppl — Annales Chirurgiae et Gynaecologiae Fenniae. Supplementum [*Helsinki*]
Ann Chir Gynaecol Suppl — Annales Chirurgiae et Gynaecologiae Fenniae. Supplementum [*Helsinki*]
Ann Chir In — Annales de Chirurgie Infantile
Ann Chir Infant — Annales de Chirurgie Infantile
Ann Chir (Paris) — Annales de Chirurgie (Paris)
Ann Chir Pl — Annales de Chirurgie Plastique
Ann Chir Plast — Annales de Chirurgie Plastique
Ann Chir Sem Hop — Annales de Chirurgie. Semaine des Hopitaux [*France*]
Ann Chir Thorac Cardio-Vasc — Annales de Chirurgie Thoracique et Cardio-Vasculaire
Ann CIRP — Annals of the CIRP
Ann Clin Biochem — Annals of Clinical Biochemistry
Ann Clin Lab Sci — Annals of Clinical and Laboratory Science
Ann Clin Med — Annals of Clinical Medicine
Ann Clin R — Annals of Clinical Research
Ann Clin Res — Annals of Clinical Research
Ann Clin Res Suppl — Annals of Clinical Research. Supplement
Ann Coll Med Antwerp — Annales Collegii Medici Antwerpiensis
Ann Coll Med (Mosul) — Annals. College of Medicine (Mosul)
Ann Coll R Med Chir Can — Annales. College Royal des Medecins et Chirurgiens du Canada
Ann Compos — Annales des Composites
Ann Conf Health Inspectors NSW — Annual Conference of Health Inspectors of New South Wales
Ann Cryptogam Exot — Annales de Cryptogamie Exotique
Ann Cryptogam Phytopathol — Annales Cryptogamici et Phytopathologici
Ann D A (J) — Annual. Department of Antiquities (Jordan)
Ann Dakar Univ Fac Sci — Annales. Dakar Universite. Faculte des Sciences
Ann Dem Hist — Annales de Demographie Historique
Ann Demogr Hist — Annales de Demographie Historique
Ann Dent — Annals of Dentistry
Ann Dermatol Syphiligr — Annales de Dermatologie et de Syphiligraphie [*Later, Annales de Dermatologie et de Venereologie*]
Ann Dermatol Venereol — Annales de Dermatologie et de Venereologie

Ann Der Syp — Annales de Dermatologie et de Syphiligraphie [*Later, Annales de Dermatologie et de Venereologie*]
Ann Dev — Annals of Development
Ann Dir Comp — Annuario di Diritto Comparato e di Studi Legislativi
Ann Discrete Math — Annals of Discrete Mathematics
Ann Dog Watch — Annual Dog Watch
Ann Dr — Annales de Droit
Ann de Droit — Annales de Droit. Revue Trimestrielle de Droit Belge
Ann de Droit Internat Med — Annales de Droit International Medical
Ann Droit Int Med — Annales de Droit International Medical
Ann Ec Natl Eaux For Stn Rech Exper For — Annales. Ecole Nationale des Eaux et Forets et de la Station de Recherches et Experiences Forestieres
Ann Ec Natl Super Agron (Montpellier) — Annales. Ecole Nationale Superieure Agronomique (Montpellier)
Ann Ecole Nat Agr Alger — Annales. Ecole Nationale d'Agriculture d'Alger
Ann Ecole Nat Super Agron — Annales. Ecole Nationale Superieure Agronomique
Ann Ecole Nat Sup Mec (Nantes) — Annales. Ecole Nationale Superieure de Mecanique (Nantes)
Ann Econ Sm — Annals of Economic and Social Measurement
Ann Econ So — Annales d'Economie et de Sociologie Rurales
Ann Ec Prat HEt — Annuaire. Ecole Pratique des Hautes Etudes, IVeme Section
Ann Ec Super Sci Inst Hautes Etud (Dakar) — Annales. Ecole Superieure des Sciences. Institut des Hautes Etudes (Dakar)
Annee Afr — Annee Africaine
Annee Agr — Annee Agricole
Annee Biol — Annee Biologique
Annee Biol (Paris) — Annee Biologique (Paris)
Annee Endocrinol — Annee Endocrinologique
Annee Polit Econ — Annee Politique et Economique
Annee Psychol — Annee Psychologique
Annee Sociol — Annee Sociologique
Annee Ther Clin Ophtalmol — Annee Therapeutique et Clinique en Ophtalmologie
Ann Embryol Morphog — Annales d'Embryologie et de Morphogenese
Ann Emerg Med — Annals of Emergency Medicine
Ann Endocr — Annales d'Endocrinologie [*Paris*]
Ann Endocrinol — Annales d'Endocrinologie [*Paris*]
Ann Endocrinol (Paris) — Annales d'Endocrinologie (Paris)
Ann Ent Fenn — Annales Entomologici Fennici
Ann Entomol Fenn — Annales Entomologici Fennici
Ann Entomol Soc Am — Annals. Entomological Society of America
Ann Entomol Soc Que — Annals. Entomological Society of Quebec
Ann Entom Soc Am — Annals. Entomological Society of America
Ann Ent S A — Annals. Entomological Society of America
Ann Ent Soc Am — Annals. Entomological Society of America
Ann Ent Soc Queb — Annals. Entomological Society of Quebec
AnnEp — L'Annee Epigraphique
Ann Epiphyt — Annales des Epiphyties [*Paris*]
Ann Epiphyt (Paris) — Annales des Epiphyties (Paris)
Ann Epiphyt Phytogenet — Annales des Epiphyties et de Phytogenetique [*Paris*]
Ann Est — Annales de l'Est
Ann Esth — Annales d'Esthetique
AnnEth — Annales d'Ethiopie
Ann Eugen — Annals of Eugenics
Ann Eur — Annuaire Europeen
Ann Exp For — Annales pro Experimentis Foresticis
Ann Fac Agrar Portici Regia Univ Napoli — Annali. Facolta di Agraria de Portici. Regia Universita di Napoli
Ann Fac Agrar Univ Bari — Annali. Facolta di Agraria. Universita di Bari
Ann Fac Agrar Univ Catt Sacro Cuore — Annali. Facolta di Agraria. Universita Cattolica del Sacro Cuore
Ann Fac Agrar Univ Pisa — Annali. Facolta di Agraria. Universita di Pisa
Ann Fac Agrar Univ Studi Milano — Annali. Facolta di Agraria. Universita degli Studi di Milano
Ann Fac Agrar Univ Stud Perugia — Annali. Facolta di Agraria. Universita degli Studi di Perugia
Ann Fac Agr (Perugia) — Annali. Facolta di Agraria (Perugia)
Ann Fac Agr Univ Cattol Sacro Cuore (Milan) — Annali. Facolta di Agraria. Universita Cattolica del Sacro Cuore (Milan)
Ann Fac Agr Univ Pisa — Annali. Facolta di Agraria. Universita di Pisa
Ann Fac Agr Univ Studii Perugia — Annali. Facolta di Agraria. Universita degli Studi di Perugia
Ann Fac Econ Commer Univ Bari — Annali. Facolta di Economia e Commercio. Universita di Bari
Ann Fac Econ Commer Univ Studi Mesina — Annali. Facolta di Economia e Commercio. Universita degli Studi di Messina
Ann Fac Lett Filosof — Annali. Facolta di Lettere e Filosofia
Ann Fac Lett Filos Univ Padova — Annali. Facolta di Lettere e Filosofia. Universita di Padova
Ann Fac Med Chir Univ Studi Perugia Atti Accad Anat Chir — Annali. Facolta di Medicina e Chirurgia. Universita degli Studi di Perugia che Pubblicano gli Atti della Accademia Anatomico-Chirurgica
Ann Fac Med Chirurg — Annali. Facolta di Medicina e Chirurgia

Ann Fac Med S Paulo — Annales. Faculdade de Medicina de Sao Paulo
Ann Fac Med Vet Torino — Annali. Facolta di Medicina Veterinaria de Torino
Ann Fac Med Vet Univ Pisa — Annali. Facolta di Medicina Veterinaria. Universita di Pisa [*Italy*]
Ann Fac Med Vet Univ Studi Pisa — Annali. Facolta di Medicina Veterinaria. Universita degli Studi di Pisa
Ann Fac Med Vet Univ Torino — Annali. Facolta di Medicina Veterinaria. Universita di Torino
Ann Fac Sci Agrar Napoli Portici — Annali. Facolta di Scienze Agrarie. Universita degli Studi di Napoli Portici
Ann Fac Sci Agrar Univ Palermo — Annali. Facolta di Scienze Agrarie. Universita di Palermo
Ann Fac Sci Agrar Univ Studi Napoli Portici — Annali. Facolta di Scienze Agrarie. Universita degli Studi di Napoli Portici
Ann Fac Sci Agr Univ Napoli Ser 3 — Annali. Facolta di Science Agrarie. Universita di Napoli. Ser 3
Ann Fac Sci Agr Univ Stud Napoli Portici — Annali. Facolta di Scienze Agrarie. Universita degli Studi di Napoli Portici
Ann Fac Sci Agr Univ Torino — Annali. Facolta di Science Agrarie. Universita di Torino
Ann Fac Sci Cameroun — Annales. Faculte des Sciences du Cameroun
Ann Fac Sci Mars — Annales. Faculte des Sciences de Marseille
Ann Fac Sci Marseille — Annales. Faculte des Sciences de Marseille
Ann Fac Sci Sect Biol Chim Sci Terre (Univ Natl Zaire) — Annales. Faculte des Sciences. Section Biologie, Chimie, et Sciences de la Terre (Universite Nationale du Zaire)
Ann Fac Sci Univ Dakar — Annales. Faculte des Sciences. Universite de Dakar
Ann Fac Sci Univ Nat Zaire (Kinshasa) Sect Math-Phys — Annales. Faculte des Sciences. Universite Nationale du Zaire (Kinshasa). Section Mathematique-Physique
Ann Fac Sci Univ Toulouse — Annales. Faculte des Sciences. Universite de Toulouse
Ann Fac Sci Univ Yaounde Ser 3 — Annales. Faculte des Sciences. Universite de Yaounde. Serie 3. Biologie-Biochimie
Ann Fac Sci Yaounde — Annales. Faculte des Sciences. Universite de Yaounde
Ann Fals Expert Chim — Annales des Falsifications et de l'Expertise Chimique [*France*]
Ann Falsif Expert Chim — Annales des Falsifications et de l'Expertise Chimique
Ann Falsif Expertise Chim — Annales des Falsifications et de l'Expertise Chimique
Ann Falsif Fraudes — Annales des Falsifications et des Fraudes [*Later, Annales des Falsifications et de l'Expertise Chimique*]
Ann Fis — Annali di Fisica
Ann Fitopatol — Annali di Fitopatologia
Ann Fond Louis Broglie — Annales. Fondation Louis de Broglie [*France*]
Ann Fond Louis de Broglie — Annales. Fondation Louis de Broglie
Ann For (Zagreb) — Annales Forestales (Zagreb)
Ann Fr Chronom Micromec — Annales Francaises de Chronometrie et de Micromecanique
Ann Fr Microtech et Chronom — Annales Francaises des Microtechniques et de Chronometrie
Ann Gastro — Annales de Gastroenterologie et d'Hepatologie
Ann Gastroenterol Hepatol — Annales de Gastroenterologie et d'Hepatologie
Ann Gembloux — Annales de Gembloux
Ann Genet — Annales de Genetique
Ann Genet Sel Anim — Annales de Genetique et de Selection Animale
Ann Genie Chimie — Annales du Genie Chimique
Ann Geofis — Annali di Geofisica
Ann Geog — Annales de Geographie
Ann Geogr — Annales de Geographie
Ann Geol Madagascar — Annales Geologiques de Madagascar
Ann Geol Peninsule Balk — Annales Geologiques de la Peninsule Balkanique
Ann Geol Serv Mines (Madagascar) — Annales Geologiques. Service des Mines (Madagascar)
Ann Geophys — Annales de Geophysique
ANNGS — Ad Novas. Norwegian Geographical Studies
Ann Guebhard — Annales Guebhard
Ann Hebert Haug — Annales. Hebert et Haug
Ann Heb Union Coll — Annals. Hebrew Union College
Ann Hist-Nat Mus Natl Hung — Annales Historico-Naturales. Musei Nationalis Hungarici
Ann Histoch — Annales d'Histochimie
Ann Histochim — Annales d'Histochimie
Ann Hist R — Annales Historiques de la Revolution Francaise
AnnHL — Annuaire d'Histoire Liegeoise
Ann Homeopath Fr — Annales Homeopathiques Francaises
Ann Human Genetics — Annals of Human Genetics
Ann Hum Bio — Annals of Human Biology
Ann Hum Gen — Annals of Human Genetics
Ann Hum Genet — Annals of Human Genetics
Ann Hydrob — Annales d'Hydrobiologie
Ann Hydrobiol — Annales d'Hydrobiologie
Ann Hydrogr — Annales Hydrographiques
Ann Hyg Lang Fr Med Nutr — Annales d'Hygiene de Langue Francaise. Medecine et Nutrition

Ann Hyg et Med Colon — Annales d'Hygiene et de Medecine Coloniales
Ann Hyg Publique Ind Soc — Annales d'Hygiene Publique. Industrielle et Sociale
Ann Hyg Pub et Med Legale — Annales d'Hygiene Publique et de Medecine Legale
Ann IA — Annals of Iowa
Ann ICRP — Annals. ICRP [*International Commission on Radiological Protection*]
Ann Idrol — Annali Idrologici
AnnIEO — Annales. Institut d'Etudes Orientales. Faculte des Lettres d'Alger
AnnIEOc — Annales. Institut d'Etudes Occidentes
Ann I Four — Annales. Institut Fourier
Ann Ig — Annali d'Igiene
Ann Ig Sper — Annali d'Igiene. Sperimentali
Ann I Hen A — Annales. Institut Henri Poincare. Section A (Physique Theorique)
Ann I Hen B — Annales. Institut Henri Poincare. Section B (Calcul des Probabilites et Statistique)
Ann Immunol — Annales d'Immunologie
Ann Immunol Hung — Annales Immunologiae Hungaricae
Ann Immunol (Paris) — Annales d'Immunologie (Paris)
Ann Indian Acad Med Sci — Annals. Indian Academy of Medical Sciences
Ann INSEE — Annales. INSEE [*Institut National de la Statistique et des Etudes Economiques*]
Ann Inst — Annales Institutorum
Ann Inst Agric Serv Rech Exp Agric Alger — Annales. Institut Agricole et des Services de Recherche et d'Experimentation Agricoles de l'Algerie
Ann Inst Belge Petrol — Annales. Institut Belge du Petrole
Ann Inst Biol (Tihany) Hung — Annales. Instituti Biologici (Tihany). Hungaricae Academiae Scientiarum
Ann Inst Biol (Tihany) Hung Acad Sci — Annales. Instituti Biologici (Tihany). Hungaricae Academiae Scientiarum
Ann Inst Cent Ampelol R Hong — Annales. Institut Central Ampelologique Royal Hongrois
Ann Inst Exp Tabac Bergerac — Annales. Institut Experimental du Tabac de Bergerac
Ann Inst Fourier (Grenoble) — Annales. Institut Fourier (Grenoble)
Ann Inst Fourier Univ Grenoble — Annales. Institut Fourier. Universite de Grenoble [*France*]
Ann Inst Geol Publ Hung — Annales. Instituti Geologici Publici Hungarici
Ann Inst Henri Poincare A — Annales. Institut Henri Poincare. Section A (Physique Theorique)
Ann Inst Henri Poincare B — Annales. Institut Henri Poincare. Section B (Calcul des Probabilites et Statistique)
Ann Inst Henri Poincare Sect A — Annales. Institut Henri Poincare. Section A (Physique Theorique)
Ann Inst Henri Poincare Sect B — Annales. Institut Henri Poincare. Section B (Calcul des Probabilites et Statistique) [*France*]
Ann Inst Hydrol Climatol — Annales. Institut d'Hydrologie et de Climatologie
Ann Inst Michel Pacha — Annales. Institut Michel Pacha
Ann Inst Nat Agron — Annales. Institut National Agronomique [*Paris*]
Ann Inst Natl Agron — Annales. Institut National Agronomique [*Paris*]
Ann Inst Natl Rech A — Annales. Institut National de la Recherche Agronomique de Tunisie
Ann Inst Natl Rech Agron Ser A — Annales. Institut National de la Recherche Agronomique. Serie A. Annales Agronomiques
Ann Inst Natl Rech Agron Ser B — Annales. Institut National de la Recherche Agronomique. Serie B. Annales de l'Amelioration des Plantes
Ann Inst Natl Rech Agron Ser C Ann Epiphyt — Annales. Institut National de la Recherche Agronomique. Serie C. Annales des Epiphyties
Ann Inst Natl Rech Agron Ser D Ann Zootech — Annales. Institut National de la Recherche Agronomique. Serie D. Annales de Zootechnie
Ann Inst Natl Rech Agron Ser E Ann Technol Agric — Annales. Institut National de la Recherche Agronomique. Serie E. Annales de Technologie Agricole
Ann Inst Natl Rech Agron Tunis — Annales. Institut National de la Recherche Agronomique de Tunisie
Ann Inst Nat Rech For Tunis — Annales. Institut National de Recherches Forestieres de Tunisie
Ann Inst Oceanogr — Annales. Institut Oceanographique
Ann Inst Pasteur — Annales. Institut Pasteur
Ann Inst Pasteur Lille — Annales. Institut Pasteur de Lille
Ann Inst Pasteur (Paris) — Annales. Institut Pasteur (Paris)
Ann Inst Phys Globe Univ Paris Bur Cent Magn Terr — Annales. Institut de Physique du Globe. Universite de Paris et Bureau Central de Magnetisme Terrestre
Ann Inst Phytopathol Benaki — Annales. Institut Phytopathologique. Benaki
Ann Inst Poincare Sect A — Annales. Institut Henri Poincare. Section A (Physique Theorique)
Ann Inst Poincare Sect B — Annales. Institut Henri Poincare. Section B (Calcul des Probabilites et Statistique)
Ann Inst Sper Enol (Asti) — Annali. Istituto Sperimentale per l'Enologia (Asti)
Ann Inst Tech Batim Trav Publics — Annales. Institut Technique du Batiment et des Travaux Publics
Ann Intern Med — Annals of Internal Medicine
Ann Int Geophys Year — Annals of the International Geophysical Year

Ann Int Med — Annals of Internal Medicine
Ann I Ocean — Annales. Institut Oceanographique
AnnION — Annali. Istituto Universitario Orientale (Napoli)
Ann Iowa — Annals of Iowa
AnnIPhO — Annuaire. Institut de Philologie et d'Histoire Orientales et Slaves [*Bruxelles*]
Ann IQSY — Annals of the IQSY [*International Quiet Sun Year*]
Ann Isnardi Auxol Norm Patol — Annali Isnardi di Auxologia Normale e Patologica
Ann Israel Phys Soc — Annals. Israel Physical Society
Ann Isr Phys Soc — Annals. Israel Physical Society
Ann I Stat — Annals. Institute of Statistical Mathematics
Ann Ist Carlo Forlanini — Annali. Istituto Carlo Forlanini
Ann Ist Orient Napoli — Annali. Istituto Orientale di Napoli
Ann Ist Sper Assestamento For Apic — Annali. Istituto Sperimentale per l'Assestamento Forestale e per l'Apicoltura
Ann Ist Sper Cereal — Annali. Istituto Sperimentale per la Cerealicoltura
Ann Ist Sper Cerealic — Annali. Istituto Sperimentale per la Cerealicoltura
Ann Ist Sper Colt Foraggere — Annali. Istituto Sperimentale per le Colture Foraggere
Ann Ist Sper Colt Ind — Annali. Istituto Sperimentale per le Colture Industriali
Ann Ist Sper Enol (Asti) — Annali. Istituto Sperimentale per l'Enologia (Asti)
Ann Ist Sper Flori — Annali. Istituto Sperimentale per la Floricoltura
Ann Ist Sper Floricolt — Annali. Istituto Sperimentale per la Floricoltura
Ann Ist Sper Frutticolt — Annali. Istituto Sperimentale per la Frutticoltura
Ann Ist Sper Nutr Piante — Annali. Istituto Sperimentale per la Nutrizione delle Piante
Ann Ist Sper Selvi — Annali. Istituto Sperimentale per la Selvicoltura
Ann Ist Sper Selvic — Annali. Istituto Sperimentale per la Selvicoltura
Ann Ist Sper Stud Dif Suolo — Annali. Istituto Sperimentale per lo Studio e la Difesa del Suolo
Ann Ist Sper Tab — Annali. Istituto Sperimentale per il Tabacco
Ann Ist Sper Vitic (Conegliano Italy) — Annali. Istituto Sperimentale per la Viticoltura (Conegliano, Italy)
Ann Ist Sper Zool Agrar — Annali. Istituto Sperimentale per la Zoologia Agraria
Ann Ist Sper Zootec — Annali. Istituto Sperimentale per la Zootecnia
Ann Ist Sper Zootec Roma — Annali. Istituto Sperimentale Zootecnico di Roma
Ann Ist Super Sanita — Annali. Istituto Superiore di Sanita
Ann Ital Chir — Annali Italiani di Chirurgia
Ann Ital Dermatol Clin Sper — Annali Italiani di Dermatologia Clinica e Sperimentale
Ann Ital Dermatol Sifilol — Annali Italiani di Dermatologia e Sifilologia
Ann Ital Pediatr — Annali Italiani di Pediatria
Anniv Bull Chuo Univ — Anniversary Bulletin. Chuo University
Ann Japan Assoc Philos Sci — Annals. Japan Association for Philosophy of Science
Ann Jpn Assoc Philos Sci — Annals. Japan Association for Philosophy of Science
Ann Kinesither — Annales de Kinesitherapie
Ann KY Nat Hist — Annals of Kentucky Natural History
Ann Laringol — Annali di Laringologia, Otologia, Rinologia, Faringologia
Ann Laringol Otol Rinol Faringol — Annali di Laringologia, Otologia, Rinologia, Faringologia
AnnLat — Annali Lateranensi
Ann Lav Pubblici — Annali dei Lavori Pubblici
Ann Leg Fr Etr — Annuaire de Legislation Francaise et Etrangere
Ann Libr Sci — Annals of Library Science and Documentation
Ann Libr Sci Docum — Annals of Library Science and Documentation
Ann Limnol — Annales de Limnologie
Ann Liv — Annals of Archaeology and Anthropology (Liverpool)
Annls Agric Fenn — Annales Agriculturae Fenniae
Annls Agric Fenniae — Annales Agriculturae Fenniae
Annls Agron — Annales Agronomiques
Annls Amel Pl — Annales de l'Amelioration des Plantes
Annls Biol — Annales de Biologie
Annls Biol Anim Biochim Biophys — Annales de Biologie Animale, Biochimie, et Biophysique
Annls Cent Rech Agron Bambey — Annales. Centre de Recherches Agronomiques de Bambey au Senegal
Annls Endocr — Annales d'Endocrinologie
Annls Epiphyt — Annales des Epiphyties et de Phytogenetique [*Paris*]
Annls Fac Sci Marseille — Annales. Faculte des Sciences de Marseille
Annls Falsif Expert Chim — Annales des Falsifications et de l'Expertise Chimique
Annls Gembloux — Annales de Gembloux
Annls Hist-Nat Mus Natn Hung — Annalis. Historico-Naturales Musei Nationalis Hungarici
Annls Inst Natn Agron (Paris) — Annales. Institut National Agronomique (Paris)
Annls Inst Natn Rech Agron Tunisie — Annales. Institut National de la Recherche Agronomique de Tunisie
Annls Inst Pasteur (Paris) — Annales. Institut Pasteur (Paris)
Annls Inst Phytopath Benaki — Annales. Institut Phytopathologique. Benaki
Annls Mines Belg — Annales des Mines de Belgique

Annls Mines (Paris) — Annales des Mines (Paris)
Annls Mus R Afr Cent Ser 8vo — Annales. Musee Royal de l'Afrique Centrale. Serie in 8vo
Annls Nutr Aliment — Annales de la Nutrition et de l'Alimentation
Annls Pharm Fr — Annales Pharmaceutiques Francaises
Annls Physiol Veg (Brux) — Annales de Physiologie Vegetale (Bruxelles)
Annls Physiol Veg (Paris) — Annales de Physiologie Vegetale (Paris)
Annls SEITA — Annales de la Direction des Etudes et de l'Equipement. Service d'Exploitation Industrielle des Tabacs et des Allumettes
Annls Soc Belge Med Trop — Annales. Societe Belge de Medecine Tropicale
Annls Soc Lit Eston Am — Annales Societatis Litterarum Estonicae in America
Annls Univ Mariae Curie-Sklodowska — Annales Universitatis Mariae Curie-Sklodowska
Ann Lyceum Nat Hist (NY) — Annals. Lyceum of Natural History (New York)
Ann M — Annales Musicologiques
AnnMAfrC — Annales. Musee Royal de l'Afrique Centrale
Ann and Mag Nat Hist — Annals and Magazine of Natural History
Ann Mag Nat Hist — Annals and Magazine of Natural History
Ann Mag Natur Hist — Annals and Magazine of Natural History
Ann Math — Annals of Mathematics
Ann of Math (2) — Annals of Mathematics. Second Series
Ann Math Logic — Annals of Mathematical Logic
Ann Math Stat — Annals of Mathematical Statistics
Ann of Math Studies — Annals of Mathematics Studies
Ann Mat Pura Appl — Annali di Matematica Pura ed Applicata
AnnMCB-L — Annales. Musee Royal du Congo Belge. Linguistique
Ann Med — Annuale Mediaevale
Ann Med Acad Cienc Med Catalunya Balears — Annals. Medicina Academia de Ciencias Mediques de Catalunya i de Balears
Ann de Med Belge — Annales de Medecine Belge et Etrangere
Ann Med Belges — Annales Medicales Belges
Ann Med et Chir Inf — Annales de Medecine et Chirurgie Infantiles
Ann Med Exp Biol Fenn — Annales Medicinae Experimentalis et Biologiae Fenniae
Ann Med Exp Biol Fenn Suppl — Annales Medicinae Experimentalis et Biologiae Fenniae. Supplementum
Ann Med (Hagerstown Maryland) — Annals of Medicine (Hagerstown, Maryland)
Ann Med Hist — Annals of Medical History
Ann Med In — Annales de Medecine Interne
Ann Med Intern — Annales de Medecine Interne
Ann Med Intern Fenn — Annales Medicinae Internae Fenniae
Ann Med Intern Fenn Suppl — Annales Medicinae Internae Fenniae. Supplementum
Ann Med Leg — Annales de Medecine Legale
Ann Med Leg Criminol — Annales de Medecine Legale et de Criminologie
Ann Med (Milan) — Annali Medici (Milan)
Ann Med Mil Fenn — Annales Medicinae Militaris Fenniae
Ann Med Nancy — Annales Medicales de Nancy
Ann Med Nav — Annali di Medicina Navale
Ann Med Nav e Colon — Annali di Medicina Navale e Coloniale
Ann Med Nav Trop — Annali di Medicina Navale e Tropicale
Ann Med (Paris) — Annales de Medecine (Paris)
Ann Med et Pharm Colon — Annales de Medecine et de Pharmacie Coloniales
Ann Med Pharm Reims — Annales de Medecine et de Pharmacie de Reims
Ann Med-Psy — Annales Medico-Psychologiques
Ann Med-Psychol — Annales Medico-Psychologiques
Ann Med Reims — Annales de Medecine de Reims
Ann Med Sect Pol Acad Sci — Annals. Medical Section. Polish Academy of Sciences
Ann Med Sondalo — Annali Medici di Sondalo
Ann Med Vet — Annales de Medecine Veterinaire
Ann Merceol Sicil — Annali di Merceol Siciliana
Ann Meteorol — Annalen der Meteorologie
Ann Microb — Annales de Microbiologie [*Institut Pasteur*] [*Paris*]
Ann Microbiol — Annali di Microbiologia
Ann Microbiol Enzimol — Annali di Microbiologia. Ed. Enzimologia
Ann Microbiol (Milan) — Annali di Microbiologia (Milan)
Ann Microbiol (Paris) — Annales de Microbiologie (Paris)
Ann Midi — Annales du Midi; Revue de la France Meridionale [*Toulouse*]
Ann Mines — Annales des Mines [*Paris*]
Ann Mines Belg — Annales des Mines de Belgique
Ann Mines Doc — Annales des Mines. Documentation
Ann Mines Geol (Tunisia) — Annales des Mines et de la Geologie (Tunisia)
Ann Mines Mem — Annales des Mines. Memoires
Ann MO Bot — Annals. Missouri Botanical Garden
Ann MO Bot Gard — Annals. Missouri Botanical Garden
Ann MO Bot Gdn — Annals. Missouri Botanical Garden
Ann Mus Civ Stor Nat "Giacomo Doria" — Annali. Museo Civico di Storia Naturale "Giacomo Doria"
Ann Mus Colon Mars — Annales. Musee Colonial de Marseille
Ann Mus Goulandris — Annales Musei Goulandris
Ann Mus Nat Arch (Plovdiv) — Annuaire. Musee National Archeologique (Plovdiv)
Ann Mus R Afr Cent Ser Quarto Zool — Annales. Musee Royal de l'Afrique Centrale. Serie in Quarto. Zoologie

Ann Mus R Congo Belge Ser 8o Sci Geol — Annales. Musee Royal du Congo Belge. Serie in Octavo. Sciences Geologiques
Ann Natal Mus — Annale. Natalse Museum
Ann Naturhist Mus Wien — Annalen des Naturhistorischen Museums in Wien
Ann Neur — Annali di Neurologia
Ann Neurol — Annals of Neurology
Ann Neuropsichiatr Psicoanal — Annali di Neuropsichiatria e Psicoanalisi
Ann Neur Psich Psic — Annali di Neuropsichiatria e Psicoanalisi
Ann New York Acad Sci — Annals. New York Academy of Sciences
AnnNorm — Annales de Normandie
Ann Normandie — Annales de Normandie
Ann N Ph — Annalen der Naturphilosophie
Ann Nuc Eng — Annals of Nuclear Energy
Ann Nucl Energy — Annals of Nuclear Energy
Ann Nucl Sci and Eng — Annals of Nuclear Science and Engineering
Ann Nucl Sci Eng — Annals of Nuclear Science and Engineering
Ann Nucl Sci Engng — Annals of Nuclear Science and Engineering
Ann Nutr Al — Annales de la Nutrition et de l'Alimentation
Ann Nutr Aliment — Annales de la Nutrition et de l'Alimentation
Ann Nutr Metab — Annals of Nutrition and Metabolism
Ann NY Acad — Annals. New York Academy of Sciences
Ann NY Acad Sci — Annals. New York Academy of Sciences
Ann NY Ac Sci — Annals. New York Academy of Sciences
Ann O — Annals of Otology, Rhinology, and Laryngology
Ann Obs Besancon — Annales. Observatoire de Besancon
Ann Obs Nat — Annales. Observatoire National d'Athenes
Ann Obstet — Annee Obstetricale
Ann Occup Hyg — Annals of Occupational Hygiene
Ann Ocul — Annales d'Oculistique [*Paris*]
Ann Oculist — Annales d'Oculistique [*Paris*]
Ann Ocul (Paris) — Annales d'Oculistique (Paris)
Ann Odonto-Stomatol — Annales Odonto-Stomatologiques
Ann Off Natl Combust Liq (France) — Annales. Office National des Combustibles Liquides (France)
Ann Oftalmol Clin Ocul — Annali di Oftalmologia e Clinica Oculistica
Ann Okla Acad Sci — Annals. Oklahoma Academy of Science
Ann Ophth — Annals of Ophthalmology
Ann Ophthalmol — Annals of Ophthalmology
Ann OR — Annals of Oriental Research. University of Madras
Ann Or (Napoli) — Annali. Istituto Universitario Orientale (Napoli)
Ann Osp Maria Vittoria Torino — Annali. Ospedale Maria Vittoria di Torino
Ann Oss Vesuviano — Annali. Osservatorio Vesuviano
Ann Ostet Ginecol — Annali di Ostetricia e Ginecologia [*Italy*]
Ann Ostet Ginecol Med Perinat — Annali di Ostetricia, Ginecologia, Medicina Perinatale
Ann Ot — Annals of Otology, Rhinology, and Laryngology
Annot Bibliogr Anim/Hum Ser Commonw Bur Anim Health — Annotated Bibliography. Animal/Human Series. Commonwealth Bureau of Animal Health
Annot Bibliography of Econ Geology — Annotated Bibliography of Economic Geology
Annot Bibliogr Commonw Bur Nutr — Annotated Bibliography. Commonwealth Bureau of Nutrition
Annot Bibliogr Med Myc — Annotated Bibliography of Medical Mycology
Annot Dokl Semin Inst Prikl Mat Tbilis Univ — Annotatsii Dokladov. Seminar Instituta Prikladnoj Matematiki. Tbilisskij Universitet
Annotness Zool Bot (Bratislava) — Annotationes Zoologicae et Botanicae (Bratislava)
Annotness Zool Jap — Annotationes Zoologicae Japonenses
Ann Oto-Lar — Annales d'Oto-Laryngologie et de Chirurgie Cervico-Faciale
Ann Oto-Laryngol — Annales d'Oto-Laryngologie [*Later, Annales d'Oto-Laryngologie et de Chirurgie Cervico-Faciale*]
Ann Oto-Laryngol Chir Cervico-Fac — Annales d'Oto-Laryngologie et de Chirurgie Cervico-Faciale
Ann Otol Rh — Annals of Otology, Rhinology, and Laryngology
Ann Otol Rhinol Laryngol — Annals of Otology, Rhinology, and Laryngology
Ann Otol Rhinol Laryngol Suppl — Annals of Otology, Rhinology, and Laryngology. Supplement
Ann Oto Rhinol Laryngol — Annals of Otology, Rhinology, and Laryngology
Ann Ottalmol Clin Ocul — Annali di Ottalmologia e Clinica Oculistica
Annot Zool Bot — Annotationes Zoologicae et Botanicae
Annot Zool Jap — Annotationes Zoologicae Japonenses
Annot Zool Japon — Annotationes Zoologicae Japonenses
Annot Zool Jpn — Annotationes Zoologicae Japonenses
Ann Paediatr — Annales Paediatrici
Ann Paediatr Fenn — Annales Paediatriae Fenniae [*Finland*]
Ann Paediatr Fenn Suppl — Annales Paediatriae Fenniae. Supplementum
Ann Paed Jap — Annales Paediatrici Japonici
Ann Paleontol — Annales de Paleontologie
Ann Paleontol Invertebr — Annales de Paleontologie Invertebre
Ann Paleontol Invertebre — Annales de Paleontologie Invertebre
Ann Paleontol Vertebr — Annales de Paleontologie Vertebre
Ann Parasitol — Annales de Parasitologie Humaine et Comparee
Ann Parasitol Hum Comp — Annales de Parasitologie Humaine et Comparee
Ann Paris — Annales. Universite de Paris
Ann Pathol — Annales de Pathologie

Ann Paulist Med e Cirurg — Annales Paulistas de Medicina e Cirurgia
Ann Ped — Annee Pediatrique
Ann Pediatr — Annales de Pediatrie [*Paris*]
Ann Pediatr Jpn Kioto Univ — Annales Paediatrici Japonici. Kioto Universitatis
Ann Pediatr (Paris) — Annales de Pediatrie (Paris)
Ann Pharm Belg — Annales Pharmaceutiques Belges
Ann Pharm F — Annales Pharmaceutiques Francaises
Ann Pharm Fr — Annales Pharmaceutiques Francaises
Ann Pharm (Lemgo Germany) — Annalen der Pharmacie (Lemgo, Germany)
Ann Pharm (Poznan) — Annales Pharmaceutici (Poznan)
Ann Phil — Annals of Philosophy
Ann Phil Hist — Brussels. Universite Libre. Institut de Philologie et d'Histoire. Annuaire
Ann Philos — Annals of Philosophy
Ann Phys — Annales de Physique
Ann Phys — Annals of Physics [*New York*]
Ann Phys Bi — Annales de Physique Biologique et Medicale
Ann Phys Biol Med — Annales de Physique Biologique et Medicale
Ann Phys (Germ) — Annalen der Physik (Germany)
Ann Physics — Annals of Physics [*New York*]
Ann Physik — Annalen der Physik
Ann Physik (7) — Annales der Physik 7 Folge
Ann Physiol Physicochim Biol — Annales de Physiologie et de Physicochimie Biologique
Ann Physiol Veg — Annales de Physiologie Vegetale [*Bruxelles*]
Ann Physiol Veg (Paris) — Annales de Physiologie Vegetale (Paris)
Ann Physiol Veg Univ Brux — Annales de Physiologie Vegetale. Universite de Bruxelles
Ann Physiq — Annales de Physique [*Paris*]
Ann Phys (Leipzig) — Annalen der Physik (Leipzig)
Ann Phys Med — Annals of Physical Medicine
Ann Phys (New York) — Annals of Physics (New York)
Ann Phys (Paris) — Annales de Physique (Paris)
Ann Phys Phys Chim — Annales de Physiologie et de Physicochimie Biologique
Ann Phytopath — Annales de Phytopathologie
Ann Phytopathol — Annales de Phytopathologie
Ann Phytopathol Soc Jap — Annals. Phytopathological Society of Japan
Ann Phytopathol Soc Jpn — Annals. Phytopathological Society of Japan
Ann Pisa — Annali. Reale Scuola Normale Superiore di Pisa. Sezione di Lettere
Ann Plast Surg — Annals of Plastic Surgery
Ann Polit Litt — Annales Politiques et Litteraires
Ann Pol et Litt — Annales Politiques et Litteraires
Ann Pol Math — Annales Polonici Mathematici
Ann Polon Math — Annales Polonici Mathematici
Ann Pontif Mus Miss Etnol (Vatican) — Annali. Pontificio Museo Missionario Etnologico (Vatican)
Ann Ponts Chaussees — Annales des Ponts et Chaussees
Ann Probab — Annals of Probability
Ann Probability — Annals of Probability
Ann Prog Rep Geol Surv West Austr — Annual Progress Report. Geological Survey. Western Australia
Ann Protist — Annales de Protistologie
AnnPsych — Annee Psychologique
Ann Psychol — Annee Psychologique
Ann Rad Diagn — Annali di Radiologia Diagnostica
Ann Radioelectr — Annales de Radioelectricite [*France*]
Ann Radiol — Annales de Radiologie
Ann Radiol Diagn — Annali di Radiologia Diagnostica
Ann Radiol Med Nucl — Annales de Radiologie. Medecine Nucleaire [*France*]
Ann Rainf Aust — Annual Rainfall, Australia [*Australia Commonwealth Bureau of Meteorology*]
Ann R Anthr — Annual Review of Anthropology
Ann R Astro — Annual Review of Astronomy and Astrophysics
Ann R Bioch — Annual Review of Biochemistry
Ann R Bioph — Annual Review of Biophysics and Bioengineering
Ann R Coll Physicians Surg Can — Annals. Royal College of Physicians and Surgeons of Canada
Ann R Coll Surg Eng — Annals. Royal College of Surgeons of England
Ann R Coll Surg Engl — Annals. Royal College of Surgeons of England
Ann RC Surg — Annals. Royal College of Surgeons of England
Ann R Earth — Annual Review of Earth and Planetary Sciences
Ann Rech For Maroc — Annales de la Recherche Forestiere au Maroc
Ann Rech Vet — Annales de Recherches Veterinaires
Ann R Ecol — Annual Review of Ecology and Systematics
Ann Reg — American Annual Register
Ann Regia Super Agric (Portici) — Annali. Regia Scuola Superiore di Agricoltura (Portici)
Ann R Entom — Annual Review of Entomology
Ann Rep Brooklyn — Annual Report. Brooklyn Museum
Ann Rep Cent Adult Dis (Osaka) — Annual Report. Center for Adult Diseases (Osaka)
Ann Rep Dep Hlth NZ — Annual Report. Department of Health [*New Zealand*]
Ann Rep DS — Annual Report. Dante Society

Ann Rep Hlth Med Serv — Annual Report. Health and Medical Services of the State of Queensland

Ann Rep Inst Med Vet Sci — Annual Report. Institute of Medical and Veterinary Science

Ann Rep Inst Vir Res — Annual Report. Institute for Virus Research [*Kyoto*]

Ann Rep Manag Adel Hosp — Annual Report. Board of Management. Royal Adelaide Hospital

Ann Rep Med Chem — Annual Reports in Medicinal Chemistry

Ann Rep NACA — Annual Report. United States National Advisory Committee for Aeronautics

Ann Rep Nat Res Counc Can — Annual Report. National Research Council of Canada

Ann Rep Past Ins SI — Annual Report. Pasteur Institute of Southern India

Ann Rep Prog Chem Sect C Phys Chem — Annual Reports on the Progress of Chemistry. Section C. Physical Chemistry

Ann Rep S Afr Inst Med Res — Annual Report. South African Institute for Medical Research

Ann Rep Smith Inst — Annual Report. Smithsonian Institution

Ann Rep Soc Libyan Stud — Annual Report. Society for Libyan Studies

Ann Rept Progr Chem — Annual Reports on the Progress of Chemistry

Ann Rept Tokyo Univ Agr Technol — Annual Report. Tokyo University of Agriculture and Technology

Ann Rep United Fruit Co Med Dept — Annual Report. United Fruit Company. Medical Department

Ann Rep Yorkshire Phil Soc — Annual Report. Yorkshire Philosophical Society

Ann Res Inst Epidemiol Microbiol — Annals. Research Institute of Epidemiology and Microbiology

Ann Res Inst Micr Dis — Annals. Research Institute for Microbial Diseases

Ann Rev Acad Nat Sci Philad — Annual Review. Academy of Natural Sciences of Philadelphia

Ann Rev Analyt Chem — Annual Review of Analytical Chemistry

Ann Rev Austr Min Ind — Annual Review. Australian Mineral Industry

Ann Rev Biochem — Annual Review of Biochemistry

Ann Rev Ecol — Annual Review of Ecology and Systematics

Ann Rev Ent — Annual Review of Entomology

Ann Rev Entomol — Annual Review of Entomology

Ann Rev Gen — Annual Review of Genetics

Ann Rev Microbiol — Annual Review of Microbiology

Ann Rev Nuclear Sci — Annual Review of Nuclear Science [*Later, Annual Review of Nuclear and Particle Science*]

Ann Rev Nucl Sci — Annual Review of Nuclear Science [*Later, Annual Review of Nuclear and Particle Science*]

Ann Rev Pharm — Annual Review of Pharmacology [*Later, Annual Review of Pharmacology and Toxicology*]

Ann Rev Phys Chem — Annual Review of Physical Chemistry

Ann Rev Phytopath — Annual Review of Phytopathology

Ann Rev Plant Physiol — Annual Review of Plant Physiology

Ann R Fluid — Annual Review of Fluid Mechanics

Ann R Genet — Annual Review of Genetics

Ann Rheum D — Annals of the Rheumatic Diseases

Ann Rheum Dis — Annals of the Rheumatic Diseases

Ann R Infor — Annual Review of Information Science and Technology

Ann R Mater — Annual Review of Materials Science

Ann R Med — Annual Review of Medicine

Ann R Micro — Annual Review of Microbiology

Ann R Nucl — Annual Review of Nuclear Science [*Later, Annual Review of Nuclear and Particle Science*]

Ann Roentg — Annals of Roentgenology

Ann Rp Ch A — Annual Reports on the Progress of Chemistry. Section A. General, Physical, and Inorganic Chemistry

Ann Rp Ch B — Annual Reports on the Progress of Chemistry. Section B. Organic Chemistry

Ann R Pharm — Annual Review of Pharmacology [*Later, Annual Review of Pharmacology and Toxicology*]

Ann R Ph Ch — Annual Review of Physical Chemistry

Ann R Physl — Annual Review of Physiology

Ann R Phyto — Annual Review of Phytopathology

Ann R Plant — Annual Review of Plant Physiology

Ann R Psych — Annual Review of Psychology

Ann R Sociol — Annual Review of Sociology

AnnS — Annales Silesiae

Ann S Afr Mus — Annals. South Africa Museum

Ann Sanita Pubblica — Annali della Sanita Pubblica

Ann Sanit Int — Annuaire Sanitaire International

Ann San Rep Prov Assam — Annual Sanitary Report of the Province of Assam

Ann Sci — Annals of Science [*London*]

Ann of Sci — Annals of Science

Ann Sci Agron — Annales de la Science Agronomique

Ann Sci Agron Fr — Annales. Science Agronomique Francaise et Etrangere

Ann Sci Ec — Annales Scientifiques. Ecole Normale Superieure

Ann Sci Ecole Norm Sup — Annales Scientifiques. Ecole Normale Superieure

Ann Sci Econ Appl — Annales des Sciences Economiques Appliquees

Ann Sci For (Paris) — Annales des Sciences Forestieres (Paris)

Ann Sci Kanazawa Univ — Annals of Science. Kanazawa University

Ann Sci Kanazawa Univ Part 2 Biol-Geol — Annals of Science. Kanazawa University. Part 2. Biology-Geology

Ann Sci Nat — Annaes de Sciencias Naturaes

Ann Sci Nat Bot — Annales des Sciences Naturelles (A) Botanique

Ann Sci Nat Bot Biol Veg — Annales des Sciences Naturelles. Botanique et Biologie Vegetale

Ann Sci Natur Bot Biol Veg — Annales des Sciences Naturelles. Botanique et Biologie Vegetale

Ann Sci Nat Zool — Annales des Sciences Naturelles (B) Zoologie

Ann Sci Nat Zool Biol Anim — Annales des Sciences Naturelles. Zoologie et Biologie Animale

Ann Sci Univ Bes — Annales Scientifiques. Universite de Besancon

Ann Sci Univ Besancon Bot — Annales Scientifiques. Universite de Besancon. Botanique

Ann Sci Univ Besancon Climatol — Annales Scientifiques. Universite de Besancon. Climatologie

Ann Sci Univ Besancon Geol — Annales Scientifiques. Universite de Besancon. Geologie

Ann Sci Univ Besancon Hydrogr — Annales Scientifiques. Universite de Besancon. Hydrographie

Ann Sci Univ Besancon Math — Annales Scientifiques. Universite de Besancon. Mathematiques

Ann Sci Univ Besancon Math 3 — Annales Scientifiques. Universite de Besancon. Mathematiques. 3e Serie

Ann Sci Univ Besancon Mec Phys Theor — Annales Scientifiques. Universite de Besancon. Mecanique et Physique Theorique

Ann Sci Univ Besancon Med — Annales Scientifiques. Universite de Besancon. Medecine

Ann Sci Univ Besancon Meteorol — Annales Scientifiques. Universite de Besancon. Meteorologie

Ann Sci Univ Besancon Physiol Biol Anim — Annales Scientifiques. Universite de Besancon. Physiologie et Biologie Animale

Ann Sci Univ Besancon Zool — Annales Scientifiques. Universite de Besancon. Zoologie

Ann Sci Univ Besancon Zool Physiol — Annales Scientifiques. Universite de Besancon. Zoologie et Physiologie

Ann Sci Univ Besancon Zool Physiol Biol Anim — Annales Scientifiques. Universite de Besancon. Zoologie, Physiologie, et Biologie Animale

Ann Sci Univ Clermont Math — Annales Scientifiques. Universite de Clermont. Serie Mathematique

Ann Sci Univ Jass Sect 1 — Annales Scientifiques. Universite de Jassy. Section 1. Mathematiques, Physique, Chimie

Ann Sci Univ Jassy Sect 2 — Annales Scientifiques. Universite de Jassy. Section 2. Sciences Naturelles

Ann Sci Univ Reims ARERS — Annales Scientifiques. Universite de Reims et ARERS [*Association Regionale pour l'Etude et la Recherche Scientifiques*]

Ann Sci Univ Reims ARERS (Assoc Reg Etude Rech Sci) — Annales Scientifiques. Universite de Reims et ARERS (Association Regionale pour l'Etude et la Recherche Scientifiques)

Ann Sclavo — Annali Sclavo

Ann Sc Nat — Annales des Sciences Naturelles

Ann Sc Nat Zool — Annales des Sciences Naturelles. Zoologie

Ann Sc Norm Super Pisa — Annali. Scuola Normale Superiore di Pisa

Ann Sc Norm Super Pisa Sci Fis Mat — Annali. Scuola Normale Superiore di Pisa. Scienze, Fisiche, e Matematiche

Ann Scu Archeol Atene — Annuario. Scuola Archeologica di Atene e delle Missioni Italiane in Oriente

Ann Scu Norm Sup — Annali. Scuola Normale Superiore

Ann Scuola Norm Sup Pisa Cl Sci — Annali. Scuola Normale Superiore di Pisa. Classe di Scienze

Ann Scuola Norm Sup Pisa Cl Sci 4 — Annali. Scuola Normale Superiore di Pisa. Classe di Scienze. Serie IV

Ann Scuola Norm Sup Pisa Sci Fis Mat — Annali. Scuola Normale Superiore di Pisa. Scienze, Fisiche, e Matematiche

Ann Sect Dendrol Soc Bot Pol — Annales. Section Dendrologique. Societe Botanique de Pologne

Ann Seism — Annuaire Seismique

Ann Seminar Metaf — Annales. Seminario de Metafisica

Ann Serv — Annales. Service des Antiquites de l'Egypte

Ann Serv Bot Agron Tunis — Annales. Service Botanique et Agronomique de Tunisie

Ann Sez Ling — Annali. Sezione Linguistica. Istituto Universitario Orientale

Ann Soc Belge Astr — Annuaire. Societe Belge d'Astronomie

Ann Soc Belge Med Trop — Annales. Societe Belge de Medecine Tropicale

Ann Soc Belge Neurol — Annales. Societe Belge de Neurologie

Ann Soc Belg Med Trop Parasitol Mycol — Annales. Societes Belges de Medecine Tropicale, de Parasitologie, et de Mycologie

Ann Soc Chim Fr — Annuaire. Societe Chimique de France

Ann Soc Ent — Annales. Societe Entomologique de France

Ann Soc Entomol Fr — Annales. Societe Entomologique de France

Ann Soc Entomol Que — Annales. Societe Entomologique du Quebec

Ann Soc I'r Econ Alp — Annuaire. Societe Francaise d'Economie Alpestre

Ann Soc Geol Belg — Annales. Societe Geologique de Belgique

Ann Soc Geol Belg Bull — Annales. Societe Geologique de Belgique. Bulletin

Ann Soc Geol Belg Mem — Annales. Societe Geologique de Belgique. Memoires

Ann Soc Geol Nord — Annales. Societe Geologique du Nord

Ann Soc Hydr Med — Annales. Societe d'Hydrologie Medicale de Paris
Ann Soc Ingeg — Annali. Societa degli Ingegneri e degli Architetti Italiani
Ann Soc Linn Lyon — Annales. Societe Linneenne de Lyon
Ann Soc Math Pol Ser IV Fundam Inf — Annales Societatis Mathematicae Polonae. Series IV. Fundamenta Informaticae
Ann Soc Med-Chir Bruges — Annales. Societe Medico-Chirurgicale de Bruges
Ann Soc Med Leg Belg — Annales. Societe de Medecine Legale de Belgique
Ann Soc Nat Hort Fr — Annales. Societe Nationale de l'Horticulture de France
Ann Soc Pol Math — Annales. Societe Polonaise de Mathematique
Ann Soc Roy Sci Med — Annales. Societe Royale des Sciences Medicales et Naturelles de Bruxelles
Ann Soc R Zool Belg — Annales. Societe Royale Zoologique de Belgique
Ann Soc Sci Bruxelles — Annales. Societe Scientifique de Bruxelles
Ann Soc Sci Bruxelles Ser 1 — Annales. Societe Scientifique de Bruxelles. Serie 1
Ann Soc Sci Bruxelles Ser 2 — Annales. Societe Scientifique de Bruxelles. Serie 2. Sciences Naturelles et Medicales
Ann Soc Sci Bruxelles Ser 3 — Annales. Societe Scientifique de Bruxelles. Serie 3. Sciences Economiques
Ann Soc Sci Brux Ser I — Annales. Societe Scientifique de Bruxelles. Serie I
Ann Soc Scient Bruxelles S B Sc Phys Nat — Annales. Societe Scientifique de Bruxelles. Serie B. Sciences Physiques et Naturelles
Ann Soc Scient Bruxelles S C Sci Med — Annales. Societe Scientifique de Bruxelles. Serie C. Sciences Medicales
Ann Soc Sci Faeroe — Annales Societatis Scientiarum Faeroensis
Ann Soc Sci Litt Cannes — Annales. Societe de Science et Litterature de Cannes
Ann Soc Sci Nat Charente-Marit — Annales. Societe des Sciences Naturelles de la Charente-Maritime
Ann Speleol — Annales de Speleologie
Ann Sper Agr — Annali della Sperimentazione Agraria
Ann Sper Agrar — Annali della Sperimentazione Agraria
AnnSR — Annales. Societa Retorumantscha
Ann Sta Chim-Agr Sper Roma Ser 3 — Annali. Stazione Chimico-Agraria Sperimentale di Roma. Ser 3
Ann Stat Belg — Annuaire Statistique de la Belgique
Ann Statist — Annals of Statistics
Ann Statist Tun — Annuaire Statistique de la Tunisie
Ann Stn Biol Besse-En-Chandesse — Annales. Station Biologique de Besse-En-Chandesse
Ann Stn Cent Hydrobiol Appl — Annales. Station Centrale d'Hydrobiologie Appliquee
Ann Stn Chim Agrar Sper Roma — Annali. Stazione Chimico-Agraria Sperimentale di Roma
Ann Stn Chim-Agrar Sper Roma Ser III Pubbl — Annali. Stazione Chimico-Agraria Sperimentale di Roma. Series III. Pubblicazione
Ann Stom — Annali di Stomatologia
Ann Stomatol — Annali di Stomatologia [*Roma*]
Ann Stomatol Ist Super Odontoiatr G Eastman — Annali di Stomatologia. Istituto Superiore di Odontoiatria G. Eastman
Ann Stomatol (Roma) — Annali di Stomatologia (Roma)
Ann Storia Nat — Annali di Storia Naturale
Ann Surg — Annals of Surgery
Ann Surv Law — Annual Survey of Law
Ann Surv of Law — Annual Survey of Law
Ann Surv Mass L — Annual Survey of Massachusetts Law
Ann Systems Res — Annals of Systems Research
Ann Syst Res — Annals of Systems Research
Ann Tab Sect 2 — Annales du Tabac. Section 2
Ann Tec Agr — Annales de Technologie Agricole [*Paris*]
Ann Technol Agr — Annales de Technologie Agricole [*Paris*]
Ann Technol Agric (Paris) — Annales de Technologie Agricole (Paris)
Ann Telecom — Annales des Telecommunications
Ann Telecomm — Annales des Telecommunications
Ann Telecommun — Annales des Telecommunications
Ann Ther — Annee Therapeutique
AnnThijm — Annalen van het Thijmgenootschap
Ann Thorac — Annals of Thoracic Surgery
Ann Thorac Surg — Annals of Thoracic Surgery
Ann Thor Surg — Annals of Thoracic Surgery
Ann Tokyo Astron Obs — Annals. Tokyo Astronomical Observatory
Ann Transvaal Mus — Annals. Transvaal Museum
Ann Transv Mus — Annals. Transvaal Museum
Ann Trav Agr Sci — Annales des Travaux Agricoles Scientifiques
Ann Trav Publics Belg — Annales des Travaux Publics de Belgique
AnnTriest — Annali Triestini
Ann Triest Cura Univ Trieste Sez 2 — Annali Triestini a Cura. Universita di Trieste. Sezione 2. Scienze ed Ingegneria
Ann Trop M — Annals of Tropical Medicine and Parasitology
Ann Trop Med Paras — Annals of Tropical Medicine and Parasitology
Ann Trop Med Parasitol — Annals of Tropical Medicine and Parasitology
Ann Tuberc — Annals of Tuberculosis
Ann Tvl Mus — Annals. Transvaal Museum
AnnUA — Annals. Ukrainian Academy of Arts and Sciences in the US
Annu A A A — Annuaire des Auditeurs et Anciens Auditeurs. Academie de Droit International de la Haye

Annu Afr Nord — Annuaire de l'Afrique du Nord
Annu Agric Suisse — Annuaire Agricole de la Suisse
Annuaire Francais Droit Int — Annuaire Francais de Droit International
Annuaire Univ Sofia Fac — Annuaire. Universite di Sofia. Faculte de Mathematiques
Annuaire Univ Sofia Fac Math Mec — Annuaire. Universite de Sofia. Faculte de Mathematiques et Mecanique
Annuaire Univ Sofia Fac Phys — Annuaire. Universite de Sofia. Faculte de Physique
Annual Law R — Annual Law Review
Annual Rep Fac Ed Iwate Univ — Iwate University. Faculty of Education. Annual Report
Annual Rep Fac Ed Univ Iwate — Annual Report. Faculty of Education. University of Iwate
Annu Amer Inst Coop — Annual. American Institute of Cooperation
Annu Anim Psychol — Annual of Animal Psychology
Annu Biol Colloq — Annual Biology Colloquium
Annu Biol Fac Sci Nat Univ Kiril Metodij (Skopje) — Annuaire. Biologie. Faculte des Sciences Naturelles. Universite Kiril. Metodij (Skopje)
Annu Book ASTM Stand — Annual Book of ASTM [*American Society for Testing and Materials*] Standards
Annu Brit Sch Athens — Annual. British School at Athens
Annu Bull Int Dairy Fed — Annual Bulletin. International Dairy Federation
Annu Bull Soc Jersiaise — Annual Bulletin. Societe Jersiaise
Annu Chim — Annuaire de Chimie
Annu Conf Hung Physiol Soc — Annual Conference. Hungarian Physiological Society
Annu Conf Res Med Educ — Annual Conference on Research in Medical Education
Annu Conf Soil Mech Found Eng — Annual Conference. Soil Mechanics and Foundation Engineering
Annu Conv Proc Wash Ass Wheat Growers — Annual Convention Proceedings. Washington Association of Wheat Growers
Annu Dr Marit Aer — Annuaire de Droit Maritime et Aerien
Annu Europ — Annuaire Europeen
Annu Fac Agric Univ Skopje — Annuaire. Faculte d'Agriculture et de Sylviculture. Universite de Skopje
Annu Fac Educ Gunma Univ Art Technol Ser — Annual Report. Faculty of Education. Gunma University. Art and Technology Seris
Annu Franc Dr Homme — Annuaire Francais des Droits de l'Homme
Annu Franc Dr Int — Annuaire Francais de Droit International
Annu Franc de Droit Internat — Annuaire Francais de Droit International
Annu Highway Geol Symp Proc — Annual Highway Geology Symposium. Proceedings
Annu Inst Europ Secur Soc — Annuaire. Institut Europeen de Securite Sociale
Annu Int Fonction Publ — Annuaire International de la Fonction Publique
Annu J Inst Eng — Annual Journal. Institution of Engineers
Ann Ukr Acad Arts Sci US — Annals. Ukrainian Academy of Arts and Sciences in the US
Ann UMCS — Annales Universitatis Mariae Curie-Sklodowska
Annu Meet Am Inst Oral Biol — Annual Meeting. American Institute of Oral Biology
Annu Meet Natl Mastitis Counc — Annual Meeting. National Mastitis Council
Annu Meet Proc Am Soc Photogramm — Annual Meeting-Proceedings. American Society of Photogrammetry
Annu Miner Symp Proc — Annual Minerals Symposium [*American Institute of Mining, Metallurgical, and Petroleum Engineers*] Proceedings
Annu Mus Natl Hist Nat — Annuaire. Museum National d'Histoire Naturelle
Annu Natl Inf Retr Colloq — Annual National Information Retrieval Colloquium
Ann Univ Abidjan Med — Annales. Universite d'Abidjan. Medecine
Ann Univ Abidjan Ser B Med — Annales. Universite d'Abidjan. Serie B. Medecine
Ann Univ Abidjan Ser C Sci — Annales. Universite d'Abidjan. Serie C. Sciences
Ann Univ Abidjan Ser E Ecol — Annales. Universite d'Abidjan. Serie E. Ecologie
Ann Univ Ankara — Annales. Universite d'Ankara
Ann Univ ARERS — Annales. Universite et de l'ARERS [*Association Regionale pour l'Etude et la Recherche Scientifiques*]
Ann Univ Bp — Annales Universitatis Scientiarum Budapestensis
Ann Univ Brazzaville — Annales. Universite de Brazzaville
Ann Univ Brazzaville Ser C Sci — Annales. Universite de Brazzaville. Serie C. Sciences
Ann Univ Fenn Abo — Annales Universitatis Fennicae Aboensis
Ann Univ Ferrara — Annali. Universita di Ferrara
Ann Univ Ferrara Sez 5 — Annali. Universita di Ferrara. Sezione 5. Chimica Pura ed Applicata
Ann Univ Ferrara Sez 6 — Annali. Universita di Ferrara. Sezione 6. Fisiologia e Chimica Biologica
Ann Univ Ferrara Sez 9 — Annali. Universita di Ferrara. Nuovo Serie. Sezione 9. Scienze Geologiche e Paleontologiche
Ann Univ Ferrara Sez I Ecol — Annali. Universita di Ferrara. Sezione I. Ecologia
Ann Univ Ferrara Sez III Biol Anim — Annali. Universita di Ferrara. Sezione III. Biologia Animale

Ann Univ Ferrara Sez IV Bot — Annali. Universita di Ferrara. Sezione IV. Botanica

Ann Univ Ferrara Sez IX Sci Geol Paleontol — Annali. Universita di Ferrara. Sezione IX. Scienze Geologiche e Paleontologiche

Ann Univ Ferrara Sez 5 Suppl — Annali. Universita di Ferrara. Sezione 5. Chimica Pura ed Applicata. Supplemento

Ann Univ Ferrara Sez VI Fisiol Chim Biol — Annali. Universita di Ferrara. Sezione VI. Fisiologia e Chimica Biologica

Ann Univ Ferrara Sez VII — Annali. Universita di Ferrara. Nuovo Serie. Sezione VII. Scienze Matematiche

Ann Univ Ferrara Sez VII NS — Annali. Universita di Ferrara. Nuovo Serie. Sezione VII

Ann Univ Ferrara Sez XI Farmacol Ter — Annali. Universita di Ferrara. Sezione XI. Farmacologia e Terapia

Ann Univ Ferrara Sez XIII Anat Comp — Annali. Universita di Ferrara. Sezione XIII. Anatomia Comparata

Ann Univ Lyon Fasc Spec — Annales. Universite de Lyon. Fascicule Special

Ann Univ Lyon Sci Med — Annales. Universite de Lyon. Sciences. Medecine

Ann Univ Lyon Sci Sect A — Annales. Universite de Lyon. Sciences. Section A. Sciences Mathematiques et Astronomie

Ann Univ Lyon Sci Sect B — Annales. Universite de Lyon. Sciences. Section B. Sciences Physiques et Chimiques

Ann Univ Lyon Sci Sect C — Annales. Universite de Lyon. Sciences. Section C. Sciences Naturelles

Ann Univ Madagascar Ser Sci Nat Math — Annales. Universite de Madagascar. Serie Sciences de la Nature et Mathematiques

Ann Univ Madagascar Ser Sci Nature Math — Annales. Universite de Madagascar. Serie Sciences de la Nature et Mathematiques

Ann Univ Mariae Curie-Sklodowska Med — Annales Universitatis Mariae Curie-Sklodowska. Sectio D. Medicina

Ann Univ Mariae Curie-Sklodowska Sect A — Annales Universitatis Mariae Curie-Sklodowska. Sectio A. Mathematica

Ann Univ Mariae Curie-Sklodowska Sect AA — Annales Universitatis Mariae Curie-Sklodowska. Sectio AA. Physica et Chemia

Ann Univ Mariae Curie-Sklodowska Sect AAA — Annales Universitatis Mariae Curie-Sklodowska. Sectio AAA. Physica [*Poland*]

Ann Univ Mariae Curie-Sklodowska Sect B — Annales Universitatis Mariae Curie-Sklodowska. Sectio B. Geographia, Geologia, Mineralogia, et Petrographia

Ann Univ Mariae Curie-Sklodowska Sect C — Annales Universitatis Mariae Curie-Sklodowska. Sectio C. Biologia

Ann Univ Mariae Curie-Sklodowska Sect C Biol — Annales Universitatis Mariae Curie-Sklodowska. Sectio C. Biologia

Ann Univ Mariae Curie-Sklodowska Sect C Suppl — Annales Universitatis Mariae Curie-Sklodowska. Sectio C. Biologia. Supplementum

Ann Univ Mariae Curie-Sklodowska Sect D — Annales Universitatis Mariae Curie-Sklodowska. Sectio D. Medicina

Ann Univ Mariae Curie-Sklodowska Sect DD — Annales Universitatis Mariae Curie-Sklodowska. Sectio DD. Medicina Veterinaria

Ann Univ Mariae Curie-Sklodowska Sect DD Med Vet — Annales Universitatis Mariae Curie-Sklodowska. Sectio DD. Medicina Veterinaria

Ann Univ Mariae Curie-Sklodowska Sect E — Annales Universitatis Mariae Curie-Sklodowska. Sectio E. Agricultura

Ann Univ Mariae Curie-Sklodowska Sect E Agric — Annales Universitatis Mariae Curie-Sklodowska. Sectio E. Agricultura

Ann Univ Mariae Curie-Sklodowska Sect EE — Annales Universitatis Mariae Curie-Sklodowska. Sectio EE. Agraria

Ann Univ M Curie-Sklodowska Sect AA — Annales Universitatis Mariae Curie-Sklodowska. Sectio AA. Physica et Chemia

Ann Univ M Curie-Sklodowska Sect AAA (Phys) — Annales Universitatis Mariae Curie-Sklodowska. Sectio AAA (Physica)

Ann Univ M Curie-Sklodowska Sect C — Annales Universitatis Mariae Curie-Sklodowska. Sectio C. Biologia

Ann Univ M Curie-Sklodowska Sect D — Annales Universitatis Mariae Curie-Sklodowska. Sectio D. Medicina

Ann Univ Montp Suppl Sci Ser Bot — Annales. Universite de Montpellier. Supplement Scientifique. Serie Botanique

Ann Univ Padova — Annale. Universita di Padova. Facolta di Economia e Commercio in Verona

Ann Univ Paris — Annales. Universite de Paris

Ann Univ Saraviensis Med — Annales Universitatis Saraviensis. Medizin

Ann Univ Sarav Math-Natur Fak — Annales Universitatis Saraviensis. Mathematisch-Naturwissenschaftliche Fakultaet

Ann Univ Sarav Med — Annales Universitatis Saraviensis. Medizin

Ann Univ Sarav (Reihe) Math-Naturwiss Fak — Annales Universitatis Saraviensis (Reihe). Mathematisch-Naturwissenschaftliche Fakultaet

Ann Univ Sci Budapest Eotvos Sect Math — Annales Universitatis Scientiarum Budapestensis de Rolando Eoetvoes Nominatae. Sectio Mathematica

Ann Univ Sci Budapest Rolando Eotvos Nominatae Sect Chim — Annales Universitatis Scientiarum Budapestensis de Rolando Eoetvoes Nominatae. Sectio Chimica

Ann Univ Sci Budap Rolando Eotvos Nominatae Sect Biol — Annales Universitatis Scientiarum Budapestensis de Rolando Eoetvoes Nominatae. Sectio Biologica

Ann Univ Sci Budap Rolando Eotvos Nominatae Sect Chim — Annales Universitatis Scientiarum Budapestensis de Rolando Eoetvoes Nominatae. Sectio Chimica

Ann Univ Sci Budap Rolando Eotvos Nominatae Sect Chim — Annales Universitatis Scientiarum Budapestensis de Rolando Eotvoes Nominatae. Sectio Chimica

Ann Univ Sci Budap Rolando Eotvos Nominatae Sect Geol — Annales Universitatis Scientiarum Budapestensis de Rolando Eoetvoes Nominatae. Sectio Geologica

Ann Univ Stellenbosch Ser A — Annale. Universiteit van Stellenbosch. Serie A

Ann Univ Stellenbosch Ser B — Annale. Universiteit van Stellenbosch. Serie B

Ann Univ Turk Ser A II Biol-Geogr — Annales Universitatis Turkuensis. Series A-II. Biologica-Geographica

Ann Univ Turk Ser A-II Biol-Geogr-Geol — Annales Universitatis Turkuensis. Series A-II. Biologica-Geographica-Geologica

Ann Univ Turku Ser A — Annales Universitatis Turkuensis. Series A

Ann Univ Turku Ser A I — Annales Universitatis Turkuensis. Series A-I. Astronomica-Chemica-Physica-Mathematica

Ann Univ Turku Ser A II — Annales Universitatis Turkuensis. Series A-II. Biologica-Geographica

Ann Uniw Marii Curie Sklodowskiej Sect E Agric — Annales. Uniwersytet Marii Curie-Sklodowskiej. Sectio E. Agricultura

Annu Ordre Souverain Mil Malte — Annuaire. Ordre Souverain Militaire de Malte

AnnUP — Annales. Universite de Paris

Annu Polit Int — Annuario di Politica Internazionale

Annu Pontif Accad Sci — Annuario. Pontificia Accademia delle Scienze

Annu Priestley Lect — Annual Priestley Lectures

Annu Proc Am Assoc Zoo Vet — Annual Proceedings. American Association of Zoo Veterinarians

Annu Proc Assoc Sci & Tech Soc S Afr — Annual Proceedings. Associated Scientific and Technical Societies of South Africa

Annu Proc Gifu Coll Pharm — Annual Proceedings. Gifu College of Pharmacy

Annu Proc Phytochem Soc — Annual Proceedings. Phytochemical Society

Annu Proc Reliab Phys (Symp) — Annual Proceedings. Reliability Physics (Symposium)

Annu Prog Child Psychiatry Chil Dev — Annual Progress in Child Psychiatry and Child Development

Annu Prog Rep SEATO Med Res Lab — Annual Progress Report. SEATO [*Southeast Asia Treaty Organization*] Medical Research Laboratories

Annu Psychoanal — Annual of Psychoanalysis

Annu R Accad Ital — Annuario. Reale Accademia d'Italia

Annu Rep Agric Exp Stn (Nebr) — Annual Report. Agricultural Experiment Station (Nebraska)

Annu Rep Agric Exp Stn Univ MD — Annual Report. Agricultural Experiment Station. University of Maryland

Annu Rep Agric Res Inst North Irel — Annual Report. Agricultural Research Institute of Northern Ireland

Annu Rep Air Resour Atmos Turbul Diffus Lab — Annual Report. Air Resources Atmospheric Turbulence and Diffusion Laboratory

Annu Rep Ala Agr Exp Sta — Annual Report. Alabama Agricultural Experiment Station

Annu Rep Am Inst Phys — Annual Report. American Institute of Physics

Annu Rep Biol Works Fac Sci Osaka Univ — Annual Report of Biological Works. Faculty of Science. Osaka University

Annu Rep Board Greenkeeping Res — Annual Report. Board of Greenkeeping Research

Annu Rep Cacao Res Univ West Indies — Annual Report on Cacao Research. University of the West Indies

Annu Rep Cancer Res Inst Kanazawa Univ — Annual Report. Cancer Research Institute. Kanazawa University

Annu Rep Can Seed Growers Ass — Annual Report. Canadian Seed Growers' Association

Annu Rep Cent Reg Arecanut Res Stn — Annual Report. Central and Regional Arecanut Research Stations

Annu Rep Clemson Agr Exp Sta — Annual Report. Clemson Agricultural Experiment Station

Annu Rep CSIR — Annual Report. CSIR [*Council for Scientific and Industrial Research*]

Annu Rep CSIRO Mar Biochem Unit — Annual Report. Commonwealth Scientific and Industrial Research Organisation. Marine Biochemistry Unit

Annu Rep Dep Agric Stock Queensl — Annual Report. Department of Agriculture and Stock. Queensland

Annu Rep Dep Agr NSW — Annual Report. Department of Agriculture. New South Wales

Annu Rep Dir Dep Terr Magn Carnegie Inst — Annual Report of the Director. Department of Terrestrial Magnetism. Carnegie Institution

Annu Rep E Afr Agr Forest Res Organ — Annual Report. East African Agriculture and Forestry Research Organization

Annu Rep Eng Res Inst Fac Eng Univ Tokyo — Annual Report. Engineering Research Institute. Faculty of Engineering. University of Tokyo

Annu Rep Eng Res Inst Tokyo Univ — Annual Report. Engineering Research Institute. Tokyo University

Annu Rep Eng Res Inst Univ Tokyo — Annual Report. Engineering Research Institute. University of Tokyo

Annu Rep Entomol Soc Ont — Annual Report. Entomological Society of Ontario

Annu Rep Fac Educ Gunma Univ Art Technol Ser — Annual Report. Faculty of Education. Gunma University. Art and Technology Series

Annu Rep Fac Educ Univ Iwate — Annual Report. Faculty of Education. University of Iwate

Annu Rep Fac Pharm Sci Nagoya City Univ — Annual Report. Faculty of Pharmaceutical Sciences. Nagoya City University

Annu Rep Fac Pharm Sci Tokushima Univ — Annual Reports. Faculty of Pharmaceutical Sciences. Tokushima University

Annu Rep Farmers Union Grain Terminal Ass — Annual Report. Farmers Union Grain Terminal Association

Annu Rep Ferment Process — Annual Reports on Fermentation Processes

Annu Rep Finan Statements Inst Corn Agr Merchants — Annual Report and Financial Statements. Institute of Corn and Agricultural Merchants

Annu Rep Fla Univ Agr Exp Sta — Annual Report. Florida University. Agricultural Experiment Station

Annu Rep Geol Surv Fed Niger — Annual Report. Geological Survey. Federation of Nigeria

Annu Rep Geol Surv Mines Dep (Swaziland) — Annual Report. Geological Survey and Mines Department (Swaziland)

Annu Rep Geol Surv West Aust — Annual Report. Geological Survey. Western Australia

Annu Rep Geophys Res Norw — Annual Report on Geophysical Research in Norway

Annu Rep Governor Kans Wheat Comm — Annual Report to the Governor. Kansas Wheat Commission

Annu Rep Hokkaido Branch Gov For Exp Stn — Annual Report. Hokkaido Branch. Government Forest Experiment Station

Annu Rep Hokusei Gakuin Jr Coll — Annual Report. Hokusei Gakuin Junior College

Annu Rep Ind Agric Exp Stn — Annual Report. Indiana Agricultural Experiment Station

Annu Rep Inorg Gen Synth — Annual Reports in Inorganic and General Syntheses

Annu Rep Inst Ferment (Osaka) — Annual Report. Institute for Fermentation (Osaka)

Annu Rep Inst Food Microbiol Chiba Univ — Annual Report. Institute of Food Microbiology. Chiba University

Annu Rep Inst Nucl Stud Univ Tokyo — Annual Report. Institute for Nuclear Study. University of Tokyo

Annu Rep Inst Phys Acad Sin — Annual Report. Institute of Physics. Academia Sinica

Annu Rep Inst Popul Probl — Annual Reports. Institute of Population Problems

Annu Rep Inst Sociol — Annual Report. Institute of Sociology

Annu Rep Inst Virus Res Kyoto Univ — Annual Report. Institute for Virus Research. Kyoto University

Annu Rep Int Assoc Milk Sanit — Annual Report. International Association of Milk Sanitarians

Annu Rep Int Crop Impr Ass — Annual Report. International Crop Improvement Association

Annu Rep Jpn Assoc Tuberc — Annual Report. Japanese Association for Tuberculosis

Annu Rep Jpn Soc Tuber — Annual Report. Japanese Society for Tuberculosis

Annu Rep Kinki Univ At Energy Res Inst — Annual Reports. Kinki University Atomic Energy Research Institute

Annu Rep Kyoritsu Coll Pharm — Annual Report. Kyoritsu College of Pharmacy

Annu Rep Lab Algol (Trebon) — Annual Report. Laboratory of Algology (Trebon)

Annu Rep Lab Exp Algol Dep Appl Algol (Trebon) — Annual Report. Laboratory of Experimental Algology and Department of Applied Algology (Trebon)

Annu Rep MAFES Miss Agric For Exp St — Annual Report. MAFES. Mississippi Agricultural and Forestry Experiment Station

Annu Rep Med Chem — Annual Reports in Medicinal Chemistry

Annu Rep Mines NS Dep Mines — Annual Report on Mines. Nova Scotia Department of Mines

Annu Rep Miss State Univ Agr Exp Sta — Annual Report. Mississippi State University. Agricultural Experiment Station

Annu Rep Nat Inst Genet (Jap) — Annual Report. National Institute of Genetics (Japan)

Annu Rep Natl Inst Genet — Annual Report. National Institute of Genetics

Annu Rep Natl Inst Nutr — Annual Report. National Institute of Nutrition

Annu Rep Natl Inst Nutr (Tokyo) — Annual Report. National Institute of Nutrition (Tokyo)

Annu Rep Natl Vet Assay Lab — Annual Report. National Veterinary Assay Laboratory

Annu Rep Natur Sci Home Econ Kinjo Gakuin Coll — Annual Report of Natural Science and Home Economics. Kinjo Gakuin College

Annu Rep Nat Veg Res Stn (Wellesbourne Eng) — Annual Report. National Vegetable Research Station (Wellesbourne, England)

Annu Rep Nebr Grain Impr Ass — Annual Report. Nebraska Grain Improvement Association

Annu Rep Nebr Wheat Comm — Annual Report. Nebraska Wheat Commission

Annu Rep N Mex Agr Exp Sta — Annual Report. New Mexico Agricultural Experiment Station

Annu Rep Noto Mar Lab — Annual Report. Noto Marine Laboratory

Annu Rep NS Fruit Grow Assoc — Annual Report. Nova Scotia Fruit Growers' Association

Annu Rep NY State Assoc Dairy Milk Insp — Annual Report. New York State Association of Dairy and Milk Inspectors

Annu Rep Ont Dep Mines — Annual Report. Ontario Department of Mines

Annu Rep Oreg State Hort Soc — Annual Report. Oregon State Horticultural Society

Annu Rep Orient Hosp (Beirut) — Annual Report. Orient Hospital (Beirut)

Annu Rep Pak Cent Jute Comm — Annual Report. Pakistan Central Jute Committee

Annu Rep Philipp Sugar Assoc — Annual Report. Philippine Sugar Association

Annu Rep Prog Chem — Annual Reports on the Progress of Chemistry [England]

Annu Rep Prog Chem Sect A — Annual Reports on the Progress of Chemistry. Section A. General, Physical, and Inorganic Chemistry

Annu Rep Prog Chem Sect A Gen Phys Inorg Chem — Annual Reports on the Progress of Chemistry. Section A. General, Physical, and Inorganic Chemistry [England]

Annu Rep Prog Chem Sect B — Annual Reports on the Progress of Chemistry. Section B. Organic Chemistry

Annu Rep Prog Chem Sect C — Annual Reports on the Progress of Chemistry. Section C. Physical Chemistry [England]

Annu Rep Prog Rubber Technol — Annual Report on the Progress of Rubber Technology

Annu Rep Radiat Cent Osaka Prefect — Annual Report. Radiation Center of Osaka Prefecture

Annu Rep Res Inst Chemobiodyn Chiba Univ — Annual Report. Research Institute for Chemobiodynamics. Chiba University

Annu Rep Res Inst Environ Med Nagoya Univ — Annual Report. Research Institute of Environmental Medicine. Nagoya University

Annu Rep Res Inst Environ Med Nagoya Univ (Engl Ed) — Annual Report. Research Institute of Environmental Medicine. Nagoya University (English Edition)

Annu Rep Res Inst Tuberc Kanazawa Univ — Annual Report. Research Institute of Tuberculosis. Kanazawa University [Japan]

Annu Rep Res React Inst Kyoto Univ — Annual Reports. Research Reactor Institute. Kyoto University

Annu Rep Res Reactor Inst Kyoto Univ — Annual Reports. Research Reactor Institute. Kyoto University

Annu Rep Res Tech Work Dep Agric North Irel — Annual Report on Research and Technical Work. Department of Agriculture for Northern Ireland

Annu Rep Sado Mar Biol Stn Niigata Univ — Annual Report. Sado Marine Biological Station. Niigata University

Annu Rep Sankyo Res Lab — Annual Report. Sankyo Research Laboratories

Annu Rep Sci Works Fac Sci Osaka Univ — Annual Report of Scientific Works. Faculty of Science. Osaka University [Japan]

Annu Rep Secr State Hortic Soc Mich — Annual Report. Secretary of the State Horticultural Society of Michigan

Annu Rep Shionogi Res Lab — Annual Report. Shionogi Research Laboratory

Annu Rep Shizuoka Public Health Lab — Annual Report. Shizuoka Public Health Laboratory [Japan]

Annu Rep Smiths Inst — Annual Report. Smithsonian Institution

Annu Rep Soc Libyan Stud — Annual Report. Society for Libyan Studies

Annu Rep Soc Plant Prot N Jap — Annual Report. Society of Plant Protection of North Japan

Annu Rep Stud Doshisha Women's Coll Lib Arts — Annual Report of Studies. Doshisha Women's College of Liberal Arts

Annu Rep Takeda Res Lab — Annual Report. Takeda Research Laboratories

Annu Rep Tanabe Seiyaku Co Ltd — Annual Report. Tanabe Seiyaku Company Limited [Japan]

Annu Rep Tob Inst PR — Annual Report. Tobacco Institute of Puerto Rico

Annu Rep Tob Res Inst — Annual Report. Tobacco Research Institute

Annu Rep Tohoku Coll Pharm — Annual Report. Tohoku College of Pharmacy

Annu Rep Tokyo Coll Pharm — Annual Report. Tokyo College of Pharmacy

Annu Rep Tokyo Metrop Labs Med Sci — Annual Report. Tokyo Metropolitan Laboratories for Medical Sciences

Annu Rep Tokyo Metrop Res Inst Environ Prot — Annual Report. Tokyo Metropolitan Research Institute for Environmental Protection

Annu Rep Tokyo Metrop Res Inst Environ Prot Engl Transl — Annual Report. Tokyo Metropolitan Research Institute for Environmental Protection. English Translation

Annu Rep Tokyo Univ Agric Technol — Annual Report. Tokyo University of Agriculture and Technology

Annu Rep Torry Res Stn (Aberdeen UK) — Annual Report. Torry Research Station (Aberdeen, UK)

Annu Rep United Dent Hosp Sydney Inst Dent Res — Annual Report. United Dental Hospital of Sydney. Institute of Dental Research

Annu Rep Univ GA Coll Agr Exp Sta — Annual Report. University of Georgia. College of Agriculture. Experiment Stations

Annu Rep Veg Growers Ass Amer — Annual Report. Vegetable Growers Association of America

Annu Rep Veg Growers Assoc Am — Annual Report. Vegetable Growers Association of America

Annu Rev Anthropol — Annual Review of Anthropology
Annu Rev Astron Astrophys — Annual Review of Astronomy and Astrophysics
Annu Rev Autom Program — Annual Review in Automatic Programming
Annu Rev Behav Ther Theory Pract — Annual Review of Behavior Therapy Theory and Practice
Annu Rev Biochem — Annual Review of Biochemistry
Annu Rev Biochem Allied Res India — Annual Review of Biochemical and Allied Research in India
Annu Rev Biophys Bioeng — Annual Review of Biophysics and Bioengineering
Annu Rev Earth Planet Sci — Annual Review of Earth and Planetary Sciences
Annu Rev Ecol Syst — Annual Review of Ecology and Systematics
Annu Rev Energy — Annual Review of Energy
Annu Rev Entomol — Annual Review of Entomology
Annu Rev Fluid Mech — Annual Review of Fluid Mechanics
Annu Rev Food Technol — Annual Review of Food Technology
Annu Rev Food Technol (Mysore) — Annual Review of Food Technology (Mysore)
Annu Rev Genet — Annual Review of Genetics
Annu Rev Ind Eng Chem — Annual Reviews of Industrial and Engineering Chemistry
Annu Rev Inf Sci Technol — Annual Review of Information Science and Technology [*Encyclopedia Britannica*]
Annu Rev Inst Plasma Phys Nagoya Univ — Annual Review. Institute of Plasma Physics. Nagoya University
Annu Rev Mater Sci — Annual Review of Materials Science
Annu Rev Med — Annual Review of Medicine
Annu Rev Microbiol — Annual Review of Microbiology
Annu Rev Neurosci — Annual Review of Neuroscience
Annu Rev Nucl Sci — Annual Review of Nuclear Science [*Later, Annual Review of Nuclear and Particle Science*]
Annu Rev Nurs Res — Annual Review of Nursing Research
Annu Rev Pharmacol — Annual Review of Pharmacology [*Later, Annual Review of Pharmacology and Toxicology*]
Annu Rev Pharmacol Toxicol — Annual Review of Pharmacology and Toxicology
Annu Rev Photochem — Annual Review of Photochemistry
Annu Rev Phys Chem — Annual Review of Physical Chemistry
Annu Rev Physiol — Annual Review of Physiology
Annu Rev Phytopathol — Annual Review of Phytopathology
Annu Rev Plant Physiol — Annual Review of Plant Physiology
Annu Rev Psychol — Annual Review of Psychology
Annu Rev Schizophr Syndr — Annual Review of the Schizophrenic Syndrome
Ann Urol — Annales d'Urologie
Annu Roum Anthropol — Annuaire Roumain d'Anthropologie
AnnUS — Annales Universitatis Saraviensis. Philosophie- Lettres
Annu Simul Symp (Rec Proc) — Annual Simulation Symposium (Record of Proceedings)
Annu Sta Chim-Agr Sper Torino — Annuario. Stazione Chimico-Agraria Sperimentale di Torino
Annu Suisse Sci Polit — Annuaire Suisse de Science Politique
Annu Surv of Afr L — Annual Survey of African Law
Annu Surv of Indian L — Annual Survey of Indian Law
Annu Symp Biomath Comput Sci Life Sci Abstr — Annual Symposium on Biomathematics and Computer Science in the Life Sciences. Abstracts
Annu Symp Found Comput Sci (Proc) — Annual Symposium on Foundations of Computer Science (Proceedings)
Annu Tech Conf Am Electroplat Soc — Annual Technical Conference. American Electroplaters' Society
Annu Tech Conf Trans Am Soc Qual Control — Annual Technical Conference Transactions. American Society for Quality Control
Annu Tiers-Monde — Annuaire du Tiers-Monde
Annu UMR-DNR Conf Energy Proc — Annual UMR-DNR [*University of Missouri, Rolla - Department of Natural Resources*] Conference on Energy. Proceedings
Annu Univ Sofia Fac Biol — Annuaire. Universite de Sofia. Faculte de Biologie
Annu Univ Sofia Fac Phys — Annuaire. Universite de Sofia. Faculte de Physique
Annu URSS — Annuaire. URSS et des Pays Socialistes Europeens
Annu Visit Lect Ser Coll Pharm Univ Tex — Annual Visiting Lecture Series. College of Pharmacy. University of Texas
Ann Vet Res — Annals of Veterinary Research
Ann Villaggio Sanat Sondalo — Annali. Villaggio Sanatoriale di Sondalo
Ann Warsaw Agric Univ SGGW-AR Anim Sci — Annals. Warsaw Agricultural University. SGGW-AR [*Szkola Glowna Gospodarstwa Wiejskiego - Akademia Rolnicza*]. Animal Science
Ann Wyo — Annals of Wyoming
Anny — Advertising News of New York [*Later, Adweek*]
Ann Zool — Annals of Zoology
Ann Zool (Agra) — Annals of Zoology (Agra)
Ann Zool Ecol Anim — Annales de Zoologie - Ecologie Animale
Ann Zool Fenn — Annales Zoologici Fennici
Ann Zool Soc Zool-Bot Fenn "Vanamo" — Annales Zoologici. Societatis Zoologicae-Botanicae Fennicae "Vanamo"
Ann Zool (Warsaw) — Annales Zoologici (Warsaw)
Ann Zootech — Annales de Zootechnie

Ann Zootech Inst Nat Rech Agron — Annales de Zootechnie. Institut National de la Recherche Agronomique
Ann Zymol — Annales de Zymologie
ANO — Air Navigation Order
An Obs Astr Met — Analele Observatorului Astronomic si Meteorologic
An Obs Buc — Anuarul. Observatorului din Bucuresti
An OCD — Analecta Ordinis Carmelitarum Discalceatorum
An O Cist — Analecta Sacri Ordinis Cisterciensis
Anodic Behav Met Semicond Ser — Anodic Behavior of Metals and Semiconductors Series
ANOH — Aarboeger foer Nordisk Oldkyndighed og Historie
ANOMA — Alluminio e Nuova Metallurgia
AnOr — Analecta Orientalia. Commentationes Scientificae de Rebus Orientis Antiqui. Pontificium Institutum Biblicum [*Rome*]
ANORA — Angle Orthodontist
An ORL Ibero-Amer — Anales Otorrinolaryngologicos Ibero-Americanos
A Norm — Annales de Normandie
A Normandie — Annales de Normandie; Revue Trimestrielle d'Etudes Regionales
An Or Res — Annals of Oriental Research
An Otorrinolaringol Iber-Am — Anales Otorrinolaringologicos Ibero-Americanos
Anot Pediatr — Anotaciones Pediatricas [*Colombia*]
An Oviedo Univ Fac Vet (Leon) — Anales. Oviedo Universidad. Facultad de Veterinaria (Leon)
AnP — Annee Propedeutique
An Paleont — Annales de Paleontologie
ANPA/RI Bull — ANPA/RI [*American Newspaper Publishers Association. Research Institute*] Bulletin
An Parques Nac (B Aires) — Anales de Parques Nacionales (Buenos Aires)
ANPA Stat — American Newspaper Publishers Association. Newsprint Statistics
An Paul Med Cir — Anais Paulistas de Medicina e Cirurgia
ANPBA — Acta Neurologica et Psychiatrica Belgica
AnPC — Annales de la Philosophie Chretienne
ANPEDD — Annual Research Reviews. Angina Pectoris
An Pediat — Anales de Pediatria
AnPh — L'Annee Philologique [*Paris*]
ANPHA — Annales de Physique
An Phil Chin Hist Asso — Annals. Philippine Chinese Historical Association
ANPHI Pap — ANPHI [*Academy of Nursing of the Philippines*] Papers
An Physik — Annalen der Physik und Chemie
ANPIA — Arquivos de Neuro-Psiquiatria
ANPQA — Annee Psychologique
AnPraem — Analecta Praemonstratensia
An Programa Acad Med Univ Nac Mayor San Marcos (Lima) — Anales. Programa Academico de Medicina. Universidad Nacional Mayor de San Marcos (Lima)
ANPSAI — Archives of Neurology and Psychiatry
AN & Q — American Notes and Queries
ANQ — American Notes and Queries
ANQ — Andover Newton Quarterly
ANQU-A — Anthropological Quarterly
An Quim — Anales de Quimica
An Quim A-Fis Tec — Anales de Quimica. Serie A. Quimica Fisica y Quimica Tecnica
An Quim B Inorg Anal — Anales de Quimica. Serie B. Quimica Inorganica y Quimica Analitica
An Quim C Org Bioquim — Anales de Quimica. Serie C. Quimica Organica y Bioquimica
An Quim Farm — Anales de Quimica y Farmacia
An Quimica — Anales de Quimica
An R Acad Farm — Anales. Real Academia de Farmacia
An R Acad Med Cir Valladolid — Anales. Real Academia de Medicina y Cirugia de Valladolid
An R Acad Nacl Med (Madr) — Anales. Real Academia Nacional de Medicina (Madrid)
An R Acad Nac Med (Madr) — Anales. Real Academia Nacional de Medicina (Madrid)
ANRCEI — Annual Review of Chronopharmacology
ANREA — Anatomical Record
An Reuniao Fitossanit Brasil — Anais. Reuniao de Fitossanitarisatas do Brasil
ANRGGSIC — Alaska. Department of Natural Resources. Division of Geological and Geophysical Surveys. Information Circular
Anritsu Tech Bull — Anritsu Technical Bulletin
ANRM — Alaska. Department of Natural Resources. Mines Geology
An Rom Sov — Analele Romino-Sovietice
An R Soc Esp Fis Quim — Anales. Real Sociedad Espanola de Fisica y Quimica
An R Soc Esp Fis Quim Ser A — Anales. Real Sociedad Espanola de Fisica y Quimica. Serie A. Fisica [*Spain*]
An R Soc Esp Fis Quim Ser B Quim — Anales. Real Sociedad Espanola de Fisica y Quimica. Serie B. Quimica
ANRTB — ANSI [*American National Standards Institute*] Reporter
ANRVA — Argonne National Laboratory. Reviews [*United States*]
ANS — Advances in Nursing Science

ANS — Archiv fuer das Studium der Neueren Sprachen
ANSA — Automatic New Structure Alert
ANS Adv Nurs Sci — ANS. Advances in Nursing Science
AnSATarrac — Analecta Sacra Tarraconensia [*Barcelona*]
An Sc (Cleveland) — Annals of Science (Cleveland)
An Sc Geol — Annales des Sciences Geologiques
An Sc Nat Zool — Annales des Sciences Naturelles. Zoologie
ANSDB — ANSI [*American National Standards Institute*] Standards Action
ANSDL — Australisch-Neuseelaendische Studien zur Deutschen Sprache und Literatur
ANSDSL — Australisch-Neuseelaendische Studien zur Deutschen Sprache und Literatur
An Sect Pedol Inst Cent Cercet Agric — Analele. Sectiei de Pedologie. Institutul Central de Cercetari Agricole
An Sect Prot Plant Inst Cent Cercet Agric (Bucharest) — Analele. Sectiei de Protectia Plantelor. Institutul Central de Cercetari Agricole (Bucharest)
An Seminar Brasil Herbic Ervas Danin — Anais. Seminario Brasileiro de Herbicidas e Ervas Daninhas
An Ser Prod Anim Inst Nac Invest Agrar — Anales. Serie Produccion Animal. Instituto Nacional de Investigaciones Agrarias
An Serv Geol Nac Salvador Bol — Anales. Servico Geologico Nacional de El Salvador. Boletin
ANSI Reptr — ANSI [*American National Standards Institute*] Reporter
ANSI Stand — ANSI [*American National Standards Institute*] Standards
ANSI Std Action — ANSI [*American National Standards Institute*] Standards Action
ANSLA — Acta Neurologica Scandinavica. Supplementum
ANSMN — American Numismatic Society. Museum Notes
ANSMusN — American Numismatic Society. Museum Notes
ANSN — American Numismatic Society. Museum Notes
ANSNNM — American Numismatic Society. Numismatic Notes and Monographs
ANSNS — American Numismatic Society. Numismatic Studies
AnSoc — Ancient Society [*Leuven*]
An Soc Biol Bogota — Anales. Sociedad de Biologia de Bogota
An Soc Biol Pernambuco — Anais. Sociedade de Biologia de Pernambuco
An Soc Bot Bras — Anais. Sociedade Botanica do Brasil
An Soc Cient Argent — Anales. Sociedad Cientifica Argentina
An Soc Cient Argent Sec S Fe — Anales. Sociedad Cientifica Argentina. Seccion Sante Fe
An Soc Entomol Bras — Anais. Sociedade Entomologica do Brasil
An Soc Esp Fis Quim — Anales. Sociedad Espanola de Fisica y Quimica [*Spain*]
An Soc Esp Hidrol Med — Anales. Sociedad Espanola de Hidrologia Medica
An Soc Geogr Hist — Anales. Sociedad de Geografia e Historia
An Soc Geogr Hist Guatem — Anales. Sociedad de Geografia e Historia de Guatemala
An Soc Med Pern — Anais. Sociedade de Medicina de Pernambuco
An Soc Med Pernambuco — Anais. Sociedade de Medicina de Pernambuco
An Soc Med-Quir Guayas — Anales. Sociedad Medico-Quirurgica del Guayas
An Soc Mex Oftalmol — Anales. Sociedad Mexicana de Oftalmologia
An Soc Mex Otorinolaringol — Anales. Sociedad Mexicana de Otorrinolaringologia
An Soc Mex Otorrinolaringol Broncoesofagol — Anales. Sociedad Mexicana de Otorrinolaringologia y Broncoesofagologia
An Soc Quim Argent — Anales. Sociedad Quimica Argentina
An Soc R Sci Med Nat Bruxelles — Annales. Societe Royale des Sciences Medicales et Naturelles de Bruxelles
An Soc Rural Argent — Anales. Sociedad Rural Argentina
An Soc Rur Argent — Anales. Sociedad Rural Argentina
An Soc Vet Zootec — Anales. Sociedad Veterinaria de Zootecnia
ANSSSR — Akademija Nauk SSSR
AnST — Analecta Sacra Tarraconensia
AnSt — Anatolian Studies. Journal of the British Institute of Archaeology at Ankara [*London*]
AnSTar — Analecta Sacra Tarraconensia [*Barcelona*]
An Staz Sper Agr M — Annali. Stazione Sperimentale Agrario di Modena
An St Casa Santos — Anais. Santa Casa de Santos
AnStEbr — Annuario di Studi Ebraici. Collegio Rabbinico Italiano [*Rome*]
An Stiint Univ Al I Cuza Iasi Sect 1 — Analele Stiintifice. Universitatii Al. I. Cuza din Iasi. Sectiunea 1. Matematica, Fizica, Chimie [*Romania*]
An Stiint Univ Al I Cuza Iasi Sect 2 — Analele Stiintifice. Universitatii Al. I. Cuza din Iasi. Sectiunea 2. Stiinte Naturale
An Stiint Univ Al I Cuza Iasi Sect 1a — Analele Stiintifice. Universitatii Al. I. Cuza din Iasi. Sectiunea 1a. Matematica [*Romania*]
An Stiint Univ Al I Cuza Iasi Sect 2a — Analele Stiintifice. Universitatii Al. I. Cuza din Iasi. Sectiunea 2a. Biologie [*Romania*]
An Stiint Univ Al I Cuza Iasi Sect 2a Biol — Analele Stiintifice. Universitatii Al. I. Cuza din Iasi. Sectiunea 2a. Biologie
An Stiint Univ Al I Cuza Iasi Sect 1b — Analele Stiintifice. Universitatii Al. I. Cuza din Iasi. Sectiunea 1b. Fizica [*Romania*]
An Stiint Univ Al I Cuza Iasi Sect 2b — Analele Stiintifice. Universitatii Al. I. Cuza din Iasi. Sectiunea 2b. Geologie
An Stiint Univ Al I Cuza Iasi Sect 2 Biol Geol Geogr — Analele Stiintifice. Universitatii Al. I. Cuza din Iasi. Sectiunea 2. Biologie, Geologie, Geografie

An Stiint Univ Al I Cuza Iasi Sect 1c — Analele Stiintifice. Universitatii Al. I. Cuza din Iasi. Sectiunea 1c. Chimie [*Romania*]
An Stiint Univ Al I Cuza Iasi Stiinte Nat Biol — Analele Stiintifice. Universitatii Al. I. Cuza din Iasi. Stiinte Naturale. Biologia [*Romania*]
An Sti Univ Al I Cuza Iasi Sect 1 Mat — Analele Stiintifice. Universitatii Al. I. Cuza din Iasi. Serie Noua. Sectiunea 1. Matematica
AnStud — Anatolian Studies. Journal of the British Institute of Archaeology at Ankara [*London*]
An Sumar (Zagreb) — Anali za Sumarstvo (Zagreb)
AnSur — Antiquity and Survival [*The Hague*]
ANT — Altalanos Nyelveszeti Tanulmanyok
ANT — Anglo-Norman Texts
Ant — Antaios
Ant — Antichthon. Journal of the Australian Society for Classical Studies
Ant — Antike
ANT — Antilliaanse Nieuwsbrief. Tweewekelijkse Uitgave van het Kabinet van de Gevolmachtigde Minister van de Nederlandse Antillen
Ant — Antiquary
Ant — Antiquity [*Gloucester*]
ANTA — Antarctic
Ant Afr — Antiquites Africaines
ANTAR — Antarctic Record [*Japan*]
Antarctic J — Antarctic Journal of the United States
Antarct J US — Antarctic Journal of the United States
Antarct Rec — Antarctic Record
Antarct Rec (Tokyo) — Antarctic Record (Tokyo)
Antarct Res Ser — Antarctic Research Series
Antar Jour US — Antarctic Journal of the United States
Antarktika Doklady Kom — Antarktika Doklady Komissii
AntAS — Antike, Alte Sprachen und Deutsche Bildung
Ant Bk — Antiquarian Bookman
AntC — Antiquite Classique
Ant Cl — Antiquite Classique
Ant Coll — Australasian Antique Collector
Ant Denk — Antike Denkmaeler
Antennas Propag Soc Int Symp — Antennas and Propagation Society. International Symposium
Ant F — Anthropological Forum
ANTF — Arbeiten zur NT Textforschung
ANTH — Anthropologica
AnThijm — Annalen van het Thijmgenootschap [*Utrecht*]
AnthL — Anthropological Linguistics
Anthol Med Santoriana — Anthologica Medica Santoriana
AnthQ — Anthropological Quarterly
Anth Quart — Anthropological Quarterly
Anthr — Anthropos
Anthr J Can — Anthropological Journal of Canada
Anthr Kozl — Anthropologiai Koezlemenyek
Anthr Ling — Anthropological Linguistics
Anthro Anz — Anthropologischer Anzeiger
Anthro Forum — Anthropological Forum
Anthro I — Anthropological Index
Anthro Ling — Anthropological Linguistics
Anthrop Gesell Wien Mitt — Anthropologische Gesellschaft in Wien. Mitteilungen
Anthrop J — Anthropological Institute. Journal
Anthropol Anz — Anthropologischer Anzeiger
Anthropol Forum — Anthropological Forum
Anthropol Koezlem — Anthropologiai Koezlemenyek
Anthropol Kozl — Anthropologiai Koezlemenyek
Anthropol Ling — Anthropological Linguistics
Anthropol Pap Am Mus Nat Hist — Anthropological Papers. American Museum of Natural History
Anthropol Pap Mus Anthropol Univ Mich — Anthropological Papers. Museum of Anthropology. University of Michigan
Anthropol Quart — Anthropological Quarterly
Anthropol Rec Univ Calif — Anthropological Records. University of California
Anthrop Q — Anthropological Quarterly
Anthrop R — Anthropological Review
Anthr Pap — Anthropological Papers. American Museum of Natural History
Anthrplgica — Anthropologica
Anthr P Mic — Anthropological Papers. Museum of Anthropology. University of Michigan
Anthr Q — Anthropological Quarterly
Anthr Rep Pap — Anthropological Report of Papua
Anthr-UCLA — Anthropology-UCLA
AntHung — Antiquitas Hungarica
ANTIB — Antincendio
Antibio Med Clin Ther — Antibiotic Medicine and Clinical Therapy
Antibiot — Antibiotiki
Antibiot Annu — Antibiotics Annual
Antibiot Chemother — Antibiotica et Chemotherapia
Antibiot and Chemother — Antibiotics and Chemotherapy
Antibiot Chemother (Basel) — Antibiotics and Chemotherapy (Basel)
Antibiot Chemother (Wash DC) — Antibiotics and Chemotherapy (Washington, DC)

Antibiot Med — Antibiotic Medicine
Antibiot Med Clin Ther (London) — Antibiotic Medicine and Clinical Therapy (London)
Antibiot Monogr — Antibiotics Monographs
Antibiot Resp Mezhved Sb — Antibiotiki Respublikanskii Mezhvedomstvennyi Sbornik
Anti-Corros — Anti-Corrosion Methods and Materials
Anti-Corros Methods Mater — Anti-Corrosion Methods and Materials
Antigon Rev — Antigonish Review
AntigR — Antigonish Review
Antike Aben — Antike und Abendland
Anti-Locust Bull — Anti-Locust Bulletin
Anti-Locust Mem — Anti-Locust Memoir
Anti-Locust Res Cent Rep — Anti-Locust Research Centre [*Later, Centre for Overseas Pest Research*] Report
Antim Ag Ch — Antimicrobial Agents and Chemotherapy
Antimicrob Agents Annu — Antimicrobial Agents Annual
Antimicrob Agents Chemother — Antimicrobial Agents and Chemotherapy
Antimicrob Newsl — Antimicrobic Newsletter
Anti Nk — Anti Nuclear
Antioch R — Antioch Review
Antioch Rev — Antioch Review
Antioquia Med — Antioquia Medica
Antiq — Antiques
Antiq — Antiquity
Antiq Afr — Antiquites Africaines
Antiq Bkman — Antiquarian Bookman
Antiq Class — Antiquite Classique
Antiq Gesell in Zuerich Mitt — Antiquarische Gesellschaft in Zuerich. Mitteilungen
Antiq Horol — Antiquarian Horology
Antiq J — Antiquaries Journal
Antiq Jnl — Antiquaries Journal
Antiq (n s) — Antiquary (New Series)
Antiq Sunderland — Antiquities of Sunderland
Antiquar J — Antiquaries Journal
Antiquary — Antiquary, Jewitt's
Antique Eng — Antique Engines
Antiques J — Antiques Journal
Antitrust B — Antitrust Bulletin
Antitrust Bull — Antitrust Bulletin
Antitrust L & Econ Rev — Antitrust Law and Economics Review
Antitrust LJ — Antitrust Law Journal
Antitrust L Sym — Antitrust Law Symposium
Antitrust & Trade Reg Rep — Antitrust and Trade Regulation Report [*Bureau of National Affairs*]
AntJ — Antiquaries Journal
AntK — Antike Kunst
Anton — Antonianum
Antonie Van Leewenhoek J Microbiol Serol — Antonie Van Leeuwenhoek Journal of Microbiology and Serology
AntP — Antike Plastik
ANTR — Antarctic Record [*New Zealand*]
Ant R — Antioch Review
An Trav Pub Belgique — Annales des Travaux Publics de Belgique
ANTRD — Anticancer Research
Antrol — Anthropological Index
Antropol Arch — Antropologicky Archiv
Antropologi — Antropologica
ANTRS — Antarctic Research Series
AntSurv — Antiquity and Survival [*The Hague*]
ANTsW — Algemeen Nederlands Tijdschrift voor Wijsbegeerte en Psychologie
ANTW — Algemeen Nederlands Tijdschrift voor Wijsbegeerte
Antw — Antwerpiensia
AntWelt — Antike Welt. Kuesschacht-Zuerich
AnU — Anales de la Universidad
AnuarioF — Anuario de Filologia
Anu Bago Invest Cient — Anuario Bago de Investigaciones Cientificas
AnUBLG — Analele. Universitatii Bucuresti. Limbi Germanice
AnUBLUC — Analele. Universitatii Bucuresti. Literatura Universala Comparata
Anu Bras Econ Florestal — Anuario Brasileiro de Economia Florestal
Anu Bras Econ Flor Inst Nac Pinho — Anuario Brasileiro de Economia Florestal. Instituto Nacional de Pinho
Anu Bras Odontol — Anuario Brasileiro de Odontologia
Anu Com Stat Geol Repub Soc Rom — Anuarul. Comitetului de Stat al Geologiei. Republica Socialista Romania
Anu Der Univ Panama — Anuario de Derecho. Universidad de Panama
Anu Ecuator Der Int — Anuario Ecuatoriano de Derecho Internacional
Anu Estad Min Mex — Anuario Estadistico de la Mineria Mexicana
Anu Estud Atl — Anuario de Estudios Atlanticos
Anu Fac Der — Anuario. Facultad de Derecho
Anu de Filos del Derecho — Anuario de Filosofia del Derecho
Anu Filosof — Anuario Filosofico
AnUG — Annales. Universite de Grenoble
Anu Hist J — Annual History Journal

ANU Hist J — ANU [*Australian National University*] Historical Journal
ANUHJ — Australian National University. Historical Journal
AnUILingv — Analele Stiintifice. Universitatii Al. I. Cuza din Iasi. Serie Noua. Sectiunea 3e (Stiinte Sociale). Lingvistica
AnUILit — Analele Stiintifice. Universitatii Al. I. Cuza din Iasi. Serie Noua. Sectiunea 3f. Literatura
Anu Indig — Anuario Indigenista
Anu Inst Cienc Pen Criminol — Anuario. Instituto de Ciencias Penales y Criminologicas
Anu Inst Geol (Rom) — Anuarul. Institutului Geologic (Romania)
Anu Inst Istor Arheologie — Anuarul. Institutului de Istorie si Arheologie
Anu Inst Patol Ig Anim — Anuarul. Institutului de Patologie si Igiena Animala
Anu Inst Patol Ig Anim Bucur — Anuarul. Institutului de Patologie si Igiena Animala Bucuresti
AnUL — Annales. Universite de Lyon
ANum — Acta Numismatica
Anu Miner Bras — Anuario Mineral Brasileiro [*Brazil*]
Anu Miner Brasil — Anuario Mineral Brasileiro
Anu Mus — Anuario Musical
ANU News — Australian National University. News
An Univ Bucur Biol Anim — Analele. Universitatii Bucuresti. Biologie Animala
An Univ Bucur Biol Veg — Analele. Universitatii Bucuresti. Biologie Vegetala
An Univ Bucur Chim — Analele. Universitatii Bucuresti. Chimie
An Univ Bucuresti Fiz — Analele. Universitatii Bucuresti. Fizica
An Univ Bucuresti Geol — Analele. Universitatii Bucuresti. Geologie
An Univ Bucuresti Mat — Analele. Universitatii Bucuresti. Matematica
An Univ Bucuresti Mat Mec — Analele. Universitatii Bucuresti. Matematica-Mecanica
An Univ Bucuresti Ser Stiint Nat Fiz — Analele. Universitatii Bucuresti. Seria Stiintele Naturii. Fizica [*Romania*]
An Univ Bucuresti Sti Natur — Analele. Universitatii Bucuresti. Stiintele Naturii
An Univ Bucur Fiz — Analele. Universitatii Bucuresti. Fizica
An Univ Bucur Geol — Analele. Universitatii Bucuresti. Geologie
An Univ Bucur Mat Mec — Analele. Universitatii Bucuresti. Matematica-Mecanica
An Univ Bucur Ser Stiint Nat Chim — Analele. Universitatii Bucuresti. Seria Stiintele Naturii. Chimie
An Univ Bucur Stiint Nat — Analele. Universitatii Bucuresti. Stiintele Naturii
An Univ Catol Valparaiso — Anales. Universidad Catolica de Valparaiso
An Univ Cent Ecuador — Anales. Universidad Central del Ecuador
An Univ Chile — Anales. Universidad de Chile
An Univ C I Parhon Ser Stiint Nat — Analele. Universitatii C. I. Parhoun. Seria Stiintele Naturii
An Univ Craiova Biol Stiinte Agric Ser A III-A — Analele. Universitatii din Craiova. Biologie Stiinte. Agricole. Seria A III-A
An Univ Craiova Mat Fiz-Chim — Analele. Universitatii din Craiova. Matematica. Fizica-Chimie
An Univ Cuenca — Anales. Universidad de Cuenca
An Univ Hispalense — Anales. Universidad Hispalense
An Univ Hispalense Ser Cienc — Anales. Universidad Hispalense. Serie de Ciencias
An Univ Hisp Ser Vet — Anales. Universidad Hispalense. Serie Veterinaria
An Univ Murcia — Anales. Universidad de Murcia
An Univ Murcia Cienc — Anales. Universidad de Murcia. Ciencias
An Univ Norte (Chile) — Anales. Universidad del Norte (Chile)
An Univ Patagonia San Juan Bosco Cienc Geol — Anales. Universidad de la Patagonia San Juan Bosco. Ciencias Geologicas
An Univ St Domingo — Anales. Universidad de Santo Domingo
An Univ Timisoara Ser Sti Fiz-Chim — Analele. Universitatii din Timisoara. Seria Stiinte Fizice-Chimice
An Univ Timisoara Ser Stiinte Fiz Chim — Analele. Universitatii din Timisoara. Seria Stiinte Fizice-Chimice
An Univ Timisoara Ser Stiinte Mat-Fiz — Analele. Universitatii din Timisoara. Seria Stiinte Matematice-Fizice [*Romania*]
An Univ Timisoara Ser Stiint Mat — Analele. Universitatii din Timisoara. Seria Stiinte Matematice
An Univ Timisoara Ser Sti Mat — Analele. Universitatii din Timisoara. Seria Stiinte Matematice
An Univ Timisoara Stiinte Fiz Chim — Analele. Universitatii din Timisoara. Seria Stiinte Fizice-Chimice
ANUOA — Actualites Neurophysiologiques
ANUPB — Advances in Nuclear Physics
ANUSDC — Annual Review of Nuclear and Particle Science
Anu Soc Broteriana — Anuario. Sociedade Broteriana
An U S S — Andrews University. Seminary Studies
ANUSSM — Australian National University. Social Science Monograph
ANUTA — Advances in Nuclear Science and Technology
Anu Tec Inst Pesqui Zootec "Francisco Osorio" — Anuario Tecnico. Instituto de Pesquisas Zootecnicas "Francisco Osorio"
AnUTFil — Analele. Universitatii din Timisoara. Seria Stiinte Filologice
ANV — Australian and New Zealand Environmental Report
ANVA — Avhandlinger Utgitt av Norsk Videnskaps-Akademi I Oslo
ANVAO — Avhandlinger Utgitt av Norsk Videnskaps-Akademi I Oslo. II
An WR — Andhra Weekly Reporter [*India*]
ANX — Annalen der Gemeinwirtschaft

ANYAA — Annals. New York Academy of Sciences
ANZAAS Congress — Australian and New Zealand Association for the Advancement of Science. Congress
ANZAAS Papers — Australian and New Zealand Association for the Advancement of Science. Papers
Anz Akad Wiss Wien Math Naturwiss Kl — Anzeiger. Akademie der Wissenschaften in Wien. Mathematisch-Naturwissenschaftliche Klasse
Anz Alt — Anzeiger fuer die Altertumswissenschaft
Anz Altertumsw — Anzeiger fuer die Altertumswissenschaft
Anz Altertumswiss — Anzeiger fuer die Altertumswissenschaft
AnzAltW — Anzeiger fuer die Altertumswissenschaft [*Innsbruck*]
ANZATVH Newsl — ANZATVH [*Australian and New Zealand Association of Teachers of the Visually Handicapped*] Newsletter
AnzAW — Anzeiger fuer die Altertumswissenschaft [*Innsbruck*]
ANZ Bank — Australia and New Zealand Bank. Quarterly Survey
ANZ Bank — Australian and New Zealand Banking Group. Quarterly Survey
ANZ Bank Q — ANZ [*Australia and New Zealand*] Bank. Quarterly
A & NZ Bank Quarterly Surv — Australia and New Zealand Bank. Quarterly Survey
ANZ Conv R — Australian and New Zealand Conveyancing Report
Anz f D Altert — Anzeiger fuer Deutsches Altertum
Anz Ger Nazionalmus — Anzeiger. Germanisches Nationalmuseum
ANZHESJ — ANZHES [*Australian and New Zealand History of Education Society*] Journal
ANZ Ind — Australia and New Zealand Bank. Business Indicators
ANZ Ind — Australian and New Zealand Banking Group. Business Indicators
ANZ Insp Sch J — Australian and New Zealand Association of Inspectors of Schools. Journal
ANZ Insurance Cases — Australian and New Zealand Insurance Cases
ANZJC — Australian and New Zealand Journal of Criminology
ANZJ Crim — Australian and New Zealand Journal of Criminology
ANZJOS — Australian and New Zealand Journal of Sociology
Anz Maschinenwes — Anzeiger fuer Maschinenwesen
Anz Oesterr Akad Wiss Math Naturwiss Kl — Anzeiger. Oesterreichische Akademie der Wissenschaften [*Wien*]. Mathematisch-Naturwissenschaftliche Klasse
Anz Orn Ges Bayern — Anzeiger. Ornithologische Gesellschaft in Bayern
Anz Ornithol Ges Bayern — Anzeiger. Ornithologische Gesellschaft in Bayern
Anz Osterr Akad Wiss Math-Naturwiss Kl — Anzeiger. Oesterreichische Akademie der Wissenschaften. Mathematisch-Naturwissenschaftliche Klasse
ANZQ — ANZ [*Australia and New Zealand*] Bank. Quarterly Survey
ANZQ Survey — ANZ [*Australia and New Zealand*] Bank. Quarterly Survey
ANZ Quart Surv — ANZ [*Australia and New Zealand*] Bank. Quarterly Survey
Anz Schaedlingskd — Anzeiger fuer Schaedlingskunde
Anz Schaedlingskd Pflanz — Anzeiger fuer Schaedlingskunde, Pflanzenschutz, Umweltschutz
Anz Schaedlingskd Pflanzenschutz — Anzeiger fuer Schaedlingskunde und Pflanzenschutz [*Later, Anzeiger fuer Schaedlingskunde, Pflanzenschutz, Umweltschutz*]
Anz Schaedlingskd Pflanzenschutz Umweltschutz — Anzeiger fuer Schaedlingskunde, Pflanzenschutz, Umweltschutz
Anz Schaedlingskd Pflanzen- und Umweltschutz — Anzeiger fuer Schaedlingskunde, Pflanzenschutz, Umweltschutz
Anz Schaedlingskd Pflanz- Umweltschutz — Anzeiger fuer Schaedlingskunde, Pflanzen- und Umweltschutz [*Later, Anzeiger fuer Schaedlingskunde, Pflanzenschutz, Umweltschutz*] [*West Germany*]
Anz Schweiz — Anzeiger fuer Schweizerische Altertumskunde
ANZ Sur — ANZ [*Australia and New Zealand*] Bank. Quarterly Survey
Anz (Wien) — Anzeiger. Akademie der Wissenschaften (Wien)
AO — Acta Orientalia
AO — Alandsk Odling: Arsbok
AO — American Oxonian
AO — Archiv Orientalni
AO — Australian Outlook
AO — Der Alte Orient. Gemeinverstaendliche Darstellungen [*Leipzig*]
AOAPA9 — Australia. Commonwealth Scientific and Industrial Research Organisation. Animal Research Laboratories. Technical Paper
AOASH — Acta Orientalia. Academiae Scientiarum Hungaricae
AOATS — Alter Orient und Altes Testament. Sonderreihe
AOAW — Anzeiger. Oesterreichische Akademie der Wissenschaften [*Wien*]. Philosophisch-Historische Klasse
AOB — Acta Orientalia [*Budapest*]
AOB — Altorientalische Bibliothek
AOBAA3 — Archivos de Oftalmologia de Buenos Aires
AOBIAR — Archives of Oral Biology
AOCCA — Annales d'Oto-Laryngologie et de Chirurgie Cervico-Faciale
AOCEDN — Archaeology in Oceania
AOCSSSR — Alaska Outer Continental Shelf Socioeconomic Studies Program. Special Reports
AOCSSTR — Alaska Outer Continental Shelf Socioeconomic Studies Program. Technical Reports
AODNS — Acta Orientalia
AOER — Arab Oil and Economic Review
AOF — Altorientalische Forschungen

AOF — Archiv fuer Orientforschung
AOFPAY — Australia. Commonwealth Scientific and Industrial Research Organisation. Division of Food Preservation. Technical Paper
AOFSA9 — Australia. Commonwealth Scientific and Industrial Research Organisation. Division of Fisheries and Oceanography. Fisheries Synopsis
AOG — Archiv fuer Oesterreichische Geschichte
AOGMA — Annali di Ostetricia, Ginecologia, Medicina Perinatale
AOGN — Alaska Oil and Gas News
AOGNAX — Archivio di Ostetricia e Ginecologia
AOGYA — Advances in Obstetrics and Gynecology
AOH — Acta Orientalia. Academiae Scientiarum Hungaricae
AOHSA — Annals of Occupational Hygiene. Supplement
AOHYA — Annals of Occupational Hygiene
AOI — Airways Operations Instructions
AOIAA — Annals of Oto-Rino-Laryngologica Ibero-Americana
AOIRAL — Australia. Commonwealth Scientific and Industrial Research Organisation. Division of Plant Industry. Field Station Record
AOJP — Australian Official Journal of Patents, Trade Marks, and Designs
AOJPTMD — Australian Official Journal of Patents, Trade Marks, and Designs
AOJTAW — American Orthoptic Journal
AOKAT — Altorientalischer Kommentar zum Alten Testament
AOKW — Annalen van de Oudheidkundige Kring van het Land van Waas
AOLAA — Acta Oto-Laryngologica
AOLPAU — Australia. Commonwealth Scientific and Industrial Research Organisation. Division of Land Research and Regional Survey. Technical Paper
AOLVA — Archivio di Oceanografia e Limnologia
AOLVAE — Archivio di Oceanografia e Limnologia
AOMCA — Advances in Organometallic Chemistry
AOMOD — AOCS Monograph
AOMPAZ — Australia. Commonwealth Scientific and Industrial Research Organisation. Division of Meteorological Physics. Technical Paper
AON — Acta Orientalia Neerlandica
AONGAD — Archives. Office du Niger
AONSEJ — Archives of Otolaryngology and Head and Neck Surgery
AOP — Analectes. Ordre de Premontre
AOP — Analyser og Problemer
AOP — Archivum Orientale Pragense
AOPA Mo Mag — AOPA [*Aircraft Owners' and Pilots' Association*] Monthly Magazine
AOPCD — Annual Report. Organization of the Petroleum Exporting Countries
AOPOCF — American Journal of Optometry and Physiological Optics
AOPRAM — Australia. Commonwealth Scientific and Industrial Research Organisation. Division of Plant Industry. Annual Report
AOR — Analecta Orientalia
AOR — Annals of Oriental Research
AOR — Anuari. Oficina Romanica
AORBA — Advances in Oral Biology
AOREDU — Archivio di Ortopedia e Reumatologia
AORHA — Annals of Otology, Rhinology, and Laryngology
AORIA — Acta Oto-Rino-Laringologica Ibero-Americana
AOrientHung — Acta Orientalia. Academiae Scientiarum Hungaricae
AORLA — Acta Oto-Rhino-Laryngologica Belgica
AORLCG — Archiv fuer Ohren-, Nasen-, und Kehlkopfheilkunde
AORLCG — Archives of Oto-Rhino-Laryngology
AORN — American Association of Operating Room Nurses. Journal
AORN J — Association of Operating Room Nurses. Journal
AOS — American Oriental Series
AOSBAN — American Orchid Society. Bulletin
AOSCA — Acta Odontologica Scandinavica
AOSG — Arbeiten aus dem Orientalischen Seminar der Universitaet Giessen
AOSGA4 — Attualita di Ostetricia e Ginecologia
AOSMAM — Archivio. Ospedale al Mare
AOSRB4 — Ambio. Special Report
AOSRD6 — Archiwum Ochrony Srodowiska
AOT — Altorientalische Texte zum Alten Testament
AOTSDE — Archives of Orthopaedic and Traumatic Surgery
AOTU — Altorientalische Texte und Untersuchungen
AOUNAZ — Archiv fuer Orthopaedische und Unfall-Chirurgie
Aoyama J Gen Educ — Aoyama Journal of General Education
AP — American Psychologist
AP — Annalen der Philosophie und Philosophischen Kritik
AP — Anthropological Papers [*Smithsonian Institution*]
Ap — April
AP — Ars Poetica
AP — Aryan Path
AP — Asian Perspectives
AP — Aurea Parma
APA — Acta Praehistorica et Archaeologica
APAA — Atti. Pontificia Accademia Romana di Archeologia
APACB — American Painting Contractor
APAD — Australian Planning Appeal Decisions
APAIS — Australian Public Affairs Information Service
APA Legisl Bull — American Pulpwood Association. Legislative Bulletin

APAOBE — Archaeology and Physical Anthropology in Oceania [*Later, Archaeology in Oceania*]
APA-PSIEP Rep — APA-PSIEP [*American Psychological Association-Project on Scientific Information Exchange in Psychology*] Report
APA Pulpwood Highl — American Pulpwood Association. Pulpwood Highlights
APA Pulpwood Statist — American Pulpwood Association. Pulpwood Statistics
APA Pulpwood Sum — American Pulpwood Association. Monthly Pulpwood Summary
APar — Aurea Parma
APARAR — Atti. Pontificia Accademia Romana di Archeologia. Rendiconti
Apar Nauk Dydakt — Aparatura Naukowa i Dydaktyczna
Apar Respir Tuberc — Aparato Respiratorio y Tuberculosis
APA Safety Alert — American Pulpwood Association. Safety Alert
APATB — Applied Atomics
APA Tech Papers — American Pulpwood Association. Technical Papers
APA Tech Release — American Pulpwood Association. Technical Release
APAVE — APAVE. Revue Technique du Groupement des Associations de Proprietaires d'Appareils a Vapeur et Electriques
APA VIC News — Australian Pre-School Association. Victorian Branch. Newsletter
APAW — Abhandlungen. Preussische Akademie der Wissenschaften
APB — Algemeen Politieblad van het Koninkrijk der Nederlanden
APBDAJ — Archiv der Pharmazie und Berichte der Deutschen Pharmazeutischen Gesellschaft
APC — Airport Forum News Services
APC — Annales de la Philosophie Chretienne
APC — Australian Personal Computer
APCA Abstr — APCA [*Air Pollution Control Association*] Abstracts
APCAD — Applied Catalysis
APCA J — APCA [*Air Pollution Control Association*] Journal
APCCBM — Annual Progress in Child Psychiatry and Child Development
APCCDO — Annual Reports on the Progress of Chemistry. Section A. Inorganic Chemistry
APCE — Annals of Public and Cooperative Economy [*Formerly, Annals of Collective Economy*]
APCEAR — Archiv for Pharmaci og Chemi
APCHA — Advances in Protein Chemistry
APCMA — Archivio di Patologia e Clinica Medica
APCMAH — Archivio di Patologia e Clinica Medica
APCOB — Archivio Putti di Chirurgia degli Organi di Movimento
APCOD — Applied Physics Communications
APCPCS — American Institute of Physics. Conference Proceedings
APD — Aslib Proceedings
APDBA — Acta Physica et Chimica (Debrecina)
APDEB — Current Problems in Dermatology
APDKA — Aktualne Problemy Informacji i Dokumentacji
APDPD — Annual Power Distribution Conference. Proceedings [*United States*]
APDTA9 — American Practitioner and Digest of Treatment
APEA J — APEA [*Australian Petroleum Exploration Association*] Journal
APE Eng — APE [*Amalgamated Power Engineering Ltd.*] Engineering
APE Engng — APE [*Amalgamated Power Engineering Ltd.*] Engineering
APEF — Annual. Palestine Exploration Fund
APEMAR — Archives Roumaines de Pathologie Experimentale et de Microbiologie
APen — Anima e Pensiero
APEND — Applied Energy
Apercus Econ Tchecosl — Apercus sur l'Economie Tchecoslovaque
APF — Acta Philosophica Fennica [*Elsevier Book Series*]
APF — Archiv fuer Papyrusforschung und Verwandte Gebiete
APFNC3 — Department of Primary Industries. Brisbane Fisheries Branch. Fisheries Notes [*New Series*]
APG — Archiv fuer Politik und Geschichte
APh — Acta Philologica. Societas Academica Dacoromana
APH — Acta Poloniae Historica
APh — Annee Philologique
APHA — American Public Health Association. Public Health Education. Section Newsletter
APhAP — Archives de Philologie. Academie Polonaise des Sciences et des Lettres
APHCA — Annales de Parasitologie Humaine et Comparee
APhD — Acta Philologica. Societas Academica Dacoromana
APhilos — Archives de Philosophie
APHRA — Ars Pharmaceutica
APHRDQ — Archives of Pharmacal Research [*Seoul*]
APhS — Acta Philologica Scandinavica. Tidskrift foer Nordisk Sprogforskning
APHYC — Applied Physics
API — Alternative Press Index
API — Annali della Pubblica Istruzione
Apiary Circ BC Dep Agric — Apiary Circular. British Columbia Department of Agriculture
Apiary Circ (Victoria) — Apiary Circular (Victoria)
Apic Abstr — Apicultural Abstracts
Apic Am — Apicultor Americano

Apic Argent — Apicultura Argentina
Apic Ital — Apicoltore d'Italia
Apicolt Ital — Apicoltore d'Italia
Apic Rom — Apicultura in Romania
Apicult Nord-Afr — Apiculteur Nord-Africain
Apic Venezol — Apicultura Venezolana
API Food Add Ref — American Paper Institute. Food Additives Reference Manual
APIJ — APIJ. Australian Planning Institute. Journal
API Journal — Australian Planning Institute. Journal
API Med Res Publ — American Petroleum Institute. Medical Research Publications
API Newsprint Bull — American Paper Institute. Newsprint Division. Bulletin
APIPAM — Australia. Commonwealth Scientific and Industrial Research Organisation. Division of Plant Industry. Technical Paper
API Publ — American Petroleum Institute. Publication
API Refining Dep Midyear Meet Prepr — American Petroleum Institute. Refining Department. Midyear Meeting. Preprints
API Statist Sum — American Paper Institute. Monthly Statistical Summary
API Wood Pulp Statist — American Paper Institute. Wood Pulp Statistics
APJ — American Paint and Coatings Journal
APJ — Appraisal Journal
APJL — Alpine Journal
APJSA — Astrophysical Journal. Supplement Series
APK — Aufsaetze zur Portugiesischen Kulturgeschichte
APKCA — Allgemeine und Praktische Chemie
APKTAA — Archeia tes Pharmakeutikes (Athens)
APL — Ancien Pays de Looz
APL — Annales Politiques et Litteraires
APL — Annales. Prince de Ligne
ApL — Approdo Letterario
APL — Archivo de Prehistoria Levantina
APLA Bull — Atlantic Provinces Library Association. Bulletin
ApLit — Apocalyptic Literature
APLMAS — Archives of Pathology and Laboratory Medicine
Apl Mat — Aplikace Matematiky
APLPB — Advances in Plasma Physics
APLSA — Annales de Chirurgie Plastique
APL Tech Dig — APL [*Applied Physics Laboratory*] Technical Digest
APM — Anuario de Prehistoria Madrilena
APM — Australian Personnel Management
ApMec — Applied Mechanics Reviews
APMHAI — Archives of Physical Medicine and Rehabilitation
ApMicrobiol — Applied Microbiology [*Later, Applied and Environmental Microbiology*]
APMNHOP — Alberta Provincial Museum. Natural History. Occasional Paper [*Canada*]
APMS — Altpreussische Monatschrift
APMSDK — Archives of Podiatric Medicine and Foot Surgery
APNAA — Arhiv za Poljoprivredne Nauke
APNAA2 — Arhiv za Poljoprivredne Nauke
APNPA — Archivio di Psicologia, Neurologia, e Psichiatria
APNPAD — Archivio di Psicologia, Neurologia, e Psichiatria
APNTAP — Arhiv za Poljoprivredne Nauke i Tehniku
APNVAV — Archiv fuer Psychiatrie und Nervenkrankheiten
APO — APO. The Australian Post Office Magazine
Apo — Apollo
APOA — APOA [*Arctic Petroleum Operators Association*] Review
APOAR — APOA [*Arctic Petroleum Operators Association*] Reports
APOCA — Acta Polytechnica. Chemistry Including Metallurgy Series
APOD — Australian Pocket Oxford Dictionary
APOJA — American Potato Journal
APOJAY — American Potato Journal
Ap Optics — Applied Optics
APORA — Advances in Physical Organic Chemistry
APP — Alternative Pink Pages. Australasian Plant Pathology
APP — Approach
Appalachia Mag — Appalachia Magazine
Appal J — Appalachian Journal
App Anal — Applicable Analysis
Appar Metody Rentgenovskogo Anal — Apparatura i Metody Rentgenovskogo Analiza
APPBD — Acta Physiologica et Pharmacologica
APPCD — Applied Physics. Part B. Photophysics and Laser Chemistry
App Econ — Applied Economics
App Environ Microbiol — Applied and Environmental Microbiology
APPHCZ — Annual Proceedings. Phytochemical Society
APPIB — American Paper Industry
APPITA — APPITA. Journal of the Australian and New Zealand Pulp and Paper Industry Technical Association
APPITA Proc — Australian Pulp and Paper Industry Technical Association. Proceedings
Appl Acoust — Applied Acoustics
Appl Anal — Applicable Analysis
Appl Anim Ethol — Applied Animal Ethology
Appl At — Applied Atomics [*England*]

Appl Biochem Bioeng — Applied Biochemistry and Bioengineering
Appl Biochem Microbiol — Applied Biochemistry and Microbiology
Appl Biochem Microbiol (Engl Transl Prikl Biokhim Mikrobiol) — Applied Biochemistry and Microbiology (English Translation of Prikladnaya Biokhimiya i Mikrobiologiya)
Appl Cryog Technol — Applications of Cryogenic Technology
Appl Econ — Applied Economics
Appl Electr Phenom — Applied Electrical Phenomena
Appl Energy — Applied Energy
Appl Entomol Zool — Applied Entomology and Zoology
Appl Ent Zool — Applied Entomology and Zoology
Appl Envir Microbiol — Applied and Environmental Microbiology
Appl Environ Microbiol — Applied and Environmental Microbiology
Appl Ergon — Applied Ergonomics
Appleton — Appleton's Journal
Appleton M — Appleton's Magazine
Appl Hydraul — Applied Hydraulics
Appliance Manuf — Appliance Manufacturer
Applicable Anal — Applicable Analysis
Applications Math — Applications of Mathematics
Applied Phil — Applied Philosophy
Applied Radiol — Applied Radiology
Applied Sc — Applied Science
Appl Mater Res — Applied Materials Research [*England*]
Appl Math — Applications of Mathematics
Appl Math Comput — Applied Mathematics and Computation
Appl Math Comput (New York) — Applied Mathematics and Computation (New York)
Appl Math Mech — Applied Mathematics and Mechanics
Appl Math Mech (English Ed) — Applied Mathematics and Mechanics (English Edition)
Appl Math Model — Applied Mathematical Modelling
Appl Math Modelling — Applied Mathematical Modelling
Appl Math Notes — Applied Mathematics Notes
Appl Math O — Applied Mathematics and Optimization
Appl Math Optim — Applied Mathematics and Optimization
Appl Math and Optimiz — Applied Mathematics and Optimization
Appl Math Sci — Applied Mathematical Sciences
Appl Mech Div Symp Ser (Am Soc Mech Eng) — Applied Mechanics Division. Symposia Series (American Society of Mechanical Engineers)
Appl Mech Rev — Applied Mechanics Reviews
Appl Mech Symp Ser — Applied Mechanics Symposia Series
Appl Mfr — Appliance Manufacturer
Appl Microb — Applied Microbiology [*Later, Applied and Environmental Microbiology*]
Appl Microbiol — Applied Microbiology [*Later, Applied and Environmental Microbiology*]
Appl Microbiol Biotechnol — Applied Microbiology and Biotechnology
Appl Mineral — Applied Mineralogy. Technische Mineralogie
Appl Moessbauer Spectrosc — Applications of Moessbauer Spectroscopy
Appl Neurop — Applied Neurophysiology
Appl Neurophysiol — Applied Neurophysiology
Appl News — Appalachian News Service
Appl Ocean Res — Applied Ocean Research
Appl Opt — Applied Optics
Appl Optics — Applied Optics
Appl Opt Suppl — Applied Optics. Supplement
Appl Ornithol — Applied Ornithology
Appl Phys — Applied Physics
Appl Phys A — Applied Physics. A [*Denmark*]
Appl Phys A — Applied Physics. A. Solids and Surfaces
Appl Phys B — Applied Physics. B [*Denmark*]
Appl Phys B — Applied Physics. B. Photophysics and Laser Chemistry
Appl Phys Comm — Applied Physics Communications
Appl Phys Commun — Applied Physics Communications
Appl Phys Eng — Applied Physics and Engineering
Appl Phys L — Applied Physics Letters
Appl Phys Lett — Applied Physics Letters
Appl Phys Part A — Applied Physics. Part A. Solids and Surfaces [*West Germany*]
Appl Phys Part B — Applied Physics. Part B. Photophysics and Laser Chemistry [*West Germany*]
Appl Phys Q — Applied Physics Quarterly
Appl Plast — Applied Plastics
Appl Polym Symp — Applied Polymer Symposia
Appl Psychol Meas — Applied Psychological Measurement
Appl Radiol — Applied Radiology
Appl Radiol Nucl Med — Applied Radiology and Nuclear Medicine [*Later, Applied Radiology*]
Appl Res Ment Retard — Applied Research in Mental Retardation
Appl Sci Dev — Applied Sciences and Development
Appl Sci Re — Applied Scientific Research
Appl Sci Res — Applied Scientific Research
Appl Sci Res Corp Thail Annu Rep — Applied Scientific Research Corporation of Thailand. Annual Report

Appl Sci Res Sect A — Applied Scientific Research. Section A. Mechanics, Heat, Chemical Engineering, Mathematical Methods [*Netherlands*]
Appl Sci Res Sect B — Applied Scientific Research. Section B. Electrophysics, Acoustics, Optics, Mathematical Methods [*Netherlands*]
Appl Sci Res (The Hague) — Applied Scientific Research (The Hague)
Appl Sci Technol Index — Applied Science and Technology Index
Appl Sol Energy — Applied Solar Energy
Appl Solid State Sci — Applied Solid State Science
Appl Spectr — Applied Spectroscopy
Appl Spectrosc — Applied Spectroscopy
Appl Spectrosc Rev — Applied Spectroscopy Reviews
Appl Spectry — Applied Spectroscopy
Appl Sp Rev — Applied Spectroscopy Reviews
Appl Stat — Applied Statistics
Appl Surf Sci — Applications of Surface Science
Appl Ther — Applied Therapeutics
App Math & Mech — Applied Mathematics and Mechanics
App Metody Rentgenovskogo Anal — Apparatura i Metody Rentgenovskogo Analiza [*USSR*]
App Microbiol — Applied Microbiology [*Later, Applied and Environmental Microbiology*]
App Op — Applied Optics
App Opt — Applied Optics
App Optics — Applied Optics
APPP — Abhandlungen zur Philosophie, Psychologie, und Paedagogik
App Phys — Applied Physics
Appraisal J — Appraisal Journal
Appraisal Jrnl — Appraisal Journal
Appretur Ztg — Appretur Zeitung
Appropriate Technol — Appropriate Technology [*England*]
App World — Apparel World
APPYA — Annual Review of Phytopathology
APPYAG — Annual Review of Phytopathology
APQ — American Philosophical Quarterly
APQPA — Acta Psiquiatrica y Psicologica de America Latina
APR — American Poetry Review
APr — Analecta Praemonstratensia
APR — Atlantic Province Reporter
APR — Australasian Photo Review
APraem — Analecta Praemonstratensia
APRAJ — Australasian Performing Right Association. Journal
APrF — Altpreussische Forschungen
APRKAI — Archiv fuer Protistenkunde
A Proc Electron Microsc Soc Am — Annual Proceedings. Electron Microscopy Society of America
A Proc Gifu Coll Pharm — Annual Proceedings. Gifu College of Pharmacy
APRSCA — Annual Progress Report. SEATO [*Southeast Asia Treaty Organization*] Medical Research Laboratories
APS — Acta Philologica Scandinavica
APS — American Philosophical Society. Proceedings
APs — American Psychologist
APS — Annals. American Academy of Political and Social Science
APS — Hsin-Li Hsueh-Pao [*Acta Psychologica Sinica*]
APSACT — Annual of Psychoanalysis
APSBAU — Archives Portugaises des Sciences Biologigues
APSCA — Acta Physiologica Scandinavica
APSE — Alternatives. Perspectives on Society and Environment [*Canada*]
APSHA — Annales de Pediatrie
APSHDH — American Journal of Pharmacy and the Sciences Supporting Public Health [*Later, American Journal of Pharmacy*]
APSID — Advances in Polymer Science
APSL — Amsterdamer Publikationen zur Sprache und Literatur
APSOA — Acta Psychologica (Amsterdam)
APSR — American Political Science Review
APSS — American Academy of Political and Social Science. Annals
APSTA — Applied Statistics
APSVC — Acta Physica Slovaca
A Psy — American Psychologist
APsyc — Archiv fuer die Gesamte Psychologie
APsych — Acta Psychologica [*Amsterdam*]
APT — Acta Psychologica Taiwanica
Aptechn Delo — Aptechnoe Delo
APTGAG — Anales. Catedra de Patologia y Clinica de la Tuberculosis. Universidad de Buenos Aires
APTKAS — Archiv fuer Physikalische Therapie
APTUA — Archives. Institut Pasteur de Tunis
APUA — Anthropological Papers. University of Alaska
A Pubbl Istr — Annali della Pubblica Istruzione
APURAK — Archivos de Pediatria del Uruguay
APYMAP — American Phytopathological Society. Monograph
APYTA — Acta Psychotherapeutica et Psychosomatica
AQ — Africa Quarterly
AQ — Amazing Stories. Quarterly
AQ — American Quarterly
AQ — Arizona Quarterly
AQ — Art Quarterly

AQ — Asiatic Quarterly
AQ — Atlantic Quarterly
AQ — Australian Quarterly
AQARD — Acqua Aria
AQBPA — Arquivos Brasileiros de Psicotecnica
AQIND — Aquatic Insects
AQPTA — Arquivos de Patologia [*Lisbon*]
AQR — Asiatic Quarterly Review
AQSZ — Aquilo Serie Zoologica
AQTOD — Aquatic Toxicology
AQTSA — Arquivos de Tisiologia
Aqua Biol Ab — Aquatic Biology Abstracts
Aquarien Mag — Aquarien Magazin
Aquarium J — Aquarium Journal
A Quart — Australian Quarterly
Aqua Sci & Fish Abstr — Aquatic Sciences and Fisheries Abstracts
Aquat Bot — Aquatic Botany
Aquat Weed Control Soc Proc — Aquatic Weed Control Society. Proceedings
Aquilo Ser Bot — Aquilo Serie Botanica
Aquilo Ser Zool — Aquilo Serie Zoologica
AR — Accounting Review
AR — Africa Report
AR — Alabama Review
AR — Alberta Reports
AR — Alliance Review [*New York*]
AR — American Record Guide
AR — American Recorder
AR — American Review [*Formerly, New American Review*]
AR — Antioch Review
AR — Antiquitaeten-Rundschau
AR — Antiviral Research
AR — Archaeological Reports
Ar — Arche
AR — Architectural Review
AR — Archiv fuer Reformationsgeschichte
Ar — Archive [*Quezon City*]
Ar — Archivio
AR — Archivum Romanicum
Ar — Arena
AR — Arizona Review
AR — Asian Review
A & R — Atene e Roma
AR — Industrial Arbitration Reports [*New South Wales*]
ARA — Aramco World Magazine
ARAA — Annual Review of Astronomy and Astrophysics
Ar A A — Arbeiten aus Anglistik und Amerikanistik
ARAAA — Annual Review of Astronomy and Astrophysics
ARABAn — Academie Royale d'Archeologie de Belgique. Annales
ARABBull — Academie Royale d'Archeologie de Belgique. Bulletin
Arab F & TV — Arab Film and Television Center News
Arab Gulf J Sci Res — Arab Gulf Journal of Scientific Research
Arabian J Sci Eng — Arabian Journal for Science and Engineering
Arabian J Sci and Eng — Arabian Journal for Science and Engineering
Arabian J Sci Engrg — Arabian Journal for Science and Engineering
Arabidopsis Inf Serv — Arabidopsis Information Service
Arab J Math — [*The*] Arab Journal of Mathematics
Arab J Nucl Sci Appl — Arab Journal of Nuclear Sciences and Applications
Arab Metall News — Arab Metallurgical News [*Algeria*]
Arab Min J — Arab Mining Journal
ArabW — Arab World
ARAC — Art and Architecture
ARACC — Archives of Acoustics
ARADAS — Annual Report. Center for Adult Diseases [*Osaka*]
ARAI — Annuario. Reale Accademia d'Italia
ARALNS — Atti. Reale Accademia dei Lincei. Notizie degli Scavi [*Rome*]
Aramco W — Aramco World Magazine
ARANA — Anales. Real Academia Nacional de Medicina [*Spain*]
ARANBP — Arctic Anthropology
Araneta J Agric — Araneta Journal of Agriculture
Araneta Res J — Araneta Research Journal
ARAOAR — Agronomia Angolana
ARAPCW — Annual Review of Anthropology
ARAR — Arctic and Alpine Research
Ar As — Arts Asiatiques
ARASC7 — Annual Reports on Analytical Atomic Spectroscopy
ARAST — Atti. Reale Accademia delle Scienze di Torino
Araucariana Ser Bot — Araucariana. Serie Botanica
Araucariana Ser Geocienc — Araucariana. Serie Geociencias
ARB — Africa Research Bulletin
ARB — Africana Research Bulletin
ARB — Arbitration Journal
Arb — Arbor
ARB — Australian Ranger Bulletin
ARBA — American Reference Books Annual
Arb Anat Inst Kais Jpn Univ Sendai — Arbeiten. Anatomisches Institut. Kaiserlich Japanischen Universitaet zu Sendai

ARBBCL — Academie Royale de Belgique. Bulletin. Classe des Lettres et des Sciences Morales et Politiques
Arb Ber Sueddtsch Ver Forschungsanst Milchwirtsch — Arbeiten und Berichte. Sueddeutsche Versuchs und Forschungsanstalt fuer Milchwirtschaft
Arb Biol Reichanst Land Forstw (Berlin) — Arbeiten. Biologischen Reichsanstalt fuer Land- und Forstwirtschaft (Berlin)
Arb Bot Inst Wurz — Arbeiten. Botanischen Instituts in Wurzburg
ARBBull — Academie Royale de Belgique. Bulletin. Classe des Lettres et des Sciences Morales et Politiques et Classe des Beaux-Arts
ARBCEY — Annual Review of Biophysics and Biophysical Chemistry
ARBDD — Arbeidervern
Arb Deut Landwirt Ges — Arbeiten. Deutsche Landwirtschafts-Gesellschaft
Arb Dritten Abt Anat Inst Kais Univ Kyoto Ser A — Arbeiten. Dritten Abteilung des Anatomischen Institutes der Kaiserlichen Universitaet Kyoto. Serie A. Untersuchungen ueber das Periphere Nervensystem
Arb Dritten Abt Anat Inst Kais Univ Kyoto Ser C — Arbeiten. Dritten Abteilung des Anatomischen Institutes der Kaiserlichen Universitaet Kyoto. Serie C. Experimentelle Tuberkuloseforschung
Arb Dritten Abt Anat Inst Kais Univ Kyoto Ser D — Arbeiten. Dritten Abteilung des Anatomischen Institutes der Kaiserlichen Universitaet Kyoto. Serie D. Lymphatologie
ArBegriffsg — Archiv fuer Begriffsgeschichte [*Bonn*]
Arbeiten Angew Statist — Arbeiten zur Angewandten Statistik
Arbeiten Niedersaechs Staats- u Universitaetsbibl — Arbeiten aus der Niedersaechsischen Staats- und Universitaetsbibliothek (Goettingen)
Arbeitsber Inst Math Masch Datenverarb Band 14 — Arbeitsberichte. Instituts fuer Mathematische Maschinen und Datenverarbeitung. Band 14
Arbeitsgem-Forsch Landes Nordrh-Westfalen — Arbeitsgemeinschaft fuer Forschung des Landes Nordrhein-Westfalen [*West Germany*]
Arbeitsmed Sozialmed Arbeitshyg — Arbeitsmedizin, Sozialmedizin, Arbeitshygiene [*Later, Arbeitsmedizin, Sozialmedizin, Praeventivmedizin*]
Arbeitsmed Sozialmed Praeventivmed — Arbeitsmedizin, Sozialmedizin, Praeventivmedizin
Arbeit und Wirt — Arbeit und Wirtschaft
Arb Gebiete Futterbaues — Arbeiten aus dem Gebiete des Futterbaues
Arb Geol Palaeontol Inst Univ Stuttgart — Arbeiten aus dem Geologisch Palaeontologischen Institut der Universitaet Stuttgart
ArbGeschAntJudUrchr — Arbeiten zur Geschichte des Antiken Judentums und des Urchristentums [*Leiden*]
Arb Gesund — Arbeit und Gesundheit
Arbit J — Arbitration Journal
Arbitration J — Arbitration Journal
Arbitration Jrnl — Arbitration Journal
Arbitrat J — Arbitration Journal
Arbitr J — Arbitration Journal
Arb J — Arbitration Journal
ARBJAH — American Rabbit Journal
Arb J of the Inst of Arbitrators — Arbitration Journal. Institute of Arbitrators
Arb J (NS) — Arbitration Journal (New Series)
Arb J (OS) — Arbitration Journal (Old Series)
Arb Leist — Arbeit und Leistung [*West Germany*]
ARBMA — Arbok fuer Universitetet i Bergen. Matematisk-Naturvitenskapelig Serie
Arb Med Fak Okayama — Arbeiten aus der Medizinischen Fakultaet Okayama
Arb Med Univ Okayama — Arbeiten aus der Medizinischen Universitaet Okayama
ARBOA — Annual Review of Biochemistry
ARBOAW — Annual Review of Biochemistry
Arbog Dan Geol Unders — Arbog-Danmarks Geologiske Undersoegelse [*Denmark*]
Arbok Univ Bergen Mat-Natur Ser — Arbok fuer Universitetet i Bergen. Matematisk-Naturvitenskapelig Serie
Arbok Univ Bergen Mat-Naturvitensk Ser — Arbok fuer Universitetet i Bergen. Matematisk-Naturvitenskapelig Serie
Arbok Univ Bergen Med Ser — Arbok fuer Universitetet i Bergen. Medisinsk Serie
Arbor Ass J — Arboricultural Association. Journal
Arbor Bull Assoc Morris Arbor — Arboretum Bulletin. Associates of the Morris Arboretum
Arboric Fruit — Arboriculture Fruitiere
Arboricult Fruit — Arboriculture Fruitiere
Arbor Kornickie — Arboretum Kornickie
Arbor Leaves — Arboretum Leaves
Arbor Sun — Ann Arbor Sun
Arb Paul-Ehrlich-Inst — Arbeiten. Paul-Ehrlich-Institut
Arb Paul Ehrlich Inst Georg Speyer Haus Ferdinand Blum Inst — Arbeiten. Paul-Ehrlich-Institut, Georg-Speyer-Haus, und Ferdinand-Blum-Institut
ARBPD4 — Annual Review of Behavior Therapy Theory and Practice
Arb Physiol Angew Entomol Berlin Dahlem — Arbeiten ueber Physiologische und Angewandte Entomologie aus Berlin Dahlem
ARBQA4 — Koninklijk Academie van Belgie. Jaarboek
ARBRA7 — Annual Review of Biochemical and Allied Research in India
Arb Reinischen Landeskunde — Arbeiten zur Reinischen Landeskunde [*West Germany*]

ARBRSI — Annual Report. Board of Regents of the Smithsonian Institution
ArbT — Arbeiten zur Theologie [*Stuttgart/Berlin-Ost*]
ARBU — Arctic Bulletin
Arb U B Mat — Arbok fuer Universitetet i Bergen. Matematisk-Naturvitenskapelig Serie
ARBUD — Arctic Bulletin
ARBUDJ — Arctic Bulletin
Arb Univ Hohenheim (Landwirtsch Hochsch) — Arbeiten. Universitaet Hohenheim (Landwirtschaftliche Hochschule)
ARBWAM — Annual Report of Biological Works. Faculty of Science. Osaka University
Arc — Arcadia [*Berlin*]
ARCAEX — Archives of Research on Industrial Carcinogenesis
ARCBE2 — Annual Review of Cell Biology
ARCCD4 — Australia. Commonwealth Scientific and Industrial Research Organisation. Division of Protein Chemistry. Annual Report
ArCCP — Arquivos. Centro Cultural Portugues [*Paris*]
ARCH — Archaeologia
Arch — Archaeology [*Cambridge, MA*]
Arch — Architecture in Australia [*Later, Architecture Australia*]
Arch — Archivio
ARCH — Archivist. Public Archives of Canada
Arch — Archivum [*Oviedo*]
Arch Acad Ecuat Med — Archivos. Academia Ecuatoriana de Medicina
Arch Acker-Pflanzenbau Bodenkd — Archiv fuer Acker-Pflanzenbau und Bodenkunde
Arch Acoust — Archives of Acoustics
Arch Aeliana — Archaeologica Aeliana
Archaeol — Archaeologia
Archaeol Aeliana 5 Ser — Archaeologia Aeliana. Series 5
Archaeol Austr — Archaeologia Austriaca
Archaeol Austriaca — Archaeologia Austriaca
Archaeol Biblio — Archaeologische Bibliographie
Archaeol Brit — Archaeology in Britain
Archaeol Cambrensis — Archaeologia Cambrensis
Archaeol J — Archaeological Journal
Archaeol J (London) — Archaeological Journal (London)
Archaeol Phy Anthrop Oceania — Archaeology and Physical Anthropology in Oceania [*Later, Archaeology in Oceania*]
Archaeol & Phys Anthropol Oceania — Archaeology and Physical Anthropology in Oceania [*Later, Archaeology in Oceania*]
Archaeol Polona — Archaeologia Polona
Archaeol Rep — Archaeological Reports
Archaeometr — Archaeometry
Arch Akust — Archiwum Akustyki
Arch Anat Cytol Pathol — Archives d'Anatomie et de Cytologie Pathologiques
Arch An Ath — Archaiologika Analekta ex Athenon
Arch Anat Histol Embryol — Archives d'Anatomie, d'Histologie, et d'Embryologie
Arch Anat Histol Embryol Norm Exp — Archives d'Anatomie, d'Histologie, et d'Embryologie; Normales et Experimentales
Arch Anat Histol Embryol (Strasb) — Archives d'Anatomie, d'Histologie, et d'Embryologie (Strasbourg)
Arch Anat M — Archives d'Anatomie Microscopique et de Morphologie Experimentale
Arch Anat Microsc Morphol Exp — Archives d'Anatomie Microscopique et de Morphologie Experimentale
Arch Anat Pathol (Paris) — Archives d'Anatomie Pathologique (Paris)
Arch Anat Pathol Sem Hop — Archives d'Anatomie Pathologique. Semaine des Hopitaux [*France*]
Arch Anat Physiol Physiol Abt — Archiv fuer Anatomie und Physiologie. Physiologische Abteilung
Arch Anat Phys Wiss Med — Archiv fuer Anatomie, Physiologie, und Wissenschaftliche Medizin
Arch Androl (New York) — Archives of Andrology (New York)
Arch Anthrop — Archiv fuer Anthropologie
Arch Antropol Crim Psichiatr Med Leg — Archivio di Antropologia Criminale, Psichiatria, e Medicina Legale
Arch Antropol Etnol — Archivio per l'Antropologia e la Etnologia
ArchAnz — Archaeologischer Anzeiger [*Berlin*]
Arch Argent Dermatol — Archivos Argentinos de Dermatologia
Arch Argent Neurol — Archivos Argentinos de Neurologia
Arch Argent Pediatr — Archivos Argentinos de Pediatria
Arch Argent Reumatol — Archivos Argentinos de Reumatologia
Arch Argent Tisiol Neumonol — Archivos Argentinos de Tisiologia y Neumonologia
ArchArm — Archeologie Armoricaine
Arch & Arts — Architecture and Arts
Arch Arzneither — Archiv fuer Arzneitherapie
Arch Atlas Norm Pathol Anat Roentgenbild — Archiv und Atlas der Normalen und Pathologischen Anatomie in Typischen Roentgenbildern
Arch ed Atti Soc Ital Chir — Archivio ed Atti. Societa Italiana di Chirurgia
Arch Augenheilkd — Archiv fuer Augenheilkunde
Arch Aujourd'hui — Architecture d'Aujourd'hui
Arch d'Aujourd'hui — Architecture d'Aujourd'hui
Arch in Aust — Architecture in Australia [*Later, Architecture Australia*]

Arch Austr — Archaeologia Austriaca
Arch Automat Telemech — Archiwum Automatyki i Telemechaniki
Arch Automat i Telemech — Archiwum Automatyki i Telemechaniki
Arch Autom Telemech — Archiwum Automatyki i Telemechaniki
Arch & B — Architecture and Building
Arch Badewes — Archiv des Badewesens
Arch Balatonicum — Archivum Balatonicum
Arch-Bat-Constr — Architecture-Batiment-Construction
Arch Begriff — Archiv fuer Begriffsgeschichte
Arch Belg Dermatol — Archives Belges de Dermatologie
Arch Belg Dermatol Syphiligr — Archives Belges de Dermatologie et de Syphiligraphie
Arch Belges Med Soc Hyg Med Trav Med Leg (Belgium) — Archives Belges de Medecine Sociale, Hygiene, Medecine du Travail, et Medecine Legale (Belgium)
Arch Belg Med Soc — Archives Belges de Medecine Sociale, Hygiene, Medecine du Travail, et Medecine Legale
Arch Belg Med Soc Hyg Med Trav Med Leg — Archives Belges de Medecine Sociale, Hygiene, Medecine du Travail, et Medecine Legale
Arch Bergbau — Archiv fuer Bergbau und Huettenwesen
ArchBg — Archaeologische Bibliographie
Arch Bibl — Archives et Bibliotheques de Belgique
Arch Bibl et Mus — Archives, Bibliotheques, et Musees de Belgique [*Later, Archives et Bibliotheques de Belgique*]
Arch Bienenk — Archiv fuer Bienenkunde
Arch Bienenkd — Archiv fuer Bienenkunde
Arch Bioch — Archives of Biochemistry and Biophysics
Arch Biochem Biophys — Archives of Biochemistry and Biophysics
Arch Biol — Archives de Biologie [*Liege*]
Arch Biol Andina — Archivos de Biologia Andina
Arch Biol M — Archivos de Biologia y Medicina Experimentales
Arch Biol Med Exp — Archivos de Biologia y Medicina Experimentales
Arch Biol Med Exp Supl — Archivos de Biologia y Medicina Experimentales. Suplemento
Arch Biol Sci — Archives of Biological Sciences
Arch Biol Sci (Engl Transl Arh Biol Nauka) — Archives of Biological Sciences (English Translation of Arhiv Bioloskih Nauka)
Arch Bioquim Quim Farm — Archivos de Bioquimica, Quimica, y Farmacia
Arch Bioquim Quim Farm (Tucuman) — Archivos de Bioquimica, Quimica, y Farmacia (Tucuman)
Arch & Bldg — Architecture and Building
Arch & BM — Architects' and Builders' Magazine [*New York*]
Arch Bodenfruchtbarkeit Pflanzenprod — Archiv fuer Bodenfruchtbarkeit und Pflanzenproduktion
Arch Bot — Archivio Botanico
Arch Bot Biogeogr Ital — Archivio Botanico e Biogeografico Italiano
Arch Brasil Med — Archivos Brasileiros de Medicina
Arch Budowy Masz — Archiwum Budowy Maszyn
Arch Budowy Maszyn — Archiwum Budowy Maszyn
Arch Build Eng — Architecture, Building, Engineering
Arch Build Eng — Architecture, Building, Structural Engineering
Arch Byz Mnem — Archeion ton Byzantinon Mnemeion tes Hellados
Arch Cal Chiro — Archives. California Chiropractic Association
Arch Camb — Archaeologia Cambrensis
Arch Cambrensis — Archaeologia Cambrensis
Arch Can — Architecture Canada
Arch Cant — Archaeologia Cantiana
Arch Cantiana — Archaeologia Cantiana. Transactions. Kent Archaeological Society
Arch Cardio y Hematol — Archivos de Cardiologia y Hematologia
Arch Cas — Archivni Casopis
Arch Chem Mikrosk — Archiv fuer Chemie und Mikroskopie
Arch Child Health — Archives of Child Health
Arch Chir Neerl — Archivum Chirurgicum Neerlandicum
Arch Chir Ortop Med — Archivio di Chirurgia Ortopedica e di Medicina
Arch Chir Torac Cardiovasc — Archivio di Chirurgia Toracica e Cardiovascolare
Arch Chir Torace — Archivio di Chirurgia del Torace
Arch Cl — Archeologia Classica
ArchClass — Archeologia Classica
Arch Clin Inst Endocrinol (Montevideo) — Archivos. Clinica e Instituto de Endocrinologia (Montevideo)
Arch Col Med El Salv — Archivos. Colegio Medico de El Salvador
Arch Col Med El Salvador — Archivos. Colegio Medico de El Salvador
Arch Concept — Architecture Concept
Arch Criminol Neuro Psiquiatr Discip Conexas — Archivos de Criminologia Neuro-Psiquiatria y Disciplinas Conexas
Arch Cubanos Cancerol — Archivos Cubanos de Cancerologia
Arch Dermat — Archives of Dermatology
Arch Dermatol — Archives of Dermatology
Arch Dermatol Exp Funct — Archivum de Dermatologia Experimentale et Functionale
Arch Dermatol Forsch — Archiv fuer Dermatologische Forschung
Arch Dermatol Res — Archives for Dermatological Research
Arch Dermatol Syphilol — Archives of Dermatology and Syphilology [*Chicago*]

Arch Dermat u Syph — Archiv fuer Dermatologie und Syphilis
Arch Dermat and Syph (Chicago) — Archives of Dermatology and Syphilology (Chicago)
Arch Derm F — Archiv fuer Dermatologische Forschung
Arch Derm R — Archives for Dermatological Research
Arch Des — Architectural Design
Arch De Vecchi Anat Patol Med Clin — Archivio "De Vecchi" per l'Anatomia Patologica e la Medicina Clinica [Italy]
Arch Diagn — Archives of Diagnosis
Arch Dis Ch — Archives of Disease in Childhood
Arch Dis Child — Archives of Disease in Childhood
Arch Dis Childhood — Archives of Disease in Childhood
Arch Druck Pap — Archiv fuer Druck und Papier
Arch Eisenbahntech — Archiv fuer Eisenbahntechnik
Arch Eisenh — Archiv fuer das Eisenhuettenwesen
Arch Eisenhuettenwes — Archiv fuer das Eisenhuettenwesen
Arch Eisenhuttenwesen — Archiv fuer das Eisenhuettenwesen [West Germany]
Arch Elektr — Archiv fuer Elektrotechnik [Berlin]
Arch Elektron Uebertragungstech — Archiv fuer Elektronik und Uebertragungstechnik
Arch Elektrotech — Archiwum Elektrotechniki [Warsaw]
Arch Elektrotech (Berlin) — Archiv fuer Elektrotechnik (Berlin)
Arch Elektr Uebertrag — Archiv der Elektrischen Uebertragung
Arch Elek Uebertragung — Archiv der Elektrischen Uebertragung
Arch "E Maragliano" Patol Clin — Archivio "E. Maragliano" di Patologia e Clinica
Arch Energ — Archiwum Energetyki
Arch Energiewirtsch — Archiv fuer Energiewirtschaft
Arch & Eng — Architect and Engineer
Arch Entwicklungsmech Org — Archiv fuer Entwicklungsmechanik der Organismen
Arch Entwicklungsmech Org (Wilhelm Roux) — Archiv fuer Entwicklungsmechanik der Organismen (Wilhelm Roux)
Arch Env He — Archives of Environmental Health
Arch Environ Contam Toxicol — Archives of Environmental Contamination and Toxicology
Arch Environ Health — Archives of Environmental Health
Arch Environ Hlth — Archives of Environmental Health
Archeol Rozhl — Archeologicke Rozhledy
Arch Eph — Archaiologike Ephemeris
Arch Ephemeris — Archaiologike Ephemeris
Arch Ert — Archaeologiai Ertesito
Arch Esp — Archivo Espanol de Arte y Arqueologia
Arch Esp Arq — Archivo Espanol de Arqueologia
Arch Esp Art — Archivo Espanol de Arte
Arch Esp Morfol — Archivo Espanol de Morfologia
Arch Esp Urol — Archivos Espanoles de Urologia
ArchEurCO — Archivum Europae Centro-Orientalis
Arch Eur So — Archives Europeennes de Sociologie
Arch Eur Sociol — Archives Europeennes de Sociologie
Arch Exp Pathol Pharmakol — Archiv fuer Experimentelle Pathologie und Pharmakologie
Arch Exp Path Pharmak — Archiv fuer Experimentelle Pathologie und Pharmakologie
Arch Exp Veterinaermed — Archiv fuer Experimentelle Veterinaermedizin
Arch Exp Vetmed — Archiv fuer Experimentelle Veterinaermedizin
Arch Fac Med Madrid — Archivos. Facultad de Medicina de Madrid
Arch Fac Med Zaragoza — Archivos. Facultad de Medicina de Zaragoza
ArchFAr — Archivo de Filologia Aragonesa
Arch Farmacol Sper Sci Affini — Archivio di Farmacologia Sperimentale e Scienze Affini
Arch Farmacol Toxicol — Archivos de Farmacologia y Toxicologia
Arch Farm (Bago) — Archivos Farmaceuticos (Bago)
Arch Farm Bioquim Tucuman — Archivos de Farmacia y Bioquimica del Tucuman
Arch Filosof — Archivio di Filosofia
Arch Fisch — Archiv fuer Fischereiwissenschaft
Arch Fischereiwiss — Archiv fuer Fischereiwissenschaft
Arch Fischereiwiss Beih — Archiv fuer Fischereiwissenschaft. Beiheft
Arch Fisiol — Archivio di Fisiologia
Arch Folk — Archives de Folklore
Arch Forstw — Archiv fuer Forstwesen
Arch Forum — Architectural Forum
Arch Freunde Naturgesch Mecklenburg — Archiv. Freunde der Naturgeschichte in Mecklenburg
Arch Fr Mal — Archives Francaises des Maladies de l'Appareil Digestif
Arch Fr Mal App Dig — Archives Francaises des Maladies de l'Appareil Digestif
Arch Fr Ped — Archives Francaises de Pediatrie
Arch Fr Pediatr — Archives Francaises de Pediatrie
Arch Fund Roux-Ocefa — Archivos. Fundacion Roux-Ocefa
Arch Gartenb — Archiv fuer Gartenbau
Arch Gartenbau — Archiv fuer Gartenbau
Arch Gefluegelk — Archiv fuer Gefluegelkunde
Arch Gefluegelkd — Archiv fuer Gefluegelkunde
Arch Gefluegelz Kleintierk — Archiv fuer Gefluegelzucht und Kleintierkunde

Arch Gefluegelzucht Kleintierk — Archiv fuer Gefluegelzucht und Kleintierkunde
Arch Geflugelkd Eur Poult Sci Rev Sci Avicole Eur — Archiv fuer Gefluegelkunde/European Poultry Science/Revue de Science Avicole Europeenne
Arch Genet — Archiv fuer Genetik [Zurich]
Arch Gen Med — Archives Generales de Medecine
Arch Gen Psychiatr — Archives of General Psychiatry
Arch Geogr — Archaeologia Geographica
Arch Geol Vietnam — Archives Geologiques du Vietnam
Arch Gesamte Naturl — Archiv fuer die Gesamte Naturlehre
Arch Gesamte Physiol Mens Tiere (Pfluegers) — Archiv fuer die Gesamte Physiologie des Menschen und der Tiere (Pfluegers)
Arch Gesamte Virusforsch — Archiv fuer die Gesamte Virusforschung
Arch Gesamte Waermetech — Archiv fuer die Gesamte Waermetechnik
Arch Gesch — Archiv fuer Geschichte der Philosophie
Arch Gesch Math Naturwiss Techn — Archiv fuer Geschichte der Mathematik, der Naturwissenschaften, und der Technik
Arch Gesch Phil — Archiv fuer Geschichte der Philosophie
Arch Geschw — Archiv fuer Geschwulstforschung
Arch Geschwulstforsch — Archiv fuer Geschwulstforschung
Arch Gewerbepathol Gewerbehyg — Archiv fuer Gewerbepathologie und Gewerbehygiene
Arch Gl It — Archivio Glottologico Italiano
Arch Gorn — Archiwum Gornictwa
Arch G Psyc — Archives of General Psychiatry
Arch G Utrecht — Archief voor de Geschiedenis van het Aartsbisdom Utrecht
Arch Gynaekol — Archiv fuer Gynaekologie
Arch Gynecol — Archives of Gynecology
Arch Helv — Archaeologia Helvetica
Arch Herald Suisses — Archives Heraldiques Suisses. Annuaire
Arch Hib — Archivium Hibernicum
Arch Hisp — Archivo Hispalense
Arch Hist Carm — Archivum Historicum Carmelitanum
Arch Hist Doctrinale Litt Moyen Age — Archives d'Histoire Doctrinale et Litteraire du Moyen-Age
Arch Hist Dom — Archives d'Histoire Dominicaine
Arch Hist E — Archive for History of Exact Sciences
Arch Hist Exact Sci — Archive for History of Exact Sciences
Arch Hist J — Archivum Histologicum Japonicum
Arch Hist Jap — Archivum Histologicum Japonicum
Arch Hist Med — Archiwum Historii Medycyny
Arch Hist Med (Warsz) — Archiwum Historii Medycyny (Warszawa)
Arch Hist Nat — Archives d'Histoire Naturelle
Arch Histol Jpn — Archivum Histologicum Japonicum
Arch Histol Norm Patol — Archivos de Histologia Normal y Patologica
Arch Hist Sci — Archives de l'Histoire des Sciences
Arch Hom — Archaeologia Homerica
Arch Hosp — Archives Hospitalieres
Arch Hosp Cruz Roja — Archivos. Hospital de la Cruz Roja de Barcelona
Arch Hosp Univ (Havana) — Archivos de Hospitales Universitarios (Havana)
Arch Hosp Vargas — Archivos. Hospital Vargas
Arch Hung — Archaeologia Hungarica
Arch Hutn — Archiwum Hutnictwa
Arch Hydrob — Archiv fuer Hydrobiologie
Arch Hydrobiol — Archiv fuer Hydrobiologie
Arch Hydrobiol u Planktonkunde — Archiv fuer Hydrobiologie und Planktonkunde
Arch Hydrobiol Rybactwa — Archivum Hydrobiologii i Rybactwa
Arch Hydrobiol Supplementb — Archiv fuer Hydrobiologie. Supplementband
Arch Hydrotech — Archiwum Hydrotechniki
Arch Hyg — Archiv fuer Hygiene
Arch Hyg (Athens) — Archives of Hygiene (Athens)
Arch Hyg Bakteriol — Archiv fuer Hygiene und Bakteriologie
ArchIA — Archivo Ibero-Americano [Madrid]
Arch Iatr Epistem — Archeion Iatrikon Epistemon
Arch Ib Am Hist Med — Archivo Iberoamericano de Historia de la Medicina y de Antropologia Medica
Arch I Card — Archivos. Instituto de Cardiologia de Mexico
Arch IE Afr — Archivos. Instituto de Estudios Africanos
Archig — Archiginnasio
Archi Hosp Rev Sci Sante Reunies — Archives Hospitalieres et Revue de Science et Sante Reunies
Archi & Manu — Archives and Manuscripts
Arch Immunol Ter Dosw — Archiwum Immunologii i Terapii Doswiadczalnej
Arch Immunol Ther Exp — Archivum Immunologiae et Therapiae Experimentalis
Arch Immunol Ther Exp (Warsz) — Archivum Immunologiae et Therapiae Experimentalis (Warszawa)
Arch Ind Hlth — Archives of Industrial Health
Arch Ind Hyg Occup Med — Archives of Industrial Hygiene and Occupational Medicine
Arch Industr Hlth — Archives of Industrial Health
Arch In Med — Archives of Internal Medicine
Arch Insect Biochem Physiol — Archives of Insect Biochemistry and Physiology

Arch Inst Aclim (Almeria Esp) — Archivos. Instituto de Aclimatacion (Almeria, Espana)
Arch Inst Biol — Archivos. Instituto Biologico
Arch Inst Biol Andina (Lima) — Archivos. Instituto de Biologia Andina (Lima)
Arch Inst Bot Univ Liege — Archives. Institut de Botanique. Universite de Liege
Arch Inst Cardiol Mex — Archivos. Instituto de Cardiologia de Mexico
Arch Inst Farmacol Exp (Madrid) — Archivos. Instituto de Farmacologia Experimental (Madrid)
Arch Inst Farmacol Exp (Med) — Archivos. Instituto de Farmacologia Experimental (Medicina)
Arch Inst Farm Exp — Archivos. Instituto de Farmacologia Experimental
Arch Inst Hessarek (Inst Razi) — Archives. Institut d'Hessarek (Institut Razi)
Arch Inst Past Alg — Archives. Institut Pasteur d'Algerie
Arch Inst Pasteur Afrique Nord — Archives. Instituts Pasteur de l'Afrique du Nord
Arch Inst Pasteur Alger — Archives. Institut Pasteur d'Algerie
Arch Inst Pasteur Algerie — Archives. Institut Pasteur d'Algerie
Arch Inst Pasteur Hell — Archives. Institut Pasteur Hellenique
Arch Inst Pasteur Madagascar — Archives. Institut Pasteur de Madagascar
Arch Inst Pasteur Tunis — Archives. Institut Pasteur de Tunis
Arch Inst Past Tunis — Archives. Institut Pasteur de Tunis
Arch Inst Prophyl — Archives. Institut Prophylactique
Arch Inst Razi — Archives. Institut Razi
Arch Int Chir — Archives Internationales de Chirurgie
Arch Interam Rheumatol — Archives of Interamerican Rheumatology [*Brazil*]
Arch Internat Histoire Sci — Archives Internationales d'Histoire des Sciences [*Paris*]
Arch Intern Med — Archives of Internal Medicine
Arch Int Etnogr Preist — Archivio Internazionale di Etnografia e Preistoria
Arch Int Hidatidosis — Archivos Internacionales de la Hidatidosis
Arch Int Hist Sci — Archives Internationales d'Histoire des Sciences
Arch Int Med Exp — Archives Internationales de Medecine Experimentale
Arch Int Neur — Archives Internationales de Neurologie
Arch Int Neurol — Archives Internationales de Neurologie
Arch Int Pharmacodyn Ther — Archives Internationales de Pharmacodynamie et de Therapie
Arch Int Physiol — Archives Internationales de Physiologie
Arch Int Physiol Biochim — Archives Internationales de Physiologie et de Biochimie
Arch Invest Med — Archivos de Investigacion Medica
Arch Inv M — Archivos de Investigacion Medica
Arch Inz Ladowej — Archiwum Inzynierii Ladowej
Arch I Phar — Archives Internationales de Pharmacodynamie et de Therapie
Arch I Phys — Archives Internationales de Physiologie et de Biochimie
Arch Ist Biochim Ital — Archivio. Istituto Biochimico Italiano
Arch Ist Osp St Corona — Archivio. Istituti Ospedalieri Santa Corona
Archit — Architecture in Australia [*Later, Architecture Australia*]
Arch Ital Anat Embriol — Archivio Italiano di Anatomia e di Embriologia
Arch Ital Anat Istol Patol — Archivio Italiano di Istologia Patologica
Arch Ital Biol — Archives Italiennes de Biologie
Arch Ital Chir — Archivio Italiano di Chirurgia
Arch Ital Clin Med — Archivio Italiano di Clinica Medica
Arch Ital Dermatol Sifilogr Venereol — Archivio Italiano di Dermatologia, Sifilografia, e Venereologia
Arch Ital Dermatol Venereol Sessuol — Archivio Italiano di Dermatologia, Venereologia, e Sessuologia
Arch Ital Laringol — Archivii Italiani di Laringologia
Arch Ital Mal Appar Dig — Archivio Italiano delle Malattie dell'Apparato Digerente [*Italy*]
Arch Ital Otol Rinol Laringol — Archivio Italiano di Otologia, Rinologia, e Laringologia
Arch Ital Patol Clin Tumori — Archivio Italiano di Patologia e Clinica dei Tumori
Arch Ital Sci Farmacol — Archivio Italiano di Scienze Farmacologiche
Arch Ital Sci Med Trop Parassitol — Archivio Italiano di Scienze Mediche Tropicali e di Parassitologia
Arch Ital Sc Med Colon — Archivio Italiano di Scienze Mediche Coloniali
Arch Ital Urol Nefrol — Archivio Italiano di Urologia e Nefrologia
Archit Archaeol Soc Durham Northumberl Trans — Architectural and Archaeological Society of Durham and Northumberland. Transactions
Archit Assoc Q — Architectural Association. Quarterly
Archit Auj — Architecture d'Aujourd'hui
Archit Aujourd — Architecture d'Aujourd'hui
Archit d'Aujourd'hui — Architecture d'Aujourd'hui
Archit Aust — Architecture Australia
Archit in Aust — Architecture in Australia [*Later, Architecture Australia*]
Arch It Bio — Archives Italiennes de Biologie
Archit Concept — Architecture Concept [*Canada*]
Archit Cronache Storia — Architettura Cronache e Storia
Archit Des — Architectural Design
Archit Dig — Architectural Digest
Architect Hist — Architectural History
Architects J — Architects' Journal
Architecture & Comportement/Archre & Behavior — Architecture et Comportement/Architecture and Behavior

Archit Eng — Architect and Engineer
Archit Forum — Architectural Forum
Archit Hist — Architectural History
Archit J — Architects' Journal
Archit Per Ind — Architectural Periodicals Index
Archit Plus — Architecture Plus
Archit R — Architectural Review
Archit Rec — Architectural Record
Archit Rev — Architectural Review
Archit Sci Rev — Architectural Science Review
Archits News — Architects News
Archit Surv — Architect and Surveyor
Archit Wohnwelt — Architektur und Wohnwelt [*West Germany*]
ArchIug — Archaeologia Iugoslavica
Archiv — Archiv fuer Reformationsgeschichte
Archiv — Archiv fuer das Studium der Neueren Sprachen und Literaturen
Archiv Anthrop — Archiv fuer Anthropologie und Voelkerforschung
Archiv Antropol Etnol — Archivio per l'Antropologia e la Etnologia
Archiv As Art — Archives of Asian Art
Archiv Diplom Consul — Archives Diplomatiques et Consulaires
ArchiveP — [*The*] Archive (Philippines)
Archives & Bibl — Archives et Bibliotheques de Belgique
Archives Environ Health — Archives of Environmental Health
Archives Eur Sociol — Archives Europeennes de Sociologie
Archives Gen Psychiat — Archives of General Psychiatry
Archives Ind Hyg & Occup Med — Archives of Industrial Hygiene and Occupational Medicine
Archives and Mss — Archives and Manuscripts
Archives Neurol — Archives of Neurology
Archives Philos — Archives de Philosophie
Archives Sci — Archives des Sciences
Archives of Science Orleans Co Soc N Sc Tr — Archives of Science. Orleans County Society of Natural Sciences. Transactions
Archives Sci Sociales Relig — Archives de Sciences Sociales des Religions
Archives Sociol Relig — Archives de Sociologie des Religions
Archives Suisses Anthrop Gen — Archives Suisses d'Anthropologie Generale
Archiv Europ Sociol — Archives Europeennes de Sociologie
Archiv Eur Sociol — Archives Europeennes de Sociologie
Archiv Gesch Buchw — Archiv fuer Geschichte des Buchwesens
Archiv Gesch Buchwes — Archiv fuer Geschichte des Buchwesens
Archiv Int Sociol Coop Develop — Archives Internationales de Sociologie de la Cooperation et du Developpement
Archiv Kommunalwiss — Archiv fuer Kommunalwissenschaften
Archiv Ling — Archivum Linguisticum
Archiv Meteorologie Geophysik u Bioklimatolgie Ser A — Archiv fuer Meteorologie, Geophysik, und Bioklimatologie. Serie A. Meteorologie und Geophysik
Archiv fuer Mus — Archiv fuer Musikwissenschaft
Archivo Esp Arq — Archivo Espanol de Arqueologia
Archivo Esp Arte — Archivo Espanol de Arte
Archiv Oesterr Gesch — Archiv fuer Oesterreichische Geschichte
Archiv f Oesterr Geschichte — Archiv fuer Oesterreichische Geschichte
Archiv Off Rechts — Archiv des Oeffentlichen Rechts
Archiv Or — Archiv Orientalni
Archiv Orientforsch — Archiv fuer Orientforschung
ArchivPhilos — Archiv fuer Philosophie
Archiv Philos Dr — Archives de Philosophie du Droit
Archiv Rechts u Soz-Philos — Archiv fuer Rechts- und Sozialphilosophie
Archiv Rom — Archivum Romanicum
Archiv Sci Soc Rel — Archives de Sciences Sociales des Religions
Archiv Sci Soc Relig — Archives de Sciences Sociales des Religions
Archiv Sex Behav — Archives of Sexual Behavior
Archiv Soc Rel — Archives de Sociologie des Religions
Archiv Stor — Archivio Storico
Archiv f Stud — Archiv fuer das Studium der Neueren Sprachen und Literaturen
Archiv Suisses Anthropol Gen — Archives Suisses d'Anthropologie Generale
Archivum Hist Soc Iesu — Archivum Historicum Societatis Iesu
Archiv Urk — Archiv fuer Urkundenforschung
Archiv Voelkerk — Archiv fuer Voelkerkunde
Archiv Volkerrechts — Archiv des Voelkerrechts
Arch J — Archaeological Journal
Arch Jpn Chir — Archiv fuer Japanische Chirurgie
Arch Juives — Archives Juives. Cahiers de la Commission des Archives Juives
ArchK — Archiv fuer Kulturgeschichte
Arch Kinderh — Archiv fuer Kinderheilkunde
Arch Kinderheilkd — Archiv fuer Kinderheilkunde
Arch Kinderheilkd Beih — Archiv fuer Kinderheilkunde. Beihefte
Arch Klin Chir — Archiv fuer Klinische Chirurgie
Arch Klin Chir Langenbecks — Archiv fuer Klinische Chirurgie. Langenbecks [*West Germany*]
Arch Klin Exp Dermatol — Archiv fuer Klinische und Experimentelle Dermatologie
Arch Klin Exp Ohren- Nasen- Kehlkopfheilkd — Archiv fuer Klinische und Experimentelle Ohren-, Nasen-, und Kehlkopfheilkunde

Arch Klin Exp Ophtalmol — Archiv fuer Klinische und Experimentelle Ophtalmologie
Arch Klin Med — Archiv fuer Klinische Medizin
Arch Kreislaufforsch — Archiv fuer Kreislaufforschung
Arch Kriminol — Archiv fuer Kriminologie
Arch Kulturgesch — Archiv fuer Kulturgeschichte
ArchL — Archivum Linguisticum
Arch Lagerstaettenforsch — Archiv fuer Lagerstaettenforschung
Arch Lagerstaettenforsch Ostalpen — Archiv fuer Lagerstaettenforschung in den Ostalpen
Arch Landtech — Archiv fuer Landtechnik
Arch Latinoamer Nutr — Archivos Latinoamericanos de Nutricion
Arch Latinoam Nutr — Archivos Latinoamericanos de Nutricion
Arch Latr Epistem — Archeion Latrikon Epistemon
Arch Lebensmittelhyg — Archiv fuer Lebensmittelhygiene
Arch Ling — Archivum Linguisticum
ArchLit — Archiv fuer Literatur und Volksdichtung
ArchLitg — Archiv fuer Liturgiewissenschaft [*Regensburg*]
Arch Mal Appar Dig Mal Nutr — Archives des Maladies de l'Appareil Digestif et des Maladies de la Nutrition
Arch Mal C — Archives des Maladies du Coeur et des Vaisseaux
Arch Mal Coeur Vaiss — Archives des Maladies du Coeur et des Vaisseaux
Arch Mal Pr — Archives des Maladies Professionnelles de Medecine du Travail et de Securite Sociale
Arch Mal Prof Hyg Toxicol Ind — Archives des Maladies Professionnelles, Hygiene, et Toxicologie Industrielles
Arch Mal Prof Med Trav Secur Soc — Archives des Maladies Professionnelles de Medecine du Travail et de Securite Sociale
Arch & Manus — Archives and Manuscripts
Arch Manuscr — Archives and Manuscripts
Arch and Manuscripts — Archives and Manuscripts
Arch Mass Spectral Data — Archives of Mass Spectral Data
Arch Math — Archiv der Mathematik
Arch Math (Basel) — Archiv der Mathematik (Basel)
Arch Math (Brno) — Archivum Mathematicum (Brno)
Arch Math Log — Archiv fuer Mathematische Logik und Grundlagenforschung
Arch Math Logik Grundlag — Archiv fuer Mathematische Logik und Grundlagenforschung [*Stuttgart*]
Arch Math Logik und Grundlagenforsch — Archiv fuer Mathematische Logik und Grundlagenforschung
Arch Mat Naturvidensk — Archiv foer Matematik og Naturvidenskab [*Norway*]
Arch Meat Fish Dairy Sci — Archives of Meat, Fish, and Dairy Science
Arch Mech — Archives of Mechanics [*Archiwum Mechaniki Stosowanej*]
Arch Mech (Arch Mech Stosow) — Archives of Mechanics (Archiwum Mechaniki Stosowanej)
Arch Mech Stosow — Archiwum Mechaniki Stosowanej [*Archives of Mechanics*]
Arch Mech Stosowanej — Archiwum Mechaniki Stosowanej [*Archives of Mechanics*]
Arch Med — Archives Medicales
Arch Med Belg — Archiva Medica Belgica
Arch Med Cuba — Archivos Medicos de Cuba
Arch Med Enf — Archives de Medecine des Enfants
Arch Med Enfants — Archives de Medecine des Enfants
Arch Med Exp — Archivos de Medicina Experimental
Arch Med Exper et Anat Path — Archives de Medecine Experimentale et d'Anatomie Pathologique
Arch Med Hydrol — Archives of Medical Hydrology
Arch Med Leg — Archivo de Medicina Legal
Arch Med (Lisbon) — Archivos de Medicina (Lisbon)
Arch Med Mex — Archivos Medicos Mexicanos [*Mexico*]
Arch Med Nav — Archives de Medecine Navale
Arch Med Vet (Valdivia) — Archivos de Medicina Veterinaria (Valdivia)
Arch Metallkd — Archiv fuer Metallkunde [*West Germany*]
Arch Meteorol Geophys Bioklimatol Ser A — Archiv fuer Meteorologie, Geophysik, und Bioklimatologie. Serie A
Arch Meteorol Geophys Bioklimatol Ser B — Archiv fuer Meteorologie, Geophysik, und Bioklimatologie. Serie B
Arch Met Geophys Bioklim Ser A Meteorologie und Geophysik — Archiv fuer Meteorologie, Geophysik, und Bioklimatologie. Serie A. Meteorologie und Geophysik
Arch Mex Anat — Archivos Mexicanos de Anatomia
Arch Mex Neurol Psiquiatr — Archivos Mexicanos de Neurologia y Psiquiatria
Arch Mex Venereol Dermatol — Archivos Mexicanos de Venereologia y Dermatologia
Arch MGB A — Archiv fuer Meteorologie, Geophysik, und Bioklimatologie. Serie A
Arch MGB B — Archiv fuer Meteorologie, Geophysik, und Bioklimatologie. Serie B
Arch Microb — Archives of Microbiology
Arch Microbiol — Archives of Microbiology
Arch Mikr Anat — Archiv fuer Mikroskopische Anatomie
Arch Mikrobiol — Archiv fuer Mikrobiologie

Arch Mikrosk Anat Entwicklungsmech — Archiv fuer Mikroskopische Anatomie und Entwicklungsmechanik
Arch Mikrosk Anat Entwmech — Archiv fuer Mikroskopische Anatomie und Entwicklungsmechanik
Arch Miner — Archiv fuer Mineralogie, Geognosie, Bergbau, und Huettenkunde
Arch Mineral — Archiwum Mineralogiczne
ArchMIran — Archaeologische Mitteilungen aus Iran. Neue Folge [*Berlin*]
Arch Miss — Archives des Missions Scientifiques et Litteraires
Arch Molluskenkd — Archiv fuer Molluskenkunde
Arch Monaldi — Archivio Monaldi
Arch Monaldi Tisiol Mal Appar Respir — Archivio Monaldi per la Tisiologia e le Malattie dell'Apparato Respiratorio
Arch Mus — Archiv fuer Musikwissenschaft
Arch Mus Hist Nat Lyon — Archives. Museum d'Histoire Naturelle de Lyon
Arch Musik — Archiv fuer Musikwissenschaft
Arch Mus Natl Hist Nat (Paris) — Archives. Museum National d'Histoire Naturelle (Paris)
Arch Mus Teyler — Archives. Musee Teyler
Arch N — Archaeological News
Arch Nachr Baden — Archaeologische Nachrichten aus Baden
Arch Naturg — Archiv fuer Naturgeschichte
Arch Naturg (Berlin) — Archiv fuer Naturgeschichte (Berlin)
Arch Naturgesch — Archiv fuer Naturgeschichte
Arch Naturkd Liv- Est- Kurlands — Archiv fuer die Naturkunde Liv-, Est-, und Kurlands [*Estonian SSR*]
Arch Naturschutz Landschaftsforsch — Archiv fuer Naturschutz und Landschaftsforschung
Arch Nauki Mater — Archiwum Nauki o Materialach [*Poland*]
Arch Neerl Phon Exp — Archives Neerlandaises de Phonetique Experimentale
Arch Neerl Physiol — Archives Neerlandaises de Physiologie
Arch Neerl Sci Exactes Nat — Archives Neerlandaises des Sciences Exactes et Naturelles [*Netherlands*]
Arch Neerl Sci Exactes Nat Ser 3A — Archives Neerlandaises des Sciences Exactes et Naturelles. Serie 3A. Sciences Exactes
Arch Neerl Zool — Archives Neerlandaises de Zoologie
Arch Neurobiol — Archivos de Neurobiologia [*Madrid*]
Arch Neurol — Archives of Neurology
Arch Neurol Psychiatry — Archives of Neurology and Psychiatry
ArchNPhonExp — Archives Neerlandaises de Phonetique Experimentale
Arch Oceanogr Limnol — Archivio di Oceanografia e Limnologia
ArchOF — Archiv fuer Orientforschung [*Graz, Austria*]
Arch Off Niger — Archives. Office du Niger
Arch Oftal Hispano-Am — Archivos de Oftalmologia Hispano-Americanos
Arch Oftalmol B Aires — Archivos de Oftalmologia de Buenos Aires
Arch Ohrenh — Archiv fuer Ohrenheilkunde
Arch Ohren- Nasen- Kehlkopfheilkd — Archiv fuer Ohren-, Nasen-, und Kehlkopfheilkunde [*West Germany*]
Arch Ohr-Nas Kehlkopfheilk — Archiv fuer Ohren-, Nasen-, und Kehlkopfheilkunde
Archo Patol Clin Med — Archivio di Patologia e Clinica Medica
Arch Ophtal — Archives d'Ophtalmologie
Arch Ophtalmol — Archives d'Ophtalmologie
Arch Ophtalmol (Paris) — Archives d'Ophtalmologie et Revue Generale d'Ophtalmologie (Paris)
Arch Ophtalmol Rev Gen Ophtalmol — Archives d'Ophtalmologie et Revue Generale d'Ophtalmologie
Arch Ophth — Archives of Ophthalmology [*Chicago*]
Arch Ophthalmol — Archives of Ophthalmology [*Chicago*]
Arch Opht (Paris) — Archives d'Ophtalmologie (Paris)
Arch Opt — Archiv fuer Optik
ArchOr — Archiv Orientalni [*Prague*]
Arch Oral B — Archives of Oral Biology
Arch Oral Biol — Archives of Oral Biology
ArchOrient — Archiv Orientalni
Arch Orthop — Archiv fuer Orthopaedische und Unfall-Chirurgie
Arch Orthop Trauma Surg — Archives of Orthopaedic and Traumatic Surgery
Arch Orthop Unfall-Chir — Archiv fuer Orthopaedische und Unfall-Chirurgie
Arch Ortop — Archivio di Ortopedia [*Later, Archivio di Ortopedia e Reumatologia*] [*Italy*]
Arch Ortop Reumatol — Archivio di Ortopedia e Reumatologia
Archos Bioquim Quim Farmac (Tucuman) — Archivos de Bioquimica, Quimica, y Farmacia (Tucuman)
Archos Bromat — Archivos de Bromatologia
Archos Inst Aclim (Almeria) — Archivos. Instituto de Aclimatacion (Almeria)
Archos Inst Antrop (Natal) — Archivos. Instituto Antropologia (Natal)
Archos Inst Biol (S Paulo) — Archivos. Instituto Biologico (Sao Paulo)
Archos Mus Paranaie — Archivos. Museu Paranaie
Arch Osp Mare — Archivio. Ospedale al Mare
Archos Soc Biol Montev — Archivos. Sociedad de Biologia de Montevideo
Arch Ostet Ginecol — Archivio di Ostetricia e Ginecologia
Archos Venez Nutr — Archivos Venezolanos de Nutricion
Archos Zootecnia — Archivos de Zootecnia
Arch Otolar — Archives of Otolaryngology
Arch Otolaryngol — Archives of Otolaryngology
Arch Oto-R — Archives of Oto-Rhino-Laryngology

Arch Oto-Rhino-Laryngol — Archives of Oto-Rhino-Laryngology
Arch Ottalmol — Archivio di Ottalmologia
Archo Vet Ital — Archivio Veterinario Italiano
Arch P — Archiv fuer Papyrusforschung
Arch Parasitol (Paris) — Archives de Parasitologie (Paris)
Arch Path — Archives of Pathology [*Later, Archives of Pathology and Laboratory Medicine*]
Arch Path Anat — Archiv fuer Pathologische Anatomie und Physiologie und fuer Klinische Medizin
Arch Path and Lab Med — Archives of Pathology and Laboratory Medicine
Arch Pathol — Archives of Pathology [*Later, Archives of Pathology and Laboratory Medicine*]
Arch Pathol Lab Med — Archives of Pathology and Laboratory Medicine
Arch Patol e Clin Med — Archivio di Patologia e Clinica Medica
Arch Patol Clin Med — Archivio di Patologia e Clinica Medica
Arch Pediat — Archives of Pediatrics
Arch Pediatr — Archives of Pediatrics
Arch Pediatr Urug — Archivos de Pediatria del Uruguay
Arch Peru Patol Clin (Lima) — Archivos Peruanos de Patologia y Clinica (Lima)
Arch Pflanzenschutz — Archiv fuer Pflanzenschutz
Arch Pflsch — Archiv fuer Pflanzenschutz
Arch Pharm — Archiv der Pharmazie
Arch Pharmacol — Archives of Pharmacology
Arch Pharmakol Exp Pathol — Archiv fuer Pharmakologie und Experimentelle Pathologie. Naunyn-Schmiedebergs [*Later, Archiv fuer Pharmakologie. Naunyn-Schmiedebergs*] [*West Germany*]
Arch Pharmakol Naunyn-Schmiedebergs — Archiv fuer Pharmakologie. Naunyn-Schmiedebergs [*Formerly, Archiv fuer Pharmakologie und Experimentelle Pathologie. Naunyn-Schmiedebergs*] [*West Germany*]
Arch Pharm (Athens) — Archeia tes Pharmakeutikes (Athens)
Arch Pharm Ber Dtsch Pharm Ges — Archiv der Pharmazie und Berichte der Deutschen Pharmazeutischen Gesellschaft
Arch Pharm Chem — Archiv for Pharmaci og Chemi
Arch Pharm Chem Sci Ed — Archiv for Pharmaci og Chemi. Scientific Edition
Arch Pharm (Weinheim Ger) — Archiv der Pharmazie (Weinheim, Germany)
Arch Phil — Archives de Philosophie
Arch Philos — Archives de Philosophie
Arch Phys Biol Chim Phys Corps Organ — Archives de Physique Biologique et de Chimie Physique des Corps Organises
Arch Phys M — Archives of Physical Medicine and Rehabilitation
Arch Phys Med Rehabil — Archives of Physical Medicine and Rehabilitation
Arch Phys Ther — Archiv fuer Physikalische Therapie
Arch Phytopathol Pflanzenschutz — Archiv fuer Phytopathologie und Pflanzenschutz
Arch Phytopath Pflschutz — Archiv fuer Phytopathologie und Pflanzenschutz
Arch Podiatr Med Foot Surg — Archives of Podiatric Medicine and Foot Surgery
Arch Pol — Archeologia Polski
Arch Polon — Archaeologia Polona
Arch Polona — Archaeologia Polona
Arch Port Sci Biol — Archives Portugaises des Sciences Biologiques
Arch Post und Fernmeldewes — Archiv fuer das Post- und Fernmeldewesen
Arch Poult Sci — Archives of Poultry Science
Arch Pract Pharm — Archives of Practical Pharmacy [*Japan*]
Arch Procesow Spalania — Archiwum Procesow Spalania [*Poland*]
Arch Protistenkd — Archiv fuer Protistenkunde. Protozoen-Algen-Pilze
Arch Psicol Neurol Psichiatr — Archivio di Psicologia, Neurologia, e Psichiatria
Arch Psych — Archiv fuer Psychologie
Arch Psychi — Archiv fuer Psychiatrie und Nervenkrankheiten
Arch Psychiat Nervenkr — Archiv fuer Psychiatrie und Nervenkrankheiten
Arch Psychiatr Nervenkr — Archiv fuer Psychiatrie und Nervenkrankheiten
Arch Psychiatr Nervenkrankh — Archiv fuer Psychiatrie und Nervenkrankheiten
Arch Psychiatry Neurol Sci — Archives of Psychiatry and Neurological Sciences
Arch Psychol (Frankf) — Archiv fuer Psychologie (Frankfurt Am Main)
Arch Putti Chir Organi Mov — Archivio Putti di Chirurgia degli Organi di Movimento
Arch R — Architectural Review
Arch Radiol — Archivio di Radiologia
Arch Radiol (Napoli) — Archivio di Radiologia (Napoli)
Arch Rass- u Ges Biol — Archiv fuer Rassen- und Gesellschafts-Biologie Einschliessend Rassen- und Gesellschaftshygiene
Arch Rass Ital Ottalmol — Archivio e Rassegna Italiana di Ottalmologia
Arch Rational Mech Anal — Archive for Rational Mechanics and Analysis
Arch Ration Mech Anal — Archive for Rational Mechanics and Analysis
Archre in Australia — Architecture in Australia [*Later, Architecture Australia*]
Archre Australia — Architecture Australia
Arch Rec — Architectural Record
Arch Rech Agron Pastorales Vietnam — Archives des Recherches Agronomiques et Pastorales au Vietnam
Arch Rechts Soz — Archiv fuer Rechts- und Sozialphilosophie
Archre East Midlands — Architecture East Midlands

Arch Reformation Hist — Archive for Reformation History
Archre in Greece — Architecture in Greece
Archre in Ireland — Architecture in Ireland
Arch Rev — Architectural Review
Arch Ricam — Archivio del Ricambio
Arch R Inst Bacteriol Camara Pestana — Archivos. Real Instituto Bacteriologico Camara Pestana
Arch R Mech — Archive for Rational Mechanics and Analysis
Arch Rom — Archivum Romanicum
Arch Roum Pathol Exp Microbiol — Archives Roumaines de Pathologie Experimentale et de Microbiologie
Arch Rozhledy — Archeologicke Rozhledy
Arch Rubber Cultiv (Bogor) — Archives of Rubber Cultivation (Bogor)
ArchRW — Archiv fuer Religionswissenschaft
Archs Anat Microsc — Archives d'Anatomie Microscopique
Archs Anat Microsc Morph Exp — Archives d'Anatomie Microscopique et de Morphologie Experimentale
Arch S A Of — Archivos. Sociedad Americana de Oftalmologia y Optometria
Archs Biochem — Archives of Biochemistry
Arch Schiffs-u Tropen-Hyg — Archiv fuer Schiffs-und Tropen-Hygiene
Arch Schlesische Kirchengesch — Archiv fuer Schlesische Kirchengeschichte
Arch Sci — Archives des Sciences
Arch Sci Avicole — Archives de Science Avicole
Arch Sci Biol — Archivio di Scienze Biologiche [*Bologna*]
Arch Sci Biol (Belgrade) — Archives des Sciences Biologiques (Belgrade)
Arch Science R — Architectural Science Review
Arch Sci Med — Archivio per le Scienze Mediche [*Torino*]
Arch Sci Ph — Archives des Sciences Physiologiques
Arch Sci Physiol — Archives des Sciences Physiologiques
Arch Sci Phys Nat — Archives des Sciences Physiques et Naturelles. Supplement a la Bibliotheque Universelle
Arch Sci Rev — Architectural Science Review
Arch Sc Med (Torino) — Archivio per le Scienze Mediche (Torino)
Arch Sc Phys Nat — Archives des Sciences Physiques et Naturelles
Arch Sex Be — Archives of Sexual Behavior
Arch Sex Behav — Archives of Sexual Behavior
Archs Inst Gr-Duc Luxemb — Archives. Institut Grand-Ducal de Luxembourg
Archs Insts Pasteur Afr N — Archives. Instituts Pasteur de l'Afrique du Nord
Archs Intern Med — Archives of Internal Medicine
Archs Int Pharmacodyn Ther — Archives Internationales de Pharmacodynamie et de Therapie
Archs Int Physiol — Archives Internationales de Physiologie
Archs Int Physiol Biochim — Archives Internationales de Physiologie et de Biochimie
Archs Med-Chir Normandie — Archives Medico-Chirurgicales de Normandie
Archs Neerl Zool — Archives Neerlandaises de Zoologie
Arch Soc Am Oftalmol Optom — Archivos. Sociedad Americana de Oftalmologia y Optometria
Arch Soc Biol Montev — Archivos. Sociedad de Biologia de Montevideo
Arch Soc Esp Oftalmol — Archivos. Sociedad Espanola de Oftalmologia
Arch Soc Estud Clin Habana — Archivos. Sociedad de Estudios Clinicos de la Habana
Arch Soc Oftalmol Hisp-Am — Archivos. Sociedad Oftalmologica Hispano-Americana
Arch Soc Zool-Bot Fenn "Vanamo" — Archivum Societatis Zoologicae-Botanicae Fennicae "Vanamo"
Arch (Sofia) — Archeologie (Sofia)
ArchSS — Archivio Storico Siciliano
Archs Sci Physiol — Archives des Sciences Physiologiques
Arch SS Rel — Archives des Sciences Sociales des Religions
Arch Stomatol — Archivio Stomatologico
Arch Stor — Archivio Storico Italiano
Arch Stor I — Archivio Storico Italiano
Arch Stor Lodigiano — Archivio Storico Lodigiano
Arch Stor Sicilia Orient — Archivio Storico per la Sicilia Orientale
Arch Stud Fisiopatol Clin Ricamb — Archivio per lo Studio della Fisiopatologia e Clinica del Ricambio
Arch Suisses Anthropol Gen — Archives Suisses d'Anthropologie Generale
Arch Suisses Neurol Neurochir Psychiatr — Archives Suisses de Neurologie, Neurochirurgie, et de Psychiatrie
Arch Surg — Archives of Surgery
Archs Virol — Archives of Virology
ArchT — Archeion Thrakes
Archt & Bldr — Architect and Builder [*South Africa*]
Arch Tech Mess Ind Messtech — Archiv fuer Technisches Messen und Industrielle Messtechnik
Arch Tech Mess Messtech Prax — Archiv fuer Technisches Messen und Messtechnische Praxis
Arch Termodyn — Archiwum Termodynamiki
Arch Termodyn Spal — Archiwum Termodynamiki i Spalania
Arch Tierernaehr — Archiv fuer Tierernaehrung
Arch Tierz — Archiv fuer Tierzucht [*East Germany*]
Arch Tisiol Mal App Resp — Archivio di Tisiologia e delle Malattie dell'Apparato Respiratorio [*Italy*]
Archtl Design — Architectural Design
Archtl History — Architectural History

Archtl Science Review — Architectural Science Review
Arch Today — Architecture Today
Arch Toxic — Archives of Toxicology [*Berlin*]
Arch Toxicol — Archives of Toxicology [*Berlin*]
Arch Toxicol (Berl) — Archives of Toxicology (Berlin)
Arch Toxicol (Suppl) — Archives of Toxicology. Supplement (Berlin)
Arch Toxikol — Archiv fuer Toxikologie [*Later, Archives of Toxicology*]
Arch Triest — Archeolgrafo Triestino
Archt Sci Rev — Architectural Science Review
Archts Jnl — Architects- Journal
Archts Trade Jnl — Architects' Trade Journal
Arch Union Med Balk — Archives. Union Medicale Balkanique
Arch Urug Med Cir Espec — Archivos Uruguayos de Medicina, Cirujia, y Especialidades
ArchV — Archiv fuer Voelkerkunde
Arch de Vecchi Anat Patol — Archivio "De Vecchi" per l'Anatomia Patologica e la Medicina Clinica
Arch Venez Med Trop Parasitol Med — Archivos Venezolanos de Medicina Tropical y Parasitologia Medica
Arch Venez Nutr — Archivos Venezolanos de Nutricion
Arch Venez Patol Trop Parasitol Med — Archivos Venezolanos de Patologia Tropical y Parasitologia Medica
Arch Venez Pueric Pediatr — Archivos Venezolanos de Puericultura y Pediatria
Arch Verdau Kr — Archiv fuer Verdauungs-Krankheiten
Arch Verdauungskr — Archiv fuer Verdauungs-Krankheiten mit Einschluss der Stoffwechselpathologie und der Diaetetik
Arch Vet — Archiva Veterinaria
Arch Vet (Buchar) — Archiva Veterinaria (Bucureşt)
Arch Vet Ital — Archivio Veterinario Italiano
Arch Virol — Archives of Virology
Arch Volkswohlfahrt — Archiv fuer Volkswohlfahrt
Arch Waermewirtsch — Archiv fuer Waermewirtschaft
Arch Waermewirtsch Dampfkesselwes — Archiv fuer Waermewirtschaft und Dampfkesselwesen [*West Germany*]
Arch Wissensch u Prakt Tierh — Archiv fuer Wissenschaftliche und Praktische Tierheilkunde
Arch Wiss Prakt Tierheilkd — Archiv fuer Wissenschaftliche und Praktische Tierheilkunde
Archwm Gorn — Archiwum Gornictwa
Archwm Hutn — Archiwum Hutnictwa
Arch Yr — Architect's Yearbook
Arch Yrbk — Architect's Yearbook
Arch Zellforsch — Archiv fuer Zellforschung
Arch Z Ges — Architectura. Zeitschrift fuer Geschichte der Baukunst
Arch Zool Exper et Gen — Archives de Zoologie Experimentale et Generale
Arch Zool Exp Gen — Archives de Zoologie Experimentale et Generale
Arch Zool Exp Gen Notes Rev — Archives de Zoologie Experimentale et Generale. Notes et Revue
Arch Zool Ital — Archivio Zoologico Italiano
Arch Zootec — Archivos de Zootecnia
ArchZtg — Archaeologische Zeitung
ARCI — Arctic Circular
Arcisp S Anna di Ferrara — Arcispedale S. Anna di Ferrara [*Italy*]
ArcP — Archeion Pontou
ARCRBD — Annual Report on Cacao Research. University of the West Indies
ARCRDF — Australia. Commonwealth Scientific and Industrial Research Organisation. Division of Forest Research. Annual Report
ARCRL Rep — Agricultural Research Council. Radiobiology Laboratory Report [*United Kingdom*]
ARCSA — Annals. Royal College of Surgeons of England
ARCSB — Archivio Stomatologico
ARCT — Arctic
Arct Aeromed Lab (US) Tech Doc Rep — Arctic Aeromedical Laboratory (United States). Technical Documentary Report
Arct Aeromed Lab (US) Tech Note — Arctic Aeromedical Laboratory (United States). Technical Note
Arct Aeromed Lab (US) Tech Rep — Arctic Aeromedical Laboratory (United States). Technical Report
Arct Alp Res — Arctic and Alpine Research
Arct Alp Res (Boulder Colo) — Arctic and Alpine Research (Boulder, Colorado)
Arct Anthropol — Arctic Anthropology
Arct Bibl — Arctic Bibliography
Arct Bull — Arctic Bulletin
Arctic Anthropol — Arctic Anthropology
Arctic Bul — Arctic Bulletin
Arctic Inst North America Research Paper — Arctic Institute of North America. Research Paper
Arctic Inst North America Special Pub — Arctic Institute of North America. Special Publication
Arctic Inst North America Tech Paper — Arctic Institute of North America. Technical Paper
Arct Inst N Am Annu Rep — Arctic Institute of North America. Annual Report
Arct Inst N Am Spec Publ — Arctic Institute of North America. Special Publication

Arct Inst N Am Tech Pap — Arctic Institute of North America. Technical Paper
Arct Inst North Am Annu Rep — Arctic Institute of North America. Annual Report
ARCU — Architektura a Urbanizmus
ARCU — Arcturus. Department of Education. Northwest Territories [*Canada*]
ARCWD — Architektur und Wohnwelt
ARD — Architectural Record
ARDAD — Army R D and A [*Research, Development, and Acquisition*] [*Later, R, D & A*] [*United States*]
ARDBA — Advances in Radiation Biology
ARDCB — Advances in Radiation Chemistry
Arden's Sydney Mag — Arden's Sydney Magazine
ARDH-A — Architecture d'Aujourd'hui
ARDRA — Australian Road Research
ARDRSP — Archivio. R. Deputazione Romana di Storia Patria
ARDS — Annual Report. Dante Society
ARDSB — American Review of Respiratory Disease
ARDSBL — American Review of Respiratory Disease
ARDVA — Army Research and Development [*Later, R, D & A*] [*United States*]
AREA — Association for Religious Education Aspects of Education. Bulletin
Area Dev — Area Development
AREAER — Annual Report on Exchange Arrangements and Exchange Restrictions
AREBA8 — Bulletin. ARERS [*Association Regionale des Amis de l'Universite et de l'Enseignement Superieur pour la Promotion de l'Etude et la Recherche Scientifiques*]
ARECB — Annual Review of Ecology and Systematics
ARECBC — Annual Review of Ecology and Systematics
AREDD — Annual Report on Energy Research, Development, and Demonstration. International Energy Agency
AREGB — Archiwum Energetyki
AREHDT — Annual Review of Public Health
ARELA — Archiwum Elektrotechniki
ARENA — Annual Review of Entomology
ARENAA — Annual Review of Entomology
Arena Rev — Arena Review
AREND — Annual Review of Energy
A Rep Natn Inst Anim Ind (Japan) — Annual Report. National Institute for Animal Industry. Ministry of Agriculture and Forestry (Japan)
A Rep Rec Res — Annual Report. Record Research. East African Agriculture and Forestry Research Organisation
ARERAM — Arerugi
ARERI — Australian Renewable Energy Resources Index
ARES — Agricultural Research
ArEspArq — Archivo Espanol de Arqueologia [*Madrid*]
Areth — Arethusa
A Rev Biochem — Annual Review of Biochemistry
A Rev Ent — Annual Review of Entomology
A Rev Genet — Annual Review of Genetics
A Rev Microbiol — Annual Review of Microbiology
A Rev Phytopath — Annual Review of Phytopathology
A Rev Pl Physiol — Annual Review of Plant Physiology
A Rev Psychol — Annual Review of Psychology
AREX — Arctic Explorer. Travel Arctic. Northwest Territories [*Canada*]
ARFAA — Academia Republicii Populare Romine. Institutul de Fizica Atomica si Institutul de Fizica. Studii si Cercetari de Fizica
ARFHA — Australian Refrigeration, Air Conditioning, and Heating
Ar Fi — Archivio di Filosofia
ARFIA — Archivio di Fisiologia
Ar Fil — Archivio di Filosofia
ARFLBA — Agricultural Research Organization. Division of Forestry. Ilanot Leaflet
ARFMA — Arhiv za Farmaciju
ARFMAC — Arhiv za Farmaciju [*Belgrade*]
ARFTAX — Annual Review of Food Technology [*Mysore*]
ARG — American Record Guide
ARG — Archiv fuer Reformationsgeschichte
Arg — Argensola
ARGAP — [*A*] Research Guide to Australian Politics
Argent Com Nac Energ At Inf — Argentina. Comision Nacional de Energia Atomica. Informe
Argent Dir Nac Geol Min Bol — Argentina. Direccion Nacional de Geologia y Mineria. Boletin
Argent Electroenerg — Argentina Electroenergetica
Argent Inst Nac Geol Min Bol — Argentina. Instituto Nacional de Geologia y Mineria. Boletin
Argent Repub Minist Agric Ganad Publ — Republica de Argentina. Ministerio de Agricultura y Ganaderia. Publicacion Miscelanea
Argent Repub Minist Agric Ganad Publ Tec — Republica de Argentina. Ministerio de Agricultura y Ganaderia. Publicacion Tecnia
Argent Repub Subsecr Min Ser Argent — Republica de Argentina. Subsecretaria de Mineria. Serie Argentina
Argent Text — Argentina Textil

ARGG — Annual Review of Gerontology and Geriatrics
ArGlottIt — Archivio Glottologico Italiano [*Florence*]
Arg LR — Argus Law Reports
ARGOA — Argosy
Argonne Natl Lab News Bull — Argonne National Laboratory. News Bulletin
Argonne Natl Lab Rev — Argonne National Laboratory. Reviews
Argonne Natl Lab Water Resour Res Program (Rep) ANL/WR — Argonne National Laboratory. Water Resources Research Program (Report) ANL/WR
Argonne Rev — Argonne Reviews
ARGPA — Archives of General Psychiatry
Arg Rep — Argus Law Reports
ARGTU — Archiv fuer Reformationsgeschichte. Texte und Untersuchungen
ARGUC9 — Agricultural Research Guyana
Argus LR — Argus Law Reports
Argus LR (CN) — Argus Law Reports (Current Notes)
Argus L Rep — Argus Law Reports
Argus (Newspr) (VIC) — Argus Reports (Newspaper) (Victoria)
ArH — Archivo Hispalense
Arh Biol Nauka — Arhiv Bioloskih Nauka
ARHEA — Arthritis and Rheumatism
Arh Farm (Belgr) — Arhiv za Farmaciju (Belgrade)
Arh Hig Rada Toksikol — Arhiv za Higijenu Rada i Toksikologiju
Arh Hig Rad Toksikol — Arhiv za Higijenu Rada i Toksikologiju
Arhitekt SSSR — Arhitektura SSSR
ARHMB — Archivus Historii Medycyny
ARHMB — Archiwum Historii Medycyny
Arh Moldovei — Arheologia Moldovei
Arh Poljopriv Nauke — Arhiv za Poljoprivredne Nauke
Arh Poljopr Nauke — Arhiv za Poljoprivredne Nauke
Arh Poljopr Nauke Teh — Arhiv za Poljoprivredne Nauke i Tehniku
ArHPont — Archivum Historiae Pontificiae [*Rome*]
ArHQ — Arkansas Historical Quarterly
Arh Rud Tehnol — Arhiv za Rudarstvo i Tehnologiju
ARHS Bull — Australian Railway Historical Society. Bulletin
ArhV — Arheoloski Vestnik
ArI — Archivo Ibero-Americano [*Madrid*]
ARI — Ariadne
ARIADS — Industrial Environmental Research Laboratory [*Research Triangle Park*]. Annual Report
ARIC — Arctic in Colour
ARID — Analecta Romana Instituti Danici
Ari D — Arion's Dolphin
Arid Lands Resour Inf Pap — Arid Lands Resource Information Paper
Arid Zone Newsl Div Land Res CSIRO — Arid Zone Newsletter. Division of Land Research. Commonwealth Scientific and Industrial Research Organisation
Arid Zone Res UNESCO — Arid Zone Research. United Nations Educational, Scientific, and Cultural Organization
Ariel E — Ariel: A Review of International English Literature
ARIFD9 — International Commission for the Northwest Atlantic Fisheries. Annual Report
ARIMDU — Annual Review of Immunology
ARINAU — Annual Report. Research Institute of Environmental Medicine. Nagoya University [*English Edition*]
ARIPUC — Annual Report. Institute of Phonetics. University of Copenhagen
ARIQD8 — Annual Report. Nigerian Institute for Oceanography and Marine Research
ARISBC — Annual Review of Information Science and Technology
Aris Phil C — Aris and Phillips Central Asian Studies
Aris Soc — Aristotelian Society. Supplementary Volume
Aristot Panepist Thessalonikis Epet Geopon Dasolog Skol — Aristoteleion Panepistemion Thessalonikis Epetiris tis Geoponikis kai Dasologikis Skolis
Arith Teach — Arithmetic Teacher
ARIVAK — Annual Report. Institute for Virus Research. Kyoto University
Ariz — Arizona Supreme Court Reports
Ariz Ag Exp — Arizona. Agricultural Experiment Station. Publications
Ariz Agric Exp Stn Bull — Arizona. Agricultural Experiment Station. Bulletin
Ariz Agric Exp Stn Res Rep — Arizona. Agricultural Experiment Station. Research Report
Ariz Agric Exp Stn Tech Bull — Arizona. Agricultural Experiment Station. Technical Bulletin
Ariz BJ — Arizona Bar Journal
Ariz Bur Mines Bull — Arizona. Bureau of Mines. Bulletin
Ariz Bur Mines Bull Geol Ser — Arizona. Bureau of Mines. Bulletin. Geological Series
Ariz Bur Mines Bull Mineral Technology Ser — Arizona. Bureau of Mines. Bulletin. Mineral Technology Series
Ariz Bur Mines Circ — Arizona. Bureau of Mines. Circular
Ariz Bur Mines Field Notes — Arizona. Bureau of Mines. Field Notes
Ariz Bus — Arizona Business
Ariz Comm Agric Hortic Annu Rep — Arizona. Commission of Agriculture and Horticulture. Annual Report
Ariz Dept Mineral Res Ann Rept — Arizona. Department of Mineral Resources. Annual Report

Ariz For Notes — Arizona Forestry Notes
Ariz For Note Sch For Nth Ariz Univ — Arizona Forestry Notes. School of Forestry. Northern Arizona University
Ariz Game Fish Dep Wildl Bull — Arizona. Game and Fish Department. Wildlife Bulletin
Ariz Geol Soc Digest Ann — Arizona Geological Society. Digest. Annual
Ariz H — Arizona Highways
Ariz His R — Arizona Historical Review
Ariz Hist Rev — Arizona Historical Review
Ariz Law R — Arizona Law Review
Ariz Legis Serv — Arizona Legislative Service
Ariz Libn — Arizona Librarian
Ariz Librn — Arizona Librarian
Ariz L Rev — Arizona Law Review
Ariz Med — Arizona Medicine
Ariz Nurse — Arizona Nurse
Arizona Acad Sci Jour — Arizona Academy of Science. Journal
Arizona Bur Mines Bull — Arizona. Bureau of Mines. Bulletin
Arizona R — Arizona Review
Arizona State LJ — Arizona State Law Journal
Ariz Q — Arizona Quarterly
Ariz R — Arizona Review
Ariz State Land Dept Water Res Rept — Arizona State Land Department. Water Resources Report
Ariz State Law J — Arizona State Law Journal
Ariz St Bur Mines B — Arizona State Bureau of Mines. Bulletin
Ariz St L J — Arizona State Law Journal
Ariz SU Ant — Arizona State University. Anthropological Research Papers
Ariz Teach — Arizona Teacher
Ariz Univ Agr Expt Bull — Arizona University. Agricultural Experiment Station. Bulletin
Ariz Univ Agr Expt Bull Phys Sci Bull — Arizona University. Agricultural Experiment Station. Bulletin. Physical Science Bulletin
Ariz Univ Lab Tree-Ring Res Pap — Arizona University. Laboratory of Tree-Ring Research. Papers
Ariz Univ Lunar Planet Lab Commun — Arizona University. Lunar and Planetary Laboratory. Communications
ArizW — Arizona and the West
Ariz Water Comm Bull — Arizona. Water Commission. Bulletin
Ariz and West — Arizona and the West
Ar J — Arbitration Journal
ARJID — Japan. Atomic Energy Research Institute. Annual Report and Account
ARJKAQ — Agricultural Research Journal of Kerala
A and R (JP) — A and R. Analysis and Research (Japan)
ARJSAG — Japanese Society for Tuberculosis. Annual Report
ARJU — Arjungnagimmat. Inuit Cultural Institute
Ark Acad Sci Proc — Arkansas Academy of Science. Proceedings
Ark Ag Exp — Arkansas. Agricultural Experiment Station. Publications
Arkansas Acad Sci Proc — Arkansas Academy of Science. Proceedings
Arkansas Agric Exp Stn Bull — Arkansas. Agricultural Experiment Station. Bulletin
Arkansas Agric Exp Stn Mimeogr Ser — Arkansas. Agricultural Experiment Station. Mimeograph Series
Arkansas Agric Exp Stn Rep Ser — Arkansas. Agricultural Experiment Station. Report Series
Arkansas Agric Exp Stn Spec Rep — Arkansas. Agricultural Experiment Station. Special Report
Arkansas Dent J — Arkansas Dental Journal
Arkansas Geol Comm Inform Circ — Arkansas. Geological and Conservation Commission. Information Circular
Arkansas Lib — Arkansas Libraries
Arkansas L Rev — Arkansas Law Review
Arkansas Univ Seismol Bull — Arkansas University. Seismological Bulletin
Arkans Fm Res — Arkansas Farm Research
Ark Astron — Arkiv foer Astronomi
Ark Bot — Arkiv foer Botanik
Ark Bus and Econ R — Arkansas Business and Economic Review
ARKEAD — Arkiv foer Kemi
ArKF — Archiv fuer Keilschriftforschung
Ark Farm Res — Arkansas Farm Research
Ark Fys — Arkiv foer Fysik
Ark Fys Semin Trondheim — Arkiv foer det Fysiske Seminar i Trondheim
Ark Geofys — Arkiv foer Geofysik
Ark G S — Arkansas. Geological Survey
Arkh Anat Gistol Embriol — Arkhiv Anatomii, Gistologii, i Embriologii
Arkh Biol Nauk — Arkhiv Biologicheskikh Nauk
Arkheologiia — Arkheologiia Organ na Arkheologicheskiia Institut i Muzei pri B'lgarskata Akademiia na Naukite
Ark His As — Arkansas Historical Association. Publications
Ark Hist Assoc Publ — Arkansas Historical Association. Publications
Ark Hist Q — Arkansas Historical Quarterly
Ark Hist Quar — Arkansas Historical Quarterly
Arkhit Stroit Leningrada — Arkhitektura i Stroitelstvo Leningrada
Arkhivi Ukr — Arkhivi Ukraini. Naukovo Informatsiinii Biuleten' Arkhivnogo Upravliniia pri Radi Ministriv URSR

Arkh Klin i Eksper Med (Moskva) — Arkhiv Klinicheskoi i Eksperimental'noi Meditsiny (Moskva)
Arkh Med Nauk — Arkhiv Meditsinskikh Nauk
Arkh Patol — Arkhiv Patologii
ArkHQ — Arkansas Historical Quarterly
Arkh Russk Protist Obsh — Arkhiv Russkogo Protistologicheskogo Obshchestva
Arkiv — Arkiv foer Nordisk Filologi
Arkiv f Nord Filologi — Arkiv foer Nordisk Filologi
ARKK-A — Arkkitehti
Ark Kemi — Arkiv foer Kemi
Ark Kemi Mineral Geol — Arkiv foer Kemi, Mineralogi, och Geologi [*Sweden*]
Ark (Kiev) — Arkheologiia (Kiev)
Ark Law — Arkansas Lawyer
Ark Law R — Arkansas Law Review
Ark Lib — Arkansas Libraries
Ark L Rev — Arkansas Law Review
Ark Mat — Arkiv foer Matematik
Ark Mat Astron Fys — Arkiv foer Matematik, Astronomi, och Fysik [*Sweden*]
Ark Matemat — Arkiv foer Matematik
Ark Mineral Geol — Arkiv foer Mineralogi och Geologi
Ark Nurse — Arkansas Nurse
Ark Otkr — Arkheologicheskie Otkrytiia
Ark Pam URSR — Arkheologichi Pamiatniki URSR
Ark Res Devel Comm Div Geology Bull Inf Circ — Arkansas. Resources and Development Commission. Division of Geology Bulletin. Information Circular
Ark Riv — Ark River Review
ARKSN — Annuarium des Roomsch-Katholieke Studenten in Nederland
Ark State Nurses Assoc Newsl — Arkansas State Nurses' Association. Newsletter
ARKT-B — Architektura
ArkUkr — Arkheologija. Publies par l'Academie des Sciences d'Ukraine
ArKulturg — Archiv fuer Kulturgeschichte
Ark Univ Inst Sci and Technology Research Ser — Arkansas University. Institute of Science and Technology. Research Series
Ark Zool — Arkiv foer Zoologi
Ark Zool (Stockholm) — Arkiv foer Zoologi (Stockholm)
ArL — Archivum Linguisticum
ARLAB — Archiv fuer Landtechnik
ARLIS Newsl — ARLIS [*Art Libraries Society/North America*] Newsletter
ARL Mins — Association of Research Libraries. Minutes
ArlQ — Arlington Quarterly
ARL/TR — Australian Radiation Laboratory. Technical Report
Ar Lw — Archiv fuer Liturgiewissenschaft
ARM — Abstracts of Research and Related Materials in Vocational and Technical Education
ARM — Archives Royales de Mari
ARM — Archives Royales de Mari. Textes Cuneiformes
ArM — Arte (Milan)
ARMC — Architecture, Mouvement, Continuite
ArmC — Arms Control and Disarmament
ARMCA — Annual Review of Medicine
ARMCAH — Annual Review of Medicine
ARMCBI — Annual Reports in Medicinal Chemistry
Armchair Det — [*The*] Armchair Detective
Arm D — [*The*] Armchair Detective
Armdale & Dist Hist Soc J & Proc — Armidale and District Historical Society. Journal and Proceedings
ARMEA — Arizona Medicine
ARMEAN — Arizona Medicine
ARMED — Armement
Armed Forces Med J India — Armed Forces Medical Journal. India
Armed Forces Soc — Armed Forces and Society
Armees Aujourd — Armees d'Aujourd'hui
Armement Bull Inf Liaison — Armement. Bulletin d'Information et de Liaison
Armenian N J — Armenian Numismatic Journal
ARMIA — Annual Review of Microbiology
ARMIAZ — Annual Review of Microbiology
Armidale Dist Hist Soc J — Armidale and District Historical Society. Journal
Armidale Hist Soc J — Armidale and District Historical Society. Journal
Armidale New Engl Univ Explor Soc Rep — Armidale. University of New England. Exploration Society. Report
Armidale Teach Coll Bull — Armidale Teachers' College. Bulletin
Armid Teach Coll Bul — Armidale Teachers' College. Bulletin
Armjan Gos Ped Inst Sb Naucn Trud Ser Fiz-Mat — Armjanskii Gosudarstvennyi Pedagogiceskii Institut Imeni H. Abovjana. Sbornik Naucnyh Trudov. Serija Fiziko-Matematiceskaja
Arm Khim Zh — Armyanskii Khimicheskii Zhurnal
ARMND — Annales de Radiologie. Medecine Nucleaire
Armored Cavalry J — Armored Cavalry Journal
Armour Res Found Rep — Armour Research Foundation. Report
Arms Explos — Arms and Explosives
ARMT — Archives Royales de Mari. Textes Administratives
ARMT — Archives Royales de Mari. Transcriptions et Traductions [*Paris*]
ARMUA3 — American Malacological Union, Incorporated. Annual Report

ARMUB — Arts et Manufactures
Army — Australian Army
Armyanskii Khim Zh — Armyanskii Khimecheskii Zhurnal
Army Law — Army Lawyer
Army Lawy — Army Lawyer
Army Logis — Army Logistician
Army Med Bull — Army Medical Bulletin
Army Med Dept Rep (London) — Army Medical Department. Reports (London)
Army Res & Devel — Army Research and Development [*Later, R, D & A*]
Army Reserv — Army Reserve Magazine
ARNAAG — Annuaire Roumain d'Anthropologie
ARNBBK — Archivos de Neurobiologia
ARNCAM — Agronomia [*La Molina*]
ARND — Arctic and Northern Development Digest
ARNE — Arctic News
ARNEA — Archives of Neurology
ARNEAS — Archives of Neurology
ARN J — American Rehabilitation Nursing Journal
ARN J — ARN [*Association of Rehabilitation Nurses*] Journal
ARNNA — Annual Report. National Institute of Nutrition
Arnold Arbor J — Harvard University. Arnold Arboretum Journal
ARNSD5 — Annual Review of Neuroscience
AR(NSW) — Industrial Arbitration Reports (New South Wales)
ARNTD8 — Annual Review of Nutrition
ARNUA — Annual Review of Nuclear Science [*Later, Annual Review of Nuclear and Particle Science*]
ARNUA8 — Annual Review of Nuclear Science [*Later, Annual Review of Nuclear and Particle Science*]
ArNVA — Arbok Det Norske Videnskapsakademi
ARNYA — Annual Report. Natural Science Research Institute. Yonsei University
ARO — Anciennes Religions Orientales
ArO — Archiv Orientalni
AROABM — Agroanimalia
AROF — Arctic Offshore. Publication of the Alaska Oil and Gas Association
AROHA8 — Archives d'Ophtalmologie et Revue Generale d'Ophtalmologie
ARom — Archivum Romanicum
Aromat Heteroaromat Chem — Aromatic and Heteroaromatic Chemistry
AROPAW — Archives of Ophthalmology
AROPDZ — Archives d'Ophtalmologie
Ar Or — Archiv Orientalni
ARORA — Archivio di Ortopedia [*Later, Archivio di Ortopedia e Reumatologia*]
AROTA — Archives of Otolaryngology
AROTAA — Archives of Otolaryngology
ARP — Arbeiten zur Romanischen Philologie
ARp — Archaeological Report Comprising the Recent Work of the Egypt Exploration Fund and the Progress of Egyptology [*London*]
ArP — Aryan Path
ARPAAQ — Archives of Pathology [*Later, Archives of Pathology and Laboratory Medicine*]
ArPapF — Archiv fuer Papyrusforschung [*Leipzig*]
ARPEA4 — Archives of Pediatrics
Ar Pf — Archiv fuer Papyrusforschung
ARPH — Annual Review of Public Health
ARPh — Archiv fuer Rechts- und Wirtschaftsphilosophie
Ar Ph — Archives de Philosophie
ARPHA — Annual Review of Physiology
ARPHAD — Annual Review of Physiology
ARPLA — Annual Review of Physical Chemistry
ARPMAS — Archiv der Pharmazie [*Weinheim, Germany*]
ARPPA — Annual Review of Plant Physiology
ARPPA3 — Annual Review of Plant Physiology
ARPR — Arctic Policy Review
ARPRD — Arbitrazni Praxe
ARPs — Archiv fuer Religionspsychologie
ARPSA — Annual Review of Psychology
ARPSAC — Annual Review of Psychology
ARPSD — Annual Review of Nuclear and Particle Science
ARPTA — Arkhiv Patologii
ARPTD — Annual Review of Pharmacology and Toxicology
ARPTDI — Annual Review of Pharmacology and Toxicology
ArQ — Arizona Quarterly
Arq Anat Antrop — Arquivo de Anatomia e Antropologia
Arq Anat Antropol — Arquivo de Anatomia e Antropologia
Arq Biol (Sao Paulo) — Arquivos de Biologia (Sao Paulo)
Arq Biol Tecnol — Arquivos de Biologia e Tecnologia
Arq Biol Tecnol (Curitiba) — Arquivos de Biologia e Tecnologia (Curitiba)
Arq Bot Estado Sao Paulo — Arquivos de Botanica do Estado de Sao Paulo
Arq Bras Cardiol — Arquivos Brasileiros de Cardiologia
Arq Bras Endocrinol Metabol — Arquivos Brasileiros de Endocrinologia e Metabologia
Arq Brasil Cardiol — Arquivos Brasileiros de Cardiologia
Arq Bras Med — Arquivos Brasileiros de Medicina
Arq Bras Med Nav — Arquivos Brasileiros de Medicina Naval

Arq Bras Nutr — Arquivos Brasileiros de Nutricao
Arq Bras Oftal — Arquivos Brasileiros de Oftalmologia
Arq Bras Oftalmol — Arquivos Brasileiros de Oftalmologia
Arq Bras Ps — Arquivos Brasileiros de Psicologia Aplicada
Arq Bras Tuberc Doencas Torax — Arquivos Brasileiros de Tuberculose e Doencas do Torax
Arq Bromatol — Arquivos de Bromatologia
Arq Catarinenses Med — Arquivos Catarinenses de Medicina
Arq Cent Estud Curso Odontol Univ Fed Minas Gerais — Arquivos. Centro de Estudos do Curso de Odontologia. Universidade Federal de Minas Gerais
Arq Cent Estud Fac Odontol Univ Fed Minas Gerais — Arquivos. Centro de Estudos da Faculdade de Odontologia. Universidade Federal de Minas Gerais
Arq Cent Estud Fac Odontol Univ Minas Gerais (Belo Horiz) — Arquivos. Centro de Estudos da Faculdade de Odontologia. Universidade de Minas Gerais (Belo Horizonte)
Arq Centro Cult Port — Arquivos. Centro Cultural Portugues
Arq Cienc Mar — Arquivos de Ciencias do Mar
Arq Cir Clin Exp (Sao Paulo) — Arquivos de Cirurgia Clinica e Experimental (Sao Paulo)
Arq Dep Assist Psicop S Paulo — Arquivos. Departamento de Assistencia a Psicopates. Estado de Sao Paulo
Arq Dermatol Sifiligr Sao Paulo — Arquivos de Dermatologia e Sifiligrafia de Sao Paulo
Arq Entomol Ser A — Arquivos de Entomologia. Serie A
Arq Entomol Ser B — Arquivos de Entomologia. Serie B
Arq Esc Super Vet Univ Rur Estado Minas Gerais — Arquivos. Escola Superior de Veterinaria. Universidade Rural. Estado de Minas Gerais
Arq Esc Vet Univ Fed Minas Gerais — Arquivos. Escola de Veterinaria. Universidade Federal de Minas Gerais
Arq Esc Vet Univ Minas Gerais — Arquivos. Escola de Veterinaria. Universidade Federal de Minas Gerais
Arq Estac Biol Mar Univ Ceara — Arquivos. Estacao de Biologia Marinha da Universidade Federal do Ceara
Arq Estac Biol Mar Univ Fed Ceara — Arquivos. Estacao de Biologia Marinha da Universidade Federal do Ceara
Arq Fac Hig Saude Publica Univ Sao Paulo — Arquivos. Faculdade de Higiene e Saude Publica. Universidade de Sao Paulo
Arq Fac Hig S Paul — Arquivos. Faculdade de Higiene e Saude Publica. Universidade de Sao Paulo
Arq Fac Nac Med — Arquivos. Faculdade Nacional de Medicina
Arq Fac Nac Med (Rio De Janeiro) — Arquivos. Faculdade Nacional de Medicina (Rio De Janeiro)
Arq Gastroenterol — Arquivos de Gastroenterologia
Arq Hig (Rio De J) — Arquivos de Higiene (Rio De Janeiro)
Arq Hig Saude Publica (Sao Paulo) — Arquivos de Higiene e Saude Publica (Sao Paulo)
Arq Inst Anat Univ Rio Grande Do Sul — Arquivos. Instituto de Anatomia. Universidade do Rio Grande Do Sul
Arq Inst Bacteriol Camara Pestana — Arquivos. Instituto Bacteriologico. Camara Pestana
Arq Inst Bacteriol Cam Pestana — Arquivos. Instituto Bacteriologico. Camara Pestana
Arq Inst Biol — Arquivos. Instituto Biologico
Arq Inst Biol Anim (Rio De J) — Arquivos. Instituto de Biologia Animal (Rio De Janeiro)
Arq Inst Biol Exerc — Arquivos. Instituto de Biologia do Exercito
Arq Inst Biol (Sao Paulo) — Arquivos. Instituto Biologico (Sao Paulo)
Arq Inst Biol Veg (Rio De J) — Arquivos. Instituto de Biologia Vegetal (Rio De Janeiro)
Arq Inst Pesqui Agron — Arquivos. Instituto de Pesquisas Agronomicas
Arq Inst Pesqui Vet Desiderio Finamor — Arquivos. Instituto de Pesquisas Veterinarias "Desiderio Finamor"
Arq Jard Bot Rio De J — Arquivos. Jardim Botanico do Rio De Janeiro
Arq Min Leprol — Arquivos Mineiros de Leprologia
Arq Mus Bocage — Arquivos. Museu Bocage
Arq Mus Hist Nat Univ Fed Minas Gerais — Arquivos. Museu de Historia Natural. Universidade Federal de Minas Gerais
Arq Mus Nac Rio De J — Arquivos. Museu Nacional do Rio De Janeiro
Arq Mus Parana — Arquivos. Museu Paranaense
Arq Neuro-Psiquiatr — Arquivos de Neuro-Psiquiatria
Arq Oncol — Arquivos de Oncologia
Arq Patol — Arquivo de Patologia
Arq Patol Geral Anat Patol Univ Coimbra — Arquivos de Patologia Geral e Anatomia Patologica. Universidade de Coimbra
Arq Patol (Lisbon) — Arquivos de Patologia (Lisbon)
Arq Pediat — Arquivos de Pediatria
Arq Port — Arqueologo Portugues
Arq Port Bioquim — Arquivos Portugueses de Bioquimica
Arq Serv Florestal (Rio De J) — Arquivos. Servico Florestal (Rio De Janeiro)
ARQT — Arquitectura
Arq Tisiol — Arquivos de Tisiologia
Arqu Bol — Arqueologia Boliviana
Arquivo Inst Gulbenkian Ci A Estud Mat Fis-Mat — Arquivo. Instituto Gulbenkian de Ciencia. A. Estudos Matematicos e Fisico-Matematicos

Arquivos Brasil Psicol Ap — Arquivos Brasileiros de Psicologia Aplicada
Arqu Mus Nac — Arquivos. Museu Nacional do Rio De Janeiro
Arq Zool Estado Sao Paulo — Arquivos de Zoologia do Estado de Sao Paulo
Arq Zool (Sao Paulo) — Arquivos de Zoologia (Sao Paulo)
ARR — American Review of Reviews
ArR — Archivi (Rome)
ARRDA — American Review of Respiratory Disease
ARREEI — Annual Review of Rehabilitation
ArRefg — Archiv fuer Reformationsgeschichte [*Guetersloh*]
Ar Rep — Argus Reports
ARRIP — Australian Road Research in Progress
ARROAA — Annual Report. Radiation Center of Osaka Prefecture
ArRW — Archiv fuer Religionswissenschaft [*Leipzig/Berlin*]
ARRWB — Argonne Reviews
ARS — Advanced Religious Studies
ARSB — Arctic Seas Bulletin. Canadian Arctic Resources Committee
Arsber Danm Fisk Havund — Arsberetning fra Danmarks Fiskeri og Havundersogelser
Arsberet Nor Fisk — Arsberetning Norges Fiskerier
Arsberet Statens Forsoegsmejeri — Arsberetning. Statens Forsoegsmejeri
Arsberet Vedkomm Nor Fisk — Arsberetning Vedkommende Norges Fiskerier
Arsber Sver Geol Unders — Arsberaettelse. Sverings Geologiska Undersoekning
Arsb Finska Vetensk Soc — Arsbok. Finska Vetenskaps Societeten
Arsb Sodermanlands Lans Hushallningssallsk — Arsbok. Sodermanlands Lans Hushallningssallskaps
Arsb Sver Met Hydrol Inst — Arsbok. Sveriges Meteorologisk och Hydrologiska Institut
Arsb Vet Soc Lund — Arsbok. Vetenskaps-Societetn i Lund
ARSC — Annals of Regional Science
ARSC — Association for Recorded Sound Collections. Journal
ARSCBS — Academie Royale des Sciences Coloniales (Brussels). Bulletin des Seances
ARSCJ — Association for Recorded Sound Collections. Journal
Ars Comb — Ars Combinatoria [*Canada*]
Ars Combin — Ars Combinatoria
Ars Curandi Odontol — Ars Curandi em Odontologia
ARSFA — Anales. Real Sociedad Espanola de Fisica y Quimica. Serie A. Fisica
ARSIA — Annuario. Regia Scuola Archeologica Italiana di Atene
Ars Islam — Ars Islamica
ARSJ — American Rocket Society. Journal
Ars J — Ars Journal
ArSK — Archiv fuer Schriftkunde
Ars Med (Ed Fr) — Ars Medici (Edition Francaise)
ARSNSP — Atti. Reale Scuola Normale Superiore di Pisa
ARSOB — Arts in Society
ArSocRel — Archives de Sociologie des Religions [*Paris*]
ArsOr — Ars Orientalis
Ars Orient — Ars Orientalis
ARSP — Archiv fuer Rechts- und Sozialphilosophie
Ars Pharm — Ars Pharmaceutica
ARSQA — Anales. Real Sociedad Espanola de Fisica y Quimica. Serie B. Quimica
Ar SR — Archives de Sociologie des Religions
Ars S — Ars Semiotica
Arsskr K Vet Landbohoejsk — Arsskrift den Kongelige Veterinaer og Landbohoejskole
Arsskr f Modersmalslararnas Foren — Arsskrift foer Modersmalslararnas Forening
Arsskr Nor Skogplanteskoler — Arsskrift foer Norske Skogplanteskoler
ARSUAX — Archives of Surgery
Art — Art/Film/Criticism
ART — Arts in Society
Art in Am — Art in America
Art Am — Art in America
Art in Amer — Art in America
Art & Arch — Art and Archaeology
ArtArch — Art and Archaeology. Technical Abstracts
Art Archaeol Res Papers — Art and Archaeology. Research Papers
Art Archaeol Tech Abstr — Art and Archaeology. Technical Abstracts
Art Asia — Arts of Asia
Art and Aust — Art and Australia
ArtB — Art Bulletin
Art Bul — Art Bulletin
Art Bull — Art Bulletin
Art Crit — Art Criticism
ARTDA — Art Direction
Art & Dec — Art and Decoration
Art Dir — Art Direction
Art Educ — Art Education
ARTEF — Arbeiter Teater Farband
Arte Mus — Arte Musical
ArteP — Arte e Poesia
Arte y Var — Arte y Variedades
Artf — Artforum
Art Gall NSW Q — Art Gallery of New South Wales. Quarterly

ArTGran — Archivo Teologico Granadino [*Granada*]
Arth — Arthaniti
Artha Vij — Artha Vijnana
Artha Vik — Artha Vikas
Art Hist — Art History
Arth Rheum — Arthritis and Rheumatism
Arthritis Rheum — Arthritis and Rheumatism
Arthropods Fla Neighboring Land Areas — Arthropods of Florida and Neighboring Land Areas
ArtI — Art Index
ARTIA2 — Archiv fuer Tierernaehrung
Artibus A — Artibus Asiae
Artic Anth — Arctic Anthropology
ARTID5 — Annual Report on Research and Technical Work. Department of Agriculture for Northern Ireland
Artif Intel — Artificial Intelligence
Artif Intell — Artificial Intelligence
Artif Organs — Artificial Organs
Artif Satell — Artificial Satellites [*Poland*]
Arti Mus — Arti Musices
Art Ind — Art Index
Art & Ind — Art and Industry
Art Int — Art International
Art J — Art Journal
Art Jnl — Art Journal
Art Jour — Art Journal
Art J P E — Art Journal. Paris Edition
Art & L — Art and the Law
Art Lib J — Art Libraries Journal
Art Libraries Jnl — Art Libraries Journal
Art Mag — Arts Magazine
Art Mthly — Art Monthly
Art N — Art News
ARTNB — Art News
Art NZ — Art New Zealand
ARTODN — Archives of Toxicology/Archiv fuer Toxikologie
ARTPA — American Review of Tuberculosis and Pulmonary Diseases
ARTPAN — American Review of Tuberculosis and Pulmonary Diseases
Art Psychot — Art Psychotherapy
ArtQ — Art Quarterly
ARTRD — Arteriosclerosis (Dallas)
Arts — Arts Magazine
Arts Afr Noire — Arts d'Afrique Noire
Arts & Arch — Arts and Architecture
Arts & Archre — Arts and Architecture
Arts As — Arts of Asia
Arts Asiat — Arts Asiatiques
Artscan — Artscanada
Arts & D — Arts and Decoration
Arts and Dec — Arts and Decoration
Arts Doc Mthly — Arts Documentation Monthly
Arts & Hum Cit Ind — Arts and Humanities Citation Index
Arts Mag — Arts Magazine
Arts Manuf — Arts et Manufactures
Arts Metiers — Arts et Metiers
Arts Reptg Ser — Arts Reporting Service
Arts Rev — Arts Review
Arts in Soc — Arts in Society
Art St — Art Stamps
ArtSt — Arte Stampa
Art Teach — Art Teacher
ARTU — Archiv fuer Reformationsgeschichte. Texte und Untersuchungen
ARUCAN — Archives of Rubber Cultivation [*Bogor*]
ARUMD — Argumente
Arup J — Arup Journal
ARV — Allgemeiner Rabbiner-Verband
ARV — Attic Red-Figure Vase Painters
ARVEBZ — Archiva Veterinaria [*Bucharest*]
ARVFA — Annual Review of Fluid Mechanics
ARVFA3 — Annual Review of Fluid Mechanics
ARVGB — Annual Review of Genetics
ARVGB7 — Annual Review of Genetics
ARVID — Archives of Virology
ARVIDF — Archives of Virology
Ar Vk — Archiv fuer Voelkerkunde
ARVPA — Annual Review of Pharmacology [*Later, Annual Review of Pharmacology and Toxicology*]
ARVPAX — Annual Review of Pharmacology [*Later, Annual Review of Pharmacology and Toxicology*]
ARVSDB — Annual Review of Sociology
ARW — Archiv fuer Religionswissenschaft
ARWBA — American Railway Engineering Association. Bulletin
ARWMA — Archiwum Mineralogiczne
ARWP — Archiv fuer Rechts- und Wirtschaftsphilosophie
ARX — Soviet and Eastern European Foreign Trade. A Journal of Translations
ARZNA — Arzneimittel-Forschung

Arznei-For — Arzneimittel-Forschung
Arzneim-Forsch — Arzneimittel-Forschung
Arzneim Forsch Drug Res — Arzneimittel-Forschung/Drug Research
Arzneimittel-Forsch — Arzneimittel-Forschung
ARZOA — Arkiv foer Zoologi
ARZOAG — Arkiv foer Zoologi
AS — Afrika Spectrum
AS — Alten Sprachen
AS — American Scholar
AS — American Speech
AS — American String Teacher
AS — Anatolian Studies
AS — Anglistisches Seminar
AS — Antiquity and Survival [*The Hague and Jerusalem*]
AS — Apostolado Sacerdotal
AS — Applied Statistics
AS — Art Scholar
A & S — Arts and Sciences
AS — Arts in Society
AS — Asbury Seminarian
AS — Asian Survey
AS — Asiatische Studien
As — Asomante
AS — Assyriological Studies. Oriental Institute. University of Chicago
ASA — Anzeiger fuer Schweizerische Altertumskunde
As A — Asie et l'Afrique
ASA — (Specification) Standards Association of Australia
ASAA — Annuario. Reale Scuola Archeologica di Atene
ASAAN — Annales. Societe Archeologique de l'Arrondissement de Nivelles
ASAB — Annales. Societe d'Archeologie de Bruxelles
ASA Bull — ASA [*Australian Society of Accountants*] Bulletin
ASAE — Annales. Service des Antiquites de l'Egypte
ASAE Tech Pap — ASAE [*American Society of Agricultural Engineers*] Technical Paper
ASAE Trans — American Society of Agricultural Engineers. Transactions
ASAI — Annales. Service Archeologique de l'Iran
ASAK — Anzeiger fuer Schweizerische Altertumskunde
ASal — Acta Salmanticensia
ASAL — Annuaire. Societe d'Histoire et d'Archeologie de la Lorraine
ASAL — Annual Survey of African Law
ASAM — Annals. South Africa Museum
As Am Geog — Association of American Geographers. Annals
As Am G Rp — Association of American Geologists and Naturalists. Reports
ASAN — Annales. Societe Archeologique de Namur
ASA Newsl — ASA [*American Society of Agronomy*] Newsletter
ASA Newsletter — American Society of Anesthesiologists. Newsletter
ASAOP — Archaeological Survey of Alberta. Occasional Papers
ASAPA3 — Archives Suisses d'Anthropologie Generale
ASA Pro Bu Ec — American Statistical Association. Proceedings of Business and Economic Statistics Section
ASA Pro So St — American Statistical Association. Proceedings of Social Statistics Section
ASA Pro St Cp — American Statistical Association. Proceedings of Statistical Computing Section
ASA Publ — ASA [*American Society of Agronomy*] Publication
ASA Spec Publ — ASA [*American Society of Agronomy*] Special Publication
ASA Tech Bul — ASA [*Australian Society of Accountants*] Technical Bulletin
ASAW — Abhandlungen. Saechsische Akademie der Wissenschaften zu Leipzig. Philosophisch-Historische Klasse
ASAWL — Abhandlungen. Saechsische Akademie der Wissenschaften zu Leipzig
ASAWL PHK — Abhandlungen. Saechsische Akademie der Wissenschaften zu Leipzig. Philosophisch-Historische Klasse
ASB — Accademia delle Scienze di Bologna. Memorie
ASB — African Studies Bulletin
ASB — American Journal of Small Business
ASB — Asia Letter. An Authoritative Analysis of Asian Affairs
ASB — Australian Stud Book
ASBA — Atas. Simposio Sobre a Biota Amazonica
ASB Bull — ASB [*Association of Southeastern Biologists*] Bulletin
ASBEB — Acta Stomatologica Belgica
ASBFC — Archivio Storico per Belluno, Feltre, e Cadore
ASBIA — Archivio di Scienze Biologiche [*Bologna*]
ASBIAL — Archivio di Scienze Biologiche
ASBLAU — Archivos. Sociedad de Biologia de Montevideo
AsbSem — [*The*] Asbury Seminarian [*Wilmore, KY*]
ASBYP — Appraisal. Science Books for Young People
ASc — American Scholar
ASc — Annals of Science [*London*]
ASC — Archivio Storico di Corsica
ASC — ASCI [*Administrative Staff College of India*] Journal of Management
ASC — Australian Consumer Sales and Credit Law Reporter
ASCA — Automatic Subject Citation Alert
ASCAA — Anales. Sociedad Cientifica Argentina
ASCAP — ASCAP [*American Society of Composers, Authors, and Publishers*] in Action

ASCAP — ASCAP [*American Society of Composers, Authors, and Publishers*] Today
ASCAP Cop L Symp — Copyright Law Symposium. American Society of Composers, Authors, and Publishers
ASCAP Copyright L Sym — ASCAP [*American Society of Composers, Authors, and Publishers*] Copyright Law Symposium
ASCAP Copyright L Symp — Copyright Law Symposium. American Society of Composers, Authors, and Publishers
ASCBull — Academie des Sciences de Cracovie. Bulletin International
ASC Commun — ASC [*American Society for Cybernetics*] Communications
ASCE Combined Sewer Separation Proj Tech Memo — ASCE [*American Society of Civil Engineers*] Combined Sewer Separation Project. Technical Memorandum
ASCE Eng Issues J Prof Activ — ASCE [*American Society of Civil Engineers*] Engineering Issues. Journal of Professional Activities
ASCE J Constr Div — ASCE [*American Society of Civil Engineers*] Journal of the Construction Division
ASCE J Eng Mech Div — ASCE [*American Society of Civil Engineers*] Journal of the Engineering Mechanics Division
ASCE J Geotech Eng Div — ASCE [*American Society of Civil Engineers*] Journal of the Geotechnical Engineering Division
ASCE J Prof Activ — ASCE [*American Society of Civil Engineers*] Journal of Professional Activities
ASCE J Sanit Eng Div — ASCE [*American Society of Civil Engineers*] Journal of the Sanitary Engineering Division
ASCE J Soil Mech Found Div — ASCE [*American Society of Civil Engineers*] Journal of the Soil Mechanics and Foundations Division
ASCE J Struct Div — ASCE [*American Society of Civil Engineers*] Journal of the Structural Division
ASCE J Surv Mapp Div — ASCE [*American Society of Civil Engineers*] Journal of the Surveying and Mapping Division
ASCE J Urban Plann Dev Div — ASCE [*American Society of Civil Engineers*] Journal of the Urban Planning and Development Division
ASCE J Waterw Harbors Coastal Eng Div — ASCE [*American Society of Civil Engineers*] Journal of the Waterways, Harbors, and Coastal Engineering Division
ASCE Man Rep Eng Pract — ASCE [*American Society of Civil Engineers*] Manuals and Reports on Engineering Practice
ASCE Proc Transp Eng J — American Society of Civil Engineers. Proceedings. Transportation Engineering Journal
ASCE Transp Eng J — ASCE [*American Society of Civil Engineers*] Transportation Engineering Journal
ASCE Urban Water Resour Res Program Tech Mem — ASCE [*American Society of Civil Engineers*] Urban Water Resources Research Program. Technical Memorandum
ASCE Urban Water Resour Res Program Tech Memo IHP — ASCE [*American Society of Civil Engineers*] Urban Water Resources Research Program. Technical Memorandum IHP [*International Hydrological Programme*]
ASCGD — Anales. Seccion de Ciencias. Colegio Universitario de Gerona. Universidad Autonoma de Barcelona
ASch — American Scholar
Aschener Bl Aufbereit Verkoken Briket — Aschener Blaetter fuer Aufbereiten Verkoken Brikettieren
ASci — American Scientist
ASCI (Admin Staff Col India) J Mgt — ASCI (Administrative Staff College of India) Journal of Management
A Sci Econ Appl — Annales des Sciences Economiques Appliquees
ASCL — Archivio Storico per la Calabria e la Lucania
ASCOA — American Scholar
ASD — Annali di Storia del Diritto
ASD — Archivio Storico per la Dalmazia
ASD — Aviation Safety Digest
As Def J — Asian Defence Journal
ASDIDY — Agricultural Science Digest
ASDMA — Advances in Structure Research by Diffraction Methods [*United States-Germany*]
ASE — Anglo-Saxon England
ASE — Annales de Sciences Economiques Appliquees
ASE — Annuario di Studi Ebraici
ASE — Archaeological Survey of Egypt
ASEA — Asiatische Studien/Etudes Asiatiques
ASEA Bul — Australian Society for Education through the Arts. Bulletin
ASEA Bull — Australian Society for Education through the Arts. Bulletin
ASEA J — ASEA [*Allmaenna Svenska Elektriska Aktiebolaget*] Journal
ASEAN (Assn Southeast Asian Nations) Bus Q — ASEAN (Association of Southeast Asian Nations) Business Quarterly
ASEAN Bus — ASEAN [*Association of Southeast Asian Nations*] Business Quarterly
ASEA Res — ASEA [*Allmaenna Svenska Elektriska Aktiebolaget*] Research
ASEA Tidn — ASEA [*Allmaenna Svenska Elektriska Aktiebolaget*] Tidning
ASEA Z — ASEA [*Allmaenna Svenska Elektriska Aktiebolaget*] Zeitschrift
ASEB — Annales. Societe d'Emulation de Bruges
As Econ — Asian Economies
ASEER — American Slavic and East European Review

ASEF — Annales. Societe d'Emulation pour l'Etude de l'Histoire et des Antiquites de Flandre
ASEG — Arquivos. Seminario de Estudos Galegos
ASEGB — Australian Society of Exploration Geophysicists. Bulletin
ASEJ — Annuaire. Societe des Etudes Juives
ASEL — Acta Semiotica et Lingvistica
ASEMC — Aviation, Space, and Environmental Medicine
As Eng Soc J — Association of Engineering Societies. Journal
ASEOAK — Archivos. Sociedad Espanola de Oftalmologia
ASEPAN — Australia. Commonwealth Scientific and Industrial Research Organisation. Division of Entomology. Technical Paper
ASET Yearb — Australian Society of Educational Technology. Yearbook
ASEU — Archivo per la Storia Ecclesiastica dell'Umbria
ASF — Analog Science Fiction
ASF — Archivio di Storia della Filosofia
ASF — Astounding Science Fiction
ASFA — Aquatic Sciences and Fisheries Abstracts [*Information Retrieval Ltd.*] [*Bibliographic database*]
ASFF — Acta Societatis pro Fauna et Flora
ASFM — Anuario. Sociedad Folklorico de Mexico
As Folk Stud — Asian Folklore Studies
As For — Asiatische Forschungen
ASFPAS — Australia. Commonwealth Scientific and Industrial Research Organisation. Division of Food Preservation and Transport. Technical Paper
ASFR — Australian Science Fiction Review
ASFR — Avon Science Fiction Reader
As Franc C R — Association Francaise pour l'Avancement des Sciences. Comptes-Rendus
ASFZA — Analele. Universitatii Bucuresti. Seria Stiintele Naturii. Fizica
ASG — Abhandlungen. Koenigliche Saechsische Gesellschaft der Wissenschaften
ASG — Abhandlungen. Philosophisch-Historische Klasse der Saechsischen Gesellschaft
ASGA — Neues Archiv fuer Saechsische Geschichte und Altertumskunde
ASGH — Anales. Sociedad de Geografia e Historia
ASGJA — American Society for Geriatric Dentistry. Journal
ASGLM — Atti. Sodalizio Glottologico Milanese
ASGM — Atti. Sodalizio Glottologico Milanese
ASGP — Annali. Seminario Giuridico di Palermo
ASGVAH — Archives des Sciences (Geneva)
ASGW — Abhandlungen. Philologisch-Historische Klasse. Koenigliche Saechsische Gesellschaft der Wissenschaften
Ash — Astonishing Stories
ASHAG — Annales. Societe d'Histoire et d'Archeologie de Gand
ASHA J Am Speech Hear Assoc — ASHA. Journal of the American Speech and Hearing Association
ASHAL — Annuaire. Societe d'Histoire et d'Archeologie de la Lorraine
ASHA Monogr — ASHA [*American Speech and Hearing Association*] Monographs
ASHA Rep — ASHA [*American Speech and Hearing Association*] Reports
ASHAT — Annales. Societe Historique et Archeologique de Tournai
ASHFY — American Swedish Historical Foundation. Yearbook
Ash G Bot Per — Asher's Guide to Botanical Periodicals
Ash M — Ashmolean Museum
ASHRAE B — American Society of Heating, Refrigerating, and Air-Conditioning Engineers. Bulletin
ASHRAE Handb Fundam — American Society of Heating, Refrigerating, and Air-Conditioning Engineers. Handbook of Fundamentals
ASHRAE Handb Prod Dir — ASHRAE [*American Society of Heating, Refrigerating, and Air-Conditioning Engineers*] Handbook and Product Directory
ASHRAE J — American Society of Heating, Refrigerating, and Air-Conditioning Engineers. Journal
ASHRAE Trans — American Society of Heating, Refrigerating, and Air-Conditioning Engineers. Transactions
ASHY — American Swedish Historical Foundation. Yearbook
ASI — Archivio Storico Italiano
ASI — Australian Science Index
Asia — Asia and the Americas
Asia Afr R — Asia and Africa Review
Asia Folkl Stud — Asian Folklore Studies
Asian Aff — Asian Affairs
Asian Aff (London) — Asian Affairs. Journal of the Royal Central Asian Society (London)
Asian Aff (New York) — Asian Affairs (New York)
Asian & African Stud (Bratislava) — Asian and African Studies (Bratislava)
Asian Arch Anaesthesiol Resusc — Asian Archives of Anaesthesiology and Resuscitation
A'sian Baker — Australasian Baker and Millers' Journal
Asian Bldg & Construction — Asian Building and Construction
A'sian Boating — Australasian Boating
Asian Bus — Asian Business and Industry
A'sian Bus Cond Bul — Australasian Business Conditions Bulletin
Asian Bus and Industry — Asian Business and Industry
A'sian Catholic R — Australasian Catholic Record

A'sian Catholic Rec — Australasian Catholic Record
A'sian Confectioner — Australasian Confectioner and Restaurant Journal
Asian Dev — Asian Development. Quarterly Newsletter
Asian Econ — Asian Economics
Asian Econ R — Asian Economic Review
A'sian Eng — Australasian Engineering
A'sian Engineer — Australasian Engineer
A'sian Exhibitor — Australasian Exhibitor
Asian Fin — Asian Finance
Asian Folk — Asian Folklore Studies
Asian Folkl Stud — Asian Folklore Studies
A'sian Grocer — Australasian Grocer
A'sian Inst Min & Metallurgy Proc — Australasian Institute of Mining and
      Metallurgy. Proceedings
A'sian Insurance & Banking Rec — Australasian Insurance and Banking
      Record
A'sian Insurance J — Australasian Insurance Journal
A'sian Irrigator — Australasian Irrigator
Asian J Infect Dis — Asian Journal of Infectious Diseases
Asian J Med — Asian Journal of Medicine
Asian J Pharm — Asian Journal of Pharmacy
A'sian J Pharmacy — Australasian Journal of Pharmacy
A'sian J Phil — Australasian Journal of Philosophy
A'sian Leather and Footwear R — Australasian Leather and Footwear Review
A'sian Leather Trades R — Australasian Leather Trades Review
Asian M — Asian Music
A'sian Manuf — Australasian Manufacturer
A'sian Manufacturer — Australasian Manufacturer
A'sian Manuf Ind Ann — Australasian Manufacturer. Industrial Annual
Asian Med J — Asian Medical Journal [Tokyo]
A'sian Meth Hist Soc J & Proc — Australasian Methodist Historical Society.
      Journal and Proceedings
Asian Mus — Asian Music
A'sian Oil & Gas J — Australasian Oil and Gas Journal
Asian Pacif Quart Cult Soc Aff — Asian Pacific Quarterly of Cultural and
      Social Affairs
Asian Pac Popul Programme News — Asian and Pacific Population Programme
      News
Asian Persp — Asian Perspectives
Asian Perspect — Asian Perspectives
A'sian Post — Australasian Post
A'sian Pr — Australasian Printer
A'sian Printer — Australasian Printer
Asian R — Asian Review
A'sian R'way & Locomotive Hist Soc Bul — Australasian Railway and
      Locomotive Historical Society. Bulletin
Asian S — Asian Survey
Asian Sch — Bulletin of Concerned Asian Scholars
Asian Stud — Asian Studies
Asian Stud Prof R — Asian Studies. Professional Review
Asian Surv — Asian Survey
A'sian Univ Mod Lang Assoc Congress Proc — Australasian Universities
      Modern Language Association. Proceedings of Congress
Asian WSJ — Asian Wall Street Journal
Asia Oceania J Obstet Gynaecol — Asia Oceania Journal of Obstetrics and
      Gynaecology
Asia Q — Asia Quarterly
Asia Quart — Asia Quarterly
Asia R — Asiatic Review
Asiatic R — Asiatic Review
Asiatic R ns — Asiatic Review. New Series
Asiatic Soc Japan Trans — Asiatic Society of Japan. Transactions
Asiat Stud — Asiatische Studien
ASIDIC News — ASIDIC [Association of Information and Dissemination
      Centers] Newsletter
Asien Afr Lateinam — Asien, Afrika, Lateinamerika
Asie Nouv — Asie Nouvelle
Asie Sud-Est Monde Insulind — Asie du Sud-Est et Monde Insulindien
ASIL — Annual Survey of Indian Law
ASILO — Adalbert Stifter Institut des Landes Oberoesterreich.
      Vierteljahresschrift
ASILS Intl LJ — ASILS [Association of Student International Law Societies]
      International Law Journal
ASIMAY — Atti. Societa Italiana di Scienze Naturali. Museo Civico di Storia
      Naturale di Milano
ASIN — Arts in Alaska. Newsletter. Alaska State Council on the Arts
ASInt — American Studies International
ASIRAF — Australia. Commonwealth Scientific and Industrial Research
      Organisation. Annual Report
ASIS — Atti. Societa Italiana di Statistica
ASISAI — Atti. Societa Italiana delle Scienze Veterinarie
ASIS Newsl — ASIS [American Society for Information Science] Newsletter
Asi St/Et As — Asiatische Studien/Etudes Asiatiques
ASJ — American Suzuki Journal
ASJPA — Australian Journal of Psychology
ASKG — Archiv fuer Schlesische Kirchengeschichte

A S e L — Acta Semiotica et Linguistica
ASL — Annual Survey of Law
ASL — Archivio Storico Lombardo
ASLA Pres Newsl — Association of State Library Agencies. President's
      Newsletter
ASLC — Australian Securities Law Cases
ASLE (Am Soc Lubr Eng) Annu Meet Prepr — ASLE (American Society of
      Lubrication Engineers) Annual Meeting. Preprints
ASLE Prepr — ASLE [American Society of Lubrication Engineers] Preprints
ASLE Trans — ASLE [American Society of Lubrication Engineers]
      Transactions
ASLF — Annales de Saint-Louis des Francais
ASLG — Atti. Societa Linguistica di Scienze e Lettere di Genova
ASLH — American Society of the Legion of Honor. Magazine
ASLHM — American Society of the Legion of Honor. Magazine
Aslib Inf — Aslib Information
Aslib Info — Aslib Information
Aslib Proc — Aslib Proceedings
ASLJD — Arizona State Law Journal
ASLL — Acta Societatis Humaniorum Litterarum Lundensis
ASLN — Australian Special Libraries News
ASLOBM — American Society of Limnology and Oceanography. Special
      Symposium
ASLod — Archivio Storico Lodigiano
ASLO (London) Rep — Australian Scientific Liaison Office (London). Report
ASLP Bul — Association of Special Libraries of the Philippines. Bulletin
ASLP Bull — Association of Special Libraries of the Philippines. Bulletin
ASLP Bulletin — Australian Society of Legal Philosophy. Bulletin
ASLP Proceedings — Australian Society of Legal Philosophy. Proceedings
ASLR — Australian Securities Law Reporter
ASL Res Rep — ASL [American Scientific Laboratories] Research Report
ASLSP — Atti. Societa Ligure di Storia Patria
ASLU — Acta Societatis Linguisticae Upsaliensis
ASLund — Arsbok Utgiven av Seminarierna i Slaviska Sprak, Jamforande
      Sprakforskning, Finsk-Ugriska Sprak och Ostasiatiska Sprak Vid Lunds
      Universitet
ASM — American Swedish Monthly
ASM — Archivio Storico Messinese
AsM — Asia Major
ASM — Asian Music
ASM — Association Management
As Ma — Asia Major
ASMA — Journal. Australian Stipendiary Magistrates' Association
Asmat Sketch Bk — Asmat Sketch Book
ASMEA — Archivio per le Scienze Mediche
ASMEAU — Archivio per le Scienze Mediche
ASME Boiler Pressure Vessel Code — American Society of Mechanical
      Engineers. Boiler and Pressure Vessel Code
ASME Pap — American Society of Mechanical Engineers. Papers
ASME Paper — American Society of Mechanical Engineers. Papers
ASME Perform Test Codes — American Society of Mechanical Engineers.
      Performance Test Codes
ASME Trans — American Society of Mechanical Engineers. Transactions
ASME Trans Ser F — American Society of Mechanical Engineers.
      Transactions. Series F
ASME Trans Ser I — American Society of Mechanical Engineers.
      Transactions. Series I.
ASMG — Atti e Memorie. Societa Magna Grecia
AS Mimeogr Circ LA State Univ Agr Exp Sta — Animal Science Mimeograph
      Circular. Louisiana State University. Agricultural Experiment Station
ASMMA — Atti. Seminario Matematico e Fisico. Universita di Modena
ASM News — American Society for Microbiology. News
ASM Trans Q — ASM [American Society for Metals] Transactions Quarterly
ASM Trans Quart — ASM [American Society for Metals] Transactions
      Quarterly
As Music — Asian Music
ASMVAD — Anais. Escola Superior de Medicina Veterinaria [Lisbon]
ASN — Annali. Scuola Normale Superiore di Pisa
ASNA Reporter — ASNA [Alabama State Nurses' Association] Reporter
ASNED — ASIS [American Society for Information Science] News
ASNMAP — Atti. Societa dei Naturalisti e Matematici di Modena
ASNOA — Astrophysica Norvegica
ASNP — Agricultural Society of Nigeria. Proceedings
ASNP — Annali. Scuola Normale Superiore di Pisa
ASNS — Archiv fuer das Studium der Neueren Sprachen und Literaturen
ASNSL — Archiv fuer das Studium der Neueren Sprachen und Literaturen
ASNSP — Annali. Scuola Normale Superiore di Pisa
ASNU — Acta Seminarii Neotestamentici Upsaliensis [Uppsala]
ASO — American Journal of Economics and Sociology
Aso — Asomante
ASOC — Analecta Sacri Ordinis Cisterciensis [Roma]
ASoc — Annales Sociologiques
ASoc — Annee Sociologique
ASoc — Arts in Society
A Soc Arch Namur — Annales. Societe Archeologique de Namur

Asoc Argent Mineral Petrol Sediment Rev — Asociacion Argentina de Mineralogia, Petrologia, y Sedimentologia. Revista
ASOCAY — Atti. Societa Italiana di Cardiologia
Asoc Colombiana Bibl Bol — Asociacion Colombiana de Bibliotecarios. Boletin
Asoc Cuba Bibl Bol — Asociacion Cubana de Bibliotecarios. Boletin
Asoc Geol Argent Monogr — Asociacion Geologica Argentina. Monografia
Asoc Ing Agron Rev — Asociacion de Ingenieros Agronomos. Revista [*Uruguay*]
Asoc Ing Uruguay Rev Ingenieria — Asociacion de Ingenieros del Uruguay. Revista de Ingenieria
A Sociol (Milano) — Annali di Sociologia (Milano)
Asoc Latinoam Entomol Publ — Asociacion Latinoamericana de Entomologia. Publicacion
Asoc Latinoam Prod Anim Mem — Asociacion Latinoamericana de Produccion Animal. Memoria
Asoc Mat Espanola — Asociacion Matematica Espanola
Asoc Med PR — Asociacion Medica de Puerto Rico
Asoc Mex Geol Pet Bol — Asociacion Mexicana de Geologos Petroleros. Boletin
Asoc Mexicana Geofisicos Explor Bol — Asociacion Mexicana de Geofisicos de Exploracion. Boletin
Asoc Mex Tec Ind Celul Pap Bol — Asociacion Mexicana de Tecnicos de las Industrias de la Celulosa y del Papel. Boletin
A Soc R — American Sociological Review
A Soc Sci Litt Cannes — Annales. Societe Scientifique Litteraire de Cannes et de l'Arrondissement de Grasse
ASOFDC — Archivos. Sociedad Canaria de Oftalmologia
ASOHAF — Archivos. Sociedad Oftalmologica Hispano-Americana
ASOL — American Symphony Orchestra League. Newsletter
ASOM — Academie des Sciences d'Outre-Mer
ASOR — American Schools of Oriental Research. Newsletter
ASORA — Australian Journal of Soil Research
ASOR Bul — American Schools of Oriental Research. Bulletin
ASOR PJSA — American Schools of Oriental Research. Publications of the Jerusalem School. Archaeology
ASOTBI — Australia. Commonwealth Scientific and Industrial Research Organisation. Division of Soil Mechanics. Technical Paper
As Outlook — Asian Outlook
A & SP — Advertising and Sales Promotion
ASP — Advertising and Sales Promotion
ASP — American Studies in Papyrology
ASP — Archiv fuer Slavische Philologie
ASP — Archivio Storico Pratese
ASP — Archivio Storico Pugliese
ASP — Australian Superannuation Practice
ASPA — Atti. Societa Piemontese di Archeologia e Belle Arti
ASPABA — Atti. Societa Piemontese di Archeologia e Belle Arti
ASPap — American Studies in Papyrology
ASPC — Academie des Sciences (Paris). Comptes Rendus
ASPCD8 — Auspicium
ASP Ctrattack — ASP Counterattack
ASPEA — Advances in Spectroscopy
Aspects Adhes — Aspects of Adhesion
Aspects Allergy Appl Immunol — Aspects of Allergy and Applied Immunology
Aspects Ed — Aspects of Education
Aspects of Ed — Aspects of Education
Aspects of Math E — Aspects of Mathematics. E
Aspects Plant Sci — Aspects of Plant Sciences
Aspects Pl Sci — Aspects of Plant Sciences
Aspects Statist Region Paris — Aspects Statistiques de la Region Parisienne
Aspen — Aspen Anthology
Aspen A — Aspen Anthology
Aspen J — Aspen Journal of the Arts
As Perspect (H) — Asian Perspectives (Honolulu)
As Perspect (S) — Asian Perspectives (Seoul)
ASPh — Archiv fuer Systematische Philosophie
ASPHAK — Archives des Sciences Physiologiques
Asphalt Inst Constr Ser — Asphalt Institute. Construction Series
Asphalt Inst Inf Ser — Asphalt Institute. Information Series
Asphalt Inst Q — Asphalt Institute. Quarterly
Asphalt Inst Res Ser — Asphalt Institute. Research Series
Asphalt Teerind Ztg — Asphalt Teerindustrie. Zeitung
Asphalt Teer Strassenbautech — Asphalt und Teer. Strassenbautechnik [*West Germany*]
Aspir Rab Nauchno Issled Inst Udobr Insektofungits (Moscow) — Aspirantskie Raboty Nauchno Issledovatel'skii Institut po Udobrenii i Insektofungitsidam (Moscow)
ASPM — Advanced Studies in Pure Mathematics [*Elsevier Book Series*]
ASPN — Archivio Storico per le Provincie Napolitane
ASPP — Archivio Storico per le Provincie Parmensi
ASPP — Asiatic Society of Pakistan. Publication
ASPR — Anglo-Saxon Poetic Records
ASPR — Australasian Small Press Review
As Profile — Asian Profile
ASPS — Atti. Societa Italiana per il Progresso delle Scienze
ASPSA — Atti. Societa Peloritana di Scienze Fisiche, Matematiche e Naturali

ASPSAJ — Atti. Societa Peloritana di Scienze Fisiche, Matematiche, e Naturali
ASPUD — ASAE [*American Society of Agricultural Engineers*] Publication
ASPZA — Avtomatizatsiya Staleplavil'nogo Proizvodstva
ASQ — Administrative Science Quarterly
As Q — Asia Quarterly
ASR — American-Scandinavian Review
ASR — American Slavic Review
ASR — American Sociological Review
ASR — Annales. Societa Retorumantscha
ASR — Archives de Sociologie des Religions
ASR — Australasian Software Report
ASR — Australian Securities Law Reporter
ASR — Avon Science Fiction Reader
ASRAB — Annales. Societe Royale d'Archeologie de Bruxelles
ASR Bull INORGA — ASR [*Automatizovane Systemy Rizeni*] Bulletin INORGA
ASRHAT — Annales. Societe Royale d'Histoire et d'Archeologie de Tournai
ASRPCM — Australia. Commonwealth Scientific and Industrial Research Organisation. Division of Soils. Report on Progress
ASRS — Archivio. Societa Romana di Storia Patria
ASRSD — Advances in Space Research
ASRSP — Archivio. Societa Romana di Storia Patria
ASRU — Archivio Storico del Risorgimento Umbrio
ASRWA7 — Agricultural Science Review. Cooperative State Research Service. US Department of Agriculture
ASS — Amazing Science Stories
ASS — Archivio Storico Siciliano
ASS — Argenteuil Symposia Series [*Elsevier Book Series*]
AsS — Asiatische Studien
Assam Rev Tea News — Assam Review and Tea News
ASSar — Archivio Storico Sardo
Ass Bibliot Fr Bull Inf — Association des Bibliothecaires Francais. Bulletin d'Informations
ASSc — Archivio di Storia della Scienza
ASSE J — ASSE Journal
Assem Autom — Assembly Automation
Assembly Eng — Assembly Engineering
Assem Eng — Assembly Engineering
Assem Fastener Eng — Assembly and Fastener Engineering
Assessment in Higher Ed — Assessment in Higher Education
Assessors J — Assessors Journal
ASSET — Abstracts of Selected Solar Energy Technology [*Japan*]
ASSF — Acta Societatis Scientiarum Fennicae
Ass Franc Avance Sc C R — Association Francaise pour l'Avancement des Sciences. Comptes-Rendus
Assignment Chil — Assignment Children
Assistant Librn — Assistant Librarian
Assistenza Soc — Assistenza Sociale
Assist Inf — Assistance Informations [*France*]
Assist Libn — Assistant Librarian
Assist Soc — Assistenza Sociale
Assiut Univ Fac Sci Bull — Assiut University. Faculty of Science. Bulletin
Assn Am Ag Coll & Exp Pro — Association of American Agricultural Colleges and Experiment Stations. Proceedings
Assn Am Col Bul — Association of American Colleges. Bulletin
Assn Am Geog Ann — Association of American Geographers. Annals
Assn Asian Stud Newsletter — Association for Asian Studies. Newsletter
Ass Naz Ing Architetti Ital Quad — Associazione Nazionale degli Ingegneri ed Architetti Italiani. Quaderni
Assn Bar City NY Rec — Association of the Bar of the City of New York. Record
Assn Bibl Francais Bull Inf — Association des Bibliothecaires Francais. Bulletin d'Informations
Assn Canadienne Bibl Langue Francaise Bul — Association Canadienne des Bibliothecaires de Langue Francaise. Bulletin
Assn Comp Mach J — Association for Computing Machinery. Journal
Assn Ed Radio J — Association for Education by Radio. Journal
Assn of Gov Bds of State Univ & Allied Insts Proc — Association of Governing Boards of State Universities and Allied Institutions. Proceedings
Assn Italiana Bibl Boll Inf — Associazione Italiana Biblioteche. Bollettino d'Informazioni
Assn Men — Association Men (Rural Manhood)
Assn Mgt — Association Management
Assn Offic Ag Chem J — Association of Official Agricultural Chemists. Journal
Assn Sch Bsns Officials US & Canada Proc — Association of School Business Officials of the United States and Canada. Proceedings
Assn Stud Teach Yrbk — Association for Student Teaching. Yearbook
Assn for Sup & Curric Develop Yearbook — Association for Supervision and Curriculum Development. Yearbook
Assn Sup & Curric Devel Yrbk — Association for Supervision and Curriculum Development. Yearbook
ASSO — Archivio Storico per la Sicilia Orientale
Assoc Am Fert Control Off Off Publ — Association of American Fertilizer Control Officials. Official Publication

Assoc Am Geographers Annals — Association of American Geographers. Annals

Assoc Am Geographers Comm Coll Geography Resource Paper — Association of American Geographers. Commission on College Geography. Resource Paper

Assoc Am Geogr Comm Coll Geogr Publ — Association of American Geographers. Commission on College Geography. Publication

Assoc Belge Dev Pac Energ At Bull Inf — Association Belge pour le Developpement Pacifique de l'Energie Atomique. Bulletin d'Information

Assoc Belge Photogr Cinematogr Bull — Association Belge de Photographie et de Cinematographie. Bulletin

Assoc Bibl Francais Bul — Association des Bibliothecaires Francais. Bulletin d'Informations

Assoc Bull Int Assoc Milk Dealers — Association Bulletin. International Association of Milk Dealers

Assoc Cadres Dir Industr B — Association de Cadres Dirigeants de l'Industrie pour le Progres Social et Economique. Bulletin

Assoc Canadienne-Francaise Av Sci Annales — Association Canadienne-Francaise pour l'Avancement des Sciences. Annales

Assoc Demographes Quebec Bul — Bulletin. Association de Demographes du Quebec

Assoc Eng Geol Ann Meet Program Abstr — Association of Engineering Geologists. Annual Meeting. Program and Abstracts

Assoc Eng Geol Annu Mtg Guideb — Association of Engineering Geologists. Annual Meeting. Guidebook

Assoc Eng Geol Annu Mtg Guide Field Trips — Association of Engineering Geologists. Annual Meeting. Guide to Field Trips

Assoc Eng Geol Bull — Association of Engineering Geologists. Bulletin

Assoc Fr Etude Quat Bull — Association Francaise pour l'Etude du Quaternaire. Bulletin

Assoc Fr Gemmol Bull — Association Francaise de Gemmologie. Bulletin

Assoc Fr Tech Pet Rev — Association Francaise des Techniciens du Petrole. Revue

Assoc Geofis Ital Atti Conv Annu — Associazione Geofisica Italiana. Atti del Convegno Annuale [*Italy*]

Assoc Geographes Francais Bull — Association de Geographes Francais. Bulletin

Assoc Geogr Fr Bull — Association de Geographes Francais. Bulletin

Assoc Geol Bassin Paris Bull — Association des Geologues du Bassin de Paris. Bulletin

Assoc Geol Bassin Paris Bull Inf — Association des Geologues du Bassin de Paris. Bulletin d'Information

Assoc Hung Telecommun Ind — Association of the Hungarian Telecommunication Industry

Assoc Ing Electr Sortis Inst Electrotech Montefiore Bull — Association des Ingenieurs Electriciens Sortis de l'Institut Electrotechnique Montefiore. Bulletin [*Belgium*]

Assoc Int Limnol Theor Appl Trav — Association Internationale de Limnologie Theoretique et Appliquee. Travaux

Assoc Int Sci Hydrol Publ — Association Internationale des Sciences Hydrologiques. Publication

Assoc Iron Steel Electr Eng Proc — Association of Iron and Steel Electrical Engineers. Proceedings

Assoc Jpn Portland Cem Eng Rev Gen Meet — Association of Japanese Portland Cement Engineers. Review of General Meeting

Assoc Latinoam Entomol Publ — Associacion Latinoamericana de Entomologia Publicacion

Assoc Manage — Association Management

Assoc Mine Mangr S Afr Circ — Association of Mine Managers of South Africa. Circulars

Assoc Mine Mangr S Afr Pap Discuss — Association of Mine Managers of South Africa. Papers and Discussions

Assoc Nat Enseign Agric Public Bull Trimest — Association des Naturalistes de l'Enseignement Agricole Public. Bulletin Trimestriel

Assoc News — Associate News

Assoc Off Anal Chem J — Association of Official Analytical Chemists. Journal

Assoc Off Analyt Chemists J — Association of Official Analytical Chemists. Journal

Assoc Official Agr Chemists Jour — Association of Official Agricultural Chemists. Journal

Assoc Pacific Coast Geographers Yearbook — Association of Pacific Coast Geographers. Yearbook

Assoc Public Analysts J — Association of Public Analysts. Journal

Assoc Recor — Association for Recorded Sound Collections. Journal

Assoc Sci Tech Soc S Afr Annu Proc — Associated Scientific and Technical Societies of South Africa. Annual Proceedings

Assoc Senegal Etud Quat Ouest Afr Bull Liaison — Association Senegalaise pour l'Etude du Quaternaire de l'Ouest Africain. Bulletin de Liaison

Assoc Soc Manager — Association and Society Manager

Assoc Tech Ind Gaz — Association Technique de l'Industrie du Gaz en France. Proceedings

Ass Off Agric Chem — Association of Official Agricultural Chemists

ASSPh — Annuaire. Societe Suisse de Philosophie

ASSRFM — Alaska Series Special Reports for Management

AssSeign — Assemblees du Seigneur [*Bruges*]

ASS Short-Circuit Test Auth Publ — Association of Short-Circuit Testing Authorities. Publication

AsSt — Asian Student

ASSTA — Acier-Stahl-Steel

Asst Libn — Assistant Librarian

Assuntos Eur — Assuntos Europeus

As Surv — Asian Survey

ASSVB — Annali. Istituto Sperimentale per la Selvicoltura

Assyr S — Assyriological Studies

AssyrSt — Assyriological Studies

A St — Aberystwyth Studies

AST — American String Teacher

AST — Analecta Sacra Tarraconensia

AST — Applied Science and Technology Index

ASt — Asian Studies

ASt — Asiatische Studien

AST — Astonishing Stories

AST — Atti e Memorie. Societa Tiburtina di Storia e d'Arte

Ast & AstroAb — Astronomy and Astrophysics. Abstracts

As Thought Soc — Asian Thought and Society

ASTI — Annual. Swedish Theological Institute

ASTI — Applied Science and Technology Index

ASTIB — Army Scientific and Technical Intelligence Bulletin

ASTic — Archivio Storico Ticinese

Astin Bull — Astin Bulletin [*Leiden*]

A S & T Ind — Applied Science and Technology Index

ASTM Book ASTM Stand — American Society for Testing and Materials. Book of ASTM Standards

ASTM Bul — American Society for Testing and Materials. Bulletin

ASTME/ASM West Metal Tool Conf — American Society of Tool and Manufacturing Engineers. ASTME/ASM Western Metal and Tool Conference

ASTME Collect Papers — American Society of Tool and Manufacturing Engineers. ASTME Collected Papers

ASTME Creative Mfg Semin Tech Papers — American Society of Tool and Manufacturing Engineers. Creative Manufacturing Seminars. Technical Papers

ASTM Geotechnical Testing Journal — American Society for Testing and Materials. Geotechnical Testing Journal

ASTM J Testing Evaln — ASTM [*American Society for Testing and Materials*] Journal of Testing and Evaluation

ASTM Meet Prepr — American Society for Testing and Materials. Meeting. Preprints

ASTM Proc — ASTM [*American Society for Testing and Materials*] Proceedings

ASTM Special Technical Publication — American Society for Testing and Materials. Special Technical Publication

ASTM Spec Tech Publ — ASTM [*American Society for Testing and Materials*] Special Technical Publications

ASTM Stand N — ASTM [*American Society for Testing and Materials*] Standardization News

ASTM Stand News — ASTM [*American Society for Testing and Materials*] Standardization News

ASTM Std — ASTM [*American Society for Testing and Materials*] Standards

ASTM Stdn News — ASTM [*American Society for Testing and Materials*] Standardization News

ASTP — Archives Suisses des Traditions Populaires

ASTPCW — Australia. Commonwealth Scientific and Industrial Research Organisation. Division of Soil Research. Technical Paper

Astro Aeron — Astronautics and Aeronautics

Astrofiz — Astrofizika

Astrofiz Issled — Astrofizicheskie Issledovaniya

Astrol 77 — Astrology '77

Astrol 78 — Astrology '78

Astrol Now — Astrology Now

Astrom Astrofiz — Astrometriya i Astrofizika

Astrometriya & Astrofiz — Astrometriya i Astrofizika

Astron — Astronomy and Astrophysics

Astron Astr — Astronomy and Astrophysics

Astron Astrophys — Astronomy and Astrophysics

Astron & Astrophys — Astronomy and Astrophysics

Astron Astrophys Suppl Ser — Astronomy and Astrophysics. Supplement Series

Astron & Astrophys Suppl Ser — Astronomy and Astrophysics. Supplement Series

Astronaut Acta — Astronautica Acta

Astronaut Aeronaut — Astronautics and Aeronautics

Astronaut Forschungsber Dtsch Raketen Ges eV — Astronautische Forschungsberichte. Deutsche Rakete Gesellschaft eV

Astronaut Forschungsber Hermann Oberth Ges — Astronautische Forschungsberichte. Hermann Oberth Gesellschaft

Astronaut Sci Rev — Astronautical Sciences Review

Astron Her — Astronomical Herald

Astron J — Astronomical Journal

Astron Jahresber — Astronomischer Jahresbericht

Astron Kal (Moscow) — Astronomicheskii Kalendar (Moscow)

Astron (Milwaukee) — Astronomy (Milwaukee)

Astronom and Astrophys — Astronomy and Astrophysics
Astronom Astrophys Ser — Astronomy and Astrophysics. Supplement Series
Astronom J — Astronomical Journal
Astronom Nachr — Astronomische Nachrichten
Astronom Z — Akademija Nauk SSSR. Astronomiceskii Zurnal
Astronom Zh — Astronomicheskii Zhurnal
Astron-Opt Inst Univ Turku Inf — Astronomia-Optika Institucio. Universitato de Turku. Informo
Astron (Paris) — Astronomie (Paris)
Astron (Paris) Suppl — Astronomie (Paris). Supplement
Astron Raumfahrt — Astronomie und Raumfahrt
Astron Soc Aust Proc — Astronomical Society of Australia. Proceedings
Astron Soc Jpn Publ — Astronomical Society of Japan. Publications
Astron Soc Pacific Pubs — Astronomical Society of the Pacific. Publications
Astron Soc Pac Leafl — Astronomical Society of the Pacific. Leaflet
Astron & Space — Astronomy and Space
Astron Tidsskr — Astronomisk Tidsskrift
Astron Tsirk — Astronomicheskii Tsirkulyar [*USSR*]
Astron Vestn — Astronomicheskii Vestnik
Astron Zh — Astronomicheskii Zhurnal
Astroph J S — Astrophysical Journal. Supplement Series
Astrophys — Astrophysics
Astrophys J — Astrophysical Journal
Astrophys J Lett Ed — Astrophysical Journal. Letters to the Editor
Astrophys J Suppl — Astrophysical Journal. Supplement
Astrophys J Suppl Ser — Astrophysical Journal. Supplement Series
Astrophys L — Astrophysical Letters
Astrophys Lett — Astrophysical Letters
Astrophys Norv — Astrophysica Norvegica [*Norway*]
Astrophys & Space Sci — Astrophysics and Space Science
Astrophys Space Sci — Astrophysics and Space Science
Astrophys Space Sci Lib — Astrophysics and Space Science Library [*Reidel, Dordrecht*]
Astrophys Space Sci Libr — Astrophysics and Space Science Library
Astro Sp Sc — Astrophysics and Space Science
ASTSC — Annals of Statistics
ASTT — Astarte. Journal of Arctic Biology
ASTYD — Aerosol, Science and Technology
ASTZA5 — Atti. Simposio Internazionale di Zootecnia
ASU — American School and University
ASu — Anthroponymica Suecana
As U A — Annales. Universite d'Abidjan
ASU Bus Tchr — Arizona State University. Business Teacher
ASUC — American Society of University Composers. Proceedings
ASUHA — Asufaruto
ASUI — Analele Stiintifice. Universitatii (Iasi)
ASULAN — Agrisul
ASUNB — American School and University
Asuntos Agr — Asuntos Agrarios
Asutustoiminnan Aikak — Asutustoiminnan Aikakauskirja
ASW — Abstracts for Social Workers
ASW — Administration in Social Work
ASW — Australian Social Welfare
ASXBA8 — Archives of Sexual Behavior
ASY — Agriculture Statistical Yearbook and Agriculture Sample [*Amman*]
ASY — Aslib Information
ASY — Association and Society Manager
ASY — Astounding Stories Yearbook
ASZ — Allgemeine Sport-Zeitung
ASZBAI — Archivum Societatis Zoologicae-Botanicae Fennicae "Vanamo"
A Szekely Nemz Muz — A Szekely Nemzeti Muzeum Ertesitoeje
A Szekely Nemz Muz Ertes — A Szekely Nemzeti Muzeum Ertesitoeje
AT — Africa Today
AT — Agronomie Tropicale
AT — Analecta Tarraconensia
AT — Antik Tanulmanyok
AT — Archeolgrafo Triestino
AT — ASCAP [*American Society of Composers, Authors, and Publishers*] in Action
At — Atenea
At — Atlantida
AT — Atlin News Miner
AT — Aufbereitungs-Technik
AT — Autumn
ATA — Abstracts on Tropical Agriculture
ATA — Alttestamentliche Abhandlungen [*Muenster*]
ATA — Annee Theologique Augustinienne
At Absorpt Newsl — Atomic Absorption Newsletter
At Acad Med S Paulo — Atos. Academia de Medicina de Sao Paulo
ATAC (Asoc Tec Azucar Cuba) — ATAC (Asociacion de Tecnicos Azucareros de Cuba)
ATACC J — ATACC [*Alberta Teachers' Association, Computer Council*] Journal
ATAC Rev Bimest Asoc Tec Azucar Cuba — ATAC. Revista Bimestral. Asociacion de Tecnicos Azucareros de Cuba
ATAEBC — Agronomie Tropicale. Agronomie Generale. Etudes Scientifiques

ATAGDK — Atualidades Agronomicas [*Sao Paulo*]
Atalanta Norv — Atalanta Norvegica
ATA Mag — ATA [*Alberta Teachers Association*] Magazine
ATA Newsletter — Alberta Teachers Association. Newsletter
ATANT — Abhandlungen zur Theologie des Alten und Neuen Testaments [*Zurich*]
Ata Reumatol Bras — Ata Reumatologica Brasileira
Atas Inst Micol Univ Fed Pernambuco — Atas. Instituto de Micologia da Universidade Federal de Pernambuco
Atas Soc Biol Rio De J — Atas. Sociedade de Biologia do Rio De Janeiro
At At Eng — Atomics and Atomic Engineering
At At Technol — Atomics and Atomic Technology
ATAVJ — Art Teachers Association of Victoria. Journal
ATAV News — Art Teachers Association of Victoria. News Sheet
ATAV News Sheet — Art Teachers Association of Victoria. News Sheet
ATB — Altdeutsche Textbibliothek
ATC — Australian Tax Cases
ATCAA — Automatica [*United States*]
ATCL — Atlin Claim
ATCSD — Annual Technical Conference. American Electroplaters' Society
ATCYA — Appropriate Technology
ATD — Acta Theologica Danica
ATD — Australasian Tax Decisions
ATD — Australian Tax Decisions
ATD — Australian Teacher of the Deaf
At Data — Atomic Data [*Later, Atomic Data and Nuclear Data Tables*]
At Data Nucl Data Tables — Atomic Data and Nuclear Data Tables
ATE — Advanced Textbooks in Economics [*Elsevier Book Series*]
Ate — Atenea [*Formerly, Nueva Atenea*]
ATE — Bedrijfsvoering, Tijdschrift voor Organisatiekunde en Arbeidskunde, Produktie, Onderhoud, Inkoop, en Logistiek
ATEHA6 — Agrotecnia
At Elektr Stn — Atomnye Elektricheskie Stantsii [*USSR*]
Atemswegs- Lungenkr — Atemswegs- und Lungenkrankheiten
ATEN — Atmospheric Environment
At En — Atomnaja Energija
Ateneo Parmense Acta Bio-Med — Ateneo Parmense. Acta Bio-Medica
Ateneo Parmense Acta Nat — Ateneo Parmense. Acta Naturalia
Ateneo Parmense Sez 1 — Ateneo Parmense. Sezione 1. Acta Bio-Medica
Ateneo Parmense Sez 2 — Ateneo Parmense. Sezione 2. Acta Naturalia [*Italy*]
At Energ — Atomnaya Energiya [*USSR*]
At Energiya (USSR) — Atomnaya Energiya (USSR)
At Energy Aust — Atomic Energy in Australia
At Energy Bull — Atomic Energy Bulletin [*Japan*]
At Energy Can Ltd AECL (Rep) — Atomic Energy of Canada Limited. AECL (Report)
At Energy Law J — Atomic Energy Law Journal
At Energy Law Rep — Atomic Energy Law Reports
At Energy Res Q Rep — Atomic Energy Research. Quarterly Report [*Japan*]
At Energy Rev — Atomic Energy Review
At Energy Rev Spec Issue — Atomic Energy Review. Special Issue
At Energy (Sydney) — Atomic Energy (Sydney) [*Australia*]
At Enerj Kom (Turkey) Bilimsel Yayin Seri — Atom Enerjisi Komisyonu (Turkey) Bilimsel Yayinlar Seri
At Eng — Atomic Energy in Australia
At Eng Tech — Atomics. Engineering and Technology
At Eng Technol — Atomic Engineering Technology
At En Newsl — Atomic Energy Newsletter
At En Rev — Atomic Energy Review
At En Yb — Atomic Energy Yearbook
Ate R — Atene e Roma
ATERD — Archiwum Termodynamiki
ATESD8 — Aristoteleion Panepistemion Thessalonikis Epistimoniki Epetiris Geoponikis kai Dasologikis Skolis
ATES Newsl — ATES [*Aquifer Thermal Energy Storage*] Newsletter
ATFCC — ATF Colada
ATF Rep — Australian Teachers' Federation. Report
ATG — Archivo Teologico Granadino
ATG — Australian Income Tax Guide
ATh — Arbeiten zur Theologie [*Stuttgart*]
Ath — Athenaeum
Ath — Athene. The American Magazine of Hellenic Thought
ATHAA — Albrecht-Thaer-Archiv
AThANT — Abhandlungen zur Theologie des Alten und Neuen Testaments [*Zurich*]
AThAug — Annee Theologique Augustinienne
ATHBA — Acta Radiologica. Therapy, Physics, Biology [*Later, Acta Radiologica. Series Two. Oncology, Radiation, Physics, and Biology*]
ATHCOM — Australasian Tertiary Handbook Collection on Microfiche
AThD — Acta Theologica Danica [*Copenhagen*]
Atheroscler — Atherosclerosis
Atheroscler Rev — Atherosclerosis Reviews
AThijmG — Annalen van het Thijmgenootschap
Ath J — Athletic Journal
Athl Adm — Athletic Administration
Athl Coach — Athletics Coach

Athl Educ Rep — Athletic Educator's Report
Athl J — Athletic Journal
Athl Train — Athletic Training
A Th M — Archeion Thessalikon Meleton
Ath Mitt — Mitteilungen. Deutsches Archaeologische Institut. Abteilung Athens
Ath Mitt-BH — Athenische Mitteilungen. Beiheft
ATHPB — Advances in Theoretical Physics
Ath Pur and Fac — Athletic Purchasing and Facilities
AThR — Anglican Theological Review
Ath Train — Athletic Training
ATI — Atomwirtschaft Atomtechnik
ATI — Australian Transport Index
At Ind — Atom Industry
A T Index — Alternative/Appropriate Technology Index
At Indones — Atom Indonesia
At-Inf — Atom-Informationen
ATIR — Atlantica and Iceland Review
At Jpn — Atoms in Japan
ATJSA — Atoms in Japan. Supplement
AtKap — Ateneum Kaplanskie [Wloclawek, Poland]
Atl — Atlantic Monthly
Atl — Atlantico
Atl — Atlantico. Revista de Cultura Contemporanea
Atl — Atlantico. Revista Luso-Brasileira
ATL — Atlantisch Perspektief
ATLA — Alternatives to Laboratory Animals
Atla — Atlantis
Atl Adv — Atlantic Advocate
Atlan — Atlantic Monthly
Atlan Adv — Atlantic Advocate
Atlan Com Q — Atlantic Community Quarterly
Atlan Insight — Atlantic Insight
Atlan Mo — Atlantic Monthly
Atlanta Econ R — Atlanta Economic Review
Atlanta Hist J — Atlanta Historical Journal
Atlanta M — Atlanta Magazine
Atlanta Med — Atlanta Medicine
Atlantic — Atlantic Monthly
Atlantic Community Q — Atlantic Community Quarterly
Atlantic Econ J — Atlantic Economic Journal
Atlantic Pap — Atlantic Papers
ATLA Pro — American Theological Library Association. Proceedings
Atlas of Aust Resources — Atlas of Australian Resources
Atlas Div Fish Oceanogr CSIRO — Atlas. Division of Fisheries and Oceanography. Commonwealth Scientific and Industrial Organisation
Atlas Jap Fossils — Atlas of Japanese Fossils
Atlas Newsl — Atlas Newsletter
Atlas Protein Sequence Struct — Atlas of Protein Sequence and Structure
Atlas Radiol Clin — Atlas de Radiologie Clinique [France]
Atl Community Quar — Atlantic Community Quarterly
Atl Econ R — Atlanta Economic Review
ATLGT — Archeion tou Thrakikou Laographikou kai Glossikou Thesaurou
ATI L J — American Trial Lawyers Journal
Atl M — Atlantic Monthly
Atl Mo — Atlantic Monthly
Atl Nat — Atlantic Naturalist
ATLPA — Arctic and Alpine Research
ATLPAV — Arctic and Alpine Research
Atl Rep — Atlantide Report
Atl Salmon J — Atlantic Salmon Journal
AtM — Atlantic Monthly
ATMAAP — Atti. Societa Toscana di Scienze Naturali Residente in Pisa. Memorie. Serie A
At Masses Fundam Constants — Atomic Masses and Fundamental Constants
ATMED6 — Atualidades Medicas
ATM Mess Pr — ATM [Archiv fuer Technisches Messen] Messtechnische Praxis
ATMNA — Automation
ATMO — Atmosphere
Atmos Envir — Atmospheric Environment
Atmos Environ — Atmospheric Environment
Atmos-Ocean — Atmosphere-Ocean [Canada]
Atmos Oceanic Phys — Atmospheric and Oceanic Physics
Atmos Oceanic Phys (Engl Ed) — Atmospheric and Oceanic Physics (English Edition)
Atmos Technol — Atmospheric Technology
Atm Poll Bull — Atmosphere Pollution Bulletin
ATMSAB — Atualidades Medico Sanitarias
ATMTas — Adabietsunaslik va Tilsunaslik Masalalari/Voprosy Literaturovedenija i Jazykoznanija (Taskent)
ATMVAK — Agronomia Tropical (Maracay, Venezuela)
ATMXAQ — Agricultura Tecnica en Mexico
ATNBAX — Atti. Societa Toscana di Scienze Naturali. Processi Verbali e Memorie. Serie B
ATNED — ATES [Aquifer Thermal Energy Storage] Newsletter

ATNMAW — Agronomie Tropicale. Serie Riz et Riziculture et Cultures Vivrieres Tropicales
At Nucl En — Atomics and Nuclear Energy
At Nucl Energy — Atomics and Nuclear Energy [England]
ATOIA — Automobil-Industrie [West Germany]
Atoll Res Bull — Atoll Research Bulletin
Atom — Atomics
Atom Absorpt Newsl — Atomic Absorption Newsletter
Atom Ener A — Atomic Energy in Australia
Atom Ener R — Atomic Energy Review
Atomic Data — Atomic Data and Nuclear Data Tables
Atomic Energy in Aust — Atomic Energy in Australia
Atomic Energy L J — Atomic Energy Law Journal
Atomic Eng LJ — Atomic Energy Law Journal
Atomic Sci — Bulletin of the Atomic Scientists
Atomkernene — Atomkernenergie
Atomkernenerg Kerntech — Atomkernenergie Kerntechnik
ATOMKI Kozl — ATOMKI [Atommag Kutato Intezet] Koezlemenyek
Atomnaya En — Atomnaya Energiya [USSR]
Atomn Energ — Atomnaya Energiya [USSR]
Atomo Petrol Elet — Atomo, Petrol, Elettricita [Italy]
Atomprax — Atompraxis
Atomtech Tajek — Atomtechnikai Tajekoztato
Atomwirtsch — Atomwirtschaft Atomtechnik
Atomwirtsch Atomtech — Atomwirtschaft Atomtechnik
Atoomenerg Haar Toepass — Atoomenergie en Haar Toepassingen
ATopPir — Actas. Primera Reunion de Toponimia Pirenaica
A Tor — Atti. Accademia delle Scienze di Torino
ATP — Archivio per lo Studio delle Tradizioni Popolari
ATP — Arts et Traditions Populaires
ATP — Australian Trade Practices Report
At Parm — Ateneo Parmense
ATPDC — Advances in Tumor Prevention, Detection, and Characterization [Elsevier Book Series]
At Phys — Atomic Physics
At Power — Atomic Power
At Pow R — Atomic Power Review
ATPR — Australian Trade Practices Reporter [Commerce Clearing House]
ATPSD — ACM [Association for Computing Machinery] Transactions on Programming Languages and Systems
ATQ — American Transcendental Quarterly
ATQK — Atuaqunik. Newsletter of Northern Quebec
ATR — Anglican Theological Review
At R — Atene e Roma
ATR — Australasian Tax Reports
ATR — Australian Telecommunication Research
At Radiat — Atomes et Radiations
ATR Aust Telecommun Res — ATR: Australian Telecommunication Research
Atrazine Inform Sheet Geigy Agr Chem Atrazine Herbic — Atrazine Information Sheet. Geigy Agricultural Chemicals. Atrazine Herbicides
ATRCA — Atlas de Radiologie Clinique
ATren — Archivio Trentino
At Res B — Atoll Research Bulletin
AT Rev — Australian Tax Review
A Trial Law Am LJ — Association of Trial Lawyers of America. Law Journal
ATriest — Archeolgrafo Triestino
ATRJ — Association of Teachers of Russian. Journal
ATRMA — Advances in Tracer Methodology
At Roma — Atene e Roma
A Trop — Acta Tropica
ATS — Arabic Translation Series
ATS — Arbeiten und Texte zur Slavistik
ATS — Australian Treaty Series
At Sci J — Atomic Scientists Journal
At Sci News — Atomic Scientists News
ATS List Transl — Associated Technical Services, Inc. List of Translations
At Spectrosc — Atomic Spectroscopy
At Stolknoveniya — Atomnye Stolknoveniya
ATS Trans — Danish Academy of Technical Sciences. Transactions
At und Strom — Atom und Strom
At Strom — Atom und Strom
ATSUDG — Archives of Toxicology. Supplement
ATSVA — Avtomatika, Telemekhanika, i Svyaz
ATSZA — Automazione e Strumentazione
Att ANL R F — Atti. Accademia Nazionale dei Lincei. Rendiconti. Classe di Scienze Fisiche, Matematiche, e Naturali
At Ass Gen — Atti. Associazione Genetica Italiana
At Tekh Rubezhom — Atomnaya Tekhnika za Rubezhom
Atti — Atti. Congresso Internazionale di Estetica
Atti Accad Fisiocrit Siena — Atti. Accademia dei Fisiocritici in Siena
Atti Accad Fisiocrit Siena Sez Agrar — Atti. Accademia dei Fisiocritici in Siena. Sezione Agraria
Atti Accad Fisiocrit Siena Sez Med-Fis — Atti. Accademia dei Fisiocritici in Siena. Sezione Medico-Fisica
Atti Accad Fis-Med-Statist Milano — Atti. Accademia Fisio-Medico-Statistica di Milano

Atti Accad Gioenia Sci Nat Catania — Atti. Accademia Gioenia di Scienze Naturali in Catania

Atti Accad Ligure Sci Lett — Atti. Accademia Ligure di Scienze e Lettere

Atti Accad Ligure Sci & Lett — Atti. Accademia Ligure di Scienze e Lettere

Atti Accad Med Lomb — Atti. Accademia Medica Lombarda

Atti Accad Med Lombarda — Atti. Accademia Medica Lombarda

Atti Accad Naz Ital Entomol Rend — Atti. Accademia Nazionale Italiana di Entomologia. Rendiconti [*Italy*]

Atti Accad Naz Lincei — Atti. Accademia Nazionale dei Lincei

Atti Accad Naz Lincei Cl Sci Fis Mat Nat Rend — Atti. Accademia Nazionale dei Lincei. Classe di Scienze Fisiche, Matematiche, e Naturali. Rendiconti

Atti Accad Naz Lincei Mem Cl Sci Fis Mat Nat — Atti. Accademia Nazionale dei Lincei. Memorie. Classe di Scienze

Atti Accad Naz Lincei Mem Cl Sci Fis Mat Nat — Atti. Accademia Nazionale dei Lincei. Memorie. Classe di Scienze Fisiche, Matematiche, e Naturali

Atti Accad Naz Lincei Mem Cl Sci Fis Mat Nat Sez 2a — Atti. Accademia Nazionale dei Lincei. Memorie. Classe di Scienze Fisiche, Matematiche, e Naturali. Sezione 2a. Fisica, Chimica, Geologia, Paleontologia, e Mineralogia

Atti Accad Naz Lincei Mem Cl Sci Fis Mat Nat Sez 3a — Atti. Accademia Nazionale dei Lincei. Memorie. Classe di Scienze Fisiche, Matematiche, e Naturali. Sezione 3a. Botanica, Zoologia, Fisiologia, Patologia

Atti Accad Naz Lincei Mem Cl Sci Fis Mat Natur Sez Ia — Atti. Accademia Nazionale dei Lincei. Memorie. Classe di Scienze Fisiche, Matematiche, e Naturali. Sezione Ia. Matematica, Meccanica, Astronomia, Geodesia, e Geofisica

Atti Accad Naz Lincei Rend Cl Sci Fis Mat & Nat — Atti. Accademia Nazionale dei Lincei. Rendiconti. Classe di Scienze Fisiche, Matematiche, e Naturali

Atti Accad Naz Lincei Rend Cl Sci Fis Mat Natur — Atti. Accademia Nazionale dei Lincei. Rendiconti. Classe di Scienze Fisiche, Matematiche, e Naturali

Atti Accad Naz Lincei Rend Cl Sci Fis Mat Natur (8) — Atti. Accademia Nazionale dei Lincei. Rendiconti. Classe di Scienze Fisiche, Matematiche, e Naturali (Serie 8)

Atti Accad Naz Lincei (Series Ottava) — Atti. Accademia Nazionale dei Lincei (Series Ottava)

Atti Accad Peloritana Pericolanti Cl Sci Fis Mat Nat — Atti. Accademia Peloritana dei Pericolanti. Classe di Scienze Fisiche, Matematiche, e Naturali

Atti Accad Peloritana Pericolanti Cl Sci Fis Mat Natur — Atti. Accademia Peloritana dei Pericolanti. Classe di Scienze Fisiche, Matematiche, e Naturali

Atti Accad Peloritana Pericolanti Cl Sci Med Biol — Atti. Accademia Peloritana dei Pericolanti. Classe di Scienze Medico-Biologiche

Atti Accad Roveretana Agiati — Atti. Accademia Roveretana degli Agiati

Atti Accad Sci Ferrara — Atti. Accademia delle Scienze di Ferrara

Atti Accad Sci Fis Mat Napoli — Atti. Accademia delle Scienze Fisiche e Matematiche di Napoli

Atti Accad Sci Ist Bologna Cl Sci Fis Mem — Atti. Accademia delle Scienze. Istituto di Bologna. Classe di Scienze Fisiche. Memorie

Atti Accad Sci Ist Bologna Cl Sci Fis Mem Ser IV — Atti. Accademia delle Scienze. Istituto di Bologna. Classe di Scienze Fisiche. Memorie. Serie IV

Atti Accad Sci Ist Bologna Cl Sci Fis Rend — Atti. Accademia delle Scienze. Istituto di Bologna. Classe di Scienze Fisiche. Rendiconti

Atti Accad Sci Ist Bologna Cl Sci Fis Rend Ser XIII — Atti. Accademia delle Scienze. Istituto di Bologna. Classe di Scienze Fisiche. Rendiconti. Serie XIII

Atti Accad Sci Ist Bologna Ren — Atti. Accademia delle Scienze. Istituto di Bologna. Rendiconti

Atti Accad Sci Istit Bologna Cl Sci Fis Rend 13 — Atti. Accademia delle Scienze. Istituto di Bologna. Classe di Scienze Fisiche. Rendiconti. Serie 13

Atti Accad Sci Lett Arti Palermo — Atti. Accademia di Scienze, Lettere, ed Arti di Palermo

Atti Accad Sci Lett Arti Palermo Parte I — Atti. Accademia di Scienze, Lettere, ed Arti di Palermo. Parte Prima. Scienze

Atti Accad Sci Lett Arti di Palermo Parte I — Atti. Accademia di Scienze, Lettere, ed Arti di Palermo. Parte Prima. Sienze

Atti Accad Sci Lett Arti Palermo Parte I 4 — Atti. Accademia di Scienze, Lettere, ed Arti di Palermo. Parte Prima. Scienze. Serie Quarta

Atti Accad Sci Lett Arti Palermo Ser Quarta Sci — Atti. Accademia di Scienze, Lettere, ed Arti di Palermo. Scienze. Serie Quarta

Atti Accad Sci Siena Fisiocrit — Atti. Accademia delle Scienze di Siena. Detta de Fisiocritici

Atti Accad Sci Torino — Atti. Accademia delle Scienze di Torino

Atti Accad Sci Torino Cl Sci Fis Mat Nat — Atti. Accademia delle Scienze di Torino. Classe di Scienze Fisiche, Matematiche, e Naturali

Atti Accad Sci Torino Cl Sci Fis Mat Natur — Atti. Accademia delle Scienze di Torino. Classe di Scienze Fisiche, Matematiche, e Naturali

Atti Accad Sci Torino I — Atti. Accademia delle Scienze di Torino. I

Atti Accad Sci Torino I Cl Sci Fis Mat Nat — Atti. Accademia delle Scienze di Torino. I. Classe di Scienze Fisiche, Matematiche, e Naturali

Atti Accad Sci Veneto-Trentino-Istriana — Atti. Accademia Scientifica Veneto-Trentino-Istriana

Atti Acc Arch N — Atti. Reale Accademia di Archeologia, Lettere, e Belle Arti di Napoli

Atti Acc Lig — Atti. Accademia Ligure di Scienze e Lettere

Atti Acc Linc — Atti. Reale Accademia dei Lincei

Atti Acc Med Lomb — Atti. Accademia Medica Lombarda

Atti Acc Olimp — Atti. Accademia Olimpica

Atti Acc Pel — Atti. Accademia Peloritana

Atti Acc Sci Torino — Atti. Accademia delle Scienze di Torino

Atti Acc Stor Arte San — Atti e Memorie. Accademia di Storia dell'Arte Sanitaria

Atti Ass Genet Ital — Atti. Associazione Genetica Italiana

Atti Assoc Genet Ital — Atti. Associazione Genetica Italiana

Atti Cent Naz Mecc Agr — Atti. Centro Nazionale Meccanico Agricolo

Atti Clin Odont — Atti. Clinica Odontoiatrica e Societa Napoletana di Stomatologia

Atti Clin Odontol Soc Napolitana Stomatol — Atti. Clinica Odontologica e Societa Napolitana di Stomatologia

Atti Clin Oto-Rino-Laringoiatr Univ Palermo — Atti. Clinica Oto-Rino-Laringoiatrica. Universita di Palermo

Atti Coll Ing Milano — Atti. Collegio deglie Ingegneri di Milano

Atti Cong Nat Ital — Atti. Congresso dei Naturalisi i Italiani

Atti Congr Int Elettron — Atti. Congresso Internazionale per l'Elettronica

Atti Congr Int Mater Plast — Atti. Congresso Internazionale delle Materie Plastiche

Atti Congr Naz Apic Ital — Atti. Congresso Nazionale della Sezione Apicultori Italiani

Atti Congr Naz Chim Ind — Atti. Congresso Nazionale di Chimica Industriale

Atti Congr Naz Chim Pura Appl — Atti. Congresso Nazionale di Chimica Pura ed Applicata

Atti Congr Naz Ital Entomol — Atti. Congresso Nazionale Italiano di Entomologia

Atti Congr Soc Ital Ortod — Atti del Congresso. Societa Italiana di Ortodonzia

Atti Convegi Lincei — Atti. Convegni Lincei [*Rome*]

Atti Conv Int Grano Duro — Atti. Convegno Internazionale del Grano Duro

Atti Conv Naz Apic — Atti. Convegno Nazionale della Apicultori

Atti Conv Naz Tec Nav — Atti. Convegno Nazionale di Tecnica Navale

Atti Conv Prev Soc — Atti. Convegno "Fiscalizzazione Oneri Sociala e Riforma della Previdenza Sociale"

Atti Conv Salute — Atti. VI Convegno della Salute

Atti C St R — Atti. Congresso Nazionale di Studi Romani

ATTID — AT Times

Atti Fac Ing Univ Bologna — Atti. Facolta d'Ingegneria. Universita di Bologna

Atti Fond Giorgio Ronchi — Atti. Fondazione Giorgio Ronchi

Atti Fond Giorgio Ronchi & Contrib Ist Naz Ottica — Atti. Fondazione Giorgio Ronchi e Contributi dell'Istituto Nazionale di Ottica

Atti Fond Ronchi — Atti. Fondazione Giorgio Ronchi

Atti Giornate Fitopatol — Atti della Giornate Fitopatologiche

Atti Ist Bot Labor Crittog Univ Pavia — Atti. Istituto Botanico e Laboratorio Crittogamico. Universita di Pavia

Atti Ist Bot Univ Pavia — Atti. Istituto Botanico. Universita di Pavia

Atti Ist Geol Univ Genova — Atti. Istituto di Geologia. Universita di Genova

Atti Ist Geol Univ Pavia — Atti. Istituto Geologico. Universita di Pavia

Atti Istr — Atti e Memorie. Societa Istriana di Archeologia e Storia Patria

Atti Ist Veneto — Atti. Istituto Veneto di Scienze, Lettere, ed Arti

Atti Ist Veneto Sci Lett Arti — Atti. Istituto Veneto di Scienze, Lettere, ed Arti

Atti Ist Veneto Sci Lett Arti Cl Sci Mat Nat — Atti. Istituto Veneto di Scienze, Lettere, ed Arti. Classe di Scienze Matematiche e Naturali

Atti Mem Accad Agric Sci Lett (Verona) — Atti e Memorie. Accademia di Agricoltura. Scienze e Lettere (Verona)

Atti Mem Accad Naz Sci Lett Arti (Modena) — Atti e Memorie. Accademia Nazionale di Scienze, Lettere, ed Arti (Modena)

Atti Mem Accad Patav Sci Lett Arti — Atti e Memorie. Accademia Patavina di Scienze, Lettere, ed Arti

Atti Mem Accad Stor Arte Sanit — Atti e Memorie. Accademia di Storia dell'Arte Sanitaria

Atti Mem Accad Virgiliana Mantova — Atti e Memorie. Accademia Virgiliana di Mantova

Atti Mem Acc Virg — Atti e Memorie. Reale Accademia Virgiliana

Atti Mem Deputazione Stor Patria Antiche Prov Modenesi — Atti e Memorie. Deputazione di Storia Patria per le Antiche Provincie Modenesi

Atti Mem M — Atti e Memorie. Reale Accademia di Mantova

Atti Memo Acad Agric Sci Lett (Verona) — Atti e Memorie. Accademia di Agricoltura, Scienze, e Lettere (Verona)

Atti Mem Soc Magna Grecia — Atti e Memorie. Societa Magna Grecia

Atti Mem Soc Tiburtina — Atti e Memorie. Societa Tiburtina di Storia e d'Arte

Atti M Grecia — Atti e Memorie. Societa Magna Grecia

Atti Mod — Atti e Memorie. Reale Accademia di Modena

Atti Mus Civ Stor Nat Triesti — Atti. Museo Civico di Storia Naturale di Triesti

Atti Not Assoc Ital Metall — Atti Notizie. Associazione Italiana di Metallurgia

Atti Ortop Traum — Atti di Ortopedia e Traumatologia

Atti Pont Acc — Atti. Pontificia Accademia Romana di Archeologia

Atti R Accad Fisiocrit Siena — Atti. Regia Accademia dei Fisiocritici in Siena

Atti R Accad Georgofili — Atti. Reale Accademia dei Georgofili

Atti R Accad Ital Rend Cl Sci Fis Mat Nat — Atti. Reale Accademia d'Italia. Rendiconti. Classe di Scienze Fisiche, Matematiche, e Naturali

Atti R Accad Lincei Mem Cl Sc Fis Mat e Nat — Atti. Reale Accademia dei Lincei. Memorie. Classe di Scienze Fisiche, Ma tematiche, e Naturali

Atti R Accad Lincei Rendic Cl Sc Fis Mat e Nat — Atti. Reale Accademia dei Lincei. Rendiconti. Classe di Scienze Fisiche, Matematiche, e Naturali

Atti R Accad Lincei (Roma) Mem Cl Sc Fis Mat e Nat — Atti. Reale Accademia dei Lincei (Roma). Memorie. Classe di Scienze Fisiche, Matematiche, e Naturali

Atti R Accad Lincei (Roma) Rendic Cl Sc Fis Mat e Nat — Atti. Reale Accademia dei Lincei (Roma). Rendiconti. Classe di Scienze Fisiche, Matematiche, e Naturali

Atti R Accad Naz Lincei (Roma) — Atti. Reale Accademia Nazional dei Lincei (Roma)

Atti R Accad Peloritana — Atti. Reale Accademia Peloritana

Atti R Accad Peloritana Cl Sci Fis Mat Biol — Atti. Reale Accademia Peloritana. Classe di Scienze Fisiche, Matematiche, e Biologiche

Atti R Accad Sci Torino Cl Sci Fis Mat Nat — Atti. Reale Accademia delle Scienze di Torino. Classe di Scienze Fisiche, Matematiche, e Naturali

Atti Rend Accad Naz Lincei Cl Sci Fis Mat Natur — Atti. Rendiconti. Accademia Nazionale dei Lincei. Classe di Scienze Fisiche, Matematiche, e Naturali

Atti R Univ Genova — Atti. Reale Universita di Genova

Atti Sci Soc Elv Sci Nat — Atti Scientifici. Societa Elvetica di Scienze Naturali

Atti Semin Mat & Fis Univ Modena — Atti. Seminario Matematico e Fisico. Universita di Modena

Atti Sem Mat Fis Univ Modena — Atti. Seminario Matematico e Fisico. Universita di Modena

Atti Simp Int Zootec — Atti. Simposio Internazionale di Zootecnia

Atti Soc Astron Ital — Atti. Societa Astronomica Italiana

Atti Soc Cultori Sc Med e Nat Cagliari — Atti. Societa fra i Cultori delle Scienze Mediche e Naturali in Cagliari

Atti Soc Elv Sci Nat Parte Sci — Atti. Societa Elvetica di Scienze Naturali. Parte Scientifica

Atti Soc Ital Cardiol — Atti. Societa Italiana di Cardiologia

Atti Soc Ital Prog Sci — Atti. Societa Italiana per il Progresso delle Scienze

Atti Soc Ital Sci Nat — Atti. Societa Italiana di Scienze Naturali. Museo Civile di Storia Naturale

Atti Soc Ital Sci Nat Mus Civ Stor Nat Milano — Atti. Societa Italiana di Scienze Naturali. Museo Civico di Storia Natu rale di Milano

Atti Soc Ital Sci Vet — Atti. Societa Italiana delle Scienze Veterinarie

Atti Soc Ital Sc Nat (Milano) — Atti. Societa Italiana di Scienze Naturali (Milano)

Atti Soc Lig Stor Patria — Atti. Societa Ligure di Storia Patria

Atti Soc Ligust Sc Nat e Geogr — Atti. Societa Ligustica di Scienze Naturali e Geografiche

Atti Soc Lomb Sci Med Biol — Atti. Societa Lombarda di Scienze Mediche e Biologiche

Atti Soc Med-Chir Padova Fac Med Chir Univ Padova — Atti. Societa Medico-Chirurgica di Padova e Facolta di Medicina e Chirurgia della Universita di Padova

Atti Soc Nat Mat Modena — Atti. Societa dei Naturalisti e Matematici di Modena

Atti Soc Oftalmol Lomb — Atti. Societa Oftalmologica Lombarda

Atti Soc Peloritana Sci Fis Mat e Nat — Atti. Societa Peloritana di Scienze Fisiche, Matematiche, e Naturali

Atti Soc Peloritana Sci Fis Mat Nat — Atti. Societa Peloritana di Scienze Fisiche, Matematiche, e Naturali

Atti Soc Peloritana Sci Fis Mat Natur — Atti. Societa Peloritana di Scienze Fisiche, Matematiche, e Naturali

Atti Soc Salernitana Med Chir — Atti. Societa Salernitana di Medicina e Chirurgia

Atti Soc Toscana Sci Nat Pisa Mem — Atti. Societa Toscana di Scienze Naturali Residente in Pisa. Memorie

Atti Soc Toscana Sci Nat Pisa P V — Atti. Societa Toscana di Scienze Naturali Residente in Pisa. Processi Verbali

Atti Soc Toscana Sci Nat Pisa P V Mem Ser A — Atti. Societa Toscana di Scienze Naturali Residente in Pisa. Processi Verbali e Memorie. Serie A

Atti Soc Toscana Sci Nat P V Mem Ser B — Atti. Societa Toscana di Scienze Naturali. Processi Verbali e Memorie. Serie B

Atti Soc Toscana Sci Nat Resid Pisa Mem Ser A — Atti. Societa Toscana di Scienze Naturali Residente in Pisa. Memorie. Serie A

Atti Tor — Atti. Reale Accademia della Scienze di Torino

Atti Ven — Atti. Istituto Veneto di Scienze, Lettere, ed Arti

Atti V Simp Int Agrochim "Zolfo in Agricoltura" — Atti. V Simposio Internazionale di Agrochimica su "Lo Zolfo in Agricoltu ra"

Attual Chemioter — Attualita di Chemioterapia

Attual Lab — Attualita di Laboratorio

Attual Med — Attualita Medica

Attual Ostet Ginecol — Attualita di Ostetricia e Ginecologia

Attual Zool — Attualita Zoologica

ATTUD — Advances in Tunnelling Technology and Subsurface Use

ATU — Altorientalische Texte und Untersuchungen [*Leiden*]

Atual Agron — Atualidades Agronomicas

Atual Agron (Sao Paulo) — Atualidades Agronomicas (Sao Paulo)

Atual Agrovet — Atualidades Agroveterinarias

Atual Med Sanit — Atualidades Medico Sanitarias

Atual Vet — Atualidades Veterinarias

Atual Vet (Sao Paulo) — Atualidades Veterinarias (Sao Paulo)

AtV — Ateneo Veneto

ATVED — Atualidades Veterinarias

ATVEDH — Atualidades Veterinarias [*Sao Paulo*]

ATW — Air Transport World

At World — Atomic World

ATX — Australian Sales Tax Guide

ATX — Business. The Magazine of Managerial Thought and Action

ATY — Automatie, Maandblad voor Meettechniek en Regeltechniek, Mechanisering, en Automatisering [*Baarn*]

ATZOAU — Attualita Zoologiche

AU — Afrika und Uebersee

AU — Annals of the University [*Grenoble*]

A & U — Architecture and Urbanism

Au — Audio

Au — Ausonia

AU — Der Altsprachliche Unterricht

AuA — Anglistik und Amerikanistik

AUA — Annals. Ukrainian Academy of Arts and Sciences in the US

AUAA J — AUAA [*American Urological Association Allied*] Journal

AUAFA — Acta Universitatis Agriculturae. Facultas Silviculturae. Series C

AUARAN — Arkansas. Agricultural Experiment Station. Special Report

AUARBO — Australia. Commonwealth Scientific and Industrial Research Organisation. Division of Animal Physiology. Annual Report

AUB — Analele. Universitatii Bucuresti

AUB — Annales Universitatis Scientiarum Budapestensis de Rolando Eoetvoes Nominatae

AUB — Annales. Universite de Besancon

A d U B — Annales. Universite de Brazzaville

AuB — Autour de la Bible [*Paris*]

AUBCB — Analele. Universitatii Bucuresti. Chimie

AUBFF — Arquivos. Universidade de Baia. Faculdade de Filosofia

AUBG — Acta Universitatis Upsaliensis

AuBiR — Australian Biblical Review [*Melbourne*]

AUBKA7 — Archives. Union Medicale Balkanique

AUB-LCO — Analele. Universitatii Bucuresti. Limbi Clasice si Orientale

AUB-LG — Analele. Universitatii Bucuresti. Limbi Germanice

AUBLL — Analele. Universitatii Bucuresti. Limba si Literatura Romana

AUB-LLR — Analele. Universitatii Bucuresti. Limba Literara

AUBLR — Analele. Universitatii Bucuresti. Limbi Romanice

AUB-LUC — Analele. Universitatii Bucuresti. Literatura Universala Comparata

AUBud — Annales Universitatis Scientiarum Budapestensis de Rolando Eoetvoes Nominatae. Sectio Philologica

Auburn Univ Eng Exp Stn Bull — Auburn University. Engineering Experiment Station. Bulletin

AUC — Acta Universitatis Carolinae

AUC — Anales. Universidad de Chile

AUC — Anuarul. Universitatea Cluj

AUC — Au Courant

AUC — Auteursrecht

AUCal — Annali. Facolta di Lettere, Filosofia, e Magistero. Universita di Cagliari

AuCaRec — Australasian Catholic Record [*Manly, NSW*]

AUCC — Annuario. Universita Cattolica del Sacro Cuore

AUCE — Anales. Universidad Central del Ecuador

AUCG-B — Acta Universitatis Carolinae: Geographica

AuChr — Antike und Christentum

AUCII — Archivio Unione Comunita Israelitiche Italiane

Auckland U L Rev — Auckland University. Law Review

Auckland Univ L Rev — Auckland University. Law Review

Auck ULR — Auckland University. Law Review

Auck UL Rev — Auckland University. Law Review

AUCMB — Acta Universitatis Carolinae: Medica. Monographia

AUCP — Acta Universitatis Carolinae Pragensis

AUCPD — Annual UMR-DNR [*University of Missouri, Rolla - Department of Natural Resources*] Conference on Energy. Proceedings

AUC-Ph — Acta Universitatis Carolinae: Philologica

AUD — Acta et Commentationes Universitatis Dorpatensis

Aud — Audience

Aud — Audubon

AUDBAO — Australia. Commonwealth Scientific and Industrial Research Organisation. Division of Building Research. Technical Paper

AUDIB — Audiology Society of Japan

Audio Engg — Audio Engineering

Audio Eng Soc J — Audio Engineering Society. Journal

Audio Eng Soc Prepr — Audio Engineering Society. Preprint

Audiol — Audiology

Audiol (Jap) — Audiology (Japan)

Audio Scene Can — Audio Scene Canada

Audiov Commun — Audio Visual Communications

Audio Video Can — Audio Video Canada

Audiov Instr — Audiovisual Instruction

Audiovis Instr — Audiovisual Instruction

Audio Visual G — Audio Visual Guide
Audio-Visual Language J — Audio-Visual Language Journal
Audio Visual Lib — Audio Visual Librarian
Auditor — Internal Auditor
AUDJDK — Audiology [*Japan*]
AUDLA — Audiology
AUDLAK — Audiology [*Basel*]
Audn — Audience
AUDTCF — Ankara Universitesi Dil ve Tarih-Cografya Fakultesi. Dergisi [*Ankara*]
AUDTCFY — Ankara Universitesi Dil ve Tarih-Cografya Fakultesi. Yayinlari
AUDUA — Audio
AUDUAD — Audubon
Audubon Mag — Audubon Magazine
Audubon Soc RI Bull — Audubon Society of Rhode Island. Bulletin
AuE — Arheologija un Etnografija
AUELA — Automatica si Electronica
AUENA — Automobile Engineer [*England*]
Auerbach Data Base Manage — Auerbach Data Base Management
Auerbach Rep — Auerbach Reporter
AUF — Archiv fuer Urkundenforschung
AUFB-A — Aufbau
Aufbereit-Tech — Aufbereitungs-Technik
Aufbereitungs-Tech — Aufbereitungs-Technik
AUFNA2 — Audubon Field Notes
AUFS — American Universities Field Staff. Reports Series
Aufschluss Sonderh — Aufschluss Sonderheft
AUFS EA — American Universities Field Staff. Reports. East Asia Series
AUFSRS — American Universities Field Staff. Reports Series
AUFS SA — American Universities Field Staff. Reports. South Asia Series
AUFS SEA — American Universities Field Staff. Reports. Southeast Asia Series
Au Fu — Ausgrabungen und Funde
AUG — Anales. Universidad de Guayaquil
AUG — Annales. Universite de Grenoble
Aug — Augustiniana
AugLv — Augustiniana (Louvain)
AugMad — Augustinus (Madrid)
AugRom — Augustinianum (Rome)
Augustana Libr Pub — Augustana Library Publications
Augustin Stud — Augustinian Studies
AUH — Anales. Universidad Hispalense
AUHisp — Anales. Universidad Hispalense
AUHJ — Australian Journal for Health, Physical Education, and Recreation
AUI — Analele. Universitatii Al. I. Cuza (Iasi)
AUIBA — Analele Stiintifice. Universitatii Al. I. Cuza din Iasi. Sectiunea 2a. Biologie
AUINA — Automotive Industries
AUJ — Aberdeen University. Journal
Aujourd'hui — Aujourd'hui: Art et Architecture
AUJSA — Australian Journal of Statistics
AUL — Acta Universitatis Latviensis
AUL — Acta Universitatis Lundensis
AUL — Annales. Universite de Lyon
AUL — Annali. Universita di Lecce
AULJA — Australian Library Journal
AULR — American University Law Review
AUM — Adelaide University. Magazine
AUM — Anales. Universidad de Murcia
AUM — Andrews University. Monographs
AUMCA4 — Archivos Uruguayos de Medicina, Cirujia, y Especialidades
AUMCS — Annales Universitatis Mariae Curie-Sklodowska. Sectio F. Nauki Filozoficzne i Humanistyczne
AUMDC — Automedica
AUMGAG — Audubon Magazine
AUMIA — Australian Mineral Industry
AUMID — Australian Miner
AUMKA — Annales Universitatis Mariae Curie-Sklodowska. Sectio D. Medicina
AUMLA — Australasian Universities Modern Language Association. Journal
AUMNA — Australian Mining
AUMTA — Automatisme
AUN — Annali. Facolta di Lettere e Filosofia. Universita di Napoli
Au N — Aufstieg und Niedergang der Roemischen Welt
AUNED — Australian Uranium News
AUNHA — Australian Natural History
A Univ Abidjan Ethnosociologie — Annales. Universite d'Abidjan. Ethnosociologie
A Univ Abidjan Histoire — Annales. Universite d'Abidjan. Histoire
A Univ Abidjan Lettres — Annales. Universite d'Abidjan. Lettres
A Univ Abidjan Linguist — Annales. Universite d'Abidjan. Linguistique
A Univ Abidjan Ser A Dr — Annales. Universite d'Abidjan. Serie A. Droit
A Univ Madagascar Ser Dr Sci Econ — Annales. Universite de Madagascar. Serie de Droit et des Sciences Economiques
A Univ M Curie-Sklodowska — Annales Universitatis Mariae Curie-Sklodowska

A Univ M Curie-Sklodowska Oecon — Annales Universitatis Mariae Curie-Sklodowska. Sectio Oeconomica
A Univ Sci Budapest Sect Geogr — Annales Universitatis Scientiarum Budapestensis de Rolando Eoetvoes Nominatae. Sectio Geographica
A Univ Sci Soc Toulouse — Annales. Universite des Sciences Sociales de Toulouse
AUOASRN — Acta Universitatis Ouluensis. Series A. Scientiae Rerum Naturalium
AUONAD — Collected Reports. Natural Science Faculty. Palacky University [*Olomouc*]
AUO-Ph — Acta Universitatis Palackianae Olomucensis. Facultas Philosophica. Philologica
AUP — Annales. Universite de Paris
AUPHB — Australian Physicist
AUPJB — Australian Paediatric Journal
AUPO — Acta Universitatis Palackianae Olomucensis
AUPRD — AUTOTESTCON [*Automatic Testing Conference*] Proceedings
AUR — Aberdeen University. Review
Aur — Aurora
AUR — Automatisering Gids
AURCA — Automation and Remote Control
AUS — Annales Universitatis Saraviensis
AUS — Annuaire. Universite de Sofia. Faculte des Lettres
Aus — Ausonia
AUS — Australian Coal Report
AUS AG & R — Acta Universitatis Szegediensis. Acta Germanica et Romanica
AUS AHLH — Acta Universitatis Szegediensis de Attila Jozsef Nominatae. Sectio Historiae Litterarum Hungaricarum
AusBiR — Australian Biblical Review [*Melbourne*]
Aus BR — Australian Biblical Review
Aus Comp J — Australian Computer Journal
AusCR — Australian Catholic Record [*Sydney*]
Aus C Rec — Australasian Catholic Record
AusCRec — Australian Catholic Record [*Sydney*]
Aus Educ Ind — Australian Education Index
AUS E & L — Acta Universitatis Szegediensis de Attila Jozsef Nominatae. Sectio: Ethnographica et Linguistica
AUSem St — Andrews University. Seminary Studies
Ausgrab Fun — Ausgrabungen und Funde
AusJBibArch — Australian Journal of Biblical Archaeology [*Sydney*]
Aus J Screen Theory — Australian Journal of Screen Theory
AusL — Australian Letters
Aus Leg Mon Dig — Australian Legal Monthly Digest
AUSLOAN — AUSLOAN: Australian Inter-Library Loans Manual
Aus Mo Motor Manual — Australian Monthly Motor Manual
Aus PAIS — Australian Public Affairs Information Service
AUS-PEAS — Acta Universitatis Szegediensis de Attila Jozsef Nominatae. Papers in English and American Studies
AusQ — Australian Quarterly
AUSQA — Australian Quarterly
Aus Quart — Australian Quarterly
AUSRA — Records. Australian Academy of Science
AUSS — Andrews University Seminary Studies
Aus Sci Ind — Australian Science Index
Aussenpol — Aussenpolitik
Aussenpoli — Aussenpolitik
Aussenwirt — Aussenwirtschaft
Aus Speleo Abstr — Australian Speleo Abstracts
Aust — [*The*] Australian
Aust Aborig — Australian Aborigines Annual Bibliography
Aust Acacias — Australian Acacias
Aust Acad H — Australian Academy of the Humanities. Proceedings
Aust Acad and Res Lib — Australian Academic and Research Libraries
Aust Acad Res Libr — Australian Academic and Research Libraries
Aust Acad Sci Rep — Australian Academy of Science. Reports
Aust Acad Sci Sci Ind Forum Forum Rep — Australian Academy of Science. Science and Industry Forum. Forum Report
Aust Accnt — Australian Accountant
Aust Accountancy Progress — Australian Accountancy Progress
Aust Accountancy Student — Australian Accountancy Student
Aust Accountant — Australian Accountant
Aust Acct — Australian Accountant
Aust Acct Stud — Australian Accountancy Student
Aust Adv Vet Sci — Australian Advances in Veterinary Science
Aust AEC AAEC/E Rep — Australian Atomic Energy Commission. AAEC/E. Report
Aust AEC AAEC/TM Rep — Australian Atomic Energy Commission. AAEC/TM. Report
Aust AEC Inf Pap — Australian Atomic Energy Commission. Information Paper
Aust AEC Res Establ Rep AAEC/S — Australian Atomic Energy Commission. Research Establishment. Report AAEC/S
Aust AEC TRG Rep — Australian Atomic Energy Commission. TRG Report
Aust Aeronaut Comm Rep ACA — Australian Aeronautical Research Committee. Report ACA

Aust Aeronaut Res Comm Rep — Australian Aeronautical Research Committee. Report
Aust Aeronaut Res Comm Rep ACA — Australian Aeronautical Research Committee. Report ACA
Aust Aeronaut Res Lab Aerodyn Rep — Australia. Aeronautical Research Laboratories. Aerodynamics. Report
Aust Aeronaut Res Lab Guided Weapons Note — Australia. Aeronautical Research Laboratories. Guided Weapons Note
Aust Aeronaut Res Lab Mater Note — Australia. Aeronautical Research Laboratories. Materials Note
Aust Aeronaut Res Lab Mater Rep — Australia. Aeronautical Research Laboratories. Materials Report
Aust Aeronaut Res Lab Mech Eng Note — Australia. Aeronautical Research Laboratories. Mechanical Engineering Note
Aust Aeronaut Res Lab Metall Note — Australia. Aeronautical Research Laboratories. Metallurgy Note
Aust Aeronaut Res Lab Metall Rep — Australia. Aeronautical Research Laboratories. Metallurgy Report
Aust Aeronaut Res Lab Metall Tech Mem — Australia. Aeronautical Research Laboratories. Metallurgy Technical Memorandum
Aust Aeronaut Res Lab Rep MET — Australia. Aeronautical Research Laboratories. Report MET (Metallurgy)
Aust Aeronaut Res Lab Struct — Australia. Aeronautical Research Laboratories. Structures and Materials Note
Aust Aeronaut Res Lab Struct Mater Note — Australia. Aeronautical Research Laboratories. Structures and Materials Note
Aust Aeronaut Res Lab Struct Mater Rep — Australia. Aeronautical Research Laboratories. Structures and Materials Report
Aust Aeronaut Res Lab Struct Note — Australia. Aeronautical Research Laboratories. Structures Note
Aust Aeronaut Res Lab Struct Rep — Australia. Aeronautical Research Laboratories. Structures Report
Aust Agric News — Australian Agricultural Newsletter
Aust Amateur Mineral — Australian Amateur Mineralogist
Aust Amateur Mineralogist — Australian Amateur Mineralogist
Aust Amat Miner — Australian Amateur Mineralogist
Aust-American Assn Canb News Bul — Australian-American Association in Canberra. News Bulletin
Aust-American J — Australian-American Journal
Aust Ann Med — Australasian Annals of Medicine
Aust Ann of Med — Australasian Annals of Medicine
Aust Arab Horse News — Australian Arabian Horse News
Aust Argus L Rep — Australian Argus Law Reports
Aust Army J — Australian Army Journal
Aust Aronaut Lab Struct Mater Rep — Australia. Aeronautical Research Laboratories. Structures and Materials Report
Aust Aronaut Res Lab Metall Tech Memo — Australia. Aeronautical Research Laboratories. Metallurgy Technical Memorandum
Aust Assoc Neurol Proc — Australian Association of Neurologists. Proceedings
Aust At Energy Symp Proc — Australian Atomic Energy Symposium. Proceedings of a Symposium on the Peaceful Uses of Atomic Energy. University of Sydney, June 2-6, 1958
Aust Auth — Australian Author
Aust Automobile Trade J — Australian Automobile Trade Journal
Aust Automot Eng & Equip — Australian Automotive Engineering and Equipment
Aust Aviation Newsletter — Australian Aviation Newsletter
Aust Aviat Newsl — Australian Aviation Newsletter
Aust Aviat Yb — Australian Aviation Yearbook
Aust Avicult — Australian Aviculture
Aust Baker — Australian Baker and Millers' Journal
Aust Bank — Australian Banker
Aust Bankr Cas — Australian Bankruptcy Cases
Aust Baptist — Australian Baptist
Aust Bar Gaz — Australian Bar Gazette
Aust Bee J — Australian Bee Journal
Aust Bib R — Australian Biblical Review
Aust Bird Bander — Australian Bird Bander
Aust Birdwatcher — Australian Birdwatcher
Aust Bldg Forum — Australia Building Forum
Aust Bldr — Australian Builder
Aust Boating — Australian Boating
Aust Book Auction Rec — Australian Book Auction Records
Aust Book R — Australian Book Review
Aust Book Rev — Australian Book Review
Aust Book Rev Children's Book & Ed Suppl — Australian Book Review. Children's Books and Educational Supplement
Aust Brewing Wine J — Australian Brewing and Wine Journal
Aust Brewing & Wine J — Australian Brewing and Wine Journal
Aust Builder — Australian Builder
Aust Build Forum — Australian Building Forum
Aust Build Sci Technol — Australian Building Science and Technology
Aust Build Technol — Australian Building Technology
Aust Bull Labour — Australian Bulletin of Labour

Aust Bur Miner Resour Geol Geophys BMR J Aust Geol Geophys — Australia. Bureau of Mineral Resources. Geology and Geophysics. BMR Journal of Australian Geology and Geophysics
Aust Bur Miner Resour Geol Geophys Bull — Australia. Bureau of Mineral Resources. Geology and Geophysics. Bulletin
Aust Bur Miner Resour Geol Geophys Pam — Australia. Bureau of Mineral Resources. Geology and Geophysics. Pamphlet
Aust Bur Miner Resour Geol Geophys Rep — Australia. Bureau of Mineral Resources. Geology and Geophysics. Report
Aust Bus — Australian Business
Aust Bush Nursing J — Australian Bush Nursing Journal
Aust Business L Rev — Australian Business Law Review
Aust Bus Law R — Australian Business Law Review
Aust Bus L Rev — Australian Business Law Review
Aust Camera — Australian Camera and Cine
Aust Canegrow — Australian Canegrower
Aust Canning Convention — Australian Canning Convention. Proceedings
Aust Canning Convention Procs — Australian Canning Convention. Proceedings
Aust Cath Hist Soc J — Australian Catholic Historical Society. Journal
Aust Catholic D — Australian Catholic Digest
Aust Catholic Truth Soc Rec — Australian Catholic Truth Society. Record
Aust Ceram Conf Proc — Australian Ceramic Conference. Proceedings
Aust Chem Abstr — Australian Chemical Abstracts
Aust Chem Eng — Australian Chemical Engineering
Aust Chem Eng Conf — Australian Chemical Engineering. Conference
Aust Chem Engineering — Australian Chemical Engineering
Aust Chem Engng — Australian Chemical Engineering
Aust Chem Inst J Proc — Australian Chemical Institute. Journal and Proceedings
Aust Chem Proc — Australian Chemical Processing
Aust Chem Process — Australian Chemical Processing
Aust Chem Process Eng — Australian Chemical Processing and Engineering
Aust Chem Process Engng — Australian Chemical Processing and Engineering
Aust Chem Processing — Australian Chemical Processing
Aust Child Fam Welfare — Australian Child and Family Welfare
Aust Child Limited — Australian Children Limited
Aust Child Ltd — Australian Children Limited
Aust Children Ltd — Australian Children Limited
Aust Christian — Australian Christian
Aust Church Q — Australian Church Quarterly
Aust Church Rec — Australian Church Record
Aust Citizen Ltd — Australian Citizen Limited
Aust Citrus News — Australian Citrus News
Aust Civ Eng — Australian Civil Engineering
Aust Civ Engng — Australian Civil Engineering
Aust Civ Engng Constr — Australian Civil Engineering and Construction
Aust Civil Eng Construc — Australian Civil Engineering and Construction
Aust Climatol Summ — Australian Climatological Summary
Aust CL Rev — Australian Current Law Review
Aust Coal Ass (Res) Rep — Australian Coal Association (Research) Limited. Report
Aust Coal & Harbour — Australian Coal, Shipping, Steel, and the Harbour
Aust Coalmining — Australian Coalmining and Mine Mechanisation
Aust Coin — Australian Coin Review
Aust Coll Educ Vic Chapter Newsl — Australian College of Education. Victorian Chapter. Newsletter
Aust Coll Speech Ther J — Australian College of Speech Therapists. Journal
Aust Commonw Advis Counc Sci Ind Bull — Australia. Commonwealth Advisory Council of Science and Industry. Bulletin
Aust Commonw Advis Counc Sci Ind Pam — Australia. Commonwealth Advisory Council of Science and Industry. Pamphlet
Aust Commonw Counc Sci Ind Res Bull — Australia. Commonwealth Council for Scientific and Industrial Research. Bulletin
Aust Commonw Counc Sci Ind Res Pam — Australia. Commonwealth Council for Scientific and Industrial Research. Pamphlet
Aust Commonw Dep Supply Aeronaut Res Comm Rep ACA — Australia. Commonwealth Department of Supply. Aeronautical Research Committee. Report ACA
Aust Commonw Dep Supply Aeronaut Res Consult Comm Rep ACA — Australia. Commonwealth Department of Supply. Aeronautical Research Consultative Committee. Report ACA
Aust Commonw Dep Supply Aeronaut Res Guided Weapons Note — Australia. Commonwealth Department of Supply. Aeronautical Research Laboratories. Guided Weapons Note
Aust Commonw Dep Supply Aeronaut Res Lab Metall Note — Australia. Commonwealth Department of Supply. Aeronautical Research Laboratories. Metallurgy Note
Aust Commonw Dep Supply Aeronaut Res Lab Metall Tech Memo — Australia. Commonwealth Department of Supply. Aeronautical Research Laboratories. Metallurgy Technical Memorandum
Aust Commonw Dep Supply Aeronaut Res Lab Rep MET — Australia. Commonwealth Department of Supply. Aeronautical Research Laboratories. Report MET (Metallurgy)

Aust Commonw Dep Supply Aeronaut Res Lab Rep SM — Australia. Commonwealth Department of Supply. Aeronautical Research Laboratories. Report SM [*Structures and Materials*]

Aust Commonw Dep Supply Def Res Lab Report — Australia. Commonwealth Department of Supply. Defence Research Laboratories. Report

Aust Commonw Dep Supply Def Stand Lab Rep — Australia. Commonwealth Department of Supply. Defence Standards Laboratories. Report

Aust Commonw Dep Supply Def Stand Lab Tech Note — Australia. Commonwealth Department of Supply. Defence Standards Laboratories. Technical Note

Aust Commonw Dep Supply Res Lab Tech Note — Australia. Commonwealth Department of Supply. Defence Research Laboratories. Technical Note

Aust Commonw Dept Supply Aeronaut Res Comm Rep — Australia. Commonwealth Department of Supply. Aeronautical Research Committee. Report

Aust Commonw Inst Sci Ind Bull — Australia. Commonwealth Institute of Science and Industry. Bulletin

Aust Commonw Inst Sci Ind Pam — Australia. Commonwealth Institute of Science and Industry. Pamphlet

Aust Commonw Sci Ind Res Organ Div Metrol Tech Pap — Australia. Commonwealth Scientific and Industrial Research Organisation. Division of Metrology. Technical Paper

Aust Comp Law Cases — Australian Company Law Cases

Aust Comput Bull — Australian Computer Bulletin

Aust Comput J — Australian Computer Journal

Aust Comput Sci Commun — Australian Computer Science Communications

Aust Conf Chem Eng — Australian Conference on Chemical Engineering

Aust Conf Nucl Tech Anal Proc — Australian Conference on Nuclear Techniques of Analysis. Proceedings

Aust Conf Nucl Tech Anal Summ Proc — Australian Conference on Nuclear Techniques of Analysis. Summary of Proceedings

Aust Conserv Found Newsl — Australian Conservation Foundation. Newsletter

Aust Conv — Australian Conveyancer and Solicitors' Journal

Aust Conveyancer — Australian Conveyancer and Solicitors' Journal

Aust Conv Sol J — Australian Conveyancer and Solicitors' Journal [*1948-59*]

Aust Cordial Maker — Australian Cordial Maker, Brewer, and Bottler's Gazette

Aust Corr Eng — Australian Corrosion Engineering

Aust Corros Eng — Australian Corrosion Engineering

Aust Corros Engng — Australian Corrosion Engineering

Aust Corrosion Eng — Australian Corrosion Engineering

Aust Cott Grow — Australian Cotton Grower

Aust Cott Grow Fmr Dairym — Australian Cotton Grower, Farmer, and Dairyman

Aust Counc Aeronaut Rep ACA — Australian Council for Aeronautics. Report ACA

Aust Country — Australian Country Magazine

Aust Country Mag — Australian Country Magazine

Aust CSIRO Abstr Publ Pap List Transl — Australia. Commonwealth Scientific and Industrial Research Organisation. Abstracts of Published Papers and List of Translations

Aust CSIRO Anim Res Lab Tech Pap — Australia. Commonwealth Scientific and Industrial Research Organisation. Animal Research Laboratories. Technical Paper

Aust CSIRO Annu Rep — Australia. Commonwealth Scientific and Industrial Research Organisation. Annual Report

Aust CSIRO Bull — Australia. Commonwealth Scientific and Industrial Research Organisation. Bulletin

Aust CSIRO Chem Res Lab Tech Pap — Australia. Commonwealth Scientific and Industrial Research Organisation. Chemical Research Laboratories. Technical Paper

Aust CSIRO Coal Res Div Locat Rep — Australia. Commonwealth Scientific and Industrial Research Organisation. Coal Research Division. Location Report

Aust CSIRO Coal Res Div Misc Rep — Australia. Commonwealth Scientific and Industrial Research Organisation. Coal Research Division. Miscellaneous Report

Aust CSIRO Coal Res Div Tech Commun — Australia. Commonwealth Scientific and Industrial Research Organisation. Coal Research Division. Technical Communication

Aust CSIRO CSIRO Wildl Res — Australia. Commonwealth Scientific and Industrial Research Organisation. CSIRO Wildlife Research

Aust CSIRO Div Anim Genet Res Rep — Australia Commonwealth Scientific and Industrial Research Organisation. Division of Animal Genetics. Research Report

Aust CSIRO Div Anim Health Annu Rep — Australia. Commonwealth Scientific and Industrial Research Organisation. Division of Animal Health. Annual Report

Aust CSIRO Div Anim Health Prod Tech Pap — Australia. Commonwealth Scientific and Industrial Research Organisation. Division of Animal Health and Production. Technical Paper

Aust CSIRO Div Anim Physiol Annu Rep — Australia. Commonwealth Scientific and Industrial Research Organisation. Division of Animal Physiology. Annual Report

Aust CSIRO Div Appl Chem Annu Rep — Australia. Commonwealth Scientific and Industrial Research Organisation. Division of Applied Chemistry. Annual Report

Aust CSIRO Div Appl Chem Tech Pap — Australia. Commonwealth Scientific and Industrial Research Organisation. Division of Applied Chemistry. Technical Paper

Aust CSIRO Div Appl Geomech Tech Memo — Australia. Commonwealth Scientific and Industrial Research Organisation. Division of Applied Geomechanics. Technical Memorandum

Aust CSIRO Div Appl Geomech Tech Pap — Australia. Commonwealth Scientific and Industrial Research Organisation. Division of Applied Geomechanics. Technical Paper

Aust CSIRO Div Appl Org Chem Res Rep — Australia. Commonwealth Scientific and Industrial Research Organisation. Division of Applied Organic Chemistry. Research Report

Aust CSIRO Div Appl Org Chem Tech Pap — Australia. Commonwealth Scientific and Industrial Research Organisation. Division of Applied Organic Chemistry. Technical Paper

Aust CSIRO Div Atmos Phys Tech Pap — Australia. Commonwealth Scientific and Industrial Research Organisation. Division of Atmospheric Physics. Technical Paper

Aust CSIRO Div Build Res Annu Rep — Australia. Commonwealth Scientific and Industrial Research Organisation. Division of Building Research. Annual Report

Aust CSIRO Div Build Res Tech Pap — Australia. Commonwealth Scientific and Industrial Research Organisation. Division of Building Research. Technical Paper

Aust CSIRO Div Chem Eng Rep — Australia. Commonwealth Scientific and Industrial Research Organisation. Division of Chemical Engineering. Report

Aust CSIRO Div Chem Technol Res Rev — Australia. Commonwealth Scientific and Industrial Research Organisation. Division of Chemical Technology. Research Review

Aust CSIRO Div Chem Technol Tech Pap — Australia. Commonwealth Scientific and Industrial Research Organisation. Division of Chemical Technology. Technical Paper

Aust CSIRO Div Coal Res Locat Rep — Australia. Commonwealth Scientific and Industrial Research Organisation. Division of Coal Research. Location Report

Aust CSIRO Div Coal Res Misc Rep — Australia. Commonwealth Scientific and Industrial Research Organisation. Division of Coal Research. Miscellaneous Report

Aust CSIRO Div Coal Res Ref LR — Australia. Commonwealth Scientific and Industrial Research Organisation. Division of Coal Research. Reference LR [*Location Report*]

Aust CSIRO Div Coal Res Tech Commun — Australia. Commonwealth Scientific and Industrial Research Organisation. Division of Coal Research. Technical Communication

Aust CSIRO Div Dairy Res Annu Rep — Australia. Commonwealth Scientific and Industrial Research Organisation. Division of Dairy Research. Annual Report

Aust CSIRO Div Entomol Tech Pap — Australia. Commonwealth Scientific and Industrial Research Organisation. Division of Entomology. Technical Paper

Aust CSIRO Div Fish Oceanogr Annu Rep — Australia. Commonwealth Scientific and Industrial Research Organisation. Division of Fisheries and Oceanography. Annual Report

Aust CSIRO Div Fish Oceanogr Circ — Australia. Commonwealth Scientific and Industrial Research Organisation. Division of Fisheries and Oceanography. Circular

Aust CSIRO Div Fish Oceanogr Fish Synop — Australia. Commonwealth Scientific and Industrial Research Organisation. Division of Fisheries and Oceanography. Fisheries Synopsis

Aust CSIRO Div Fish Oceanogr Rep — Australia. Commonwealth Scientific and Industrial Research Organisation. Division of Fisheries and Oceanography. Report

Aust CSIRO Div Fish Oceanogr Tech Pap — Australia. Commonwealth Scientific and Industrial Research Organisation. Division of Fisheries and Oceanography. Technical Paper

Aust CSIRO Div Fish Tech Pap — Australia. Commonwealth Scientific and Industrial Research Organisation. Division of Fisheries. Technical Paper

Aust CSIRO Div Food Preserv Rep Res — Australia. Commonwealth Scientific and Industrial Research Organisation. Division of Food Preservation. Report of Research

Aust CSIRO Div Food Preserv Tech Pap — Australia. Commonwealth Scientific and Industrial Research Organisation. Division of Food Preservation. Technical Paper

Aust CSIRO Div Food Preserv Transp Tech Pap — Australia. Commonwealth Scientific and Industrial Research Organisation. Division of Food Preservation and Transport. Technical Paper

Aust CSIRO Div Food Res Rep Res — Australia. Commonwealth Scientific and Industrial Research Organisation. Division of Food Research. Report of Research

Aust CSIRO Div Food Res Tech Pap — Australia. Commonwealth Scientific and Industrial Research Organisation. Division of Food Research. Technical Paper

Aust CSIRO Div For Prod For Prod Newsl — Australia. Commonwealth Scientific and Industrial Research Organisation. Division of Forest Products. Forest Products Newsletter

Aust CSIRO Div For Prod Technol Pap — Australia. Commonwealth Scientific and Industrial Research Organisation. Division of Forest Products. Technological Paper

Aust CSIRO Div Hortic Res Rep — Australia. Commonwealth Scientific and Industrial Research Organisation. Division of Horticulture. Research Report

Aust CSIRO Div Ind Chem Tech Pap — Australia. Commonwealth Scientific and Industrial Research Organisation. Division of Industrial Chemistry. Technical Paper

Aust CSIRO Div Irrig Res Annu Rep — Australia. Commonwealth Scientific and Industrial Research Organisation. Division of Irrigation Research. Annual Report

Aust CSIRO Div Land Resour Manage Tech Pap — Australia. Commonwealth Scientific and Industrial Research Organisation. Division of Land Resources Management. Technical Paper

Aust CSIRO Div Land Res Reg Surv Tech Pap — Australia. Commonwealth Scientific and Industrial Research Organisation. Division of Land Research and Regional Survey. Technical Paper

Aust CSIRO Div Land Res Tech Pap — Australia. Commonwealth Scientific and Industrial Research Organisation. Division of Land Research. Technical Paper

Aust CSIRO Div Land Use Res Tech Pap — Australia. Commonwealth Scientific and Industrial Research Organisation. Division of Land Use Research. Technical Paper

Aust CSIRO Div Math Stat Tech Pap — Australia. Commonwealth Scientific and Industrial Research Organisation. Division of Mathematical Statistics. Technical Paper

Aust CSIRO Div Mech Eng Annu Rep — Australia. Commonwealth Scientific and Industrial Research Organisation. Division of Mechanical Engineering. Annual Report

Aust CSIRO Div Meteorol Phys Tech Pap — Australia. Commonwealth Scientific and Industrial Research Organisation. Division of Meteorological Physics. Technical Paper

Aust CSIRO Div Metrol Tech Pap — Australia. Commonwealth Scientific and Industrial Research Organisation. Division of Metrology. Technical Paper

Aust CSIRO Div Mineral Tech Commun — Australia. Commonwealth Scientific and Industrial Research Organisation. Division of Mineralogy. Technical Communication

Aust CSIRO Div Miner Chem Invest Rep — Australia. Commonwealth Scientific and Industrial Research Organisation. Division of Mineral Chemistry. Investigation Report

Aust CSIRO Div Miner Chem Locat Rep — Australia. Commonwealth Scientific and Industrial Research Organisation. Division of Mineral Chemistry. Location Report

Aust CSIRO Div Miner Chem Tech Commun — Australia. Commonwealth Scientific and Industrial Research Organisation. Division of Mineral Chemistry. Technical Communication

Aust CSIRO Div Nutr Biochem Res Rep — Australia. Commonwealth Scientific and Industrial Research Organisation. Division of Nutritional Biochemistry. Research Report

Aust CSIRO Div Plant Ind Annu Rep — Australia. Commonwealth Scientific and Industrial Research Organisation. Division of Plant Industry. Annual Report

Aust CSIRO Div Plant Ind Field Stn Rec — Australia. Commonwealth Scientific and Industrial Research Organisation. Division of Plant Industry. Field Station Record

Aust CSIRO Div Plant Ind Tech Pap — Australia. Commonwealth Scientific and Industrial Research Organisation. Division of Plant Industry. Technical Paper

Aust CSIRO Div Soil Mech Tech Pap — Australia. Commonwealth Scientific and Industrial Research Organisation. Division of Soil Mechanics. Technical Paper

Aust CSIRO Div Soils Div Rep — Australia. Commonwealth Scientific and Industrial Research Organisation. Division of Soils. Divisional Report

Aust CSIRO Div Soils Notes Soil Tech — Australia. Commonwealth Scientific and Industrial Research Organisation. Division of Soils. Notes on Soil Techniques

Aust CSIRO Div Soils Rep Prog — Australia. Commonwealth Scientific and Industrial Research Organisation. Division of Soils. Report on Progress

Aust CSIRO Div Soils Soils Land Use Ser — Australia. Commonwealth Scientific and Industrial Research Organisation. Division of Soils. Soils and Land Use Series

Aust CSIRO Div Soils Tech Pap — Australia. Commonwealth Scientific and Industrial Research Organisation. Division of Soils. Technical Paper

Aust CSIRO Div Text Ind Rep — Australia. Commonwealth Scientific and Industrial Research Organisation. Division of Textile Industry. Report

Aust CSIRO Div Trop Agron Tech Pap — Australia. Commonwealth Scientific and Industrial Research Organisation. Division of Tropical Agronomy. Technical Paper

Aust CSIRO Div Trop Crops Pastures Tech Pap — Australia. Commonwealth Scientific and Industrial Research Organisation. Division of Tropical Crops and Pastures. Technical Paper

Aust CSIRO Div Trop Crops Pastures Trop Agron Tech Memo — Australia. Commonwealth Scientific and Industrial Research Organisation. Division of Tropical Crops and Pastures. Tropical Agronomy. Technical Memorandum

Aust CSIRO Div Trop Pastures Annu Rep — Australia. Commonwealth Scientific and Industrial Research Organisation. Division of Tropical Pastures. Annual Report

Aust CSIRO Div Trop Pastures Tech Pap — Australia. Commonwealth Scientific and Industrial Research Organisation. Division of Tropical Pastures. Technical Paper

Aust CSIRO Div Wildl Res Rep — Australia. Commonwealth Scientific and Industrial Research Organisation. Division of Wildlife. Research Report

Aust CSIRO For Prod Lab Div Appl Chem Technol Pap — Australia. Commonwealth Scientific and Industrial Research Organisation. Forest Products Laboratory. Division of Applied Chemistry. Technological Paper

Aust CSIRO For Prod Lab Div Build Res Technol Pap — Australia. Commonwealth Scientific and Industrial Research Organisation. Forest Products Laboratory. Division of Building Research. Technological Paper

Aust CSIRO For Prod Lab Technol Pap — Australia. Commonwealth Scientific and Industrial Research Organisation. Forest Products Laboratory. Technological Paper

Aust CSIRO Irrig Res Stn Techn Pap — Australia. Commonwealth Scientific and Industrial Research Organisation. Irrigation Research Stations. Technical Paper

Aust CSIRO Irrig Res Stn Tech Pap — Australia. Commonwealth Scientific and Industrial Research Organisation. Irrigation Research Stations. Technical Paper

Aust CSIRO Land Resour Lab Div Soils Bienn Rep — Australia. Commonwealth Scientific and Industrial Research Organisation. Land Resources Laboratories. Division of Soils. Biennial Report

Aust CSIRO Land Res Ser — Australia. Commonwealth Scientific and Industrial Research Organisation. Land Research Series

Aust CSIRO Min Dep Univ Melbourne Ore Dressing Invest Rep — Australia. Commonwealth Scientific and Industrial Research Organisation. Mining Department. University of Melbourne. Ore Dressing Investigations. Report

Aust CSIRO Mineragraphic Invest Tech Pap — Australia. Commonwealth Scientific and Industrial Research Organisation. Mineragraphic Investigations. Technical Paper

Aust CSIRO Miner Res Lab Annu Rep — Australia. Commonwealth Scientific and Industrial Research Organisation. Minerals Research Laboratories. Annual Report

Aust CSIRO Miner Res Lab Invest Rep — Australia. Commonwealth Scientific and Industrial Research Organisation. Minerals Research Laboratories. Investigation Report

Aust CSIRO Natl Meas Lab Tech Pap — Australia. Commonwealth Scientific and Industrial Research Organisation. National Measurement Laboratory. Technical Paper

Aust CSIRO Natl Stand Lab Tech Pap — Australia. Commonwealth Scientific and Industrial Research Organisation. National Standards Laboratory. Technical Paper

Aust CSIRO Nat Stand Lab Tech Pap — Australia. Commonwealth Scientific and Industrial Research Organisation. National Standards Laboratory. Technical Paper

Aust CSIRO Soil Mech Sect Tech Memo — Australia. Commonwealth Scientific and Industrial Research Organisation. Soil Mechanics Section. Technical Memorandum

Aust CSIRO Soil Mech Sect Tech Pap — Australia. Commonwealth Scientific and Industrial Research Organisation. Soil Mechanics Section. Technical Paper

Aust CSIRO Soil Publ — Australia. Commonwealth Scientific and Industrial Research Organisation. Soil Publication

Aust CSIRO Soils Land Use Ser — Australia. Commonwealth Scientific and Industrial Research Organisation. Soils and Land Use Series

Aust CSIRO Wildl Surv Sect Tech Pap — Australia. Commonwealth Scientific and Industrial Research Organisation. Wildlife Survey Section. Technical Paper

Aust Ctry Mag — Australian Country Magazine

Aust Culturist — Australian Culturist

Aust Curr Law Rev — Australian Current Law Review

Aust Curr L Rev — Australian Current Law Review

Aust Dairy R — Australian Dairy Review

Aust Dairy Rev — Australian Dairy Review

Aust Def Res Lab Paint Notes — Australia. Defence Research Laboratories. Paint Notes

Aust Def Res Lab Plat Notes — Australia. Defence Research Laboratories. Plating Notes

Aust Def Sci Serv Mater Res Lab Tech Note — Australian Defence Scientific Service. Materials Research Laboratory. Technical Note

Aust Def Sci Serv Weapons Res Est Tech Note — Australian Defence Scientific Service. Weapons Research Establishment. Technical Note

Aust Def Sc Serv ARL Report — Australian Defence Scientific Service. Aeronautical Research Laboratories. Report

Aust Def Stand Lab Rep — Australia. Defence Standards Laboratories. Report

Aust Def Stand Lab Tech Mem — Australia. Defence Standards Laboratories. Technical Memorandum
Aust Def Stand Lab Tech Memo — Australia. Defence Standards Laboratories. Technical Memorandum
Aust Def Stand Lab Tech Note — Australia. Defence Standards Laboratories. Technical Note
Aust Demographic R — Australian Demographic Review
Aust Dental J — Australian Dental Journal
Aust Dent J — Australian Dental Journal
Aust Dent Mirr — Australian Dental Mirror
Aust Dent Summ — Australian Dental Summary
Aust Dep Agric Biol Branch Tech Pap — Australia. Department of Agriculture. Biology Branch. Technical Paper
Aust Dep Def Mater Res Lab Rep — Australia. Department of Defence. Materials Research Laboratories. Report
Aust Dep Def Mater Res Lab Tech Note — Australia. Department of Defence. Materials Research Laboratories. Technical Note
Aust Dep Def Weapons Res Establ Tech Rep — Australia. Department of Defence. Weapons Research Establishment. Technical Report
Aust Dep Health Aust Radiat Lab Tech Rep ARL/TR — Australia. Department of Health. Australian Radiation Laboratory. Technical Report ARL/TR
Aust Dep Health Aust Radiat Lab Tech Rep Ser ARL/TR — Australia. Department of Health. Australian Radiation Laboratory. Technical Report Series ARL/TR
Aust Dep Munitions Paint Notes — Australia. Department of Munitions. Paint Notes
Aust Dep Supply Aeronaut Res Lab Mech Eng Note — Australia. Department of Supply. Aeronautical Research Laboratories. Mechanical Engineering Note
Aust Dep Supply Aeronaut Res Lab Struct Mater Note — Australia. Department of Supply. Aeronautical Research Laboratories. Structures and Materials Note
Aust Dep Supply Def Res Lab Paint Notes — Australia. Department of Supply. Defence Research Laboratories. Paint Notes
Aust Dep Supply Def Res Lab Plat Notes — Australia. Department of Supply. Defence Research Laboratories. Plating Notes
Aust Digest — Australian Digest
Aust Dir — Australian Director
Aust Director — Australian Director
Aust Dirt Bike — Australasian Dirt Bike
Aust Draftsmen — Australian Draftsmen
Aust Dried Fruit News — Australian Dried Fruit News
Aust Early Child Resource Booklets — Australian Early Childhood Resource Booklets
Aust Econ — Australian Economic Papers
Aust Econ H — Australian Economic History Review
Aust Econ Hist R — Australian Economic History Review
Aust Econ Hist Rev — Australian Economic History Review
Aust Econ News Dig — Australian Economic News Digest
Aust Econ Pap — Australian Economic Papers
Aust Econ Rev — Australian Economic Review
Aust Educ R — Australian Education Review
Aust Educ Res — Australian Education Researcher
Aust Educ Rev — Australian Education Review
Aust Electrochem Conf — Australian Electrochemistry Conference
Aust Electron Bull — Australian Electronics Bulletin
Aust Electron Eng — Australian Electronics Engineering
Aust Electron Engng — Australian Electronics Engineering
Aust Electr World — Australian Electrical World
Aust Elect Wld — Australian Electrical World
Aust Elec World — Australian Electrical World
Aust Encycl — Australian Encyclopaedia
Aust Endeavourer — Australian Endeavourer
Aust Engineer — Australasian Engineer
Aust Engr — Australasian Engineer
Aust Ent Mag — Australian Entomological Magazine
Aust Entomol Mag — Australian Entomological Magazine
Aust Entomol Soc J — Australian Entomological Society. Journal
Aust Entomol Soc Misc Publ — Australian Entomological Society. Miscellaneous Publication
Aust Exporter — Australian Exporter
Aust External Terr — Australian External Territories
Aust Ext Terr — Australian External Territories
Aust Fact — Australian Factory
Aust Factory — Australian Factory
Aust Fam Physician — Australian Family Physician
Aust Fam Safe — Australian Family Safety
Aust Fashion News — Australian Fashion News
Aust Fd Manuf — Australian Food Manufacturer and Distributor
Aust Fd Mf — Australian Food Manufacturer and Distributor
Aust Fd Mfr — Australian Food Manufacturer and Distributor
Aust Financial R — Australian Financial Review
Aust Financial Rev — Australian Financial Review
Aust Financial Times — Australian Financial Times
Aust Financ Rev — Australian Financial Review

Aust Finish — Australian Finishing
Aust Finish Rev — Australian Finishing Review
Aust Fin Rev — Australian Financial Review
Aust Fish — Australian Fisheries
Aust Fish Educ Leafl — Australian Fisheries Education Leaflet
Aust Fish Newsl — Australian Fisheries Newsletter
Aust Fish Pap — Australian Fisheries Paper
Aust Fm Mgmt J — Australian Farm Management Journal
Aust Food Manuf — Australian Food Manufacturer and Distributor
Aust Food Manuf Distrib — Australian Food Manufacturer and Distributor
Aust Food Mfr Distrib — Australian Food Manufacturer and Distributor
Aust For — Australian Forestry
Aust For Aff R — Australian Foreign Affairs Record
Aust Foreign Aff Rec — Australian Foreign Affairs Record
Aust Forester — Australian Forester
Aust Forest Inds J — Australian Forest Industries Journal
Aust Forest Res — Australian Forest Research
Aust Forestry — Australian Forestry
Aust For Grow — Australian Forest Grower
Aust For Ind J — Australian Forest Industries Journal
Aust For Ind J Aust Log — Australian Forest Industries Journal and Australian Logger
Aust For J — Australian Forest Journal
Aust For (Perth) — Australian Forestry (Perth)
Aust For Res — Australian Forest Research
Aust For Resour — Australian Forest Resources
Aust For Tree Nutr Conf Contrib Pap — Australian Forest Tree Nutrition Conference. Contributed Papers
Aust Foundry Trade J — Australian Foundry Trade Journal
Aust Found Trade J — Australian Foundry Trade Journal
Aust Fract Group Conf — Australian Fracture Group Conference
Aust Fract Group Conf Proc — Australian Fracture Group Conference. Proceedings
Aust Furn Trade J — Australian Furnishing Trade Journal
Aust Gas Bull — Australian Gas Bulletin
Aust Gas J — Australian Gas Journal
Aust Gem — Australian Gem and Treasure Hunter
Aust Gemmol — Australian Gemmologist
Aust Gemmologist — Australian Gemmologist
Aust Gems — Australian Gems and Crafts
Aust Geneal — Australian Genealogist
Aust Genealogist — Australian Genealogist
Aust Geog — Australian Geographer
Aust Geogr — Australian Geographer
Aust Geographer — Australian Geographer
Aust Geog Rec — Australian Geographical Record
Aust Geog Record — Australian Geographical Record
Aust Geogr Rec — Australian Geographical Record
Aust Geogr Stud — Australian Geographical Studies
Aust Geogr Studies — Australian Geographical Studies
Aust Geog S — Australian Geographical Studies
Aust Geog Stud — Australian Geographical Studies
Aust Geog Studies — Australian Geographical Studies
Aust Geol — Australian Geologist
Aust Geomechanics J — Australian Geomechanics Journal
Aust Geomech J — Australian Geomechanics Journal
Aust Gliding — Australian Gliding
Aust Goat World — Australian Goat World
Aust Gourmet — Australian Gourmet
Aust Gov Anal Lab Rep Invest — Australian Government Analytical Laboratories. Report of Investigations
Aust Gov Publ — Australian Government Publications
Aust Grade Teach — Australian Grade Teacher
Aust Grapegr — Australian Grapegrower [*Later, Australian Grapegrower and Winemaker*]
Aust Grapegrow — Australian Grapegrower and Winemaker
Aust Hand Weaver — Australian Hand Weaver and Spinner
Aust Hardware J — Australian Hardware Journal
Aust Hereford A — Australian Hereford Annual
Aust Hereford Ann — Australian Hereford Annual
Aust Hereford Annu — Australian Hereford Annual
Aust Hereford J — Australian Hereford Journal
Aust Hereford Soc Q — Hereford Quarterly. Australian Hereford Society
Aust Hi-Fi — Australian Hi-Fi
Aust Highway — Australian Highway
Aust Hist Teach — Australian History Teacher
Aust Home Beaut — Australian Home Beautiful
Aust Home J — Australian Home Journal
Aust Homemaker — Australian Homemaker
Aust Hosp — Australian Hospital
Aust Hospital — Australian Hospital
Aust House Gard — Australian House and Garden
Aust House and Garden — Australian House and Garden
Aust Housing — Australian Housing
Aust Human Res Cncl A Rept — Australian Humanities Research Council. Annual Report

Aust Hwy — Australian Highway
Aust Immigr Consol Stat — Australian Immigration: Consolidated Statistics
Aust Ind Dev Assoc Dir Repts — Australian Industries Development Association. Director Reports
Aust Ind Development Assn Director Report — Australian Industries Development Association. Director Reports
Aust Ind LR — Australian Industrial Law Review
Aust Ind Min Stand — Australian Industrial and Mining Standard
Austin Sem Bul — Austin Seminary Bulletin. Faculty Edition
Aust Inst Internat Aff NSW Br — Australian Institute of International Affairs. New South Wales Branch
Aust Intercollegian — Australian Intercollegian
Aust Irrig — Australasian Irrigator
Aust Irrig — Australasian Irrigator and Pasture Improver
Aust Irrig Past Improver — Australasian Irrigator and Pasture Improver
Aust J — Australian Journal
Aust J Adult Ed — Australian Journal of Adult Education
Aust J Adult Educ — Australian Journal of Adult Education
Aust J Adv Nurs — Australian Journal of Advanced Nursing
Aust J Ag E — Australian Journal of Agricultural Economics
Aust J Ag Econ — Australian Journal of Agricultural Economics
Aust J Ag R — Australian Journal of Agricultural Research
Aust J Agr — Australian Journal of Agricultural Research
Aust J Agr Econ — Australian Journal of Agricultural Economics
Aust J Ag Res — Australian Journal of Agricultural Research
Aust J Agric Econ — Australian Journal of Agricultural Economics
Aust J Agric Res — Australian Journal of Agricultural Research
Aust J Agr Res — Australian Journal of Agricultural Research
Aust J Alcohol & Drug Depend — Australian Journal of Alcohol and Drug Dependence
Aust J Appl Sci — Australian Journal of Applied Science
Aust J Arch & Arts — Australian Journal of Architecture and Arts
Aust J Biblical Archaeol — Australian Journal of Biblical Archaeology
Aust J Biol — Australian Journal of Biological Sciences
Aust J Biol Sci — Australian Journal of Biological Sciences
Aust J Bot — Australian Journal of Botany
Aust J Botany — Australian Journal of Botany
Aust J Bot Supplry Ser Suppl — Australian Journal of Botany. Supplementary Series. Supplement
Aust J Bot Suppl Ser — Australian Journal of Botany. Supplementary Series
Aust J Bot Suppl Ser Suppl — Australian Journal of Botany. Supplementary Series. Supplement
Aust J Chem — Australian Journal of Chemistry
Aust J Chem Eng — Australian Journal of Chemical Engineers
Aust J Coal Min Technol Res — Australian Journal of Coal Mining Technology and Research
Aust J Dair — Australian Journal of Dairy Technology
Aust J Dairy Tech — Australian Journal of Dairy Technology
Aust J Dairy Technol — Australian Journal of Dairy Technology
Aust J Dairy Technology — Australian Journal of Dairy Technology
Aust J Dairy Technol Suppl — Australian Journal of Dairy Technology. Supplement
Aust J Dent — Australian Journal of Dentistry
Aust J Dentistry — Australian Journal of Dentistry
Aust J Derm — Australasian Journal of Dermatology
Aust J Derm — Australian [later, Australasian] Journal of Dermatology
Aust J Dermatol — Australasian Journal of Dermatology
Aust J Dermatol — Australian [later, Australasian] Journal of Dermatology
Aust J Dev Disabilities — Australian Journal of Developmental Disabilities
Aust J Early Child — Australian Journal of Early Childhood
Aust J Earth Sci — Australian Journal of Earth Sciences
Aust J Ecol — Australian Journal of Ecology
Aust J Ed — Australian Journal of Education
Aust J Educ — Australian Journal of Education
Aust Jewish Herald — Australian Jewish Herald
Aust Jewish Hist Soc J & Proc — Australian Jewish Historical Society. Journal and Proceedings
Aust Jewish Hist Soc J Proc — Australian Jewish Historical Society. Journal and Proceedings
Aust Jewish News — Australian Jewish News
Aust Jewish Outlook — Australian Jewish Outlook
Aust J Ex A — Australian Journal of Experimental Agriculture and Animal Husbandry
Aust J Ex B — Australian Journal of Experimental Biology and Medical Science
Aust J Exp Agr Anim Husb — Australian Journal of Experimental Agriculture and Animal Husbandry
Aust J Exp Agric An Husb — Australian Journal of Experimental Agriculture and Animal Husbandry
Aust J Exp Agric Anim Husb — Australian Journal of Experimental Agriculture and Animal Husbandry
Aust J Exp Agric & Anim Husb — Australian Journal of Experimental Agriculture and Animal Husbandry
Aust J Exp B — Australian Journal of Experimental Biology and Medical Science

Aust J Exp Biol — Australian Journal of Experimental Biology and Medical Science
Aust J Exp Biol Med Sci — Australian Journal of Experimental Biology and Medical Science
Aust J Exper Agric — Australian Journal of Experimental Agriculture
Aust J Exper Agric — Australian Journal of Experimental Agriculture and Animal Husbandry
Aust J Expl Biol Med Sci — Australian Journal of Experimental Biology and Medical Science
Aust J Fam Ther — Australian Journal of Family Therapy
Aust J Forensic Sci — Australian Journal of Forensic Sciences
Aust J For Sci — Australian Journal of Forensic Sciences
Aust J French Stud — Australian Journal of French Studies
Aust J Fr S — Australian Journal of French Studies
Aust J Fr Stud — Australian Journal of French Studies
Aust J Geod Photogramm and Surv — Australian Journal of Geodesy, Photogrammetry, and Surveying
Aust J Health Phys Educ Recreation — Australian Journal for Health, Physical Education, and Recreation
Aust J Health Phys Edu Recreation — Australian Journal for Health, Physical Education, and Recreation
Aust J Higher Ed — Australian Journal of Higher Education
Aust J Higher Educ — Australian Journal of Higher Education
Aust J Hosp Pharm — Australian Journal of Hospital Pharmacy
Aust J Inst — Australian Journal of Instrumentation and Control
Aust J Instrum Control — Australian Journal of Instrumentation and Control
Aust J Instrum & Control — Australian Journal of Instrumentation and Control
Aust J Instrument Tech — Australian Journal of Instrument Technology
Aust J Instrument Technology — Australian Journal of Instrument Technology
Aust J Instrum Tech — Australian Journal of Instrument Technology
Aust J Instrum Technol — Australian Journal of Instrument Technology
Aust J Inst Trans — Australian Journal. Institute of Transport
Aust JL & Soc — Australian Journal of Law and Society
Aust J Manage — Australian Journal of Management
Aust J Mar — Australian Journal of Marine and Freshwater Research
Aust J Mar Freshwater Res — Australian Journal of Marine and Freshwater Research
Aust J Mar Freshwat Res — Australian Journal of Marine and Freshwater Research
Aust J Mar Freshw Res — Australian Journal of Marine and Freshwater Research
Aust J Med Lab Sci — Australian Journal of Medical Laboratory Science
Aust J Med Technol — Australian Journal of Medical Technology
Aust J Ment Retard — Australian Journal of Mental Retardation
Aust J Music Ed — Australian Journal of Music Education
Aust J Music Educ — Australian Journal of Music Education
Aust Jnl of Forensic Sciences — Australian Journal of Forensic Sciences
Aust J Ophthalmol — Australian Journal of Ophthalmology
Aust J Optom — Australian Journal of Optometry
Aust J Optometry — Australian Journal of Optometry
Aust J Pharm — Australian Journal of Pharmacy
Aust J Pharmacy — Australian Journal of Pharmacy
Aust J Pharm Sci — Australian Journal of Pharmaceutical Sciences
Aust J Pharm Suppl — Australian Journal of Pharmacy. Supplement
Aust J Phil — Australasian Journal of Philosophy
Aust J Phys — Australian Journal of Physics
Aust J Phys Astrophys Suppl — Australian Journal of Physics. Astrophysical Supplement
Aust J Phys Ed — Australian Journal of Physical Education
Aust J Phys Educ — Australian Journal of Physical Education
Aust J Physical Educ — Australian Journal of Physical Education
Aust J Physiother — Australian Journal of Physiotherapy
Aust J Physiotherapy — Australian Journal of Physiotherapy
Aust J Plan — Australian Journal of Plant Physiology
Aust J Plant Physiol — Australian Journal of Plant Physiology
Aust J Pl Physiol — Australian Journal of Plant Physiology
Aust J Pol Hist — Australian Journal of Politics and History
Aust J Pol and Hist — Australian Journal of Politics and History
Aust J Poli — Australian Journal of Politics and History
Aust J Poli & Hist — Australian Journal of Politics and History
Aust J Polit Hist — Australian Journal of Politics and History
Aust J Politics Hist — Australian Journal of Politics and History
Aust J Politics & History — Australian Journal of Politics and History
Aust J Ps Phil — Australasian Journal of Psychology and Philosophy
Aust J Psyc — Australian Journal of Psychology
Aust J Psych — Australian Journal of Psychology
Aust J Psychol — Australian Journal of Psychology
Aust J Psychological Research — Australian Journal of Psychological Research
Aust J Psychology — Australian Journal of Psychology
Aust J Psych Res — Australian Journal of Psychological Research
Aust J Pub Admin — Australian Journal of Public Administration
Aust J Publ — Australian Journal of Public Administration
Aust Jr — Australian Jurist
Aust J Reading — Australian Journal of Reading
Aust J Rem Educ — Australian Journal of Remedial Education

Aust Jr R — Australian Jurist Reports [*1870-74*]
Aust J Sci — Australian Journal of Science
Aust J Science — Australian Journal of Science
Aust J Scientific Research — Australian Journal of Scientific Research
Aust J Scient Res — Australian Journal of Scientific Research
Aust J Sci Res B — Australian Journal of Scientific Research. Series B.
    Biological Sciences
Aust J Sci Res Ser A — Australian Journal of Scientific Research. Series A.
    Physical Sciences
Aust J Sci Res Ser B — Australian Journal of Scientific Research. Series B
Aust J of Screen Th — Australian Journal of Screen Theory
Aust J Soc — Australian Journal of Social Issues
Aust J Social Iss — Australian Journal of Social Issues
Aust J Social Issues — Australian Journal of Social Issues
Aust J Social Work — Australian Journal of Social Work
Aust J Soc Issues — Australian Journal of Social Issues
Aust J Soc Work — Australian Journal of Social Work
Aust J Soil — Australian Journal of Soil Research
Aust J Soil Res — Australian Journal of Soil Research
Aust J Stat — Australian Journal of Statistics
Aust J Statist — Australian Journal of Statistics
Aust J Stats — Australian Journal of Statistics
Aust J Teach Educ — Australian Journal of Teacher Education
Aust J Teach Pract — Australian Journal of Teaching Practice
Aust Junior Farmer — Australian Junior Farmer
Aust Jur — Australian Jurist
Aust Jur — Australian Jurist Reports
Aust Jur Rep — Australian Jurist Reports [*1870-74*]
Aust J Zool — Australian Journal of Zoology
Aust J Zool Supplry Ser — Australian Journal of Zoology. Supplementary
    Series
Aust J Zool Supplry Ser Suppl — Australian Journal of Zoology.
    Supplementary Series. Supplement
Aust J Zool Suppl Ser — Australian Journal of Zoology. Supplementary Series
Aust Lapidary — Australian Lapidary Magazine
Austl Argus LR — Australian Argus Law Reports
Aust Law — Australian Lawyer
Aust Law J — Australian Law Journal
Aust Law News — Australian Law News
Aust Law Rev — Australian Law Review
Aust Lawyer — Australian Lawyer
Austl Bankr Cas — Australian Bankruptcy Cases
Austl Bus L Rev — Australian Business Law Review
Austl Com J — Australian Commercial Journal
Aust Leather J — Australian Leather Journal. Boot and Shoe Recorder
Aust Leath Footwear Rev — Australasian Leather and Footwear Review
Aust Leath J — Australian Leather Journal. Boot and Shoe Recorder
Aust Leath Tr Rev — Australasian Leather Trades Review
Aust Lett — Australian Letters
Aust Liberal — Australian Liberal
Aust Lib J — Australian Library Journal
Aust Libr J — Australian Library Journal
Aust Libr J Suppl — Australian Library Journal. Supplement
Aust Literary Letter — Australian Literary Letter
Aust Lit S — Australian Literary Studies
Aust Lit St — Australian Literary Studies
Aust Lit Stud — Australian Literary Studies
Aust L J — Australian Law Journal
Austl J For Sci — Australian Journal of Forensic Sciences
Austl J Phil — Australasian Journal of Philosophy
Austl LJ Rep — Australian Law Journal. Reports
Austl Jur R — Australian Jurist Reports [*1870-74*]
Austl LJ — Australian Law Journal
Austl LJ Rep — Australian Law Journal. Reports
Aust LN — Australian Law News
Austl & NZJ Criminology — Australian and New Zealand Journal of
    Criminology
Aust L Rep — Australian Law Reports
Aust LT — Australian Law Times
Austl Tax — Australian Tax Decisions
Austl Tax Rev — Australian Tax Review
Austl YB Int'l L — Australian Yearbook of International Law
Aust Machinery & Prod Eng — Australian Machinery and Production
    Engineering
Aust Mach Prod Eng — Australian Machinery and Production Engineering
Aust Mach Prod Engng — Australian Machinery and Production Engineering
Aust Mag — Australian Magazine
Aust Mammal — Australian Mammalogy
Aust Man — Australian Manager
Aust Manager — Australian Manager
Aust Manag R — Australian Management Review
Aust Manuf — Australasian Manufacturer
Aust Mar Sci Bull — Australian Marine Science Bulletin
Aust Mar Sci Newsl — Australian Marine Sciences Newsletter
Aust Marxist Rev — Australian Marxist Review

Aust Mater Res Lab Rep — Australia. Materials Research Laboratories.
    Report
Aust Mater Res Lab Tech Note — Australia. Materials Research Laboratories.
    Technical Note
Aust Maths Teach — Australian Mathematics Teacher
Aust Math Teach — Australian Mathematics Teacher
Aust Mech Eng — Australian Mechanical Engineering
Aust Mech Engng — Australian Mechanical Engineering
Aust Mech Engr — Australian Mechanical Engineering
Aust Med J — Australian Medical Journal
Aust Merino Wool Campaign — Australian Merino Wool Campaign
Aust Meteorol Mag — Australian Meteorological Magazine
Aust Methodist Hist Soc J Proc — Australasian Methodist Historical Society.
    Journal and Proceedings
Aust Methods Eng — Australian Methods Engineer
Aust Met Mag — Australian Meteorological Magazine
Aust Mgr — Australian Manager
Aust Milk Dairy Prod J — Australian Milk and Dairy Products Journal
Aust Min — Australian Mining
Aust Min Counc Newsl — Australian Mining Council. Newsletter
Aust Min Dev Lab Bull — Australian Mineral Development Laboratories
    [*AMDEL*]. Bulletin
(Aust Min Dev Labs) Bull — AMDEL (Australian Mineral Development
    Laboratories) Bulletin
Aust Min Engng Rev — Australian Mining and Engineering Review
Aust Min Eng Rev — Australian Mining and Engineering Review
Aust Miner Dev Lab Bull — Australian Mineral Development Laboratories
    [*AMDEL*]. Bulletin
Aust Miner Dev Lab Rep — Australian Mineral Development Laboratories.
    Report
Aust Miner Ind — Australian Mineral Industry
Aust Miner Ind Annu Rev — Australian Mineral Industry. Annual Review
Aust Miner Ind Rev — Australian Mineral Industry. Review
Aust Miner Ind Stat — Australian Mineral Industry. Statistics
Aust Min Ind — Australian Mineral Industry
Aust Min Ind Stat — Australian Mineral Industry. Statistics
Aust Mining — Australian Mining
Aust Min Pet Law J — Australian Mining and Petroleum Law Journal
Aust Min Stand — Australian Mining Standard
Aust Mod Rail — Australian Model Railway Magazine
Aust Mon Weath Rep — Australian Monthly Weather Report and
    Meteorological Abstract
Aust Mot Cycle News — Australian Motor Cycle News
Aust Motorist — Australian Motorist
Aust Motor Sports — Australian Motor Sports
Aust Munic J — Australian Municipal Journal
Aust Museum Mag — Australian Museum. Magazine
Aust Musical News & D — Australian Musical News and Musical Digest
Aust Mus Mag — Australian Museum. Magazine
Aust Mus Rec — Australian Museum. Records
Aust Mus (Sydney) Mem — Australian Museum (Sydney). Memoirs
Aust Nat — Australian Naturalist
Aust Nat Bibliogr — Australian National Bibliography
Aust Nat Clay — Australian National Clay
Aust Nat H — Australian Natural History
Aust Nat Hist — Australian Natural History
Aust Natl Meas Lab Tech Pap — Australia. National Measurement
    Laboratory. Technical Paper
Aust Natl Univ Res Sch Phys Sci Dep Eng Phys Publ — Australian National
    University. Research School of Physical Sciences. Department of
    Engineering Physics. Publication
Aust Natn Clay — Australian National Clay
Aust Nat Univ News — Australian National University. News
Aust Nat Univ Res Sch Pacif Stud Geog Pub — Australian National University.
    Research School of Pacific Studies. Department of Geography.
    Publication
Aust Natural History — Australian Natural History
Aust Natur His — Australian Natural History
Aust Natur Hist — Australian Natural History
Aust Neigh — Australia's Neighbours
Aust Neighb — Australia's Neighbours
Aust Neighbours — Australia's Neighbours
Aust News — Austral News
Aust News (Johannesburg) — Austral News (Johannesburg)
Aust News (Montreal) — Austral News (Montreal)
Aust News R — Australian News Review
Aust News (Singapore) — Austral News (Singapore)
Aust News (Wellington) — Austral News (Wellington)
Aust New Zeal Environ Rep — Australian and New Zealand Environmental
    Report
Aust Now — Australia Now
Aust Numismatic J — Australian Numismatic Journal
Aust Numismatic Soc Rep — Australian Numismatic Society. Report
Aust Num J — Australian Numismatic Journal
Aust Num Meteor Res Centr (Melb) Ann Rep — Australian Numerical
    Meteorology Research Centre (Melbourne). Annual Report

Aust Num Soc Rept — Australian Numismatic Society. Report
Aust Nurses J — Australian Nurses' Journal
Aust Nurses J (Melbourne) — Australian Nurses' Journal (Melbourne)
Aust NZ Assoc Adv Sci Congr Pap — Australian and New Zealand Association for the Advancement of Science. Congress. Papers
Aust NZ Conf Geomech Proc — Australian-New Zealand Conference on Geomechanics. Proceedings
Aust & NZ Environ Rep — Australian and New Zealand Environmental Report
Aust & NZ General Practitioner — Australian and New Zealand General Practitioner
Aust NZ Gen Practnr — Australian and New Zealand General Practitioner
Aust NZ J C — Australian and New Zealand Journal of Criminology
Aust & NZ J Criminol — Australian and New Zealand Journal of Criminology
Aust NZ J M — Australian and New Zealand Journal of Medicine
Aust & NZ J Med — Australian and New Zealand Journal of Medicine
Aust NZ J Med — Australian and New Zealand Journal of Medicine
Aust NZ J Med Suppl — Australian and New Zealand Journal of Medicine. Supplement
Aust NZ J O — Australian and New Zealand Journal of Obstetrics and Gynaecology
Aust NZ J Obstet Gynaec — Australian and New Zealand Journal of Obstetrics and Gynaecology
Aust NZ J Obstet Gynaecol — Australian and New Zealand Journal of Obstetrics and Gynaecology
Aust & NZ J Obstet & Gynaecol — Australian and New Zealand Journal of Obstetrics and Gynaecology
Aust NZ J Obstet Gynaecol (Suppl) — Australian and New Zealand Journal of Obstetrics and Gynaecology (Supplement)
Aust NZ J P — Australian and New Zealand Journal of Psychiatry
Aust NZ J Psychiat — Australian and New Zealand Journal of Psychiatry
Aust & NZ J Psychiatry — Australian and New Zealand Journal of Psychiatry
Aust NZ J Psychiatry — Australian and New Zealand Journal of Psychiatry
Aust NZ J S — Australian and New Zealand Journal of Surgery
Aust NZ J Soc — Australian and New Zealand Journal of Sociology
Aust & NZ J Soc — Australian and New Zealand Journal of Sociology
Aust NZ J Sociol — Australian and New Zealand Journal of Sociology
Aust & NZ J Sociol — Australian and New Zealand Journal of Sociology
Aust NZ J Surg — Australian and New Zealand Journal of Surgery
Aust & NZ J Surgery — Australian and New Zealand Journal of Surgery
Aust NZ Rose A — Australian and New Zealand Rose Annual
Aust NZ Soc — Australian and New Zealand Journal of Sociology
Aust & NZ W — Australia and New Zealand Weekly
Aust NZ W — Australian and New Zealand Weekly
Aust OCCA Proc News — Australian OCCA [*Oil and Colour Chemists Association*] Proceedings and News
Aust Occupational Ther J — Australian Occupational Therapy Journal
Aust Occup Ther J — Australian Occupational Therapy Journal
Aust Off J Pat — Australian Official Journal of Patents, Trade Marks, and Designs
Aust Off J Pat Trade Marks Des Pat Abr Suppl — Australian Official Journal of Patents, Trade Marks, and Designs. Patent Abridgments Supplement
Aust Oil Colour Chem Assoc Proc News — Australian Oil and Colour Chemists Association. Proceedings and News
Aust Oil Gas J — Australasian Oil and Gas Journal
Aust Oil Seed Gr — Australian Oil Seed Grower
Aust Orchid Rev — Australian Orchid Review
Aust Orthod J — Australian Orthodontic Journal
Aust Out — Australian Outlook
Aust Outdoors — Australian Outdoors
Aust Outl — Australian Outlook
Aust Outloo — Australian Outlook
Aust Outlook — Australian Outlook
Aust & Pac Book Prices Curr — Australian and Pacific Book Prices Current
Aust Packaging — Australian Packaging
Aust Paedia — Australian Paediatric Journal
Aust Paediat J — Australian Paediatric Journal
Aust Paediatric J — Australian Paediatric Journal
Aust Paediatr J — Australian Paediatric Journal
Aust Paint J — Australian Paint Journal
Aust Parks — Australian Parks
Aust Parks — Australian Parks and Recreation
Aust Parks & Recreat — Australian Parks and Recreation
Aust Parl Deb House Rep — Australia. House of Representatives. Parliamentary Debates
Aust Parl Deb Senate — Australia. Parliament. Senate. Parliamentary Debates
Aust Parl H of R Parl Deb — Australia. Parliament. House of Representatives. Parliamentary Debates
Aust Parl Sen Parl Deb — Australia. Parliament. Senate. Parliamentary Debates
Aust Past — Australian Pastoralist
Aust Pat Doc — Australian (Patent Document)
Aust Pat Off Aust Off J Pat Trade Marks Des — Australia. Patent Office. Australian Official Journal of Patents, Trade Marks, and Designs
Aust Pet Explor Assoc J — Australian Petroleum Exploration Association. Journal

Aust Phot — Australian Photography
Aust Photogr J — Australian Photographic Journal
Aust Phys — Australian Physicist
Aust Physicist — Australian Physicist
Aust Physiol Pharmacol Soc Proc — Australian Physiological and Pharmacological Society. Proceedings
Aust Pl — Australian Plants
Aust Plan Inst J — Australian Planning Institute. Journal
Aust Plann Inst J — Australian Planning Institute. Journal
Aust Plant Dis Rec — Australian Plant Disease Recorder
Aust Plant Introd Rev — Australian Plant Introduction Review
Aust Plant Pathol Soc Newsl — Australian Plant Pathology Society. Newsletter
Aust Plants — Australian Plants
Aust Plas Rubb J — Australian Plastics and Rubber Journal
Aust Plast — Australian Plastics
Aust Plast All Trades Rev — Australian Plastics and Allied Trades Review
Aust Plastics J — Australian Plastics Journal
Aust Plastics & Rubber J — Australian Plastics and Rubber Journal
Aust Plastics Yrbk — Australian Plastics Year Book
Aust Plast J — Australian Plastics Journal
Aust Plast Rubb — Australian Plastics and Rubber
Aust Plast Rubber — Australian Plastics and Rubber
Aust Plast & Rubber — Australian Plastics and Rubber
Aust Plast & Rubber Buy Guide — Australian Plastics and Rubber Buyers Guide
Aust Plast Rubber J — Australian Plastics and Rubber Journal
Aust Plast Yb — Australian Plastics Year Book
Aust Pl Dis Rec — Australian Plant Disease Recorder
Aust Police J — Australian Police Journal
Aust Pop Phot — Australian Popular Photography
Aust Post Office Res Lab Rep — Australian Post Office Research Laboratories. Report
Aust Power Eng — Australian Power Engineering
Aust Pr — Australian Printer
Aust Pre-School Assn Biennial Conf — Australian Pre-School Association. Biennial Conference
Aust Pre-School Q — Australian Pre-School Quarterly
Aust Pre-School Quart — Australian Pre-School Quarterly
Aust Pre-Sch Quart — Australian Pre-School Quarterly
Aust Press Statement — Australia. Government Public Relations Office. Ministerial Press Statements
Aust Printer — Australasian Printer
Aust Process Eng — Australian Process Engineering
Aust Processs Engng — Australian Process Engineering
Aust Prod — Australia. Commonwealth Bureau of Census and Statistics. Monthly Bulletin of Production Statistics
Aust Psych — Australian Psychologist
Aust Psychl — Australian Psychologist
Aust Psychol — Australian Psychologist
Aust Pulp Pap Ind Tech Assoc Proc — Australian Pulp and Paper Industry Technical Association. Proceedings
Aust Pump J — Australian Pump Journal
Aust Pwr Engng — Australian Power Engineering
Aust Q — Australian Quarterly
Aust Qly — Australian Quarterly
Aust Quart — Australian Quarterly
Aus Trade — Austrian Trade News
Aust Radiat Lab Tech Rep ARL/TR — Australian Radiation Laboratory. Technical Report ARL/TR
Aust Radiat Lab Tech Rep Ser ARL/TR — Australian Radiation Laboratory. Technical Report Series ARL/TR
Aust Radiat Rec — Australian Radiation Records
Aust Radio — Australasian Radiology
Aust Radiol — Australasian Radiology
Aust Railway Hist Soc Bul — Australian Railway Historical Society. Bulletin
Australas Ann Med — Australasian Annals of Medicine
Australas Baker — Australasian Baker and Millers' Journal
Australas Baker Millers J — Australasian Baker and Millers' Journal
Australas Beekpr — Australasian Beekeeper
Australas Bull Med Phys Biophy — Australasian Bulletin of Medical Physics and Biophysics
Australas Bull Med Phys Biophys — Australasian Bulletin of Medical Physics and Biophysics
Australas Chem Metall — Australasian Chemist and Metallurgist
Australas Conf Heat Mass Transfer — Australasian Conference on Heat and Mass Transfer
Australas Conf Heat Mass Transfer Proc — Australasian Conference on Heat and Mass Transfer. Proceedings
Australas Corros — Australasian Corrosion Engineering
Australas Corros Assoc Prepr Pap Annu Conf — Australasian Corrosion Association. Preprinted Papers of the Annual Conference
Australas Corros Assoc Tech Pap Annual Conf — Australasian Corrosion Association. Technical Paper of the Annual Conference
Australas Corros Eng — Australasian Corrosion Engineering
Australas Corros Engng — Australasian Corrosion Engineering
Australas Eng — Australasian Engineer

Australas Engng Mach — Australasian Engineering and Machinery
Australas Engr — Australasian Engineer
Australas Environ — Australasian Environment
Australas Hardware Machinery — Australasian Hardware and Machinery
Australas Herb News — Australasian Herbarium News
Australasian As Rp — Australasian Association for the Advancement of Science. Reports
Australasian Bk News — Australasian Book News and Library Journal
Australas IMM Conf — Australasian Institute of Mining and Metallurgy. Conference
Australas Inst Met Annu Conf — Australasian Institute of Metals. Annual Conference
Australas Inst Met J — Australasian Institute of Metals. Journal
Australas Inst Met Met Congr — Australasian Institute of Metals. Metals Congress
Australas Inst Mining Met Proc — Australasian Institute of Mining and Metallurgy. Proceedings
Australas Inst Min Metall Conf — Australasian Institute of Mining and Metallurgy. Conference
Australas Inst Min Metall Conf Ser — Australasian Institute of Mining and Metallurgy. Conference Series
Australas Inst Min Metall Monogr Ser — Australasian Institute of Mining and Metallurgy. Monograph Series
Australas Inst Min Metall Proc — Australasian Institute of Mining and Metallurgy. Proceedings
Australas Inst Min Metall Symp Ser — Australasian Institute of Mining and Metallurgy. Symposia Series
Australas Irrig — Australasian Irrigator and Pasture Improver
Australas J Dermatol — Australasian Journal of Dermatology
Australas J Med Technol — Australasian Journal of Medical Technology
Australas J Phar — Australasian Journal of Pharmacy
Australas J Pharm — Australasian Journal of Pharmacy
Australas J Pharm Sci Suppl — Australasian Journal of Pharmacy. Science Supplement
Australas Leath Footwear Rev — Australasian Leather and Footwear Review
Australas Leath Trades Rev — Australasian Leather Trades Review
Australas Manuf — Australasian Manufacturer
Australas Manuf Eng — Australasian Manufacturing Engineer
Australas Med Congr — Australasian Medical Congress. Transactions
Australas Med Gaz — Australasian Medical Gazette
Australas Mfr — Australasian Manufacturer
Australas Mfr Plast Rev — Australasian Manufacturer. Plastics Review
Australas Nurses J — Australasian Nurses Journal
Australas Nurs J (Port Adelaide) — Australasian Nursing Journal (Port Adelaide)
Australas Oil Gas J — Australasian Oil and Gas Journal
Australas Oil Gas Rev — Australasian Oil and Gas Review
Australas Oil & Gas Rev — Australasian Oil and Gas Review
Australas Past Rev — Australasian Pastoralists' Review
Australas Pharm Notes News — Australasian Pharmaceutical Notes and News
Australas Photogr Rev — Australasian Photographic Review
Australas Photo Rev — Australasian Photo Review
Australas Photo Review — Australasian Photo Review
Australas Phys and Eng Sci Med — Australasian Physical and Engineering Sciences in Medicine
Australas Phys Eng Sci Med — Australasian Physical and Engineering Sciences in Medicine
Australas Phys Sci Med — Australasian Physical Sciences in Medicine [*Later, Australasian Physical and Engineering Sciences in Medicine*]
Australas Plant Pathol — APP. Australasian Plant Pathology
Australas Plat Finish — Australasian Plating and Finishing
Australas Print — Australasian Printer
Australas Printer — Australasian Printer
Australas Radiol — Australasian Radiology
Australas Trade Rev — Australasian Trade Review and Manufacturers Journal
Australas Typogr J — Australasian Typographical Journal
Austral Comput J — Australian Computer Journal
Austral Econ Hist R — Australian Economic History Review
Austral Econ Pap — Australian Economic Papers
Austral Fam Physician — Australian Family Physician
Austral For Aff Rec — Australian Foreign Affairs Record
Australian Acad and Res Lib — Australian Academic and Research Libraries
Australian For J — Australian Forestry Journal
Australian Inst Libn Proc — Australian Institute of Librarians. Proceedings
Australian J Mus Ed — Australian Journal of Music Education
Australian J Psychol — Australian Journal of Psychology
Australian Lib J — Australian Library Journal
Australian and New Zealand Assoc Adv Sci Rept — Australian and New Zealand Association for the Advancement of Science. Report
Australian and NZ J Sociol — Australian and New Zealand Journal of Sociology
Austral J Agr Econ — Australian Journal of Agricultural Economics
Austral J Agric Econ — Australian Journal of Agricultural Economics
Austral J Biol Sci — Australian Journal of Biological Sciences
Austral J Bot — Australian Journal of Botany
Austral J Chem — Australian Journal of Chemistry

Austral J High Educ — Australian Journal of Higher Education
Austral J Hum Commun Dis — Australian Journal of Human Communication Disorders
Austral J Phys — Australian Journal of Physics
Austral J Polit Hist — Australian Journal of Politics and History
Austral J Soc Issues — Australian Journal of Social Issues
Austral J Statist — Australian Journal of Statistics
Austral M — Australian Mining
Austral Math Soc Gaz — Australian Mathematical Society. Gazette
Austral Med J — Australian Medical Journal
Austral N Zealand J Sociol — Australian and New Zealand Journal of Sociology
Austral O — Australian Outlook
Austral Off J Pat — Australian Official Journal of Patents
Austral Outlook — Australian Outlook
Austral Paint J — Australian Paint Journal
Austral Pkg — Australian Packaging
Austral Plan Inst J — Australian Planning Institute. Journal
Austral Publ Aff Inform Serv — Australian Public Affairs Information Service
Austral Quart — Australian Quarterly
Austral Sci Index — Australian Science Index
Austral Teacher Deaf — Australian Teacher of the Deaf
Austr Beek — Australasian Beekeeper
Austr Brew Wi J — Australian Brewing and Wine Journal
Austr Chem Abstr — Australian Chemical Abstracts
Austr Chem Inst J Pr — Australian Chemical Institute. Journal and Proceedings
Austr Chem Met — Australasian Chemist and Metallurgist
Austr Civ Eng Constr — Australian Civil Engineering and Construction
Austr Cott Grow — Australian Cotton Grower
Austr Cott Grow Farm Dairym — Australian Cotton Grower, Farmer, and Dairyman
Austr Dent J — Australian Dental Journal
Austr Dent Mirr — Australian Dental Mirror
Aust Rd Index — Australian Road Index
Aust Rd Res — Australian Road Research
Aust Rd Res Progress — Australian Road Research in Progress
Aust Rd Res Rep — Australian Road Research. Reports
AUSTRE — Australian Scientific and Technological Reports
AUSTRE on COM — Australian Scientific and Technological Reports on COM
Aust Red Cross Q — Australian Red Cross Quarterly
Aust Refrig Air Cond & Heat — Australian Refrigeration, Air Conditioning, and Heating
Aust Refrig Air Cond Heat — Australian Refrigeration, Air Conditioning, and Heating
Aust Refrig Air Condit — Australian Refrigeration, Air Conditioning, and Heating
Aust Refrig Air Condit Heat — Australian Refrigeration, Air Conditioning, and Heating
Aust Refrig Air Con Heat — Australian Refrigeration, Air Conditioning, and Heating
Aust Refrig Rev — Australian Refrigeration Review
Austr Eng — Australasian Engineer
Aust Rep — Australian Reporter
Aust Reptile Park Rec — Australian Reptile Park. Records
Austr For — Australian Forestry
Austr For J — Australian Forestry Journal
Austr Geogr — Australian Geographer
Austr Geogr Soc Rep — Australian Geographical Society. Report
Austr Herb News — Australasian Herbarium News
Aust Rhodes R — Australian Rhodes Review
Austria Geol Bundesanst Verh — Austria. Geologische Bundesanstalt. Verhandlungen
Austria Mach Steel — Austria. Machinery and Steel
Austrian J Oncol — Austrian Journal of Oncology
Austria Zentralanst Meteorol Geodynamik Arb — Austria. Zentralanstalt fuer Meteorologie und Geodynamik. Arbeiten
Austr Inst Aborig Stud Newsletter — Australian Institute of Aboriginal Studies. Newsletter
Austr J Agric Res — Australian Journal of Agricultural Research
Austr J Appl Sci — Australian Journal of Applied Science
Austr J Biol Sci — Australian Journal of Biological Sciences
Austr J Bot — Australian Journal of Botany
Austr J Chem — Australian Journal of Chemistry
Austr J Dent — Australian Journal of Dentistry
Austr J Derm — Australian [*later, Australasian*] Journal of Dermatology
Austr J Exp Biol Med Sci — Australian Journal of Experimental Biology and Medical Science
Austr J Instr Techn — Australian Journal of Instrument Technology
Austr J Mar Freshwat Res — Australian Journal of Marine and Freshwater Research
Austr J Pharm — Australian Journal of Pharmacy
Austr J Phys — Australian Journal of Physics
Austr J Psychol — Australian Journal of Psychology
Austr J Sci — Australian Journal of Science

Austr J St — Australian Journal of Statistics
Austr J Zool — Australian Journal of Zoology
Austr Leath J — Australian Leather Journal
Austrl Fin — Australian Financial Review
Austr LJ — Australian Law Journal
Austr LT — Australian Law Times
Austr Mach Prod Eng — Australian Machinery and Production Engineering
Austr Mech Eng — Australian Mechanical Engineering
Austr Med Congr — Australasian Medical Congress
Austr Med Gaz — Australasian Medical Gazette
Austr Med J — Australian Medical Journal
Austr Min Ind Rev — Australian Mineral Industry. Review
Austr Min Ind Stat — Australian Mineral Industry. Statistics
Austr Mth Weath Rep — Australian Monthly Weather Report
Austr Mus Mag — Australian Museum. Magazine
Austr Nat — Australian Naturalist
Austr Neighb — Australia's Neighbours
Austr NZ Gen Pract — Australian and New Zealand General Practitioner
Austr NZ J Obst Gynaec — Australian and New Zealand Journal of Obstetrics and Gynaecology
Austr NZ J Surg — Australian and New Zealand Journal of Surgery
Aust Road Haulage J — Australian Road Haulage Journal
Aust Road Res — Australian Road Research
Aust Road Res Bd Bull — Australian Road Research Board. Bulletin
Aust Road Res Board AIR Rep — Australian Road Research Board. AIR Reports
Aust Road Res Board ARR Rep — Australian Road Research Board. ARR Reports
Aust Road Res Board Bull — Australian Road Research Board. Bulletin
Aust Road Res Board Conf — Australian Road Research Board. Conference
Aust Road Res Board Proc Conf — Australian Road Research Board. Proceedings of the Conference
Aust Road Res Bp Spec Rep — Australian Road Research Board. Special Report
Aust Road Research — Australian Road Research
Austr Off J Pat — Australian Official Journal of Patents, Trade Marks, and Designs
Aust Rose A — Australian Rose Annual
Aust Rose Annu — Australian Rose Annual
Austr Past — Australian Pastoralist
Austr Past Rev — Australasian Pastoralists' Review
Austr Photogr J — Australian Photographic Journal
Austr Plast — Australian Plastics
Austr Plast All Trade Rev — Australian Plastics and Allied Trades Review
Austr Plast Rubb J — Australian Plastics and Rubber Journal
Austr Pl Dis Rec — Australian Plant Disease Recorder
Austr Q — Australian Quarterly
Austr Rad Rec — Australian Radiation Records
Austr Sci Abstr — Australian Science Abstracts
Austr Sci Ind — Australian Science Index
Austr Stand Q — Australian Standards Quarterly
Austr Statesm Min Stand — Australian Statesman and Mining Standard
Austr Sug J — Australian Sugar Journal
Austr Surv — Australian Surveyor
Austr Tax D — Australian Tax Decisions
Austr Terr — Australian Territories
Austr Timb J — Australian Timber Journal
Austr Tob J — Australian Tobacco Journal
Aust Rubber — Australian Rubber
Austr Vet J — Australian Veterinary Journal
Austr Weld Eng — Australian Welding Engineer
Austr Wild Life — Australian Wild Life
Aust Saf News — Australian Safety News
Aust Sch L — Australian School Librarian
Aust Sch Lib — Australian School Librarian
Aust Sch Libr — Australian School Librarian
Aust Sch Librn — Australian School Librarian
Aust School Libr — Australian School Librarian
Aust Sci — Australian Scientist
Aust Sci Abstr — Australian Science Abstracts
Aust Science Teachers J — Australian Science Teachers' Journal
Aust Scient — Australian Scientist
Aust Scientist — Australian Scientist
Aust Sci Index — Australian Science Index
Aust Sci Newsl — Australian Science Newsletter
Aust Sci Teach J — Australian Science Teachers' Journal
Aust Seacraft — Australian Seacraft Magazine
Aust Seacraft — Australian Seacraft, Power, and Sail
Aust Seacraft Mag — Australian Seacraft Magazine
Aust Shell News — Australian Shell News
Aust's Heritage — Australia's Heritage
Aust Shorthorn — Australian Shorthorn
Aust Ski — Australian Ski Year Book
Aust Ski YB — Australian Ski Year Book
Austsn Cath Rec — Australasian Catholic Record
Austsn J Pharm — Australasian Journal of Pharmacy

Austsn J Philos — Australasian Journal of Philosophy
Austsn Meth Hist Soc J — Australasian Methodist Historical Society. Journal and Proceedings
Austsn Pr — Australasian Printer
Aust Soc Accountants SA Convention — Australian Society of Accountants. South Australian Division. Convention Reports
Aust Soc Anim Prod Victorian Branch Fed Counc Bull — Australian Society of Animal Production. Victorian Branch. Federal Council. Bulletin
Aust Soc Dairy Technol Tech Pub — Australian Society of Dairy Technology. Technical Publication
Aust Soc Dairy Technol Tech Publ — Australian Society of Dairy Technology. Technical Publication
Aust Soc Dairy Techn Tech Publ — Australian Society of Dairy Technology. Technical Publication
Aust Soc Dairy Tech Tech Pub — Australian Society of Dairy Technology. Technical Publication
Aust Soc Explor Geophys Bull — Australian Society of Exploration Geophysicists. Bulletin
Aust Soc Study Lab Hist Bull — Australian Society for the Study of Labour History. Bulletin
Aust Soc Sugar Cane Technol Proc Conf — Australian Society of Sugar Cane Technologists. Proceedings of the Conference
Aust Soc Welfare — Australian Social Welfare
Aust South Dep Mines Geol Sur Bull — South Australia. Department of Mines. Geological Survey. Bulletin
Aust South Dep Mines Geol Surv Rep Invest — South Australia. Department of Mines. Geological Survey. Report of Investigations
Aust South Dep Mines Min Rev — South Australia. Department of Mines. Mining Review
Aust Spec Libr News — Australian Special Libraries News
Aust Stamp Bull — Australian Stamp Bulletin
Aust Stamp M — Australian Stamp Monthly
Aust Stamp Mo — Australian Stamp Monthly
Aust Stand Q — Australian Standards Quarterly
Aust Stand Specif — Australian Standard Specifications
Aust Stand Specif Stand Ass Aust — Australian Standard Specifications. Standards Association of Australia
Aust Statesm Min Stand — Australian Statesman and Mining Standard
Aust Stock Exchange J — Australian Stock Exchange Journal
Aust Stock Exch J — Australian Stock Exchange Journal
Aust Stud — Australian Student
Aust Stud & Farm M — Australian Stud and Farm Monthly
Aust Stud Legal Philos — Australian Studies in Legal Philosophy
Aust Sugar J — Australian Sugar Journal
Aust Sugar Yr Bk — Australian Sugar Year Book
Aust Sug J — Australian Sugar Journal
Aust Sug Yb — Australian Sugar Yearbook
Aust Surv — Australian Surveyor
Aust Survey — Australian Surveyor
Aust Surveyor — Australian Surveyor
Aust TAFE Teach — Australian TAFE [*Department of Technical and Further Education*] Teacher
Aust Tax D — Australasian Tax Decisions
Aust Tax Rev — Australasian Tax Review
Aust Tax Rev — Australasian Tax Review
Aust T Deaf — Australian Teacher of the Deaf
Aust Teach — Australian Teacher
Aust Teach Deaf — Australian Teacher of the Deaf
Aust Teacher of the Deaf — Australian Teacher of the Deaf
Aust Teach Fed Rep — Australian Teachers' Federation. Report
Aust Teach J — Australian Technical Journal
Aust Telecomm Res — Australian Telecommunication Research
Aust Telecomm Research — Australian Telecommunication Research
Aust Telecommun Dev Assoc — Australian Telecommunications Development Association. Annual Report
Aust Telecommun Res — Australian Telecommunication Research
Aust Terr — Australian Territories
Aust Territ — Australian Territories
Aust Territories — Australian Territories
Aust Theatre Yrbk — Australian Theatre Yearbook
Aust Timber J — Australian Timber Journal
Aust Timb J — Australian Timber Journal
Aust Timb J — Australian Timber Journal and Building Products Merchandiser
Aust Tobacco J — Australian Tobacco Journal
Aust Tob Grow Bull — Australian Tobacco Grower's Bulletin
Aust Tob J — Australian Tobacco Journal
Aust Today — Australia Today
Aust Tract Test — Australian Tractor Test
Aust Tract Test Comm Aust Tract Test — Australian Tractor Testing Committee. Australian Tractor Test
Aust Trade Chronicle — Australian Trade Chronicle
Aust Transp — Australian Transport
Aust Transport — Australian Transport
Aust Travel Goods — Australian Travel Goods and Handbags and Accessories
Aust Traveller — Australian Traveller

Aust Univ — Australian University
Aust Urban Stud — Australian Urban Studies
Aust Vet J — Australian Veterinary Journal
Aust Vet Pr — Australian Veterinary Practitioner
Aust Waste Conf — Australian Waste Conference
Aust Waste Disposal Conf — Australian Waste Disposal Conference
Aust Waste Manage Control Conf Pap — Australian Waste Management and Control Conference. Papers
Aust Water Resour Counc Hydrol Ser — Australian Water Resources Council. Hydrological Series
Aust Water Resour Counc Stream Gauging Inf — Australian Water Resources Council. Stream Gauging Information
Aust Water Resour Counc Tech Pap — Australian Water Resources Council. Technical Paper
Aust Water Resour Coun Tech Pap — Australian Water Resources Council. Technical Paper
Aust Water Wastewater Assoc Fed Conv — Australian Water and Wastewater Association. Federal Convention
Aust Water Wastewater Assoc Summer Sch — Australian Water and Wastewater Association. Summer School
Aust Water Well J — Australasian Water Well Journal
Aust Wat Resour Coun Hydrol Ser — Australian Water Resources Council. Hydrological Series
Aust Weapons Res Establ Tech Rep — Australia. Weapons Research Establishment. Technical Report
Aust Weed Control Handb — Australian Weed Control Handbook
Aust Weeds — Australian Weeds
Aust Weeds Conf Proc — Australian Weeds Conference. Proceedings
Aust Weld — Australian Welder
Aust Weld Engr — Australian Welding Engineer
Aust Welding J — Australian Welding Journal
Aust Weld J — Australian Welding Journal
Aust Weld Res — Australian Welding Research
Aust Weld Res Ass Bull — Australian Welding Research Association. Bulletin
Aust West Dep Mines Annu Rep — Western Australia. Department of Mines. Annual Report
Aust West Dep Mines Annu Rep Geol Surv — Western Australia. Department of Mines. Annual Report of the Geological Survey
Aust West Dep Mines Bull — Western Australia. Department of Mines. Bulletin
Aust (West) Dep Mines Rep Mineral Anal Chem — Australia (Western). Department of Mines. Report of the Mineralogist, Analyst, and Chemist
Aust West Geol Surv Bull — Western Australia. Geological Survey. Bulletin
Aust West Geol Surv Miner Resour Bull — Western Australia. Geological Survey. Mineral Resources Bulletin
Aust (West) Rep Dir Gov Chem Lab — Australia (Western). Report of the Director of Government Chemical Laboratories
Aust Wildl Res — Australian Wildlife Research
Aust Wild R — Australian Wildlife Research
Aust Wine Brewing Spir Rev — Australian Wine, Brewing, and Spirit Review
Aust Wine Brewing and Spir Rev — Australian Wine, Brewing, and Spirit Review
Aust Wine Brew Spirit Rev — Australian Wine, Brewing, and Spirit Review
Aust Womens W — Australian Women's Weekly
Aust Wool Bd Rep — Australian Wool Board. Report
Aust Wool Bur Wool Stat Service — Australian Wool Bureau. Wool Statistical Service
Aust Wool Bur Wool Stat Service Aust Wool Stat Analysis — Australian Wool Bureau. Wool Statistical Service. Australian Wool. Statistical Analysis
Aust Wool Stat Analysis — Australian Wool. Statistical Analysis
Aust Wool Test Auth Text Test Bull — Australian Wool Testing Authority. Textile Testing Bulletin
Aust Workshop Coal Hydrogenation — Australian Workshop on Coal Hydrogenation
Aust YB Intl L — Australian Yearbook of International Law
Aust Yearbook Int L — Australian Yearbook of International Law
Aust Yr Bk IL — Australian Yearbook of International Law
Aust Yr Book Int Law — Australian Yearbook of International Law
Aust Zoo — Australian Zoologist
Aust Zool — Australian Zoologist
Aust Zoologist — Australian Zoologist
AUT — Analele. Universitatii din Timisoara. Seria Stiinte Filologice
AUT — Annales Universitatis Turkuensis
AUT — Annali. Universita Toscane
Aut — Authentic Science Fiction
AUT — Auto + Motortechniek
Aut Eng — Automotive Engineering
AUTMA — Automatizace
Auto Age — Automotive Age
Auto Chn S — Automotive Chain Store
Auto and Con — Automation and Control
Auto Eng — Automobile Engineer
Autogene Metallbearb — Autogene Metallbearbeitung
Autogestion et Social — Autogestion et Socialisme
Auto Highwy — Automotive Industries. Truck and Off Highway
Auto Housg — Automation in Housing and Systems Building News

Auto Ind — Automotive Industries
Auto Ind Rep — Autotransaction Industry Report
Automat Control and Computer Sci — Automatic Control and Computer Sciences
Automat Control Comput Sci — Automatic Control and Computer Sciences
Automat Control Theory Appl — Automatic Control Theory and Applications
Automat Data Process Inform B — Automatic Data Processing Information Bulletin
Automat Document and Math Linguistics — Automatic Documentation and Mathematical Linguistics
Automat Elec Tech J — Automatic Electric Technical Journal
Automatica-J IFAC — Automatica: The Journal of IFAC [*International Federation of Automatic Control*]
Automatic Control Theory Appl — Automatic Control Theory and Applications
Automation (Cleve) — Automation (Cleveland)
Automatisierungspraxis — Automatisierungspraxis fuer Grundlagen Geratebau und Betrieberfahrungen
Automat Monit Mea — Automatic Monitoring and Measuring
Automat Programming — Automatic Programming
Automat Remote Contr — Automation and Remote Control [*USSR*]
Automat Remote Control — Automation and Remote Control
Automat Weld (USSR) — Automatic Welding (USSR)
Autom Control — Automatic Control [*Japan*]
Autom and Control — Automation and Control
Autom Control Comput Sci — Automatic Control and Computer Sciences
Autom Control and Comput Sci — Automatic Control and Computer Sciences
Autom Control Theory & Appl — Automatic Control Theory and Applications
Autom Data Process Inf Bull — Automatic Data Processing Information Bulletin
Autom Doc Math Linguist — Automatic Documentation and Mathematical Linguistics
Autom Elec Tech J — Automatic Electric Technical Journal
Autom si Electron — Automatica si Electronica
Auto Merch — Auto Merchandising News
Autom et Inf Ind — Automatique et Informatique Industrielles
Autom Mach — Automatic Machining
Autom Monit and Meas — Automatic Monitoring and Measuring
Automobile Abs — Automobile Abstracts
Automobiltech Z — Automobiltechnische Zeitschrift
Automob Q — Automobile Quarterly
Automob Technol — Automobile Technology [*Japan*]
Automot Abstr — Automotive Abstracts
Automot Aviat Ind — Automotive and Aviation Industries
Automot Des Eng — Automotive Design Engineering
Automot Eng — Automotive Engineering
Automot Eng (Lond) — Automotive Engineer (London)
Automot Engng — Automotive Engineering
Automot Eng (Pittsb) — Automotive Engineering (Pittsburgh)
Automot Engr — Automotive Engineer
Automot Ind — Automotive Industries
Automotive & Aviation Ind — Automotive and Aviation Industries
Automotive Ind — Automotive Industry
Automot N — Automotive News
Automot News — Automotive News
Automot Serv News — Automotive Service News [*Japan*]
Automot Top — Automotive Topics
Autom Remote Control — Automation and Remote Control [*USSR*]
Autom & Remote Control — Automation and Remote Control [*USSR*]
Autom & Strum — Automazione e Strumentazione
Autom Strum — Automazione e Strumentazione
Autom Syst Rizeni — Automatizovane Systemy Rizeni - Bulletin INORGA
Autom Weld — Automatic Welding [*USSR*]
Auto News — Automotive News
Auto Rbldr — Automotive Rebuilder
Auto Tech — Auto Technik
AUTRB — Australian Transport
Aut Remot R — Automation and Remote Control (USSR)
AUTUA — Annales Universitatis Turkuensis. Series A-I. Astronomica-Chemica-Physica-Mathemtica
Aut Weld R — Automatic Welding (USSR)
AuU — Afrika und Uebersee
AUUASLU — Acta Universitatis Upsaliensis. Acta Societatis Linguisticae Upsaliensis
AUUHL — Acta Universitatis Upsaliensis. Historia Litterarum
AUUSAU — Acta Universitatis Upsaliensis. Studia Anglistica Upsaliensia
AUUSEU — Acta Universitatis Upsaliensis. Studia Ethnologica Upsaliensia
AUUSGU — Acta Universitatis Upsaliensis. Studia Germanistica Upsaliensia
AUUSRU — Acta Universitatis Upsaliensis. Studia Romanica Upsaliensia
AUV — Anales. Universidad de Valencia
Auvergne Litt — L'Auvergne Litteraire, Artistique, et Historique
AUVJA — Australian Veterinary Journal
AUW — Acta Universitatis Wratislaviensis
AUW — Aussenwirtschaft. Zeitschrift fuer Internationale Wirtschaftsbeziehungen
AUWEA — Automatic Welding (English Translation)
AUWJA — Australian Welding Journal

AUWMD — ASCE [*American Society of Civil Engineers*] Urban Water Resources Program. Technical Memorandum IHP [*International Hydrological Programme*]
AUWPET — Agricultural University (Wageningen). Papers
AUWTB — ASCE [*American Society of Civil Engineers*] Urban Water Resources Research Program. Technical Memorandum
AUZ — Australian Packaging [*Sydney*]
AUZCA — Analele Stiintifice. Universitatii Al. I. Cuza din Iasi. Sectiunea 1c. Chimie
AUZFA — Analele Stiintifice. Universitatii Al. I. Cuza din Iasi. Sectiunea 1b. Fizica
AUZMA — Analele Stiintifice. Universitatii Al. I. Cuza din Iasi. Sectiunea 1a. Matematica
AV — Annales Valaisannes
AV — Archaeologische Veroeffentlichungen. Deutsches Archaeologisches Institut Cairo
AV — Archivio Veneto
AV — Arheoloski Vestnik
AV — Artha Vijnana
AV — Ateneo Veneto
AV — Audio Visual
AV — Aus Aachens Vorzeit
AV — AV Communication Review
AVAGA — Avvenire Agricolo
Av Aliment Mejora Anim — Avances en Alimentacion y Mejora Animal
Av Aliment Mejora Anim Supl — Avances en Alimentacion y Mejora Animal. Suplemento
Avances Aliment Mejora Anim — Avances en Alimentacion y Mejora Animal
A Van Leeuw — Antonie Van Leeuwenhoek Journal of Microbiology and Serology
Avant Sc C — Avant-Scene Cinema
Avant Scene — Avant-Scene Cinema
Avant Sc Th — Avant Scene Theatre
AVAPA — Archivio "De Vecchi" per l'Anatomia Patologica e la Medicina Clinica
AVBAAI — Agronomia y Veterinaria
AVBIB — Advances in the Biosciences
AVBNA — Arhiv Bioloskih Nauka
AVBNAN — Archives des Sciences Biologiques [*Belgrade*]
AVBNAN — Arhiv Bioloskih Nauka
AVBWKN — Annalen der Vereeniging tot het Hevorderen van de Beoefening der Wetenschap Onder de Katholieken in Nederland
Avco Corp Res Rep — Avco Corporation. Research Reports
AV Comm R — AV Communication Review
AV Commun Rev — AV Communication Review
AVCR — AV Communication Review
AVDIA — Avian Diseases
AVEIA — Archivio Veterinario Italiano
AVEIAN — Archivio Veterinario Italiano
AVen — Archivio Veneto
Avenir Agr — Avenir Agriculture
Avenir Med — Avenir Medical
Av Ensenanza Invest Esc Nac Agric (Chapingo) — Escuela Nacional de Agricultura (Chapingo). Avances en la Ensenanza y la Investigacion
Avery Ind Archit Per — Avery Index to Architectural Periodicals of Columbia University
Avesta Stainless Bull — Avesta Stainless Bulletin
AVETD — Atomno-Vodorodnaya Energetika i Tekhnologiya
AVF — Archivos Venezolanos de Folklore
AVG — Educational Screen and Audiovisual Guide [*Later, A V Guide: The Learning Media Magazine*]
Av Hist Soc Aust J — Aviation Historical Society of Australia. Journal
Avh Norske Vid-Akad Oslo I NS — Avhandlinger Utgitt av Norske Videnskaps-Akademi I Oslo. I. Matematisk-Naturvidenskapelig Klasse. Ny Serie
Avh Nor Vidensk-Akad Oslo I — Avhandlinger Utgitt av Norsk Videnskaps-Akademi I Oslo. I. Matematisk-Naturvidenskapelig Klasse
Avh Utgitt Nor Vidensk-Akad Oslo Mat-Naturvidensk Kl — Avhandlinger Utgitt av Norsk Videnskaps-Akademie I Oslo. Matematisk-Naturvidenskapelig Klasse
Av I — Audiovisual Instruction
AVIAA — Aviation Age
Avian Dis — Avian Diseases
Avian Pathol — Avian Pathology
Avian Res — Avian Research
Aviat Age — Aviation Age
Aviation N — Aviation News
Aviation W — Aviation Week
Aviat Kosmonavt — Aviatsiya i Kosmonavtika [*USSR*]
Aviat Med — Aviation Medicine
Aviat Res Monogr — Aviation Research Monographs
Aviat Rev — Aviation Review
Aviats Khim — Aviatsiya i Khimiya
Aviat Space Environ Med — Aviation, Space, and Environmental Medicine
Aviat Spac Environ Med — Aviation, Space, and Environmental Medicine
Aviat Sp En — Aviation, Space, and Environmental Medicine

Aviats Promst — Aviatsionnaya Promyshlennost
Aviat Week Space Technol — Aviation Week and Space Technology
Avia Week — Aviation Week and Space Technology
Avic Mag — Avicultural Magazine
Avicult Mag — Avicultural Magazine
Avicult Tec — Avicultura Tecnica
AVINB — Advances in Instrumentation
A-V Ind — Audio-Visual Index
AV Inst — Audiovisual Instruction
Av Instr — Audiovisual Instruction
AVISD — Avishkar
AVKOA — Aviatsiya i Kosmonavtika
AV Libn — Audiovisual Librarian
A-V L J — Audio-Visual Language Journal
AVMED — Aviation Medicine
A-V Media — Audio-Visual Media
AVMHB — Archives of Mechanics
AVMPAG — Archivos Venezolanos de Medicina Tropical y Parasitologia Medica
AVN — Aviation News
AVNAG — Annalen des Vereins fuer Nassauische Altertumskunde und Geschichtsforschung
AVNAKGF — Annalen des Vereins fuer Nassauische Altertumskunde und Geschichtsforschung
AVNDA — Avtomobil'nye Dorogi
AVNP — Arviap Nipinga. Eskimo Point
AVNUA2 — Archivos Venezolanos de Nutricion
Avocado Grow — Avocado Grower
AvP — Altertuemer von Pergamon
AVPBC — Advances in Psychobiology
AVPCA — Advances in Pharmacology and Chemotherapy
AVPCCS — Archiv for Pharmaci og Chemi. Scientific Edition
AVPMAM — American Veterinary Medical Association. Scientific Proceedings of the Annual Meeting
AVPPAV — Archivos Venezolanos de Puericultura y Pediatria
AVPRA — Avtomobil'naya Promyshlennost
Av Prod Anim — Avances en Produccion Animal
AVPTA9 — Archivos Venezolanos de Patologia Tropical y Parasitologia Medica
AVPZAR — Archiv fuer Pflanzenschutz
AVR — Australian Video Review
AVSCB — Advances in Veterinary Science and Comparative Medicine
AVSLK — Archiv des Vereins fuer Siebenbuergische Landeskunde
AVsLund — Vetenskaps-Societeten i Lund. Aarsbok
AVSTA — Advances in Space Science and Technology
AVSVA — Avtomaticheskaya Svarka
AVT — Archivio Veneto-Tridentino
AVTEA — Avtomatika i Telemekhanika
AVThRw — Aufsaetze und Vortraege zur Theologie und Religionswissenschaft [*Berlin*]
Avtodorozhnik Ukr — Avtodorozhnik Ukrainy
Avtog Delo — Avtogennoe Delo
Avtomatika — Akademija Nauk Ukrainskoi RSR. Institut Elektrotehniki Avtomatika [*Kiev*]
Avtomat Izchisl Tekhn — Avtomatika i Izchislitelna Tekhnika
Avtomat Sistemy Upravlen — Leningradskii Gosudarstvennyi Universitet Avtomatizirovannye Sistemy Upravlenija
Avtomat Sistemy Upravlenija i Pribory Avtomat — Avtomatizirovannye Sistemy Upravlenija i Pribory Avtomatiki
Avtomat i Telemeh — Akademija Nauk SSSR. Avtomatika i Telemehanika [*Moscow*]
Avtomat i Telemekh — Akademiya Nauk SSSR. Avtomatika i Telemekhanika
Avtomat i Telemekh — Avtomatika i Telemekhanika
Avtomat Upravlenie i Vychisl Tekhn — Avtomaticheskoe Upravlenie i Vychislitel'naya Tekhnika
Avtomat Upravl i Vycisl Tehnika — Avtomaticeskoe Upravlenie i Vycislitel'naja Tehnika
Avtomat i Vychisl Tekhn — Avtomatika i Vychislitel'naya Tekhnika. Akademiya Nauk Latviiskoi SSR
Avtomat i Vychisl Tekhn — Avtomatika i Vychislitel'naya Tekhnika. Minskii Radiotekhnicheskii Institut
Avtomat i Vycisl Tehn (Riga) — Avtomatika i Vychislitel'naja Tehnika (Riga)
Avtometrija — Avtometrija Akademija Nauk SSSR
Avtom Khim Proizvod (Kiev) — Avtomatizatsiya Khimicheskikh Proizvodstv (Kiev)
Avtom Khim Proizvod (Moscow) — Avtomatizatsiya Khimicheskikh Proizvodstv (Moscow)
Avtomob Dorogi — Avtomobil'nye Dorogi
Avtomob Dorogi Dorozhne Budiv — Avtomobil ni Dorogi i Dorozhne Budivnitstvo
Avtomob Prom-st — Avtomobil'naya Promyshlennost [*USSR*]
Avtomob Trakt Promst — Avtomobil'naya i Traktornaya Promyshlennost
Avtomob Transp (Kiev) — Avtomobil'nyi Transport (Kiev)
Avtomob Transp (Moscow) — Avtomobil'nyi Transport (Moscow)
Avtomon Transp Kaz — Avtomobil'nyi Transport Kazakhstana [*Kazakh SSR*]
Avtom Priborostr — Avtomatizatsiya i Priborostroenie

Avtom Priborostr Inf Nauchno Tekh — Avtomatika i Priborostroenie. Informasionnyi Nauchno-Tekhnicheskii

Avtom Proizvod Protsessov — Avtomatizatsiya Proizvodstvennykh Protsessov

Avtom Proizvod Protsessov Mashinostr Priborostr (Lvov) — Avtomatizatsiya Proizvodstvennykh Protsessov v Mashinostroenii i Priborostroenii (Lvov)

Avtom Staleplavil'n Proizvod — Avtomatizatsiya Staleplavil'nogo Proizvodstva [*USSR*]

Avtom Svarka — Avtomaticheskaya Svarka

Avtom Telemekh — Avtomatika i Telemekhanika

Avtom & Telemekh — Avtomatika i Telemekhanika

Avtom Telemekh Svyaz — Avtomatika, Telemekhanika, i Svyaz

Avtom & Vychisl Tekh — Avtomatika i Vychislitel'naya Tekhnika

Avtotrakt Delo — Avtotraktornoe Delo

AVTRA — Avtomobil'nyi Transport

Avven Agr — Avvenire Agricolo

AVVTA — Avtomatika i Vychislitel'naya Tekhnika (1961-66)

AW — Air Wonder Stories

AW — All-Alaska Weekly

AW — Allgemeine Wochenzeitung der Juden in Deutschland

AW — Alliance Witness

AW — American West

AW — Annals of Wyoming

AW — Antike Welt

AW — Aviation Week

Awamia Rev Rech Agron Maroc — Awamia Revue de la Recherche Agronomique Marocaine

AWAN — AWA [*Alberta Wilderness Association*] Newsletter

Awards Nucl Med Radiopharmacol — Awards in Nuclear Medicine and Radiopharmacology

Awas — Awasis

AWAT — Archiv fuer Wissenschaftliche Erforschung des Alten Testaments [*Halle*]

AWA Tech Rev — AWA [*Amalgamated Wireless Australasia*] Technical Review

AWBAbh — Koeniglich-Preussische Akademie der Wissenschaften (Berlin). Abhandlungen

AWBMA — Archiwum Budowy Maszyn

AWBSb — Koeniglich-Preussische Akademie der Wissenschaften (Berlin). Sitzungsberichte

AWCH NSW Newsletter — Association for the Welfare of Children in Hospital. New South Wales. Newsletter

AWD — Recht der Internationalen Wirtschaft Aussenwirtschaftsdienst des Betriebsberaters

AWG Phk — Akademie der Wissenschaften in Goettingen. Philologisch-Historische Klasse

AWIFA — Angewandte Informatik/Applied Informatics

AWJ — Allgemeine Wochenzeitung der Juden in Deutschland

AWJD — Allgemeine Wochenzeitung der Juden in Deutschland

AWLMA9 — Akademie der Wissenschaften und der Literatur in Mainz. Abhandlungen der Mathematisch-Naturwissenschaftlichen Klasse

AWLM AGSK — Akademie der Wissenschaften und der Literatur in Mainz. Abhandlungen der Geistes- und Sozialwissenschaftlichen Klasse

AWLMGS — Akademie der Wissenschaften und der Literatur in Mainz. Abhandlungen der Geistes- und Sozialwissenschaftlichen Klasse

AWLML — Akademie der Wissenschaften und der Literatur in Mainz. Klasse der Literatur

AWM — Auskunftsblatt [*Bern*]

AWMAbh — Akademie der Wissenschaften in Muenchen. Abhandlungen

AWMADF — Agricultural Water Management

AWMMAE — Akademie der Wissenschaften und der Literatur in Mainz. Mathematisch-Naturwissenschaftlichen Klasse. Mikrofauna des Meeresbodens

AWMSb — Akademie der Wissenschaften in Muenchen. Philosophisch-Historische Klasse. Sitzungsberichte

AWO — Afrique Industrie Infrastructures

AWO — Average Monthly Weather Outlook

AWPAA — Angewandte Parasitologie

AWPOA — Air and Water Pollution

AWPOAZ — Air and Water Pollution

AWR — Anglo-Welsh Review

AWRHA — Australian Water Resources Council. Hydrological Series

AWS — Air Wonder Stories

AWSJ — Asian Wall Street Journal

AWSTA — Aviation Week and Space Technology

AWTEA — Allgemeine Waermetechnik

AWW — Australian Women's Weekly

AWW — Australian Writer's Workshop

AWWDs — Koenigliche Akademie der Wissenschaften (Wien). Denkschriften

AWWSb — Akademie der Wissenschaften in Wien. Sitzungsberichte

AXB — Artha Vijnana

Axel Heiberg Isl Res Rep Geol McGill Univ — Axel Heiberg Island Research Reports. Geology. McGill University

AXL — Cartonnages et Emballages Modernes

AXVMA — Archiv fuer Experimentelle Veterinaermedizin

AYBIL — Australian Yearbook of International Law

AYLR — Aylesford Review

AYR — American Year Review

Ayrshire Archaeol Natur Hist Collect 2 Ser — Ayrshire Archaeological and Natural History Collections. Series 2

AZ — Archaeologische Zeitung

AZ — Archivalische Zeitschrift

AZ — Arizona Reports

Azabu Juika Daigaku Kenkyu Hokoku Bull — Azabu Juika Daigaku Kenkyu Hokoku/Bulletin. Azabu Veterinary College

AZARAO — Arizona. Agricultural Experiment Station. Research Report

AZATAU — Arizona. Agricultural Experiment Station. Technical Bulletin

AZDJ — Allgemeine Zeitung des Judentums

AZEGAB — Archives de Zoologie Experimentale et Generale

Azerbaidzan Gos Univ Ucen Zap — Azerbaidzanskii Gosudarstvennyi Universitet Imeni M. Kirova. Ucenyi Zapiski

Azerbaidzan Gos Univ Ucen Zap Ser Fiz-Mat Nauk — Azerbaidzanskii Gosudarstvennyi Universitet Imeni S. M. Kirova. Ucenye Zapiski. Serija Fiziko-Matematiceskih Nauk

Azerbaidzhan Med Zhurnal — Azerbaidzhanskii Meditsinskii Zhurnal

Azerb Khim Zh — Azerbajdzhanskij Khimicheskij Zhurnal

Azerb Med Zh — Azerbaidzhanskii Meditsinskii Zhurnal

Azerb Neft Khoz — Azerbajdzhanskoe Neftyanoe Khozyajstvo

AZHIA — Arizona Highways

AZIH — Archiwum Zydowskiego Instytutu Historycznego

AZJ — Allgemeine Zeitung des Judentums

AZKZA — Azerbaidzhanskii Khimicheskii Zhurnal

AZ L — Arizona Law Review

AZ LR — Arizona Law Review

AZMZA — Azerbaidzhanskii Meditsinskii Zhurnal

AZO — Allgemeine Zionistische Organisation

AZOF — Annales Zoologica Fennici

AZOGB — Australian and New Zealand Journal of Obstetrics and Gynaecology

AZOIAX — Archivio Zoologico Italiano

AZOTAW — Archivos de Zootecnia

AZTh — Arbeiten zur Theologie [*Stuttgart/Berlin*]

AZWBAI — Arizona. Game and Fish Department. Wildlife Bulletin

AZXNAP — Archives de Zoologie Experimentale et Generale. Notes et Revue

B

B — Banker
B — Barcelona
B — Bibliofilia
B — Bibliotekarz
B — Biekorf
B — Bigaku
B — Brazda
B — Broadcasting
B — [*The*] Bulletin
Ba — Babel. International Journal of Translation [*Budapest*]
BA — Bach
Ba — Baconiana
BA — Balkan Archiv
BA — Beitraege zur Assyriologie und Semitischen Sprachwissenschaft
BA — Biblical Archaeologist
BA — Biological Abstracts
BA — Bollettino d'Arte
BA — Books Abroad
BA — Buenos Aires
BA — Business Administration
BA — Die Botschaft des Alten Testaments [*Stuttgart*]
BAA — Braunschweiger Anglistische Arbeiten
BAA — Bulletin d'Archeologie Algerienne
BAA — Bulletin des Archives d'Anvers
BAA — Technisch Weekblad
BAAAC — Bulletin. Association des Amis de l'Art Copte
BAABL — Boletin. Academia Argentina de Buenas Letras
BAAFB — Bulletin. Academie des Sciences Agricoles et Forestieres (Bucharest)
BAAFBT — Bulletin. Academie des Sciences Agricoles et Forestieres
BAAFLP — Bulletin. Association Amicale des Anciens Eleves de la Faculte des Lettres de Paris
BAAI — Bollettino. Associazione degli Africanisti Italiani
BAAJ — British Archaeological Association. Journal
BAAL — Boletin. Academia Argentina de Letras
BAALA — Societe des Agricultures d'Algerie. Bulletin
BAAPA — Bulletin. American Association of Petroleum Geologists
BAAR — Bollettino. Associazione Archeologica Romana
BAARD — Bulletin. Association des Amis de Rabelais et de la Deviniere
BAASB — British Association for American Studies. Bulletin
BAB — Academie Royale de Belgique. Bulletin. Classe des Lettres et des Sciences Morales et Politiques
Bab — Babyloniaca. Etudes de Philologie Assyro-Babylonienne [*Paris*]
BABA — Boletin. Academia de Bellas Artes de Valladolid
BABAB — Bauplanung-Bautechnik
BABAT — Boletin. Academia de Bellas Artes y Ciencias Historicas de Toledo
BABC — Boletin. Academia de Bellas Artes de Cordoba
B Aberdeen Univ Afr Stud Group — Bulletin. Aberdeen University. African Studies Group
B A Besch — Bulletin van de Vereeniging tot Bevordering der Kennis van de Antike Beschaving
Bab J A — Babel. Journal of the Australian Federation of Modern Language Teachers Association [*Darlinghurst, New South Wales*]
BABL — Boletin. Real Academia de Buenas Letras de Barcelona
BABLB — Boletin. Real Academia de Buenas Letras de Barcelona

BABN — Bollettino. Archivio Storico del Banco di Napoli
BABSD — South African Bureau of Standards. Bulletin
BAC — Biblioteca de Autores Cristianos
BAC — Boletin. Academia Colombiana
BAC — Boletin. Real Academia de Cordoba
BAC — Bulletin Archeologique. Comite des Travaux Historiques et Archeologiques
BACA — Bulleti. Associacio Catalana d'Antropologia
B Acad Roy Belg — Bulletin. Classe des Lettres et des Sciences Morales et Politiques. Academie Royale de Belgique
B Acad Sci — Bulletin. Academy of Sciences of the USSR. Division of Chemical Science
BACBLNAC — Boletin. Academia de Ciencias, Bellas Letras, y Nobles Artes de Cordoba
Bach of Arts — Bachelor of Arts
Backgr Collect — Background to Collecting
Backgr Notes — Background Notes
Back Notes — Background Notes on the Countries of the World. US Department of State
Backyard — Your Big Backyard
BACL — Boletin. Academia Cubana de la Lengua
BAClLg — Bulletin Semestriel. Association des Classiques de l'Universite de Liege
BACM — Bulletin. Academie pour l'Histoire de la Culture Materielle
BACOAV — Bulletin. Agricultural Chemical Society of Japan
BACol — Boletin. Academia Colombiana
BA Coll Agric Mag — BA [*Bansilal Amritlal*] College of Agriculture Magazine [*India*]
B A Crist — Bullettino di Archeologia Cristiana
Bacteriol Proc — Bacteriological Proceedings
Bacteriol Rev — Bacteriological Reviews
Bacteriol Virusol Parazitol Epidemiol (Buchar) — Bacteriologia, Virusologia, Parazitologia, Epidemiologia (Bucharest)
BACTH — Bulletin Archeologique. Comite des Travaux Historiques et Scientifiques [*Paris*]
BACTHS — Bulletin Archeologique. Comite des Travaux Historiques et Scientifiques [*Paris*]
Bact Proc — Bacteriological Proceedings
Bact R — Bacteriological Reviews
Bact Rev — Bacteriological Reviews
Bact Rs — Bacteriological Reviews
BAD — Bangkok Bank. Monthly Review
Bad Hersfelder Jh — Bad Hersfelder Jahresheft
Badische Hist Komm Neujahrsbl — Badische Historische Kommission. Neujahrsblaetter
BADL — Bonner Arbeiten zur Deutschen Literatur
Bad M — Badminton Magazine
BADWS — Bayerische Akademie der Wissenschaften. Philosophisch Historische Klasse. Sitzungsberichte
BAE — Bank of Jamaica. Bulletin
BAE — Biblioteca de Autores Espanoles
BAE — Boletin. Real Academia Espanola
BAEAD2 — Alabama. Agricultural Experiment Station. Auburn University. Bulletin
BAEC — Bolletino. Amicizia Ebraico-Cristiana di Firenze

BAEC — Bulletin. Association des Amis des Eglises et de l'Art Coptes
BAEO — Boletin. Asociacion Espanola de Orientalistas
BAEPE — Boletin. Asociacion Europea de Profesores de Espanol
Baer Berl — Baer von Berlin
Baessler-Arch — Baessler-Archiv. Beitraege zur Voelkerkunde
BAF — Bamberger Abhandlungen und Forschungen
BAF — Bulletin. Association des Amis de Flaubert
BAFA — Boletin. Asociacion Folklorica (Argentina)
BAfO — Beiheft. Archiv fuer Orientforschung [*Graz*]
BAFPD — Biogas and Alcohol Fuels Production
BAG — Beitraege zur Alten Geschichte
BAG — Boletin. Academia Gallega
BAG — Bovagblad
BAGB — Bulletin. Association Guillaume Bude
BAGB SC — Bulletin. Association Guillaume Bude. Supplement Critique
B Agenc Int Energie Atom — Bulletin. Agence Internationale de l'Energie Atomique
BAGF — Bulletin. Association des Geographes Francais
Baghdad Univ Coll Sci Bull — Baghdad University. College of Science. Bulletin
BaghMitt — Baghdader Mitteilungen des Deutschen Archaeologischen Instituts. Abteilung Baghdad [*Berlin*]
BAGS — Bulletin. American Geographical Society
BAH — Biological Agriculture and Horticulture
BAH — Boletin. Academia de la Historia
BAH — Bulletin. Academie d'Hippone
BAH — Business Archives and History
BAHAD — Bulletin of Animal Health and Production in Africa
BAHD — Bulletin d'Archeologie et d'Histoire Dalmate
BAHID — Basic and Applied Histochemistry
BAHIFAI — Bibliotheque Archeologique et Historique de l'Institut Francais d'Archeologie d'Istanbul
BAHist — Boletin. Real Academia de la Historia
BAI — Biological and Agricultural Index
BAI — Bulletin. American Institute of Swedish Arts, Literature, and Science
BAIBL — Bulletin. Academie des Inscriptions et Belles-Lettres
BAINB — Bulletin. Astronomical Institutes of the Netherlands. Supplement Series
BAIU — Bulletin. Alliance Israelite Universelle
BAK — Bakker. Actueel Vakblad voor de Broodbakkerij. Banketbakkerij [*Nijmegen*]
Bakelite Rev — Bakelite Review
Baker J T Chem Co Prod Bull — Baker, J. T., Chemical Company. Product Bulletin
Baker Millers J — Baker and Millers' Journal
Baker Millr J — Baker and Millers' Journal
Baker Prod — Bakery Production and Marketing
Baker's — Baker's Digest
Baker's Dig — Baker's Digest
Baker's Rev — Baker's Review
Baker's Tech Dig — Baker's Technical Digest
Baking Ind — Baking Industry
Baking Technol — Baking Technology
Bakish Mater Corp Publ — Bakish Materials Corporation. Publication
Bakkerij Wet — Bakkerij Wetenschap
BAL — Berichte. Verhandlungen der Saechsischen Akademie der Wissenschaften zu Leipzig [*Berlin*]
BAL — Buenos Aires Literaria
BAL — Bulletin des Antiquites Luxembourgeoises
BALA — Bulletin. American Library Association
BALA — Bulletin. Association Lyonnaise de Recherches Archeologiques
BALAC — Bulletin d'Ancienne Litterature et d'Archeologie Chretienne
Balasov Gos Ped Inst Ucen Zap — Balasovkii Gosudarstvennyi Pedagogiceskii Institut. Ucenye Zapiski
BALB — Boletin. Real Academia de Buenas Letras de Barcelona
BALC — Bulletin d'Ancienne Litterature Chretienne Latine [*Maredosous*]
BALF — Black American Literature Forum
BALF — Bulletin. Academie Royale de Langue et de Litterature Francaises
Balgarska M — Balgarska Muzyka
BALI — Bollettino dell'Atlante Linguistico Italiano
BALit — Biblioteka Analiz Literackich
Balkan Stud — Balkan Studies
BalkE — Balkansko Ezikoznanije
Balk Stud — Balkan Studies
Ballade — Ballade Tidsskrift for Ny Musikk
Ball Bear J — Ball Bearing Journal
Ballet N — Ballet News
Ballet Rev — Ballet Review
Ball Roller Bear Eng — Ball and Roller Bearing Engineering
Ball & Roller Bear Engng — Ball and Roller Bearing Engineering
Ball State J — Ball State Journal for Business Educators
Ball St Uni — Ball State University Forum
BALM — Bollettino dell'Atlante Linguistico Mediterraneo
Balneol Pol — Balneologia Polska
Balneol Soc Japan Jour — Balneological Society of Japan. Journal
Bal R — Baltic Review
Ba LR — University of Baltimore. Law Review

Bal Sheet — Balance Sheet
Bal St — Balkan Studies
Baltimore B of Ed — Baltimore Bulletin of Education
Baltimore Mus Art N — Baltimore Museum of Art. News
Baltimore Mus N — Baltimore Museum of Art. News
Balwant Vidyapeeth J Agric Sci Res — Balwant Vidyapeeth Journal of Agricultural and Scientific Research
Balwant Vidyapeeth J Agr Sci Res — Balwant Vidyapeeth Journal of Agricultural and Scientific Research
BaM — Baghdader Mitteilungen [*Berlin*]
BAM — Buenos Aires Musical
BAM — Bulletin d'Archeologie Marocaine
BAMAB — Battery Man
BAMalgache — Bulletin. Academie Malgache
BAM Amtsbl Mitteilungsbl — BAM Berlin Amtsblatt und Mitteilungsblatt der Bundesanstalt fuer Materialpruefung
B Am Anth A — Bulletin. American Anthropological Association
BAM-Ber — BAM-Berichte. Forschung und Entwicklung in der Bundesanstalt fuer Materialpruefung
BAMEG — Bulletin Annuel. Musee d'Ethnographie de la Ville de Geneve
B Amer School Orient — Bulletin. American Schools of Oriental Research
B Am Hist Col — Bulletin. American Historical Collection
BAMIA — Bulletin. American Meteorological Society
BAmicEbrCr — Bolletino. Amicizia Ebraico-Cristiana di Firenze
B Am Math S — Bulletin. American Mathematical Society
B Am Meteor — Bulletin. American Meteorological Society
BAMOA — Bulletin. American Mathematical Society
B Am Pal — Bulletins of American Paleontology
B Am Phys S — Bulletin. American Physical Society
BAMRAM — Bulletin. Academie de Medecine de Roumanie
BAMS — Bulletin. American Mathematical Society
BAMS — Bulletin. American Musicological Society
B Am S Pap — Bulletin. American Society of Papyrologists
BAN — Banking Law Journal
BAN — Bulletin de l'Afrique Noire
Banach Center Publ — Banach Center. Publications [*Warsaw*]
Banaras Metall — Banaras Metallurgist
BANAZ — Boletin. Academia Aragonesa de Nobles y Bellas Artes de San Luis de Zaragoza
Banb Erev Hamal — Banber Erevani Hamalsarani-Vestnik Erevanskogo Universiteta
Banbury Rep — Banbury Report
Banca d'Italia Bol — Banca d'Italia. Bollettino
Banca Nazionale del Lavoro Q R — Banca Nazionale del Lavoro. Quarterly Review
Banca Naz Lav Quart R — Banca Nazionale del Lavoro. Quarterly Review
B Anc Lit — Bulletin d'Ancienne Litterature et d'Archeologie Chretienne
Banco Angola Bol Trim — Banco de Angola. Boletim Trimestral
Banco Brasil Bol Trim — Banco do Brasil. Boletim Trimestral
Banco Central Bolivia Bol Estadistico — Banco Central de Bolivia. Boletin Estadistico
Banco Nacl — Banco Nacional de Comercio Exterior, SA, Mexico. Annual Report
Banco Roma — Banco Roma. Review of the Economic Conditions in Italy
BANE — Bible and the Ancient Near East
BANGA — Bauingenieur
Bangabasi College Mag — Bangabasi College Magazine [*Calcutta*]
Bangabasi Morning College Mag — Bangabasi Morning College Magazine [*Calcutta*]
Bangalore Th F — Bangalore Theological Forum
Bangkok Bank Mo R — Bangkok Bank. Monthly Review
Bangkok R — Monthly Review (Bangkok)
Bangladesh Agr Sci Abstr — Bangladesh Agricultural Sciences Abstracts
Bangladesh Devel Stud — Bangladesh Development Studies
Bangladesh Geol Surv Rec — Bangladesh Geological Survey. Records
Bangladesh Hortic — Bangladesh Horticulture
Bangladesh J Agric Sci — Bangladesh Journal of Agricultural Sciences
Bangladesh J Anim Sci — Bangladesh Journal of Animal Sciences
Bangladesh J Biol Agric Sci — Bangladesh Journal of Biological and Agricultural Sciences
Bangladesh J Bot — Bangladesh Journal of Botany
Bangladesh J Sci & Ind Res — Bangladesh Journal of Scientific and Industrial Research
Bangladesh J Sci Ind Res — Bangladesh Journal of Scientific and Industrial Research
Bangladesh J Zool — Bangladesh Journal of Zoology
Bangladesh Med Res Counc Bull — Bangladesh Medical Research Council. Bulletin
Bangladesh Pharm J — Bangladesh Pharmaceutical Journal
Bangladesh Vet J — Bangladesh Veterinary Journal
Bangla Dev Stud — Bangladesh Development Studies
Bangla Hist Stud — Bangladesh Historical Studies
BANHQ — Boletin. Academia Nacional de la Historia (Quito)
Bank — Bankers' Magazine
Bank Admin — Magazine of Bank Administration
Bank-Betr — Bank-Betrieb

Bank Can R — Bank of Canada. Review
Bank England Q Bul — Bank of England. Quarterly Bulletin
Bank Eng QB — Bank of England. Quarterly Bulletin
Bank Eng Q Bull — Bank of England. Quarterly Bulletin
Banker-F — Banker-Farmer
Bankers J — Bankers' Journal
Bankers' M — Bankers' Magazine
Bankers M — Bankers' Monthly
Bankers' Mag — Bankers' Magazine
Bankers Mag A'sia — Bankers Magazine of Australasia
Bankers Mag Aust — Bankers Magazine of Australasia
Bankers Mag Australas — Bankers Magazine of Australasia
Bankers M Australasia — Bankers' Magazine of Australasia
Bankers' Mo — Bankers' Monthly
Bankers' Mon — Bankers' Monthly
Bank Finland Mo Bul — Bank of Finland. Monthly Bulletin
Bank Finland Mthly B — Bank of Finland. Monthly Bulletin
Banking Am Bankers Assn — Banking. American Bankers Association
Banking Law J — Banking Law Journal
Banking LJ — Banking Law Journal
Bank Law J — Banking Law Journal
Bank LJ — Banking Law Journal
Bank London South Amer R — Bank of London and South America. Review
Bank London and South Am R — Bank of London and South America. Review
Bank Mag — Bankers' Magazine
Bank Mag A/sia — Bankers' Magazine of Australasia
Bank M (L) — Bankers' Magazine (London)
Bank M (Lond) — Bankers' Magazine (London)
Bank M (NY) — Bankers' Magazine (New York)
Bank Montreal Bus R — Bank of Montreal. Business Review
Bank NSW R — Bank of New South Wales. Review
Bank of NSW R — Bank of New South Wales. Review
Bank NSW Re — Bank of New South Wales. Review
Bank NSW Rev — Bank of New South Wales. Review
Bankr L Rep — Bankruptcy Law Reports [*Commerce Clearing House*]
Bank Sudan Ec Fin Bull — Bank of Sudan. Economic and Financial Bulletin
Bank Sys — Bank Systems and Equipment
Bank Syst and Equip — Bank Systems and Equipment
Bank Thailand Mo Bul — Bank of Thailand. Monthly Bulletin
Bank Thailand Q Bul — Bank of Thailand. Quarterly Bulletin
BANLE — Boletin. Academia Norteamericana de la Lengua Espanola
Ban LJ — Banking Law Journal
BANMAC — Bulletin. Academie Nationale de Medecine [*Paris*]
B Annu Mus Ethnogr Geneve — Bulletin Annuel. Musee d'Ethnographie de la Ville de Geneve
BANQ — Biblionews and Australian Notes and Queries
Banque Centrale Etats Afr Ouest Notes Info et Statis — Banque Centrale des Etats de l'Afrique de l'Ouest. Notes d'Information et Statistiques
Banque Centrale Madagascar Bul Mensuel Statis — Banque Centrale de Madagascar. Bulletin Mensuel de Statistiques
Banque Fr Bul Trim — Banque de France. Bulletin Trimestriel
Banque Marocaine du Commerce Exterieur Mo Info R — Banque Marocaine du Commerce Exterieur. Monthly Information Review
Banque Nationale de Belgique Bul — Banque Nationale de Belgique. Bulletin
Banque Repub Burundi Bul Mensuel — Banque de la Republique du Burundi. Bulletin Mensuel
Banque Zaire Bul Trim — Banque du Zaire. Bulletin Trimestriel
Bansilal Amritlal Agric Coll Mag — Bansilal Amritlal Agricultural College. Magazine
Bansk Obz — Bansky Obzor
B Ant Fr — Bulletin. Societe Nationale des Antiquaires de France
B Anthropol Inst — Bulletin. Anthropological Institute [*Nagoya*]
Banyasz Kohasz Lap Banyasz — Banyaszati es Kohaszati Lapok. Banyaszat
Banyasz Kohasz Lapok — Banyaszati es Kohaszati Lapok
Banyasz Kohasz Lapok Banyasz — Banyaszati es Kohaszati Lapok. Banyaszat
Banyasz Kohasz Lapok Koeolaj Foeldgaz — Banyaszati es Kohaszati Lapok. Koeolaj es Foeldgaz
Banyasz Kohasz Lapok Kohasz — Banyaszati es Kohaszati Lapok. Kohaszat
Banyasz Kohasz Lapok Ontode — Banyaszati es Kohaszati Lapok. Ontode
Banyasz Kut Intez Kozl — Banyaszati Kutato Intezet Kozlemenyei
Banyasz Kut Intez Kozlem — Banyaszati Kutato Intezet Kozlemenyei [*Hungary*]
Banyasz Lapok — Banyaszati Lapok
BANYB — Banyaszat
BANZ Antarct Exped Rep Ser B — BANZ [*British-Australian-New Zealand*] Antarctic Research Expedition. Report. Series B
BAPBAN — Bulletin. Academie Polonaise des Sciences. Serie des Sciences Biologiques
BAPC — Bulletin. Academie Polonaise de Cracovie
BAPE — Boletim. Academia Portuguesa do Ex-Libris
BAPEL — Boletim. Academia Portuguesa do Ex-Libris
BAPI — Bollettino. Archivio Paleografico Italiano
BAPSA — Bulletin. American Physical Society
BAPSL — Bulletin. Academie Polonaise des Sciences et des Lettres
Bapt B — Baptist Bulletin

Bapt H Heri — Baptist History and Heritage
Bapt Hist and Heritage — Baptist History and Heritage
Bapt Q — Baptist Quarterly [*London*]
Bapt Q — Baptist Quarterly Review [*London*]
Bapt Ref R — Baptist Reformation Review
BAPXB — Baupraxis
BAQ — Barclays Review
Bar — Baretti
Bar — Barrister
BAR — Barron's
BAR — Biblical Archaeology Review
BAR — Biblioteca dell'Archivum Romanicum
BAR — Book Arts Review
BAR — Bulletin. Association des Amis de Rabelais et de la Deviniere
BARAB — Bulletin. Academie Royale d'Archeologie de Belgique
Barat R — Barat Review
BARB — Academie Royale de Belgique. Bulletin. Classe des Lettres et des Sciences Morales et Politiques et Classe des Beaux-Arts
BARB — Bulletin. Academie Royale de Belgique [*Brussels*]
Barbados Annu Rep Dep Sci Agric — Barbados. Annual Report. Department of Science and Agriculture
Barbados Nurs J — Barbados Nursing Journal
Bar Bull Boston — Bar Bulletin of the Boston Bar Association
Bar Bull (NY County Law A) — New York County Lawyers Association. Bar Bulletin
BArchAlex — Bulletin. Societe Archeologique d'Alexandrie
Barc Inst Invest Geol Publ — Barcelona. Instituto de Investigaciones Geologicas. Publicaciones
Barc Inst Prov Paleontol Actividades — Barcelona. Instituto Provincial de Paleontologia. Actividades
Barc Inst Prov Paleontol Bol Inf — Barcelona. Instituto Provincial de Paleontologia. Boletin Informativo [*Sabadell*]
Barc Inst Prov Paleontol Paleontol Evol — Barcelona. Instituto Provincial de Paleontologia. Paleontologia y Evolucion
Barclays R — Barclays Review
Barclays Rev — Barclays Review
Barc Univ Fac Cienc Misc Alcobe — Barcelona Universidad. Facultad de Ciencias. Miscellanea Alcobe
Barc Univ Inst Geol Mem Commun — Barcelona Universidad. Instituto Geologia. Memorias y Communicaciones
BARD — Bulletin. Association des Amis de Rabelais et de la Deviniere
BAREA — Bacteriological Reviews
BA Rev — Black Academy Review
Bar Exam — Bar Examiner
Bargaining Rep — Bargaining Report
Bar Gaz — Bar Gazette
BARIDN — Agricultural Research Council. Meat Research Institute [*Bristol*]. Biennial Report
BARLLF — Bulletin. Academie Royale de Langue et de Litterature Francaises
BARMAW — Bulletin. Academie Royale de Medecine de Belgique
Bar Mus Hist Soc J — Barbados Museum and Historical Society. Journal
B Arn — Bibliotheca Arnamagnaeana
Barnaul Gos Ped Inst Ucen Zap — Barnaul'skii Gosudarstvennyi Pedagogiceskii Institut. Ucenye Zapiski
Barn Nob Cr — Barnes and Noble Critical Study Series
Baroda J Nutr — Baroda Journal of Nutrition
Baroid News Bull — Baroid News Bulletin
Barossa Hist Bull — Barossa Historical Bulletin
BA/RRM — Biological Abstracts/Reports, Reviews, Meetings [*Formerly, BIOI*]
Barrow (W J) Res Lab Publ — Barrow (W. J.) Research Laboratory. Publication
Bartlett Tree Res Lab Bull — Bartlett Tree Research Laboratory. Bulletin
BAS — Bancaria
BAS — Bochumer Anglistische Studien
BAS — Bulletin of the Atomic Scientists
BAS — Business and Society
BASB — British Antarctic Survey. Bulletin
BASD — Bollettino di Archeologia e Storia Dalmata
BASD — British Antarctic Survey. Data
BASF Inf — BASF [*Badische Anilin- und Sodafabrik*] Information
BASF Rev — BASF [*Badische Anilin- und Sodafabrik*] Review
BASI — Bulletin. American Swedish Institute
B Asian Schol — Bulletin of Concerned Asian Scholars
BASIC — Bulletin. American Society for Information Science
Basic Appl Histochem — Basic and Applied Histochemistry
Basic Biol Color Ser — Basic Biology in Color Series
Basic Life Sci — Basic Life Sciences
Basic Pharmacol Ther — Basic Pharmacology Therapeutics [*Japan*]
Basic Rec Rep LA Dep Public Works — Basic Records Report. Louisiana Department of Public Works
Basic Rec Rep US Dep Inter Geol Surv — Basic Record Report. United States Department of Interior. Geological Survey
Basic Res Cardiol — Basic Research in Cardiology
BASIS — Bulletin. American Society for Information Science
Baskerville Chem J — Baskerville Chemical Journal

Baskir Gos Univ Ucen Zap — Baskirskii Gosudarstvennyi Universitet. Ucenye Zapiski
BASL — Bochumer Arbeiten zur Sprach- und Literaturwissenschaft
BASLAY — Bulletin. Academie et Societe Lorraines des Sciences
Basler Beitr Ethnol — Basler Beitraege zur Ethnologie
Basler Beitr Geogr — Basler Beitraege zur Geographie
Basler Z Gesch & Altertumsk — Basler Zeitschrift fuer Geschichte und Altertumskunde
BASM — Bollettino. Associazione per gli Studi Mediterranei
BASO — Bulletin. American Schools of Oriental Research in Jerusalem and Bagdad
BASOR — Bulletin. American Schools of Oriental Research
BASORSS — Bulletin. American Schools of Oriental Research. Supplementary Series
BASP — Bollettino. R. Accademia de Scienze, Lettere, e Belle Arti di Palermo
BASP — Bulletin. Academie de Science de St. Petersbourg
BASP — Bulletin. American Society of Papyrologists
BASPR — Bulletin. American School of Prehistoric Research
BASR — Bulletin. Academie des Sciences de Russie
Bas R Card — Basic Research in Cardiology
BASS — Beitraege zur Assyriologie und Semitischen Sprachwissenschaft
BAssBude — Bulletin. Association Guillaume Bude [*Paris*]
B Ass Geogr Franc — Bulletin. Association des Geographes Francais
B Assoc Cadres Dir Industr Progres Soc Econ — Bulletin. Association de Cadres Dirigeants de l'Industrie pour le Progres Social et Economique
BASSR — British Antarctic Survey. Scientific Reports
Bass Sound — Bass Sound Post
B Astr I Cz — Bulletin. Astronomical Institutes of Czechoslovakia
BASU — Balkan Studies
BASURSS — Bulletin. Academie des Sciences de l'URSS
BAT — Bataille
BAT — Boletin Arqueologico de Tarragona
Bateman E — Bateman Eichler and Hill Richards. Research Report
BATF — Boletin. Asociacion Tucumana de Folklore
Baths Bath Eng — Baths and Bath Engineering
Baths Serv Rec Mgmt — Baths Service and Recreation Management
Batim Int — Batiment International [*France*]
Batim Int Build Res Pract — Batiment International/Building Research and Practice
BATMA — Bulletin. Association Technique Maritime et Aeronautique
B Atom Sci — Bulletin of the Atomic Scientists
BATRA — Battelle Technical Review
Bat Res News — Bat Research News
Battelle Inf (Frankfurt) — Battelle Information (Frankfurt)
Battelle Mem Inst DCIC Rep — Battelle Memorial Institute. Defense Ceramic Information Center. DCIC Report
Battelle Mem Inst DMIC Memo — Battelle Memorial Institute. Defense Metals Information Center. DMIC Memorandum
Battelle Mem Inst DMIC Rep — Battelle Memorial Institute. Defense Metals Information Center. DMIC Report
Battelle Mg — Battelle Monographs
Battelle Res Outlook — Battelle Research Outlook
Battelle T — Battelle Today
Battelle Tech R — Battelle Technical Review
Battel R & D — Battelle Memorial Institute. Probable Levels of R and D Expenditures
Battery Mn — Battery Man
Bau Betr — Bau und Betrieb
B Auckland Inst Mus — Bulletin. Auckland Institute and Museum
Bauelem Elektrotech — Bauelemente der Elektrotechnik
Bauen Landwirtsch — Bauen fuer die Landwirtschaft
BAUGA — Buecherei des Augenarztes
Bauginia Z Basler Botan Ges — Bauginia. Zeitschrift. Basler Botanische Gesellschaft
Bauinf Wiss Tech — Bauinformation. Wissenschaft und Technik [*East Germany*]
Bauing Prax — Bauingenieur Praxis
BAUMA — Baumeister
Baumasch Bautech — Baumaschine und Bautechnik
BaumB — Baum Bugle: A Journal of Oz
Bauplanung Bautech — Bauplanung-Bautechnik
Baustoffind Ausg B — Baustoffindustrie. Ausgabe B. Bauelemente
Bautech-Arch — Bautechnik-Archiv
Bautechnik Ausg A — Bautechnik. Ausgabe A
Bauteile Rep — Bauteile Report
BAUVA — Bauverwaltung
Bau & Werk — Baukunst und Werkform
BAV — Boletin. Academia Venezolana
BAVED — Bayerische Verwaltungsblaetter
BAVFAV — Bulletin. Academie Veterinaire de France
BAW — Banco Central. Boletin Informativo [*Madrid*]
BAWOA — Bauen und Wohnen
BAW PHK — Bayerische Akademie der Wissenschaften. Philosophisch Historische Klasse. Sitzungsberichte
BAWS — Bayerische Akademie der Wissenschaften. Philosophisch Historische Klasse. Sitzungsberichte

BAWTA — Bauwelt
BAX — Management Facetten
Bax S — Arnold Bax Society. Bulletin
BAYED — Bayerland
Bayer Aerztebl — Bayerisches Aerzteblatt
Bayer Akad Wiss Jahrb — Bayerische Akademie der Wissenschaften. Jahrbuch
Bayer Akad Wiss Math-Natur Kl Abh — Bayerische Akademie der Wissenschaften. Mathematisch-Naturwissenschaftliche Klasse. Abhandlungen
Bayer Akad Wiss Math-Natur Kl Abh NF — Bayerische Akademie der Wissenschaften. Mathematisch-Naturwissenschaftliche Klasse. Abhandlungen. Neue Folge [*Munich*]
Bayer Akad Wiss Math-Natur Kl S-B — Bayerische Akademie der Wissenschaften. Mathematisch-Naturwissenschaftliche Klasse. Sitzungsberichte
Bayer Akad Wiss Math-Natur Kl Sitzungsber — Bayerische Akademie der Wissenschaften. Mathematisch-Naturwissenschaftliche Klasse. Sitzungsberichte
Bayer Akad Wiss Math-Naturw Abt Abh — Bayerische Akademie der Wissenschaften. Mathematisch-Naturwissenschaftliche Abteilung. Abhandlungen
Bayer Akad Wiss Math-Naturwiss Kl Abh — Bayerische Akademie der Wissenschaften. Mathematisch-Naturwissenschaftliche Klasse. Abhandlungen
Bayer Akad Wiss Math-Naturwiss Kl Sitzungsber — Bayerische Akademie der Wissenschaften. Mathematisch-Naturwissenschaftliche Klasse. Sitzungsberichte
Bayer Akad Wiss Philos-Hist Abt Abh — Bayerische Akademie der Wissenschaften. Philosophisch-Historische Abteilung. Abhandlungen
Bayer Akad d Wiss Philos-Philol u Hist Kl Abhandl — Bayerische Akademie der Wissenschaften. Philosophisch-Philologische und Historische Klasse. Abhandlungen
Bayer Color — Bayer Colorist
Bayer Farben Rev Spec Ed (USA) — Bayer Farben Revue. Special Edition (USA)
Bayerische Akad Wiss Jahrbuch — Bayerische Akademie der Wissenschaften. Jahrbuch
Bayer Landwirt Jahrb — Bayerisches Landwirtschaftliches Jahrbuch
Bayer Landwirtschaftsrat Vierteljahresschr — Bayerischer Landwirtschaftsrat Vierteljahresschrift
Bayer Landwirtsch Jahrb — Bayerisches Landwirtschaftliches Jahrbuch
Bayer Landwirtsch Jahrb Sonderh — Bayerisches Landwirtschaftliches Jahrbuch. Sonderheft
Bayer Landw Jb — Bayerisches Landwirtschaftliches Jahrbuch
Bayer Sitzb — Bayerische Akademie der Wissenschaften. Sitzungsberichte
Bayer Staatssaml Palaeontol Hist Geol Mitt — Bayerische Staatssammlung fuer Palaeontologie und Historische Geologie. Mitteilungen
Bayer Staatsztg Bayer Staatsanz — Bayerische Staatszeitung und Bayerischer Staatsanzeiger
Bayer-Symp — Bayer-Symposium
Bayer Verwaltungsbl — Bayerische Verwaltungsblaetter
Bayer Vorgeschbl — Bayerische Vorgeschichtsblaetter
Baylor Bus Studies — Baylor Business Studies
Baylor Geol Stud Bull — Baylor Geological Studies. Bulletin
Baylor Law — Baylor Law Review
Baylor Law R — Baylor Law Review
Baylor L Rev — Baylor Law Review
Baylor Nurs Educ — Baylor Nursing Educator
Bay LR — Baylor Law Review
Bayreuth Math Schr — Bayreuther Mathematische Schriften
Bay State Libn — Bay State Librarian
Bay State Mo — Bay State Monthly
Bay St Librn — Bay State Librarian
Bay Workr — Bay Area Worker
BAZTA — Bauzeitung
BB — Bayreuther Blaetter
B & B — Bench and Bar
BB — Bezzenbergers Beitraege
BB — Bibliographie de Belgique
BB — Biblische Beitraege
BB — Billboard
BB — Bonner Beitraege
BB — Books and Bookmen
B & B — Books and Bookmen
BB — Bossche Bijdragen
BB — British Business
BB — Bulletin of Bibliography
BB — Bulletin du Bibliophile et du Bibliothecaire
BBA — Berliner Byzantinistische Arbeiten
BBA — Biochimica et Biophysica Acta
BBAA — Boletin Bibliografico de Antropologia Americana
BBACA — Biochimica et Biophysica Acta
BBAE — Bulletin. Bureau of American Ethnology
BBA Libr — BBA [*Biochimica et Biophysica Acta*] Library
B Banque Nat Belgique — Bulletin. Banque Nationale de Belgique
B & Bar — Bench and Bar

B Bar — Bench and Bar
BBASA6 — Chung Yang Yen Chiu Yuan Chih Wu Hsueh Hui K'an
B Baud — Bulletin Baudelairien
BBB — Banque de France. Bulletin Trimestriel
BBB — Boletin de Bibliotecas y Bibliografia
BBB — Bonner Biblische Beitraege
BBB — Bulletin du Bibliophile et du Bibliothecaire
BBBMB — Biochimica et Biophysica Acta. Biomembranes
BBBNS — Biblioteca Bio-Bibliografica della Terra Santa. Nova Serie
BBBr — Boletim Bibliografico Brasileiro
BBBRD — BBR. Brunnenbau, Bau von Wasserwerken, Rohrleitungsbau
BB Bul — BB [*B'nai Brith in Australia*] Bulletin
BBCBB — Berichte Biochemie und Biologie
BBC Eng — BBC [*British Broadcasting Corporation*] Engineering
BBC Eng Div Monogr — BBC [*British Broadcasting Corporation*] Engineering Division. Monograph
BBCNA — BBC [*Brown, Boveri, und Cie.*] Nachrichten
BBC Nachr — BBC [*Brown, Boveri, und Cie.*] Nachrichten
BBCS — Bulletin. Board of Celtic Studies
BBDAA — Bulletin d'Information. Association Belge pour le Developpement Pacifique de l'Energie Atomique
B Bd Celt S — Bulletin. Board of Celtic Studies/Bwletin y Bwrdd Gwybodau Celtaidd
BBDI — Bulletin of Bibliography and Dramatic Index
BBEZA — Biochimica et Biophysica Acta. Enzymology
BBF — Bulletin des Bibliotheques de France
BBG — Basler Beitraege zur Geschichtswissenschaft
BBG — Blaetter fuer das Bayerische Gymnasial-Schulwesen
BBGG — Bollettino della Badia Greca di Grottaferrata
BBGSB — Biochimica et Biophysica Acta. General Subjects
BBH — Bulletin Analytique de Bibliographie Hellenique
BBH — Notities over Europa
BBHCD — Bangason Bango Hakhoe Chi
BBib — Beschreibende Bibliographien
BBibl — Bulletin du Bibliophile
BBICAW — BSBI [*Botanical Society of the British Isles*] Conference Reports
BBIJM — B'nai B'rith International Jewish Monthly
B Bimestr Soc Comptabil France — Bulletin Bimestriel. Societe de Comptabilite de France
BBJ — Boston Bar Journal
BBK — Bibliotekininkystes ir Bibliografijos Klausimai
BBK — Business Review (Bangkok)
BBKCA — Bruns' Beitraege zur Klinischen Chirurgie
BBKCA8 — Bruns' Beitraege zur Klinischen Chirurgie
BBKG — Beitraege zur Bayerischen Kirchengeschichte
Bbl — Biblica [*Rome*]
BBL — Biblioteksbladet
BBLA — Beitraege zur Biblischen Landes- und Altertumskunde
BBLAK — Beitraege zur Biblischen Landes- und Altertumskunde
BBLG — Basler Beitraege zur Deutschen Literatur- und Geistesgeschichte
BBM — Betriebs-Berater. Zeitschrift fuer Recht und Wirtschaft
BBM — Boletin Bibliografico Mexicano
BBM — Bulletin. Brooklyn Museum
BBMB — Bulletin Bibliographique. Musee Belge
BBMP — Boletin. Biblioteca de Menendez Pelayo
BBMPG — Baroda Museum and Picture Gallery. Bulletin
BBN — Berliner Beitraege zur Namenforschung
BBN — British Book News
BBNL — Boletin. Biblioteca National (Lima)
BBNM — Boletin. Biblioteca National (Mexico)
BBNPA — Biochimica et Biophysica Acta. Nucleic Acids and Protein Synthesis
BBOJ — Berks, Bucks, and Oxon. Archaeological Journal
BBP — Bank of Papua New Guinea. Quarterly Economic Bulletin
BBPAD — Bano Biggyan Patrika
BBPCA — Berichte. Bunsengesellschaft fuer Physikalische Chemie
BBPMAT — Buletin Balai Penelitian Perkebunan Bedan
BBPMB — Bulletin Bibliographique. Musee Belge
BBPTB — Biochimica et Biophysica Acta. Protein Structure
BBR — Beitraege zur Kenntnis der Babylonischen Religion
BBr — Books at Brown
BBR — Buletinul Bibliotecii Romane
BBRCA — Biochemical and Biophysical Research Communications
BBROA — Baender, Bleche, Rohre
BBRP — Berliner Beitraege zur Romanischen Philologie
B Br Psycho — Bulletin. British Psychological Society
BBS — Bulletin of Baltic Studies
BBSAJ — Bulletin. British School of Archaeology, Jerusalem [*1922-25, after 1927 included in PEFOS*]
BBSIA — Bulletin Bibliographique. Societe Internationale Arthurienne
BBSP — Botetourt Bibliographical Society. Publications
BBSPA — Biochimica e Biologia Sperimentale
BBST — Bibliotheque Bonaventurienne. Series "Textes"
BBT — Bulletin of Black Theatre
B Buddhist Cult Inst Ryukoku Univ — Bulletin. Buddhist Cultural Institute. Ryukoku University

BBude — Bulletin. Association Guillaume Bude [*Paris*]
BBY — Bankbedrijf en Effectenbedrijf
BBY — Britannica Book of the Year
BByzA — Berliner Byzantinistische Arbeiten. Deutsche Akademie der Wissenschaften zu Berlin
BByzI — Bulletin. Byzantine Institute
BBZ — Baylor Business Studies
BbZ — Biblische Zeitschrift
BC — Bibliographia Cartographica
BC — Bibliotheca Celtica
BC — Boletim Cultural. Camara Municipal do Porto
BC — Bollettino della Capitale
BC — Book Collector
BC — Brisbane Courier
B/C — Broadcasting
BC — Bulletin of the Comediantes
BC — Bulletin Critique
BC — Bulletin de Nos Communautes
BC — New South Wales Bankruptcy Cases
BCA — Blaetter fuer Christliche Archaeologie und Kunst
BCAC — Bollettino. Commissione Archeologica Comunale di Roma
BCACR — Bollettino. Commissione Archeologica Comunale di Roma
BC Admin — British Columbia Administrator
BCAM — Bulletin. Cercle Archeologique, Litteraire, et Artistique de Malines
BCAN — Bulletin. Commission Archeologique de Narbonne
BCANA — Bulletin. International Union Against Cancer
B Cancer — Bulletin du Cancer [*Paris*]
BCA News — BCA [*Business Committee for the Arts*] News
BCAR — Bollettino. Commissione Archeologica Comunale di Roma
BCARDD — Connecticut Arboretum Bulletin
BC Art Teach Assn J — British Columbia Art Teachers' Association. Journal
BCASSI News — British Columbia Association of School Supervisors of Instruction. News
Bcast — Broadcast [*United Kingdom*]
BCB — Boletin Cultural y Bibliografico [*Bogota*]
BCB — Brinkman's Cumulatieve Catalogus van Boeken in Nederland en Vlaanderen Uitgegeven of Herdrukt met Aanvullingen over Voorafgaande Jaren
BCBA — Academie Royale de Belgique. Bulletin. Classe des Beaux-Arts
BCBJ — Monthly Bulletin. Central Bank of Jordan
BCBL — Bulletin. Cercle Belge de Linguistique
BC Bus Ed Assn News — British Columbia Business Educators' Association. Newsletter
BCCCD — Biweekly Cryogenics Current Awareness Service
BCCCN — Bollettino. Commemorazione del XVI Centenario del Concilio di Nicea
BCCF — Bollettino Critico di Cose Francescane
BCCMP — Boletim Cultural. Camara Municipal do Porto
BC Couns — British Columbia Counsellor
BCD — Bank fuer Gemeinwirtschaft. Aussenhandelsdienst
BCD — Bankruptcy Court Decisions
BCD — Business Conditions Digest
BC Dep Mines Bull — British Columbia. Department of Mines. Bulletin
BC Dep Mines Non Met Miner Invest Rep — British Columbia. Department of Mines. Non Metallic Mineral Investigations Report
BC Dep Mines Pet Resour Bull — British Columbia. Department of Mines and Petroleum Resources. Bulletin
BC Dep Recreat Conserv Annu Rep — British Columbia. Department of Recreation and Conservation. Annual Report
BCDI — Bollettino della Carta dei Dialetti Italiani
BCE — Bulletin des Communautes Europeennes
BCECC — Bulletin de Cultures Ethniques et de Civilisations Comparees
BCEDLFB — Bulletin. Centre d'Etudes et de Discussion de Litterature Francaise. Universite de Bordeaux
BCELA — British Communications and Electronics
BC Engl Teach J — British Columbia English Teachers' Association. Journal
B Centre Docum Et Jur Econ Soc — Bulletin. Centre de Documentation d'Etudes Juridiques, Economiques, et Sociales
B Centre Europ Cult — Bulletin. Centre Europeen de la Culture
B Centre Inform Et Credit — Bulletin. Centre d'Information et d'Etude du Credit
BC Env Aff LR — Boston College. Environmental Affairs Law Review
BC Environ Aff Law R — Boston College. Environmental Affairs Law Review
BC Envtl Aff L Rev — Boston College. Environmental Affairs Law Review
BCER — Bank of China. Economic Review
B Ceram RA Spec Publ — British Ceramic Research Association. Special Publications
B Ceram RA Tech Note — British Ceramic Research Association. Technical Notes
BCESS — Bibliotheque des Centres d'Etudes Superieures Specialisees
BCETB — Bulletin d'Information. CETAMA
BCETCEHRS — Bibliotheque des Centres d'Etudes Superieures Specialisees. Travaux du Centre d'Etudes Superieures Specialisees d'Histoire de Religions de Strasbourg

BCF — Boletim Trimestral Subcomissao Catarinense de Folclore da Comissao Nacional Brasileira de Folclore do Instituto Brasileiro de Educacao, Ciencia, e Cultura
BCF — Business China
BCFF — Bulletin. Comite Flamand de France
BC For Serv Annu Rep — British Columbia. Forest Service. Annual Report
BC For Serv For Res Rev — British Columbia. Forest Service. Forest Research Review
BC For Serv Res Notes — British Columbia. Forest Service. Research Notes
BC For Serv Tech Publ — British Columbia. Forest Service. Technical Publication
BCGuineP — Boletim Cultural da Guine Portuguesa
BCH — Bulletin de Correspondance Hellenique
BCHAC — Bulletin. Cercle Historique et Archeologique de Courtrai
B Chem S J — Bulletin. Chemical Society of Japan
BC His Q — British Columbia Historical Quarterly
BCHS — Bulletin. Cincinnati Historical Society
BCH Supp — Bulletin de Correspondance Hellenique. Supplement
BCI — Nederlandse Chemische Industrie
BCIA — [A] Critical Introduction to the Apocrypha [L. H. Brockinton]
BCIIS — Bulletin. Christian Institutes of Islamic Studies
BC Ind Com'l L Rev — Boston College. Industrial and Commercial Law Review
BC Ind & Com L R — Boston College. Industrial and Commercial Law Review
BC Ind & Com L Rev — Boston College. Industrial and Commercial Law Review
BC Indus & Com L Rev — Boston College. Industrial and Commercial Law Review
BC Int'l and Comp LJ — Boston College. International and Comparative Law Journal
BC Int'l and Comp L Rev — Boston College. International and Comparative Law Review
BCIRA J — BCIRA [British Cast Iron Research Association] Journal
BCKGD — Backgrounder
BCLA Rept — BCLA [British Columbia Library Association] Reporter
BCLC — Bulletin. Cercle Linguistique de Copenhague
B Cleveland Mus Art — Bulletin. Cleveland Museum of Art
B Clev Mus — Bulletin. Cleveland Museum of Art
BCLF — Bulletin Critique du Livre Francais
BC Lib Q — British Columbia Library Quarterly
BCLQ — British Columbia Library Quarterly
BCL Rev — Boston College. Law Review
BCLRS — Building and Construction Legal Reporting Service
BCLSMP — Academie Royale de Belgique. Bulletin. Classe des Lettres et des Sciences Morales et Politiques
BC Lumberm — British Columbia Lumberman
BCM — Banque Centrale des Etats de l'Afrique de l'Ouest. Notes d'Information et Statistiques
BCM — Book Collector's Market
BCM — Buletinul. Comisiunii Monumentelor Istorice
BCMA — Bulletin. Cleveland Museum of Art
BCMB — Boletin. Comision de Monumentos de Burgos
BC Minist Agric Publ — British Columbia. Ministry of Agriculture. Publications
BC Minist Mines Pet Resour Annu Rep — British Columbia. Minister of Mines and Petroleum Resources. Annual Report
BCML — Boletin. Comision de Monumentos de Lugo
BCMSB — Bulletin. Calcutta Mathematical Society
BCMU — BC [British Columbia] Musher [Canada]
BCMV — Boletin. Comision de Monumentos de Valladolid
BCMVASA — Bulletin. Central Mississippi Valley American Studies Association
BC (Newspr) (Q) — Brisbane Courier Reports (Newspaper) (Queensland)
BC (NSW) — New South Wales Bankruptcy Cases
BCO — Bibliotheca Classica Orientalis
BCOD — BC [British Columbia] Outdoors [Canada]
BCol — Book Collector
B Co Leg J'nal — Beaver County Legal Journal [Pennsylvania]
B Com — Bulletin of the Comediantes
B Comediant — Bulletin of the Comediantes
BComEtSulp — Bulletin. Comite des Etudes. Compagnie de S. Sulpice [Paris]
B Commun Europ — Bulletin des Communautes Europeennes
BCON — British Commonwealth Occupation News
B Con As Sc — Bulletin of Concerned Asian Scholars
B Concern As Schol — Bulletin of Concerned Asian Scholars
B Concerned Asian Scholars — Bulletin of Concerned Asian Scholars
B Conjonct Region — Bulletin de Conjoncture Regionale
B Conjoncture Suppl — Bulletin de Conjoncture Regionale. Supplement
B Copyrgt S — Bulletin. Copyright Society of the USA
BCPAA — Beitraege zur Chemischen Physiologie und Pathologie
BCPCA — Biochemical Pharmacology
BCPCB7 — Buletinul de Cercetari Piscicole
BCPE — Bollettino. Centro Internazionale per lo Studio dei Papiri Ercolanesi [Cronache Ercolanesi] [Napoli]
BCPE — Bulletin. Centre Protestant d'Etudes
BCPEA — British Columbia Professional Engineer
BCPG — Bulletin of Canadian Petroleum Geology

BCPGA — Bulletin of Canadian Petroleum Geology
BCPHBM — British Journal of Clinical Pharmacology
BCPN — Boletin. Comision Provincial de Monumentos de Navarra
BCPO — Boletin. Comision Provincial de Monumentos de Orense
BCPOrense — Boletin. Comision Provincial de Monumentos de Orense
BCPPAB — Buletinul. Institutului de Cercetari si Proiectari Piscicole
BC Prof Eng — British Columbia Professional Engineer
BC Prov Mus Nat Hist Anthropol Handb — British Columbia Provincial Museum of Natural History and Anthropology. Handbook
BC Prov Mus Nat Hist Anthropol Rep — British Columbia Provincial Museum of Natural History and Anthropology. Report
BCPTA — British Chemical Engineering and Process Technology
BCQ — Book Collector's Quarterly
BCR — Bolletino. Commissione Archeologica Communale di Roma
BCr — Bulletin Critique du Livre Francais
BCRAA — Bulletin. Commissions Royales d'Art et d'Archeologie
BCRAD — BCRA [British Carbonization Research Association] Review
BCRA Rev — BCRA [British Carbonization Research Association] Review
BCRBD — Boletim. Casa Regional da Beira-Douro
BCRCA — Boletim. Comissao Reguladora de Cereais do Arquipelago dos Acores
BCREA — Bulletin. Centre de Recherches et d'Essais de Chatou
B & C Rec — Brick and Clay Record
BCRED — Bulletin. Centres de Recherches Exploration-Production ELF [Essences et Lubrifiants de France] - Aquitaine
BC Res — BC [British Columbia] Research
BC Res — British Columbia Research
BC Res Counc Annu Rep — British Columbia. Research Council. Annual Report
BC Res Counc Tech Bull — British Columbia. Research Council. Technical Bulletin
B C Res Mus — Bulletin. Council for Research in Music Education
BCRH — Bulletin. Commission Royale d'Histoire
BCRTD — Bulletin. Commission Royale de Toponymie et de Dialectologie
BCS — Bulletin of Chinese Studies
B CSAR Belg — Bulletin. Classe des Sciences. Academie Royale de Belgique
BCSCA — Bibliotheca Cardiologica (Switzerland)
BCSFLS — Bollettino. Centro di Studi Filologici e Linguistici Siciliani
BCSic — Bollettino. Centro di Studi Filologici e Linguistici Siciliani
BCSJA — Bulletin. Chemical Society of Japan
BCSLA R — BCSLA [British Columbia School Librarians' Association] Reviews
BCSO — Bollettino. Centro di Studi Onomastici [G. D. Serra]
BCSP — Bollettino. Centro di Studi di Poesia Italiana e Straniera [Roma]
BCSS — Bollettino. Centro di Studi Filologici e Linguistici Siciliani
BCST — BC [British Columbia] Studies [Canada]
BCSTA — Bulletin. Calcutta School of Tropical Medicine
BCSTB — Biochemical Society. Transactions
BCSV — Bollettino. Centro di Studi Vichiani
BCSYDM — Bristol-Myers Cancer Symposia
BCTD — Bulletin. Commission Royale de Toponymie et de Dialectologie
BCTF News — British Columbia Teachers' Federation. Newsletter
BCTH — Bulletin Archeologique. Comite des Travaux Historiques
BCTH — Bulletin. Comite des Travaux Historiques et Scientifiques
BCTKA — Bromatologia i Chemia Toksykologiczna
BCTKAG — Bromatologia i Chemia Toksykologiczna
BCTRD6 — Breast Cancer Research and Treatment
BCu — Boletim Cultural
BC Univ Dep Geol Rep — British Columbia University. Department of Geology. Report
BCURA — British Coal Utilisation Research Association. Monthly Bulletin
BCURA Gaz — BCURA [British Coal Utilization Research Association] Gazette
BCWL — Bulletin of Canadian Welfare Law
BC-X Can For Serv Pac For Res Cent — BC-X. Canadian Forestry Service. Pacific Forest Research Centre
BCYCD — BioCycle
BD — Bulletin du Cange
BDA — Bollettino d'Arte
Bd Agric and Fish Ann Rep Proc Dis Anim Acts (London) — Board of Agriculture and Fisheries. Annual Reports of Proceedings under the Diseases of Animals Acts (London)
BDAPC — Bulletin. Debating Association of Pennsylvania Colleges
BDASI — Bulletin. Department of Antiquities of the State of Israel
BDB — Borsenblatt fuer den Deutschen Buchhandel
BDBAD — Baumaschinendienst
BDBBDB — Departement de Biologie. College Bourget Rigaud. Bulletin
BDBHA — Boersenblatt fuer den Deutschen Buchhandel
BDC — Bulleti de Dialectologia Catalana
BDC — Bulletin. Deccan College Research Institute
BDCDA — Bulletin de Documentation. Centre d'Information du Chrome Dur
BDCGA — Berichte. Deutsche Chemische Gesellschaft
BDCNB — Bulletin. Centre de Compilation de Donnees Neutroniques
BDCSB — Building Design and Construction
BDE — Boletin de Dialectologia Espanola
BDEC — Bulletin. Department of English (Calcutta)

B Deccan Coll Res Inst — Bulletin. Deccan College Research Institute

B Dept Ag (Trinidad) — Bulletin. Department of Agriculture (Trinidad and Tobago)

B Dept Archaeol Anthropol — Bulletin. Department of Archaeology and Anthropology [*Taipei*]

B Dept Sociol (Okinawa) — Bulletin. Department of Sociology (Okinawa)

BDEVDI — Brain and Development

BdF — Boletim de Filologia

BDG — Scandinavian Economies. A Business Economic Report on Denmark, Finland, Norway, and Sweden

BDGAA — Bilten Dokumentacije

BDGAB — Boletin. Direccion General de Archivos y Bibliotecas

BDGHA — Bundesgesundheitsblatt

BDI — Beyond Infinity

BdI — Bullettino. Istituto di Corrispondenza Archeologica

BDial — Balgarska Dialektologija

BDIPD — Blaetter fuer Deutsche und Internationale Politik

B Divis Hum Relat — Bulletin. Division of Human Relations

BdJ — Barre du Jour

BDJOA — British Dental Journal

BDK — Beitraege zur Deutschen Klassik

BDKA — Beitraege zur Deutschen Klassik. Abhandlungen

BDKGA — Berichte. Deutsche Keramische Gesellschaft

BDL — Beleid en Maatschappij

BDLG — Blaetter fuer Deutsche Landesgeschichte

BDLIC — Bolleti del Diccionari de la Llengua Catlana

BDLM — Bibliographien zur Deutschen Literatur des Mittelalters

BDM — Bollettino del Domus Mazziniana

BDN — Bausteine zum Deutschen Nationaltheater

BDN — Bulletin d'Information. Office de Commercialisation

BDNKA — Busushchee Nauki

BDO — Business Eastern Europe

B Docum Prat Secur Soc Legisl Trav — Bulletin de Documentation Pratique de Securite Sociale et de Legislation du Travail

BDOGA — Bericht. Deutsche Ophthalmologische Gesellschaft

BDP — Beitraege zur Deutschen Philologie

BDPH — Blaetter fuer Deutsche Philosophie. Zeitschrift der Deutsche Philosophische Gesellschaft

BDR — Bedrijfsdocumentaire; Magazine op het Gebied van Praktisch Management

B Dr Tchecosl — Bulletin de Droit Tchecoslovaque

BDSekt — Bjulleten Dialektologiceskogo Sektora Instituta Russkogo Jazyka

BDSPU — Bollettino. Deputazione di Storia Patria per l'Umbria

Bd Trade Metropolitan Toronto J — Journal. Board of Trade of Metropolitan Toronto

BDVA — Beitraege zur Deutschen Volks- und Altertumskunde

BDW — Bulletin du Dictionnaire Wallon

BDZ — Business Europe. A Weekly Report to Managers. Europe, Middle-East, and Africa

BE — [*The*] Babylonian Expedition of the University of Pennsylvania. Series A: Cuneiform Texts

BE — Balgarski Ezik

BE — Basic Education

Be — Bealoideas

Be — Belgrade

BE — Business Economist

BEA — Boletin de Estudios Asturianos

BEA — Bulletin des Etudes Arabes

BEAD (Ankara Turkey) — Bati Edebiyatlari Arastirma Dergisi (Ankara, Turkey)

Bead J — Bead Journal

BEA J — Business Education Association of Metropolitan New York. Journal

BEAJA — BEAMA [*British Electrical and Allied Manufacturers Association*] Journal

BEAMA J — BEAMA [*British Electrical and Allied Manufacturers Association*] Journal

Bears Bluff Lab Prog Rep — Bears Bluff Laboratories. Progress Report

Beaufortia Ser Misc Publ Zool Mus Univ Amsterdam — Beaufortia Series of Miscellaneous Publications. Zoological Museum. University of Amsterdam

Beaux-Arts Inst Des Bul — Beaux-Arts Institute of Design. Bulletin

BEAV — Beaver [*Canada*]

Beaver — Beaver County Legal Journal [*Pennsylvania*]

Beaver County LJ — Beaver County Legal Journal [*Pennsylvania*]

Beaver County LJ (PA) — Beaver County Legal Journal (Pennsylvania)

BEBIM — Bulletin of Experimental Biology and Medicine

BEBMA — Byulleten' Eksperimental'noi Biologii i Meditsiny

BEBR — Bechtel Briefs

BEC — Bibliotheque de l'Ecole des Chartes

BEC — Boletim de Estudos Classicos

BECAN — Biomedical Engineering Current Awareness Notification

BECD — Behavioural Sciences and Community Development

BECh — Bibliotheque de l'Ecole des Chartes

BeCHS — Berks County Historical Society. Papers

Bechuanaland Prot Geol Surv Dep Miner Resour Rep — Bechuanaland Protectorate. Geological Survey Department. Mineral Resources Report

Beckacite Nachr — Beckacite Nachrichten

Beck Isoliertech — Beck Isoliertechnik

Beckman Bull — Beckman Bulletin

Beckman Instrum Inc Tech Rep — Beckman Instruments, Incorporated. Technical Report

Beckman Rep — Beckman Report

B Ecole Fr Ex Or — Bulletin. Ecole Francaise d'Extreme-Orient

B Econ Europe — Bulletin Economique pour l'Europe

B Econ Res — Bulletin of Economic Research

B Econ Soc Maroc — Bulletin Economique et Social du Maroc

BECRB — Beckman Report

BECSB — Bulletin. European Communities. Supplement

BECTA — Bulletin of Environmental Contamination and Toxicology

BEDBA — Berichte. Deutsche Botanische Gesellschaft

Bedfordshire Archaeol J — Bedfordshire Archaeological Journal

Bedi Kart — Bedi Karthlisa

Bedrijfsontwikkeling Ed Akkerbouw — Bedrijfsontwikkeling. Editie Akkerbouw. Maandblad voor Agrarische Produktie. Verwerking en Afzet

Bedrijfsontwikkeling Ed Tuinbouw — Bedrijfsontwikkeling. Editie Tuinbouw

Bedrijfsontwikkeling Ed Veehouderij — Bedrijfsontwikkeling. Editie Veehouderij

BEDS — Beitraege zur Erforschung der Deutschen Sprache

BEE — Berichten over de Buitenlandse Handel

BEE — Bulletin of Environmental Education

Beef Cattle Sci Handb — Beef Cattle Science Handbook

Beef Res Rep — Beef Research Report

Beef Res Rep (Bur Agric Econ) — Beef Research Report (Bureau of Agricultural Economics)

Bee Genet Inf Bull — Bee Genetics Information Bulletin

BEEIA — Edison Electric Institute. Bulletin

Beekeep A — Bee-Keeping Annual

Beekeep Div Leafl (Tanganyika) — Beekeeping Division Leaflet. Forest Department (Tanganyika)

Beekeep Inf Coop Ext Serv (Ohio) — Beekeeping Information. Cooperative Extension Service (Ohio)

Beekeep (QD) — Beekeeping (Queensland)

Bee Kingdom Leafl — Bee Kingdom Leaflet

Beekprs Bull — Beekeepers Bulletin

Beekprs Mag — Bee-Keepers Magazine

Beekprs News — Bee-Keepers News

Beekprs Rec — Bee-Keepers Record

BEEMA — Association des Ingenieurs Electriciens Sortis de l'Institut Electrotechnique Montefiore. Bulletin

BEENA — Bergbau und Energiewirtschaft

BeethovenJb — Beethoven-Jahrbuch

Bee Wld — Bee World

BEF — Bank of England. Quarterly Bulletin

BEF — Boletin Eclesiastico de Filipinas

BEF — Bulletin des Etudes Francaises

BEFAR — Bibliotheque des Ecoles Francaises d'Athenes et de Rome

BEFEO — Bulletin. Ecole Francaise d'Extreme-Orient

BEFPA — Bollettino. Istituto di Entomologia Agraria e Osservatorio di Fitopatologia di Palermo

BEFT — Beaufort. Dome Petroleum Ltd.

BEG — Belgische Kleding

BEG — Boletin de Estudios Germanicos

BEGAA — Bergbau-Archiv

BEGBA — Bulletin. Eidgenoessisches Gesundheitsamt. Beilage B

BEGHA — Bulletin of Engineering Geology and Hydrogeology [*English Translation*] [*Yugoslavia*]

BEGIA — Bulletin. Institution of Engineers (India)

BEGMA — Beitraege zur Gerichtliche Medizin

BEGOA — Gerlands Beitraege zur Geophysik

BEGUB — Bulletin EGU

Behav — Behaviour

Behav Biol — Behavioral Biology

Behav Brain Res — Behavioural Brain Research

Behav Ecol Sociobiol — Behavioral Ecology and Sociobiology

Behav Genet — Behavior Genetics

Behav and Inf Technol — Behaviour and Information Technology

Behavioral Bio — Behavioral Biology

Behavioral Sci — Behavioral Science

Behavioral & Social Sci Libn — Behavioral and Social Sciences Librarian

Behavior Sci Notes — Behavior Science Notes

Behavior Ther — Behavior Therapy

Behaviour Inf Tech — Behaviour and Information Technology

Behaviour Res & Ther — Behaviour Research and Therapy

Behav Modif — Behavior Modification

Behav Neural Biol — Behavioral and Neural Biology

Behav Neuropsychiatry — Behavioral Neuropsychiatry

Behav Processes — Behavioural Processes

Behav Psychother — Behavioural Psychotherapy

Behav Res M — Behavior Research Methods and Instrumentation

Behav Res Methods Instrum — Behavior Research Methods and Instrumentation

Behav Res Methods & Instrum — Behavior Research Methods and Instrumentation
Behav Res T — Behaviour Research and Therapy
Behav Res Ther — Behaviour Research and Therapy
Behav Sci — Behavioral Science
Behav Sci Com Dev — Behavioural Sciences and Community Development
Behav Sci Community Develop — Behavioural Sciences and Community Development
Behav Sci N — Behavior Science Notes
Behav Sci R — Behavior Science Research
Behav and Soc Sci Libr — Behavioral and Social Sciences Librarian
Behav Soc Sci Libr — Behavioral and Social Sciences Librarian
Behav Ther — Behavior Therapy
Behav Today — Behavior Today
BEHE — Bibliotheque de l'Ecole des Hautes Etudes Belfagor
BEHMA — Berg- und Huettenmaennische Monatshefte. Montanistische Hochschule in Leoben
Behring Inst Mitt — Behring Institute Mitteilungen [*West Germany*]
Behringwerk Mitt — Behringwerk Mitteilungen
BEHSA — Behavioral Science
Bei — Beiblatt zur Anglia
BEI — Benefits International
BEI — British Education Index [*Bibliographic database*] [*British Library*]
BEI — Review of the Economic Conditions in Italy
Beibl — Beiblatt zur Anglia
Beibl Ann Phys — Beiblaetter zu den Annalen der Physik
Beiblatt — Beiblatt zur Anglia
Beih Ber Naturhist Ges Hannover — Beihefte. Berichten der Naturhistorischen Gesellschaft zu Hannover
Beihefte Arch Schiffs- u Tropen-Hyg — Beihefte. Archiv fuer Schiffs und Tropen-Hygiene
Beihefte Elem Math — Beihefte. Zeitschrift Elemente der Mathematik
Beih Int Z Vitam-Ernaehrungsforsch — Beiheft. Internationale Zeitschrift fuer Vitamin- und Ernaehrungsforschung
Beih Schweiz Bienenztg — Beihefte. Schweizerische Bienenzietung
Beih Sydowia Ann Mycol Ser II — Beihefte. Sydowia Annales. Mycologici. Ser II
Beih Tueb Atlas Vorderen Orients Reihe A Naturwiss — Beihefte. Tuebinger Atlas des Vorderen Orients. Reihe A. Naturwissenschaft
Beih Zentralbl Gewerbehyg Unfallverhuet — Beihefte. Zentralblatt fuer Gewerbehygiene und Unfallverhuetung
Beih Z Schweiz Forstver — Beiheft. Zeitschriften des Schweizerischen Forstvereins
Beijing R — Beijing Review
BEIND — Beratende Ingenieure
Beispiele Angew Forsch Fraunhofer Ges Foerd Angew Forsch — Beispiele Angewandter Forschung. Fraunhofer Gesellschaft zur Foerderung der Angewandten Forschung
Beitr — Beitraege zur Geschichte der Deutschen Sprache und Literatur [*Halle*]
Beitraege Algebra Geom — Beitraege zur Algebra und Geometrie
Beitraege Anal — Beitraege zur Analysis
Beitraege Gesch Buchw — Beitraege zur Geschichte des Buchwesens
Beitraege Namen — Beitraege zur Namenforschung
Beitraege Numer Math — Beitraege zur Numerischen Mathematik
Beitrage Bf — Beitraege zur Aegyptischen Bauforschung und Altertumskunde [*Cairo*]
Beitr Agrarwiss — Beitraege zur Agrarwissenschaft
Beitr Biol Pfl — Beitraege zur Biologie der Pflanzen
Beitr Biol Pflanz — Beitraege zur Biologie der Pflanzen
Beitr Chem Physiol Pathol — Beitraege zur Chemischen Physiologie und Pathologie [*West Germany*]
Beitr Datenverarb Unternehmensforsch — Beitraege Datenverarbeitung und Unternehmensforschung
Beitr Deutsch Volks Altertumskunde — Beitraege zur Deutschen Volks- und Altertumskunde
Beitr Engl u Nordamerikas — Beitraege zur Erforschung der Sprache und Kultur Englands und Nordamerikas
Beitr Ent — Beitraege zur Entomologie
Beitr Entomol — Beitraege zur Entomologie
Beitr Entwicklungsmech Anat Pflanz — Beitraege zur Entwicklungsmechanischen Anatomie der Pflanzen
Beitr Forschungstech — Beitraege zur Forschungstechnologie [*Berlin*]
Beitr Forschungstechnol — Beitraege zur Forschungstechnologie
Beitr Forstwirtsch — Beitraege fuer die Forstwirtschaft [*West Germany*]
Beitr Geobot Landesaufn Schweiz — Beitraege Geobotanischen Landesaufnahme der Schweiz
Beitr Geol Karte Schweiz — Beitraege zur Geologischen Karte der Schweiz
Beitr Geol Schweiz Geotech Ser — Beitraege zur Geologie der Schweiz. Geotechnische Serie
Beitr Geol Schweiz Kleinere Mitt — Beitraege zur Geologie der Schweiz. Kleinere Mitteilungen
Beitr Geol Thueringen — Beitraege zur Geologie von Thueringen
Beitr Geoph — Beitraege zur Geophysik
Beitr Geophysik — Beitraege zur Geophysik
Beitr Gerichtl Med — Beitraege zur Gerichtlichen Medizin

Beitr Gesch Dtsch Sprache — Beitraege zur Geschichte der Deutschen Sprache und Literatur
Beitr Gesch Pharm — Beitraege zur Geschichte der Pharmazie
Beitr Gesch Pharm Ihrer Nachbargeb — Beitraege zur Geschichte der Pharmazie und Ihrer Nachbargebiete
Beitr Gesch Univ Erfurt — Beitraege zur Geschichte der Universitaet Erfurt
BeitrHistTh — Beitraege zur Historischen Theologie [*Tuebingen*]
Beitr Hyg Epidemiol — Beitraege zur Hygiene und Epidemiologie
Beitr Infusionsther Klin Ernaehr — Beitraege zur Infusionstherapie und Klinische Ernaehrung
Beitr Klin Chir — Beitraege zur Klinischen Chirurgie
Beitr Klin Erforsch Tuberk Lungenkr — Beitraege zur Klinik und Erforschung der Tuberkulose und der Lungenkrankheiten
Beitr Klin Tuberk Spezif Tuber-Forsch — Beitraege zur Klinik der Tuberkulose und Spezifischen Tuberkulose-Forschung
Beitr Konfl — Beitraege zur Konfliktforschung
Beitr Konfliktforsch — Beitraege zur Konfliktforschung
Beitr Kryptogamenflora Schweiz — Beitraege zur Kryptogamenflora der Schweiz
Beitr Krystallogr Mineral — Beitraege zur Krystallographie und Mineralogie
Beitr z Land u Volk v Elsass-Loth — Beitraege zur Landes und Volkeskunde von Elsass-Lothringen
Beitr Math Informatik Nachrichtentech — Beitraege zur Mathematik, Informatik, und Nachrichtentechnik
Beitr Math-Naturwiss Unterr — Beitraege zum Mathematisch-Naturwissenschaftlichen Unterricht
Beitr Meer — Beitraege zur Meereskunde
Beitr Mineralogie u Petrographie — Beitraege zur Mineralogie und Petrographie
Beitr Miner Petrogr — Beitraege zur Mineralogie und Petrographie
Beitr Musik — Beitraege zur Musikwissenschaft
BeitrMw — Beitraege zur Musikwissenschaft [*DDR*]
Beitr Naturkd Forsch Suedwestdtsch — Beitraege zur Naturkundlichen Forschung in Suedwestdeutschland
Beitr Naturkd Forsch Suedwestdtsch Beih — Beitraege zur Naturkundlichen Forschung in Suedwestdeutschland. Beihefte
Beitr Naturkd Niedersachsens — Beitraege zur Naturkunde Niedersachsens
Beitr Naturk Forsch Suedwdtl — Beitraege zur Naturkundlichen Forschung in Suedwestdeutschland
Beitr Neotrop Fauna — Beitraege zur Neotropischen Fauna
Beitr Neurochir — Beitraege zur Neurochirurgie
Beitr Numer Math — Beitraege zur Numerischen Mathematik
Beitr Onkol — Beitraege zur Onkologie
Beitr Orthop Traumatol — Beitraege zur Orthopaedie und Traumatologie
Beitr Path — Beitraege zur Pathologie
Beitr Path Anat u Allg Path — Beitraege zur Pathologischen Anatomie und zur Allgemeinen Pathologie
Beitr Pathol — Beitraege zur Pathologie
Beitr Pathol Anat Allg Pathol — Beitraege zur Pathologischen Anatomie und zur Allgemeinen Pathologie
Beitr Phys Atmos — Beitraege zur Physik der Atmosphaere
Beitr Plasmaphys — Beitraege aus der Plasmaphysik
Beitr Pl Physik — Beitraege aus der Plasmaphysik
Beitr Radioastron — Beitraege zur Radioastronomie
Beitr Rheumatol — Beitraege zur Rheumatologie
Beitr Sexualforsch — Beitraege zur Sexualforschung
Beitr Silikose-Forsch — Beitraege zur Silikose-Forschung
Beitr Silikose-Forsch (Pneumokoniose) — Beitraege zur Silikose-Forschung (Pneumokoniose)
Beitr Silikose-Forsch Sonderb — Beitraege zur Silikose-Forschung. Sonderband
Beitr Tabakforsch — Beitraege zur Tabakforschung
Beitr Tabakforsch Int — Beitraege zur Tabakforschung International
Beitr Trop Landwirtsch Veterinaermed — Beitraege zur Tropischen Landwirtschaft und Veterinaermedizin
Beitr Trop Subtrop Landwirtsch Tropenveterinaermed — Beitraege zur Tropischen und Subtropischen Landwirtschaft und Tropenveterinaermedizin
Beitr Vogelkd — Beitraege zur Vogelkunde
Beitr Wuerttemb Apothekengesch — Beitraege zur Wuerttembergischen Apothekengeschichte
Be Jb — Beethoven-Jahrbuch
BEJUA — Behavioral Engineering
Beke es Szocial — Beke es Szocializmus
BEKOA — Berichte. Gesellschaft fuer Kohlentechnik
BEL — Balgarski Ezik i Literatura
Bel — Belfagor
BEL — Bell Journal of Economics
BEL — Mededelingen. Verbond van Belgische Ondernemingen
Belarusk Med Dumka — Belaruskaia Medychnaia Dumka
Beleid en Mij — Beleid en Maatschappij
Belg Apic — Belgique Apicole
Belg Econ — Belgium. Economic and Technical Information. English Edition
Belg E & T — Belgium Economy and Technique
Belgian R Internat Law — Belgian Review of International Law
Belgicatom Bull — Belgicatom Bulletin [*Belgium*]

Belgicatom Bull Inf — Belgicatom Bulletin d'Information
Belg Inst Verbetering Beit Driemaand Publ — Belgisch Institut tot Verbetering van de Beit Driemaandelijkse Publikatie
Belgique Med — Belgique Medicale
Belg Memo — Business Memo from Belgium
Belg Ned Tijdschr Oppervlatke Tech Met — Belgisch-Nederlands Tijdschrift voor Oppervlatketechnieken van Metalen
Belg Plast — Belgian Plastics
Belgra — Belgravia
Belg Rev — Belgian American Trade Review
Belg Serv Geol Mem — Belgium. Service Geologique. Memoire
Belg Serv Geol Prof Pap — Belgium. Service Geologique. Professional Paper
Belg Tijdschr Geneeskd — Belgisch Tijdschrift voor Geneeskunde
Belg Tijdschr Radiol — Belgisch Tijdschrift voor Radiologie
Belg Tijdschr Reumatol Fys Geneeskd — Belgisch Tijdschrift voor Reumatologie en Fysische Geneeskunde
Bel L — Belaruskaja Linhvistyka
BELL — Bulletin. Societe des Etudes de Lettres (Lausanne)
Belle Glade AREC Res Rep EV Fla Univ Agric Res Educ Cent — Belle Glade AREC. Research Report EV. Florida University. Agricultural Research and Education Center
Belleten — Belleten Tuerk Tarih Kurumu
Belle W Baruch Libr Mar Sci — Belle W. Baruch Library in Marine Science
Bell J Econ — Bell Journal of Economics
Bell J Econ Manage Sci — Bell Journal of Economics and Management Science [Later, Bell Journal of Economics]
Bell J Econ and Manage Sci — Bell Journal of Economics and Management Science [Later, Bell Journal of Economics]
Bell J Econom — Bell Journal of Economics
Bell Lab Re — Bell Laboratories Record
Bell Lab Rec — Bell Laboratories Record
Bell System Tech J — Bell System Technical Journal
Bell Syst T — Bell System Technical Journal
Bell Syst Tech J — Bell System Technical Journal
Bell Telephone Mag — Bell Telephone Magazine
Bell Teleph Syst Tech Publ Monogr — Bell Telephone System. Technical Publications. Monographs
Beloit — Beloit Poetry Journal
Beloit Poet — Beloit Poetry Journal
Beloruss Nauchno Issled Inst Melior Vodn Khoz Tr — Belorusskii Nauchno-Issledovatel'skii Institut Melioratsii i Vodnogo Khozyaistva. Trudy
Beloruss Nauchno Issled Kozhno Venerol Inst Sb Nauchn Tr — Belorusskii Nauchno-Issledovatel'skii Kozhno-Venerologicheskii Institut. Sbornik Nauchnykh Trudov
Bel Po J — Beloit Poetry Journal
BELR — Bell Laboratories Record
Beltsville Symp Agric Res — Beltsville Symposia in Agricultural Research
BEM — Bulletin Economique et Social du Maroc
BEMBA — Boletin de Estudios Medicos y Biologicos
BEMID — Bulletin. Electron Microscope Society of India
BEMTA — Berliner und Muenchener Tieraerztliche Wochenschrift
Ben — Benedictina
BEN — Benelux
BEn — Black Enterprise
Bench & B — Bench and Bar
Bench and B Minn — Bench and Bar of Minnesota
Benchmark Pap Energy — Benchmark Papers on Energy
Benchmark Papers Electrical Engrg Comput Sci — Benchmark Papers in Electrical Engineering and Computer Science
Benchmark Pap Opt — Benchmark Papers in Optics
Bendix Tech J — Bendix Technical Journal
Benelux (The Hague) — Union Economique Benelux (The Hague)
Bengal Agric J — Bengal Agricultural Journal
Bengal Public Health J — Bengal Public Health Journal
Bengal Vet — Bengal Veterinarian
Benin R — Benin Review
BENPD — Building Energy Progress
BENSD — Biomass Energy Institute. Newsletter
B Ent — Black Enterprise
Bentley — Bentley's Miscellany
Bent Q — Bentley's Quarterly Review
B Ent Res — Bulletin of Entomological Research
B Envir Con — Bulletin of Environmental Contamination and Toxicology
Benzole Dig — Benzole Digest
Benzole Prod Ltd Inf Circ — Benzole Producers Limited. Information Circular
Benzole Prod Ltd Res Pap — Benzole Producers Limited. Research Paper
BEO — Bulletin d'Etudes Orientales
BEOD — Bulletin d'Etudes Orientales (Damascus)
Beor — Queensland Law Reports (Beor)
BEP — Beitraege zur Englischen Philologie
BEP — Bulletin des Etudes Parnassiennes
BEP — Bulletin des Etudes Portugaises et de l'Institut Francais au Portugal
BEPFA — Beitraege zur Biologie der Pflanzen
BEPh — Beitraege zur Englischen Philologie
BEPIF — Bulletin des Etudes Portugaises et de l'Institut Francais au Portugal
BEPRD — Bulletin Europeen de Physiopathologie Respiratoire

BEQB — Bank of England. Quarterly Bulletin
Ber — Berichte. Deutsche Chemische Gesellschaft
BeR — Berkeley Review
BER — Bulletin of Economic Research
Ber Abwassertech Ver — Berichte. Abwassertechnische Vereinigung
Ber Afd Trop Prod K Inst Trop — Berichten. Afdeling Tropische Producten van het Koninklijke Institut ? por de Tropen
Ber Akad Wiss Wien — Sitzungsberichte. Akademie der Wissenschaften in Wien
Ber Alg Proefst AVROS — Bericht van het Algemeen Proefstation der AVROS
Ber Arbeitsgem Ferromagn — Berichte. Arbeitsgemeinschaft Ferromagnetismus
Ber Arbeitsgem Saechs Bot — Berichte. Arbeitsgemeinschaft Saechsischer Botaniker
Ber Arbeitstag Arbeitsgem Saatzuchtleiter — Bericht. Arbeitstagung der Arbeitsgemeinschaft der Saatzuchtleiter
Beratende Ing — Beratende Ingenieure [West Germany]
Ber Bayer Bot Ges Erforsch Heim Flora — Berichte. Bayerische Botanische Gesellschaft zur Erforschung der Heimischen Flora
Ber Biochem Biol — Berichte Biochemie und Biologie
Ber Bun Ges — Berichte. Bunsengesellschaft fuer Physikalische Chemie
Ber Bunsen Ges — Berichte. Bunsengesellschaft fuer Physikalische Chemie
Ber Bunsenges Phys Chem — Berichte. Bunsengesellschaft fuer Physikalische Chemie
Berc — Berceo
Ber Deu Bot — Berichte. Deutsche Botanische Gesellschaft
Ber Deut Ausschusses Stahlbau — Berichte. Deutscher Ausschuss fuer Stahlbau
Ber Deut Bot Ges — Berichte. Deutsche Botanische Gesellschaft
Ber Deut Chem Ges — Berichte. Deutsche Chemische Gesellschaft
Ber Deut Keram Gesell — Berichte. Deutsche Keramische Gesellschaft
Ber Deut Wetterdienst — Berichte. Deutscher Wetterdienst
Ber Dt Bot Ges — Berichte. Deutsche Botanische Gesellschaft
Ber Dt Chem Ges — Berichte. Deutsche Chemische Gesellschaft
Ber Dtsch Bot Ges — Berichte.Deutsche Botanische Gesellschaft
Ber Dtsch Chem Ges — Berichte. Deutsche Chemische Gesellschaft [West Germany]
Ber Dtsch Chem Ges A — Berichte. Deutsche Chemische Gesellschaft. Abteilung A. Vereins Nachrichten
Ber Dtsch Chem Ges B — Berichte. Deutsche Chemische Gesellschaft. Abteilung B. Abhandlungen
Ber Dtsch Ges Geol Wiss Reihe A — Berichte. Deutsche Gesellschaft fuer Geologische Wissenschaften. Reihe A. Geologie und Palaeontologie
Ber Dtsch Ges Geol Wiss Reihe B — Berichte. Deutsche Gesellschaft fuer Geologische Wissenschaften. Reihe B. Mineralogie und Lagerstaettenforschung
Ber Dtsch Ges Holzforsch — Bericht. Deutsche Gesellschaft fuer Holzforschung
Ber Dtsch Keram Ges — Berichte. Deutsche Keramische Gesellschaft
Ber Dtsch Landeskd — Bericht zur Deutschen Landeskunde
Ber Dtsch Ophthalmol Ges — Bericht. Deutsche Ophthalmologische Gesellschaft.[West Germany]
Ber Dtsch Pharm Ges — Berichte. Deutsche Pharmazeutische Gesellschaft
Ber Dtsch Phys Ges — Berichte. Deutsche Physikalische Gesellschaft
Ber Dtsch Wetterdienstes — Berichte. Deutscher Wetterdienst
Ber Dtsch Wiss Komm Meeresforsch — Berichte. Deutscher Wissenschaftliche Kommission fuer Meeresforschung
Ber D W Meer — Berichte. Deutsche Wissenschaftliche Kommission fuer Meeresforschung
Berdyanskii Opytn Neftemaslozavod Tr — Berdyanskii Opytnyi Neftemaslozavod. Trudy
BEREA — Bulletin of Entomological Research
Ber Eidg Anst Forstl Versuchswes — Berichte. Eidgenoessische Anstalt fuer das Forstliche Versuchswesen
Ber Ernst-Mach-Inst — Bericht. Ernst-Mach-Institut [Freiburg]
Beret Faellesudvalget Statens Planteavls- Husdyrbrugsfors — Beretning fra Faellesudvalget foer Statens Planteavls- og Husdyrbrugsforsog
Beret Forsogslab — Beretning fra Forsogslaboratoriet
Beretn Statsfrokontr (Denmark) — Beretning fra Statsfrokontrollen (Denmark)
Beret Statens Forogsmejeri — Beretning fra Statens Forogsmejeri
Beret Statens Husdyrbrugsfors — Beretning fra Statens Husdyrbrugsforsog
Ber Fachausschuesse Dtsch Glastech Ges — Berichte der Fachausschuesse. Deutsche Glastechnische Gesellschaft
Ber Forschungsinst Cech Zuckerind Prag — Bericht. Forschungsinstitut der Cechoslavakischen Zuckerindustrie in Prag
Ber Forschungsinst Zuckerind Boehm Machren Prag — Bericht. Forschungsinstitut der Zuckerindustrie fuer Boehmen und Machren in Prag
Berg — Bergonum
BERGA — Bergakademie
Bergbau-Arch — Bergbau-Archiv [West Germany]
Bergbau Energiewirtsch — Bergbau und Energiewirtschaft [West Germany]
Bergbau Rohst Energ — Bergbau Rohstoffe Energie
Bergbau Rundsch — Bergbau Rundschau
Bergbau Wirtsch — Bergbau und Wirtschaft
Bergbauwiss — Bergbauwissenschaften

Bergbauwissen Verfahrenstech Bergbau Huettenwes — Bergbauwissenschaften und Verfahrenstechnik im Bergbau und Huettenwesen
Bergbauwiss Verfahrenstech Bergbau Huettenwes — Bergbauwissenschaften und Verfahrenstechnik im Bergbau und Huettenwesen
BERGD — Bergbau
Bergens Mus Arbok Naturvitensk Rekke — Bergens Museums. Aarbok. Naturvitenskapelig Rekke
Bergens Mus Skr — Bergens Museums. Skrifter
Ber Geobot Forschungsinst Ruebel Zuerich — Bericht. Geobotanische Forschungsinstitut Ruebel in Zuerich
Ber Geobot Inst Eidg Tech Hochsch Stift Ruebel Zuer — Berichte. Geobotanische Institute der Eidgoessischen Technischen Hochschule Stiftung Ruebel Zuerich
Ber Geobot Inst Eidg Tech Hochsch Stift Ruebel Zuerich — Berichte. Geobotanische Institut der Eidgenoessischen Technischen Hochschule Stiftung Ruebel Zuerich
Ber Geol Ges DDR Gesamtgeb Geol Wiss — Berichte. Geologische Gesellschaft in der Deutschen Demokratischen Republik fuer das Gesamtgebiet der Geologischen Wissenschaft
Ber Geol Ges Dtsch Repub Gesamtgeb Geol Wiss — Berichte. Geologische Gesellschaft in der Deutschen Demokratischen Republik fuer das Gesamtgebiet der Geologischen Wissenschaft [*East Germany*]
Ber Gesamte Physiol Exp Pharmakol — Berichte ueber die Gesamte Physiologie und Experimentelle Pharmakologie
Ber Ges Inn Med DDR — Bericht. Gesellschaft fuer Innere Medizin der Deutschen Demokratischen Republik
Ber Ges Kohlentech — Berichte. Gesellschaft fuer Kohlentechnik [*East Germany*]
Ber Getreidechem-Tag (Detmold) — Bericht ueber die Getreidechemiker-Tagung (Detmold) [*West Germany*]
Ber Getreidetag (Detmold) — Bericht ueber die Getreidetagung (Detmold)
Berg Heuttenmaenn Monatsh — Berg- und Huettenmaennische Monatshefte
Berg Huettenmaenn Jahrb Montan Hochsch Leoben — Berg und Huettenmaennisches Jahrbuch. Montanistische Hochschule in Leoben
Berg Huettenmaenn Monatsh Montan Hochsch Leoben — Berg und Huettenmaennische Monatshefte. Montanistische Hochschule in Leoben [*Austria*]
Berg Huettenmaenn Monatsh Suppl — Berg und Huettenmaennische Monatshefte. Supplementum
Berg u Huettenm Ztg — Berg und Huettenmaennische Zeitung
Berg Huttenmann Monatsh — Berg- und Huettenmaennische Monatshefte [*Austria*]
Berg Tech — Berg Technik
Berichte — Muenzen- und Medaillensammler Berichte aus allen Gebieten der Geld-, Muenzen-, und Medaillenkunde
Berichte Dtsch Wiss Komm Meeresforsch — Berichte. Deutsche Wissenschaftliche Kommission fuer Meeresforschung
Ber Inf Europ Gem — Berichte und Informationen. Europaeische Gemeinschaften
Ber Inf KEG — Berichte und Informationen. Kommission der Europaeischen Gemeinschaften
Ber Inst Festkoerpermech Fraunhofer-Ges — Bericht. Institut fuer Festkoerpermechanik der Fraunhofer-Gesellschaft
Ber Inst Hochenergiephys (Wien) — Bericht. Institut fuer Hochenergiephysik der Osterreichischen Akademie der Wissenschaften (Wien)
Ber Inst Tabakforsch (Dresden) — Berichte. Institut fuer Tabakforschung (Dresden) [*East Germany*]
Ber Inst Tabakforsch Wohlsdorf-Biendorf — Berichte. Institut fuer Tabakforschung. Wohlsdorf-Biendorf
Ber Int Ges Getreidechem — Berichte. Internationale Gesellschaft fuer Getreidechemie
Berita Biol — Berita Biologi
Ber J Soc — Berkeley Journal of Sociology
Berk — Berkeley
Berkala Ilmu Kedokt — Berkala Ilmu Kedokteran [*Indonesia*]
Berk Bud St — Berkeley Buddhist Studies Series
Berk Co LJ — Berks County Law Journal
Berkeley J Sociol — Berkeley Journal of Sociology
Ber Kernforschungsanlage Juelich — Berichte. Kernforschungsanlage Juelich
Ber Kernforschungszentr Karlsruhe — Bericht. Kernforschungszentrum Karlsruhe
Ber Kfa Juelich — Berichte. Kernforschungsanlage Juelichgesellschaft mit Beschraenkter Haftung
Berk Relig — Berkeley Religious Studies Series
Berks — Berks County Law Journal
Berks Co — Berks County Law Journal
BerksCoHS — Berks County Historical Society. Papers
Berkshire Archaeol J — Berkshire Archaeological Journal
Berkshire Arch J — Berkshire Archaeological Journal
Berkshire Hist Sc Soc — Berkshire Historical and Scientific Society
BERLA — Bericht ueber Landwirtschaft
Ber Landwirt N F — Berichte ueber Landwirtschaft. Neue Folge
Ber Landwirtsch — Berichte ueber Landwirtschaft
Ber Landwirtsch Sonderh — Berichte ueber Landwirtschaft. Sonderheft
Berl Ent Z — Berliner Entomologische Zeitschrift

Berl Freie Univ FU Pressedienst Wiss — Berlin Freie Universitaet. FU Pressedienst Wissenschaft
Ber Limnol Flusst Freudenthal Munden — Berichte. Limnologische Flusstation Freudenthal Munden
Berliner Num Z — Berliner Numismatische Zeitschrift
Berl Jahrb Pharm — Berlinisches Jahrbuch fuer die Pharmacie
Berl Klin Wchnschr — Berliner Klinische Wochenschrift
Berl Muench Tieraerztl Wochenschr — Berliner und Muenchener Tieraerztliche Wochenschrift
Berl Muench Tieraerztl Wschr — Berliner und Muenchener Tieraerztliche Wochenschrift
Berl Mus — Berliner Museen
Berl Tieraerztl Wchnschr — Berliner Tieraerztliche Wochenschrift
Berl Wetterkarte Suppl — Berliner Wetterkarte. Supplement [*West Germany*]
Berl Winck Prog — Berlin. Winckelmannsprogramm der Archaeologischen Gesellschaft
Ber Math-Statist Sekt Forschungszentrum (Graz) — Berichte. Forschungszentrum. Mathematisch-Statistische Sektion (Graz)
Ber Max-Planck-Inst Stroemungsforsch — Bericht. Max-Planck-Institut fuer Stroemungsforschung [*West Germany*]
Berm Hist Q — Bermuda. Historical Quarterly
Ber MPI Kernphys (Heidelberg) — Bericht. Max-Planck-Institut fuer Kernphysik (Heidelberg)
Ber MPI Phys Astrophys Inst Extraterr Phys — Bericht. Max-Planck-Institut fuer Physik und Astrophysik. Institut fuer Extraterrestrische Physik
Ber MPI Plasmaphys Garching — Bericht. Max-Planck-Institut fuer Plasmaphysik. Garching bei Muenchen
Ber MPI Stroemungsforsch — Bericht. Max-Planck-Institut fuer Stroemungsforschung
Bermuda Biol Stn Res Spec Publ — Bermuda. Biological Station for Research. Special Publication
Bermuda Rep Dir Agric Fish — Bermuda. Report of the Director of Agriculture and Fisheries
Ber Naturforsch Ges (Augsb) — Berichte. Naturforschende Gesellschaft (Augsburg)
Ber Naturforsch Ges Freiburg — Berichte. Naturforschende Gesellschaft zu Freiburg
Ber Naturforsch Ges Freiburg Breisgau — Berichte. Naturforschende Gesellschaft zu Freiburg im Breisgau
Ber Naturhist Ges Hannover — Bericht. Naturhistorische Gesellschaft zu Hannover
Ber Naturwiss-Med Ver Innsb — Berichte. Naturwissenschaftlich-Medizinischer Verein in Innsbruck
Ber Naturw Med Ver Innsbruck — Berichte. Naturwissenschaftlich-Medizinischer Verein in Innsbruck
BERND — Bio-Energy Re-News
Bernice Pauahi Bishop Museum Bull — Bernice Pauahi Bishop Museum. Bulletin
Bernice Pauahi Bishop Museum Bull Special Pub — Bernice Pauahi Bishop Museum. Bulletin. Special Publication
Bernice Pauahi Bishop Mus Oc P — Bernice Pauahi Bishop Museum. Occasional Papers
Bernice P Bishop Mus Spec Publ — Bernice Pauahi Bishop Museum. Special Publication
BEROA — Better Roads
Ber Oberhess Ges Nat Heikd Giessen Naturwiss Abt — Bericht. Oberhessische Gesellschaft fuer Natur und Heilkunde zu Giessen. Naturwissenschaftliche Abteilung
Ber Oesterr Studienges Atomenerg — Berichte. Oesterreichische Studiengesellschaft fuer Atomenergie
Ber Ohara Inst Landw Biol — Berichte. Ohara Institut fuer Landwirtschaftliche Biologie
Ber Ohara Inst Landwirtsch Biol Okayama Univ — Berichte. Ohara Institut fuer Landwirtschaftliche Biologie. Okayama Universitaet
Ber Ohara Inst Landwirtsch Forsch Kurashiki — Berichte. Ohara Institut fuer Landwirtschaftliche Forschungen in Kurashiki
Ber Ohara Inst Landwirtsch Forsch Okayama Univ — Berichte. Ohara Institut fuer Landwirtschaftliche Forschungen. Okayama Universitaet
Ber Pet Ind — Berichte ueber die Petroleum Industrie
Ber Physiol Lab Versuchsanst Landwirtsch Inst Univ Halle — Berichte. Physiologisches Laboratorium und der Versuchsanstalt des Landwirtschaftlichen Instituts der Universitaet Halle
Ber Phys-Med Ges Wuerzb — Berichte. Physikalisch-Medizinische Gesellschaft zu Wuerzburg
Ber Rassenkeuze — Bericht ueber Rassenkeuze
Ber Schweiz Bot Ges — Berichte. Schweizerische Botanische Gesellschaft
Ber Staat Denkmaf Saarland — Bericht. Staatliche Denkmalpflege im Saarland. Beitraege zur Archaeologie und Kunstgeschichte
Ber Tag Nordwestdtsch Forstver — Berichte ueber die Tagung im Nordwestdeutscher Forstverein
Ber Tech Akad Wuppertal — Berichte. Technische Akademie Wuppertal
Ber Tech Wiss Abt Verb Keram Gewerke Dtschl — Berichte. Technisch Wissenschaftliche Abteilung des Verbandes Keramischer Gewerke in Deutschland
BERUA — Berufs-Dermatosen
BERUAG — Dermatoses Professionnelles

Berufs-Derm — Berufs-Dermatosen
Ber Ukr Wiss Forsch Inst Phys Chem — Berichte. Ukrainische Wissenschaftliche Forschungs Institut fuer Physikalische Chemie
Ber Univ Jyvaeskyla Math Inst — Bericht. Jyvaeskylae Universitaet. Mathematisches Institut
Ber Verh Saechs Akad Wiss Leipzig Math-Naturwiss Kl — Berichte. Verhandlungen der Saechsischen Akademie der Wissenschaften zu Leipzig. Mathematisch-Naturwissenschaftliche Klasse [East Germany]
Ber Verh Saechs Akad Wiss Leipzig Math Phys Kl — Berichte. Verhandlungen der Saechsischen Akademie der Wissenschaften zu Leipzig. Mathematisch-Physische Klasse
Ber Wiss Biol — Berichte ueber die Wissenschaftliche Biologie
Ber Wissenschaftsgesch — Berichte zur Wissenschaftsgeschichte
Ber Zusammenkunft Dtsch Ophthalmol Ges — Bericht ueber die Zusammenkunft der Deutschen Ophthalmologischen Gesellschaft
Besancon Univ Ann Sci Ser 3 — Besancon Universite Annales Scientifiques. Serie 3. Geologie
BESID — BS. Betriebssicherheit [Austria]
Beskontaktn Elektr Mash — Beskontaktnye Elektricheskie Mashiny
BESM — Bulletin Economique et Social du Maroc
Bess — Bessarione
Best — Best Sellers
BESTA — Beton- und Stahlbetonbau
Best Life — Best's Review. Life/Health Insurance Edition
Best Sell — Best Sellers
Best's Ins N — Best's Insurance News
Best's Life — Best's Review. Life/Health Insurance Edition
Bests Prop — Best's Review. Property/Liability Edition
Bests R — Best's Review. Life/Health Insurance Edition
Best's Rev Life Health Insur Ed — Best's Review. Life/Health Insurance Edition
Best's Rev Prop/Casualty Insur Ed — Best's Review. Property/Casualty Insurance Edition
Bests R Life Ed — Best's Review. Life/Health Insurance Edition
Bests R Prop Ed — Best's Review. Property/Liability Edition
Best's R (Property Ed) — Best's Review (Property/Liability Edition)
Beszamolo Vizgazdalkodasi Tud Kut Intez Munkajarol — Beszamolo a Vizgazdalkodasi Tudomanyos Kutato Intezet Munkajarol
BET — Bedrijf en Techniek [Amsterdam]
Beta Phi Research Exch — Beta Phi Research Exchange
Beth Hamikra — Beth Hamikra. Bulletin of the Israel Society for Biblical Research and the World Jewish Biblical Society
Beth Isr Hosp Semin Med — Beth Israel Hospital. Seminars in Medicine
Bet Hom & Gard — Better Homes and Gardens
BETKA — Bergbautechnik
Bet Libns — Between Librarians
Betongtek Publ — Betongtekniske Publikasjoner
Beton Herstellung Verwend — Beton, Herstellung, Verwendung
Betons Ind — Betons Industriels [France]
Betonstein Zig — Betonstein Zeitung
Betontech Ber — Betontechnische Berichte [West Germany]
Betonwerk Fertigteil-Tech — Betonwerk und Fertigteil-Technik [West Germany]
B Et Orient — Bulletin d'Etudes Orientales
Betr-Berat — Betriebs-Berater. Zeitschrift fuer Recht und Wirtschaft
BETRC — British Engine Technical Reports
BETRD — Betrieb (Duesseldorf)
Betr Erz — Betrifft Erziehung [West Germany]
Betriebswirt Mitt Wirtberater — Betriebswirtschaftliche Mitteilungen fuer den Wirtschaftsberater
Betriebswirtsch Forsch Praxis — Betriebswirtschaftliche Forschung und Praxis
Betr-Oekon — Betriebs-Oekonom
Betr-Tech — Betriebs-Technik
BETS — Bulletin. Evangelical Theological Society [Later, Journal. Evangelical Theological Society]
Betterave Ind Agr — Betterave et les Industries Agricoles
Better Bus — Better Business
Better F — Better Farming
BETUA — Toyama Daigaku Kogakubu Kiyo
Betw Libns — Between Librarians
Betz Indic — Betz Indicator
BEUP — [The] Babylonian Expedition of the University of Pennsylvania: Cuneiform Texts
B Eur S Hum — Bulletin. European Society of Human Genetics
Beverage — Beverage Industry
Beverage Ind — Beverage Industry
BEVOA — Beitraege zur Vogelkunde
BEVSA — Berichte. Verhandlungen der Saechsischen Akademie der Wissenschaften zu Leipzig. Mathematisch-Naturwissenschaftliche Klasse
BEvTh — Beitraege zur Evangelischen Theologie [Munich]
BEvTSoc — Bulletin. Evangelical Theological Society [Wheaton, IL] [Later, Journal. Evangelical Theological Society]
Bev Wld — Beverage World
B Exam — Bar Examiner

BEXBA — Bulletin of Experimental Biology and Medicine [English Translation]
BEXBB — Biochemistry and Experimental Biology
B Exp B Med — Bulletin of Experimental Biology and Medicine
Bey B — Beyond Baroque
B Ez — Balkansko Ezikoznanije
BEZEA — Betonstein Zeitung
Bezop Tr Prom-st — Bezopasnost' Truda v Promyshlennosti
BF — Bibliofilia
BF — Boletin de Filologia
BF — Book Forum
BF — Books from Finland
BFA — Benelumat Revue
BFA — Bulletin. Faculty of Arts. University of Egypt [Cairo]
BFAC — Bulletin. Faculty of Arts. University of Egypt (Cairo)
BFAM — Bulletin. Fogg Art Museum
BFBU — Beaufort Bulletin. Dome Petroleum Ltd.
BFC — Boletin. Instituto de Filologia de la Universidad de Chile
BFC — Bollettino di Filologia Classica
BFChTh — Beitraege zur Foerderung Christlicher Theologie [Guetersloh]
BFCL — Bulletin. Facultes Catholiques de Lyon
BFCTL — Bibliotheque de la Faculte Catholique de Theologie de Lyon
BFD — Bulletin for International Fiscal Documentation
BFE — Boletin de Filologia Espanola
BFF — Beyond Fiction
BFH — Bouwmarkt
BFHA — Bulletin. Friends Historical Association
BFIF — Bulletin Folklorique d'Ile-De-France
BFL — Bulletin. Faculte des Lettres de Lille
BFLAV — Bulletin. Foreign Language Association of Virginia
BFLS — Bulletin. Faculte des Lettres de Strasbourg
BFM — Boletin de Filologia (Montevideo)
BFM — Business Conditions Digest
BFMB — Bank of Finland. Monthly Bulletin
BFNJ — Bijdragen Uitgegeven door en Philosophische en Theologische Faculteiten der Noord- en Zuid-Nederlandse Jezuieten
BFo — Biuletyn Fonograficzny
BFO — Steel News
BFOL — Beaufort Outlook. Newsletter from the Northern Office of the Beaufort Sea Alliance
B Fon — Biuletyn Fonograficzny
BFOO — Berichte. Forschungsinstitut fuer Osten und Orient [Vienna]
B Forum — Book Forum
BFPhLL — Bibliotheque de la Faculte de Philosophie et Lettres de l'Universite de Liege
BFPLUL — Bibliotheque de la Faculte de Philosophie et Lettres de l'Universite de Liege
BFR — Bibliotheque Francaise et Romane
BFR — Boletin de Filologia (Rio De Janeiro)
BFRPD — Biofuels Report
BFS — Bulletin. Faculte des Lettres de Strasbourg
BFSGA — Bulletin. Federation des Societes de Gynecologie et d'Obstetrique de Langue Francaise
BFT — Bizarre Fantasy Tales
BFT — Bulgarian Foreign Trade
BFTh — Beitraege zur Foerderung Christlicher Theologie [Guetersloh]
BFTMB — Bundesministerium fuer Forschung und Technologie. Mitteilungen
BFTRA — Bois et Forets des Tropiques
BFU — Boletin de Filologia. Instituto de Estudios Superiores del Uruguay
BFUCH — Boletin de Filologia. Instituto de Filologia. Universidade de Chile
BFX — Overseas Business Reports
BG — Bijdragen tot de Geschiedenis
BG — Blue Guitar
BG — Bogoslovski Glasnik
BG — Bungaku
BGAOAT — Breviora Geologica Asturica
BGB — Bulletin. Association Guillaume Bude
BGBH — Bijdragen voor de Geschiedenis van het Bisdom van Haarlem
BGBWD — Blaetter fuer Grundstuecks, Bau-, und Wohnungsrecht
BGCTH — Bulletin. Section de Geographie. Comite des Travaux Historiques et Scientifiques
BGDSL — Beitraege zur Geschichte der Deutschen Sprache und Literatur [Halle]
BGDSLH — Beitraege zur Geschichte der Deutschen Sprache und Literatur (Halle)
BGDSLT — Beitraege zur Geschichte der Deutschen Sprache und Literatur (Tuebingen)
BGENA — Biologie et Gastro-Enterologie
BGFND — Bulletin. Groupe Francais d'Humidimetrie Neutronique
BGGPB — Biofeedback and Self-Regulation
BGGUA — Bulletin. Groenlands Geologiske Undersoegelse
BGH — Beleggers Belangen
BGHB — Bijdragen tot de Geschiedenis Bijzonderlijk van het Aloude Hertogdom Brabant
BGHD — Bulletin de Geographie Historique et Descriptive
BGIGA — Biuletyn Glownego Instytutu Gornictwa

BGLE — Bangladesh Development Studies
BGLRK — Beitraege zur Geschichte und Lehre der Reformierten Kirche [*Neukirchen*]
BGLS — Bausteine zur Geschichte der Literatur bei den Slaven
BGMIA — Boletin Geologico y Minero
BGN — Bijdragen voor de Geschiedenis der Nederlanden
BGNSA — Berufsgenossenschaft
BGPMN — Bijdragen voor de Geschiedenis van de Provincie der Minderbroeders in de Nederlanden
BGPTM — Beitraege zur Geschichte der Philosophie und Theologie des Mittelalters
BGROD — Bundesgesetzblatt fuer die Republik Oesterreich
BGRS — Bungaku Ronshu [*Studies on Literature*]
BGRSA — Bulletin. Groupement International pour la Recherche Scientifique en Stomatologie
BGSA — Bulletin. Geological Society of America
BGSGB — Bibliotheca Gastroenterologica
BGSPD — Bulgarsko Geofizichno Spisanie
BGSSE — Beitraege zur Geschichte von Stadt und Stift Essen
BGSTB — Biologist [*Champaign, IL*]
BGU — Bluegrass Unlimited
BGWK — Boekenschouw voor Godsdienst, Wetenschap en Kunst
BGWVAO — George Washington University. Bulletin
BH — Bear Hills Native Voice [*Hobbema, Alberta*]
BH — Bibliografia Hispanica
BH — Bibliotheque Historique
BH — Bulletin Hispanique
BH — Business History
BHAG — Bulletin. Societe d'Histoire et d'Archeologie de Gand
BHAGA — Bhagirath
BHAR — Bulletin. Section Historique. Academie Roumaine
Bhar Ma Q — Bharata Manisha Quarterly
Bhavan's J — Bhavan's Journal
BHB — Nouvelles Economiques de Suisse
BHBLA — Behavioral Biology
BHBSA — Harvard Business School. Bulletin
BHC — Business in Thailand
BHDEA — Bulletin of the History of Dentistry
BHDL — Bulletin Historique. Diocese de Lyon
B He — Baltische Hefte
BHE — Barid Hollanda
BHEAT — Bulletin d'Histoire et Exegese de l'Ancien Testament [*Louvain*]
BHET — Bulletin d'Histoire et Exegese de l'Ancien Testament [*Louvain*]
BHEW — Bulletin. Societe pour l'Histoire des Eglises Wallonnes
BHF — Bonner Historische Forschungen
BHFIA — Bulletin. Haffkine Institute
BHGDA — Better Homes and Gardens
BHGNA — Behavior Genetics
BHH — Baptist History and Heritage
BHI — British Humanities Index [*Library Association Publishing Ltd.*] [*London*]
BHi — Bulletin Hispanique
BHI — Business History
BHI — Europe Outremer. Revue Internationale
BHIJA — Bulletin. Heart Institute (Japan)
BHis — Biblioteca Hispana
BHisp — Bibliografia Hispanica
BHisp — Bulletin Hispanique
B Hispan — Bulletin Hispanique
B Hispan S — Bulletin of Hispanic Studies
B Hist Med — Bulletin of the History of Medicine
BHM — Bibliography of the History of Medicine
BHM — Bulletin of the History of Medicine
BHM — Bulletin. Societe Francaise d'Histoire de la Medecine
BHM Berg u Huttenm Mh — BHM. Berg- und Huttenmaennische Monatshefte
BHMMA — Berg- und Huettenmaennische Monatshefte
BHNNA — Societe d'Histoire Naturelle de l'Afrique du Nord. Bulletin
BHO — Business Horizons
B Hor — Business Horizons
BHPAS — Bulletin. National Research Institute of History and Philology. Academia Sinica
BHPCTHS — Bulletin Historique et Philologique. Comite des Travaux Historiques et Scientifiques
BHPF — Bulletin Historique et Litteraire. Societe de l'Histoire du Protestantisme Francais
BHP J — BHP [*Broken Hill Proprietary Ltd.*] Journal
BHP Jo — BHP [*Broken Hill Proprietary Ltd.*] Journal
B H Points — Bulletin of High Points
BHP R — BHP [*Broken Hill Proprietary Ltd.*] Review
BHP Res Div Inf Circ — Broken Hill Proprietary Ltd. Research Division. Information Circular
BHP Rev — BHP [*Broken Hill Proprietary Ltd.*] Review
BHPSO — Bulletin. Historical and Philosophical Society of Ohio
BHP Tech Bull — BHP [*Broken Hill Proprietary Ltd.*] Technical Bulletin
BHR — Bibliotheque d'Humanisme et Renaissance

BHR — British Hotelier and Restaurateur
BHR — Business History Review
BHS — Biuletyn Historii Sztuki
BHS — Bulletin of Hispanic Studies
BHSAM — Bulletin Historique. Societe des Antiquitaires de la Morinie
BHSM — Bulletin. Historical Society of Montgomery County
BHSMCo — Bulletin. Historical Society of Montgomery County
BHTh — Beitraege zur Historischen Theologie [*Tuebingen*]
BHTP — Bulletin d'Histoire du Theatre Portugais
BhV — Bharatiya Vidya
BHV — Business History Review
BHVBamberg — Bericht. Historischer Verein fuer das Fuerstbistum (Bamberg)
BHVFB — Bericht. Historischer Verein fuer das Fuerstbistum (Bamberg)
BHZ — Business Horizons
Bi — Biblica
Bi — Bibliofilia
BI — Bibliografia Italiana
BI — Bibliotheca Islamica
Bi — Biblos
Bi — Bijdragen
BI — Books at Iowa
BI — Bulletin Italien
BI — Business Index
BI — Business Insurance
BiA — Biblical Archaeologist
BIA — Bollettino. Reale Istituto di Archeologia e Storia dell'Arte
BIA — Bulletin. Institute of Archaeology
BIAA — Bollettino. Reale Istituto di Archeologia e Storia dell'Arte
BIAAD4 — Buletinul. Institutului Agronomic Cluj-Napoca. Seria Agricultura
BIAB — Bulletin. Institut Archeologique Bulgare
BIABE — Biomass Abstracts
BIA Bulg — Bulletin. Institut Archeologique Bulgare
BIACDA — Buletinul. Institutului Agronomic Cluj-Napoca
Biafra R — Biafra Review
BIAHA — Bulletin. International Association of Scientific Hydrology
BIAL — Bulletin. Institut Archeologique Liegeois
BIAL — Bulletin. Institute of Archaeology. University of London
BIALB — Boletim. Instituto de Tecnologia de Alimentos [*Campinas, Brazil*]
BIAMA — Bulletin International. Academie Polonaise des Sciences et des Lettres. Classe des Sciences Mathematiques et Naturelles. Serie A. Sciences Mathematiques
BIANA — Bibliotheca Anatomica
Bian & Nero — Bianco e Nero
BIAO — Bulletin. Institut Francais d'Archeologie Orientale
BIAP — Bulletin International. Academie Polonaise des Sciences et des Lettres
BIAPSL — Bulletin International. Academie Polonaise des Sciences et des Lettres
BIAS — Bulletin in Applied Statistics
BIAVDX — Buletinul. Institutului Agronomic Cluj-Napoca. Seria Zootehnie si Medicina Veterinara
BIB — Bank of Israel. Bulletin [*Jerusalem*]
Bib — Biblica
Bib — Biblos
BIB — Bulletin. Institut International de Bibliographie
BIB — Open; Vaktijdschrift voor Bibliothecarissen, Literatuuronderzoekers, Bedrijfsarchivarissen, en Documentalisten
Bib A — Biblical Archeologist
BibAg — Bibliography of Agriculture
Bib Arch — Biblical Archaeologist
Bib Arch Rev — Biblical Archaeology Review
BIBIA — Biotechnology and Bioengineering
Bib Inz Oprogram — Biblioteka Inzynierii Oprogramowania
Bibl — Biblica [*Rome*]
Bibl — Bibliographic Index
Bibl — Bibliographie Linguistique
Bibl Anat — Bibliotheca Anatomica
Bibl Anatom — Bibliotheca Anatomica
Bibl Arch — Biblical Archaeologist
Bibl Archaeolo — Biblical Archaeologist
Bibl Archeol — Biblical Archeologist
Bibl Arch Roman Ser II Linguistica — Biblioteca. Archivum Romanicum. Serie II. Linguistica
Bibl Asiatica — Bibliographia Asiatica
BIBLB — Boletim Internacional de Bibliografia Luso-Brasileira [*Lisboa*]
Bibl Biotheor — Bibliotheca Biotheoretica
Bibl Br Sci Arts — Bibliotheque Britannique. Sciences et Arts
Bibl Cardio — Bibliotheca Cardiologica
Bibl Cardiol — Bibliotheca Cardiologica
Bibl Dedalo — Biblioteca Dedalo
Bibl Docum Terminology — Bibliography, Documentation, Terminology
Bibl Ec Chartes — Bibliotheque de l'Ecole des Chartes
Bibl Ecole Chartes — Bibliotheque de l'Ecole des Chartes
Bibl Engl Lang & Lit — Bibliography of English Language and Literature
Bible T — Bible Today
Bibl Filol — Bibliografia Filologica do Centro de Estudos Filologica de Lisboa

Bibl Gastro — Bibliotheca Gastroenterologica
Bibl Gastroenterol — Bibliotheca Gastroenterologica
BiblGeo — Bibliography and Index of Geology
Bibl Gesch Dt Arbeiterbewegung — Bibliographie zur Geschichte der Deutschen Arbeiterbewegung
Bibl Gynaecol — Bibliotheca Gynaecologica
Bibl Haem — Bibliotheca Haematologica
Bibl Haematol — Bibliotheca Haematologica
Bibl Hist Vaudoise — Bibliotheque Historique Vaudoise
BiblH & R — Bibliotheque d'Humanisme et Renaissance
Bibl Hum R — Bibliotheque d'Humanisme et Renaissance
Bibl Hum Renaissance — Bibliotheque d'Humanisme et Renaissance
Bibl Ind — Bibliographic Index
Bibl & Ind Geol — Bibliography and Index of Geology
Biblio — Bibliofilia
Biblio France — Bibliographie de la France
Bibliog — Bibliographer
Bibliog Doc Terminology — Bibliography, Documentation, Terminology
Bibliogr Annu Madagascar — Bibliographie Annuelle de Madagascar
Bibliogr Bestrahlung Lebensm — Bibliographie zur Bestrahlung von Lebensmitteln [*West Germany*]
Bibliogr Bibl Conmem Orton Inst Interamer Cienc Agr — Bibliografias. Biblioteca Conmemorativa Orton. Instituto Interamericano de Ciencias Agricolas
Bibliogr Bras Odontol — Bibliografia Brasileira Odontologia
Bibliogr Bur Soils — Bibliography. Commonwealth Bureau of Soils
Bibliogr Chim — Bibliographia Chimica
Bibliogr Farm — Bibliografica Farmaceutica
Bibliogr For Bur (Oxf) — Annotated Bibliography. Commonwealth Forestry Bureau (Oxford)
Bibliogr Genet — Bibliographia Genetica
Bibliogr Genet Med — Bibliographica Genetica Medica
Bibliogr High Temp Chem Phys Gases Plasmas — Bibliography on the High Temperature Chemistry and Physics of Gases and Plasmas
Bibliogr High Temp Chem Phys Mater — Bibliography on the High Temperature Chemistry and Physics of Materials
Bibliogr High Temp Chem Phys Mater Condens State — Bibliography on the High Temperature Chemistry and Physics of Materials in the Condensed State
Bibliogr Irradiat Foods — Bibliography in Irradiation of Foods [*West Germany*]
Bibliogr Lit Agric US Dep Agric Econ Stat Serv — Bibliographies and Literature of Agriculture. United States Department of Agriculture. Economics and Statistics Service
Bibliogr Paint Technol — Bibliographies in Paint Technology
Bibliogr Reihe Kernforschungsanlage Juelich — Bibliographische Reihe der Kernforschungsanlage Juelich
Bibliogr Rev Chem — Bibliography of Reviews in Chemistry
Bibliogr Sci Ind Rep — Bibliography of Scientific and Industrial Reports
Bibliogr Ser IAEA — Bibliographical Series. International Atomic Energy Agency
Bibliogr Ser Ore For Res Lab — Bibliographical Series. Oregon State University. Forest Research Laboratory
Bibliogr Tech Rep — Bibliography of Technical Reports
Bibliogr Umweltradioakt Lebensm — Bibliographie zur Umweltradioaktivitaet in Lebensmitteln [*West Germany*]
Bibliog Soc Am Pa — Bibliographical Society of America. Papers
Biblio Ital Educ Sordi — Bibliografia Italiana sull'Educazione dei Sordi
Biblio Sci Nat Helv — Bibliographia Scientiae Naturalis Helvetica [*Bern*]
Biblio Soc Am — Bibliographical Society of America. Papers
Biblioteca Nac Jose Marti R — Biblioteca Nacional Jose Marti. Revista
Biblioth Med Cassel — Bibliotheca Medica Cassel
Bibliot Vrach — Biblioteka Vracha
Bibl Laeger — Bibliotek for Laeger
Bibl Liberta — Biblioteca della Liberta
Bibl Mat — Biblioteka Matematyczna
Bibl Microbiol — Bibliotheca Microbiologica
Bibl Nutr D — Bibliotheca Nutrito et Dieta
Bibl Nutr Dieta — Bibliotheca Nutrito et Dieta
Bibl Ophthalmol — Bibliotheca Ophthalmologica
Bibl Orient — Bibliotheca Orientalis
Bibl Oto-Rhino-Laryngol — Bibliotheca Oto-Rhino-Laryngologica
Bibl Paediatr — Bibliotheca Paediatrica
Bibl Pflanz — Bibliographie der Pflanzenschutzliteratur
Biblphical Bull US Dep Agric Libr — Bibliographical Bulletin. United States Department of Agriculture. Library
Biblphical Contr US Dep Agric Libr — Bibliographical Contributions. United States Department of Agriculture. Library
Biblphie Anat — Bibliographie Anatomique
Biblphien Dt Wetterd — Bibliographien des Deutschen Wetterdienstes
Bibl Phonet — Bibliotheca Phonetica
Bibl Phonetica — Bibliotheca Phonetica
Biblphy Agric (Wash) — Bibliography of Agriculture (Washington)
Biblphy Bee Research Ass — Bibliography. Bee Research Association
Biblphy Int Bee Res Ass — Bibliography. International Bee Research Association

Bibl Primatol — Bibliotheca Primatologica
Bibl Problem — Biblioteka Problemow
Bibl Psych — Bibliotheca Psychiatrica
Bibl Psychiatr — Bibliotheca Psychiatrica
Bibl Psychiatr Neurol — Bibliotheca Psychiatrica et Neurologica
Bibl Radiol — Bibliotheca Radiologica
Bibl Repro — Bibliography of Reproduction
BiblRes — Biblical Research. Papers of the Chicago Society of Biblical Research [*Amsterdam*]
Bibl Sac — Bibliotheca Sacra
Bibl Selective Pubns Officielles Fr — Bibliographie Selective des Publications Officielles Francaises
Bibl Sel'sk Profsoiuznogo Akt — Bibliotechka Sel'skogo Profsoiuznogo Aktivista
Bibl Soc Am Pa — Bibliographical Society of America. Papers
Bibl Stor T — Biblioteca Storica Toscana. Sezione di Storia del Risorgimento
BiblStud — Biblische Studien [*Neukirchen*]
Bibl Tuberc — Bibliotheca Tuberculosea
Bibl Tuberc Med Thorac — Bibliotheca Tuberculosea et Medicinae Thoracalis
Bibl Tub Me T — Bibliotheca Tuberculosea et Medicinae Thoracalis
Bibl Univers Geneve — Bibliotheque Universelle de Geneve
Bibl Univers Rev Gen — Bibliotheque Universelle et Revue de Geneve
Bibl Univers Rev Suisse — Bibliotheque Universelle et Revue Suisse
Bibl Univers Rev Suisse Etrang Nouv Periode — Bibliotheque Universelle. Revue Suisse et Etrangere. Nouvelle Periode
Bibl Univers Sci B L Arts Sci Arts — Bibliotheque Universelle des Sciences, Belles Lettres, et Arts. Sciences et Arts
Bibl "Vita Hum" — Bibliotheca "Vita Humana"
Bibl Wirtschaftspresse — Bibliographie der Wirtschaftspresse
BiblZ — Biblische Zeitschrift
BibO — Bibliotheca Orientalis
Bib Or — Bibbia e Oriente
Bib R — Biblical Review
BIBR — Bulletin. Institut Historique Belge de Rome
BIBRA Bull — BIBRA [*British Industrial Biological Research Association*] Bulletin
Bib Res — Biblical Research
Bib Sac — Bibliotheca Sacra
Bib Sacra — Bibliotheca Sacra
Bibs of Aust Writers — Bibliographies of Australian Writers [*State Library of South Australia*]
Bib Soc Am — Bibliographical Society of America. Papers
BibTB — Biblical Theology Bulletin [*Rome*]
Bib Th Bul — Biblical Theology Bulletin
Bib World — Biblical World
Bib Z — Biblische Zeitschrift
BIC — Books in Canada
BIC — Bulletin Interieur des Cadres
BICA — Bullettino. Istituto di Corrispondenza Archeologica
BICAER — Bulletin. International Committee on Urgent Anthropological and Ethnological Research
BICB — Institut Royal Colonial Belge. Bulletin des Seances
BICByz — Bulletin d'Information et de Coordination. Association Internationale des Etudes Byzantines
BICC — Boletin. Instituto Caro y Cuervo
BICEB — Bulletin d'Information des Centrales Electriques
BICED — Biologie Cellulaire
Bic Forum — Bicycle Forum
BICH — Bulletin. International Committee of Historical Sciences
BICHA — Biochemistry
BICHB — Bioinorganic Chemistry
BICHS — Bulletin. International Committee of Historical Sciences
Bickel C M N — Bickel's Coin and Medal News. Munt en Medaljenuus
BICMA — Bulletin. Institute of Chemistry. Academia Sinica [*Taiwan*]
BICOB — Biological Conservation
BICR — Bollettino. Istituto Centrale di Restauro
BICRA — Bulletin. Institute for Chemical Research. Kyoto University
BICS — Bulletin. Institute of Classical Studies. University of London
BICTA — Bibliotheca Tuberculosea
BICYA — Biological Cybernetics
Bicycles Bull — Bicycles Bulletin
BIDCUS — Bibliotheque de l'Institut de Droit Canonique de l'Universite de Strasbourg
BIDFD — Bulletin. International Dairy Federation
BIDICS (Bond Index Determinations Inorg Cryst Struct) — BIDICS (Bond Index to the Determinations of Inorganic Crystal Structures)
BIDID — Biosources Digest
BIDR — Bollettino. Istituto di Diritto Romano
BIDZD — Boei Ika Daigakko Zasshi
BIE — Boletin. Instituto de las Espanas
BIE — Boletin. Instituto Espanol de Londres
BIE — Bulletin. Institut d'Egypte
BIEA — Boletin. Instituto de Estudios Asturianos
Biedermanns Zentralbl — Biedermanns Zentralblatt
Biedermanns Zentralbl Abt A — Biedermanns Zentralblatt. Abteilung A. Allgemeiner und Referierender Teil

Biedermanns Zentralbl Abt B — Biedermanns Zentralblatt. Abteilung B. Tierernaehrung
BIEGB — Bulletin. International Association of Engineering Geology
BIEH — Boletin. Instituto de Estudios Helenicos
Bienenbl Bundesgebiet — Bienen-Blatt fuer des Bundesgebiet
Bienenw Zbl — Bienenwirtschaftliches Zentralblatt
Bienen Ztg — Bienen-Zeitung
Bienn Rep Hawaii Inst Geophys — Biennial Report. Hawaii Institute of Geophysics
Bienn Rev Anthropol — Biennial Review of Anthropology
Bienn Studi Stor Arte Med — Biennial. Studi Storia Arte Medicina
Bien Rep Hawaii Agr Exp Sta — Biennial Report. Hawaii Agricultural Experiment Station
Bien Rep Iowa Book Agr — Biennial Report. Iowa. Book of Agriculture. Iowa State Department of Agriculture
Bien Rep Nev State Dept Agr — Biennial Report. Nevada State Department of Agriculture
BIES — Bulletin. Israel Exploration Society [*Formerly, BJPES*] [*Jerusalem*]
BIF — Boletin. Instituto Frances
BIFAO — Bulletin. Institut Francais d'Archeologie Orientale
BIFD — Bulletin for International Fiscal Documentation
BIFG — Boletin. Instituto Fernan Gonzalez
BIFG — Bollettino. Istituto di Filologia Greca. Universita di Padova
BIFLTA — Bulletin. Illinois Foreign Language Teachers Association
BIFP — Boletin. Instituto de Investigaciones Folkloricas. Universidad Interamericana (Panama)
BIFP — Bulletin et Memoires. Institut des Fouilles de Provence et des Prealpes
BIFR — Buletinul. Institutului de Filologie Romana "Alexandru Philippide" [*Iasi*]
BIFRI — Buletinul. Institutului de Filologie Romana "Alexandru Philippide" (Iasi)
BIFV — Boletin. Instituto de Folklore
BIGBA — Buletinul. Institutului Politehnic "Gheorghe Gheorghiu-Dej" Bucuresti
Big D — Big Deal
BIGEB — Biochemical Genetics
BIGENA — Bibliography and Index of Geology Exclusive of North America
Big Farm Manage — Big Farm Management
BIGLA — Bioloski Glasnik
Big Mama — Big Mama Rag
Big Sky Econ Mont Stat Univ Coop Ext Serv — Big Sky Economics. Montana State University. Cooperative Extension Service
BiH — Bibliografia Hispanica
BIHAA — Bibliotheca Haematologica
Bihang K Svensk Vetensk-Akad Handl (Stockholm) — Bihang till Kongliga Svenska Vetenskaps-Akademiens Handlingar (Stockholm)
Bihar Acad Agr Sci Proc — Bihar Academy of Agricultural Sciences. Proceedings
BIHBR — Bulletin. Institut Historique Belge de Rome
B I Hist R — Bulletin. Institute of Historical Research
BI Hochschultaschenb — BI [*Bibliographisches Institut*] Hochschultaschenbuecher
BIHP — Bulletin. Institute of History and Philology. Academia Sinica
BiHR — Bibliotheque d'Humanisme et Renaissance
BIHR — Bulletin. Institute of Historical Research
BIIDD — Bulletin. Institute for Industrial and Social Development [*South Korea*]
BIIH — Boletin. Instituto de Investigaciones Historicas
BIIL — Boletin. Instituto de Investigaciones Literarias
BIINA — Biuletyn Instytutu Naftowego
BIIRHT — Bulletin d'Information. Institut de Recherche et d'Histoire des Textes
BIIZDH — Instytut Zootechnik. Biuletyn Informacyjny
Bijdr — Bijdragen. Tijdschrift voor Filosofie en Theologie [*Nijmegen/Brugge*]
Bijdragen Dialectencommissie — Bijdragen en Mededeelingen der Dialectencommissie van de Koninklijke Akademie van Wetenschappen te Amsterdam
Bijdragen Nederl-Indie — Bijdragen tot de Taal-Land- en Volkenkunde van Nederlandsche-Indie
Bijdrag Taal-Land- Volkenk — Bijdragen tot de Taal-Land- en Volkenkunde
Bijdr Dierk — Bijdragen tot de Dierkunde
Bijdr Gesch Ndl — Bijdragen voor de Geschiedenis der Nederlanden
Bijdr Taal- Land-en Volkenk Nederl-Indie — Bijdragen tot de Taal-Land- en Volkenkunde van Nederlandsche-Indie
BijdrTLV — Bijdragen tot de Taal-Land- en Volkenkunde
BIJOA — Biochemical Journal
BIJS — Bulletin. Institute of Jewish Studies
BIK — Biergrosshandel. Zeitschrift fuer den Gesamten Biergrosshandel und Getrankegrosshandel
Biken J — Biken Journal
BIKHD — Bioorganicheskaya Khimiya
BiKi — Bibel und Kirche [*Stuttgart*]
BIKJA — Biken Journal
BIKOA — Biologiai Koezlemenyek
Bil — Bilychnis
BIL — Bollettino Internazionale di Informazioni sul Latino

BILAL — Bulletin d'Information. Laboratoire d'Analyse Lexicologique
BILC — Boletim. Instituto Luis de Camoes
Bild Wiss — Bild der Wissenschaft
Bild der Wissenschaft — Bild der Wissenschaft. Zeitschrift ueber die Wissenschaften und die Technik in Unserer Zeit
BILE — Bollettino. Istituto di Lingue Estere [*Genova*]
BiLeb — Bibel und Leben [*Duesseldorf*]
BILEG — Bollettino. Istituto di Lingue Estere (Genova)
BILIA — Biologicke Listy
Biling Rev — Bilingual Review/Revista Bilingue
BiLit — Bibel und Liturgie [*Klosterneuburg, Austria*]
Biljeske Inst Oceanogr Ribar (Split) — Biljeske. Institut za Oceanografiju i Ribarstvo (Split)
BILLA — Billboard
Billings Geol Soc Annu Field Conf Guideb — Billings Geological Society. Annual Field Conference. Guidebook
BILPatr — Bulletin d'Information et de Liaison. Association Internationale des Etudes Patristiques
Bilt Dok — Bilten Dokumentacije [*Yugoslavia*]
Bilt Farm Drus Maked — Bilten za Farmaceutskoto Drustvo za Makedonija
Bilt Farm Drus Soc Repub Makedonija — Bilten za Farmaceutskoto Drustvo za Socijalisticka Republika Makedonija
Bilt Hematol Transfuz — Bilten za Hematologiju i Transfuziju
Bilt Hmelj Sirak — Bilten za Hmelj i Sirak
Bilt Sojuzot Zdruzenijata Farm Farm Teh SR Maked — Bilten za Sojuzot za Zdruzenijata za Farmacevtite i Farmacevtskite Tehnicari za SR Makedonija
BIM — Brookings Papers on Economic Activity
Bi-M Bull N Dak Agric Exp Stn — Bi-Monthly Bulletin. North Dakota Agricultural Experiment Station
BIMDA — Biochemical Medicine
BIMDB — Biomedicine
BIMEA — Biologie Medicale
BIMEB — Biomedical Engineering
BIMOA — Biologiya Morya [*Kiev*]
Bi-M Res Notes Canada Dep For — Bi-Monthly Research Notes. Canada Department of Forestry
BIN — Bollettino Italiano di Numismatica
B Indo Econ Stud — Bulletin of Indonesian Economic Studies
B Indones Econ Stud — Bulletin of Indonesian Economic Studies
BINEA — Biologia Neonatorum [*Later, Biology of the Neonate*]
BINED — BIOP [*Board on International Organizations and Programs*] Newletter [*United States*]
B Inform Centre Docum Educ Europe — Bulletin d'Information. Centre de Documentation pour l'Education en Europe
B Inform C N C — Bulletin d'Information. Centre National de la Cinematographie
B Inform Dept Econ Sociol Rur — Bulletin d'Information. Departement d'Economie et de Sociologie Rurales
B Inform Econ — Bulletin d'Informations Economiques
B Inform Econ Caisse Nat Marches Etat — Bulletin d'Information Economique de la Caisse Nationale des Marches de l'Etat
B Inform Haut Comite Et Inform Alcool — Bulletin d'Information. Haut Comite d'Etude et d'Information sur l'Alcoolisme
B Inform Region Champagne-Ardenne — Bulletin d'Information Regionale Champagne-Ardenne
B Inform Region Paris — Bulletin d'Information de la Region Parisienne
B Inf Zak Narod — Biuletyn Informacyjny. Zakladu Narodowego Ossolinskich Biblioteki Polskiej Akademii Nauk
Binnenschiffahrts-Nachr — Binnenschiffahrts-Nachrichten
B Inostr Kommerc Inform Priloz — Bjulleten Inostrannoj Kommerceskoj Informacii Prilozenie
B In Sci T — Bulletin d'Informations Scientifiques et Techniques. Commissariat a l'Energie Atomique
BINSCS — Boreal Institute for Northern Studies. Contribution Series
BINSOP — Boreal Institute for Northern Studies. Occasional Publication
BInstArch — Bulletin. Institute of Archaeology [*London*]
B Inst Archaeol — Bulletin. Institute of Archaeology. University of London
B Inst Communication Res — Bulletin. Institute of Communication Research
B Inst Develop Stud — Bulletin. Institute of Development Studies
B Inst Ethnol Acad Sinica — Bulletin. Institute of Ethnology. Academia Sinica
B Inst Fondam Afr Noire — Bulletin. Institut Fondamental d'Afrique Noire
B Inst Franc Et Andines — Bulletin. Institut Francais d'Etudes Andines
B Inst Hist Med (Hyderabad) — Bulletin. Institute of History of Medicine (Hyderabad)
B Inst Int Adm Publ — Bulletin. Institut International d'Administration Publique
B Inst Rech Econ — Bulletin. Institut de Recherches Economiques
B Inst Trad Cult — Bulletin. Institute of Traditional Culture
Binsurance — Business Insurance
B Int Assoc Educ Vocat Guidance — Bulletin. International Association for Educational and Vocational Guidance
B Int Committee on Urg Anthropol Ethnol Res — Bulletin. International Committee on Urgent Anthropological and Ethnological Research
B Interminist Rational Choix Budget — Bulletin Interministeriel pour la Rationalisation des Choix Budgetaires

B Interparl — Bulletin Interparlementaire
B Int Fisc Docum — Bulletin for International Fiscal Documentation
B Int Fis D — Bulletin for International Fiscal Documentation
BINUA — Bulletin d'Instrumentation Nucleaire
BioAb — Biological Abstracts
BioAg — Biological and Agricultural Index
BioC — Biologia Culturale
Bioc Biop A — Biochimica et Biophysica Acta
Bioc Biop R — Biochemical and Biophysical Research Communications
BIOCC — Bedford Institute of Oceanography. Collected Contributions
Biochem — Biochemistry
Biochem Biophys Perspect Mar Biol — Biochemical and Biophysical Perspectives in Marine Biology
Biochem Biophys Res Commun — Biochemical and Biophysical Research Communications
Biochem Bull (NY) — Biochemical Bulletin (New York)
Biochem Centralbl — Biochemisches Centralblatt
Biochem Clin Bohemoslov — Biochemia Clinica Bohemoslovaca
Biochem Educ — Biochemical Education [*England*]
Biochem Exp Biol — Biochemistry and Experimental Biology
Biochem Gen — Biochemical Genetics
Biochem Genet — Biochemical Genetics
Biochem J — Biochemical Journal
Biochem Med — Biochemical Medicine
Biochem Pharmacol — Biochemical Pharmacology
Biochem Physiol Pflanz — Biochemie und Physiologie der Pflanzen
Biochem Prep — Biochemical Preparations
Biochem Rev (Bangalore) — Biochemical Reviews (Bangalore)
Biochem Soc Spec Publ — Biochemical Society. Special Publications
Biochem Soc Symp — Biochemical Society. Symposia
Biochem Soc Trans — Biochemical Society. Transactions
Biochem SSR — Biochemistry-USSR
Biochem Syst Ecol — Biochemical Systematics and Ecology
Biochem Z — Biochemische Zeitschrift
Biochim Appl — Biochimica Applicata
Biochim Biol Sper — Biochimica e Biologia Sperimentale
Biochim Biophys Acta — Biochimica et Biophysica Acta
Biochim Biophys Acta B -- Biochimica et Biophysica Acta. B. Bioenergetics
Biochim Biophys Acta Bioenerg — Biochimica et Biophysica Acta. B. Bioenergetics
Biochim Biophys Acta Biomembranes — Biochimica et Biophysica Acta. Biomembranes
Biochim Biophys Acta BR — Biochimica et Biophysica Acta. BR. Reviews on Bioenergetics
Biochim Biophys Acta Enzymol — Biochimica et Biophysica Acta. Enzymology
Biochim Biophys Acta G — Biochimica et Biophysica Acta. G. General Subjects
Biochim Biophys Acta General Subjects — Biochimica et Biophysica Acta. General Subjects
Biochim Biophys Acta Libr — Biochimica et Biophysica Acta. Library
Biochim Biophys Acta Lipids Lipid Metab — Biochimica et Biophysica Acta. Lipids and Lipid Metabolism
Biochim Biophys Acta M — Biochimica et Biophysica Acta. M. Biomembranes
Biochim Biophys Acta MR — Biochimica et Biophysica Acta. MR. Reviews on Biomembranes
Biochim Biophys Acta Nucl Acids Protein Synth — Biochimica et Biophysica Acta. Nucleic Acids and Protein Synthesis
Biochim Biophys Acta P — Biochimica et Biophysica Acta. P. Protein Structure
Biochim Biophys Acta Protein Struct — Biochimica et Biophysica Acta. P. Protein Structure
Bioch Pharm — Biochemical Pharmacology
Bioch Soc T — Biochemical Society. Transactions
Bioclimat Numero Spec — Bioclimat Numero Special
Bioc Phy Pf — Biochemie und Physiologie der Pflanzen
BIODA — Biodynamica
BIOEA — Biomedical Engineering [*English Translation*]
Bioelectr B — Bioelectrochemistry and Bioenergetics
Bioelectrochem Bioenerg — Bioelectrochemistry and Bioenergetics
BIOFA — Biofizika
BIOFDL — Annual Research Reviews. Biofeedback
Biofeedback Self-Regul — Biofeedback and Self-Regulation
Biofiz — Biofizika
Biofiz Zhivoi Kletki — Biofizika Zhivoi Kletki
Biofuels Rep — Biofuels Report
Biogas Alcohol Fuels Prod — Biogas and Alcohol Fuels Production
Biog Ind — Biography Index
Biogr Hervorragender Naturwiss Tech Med — Biographien Hervorragender Naturwissenschaftler, Techniker, und Mediziner
Biogr Mem Fellows R Soc — Biographical Memoirs. Fellows of the Royal Society
Biogr Mem Nat Acad Sci USA — Biographical Memoirs. National Academy of Sciences. United States of America
Biogr Mem Natl Acad Sci — Biographical Memoirs. National Academy of Sciences
BIOHA — Biokhimiya [*Moscow*]

BioI — Biography Index
BIOI — BioResearch Index [*Superseded by BA/RRM*]
Bioinorg Ch — Bioinorganic Chemistry
Bioinorg Chem — Bioinorganic Chemistry
BIOJA — Biophysical Journal
Bio-Joule Newsl — Bio-Joule Newsletter [*Canada*]
BIOKA — Biometrika
Biokhim — Biokhimiya
Biokhim Chain Prozvod — Biokhimiya Chainogo Proizvodstva
Biokhim Kul't Rast Mold — Biokhimiya Kul'turnykh Rastenii Moldavu
Biokhim Nasekomykh — Biokhimiya Nasekomykh
Biokhim Plodov Ovoshchei — Biokhimiya Plodov i Ovoshchei
Biokhim Vinodel — Biokhimiya Vinodeliya
Biokhim Zerna Khlebopeeh — Biokhimiya Zerna i Khlebopeeheniya
Biokhim Zh — Biokhimichna Zhurnal
Biokon Rep — Biokon Reports
Biol — Biologia
Biol — O Biologico
Biol Abh — Biologische Abhandlungen
Biol Abs — Biological Abstracts
Biol Abstr — Biological Abstracts
Biol & Agr Ind — Biological and Agricultural Index
Biol Akt Veshchestva Mikroorg — Biologicheski Aktivnye Veshchestva Mikroorganizmov
Biol B — Biological Bulletin
Biol Board Can Bull — Biological Board of Canada. Bulletin
Biol Brain Dysfunction — Biology of Brain Dysfunction
Biol (Bratislava) — Biologia (Bratislava)
Biol Bul — Biological Bulletin
Biol Bull — Biological Bulletin
Biol Bull Acad Sci USSR — Biology Bulletin. Academy of Sciences of the USSR
Biol Bull Dep Biol Coll Sci Tunghai Univ — Biological Bulletin. Department of Biology. College of Science. Tunghai University
Biol Bull Mar Biol Lab (Woods Hole) — Biological Bulletin. Marine Biological Laboratory (Woods Hole) [*Massachusetts*]
Biol Bull (Woods Hole) — Biological Bulletin (Woods Hole)
Biol Chem Zivocisne Vyroby Vet — Biologizace a Chemizace Zivocisne Vyroby-Veterinaria
Biol Conf "Oholo" Annu Meet — Biological Conference "Oholo." Annual Meeting
Biol Conser — Biological Conservation
Biol Conserv — Biological Conservation
Biol Culturale — Biologia Culturale
Biol Cybern — Biological Cybernetics
Biol Cybernet — Biological Cybernetics
Biol Cybernetics — Biological Cybernetics
Biol Deistvie Bystrykh Neitronov — Biologicheskoe Deistvie Bystrykh Neitronov
Biol Deistvie Gig Znach Atmos Zagryaz — Biologicheskoe Deistvie i Gigienicheskoe Znachenie Atmosfernykh Zagryaznenii
Biol Deistvie Radiats — Biologicheskoe Deistvie Radiatsii [*Ukrainian SSR*]
Biol Dig — Biology Digest
Biol Gabonica — Biologia Gabonica
Biol Gallo-Hell — Biologia Gallo-Hellenica
Biol Gallo-Hellenica — Biologia Gallo-Hellenica
Biol Gastro — Biologie et Gastro-Enterologie
Biol Gastro-Enterol — Biologie et Gastro-Enterologie
Biol Gen — Biologia Generalis
Biol Glas — Bioloski Glasnik
Biol Handb — Biological Handbooks
Biol Hum Aff — Biology and Human Affairs
Biol Ind — Biologia et Industria
Biol J — Biological Journal
Biol Jaarb — Biologisch Jaarboek
Biol Jb — Biologisch Jaarboek [*Gent*]
Biol J Linn — Biological Journal. Linnean Society
Biol J Linn Soc — Biological Journal. Linnean Society
Biol J Linn Soc Lond — Biological Journal. Linnean Society of London
Biol J Nara Women's Univ — Biological Journal. Nara Women's University
Biol J Okayama Univ — Biological Journal. Okayama University
Biol Khim — Biologiya i Khimiya
Biol Koezl — Biologiai Koezlemenyek
Biol Koezlem — Biologiai Koezlemenyek
Biol Lab Zhivotn — Biologiya Laboratornykh Zhivotnykh
Biol Lat — Biologica Latina
Biol Listu — Biologickych Listu
Biol Listy — Biologicke Listy
Biol Macromol — Biological Macromolecules
Biol Macromol Assem — Biological Macromolecules and Assemblies
Biol Medd K Dan Vidensk Selsk — Biologiske Meddelelser Kongelige Danske Videnskabernes Selskab
Biol Meddr — Biologiske Meddelelser
Biol Med Milano Ed Ital — Biologie Medical Milano. Edizione per l'Italia [*Milano*]
Biol Med (Niteroi Brazil) — Biologia Medica (Niteroi, Brazil)

Biol Med (Paris) — Biologie Medicale (Paris)
Biol Membr — Biological Membranes
Biol Mikroorg Ikh Ispol'z Nar Khoz — Biologiya Mikroorganizmov i Ikh Ispol'zovanie v Narodnom Khozyaistve
Biol Moria — Biologiia Moria
Biol Morya (Vladivost) — Biologiya Morya (Vladivostok)
Biol Nauka Sel'sk Lesn Khoz — Biologicheskaya Nauka. Sel'skomu i Lesnomu Khozyatsteu
Biol Nauki — Biologicheskie Nauki [*Moscow*]
Biol Neonat — Biology of the Neonate
Biol Neonatorum — Biologia Neonatorum [*Later, Biology of the Neonate*]
Biol Notes Ill Nat Hist Surv — Biological Notes. Illinois Natural History Survey
Biologia Bratisl — Biologia. Casopis Slovenskej Akademie vied Bratislava
Biologia Pl — Biologia Plantarum
Biologica Lat — Biologica Latina
Biol Pap Univ Alaska — Biological Papers. University of Alaska
Biol Pap Univ Alaska Spec Rep — Biological Papers. University of Alaska. Special Report
Biol Pesq — Biologia Pesquera
Biol Plant — Biologia Plantarum
Biol Pr — Biologicke Prace
Biol Psychi — Biological Psychiatry
Biol Psychiatry — Biological Psychiatry
Biol Psychol — Biological Psychology
Biol R — Biological Reviews
Biol Rdsch — Biologische Rundschau
Biol Reprod — Biology of Reproduction
Biol Reprod Kletok — Biologiya Reprodakisii Kletok
Biol Reprod Suppl — Biology of Reproduction. Supplement
Biol Res Rep Univ Jyvaeskylae — Biological Research Reports. University of Jyvaeskylae
Biol Resur Bodoemov Mold — Biologicheskie Resursy Bodoemov Moldavii
Biol Rev — Biological Reviews. Cambridge Philosophical Society
Biol Rev Camb Philos Soc — Biological Reviews. Cambridge Philosophical Society
Biol Rev Cambridge Phil Soc — Biological Reviews. Cambridge Philosophical Society
Biol Rev City Coll NY — Biological Review. City College of New York
Biol Rs — Biological Reviews
Biol Rundsch — Biologische Rundschau
Biol Rundschau — Biologische Rundschau
Biol Sci — Biological Science
Biol Sci Curriculum Study Bull — Biological Sciences Curriculum Study. Bulletin
Biol Sci (Tokyo) — Biological Science (Tokyo)
Biol Shk — Biologiya Shkole
Biol Soc Nev Mem — Biological Society of Nevada. Memoirs
Biol Soc Nev Occas Pap — Biological Society of Nevada. Occasional Papers
Biol Soc Pak Monogr — Biological Society of Pakistan. Monograph
Biol Soc Washington Proc — Biological Society of Washington. Proceedings
Biol Soc Wash Proc — Biological Society of Washington. Proceedings
Biol Sol — Biologie du Sol. Bulletin International d'Informations
Biol Sol Microbiol — Biologie du Sol. Microbiologie
Biol Svoistva Khim Soedin — Biologicheskie Svoistva Khimicheskikh Soedinenii
Biol Symp — Biological Symposia
Biol Trab Inst Biol "Juan Noe" Fac Med Univ Chile — Biologica. Trabajos. Instituto de Biologia "Juan Noe." Facultad de Medicina de la Universidad de Chile
Biol Trace Elem Res — Biological Trace Element Research
Biol Unserer Zeit — Biologie in Unserer Zeit
Biol Vestn — Bioloski Vestnik
Biol Vnutr Vod — Biologiia Vnutrennikh Vod
Biol Vnutr Vod Inf Byull — Biologiya Vnutrennykh Vod. Informatsionii Byulleten
Biol Vses Inst Eksp Vet — Biologischeskii i Vsesoyuzni Institut Eksperimental'noi Veterinarii
Biol Zakl Pol'nohospod — Biologike Zaklad Pol'nohospodarstva
Biol Zbl — Biologisches Zentralblatt
Biol Zb L'viv Derzh Univ — Biologichnii Zbirnik. L'vivs'kii Derzhaenii Universitet
Biol Zentralbl — Biologisches Zentralblatt
Biol Zh — Biologicheskii Zhurnal
Biol Zh Arm — Biologicheskii Zhurnal Armenii
Biol Zh Armenii — Biologicheskii Zhurnal Armenii
Biom — Biometrics
Biom — Biometrika
BIOMA — Biometrics
Biomass Dig — Biomass Digest
Biomass Energy Inst Newsl — Biomass Energy Institute. Newsletter [*Canada*]
Biomater Med Devices Artif Organs — Biomaterials, Medical Devices, and Artificial Organs
Biomater Med Devices and Artif Organs — Biomaterials, Medical Devices, and Artificial Organs
Biomat Med — Biomaterials, Medical Devices, and Artificial Organs
Biom Bull — Biometrae Bulletin

Biomed Appl Gas Chromatogr — Biomedical Applications of Gas Chromatography
Biomed Appln Polym — Biomedical Applications of Polymers
Biomed Biochim Acta — Biomedica Biochimica Acta
Biomed Commun — Biomedical Communications
Biomed Eng — Biomedical Engineering [*New York*]
Biomed Eng (Engl Transl) — Biomedical Engineering (English Translation)
Biomed Eng (Lond) — Biomedical Engineering (London)
Biomed Engng Curr Aware Notif — Biomedical Engineering Current Awareness Notification
Biomed Eng (NY) — Biomedical Engineering (New York)
Biomed Eng (USSR) — Biomedical Engineering (USSR)
Biomed Expr — Biomedicine Express [*Paris*]
Biomed Express (Paris) — Biomedicine Express (Paris)
Biomed Mass — Biomedical Mass Spectrometry
Biomed Mass Spectrom — Biomedical Mass Spectrometry
Biomed Mater Symp — Biomedical Materials Symposium
Biomed Pharmacother — Biomedicine Pharmacotherapy
Bio-Med Purv — Bio-Medical Purview
Bio-Med Rep 406 Med Lab — Bio-Medical Reports of the 406 Medical Laboratory
Biomed Res — Biomedical Research
Biomed Sci Instrum — Biomedical Sciences Instrumentation
Biomed Sci (Tokyo) — Biomedical Sciences (Tokyo)
Biomed Tech — Biomedizinische Technik [*Berlin*]
Biomed Tech (Berlin) — Biomedizinische Technik (Berlin)
Biomed Tech Biomed Eng — Biomedizinische Technik. Biomedical Engineering
Biometeorol Res Cent (Leiden) Monogr Ser — Biometeorological Research Centre (Leiden). Monograph Series
Biomet-Praximet — Biometrie-Praximetrie
Biometrical J — Biometrical Journal
Biometrie Hum — Biometrie Humaine
Biometr-Praxim — Biometrie-Praximetrie
Biometr Z — Biometrische Zeitschrift
Biom J — Biometrical Journal
Biom Z — Biometrische Zeitschrift
Biom Zeit — Biometrische Zeitschrift
Bionika Mat Model Biol — Bionika i Matematicheskoe Modelirovanie v Biologii
Bioorg Chem — Bioorganic Chemistry
Bioorg Khim — Bioorganicheskaya Khimiya
BIOPA — Biophysics [*English Translation*]
Biopharm Drug Dispos — Biopharmaceutics and Drug Disposition
Biophys — Biophysics
Biophys Centralbl — Biophysikalisches Centralblatt
Biophys Ch — Biophysical Chemistry
Biophys Chem — Biophysical Chemistry
Biophys J — Biophysical Journal
Biophys J Suppl — Biophysical Journal. Supplement
Biophys Soc Annu Meet Abstr — Biophysical Society. Annual Meeting. Abstracts
Biophys Soc Symp — Biophysical Society. Symposium
Biophys Str — Biophysics of Structure and Mechanism
Biophys Struct & Mech — Biophysics of Structure and Mechanism
Biophys Struct Mech — Biophysics of Structure and Mechanism
BIOP Newsl — BIOP [*Board of International Organizations and Programs*] Newsletter
Biopolym Symp — Biopolymers Symposia
Bioquim Clini — Bioquimica Clinica
BiOr — Bibliotheca Orientalis
BIORA — Biochemistry [*English Translation*]
BIORS — Bedford Institute of Oceanography. Report Series
BioSci — BioScience
Biosci Commun — Biosciences Communications
Biosci Rep — Bioscience Reports
Biosci Rep Abo Akad — Bioscience Report. Abo Akademi
BIOSE — Bio-Sciences
Biosources Dig — Biosources Digest
BIOSW — BIOS. Baffin Island Oil Spill Project Working Report
Bio Syst — Bio Systems
Biotech Bio — Biotechnology and Bioengineering
Biotech Bioeng — Biotechnology and Bioengineering
Biotechnol Adv — Biotechnology Advances
Biotechnol Bioeng — Biotechnology and Bioengineering
Biotechnol Bioeng Symp — Biotechnology and Bioengineering. Symposium
Biotechnol Genet Eng Rev — Biotechnology and Genetic Engineering Reviews
Biotechnol Lett — Biotechnology Letters [*England*]
Biotechnol Ser — Biotechnology Series
Biotelemetr — Biotelemetry [*Later, Biotelemetry and Patient Monitoring*]
Biotelem Patient Monit — Biotelemetry and Patient Monitoring
Biotest Bull — Biotest Bulletin
BioV — Bioloski Vestnik
BIOVD — Biovigyanam
BIP — Bulletin de l'Industrie Petroliere
BIPAA — Bulletin. Institut Pasteur [*Paris*]
B I Pasteur — Bulletin. Institut Pasteur [*Paris*]

BIPCB — Biological Psychiatry
BIPED — Buletinul. Institutului Politehnic "Gheorghe Gheorghiu-Dej" Bucuresti. Seria Electrotehnica
BIPG — Bulletin. Institut de Phonetique de Grenoble
BIPGA — Buletinul. Institutului de Petrol, Gaze, si Geologie
BIPID — Bits and Pieces
BIPMA — Biopolymers
BIPNA — Bibliotheca Phonetica
BiR — Biblical Research [*Chicago*]
B Iran Inst — Bulletin. Iranian Institute
Birbal Sahni Inst Palaeobot Spec Publ — Birbal Sahni Institute of Palaeobotany. Special Publication
BIR Bull — BIR [*British Institute of Radiology*] Bulletin
Bird-Band — Bird-Banding
Bird E — Bird Effort
Bird Keeping — Bird Keeping in Australia
Bird L — Bird Lore [*Pennsylvania*]
BIREB — Biology of Reproduction
BiRes — Biblical Research [*Chicago*]
BIRESUL — Bulletin. Institut de Recherches Economiques et Sociales. Universite de Louvain
Birla Archaeol Cult Res Inst Res Bull — Birla Archaeological and Cultural Research Institute. Research Bulletin
BIRMA — Birmingham University. Chemical Engineer
Birmingham Ph Soc Pr — Birmingham [*England*] Philosophical Society. Proceedings
Birmingham Univ Chem Eng — Birmingham University. Chemical Engineer
Birmingham Univ Hist — Birmingham University. Historical Journal
BIRPA — Bulletin. Institut Royal du Patrimoine Artistique
BIRS — British Institute of Recorded Sound. Bulletin
BIRSC — Bulletin. Institut de Recherches Scientifiques au Congo
BIRT — Bulletin d'Information. Institut de Recherche et d'Histoire des Textes
Birth Defects — Birth Defects. Original Article Series
Birth Family J — Birth and the Family. Journal
BIRUA — Biologische Rundschau
BIS — Bulletin of Indonesian Economic Studies
BIS — Bulletin. Institute for the Study of the USSR
BISchk — Buletin i Institutit te Shkecave
BISDP — Boletin Informativo. Seminario de Derecho Politico
BISDSL — Britische und Irische Studien zur Deutschen Sprache und Literatur
BISGM — Boletin Informativo. Secretaria General del Movimiento
BISI — Bollettino. Istituto Storico Italiano
BISIAM — Bollettino. Istituto Storico Italiano e Archivio Muratoriano
BISIMAM — Bollettino. Istituto Storico Italiano per il Medioevo e Archivio Muratoriano
BISNA — BioScience
BISO — Bulletin. Institut pour l'Etude de l'Europe Sud-Orientale
BISRD — Boletim Informativo. Sociedade Brasileira de Radiologia
BISS — Bibliographie Internationale des Sciences Sociales
B Ist Sier — Bollettino. Istituto Sieroterapico Milanese
BISV — Bollettino. Istituto di Storia della Societa e dello Stato Veneziano
BISWA — Biuletyn Instytuta Spawalnictwa. Gliwice
BITAA — Bitumen, Teere, Asphalte, Peche
BItal — Bulletin Italien
B Ital Biol — Bollettino. Societa Italiana di Biologia Sperimentale
BiTerS — Bible et Terre Sainte (Nouvelle Serie) [*Paris*]
BITJA — Journal. Birla Institute of Technology and Science
Bitki Koruma Bul — Bitki Koruma Bulteni
Bitki Koruma Bul Ek Yayin — Bitki Koruma Bulteni. Ek Yayin
Bitki Koruma Bul Plant Prot Bull — Bitki Koruma Bulteni. Plant Protection Bulletin
Bit Nord Tidskr Informationsbehandl — Bit Nordisk Tidskrift fuer Informationsbehandling
BITOA — Bild und Ton
BiTod — Bible Today [*Collegeville, MN*]
BiTr — Bible Translator [*London*]
BiTrans — Bible Translator [*London*]
BITUA — Bitumen
Bitumen Teere Asphalte Peche — Bitumen, Teere, Peche, und Verwandte Stoffe
BITYA — Byulleten' Informatsionnogo Tsentra po Yadernym Dannym
BIUGA — Biuletyn Instytutu Geologicznego
Biul Geol — Biuletyn Geologiczny
Biul Gl Inst Gorn — Biuletyn Glownego Instytutu Gornictwa [*Poland*]
Biul Gos Nikitsk Bot Sad — Biulleten'. Gosudarstvennyi Nikitskii Botanicheskii Sad
Biul IB — Biuletyn. Instytutu Bibliograficznego
Biul IGS — Biuletyn. Instytutu Gospodarstwa Spolecznego
Biul Inf Geol Geofiz Ekon Tech Prac Geol — Biuletyn Informacyjny. Geologia. Geofizyka oraz Ekonomika i Technika Prac Geologicznych
Biul Inf Inst Badaw Proj Przem Farb Lakierow — Biuletyn Informacyjny. Instytut Badawezo Projektowy Przemyslu Farb i Lakierow
Biul Inf Inst Lekow — Biuletyn Informacyjny. Instytutu Lekow
Biul Inf Inst Mater Ogniotrwalych — Biuletyn Informacyjny. Instytutu Materialow Ogniotrwalych

Biul Inf Inst Zbozowego Warszawie — Biuletyn Informacyjny. Instytutu Zbozowego w Warszawie
Biul Inf Mater Ogniotrwalych — Biuletyn Informacyjny. Materialow Ogniotrwalych
Biul Inf Nauk Tech Inst Tech Budow — Biuletyn Informacyjny. Naukowo Technicznej. Instytut Techniki Budowlanej
Biul Inform Inst Zboz Warszawie — Biuletyn Informacyjny. Instytutu Zbozowego w Warszawie
Biul Inst Energ — Biuletyn. Instytutu Energetyki
Biul Inst Genet Hodowli Zwierzat Pol Akad Nauk — Biuletyn. Instytutu Genetyki i Hodowli Zwierzat Polskiej Akademii Nauk [*Poland*]
Biul Inst Geol (Warsaw) — Biuletyn. Instytut Geologiczny (Warsaw)
Biul Inst Hodowli Aklimat Ros (Warszawa) — Biuletyn. Instytutu Hodowli i Aklimatyzacji Roslin (Warszawa)
Biul Inst Hodowli Aklim Rosl — Biuletyn. Instytutu Hodowli i Aklimatyzacji Roslin
Biul Inst Mech Precyz — Biuletyn Instytutu Mechaniki Precyzyjnej
Biul Inst Med Morsk Gdansk — Biuletyn. Instytutu Medycyny Morskiej w Gdansku
Biul Inst Med Morsk Trop Gdyni — Biuletyn. Instytutu Medycyny Morskiej i Tropikalne w Gdyni
Biul Inst Naftowego — Biuletyn. Instytutu Naftowego
Biul Inst Ochr Rosl — Biuletyn. Instytutu Ochrony Roslin [*Poznan*]
Biul Inst Spawalnictwa — Biuletyn. Instytutu Spawalnictwa
Biul Inst Tech Drewna — Biuletyn. Instytutu Technologii Drewna
Biul Inst Weglowego Komun — Biuletyn Instytutu Weglowego. Komunikat
Biul Inst Ziemniaka — Biuletyn. Instytutu Ziemniaka
Biul Kwarant Ochr Ros Min Roln (Warszawa) — Biuletyn. Kwarantanny i Ochrony Roslin Ministerstwo Rolnictwa (Warszawa)
Biull Eksp Biol Med — Biulleten Eksperimentalnoi Biologii i Meditsiny
Biull Izobret — Biulleten Izobretenii [*USSR*]
Biul Lubel Towarz Nauk Mat Fiz Chem — Biuletyn Lubeldkiego Towarzystwa Naukowego. Matematyka, Fizka, Chemia
Biul Lubel Tow Nauk Wydz 2 — Biuletyn Lubelskiego Towarzystwa Naukowego. Wydzial 2. Biologia
Biull Vses Nauchno-Issled Inst Kukuruzy — Biulleten' Vsesoiuznogo Nauchno-Issledovatel'skogo Instituta Kukuruzy
Biul Nauchno Tekh Inf Agron Fiz — Biulleten' Nauchno. Tekhnicheskoi Informatsii po Agronomicheskoi Fizike
Biul Nauchno-Tekh Inf Vses Nauchno-Issled Inst Risa — Biulleten' Nauchno-Tekhnicheskoi Informatsii Vsesoiuznyi Nauchno-Issledovatel'skii Instituta Risa
Biul Panst Inst Nauk Leczn Surow Ros Poznaniu — Biuletyn Panstwowy Instytut Naukowy Leczniczych Surowcow Roslinnych w Poznaniu
Biul Peryglac — Biuletyn Peryglacjalny
Biul PIK — Biuletyn Panstwowego Instytutu Ksiazki
Biul Prod Pieczarek — Biuletyn Producenta Pieczarek
Biul Sluzby Sanit Epidemiol Wojewodztwa Katowickiego — Biuletyn Sluzby Sanitarno Epidemiologiczej Wojewodztwa Katowickiego
Biul Tech Elektrownie Elektrocieplownie — Biuletyn Techniczny, Elektrownie, i Elektrocieplownie [*Poland*]
Biul Vses Nauchno Issled Inst Zashch Rast — Biulletin' Vsesoiuznyi Nauchno Issledovatel'skii Institut Zashchity Rastenii
Biul Warzywniczy — Biuletyn Warzywniczy
Biul Wojsk Akad Med — Biuletyn Wojskowej Akademii Medycznej
Biul Wojsk Akad Tech — Biuletyn Wojskowej Akademii Technicznej Imienia Jaroslawa Dabrowskiego
Biul Zakl Ochr Srodowiska Reg Przem Pol Akad Nauk — Biuletyn Zaklad Ochrony Srodowiska Regionow Przemyslowych Polskiej Akademii Nauk
Biul Zydowskiego Inst Hist — Biuletyn Zydowskiego Instytutu Historycznego
BIUNA — Biologieunterricht
BIV — Boletin Indigenista Venezolano
BiViChr — Bible et Vie Chretienne [*Maredsous*]
BiVieChr — Bible et Vie Chretienne [*Maredsous*]
BiWelt — Die Bibel in der Welt [*Ruhr*]
BIWIA — Bild der Wissenschaft
Biwkly Cryog Curr Aware Serv — Biweekly Cryogenics Current Awareness Service
BiZ — Biblische Zeitschrift
Biz — Bizarre Mystery Magazine
BIZEA — Biochemische Zeitschrift
BIZEB — Biometrische Zeitschrift
BIZNA — Biologisches Zentralblatt
B I Zool AS — Bulletin. Institute of Zoology. Academia Sinica [*Taipei*]
BIZYAS — Chung Yang Yen Chiu Yuan T'ung Wu Yen Chiu So Chi K'an
BJ — Bonner Jahrbuecher
BJ — Bookman's Journal
BJ — La Sainte Bible. Traduit en Francais sous la Direction de l'Ecole Biblique de Jerusalem
BJA — British Journal of Administrative Management
BJA — British Journal of Aesthetics
BJANA — British Journal of Anaesthesia
B Jap S S F — Bulletin. Japanese Society of Scientific Fisheries
BJAY — Blue Jay
BJAYAC — British Journal of Audiology

B JB — Bach Jahrbuch
BJB — Bonner Jahrbuecher
BJBE — Bulletin. Jardin Botanique de l'Etat a Bruxelles
BJBTB — Bangladesh Journal of Botany
BJCAAI — British Journal of Cancer
BJCEA — Boletin. Junta do Control de Energia Atomica
BJCPB — British Journal of Social and Clinical Psychology
BJCPBU — British Journal of Social and Clinical Psychology
BJCPDW — British Journal of Clinical Psychology
BJ Crim — British Journal of Criminology
B J Criminology — British Journal of Criminology
BJDCA — British Journal of Diseases of the Chest
BJDCAT — British Journal of Diseases of the Chest
BJDEAZ — British Journal of Dermatology
BJDEB — British Journal of Disorders of Communication
BJ Delinq — British Journal of Delinquency
B J Disorders of Communication — British Journal of Disorders of
    Communication
BJDPE4 — British Journal of Developmental Psychology
BJDSA9 — British Journal of Dermatology. Supplement
BJEBA — British Journal of Experimental Biology
BJECD — Bell Journal of Economics
B J Ednl Psych — British Journal of Educational Psychology
B J Ednl Studies — British Journal of Educational Studies
B J Ednl Technology — British Journal of Educational Technology
BJEMA — Bell Journal of Economics and Management Science [*Later, Bell
    Journal of Economics*]
BJEMA — British Journal of Aesthetics
BJEP — British Journal of Educational Psychology
BJEPA — British Journal of Experimental Pathology
BJEPA5 — British Journal of Experimental Pathology
BJES — British Journal of Educational Studies
BJESA — British Journal of Educational Psychology
BJESAE — British Journal of Educational Psychology
BJewPES — Bulletin. Jewish Palestine Exploration Society
BJF — Biblioteka Juznoslovenskog Filologa
BJFPDD — British Journal of Family Planning
BJG — Bank of Japan. Monthly Economic Review
BJGL — Blaetter fuer Juedische Geschichte und Literatur
B J Guidance & Counseling — British Journal of Guidance and Counseling
BJGZ — Berliner Juedische Gemeinde-Zeitung
BJHEA — British Journal of Haematology
BJHEAL — British Journal of Haematology
BJHIL — Bibliographie zur Juedisch-Hellenistischen und
    Intertestamentarischen Literatur
BJHMA — British Journal of Hospital Medicine
BJHMAB — British Journal of Hospital Medicine
BJHSAT — British Journal for the History of Science
BJI — British Journal of Industrial Relations
BJIMA — British Journal of Industrial Medicine
BJIMAG — British Journal of Industrial Medicine
BJ Ind Rel — British Journal of Industrial Relations
B J In-Service Ed — British Journal of In-Service Education
BJIR — British Journal of Industrial Relations
BJLS — British Journal of Law and Society
B J Ma St Ps — British Journal of Mathematical and Statistical Psychology
B J Math & Stat Psych — British Journal of Mathematical and Statistical
    Psychology
BJMEAC — British Journal of Medical Education
BJMEDF — British Journal of Sexual Medicine
BJ Mental Subnormality — British Journal of Mental Subnormality
BJMPA — British Journal of Medical Psychology
BJMPAB — British Journal of Medical Psychology
BJMPs — British Journal of Medical Psychology
BJMRDK — Brazilian Journal of Medical and Biological Research
BJMSA — British Journal of Mathematical and Statistical Psychology
BJMSBL — British Journal of Mental Subnormality
BJMTD — British Journal of Music Therapy
BJNTA — British Journal of Non-Destructive Testing
BJNUA — British Journal of Nutrition
BJNUAV — British Journal of Nutrition
BJOCA — British Journal of Occupational Safety
BJOGA — British Journal of Obstetrics and Gynaecology
BJOGAS — British Journal of Obstetrics and Gynaecology
B John Ryl — Bulletin. John Rylands Library. University of Manchester
BJOPA — British Journal of Ophthalmology
BJOPAL — British Journal of Ophthalmology
BJOSA — British Journal of Sociology
BJOSB — British Journal of Oral Surgery [*Later, British Journal of Oral and
    Maxillofacial Surgery*]
BJOSBV — British Journal of Oral Surgery [*Later, British Journal of Oral and
    Maxillofacial Surgery*]
BJOSEY — British Journal of Oral and Maxillofacial Surgery
BJOTA — Begg Journal of Orthodontic Theory and Treatment
BJP — British Journal of Psychology

BJPCA — British Journal of Pharmacology and Chemotherapy [*Later, British
    Journal of Pharmacology*]
BJPCAL — British Journal of Pharmacology and Chemotherapy [*Later,
    British Journal of Pharmacology*]
BJPCB — British Journal of Pharmacology
BJPCBM — British Journal of Pharmacology
BJPEBS — British Journal of Physical Education
BJPES — Bulletin. Jewish Palestine Exploration Society
B J Physical Ed — British Journal of Physical Education
BJPIA5 — British Journal for the Philosophy of Science
BJPOAN — British Journal of Physiological Optics
BJPs — British Journal of Psychology
BJPSA — British Journal of Plastic Surgery
BJPSAZ — British Journal of Plastic Surgery
BJPSB — British Journal of Psychiatry
BJPSB2 — British Journal of Psychiatry. Special Publication
B J Psych — British Journal of Psychology
BJ Psychiatry — British Journal of Psychiatry
BJPVA — British Journal of Preventive and Social Medicine
BJPVAA — British Journal of Preventive and Social Medicine
BJPYA — British Journal of Psychiatry
BJPYAJ — British Journal of Psychiatry
BJR — Bulletin des Jeunes Romanistes
BJR — Bulletin. John Rylands Library. University of Manchester
BJRAA — British Journal of Radiology
BJRAAP — British Journal of Radiology
BJ Religious Ed — British Journal of Religious Education
BJRHDF — British Journal of Rheumatology
BJRL — Bulletin. John Rylands Library. University of Manchester
BJRLM — Bulletin. John Rylands Library. University of Manchester
BJRSAB — British Journal of Radiology. Supplement
BJS — British Journal of Sociology
BJSCP — British Journal of Social and Clinical Psychology
BJSGA — British Journal of Psychology. General Section
BJSGAE — British Journal of Psychology
BJSIB — Bangladesh Journal of Scientific and Industrial Research
BJSMAW — British Journal of Social Medicine
B JSME — Bulletin. JSME [*Japan Society of Mechanical Engineers*]
B J Social and Clinical Psych — British Journal of Social and Clinical
    Psychology
B J Sociology — British Journal of Sociology
BJSPDA — British Journal of Social Psychology
B J Stat Psych — British Journal of Statistical Psychology
BJSUA — British Journal of Surgery
BJSUAM — British Journal of Surgery
BJTBA4 — British Journal of Tuberculosis
BJ Teach Ed — British Journal of Teacher Education
BJTUAR — British Journal of Tuberculosis and Diseases of the Chest
Bjull Akad Nauk Uz SSR — Bjulleten Akademiji Nauk Uzbekskoj SSR
Bjull Glavn Bot Sada — Bjulleten Glavnogo Botaniceskogo Sada
Bjull Gos Nikit Bot Sada — Bjulleten Gosudarstvennogo Nikitskogo
    Botaniceskogo Sada
Bjull Inst Teoret Astronom — Bjulleten Instituta Teoreticeskoi Astronomii
Bjull Inst Teoret Astronom — Bjulleten Instituta Teoreticeskoi Astronomii.
    Akademija Nauk Sojuza Sovetskih Socialisticeskih Respublik
Bjull Mosk Obsc Ispyt Prir Otd Biol — Bjulleten' Moskovskogo Obscestva
    Ispytatelej Prirody. Otdel Biologiceskij
BJURA — British Journal of Urology
BJURAN — British Journal of Urology
BJV — Berliner Jahrbuch fuer Vor- und Fruehgeschichte
BJVDA — British Journal of Venereal Diseases
BJVDAK — British Journal of Venereal Diseases
BK — Bedi Karthlisa
Bk — Bookman
Bk Abroad — Books Abroad
BKAT — Biblischer Kommentar. Altes Testament
BKB — Bank of Israel. Economic Review
BKBCB — Bulletin. Boris Kidric Institute of Nuclear Sciences. Chemistry
BKBGA4 — Brooklyn Botanic Garden. Annual Report
Bkbinding & Bk Production — Bookbinding and Book Production
Bkbird — Bookbird
Bk & Bkmen — Books and Bookmen
BKBR — Beitraege zur Kenntnis der Babylonischen Religion
Bk Buyer — Book Buyer [*Later, Lamp*]
Bk Coll — Book Collector
Bk Collec — Book Collector
Bk Collecting & Lib Mo — Book Collecting and Library Monthly
Bk Collector — Book Collector
BKCSD — Bulletin. Korean Chemical Society [*South Korea*]
BKEJA — Berichte. Kernforschungsanlage Juelich
Bk Forum — Book Forum
BKFSD — Bulletin. Korean Fisheries Technological Society [*South Korea*]
BKGP — Blaetter fuer Kirchengeschichte Pommerns
BKH — Baksteen. Tweemaandelijks Tijdschrift Gewijd aan de Technische en
    Esthetische Eigenschappen van Gebakken Kleiprodukten
Bk Hawaii — Bank of Hawaii. Monthly Review

BkIA — Books at Iowa
BKISA — Bulletin. Boris Kidric Institute of Nuclear Sciences. Supplement
BKJ — Beitraege zur Kinder- und Jugendliteratur
BKK — Expovisie. Beurzen, Tentoonstellingen, Congressen, Hotellerie
Bkl — Booklist
BkL — Bookman (London)
Bklegger — Booklegger Magazine
Bklist — Booklist and Subscription Books Bulletin [*Later, Booklist*]
Bk LJ — Banking Law Journal
BKLKB — Banyaszati es Kohaszati Lapok. Kohaszat
BKM — Bankers' Monthly
Bkman (Lond) — Bookman (London)
Bkmark — Bookmark
Bkmark (Idaho) — Bookmark. University of Idaho
BKMGA — Blackwood's Magazine
BKMR — Beitraege zur Kulturgeschichte des Mittelalters und der Renaissance
BKN — Bank Negara Malaysia. Quarterly Economic Bulletin
Bk-News — Book-News
BKO — Bank of Korea. Quarterly Economic Review
BKO — Beitraege zur Kenntnis des Orients
BKOAA — Byulleten' Komissii po Opredeleniyu Absolyutnogo Vozrasta Geologicheskikh Formatsii
B Konan Women Coll — Bulletin. Konan Women's College
BKQ — Bakery Production and Marketing
BKR — Banker
BKRC — Bulletin. Korean Research Center
Bk Rev Dig — Book Review Digest
Bk Rev Ind — Book Review Index
Bk Rev Mo — Book Reviews of the Month
Bks Abroad — Books Abroad
Bks & Bkmn — Books and Bookmen
BKSCA — Black Scholar
Bks in Can — Books in Canada
Bks & Libs — Books and Libraries at the University of Kansas
Bks Today — Books Today [*Sunday Chicago Tribune*]
BKSTS J — BKSTS [*British Kinematograph Sound and Television Society*] Journal
BK Tech Rev — BK Technical Review
BKTLA — Book Trolley
Bk Trolley — Book Trolley
BKW — Bakkerswereld
BKW — [*A*] Book of Weird Tales
BkW — Book World
Bk Wk — Book Week
Bk World — Book World
BL — Bibel und Leben [*Duesseldorf*]
BL — Bibliographie Linguistique
BL — Bibliotheekleven
Bl — Black Perspective in Music
BL — Book List. Society for Old Testament Studies [*Manchester*]
BL — Booklist
B & L — Brain and Language
BL — Bulletin des Lettres
BL — Bulletin Linguistique. Faculte des Lettres de Bucarest
BL — Business Lawyer
BLA — Black Art [*London*]
BLA — Business Latin America
Black — Blackwood's Magazine
Black Am L — Black American Literature Forum
Black Bus News — Black Business News
BlackCh — Black Church
Black Coll — Black Collegian
Black Ent — Black Enterprise
Black F — Black Forum
Black Fox Mag — Black Fox Magazine
Black Hills Eng — Black Hills Engineer
BlackI — Black Images: A Critical Quarterly on Black Arts and Culture
BlackIC — Black I: A Canadian Journal of Black Expression
Black L J — Black Law Journal
Black Mag — Blackwood's Magazine
Black N Dig — Black News Digest
Black Perspective M — Black Perspective in Music
Black Pol Econ — Review of Black Political Economy
BlackR — Black Review
Black Rock For Bull — Black Rock Forest. Bulletin
Black Rock For Pap — Black Rock Forest. Papers
Black Sch — Black Scholar
Black W — Black World
Blackw — Blackwood's Magazine
Blackwood's Mag — Blackwood's Magazine
Blaett Dtsche u Int Polit — Blaetter fuer Deutsche und Internationale Politik
Blaett Technikgesch — Blaetter fuer Technikgeschichte
Blagoveshch Gos Med Inst Tr — Blagoveshchenskii Gosudarstvennyi Meditsinskii Institut. Trudy
Bl Agric Chem Soc Jap — Bulletin. Agricultural Chemical Society of Japan
Blair & Ketchum's — Blair and Ketchum's Country Journal

Blake Ill Q — Blake. An Illustrated Quarterly
BlakeN — Blake Newsletter
BlakeS — Blake Studies
Blake Stud — Blake Studies
BLAM — Boletin Latino-Americano de Musica
BLAM — Bulletin. Librairie Ancienne et Moderne
Bl Amer Lit Forum — Black American Literature Forum
Bl Am Phys Soc — Bulletin. American Physical Society
Bl Assoc Chim — Bulletin. Association des Chimistes
Blast F & Steel Pl — Blast Furnace and Steel Plant
Blast Furn Coke Oven Raw Mater Proc — Blast Furnace, Coke Oven, and Raw Materials. Proceedings
Blast Furn Steel Plant — Blast Furnace and Steel Plant
BLB — Bloembollenexport
BLB — Bulletin Linguistique. Faculte des Lettres de Bucarest
Bl Belt Mag — Black Belt Magazine
Bl Bergshandteringens Vaenner — Blad foer Bergshandteringens Vaenner
BLBI — Bulletin. Leo Baeck Institute
BLBIA — Bluegrass
Bl Bks B — Black Books Bulletin
BLC — Bulletin de Litterature Chretienne
BLCED — Blood Cells
Bl Chem Soc Jap — Bulletin. Chemical Society of Japan
Bl Deutsche Landesgesch — Blaetter fuer Deutsche Landesgeschichte
Bldg — Building
BLDGA — Buildings
Bldg Age — Building Age and National Builder
Bldg Conserv — Building Conservation
Bldg Conservation — Building Conservation
Bldg Des — Building Design
Bldg Design — Building Design
Bldg Econ — Building Economist
Bldg Economist — Building Economist
Bldg Env — Building and Environment
Bldg Envir — Building and Environment
Bldg Environ — Building and Environment
Bldg & Environment — Building and Environment
Bldg Forum — Building Forum
Bldg Mater — Building Materials
Bldg Mater — Building Materials and Equipment
Bldg Mats List — Building Materials List
Bldg Mgmt Abs — Building Management Abstracts
Bldg Opr — Building Operating Management
Bldg Products — Building Products
Bldg Refurb — Building Refurbishment
Bldg Refurbishment & Maintenance — Building Refurbishment and Maintenance
Bldg Research Assocn New Zealand Bldg Information Bull — Building Research Association of New Zealand. Building Information Bulletin
Bldg Research & Practice — Building Research and Practice
Bldg Res Practice — Building Research and Practice
Bldg Res (Washington DC) — Building Research (Washington, DC)
Bldgs — Buildings: The Construction and Building Management Journal
Bldg Sci — Building Science
Bldg Serv — Building Services
Bldg Serv Engr — Building Services Engineer
Bldg Serv Environ Engr — Building Services and Environmental Engineer
Bldg Services — Building Services
Bldg Services Engineer — Building Services Engineer
Bldg Services Environ Engnr — Building Services and Environmental Engineer
Bldg Services & Environmental Engineer — Building Services and Environmental Engineer
Bldg Soc Gaz — Building Societies Gazette
Bldg Specif — Building Specification
Bldg Specification — Building Specification
Bldg with Steel — Building with Steel
Bldg Study Div Bldg Res CSIRO — Building Study. Division of Building Research. Commonwealth Scientific and Industrial Research Organisation
Bldg Systems Design — Building Systems Design
Bldg Tech File — Building Technical File
Bldg Tech Mgmt — Building Technology and Management
Bldg Technol Mgmt — Building Technology and Management
Bldg Trades J — Building Trades Journal
Bldg Trades Jnl — Building Trades Journal
BLDIA — Black Diamond
Bl D Lg — Blaetter fuer Deutsche Landesgeschichte
Bl D Ph — Blaetter fuer Deutsche Philosophie
Bld Res Prac — Building Research and Practice
Bld Serv Enging Res Tech — Building Services Engineering Research and Technology
Bld Technol Mgmnt — Building Technology and Management
Bl Dt und Internat Pol — Blaetter fuer Deutsche und Internationale Politik
Bl Dtsch Int Polit — Blaetter fuer Deutsche und Internationale Politik
BLE — Bulletin Linguistique et Ethnologique
BLE — Bulletin de Litterature Ecclesiastique

Bleacher Finish Tex Chem — Bleacher, Finisher, and Textile Chemist

BLEND — Black Enterprise

BLESA — Bollettino. Laboratorio di Entomologia Agraria "Filippo Silvestri" di Portici

BLF — Bank of London and South America. Review

BLFSA — Blast Furnace and Steel Plant

BLFSB — Basic Life Sciences

Bl Grundstuecks Bau-Wohnungsrecht — Blaetter fuer Grundstuecks, Bau- und Wohnungsrecht [*West Germany*]

BLGTB — Biologist [*London*]

BLH — Best's Review. Life/Health Insurance Edition

BLH — Boletin de Estudios Latinamericanos y del Caribe

BlH — Bulletin Hispanique

Bl Heimatkd — Blaetter fuer Heimatkunde

BLI — Beitraege zur Linguistik und Informationsverarbeitung

B Liaison Inform Adm Centr Econ Finances — Bulletin de Liaison et d'Information. Administration Centrale de l'Economie et des Finances

B Lit E — Bulletin de Litterature Ecclesiastique

BLJ — British Library Journal

Blk Lib — Black Liberation

Blk Panth — Black Panther

Blk Schol — Black Scholar

BLL — Belaruskaia Litaratura

BLLIAX — Bratislavske Lekarske Listy

Bl LJ — Black Law Journal

BLL Rev — BLL [*British Library Lending Division*] Review

BLL Review — British Library. Lending Division. Review

Bll Univ Tenn Agr Exp Sta — Bulletin. University of Tennessee. Agricultural Experiment Station

BLM — Bolletini di Litteratura Moderna

BLM — Bonniers Litteraera Magasin

BLM — Book League Monthly

BLMag — Bonniers Litteraera Magasin

BLM (Bon Lit) — BLM (Bonniers Litterara Magasin)

BLMNR — Bureau of Land Management. Alaska. News Release

BLMRA J — BLMRA [*British Leather Manufacturers' Research Association*] Journal

BLN — Banca Nazionale del Lavoro. Quarterly Review

BLN — Bottomline

BLOAA — Biologia [*Bratislava*]

Blood Purif — Blood Purification

Blood Ther J — Blood Therapy Journal

Blood Vess — Blood Vessels

Bl Orcl — Black Oracle

BLOT — Book List. Society for Old Testament Studies

BLPYA — Biological Psychology

BLR — Baylor Law Review

BLR — Belorussian Review [*Munich*]

BLR — Bodleian Library Record

BLR — Business Law Review

BLRCA — Bell Laboratories Record

BlS — Black Scholar

BLS — Business Lawyer. Special Issue

BLS — Employee Relations

BLS CPI — United States. Bureau of Labor Statistics. CPI [*Consumer Price Index*] Detailed Report

BLSCR — Bollettino Linguistico per la Storia e la Cultura Regionale

Bl Soc Chim Belg — Bulletin. Societe Chimique de Belgique

Bl Soc Chim Ind — Bulletin. Societe de Chimie Industrielle

BLS PPI — United States. Bureau of Labor Statistics. Producer Prices and Price Indexes

BLS Review — United States. Bureau of Labor Statistics. Monthly Labor Review

BLT — Belgie/Economische en Handelsvoorlichting

BLT — Brethren Life and Thought

BLTBAI — Folia Societatis Scientiarum Lublinensis Biologia

BLTND — [*The*] Bulletin

BLTSG — Bulletin. Lutheran Theological Seminary [*Gettysburg*]

Blue Cross Assoc Res Ser — Blue Cross Association. Research Series

Bluegrass — Bluegrass Unlimited

Blues — Blues Unlimited

BLUMA — Bollettino. Unione Matematica Italiana

B Lund — Bulletin. Societe de Lettres de Lund

BLux — Bulletin Linguistique et Ethnologique. Institut Granducal (Luxembourg)

BLVS — Bibliothek des Literarischen Vereins (Stuttgart)

BL W — Black World

Bl Wuerttemb Kirchengesch — Blaetter fuer Wuerttembergische Kirchengeschichte

Bl Zuckerruebenbau — Blaetter fuer Zuckerruebenbau

BM — Baghdader Mitteilungen

BM — Baltische Monatsschrift

BM — Banber Matenadarani

BM — Bankers' Magazine

BM — Benediktinische Monatshefte [*Beuron*]

BM — Beth Mikra

BM — Blackwood's Magazine

BM — Bluegrass Music News

BM — Bonniers Maenadstidning [*Stockholm*]

Bm — Bookman

B of M — Books of the Month

BM — British Museum. Quarterly

BM — Bulletin Monumental

BM — Burlington Magazine

BMA — Bergens Museums. Aarbok

BM Aa — Bergens Museums. Aarbok

BMAAA — Byuleten' Mezhdunarodnykh Agenstv Atomnoi Energii

B Mad — Bulletin de Madagascar

BMAD — Bulletin Mensuel. Academie Delphinale

BMadagascar — Bulletin de Madagascar

BMAEA7 — Montana. Agricultural Experiment Station. Bulletin

BMAH — Bulletin. Musees Royaux d'Art et d'Histoire

BMAIU — Bulletin Mensuel. Alliance Israelite Universelle

BMARB — Bergens Museums. Aarbok

B Marin Sci — Bulletin of Marine Science

B Math Biol — Bulletin of Mathematical Biology

B Math Stat — Bulletin of Mathematical Statistics

BMB — Boston Museum. Bulletin

BMB — British Medical Bulletin

BMB — Bulletin Bibliographique. Musee Belge

BMB — Bulletin. Musee Basque

BMB — Bulletin. Musee de Beyrouth

BMBAB — Bulletin. Musees Royaux des Beaux-Arts de Belgique

BM Beyrouth — Bulletin. Musee de Beyrouth

BMBIA — Bulletin of Mathematical Biophysics

BMBL — Berliner Munzblaetter

BMBTA — Baumaschine und Bautechnik

BMBUA — British Medical Bulletin

BMBUAQ — British Medical Bulletin

BMCL — Bulletin of Medieval Canon Law

BMCN — Book of the Month Club. News

BMCR — Bollettino. Museo della Civilta Romana

BMD — Bijdragen en Mededeelingen der Dialectencommissie van de Koninklijke Akademie van Wetenschappen te Amsterdam

BMDIA — Bulletin. Mount Desert Island Biological Laboratory

BMDial — Bijdragen en Mededeelingen der Dialectencommissie van de Koninklijke Akademie van Wetenschappen te Amsterdam

BMDJA — Burma Medical Journal

BMDOA — Biomaterials, Medical Devices, and Artificial Organs

BM/E — Broadcast Management/Engineering

B Med Lib A — Bulletin. Medical Library Association

BMEEB — Bulletin of Mechanical Engineering Education

BMEGA — Bulletin. Mechanical Engineering Laboratory of Japan

B Mem Soc Anthr — Bulletins et Memoires. Societe d'Anthropologie de Paris

B Mem Soc Arch Bordeaux — Bulletin et Memoires. Societe Archeologique de Bordeaux

B Menninger — Bulletin. Menninger Clinic

B Mens Statist Trav Suppl — Bulletin Mensuel des Statistiques du Travail. Supplement

B Mens Stat O-Mer — Bulletin Mensuel de Statistique d'Outre-Mer

BMEPAQ — British Museum (Natural History). Economic Series

B Metr Mus A — Bulletin. Metropolitan Museum of Art [*New York*]

BMF — Bulletin. Musees de France

BMFA — Bulletin. Museum of Fine Arts [*Boston*]

BMFAAK — British Museum (Natural History). Fossil Mammals of Africa

BMFEA — Bulletin. Museum of Far Eastern Antiquities [*Stockholm*]

BMFJ — Bulletin. Maison Franco-Japonais

BMFR — Blaetter fuer Muenzfreunde

BMFT Mitt — BMFT [*Bundesministerium fuer Forschung und Technologie*] Mitteilungen

BMFT Mitteilungen — Bonn. Pressereferat des Bundesministeriums fuer Forschung und Technologie. Mitteilungen

BMGC — British Museum. General Catalogue of Printed Books

BMGeire — Bijdragen en Mededeelingen Uitgegeven door de Vereeniging Geire

BMGHA — Bamidgeh

BMGJW — Bijdragen en Mededeelingen van het Genootschap voor de Joodsche Wetenschap in Nederland

BMGLA — Bulletin. Societe des Sciences Medicales du Grand-Duche de Luxembourg

BMGS — Byzantine and Modern Greek Studies

BMH — Bulletin. Museum Haaretz [*Tel Aviv*]

BMH — Handelsvoorlichting Bank Mees en Hope

BMHA — Bulletin pour la Conservation des Monuments Historiques d'Alsace

BMHBA — Bulletin. Musee Hongrois des Beaux Arts

BMHG — Bijdragen en Mededeelingen van het Historisch Genootschap

BMHM — Bulletin. Musee Historique de Mulhouse

BMHNAZ — Museo Nacional de Historia Natural. Boletin [*Santiago*]

BMHS — Bulletin. Missouri Historical Society

BMI — BMI: The Many Worlds of Music

BMIB — Bank Markazi Iran. Bulletin

B Midwest M — Bulletin. Midwest Modern Language Association

BMIR — Bollettino. Museo dell'Impero Romano
B Miss Hist Soc — Bulletin. Missouri Historical Society
BMJA — Bulletin. Museum of Jewish Antiquities
BMJE — British Medical Journal Epitome
BMJH — Boletin. Museo de Motivos Populares Argentinos Jose Hernandez
BMJOA — British Medical Journal
BMJOAE — British Medical Journal
BML — Bibliotheque du Museon (Louvain)
BMLA — Bulletin. Medical Library Association
BMM — Belaruskaia Mova. Mizhvuzauski Zbornik
BMM — Bibliography of Manichaean Materials
BMM — Biblioteca Moderna Mondadori
BMM — Bulletin. Metropolitan Museum of Art
BMMA — Bulletin. Metropolitan Museum of Art
BMMLA — Bulletin. Midwest Modern Language Association
BMN — Building Material News
BMNB — Bulletin. Musee National de Burgas
BMNE — Bulletin. Museum of Mediterranean and Near Eastern Antiquities
BMNPA3 — British Museum (Natural History). Publication
BMNRBA — British Museum (Natural History). Report
BMod — Bibliographie Moderne
BMOGA — Bollettino delle Malattie dell'Orecchio, della Gola, del Naso
B Mon — Bulletin Monumental
B (Montreal) — Business Review (Montreal)
B Monument — Bulletin Monumental
BMP — Birmingham Post
BMP — Boletim Mensal. Sociedade de Lingua Portuguesa
BMPBA — British Columbia. Department of Mines and Petroleum Resources. Bulletin
BMPGA — Byulleten' Moskovskogo Obshchestva Ispytatelei Prirody Otdel Geologicheskii
BMPMB — Bibliotheca Microbiologica
BMPSEQ — Brunner/Mazel Psychosocial Stress Series
BMQ — Boston Medical Quarterly
BMQ — British Museum. Quarterly
BMR — Bank Marketing
BMR — Black Music Research Journal
BMR — Monthly Bibliography of Medical Reviews
BMRAH — Bulletin. Musees Royaux d'Art et d'Histoire
BMRBA — Bulletin. Musees Royaux des Beaux-Arts
BMRED — Bureau of Mines. Research [United States]
BMR J Aust Geol Geophys — BMR [Australia. Bureau of Mineral Resources. Geology and Geophysics] Journal of Australian Geology and Geophysics
BMR J Aust Geol & Geophys — BMR [Australia. Bureau of Mineral Resources. Geology and Geophysics] Journal of Australian Geology and Geophysics
BMRN — Bimonthly Research Notes. Canada Department of Environment
BMRSA — Bulletin of Marine Science
BMS — Babylonian Magic and Sorcery
BMS — Benedictiner Monatsschrift
BMSA — Bulletins et Memoires. Societe d'Anthropologie
B M S Anthr — Bulletins et Memoires. Societe d'Anthropologie de Paris
BMSAO — Bulletin et Memoires. Societe des Antiquaires de l'Ouest
BMSIA — Biomedical Sciences Instrumentation
BMSLP — Boletim Mensal. Sociedade de Lingua Portuguesa
BMSMA — Bulletins et Memoires. Societe Medicale des Hopitaux de Paris
BMSQ — Boston Medical and Surgical Quarterly
BMSSB — Bulletin Mathematique [Romania]
BMSSD — Biomass Digest
BMSTA — Transactions. British Mycological Society
BMSYA — Biomedical Mass Spectrometry
BMTBA — Bulletin of Mathematical Biology
BMTFA — Buletinul. Institutului Politehnic din Iasi. Sectia 1. Matematica, Mecanica Teoretica, Fizica
BMus — Berliner Museen
B Mus Anthropol Prehist — Bulletin. Musee d'Anthropologie Prehistorique
B Mus Art — Bulletin. Musees Royaux d'Art et d'Histoire
BMusB — Bulletin. Museum of Fine Arts (Boston)
BMusBeyr — Bulletin. Musee de Beyrouth
B Mus FA — Museum of Fine Arts. Bulletin [Boston]
B Mus Far East Antiq — Bulletin. Museum of Far Eastern Antiquities
BMusFr — Bulletin. Musees de France
BMusHongr — Bulletin. Musee Hongrois des Beaux Arts
B Mus Imp — Bollettino. Museo dell'Impero Romano
B Muz — Belgarsko Muzikoznanie
B Mw — Beitraege zur Musikwissenschaft
BMYBA — British Mycological Society. Bulletin
BMYSD2 — British Mycological Society. Symposium
BMZTA — Biomedizinische Technik
BN — Beitraege zur Namenforschung
BN — Bibliotheque Nationale
BN — Bibliotheque Norbertine
BN — Biography News
BN — Biuletyn Numizmatyczny
BN — Book Notes

BN — Borsen
BN — Browning Newsletter
BN — Burke's Newsletter
BNA — Tijdschrift. Nationale Bank van Belgie
BNAMC — Bulletin. National Association for Music Therapy
BNAP — Bulletin. National Association of Secondary-School Principals
B Narcotics — Bulletin on Narcotics
BNA Sec Reg — Securities Regulation and Law Reports (Bureau of National Affairs)
B Nat Geogr Soc India — Bulletin. National Geographical Society of India
B Nauk Inst Nauk Ekon Univ Warszaw — Biuletyn Naukowy Instytutu Nauk Ekonomicznych Universytetu Warszawskiego
BNB — British National Bibliography
BNBE — Economic Bulletin. National Bank of Egypt
BN (Bian Ner) — BN (Bianco e Nero)
BNBID — Behavioral and Neural Biology
BNBUD — Baroid News Bulletin
BNC — Business and Finance
Bnc Angola — Boletin Trimestral. Banco de Angola
Bnc Lavoro — Italian Trends. Banco Lavoro
BndM — Benediktinische Monatsschrift
BNDSA — Bibliotheca Nutrito et Dieta (Switzerland)
BNDSD — Bundesarbeitsblatt
BNEOB — Biology of the Neonate
BNEPB — Behavioral Neuropsychiatry
BNF — Beitraege zur Namenforschung
BNF Nutr Bull — BNF [British Nutrition Foundation] Nutrition Bulletin
BNGrJb — Byzantinisch-Neugriechische Jahrbuecher
BNI — Bank van de Nederlandse Antillen. Quarterly Bulletin
BNI — Bibliografia Nazionale Italiana
BNIAA — Norinsho Kachiku Eisei Shikenjo Kenkyu Hokoku
BNIST Rapp Annu — BNIST [Bureau National de l'Information Scientifique et Technique] Rapport Annuel
BNJ — British Numismatic Journal, Including the Proceedings of the British Numismatic Society
BNJ — Business News. Facts, Analysis, Information
BNJ — Byzantinisch-Neugriechische Jahrbuecher
B NJ Acad S — Bulletin. New Jersey Academy of Science
BNK — Bank Reports
BNKAB — Bionika
BNKRB — Banker
BNL — Banca Nazionale del Lavoro. Quarterly Review
BNL — Beitraege zur Neueren Literaturgeschichte
BNLVAI — Brookhaven National Laboratory. Lectures in Science. Vistas in Research
BNMB — Bank Negara Malaysia. Bulletin
BNN — Buggalo Nam Newsletter
BNO — Biuletyn Nauczyciela Opolskiego
BNOB — Bulletin. Nederlandse Oudheidkundige Bond
BNOTA — Belgisch-Nederlands Tijdschrift voor Oppervlaktetechnieken van Metalen
BNPL — Bulletin. New York Public Library
BNR — Bank Note Reporter
BNR — Botswana Notes and Records
BN & R — Botswana Notes and Records
BNS — Banque Nationale Suisse. Bulletin Mensuel
BNSCDX — Braunschweiger Naturkundliche Schriften
BNSDA — Bulletin. New York State Society of Dentistry for Children
BNSKA — Bunseki Kagaku
BNSMR — Bank of Nova Scotia. Monthly Review
B Num — Bulletin de Numismatique
BNUNA — Bulletin on Narcotics [Switzerland]
BNV — Business Asia. Weekly Report to Managers of Asia/Pacific Operations
B NY Ac Med — Bulletin. New York Academy of Medicine
BNYPL — Bulletin. New York Public Library
BNZED — Bulletin. New Zealand National Society for Earthquake Engineering
B e O — Bibbia e Oriente
BO — Bibliotheca Orientalis
BO — Black Orpheus
Bo — Bolivar
BOA — Bibliography of Agriculture
BoAb — Boating Abstracts
Board Environ Stud Res Pap Univ Newcastle — University of Newcastle. Board of Environmental Studies. Research Paper
Board Mfr — Board Manufacture and Practice
Board of Review Decisions — Decisions. Income Tax Board of Review
Boardroom — Boardroom Reports
BOAS — Bulletin. School of Oriental and African Studies
Bo B — Bok og Bibliotek
BOB — By og Bygd. Norsk Folkemuseums Arbok
BOCDA — Building Official and Code Administrator [United States]
BOCES XVIII — Boletin. Centro de Estudios del Siglo XVIII, Oviedo
BOCKA — Bochu Kagaku
BOCVA — Boletin. Academia de Ciencias Fisicas, Matematicas, y Naturales (Caracas, Venezuela)

BODEA — Bodenkultur
Bodenbiol Microbiol — Bodenbiologie Microbiologie
Bodleian Lib Rec — Bodleian Library Record
Bodleian Libr Rec — Bodleian Library Record
Bodl Libr Rec — Bodleian Library Record
Body Pol — Body Politic
BOEIA — Boei Eisei
Boek — Het Boek
BOEMA — Boletin. Instituto de Estudios Medicos y Biologicos. Universidad Nacional Autonoma de Mexico
Boergyogy Venerol Sz — Boergyogyaszati es Venerologiai Szemle
Boersenbl Dtsch Buchhandel — Boersenblatt fuer den Deutschen Buchhandel [*East Germany*]
Boersen-Ztg — Boersen-Zeitung
BOF — Bank of Finland. Monthly Bulletin
B Offic Ch Com (Bruxelles) — Bulletin Officiel. Chambre de Commerce (Bruxelles)
B Off Int — Bulletin. Office International des Instituts d'Archeologie et d'Histoire de l'Art
B Off Int Vitic — Bulletin. Office International de la Viticulture
Bo Fi Cl — Bollettino di Filologia Classica
B Of San Pa — Boletin. Oficina Sanitaria Panamericana
BOGIA — Bollettino. Societa Geologica Italiana
Bohrtech Ztg — Bohrtechniker Zeitung
BOIA — Bulletin. Office International des Instituts d'Archeologie et d'Histoire de l'Art
BOIID — Boletin IIE [*Instituto de Investigaciones Electricas*]
Boiler Eng — Boiler Engineer [*Japan*]
Boiler Maker Plate Fabr — Boiler Maker and Plate Fabricator
Bois Forets Trop — Bois et Forets des Tropiques
Bois For Trop — Bois et Forets des Tropiques
BOK — Boekverkoper
Bok og Bibl — Bok og Bibliotek
Bol — Bolivar
Bol Acad Cienc Exactas Fis Nat — Boletin. Academia de Ciencias Exactas, Fisicas, y Naturales
Bol Acad Cienc Fis Mat Nat (Caracas) — Boletin. Academia de Ciencias Fisicas, Matematicas, y Naturales (Caracas)
Bol Acad Cienc Fis Mat Natur — Boletin. Academia de Ciencias Fisicas, Matematicas, y Naturales [*Caracas*]
Bol Acad Nac Cienc (Cordoba) — Boletin. Academia Nacional de Ciencias (Cordoba)
Bol Acad Nac Farm — Boletim. Academia Nacional de Farmacia
Bol Acad Nac Med — Boletim. Academia Nacional de Medicina
Bol Acad Nac Med (B Aires) — Boletin. Academia Nacional de Medicina (Buenos Aires)
Bol Acad Nac Med (Rio De J) — Boletim. Academia Nacional de Medicina (Rio De Janeiro)
Bol Agr — Boletin de Agricultura, Mineria, e Industrias
Bol Agr Dept Prod Veg (Minas Gerais) — Boletim de Agricultura. Departmento de Producao Vegetal (Minas Gerais)
Bol Agr Dir Publ Agr (Sao Paulo) — Boletim de Agricultura. Directoria de Publicidade Agricola (Sao Paulo)
Bol Agric Asoc Agric Rio Culiacan — Boletin Agricola. Asociacion de Agricultores del Rio Culiacan
Bol Agric (Belo Horizonte Brazil) — Boletim de Agricultura (Belo Horizonte, Brazil)
Bol Agric Zootech e Vet Bello Horizonte — Boletim de Agricultura, Zootechnia, e Veterinaria. Bello Horizonte
Bol Agro-Pec — Boletin Agro-Pecuario
Bol Agropecu Com Colomb Aliment Lacteos — Boletin Agropecuario. Compania Colombiana de Alimentos Lacteos
Bol Argent For — Boletin Argentino Forestal
Bol Arq — Boletin Arqueologico de Tarragona
Bol Asoc Argent Electrotec — Boletin. Asociacion Argentina de Electrotecnicos
Bol Asoc Argent Odontol Ninos — Boletin. Asociacion Argentina de Odontologia para Ninos
Bol Asoc Chil Prot Fam — Boletin. Asociacion Chilena de Proteccion de la Familia
Bol Asoc Med PR — Boletin. Asociacion Medica de Puerto Rico
Bol Asoc Med Puerto Rico — Boletin. Asociacion Medica de Puerto Rico
Bol Asoc Mex Geofis Explor — Boletin. Asociacion Mexicana de Geofisicos de Exploracion
Bol Asoc Mex Geol Pet — Boletin. Asociacion Mexicana de Geologos Petroleros
Bol Asoc Mex Geol Petrol — Boletin. Asociacion Mexicana de Geologos Petroleros
Bol Asoc Nac Ing Agron — Boletin. Asociacion Nacional de Ingenieros Agronomos
Bol Asoc Nac Ingen Agron — Boletin. Asociacion Nacional de Ingenieros Agronomos
Bol Asoc Urug Prog Cienc — Boletin. Asociacion Uruguaya para el Progreso de la Ciencia
Bol Asoc Venez Enferm Prof — Boletin. Asociacion Venezolana de Enfermeras Profesionales

Bol Asoc Venez Geol Min Pet — Boletin. Asociacion Venezolana de Geologia, Mineria, y Petroleo
Bol Assist Med Indigen (Luanda) — Boletim de Assistencia Medicaos Indigenas e da Luta Contra a Moleatia do Sono (Luanda)
Bol Assoc Bras Fis Med — Boletim. Associacao Brasileira de Fisicos em Medicina [*Brazil*]
Bol Assoc Bras Quim — Boletim. Associacao Brasileira de Quimica
Bol Assoc Filos Nat (Portugal) — Boletim. Associacao de Filosofia Natural (Portugal)
Bol AVGMP — Boletin. AVGMP [*Asociacion Venezolana de Geologia, Mineria, y Petroleo*]
Bol Azucar Mex — Boletin Azucarero Mexicano
Bol Bibl — Boletin Bibliografico Forestal [*Chile*]
Bol Bibl Agric — Boletin para Bibliotecas Agricolas
Bol Bibl Antropol Amer — Boletin Bibliografico de Antropologia Americana
Bol Bibliog Geofisica y Oceanografia Am — Boletin. Bibliografico de Geofisica y Oceanografia Americanas
Bol Bibliogr Fac Agron Univ Cent Venez — Boletin Bibliografico. Facultad de Agronomia. Universidad Central de Venezuela
Bol Biblio (Peru) — Boletin Bibliografico (Peru)
Bol Biblioteca — Boletin de Biblioteca
Bol Bibl Menendez Pelayo — Boletin. Biblioteca de Menendez Pelayo
Bol Biol — Boletin Biologico
Bol Biol (S Paulo) — Boletim Biologica (Sao Paulo)
Bol Cam Com (Caracas) — Boletin. Camara de Comercio (Caracas)
Bol Cear Agron — Boletim Cearense de Agronomia
Bol Cent Estud Hosp Servidores Estado (Rio De J) — Boletim. Centro de Estudos do Hospital dos Servidores do Estado (Rio De Janeiro)
Bol Cent Invest Biol Univ Zulia — Boletin. Centro de Investigaciones Biologicas. Universidad del Zulia
Bol Cent Nav — Boletin. Centro Naval
Bol Cent Panam Fiebre Aftosa — Boletin. Centro Panamericano de Fiebre Aftosa
Bol Chil Parasitol — Boletin Chileno de Parasitologia
Bol Cia Adm Guano — Boletin. Compania Administradora del Guano
Bol Ciencias Econs — Boletim de Ciencias Economicas
Bol Ciencias Pol y Socs — Boletin de Ciencias Politicas y Sociales
Bol Cienc Mar — Boletim de Ciencias do Mar
Bol Cienc Tecnol Dep Asuntos Cult Union Panam — Boletin de Ciencia y Tecnologia. Departamento de Asuntos Culturales. Union Panamericana
Bol Clin Endocrinol Metab — Boletin. Clinica de Endocrinologia y Metabolismo
Bol Clin Hosp Civis Lisb — Boletim Clinico dos Hospitals Civis de Lisboa
Bol Col Prof Enferm PR — Boletin. Colegio de Profesionales de la Enfermeria de Puerto Rico
Bol Col Quim PR — Boletin. Colegio de Quimicos de Puerto Rico
Bol Combust Petroquim — Boletin de Combustibles y Petroquimica
Bol Com Geogr Geol Estado Sao Paulo — Boletim. Comissao Geografica e Geologica do Estado de Sao Paulo
Bol Com Nac Energ Nucl (Braz) — Boletim. Comissao Nacional de Energia Nuclear (Brazil)
Bol Comp Admin Guano — Boletin. Compania Administradora del Guano
Bol Cons Nac Pesqui (Brazil) — Boletin. Conselho Nacional de Pesquisas (Brazil)
Bol Cuerpo Ing Minas Peru — Boletin. Cuerpo de Ingenieros de Minas del Peru
Bol Cult Guine Portug — Boletim Cultural da Guine Portuguesa
Bol Demografico (Brazil) — Boletim Demografico (Brazil)
Bol Dent Oper — Boletim de Dentistica Operatoria
Bol Dep For (Uruguay) — Boletin. Departamento Forestal (Montevideo, Uruguay)
Bol Dep Geol Uni Son — Boletin. Departamento de Geologia. Universidad de Sonora
Bol Dept Eng Quim Esc Politec Univ Sao Paulo — Boletim. Departamento de Engenharia Quimica da Escola Politecnica. Universidade de Sao Paulo
Bol Dermatol Sanit — Boletin Dermatologico Sanitario
Bol Didat Esc Agron Eliseu Maciel (Pelotas Brazil) — Boletim Didatico da Escola de Agronomia Eliseu Maciel (Pelotas, Brazil)
Bol Dir Agric Ganad (Peru) — Boletin. Direccion de Agricultura y Ganaderia (Peru)
Bol Dir Malariol Saneamiento Ambiental — Boletin. Direccion de Malariologia y Saneamiento Ambiental
Bol Dir Nac Geol Min (Argent) — Boletin. Direccion Nacional de Geologia y Mineria (Argentina)
Bol Div Nac Dermatol Sanit — Boletim. Divisao Nacional de Dermatologia Sanitaria
Bol Div Nac Lepra — Boletim. Divisao Nacional de Lepra
Bol Divulg Inst Nac Invest For (Mex) — Boletin Divulgativo. Instituto Nacional de Investigaciones Forestales (Mexico)
Bol Divulg Tec Inst Patol Veg (B Aires) — Boletin de Divulgacion Tecnica Instituto de Patologia Vegetal (Buenos Aires)
Bol Docum Fondo Invest Econ Soc — Boletin de Documentacion. Fondo para la Investigacion Economica y Social
Bol Eclesias Fil — Boletin Eclesiastico de Filipinas
Bol Econ Pubblica — Bollettino dell'Economia Pubblica
Bol Entomol Venez — Boletin de Entomologia Venezolana
Bol Epidemiol — Boletin Epidemiologico

Bol Epidemiol (Rio De J) — Boletim Epidemiologico (Rio De Janeiro)

Bol Equipe Odontol Sanit — Boletim da Equipe de Odontologia Sanitaria

Bol Esc Farm (Coimbra) — Boletim. Escola de Farmacia (Coimbra)

Bol Esc Farm Univ Coimbra Ed Cien — Boletim. Escola de Farmacia. Universidade de Coimbra. Edicao Cientifica

Bol Esc Farm Univ Coimbra Ed Didact Not Farm — Boletim. Escola de Farmacia. Universidade de Coimbra. Edicao Didactica. Noticias Farmaceuticas

Bol Esc Nac Agr (Lima) — Boletin. Escuela Nacional de Agricultura (Lima)

Bol Esc Super Agric "Luiz De Queiroz" Univ Sao Paulo — Boletim. Escola Superior de Agricultura "Luiz De Queiroz." Universidade de Sao Paulo

Bol Estac Biol Mar Univ Fed Ceara — Boletim. Estacao de Biologia Marinha. Universidade Federal do Ceara

Bol Estac Cent Ecol — Boletin. Estacion Central de Ecologia

Bol Estac Exp Agric "La Molina" — Boletin. Estacion Experimental Agricola "La Molina"

Bol Estac Exp Agr "La Molina" — Boletin. Estacion Experimental Agricola "La Molina"

Bol Estac Exp Agropec Pres Roque Saenz Pena (Argentina) — Boletin. Estacion Experimental Agropecuaria de Presidencia Roque Saenz Pena (Argentina)

Bol Estac Exp Agr "Tingo Maria" — Boletin. Estacion Experimental Agricola "Tingo Maria"

Bol Estadistica — Boletin de Estadistica

Bol Estadistico Trim (Bolivia) — Boletin Estadistico Trimestral (Bolivia)

Bol Estud Econ — Boletin de Estudios Economicos

Bol Estud Geogr Univ Nac Cuyo — Boletin de Estudios Geograficos de la Universidad Nacional de Cuyo

Bol Estud Latinoamer — Boletin de Estudios Latinamericanos y del Caribe

Bol Estud Med Biol — Boletin de Estudios Medicos y Biologicos

Bol Estud Med Biol Univ Nac Auton Mex — Boletin de Estudios Medicos y Biologicos. Universidad Nacional Autonoma de Mexico

Bol Estud Pesca — Boletim de Estudos de Pesca

Bol Estud Supt Desenvolvimento Nordeste Div Geol (Braz) — Boletim de Estudos. Superintendencia do Desenvolvimento do Nordeste. Divisao de Geologia (Brazil)

Boletin IF — Boletin. Instituto de Folklore

Bol Exp Serv Agric Interam (La Paz) — Boletin. Experimental Servicio Agricola Interamericano (La Paz)

Bolex Rep — Bolex Reporter

Bol Fac Agron Univ San Carlos Guatemala — Boletin. Facultad de Agronomia. Universidad de San Carlos de Guatemala

Bol Fac Cienc Agrar Para — Boletim. Faculdade de Ciencias Agrarias do Para

Bol Fac Cienc For Univ Los Andes — Boletin. Facultad de Ciencias Forestales. Universidad de Los Andes

Bol Fac Der Cienc Soc (Cordoba) — Boletin. Facultad de Derecho y Ciencias Sociales (Cordoba)

Bol Fac Dir (Coimbra) — Boletim. Faculdade de Direito (Coimbra)

Bol Fac Farm Univ Coimbra Ed Cient — Boletim. Faculdade de Farmacia. Universidade de Coimbra. Edicao Cientifica

Bol Fac Farm Univ Coimbra Ed Didact Not Farm — Boletim. Faculdade de Farmacia. Universidade de Coimbra. Edicao Didactica. Noticias Farmaceuticas

Bol Fac Farm Univ Lisboa — Boletim. Faculdade de Farmacia. Universidade de Lisboa

Bol Fac Filos Cienc Let Univ Sao Paulo Ser Bot — Boletim. Faculdade de Filosofia, Ciencias, e Letras. Universidade de Sao Paulo. Serie Botanica

Bol Fac Filos Cienc Let Univ Sao Paulo Ser Zool — Boletim. Faculdade de Filosofia, Ciencias, e Letras. Universidade de Sao Paulo. Serie Zoologia

Bol Fac Ing Agrimens Univ Repub — Boletim. Facultad de Ingenieria y Agrimensura. Universidad de la Republica

Bol Fac Ing y Agrimensura Montevideo — Boletin. Facultad de Ingenieria y Agrimensura de Montevideo

Bol Fac Ing Agrimensura Montevideo — Boletin. Facultad de Ingenieria y Agrimensura de Montevideo

Bol Fac Ing Montevideo — Boletin. Facultad de Ingenieria de Montevideo

Bol Fac Ing Univ Repub — Boletin. Facultad de Ingenieria. Universidad de la Republica

Bol Fac Odontol Piracicaba Univ Estadual Campinas — Boletim. Faculdade de Odontologia de Piracicaba. Universidade Estadual de Campinas

Bol Farm Mil — Boletin de Farmacia Militar

Bol Fed Med Ecuador — Boletin. Federacion Medica del Ecuador

Bol Fitossanit — Boletim Fitossanitario

Bol For Ind For Amer Lat FAO — Boletin Forestal y de Industrias Forestales para America Latina. Oficina Forestal Regional de la FAO [*Food and Agriculture Organization*]

Bol Fund Goncalo Moniz — Boletim. Fundacao Goncalo Moniz

Bol Genet — Boletin Genetico

Bol Geo Dir Geol (Venez) — Boletin de Geologia. Direccion de Geologia (Venezuela)

Bol Geog — Boletim Geografico

Bol Geogr — Boletim Geografico

Bol Geol (Caracas) — Boletin de Geologia (Caracas)

Bol Geol (Caracas) Publ Espec — Boletin de Geologia (Caracas). Publicacion Especial

Bol Geol Dir Geol (Venez) — Boletin de Geologia. Direccion de Geologia (Venezuela)

Bol Geol Miner — Boletin Geologico y Minero

Bol Geol Min (Esp) — Boletin Geologico y Minero (Espana)

Bol Geol Publ Espec — Boletin de Geologia. Publicacion Especial

Bol Geol Publ Espec Dir Geol (Venez) — Boletin de Geologia. Publicacion Especial. Direccion de Geologia (Venezuela)

Bol Geol Univ Ind Santander — Boletin de Geologia. Universidad Industrial de Santander

Bolg Fiz Zh — Bolgarskii Fizicheskii Zhurnal [*Bulgaria*]

Bol Hig Epidemiol — Boletin de Higiene y Epidemiologia

Bol Hist Nat Soc "Felipe Poey" — Boletin de Historia Natural. Sociedad "Felipe Poey"

Bol Historia Nat — Boletin de Historia Natural

Bol Hosp Civ San Juan De Dios (Quito) — Boletin. Hospital Civil de San Juan De Dios (Quito)

Bol Hosp Clin Fac Med Univ Bahia — Boletim. Hospital das Clinicas. Faculdade de Medicina. Universidade da Bahia

Bol Hosp Fac Med Univ Bahia — Boletim. Hospital da Faculdade de Medicina. Universidade da Bahia

Bol Hosp Oftalmol Nuestra Senora de la Luz — Boletin. Hospital Oftalmologico de Nuestra Senora de la Luz

Bol Iberoam Cult Tec — Boletin Iberoamericano de Cultura Tecnica

Bol Ind Anim — Boletim de Industria Animal

Bol Inf Asoc Venez Geol Min Pet — Boletin Informativo. Asociacion Venezolana de Geologia, Mineria, y Petroleo

Bol Inf Bromatol — Boletin de Informacion Bromatologica

Bol Inf Cient Nac — Boletin de Informaciones Cientificas Nacionales

Bol Inf Dent (Madr) — Boletin de Informacion Dental (Madrid)

Bol Inf Estac Exp Agri Tucuman — Boletin Informativo. Estacion Experimental Agricola de Tucuman

Bol Inf Inst Biol Marit — Boletim Informativo. Instituto de Biologia Maritima

Bol Inf Inst Cubano Invest Tecnol — Boletin Informativo. Instituto Cubano de Investigaciones Tecnologicas

Bol Inform Inst Cacau Bahia — Boletim Informativo. Instituto de Cacau da Bahia

Bol Inform Inst For (Chile) — Boletin Informativo. Instituto Forestal (Santiago-De-Chile)

Bol Inform Inst Nac Tec Agropec Inst Fitotec — Boletin Informativo. Instituto Nacional de Tecnologia Agropecuaria. Instituto de Fitotecnia

Bol Inform Minist Agric (Madrid) — Boletin de Informacion. Ministerio de Agricultura (Madrid)

Bol Inform Tec Asoc Invest Tec Ind Madera — Boletin. Informacion Tecnica. Asociacion de Investigacion Tecnica de las Industrias de la Madera y Corcho

Bol Inf Pet — Boletin de Informaciones Petroleras

Bol Inf Soc Bras Radiol — Boletim Informativo. Sociedade Brasileira de Radiologia

Bol Inf Tec Dep Met No Ferreos CSIC (Spain) — Boletin de Informacion Tecnica. Departamento de Metales No Ferreos. Consejo Superior de Investigaciones Cientificas (Spain)

Bol INPA Bot — Boletim. INPA [*Instituto Nacional de Pesquisas da Amazonia*]. Botanica

Bol INPA Patol Trop — Boletim. INPA [*Instituto Nacional de Pesquisas da Amazonia*]. Patologia Tropical

Bol INPA Pat Trop — Boletim. INPA [*Instituto Nacional de Pesquisas da Amazonia*]. Patologia Tropical

Bol INPA Pesqui Florestais — Boletim. INPA [*Instituto Nacional de Pesquisas da Amazonia*]. Pesquisas Florestais

Bol INPA Tecnol — Boletim. INPA [*Instituto Nacional de Pesquisas da Amazonia*]. Tecnologia

Bol Inseminacao Artif — Boletim de Inseminacao Artificial

Bol Inst Agric Trop Univ PR — Boletin. Instituto de Agricultura Tropical. Universidad de Puerto Rico

Bol Inst Agron Campinas — Boletim. Instituto Agronomico Campinas

Bol Inst Angola — Boletim. Instituto de Angola

Bol Inst Antropol Univ Antioquia Medellin — Boletin. Instituto de Antropologia. Universidad de Antioquia, Medellin

Bol Inst Bacteriol Chile — Boletin. Instituto Bacteriologico de Chile

Bol Inst Biol Bahia — Boletim. Instituto Biologico da Bahia

Bol Inst Biol Mar (Mar Del Plata) — Boletin. Instituto de Biologia Marina (Mar Del Plata)

Bol Inst Biol Mar Univ Fed Rio Grande Do Norte — Boletim. Instituto de Biologia Marinha. Universidade Federal do Rio Grande Do Norte

Bol Inst Boliv Pet — Boletin. Instituto Boliviano del Petroleo

Bol Inst Bot (Sao Paulo) — Boletim. Instituto de Botanica (Sao Paulo)

Bol Inst Bot Univ Quito — Boletin. Instituto Botanica. Universidad de Quito

Bol Inst Cent Biocienc Ser Bot — Boletim. Instituto Central de Biociencias. Serie Botanica

Bol Inst Cienc Biol Geocienc Commun Malacol — Boletim. Instituto de Ciencias Biologicas e de Geociencias. Communicacoes Malacologicas

Bol Inst Cienc Nat Univ Cent Ecuador — Boletin. Instituto de Ciencias Naturales. Universidad Central del Ecuador

Bol Inst Cienc Nat Univ Rio Grande Do Sul — Boletim. Instituto de Ciencias Naturais. Universidade do Rio Grande Do Sul

Bol Inst Clin Quir — Boletin. Instituto de Clinica Quirurgica

Bol Inst Ecol Exp Agric — Boletim. Instituto de Ecologia e Experimentacao Agricolas
Bol Inst Esp Oceanogr — Boletin. Instituto Espanol de Oceanografia
Bol Inst Estud Med Biol — Boletin. Instituto de Estudios Medicos y Biologicos
Bol Inst Estud Med Biol Univ Nac Mex — Boletin. Instituto de Estudios Medicos y Biologicos. Universidad Nacional de Mexico
Bol Inst Estud Polit — Boletin. Instituto de Estudios Politicos
Bol Inst For Invest Exp (Madrid) — Boletin. Instituto Forestal de Investigaciones y Experiencias (Madrid)
Bol Inst For Lat-Am Invest Capac — Boletin. Instituto Forestal Latino-Americano de Investigacion y Capacitacion
Bol Inst Genet Soc Nac Agrar (Lima) — Boletin. Instituto de Genetica. Sociedad Nacional Agraria (Lima)
Bol Inst Geocienc Astron Univ Sao Paulo — Boletim. Instituto de Geociencias e Astronomia. Universidade de Sao Paulo
Bol Inst Geogr Geol (Sao Paulo State) — Boletim. Instituto Geografico e Geologico (Sao Paulo State)
Bol Inst Geol — Boletin. Instituto de Geologia
Bol Inst Geol (Mex) — Boletin. Instituto de Geologia (Mexico)
Bol Inst Geol Min Esp — Boletin. Instituto Geologico y Minero de Espana
Bol Inst Geol Univ Recife Mineral — Boletin. Instituto de Geologia. Universidade de Recife. Mineralogia
Bol Inst Hist Nat Curitiba Bot — Boletim. Instituto de Historia Natural Curitiba Botanica
Bol Inst Int Am Prot Infanc — Boletin. Instituto Internacional Americano de Proteccion a la Infancia
Bol Inst Interam Nino — Boletin. Instituto Interamericano del Nino
Bol Inst Invest Bibliogr — Boletin. Instituto de Investigaciones Bibliograficas
Bol Inst Invest Cient Angola — Boletin. Instituto de Investigacao Cientifica de Angola
Bol Inst Invest Cient Univ Nuevo Leon — Boletin. Instituto de Investigaciones Cientificas. Universidad de Nuevo Leon
Bol Inst Invest Geol (Chile) — Boletin. Instituto de Investigaciones Geologicas (Chile)
Bol Inst Investig Cient Angola — Boletim. Instituto de Investigacao Cientifica de Angola
Bol Inst Invest Recur Mar (Callao) — Boletin. Instituto de Investigacion de los Recursos Marinos (Callao)
Bol Inst Invest Vet (Maracay) — Boletin. Instituto de Investigaciones Veterinarias (Maracay)
Bol Inst Mar Peru (Callao) — Boletin. Instituto del Mar del Peru (Callao)
Bol Inst Mat Astron Fis — Boletin. Instituto de Matematica, Astronomia, y Fisica
Bol Inst Med Exp Estud Trat Cancer (Buenos Aires) — Boletin. Instituto de Medicina Experimental para el Estudio y Tratamiento del Cancer (Buenos Aires)
Bol Inst Microbiol Univ Fed Rio Grande Do Sul — Boletim. Instituto de Microbiologia. Universidade Federal do Rio Grande Do Sul
Bol Inst Nac Antropol Hist Mexico — Boletin. Instituto Nacional de Antropologia e Historia de Mexico
Bol Inst Nac Hig Alfonso XIII — Boletin. Instituto Nacional de Higiene de Alfonso XIII
Bol Inst Nac Hig (Caracas) — Boletin. Instituto Nacional de Higiene (Caracas)
Bol Inst Nac Invest Agron (Madr) — Boletin. Instituto Nacional de Investigaciones Agronomicas (Madrid)
Bol Inst Nac Neumol (Mex) — Boletin. Instituto Nacional de Neumologia (Mexico)
Bol Inst Nac Pesqui Amazonia Pesqui Florestais — Boletim. Instituto Nacional de Pesquisas da Amazonia. Pesquisas Florestais
Bol Inst Num Hist San Nicolas — Boletin. Instituto de Numismatica e Historia de San Nicolas de los Arroyos [*Argentina*]
Bol Inst Oceanogr — Boletin. Instituto Oceanografico
Bol Inst Oceanogr Univ Oriente (Cumana) — Boletin. Instituto Oceanografico. Universidad de Oriente (Cumana)
Bol Inst Patol Med (Madrid) — Boletin. Instituto de Patologia Medica (Madrid)
Bol Inst Pesqui Cir (Rio De J) — Boletin. Instituto de Pesquisas Cirurgicas (Rio De Janeiro)
Bol Inst Pesqui Vet "Desiderio Finamor" — Boletin. Instituto de Pesquisas Veterinarias "Desiderio Finamor"
Bol Inst Quim Agric (Rio De Janeiro) — Boletin. Instituto de Quimica Agricola (Rio De Janeiro)
Bol Inst Quim Univ Nac Auton Mex — Boletin. Instituto de Quimica. Universidad Nacional Autonoma de Mexico
Bol Inst Sudam Pet (Montevideo) — Boletin. Instituto Sudamericano del Petroleo (Montevideo)
Bol Inst Tecnol Aliment — Boletin. Instituto de Tecnologia de Alimentos
Bol Inst Tecnol Rural Univ Ceara — Boletim. Instituto de Tecnologia Rural. Universidade do Ceara
Bol Inst Tonantzintla — Boletin. Instituto de Tonantzintla
Bol Interamer M — Boletin Interamericano de Musica/Inter-American Music Bulletin
Bol IPA PSM — Boletim. IPA [*Instituto de Pesquisas Agronomicas*]. PSM [*Programa de Sorgo e Milheto*]

Bol Ist Pato Lib — Bollettino. Istituto di Patologia del Libro
Bol Ist Stud Verdiani — Bollettino. Istituto di Studi Verdiani
Bolivia Dep Nac Geol Bol — Bolivia. Departamento Nacional de Geologia. Boletin
Bol Junta Control Energ At — Boletin. Junta do Control de Energia Atomica [*Peru*]
Bol Junta Geral Distr Auton Ponta Delgada — Boletim. Junta Geral Distrito Autonomo Ponta Delgada
Bol Junta Nac Cortica — Boletim. Junta Nacional da Cortica
Bol Lab Clin "Luis Razetti" — Boletin. Laboratorio de la Clinica "Luis Razetti"
Bol Lab Paleontol Vertebr — Boletin. Laboratorio de Paleontologia de Vertebrados
Bol Lab Quim Nac (Colombia) — Boletin. Laboratorio Quimico Nacional (Colombia)
Boll Accad Med-Chir Bologna — Bollettino. Accademia Medico-Chirurgica di Bologna
Boll Accad Med Genova — Bollettino. Accademia Medica de Genova
Boll Accad Med Pistoiese Filippo Pacini — Bollettino. Accademia Medica Pistoiese Filippo Pacini
Boll Accad Svizz Sci Med — Bollettino. Accademia Svizzera delle Scienze Mediche
Boll Arte — Bollettino d'Arte
Boll Assoc African Ital — Bollettino. Associazione degli Africanisti Italiani
Boll Assoc Ital Chim Tess Color — Bollettino. Associazione Italiana de Chimica Tessile e Colloristica
Boll Assoc Ital Ind Zucchero Alcool — Bollettino. Associazione Italiana delle Industrie delle Zucchero e dell'Alcool
Boll Assoc Ital Piante Med Aromat Altre Piante Utili — Bollettino. Associazione Italiana pro Piante Medicinal Aromatiche ed Altre Piante Utili
Boll Assoc Rom Entomol — Bollettino. Associazione Romana di Entomologia
Boll Atti Accad Med Roma — Bollettino ed Atti. Accademia Medica di Roma
Boll Atti Soc Ital Endocrinol — Bollettino ed Atti. Societa Italiana de Endocrinologia
Boll Centro Camuno — Bollettino. Centro Camuno di Studii Preistorici
Boll Centro Stud Vichiani — Bollettino. Centro di Studi Vichiani
Boll Chim Farm — Bollettino Chimico Farmaceutico
Boll Chim Ig Parte Sci — Bollettino dei Chimici Igienisti. Parte Scientifica
Boll Chim Unione Ital Parte Sci — Bollettino dei Chimici. Unione Italiana dei Laboratori Provinciali. Parte Scientifica
Boll Circ Num Napoletano — Bollettino del Circolo Numismatico Napoletano
Boll Clin — Il Bollettino delle Cliniche
Boll Coton — Bollettino della Cotoniera
Bol Leite — Boletim do Leite
Bol Leite Seus Deriv — Boletim do Leite e Seus Derivados
Boll Fond Sen Pascale Cent Diagn Cura Tumori — Bollettino. Fondazione Sen Pascale Centro per la Diagnosi e la Cura dei Tumori
Boll Geod Sci Affini — Bollettino di Geodesia e Scienze Affini [*Florence*]
Boll Geofis Teor Appl — Bollettino di Geofisica. Teorica ed Applicata
Boll Geofis Teorica Appl — Bollettino di Geofisica. Teorica ed Applicata
Bol Liga Cancer — Boletin de la Liga Contra el Cancer
Boll Inf Ind Olearia Sapon — Bollettino d'Informazioni per l'Industria Olearia e Saponiera
Boll Int Opere Sci Med — Bollettino Internazionale delle Opere Scientifiche Medicina
Boll Ist Agrar Scandicci — Bollettino. Istituto Agrario di Scandicci
Boll Ist Aliment Dietol — Bollettino. Istituto di Alimentazione e Dietologia
Boll Ist Ent Agr Oss Fitopat Palermo — Bollettino. Istituto di Entomologia Agraria e Osservatorio di Fitopatologia di Palermo
Boll Ist Entomol — Bollettino. Istituto di Entomologia
Boll Ist Entomol Agrar Osse Fitopatol Palermo — Bollettino. Istituto di Entomologia Agraria e Osservatorio di Fitopatologia di Palermo
Boll Ist Entomol Agrar Oss Fitopatol Palermo — Bollettino. Istituto di Entomologia Agraria e Osservatorio di Fitopatologia di Palermo
Boll Ist Entomol Univ Studi Bologna — Bollettino. Istituto dei Entomologia. Universita degli Studi di Bologna
Boll Ist Ent Univ Bologna — Bollettino. Istituto di Entomologia. Universita degli Studia di Bologna
Boll Ist Patol Libr — Bollettino. Istituto di Patologia del Libro Alfonso Gallo
Boll Ist Patol Libro — Bollettino. Istituto di Patologia del Libro
Boll Ist Patologia Lib — Bollettino. Istituto di Patologia del Libro
Boll Ist Sieroter Milan — Bollettino. Istituto Sieroterapico Milanese
Boll Lab Chim Prov — Bollettino. Laboratori Chimici Provinciali
Boll Lab Entol Agr — Bollettino. Laboratorio di Entomologia Agraria
Boll Lab Entomol Agrar Portici — Bollettino. Laboratorio di Entomologia Agraria "Filippo Silvestri" di Portici [*Italy*]
Boll Laboratori Chim Prov — Bollettino. Laboratori Chimici Provinciali
Boll Laniera — Bollettino della Laniera
Boll Mal Orecch Gola Naso — Bollettino delle Malattie dell'Orecchio, della Gola, del Naso
Boll Mal Orecchio Gola Naso — Bollettino delle Malattie dell'Orecchio, della Gola, del Naso [*Italy*]
Boll Med Svizz — Bollettino del Medici Svizzeri
Boll Mem Soc Piemont Chir — Bollettino e Memorie. Societa Piemontese de Chirurgia

Boll Mem Soc Tosco Umbro Emiliana Med Interna — Bollettino e Memorie. Societa Tosco Umbro Emiliana di Medicina Interna

Boll Mens Cam Com Ind Agr (Perugia) — Bollettino Mensile. Camera di Commercio Industria e Agricoltura (Perugia)

Boll Metallogr — Bollettino Metallografico

Boll Meteorol Idrol Agrar — Bollettino di Meteorologia e di Idrologia Agraria

Boll Mus Civ Stor Nat Ven — Bollettino. Museo Civico di Storia Naturale di Venezia

Boll Mus Civ Stor Nat Venezia — Bollettino. Museo Civico di Storia Naturale di Venezia

Boll Mus Civ Stor Nat Verona — Bollettino. Museo Civico di Storia Naturale di Verona

Boll dei Mus Is Biol Univ Genova — Bollettino. Musei e degli Istituti Biologici. Universita di Genova

Boll Mus Ist Biol Univ Genova — Bollettino. Musei e degli Istituti Biologici. Universita di Genova

Boll Mus Zool Univ Torino — Bollettino. Museo di Zoologia. Universita di Torino

BollN — Bollettino Numismatico di Luigi Simonetti

Boll Oceanol Teor ed Appl — Bollettino di Oceanologia Teorica ed Applicata

Boll Ocul — Bollettino d'Oculistica

Boll Pesca Piscic Idrobiol — Bollettino di Pesca, Piscicoltura, e Idrobiologia

Boll Psicol App — Bollettino di Psicologia Applicata

Boll Psicol Appl — Bollettino di Psicologia Applicata

Boll Psicol Appl Inserto — Bollettino di Psicologia Applicata. Inserto

Boll Regia Stn Sper Ind Carta Stud Fibre Tess Veg — Bollettino. Regia Stazione Sperimentale per l'Industria della Carta e lo Studio delle Fibre Tessili Vegetali

Boll Regia Stn Sper Ind Pelli Mater Concianti Napoli — Bollettino. Regia Stazione Sperimentale per l'Industria delle Pelli e delle Materie Concianti Napoli

Boll Regio Is Super Agrar Pisa — Bollettino. Regio Istituto Superiore Agrario di Pisa

Boll Ric Inf Cent Reg Sper Ind Enol F Paulsen (Marsala) — Bollettino di Ricerche e Informazioni. Centro Regionale Sperimentale per l'Industria Enologia F. Paulsen (Marsala)

Boll Ric Reg Sicil Cent Sper Enol F Paulsen (Marsala) — Bollettino di Ricerche. Regione Siciliana. Centro Sperimentale Enologia F. Paulsen (Marsala)

Boll Riv — Bollettino delle Riviste

Boll Schermogr — Bollettino Schermografico

Boll Scient — Bollettino Scientifico

Boll Sci Fac Chim Ind Bologna — Bollettino Scientifico. Facolta di Chimica Industriale di Bologna [*Italy*]

Boll Sci Med — Bollettino delle Scienze Mediche [*Italy*]

Boll Sedute Accad Gioenia Sci Nat Catania — Bollettino. Sedute della Accademia Gioenia di Scienze Naturali in Catania

Boll Serv Geol Ital — Bollettino. Servizio Geologico d'Italia

Boll Soc Adriat Sci (Trieste) — Bollettino. Societa Adriatica di Scienze (Trieste)

Boll Soc Adriat Sci (Trieste) Suppl — Bollettino. Societa Adriatica di Scienze (Trieste). Supplemento

Boll Soc Biol Sper — Bollettino. Societa di Biologia Sperimentale

Boll Soc Ent Ital — Bollettino. Societa Entomologica Italiana

Boll Soc Entomol Ital — Bollettino. Societa Entomologica Italiana

Boll Soc Eustachiana — Bollettino. Societa Eustachiana

Boll Soc Geog — Bollettino. Societa Geografica Italiana

Boll Soc Geogr Ital — Bollettino. Societa Geografica Italiana

Boll Soc Geol Ital — Bollettino. Societa Geologica Italiana

Boll Soc Ital Biol Sper — Bollettino. Societa Italiana di Biologia Sperimentale

Boll Soc Ital Cardiol — Bollettino. Societa Italiana di Cardiologia

Boll Soc Ital Ematol — Bollettino. Societa Italiana di Ematologia

Boll Soc Ital Farm Osp — Bollettino. Societa Italiana di Farmacia Ospedaliera

Boll Soc Ital Fis — Bollettino. Societa Italiana di Fisica

Boll Soc Ital Patol — Bollettino. Societa Italiana di Patologia

Boll Soc Med-Chir Osp Prov Cremona — Bollettino. Societa Medico-Chirurgica e Ospedali Provincia di Cremona

Boll Soc Med-Chir Pavia — Bollettino. Societa Medico-Chirurgica di Pavia

Boll Soc Med Lazzaro Spallanzani Reggio Emilia — Bollettino. Societa Medica Lazzaro Spallanzani con Sede in Reggio Emilia

Boll Soc Nat Napoli — Bollettino. Societa di Naturalisti di Napoli

Boll Soc Paleontol Ital — Bollettino. Societa Paleontologica Italiana

Boll Soc Rom Stud Zool — Bollettino. Societa Romana per gli Studi Zoologici

Boll Soc Zool Ital — Bollettino. Societa Zoologica Italiana

Boll S P — Bollettino Storico Piacentino

Boll Sta Patol Veg — Bollettino. Stazione di Patologia Vegetale di Roma

Boll Stn Patol Veg Roma — Bollettino. Stazione di Patologia Vegetale di Roma

Boll Stor Cat — Bollettino Storico Catanese

Boll Storia Sci Mat — Bollettino di Storia delle Scienze Matematiche

Boll Stor Svizz Ital — Bollettino Storico della Svizzera Italiana

Boll Stran — Bollettino Universitario Italiano per Stranieri

Boll Tec FINSIDER — Bollettino Tecnico FINSIDER [*Italy*]

Boll Tec Regio Ist Sper Coltiv Tab Leonardo Angeloni — Bollettino Tecnico. Regio Istituto Sperimentale per la Coltivazione dei Tabacchi Leonardo Angeloni

Boll Uffic Cam Com Ind Agr Udine — Bollettino Ufficiale. Camera di Commercio, Industria, e Agricoltura di Udine

Boll Uffic Stn Sper Ind Essenze Deriv Agrumi Reggio Calabria — Bollettino Ufficiale. Stazione Sperimentale per l'Industria delle Essenze e dei Derivati degli Agrumi in Reggio Calabria

Boll Unione Mat Ital Ser IV — Bollettino. Unione Matematica Italiana. Series IV [*Italy*]

Boll Un Mat Ital — Bollettino. Unione Matematica Italiana

Boll Un Mat Ital A — Bollettino. Unione Matematica Italiana. A

Boll Un Mat Ital A V — Unione Matematica Italiana. Bollettino. A. Serie V [*Bologna*]

Boll Un Mat Ital A VI — Unione Matematica Italiana. Bollettino. A. Serie VI

Boll Un Mat Ital B — Bollettino. Unione Matematica Italiana. B

Boll Un Mat Ital B VI — Unione Matematica Italiana. Bollettino. B. Serie VI

Boll Un Mat Ital C 5 — Bollettino. Unione Matematica Italiana. C. Serie V. Analisi Funzionale e Applicazioni

Boll Un Mat Ital Suppl — Unione Matematica Italiana. Bollettino. Supplemento

Boll Zool — Bollettino di Zoologia

Boll Zool Agrar Bachic — Bollettino di Zoologia Agraria e di Bachicoltura

Boll Zool Agrar Bachicolt — Bollettino di Zoologia Agraria e di Bachicoltura

Boll Zool Agr Bachic — Bollettino di Zoologia Agraria e di Bachicoltura

Boll Zool Agr Bachicolt — Bollettino di Zoologia Agraria e di Bachicoltura

Boll Zool (Napoli) — Bollettino di Zoologia (Napoli)

Bolm Apic — Boletim Apicola

Bol Mat — Boletin de Matematicas

Bol Mat Estat Fis (Araraquara Brazil) — Boletim de Matematica, Estatistica, e Fisica (Araraquara, Brazil)

Bol Mat Estatist Fis — Boletim de Matematica, Estatistica, e Fisica

Bol Med Brit — Boletin Medico Britanico

Bol Med Chile — Boletin Medico de Chile

Bol Med Cirug y Farm (Madrid) — Boletin de Medicina, Cirugia, y Farmacia (Madrid)

Bol Med Hosp Inf — Boletin Medico. Hospital Infantil

Bol Med Hosp Infant Mex — Boletin Medico. Hospital Infantil de Mexico

Bol Med Inf — Boletin Medico Informativo

Bol Med Inst Mex Seg Soc — Boletin Medico. Instituto Mexicano del Seguro Social

Bol Med Quir — Boletin Medico-Quirurgico

Bol Med Soc — Boletin Medico-Social. Caja de Seguro Obligatorio

Bol Med Univ Auton Guadalajara — Boletin Medico. Universidad Autonoma de Guadalajara

Bol Med Univ Guad — Boletin Medico. Universidad Autonoma de Guadalajara

Bol Mensal Estatistica (Portugal) — Boletim Mensal de Estatistica (Portugal)

Bol Mens Estadist — Boletin Mensual de Estatistica

Bol Mensile Statis — Bollettino Mensile di Statistica

Bol Mens Obs Ebro — Boletin Mensual. Observatorio del Ebro

Bol Mensual Estadistica — Boletin Mensual de Estadistica

Bol Mensual Estadistica Agraria — Boletin Mensual de Estadistica Agraria

Bol Mensual Estadisticas Agrics — Boletin Mensual de Estadisticas Agricolas

Bolm Esc Agric "Luiz Queiroz" — Boletim. Escola Agricola "Luiz De Queiroz"

Bol Met (Ecuad) — Boletin Meteorologico (Ecuador)

Bol Met Seism — Boletin Meteorologico y Seismologico

Bol Mexic Der Comp — Boletin Mexicano de Derecho Comparado

Bol Mex Reumatol — Boletin Mexicano de Reumatologia

Bol Minas — Boletin de Minas

Bol Minas y Energia — Boletin de Minas y Energia

Bol Minas y Petroleo — Boletin de Minas y Petroleo

Bol Minas (Port Dir-Geral Minas Serv Geol) — Boletim de Minas (Portugal Direccao-Geral de Minas e Servicos Geologicos)

Bolm Ind Anim — Boletim de Industria Animal

Bol Mineral — Boletim Mineralogico

Bol Minero — Boletin Minero

Bol Min Ind — Boletin Minero e Industrial

Bol Minist Sanid Asist Soc (Venez) — Boletim. Ministerio de Sanidad y Asisteneta Social (Venezuela)

Bol Min Petr — Boletin de Miras y Petroleo [*Chile*]

Bolm Inst Angola — Boletim. Instituto de Angola

Bolm Mus Para Emilio Goeldi Bot — Boletim. Museu Paraense Emilio Goeldi. Nova Serie. Botanica

Bolm Real Soc Esp Hist Nat Secc — Boletim. Real Sociedad Espanola de Historia Natural. Seccion Biologica

Bolm Soc Bras Ent — Boletim. Sociedade Brasileira de Entomologia

Bolm Soc Broteriana — Boletim. Sociedade Broteriana

Bolm Soc Cearense Agron — Boletim. Sociedade Cearense de Agronomia

Bolm Tec Inst Agron N — Boletim Tecnico. Instituto Agronomico do Norte

Bolm Tec Inst Pesq Exp Agropecuar N — Boletim Tecnico. Instituto de Pesquisas e Experimentacao Agropecuarias do Norte

Bolm Univ Parana Zool — Boletim. Universidade Federal do Parana. Zoologia

Bol Mus Bot Munic (Curitiba) — Boletim. Museu Botanico Municipal (Curitiba)

Bol Mus Cienc Nat — Boletin. Museo de Ciencias Naturales

Bol Mus Hist Nat UFMG Bot — Boletim. Museu de Historia Natural UFMG [*Universidade Federal de Minas Gerais*]. Botanica

Bol Mus Hist Nat UFMG Geol — Boletim. Museu de Historia Natural UFMG [*Universidade Federal de Minas Gerais*]. Geologia

Bol Mus Hist Nat UFMG Zool — Boletim. Museu de Historia Natural UFMG [*Universidade Federal de Minas Gerais*]. Zoologia

Bol Mus Lab Mineral Geol Fac Cienc Univ Lisboa — Boletim. Museu e Laboratorio Mineralogico e Geologicao. Faculdade de Ciencias. Universidade de Lisboa

Bol Mus Munic Funchal — Boletim. Museu Municipal do Funchal

Bol Mus Nac (Rio De Janeiro) Geol — Boletim. Museu Nacional (Rio De Janeiro). Geologia

Bol Mus Nac (Rio De J) Antropol — Boletim. Museu Nacional (Rio De Janeiro). Antropologia

Bol Mus Nac (Rio De J) Bot — Boletim. Museu Nacional (Rio De Janeiro). Botanica

Bol Mus Nac (Rio De J) Zool — Boletim. Museu Nacional (Rio De Janeiro). Zoologia

Bol Mus Para Emilio Goeldi Nova Ser Bot — Boletim. Museu Paraense Emilio Goeldi. Nova Serie. Botanica

Bol Mus Para Emilio Goeldi Nova Ser Geol — Boletim. Museu Paraense Emilio Goeldi. Nova Serie. Geologia

Bol Mus Para Emilio Goeldi Nova Ser Zool — Boletim. Museu Paraense Emilio Goeldi. Nova Serie. Zoologia

Bol Mus Paraense Emilio Goeldi — Boletim. Museu Paraense Emilio Goeldi

Bol Mus Paraense Emilio Goeldi Nova Ser Antropol — Boletim. Museu Paraense Emilio Goeldi. Nova Serie. Antropologia

Bol Mus Paraense Emilio Goeldi Nova Ser Bot — Boletim. Museu Paraense Emilio Goeldi. Nova Serie. Botanica

Bol Mus Paraense Emilio Goeldi Nova Ser Geol — Boletim. Museu Paraense Emilio Goeldi. Nova Serie. Geologia

Bol Mus Soc Argent — Boletin. Museo Social Argentino

Bol Mus Soc Arqueol la Serena — Boletin. Publicaciones del Museo y de la Sociedad Arqueologica de la Serena

Bol Mus Valp — Boletin. Museo de Valparaiso

Bolm Zool Univ S Paulo — Boletim de Zoologia. Universidade de Sao Paulo

Bol Nac Minas — Boletin Nacional de Minas

Boln Divulg Ganad — Boletin de Divulgacion Ganaderia

Boln Divulg (Pergamino) — Boletin de Divulgacion (Pergamino)

Boln Estac Exp Agric "Tingo Maria" — Boletin. Estacion Experimental Agricola "Tingo Maria"

Boln Geol (Bogota) — Boletin Geologico. Instituto Geologico Nacional (Bogota, Colombia)

Boln Mus Hist Nat Javier Prado — Boletin. Museo de Historia Natural "Javier Prado"

Boln Mus Nac Hist Nat (Chile) — Boletin. Museo Nacional de Historia Natural (Chile)

Boln Of Estado — Boletin Oficial del Estado

Bol Not Inst Fom Algodonero (Bogota) — Boletin de Noticias. Instituto de Fomento Algodonero (Bogota)

Boln Patol Veg Ent Agric — Boletin de Patologia Vegetal y Entomologia Agricola

Boln R Soc Esp Hist Nat — Boletin. Real Sociedad Espanola de Historia Natural

Boln Rur Inst Nac Tecnol Agropec — Boletin Rural. Instituto Nacional de Tecnologia Agropecuaria

Boln Soc Venez Cienc Nat — Boletin. Sociedad Venezolana de Ciencias Naturales

Boln Tec Fac Agron Univ Chile — Boletin Tecnico. Facultad de Agronomia. Universidad de Chile

Bol Nucl — Boletin Nucleo

Bol Num (Brasil) — Boletim de Numismatica (Brasil)

Boln Univ Montevideo Fac Agron — Boletin. Universidad de la Republica. Facultad de Agronomia (Montevideo)

Bol Obras Sanit Nac (Argent) — Boletin de Obras Sanitarias de la Nacion (Argentina)

Bol Obs Ebro Ser A — Boletin. Observatorio del Ebro. Serie A

Bol Oceanogr Pesc — Boletin de Oceanografia y Pescas

Bol Odont — Boletin de Odontologia

Bol Odont Mex — Boletin Odontologico Mexicano

Bol Odont Paul — Boletim Odontologico Paulista

Bol Of Asoc Tec Azucar Cuba — Boletin Oficial. Asociacion de Tecnicos Azucareros de Cuba

Bol Of Col Quim PR — Boletin Oficial. Colegio Quimicos de Puerto Rico

Bol Of Estado — Boletin Oficial del Estado [*Spain*]

Bol Ofic Sanit Panam Engl Ed — Boletin. Oficina Sanitaria Panamericana. English Edition

Bol Ofic Sanit Panamer — Boletin. Oficina Sanitaria Panamericana

Bol Of Sanit Panam — Boletin. Oficina Sanitaria Panamericana

Bol Oftal — Boletin Oftalmologico

Bologna Med — Bologna Medica

Bol Oncol — Boletim de Oncologia

Bol Ord Med — Boletim. Ordem dos Medicos

Bol Paleontol B Aires — Boletin Paleontologico de Buenos Aires

Bol Parana Geocienc — Boletim Paranaense de Geociencias

Bol Parana Geogr — Boletim Paranaense de Geografia

Bol Par Geogr — Boletim Paranaense de Geografia

Bol Patol Med (Madr) — Boletin de Patologia Medica (Madrid)

Bol Patol Veg Entomol Agric — Boletin de Patologia Vegetal y Entomologia Agricola

Bol Paul Geogr — Boletim Paulista de Geografia

Bol Pecuar Dir Geral Serv Pecuar (Portugal) — Boletim Pecuario. Direccao Geral dos Servicios Pecuarios (Portugal)

Bol Pecu (Lisb) — Boletim Pecuario (Lisbon)

Bol Petroleo — Boletin del Petroleo

Bol Planificacion — Boletin de Planificacion

Bol Popular Min Agric (Guatemala) — Boletin Popular. Direccion General de Agricultura de Guatemala. Ministerio de Agricultura (Guatemala)

Bol Prod Anim — Boletin de Produccion Animal

Bol Prod Fom Agric — Boletin de Produccion y Fomento Agricola

Bol Psicol — Boletim de Psicologia

Bol Psiquiatr — Boletim de Psiquiatria

Bol Quim Peru — Boletin del Quimico Peruano

Bol R Ac Hist — Boletin. Real Academia de la Historia [*Madrid*]

Bol Radiact — Boletin de Radiactividad

Bol Real Ac — Boletin. Real Academia de la Historia

Bol Real Soc Geogr — Boletin. Real Sociedad de Geografia [*Madrid*]

Bol Resenas Ser Ganad — Boletin de Resenas. Serie Ganaderia (Havana)

Bol Rev Peru Pediat — Boletin. Revista Peruana de Pediatria

Bol R Soc Espan Hist Nat — Boletin. Real Sociedad Espanola de Historia Natural

Bol R Soc Esp Hist Nat — Boletin. Real Sociedad Espanola de Historia Natural

Bol R Soc Esp Hist Nat Secc Biol — Boletin. Real Sociedad Espanola de Historia Natural. Seccion Biologica

Bol R Soc Esp Hist Nat Secc Geol — Boletin. Real Sociedad Espanola de Historia Natural. Seccion Geologica

BOLS — Boreales. Revue du Centre de Recherches Inter-Nordiques

BOLSA — Bank of London and South America. Review

Bol Salubr Hig — Boletin de Salubridad e Higiene

Bol Salud Publica — Boletin de Salud Publica

Bol Sanat (Sao Lucas) — Boletim do Sanatorio (Sao Lucas)

Bol Secr Sal Publ — Boletin Administrativo. Secretaria de Salud Publica de la Nacion

Bol Ser D Estud Espec Inst Geol Miner Repub Peru — Boletin. Serie D. Estudios Especiales. Instituto de Geologia y Mineria. Republica del Peru [*Lima*]

Bol Serv Def Contra Plagas Inspeccion Fitopatol (Spain) — Boletin. Servicio de Defensa Contra Plagas e Inspeccion Fitopatologica (Spain)

Bol Serv Geol Minas (Mocambique) — Boletim dos Servicos de Geologia e Minas (Mocambique)

Bol Serv Geol Nac Nicaragua — Boletin. Servicio Geologico Nacional de Nicaragua

Bol Serv Med Nac Empl (Ch) — Boletin. Servicio Medico Nacional de Empleados (Chile)

Bol Serv Nac Sal (Ch) — Boletin. Servicio Nacional de Salud (Chile)

Bol Serv Plagas For — Boletin. Servicio de Plagas Forestales

Bol Soc Arg Angiol — Boletines. Sociedad Argentina de Angiologia

Bol Soc Arg Bot — Boletin. Sociedad Argentina de Botanica

Bol Soc Arg Ciruj — Boletines y Trabajos. Sociedad Argentina de Cirujanos

Bol Soc Argent Angiol — Boletin. Sociedad Argentina de Angiologia

Bol Soc Argent Bot — Boletin. Sociedad Argentina de Botanica

Bol Soc Arg Est Gaea — Boletin. Sociedad Argentina de Estudios Geograficos Gaea

Bol Soc Astr Mex — Boletin. Sociedad Astronomica de Mexico

Bol Soc Biol Concepcion — Boletin. Sociedad de Biologia de Concepcion

Bol Soc Boliv Pediat — Boletin. Sociedad Boliviana de Pediatria

Bol Soc Bot Estado Jalisco — Boletin. Sociedad Botanica del Estado de Jalisco

Bol Soc Bot Mex — Boletin. Sociedad Botanica de Mexico

Bol Soc Bras Agron — Boletim. Sociedade Brasileira de Agronomia

Bol Soc Bras Ent — Boletim. Sociedade Brasileira de Entomologia

Bol Soc Bras Geol — Boletim. Sociedade Brasileira de Geologia

Bol Soc Brasil Mat — Boletim. Sociedade Brasileira de Matematica

Bol Soc Bras Mat — Boletim. Sociedade Brasileira de Matematica

Bol Soc Bras Med Vet — Boletim. Sociedade Brasileira de Medicina Veterinaria

Bol Soc Bras Tuberc — Boletim. Sociedade Brasileira de Tuberculose

Bol Soc Broteriana — Boletim. Sociedade Broteriana

Bol Soc Castell Cult — Boletin. Sociedad Castellonense de Cultura

Bol Soc Cast Leon Pediat — Boletin. Sociedad Castellanoleonesa de Pediatria

Bol Soc Catal Pediat — Boletin. Sociedad Catalana de Pediatria

Bol Soc Cear Agron — Boletim. Sociedade Cearense de Agronomia

Bol Soc Cearense Agron — Boletim. Sociedade Cearense de Agronomia

Bol Soc Chil Obstet Ginec — Boletin. Sociedad Chilena de Obstetricia y Ginecologia

Bol Soc Chil Obstet Ginecol — Boletin. Sociedad Chilena de Obstetricia y Ginecologia

Bol Soc Chil Quim — Boletin. Sociedad Chilena Quimica

Bol Soc Chim Sao Paulo — Boletin. Sociedad de Chimica de Sao Paulo

Bol Soc Cirug Chile — Boletin. Sociedad de Cirugia de Chile

Bol Soc Cirug Cord — Boletines y Trabajos. Sociedad de Cirugia de Cordoba

Bol Soc Cirug Urug — Boletin. Sociedad de Cirugia del Uruguay

Bol Soc Cir Urug — Boletin. Sociedad de Cirugia del Uruguay

Bol Soc Col Cienc Nat — Boletin. Sociedad Colombiana de Ciencias Naturales

Bol Soc Colomb Quim Farm — Boletin. Sociedad Colombiana de Quimicos Farmaceuticos

Bol Soc Cubana Dermatol Sifilogr — Boletin. Sociedad Cubana de Dermatologia y Sifilografia

Bol Soc Cub Derm Sif — Boletin. Sociedad Cubana de Dermatologia y Sifilografia

Bol Soc Eng Rio Grande Do Sul — Boletim. Sociedade de Engenharia do Rio Grande Do Sul

Bol Soc Esp Ceram — Boletin. Sociedad Espanola de Ceramica

Bol Soc Esp Ceram Vidrio — Boletin. Sociedad Espanola de Ceramica y Vidrio

Bol Soc Esp Hist Farm — Boletin. Sociedad Espanola de Historia de la Farmacia

Bol Soc Esp Hist Med — Boletin. Sociedad Espanola de Historia de la Medicina

Bol Soc Fom Fabril — Boletin. Sociedad de Fomento Fabril

Bol Soc Geol Boliv — Boletin. Sociedad Geologica Boliviana

Bol Soc Geol Mex — Boletin. Sociedad Geologica Mexicana

Bol Soc Geol Peru — Boletin. Sociedad Geologica del Peru

Bol Soc Geol Port — Boletim. Sociedade Geologica de Portugal

Bol Soc Ital Fis — Bollettino. Societa Italiana di Fisica

Bol Soc Mat Mexicana — Boletin. Sociedad Matematica Mexicana

Bol Soc Mat Mexicana 2 — Boletin. Sociedad Matematica Mexicana. Segunda Serie [*Mexico City*]

Bol Soc Med Cent Materno Infant Gral Maximino Avila Camacho — Boletin. Sociedad Medica del Centro Materno Infantil Gral Maximino Avila Camacho [*Mexico*]

Bol Soc Med e Cirug S Paulo — Boletim. Sociedade de Medicina e Cirugia de Sao Paulo

Bol Soc Mex Hist Filos Med — Boletin. Sociedad Mexicana de Historia y Filosofia de la Medicina

Bol Soc Mex Micol — Boletin. Sociedad Mexicana de Micologia

Bol Soc Nac Mineria Petrol — Boletin. Sociedad Nacional de Mineria y Petroleo

Bol Soc Paran Mat 2 — Boletim. Sociedade Paranaense de Matematica. 2 Serie [*Panama*]

Bol Soc Paul Med Vet — Boletim. Sociedade Paulista de Medicina Veterinaria

Bol Soc Port Cienc Nat — Boletim. Sociedade Portuguesa de Ciencias Naturais

Bol Soc Quim Peru — Boletin. Sociedad Quimica del Peru

Bol Soc St Vald — Bollettino. Societa di Studi Valdesi

Bol Soc Valencia Pediatr — Boletin. Sociedad Valenciana de Pediatria

Bol Soc Venez Cienc Nat — Boletin. Sociedad Venezolana de Ciencias Naturales

Bol Soc Venez Cir — Boletin. Sociedad Venezolana de Cirugia

Bol Soc Venez Espeleol — Boletin. Sociedad Venezolana de Espeleologia

Bol Soc Venez Geol — Boletin. Sociedad Venezolana de Geologos

Bol Suelos Deriv Cenizas Volcanicas — Boletin sobre Suelos Derivados de Cenizas Volcanicas

Bol Supt Serv Cafe (Sao Paulo) — Boletim. Superintendencia dos Servicos do Cafe (Sao Paulo)

Bol Tec Arpel — Boletin Tecnico Arpel

Bol Tec Asoc Interam Bibl Doc Agric — Boletin Tecnico. Asociacion Interamericana de Bibliotecarios y Documentalistas Agricolas

Bol Tec Braz Dep Nac Obras Contra Secas — Boletim Tecnico. Brazil Departamento Nacional de Obras Contra as Secas

Bol Tec Cent Pesqui Desenvolvimento (Estado Bahia) — Boletim Tecnico. Centro de Pesquisas e Desenvolvimento (Estado da Bahia)

Bol Tec Cent Tecnol Agric Aliment — Boletim Tecnico. Centro de Tecnologia Agricola e Alimentar

Bol Tec Cent Tecnol Agric Aliment (Rio De Janeiro) — Boletim Tecnico. Centro de Tecnologia Agricola e Alimentar (Rio De Janeiro)

Bol Tec Dep Nac Obras Contra Secas — Boletim Tecnico. Departamento Nacional de Obras Contra as Secas

Bol Tec Dep Prod Veg Secr Agric Parana — Boletim Tecnico. Departamento de Producao Vegetal Secretaria de Agricultura do Parana

Bol Tec Div Tecnol Agric Aliment (Brazil) — Boletim Tecnico. Divisao de Tecnologia Agricola e Alimentar (Brazil)

Bol Tec Equipe Pedol Fertil Solo (Brazil) — Boletim Tecnico. Equipe de Pedologia e Fertilidade do Solo (Brazil)

Bol Tec Esc Ingen For Univ Chile — Boletin Tecnico. Escuela de Ingenieria Forestal. Universidad de Chile

Bol Tec Esc Nac Agr Chapingo — Boletin Tecnico. Escuela Nacional de Agricultura Chapingo

Bol Tec Esc Super Agric Antonio Narro Univ Coahuila Saltillo — Boletin Tecnico. Escuela Superior de Agricultura "Antonio Narro." Universidad de Coahuila (Saltillo)

Bol Tec Es Super Agric Antonio Narro Univ Coahuila Saltillo — Boletin Tecnico. Escuela Superior de Agricultura "Antonio Narro." Universidad de Coahuila (Saltillo)

Bol Tec Feder Nac Cafeteros (Colombia) — Boletin Tecnico. Federacion Nacional de Cafeteros (Colombia)

Bol Tec Inst Agron — Boletim Tecnico. Instituto Agronomico

Bol Tec Inst Agron Leste (Cruz Das Almas) — Boletim Tecnico. Instituto Agronomico do Leste (Cruz Das Almas)

Bol Tec Inst Agron Nordeste — Boletim Tecnico. Instituto Agronomico do Nordeste

Bol Tec Inst Agron Norte — Boletim Tecnico. Instituto Agronomico do Norte

Bol Tec Inst Agron Norte Belem — Boletim Tecnico. Instituto Agronomico do Norte Belem

Bol Tec Inst Agron Sul — Boletim Tecnico. Instituto Agronomico do Sul

Bol Tec Inst Agron Sul (Pelotas) — Boletim Tecnico. Instituto Agronomico do Sul (Pelotas)

Bol Tec Inst Agron Sul (Pelotas Brazil) — Boletim Tecnico. Instituto Agronomico do Sul (Pelotas, Brazil)

Bol Tec Inst Fom Algodonero (Bogota) — Boletin Tecnico. Instituto de Fomenta Algodonero (Bogota)

Bol Tec Inst For Chile — Boletin Tecnico. Instituto Forestal. Santiago-De-Chile

Bol Tec Inst Form Algodonero (Bogota) — Boletin Tecnico. Instituto de Fomenta Algodonero (Bogota)

Bol Tec Inst Nac Invest For (Mex) — Boletin Tecnico. Instituto Nacional de Investigaciones Forestales (Mexico)

Bol Tec Inst Pesqui Exp Agropecu Norte — Boletim Tecnico. Instituto Pesquisas e Experimentacao Agropecuarias do Norte

Bol Tec Inst Prov Agropecu (Mendoza) — Boletin Tecnico. Instituto Provincial Agropecuario (Mendoza)

Bol Tec IPEAN — Boletim Tecnico. Instituto Pesquisas e Experimentacao Agropecuarias do Norte

Bol Tec Min Agr (Colombia) — Boletin Tecnico. Ministerio de Agricultura (Colombia)

Bol Tec Min Agr (Guatemala) — Boletin Tecnico. Ministerio de Agricultura (Guatemala)

Bol Tec Minist Agric Ganad (Costa Rica) — Boletin Tecnico. Ministerio de Agricultura y Ganaderia (Costa Rica)

Bol Tec Minist Agric Ind (San Jose Costa Rica) — Boletin Tecnico. Ministerio de Agricultura e Industrias (San Jose, Costa Rica)

Bol Tec Peru Serv Invest Promoc Agr — Boletin Tecnico. Peru Servicio de Investigacion y Promocion Agraria

Bol Tec Petrobras — Boletim Tecnico. Petrobras [*Centro de Pesquisas e Desenvolvimento*]

Bol Tec Univ Chile Fac Cienc For — Boletin Tecnico. Universidad de Chile. Facultad de Ciencias Forestales

Bol Trab Soc Argent Cir — Boletines y Trabajos. Sociedad Argentina de Cirujanos

Bol y Trab Soc Cirug Buenos Aires — Boletines y Trabajos. Sociedad de Cirugia de Buenos Aires

Bol Univ Chile — Boletin. Universidad de Chile

Bol Univ Fed Parana Bot — Boletim. Universidade Federal do Parana. Botanica

Bol Univ Fed Parana Fis Teor — Boletim. Universidade Federal do Parana. Fisica Teorica [*Brazil*]

Bol Univ Fed Parana Zool — Boletim. Universidade Federal do Parana. Zoologia

Bol Univ Parana Farm — Boletim. Universidade do Parana. Farmacognosia

Bol Univ Parana Geol — Boletim. Universidade do Parana. Geologia

Bol Urug Sociol — Boletin Uruguayo de Sociologia

Bol Zool — Boletim de Zoologia

Bol Zool Biol Mar (Nova Ser) — Boletim de Zoologia e Biologia Marinha (Nova Serie)

Bol Zool Mus Para Emilio Goeldi — Boletim de Zoologia. Museu Paraense Emilio Goeldi

Bombay Geogr Mag — Bombay Geographical Magazine

Bombay Hosp J — Bombay Hospital Journal

Bombay Technol — Bombay Technologist

BOMBB — Biomembranes

BOMDD — Bio Med

Bome S-Afr — Bome in Suid-Afrika

BOMXA — Boletin. Asociacion Mexicana de Geologos Petroleros

Bone Metab — Bone Metabolism [*Japan*]

BONNA — Bollettino. Societa di Naturalisti di Napoli

Bonner Energ-Rep — Bonner Energie-Report

Bonner Jb — Bonner Jahrbuecher

Bonner Math Schriften — Bonner Mathematische Schriften [*Bonn*]

Bonn Jb — Bonner Jahrbuecher

Bonn Math Schr — Bonner Mathematische Schriften

Bonn Zool Beitr — Bonner Zoologische Beitraege

Bonn Zool Monogr — Bonner Zoologische Monographien

Bonsai J — Bonsai Journal

BOO — Banco de Guatemala. Informe Economico

BOOCA — Bollettino d'Oculistica

Book Collec — Book Collector

Book Collect — Book Collector

Bookl For Comm (Lond) — Booklet. Forestry Commission (London)

Booklist — American Library Association. Booklist

Booklist — Booklist and Subscription Books Bulletin [*Later, Booklist*]

Booklist and SBB — Booklist and Subscription Books Bulletin [*Later, Booklist*]

Booklover's M — Booklover's Magazine

Bookl Timb Pres Assoc Aust — Booklet. Timber Preservers' Association of Australia

Bookm — Bookman

Bookmark — Bookmark. New York State Library

Bookm (Lond) — Bookman (London)

Book Prod — Book Production Industry

Book R — Book Reviews

Books — New York Herald Tribune Books

Books in Library and Information Sci — Books in Library and Information Science [*New York*]
Books in Scot — Books in Scotland
Book Suppl J Child Psychol Psychiatr — Book Supplement. Journal of Child Psychology and Psychiatry
BOP — Bibliographique Officiel des Imprimes Publies en Pologne. Bulletin
BOP — Bouwbedrijf
BOPSA — Bibliotheca Ophthalmologica
BOR — Babylonian and Oriental Record
BOR — Biserica Orthodoxa Romana
BOran — Bulletin Trimestriel des Antiquites Africaines Recueillies par les Soins de la Societe de Geographie et d'Archeologie de la Province d'Oran
Bor Cipotech — Bor es Cipotechnika
Bordeaux Chir — Bordeaux Chirurgicale [*France*]
Bordeaux Med — Bordeaux Medical
Borden's Rev Nutr Res — Borden's Review of Nutrition Research
Borderl Neurol — Borderlands of Neurology
Bord Med — Bordeaux Medical
Boreal Inst North Stud Univ Alberta Annu Rep — Boreal Institute for Northern Studies. University of Alberta. Annual Report
Boreal Inst North Stud Univ Alberta Occas Publ — Boreal Institute for Northern Studies. University of Alberta. Occasional Publication
Borgyogy Venerol Sz — Borgyogyaszati es Venerologiai Szemle
BORL — Boreal
Bornholm Sam — Bornholmske Samlinger
Bor Res B — Borneo Research Bulletin
Borsod Szle — Borsodi Szemle
BoRv — Book Review Digest
BOS — Bonner Orientalistische Studien
Bosbou S-Afr — Bosbou in Suid-Afrika
Bosbouwproefstn TNO Korte Meded — Bosbouwproefstation TNO. Korte Mededeling
Bosb Suid-Afr — Bosbou in Suid-Afrika
Bosch Tech Ber — Bosch Technische Berichte
BOSFA — Bollettino. Societa Italiana di Fisica
BOSGA — Bollettino. Servizio Geologico d'Italia
Bos Pub Lib Q — Boston Public Library. Quarterly
Bost — Bostonian
Bost Coll Ind L Rev — Boston College. Industrial and Commercial Law Review
Bost Mo — Boston Monthly Magazine
Boston BJ — Boston Bar Journal
Boston Col Environmental Affairs Law R — Boston College. Environmental Affairs Law Review
Boston Col Ind Com L Rev — Boston College. Industrial and Commercial Law Review
Boston Col Int Comp L Rev — Boston College. International and Comparative Law Review
Boston Col Internat and Comparative Law R — Boston College. International and Comparative Law Review
Boston Col Int'l & Comp LJ — Boston College. International and Comparative Law Journal
Boston Coll Environ Aff Law Rev — Boston College. Environmental Affairs Law Review
Boston Col Stud Phil — Boston College. Studies in Philosophy
Boston J N H — Boston Journal of Natural History
Boston J Ph — Boston Journal of Philosophy and the Arts
Boston M — Boston Magazine
Boston Med Q — Boston Medical Quarterly
Boston Med and S J — Boston Medical and Surgical Journal
Boston Mus Bul — Boston Museum of Fine Arts. Bulletin
Boston Pub Lib Quar — Boston Public Library. Quarterly
Boston R — Boston Review
Boston Soc C E J — Boston Society of Civil Engineers. Journal
Boston Soc of Nat Hist Memoirs — Boston Society of Natural History. Memoirs
Boston Soc of Nat Hist Occ Papers — Boston Society of Natural History. Occasional Papers
Boston Soc of Nat Hist Proc — Boston Society of Natural History. Proceedings
Boston State Hosp Monogr Ser — Boston State Hospital. Monograph Series
Boston Stud Philos Sci — Boston Studies in the Philosophy of Science
Boston U LR — Boston University. Law Review
Boston UL Rev — Boston University. Law Review
Boston U St — Boston University. Studies in Philosophy and Religion
Bost Q — Boston Quarterly
Bost R — Boston Review
Bost Soc Natur Hist Occ Pa — Boston Society of Natural History. Occasional Papers
Bost Soc Natur Hist Proc — Boston Society of Natural History. Proceedings
Bost Sym — Boston Symphony Orchestra. Program Notes
Bost Sym Concert Bul — Boston Symphony Orchestra. Concert Bulletin
Bo Stud — Bonner Studien zur Englischen Philologie
Bost UL Rev — Boston University. Law Review
BOSUAN — Forestry in South Africa
Bos U J — Boston University. Journal
Bos U Law Rev — Boston University. Law Review

BOSYA — Bulletin. Ophthalmological Society of Egypt
Bot Abstr — Botanical Abstracts
Botan B A S — Botanical Bulletin. Academia Sinica
Botan Gaz — Botanical Gazette
Botan J Lin — Botanical Journal. Linnean Society [*London*]
Botan Mag — Botanical Magazine [*Tokyo*]
Botan Marin — Botanica Marina
Botan Notis — Botaniska Notiser
Botan Rev — Botanical Review
Botan Tids — Botanisk Tidsskrift
Bot Arch — Botanisches Archiv
Bot Bull Acad Sinica — Botanical Bulletin. Academia Sinica
Bot Bull Acad Sinica Inst Bot New Ser — Botanical Bulletin. Academia Sinica. Institute of Botany. New Series
Bot Bull Acad Sin (Taipei) — Botanical Bulletin. Academia Sinica (Taipei)
Bot Gard (Singapore) Annu Rep — Botanic Gardens (Singapore). Annual Report
Bot Gaz — Botanical Gazette
Bot Gothob Acta Univ Gothob — Botanica Gothoburgensia. Acta Universitatis Gothoburgensis
Bot Haves Virksomhed Beret — Botanisk Haves Virksomhed Beretning
Bot Issled Beloruss Otd Vses Bot O-va — Botanika. Issledovaniya. Belorusskoe Otdelenie Vsesoyuznogo Botanicheskogo Obshchestva
Bot Jahrb Syst Pflanzengesch Pflanzengeogr — Botanische Jahrbuecher fuer Systematik Pflanzengeschichte und Pflanzengeographie
BOTJAT — British Orthoptic Journal
Bot J Linn Soc — Botanical Journal. Linnean Society [*London*]
Bot J Linn Soc (Lond) — Botanical Journal. Linnean Society (London)
Bot Klausimai — Botanikos Klausimai
Bot Koezl — Botanikai Koezlemenyek
Bot Koezlem — Botanikai Koezlemenyek
BOTLA — Bollettino. Societa Italiana di Cardiologia
Bot Mag (Tokyo) — Botanical Magazine (Tokyo)
Bot Mar — Botanica Marina
Bot Mar Suppl — Botanica Marina. Supplement
Bot Mater Gerb Bot Inst Akad Nauk — Botanicheskie Materialy Gerbariya Botanicheskogo Instituta. Akademii Nauk
Bot Mater Gerb Inst Bot Akad Nauk Kaz — Botanicheskie Materialy Gerbariya Instituta Botaniki. Akademii Nauk Kazakhskoi
Bot Mater Gerb Inst Bot Akad Nauk Kaz SSR — Botanicheskie Materialy Gerbariya Instituta Botaniki. Akademii Nauk Kazakhskoi SSR
Bot Monogr (New Delhi) — Botanical Monographs (New Delhi)
Bot Monogr (Oxf) — Botanical Monographs (Oxford)
Bot Mus Leafl — Botanical Museum Leaflets. Harvard University
Bot Mus Leafl Harv Univ — Botanical Museum Leaflets. Harvard University
BOT (New York) — Books of the Times (New York)
Bot Not — Botaniska Notiser
Bot Notis — Botaniska Notiser
Bot Notiser — Botaniska Notiser
Bot Not Suppl — Botaniska Notiser. Supplement
Bot R — Botanical Review
BOTRA — Beitraege zur Orthopaedie und Traumatologie
Bot Rev — Botanical Review
Bot Rhedonica Ser A — Botanica Rhedonica. Serie A
Bot Soc Edinb Trans — Botanical Society of Edinburgh. Transactions
Bot Stud — Botanische Studien
Bot Surv S Afr Mem — Botanical Survey of South Africa. Memoir
Botswana Geol Sur Dep Miner Resour Rep — Botswana. Geological Survey Department. Mineral Resources Report
Botswana Geol Surv Dist Mem — Botswana. Geological Survey. District Memoir
Botswana Geol Surv Mines Dep Annu Rep — Botswana. Geological Survey and Mines Department. Annual Report
Botswana Mag — Botswana Magazine
Botswana Notes Rec — Botswana Notes and Records
Bot Tidsskr — Botanisk Tidsskrift
Bot Z — Botaniceskij Zurnal
Bot Zblt — Botanisches Zentralblatt
Bot Zh (Kiev) — Botanichnyi Zhurnal (Kiev)
Bot Zh (Leningr) — Botanicheskii Zhurnal (Leningrad)
Bot Zh (Moscow) — Botanicheskii Zhurnal (Moscow)
Bot Zh (SSSR) — Botanicheskii Zhurnal (SSSR)
Bound — Boundary 2
Boundary-Layer Meteorol — Boundary-Layer Meteorology
Bourne Soc Local Hist Rec — Bourne Society. Local History Records
Bouwsteenen J V N M — Bouwsteenen. Jaarboek der Vereeniging voor Nederlandsche Muziekgeschiedenis
BoV — Bockernas Varld
Bovine Pract — Bovine Practitioner
BOW — Kappersbondsnieuws
Box — Boxspring
Boxbrd Con — Boxboard Containers
Boyce Thompson Inst Contrib — Boyce Thompson Institute. Contributions
Boyce Thompson Inst Plant Res Prof Pap — Boyce Thompson Institute for Plant Research. Professional Papers
Boyer Mus Coll — Boyer Museum Collection

BOZAA — Bollettino di Zoologia Agraria e di Bachicoltura
Bozart — Bozart and Contemporary Verse
BOZED — Boersen-Zeitung
BP — Banasthali Patrika
BP — Bibliographie Philosophie
B de P — Bibliotheque de la Pleiade
BP — Bijdragen van de Philosophische en Theologische Faculteiten der Nederlandsche Jezuieten
BPAAA — Beitraege zur Pathologischen Anatomie und zur Allgemeinen Pathologie
BPABA — Biologia Plantarum [*Prague*]
BP Accel — BP [*British Petroleum*] Accelerator
BPAH — Bulletin. Pan American Health Organization
BPAIA — Bulletin of Pathology (Chicago, Illinois)
BPAU — Bulletin. Pan American Union
BPCMUS — Bulletin. Post-Graduate Committee in Medicine. University of Sydney
BPCTH — Bulletin Philologique et Historique. Comite des Travaux Historiques et Scientifiques [*Paris*]
BPE — Brookings Papers on Economic Activity
BPEA — Brookings Papers on Economic Activity
B Peace Propos — Bulletin of Peace Proposals
BPEAD — Brookings Papers on Economic Activity
BPEC — Bollettino. Comitato per la Preparazione dell'Edizione Nazionale dei Classici Greci e Latini
BPEFA — Buletinul. Institutului Politehnic din Brasov. Seria B. Economie Forestiera
BPES — Bulletin. Palestine Exploration Society
BPF — Bulletin du Protestantisme Francais
BPGGA — Bulletin. Academie Polonaise des Sciences. Serie des Sciences Geologiques et Geographiques
BPGMD — Buletinul. Institutului Politehnic "Gheorghe Gheorghiu-Dej" Bucuresti. Seria Mecanica
BPh — Bibliographie de la Philosophie
BPH — Bulletin Philologique et Historique
BPHBA — BHP [*Broken Hill Proprietary Ltd.*] Technical Bulletin (Australia)
BPhC — Bibliotheca Philologica Classica
BPHCTHS — Bulletin Philologique et Historique. Comite des Travaux Historiques et Scientifiques [*Paris*]
B Phila Mus — Bulletin. Philadelphia Museum of Art
BPHist — Bulletin Philologique et Historique
BPHJA — British Phycological Journal
BPHJAA — British Phycological Journal
BPhM — Bulletin. Societe Internationale pour l'Etude de la Philosophie Medievale
BPHP — Bulletin Philologique et Historique. Comite des Travaux Historiques et Scientifiques (Paris)
BPhSC — Bulletin. Philological Society of Calcutta
BPhSJ — Bulletin. Phonetic Society of Japan
BPHUED — Buletin Penelitian Hutan
BPhW — Berliner Philologische Wochenschrift
B Physiopa — Bulletin de Physiopathologie Respiratoire
BPI — Bollettino Paleontologico Italiano
BPI — Bollettino delle Publicatione Italiane
BPI — Book Production Industry
BPI — Business Periodicals Index [*H. W. Wilson Co.*] [*Bronx, NY*]
BPJ — Beloit Poetry Journal
BPJSA — Biophysical Journal. Supplement
BPK — Berichte. Preussische Kunstsammlungen [*Berlin*]
BPKG — Blaetter fuer Pfaelzische Kirchengeschichte
BPKS — Berichte [*Amtliche*]. Preussische Kunstsammlungen
BPKUD — BP [*Benzin und Petroleum AG Hamburg*] Kurier
BP Kur — BP [*Benzin und Petroleum AG Hamburg*] Kurier
BPLQ — Boston Public Library. Quarterly
BPM — Bulletin. Palestine Museum
BPMGA — Berichte. Physikalisch-Medizinische Gesellschaft zu Wuerzburg
BPN — Building Products News
BPNSA — Bibliotheca Psychiatrica et Neurologica (Switzerland)
BPNSAX — Aktuelle Fragen der Psychiatrie und Neurologie
BPNSB — Bulletin. Psychonomic Society
BPOEA — British Power Engineering
BPOJA — British Polymer Journal
B Pol Biol — Bulletin. Academie Polonaise des Sciences. Serie des Sciences Biologiques
B Pol Chim — Bulletin. Academie Polonaise des Sciences. Serie des Sciences Chimiques
B Pol Math — Bulletin. Academie Polonaise des Sciences. Serie des Sciences Mathematiques, Astronomiques, et Physiques
B Pol Sci T — Bulletin. Academie Polonaise des Sciences. Serie des Sciences de la Terre
B Pol Techn — Bulletin. Academie Polonaise des Sciences. Serie des Sciences Techniques
BPOPD — British Public Opinion
BPOSA — British Poultry Science
BPOSA4 — British Poultry Science
BPP — Bengal Past and Present

BPP — Biochemie und Physiologie der Pflanzen
BPPHA — Beitraege aus der Plasmaphysik
BPPRA — Bulletin de Physio-Pathologie Respiratoire
BPPRD — Bulletin of Peace Proposals
BPR — American Book Publishing Record
BP & R — British Plastics and Rubber
BPR — Bulletin of Prosthetics Research
BPR — Butterworth's Property Reports
B Prince of Wales Mus West India — Bulletin. Prince of Wales Museum of Western India
BPRMA — Bibliotheca Primatologica
BPRRB — Bulletin of Prosthetics Research
BPS — Bulletin. Psychonomic Society
BPSBA7 — British Pteridological Society. Bulletin
BPSC — Bulletin. Philological Society of Calcutta
BP Shield Int — BP [*British Petroleum*] Shield International
B Psic Appl — Bollettino di Psicologia Applicata
BPSMLA — Bulletin. Pennsylvania State Modern Language Association
BPSP — Bollettino. Societa Pavese di Storia Patria
BPSTBS — Bulletin. Academie Polonaise des Sciences. Serie des Sciences de la Terre
B Psychol — Bulletin de Psychologie
B Psychon S — Bulletin. Psychonomic Society
BPT — Journal of Contemporary Business
BPTJ — Biuletyn Polskiego Towarzystwa Jezykoznawczego
BPUA — Biological Papers. University of Alaska
BPUASR — Biological Papers. University of Alaska. Special Report
BPW — Berliner Philologische Wochenschrift
BPYBA3 — British Phycological Bulletin [*Later, British Phycological Journal*]
BPYCA — Rikagaku Kenkyusho Iho
BPYKA — Biophysik [*Berlin*]
BPZBA — Bulletin. Societe des Amis des Sciences et des Lettres de Poznan. Serie B. Sciences Mathematiques et Naturelles
BQ — Banknote Quarterly
BQ — Baptist Quarterly
BQL — Bank Markazi Iran. Bulletin
BQO — Belgian Business
BQR — Bodleian Quarterly Record
BQU — Bangladesh Bank. Bulletin
BQU — Business Quarterly
BR — Baltic Review [*New York*]
BR — Benedictine Review
BR — Bennington Review
BR — Biblical Research
BR — Biblical Review
BR — Bibliotheca Romana
BR — Brooklyn Law Review
BR — Bucknell Review
BR — Budapest Regisegei
BR — Business Review
BRA — Beitraege zur Religionsgeschichte des Altertums [*Halle/S.*]
BrA — Brasil Acucareiro
Brabantse Folkl — De Brabantse Folklore
BRABLB — Boletin. Real Academia de Buenas Letras de Barcelona
Br Abstr — British Abstracts
Br Abstr A1 — British Abstracts A1. General, Physical, and Inorganic Chemistry
Br Abstr A2 — British Abstracts A2. Organic Chemistry
Br Abstr A3 — British Abstracts A3. Physiology and Biochemistry
Br Abstr B1 — British Abstracts B1. Chemical Engineering, Fuels, Metallurgy, Applied Electrochemistry, and Industrial Inorganic Chemistry
Br Abstr B2 — British Abstracts B2. Industrial Organic Chemistry
Br Abstr B3 — British Abstracts B3. Agriculture, Foods, Sanitation
Br Abstr C — British Abstracts C. Analysis and Apparatus
Br Abstr Med Sci — British Abstracts of Medical Sciences
BRAC — Boletin. Real Academia de Cordoba
BRACA2 — Brasil Acucareiro
Brac LJ — Bracton Law Journal
Bracton LJ — Bracton Law Journal
Bradea Bol Herb Bradeanum — Bradea. Boletim do Herbarium Bradeanum
Bradford Antiq — Bradford Antiquary
BRAE — Boletin. Real Academia Espanola
Br Agric Bull — British Agricultural Bulletin
BRAH — Boletin. Real Academia de la Historia
Brahms-Stud — Brahms-Studien
BRAIA — Brain. Journal of Neurology
Brain Behav — Brain, Behavior, and Evolution
Brain Behav Evol — Brain, Behavior, and Evolution
Brain Behav Res Monogr Ser — Brain and Behavior Research Monograph Series
Brain Dev — Brain and Development
Brain Lang — Brain and Language
Brain/Mind — Brain/Mind Bulletin
Brain Pep — Brain Peptides
Brain Res — Brain Research
Brain Res Bull — Brain Research Bulletin

Brain Res Rev — Brain Research Reviews
Brake FE — Brake and Front End
Br Alma Comp — British Almanac Companion
B Rama Miss Inst Cult — Bulletin. Ramakrishna Mission Institute of Culture
Brandschutz Dtsch Feuerwehrztg — Brandschutz Deutsche Feuerwehrzeitung
Brandstofnavorsingsinst S Afr Bull — Brandstofnavorsingsinstituut van Suid-Afrika. Bulletein
Branntweinwirt — Branntweinwirtschaft
Br Antarct Surv Bull — British Antarctic Survey. Bulletin
Br Antarct Surv Sci Rep — British Antarctic Survey. Scientific Reports
Br Archaeol Abstr — British Archaeological Abstracts
Bras — Brasilia
Bras Acucareiro — Brasil Acucareiro
Bras Flores — Brasil Florestal
Brasil Acucar — Brasil Acucareiro
Brasil Apic — Brasil Apicola
Bras-Med — Brasil-Medico
Brass B — Brass Bulletin
Brass Founder Finsh — Brass Founder and Finisher
Brass Fr — Brasseur Francais
Brass Malt — Brasserie et Malterie
Brass W — Brass World and Plater's Guide
Brass & Wood Q — Brass and Woodwind Quarterly
Bras Text — Brasil Textil
Br Astron Assoc Circ — British Astronomical Association. Circular
Bratisl Lek Listy — Bratislavske Lekarske Listy
Brauerei Wiss Beil — Brauerei. Wissenschaftliche Beilage
Brau Malzind — Brau- und Malzindustrie
Braunkohle Waerme Energ — Braunkohle, Waerme, und Energie
Braunschweig Wiss Ges Abh — Braunschweigische Wissenschaftliche Gesellschaft. Abhandlungen
Braunschw Konserv Z — Braunschweigische Konserven-Zeitung
Brauwiss — Brauwissenschaft
Braz Com Nac Energ Nucl Bol — Brazil. Comissao Nacional de Energia Nuclear. Boletim
Braz Dep Nac Obras Secas Serv Piscic Publ Ser 1 C — Brazil. Departamento Nacional de Obras Contra as Secas. Servico de Piscicultura. Publicacao. Serie 1 C
Braz Dep Nac Prod Miner Anu Miner Bras — Brazil. Departamento Nacional da Producao Mineral. Anuario Mineral Brasileiro
Braz Dep Nac Prod Miner Bol — Brazil. Departamento Nacional da Producao Mineral. Boletim
Braz Dep Nac Prod Miner Div Aguas — Brazil. Departamento Nacional da Producao Mineral. Divisao de Aguas. Boletim
Braz Div Fom Prod Miner Avulso — Brazil. Divisao de Fomento da Producao Mineral. Avulso
Braz Div Fom Prod Miner Bol — Brazil. Divisao de Fomento da Producao Mineral. Boletim
Braz Div Fom Prod Miner Mem — Brazil. Divisao de Fomento da Producao Mineral. Memoria
Braz Div Geol Mineral Avulso — Brazil. Divisao de Geologia e Mineralogia. Avulso
Braz Div Geol Mineral Notas Prelim Estud — Brazil. Divisao de Geologia e Mineralogia. Notas Preliminares e Estudos
Braz Econ — Brazilian Economy. Trends and Perspectives
Braz Escritorio Pesqui Exp Equipe Pedol Fertil Solo Bol Tec — Brazil. Escritorio de Pesquisas e Experimentacao. Equipe de Pedologia e Fertilidade da Solo. Boletim Tecnico
Brazil Camara Deput Bibl Bol — Brazil. Camara dos Deputados. Biblioteca. Boletim
Brazil Cons Nac Petrol Relat — Brazil. Conselho Nacional do Petroleo. Relatorio
Brazil Dep Nac Prod Miner Lab Prod Miner Avulso — Brazil. Departmento Nacional da Producao Mineral. Laboratorio da Producao Mineral. Avulso
Brazil Div Geol Mineral Bol — Brazil. Divisao de Geologia e Mineralogia. Boletim
Brazil Div Geol Mineral Notas Prelim Estud — Brazil. Divisao de Geologia e Mineralogia. Notas Preliminares e Estudos
Brazilian Bus — Brazilian Business
Brazilian Econ Studies — Brazilian Economic Studies
Brazil-Med — Brazil-Medico
Brazil Minist Minas Energ Dep Nac Prod Miner Bol — Brazil. Ministerio das Minas e Energia. Departamento Nacional da Producao Mineral. Boletim
Brazil S — Brazilian Studies
Braz Inst Agron Nordeste Bol Tec — Brazil. Instituto Agronomico da Nordeste. Boletim Tecnico
Braz Inst Oleos Bol — Brazil. Instituto de Oleos. Boletim
Braz J Med Biol Res — Brazilian Journal of Medical and Biological Research
Braz Lab Prod Miner Avulso — Brazil. Laboratorio da Producao Mineral. Avulso
Braz Lab Prod Miner Bol — Brazil. Laboratorio da Producao Mineral. Boletim
Braz Minist Agric Cent Tecnol Agric Aliment Bol Tec — Brazil. Ministerio da Agricultura. Centro de Tecnologia Agricola e Alimentar. Boletim Tecnico

Braz Serv Inf Agric Estud Tee — Brazil. Servico de Informacao Agricola. Estudos Teemcos
Braz Supt Desenvolvimento Nordeste Div Geol Bol Estud — Brazil. Superintendencia do Desenvolvimento do Nordeste. Divisao de Geologia. Boletim de Estudos
Braz Supt Desenvolvimento Nordeste Div Geol Ser Geol Econ — Brazil. Superintendencia do Desenvolvimento do Nordeste. Divisao de Geologia. Serie Geologia Economica
Braz Supt Desenvolvimento Nordeste Div Geol Ser Geol Espec — Brazil. Superintendencia do Desenvolvimento do Nordeste. Divisao de Geologia. Serie Geologia Especial
BRBEBE — Brain, Behavior, and Evolution
Br Bee J — British Bee Journal
BRBIDS — Bryophytorum Bibliotheca
Br Birds — British Birds
Br Bks Print — British Books in Print
BRBOA — Brown Boveri Review
Br Br — Brunn-Bruckmann
BRBUD — Brain Research Bulletin
BRBUDU — Brain Research Bulletin
Br Bus — British Business [England]
Br Business — British Business
BRC — Banco de la Republica. Revista
Br Cast Iron Res Assoc Jrna Res Dev — British Cast Iron Research Association. Journal of Research and Development
Br Cave Res Assoc Trans — British Cave Research Association. Transactions
Br Ceram Abstr — British Ceramic Abstracts
Br Ceram Rev — British Ceramic Review [England]
Br Ceram Trans J — British Ceramic Transactions and Journal
Br Cer Res Assoc Spec Publ — British Ceramic Research Association. Special Publications
Br Chem Abstr A — British Chemical Abstracts. A. Pure Chemistry
Br Chem Abstr B — British Chemical Abstracts. B. Applied Chemistry
Br Chem Eng — British Chemical Engineering
Br Chem Engng — British Chemical Engineering
Br Chem Engng Process Technol — British Chemical Engineering and Process Technology
Br Chem Eng Process Technol — British Chemical Engineering and Process Technology
BRCI — Bulletin. Research Council of Israel
Br Claywkr — British Clayworker
Br Coal Util Res Ass Mon Bull — British Coal Utilisation Research Association. Monthly Bulletin
Br Colon Drug — British and Colonial Druggist
Br Columbia Med J — British Columbia Medical Journal
Br Columb Libr Q — British Columbia Library Quarterly
Br Commun Electron — British Communications and Electronics [England]
Br Constr Eng — British Constructional Engineer
Br Corrosion J — British Corrosion Journal
Br Corros J — British Corrosion Journal
BRCPA — Biological Reviews. Cambridge Philosophical Society
BRD — Book Review Digest
BRDAA — Beitraege zur Radioastronomie
Brdcstng — Broadcasting
Br Decorator — British Decorator
Br Den Annu — British Dental Annual
Br Dental J — British Dental Journal
Br Dent J — British Dental Journal
Br Dent Surg Assist — British Dental Surgery Assistant
BRDGAT — Brewers Digest
BRDIA — Bulletin on Rheumatic Diseases
BRDSPL — Bollettino. Regia Deputazione di Storia Patria per la Liguria
BRDSPU — Bollettino. Regia Deputazione di Storia Patria per l'Umbria
Bread Manuf WA — Bread Manufacturer and Pastrycook of Western Australia
B Real Acad — Boletin. Real Academia de la Historia
BrechtH — Brecht Heute - Brecht Today
Brecht J — Brecht-Jahrbuch
Br Ecol Soc Symp — British Ecological Society. Symposium
BRE Dig — BRE [Building Research Establishment] Digest
Breeder's Gaz — Breeder's Gazette
Br Engine Tech Rep — British Engine Technical Reports
Br Eng Tech Rep — British Engine Technical Reports
Brennerei Ztg — Brennerei Zeitung
Brennst-Chem — Brennstoff-Chemie
Brennst-Waerme-Kraft — Brennstoff-Waerme-Kraft [Fuel, Heat, Power]
Brennst Waermewirtsch — Brennstoff- und Waermewirtschaft [East Germany]
Brenns-Waerme-Kraft — Brennstoff-Waerme-Kraft [Fuel, Heat, Power]
Brenn-Waerme — Brennstoff-Waerme-Kraft [Fuel, Heat, Power]
Bren-S — Brenner-Studien
Brent Unempl Bull — Brent Unemployment Bulletin
BRERD — Brain Research Reviews
BRERD2 — Brain Research Reviews
BResClsr — Bulletin. Research Council of Israel [Jerusalem]
BRESD — Biomedical Research
B Res Hum — Bulletin of Research in the Humanities

Breth Life — Brethren Life and Thought
Breviora Geol Asturica — Breviora Geologica Asturica
Brew Dig — Brewers Digest
Brew Distill Int — Brewing and Distilling International
Brew Guardian — Brewers' Guardian
Brew Guild J — Brewers' Guild Journal
Brew J — Brewers Journal
Brew Rev — Brewing Review
Brew Tech Rev — Brewers Technical Review
Brew Trade Rev — Brewing Trade Review
BRF — Bulletin. Rabinowitz Fund for the Exploration of Ancient Synagogues
Br Farmer Stockbreed — British Farmer and Stockbreeder
Br Fern Gaz — British Fern Gazette
Br Food J — British Food Journal
Br Foundryman — British Foundryman
BRG — Blaetter der Rilke-Gesellschaft
Br Geol — British Geologist
BRGIAG — Brewers' Guild Journal
BRGK — Bericht. Roemisch-Germanische Kommission
Br Grassl Soc Occas Symp — British Grassland Society. Occasional Symposium
BRGTAF — Bragantia
BRGUAI — Brewers' Guardian
Br Guiana Geol Surv Dep Bull — British Guiana. Geological Survey Department. Bulletin
Br Guiana Geol Surv Dep Miner Resour Pam — British Guiana. Geological Survey Department. Mineral Resources Pamphlet
BRH — Bulletin of Research in the Humanities
BRH Bull — BRH [Bureau of Radiological Health] Bulletin
Br Heart J — British Heart Journal
Br H I — British Humanities Index
Br Hist Illus — British History Illustrated
BRHLA — Biorheology [England]
Br Honduras Dep Agric Annu Rep — British Honduras. Department of Agriculture. Annual Report
BRI — BioResearch Index [Superseded by BA/RRM]
BRI — British Journal of Industrial Relations [United Kingdom]
BRI — Buddhist Research Information
Briar Q — Briarcliff Quarterly
BRICA — Bulletin. Research Council of Israel. Section C. Technology
Brickb — Brickbuilder
Brick Bull — Brick Bulletin
Brick Clay Rec — Brick and Clay Record
Brick Dev Res Inst Tech Notes Clay Prod — Brick Development Research Institute. Technical Notes on Clay Products
Brick Tech Note — Brick Technical Note
Brief Case — Legal Aid Brief Case
BRIFB — Berichte und Informationen. Europaeische Gemeinschaften
Brigham You — Brigham Young University. Studies
Brigham Young U L Rev — Brigham Young University. Law Review
Brigham Young Univ Geol Stud — Brigham Young University. Geology Studies
Brigham Young Univ L Rev — Brigham Young University. Law Review
Brigham Young Univ Res Stud Geol Ser — Brigham Young University. Research Studies. Geology Series
Brigham Young Univ Sci Bull Biol Ser — Brigham Young University. Science Bulletin. Biological Series
Brigham YULR — Brigham Young University. Law Review
Brig Yo ULR — Brigham Young University. Law Review
BRIMD7 — Brimleyana
Br Ind Finish (Leighton Buzzard Engl) — British Industrial Finishing (Leighton Buzzard, England)
Br Ink Mkr — British Ink Maker
Br Isles Bee Breeders' News — British Isles Bee Breeders' Association. News
Bristol Med-Chir J — Bristol Medico-Chirurgical Journal
Bristol-Myers Nutr Symp — Bristol-Myers Nutrition Symposia
Bristol Univ Dep Agric Hortic Bull — Bristol University. Department of Agriculture and Horticulture. Bulletin
Bristol Univ Spelaeol Soc Proc — Bristol University. Spelaeological Society. Proceedings
Brit Acad Proc — British Academy, London. Proceedings
Britannica R For Lang Educ — Britannica Review of Foreign Language Education
Brit Arch Ab — British Archaeological Abstracts
Brit Archaeol Rep — British Archaeological Reports
Brit As Rp — British Association for the Advancement of Science. Report
Brit Assoc Am Studies Bull — British Association for American Studies. Bulletin
Brit Bee J — British Bee Journal and Beekeepers' Adviser
Brit Birds — British Birds
Brit Bk N — British Book News
Brit Bk N C — British Book News. Children's Supplement
Brit Bk News — British Book News
Brit Bk Yr — Britannica Book of the Year
Brit Busn — British Business
Brit Chem Eng — British Chemical Engineering

Brit Columbia Dep Mines Petrol Resour Bull — British Columbia. Department of Mines and Petroleum Resources. Bulletin
Brit Columbia Lib Q — British Columbia Library Quarterly
Brit Constr Steelworks Ass Publ — British Constructional Steelworks Association. Publications
Brit Corrosion J — British Corrosion Journal
Brit Corros J — British Corrosion Journal
Brit Deaf News — British Deaf News
Brit Ecol Soc Symp — British Ecological Society. Symposium
BritEdI — British Education Index
Brit Engine Boiler Elec Ins Co Tech Rep — British Engine, Boiler, and Electrical Insurance Company. Technical Report
Brit & For Evang R — British and Foreign Evangelical Review
Brit & For R — British and Foreign Review
Brit Granite Whinstone Fed J — British Granite and Whinstone Federation. Journal
Brit Grassland Soc J — British Grassland Society. Journal
Brit Heart J — British Heart Journal
Brit Hosp Soc Serv J — British Hospital and Social Service Journal
Brit Hum — British Humanities Index
Brit Ink Maker — British Ink Maker
British Archaeological Assocn Conference Trans — British Archaeological Association. Conference Transactions
British Ceramic Soc Trans — British Ceramic Society. Transactions
British Columbia Dept Mines Ann Rept Bull — British Columbia. Department of Mines. Annual Report. Bulletin
British Columbia Univ Dept Geology Rept — British Columbia University. Department of Geology. Report
British J Math Statist Psychology — British Journal of Mathematical and Statistical Psychology [London]
British J Pol Science — British Journal of Political Science
British Mus (Nat History) Bull Geology — British Museum (Natural History). Bulletin. Geology
British Nat Biblio — British National Bibliography [London]
British Reports Transl & Theses — British Reports, Translations, and Theses
British Tax R — British Tax Review
Brit J Addict — British Journal of Addiction
Brit J Aes — British Journal of Aesthetics
Brit J Aesth — British Journal of Aesthetics
Brit J Aesthetics — British Journal of Aesthetics
Brit J Ap Phys — British Journal of Applied Physics
Brit J Audiol — British Journal of Audiology
Brit J Child Dis — British Journal of Children's Diseases
Brit J Crim — British Journal of Criminology
Brit J of Crimin — British Journal of Criminology
Brit J Criminol — British Journal of Criminology
Brit J Criminol — British Journal of Criminology, Delinquency, and Deviant Social Behavior
Brit J Criminology — British Journal of Criminology
Brit J Delinq — British Journal of Delinquency
Brit J Dis Commun — British Journal of Disorders of Communication
Brit J Ed Psychol — British Journal of Educational Psychology
Brit J Ed Studies — British Journal of Educational Studies
Brit J Educ Psychol — British Journal of Educational Psychology
Brit J Educ Stud — British Journal of Educational Studies
Brit J Hist Sci — British Journal for the History of Science
Brit J Hosp Med — British Journal of Hospital Medicine
Brit J Ind Rel — British Journal of Industrial Relations
Brit J Industr Med — British Journal of Industrial Medicine
Brit J Industr Relat — British Journal of Industrial Relations
Brit J Int Stud — British Journal of International Studies
Brit J Law & Soc — British Journal of Law and Society
Brit Jl Photogr — British Journal of Photography
Brit J L & Soc — British Journal of Law and Society
Brit JL & Soc'y — British Journal of Law and Society
Brit J Math & Stat Psychol — British Journal of Mathematical and Statistical Psychology
Brit J Med Psychol — British Journal of Medical Psychology
Brit J Ment Subnorm — British Journal of Mental Subnormality
Brit J Non-Destruct Test — British Journal of Non-Destructive Testing
Brit J Nutr — British Journal of Nutrition
Brit J Nutr Proc Nutr Soc — British Journal of Nutrition. Proceedings of the Nutrition Society
Brit Jour Sociol — British Journal of Sociology
Brit J Pharmacol — British Journal of Pharmacology
Brit J Pharmacol Chemother — British Journal of Pharmacology and Chemotherapy [Later, British Journal of Pharmacology]
Brit J Philos Sci — British Journal for the Philosophy of Science
Brit J Phil Sci — British Journal for the Philosophy of Science
Brit J Photo — British Journal of Photography
Brit J Pol Sci — British Journal of Political Science
Brit J Prev Soc Med — British Journal of Preventive and Social Medicine
Brit J Psychiat — British Journal of Psychiatry
Brit J Psychol — British Journal of Psychology
Brit J Psych Soc Work — British Journal of Psychiatric Social Work
Brit J Radiol — British Journal of Radiology

Brit J Social & Clin Psychol — British Journal of Social and Clinical Psychology
Brit J Social Psychiat — British Journal of Social Psychiatry
Brit J Sociol — British Journal of Sociology
Brit Kinematogr Sound Telev — British Kinematography, Sound, and Television
Brit Kinemat Sound and Telev — British Kinematography, Sound, and Television
Brit Lib Assoc — Library Association of the United Kingdom. Monthly Notes
Brit Lib J — British Library Journal
Brit Lib Res Dev Newsletter — British Library Research and Development Newsletter
Brit Med J — British Medical Journal
Brit Mus (Nat Hist) Econom Ser — British Museum (Natural History). Economic Series
Brit Mus Subj Index — British Museum. Subject Index
Brit Mus Yearb — British Museum. Yearbook
Brit Mycol Soc Trans — British Mycological Society. Transactions
Brit Numis J — British Numismatic Journal
Brit Pat Abs Sect CH Chem — British Patent Abstracts. Section CH. Chemical
Brit Plast — British Plastics [*Later, European Plastics News*]
Brit Plast Rubb — British Plastics and Rubber
Brit Polit Sociol Yb — British Political Sociology. Yearbook
Brit Polym J — British Polymer Journal
Brit Poultry Sci — British Poultry Science
Brit Printer — British Printer
Brit Q — British Quarterly Review
Brit Quar Rev — British Quarterly Review
Brit Repts Transl Theses — British Reports, Translations, and Theses
Brit Sch Athens Ann — British School at Athens. Annual
Brit Sch at Rome Papers — British School at Rome. Papers
Britsh Ink — British Ink Maker
Brit Stand — British Standard Specification
Brit Stand Inst Brit Stand — British Standards Institution. British Standard
Brit Steelmaker — British Steelmaker
Brit Tax Rev — British Tax Review
Brit Techl — British Technology Index
Brit Weld J — British Welding Journal
Brit Yb Int Law — British Yearbook of International Law
Brit Yb Int'l L — British Yearbook of International Law
Brit Yearbook Int L — British Yearbook of International Law
Br J Actinother Physiother — British Journal of Actinotherapy and Physiotherapy
Br J Addict — British Journal of Addiction
Br J Aesth — British Journal of Aesthetics
Br J Alcohol Alcohol — British Journal on Alcohol and Alcoholism
Br J Anaest — British Journal of Anaesthesia
Br J Anaesth — British Journal of Anaesthesia
Br J Anim Behav — British Journal of Animal Behaviour
Br J Appl Phys — British Journal of Applied Physics
Br J Appl Phys Suppl — British Journal of Applied Physics. Supplement
Br J Audiol — British Journal of Audiology
Br J Audiology — British Journal of Audiology
Br J Audiol Suppl — British Journal of Audiology. Supplement
Br J Canc — British Journal of Cancer
Br J Cancer — British Journal of Cancer
Br J Cancer Suppl — British Journal of Cancer. Supplement
Br J Clin Equip — British Journal of Clinical Equipment
Br J Clin P — British Journal of Clinical Practice
Br J Clin Pharmacol — British Journal of Clinical Pharmacology
Br J Clin Psychol — British Journal of Clinical Psychology
Br J Cl Ph — British Journal of Clinical Pharmacology
Br J Crimin — British Journal of Criminology
Br J Dent Sci Prosthetics — British Journal of Dental Science and Prosthetics
Br J Derm — British Journal of Dermatology
Br J Dermatol — British Journal of Dermatology
Br J Dermatol Suppl — British Journal of Dermatology. Supplement
Br J Dermatol Syph — British Journal of Dermatology and Syphilis
Br J Dis Ch — British Journal of Diseases of the Chest
Br J Dis Chest — British Journal of Diseases of the Chest
Br J Dis Co — British Journal of Disorders of Communication
Br J Ed Psy — British Journal of Educational Psychology
Br J Educ Psychol — British Journal of Educational Psychology
Br J Educ S — British Journal of Educational Studies
Br J Educ Stud — British Journal of Educational Studies
Br J Educ T — British Journal of Educational Technology
Br J Eighteenth Century Stud — British Journal for Eighteenth Century Studies
Br J Ex Pat — British Journal of Experimental Pathology
Br J Exp Bio — British Journal of Experimental Biology
Br J Exp Biol — British Journal of Experimental Biology
Br J Exp Path — British Journal of Experimental Pathology
Br J Exp Pathol — British Journal of Experimental Pathology
BRJFA — British Journal of Photography
Br J Haem — British Journal of Haematology
Br J Haematol — British Journal of Haematology
Br J Hist S — British Journal for the History of Science

Br J Hist Sci — British Journal for the History of Science
Br J Hosp Med — British Journal of Hospital Medicine
Br J Ind Me — British Journal of Industrial Medicine
Br J Ind Med — British Journal of Industrial Medicine
Br J Ind Medicine — British Journal of Industrial Medicine
Br J Ind Saf — British Journal of Industrial Safety
Br J Inebriety — British Journal of Inebriety
Br J Int Stud — British Journal of International Studies
Br J Law Soc — British Journal of Law and Society
Br J Math S — British Journal of Mathematical and Statistical Psychology
Br J Med Educ — British Journal of Medical Education
Br J Med Ps — British Journal of Medical Psychology
Br J Med Psychol — British Journal of Medical Psychology
Br J Ment S — British Journal of Mental Subnormality
BRJNA — Building Research
Br J Non-Destr Test — British Journal of Non-Destructive Testing
Br J Nutr — British Journal of Nutrition
Br J Obstet Gynaecol — British Journal of Obstetrics and Gynaecology
Br J Obst G — British Journal of Obstetrics and Gynaecology
Br J Occup Saf — British Journal of Occupational Safety
Br J Ophth — British Journal of Ophthalmology
Br J Ophthalmol — British Journal of Ophthalmology
Br J Oral S — British Journal of Oral Surgery [*Later, British Journal of Oral and Maxillofacial Surgery*]
Br J Oral Surg — British Journal of Oral Surgery [*Later, British Journal of Oral and Maxillofacial Surgery*]
Br J Orthod — British Journal of Orthodontics
Br J Pharm — British Journal of Pharmacology
Br J Pharmac — British Journal of Pharmacology
Br J Pharmac Chemother — British Journal of Pharmacology and Chemotherapy [*Later, British Journal of Pharmacology*]
Br J Pharmacol — British Journal of Pharmacology
Br J Pharmacol Chemother — British Journal of Pharmacology and Chemotherapy [*Later, British Journal of Pharmacology*]
Br J Philos Sci — British Journal for the Philosophy of Science
Br J Phil S — British Journal for the Philosophy of Science
Br J Photogr — British Journal of Photography
Br J Photogr Ann — British Journal of Photography. Annual
Br J Phys Ed — British Journal of Physical Education
Br J Physiol Opt — British Journal of Physiological Optics
Br J Phys Med — British Journal of Physical Medicine
Br J Phys O — British Journal of Physiological Optics
Br J Plast Surg — British Journal of Plastic Surgery
Br J Pl Sur — British Journal of Plastic Surgery
Br J Poli S — British Journal of Political Science
Br J Polit Sci — British Journal of Political Science
Br J Prev S — British Journal of Preventive and Social Medicine
Br J Prev Soc Med — British Journal of Preventive and Social Medicine
Br J Psychi — British Journal of Psychiatry
Br J Psychiatry — British Journal of Psychiatry
Br J Psychiatry Spec Publ — British Journal of Psychiatry. Special Publication
Br J Psycho — British Journal of Psychology
Br J Psychol — British Journal of Psychology
Br J Radiol — British Journal of Radiology
Br J Radiol Suppl — British Journal of Radiology. Supplement
Br J Soc Cl — British Journal of Social and Clinical Psychology
Br J Soc Clin Psychol — British Journal of Social and Clinical Psychology
Br J Sociol — British Journal of Sociology
Br J Soc Med — British Journal of Social Medicine
Br J Soc Ps — British Journal of Social Psychiatry
Br J Soc W — British Journal of Social Work
Br J Soc Wk — British Journal of Social Work
Br J Sports Med — British Journal of Sports Medicine
Br J Surg — British Journal of Surgery
Br J Tuberc — British Journal of Tuberculosis
Br J Tuberc Dis Chest — British Journal of Tuberculosis and Diseases of the Chest
Br J Urol — British Journal of Urology
Br J Ven Dis — British Journal of Venereal Diseases
Br J Vener Dis — British Journal of Venereal Diseases
BRKIA — British Kinematography
Br Kinematogr — British Kinematography
Br Kinematogr — British Kinematography, Sound, and Television
Br Kinematogr Sound and Telev — British Kinematography, Sound, and Television
Br Knitting Ind — British Knitting Industry
BRL — Bulletin. John Rylands Library. University of Manchester
BRLGA — Brain and Language
Br Libr News — British Library News
Br LR — Brooklyn Law Review
BRLTD — Bulletin. Research Laboratory for Nuclear Reactors. Tokyo Institute of Technology
BRM — Bulletin. Council for Research in Music Education
BRMA Rev — BRMA [*British Rubber Manufacturers' Association Ltd.*] Review
BRMEA — Bruxelles Medical

BRMEAY — Bruxelles Medical
Br Med B — British Medical Bulletin
Br Med Bull — British Medical Bulletin
Br Med J — British Medical Journal
BRMIA — Behavior Research Methods and Instrumentation
BRMIC — Ramarkrishna Mission Institute of Culture [*Calcutta*]. Bulletin
Br Min — British Mining
BRMMLA — Bulletin. Rocky Mountain Modern Language Association
BRMRA5 — Brasil-Medico
Br Mus (Nat Hist) Bull — British Museum (Natural History). Bulletin. Geology
Br Mus (Nat Hist) Bull Geol — British Museum (Natural History). Bulletin. Geology
Br Mus (Nat Hist) Bull Zool — British Museum (Natural History). Bulletin. Zoology
Br Mus (Nat Hist) Econ Ser — British Museum (Natural History). Economic Series
Br Mus (Nat Hist) Fossil Mammals Afr — British Museum (Natural History). Fossil Mammals of Africa
Br Mus (Nat Hist) Mineral Leafl — British Museum (Natural History). Mineralogy Leaflet
Br Mus (Nat Hist) Palaeontol Leafl — British Museum (Natural History). Palaeontology Leaflet
Br Mus (Nat Hist) Publ — British Museum (Natural History). Publication
Br Mus (Nat Hist) Rep — British Museum (Natural History). Report
Br Mycol Soc Trans — British Mycological Society. Transactions
Br Nat Bibliography — British National Bibliography
BRNNRC — Building Research News. National Research Council of Canada
Br Non Ferrous Met Res Assoc Ann Rep — British Non-Ferrous Metals Research Association. Annual Report
Brno Univ Prirod Fak Scr Geol — Brno. Universita. Prirodovedecka Fakulta. Scripta Geologia
BRNSBE — Brenesia
BRNWA — Brennstoff- und Waermewirtschaft
Broad — Broadside Series
Broadcast — Broadcasting Magazine
Broadcast Equip Today — Broadcast Equipment Today
Broadcasting Bus — Broadcasting Business
Broadcast Technol — Broadcast Technology
Broadw — Broadway
Broad Way Clin Suppl — Broad Way Clinical Supplement [*England*]
BROB — Berichten. Rijksdienst voor het Oudheidkundig Bodemonderzoek
BROBA — Brookings Bulletin
Brock Univ Dep Geol Sci Res Rep Ser — Brock University. Department of Geological Sciences. Research Report Series
Brolga R — Brolga Review
Bromatol Chem Toksykol — Bromatologia i Chemia Toksykologiczna
Bromley Local Hist — Bromley Local History
Bromma Hembygds-Foren Arsskr — Bromma Hembygds-Forenings Arsskrift
BRONA — Bronches
BRONA3 — Bronches
Brook Bul — Brookings Bulletin
Brookhaven Natl Lab Lect Sci Vistas Res — Brookhaven National Laboratory. Lectures in Science. Vistas in Research
Brookhaven Symp Biol — Brookhaven Symposia in Biology
Brookings Bull — Brookings Bulletin
Brookings P — Brookings Papers on Economic Activity
Brookings Pa Econ Activ — Brookings Papers on Economic Activity
Brookings Pas Econ Activity — Brookings Papers on Economic Activity
Brookings R — Brookings Review
Brook J Int L — Brooklyn Journal of International Law
Brookl J Int L — Brooklyn Journal of International Law
Brookl L Rev — Brooklyn Law Review
Brookl Mus Bull — Brooklyn Museum. Bulletin
Brookl Mus J — Brooklyn Museum. Journal
Brookl Mus Quart — Brooklyn Museum. Quarterly
Brook LR — Brooklyn Law Review
Brooklyn Bar — Brooklyn Barrister
Brooklyn Bot Gard Annu Rep — Brooklyn Botanic Garden. Annual Report
Brooklyn Bot Gard Mem — Brooklyn Botanic Garden. Memoirs
Brooklyn Bot Gard Rec — Brooklyn Botanic Garden. Record
Brooklyn Bot Gard Rec Plants Gard — Brooklyn Botanic Garden. Record. Plants and Gardens
Brooklyn Hosp J — Brooklyn Hospital. Journal
Brooklyn J Int L — Brooklyn Journal of International Law
Brooklyn J Intl L — Brooklyn Journal of International Law
Brooklyn L Rev — Brooklyn Law Review
Brooklyn Mus Ann — Brooklyn Museum. Annual
Brooklyn Mus Bul — Brooklyn Institute of Arts and Sciences. Museum Bulletin
Brook Mus Q — Brooklyn Museum. Quarterly
Brook Pap Econ Act — Brookings Papers on Economic Activity
Brook S Bio — Brookhaven Symposia in Biology
Brookville Soc N H B — Brookville Society of Natural History. Bulletin
BROPD — Bjulleteni Rukopisnogo Otdela Puskinskogo Doma
BRORAF — Broteria. Serie Trimestral. Ciencias Naturais
Br Orthopt J — British Orthoptic Journal

Brot — Broteria
BROTA — Brot und Gebaeck
BROTAL — Brot und Gebaeck
Broteria Ser Trimest Cienc Nat — Broteria. Serie Trimestral. Ciencias Naturais
Brown Am — Brown American
Brown Boveri Mitt — Brown Boveri Mitteilungen [*Brown Boveri Review*]
Brown Boveri Rev — Brown Boveri Review
Brown Bov R — Brown Boveri Review
Browning In — Browning Institute. Studies
Browning Inst Stud — Browning Institute. Studies
Brownson — Brownson's Quarterly Review
Brown Sup Dec — Brown's Supplement to Morison's Dictionary, Sessions Cases [*Scotland*]
BRP — Beitraege zur Romanischen Philologie
BRP — Bollettino. R. Universita Italiana per Stranieri di Perugia
Br Pet Equip News — British Petroleum Equipment News
BRPFD — Blech, Rohre, Profile
BRPGDO — Brooklyn Botanic Garden. Record. Plants and Gardens
BRPh — Beitraege zur Romanischen Philologie
Br Phycol Bull — British Phycological Bulletin [*Later, British Phycological Journal*]
Br Phycol J — British Phycological Journal
BRPLA — British Plastics [*Later, European Plastics News*]
Br Plast — British Plastics [*Later, European Plastics News*]
Br Plast Rubber — British Plastics and Rubber
BRPNDB — Broncho-Pneumologie
Br Polym J — British Polymer Journal
Br Portland Cem Res Assoc Pam — British Portland Cement Research Association. Pamphlets
Br Poult Sc — British Poultry Science
Br Poult Sci — British Poultry Science
Br Power Eng — British Power Engineering [*England*]
BRPRA Techn Bull — BRPRA [*British Rubber Producers' Research Association*] Technical Bulletin
BRPRD — Bulletin of Radiation Protection
Br Print — British Printer
Br Psych Soc Bull — British Psychological Society. Bulletin
BRPT — Briarpatch. Saskatchewan's Independent Monthly Newsmagazine [*Canada*]
Br Pteridol Soc Bull — British Pteridological Society. Bulletin
Br Public Opin — British Public Opinion
BRR — Barron's Financial Weekly
BRR — Brazilian Economic Studies
BRRAB — Brain Research Bulletin
Br Rayon Silk J — British Rayon and Silk Journal
BR/RB — Bilingual Review/Revista Bilingue
BRREA — Brain Research
BRREAP — Brain Research
Br Reg Geol — British Regional Geology
BRRUD — Brauerei-Rundschau
Br S Afr Co Publ Mazoe Citrus Exp Stn — British South Africa Company. Publication. Mazoe Citrus Experimental Station
BRS Bull — BRS [*Bibliographic Retrieval Services*] Bulletin
BRSCB — Building Research Station. Current Papers
Br Sci News — British Science News
BRSG — Boletin. Real Sociedad Geografica
BRSGI — Bollettino. Reale Societa Geografica Italiana
Br Small Anim Vet Assoc Congr Proc — British Small Animal Veterinary Association. Congress. Proceedings
BRSOA — British Steel Corporation. Open Report
Br Soap Manuf — British Soap Manufacturer
BRSRA — Bibliotheca Radiologica [*Switzerland*]
BRSTB — British Steel
Br Steel — British Steel
Br Steel Corp Rep — British Steel Corporation. Reports
Br Steelmaker — British Steelmaker
Br Stud Monit — British Studies Monitor
BRSUAA — British Sugar Beet Review
Br Sugar Beet Rev — British Sugar Beet Review
Br Sug Beet Rev — British Sugar Beet Review
Br Sulphur Corp Q Bull — British Sulphur Corporation. Quarterly Bulletin
BRSV — Boletin. Real Sociedad Vascongada de Amigos del Pais
Brs Z — Breslauer Zeitung
BRT — Behavior Research and Therapy
BRTAAN — Brittonia
BR Tax R — British Tax Review
Br Technol Index — British Technology Index
Br Telecom Engng — British Telecommunications Engineering
Br Telecom J — British Telecom Journal
Br Telecommun Eng — British Telecommunications Engineering
Br Territ Borneo Annu Rep Geol Sur Dep — British Territories in Borneo. Annual Report. Geological Survey Department
Br Territ Borneo Geol Surv Dep Rep — British Territories in Borneo. Geological Survey Department. Report
BRTHA — Behavior Research and Therapy

Brt Lgts — Bright Lights
Br Travel News — British Travel News
Bruel & Kjaer Tech Rev — Bruel and Kjaer Technical Review
Bruker Rep — Bruker Report
BRUND2 — Brunonia
BR UNESCO — Bulletin. Commission Nationale de la Republique Populaire Roumaine pour l'UNESCO
Brun Mus J — Brunei Museum. Journal
Brunnenbau Bau Rohrleitungsbau — Brunnenbau Bau von Wasserwerken Rohrleitungsbau
Bruns' Beitr Klin Chir — Bruns' Beitraege zur Klinischen Chirurgie
Brush & P — Brush and Pencil
Brus Museum — Brussels Museum of Musical Instruments. Bulletin
Brus Mus Roy Beaux Arts Bull — Brussels. Musees Royaux des Beaux-Arts Belgiques. Bulletin
B Russell Mem Lect Phil Sci — Bertrand Russell Memorial Lecture in Philosophy and Science
Brussels Museum M Instruments Bul — Brussels Museum of Musical Instruments. Bulletin
Brussels Mus Roy Bul — Brussels. Musees Royaux d'Art et d'Histoire. Bulletin
Brux Med — Bruxelles Medical
Br Vest — Bratskij Vestnik
Br Vet J — British Veterinary Journal
BRVRAG — Breviora
BRVWA — Business Review. University of Washington
BRW — Business Review Weekly
Br Wat Supply — British Water Supply
BRWJA — British Welding Journal
BRX — Brazil. A Monthly Publication on Trade and Industry
BRYGAW — Brygmesteren
BRYOA — Bryologist
BRYOAM — Bryologist
Bryol — Bryologist
BS — Bantu Studies
BS — Best Sellers
BS — Biblioteka Slovesnika
BS — Bibliotheca Sacra
BS — Bogoslovska Smotra
BS — Bollettino Senese
BS — Bollingen Series
BS — Botanische Studien
BS — Brixia Sacra
BS — Building Science
BS — Bukowiner Schule
BS — Bulletin Signaletique
BS — Bulletin. Sommaires des Periodiques Francais et Etrangers
BS — Byzantino-Slavica
BS 101 — Bulletin Signaletique 101. Sciences de l'Information. Documentation
BSa — Bibliotheca Sacra
BSA — British School at Athens. Annual
BSAA — Boletin. Seminario de Estudios de Arte y Arqueologia
BSAA — Bulletin Signaletique. Art et Archeologie
BSAA — Bulletin. Societe Archeologique d'Alexandrie
BSAAV — Boletin. Seminario de Estudios de Arte y Arqueologia. Universidad de Valladolid
BSAB — Bulletin. Societe d'Anthropologie (Brussels)
BSAB — Bulletin. Societe Archeologique de Bordeaux
BSAB — Bulletin. Societe Archeologique Bulgare
BSAC — Bulletin. Societe d'Archeologie Copte
BSACorreze — Bulletin. Societe Archeologique de la Correze
BSAE — British School of Archaeology in Egypt. Publications
BSAF — Bulletin. Societe Nationale des Antiquaires de France
BSAFrance — Bulletin. Societe Nationale des Antiquaires de France
BSAHDL — Bulletin. Societe d'Art et d'Histoire du Diocese de Liege
BSAHL — Bulletin. Societe Archeologique et Historique du Limousin
BSAHLimousin — Bulletin. Societe Archeologique et Historique du Limousin
BSAHNantes — Bulletin. Societe Archeologique et Historique de Nantes et de Loire-Atlantique
BSAIO — Boletin. Sociedad Argentina de Investigacion Operativa
BSAL — Bolleti. Societat Arqueologica Lubliana
BSAL — Bulletin. Societe d'Anthropologie (Lyon)
BSAL — Bulletin. Societe Archeologique du Limousin
BSAM — Bulletin. Societe des Amis de Montaigne
BSAM — Bulletin. Societe Archeologique du Midi de la France
BSAM — Bulletin Trimestriel. Societe Academique des Antiquaires de la Morinie
BSAMA — Bulletin. Schweizerische Akademie der Medizinischen Wissenschaften
BSAMA5 — Bulletin. Academie Suisse des Sciences Medicales
BSAMorinie — Bulletin Trimestriel. Societe Academique des Antiquaires de la Morinie
BSAN — Bulletin. Societe des Antiquaires de Normandie
BSANormandie — Bulletin. Societe des Antiquaires de Normandie
BSAO — Bulletin. Societe des Antiquaires de l'Ouest et des Musees de Poitiers
BSAOuest — Bulletin. Societe des Antiquaires de l'Ouest et des Musees de Poitiers

BSAP — Bibliographical Society of America. Papers
BSAP — Bulletin. Societe des Amis de Marcel Proust et de Combray
BSAP — Bulletin Trimestriel. Societe des Antiquaires de Picardie
BSAPicardie — Bulletin Trimestriel. Societe des Antiquaires de Picardie
BSAPR — Bulletin. Societe des Amis de Port-Royal
BSARPR — Buletin Stiintific. Academia Republicii Populare Romine
BSAS — Bulletin. Societe Archeologique de Sens
BSASD — Bulletin. Societe d'Archeologique et de Statistique de la Drome
BSAT — Bulletin. Societe Archeologique de Touraine
BSA Touraine — Bulletin Trimestriel. Societe Archeologique de Touraine
BSAV — Boletin. Seminario de Estudios de Arte y Arqueologia. Universidad de Valladolid
BSAW — Berichte. Saechsische Akademie der Wissenschaften
BSAW — Berichte. Verhandlungen der Saechsischen Akademie der Wissenschaften
BSBB — Bulletin. Societe des Bibliophiles Belges Seant a Mons
BSBBM — Bulletin. Societe des Bibliophiles Belges Seant a Mons
BSBF — Bulletin. Societe des Bibliolatres de France
BSBFA — Bulletin. Societe Botanique de France
BSBG — Berichte. Schweizerische Botanische Gesellschaft
BSBGA — Berichte. Schweizerische Botanische Gesellschaft
BSBGD — Bulletin. Societe Belge de Geologie
BSBIA — Brookhaven Symposia in Biology
BSBIAW — Brookhaven Symposia in Biology
BSBI Conf Rep — BSBI [*Botanical Society of the British Isles*] Conference Reports
BSBL — Bulletin. Societe des Bibliophiles Liegeois
BS Bl — Bundessteuerblatt
B S Bot Fr I — Bulletin. Societe Botanique de France. Premiere Partie
BSBPA — Bulletin. Societe Belge de Geologie, de Paleontologie, et d'Hydrologie [*Later, Bulletin. Societe Belge de Geologie*]
BSBPP — Bulletin. Societe Bibliographique des Publications Populaires
BSBQA — Bulletin. Societes Chimiques Belges
BSBR — Bollettino Sistematico di Bibliografia Romana
BSBS — Bollettino Storico-Bibliografico Subalpino
BSB Subalpino — Bollettino Storico-Bibliografico Subalpino
BSC — Bibliotheque de Sociologie Contemporaine
BSC — Bollettino Storico Catanese
BSC — Bollettino Storico Cremonese
BSC — Bulletin. Societe Chateaubriand
B Sc Ak Med — Bulletin. Schweizerische Akademie der Medizinischen Wissenschaften
BSCAM — Bulletin des Seances. Cercle Archeologique de Mons
BSCat — Bollettino Storico Catanese
BSCC — Boletin. Sociedad Castellonense de Cultura
BSCFA — Bulletin. Societe Chimique de France
B S Ch Fr I — Bulletin. Societe Chimique de France. Premiere Partie
B S Ch Fr II — Bulletin. Societe Chimique de France. Deuxieme Partie
B S Chim Be — Bulletin. Societes Chimiques Belges
B Sch Or Afr Stud — Bulletin. School of Oriental and African Studies
B Sch Orien — Bulletin. School of Oriental and African Studies. University of London
B Sch Orient Afr Stud — Bulletin. School of Oriental and African Studies
BSci — Behavioral Science
BSCIA — Bulletin. Societe de Chimie Biologique
B Sci Math — Bulletin des Sciences Mathematiques
BSCJ — Ball State Commerce Journal
BSCJA — Bristol Chamber of Commerce. Journal
BSCL — Business Service Checklist
BSCLA — Bulletin Annuel. Societe Suisse de Chronometrie et Laboratoire Suisse de Recherches Horlogeres
BSCNA — Bulletin. Societe de Chimie Industrielle
B Sc Nat — Bulletin des Sciences Naturelles et de Geologie
BSCP Commun — BSCP [*Biological Sciences Communication Project*] Communique
BSCSD2 — British Society for Cell Biology. Symposium
BSC Stat — British Sulphur Corporation Ltd. Statistical Supplement
BSDSL — Basler Studien zur Deutschen Sprache und Literatur
BSE — Brno Studies in English
BSE — Recherches Economiques de Louvain
BSEA — Boletin. Seminario de Estudios de Arte y Arqueologia
BSEAA — Boletin. Seminario de Estudios de Arte y Arqueologia
B Seances Acad Roy Sci O-Mer — Bulletin des Seances. Academie Royale des Sciences d'Outre-Mer
BSE Bourbonn — Bulletin. Societe d'Emulation du Bourbonnais
BSEBourbonnais — Bulletin. Societe d'Emulation du Bourbonnais
B Sect Geogr Soc Sav — Bulletin. Section de Geographie. Actes du 96e Congres National des Societes Savantes
BSED — Bulletin. Societe d'Etudes Dantesques. Centre Universitaire Mediterraneen
BSEDEIS — Bulletin SEDEIS [*Societe d'Etudes et de Documentation Economiques, Industrielles, et Sociales*]
BSEE — Boletin. Societe Espanola de Excursiones
BSEF — Boletim. Sociedade de Estudios Filologicos
BSEIC — Bulletin. Societe des Etudes Indochinoises
B Seis S Am — Bulletin. Seismological Society of America

BSELB — Berita Selulosa
BSELot — Bulletin. Societe des Etudes Litteraires, Scientifiques, et Artistiques du Lot
BSEM — Boletin. Sociedade do Estudos de Mocambique Byzantinoslavica
BSEND — Building Services and Environmental Engineer
BSEO — Bulletin. Societe d'Etudes Oceaniennes
BSEPC — Bulletin. Societe d'Etudes de la Province de Cambrai
BSEPT — Bulletin Scientifique. Ecole Politechnique de Timisoara
BSEQA — Business Systems and Equipment
BSER — Bulletin. Societe Ernest Renan
B Serv Carte Geol — Bulletin. Service de la Carte Geologique de la France
B Serv Carte Geol Alg — Bulletin. Service de la Carte Geologique de l'Algerie
B Serv Carte Phytogeogr — Bulletin. Service de la Carte Phytogeographique
B Serv Soc Caisses Assur Malad — Bulletin. Service Social des Caisses d'Assurance Maladie
B Serv Tunis Statist — Bulletin. Service Tunisien des Statistiques
BSESD — Bulletin. School of Engineering and Architecture of Sakarya
BSES News — British Schools Exploring Society. News
BSFA Bull — BSFA [*British Steel Founders' Association*] Bulletin
BSFCA — Bollettino Scientifico. Facolta di Chimica Industriale di Bologna
BSFE — Bulletin. Societe Francaise d'Egyptologie [*Paris*]
BSFEA — Bulletin. Societe Francaise des Electriciens
BSFEM — Bulletin. Societe Francaise d'Etudes Mariales
BSFF — Bollettino. Societa Filologica Friulana
BSFIA — Bulletin. Sport Fishing Institute
BSFN — Bulletin. Societe Francaise de Numismatique
B S Fr Cer — Bulletin. Societe Francaise de Ceramique
B S Fr D Sy — Bulletin. Societe Francaise de Dermatologie et de Syphiligraphie
B S Fr Min — Bulletin. Societe Francaise de Mineralogie et de Cristallographie
BSGAE — Boletin. Sociedad General de Autores de Espana
BSGAO — Bulletin. Societe de Geographie et d'Archeologie d'Oran
BSGF — Bulletin. Societe Geologique de France
BSGIA — Bollettino. Societa Geografica Italiana
BSGW — Berichte. Verhandlungen der Saechsischen Gesellschaft der Wissenschaften [*Berlin*]
BSHAF — Bulletin. Societe de l'Histoire de l'Art Francais
BSHAP — Provincia. Bulletin de la Societe d'Histoire et d'Archeologie de Marseille et de la Provence
BSHAPerigord — Bulletin. Societe Historique et Archeologique du Perigord
BSHEW — Bulletin. Societe pour l'Histoire des Eglises Wallonnes
BSHM — Bulletin. Societe d'Histoire de la Medecine
BSHM — Bulletin. Societe d'Histoire Moderne
BSHNAN — Bulletin. Societe d'Histoire Naturelle de l'Afrique du Nord
BSHPF — Bulletin. Societe de l'Histoire du Protestantisme Francais
BSHPIF — Bulletin. Societe Historique de Paris et de l'Ile de France
BSHS — Bulletin. Societe d'Histoire et de Geographie de la Region de Setif
BSHSL — Bulletin Signaletique. Histoire et Science de la Litterature
BSHST — Bulletin Signaletique. Histoire des Sciences et des Techniques
BSHY — Bulletin. Societe des Sciences Historiques de l'Yonne
BSIAD — Bulletin. South African Institute of Assayers and Analysts
BSIBA — Bollettino. Societa Italiana di Biologia Sperimentale
BSignHum — Bulletin Signaletique. Sciences Humaines, Etc. [*Paris*]
BSII — Bollettino degli Studi Inglesi in Italia
BSINA — BSI [*British Standards Institution*] News
BSI News — BSI [*British Standards Institution*] News
BSIPA — Buletinul Stiintific. Institutului Politehnic [*Cluj*]
BSI Sales Bull — BSI [*British Standards Institution*] Sales Bulletin
BSJ — Baker Street Journal
BSKG — Beitraege zur Saechsischen Kirchengeschichte
BSL — Bollettino Storico Livornese
BSL — Bulletin. Societe de Linguistique de Paris
BSL — Bulletin. Societe Scientifique et Litteraire du Limbourg
BSL — Byzantino-Slavica
BSLELEP — Bulletin. Societe Lorraine des Etudes Locales dans l'Enseignement Public
BSLLW — Bulletin. Societe de Langue et Litterature Wallonnes
BSLP — Bulletin. Societe de Linguistique de Paris
BSM — Beitraege zur Schweizerdeutschen Mundartforschungen
BSM — Bollettino Storico Mantovano
BSM — Bollettino di Studi Mediterranei
BSM — British Studies Monitor
BSM — Bulletin Statistique Mensuel [*Beirut*]
B S Math Fr — Bulletin. Societe Mathematique de France
BSMHA — Bulletins et Memoires. Societe Medicale des Hopitaux de Paris
BSMHB — Biophysics of Structure and Mechanism
BSNA — Bulletin. Societe Nationale des Antiquaires de France
BSNAF — Bulletin. Societe Nationale des Antiquaires de France
BSNG — Bulletin. Societe Neuchateloise de Geographie
BSNotes — Browning Society. Notes
BSNR — Buletinul. Societatii Numismatice Romane
BSNRB — Binnenschiffahrts-Nachrichten
BSNS — Bollettino della Sezione di Novara della R. Deputazione Subalpina di Storia Patria
Bsns Abroad — Business Abroad
Bsns Automation — Business Automation

Bsns Ed Forum — Business Education Forum
Bsns Ed World — Business Education World
Bsns Hist R — Business History Review
Bsns Lit — Business Literature
Bsns Mgt — Business Management
Bsns Mgt (London) — Business Management (London)
Bsns & Tech Sources — Business and Technology Sources
Bsns W — Business Week
Bsns W — Business World
BSO — Monthly Bulletin of Statistics
BSOA — Bulletin. School of Oriental and African Studies
BSOAS — Bulletin. School of Oriental and African Studies
B Soc Anthropol Paris — Bulletins et Memoires. Societe d'Anthropologie de Paris
B Soc Archeol Hist Limousin — Bulletin. Societe Archeologique et Historique du Limousin
B Soc Arch Eure-Et-Loir — Bulletin. Societes Archeologiques d'Eure-Et-Loir
B Soc Arch HCH — Bulletin. Societe Archeologique et Historique des Hauts Cantons de l'Herault
B Soc Bulg — Bulletin. Societe Archeologique Bulgare
B Soc Ethnogr Limousin Marche — Bulletin. Societe d'Ethnographie du Limousin et de la Marche
B Soc Et Indochinoises — Bulletin. Societe des Etudes Indochinoises
B Soc Et Ocean — Bulletin. Societe d'Etudes Oceaniennes
B Soc Et Sci Aude — Bulletin. Societe d'Etudes Scientifiques de l'Aude
B Soc Franc Sociol — Bulletin. Societe Francaise de Sociologie
BSocFrEg — Bulletin. Societe Francaise d'Egyptologie [*Paris*]
B Soc Linguist Paris — Bulletin. Societe de Linguistique de Paris
B Soc Linn — Bulletin. Societe Linneenne
B Soc Litt Hist Brie — Bulletin. Societe Litteraire et Historique de la Brie
B Soc Neuch Geogr — Bulletin. Societe Neuchatelloise de Geographie
B Soc Prehist Franc C R Mens — Bulletin. Societe Prehistorique Francaise. Comptes Rendus Mensuels
B Soc Roy Belge Anthropol — Bulletin. Societe Royale Belge d'Anthropologie
B Soc Suisse American — Bulletin. Societe Suisse des Americanistes
B Soc Thanatologie — Bulletin. Societe de Thanatologie
BSONA — Byulleten' Stantsii Opticheskogo Nablyudeniya Iskusstvennykh Sputnikov Zemli
BSOS — Bulletin. School of Oriental and African Studies
BSOS — Bulletin. School of Oriental Studies
BSP — Bibliographical Society of America. Papers
BSP — Bibliographical Society [*London*]. Publications
BSP — Bollettino Storico Piacentino
BSP — Bollettino Storico Pistoiese
BSP — British Space Fiction Magazine
BSPA — Bollettino. Societa Piemontese di Archeologia
BSPABA — Bollettino. Societa Piemontese di Archeologia e Belle Arti
BSPBA — Bulletin. Societe de Pharmacie de Bordeaux
BSPEA — Bulletin. Societe de Pathologie Exotique et de Ses Filiales
BSPF — Bulletin. Societe Prehistorique Francaise
B S Ph — Bulletin. Societe Francaise de Philosophie
BSPi — Bollettino Storico Pistoiese
BSPIA — Bollettino. Societa Paleontologica Italiana
BSPiac — Bollettino di Storia Piacentina
BSPis — Bollettino Storico Pisano
BSPL — Bulletin. Societe Polonaise de Linguistique
BSPN — Bollettino Storico per la Provincia de Novara
BSPS — Bollettino. Societa Pavese di Storia Patria
BSPSP — Bollettino. Societa Pavese di Storia Patria
BSPTA — Buletinul Stiintific si Tehnic. Institutului Politehnic (Timisoara)
BSPTR — Beaufort Sea Project. Technical Report
BSPU — Bollettino. Regia Deputazione di Storia Patria per l'Umbria
BSQ — Business Quarterly [*Canada*]
BSR — British School of Archaeology at Rome. Papers
BSRAA — Bulletin. Societe Royale d'Archeologie d'Alexandrie
BSRBB — Bulletin. Societe Royale de Botanique de Belgique
BSRGE — Bulletin. Societe Royale de Geographie d'Egypte
BSRIA — Southern Research Institute. Bulletin [*United States*]
BSRMA — Bulletin. Institut National de la Sante et de la Recherche Medicale
BSRV-L — Bulletin. Societe Royale de Vieux-Liege
BSS — Birger Sjoberg Sallskapet
BSS — Buletin per Shkencat Shoqerore
BSS — Bulletin of Spanish Studies
BSS — Bulletin de Statistique Suisse
BSSAD — Business SA [*South Africa*]
BSSAT — Bollettino di Studi Storici ed Archeologici di Tivoli e Regione
BS Sci Ed — Bulletin Signaletique. Sciences de l'Education
BS Sci L — Bulletin Signaletique. Sciences du Langage
B S Sci Med — Bulletin. Societe des Sciences Medicales du Grand-Duche de Luxembourg
BS Sci R — Bulletin Signaletique. Sciences Religieuses
BSSGC — Buletinul. Societatii de Stiinte Geologice din Republica Socialista Romania
BSSHNY — Bulletin. Societe des Sciences Historiques et Naturelles de l'Yonne
BSSI — Bollettino Storico della Svizzera Italiana

BSSIA — Byulleten' Sovet po Seismologii
BSSL — Bibliographien zum Studium der Deutschen Sprache und Literatur
BSSL — Bulletin. Societe des Sciences et des Lettres de Lodz
BSSLL — Bulletin. Societe Scientifique et Litteraire du Limbourg
BSSNB — National Bureau of Standards. Building Science Series
BS Soc Ethn — Bulletin Signaletique. Sociologie - Ethnologie
BSSP — Bollettino Senese di Storia Patria
BSSS — Bulletin Mensuel. Societe des Sciences de Semur
BSSY — Bulletin. Societe des Sciences Historiques de l'Yonne
BSSYA — Biochemical Society. Symposia
BSt — Biblische Studien [*Neukirchen*]
BST — Bronte Society. Transactions
B Statist (Bruxelles) — Bulletin de Statistique (Bruxelles)
BSTCA — Bulletin. Standard Oil Company of California
BSTCF — Ball State Teachers College Forum [*Later, BSUF*]
BSTEA — British Steelmaker
BSTEC — Bulletin. Societe Toulousaine d'Etudes Classiques
BSt(F) — Biblische Studien (Freiburg)
BSTGA — Bulletin. South Texas Geological Society
BSTIS — Biweekly Scientific and Technical Intelligence Summary
BSTJ — Bell System Technical Journal
BSTJA — Bell System Technical Journal
BStM — Bollettino. Associazione Internazionale degli Studi Mediterranei
BStud Lat — Bollettino do Studi Latini
B Stupefiants — Bulletin des Stupefiants
BSU — Transport Echo. The Benelux Transport Magazine
BSUCA — Buletinul Stiintific al Universitatii Craiova
BSUF — Ball State University Forum
BSUSSR — Bulletin. Institute for the Study of the USSR
BSVAH — Bulletin. Societe Veric toise d'Archeologie et d'Histoire
BSVasc — Boletin. Real Sociedad Vascongada de Amigos del Pais
BSVPB — Bulletin. Slovenskej Pol'nohospodarskej Akademie. Vyskumneho Ustavu Potravinarskeho
BSVSAQ — Kongelige Danske Videnskabernes Selskab. Biologiske Skrifter
BSW — Bank of New South Wales. Review
BSYSA — Bulletin Scientifique. Conseil des Academies des Sciences et des Arts de la RSF de Yougoslavie. Section A. Sciences Naturelles, Techniques, et Medicales
B S Zool Fr — Bulletin. Societe Zoologique de France
BT — Bible Today
BT — Bible Translator
BT — Bibliotheque de Theologie
BT — Big Table
BT — Bio/Technology
BT — Black Times. Voices of the National Community
BTAED — BMWI Tagesnachrichten
BTA J — Business Teachers Association of New York State. Journal
BTAM — Bulletin de Theologie Ancienne et Medievale
BTAPB — Bitumen, Teere, Asphalte, Peche, und Verwandte Stoffe
BTAS — Bulletin. Texas Archaeological Society
BTB — Biblical Theology Bulletin
BTBCA — Bulletin. Torrey Botanical Club
BTBib — Bulletin de Theologie Biblique [*Rome*]
BTBVA — Bulletin Technique. Bureau Veritas [*France*]
BTCAB — Boletim Tecnico. Centro de Tecnologia Agricola e Alimentar (Brazil)
BTCCDT — Centro Nacional de Investigaciones de Cafe. Boletin Tecnico [*Chinchina*]
BTD — Bank of Thailand. Monthly Bulletin
BTD — Bulletin. Commission Royale de Toponymie et de Dialectologie
BTE — Belfast Telegraph
BTEKA — Byulleten' Tekhniko-Ekonomicheskoi Informatsii
BTERD — Biological Trace Element Research
BTF — Betriebswirtschaftliche Forschung und Praxis
BTFCA — Bulletin Technique. Societe Francaise des Constructions Babcock et Wilcox
BTFFA — Bulletin Technique des Mines de Fer de France
BTFIA — Bollettino Tecnico FINSIDER [*Societa Finanziaria Siderurgica*]
BTH — Bibliotheque de Theologie Historique
BTh — Bulletin de Theologie Ancienne et Medievale
BTHDA — Birth Defects. Original Article Series
BTHDAK — March of Dimes Birth Defects Foundation. Birth Defects Original Article Series
BThom — Bulletin Thomiste
BTI — British Technology Index
BTI — Buddhist Text Information
BTIAL — Bulletin Trimestriel. Institut Archeologique du Luxembourg
BTIALux — Bulletin Trimestriel. Institut Archeologique du Luxembourg
B Tibetol — Bulletin of Tibetology
BTIDA — Byulleten' Tsentra po Yadernym Dannym
BTITA — Bulletin. Tokyo Institute of Technology
BTJ — British Business
BTLV — Bijdragen tot de Taal-Land- en Volkenkunde
BTLVNI — Bijdragen tot de Taal-Land- en Volkenkunde van Nederlandsche-Indie
BTMDA — Bulletin. Tokyo Medical and Dental University

BTMG — Blaetter der Thomas Mann Gesellschaft
BTMNA — Bitamin
BTMSD — Bio Times
BTN — British Travel News
BTNKA — Biotechniek [*The Netherlands*]
BTNQA — Botanique
BTONA — Beton, Herstellung, Verwendung
B Tor Bot C — Bulletin. Torrey Botanical Club
BTP — Bibliotheque des Textes Philosophiques
BTPGA — Beitraege zur Pathologie
BTQSA — Bulletin Technique de la Suisse Romande
BTR — British Tax Review
BTR — Business Trends. A Concise and Systematic Weekly Report to Management on the Argentine Economy
B Trim Banque France — Bulletin Trimestriel. Banque de France
B Trim Ecole Nat Sante Publ — Bulletin Trimestriel. Ecole Nationale de la Sante Publique
BTROA — Biotropica
BTS — Business Times. An Economic and Business Review
BTSAAM — Bulletin Trimestriel. Societe Academique des Antiquaires de la Morinie
BTSAP — Bulletin Trimestriel. Societe des Antiquaires de Picardie
BTSCB — Bulletin Technique de Securite et Salubrite. Institut National des Industries Extractives
BTSEAA — El Salvador. Direccion General de Investigaciones Agronomicas. Seccion de Entomologia. Boletin Tecnico
BTTA — Journal. British Thoracic and Tuberculosis Association
BTTA Rev — BTTA [*British Thoracic and Tuberculosis Association*] Review [*Scotland*]
BTTCA9 — Comision Interamericana del Atun Tropical. Boletin
BTTCA9 — Inter-American Tropical Tuna Commission. Bulletin
BTUPA — Bulletin. Union des Physiciens
BTVVA — Bulletin Technique Vevey
BTZBA — Beton i Zhelezobeton
BU — Blues Unlimited
BUAMD — Business America
BuB — Buch und Bibliothek
BuB — Buecherei und Bildung
BUBBA — Bundesbaublatt
BUBEA — Bulletin Belgicatom
BUBFA — Bulletin Biologique de la France et de la Belgique
BUCAB — Bulletin du Cancer
BUCDA — Bulletin. Georgia Academy of Science
Buchar- Univ- An Geol — Bucharest. Universitatea. Analele. Geologie
Buchar Univ An Ser Stiint Nat — Bucharest. Universitatea. Analele. Seria Stiintele Naturii
Buch und Bibl — Buch und Bibliothek
Buchr Atomkernenerg — Buchreihe Atomkernenergie
BuCHS — Bucks County Historical Society. Papers
Bucknell Re — Bucknell Review
BucksCoHS — Bucks County Historical Society. Papers
Budapesti Musz Egy Elemiszerkem Tansz Kozl — Budapesti Muszaki Egyetem Elemiszerkemiai Tanszekenek Kozlemenyei
Budapesti Musz Egy Mezogazd Kem Technol Tansz Evk — Budapesti Muszaki Egyetem Mezogazdasagi Kemiai Technologiai Tanszekenek Evkonyve
Budapesti Musz Egy Mezogazd Kem Technol Tansz Kozl — Budapesti Muszaki Egyetem Mezogazdasagi Kemiai Technologiai Tanszekenek Kozlemenyei
Budapest Reg — Budapest Regisegei
Budavox Telecommun Rev — Budavox Telecommunication Review
Budget Program Newsl — Budget and Program Newsletter
Budiv Mater Konstr — Budivel'ni Materialy i Konstruktsii
Budownictwo Roln — Budownictwo Rolnicze
BUE — Bulletin. Faculty of Arts. University of Egypt [*Cairo*]
BUECD — Bulletin d'Ecologie
Buech Augenarzt — Buecherei des Augenarztes
Buecher Arch Bienenk — Buecher des Archiv fuer Bienenkunde
Buecherei Bienenk — Buecherei fuer Bienenkunde
Buecher Wirt — Buecher fuer die Wirtschaft
Buenos Aires Mus — Buenos Aires Musical
Buenos Aires (Prov) Com Invest Cient Monogr — Buenos Aires (Province). Comision de Investigaciones Cientificas. Monografias
Buerotech Autom & Organ — Buerotechnik Automation und Organisation
Buerotech und Org — Buerotechnik und Organisation
BUESD — Buerger im Staat
Buffalo Gal Notes — Buffalo Fine Arts Academy. Albright Art Gallery. Notes
Buffalo Hist Soc Publ — Buffalo Historical Society. Publications
Buffalo L Rev — Buffalo Law Review
Buffalo Phil — Buffalo Philharmonic. Program Notes
Buffalo Soc Nat Sci Bull — Buffalo Society of Natural Sciences. Bulletin
Buffalo Soc N Sc B — Buffalo Society of Natural Sciences. Bulletin
BUFFB — Boletim. Universidade Federal do Parana. Fisica Teorica (Brazil)
Buff Law R — Buffalo Law Review
Buff LR — Buffalo Law Review
Buff L Rev — Buffalo Law Review
BUFSA — Bulletin. Association Francaise pour l'Etude du Sol

BUG — Boletin. Universidad de Granada
BUGGA — Bulletin. Geological Survey of Great Britain
BUGMAF — Geological Society of America. Bulletin
BUGTA — Bulletin of Grain Technology [India]
BUI — Nederland USSR Instituut. Maandberichten
BUIAA — Bulletin d'Informations Scientifiques et Techniques. Commissariat a l'Energie Atomique [France]
BUIDD — Building Ideas
Build — Builder
Build — Building
Build & Archit — Building and Architecture
Build Briefs Div Build Res CSIRO — Building Briefs. Division of Building Research. Commonwealth Scientific and Industrial Research Organisation
Build & Cons — Building and Construction
Build & Cons (VIC) — Building and Construction and Cazaly's Contract Reporter (Melbourne, Victoria)
Build Decorating Mat — Building and Decorating Materials
Build & Decorating Materials — Building and Decorating Materials
Build Des Constr — Building Design and Construction
Build Econ — Building Economist
Build Energy Prog — Building Energy Progress
Build & Eng — Building and Engineering
Build Environ — Building and Environment [England]
Builder (NSW) — Builder (New South Wales)
Builders Timber Merchants J — Builders and Timber Merchants Journal
Build Forum — Building Forum
Build (Hobart) — Building (Hobart)
Build Ideas — Building Ideas
Build Inf Bull — Building Information Bulletin [New Zealand]
Building & Arch — Building and Architecture
Building Ltg Engng — Building, Lighting, and Engineering
Building Ltg and Engng — Building, Lighting, and Engineering
Building Sci Ser Nat Bur Stand US — Building Science Series. United States National Bureau of Standards
Build Int (Engl Ed) — Build International (English Edition)
Build Light Eng — Building, Lighting, and Engineering
Build Ltg Engng — Building, Lighting, and Engineering
Build & Manuf — Building and Manufacturing
Build Mater — Building Materials [Sydney]
Build Mater — Building Materials and Equipment
Build Mater & Equip — Building Materials and Equipment
Build Mater Equip (Syd) — Building Materials and Equipment (Sydney)
Build Materials — Building Materials
Build Mater Mag — Building Materials Magazine [Australia]
Build NSW — Builder NSW [New South Wales]
Build Off Code Adm — Building Official and Code Administrator [United States]
Build Oper Manage — Building Operating Management
Build Perm — Building-Permit Activity [Florida]
Build Prod News — Building Products News
Build Res — Building Research
Build Res Establ Dig — Building Research Establishment. Digest
Build Res Estab (Sta) Digest — Building Research Establishment (Station). Digest
Build Res Pract — Building Research and Practice
Build Res Stn Curr Pap — Building Research Station. Current Papers [England]
Build Sci — Building Science
Build Serv — Building Services
Build Serv Eng — Building Services Engineer
Build Serv Eng Res — Building Services Engineering Research and Technology
Build Serv Eng Res and Technol — Building Services Engineering Research and Technology
Build Serv Environ Eng — Building Services and Environmental Engineer [England]
Build Stand — Building Standards [United States]
Build Steel — Building with Steel
Build Syst Des — Building Systems Design
Build Technol Manage — Building Technology and Management [England]
Build Worker — Building Worker
Built Env — Built Environment
Built Envir — Built Environment
BUIMB — Bollettino. Unione Matematica Italiana. Series IV
BUIND — Business India
BUJ — Boston University. Journal
BUJ — Business Japan
BUJPA — Bulletin. Japan Petroleum Institute
Bujq Soc — Bujqesia Socialiste
BUKEA — Busseiron Kenkyu
BUKKA — Bunko Kenkyu
BUL — B + U. Bouw en Uitvoering van Gemeentewerken; Maandblad voor Functionarissen van de Diensten van Publieke en Openbare Werken
BUL — Boston University. Law Review
Bul — [The] Bulletin
Bul Admin Penitentiaire — Bulletin. Administration Penitentiaire

Bul Afr Noire — Bulletin de l'Afrique Noire
Bul Akad Stiince RSS Moldoven — Buletinul Akademiei. Stiince a RSS Moldovenest
Bul Am Acad Psy and L — Bulletin. American Academy of Psychiatry and the Law
Bul/AMQ — Bulletin. Association Mathematique du Quebec
Bul Am Repub — Bulletin. International Bureau of the American Republics
Bul Analytique Docum — Bulletin Analytique de Documentation Politique, Economique, et Sociale Contemporaine
Bul Arch Maroc — Bulletin d'Archeologie Marocaine
Bul Atomic Sci — Bulletin of the Atomic Scientists
Bul Aust Asian Assn of Vic — Bulletin. Australian-Asian Association of Victoria
Bul Aust Assn Occupational Therapists — Bulletin. Australian Association of Occupational Therapists
Bul Aust Ind — Bulletin for Australian Industry
Bul Aust Industry — Bulletin for Australian Industry
Bul Aust Soc Stud Lab Hist — Bulletin. Australian Society for the Study of Labour History
Bul B — Bulletin of Bibliography
Bul Belg — Bulletin. Banque Nationale de Belgique
Bul Bibl — Bulletin Bibliographique
Bul Bibl de France — Bulletin des Bibliotheques de France
Bul Bibliog — Bulletin of Bibliography
Bul of Bibliography — Bulletin of Bibliography and Dramatic Index
Bul Black Theatre — Bulletin of Black Theatre
Bul Bus Research Ohio State Univ — Bulletin of Business Research. Ohio State University
Bul Cercet Piscic — Buletinul de Cercetari Piscicole
Bul Chambre Com Francaise — Bulletin. Chambre de Commerce Francaise et Organe Officiel du Tourisme Francaise en Australie
Bul Child Bks — Bulletin. Center for Children's Books
Bul Chr Inst Islamic St — Bulletin. Christian Institutes of Islamic Studies
Bul Corresp Hellenique — Bulletin de Correspondance Hellenique
BULDB — Building
Bul Doc Bibliog — Bulletin de Documentation Bibliographique
Bul Docum — Bulletin de Documentation
Bul Docum Econ — Bulletin de Documentation Economique
Bul Econ et Fin — Bulletin Economique et Financier
Bul Econ Research (England) — Bulletin of Economic Research (England)
Bul Econ et Soc Maroc — Bulletin Economique et Social du Maroc
Buletin Univ Shtet Tiranes Shkencat Nat — Buletin. Universiteti Shteteror te Tiranes. Shkencat Natyrore
Bul Fac Stiinte Cernauti — Buletinul Facultatii de Stiinte din Cernauti
Bul Fiz — Buletin Fizik
Bulg Acad Sci Commun Dep Chem — Bulgarian Academy of Sciences. Communications. Department of Chemistry
Bulg Akad Nauk Dokl — Bulgarska Akademiya na Naukite. Doklady
Bulg Akad Nauk Geol Inst Izv Ser Inzh Geol Khidrogeol — Bulgarska Akademiya na Naukite. Geologicheski Institut. Izvestiya. Seriya Inzhenerna Geologiya i Khidrogeologiya
Bulg Akad Nauk Geol Inst Izv Ser Paleontol — Bulgarska Akademiya na Naukite. Geologicheski Institut. Izvestiya. Seriya Paleontologiya
Bulg Akad Nauk Zool Inst Muz Izv — Bulgarska Akademiya na Naukite. Otdeleniye za Biologichni Nauki. Zoologicheski Institut si Muzey. Izvestiya
Bulgar J Phys — Bulgarian Journal of Physics
Bulgar Math Monographs — Bulgarian Mathematical Monographs
Bulgar Muz — Bulgarska Muzika
Bulg F — Bulgarian Films
Bulg Geofiz Spis — Bulgarsko Geofizichno Spisanie [Bulgaria]
Bulg Geol Druzh Spis — Bulgarsko Geologichesko Druzhestvo. Spisanie
Bulg Hist — Bulgarian Historical Review/Revue Bulgare d'Histoire
Bulg J Phys — Bulgarian Journal of Physics
Bulg Tiutiun — Bulgarski Tiutiun
BULIB — Bulletin on Inventions
BULID — Business Librarian
Bul Indonesian Econ Studies — Bulletin of Indonesian Economic Studies
Bul Ind Psychol — Bulletin for Industrial Psychology and Personnel Practice
Bul Inf Lab Cent Color — Buletin Information. Laboratorul Central Coloristic
Bul Info — Bulletin d'Information. Departement d'Economie et de Sociologie Rurales [Paris]
Bul Info Region Parisienne — Bulletin d'Information de la Region Parisienne
Bul Inst Agron Cluj-Napoca — Buletinul. Institutului Agronomic Cluj-Napoca
Bul Inst Agron Cluj Napoca Inst Agron Dr Petru Groza — Buletinul. Institutului Agronomic Cluj-Napoca. Institutul Agronomic "Dr. Petru Groza"
Bul Inst Agron Cluj Napoca Ser Agric — Buletinul. Institutului Agronomic Cluj-Napoca. Seria Agricultura
Bul Inst Cercet Proiect Piscic — Buletinul. Institutului de Cercetari si Proiectari Piscicole
Bul Inst Pet Gaze Geol — Buletinul. Institutului de Petrol, Gaze, si Geologie [Romania]
Bul Inst Polit Brasov Ser B Econ For — Buletinul. Institutului Politehnic din Brasov. Seria B. Economie Forestiera

Bul Inst Politeh Brasov A — Buletinul. Institutului Politehnic din Brasov. Seria A. Mecanica

Bul Inst Politeh Bucur — Buletinul. Institutului Politehnic Bucuresti

Bul Inst Politeh Bucuresti — Buletinul. Institutului Politehnic Bucuresti

Bul Inst Politeh Bucuresti Ser Chim Metal — Buletinul. Institutului Politehnic "Gheorghe Gheorghiu-Dej" Bucuresti. Seria Chimie-Metalurgie

Bul Inst Politeh Bucuresti Ser Mec — Buletinul. Institutului Politehnic "Gheorghe Gheorghiu-Dej" Bucuresti. Seria Mecanica

Bul Inst Politeh (Chim-Metal) — Buletinul. Institutului Politehnic "Gheorghe Gheorghiu-Dej" Bucuresti. Seria Chimie-Metalurgie

Bul Inst Politeh "Gheorghe Gheorghiu Dej" Bucur — Buletinul. Institutului Politehnic "Gheorghe Gheorghiu-Dej" Bucuresti

Bul Inst Politeh "Gheorghe Gheorghiu Dej" Bucuresti — Buletinul. Institutului Politehnic "Gheorghe Gheorghiu-Dej" Bucuresti

Bul Inst Politeh Gheorghe Gheorghiu-Dej Bucuresti Ser Chim — Buletinul. Institutului Politehnic "Gheorghe Gheorghiu-Dej" Bucuresti. Seria Chimie

Bul Inst Politeh Gheorghe Gheorghiu-Dej Bucuresti Ser Mec — Buletinul. Institutului Politehnic "Gheorghe Gheorghiu-Dej" Bucuresti. Seria Mecanica

Bul Inst Politeh Gheorghe Gheorghiu Dej Chim-Metal — Buletinul. Institutului Politehnic "Gheorghe Gheorghiu-Dej." Seria Chimie-Metalurgie [Romania]

Bul Inst Politeh Gheorghe Gheorghiu Dej Electroteh — Buletinul. Institutului Politehnic "Gheorghe Gheorghiu-Dej." Seria Electrotehnica [Romania]

Bul Inst Politeh Gheorghe Gheorghiu Dej Mec — Buletinul. Institutului Politehnic "Gheorghe Gheorghiu-Dej." Seria Mecanica [Romania]

Bul Inst Politeh Iasi — Buletinul. Institutului Politehnic din Iasi

Bul Inst Politeh Iasi I — Buletinul. Institutului Politehnic din Iasi. Sectia I. Matematica, Mecanica Teoretica, Fizica

Bul Inst Politeh Iasi III — Buletinul. Institutului Politehnic din Iasi. Sectia III. Electrotehnica, Electronica Automatizari

Bul Inst Politeh Iasi Sect I — Buletinul. Institutului Politehnic din Iasi. Sectia I. Matematica, Mecanica Teoretica, Fizica

Bul Inst Politeh Iasi Sect II — Buletinul. Institutului Politehnic din Iasi. Sectia II. Chimie

Bul Inst Politeh Iasi Sect III — Buletinul. Institutului Politehnic din Iasi. Sectia III. Electrotehnica, Electronica Automatizari

Bul Inst Politeh Iasi Sect IV — Buletinul. Institutului Politehnic din Iasi. Sectia IV. Mecanica Tehnica

Bul Inst Politeh (Mec) — Buletinul. Institutului Politehnic "Gheorghe Gheorghiu-Dej" Bucuresti. Seria Mecanica

Bul Inst Politehn Bucuresti — Buletinul. Institutului Politehnic Bucuresti

Bul Inst Politehn Bucuresti Ser Chim-Metal — Buletinul. Institutului Politehnic "Gheorghe Gheorghiu-Dej." Bucuresti. Seria Chimie-Metalurgie [Bucharest]

Bul Inst Politehn Bucuresti Ser Electrotehn — Buletinul. Institutului Politehnic "Gheorghe Gheorghiu-Dej." Bucuresti. Seria Electrotehnica

Bul Inst Politehn Bucuresti Ser Mec — Institutului Politehnic Gheorghe Gheorghiu Dej Bucuresti. Buletinul. Seria Mecanica [Bucharest]

Bul Inst Politehn Iasi — Buletinul. Institutului Politehnic din Iasi. Seria Noua

Bul Inst Politehn Iasi NS — Buletinul. Institutului Politehnic din Iasi. Seria Noua

Bul Inst Politehn Iasi Sect I — Institutului Politehnic din Iasi. Buletinul. Sectia I [Iasi]

Bul Inst Stud si Project Energ — Buletinul. Institutului de Studii si Projectari Energetice

Bul Inst Stud & Proj Energ — Buletinul. Institutului de Studii si Projectari Energetice

Bul Internat Fiscal Docum — Bulletin for International Fiscal Documentation

Bul Internat Fiscal Documentation — Bulletin for International Fiscal Documentation

Bul Int Fiscal Doc — Bulletin for International Fiscal Documentation

Bul Kebun Raya Bot Gard Indones — Buletin Kebun Raya. Botanical Gardens of Indonesia

Bulk Solids Handl — Bulk Solids Handling

Bulk Syst Int — Bulk Systems International

Bull A Ariz Univ Ext Serv — Bulletin A. University of Arizona. Extension Service

Bull Acad Chir Dent (Paris) — Bulletin. Academie de Chirurgie Dentaire (Paris)

Bull Acad Ebroic — Bulletin. Academie Ebroicienne

Bull Acad Imp Sc St Petersb — Bulletin. Academie Imperiale des Sciences de St. Petersbourg

Bull Acad M — Bulletin. American Academy of Medicine

Bull Acad Malgache — Bulletin. Academie Malgache

Bull Acad Med (Paris) — Bulletin. Academie de Medecine (Paris)

Bull Acad Med Roum — Bulletin. Academie de Medecine de Roumanie

Bull Acad Med Toledo — Bulletin. Academy of Medicine of Toledo and Lucas County [Ohio]

Bull Acad Med Toronto — Bulletin. Academy of Medicine of Toronto

Bull Acad Natl Med — Bulletin. Academie Nationale de Medecine [Paris]

Bull Acad Natl Med (Paris) — Bulletin. Academie Nationale de Medecine (Paris)

Bull Acad Polon Sci Ser Sci Biol — Bulletin. Academie Polonaise des Sciences. Serie des Sciences Biologiques

Bull Acad Polon Sci Ser Sci Math Astronom Phys — Bulletin. Academie Polonaise des Sciences. Serie des Sciences Mathematiques, Astronomiques, et Physiques

Bull Acad Polon Sci Ser Sci Phys Astronom — Academie Polonaise des Sciences. Bulletin. Serie des Sciences Physiques et Astronomiques [Warsaw]

Bull Acad Polon Sci Ser Sci Tech — Bulletin. Academie Polonaise des Sciences. Serie des Sciences Techniques

Bull Acad Pol Sci — Bulletin. Academie Polonaise des Sciences

Bull Acad Pol Sci Biol — Bulletin. Academie Polonaise des Sciences. Serie des Sciences Biologiques

Bull Acad Pol Sci Ser Sci Biol — Bulletin. Academie Polonaise des Sciences. Serie des Sciences Biologiques

Bull Acad Pol Sci Ser Sci Chim — Bulletin. Academie Polonaise des Sciences. Serie des Sciences Chimiques

Bull Acad Pol Sci Ser Sci Math Astron et Phys — Bulletin. Academie Polonaise des Sciences. Serie des Sciences Mathematiques, Astronomiques, et Physiques

Bull Acad Pol Sci Ser Sci Math Astron Phys — Bulletin. Academie Polonaise des Sciences. Serie des Sciences Mathematiques, Astronomiques, et Physiques

Bull Acad Pol Sci Ser Sci Phys et Astron — Bulletin. Academie Polonaise des Sciences. Serie des Sciences Physiques et Astronomiques

Bull Acad Pol Sci Ser Sci Tech — Bulletin. Academie Polonaise des Sciences. Serie des Sciences Techniques

Bull Acad Pol Sci Ser Sci Terre — Bulletin. Academie Polonaise des Sciences. Serie des Sciences de la Terre

Bull Acad R Belg Cl Sci — Bulletin. Academie Royale de Belgique. Classe des Sciences

Bull Acad R Med Belg — Bulletin. Academie Royale de Medecine de Belgique

Bull Acad Roy Med Belgique — Bulletin. Academie Royale de Medecine de Belgique

Bull Acad Sci Agric For — Bulletin. Academie des Sciences Agricoles et Forestieres

Bull Acad Sci Ga SSR — Bulletin. Academy of Sciences of the Georgian SSR

Bull Acad Sci Math Nat Acad R Serbe A — Bulletin. Academie des Sciences Mathematiques et Naturelles. Academie Royale Serbe. Serie A. Sciences Mathematiques et Physiques

Bull Acad Sci Math Nat Acad R Serbe B — Bulletin. Academie des Sciences Mathematiques et Naturelles. Academie Royale Serbe. Serie B. Sciences Naturelles

Bull Acad Sci United Prov Agra Oudh India — Bulletin. Academy of Sciences of the United Provinces of Agra and Oudh, India

Bull Acad Sci URSS — Bulletin. Academie des Sciences de l'URSS

Bull Acad Sci USSR Div Chem Sci — Bulletin. Academy of Sciences of the USSR. Division of Chemical Science

Bull Acad Sci USSR Geol Ser — Bulletin. Academy of Sciences of the USSR. Geologic Series

Bull Acad Sci USSR Phys Sci — Bulletin. Academy of Sciences of the USSR. Physical Sciences

Bull Acad Sci USSR Phys Ser — Bulletin. Academy of Sciences of the USSR. Physical Series

Bull Acad Sci USSR Phys Ser (Columbia Tech Transl) — Bulletin. Academy of Sciences of the USSR. Physical Series (Columbia Technical Translations)

Bull Acad Serbe Sci Arts Cl Sci Math Nat — Bulletin. Academie Serbe des Sciences et des Arts. Classe des Sciences Mathematiques et Naturelles

Bull Acad Serbe Sci Arts Cl Sci Math Nat Sci Nat — Bulletin. Academie Serbe des Sciences et des Arts. Classe des Sciences Mathematiques et Naturelles. Sciences Naturelles

Bull Acad Serbe Sci Arts Cl Sci Math Natur — Bulletin. Academie Serbe des Sciences et des Arts. Classe des Sciences Mathematiques et Naturelles

Bull Acad Serbe Sci Arts Cl Sci Math Natur Sci Math — Bulletin. Academie Serbe des Sciences et des Arts. Classe des Sciences Mathematiques et Naturelles. Sciences Mathematiques

Bull Acad Serbe Sci et Arts Cl Sci Tech — Bulletin. Academie Serbe des Sciences et des Arts. Classe des Sciences Techniques

Bull Acad Serbe Sci Cl Sci Math Nat — Bulletin. Academie Serbe des Sciences. Classe des Sciences Mathematiques et Naturelles

Bull Acad Soc Lorraines Sci — Bulletin. Academie et Societe Lorraines des Sciences

Bull Acad Sui Sci Med — Bulletin. Academie Suisse des Sciences Medicales

Bull Acad Suisse Sci Med — Bulletin. Academie Suisse des Sciences Medicales

Bull Acad Vet Fr — Bulletin. Academie Veterinaire de France

Bull Acad Vet France — Bulletin. Academie Veterinaire de France

Bull ACLS — Bulletin. American Council of Learned Societies

Bull Ac Malg — Bulletin. Academie Malgache

Bull Ac Polon Sci — Bulletin. Academie Polonaise des Sciences

Bull Advis Counc Sci Ind Res (Can) — Bulletin. Advisory Council for Scientific and Industrial Research (Canada)

Bull Aeronaut Res Inst Univ Tokyo — Bulletin. Aeronautical Research Institute. University of Tokyo

Bull AFG — Bulletin. Association Francaise de Gemmologie

Bull Agence Gen Colon (Fr) — Bulletin. Agence Generale des Colonies (France)

Bull Agr CB — Bulletin Agricole du Congo Belge

Bull Agr Chem Soc Jap — Bulletin. Agricultural Chemical Society of Japan

Bull Acad Polon Sci Ser Sci Biol — Bulletin. Academie Polonaise des Sciences. Serie des Sciences Biologiques

Bull Agr Congo — Bulletin Agricole du Congo
Bull Agric Chem Insp Stn — Bulletin. Agricultural Chemicals Inspection Station
Bull Agric Chem Insp Stn (Tokyo) — Bulletin. Agricultural Chemicals Inspection Station (Tokyo)
Bull Agric Chem Soc Jpn — Bulletin. Agricultural Chemical Society of Japan
Bull Agric Cong Belg — Bulletin Agricole du Congo Belge
Bull Agric Congo Belg — Bulletin Agricole du Congo Belge
Bull Agric Dep (Assam) — Bulletin. Agricultural Department (Assam)
Bull Agric Dep (Tasm) — Bulletin. Agricultural Department (Tasmania)
Bull Agric Exp Stn (Rehovoth) — Bulletin. Agricultural Experiment Station (Rehovoth)
Bull Agric Exp Stn (Tahreer Prov) — Bulletin. Agricultural Experiment Station (Tahreer Province)
Bull Agric Hort — Bulletin de l'Agriculture et de l'Horticulture
Bull Agric Mech Coll Texas — Bulletin. Agricultural and Mechanical College of Texas
Bull Agric Res Inst Kanagawa Prefect — Bulletin. Agricultural Research Institute of Kanagawa Prefecture
Bull Agric Rwanda — Bulletin Agricole du Rwanda
Bull Agri Eng Res Stn — Bulletin. Agricultural Engineering Research Station. Nogyo Doboku Shikenjo Hokou [*Japan*]
Bull Agron Inst Rech Agron Trop Cult Vivrieres — Bulletin Agronomique. Institut de Recherches Agronomiques Tropicales et des Cultures Vivrieres
Bull Agr Res Inst (Pusa) — Bulletin. Agricultural Research Institute (Pusa)
Bull Agr Res Sta (Rehovat) — Bulletin. Agricultural Research Station (Rehovat)
Bull Aichi Agr Exp Sta — Bulletin. Aichi Agricultural Experiment Station
Bull Aichi Gakugei Univ — Bulletin. Aichi Gakugei University
Bull Aichi Inst Technol — Bulletin. Aichi Institute of Technology
Bull Aichi Univ Ed Natur Sci — Bulletin. Aichi University of Education. Natural Science [*Kariya*]
Bull AIEMA — Bulletin d'Information. Association Internationale pour l'Etude de la Mosaique Antique
Bull AI Et SE Eur — Bulletin. Association Internationale d'Etudes du Sud-Est Europeen
Bull Ala Agr Exp Sta — Bulletin. Alabama Agricultural Experiment Station. Auburn University
Bull Ala Agric Exp Sta — Bulletin. Alabama Agricultural Experiment Station. Auburn University
Bull Ala Agric Exp Stn — Bulletin. Alabama Agricultural Experiment Station. Auburn University
Bull Alameda-Contra Costa Med Assoc — Bulletin. Alameda-Contra Costa Medical Association [*California*]
Bull Alameda Cty Dent Soc — Bulletin. Alameda County Dental Society
Bull Alaska Agr Exp Sta — Bulletin. Alaska Agricultural Experiment Station
Bull Alaska Agric Exp Stn — Bulletin. Alaska Agricultural Experiment Station
Bull Alex — Bulletin. Societe Archeologique d'Alexandrie
Bull Alger Carcinol — Bulletin Algerien de Carcinologie
Bull Allegheny County Med Soc — Bulletin. Allegheny County Medical Society [*Pennsylvania*]
Bull ALLF — Bulletin. Academie Royale de Langue et de Litterature Francaises
Bull Alloy Phase Diagrams — Bulletin of Alloy Phase Diagrams
Bull Allyn Mus — Bulletin. Allyn Museum
Bull Am Acad Dermatol — Bulletin. American Academy of Dermatology
Bull Am Acad Orthopaedic Surg — Bulletin. American Academy of Orthopaedic Surgeons
Bull Am Acad Psychiatr Law — Bulletin. American Academy of Psychiatry and the Law
Bull Am Acad Psychiatry Law — Bulletin. American Academy of Psychiatry and the Law
Bull Am Acad Rel — Bulletin. American Academy of Religion
Bull Am Anthr Ass — Bulletin. American Anthropological Association
Bull Am Assoc Bot Gard Arboreta — Bulletin. American Association of Botanical Gardens and Arboreta
Bull Am Assoc Nurse Anesth — Bulletin. American Association of Nurse Anesthetists
Bull Am Assoc Pet Geol — Bulletin. American Association of Petroleum Geologists
Bull Am Assoc Variable Star Obs — Bulletin. American Association of Variable Star Observers
Bull Am Ass Petrol Geol — Bulletin. American Association of Petroleum Geologists
Bull Am Ass Publ Hlth Dent — Bulletin. American Association of Public Health Dentists
Bull Am Ass Publ Hlth Phys — Bulletin. American Association of Public Health Physicians
Bull Am Ass Univ Prof — Bulletin. American Association of University Professors
Bull Am Astron Soc — Bulletin. American Astronomical Society
Bull Am Cer Soc — Bulletin. American Ceramic Society
Bull Am Coll Surg — Bulletin. American College of Surgeons
Bull Am Dahlia Soc — Bulletin. American Dahlia Society
Bull Am Dent Ass — Bulletin. American Dental Association

Bull Amer Math Soc — Bulletin. American Mathematical Society
Bull Amer Math Soc NS — American Mathematical Society. Bulletin. New Series
Bull Amer Meteorol Soc — Bulletin. American Meteorological Society
Bull Amer Soc Bakery Eng — Bulletin. American Society of Bakery Engineers
Bull Am Foundrymen's Assoc — Bulletin. American Foundrymen's Association
Bull Am Game Protect Ass — Bulletin. American Game Protective Association
Bull Am Group IIC — Bulletin. American Group. International Institute for Conservation of Historic and Artistic Works
Bull Am Hosta Soc — Bulletin. American Hosta Society
Bull Am Inst Min Metall Eng — Bulletin. American Institute of Mining and Metallurgical Engineers
Bull Am Malacol Union Inc — Bulletin. American Malacological Union, Incorporated
Bull Am Math Soc — Bulletin. American Mathematical Society
Bull Am Meteorol Soc — Bulletin. American Meteorological Society
Bull Am Mus Nat Hist — Bulletin. American Museum of Natural History
Bull Am Orchid Soc — Bulletin. American Orchid Society
Bull Am Paleontol — Bulletins of American Paleontology
Bull Am Paleontology — Bulletins of American Paleontology
Bull Am Pharm Assoc — Bulletin. American Pharmaceutical Association
Bull Am Phys Soc — Bulletin. American Physical Society
Bull Am Prot Hosp Assoc — Bulletin. American Protestant Hospital Association
Bull Am Sch Prehist Res — Bulletin. American School of Prehistoric Research
Bull Am Soc Hosp Pharm — Bulletin. American Society of Hospital Pharmacists
Bull Am Soc Inform Sci — Bulletin. American Society for Information Science
Bull Am Soc Inf Sci — Bulletin. American Society for Information Science
Bull Am Zinc Inst — Bulletin. American Zinc Institute
Bull Anal Ent Med Vet — Bulletin Analytique d'Entomologie Medical et Veterinaire
Bull Anc Eleves Ec Fr Meun — Bulletin. Anciens Eleves de l'Ecole Francaise de Meunerie
Bull Anciens Eleves Ecole Franc Meun — Bulletin. Anciens Eleves de l'Ecole Francaise de Meunerie
Bull Anim Behav — Bulletin of Animal Behavior
Bull Anim Health Prod Afr — Bulletin of Animal Health and Production in Africa
Bull Annls Soc R Ent Belg — Bulletin et Annales. Societe Royale Entomologique de Belgique
Bull Ann Soc Entomol Belg — Bulletin et Annales. Societe Entomologique de Belgique
Bull Ann Soc R Belge Entomol — Bulletin et Annales. Societe Royale Belge d'Entomologie
Bull Ann Soc R Entomol Belg — Bulletin et Annales. Societe Royale d'Entomologie de Belgique
Bull Ann Soc Roy Entomol Belg — Bulletin et Annales. Societe Royale d'Entomologie de Belgique
Bull Ann Soc Suisse Chronom et Lab Suisse Rech Horlogeres — Bulletin Annuel. Societe Suisse de Chronometrie et Laboratoire Suisse de Recherches Horlogeres
Bull Annu Soc Suisse Chronom Lab Suisse Rech Horlog — Bulletin Annuel. Societe Suisse de Chronometrie et Laboratoire Suisse de Recherches Horlogeres
Bull Antivenin Inst Am — Bulletin. Antivenin Institute of America
Bull Aomori Agr Exp Sta — Bulletin. Aomori Agricultural Experiment Station
Bull Aomori Agric Exp Stn — Bulletin. Aomori Agricultural Experiment Station
Bull Aomori Apple Exp Stn — Bulletin. Aomori Apple Experiment Station
Bull A Phys Soc — Bulletin. American Physical Society
Bull Apic — Bulletin Apicole
Bull Apic Doc Sci Tech Inf — Bulletin Apicole de Documentation Scientifique et Technique et d'Information
Bull APM Forests — Bulletin. APM [*Australian Paper Manufacturers*] Forests Proprietary Ltd.
Bull Aquat Biol — Bulletin of Aquatic Biology
BullArch — Bulletin Archeologique. Comite des Travaux Historiques et Scientifiques [*Paris*]
Bull Arch Alg — Bulletin d'Archeologie Algerienne
Bull Arch Maroc — Bulletin d'Archeologie Marocaine
Bull ARERS — Bulletin. Association Regionale pour l'Etude et la Recherche Scientifiques
Bull Ariz Agr Exp Sta — Bulletin. Arizona Agricultural Experiment Station
Bull Ariz Agr Exp Sta Coop Ext Serv — Bulletin. Arizona Agricultural Experiment Station. Cooperating Extension Service
Bull Ariz Agric Exp Stn — Bulletin. Arizona Agricultural Experiment Station
Bull Ark Agr Exp Sta — Bulletin. Arkansas Agricultural Experiment Station
Bull Ark Agric Exp Stn — Bulletin. Arkansas Agricultural Experiment Station
Bull Arkansas Agric Exp Stn — Bulletin. Arkansas Agricultural Experiment Station
Bull Arts Sci Div Univ Ryukyus Math Natur Sci — Bulletin. Arts and Science Division. University of the Ryukyus. Mathematics and Natural Sciences

Bull Ass Anat (Paris) — Bulletin. Association des Anatomistes (Paris)
Bull Ass Can Bibliot Lang Fr — Bulletin. Association Canadienne des Bibliothecaires de Langue Francaise
Bull Ass Dipl Microbiol Nancy — Bulletin. Association des Diplomes de Microbiologie. Faculte de Pharmacie de Nancy
Bull Ass Diplomes Microbiol Fac Pharm Nancy — Bulletin. Association des Diplomes de Microbiologie. Faculte de Pharmacie de Nancy
Bull Ass Fr Etude Sol — Bulletin. Association Francaise pour l'Etude du Sol
Bull Ass Geogr Fr — Bulletin. Association des Geographes Francais
Bull Assoc Anat — Bulletin. Association des Anatomistes
Bull Assoc Anat (Nancy) — Bulletin. Association des Anatomistes (Nancy)
Bull Assoc Anc Eleves Inst Ind Ferment Bruxelles — Bulletin. Association des Anciens Eleves de l'Institut des Industries de Fermentation de Bruxelles [*Belgium*]
Bull Assoc Anc Eleves Super Ferment Gand — Bulletin. Association des Anciens Eleves de l'Institut Superieur des Fermentations de Gand
Bull Assoc Anc Etud Brass Univ Louv — Bulletin. Association des Anciens Etudiants de l'Ecole Superieure de Brasserie de l'Universite de Louvain
Bull Assoc Anc Etud Ec Super Brass Univ Louv — Bulletin. Association des Anciens Etudiants de l'Ecole Superieure de Brasserie de l'Universite de Louvain
Bull Assoc Anc Etud Ec Super Brass Univ Louvain — Bulletin. Association des Anciens Etudiants de l'Ecole Superieure de Brasserie de l'Universite de Louvain
Bull Assoc Anciens Eleves Ecole Fr Meun — Bulletin. Association des Anciens Eleves de l'Ecole Francaise de Meunerie [*France*]
Bull Assoc Chim — Bulletin. Association des Chimistes
Bull Assoc Chim Sucr Distill Fr Colon — Bulletin. Association des Chimistes de Sucrerie et de Distillerie de France et des Colonies
Bull Assoc Chim Sucr Distill Ind Agric Fr Colon — Bulletin. Association des Chimistes de Sucrerie, de Distillerie, et des Industries Agricoles de France et des Colonies
Bull Assoc Diplomes Microbiol Fac Pharm Nancy — Bulletin. Association des Diplomes de Microbiologie. Faculte de Pharmacie de Nancy
Bull Assoc Eng Geol — Bulletin. Association of Engineering Geologists
Bull Assoc Engng Geol — Bulletin. Association of Engineering Geologists
Bull Assoc Fr Etude Cancer — Bulletin. Association Francaise pour l'Etude du Cancer
Bull Assoc Fr Etude Sol — Bulletin. Association Francaise pour l'Etude du Sol
Bull Assoc Fr Etud Sol — Bulletin. Association Francaise pour l'Etude du Sol
Bull Assoc Fr Ing Chim Tech Ind Cuir Doc Inf Cent Tech Cuir — Bulletin. Association Francaise des Ingenieurs, Chimistes, et Techniciens des Industries du Cuir et Documents et Informations du Centre Technique du Cuir
Bull Assoc Fr Ing Tech Cinema — Bulletin. Association Francaise des Ingenieurs et Techniciens du Cinema
Bull Assoc Fr Tech Pet — Bulletin. Association Francaise des Techniciens du Petrole [*France*]
Bull Assoc Guillaume Bude — Bulletin. Association Guillaume Bude
Bull Assoc Kinet India — Bulletin. Association of Kineticists of India
Bull Assoc Minn Entomol — Bulletin. Association of Minnesota Entomologists
Bull Assoc R Anc Etud Brass Univ Louv — Bulletin. Association Royal des Anciens Etudiants en Brasserie de l'Universite de Louvain
Bull Assoc State Eng Soc — Bulletin. Associated State Engineering Societies
Bull Assoc Suisse Electr — Bulletin. Association Suisse des Electriciens
Bull Assoc Tech Fonderie — Bulletin. Association Technique de Fonderie
Bull Assoc Tech Mar Aeronaut — Bulletin. Association Technique Maritime et Aeronautique [*France*]
Bull Assoc Tech Marit Aeronaut — Bulletin. Association Technique Maritime et Aeronautique
Bull Assoc Trop Biol — Bulletin. Association for Tropical Biology
Bull Ass Oper Millers — Bulletin. Association of Operative Millers
Bull Ass Philomath Alsace et Lorraine — Bulletin. Association Philomathique d'Alsace et de Lorraine
Bull Ass Suisse Elec — Bulletin. Association Suisse des Electriciens
Bull Astron — Bulletin Astronomique [*France*]
Bull Astron Inst Czech — Bulletin. Astronomical Institutes of Czechoslovakia
Bull Astron Inst Neth — Bulletin. Astronomical Institutes of the Netherlands
Bull Astron Inst Neth Suppl Ser — Bulletin. Astronomical Institutes of the Netherlands. Supplement Series
Bull Astronom Inst of Czechoslovakia — Bulletin. Astronomical Institutes of Czechoslovakia
Bull Astronom Soc India — Bulletin. Astronomical Society of India
Bull At Energy Res Inst Korea — Bulletin. Atomic Energy Research Institute of Korea
Bull Atmos Radioactiv — Bulletin of Atmospheric Radioactivity [*Japan*]
Bull Atom Sci — Bulletin of the Atomic Scientists
Bull Atom Scient — Bulletin of the Atomic Scientists
Bull At Sci — Bulletin of the Atomic Scientists
Bull Auckl Inst Mus — Bulletin. Auckland Institute and Museum
Bull Audiophonol — Bulletin d'Audiophonologie
Bull Aust Math Soc — Bulletin. Australian Mathematical Society
Bull Aust Miner Dev Lab — Bulletin. Australian Mineral Development Laboratories
Bull Australas Inst Min Metall — Bulletin. Australasian Institute of Mining and Metallurgy

Bull Austral Math Soc — Bulletin. Australian Mathematical Society
Bull Aust Road Res Bd — Bulletin. Australian Road Research Board
Bull Aust Soc Explor Geophys — Bulletin. Australian Society of Exploration Geophysicists
Bull Aust Soc Stud Lab Hist — Bulletin. Australian Society for the Study of Labour History
Bull Aust Weld Res Assoc — Bulletin. Australian Welding Research Association
Bull Ayer Clin Lab PA Hosp — Bulletin. Ayer Clinical Laboratory of the Pennsylvania Hospital
Bull Azabu Vet Coll — Bulletin. Azabu Veterinary College
Bull Balai Penelitian Perkebunan Medan — Bulletin Balai Penelitian Perkebunan Medan
Bull Basic Sci Res — Bulletin of Basic Science Research
Bull Basrah Nat Hist Mus — Bulletin. Basrah Natural History Museum
Bull Belgicatom — Bulletin Belgicatom
Bull Belg Phys Soc — Bulletin. Belgian Physical Society
Bull Bell Mus Pathobiol — Bulletin. Bell Museum of Pathobiology
Bull Bernice P Bishop Mus — Bulletin. Bernice P. Bishop Museum
Bull Bibl — Bulletin of Bibliography
Bull Bibl de France — Bulletin des Bibliotheques de France
Bull Bibl France — Bulletin des Bibliotheques de France
Bull Bibliog — Bulletin of Bibliography
Bull Biblioth Fr — Bulletin des Bibliotheques de France
Bull Biblphique Pedol ORSTOM — Bulletin Bibliographique de Pedologie. Office de la Recherche Scientifique et Technique d'Outre-Mer
Bull Bime — Bulletin Bimestriel
Bull Bimest INACOL — Bulletin Bimestriel. INACOL [*Institut National pour l'Amelioration des Conserves de Legumes*]
Bull Bingham Oceanogr Collect Yale Univ — Bulletin. Bingham Oceanographic Collection. Yale University
Bull Biogeogr Soc Jpn — Bulletin. Biogeographical Society of Japan
Bull Biol France et Belgique — Bulletin Biologique de la France et de la Belgique
Bull Biol Fr Belg — Bulletin Biologique de la France et de la Belgique
Bull Biol Pharm — Bulletin des Biologistes Pharmaciens
Bull Biol Res Cent (Baghdad) — Bulletin. Biological Research Centre (Baghdad)
Bull Biol Res Cent Publ (Baghdad) — Bulletin. Biological Research Centre. Publication (Baghdad)
Bull Biol Soc Wash — Bulletin. Biological Society of Washington
Bull Bismuth Inst — Bulletin. Bismuth Institute
Bull Board Celtic Stud — Bulletin. Board of Celtic Studies
Bull B Okla Agric Exp Stn — Bulletin B. Oklahoma Agricultural Experiment Station
Bull Boris Kidric Inst Nucl Sci — Bulletin. Boris Kidric Institute of Nuclear Sciences
Bull Boris Kidric Inst Nucl Sci Biol — Bulletin. Boris Kidric Institute of Nuclear Sciences. Biology
Bull Boris Kidric Inst Nucl Sci Ceram Metall — Bulletin. Boris Kidric Institute of Nuclear Sciences. Ceramics and Metallurgy
Bull Boris Kidric Inst Nucl Sci Chem — Bulletin. Boris Kidric Institute of Nuclear Sciences. Chemistry
Bull Boris Kidric Inst Nucl Sci Electron — Bulletin. Boris Kidric Institute of Nuclear Sciences. Electronics
Bull Boris Kidric Inst Nucl Sci Nucl Eng — Bulletin. Boris Kidric Institute of Nuclear Sciences. Nuclear Engineering
Bull Boris Kidric Inst Nucl Sci Phys — Bulletin. Boris Kidric Institute of Nuclear Sciences. Physics
Bull Boris Kidric Inst Nucl Sci Suppl — Bulletin. Boris Kidric Institute of Nuclear Sciences. Supplement
Bull Bot Gard Buitenzorg — Bulletin. Botanic Gardens of Buitenzorg
Bull Bot Soc Bengal — Bulletin. Botanical Society of Bengal
Bull Bot Soc Coll Sci (Nagpur) — Bulletin. Botanical Society. College of Science (Nagpur)
Bull Bot Soc Gov Sci Coll (Jabalpur (MP) India) — Bulletin. Botanical Society. Government Science College (Jabalpur (MP) India)
Bull Bot Soc Univ Saugar — Bulletin. Botanical Society. University of Saugar
Bull Bot Surv India — Bulletin. Botanical Survey of India
Bull B Psych Soc — Bulletin. British Psychological Society
Bull Br Beekprs Ass Res Comm — Bulletin. British Bee-Keepers Association. Research Committee
Bull Br Cast Iron Res Assoc — Bulletin. British Cast Iron Research Association
Bull Brew Sci — Bulletin of Brewing Science
Bull Br Interplanet Soc — Bulletin. British Interplanetary Society
Bull Brit Mus Natur Hist — Bulletin. British Museum (Natural History)
Bull Brit Mus Natur Hist Geol — Bulletin. British Museum (Natural History). Geology
Bull Br Mus (Nat Hist) Bot — Bulletin. British Museum (Natural History). Botany
Bull Br Mus (Nat Hist) Entomol — Bulletin. British Museum (Natural History). Entomology
Bull Br Mus (Nat Hist) Entomol Suppl — Bulletin. British Museum (Natural History). Entomology. Supplement
Bull Br Mus (Nat Hist) Geol — Bulletin. British Museum (Natural History). Geology

Bull Br Mus (Nat Hist) Geol Suppl — Bulletin. British Museum (Natural History). Geology. Supplement

Bull Br Mus (Nat Hist) Hist Ser — Bulletin. British Museum (Natural History). Historical Series

Bull Br Mus Nat Hist Mineral — Bulletin. British Museum (Natural History). Mineralogy

Bull Br Mus (Nat Hist) Zool — Bulletin. British Museum (Natural History). Zoology

Bull Br Mus (Nat Hist) Zool Suppl — Bulletin. British Museum (Natural History). Zoology. Supplement

Bull Br Mycol Soc — Bulletin. British Mycological Society

Bull Brooklyn Entomol Soc — Bulletin. Brooklyn Entomological Society

Bull Brooklyn Ent Soc — Bulletin. Brooklyn Entomological Society

Bull Br Ornithol Club — Bulletin. British Ornithologists' Club

Bull Br Soc Rheol — Bulletin. British Society of Rheology

Bull Buffalo Gen Hosp — Bulletin. Buffalo General Hospital

Bull Buffalo Soc Nat Sci — Bulletin. Buffalo Society of Natural Sciences

Bull Bur Agric Intell Plant Des — Bulletin. Bureau of Agricultural Intelligence and Plant Diseases

Bull Bur Bio Technol — Bulletin. Bureau of Bio Technology

Bull Bur Chem US Dep Agric — Bulletin. Bureau of Chemistry. United States Department of Agriculture

Bull Bureau Animal Indust US Dept Agric — Bulletin. Bureau of Animal Industry. United States Department of Agriculture

Bull Bur Ent US Dep Agric — Bulletin. Bureau of Entomology. United States Department of Agriculture

Bull Bur Geol Topogr (NJ) — Bulletin. Bureau of Geology and Topography (New Jersey)

Bull Bur Miner Resour Geol Geophys — Australia. Bureau of Mineral Resources. Geology and Geophysics. Bulletin

Bull Bur Miner Resour Geol Geophys Aust — Australia. Bureau of Mineral Resources. Geology and Geophysics. Bulletin

Bull Bur Miner Resour Geol Geophys (Aust) — Bulletin. Bureau of Mineral Resources. Geology and Geophysics (Australia)

Bull Bur Rech Geol Minieres — Bulletin. Bureau de Recherches Geologiques et Minieres [France]

Bull Bur Rech Geol Minieres Deuxieme Ser Sect 2 — Bulletin. Bureau de Recherches Geologiques et Minieres. Deuxieme Serie. Section 2. Geologie des Gites Mineraux

Bull Bur Rech Geol Minieres Deuxieme Ser Sect 3 — Bulletin. Bureau de Recherches Geologiques et Minieres. Deuxieme Serie. Section 3. Hydrogeologie - Geologie de l'Ingenieur

Bull Bur Rech Geol Minieres (Fr) Sect 1 — Bulletin. Bureau de Recherches Geologiques et Minieres (France). Section 1. Geologie de la France

Bull Bur Rech Geol Minieres (Fr) Sect 2 — Bulletin. Bureau de Recherches Geologiques et Minieres (France). Section 2. Geologie Appliquee

Bull Bur Rech Geol Minieres (Fr) Sect 3 — Bulletin. Bureau de Recherches Geologiques et Minieres (France). Section 3. Hydrogeologie - Geologie de l'Ingenieur

Bull Bur Rech Geol Minieres (Fr) Sect 4 — Bulletin. Bureau de Recherches Geologiques et Minieres (France). Section 4. Geologie Generale

Bull Bur Rech Geol Minieres Sec 2 Geol Appl — Bulletin. Bureau de Recherches Geologiques et Minieres. Section 2. Geologie Appliquee

Bull Bur Rech Geol Minieres Ser 2 Sect 2 — Bulletin. Bureau de Recherches Geologiques et Minieres. Serie 2. Section 2 (France)

Bull Bur Rech Geol Min Sect 3 (Fr) — Bulletin. Bureau de Recherches Geologiques et Minieres. Section 3. Hydrogeologie - Geologie de l'Ingenieur (France)

Bull Bus Archs Coun Aust — Business Archives Council of Australia. Bulletin

Bull Bussey Inst — Bulletin. Bussey Institution

Bull B Wyo Agric Exp Stn — Bulletin B. Wyoming Agricultural Experiment Station

Bull Calcutta Math Soc — Bulletin. Calcutta Mathematical Society

Bull Calcutta Sch Trop Med — Bulletin. Calcutta School of Tropical Medicine

Bull Calif Agr Exp Sta — Bulletin. California Agricultural Experiment Station

Bull Calif Agric Exp Stn — Bulletin. California Agricultural Experiment Station

Bull Calif Dep Agric — Bulletin. California Department of Agriculture

Bull Calif Dept Agr — Bulletin. California Department of Agriculture

Bull Calif Insect Surv — Bulletin of the California Insect Survey

Bull Canada Dept Agric — Bulletin. Dominion of Canada. Department of Agriculture

Bull Cancer — Bulletin du Cancer [Paris]

Bull Cancer Inst Okayama Univ Med Sch — Bulletin. Cancer Institute. Okayama University Medical School

Bull Cancer (Paris) — Bulletin du Cancer (Paris)

Bull Can Pet Geol — Bulletin of Canadian Petroleum Geology

Bull Can Petrol Geol — Bulletin of Canadian Petroleum Geology

Bull Can Welfare L — Bulletin of Canadian Welfare Law

Bull Can Wheat Board — Bulletin. Canadian Wheat Board

Bull Caoutch Inst Fr Outre Mer — Bulletin. Caoutchoucs de l'Institut Francais d'Outre-Mer

Bull Carnegie Mus Nat Hist — Bulletin. Carnegie Museum of Natural History

Bull Carte Veg Provence Alpes Sud — Bulletin de la Carte et de la Vegetation de la Provence et des Alpes du Sud

Bull CCB — Bulletin. Center for Children's Books

Bull Cent Compilation Donnees Neutroniques — Bulletin. Centre de Compilation de Donnees Neutroniques [France]

Bull Cent Etud Rech Sci (Biarritz) — Bulletin. Centre d'Etudes et de Recherches Scientifiques (Biarritz)

Bull Cent Food Technol Res Inst (Mysore) — Bulletin. Central Food Technological Research Institute (Mysore)

Bull Cent Insp Inst Weights Meas (Tokyo) — Bulletin. Central Inspection Institute of Weights and Measures (Tokyo)

Bull Cent Int Engrais Chim — Bulletin. Centre International des Engrais Chimiques

Bull Cent Leather Res Inst (Madras) — Bulletin. Central Leather Research Institute (Madras)

Bull Cent Mar Fish Res Inst — Bulletin. Central Marine Fisheries Research Institute

Bull Cent Phys Nucl Univ Lib Bruxelles — Bulletin. Centre de Physique Nucleaire. Universite Libre de Bruxelles

Bull Cent Phys Nucl Univ Libre Bruxelles — Bulletin. Centre de Physique Nucleaire. Universite Libre de Bruxelles

Bull Central Res Lab OIT — Bulletin. Central Research Laboratory. Osaka Institute of Technology

Bull Cent Rech Essais Chatou — Bulletin. Centre de Recherches et d'Essais de Chatou [France]

Bull Cent Rech Explor ELF Aquitaine — Bulletin. Centres de Recherches Exploration-Production ELF [Essences et Lubrifiants de France] - Aquitaine

Bull Cent Rech Pau — Bulletin. Centre de Recherches de Pau

Bull Cent Res Inst Univ Kerala (India) Ser C Nat Sci — Bulletin. Central Research Institute. University of Kerala (India). Series C. Natural Science

Bull Cent Res Inst Univ Kerala (Trivandrum) Ser C — Bulletin. Central Research Institute. University of Kerala (Trivandrum). Series C. Natural Science

Bull Centres Rech Explor-Prod ELF-Aquitaine — Bulletin. Centres de Recherches Exploration-Production ELF [Essences et Lubrifiants de France] - Aquitaine

Bull Cent Text Controle Rech Sci — Bulletin. Centre Textile de Controle et de Recherche Scientifique

BullCER — Bulletin. Cercle Ernest Renan [Paris]

Bull Cerc Arch Hesbaye-Condroz — Bulletin. Cercle Archeologique Hesbaye-Condroz

Bull Cercle Benelux Hist Pharm — Bulletin. Cercle Benelux d'Histoire de la Pharmacie

Bull Cercle Etud Met — Bulletin. Cercle d'Etudes des Metaux

Bull Cercle Etud Metaux — Bulletin. Cercle d'Etudes des Metaux

Bull des Cereales Plant Fecule — Bulletin des Cereales et des Plantes a Fecule

Bull CETA — Bulletin. Centres d'Etudes Techniques Agricoles

Bull Chem Res Inst Non-Aqueous Solutions Tohoku Univ — Bulletin. Chemical Research Institute of Non-Aqueous Solutions. Tohoku University [Japan]

Bull Chem Soc Japan — Bulletin. Chemical Society of Japan

Bull Chem Technol Macedonia — Bulletin. Chemists and Technologists of Macedonia

Bull Chest Dis Res Inst Kyoto Univ — Bulletin. Chest Disease Research Institute. Kyoto University

Bull Chiba-ken Agr Exp Sta — Bulletin. Chiba-ken Agricultural Experiment Station

Bull Chiba Prefect Agri Exp Stn — Bulletin. Chiba Prefecture Agricultural Experiment Station [Japan]

Bull Chic Acad Sci — Bulletin. Chicago Academy of Sciences

Bull Chic Herpetol Soc — Bulletin. Chicago Herpetological Society

Bull Chichibu Mus Nat Hist — Bulletin. Chichibu Museum of Natural History

Bull Chin Assoc Adv Sci — Bulletin. Chinese Association for the Advancement of Science

Bull Chin Bot Soc — Bulletin. Chinese Botanical Society

Bull Chubu Inst Technol — Bulletin. Chubu Institute of Technology

Bull Chugoku Agr Exp Sta — Bulletin. Chugoku National Agricultural Experiment Station

Bull Chugoku Agr Exp Sta Ser A Ser D Ser E — Bulletin. Chugoku Agricultural Experiment Station. Series A, D, and E

Bull Chugoku Natl Agric Exp Stn Ser A — Bulletin. Chugoku National Agricultural Experiment Station. Series A (Crop Division)

Bull Chugoku Natl Agric Exp Stn Ser A (Crop Div) — Bulletin. Chugoku National Agricultural Experiment Station. Series A (Crop Division)

Bull Chugoku Natl Agric Exp Stn Ser B — Bulletin. Chugoku National Agricultural Experiment Station. Series B (Livestock Division)

Bull Chugoku Natl Agric Exp Stn Ser B (Livest Div) — Bulletin. Chugoku National Agricultural Experiment Station. Series B (Livestock Division)

Bull Chugoku Natl Agric Exp Stn Ser E — Bulletin. Chugoku National Agricultural Experiment Station. Series E (Environment Division)

Bull Chugoku Natl Agric Exp Stn Ser E (Environ Div) — Bulletin. Chugoku National Agricultural Experiment Station. Series E (Environment Division)

Bull Chukyo Women's Coll — Bulletin. Chukyo Women's College

Bull Chukyo Women's Univ — Bulletin. Chukyo Women's University

Bull CIMAB — Bulletin. Centre d'Information du Material et des Articles de Bureau

Bull Cinci Dent Soc — Bulletin. Cincinnati Dental Society

Bull Classe Sci Acad Roy Belg — Bulletin. Classe des Sciences. Academie Royale de Belgique

Bull Clemson Agr Exp Sta — Bulletin. Clemson Agricultural Experiment Station

Bull Cleve Med Libr Assoc — Bulletin. Cleveland Medical Library Association

Bull Cl Sci Acad R Belg — Bulletin. Classe des Sciences. Academie Royale de Belgique

Bull Cl Sci Acad R Belg 5e Ser — Bulletin. Classe des Sciences. Academie Royale de Belgique. 5e Serie

Bull Cl Sci Acad Royale Belg — Bulletin. Classe des Sciences. Academie Royale de Belgique

Bull Cocon Res Inst (Ceylon) — Bulletin. Coconut Research Institute (Ceylon)

Bull Coll Agr Forest Univ Nanking — Bulletin. College of Agriculture and Forestry. University of Nanking

Bull Coll Agric Res Cent Wash State Univ — Bulletin. College of Agriculture. Research Center. Washington State University

Bull Coll Agric Res Cent Wash St Univ — Bulletin. College of Agriculture. Research Center. Washington State University

Bull Coll Agric Sci (Mosonmagyarovar Hung) — Bulletin. College of Agricultural Sciences (Mosonmagyarovar, Hungary)

Bull Coll Agric Univ Teheran — Bulletin. College of Agriculture. University of Teheran

Bull Coll Agric Utsunomiya Univ — Bulletin. College of Agriculture. Utsunomiya University

Bull Coll Agric Vet Med Nihon Univ — Bulletin. College of Agriculture and Veterinary Medicine. Nihon University

Bull Coll Agr Utsunomiya Univ — Bulletin. College of Agriculture. Utsunomiya University

Bull College Sci (Baghdad) — Bulletin. College of Science (Baghdad)

Bull College Sci Univ Ryukyus — University of the Ryukyus. College of Science. Bulletin [*Naha*]

Bull Coll Eng Natl Taiwan Univ — Bulletin. College of Engineering. National Taiwan University

Bull Coll Foreign Stud (Yokohama) Nat Sci — Bulletin. College of Foreign Studies (Yokohama). Natural Science

Bull Coll Gen Educ Nagoya City Univ Nat Sci Sect — Bulletin. College of General Education. Nagoya City University. Natural Science Section

Bull Coll Sci 1 — Bulletin. College of Science. Part 1 [*Baghdad*]

Bull Coll Sci Univ Baghdad — Bulletin. College of Science. University of Baghdad

Bull Coll Sci Univ Ryukyus — Bulletin. College of Science. University of the Ryukyus

Bull Colo Agr Exp Sta — Bulletin. Colorado Agricultural Experiment Station

Bull Colo Agric Exp Stn — Bulletin. Colorado Agricultural Experiment Station

Bull Colo Dept Agr — Bulletin. Colorado Department of Agriculture

Bull Colo State Univ Agr Exp Sta — Bulletin. Colorado State University. Agricultural Experiment Station

Bull Colo State Univ Exp Stn — Bulletin. Colorado State University. Experiment Station

Bull Colo St Univ Agric Exp Stn — Bulletin. Colorado State University. Agricultural Experiment Station

Bull Colo Vet Med Assoc — Bulletin. Colorado Veterinary Medical Association

BullComEt — Bulletin. Comite d'Etudes [*Paris*]

Bull Com For — Bulletin. Comite des Forets

Bull Comm — Bullettino. Commissione Archeologica Comunale di Roma

Bull Comm Arch Narbonne — Bulletin. Commission Archeologique de Narbonne

Bull Comm Geol Finl — Bulletin. Commission Geologique de Finlande

Bull Commonw Bur Past Fld Crops — Bulletin. Commonwealth Bureau of Pastures and Field Crops

Bull Commonw Scient Ind Res Org — Bulletin. Commonwealth Scientific and Industrial Research Organisation

Bull Commonw Sci Industr Res Organ (Aust) — Bulletin. Commonwealth Scientific and Industrial Research Organisation (Australia)

Bull of Computer Aided Archtl Design — Bulletin of Computer Aided Architectural Design

Bull Conn Agr Exp Sta — Bulletin. Connecticut Agricultural Experiment Station

Bull Conn Agric Exp Sta — Bulletin. Connecticut Agricultural Experiment Station

Bull Conn Hist Soc — Bulletin. Connecticut Historical Society

Bull Co-Op Ext Serv Coll Agric Univ Idaho — Bulletin. Co-Operative Extension Service. College of Agriculture. University of Idaho

Bull Coop Ext Serv Colo State Univ — Bulletin. Cooperative Extension Service. Colorado State University

Bull Coop Ext Serv Montana State Univ — Montana State University. Cooperative Extension Service. Bulletin

Bull Coop Ext Serv Mont State Univ — Bulletin. Cooperative Extension Service. Montana State University

Bull Co-Op Ext Serv Ohio St Univ — Bulletin. Cooperative Extension Service. Ohio State University

Bull Coop Ext Serv Univ Conn — Bulletin. Cooperative Extension Service. University of Connecticut

Bull Coop Ext Serv Univ GA Coll Agric — Bulletin. Cooperative Extension Service. University of Georgia. College of Agriculture

Bull Cop Soc — Bulletin. Copyright Society of the USA

Bull Copyright Soc'y — Bulletin. Copyright Society of the USA

Bull Cornell Univ Agric Exp Stn — Bulletin. Cornell University Agricultural Experiment Station

Bull Council Res Mus Educ — Bulletin. Council for Research in Music Education

Bull C'right Soc'y — Bulletin. Copyright Society of the USA

Bull Crimean Astrophys Obs — Bulletin. Crimean Astrophysical Observatory

Bull Cr Soc — Bulletin. Copyright Society of the USA

Bull CSIRO — Australia. Commonwealth Scientific and Industrial Research Organization. Bulletin

Bull Daito Bunka Univ — Bulletin. Daito Bunka University [*Japan*]

Bull Del Agric Exp Stn — Bulletin. Delaware Agricultural Experiment Station

Bull Delaware County Med Soc — Bulletin. Delaware County Medical Society [*Pennsylvania*]

Bull Dep Agric (Br Columb) — Bulletin. Department of Agriculture (British Columbia)

Bull Dep Agric For (Un S Afr) — Bulletin. Department of Agriculture and Forestry (Union of South Africa)

Bull Dep Agric (Madras) — Bulletin. Department of Agriculture (Madras)

Bull Dep Agric NW Terr — Bulletin. Department of Agriculture. North-West Territories

Bull Dep Agric Res R Trop Inst (Amsterdam) — Bulletin. Department of Agricultural Research. Royal Tropical Institute (Amsterdam)

Bull Dep Agric Res Trop Inst (Amst) — Bulletin. Department of Agricultural Research. Royal Tropical Institute (Amsterdam)

Bull Dep Agric (Tas) — Bulletin. Department of Agriculture (Tasmania)

Bull Dep Agric (Tasm) — Bulletin. Department of Agriculture (Tasmania)

Bull Dep Agric Tech Serv (Transv) — Bulletin. Department of Agricultural Technical Services (Transvaal)

Bull Dep Agric (West Aust) — Bulletin. Department of Agriculture (Western Australia)

Bull Dep Civ Engng QD Univ — Bulletin. Department of Civil Engineering. University of Queensland

Bull Dep Civ Eng Queensl Univ — Bulletin. Department of Civil Engineering. University of Queensland

Bull Dep For (S Afr) — Bulletin. Department of Forestry (Pretoria, South Africa)

Bull Dep For Univ Ibadan — Bulletin. Department of Forestry. University of Ibadan

Bull Dep Gen Educ Tokyo Med Dent Univ — Bulletin. Department of General Education. Tokyo Medical and Dental University

Bull Dep Geol Heb Univ (Jerusalem) — Bulletin. Department of Geology. Hebrew University (Jerusalem)

Bull Dep Sci Ind Res (NZ) — Bulletin. Department of Scientific and Industrial Research (New Zealand)

Bull Dept Agr Econ Univ Manchester — Bulletin. Department of Agricultural Economics. University of Manchester

Bull Dept Agric and Indust (West Australia) — Bulletin. Department of Agriculture and Industries (Western Australia)

Bull Dept Agr (Mysore) Entomol Ser — Bulletin. Department of Agriculture (Mysore State). Entomology Series

Bull Dept Agron Mosonmagyarovar Coll Agr Sci — Bulletin. Department of Agronomy. Mosonmagyarovar College of Agricultural Sciences

Bull Dept Agr (Tanganyika) — Bulletin. Department of Agriculture (Tanganyika)

Bull Dept Agr Tech Serv (Repub S Afr) — Bulletin. Department of Agricultural Technical Services (Republic of South Africa)

Bull Dept Gen Ed College Sci Tech Nihon Univ — Bulletin. Department of General Education. College of Science and Technology. Nihon University

Bull Dept Gen Educ Nagoya City Univ Nat Sci Sect — Bulletin. Department of General Education. Nagoya City University. Natural Science Section

Bull Dep Zool Univ Punjab — Bulletin. Department of Zoology. University of the Punjab

Bull Direction Etudes Recherches Ser C Math Informat — Bulletin. Direction des Etudes et Recherches. Serie C. Mathematiques. Informatique

Bull Direction Etudes Rech Ser C Math Inform — Electricite de France. Bulletin de la Direction des Etudes et Recherches. Serie C. Mathematiques-Informatique [*Grenoble*]

Bull Dir Etud & Rech A — Bulletin. Direction des Etudes et Recherches. Serie A

Bull Dir Etud & Rech B — Bulletin. Direction des Etudes et Recherches. Serie B

Bull Dir Etud & Rech C — Bulletin. Direction des Etudes et Recherches. Serie C

Bull Dir Etud Rech Electr Fr Ser A — Bulletin. Direction des Etudes et Recherches. Electricite de France. Serie A. Nucleaire, Hydraulique, Thermique

Bull Dir Etud & Rech Ser A — Bulletin. Direction des Etudes et Recherches. Serie A

Bull Dir Etud & Rech Ser B — Bulletin. Direction des Etudes et Recherches. Serie B

Bull Dir Etud & Rech Ser C — Bulletin. Direction des Etudes et Recherches. Serie C

Bull Dir Mines Geol (Afr Equa) — Bulletin. Direction des Mines et de la Geologie (Afrique Equatoriale)

Bull Div Miner Resour (VA) — Bulletin. Division of Mineral Resources (Virginia)

Bull Div Plant Ind NSW Dept Agr — Bulletin. Division of Plant Industry. New South Wales Department of Agriculture

Bull Div Silv Dep For Papua & N Guinea — Bulletin. Division of Silviculture. Department of Forests of Papua and New Guinea

Bull Div Veg Physiol Path US Dep Agric — Bulletin. Division of Vegetable Physiology and Pathology. United States Department of Agriculture

Bull Doc Bibliog — Bulletin de Documentation Bibliographique

Bull Doc Cent Inf Chrome Dur — Bulletin de Documentation. Centre d'Information du Chrome Dur [*France*]

Bull Doc Int Superphosphate Mfr Ass Agr Comm — Bulletin. Documentation of the International Superphosphate Manufacturer's Association. Agricultural Committee

Bull Docum Ass Int Fabr Superphos — Bulletin de Documentation. Association Internationale des Fabricants de Superphosphates

Bull Dosente — Bulletin vir Dosente

Bull de Droit Nucl — Bulletin de Droit Nucleaire

Bull Droit Nucl — Bulletin de Droit Nucleaire

Bull de Droit Tchecoslovaque — Bulletin de Droit Tchecoslovaque

Bull Duke Univ Sch For — Bulletin. Duke University School of Forestry

Bull Earth Miner Sci Exp Sta PA State Univ — Bulletin. Earth and Mineral Sciences Experiment Station. Pennsylvania State Univ

Bull Earth Miner Sci Exp Stn PA State Univ — Bulletin. Earth and Mineral Sciences Experiment Station. Pennsylvania State University

Bull Earthquake Res Inst Univ Tokyo — Bulletin. Earthquake Research Institute. University of Tokyo

Bull Earth Sci Fac Ege Univ (Izmir) — Bulletin. Earth Science Faculty. Ege University (Izmir)

Bull East Scotl Coll Agric — Bulletin. East of Scotland College of Agriculture

Bull Ec Meun Belge — Bulletin. Ecole de la Meunerie Belge

Bull Ec Natl Super Agron Ind Aliment — Bulletin. Ecole Nationale Superieure d'Agronomie et des Industries Alimentaires

Bull Ec Natl Super Agron Nancy — Bulletin. Ecole Nationale Superieure Agronomique de Nancy

Bull Ec Natn Sup Agron Nancy — Bulletin. Ecole Nationale Superieure Agronomique de Nancy

Bull Ec Nat Super Agron Ind Aliment — Bulletin. Ecole Nationale Superieure d'Agronomie et des Industries Alimentaires

Bull Ecol — Bulletin d'Ecologie

Bull Ecole Nat Super Agron Nancy — Bulletin. Ecole Nationale Superieure Agronomique de Nancy

Bull Ecole Super Agr Tunis — Bulletin. Ecole Superieure d'Agriculture de Tunis

Bull Ecol Res Comm-NFR (Statens Naturvetensk Forskningsrad) — Bulletins. Ecological Research Committee-NFR (Statens Naturvetenskapliga Forskningsrad)

Bull Ecol Soc Amer — Bulletin. Ecological Society of America

Bull Econom — Bulletin Economique Mensuelle

Bull Edinburgh Sch Agr — Bulletin. Edinburgh School of Agriculture

Bull Ehime Agr Exp Sta — Bulletin. Ehime Agricultural Experiment Station

Bull Ehime Univ For — Bulletin. Ehime University Forest

Bull Eidgenoess Gesundh Beil B — Bulletin. Eidgenoessisches Gesundheitsamt. Beilage B [*Switzerland*]

Bulleid Mem Lect — Bulleid Memorial Lectures

Bull Electron Microsc Soc India — Bulletin. Electron Microscope Society of India

Bull Electrotech Lab — Bulletin. Electrotechnical Laboratory [*Japan*]

Bull Electrotech Lab (Tokyo) — Bulletin. Electrotechnical Laboratory (Tokyo)

Bull Endem Dis — Bulletin of Endemic Diseases

Bull Endem Dis (Baghdad) — Bulletin of Endemic Diseases (Baghdad)

Bull Eng Geol Hydrogeol (Engl Transl) — Bulletin of Engineering Geology and Hydrogeology (English Translation) [*Yugoslavia*]

Bull Engrais — Bulletin des Engrais

Bull Eng Res Inst Kyoto Univ — Bulletin. Engineering Research Institute of Kyoto University [*Japan*]

Bull Entomol — Bulletin of Entomology

Bull Entomol Res — Bulletin of Entomological Research

Bull Entomol Soc Am — Bulletin. Entomological Society of America

Bull Entomol Soc Amer — Bulletin. Entomological Society of America

Bull Entomol Soc Egypt Econ Ser — Bulletin. Entomological Society of Egypt. Economic Series

Bull Entomol Soc Nigeria — Bulletin. Entomological Society of Nigeria

Bull Ent Res — Bulletin of Entomological Research

Bull Ent Soc Am — Bulletin. Entomological Society of America

Bull Envir Contam Toxic — Bulletin of Environmental Contamination and Toxicology

Bull Environ Contam Toxicol — Bulletin of Environmental Contamination and Toxicology

Bull Environ Sci — Bulletin of Environmental Sciences [*South Korea*]

Bull Epizoot Dis Afr — Bulletin of Epizootic Diseases of Africa

Bull Escher Wyss — Bulletin Escher Wyss

BullETHS — Bulletin. Evangelical Theological Society [*Wheaton, IL*] [*Later, Journal. Evangelical Theological Society*]

Bulletin-AQQUA — Bulletin. Association Quebecoise pour l'Etude du Quaternaire

Bulletin Singapore Natl Inst Chem — Bulletin. Singapore National Institute of Chemistry

Bull Etud Commun Mediter — Bulletin de l'Etude en Commun de la Mediterranee

Bull Etud Rech Tech — Bulletin d'Etudes et de Recherches Techniques

Bull Eur Communities — Bulletin. European Communities [*Luxembourg*]

Bull Eur Communities Suppl — Bulletin. European Communities. Supplement [*Luxembourg*]

Bull Eur Physiopathol Respir — Bulletin Europeen de Physiopathologie Respiratoire

Bull Eur South Obs — Bulletin. European Southern Observatory [*West Germany*]

Bull Exp Biol Med — Bulletin of Experimental Biology and Medicine

Bull Exp Biol Med (Eng Transl Byull Eksp Biol Med) — Bulletin of Experimental Biology and Medicine (English Translation of Byulleten' Eksperimental'noi Biologii i Meditsiny)

Bull Exp Farm Coll Agr Ehime Univ — Bulletin. Experimental Farm College of Agriculture. Ehime University

Bull Exp Fms Brch Dep Agric (Can) — Bulletin. Experimental Farms Branch. Department of Agriculture (Canada)

Bull Exp For Tokyo Univ Agric Technol — Bulletin of the Experiment Forest. Tokyo University of Agriculture and Technology

Bull Exp Stn Horse Breed (Slatinany) — Bulletin. Experimental Station for Horse Breeding (Slatinany)

Bull Fac Agric Cairo Univ — Bulletin. Faculty of Agriculture. Cairo University

Bull Fac Agric Hirosaki Univ — Bulletin. Faculty of Agriculture. Hirosaki University

Bull Fac Agric Kagoshima Univ — Bulletin. Faculty of Agriculture. Kagoshima University

Bull Fac Agric Meiji Univ — Bulletin. Faculty of Agriculture. Meiji University

Bull Fac Agric Mie Univ — Bulletin. Faculty of Agriculture. Mie University

Bull Fac Agric Miyazaki Univ — Bulletin. Faculty of Agriculture. Miyazaki University

Bull Fac Agric Niigata Univ — Bulletin. Faculty of Agriculture. Niigata University

Bull Fac Agric Sci (Mosonmagyarovar Hung) — Bulletin. Faculty of Agricultural Sciences (Mosonmagyarovar, Hungary)

Bull Fac Agric Shimane Univ — Bulletin. Faculty of Agriculture. Shimane University

Bull Fac Agric Shizuoka Univ — Bulletin. Faculty of Agriculture. Shizuoka University

Bull Fac Agric Tamagawa Univ — Bulletin. Faculty of Agriculture. Tamagawa University

Bull Fac Agric Tokyo Univ Agric Technol — Bulletin. Faculty of Agriculture. Tokyo University of Agriculture and Technology

Bull Fac Agric Tottori Univ — Bulletin. Faculty of Agriculture. Tottori University

Bull Fac Agric Univ Miyazaki — Bulletin. Faculty of Agriculture. University of Miyazaki

Bull Fac Agric Yamaguti Univ — Bulletin. Faculty of Agriculture. Yamaguti University

Bull Fac Agr Kagoshima Univ — Bulletin. Faculty of Agriculture. Kagoshima University

Bull Fac Agr Meiji Univ — Bulletin. Faculty of Agriculture. Meiji University

Bull Fac Agr Niigata Univ — Bulletin. Faculty of Agriculture. Niigata University

Bull Fac Agr Shimane Univ — Bulletin. Faculty of Agriculture. Shimane University

Bull Fac Agr Shizuoka Univ — Bulletin. Faculty of Agriculture. Shizuoka University

Bull Fac Agr Univ Miyazaki — Bulletin. Faculty of Agriculture. University of Miyazaki

Bull Fac Agr Yamaguchi Univ — Bulletin. Faculty of Agriculture. Yamaguchi University

Bull Fac Educ Chiba Univ — Bulletin. Faculty of Education. Chiba University

Bull Fac Educ Hirosaki Univ — Bulletin. Faculty of Education. Hirosaki University

Bull Fac Educ Hiroshima Univ — Bulletin. Faculty of Education. Hiroshima University

Bull Fac Educ Hiroshima Univ Part 3 (Sci Tech) — Bulletin. Faculty of Education. Hiroshima University. Part 3 (Science and Technology)

Bull Fac Educ Kanazawa Univ Nat Sci — Bulletin. Faculty of Education. Kanazawa University. Natural Science

Bull Fac Educ Kobe Univ — Bulletin. Faculty of Education. Kobe University

Bull Fac Educ Kochi Univ Ser 3 — Bulletin. Faculty of Education. Kochi University. Series 3

Bull Fac Educ Univ Kagoshima Nat Sci — Bulletin. Faculty of Education. University of Kagoshima. Natural Science

Bull Fac Educ Utsunomiya Univ Sect 2 — Bulletin. Faculty of Education. Utsunomiya University. Section 2

Bull Fac Educ Wakayama Univ Nat Sci — Bulletin. Faculty of Education. Wakayama University. Natural Science

Bull Fac Educ Yamaguchi Univ — Bulletin. Faculty of Education. Yamaguchi University

Bull Fac Ed Univ Kagoshima — Bulletin. Faculty of Education. University of Kagoshima

Bull Fac Ed Utsunomiya Univ Sect 2 — Bulletin. Faculty of Education. Utsunomiya University. Section 2

Bull Fac Ed Wakayama Univ Natur Sci — Wakayama University. Faculty of Education. Bulletin. Natural Science

Bull Fac Eng Alexandria Univ — Bulletin. Faculty of Engineering. Alexandria University [*Egypt*]

Bull Fac Eng Hiroshima Univ — Bulletin. Faculty of Engineering. Hiroshima University

Bull Fac Eng Hokkaido Univ — Bulletin. Faculty of Engineering. Hokkaido University

Bull Fac Eng Ibaraki Univ — Bulletin. Faculty of Engineering. Ibaraki University

Bull Fac Eng Miyazaki Univ — Bulletin. Faculty of Engineering. Miyazaki University

Bull Fac Engrg Hiroshima Univ — Bulletin. Faculty of Engineering. Hiroshima University

Bull Fac Engrg Miyazaki Univ — Bulletin. Faculty of Engineering. Miyazaki University

Bull Fac Eng Tokushima Univ — Bulletin. Faculty of Engineering. Tokushima University

Bull Fac Eng Toyama Univ — Bulletin. Faculty of Engineering. Toyama University [*Japan*]

Bull Fac Eng Univ Alexandria Chem Eng — Bulletin. Faculty of Engineering. University of Alexandria. Chemical Engineering [*Egypt*]

Bull Fac Eng Univ Alexandria Eng Chem Eng — Bulletin. Faculty of Engineering. University of Alexandria. Engineering. Chemical Engineering

Bull Fac Eng Yokohama Natl Univ — Bulletin. Faculty of Engineering. Yokohama National University

Bull Fac Eng Yokohama Univ — Bulletin. Faculty of Engineering. Yokohama University

Bull Fac Fish Hokkaido Univ — Bulletin. Faculty of Fisheries. Hokkaido University

Bull Fac Fish Nagasaki Univ — Bulletin. Faculty of Fisheries. Nagasaki University [*Japan*]

Bull Fac For Univ BC — Bulletin. Faculty of Forestry. University of British Columbia

Bull Fac Gen Ed Gifu Univ — Gifu University. Faculty of General Education. Bulletin

Bull Fac Gen Educ Utsunomiya Univ Sect 2 — Bulletin. Faculty of General Education. Utsunomiya University. Section 2

Bull Fac Lib Arts Ibaraki Univ (Nat Sci) — Bulletin. Faculty of Liberal Arts. Ibaraki University (Natural Science)

Bull Fac Med Istanbul — Bulletin. Faculte de Medecine d'Istanbul

Bull Fac Pharm Cairo Univ — Bulletin. Faculty of Pharmacy. Cairo University

Bull Fac Pharm Kinki Univ — Bulletin. Faculty of Pharmacy. Kinki University

Bull Fac School Ed Hiroshima Univ Part II — Bulletin. Faculty of School Education. Hiroshima University. Part II

Bull Fac Sci Alexandria Univ — Bulletin. Faculty of Science. Alexandria University

Bull Fac Sci Assiut Univ — Bulletin. Faculty of Science. Assiut University

Bull Fac Sci (Cairo) — Bulletin. Faculty of Science (Cairo)

Bull Fac Sci Cairo Univ — Bulletin. Faculty of Science. Cairo University

Bull Fac Sci Eng Chuo Univ — Bulletin. Faculty of Science and Engineering. Chuo University

Bull Fac Sci Engrg Chuo Univ — Bulletin. Faculty of Science and Engineering. Chuo University

Bull Fac Sci Ibaraki Univ Ser A — Bulletin. Faculty of Science. Ibaraki University. Series A. Mathematics

Bull Fac Sci Ibaraki Univ Series A — Bulletin. Faculty of Science. Ibaraki University. Series A. Mathematics

Bull Fac Sci King Abdul Aziz Univ — Bulletin. Faculty of Science. King Abdul Aziz University

Bull Fac Sci Riyad Univ — Bulletin. Faculty of Science. Riyad University. Series II

Bull Fac Sci Univ Fr Chin Peiping — Bulletin. Faculte des Sciences. Universite Franco-Chinoise de Peiping

Bull Far Eastern Antiquities — Bulletin. Museum of Far Eastern Antiquities [*Stockholm*]

Bull Farm Manage Land Util Ser H — Bulletin. Farm Management and Land Utilization. Series H

Bull Far Seas Fish Res Lab (Shimizu) — Bulletin. Far Seas Fisheries Research Laboratory (Shimizu)

Bull Fed Ind Chim Bel — Bulletin. Federation des Industries Chimiques de Belgique

Bull Fed Int Assoc Chim Text Couleur — Bulletin. Federation Internationale des Associations des Chimistes du Textile et de la Couleur

Bull Fed Min Agr (Salisbury) — Bulletin. Federal Ministry of Agriculture (Salisbury)

Bull Fed Soc Gynecol Obstet Lang Fr — Bulletin. Federation des Societes de Gynecologie et d'Obstetrique de Langue Francaise

Bull Fed Soc Hist Nat Franche-Comte — Bulletin. Federation des Societes d'Histoire Naturelle de Franche-Comte

Bull Fil Soc Biol Paris — Bulletin. Filiales de la Societe de Biologie de Paris

Bull First Agron Div Tokai-Kinki Nat Agr Exp Sta — Bulletin. First Agronomy Division. Tokai-Kinki National Agricultural Experiment Station

Bull First Agron Div Tokai-Kinki Natl Agric Exp Stn — Bulletin. First Agronomy Division. Tokai-Kinki National Agricultural Experiment Station

Bull Fish Exp Stn Gov Gen Chosen Ser B — Bulletin. Fishery Experiment Station. Government General of Chosen. Series B

Bull Fish Res Board Can — Bulletin. Fisheries Research Board of Canada

Bull Fish Res Stn (Ceylon) — Bulletin. Fisheries Research Station (Ceylon)

Bull Fla Agr Exp Sta — Bulletin. Florida Agricultural Experiment Station

Bull Fla Agric Exp Stn — Bulletin. Florida Agricultural Experiment Station

Bull Fla Agric Ext Serv — Bulletin. Florida Agricultural Extension Service

Bull Fla Dep Agric — Bulletin. Florida Department of Agriculture

Bull Fla Dept Agr Div Plant Ind — Bulletin. Florida Department of Agriculture. Division of Plant Industry

Bull Fla State Mus Biol Sci — Bulletin. Florida State Museum. Biological Sciences

Bull Fla Univ Agr Exp Sta — Bulletin. Florida University. Agricultural Experiment Station

Bull Fonds Rech For Univ Laval — Bulletin. Fonds de Recherches Forestieres. Universite Laval

Bull Food Ind Exp Stn Hiroshima Prefect — Bulletin. Food Industrial Experiment Station. Hiroshima Prefecture

Bull For Comm (Lond) — Bulletin. Forestry Commission (London)

Bull For Comm Tasm — Bulletin. Forestry Commission of Tasmania

Bull For Comm Vict — Bulletin. Forests Commission of Victoria

Bull For Dep (Uganda) — Bulletin. Forest Department. Kampala (Uganda)

Bull For Dep W Aust — Bulletin. Forests Department of Western Australia

Bull For Dep West Aust — Bulletin. Forests Department of Western Australia

Bull For Dep West Aust — Western Australia. Forests Department. Bulletin

Bull Ford For Cent — Bulletin. Ford Forestry Center

Bull Forest Comm Vict — Bulletin. Forests Commission of Victoria

Bull Forest Dep WA — Bulletin. Forests Department of Western Australia

Bull Forests Comm Tasm — Bulletin. Forests Commission of Tasmania

Bull Forests Dep West Aust — Bulletin. Forests Department of Western Australia

Bull For Exp Sta (Meguro) — Bulletin. Government Forest Experiment Station (Meguro)

Bull For Prod Res (Lond) — Bulletin. Forest Products Research. Ministry of Technology (London)

Bull For Timb Bur — Bulletin. Forestry and Timber Bureau

Bull For Timb Bur (Aust) — Bulletin. Forestry and Timber Bureau (Canberra, Australia)

Bull Foundry Abstr Br Cast Iron Res Assoc — Bulletin and Foundry Abstracts. British Cast Iron Research Association

Bull Freshw Fish Res Lab (Tokyo) — Bulletin. Freshwater Fisheries Research Laboratory (Tokyo)

Bull Frnds Hist Assn — Bulletin. Friends Historical Association [*Philadelphia*]

Bull Fr Piscic — Bulletin Francais de Pisciculture

Bull Fruit Tree Res Stn Minist Agric For Ser E (Akitsu) — Bulletin. Fruit Tree Research Station. Ministry of Agriculture and Forestry. Series E (Akitsu)

Bull Fruit Tree Res Stn Ser A (Hiratsuka) — Bulletin. Fruit Tree Research Station. Series A (Hiratsuka)

Bull Fruit Tree Res Stn Ser B (Okitsu) — Bulletin. Fruit Tree Research Station. Series B (Okitsu)

Bull Fruit Tree Res Stn Ser C (Morioka) — Bulletin. Fruit Tree Research Station. Series C (Morioka)

Bull Ft Wayne Med Soc — Bulletin. Fort Wayne Medical Society [*Indiana*]

Bull Fuel Res Inst S Afr — Bulletin. Fuel Research Institute of South Africa

Bull Fuji Women's Coll — Bulletin. Fuji Women's College

Bull Fukuoka Agr Exp Stn — Bulletin. Fukuoka Agricultural Experiment Station

Bull Fukuokaken For Exp Sta — Bulletin. Fukuokaken Forest Experiment Station

Bull Fukuoka Pref Agr Exp Sta — Bulletin. Fukuoka Prefectural Agricultural Experiment Station

Bull Fukuoka Ringyo Shikenjo — Bulletin. Fukuoka. Ringyo Shikenjo

Bull Fukuoka Univ Ed III — Bulletin. Fukuoka University of Education. Part III. Natural Sciences

Bull Fukuoka Univ Educ Part 3 Nat Sci — Bulletin. Fukuoka University of Education. Part 3. Natural Sciences

Bull Fukushima Prefect Fish Exp Stn — Bulletin. Fukushima Prefectural Fisheries Experimental Station

Bull GA Acad Sci — Bulletin. Georgia Academy of Science

Bull GA Agr Exp Sta — Bulletin. Georgia Agricultural Experiment Station

Bull GA Agric Exp Stn — Bulletin. Georgia Agricultural Experiment Station

Bull Galenica — Bulletin Galenica

Bull GB For Prod Res — Bulletin. Great Britain Forest Products Research

Bull Geisinger Med Cent — Bulletin. Geisinger Medical Center

Bull Gen Ed Dokkyo Univ School Medicine — Bulletin of General Education. Dokkyo University. School of Medicine

Bull Genessee County Med Soc — Bulletin. Genessee County Medical Society [*Michigan*]

Bull Genet — Bulletin of Genetics [*China*]

Bull Gen Therap (Paris) — Bulletin General. Therapeutique Medicale, Chirurgicale, et Obstetricale (Paris)

Bull Geochem Soc India — Bulletin. Geochemical Society of India

Bull Geod — Bulletin Geodesique

Bull Geodesique — Bulletin Geodesique

Bull Geogr Surv Inst — Bulletin. Geographical Survey Institute

Bull Geol Inst Bulg Acad Sci Ser Geotecton — Bulletin. Geological Institute. Bulgarian Academy of Sciences. Series Geotectonics

Bull Geol Inst Univ Upps — Bulletin. Geological Institutions of the University of Uppsala

Bull Geol Inst Univ Ups — Bulletin. Geologiska Institut. Universitet Upsala

Bull Geol Min Metall Soc India — Bulletin. Geological, Mining, and Metallurgical Society of India

Bull Geol Min Metall Soc Liberia — Bulletin. Geological, Mining, and Metallurgical Society of Liberia

Bull Geol Soc Am — Bulletin. Geological Society of America

Bull Geol Soc China — Bulletin. Geological Society of China

Bull Geol Soc Den — Bulletin. Geological Society of Denmark

Bull Geol Soc Denmark — Bulletin. Geological Society of Denmark

Bull Geol Soc Finl — Bulletin. Geological Society of Finland

Bull Geol Soc Malays — Bulletin. Geological Society of Malaysia

Bull Geol Soc Turk — Bulletin. Geological Society of Turkey

Bull Geol Surv Can — Bulletin. Geological Survey of Canada

Bull Geol Surv G — Bulletin. Geological Survey of Georgia

Bull Geol Surv GB — Bulletin. Geological Survey of Great Britain

Bull Geol Surv Gr Brit — Bulletin. Geological Survey of Great Britain

Bull Geol Surv Greenland — Bulletin. Geological Survey of Greenland

Bull Geol Surv Guyana — Bulletin. Geological Survey of Guyana

Bull Geol Surv India A — Bulletin. Geological Survey of India. Series A. Economic Geology

Bull Geol Surv India Ser B — Bulletins. Geological Survey of India. Series B. Engineering Geology and Ground Water

Bull Geol Surv Indones — Bulletin. Geological Survey of Indonesia

Bull Geol Surv Israel — Bulletin. Geological Survey of Israel

Bull Geol Surv Jap — Bulletin. Geological Survey of Japan

Bull Geol Surv Jpn — Bulletin. Geological Survey of Japan

Bull Geol Surv NSW — Geological Survey of New South Wales. Bulletin

Bull Geol Surv Prague — Bulletin. Geological Survey of Prague

Bull Geol Surv Rhod — Bulletin. Geological Survey of Rhodesia

Bull Geol Surv S Afr — Bulletin. Geological Survey of South Africa

Bull Geol Surv S Aust — Bulletin. Geological Survey of South Australia

Bull Geol Surv South Aust — Geological Survey of South Australia. Bulletin

Bull Geol Surv Taiwan — Bulletin. Geological Survey of Taiwan

Bull Geol Surv Tanz — Bulletin. Geological Survey of Tanzania

Bull Geol Surv Tas — Geological Survey of Tasmania. Bulletin

Bull Geol Surv Tasm — Geological Survey of Tasmania. Bulletin

Bull Geol Surv Vic — Geological Survey of Victoria. Bulletin

Bull Geol Surv Vict — Geological Survey of Victoria. Bulletin

Bull Geol Surv West Aust — Bulletin. Geological Survey of Western Australia

Bull Geol Surv West Aust — Geological Survey of Western Australia. Bulletin

Bull Geophys — Bulletin de Geophysique

Bull Geophys Obs Haile Sellassie I Univ — Bulletin. Geophysical Observatory. Haile Sellassie I University [Ethiopia]

Bull Georgetown Univ Med Cent — Bulletin. Georgetown University Medical Center

Bull Geotherm Resour Counc (Davis Calif) — Bulletin. Geothermal Resources Council (Davis, California)

Bull Ghana Geol Surv — Bulletin. Ghana Geological Survey

Bull Gifu College E — Bulletin. Gifu College of Education

Bull Gifu College Ed — Bulletin. Gifu College of Education

Bull Gov — Bullettino. Commissione Archeologica de Governatorato di Roma

Bull Gov Chem Lab West Aust — Western Australia. Government Chemical Laboratories. Bulletin

Bull Gov For Exp Stn (Tokyo) — Bulletin. Government Forest Experiment Station (Tokyo)

Bull Gov Ind Res Inst (Osaka) — Bulletin. Government Industrial Research Institute (Osaka)

Bull Govt Chem Labs West Aust — Western Australia. Government Chemical Laboratories. Bulletin

Bull Govt Forest Expt Sta — Bulletin. Government Forest Experiment Station [Tokyo]

Bull Grain Technol — Bulletin of Grain Technology

Bull Greene County Med Soc — Bulletin. Greene County Medical Society [Missouri]

Bull Greenville County Med Soc — Bulletin. Greenville County Medical Society [South Carolina]

Bull Groenl Geol Unders — Bulletin. Groenlands Geologiske Undersoegelse [Denmark]

Bull Groupe Fr Humidimetrie Neutron — Bulletin. Groupe Francais d'Humidimetrie Neutronique

Bull Groupe Fr Humidimetrie Neutronique — Bulletin. Groupe Francais d'Humidimetrie Neutronique [France]

Bull Groupe Trav Etud Equilibre Foret-Gibier — Bulletin. Groupe de Travail pour l'Etude de l'Equilibre Foret-Gibier

Bull Group Eur Rech Sci Stomatol Odontol — Bulletin. Groupement Europeen pour la Recherche Scientifique en Stomatologie et Odontologie

Bull Group Int Rech Sci Stomatol — Bulletin. Groupement International pour la Recherche Scientifique en Stomatologie

Bull Group Int Rech Sci Stomatol Odontol — Bulletin. Groupement International pour la Recherche Scientifique en Stomatologie et Odontologie

Bull Grpe Fr Argiles — Bulletin. Groupe Francais des Argiles

Bull GTV (Group Tech Vet) Dossiers Tech Vet — Bulletin des GTV (Groupements Techniques Veterinaires). Dossiers Techniques Veterinaires

Bull Guerre Biol Pharm — Bulletin de Guerre des Biologistes Pharmaciens

Bull Haffkine Inst — Bulletin. Haffkine Institute

Bull Hatano Tob Exp Stn — Bulletin. Hatano Tobacco Experiment Station

Bull Hear Inst (Jpn) — Bulletin. Heart Institute (Japan)

Bull Hell Vet Med Soc — Bulletin. Hellenic Veterinary Medical Society

Bull Hennepin County Med Soc — Bulletin. Hennepin County Medical Society [Minnesota]

Bull Highw Res Bd — Bulletin. Highway Research Board

Bull Hiroshima Agric Coll — Bulletin. Hiroshima Agricultural College

Bull Hiroshima Food Res Inst — Bulletin. Hiroshima Food Research Institute

Bull Hiroshima Jogakuin Coll — Bulletin. Hiroshima Jogakuin College

Bull Hiroshima Prefect Agric Exp Stn — Bulletin. Hiroshima Prefectural Agricultural Experiment Station

Bull Hiroshima Prefect Inst Public Health — Bulletin. Hiroshima Prefectural Institute of Public Health

Bull Hisp — Bulletin Hispanique

Bull Hist Dent — Bulletin of the History of Dentistry

Bull Hist Med — Bulletin of the History of Medicine

Bull Hist Metal Group — Bulletin. Historical Metallurgy Group

Bull Histol Appl — Bulletin d'Histologie Appliquee

Bull Hoblitzelle Agric Lab Tex Res Found — Bulletin. Hoblitzelle Agricultural Laboratory. Texas Research Foundation

Bull Hoblitzelle Agr Lab Tex Res Found — Bulletin. Hoblitzelle Agricultural Laboratory. Texas Research Foundation

Bull Hokkaido For Exp Stn — Bulletin. Hokkaido Forest Experiment Station

Bull Hokkaido Pref Agr Exp Sta — Bulletin. Hokkaido Prefectural Agricultural Experiment Station

Bull Hokkaido Prefect Agric Exp Stn — Bulletin. Hokkaido Prefectural Agricultural Experiment Station

Bull Hokkaido Reg Fish Res Lab — Bulletin. Hokkaido Regional Fisheries Research Laboratories

Bull Hokkaido Underground Resour Invest — Bulletin of Hokkaido Underground Resource Investigation [Japan]

Bull Hokuriku Natl Agric Exp Stn — Bulletin. Hokuriku National Agricultural Experiment Station

Bull Hortic (Liege) — Bulletin Horticole (Liege)

Bull Hortic Res Stn (Minist Agric For) Ser A (Hiratsuka) — Bulletin. Horticultural Research Station (Ministry of Agriculture and Forestry). Series A (Hiratsuka)

Bull Hortic Res Stn (Minist Agric For) Ser B (Okitsu) — Bulletin. Horticultural Research Station (Ministry of Agriculture and Forestry). Series B (Okitsu)

Bull Hortic Res Stn (Minist Agric For) Ser C (Morioka) — Bulletin. Horticultural Research Station (Ministry of Agriculture and Forestry). Series C (Morioka)

Bull Hortic Res Stn (Minist Agric For) Ser D (Kurume) — Bulletin. Horticultural Research Station (Ministry of Agriculture and Forestry). Series D (Kurume)

Bull Hosp Joint Dis — Bulletin. Hospital for Joint Diseases

Bull Hosp Jt Dis — Bulletin. Hospital for Joint Diseases

Bull Hot Spring Res Inst Kanagawa Prefect — Bulletin. Hot Spring Research Institute. Kanagawa Prefecture

Bull Hudson Cty Dent Soc — Bulletin. Hudson County Dental Society

Bull Hum Body Meas — Bulletin of Human Body Measurement

Bull Hyg — Bulletin of Hygiene

Bull Hyg Lab US Mar Hosp Serv — Bulletin. Hygienic Laboratory. United States Marine Hospital Service

Bull Hyg Lab US Pub Health and Mar Hosp Serv — Bulletin. Hygienic Laboratory. United States Public Health and Marine Hospital Service

Bull Hyg Lab US Pub Health Serv — Bulletin. Hygienic Laboratory. United States Public Health Service

Bull Hyg Prof — Bulletin de l'Hygiene Professionnelle

Bull Hyogo Pref Agr Exp Sta — Bulletin. Hyogo Prefectural Agricultural Experiment Station

Bull Hyogo Prefect Agric Cent Exp Ext Educ — Bulletin. Hyogo Prefectural Agricultural Center for Experiment, Extension, and Education

Bull Hyogo Prefect For Exp Stn — Bulletin. Hyogo Prefectural Forest Experiment Station

Bul Liaison et Info — Bulletin de Liaison et d'Information

Bull Ibaraki Prefect For Exp Stn — Bulletin. Ibaraki Prefectural Forest Experiment Station

Bull Idaho Agr Exp Sta — Bulletin. Idaho Agricultural Experiment Station

Bull Idaho Bur Mines Geol — Bulletin. Idaho Bureau of Mines and Geology

Bull Idaho For Wildl Range Exp Stn — Bulletin. Idaho Forest, Wildlife, and Range Experiment Station

Bull Ill Agr Exp Sta — Bulletin. Illinois Agricultural Experiment Station

Bull Ill Agric Exp Sta — Bulletin. University of Illinois. Agricultural Experiment Station

Bull Ill State Geol Surv — Bulletin. Illinois State Geological Survey

Bull Ill St Lab Nat Hist — Bulletin. Illinois State Laboratory of Natural History

Bull Imp Bur Pastures Forage Crops — Bulletin. Imperial Bureau of Pastures and Forage Crops

Bull Imp Inst (London) — Bulletin. Imperial Institute (London)

Bull Indep Biol Lab (Kefar-Malal) — Bulletin. Independent Biological Laboratories (Kefar-Malal)

Bull Indian Coun Agric Res — Bulletin. Indian Council of Agricultural Research

Bull Indian Ind Res — Bulletins. Indian Industrial Research

Bull Indian Inst Hist Med — Bulletin. Indian Institute of the History of Medicine

Bull Indian Natl Sci Acad — Bulletin. Indian National Science Academy

Bull Indian Phytopathol Soc — Bulletin. Indian Phytopathological Society

Bull Indian Soc Earthqu Technol — Bulletin. Indian Society of Earthquake Technology

Bull Indian Soc Malar Commun Dis — Bulletin. Indian Society for Malaria and Other Communicable Diseases

Bull Indian Soc Soil Sci — Bulletin. Indian Society of Soil Science

Bull India Sect Electrochem Soc — Bulletin. India Section. Electrochemical Society

Bull Ind Res Cent Ehime Prefect — Bulletin. Industrial Research Center of Ehime Prefecture

Bull Ind Res Inst Ehime Prefect — Bulletin. Industrial Research Institute of Ehime Prefecture

Bull Ind Res Inst Kanagawa Prefect — Bulletin. Industrial Research Institute of Kanagawa Prefecture [*Japan*]

Bull Inf Appl Ind Radioelem — Bulletin d'Information sur les Applications Industrielles des Radioelements

Bull Inf Assoc Belge Dev Pac Energ At — Bulletin d'Information. Association Belge pour le Developpement Pacifique de l'Energie Atomique [*Belgium*]

Bull Inf Assoc Nat Serv Eau (Belg) — Bulletin d'Information. Association Nationale des Services d'Eau (Belgium)

Bull Inf Assoc Tech Energ Nucl — Bulletin d'Information. Association Technique pour l'Energie Nucleaire

Bull Inf ATEN — Bulletin d'Information. ATEN [*Association Technique pour l'Energie Nucleaire*] [*France*]

Bull Inf ATEN Suppl — Bulletin d'Information. ATEN [*Association Technique pour l'Energie Nucleaire*]. Supplement [*France*]

Bull Inf Bur Natl Metrol — Bulletin d'Information. Bureau National de Metrologie

Bull Inf Cent Electr — Bulletin d'Information des Centrales Electriques [*France*]

Bull Inf Centre Donnees Stellaires — Bulletin d'Information. Centre de Donnees Stellaires

Bull Inf CNEEMA (Cent Natl Etud Exp Mach Agric) — Bulletin d'Information. CNEEMA (Centre National d'Etudes et d'Experimentation de Machinisme Agricole)

Bull Inf Generateurs Isot — Bulletin d'Information sur les Generateurs Isotopiques

Bull Inf INEAC — Bulletin d'Information. Institut National pour l'Etude Agronomique du Congo Belge

Bull Inf Inst Text Fr Nord — Bulletin d'Information. Institut Textile de France - Nord

Bull Infirm Cathol Can — Bulletin. Infirmieres Catholiques du Canada

Bull Inf ITF Nord — Bulletin d'Information. ITF [*Institut Textile de France*] Nord

Bull Inf Minist Agric — Bulletin d'Information. Ministere de l'Agriculture

Bull Inform Inst Nat Etud Agron Congo (INEAC) — Bulletin d'Information. Institut National pour l'Etude Agronomique du Congo Belge (INEAC)

Bull Inform Inst Rebois Tunis — Bulletin d'Information. Institut de Reboisement de Tunis

Bull Inform Tech Centre Tech Bois — Bulletin d'Informations Techniques. Centre Technique du Bois

Bull Inf Rizic Fr — Bulletin d'Information des Riziculteurs de France

Bull Inf Sci Tech — Bulletin d'Informations Scientifiques et Techniques

Bull Inf Sci Tech Commis Energ At — Bulletin d'Informations Scientifiques et Techniques. Commissariat a l'Energie Atomique [*France*]

Bull Inf Sci & Tech (Paris) — Bulletin d'Informations Scientifiques et Techniques (Paris)

Bull Inf Stn Exp Avic Ploufragan — Bulletin d'Information. Station Experimentale d'Aviculture de Ploufragan

Bull Inf Tech Charbon Fr — Bulletin d'Informations Techniques. Charbonages de France

Bull Inst Agric Res Rolling Land (Tokyo) — Bulletin. Institute for Agricultural Research on Rolling Land (Tokyo)

Bull Inst Agric Res Tohoku Univ — Bulletin. Institute for Agricultural Research. Tohoku University

Bull Inst Agron Sta Rech Gembloux — Bulletin. Institut Agronomique et Stations de Recherches de Gembloux

Bull Inst Agron Stn Rech Gembloux — Bulletin. Institut Agronomique et Stations de Recherches de Gembloux

Bull Inst Agron Stn Rech Gembloux Hors Ser — Bulletin. Institut Agronomique et Stations de Recherches de Gembloux. Hors Serie

Bull Inst Agron Stns Rech Gembloux — Bulletin. Institut Agronomique et Stations de Recherches de Gembloux

Bull Inst Agr Res Tohoku Univ — Bulletin. Institute for Agricultural Research. Tohoku University

Bull Inst Archaeol Univ London — Bulletin. Institute of Archaeology. University of London

Bull Inst Archeol Liegeois — Bulletin. Institut Archeologique Liegeois

Bull Inst Arch Liegeois — Bulletin. Institut Archeologique Liegeois

Bull Inst At Energ Kyoto Univ — Bulletin. Institute of Atomic Energy. Kyoto University [*Japan*]

Bull Inst At Energy Kyoto Univ — Bulletin. Institute of Atomic Energy. Kyoto University

Bull Inst Balneother — Bulletin. Institute of Balneotherapeutics [*Japan*]

Bull Inst Basic Sci Inha Univ — Bulletin. Institute for Basic Science. Inha University

Bull Inst Chem Acad Sin — Bulletin. Institute of Chemistry. Academia Sinica [*Taiwan*]

Bull Inst Chem Res Kyoto Univ — Bulletin. Institute for Chemical Research. Kyoto University

Bull Inst Classic Stud — Bulletin. Institute of Classical Studies. University of London

Bull Inst Const Med Kumamoto Univ — Bulletin. Institute of Constitutional Medicine. Kumamoto University

Bull Inst Corros Sci Technol — Bulletin. Institute of Corrosion Science and Technology

Bull Inst Desert Egypte — Bulletin. Institut du Desert d'Egypte

Bull Inst Egypt — Bulletin. Institut d'Egypte

Bull Inst Email Vitrifie — Bulletin. Institut de l'Email Vitrifie

Bull Inst Eng — Bulletin. Institution of Engineers

Bull Inst Eng (India) — Bulletin. Institution of Engineers (India)

Bull Inst Filip Geol — Bulletin. Institute of Filipino Geologists

Bull Inst Fondam Afr Noire Ser A Sci Nat — Bulletin. Institut Fondamental d'Afrique Noire. Serie A. Sciences Naturelles

Bull Inst Fr Archeol Orient — Bulletin. Institut Francais d'Archeologie Orientale

Bull Inst Fr Cafe Cacao — Bulletin. Institut Francais du Cafe et du Cacao

Bull Inst Gen Psychol — Bulletin. Institut General Psychologique

Bull Inst Geol Bassin Aquitaine — Bulletin. Institut de Geologie du Bassin d'Aquitaine

Bull Inst Geol Geophys Res (Belgrade) Ser A — Bulletin. Institute for Geological and Geophysical Research (Belgrade). Series A. Geology

Bull Inst Geol Geophys Res (Belgrade) Ser B — Bulletin. Institute for Geological and Geophysical Research (Belgrade). Series B. Engineering Geology and Hydrogeology

Bull Inst Geol Geophys Res (Belgrade) Ser C — Bulletin. Institute for Geological and Geophysical Research (Belgrade). Series C. Applied Geophysics

Bull Inst Geol Geophys Res Ser A (Engl Transl) — Bulletin. Institute for Geological and Geophysical Research. Series A. Geology (English Translation)

Bull Inst Geol Geophys Res Ser B (Engl Trans) — Bulletin. Institute for Geological and Geophysical Research. Series B. Engineering Geology and Hydrogeology (English Translation)

Bull Inst Geol Geophys Res Ser C (Eng Trans) — Bulletin. Institute for Geological and Geophysical Research. Series C. Applied Geophysics (English Translation)

Bull Inst Geol Sci — Bulletin. Institute of Geological Sciences

Bull Inst Geol Univ Louis Pasteur Strasbourg — Bulletin. Institut de Geologie. Universite Louis Pasteur de Strasbourg

Bull Inst Geophys Natl Cent Univ — Bulletin. Institute of Geophysics. National Central University [*Taiwan*]

Bull Inst Hist Res — Bulletin. Institute of Historical Research

Bull Inst Immunol Sci Hokkaido Univ — Bulletin. Institute of Immunological Science. Hokkaido University

Bull Inst Ind Soc Dev — Bulletin. Institute for Industrial and Social Development [*South Korea*]

Bull Inst Internat Statist — Bulletin. Institut International de Statistique

Bull Inst Int Froid — Bulletin. Institut International du Froid

Bull Inst Int Froid Annexe — Bulletin. Institut International du Froid. Annexe [*France*]

Bull Inst Jam Sci Ser — Bulletin. Institute of Jamaica. Science Series

Bull Inst Marit Trop Med Gdynia — Bulletin. Institute of Maritime and Tropical Medicine in Gdynia

Bull Inst Mar Med Gdansk — Bulletin. Institute of Marine Medicine in Gdansk

Bull Inst Mar Trop Med Gdynia — Bulletin. Institute of Maritime and Tropical Medicine in Gdynia

Bull Inst Math Acad Sinica — Bulletin. Institute of Mathematics. Academia Sinica

Bull Inst Math Appl — Bulletin. Institute of Mathematics and Its Applications

Bull Inst Med Research FMS — Bulletin. Institute for Medical Research. Federated Malay States

Bull Inst Med Res (Kuala Lumpur) — Bulletin. Institute for Medical Research (Kuala Lumpur)

Bull Inst Med Res Univ Madr — Bulletin. Institute for Medical Research. University of Madrid

Bull Inst Met — Bulletin. Institute of Metals
Bull Inst Met Finish — Bulletin. Institute of Metal Finishing
Bull Inst Min Metall — Bulletin. Institution of Mining and Metallurgy
Bull Inst Nat Educ Shiga Heights — Bulletin. Institute of Natural Education in Shiga Heights
Bull Inst Natl Hyg (Paris) — Bulletin. Institut National d'Hygiene (Paris)
Bull Inst Natl Sante Rech Med (Paris) — Bulletin. Institut National de la Sante et de la Recherche Medicale (Paris)
Bull Inst Natl Sci Rech Oceanogr Peche — Bulletin. Institut National Scientifique et Technique d'Oceanographie et de Peche
Bull Inst Nutr Bulg Acad Sci — Bulletin. Institute of Nutrition. Bulgarian Academy of Sciences
Bull Inst Obs Phys Globe Puy De Dome — Bulletin. Institut et Observatoire Physique du Globe du Puy De Dome
Bull Inst Oceanogr Fish — Bulletin. Institute of Oceanography and Fisheries
Bull Inst Oceanogr (Monaco) — Bulletin. Institut Oceanographique (Monaco)
Bull Inst Pap Chem — Bulletin. Institute of Paper Chemistry
Bull Inst Pasteur — Bulletin. Institut Pasteur [*Paris*]
Bull Inst Pasteur (Paris) — Bulletin. Institut Pasteur (Paris)
Bull Inst Peches Marit Maroc — Bulletin. Institut des Peches Maritimes du Maroc
Bull Inst Phys Chem Res — Bulletin. Institute of Physical and Chemical Research
Bull Inst Phys (Malays) — Bulletin. Institute of Physics (Malaysia)
Bull Inst Phys Univ Libre Bruxelles — Bulletin. Institut de Physique. Universite Libre de Bruxelles [*Belgium*]
Bull Inst Post Grad Med Educ Res — Bulletin. Institute of Post Graduate Medical Education and Research
Bull Inst Prov Coop Agr — Bulletin. Institut Provincial de Cooperation Agricole
Bull Inst Public Health (Tokyo) — Bulletin. Institute of Public Health (Tokyo)
Bull Inst Radiat Breed — Bulletin. Institute of Radiation Breeding [*Japan*]
Bull Inst R Sci Nat Belg — Bulletin. Institut Royal des Sciences Naturelles de Belgique
Bull Inst R Sci Nat Belg Biol — Bulletin. Institut Royal des Sciences Naturelles de Belgique. Biologie
Bull Inst R Sci Nat Belg Entomol — Bulletin. Institut Royal des Sciences Naturelles de Belgique. Entomologie
Bull Inst R Sci Nat Belg Sci Terre — Bulletin. Institut Royal des Sciences Naturelles de Belgique. Sciences de la Terre
Bull Instrum Nucl — Bulletin d'Instrumentation Nucleaire
Bull Inst Sanit Eng — Bulletin. Institution of Sanitary Engineers
Bull Inst Space Aeronaut Sci Univ Tokyo — Bulletin. Institute of Space and Aeronautical Science. University of Tokyo
Bull Inst Space & Aeronaut Sci Univ Tokyo A — Bulletin. Institute of Space and Aeronautical Science. University of Tokyo. A
Bull Inst Space & Aeronaut Sci Univ Tokyo B — Bulletin. Institute of Space and Aeronautical Science. University of Tokyo. B
Bull Inst Verre — Bulletin. Institut du Verre
Bull Inst Vitreous Enamellers — Bulletin. Institute of Vitreous Enamellers
Bull Inst Zool Acad Sin (Taipei) — Bulletin. Institute of Zoology. Academia Sinica (Taipei)
Bull Int Acad Pol Sci Lett Cl Sci Math Nat Ser A — Bulletin International. Academie Polonaise des Sciences et des Lettres. Classe des Sciences Mathematiques et Naturelles. Serie A. Sciences Mathematiques [*Poland*]
Bull Int Acad Pol Sci Lett Cl Sci Math Nat Ser B 1 — Bulletin International. Academie Polonaise des Sciences et des Lettres. Classe des Sciences Mathematiques et Naturelles. Serie B 1. Botanique
Bull Int Acad Sci Cracovie — Bulletin International. Academie des Sciences de Cracovie
Bull Int Acad Yougoslave Sci Beaux-Arts Cl Sci Math Nat — Bulletin International. Academie Yougoslave des Sciences et des Beaux-Arts. Classe des Sciences Mathematiques et Naturelles [*Yugoslavia*]
Bull Int Assoc Eng Geol — Bulletin. International Association of Engineering Geology
Bull Int Assoc Med Mus — Bulletin. International Association of Medical Museums
Bull Int Assoc Sci Hydrol — Bulletin. International Association of Scientific Hydrology
Bull Int Assoc Shell Spat Struct — Bulletin. International Association for Shell and Spatial Structures
Bull Int Ass Sci Hydrol — Bulletin. International Association of Scientific Hydrology
Bull Int Ass Shell Struct — Bulletin. International Association for Shell Structures
Bull Int Ass Wood Anatomists — Bulletin. International Association of Wood Anatomists
Bull Intern Assocn Paper Hist — Bulletin. International Association of Paper Historians
Bull for Internat Fiscal Docum — Bulletin for International Fiscal Documentation
Bull Int Fisc Doc — Bulletin for International Fiscal Documentation
Bull Int Inst Ref — International Institute of Refrigeration. Bulletin [*Paris*]
Bull Int Inst Refrig — Bulletin. International Institute of Refrigeration
Bull for Int'l Fisc Doc — Bulletin for International Fiscal Documentation
Bull Int Off Epizoot — Bulletin. International Office of Epizootics

Bull Int Peat Soc — Bulletin. International Peat Society
Bull Int Potash Inst — Bulletin. International Potash Institute
Bull Int Ry Congr Ass — Bulletin. International Railway Congress Association
Bull Int Ser Sante Armees Terre Mer Air — Bulletin International. Services de Sante des Armees de Terre, de Mer, et de l'Air
Bull Int Soc Trop Ecol — Bulletin. International Society for Tropical Ecology
Bull Int Union Cancer — Bulletin. International Union Against Cancer [*Switzerland*]
Bull Int Union Tuberc — Bulletin. International Union Against Tuberculosis
Bull Invent — Bulletin on Inventions [*United States*]
Bull Iowa Agr Exp Sta — Bulletin. Iowa Agricultural Experiment Station
Bull Iowa Nurses Assoc — Bulletin. Iowa Nurses Association
Bull Iowa State Univ Sci Technol Eng Exp Stn — Bulletin. Iowa State University of Science and Technology. Engineering Experiment Station
Bull Iranian Math Soc — Bulletin. Iranian Mathematical Society
Bull Iranian Petrol Inst — Bulletin. Iranian Petroleum Institute
Bull Iran Pet Inst — Bulletin. Iranian Petroleum Institute
Bull Iraq Nat Hist Mus (Univ Baghdad) — Bulletin. Iraq Natural History Museum (University of Baghdad)
Bull IRO (Aust) — Bulletin. Commonwealth Scientific and Industrial Research Organisation (Australia)
Bull Ishikawa Prefect Coll Agric — Bulletin. Ishikawa Prefecture College of Agriculture
Bull Isr Phys Soc — Bulletin. Israel Physical Society
Bull Isr Soc Spec Libr & Inf Cent — Bulletin. Israel Society of Special Libraries and Information Centres
Bull Iwate-Ken Agr Exp Sta — Bulletin. Iwate-Ken Agricultural Experiment Station
Bull Iwate Univ For — Bulletin. Iwate University Forests
Bull Jam Geol Surv — Bulletin. Jamaica Geological Survey
Bull Japan Soc Precis Engng — Bulletin. Japan Society of Precision Engineering
Bull Jap Pet Inst — Bulletin. Japan Petroleum Institute
Bull Jap Soc Grinding Eng — Bulletin. Japan Society of Grinding Engineers
Bull Jap Soc Mech E — Japan Society of Mechanical Engineers. Bulletin
Bull Jap Soc Precis Eng — Bulletin. Japan Society of Precision Engineering
Bull Jard Bot Buitenzorg — Bulletin. Jardin Botanique de Buitenzorg
Bull Jard Bot Etat Brux — Bulletin. Jardin Botanique de l'Etat a Bruxelles
Bull Jard Bot Natl Belg — Bulletin. Jardin Botanique National de Belgique
Bull Jard Bot Natn Belg — Bulletin. Jardin Botanique National de Belgique
Bull Jealott's Hill Res St — Bulletin. Jealott's Hill Research Station
Bull Johns Hopk Hosp — Bulletin. Johns Hopkins Hospital
Bull Johns Hopkins Hosp — Bulletin. Johns Hopkins Hospital
Bull Josai Dent Univ — Bulletin. Josai Dental University
Bull Jpn Electron Mater Soc — Bulletin. Japan Electronic Materials Society
Bull Jpn Entomol Acad — Bulletin. Japan Entomological Academy
Bull Jpn Inst Met — Bulletin. Japan Institute of Metals
Bull Jpn Min Ind Assoc — Bulletin. Japan Mining Industry Association
Bull Jpn Pet Inst — Bulletin. Japan Petroleum Institute
Bull Jpn Sea Reg Fish Res Lab — Bulletin. Japan Sea Regional Fisheries Research Laboratories
Bull Jpn Soc Mech Eng — Bulletin. Japan Society of Mechanical Engineers
Bull Jpn Soc Phycol — Bulletin. Japanese Society of Phycology
Bull Jpn Soc Precis Eng — Bulletin. Japan Society of Precision Engineering
Bull Jpn Soc Sci Fish — Bulletin. Japanese Society of Scientific Fisheries
Bull Jpn Soc Tuberc — Bulletin. Japanese Society of Tuberculosis
Bull JSAE — Bulletin. JSAE [*Japan Society of Automotive Engineers*]
Bull JSME — Bulletin. JSME [*Japan Society of Mechanical Engineers*]
Bull Kagawa Agr Exp Sta — Bulletin. Kagawa Agricultural Experiment Station
Bull Kagawa Agric Exp Stn — Bulletin. Kagawa Agricultural Experiment Station
Bull Kagoshima Univ For — Bulletin. Kagoshima University Forest
Bull Kanagawa Agric Exp Stn — Bulletin. Kanagawa Agricultural Experiment Station
Bull Kanagawa Hort Exp Stn — Bulletin. Kanagawa Horticultural Experiment Station
Bull Kanagawa Hortic Exp Stn — Bulletin. Kanagawa Horticultural Experiment Station
Bull Kans Agr Exp Sta — Bulletin. Kansas Agricultural Experiment Station
Bull Kans Agric Exp Stn — Bulletin. Kansas Agricultural Experiment Station
Bull Kansas City Vet Coll Quart — Bulletin. Kansas City Veterinary College. Quarterly
Bull Kans Eng Exp Stn — Bulletin. Kansas Engineering Experiment Station
Bull Kans State Geol Surv — Bulletin. Kansas State Geological Survey
Bull K Belg Inst Natuurwet Aardwet — Bulletin van het Koninklijke Belgische Instituut voor Natuurwetenschappen. Aardwetenschappen
Bull K Belg Inst Natuurwet Biol — Bulletin van het Koninklijke Belgische Instituut voor Natuurwetenschappen. Biologie
Bull K Belg Inst Natuurwet Entomol — Bulletin van het Koninklijke Belgische Instituut voor Natuurwetenschappen. Entomologie
Bull Kent County Med Soc — Bulletin. Kent County Medical Society [*California*]
Bull Kesennuma Miyagi Prefect Fish Exp Stn — Bulletin. Kesennuma Miyagi Prefectural Fisheries Experiment Station

Bull King County Med Soc — Bulletin. King County Medical Society [*Washington*]
Bull Kisarazu Tech Coll — Bulletin. Kisarazu Technical College
Bull Kobayasi Inst Phys Res — Bulletin. Kobayasi Institute of Physical Research
Bull Kobe Med Coll — Bulletin. Kobe Medical College
Bull Kochi Tech Coll — Bulletin. Kochi Technical College
Bull Korean Chem Soc — Bulletin. Korean Chemical Society [*South Korea*]
Bull Korean Fish Soc — Bulletin. Korean Fisheries Society
Bull KY Agr Exp Sta — Bulletin. Kentucky Agricultural Experiment Station
Bull KY Agric Exp Stn — Bulletin. Kentucky Agricultural Experiment Station
Bull Kyoto Daigaku Inst Chem Res — Bulletin. Kyoto Daigaku Institute for Chemical Research
Bull Kyoto Gakugei Univ Ser B Math Nat Sci — Bulletin. Kyoto Gakugei University. Series B. Mathematics and Natural Science
Bull Kyoto Prefect Univ For — Bulletin. Kyoto Prefectural University Forests
Bull Kyoto Univ Ed Ser B — Bulletin. Kyoto University of Education. Series B. Mathematics and Natural Science
Bull Kyoto Univ Educ Ser B Math Nat Sci — Bulletin. Kyoto University of Education. Series B. Mathematics and Natural Science
Bull Kyoto Univ For — Bulletin. Kyoto University Forests
Bull Kyushu Agr Exp Sta — Bulletin. Kyushu Agricultural Experiment Station
Bull Kyushu Agric Exp Stn — Bulletin. Kyushu Agricultural Experiment Station
Bull Kyushu Inst Tech Math Natur Sci — Bulletin. Kyushu Institute of Technology. Mathematics and Natural Science
Bull Kyushu Inst Technol Math Nat Sci — Bulletin. Kyushu Institute of Technology. Mathematics and Natural Science
Bull Kyushu Inst Technol Sci & Technol — Bulletin. Kyushu Institute of Technology. Science and Technology
Bull Kyushu Univ For — Bulletin. Kyushu University Forests
Bull LA Agr Exp Sta — Bulletin. Louisiana Agricultural Experiment Station
Bull LA Agric Exp Stn — Bulletin. Louisiana Agricultural Experiment Station
Bull Lab Biol Appl (Paris) — Bulletin. Laboratoire de Biologie Appliquee (Paris)
Bull Lab Geol Mineral Geophys Mus Geol Univ Laus — Bulletin. Laboratoires de Geologie, Mineralogie, Geophysique, et Musee Geologique. Universite de Lausanne
Bull Lab Geol Mineral Geophys Mus Geol Univ Lausanne — Bulletin. Laboratoires de Geologie, Mineralogie, Geophysique, et Musee Geologique. Universite de Lausanne
Bull Lab Marit Dinard — Bulletin. Laboratoire Maritime de Dinard
Bull Lab Prof — Bulletin du Laboratoire Professionnel
Bull LA Co-Op Ext Serv — Bulletin. Louisiana Cooperative Extension Service
Bull Landbproefstn Suriname — Bulletin. Landbouwproefstation in Suriname
Bull LA Neurol Soc — Bulletin. Los Angeles Neurological Societies
Bull Liaison Lab Lab Prof Pein Bitry Thiais (Fr) — Bulletin de Liaison du Laboratoire. Laboratoire de la Profession des Peintures Bitry Thiais (France)
Bull Liaison Lab Ponts Chaussees — Bulletin de Liaison des Laboratoires des Ponts et Chaussees
Bull Liaison Rech Inform Automat — Bulletin de Liaison de la Recherche en Informatique et Automatique [*Rocquencourt*]
Bull Liberia Geol Surv — Bulletin. Liberia Geological Survey
Bull London Math Soc — Bulletin. London Mathematical Society
Bull Los Ang Cty Mus Nat Hist Sci — Bulletin. Los Angeles County Museum of Natural History. Contributions in Science
Bull Los Angeles Dent Soc — Bulletin. Los Angeles Dental Society
Bull Los Angeles Neurol Soc — Bulletin. Los Angeles Neurological Societies
Bull Los Ang Neurol Soc — Bulletin. Los Angeles Neurological Societies
Bull L Sci and Tech — Bulletin of Law, Science, and Technology
Bull Madhya Pradesh Agric Dep — Bulletin. Madhya Pradesh Agriculture Department
Bull Madras Gov Mus (Nat Hist Sect) — Bulletin. Madras Government Museum (Natural History Section)
Bull Malaysian Math Soc — Bulletin. Malaysian Mathematical Society
Bull Malaysian Math Soc (2) — Bulletin. Malaysian Mathematical Society. Second Series [*Kuala Lumpur*]
Bull Malays Kementerian Pertanian — Bulletin. Malaysia Kementerian Pertanian
Bull Malays Minist Agric Rural Dev — Bulletin. Malaysia Ministry of Agriculture and Rural Development
Bull Manila Med Soc — Bulletin. Manila Medical Society
Bull Mar Biol Stn Asamushi — Bulletin. Marine Biological Station of Asamushi
Bull Mar Ecol — Bulletins of Marine Ecology
Bull Marine Sci — Bulletin of Marine Science
Bull Marine Sci Gulf and Caribbean — Bulletin. Marine Science of the Gulf and Caribbean [*Later, Bulletin of Marine Science*]
Bull Mar Sci — Bulletin of Marine Science
Bull Mar Sci Gulf Caribb — Bulletin. Marine Science of the Gulf and Caribbean [*Later, Bulletin of Marine Science*]
Bull Mason Clinic — Bulletin. Mason Clinic
Bull Mass Agr Exp Sta — Bulletin. Massachusetts Agricultural Experiment Station
Bull Mass Agric Exp Sta — Bulletin. Massachusetts Agricultural Experiment Station

Bull Mass Audubon Soc — Bulletin. Massachusetts Audubon Society
Bull Mass Nurses Assoc — Bulletin. Massachusetts Nurses Association
Bull Mat Biophys — Bulletin of Mathematical Biophysics
Bull Mater Sci — Bulletin of Materials Science [*India*]
Bull Mater Sci (India) — Bulletin of Materials Science (India)
Bull Math — Bulletin Mathematique [*Romania*]
Bull Math Biol — Bulletin of Mathematical Biology
Bull Math Biology — Bulletin of Mathematical Biology
Bull Math Soc Sci Math RS Roumanie — Bulletin Mathematique. Societe des Sciences Mathematiques de la Republique Socialiste de Roumanie
Bull Math Statist — Bulletin of Mathematical Statistics
Bull MD Agr Exp Sta — Bulletin. Maryland Agricultural Experiment Station
Bull MD Agric Exp Stn — Bulletin. Maryland Agricultural Experiment Station
Bull MD Herpetol Soc — Bulletin. Maryland Herpetological Society
Bull ME Agric Exp Sta — Bulletin. Maine University Agricultural Experiment Station
Bull ME Agric Exp Stn — Bulletin. Maine Agricultural Experiment Station
Bull Mech Eng Educ — Bulletin of Mechanical Engineering Education
Bull Mech Eng Lab — Bulletin. Mechanical Engineering Laboratory
Bull Mech Engng Educ — Bulletin of Mechanical Engineering Education
Bull Med Coll VA — Bulletin. Medical College of Virginia
Bull Med Leg Toxicol Med — Bulletin de Medecine Legale et de Toxicologie Medicale
Bull Med Libr Ass — Bulletin. Medical Library Association
Bull Med Libr Assoc — Bulletin. Medical Library Association
Bull Med Nord — Bulletin Medical du Nord
Bull Med (Paris) — Bulletin Medical (Paris)
Bull Med Res Natl Soc Med Res — Bulletin for Medical Research. National Society for Medical Research
Bull Med Staff Methodist Hosp Dallas — Bulletin. Medical Staff of Methodist Hospitals of Dallas
Bull Med Suisses — Bulletin des Medecins Suisses
Bull ME For Dep — Bulletin. Maine Forestry Department
Bull Meiji Coll Pharm — Bulletin. Meiji College of Pharmacy [*Japan*]
Bull Mem Acad R Med Belg — Bulletin et Memoires. Academie Royale de Medecine de Belgique
Bull Mem Ec Prep Med Pharm Dakar — Bulletins et Memoires. Ecole Preparatoire de Medecine et de Pharmacie de Dakar
Bull Mem Fac Med Pharm Dakar — Bulletins et Memoires. Faculte de Medecine et de Pharmacie de Dakar
Bull et Mem Soc Anat Paris — Bulletins et Memoires. Societe Anatomique de Paris
Bull Mem Soc Anthropol Paris — Bulletins et Memoires. Societe d'Anthropologie de Paris
Bull et Mem Soc Centr Med Vet — Bulletins et Memoires. Societe Centrale de Medecine Veterinaire
Bull Mem Soc Chir Paris — Bulletin et Memoires. Societe des Chirurgiens de Paris
Bull et Mem Soc Chir Paris — Bulletin et Memoires. Societe de Chirurgie de Paris
Bull Mem Soc Fr Ophtalmol — Bulletins et Memoires. Societe Francaise d'Ophtalmologie
Bull et Mem Soc Med Hop Bucarest — Bulletins et Memoires. Societe Medicale des Hopitaux de Bucarest
Bull et Mem Soc Med Hop Paris — Bulletins et Memoires. Societe Medicale des Hopitaux de Paris
Bull Mem Soc Med Paris — Bulletin et Memoires. Societe de Medecine de Paris
Bull et Mem Soc Nat Chir (Paris) — Bulletins et Memoires. Societe Nationale de Chirurgie (Paris)
Bull Mem Soc Natl Chir — Bulletins et Memoires. Societe Nationale de Chirurgie
Bull et Mem Soc Therap — Bulletins et Memoires. Societe de Therapeutique
Bull Menninger Clin — Bulletin. Menninger Clinic
Bull Mens Ecole Super Agr Viticult Angers — Bulletin Mensuel. Ecole Superieure d'Agriculture et de Viticulture d'Angers
Bull Mens Nat Belg — Bulletin Mensuel des Naturalistes Belges
Bull Mens Soc Linn Lyon — Bulletin Mensuel. Societe Linneenne de Lyon
Bull Mens Soc Vet Prat France — Bulletin Mensuel. Societe Veterinaire Pratique de France
Bull Met Mus — Bulletin. Metals Museum [*Japan*]
Bull Metrol — Bulletin de Metrologie
Bull Meun Fr — Bulletin Meunerie Francaise
Bull Mich Agric Coll — Bulletin. Michigan Agricultural College
Bull Mich Agric Coll Exp Stn — Bulletin. Michigan Agricultural College. Experiment Station
Bull Mich State Dent Soc — Bulletin. Michigan State Dental Society
Bull Mich St Univ — Bulletin. Michigan State University
Bull Microscopie Appl — Bulletin de Microscopie Appliquee
Bull Millard Fillmore Hosp — Bulletin. Millard Fillmore Hospital
Bull Min Agr Land (Jamaica) — Bulletin. Ministry of Agriculture and Lands (Jamaica)
Bull Mineral — Bulletin de Mineralogie [*France*]
Bull Mineral Res Explor Inst (Turkey) — Bulletin. Mineral Research and Exploration Institute (Turkey). Foreign Edition

Bull Miner Ind Exp Stn PA State Univ — Bulletin. Mineral Industries Experiment Station. Pennsylvania State University

Bull Miner Res Explor Inst (Turk) — Bulletin. Mineral Research and Exploration Institute (Turkey)

Bull Miner Res Explor Inst (Turk) Foreign Ed — Bulletin. Mineral Research and Exploration Institute (Turkey). Foreign Edition

Bull Minist Agric Egypt Tech Scient Serv — Bulletin. Ministry of Agriculture. Egypt Technical and Scientific Service

Bull Minist Agric Fish Fd — Bulletin. Ministry of Agriculture, Fisheries, and Food

Bull Minist Agric Fish Fd (Lond) — Bulletin. Ministry of Agriculture, Fisheries, and Food (London)

Bull Minist Agric Fish Food (GB) — Bulletin. Ministry of Agriculture, Fisheries, and Food (Great Britain)

Bull Minist Agric Fish (NZ) — Bulletin. Ministry of Agriculture and Fisheries (New Zealand)

Bull Minist Agric (Queb) — Bulletin. Ministry of Agriculture (Quebec)

Bull Minist Agric Rural Dev (Malays) — Bulletin. Ministry of Agriculture and Rural Development (Malaysia)

Bull Minn Geol Surv — Bulletin. Minnesota Geological Survey

Bull Misaki Mar Biol Inst Kyoto Univ — Bulletin. Misaki Marine Biological Institute. Kyoto University

Bull Misc Inf R Bot Gard — Bulletin of Miscellaneous Information. Royal Botanic Garden

Bull Miss Agric Exp Sta — Bulletin. Mississippi State University. Agricultural Experiment Station

Bull Miss Agric Exp Stn — Bulletin. Mississippi Agricultural Experiment Station

Bull Miss State Univ Agr Exp Sta — Bulletin. Mississippi State University. Agricultural Experiment Station

Bull Miyagi Agr Coll — Bulletin. Miyagi Agricultural College

Bull Miyagi Agric Coll — Bulletin. Miyagi Agricultural College

Bull Miyazaki Agr Exp Sta — Bulletin. Miyazaki Agricultural Experiment Station

Bull Mizunami Fossil Mus — Bulletin. Mizunami Fossil Museum

Bull MO Acad Sci Suppl — Bulletin. Missouri Academy of Science. Supplement

Bull MO Bot Gdn — Bulletin. Missouri Botanical Garden

Bull MO Hist Soc — Bulletin. Missouri Historical Society

Bull Mol Biol Med — Bulletin of Molecular Biology and Medicine

Bull Mon — Bulletin Monumental

Bull Monroe County Med Soc — Bulletin. Monroe County Medical Society [*New York*]

Bull Mont Agr Exp Sta — Bulletin. Montana Agricultural Experiment Station

Bull Montana Agric Exp Stn — Bulletin. Montana Agricultural Experiment Station

Bull Montg-Bucks Dent Soc — Bulletin. Montgomery-Bucks Dental Society

Bull Mont State Coll Coop Ext Serv — Bulletin. Montana State College. Cooperative Extension Service

Bull Morioka Tob Exp Stn — Bulletin. Morioka Tobacco Experiment Station

Bull Mt Desert Isl Biol Lab — Bulletin. Mount Desert Island Biological Laboratory

Bull Mukogawa Women's Univ Nat Sci — Bulletin. Mukogawa Women's University. Natural Science [*Japan*]

Bull Murithienne — Bulletin de la Murithienne

Bull Mus Comp Zool — Bulletin. Museum of Comparative Zoology

Bull Mus Comp Zool Harv — Bulletin. Museum of Comparative Zoology at Harvard University

Bull Mus Comp Zool Harv Univ — Bulletin. Museum of Comparative Zoology at Harvard University

Bull Mus Hist Nat Mars — Bulletin. Museum d'Histoire Naturelle de Marseille

Bull Mus Hist Nat Marseille — Bulletin. Musee d'Histoire Naturelle de Marseille

Bull Mus Hist Nat Pays Serbe — Bulletin. Museum d'Histoire Naturelle du Pays Serbe

Bull Mus Hong — Bulletin. Musee Hongrois des Beaux-Arts

Bull Mus Nat Hist Nat (Paris) — Bulletin. Museum National d'Histoire Naturelle (Paris)

Bull Mus Natl Hist Nat — Bulletin. Museum National d'Histoire Naturelle [*Paris*]

Bull Mus Natl Hist Nat Bot — Bulletin. Museum National d'Histoire Naturelle. Botanique [*Paris*]

Bull Mus Natl Hist Nat Ecol Gen — Bulletin. Museum National d'Histoire Naturelle. Ecologie Generale [*Paris*]

Bull Mus Natl Hist Nat Sci Terre — Bulletin. Museum National d'Histoire Naturelle. Sciences de la Terre [*Paris*]

Bull Mus Natl Hist Nat Ser 3 Sci Terre — Bulletin. Museum National d'Histoire Naturelle. Serie 3. Sciences de la Terre [*Paris*]

Bull Mus Natl Hist Nat Zool — Bulletin. Museum National d'Histoire Naturelle. Zoologie [*Paris*]

Bull Mus R Hist Nat Belg — Bulletin. Musee Royal d'Histoire Naturelle de la Belgique

Bull Mus Roy Beaux Arts Belg — Bulletin. Musees Royaux des Beaux-Arts de Belgique

Bull Mysore Geol Assoc — Bulletin. Mysore Geologists Association

Bull Nagano Agr Exp Sta — Bulletin. Nagano Agricultural Experiment Station

Bull Nagaoka Munic Sci Mus — Bulletin. Nagaoka Municipal Science Museum

Bull Nagoya City Univ Dep Gen Educ Nat Sci Sect — Bulletin. Nagoya City University. Department of General Education. Natural Science Section

Bull Nagoya Inst Tech — Bulletin. Nagoya Institute of Technology

Bull Nagoya Inst Technol — Bulletin. Nagoya Institute of Technology

Bull Naikai Reg Fish Res Lab — Bulletin. Naikai Regional Fisheries Research Laboratory [*Japan*]

Bull N Am Gladiolus Counc — Bulletin. North American Gladiolus Council

Bull Naniwa Univ Ser A — Bulletin. Naniwa University. Series A. Engineering and Natural Sciences

Bull Naniwa Univ Ser B — Bulletin. Naniwa University. Series B. Agricultural and Natural Science

Bull Nansei Reg Fish Res Lab — Bulletin. Nansei Regional Fisheries Research Laboratories

Bull Nara Univ Ed Natur Sci — Bulletin. Nara University of Education. Natural Science

Bull Nara Univ Educ Nat Sci — Bulletin. Nara University of Education. Natural Science

Bull Narc — Bulletin on Narcotics

Bull Narcotics — Bulletin on Narcotics

Bull Nat Assoc Wool Manuf — Bulletin. National Association of Wool Manufacturers

Bull Nat Dist Heat Assoc — Bulletin. National District Heating Association

Bull Nat Formul Comm — Bulletin. National Formulary Committee

Bull Nat Geophys Res Inst (India) — Bulletin. National Geophysical Research Institute (India)

Bull Nat His Mus Belgr Ser A Mineral Geol Paleontol — Bulletin. Natural History Museum in Belgrade. Series A. Mineralogy, Geology, Paleontology

Bull Nat Hist Mus Belgrade B — Bulletin. Natural History Museum in Belgrade. Series B. Biological Sciences

Bull Nat Hist Mus Belgr Ser B Biol Sci — Bulletin. Natural History Museum in Belgrade. Series B. Biological Sciences

Bull Nat Hist Res Cent Univ Baghdad — Bulletin. Natural History Research Center. University of Baghdad

Bull Nat Inst Anim Ind — Bulletin. National Institute of Animal Industry

Bull Nat Inst Geol Min (Bandung Indonesia) — Bulletin. National Institute of Geology and Mining (Bandung, Indonesia)

Bull Nat Inst Hyg Sci — Bulletin. National Institute of Hygienic Sciences

Bull Natl Bot Gard — Bulletin. National Botanic Garden [*Lucknow, India*]

Bull Natl Fish Univ Busan (Nat Sci) — Bulletin of National Fisheries. University of Busan (Natural Sciences)

Bull Natl Geophys Res Inst (India) — Bulletin. National Geophysical Research Institute (India)

Bull Natl Grassl Res Inst — Bulletin. National Grassland Research Institute [*Japan*]

Bull Natl Hyg Lab (Tokyo) — Bulletin. National Hygienic Laboratory (Tokyo)

Bull Natl Inst Agric Sci Ser A — Bulletin. National Institute of Agricultural Sciences. Series A (Physics and Statistics)

Bull Natl Inst Agric Sci Ser A (Phys Stat) — Bulletin. National Institute of Agricultural Sciences. Series A (Physics and Statistics) (Japan)

Bull Natl Inst Agric Sci Ser B (Soils Fert) (Japan) — Bulletin. National Institute of Agricultural Sciences. Series B (Soils and Fertilizers) (Japan)

Bull Natl Inst Agric Sci Ser D (Physiol Genet) (Japan) — Bulletin. National Institute of Agricultural Sciences. Series D (Physiology and Genetics) (Japan)

Bull Natl Inst Agric Sci Ser G (Anim Husb) — Bulletin. National Institute of Agricultural Sciences. Series G (Animal Husbandry) (Japan)

Bull Natl Inst Agri Sci Ser C — Bulletin. National Institute of Agricultural Sciences. Series C [*Japan*]

Bull Natl Inst Anim Health (Jpn) — Bulletin. National Institute of Animal Health (Japan)

Bull Natl Inst Anim Ind (Chiba) — Bulletin. National Institute of Animal Industry (Chiba)

Bull Natl Inst Hyg Sci (Tokyo) — Bulletin. National Institute of Hygienic Sciences (Tokyo)

Bull Natl Inst Oceanogr (India) — Bulletin. National Institute of Oceanography (India)

Bull Natl Inst Pollut Resour — Bulletin. National Research Institute for Pollution and Resources [*Japan*]

Bull Natl Inst Sci India — Bulletin. National Institute of Sciences of India

Bull Natl Mus (Singapore) — Bulletin. National Museum (Singapore)

Bull Natl Pearl Res Lab — Bulletin. National Pearl Research Laboratory [*Japan*]

Bull Natl Plant Belg — Bulletin. Nationale Plantentuin van Belgie

Bull Natl Res Counc Philipp — Bulletin. National Research Council of the Philippines

Bull Natl Res Inst Tea — Bulletin. National Research Institute of Tea [*Japan*]

Bull Natl Res Lab Metrol — Bulletin. National Research Laboratory of Metrology [*Japan*]

Bull Natl Res Lab Metrology — Bulletin. National Research Laboratory of Metrology [*Japan*]

Bull Natl Sci Found — Bulletin. National Science Foundation

Bull Natl Sci Mus Ser A (Zool) — Bulletin. National Science Museum. Series A (Zoology) (Japan)

Bull Natl Sci Mus Ser B (Bot) — Bulletin. National Science Museum. Series B (Botany) (Japan)

Bull Natl Sci Mus Ser C (Geol) — Bulletin. National Science Museum. Series C (Geology) [*Later, Bulletin. National Science Museum. Series C. (Geology and Paleontology)*] (Japan)

Bull Natl Sci Mus Ser C (Geol Paleontol) — Bulletin. National Science Museum. Series C (Geology and Paleontology) (Japan)

Bull Natl Sci Mus Ser D (Anthropol) — Bulletin. National Science Museum. Series D (Anthropology) (Japan)

Bull Natl Sci Mus (Tokyo) — Bulletin. National Science Museum (Tokyo)

Bull Natl Speleol Soc — Bulletin. National Speleological Society [*United States*]

Bull Natn Inst Agric Sci (Tokyo) — Bulletin. National Institute of Agricultural Sciences (Tokyo)

Bull Natn Inst Hyg Sci (Tokyo) — Bulletin. National Institute of Hygienic Sciences (Tokyo) [*Japan*]

Bull Natn Inst Sci India — Bulletin. National Institute of Sciences of India

Bull Natn Sci Mus (Tokyo) — Bulletin. National Science Museum (Tokyo)

Bull Nat Pearl Res Lab (Jpn) — Bulletin. National Pearl Research Laboratory (Japan)

Bull Nat Res Counc (US) — Bulletin. National Research Council (US)

Bull Nat Res Lab Metrology — Bulletin. National Research Laboratory of Metrology [*Japan*]

Bull Nat Sci (Wellington) — Bulletin of Natural Sciences (Wellington)

Bull N Carol Dep Conserv Dev — Bulletin. North Carolina Department of Conservation and Development

Bull N Carol St Univ Agric Exp Stn — Bulletin. North Carolina State University. Agricultural Experiment Station

Bull NC Div Miner Resour — Bulletin. North Carolina Division of Mineral Resources

Bull NC Div Resour Plann Eval Miner Resour Sect — Bulletin. North Carolina Division of Resource Planning and Evaluation. Mineral Resources Section

Bull N Dak Agr Exp Sta — Bulletin. North Dakota Agricultural Experiment Station

Bull N Dak Agric Exp St — Bulletin. North Dakota Agricultural Experimental Station

Bull N Dak Agric Exp Stn — Bulletin. North Dakota Agricultural Experiment Station

Bull Nebr Agric Exp St — Bulletin. Nebraska Agricultural Experiment Station

Bull Neurol Inst NY — Bulletin. Neurological Institute of New York

Bull Nev Agr Exp St — Bulletin. Nevada Agricultural Experiment Station

Bull New Engl Med Cent — Bulletin. New England Medical Center

Bull New Hamps Agric Exp Stn — Bulletin. New Hampshire Agricultural Experiment Station

Bull New Jers Agric Exp St — Bulletin. New Jersey Agricultural Experiment Station

Bull New Jers Agric Exp Stn — Bulletin. New Jersey Agricultural Experiment Station

Bull New Jers St Soil Conserv Comm — Bulletin. New Jersey State Soil Conservation Committee

Bull New Mex Agric Exp Stn — Bulletin. New Mexico Agricultural Experiment Station

Bull NH Agric Exp Stn — Bulletin. New Hampshire Agricultural Experiment Station

Bull N Hampshire Agric Exper Station — Bulletin. New Hampshire Agricultural Experiment Station

Bull Niger For Dep — Bulletin. Nigerian Forestry Departments

Bull Niigata Univ For — Bulletin. Niigata University Forests

Bull Nippon Dent Coll Gen Educ — Bulletin. Nippon Dental College. General Education

Bull Nippon Dent Univ Gen Educ — Bulletin. Nippon Dental University. General Education

Bull Nippon Vet Zootech Coll — Bulletin. Nippon Veterinary and Zootechnical College

Bull NJ Acad Sci — Bulletin. New Jersey Academy of Science

Bull NJ Agr Exp Sta — Bulletin. New Jersey Agricultural Experiment Station

Bull NJ Bur Geol Topogr — Bulletin. New Jersey Bureau of Geology and Topography

Bull N Mex Agr Exp Sta — Bulletin. New Mexico Agricultural Experiment Station

Bull Norg Geol Unders — Bulletin. Norges Geologiske Undersokelse

Bull North Carolina Bd Health — Bulletin. North Carolina Board of Health

Bull North Scotl Coll Agric — Bulletin. North of Scotland College of Agriculture

Bull NRDC — Bulletin. National Research Development Corporation [*England*]

Bull N Rhodesia Dept Agr — Bulletin. Northern Rhodesia Department of Agriculture

Bull NRLM — Bulletin. NRLM [*National Research Laboratory of Metrology*]

Bull N Scot Coll Agr — Bulletin. North of Scotland College of Agriculture

Bull N Scotl Coll Agric — Bulletin. North of Scotland College of Agriculture

Bull N Scotl Coll Agric Beekeep Dep — Bulletin. North of Scotland College of Agriculture. Beekeeping Department

Bull Nth Terr Austr — Bulletin of the Northern Territory of Australia

Bull Number Theory Related Topics — Bulletin of Number Theory and Related Topics

Bull Nutr Inst UAR — Bulletin. Nutrition Institute of the United Arab Republic

Bull NY Acad Med — Bulletin. New York Academy of Medicine

Bull NY Agr Exp Sta — Bulletin. New York Agricultural Experiment Station

Bull NY Med Coll Flower Fifth Ave — Bulletin. New York Medical College. Flower and Fifth Avenue

Bull NYPL — Bulletin. New York Public Library

Bull NY Pub Lib — Bulletin. New York Public Library

Bull NY St Agric Exp St — Bulletin. New York State Agricultural Experiment Station

Bull NY St Agric Exp Stn — Bulletin. New York State Agricultural Experiment Station

Bull NY State Flower Ind — Bulletin. New York State Flower Industries

Bull NY State Mus — Bulletin. New York State Museum

Bull NY State Mus Sci Serv — Bulletin. New York State Museum and Science Service

Bull NY St Conserv Dep — Bulletin. New York State Conservation Department

Bull NY St Dep Agric — Bulletin. New York State Department of Agriculture

Bull NY St Mus — Bulletin. New York State Museum

Bull NY St Mus Sci Serv — Bulletin. New York State Museum and Science Service

Bull NY Zool Soc — Bulletin. New York Zoological Society

Bull NZ Astr Soc — Bulletin. New Zealand Astronomical Society. Variable Star Section

Bull NZ Dep Scient Ind Res — Bulletin. New Zealand Department of Scientific and Industrial Research

Bull NZ Dept Sci Ind Res — Bulletin. New Zealand Department of Scientific and Industrial Research

Bull NZ Geol Surv — Bulletin. New Zealand Geological Survey

Bull NZ Natl Soc Earthq Eng — Bulletin. New Zealand National Society for Earthquake Engineering

Bull NZ Soc Earthquake Eng — Bulletin. New Zealand Society of Earthquake Engineering

Bull NZ Soc Periodontol — Bulletin. New Zealand Society of Periodontology

Bull Obs Puy De Dome — Bulletin. Observatoire du Puy De Dome

Bull Oceanogr Inst — Bulletin. Oceanographical Institute of Taiwan

Bull Ocean Res Inst Univ Tokyo — Bulletin. Ocean Research Institute. University of Tokyo

Bull OEPP — Bulletin OEPP [*Organisation Europeenne et Mediterraneenne pour la Protection des Plantes*]

Bull Oerlikon — Bulletin Oerlikon [*Switzerland*]

Bull Off Ass Med Dent Fr — Bulletin Officiel. Association des Medecins Dentistes de France

Bull Off Dir Rech Sci Ind Inv (Fr) — Bulletin Officiel. Direction des Recherches Scientifiques et Industrielles et des Inventions (France)

Bull Offic — Bulletin Officiel de la Propriete Industrielle [*Berne*]

Bull Office Exper Stations US Dept Agric — Bulletin. Office of Experiment Stations. United States Department of Agriculture

Bull Office Surg Gen US War Dept — Bulletins. Office of the Surgeon General. United States War Department

Bull Offic Propriete Ind (Fr) — Bulletin Officiel de la Propriete Industrielle (France)

Bull Off Int Epizoot — Bulletin. Office International des Epizooties

Bull Off Int Hyg Publ — Bulletin Mensuel. Office International d'Hygiene Publique

Bull Off Off Int Cacao Choc — Bulletin Officiel. Office International du Cacao et du Chocolat

Bull Off Propr Ind Abr — Bulletin Officiel de la Propriete Industrielle. Abreges

Bull Off Propr Ind Brev Invent Abr Listes — Bulletin Officiel de la Propriete Industrielle. Brevets d'Invention, Abreges, et Listes

Bull Off Soc Int Psycho Proph Obstet — Bulletin Officiel. Societe Internationale de Psychoprophylaxie Obstetricale

Bull Ogata Inst Med Chem Res — Bulletin. Ogata Institute for Medical and Chemical Research

Bull Ohio Agr Exp Sta — Bulletin. Ohio Agricultural Experiment Station

Bull Ohio Agric Exp St — Bulletin. Ohio Agricultural Experiment Station

Bull Ohio Agric Exp Stn — Bulletin. Ohio Agricultural Experiment Station

Bull Ohio Biol Surv — Bulletin. Ohio Biological Survey

Bull Ohio Eng Exp St — Bulletin. Ohio Engineering Experiment Station

Bull Ohio St Univ Co-Op Ext Serv — Bulletin. Ohio State University. Co-Operative Extension Service

Bull Oil Nat Gas Comm — Bulletin. Oil and Natural Gas Commission [*India*]

Bull Oil Natur Gas Comm (India) — Bulletin. Oil and Natural Gas Commission (India)

Bull OIV — Bulletin de l'OIV [*Office International de la Vigne et du Vin*]

Bull Oji Inst For Tree Impr — Bulletin. Oji Institute for Forest Tree Improvement

Bull Okayama Coll Sci — Bulletin. Okayama College of Science

Bull Okayama Tob Exp Stn — Bulletin. Okayama Tobacco Experiment Station

Bull Okla Agric Exp St — Bulletin. Oklahoma Agricultural Experiment Station

Bull Okla Agric Exp Stn — Bulletin. Oklahoma Agricultural Experiment Station

Bull Okla Anthrop Soc — Bulletin. Oklahoma Anthropological Society

Bull Okla Dent Ass — Bulletin. Oklahoma State Dental Association
Bull Okla Geol Surv — Bulletin. Oklahoma Geological Survey
Bull Okla Ornithol Soc — Bulletin. Oklahoma Ornithological Society
Bull Okla State Univ Agr Exp Sta — Bulletin. Oklahoma State University. Agricultural Experiment Station
Bull Ont Agric Coll — Bulletin. Ontario Agricultural College
Bull Ont Coll Pharm — Bulletin. Ontario College of Pharmacy
Bull Ont Dep Agric — Bulletin. Ontario Department of Agriculture
Bull Ont Med Ass — Bulletin. Ontario Medical Association
Bull Oper Res Soc Am — Bulletin. Operations Research Society of America
Bull Ophthalmol Soc Egypt — Bulletin. Ophthalmological Society of Egypt
Bull Ophth Soc Eg — Bulletin. Ophthalmological Society of Egypt
Bull Op Res Soc Am — Bulletin. Operations Research Society of America
Bull Orange County Med Assoc — Bulletin. Orange County Medical Association [California]
Bull Ordre Natl Pharm — Bulletin. Ordre National des Pharmaciens
Bull Ordre Pharm (Brussels) — Bulletin. Ordre des Pharmaciens (Brussels)
Bull Ore Agric Coll — Bulletin. Oregon Agricultural College
Bull Ore Agric Exp Stn — Bulletin. Oregon Agricultural Experiment Station
Bull Ore Ent Soc — Bulletin. Oregon Entomological Society
Bull Ore For Res Lab — Bulletin. Oregon State University. Forest Research Laboratory
Bull Oreg Agr Exp Sta — Bulletin. Oregon Agricultural Experiment Station
Bull Oreg Agric Exp St — Bulletin. Oregon Agricultural Experiment Station
Bull Organ Int Metrol Leg — Bulletin. Organisation Internationale de Metrologie Legale
Bull Org Mond Sante — Bulletin. Organisation Mondiale de la Sante
Bull Orn Soc NZ — Bulletin. Ornithological Society of New Zealand
Bull ORSA — Bulletin. Operations Research Society of America
Bull Orton Soc — Bulletin. Orton Society
Bull Osaka Agric Res Cent — Bulletin. Osaka Agricultural Research Center
Bull Osaka Med Sch — Bulletin. Osaka Medical School
Bull Osaka Med Sch Suppl — Bulletin. Osaka Medical School. Supplement
Bull Osaka Munic Tech Res Inst — Bulletin. Osaka Municipal Technical Research Institute [Japan]
Bull Osaka Mus Nat Hist — Bulletin. Osaka Museum of Natural History
Bull Osaka Prefect Tech College — Bulletin. Osaka Prefectural Technical College
Bull Os Med Sch — Bulletin. Osaka Medical School
Bull Otago Catchm Bd — Bulletin. Otago Catchment Board
Bull Oxf Univ Inst Stat — Bulletin. Oxford University. Institute of Statistics
Bull PA Agr Exp Sta — Bulletin. Pennsylvania Agricultural Experiment Station
Bull PA Agric Exp Stn — Bulletin. Pennsylvania Agricultural Experiment Station
Bull Pacif Orchid Soc Haw — Bulletin. Pacific Orchid Society of Hawaii
Bull Pac Orchid Soc Hawaii — Bulletin. Pacific Orchid Society of Hawaii
Bull Pac Trop Bot Gard — Bulletin. Pacific Tropical Botanical Garden
Bull Pan Am Health Organ — Bulletin. Pan American Health Organization
Bull Parenter Drug Assoc — Bulletin. Parenteral Drug Association
Bull Passaic Cty Dent Soc — Bulletin. Passaic County Dental Society
Bull PA State Univ Agr Exp Sta — Bulletin. Pennsylvania State University. Agricultural Experiment Station
Bull Pathol (Chicago) — Bulletin of Pathology (Chicago)
Bull Peab Mus Nat Hist — Bulletin. Peabody Museum of Natural History
Bull Peace Propos — Bulletin of Peace Proposals
Bull Penns Agric Exp St — Bulletin. Pennsylvania Agricultural Experiment Station
Bull Penns St Dent Soc — Bulletin. Pennsylvania State Dental Society
Bull Perma Int Ass Navig Congr — Bulletin. Permanent International Association of Navigation Congresses
Bull Permanent Int Assoc Navigation Congresses — Bulletin. Permanent International Association of Navigation Congresses
Bull Perm Int Assoc Navig Congr — Bulletin. Permanent International Association of Navigation Congresses
Bull Pharm — Bulletin of Pharmacy
Bull Pharm (Istanbul) — Bulletin of Pharmacy (Istanbul)
Bull Pharm Res Inst (Osaka) — Bulletin. Pharmaceutical Research Institute (Osaka)
Bull Phila Cty Dent Soc — Bulletin. Philadelphia County Dental Society
Bull Philadelphia Astronaut Soc — Bulletin. Philadelphia Astronautical Society
Bull Phila Herpetol Soc — Bulletin. Philadelphia Herpetological Society
Bull Phys Fitness Res Inst — Bulletin. Physical Fitness Research Institute
Bull Physio Pathol Respir — Bulletin de Physio-Pathologie Respiratoire
Bull Physiopathol Respir (Nancy) — Bulletin de Physiopathologie Respiratoire (Nancy)
Bull Pittsb Univ — Bulletin. Pittsburgh University
Bull Plankton Soc Jpn — Bulletin. Plankton Society of Japan
Bull Plant Bd Fla — Bulletin. Plant Board of Florida
Bull Plant Physiol (Beijing) — Bulletin. Plant Physiology (Beijing)
Bull P NSW Dep Agric Div Plant Ind — Bulletin P. New South Wales Department of Agriculture. Division of Plant Industry
Bull Pol Acad Sci Biol — Bulletin. Polish Academy of Sciences. Biology
Bull Pol Acad Sci Chem — Bulletin. Polish Academy of Sciences. Chemistry
Bull Pol Acad Sci Earth Sci — Bulletin. Polish Academy of Sciences. Earth Sciences

Bull Pol Med Sci Hist — Bulletin of Polish Medical Science and History
Bull Postgrad Inst Med Educ Res (Chandigarh) — Bulletin. Postgraduate Institute of Medical Education and Research (Chandigarh)
Bull Poznan Tow Przyjaciol Nauk Ser D — Bulletin. Poznanskie Towarzystwo Przyjaciol Nauk. Serie D
Bull Presse- Informationsamt Bundesregier — Bulletin. Presse- und Informationsamt der Bundesregierung
Bull Press Exchange Documn Cent Apimondia — Bulletin. Press Exchange and Documentation Centre of Apimondia
Bull Primary Tungsten Assoc — Bulletin. Primary Tungsten Association
Bull Prosthet Res — Bulletin of Prosthetics Research
Bull Psychon Soc — Bulletin. Psychonomic Society
Bull Public Health Inst Hyogo Prefect — Bulletin. Public Health Institute of Hyogo Prefecture
Bull Puerto Rico Agric Exp Stn Insular Stn (Rio Piedras) — Bulletin. Puerto Rico Agricultural Experiment Station. Insular Station (Rio Piedras)
Bull Punjab Agric Univ — Bulletin. Punjab Agricultural University
Bull Pure Appl Sci — Bulletin of Pure and Applied Sciences
Bull Pusan Fish Coll (Nat Sci) — Bulletin. Pusan Fisheries College (Natural Sciences)
Bull R Accad Med Roma — Bullettino. Reale Accademia Medica di Roma
Bull Radiat Prot — Bulletin of Radiation Protection [India]
Bull Radio Electr Eng Div Natl Res Counc Can — Bulletin. Radio and Electrical Engineering Division. National Research Council of Canada
Bull Radio Electr Eng Div Nat Res Counc Can — Bulletin. Radio and Electrical Engineering Division. National Research Council of Canada
Bull Raffles Mus — Bulletin. Raffles Museum
Bull Rech Agron Gembloux — Bulletin des Recherches Agronomiques de Gembloux
Bull Reg Res Lab (Jammu) — Bulletin. Regional Research Laboratory (Jammu)
Bull Rem Sens Soc Aust — Remote Sensing Association of Australia. Bulletin
Bull Repub Inst Prot Nat Mus Nat Hist Titograd — Bulletin. Republic Institution for the Protection of Nature and the Museum of Natural History in Titograd
Bull Res Coll Agric Vet Sci Nihon Univ — Bulletin of Research. College of Agriculture and Veterinary Science. Nihon University
Bull Res Coll Agr Vet Med Nihon Univ — Bulletin of Research. College of Agriculture and Veterinary Medicine. Nihon University
Bull Res Counc Isr — Bulletin. Research Council of Israel
Bull Res Counc Isr Sect A Chem — Bulletin. Research Council of Israel. Section A. Chemistry
Bull Res Counc Isr Sect A Math Phys Chem — Bulletin. Research Council of Israel. Section A. Mathematics, Physics, and Chemistry
Bull Res Counc Isr Sect B Biol Geol — Bulletin. Research Council of Israel. Section B. Biology and Geology
Bull Res Counc Isr Sect B Zool — Bulletin. Research Council of Israel. Section B. Zoology
Bull Res Counc Isr Sect C Technol — Bulletin. Research Council of Israel. Section C. Technology
Bull Res Counc Isr Sect D Bot — Bulletin. Research Council of Israel. Section D. Botany
Bull Res Counc Isr Sect E Exp Med — Bulletin. Research Council of Israel. Section E. Experimental Medicine
Bull Res Counc Isr Sect G Geo-Sci — Bulletin. Research Council of Israel. Section G. Geo-Sciences
Bull Res Coun Israel — Bulletin. Research Council of Israel
Bull Res Hum — Bulletin of Research in the Humanities
Bull Res Humanit — Bulletin of Research in the Humanities
Bull Res Inst Appl Electr — Bulletin. Research Institute of Applied Electricity
Bull Res Inst Appl Mech Kyushu Univ — Bulletin. Research Institute for Applied Mechanics. Kyushu University [Japan]
Bull Res Inst Diathetic Med Kumamoto Univ — Bulletin. Research Institute for Diathetic Medicine. Kumamoto University
Bull Res Inst Electron Shizuoka Univ — Bulletin. Research Institute of Electronics. Shizuoka University
Bull Res Inst Ferment Yamanashi Univ — Bulletin. Research Institute of Fermentation. Yamanashi University [Japan]
Bull Res Inst Food Sci Kyoto Univ — Bulletin. Research Institute for Food Science. Kyoto University
Bull Res Inst Miner Dressing Metall Tohoku Univ — Bulletin. Research Institute of Mineral Dressing and Metallurgy. Tohoku University [Japan]
Bull Res Inst Polymers Textiles — Bulletin. Research Institute for Polymers and Textiles
Bull Res Inst Sci Meas Tohoku Univ — Bulletin. Research Institute for Scientific Measurements. Tohoku University
Bull Res Inst Sumatra Plant Assoc — Bulletin. Research Institute. Sumatra Plantations Association
Bull Res Inst Univ Kerala (Trivandrum) Ser A — Bulletin. Research Institute. University of Kerala (Trivandrum). Series A. Physical Sciences
Bull Res Lab Nucl React Tokyo Inst Technol — Bulletin. Research Laboratory for Nuclear Reactors. Tokyo Institute of Technology
Bull Res Lab Precis Mach Electron — Bulletin. Research Laboratory of Precision Machinery and Electronics

Bull Res Lab Precis Mach and Electron — Bulletin. Research Laboratory of Precision Machinery and Electronics

Bull Res Lab Precis Mach Electron (Tokyo Inst Technol) — Bulletin. Research Laboratory of Precision Machinery and Electronics. (Tokyo Institute of Technology)

Bull Rheum Dis — Bulletin on Rheumatic Diseases

Bull Rhode Isl Agric Exp Stn — Bulletin. Rhode Island Agricultural Experiment Station

Bull RI Agric Exp Stn — Bulletin. Rhode Island Agricultural Experiment Station

Bull Richmond County Med Soc — Bulletin. Richmond County Medical Society [*Georgia*]

Bull Rijksmus — Bulletin. Rijksmuseum

Bull Riverside County Med Assoc — Bulletin. Riverside County Medical Association [*California*]

Bull Roum — Academie Roumaine. Bulletin de la Section Historique

Bull Rubber Grow Assoc — Bulletin. Rubber Growers Association

Bull S Afr Cult Hist Mus — Bulletin. South African Cultural History Museum

Bull S Afr Inst Assayers Anal — Bulletin. South African Institute of Assayers and Analysts

Bull Saga Agr Exp Sta — Bulletin. Saga Agricultural Experiment Station

Bull Saginaw County Med Soc — Bulletin. Saginaw County Medical Society [*Michigan*]

Bull Saitama Hortic Exp Stn — Bulletin. Saitama Horticultural Experiment Station

Bull Salesian Polytech — Bulletin. Salesian Polytechnic

Bulls Am Paleontology — Bulletins of American Paleontology

Bull San Mateo County Med Soc — Bulletin. San Mateo County Medical Society [*California*]

Bull Sante Prod Anim Afr — Bulletin des Sante et Production Animales en Afrique

Bull SC Acad Sci — Bulletin. South Carolina Academy of Science

Bull Sch For Mont St Univ — Bulletin. School of Forestry. Montana State University

Bull Sch For S F Austin St Coll — Bulletin. School of Forestry. Stephen F. Austin State College

Bull School Eng Archit Sakarya — Bulletin. School of Engineering and Architecture of Sakarya

Bull Sch Orient Afr Stud — Bulletin. School of Oriental and African Studies. University of London

Bull Schweiz Akad Med Wiss — Bulletin. Schweizerische Akademie der Medizinischen Wissenschaften

Bull Schweiz Electrotech Ver — Bulletin. Schweizerischer Elektrotechnischer Verein [*Switzerland*]

Bull Schweiz Ges Anthropol Ethnol — Bulletin. Schweizerische Gesellschaft fuer Anthropologie und Ethnologie

Bull Sci Assoc Ing Electr Inst Electrotech (Montefiore) — Bulletin Scientifique. Association des Ingenieurs Electriciens Sortis de l'Institut Electrotechnique (Montefiore)

Bull Sci Cons Acad RSF Yougosl — Bulletin Scientifique. Conseil des Academies de la RSF de Yougoslavie

Bull Sci Cons Acad RSF Yougosl Sect A Sci Nat Tech Med — Bulletin Scientifique. Conseil des Academies de la RSF de Yougoslavie. Section A. Sciences Naturelles, Techniques, et Medicales

Bull Sci Cons Acad Sci Arts RSF Yougosl Sect A — Bulletin Scientifique. Conseil des Academies des Sciences et des Arts de la RSF de Yougoslavie. Section A. Sciences Naturelles, Techniques, et Medicales

Bull Sci Conseil Acad RSF Yougoslav Sect A — Bulletin Scientifique. Conseil des Academies de la RSF de Yougoslavie. Section A [*Zagreb*]

Bull Sci Eng Res Lab Waseda Univ — Bulletin. Science and Engineering Research Laboratory. Waseda University

Bull Sci Engrg Div Univ Ryukyus Math Natur Sci — Bulletin. University of the Ryukyus. Science and Engineering Division. Mathematics and Natural Sciences

Bull Scient France et Belgique — Bulletin Scientifique de la France et de la Belgique

Bull Sci Hist Auvergne — Bulletin Scientifique et Historique de l'Auvergne

Bull Sci Ind Maison Roure Bertrand Fils — Bulletin Scientifique et Industriel de la Maison Roure Bertrand Fils

Bull Sci Inst Text Fr — Bulletin Scientifique. Institut Textile de France

Bull Sci ITF — Bulletin Scientifique. Institut Textile de France

Bull Sci Math — Bulletin des Sciences Mathematiques

Bull Sci Math (2) — Bulletin des Sciences Mathematiques (2e Serie) [*Paris*]

Bull Sci Med — Bullettino delle Scienze Mediche

Bull Sci Pharmacol — Bulletin des Sciences Pharmacologiques

Bull Sci Sect A — Bulletin Scientifique. Section A. Sciences Naturelles, Techniques, et Medicales

Bull Sci Tech Doc Cent (Egypt) — Bulletin. Scientific and Technical Documentation Centre (Egypt)

Bull Sci Technol Agency — Bulletin. Science and Technology Agency [*Japan*]

Bull Sci Terre Univ Poitiers — Bulletin. Sciences de la Terre. Universite de Poitiers

Bull Sc Med Bologna — Bullettino delle Scienze Mediche di Bologna

Bull Scott Assoc Geogr Teach — Bulletin. Scottish Association of Geography Teachers

Bull Scott Georgian Soc — Bulletin. Scottish Georgian Society

Bull Scripps Inst Oceanogr Univ Calif — Bulletin. Scripps Institution of Oceanography of the University of California

Bull Sc Soc Philomat Paris — Bulletin des Sciences. Societe Philomathique de Paris

Bull S Dak Agr Exp Sta — Bulletin. South Dakota Agricultural Experiment Station

Bull SD Geol Surv — Bulletin. South Dakota Geological Survey

Bull Seances Acad R Sci Outre-Mer (Brussels) — Bulletin des Seances. Academie Royale des Sciences d'Outre-Mer (Brussels)

Bull Seanc Soc Sci Nancy — Bulletin des Seances. Societe des Sciences de Nancy et Reunion Biologique de Nancy

Bull Sec Agron Div Tokai-Kinki Natl Agric Exp Stn — Bulletin. Second Agronomy Division. Tokai-Kinki National Agricultural Experiment Station

Bull Second Agron Div Tokai-Kinki Nat Agr Exp Sta — Bulletin. Second Agronomy Division. Tokai-Kinki National Agricultural Experiment Station

Bull Sect Log — Bulletin. Section of Logic

Bull Sect Sci Acad Roum — Bulletin. Section Scientifique. Academie Roumaine

Bull Seikai Reg Fish Res Lab — Bulletin. Seikai Regional Fisheries Research Laboratory

Bull Seishin-Igaku Inst — Bulletin. Seishin-Igaku Institute

Bull Seishin Igaku Inst (Seishin Igaku Kenkyusho Gyosekishu) — Bulletin. Seishin Igaku Institute (Seishin Igaku Kenkyusho Gyosekishu)

Bull Seismol Soc Am — Bulletin. Seismological Society of America

Bull Seismol Soc Amer — Bulletin. Seismological Society of America

Bull Seismol (Warsaw) — Bulletin Seismologique (Warsaw)

Bull Seoul Natl Univ For Seoul Taehakyo Yonsuplim Pogo — Bulletin. Seoul National University Forests/Seoul Taehakkyo Yonsuplim Pogo

Bull Ser C Soc Geol Mineral Bretagne — Bulletin. Serie C. Societe Geologique et Mineralogique de Bretagne

Bull Ser Exp Stn Gov Gen Chosen — Bulletin. Sericultural Experiment Station. Government General of Chosen

Bull Seric Exp Stn (Tokyo) — Bulletin. Sericultural Experiment Station (Tokyo)

Bull Serv Carte Geol Alger — Bulletin. Service de la Carte Geologique de l'Algerie

Bull Serv Carte Geol Alger Ser 2 — Bulletin. Service de la Carte Geologique de l'Algerie. Serie 2. Stratigraphie

Bull Serv Carte Geol Alger Ser 3 — Bulletin. Service de la Carte Geologique de l'Algerie. Serie 3. Geologie Appliquee

Bull Serv Carte Geol Alger Ser 5 — Bulletin. Service de la Carte Geologique de l'Algerie. Serie 5. Petrographie

Bull Serv Carte Geol Alger Ser 6 — Bulletin. Service de la Carte Geologique de l'Algerie. Serie 6. Metallogenie

Bull Serv Carte Geol Als Lorr — Bulletin. Service de la Carte Geologique d'Alsace et de Lorraine

Bull Serv Carte Geol Fr — Bulletin. Service de la Carte Geologique de la France

Bull Serv Cult Etud Peuplier et Saule — Bulletin. Service de Culture et d'Etudes du Peuplier et du Saule

Bull Serv Geol Luxemb — Bulletin. Service Geologique du Luxembourg

Bull Shanghai Sci Inst — Bulletin. Shanghai Science Institute

Bull Shemane Agric Exp Stn — Bulletin. Shemane Agricultural Experiment Station

Bull Shiga Pref Agr Exp Sta — Bulletin. Shiga Prefectural Agricultural Experiment Station

Bull Shih Yen Pao Kao Taiwan For Res Inst — Bulletin. Shih Yen Pao Kao. Taiwan Forest Research Institute

Bull Shikoku Agr Exp Sta — Bulletin. Shikoku Agricultural Experiment Station

Bull Shikoku Agric Exp Stn — Bulletin. Shikoku Agricultural Experiment Station

Bull Shimane Agr Coll — Bulletin. Shimane Agricultural College

Bull Shimane Agr Exp Sta — Bulletin. Shimane Agricultural Experiment Station

Bull Shimane Agric Coll — Bulletin. Shimane Agricultural College

Bull Shimane Agric Exp Stn — Bulletin. Shimane Agricultural Experiment Station

Bull Shimane Univ Nat Sci — Bulletin. Shimane University. Natural Science [*Japan*]

Bull Shinshu Univ For — Bulletin. Shinshu University Forests

Bull Shizuoka Agr Exp Sta — Bulletin. Shizuoka Agricultural Experiment Station

Bull Shizuoka Daigaku Nogaku-Bu — Bulletin. Shizuoka Daigaku Nogaku-Bu

Bull Shizuoka Pref Agr Exp Sta — Bulletin. Shizuoka Prefectural Agricultural Experiment Station

Bull Shizuoka Prefect Fish Exp Stn — Bulletin. Shizuoka Prefectural Fisheries Experiment Station

Bull SHPF — Bulletin. Societe de l'Histoire du Protestantisme Francais

Bull Shrimp Cult Res Cent — Bulletin. Shrimp Culture Research Center

Bull Signal — Bulletin Signaletique

Bull Sign Polym Peint Bois Cuirs — Bulletin Signaletique. Polymeres, Peintures, Bois, Cuirs

Bull Sinai Hosp Detroit — Bulletin. Sinai Hospital of Detroit

Bull Sloane Hosp Women Columbia-Presbyt Med Cent — Bulletin. Sloane Hospital for Women in the Columbia-Presbyterian Medical Center

Bull Slov Pol'nohospod Akad Vysk Ustavu Potravin — Bulletin. Slovenskej Pol'nohospodarskej Akademie. Vyskumneho Ustavu Potravinarskeho

Bull Soc Agric Fr — Bulletin. Societe des Agriculteurs de France

Bull Soc Agricrs Fr — Bulletin. Societe des Agriculteurs de France

Bull Soc Amis Sci Lett Poznan Ser B — Bulletin. Societe des Amis des Sciences et des Lettres de Poznan. Serie B. Sciences Mathematiques et Naturelles

Bull Soc Amis Sci Lett Poznan Ser C — Bulletin. Societe des Amis des Sciences et des Lettres de Poznan. Serie C. Medecine

Bull Soc Amis Sci Lett Poznan Ser D — Bulletin. Societe des Amis des Sciences et des Lettres de Poznan. Serie D. Sciences Biologiques

Bull Soc Amis Sci Lett Poznan Ser D Sci Biol — Bulletin. Societe des Amis des Sciences et des Lettres de Poznan. Serie D. Sciences Biologiques

Bull Soc Anat Paris — Bulletin. Societe Anatomique de Paris

Bull Soc Antiq Picardie — Bulletin. Societe des Antiquaires de Picardie

Bull Soc Apic Alpes-Marit — Bulletin. Societe d'Apiculture des Alpes-Maritimes

Bull Soc Archeol Finistere — Bulletin. Societe Archeologique du Finistere

Bull Soc Archeol Hist Artist Vieux Pap — Bulletin. Societe Archeologique, Historique, et Artistique de Vieux Papier

Bull Soc Belge Etud Napoleon — Bulletin. Societe Belge d'Etudes Napoleoniennes

Bull Soc Belge Geol — Bulletin. Societe Belge de Geologie [Belgium]

Bull Soc Belge Ing Ind — Bulletin. Societe Belge des Ingenieurs et des Industriels

Bull Soc Belge Ophtalmol — Bulletin. Societe Belge d'Ophtalmologie

Bull Soc Belge Phys — Bulletin. Societe Belge de Physique

Bull Soc Belg Geol Paleontol Hydrol — Bulletin. Societe Belge de Geologie, de Paleontologie, et d'Hydrologie [Later, Bulletin. Societe Belge de Geologie]

Bull Soc Borda — Bulletin. Societe de Borda

Bull Soc Bot Belg — Bulletin. Societe Royale de Botanique de Belgique

Bull Soc Bot Fr — Bulletin. Societe Botanique de France

Bull Soc Bot France — Bulletin. Societe Botanique de France

Bull Soc Bot Geneve — Bulletin. Societe Botanique de Geneve

Bull Soc Bot N Fr — Bulletin. Societe de Botanique du Nord de la France

Bull Soc Bot Nord Fr — Bulletin. Societe de Botanique du Nord de la France

Bull Soc Bot Suisse — Bulletin. Societe Botanique Suisse

Bull Soc Cent For Belg — Bulletin. Societe Centrale Forestiere de Belgique

Bull Soc Centr Med Vet — Bulletin. Societe Centrale de Medecine Veterinaire

Bull Soc Chim Belg — Bulletin. Societes Chimiques Belges

Bull Soc Chim (Beograd) — Bulletin. Societe Chimique (Beograd)

Bull Soc Chim Biol — Bulletin. Societe de Chimie Biologique [France]

Bull Soc Chim Fr — Bulletin. Societe Chimique de France

Bull Soc Chim de France — Bulletin. Societe Chimique de France

Bull Soc Chim France — Bulletin. Societe Chimique de France

Bull Soc Chim Fr Doc — Bulletin. Societe Chimique de France. Documentation

Bull Soc Chim Fr I — Bulletin. Societe Chimique de France. Premiere Partie. Chimie Analytique, Chimie Minerale, Chimie Physique

Bull Soc Chim Fr II — Bulletin. Societe Chimique de France. Deuxieme Partie

Bull Soc Chim Fr Mem — Bulletin. Societe Chimique de France. Memoires

Bull Soc Chim Fr Part 1 — Bulletin. Societe Chimique de France. Premiere Partie. Chimie Analytique, Chimie Minerale, Chimie Physique

Bull Soc Chim Fr Part 2 — Bulletin. Societe Chimique de France. Deuxieme Partie. Chimie Organique, Biochimie

Bull Soc Chim Ind — Bulletin. Societe de Chimie Industrielle [France]

Bull Soc Chir Paris — Bulletin. Societe de Chirurgie de Paris

Bull Soc Encour Ind Natl — Bulletin. Societe d'Encouragement pour l'Industrie Nationale

Bull Soc Ent Egypte — Bulletin. Societe Entomologique d'Egypte

Bull Soc Ent Fr — Bulletin. Societe Entomologique de France

Bull Soc Ent Mulhouse — Bulletin. Societe Entomologique de Mulhouse

Bull Soc Entomol Egypte — Bulletin. Societe Entomologique d'Egypte

Bull Soc Entomol Fr — Bulletin. Societe Entomologique de France

Bull Soc Entomol Suisse — Bulletin. Societe Entomologique Suisse

Bull Soc Et Lot — Bulletin. Societe des Etudes du Lot

Bull Soc Etud Oceaniennes — Bulletin. Societe d'Etudes Oceaniennes

Bull Soc For Belg — Bulletin. Societe Royale Forestiere de Belgique

Bull Soc For Franche-Comte — Bulletin. Societe Forestiere de Franche-Comte et Belfort

Bull Soc For Franche-Comte — Bulletin Trimestriel. Societe Forestiere de Franche-Comte et des Provinces de l'Est [Salins-Les-Bains]

Bull Soc Franc Hyg — Bulletin. Societe Francaise d'Hygiene

Bull Soc Franc Phot — Bulletin. Societe Francaise de Photographie

Bull Soc Franc Physiol Veg — Bulletin. Societe Francaise de Physiologie Vegetale

Bull Soc Fr Ceram — Bulletin. Societe Francaise de Ceramique

Bull Soc Fr Dermatol Syphiligr — Bulletin. Societe Francaise de Dermatologie et de Syphiligraphie

Bull Soc Fr Electr — Bulletin. Societe Francaise des Electriciens [France]

Bull Soc Fr Hist Hop — Bulletin. Societe Francaise d'Histoire des Hopitaux

Bull Soc Frib Sci Nat — Bulletin. Societe Fribourgeoise des Sciences Naturelles

Bull Soc Fr Micros — Bulletin. Societe Francaise de Microscopie

Bull Soc Fr Miner Cristallogr — Bulletin. Societe Francaise de Mineralogie et de Cristallographie

Bull Soc Fr Mycol Med — Bulletin. Societe Francaise de Mycologie Medicale

Bull Soc Fr Phil — Bulletin. Societe Francaise de Philosophie

Bull Soc Fr Photogramm — Bulletin. Societe Francaise de Photogrammetrie [Later, Bulletin. Societe Francaise de Photogrammetrie et de Teledetection]

Bull Soc Fr Photogramm et Teledetect — Bulletin. Societe Francaise de Photogrammetrie et de Teledetection

Bull Soc Fr Physiol Veg — Bulletin. Societe Francaise de Physiologie Vegetale

Bull Soc Geol Fr — Bulletin. Societe Geologique de France

Bull Soc Geol France — Bulletin. Societe Geologique de France

Bull Soc Geol Mineral Bretagne Ser C — Bulletin. Societe Geologique et Mineralogique de Bretagne. Serie C

Bull Soc Geol Normandie — Bulletin. Societe Geologique de Normandie

Bull Soc Hist Nat Afr Nord — Bulletin. Societe d'Histoire Naturelle de l'Afrique du Nord

Bull Soc Hist Nat Doubs — Bulletin. Societe d'Histoire Naturelle du Doubs

Bull Soc Hist Nat Toulouse — Bulletin. Societe d'Histoire Naturelle de Toulouse

Bull Soc Hist Natur Afr Nord — Bulletin. Societe d'Histoire Naturelle de l'Afrique du Nord

Bull Soc Ind Amiens — Bulletin. Societe Industrielle d'Amiens

Bull Soc Ind Miner St Etienne — Bulletin. Societe de l'Industrie Minerale de St. Etienne

Bull Soc Ind Rouen — Bulletin. Societe Industrielle de Rouen

Bull Soc Int Chir — Bulletin. Societe Internationale de Chirurgie

Bull Soc Int Electr — Bulletin. Societe Internationale des Electriciens

Bull Soc Lat Am Stud — Bulletin. Society for Latin American Studies

Bull Soc Linn Bord — Bulletin. Societe Linneenne de Bordeaux

Bull Soc Linn Lyon — Bulletin Mensuel. Societe Linneenne de Lyon

Bull Soc Linn Lyon — Bulletin. Societe Linneenne de Lyon

Bull Soc Linn Normandie — Bulletin. Societe Linneenne de Normandie

Bull Soc Linn Provence — Bulletin. Societe Linneenne de Provence

Bull Soc Lorraine Sci — Bulletin. Societe Lorraine des Sciences

Bull Soc Math Belg — Bulletin. Societe Mathematique de Belgique

Bull Soc Math Fr — Bulletin. Societe Mathematique de France

Bull Soc Math Grece — Bulletin. Societe Mathematique de Grece

Bull Soc Math Grece NS — Bulletin. Societe Mathematique de Grece. Nouvelle Serie

Bull Soc Math Phys Macedoine — Bulletin. Societe des Mathematiciens et des Physiciens de la Republique Populaire de Macedoine

Bull Soc Med Afr Noire — Bulletin. Societe Medicale d'Afrique Noire de Langue Francaise

Bull Soc Med Afr Noire Lang Fr — Bulletin. Societe Medicale d'Afrique Noire de Langue Francaise

Bull Soc Med-Chir Indo-Chine — Bulletin. Societe Medico-Chirurgicale de l'Indo-Chine

Bull Soc Med Hop Lyon — Bulletin. Societe Medicale des Hopitaux de Lyon

Bull Soc Med Hop Pa — Bulletins et Memoires. Societe Medicale des Hopitaux de Paris

Bull Soc Med Hop Paris — Bulletins et Memoires. Societe Medicale des Hopitaux de Paris

Bull Soc Med Par — Bulletin et Memoires. Societe de Medecine de Paris

Bull Soc Microsc Can — Bulletin. Societe de Microscopie du Canada

Bull Soc Mycol — Bulletin. Societe Mycologique de Geneve

Bull Soc Mycol Fr — Bulletin. Societe Mycologique de France

Bull Soc Nat Antiq Fr — Bulletin. Societe Nationale des Antiquaires de France

Bull Soc Nat Archeol Ain — Bulletin. Societe des Naturalistes et des Archeologues de l'Ain

Bull Soc Nat Fr — Bulletin. Societe Nationale des Antiquaires de France

Bull Soc Nat Lux — Bulletin. Societe des Naturalistes Luxembourgeois

Bull Soc Nat Voroneje — Bulletin. Societe des Naturalistes de Voroneje

Bull Soc Nav Archit Mar Eng — Bulletin. Society of Naval Architects and Marine Engineers

Bull Soc Neuchatel Sci Nat — Bulletin. Societe Neuchatelloise des Sciences Naturelles

Bull Soc NZ — Bulletin. Royal Society of New Zealand

Bull Soc Obst Gynec — Bulletin. Societe d'Obstetrique et de Gynecologie de Paris

Bull Soc Ophtal Egy — Bulletin. Societe d'Ophtalmologie d'Egypte

Bull Soc Ophtal Fr — Bulletin. Societes d'Ophtalmologie de France

Bull Soc Ophtalmol Fr — Bulletin. Societes d'Ophtalmologie de France

Bull Soc Ophtalmol Paris — Bulletin. Societe d'Ophtalmologie de Paris

Bull Soc Path Exot — Bulletin. Societe de Pathologie Exotique et de Ses Filiales

Bull Soc Pathol Exot — Bulletin. Societe de Pathologie Exotique

Bull Soc Pathol Exot Filiales — Bulletin. Societe de Pathologie Exotique et de Ses Filiales

Bull Soc Pediat Paris — Bulletin. Societe de Pediatrie de Paris

Bull Soc Pharmacol Environ Pathol — Bulletin. Society of Pharmacological and Environmental Pathologists

Bull Soc Pharm Bord — Bulletin. Societe de Pharmacie de Bordeaux

Bull Soc Pharm Lille — Bulletin. Societe de Pharmacie de Lille

Bull Soc Pharm Mars — Bulletin. Societe de Pharmacie de Marseille

Bull Soc Pharm Marseille — Bulletin. Societe de Pharmacie de Marseille

Bull Soc Pharm Nancy — Bulletin. Societe de Pharmacie de Nancy

Bull Soc Pharm Strasb — Bulletin. Societe de Pharmacie de Strasbourg

Bull Soc Philomat Paris — Bulletin. Societe Philomathique de Paris
Bull Soc Philom Vosg — Bulletin. Societe Philomatique Vosgienne
Bull Soc Photogr Sci Technol Jpn — Bulletin. Society of Photographic Science and Technology of Japan
Bull Soc Phycol Fr — Bulletin. Societe Phycologique de France
Bull Soc Port Sci Nat — Bulletin. Societe Portugaise des Sciences Naturelles
Bull Soc Portugaise Sc Nat — Bulletin. Societe Portugaise des Sciences Naturelles
Bull Soc Prehist Fr — Bulletin. Societe Prehistorique Francaise
Bull Soc Promot Eng Educ — Bulletin. Society for the Promotion of Engineering Education
Bull Soc R Belge Electr — Bulletin. Societe Royale Belge des Electriciens
Bull Soc R Belge Gynecol Obstet — Bulletin. Societe Royale Belge de Gynecologie et d'Obstetrique
Bull Soc R Bot Belg — Bulletin. Societe Royale de Botanique de Belgique
Bull Soc R For Belg — Bulletin. Societe Royale Forestiere de Belgique
Bull Soc R For Belg Tijdschr K Belg Bosbouwmaatsch — Bulletin. Societe Royale Forestiere de Belgique/Tijdschrift van de Koninklijke Belgische Bosbouwmaatschappij
Bull Soc Romande Apic — Bulletin. Societe Romande d'Apiculture
Bull Soc Roum Neurol Psychiatr Psychol Endocrinol — Bulletin. Societe Roumaine de Neurologie, Psychiatrie, Psychologie, et Endocrinologie
Bull Soc Roy Belg Elec — Bulletin. Societe Royale Belge des Electriciens
Bull Soc Roy Sci Liege — Bulletin. Societe Royale des Sciences de Liege
Bull Soc R Pharm Bruxelles — Bulletin. Societe Royale de Pharmacie de Bruxelles
Bull Soc R Sci Liege — Bulletin. Societe Royale des Sciences de Liege
Bull Soc Sci Bretagne — Bulletin. Societe Scientifique de Bretagne
Bull Soc Scient Bretagne — Bulletin. Societe Scientifique de Bretagne
Bull Soc Scient Med Ouest — Bulletin. Societe Scientifique et Medicale de l'Ouest
Bull Soc Sci Hyg Aliment Aliment Ration — Bulletin. Societe Scientifique d'Hygiene Alimentaire et Alimentation Rationnelle
Bull Soc Sci Hyg Aliment Aliment Ration Homme — Bulletin. Societe Scientifique d'Hygiene Alimentaire et d'Alimentation Rationnelle de l'Homme
Bull Soc Sci Lett Lodz — Bulletin. Societe des Sciences et des Lettres de Lodz
Bull Soc Sci Lett Lodz Cl 4 — Bulletin. Societe des Sciences et des Lettres de Lodz. Classe 4. Sciences Medicales
Bull Soc Sci Lettres Lodz — Bulletin. Societe des Sciences et des Lettres de Lodz
Bull Soc Sci Med Grand-Duche Luxemb — Bulletin. Societe des Sciences Medicales du Grand-Duche de Luxembourg
Bull Soc Sci Med Gr-Duche Luxemb — Bulletin. Societe des Sciences Medicales du Grand-Duche de Luxembourg
Bull Soc Sci Nancy — Bulletin. Societe des Sciences de Nancy
Bull Soc Sci Nat Maroc — Bulletin. Societe des Sciences Naturelles du Maroc
Bull Soc Sci Nat Ouest Fr — Bulletin. Societe des Sciences Naturelles de l'Ouest de la France
Bull Soc Sci Nat Phys Maroc — Bulletin. Societe des Sciences Naturelles et Physiques du Maroc
Bull Soc Sci Nat Tunis — Bulletin. Societe des Sciences Naturelles de Tunisie
Bull Soc Sci Photogr Jpn — Bulletin. Society of Scientific Photography of Japan
Bull Soc Sci Vet Med Comp Lyon — Bulletin. Societe des Sciences Veterinaires et de Medecine Comparee de Lyon
Bull Soc Sc Vet Lyon — Bulletin. Societe des Sciences Veterinaires de Lyon
Bull Soc Sea Water Sci (Jpn) — Bulletin. Society of Sea Water Science (Japan)
Bull Soc Stiinte Geol Repub Soc Rom — Buletinul. Societatii de Stiinte Geologice din Republica Socialista Romania
Bull Soc Vaudoise Sci Nat — Bulletin. Societe Vaudoise des Sciences Naturelles
Bull Soc Vaud Sci Nat — Bulletin. Societe Vaudoise des Sciences Naturelles
Bull Soc Vector Ecol — Bulletin. Society of Vector Ecologists
Bull Soc Vieux Papier — Bulletin. Societe de Vieux Papier
Bull Soc Zool Anvers — Bulletins. Societe de Zoologie d'Anvers
Bull Soc Zool Fr — Bulletin. Societe Zoologique de France
Bull Soc Zool France — Bulletin. Societe Zoologique de France
Bull Soil Bur (NZ) — Bulletin. Soil Bureau Department of Scientific and Industrial Research (New Zealand)
Bull Soil Surv Gt Br — Bulletin. Soil Survey of Great Britain
Bull Sonoma County Med Assoc — Bulletin. Sonoma County Medical Association [*California*]
Bull South Calif Acad Sci — Bulletin. Southern California Academy of Sciences
Bull South Pac Gen Hosp — Bulletin. Southern Pacific General Hospital
Bull South Tex Geol Soc — Bulletin. South Texas Geological Society
Bull Spec Astrophys Obs (North Caucasus) — Bulletin. Special Astrophysical Observatory (North Caucasus)
Bull Spec Libr Coun Phila — Bulletin. Special Libraries Council of Philadelphia and Vicinity
Bull Speleol Soc DC — Bulletin. Speleological Society of the District of Columbia
Bull Spokane County Med Soc — Bulletin. Spokane County Medical Society [*Washington*]
Bull Sport Fish Inst — Bulletin. Sport Fishing Institute

Bull Stand Oil Co Calif — Bulletin. Standard Oil Company of California
Bull State Biol Surv Kans — Bulletin. State Biological Survey of Kansas
Bull State Fruit Exp Stn Southwest MO State Univ (Mt Grove) — Bulletin. State Fruit Experiment Station. Southwest Missouri State University (Mountain Grove)
Bull State Inst Mar Trop Med Gdansk — Bulletin. State Institute of Marine and Tropical Medicine in Gdansk
Bull State Plant Board Fla — Bulletin. State Plant Board of Florida
Bull State Univ Iowa — Bulletin. State University of Iowa
Bull Statist Soc NSW — Bulletin. Statistical Society of New South Wales
Bull S Tex Geol Soc — Bulletin. South Texas Geological Society
Bull St Marianna Univ Sch Med Gen Educ — Bulletin. St. Marianna University. School of Medicine. General Education
Bull Stn Exp Agric Hong A — Bulletin. Stations d'Experimentation Agricole Hongroises. A. Production Vegetale
Bull Stn Exp Agric Hong C — Bulletin. Stations d'Experimentation Agricole Hongroises. C. Horticulture
Bull Stomatol Kyoto Univ — Bulletin of Stomatology. Kyoto University
Bull Sugadaira Biol Lab — Bulletin. Sugadaira Biological Laboratory
Bull Sugar Beet Res — Bulletin of Sugar Beet Research
Bull Sugar Beet Res Suppl — Bulletin of Sugar Beet Research. Supplement
Bull Suicidol — Bulletin of Suicidology
Bull Suisse Mycol — Bulletin Suisse de Mycologie
Bull Suzugamine Women's Coll Nat Sci — Bulletin. Suzugamine Women's College. Natural Science
Bull Swazild Dep Agric — Bulletin. Swaziland Department of Agriculture
Bull Synd Apic — Bulletin. Union Syndicale des Apiculteurs
Bull Taiwan Agric Res Inst — Bulletin. Taiwan Agricultural Research Institute
Bull Taiwan Forestry Res Inst — Bulletin. Taiwan Forestry Research Institute
Bull Taiwan For Res Inst — Bulletin. Taiwan Forestry Research Institute
Bull Tall Timbers Res Stn — Bulletin. Tall Timbers Research Station
Bull Tas For Comm — Tasmanian Forest Commission. Bulletin
Bull Tea Res Stn Minist Agric For — Bulletin. Tea Research Station. Ministry of Agriculture and Forestry [*Japan*]
Bull Tech AIBr — Bulletin Technique AIBr [*Association des Ingenieurs Sortis de l'Universite Libre de Bruxelles*]
Bull Tech Api — Bulletin Technique Apicole
Bull Tech Bur Veri — Bulletin Technique. Bureau Veritas
Bull Tech Chambre Synd Mines Fer Fr — Bulletin Technique. Chambre Syndicale des Mines de Fer de France
Bull Tech Dep Genet Anim — Bulletin Technique. Departement de Genetique Animale [*France*]
Bull Tech Div Sols Queb Minist Agric — Bulletin Technique. Division des Sols. Province du Quebec - Ministere de l'Agriculture
Bull Tech Genie Rural — Bulletin Technique du Genie Rural [*France*]
Bull Tech Houille Deriv Inst Natl Ind Charbon — Bulletin Technique de l'Houille et Derives. Institut National de l'Industrie Charbonniere
Bull Tech Inf — Bulletin Technique d'Information
Bull Tech Inf Ingrs Servs Agric — Bulletin Technique d'Information des Ingenieurs des Services Agricoles
Bull Tech Inf Min Agric (France) — Bulletin Technique d'Information. Ministere de l'Agriculture (France)
Bull Tech Inform Min Agr (France) — Bulletin Technique d'Information. Ministere de l'Agriculture (France)
Bull Tech Mines Fer Fr — Bulletin Technique des Mines de Fer de France
Bull Tech Secur Salubr Inst Natl Ind Extr — Bulletin Technique de Securite et Salubrite. Institut National des Industries Extractives
Bull Tech Soc Fr Constr Babcock Wilcox — Bulletin Technique. Societe Francaise des Constructions Babcock et Wilcox
Bull Tech Soc Fr Constr Babcock et Wilcox — Bulletin Technique. Societe Francaise des Constructions Babcock et Wilcox [*France*]
Bull Tech Suisse Romande — Bulletin Technique de la Suisse Romande
Bull Tech Univ Istanbul — Bulletin. Technical University of Istanbul
Bull Tech Valorisation Util Combust Inst Natl Ind Extr — Bulletin Technique. Valorisation et Utilisation des Combustibles. Institut National des Industries Extractives
Bull Tech Vevey — Bulletin Technique Vevey
Bull Tenn Agric Exp Stn — Bulletin. Tennessee Agricultural Experiment Station
Bull Tenn Nurses Assoc — Bulletin. Tennessee Nurses Association
Bull Tex Agr Exp Sta — Bulletin. Texas Agricultural Experiment Station
Bull Tex Agric Exp Stn — Bulletin. Texas Agricultural Experiment Station
Bull Tex Mem Mus — Bulletin. Texas Memorial Museum
Bull Tex Ornithol Soc — Bulletin. Texas Ornithological Society
Bull Thermodyn & Thermochem — Bulletin of Thermodynamics and Thermochemistry
Bull Tob Res Inst — Bulletin. Tobacco Research Institute
Bull Tob Res Inst Taiwan Tob Wine Monop Bur — Bulletin. Tobacco Research Institute. Taiwan Tobacco and Wine Monopoly Bureau
Bull Tochigi Agr Exp Sta — Bulletin. Tochigi Agricultural Experiment Station
Bull Tohoku Inst Technol Sect B — Bulletin. Tohoku Institute of Technology. Section B. Sciences
Bull Tohoku Nat Agr Exp Sta — Bulletin. Tohoku National Agricultural Experiment Station
Bull Tohoku Natl Agric Exp Stn — Bulletin. Tohoku National Agricultural Experiment Station

Bull Tohoku Natol Agr Exp Stn (Morioka) — Bulletin. Tohoku National Agricultural Experiment Station (Morioka)

Bull Tohoku Reg Fish Res Lab — Bulletin. Tohoku Regional Fisheries Research Laboratory

Bull Tokai-Kinki Agr Exp Sta — Bulletin. Tokai-Kinki National Agricultural Experiment Station

Bull Tokai-Kinki Nat Agr Exp Sta — Bulletin. Tokai-Kinki National Agricultural Experiment Station

Bull Tokai-Kinki Natl Agric Exp Stn — Bulletin. Tokai-Kinki National Agricultural Experiment Station

Bull Tokai Reg Fish Res Lab — Bulletin. Tokai Regional Fisheries Research Laboratory

Bull Tokyo Coll Domest Sci — Bulletin. Tokyo College of Domestic Science

Bull Tokyo Dent Coll — Bulletin. Tokyo Dental College

Bull Tokyo Gakugei Univ — Bulletin. Tokyo Gakugei University

Bull Tokyo Gakugei Univ Ser 4 — Bulletin. Tokyo Gakugei University. Series 4

Bull Tokyo Inst Technol — Bulletin. Tokyo Institute of Technology

Bull Tokyo Kasei Daigaku — Bulletin. Tokyo Kasei Daigaku

Bull Tokyo Med Dent Univ — Bulletin. Tokyo Medical and Dental University

Bull Tokyo Metro Rehab Cent Phys Ment Handcp — Bulletin. Tokyo Metropolitan Rehabilitation Center of the Physically and Mentally Handicapped

Bull Tokyo Sci Mus — Bulletin. Tokyo Science Museum

Bull Tokyo Univ For — Bulletin. Tokyo University Forests

Bull Torrey Bot Club — Bulletin. Torrey Botanical Club

Bull Tottori Agr Exp Sta — Bulletin. Tottori Agricultural Experiment Station

Bull Tottori Tree Fruit Exp Stn — Bulletin. Tottori Tree Fruit Experiment Station

Bull Tottori Univ For — Bulletin. Tottori University Forests

Bull Train — Bulletin on Training

Bull Tra Soc Pharm Lyon — Bulletin des Travaux. Societe de Pharmacie de Lyon

Bull Trav Soc Pharm Bordeaux — Bulletin des Travaux. Societe de Pharmacie de Bordeaux

Bull Trimest INACOL — Bulletin Trimestriel INACOL [*Institut National pour l'Amelioration des Conserves de Legumes*]

Bull Trimest Inst Natl Amelior Conserves Legumes (Belg) — Bulletin Trimestriel. Institut National pour l'Amelioration des Conserves de Legumes (Belgium)

Bull Trimest Soc Hist Nat Amis Mus Autun — Bulletin Trimestriel. Societe d'Histoire Naturelle des Amis de la Museum d'Autun

Bull Trimest Soc Mycol Fr — Bulletin Trimestriel. Societe Mycologique de France

Bull Tufts N Engl Med Cent — Bulletin. Tufts New England Medical Center

Bull Tulane Med Fac — Bulletin. Tulane Medical Faculty

Bull Tulane Univ Med Fac — Bulletin. Tulane University Medical Faculty

Bull Union Agric Egypte — Bulletin. Union des Agriculteurs d'Egypte

Bull Union Oceanogr Fr — Bulletin. Union des Oceanographes de France

Bull Union Physiciens — Bulletin. Union des Physiciens

Bull Union Synd Agric Egypte — Bulletin. Union Syndicale des Agriculteurs d'Egypte

Bull Union Synd Apic Picards — Bulletin. Union Syndicale des Apiculteurs Picards

Bull United Plant Assoc South Ind Sci Dep — Bulletin. United Planters' Association of Southern India. Scientific Department

Bull Univ Alberta — Bulletin. University of Alberta

Bull Univ Coll Med (Calcutta) — Bulletin. University College of Medicine (Calcutta)

Bull Univ Coll Med Calcutta Univ — Bulletin. University College of Medicine. Calcutta University

Bull Univ GA Coll Agr Coop Ext Serv — Bulletin. University of Georgia. College of Agriculture. Cooperative Extension Service

Bull Univ Idaho Coll Agr Ext Serv — Bulletin. University of Idaho. College of Agriculture. Extension Service

Bull Univ Iowa Inst Agr Med — Bulletin. University of Iowa. Institute of Agricultural Medicine

Bull Univ KY Off Res Eng Serv — Bulletin. University of Kentucky. Office of Research and Engineering Services

Bull Univ MD Coop Ext Serv — Bulletin. University of Maryland. Cooperative Extension Service

Bull Univ MD Sch Med — Bulletin. University of Maryland. School of Medicine

Bull Univ Miami Sch Med Jackson Mem Hosp — Bulletin. University of Miami School of Medicine and Jackson Memorial Hospital

Bull Univ MO Coll Agr Exp Sta — Bulletin. University of Missouri. College of Agriculture. Experiment Station

Bull Univ MO Rolla Tech Ser — Bulletin. University of Missouri at Rolla. Technical Series

Bull Univ Nebr State Mus — Bulletin. University of Nebraska State Museum

Bull Univ Neb St Mus — Bulletin. University of Nebraska State Museum

Bull Univ Osaka Prefect Ser A — Bulletin. University of Osaka Prefecture. Series A. Sakai

Bull Univ Osaka Prefect Ser B Agric Biol — Bulletin. University of Osaka Prefecture. Series B. Agriculture and Biology

Bull Univ Osaka Prefecture Ser A — Bulletin. University of Osaka Prefecture. Series A. Engineering and Natural Sciences

Bull Univ Osaka Pref Ser B — Bulletin. University of Osaka Prefecture. Series B

Bull Univ RI Agric Exp Stn — Bulletin. University of Rhode Island. Agricultural Experiment Station

Bull US Bur Mines — Bulletin. United States Bureau of Mines

Bull US Dept Agric — Bulletin. United States Department of Agriculture

Bull US Geol Surv — Bulletin. United States Geological Survey

Bull US Natl Mus — Bulletin. United States National Museum

Bull US Natn Mus — Bulletin. United States National Museum

Bull Utah Agr Exp Sta — Bulletin. Utah Agricultural Experiment Station

Bull Utah Agric Exp Stn — Bulletin. Utah Agricultural Experiment Station

Bull Utah Eng Exp Stn — Bulletin. Utah Engineering Experiment Station

Bull Utsunomiya Tob Exp Stn — Bulletin. Utsunomiya Tobacco Experiment Station

Bull Utsunomiya Univ For — Bulletin. Utsunomiya University Forests

Bull Utsunomiya Univ Sect 2 — Bulletin. Utsunomiya University. Section 2

Bull VA Agr Exp Sta — Bulletin. Virginia Agricultural Experiment Station

Bull VA Agric Exp Stn — Bulletin. Virginia Agricultural Experiment Station

Bull VA Agric Ext Serv — Bulletin. Virginia Agricultural Extension Service

Bull VA Geol Surv — Bulletin. Virginia Geological Survey

Bull Vancouver Med Assoc — Bulletin. Vancouver Medical Association

Bull VA Polytech Inst Agr Ext Serv — Bulletin. Virginia Polytechnic Institute. Agricultural Extension Service

Bull VA Polytech Inst State Univ VA Water Resources Cent — Bulletin. Virginia Polytechnic Institute and State University. Virginia Water Resources Research Center

Bull VA Sect Amer Chem Soc — Bulletin. Virginia Sections of the American Chemical Society

Bull VA Water Resour Res Cent — Bulletin. Virginia Water Resources Research Center

Bull Veg Ornamental Crops Res Stn Ser A — Bulletin. Vegetable and Ornamental Crops Research Station. Series A

Bull Veg Ornamental Crops Res Stn Ser C (Kurume) — Bulletin. Vegetable and Ornamental Crops Research Station. Series C (Kurume)

Bull Ver Schweiz Pet-Geol Ing — Bulletin. Vereinigung der Schweizerischen Petroleum-Geologen und -Ingenieure

Bull Ver Schweiz Petrol Geol-Ing — Bulletin. Vereinigung der Schweizerischen Petroleum-Geologen und -Ingenieure

Bull Vet Inst Pulawy — Bulletin. Veterinary Institute in Pulawy

Bull Vet (Lisb) — Bulletin Veterinaire (Lisbon)

Bull Vict Inst Educ Res — Bulletin. Victorian Institute of Educational Research

Bull V Luna Gen Hosp Med Soc — Bulletin V. Luna General Hospital Medical Society

Bull Volcanic Eruptions (Tokyo) — Bulletin of Volcanic Eruptions (Tokyo)

Bull Volcanol — Bulletin Volcanologique

Bull VT Agric Exp Stn — Bulletin. Vermont Agricultural Experiment Station

Bull Vysk Ustavu Pap Celul — Bulletin. Vyskumneho Ustavu Papieru a Celulozy

Bull Vysk Ustavu Potravin — Bulletin. Vyskumneho Ustavu Potravinarskeho

Bull Vysk Ustavu Priem Celul — Bulletin. Vyskumneho Ustavu Priemyslu Celulozy

Bull Wagner Free Inst Sci — Bulletin. Wagner Free Institute of Science

Bull Wakayama Fruit Tree Exp Stn — Bulletin. Wakayama Fruit Tree Experiment Station

Bull War Med — Bulletin of War Medicine

Bull Waseda Appl Chem Soc — Bulletin. Waseda Applied Chemical Society

Bull Wash Agr Exp Sta — Bulletin. Washington Agricultural Experiment Station

Bull Wash Agric Exp Stn — Bulletin. Washington Agricultural Experiment Station

Bull Washington Agric Exp Stn — Bulletin. Washington Agricultural Experiment Station

Bull Wash St Coll Ext Serv — Bulletin. Washington State College Extension Service

Bull Wat Res Fdn Aust — Bulletin. Water Research Foundation of Australia

Bull Wds For Dep S Aust — Bulletin. Woods and Forests Department of South Australia

Bull Welsh Pl Breed Stn — Bulletin. Welsh Plant Breeding Station. University College of Wales

Bull West Soc Eng — Bulletin. Western Society of Engineers

Bull WHO — Bulletin. World Health Organization

Bull Wildl Dis Assoc — Bulletin. Wildlife Disease Association

Bull Wis Agr Exp Sta — Bulletin. Wisconsin Agricultural Experiment Station

Bull Wis Agric Exp Stn — Bulletin. Wisconsin Agricultural Experiment Station

Bull Wld Hlth Org — Bulletin. World Health Organization

Bull Wollongong Univ Coll — Wollongong University College. Bulletin

Bull Wood Res Lab VA Polyt Inst — Bulletin. Wood Research Laboratory. Virginia Polytechnic Institute

Bull Woods For Dep South Aust — South Australia. Woods and Forests Department. Bulletin

Bull Woo:s Forests Dep S Aust — South Australia. Woods and Forests Department. Bulletin

Bull World Health Organ — Bulletin. World Health Organization

Bull W Va Agric Exp Sta — Bulletin. West Virginia University. Agricultural Experiment Station

Bull W Va Univ Agr Exp Sta — Bulletin. West Virginia University. Agricultural Experiment Station
Bull Wyo Agr Exp Sta — Bulletin. Wyoming Agricultural Experiment Station
Bull Wyo Agric Exp Stn — Bulletin. Wyoming Agricultural Experiment Station
Bull Wyo Dept Agr Div Statist Inform — Bulletin. Wyoming Department of Agriculture. Division of Statistics and Information
Bull Yale Sch For — Bulletin. Yale University School of Forestry
Bull Yamagata Univ (Agric Sci) — Bulletin. Yamagata University (Agricultural Science)
Bull Yamagata Univ (Eng) — Bulletin. Yamagata University (Engineering)
Bull Yamagata Univ (Nat Sci) — Bulletin. Yamagata University (Natural Science)
Bull Yamagata Univ (Natur Sci) — Bulletin. Yamagata University (Natural Science)
Bull Yamaguchi Agric Exp Stn — Bulletin. Yamaguchi Agricultural Experiment Station
Bull Yamaguchi Med Sch — Bulletin. Yamaguchi Medical School
Bull Yamaguchi Prefect Poult Breed Stn — Bulletin. Yamaguchi Prefectural Poultry Breeding Station
Bull Yamanashi Agric Exp Stn — Bulletin. Yamanashi Agricultural Experiment Station
Bull Yamanashi For Exp Sta — Bulletin. Yamanashi Prefectural Forest Experiment Station
Bull Yamanashi Pref Agr Exp Sta — Bulletin. Yamanashi Prefectural Agricultural Experiment Station
Bull Y Natl Fert Dev Cent (US) — Bulletin Y. National Fertilizer Development Center (United States)
Bull (Zagreb) — Bulletin International. Academie Yugoslave (Zagreb)
Bull Zool — Bulletin of Zoology
Bull Zool Nomencl — Bulletin of Zoological Nomenclature
Bull Zool Soc Coll Sci (Nagpur) — Bulletin. Zoological Society College of Science (Nagpur)
Bull Zool Soc Egypt — Bulletin. Zoological Society of Egypt
Bull Zool Surv India — Bulletin. Zoological Survey of India
Bul si Mem Soc Med Vet Bucuresti — Buletinul si Memorie. Societatii de Medicina Veterinaria din Bucuresti
Bul Mensuel Statis (Cameroon) — Bulletin Mensuel des Statistiques (Cameroon)
Bul Mensuel Statis (Congo People's Republic) — Bulletin Mensuel des Statistiques (Congo People's Republic)
Bul Mensuel Statis (France) — Bulletin Mensuel de Statistique (France)
Bul Mensuel Statis (Gabon) — Bulletin Mensuel de Statistique (Gabon)
Bul Mon Ist — Buletinul Monumentelor Istorica
Bul Narcotics (UN) — Bulletin on Narcotics (United Nations)
Bul Nat Gallery of SA — Bulletin. National Gallery of South Australia
Bul NHPL — Bulletin. New Hampshire Public Libraries
Bul NYPL — Bulletin. New York Public Library
Bul Pan Am Union — Bulletin. Pan American Union
Bul Penelitian Teknol Hasil Pertanian — Buletin Penelitian Teknologi Hasil Pertanian
Bul Post-Graduate Ctee in Medicine Univ of Syd — Bulletin. Post-Graduate Committee in Medicine. University of Sydney
Bul for Psych — Bulletin for Psychologists
Bu LR — Buffalo Law Review
BU L Rev — Boston University. Law Review
Bul Sci AIM — Bulletin Scientifique. Association des Ingenieurs Electriciens Sortis de l'Institut Electrotechnique (Montefiore)
BulSNTS — Bulletin. Studiorum Novi Testamenti Societas
Bul Soc Stiinte Cluj — Buletinul. Societatii de Stiinte din Cluj
Bul Stand — Buletinul de Standardizare
Bul Stat Agr — Bulletin des Statistiques Agricoles
Bul Statis Agric — Bulletin Statistique Agricole
Bul Statis (Belgium) — Bulletin de Statistique (Belgium)
Bul Statis et Docum — Bulletin de Statistique et de Documentation
Bul Sti Inst Politehn (Cluj) — Buletinul Stiintific. Institutului Politehnic (Cluj)
Bul Sti Inst Politehn (Cluj) Ser Construc — Buletinul Stiintific. Institutului Politehnic (Cluj). Seria Constructii
Bul Sti Inst Politehn (Cluj) Ser Electromec — Buletinul Stiintific. Institutului Politehnic (Cluj). Seria Electromecanica
Bul Sti Inst Politehn (Cluj) Ser Mec — Buletinul Stiintific. Institutului Politehnic (Cluj). Seria Mecanica
Bul Stiint Inst Constr (Bucuresti) — Buletinul Stiintific. Institutul de Constructii (Bucuresti)
Bul Stiint Inst Pedagog (Baia Mare) Ser B — Buletin Stiintific. Institutul Pedagogic (Baia Mare). Seria B. Biologie, Fizico- Chimie, Matematica
Bul Stiint Inst Politeh (Cluj) — Buletinul Stiintific. Institutului Politehnic (Cluj)
Bul Stiint Inst Politeh (Cluj-Napoca) — Buletinul Stiintific. Institutului Politehnic (Cluj-Napoca)
Bul Stiint Inst Politeh (Cluj) Ser Electromec — Buletinul Stiintific. Institutului Politehnic (Cluj). Seria Electromecanica
Bul Stiint Inst Politehn (Cluj) Ser Electromec — Buletinul Stiintific. Institutului Politehnic (Cluj). Seria Electromecanica
Bul Stiint Inst Politehn (Cluj) Ser Mec — Buletinul Stiintific. Institutului Politehnic (Cluj). Seria Mecanica

Bul Stiint Teh Inst Politeh (Timisoara) — Buletinul Stiintific si Tehnic. Institutului Politehnic (Timisoara)
Bul Stiint Univ Craiova — Buletinul Stiintific al Universitat. Universitatii Craiova [*Romania*]
Bul Sti Tehn Inst Politehn "Traian Vuia" (Timisoara) — Buletinul Stiintific si Tehnic. Institutului Politehnic "Traian Vuia" (Timisoara)
Bul Suicidol — Bulletin of Suicidology
Bul Teh Inf Cent Cercet Mater Prot — Buletin Tehnico-Informativ. Central de Cercetari pentru Materiale de Protectie
Bul Teh Inf Lab Cent Cercet Lacuri Cerneluri Bucuresti — Buletin Tehnico-Informativ. Laboratorului Central de Cercetari pentru Lacuri si Cerneluri Bucuresti
Bul Univ Brasov — Buletinul. Universitatea din Brasov
Bul Univ Brasov Ser A Mec Apl — Buletinul. Universitatii din Brasov. Seria A. Mecanica Aplicata Constructii de Masini
Bul Univ Brasov Ser C — Buletinul. Universitatea din Brasov. Seria C
Bul Univ Brasov Ser C Mat Fiz Chim Sti Natur — Buletinul. Universitatii din Brasov. Seria C. Matematica, Fizica, Chimie, Stiinte Naturale
Bul Univ Shteteror Tiranes Shk Nat — Buletin. Universiteti Shteteror te Tiranes. Fakulteti i Shkencave te Natyres
Bul VIER — Bulletin. Victorian Institute of Educational Research
BUM — Boletin. Universidad de Madrid
Bumagodel Mashinostr — Bumagodelatel'noe Mashinostroenie
Bumazh Prom — Bumazhnaya Promyslennost
Bumaz Prom — Bumazhnaya Promyslennost
Bum Derevoobrab Promst — Bumazhnaya i Derevoobrabatyvayushchaya Promyshlennost
BUMMB — Building Materials Magazine [*Australia*]
BUMPA — Bumazhnaya Promyshlennost
BUMSD — Bulletin of Materials Science
BUMTAW — Bulletin. Academie Malgache
BUNDD — Bundesrat - Drucksache
Bundesanzeiger Beil — Bundesanzeiger. Beilage
Bundesges — Bundesgesundheitsblatt [*West Germany*]
Bundesgesetzbl Repub Oesterr — Bundesgesetzblatt fuer die Republik Oesterreich
Bundesminist Bild Wiss Forschungsber — Bundesministerium fuer Bildung und Wissenschaft. Forschungsbericht
Bundesminist Forsch Technol Forschungsber DV — Bundesministerium fuer Forschung und Technologie. Forschungsbericht DV. Datenverarbeitung
Bundesminist Forsch Technol Forschungsber K — Bundesministerium fuer Forschung und Technologie. Forschungsbericht K. Kernforschung
Bundesminist Forsch Technol Forschungsber M — Bundesministerium fuer Forschung und Technologie. Forschungsbericht M. Meeresforschung
Bundesminist Forsch Technol Forschungsber T — Bundesministerium fuer Forschung und Technologie. Forschungsbericht T. Technologische Forschung und Entwicklung
Bundesminist Forsch Technol Forschungsber W — Bundesministerium fuer Forschung und Technologie. Forschungsbericht W. Weltraumforschung
Bundesminist Forsch Technol Forschungsber Weltraumforsch — Bundesministerium fuer Forschung und Technologie. Forschungsbericht W. Weltraumforschung
Bundes Vers Inst Kulturtech Tech Bodenk — Bundesversuchsinstitut fuer Kulturtechnik und Technische Bodenkunde
BundJb — Bunder Jahrbuch
BUNDMB — Bundnerisches Monatsblatt
B Universities Annual — British Universities Annual
Bunseki Kag — Bunseki Kagaku
BUnt — Biblische Untersuchungen [*Regensburg*]
BUP — Bulletin. University of Pittsburgh
BUPFA5 — Commonwealth Bureau of Pastures and Field Crops. Hurley Berkshire Bulletin
BUPRD — Budget and Program Newsletter [*United States*]
BuR — Bucknell Review
BUR — Bureaucrat
Bur Am Ethn — Bureau of American Ethnology. Bulletin
Bur Am Ethnol Annual Report — Bureau of American Ethnology. Annual Report
Burdekin-Townsville Reg QD Resour Ser — Burdekin-Townsville Region, Queensland. Resource Series
Bureau of Steel Manuf — Bureau of Steel Manufacturers of Australia. Paper Presented at the Annual Meeting
Buren Ispyt Neft Gazov Skvazhin Oslozhennykh Usloviyakh Uzb — Burenie i Ispytanie Neftyanykh i Gazovykh Skvazhin v Oslozhennykh Usloviyakh Uzbekistana
Bur Farmer — Bureau Farmer
Burgenlaend Bienenzucht — Burgenlaendische Bienenzucht
Burgenl Heimatbl — Burgenlaendische Heimatblaetter
BurgHb — Burgenlaendische Heimatblaetter
Burg Monographs in Sci — Burg Monographs in Science [*Basel*]
Buridava — Buridava Studii si Materiale
Bur Insp Test Commer Commod (China) Bull — Bureau for Inspecting and Testing Commercial Commodities (China). Bulletin
BURJL — Bulletin Ustavu Russkeho Jazyka a Literatury
Burlington Mag — Burlington Magazine
Burl M — Burlington Magazine

Burl Mag — Burlington Magazine
Burma Med J — Burma Medical Journal
Bur Mines Inf Circ — Bureau of Mines. Information Circular [*United States*]
Bur Mines Rep Invest — Bureau of Mines. Report of Investigations [*United States*]
Bur Mines Technol News — Bureau of Mines. Technology News [*United States*]
Burns Chron — Burns Chronicle
Bur Rech Geol Min Bull Sect 2 Geol Gites Miner (Fr) — Bureau de Recherches Geologiques et Minieres. Bulletin. Section 2. Geologie des Gites Mineraux (France)
Bur River — Burning River News
Burroughs Clear House — Burroughs Clearing House
BURS — Bibliotheque Universelle et Revue Suisse
Bur Stand (US) Cir — Bureau of Standards (US). Circular
Bur Sugar Exp Stn (Brisbane) Annu Rep — Bureau of Sugar Experiment Stations (Brisbane). Annual Report
Bur Sugar Exp St Queensl Tech Commun — Bureau of Sugar Experiment Stations. Queensland Technical Communications
Bur Sug Exp Sta Tech Commun — Queensland. Bureau of Sugar Experiment Stations. Technical Communication
Bur Sug Exp Stat Tech Commun — Queensland. Bureau of Sugar Experiment Stations. Technical Communication
BUS — Brown University. Studies
BUS — Bulletin. Universite de Strasbourg
BUS — Industrial Management [*London*]
BUSAB — Business Administration [*England*]
Bus Adm — Business Administration
Bus Am — Business America
Bus Am — Business American. The Journal of Industry and Trade
Busan Women's Univ J — Busan Women's University. Journal [*South Korea*]
Bus Arch Cncl Aust Bull — Business Archives Council of Australia. New South Wales Branch. Bulletin
Bus Arch & Hist — Business Archives and History
Bus Archives Council Aust Bul — Business Archives Council of Australia. Bulletin
Bus Archives Council Aust Pub — Business Archives Council of Australia. Publications
Bus Archs Hist — Business Archives and History
Bus in Brief — Business in Brief
BUSC — Boletin. Universidad de Santiago de Compostela
BUSCA — Bollettino delle Scienze Mediche
BUSCB — Building Science
Bus Cond Dig — Business Conditions Digest
Bus Conditions Dig — Business Conditions Digest
BUSE — Boston University. Studies in English
BUSEB — Byulleten' Sovetskoi Antarkticheskoi Ekspeditsii
Bus Econ — Business Economics
Bus and Econ Dim — Business and Economic Dimensions [*Florida*]
Bus and Econ Dimensions — Business and Economic Dimensions
Bus Economist — Business Economist
BUSED — Base and User
Bus Ed Forum — Business Education Forum
Bus Ed J — Business Education Journal
Bus Ed Observer — New Jersey Business Education Observer
Bus Educ Ind — Business Education Index
Bus Ed World — Business Education World
Bus and Fin (Ireland) — Business and Finance (Ireland)
Bus Forum — Business Forum
Bus History — Business History
Bus Hist R — Business History Review
Bus Hist Soc Bull — Business History Society. Bulletin
Bus Horiz — Business Horizons
Bus Horizons — Business Horizons
BusI — Business Periodicals Index
BUSIB — Bussei
Bus India — Business India
Busin Econ — Business Economics
Busin Economist — Business Economist
Business Insur — Business Insurance
Business LR — Business Law Review
Business Q — Business Quarterly
Business R — Business Review
Business Rev — Business Review
Bus Inf Technol — Business Information Technology
Busin Monitor Rubb — Business Monitor. Rubber
Busin Monitor Synth — Business Monitor. Synthetic Resins and Plastics Materials
Busin R — Business Review
Busin Soc R — Business and Society Review
Bus Insur — Business Insurance
Bus Jap — Business Japan
Bus J (Manila) — Business Journal (Manila)
Bus Jpn — Business Japan
BUSKA — Bulletin. Schweizerischer Elektrotechnischer Verein
BUSKB — Bussei Kenkyu

Bus L — Business Lawyer
BUSL — Business Life [*Canada*]
BUSLA — Bulletin International. Academie Yougoslave des Sciences et des Beaux-Arts. Classe des Sciences Mathematiques et Naturelles
Bus Law — Business Lawyer
Bus LR — Business Law Review
Bus L Rev — Business Law Review
Bus L Rev (Butterworths) — Business Law Review (Butterworths)
Bus Mag — Business Magazine
Bus Mark — Business Marketing
Bus Matters — Business Matters
Bus Period Index — Business Periodicals Index
Bus Prof Ethics J — Business and Professional Ethics Journal
Bus and Public Affairs — Business and Public Affairs
Bus Q — Business Quarterly
Bus R (Bangkok) — Business Review (Bangkok)
Bus Rev — Business Review
Bus Rev Wash Univ — Business Review. Washington University
Bus Scr — Business Screen
Bus & Soc R — Business and Society Review
Bus & Soc R — Business and Society Review/Innovation
Bus Soc Rev — Business and Society Review
Bus & Soc'y Rev — Business and Society Review
Bus Syst — Business Systems
Bus Syst & Equip — Business Systems and Equipment
Bus Taiwan — Business and Industry Taiwan
Bus Transp — Bus Transportation
Bus Venezuela — Business Venezuela
Bus W — Business Week
Bus Week — Business Week
BUT — Buletin. Universiteti Shteteror te Tiranes. Seria Shkencat Shoqerore
BUT — Bulletin. Universite de Toulouse
BUT — Business International
Butler Univ Bot Stud — Butler University Botanical Studies
Butl Sec Mat Soc Catalana Cienc Fis Quim Mat — Butlleti. Seccio de Matematiques. Societat Catalana de Ciencies Fisiques, Quimiques, i Matematiques
Butl Soc Catalana Cienc Fis Quim Mat 2 — Butlleti. Societat Catalana de Ciencies Fisiques, Quimiques, i Matematiques. Segona Epoca
BUTMB — Building Technology and Management
BUTPA — Butane Propane
Butsuri Phys Soc Jap — Butsuri. Physical Society of Japan
Butter & Cheese J — Butter and Cheese Journal
Butter Cheese Milk Prod J — Butter, Cheese, and Milk Products Journal
BUVOA — Bulletin Volcanologique
BUVSA — Bulletin. Vereinigung der Schweizerischen Petroleum-Geologen und -Ingenieure
BUW — Business Week
BUWEA — Business Week
BUX — Greece's Weekly for Business and Finance
BUYRA — Bulletin. Parenteral Drug Association
BV — Biblical Viewpoint
BV — Bogens Verden
BV — Bogoslovni Vestnik
BVAB — Bulletin van de Vereeniging tot Bevordering der Kennis van de Antike Beschaving
BVAOD — Byulleten' Vil'nyusskoi Astronomicheskoi Observatorii
BVB — Bont. Maandblad voor het Bontbedrijf
BVC — Bible et Vie Chretienne [*Paris*]
BVG — Bijdragen voor Vaderlandsche Geschiedenis en Oudheidskunde
BVGO — Bijdragen voor Vaderlandsche Geschiedenis en Oudheidskunde
BVGPA — Boletin Informativo. Asociacion Venezolana de Geologia, Mineria, y Petroleo
BVHUA — Bibliotheca "Vita Humana"
BVI — Venezolaans Nederlandse Kamer van Koophandel en Industrie. Bulletin
BVIBA — Biologiya Vnutrennikh Vod. Informatsionnyi Byulleten
BVIRA — Byulleten' Vsesoyuznogo Nauchno-Issledovatel'skogo Instituta Rastenievodstva Imeni N. I. Vavilova
BVJOA — British Veterinary Journal
BVJOA9 — British Veterinary Journal
BVM — Buvoha Mededelingen
BVP — Personenvervoer
BVR — Beroepsvervoer
BVSAW — Berichte. Verhandlungen der (Koeniglich) Saechsischen Akademie der Wissenschaften zu Leipzig
BVSAWL — Berichte. Verhandlungen der Saechsischen Akademie der Wissenschaften zu Leipzig
BVSGW — Berichte. Verhandlungen der Saechsischen Gesellschaft der Wissenschaften
BVSRJL — Bulletin Vysoke Skoly Russkeho Jazyka a Literatury
BVUPD — Bulletin. Vyskumneho Ustavu Potravinarskeho
BW — Between Worlds
BW — Biblical World [*Chicago*]
BW — Blick durch die Wirtschaft
BW — Blues World
BW — Book World [*Chicago Tribune*]

BW — Brass and Wind News
BW — Business Week
BWA — Business Venezuela
BWANT — Beitraege zur Wissenschaft vom Alten und Neuen Testament [*Leipzig/Stuttgart*]
BWAT — Beitraege zur Wissenschaft vom Alten Testament
BWATA — Biuletyn Wojskowej Akademii Technicznej Imienia Jaroslawa Dabrowskiego
BWAuNT — Beitraege zur Wissenschaft vom Alten und Neuen Testament [*Leipzig/Stuttgart*]
BWCSA — Broad Way Clinical Supplement
BWDEB — Boden Wand und Decke
BWE — Business Week
BWESA — Berliner Wetterkarte. Supplement
BWG — Bouw. Onafhankelijk Weekblad voor de Bouw
B WHO — Bulletin. World Health Organization
BWK — Brennstoff-Waerme-Kraft [*Fuel, Heat, Power*]
BWKG — Blaetter fuer Wuerttembergische Kirchengeschichte
BWL — Bouwbelangen
BWO — Bibliographie der Wirtschaftspresse
BWPA News Sheet — BWPA [*British Wood Preserving Association*] News Sheet
BWR — Black Warrior Review
BWR — Bouwkroniek. Weekblad voor de Bouwvakken en Aanverwante Vakken. Aanbestedingsbulletin voor Alle Werken en Leveringen
BWT — Bestuurswetenschappen
BWTSA — Bauwirtschaft
BWUJD — Busan Women's University. Journal
BWVACET — Bulletin. West Virginia Association of College English Teachers
BW (WP) — Book World (Washington Post)
BWWSAP — Branntweinwirtschaft
BWX — Berliner Wirtschaft; Mitteilungen der Industriekammer und Handelskammer zu Berlin
BWY — Bouw/Werk. De Bouw in Feiten, Cijfers, en Analyses
BXD — Bulletin de Documentation Rhenane
BXK — Bank Leumi Le-Israel. Economic Review
BXTJA — Bendix Technical Journal
BXV — Boxboard Containers
BYA — Beleidsanalyse
BYB — Maandstatistiek Bouwnijverheid
BYBBA — Brigham Young University. Science Bulletin. Biological Series
BYBBAJ — Brigham Young University. Science Bulletin. Biological Series
BYDAA — Baylor Dental Journal
ByF — Biblia y Fe [*Madrid*]
BYGEA — Byggmestern
Bygnin Medd — Bygningsstatiske Meddelelser
BYGSA — Brigham Young University. Geology Studies
BYH — Bulletin. Europese Gemeenschappen. Europese Gemeenschap voor Kolen en Staal, Europese Economische Gemeenschap, Europese Gemeenschap voor Atoomenergie
BYIL — British Yearbook of International Law
ByJ — Byzantinisch-Neugriechische Jahrbuecher
BYL — Bulletin van de Generale Bankmaatschappij
BYLJA — Bayerisches Landwirtschaftliches Jahrbuch
By LR — Baylor Law Review
BYM — Bell Journal of Economics
BYMEA — Bygningsstatiske Meddelelser
BYMOA — Byulleten' Moskovskogo Obshchestva Ispytatelei Prirody Otdel Biologicheskii
B Yokohama City Univ — Bulletin. Yokohama City University
Byron J — Byron Journal
Byrsa — Cahiers de Byrsa
BYSTA — Byulleten' Stroitel'noi Tekhniki
ByT — Barrasiha-Ye Tarikhi
BYU — BYU [*Brigham Young University*] Law Review
Byull Abastumanskaya Astrofiz Obs Akad Nauk Gruz SSR — Byulleten' Abastumanskaya Astrofizicheskaya Observatoriya Akademiya Nauk Gruzinskoi SSR [*Georgian SSR*]
Byull Akad Nauk Gruz SSR Abastumanskaya Astrofiz Obs — Byulleten' Akademiya Nauk Gruzinskoi SSR Abastumanskaya Astrofizicheskaya Observatoriya [*Georgian SSR*]
Byull Akad Nauk Uzb SSR — Byulleten' Akademii Nauk Uzbekskoi SSR
Byull Azerb Nauchno Issled Inst Khlopkovod — Byulleten' Azerbaidzhanskogo Nauchno Issledovatel'skogo Instituta Khlopkovodstva
Byull Belogo Morya — Byulleten' Belogo Morya
Byull Bot Sada Akad Nauk Arm SSR — Byulleten' Botanicheskogo Sada Akademii Nauk Armyanskoi SSR
Byull Bot Sada Erevan — Byulleten' Botanicheskogo Sada Erevan
Byull Eksp Biol Med — Byulleten' Eksperimental'noi Biologii i Meditsiny
Byull Fiziol Rast — Byulleten' po Fiziologii Rastenii
Byull Glavn Bot Sada (Leningr) — Byulleten' Glavnogo Botanicheskogo Sada (Leningrad)
Byull Gl Bot Sada — Byulleten' Glavnogo Botanicheskogo Sada [*Leningrad*]
Byull Gos Nikitsk Bot Sada — Byulleten' Gosudarstvennogo Nikitskogo Botanicheskogo Sada

Byull Inf Tsentra Yad Dannym — Byulleten' Informatsionnogo Tsentral'nogo po Yadernym Dannym
Byull Inf Tsentr Genet Lab Im I V Michurina — Byulleten' Informatsii Tsentralnoi Geneticheskoi Laboratorii Imeni I. V. Michurina
Byull Inst Astrofiz Akad Nauk Tadzh — Byulleten' Instituta Astrofiziki Akademiya Nauk Tadzhikskoi SSR
Byull Inst Astrofiz Akad Nauk Tadzh SSR — Byulleten' Instituta Astrofiziki Akademiya Nauk Tadzhikskoi SSR
Byull Inst Biol Akad Nauk B SSR — Byulleten' Instituta Biologiya Akademii Nauk Belorusskoi SSR
Byull Inst Biol Vodokhran — Byulleten' Instituta Biologii Vodokhranilishcha
Byull Inst Metallokeram Spets Splavov Akad Nauk Ukr SSR — Byulleten' Instituta Metallokeramiki i Spetsial'nykh Splavov Akademiya Nauk Ukrainskoi SSR
Byull Inst Teor Astron — Byulleten' Instituta Teoreticheskoi Astronomii [*USSR*]
Byull Inst Teor Astron Akad Nauk SSSR — Byulleten' Instituta Teoreticheskoi Astronomii Akademiya Nauk SSSR
Byull Inst Teoret Astronom — Akademiya Nauk SSSR. Byulleten Instituta Teoreticheskoi Astronomii
Byull Kavk Inst Miner Syrya — Byulleten' Kavkazskogo Instituta Mineral'nogo Syr'ya
Byull Kirgiz Nauch Issled Inst Zemled — Byulleten' Kirgizskogo Nauchno-Issledovatel'skogo Instituta Zemledeliya
Byull Kirgiz Nauchno-Issled Inst Zeml — Byulleten' Kirgizskogo Nauchno-Issledovatel'skogo Instituta Zemledeliya
Byull Kirg Nauchno Issled Inst Zemled — Byulleten' Kirgizskogo Nauchno-Issledovatel'skogo Instituta Zemledeliya
Byull Kom Izuch Chetvertichn Perioda Akad Nauk SSSR — Byulleten' Komissii po Izucheniyu Chetvertichnogo Perioda Akademiya Nauk SSSR
Byull Kom Kometam Meteoram Astron Sov Akad Nauk SSSR — Byulleten' Komissii po Kometam i Meteoram Astronomicheskogo Sovieta Akademii Nauk SSSR
Byull Kom Opred Absol Geol Form — Byulleten' Komissii po Opredeleniyu Absolyutnogo Vozrasta Geologicheskikh Formatsii [*USSR*]
Byull Kom Opred Absol Vozrasta Geol Form Akad Nauk SSSR — Byulleten' Komissii po Opredeleniyu Absolyutnogo Vozrasta Geologicheskikh Formatsii Akademiya Nauk SSSR
Byull Leningr Inst Organ Okhr Tr — Byulleten' Leningradskii Institut Organizatsii i Okhrany Truda
Byull Leningr Otd Inst Udobr Agropochvoved — Byulleten' Leningradskogo Otdeleniya Institut Udobrenii i Agropochvovedeniya
Byull Mezhdunar O-va Torfu — Byulleten' Mezhdunarodnogo Obshchestva po Torfu
Byull Mosk Obshch Ispyt Prir — Byulleten' Moskovskogo Obshchestva Ispytatelei Prirody Otdel Biologicheskii
Byull Mosk Ova Ispyt Prir Kalinin Otd — Byulleten' Moskovskogo Obshchestva Ispytatelei Prirody Kalininskii Otdel
Byull Mosk Ova Ispyt Prir Otd Biol — Byulleten' Moskovskogo Obshchestva Ispytatelei Prirody Otdel Biologicheskii
Byull Mosk Ova Ispyt Prir Otd Geol — Byulleten' Moskovskogo Obshchestva Ispytatelei Prirody Otdel Geologicheskii
Byull Nauch-Issled Inst Malyarii Med Parazitol — Byulleten' Nauchno-Issledovatel'skogo Instituta Malyarii i Meditsinskoi Parazitologii
Byull Nauchno Issled Inst Malyarii Med Parazitol — Byulleten' Nauchno Issledovatel'skogo Instituta Malyarii i Meditsinskoi Parazitologii
Byull Nauchno Issled Khim Farm Inst — Byulleten' Nauchno Issledovatel'skogo Khimiko Farmatsevticheskogo Instituta
Byull Nauchno-Tekh Inf — Byulleten' Nauchno-Tekhnicheskoi Informatsii
Byull Nauchno-Tekh Inf Agron Fiz — Byulleten' Nauchno-Tekhnicheskoi Informatsii po Agronomicheskoi Fizike
Byull Nauchno Tekh Inf Arm Nauchno Issled Inst Zemled — Byulleten' Nauchno-Tekhnicheskoi Informatsii Armyanskogo Nauchno-Issledovatel'skogo Instituta Zemledeliya
Byull Nauchno Tekh Inf Beloruss Nauchno Issled Inst Zemled — Byulleten' Nauchno-Tekhnicheskoi Informatsii Belorusskogo Nauchno-Issledovatel'skogo Instituta Zemledeliya
Byull Nauchno Tekh Inf Gos Geol Kom SSSR — Byulleten' Nauchno-Tekhnicheskoi Informatsii Gosudarstvennyi Geologicheskii Komitet SSSR
Byull Nauchno Tekh Inf Inst — Byulleten' Nauchno-Tekhnicheskoi Informatsii Nauchno-Issledovatel'skogo Instituta Pchelovodstva
Byull Nauchno Tekh Inf Litov Nauchno Issled Inst Zhivotnovod — Byulleten' Nauchno-Tekhnicheskoi Informatsii Litovskogo Nauchno-Issledovatel'skogo Instituta Zhivotnovodstva
Byull Nauchno Tekh Inf Maslichn Kult — Byulleten' Nauchno-Tekhnicheskoi Informatsii po Maslichnym Kulturam
Byull Nauchno Tekh Inf Minist Geol Okhr Nedr SSSR — Byulleten' Nauchno-Tekhnicheskoi Informatsii Ministerstvo Geologii i Okhrany Nedr SSSR
Byull Nauchno Tekh Inf Minist Geol SSSR — Byulleten' Nauchno-Tekhnicheskoi Informatsii Ministerstvo Geologii SSSR
Byull Nauchno-Tekh Inf S-kh Mikrobiol — Byulleten' Nauchno-Tekhnicheskoi Informatsii po Sel'skokhozyaistvennoi Mikrobiologii
Byull Nauchno-Tekh Inf (Sumskaya Gos Skh Opytn Stn) — Byulleten' Nauchno-Tekhnicheskoi Informatsii (Sumskaya Gosudarstvennaya Sel'skokhozyaistvennaya Opytnaya Stantsiya)

Byull Nauchno Tekh Inf Tadzh Nauchno Issled Inst Sel'sk Khoz — Byulleten' Nauchno-Tekhnicheskoi Informatsii Tadzhikskogo Nauchno-Issledovatel'skogo Instituta Sel'sk Khozyaistva

Byull Nauchno Tekh Inf Tsentr Torfobolotnoi Opytn Stant — Byulleten' Nauchno-Tekhnicheskoi Informatsii Tsentralnoi Torfobolotnoi Opytnoi Stantsii

Byull Nauchno Tekh Inf Turkm Nauchno Issled Inst Zemled — Byulleten' Nauchno-Tekhnicheskoi Informatsii Turkmenskogo Nauchno-Issledovatel'skogo Instituta Zemledeliya

Byull Nauchno Tekh Inf Ukr Nauchno Issled Inst Met — Byulleten' Nauchno-Tekhnicheskoi Informatsii Ukrainskii Nauchno-Issledovatel'skii Institut Metallov

Byull Nauchno Tekh Inf Ukr Nauchno Issled Inst Ogneuporov — Byulleten' Nauchno-Tekhnicheskoi Informatsii Ukrainskogo Nauchno-Issledovatel'skogo Instituta Ogneuporov

Byull Nauchno Tekh Inf Ukr Nauchno Issled Uglekhim Inst — Byulleten' Nauchno-Tekhnicheskoi Informatsii Ukrainskii Nauchno-Issledovatel'skii Uglekhimicheskii Institut

Byull Nauchno Tekh Inf Ural Nauchno Issled Inst Chern Met — Byulleten' Nauchno-Tekhnicheskoi Informatsii Ural'skogo Nauchno-Issledovatel'skogo Instituta Chernykh Metallov

Byull Nauchno Tekh Sov Metall Legk Met — Byulleten' Nauchno-Tekhnicheskogo Soveta po Metallurgii Legkikh Metallov

Byull Nauchn Stud Ova Kaz Gos Univ — Byulleten' Nauchnogo Studencheskogo Obshchestva Kazakhskii Gosudarstvennyi Universitet

Byull Obmena Opytom Lakokras Promsti — Byulleten' Obmena Opytom Lakokrasochnoi Promyshlennosti

Byull Ova Estestvoispyt Voronezh Gos Univ — Byulleten' Obshchestva Estestvoispytatelei pri Voronezhskom Gosudarstvennom Universitete

Byull Pochvoveda — Byulleten' Pochvoveda

Byull Sakharotresta — Byulleten' Sakharotresta

Byull Sov Antarkt Eksped — Byulleten' Sovetskoi Antarkticheskoi Ekspeditsii [*USSR*]

Byull Sov Seismol — Byulleten' Sovet po Seismologii [*USSR*]

Byull Sredneaziat Gos Univ — Byulleten' Sredneaziatskogo Gosudarstvennogo Universiteta

Byull Stn Opt Nablyudeniya Iskusstvennykh Sputnikov Zemli — Byulleten' Stantsii Opticheskogo Nablyudeniya Iskusstvennykh Sputnikov Zemli [*USSR*]

Byull Stroit Tekh — Byulleten' Stroitel'noi Tekhniki [*USSR*]

Byull Stud Nauchn Ova Kaz Gos Univ — Byulleten' Studencheskogo Nauchnogo Obshchestva Kazakhskii Gosudarstvennyi Universitet

Byull Stud Nauchn Ova Leningr Gos Univ — Byulleten' Studencheskogo Nauchnogo Obshchestva Leningradskii Gosudarstvennyi Universitet

Byull Tekh-Ehkon Inf Gos Nauchno-Issled Inst Nauchn Tekh Inf — Byulleten' Tekhniko-Ehkonomicheskoj Informatsii. Gosudarstvennyj Nauchno-Issledovatel'skij Institut Nauchnoj i Tekhnicheskoj Informatsii

Byull Tekh-Ehkon Inf Gos Nauchno-Issled Inst Nauchn Tekn Inf — Byulleten' Tekhniko-Ehkonomicheskoj Informatsii. Gosudarstvennyj Nauchno-Issledovatel'skij Institut Nauchnoj i Tekhnicheskoj Informatsii

Byull Tekh Ekon Inf — Byulleten' Tekhniko-Ekonomicheskoi Informatsii

Byull Tekh-Ekon Inf Gos Nauchno-Issled Inst Nauchn Tekh Inf — Byulleten' Tekhniko-Ekonomicheskoi Informatsii Gosudarstvennyi Nauchno-Issledovatel'skii Institut Nauchnoi i Tekhnicheskoi Informatsii [*USSR*]

Byull Tsentra Yad Dannym — Byulleten' Tsentra po Yadernym Dannym [*USSR*]

Byull Tsvetn' Metall — Byulleten' Tsvetnoi Metallurgii

Byull Ural Otd Mosk Ova Ispyt Prir — Byulleten' Ural'skogo Otdeleniya Moskovskogo Obshchestva Ispytatelei Prirody

Byull Vil'nyus Astron Obs — Byulleten' Vil'nyusskoi Astronomicheskoi Observatorii [*Lithuanian SSR*]

Byull Vost Sib Fenol Kom — Byulleten' Vostochno Sibirskoi Fenologicheskoi Komissii

Byull Vses Astron Geod Ova — Byulleten' Vsesoyuznogo Astronomo-Geodezicheskogo Obshchestva

Byull Vses Inst Eksp Vet — Byulleten' Vsesoyuznogo Instituta Eksperimental'noi Veterinarii

Byull Vses Inst Gel'mintol — Byulleten' Vsesoyuznogo Instituta Gel'mintologii

Byull Vses Inst Rastenievod — Byulleten' Vsesoyuznogo Instituta Rastenievodstva

Byull Vses Kardiol Nauchn Tsentra AMN SSSR — Byulleten' Vsesoyuznogo Kardiologicheskogo Nauchnogo Tsentra AMN SSSR

Byull Vses Koord Kom Mikroelem — Byulleten' Vsesoyuznoi Koordinatsionnoi Komissee po Mikroelementam

Byull Vses Nauchno Issled Geol Inst — Byulleten' Vsesoyuznogo Nauchno-Issledovatel'skogo Geologicheskogo Instituta

Byull Vses Nauchno-Issled Inst Agrolesomelior — Byulleten' Vsesoyuznogo Nauchno-Issledovatel'skogo Instituta Agrolesomelioratsii

Byull Vses Nauchno Issled Inst Chain Promsti — Byulleten' Vsesoyuznogo Nauchno-Issledovatel'skogo Instituta Chainoi Promyshlennosti

Byull Vses Nauchno-Issled Inst Chaya Subtrop Kul't — Byulleten' Vsesoyuznogo Nauchno-Issledovatel'skogo Instituta Chaya i Subtropicheskikh Kul'tur

Byull Vses Nauchno Issled Inst Eksp Vet Im Ya R Kovalenko — Byulleten' Vsesoyuznogo Nauchno-Issledovatel'skogo Instituta Eksperimental'noi Veterinarii Imeni Ya. R. Kovalenko

Byull Vses Nauchno-Issled Inst Kukuruzy — Byulleten' Vsesoyuznogo Nauchno-Issledovat'skogo Instituta Kukuruzy

Byull Vses Nauchno-Issled Inst Rastenievod Im N I Vavilova — Byulleten' Vsesoyuznogo Nauchno-Issledovatel'skogo Instituta Rastenievodstva Imeni N. I. Vavilova [*USSR*]

Byull Vses Nauchno Issled Inst Tsem — Byulleten' Vsesoyuznogo Nauchno-Issledovatel'skogo Instituta Tsementov

Byull Vses Nauchno Issled Inst Udobr Agropochvoved — Byulleten' Vsesoyuznogo Nauchno-Issledovatel'skogo Instituta Udobrenii i Agropochvovedeniya

Byull Vses Nauchno-Issled Inst Zashch Rast — Byulleten' Vsesoyuznogo Nauchno-Issledovatel'skogo Instituta Zashchity Rastenii

Byull Vses Ordena Lenina Inst Eksp Vet — Byulleten' Vsesoyuznogo Ordena Lenina Instituta Eksperimental'noi Veterinarii

Byull Vulkanol Stn Akad Nauk SSSR — Byulleten' Vulkanologicheskikh Stantsii Akademiya Nauk SSSR

Byull Vulkanol Stn Kamchatke Akad Nauk SSSR — Byulleten' Vulkanologicheskikh Stantsii na Kamchatke Akademiya Nauk SSSR

BYU LR — Brigham Young University. Law Review

BYU L Rev — Brigham Young University. Law Review

BYUS — Brigham Young University. Studies

ByZ — Byzantinische Zeitschrift

Byz — Byzantion

Byzantinak — Byzantina kai Metabyzantina

Byzantine M — Byzantine and Modern Greek Studies

Byzantine S — Byzantine Studies

Byzantinische Z — Byzantinische Zeitschrift

Byzantin Z — Byzantinische Zeitschrift

Byz Arch — Byzantinisches Archiv

Byz-Bulg — Byzantino-Bulgarica

Byz F — Byzantinische Forschungen

Byz Forsch — Byzantinische Forschungen

Byz-Met — Byzantina-Metabyzantina

ByzMetabyz — Byzantina-Metabyzantina

Byz-Neugr Jahrb — Byzantinisch-Neugriechische Jahrbuecher

BYZNGJB — Byzantinisch-Neugriechische Jahrbuecher

BYZOA — Byulleten' Izobretenii

ByzS — Byzantino-Slavica

ByzSl — Byzantino-Slavica

Byz Slav — Byzantino-Slavica. Sbornik pro Studium Byzantskoslovanskych Vztahu

ByzZ — Byzantinische Zeitschrift

BZ — Biblische Zeitschrift

BZ — Borsen Zeitung

BZ — Byzantinische Zeitschrift

BZA — Berichte ueber Landwirtschaft. Zeitschrift fuer Agrarpolitik und Landwirtschaft

B Zambia Lang Group — Bulletin of the Zambia Language Group

BZAW — Beihefte. Zeitschrift fuer die Alttestamentliche Wissenschaft [*Giessen/Berlin*]

B Zb — Bayerisches Zahnaerzteblatt

BzDB — Bibliographien zur Deutsche Barockliteratur

BZE — Bankers' Magazine

BZF — Biblische Zeitfragen [*Muenster*]

B Zfr — Biblische Zeitfragen

BZG — Basler Zeitschrift fuer Geschichte und Altertumskunde

BZG — Beitraege zur Geschichte der Deutschen Arbeiterbewegung

BZGA — Basler Zeitschrift fuer Geschichte und Altertumskunde

BZGAK — Basler Zeitschrift fuer Geschichte und Altertumskunde

BZHM — Berliner Zahnaerztliche Halbmonatsschrift

BZIH — Biuletyn Zydowskiego Instytutu Historycznego

BzJA — Beihefte zum Ja

BZM — Berliner Zeitung am Mittag

BZM — Beton, Herstellung, Verwendung

BzMW — Beitraege zur Musikwissenschaft

BZN — Beitraege zur Namenforschung [*Heidelberg*]

BzNH — Bizantion-Nea Hellas

BZNW — Beihefte. Zeitschrift fuer die Neutestamentliche Wissenschaft und die Kunde der Alteren Kirche [*Giessen/Berlin*]

BZR Gg — Beihefte. Zeitschrift fuer Religions und Geistesgeschichte

B Ztfr — Biblische Zeitfragen

BZThS — Bonner Zeitschrift fuer Theologie und Seelsorge

BZTS — Bonner Zeitschrift fuer Theologie und Seelsorge

BZWW — Beihefte. Zeitschrift Wirkendes Wort

BZX — Bank of Tanzania. Economic Bulletin

C

C — Campaign
C — Canada. Department of the Environment. Fisheries and Marine Service. Technical Report Series
C — Candela
C — Castrum Peregrini
C — Cenobio
C — Century
C — Chemisches Zentralblatt
C — Coimbra
C — Collier's
C — Columbia Journalism Review
C — Commonweal
C — Correspondent
C — Critica
C — Critique
C77 — Cinema 77
C 83 — Cinema 83
CA — CA. A Bulletin of Cancer Progress
CA — CA. A Cancer Journal for Clinicians
Ca — Cancer Journal for Clinicians
CA — Cercetari Arheologice
CA — Chemical Abstracts [Chemical Abstracts Service] [Database]
C A — Chemical Age
CA — Church Administration
CA — Communication Arts
CA — Critica d'Arte
CA — Cuadernos Americanos
CA — Current Anthropology
CAA — Camara de Industria y Comercio Argentino-Alemana
CAA — Chinese Astronomy and Astrophysics
CAA — Commonwealth Arbitration Awards and Determinations
CAAB — Canadian Archaeological Association. Bulletin
CAAGB — Canada Agriculture
CAAH — Cahiers Alsaciens d'Archeologie, d'Art, et d'Histoire
CAAJ — CAA [Civil Aeronautics Administration] Journal
CAA J — Civil Aeronautics Administration. Journal
CAANA — Comptes Rendus. Association des Anatomistes
CAANB — Cahiers d'Anesthesiologie
Ca Ar — Cahiers Archeologiques
CAAR — Calgary Archaeologist. University of Calgary [Canada]
CAARA — Canadian Architect
CAAS Bull — Canadian Association for American Studies. Bulletin
CAB — Cahiers d'Archeologie Biblique
CAB — Current Affairs Bulletin
CAB — Current Awareness Bulletin
CAB Annot Bibliogr — Commonwealth Agricultural Bureaux. Annotated Bibliography [Database]
CABCD — Cancer Biochemistry - Biophysics
CABD — Canadian Building Digest
Ca Bi Q — Catholic Biblical Quarterly
Cablecast Cable TV Eng — Cablecasting, Cable TV Engineering
Cable Rpt — Cable Report
Cables Transm — Cables et Transmission
Cables & Transm — Cables et Transmission
Cable Telev Eng — Cable Television Engineering

Cabl Transm — Cables et Transmission
CABN — Caribou News [Canada]
CaboV — Cabo Verde
C A Brescia — Commentari. Accademia di Brescia
CABSAF — Catholic University of America. Biological Studies
CABUA — Canadian Business
CA Bull — CA. A Bulletin of Cancer Progress
CA Bull Cancer Prog — CA. A Bulletin of Cancer Progress
CAC — Current Abstracts of Chemistry [Institute for Scientific Information] [Database]
CACAA — Cafe, Cacao, The
CA Cancer J Clin — CA. A Cancer Journal for Clinicians
Cacao Bol Inf — Cacao Boletin Informacion
Cacao Choc Suikerwerken — Cacao Chocolade en Suikerwerken
Cacao Colomb — Cacao en Colombia
Cacau Atual — Cacau Atualidades
CACBB — Annual Reports on the Progress of Chemistry. Section B. Organic Chemistry
CACBB4 — Annual Reports on the Progress of Chemistry. Section B. Organic Chemistry
Cacciat Ital — Cacciatore Italiano
Cacciat Trent — Cacciatore Trentino
CACH — Canadian Churchman
CAC & IC — Current Abstracts of Chemistry and Index Chemicus
CACM — Communications. ACM [Association for Computing Machinery]
CACO — Canadian Conservationist
CACOD — Canadian Consumer
CACP — Cahiers de l'Amitie Charles Peguy
CACS — Canada. Climatological Studies
Cact J — Cactus Journal
Cact Succ J — Cactus and Succulent Journal
Cact Succ J Gr Br — Cactus and Succulent Journal of Great Britain
Cact Suc Mex — Cactaceas y Suculentas Mexicanas
Cact Suculentas Mex — Cactaceas y Suculentas Mexicanas
Cactus Succ J — Cactus and Succulent Journal [United States]
Cactus Succ J Gt Br — Cactus and Succulent Journal of Great Britain
Cactus Succulent J — Cactus and Succulent Journal
Cactus Succulent J GB — Cactus and Succulent Journal of Great Britain
Ca Cu — Boletin. Instituto Caro y Cuervo
CACYA4 — Cancer Cytology
Cad — Caducee
Cad — Caduceo. Revista Grafica Espanola Economico Financiera
Cad — Caduceus
CAD — Computer Applications Digest
Cad Amazonia — Cadernos da Amazonia
CadB — Cadernos Brasileiros
CAD/CAM Tech — CAD/CAM [Computer-Aided Design/Computer-Aided Manufacturing] Technology
Cad Cient — Cadernos Cientificos
Cad Cient — Cadernos Cientificos Instituto Pasteur de Lisboa
CADEC — Computer-Aided Design of Electronic Circuits [Elsevier Book Series]
Cadence — Cadence Magazine
CADIDW — Cardiovascular Diseases Bulletin. Texas Heart Institute
Cad Med — Cadiz Medico

Cad Mens Estat Inf Inst Vinho Porto — Cadernos Mensais de Estatistica e Informacao. Editados pelo Instituto da Vinho da Porto
CADOD — Cahiers de l'Analyse des Donnees
Cad Omega — Caderno Omega
Cad Omega Univ Fed Rural Pernambuco — Caderno Omega. Universidade Federal Rural de Pernambuco
CADRDP — Cardiovascular Drugs
Cadres et Profes — Cadres et Professions
CAE — Canadian Entomologist
CAE — Cercle Archeologique d'Enghien. Annales
CAEAn — Cercle Archeologique d'Enghien. Annales
CAEEA — Canadian Electronics Engineering
CAEF — Cahiers. Association Internationale des Etudes Francaises
CAELB — Atomic Energy Law Reports
CAEN — Canadian Energy News
CAENA — Canadian Entomologist
CAES — Canadian Ethnic Studies
CAETB — Canadian Aeronautic and Space Institute. Transactions
CAF — Captain Future
Cafe — Cafe Solo
Cafe Peru Cent Coop Agrar Cafe Peru — Cafe Peru. Central de Cooperativas Agrarias Cafe Peru
CAFGA — California Fish and Game
CAFN — Canadian Field-Naturalist
CAFNA — Canadian Field-Naturalist
CAFO — Canadian Forum
CAFODQ — Cancer Forum
CAFOER — Cancer Focus
CAfr — Congo-Afrique
C Afr Adm Publ — Cahiers Africains d'Administration Publique
C Afr Secur Soc — Cahiers Africains de la Securite Sociale
CAFSB2 — Congres. Association Francaise pour l'Avancement des Sciences [*Nancy*]
CAGIB — Chemical Age International
CAGQ — Cahiers de Geographie de Quebec
CAGRA — California Agriculture
CAGYAO — Cardiology
Ca H — Cahiers d'Histoire
CAHA — Cahiers d'Archeologie et d'Histoire d'Alsace
Cah Acoust — Cahiers d'Acoustique
Cah Aerod — Cahiers d'Aerodynamique
Cah Albert Le Grand — Cahiers Albert Le Grand
Cah Albert Roussel — Cahiers Albert Roussel
Cah Alg San — Cahiers Algeriens de la Sante
Cah Als Arch — Cahiers Alsaciens d'Archeologie, d'Art, et d'Histoire
Cah Am Lat — Cahiers des Ameriques Latines
Cah Am Latines Ser Sciences Homme — Cahiers des Ameriques Latines. Serie Sciences de l'Homme
Cah Anal — Cahiers pour l'Analyse
Cah Anal Text — Cahiers d'Analyse Textuelle
Cah Anesth — Cahiers d'Anesthesiologie
Cah Anesthesiol — Cahiers d'Anesthesiologie
Cah Ann — Cahiers des Annales
Cah Ann Norm — Cahier des Annales de Normandie
Cah Apic — Cahiers Apicoles
Cah A R — Cahiers de l'Actualite Religieuse
Cah Arch — Cahiers Archeologiques
Cah Archeol Hist Berry — Cahiers d'Archeologie et d'Histoire du Berry
Cah Arch Hist Berry — Cahiers d'Archeologie et d'Histoire du Berry
Cah Arch Subaqu — Cahiers d'Archeologie Subaquatique
Cah Art — Cahiers d'Art
Cah Art Sacre — Cahiers de l'Art Sacre
Cah As Se — Cahiers de l'Asie du Sud-Est
Cah Ass Int Et Fr — Cahiers. Association Internationale des Etudes Francaises
Cah Biloque — Cahiers de la Biloque
Cah Biol Mar — Cahiers de Biologie Marine
Cah Bio Mar — Cahiers de Biologie Marine
Cah Bleus Vet — Cahiers Bleus Veterinaires
Cah Brux — Cahiers Bruxellois
CAHC — Cuadernos de Arqueologia e Historia de la Ciudad
Cah Canadiens M — Cahiers Canadiens de Musique [*Canada Music Book*]
Cah Cent Etud Rech Oper — Cahiers. Centre d'Etudes de Recherche Operationnelle
Cah Centre Tech Bois — Cahier. Centre Technique du Bois
Cah CERBOM — Cahiers. CERBOM [*Centre d'Etudes et de Recherche de Biologie et d'Oceanographie Medicale*]
CahCerclERenan — Cahiers. Cercle Ernest Renan [*Paris*]
Cah Ch Foucauld — Cahiers Charles De Foucauld
Cah Chir — Cahiers de Chirurgie
Cah Cinema — Cahiers du Cinema
Cah Civ Med — Cahiers de Civilisation Medievale
Cah Coll Med Hop Paris — Cahiers. College de Medecine des Hopitaux de Paris
Cah Communisme — Cahiers du Communisme
Cah Com Prev Batim Trav Publics — Cahiers. Comites de Prevention du Batiment et des Travaux Publics [*France*]

Cah Debussy — Cahiers Debussy
Cah Docum — Cahiers de la Documentation
Cah de Droit Eur — Cahiers de Droit Europeen
Cah de Droit (Quebec) — Cahiers de Droit (Quebec) [*Canada*]
CAHE — Canadian Heritage
Cah Econ Br — Cahiers Economiques de Bruxelles
Cah Econs Bruxelles — Cahiers Economiques de Bruxelles
Cah Econs et Monetaires — Cahiers Economiques et Monetaires
Cah Econs et Soc — Cahiers Economiques et Sociaux
Cah Elis — Cahiers Elisabethains
Cah Enf — Cahiers de l'Enfrance
Cah Et Afr — Cahiers d'Etudes Africaines
Cah d'Et Afr — Cahiers d'Etudes Africaines. Revue Trimestrielle
Cah Et Cath — Cahiers d'Etudes Cathares
Cah Etud Af — Cahiers d'Etudes Africaines
Cah Etud Anc — Cahiers des Etudes Anciennes
Cah Etud Biol — Cahiers d'Etudes Biologiques
Cah Etud Mediev — Cahier d'Etudes Medievales
Cah Expansion Reg — Cahiers de l'Expansion Regionale
Cah Fac Sci Univ Mohammed Ser Bio Anim — Cahiers. Faculte des Sciences. Universite Mohammed 5. Serie Biologie Animale
Cah Fr — Cahiers Francais
Cah Geogr Phys — Cahiers de Geographie Physique
Cah Geol — Cahiers Geologiques
Cah Geol Thoiry — Cahiers Geologiques de Thoiry
Cah Groupe Fr Rheol — Cahiers. Groupe Francais de Rheologie
Cah Haut Marnais — Cahiers Haut-Marnais
Cah Hist — Cahiers d'Histoire
Cah Hist Arch — Cahiers d'Histoire et d'Archeologie
Cah Hist Eg — Cahiers d'Histoire Egyptienne
Cah Hist Mond — Cahiers d'Histoire Mondiale/Journal of World History
Cah Hist Soc Hist Que — Cahiers d'Histoire. Societe Historique de Quebec
Cahiers — Cahiers du Cinema
Cahiers — Cahiers de Droit
Cahiers C — Cahiers Cesairiens
Cahiers Centre Etudes Recherche Oper — Cahiers. Centre d'Etudes de Recherche Operationnelle
Cahiers Centre Etudes Rech Oper — Cahiers. Centre d'Etudes de Recherche Operationnelle [*Brussels*]
Cahiers Cinematheque — Cahiers de la Cinematheque
Cahiers CSTB — Cahiers. Centre Scientifique et Technique du Batiment
Cahiers Droit — Quebec [*City*]. Universite Laval. Faculte de Droit. Cahiers de Droit
CahiersE — Cahiers Elisabethains
Cahiers in Eng — Cahiers du Cinema in English
CahiersF — Cahiers Francophones
Cahiers Geog Quebec — Cahiers de Geographie de Quebec
Cahiers Geol — Cahiers Geologiques
Cahiers Herne — Cahiers de l'Herne
Cahiers I — Cahiers Irlandais
Cahiers Math Montpellier — Cahiers Mathematiques Montpellier. Universite des Sciences et Techniques du Languedoc
Cahiers ORSTOM Pedologie — Cahiers. ORSTOM [*Office de la Recherche Scientifique et Technique d'Outre-Mer*]. Serie Pedologie
Cahiers R — Cahiers Renaniens
Cahiers S — Cahiers Staeliens
Cahiers Sci — Cahiers Scientifiques
Cahiers Sci (Suppl Bois Forets Trop) — Cahiers Scientifiques (Supplement to Bois et Forets des Tropiques)
Cahiers Topologie Geom Differentielle — Cahiers de Topologie et Geometrie Differentielle
Cah I F A L — Cahiers. Institut Francais d'Amerique Latine
Cah Inf Stn Biol Mar Grande-Riviere — Cahiers d'Information Station de Biologie Marine de Grande-Riviere
Cah Ing Agron — Cahiers des Ingenieurs Agronomes
Cah Ingnrs Agron — Cahiers des Ingenieurs Agronomes
Cah Int — Cahiers Internationaux
Cah Internat Sociol — Cahiers Internationaux de Sociologie
Cah Int Soc — Cahiers Internationaux de Sociologie
Cah Iroise — Cahiers de l'Iroise
Ca Hist — Cahiers d'Histoire
Cah Ivoiriens Rech Econ et Soc — Cahiers Ivoiriens de Recherche Economique et Sociale
CAHJ — CAHPER [*Canadian Association for Health, Physical Education, and Recreation*] Journal
Cah Juridiques Electr Gaz — Cahiers Juridiques de l'Electricite et du Gaz
Cah Kinesither — Cahiers de Kinesitherapie
Cah Lab Hydrobiol Montereau — Cahiers. Laboratoire d'Hydrobiologie de Montereau [*France*]
Cah Leopold Delisle — Cahiers Leopold Delisle
Cah Lex — Cahiers de Lexicologie
Cah Ling — Cahiers de Linguistique Theorique et Appliquee
Cah Ling As Or — Cahiers de Linguistique Asie Orientale
Cah Maboke — Cahiers de la Maboke
CAHMB — Cahiers de Medecine [*Paris*]
Cah Med — Cahiers de Medecine

Cah Med — Cahiers Medicaux
Cah Med Assises Med — Cahiers de Medecine Assises de Medecine
Cah Med Eur Med — Cahiers de Medecine Europa Medica
Cah Med Interprof — Cahiers de Medecine Interprofessionnelle [*France*]
Cah Med Lyon — Cahiers Medicaux Lyonnais
Cah Med Trav — Cahiers de Medecine du Travail
Cah Med Vet — Cahiers de Medecine Veterinaire
Cah Micropaleontol — Cahiers de Micropaleontologie
Cah Monde Hisp Luso-Bresil — Cahiers du Monde Hispanique et Luso-Bresilien
Cah Mon Rus — Cahiers du Monde Russe et Sovietique
Cah Mus Forezien — Cahiers. Musee Forezien
CahN — Cahiers Numismatiques
Cah Nat — Cahiers des Naturalistes
Cah Notes Doc — Cahiers de Notes Documentaires
Cah Notes Doc Secur Hyg Trav — Cahiers de Notes Documentaires. Securite et Hygiene du Travail
Cah Nouv Journee — Cahiers de la Nouvelle Journee
Cah Num — Cahiers Numismatiques
Cah Nutr Diet — Cahiers de Nutrition et de Dietetique
CAHOA — Canadian Hospital
Cah Oceanogr — Cahiers Oceanographiques
Cah Oceanogr Suppl — Cahiers Oceanographiques. Supplement
Cah Odonto-Stomatol — Cahiers d'Odonto-Stomatologie
Cah Odontostomatol (Touraine) — Cahiers Odontostomatologiques (Touraine)
Cah Off Rech Sci Tech Outre-Mer Ser Pedol — Cahiers. Office de la Recherche Scientifique et Technique d'Outre-Mer. Serie Pedologie
Cah O-Mer — Cahiers d'Outre-Mer
Cah ORST Hy — Cahiers. ORSTOM [*Office de la Recherche Scientifique et Technique d'Outre-Mer*]. Hydrobiologie
Cah ORST Oc — Cahiers. ORSTOM [*Office de la Recherche Scientifique et Technique d'Outre-Mer*]. Oceanographie
Cah ORSTOM Physiol Plant Trop Cult — Cahiers. ORSTOM [*Office de la Recherche Scientifique et Technique d'Outre-Mer*]. Physiologie des Plantes Tropicales Cultivees
Cah ORSTOM Ser Biol — Cahiers. ORSTOM [*Office de la Recherche Scientifique et Technique d'Outre-Mer*]. Serie Biologie
Cah ORSTOM Ser Entomol Med — Cahiers. ORSTOM [*Office de la Recherche Scientifique et Technique d'Outre-Mer*]. Serie Entomologie Medicale
Cah ORSTOM Ser Entomol Med Parasitol — Cahiers. ORSTOM [*Office de la Recherche Scientifique et Technique d'Outre-Mer*]. Serie Entomologie Medicale et Parasitologie
Cah ORSTOM Ser Hydrobiol — Cahiers. ORSTOM [*Office de la Recherche Scientifique et Technique d'Outre-Mer*]. Serie Hydrobiologie
Cah ORSTOM Ser Hydrol — Cahiers. ORSTOM [*Office de la Recherche Scientifique et Technique d'Outre-Mer*]. Serie Hydrologie
Cah ORSTOM Ser Oceanogr — Cahiers. ORSTOM [*Office de la Recherche Scientifique et Technique d'Outre-Mer*]. Serie Oceanographie
Cah ORSTOM Ser Pedol — Cahiers. ORSTOM [*Office de la Recherche Scientifique et Technique d'Outre-Mer*]. Serie Pedologie
Cah ORSTOM Ser Sci Hum — Cahiers. ORSTOM [*Office de la Recherche Scientifique et Technique d'Outre-Mer*]. Serie Sciences Humaines
Cah Outre-Mer — Cahiers d'Outre-Mer
Cah Pac — Cahiers du Pacifique
Cah Pedol ORSTOM — Cahiers de Pedologie. Office de la Recherche Scientifique et Technique d'Outre-Mer
CAHPER J — CAHPER [*Canadian Association for Health, Physical Education, and Recreation*] Journal
Cah Phys — Cahiers de Physique [*France*]
Cah P L — Cahiers Pierre Loti
Cah Presse Fr — Cahiers de la Presse Francaise
Cah Prot — Cahiers Protestants
Cah Prothese — Cahiers de Prothese
Cah Psych — Cahiers de Psychiatrie
Cah Quebecois Demographie — Cahiers Quebecois de Demographie
Cah Rac — Cahiers Raciniens
Cah Rech Agron — Cahiers de la Recherche Agronomique
Cah Rech Agron Inst Rech Agron (Morocco) — Cahiers de la Recherche Agronomique. Institut National de la Recherche Agronomique (Morocco)
Cah Relig Afr — Cahiers des Religions Africaines
Cah Rene de Lucinge — Cahiers Rene de Lucinge
CAHS — CAHS [*Canadian Aviation Historical Society*] Journal
Cah Sci Appl — Cahiers de Science Appliquee
Cah Sem Econ — Cahiers du Seminaire d'Econometrie
CahSion — Cahiers Sioniens [*Paris*]
Cah Soc Ec — Cahiers de Sociologie Economique
Cah Sociol Demogr Med — Cahiers de Sociologie et de Demographie Medicales
Cah Sticht Bio-Wet Maatsch — Cahiers van de Stichting Bio-Wetenschappen en Maatschappij
Cah Synth Org — Cahiers de Synthese Organique
CAHT — Cahiers de Tunisie
CahTD — Cahiers. Groupe Francois-Thureau-Dangin. I [*Paris, 1960*]
Cah Tech — Cahiers Techniques de l'Art

Cah Tech Cent Nat Coord Etud Rech Nutr Aliment — Cahiers Techniques. Centre National de Coordination des Etudes et Recherches sur la Nutrition et l'Alimentation
Cah Therm — Cahiers de la Thermique
Cah Tun — Cahiers de Tunisie
Cah Tunisie — Cahiers de Tunisie
Cah Vict Ed — Cahiers Victoriens et Edouardiens
Cah V Paret — Cahiers Vilfredo Pareto
Cah Zair Et Polit Soc — Cahiers Zairois d'Etudes Politiques et Sociales
Cah Zairois Etud Pol et Soc — Cahiers Zairois d'Etudes Politiques et Sociales
CAI — CAIC [*Computer Assisted Instruction Center*] Technical Memo. Florida State University
CAIEF — Cahiers. Association Internationale des Etudes Francaises
CAIIAK — Centro de Investigaciones Agricolas del Noreste. Informe de Investigacion Agricola
CAIL — Academie des Inscriptions et Belles Lettres. Comptes Rendus des Seances [*Paris*]
CAIN — Cancer Investigation
CAIN — Comite Arctique. International Newsletter
CAIRDG — Cardiovascular and Interventional Radiology
Cairo St Engl — Cairo Studies in English
Cairo Univ Fac Sci Bull — Cairo University. Faculty of Science. Bulletin
Cairo Univ Herb Publ — Cairo University. Herbarium. Publications
CaiSE — Cairo Studies in English
CAIU — Cahiers. Alliance Israelite Universelle
CAIUM — Cahiers. Alliance Israelite Universelle [*Mahberet*]
CAJ — Central Asiatic Journal
CAJ — College Art Journal
CAJMA3 — Central African Journal of Medicine
CAJOB — Canadian Journal of Ophthalmology
CAJOD — Cato Journal
CAKCAC — Communications. Faculte des Sciences. Universite d'Ankara. Serie C. Sciences Naturelles
C A L — Cahiers. Academie Luxembourgeoise
CAL — Cahiers des Ameriques Latines
Cal — Caliche
CaL — Campus Life
CAL — Current Antarctic Literature
Cal Ac Sc — California Academy of Sciences
Cal Ac Sc Mem — California Academy of Sciences. Memoirs
Cal Ac Sc Oc P — California Academy of Sciences. Occasional Papers
Cal Ac Sc Pr — California Academy of Sciences. Proceedings
Cal Ag Exp — University of California. College of Agriculture. Agricultural Experiment Station. Publications
Cal Agr — California Agriculture
CALC — Cahiers Algeriens de Litterature Comparee
Calcif Tiss — Calcified Tissue Research [*Later, Calcified Tissue International*]
Calcif Tissue Int — Calcified Tissue International
Calcif Tissue Res — Calcified Tissue Research [*Later, Calcified Tissue International*]
Calcif Tissues Proc Eur Symp — Calcified Tissues. Proceedings of the European Symposium
Calcitonin Proc Int Symp — Calcitonin Proceedings. International Symposium
Cal Citrograph — California Citrograph
Calc J M — Calcutta Journal of Medicine
Calc Med Rev — Calcutta Medical Review
Cal Countryman — California Countryman
Calc Rev — Calcutta Review
Calc Tiss Res — Calcified Tissue Research [*Later, Calcified Tissue International*]
Cal Cultivator — California Cultivator
Calcut St — Calcutta Statistical Association. Bulletin
Calcutta Hist J — Calcutta Historical Journal
Calcutta Med J — Calcutta Medical Journal
Calcutta R — Calcutta Review
Cal Dairym — California Dairyman
CALEDQ — Cancer Letters
CALF News Concern Am Livest Feeders — CALF News. Concerning America's Livestock Feeders
CALGIR — Community and Local Government Information Review
Calif Acad Sci Mem — California Academy of Sciences. Memoirs
Calif Acad Sci Occasional Paper Proc — California Academy of Sciences. Occasional Papers and Proceedings
Calif Ag Bul — California. Department of Agriculture. Bulletin
Calif Agr — California Agriculture
Calif Agric — California Agriculture
Calif Agric Calif Agric Exp Stn — California Agriculture. California Agricultural Experiment Station
Calif Agric Exp Stn Bull — California. Agricultural Experiment Station. Bulletin
Calif Agric Ext Serv Circ — California. Agricultural Extension Service. Circular
Calif Air Qual Data — California Air Quality Data
Calif Anthropol — California Anthropologist
Calif Bee Times — California Bee Times
Calif Birds — California Birds

Calif Bus — California Business
Calif Bus Ed J — California Business Education Journal
Calif Cattleman — California Cattleman
Calif Citrogr — California Citrograph
Calif Coop Oceanic Fish Invest Atlas — California Cooperative Oceanic Fisheries Investigations. Atlas
Calif Coop Oceanic Fish Invest Rep — California Cooperative Oceanic Fisheries Investigations. Reports
Calif Dep Agric Bienn Rep — California. Department of Agriculture. Biennial Report
Calif Dep Agric Bull — California. Department of Agriculture. Bulletin
Calif Dep Agric Bur Entomol Occas Pap — California. Department of Agriculture. Bureau of Entomology. Occasional Papers
Calif Dep Fish Game Fish Bull — California. Department of Fish and Game. Fish Bulletin
Calif Dep Fish Game Game Bull — California. Department of Fish and Game. Game Bulletin
Calif Dep Food Agric Lab Serv-Entomol Occas Pap — California. Department of Food and Agriculture. Laboratory Services-Entomology. Occasional Papers
Calif Dep Nat Resour Div Mines Bull — California. Department of Natural Resources. Division of Mines. Bulletin
Calif Dep Nat Resour Div Mines Spec Rep — California. Department of Natural Resources. Division of Mines. Special Reports
Calif Dep Nat Resour Div Soil Conserv Bull — California. Department of Natural Resources. Division of Soil Conservation. Bulletin
Calif Dept Agric Bur Entomol Occas Pap — California. Department of Agriculture. Bureau of Entomology. Occasional Papers
Calif Dept Nat Res Div Mines Bull — California. Department of Natural Resources. Division of Mines. Bulletin
Calif Dept Nat Res Div Mines Econ Mineral Map — California. Department of Natural Resources. Division of Mines. Economic Mineral Map
Calif Dept Nat Res Div Mines Mineral Inf Service — California. Department of Natural Resources. Division of Mines. Mineral Information Service
Calif Dept Nat Res Div Mines Rept State Mineralogist — California. Department of Natural Resources. Division of Mines. Report of State Mineralogist
Calif Dept Nat Res Div Mines Special Rept — California. Department of Natural Resources. Division of Mines. Special Report
Calif Dept Public Works Div Water Res Bull — California. Department of Public Works. Division of Water Resources. Bulletin
Calif Dept Public Works Div Water Res Water Quality Inv Rept — California. Department of Public Works. Division of Water Resources. Water Quality Investigations Report
Calif Dept Water Res Bull — California. Department of Water Resources. Bulletin
Calif Dept Water Res Div Res Plan Bull — California. Department of Water Resources. Division of Resources. Planning Bulletin
Calif Dept Water Res Rept — California. Department of Water Resources. Report
Calif Div For Fire Control Notes — California. Division of Forestry. Fire Control Notes
Calif Div Mines Geol Bull — California. Division of Mines and Geology. Bulletin
Calif Div Mines Geol Geol Data Map — California. Division of Mines and Geology. Geologic Data Map
Calif Div Mines Geol Map Sheet Ser — California. Division of Mines and Geology. Map Sheet Series
Calif Div Mines Geol Rep — California. Division of Mines and Geology. County Report
Calif Div Mines Geol Rep State Geol — California. Division of Mines and Geology. Report of the State Geologist
Calif Div Mines Geol Spec Publ — California. Division of Mines and Geology. Special Publication
Calif Div Mines Geol Spec Rep — California. Division of Mines and Geology. Special Report
Calif Ed — California Education
Calif El Sch Adm Assn Mon — California Elementary School Administrators Association. Monographs
Calif El Sch Adm Assn Yearbook — California Elementary School Administrators Association. Yearbook
Calif Feeders Day — California Feeders' Day
Calif Fire Control Note Calif Div For — California Fire Control Notes. California Division of Forestry
Calif Fire Prev Note Calif Div For — California Fire Prevention Notes. California Division of Forestry
Calif Fish — California Fish and Game
Calif Fish Game — California Fish and Game
Calif Folklore Qu — California Folklore Quarterly
Calif For & For Prod Calif For Prod Lab — California Forestry and Forest Products. University of California. Forest Products Laboratory
Calif Geol — California Geology
Calif Health — California's Health
Calif Hist Q — California Historical Quarterly
Calif Hist Soc Q — California Historical Society. Quarterly [*San Francisco*]

Calif Hist Soc Quar — California Historical Society. Quarterly [*San Francisco*]
Calif Hortic J — California Horticultural Journal
Calif Inst Technol Earthquake Eng Res Lab (Rep) EERL — California Institute of Technology. Earthquake Engineering Research Laboratory (Report) EERL
Calif Inst Technol Jet Propul Lab Tech Memo — California Institute of Technology. Jet Propulsion Laboratory. Technical Memorandum
Calif Inst Technology Div Geol Sci Contr — California Institute of Technology. Division of Geological Sciences. Contributions
Calif J Ed Res — California Journal of Educational Research
Calif J Edu — California Journal of Educational Research
Calif J El Ed — California Journal of Elementary Education
Calif Jour Mines and Geology — California Journal of Mines and Geology
Calif J Sec Ed — California Journal of Secondary Education
Calif Libn — California Librarian
Calif Librn — California Librarian
Calif L Rev — California Law Review
Calif M — Californian Illustrated Magazine
Calif Manag — California Management Review
Calif Management Rev — California Management Review
Calif Manage Rev — California Management Review
Calif Manag R — California Management Review
Calif Med — California Medicine
Calif Mgt R — California Management Review
Calif Min J — California Mining Journal
Calif Mosq Control Assoc Proc Pap Annu Conf — California Mosquito Control Association. Proceedings and Papers of the Annual Conference
Calif Mosq Vector Control Assoc Proc Pap Annu Conf — California Mosquito and Vector Control Association. Proceedings and Papers of the Annual Conference
Calif Nat Hist Guides — California Natural History Guides
Calif Nurs — California Nurse
Calif Oil Fields — California Oil Fields
Calif Oil World — California Oil World
Calif Oil World Pet Ind — California Oil World and Petroleum Industry
California Acad Sci Proc — California Academy of Sciences. Proceedings
California Dept Water Resources Bull — California. Department of Water Resources. Bulletin
California Div Mines and Geology Bull — California. Division of Mines and Geology. Bulletin
California Div Mines and Geology Map Sheet — California. Division of Mines and Geology. Map Sheet
California Div Mines and Geology Mineral Inf Service — California. Division of Mines and Geology. Mineral Information Service
California Div Mines and Geology Spec Rept — California. Division of Mines and Geology. Special Report
California Geol — California Geology
California Univ Pubs Geol Sci — California University. Publications in Geological Sciences
California Univ Water Resources Center Rept — California University. Water Resources Center. Report
California West L Rev — California Western Law Review
Californium 252 Prog — Californium-252 Progress
Calif Pal Leg Hon Bul — California Palace of the Legion of Honor. Museum Bulletin
Calif Poult Lett Univ Calif Coop Ext — California Poultry Letter. University of California Cooperative Extension
Calif Q — California Quarterly
Calif S B — State Bar of California. Journal
Calif SBJ — State Bar of California. Journal
Calif Sch — California Schools
Calif Sch Lib — California School Libraries
Calif Sch Libr — California School Libraries
Calif Sewage Works J — California Sewage Works Journal
Calif Slavic Stud — California Slavic Studies
Calif State Dep Public Health Wkly Bull — California. State Department of Public Health. Weekly Bulletin
Calif State Dept Education Bull — California State Department of Education. Bulletin
Calif State J Med — California State Journal of Medicine
Calif State Univ (Chico) Reg Programs Monogr — California State University (Chico). Regional Programs Monograph
Calif State Water Pollut Control Board Publ — California State Water Pollution Control Board. Publication
Calif State Water Pollution Control Board Pub — California State Water Pollution Control Board. Publication
Calif State Water Res Board Bull — California State Water Resources Board. Bulletin
Calif State Water Resour Control Board Publ — California. State Water Resources Control Board. Publication
Calif Turfgrass Cult Calif Univ Berkeley Coop Ext Serv — California Turfgrass Culture. California University. Berkeley Cooperative Extension Service
Calif Univ Agr Expt Sta Ground Water Studies — California University. Agricultural Experiment Station. Ground Water Studies

Calif Univ (Berkeley) Water Resour Cent Desalin Rep — California University (Berkeley). Water Resources Center. Desalination Report

Calif Univ Chron — California University. Chronicle

Calif Univ Inst Transp and Traffic Eng Inf Circ — California University. Institute of Transportation and Traffic Engineering. Information Circular

Calif Univ Mem — California University. Memoirs

Calif Univ Publ Geol Sci — California University. Publications in Geological Sciences

Calif Univ Pubs Astronomy — California University. Publications in Astronomy

Calif Univ Pubs Geography — California University. Publications in Geography

Calif Univ Pubs Geol Sci — California University. Publications in Geological Sciences

Calif Univ Pubs Zoology — California University. Publications in Zoology

Calif Univ (Riverside) Campus Mus Contrib — California University (Riverside). Campus Museum. Contributions

Calif Univ Scripps Inst — California University. Scripps Institution of Oceanography. Reference Series

Calif Univ Scripps Inst Oceanogr Annu Rep — California University. Scripps Institution of Oceanography. Annual Report

Calif Univ Scripps Inst Oceanography Bull — California University. Scripps Institution of Oceanography. Bulletin

Calif Univ Scripps Inst Oceanography SIO Reference — California University. Scripps Institution of Oceanography. SIO Reference

Calif Univ Scripps Inst Oceanography Submarine Geology Rept — California University. Scripps Institution of Oceanography. Submarine Geology Report

Calif Univ Scripps Inst Oceanogr Contrib — California University. Scripps Institution of Oceanography. Contributions

Calif Univ Scripps Inst Oceanogr Ref Ser — California University. Scripps Institution of Oceanography. Reference Series

Calif Univ Water Res Center Archives Archives Ser Rept Contr — California University. Water Resources Center Archives. Archives Series Report. Contributions

Calif Univ Water Resour Cent Rep — California University. Water Resources Center. Report

Calif Vector Views — California Vector Views

Calif Vet — California Veterinarian

Calif Water Pollut Control Assoc Bull — California Water Pollution Control Association. Bulletin

Calif Western Int L J — California Western International Law Journal

Calif Western L Rev — California Western Law Review

Calif West Int'l LJ — California Western International Law Journal

Calif West L Rev — California Western Law Review

Calif West Med — California and Western Medicine

Calif West States Grape Grow — California and Western States Grape Grower

Calif W Int Law J — California Western International Law Journal

Calif W Int'l LJ — California Western International Law Journal

Calif WL Rev — California Western Law Review

Cali His Nugget — California History Nugget

Calitatea Prod & Metrol — Calitatea Productiei si Metrologie

Cal J — California Journal

CALJ — Canadian Alpine Journal

Cal J Tech — California Journal of Technology

CALL — Current Awareness. Library Literature

Cal Law R — California Law Review

Cal L Rev — California Law Review

Cal M As — California Miners' Association

Cal Mgmt Rev — California Management Review

Cal Mgt R — California Management Review

CalN — Calabria Nobilissima

Cal Neva TL — Cal-Neva Token Ledger

CALOA — Calore

CALOD — Calorie

Calore Tecnol — Calore e Tecnologia

Calorim Therm Anal — Calorimetry and Thermal Analysis

Cal Phys Geog Club B — California Physical Geography Club. Bulletin

Cal Q — California Quarterly

Cal Q Sec Ed — California Quarterly of Secondary Education

CalR — Calcutta Review

CA LR — California Law Review

Cal SS — California Slavic Studies

Cal State Comm Hort B — California State Commission of Horticulture. Monthly Bulletin

Cal St M Bur — California State Mining Bureau

Cal St M Bur An Rp B — California State Mining Bureau. Annual Report. Bulletin

Cal Th J — Calvin Theological Journal

Cal Univ Dp G B — California University. Publications. Department of Geology. Bulletin

Cal Univ Pub — California University [*Berkeley*]. Publications in Agricultural Science

Cal Univ Pub Geog — California University. Publications in Geography

Cal Univ Seism Sta B — California University. Publications. Seismography Stations. Bulletin

CalvTJ — Calvin Theological Journal [*Grand Rapids, MI*]

CalwerH — Calwer Hefte zur Foerderung Biblischen Glaubens und Christlichen Lebens

Cal W Int'l LJ — California Western International Law Journal

Cal WL Rev — California Western Law Review

CAm — Casa de las Americas

CAM — Contemporary Australian Management

Cam Abs — Cambridge Abstracts

CA Mag — CA [*Chartered Accountant*] Magazine [*Canada*]

CA Magazin — CA [*Chemical Abstracts*] Magazine

CA Mag J Commer Art — CA Magazine. Journal of Commercial Art

CAMAn — Cercle Archeologique de Mons. Annales

Camara Comer Bogota R — Camara de Comercio de Bogota. Revista

Camara Text Mex Rev Tec — Camara Textil de Mexico. Revista Tecnica

Camb J — Cambridge Journal

Camb L J — Cambridge Law Journal

Camb Monogr Exp Biol — Cambridge Monographs in Experimental Biology

Camb Philos Soc Trans — Cambridge Philosophical Society. Transactions

Camb Q — Cambridge Quarterly

Cambrian Archaeol Ass Monogr Collect — Cambrian Archaeological Association. Monographs and Collections

Cambrian Law R — Cambrian Law Review

Cambrian LR — Cambrian Law Review

Cambrian L Rev — Cambrian Law Review

Cambridge Anthropol — Cambridge Anthropology

Cambridge Comput Sci Texts — Cambridge Computer Science Texts

Cambridge Econ Policy Rev — Cambridge Economic Policy Review

Cambridge Inst Ed Bulletin — Cambridge Institute of Education. Bulletin

Cambridge J Econ — Cambridge Journal of Economics

Cambridge J Economics — Cambridge Journal of Economics

Cambridge J Ed — Cambridge Journal of Education

Cambridge J Educ — Cambridge Journal of Education

Cambridge LJ — Cambridge Law Journal

Cambridge Medieval Celtic Stud — Cambridge Medieval Celtic Studies

Cambridge Monographs Math Phys — Cambridge Monographs on Mathematical Physics

Cambridge Monographs Mech Appl Math — Cambridge Monographs on Mechanics and Applied Mathematics

Cambridge Philos Soc Biol Rev — Cambridge Philosophical Society. Biological Reviews

Cambridge Ph Soc Pr — Cambridge Philosophical Society. Proceedings

Cambridge Q — Cambridge Quarterly

Cambridge Stud Math Biol — Cambridge Studies in Mathematical Biology

Cambridge Tracts in Math — Cambridge Tracts in Mathematics

Cambridge Univ Med Soc Mag — Cambridge University Medical Society. Magazine

CAMBull — Cercle Archeologique de Malines. Bulletin

CAMCA — CA. A Cancer Journal for Clinicians

Cam Club — Camera Club

CAMEA — California Medicine

CAMEEW — Cardiovascular Medicine

Camellia J — Camellia Journal

Camera — Camera and Cine

Camera Obsc — Camera Obscura

C Amer Lat — Cahiers des Ameriques Latines

C Amer Lat Ser Sci Homme — Cahiers des Ameriques Latines. Serie Sciences de l'Homme

Cameron Synth Fuels Rep — Cameron Synthetic Fuels Report

Cameroun Agric Pastor For — Cameroun Agricole, Pastoral, et Forestier

Cameroun Dir Mines Geol Act Minieres Cameroun — Cameroun. Direction des Mines et de la Geologie. Activites Minieres au Cameroun

Cameroun Territ Bull Dir Mines Geol — Cameroun Territoire. Bulletin de la Direction des Mines et de la Geologie

CAMI — Canadian Mineralogist

CAMIA — Canadian Mineralogist

CamJ — Cambridge Journal

CAMJ — Canadian Mining Journal

CAMJA — Canadian Mining Journal

Cam Obs — Camera Obscura

Campaign — Campaigner

CAMPB — Comments on Atomic and Molecular Physics

Campbell L Rev — Campbell Law Review

Campbell Soup Dep Agric Res Bull — Campbell Soup Company. Department of Agricultural Research. Bulletin

Campbell Soup Dep Agric Res Res Monogr — Campbell Soup Company. Department of Agricultural Research. Research Monograph

Camp Mag — Camping Magazine

Campo Suelo Argent — Campo y Suelo Argentino

CamQ — Cambridge Quarterly

CAMQA — Canadian Metallurgical Quarterly

CamR — Cambridge Review

CAMT — Canada. Meteorological Translations

CAMZA — CA Magazine. Journal of Commercial Art

CAN — Cahiers Francais; Revue Periodique de l'Actualite Politique, Economique, Sociale, et Culturelle de la France

CaN — Calabria Nobilissima

Can — Canadiana
Can — Canoniste
CAN — Canticle
CANA — California Association of Nurse Anesthetists
Can Acoust Acoust Can — Canadian Acoustics/Acoustique Canadienne
Canada Ag — Canada. Department of Agriculture. Publication
Canada Bus — Canadian Business Magazine
Canada Defence Research Board Handb — Canada Defence Research Board. Handbook
Canada Dept Mines and Tech Surveys Geog Br Bibl Ser — Canada. Department of Mines and Technical Surveys. Geographical Branch. Bibliographical Series
Canada Dept Mines and Tech Surveys Geog Bull — Canada. Department of Mines and Technical Surveys. Geographical Bulletin
Canada Dept Mines and Tech Surveys Geog Paper — Canada. Department of Mines and Technical Surveys. Geographical Paper
Canada Dept Mines and Tech Surveys Mem — Canada. Department of Mines and Technical Surveys. Memoir
Canada Dept Mines and Tech Surveys Misc Paper Ser — Canada. Department of Mines and Technical Surveys. Miscellaneous Paper Series
Canada Dominion Observatory Contr Pub — Canada Dominion Observatory Contributions. Publications
Canada Geol Survey Bull — Canada. Geological Survey. Bulletin
Canada Geol Survey Econ Geology Rept — Canada. Geological Survey. Economic Geology Report
Canada Geol Survey Geophysics Paper — Canada. Geological Survey. Geophysics Paper
Canada Geol Survey Map — Canada. Geological Survey. Map
Canada Geol Survey Mem — Canada. Geological Survey. Memoir
Canada Geol Survey Paper — Canada. Geological Survey. Paper
Canada Geol Survey Prelim Ser Map — Canada. Geological Survey. Preliminary Series. Map
Canada Med J — Canada Medical Journal and Monthly Record of Medical and Surgical Science
Canada Natl Mus Bull Nat History Paper Special Contr — Canada. National Museum Bulletin. Natural History Paper. Special Contributions
Canad Bar Rev — Canadian Bar Review
Canad Bookm — Canadian Bookman
Canad Chem Process — Canadian Chemical Processing
Canad Doctor — Canadian Doctor
Canad Ent — Canadian Entomologist
Canad Entom — Canadian Entomologist
Canad Fam Physician — Canadian Family Physician
Canad Fld-Nat — Canadian Field-Naturalist
Canad For Ind — Canadian Forest Industries
Canad Forum — Canadian Forum
Canad Geog J — Canadian Geographical Journal [*Later, Canadian Geographic*]
Canad Hist Assn Rep — Canadian Historical Association. Reports
Canad Hist Rev — Canadian Historical Review
Canad Hosp — Canadian Hospital
Canadian Alpine Jour — Canadian Alpine Journal
Canadian Archt — Canadian Architect
Canadian Assoc Geographers Education Comm Bull — Canadian Association of Geographers. Education Committee. Bulletin
Canadian Bldg Digest — Canadian Building Digest
Canadian Ceramic Soc Jour — Canadian Ceramic Society. Journal
Canadian Geotech Jour — Canadian Geotechnical Journal
Canadian Inst Mining and Metallurgy Trans — Canadian Institute of Mining and Metallurgy. Transactions
CanadianJTH — Canadian Journal of Theology [*Toronto*]
Canadian Lib Assn Bul — Canadian Library Association. Bulletin
Canadian Shipp & Mar Engng — Canadian Shipping and Marine Engineering
Canad J — Canadian Journal of Industry
Canad J Afr Stud — Canadian Journal of African Studies
Canad J Biochem — Canadian Journal of Biochemistry and Physiology
Canad J Bot — Canadian Journal of Botany
Canad J Chem — Canadian Journal of Chemistry
Canad J Chem Engng — Canadian Journal of Chemical Engineering
Canad J Econ — Canadian Journal of Economics
Canad J Math — Canadian Journal of Mathematics [*Ottawa, Ontario*]
Canad J Med Sc — Canadian Journal of Medical Science
Canad J Med Tech — Canadian Journal of Medical Technology
Canad J Med Technol — Canadian Journal of Medical Technology
Canad J Microbiol — Canadian Journal of Microbiology
Canad J Phys — Canadian Journal of Physics
Canad J Pl Sci — Canadian Journal of Plant Science
Canad J Polit Sci — Canadian Journal of Political Science
Canad J Psychiatr — Canadian Journal of Psychiatry
Canad J Psychiatr Nurs — Canadian Journal of Psychiatric Nursing
Canad J Psychol — Canadian Journal of Psychology
Canad J Public Health — Canadian Journal of Public Health
Canad J Radiogr Radiother Nucl Med — Canadian Journal of Radiography, Radiotherapy, Nuclear Medicine

Canad J Soil Sci — Canadian Journal of Soil Science
Canad J Statist — Canadian Journal of Statistics
CanadJT — Canadian Journal of Theology [*Toronto*]
Canad J Zool — Canadian Journal of Zoology
Canad Lib — Canadian Library
Canad Lib Assn Bul — Canadian Library Association. Bulletin
Canad Lib Assn Feliciter — Canadian Library Association. Feliciter
Canad Lib J — Canadian Library Journal
Canad M — Canadian Magazine
Canad Med Assoc J — Canadian Medical Association. Journal
Can Admin — Canadian Administrator
Canad Mo — Canadian Monthly
Canad Nurse — Canadian Nurse
Canad Person Industr Relat J — Canadian Personnel and Industrial Relations Journal (Including the Canadian Training Digest)
Canad Plast — Canadian Plastics
Canad Pract — Canadian Practitioner
Canad Pract and Rev — Canadian Practitioner and Review
Canad Psychiat Ass J — Canadian Psychiatric Association. Journal
Canad Publ Adm — Canadian Public Administration/Administration Publique du Canada
Canad R Sociol Anthropol — Canadian Review of Sociology and Anthropology
Canad Slavonic Pap — Canadian Slavonic Papers
Canad Soc Lab Technol Bull — Canadian Society of Laboratory Technologists. Bulletin
Canad Vet Rec — Canadian Veterinary Record
Canad Yb Int Law — Canadian Yearbook of International Law
Can Aeronaut J — Canadian Aeronautical Journal
Can Aeronaut Space Inst Trans — Canadian Aeronautic and Space Institute. Transactions
Can Aeronaut and Space J — Canadian Aeronautics and Space Journal
Can Aeronaut Space J — Canadian Aeronautics and Space Journal
Can Aer Spa — Canadian Aeronautics and Space Journal
Can Agr Eng — Canadian Agricultural Engineering
Can Agric — Canada Agriculture
Can Agric Eng — Canadian Agricultural Engineering
Can Agric Insect Pest Rev — Canadian Agricultural Insect Pest Review
Can Al J — Canadian Alpine Journal
Can-Am Slav — Canadian-American Slavic Studies
Can Anae S J — Canadian Anaesthetists' Society. Journal
Can Anaesth Soc J — Canadian Anaesthetists' Society. Journal
Can Ant Coll — Canadian Antiques Collector
Can Arch — Canadian Architect
Can Arct Land Use Res Prog Rep — Canada. Arctic Land Use Research Program Report
Can Art — Canadian Art
Can Aud — Canadian Audubon
Can Audubon — Canadian Audubon
Can Auth & Book — Canadian Author and Bookman
Can Automot Trade — Canadian Automotive Trade
Can Av — Canadian Aviation
Can Bank — Canadian Banker [*Formerly, Canadian Banker and ICB Review*]
Can Banker — Canadian Banker [*Formerly, Canadian Banker and ICB Review*]
Can Banker & ICB R — Canadian Banker and ICB [*Institute of Canadian Bankers*] Review
Can Banker ICB Rev — Canadian Banker and ICB [*Institute of Canadian Bankers*] Review
Can Bank R — Canadian Bankruptcy Reports
Can Bankr — Canadian Bankruptcy Reports
Can Bankr Rep — Canadian Bankruptcy Reports
Can Bar AJ — Journal. Canadian Bar Association
Can Bar J — Canadian Bar Journal
Can Bar J (NS) — Canadian Bar Journal. New Series
Can Bar R — Canadian Bar Review
Can Bar Rev — Canadian Bar Review
Canb Comments — Canberra Comments
Can Bee J — Canadian Bee Journal
Can Beekeep — Canadian Beekeeping
Canberra Anthropol — Canberra Anthropology
Canb Hist Soc Add — Canberra and District Historical Society. Addresses
Canb Hist Soc News — Canberra and District Historical Society. Newsletter
Can B J — Canadian Bar Journal
Can Bkman — Canadian Bookman
Canb Letter — Canberra Letter
Can Board Grain Comm Grain Res Lab Annu Rep — Canada. Board of Grain Commissioners. Grain Research Laboratory. Annual Report
Can BPI — Canadian Business Periodicals Index [*Later, Canadian Business Index*]
Can BR — Canadian Bar Review
Can B Rev — Canadian Bar Review
Canb Survey — Canberra Survey
Can Build Dig — Canadian Building Digest
Can Bull Nutr — Canadian Bulletin on Nutrition
Canb Univ Col Gaz — Canberra University College. Gazette
Canb Univ Coll Gaz — Canberra University College. Gazette

Can Bus — Canadian Business
Can Bus Econ — Canadian Business Economics
Can Bus LJ — Canadian Business Law Journal
Can Bus Mag — Canadian Business Magazine
Can Bus R — Canadian Business Review
Can Bus Rev — Canadian Business Review
Canb Viewpoint — Canberra Viewpoint
Canb Weekly — Canberra Weekly
Can B Year Book — Canadian Bar Association. Year Book
Can C — Canoniste Contemporain
CANCAM Proc Can Congr Appl Mech — CANCAM Proceedings. Canadian Congress of Applied Mechanics
Can Cancer Conf — Canadian Cancer Conference
Can Cartogr — Canadian Cartographer
Can Cases L Torts — Canadian Cases on the Law of Torts
Can Cattlemen — Canadian Cattlemen
Canc Bioc B — Cancer Biochemistry - Biophysics
Canc Bull — Cancer Bulletin
Can CC — Canadian Criminal Cases
Canc Chemoth Abstr — Cancer Chemotherapy Abstracts
Canc Chemother Rep — Cancer Chemotherapy Reports
Canc Chemother Rep Suppl — Cancer Chemotherapy Reports. Supplement
Canc Ch P 1 — Cancer Chemotherapy Reports. Part 1
Canc Ch P 2 — Cancer Chemotherapy Reports. Part 2
Canc Ch P 3 — Cancer Chemotherapy Reports. Part 3
Canc Curr Lit Ind — Cancer Current Literature Index
Can Cem Concr Rev — Canadian Cement and Concrete Review
Can Cent Miner Energy Technol Publ — Canada. Centre for Mineral and Energy Technology. Publications
Can Cent Miner Energy Technol Sci Bull — Canada. Centre for Mineral and Energy Technology. Scientific Bulletin
Can Cent Ser — Canadian Centenary Series
Can Cent Terminol Bull Terminol — Canada. Centre de Terminologie. Bulletin de Terminologie
Cancer Biochem Biophys — Cancer Biochemistry - Biophysics
Cancer Bull — Cancer Bulletin
Cancer Chemother Pharmacol — Cancer Chemotherapy and Pharmacology
Cancer Chemother Rep — Cancer Chemotherapy Reports
Cancer Chemother Rep Part 1 — Cancer Chemotherapy Reports. Part 1
Cancer Chemother Rep Part 2 — Cancer Chemotherapy Reports. Part 2
Cancer Chemother Rep Part 3 — Cancer Chemotherapy Reports. Part 3
Cancer Chemother Screening Data — Cancer Chemotherapy Screening Data
Cancer Chem Rep — Cancer Chemotherapy Reports
Cancer Clin Trials — Cancer Clinical Trials
Cancer Cytol — Cancer Cytology
Cancer Detect Prev — Cancer Detection and Prevention
Cancer Genet Cytogenet — Cancer Genetics and Cytogenetics
Cancer Immunol Immunother — Cancer Immunology and Immunotherapy
Cancer Lett — Cancer Letters
Cancer Nurs — Cancer Nursing
Cancer Rehabil — Cancer Rehabilitation
Cancer Res — Cancer Research
Cancer Res Inst Slovak Acad Sci Annu Rep — Cancer Research Institute. Slovak Academy of Sciences. Annual Report
Cancer Semin — Cancer Seminar
Cancer Suppl — Cancer Supplement
Cancer T R — Cancer Treatment Reviews
Cancer Treat Rep — Cancer Treatment Reports
Cancer Treat Rev — Cancer Treatment Reviews
Can Chart Acc — Canadian Chartered Accountant [*Later, CA Magazine*]
Can Chart Account — Canadian Chartered Accountant [*Later, CA Magazine*]
Can Chart Acct — Canadian Chartered Accountant [*Later, CA Magazine*]
Can Chem Educ — Canadian Chemical Education
Can Chem J — Canadian Chemical Journal
Can Chem J — Cancer Chemical Journal
Can Chem & Met — Canadian Chemistry and Metallurgy
Can Chem Met — Canadian Chemistry and Metallurgy
Can Chem News — Canadian Chemical News
Can Chem Proc — Canadian Chemical Processing
Can Chem Process — Canadian Chemical Processing
Can Chem & Process Ind — Canadian Chemistry and Process Industries
Can Child Lit — Canadian Children's Literature
Can CL — Canadian Current Law
Can Collector — Canadian Collector
Can Color Text Process — Canadian Colorist and Textile Processor
Can Commerce — Canada Commerce
Can Commun Power Conf Proc — Canadian Communications and Power Conference. Proceedings
Can Comp — Canadian Composer
Can Composer — Canadian Composer
Can Consum — Canadian Consumer
Can Consumer — Canadian Consumer
Can Controls Instrum — Canadian Controls and Instrumentation
Can Controls & Instrum — Canadian Controls and Instrumentation
Can Copper — Canadian Copper
Can Crafts — Canada Crafts

Canc Res — Cancer Research
Canc Res Campaign Annu Rep — Cancer Research Campaign. Annual Report
Canc Res Inst Slovak Acad Annu Rep — Cancer Research Institute. Slovak Academy of Sciences. Annual Report
Canc Rev — Cancer Review
Can Crim — Criminal Reports (Canada)
Can Dairy Ice Cream J — Canadian Dairy and Ice Cream Journal
Can Datasyst — Canadian Datasystems
C and EN — Chemical and Engineering News
Can Dep Agric Annu Rep — Canada. Department of Agriculture. Annual Report
Can Dep Agric Bull — Canada. Department of Agriculture. Bulletin
Can Dep Agric Circ — Canada. Department of Agriculture. Circular
Can Dep Agric Farmers Bull — Canada. Department of Agriculture. Farmers' Bulletin
Can Dep Agric Plant Res Inst Agro-Meteorol Sect Tech Bull — Canada. Department of Agriculture. Plant Research Institute. Agrometeorology Section. Technical Bulletin
Can Dep Agric Publ — Canada. Department of Agriculture. Publication
Can Dep Agric Res Branch Monogr — Canada. Department of Agriculture. Research Branch Monograph
Can Dep Agric Res Branch Rep — Canada. Department of Agriculture. Research Branch Report
Can Dep Agric Tech Bull — Canada. Department of Agriculture. Technical Bulletin
Can Dep Energy Mines Resources Earth Phys Br Mem — Canada. Department of Energy. Mines and Resources. Earth Physics Branch. Memoir
Can Dep Energy Mines Resources Earth Phys Br Mineral Rep — Canada. Department of Energy. Mines and Resources. Earth Physics Branch. Mineral Report
Can Dep Energy Mines Resources Earth Sci Br Inform Circ — Canada. Department of Energy. Mines and Resources. Earth Science Branch. Information Circular
Can Dep Environ Can For Ser North For Res Cent Inf Rep — Canada. Department of the Environment. Canadian Forestry Service. Northern Forest Research Centre. Information Report
Can Dep Environ Mar Sci Dir Manuscr Rep Ser — Canada. Department of the Environment. Marine Sciences Directorate. Manuscript Report Series
Can Dep Fish Annu Rep — Canada. Department of Fisheries. Annual Report
Can Dep Fish For Annu Rep — Canada. Department of Fisheries and Forestry. Annual Report
Can Dep Fish For Bimon Res Notes — Canada. Department of Fisheries and Forestry. Bimonthly Research Notes
Can Dep Fish For Can For Ser Inf Rep — Canada. Department of Fisheries and Forestry. Canadian Forestry Service. Information Report
Can Dep Fish For Can For Serv Inf Rep FF-X — Canada. Department of Fisheries and Forestry. Canadian Forestry Service. Information Report FF-X
Can Dep Fish For Can For Serv Publ — Canada. Department of Fisheries and Forestry. Canadian Forestry Service Publication
Can Dep Fish For For Branch Dep Publ — Canada. Department of Fisheries and Forestry. Forestry Branch Departmental Publication
Can Dep For For Entomol Pathol Branch Bi-Mon Prog Rep — Canada. Department of Forestry. Forest Entomology and Pathology Branch. Bi-Monthly Progress Report
Can Dep For Rural Dev Annu Rep — Canada. Department of Forestry and Rural Development. Annual Report
Can Dep For Rural Dev Annu Rep For Insect Dis Surv — Canada. Department of Forestry and Rural Development. Annual Report. Forest Insect and Disease Survey
Can Dep For Rural Dev Bi-Mon Res Notes — Canada. Department of Forestry and Rural Development. Bi-Monthly Research Notes
Can Dep For Rural Dev For Branch Dep Publ — Canada. Department of Forestry and Rural Development. Forestry Branch. Department Publication
Can Dep For Rural Dev For Branch Inf Rep FF-X — Canada. Department of Forestry and Rural Development. Forestry Branch. Information Report FF-X
Can Dep Indian North Aff Arct Land Use Res Program Rep ALUR — Canada. Department of Indian and Northern Affairs. Arctic Land Use Research Program. Report ALUR
Can Dept Forestry Bimo Res Note — Canada. Department of Fisheries and Forestry. Bimonthly Research Notes
Can Dept Forestry Disease Surv — Canada. Department of Fisheries and Forestry. Annual Report of the Forest Insect and Disease Survey
Can Dept Forestry Publ — Canada. Department of Fisheries and Forestry. Departmental Publications
Can Dept Forestry Res News — Canada. Department of Fisheries and Forestry. Research News
Candid — Candid Quarterly Review of Public Affairs
Can Dimen — Canadian Dimension
Cand J St — Canadian Journal of Statistics
Can Doct — Canadian Doctor
Can Dp Interior Rp Chief Astronomer — Canada. Department of the Interior. Report of the Chief Astronomer

Can Dp Interior Sup Mines Rp — Canada. Department of the Interior. Superintendent of Mines. Report
Can Drug — Canadian Druggist
Can Dyer Color User — Canadian Dyer and Color User
Candy Ind — Candy and Snack Industry
Candy Ind Confect J — Candy Industry and Confectioners Journal
Candy Snack Ind — Candy and Snack Industry
Can Earth Phys Branch Publ — Canada. Earth Physics Branch. Publications
CanEdI — Canadian Education Index
Can Ed Res Digest — Canadian Education and Research Digest
Can Educ Res Dig — Canadian Education and Research Digest
Cane Growers Q Bul — Cane Growers Quarterly Bulletin
Cane Grow Q Bull — Cane Growers Quarterly Bulletin
Cane Gr Quart Bull — Cane Growers Quarterly Bulletin
Can Electr Assoc Trans Eng Oper Div — Canadian Electrical Association. Transactions of the Engineering and Operating Division
Can Electr Eng J — Canadian Electrical Engineering Journal
Can Electron Eng — Canadian Electronics Engineering
Can Energy News — Canadian Energy News
Can Eng — Canadian Engineer
Can Ent — Canadian Entomologist
Can Entm — Canadian Entomologist
Can Entom — Canadian Entomologist
Can Entomol — Canadian Entomologist
Can Environ Prot Serv Econ Tech Rev Rep — Canada. Environmental Protection Service. Economic and Technical Review Report
Can Environ Prot Serv Technol Dev Rep — Canada. Environmental Protection Service. Technology Development Report
Can F — Canadian Forum
Can Farm Ec — Canadian Farm Economics
Can Farm Econ — Canadian Farm Economics
Can Fd J — Canadian Food Journal
Can Feed Grain J — Canadian Feed and Grain Journal
Can Fic Mag — Canadian Fiction Magazine
Can Fi Cu — Canadian Fish Culturist
Can Field-Nat — Canadian Field-Naturalist
Can Field-Natur — Canadian Field-Naturalist
Can Fie Nat — Canadian Field-Naturalist
Can Fish Cult — Canadian Fish Culturist
Can Fisherm — Canadian Fisherman
Can Fisherman — Canadian Fisherman
Can Fish Mar Serv Data Rep Ser Cen-D — Canada. Fisheries and Marine Service. Data Report. Series Cen-D
Can Fish Mar Serv Misc Spec Publ — Canada. Fisheries and Marine Service. Miscellaneous Special Publication
Can Fish Mar Serv Resour Branch Marit Reg Inf Publ MAR-N — Canada. Fisheries and Marine Service Resource Branch. Maritimes Region. Information Publication MAR-N
Can Fish Mar Serv Resour Dev Branch Halifax Prog Rep — Canada. Fisheries and Marine Service Resource Development Branch. Halifax Progress Report
Can Fish Mar Serv Resour Dev Branch Marit Reg Rep — Canada. Fisheries and Marine Service Resource Development Branch. Maritimes Region. Report
Can Fish Mar Serv Tech Rep — Canada. Fisheries and Marine Service. Technical Report
Can Fish Mar Serv Tech Rep Ser Cen-T — Canada. Fisheries and Marine Service. Technical Report. Series Cen-T
Can Fish Rep — Canadian Fisheries Reports
Can Fish Serv Resour Dev Branch Halifax Prog Rep — Canada. Fisheries Service. Resource Development Branch. Halifax Progress Report
Can Fld Nat — Canadian Field-Naturalist
Can Folk Mus — Canadian Folk Music Journal
Can Food Bull — Canadian Food Bulletin
Can Food Ind — Canadian Food Industries
Can Food Pack — Canadian Food Packer
Can For Branch Dep Publ — Canada. Forestry Branch. Departmental Publication
Can Forces Dent Serv Q — Canadian Forces Dental Services Quarterly
Can For Entomol Pathol Branch Annu Rep — Canada. Forest Entomology and Pathology Branch. Annual Report
Can For Ind — Canadian Forest Industries
Can For J — Canadian Forestry Journal
Can For M — Canadian Forestry Magazine
Can For Prod Res Branch Annu Rep — Canada. Forest Products Research Branch. Annual Report
Can For Prod Res Branch Tech Note — Canada. Forest Production Research Branch. Technical Note
Can For Res Branch Annu Rep — Canada. Forest Research Branch. Annual Report
Can For Ser For Fire Res Inst Info Rep — Canada. Forestry Service. Forest Fire Research Institute. Information Report
Can For Serv Annu Rep For Insect Dis Surv — Canadian Forestry Service. Annual Report of the Forest Insect and Disease Survey
Can For Serv Bi-Mon Res Notes — Canada. Forestry Service. Bi-Monthly Research Notes

Can For Serv Chem Control Res Inst File Rep — Canadian Forestry Service. Chemical Control Research Institute. File Report
Can For Serv Chem Control Res Inst Rep CC-X — Canadian Forestry Service. Chemical Control Research Institute. Report CC-X
Can For Serv For Fire Res Inst Inf Rep FF-X — Canadian Forestry Service. Forest Fire Research Institute. Information Report FF-X
Can For Serv For Fire Res Inst Misc Rep FF-X — Canadian Forestry Service. Forest Fire Research Institute. Miscellaneous Report FF-X
Can For Serv For Manage Inst Inf Rep FMR-X — Canadian Forestry Service. Forest Management Institute. Information Report FMR-X
Can For Serv For Tech Rep — Canadian Forestry Service. Forestry Technical Report
Can For Serv North For Res Cent For Rep — Canadian Forestry Service. Northern Forest Research Centre. Forestry Report
Can For Serv North For Res Cent Inf Rep NOR-X — Canadian Forestry Service. Northern Forest Research Centre. Information Report NOR-X
Can For Serv Pac For Res Cent BC-P — Canadian Forestry Service. Pacific Forest Research Centre BC-P
Can For Serv Pac For Res Cent For Pest Leafl — Canadian Forestry Service. Pacific Forest Research Centre. Forest Pest Leaflet
Can For Serv Pac For Res Cent Inf Rep BC-X — Canadian Forestry Service. Pacific Forest Research Centre. Information Report BC-X
Can For Serv Pac For Res Cent Rep BC-X — Canadian Forestry Service. Pacific Forest Research Centre. Report BC-X
Can For Serv Publ — Canadian Forestry Service. Publication
Can Forum — Canadian Forum
Can Foundry J — Canada's Foundry Journal
Can Franc — Canada Francais
Can Gas J — Canadian Gas Journal
Can Geog — Canadian Geographer
Can Geog J — Canadian Geographical Journal [*Later, Canadian Geographic*]
Can Geogr — Canadian Geographer
Can Geogr — Canadian Geography
Can Geographic — Canadian Geographic
Can Geogr J — Canadian Geographical Journal [*Later, Canadian Geographic*]
Can Geol Surv Bull — Canada. Geological Survey. Bulletin
Can Geol Surv Map — Canada. Geological Survey. Map
Can Geol Surv Mem — Canada. Geological Survey. Memoir
Can Geol Surv Misc Rep — Canada. Geological Survey. Miscellaneous Report
Can Geol Surv Pap — Canada. Geological Survey. Paper
Can Geoph Bull — Canadian Geophysical Bulletin
Can Geophys Bull — Canadian Geophysical Bulletin
Can Geotech J — Canadian Geotechnical Journal
Can Gov Publ Q — Canadian Government Publications Quarterly
Can Grain Res Lab Annu Rep — Canadian Grain Research Laboratory. Annual Report
Can Grow Q Bull — Cane Growers Quarterly Bulletin
Can G S — Canada. Geological Survey
Can G S An Rp — Canada. Geological Survey. Annual Report
Can G S Mem — Canada. Geological Survey. Memoir
Can G S Mus B — Canada. Geological Survey. Museum Bulletin
Can G S Sum Rp — Canada. Geological Survey. Summary Report
Can Heritage — Canadian Heritage
Can His R — Canadian Historical Review
Can Hist Ass Ann Rep — Canadian Historical Association. Annual Report
Can Hist Assn — Canadian Historical Association. Historical Papers
Can Hist Assn Rep — Canadian Historical Association. Report
Can Hist Assoc Ann Rep — Canadian Historical Association. Annual Report
Can Hist Mag — Canada. An Historical Magazine
Can Hist R — Canadian Historical Review
Can Hist Rev — Canadian Historical Review
Can Home Ec J — Canadian Home Economics Journal
Can Home Econ J Rev Can Econ Familiale — Canadian Home Economics Journal/Revue Canadienne d'Economie Familiale
Can Hort — Canadian Horticulture and Home Magazine
Can Hort Beek — Canadian Horticulturist and Beekeeper
Can Hosp — Canadian Hospital
CanHR — Canadian Historical Review
CanI — Canadian Periodical Index
Can I Food — Canadian Institute of Food Science and Technology. Journal
Can Ind — Canadian Periodical Index
Can Ind Geosci Data — Canadian Index to Geoscience Data
Canine Pract — Canine Practice
Can Inland Waters Branch Rep Ser — Canada. Inland Waters Branch. Report Series
Can Inland Waters Branch Sci Ser — Canada. Inland Waters Branch. Scientific Series
Can Inland Waters Dir Rep Ser — Canada. Inland Waters Directorate. Report Series
Can Inland Waters Dir Sediment Data Can Rivers — Canada. Inland Waters Directorate. Sediment Data for Canadian Rivers
Can Insect Pest Rev — Canadian Insect Pest Review
Can Inst Food Sci Technol J — Canadian Institute of Food Science and Technology. Journal
Can Inst Food Technol J — Canadian Institute of Food Technology. Journal

Can Inst Min Metall Min Soc NS Trans — Canadian Institute of Mining and Metallurgy and the Mining Society of Nova Scotia. Transactions
Can Inst Min Met Spec Vol — Canadian Institute of Mining and Metallurgy. Special Volume
Can Inst Pr — Canadian Institute Proceedings
Can Int Educ — Canadian and International Education
Can J — Canadian Journal [*Toronto*]
CANJA — Canadian Anaesthetists' Society. Journal
Can J Afr S — Canadian Journal of African Studies
Can J Afr Stud — Canadian Journal of African Studies
Can J Afr Studies — Canadian Journal of African Studies
Can J Agr Econ — Canadian Journal of Agricultural Economics
Can J Agric Econ — Canadian Journal of Agricultural Economics
Can J Agric Econ Rev Can Econ Rurale — Canadian Journal of Agricultural Economics/Revue Canadienne d'Economie Rurale
Can J Agric Sci — Canadian Journal of Agricultural Science
Can J Agr Sci — Canadian Journal of Agricultural Science
Can J Ag Sci — Canadian Journal of Agricultural Science
Can J Anim — Canadian Journal of Animal Science
Can J Anim Sci — Canadian Journal of Animal Science
Can J Appl Sport Sci — Canadian Journal of Applied Sport Sciences
Can J Appl Sport Sciences — Canadian Journal of Applied Sport Sciences
Can J Behav Sci — Canadian Journal of Behavioural Science
Can J Beh S — Canadian Journal of Behavioural Science
Can J Bioch — Canadian Journal of Biochemistry
Can J Biochem — Canadian Journal of Biochemistry
Can J Biochem Physiol — Canadian Journal of Biochemistry and Physiology
Can J Bot — Canadian Journal of Botany
Can J Chem — Canadian Journal of Chemistry
Can J Chem Eng — Canadian Journal of Chemical Engineering
Can J Chem Engng — Canadian Journal of Chemical Engineering
Can J Ch En — Canadian Journal of Chemical Engineering
Can J Civ Eng — Canadian Journal of Civil Engineering
Can J Civ Engng — Canadian Journal of Civil Engineering
Can J Civ Eng/Rev Can Genie Civ — Canadian Journal of Civil Engineering/ Revue Canadienne de Genie Civil
Can J Clin — Cancer Journal for Clinicians
Can J Com M — Canadian Journal of Comparative Medicine
Can J Comp Med — Canadian Journal of Comparative Medicine
Can J Comp Med Vet Sci — Canadian Journal of Comparative Medicine and Veterinary Science [*Later, Canadian Journal of Comparative Medicine*]
Can J Corr — Canadian Journal of Corrections
Can J Correction — Canadian Journal of Corrections
Can J Crim — Canadian Journal of Criminology and Corrections
Can J Crim & Correct — Canadian Journal of Criminology and Corrections
Can J Criminology & Corr — Canadian Journal of Criminology and Corrections
Can J Development Studies — Canadian Journal of Development Studies
Can J Development Studies (Ottawa) — Canadian Journal of Development Studies (Ottawa)
Can J Earth — Canadian Journal of Earth Sciences
Can J Earth Sci — Canadian Journal of Earth Sciences
Can J Ec — Canadian Journal of Economics
Can J Econ — Canadian Journal of Economics
Can J Econ Polit Sci — Canadian Journal of Economics and Political Science [*Later, Canadian Journal of Economics*]
Can J Econ Pol Sci — Canadian Journal of Economics and Political Science [*Later, Canadian Journal of Economics*]
Can J Econ & Pol Sci — Canadian Journal of Economics and Political Science [*Later, Canadian Journal of Economics*]
Can J Econ Rev Can Econ Univ Toronto Press Can Econ Assoc — Canadian Journal of Economics/Revue Canadienne d'Economique. University of Toronto Press. Canadian Economics Association
Can J Fabr — Canadian Journal of Fabrics
Can J Fish Aquatic Sci — Canadian Journal of Fisheries and Aquatic Sciences
Can J Fish Aquat Sci — Canadian Journal of Fisheries and Aquatic Sciences
Can J Fish Aquat Sci J Can Sci Halieutiques Aquat — Canadian Journal of Fisheries and Aquatic Sciences. Journal Canadien des Sciences Halieutiques et Aquatiques
Can J Forest Res — Canadian Journal of Forest Research
Can J For Res — Canadian Journal of Forest Research
Can J Gen Cyt — Canadian Journal of Genetics and Cytology
Can J Genet — Canadian Journal of Genetics and Cytology
Can J Genet Cytol — Canadian Journal of Genetics and Cytology
Can J His — Canadian Journal of History
Can J Hist — Canadian Journal of History
Can J Hist Sport Phys Educ — Canadian Journal of History of Sport and Physical Education
Can J Hosp Pharm — Canadian Journal of Hospital Pharmacy
Can J Info Science — Canadian Journal of Information Science
Can J Ital — Canadian Journal of Italian Studies
Can J L — Canadian Journal of Linguistics
Can J Ling — Canadian Journal of Linguistics
Can J Lingu — Canadian Journal of Linguistics
Can J Math — Canadian Journal of Mathematics
Can J Med Sci — Canadian Journal of Medical Science

Can J Med Surg — Canadian Journal of Medicine and Surgery
Can J Med T — Canadian Journal of Medical Technology
Can J Med Techn — Canadian Journal of Medical Technology
Can J Med Technol — Canadian Journal of Medical Technology
Can J Micro — Canadian Journal of Microbiology
Can J Microb — Canadian Journal of Microbiology
Can J Microbiol — Canadian Journal of Microbiology
Can J Neurol Sci — Canadian Journal of Neurological Science
Can J Occup Ther — Canadian Journal of Occupational Therapy
Can J Ophth — Canadian Journal of Ophthalmology
Can J Ophthalm — Canadian Journal of Ophthalmology
Can J Ophthalmol — Canadian Journal of Ophthalmology
Can J Optom — Canadian Journal of Optometry
Can J Otolaryngol — Canadian Journal of Otolaryngology
Can Jour Hist — Canadian Journal of History
Can J Pharm Sci — Canadian Journal of Pharmaceutical Sciences
Can J Phil — Canadian Journal of Philosophy
Can J Ph Sc — Canadian Journal of Pharmaceutical Sciences
Can J Phys — Canadian Journal of Physics
Can J Physiol Pharm — Canadian Journal of Physiology and Pharmacology
Can J Physiol Pharmacol — Canadian Journal of Physiology and Pharmacology
Can J Physl — Canadian Journal of Physiology and Pharmacology
Can J Plant — Canadian Journal of Plant Science
Can J Plant Pathol — Canadian Journal of Plant Pathology
Can J Plant Sci — Canadian Journal of Plant Science
Can J Pl Sci — Canadian Journal of Plant Science
Can J Poli — Canadian Journal of Political Science
Can J Pol Sc — Canadian Journal of Political Science
Can J Pol Sci — Canadian Journal of Political Science
Can J Pol Science — Canadian Journal of Political Science
Can J Pol Science (Ont) — Canadian Journal of Political Science (Ontario)
Can J Pol and Soc Theory — Canadian Journal of Political and Social Theory
Can J Psych — Canadian Journal of Psychology
Can J Psychiatr Nurs — Canadian Journal of Psychiatric Nursing
Can J Psychiatry — Canadian Journal of Psychiatry
Can J Psychol — Canadian Journal of Psychology
Can J Publ — Canadian Journal of Public Health
Can J Publ Hlth — Canadian Journal of Public Health
Can J Public Health — Canadian Journal of Public Health
Can J Radiogr Radiother Nucl Med (Engl Ed) — Canadian Journal of Radiography, Radiotherapy, Nuclear Medicine (English Edition)
Can J Rel Thought — Canadian Journal of Religious Thought
Can J Remote Sens — Canadian Journal of Remote Sensing
Can J Remote Sensing — Canadian Journal of Remote Sensing
Can J Res — Canadian Journal of Research
Can J Res Sect A — Canadian Journal of Research. Section A. Physical Sciences
Can J Res Sect B — Canadian Journal of Research. Section B. Chemical Sciences
Can J Res Sect C Bot Sci — Canadian Journal of Research. Section C. Botanical Sciences
Can J Res Sect D Zool Sci — Canadian Journal of Research. Section D. Zoological Sciences
Can J Res Sect E Med Sci — Canadian Journal of Research. Section E. Medical Sciences
Can J Res Sect F — Canadian Journal of Research. Section F. Technology
Can J Sci — Canadian Journal of Science, Literature, and History
Can J Soil — Canadian Journal of Soil Science
Can J Soil Sci — Canadian Journal of Soil Science
Can J Spect — Canadian Journal of Spectroscopy
Can J Spectrosc — Canadian Journal of Spectroscopy
Can J Spectry — Canadian Journal of Spectroscopy
Can J Statis — Canadian Journal of Statistics
Can J Surg — Canadian Journal of Surgery
Can JT — Canadian Journal of Theology
Can J Technol — Canadian Journal of Technology
Can J Th — Canadian Journal of Theology
Can J Zool — Canadian Journal of Zoology
Can L — Canadian Literature
Can Lab — Canadian Labour
Can Labour — Canadian Labour
Can Lanc — Canada Lancet and Practitioner
Can Law — Canadian Lawyer
Can Lawyer — Canadian Lawyer
Can Lbr — Canadian Labour
Can Legal Aid Bul — Canadian Legal Aid Bulletin
Can Lib — Canadian Library
Can Lib Assn Bul — Canadian Library Association. Bulletin
Can Lib Bull — Canadian Library Bulletin
Can Lib J — Canadian Library Journal
Can Libr J — Canadian Library Journal
Can Lit — Canadian Literature
Can Lit Mag — Canadian Literary Magazine
Can M — Canadian Magazine
Can Mach Metalwork — Canadian Machinery and Metalworking

Can MAJ — Canadian Medical Association. Journal
CANMAN — Casopis Narodniho Muzea [*Prague*]
Can Math B — Canadian Mathematical Bulletin
Can Math Bull — Canadian Mathematical Bulletin
Can Math Teach — Canadian Mathematics Teacher
Can Med A J — Canadian Medical Association. Journal
Can Med Ass J — Canadian Medical Association. Journal
Can Med Assn J — Canadian Medical Association. Journal
Can Med Assoc J — Canadian Medical Association. Journal
Can Mental Health — Canada's Mental Health
Can Ment He — Canada's Mental Health
Can Ment Health — Canada's Mental Health
Can Ment Hlth — Canada's Mental Health
Can Metall Q — Canadian Metallurgical Quarterly
Can Metal Q — Canadian Metallurgical Quarterly
Can Metalwork/Mach Prod — Canadian Metalworking/Machine Production
Can Metalwork Prod — Canadian Metalworking Production
Can Met Quart — Canadian Metallurgical Quarterly
Can Milling Feed — Canadian Milling and Feed
Can Mineral — Canadian Mineralogist
Can Miner Ind Rev — Canadian Mineral Industry. Review
Can Miner Resour Branch Miner Bull — Canada. Mineral Resources Branch. Mineral Bulletin
Can Miner Resour Branch Miner Inf Bull — Canada. Mineral Resources Branch. Mineral Information Bulletin
Can Miner Resour Branch Miner Rep — Canada. Mineral Resources Branch. Mineral Report
Can Miner Resour Div Miner Bull — Canada. Mineral Resources Division. Mineral Bulletin
Can Miner Yearb — Canadian Minerals Yearbook
Can Mines Branch Memo Ser — Canada. Mines Branch. Memorandum Series
Can Mines Branch Monogr — Canada. Mines Branch. Monograph
Can Mines Branch Radioact Div Top Rep — Canada. Mines Branch. Radioactivity Division. Topical Report
Can Mines Branch Rep — Canada. Mines Branch. Report
Can Mines Branch Res Rep — Canada. Mines Branch. Research Report
Can Mines Branch Tech Bull — Canada. Mines Branch. Technical Bulletin
Can Mines Branch Tech Pap — Canada. Mines Branch. Technical Paper
Can Mines Br Sum Rp — Canada. Department of Mines. Mines Branch. Summary Report
Can Mining J — Canadian Mining Journal
Can Mining Met Bul — Canadian Mining and Metallurgical Bulletin
Can Min J — Canadian Mining Journal
Can Min Met — Canadian Mining and Metallurgical Bulletin
Can Min Metall Bull — Canadian Mining and Metallurgical Bulletin
Can Min & Metallurg Bull — Canadian Mining and Metallurgical Bulletin
Can Min & Met Bul — Canadian Mining and Metallurgical Bulletin
Can-Mong R — Canada-Mongolia Review
Can M Rv — Canadian Mining Review
Can Munic Util — Canadian Municipal Utilities
Can Mus — Canadian Musician
Can Mus Bk — Canada Music Book
Can Mus Ed — Canadian Music Educator
Can Mus J — Canadian Music Journal
Can Nat — Canadian Naturalist and Geologist and Proceedings of the Natural History Society of Montreal
Can Natl Aeronaut Establ Mech Eng Rep — Canada. National Aeronautical Establishment. Mechanical Engineering Report
Can Natl Res Counc Div Mech Eng Lab Tech Rep — Canada. National Research Council. Division of Mechanical Engineering. Laboratory Technical Report
CANNB — Canadian Nurse
Cann Pack — Canning and Packing
Cann Trade — Canning Trade
Can Nucl — Canada Nucleaire
Can Nucl Assoc Annu Int Conf — Canadian Nuclear Association. Annual International Conference
Can Nucl Assoc Annu Int Conf (Pro) — Canadian Nuclear Association. Annual International Conference (Proceedings)
Can Nucl Assoc Report — Canadian Nuclear Association. Report
Can Nucl Soc Annu Conf Trans — Canadian Nuclear Society. Annual Conference. Transactions
Can Nucl Soc Trans — Canadian Nuclear Society. Transactions
Can Nucl Technol — Canadian Nuclear Technology
Can Nurse — Canadian Nurse
CANO — Canoma. Canada Department of Energy, Mines, and Resources
Canon Law — Canon Law Abstracts
Can Oper Res Soc J — Canadian Operational Research Society. Journal
CANP — Canadian Association of Native Peoples. Bulletin
Can Pac For Res Cent Rep BC X — Canada. Pacific Forest Research Centre. Report. BC X
Can Paint Finish — Canadian Paint and Finishing
Can Paint Varn — Canadian Paint and Varnish
Can Pap Rural Hist — Canadian Papers in Rural History
Can Pat Office Rec — Canadian Patent Office. Record
Can Pat Office Recd — Canadian Patent Office. Record

Can Pat Rep — Canadian Patent Reporter
Can Peat Soc B — Canadian Peat Society. Bulletin
Can Pers — Canadian Personnel and Industrial Relations Journal (Including the Canadian Training Digest)
Can Pet — Canadian Petroleum
Can Petro Eng — Canadian Petro Engineering
Can Petrol — Canadian Petroleum
Can Pharm J — Canadian Pharmaceutical Journal
Can Phil Rev — Canadian Philosophical Reviews
Can Pkg — Canadian Packaging
Can Plant Dis Surv — Canadian Plant Disease Survey
Can Plastics — Canadian Plastics
Can Po — Canadian Poetry
Can Poetry — Canadian Poetry
Can Poult Rev — Canadian Poultry Review
Can Poultry Rev — Canadian Poultry Review
Can Power Eng — Canadian Power Engineering
Can Power Eng Plant Maint — Canadian Power Engineering and Plant Maintenance
Can P R — Canadian Patent Reporter
Can Printer Publ — Canadian Printer and Publisher
Can Psl & Ind Rel J — Canadian Personnel and Industrial Relations Journal (Including the Canadian Training Digest)
Can Psychi — Canadian Psychiatric Association. Journal
Can Psychiatr Assoc J — Canadian Psychiatric Association. Journal
Can Psychol — Canadian Psychologist
Can Psychology — Canadian Psychology
Can Psychol Rev — Canadian Psychological Review
Can Psych Psych Can — Canadian Psychology/Psychologie Canadienne
Can Psych R — Canadian Psychological Review
Can Pub Admin — Canadian Public Administration/Administration Publique du Canada
Can Publ Ad — Canadian Public Administration/Administration Publique du Canada
Can Public Admin — Canadian Public Administration
Can Public Policy — Canadian Public Policy
Can Public Policy (Guelph) — Canadian Public Policy (Guelph)
Can Pub Pol — Canadian Public Policy
Can Pub Policy — Canadian Public Policy
Can Pulp Paper Ind — Canadian Pulp and Paper Industry
Can Quill — Canadian Quill
Can R Am St — Canadian Review of American Studies
Can R Com L — Canadian Review of Comparative Literature/Revue Canadienne de Litterature Comparee
Can Rec N H — Canadian Record of Natural History and Geology
Can Rec Sc — Canadian Record of Science
Can Renewable Energy News — Canadian Renewable Energy News
Can Res — Canadian Research
Can Res Dev — Canadian Research and Development [*Later, Canadian Research*]
Can Res Inst Launders Clean Tech — Canadian Research Institute of Launderers and Cleaners. Technical Report
Can Resour Dev Branch Fish Ser Halifax Prog Rep — Canada. Resource Development Branch. Fisheries Service. Halifax Progress Report
Can Rev — Canadian Review
Can Rev Am Stud — Canadian Review of American Studies
Can Rev Comp Lt — Canadian Review of Comparative Literature/Revue Canadienne de Litterature Comparee
Can Rev Sociol Anthropol — Canadian Review of Sociology and Anthropology
Can Rev Stud Natl — Canadian Review of Studies in Nationalism
Can R Soc — Canadian Review of Sociology and Anthropology
Can R Soc A — Canadian Review of Sociology and Anthropology
Can R Sociol Anth — Canadian Review of Sociology and Anthropology
Can R Sociol & Anthrop — Canadian Review of Sociology and Anthropology
Can R Studies Nationalism — Canadian Review of Studies in Nationalism
Can R Stud Nat — Canadian Review of Studies in Nationalism
CANS — Canada - North of 60
Can Sci — Canadian Scientist
Can Sc Mo — Canadian Science Monthly
Can Serv Med J — Canadian Services Medical Journal
Can Slav P — Canadian Slavonic Papers
Can Slav Stud — Canadian-American Slavic Studies
Can's Mental Health — Canada's Mental Health
CANSN — Canada - North of 60. Newsletter
Can Soc Pet Geol Mem — Canadian Society of Petroleum Geologists. Memoir
CanSP — Canadian Slavonic Papers
Can Spec Publ Fish Aquat Sci — Canadian Special Publication of Fisheries and Aquatic Sciences
Can Spectrosc — Canadian Spectroscopy
Can Spectry — Canadian Spectroscopy
CanSS — Canadian-American Slavic Studies
Can Stand Ass CSA Stand — Canadian Standards Association. CSA Standard
Can Statis R — Canadian Statistical Review
Can Struct Eng Conf — Canadian Structural Engineering Conference
Can Studies Population — Canadian Studies in Population
Can Surv — Canadian Surveyor

Can Symp Remote Sensing Proc — Canadian Symposium of Remote Sensing. Proceedings
Can Taxation — Canadian Taxation
Can Tax J — Canadian Tax Journal
Canteras Explot — Canteras y Explotaciones
Canterbury Chamber Commer Agric Bull — Canterbury Chamber of Commerce. Agricultural Bulletin
Canterbury Eng J — Canterbury Engineering Journal
Can Text J — Canadian Textile Journal
CAnth — Current Anthropology
Can Theat R — Canadian Theatre Review
Can Theatre R — Canadian Theatre Review
CAnthr — Current Anthropology
C Anthropol Ecol Hum — Cahiers d'Anthropologie et d'Ecologie Humaines
C Antiq FPL — Coins and Antiquities Ltd. Fixed Price List [London]
Cant Mount — Canterbury Mountaineer [New Zealand]
Can Tob Grower — Canadian Tobacco Grower
Canto Greg — Canto Gregoriano
Can Transp — Canadian Transportation
Cantrill's Fmnts — Cantrill's Filmnotes
CANUA — Canadian Nurse
CANUDG — Comparative Animal Nutrition
Ca Nurs — Cancer Nursing
Can Vet J — Canadian Veterinary Journal
Can Vet Record — Canadian Veterinary Record
Can Victoria Mem Mus B — Canada. Victoria Memorial Museum. Bulletin
CANW — Canada Now! Social Studies Magazine for Schools
CANWA — Chemia Analityczna (Warsawa)
Can Water Resour Branch Water Resour Pap S — Canada. Water Resources Branch. Water Resources Paper S. Sediment
Can Wel — Canadian Welfare
Can Welder Fabr — Canadian Welder and Fabricator
Can Welfare — Canadian Welfare
Can Wildl Serv — Canadian Wildlife Service
Can Wildl Serv Occas Pap — Canadian Wildlife Service. Occasional Papers
Can Wildl Serv Prog Notes — Canadian Wildlife Service. Progress Notes
Can Wildl Serv Rep Ser — Canadian Wildlife Service. Report Series
Can & World — Canada and the World
CANWP — Canadian Network Papers. National Library of Canada
Can YBIL — Canadian Yearbook of International Law
Can Yb of Internat — Canadian Yearbook of International Law
Can YB Int'l L — Canadian Yearbook of International Law
Cany C News — Canyon Cinema News
Can Yearb Int Law — Canadian Yearbook of International Law
Can Yearbook Int L — Canadian Yearbook of International Law
CANZLLI — Current Australian and New Zealand Legal Literature Index
CAO — Cabinet Maker and Retail Furnisher
Caoutch Gutta Percha — Caoutchouc et la Gutta Percha
Caoutch Latex Artif — Caoutchoucs et Latex Artificiels
Caoutch Mod — Caoutchouc Moderne
Cap — Capitoli
Cap — Capitolium
CAP — Computers and People
CAPBAY — Catalogue of American Amphibians and Reptiles
CAPBBZ — Colorado. Agricultural Experiment Station. Bulletin
Cap Chem — Capital Chemist
CAPE — Canadian Petroleum
Cape Good Hope Dep Nat Conserv Rep — Cape Of Good Hope. Department of Nature Conservation. Report
Cape Librn — Cape Librarian
Cape Of Good Hope Dep Nat Conserv Invest Rep — Cape Of Good Hope. Department of Nature Conservation. Investigational Report
Cape Of Good Hope Dep Nat Conserv Rep — Cape Of Good Hope. Department of Nature Conservation. Report
Cape Town Univ Dep Geol Precambrian Res Unit Annu Rep — Cape Town. University. Department of Geology. Precambrian Research Unit. Annual Report
Capit — Capitolium
Capital — Capital and Class
Capital Goods R — Capital Goods Review
Capital ULR — Capital University. Law Review
Capital U L Rev — Capital University Law Review
Capital Univ L Rev — Capital University. Law Review
Capita Zool — Capita Zoologica
Capitol Stud — Capitol Studies
CaPL — Cahiers de la Pleiade
CAPL — Chronique Archeologique du Pays de Liege
CAPLD — Carolina Planning
Cap Libn — Cape Librarian
Cap Stud — Capitol Studies
Captv Insur — Captive Insurance Concept
Cap U LR — Capital University. Law Review
Cap UL Rev — Capital University. Law Review
CAPWAn — Cercle Archeologique du Pays de Waes. Annales
CaQ — California Quarterly
CAQDA — California Air Quality Data

CaR — Cakavska Ric
CAR — Canadian Annual Review
CAR — Caravan Kampeersport. Maandblad voor Caravan/ Kampeerliefhebbers
Car — Caravelle
Car — Carmelus
Car — Carovana
CAR — Central Asian Review
CAR — Commonwealth Arbitration Reports
Car A and E J — Cardozo Arts and Entertainment Journal
Carbide J — Carbide Journal
Carbide Tool J — Carbide and Tool Journal
Carbohydr Chem — Carbohydrate Chemistry
Carbohyd Res — Carbohydrate Research
Carbohydr Metab Quant Physiol Math Model — Carbohydrate Metabolism. Quantitative Physiology and Mathematical Modeling
Carbohydr Res — Carbohydrate Research
Carbohy Res — Carbohydrate Research
CARCBE — Annual Report. Central and Regional Arecanut Research Stations
CArch — Cahiers Archeologiques
Carcinog Compr Surv — Carcinogenesis: A Comprehensive Survey
Carcinog Tech Rep Ser US Natl Cancer Inst — Carcinogenesis Technical Report Series. United States National Cancer Institute
CARCMYS — Canadian Arctic Resources Committee. Monograph. Yukon Series
CARDAG — Cardiologia
CARDDJ — Cardiologia [Rome]
Cardil Hung — Cardiologia Hungarica
Cardiol Bull — Cardiologisches Bulletin
Cardiol Prat — Cardiologia Pratica
Cardio Res — Cardiovascular Research
Cardiovasc Clin — Cardiovascular Clinics
Cardiovasc Dis Bull Tex Heart Inst — Cardiovascular Diseases Bulletin. Texas Heart Institute
Cardiovasc Flow Dyn Meas (NATO Adv Study Inst) — Cardiovascular Flow Dynamics and Measurements (North Atlantic Treaty Organization. Advanced Study Institute on Cardiovascular Flow Dynamics)
Cardiovasc Intervent Radiol — Cardiovascular and Interventional Radiology
Cardiovasc Med — Cardiovascular Medicine
Cardiovasc Nurs — Cardiovascular Nursing
Cardiovasc Radiol — Cardiovascular Radiology
Cardiovasc Res — Cardiovascular Research
Cardiovasc Res Cent Bull — Cardiovascular Research Center. Bulletin [Houston]
Cardiovasc Res Cent Bull (Houston) — Cardiovascular Research Center. Bulletin (Houston)
Cardiovas Res Suppl — Cardiovascular Research. Supplement
Cardiovas Rev — Cardiovascular Review
Cardozo L Rev — Cardozo Law Review
Car & Dr — Car and Driver
CAREBK — Caries Research
Career Dev Bul — Career Development Bulletin
CAREL — Cascadian Regional Library
Car Eng — Carbide Engineering
Carey's Mus — Carey's American Museum
Cargese Lect Phys — Cargese Lectures in Physics
Cargill Crop Bull — Cargill Crop Bulletin
Cargo Syst Int — Cargo Systems International
CARHS — Canadian-American Review of Hungarian Studies
CARIAV — Caribbean Forester
Caribb Agr — Caribbean Agriculture
Caribb Agric — Caribbean Agriculture
Carib Basin Econ Surv — Caribbean Basin Economic Survey
Caribbean Jour Sci — Caribbean Journal of Science
Caribbean J Sci Math — Caribbean Journal of Science and Mathematics
Caribbean R — Caribbean Review
Caribbean S — Caribbean Studies
Caribbean Stud — Caribbean Studies
Caribb For — Caribbean Forester
Carib J Sci — Caribbean Journal of Science
Caribb Med J — Caribbean Medical Journal
Carib J Rel St — Caribbean Journal of Religious Studies
Carib Q — Caribbean Quarterly
Carib Stud — Caribbean Studies
Caries Res — Caries Research
Carinthia — Carinthia Mitteilungen des Geschichtsverein fuer Kaernten
Carinthia 2 Sonderh — Carinthia 2. Sonderheft
CarJos — Cahiers de Josephologie [Montreal, PQ]
CARLD — Chicorel Abstracts to Reading and Learning Disabilities
Carleton Misc — Carleton Miscellany
Carleton Univ Dep Geol Geol Pap — Carleton University. Department of Geology. Geological Paper
Carleton Univ Dept Geology Geol Paper — Carleton University. Department of Geology. Geological Paper
Carl Mis — Carleton Miscellany
CarlN — Carleton Newsletter

Carlsberg Res Commun — Carlsberg Research Communications
Carmarthenshire Antiq — Carmarthenshire Antiquary
CARN — Cairn. Archives of the Canadian Rockies Newsletter
CARN — Carnets de l'Enfance
Carnegie Coll Physical Ed Research Papers — Carnegie College of Physical Education. Leeds. Research Papers in Physical Education
Carnegie Inst Technol Coal Res Lab Contri — Carnegie Institute of Technology. Coal Research Laboratory. Contribution
Carnegie Inst Washington Pap Geophys Lab — Carnegie Institution of Washington. Papers from the Geophysical Laboratory
Carnegie Inst Wash Pap Geophys Lab — Carnegie Institution of Washington. Papers from the Geophysical Laboratory
Carnegie Inst Wash Publ — Carnegie Institution of Washington. Publication
Carnegie Inst Wash Year Book — Carnegie Institution of Washington. Year Book
Carnegie Mag — Carnegie Magazine
Carnegie-Mellon Univ TRI Res Rep — Carnegie-Mellon University, Pittsburgh. Transportation Research Institute. TRI Research Report
Carnegie Mus An Mem — Carnegie Museum of Natural History. Annals. Memoirs
Carnegie Mus Annals — Carnegie Museum of Natural History. Annals
Carnegie Mus Nat Hist Annu Rep — Carnegie Museum of Natural History. Annual Report
Carnegie Mus Nat Hist Spec Publ — Carnegie Museum of Natural History. Special Publication
Carnegie Res Papers — Carnegie Research Papers
Carn Enfance — Carnets de l'Enfance
Carnes Merc — Carnes y Mercados
Carnet Mus — Carnet Musical
Carnets Enfance — Carnets de l'Enfance
Carnets Zool — Carnets de Zoologie
Carnivore Genet Newsl — Carnivore Genetics Newsletter
CarnM — Carnegie Magazine
CAROEJ — Carolinea
Carol Biol Readers — Carolina Biology Readers
Carol Camellias — Carolina Camellias
Carolina Q — Carolina Quarterly
Carol J Pharm — Carolina Journal of Pharmacy
Carol Plann — Carolina Planning
Carol Q — Carolina Quarterly
Carol Tips — Carolina Tips
Carousel Q — Carousel Quarterly
CarP — Carolina Playbook
CAR Q — Carolina Quarterly
Carroll Bus Bul — Carroll Business Bulletin
Carswell's Prac — Carswell's Practice Cases
Carta Geol Chile Inst Invest Geol — Carta Geologica de Chile. Instituto de Investigaciones Geologicas
Carte — Carte Segrete
Cartogr — Cartography
Cartogr J — Cartographic Journal
CARV — Carnivore. Carnivore Research Institute [*Petersburg, IL*]
CARYAB — Caryologia
CAS — Canadian Business Review
CAS — Central Asiatic Studies
CAS — Chemical Abstracts Service. Report
CAS — Current Australian Serials
CasaA — Casa de las Americas
CASAE — Cahier. Supplement aux Annales du Service des Antiquites de l'Egypte [*Cairo*]
Cas Cesk Lek — Casopis Ceskenho Lekarstnitva
Cas Cesk Spolecnosti Entomol — Casopis Ceskoslovenske. Spolecnosti Entomologicke
CaSE — Carnegie Series in English
CASEA — Cancer Seminar
Case & Com — Case and Comment
Case Stud At Phys — Case Studies in Atomic Physics
Case West J Int Law — Case Western Reserve. Journal of International Law
Case West Reserve — Case Western Reserve University. Studies in Anthropology
Case West Reserve L Rev — Case Western Reserve. Law Review
Case West Res J Int'l L — Case Western Reserve. Journal of International Law
Case West Res L Rev — Case Western Reserve. Law Review
Case W Res — Case Western Reserve. Journal of International Law
Case W Reserve Law R — Case Western Reserve. Law Review
Case W Reserve L Rev — Case Western Reserve. Law Review
Case W Res J Int L — Case Western Reserve. Journal of International Law
Case W Res L Rev — Case Western Reserve. Law Review
CASI Trans — CASI [*Canadian Aeronautics and Space Institute*] Transactions
CAsJ — Central Asiatic Journal
Cas Lek Cesk — Casopis Lekaru Ceskych
Cas Mineral Geol — Casopis pro Mineralogii a Geologii
Cas Morav Mus (Brne) — Casopis Moravskeho Musea (Brne)
Cas Morav Mus Vedy Prir — Casopis Moravskeho Musea. Vedy Prirodni
CASNAH — Casopis Slezskeho Muzea. Serie A. Vedy Prirodni

Cas Nar Muz Oddil Priroddoved — Casopis Narodniho Muzea. Oddil Priroddovedny [*Prague*]
Cas Nar Muz (Prague) — Casopis Narodniho Muzea (Prague)
Cas Nar Muz Praze Rada Prirodoved — Casopis Narodniho Muzea v Praze. Rada Prirodovedna
Cas Narod Muz — Casopis Narodniho Muzea. Historicke Muzeum Rocnik [*Prague*]
Casopis Pest Mat — Ceskoslovenska Akademie Ved. Casopis pro Pestovani Matematiky
C A Source Index — Chemical Abstracts Service. Source Index Quarterly
CASPA — Canadian Spectroscopy
Cas Prum Chem — Casopis pro Prumysl Chemicky
CAsR — Central Asian Review
CASRAT — Colorado State University. Annual Report
CASRBU — Connecticut. Storrs Agricultural Experiment Station. Research Report
CASS — Canadian-American Slavic Studies
CASS — Computer Applications in Shipping and Shipbuilding [*Elsevier Book Series*]
CASSAW — Cassinia
Cassier — Cassier's Magazine
Cassinia J Ornithol East Penn South NJ Del — Cassinia. A Journal of Ornithology of Eastern Pennsylvania, Southern New Jersey, and Delaware
Cas Slezskeho Muz Ser A Sci Nat — Casopis Slezskeho Muzea. Serie A. Scientiae Naturales
Cas Slezskeho Muz Vedy Prir Acta Mus Silesiae Ser A Sci Nat — Casopis Slezskeho Muzea. Vedy Prirodni (Acta Musei Silesiae. Series A. Scientiae Naturales)
Cas Slezske Muz — Casopis Slezskeho Muzea
Cass M — Cassier's Magazine
Cassoe Nesl — Cassoe Newsletter
CASTA — Colorado State University. Agricultural Experiment Station. Technical Bulletin
CASTAZ — Colorado State University. Experiment Station. Technical Bulletin
Cast Eng — Casting Engineering
Cast Eng/Foundry World — Casting Engineering/Foundry World
Cast Forg — Casting and Forging [*Japan*]
Cast Forg Steel — Casting and Forging of Steel [*Japan*]
Cast Met Res J — Cast Metals Research Journal
CASU — Canadian Surveyor
CASUA — Canadian Surveyor
CASUD7 — Cancer Surveys
CASURSS — Comptes Rendus. Academie des Sciences de l'Union des Republiques Sovietiques Socialistes
Cas W Res L Rev — Case Western Reserve. Law Review
CAT — Cahiers d'Analyse Textuelle. Les Belles Lettres [*Liege*]
Cat — Catalyst
Cat — Catechistes [*Paris*]
CAT — Commentaire de l'Ancien Testament [*Neuchatel*]
CaT — Computers and Translation
Catal Chem — Catalysts in Chemistry
Catal Environ Qual — Catalyst for Environmental Quality
Catal Rev — Catalysis Reviews
Catal Rev Sci Eng — Catalysis Reviews. Science and Engineering
Catalyst Envir Qual — Catalyst for Environmental Quality
Cat Am Amphib Reptiles — Catalogue of American Amphibians and Reptiles
Cat Br Off Publications — Catalogue of British Official Publications
Cat Calcareous Nannofossils — Catalogue of Calcareous Nannofossils. Edizioni Tecnoscienza [*Rome*]
Cateques Latinoamer — Catequesis Latinoamericana
Cater — Catering
Cat Faunae Austriae — Catalogus Faunae Austriae
Cat Faunae Pol — Catalogus Faunae Poloniae
Cat Fossilium Austriae — Catalogus Fossilium Austriae
CATGD4 — Centro Internacional de Agricultura Tropical [*CIAT*]. Series GE
Cath — Catholicisme. Hier, Aujourd'hui, Demain [*Paris*]
CATHA4 — Carinthia 2
Cath Bibl Q — Catholic Biblical Quarterly
Cath Bib Q — Catholic Biblical Quarterly
Cath Charis — Catholic Charismatic
Cath Choirmaster — Catholic Choirmaster
Cath Doc — Catholic Documentation
Cath Ed R — Catholic Educational Review
Cathet Cardiovasc Diagn — Catheterization and Cardiovascular Diagnosis
Catheterization Cardiovasc Diagn — Catheterization and Cardiovascular Diagnosis
Cath His R — Catholic Historical Review
Cath Hist R — Catholic Historical Review
Cath Hist Rev — Catholic Historical Review
Cath Hosp — Catholic Hospital
CathHR — Catholic Historical Review
Cathl — Catholic Periodical and Literature Index
Cath Law — Catholic Lawyer
Cath Lawyer — Catholic Lawyer
Cath Libr Wld — Catholic Library World

Cath Lib W — Catholic Library World
Cath Lib World — Catholic Library World
Cath M — Catholic Mind
Cathol Hist Rev — Catholic Historical Review
Cathol Hosp — Catholic Hospital
Catholic Doc — Catholic Documentation
Catholic Law — Catholic Lawyer
Catholic UALR — Catholic University of America. Law Review
Catholic ULR — Catholic University. Law Review
Catholic U L Rev — Catholic University. Law Review
Catholic Univ L Rev — Catholic University. Law Review
Catholic W — Catholic Weekly
Cathol Nurse (Wallsend) — Catholic Nurse (Wallsend)
Cath-Presb — Catholic-Presbyterian
Cath Rec Soc Pub — Catholic Record Society. Publications
Cath Sch J — Catholic School Journal
Cath UALR — Catholic University of America. Law Review
Cath U Law — Catholic University of America. Law Review
Cath ULR — Catholic University. Law Review
Cath UL Rev — Catholic University. Law Review
Cath Univ Am Biol Stud — Catholic University of America. Biological Studies
Cath Univ Bull — Catholic University. Bulletin
Cath Univ Law Rev — Catholic University of America. Law Review
CathW — Catholic World
Cath Work — Catholic Worker
Cat Index — Catalogue and Index
Cat Index — Catalogue and Index. Library Association Cataloguing and Indexing Group
Cat Invertebres Suisse Mus Hist Nat Geneve — Catalogue des Invertebres de la Suisse Museum d'Histoire Naturelle de Geneve
Cato J — Cato Journal
CATRAY — Canning Trade
CATRB — Calcified Tissue Research [Later, Calcified Tissue International]
Cattlemen Beef Mag — Cattlemen. The Beef Magazine
Cat Trans C — Catalogus Translationum et Commentariorum/Medieval and Renaissance Latin Translations and Commentaries
CATUA — Chimica Acta Turcica
CAU — Construccion Arquitectura Urbanismo
CAUTA — Canadian Automotive Trade
CAUT ACPU Bul — Canadian Association of University Teachers/Association Canadienne des Professeurs d'Universite. Bulletin
CAV — Chambre de Commerce et d'Industrie d'Anvers. Bulletin
Caveat — Caveat Emptor
Cave Geol — Cave Geology
Cave Res Group GB Trans — Cave Research Group of Great Britain. Transactions
Cave Res Group Great Britain Trans — Cave Research Group of Great Britain. Transactions
Cave Sci — Cave Science
CAVOAZ — Contribuicoes Avulsas. Instituto Oceanografico Sao Paulo
CaVS — Cahiers du Vingtieme Siecle
CaW — Catholic World
CAW — China Aktuell
CAWE — Canada West
CA WILJ — California Western International Law Journal
CA WLR — California Western Law Review
Cawthron Inst (Nelson NZ) Rep — Cawthron Institute (Nelson, New Zealand). Report
Cawthron Inst Publs — Cawthron Institute. Publications
Cax — Caxton Magazine
CAXPAE — Connecticut. Storrs Agricultural Experiment Station. Progress Report
CB — Cahiers de Byrsa
CB — Classical Bulletin
CB — Commentationes Balticae
CB — Cuadernos Bibliograficos [Madrid]
CB — Cultura Biblica
CB — Cumulative Bulletin [United States Internal Revenue Service]
CB — Current Bibliography on African Affairs
CB — Customs Bulletin
CB — US Consulate [Hong Kong]. Current Background
CBA — Cronaca delle Belle Arti
CBA — Maandstatistiek van Bevolking en Volksgezondheid
CBAA — Current Bibliography on African Affairs
CBA Handbook — Commonwealth Broadcasting Association. Handbook
CBAIAL — Contributions. Arctic Institute. Catholic University of America
CBalt — Commentationes Balticae
CBAQAB — Contribuciones Cientificas. Facultad de Ciencias Exactas y Naturales. Universidad de Buenos Aires. Serie Quimica
CBASA — Ciba Symposia
CBASF — Current Bibliography for Aquatic Sciences and Fisheries
CBB — Commercial Bank of Greece. Economic Bulletin
CBBAA2 — Communications in Behavioral Biology. Part A. Original Articles
CBBMC — Ciencia Biologica
CB Bul — Conference Board. Information Bulletin
CBC — Cahiers Benjamin Constant

CBC — Cesare Barbieri Courier
CB Cap A — Conference Board. Manufacturing Investment Statistics. Capital Appropriations
CB Cap Inv — Conference Board. Manufacturing Investment Statistics. Capital Investment and Supply Conditions
CBC (Citizens Budget Comm) Q — CBC (Citizens Budget Commission) Quarterly
CBCPA — Comparative Biochemistry and Physiology
CBCPAI — Comparative Biochemistry and Physiology
CBD — Commerce Business Daily [Department of Commerce] [Chicago, IL] [Database]
CBE — Sociale Maandstatistiek
CBEMR — Commercial Bank of Ethiopia. Market Report
CBESD — Caribbean Basin Economic Survey
CBF — Cell Biochemistry and Function
CBFAS — Canadian Bulletin of Fisheries and Aquatic Sciences
CBFMA — Combustion and Flame
CBFMAO — Combustion and Flame
CBFUDH — Cell Biochemistry and Function
CBG — Collationes Brugenses et Gandavenses
CBI — Canadian Banker [Formerly, Canadian Banker and ICB Review]
CBI — Canadian Business Index [Micromedia Ltd.] [Database] [Toronto, ON]
CBI — Cumulative Book Index
CBI — Current Bibliographic Information
CBI (Confederation British Industry) R — CBI (Confederation of British Industry) Review
CBI Forsk — CBI [Cement-och Betonginstitutet] Forskning
CBI Ind Trends — CBI [Confederation of British Industry] Industrial Trends
CBI Ind Trends Surv — CBI [Confederation of British Industry] Industrial Trends Survey
CBIMA — Cahiers de Biologie Marine
CBINA — Chemico-Biological Interactions
CBI News — Confederation of British Industry. News
CBIOD — Cell Biophysics
CBIP — Canadian Books in Print
CBJ — Connecticut Bar Journal
CBJ — Koopkracht. Blad voor de Konsument
CBJNA — Carbide Journal
CBK — Economies et Societes
CBKK — Chuban Kenkyu [Studies on Chinese Language and Literature]
CBL — Canadian Business Law Journal
CBL — Collectanea Biblica Latina [Rome]
CBL — Cumulative Book List
CBL — Journal of Commercial Bank Lending
CBLBA — Ciba Lectures in Microbial Biochemistry
CBLGA2 — Chronobiologia
Cbl Ges Forstw — Centralblatt fuer das Gesamte Forstwesen
CBLKAE — Contributions. Biological Laboratory. Kyoto University
CBLLAH — Contributions. Bears Bluff Laboratories
Cb LR — Columbia Law Review
CBMDAW — Computers in Biology and Medicine
CB Merger — Conference Board. Announcements of Mergers and Acquisitions
CBMODY — Cell Biology Monographs
CBMRB7 — Computers and Biomedical Research
CBP — CB Review (Philippines)
CBPAB5 — Comparative Biochemistry and Physiology. A. Comparative Physiology
CBPBB — Comparative Biochemistry and Physiology. B. Comparative Biochemistry
CBPBB8 — Comparative Biochemistry and Physiology. B. Comparative Biochemistry
CBPCBB — Comparative Biochemistry and Physiology. C. Comparative Pharmacology [Later, Comparative Biochemistry and Physiology. C. Comparative Pharmacology and Toxicology]
CBPCD — Ciments, Betons, Platres, Chaux
CBPCEE — Comparative Biochemistry and Physiology. C. Comparative Pharmacology and Toxicology
CBPI — Canadian Business Periodicals Index [Later, Canadian Business Index]
CBPRA — Cerebral Palsy Review
CBQ — Catholic Biblical Quarterly
CBr — Cadernos Brasileiros
CBR — Canadian Bar Review
CBR — China Business Report
CBRA — Canadian Book Review Annual
CBRBAH — Comunicaciones. Museo Argentino de Ciencias Naturales "Bernardino Rivadavia" e Instituto Nacional de Investigacion de las Ciencias Naturales. Ciencias Botanicas
CBRC — Current Book Review Citations
CB Review — Canadian Business Review
CBRI — Children's Book Review Index
CBRPDS — Cell Biology International Reports
CBRS — Children's Book Review Service
CBS — Canadian Business Magazine
CBS — Chugoku No Bunka To Shakai [Chinese Culture and Society]

CB Stat — Conference Board. Statistical Bulletin
CBSTB — Combustion Science and Technology
CBTIAE — Contributions. Boyce Thompson Institute
CBTNAT — Comunicari de Botanica
CBU — Canadian Business Review
CBU — Coal Age
C Bun H — Chugoku Bungaku Ho
CBV — Comenius-Blaetter fuer Volkserziehung
CBW — Centralblatt fuer Bibliothekwesen
CBW — Congress Bi-Weekly
C B Worldbus — Conference Board Worldbusiness
CC — Cahiers du Cinema
C & C — Cameron and Carroll
C & C — Case and Comment
CC — Christian Century
C & C — Christianity and Crisis
CC — Civilta Cattolica
CC — Codrul Cosminului
CC — Contemporary China
CC — Corpus Christianorum
CC — Cross Currents
CC — Currency Collector
CC — Current Contents
CC — Current Contents/Social and Behavioral Sciences
CCA — Cancer Chemotherapy Abstracts
CCA — Cancer Chemotherapy Annual [*Elsevier Book Series*]
CCa — Civilta Cattolica
CCA — Computer and Control Abstracts [*IEE*]
CCAB — Corsi di Cultura sull'Arte Ravennate e Bizantina
CC/AB & ES — Current Contents/Agriculture, Biology, and Environmental Sciences
CCACA — Croatica Chemica Acta
CCACB — CRC [*Chemical Rubber Company*] Critical Reviews in Analytical Chemistry
CC/A & H — Current Contents/Arts and Humanities
CCALA — Cry California
C Can — Cinema Canada
CCanC — Cahier Canadien Claudel
CCARY — CCAR [*Central Conference of American Rabbis*] Yearbook
CCatt — Civilta Cattolica
CCB — Center for Children's Books. Bulletin
CCB-B — Center for Children's Books. Bulletin
CCBCAF — Computers in Chemical and Biochemical Research
CCBEA — Contamination Control. Biomedical Environments
CCBEAL — Contamination Control. Biomedical Environments
CCB Rev Choc Confect Bakery — CCB. Review for Chocolate Confectionery and Bakery
CCBUC — Cursos e Conferencias da Biblioteca de Universidade de Coimbra
CCBZAG — Contribuciones Cientificas. Facultad de Ciencias Exactas y Naturales. Universidad de Buenos Aires. Serie Zoologia
CCC — Chinese Cooperative Catalog [*Library of Congress*]
CCC — Citeaux. Commentarii Cistercienses
CCC — College Composition and Communication
CCCBAH — Canterbury Chamber of Commerce. Agricultural Bulletin
CCC Bul — Canterbury Chamber of Commerce. Bulletin [*New Zealand*]
CCC Hist Bldg Ctee Min — Cumberland County Council. Historic Buildings Committee. Minutes
CCCist — Citeaux. Commentarii Cistercienses
CCCQDV — CCQ. Critical Care Quarterly
CCD — Chambre de Commerce de Tunis. Bulletin
CCD — Commonwealth Employees Compensation Decisions
CCDIDC — Catheterization and Cardiovascular Diagnosis
CCE — Contributions to Canadian Economics
CCE — Cuadernos de Cultura Espanola
CCEA Newsl — Commonwealth Council for Educational Administration. Newsletter
CCEA SEA — Commonwealth Council for Educational Administration. Studies in Educational Administration
CCECA — CRC [*Chemical Rubber Company*] Critical Reviews in Environmental Control
CCEI — Cahiers. Centre d'Etudes Irlandaises
CCELCN — Canadian Committee on Ecological Land Classification. Newsletter
C Cent — Christian Century
C Centre Et Coutumes — Cahiers. Centre d'Etudes des Coutumes
CCER — Cahiers. Cercle Ernest Renan pour Libres Recherches d'Histoire du Christianisme [*Paris*]
CCERO — Cahiers. Centre d'Etudes de Recherche Operationnelle
CCF — Cahiers Economiques et Monetaires
CCF — Cesky Casopis Filologicky
CCFCSP — Canadian Centre for Folk Culture Studies Papers. National Museum of Man Mercury Series
CCFDD — CFI. Ceramic Forum International/Berichte der DKG
CCFFAA — Contributions. Cushman Foundation for Foraminiferal Research
CCH — Ceskoslovensky Casopis Historicky
CCH — Cesky Casopis Historicky

CCHCDE — Chinese Journal of Tuberculosis and Respiratory Diseases
CCHCDE — Chung-Hua Chieh Heh Heh Hu Hsi Hsi Chi Ping Tsa Chih
(CCH) CLC — Company Law Cases (Commerce Clearing House) [*Australia*]
CCHHAQ — Chishitsu Chosajo Hokoku
CCHHAQ — Geological Survey of Japan. Report
CCH Inh Est & Gift Tax Rep — Inheritance, Estate, and Gift Tax Reports (Commerce Clearing House)
CCHMD — Clinics in Chest Medicine
CCHNDD — Cell and Chromosome Newsletter
CCHP — Chung Chi Hsueh-Pao
CCHPA — Jianzhu Xuebao
C Cinema — Cahiers du Cinema
CCISA — Canadian Controls and Instrumentation
CCist — Collectanea Cisterciensa
CCIWD — Canada. Centre for Inland Waters. Data Report Series
CCIWF — Canada. Centre for Inland Waters. Filed Report Series
CCIWM — Canada. Centre for Inland Waters. Manuscript Report Series
CCIWT — Canada. Centre for Inland Waters. Technical Note Series
CCJ — Chung Chi Journal
CCJDA — Journal. Chemical Society. Section D. Chemical Communications
CCL — Management Accounting
CCLA Record — CCLA [*Correspondence Chess League of Australia*] Record
CCLat — Corpus Christianorum. Series Latina [*Turnhout*]
CCLC — Cuadernos del Congreso por la Libertad de la Cultura
CCLCDY — Chinese Journal of Oncology
CCLIB — Cardiovascular Clinics
CCLP — Contents of Current Legal Periodicals
CCM — Cahiers de Civilisation Medievale
CCM — Casopis Ceskenho Musea
CCM — Clays and Clay Minerals
CCM — Colby College. Monographs
CCM — Conseiller du Commerce Exterieur [*Paris*]
CCM — Critical Care Medicine
CCMDA — Cahiers. College de Medecine des Hopitaux de Paris
CCMDC — Critical Care Medicine
CCMe — Cahiers de Civilisation Medievale
CCMJ — Contents of Contemporary Mathematical Journals
CCN — Christian College News
CCN — Commonwealth Employees Compensation Notes
CCNED — Chishitsu Chosasho Nenpo
CCNS — Christian College News Service
CCNTB — Current Concepts in Nutrition
CCOMA — Chemical Communications
C Communisme — Cahiers du Communisme
C-CORE — C-CORE [*Centre for Cold Ocean Resources Engineering*] Publications
CCP — Checkout. Management im Modernen Handel
CCP — Current Commonwealth Publications
CCPBA — Cahiers. Comites de Prevention du Batiment et des Travaux Publics
CCPPD — Canadian Communications and Power Conference. Proceedings
CCPRA — Canadian Chemical Processing
CCPTAY — Contraception
CCPYAF — Comments on Contemporary Psychiatry
CCQ — Critical Care Quarterly
CCQUD — Cataloging and Classification Quarterly
CCR — Claflin College. Review
CCRB — Cahiers de la Compagnie Madeleine Renaud-Jean Louis Barrault
CCRCDU — Contributions. Central Research Institute for Food Crops [*Bogor*]
CCREE3 — Cell and Chromosome Research
C C Rev — Comparative Civilizations Review
CCRHOS — Canadian Contractor Report of Hydrography and Ocean Sciences
C Crit — Comparative Criticism
CCR (VIC) — County Court Reports (Victoria)
CCS — Collectanea Commissionis Synodalis [*Peking*]
CCSUDL — Carcinogenesis: A Comprehensive Survey
CCT — Cuadernos de Cultura Teatral
CCTE — Conference of College Teachers of English of Texas. Proceedings
CCT Occ Pap — Canadian College of Teachers. Occasional Papers
CCU — Cuadernos de la Catedra de Unamuno
C Cubano — Cine Cubano
CCUHCL — Cahiers. Centre Universitaire d'Histoire Contemporaine de Louvain
C Cul — Chinese Culture
CCult — Cronache Culturali
CCV — Centro de Cultura Valenciana
CCX — Cinquante Millions de Consommateurs
CCZ — Camara de Comercio de Bogota. Revista
C de D — Cahiers de Droit
CD — Cairo Document
C/D — Car and Driver
CD — Child Development
CD — Ciudad de Dios
CD — Climatological Data
CD — Comparative Drama
CD — Computer Design

CD — Cuadernos para el Dialogo
CdA — Camp de l'Arpa
CDAB — Child Development Abstracts and Bibliography
CDA J — California Dental Association. Journal
CDAPAM — Conserve e Derivati Agrumari
CDAS — Computer Design and Architecture Series [*Elsevier Book Series*]
CDB — Colecao Documentos Brasileiros
CDB — Community Development Bulletin
CDC — Centers for Disease Control. Publications
CDCP — Comparative Drama Conference. Papers
CdD — Ciudad de Dios
CDDED7 — Cancer Drug Delivery
CDE — Cahiers de Droit Europeen
CdE — Chronique d'Egypte
CDEGA — Chiba Daigaku Engeigakubu Gakujutsu Hokoko
CDESDK — Contraceptive Delivery Systems
CdF — Cuadernos de Filologia
CDFKAW — Annual Report. Institute of Food Microbiology. Chiba University
C Dgst — Catholic Digest
CDHS — Canberra Historical Journal
CDI — Commander's Digest
CdIL — Cahiers. Institut de Linguistique de Louvain
CDJM — Canadian Journal of Mathematics
CDKKA — Chiba Daigaku Kogakubu Kenkyu Hokoko
CdL — Cahiers de Lexicologie
CDL — Canadian Labour
CDL — Le Commerce du Levant [*Beirut*]
CDMBA — California. Division of Mines and Geology. Bulletin
CDMI Bul — Centre de Documentation de Musique Internationale. Bulletin
CDN — Chicago Daily News
Cdn Bnk Rv — Canadian Banker and ICB [*Institute of Canadian Bankers*] Review [*Later, Canadian Banker*]
Cdn Chem P — Canadian Chemical Processing
Cdn Contrl — Canadian Controls and Instrumentation
Cdn Data — Canadian Datasystems
Cdn Elec E — Canadian Electronics Engineering
Cdn Forest — Canadian Forest Industries
Cdn J ECE — Canadian Journal of Early Childhood Education
Cdn Machin — Canadian Machinery and Metalworking
CDNP — Chicago Daily News. Panorama
Cdn Pkg — Canadian Packaging
Cdn Plast — Canadian Plastics
Cdn P & P — Canadian Pulp and Paper Industry
C Docum Ch Com Marseille — Cahiers de Documentation de la Chambre de Commerce et d'Industrie de Marseille
CDOEAP — Community Dentistry and Oral Epidemiology
CDPRD — Cancer Detection and Prevention
CDPRD4 — Cancer Detection and Prevention
C Dr Entreprise — Cahiers de Droit de l'Entreprise
CDREOR — Canada. Defence Research Establishment. Ottawa. Reports
C Dr Europ — Cahiers de Droit Europeen
CdS — Corriere della Sera
CDS — Country Dance and Song
CDSEA — Chuo Daigaku Rikogakubu Kiyo
CDSKAT — Annual Report. Research Institute for Chemobiodynamics. Chiba University
CDSP — Current Digest of the Soviet Press
CDS Rev — Chicago Dental Society. Review
CDSS N — Country Dance and Song Society. News
CDU — Centre de Documentation Universitaire
CDX — WVC Documentatie. Systematisch Overzicht met Samenvattingen van Nieuwe Boeken, Tijdschriftartikelen, Parlementaire Stukken
CE — Cahiers Evangiles
Ce — Celtica
CE — Central Opera Service. Bulletin
CE — Ceylon Economist
CE — Chemistry in Ecology
CE — Chief Executive
CE — Childhood Education
CE — Christian East
CE — Chronique d'Egypte
CE — College English
CE — Comptes Economiques [*Beirut*]
C & E — Conferences and Exhibitions [*Later, Conferences and Exhibitions International*]
CE — Construction and Engineering [*Philippines*]
CE — Consumer Electronics
CE — Corno Emplumado
CE — Correo Erudito
C/E — Creation/Evolution
CE — Current Endocrinology [*Elsevier Book Series*]
CEA — Cahiers d'Etudes Africaines
CEA — Cahiers des Etudes Anciennes
CEA — CEA [*College English Association*] Critic
CEA — Contributions to Economic Analysis [*Elsevier Book Series*]
CEAAN — Center for Editions of American Authors [*Later, CSE*]. Newsletter

CEAC — CEA [*College English Association*] Chap Book
CEACrit — CEA [*College English Association*] Critic
CEAEA — Canadian Electrical Association. Transactions. Engineering and Operating Division
CEAF — CEA [*College English Association*] Forum
CEAfr — Cahiers d'Etudes Africaines
CEAGD5 — Centro Agricola
CEAL — Centro Editor de America Latina
CEA News — Canadian Education Association. Newsletter
CEA Notes Inf — CEA [*Cahiers d'Etudes Anciennes*] Notes d'Information [*France*]
CEAZD — Centro Azucar
CEBAL — Copenhagen School of Economics and Business Administration. Language Department Publications
CEBEA — Centre Belge d'Etude et de Documentation des Eaux. Bulletin Mensuel
CEBIEH — Cell Biology. Monographs
CEBUD — Ceramika Budowlana
CEC — Cahiers d'Etudes Cathares
CEC — Conselho Estadual de Cultura
CECEB — Chemical Economy and Engineering Review
CECED9 — Commission des Communautes Europeennes/Commissione delle Comunita Europee/Commission of the European Communities. Eur Report
CECIAI — Cecidologia Indica
Cecidol Indica — Cecidologia Indica
CECJA — Civil Engineering, Construction, and Public Works Journal [*India*]
CECN — Canadian Environmental Control Newsletter
CECOB — Cement and Concrete
C Econ Bruxelles — Cahiers Economiques de Bruxelles
C Econ Soc — Cahiers Economiques et Sociaux [*Kinshasa*]
CECRA — CEC [*Consolidated Electrodynamics Corporation*] Recordings [*United States*]
CECTA — Cellulose Chemistry and Technology
C Ed — Childhood Education
CEd — Communication Education
CEE — Commerce Exterieur Albanais
CEER — Chemical Economy and Engineering Review
CeF — Ce Fastu?
CE Focus — Continuing Education in Nursing Focus
CEG — Cuadernos de Estudios Gallegos
CEGB Dig — CEGB [*Central Electricity Generating Board*] Digest [*England*]
CEGB Res — CEGB [*Central Electricity Generating Board*] Research
CEGB Tech Disclosure Bull — CEGB [*Central Electricity Generating Board*] Technical Disclosure Bulletin [*England*]
CEGFA — Centralblatt fuer das Gesamte Forstwesen [*Austria*]
CEGJB — Canterbury Engineering Journal
CEGPAP — CEGS [*Council on Education in the Geological Sciences*] Programs Publication
CEGS Programs Publ — CEGS [*Council on Education in the Geological Sciences*] Programs Publication
CEGYA — Ceskoslovenska Gynekologie
CEH — Central European History
CEH — Chromatography of Environmental Hazards [*Elsevier Book Series*]
C of E Hist Soc J — Church of England Historical Society. Journal
CEI — Canadian Education Index [*See also RCE*]
CEI — Chemical Engineering Index
CEI — Conferences and Exhibitions International
CEIAA — Centro di Studi per l'Ingegneria Agraria. Memorie ed Atti
CEIADR — Commission of the European Communities. Information on Agriculture
CEIED — Chemical Engineering (International Edition)
CEIND — Ceramurgia International
CEINEX — Cecidologia Internationale
CEJ — California English Journal
CEJ — Christian Educators Journal
CEJL — Current Events in Jewish Life [*New York*]
CEK — Cahiers Economiques de Bruxelles
CEL — China Trade and Economic Newsletter [*London*]
CELBA — Conti Elektro Berichte
CELCA — Commutation et Electronique
Celest Mech — Celestial Mechanics
Celjabinsk Gos Ped Inst Trudy — Celjabinskii Gosudarstvennyi Pedagogiceskii Institut. Trudy
CELLA4 — Cellule
Cell Biol Int Rep — Cell Biology International Reports
Cell Biol Monogr — Cell Biology Monographs
Cell Biophys — Cell Biophysics
Cell Differ — Cell Differentiation
Cell Immun — Cellular Immunology
Cell Immunol — Cellular Immunology
Cell Mol Biol — Cellular and Molecular Biology
Cell Senescence Somatic Cell Genet — Cellular Senescence and Somatic Cell Genetics
Cell Struct Funct — Cell Structure and Function
Cell Surf Rev — Cell Surface Reviews

Cell Tis Re — Cell and Tissue Research
Cell Tiss K — Cell and Tissue Kinetics
Cell Tissue Kinet — Cell and Tissue Kinetics
Cell Tissue Res — Cell and Tissue Research
Cellul Carta — Cellulosa e Carta
Celluloid Ind — Celluloid Industrie
Celluloid Plast Massen — Celluloid und Plastische Massen
Cellulose Chem Technol — Cellulose Chemistry and Technology
Celosloven Geol Konf Mater — Celoslovenska Geologicka Konferencia. Materialy
Celostatna Konf Term Anal — Celostatna Konferencia o Termickej Analyze
Celovek i Obsc — Celovek i Obscestvo
Celt — Celtiberia
Celtic R — Celtic Review
Celul Hirtie — Celuloza si Hirtie
Celuloza Hirt — Celuloza si Hirtie
Celul Pap Grafika — Celuloza, Papir, Grafika
CEM — Cahiers d'Etudes Medievales
CEM — Chemical Engineering Monographs [*Elsevier Book Series*]
CEM — Clinical and Experimental Metastasis
CEM — Cuadernos de Estudios Manc\hegos
Cem Betong — Cement och Betong
CEMC — Centro de Estudios Mayas-Cuadernos
Cem Cem Manuf — Cement and Cement Manufacture
Cem Concr (Delhi) — Cement and Concrete (Delhi)
Cem Concrete Ass Res Rep — Cement and Concrete Association. Research Report
Cem Concr Res — Cement and Concrete Research
Cem Concr (Tokyo) — Cement and Concrete (Tokyo)
Cem Era — Cement Era
Cem Ind (Tokyo) — Cement Industry (Tokyo)
Cem Lime Grav — Cement, Lime, and Gravel
Cem Lime Mf — Cement and Lime Manufacture
Cem Mill Quarry — Cement Mill and Quarry
Cem Technol — Cement Technology
Cem Vapno Azbestocem Sadra — Cement. Vapno, Azbestocement, Sadra
CEMW — Columbia Essays on Modern Writers
Cem Wapno Gips — Cement Wapno Gips
CEN — Canada. Department of the Environment. Fisheries and Marine Service. Data Report Series
C & EN — Chemical and Engineering News
CEN — Chemische Industrie. Zeitschrift fuer die Deutsche Chemiewirtschaft
CEn — Colecao Ensaio
CEN — Construction Equipment News
CENB — Cercle d'Etudes Numismatiques. Bulletin
CENCBM — Carnets de l'Enfance/Assignment Children
CENCN — Centre d'Etudes Nordiques. Collection Nordicana. University of Laval
CEN Constr Equip News — CEN. Construction Equipment News
CENEA — Chemical and Engineering News
Cen Eur Hist — Central European History
C & E News — Chemical and Engineering News
CENIA5 — Cenicafe
CENMD — Chemical Engineering Monographs
Cent — Century Magazine
Cent Afr J Med — Central African Journal of Medicine
Cent Agric — Centro Agricola
Cent Agric Publ Doc (Wageningen) Annu Rep — Centre for Agricultural Publications and Documentation (Wageningen). Annual Report
Cent Arecanut Res St Tech Bull — Central Arecanut Research Station. Technical Bulletin
Cent Asia J — Central Asiatic Journal
Cent Belge Etude Corros Rapp Tech — Centre Belge d'Etude de la Corrosion. Rapport Technique
Cent Belge Etude Doc Eaux Bull Mens — Centre Belge d'Etude et de Documentation des Eaux. Bulletin Mensuel [*Belgium*]
Cent Doc Sider Cir Inf Tech — Centre de Documentation Siderurgique. Circulaire d'Information Techniques
Cent Edafol Biol Apl Salamanca Anu — Centro de Edafologia y Biologia Aplicada de Salamanca. Anuario
Centennial Mag — Centennial Magazine
Center — Center Magazine
Center Child Bk Bull — Center for Children's Books. Bulletin
Center Mag — Center Magazine
Cent Estud Zool Univ Brasil Avulso — Centro de Estudos Zoologicos. Universidade do Brasil. Avulso
Cent Etude Azote — Centre d'Etude de l'Azote
Cent Etude Rech Essais Sci Genie Univ Liege Mem — Centre d'Etude, de Recherches, et d'Essais Scientifiques du Genie Civil. Universite de Liege. Memoires
Cent Etud Rech Essais Sci Genie Civ Univ Liege Mem — Centre d'Etudes de Recherches et d'Essais Scientifiques du Genie Civil. Universite de Liege. Memoires
Cent Eur Fed — Central European Federalist
Cent Eur H — Central European History
Cent Eur Hist — Central European History

Cent Form Tech Perfect Bull — Centre de Formation Technique et de Perfectionnement. Union des Fabricants de Biscuits, Biscottes, Aliment Dietetiques, et Divers. Bulletin
Cent Geomorphol Caen Bull — Centre de Geomorphologie de Caen. Bulletin
Cent Glass Ceram Res Inst Bull — Central Glass and Ceramic Research Institute. Bulletin
Cent High-Energy Form Pro — Center for High-Energy Forming. Proceedings International Conference
Cent High Res Res Rep Tex Austin — Center for Highway Research. Research Report. University of Texas at Austin
Cent Inf Chrome Dur Bull Doc — Centre d'Information du Chrome Dur. Bulletin de Documentation
Cent Inf Nickel Toutes Appl Tech Ind Ser A — Centre d'Information du Nickel pour Toutes Applications Techniques et Industrielles. Serie A. Alliages
Cent Inf Nickel Toutes Appl Tech Ind Ser C — Centre d'Information du Nickel pour Toutes Applications Techniques et Industrielles. Serie C. Fontes au Nickel
Cent Inf Nickel Toutes Appl Tech Ind Ser D — Centre d'Information du Nickel pour Toutes Applications Techniques et Industrielles. Serie D. Nickelage
Cent Inf Nickel Toutes Appl Tech Ind Ser X — Centre d'Information du Nickel pour Toutes Applications Techniques et Industrielles. Serie X. Applications du Nickel
Cent Inland Fish Res Inst (Barrackpore) Annu Rep — Central Inland Fisheries Research Institute (Barrackpore). Annual Report
Cent Inland Fish Res Inst (Barrackpore) Bull — Central Inland Fisheries Research Institute (Barrackpore). Bulletin
Cent Inland Fish Res Inst (Barrackpore India) Surv Rep — Central Inland Fisheries Research Institute (Barrackpore, India). Survey Report
Cent Inland Fish Res Inst (Barrackpore) Misc Contri — Central Inland Fisheries Research Institute (Barrackpore). Miscellaneous Contribution
Cent Inland Fish Res Inst (Barrackpore) Misc Contrib — Central Inland Fisheries Research Institute (Barrackpore). Miscellaneous Contribution
Cent Inland Fish Res Inst (Barrackpore) Surv Rep — Central Inland Fisheries Research Institute (Barrackpore). Survey Report
Cent Inst Mater Onderz Afd Corr Medede — Centraal Instituut voor Materiaal Onderzoek. Afdeling Corrosie. Mededeling
Cent Inst Mater Onderz Afde Corros Circ — Centraal Instituut voor Materiaal Onderzoek. Afdeling Corrosie. Circulaire
Cent Inst Mater Onderz Afd Hout Circ — Centraal Instituut voor Materiaal Onderzoek. Afdeling Hout. Circulaire
Cent Inst Mater Onderz Afd Verf Circ — Centraal Instituut voor Materiaal Onderzoek. Afdeling Verf. Circulaire
Cent Inst Phys Inst Phys Nucl Eng Rep (Romania) — Central Institute of Physics. Institute for Physics and Nuclear Engineering. Report (Romania)
Cent Int Agric Trop Annu Rep — Centro Internacional de Agricultura Tropical [*CIAT*]. Annual Report
Cent Int Agric Trop Ser CE — Centro Internacional de Agricultura Tropical [*CIAT*]. Series CE
Cent Int Agric Trop Ser EE — Centro Internacional de Agricultura Tropical [*CIAT*]. Series EE
Cent Int Agric Trop Ser FE — Centro Internacional de Agricultura Tropical [*CIAT*]. Series FE
Cent Int Agric Trop Ser GE — Centro Internacional de Agricultura Tropical [*CIAT*]. Series GE
Cent Int Agric Trop Ser Semin — Centro Internacional de Agricultura Tropical [*CIAT*]. Series Seminars
Cent Int Agric Trop Tech Bull — Centro Internacional de Agricultura Tropical [*CIAT*]. Technical Bulletin
Cent Invest Agric Noreste Inf Invest Agric — Centro de Investigaciones Agricolas del Noreste. Informe de Investigacion Agricola
Cent Invest Agron Maracay Monogr — Centro de Investigaciones Agronomicas Maracay. Monografia
Cent Invest Biol Mar Contrib Tec — Centro de Investigacion de Biologia Marina. Contribucion Tecnica
Cent Invest Tecnol (Pando Urug) Inf Invest — Centro de Investigaciones Tecnologicas (Pando, Uruguay). Informe de Investigacion
Cent Jpn J Orthop Traumatic Surg — Central Japan Journal of Orthopaedic and Traumatic Surgery
Cent Lab Ochron Radiol Rap — Centralne Laboratorium Ochrony Radiologiczncj Raport
Cent Landbouwpubl Landbouwdoc Literatuuroverz — Centrum voor Landbouwpublikates en Landbouwdocumentatie Literatuuroverzicht
Cent Mar Fish Res Inst Bull — Central Marine Fisheries Research Institute. Bulletin
Cent Med J Semin Rep (Moscow) — Central Medical Journal. Seminar Reports (Moscow)
Cent Nac Invest Cient Rev CENIC Cienc Biol — Centro Nacional de Investigaciones Cientificas. Revista CENIC. Ciencias Biologicas
Cent Nat Exploit Oceans Publ Ser Rapp Sci Tech (Fr) — Centre National pour l'Exploitation des Oceans. Publications. Serie. Rapports Scientifiques et Techniques (France)
Cent Natl Doc Sci Tech Rap Act — Centre National de Documentation Scientifique et Technique. Rapport d'Activite

Cent Natl Rech Sci Tech Ind Cimentiere Rapp Rech — Centre National de Recherches Scientifiques et Techniques pour l'Industrie Cimentiere. Rapport de Recherche

Cent Nat Rech Sci Groupe Fr Argiles R Reun Etude — Centre National de la Recherche Scientifique. Groupe Francais des Argiles. Compte Rendu des Reunions d'Etudes

CENTO Conf Ld Classif Non-Irrig Lds — CENTO [*Central Treaty Organization*] Conference on Land Classification for Non-Irrigated Lands

Cent Overseas Pest Res Misc Rep — Centre for Overseas Pest Research. Miscellaneous Report

Cent Overseas Pest Res Rep — Centre for Overseas Pest Research. Report

Cent Pesqui Agropecu Trop Umido — Centro de Pesquisa Agropecuaria do Tropico Umido EMBRAPA

Cent Pesqui Desenvolvimento Bol Tec (Estado Bahia) — Centro de Pesquisas e Desenvolvimento. Boletim Tecnico (Estado da Bahia)

Cent Phar J — Central Pharmaceutical Journal

Cent Plant Crops Res Inst (Kasaragod) Annu Rep — Central Plantation Crops Research Institute (Kasaragod). Annual Report

CentR — Centennial Review

Central Bank Barbados Q Rept — Central Bank of Barbados. Quarterly Report

Central Bank Ireland Q Bul — Central Bank of Ireland. Quarterly Bulletin

Central Bank Libya Econ Bul — Central Bank of Libya. Economic Bulletin

Central Bank Malta QR — Central Bank of Malta. Quarterly Review

Central Bank Nigeria Econ and Fin R — Central Bank of Nigeria. Economic and Financial Review

Central Bank Trinidad and Tobago Q Econ Bul — Central Bank of Trinidad and Tobago. Quarterly Economic Bulletin

Centralbl Allg Path u Path Anat — Centralblatt fuer Allgemeine, Pathologie, und Pathologische Anatomie

Centralbl Bakteriol — Centralblatt fuer Bakteriologie und Parasitenkunde

Centralbl Chir — Centralblatt fuer Chirurgie

Centralbl Gesamte Forstwes — Centralblatt fuer das Gesamte Forstwesen

Centralbl Innere Med — Centralblatt fuer Innere Medicin

Centralbl Miner — Centralblatt fuer Mineralogie, Geologie, und Palaeontologie

Central Opera — Central Opera Service. Bulletin

Central Q Herald — Central Queensland Herald

Centr Asiat J — Central Asiatic Journal

Centr Bank Ireland Annu Rep — Central Bank of Ireland. Annual Report

Centr Bank Ireland Quart B — Central Bank of Ireland. Quarterly Bulletin

Cent Rech Ecol Phytosociol Gembloux Commun — Centre de Recherches Ecologiques et Phytosociologiques de Gembloux. Communication

Cent Rech Oceanogr (Abidjan) Doc Sci — Centre de Recherches Oceanographiques (Abidjan). Documents Scientifiques

Cent Rech Oceanogr (Abidjan) Doc Sci Provisoire — Centre de Recherches Oceanographiques (Abidjan). Document Scientifique Provisoire

Cent Rech Pau Bull — Societe Nationale des Petroles d'Aquitaine. Centre de Recherches de Pau. Bulletin. [*Later, Bulletin. Centres de Recherches Exploration-Production ELF Aquitaine*]

Cent Rech Sci Tech Ind Fabr Met Sect Plast Rep PL — Centre de Recherches Scientifiques et Techniques de l'Industrie des Fabrications Metalliques. Section Plastiques. Report PL

Centr Econ Plan — Centraal Economisch Plan

Centre Et Docum Soc (Liege) — Centre d'Etudes et de Documentation Sociales (Liege)

Centre Etud et Docum Socs Bul — Centre d'Etudes et de Documentation Sociales. Bulletin Mensuel

Centre Etud Emploi Cah — Centre d'Etudes de l'Emploi. Cahiers

Centre Info et Etud Credit Bul — Centre d'Information et d'Etudes du Credit. Bulletin

Centre Inform Chrome Dur Bull Doc — Centre d'Information du Chrome Dur. Bulletin de Documentation

Centre Nat Rech Sci Tech Ind Cimentiere Rapp Rech — Centre National de Recherches Scientifique et Techniques pour l'Industrie Cimentiere. Rapport de Recherche

Centre Recherches Pau Bull — Centre de Recherches de Pau. Bulletin

Centre Sci & Tech Constr Note Inf Tech — Centre Scientifique et Technique de la Construction. Note d'Information Technique

Centro Estud Demograficos R — Centro de Estudos Demograficos. Revista

Centro Estud Rurais e Urbanos Cad — Centro de Estudos Rurais e Urbanos. Cadernos

Centro Investigacion y Accion Soc R — Centro de Investigacion y Accion Social. Revista

Centro Pirenaico Biolog Exp — Publicaciones. Centro Pirenaico de Biologia Experimental

Centro pro Un Bul — Centro pro Unione. Bulletin

Cent SS RR — Center for Settlement Studies. University of Manitoba. Research Reports

Cent St Spe — Central States Speech Journal

Cent Studi Lotta Antitermitica Pubbl — Centro di Studi per la Lotta Antitermitica. Pubblicazione

Cent Stud Ing Agrar Mem Atti — Centro di Studi per l'Ingegneria Agraria. Memorie ed Atti [*Italy*]

Cent Tech For Trop (Nogent Sur Marne Fr) Note Tech — Centre Technique Forestier Tropical (Nogent Sur Marne, France). Note Technique

Cent Tech For Trop (Nogent Sur Marne Fr) Publ — Centre Technique Forestier Tropical (Nogent Sur Marne, France). Publication

Cent Tech Union Bull — Centre Technique de l'Union. Bulletin

CENUA — Courrier des Etablissements Neu

CEO — Courrier de l'Extreme-Orient

CEOABL — Centre National pour l'Exploitation des Oceans. Rapport Annuel

CEOFA — Ceskoslovenska Oftalmologie

Ceol — Ceol. Journal of Irish Music

CEOTA — Ceskoslovenska Otolaryngologie

CEP — Chemical Engineering Progress

CEP — Czechoslovak Economic Papers

CEPBA — Cerebral Palsy Bulletin

CEPCAV — Centre de Recherches Ecologiques et Phytosociologiques de Gembloux. Communication

CEPEA — Ceskoslovenska Pediatrie

CEPEC Inf Tec — CEPEC [*Centro de Pesquisas do Cacau*] Informe Tecnico

CEPED — Civil Engineering for Practicing and Design Engineers

CEPLAC Bol Tec — CEPLAC [*Comissao Executiva do Plano da Lavoura Cacaueira*] Boletim Tecnico

CEPLAC Comun Tec — CEPLAC [*Comissao Executiva do Plano da Lavoura Cacaueira*] Comunicacao Tecnica

CEPND — CEP [*Council on Economic Priorities*] Newsletter

CEP Newsl — CEP [*Council on Economic Priorities*] Newsletter

CEPRA — Chemical Engineering Progress

CEPSA — Chemical Engineering Progress. Symposium Series

CEPSB — Ceskoslovenska Psychologie

CEPYA — Ceskoslovenska Psychiatrie

CEQ — Central Bank of Barbados. Quarterly Report

CER — Cahiers d'Etudes Romanes

CER — Catholic Educational Review

CER — Comparative Education Review

CERAB — Ceskoslovenska Radiologie

Ceram Abstr — Ceramic Abstracts

Ceram Age — Ceramic Age

Ceram Awareness Bull — Ceramic Awareness Bulletin

Ceram Budow — Ceramika Budowlana

Ceram Bull — Ceramic Bulletin

Ceram Crist — Ceramica y Cristal

Ceram Eng Sci Proc — Ceramic Engineering and Science Proceedings

Ceram Forum Int — Ceramic Forum International [*West Germany*]

Ceramic Abstr — Ceramic Abstracts

Ceramic R — Ceramic Review

Ceramic S B — American Ceramic Society. Bulletin

Ceramics Int — Ceramics International [*United Kingdom*]

Ceramics Mo — Ceramics Monthly

Ceram Ind — Ceramic Industry

Ceram Ind J — Ceramics Industries Journal

Ceram Ind (Sevres Fr) — Ceramiques Industrielles (Sevres, France)

Ceram Int News — Ceramics International News [*Italy*]

Ceram Jap — Ceramics Japan

Ceram Jpn — Ceramics Japan

Ceram Laterizi — Ceramichte e Laterizi

Ceram Mo — Ceramics Monthly

Ceramurgia Int — Ceramurgia International

Ceramurgia Tec Ceram — Ceramurgia, Tecnologia Ceramica

Ceramurg Int — Ceramurgia International

Ceram Verrerie — Ceramique et Verrerie

Ceram Verrerie Emaill — Ceramique, Verrerie, Emaillerie

CERBD — Chemical Engineering Research Bulletin (Dacca)

Cerberus Elektron — Cerberus Elektronik

CERBOM Rapp Act — CERBOM [*Centre d'Etudes et de Recherches de Biologie et d'Oceanographie Medicale*] Rapport d'Activite [*France*]

Cercet Agron Moldova — Cercetari Agronomice in Moldova

Cercetari Muzicol — Cercetari de Muzicologie

Cercet Ist — Cercetari Istorice

Cercet Metal — Cercetari Metalurgice

Cercet Metal Inst Cercet Metal (Bucharest) — Cercetari Metalurgice. Institutul de Cercetari Metalurgice (Bucharest)

Cercet Miniere Inst Cercet Miniere — Cercetari Miniere. Institutul de Cercetari Miniere

Cercet Num — Cercetari Numismatice

CERDA — Chemie der Erde

Cerdic — Cerdic. Universite des Sciences Humaines de Strasbourg

Cereal Chem — Cereal Chemistry

Cereal Chem Bull — Cereal Chemists Bulletin

Cereal Crop Ser Indian Counc Agr Res — Cereal Crop Series. Indian Council of Agricultural Research

Cereal Foods World — Cereal Foods World

Cereal F W — Cereal Foods World

Cereal Res Commun — Cereal Research Communications

Cereal Rusts Bull — Cereal Rusts Bulletin

Cereal Sci Today — Cereal Science Today

Cereb Circ Metab — Cerebral Circulation and Metabolism

Cerebrovasc Dis — Cerebrovascular Diseases

Cereb Vas Dis — Cerebral Vascular Diseases

Cereb Vas Dis Int Conf — Cerebral Vascular Diseases. International
Conference
CERED — CEGB [*Central Electricity Generating Board*] Research [*England*]
Cere Vasc Dis Trans Conf — Cerebral Vascular Diseases. Transactions of the
Conference
Cer Ind — Ceramic Industry
CERMA — Cermica
CERMB — Cercetari Metalurgice
CERN High Energy React Anal Group Rep — CERN [*Conseil Europeen pour
la Recherche Nucleaire*] High Energy Reaction Analysis Group Report
CER-T — Cahiers d'Etudes de Radio-Television
CERT — CERT. Civil Engineering and Road Transport [*New Zealand*]
Certifd Engr — Certificated Engineer
Certif Dent Tec — Certified Dental Technician
Certif Eng — Certificated Engineer
Certif Eng — Certified Engineer
CES — Cahiers Economiques et Sociaux [*Kinshasa*]
CES — Chinese Economic Studies
CE and S — Commonwealth Essays and Studies
CES — Computer Enhanced Spectroscopy
CeS — Cultura e Scuola
CES A — Ceskoslovenska Stomatologie
CESBBA — Connecticut. Agricultural Experiment Station. Department of
Entomology. Special Bulletin
CESCA — Chemical Engineering Science
CES (Centre Environmental Studies) R — CES (Centre Environmental Studies)
Review
CES Conf Paps — Centre for Environmental Studies. Conference Papers
CESGA — Comments on Earth Sciences. Geophysics
CES Inf Paps — Centre for Environmental Studies. Information Papers
Cesk Akad Ved Geogr Ustav Zpr — Ceskoslovenska Akademie Ved.
Geograficky Ustav Zpravy [*Brno*]
Cesk Akad Ved Ved Inf CSAV — Ceskoslovenska Akademie Ved. Vedecke
Informace CSAV
Ceska Mykol — Ceska Mykologie
Cesk Biol — Ceskoslovenska Biologie
Cesk Cas Fys A — Ceskoslovensky Casopis pro Fysiku. Sekce A
Cesk Cas Fyz — Ceskoslovensky Casopis pro Fyziku. Sekce A (Prague)
Cesk Cas Fyz Sekce A — Ceskoslovensky Casopis pro Fyziku. Sekce A
Cesk Cas Hist — Ceskoslovensky Casopis Historicky
Cesk C Fys — Ceskoslovensky Casopis pro Fysiku. Sekce A
Cesk Dermatol — Ceskoslovenska Dermatologie
Cesk Epidemiol Mikrobiol Immunol — Ceskoslovenska Epidemiologie,
Mikrobiologie, Immunologie
Cesk Farm — Ceskoslovenska Farmacie
Cesk Fysiol — Ceskoslovenska Fysiologie
Cesk Gastroenterol Vyz — Ceskoslovenska Gastroenterologie a Vyziva
Cesk Gynekol — Ceskoslovenska Gynekologie
Cesk Hyg — Ceskoslovenska Hygiena
Cesk Hyg Epidemiol Mikrobiol Imunol — Ceskoslovenska Hygiena
Epidemiologie, Mikrobiologie, Imunologie
Cesk Inf — Ceskoslovenska Informatika. Teorie a Praxe
Cesk Inf Teor and Praxe — Ceskoslovenska Informatika Teorie a Praxe
Cesk Kozarstvi — Ceskoslovenska Kozarstvi
Cesk Lit — Ceska Literatura
Cesk Mikrobiol — Ceskoslovenska Mikrobiologie
Cesk Morfol — Ceskoslovenska Morfologie
Cesk Neurol — Ceskoslovenska Neurologie [*Later, Ceskoslovenska Neurologie
a Neurochirurgie*]
Cesk Neurol Neurochir — Ceskoslovenska Neurologie a Neurochirurgie
Cesk Oftalmol — Ceskoslovenska Oftalmologie
Cesk Onkol — Ceskoslovenska Onkologie
Ceskoslovensk Akad Ved Geog Ustav (Brno) Studia Geog — Ceskoslovenska
Akademie Ved. Geograficky Ustav (Brno). Studia Geographica
Cesk Otolaryngol — Ceskoslovenska Otolaryngologie
Cesk Parasitol — Ceskoslovenska Parasitologie
Cesk Patol — Ceskoslovenska Patologie
Cesk Pediatr — Ceskoslovenska Pediatrie
Cesk Psychiatr — Ceskoslovenska Psychiatrie
Cesk Psycho — Ceskoslovenska Psychologie
Cesk Psychol — Ceskoslovenska Psychologie
Cesk Radiol — Ceskoslovenska Radiologie
Cesk Rentgenol — Ceskoslovenska Rentgenologie
Cesk Stand — Ceskoslovenska Standardizace
Cesk Stomatol — Ceskoslovenska Stomatologie
Cesky Vcel — Cesky Vcelar
Cesk Zdrav — Ceskoslovenske Zdravotnictvi
CES Res Series — Centre for Environmental Studies. Research Series
CESRL Rep Univ Tex Austin Dep Civ Eng Struct Res Lab — CESRL Report.
University of Texas at Austin. Department of Civil Engineering.
Structures Research Laboratory
Ce Sta — Ceskoslovenska Stomatologie
CESTD — Ceskoslovenska Standardizace
CEStudies — Canadian Ethnic Studies
CES Univ Wkng Paps — Centre for Environmental Studies. University
Working Papers

C Et Afr — Cahiers d'Etudes Africaines
CETDA — CEGB [*Central Electricity Generating Board*] Technical
Disclosure Bulletin [*England*]
CEU — Consensus. Informatietijdschrift over Energie Mol
CEUFA — Central European Federalist
C Europ — Cahiers Europeens
CEWOA — Chemical Engineering World
CEXIA — Clinical and Experimental Immunology
CEXPB — Clinical and Experimental Pharmacology and Physiology
CEXSBI — Colorado State University. Experiment Station. Bulletin
CEY — Cuba Economic News
Cey J Hist Soc Stud — Ceylon Journal of Historical and Social Studies
Ceylon Assoc Adv Sci Proc Annu Sess — Ceylon Association for the
Advancement of Science. Proceedings of the Annual Session
Ceylon Coconut Plant Rev — Ceylon Coconut Planters' Review
Ceylon Coconut Q — Ceylon Coconut Quarterly
Ceylon Dent J — Ceylon Dental Journal
Ceylon Fish Res St Prog Rep Biol Technol — Ceylon. Fisheries Research
Station. Progress Reports. Biological and Technological
Ceylon For — Ceylon Forester
Ceylon J Med Sci — Ceylon Journal of Medical Science
Ceylon J Sci Anthropol — Ceylon Journal of Science. Anthropology
Ceylon J Sci Biol Sci — Ceylon Journal of Science. Biological Sciences
Ceylon J Sci Sect A Bot — Ceylon Journal of Science. Section A. Botany
Ceylon J Sci Sect B Zool — Ceylon Journal of Science. Section B. Zoology
Ceylon J Sci Sect C Fish — Ceylon Journal of Science. Section C. Fisheries
Ceylon J Sci Sect D Med Sci — Ceylon Journal of Science. Section D. Medical
Science
Ceylon Med J — Ceylon Medical Journal
Ceylon Natl Mus Adm Rep Dir Part IV Educ Sci Art (E) — Ceylon. National
Museums Administration. Report of the Director. Part IV. Education,
Science, and Art (E)
Ceylon Natl Mus Ethnogr Ser — Ceylon National Museums. Ethnographic
Series
Ceylon Nat Mus Adm Rep Dir Part IV Educ Sci Art — Ceylon. National
Museums Administration. Report of the Director. Part IV. Education,
Science, and Art
Ceylon Rubber Res Scheme Q Circ — Ceylon Rubber Research Scheme.
Quarterly Circular
Ceylon Vet J — Ceylon Veterinary Journal
CF — Canada Francais
CF — Canadian Forum
CF — Captain Future
CF — Ce Fastu?
CF — Classical Folia
CF — Collectanea Franciscana
CF — Confluence
CFA — Central Bank of the Bahamas. Quarterly Review
CFABEW — Communications. Faculte des Sciences. Universite d'Ankara.
Serie C. Biologie
C Fantas — Cinefantastique
CFB — Across the Board
CFBTAJ — Commonwealth Forestry Bureau. Technical Communication
CFC — Contemporary French Civilization
CFC — Cuadernos de Filologia Clasica
CFCA — Challenge for Change. Access. National Film Board of Canada
CFE — Economic Road Maps
CFEKA7 — Chirurgisches Forum fuer Experimentelle und Klinische
Forschung
CFEM Ser Tec — CFEM [*Comision Forestal del Estado de Michoacan*] Serie
Tecnica
CFeng — Ching Feng
CFFAn — Comite Flamand de France. Annales
CFI — CBI Newsbulletin
CFIAAV — Conferencia Interamericana de Agricultura [*Caracas*]
CFI Ceram Forum Int/Ber DKG — CFI. Ceramic Forum International/
Berichte der DKG [*West Germany*]
CFI (Ceram Forum Int) Ber Dtsch Keram Ges — CFI (Ceramic Forum
International) Berichte der Deutschen Keramischen Gesellschaft
CFIRBF — Colorado Fisheries Research Review
CFKEA — Commercial Fisheries Review
Cfl — Confluence
CFM — Canadian Fiction Magazine
CFM — Club Francais de la Medaille
CFM — Credit and Financial Management
CFMA — Classiques Francais du Moyen Age
CFMCBO — Central Inland Fisheries Research Institute (Barrackpore).
Miscellaneous Contribution
C F Mgmt — Credit and Financial Management
CFMJ — Canadian Folk Music Journal
CFMSMSP — Canada. Department of the Environment. Fisheries and Marine
Service. Miscellaneous Special Publication
CFMSTR — Canada. Department of the Environment. Fisheries and Marine
Service. Technical Report
CFOCCRH — Canada. Fisheries and Oceans. Canadian Contractor Report of
Hydrography and Ocean Sciences

CFOI — Canadian Forest Industries
CFO J — CFO [*Colorado Field Ornithologists*] Journal
CFol — Classical Folia
CFORAA — Colorado Field Ornithologist
C Forum — Cineforum
CForum — Cultural Forum [*New Delhi*]
CFPOB — Chaud-Froid-Plomberie
CFPQAC — Food Preservation Quarterly
CFPSA — Confinia Psychiatrica
CFPSAI — Confinia Psychiatrica/Confins de la Psychiatrie
CFQ — California Folklore Quarterly
CFR — Commerce Franco-Suisse
C Franc — Cahiers Francais
CFREAK — Commercial Fisheries Review
CFRMB — Chantiers de France
CFS — Cahiers Ferdinand de Saussure
CFSBDJ — Communications. Faculte des Sciences. Universite d'Ankara. Serie
    C2. Botanique
CFSFP — Canadian Forestry Service. Forestry Publication
CFSFTR — Canadian Forestry Service. Forestry Technical Report
CFSGDY — Communications. Faculte des Sciences. Universite d'Ankara.
    Serie C1. Geologie
CFSR — Canadian Forestry Service. Research News
CFSXAE — Contraception-Fertilite-Sexualite
CFSZDN — Communications. Faculte des Sciences. Universite d'Ankara.
    Serie C3. Zoologie
CFT — China's Foreign Trade
CFTPB — Californium-252 Progress
CFTTA — Chemiefasern und Textil-Anwendungstechnik/Textil-Industrie
CFTXA — Chemiefasern/Textil-Industrie
CFX — Confectie. Sociaal, Economisch, en Technisch Maandblad voor de
    Confectie Industrie in de Beneluxlanden
CG — Canadian Geographic
CG — Chugoku Gogaku
CG — Classiques Garnier
CG — Common Ground
CG — Courrier Graphique
CGB — Colecao General Benicio
CGB — Global Church Growth Bulletin
CGBCA9 — Colloquium. Gesellschaft fuer Biologische Chemie in Mosbach
CGBLB — Colorado. Geological Survey. Bulletin
CGBMA — Coal, Gold, and Base Minerals of Southern Africa
CGBUA — Canadian Geophysical Bulletin
CGCPA — Geological Survey of Canada. Paper
CGCPAJ — Geological Survey of Canada. Paper
CGCYD — Cancer Genetics and Cytogenetics
CGCYDF — Cancer Genetics and Cytogenetics
CGEJ — Canadian Geographical Journal [*Later, Canadian Geographic*]
CGEPAT — Comunicacoes. Servicos Geologicos de Portugal
CGF — Computer Graphics Forum
CGFE — Commission Geologique de Finlande. Bulletin
CGFPAY — Colorado. Division of Game, Fish, and Parks. Special Report
CGFTD — Cahiers. Groupe Francois-Thureau-Dangin
CGGFA9 — Congres pour l'Avancement des Etudes de Stratigraphie et de
    Geologie du Carbonifere. Compte Rendu
CGHCA — Chongi Hakhoe Chi
CGHRBH — Cape Of Good Hope. Department of Nature Conservation.
    Report
CGI — Creative Guitar International
CGIB — Comitato Glaciologico Italiano. Bollettino
CGIJD — Chinetsu Gijutsu
CGIRAL — Cape Of Good Hope. Department of Nature Conservation.
    Investigational Report
CGJ — Canadian Geographic
CGJO — Canadian Geotechnical Journal
CGJOA — Canadian Geotechnical Journal
CGLIA9 — Conchiglie [*Milan*]
CGNWAR — Carnivore Genetics Newsletter
CGOMA — Canada. Geological Survey. Map
CGP — Carleton Germanic Papers
CGP — Current Geographical Publications
CGPCAB — Colloquium. Gesellschaft fuer Physiologische Chemie
CGPQA — Canadian Government Publications Quarterly
CGRRAW — Colorado Game Research Review
CGSTA — Clinics in Gastroenterology
CGSTB — Cognition
CH — Cahiers d'Histoire
CH — Church History
CH — Community Health
CH — Critica Hispanica
CH — Cuadernos Hispanoamericanos [*Madrid*]
CH — Current History
CHA — Cahiers d'Histoire et d'Archeologie
CHA — Challenge. Magazine of Economic Affairs
CHA — Commerce International
CHA — Cuadernos Hispanoamericanos [*Madrid*]

CHAC — Cercle Historique et Archeologique de Courtrai. Bulletin
Chacaras Quint — Chacaras e Quintais
CHACBull — Cercle Historique et Archeologique de Courtrai. Bulletin
CHAGA — Chemical Age
Ch Agric — Chambres d'Agriculture
Chagyo Shikenjo Kenkyu Hokoku Bull Natl Res Inst Tea — Chagyo Shikenjo
    Kenkyu Hokoku. Bulletin. National Research Institute of Tea
CHAIA — Chemical Age of India
Cha Ind — Chaleur et Industrie
Chain React — Chain Reaction
Chain Store Age Adm Ed — Chain Store Age. Administration Edition
Chain Store Age Exec — Chain Store Age. Executive Edition
Chain Store Age Exec — Chain Store Age Executive with Shopping Center Age
Chain Store Age Gen Merch Ed — Chain Store Age. General Merchandise
    Edition
Chain Store Age Supermark — Chain Store Age Supermarkets
Chal Clim — Chaleur et Climats
Chal Climats — Chaleur et Climats
Chal Ind — Chaleur et Industrie [*France*]
Challenge in Ed Admin — Challenge in Educational Administration
Challenges Mont Agr — Challenges to Montana Agriculture
Chalmers Tek Hoegsk Handl — Chalmers Tekniska Hoegskola. Handlingar
Chalmers Tek Hogsk Doktorsavh — Chalmers Tekniska Hoegskola.
    Doktorsavhandlingar
Chamber of Ag Vic Yrbk — Chamber of Agriculture of Victoria. Yearbook
Chamber Mines J — Chamber of Mines. Journal
Chamb J — Chamber's Edinburgh Journal
Chamb Mines Newsl — Chamber of Mines. Newsletter
Chambre de Commerce Francaise Bul — Chambre de Commerce Francaise en
    Australie. Bulletin
Chambre Commer Fr Can R — Chambre de Commerce Francaise au Canada.
    Revue
Chambre Commer Gabon Bul — Bulletin. Chambre de Commerce
    d'Agriculture, d'Industrie, et des Mines du Gabon
Chambre Commer Repub Cote D'Ivoire Bul Mensuel — Chambre de Commerce.
    Republique de Cote D'Ivoire. Bulletin Mensuel
CHANA — Chemist-Analyst
Chang Ed — Changing Education
Change (Par) — Change (Paris)
Changes — Changes Socialist Monthly
Changing T — Changing Times
Chang Times — Changing Times
Chanoyu Q — Chanoyu Quarterly
Chantiers Fr — Chantiers de France
Chantiers Mag — Chantiers Magazine [*France*]
Char — Charities
CHAR — Committee for High Arctic Scientific Research Liaison and
    Information Exchange [*CHARLIE*]. News Bulletin
Charged React Polym — Charged and Reactive Polymers
Charlotte Med J — Charlotte Medical Journal
Char R — Charities Review
Chart Acc in Aust — Chartered Accountant in Australia
Chart Accnt in Aust — Chartered Accountant in Australia
Chart Accountant in Aust — Chartered Accountant in Australia
Chart Acct — Chartered Accountant in Australia
Chart Build — Chartered Builder
Chart Builder — Chartered Builder
Chart Eng — Chartered Engineer
Chartered Accountant Aust — Chartered Accountant in Australia
Chartered Surveyor Urban Qly — Chartered Surveyor. Urban Quarterly
Chart Inst Transp J — Chartered Institute of Transport. Journal [*England*]
Chart Mech Eng — Chartered Mechanical Engineer
Chart Mech Engr — Chartered Mechanical Engineer
Chart Munic Eng — Chartered Municipal Engineer
Chart Quant Surv — Chartered Quantity Surveyor
Chart Sec — Chartered Secretary
Chart Surv — Chartered Surveyor [*Later, Chartered Surveyor Weekly*]
Chart Surv Land Hydrogr Miner Q — Chartered Surveyor. Land Hydrographic
    and Minerals Quarterly [*England*]
Chart Surv Rural Q — Chartered Surveyor. Rural Quarterly [*England*]
Chart Surv Wkly — Chartered Surveyor Weekly
CHAS — Cambridgeshire and Huntingdonshire Archaeological Society
Chase Econ Bul — Chase Economic Bulletin
Chase Fin — Chase Manhattan Bank. International Finance
Chase Obsv — Chase Economic Observer
Cha Ti — Changing Times
Chaucer R — Chaucer Review
Chaucer Rev — Chaucer Review
Chaucer Soc — Chaucer Society
Chauf Vent Cond — Chauffage, Ventilation, Conditionnement [*France*]
ChauR — Chaucer Review
Chaut — Chautauquan
CHAVB — Chemie-Anlagen und Verfahren
CHBEA — Chemische Berichte
CHBIE4 — Chronobiology International
CHC — Chile Economic Report

ChC — Chinese Culture
ChC — Christian Century
ChCen — Christian Century
CHCGA — Chishitsu Chosajo Geppo
CHCGAX — Chishitsu Chosajo Geppo
CHC J — Children's Health Care. Journal of the Association for the Care of Children's Health
CHCLG — Cahiers d'Histoire Publies par les Universites de Clermont-Lyon-Grenoble
CHCOD — Chemical Concepts
Ch D — Christian Doctrine
CHDCA — Comptes Rendus des Seances. Academie des Sciences. Serie C. Sciences Chimiques
CHDDA — Comptes Rendus des Seances. Academie des Sciences. Serie D. Sciences Naturelles
CHDEA — Child Development
CHDID — Chimica Didactica
CHE — Cahiers d'Histoire Egyptienne [*Cairo*]
ChE — Chiake Epitheoresis
CHE — Chronicle of Higher Education
CHE — Cuadernos de Historia de Espana
C H Ed — Chronicle of Higher Education
CHEDA — Chemical Engineering Education
CHEDC — Chemie. Experiment und Didaktic
CHEEA — Chemical Engineering [*New York*]
Cheiron Tamil Nadu J Vet Sci Anim Husb — Cheiron. The Tamil Nadu Journal of Veterinary Science and Animal Husbandry
CHEJ — Canadian Home Economics Journal
Cheju Univ J — Cheju University. Journal
CHEKAL — Chung-Hua Min Kuo Hsiao Erh K'o I Hsueh Hui Tsa Chi
Chekh Biol — Chekhoslovatskaya Biologiya
Chekh Fiziol — Chekhoslovatskaya Fiziologiya
Chekh Med Obozr — Chekhoslovatskoe Meditsinskoe Obozrenie
Chekhoslov Biol — Chekhoslovatskaya Biologiya
Chel — Chelsea
Chelates Anal Chem — Chelates in Analytical Chemistry
Chel Biosfera — Chelovek i Biosfera
CHEM — Community Health Education Monographs
ChemAb — Chemical Abstracts
Chem Abs Macromol — Chemical Abstracts. Macromolecular Sections
Chem Abstr — Chemical Abstracts
Chem Abstr Cum Subj Index — Chemical Abstracts. Decennial Cumulative Subject Index
Chem Abstr Jpn — Chemical Abstracts of Japan
Chem Abstr Serv Source Index — Chemical Abstracts Service. Source Index
Chem Abstr Subj Ind — Chemical Abstracts. Annual Subject Index
Chem Ackersmann — Chemische Ackersmann
Chem Age — Chemical Age
Chem Age India — Chemical Age of India
Chem Age Int — Chemical Age International
Chem Age (Lond) — Chemical Age (London)
Chem Agric Int Congr — Chemistry in Agriculture. International Congress
Chem Ag Sv — Chemical Age Survey
Chem Anal (New York) — Chemical Analysis. A Series of Monographs on Analytical Chemistry and Its Applications (New York)
Chem Anal Ser Monogr Anal Chem Appl — Chemical Analysis. A Series of Monographs on Analytical Chemistry and Its Applications
Chem Anal (Warszawa) — Chemia Analityczna (Warszawa)
Chem Analyse — Chemische Analyse
Chem-Anlagen Verfahren — Chemie-Anlagen und Verfahren
Chem Appar — Chemische Apparatur
Chem Arb Werk Labor — Chemie Arbeit in Werk und Labor
Chem Aust — Chemistry in Australia
Chem Ber — Chemische Berichte
Chem Biochem Amino Acids Pept Proteins — Chemistry and Biochemistry of Amino Acids, Peptides, and Proteins
Chem-Bio In — Chemico-Biological Interactions
Chem-Biol Interact — Chemico-Biological Interactions
Chem-Biol Interactions — Chemico-Biological Interactions
Chem Biol (Tokyo) — Chemistry and Biology (Tokyo)
Chem Biomed Environ Inst — Chemical, Biomedical, and Environmental Instrumentation
Chem Biomed and Environ Instrum — Chemical, Biomedical, and Environmental Instrumentation
Chem Biomed Environ Instrum — Chemical, Biomedical, and Environmental Instrumentation
Chem Bk Econ — Chemical Bank. Weekly Economic Package
Chem Bk Frct — Chemical Bank. Economic Forecast Summary
Chem in Br — Chemistry in Britain
Chem Br — Chemistry in Britain
Chem Brit — Chemistry in Britain
Chem Bull — Chemical Bulletin
Chem Bus — Chemical Business
Chem Can — Chemistry in Canada
Chem Cda — Chemistry in Canada
Chem Chem Ind — Chemistry and Chemical Industry [*North Korea*]

Chem Chron A — Chemika Chronika. Section A
Chem Chron B — Chemika Chronika. Section B
Chem Chron Epistem Ekdosis — Chemika Chronika. Epistemonike Ekdosis [*Greece*]
Chem Chron Genike Ekdosis — Chemika Chronika. Genike Ekdosis
Chem Color Oil Daily — Chemical, Color, and Oil Daily
Chem Color Oil Rec — Chemical, Color, and Oil Record
Chem Commun — Chemical Communications [*Journal of the Chemical Society. Section D*]
Chem Communs — Chemical Communications
Chem Commun Univ Stockholm — Chemical Communications. University of Stockholm
Chem Concepts — Chemical Concepts
Chem Control Res Inst (Ottawa) Inf Rep — Chemical Control Research Institute (Ottawa). Information Report
Chem Corps J — Chemical Corps Journal
CHEMD — Chemsa
Chem Depend — Chemical Dependencies
Chem Digest — Chemurgic Digest
Chem Div Trans Am Soc Qual Control — Chemical Division Transactions. American Society for Quality Control
Chem Drug — Chemist and Druggist
Chem Econ — Chemical Economy and Engineering Review
Chem Econ Eng Rev — Chemical Economy and Engineering Review
Chem Educ — Chemical Education [*Japan*]
Chem Eng — Chemical Engineer
Chem Eng — Chemical Engineering
Chem Eng (Aust) — Chemical Engineering (Australia)
Chem Eng Comm — Chemical Engineering Communications
Chem Eng Commun — Chemical Engineering Communications
Chem Eng Costs Q — Chemical Engineering Costs Quarterly
Chem Eng Data Ser — Chemical and Engineering Data Series
Chem Eng Educ — Chemical Engineering Education
Chem Eng Fundam — Chemical Engineering Fundamentals
Chem and Engin News — Chemical and Engineering News
Chem Eng J — Chemical Engineering Journal
Chem Eng & Min R — Chemical Engineering and Mining Review
Chem Eng and Min Rev — Chemical Engineering and Mining Review
Chem Eng Monogr — Chemical Engineering Monographs [*Netherlands*]
Chem & Eng N — Chemical and Engineering News
Chem Eng News — Chemical and Engineering News
Chem Engng — Chemical Engineering
Chem Engng (Aust) — Chemical Engineering (Australia)
Chem Engng Commun — Chemical Engineering Communications
Chem Engng J — Chemical Engineering Journal
Chem Engng Min Rev — Chemical Engineering and Mining Review
Chem & Engng News — Chemical and Engineering News
Chem Engng Prog — Chemical Engineering Progress
Chem Engng Res Des — Chemical Engineering Research and Design
Chem Engng Sci — Chemical Engineering Science
Chem Engng World — Chemical Engineering World
Chem Engn News — Chemical and Engineering News
Chem Eng (NY) — Chemical Engineering (New York)
Chem Eng Pr — Chemical Engineering Progress
Chem Eng Process — Chemical Engineering and Processing
Chem Eng Prog — Chemical Engineering Progress
Chem Eng Prog Monogr Ser — Chemical Engineering Progress. Monograph Series
Chem Eng Progr — Chemical Engineering Progress
Chem Eng Progr Symp Ser — Chemical Engineering Progress. Symposium Series
Chem Eng Prog Symp Ser — Chemical Engineering Progress. Symposium Series
Chem Engr — Chemical Engineer
Chem Engr Diary & Process Ind News — Chemical Engineer Diary and Process Industries News
Chem Eng Res and Des — Chemical Engineering Research and Design
Chem Engrg J — Chemical Engineering Journal
Chem Engr (Lond) — Chemical Engineer (London)
Chem Engr (Rugby) — Chemical Engineer (Rugby)
Chem Eng Sc — Chemical Engineering Science
Chem Eng Sci — Chemical Engineering Science
Chem Eng (Tokyo) — Chemical Engineering (Tokyo)
Chem Eng Works Chem — Chemical Engineering and the Works Chemist
Chem Eng World — Chemical Engineering World
Chem Equip News — Chemical Equipment News
Chem Equip Preview — Chemical Equipment Preview
Chem Era — Chemical Era [*India*]
Chem Erde — Chemie der Erde
Chem Exp Didakt — Chemie. Experiment und Didaktik
Chem Exp + Technol — Chemie. Experiment und Technologie
Chem Exp Technol — Chemie. Experiment und Technologie
Chem Fab — Chemische Fabrik
Chem Fabr — Chemische Fabrik [*West Germany*]
Chem Fact (Tokyo) — Chemical Factory (Tokyo)
Chem Farming — Chemical Farming

Chemfasern — Chemiefasern/Textil-Industrie
Chem Geol — Chemical Geology
Chem Geology — Chemical Geology
Chem Heterocycl Comp — Chemistry of Heterocyclic Compounds
Chem Heterocycl Comp (USSR) — Chemistry of Heterocyclic Compounds (USSR)
Chem High Polym — Chemistry of High Polymers [*Japan*]
Chemia Analit — Chemia Analityczna [*Warszawa*]
Chemica Scr — Chemica Scripta
Chemico-Biol Interactions — Chemico-Biological Interactions
Chemiefasern Text-Anwendungstech — Chemiefasern und Textil-Anwendungstechnik [*Later, Chemiefasern/Textil-Industrie*]
Chemiefasern + Text-Anwendungstech Text Ind — Chemiefasern und Textil-Anwendungstechnik/Textil Industrie
Chemiefasern/Text-Ind — Chemiefasern/Textil-Industrie
Chemie-Ingr-Tech — Chemie-Ingenieur-Technik
Chemie Tech Landw — Chemie und Technik in der Landwirtschaft
Chem Ind — Chemical Industries
Chem Ind — Chemical Industry and Engineering
Chem Ind — Chemistry and Industry
Chem & Ind — Chemistry and Industry
Chem Ind (Berlin) — Chemische Industrie (Berlin)
Chem Ind (Berlin) Gemeinschaftsausg — Chemische Industrie (Berlin). Gemeinschaftsausgabe
Chem Ind (Berlin) Nachrichtenausg — Chemische Industrie (Berlin). Nachrichtenausgabe
Chem Ind Dev — Chemical Industry Developments
Chem Ind (Duesseldorf) — Chemische Industrie (Duesseldorf)
Chem Ind Eng — Chemical Industry and Engineering
Chem Ind and Engng — Chemical Industry and Engineering
Chem Ind Int — Chemische Industrie International
Chem Ind Int (Engl Transl) — Chemische Industrie International (English Translation) [*West Germany*]
Chem Ind (Jpn) — Chemical Industry (Japan)
Chem Ind (Jpn) Suppl — Chemical Industry (Japan). Supplement
Chem Ind NZ — Chemistry and Industry in New Zealand
Chem Ind (Tenali India) — Chemical Industry (Tenali, India)
Chem Ind Week — Chemical Industries Week
Chem Infd — Chemischer Informationsdienst
Chem Info — Chemical Information and Computer Sciences. Journal
ChemInform — Chemischer Informationsdienst
Chem Informationsdienst Anorg Phys Chem — Chemischer Informationsdienst. Anorganische und Physikalische Chemie
Chem Informationsdienst Org Chem — Chemischer Informationsdienst. Organische Chemie
Chem-Ing-T — Chemie-Ingenieur-Technik
Chem-Ing-Tech — Chemie-Ingenieur-Technik
Chem Inst Can J Conf Am Chem Soc Abstr Pap — Chemical Institute of Canada. Joint Conference with the American Chemical Society. Abstracts of Papers
Chem Instr — Chemical Instrumentation
Chem Instrum — Chemical Instrumentation
Chem Int — Chemistry International
Chemische — Chemische Industrie
Chemistry (Kyoto) Suppl — Chemistry (Kyoto). Supplement [*Japan*]
Chem J Freunde Natur — Chemisches Journal fuer die Freunde der Naturlehre
Chem Jrl — Chemicals and Petro-Chemicals Journal
Chem Kunst Aktuell — Chemie Kunststoffe Aktuell
Chem Lab Betr — Chemie fuer Labor und Betrieb
Chem Lab Rep Dep Mines (NSW) — Chemical Laboratory Report. Department of Mines (New South Wales)
Chem Lab Rep NSW Dep Mines — Chemical Laboratory Report. New South Wales Department of Mines
Chem Leafl — Chemistry Leaflet
Chem Lett — Chemistry Letters
Chem Lide — Chemie a Lide
Chem Listy — Chemicke Listy
Chem Listy Vedu Prum — Chemicke Listy pro Vedu a Prumysl
Chem Mag — Chemie Magazine [*Belgium*]
Chem Mark — Chemical Markets
Chem Market Reptr — Chemical Marketing Reporter
Chem Mark Rep — Chemical Marketing Reporter
Chem Metall Z — Chemisch Metallurgische Zeitschrift
Chem & Met Eng — Chemical and Metallurgical Engineering
Chem Mikrobiol Technol Lebensm — Chemie, Mikrobiologie, Technologie der Lebensmittel
Chem Mktg Rep — Chemical Marketing Reporter
Chem Mkt R — Chemical Marketing Reporter
Chem Mkt Rept — Chemical Marketing Reporter
Chem Mutagens — Chemical Mutagens
Chem Nat Compd — Chemistry of Natural Compounds
Chem Nat Compounds — Chemistry of Natural Compounds
Chem News — Chemical News
Chem News — Chemical News and Journal of Industrial Science
Chem NZ — Chemistry in New Zealand
Chem Obz — Chemicke Obzor

Chem Oil Gas Rom — Chemistry, Oil, and Gas in Romania
Chemothera — Chemotherapy
Chemother Fact Sheet — Chemotherapy Fact Sheet
Chemother Pro Int Congr Chemother — Chemotherapy. Proceedings of the International Congress of Chemotherapy
Chem Pet Eng — Chemical and Petroleum Engineering
Chem & Pet Engng — Chemical and Petroleum Engineering
Chem Petro-Chem J — Chemicals and Petro-Chemicals Journal
Chem Pharm — Chemical and Pharmaceutical Bulletin
Chem Pharm Bull (Tokyo) — Chemical and Pharmaceutical Bulletin (Tokyo)
Chem Pharm Tech (Dordrecht Neth) — Chemische en Pharmaceutische Technik (Dordrecht, Netherlands)
Chem Phys — Chemical Physics
Chem Phys Carbon — Chemistry and Physics of Carbon
Chem Phys L — Chemistry and Physics of Lipids
Chem Phys Lett — Chemical Physics Letters
Chem Phys Lipids — Chemistry and Physics of Lipids
Chem Phys Solids Their Surf — Chemical Physics of Solids and Their Surfaces
Chem Phys Technol Kunst Einzeldarst — Chemie, Physik, und Technologie der Kunststoffe in Einzeldarstellungen
Chem Plant (Tokyo) — Chemical Plant (Tokyo)
Chem P Lett — Chemical Physics Letters
Chem Prax — Chemische Praxis
Chem Preview — Chemical Preview
Chem Process — Chemical Processing
Chem Process Eng — Chemical and Process Engineering
Chem and Process Eng — Chemical and Process Engineering
Chem Process Eng At World — Chemical and Process Engineering and Atomic World
Chem & Process Engng — Chemical and Process Engineering [*Later, Process Engineering*]
Chem Processing — Chemical Processing
Chem Process (London) — Chemical Processing (London)
Chem Process Rev — Chemical Processing Review
Chem Proc (Sydney) — Chemical Processing (Sydney) [*Australia*]
Chem Prod — Chemische Produktion
Chem Prod Aerosol News — Chemical Products and Aerosol News
Chem Prod Chem News — Chemical Products and the Chemical News [*England*]
Chem Progr — Chemical Progress
Chem Prum — Chemicky Prumysl
Chem Purch — Chemical Purchasing
Chem Q — Chemists Quarterly
Chem R — Chemical Reviews
Chem Rdsch Mitteleur — Chemische Rundschau fuer Mitteleuropa und der Balkan
Chem Rec-Age — Chemical Record-Age
Chem Reihe — Chemische Reihe
Chem Rev — Chemical Reviews
Chem Rev Fett Harz Ind — Chemische Revue ueber die Fett und Harz Industrie
Chem Rundschau — Chemische Rundschau
Chem Rundsch Farbbeilage — Chemische Rundschau. Farbbeilage
Chem Rundsch Mag — Chemische Rundschau Magazine
Chem Rundsch (Solothurn) — Chemische Rundschau (Solothurn) [*Switzerland*]
Chem Saf Data Sheet — Chemical Safety Data Sheet
CHEMSAFE — Chemical Industry Scheme for Assistance in Freight Emergencies
Chem Scr — Chemica Scripta
Chem Scripta — Chemica Scripta
Chem Senses — Chemical Senses and Flavor
Chem Soc J — Chemical Society. Journal [*London*]
Chem Soc Re — Chemical Society. Reviews [*London*]
Chem Soc Rev — Chemical Society. Reviews [*London*]
Chem Soc Spec Publ — Chemical Society. Special Publication [*London*]
Chem Spec Manuf Assoc Proc Mid-Year Meet — Chemical Specialties Manufacturers Association. Proceedings of the Mid-Year Meeting
Chem Stosow — Chemia Stosowana
Chem Stosow Ser A — Chemia Stosowana. Seria A
Chem Stosow Ser B — Chemia Stosowana. Seria B
Chem Strojir Stavitelstvi Pristrojova Tech — Chemicke Strojirenstvi. Stavitelstvi a Pristrojova Technika
Chem Szk — Chemia Szkole
Chem Take-Off — Chemical Take-Off
Chem Tech — Chemical Technology
Chem Tech — Chemische Technik
Chem Tech (Amsterdam) — Chemie en Techniek (Amsterdam)
Chem Tech Fabr — Chemisch Technische Fabrikant
Chem Tech Landwirt — Chemie und Technik in der Landwirtschaft
Chem Technol — Chemical Technology
Chem Technol Fuels Oils — Chemistry and Technology of Fuels and Oils
Chem Tech Rev — Chemie und Technik Revue
Chem Tech Rundsch Anz Chem Ind — Chemisch Technische Rundschau und Anzeiger der Chemischen Industrie
Chem Tech Uebers — Chemisch Technische Uebersicht

Chemtech (US) — Chemtech (United States) [*Formerly, Chemical Technology*]
Chem Thermodyn — Chemical Thermodynamics
Chem Titles — Chemical Titles
Chem Trade J Chem Eng — Chemical Trade Journal and Chemical Engineer
Chem Umsch Geb Fette Oele Wachse Harze — Chemische Umschau auf dem Gebiete der Fette, Oele, Wachse, und Harze
Chem Unserer Zeit — Chemie in Unserer Zeit
Chemurgic Dig — Chemurgic Digest
Chem W — Chemical Week
Chem Warf Bull — Chemical Warfare Bulletin
Chem Week — Chemical Week
Chem Weekbl — Chemisch Weekblad [*Later, Chemisch Weekblad/Chemische Courant*]
Chem Weekb Mag — Chemisch Weekblad Magazine [*Later, Chemisch Magazine*]
Chem Wkly — Chemical Weekly
Chem Wkr — Chemical Worker
Chemy Ind — Chemistry and Industry
Chemy Life — Chemistry and Life
Chem-Zeitun — Chemiker-Zeitung
Chem Zelle Gewebe — Chemie der Zelle und Gewebe
Chem Zent Bl — Chemisches Zentralblatt
Chem Zool — Chemical Zoology
Chem-Ztg — Chemiker-Zeitung
Chem-Ztg Chem Appar — Chemiker-Zeitung. Chemische Apparatur
Chem Zvesti — Chemicke Zvesti
CHERD — Chemical Era
Chesapeake Bay Inst Johns Hopkins Univ Tech Rep — Chesapeake Bay Institute. Johns Hopkins University. Technical Report
Chesapeake Sci — Chesapeake Science
Chesterton Rev — Chesterton Review
Chest Heart Stroke J — Chest, Heart, and Stroke Journal
CHETA — Chung-Hua Erh K'o Tsa Chih
CHETAE — Chinese Journal of Pediatrics
CHETAE — Chung-Hua Erh K'o Tsa Chih
ChET Chem Exp Technol — ChET. Chemie. Experiment und Technologie [*West Germany*]
Chet Soc — Chetham Society
Chetvertichn Period — Chetvertichnyi Period
CHEYAT — Chung-Hua Erh Pi Yen Hou K'o Tsa Chih
CHF — Cahiers d'Histoire et de Folklore
CHFCA — Chung-Hua Fu Ch'an K'o Tsa Chih
CHFCA2 — Chinese Journal of Obstetrics and Gynecology
CHFCA2 — Chung-Hua Fu Ch'an K'o Tsa Chih
CHFSAG — Chung-Hua Fang She Hsueh Tsa Chih
CHGEA — Chemical Geology
CHGLA — Chemik
CHGSAL — Chromatographic Science Series
CHH — Chronos. Vakblad voor de Uurwerkbranche
ChH — Church History
Ch & H — Church and Home
CHHCDF — Chung-Hua Hsin Hsuch Kuan Ping Tsa Chih
Ch Hist — Church History
CHHNA — Chung-Hua Nei K'o Tsa Chih
CHHNAB — Chinese Journal of Internal Medicine
CHHOAE — Chronica Horticulturae
CHHPA — Ch'ing Hua Ta Hsueh Hsueh Pao
CHHTAT — Chinese Medical Journal [*Peking*]
CHHTAT — Chung-Hua I Hsueh Tsa Chih
CHI — China Newsletter
Chiang Mai Med Bull — Chiang Mai Medical Bulletin
Chiba Found Colloq Ageing — Chiba Foundation. Colloquia on Ageing
Chiba Med J — Chiba Medical Journal
Chi B Rec — Chicago Bar Record
Chicag Chem Bull — Chicago Chemical Bulletin
Chicago Acad Sci Bull Nat History Misc — Chicago Academy of Sciences. Bulletin. Natural History Miscellanea
Chicago Archtl Jnl — Chicago Architectural Journal
Chicago Art Inst Bul — Chicago Art Institute. Bulletin
Chicago Art Inst Cal — Chicago Art Institute. Calendar
Chicago Art Inst Q — Chicago Art Institute. Quarterly
Chicago Bar Rec — Chicago Bar Record
Chicago B Rec — Chicago Bar Record
Chicago Dairy Prod — Chicago Dairy Produce
Chicago His — Chicago History of Science and Medicine
Chicago-Kent L Rev — Chicago-Kent Law Review
Chicago Med — Chicago Medicine
Chicago Med Exam — Chicago Medical Examiner
Chicago Nat — Chicago Naturalist
Chicago Psychoanal Lit Ind — Chicago Psychoanalytic Literature Index
Chicago R — Chicago Review
Chicago Rev — Chicago Review
Chicago Sch J — Chicago Schools Journal
Chicago Stds — Chicago Studies
Chicago Studs — Chicago Studies

Chicago Trib — Chicago Tribune
Chicago Univ Dept Geography Research Paper — Chicago. University. Department of Geography. Research Paper
Chicano L Rev — Chicano Law Review
Chic Med Sch Q — Chicago Medical School Quarterly
Chic Nat Hist Mus Annu Rep — Chicago Natural History Museum. Annual Report
Chic R — Chicago Review
ChicSt — Chicago Studies [*Mundelein, IL*]
ChicTSemReg — Chicago Theological Seminary. Register
Chic Univ Dep Geogr Res Pap — Chicago. University. Department of Geography. Research Paper
Chief Executive Mon — Chief Executive Monthly
CHIHA — Chi'i Hsiang Hsueh Pao
Chih Wu Hsueh Pao Acta Bot Sin — Chih Wu Hsueh Pao. Acta Botanica Sinica
CHIIA — Chemische Industrie International [*English Translation*]
Chi Jrl R — Chicago Journalism Review
CHIKD — Chi Kuang
Chi-Kent LR — Chicago-Kent Law Review
Chi-Kent L Rev — Chicago-Kent Law Review
Chi-Kent Rev — Chicago-Kent Law Review
Chikyukagaku (Geochem) — Chikyukagaku (Geochemistry) Nagoya
Child Care — Child Care Quarterly
Child Care Health Dev — Child Care Health and Development
Child Care Q — Child Care Quarterly
Child Contemp Soc — Children in Contemporary Society
Child D — Children's Digest
Child Dev — Child Development
ChildDevAb — Child Development Abstracts
Child Devel — Child Development
Child Developm Absts Biblio — Child Development Abstracts and Bibliography
Child Ed — Childhood Education
Child Health Care — Children's Health Care
Childh Educ — Childhood Education
ChildL — Children's Literature
Child Legal Rights J — Children's Legal Rights Journal
Child Lib News — Children's Libraries Newsletter
Child Lit — Children's Literature
Child Lit Educ — Children's Literature in Education
Child Par M — Children. The Parents' Magazine
Child Psych — Child Psychiatry and Human Development
Child Psych & Human Devel — Child Psychiatry and Human Development
Child Psychiatry Hum Dev — Child Psychiatry and Human Development
Child Psy Q — Child Psychiatry Quarterly
Childrens Lib News — Children's Libraries Newsletter
Child St J — Child Study Journal
Child Stud J — Child Study Journal
Child Today — Children Today
Child Trop (Engl Ed) — Children in the Tropics (English Edition)
Child Wel — Child Welfare
Chile Econ — Chile Economic Report
Chillan Chile Estac Exp Bol Tec — Chillan, Chile. Estacion Experimental. Boletin Tecnico
Chil Nitrate Agric Serv Inf — Chilean Nitrate Agricultural Service. Information
Chim — Chimica
Chim Acta Turc — Chimica Acta Turcica
Chim Actual — Chimie Actualites [*France*]
Chim Agric — Chimizarea Agriculturii
Chim Anal (Bucharest) — Chimie Analitica (Bucharest) [*Romania*]
Chim Anal (Paris) — Chimie Analytique (Paris)
Chim Analyt — Chimie Analytique
Chim Chron (Athens) — Chimika Chronika (Athens)
Chim Didact — Chimica Didactica
Chimica Ind (Milano) — Chimica e l'Industria (Milano)
Chimie Act — Chimie Actualites
Chimie & Ind — Chimie et Industrie
Chimie Peint — Double Liason. Chimie des Peintures
Chim Ind — Chimica e l'Industria
Chim Ind - Genie Chim — Chimie et Industrie - Genie Chimique
Chim Ind (Paris) — Chimie et Industrie (Paris)
Chim Microbiol Technol Aliment — Chimie, Microbiologie, Technologie Alimentaire
Chim Mod — Chimie Moderne [*France*]
Chim Nouv — Chimie Nouvelle
Chim Pure Appl — Chimie Pure et Appliquee
Chim Tech — Chimie et Technique
Chim Ther — Chimica Therapeutica
Chim Ther — Chimie Therapeutique
China Bus R — China Business Review
China Clay Trade Rev — China Clay Trade Review
China For Tr — China's Foreign Trade [*Peking*]
China Geog — China Geographer [*Los Angeles*]
Chin Agric Sci — Chinese Agricultural Science [*People's Republic of China*]
China Internat Bus — China International Business

China J — China Journal
China L Rep — China Law Reporter
China Med — China's Medicine
China Med J — China Medical Journal
China Med Miss J — China Medical Missionary Journal
Chin Am J Comm Rural Reconstr Plant Ind Ser — Chinese-American Joint Commission on Rural Reconstruction. Plant Industry Series
Chin Am J Comm Rural Reconstr (Taiwan) Spec Bull — Chinese-American Joint Commission on Rural Reconstruction (Taiwan). Special Bulletin
China News Anal — China News Analysis [*Hong Kong*]
Chin Anim Husb Vet Med — Chinese Animal Husbandry and Veterinary Medicine [*People's Republic of China*]
China Q — China Quarterly [*London*]
China Quart — China Quarterly
China Reconstr — China Reconstructs
China Rep — China Report
China's — China's Screen
China Sci Tech Abstracts Ser I Math Astronom Phys — China Science and Technology Abstracts. Series I. Mathematics, Astronomy, Physics
China Sci & Technol Abstr Ser 3 — China Science and Technology Abstracts. Series III. Industry Technology
China's Med (Peking) — China's Medicine (Peking)
Chin Astron — Chinese Astronomy [*Later, Chinese Astronomy and Astrophysics*]
China W R — China Weekly Review
CHINB — Chemical Instrumentation [*New York*]
Chin Bee J — Chinese Bee Journal [*Taiwan*]
Chin Cult — Chinese Culture
Chin Econ S — Chinese Economic Studies
Chin Educ — Chinese Education
Chinese Ann Math — Chinese Annals of Mathematics [*Shanghai*]
Chinese Astronom — Chinese Astronomy [*Later, Chinese Astronomy and Astrophysics*] [*Oxford*]
Chinese Astronom Astrophys — Chinese Astronomy and Astrophysics [*Oxford*]
Chinese Cult — Chinese Culture
Chinese Econ Studies — Chinese Economic Studies
Chinese J Math — Chinese Journal of Mathematics
Chinese J Phys (Peking) — Chinese Journal of Physics (Peking)
Chinese Law Gvt — Chinese Law and Government
Chinese L & Govt — Chinese Law and Government
Chinese M — Chinese Music
Chin J Appl Chem — Chinese Journal of Applied Chemistry
Chin J Archaeol — Chinese Journal of Archaeology
Chin J Dermatol — Chinese Journal of Dermatology [*People's Republic of China*]
Chin J Gynecol Obstet — Chinese Journal of Gynecology and Obstetrics [*People's Republic of China*]
Chin J Intern Med — Chinese Journal of Internal Medicine [*People's Republic of China*]
Chin J Lasers — Chinese Journal of Lasers
Chin J Mech — Chinese Journal of Mechanics [*People's Republic of China*]
Chin J Mech Eng — Chinese Journal of Mechanical Engineering
Chin J Microbiol — Chinese Journal of Microbiology [*Later, Chinese Journal of Microbiology and Immunology*]
Chin J Ophthalmology — Chinese Journal of Ophthalmology [*People's Republic of China*]
Chin J Otorhinolaryngol — Chinese Journal of Otorhinolaryngology [*People's Republic of China*]
Chin J Pediatr — Chinese Journal of Pediatrics [*People's Republic of China*]
Chin J Phys — Chinese Journal of Physics
Chin J Physiol — Chinese Journal of Physiology
Chin J Physiol Rep Ser — Chinese Journal of Physiology. Report Series
Chin J Phys (New York) — Chinese Journal of Physics (New York)
Chin J Phys (Taipei) — Chinese Journal of Physics (Taipei)
Chin J Sci Agr — Chinese Journal of the Science of Agriculture
Chin J Surg — Chinese Journal of Surgery [*People's Republic of China*]
ChinL — Chinese Literature
Chin Law G — Chinese Law and Government
Chin Law Govt — Chinese Law and Government [*New York*]
Chin L and Gov — Chinese Law and Government
Chin Lit — Chinese Literature [*Peking*]
Chin Lit Es — Chinese Literature. Essays, Articles, Reviews
Chin Med J — Chinese Medical Journal
Chin Pen — Chinese Pen [*Taipei*]
Chin Phys — Chinese Physics [*United States*]
Chin Repub Stud — Chinese Republic Studies. Newsletter
Chin Soc A — Chinese Sociology and Anthropology
Chin Social & Pol Sci R — Chinese Social and Political Science Review
Chin Sociol Anthro — Chinese Sociology and Anthropology [*New York*]
Chin St Lit — Chinese Studies in Literature
Chin St Ph — Chinese Studies in Philosophy
Chin Stud — Chinese Studies in History
Chin Stud Hist — Chinese Studies in History [*New York*]
Chin Stud Phil — Chinese Studies in Philosophy
Chin Stud Philo — Chinese Studies in Philosophy [*New York*]
CHIQ — Concordia Historical Institute Quarterly

ChiR — Chicago Review
Chir Aktuell — Chirurgie Aktuell
CHIRAS — Chirurg
Chir-Dent Fr — Chirurgien-Dentiste de France
Chir Forum Exp Klin Forsch — Chirurgisches Forum fuer Experimentelle und Klinische Forschung
Chir Gastroenterol (Engl Ed) — Chirurgia Gastroenterologica (English Edition)
Chir Gen — Chirurgia Generale
Chir Ital — Chirurgia Italiana
Chir Maxillofac Plast — Chirurgia Maxillofacialis et Plastica
Chir Narzadow Ruchu Ortop Pol — Chirurgia Narzadow Ruchu i Ortopedia Polska
Chiro Hist — Chiropractic History
Chir Organi Mov — Chirurgia degli Organi di Movimento
Chir Org Movimento — Chirurgia degli Organi di Movimento
Chir Patol Sper — Chirurgia e Patologia Sperimentale
Chir Pediatr — Chirurgie Pediatrique
Chir Plast — Chirurgia Plastica
Chir Plast Reconstr — Chirurgia Plastica et Reconstructiva
Chir Torac — Chirurgia Toracica
Chir Vet Ref Abstr — Chirurgia Veterinaria Referate. Abstracts
Chislennye Metody Din Razrezh Gazov — Chislennye Metody v Dinamike Razrezhennykh Gazov
Chislennye Metody Mekh Sploshnoi Sredy — Chislennye Metody Mekhaniki Sploshnoi Sredy [*USSR*]
Chisl Metody Mekh Sploshn Sredy — Akademiya Nauk SSSR. Sibirskoe Otdelenie. Vychislitelnyi Tsentr. Chislennye Metody Mekhaniki Sploshnoi Sredy
C Hist — Catholic Historical Review
CHist — Church History
CHist — Corse Historique
C Hist Inst Maurice Thorez — Cahiers d'Histoire. Institut Maurice Thorez
Chi Sym — Chicago Symphony Orchestra. Program Notes
CHITAY — Chirurgia Italiana
Chi T M — Chicago Tribune Magazine
Chittagong Univ Stud Part II Sci — Chittagong University. Studies. Part II. Science
Chitty LJ — Chitty's Law Journal
Chitty's L J — Chitty's Law Journal
CHIUA — Chemische Industrie [*Duesseldorf*]
CHJ — Cambridge Historical Journal
CHJIA — Chitaniumu Jirukoniumu
CHJPB — Chinese Journal of Physics [*Peking*] [*English translation*]
CHK — Caterer and Hotelkeeper
CHKAD — Chiiki Kaihatsu
CHKWA — Chijil Kwa Chiri
ChL — Christian Liberty
Ch L — University of Chicago. Law Review
Ch L B — Charles Lamb Bulletin
CHLBA — Chemie fuer Labor und Betrieb
CHLGB — Challenge
Ch Lib Newsl — Children's Libraries Newsletter
ChLit — Chinese Literature
Ch LR — University of Chicago. Law Review
CHLSA — Chemicke Listy
CHLSSF — Commentationes Humanarum Litterarum. Societas Scientiarum Fennica
CHM — Cahiers d'Histoire Mondiale/Journal of World History
CHM — Chemisch Magazine
Chm — Churchman
CHMAD — Chemie Magazine
CHMEB — China's Medicine
CHMEBA — China's Medicine [*Peking*]
CHMEBA — Chung-Kuo I Hsueh
CHMGA — Chartered Mechanical Engineer
Ch Mis I — Church Missionary Intelligencer
CHMJB — Chamber of Mines. Journal
Chmn — Churchman
CHMNA — Chantiers Magazine
CHMond — Cahiers d'Histoire Mondiale/Journal of World History [*Paris*]
CHMTB — Chemical Technology
CHNCDB — Journal of Agricultural Research of China
CHNHA — Chung-Hua Nung Hsueh Hui Pao
CHNHAN — Journal. Agricultural Association of China. New Series
Chn Store — Chain Store Age
CHNYB — Chishitsu Nyusu
CHO — Choice
Choc Confiserie Fr — Chocolaterie. Confiserie de France
CHOMA9 — Chirurgia degli Organi di Movimento
C Home — Christian Home
CHONDF — Contemporary Hematology/Oncology
Chonnam Med J — Chonnam Medical Journal
Choral G — Choral and Organ Guide
Choral J — Choral Journal

CHOVA2 — Commissie voor Hydrologisch Onderzoek TNO [*Nederlandse Centrale Organisatie voor Toegepast Natuurwetenschappelijk Onderzoek*]
Chowder — Chowder Review
CHPAAC — Chirurgia e Patologia Sperimentale
CHPAD — Journal. Korean Academy of Maxillofacial Radiology
CHPCA — Chemical Processing (Chicago)
CHPHD — Chinese Physics
CHPI — Christian Periodical Index
CHPLB — Chemical Physics Letters
CHPRD — Chemische Produktion
CHPUA — Chemicky Prumysl
CHPXBE — Chirurgische Praxis
CHQ — California Historical Quarterly [*San Francisco*]
Ch Q — Church Quarterly
Ch Q — Church Quarterly Review
Ch Q R — Church Quarterly Review
CHR — Canadian Historical Review
CHR — Canadian Hotel and Restaurant
CHR — Catholic Historical Review
CHR — China Business Review
CHR — Current Housing Reports
CHRAQ — Cornell Hotel and Restaurant Administration Quarterly
CHRA Rec — CHRA [*Canadian Health Record Association*] Recorder
CHRBAP — Chronica Botanica
Chr C — Christian Century
Chr Cent — Christian Century
Chr & Cr — Christianity and Crisis
Chr Cris — Christianity and Crisis
Chr & Crisis — Christianity and Crisis
Chr Disc — Christian Disciple
ChrE — Chronique d'Egypte
CHREA — Chemical Reviews
Chr Eg — Chronique d'Egypte
Chr Exam — Christian Examiner
CHRF — Cahiers d'Histoire de la Revolution Francaise
CHRGA6 — Chirurgia Gastroenterologica [*English Edition*]
CHRGB7 — Chromatographia
ChrGem — Die Christengemeinschaft [*Stuttgart*]
Chris Art — Christian Art [*Boston*]
Chris Q — Christian Quarterly Review
Chris Sc Mon — Christian Science Monitor
Christ Brothers Stud — Christian Brothers Studies
Christ Cen — Christian Century
ChristCent — Christian Century [*Chicago*]
Christiana Albertina Kiel Univ Z — Christiana Albertina. Kieler Universitaets Zeitschrift
Christian Cent — Christian Century
Christian Sci Mon — Christian Science Monitor
Christian Sci Mon Mag — Christian Science Monitor. Magazine Section
Christ Libr — Christian Librarian
Christ Lit — Christianity and Literature
Christmas Tree Grow J — Christmas Tree Growers Journal
Christ Nurse — Christian Nurse
Christ Sci Mon — Christian Science Monitor
ChristTod — Christianity Today [*Washington, DC*]
ChrJF — Christlich-Juedisches Forum
Chr Lit — Christian Literature
Chr Ministry — Christian Ministry
Chr Mo Spec — Christian Monthly Spectator
ChrNIsrael — Christian News from Israel [*Jerusalem*]
CHROAU — Chromosoma [*Berlin*]
Chr Obs — Christian Observer
CHROD — Chronolog
Chromatin Chromosomal Protein Res — Chromatin and Chromosomal Protein Research
Chromatogr — Chromatographia
Chromatogr Methods — Chromatographic Methods
Chromatogr Newsl — Chromatography Newsletter
Chromatogr Rev — Chromatographic Reviews
Chromatogr Sci — Chromatographic Science
Chromatogr Sci Ser — Chromatographic Science Series
Chromat Rev — Chromatographic Reviews
Chromo Inf Serv — Chromosome Information Service
Chromos — Chromosoma
Chromos Inform Serv (Tokyo) — Chromosome Information Service (Tokyo)
Chromosome Inf Serv (Tokyo) — Chromosome Information Service (Tokyo)
Chromosome Var Hum Evol — Chromosome Variations in Human Evolution
Chron Actual — Chroniques d'Actualite
Chron Alum — Chronique Aluminum
Chron Aust Ed — Chronicle of Australian Education
Chron Bot — Chronica Botanica
Chron Chim — Chronache di Chimica [*Italy*]
Chron Egypte — Chronique d'Egypte
Chron Higher Educ — Chronicle of Higher Education
Chron Hortic — Chronica Horticulturae

Chronicles Okla — Chronicles of Oklahoma
Chron Nat — Chronica Naturae
Chronobiologia Organ Int Soc Chronobiology — Chronobiologia. Organ of the International Society for Chronobiology
ChronOkla — Chronicles of Oklahoma
Chron OMS — Chronique. Organisation Mondiale de la Sante
Chron Pol Etrangere — Chronique de Politique Etrangere
Chron Polit Etr — Chronique de Politique Etrangere
Chron Przyr Ojczysta — Chronmy Przyrode Ojczysta
Chron Rech Min — Chronique de la Recherche Miniere [*Paris*]
Chron Rech Miniere — Chronique de la Recherche Miniere [*France*]
Chron Soc France — Chronique Sociale de France
ChrOost — Het Christelijk Oosten [*Nijmegen*]
ChrPer — Christian Perspectives
Chr Per Ind — Christian Periodical Index
Chr Q — Christian Quarterly
Chr Q Spec — Christian Quarterly Spectator
Chr R — Christian Review
Chr Rem — Christian Remembrance
Chr Sch R — Christian Scholar's Review
Chr Sci Mon — Christian Science Monitor
Chr Sci Monitor — Christian Science Monitor
Chr T — Christianity Today
CHRTB — Chromosomes Today
CHRTBC — Chromosomes Today
Chr Today — Christianity Today
CHRU — Christian Union [*New York*]
CHRUA — Chemische Rundschau [*Solothurn, Switzerland*]
Chr Un — Christian Union
CHRYA — Chemistry
CHS — Baghdad Chamber of Commerce. Commercial Bulletin. Bi-Weekly
ChS — Christian Scholar
CHSB — Cincinnati Historical Society. Bulletin
CHSB — Connecticut Historical Society. Bulletin
CHSCD — Changing Scene
Ch Soc — Church and Society
C H Soc Q — California Historical Society Quarterly
CHSOP — Canadian Historic Sites. Occasional Papers in Archaeology and History
CHSQ — California Historical Society. Quarterly [*San Francisco*]
Ch S R — Christian Scholar's Review
CHSTA — Child Study Journal
CHSUA — Chartered Surveyor [*Later, Chartered Surveyor Weekly*]
ChT — Church Teachers
CHTED — Chemtech
CHTHA — Chung-Shan Ta Hsueh Hsueh Pao. Tzu Jan K'o Hsueh
CHTRD — Chicago Tribune
CHTTA — Chuko To Tanko
CHTZA — Chishitsugaku Zasshi
CHTZA5 — Chishitsugaku Zasshi
Chu — Church Music
Chugoku Shikoku Dist J Jpn Soc Obstet Gynecol — Chugoku and Shikoku Districts Journal. Japan Society of Obstetrics and Gynecology
CHUIAR — Chung-Ang Uihak
CHum — Computers and the Humanities [*Database*]
Chung-Ang J Med — Chung-Ang Journal of Medicine [*South Korea*]
Chung Hua Lin Hsueh Chi K'an Q J Chin For — Chung-Hua Lin Hsueh Chi K'an. Quarterly Journal of Chinese Forestry
Chung-Hua Nung Yeh Yen Chiu J Agric Res China — Chung-Hua Nung Yeh Yen Chiu/Journal of Agriculture Research of China
Chung-Kuo Lin Yeh K'o Hsueh Chin For Sci — Chung-Kuo Lin Yeh K'o Hsueh/Chinese Forestry Science
Chung-Kuo Nung Yeh Hua Hsueh Hui Chih J Chin Agric Chem Soc — Chung-Kuo Nung Yeh Hua Hsueh Hui Chih/Journal of the Chinese Agriculture Chemical Society
Chung-Kuo Nung Yeh K'o Hsueh Sci Agric Sin — Chung-Kuo Nung Yeh K'o Hsueh/Scientia Agriculture Sinica
Chungnam J Sci — Chungnam Journal of Sciences [*South Korea*]
Chung-Shan Univ J Nat Sci Ed — Chung-Shan University Journal. Natural Sciences Edition [*People's Republic of China*]
Church Eng Hist Soc J — Church of England Historical Society. Journal
Church Hist — Church History
Church Mus (London) — Church Music (London)
Church Mus (St L) — Church Music (St. Louis)
Church Q — Church Quarterly Review
Church Q R — Church Quarterly Review
Church R — Church Review
CHVCA — Chauffage, Ventilation, Conditionnement
CHW — Chemisch Weekblad/Chemische Courant
CHWCA — Chung-Hua Wai K'o Tsa Chih
CHWCAJ — Chinese Journal of Surgery
CHWEA — Chemisch Weekblad [*Later, Chemisch Weekblad/Chemische Courant*]
CHWHA — Chih Wu Hsueh Pao
CHWKA — Chemical Week
CHWOD — Chevron World

CHX — Chemische Rundschau. Europaeische Wochenzeitung fuer Chemie, Pharmazeutik, und die Lebensmittelindustrie
CHYCDW — Chinese Journal of Preventive Medicine
CI — Canadian Insurance
CI — Canadian Interiors
CI — Cancer Investigation
CI — Chemistry International
CI — City Invincible
CI — Commercial Intelligencer
CI — Critical Inquiry
CI — Cuadernos del Idioma
CIA — Corpus Inscriptionum Atticarum
CIAC — Canadian Indian Artcrafts. National Indian Arts and Crafts Advisory Committee
CIACDL — Centro Internacional de Agricultura Tropical [*CIAT*]. Series CE
CIADI — Clinically Important Adverse Drug Interactions [*Elsevier Book Series*]
CIAH — Culture, Illness, and Healing
CIAMAE — Centro de Investigaciones Agronomicas Maracay. Monografia
CIARAT — Cawthron Institute [*Nelson, New Zealand*]. Report
CIAT Annu Rep — CIAT [*Centro Internacional de Agricultura Tropical*] Annual Report
CIATB2 — Centro Internacional de Agricultura Tropical [*CIAT*]. Annual Report
CIATC3 — Centro Internacional de Agricultura Tropical [*CIAT*]. Technical Bulletin
CIAT Ser Semin — CIAT [*Centro Internacional de Agricultura Tropical*] Series Seminars
Ciba — Ciba Symposia
Ciba Clin Symp — Ciba Clinical Symposia
Ciba Collect Med Illus — Ciba Collection of Medical Illustrations
Ciba Found Colloq Endocrinol — Ciba Foundation. Colloquia on Endocrinology
Ciba Found Study Group — Ciba Foundation. Study Group
Ciba Found Symp — Ciba Foundation. Symposium
Ciba-Geigy Tech Notes — Ciba-Geigy Technical Notes
Ciba J — Ciba Journal
Ciba Lect Microb Biochem — Ciba Lectures in Microbial Biochemistry
Ciba R — Ciba Review
Ciba Rundsch — Ciba Rundschau
Ciba Symp — Ciba Symposia
CIBMAJ — Centro de Investigacion de Biologia Marina. Contribucion Tecnica
CIBMBK — Commonwealth Institute of Biological Control. Miscellaneous Publication
CIBSB — Ciba Foundation. Symposium
CICF — Current Issues in Commerce and Finance
CICIAMS Nouv — CICIAMS [*Comite International Catholique des Infirmieres et Assistantes Medico-Sociales*] Nouvelles
CIC Inform B Inform Gen — CIC Informations. Bulletin d'Informations Generales
CICNEV — Contemporary Issues in Clinical Nutrition
CICRD8 — Colloque Scientifique International sur le Cafe
CICSA — Clinical Symposia
CIDE — Caisse Israelite de Demarrage Economique
CIDG — Current Intelligence Digest
CIDS — Centro Intercultural de Documentacion Sondeos
CIE — Catering Industry Employee
CIE — Corpus Inscriptionum Etruscarum
CIEA Preclin Rep — CIEA [*Central Institute for Experimental Animals*] Preclinical Reports
Cie Fr Pet Notes Mem — Compagnie Francaise des Petroles. Notes et Memoires
Cienc — Ciencia
Cienc Adm — Ciencias Administrativas
Cienc Agron — Ciencia Agronomica
Cienc Biol B — Ciencia Biologica. B. Ecologia e Sistematica
Cienc Biol Biol Mol Cel — Ciencia Biologica. Biologia Molecular e Cellular
Cienc Biol (Coimbra) — Ciencia Biologica (Coimbra) [*Portugal*]
Cienc Biol Ecol Sist — Ciencia Biologica, Ecologia, e Sistematica
Cienc Biol (Luanda) — Ciencias Biologicas (Luanda)
Cienc Biol Mol Cell Biol — Ciencia Biologica. Molecular and Cellular Biology
Cienc Cult (Maracaibo) — Ciencia y Cultura (Maracaibo)
Cienc Cult (Sao Paulo) — Ciencia e Cultura (Sao Paulo)
Cienc Cult Saude — Ciencia, Cultura, Saude
Cienc Cult Soc Bras Progr Cienc — Ciencia e Cultura. Sociedade Brasileira para o Progresso da Ciencia
Cienc For — Ciencia Forestal
Ciencia Info — Ciencia da Informacao
Ciencia y Soc — Ciencia y Sociedad
Ciencias Ser 5 — Ciencias. Serie 5. Bioquimica Farmaceutica
Ciencias Ser 1 Mat — Ciencias. Serie 1. Matematica [*Havana*]
Ciencia e Tec Fiscal — Ciencia e Tecnica Fiscal
Ciencia Tecnol — Ciencia y Tecnologia
Cienc Interam — Ciencia Interamericana
Cienc Invest — Ciencia e Investigacion
Cienc Invest Agrar — Ciencia e Investigacion Agraria
Cienc Invest (B Aires) — Ciencia e Investigacion (Buenos Aires)

Cienc Mat — Ciencias Matematicas [*Havana*]
Cienc Nat — Ciencia y Naturaleza
Cienc Neurol — Ciencias Neurologicas
Cienc Ser 10 Bot (Havana) — Ciencias. Serie 10. Botanica (Havana)
Cienc Ser 4 Cienc Biol (Havana) — Ciencias. Serie 4. Ciencias Biologicas (Havana)
Cienc Ser 8 Invest Mar (Havana) — Ciencias. Serie 8. Investigaciones Marinas (Havana)
Cienc & Tec — Ciencia y Tecnica
Cienc Tec (Buenos Aires) — Ciencia y Tecnica (Buenos Aires)
Cienc Tec Fis Mat — Ciencias Tecnicas Fisicas y Matematicas
Cienc Tec Mar — Ciencia y Tecnologia del Mar. Comite Oceanografico Nacional [*Valparaiso, Chile*]
Cienc Tec Mundo — Ciencia y Tecnica en el Mundo
Cienc Tecn — Ciencia y Tecnologia
Cienc Tec Soldadura (Madrid) — Ciencia y Tecnica de la Soldadura (Madrid)
Cienc Terra — Ciencias da Terra
Cienc Vet — Ciencias Veterinarias
Cienc Vet Aliment Nutr Anim — Ciencias Veterinarias y Alimentas y Nutricion Animal
Ci Eng — Civil Engineering
Cien Tom — Ciencia Tomista
Ciep Ogrz Went — Cieplownictwo, Ogrzewnictwo, Wentylacja
CIETD — Ciencias da Terra
CIFBA6 — Central Inland Fisheries Research Institute (Barrackpore). Bulletin
CIFCA9 — Communications. Instituti Forestalis Cechosloveniae
CiFe — Ciencia y Fe
CIFM — Contributi. Istituto di Filologia Moderna
CIFRBL — Central Inland Fisheries Research Institute (Barrackpore). Annual Report
CIFRI (Cent Inland Fish Res Inst) Semin — CIFRI (Central Inland Fisheries Research Institute) Seminar
CIFSBO — Central Inland Fisheries Research Institute (Barrackpore). Survey Report
CIF-SP — Congresso Internacional de Filosofia. Anais (Sao Paulo)
CIG — Corpus Inscriptionum Graecarum [*A collection of Greek inscriptions*] [*Latin*]
CIG Cryog Indus Gases — CIG. Cryogenics and Industrial Gases
CIHMBG — Congreso Internacional de Hematologia. Conferencias
CIHMBG — International Congress of Hematology. Lectures
CIIG Bull — CIIG [*Construction Industry Information Group*] Bulletin
CIIMDN — Cancer Immunology and Immunotherapy
CIJ — Canada Commerce
CIJE — Current Index to Journals in Education [*United States Office of Education*]
CIJED4 — Centro Internacional de Agricultura Tropical [*CIAT*]. Series JE
CIL — Contemporary Indian Literature
CIL — Corpus Inscriptionum Latinarum [*A collection of Latin inscriptions*] [*Latin*]
CIL — Crain's Illinois Business
CILA B — CILA [*Centre Internationale de Linguistique Appliquee*] Bulletin
CILJDT — Contact and Intraocular Lens Medical Journal
CILL — Current Inquiry into Language and Linguistics
CILP — Conferences. Institut de Linguistique de Paris
Ci LR — Cincinnati Law Review
CILT — Amsterdam Studies in the Theory and History of Linguistic Science. Series IV. Current Issues in Linguistic Theory
CIMAGL — Cahiers. Institut du Moyen Age Grec et Latin
Cimbebasia Mem — Cimbebasia. Memoir
Cimbebasia Ser A — Cimbebasia. Series A
Cim Beton — Ciment si Beton
Cim Betons Platres Chaux — Ciments, Betons, Platres, Chaux [*France*]
CIM Bull — CIM [*Canadian Institute of Mining and Metallurgy*] Bulletin
CIM Bulletin — Canadian Institute of Mining and Metallurgy. Bulletin [*Montreal*]
Cimento Mustahsilleri Bul — Cimento Mustahsilleri Bulteni
CIMIDV — Comparative Immunology, Microbiology, and Infectious Diseases
CIMMYT News — Centro Internacional de Mejoramiento de Maiz y Trigo. News
CIMOA — Chimie Moderne
CimR — Cimarron Review
CIMS — Canada. Industrial Meteorology Studies. Environment Canada. Atmospheric Environment
CIN — Canadian Insurance
CIN — Chemical Industry Notes [*Chemical Abstracts Service*] [*Bibliographic database*]
Cin BAJ — Cincinnati Bar Association. Journal
Cincinnati J Med — Cincinnati Journal of Medicine
Cincinnati Med — Cincinnati Medicine
Cincinnati Mus Bull — Cincinnati Art Museum. Bulletin
Cincinnati Mus Bul ns — Cincinnati Art Museum. Bulletin. New Series
Cincinnati Mus N — Cincinnati Art Museum. News
Cinc Sym Prog Notes — Cincinnati Symphony Orchestra. Program Notes
Cinegram — Cinegram Magazine
Cinema Can — Cinema Canada
Cinema J — Cinema Journal

Cinema P — Cinema Papers
Cinemateca Rev — Cinemateca Revista
Cinematgr — Cinematographe
C Inform Chef Personnel — Cahiers d'Information du Chef de Personnel
C Ingen Agron — Cahiers des Ingenieurs Agronomes
CINL — Cumulative Index to Nursing and Allied Health Literature
Cin Law Rev — University of Cincinnati. Law Review
Cin L Rev — University of Cincinnati. Law Review
CINMDE — Colloque. INSERM [*Institut National de la Sante et de la Recherche Medicale*]
CINND — Ceramics International
CINP — CINEP/PLUS. Bulletin du Centre d'Ingenierie Nordique de l'Ecole Polytechnique
C Inst Amenag Urb Region Paris — Cahiers. Institut d'Amenagement et d'Urbanisation de la Region Parisienne
Cin Sym — Cincinnati Symphony Orchestra. Program Notes
CINTD — Communications International
C Int Sociol — Cahiers Internationaux de Sociologie
CINUD — Computers in Industry
CINVD7 — Cancer Investigation
CIOVD — Cistota Ovzdusia
CIP Circ Int Potato Cent — CIP Circular. International Potato Center
CIPED — Carvao, Informacao, e Pesquisa [*Brazil*]
CIPS Rev — CIPS [*Canadian Information Processing Society*] Review
CIPVDH — Comunicaciones. INIA [*Instituto Nacional de Investigaciones Agrarias*]. Serie Produccion Vegetal
CIRAA — CIRP [*College International pour l'Etude Scientifique des Techniques de Production Mecanique*] Annals
CIRADW — Contributions. Central Research Institute for Agriculture [*Bogor*]
Cir Bucal — Cirugia Bucal
Circ Agric Ext Serv Univ Ark — Circular. Agricultural Extension Service. University of Arkansas
Circ Agric Ext Serv Wash St Univ — Circular. Agricultural Extension Service. Washington State University
Circ Ala Agr Exp Sta — Circular. Alabama Agricultural Experiment Station
Circ Ala Geol Surv — Circular. Alabama Geological Survey
Circ Ala Polytech Inst Ext Serv — Circular. Alabama Polytechnic Institute. Extension Service
Circ Ariz Agric Ext Serv — Circular. Arizona Agricultural Extension Service
Circ Ark St Pl Bd — Circular. Arkansas State Plant Board
Circ Assoc Mine Managers S Afr — Circular. Association of Mine Managers of South Africa
Circ Auburn Univ Agr Ext Serv — Circular. Auburn University. Agricultural Extension Service
Circ Bur Ent US Dep Agric — Circular. Bureau of Entomology. United States Department of Agriculture
Circ Calif Agr Ext Serv — Circular. California Agricultural Extension Service
Circ Cent Invest Agr El Bajio (CIAB) — Circular. Centro de Investigaciones Agricolas de El Bajio (CIAB)
Circ Cent Invest Agr Noroeste (CIANO) — Circular. Centro de Investigaciones Agricolas del Noroeste (CIANO)
Circ Cent Invest Agr Sudeste — Circular. Centro de Investigaciones Agricolas del Sudeste
Circ Cent Invest Basicas (CIB) — Circular. Centro de Investigaciones del Basicas (CIB)
Circ Clemson Agr Coll Ext Serv — Circular. Clemson Agricultural College. Extension Service
Circ Coop Ext Serv Univ Ill — Circular. Cooperative Extension Service. University of Illinois
Circ Div Fd Res CSIRO — Circular. Division of Food Research. Commonwealth Scientific and Industrial Research Organisation
Circ Div Fish Oceanogr CSIRO — Circular. Division of Fisheries and Oceanography. Commonwealth Scientific and Industrial Research Organisation
Circ Div Mech Eng CSIRO — Circular. Division of Mechanical Engineering. Commonwealth Scientific and Industrial Research Organisation
Circ Electrotech Lab (Tokyo) — Circulars. Electrotechnical Laboratory (Tokyo)
Circ Electrotech Lab (Tokyo Japan) — Circulars. Electrotechnical Laboratory (Tokyo, Japan)
Circ Eng Sec CSIRO — Circular. Engineering Section. Commonwealth Scientific and Industrial Research Organisation
Circ Estac Exp Agric Tucuman — Circular. Estacion Experimental Agricola de Tucuman
Circ Farm — Circular Farmaceutica
Circ Fla Agric Exp Stn — Circular. Florida Agricultural Experiment Station
Circ Fla Agric Ext Serv — Circular. Florida Agricultural Extension Service
Circ Fla Univ Agr Ext Serv — Circular. Florida University. Agricultural Extension Service
Circ GA Agr Exp Sta — Circular. Georgia Agricultural Experiment Stations
Circ Geol Surv GA — Circular. Geological Survey of Georgia
Circ Hort Biol Serv Nova Scot Dep Agric Mktg — Circular. Horticulture and Biology Service. Nova Scotia Department of Agriculture and Marketing
Circ Ill Dep Agric — Circular. Illinois Department of Agriculture
Circ Ill Nat Hist Surv — Circular. Illinois Natural History Survey

Circ Ill Natur Hist Surv — Circular. Illinois Natural History Survey
Circ Ill State Geol Surv Div — Circular. Illinois State Geological Survey Division
Circ Inf Agric Exp Stn Oreg State Univ — Circular of Information. Agricultural Experiment Station. Oregon State University
Circ Inform Oreg State Coll Agr Exp Sta — Circular of Information. Oregon State College. Agricultural Experiment Station
Circ Inst Agron — Circular. Instituto Agronomico
Circ Inst Agron Norte (Brazil) — Circular. Instituto Agronomica do Norte (Brazil)
Circ Inst Agron Sul (Pelotas) — Circular. Instituto Agronomico do Sul (Pelotas)
Circ Inst Pesq Exp Agropecuar N — Circular. Instituto de Pesquisas e Experimentacao Agropecuarias do Norte
Circ Inst Pesqui Agropecu Norte — Circular. Instituto de Pesquisas Agropecuarias do Norte
Circ Inst Pesqui Agropecu Sul — Circular. Instituto de Pesquisas Agropecuarias do Sul
Cir Cir — Cirugia y Cirujanos
Cir Cirujanos — Cirugia y Cirujanos [*Mexico*]
Circ Kans Agr Exp Sta — Circular. Kansas Agricultural Experiment Station
Circ Kans Agric Exp Stn — Circular. Kansas Agricultural Experiment Station
Circ Kans State Univ Agr Appl Sci Ext Serv — Circular. Kansas State University of Agriculture and Applied Science. Extension Service
Circ KY Agric Exp Stn — Circular. Kentucky Agricultural Experiment Station
Circ KY Univ Agr Ext Serv — Circular. Kentucky University. Agricultural Extension Service
Circ LA Agr Exp Sta — Circular. Louisiana Agricultural Experiment Station
Circ Line Elevators Farm Serv — Circular. Line Elevators Farm Service
Circ Metab Cerveau — Circulation et Metabolisme du Cerveau
Circ Mont Agr Exp Sta — Circular. Montana Agricultural Experiment Station
Circ Mont State Coll Coop Ext Serv — Circular. Montana State College. Cooperative Extension Service
Circ MO Univ Coll Agr Ext Serv — Circular. Missouri University. College of Agriculture. Extension Service
Circ N Dak Agr Coll Agr Ext Serv — Circular. North Dakota Agricultural College. Agricultural Extension Service
Circ New Jers Agric Exp Stn — Circular. New Jersey Agricultural Experiment Station
Circ New Mex St Bur Mines Miner Resour — Circular. New Mexico State Bureau of Mines and Mineral Resources
Circ NJ Agr Exp Sta — Circular. New Jersey Agricultural Experiment Station
Circ NJ Agric Exp Stn — Circular. New Jersey Agricultural Experiment Station
Circ N Mex State Univ Agr Ext Serv — Circular. New Mexico State University. Agricultural Extension Service
Circ Okla State Univ Agr Appl Sci Agr Ext Serv — Circular. Oklahoma State University of Agriculture and Applied Science. Agricultural Extension Service
Circ Ont Dep Agric — Circular. Ontario Department of Agriculture
Circ Ore Agric Exp Stn — Circular. Oregon Agricultural Experiment Station
Circ Oreg State Coll Eng Exp — Circular. Oregon State College. Engineering Experiment Station
Circ Oreg State Univ Eng Exp St — Circular. Oregon State University. Engineering Experiment Station
Circ PA Agric Exp Stn — Circular. Pennsylvania Agricultural Experiment Station
Circ PA State Univ Earth Miner Sci Exp St — Circular. Pennsylvania State University. Earth and Mineral Sciences Experiment Station
Circ PA Univ Ext Serv — Circular. Pennsylvania University Extension Service
Circ Res — Circulation Research
Circ Res Suppl — Circulation Research. Supplement
Circ to Sch — Circular to Schools
Circ S Dak Agr Exp Sta — Circular. South Dakota Agricultural Experiment Station
Circ Secr Agr Secc Inform Publ Agr (Porto Alegre) — Circular. Secretaria da Agricultura. Seccao de Informacoes e Publicidade Agricola (Porto Alegre)
Circ Ser W Va Geol Econ Sur — Circular Series. West Virginia Geological and Economic Survey
Circ S Fla Agric Exp Stn — Circular. South Florida Agricultural Experiment Station
Circ Shock — Circulatory Shock
Circ Shock (Suppl) — Circulatory Shock (Supplement)
Circ Speleol Rom Not — Circolo Speleologico Romano. Notiziario
Circ Suppl — Circulation. Supplement
Circuits Manuf — Circuits Manufacturing
Circuits Mfg — Circuits Manufacturing
Circuits Syst — Circuits and Systems
Circular Com Parasitol Agric (Mexico) — Circular. Comision de Parasitologia Agricola (Mexico)
Circular Illinois Agric Exper Station — Circular. Illinois Agricultural Experiment Station
Circular West Virginia Agric Exper Station — Circular. West Virginia Agricultural Experiment Station
Circulation Res — Circulation Research

Circ Univ GA Coll Agr Coop Ext Serv — Circular. University of Georgia. College of Agriculture. Cooperative Extension Service
Circ Univ Ill Coll Agr Coop Ext Serv — Circular. University of Illinois. College of Agriculture. Cooperative Extension Service
Circ Univ KY Agr Ext Serv — Circular. University of Kentucky. Agricultural Extension Service
Circ Univ Nebr Coll Agr Home Econ Agr Exp Sta — Circular. University of Nebraska. College of Agriculture and Home Economics. Agricultural Experiment Station
Circ Univ Nev Max C Fleischmann Coll Agr Agr Ext Serv — Circular. University of Nevada. Max C. Fleischmann College of Agriculture. Agricultural Extension Service
Circ Univ Wis Coll Agr Ext Serv — Circular. University of Wisconsin. College of Agriculture. Extension Service
Circ Utah Agric Exp Stn — Circular. Utah Agricultural Experiment Station
Circ VA Polytech Inst Agr Ext Serv — Circular. Virginia Polytechnic Institute. Agricultural Extension Service
Circ Wash Agr Exp Sta — Circular. Washington Agriculture Experiment Station
Circ Wis Univ Agric Ext Serv — Circular. Wisconsin University of Agriculture. Extension Service
Circ Wyo Agric Ext Serv — Circular. Wyoming Agricultural Extension Service
Cir Div Food Res CSIRO — Circular. Division of Food Research. Commonwealth Scientific and Industrial Research Organisation
Cir Esp — Cirugia Espanola
CIRFAS — Canadian Industry Report of Fisheries and Aquatic Sciences
CIRIBK — Congres International de Reproduction Animale et Insemination Artificielle
Cirk Jordbrukstek Inst — Cirkulaer. Jordbrukstekniska Institutet
CIRND3 — Comunicaciones. INIA [*Instituto Nacional de Investigaciones Agrarias*]. Serie Recursos Naturales
CIRPHO — CIRPHO [*Cercle International de Recherches Philosophiques par Ordinateur*] Review
CIRQNS — Centre for International Relations. Queen's University. Northern Studies Series
CIRQNSS — Centre for International Relations. Queen's University. Northern Studies Series
Cir Ser Oreg State Coll Eng Exp Stn — Circular Series. Oregon State College. Engineering Experiment Station
Cir Urug — Cirugia del Uruguay
CIS — Cahiers Internationaux de Sociologie
CIS — Computer and Information Systems
CIS — Corpus Inscriptionum Semiticarum
CIS Abstr — CIS [*Congressional Information Service*] Abstracts on Cards
CISE Newsl — Library Association. University and Research Section. Colleges, Institutes, and Schools of Education Subsection. Newsletter
CISGDL — Comunicaciones. INIA [*Instituto Nacional de Investigaciones Agrarias*]. Serie General
CISI — CIS [*Congressional Information Service*] Index
CISIDR — Comunicaciones. INIA [*Instituto Nacional de Investigaciones Agrarias*]. Serie Proteccion Vegetal
CIS Ind — CIS [*Congressional Information Service*] Index
Cisl Metody Meh Splosn Stredy — Cislennye Metody Mehaniki Splosnoi Stredy
CistC — Cistercienserchronik
CISTDQ — Comunicaciones. INIA [*Instituto Nacional de Investigaciones Agrarias*]. Serie Tecnologia Agraria
Cist Stud — Cistercian Studies
CiT — Ciencia Tomista
Cit — Citeaux
CIT — Commerce International
CITE — CITES Reports. Convention on International Trade in Endangered Species of Wild Fauna and Flora
CITEA — Chemie-Ingenieur-Technik
Cit God — City of God
Citibank — Citibank. Monthly Economic Letter
Citibank Mo Econ Letter — Citibank. Monthly Economic Letter
Citin Gos Ped Inst Ucen Zap — Citinskii Gosudarstvennyi Pedagogiceskii Institut. Ucenye Zapiski
CITJD — Chartered Institute of Transport. Journal
CITMD — Cahiers d'Informations Techniques/Revue de Metallurgie
CitN — Citeaux in de Nederlande
CiTom — La Ciencia Tomista [*Salamanca*]
Citrus Grow — Citrus Grower
Citrus Grow Sub-Trop Fruit J — Citrus Grower and Sub-Tropical Fruit Journal
Citrus Ind — Citrus Industry
Citrus Mag — Citrus Magazine
Citrus Subtrop Fruit J — Citrus and Subtropical Fruit Journal [*South Africa*]
Citrus Veg Mag — Citrus and Vegetable Magazine
City Adelaide Munic Yb — Adelaide. City. Municipal Year Book
City Stoke-On-Trent Mus Archaeol Soc Rep — City of Stoke-On-Trent Museum. Archaeological Society. Reports
CIV — Civilisations
CivCatt — La Civilta Cattolica [*Rome*]
Civ Def Bull — Civil Defence Bulletin
Civ Develop — Civic Development

Civ Eng — Civil Engineering
Civ Eng Constr Public Works J — Civil Engineering, Construction, and Public Works Journal [*India*]
Civ Eng Contract — Civil Engineering Contractor
Civ Eng Jpn — Civil Engineering in Japan
Civ Engng — Civil Engineering [*London*]
Civ Engng ASCE — Civil Engineering. American Society of Civil Engineers
Civ Engn (GB) — Civil Engineering (Great Britain)
Civ Engng (Lond) — Civil Engineering (London)
Civ Engng Pract & Des Engrs — Civil Engineering for Practicing and Design Engineers
Civ Engng Publ Wks Rev — Civil Engineering and Public Works Review
Civ Engng Trans — Civil Engineering Transactions. Institution of Engineers of Australia
Civ Engng Trans Instn Engrs Aust — Civil Engineering Transactions. Institution of Engineers of Australia
Civ Eng (NY) — Civil Engineering (New York)
Civ Eng Public Works Rev — Civil Engineering and Public Works Review
Civ Eng Pub Works Rev — Civil Engineering and Public Works Review
Civ Eng S Afr — Civil Engineering in South Africa
Civ Eng Trans Inst Eng Aust — Civil Engineering Transactions. Institution of Engineers of Australia
Civic Dev — Civic Development
Civil Aero J — Civil Aeronautics Administration. Journal
Civil Defence Bul — Civil Defence Bulletin
Civil Eng — Civil Engineering
Civil Engineering ASCE — Civil Engineering. American Society of Civil Engineers
Civil Enging — Civil Engineering
Civil Enging Practicing Des Engrs — Civil Engineering for Practicing and Design Engineers
Civil Enging Surv — Civil Engineering Surveyor
Civil Liberties R — Civil Liberties Review
Civil Liberties Rev — Civil Liberties Review
Civil Rights Dig — Civil Rights Digest
Civil Rights Research R — Civil Rights Research Review
Civilta Catt — Civilta Cattolica
Civilta Macch — Civilta delle Macchine
Civil War H — Civil War History
Civil War Hist — Civil War History
Civ Lib Rev — Civil Liberties Review
Civ Lib Rptr — Civil Liberties Reporter
Civ & Military LJ — Civil and Military Law Journal
Civ and Mil LJ — Civil and Military Law Journal
Civ Rights Digest — Civil Rights Digest
Civ Rts Dig — Civil Rights Digest
Civ Serv J — Civil Service Journal
CIVTA4 — Congres International de la Vigne du Vin
Civ War Times Illus — Civil War Times Illustrated
CIWDSS — Canada. Inland Waters Directorate. Scientific Series
CIWDSSS — Canada. Inland Waters Directorate. Social Science Series
CIWDTB — Canada. Inland Waters Directorate. Technical Bulletin
CIWPAV — Carnegie Institution of Washington. Publication
CIWQIR — Canada. Inland Waters Directorate. Water Quality Interpretive Reports
CIWYAO — Carnegie Institution of Washington. Year Book
CIZSAL — Conseil International pour l'Exploration de la Mer. Zooplankton Sheet
CJ — Cambridge Journal
CJ — Canadian Journal of Economics
CJ — Chamber's Journal
CJ — Choral Journal
CJ — Cinema Journal
CJ — Classical Journal
CJ — Computer Journal [*British*]
CJ — Concordia Journal
CJ — Conservative Judaism
CJ — Coyote's Journal
CJA — Canadian Journal of Archaeology
CJA — Christlich-Juedische Arbeitsgemeinschaft
CJa — Cizi Jazyky ve Skole
CJAfS — Caribbean Journal of African Studies
CJap — Contemporary Japan
CJAS — Canadian Journal of African Studies
CJB — Columbia Journal of World Business
CJBIA — Canadian Journal of Biochemistry
CJBO — Canadian Journal of Botany
CJBOA — Canadian Journal of Botany
CJC — Cahiers Jean Cocteau
CJCE — Canadian Journal of Civil Engineering
CJCEA — Canadian Journal of Chemical Engineering
CJCHA — Canadian Journal of Chemistry
CJCMA — Canadian Journal of Comparative Medicine
CJD — Canadian Journal of Economics
CJE — Canadian Journal of Economics

CJE — Canadian Journal of Economics and Political Science [*Later, Canadian Journal of Economics*]
CJECB — Canadian Journal of Economics
CJEPS — Canadian Journal of Economics and Political Science [*Later, Canadian Journal of Economics*]
CJES — Canadian Journal of Earth Sciences
CJESA — Canadian Journal of Earth Sciences
CJF — Chicago Jewish Forum
CJFA — Canadian Journal of Fisheries and Aquatic Sciences
CJFR — Canadian Journal of Forest Research
CJG — Cahiers Jean Giraudoux
CJH — Canadian Journal of History
C J It S — Canadian Journal of Italian Studies
CJL — Canadian Journal of Linguistics
CJL — Cesky Jazyk a Literatura
CJL — Columbia Journal of Law and Social Problems
CJLit — Cesky Jazyk a Literatura
CJMAA — Canadian Journal of Mathematics
CJ(Malta) — Classical Journal (Malta)
CJMBAE — Chinese Journal of Microbiology [*Later, Chinese Journal of Microbiology and Immunology*]
CJMED — Chung-Ang Journal of Medicine
CJMEDQ — Chung-Ang Journal of Medicine
CJMGA — California Journal of Mines and Geology
CJMIA — Canadian Journal of Microbiology
CJMTA — Canadian Journal of Medical Technology
CJN — Canadian Jewish News
CJN — Canadian Journal of Anthropology
CJNE — Canadian Journal of Native Education
CJNS — Canadian Journal of Native Studies
CJOA — Canadian Journal on Aging
CJOL — Chinese Journal of Oceanology and Limnology
CJOPA — Chinese Journal of Physics [*Taipei*]
CJORD — Columbia Journalism Review
CJOSD — Chungnam Journal of Sciences
CJP — Canadian Journal of Psychology
CJPEA — Canadian Journal of Public Health
CJPH — Canadian Journal of Public Health
CJPHA — Canadian Journal of Physics
CJPhil — Canadian Journal of Philosophy
CJPI — Criminal Justice Periodical Index [*University Microfilms International*] [*Ann Arbor, MI*] [*Bibliographic database*]
CJPPA — Canadian Journal of Physiology and Pharmacology
CJPs — Canadian Journal of Psychology
CJPSA — Canadian Journal of Psychology
CJPYA — Chinese Journal of Physiology
CJR — Chicago Journalism Review
CJR — Columbia Journalism Review
CJR — Contemporary Jewish Record [*New York*]
CJS — Cizi Jazyky ve Skole
CJSSA — Canadian Journal of Soil Science
CJSUA — Canadian Journal of Surgery
CJT — Canadian Journal of Theology
CJU — Conjuntura Economica
CJUADK — Contact. Journal of Urban and Environmental Affairs
CJVS — Cizi Jazyky ve Skole
CJW — Columbia Journal of World Business
CJZ — Canadian Journal of Zoology
CJZOA — Canadian Journal of Zoology
CK — Chicago-Kent Law Review
CKCFA — Ceskoslovensky Casopis pro Fysiku
CKCKD — Chung-Kuo Kung Ch'eng Hsueh K'an
CKD — Casopis Katolickeko Duckovenstva a Prilohou
CKD — Chambre de Commerce et d'Industrie. Republique Populaire du Benin. Bulletin Hebdomadaire d'Information et de Documentation
CKHMA — Chung-Kuo Hsu Mu Shou I
CKI — Central Bank of Ireland. Quarterly Bulletin
CKKKA — Cho-Koon Kenkyu
CKLR — Chicago-Kent Law Review
CKN — Chambre de Commerce, d'Agriculture, et d'Industrie du Niger. Bulletin
CKNHA — Chung-Kuo Nung Yeh Hua Hsueh Hui Chih
CKNKD — Chikyukagaku (Nippon Chikyu Kagakkai)
CKNKDM — Geochemistry [*Later, Geochemistry International*]
CKNSA — Chiba-Ken Nogyo Shikenjo Kenkyu Hokoku
CKNYA — Chung-Kuo Nung Yeh K'o Hsueh
CKP — Central Bank of Cyprus. Bulletin
CKTND — Chayon Kwahak Taehak Nomunjip
CKWCD9 — Chinese Journal of Microbiology and Immunology [*Taipei*]
CKYW — Chung-Kuo Yu-Wen
CL — Ceska Literatura
C and L — Christianity and Literature
Cl — Clavier
Cl — Clavileno
CL — Comparative Literature
CL — Cuadernos de Literatura

CL — Current Law Year Book
CLA — Children's Literature Abstracts
CLA — Collections Litteratures Africaines
CLA — College Language Association. Journal
CLAB — Commercial Law Association. Bulletin
CLA Bull — Colorado Library Association. Bulletin
CLA Bulletin — Commercial Law Association. Bulletin
CLADA — Crystal Lattice Defects
CLAGB — Clinical Allergy [*England*]
CLAJ — CLA [*College Language Association*] Journal
CLAND — Computer Languages
Clan Gunn Soc Mag — Clan Gunn Society. Magazine
Clan MacLeod Mag — Clan MacLeod Magazine
Clan Munro Mag — Clan Munro Magazine
Clare Q — Claremont Quarterly
Clarke Inst Psychiatry Monogr Ser — Clarke Institute of Psychiatry. Monograph Series
Class B — Classical Bulletin
ClassBull — Classical Bulletin [*St. Louis, MO*]
Classic — Classic Images
Classical J — Classical Journal
Classical Philol — Classical Philology
Classical Q — Classical Quarterly
Classic F Col — Classic Film Collector
Classic Jnl — Classical Journal
Classic World — Classical World
Class J — Classical Journal
ClassMed — Classica et Mediaevalia [*Aarhus*]
Class Mod L — Classical and Modern Literature
Class Out — Classical Outlook
ClassPh — Classical Philology [*Chicago*]
Class Phil — Classical Philology
Class Philol — Classical Philology
Class Q — Classical Quarterly
Class R — Classical Review
Class Rev — Classical Review
Class Rev N Ser — Classical Review. New Series
Class R ns — Classical Review. New Series
Class Soc Bull — Classification Society. Bulletin
ClassW — Classical Weekly [*New York*]
Class W — Classical World
Class World — Classical World
CLATDP — Compendium de Investigaciones Clinicas Latinoamericanas
ClaudelS — Claudel Studies
Claudel St — Claudel Studies
Clausthaler Geol Abh — Clausthaler Geologische Abhandlungen
Clausthaler Hefte Lagerstaettenk Geochemie Miner Rohst — Clausthaler Hefte zur Lagerstaettenkund und Geochemie der Mineralischen Rohstoffe
Clav — Clavileno
CLAVA — Clavier
CLAWA — Clarinet
Clay Clay M — Clays and Clay Minerals
Claycraft Struct Ceram — Claycraft and Structural Ceramics
Clay Miner — Clay Minerals
Clay Miner Bull — Clay Minerals. Bulletin [*Later, Clay Minerals*]
Clay Prod J — Clay Products Journal of Australia
Clay Prod J Aust — Clay Products Journal of Australia
Clay Prod J Austr — Clay Products Journal of Australia
Clay Sci (Tokyo) — Clay Science (Tokyo)
Clays Clay Miner — Clays and Clay Minerals
CLB — Commonwealth Law Bulletin
CLB — Communications Law Bulletin
CLBCBB — Cardiologisches Bulletin
CLBIA — Clinical Biochemistry [*Ottawa*]
CLBUA — Clinical Bulletin
CLC — Columbia Library. Columns
CLC — Company Law Cases
CLC — Cuadernos de Literatura Contemporanea
CLCAA9 — Cellulosa e Carta
CLCEA — Casopis Lekaru Ceskych
CLCEAL — Casopis Lekaru Ceskych
CLCHA — Clinical Chemistry [*Winston-Salem, North Carolina*]
CLCHD — Climatic Change
CLCL — Computational Linguistics and Computer Languages
CL & CL Comput Linguist Comput Lang — CL & CL. Computational Linguistics and Computer Languages [*Budapest*]
CLCNB — Clinician [*Panjim-Goa, India*]
CLD — California Library Directory
CLD — Central Bank of Malta. Quarterly Review
CLDFAT — Cell Differentiation
CLe — Cahiers de Lexicologie
CLE — Cahiers. Ligue Catholique de l'Evangile
Clean Air J — Clean Air Journal
Clean Air Spec Ed — Clean Air. Special Edition
Clean Fuels Biomass Wastes Symp Pap — Clean Fuels from Biomass and Wastes. Symposium Papers

Cleaning Maint Big Bldg Mgmt — Cleaning Maintenance and Big Building Management
CLEAR — Chinese Literature. Essays, Articles, Reviews
Clear H — Clearing House
Clearing H — Clearing House
Clearing House J — Clearing House Journal
Clearinghouse Rev — Clearinghouse Review
CLEB — Comunidad Latinoamericana de Escritores. Boletin
CLECA — Clinical Endocrinology
Clef Pal J — Cleft Palate Journal
CleM — [The] Clergy Monthly [Ranchi, Bihar, India]
CLEM — Contact List of Electronic Music [Canada]
Clemson Univ Coll Eng Eng Exp Sta Bull — Clemson University [Clemson, South Carolina]. College of Engineering. Engineerig Experiment Station. Bulletin
Clemson Univ Coll For Recreat Resour Dep For For Res Ser — Clemson University. College of Forest and Recreation Resources. Department of Forestry. Forest Research Series
Clemson Univ Dep For For Bull — Clemson University. Department of Forestry. Forestry Bulletin
Clemson Univ Dep For For Res Ser — Clemson University. Department of Forestry. Forest Research Series
Clemson Univ Dep For Tech Pap — Clemson University. Department of Forestry. Technical Paper
Clemson Univ Rev Ind Manage Text Sci — Clemson University. Review of Industrial Management and Textile Science
ClergyM — [The] Clergy Monthly [Ranchi, Bihar, India]
ClergyR — [The] Clergy Review [London]
Clermont Univ Ann Sci Geol Mineral — Clermont. Universite. Annales Scientifiques. Geologie et Mineralogie
C Let Dram — Cineschedario-Letture Drammatiche
Clev B A J — Cleveland Bar Association. Journal
Clev Bar Ass'n J — Cleveland Bar Association. Journal
Clev B Assn J — Cleveland Bar Association. Journal
Cleve Busn — Crain's Cleveland Business
Cleve Clin Q — Cleveland Clinic. Quarterly
Cleveland Clin Cardiovasc Consult — Cleveland Clinic. Cardiovascular Consultations
Cleveland Clin Q — Cleveland Clinic. Quarterly
Cleveland Inst Eng Proc — Cleveland Institution of Engineers. Proceedings
Cleveland Med J — Cleveland Medical Journal
Cleveland Mus Bull — Cleveland Museum of Art. Bulletin
Cleveland Mus Nat History Mus News — Cleveland Museum of Natural History. Museum News
Cleveland Mus Nat History Sci Pubs — Cleveland Museum of Natural History. Science Publications
Cleveland Symp Macromol — Cleveland Symposium on Macromolecules
Clev-Mar L Rev — Cleveland-Marshall Law Review
Clev Orch — Cleveland Orchestra. Program Notes
Clev St L R — Cleveland State Law Review
Clev St L Rev — Cleveland State Law Review
CLex — Cahiers de Lexicologie
CLF — Chronique des Lettres Francaises
CLF — Club du Livre Francais
CLGAAT — Colorado. Agricultural Experiment Station. Annual Report
CLGNA — Clinical Genetics
CLGR — Clinical Gerontologist
CLGUA — Colliery Guardian [England]
CLH — Canadian Library Handbook
CLHMD — Cahiers. Laboratoire d'Hydrobiologie de Montereau
CLi — Christian Librarian
CLi — Cuadernos de Literatura
CLid — Cesky Lid
C Life — Christian Life
C Ligures Prehist Archeol — Cahiers Ligures de Prehistoire et d'Archeologie
CLIIA — Clinical Immunology and Immunopathology
Clima Comm Internat — Clima Commerce International
Climat Data — Climatological Data
CLIMB8 — Cellular Immunology
Clim Change — Climatic Change
Clim Control — Climate Control [India]
CLin — Cercetari de Linguistica
Clin Allergy — Clinical Allergy
Clin All-Round — Clinic All-Round [Japan]
Clin Anaesthesiol — Clinics in Anaesthesiology
Clin Anesth — Clinical Anesthesia
Clin Approaches Probl Child — Clinical Approaches to Problems of Childhood
Clin Bacteriol (Tokyo) — Clinical Bacteriology (Tokyo)
Clin Bioch — Clinical Biochemistry
Clin Biochem — Clinical Biochemistry
Clin Biochem Anal — Clinical and Biochemical Analysis
Clin Bull — Clinical Bulletin
Clin Bull (Mem Sloan-Kettering Cancer Cent) — Clinical Bulletin (Memorial Sloan-Kettering Cancer Center)
Clin Cardiol — Clinical Cardiology
Clin Chem — Clinical Chemistry

Clin Chem (Winston Salem North Carolina) — Clinical Chemistry (Winston-Salem, North Carolina)
Clin Chest Med — Clinics in Chest Medicine
Clin Chim A — Clinica Chimica Acta
Clin Chim Acta — Clinica Chimica Acta
Clin Cytol Ser Monogr — Clinical Cytology: A Series of Monographs
Clin EEG — Clinical Electroencephalography
Clin Electr — Clinical Electroencephalography
Clin Electroencephalogr — Clinical Electroencephalography
Clin End Me — Clinics in Endocrinology and Metabolism
Clin Endocr — Clinical Endocrinology
Clin Endocrinol — Clinical Endocrinology
Clin Endocrinol Metab — Clinical Endocrinology and Metabolism
Clin Eng — Clinical Engineering
Clin Engineer — Clinical Engineer
Clin Eur — Clinica Europa
Clin Exp Dermatol — Clinical and Experimental Dermatology
Clin Exp Dial Apheresis — Clinical and Experimental Dialysis and Apheresis
Clin Exp Hypertens — Clinical and Experimental Hypertension
Clin Exp Im — Clinical and Experimental Immunology
Clin Exp Immunol — Clinical and Experimental Immunology
Clin Exp Immunoreprod — Clinical and Experimental Immunoreproduction
Clin Exp Neurol — Clinical and Experimental Neurology
Clin Exp Nutr — Clinical and Experimental Nutrition
Clin Exp Obstet Gynecol — Clinical and Experimental Obstetrics and Gynecology
Clin Exp Ph — Clinical and Experimental Pharmacology and Physiology
Clin Exp Pharmacol Physiol Suppl — Clinical and Experimental Pharmacology and Physiology. Supplement
Clin Exp Pharmcol Physiol — Clinical and Experimental Pharmacology and Physiology
C Ling — Cercetari de Linguistica
Clin Gastro — Clinics in Gastroenterology
Clin Genet — Clinical Genetics
Clin Geral (Sao Paulo) — Clinica Geral (Sao Paulo)
Clin Ginecol — Clinica Ginecologica
Clin Haemat — Clinics in Haematology
Clin Haematol — Clinics in Haematology
Clin Hig Hidrol — Clinica Higiene e Hidrologia
Clinica Chim Acta — Clinica Chimica Acta
Clinica Pediat — Clinica Pediatrica
Clinica Terap — Clinica Terapeutica
Clin Immun — Clinical Immunology and Immunopathology
Clin Immunol Immunopathol — Clinical Immunology and Immunopathology
Clin Invest Med — Clinical and Investigative Medicine
Clin Lab — Clinica y Laboratoria
Clin Lab Haematol — Clinical and Laboratory Haematology
Clin Latina — Clinica Latina
Clin Libr Q — Clinical Librarian Quarterly
Clin Manage Phys Ther — Clinical Management in Physical Therapy
Clin Med — Clinical Medicine
Clin Med Ital — Clinica Medical Italiana
Clin Med Surg — Clinical Medicine and Surgery
Clin Nephrol — Clinical Nephrology
Clin Neurol — Clinical Neurology and Neurosurgery
Clin Neurol Neurosurg — Clinical Neurology and Neurosurgery
Clin Neurol (Tokyo) — Clinical Neurology (Tokyo)
Clin Neuropharmacol — Clinical Neuropharmacology
Clin Neurosurg — Clinical Neurosurgery
Clin Notes Respir Dis — Clinical Notes on Respiratory Diseases
Clin Nucl Med — Clinical Nuclear Medicine
Clin Nutr — Clinical Nutrition
Clin Obstet Gynecol — Clinical Obstetrics and Gynecology
Clin Oncol — Clinical Oncology
Clin Oncol (Tianjin) — Clinical Oncology (Tianjin)
Clin Ophtalmol — Clinique Ophtalmologique
Clin Orthop — Clinical Orthopaedics
Clin Orthop — Clinical Orthopaedics and Related Research
Clin Orthop Relat Res — Clinical Orthopaedics and Related Research
Clin Orthop Surg — Clinical Orthopedic Surgery [Japan]
Clin Ortop — Clinica Ortopedica
Clin Ostet Ginecol — Clinica Ostetrica e Ginecologica
Clin Otolaryngol — Clinical Otolaryngology
Clin Otorinolaringoiatr (Catania) — Clinica Otorinolaringoiatrica (Catania)
Clin Pediat — Clinica Pediatrica
Clin Pediat — Clinical Pediatrics [Philadelphia]
Clin Pediatr — Clinical Pediatrics
Clin Pediatr (Phila) — Clinical Pediatrics (Philadelphia)
Clin Pediatr (Philadelphia) — Clinical Pediatrics (Philadelphia)
Clin Perinatol — Clinics in Perinatology
Clin Pharm — Clinical Pharmacology and Therapeutics
Clin Pharmacokinet — Clinical Pharmacokinetics
Clin Pharmacol Ther — Clinical Pharmacology and Therapeutics
Clin Phys and Physiol Meas — Clinical Physics and Physiological Measurement
Clin Plast Surg — Clinics in Plastic Surgery

Clin Proc Child Hosp DC — Clinical Proceedings. Children's Hospital of the District of Columbia [*Later, Children's Hospital National Medical Center*]. Clinical Proceedings
Clin Proc Child Hosp Natl Med Cent — Clinical Proceedings. Children's Hospital National Medical Center
Clin Psychiatr — Clinical Psychiatry [*Japan*]
Clin Radiol — Clinical Radiology
Clin Rep — Clinical Report [*Japan*]
Clin Reprod Neuroendocrinol Int Semin — Clinical Reproductive Neuroendocrinology. International Seminar on Reproductive Physiology and Sexual Endocrinology
Clin Res — Clinical Research
Clin Res Cent Symp (Harrow Engl) — Clinical Research Centre. Symposium (Harrow, England)
Clin Rheum Dis — Clinics in Rheumatic Diseases
Clin Sci — Clinical Science [*Oxford*] [*Later, Clinical Science and Molecular Medicine*]
Clin Sci Mol Med — Clinical Science and Molecular Medicine [*Oxford*]
Clin Sci Mol Med Suppl — Clinical Science and Molecular Medicine. Supplement
Clin Sci (Oxf) — Clinical Science (Oxford) [*Later, Clinical Science and Molecular Medicine*]
Clin Sci Suppl — Clinical Science. Supplement
Clin Sc Mol — Clinical Science and Molecular Medicine [*Oxford*]
Clin Surg — Clinical Surgery [*Japan*]
Clin S Work — Clinical Social Work Journal
Clin Symp — Clinical Symposia
Clin Ter — Clinica Terapeutica
Clin Ther — Clinical Therapeutics
Clin Toxic — Clinical Toxicology
Clin Toxicol — Clinical Toxicology
Clin Toxicol Bull — Clinical Toxicology. Bulletin
Clin Vet (Milan) — Clinica Veterinaria (Milan)
Clio Med — Clio Medica
CLit — Ceska Literatura
CLit — Convorbiri Literare
CLit — Correo Literario
CLJ — Cambridge Law Journal
CLJ — Canadian Library Journal
CLJ — Classical Journal
CLJ — Cornell Library Journal
CLJ — Criminal Law Journal
CLJ — Criminal Law Journal of India
CLLA — Cahiers de Litterature et de Linguistique Appliquee
CLLAN — Collection Langues et Litteratures de l'Afrique Noire
CLLR — Crown Lands Law Reports
CLM — Chinese Literature Monthly
ClM — [*The*] Clergy Monthly [*Ranchi, Bihar, India*]
CLMBB — College Music Symposium
Cl Med — Classica et Mediaevalia
CLMJA — California Mining Journal
CLMO — Climate Monitor. Climatic Research Unit. University of East Anglia
ClMthly — Clergy Monthly
CLN — Chemical and Engineering News
CLN — Children's Libraries Newsletter
CLNEA — Clinical Neurosurgery
CLNL — Comparative Literature News-Letter
CLO — Cahiers Linguistiques d'Ottawa
CLOND — Clinical Oncology
CLP — Classical Philology
CLP — Current Legal Problems
CLPCA — Chung-Kuo K'o-Hsueh-Yuan Lan-Chou Hua-Hsueh Wu-Li Yen-Chiu-So Yen-Chiu Pao-Kao Chi-K An
CLPED — Clinics in Perinatology
CLPJA — Cleft Palate Journal
CLPNAB — Collective Phenomena [*London*]
CLPTA — Clinical Pharmacology and Therapeutics
Cl Q — Classical Quarterly
CLQ — Colby Library. Quarterly
CLQ — Cornell Law Quarterly
CL (Q) — Crown Lands Law Reports (Queensland)
CLR — Children's Literature Review
Cl R — Classical Review
ClR — [*The*] Clergy Review [*London*]
CLR — Columbia Law Review
CLR — Commonwealth Law Reports
CLR — Crown Lands Law Reports
CLRAA — Clinical Radiology
CLR (Aust) — Commonwealth Law Reports (Australia)
CLRDA — CLR [*Council on Library Resources*] Recent Developments
CLREA — Clinical Research
CL Rev — California Law Review
ClRh — Clara Rhodos
CLR Recent Devt — CLR [*Council on Library Resources*] Recent Developments
CLS — California Library Statistics

CLS — Charles Lamb Society. Bulletin
CLS — Comparative Literature Studies
CLSAP — Canon Law Society of America. Proceedings
CLSB — Charles Lamb Society. Bulletin
CLSJ — Company and Securities Law Journal
CLSOAT — Contact Lens Society of America. Journal
CLS Q — CLS [*Christian Legal Society*] Quarterly
Clt — Culture
CLTA — Cahiers de Linguistique Theorique et Appliquee
CLTPD — Chi Lin Ta Hsueh Hsueh Pao. Tzu Jan K'o Hsueh Pan
CLTS — Contributions. Institute of Low Temperature Science [*Japan*]
CLU — CLU [*Chartered Life Underwriters*] Journal
Club Ser Univ NC State Coll Agr Eng Agr Ext Serv — Club Series. University of North Carolina. State College of Agriculture and Engineering. Agricultural Extension Service
CLU J — CLU [*Chartered Life Underwriters*] Journal
Cluj Med — Clujul Medical
CLUQ — Cahiers de Linguistique. Universite du Quebec
Clustering Phenom Nuclei — Clustering Phenomena in Nuclei [*Vieweg, Braunschweig*]
CLW — Catholic Library World
Cl Weekly — Classical Weekly
CLYB — Current Law Year Book
CM — Cahiers Maynard
CM — Canadian Materials
CM — Canadian Mining Journal
CM — Carleton Miscellany
CM — Century Magazine
CM — Church Musician
CM — Civilta Moderna
C & M — Classica et Mediaevalia
CM — Classica et Mediaevalia
CM — Cleveland-Marshall Law Review
CM — Clio Medica
CM — Coins, Incorporating Coins and Medals
CM — Colloquia Mathematica. Societatis Janos Bolyai [*Elsevier Book Series*]
CM — Colorado Magazine
CM — Construction Management [*A publication*]
CM — Cornhill Magazine
CMAGD — Chemisch Magazine
C Magic — Cinemagic
CMAJ — Canadian Medical Association. Journal
CMAJA — Canadian Medical Association. Journal
CMAnnual — Coins Annual
CMAUA — Chemoautomatyka
CMAZAD — Comunicaciones. Museo Argentino de Ciencias Naturales "Bernardino Rivadavia" e Instituto Nacional de Investigacion de las Ciencias Naturales. Zoologia
CMBI — Commentationes Biologicae. Societas Scientiarum Fennica
CMBID4 — Cellular and Molecular Biology
CMBUA — Canadian Mathematical Bulletin
CMC — Coins, Medals, and Currency Weekly
CMC — Crosscurrents/Modern Critiques
C Mc — Current Musicology
CMCB — Comments on Molecular and Cellular Biophysics
CMCD — Coins, Medals, and Currency Digest and Monthly Catalogue
CMCEA — Commerce [*India*]
CMCHA — Canadian Machinery and Metalworking
Cmcl Law Assoc Bull — Commercial Law Association. Bulletin
CMCPDU — Comunicacoes. Museu de Ciencias. PUCRGS [*Pontificia Universidade Catolica do Rio Grande Do Sul*]
CMCYEO — Cell Motility and the Cytoskeleton
CMD — California Management Review
CMDCDU — Congressi Italiani di Medicina
CME — Chartered Mechanical Engineer
CMEDD4 — Cardiovascular Medicine
CMEDSTR — Canada. Marine Environmental Data Service. Technical Report
CMENA — Chemical and Metallurgical Engineering
CMEW — Comparative Medicine East and West
CMEWDR — Comparative Medicine East and West
CMF — Casopis pro Moderni Filologii
CMF — Crosscurrents/Modern Fiction
CMF — Yugoslavia Export
CMFAAV — Communications. Faculte des Sciences. Universite d'Ankara
CMFL — Casopis pro Moderni Filologii a Literatury
CMFRI Bull — CMFRI [*Central Marine Fisheries Research Institute*] Bulletin
CMG — Consumentengids
CMGEA — Geological Survey of Canada. Bulletin
CMGEAE — Geological Survey of Canada. Bulletin
CMGPA — Centralblatt fuer Mineralogie, Geologie, und Palaeontologie
CMH — Cambridge Mediaeval History
CMHJAY — Community Mental Health Journal
CMI — Chemical Week
CMI — Coping with Medical Issues [*Elsevier Book Series*]
CMICA — Canada. Mines Branch. Information Circular

CMIDB — Chemischer Informationsdienst
CMI Descr Pathog Fungi Bact — CMI [*Commonwealth Mycological Institute*] Descriptions of Pathogenic Fungi and Bacteria
CMIMAE — Commonwealth Mycological Institute. Mycological Papers
CMIPB — Cahiers de Medecine Interprofessionnelle
CMIS — Change to Metric Information Service
CMJ — Canadian Mining Journal
CMJ — Czechoslovak Mathematical Journal
CMJODS — Chinese Medical Journal [*English Edition*]
CMJPB — Community and Junior College Journal
CMJUA9 — Caribbean Medical Journal
CMK — Compendium. Dagelijks Overzicht van de Buitenlandse Pers
CMKRA — Chemical Marketing Reporter
CMKZA — Chemiker-Zeitung
CML — Chambre de Commerce France Amerique Latine
CML — Classical and Modern Literature: A Quarterly
CML — Club du Meilleur Livre
CML — Commercial Law Journal
CMLR — Canadian Modern Language Review
CMLR — Cleveland-Marshall Law Review
CMLR — Common Market Law Reports
CMM — Casopis Matice Moravske
CMM — Chemical Engineering. Chemical Technology for Profit Minded Engineers
CMMBA — Canadian Mining and Metallurgical Bulletin
CMMBE5 — Cell Culture Methods for Molecular and Cell Biology
CMMSC — Chislennye Metody Mekhaniki Sploshnoi Sredy
Cmmty Serv — Community Service Newsletter
CMN — Cellular and Molecular Neurobiology
CMN — Common Market News [*London*]
CMNEDI — Cellular and Molecular Neurobiology
CMNLD — Chamber of Mines. Newsletter [*South Africa*]
CMO — Computers and Operations Research
CMo — Creative Moment
C₁ Mol Chem — C₁ Molecule Chemistry
C Monde Hisp Luso-Bresil — Cahiers du Monde Hispanique et Luso-Bresilien
C Monde Russe Sov — Cahiers du Monde Russe et Sovietique
CMONDG — Computer Monographs
CMonth — Coin Monthly
CMOPAJ — Casopis Narodniho Muzea v Praze. Rada Prirodovedna
CMORA — Computers and Operations Research
CMORAP — Computers and Operations Research
CMOTDY — Cell Motility
CMP — CMP Newsletter
CMPBEK — Computer Methods and Programs in Biomedicine
CMPHA — Communications in Mathematical Physics
CMPLDF — Complement
CMPMA — Compositio Mathematica
CMPRB — Coal Mining and Processing
CMPSD — Culture, Medicine, and Psychiatry
CMPYAH — Commonwealth Mycological Institute. Phytopathological Papers
CMPZBL — Comunicacoes. Museu de Ciencias. PUCRGS [*Pontificia Universidade Catolica do Rio Grande Do Sul*]. Serie Zoologia
CMQ — Tijdschrift voor Marketing
CMR — California Management Review
CMR 17 — Centre Meridional de Recherche sur le Dix-Septieme Siecle
CMRAD — Camera
CMR Chem Bus — Chemical Business (Supplement to Chemical Marketing Reporter)
CMRDM — Corpus Monumentorum Religionis Dei Menis
CMRFAS — Canadian Manuscript Report of Fisheries and Aquatic Sciences
CMRPD3 — Cardiovascular Medicine [*New York*]
CMRS — Cahiers du Monde Russe et Sovietique
CMS — College Music Symposium
CMSCA — Contributions in Marine Science
CMSDMR — Canada. Marine Sciences Directorate. Department of Fisheries and Oceans. Manuscript Report
CMSRAB — Communications. Research Institute of the Sumatra Planters' Association. Rubber Series
CMTBB — Canada. Mines Branch. Technical Bulletin
CMTLBX — Food Chemistry, Microbiology, Technology
CMTS — Clarendon Medieval and Tudor Series
CMUC — Commentationes Mathematicae. Universitatis Carolinae
CMUE B — Council for Research in Music Education. Bulletin
CMUED — Contributions to Music Education
CMUMD9 — Cell and Muscle Motility
CMUTB — Chemieunterricht
CMXPAU — Chirurgia Maxillofacialis et Plastica
CMYBA — Canadian Minerals Yearbook
CN — Calcoin News
Cn — Center Magazine
CN — Clinical Nephrology
CN — Consultants News
CN — Cornishman
CN — Cultura Neolatina
CNA — Canadian Advertising Rates and Data

CNABAG — Connecticut. Agricultural Experiment Station. Bulletin [*New Haven*]
CNACAJ — Connecticut. Agricultural Experiment Station. Circular [*New Haven*]
CNAIB — Clean Air (Brighton, England)
CNASAX — Chugoku Nogyo Shikenjo Hokoku. A. Sakumotsu-Bu
CNat — Cahiers des Naturalistes
CNBUAA — Connecticut. Storrs Agricultural Experiment Station. Bulletin
CNCBAQ — Comunicaciones. Instituto Nacional de Investigacion de las Ciencias Naturales. Ciencias Botanicas
CNCCA — Canadian Cancer Conference
CNCNAS — Contamination Control
CNDBA — Bulletin. Cincinnati Dental Society
CNDIB — Cahiers de Notes Documentaires
CNDLAR — Candollea
CNE Commun Navig Electron — CNE. Communication/Navigation Electronics
CNEKAT — Chugoku Nogyo Shikenjo Hokoku. E. Kankyo-Bu
CNEP Bol — CNEP [*Comision Nacional para la Erradicacion del Paludismo*] Boletin
CNew — Carlyle Newsletter
CNEWA — Chemical News
C News — Cinemanews
CNF — Consudel. Maandblad voor de Benelux, Gewijd aan de Belangen van Industrie en Handel op het Gebied van Cacao, Chocolade, Suikerwerken, Koek, Banket, Biscuit Enz
CNFI — Christian News from Israel
CNFRA Com Nat Fr Rech Antarct — CNFRA. Comite National Francais des Recherches Antarctiques
CNFS Commer News For Serv — CNFS. Commercial News for the Foreign Service
CNG — Change
CNGGA — Canadian Geographer
CNGGAR — Geographe Canadien
CNGTA — Changing Times
CNH — Courier. European Community, Africa, Caribbean, Pacific
CNHABF — Carnegie Museum of Natural History. Annual Report
CNI — Christian News from Israel
CNIE — Commonwealth Novel in English
CNJ — Canadian Numismatic Journal
CNJGA — Canadian Journal of Genetics and Cytology
CNJNA — Canadian Journal of Animal Science
CNJPA — Canadian Journal of Pharmaceutical Sciences
CNL — Central Bank of Nigeria. Economic and Financial Review (Lagos)
CNLB — Canadian Native Law Bulletin. Native Law Centre. University of Saskatchewan
CNLMA2 — Contact Lens Medical Bulletin
CNLR — Canadian Native Law Reporter. Native Law Centre. University of Saskatchewan
CNLR — Council on National Literatures/Quarterly World Report
CNM — Canadian Manager
CNM — Casopis Narodniho Muzea [*Prague*]
CNM — Contemporary Poland
CNMAD — Construction News Magazine
CNMBB — Canada. Mineral Resources Branch. Mineral Bulletin
CNMEAH — Connecticut Medicine
CNMED — Clinical Nuclear Medicine
CNN — Common Market Business Reports
CNNS — Canadian Native News Service
CNOR — Canada. Northern Forest Research Centre. Information Reports
CNP — France Pays Bas
CNPIA — Canadian Pulp and Paper Industry
CNPPA — Comments on Nuclear and Particle Physics
CNQBAS — Cane Growers Quarterly Bulletin
CNRCB — Clinical Notes on Respiratory Diseases
CNREA8 — Cancer Research
C N Report — Computer Negotiations Report
CNRM — CNRM [*Centre National de Recherches Metallurgiques*]. Metallurgical Reports
CNRM — CONRIM [*Committee on Natural Resource Information Management*] Newsletter [*Anchorage, Alaska*]
CNRM (Cent Natl Rech Metall) Metall Rep — CNRM (Centre National de Recherches Metallurgiques). Metallurgical Reports [*Belgium*]
CNROA4 — Chirurgia Narzadow Ruchu i Ortopedia Polska
CNRS Groupe Fr Argiles Bull — Centre National de la Recherche Scientifique. Groupe Francais des Argiles. Bulletin
CNSBB5 — Chugoku Nogyo Shikenjo Hokoku. B. Chikusan-Bu
CNSLAY — Consultant [*Philadelphia*]
CNSRG — Canada. Northern Science Research Group. Reports
CNSRGSSN — Canada. Northern Science Research Group. Social Science Notes
CNSSEP — Central Nervous System. Pharmacology Series
CNSVAU — Conservationist
CNTA — Contact
CNTEBJ — Congreso Nacional de Tuberculosis y Enfermedades Respiratorias
CNTIB — Constructii (Bucharest)

Cntry Wom — Country Women
CNU — Financial Executive
C Nuovo — Cinema Nuovo
CNUTA — Canadian Nuclear Technology
CO — Cahiers de l'Ouest
CO — Chronicles of Oklahoma
CO — Classical Outlook
CO — Colorado Journal of Research in Music Education
Co — Conference
Co — Corona
COA — Coal Miner
CoA — Coat of Arms
COABER — Computer Applications in the Biosciences
Coach and Athl — Coach and Athlete
Coach Clin — Coaching Clinic
Coaching J Bus Rev — Coaching Journal and Bus Review
Coach Rev — Coaching Review
Coach Women's Athl — Coaching Women's Athletics
Coach Women's Athletics — Coaching Women's Athletics
Coal Abstr — Coal Abstracts [England]
Coal Conference and Expo — Coal Conference and Exposition
Coal Energy Q — Coal and Energy Quarterly
Coal Geol Bull WV Geol Econ Surv — Coal Geology Bulletin. West Virginia Geological and Economic Survey
Coal Gold Base Miner South Afr — Coal, Gold, and Base Minerals of Southern Africa
Coal Ind N — Coal Industry News
Coal Manage Tech Symp — Coal Management Techniques Symposia
Coal Mine Drain Res Symp — Coal Mine Drainage Research Symposia
Coal Min Process — Coal Mining and Processing
Coal M & P — Coal Mining and Processing
Coal Obs — Coal Observer
Coal Oper — Coal Operator
Coal Outlk — Coal Outlook
Coal Prep — Coal Preparation
Coal Prep (Gordon & Breach) — Coal Preparation (Gordon & Breach)
Coal Prep Symp — Coal Preparation Symposia
Coal Process Technol — Coal Processing Technology
Coal Q — Coal Quarterly
Coal Res CSIRO — Coal Research in CSIRO [Commonwealth Scientific and Industrial Research Organisation]
Coal Sci Technol (Peking) — Coal Science Technology (Peking)
Coal Situat — Coal Situation
Coal Technol — Coal Technology
Coal Technol (Houston) — Coal Technology (Houston)
Coal Util — Coal Utilization
Coal Util Symp — Coal Utilization Symposia
Coal Wk I — Coal Week International
COANB — Coal News [London]
COASB — Comments on Astrophysics and Space Physics [Later, Comments on Astrophysics]
COAST — Canada. Ocean and Aquatic Sciences Central Region. Technical Notes
Coastal Bend Med — Coastal Bend Medicine [Texas]
Coastal Eng — Coastal Engineering
Coastal Eng Japan — Coastal Engineering in Japan
Coastal Eng Jpn — Coastal Engineering in Japan
Coastal Engng — Coastal Engineering
Coastal Engng Japan — Coastal Engineering in Japan
Coastal Res Notes — Coastal Research Notes
Coastal Zone Manage J — Coastal Zone Management Journal
Coastal Zone Mgt J — Coastal Zone Management Journal
Coast Zone Manage J — Coastal Zone Management Journal
COB — Cobouw. Dagblad voor de Bouwwereld
COBAA — Cobalt
Cobalt Cobalt Abstr — Cobalt and Cobalt Abstracts
Cobble — Cobblestone
COBD — Commerce Business Daily
COBGA — Commentationes Biologicae. Societas Scientiarum Fennica
COBGA9 — Commentationes Biologicae. Societas Scientiarum Fennica
COBIEJ — Comunicaciones Biologicas
COBLES — Continental Birdlife
COBRD — Communication and Broadcasting
COC — Computer Communications
COCA — Conservation Canada
COCHDK — Computers in Chemistry
Cockerill — Cockerill Sambre Acier [Belgium]
Cocoa Res Inst (CSIR) Annu Rep — Cocoa Research Institute (Council for Scientific and Industrial Research). Annual Report
Cocoa Res Inst (Ghana Acad Sci) Annu Rep — Cocoa Research Institute (Ghana Academy of Sciences). Annual Report
Coconut Bull — Coconut Bulletin
Coconut Res Inst Bull — Coconut Research Institute. Bulletin
COCR — Collectanea Ordinis Cisterciensium Reformatorum
CODATA Bull — CODATA [Committee on Data for Science and Technology] Bulletin

CODATA Newsl — CODATA [Committee on Data for Science and Technology] Newsletter [France]
CODEDG — Contact Dermatitis
Code Fed Reg — Code of Federal Regulations
Cod Man — Codices Manuscripti
CODSBM — Centre de Recherches Oceanographiques [Abidjan]. Document Scientifique Provisoire
Co Engl — College English
COEQD — CoEvolution Quarterly
Coeur Med I — Coeur et Medecine Interne
Coeur Med Interne — Coeur et Medecine Interne
Coevolutn — Coevolution Quarterly
CoEv Q — CoEvolution Quarterly
Coffee Brew Inst Publ — Coffee Brewing Institute. Publication
Coffee Cacao J — Coffee and Cacao Journal
Coffee Res Found (Kenya) Annu Rep — Coffee Research Foundation (Kenya). Annual Report
COFR — Commercial Fisheries Review
CO & G — Clinical Obstetrics and Gynecology
Cog — Cognition [The Hague]
COGCA — Chemistry, Oil, and Gas in Romania
COGLAC Newsl — COGLAC [Coal Gasification, Liquefaction, and Conversion to Electricity] Newsletter
Cognitive Psychol — Cognitive Psychology
Cog Psyc — Cognitive Psychology
Cog Psychol — Cognitive Psychology
COGYA — Clinical Obstetrics and Gynecology
COH — Christelijk Oosten en Hereniging
COHAJ — Canadian Oral History Association. Journal/Societe Canadienne d'Histoire Orale. Journal
COHEB — Community Health (Bristol)
COHEBY — Community Health [Bristol]
COI — Coin Slot Location
Coil Winding Int — Coil Winding International
Coimbra Med — Coimbra Medica
Coimbra Univ Mus Lab Mineral Geol Mem Not — Coimbra. Universidade. Museu e Laboratorio Mineralogico e Geologico. Memorias e Noticias. [Coimbra, Portugal]
COIMDV — Comprehensive Immunology
COIMEW — Concepts in Immunopathology
COINAV — Colloques Internationaux. Centre National de la Recherche Scientifique
Coin Medal Bull — Seaby's Coin and Medal Bulletin
Coin Rev — Coin Review
COJ — Commodity Journal
COJOA — Colloid Journal of the USSR [English Translation]
COJPA8 — Colorado Journal of Pharmacy
COKCA — Coke and Chemistry USSR [English Translation]
Coke Chem R — Coke and Chemistry USSR
Coke Chem USSR — Coke and Chemistry USSR
Coke Res Rep — Coke Research Report [England]
COKRA — Coke Research Report
Col — Colloquium. Freien Universitaet
COL — Colorado Music Educator
COL — Cornell Linguistic Contributions
ColA — Coloquio Artes
COLAA — Coal Age
ColBG — Collationes Brugenses et Gandavenses [Brugge]
ColBiQ — College of the Bible. Quarterly [Lexington, KY]
Colburn — Colburn's New Monthly Magazine
Colby Libr — Colby Library. Quarterly
ColcFranc — Collectanea Franciscana [Rome]
Colchester Archaeol Group Annu Bull — Colchester Archaeological Group. Annual Bulletin
ColCM — Colby College. Monographs
Col Comp & Comm — College Composition and Communication
ColctCist — Collectanea Cisterciensia [Forges, Belgique]
ColcTFujen — Collectanea Theologica Universitatis Fujen [T'aipei, Taiwan]
ColctMech — Collectanea Mechlinensia [Mechelen]
ColctT — Collectanea Theologica [Warsaw]
Cold Reg Sci Technol — Cold Regions Science and Technology [Netherlands]
Cold S Harb — Cold Spring Harbor Symposia on Quantitative Biology
Cold Spr Harb Symp — Cold Spring Harbor Symposia on Quantitative Biology
Cold Spring Harbor Conf Cell Proliferation — Cold Spring Harbor Conference on Cell Proliferation
Cold Spring Harbor Symp Quant Biol — Cold Spring Harbor Symposia on Quantitative Biology
Cold Spring Harbor Symp Quantit Biol — Cold Spring Harbor Symposia on Quantitative Biology
Cold Spring Harb Symp Quant Biol — Cold Spring Harbor Symposia on Quantitative Biology
Colec Agropec Inst Nac Tec Agropec (Argentina) — Coleccion Agropecuaria. Instituto Nacional de Tecnologia Agropecuaria (Argentina)
Colec Monograf Mem Mat — Coleccion de Monografias y Memorias de Matematicas

Colect Monogr Bot Biol Veg — Collection de Monographies de Botanique et de Biologie Vegetale

ColeFranc — Collectanea Franciscana [*Rome*]

ColEng — College English

Coleopt Bull — Coleopterists' Bulletin

Coleopts Bull — Coleopterists' Bulletin

ColeT — Collectanea Theologica [*Warsaw*]

Coletanea Inst Tecnol Aliment — Coletanea. Instituto de Tecnologia de Alimentos

Colet Inst Tecnol Aliment — Coletanea. Instituto de Tecnologia de Alimentos

ColetMech — Collectanea Mechlinensia [*Mechelen, Belgium*]

ColF — Columbia Forum

Col Farm — Colegio Farmaceutico

ColG — Collationes Gandavenses

ColGer — Colloquia Germanica

Col Hist Soc Rec — Columbia Historical Society. Records

Col Hum RL Rev — Columbia Human Rights Law Review

Col Hu Ri LR — Columbia Human Rights Law Review

CoLi — Comparative Literature

Col Interam Defensa R — Colegio Interamericano de Defensa Revista

Col J Environ L — Columbia Journal of Environmental Law

Col J Env L — Columbia Journal of Environmental Law

Col J L and Soc Prob — Columbia Journal of Law and Social Problems

Col JL & Soc Probl — Columbia Journal of Law and Social Problems

Col Jour Rev — Columbia Journalism Review

ColJR — Columbia Journalism Review

Col J Transnat'l L — Columbia Journal of Transnational Law

Col J Tr L — Columbia Journal of Transnational Law

Col J World Bus — Columbia Journal of World Business

Col(L) — Coloquio (Lisbon)

Collab Proc Ser Int Inst Appl Syst Anal — Collaborative Proceedings Series. International Institute for Applied Systems Analysis

Coll Agric (Nagpur) Mag — College of Agriculture (Nagpur). Magazine

Coll Amis Hist — Collection. Amis de l'Histoire

Coll Am Statis Assn — Collections. American Statistical Association

Collana Accad Accad Patav Sci Lett Arti — Collana Accademica. Accademia Patavina di Scienze, Lettere, ed Arti

Collana Monogr Ateneo Parmense — Collana di Monografie. Ateneo Parmense

Collana Monogr Oli Essenz Sui Deri Agrum — Collana di Monografie sugli Oli Essenziali e Sui Derivati Agrumari

Collana Monogr Rass Med Sarda — Collana di Monografie di Rassegna Medica Sarda

Coll Art J — College Art Journal

CollLat — Collection Latomus

Col Law Review — Columbia Law Review

Coll Bd R — College Board Review

CollBrugGand — Collationes Brugenses et Gandavenses [*Gent, Belgium*]

Coll Cist — Collectanea Cisterciensa

Coll Comp & Comm — College Composition and Communication

Coll Composition & Commun — College Composition and Communication

Coll Courant — College Courant

Coll Czech — Collection of Czechoslovak Chemical Communications

Coll Dir Etudes Rech Elec France — Collection. Direction des Etudes et Recherches d'Electricite de France

CollE — College English

Collec Czechosl Chem Commun — Collection of Czechoslovak Chemical Communications

Coll Ecole Norm Sup Jeunes Filles — Collection. Ecole Normale Superieure de Jeunes Filles

Collect Biol Evol — Collection de Biologie Evolutive

Collect Bot (Barc) — Collectanea Botanica (Barcelona)

Collect Breed — Collecting and Breeding

Collect Colloq Semin Inst Fr Pet — Collection. Colloques et Seminaires. Institut Francais du Petrole

Collect Czech Chem Commun — Collection of Czechoslovak Chemical Communications

Collect Czechoslovak Chem Commun — Collection of Czechoslovak Chemical Communications

Collect Ecole Norm Sup Jeunes Filles — Collection. Ecole Normale Superieure de Jeunes Filles

Collect Ecologie — Collection d'Ecologie

Collected Studies Ser — Collected Studies Series [*London*]

Collect Enseignement Sci — Collection Enseignement des Sciences

Collect Grands Probl Biol Monogr — Collection "Les Grands Problemes de la Biologie." Monographie

Collect Math — Collectanea Mathematica

Collect Monogr Bot Biol Veg — Collection de Monographies de Botanique et de Biologie Vegetale

Collect Pap Annu Symp Fundam Cancer Res — Collection of Papers Presented at the Annual Symposium on Fundamental Cancer Research

Collect Pap Changchun Inst Appl Chem Acad Sin — Collected Papers. Changchun Institute of Applied Chemistry. Academia Sinica

Collect Pap Earth Sci Nagoya Univ Dep Earth Sci — Collected Papers on Earth Sciences. Nagoya University. Department of Earth Sciences

Collect Papers Lister Inst Prevent Med — Collected Papers. Lister Institute of Preventive Medicine

Collect Papers Math Soc Wakayama Univ — Collected Papers. Mathematical Society. Wakayama University

Collect Papers School Hyg and Pub Health Johns Hopkins Univ — Collected Papers. School of Hygiene and Public Health. Johns Hopkins University

Collect Pap Fac Sci Osaka Imp Univ Ser A — Collected Papers. Faculty of Science. Osaka Imperial University. Series A. Mathematics

Collect Pap Fac Sci Osaka Imp Univ Ser B — Collected Papers. Faculty of Science. Osaka Imperial University. Series B. Physics

Collect Pap Fac Sci Osaka Imp Univ Ser C — Collected Papers. Faculty of Science. Osaka Imperial University. Series C. Chemistry

Collect Pap Fac Sci Osaka Univ Ser B — Collected Papers. Faculty of Science. Osaka University. Series B. Physics

Collect Pap Fac Sci Osaka Univ Ser C — Collected Papers. Faculty of Science. Osaka University. Series C. Chemistry

Collect Pap Inst Appl Chem Acad Sin — Collected Papers. Institute of Applied Chemistry. Academia Sinica

Collect Pap Inst Appl Chem Chin Acad Sci — Collected Papers. Institute of Applied Chemistry. Chinese Academy of Sciences

Collect Pap Jpn Soc Civ Eng — Collected Papers. Japan Society of Civil Engineers

Collect Pap Mayo Clin Mayo Found — Collected Papers. Mayo Clinic and Mayo Foundation

Collect Pap Med Mayo Clin Mayo Found — Collected Papers in Medicine. Mayo Clinic and Mayo Foundation

Collect Pap Med Sci Fukuoka Univ — Collected Papers on Medical Science. Fukuoka University

Collect Pap Res Lab Parke Davis Co — Collected Papers. Research Laboratory of Parke, Davis & Company

Collect Pap Surg Mayo Clin Mayo Found — Collected Papers in Surgery. Mayo Clinic and Mayo Foundation

Collect Pap Technol Sci Fukuoka Univ — Collected Papers on Technological Sciences. Fukuoka University

Collect Pharm Suec — Collectanea Pharmaceutica Suecica

Collect Phenom — Collective Phenomena

Collect Rep Nat Sci Fac Palacky Univ (Olomouc) — Collected Reports. Natural Science Faculty. Palacky University (Olomouc)

Collect Sci Pap Econ Agric Univ (Ceske Budejovice) Biol Part — Collection of Scientific Papers. Economic Agricultural University (Ceske Budejovice). Biological Part

Collect Sci Works Fac Med Charles Univ (Hradec Kralove) — Collection of Scientific Works. Faculty of Medicine. Charles University (Hadec Kralove)

Collect Studies Ser — Collected Studies Series

Collect Tech Pap AIAA/ASME/SAE Struct Dyn Mater Conf — Collection of Technical Papers. AIAA/ASME/SAE Structural Dynamics and Materials Conference

Collect Theses Kwang Woon Inst Technol — Collection of Theses. Kwang Woon Institute of Technology [*Republic of Korea*]

Collect Trav Acad Int Hist Sci — Collection des Travaux. Academie Internationale d'Histoire des Sciences

Collect Treatises Fac Hum Univ Fukuoka — Collection of Treatises Published by the Faculty of Humanity. University of Fukuoka [*Japan*]

Collect Works Cardio-Pulm Dis — Collected Works on Cardio-Pulmonary Disease

College Mus — College Music Symposium

College & Research Lib — College and Research Libraries

Coll Eng — College English

Coll Engl — College English

Coll Enseignement Sci — Collection Enseignement des Sciences [*Paris*]

Coll Fr — Collectionneur Francais

Coll Fran — Collectanea Franciscana

Coll G — Colloquia Germanica

Coll Hist Sci — Collection d'Histoire des Sciences [*Paris*]

Collier Bankr — Collier's Law of Bankruptcy

Collier's — Collier's National Weekly

Collier's Yrbk — Collier's Encyclopedia Yearbook

Colliery Eng — Colliery Engineering

Colliery Eng (London) — Colliery Engineering (London)

Colliery Eng (Scranton PA) — Colliery Engineer (Scranton, Pennsylvania)

Colliery Guard — Colliery Guardian

Colliery Guardian J Coal Iron Trades — Colliery Guardian and Journal of the Coal and Iron Trades

Col Lit — College Literature

Coll L — College Literature

Coll Latomus — Collection Latomus

Coll Lit — College Literature

Coll Mass Hist Soc — Collections. Massachusetts Historical Society

Coll Math — Colloquium Mathematicum

CollMech — Collectanea Mechlinensia [*Mechelen, Belgium*]

Coll Med Ann (Mosul) — College of Medicine. Annals (Mosul)

Coll Mgt — College Management

Coll Music — College Music Symposium

Colln Czech Chem Commun — Collection of Czechoslovak Chemical Communications

Colln Etud Mus Vie Wallonne — Collection d'Etudes Publiee par le Musee de la Vie Wallonne

Coll News — College News
Collns INSEE Ser R — Collections. Institut Nationale de la Statistique et des Etudes Economiques. Serie R. Regions
Coll N & V — Collegiate News and Views
Colloid Chem — Colloid Chemistry
Colloides Biol Clin Ther — Colloides en Biologie. Clinique et Therapeutique
Colloid Interface Sci Pro Int Conf — Colloid and Interface Science. Proceedings of the International Conference on Colloids and Surfaces
Colloid J — Colloid Journal of the USSR
Colloid J USSR — Colloid Journal of the USSR
Colloid Polymer Sci — Colloid and Polymer Science
Colloid Polym Sci — Colloid and Polymer Science
Colloid P S — Colloid and Polymer Science
Colloid Sci — Colloid Science
Colloids Surf — Colloids and Surfaces
Colloids and Surf — Colloids and Surfaces
Colloid Surf Sci Symp — Colloid Surface Science Symposium
Colloid Symp Monogr — Colloid Symposium Monograph
Colloq Art — Colloquies on Art and Archaeology in Asia
Colloq Club Jules Gonin — Colloque. Club Jules Gonin
Colloq Ger — Colloquia Germanica
Colloq Ges Biol Chem Mosbach — Colloquium. Gesellschaft fuer Biologische Chemie in Mosbach
Colloq Ges Physiol Chem — Colloquium. Gesellschaft fuer Physiologische Chemie
Colloq Inst Natl Sante Rech Med — Colloque. Institut National de la Sante et de la Recherche Medicale [*France*]
Colloq Int Blennorragie — Colloque International sur la Blennorragie. Comptes Rendus
Colloq Int Cent Natl Rech Sci — Colloques Internationaux. Centre National de la Recherche Scientifique
Colloq Int Chim Cafes C R — Colloque International sur la Chimie des Cafes. Comptes Rendus
Colloq Int CNRS — Colloques Internationaux. Centre National de la Recherche Scientifique
Colloq Int Electr Sol — Colloque International sur l'Electricite Solaire. Comptes Rendus
Colloq Internat CNRS — Colloques Internationaux. Centre National de la Recherche Scientifique
Colloq Int Potash Inst — Colloquium. International Potash Institute
Colloq Math — Colloquium Mathematicum [*Warsaw*]
Colloq Math Soc Janos Bolyai — Colloquia Mathematica. Societatis Janos Bolyai
Colloq Metall — Colloque de Metallurgie
Colloq Pflanzenphysiol Humboldt Univ Berlin — Colloquia Pflanzenphysiologie. Humboldt-Universitaet zu Berlin
Colloq Spectro Int Pro — Colloquium Spectroscopicum Internationale. Proceedings
Colloq Spectrosc Int Acta — Colloquium Spectroscopicum Internationale. Acta
Colloques Int Cent Natn Rech Scient — Colloques Internationaux. Centre National de la Recherche Scientifique
Colloques Internat CNRS — Colloques Internationaux. Centre National de la Recherche Scientifique
Colloques Int Path Insectes — Colloques Internationales de la Pathologie des Insectes
Colloques Nat CNRS — Colloques Nationaux. Centre National de la Recherche Scientifique
Colloquiumsber Inst Gerbereichem Tech Hochsch (Darmstadt) — Colloquiumsberichte. Instituts fuer Gerbereichemie. Technischen Hochschule (Darmstadt)
Coll Phil — Collection Philosophica
Coll Polym Sci — Colloid and Polymer Science
Coll Press — College Press Service
Coll Programmation Rech Oper Appl — Collection. Programmation Recherche Operationnelle Appliquee
Col LR — Columbia Law Review
Coll Res Li — College and Research Libraries
Coll & Res Lib — College and Research Libraries
Coll & Res Lib N — College and Research Library News
Coll Res Libr — College and Research Libraries
Col L Rev — Columbia Law Review
Coll Sci Mat — Collana di Scienze Matematiche
Coll Statist Agric Et — Collections de Statistique Agricole. Etudes
Coll Stud J — College Student Journal
Coll Stud Pers Abstr — College Student Personnel Abstracts
Coll Surfaces — Colloids and Surfaces
Coll Travaux Acad Internat Hist Sci — Collection des Travaux. Academie Internationale d'Histoire des Sciences
Coll & Univ — College and University
Coll & Univ Bus — College and University Business
Coll & Univ J — College and University Journal
Coll Works Cardio-Pulm Dis — Collected Works on Cardio-Pulmonary Disease
ColM — Colorado Magazine
COLMA9 — Colorado Medicine
ColMech — Collectanea Mechlinensia [*Mechelen, Belgium*]
Col Med — Colegio Medico

Col Med Vida Med — Colegio Medico Vida Medica
Colmen Esp — Colmenero Espanol
Col Mgt — College Management
Col Monograf Mem Mat — Coleccion de Monografias y Memorias de Matematicas [*Madrid*]
ColN — Colonial Newsletter
Col Nac Mem — Memoria. El Colegio Nacional
Colo Ag Exp — Colorado. Agricultural Experiment Station. Publications
Colo Agric Exp Stn Annu Rep — Colorado. Agricultural Experiment Station. Annual Report
Colo Agric Exp Stn Bull — Colorado. Agricultural Experiment Station. Bulletin
Colo Agric Exp Stn Tech Bull — Colorado. Agricultural Experiment Station. Technical Bulletin
COLOB — Colourage
Colo Bur Mines Ann Rept — Colorado. Bureau of Mines. Annual Report
Colo Bus R — Colorado Business Review
Colo Country Life — Colorado Country Life
Colo Dep Game Fish Parks Spec Rep — Colorado. Department of Game, Fish, and Parks. Special Report
Colo Div Game Fish Parks Fish Res Rev — Colorado. Division of Game, Fish, and Parks. Fisheries Research Review
Colo Div Game Fish Parks Spec Rep — Colorado. Division of Game, Fish, and Parks. Special Report
Colo Div Game Parks Game Res Rev — Colorado. Division of Game, Fish, and Parks. Game Research Review
Colo Div Wildl Div Rep — Colorado. Division of Wildlife. Division Report
Colo Div Wildl Spec Rep — Colorado. Division of Wildlife. Special Report
Colo Div Wildl Tech Publ — Colorado. Division of Wildlife. Technical Publication
Colo Energy Factbook — Colorado Energy Factbook
Colo Engineer — Colorado Engineer
Colo Farm & Home Res — Colorado Farm and Home Research
Colo Field Ornithol — Colorado Field Ornithologist
Colo Fish Res Rev — Colorado Fisheries Research Review
Colo Game Fish Parks Dep Spec Rep — Colorado. Game, Fish, and Parks Department. Special Report
Colo Game Res Rev — Colorado Game Research Review
Colo Geol Surv Bull — Colorado. Geological Survey. Bulletin
Colo Geol Surv Map Ser — Colorado. Geological Survey. Map Series
Colo Geol Surv Spec Publ — Colorado. Geological Survey. Special Publication
Colo Ground Water Basic Data Rep — Colorado Ground Water Basic Data Report
Colo J Pharm — Colorado Journal of Pharmacy
Colo J Res Mus Ed — Colorado Journal of Research in Music Education
Colo Law — Colorado Lawyer
Colo Lib Assn Bul — Colorado Library Association. Bulletin
ColoM — Colorado Magazine
Colo Mag — Colorado Magazine
Colomb Inst Geogr "Agustin Codazzi" Dep Agrol (Publ) — Colombia. Instituto Geografico "Agustin Codazzi." Departamento Agrologico (Publicaciones)
Colomb Inst Geogr Agustin Codazzi Dir Agrol Publ — Colombia. Instituto Geografico "Agustin Codazzi." Direccion Agrologica. Publicaciones
Colomb Inst Geol Nac Compil Estud Geol Of Colomb — Colombia. Instituto Geologica Nacional. Compilacion de los Estudios Geologicos Oficiales en Colombia
Colomb Minist Agric Div Invest Inf Tec — Colombia. Ministerio de Agricultura. Division de Investigacion. Informacion Tecnica
Colomb Minist Minas Energ Mem — Colombia. Ministro de Minas y Energia. Memoria
Colombo L Rev — Colombo Law Review
Colomb Repub Minist Minas Pet Bol Minas — Republica de Colombia. Ministerio de Minas y Petroleos. Boletin de Minas
Colomb Repub Minist Minas Pet Bol Nac Minas — Republica de Colombia. Ministerio de Minas y Petroleos. Boletin Nacional de Minas
Colo Med — Colorado Medicine
Colon Auton — Colonies Autonomes
Colon Geol Miner Resour Suppl Bull Suppl — Colonial Geology and Mineral Resources Supplement Series. Bulletin Supplement
Colonial Geology and Mineral Res — Colonial Geology and Mineral Resources
Colonial Research Pub — Colonial Research Publications
Colon Pl Anim Prod — Colonial Plant and Animal Products
Colon Plant Anim Prod — Colonial Plant and Animal Products
Colo Nurse — Colorado Nurse
Colo Outdoors — Colorado Outdoors
ColoQ — Colorado Quarterly
Coloquio — Coloquio Letras
Colorado Med — Colorado Medicine
Colorado School Mines Prof Contr — Colorado School of Mines. Professional Contributions
Colorado-Wyoming Acad Sci Jour — Colorado-Wyoming Academy of Science. Journal
Colo Rancher Farmer — Colorado Rancher and Farmer
Color Eng — Color Engineering
Color Mater — Color Materials [*Japan*]

Color Res and Appl — Color Research and Application
Color Res Appl — Color Research and Application
Color Sch Mines Q Bull — Colorado School of Mines. Quarterly Bulletin
Color Tr J — Color Trade Journal and Textile Chemist
Colo Sch Mines Mag — Colorado School of Mines. Magazine
Colo Sch Mines Mineral Energy Resources Bul — Colorado School of Mines. Mineral and Energy Resources Bulletin
Colo Sch Mines Miner Ind Bull — Colorado School of Mines. Mineral Industries Bulletin
Colo Sch Mines Q — Colorado School of Mines. Quarterly
Colo Sch Mines Quart — Colorado School of Mines. Quarterly
Colo Sci Soc Proc — Colorado Scientific Society. Proceedings
Colo State Univ Annu Rep — Colorado State University. Annual Report
Colo State Univ Exp Stn Bull — Colorado State University. Experiment Station. Bulletin
Colo State Univ Exp Stn Tech Bull — Colorado State University. Experiment Station. Technical Bulletin
Colo State Univ Expt Sta Bull — Colorado State University. Experiment Station. Bulletin
Colo State Univ (Fort Collins) Hydrol Pap — Colorado State University (Fort Collins). Hydrology Papers
Colo State Univ Range Sci Dep Range Sci Ser — Colorado State University. Range Science Department. Range Science Series
Colo-Wyo Acad Sci Jour — Colorado-Wyoming Academy of Science. Journal
Col Phys Ed Assn Proc — College Physical Education Association. Proceedings
COLPS — Center for Oceans Law and Policy. University of Virginia. Oceans Policy Studies
ColQ — Colorado Quarterly
Col Quim-Farm — Colegio Quimico-Farmaceutico
Col Quim Ing Quim Costa Rica Rev — Colegio de Quimicos e Ingenieros Quimicos de Costa Rica. Revista
Col & Res Lib — College and Research Libraries
Col Soc Mass Publ — Colonial Society of Massachusetts. Publications
Col Soc Mass Trans — Colonial Society of Massachusetts. Transactions
ColStuAb — College Student Personnel Abstracts
Colt G Vinic Ital — Coltivatore e Giornale Vinicolo Italiano
Coltiv G Vinic Ital — Coltivatore e Giornale Vinicolo Italiano
Colt News — Colt Newsletter
Colt Prot — Colture Protette
Colt Protette — Colture Protette
Columbia Hist Soc Rec — Columbia Historical Society. Records
Columbia J-ism R — Columbia Journalism Review
Columbia J Law and Social Problems — Columbia Journal of Law and Social Problems
Columbia J of L and Soc Probl — Columbia Journal of Law and Social Problems
Columbia Journalism Rev — Columbia Journalism Review
Columbia J Transnat Law — Columbia Journal of Transnational Law
Columbia J Wld Busin — Columbia Journal of World Business
Columbia J World Bus — Columbia Journal of World Business
Columbia Law R — Columbia Law Review
Columbia Law Rev — Columbia Law Review
Columbia Lib C — Columbia Library. Columns
Columbia Libr Col — Columbia Library. Columns
Columbia Libr Columns — Columbia Library. Columns
Columbia U Q — Columbia University. Quarterly
Columb J L — Columbia Journal of Law and Social Problems
Columb Jrl — Columbia Journal of World Business
Columb J Tr — Columbia Journal of Transnational Law
Columb J W — Columbia Journal of World Business
Columb Law — Columbia Law Review
Columbus Gal Bul — Columbus, Ohio. Columbus Gallery of Fine Arts. Bulletin
Colum Forum — Columbia Forum
Colum His S — Columbia Historical Society. Records
Colum Human Rights L Rev — Columbia Human Rights Law Review
Colum Hum Rts L Rev — Columbia Human Rights Law Review
Colum J Environ L — Columbia Journal of Environmental Law
Colum J Envtl L — Columbia Journal of Environmental Law
Colum J Law & Soc Prob — Columbia Journal of Law and Social Problems
Colum J L & Soc Prob — Columbia Journal of Law and Social Problems
Colum Journalism R — Columbia Journalism Review
Colum J Transnat L — Columbia Journal of Transnational Law
Colum J Transnat'l Law — Columbia Journal of Transnational Law
Colum J World Bus — Columbia Journal of World Business
Colum L Rev — Columbia Law Review
Colum Univ Q — Columbia University. Quarterly
Col Univ — College and University
Col & Univ — College and University
Col & Univ Bsns — College and University Business
Col Univ Gerona Secc Cien An — Colegio Universitario de Gerona. Seccion de Ciencias. Anales
Col & Univ J — College and University Journal
COM — Cahiers d'Outre-Mer
COM — Comet Stories
COM — Commentary
COM — Composer

COM — Cost and Management
ComAb — Computer Abstracts
Com Amer — Commerce America
COMBA — Combustion
Comb Eng — Combustion Engineering
Comb Expl (R) — Combustion, Explosion, and Shock Waves (USSR)
Comb Flame — Combustion and Flame
Comb Proc Int Plant Propagators Soc — Combined Proceedings. International Plant Propagators' Society
Comb Sci T — Combustion Science and Technology
Combust Combust — Combustione e Combustibile
Combust Eng Assoc Doc — Combustion Engineering Association. Document [*England*]
Combust Explos and Shock Waves — Combustion, Explosion, and Shock Waves
Combust Explos Shock Waves — Combustion, Explosion, and Shock Waves [*USSR*]
Combust and Flame — Combustion and Flame
Combust Flame — Combustion and Flame
Combust Sci Technol — Combustion Science and Technology
Combust Sci Technol Book Ser — Combustion Science and Technology. Book Series
Com Canada — Commerce Canada
Com Challenges of Mod Soc Air Pollution — Committee on the Challenges of Modern Society. Air Pollution
Com Coll Front — Community College Frontiers
Com Coll R — Community College Review
Com Com — Journal of Community Communications
Com Con Psy — Comments on Contemporary Psychiatry
COMD — Countermedia. Alaska Journalism Review and Supplement
Com Develop J — Community Development Journal
Com Dev J — Community Development Journal
Com Dev Pancha Raj D — Community Development and Panchayati Raj Digest
COMEAO — Concours Medical
Com & Electronics — Communication and Electronics
C O-Mer — Cahiers d'Outre-Mer
Comercio Exterior de Mexico — Comercio Exterior de Mexico
Comercio Prod — Comercio y Produccion
ComErm — Communications. Musee National de l'Ermitage
Com Ext Mexico — Comercio Exterior de Mexico
Com Ext Tchecosl — Commerce Exterieur Tchecoslovaque
Com Fac Sci Univ Ankara Ser A₃ Astronom — Universite d'Ankara. Faculte des Sciences. Communications. Serie A₃. Astronomie
Com and Fin Chr — Commercial and Financial Chronicle. Statistical Section
Com For Rev — Commonwealth Forestry Review
Com Glaciol Ital Boll Ser 2 — Comitato Glaciologico Italiano. Bollettino. Serie Seconda
Com Inst Agron Sul — Comunicado. Instituto Agronomico do Sul
Com Interam Atun Trop Bol — Comision Interamericana del Atun Tropical. Boletin
Com Internaz — Communita Internazionale
Com Int Etude Bauxites Alumine Alum Trav — Comite International pour l'Etude des Bauxites, de l'Alumine, et d'Aluminium. Travaux
Com Int Etude Bauxites Oxydes Hydroxydes Alum Trav — Comite International pour l'Etude des Bauxites, des Oxydes, et des Hydroxydes d'Aluminium. Travaux
Com Int Poids Mes Com Consult Def Metre Trav — Comite International des Poids et Mesures. Comite Consultatif pour la Definition du Metre. Travaux
Com Int Poids Mes Com Consult Electr Trav — Comite International des Poids et Mesures. Comite Consultatif d'Electricite. Travaux
Com Int Poids Mes Com Consult Etalons Mes Radiat Ionis Trav — Comite International des Poids et Mesures. Comite Consultatif pour les Etalons de Mesure des Radiations Ionisantes. Travaux
Com Int Poids Mes Com Consult Photom Trav — Comite International des Poids et Mesures. Comite Consultatif de Photometrie. Travaux
Com Int Poids Mes Com Consult Thermom Trav — Comite International des Poids et Mesures. Comite Consultatif de Thermometrie. Travaux
Com Invest Cient Prov Buenos Aires Inf — Comision de Investigaciones Cientificas de la Provincia de Buenos Aires. Informes
Comitato Naz Energia Nucleare Notiz — Comitato Nazionale per l'Energia Nucleare. Notiziario
COMJD — Commodity Journal
Com & Jr Coll — Community and Junior College Journal
Com & Jr Coll J — Community and Junior College Journal
Com and L — Communications and the Law
Com L Assoc Bull — Commercial Law Association. Bulletin
Com & Law — Communications and the Law
Com Law — Communications and the Law
Com L J — Commercial Law Journal
Comm — Commonweal
Comm — Communication. Kodak Research Laboratories
Com M — Communication Monographs
Comm ACM — Communications. ACM [*Association for Computing Machinery*]

Comm Algeb — Communications in Algebra

Comm Algebra — Communications in Algebra

Comm Alkali React Concr Nat Prog Rep H — Committee on Alkali Reactions in Concrete. Danish National Institute of Building Research and the Academy of Technical Sciences. Progress Report. Series H. Methods of Evaluation of Alkali Reactions

Comm Alkali React Concr Prog Rep A — Committee on Alkali Reactions in Concrete. Danish National Institute of Building Research and the Academy of Technical Sciences. Progress Report. Series A. Alkali Reactions in Concrete. General

Comm Alkali React Concr Prog Rep D — Committee on Alkali Reactions in Concrete. Danish National Institute of Building Research and the Academy of Technical Sciences. Progress Report. Series D. Aggregate Types of Denmark

Comm Alkali React Concr Prog Rep F — Committee on Alkali Reactions in Concrete. Danish National Institute of Building Research and the Academy of Technical Sciences. Progress Report. Series F. Alkali Contents of Concrete Components

Comm Alkali React Concr Prog Rep I — Committee on Alkali Reactions in Concrete. Danish National Institute of Building Research and the Academy of Technical Sciences. Progress Report. Series I. Inhibition of Alkali Reactions by Admixtures

Comm Alkali React Concr Prog Rep N — Committee on Alkali Reactions in Concrete. Danish National Institute of Building Research and the Academy of Technical Sciences. Progress Report. Series N. Observed Symptoms of Deterioration

Comman Dig — Commander's Digest

Comm AR — Commonwealth Arbitration Reports

Comm Archives Centrales Orgue — Communications. Archives Centrales de l'Orgue/Mededelingen. Centraal Orgelarchief

Comm Bibl Hist Med Hungar — Communicationes. Bibliotheca Historiae Medicae Hungarica

Comm Broadc — Communication and Broadcasting

Comm Bul — Commercial Bulletin for Teachers in Secondary Schools

Comm Data Sci Technol Spec Rep (ICSU) — Committee on Data for Science and Technology. Special Report (International Council of Scientific Unions)

Comm Den Or — Community Dentistry and Oral Epidemiology

Comm Dev J — Community Development Journal

Comm Dublin Inst Adv Studies Ser A — Communications. Dublin Institute for Advanced Studies. Series A

Comm Ed — Commercial Education

Comm Educ — Communication Education

Commen — Commentary

Comm Energie At (Fr) Serv Doc Ser Bibliogr — Commisariat a l'Energie Atomique (France). Service de Documentation. Serie Bibliographie

Com Men Health J — Community Mental Health Journal

Commentat Biol — Commentationes Biologicae

Commentat Biol Soc Sci Fenn — Commentationes Biologicae. Societas Scientiarum Fennica

Commentat Phys-Math — Commentationes Physico-Mathematicae

Commentat Phys-Math Suppl — Commentationes Physico-Mathematicae. Supplement

Commentat Pontif Acad Sci — Commentationes Pontificiae. Academiae Scientiarum

Com Ment Health J — Community Mental Health Journal

Comment Math Helv — Commentarii Mathematici Helvetici

Comment Math Prace Mat — Roczniki Polskiego Towarzystwa Matematycznego. Seria I. Commentationes Mathematicae Prace Matematyczne

Comment Math Special Issue — Commentationes Mathematicae. Special Issue

Comment Math Univ Carolin — Commentationes Mathematicae. Universitatis Carolinae

Comment Math Univ Carolinae — Commentationes Mathematicae. Universitatis Carolinae

Comment Math Univ St Paul — Commentarii Mathematici. Universitatis Sancti Pauli

Comment Phys Math Soc Sci Fenn — Commentationes Physico-Mathematicae. Societas Scientiarum Fennica

Comment Plant Sci — Commentaries in Plant Science

Comment Pontif Acad Sci — Commentario. Pontificia Academia Scientiarum

Comments Astrophys — Comments on Astrophysics [United States, England]

Comments Astrophys Comments Mod Phys Part C — Comments on Astrophysics. Comments on Modern Physics. Part C

Comments Astrophys Space Phys — Comments on Astrophysics and Space Physics [Later, Comments on Astrophysics]

Comments At Mol Phys — Comments on Atomic and Molecular Physics

Comments Contemp Psychiatry — Comments on Contemporary Psychiatry

Comments Earth Sci Geophys — Comments on Earth Sciences. Geophysics

Comments Mol and Cell Biophys Comments Mod Biol Part A — Comments on Molecular and Cellular Biophysics. Comments on Modern Biology. Part A

Comments Nucl Part Phys — Comments on Nuclear and Particle Physics

Comments Nucl & Part Phys — Comments on Nuclear and Particle Physics

Comments Nucl Part Phys Suppl — Comments on Nuclear and Particle Physics. Supplement

Comments Plasma Phys & Controlled Fusion — Comments on Plasma Physics and Controlled Fusion

Comments Plasma Phys Controlled Fusion — Comments on Plasma Physics and Controlled Fusion [England]

Comments Solid State Phys — Comments on Solid State Physics

Commer Am — Commerce America

Commer Bank Australia Econ R — Commercial Bank of Australia. Economic Review

Commerce et Coop — Commerce et Cooperation

Commerce Ind & Min R — Commerce, Industrial, and Mining Review

Commerce Int — Commerce International

Commercium Lit Rei Med et Sc Nat — Commercium Litterarium ad Rei Medicae et Scientiae Naturali Incrementum Institutum

Commer Fert Plant Food Ind — Commercial Fertilizer and Plant Food Industry

Commer Fert Yearb — Commercial Fertilizer. Yearbook

Commer Fin J — Commercial Finance Journal

Commer Fish Abstr — Commercial Fisheries Abstracts

Commer Fish Rev — Commercial Fisheries Review

Commer Ind — Commercial Index

Commer Ind & Min Rev — Commerce, Industrial, and Mining Review

Commer Letter Can Imperial Bank Commer — Commercial Letter. Canadian Imperial Bank of Commerce

Commer Levant — Commerce du Levant

Commer Motor — Commercial Motor

Commer News USA — Commercial News USA

Commer Rabbit — Commercial Rabbit

Comm Fac Sci Univ Ankara Ser A — Communications. Faculte des Sciences. Universite d'Ankara. Serie A. Mathematiques-Physique-Astronomie

Comm Fert — Commercial Fertilizer

Comm & Fin — Commerce and Finance

Comm & Fin Chron — Commercial and Financial Chronicle

Comm Heal S — Community Health Studies

Comm Health — Community Health

Comm Hist Art Med — Communicationes de Historia Artis Medicinae

Comm Hydrol Onderz TNO Versl Meded — Commissie voor Hydrologisch Onderzoek TNO [Nederlandse Centrale Organisatie voor Toegepast Natuurwetenschappelijk Onderzoek]. Verslagen en Mededelingen

Comm Hydrol Onderz TNO Versl Tech Bijeenkomst — Commissie voor Hydrologisch Onderzoek TNO [Nederlandse Centrale Organisatie voor Toegepast Natuurwetenschappelijk Onderzoek]. Verslag van de Technische Bijeenkomst

Comm Hydrol Res TNO (Cent Organ Appl Sci Res Neth) Proc Inf — Committee for Hydrological Research TNO (Central Organization for Applied Scientific Research in the Netherlands). Proceedings and Informations

Comm (India) — Commerce (India)

Comm Intnl — Communications International

Comm L Assoc Bull — Commercial Law Association. Bulletin

Comm LB — Commonwealth Law Bulletin

Comm L Law — Common Law Lawyer

Comm LR — Commonwealth Law Reports

Comm M — Commerce Monthly

Comm Math H — Commentarii Mathematici Helvetici

Comm Math P — Communications in Mathematical Physics

Comm Ment H — Community Mental Health Journal

Comm Mkt LR — Common Market Law Reports

Comm Mkt L Rep — Common Market Law Reports

Comm Monogr — Communication Monographs

Comm Mot — Commercial Motor

Comm News — Communications News

Com Mod — Commerce Moderne

Commod Bul Dep Agric NSW Div Mark Econ — Commodity Bulletin. Department of Agriculture of New South Wales. Division of Marketing and Economics

Commodities M — Commodities Magazine

Commod J — Commodity Journal

Commod Jrl — Commodity Journal

Commod Mag — Commodities Magazine

Common — Common Sense

Common Agric — Commonwealth Agriculturist

Common Cause M — Common Cause Membership

Common Exp Build Stn NSB — Australia. Commonwealth Experimental Building Station. Notes on the Science of Building

Commonw Agric — Commonwealth Agriculturist

Commonw Bur Anim Breed Genet Tech Commun — Commonwealth Bureau of Animal Breeding and Genetics. Technical Communication

Commonw Bur Anim Health Rev Ser — Commonwealth Bureau of Animal Health. Review Series

Commonw Bur Anim Nutr Tech Commun — Commonwealth Bureau of Animal Nutrition. Technical Communication

Commonw Bur Hortic Plant Crops (GB) Tech Commun — Commonwealth Bureau of Horticulture and Plantation Crops (Great Britain). Technical Communication

Commonw Bur Nutr Tech Commun — Commonwealth Bureau of Nutrition. Technical Communication

Commonw Bur Pastures Field Crops Bull — Commonwealth Bureau of Pastures and Field Crops. Bulletin

Commonw Bur Pastures Field Crops (GB) Rev Ser — Commonwealth Bureau of Pastures and Field Crops (Great Britain). Review Series

Commonw Bur Pastures Field Crops Hurley Berkshire Bull — Commonwealth Bureau of Pastures and Field Crops. Hurley Berkshire Bulletin

Commonw Bur Plant Breed Genet Tech Commun — Commonwealth Bureau of Plant Breeding and Genetics. Technical Communication

Commonw Bur Soils Spec Publ — Commonwealth Bureau of Soils. Special Publication

Commonw Bur Soils Tech Commun — Commonwealth Bureau of Soils. Technical Communication

Commonwealth Club Cal Transactions — Commonwealth Club of California. Transactions

Commonwealth Phytopathol — Commonwealth Phytopathological News

Commonwealth Road Trans Index — Commonwealth Road Transport Index

Commonw Eng — Commonwealth Engineer

Commonw Engr — Commonwealth Engineer

Commonw Exp Build Stat Bull — Australia. Commonwealth Experimental Building Station. Bulletin

Commonw Exp Build Stat RF — Australia. Commonwealth Experimental Building Station. CEBS Researchers and Facilities

Commonw Exp Build Stat SR — Australia. Commonwealth Experimental Building Station. Special Report

Commonw Exp Build Stat TS — Australia. Commonwealth Experimental Building Station. Technical Study

Commonw Fert — Commonwealth Fertilizer

Commonw For Bur Tech Commun — Commonwealth Forestry Bureau. Technical Communication

Commonw For Rev — Commonwealth Forestry Review

Commonw Geol Liaison Off Liaison Rep — Commonwealth Geological Liaison Office. Liaison Report

Commonw Geol Liaison Off Spec Liaison Rep — Commonwealth Geological Liaison Office. Special Liaison Report [*London*]

Commonw Inst Biol Control Misc Publ — Commonwealth Institute of Biological Control. Miscellaneous Publication

Commonw Inst Helminthol Albans Tech Commun — Commonwealth Institute of Helminthology. Saint Albans Technical Communication

Commonw L Rep — Commonwealth Law Reports

Commonw Min Metall Congr Proc — Commonwealth Mining and Metallurgical Congress. Proceedings

Commonw Mycol Inst Descr Pathog Fungi Bact — Commonwealth Mycological Institute. Descriptions of Pathogenic Fungi and Bacteria

Commonw Mycol Inst Mycol Pap — Commonwealth Mycological Institute. Mycological Papers

Commonw Mycol Inst Phytopathol Pap — Commonwealth Mycological Institute. Phytopathological Papers

Commonw Phytopath News — Commonwealth Phytopathological News

Comm Partial Differential Equations — Communications in Partial Differential Equations

Comm Phys-M — Commentationes Physico-Mathematicae

Comm Phytopathol News — Commonwealth Phytopathological News

Comm Probl Drug Depend Proc Annu Sci Meet US Nat Res Counc — Committee on Problems of Drug Dependence. Proceedings of the Annual Scientific Meeting. United States National Research Council

Comm Prop J — Community Property Journal

Comm Pure Appl Math — Communications on Pure and Applied Mathematics

Comm Q — Communication Quarterly

Comm Rep — Commerce Reports

Comm Res — Communication Research

Comm Res Trends — Communication Research Trends

Comm Roy Soc Edinburgh Phys Sci — Communications. Royal Society of Edinburgh. Physical Sciences

Comms N — Communications News

Comm Soil S — Communications in Soil Science and Plant Analysis

Comm St A — Communications in Statistics. Part A. Theory and Methods

Comm Statis — Communications in Statistics

Comm Statist A Theory Methods — Communications in Statistics. Part A. Theory and Methods

Comm Statist B Simulation Comput — Communications in Statistics. Part B. Simulation and Computation

Comm Statist Econometric Rev — Communications in Statistics. Econometric Reviews

Comm Statist Sequential Anal — Communications in Statistics. Part C. Sequential Analysis

Comm Statist Simulation Comput — Communications in Statistics. Part B. Simulation and Computation

Comm Statist Theory Methods — Communications in Statistics. Part A. Theory and Methods

Comm St B — Communications in Statistics. Part B. Simulation and Computation

Comm Today — Commerce Today

Commun — Communion

Commun ACM — Communications. ACM [*Association for Computing Machinery*]

Commun Action — Community Action

Commun Algebra — Communications in Algebra

Commun Arts Mag — Communication Arts Magazine

Commun Assoc Int Limnol Theor Appl — Communications. Association Internationale de Limnologie Theorique et Appliquee

Commun Aust — Communications Australia

Commun Balai Penjelidikan Pemakaian Karet — Communication. Balai Penjelidikan dan Pemakaian Karet

Commun Behav Biol Part A Orig Artic — Communications in Behavioral Biology. Part A. Original Articles

Commun Biohist — Occasional Communications. Utrecht University. Biohistorical Institute

Commun Broadc — Communication and Broadcasting

Commun Broadcast — Communication and Broadcasting [*England*]

Commun Care — Community Care

Commun Cent Rech Zootech Univ Louv — Communication. Centre de Recherches Zootechniques. Universite de Louvain

Commun Cybern — Communication and Cybernetics

Commun and Cybernet — Communication and Cybernetics

Commun Dep Agric Res R Trop Inst (Amst) — Communication. Department of Agricultural Research. Royal Tropical Institute (Amsterdam)

Commun Dep Anat Univ Lund (Swed) — Communication. Department of Anatomy. University of Lund (Sweden)

Commun Dev J — Community Development Journal

Commun Dublin Inst Adv Stud A — Communications. Dublin Institute for Advanced Studies. Series A

Commun Dublin Inst Adv Stud Ser A — Communications. Dublin Institute for Advanced Studies. Series A

Commun Dublin Inst Adv Stud Ser D — Communications. Dublin Institute for Advanced Studies. Series D. Geophysical Bulletin

Commun Electron — Communications and Electronics [*England*]

Commun Eng — Communication Engineering

Commun Eng Int — Communications Engineering International

Commun Equip & Syst Des — Communications Equipment and Systems Design

Commun Fac Med Vet Univ Etat Gand — Communications. Faculte de Medecine Veterinaire. Universite de l'Etat Gand

Commun Fac Sci Univ Ankara — Communications. Faculte des Sciences. Universite d'Ankara

Commun Fac Sci Univ Ankara Ser A2 — Communications. Faculte des Sciences. Universite d'Ankara. Serie A2. Physique

Commun Fac Sci Univ Ankara Ser B — Communications. Faculte des Sciences. Universite d'Ankara. Serie B. Chimie

Commun Fac Sci Univ Ankara Ser C — Communications. Faculte des Sciences. Universite d'Ankara. Serie C. Sciences Naturelles

Commun Fac Sci Univ Ankara Ser C Sci Nat — Communications. Faculte des Sciences. Universite d'Ankara. Serie C. Sciences Naturelles

Commun Fac Vet Med State Univ (Ghent) — Communications. Faculty of Veterinary Medicine. State University (Ghent)

Communicable Disease Rep — Communicable Disease Report

Communic Afr — Communications Africa

Communication Studies Bull — Communication Studies Bulletin [*United Kingdom*]

Communication Tech Impact — Communications Technology Impact

Communic et Lang — Communication et Langages

Commun Inst For Cech — Communicationes. Instituti Forestalis Cechosloveniae

Commun Inst For Csl — Communicationes. Instituti Forestalis Cechosloveniae

Commun Inst For Fenn — Communicationes. Instituti Forestalis Fenniae

Commun Inst For Res Agric Univ (Wageningen) — Communication. Institute of Forestry Research. Agricultural University (Wageningen) [*Netherlands*]

Commun Inst Therm Appl Ec Polytech Fed Lausanne — Communication. Institut de Thermique Appliquee. Ecole Polytechnique Federale de Lausanne [*Switzerland*]

Commun Int — Communications International

Commun Int Assoc Theor Appl Limnol — Communications. International Association of Theoretical and Applied Limnology

Communist China Dig — Communist China Digest

Communist Chin Sci Abstr — Communist Chinese Scientific Abstracts

Communist R — Communist Review

Communist Rev — Communist Review

Communit — Communities

Communit Health S Afr — Community Health in South Africa

Community Dent Oral Epidemiol — Community Dentistry and Oral Epidemiology

Community Devel J — Community Development Journal

Community Develop J — Community Development Journal

Community Development J — Community Development Journal

Community Dev J — Community Development Journal

Community Jr Coll J — Community and Junior College Journal

Community Med — Community Medicine

Community Ment Health J — Community Mental Health Journal

Community Ment Health Rev — Community Mental Health Review [*Later, Prevention in Human Services*]

Community Ment Hlth J — Community Mental Health Journal

Community Prop J — Community Property Journal

Commun Jajasan Penjelidikan Pemakain Karet — Communications. Jajasan Penjelidikan dan Pemakain Karet

Commun J Inst Nucl Res (Dubna) — Communications. Joint Institute for Nuclear Research (Dubna)
Commun Kamerlingh Onnes Lab Univ Leiden — Communications. Kamerlingh Onnes Laboratory. University of Leiden
Commun Kamerlingh Onnes Lab Univ Leiden Suppl — Communications. Kamerlingh Onnes Laboratory. University of Leiden. Supplement
Commun & Law — Communications and the Law
Commun Lunar & Planet Lab — Communications. Lunar and Planetary Laboratory
Commun Math Inst Rijksuniv Utrecht — Communications. Mathematical Institute. Rijksuniversiteit Utrecht
Commun Math Phys — Communications in Mathematical Physics
Commun News — Communications News
Commun Nurs Res — Communicating Nursing Research
Commun NV K Ned Springstoffenfabr — Communication. NV [*Naamloze Vennootschap*] Koninklijke Nederlandsche Springstoffenfabrieken
Commun Part Differ Equ — Communications in Partial Differential Equations
Commun Phys — Communications on Physics
Commun Phys Lab Univ Leiden — Communications. Physical Laboratory. University of Leiden
Commun Psychopharmacol — Communications in Psychopharmacology
Commun Pure Appl Math — Communications on Pure and Applied Mathematics
Commun Quart — Communication Quarterly
Commun Res Inst Sumatra Plant Assoc Rubber Ser — Communications. Research Institute of the Sumatra Planters' Association. Rubber Series
Commun R Soc Edinburgh Phys Sci — Communications. Royal Society of Edinburgh. Physical Sciences
Commun Sci & Tech Inf — Communicator of Scientific and Technical Information
Communs Electron (Lond) — Communications and Electronics (London)
Communs Fac Sci Univ Ankara — Communications. Faculte des Sciences. Universite d'Ankara. Serie C
Commun Soil Sci Plant Anal — Communications in Soil Science and Plant Analysis
Commun Stat — Communications in Statistics
Commun Stat A — Communications in Statistics. Part A. Theory and Methods
Commun Stat B — Communications in Statistics. Part B. Simulation and Computation
Commun Stat Part A Theory Methods — Communications in Statistics. Part A. Theory and Methods
Commun Stat Part B — Communications in Statistics. Part B. Simulation and Computation
Commun Swed Sugar Corp — Communications. Swedish Sugar Corporation
Commun Transport Q — Community Transport Quarterly
Commun Vet — Communicationes Veterinariae
Commutat & Electron — Commutation et Electronique
Commutation Electron — Commutation et Electronique
Commutat and Transm — Commutation and Transmission
Comm Veh — Commercial Vehicles
CommViat — Communio Viatorum. A Theological Quarterly [*Prague*]
Commw Arb — Commonwealth Arbitration Reports
Commw Art — Commonwealth Arbitration Reports
Commw Exp Build Stat NSB — Commonwealth Experimental Building Station. Notes on the Science of Building
Commw LB — Commonwealth Law Bulletin
Commw LR — Commonwealth Law Reports
Commwth Eng — Commonwealth Engineer
Com Nac Energ Nucl (Braz) Bol — Comissao Nacional de Energia Nuclear (Brazil). Boletim
Com Nac Energ Nucl (Mex) Publ — Comision Nacional de Energia Nuclear (Mexico). Publicacion
Com Naz Energ Nucl Not — Comitato Nazionale per l'Energia Nucleare. Notiziario
Com Naz Energ Nucl Repr — Comitato Nazionale per l'Energia Nucleare. Reprints
Com Naz Ric Nucl (Italy) Not — Comitato Nazionale per le Ricerche Nucleari (Italy). Notiziario
COMNB — Commentary
Comnty — Community Newspapers
Comp — Compass
COMPA — Compost Science [*Later, Bio Cycle*]
Compagn Franc Petrol Notes Mem — Compagnie Francaise des Petroles. Notes et Memoires
Comp Air Mag — Compressed Air Magazine
Com P A Math — Communications on Pure and Applied Mathematics
COMPAN — Compost Science [*Later, Bio Cycle*]
Comp Anim Nutr — Comparative Animal Nutrition
Company Law — Company Lawyer
Comparative Ed — Comparative Education
Comparative Educ R — Comparative Education Review
Compare — Journal. Comparative Education Society in Europe (British Section)
Compar Pol Stud — Comparative Political Studies
Comp & Automation — Computers and Automation [*Later, Computers and People*]

Comp Bioc A — Comparative Biochemistry and Physiology. A
Comp Bioc B — Comparative Biochemistry and Physiology. B
Comp Bioc C — Comparative Biochemistry and Physiology. C
Comp Biochem Physiol — Comparative Biochemistry and Physiology
Comp Biochem Physiol A Comp Physiol — Comparative Biochemistry and Physiology. A. Comparative Physiology
Comp Biochem Physiol B — Comparative Biochemistry and Physiology. B. Comparative Biochemistry
Comp Biochem Physiol B Comp Biochem — Comparative Biochemistry and Physiology. B. Comparative Biochemistry
Comp Biochem Physiol C — Comparative Biochemistry and Physiology. C. Comparative Pharmacology [*Later, Comparative Biochemistry and Physiology. C. Comparative Pharmacology and Toxicology*]
Comp Biochem Physiol C Comp Pharmacol — Comparative Biochemistry and Physiology. C. Comparative Pharmacology [*Later, Comparative Biochemistry and Physiology. C. Comparative Pharmacology and Toxicology*]
Comp Biochem Physiol C Comp Pharmacol Toxicol — Comparative Biochemistry and Physiology. C. Comparative Pharmacology and Toxicology
Comp Bul — Computer Bulletin
Comp Chem — Computers and Chemistry
Comp Civ R — Comparative Civilizations Review
Comp Comm — Computer Communications
Comp Compacts — Computer Compacts
CompD — Comparative Drama
Comp Data — Computer Data
Comp Dec — Computer Decisions
Comp Decisions — Computer Decisions
Comp Des — Computer Design
CompDr — Comparative Drama
Comp Drama — Comparative Drama
Comp Ed — Comparative Education
Comp Ed R — Comparative Education Review
Comp Educ — Comparative Education
Comp & Educ — Computers and Education
Comp Educ R — Comparative Education Review
Comp Edu Re — Comparative Education Review
Compend Dtsch Ges Mineraloelwiss Kohlechem — Compendium. Deutsche Gesellschaft fuer Mineraloelwissenschaft und Kohlechemie [*East Germany*]
Compend Tech Pap Annu Meet Inst Transp Eng — Compendium of Technical Papers. Annual Meeting. Institute of Transportation Engineers
Compens Med — Compensation Medicine
Compens R — Compensation Review
Compens Rev — Compensation Review
Comp Fluids — Computers and Fluids
Comp Gen Pharmacol — Comparative and General Pharmacology
Comp Gra Forum — Computer Graphics Forum
Comp Graphics — Computer Graphics
Comp Graph Wrld — Computer Graphics World
Compil Res Work Accomplished Weld Res Inst (Bratislava) — Compilation of Research Work Accomplished in the Welding Research Institute (Bratislava)
Comp Immunol Microbiol Infect Dis — Comparative Immunology, Microbiology, and Infectious Diseases
Comp Int Law J South Afr — Comparative and International Law Journal of Southern Africa
Comp & Int LJ South Africa — Comparative and International Law Journal of Southern Africa
Comp & Int'l LJS Afr — Comparative and International Law Journal of Southern Africa
Comp J — Computer Journal
Comp Jurid Rev — Comparative Juridical Review
Comp Jur Rev — Comparative Juridical Review
Comp L — Comparative Literature
CompL — Computational Linguistics
Comp Lab Law — Comparative Labor Law
Com Plan R — Community Planning Review
Comp Law — Computer Law and Tax Report
Comp Lawy — Company Lawyer
Comp Lit — Comparative Literature
Comp Lit St — Comparative Literature Studies
Comp Lit Stud — Comparative Literature Studies
Comp L Rev — Comparative Law Review
Comp L Rev Japan Inst — Comparative Law Review. Japan Institute of Comparative Law
Comp L Ser — Comparative Law Series. United States Bureau of Foreign and Domestic Commerce. General Legal Bulletin
Comp Master Marin Aust J — Company of Master Mariners of Australia. Journal
Comp Math — Compositio Mathematica
Comp & Med — Computers and Medicine
Comp Med East West — Comparative Medicine East and West
Comp Methods Appl Mech Eng — Computer Methods in Applied Mechanics and Engineering

Comp Mgmt — Computer Management
Comp Net — Computer Networks
Comp News-Rec — Composers News-Record
Components Rep — Components Report
Component Technol — Component Technology
Comp Oper Res — Computers and Operations Research
Composites Technol Rev — Composites Technology Review
Compositio Math — Compositio Mathematica
Compos Mater — Composite Materials
Compos Technol Rev — Composites Technology Review
Compost Sci — Compost Science [*Later, Bio Cycle*]
Compost Sci Land Util — Compost Science/Land Utilization [*Later, Bio Cycle*]
Comp Pathol Bull — Comparative Pathology Bulletin
Comp & People — Computers and People
Comp Pers — Computer Personnel
Comp Phys Comm — Computer Physics Communications
Comp Physiol Ecol — Comparative Physiology and Ecology
Comp Pol — Comparative Politics
Comp Poli S — Comparative Political Studies
Comp Polit — Comparative Politics
Comp Polit Stud — Comparative Political Studies
Comp Pol Stud — Comparative Political Studies
Comp Psychi — Comprehensive Psychiatry
Compr Anal Chem — Comprehensive Analytical Chemistry
Comprehensive Ed — Comprehensive Education
Comprehensive Nurs Mon (Tokyo) — Comprehensive Nursing Monthly (Tokyo)
Compres Air — Compressed Air
Compress Air — Compressed Air
Comp Rev — Compensation Review
Comp Rev — Computing Reviews
Compr Immunol — Comprehensive Immunology
Compr Nurs Q — Comprehensive Nursing Quarterly
Compr Pediatr Nurs — Comprehensive Pediatric Nursing
Compr Psychiatry — Comprehensive Psychiatry
Compr Ther — Comprehensive Therapy
Comp Stud S — Comparative Studies in Society and History
Comp Stud Soc Hist — Comparative Studies in Society and History
Comp Stud Soc & Hist — Comparative Studies in Society and History
Comp Surv — Computing Surveys
Comp Talk — Computer Talk
Comp Tech Rev — Composites Technology Review
Comptes Rend — Comptes Rendus. Academie des Sciences
Comptes Rendus — Comptes Rendus Hebdomadaires des Seances. Academie des Sciences
Compt Rend Acad — Comptes Rendus des Seances. Academie des Inscriptions et Belles-Lettres
Compt Rend Acad Agr France — Comptes Rendus. Academie d'Agriculture de France
Compt Rend Acad Bulg Sci — Comptes Rendus. Academie Bulgare des Sciences
Compt Rend Acad Sci — Comptes Rendus. Academie des Sciences
Compt Rend Acad Sci Outre-Mer — Comptes Rendus Trimestriels des Seances. Academie des Sciences d'Outre-Mer
Compt Rend Acad Sc (Paris) — Comptes Rendus Hebdomadaires des Seances. Academie des Sciences (Paris)
Compt Rend Cong Internat Med Trop et Hyg — Comptes Rendus. Congres International de Medecine Tropicale et d'Hygiene
Compt Rend Soc Biol (Paris) — Comptes Rendus des Seances. Societe de Biologie et de Ses Filiales et Associees (Paris)
Comp Urb Res — Comparative Urban Research
Comput — Computer
Comput Abstr — Computer Abstracts
Comput Acquis Syst Ser — Computerized Acquisitions Systems Series
Comput Aided Des — Computer-Aided Design
Comput Appl — Computer Applications
Comput Appl — Computers and Their Applications
Comput Appl Archaeol — Computer Applications in Archaeology
Comput Appl Chem (China) — Computers and Applied Chemistry (China)
Comput Appl Nat and Soc Sci — Computer Applications in the Natural and Social Sciences
Comput Appl Serv — Computer Applications Service
Comput Arch Elektron Rechn — Computing. Archiv fuer Elektronisches Rechnen
Comput Arch Inf Num — Computing. Archiv fuer Informatik und Numerik
Comput Archit News — Computer Architecture News
Comput Autom — Computers and Automation [*Later, Computers and People*]
Comput and Autom and People — Computers and Automation and People
Comput Biol and Med — Computers in Biology and Medicine
Comput Biol Med — Computers in Biology and Medicine
Comput Biom — Computers and Biomedical Research
Comput Biomed Res — Computers and Biomedical Research
Comput and Biomed Res — Computers and Biomedical Research
Comput Bull — Computer Bulletin
Comput Busn — Computer Business News
Comput Bus News — Computer Business News

Comput Cardiol — Computers in Cardiology
Comput Cat Syst Ser — Computerized Cataloging Systems Series
Comput Chem — Computers and Chemistry
Comput Chem Biochem Res — Computers in Chemical and Biochemical Research
Comput & Chem Eng — Computers and Chemical Engineering
Comput Chem Eng — Computers and Chemical Engineering
Comput Chem Instrum — Computers in Chemistry and Instrumentation
Comput Circ Syst Ser — Computerized Circulation Systems Series
Comput Commun — Computer Communications
Comput Commun Rev — Computer Communication Review
Comput & Contr Abstr — Computer and Control Abstracts [*IEE*]
Comput Contrib — Computer Contributions
Comput Control Abstr — Computer and Control Abstracts [*IEE*]
Comput Control Abstracts — Computer and Control Abstracts [*IEE*]
Comput Control Inf Theory — Computers, Control, and Information Theory
Comput Data — Computer Data
Comput and Data Process Technol — Computer and Data Processor Technology
Comput Decis — Computer Decisions
Comput Des — Computer Design
Comput Educ — Computer Education
Comput and Educ — Computers and Education
Comput Electr Eng — Computers and Electrical Engineering
Comput & Electr Eng — Computers and Electrical Engineering
Comput Electr Engrg — Computers and Electrical Engineering
Comput Elem Syst — Computer Elements and Systems
Comput Engrg Ser — Computer Engineering Series
Comput Enhanc Spectrosc — Computer Enhanced Spectroscopy
Comput Environ Urban Syst — Computers, Environment, and Urban Systems [*England*]
Comput Equip Rev — Computer Equipment Review
Computer Aided Des — Computer-Aided Design
Computer Ed — Computer Education Conference
Computer Engrg Ser — Computer Engineering Series
Computer Hu — Computers and the Humanities [*Database*]
Computer J — Computer Journal
Computer LJ — Computer-Law Journal
Computer Mus J — Computer Music Journal
Computer Pe — Computers and People
Computer Ph — Computer Physics Communications
Computer Pr — Computer Programs in Biomedicine
Computers Geosci — Computers and Geosciences
Computer Wkly — Computer Weekly
Comput and Fluids — Computers and Fluids
Comput Fraud and Secur Bull — Computer Fraud and Security Bulletin
Comput & Geosci — Computers and Geosciences
Comput Geosci — Computers and Geosciences
Comput Graphics — Computers and Graphics
Comput & Graphics — Computers and Graphics
Comput Graphics and Art — Computer Graphics and Art
Comput Graphics and Image Process — Computer Graphics and Image Processing
Comput Graphics Image Process — Computer Graphics and Image Processing
Comput Graphics World — Computer Graphics World
Comput Hum — Computers and the Humanities [*Database*]
Comput & Humanities — Computers and the Humanities [*Database*]
Comput Ind — Computers in Industry [*Netherlands*]
Comput Ind Eng — Computers and Industrial Engineering
Comput Inf — Computer Information
Comput & Info Sys — Computer and Information Systems
Computing J Abs — Computing Journal Abstracts
Comput J — Computer Journal
Comput L — Computational Linguistics
Comput Lang — Computer Languages
Comput Manage — Computer Management
Comput Math Appl — Computers and Mathematics with Applications
Comput & Math with Appl — Computers and Mathematics with Applications
Comput Med — Computers and Medicine
Comput Methods Appl Mech & Eng — Computer Methods in Applied Mechanics and Engineering
Comput Methods Appl Mech Eng — Computer Methods in Applied Mechanics and Engineering
Comput Methods Appl Mech & Engng — Computer Methods in Applied Mechanics and Engineering
Comput Methods Appl Mech Engrg — Computer Methods in Applied Mechanics and Engineering
Comput Mgmt — Computer Management
Comput Mus — Computer Music Journal
Comput Music J — Computer Music Journal
Comput Networks — Computer Networks
Comput Newsl Schools Bus — Computing Newsletter for Schools of Business
Comput Oper Res — Computers and Operations Research
Comput & Oper Res — Computers and Operations Research
Comput and People — Computers and People
Comput Performance — Computer Performance

Comput Peripherals Rev — Computer Peripherals Review
Comput Pers — Computer Personnel
Comput Phys Comm — Computer Physics Communications
Comput Phys Commun — Computer Physics Communications
Comput Phys Rep — Computer Physics Reports
Comput Prax — Computer Praxis
Comput Program Abstr — Computer Program Abstracts
Comput Programs Biomed — Computer Programs in Biomedicine
Comput Programs Chem — Computer Programs for Chemistry
Comput Rep Dep Archit Sci Syd Univ — Computer Report. Department of
  Architectural Science. University of Sydney
Comput Rev — Computing Reviews
Comput S Afr — Computing South Africa
Comput Sci Appl Math — Computer Science and Applied Mathematics
Comput Sci Monographs (Tokyo) — Computer Science Monographs (Tokyo)
Comput and Secur — Computers and Security
Comput Ser Syst Ser — Computerized Serials Systems Series
Comput and Soc — Computers and Society
Comput Stat and Data Anal — Computational Statistics and Data Analysis
Comput and Struct — Computers and Structures
Comput Struct — Computers and Structures
Comput and Structures — Computers and Structures
Comput Stud Hum & Verbal Behav — Computer Studies in the Humanities
  and Verbal Behavior
Comput Suppl — Computing. Supplementum [*Vienna*]
Comput Surv — Computer Survey
Comput Surv — Computing Surveys
Comput Survey — Computing Surveys
Comput Talk — Computer Talk
Comput Terminals Rev — Computer Terminals Review
Comput Times with Computacards — Computer Times with Computacards
Comput Today — Computing Today
Comput Tomogr — Computerized Tomography
Comput Vision Graphics and Image Process — Computer Vision. Graphics and
  Image Processing
Comput Week — Computer Week
Comput Wkly — Computer Weekly
Comput Wkly Int — Computer Weekly International
Comput World — Computer World
Computwrld — Computerworld
Comp Wkly — Computer Weekly
Compwrld on Comm — Computerworld on Communications
Compwrld OA — Computerworld Office Automation
ComQ — Commonwealth Quarterly
COMRDW — Computerized Radiology
ComRev — Computing Reviews
COMSAT Tech Rev — COMSAT [*Communications Satellite Corp.*]
  Technical Review
Com Spec Katanga Ann Ser Mines Ser Geogr Geol — Comite Special du
  Katanga. Annales du Service des Mines et du Service Geographique et
  Geologique
Com Stat Energ Nucl Inst Fiz At Rep (Rom) — Comitetul de Stat pentru
  Energia Nucleara. Institutul de Fizica Atomica. Report (Romania)
Comt — Commentary
Com Today — Commerce Today
Comun Acad Rep Pop Romine — Comunicarile. Academiei Republicii Populare
  Romine
Comun Acad Repub Pop Rom — Comunicarile. Academiei Republicii Populare
  Romine
Comun Bot — Comunicari de Botanica
Comun Bot Mus Hist Nat Montev — Comunicaciones Botanicas. Museo de
  Historia Natural de Montevideo
Comun Coloq Invest Agua — Comunicaciones Presentadas al Coloquio de
  Investigaciones sobre el Agua
Comun y Cult — Comunicacion y Cultura
Comunicacao e Soc — Comunicacao e Sociedade
Comunicari Bot — Comunicari de Botanica
Comun INIA (Inst Nac Invest Agrar) Ser Tecnol — Comunicaciones. INIA
  (Instituto Nacional de Investigaciones Agrarias). Serie Tecnologia
Comun INIA Prot Veg — Comunicaciones. INIA [*Instituto Nacional de
  Investigaciones Agrarias*]. Serie Proteccion Vegetal
Comun INIA Ser Prod Veg — Comunicaciones. INIA [*Instituto Nacional de
  Investigaciones Agrarias*]. Serie Produccion Vegetal
Comun INIA Ser Prod Veg Inst Nac Invest Agrar — Comunicaciones INIA
  [*Instituto Nacional de Investigaciones Agrarias*]. Serie Production
  Vegetal
Comun INIA Ser Prot Veg — Comunicaciones. INIA [*Instituto Nacional de
  Investigaciones Agrarias*]. Serie Proteccion Vegetal
Comun INIA Ser Pro Veg (Spain) — Comunicaciones. INIA [*Instituto
  Nacional de Investigaciones Agrarias*]. Serie Proteccion Vegetal
  (Spain)
Comun INIA Ser Recur Nat — Comunicaciones. INIA [*Instituto Nacional de
  Investigaciones Agrarias*]. Serie Recursos Naturales
Comun Inst Cienc Nat Mat Univ El Salvador — Comunicaciones. Instituto de
  Ciencias Naturales y Matematicas. Universidad de El Salvador

Comun Inst For Invest Exp (Madrid) — Comunicacion. Instituto Forestal de
  Investigaciones y Experiencias (Madrid)
Comun Inst Nac Invest Cienc Nat Cienc Bot — Comunicaciones. Instituto
  Nacional de Investigacion de las Ciencias Naturales. Ciencias Botanicas
Comun Inst Trop Invest Cient — Comunicaciones. Instituto Tropical de
  Investigaciones Cientificas
Comunita Int — Comunita Internazionale
Comunita Internaz — Comunita Internazionale
Comun Missao Estud Agron Ultramar (Lisb) — Comunicacao-Missao de
  Estudos Agronomicos do Ultramar (Lisbon)
Comun Mus Cienc PUCRGS (Pontif Univ Catol Rio Grande Do Sul) —
  Comunicacoes. Museu de Ciencias. PUCRGS (Pontificia Universidade
  Catolica do Rio Grande Do Sul)
Comun Paleontol Mus Hist Nat Montev — Comunicaciones Paleontologicas.
  Museo de Historia Natural de Montevideo
Comun Serv Geol Port — Comunicacoes. Servicos Geologicos de Portugal
Comun Soc Malacol Urug — Comunicaciones. Sociedad Malacologica del
  Uruguay
Comun Stiint Simp Biodeterior Clim — Comunicari Stiintifice. Simpozion de
  Biodeteriorare si Climatizare
Comun Tec Empresa Pesqui Agropecu Bahia — Comunicado Tecnico. Empresa
  de Pesquisa Agropecuaria da Bahia
Comun Tec Empresa Pesqui Agropecu Estado Rio De J — Comunicado
  Tecnico. Empresa de Pesquisa Agropecuaria do Estado do Rio De
  Janeiro
Comun Tec Inst Ecol Exp Agric — Comunicados Tecnicos. Instituto de
  Ecologia e Experimentacao Agricolas
Comun Univ El Salvador Inst Cienc Nat Mat — Comunicaciones. Universidad
  de El Salvador. Instituto de Ciencias Naturales y Matematicas
Comun Zool — Comunicari de Zoologie
Comun Zool Mus Hist Nat Montev — Comunicaciones Zoologicas. Museo de
  Historia Natural de Montevideo
Com Via — Communio Viatorum
Comw — Commonweal
CON — Conservator. Vaktijdschrift voor de Iisfrica Branche
Con — Contact
Con — Contour
Con — Convivium
CONAEL — Contaminacion Ambiental
Con BJ — Connecticut Bar Journal
Conc — Concilium. Internationale Zeitschrift fuer Theologie [*Einsiedeln/
  Zurich/Mainz*]
Concimi Concimaz — Concimi e Concimazione
Conc Milk Ind — Concentrated Milk Industries
Concor — Concordia Theological Monthly
Concours Med — Concours Medical
ConcPo — Concerning Poetry
Conc Poet — Concerning Poetry
Concr Cem Age — Concrete Cement Age
Concr Constr — Concrete Construction
Concr Constru Eng — Concrete and Constructional Engineering
Concr Eng — Concrete Engineering
Concrete P — Concrete Products
Concr Inst Aust News — Concrete Institute of Australia. News
Concr J — Concrete Journal [*Japan*]
Concr Soc Tech Rep — Concrete Society. Technical Report
ConcTM — Concordia Theological Monthly [*St. Louis, MO*]
Condition — Conditions
Condotta Med — Condotta Medica
Cond Reflex — Conditional Reflex
CONEAT — Confinia Neurologica
Conf — Conferencia
Conf — Confluence
CONFA — Confructa
Conf Adrenal Cortex Trans — Conference on Adrenal Cortex. Transactions
Conf Adv Magn Mater Their Appl — Conference on Advances in Magnetic
  Materials and Their Applications
Conf Aust Fract Group (Proc) — Australian Fracture Group Conference
  (Proceedings)
CONFAW — Confructa
Conf Bd Bsns Mgt Rec — Conference Board. Business Management Record
Conf Bd Bsns Rec — Conference Board. Business Record
Conf Bd Rec — Conference Board. Record
Conf Biol Antioxid Trans — Conference on Biological Antioxidants.
  Transactions
Conf Blood Clotting Allied Probl Trans — Conference on Blood Clotting and
  Allied Problems. Transactions
Conf Board Rec — Conference Board. Record
Conf Capturing Sun Bioconver Pro — Conference on Capturing the Sun
  through Bioconversion. Proceedings
Conf Char and Correc — National Conference of Charities and Correction.
  Proceedings
Conf Circompolaire Ecol Nord R — Conference Circompolaire sur l'Ecologie
  du Nord. Compte Rendu
Conf City Govt — National Conference for Good City Government.
  Proceedings

Conf City Planning — National Conference on City Planning. Proceedings

Conf Compat Propellants Explos Pyrotech Plast Addit — Conference on Compatibility of Propellants, Explosives, and Pyrotechnics with Plastics and Additives

Conf Connect Tissues Trans — Conference on Connective Tissues. Transactions

Conf Control Gaseous Sulphur Nitrogen Comp Emiss — Conference on the Control of Gaseous Sulphur and Nitrogen Compound Emission

Conf Cult Mar Invertebr Anim Proc — Conference on Culture of Marine Invertebrate Animals. Proceedings

Conf Dig Int Electr Electron Conf Expo — Conference Digest. International Electrical, Electronics Conference Exposition

Confect Manuf — Confectionery Manufacture

Confed Nac Com — Confederacao Nacional do Comercio

Confed Nat Mutualite Coop Cred Agric Congres — Confederation Nationale de la Mutualite de la Cooperation et du Credit Agricoles Congres

Conf Environ Chem Hum Anim Health Proc — Conference on Environmental Chemicals. Human and Animal Health. Proceedings

Confer Sem Mat Univ Bari — Conferenze. Seminario di Matematica. Universita di Bari

Conf Eur Microcirc — Conference Europeenne sur la Microcirculation

Conf Great Lakes Res Proc — Conference on Great Lakes Research. Proceedings

Confin Neurol — Confinia Neurologica

Confin Psychiatr — Confinia Psychiatrica

Conf Inst Nac Invest Agron Min Agr (Spain) — Conferencias. Instituto Nacional de Investigaciones Agronomicas. Ministerio Agricultura (Spain)

Conf Inst Nac Invest Agron (Spain) — Conferencias. Instituto Nacional de Investigaciones Agronomicas (Spain)

Conf Interam Agric (Caracas) — Conferencia Interamericana de Agricultura (Caracas)

Conf Int Grands Reseaux Elec Haute Tension — Conference Internationale des Grands Reseaux Electriques a Haute Tension

Conflict Mgt and Peace Science — Conflict Management and Peace Science

Conflict Q — Conflict Quarterly

Conf Liver Inj Trans — Conference on Liver Injury. Transactions

Conf Metab Interrelat Trans — Conference on Metabolic Interrelations. Transactions

Conform Anal Pap Int Symp — Conformational Analysis. Scope and Present Limitations Papers Presented at the International Symposium

Conf Palais Decouverte Ser A — Conferences. Palais de la Decouverte. Serie A

Conf Pap Inst Metall Tech (London) — Conference Papers. Institute of Metallurgical Technicians (London)

Conf Pap Int Cosmic Ray Conf — Conference Papers. International Cosmic Ray Conference

Conf Pers Fin LQR — Conference on Personal Finance Law. Quarterly Report

Conf Pers Fin L Q Rep — Conference on Personal Finance Law. Quarterly Report

Conf Probl Aging Trans — Conference on Problems of Aging. Transactions

Conf Probl Conscious Trans — Conference on Problems of Consciousness. Transactions

Conf Probl Early Infancy Trans — Conference on Problems of Early Infancy. Transactions

Conf Probl Infancy Child Trans — Conference on Problems of Infancy and Childhood. Transactions

Conf Proc Annu Symp Comput Archit — Conference Proceedings. Annual Symposium on Computer Architecture

Conf Proc Int Conf Fire Saf — Conference Proceedings. International Conference on Fire Safety

Conf Proc Intersoc Energy Convers Eng Conf — Conference Proceedings. Intersociety Energy Conversion Engineering Conference

Conf Proc Recycl World Congr — Conference Proceedings. Recycling World Congress

Conf Prod Prop Test Aggregates Pap — Conference on the Production, Properties, and Testing of Aggregates. Papers

Conf Psych — Confinia Psychiatrica

Conf Publ Inst Mech Eng — Conference Publications. Institution of Mechanical Engineers

Conf Publiques Univ Damas — Conferences Publiques. Universite de Damas

Confr — Confrontation

Conf Read (Univ Chicago) — Conference on Reading (University of Chicago). Proceedings

Conf on Read (Univ Pittsburgh) Rep — Conference on Reading (University of Pittsburgh). Report

Conf Rec Annu Pulp Pap Ind Tech Conf — Conference Record. Annual Pulp and Paper Industry Technical Conference

Conf Rec Asilomar Conf Circuits Syst Comput — Conference Record. Asilomar Conference on Circuits Systems and Computers

Conf Rec IAS Annu Meet — Conference Record. IAS [*IEEE Industry Applications Society*] Annual Meeting

Conf Rec IEEE Photovoltaic Spec Conf — Conference Record. IEEE [*Institute of Electrical and Electronics Engineers*] Photovoltaic Specialists Conference

Conf Renal Funct Trans — Conference on Renal Function. Transactions

Conf Rep R Aust Inst Parks Rec — Conference Report. Australian Institute of Parks and Recreation

Confrontat — Confrontation

Confront Radio-Anatomo-Clin — Confrontations Radio-Anatomo-Cliniques [*France*]

Conf Solid State Devices Mater — Conference on Solid State Devices and Materials

Conf Solid State Devices Proc — Conference on Solid State Devices. Proceedings

Conf e Studi Accad Polacca Sci Bibl Centro Studi Roma — Conferenze e Studi. Accademia Polacca delle Scienze. Biblioteca e Centro di Studi a Roma

Conf Superionic Conduct Chem Phys Appl Pro — Conference on Superionic Conductors. Chemistry, Physics, and Applications. Proceedings

Cong — Congregationalist

Cong Cient Mexicano Mem Cienc Fisicas y Matematicas — Congreso Cientifico Mexicano. Memoria. Ciencias Fisicas y Matematicas

Cong Dig — Congressional Digest

Cong Digest — Congressional Digest

Cong Internat Med C R — Congres International de Medecine. Comptes Rendus

Congiunt Econ Lombarda — Congiuntura Economica Lombarda

Congiuntura Econ Laziale — Congiuntura Economica Laziale

Congiuntura Ital — Congiuntura Italiana

Cong M — Congregational Magazine

Cong Mo — Congregationalist Monthly Review

Cong and Presidency — Congress and the Presidency

Cong Q — Congregational Quarterly

Cong of Q Coop — Congress of Queensland Cooperatives. Papers and Proceedings

Cong Q W Rept — Congressional Quarterly. Weekly Report

Cong R — Congregational Review

Congr Assoc Fr Av Sci (Nancy) — Congres. Association Francaise pour l'Avancement des Sciences (Nancy)

Congr Assoc Geol Carpatho-Balkan Bull — Congres. Association Geologique Carpatho-Balkanique. Bulletin

Congr Av Etud Stratigr Geol Carbonifere C R — Congres pour l'Avancement des Etudes de Stratigraphie et de Geologie du Carbonifere. Compte Rendu

Congr Bras Apic — Congresso Brasileiro de Apicultura

Congr Conv Simp Sci CNR — Congressi. Convegni e Simposi Scientifici. Consiglio Nazionale delle Richerche

Congr Dig — Congressional Digest

Cong Rec — Congressional Record

Congres Archeol — Congres Archeologique de France

Congres Archeol de France — Congres Archeologique de France

Congresb Wereldcongr Oppervlaktebehandel Met — Congresboek. Wereldcongres voor Oppervlaktebehandeling van Metalen

Congres Pomol — Congres Pomologique

Congres des Rel Ind — Congres des Relations Industrielles. Universite Laval. Rapport

Congress Numer — Congressus Numerantium

Congress St — Congressional Studies

Congr Geol Argent Relat — Congreso Geologico Argentino. Relatorio

Congr Group Av Methodes Anal Spectrogr Prod Metall — Congres du Groupement pour l'Avancement des Methodes d'Analyse Spectrographique des Produits Metallurgiques

Congr Hung Pharmacol Soc Pro — Congress. Hungarian Pharmacological Society. Proceedings

Congr Ibero-Am Geol Econ — Congreso Ibero-Americano de Geologia Economica

Congr Industr Chem — Compte Rendu. Congres International de Chemie Industrielle

Congr Int Annu Assoc Nucl Can — Congres International Annuel. Association Nucleaire Canadienne

Congr Int Bot Rapp Commun — Congres International de Botanique. Rapports et Communications

Congr Int Cybern Actes — Congres International de Cybernetique. Actes

Congr Int Estud Pirenaicos Resumen Comun — Congreso Internacional de Estudios Pirenaicos. Resumen de las Comunicaciones

Congr Int Fed Soc Cosmet Chem Prepr Sci Pap — Congress of International Federation of Societies of Cosmetic Chemists. Preprint of Scientific Papers

Congr Int Hematol Conf — Congreso Internacional de Hematologia. Conferencias

Congr Int Jus Fruits — Congres International des Jus de Fruits

Congr Int Potash Inst — Congress. International Potash Institute

Congr Int Reprod Anim Insemination Artif — Congres International de Reproduction Animale et Insemination Artificielle

Congr Int Stratigr Geol Carbonifere C R — Congres International de Stratigraphie et de Geologie du Carbonifere. Compte Rendu

Congr Int Vigne Vin — Congres International de la Vigne du Vin

Congr Mond Recyclage Textes Conf — Congres Mondial du Recyclage. Textes de la Conference

Congr Nac Tuberc Enferm Respir — Congreso Nacional de Tuberculosis y Enfermedades Respiratorias

Congr Natl Soc Savantes Sect Sci C R — Congres National. Societes Savantes. Section des Sciences. Comptes Rendus

Congr Numer — Congressus Numerantium
Congr Print — Congress in Print
Congr Proc Recycl World Congr — Congress Proceedings. Recycling World Congress
Congr Venez Cir — Congreso Venezolano de Cirugia
Congr Yellow Book — Congressional Yellow Book
Con Int Explor Mer Bull Stat Peches Marit — Conseil International pour l'Exploration de la Mer. Bulletin Statistique des Peches Maritimes
Conjoncture Econ Maroc — Conjoncture Economique au Maroc
Conjuntura Econ — Conjuntura Economica
ConL — Contemporary Literature
Con Life — Consecrated Life
ConLit — Contemporary Literature
ConLit — Convorbiri Literare
Con LR — Connecticut Law Review
Con L Rev — Connecticut Law Review
Con Mus Ed — Contribution to Music Education
Conn — Connexions
Conn — Connoisseur
Conn — Connotation
Conn Acad Arts & Sci Trans — Connecticut Academy of Arts and Sciences. Transactions
Conn Agr Expt Sta Bull — Connecticut. Agricultural Experiment Station. Bulletin [*New Haven*]
Conn Agric Exp Stn Bull (New Haven) — Connecticut. Agricultural Experiment Station. Bulletin (New Haven)
Conn Agric Exp Stn Dep Entomol Spec Bull — Connecticut. Agricultural Experiment Station. Department of Entomology. Special Bulletin
Conn Agric Exp Stn (New Haven) Circ — Connecticut. Agricultural Experiment Station. Circular (New Haven)
Conn Agric Exp Stn Storrs Misc Publ — Connecticut. Agricultural Experiment Station. Storrs. Miscellaneous Publication
Conn Agric Exp Stn Storrs Res Rep — Connecticut. Agricultural Experiment Station. Storrs. Research Report
Connais Art — Connaissance des Arts
Connaiss Arts — Connaissance des Arts
Connaiss Loire — Connaissance de la Loire
Connaiss Plast — Connaissance des Plastiques
Conn Bar J — Connecticut Bar Journal
Conn B J — Connecticut Bar Journal
Connecticut L Rev — Connecticut Law Review
Connecticut Water Resources Bull — Connecticut Water Resources Bulletin
Connections J — Connections Journal
Connector Symp Proc — Connector Symposium. Proceedings
Connect Tis — Connective Tissue Research
Connect Tissue Res — Connective Tissue Research
Conn Geol Natur Hist Surv Bull — Connecticut. Geological and Natural History Survey. Bulletin
Conn Govt — Connecticut Government
Conn Greenhouse Newsl Univ Conn Coop Ext Ser — Connecticut Greenhouse Newsletter. University of Connecticut. Cooperative Extension Service
Conn G S — Connecticut. Geological and Natural History Survey
Conn Health Bull — Connecticut Health Bulletin
Conn His S — Connecticut Historical Society. Collections
Conn Hist Soc Bull — Connecticut Historical Society. Bulletin
Conn Hist Soc Coll — Connecticut Historical Society. Collections
ConnHSB — Connecticut Historical Society. Bulletin
Conn Ind — Connecticut Industry
Conn Lib — Connecticut Libraries
Conn Lib Assn Bul — Connecticut Library Association. Bulletin
Conn LJ — Connecticut Law Journal
Conn LR — Connecticut Law Review
Conn L Rev — Connecticut Law Review
Conn M — Connecticut Magazine [*New Haven*]
Conn Med — Connecticut Medicine
Conn Med J — Connecticut Medicine Journal
Conn Mineral Folio — Connecticut. Mineral Folios
Conn Nurs News — Connecticut Nursing News
Conn R — Connecticut Review
Conn Rev — Connecticut Review
Con(NS) — Convivium (New Series)
Conn State Ag Exp — Connecticut. State Agricultural Experiment Station. Publications
Conn State Geol Nat Hist Surv Bull — Connecticut. State Geological and Natural History Survey. Bulletin
Conn State Geol Nat Hist Surv Misc Ser — Connecticut. State Geological and Natural History Survey. Miscellaneous Series
Conn State Geol Nat Hist Surv Quadrangle Rep — Connecticut. State Geological and Natural History Survey. Quadrangle Report
Conn State Geol Nat Hist Surv Rep Invest — Connecticut. State Geological and Natural History Survey. Report of Investigations
Conn State Med J — Connecticut State Medical Journal
Conn Storrs Agric Exp Stn Bull — Connecticut. Storrs Agricultural Experiment Station. Bulletin
Conn Storrs Agric Exp Stn Res Rep — Connecticut. Storrs Agricultural Experiment Station. Research Report

Conn Univ Eng Exp Stn Bull — Connecticut. University Engineering Experiment Station. Bulletin
Conn Veg Grow Assoc Proc Annual Meet — Connecticut Vegetable Growers' Association. Proceedings. Annual Meeting
Conn Water Res Comm Conn Water Res Bull — Connecticut Water Resources Commission. Connecticut Water Resources Bulletin
Conn Water Resour Bull — Connecticut Water Resources Bulletin
Conn Woodl — Connecticut Woodlands
Conn Woodlands — Connecticut Woodlands
Con P — Contemporary Poetry
CONQAV — Conquest
Conquest J Res Def Soc — Conquest. Journal of the Research Defence Society
ConR — Contemporary Review
Con Res Mag — Consumers' Research Magazine
CONS — Conservation News. National Wildlife Federation
Cons — Consigna
Cons Com Ext — Conseiller du Commerce Exterieur
Consejo Sup Invest Cient Bibl Bol — Consejo Superior de Investigaciones Cientificas. Biblioteca General. Boletin [*Madrid*]
Conser Ser Dep Cap T — Conservation Series. Department of the Capital Territory
Conserv — Conservationist
Conserve Deriv Agrum — Conserve e Derivati Agrumari
Conserver Soc Notes — Conserver Society Notes [*Canada*]
Conserv Found Lett — Conservation Foundation Letter
Conserv Nat — Conservation of Nature [*Japan*]
Conserv News — Conservation News
Conserv R — Conservative Review
Conserv Recycling — Conservation and Recycling [*England*]
Conserv & Recycling — Conservation and Recycling
Conserv Res Rep US Dep Agric Agric Res Serv — Conservation Research Report. United States Department of Agriculture. Agricultural Research Service
Conserv Ser Dep Cap T — Conservation Series. Department of the Capital Territory
Conserv Volunteer — Conservation Volunteer
Cons Int Explor Mer Bull Stat Peches Marit — Conseil International pour l'Exploration de la Mer. Bulletin Statistique des Peches Maritimes
Cons Int Explor Mer Zooplankton Sheet — Conseil International pour l'Exploration de la Mer. Zooplankton Sheet
Cons L Today — Consumer Law Today
Consmr Rpt — Consumer Reports
Cons N — Consumer News
Cons Natl Rech Can Bull — Conseil National de Recherches du Canada. Bulletin
Cons Natl Rech Can Div Genie Mec Rapp Tech Lab — Conseil National de Recherches du Canada. Division de Genie Mecanique. Rapport Technique de Laboratoire
Consol Frt Classif — Consolidated Freight Classification
Cons Rech Dev For Que Etude — Conseil de la Recherche et du Developpement Forestiers du Quebec. Etude
Cons Recur Nat No Renov Publ (Mex) — Consejo de Recursos Naturales No Renovables. Publicacion (Mexico)
Cons Rep — Consumer Reports
Cons Sci Int Rech Trypanosomiases — Conseil Scientifique International de Recherches sur les Trypanosomiases
Constitutional and Parliamentary Info — Constitutional and Parliamentary Information
Constr — Construction
Constr Contracting — Construction Contracting
Constrl Rev — Constructional Review
Constrl Rev Tech Suppl — Constructional Review. Technical Supplement
Constr Mach — Construction Machinery [*Japan*]
Constr Mach Equip — Construction Machinery and Equipment
Constr Mech (Tokyo) — Construction Mechanization (Tokyo)
Constr Met — Construction Metallique
Constr Metal — Construction Metallique
Constr Meth — Construction Methods
Constr Methods Equip — Construction Methods and Equipment
Constr News — Construction News
Constr News (London) — Construction News (London)
Constr News Mag — Construction News Magazine [*England*]
Constr News Magazine — Construction News Magazine
Constr Paps — Construction Papers
Constr Plant & Equip — Construction Plant and Equipment
Constr Plant Equip — Construction Plant and Equipment
Constr Q — Constructive Quarterly
Constr R — Construction Review
Constr Ref — Construction References
Constr Rev — Constructional Review
Constr Road Trans — Construction and Road Transport
Constr S Afr — Construction in Southern Africa
Constr Specifier — Construction Specifier
Constr Tech Bull — Construction Technical Bulletin
Construct-Amenag — Construction-Amenagement
Constructional R — Constructional Review

Construction Law — Construction Lawyer
Constru Masini — Constructia de Masini
Consult Eng (London) — Consulting Engineer (London)
Consult Engr — Consulting Engineer
Consult Eng (St Joseph Mich) — Consulting Engineer (St. Joseph, Michigan)
Consum Brief Summ — Consumer Briefing Summary
Consumer Buying Prosp — Consumer Buying Prospects
Consumer Rep — Consumer Reports
Consum Health Perspect — Consumer Health Perspectives
Consum Ind — Consumer's Index
Consum Rep — Consumer Reports
Cont — Contact [*Canadian Studies Foundation*]
CONT — Contact. Journal of Urban and Environmental Affairs
Contabilidad Admin — Contabilidad. Administracion
Contact — 3-2-1 Contact
Contact Intraocul Lens Med J — Contact and Intraocular Lens Medical
    Journal
Contact J Urban Environ Aff — Contact. Journal of Urban and Environmental
    Affairs
Contact Lens Med Bull — Contact Lens Medical Bulletin
Contact Lens Soc Am J — Contact Lens Society of America. Journal
Containerisation Int — Containerisation International
Contam Control — Contamination Control
Contam Control Biomed Environ — Contamination Control. Biomedical
    Environments
Cont Appl St — Contributions to Applied Statistics
Cont Drug P — Contemporary Drug Problems
Cont Ed — Contemporary Education
Cont Educ — Contemporary Education
Contemp — Contemporaneo
Contemp — Contemporary Review
Contemp Agric — Contemporary Agriculture
Contemp Anesth Pract — Contemporary Anesthesia Practice
Contemp As R — Contemporary Asia Review
Contemp China — Contemporary China
Contemp Crisis — Contemporary Crisis
Contemp Drug — Contemporary Drug Problems
Contemp Drug Prob — Contemporary Drug Problems
Contemp Ed — Contemporary Education
Contemp Educ — Contemporary Education
Contemp Educ Psychol — Contemporary Educational Psychology
Contemp Issues Clin Nutr — Contemporary Issues in Clinical Nutrition
Contemp Issues Infect Dis — Contemporary Issues in Infectious Diseases
Contemp Jewish Rec — Contemporary Jewish Record
Contemp Lit — Contemporary Literature
Contemp M — Contemporary Marxism
Contemp Neurol Ser — Contemporary Neurology Series
Contemp Pharm Pract — Contemporary Pharmacy Practice
Contemp Phys — Contemporary Physics
Contemp Poland — Contemporary Poland
Contemp Polit — Contemporary Politics
Contemp Probl Cardiol — Contemporary Problems in Cardiology
Contemp Psychoanal — Contemporary Psychoanalysis
Contemp Psychol — Contemporary Psychology
Contemp R — Contemporary Review
Contemp Rev — Contemplative Review
Contemp Sociol — Contemporary Sociology
Contemp Sociology — Contemporary Sociology
Contemp Surg — Contemporary Surgery
Contemp Top Anal Clin Chem — Contemporary Topics in Analytical and
    Clinical Chemistry
Contemp Top Immunobiol — Contemporary Topics in Immunobiology
Contemp Top Mol Immunol — Contemporary Topics in Molecular Immunology
Cont Fr Civ — Contemporary French Civilization
Cont Hum De — Contributions to Human Development
Conti Elektro Ber — Conti Elektro Berichte [*West Germany*]
Contin Educ — Continuing Education in New Zealand
Contin Edu Lect (Soc Nucl Med Southeast Chapter) — Continuing Education
    Lectures (Society of Nuclear Medicine. Southeastern Chapter)
Continentl — Continental Comment
Contin Mo — Continental Monthly
Continuing Ed Fam Physician — Continuing Education for the Family
    Physician
Continuing Educ for the Fam Physician — Continuing Education for the Family
    Physician
Continuing Med Educ Newsletter — Continuing Medical Education Newsletter
Cont Jew Rec — Contemporary Jewish Record
Cont Keybd — Contemporary Keyboard
Cont Learning — Continuous Learning
Contl & I — Control and Instrumentation
Cont Lit — Contemporary Literature
ConTM — Concordia Theological Monthly
Cont Marx — Contemporary Marxism
Cont Metall Chem Eng — Continental Metallurgical and Chemical
    Engineering
Cont P — Contemporary Poetry

Cont & Packag — Containers and Packaging
Cont Paint Resin News — Continental Paint and Resin News [*England*]
Cont Philos — Contemporary Philosophy
Cont Phys — Contemporary Physics
Cont Psycha — Contemporary Psychoanalysis
Cont Psycho — Contemporary Psychology
Cont R — Contemporary Review
Contracept — Contraception
Contracept-Fertil-Sex — Contraception-Fertilite-Sexualite
Contract — Contractor
Contract & Constr Eng — Contracting and Construction Engineer
Contracting — Contracting and Construction Equipment
Contracting — Contracting and Public Works
Contract Int — Contract Interiors
Contract Inter — Contract Interiors
Contract J — Contract Journal [*England*]
Contract Jnl — Contract Journal
Contract Rec Eng Rev — Contract Record and Engineering Review [*Canada*]
Contract Rep Eur Space Res Organ — Contractor Report. European Space
    Research Organization
Contract Rep US Army Eng Waterw Exp Stn — Contract Report. US Army
    Engineer Waterways Experiment Station
Contr Boyce Thompson Inst Pl Res — Contributions. Boyce Thompson Institute
    for Plant Research
Contr Canada Dep For Forest Res Brch — Contribution. Canada Department
    of Forestry. Forest Research Branch
Contr Dep Hort Univ Ill — Contributions. Department of Horticulture.
    University of Illinois
Contr Drama — Contributions in Drama and Theatre Studies
Contr Eng — Control Engineering
Contr Fonds Rech For Univ Laval — Contribution. Fonds de Recherches
    Forestieres. Universite Laval
Contr Herb Aust — Contributions. Herbarium Australiense
Contrib Am Entomol Inst (Ann Arbor) — Contributions. American
    Entomological Institute (Ann Arbor)
Contrib Arct Inst Cathol Univ Am — Contributions. Arctic Institute. Catholic
    University of America
Contrib As Stud — Contributions to Asian Studies
Contrib Atmos Phys — Contributions to Atmospheric Physics
Contrib Avulsas Inst Oceanogr Sao Paulo — Contribuicoes Avulsas. Instituto
    Oceanografico Sao Paulo
Contrib Bears Bluff Lab — Contributions. Bears Bluff Laboratories
Contrib Biol Lab Sci Soc China Bot Ser — Contributions. Biological
    Laboratory. Science Society of China. Botanical Series
Contrib Biol Lab Sci Soc China Zool Ser — Contributions. Biological
    Laboratory. Science Society of China. Zoological Series
Contrib Bot — Contributii Botanice
Contrib Boyce Thompson Inst — Contributions. Boyce Thompson Institute for
    Plant Research
Contrib Can Biol Fish — Contributions to Canadian Biology and Fisheries
Contrib Cent Res Inst Agric (Bogor) — Contributions. Central Research
    Institute for Agriculture (Bogor)
Contrib Centro Linceo Interdisc Sci Mat Appl — Contributi. Centro Lindeo
    Interdisciplinare di Scienze Matematiche e loro Applicazioni [*Rome*]
Contrib Cient Fac Cienc Exactas Nat Univ B Aires Ser Bot — Contribuciones
    Cientificas. Facultad de Ciencias Exactas y Naturales. Universidad de
    Buenos Aires. Serie Botanica
Contrib Cient Fac Cienc Exactas Nat Univ B Aires Ser Geol — Contribuciones
    Cientificas. Facultad de Ciencias Exactas y Naturales. Universidad de
    Buenos Aires. Serie Geologia
Contrib Cient Fac Cienc Exactas Nat Univ B Aires Ser Quim — Contribuciones
    Cientificas. Facultad de Ciencias Exactas y Naturales. Universidad de
    Buenos Aires. Serie Quimica
Contrib Cient Fac Cienc Exactas Nat Univ B Aires Ser Zool — Contribuciones
    Cientificas. Facultad de Ciencias Exactas y Naturales. Universidad de
    Buenos Aires. Serie Zoologia
Contrib Cient Univ Buenos Aires Fac Cienc Exactas Nat Ser C —
    Contribuciones Cientificas. Facultad de Ciencias Exactas y Naturales.
    Universidad de Buenos Aires. Serie C. Quimica
Contrib Curr Res Geophys — Contributions to Current Research in Geophysics
Contrib Cushman Found Foraminiferal Res — Contributions. Cushman
    Foundation for Foraminiferal Research
Contrib Dan Pharmacopoeia Comm — Contributions. Danish Pharmacopoeia
    Commission
Contrib Dep Biol Univ Laval (Que) — Contributions. Departement de Biologie.
    Universite Laval (Quebec)
Contrib Dep Geol Mineral Niigata Univ — Contributions. Department of
    Geology and Mineralogy. Niigata University
Contrib Dep Limnol Acad Nat Sci Phila — Contributions. Department of
    Limnology. Academy of Natural Sciences of Philadelphia
Contrib Dudley Herb — Contributions. Dudley Herbarium
Contrib Dudley Mus — Contributions. Dudley Museum
Contrib Econom Anal — Contributions to Economic Analysis [*Amsterdam*]
Contrib Estud Cienc Fis Mat Ser Mat Fis — Contribucion al Estudio de las
    Ciencias Fisicas y Matematicas. Serie Matematico Fisica

Contrib Estud Cienc Fis Mat Ser Tec — Contribucion al Estudio de las Ciencias Fisicas y Matematicas. Serie Tecnica
Contrib Estudo Antropol Port — Contribuicoes para o Estudo da Antropologia Portuguesa
Contrib Fac Sci Haile Selassie I Univ Ser C Zool — Contributions. Faculty of Science. Haile Selassie I University. Series C. Zoology
Contrib Fac Sci Univ Coll Addis Ababa (Ethiop) Ser C (Zool) — Contributions. Faculty of Science. University College of Addis Ababa (Ethiopia). Series C (Zoology)
Contrib Gen Agric Res Stn (Bogor) — Contributions. General Agricultural Research Station (Bogor)
Contrib Geol — Contributions to Geology
Contrib Geol Spec Pap — Contributions to Geology. Special Paper
Contrib Geol Univ Wyo — Contributions to Geology. University of Wyoming
Contrib Geophys Inst Kyoto Univ — Contributions. Geophysical Institute. Kyoto University
Contrib Geophys Inst Slovak Acad Sci — Contributions. Geophysical Institute. Slovak Academy of Sciences
Contrib Geophys Inst Slovak Acad Sci Ser Meteorol — Contributions. Geophysical Institute. Slovak Academy of Sciences. Series of Meteorology
Contrib Geophys Obs Haile Sellassie I Univer Ser A — Contributions. Geophysical Observatory. Haile Sellassie I University. Series A
Contrib Gray Herb Harv Univ — Contributions. Gray Herbarium. Harvard University
Contrib Gynecol Obstet — Contributions to Gynecology and Obstetrics
Contrib Herb Aust — Contributions. Herbarium Australiense
Contrib Hum Dev — Contributions to Human Development
Contrib Ind Sociol — Contributions to Indian Sociology
Contrib Inst Antart Argent — Contribuciones. Instituto Antartico Argentino
Contrib Inst Bot Univ Montreal — Contributions. Institut de Botanique. Universite de Montreal
Contrib Inst Chem Nat Acad Peiping — Contributions. Institute of Chemistry. National Academy of Peiping
Contrib Inst Geol Paleontol Tohoku Univ — Contributions. Institute of Geology and Paleontology. Tohoku University
Contrib Inst Low Temp Sci A — Contributions. Institute of Low Temperature Science. Series A
Contrib Inst Low Temp Sci Hokkaido Univ — Contributions. Institute of Low Temperature Science. Hokkaido University
Contrib Inst Low Temp Sci Hokkaido Univ — Contributions. Institute of Low Temperature Science. Hokkaido University. Series B
Contrib Inst Low Temp Sci Hokkaido Univ B — Contributions. Institute of Low Temperature Science. Hokkaido University. Series B
Contrib Inst Low Temp Sci Hokkaido Univ Ser A — Contributions. Institute of Low Temperature Science. Hokkaido University. Series A
Contrib Inst Low Temp Sci Hokkaido Univ Ser B — Contributions. Institute of Low Temperature Science. Hokkaido University. Series B
Contrib Inst Low Temp Sci Ser A — Contributions. Institute of Low Temperature Science. Series A
Contrib Inst Phys Nat Acad Peiping — Contributions. Institute of Physics. Natural Academy of Peiping
Contrib Iowa Corn Res Inst — Contributions. Iowa Corn Research Institute
Contrib Istanbul Sci Clin — Contributions d'Istanbul a la Science Clinique
Contrib Ist Ric Agrar Milano — Contributi. Istituto di Ricerche Agrarie Milano
Contrib Lab Vertebr Biol Univ Mich — Contributions. Laboratory of Vertebrate Biology. University of Michigan
Contrib Lunar Sci Inst — Contributions. Lunar Science Institute
Contrib Mar Sci — Contributions in Marine Science
Contrib Meteorit Soc — Contributions. Meteoritical Society
Contrib Microbiol Immunol — Contributions to Microbiology and Immunology
Contrib Mineral & Petrol — Contributions to Mineralogy and Petrology
Contrib Mineral Petrol — Contributions to Mineralogy and Petrology
Contrib Mineral Petrol Beitr Mineral Petrol — Contributions to Mineralogy and Petrology - Beitraege zur Mineralogie und Petrologie [Berlin-Heidelberg-New York]
Contrib Mineral Petrology — Contributions to Mineralogy and Petrology
Contrib Mus Paleontol Univ Mich — Contributions. Museum of Paleontology. University of Michigan
Contrib Nat Res Inst Geol Acad Sin — Contributions. National Research Institute of Geology. Academia Sinica
Contrib Nepal Stud — Contributions to Nepalese Studies
Contrib Nephrol — Contributions to Nephrology
Contrib NSW Herb — Contributions. New South Wales National Herbarium
Contrib NSW Natl Herb — Contributions. New South Wales National Herbarium
Contrib NSW Natl Herb Flora Ser — Contributions. New South Wales National Herbarium. Flora Series
Contrib Oncol — Contributions to Oncology
Contrib Paleolimnol Lake Biwa Jpn Pleistocene — Contribution on the Paleolimnology of Lake Biwa and the Japanese Pleistocene
Contrib Perkins Obs — Contributions. Perkins Observatory
Contrib Perkins Obs Ser 1 — Contributions. Perkins Observatory. Series 1
Contrib Perkins Obs Ser 2 — Contributions. Perkins Observatory. Series 2
Contrib Primatol — Contributions to Primatology

Contrib Qd Herb — Contributions. Queensland Herbarium
Contrib Queensl Herb — Contributions. Queensland Herbarium
Contrib Sedimentology — Contributions to Sedimentology
Contrib Sens Physiol — Contributions to Sensory Physiology
Contrib Shanghai Inst Entomol — Contributions. Shanghai Institute of Entomology
Contrib Soc Res Meteorites — Contributions. Society for Research on Meteorites
Contrib Symp Immunol Ges Allerg Immunitaetsforsch — Contributions. Symposium on Immunology. Gesellschaft fuer Allergie und Immunitaetsforschung
Contrib Univ Mich Herb — Contributions. University of Michigan Herbarium
Contrib US Natl Herb — Contributions. United States National Herbarium
Contrib Vertebr Evol — Contributions to Vertebrate Evolution
Contrib Welder Wildl Found — Contribution. Welder Wildlife Foundation
Contr Inst Bot Univ Montreal — Contributions. Institut de Botanique. Universite de Montreal
Contr Inst For Prod Univ Wash — Contribution. Institute of Forest Products. University of Washington. College of Forest Resources
Contr Instr — Control and Instrumentation
Contr Instrum — Control and Instrumentation
Contrl Eng — Control Engineering
Contr Marine Sci — Contributions in Marine Science
Contr Mar S — Contributions in Marine Science
Contr Min P — Contributions to Mineralogy and Petrology
Contr NSW Natn Herb — Contributions. New South Wales National Herbarium
Control Automat Process — Control and Automation Process [England]
Control Cibern & Autom — Control Cibernetica y Automatizacion
Control & Cybern — Control and Cybernetics
Control Cybern — Control and Cybernetics
Control Eng — Control Engineering
Control Engng — Control Engineering
Control Feed Behav Biol Brain Protein-Calorie Malnutr — Control of Feeding Behavior and Biology of the Brain in Protein-Calorie Malnutrition
Control Instrum — Control and Instrumentation
Controlled Clin Trials — Controlled Clinical Trials
Control Power Syst Conf Expo Conf Rec — Control of Power Systems Conference and Exposition. Conference Record
Control Rev — Control Review
Control Sys — Control Systems
Contr Prim — Contributions to Primatology
Contr Qd Herb — Contributions. Queensland Herbarium
Contr Sc — Contributions to Science
Contr Sci Prat Migl Conosc Util Legno — Contributi Scientifico. Pratici per una Migliore Conoscenza ed Utilizzazione del Legno
Cont Shelf Res — Continental Shelf Research
Cont Sociol — Contemporary Sociology
conv — Conveyancer and Property Lawyer
Conv — Convivium
Conven Proc Agric Vet Chem Assoc Aust — Convention Proceedings. Agricultural and Veterinary Chemicals Association of Australia
Convey — Conveyancer and Property Lawyer
Convey NS — Conveyancer and Property Lawyer. New Series
Conv IICA-ZN-ROCAP Bibliogr — Convenio IICA-ZN-ROCAP [Instituto Interamericano de Ciencias Agricolas-Zona Norte-Regional Organization for Central America and Panama] Bibliografia
Conv IICA-ZN-ROCAP Publ Misc — Convenio IICA-ZN-ROCAP [Instituto Interamericano de Ciencias Agricolas-Zona Norte-Regional Organization for Central America and Panama] Publication Miscelanea
Conv Int Acque Sotterranee Atti — Convegno Internazionale sulle Acque Sotterranee. Atti. Ente Sviluppo Agricolo in Sicilia [Palermo]
Conv Ital Sci Macromol Atti — Convegno Italiano di Scienza delle Macromolecole. Atti
ConvLit — Convorbiri Literare
Conv (NS) — Conveyancer and Property Lawyer. New Series
Conv and Prop Law — Conveyancer and Property Lawyer
COO — Chronicles of Oklahoma
COOFA — Cahiers Oceanographiques (France)
COOP — Co-Op North
Coop — Cooperation
Coop Agr — Cooperation Agricole
Coop Agric — Cooperation Agricole
Coop Agric Coop Fed Que — Cooperateur Agricole la Cooperative Federee de Quebec
Co-Op Bull Taiwan For Res Inst — Co-Operative Bulletin. Taiwan Forestry Research Institute
Coop Can — Cooperation Canada
Coop and Conflict — Cooperation and Conflict
Coop Consum — Cooperative Consumer
Coop y Desarrollo — Cooperativesmo y Desarrollo
Coop et Development — Cooperation et Developpement
Coop-Distrib-Consom — Cooperation-Distribution-Consommation
Co-Op Econ Insect Rep — Cooperative Economic Insect Report
Co-Op Electr Res — Co-Operative Electrical Research
Cooper Union Chron — Cooper Union Museum Chronicle

Coop Grain Quart — Coop Grain Quarterly
Coop Inf — Cooperation Information
Coop Manager & F — Cooperative Manager and Farmer
Coop Meat Trade D — Cooperatives Meat Trade Digest
Coop Mediterr Energ Sol Rev Int Heliotech — Cooperation Mediterraneenne pour l'Energie Solaire. Revue Internationale d'Heliotechnique [*France*]
Coop News — Co-Operative News and Digest
Coop Resour Rep Ill State Water Survey Ill State Geol Surv — Cooperative Resources Report. Illinois State Water Survey and Illinois State Geological Survey
Coop Res Rep Int Counc Explor Sea Ser A — Cooperative Research Report. International Council for the Exploration of the Sea. Series A
Coop Tech — Cooperation Technique
Coord Ch Re — Coordination Chemistry Reviews
Coord Guidel Wildl Habitats US For Serv Calif Reg — Coordination Guidelines for Wildlife Habitats. United States Forest Service. California Region
Coord Res Counc CRC Rep — Coordinating Research Council. CRC Report
COOUA — Colorado Outdoors
COP — Computermarkt
Copenhagen Univ Mineralog Geol Mus Contr Mineralogy — Copenhagen University. Mineralogical and Geological Museum. Contributions to Mineralogy
COPMBU — Computer Programs in Biomedicine
COPNDZ — Concepts in Pediatric Neurosurgery
Copper Abstr — Copper Abstracts
Copper Dev Assoc Tech Rep — Copper Development Association. Technical Report
Copper Dev Assoc Tech Sur — Copper Development Association. Technical Survey
Copper Development Assocn Information Sheet — Copper Development Association. Information Sheet
Copper Stud — Copper Studies
COPYA — Comprehensive Psychiatry
COPYAV — Comprehensive Psychiatry
Copy Rep — Copyright Reporter
Copyright L Sym (ASCAP) — Copyright Law Symposium. American Society of Composers, Authors, and Publishers
Copy Soc Aust News — Copyright Society of Australia. Newsletter
Copy Soc Bull — Bulletin. Copyright Society of the USA
COR — Business America
CoR — Contemporary Review
Cor — Cornell Law Review
COR — Corona
Cor — Correspondent
Cor-Bl Naturf-Ver Riga — Correspondenzblatt. Naturforscher-Verein zu Riga
Cord — Corduroy
CORE — Construction Review
COREBG — Conditional Reflex
CorL — Correo Literario
Cor LQ — Cornell Law Quarterly
Cormosea Newsl — Cormosea Newsletter
Corn Ann — Corn Annual
Cornell Ag Exp — Cornell University. Agricultural Experiment Station. Publications
Cornell Eng — Cornell Engineer
Cornell Ext Bull — Cornell Extension Bulletin
Cornell Feed Serv NY State Coll Agr Ext Serv — Cornell Feed Service. New York State College of Agriculture. Extension Service [*Cornell University*]
Cornell Hotel & Rest Adm Q — Cornell Hotel and Restaurant Administration Quarterly
Cornell Hotel & Restau Adm Q — Cornell Hotel and Restaurant Administration Quarterly
Cornell Hotel Restaur Adm Q — Cornell Hotel and Restaurant Administration Quarterly
Cornell Hotel and Restaurant Admin Q — Cornell Hotel and Restaurant Administration Quarterly
Cornell Hotel Restaurant Adm Q — Cornell Hotel and Restaurant Administration Quarterly
Cornell I J — Cornell International Law Journal
Cornell Internat Law J — Cornell International Law Journal
Cornell Internat LJ — Cornell International Law Journal
Cornell Int L J — Cornell International Law Journal
Cornell Intl LJ — Cornell International Law Journal
Cornell Int Symp Workshop Hydrogen Econ — Cornell International Symposium and Workshop on the Hydrogen Economy
Cornell J S — Cornell Journal of Social Relations
Cornell J Soc Relat — Cornell Journal of Social Relations
Cornell Law Q — Cornell Law Quarterly
Cornell Law R — Cornell Law Review
Cornell Law Rev — Cornell Law Review
Cornell LF — Cornell Law Forum
Cornell Lib J — Cornell Library Journal
Cornell L Q — Cornell Law Quarterly
Cornell L R — Cornell Law Review
Cornell L Rev — Cornell Law Review

Cornell Med J — Cornell Medical Journal
Cornell Plant — Cornell Plantations
Cornell Plantat — Cornell Plantations
Cornell Univ Dep Struc Eng Rep — Cornell University. Department of Structural Engineering. Report
Cornell Univ Lib Bull — Cornell University Libraries. Bulletin
Cornell Vet — Cornell Veterinarian
Cornell Vet Suppl — Cornell Veterinarian. Supplement
Cornh — Cornhill Magazine
Corning Res — Corning Research
Corn Inst Eng Trans — Cornish Institute of Engineers. Transactions
Cornish Arch — Cornish Archaeology
Cornish Archaeol — Cornish Archaeology
CORPA — Clinical Orthopaedics
Corp Bulletin — Bureau of Corporate Affairs. Bulletin
Corp Counsel Rev J Corp Counsel Section St B Tex — Corporate Counsel Review. Journal of the Corporate Counsel Section. State Bar of Texas
Corp Fit and R — Corporate Fitness and Recreation
Corp Forms (P-H) — Corporation Forms (Prentice-Hall, Inc.)
Corp J — Corporation Journal
Corp L Guide — Corporation Law Guide [*Commerce Clearing House*]
Corp LR — Corporation Law Review
Corp L Rev — Corporation Law Review
Corporate Rept — Corporate Report
Corp Prac Com — Corporate Practice Commentator
Corp Prac Comm — Corporate Practice Commentator
Corp Prac Comment — Corporate Practice Commentator
Corp Prac Ser (BNA) — Corporate Practice Series (Bureau of National Affairs)
Corp Pract Comment — Corporate Practice Commentator
Corpus Christi Geol Soc Bull — Corpus Christi Geological Society. Bulletin
Correct Mag — Corrections Magazine
Correct Today — Corrections Today
Correio Agric — Correio Agricola
Correio Med Lisb — O Correio Medico de Lisboa
Corresp Orient Et — Correspondance d'Orient. Etudes
Corr Fotogr — Corriere Fotografico
Corr Fotogr Sudam — Correo Fotografico Sudamericano
Corr Mater Prot — Corrosion and Material Protection
Corr Met Finish (S Afr) — Corrosion and Metal Finishing (South Africa)
Corros Abstr — Corrosion Abstracts
Corros Anti-Corros — Corrosion et Anti-Corrosion [*France*]
Corros Australas — Corrosion Australasia
Corros Bull — Corrosion Bulletin
Corros Coat S Afr — Corrosion and Coatings South Africa
Corros Eng (Tokyo) — Corrosion Engineering (Tokyo)
Corrosion Sci — Corrosion Science
Corros Maint — Corrosion and Maintenance [*India*]
Corros Mar Environ — Corrosion in Marine Environment
Corros Pre Contr — Corrosion Prevention and Control
Corros Prev Control — Corrosion Prevention and Control
Corros Prot — Corrosion y Proteccion
Corros Prot Mater — Corrosao e Proteccao de Materiais
Corros Sci — Corrosion Science
Corros Technol — Corrosion Technology [*England*]
Corros Trait Prot Finition — Corrosion, Traitements, Protection, Finition
Corr Soc Ps — Corrective and Social Psychiatry
Corrugated Newsl — Corrugated Newsletter
Corse Hist — Corse Historique. Etudes et Documents
Corse Med — Corse Medicale
Corse Mediterr Med — Corse Mediterranee Medicale
Corsi Semin Chim — Corsi e Seminari di Chimica. Consiglio Nazionale delle Ricerche e Fondazione "F. Giordani"
CORS J — CORS [*Canadian Operational Research Society*] Journal
C ORSTOM Ser Sci Hum — Cahiers. ORSTOM [*Office de la Recherche Scientifique et Technique d'Outre-Mer*]. Serie Sciences Humaines
CORTB — Clinical Orthopaedics and Related Research
CORTDT — Contemporary Orthopaedics
Cos — Cosmic Stories
COS — Cosmopolitan
Cos — Cosmos Science Fiction and Fantasy Magazine
Cos Chem — Cosmetic Chemists. Journal of the Society
COSE — Common Sense. Journal of Information for Environmentally Concerned Citizens. Kootenay Environmental Institute [*Galena Bay, British Columbia*]
COSHB — Cahiers. ORSTOM [*Office de la Recherche Scientifique et Technique d'Outre-Mer*]. Hydrologie
Cosm — Cosmic Science Fiction
Cosmet J — Cosmetic Journal
Cosmet News — Cosmetic News
Cosmet Technol — Cosmetic Technology
Cosmet & Toiletries — Cosmetics and Toiletries
Cosmet Toiletry Fragrance Assoc Cosmet J — Cosmetic, Toiletry, and Fragrance Association. Cosmetic Journal
Cosmic Electrodyn — Cosmic Electrodynamics
Cosmic Res — Cosmic Research

Cosmop — Cosmopolitan
Cosmopol — Cosmopolitan
COSPAR Inf Bull — COSPAR [*Committee on Space Research*] Information Bulletin [*Netherlands*]
COSPB — Comments on Solid State Physics
Costa Rica B Fomento — Costa Rica. Boletin de Fomento
Costa Rica Centro de Estudios Sismologicos An — Costa Rica. Centro de Estudios Sismologicos. Anales
Costa Rica Inst Geog Informe Semestral Informe Trimestral — Costa Rica. Instituto Geografico. Informe Semestral. Informe Trimestral
Costa Rica Minist Agric Ganad Bol Misc — Costa Rica. Ministerio de Agricultura y Ganaderia. Boletin Miscelaneo
Costa Rica Minist Agric Ganad Bol Tec — Costa Rica. Ministerio de Agricultura y Ganaderia. Boletin Tecnico
Cost Bul — Cost Bulletin
Cost Eng — Cost Engineering
Cost and Man — Cost and Management
Cost Manage — Cost and Management
Cost & Mgt — Cost and Management
Cos & Toil — Cosmetics and Toiletries
Costr Met — Costruzioni Metalliche
COSUD — Colloids and Surfaces
COSUD3 — Colloids and Surfaces
COT — Colombia Today
COTED — Coal Technology
COTHD3 — Comprehensive Therapy
COTH Rep — COTH [*Council of Teaching Hospitals*] Report
COTOEP — Concepts in Toxicology
Coton Fibres Trop — Coton et Fibres Tropicales
Coton Fibres Trop Bull Anal — Coton et Fibres Tropicales. Bulletin Analytique
Coton Fibres Trop Engl Ed — Coton et Fibres Tropicales. English Edition
Coton Fibr Trop — Coton et Fibres Tropicales
Cott Impr Conf — Cotton Improvement Conference
Cotton Dev — Cotton Development
Cotton Dig — Cotton Digest
Cotton Grow Rev — Cotton Growing Review
Cotton Int Ed — Cotton International Edition
Cotton Res Corp Cotton Res Rep — Cotton Research Corporation. Cotton Research Reports
Cotton Res Corp Prog Rep Exp Stn — Cotton Research Corporation. Progress Reports from Experiment Stations
Cotton Res Inst Sindos Sci Bull New Ser — Cotton Research Institute. Sindos Science Bulletin. New Series
Cotton Rev — Cotton. Monthly Review of the World Situation
Cotton Wool Situat CWS US Dep Agric Econ Stat Serv — Cotton and Wool Situation. CWS. United States Department of Agriculture. Economics and Statistics Service
COU — Courrier des Pays de l'Est. Mensuel d'Informations Economiques
Counc Agric Sci Technol Rep — Council for Agricultural Science and Technology. Report
Counc Brit Archaeol Annu Rep — Council for British Archaeology. Annual Report
Counc Brit Archaeol Res Rep — Council for British Archaeology. Research Reports
Counc Econ Prior Newsl — Council on Economic Priorities. Newsletter
Council Anthropol Educ Qu — Council on Anthropology and Education. Quarterly
Council Eur Inf Bull — Council of Europe. Information Bulletin
Counc Notes — Council Notes
Counc Sci Indones Publ — Council for Sciences of Indonesia. Publication
Couns Ed Su — Counselor Education and Supervision
Counsel Ed & Sup — Counselor Education and Supervision
Counsel Educ & Superv — Counselor Education and Supervision
Counsel Val — Counseling and Values
Counsel & Values — Counseling and Values
Couns Psych — Counseling Psychologist
Counterpt — Counterpoint
Countrmsrs — Electronic, Electro-Optic, and Infrared Countermeasures
Country — Country Kids
Country Cal — Country Calendar
Country Gent — Country Gentleman
Country Hour J — Country Hour Journal
Countryman's Mag — (Western Mail) Countryman's Magazine
Countryside Comm J — Countryside Commission. Journal
Countryside M — Countryside Magazine
Countryside M — Countryside Magazine and Suburban Life
Country Traders R — Country Traders' Review
County Newsl — County Newsletter
COURA — Clinica Otorinolaringoiatrica
Cour Forschungsinst Senckenb — Courier Forschungsinstitut Senckenberg
Cour Mus France — Courrier Musical de France
Courr Apic — Courrier Apicole
Courr Centre Int Enfance — Courrier. Centre International pour l'Enfance
Courr Etabl Neu — Courrier des Establissements Neu [*France*]
Courr Extr-Orient — Courrier de l'Extreme-Orient/Berichten uit het Verre Oosten

Courrier — Courrier Revue Medico-Sociale de l'Enfance
Courrier Pays Est — Courrier des Pays de l'Est
Courr Nat — Courrier de la Nature
Courr Norm — Courrier de la Normalisation
Courr Pays Est — Courrier des Pays de l'Est
Courr UNESCO — Courrier. UNESCO
Cours Doc Bil — Cours et Documents de Biologie
Cours Perfect Pediatr Prat — Cours de Perfectionnement en Pediatrie pour le Practicien
Cours Perfect Soc Suisse Psychiatr — Cours de Perfectionnement. Societe Suisse de Psychiatrie
Court Mgt J — Court Management Journal
COUTA — Coal Utilization
Coventry Eng Soc J — Coventry Engineering Society. Journal
COVPAY — Centre for Overseas Pest Research. Report
Cov Q — Covenant Quarterly
Covrt Act — Covert Action
COWA — Surveys and Bibliographies. Council for Old World Archaeology. Department of Sociology and Anthropology. Boston University
COWAEW — Colonial Waterbirds
COWPA — California Oil World and Petroleum Industry
Coyuntura Econ — Coyuntura Economica
COZE — Coastal Zone. Informal Newsletter of the Resources of the Pacific and Western Arctic Coasts of Canada
COZOAH — Comunicari de Zoologie
CP — Castrum Peregrini
CP — China Pictorial
CP — Classical Philology
CP — Clinical Physiology
CP — Concerning Poetry
CP — Contemporary Psychology
CP — Coyoti Prints. Caribou Tribal Council Newsletter
CP — Crop Protection
CP — Cultura Politica [*Rio De Janeiro*]
CPA — Computer Program Abstracts [*NASA*]
CPA — CPA [*American Institute of Certified Public Accountants*] Journal
CPA — Criminology and Penology Abstracts
CPAA — Current Physics Advance Abstracts
CPAJ — CPA [*American Institute of Certified Public Accountants*] Journal
CPAJA — Canadian Psychiatric Association. Journal
CPAMA — Communications on Pure and Applied Mathematics
CPAOD — Chongqing Daxue Xuebao
CPAPA4 — Colonial Plant and Animal Products
C Papers — Cinema Papers
CPARD — Cerpadla Potrubi Armatury
CPASAD — Commentationes Pontificiae. Academiae Scientiarum
CPB — Clinical Physiology and Biochemistry
CPB — Cyprus Popular Bank Newsletter
CPBLAV — Comparative Pathology Bulletin
CPBTA — Chemical and Pharmaceutical Bulletin (Tokyo)
CPC — Canadian Packaging
CPC — Canadian Public Administration
CPC — Carswell's Practice Cases
CPC — Current Papers on Computers and Control
CPCEAF — Canine Practice
CPCIAR — CEPEC [*Centro de Pesquisas do Cacau*] Informe Tecnico
CPCJD — Chemicals and Petro-Chemicals Journal
CPCP — University of California. Publications in Classical Philology
CPD — Commonwealth Parliamentary Debates
CPDE — Clinical Pharmacology and Drug Epidemiology [*Elsevier Book Series*]
CPD (HR) — Commonwealth Parliamentary Debates (House of Representatives)
CPD (R) — Commonwealth Parliamentary Debates (House of Representatives)
CPDRD — Current Problems in Diagnostic Radiology
CPD (S) — Commonwealth Parliamentary Debates (Senate)
CPDSAS — Inventaire des Maladies des Plantes au Canada
CPe — Castrum Peregrini
CPE — Current Papers in Electrical and Electronics Engineering
CPECD — Comparative Physiology and Ecology
CPECDM — Comparative Physiology and Ecology
CPEDA — Clinical Pediatrics [*Philadelphia*]
C Pedag — Cahiers Pedagogiques
C Pedag Inst Et Occitanes — Cahiers Pedagogiques. Institut d'Etudes Occitanes
CPEDDP — Chirurgie Pediatrique
CPEGA — Canadian Petro Engineering
CPENA — Chemical and Process Engineering [*London*]
CPENB — Chemical Processing and Engineering
CPETA — Canadian Petroleum
CPFLBI — Computers and Fluids
CPG — Canadian Plastics
CPGPAY — Comparative and General Pharmacology
CPh — Classical Philology
CPH — Colecao Poetas de Hoje
CPHCA — Chemistry and Physics of Carbon

CPHCC — Computers and the Humanities [*Database*]
CPHMA — Commentationes Physico-Mathematicae
CPHPA — Chieh P'ou Hsueh Pao
CPHRDE — International Journal of Clinical Pharmacology Research
CPHYDZ — Colloques Phytosociologiques
CPI — Conference Papers Index [*Cambridge Scientific Abstracts*] [*Bethesda, MD*]
CPI — Current Physics Index
CPIAAX — Central Plantation Crops Research Institute [*Kasaragod*]. Annual Report
CPI Mgmt — CPI [*Current Physics Index*] Management Service
CPJ — Chambre de Commerce et d'Industrie de Nouvelle Caledonie. Bulletin
CPL — Conveyancer and Property Lawyer. New Series
CPLI — Catholic Periodical and Literature Index
C Pl Phys C Fus — Comments on Plasma Physics and Controlled Fusion
CPLRBW — Chirurgia Plastica et Reconstructiva
CPLSA — Canadian Journal of Plant Science
CPM — Current Physics Microform
CPMAA — Cuoio, Pelli, Materie Concianti
pMF — Casopis pro Moderni Filologii
CPMHA6 — Comunicaciones Paleontologicas. Museo de Historia Natural de Montevideo
CPMJ — Canadian Paper Money Journal
CPMMAL — Collected Papers in Medicine. Mayo Clinic and Mayo Foundation
CPMSB6 — Colloid and Polymer Science
CPMSR — Canada. Fisheries and Marine Service. Pacific Marine Science Report
CP du N — Cours de Perfectionnement du Notariat
CPo — Comparative Politics
CPOEA — Canadian Power Engineer
CPOEB — Canadian Power Engineering and Plant Maintenance
CPP — Commonwealth Parliamentary Papers
CPP — Conference of Actuaries in Public Practice Proceedings
CPP — Current Papers in Physics
CPPA Newsprint Data — CPPA [*Canadian Pulp and Paper Association*] Newsprint Data
CPPA Newsprint Rept — CPPA [*Canadian Pulp and Paper Association*] Monthly Newsprint Report
CPPA Press Dig — CPPA [*Canadian Pulp and Paper Association*] Press Digest
CPPA Ref Tables — CPPA [*Canadian Pulp and Paper Association*] Reference Tables
CPPA Tech Sect Proc — CPPA [*Canadian Pulp and Paper Association*] Technical Section. Proceedings
CPPM — Clinical Physics and Physiological Measurement
CPPSBL — Contemporary Psychoanalysis
CPR — Canadian Patent Reporter
CPR — Copper. Quarterly Report
CPR — Current Population Reports
C Pratiq — Cinema Pratique
CPRMBD — Centre for Overseas Pest Research. Miscellaneous Report
CPROA — Chemical Processing [*London*]
CPR Proc — Computer Personnel Research Proceedings
CPS — Comparative Political Studies
CPSAR — Commonwealth Public Service Arbitration Reports
CPSMBI — Collected Papers in Surgery. Mayo Clinic and Mayo Foundation
CPSOA — Composites
CPSR — Commonwealth Public Service Arbitration Reports
CPSTB — Current Psychiatric Therapies
CPSUA — Current Problems in Surgery
CPsy — Cognitive Psychology
CPSZDP — Communications in Psychopharmacology
CPTEA — Chemical and Petroleum Engineering [*English Translation*]
CPTHA — Component Technology
CPW — Confectionery Production
CPZOAO — Chronmy Przyrode Ojczysta
CQ — Cambridge Quarterly
CQ — Caribbean Quarterly
CQ — Carolina Quarterly
CQ — China Quarterly
CQ — Classical Quarterly
CQ — Critical Quarterly
CQB — Cornell Hotel and Restaurant Administration Quarterly
CQCQA — CQ Radio Amateur's Journal
CQG — Chain Store Age
CQK — Conjunctuur
CQMTA — Colloque de Metallurgie
CQO — China Quarterly
CQR — Church Quarterly Review
CQR — Classical Quarterly Review
CQ Radio Amat J — CQ Radio Amateur's Journal
C Quebec — Cinema Quebec
CR — Calcutta Review
CR — Carnegie-Rochester Conference Series on Public Policy [*Elsevier Book Series*]

CR — Centennial Review
CR — China Reconstructs
CR — Classical Review
CR — Columbia Law Review
CR — Computing Reviews
CR — Congressional Record [*United States*]
CR — Consumer Reports
CR — Consumer Research Bulletin
CR — Contemporary Review
CR — Criminal Reports
Cr — Criterion
CR — Critical Review
CR — Crop Research
Cr — Crux
CRa — Cahiers Raciniens
CRAABull — Commissions Royales d'Art et d'Archeologie. Bulletin
CRABB — Current Affairs Bulletin
C R Acad Agric France — Comptes Rendus Hebdomadaires des Seances. Academie d'Agriculture de France
C R Acad Agric Georgi Dimitrov — Comptes Rendus. Academie Agricole Georgi Dimitrov
C R Acad Bulgare Sci — Comptes Rendus. Academie Bulgare des Sciences
C R Acad Bulg Sci — Comptes Rendus. Academie Bulgare des Sciences
C R Acad Sci — Comptes Rendus Hebdomadaires des Seances. Academie des Sciences
C R Acad Sci Agric Bulg — Comptes Rendus. Academie des Sciences Agricoles en Bulgarie
C R Acad Sci (Paris) — Comptes Rendus. Academie des Sciences (Paris)
CR Acad Sci (Paris) Ser A-B — Comptes Rendus Hebdomadaires des Seances. Academie des Sciences (Paris). Serie A et B
CR Acad Sci (Paris) Ser III Sci Vie — Comptes Rendus des Seances. Academie des Sciences (Paris). Serie III. Sciences de la Vie
CR Acad Sci (Paris) Ser II Mec Phys Chim Sci — Comptes Rendus des Seances. Academie des Sciences (Paris). Serie II. Mecanique, Physique, Chimie, Sciences de la Terre, Sciences de l'Univers
CR Acad Sci (Paris) Ser I Math — Comptes Rendus des Seances. Academie des Sciences (Paris). Serie I. Mathematique
C R Acad Sci (Paris) Vie Academique — Comptes Rendus Hebdomadaires des Seances. Academie des Sciences. Vie Academique (Paris) [*Later, Comptes Rendus des Seances. Academie des Sciences. Vie Academique*]
C R Acad Sci Ser 2 — Comptes Rendus. Academie des Sciences. Serie 2. Mecanique, Physique, Chimie, Sciences de l'Univers, Sciences de la Terre
C R Acad Sci Ser 3 — Comptes Rendus. Academie des Sciences. Serie 3. Sciences de la Vie
C R Acad Sci Ser Gen Vie Sci — Comptes Rendus. Academie des Sciences. Serie Generale. La Vie des Sciences
CR Ac Inscr — Comptes Rendus des Seances. Academie des Inscriptions et Belles Lettres
C R Ac Sci A — Comptes Rendus Hebdomadaires des Seances. Academie des Sciences. Serie A
C R Ac Sci B — Comptes Rendus Hebdomadaires des Seances. Academie des Sciences. Serie B
C R Ac Sci C — Comptes Rendus Hebdomadaires des Seances. Academie des Sciences. Serie C
C R Ac Sci D — Comptes Rendus Hebdomadaires des Seances. Academie des Sciences. Serie D
Craft A — Craft Australia
Craft Aust — Craft Australia
Craft Horiz — Craft Horizons
CRAGAP — Caribbean Agriculture
CRAI — Comptes Rendus. Academie des Inscriptions et Belles Lettres
CRAIBL — Comptes Rendus. Academie des Inscriptions et Belles Lettres
CRAL — Compte Rendu. Association Lyonnaise de Recherches Archeologiques
Cramp Mag — Crampton's Magazine
Cranbrook Inst Sci Bull — Cranbrook Institute of Science. Bulletin
Cranbrook Inst Sci Bull News Letter — Cranbrook Institute of Science. Bulletin. News Letter
CraneR — Crane Review
CRAP — Comptes Rendus. Academie Polonaise des Sciences et des Lettres
CRAS — Centennial Review of Arts and Sciences [*Later, Centennial Review*]
CRASR — Comptes Rendus. Academie des Sciences de Russie
C R Assoc Anat — Comptes Rendus. Association des Anatomistes
C R Assoc Int Essais Semences — Comptes Rendus. Association Internationale d'Essais de Semences
CRB — Cahiers de la Compagnie Madeleine Renaud-Jean Louis Barrault
CRB — Cahiers de la Revue Biblique [*Paris*]
CRB — China Report
CRB — Courier de la Bourse et de la Banque
CrB — Critisch Bulletin
CRBDDO — Commentaries on Research in Breast Disease
CRBRAT — Carbohydrate Research
CRC — World Development
CRCBAK — Cardiovascular Research Center. Bulletin [*Houston*]

CRC Critical Reviews in Environmental Control — Chemical Rubber Company. Critical Reviews in Environmental Control
CRC Crit Rev Anal Chem — CRC [*Chemical Rubber Company*] Critical Reviews in Analytical Chemistry
CRC Crit Rev Biochem — CRC [*Chemical Rubber Company*] Critical Reviews in Biochemistry
CRC Crit Rev Bioeng — CRC [*Chemical Rubber Company*] Critical Reviews in Bioengineering
CRC Crit Rev Biomed Eng — CRC [*Chemical Rubber Company*] Critical Reviews in Biomedical Engineering
CRC Crit Rev Clin Lab Sci — CRC [*Chemical Rubber Company*] Critical Reviews in Clinical Laboratory Sciences
CRC Crit Rev Clin Neurobiol — CRC [*Chemical Rubber Company*] Critical Reviews in Clinical Neurobiology
CRC Crit Rev Clin Radiol Nucl Med — CRC [*Chemical Rubber Company*] Critical Reviews in Clinical Radiology and Nuclear Medicine
CRC Crit Rev Environ Control — CRC [*Chemical Rubber Company*] Critical Reviews in Environmental Control
CRC Crit Rev Food Sci Nutr — CRC [*Chemical Rubber Company*] Critical Reviews in Food Science and Nutrition
CRC Crit Rev Food Technol — CRC [*Chemical Rubber Company*] Critical Reviews in Food Technology
CRC Crit Rev Radiol Sci — CRC [*Chemical Rubber Company*] Critical Reviews in Radiological Sciences
CRC Crit Rev Solid Sci — CRC [*Chemical Rubber Company*] Critical Reviews in Solid State Sciences
CRC Crit Rev Solid State Mater Sci — CRC [*Chemical Rubber Company*] Critical Reviews in Solid State and Materials Sciences
CRC Crit Rev Toxicol — CRC [*Chemical Rubber Company*] Critical Reviews in Toxicology
CRC Crit R Microbiol — CRC [*Chemical Rubber Company*] Critical Reviews in Microbiology
CRCFA — Crescendo International
CRCFBSR — Community Research Center. Fairbanks North Star Borough. Special Report
CRC Handb Exp Aspects Oral Biochem — CRC [*Chemical Rubber Company*] Handbook of Experimental Aspects of Oral Biochemistry
CRC Handb Nat Occurring Food Toxicants — CRC [*Chemical Rubber Company*] Handbook of Naturally Occurring Food Toxicants
CRC Handb Nutr Suppl — CRC [*Chemical Rubber Company*] Handbook of Nutritional Supplements
CRC Handb Stereoisomers Drugs Psychopharmacol — CRC [*Chemical Rubber Company*] Handbook of Stereoisomers. Drugs in Psychopharmacology
CRCMC — Creem Magazine
CRCODS — Carlsberg Research Communications
CR Congr Ind Gaz — Compte Rendu. Congres de l'Industrie du Gaz [*France*]
CR Congr Int Chim Ind — Comptes Rendus. Congres Internationaux de Chimie Industrielle
C R Congr Int Psychother — Comptes Rendus. Congres International de Psychotherapie
C R Congr Union Phytopathol Mediterr — Comptes Rendus. Congres de l'Union Phytopathologique Mediterraneenne
Cr Crafts — Creative Crafts
Cr Cu — Cross Currents
CR 3d — Criminal Reports. Third Series . Annotated
CRdGLECS — Comptes Rendus. Groupe Linguistique d'Etudes Chamito-Semitiques [*Paris*]
CRDMBP — Chronica Dermatologica
CRD Newsl US Dep Agric Ext Community Rural Dev — CRD Newsletter. United States Department of Agriculture. Science and Education Administration. Extension, Community, and Rural Development
CR (Dokl) Acad Sci URSS — Comptes Rendus (Doklady). Academie des Sciences de l'Union des Republiques Sovietiques Socialistes
CRDVA — Canadian Research and Development [*Later, Canadian Research*]
Creat Crafts — Creative Crafts
Creation Res Soc Q — Creation Research Society. Quarterly
Creat Res Soc Q — Creation Research Society. Quarterly
Creatv Comp — Creative Computing
CRECD — Conservation and Recycling
CRECD2 — Conservation and Recycling
CREDIF — Bulletin Bibliographique de CREDIF [*Centre de Recherche et d'Etude pour la Diffusion du Francais*] Service de Documentation
Creditanst-Bankverein Wirtschaftsber — Creditanstalt-Bankverein. Wirtschaftsberichte
Credit Communal Belgique Bul Trim — Credit Communal de Belgique. Bulletin Trimestriel
Credit Financ Manage — Credit and Financial Management
Credit & Fin Mgt — Credit and Financial Management
Credit M — Credit Monthly
Credit Wld — Credit World
Cred Rur — Credito Rural
Cred Suisse Bul — Credit Suisse. Bulletin
Creighton L Rev — Creighton Law Review
CREJ — Contents of Recent Economics Journals
CREL — Cahiers Roumains d'Etudes Litteraires
Cres — Cresset

Crescendo Int — Crescendo International
Crest Colect — Cresterea Colectiilor. Caiet Selectiv de Informare Bibliotecii Academii Republicii Socialist Romania
Crest Patr Muz Bul — Cresterea Patrimoniului Muzeal Buletin
CRETB — Current [*New York*]
C Rev — Chesterton Review
C Rev AS — Canadian Review of American Studies
C Rev B — Conch Review of Books
C Revue — Cine Revue
CRF — Consumer Reports
CRGAA3 — Chirurgia [*Bucharest*]
CRGIA — Ceramurgia, Tecnologia Ceramica
Cr H — Craft Horizons
CRH Acad Sci Ser A Sci Math — Comptes Rendus Hebdomadaires des Seances. Academie des Sciences. Serie A. Sciences Mathematiques
CRH Acad Sci Ser B Sci Phys — Comptes Rendus Hebdomadaires des Seances. Academie des Sciences. Serie B. Sciences Physiques
CRH Acad Sci Ser C Sci Chim — Comptes Rendus Hebdomadaires des Seances. Academie des Sciences. Serie C. Sciences Chimiques
CRH Acad Sci Ser D Sci Natur — Comptes Rendus Hebdomadaires des Seances. Academie des Sciences. Serie D. Sciences Naturelles
CRHBull — Commission Royale d'Histoire. Bulletin
CR Hebd Acad Sci Ser 2 — Comptes Rendus Hebdomadaires des Seances. Academie des Sciences. Serie 2
CR Hebd Acad Sci Ser D — Academie des Sciences. Comptes Rendus Hebdomadaires des Seances. Serie D. Sciences Naturelles [*Paris*]
CR Hebd Seanc Acad Sci Jekaterinoslaw — Compte Rendu Hebdomadaire des Seances. Academie des Sciences de Jekaterinoslaw
CR Hebd Seanc Acad Sci (Paris) D — Comptes Rendus Hebdomadaires des Seances. Academie des Sciences (Paris). D. Sciences Naturelles
C R Hebd Seances Acad Agric Fr — Comptes Rendus Hebdomadaires des Seances. Academie d'Agriculture de France
C R Hebd Seances Acad Sci — Comptes Rendus Hebdomadaires des Seances. Academie des Sciences
C R Hebd Seances Acad Sci Ser 2 — Comptes Rendus Hebdomadaires des Seances. Academie des Sciences. Serie 2. Mecanique-Physique, Chimie Sciences de l'Univers, Sciences de la Terre
C R Hebd Seances Acad Sci Ser 3 — Comptes Rendus Hebdomadaires des Seances. Academie des Sciences. Serie 3. Sciences de la Vie
C R Hebd Seances Acad Sci Ser A Sci Math — Comptes Rendus Hebdomadaires des Seances. Academie des Sciences. Serie A. Sciences Mathematiques
C R Hebd Seances Acad Sci Ser C — Comptes Rendus Hebdomadaires des Seances. Academie des Sciences. Serie C. Sciences Chimiques
C R Hebd Seances Acad Sci Ser D — Comptes Rendus Hebdomadaires des Seances. Academie des Sciences. Serie D. Sciences Naturelles
C R Hebd Seances Acad Sci Ser D Sci Nat — Comptes Rendus Hebdomadaires des Seances. Academie des Sciences. Serie D. Sciences Naturelles
CRHPR — Cahiers de la Revue d'Histoire et de Philosophie Religieuses
CRI — Ceramic Industry
CRI — Credit
Cri — Criterion
CRI Abstr — Cement Research Institute of India. Abstracts
CRIEH — Centre de Recherches. Institut d'Etudes Hispaniques
CRIGB — Cryogenic and Industrial Gases
CRIJA — Ceramic Industries Journal
CRIL — Colorado Research in Linguistics
Crim — Criminology
CrimAb — Abstracts on Criminology and Penology
Crim Def — Criminal Defense
Crim & Delin — Crime and Delinquency
Crime & Delin — Crime and Delinquency
Crime Delin — Crime and Delinquency
Crime & Delin'cy — Crime and Delinquency
Crime & Delinq — Crime and Delinquency
Crime Delinq Abstr — Crime and Delinquency Abstracts
Crime and Just — Crime and Justice
Crime Prev News — Crime Prevention News
Crime & Soc Just — Crime and Social Justice
Crimin — Criminology
Criminal Justice Q — Criminal Justice Quarterly
Criminal Justice R — Criminal Justice Review
Criminal Law Bul — Criminal Law Bulletin
Criminal LQ — Criminal Law Quarterly
Crim J and Beh — Criminal Justice and Behavior
Crim Just — Crime and Social Justice
Crim Just B — Criminal Justice and Behavior
Crim Just & Behav — Criminal Justice and Behavior
Crim Just Ethics — Criminal Justice Ethics
Crim Just J — Criminal Justice Journal
Crim Just Newsl — Criminal Justice Newsletter
Crim Law Bul — Criminal Law Bulletin
Crim Law Q — Criminal Law Quarterly
Crim Law R — Criminal Law Review
Crim L Bul — Criminal Law Bulletin
Crim L Bull — Criminal Law Bulletin

rim LJ — Criminal Law Journal
rim LJI — Criminal Law Journal of India
rim LJ Ind — Criminal Law Journal of India
rim LJ (Sydney) — Criminal Law Journal (Sydney) [*Australia*]
rim L Q — Criminal Law Quarterly
rim L R — Criminal Law Review
rim L Rep — Criminal Law Reporter
rim L Rev — Criminal Law Review
rim L Rev (England) — Criminal Law Review (England)
rim L Rptr — Criminal Law Reporter
rim R (Can) — Criminal Reports (Canada)
rim Rep — Criminal Reports
rim Rep NS — Criminal Reports. New Series
RINBJ — Annual Report. Nigeria Cocoa Research Institute
RIPEL — Cahiers de Recherches. Institut de Papyrologie et d'Egyptologie de Lille
risia — Crisia Culegere de Materiale si Studii
riss-Cross — Criss-Cross Art Communications
rist y Soc — Cristianismo y Sociedad
rit — Criterion
rit — Criterium. Letterkundig Maandblad
rit — Critic
rit — Critica
rit — Criticism. A Quarterly for Literature and the Arts
rit — Critique. A Review of Contemporary Art
rit — Critique: Studies in Modern Fiction
rit d A — Critica d'Arte
rit Arte — Critica d'Arte
rit Arts — Critical Arts
rit Care Med — Critical Care Medicine
rit Care Update — Critical Care Update
rit C Nurse — Critical Care Nurse
rit Econ Polit — Critiques de l'Economie Politique
rit Eval Some Equil Constants Involv Alkylammonium Extr — Critical Evaluation of Some Equilibrium Constants Involving Alkylammonium Extractants
rit I — Critical Inquiry
rit Inq — Critical Inquiry
ritiq — Critique
ritique of Anthropol — Critique of Anthropology
ritique S — Critique: Studies in Modern Fiction
ritiques Econ Pol — Critiques de l'Economie Politique
ritm — Criticism
rit Marx — Critica Marxista
rit Mass J — Critical Mass Journal
rit Pen — Critica Penale
rit Perspe — Critical Perspectives
rit Pol — Critica Politica
rit Q — Critical Quarterly
ritq — Critique
rit Quart — Critical Quarterly
rit R — Critical Review
rit Rev — Critical Review
rit Rev Anal Chem — Critical Reviews in Analytical Chemistry
rit Rev Biochem — Critical Reviews in Biochemistry
rit Rev Bioeng — Critical Reviews in Bioengineering
rit Rev Biotechnol — Critical Reviews in Biotechnology
rit Rev Clin Lab Sci — Critical Reviews in Clinical Laboratory Sciences
rit Rev Clin Neurobiol — Critical Reviews in Clinical Neurobiology
rit Rev Clin Radiol Nucl Med — Critical Reviews in Clinical Radiology and Nuclear Medicine
rit Rev Environ Control — Critical Reviews in Environmental Control
rit Rev Food Sci Nutr — Critical Reviews in Food Science and Nutrition
rit Rev Food Technol — Critical Reviews in Food Technology
rit Rev Microbiol — Critical Reviews in Microbiology
rit Rev Solid State Sci — Critical Reviews in Solid State Sciences
rit Rev Toxicol — Critical Reviews in Toxicology
ritS — Critical Survey
rit Soc — Critica Sociale
rit Social (Paris) — Critique Socialiste (Paris)
rit Sociol (Roma) — Critica Sociologica (Roma)
rit Stor — Critica Storica
RJ — Contemporary Religions in Japan
R Journ Natl Compos — Comptes Rendus des Journees Nationales sur les Composites
RJSA4 — Caribbean Journal of Science
r Just — Criminal Justice
RL — College and Research Libraries
RL — Critical Review of Theological and Philosophical Literature
r Law Rep — Criminal Law Reporter
r LJ — Criminal Law Journal of India
RLM — CRREL [*Cold Regions Research and Engineering Laboratory*] Monograph Series [*United States*]
RLN — Comparative Romance Linguistics Newsletter
r LR — Criminal Law Reporter
R Mag — CR [*Chemische Rundschau*] Magazin

CRM Boletin de Informacion — Consejo de Recursos Minerales. Boletin de Informacion
CRME — Council for Research in Music Education. Bulletin
CRNGDP — Carcinogenesis [*London*]
CRNIA — Current Notes on International Affairs [*Australia*]
CRNS — Criminal Reports. New Series
CRNSBP — Chironomus
CRNVD2 — Carnivore [*Seattle*]
Croat Chem — Croatica Chemica Acta
Croat Chem A — Croatica Chemica Acta
Croat Chem Acta — Croatica Chemica Acta
CROCB — Chronache di Chimica
CRODAI — Centre de Recherches Oceanographiques [*Abidjan*]. Documents Scientifiques
CRodSpol — Casopis Rodopisne Spolecnosti Ceskoslovenske
CROEA — Cronache Economiche
CRom — Cuget Romanesc
C (Romania) — Cinema (Romania)
Cron — Cronos
Cron Agric — Cronica Agricola
Cron Catania — Cronache di Archeologia e di Storia dell'Arte. Universita de Catania
Cron Chim — Cronache de Chimica
Cron Dent — Cronica Dental
Cron Econ — Cronache Economiche
Cron Erc — Cronache Ercolanesi
Croner's — Croner's Export Digest
Croner's Ref Book Employ — Croner's Reference Book for Employers
Croner's Ref Book Export — Croner's Reference Book for Exporters
Cron Farm — Cronache Farmaceutiche
Cron Med (Lima) — Cronica Medica (Lima)
Cron Med Mex — Cronica Medica Mexicana
Cron Med Mexicana — Cronica Medica Mexicana
Cron Med-Quir Habana — Cronica Medico-Quirurgica de La Habana
Cron Vin Cer — Cronica de Vinos y Cereales
Crop Bull Can Board Grain Comm — Crop Bulletin. Canada Board of Grain Commissioners
Crop Bull Grain Res Lab (Can) — Crop Bulletin. Grain Research Laboratory (Canada)
Crop Improv — Crop Improvement
Crop Prod — Crop Production
Crop Res ARS — Crops Research ARS [*Agricultural Research Service*]
Crop Res News Dep Sci Ind Res (NZ) — Crop Research News. New Zeealand Department of Scientific and Industrial Research
Crop Res News NZ Dep Sci Ind Res — Crop Research News. New Zealand Department of Scientific and Industrial Research
Crop Sci — Crop Science
Crop Soil NC State Univ — Crop Soils. North Carolina State University
Cross C — Cross Currents
Cross & Cr — Cross and Crown
Cross Cur — Cross Currents
Cross Curr — Cross Currents
Crown Agents QR — Crown Agents Quarterly Review
Crown Ag R — Crown Agents Review
Crown Col — Crown Colonist
Crown C Rev — Crown Counsel's Review
Crowther FPL — D. J. Crowther Ltd. Fixed Price List
CRPD — Clinical Research Practices and Drug Regulatory Affairs
C R (Petersb) — Compte Rendu. Commission Imperiale Archeologique (St. Petersbourg)
CRPSA — Crop Science
CR P v Mem Ass Breton — Compte Rendu. Proces-Verbaux et Memoires. Association Bretonne
CrQ — Critical Quarterly
CRR — Compte Rendu. Rencontre Assyriologique Internationale
Cr R — Criminal Reports
CRRA — Compte Rendu. Rencontre Assyriologique Internationale
CRRDB — CRC [*Chemical Rubber Company*] Critical Reviews in Radiological Sciences
C R Rech Bibl Immigr — Comptes Rendus de Recherches et Bibliographie sur l'Immigration
CR Rech Inst Encour Rech Sci Ind Agric — Comptes Rendus de Recherches. Institut pour l'Encouragement de la Recherche Scientifique dans l'Industrie et l'Agriculture [*Belgium*]
CRRED — Carbonization Research Report
CRREL — CRREL [*Cold Regions Research and Engineering Laboratory*] Report [*United States*]
CRRELDT — CRREL [*Cold Regions Research and Engineering Laboratory*] Draft Translation [*United States*]
CRREL Monograph — Cold Regions Research and Engineering Laboratory. Monograph
CRRELR — CRREL [*Cold Regions Research and Engineering Laboratory*] Report [*United States*]
CRREL Report — Cold Regions Research and Engineering Laboratory. Report
CRRELRR — CRREL [*Cold Regions Research and Engineering Laboratory*] Research Reports [*United States*]

CRRELSR — CRREL [*Cold Regions Research and Engineering Laboratory*] Special Report [*United States*]
CRRELTR — CRREL [*Cold Regions Research and Engineering Laboratory*] Technical Reports [*United States*]
Cr Rep — Criminal Reports
CRRERI — Commonwealth Regional Renewable Energy Resources Index
CRRVAJ — Chromatographic Reviews
CrS — Cristianesimo nella Storia
CrS — Critica Storica
CRSA — Canadian Review of Sociology and Anthropology
CRSAIBL — Comptes Rendus des Seances. Academie des Inscriptions et Belles-Lettres
CRSBA — Comptes Rendus des Seances. Societe de Biologie et de Ses Filiales
CR Seance Publ Ann Acad Pharm — Comptes Rendus de la Seance Publique Annuelle. Academie de la Pharmacie
C R Seances Acad Agric Fr — Comptes Rendus des Seances. Academie d'Agriculture de France
CR Seances Acad Sci Roum — Comptes Rendus des Seances. Academie des Sciences de Roumanie
CR Seances Acad Sci Ser 2 — Comptes Rendus des Seances. Academie des Sciences. Serie 2. Mecanique, Physique, Chimie, Sciences de la Terre, Sciences de l'Univers [*France*]
C R Seances Acad Sci Ser 3 — Comptes Rendus des Seances. Academie des Sciences. Serie 3. Sciences de la Vie
CR Seances Acad Sci Ser A — Comptes Rendus des Seances. Academie des Sciences. Serie A. Sciences Mathematiques [*France*]
CR Seances Acad Sci Ser B — Comptes Rendus des Seances. Academie des Sciences. Serie B. Sciences Physiques [*France*]
CR Seances Acad Sci Ser C — Comptes Rendus des Seances. Academie des Sciences. Serie C. Sciences Chimiques [*France*]
CR Seances Acad Sci Ser D — Comptes Rendus des Seances. Academie des Sciences. Serie D. Sciences Naturelles [*France*]
CR Seances Acad Sci Ser I — Comptes Rendus de Seances. Academie des Sciences. Serie I. Mathematique
C R Seances Acad Sci Vie Acad — Comptes Rendus des Seances. Academie des Sciences. Vie Academique
CR Seances Inst Geol Roum — Comptes Rendus des Seances. Institut Geologique de Roumanie
C R Seances Mens Soc Sci Nat Phys Maroc — Comptes Rendus des Seances Mensuelles. Societe des Sciences Naturelles et Physiques du Maroc
C R Seances Soc Biogeogr — Compte Rendu des Seances. Societe de Biogeographie
C R Seances Soc Biol Fil — Comptes Rendus des Seances. Societe de Biologie et de Ses Filiales
CR Seances Soc Biol (Paris) — Comptes Rendus des Seances. Societe de Biologie (Paris)
C R Seances Soc Phys Hist Nat Geneve — Compte Rendu des Seances. Societe de Physique et d'Histoire Naturelle de Geneve
CR Seanc Mens Soc Sci Nat Phys Maroc — Comptes Rendus des Seances Mensuelles. Societe des Sciences Naturelles et Physiques du Maroc
CR Seanc Soc Biol — Comptes Rendus des Seances. Societe de Biologie
CR Seanc Soc Biol Fil — Comptes Rendus des Seances. Societe de Biologie et de Ses Filiales
CR Sem Geol Com Nat Malgache Geol — Comptes Rendus de la Semaine Geologique. Comite National Malgache de Geologie
CRSHA — Circulatory Shock
CRSIGR — Comptes Rendus des Seances. Institut de Geologie Roumaine
CRSL — Comptes-Rendus. Societe des Sciences et des Lettres
CRSL — Comptes Rendus. Societe des Sciences et des Lettres de Lodz
CRSLub — Comptes Rendus. Societe des Sciences et des Lettres. Universite Catholique de Lublin
CRSOA — Crops and Soils
C R Soc Biol — Comptes Rendus des Seances. Societe de Biologie et de Ses Filiales
C R Soc Biol (Paris) — Comptes Rendus des Seances. Societe de Biologie (Paris)
CR Soc Franc Gynec — Comptes Rendus. Societe Francaise de Gynecologie
C R Soc Fr Gynecol — Comptes Rendus. Societe Francaise de Gynecologie
CR Soc Geol Fr — Comptes Rendus Sommaire des Seances. Societe Geologique de France
CR Soc Roy Econ Pol — Comptes Rendus des Travaux. Societe Royale d'Economie Politique de Belgique
C R Soc Sci Nat Phys Maroc — Comptes Rendus des Seances Mensuelles. Societe des Sciences Naturelles et Physiques du Maroc
CR Somm Seances Soc Geol Fr — Compte Rendu Sommaire des Seances. Societe Geologique de France
CR Somm Seanc Soc Biogeogr — Compte Rendu Sommaire des Seances. Societe de Biogeographie
C R Som Seances Soc Geol Fr — Comptes Rendus Sommaire des Seances. Societe Geologique de France
CRSP — Comptes Rendus. Societe des Sciences et des Lettres de Poznan
CRSQ — Creation Research Society. Quarterly

CRST — Cold Regions Science and Technology
CRSTB — Proceedings. Conference on Remote Systems Technology
CRSTD — Cold Regions Science and Technology
CRSVa — Comptes Rendus. Societe des Sciences et des Lettres de Varsovie
CRSW — Comptes Rendus. Societe des Sciences et des Lettres de Wroclaw
C R Symp Int Jets Mol — Comptes Rendus. Symposium International sur les Jets Moleculaires
CRTD — Cold Regions Technical Digest
CRTED — Crystal Research and Technology
Cr Trav Carlsb — Comptes Rendus des Travaux. Laboratoire Carlsberg
CR Trav Fac Sci Univ Aix Marseille — Comptes Rendus des Travaux. Faculte des Sciences. Universite de l'Aix Marseille
C R Trav Lab Carlsberg — Comptes Rendus des Travaux. Laboratoire Carlsberg
C R Trav Lab Carlsberg Ser Chim — Comptes Rendus des Travaux. Laboratoire Carlsberg. Serie Chimique
C R Trav Lab Carlsberg Ser Physiol — Comptes Rendus des Travaux. Laboratoire Carlsberg. Serie Physiologique
C R Trim Acad Sci O-Mer — Comptes Rendus Trimestriels. Academie des Sciences d'Outre-Mer
C R Tr Lab C — Comptes Rendus des Travaux. Laboratoire Carlsberg
CRTXA — Cortex
CRu — Ceskoslovenska Rusistika
CRus — Ceskoslovenska Rusistika
CRUSA — Crustaceana [*Leiden*]
Crush Grind Min Quarr J — Crushing, Grinding, Mining, and Quarrying Journal
Crushing Grinding Min Quarrying J — Crushing, Grinding, Mining, and Quarrying Journal
Crustaceana Suppl (Leiden) — Crustaceana. Supplement (Leiden)
CRV — Creditanstalt-Bankverein. Wirtschaftsberichte
Cr Wtg — Creative Writing
CRYBA — Cryobiology
Cry Calif — Cry California
CRYOA — Cryogenics [*England*]
Cryog — Cryogenics
Cryog Eng — Cryogenic Engineering [*Japan*]
Cryog Eng News — Cryogenic Engineering News
Cryog & Ind Gases — Cryogenics and Industrial Gases
Cryog Suppl — Cryogenics. Supplement
Cryog Technol — Cryogenic Technology
Crys Lattice Defects — Crystal Lattice Defects
Crystallogr Comput Tech Proc Int Summer Sch — Crystallographic Computing Techniques. Proceedings of an International Summer School
Crystallogr (Sov Phys) — Crystallography (Soviet Physics)
Cryst Chem Non-Met Mater — Crystal Chemistry of Non-Metallic Materials
Cryst Field Eff Met Alloys (Proc Int Conf) — Crystal Field Effects in Metals and Alloys (Proceedings of the International Conference on Crystal Field Effects in Metals and Alloys)
Cryst Latt — Crystal Lattice Defects
Cryst Lattice Defects — Crystal Lattice Defects
Cryst Lattice Defects Amorphous Mater — Crystal Lattice Defects and Amorphous Materials [*Formerly, Crystal Lattice Defects*]
Cryst Lattice Defects and Amorphous Mater — Crystal Lattice Defects and Amorphous Materials [*Formerly, Crystal Lattice Defects*]
Cryst Res Technol — Crystal Research and Technology
Cryst Res and Technol — Crystal Research and Technology
Cryst Struct Commun — Crystal Structure Communications [*Italy*]
CRZLAT — Communication. Centre de Recherches Zootechniques. Universite de Louvain
CS — Cahiers Sioniens [*Paris*]
CS — Cahiers du Sud
CS — Christopher Street
CS — Clinical Studies [*Elsevier Book Series*]
CS — Computers and Standards
CS — Contemporary Sociology
CS — Cornish Studies
CS — Corriere della Sera
CS — Critica Storica
CS — Croatia Sacra
C & S — Cultura e Scuola
CS — Current Scene [*Hong Kong*]
CSA — Cahiers. Societe Asiatique
CSA — Central Bank of Trinidad and Tobago. Quarterly Economic Report
CSAAA — Annual Reports on the Progress of Chemistry. Section A. General, Physical, and Inorganic Chemistry
2CSAB — Two Complete Science Adventure Books
CSAKA — Chemia Stosowana. Seria A. Kwartalnik Poswiecony Zagadnieniom Technologii Chemicznej
CSAN — Coin, Stamp, and Antique News
CSAPC — Case Studies in Atomic Physics
CSARCX — Cancer Research Institute. Slovak Academy of Sciences. Annual Report
CSATD6 — Department of the Capital Territory. Conservation Series [*Canberra*]
Csatornamue Inf — Csatornamue Informacio

CSAV — Ceskoslovenska Akademie Ved

CSB — Cataloging Service Bulletin

CSB — Cathedral Service Book

CSB — Common Market Business Reports (Spain)

CSB — Companies and Securities Bulletin

CSBKA — Chemia Stosowana. Seria B. Kwartalnik Poswiecony Zagadnieniom Inzynierii i Aparatury Chemicznej

CSBL-A — Casabella

CSBW — Chicago Sun Book Week

C Sc — Cognitive Science

CSC — Coins, Stamps, and Collecting

CSCA — California Studies in Classical Antiquity

CSCH — Ceskoslovensky Casopis Historicky

CSCO — Corpus Scriptorum Christianorum Orientalium

CSCPC3 — Australia. Commonwealth Scientific and Industrial Research Organisation. Division of Chemical Physics. Annual Report

CSCRS — Calcutta Sanskrit College Research Series

CSDIR — Centro Studi e Documentazione sull'Italia Romana

CSE — Cornell Studies in English

CSE — Cosmetics International

CSE — Cost Engineering

CSEB — Canadian Society of Environmental Biologists. Newsletter/Bulletin

CSEL — Corpus Scriptorum Ecclesiasticorum Latinorum

CSELT Rappo Tec — CSELT [*Centro Studi e Laboratori Telecomunicazioni*] Rapporti Tecnici

CSELT Rapp Tec — CSELT [*Centro Studi e Laboratori Telecomunicazioni*] Rapporti Tecnici

CSEV — Climatological Studies. Environment Canada. Atmospheric Environment

CSF — Cambridge Studies in French

CS Faraday Transactions 1 — Chemical Society. Faraday Transactions 1

CSFJA — Citrus and Subtropical Fruit Journal

CSFRD — Cameron Synthetic Fuels Report

CSFSD — Ciencias Forestales

CSFUDY — Cell Structure and Function

CSGCAG — Congres International de Stratigraphie et de Geologie du Carbonifere. Compte Rendu

CSGEA — Compass. Sigma Gamma Epsilon

CSGH — Chosen Gakuno

CSGLL — Canadian Studies in German Language and Literature

CSGYAF — Contemporary Surgery

CSHSA — Cold Spring Harbor Symposia on Quantitative Biology

CSHVB — Computer Studies in the Humanities and Verbal Behavior

CSI — CSIRO [*Commonwealth Scientific and Industrial Research Organisation*] Index

CSIC — Consejo Superior de Investigaciones Cientificas [*Madrid, Spain*]

CSIC Cent Edafol Biol Apl Anu — Consejo Superior de Investigaciones Cientificas. Centro de Edafologia y Biologia Aplicada. Anuario

CSIC Estud Geol — Consejo Superior de Investigaciones Cientificas. Estudios Geologicos [*Madrid*]

CSIC Patronato Juan De La Cierva Invest Tec Cuad — Consejo Superior de Investigaciones Cientificas. Patronato Juan De La Cierva de Investigaciones Tecnicas. Cuaderno

CSIO Commun — CSIO [*Central Scientific Instruments Organisation*] Communications [*India*]

CSion — Cahiers Sioniens [*Paris*]

CSIR Air Pollut Res Group Rep APRG (S Afr) — Council for Scientific and Industrial Research. Air Pollution Research Group. Report APRG (South Africa)

CSIR Dep Mines Asbestos Min Ind Asbestosis Res Proj Annu Rep — Council for Scientific and Industrial Research and Department of Mines and the Asbestos Mining Industry. Asbestosis Research Project. Annual Report

CSIR News (India) — CSIR [*Council for Scientific and Industrial Research*] News (India)

CSIRO Abstr — CSIRO [*Commonwealth Scientific and Industrial Research Organisation*] Abstracts

CSIRO An Health Div TP — CSIRO [*Commonwealth Scientific and Industrial Research Organisation*] Division of Animal Health and Production. Technical Paper

CSIRO Annu Rep — CSIRO [*Commonwealth Scientific and Industrial Research Organisation*] Annual Report

CSIRO An Res Labs TP — CSIRO [*Commonwealth Scientific and Industrial Research Organisation*] Animal Research Laboratories. Technical Paper

CSIRO Aust Div Trop Crops Pastures Tech Pap — Australia. Commonwealth Scientific and Industrial Research Organisation. Division of Tropical Crops and Pastures. Technical Paper

CSIRO Aust Div Trop Crops Pastures Tech Pap — CSIRO [*Commonwealth Scientific and Industrial Research Organisation*] Australia. Division of Tropical Crops and Pastures. Technical Paper

CSIRO Bio Mem News — Bio Membrane News CSIRO [*Commonwealth Scientific and Industrial Research Organisation*] Biomembrane Committee

CSIRO Build Res Div Building Study — CSIRO [*Commonwealth Scientific and Industrial Research Organisation*] Division of Building Research. Building Study

CSIRO Build Res Div Rep — CSIRO [*Commonwealth Scientific and Industrial Research Organisation*] Division of Building Research. Report

CSIRO Build Res Div Tech Pap — CSIRO [*Commonwealth Scientific and Industrial Research Organisation*] Division of Building Research. Technical Paper

CSIRO Build Res Div TP — CSIRO [*Commonwealth Scientific and Industrial Research Organisation*] Division of Building Research. Technical Paper

CSIRO Bull — CSIRO [*Commonwealth Scientific and Industrial Research Organisation*] Bulletin [*Australia*]

CSIRO Chem Res Labs TP — CSIRO [*Commonwealth Scientific and Industrial Research Organisation*] Chemical Research Laboratories. Technical Paper

CSIRO Chem Res Lab Tech Pap — CSIRO [*Commonwealth Scientific and Industrial Research Organisation*] Chemical Research Laboratories. Technical Paper

CSIRO Coal Res Div Ref TC — CSIRO [*Commonwealth Scientific and Industrial Research Organisation*] Division of Coal Research. Reference TC [*Technical Communication*]

CSIRO Coal Res Div Tech Commun — CSIRO [*Commonwealth Scientific and Industrial Research Organisation*] Division of Coal Research. Technical Communication

CSIRO Coal Res Lab Invest Rep — CSIRO [*Commonwealth Scientific and Industrial Research Organisation*] Coal Research Laboratory. Division of Mineral Chemistry. Investigation Report

CSIRO Coal Res Lab Tech Commun — CSIRO [*Commonwealth Scientific and Industrial Research Organisation*] Coal Research Laboratory. Division of Mineral Chemistry. Technical Communication

CSIRO Computing Res Sect Memo — CSIRO [*Commonwealth Scientific and Industrial Research Organisation*] Computing Research Section. Memorandum

CSIRO Consumer Liaison Ser Leaflet — Consumer Liaison Service Leaflet CSIRO [*Commonwealth Scientific and Industrial Research Organisation*]. Division of Food Research

CSIRO Dig of Curr Act — CSIRO [*Commonwealth Scientific and Industrial Research Organisation*] Digest of Current Activities

CSIRO Div Appl Geomech Prog Circ — Computer Program Users Manual CSIRO [*Commonwealth Scientific and Industrial Research Organisation. Division of Applied Geomechanics*]

CSIRO Div Appl Organic Chem Res Rep — CSIRO [*Commonwealth Scientific and Industrial Research Organisation*] Division of Applied Organic Chemistry. Research Report

CSIRO Div Atmos Phys Tech Pap — CSIRO [*Commonwealth Scientific and Industrial Research Organisation*] Division of Atmospheric Physics. Technical Paper [*Australia*]

CSIRO Div Build Res Publ — CSIRO [*Commonwealth Scientific and Industrial Research Organisation*] Division of Building Research. Publications

CSIRO Div Chem Phys Ann Rep — CSIRO [*Commonwealth Scientific and Industrial Research Organisation*] Division of Chemical Physics. Annual Report

CSIRO Div Chem Phys Annu Rep — CSIRO [*Commonwealth Scientific and Industrial Research Organisation*] Division of Chemical Physics. Annual Report

CSIRO Div Chem Technol Tech Pap — CSIRO [*Commonwealth Scientific and Industrial Research Organisation*] Division of Chemical Technology. Technical Paper

CSIRO Div Entomol Annu Rep — CSIRO [*Commonwealth Scientific and Industrial Research Organisation*] Division of Entomology. Annual Report

CSIRO Div Fish Oceanogr Rep — CSIRO [*Commonwealth Scientific and Industrial Research Organisation*] Division of Fisheries and Oceanography. Report

CSIRO Div Fish Oceanogr Rep (Aust) — CSIRO [*Commonwealth Scientific and Industrial Research Organisation*] Division of Fisheries and Oceanography. Report (Australia)

CSIRO Div Food Res Rep Res — CSIRO [*Commonwealth Scientific and Industrial Research Organisation*] Division of Food Research. Report of Research

CSIRO Div Forest Prod Technol Paper — CSIRO [*Commonwealth Scientific and Industrial Research Organisation*] Division of Forest Products. Technological Paper

CSIRO Div For Res Ann Rep — CSIRO [*Commonwealth Scientific and Industrial Research Organisation*] Division of Forest Research. Annual Report

CSIRO Div Land Use Res Publ — CSIRO [*Commonwealth Scientific and Industrial Research Organisation*] Division of Land Use Research. Publications

CSIRO Div Mech Eng Info Serv Leafl — CSIRO [*Commonwealth Scientific and Industrial Research Organisation*] Division of Mechanical Engineering. Information Service Leaflet

CSIRO Div Mineral Invest Rep — CSIRO [*Commonwealth Scientific and Industrial Research Organisation*] Division of Mineralogy. Investigation Report

CSIRO Div Mineral Tech Commun — CSIRO [*Commonwealth Scientific and Industrial Research Organisation*] Division of Mineralogy. Technical Communication

CSIRO Div Miner Chem Invest Rep — CSIRO [*Commonwealth Scientific and Industrial Research Organisation*] Division of Mineral Chemistry. Investigation Report

CSIRO Div Miner Phys Invest Rep — CSIRO [*Commonwealth Scientific and Industrial Research Organisation*] Division of Mineral Physics. Investigation Report

CSIRO Div Plant Ind Field Stn Rec Aust — Australia. Commonwealth Scientific and Industrial Research Organisation. Division of Plant Industry. Field Station Record

CSIRO Div Text Phys Ann Rep — CSIRO [*Commonwealth Scientific and Industrial Research Organisation*] Division of Textile Physics. Annual Report

CSIRO Div Trop Agron Annu Rep — CSIRO [*Commonwealth Scientific and Industrial Research Organisation*] Division of Tropical Agronomy. Annual Report

CSIRO Div Trop Crops Pastures Trop Agron Tech Memo — CSIRO [*Commonwealth Scientific and Industrial Research Organisation*] Division of Tropical Crops and Pastures. Tropical Agronomy Technical Memorandum

CSIRO Engng Sect C — CSIRO [*Commonwealth Scientific and Industrial Research Organisation*] Engineering Section. Circular

CSIRO Engng Sect Int Rept — CSIRO [*Commonwealth Scientific and Industrial Research Organisation*] Engineering Section. Internal Report

CSIRO Entomol Div Tech Pap — CSIRO [*Commonwealth Scientific and Industrial Research Organisation*] Division of Entomology. Technical Paper

CSIRO Entomol Div TP — CSIRO [*Commonwealth Scientific and Industrial Research Organisation*] Division of Entomology. Technical Paper

CSIRO Fd Pres Div Circ — CSIRO [*Commonwealth Scientific and Industrial Research Organisation*] Division of Food Preservation. Circular

CSIRO Fd Preserv Div Tech Pap — CSIRO [*Commonwealth Scientific and Industrial Research Organisation*] Division of Food Preservation. Technical Paper

CSIRO Fd Preserv Q — CSIRO [*Commonwealth Scientific and Industrial Research Organisation*] Food Preservation Quarterly

CSIRO Fd Res Q — CSIRO [*Commonwealth Scientific and Industrial Research Organisation*] Food Research Quarterly

CSIRO Fish Div C — CSIRO [*Commonwealth Scientific and Industrial Research Organisation*] Division of Fisheries and Oceanography. Circular

CSIRO Fish Div Fish Synopsis — CSIRO [*Commonwealth Scientific and Industrial Research Organisation*] Division of Fisheries and Oceanography. Fisheries Synopsis

CSIRO Fish Div Oceanogrl Cruise Rep — CSIRO [*Commonwealth Scientific and Industrial Research Organisation*] Division of Fisheries and Oceanography. Oceanographical Cruise Report

CSIRO Fish Div Oceanogrl Stn List — CSIRO [*Commonwealth Scientific and Industrial Research Organisation*] Division of Fisheries and Oceanography. Oceanographical Station List

CSIRO Fish Div Oceanogr Station List — CSIRO [*Commonwealth Scientific and Industrial Research Organisation*] Division of Fisheries and Oceanography. Oceanographical Station List

CSIRO Fish Div Rep — CSIRO [*Commonwealth Scientific and Industrial Research Organisation*] Division of Fisheries and Oceanography. Report

CSIRO Fish Div Tech Pap — CSIRO [*Commonwealth Scientific and Industrial Research Organisation*] Division of Fisheries and Oceanography. Technical Paper

CSIRO Fish Div TP — CSIRO [*Commonwealth Scientific and Industrial Research Organisation*] Division of Fisheries and Oceanography. Technical Paper

CSIRO Food Pres Div C — CSIRO [*Commonwealth Scientific and Industrial Research Organisation*] Division of Food Preservation. Circular

CSIRO Food Pres Div TP — CSIRO [*Commonwealth Scientific and Industrial Research Organisation*] Division of Food Preservation. Technical Paper

CSIRO Food Preserv Q — CSIRO [*Commonwealth Scientific and Industrial Research Organisation*] Food Preservation Quarterly

CSIRO Food Res Q — CSIRO [*Commonwealth Scientific and Industrial Research Organisation*] Division of Food Research. Food Research Quarterly

CSIRO Food Res Q Suppl Ser — CSIRO [*Commonwealth Scientific and Industrial Research Organisation*] Division of Food Research. Food Research Quarterly. Supplementary Series

CSIRO Forest Prod Newsl — CSIRO [*Commonwealth Scientific and Industrial Research Organisation*] Forest Products Newsletter

CSIRO For Prod Div Technol P — CSIRO [*Commonwealth Scientific and Industrial Research Organisation*] Division of Forest Products. Technological Paper

CSIRO For Prod Div Technol Pap — CSIRO [*Commonwealth Scientific and Industrial Research Organisation*] Division of Forest Products. Technological Paper

CSIRO For Prod Newsl — CSIRO [*Commonwealth Scientific and Industrial Research Organisation*] Division of Forest Products. Forest Products Newsletter

CSIRO For Prod Newslett — CSIRO [*Commonwealth Scientific and Industrial Research Organisation*] Forest Products Newsletter

CSIRO For Prod Newsletter — CSIRO [*Commonwealth Scientific and Industrial Research Organisation*] Forest Products Newsletter

CSIRO For Prod Tech Notes — CSIRO [*Commonwealth Scientific and Industrial Research Organisation*] Division of Forest Products. CSIRO Forest Products Technical Notes

CSIRO Ind Res News — CSIRO [*Commonwealth Scientific and Industrial Research Organisation*] Industrial Research News

CSIRO Inst Earth Resour Invest Rep — CSIRO [*Commonwealth Scientific and Industrial Research Organisation*] Institute of Earth Resources. Investigation Report

CSIRO Inst Earth Resour Tech Commun — CSIRO [*Commonwealth Scientific and Industrial Research Organisation*] Institute of Earth Resources. Technical Communication

CSIRO Irrig Res Stat TP — CSIRO [*Commonwealth Scientific and Industrial Research Organisation*] Irrigation Research Stations. Technical Paper

CSIRO Land Res Regional Surv Div Tech Pap — CSIRO [*Commonwealth Scientific and Industrial Research Organisation*] Division of Land Research and Regional Survey. Technical Paper

CSIRO Land Res Regional Surv Div TP — CSIRO [*Commonwealth Scientific and Industrial Research Organisation*] Division of Land Research and Regional Survey. Technical Paper

CSIRO Land Res Ser — CSIRO [*Commonwealth Scientific and Industrial Research Organisation*] Land Research Series

CSIRO Leaflet Ser — CSIRO [*Commonwealth Scientific and Industrial Research Organisation*] Leaflet Series

CSIRO Mar Biochem Unit Annu Rep — CSIRO [*Commonwealth Scientific and Industrial Research Organisation*] Marine Biochemistry Unit. Annual Report

CSIRO Marine Biochem Unit Ann Rep — CSIRO [*Commonwealth Scientific and Industrial Research Organisation*] Marine Biochemistry Unit. Annual Report

CSIRO Math Statist Div Tech Pap — CSIRO [*Commonwealth Scientific and Industrial Research Organisation*] Division of Mathematical Statistics. Technical Paper

CSIRO Math Statist Div TP — CSIRO [*Commonwealth Scientific and Industrial Research Organisation*] Division of Mathematical Statistics. Technical Paper

CSIRO Mech Engng Div Circ — CSIRO [*Commonwealth Scientific and Industrial Research Organisation*] Division of Mechanical Engineering. Circular

CSIRO Mech Engng Div Rep — CSIRO [*Commonwealth Scientific and Industrial Research Organisation*] Division of Mechanical Engineering. Report

CSIRO Met Phys Div Tech Pap — CSIRO [*Commonwealth Scientific and Industrial Research Organisation*] Division of Meteorological Physics. Technical Paper

CSIRO Minerag Investig TP — CSIRO [*Commonwealth Scientific and Industrial Research Organisation*] Mineragraphic Investigations. Technical Paper

CSIRO Minerag Invest Tech Pap — CSIRO [*Commonwealth Scientific and Industrial Research Organisation*] Mineragraphic Investigations. Technical Paper

CSIRO Miner Phys Sect Invest Rep — CSIRO [*Commonwealth Scientific and Industrial Research Organisation*] Mineral Physics Section. Investigation Report

CSIRO Miner Res Lab Ann Rep — CSIRO [*Commonwealth Scientific and Industrial Research Organisation*] Minerals Research Laboratories. Annual Report

CSIRO Miner Res Lab Annu Rep — CSIRO [*Commonwealth Scientific and Industrial Research Organisation*] Minerals Research Laboratories. Annual Report

CSIRO Miner Res Lab Div Mineral Tech Commun — CSIRO [*Commonwealth Scientific and Industrial Research Organisation*] Minerals Research Laboratories. Division of Mineralogy. Technical Communication

CSIRO Miner Res Lab Invest Rep — CSIRO [*Commonwealth Scientific and Industrial Research Organisation*] Minerals Research Laboratories. Investigation Report

CSIRO Miner Res Lab Res Rev — CSIRO [*Commonwealth Scientific and Industrial Research Organisation*] Minerals Research Laboratories. Research Review

CSIRO Miner Res Lab Tech Commun — CSIRO [*Commonwealth Scientific and Industrial Research Organisation*] Minerals Research Laboratories. Technical Communication

CSIRO Natl Meas Lab Bienn Rep — CSIRO [*Commonwealth Scientific and Industrial Research Organisation*] National Measurement Laboratory. Biennial Report

CSIRO Natl Meas Lab Tech Pap — CSIRO [*Commonwealth Scientific and Industrial Research Organization*] National Measurement Laboratory. Technical Paper

CSIRO Natl Measure Lab Biennial Rep — CSIRO [*Commonwealth Scientific and Industrial Research Organisation*] National Measurement Laboratory. Biennial Report

CSIRO Natl Stand Lab Bienn Rep — CSIRO [*Commonwealth Scientific and Industrial Research Organisation*] National Standards Laboratory. Biennial Report

CSIRO Nat Stand Lab Div Appl Phys Test Pamph — CSIRO [*Commonwealth Scientific and Industrial Research Organisation*] National Standards Laboratory. Division of Applied Physics. Test Pamphlet

CSIRO Nat Stands Lab Circ — CSIRO [*Commonwealth Scientific and Industrial Research Organisation*] National Standards Laboratory. Circular

CSIRO Nat Stands Lab Tech Pap — CSIRO [*Commonwealth Scientific and Industrial Research Organisation*] National Standards Laboratory. Technical Paper

CSIRO Nat Stands Lab Test Pamphl — CSIRO [*Commonwealth Scientific and Industrial Research Organisation*] National Standards Laboratory. Test Pamphlet

CSIRO Nat Stands Lab TP — CSIRO [*Commonwealth Scientific and Industrial Research Organisation*] National Standards Laboratory. Technical Paper

CSIROOA Bul — CSIROOA Bulletin. Journal of the Association of Officers of the Commonwealth Scientific and Industrial Research Organisation

CSIRO Phys Met Sec Tech Pap — CSIRO [*Commonwealth Scientific and Industrial Research Organisation*] Physical Metallurgy Section. Technical Paper

CSIRO Plant Ind Div Field Sta Rec — CSIRO [*Commonwealth Scientific and Industrial Research Organisation*] Division of Plant Industry. Field Station Record

CSIRO Plant Ind Div Field Stn Rec — CSIRO [*Commonwealth Scientific and Industrial Research Organisation*] Division of Plant Industry. Field Station Record

CSIRO Plant Ind Div Tech Pap — CSIRO [*Commonwealth Scientific and Industrial Research Organisation*] Division of Plant Industry. Technical Paper

CSIRO Plant Ind Div TP — CSIRO [*Commonwealth Scientific and Industrial Research Organisation*] Division of Plant Industry. Technical Paper

CSIRO Plant Ind TP — CSIRO [*Commonwealth Scientific and Industrial Research Organisation*] Division of Plant Industry. Technical Paper

CSIRO Radiophys Div Rept — CSIRO [*Commonwealth Scientific and Industrial Research Organisation*] Division of Radiophysics. Report

CSIRO Sci Index — CSIRO [*Commonwealth Scientific and Industrial Research Organisation*] Science Index

CSIRO Soil Mechanics Sect Geotech Rep — CSIRO [*Commonwealth Scientific and Industrial Research Organisation*] Soil Mechanics Section. Geotechnical Report

CSIRO Soil Mechanics Sect Tech Rep — CSIRO [*Commonwealth Scientific and Industrial Research Organisation*] Soil Mechanics Section. Technical Report

CSIRO Soil Mech Div Tech Pap — CSIRO [*Commonwealth Scientific and Industrial Research Organisation*] Division of Soil Mechanics. Technical Paper

CSIRO Soil Mech Div Tech Rep — CSIRO [*Commonwealth Scientific and Industrial Research Organisation*] Division of Soil Mechanics. Technical Report

CSIRO Soil Mech Sect Tech Rep — CSIRO [*Commonwealth Scientific and Industrial Research Organisation*] Soil Mechanics Section. Technical Report

CSIRO Soil Pub — CSIRO [*Commonwealth Scientific and Industrial Research Organisation*] Soil Publications

CSIRO Soils Div SLU — CSIRO [*Commonwealth Scientific and Industrial Research Organisation*] Division of Soils. Soils and Land Use Series

CSIRO Text Ind Div Rep — CSIRO [*Commonwealth Scientific and Industrial Research Organisation*] Division of Textile Industry. Report

CSIRO Text News — CSIRO [*Commonwealth Scientific and Industrial Research Organisation*] Wood Research Laboratory. Textile News

CSIRO Text Phys Div Rep — CSIRO [*Commonwealth Scientific and Industrial Research Organisation*] Division of Textile Physics. Report

CSIRO Trop Pastures Div TP — CSIRO [*Commonwealth Scientific and Industrial Research Organisation*] Division of Tropical Pastures. Technical Paper

CSIRO Wheat Res Unit Annu Rep — CSIRO [*Commonwealth Scientific and Industrial Research Organisation*] Wheat Research Unit. Annual Report

CSIRO Wildl Res — CSIRO [*Commonwealth Scientific and Industrial Research Organisation*] Wildlife Research

CSIRO Wildl Res Div Tech Pap — CSIRO [*Commonwealth Scientific and Industrial Research Organisation*] Division of Wildlife Research. Technical Paper

CSIRO Wildl Res Div TP — CSIRO [*Commonwealth Scientific and Industrial Research Organisation*] Division of Wildlife Research. Technical Paper

CSIRO Wildl Surv Sect TP — CSIRO [*Commonwealth Scientific and Industrial Research Organisation*] Wildlife Survey Section. Technical Paper

CSIRO Wool Text News — CSIRO [*Commonwealth Scientific and Industrial Research Organisation*] Division of Textile Industry. Wool Textile News

CSIRO Wool Text Res Labs Rep — CSIRO [*Commonwealth Scientific and Industrial Research Organisation*] Wool Textile Research Laboratories. Report

CSIRO Wool Text Res Labs TC — CSIRO [*Commonwealth Scientific and Industrial Research Organisation*] Wool Textile Research Laboratories. Trade Circular

CSIRO Wool Text Res Labs TP — CSIRO [*Commonwealth Scientific and Industrial Research Organisation*] Wool Textile Research Laboratories. Technical Paper

CSIR Res Rep — CSIR [*Council for Scientific and Industrial Research*] Research Report

CSIR Res Rev — CSIR [*Council for Scientific and Industrial Research*] Research Review

CSIR Spec Rep FIS — CSIR [*Council for Scientific and Industrial Research*] Special Report FIS

CSIR Zool Monogr — CSIR [*Council for Scientific and Industrial Research*] Zoological Monograph

CSJ — Casopis pro Slovanske Jazyky, Literaturu, a Dejiny SSSR

CSJ — Civil Service Journal

CSJP — Cahiers Saint-John Perse

CSKKA — Chikusan Shikenjo Kenkyu

CSKNA — Ceskoslovenska Neurologie [*Later, Ceskoslovenska Neurologie a Neurochirurgie*]

CSL — Cambridge Studies in Linguistics

CSL — Scanshore

CSLBull — C. S. Lewis Society. Bulletin [*New York*]

CSLHA — Chartered Surveyor. Land Hydrographic and Minerals Quarterly

C & SLib — Church and Synagogue Libraries

CSLJa — Casopis pro Slovanske Jazyky, Literaturu, a Dejiny SSSR

Cslka Derm — Ceskoslovenska Dermatologie

Cslka Farm — Ceskoslovenska Farmacie

Cslka Fysiol — Ceskoslovenska Fysiologie

Cslka Stomat — Ceskoslovenska Stomatologie

CSLN — California State Library Newsletter

CSLP — Canadian Slavonic Papers

CSLR — Cleveland State Law Review

CSM — Christian Science Monitor

CSMDA — Canadian Services Medical Journal

CSMIA — Mineral Industries Bulletin. Colorado School of Mines

CSMJAX — Connecticut State Medical Journal

CSMLA5 — Comunicaciones. Sociedad Malacologica del Uruguay

CSMLT — Cambridge Studies in Medieval Life and Thought

CSMMS — Christian Science Monitor. Magazine Section

C S Mon Mag — Christian Science Monitor. Magazine Section

CSMQD — Colorado School of Mines. Quarterly

CSO — Maandstatistiek Financiewezen

C Societa — Cinema Societa

C Sociol Demogr Medic — Cahiers de Sociologie et de Demographie Medicales

C Sol St Phys — Comments on Solid State Physics

Cs Onkol — Ceskoslovenska Onkologie

CSOPAR — Casopis Ceskoslovenske. Spolecnosti Entomologicke

CSOSA — Communications in Soil Science and Plant Analysis

CSOSA2 — Communications in Soil Science and Plant Analysis

CSP — Cahiers du Seminaire Ch. Gide

CSP — Cahiers Sextil Puscariu

CSP — California State Publications

CSP — Canadian Slavonic Papers

CSP — Catholic School Paper

CSp — Ceskoslovensky Spisovatel

CSP — Contents of Selected Periodicals

CSPADO — Comunicaciones. INIA [*Instituto Nacional de Investigaciones Agrarias*]. Serie Produccion Animal

Cs Parasit — Ceskoslovenska Parasitologie

Cs Pediat — Ceskoslovenska Pediatrie

CSPG Mem — CSPG [*Canadian Society of Petroleum Geologists*] Memoir

CSPG Reservoir — Canadian Society of Petroleum Geologists. Reservoir

CSPh — Cornell Studies in Classical Philology

CSPHA — Contributions to Sensory Physiology

CSPJA — Canadian Aeronautics and Space Journal

CSPMBO — Conseil International pour l'Exploration de la Mer. Bulletin Statistique des Peches Maritimes

CSPSD — Canadian Special Publication of Fisheries and Aquatic Sciences

Cs Psych — Ceskoslovenska Psychiatrie

Cs Psych — Ceskoslovenska Psychologie

CSP-T — Contents of Selected Periodicals - Technical

CSQ — Christian Science Quarterly

CSR — Cell Surface Reviews [*Elsevier Book Series*]

CsR — Ceskoslovenska Rusistika

CSR — Christian Scholar's Review

CSR — Continental Shelf Research

CSR Agric Circ — CSR [*Colonial Sugar Refining Company Limited*] Agricultural Circular

C S R Bul — Council on the Study of Religion. Bulletin

CSREDC — Cell Surface Reviews

Cs Rentgen — Ceskoslovenska Rentgenologie

CSRG — Commission for Scientific Research in Greenland. Newsletter

CSRPB — Chemica Scripta

CSRQA — Chartered Surveyor. Rural Quarterly

CSRSAH — Colorado State University. Range Science Department. Range Science Series
CSRVB — Chemical Society. Reviews
CSS — California Slavic Studies
CSS — Canadian Slavic Studies
CSSA Spec Publ — CSSA [*Crop Science Society of America*] Special Publication
CSSCD — Communications in Statistics. Part B. Simulation and Computation
CSSH — Comparative Studies in Society and History
CSSJ — Central States Speech Journal
CSSOP — Center for Settlement Studies. University of Manitoba. Series 5. Occasional Papers
CSSP — Circuits, Systems, and Signal Processing
CSSRR — Center for Settlement Studies. University of Manitoba. Series 2. Research Reports
CST — Chicago Sunday Tribune
CST — Coal Science and Technology [*Elsevier Book Series*]
CSt — Colecao Studium
C St — Comunicazioni i Studi
CST — Contemporary Studies in Theology [*London*]
CST — Cost and Management
CSTA R — CSTA [*Canadian Society of Technical Agriculturists*] Review
CSTA Rev — CSTA [*Canadian Society of Technical Agriculturists*] Review
CSTB — Cahiers. Centre Scientifique et Technique du Batiment
CSTC — Ceskoslovensky Terminologicky Casopis
CSTC Rev — CSTC [*Centre Scientifique et Technique de la Construction*] Revue
CSTNAC — Castanea
CSTRC — COMSAT [*Communications Satellite Corp.*] Technical Review
CSTWA — Chemia Stosowana
CSU — Consumer's Research Magazine
Csud — Cinemasud
CSVAH — Chronique. Societe Vervietoise d'Archeologie et d'Histoire
CSW — Chartered Surveyor Weekly
CSWPA — Chung-Kuo Shui Sheng Wu Hui Pao
CSY — CSCE [*Centre Senegalais du Commerce Exterieur*] Informations
CSYIB — Cargo Systems International
Cs Zdrav — Ceskoslovenske Zdravotnictvi
CT — Cahiers Thomistes
CT — Cahiers de Tunisie
CT — Cameroon Tribune
CT — Canadian Token
CT — Canberra Times
CT — Chemical Titles
CT — Children Today
CT — China To-Day
CT — Christianity Today
CT — Ciencia Tomista
CT — Collectanea Theologica
C & T — Culture and Tradition
CT — Journal of Computed Tomography
CTA J — CTA [*Cine Technicians' Association*] Journal [*India*]
Ctary — Commentary
CTASD — China Science and Technology Abstracts
CTBR — Commonwealth Taxation Board of Review Decisions
CTBR NS — Commonwealth Taxation Board of Review Decisions. New Series
CTC — Ceskoslovensky Terminologicky Casopis
CTC — Contract Journal
CTCEA — Current Therapeutic Research. Clinical and Experimental
CTCP — Clinical Toxicology of Commercial Products [*Dartmouth Medical School; University of Rochester*] [*Database*]
CTCPD — Changchun Dizhi Xueyuan Xuebao
CTCRA — Current Topics in Cellular Regulation
CTD — Cahiers. Groupe Francois-Thureau-Dangin [*Paris*]
C Td — Ceylon Today
CTD — Commission de Toponymie et Dialectologie
CTDBA — Current Topics in Developmental Biology
CTEAA7 — Comunicados Tecnicos. Instituto de Ecologia e Experimentacao Agricolas
CTEEA — Current Topics in Experimental Endocrinology
CTEGA — Cutting Tool Engineering
CTF — Continentaler Stahlmarkt (Frankfurt Am Main)
CTFA Cosmet J — CTFA [*Cosmetic, Toiletry, and Fragrance Association*] Cosmetic Journal
CTFMD — Ciencias Tecnicas Fisicas y Matematicas
CTHBAr — Comite des Travaux Historiques et Scientifiques. Bulletin Archeologique
CTHBull — Comite des Travaux Historiques et Scientifiques. Bulletin Archeologique
CTHBullH — Comite des Travaux Historiques et Scientifiques. Bulletin Historique et Philologique
CThM — Concordia Theological Monthly
CTI — Current Technology Index [*Library Association Publishing Ltd.*] [*London, England*]
CTI — Documentatieblad van het Centraal Orgaan van de Landelijke Opleidingsorganen van het Bedrijfsleven

CTIBBV — Contemporary Topics in Immunobiology
CTICD2 — Catalogue of Type Invertebrate Fossils. Geological Survey of Canada
CTI Commun Technol Impact — CTI. Communication Technology Impact
CTIPB5 — Carolina Tips
CTJ — Calvin Theological Journal
CTJ — Canadian Textile Journal
CT J Comput Tomography — CT. Journal of Computed Tomography
CTJOA — Canadian Textile Journal
CTKIAR — Cell and Tissue Kinetics
CTL — Cahiers - Theatre Louvain
CTLF — Cuttlefish. Unalaska City School. Unalaska
CTLMAA — Cattleman
CTM — Concordia Theological Monthly
CTMIA — Current Topics in Microbiology and Immunology
CTMIB4 — Contemporary Topics in Molecular Immunology
CTMS — Current Topics in Materials Science [*Elsevier Book Series*]
CTN — China Trade Report
CTNOR — Canada. Task Force on Northern Oil Development. Report
C Tom — Ciencia Tomista
CTOMD — Computerized Tomography
CTOMDS — Computerized Tomography
CTOXA — Clinical Toxicology
CTP — Customs Tariff Proposals
CTQ — Computable. Automatiseringsvakblad voor de Benelux
CTQ — Contemporary Thought Quarterly
CTR — COMSAT [*Communications Satellite Corp.*] Technical Review
C Tracts — Cine Tracts
CTRED — Cancer Treatment Reviews
CTREDJ — Cancer Treatment Reviews
CTRFAS — Canadian Technical Report of Fisheries and Aquatic Sciences
CTRHOS — Canadian Technical Report of Hydrography and Ocean Sciences
CTRQA — Current Topics in Radiation Research. Quarterly
CTRR — Current Topics in Radiation Research [*Elsevier Book Series*]
CTRRA — Current Topics in Radiation Research
CTRRD — Cancer Treatment Reports
CTRRDO — Cancer Treatment Reports
Ctry Demogr Profiles — Country Demographic Profiles
Ctry Gentleman — Country Gentleman
Ctry Landowner — Country Landowner
Ctry Life — Country Life
Ctry Life Am — Country Life in America
Ctry Profiles — Country Profiles
Ctry Women — Country Women
CTS — Centralized Title Service
CTSRC — Cell and Tissue Research
CTSRCS — Cell and Tissue Research
CTS Reg — Chicago Theological Seminary. Register
CTSYEH — Cancer Treatment Symposia
CTUBDP — Collection des Travaux. Universite de Brazzaville
C Tunisie — Cahiers de Tunisie
CTUSA5 — Comunicaciones. Instituto Tropical de Investigaciones Cientificas
CTV — Cotton. Monthly Review of the World Situation
CTYKA — Ch'uan-Kuo Ti-I-Chieh Yeh-Chin Kuo-Ch Eng Wu-Li Hua-Hsueh Hsueh-Shu Pao-Kao-Hui Lun-Wen Chi
CTZ — Capital. Das Deutsche Wirtschaftsmagazin
CU — Canadian Underwriter
C & U — College and University
Cu A — Cuadernos Americanos
CUAB — Catholic University of America. Bulletin
Cuad Actual Tec Asoc Argent Consorcios Reg Exp Agric — Cuaderno de Actualizacion Tecnica. Asociacion Argentina de Consorcios Regionales de Experimentacion Agricola
Cuad Amer — Cuadernos Americanos
Cuad Arquit Urban — Cuadernos de Arquitectura y Urbanismo
Cuad Cienc Biol Univ Granada — Cuadernos de Ciencias Biologicas. Universidad de Granada
Cuad Cirug — Cuadernos de Cirugia
Cuad CVF — Cuadernos de la Corporacion Venezolana de Fomento
Cuad Econ (Barcelona) — Cuadernos de Economia (Barcelona)
Cuad Econ (Santiago) — Cuadernos de Economia (Santiago)
Cuadern Inst Mat Beppo Levi — Cuadernos. Instituto de Matematica Beppo Levi
Cuadernos H — Cuadernos Hispanoamericanos
Cuadern Teorema — Cuadernos Teorema
Cuad Filol Cl — Cuadernos de Filologia Clasica
Cuad Filosof — Cuadernos de Filosofia
Cuad Gall — Cuadernos de Estudios Gallegos
Cuad Geogr Colom — Cuadernos de Geografia de Colombia
Cuad Geol Iber — Cuadernos de Geologia Iberica
Cuad Geol Univ Granada — Cuadernos de Geologia. Universidad de Granada
Cuad Hisp — Cuadernos Hispanoamericanos
Cuad Hist Econ Cataluna — Cuadernos de Historia de la Economia Catuluna
Cuad Hist Espan — Cuadernos de Historia de Espana
Cuad Hist Primit — Cuadernos de Historia Primitiva
Cuad Hist Salud Publica — Cuadernos de Historia de la Salud Publica

Cuad Hist Sanit — Cuadernos de Historia Sanitaria
Cuad Inform Econ Sociol — Cuadernos de Informacion Economica y Sociologica
Cuad Inst Hist (Mex) — Cuadernos. Instituto de Historia (Mexico)
Cuad Inst Hist Ser Antr — Cuadernos. Instituto de Historia. Seria Antropologica [Mexico]
Cuad Inst Nac Antropol — Cuadernos. Instituto Nacional de Antropologia
Cuad Manch — Cuadernos de Estudios Manchegos
Cuad Med — Cuadernos Medicos
Cuad Med Divulg Cient — Cuadernos Medicos y de Divulgacion Cientifico
Cuad Min Geol Univ Tuc — Cuadernos de Mineralogia y Geologia. Universidad de Tucuman
Cuad Num — Cuadernos de Numismatica
Cuad Oceanogr Univ Oriente (Cumana) — Cuadernos Oceanograficos. Universidad de Oriente (Cumana)
Cuad P Arq Cast — Cuadernos de Prehistoria y Arqueologia Castellonense
Cuad Realidades Socs — Cuadernos de Realidades Sociales
Cuad Ruedo Iber — Cuadernos de Ruedo Iberico
Cuad Sind — Cuadernos. Centro de Estudios Sindicales
Cuad Teol — Cuadernos Teologicos
CUALR — Catholic University of America. Law Review
CUAN — Current Anthropology
CUAPS — Catholic University of America. Patristic Studies
CUASRL — Catholic University of America. Studies in Romance Languages and Literatures
CUASRLL — Catholic University of America. Studies in Romance Languages and Literatures
CUB — Catholic University. Bulletin
Cuba — Cubatimes
Cuba Bibl — Cuba Bibliotecologica
Cuba Dir Montes B Minas — Cuba. Direccion de Montes y Minas. Boletin de Minas
Cuban J Agric Sci — Cuban Journal of Agricultural Science
Cuba Revw — Cuba Review
Cuba Soc — Cuba Socialista
CUBBA2 — Contribuciones Cientificas. Facultad de Ciencias Exactas y Naturales. Universidad de Buenos Aires. Serie Botanica
Cu Bi — Cultura Biblica
CuBib — Cultura Biblica [Segovia, Spain]
CUC — Cahiers Universitaires Catholiques
CUC — Cultura Universitaria (Caracas)
CUCA — Columbia University. Contributions to Anthropology
CuCanI — Cuadernos Canarios de Investigacion
CUC Gaz — Canberra University College. Gazette
CuCo — Cursos y Conferencias
CUDPB — Chile. Universidad. Departamento de Astronomia. Publicaciones
Cu EG — Cuadernos de Estudios Gallegos
CUE J — Computer Using Educators of BC [British Columbia] Journal [Canada]
Cu EM — Cuadernos de Estudios Manchegos
CUF — Columbia University. Forum
CUGS — Columbia University. Germanic Studies
CuH — Cuadernos Hispanoamericanos [Madrid]
Cu H — Current History
CUIVA — Cuivre, Laitons, Alliages
CUJ — CPCU [Chartered Property and Casualty Underwriters] Journal
CUJSD — Cheju University. Journal (South Korea)
CUK — Cuir. Journal Trihebdomadaire d'Informations du Cuir et de la Chaussure
CUKOA — Cukoripar
Cul Dair Prod J — Cultured Dairy Products Journal
CulEA — Cultural Events in Africa
CULR — Catholic University. Law Review
Cul Stud Cerc (Brasov) — Culegere de Studii si Cercetari (Brasov)
Cult — Cultura
Cult — Culture
Cult Atesina — Cultura Atesina
Cult B — Cultura Biblica
CultBib — Cultura Biblica [Segovia, Spain]
CultBibl — Cultura Biblica [Segovia, Spain]
Cult Corr — Cultural Correspondence
Cult Dairy Prod J — Cultured Dairy Products Journal
Cult et Devel — Cultures et Developpement
Cult Esp — Cultura Espanola
Cult Fr — Culture Francaise
Cult Franc — Culture Francaise
Cult Hermen — Cultural Hermeneutics
Cult Med — Cultura Medica
Cult Med Mod — Cultura Medica Moderna
Cult Med Psychiatry — Culture, Medicine, and Psychiatry
Cult Mod — Cultivador Moderno
Cult Neol — Cultura Neolatina
Cult Neolat — Cultura Neolatina
Cult Resour Rep US For Serv Southwest Reg — Cultural Resource Report. United States Forest Service. Southwestern Region
Cult Scuol — Cultura e Scuola

Cult Stomat — Cultura Stomatologica
Cult Univ — Cultura Universitaria
Cultura Med Mod — Cultura Medica Moderna
Cumana Univ Oriente Inst Oceanogr Bol — Cumana. Universidad de Oriente. Instituto Oceanografico. Boletin
CUMBB — Currents in Modern Biology [The Netherlands]
Cumberland L Rev — Cumberland Law Review
Cumberland-Samford — Cumberland-Samford Law Review
Cumberland-Samford L Rev — Cumberland-Samford Law Review
Cumber-Sam L Rev — Cumberland-Samford Law Review
Cum B Ind — Cumulative Book Index
Cumb L Rev — Cumberland Law Review
Cum Book — Cumulative Book Index
Cumb Q — Cumberland Presbyterian Quarterly Review
Cum Bull — Cumulative Bulletin [United States Internal Revenue Service]
Cum Comput Abstr — Cumulative Computer Abstracts
CUMIA — Coeur et Medecine Interne
Cumidava — Cumidava Culegere de Studii si Cercetari
Cum L Rev — Cumberland Law Review
CUMOA — Cultivador Moderno
Cum-Sam — Cumberland-Samford Law Review
Cumul Index Med — Cumulated Index Medicus
Cu N — Cultura Neolatina
Cunobelin — Cunobelin Yearbook. British Association of Numismatic Societies
CUNZA — Chemie in Unserer Zeit
CUO — Current Sociology
Cuore Circ — Cuore e Circolazione
Cuore Circol — Cuore e Circolazione
CUPAD — Current Energy Patents
CUQ — Columbia University. Quarterly
CUR — University of Colorado. Law Review
CURABA — Current Archives Bibliography Australia
Cur Accts — Current Accounts
Cur Anthrop — Current Anthropology
Cur Anthropol — Current Anthropology
Cur Bibliog African Affairs — Current Bibliography on African Affairs
Cur Biog — Current Biography
Cur Biog Yrbk — Current Biography Yearbook
Cur Ev — Current Events
Cur Health — Current Health
Cur Hist — Current History
Cur Hist M NY Times — Current History Magazine of the New York Times
Cur Issues Higher Ed — Current Issues in Higher Education
Cur Issues Higher Educ Ann Ser — Current Issues in Higher Education. Annual Series
CURL — Children's Understanding of Reading Language
Cur Lit — Current Literature
Cur Opinion — Current Opinion
Cur R — Curriculum Review
Curr Affairs Bull — Current Affairs Bulletin
Curr Aff B — Current Affairs Bulletin
Curr Aff Bull — Current Affairs Bulletin
Curr Agric — Current Agriculture
Curr Alcohol — Currents in Alcoholism
Curr Anthr — Current Anthropology
Curr Anthrop — Current Anthropology
Curr Anthropol — Current Anthropology
Curr Archaeol — Current Archaeology
Curr Aus NZ Leg Lit Ind — Current Australian and New Zealand Legal Literature Index
Curr Awareness Bull — Current Awareness Bulletin
Curr Bibl Aquatic Sci & Fish — Current Bibliography for Aquatic Sciences and Fisheries
Curr Bus — Survey of Current Business [United States]
Curr Chem Pap — Current Chemical Papers
Curr Concepts Cerebrovasc Dis Stroke — Current Concepts of Cerebrovascular Disease: Stroke
Curr Concepts Emerg Med — Current Concepts in Emergency Medicine
Curr Concepts Nutr — Current Concepts in Nutrition
CurrCont — Current Contents
CURRD — Current
Curr Dev Psychopharmacol — Current Developments in Psychopharmacology
Curr Dig Sov Press — Current Digest of the Soviet Press
Curr Econ Bus Aspects Wine Ind Symp — Current Economics and Business Aspects of the Wine Industry. Symposium
Curr Energy Pat — Current Energy Patents
Curr Eng Pract — Current Engineering Practice
Current Accts — Current Accounts
Current Adv Plant Sci — Current Advances in Plant Science
Current Affairs Bul — Current Affairs Bulletin
Current Chem Transl — Current Chemical Translations
Current Dig Soviet Pr — Current Digest of the Soviet Press
Current Hist — Current History
Current Ind Rept — Current Industrial Reports
Current L — Current Law
Current Law — Current Law and Social Problems

Current L & Soc Probl — Current Law and Social Problems
Current LYB — Current Law Year Book
Current Math Publ — Current Mathematical Publications
Current Med — Current Medicine for Attorneys
Current Mus — Current Musicology
Current Notes — Current Notes on International Affairs
Curr Eye Res — Current Eye Research
Curr Genet — Current Genetics
Curr Hist — Current History
Curric Inquiry — Curriculum Inquiry
Curric News — Curriculum News
Curric R — Curriculum Review
Curric & Research Bul — Curriculum and Research Bulletin
Curric Stud and Ed Res B — Curriculum Study and Educational Research Bulletin
Curric Theo — Curriculum Theory Network
Curriculum Perspect — Curriculum Perspective
Curriculum Res Bull — Curriculum and Research Bulletin
Curr Ind Commonw Leg Per — Current Index to Commonwealth Legal Periodicals
Curr Indian Stat — Current Indian Statutes
Curr Ind Rept Footwear — Current Industrial Reports. Footwear
Curr Ind Rept Plast Bottles — Current Industrial Reports. Plastic Bottles
Curr Inf Ser Idaho Agric Exp Stn — Idaho. Agricultural Experiment Station. Current Information Series
Curr Lab Pract — Current Laboratory Practice
Curr Leather Lit — Current Leather Literature
Curr Leg Probl — Current Legal Problems
Curr Lit Blood — Current Literature of Blood
Curr LYB — Current Law Year Book
Curr Med Pract — Current Medical Practice
Curr Med Pract (India) — Current Medical Practice (India)
Curr Med Res Opin — Current Medical Research and Opinion
Curr Microbiol — Current Microbiology
Curr Mod Biol — Currents in Modern Biology
Curr Mod Biol Biosyst — Currents in Modern Biology. Biosystems
Curr Mun Pr — Current Municipal Problems
Curr Music — Current Musicology
Curr Nephrol — Current Nephrology
Curr Notes — Current Notes on International Affairs
Curr Notes Int Aff — Current Notes on International Affairs
Curr Notes Int Affairs — Current Notes on International Affairs
Curr Pap Aeronaut Res Counc (UK) — Current Papers. Aeronautical Research Council (United Kingdom)
Curr Papers Phys — Current Papers in Physics
Curr Pap Phys — Current Papers in Physics
Curr Pop Rep — Current Population Reports. United States Census Bureau
Curr Pop Rep Special Studies — Current Population Reports. Special Studies. United States Census Bureau
Curr Popul Rep Consum Income — Current Population Reports. Consumer Income. Series P-60 [United States]
Curr Popul Rep Popul Charact — Current Population Reports. Population Characteristics. Series P-20 [United States]
Curr Popul Rep Popul Estim Proj — Current Population Reports. Population Estimates and Projections. Series P-25 [United States]
Curr Popul Rep Spec Censuses — Current Population Reports. Special Censuses. Series P-28 [United States]
Curr Popul Rep Spec Stud — Current Population Reports. Special Studies. Series P-23 [United States]
Curr Pract Gerontol Nurs — Current Practice in Gerontological Nursing
Curr Pract Obstet Gynecol Nurs — Current Practice in Obstetric and Gynecologic Nursing
Curr Pract Orthop Surg — Current Practice in Orthopaedic Surgery
Curr Prob Dermatol — Current Problems in Dermatology
Curr Probl Cancer — Current Problems in Cancer
Curr Probl Cardiol — Current Problems in Cardiology
Curr Probl Clin Biochem — Current Problems in Clinical Biochemistry
Curr Probl Dermatol — Current Problems in Dermatology
Curr Probl Diagn Radiol — Current Problems in Diagnostic Radiology
Curr Probl Epilepsy — Current Problems in Epilepsy
Curr Probl Pediatr — Current Problems in Pediatrics
Curr Probl Surg — Current Problems in Surgery
Curr Psychiatr Ther — Current Psychiatric Therapies
Curr Radiol — Current Radiology
Curr Rep W Va Univ Agr Exp Sta — Current Report. West Virginia University. Agricultural Experiment Station
Curr Res — Current Research
Curr Res Anesth Analg — Current Researches in Anesthesia and Analgesia
Curr Res Neth Biol — Current Research in the Netherlands. Biology
Curr Rev Agr Cond Can — Current Review of Agricultural Conditions in Canada
Curr Rev Nurse Anesth — Current Reviews for Nurse Anesthetists
Curr Rev Recov Room Nurses — Current Reviews for Recovery Room Nurses
Curr Rev Respir Ther — Current Reviews in Respiratory Therapy
Curr Sci — Current Science [Bangalore, India]
Curr Sociol — Current Sociology

Curr Surg — Current Surgery
Curr Swed — Current Sweden
Curr Theory Res Motiv Nebr Symp Motiv — Current Theory and Research in Motivation. Nebraska Symposium on Motivation
Curr Ther R — Current Therapeutic Research. Clinical and Experimental
Curr Ther Res Clin Exp — Current Therapeutic Research. Clinical and Experimental
Curr Tit Electrochem — Current Titles in Electrochemistry
Curr Titles Turk Sci — Current Titles in Turkish Science
Curr T M — Currents in Theology and Mission
Curr Top Bioenerg — Current Topics in Bioenergetics
Curr Top Cell Regul — Current Topics in Cellular Regulation
Curr Top Clin Chem — Current Topics in Clinical Chemistry
Curr Top Comp Pathobiol — Current Topics in Comparative Pathobiology
Curr Top Crit Care Med — Current Topics in Critical Care Medicine
Curr Top Dev Biol — Current Topics in Developmental Biology
Curr Top Exp Endocrinol — Current Topics in Experimental Endocrinology
Curr Top Eye Res — Current Topics in Eye Research
Curr Top Hematol — Current Topics in Hematology
Curr Top Immunol Ser — Current Topics in Immunology Series
Curr Top Membranes Transp — Current Topics in Membranes and Transport
Curr Top Microbiol Immunol — Current Topics in Microbiology and Immunology
Curr Top Mol Endocrinol — Current Topics in Molecular Endocrinology
Curr Top Neurobiol — Current Topics in Neurobiology
Curr Top Nutr Dis — Current Topics in Nutrition and Disease
Curr Top Pathol — Current Topics in Pathology
Curr Top Radiat Res — Current Topics in Radiation Research
Curr Top Radiat Res Q — Current Topics in Radiation Research. Quarterly
Curr Top Reprod Endocrinol — Current Topics in Reproductive Endocrinology
Curr Top Surg Res — Current Topics in Surgical Research
Curr Top Thyroid Res Proc Int Thyroid Conf — Current Topics in Thyroid Research. Proceedings of the International Thyroid Conference
Curr Top Vet Med Anim Sci — Current Topics in Veterinary Medicine and Animal Science
Curr US Gov Per Mfiche — Current US Government Periodicals on Microfiche
Cur Scene — Current Scene
Cur Sci — Current Science
Cursos Congr Univ Santiago De Compostela — Cursos y Congresos. Universidad de Santiago De Compostela
Curtis's Bot Mag New Ser — Curtis's Botanical Magazine. New Series
C (US) — Cinema (United States)
CUSCA — Current Science [India]
CUSCDP — Chittagong University. Studies. Part II. Science
Cushman Found Foraminifer Res Spec Publ — Cushman Foundation for Foraminiferal Research. Special Publication
Cushman Found Foram Research Contr — Cushman Foundation for Foraminiferal Research. Contributions
CUSQ — Cultural Survival Quarterly
CUTBA — Current Topics in Bioenergetics
CuTM — Currents in Theology and Mission
Cuttington Res J — Cuttington Research Journal
Cutting Tool Eng — Cutting Tool Engineering
Cut Tool En — Cutting Tool Engineering
CUUCV — Cultura Universitaria. Universidad Central de Venezuela
Cuvas Gos Ped Inst Ucen Zap — Cuvasskii Gosudarstvennyi Pedagogiceskii Institut Imeni I. Ja. Jakovleva Ucenye Zapiski [Cheboksary]
Cuvas Gos Univ I Cuvas Gos Ped Inst Ucen Zap — Cuvasskii Gosudarstvennyi Universitet Imeni I. N. Ul'janova Cuvasskii Gosudarstvennyi Pedagogiceskii Institut Imeni I. Ja. Jakovleva Ucenyi Zapiski
CuW — Christentum und Wissenschaft [Leipzig]
CUWPL — Columbia University. Working Papers in Linguistics
CV — Cerf-Volant
CV — Citta di Vita
CV — Civilta Fascista
CV — Commentationes Vindobonenses
CV — Communio Viatorum [Prague]
C and V — Counseling and Values
CV — Crkoven Vestnik
CVA — Corpus Vasorum Antiquorum
CVCHD — Chonnam Medical Journal
CVE — Cahiers Victoriens et Edouardiens
CVEGA — Civil Engineering
CVETAA — Communicationes Veterinariae
CVETB — Civil Engineering Transactions. Institution of Engineers of Australia
CVI — Printing World
C Vind — Commentationes Vindobonenses
CVNS — Conveyance News
CVP — Cardiovascular and Pulmonary Technology. Journal
CVP J Cardiovasc Pulm Technol — CVP. Journal of Cardiovascular and Pulmonary Technology
CVREAU — Cardiovascular Research
CVS — Classiques du XXe Siecle
CVSMO — Casopis Vlasteneckeho Spolku Musejniho v Olomouci
CVSMOL — Casopis Vlasteneckeho Spolku Musejniho v Olomouci

VTJA — Ceylon Veterinary Journal
VTRBC — Connective Tissue Research
VVIDV — Connaissance de la Vigne et du Vin
VZOAW — Congreso Venezolano de Cirugia
W — Canadian Welfare
W — Catholic World
' & W — Christentum und Wissenschaft
W — Classical Weekly
W — Classical World
W — Coin World
W — Computerworld
WA — Container News
WAHAT — Commonwealth Bureau of Animal Health. Review Series
WAPAJ — Commonwealth Bureau of Horticulture and Plantation Crops.
   Technical Communication
WB — Canadian Weekly Bulletin
WBSAX — Commonwealth Bureau of Soils. Technical Communication
W-Can Welf — CW-Canadian Welfare
WCBAL — Connecticut Water Resources Bulletin
WCDA — Collected Works on Cardio-Pulmonary Disease
WCDAR — Collected Works on Cardio-Pulmonary Disease
WCP — Contemporary Writers in Christian Perspective
wd — Catholic World
WD — Credit World
WE — Chemical Week
weal — Commonweal
wealth — Commonwealth
wealth Agriculturist — Commonwealth Agriculturist
wealth Eng — Commonwealth Engineer
wealth Jeweller — Commonwealth Jeweller and Watchmaker
wealth Jeweller and Watchmaker — Commonwealth Jeweller and
   Watchmaker
wealth Pub Serv Board Bul — Commonwealth Public Service Board. Bulletin
WFN — Canadian Wildlife and Fisheries Newsletter
WFRA — Commonwealth Forestry Review
WFRAG — Commonwealth Forestry Review
WGV — Chronik. Wiener Goetheverein
WH — Civil War History
WHM — Current Works in the History of Medicine
WI — Commerce
WL — Case Western Reserve. Law Review
WLM — Chung-Wai Literary Monthly
WLR — California Western Law Review
WM — Cashflow Magazine
WN — Cosmetic World News
WODAJ — Connecticut Woodlands
WPBA — California Water Pollution Control Association. Bulletin
WPL — Cornell Working Papers in Linguistics
WRJ — Canadian Water Resources Journal
WR J Int L — Case Western Reserve. Journal of International Law
WR LR — Case Western Reserve. Law Review
WS — Metropolitan Chamber of Commerce and Industry. Chamber News
WSOP — Canadian Wildlife Service. Occasional Paper
WSPA7 — Colorado. Division of Wildlife. Special Report
WSPN — Canadian Wildlife Service. Progress Notes
WSRS — Canadian Wildlife Service. Report Series
XA — Chambre de Commerce, d'Agriculture, et d'Industrie de la Republique
   Togolaise. Bulletin Mensuel
XE — China Informatie
XG — Commerce in Belgium
XT — Banco Nacional de Comercio Exterior. Comercio de Exterior
y — Crawdaddy
yanamid Int Mitt — Cyanamid International. Mitteilungen
yanamid Int Vet Bull — Cyanamid International. Veterinary Bulletin
yanamid Mag — Cyanamid Magazine
ybernet Systems — Cybernetics and Systems
ybern and Syst — Cybernetics and Systems
YBNA — Cybernetics [English Translation]
yC — Cursos y Conferencias
YCLA — Cycles
ycl Anat and Physiol — Cyclopaedia of Anatomy and Physiology
ycle Aust — Cycle Australia
YENA — Cryogenic Engineering News
ym Trans — Honourable Society of Cymmrodorion. Transactions
yP — Contaminacion y Prevencion
yp — Cypher
Cyprus Agric J — Cyprus Agricultural Journal
Cyprus Agric Res Inst Annu Rep — Cyprus Agricultural Research Institute.
   Annual Report
Cyprus Agric Res Inst Misc Publ — Cyprus Agricultural Research Institute.
   Miscellaneous Publications
Cyprus Agric Res Inst Prog Rep — Cyprus Agricultural Research Institute.
   Progress Report
Cyprus Agric Res Inst Tech Bull — Cyprus Agricultural Research Institute.
   Technical Bulletin

Cyprus Agric Res Inst Tech Pap — Cyprus Agricultural Research Institute.
   Technical Paper
Cyprus Dep Agric Annu Rep — Cyprus Department of Agriculture. Annual
   Report
Cyprus Geol Surv Dep Bull — Cyprus. Geological Survey Department. Bulletin
Cyprus Geol Surv Dep Mem — Cyprus. Geological Survey Department.
   Memoir
Cyprus Ind — Cyprus Industrial Journal
CyR — Cruz y Raya
CYTBA — Cytobios
CYTEA — Cryogenic Technology
CYTGA — Cytogenetics [Switzerland]
CYTOA — Cytologia
Cytog C Gen — Cytogenetics and Cell Genetics
Cytogenet Cell Genet — Cytogenetics and Cell Genetics
Cytol — Cytologia
Cytol Genet — Cytology and Genetics [English Translation of Tsitologiya i
   Genetika]
Cytol Genet (Engl Transl Tsitol Genet) — Cytology and Genetics (English
   Translation of Tsitologiya i Genetika)
Cytol Neurol Stud Fac Med Univ Kanazawa — Cytological and Neurological
   Studies. Faculty of Medicine. University of Kanazawa
CYTZA — Cytobiologie
CZ — Cela Zimes
Cz — Czytelnik
C Zair Et Polit Soc — Cahiers Zairois d'Etudes Politiques et Sociales
C Zair Rech Develop — Cahiers Zairois de la Recherche et du Developpement
Czas Stomatol — Czasopismo Stomatologiczne
Czas Tech (Krakow) — Czasopismo Techniczne (Krakow)
CZCAA — Chemiker-Zeitung. Chemische Apparatur
CZ Chem-Tech — CZ Chemie-Technik
CZE — Czechoslovak Foreign Trade
Czech Acad Sci Bot Inst Hydrobiol Lab Annu Rep — Czechoslovak Academy of
   Sciences. Botanical Institute. Hydrobiological Laboratory. Annual
   Report
Czech Bibliogr Ind Hyg Occup Dis — Czechoslovak Bibliography on Industrial
   Hygiene and Occupational Diseases
Czech Congr Gastroenterol — Czechoslovak Congress of Gastroenterology
Czech F — Czechoslovak Film
Czech Heavy Ind — Czechoslovak Heavy Industry
Czech J Phys — Czechoslovak Journal of Physics
Czech Med — Czechoslovak Medicine
Czechosl Econ Pap — Czechoslovak Economic Papers
Czechoslovak Econ Dig — Czechoslovak Economic Digest
Czechoslovak J Phys — Czechoslovak Journal of Physics
Czech Res Inst Crop Prod Annu Rep — Czechoslovakia. Research Institutes for
   Crop Production. Annual Report
Czech Urad Vynalezy Objevy Vestn — Czechoslovakia. Urad pro Vynalezy a
   Objevy. Vestnik
Czec J Phys — Czechoslovak Journal of Physics. Section B
Czec Math J — Czechoslovak Mathematical Journal
CZHIA — Czechoslovak Heavy Industry
CZI — Chemiker-Zeitung. Chemie, Technische Chemie, Chemiewirtschaft;
   mit Chemie-Borse und Bezugsquellen fuer die Chemische Industrie
CZMJA — Czechoslovak Mathematical Journal
CZMJB — Coastal Zone Management Journal
CZMMAN — Comunicaciones Zoologicas. Museo de Historia Natural de
   Montevideo
CZN — Casopis za Zgodovino in Narodpisje
CZOOA5 — Carnets de Zoologie
CZSTA — Czasopismo Stomatologiczne
C (Zurich) — Cinema (Zurich)
CZYPA — Czechoslovak Journal of Physics

D

D — Dacoromania
D — Dance
D — December
D — Dialectica
D — Dickensian
D — Drammaturgia
D & A — Defense & Armament Magazine
DA — Deutsche Aussenpolitik
DA — Deutsches Archiv
DA — Direct Action
d/a — Direct Advertising [*Later, Printing Paper Quarterly*]
DA — Dissertation Abstracts [*Later, Dissertation Abstracts International*]
DA — Documentation Abstracts
D d A — Droit d'Auteur
DAAL — Directory of Australian Academic Libraries
DAb — Dissertation Abstracts [*Later, Dissertation Abstracts International*]
DABAA — Dissertation Abstracts International. Section A
DABBB — Dissertation Abstracts International. Section B
Dac — Dacia
Dac — Dacoromania
DAC — Dictionnaire d'Archeologie Chretienne et de Liturgie
DACAS — Drug Abuse Current Awareness System
Dacca Univ Stud Part B — Dacca University. Studies. Part B
Dacia — Dacia. Revue d'Archeologie et d'Histoire Ancienne
DACL — Dictionnaire d'Archeologie Chretienne et de Liturgie
Dacor — Dacoromania
Dac Terr — Dacotah Territory
DAD — Data Automation Digest
DADE — Drugs and Drug Abuse Education
DADG — Danish Arctic Station of Disko Island, Greenland. Publications
DAEDA — Daedalus
DAEM — Deutsches Archiv fuer Erforschung des Mittelalters
DAENDT — Developments in Agricultural Engineering
DAE Res Rep Dep Agric Econ Agribusiness LA State Univ — DAE Research Report. Department of Agricultural Economics and Agribusiness. Louisiana State University
DaF — Deutsch als Fremdsprache
DAFT — Dansk Ornithologisk Forenings Tidsskrift
Dagestan Gos Univ Ucen Zap — Dagestanskii Gosudarstvennyi Universitet Imeni V. I. Lenina Ucenyi Zapiski [*Makhachkala*]
DAGM — Deutsches Archiv fuer Geschichte des Mittelalters
DAI — Dairy Industries International
DAI — Dissertation Abstracts International
Dainichi-Nippon Cables Rev — Dainichi-Nippon Cables Review [*Japan*]
DAIRI — Dissertation Abstracts International. Retrospective Index
Dairy F — Dairy Farmer
Dairyfarm Annu — Dairyfarming Annual
Dairyfmg Dig — Dairyfarming Digest
Dairy Goat J — Dairy Goat Journal
Dairy Herd Manage — Dairy Herd Management
Dairy Herd Mgt — Dairy Herd Management
Dairy Ind — Dairy Industries International
Dairy Ind Int — Dairy Industries International
Dairy Indus — Dairy Industries [*Later, Dairy Industries International*]

Dairymen's Digest South Reg Ed — Dairymen's Digest. Southern Region Edition
Dairymen's Dig North Cent Reg Ed — Dairymen's Digest. North Central Region Edition
Dairy Res Rep — Dairy Research Report
Dairy Res Rep (Dep Agric Fish) — Dairy Research Report (South Australia Department of Agriculture and Fisheries)
Dairy Sci Abstr — Dairy Science Abstracts
Dairy Sci Handb — Dairy Science Handbook
Dairy Tales Calif Univ Berkeley Coop Ext Serv — Dairy Tales. California University, Berkeley. Cooperative Extension Service
Daiwa — Daiwa Investment Monthly
DAJ — Derbyshire Archaeological Journal
DAJO — Danish Journal
DAKEA — Dansk Kemi
Dak Law Rev — Dakota Law Review
Dak L Rev — Dakota Law Review
Dakota F — Dakota Farmer
Dakota Law Rev — Dakota Law Review
DALB — Dictionary of American Library Biography
Dalgetys Annual Wool D — Dalgetys Annual Wool Digest
Dalgetys Annual Wool R — Dalgetys Annual Wool Review
Dalhousie L J — Dalhousie Law Journal
Dalhousie R — Dalhousie Review
Dalhousie Rev — Dalhousie Review
Dalhous Rev — Dalhousie Review
DALIS — Directory of Automated Library and Information Systems in Australia
Dallas Med J — Dallas Medical Journal
Dallas Sym — Dallas Symphony Orchestra. Program Notes
Dal LJ — Dalhousie Law Journal
Dall Med J — Dallas Medical Journal
Dall R — Dallas Reports
Dal'nevost Fiz Sb — Dal'nevostochnyi Fizicheskii Sbornik
Dal'nevost Nauchno Issled Inst Stroit Sb Nauchn Rab — Dal'nevostochnyi Nauchno-Issledovatel'skii Institut po Stroitel'stvu Sbornik Nauchnykh Rabot
Dal Nevostocn Gos Univ Ucen Zap — Dal'nevostocnyi Gosudarstvennyi Universitet Ucenyi Zapiski Serija Fiziko-Matematiceskih Nauk
Dal'nevostocn Mat Sb — Dal'nevostochnyi Matematiceskii Sbornik
Dal R — Dalhousie Review
Dal Rev — Dalhousie Review
DALV — Deutsches Archiv fuer Landes und Volksforschung
DAME — Developments in Agricultural and Managed-Forest Ecology [*Elsevier Book Series*]
DAMJA — Dallas Medical Journal
DAMSEL — Directory of Australian Manufactured Scientific Equipment and Laboratoryware
DAN — Doklady Akademii Nauk SSSR
Dan AEC Res Establ Riso Rep — Danish Atomic Energy Commission. Research Establishment. Risoe Report
Dan Arct Res — Danish Arctic Research
Dana-Rep Carlsberg Found — Dana-Report. Carlsberg Foundation
DAN Bolg — Doklady Bolgarskoi Akademii Nauk
Dan Bot Ark — Dansk Botanisk Arkiv

Dan Brygg Tid — Dansk Bryggeritidende
Dance in Can — Dance in Canada
Dance Chron — Dance Chronicle
Dance Mag — Dance Magazine
Dance N — Dance News
Dance Per — Dance Perspectives
Dance Res A — Dance Research Annual
Dance Res An — Dance Research Annual
Dance Res J — Dance Research Journal
Dance Sco — Dance Scope
Dancing Tim — Dancing Times
Dan Dendrol Arsskr — Dansk Dendrologisk Arsskrift
Dan Erhvervsfjerkrae — Dansk Erhvervsfjerkrae
DanF — Danske Folkemaal
Dan Farm Aarb — Dansk Farmaceutisk Aarbog
Dan Fisk Tid — Dansk Fiskeritidende
Danfoss J — Danfoss Journal
Dan Geol Unders Arbog — Danmarks Geologiske Undersoegelse. Arbog
Dan Geol Unders III Raekke — Danmarks Geologiske Undersoegelse. III Raekke
Dan Geol Unders II Raekke — Danmarks Geologiske Undersoegelse. II Raekke
Dan Geol Unders IV Raekke — Danmarks Geologiske Undersoegelse. IV Raekke
Dan Geol Unders Raekke 2 — Danmarks Geologiske Undersoegelse. Raekke 2
Dan Geol Unders Raekke 3 — Danmarks Geologiske Undersoegelse. Raekke 3
Dan Geol Unders Rapp — Danmarks Geologiske Undersoegelse. Rapport
Dan Geol Unders Ser A — Danmarks Geologiske Undersoegelse. Serie A
Dan Geol Unders Ser B — Danmarks Geologiske Undersoegelse. Serie B
Dan Haveb — Dansk Havebrug
Dan Havetid — Dansk Havetidende
Dan Ingeniorforen Spildevandskom Skr — Dansk Ingeniorforening Spildevandskomiteen Skrift
DANKA — Doklady Akademii Nauk SSR
Dan Kemi — Dansk Kemi
Dan Landbr — Dansk Landbrug
Danmarks Geol Undersoegelse — Danmarks Geologiske Undersoegelse
Dan Med B — Danish Medical Bulletin
Dan Med Bull — Danish Medical Bulletin
Dan Med Bull Suppl — Danish Medical Bulletin. Supplement
Dan Naturfr — Dansk Naturfredning
Dan Naturfredning — Dansk Naturfredning
Dan Naturfredningsforen Arsskr — Danmarks Naturfredningsforenings Arsskrift
Dan Ornithol Foren Feltornithol — Dansk Ornithologisk Forening. Feltornithologen
Dan Ornithol Foren Fuglevaern — Dansk Ornithologisk Forening. Fuglevaern
Dan Ornithol Foren Tidsskr — Dansk Ornithologisk Forenings Tidsskrift
Dan Pest Infest Lab Annu Rep — Danish Pest Infestation Laboratory. Annual Report
Dan Rev Game Biol — Danish Review of Game Biology
Dan Selsk Bygningsstatik Bygningsstatiske Medd — Dansk Selskab foer Bygningsstatik, Bygningsstatiske Meddelelser
Dansk Audiol — Dansk Audiologopaedi
Dansk Bog — Dansk Bogfortegnelse
Dansk Botan — Dansk Botanisk Arkiv
Danske Vid Selsk Mat-Fys Medd — Det Kongelige Danske Videnskabernes Selskab. Matematisk-Fysiske Meddelelser
Dansk Geol Foren Medd — Dansk Geologisk Forening Meddelelser
Dansk Geol Foren Meddel — Dansk Geologisk Forening Meddelelser
Dansk Mus — Dansk Musiktidsskrift
Dan Skovforen Tidsskr — Dansk Skovforenings Tidsskrift
Dansk Rad Ind — Dansk Radio Industri
Dansk Tekn Tidsskr — Dansk Teknisk Tidsskrift
Dansk T Farm — Dansk Tidsskrift foer Farmaci
Dansk Tidssk Farm — Dansk Tidsskrift foer Farmaci
DAN SSSR — Doklady Akademii Nauk SSSR
Dan Tdsskr Farm — Dansk Tidsskrift foer Farmaci
Dan Tek Tidsskr — Dansk Teknisk Tidsskrift [*Denmark*]
Dan Tidsskr Farm Supple — Dansk Tidsskrift foer Farmaci. Supplementum
DanTTs — Dansk Teologisk Tidsskrift [*Copenhagen*]
DanU — Dansk Udsyn
Danv Q — Danville Quarterly Review
Dan Yrbk Phil — Danish Yearbook of Philosophy
DAOD — Defending All Outdoors. Alberta Fish and Game Association
DAOREO — Diseases of Aquatic Organisms
DAP — Deutsche Aussenpolitik
DAP — Quarterly. Department of Antiquities in Palestine
DAPBAB — Data Acquisition and Processing in Biology and Medicine
Daphn — Daphnis. Zeitschrift fuer Mittlere Deutsche Literatur
DAPJD4 — Date Palm Journal
DAPNA — Doklady Akademii Pedagogicheskikh Nauk RSFSR
D Apoth Ztg — Deutsche Apotheker-Zeitung
DAPSAS — Developments in Applied Spectroscopy
Da R — Dalhousie Review
D Arch — Dialoghi di Archeologia
D Arch — Dodekanesiakon Archeion

D Arch Klin Med — Deutsches Archiv fuer Klinische Medizin
DArChr — Dictionnaire d'Archeologie Chretienne et de Liturgie
DArChrL — Dictionnaire d'Archeologie Chretienne et de Liturgie
Daresbury Lab Prepr DL/P — Daresbury Laboratory. Preprint DL/P
Daresbury Lab Prepr DL/SRF/P — Daresbury Laboratory. Preprint DL/SRF/P
Daresbury Lab Tech Memo — Daresbury Laboratory. Technical Memorandum
Daresbury Nucl Phys Lab Rep — Daresbury Nuclear Physics Laboratory. Report
Daresbury Nucl Phys Lab Tech Memo — Daresbury Nuclear Physics Laboratory. Technical Memorandum
Dar Es Salaam Med J — Dar Es Salaam Medical Journal
Dari Seama Sedintelor Com Stat Geol (Rom) — Dari de Seama ale Sedintelor. Comitetul de Stat al Geologiei (Romania)
Dari Seama Sedintelor Inst Geol (Rom) — Dari de Seama ale Sedintelor. Institutul Geologie (Romania)
Dari Seama Sedint RPR Com Geol — Dari de Seama ale Sedintelor. Republica Populara Romana Comitetul Geologic
Dar Sag — Dictionnaire des Antiquites Grecques et Romaines (Daremberg and Saglio)
Darshana Int — Darshana International
Dart Bi-Mo — Dartmouth Bi-Monthly
Dartm Coll Bull — Dartmouth College. Bulletin
Dartmouth Alumni Mag — Dartmouth Alumni Magazine
DARWAG — Darwiniana [*Buenos Aires*]
Darwin — Darwiniana. Revista del Instituto de Botanica Darwinion
DAS — Developments in Atmosphere Science [*Elsevier Book Series*]
Das Chron — Dasika Chronika
DASD — Deutsche Akademie fuer Sprache und Dichtung (Darmstadt). Jahrbuch
DASDJ — Deutsche Akademie fuer Sprache und Dichtung (Darmstadt). Jahrbuch
DASJA — Journal. Dental Association of South Africa
DaSt — Dante Studies
Data Acquis Process Biol Med — Data Acquisition and Processing in Biology and Medicine
Data Acquis Process Biol Med Proc Rochester Conf — Data Acquisition and Processing in Biology and Medicine. Proceedings of the Rochester Conference
Data At Power — Data of Atomic Power [*Japan*]
Database J — Database Journal
Database Jrnl — Database Journal
Data Bus — Data Business
Data C — Data Communications
Data Chan — Data Channels
Data Comm — Data Communications
Data Commun — Data Communications
Data Dyn — Data Dynamics
Data Ed — Data Education
Data Manage — Data Management
Data Mgmt — Data Management
Data Mgt — Data Management
Data Proc — Data Processing
Data Proc Dig — Data Processing Digest
Data Proces — Data Processing
Data Process — Data Processing Digest
Data Process Educ — Data Processing for Education [*North American Publishing Co.*]
Data Process Mag — Data Processing Magazine
Data Process Med — Data Processing in Medicine
Data Process Pract — Data Processing Practitioner
Datapro Rep Data Commun — Datapro Reports on Data Communications
Datapro Rep Minicomput — Datapro Reports on Minicomputers
Datapro Rep Office Syst — Datapro Reports on Office Systems
Data Rec Oceanogr Obs Explor Fish (Hokkaido) — Data Record of Oceanographic Observations and Exploratory Fishing (Hokkaido)
Data Rep — Data Report
Data Sys — Data Systems
Data Syst — Data Systems
Data Systems N — Data Systems News
Data Trng — Data Training
Data User Ns — Data Users News
DATE — Directory of Australian Tertiary Education
Date Grow Inst Rep — Date Growers' Institute. Report
Datenverarb Med — Datenverarbeitung in der Medizin
Datenverarb Recht — Datenverarbeitung im Recht
DATJBM — Datenjournal
DATPR — Domestic Air Transport Policy Review
Datum Collect Tokai Reg Fish Res Lab — Datum Collection. Tokai Regional Fisheries Research Laboratory
DAU — Datamation
DAUK — Deutsche Arbeiten der Universitaet Koeln
Dauph Med — Dauphine Medical
Dav — Davar. Revista Literaria
DAVEDJ — Dansk Veterinaertidsskrift

DAVS — Developments in Animal and Veterinary Sciences [*Elsevier Book Series*]
DAVSDR — Developments in Animal and Veterinary Sciences
DAW — Denkschriften der Akademie der Wissenschaften in Wien
DAWB — Deutsche Akademie der Wissenschaften zu Berlin
DAWBIDSL — Deutsche Akademie der Wissenschaften zu Berlin. Institut fuer Deutsche Sprache und Literatur
Dawe Dig — Dawe Digest
DAWW — Denkschriften der Akademie der Wissenschaften in Wien
Day Care & Early Educ — Day Care and Early Education
Dayton Med — Dayton Medicine
DAZ — Deutsche Allgemeine Zeitung
DAZ — Deutsche Angler-Zeitung
DAZ — Deutsche Apotheker-Zeitung
DB — Deutsche Bibliographie
DB — Developments in Biochemistry [*Elsevier Book Series*]
DB — Dialektolohicnyi Bjuleten
DB — Doitsu Bungaku
DBA — Baumarkt. Zeitschrift fuer Wirtschaftliche Unternehmensfuehrung
DBA — Dansk Botanisk Arkiv
DBB — Deutsche Bibliographie. Das Deutsche Buch. Auswahl Wichtiger Neuerscheinungen
DBB — Developments in Bioenergetics and Biomembranes [*Elsevier Book Series*]
DBCRB2 — Diabetologia Croatica
DBDK — Daito Bunka Daigaku Kiyo
DBDKK — Daito Bunka Daigaku Kangakkaishi
DBED — Diabetes Educator
D Bei — Deutsche Beitraege
DBF — Dictionnaire de Biographie Francaise
DBF — Distributie Vandaag. Maandblad over Verkooppromotie en Moderne Handelstechniek
DBGGA — Dopovidi Akademii Nauk Ukrains'koi RSR. Seriya B. Geologiya, Geofizika, Khimiya, ta Biologiya
DBGU — Deutsche Beitraege zur Geistigen Ueberlieferung
DBHVA — Deutsche Bibliographie. Halbjahres-Verzeichnis
D Bien Zt — Deutsche Bienenzeitung
DBIOA — Doklady Biochemistry [*English Translation*]
DBJ — Duke Bar Journal
DBJb — Deutsches Biographisches Jahrbuch
Dble Dealer — Double Dealer
DBLRA — Doklady Akademii Nauk BSSR
DBM — Dun's Business Month
DBMAD — Auerbach Data Base Management
DBNM — Darmstaedter Beitraege zur Neuen Musik
DBO — Directors and Boards
D Bot Ms — Deutsche Botanische Monatsschrift
DBR — Dialectes Belgo-Romans
D & B Rpts — D and B [*Dun and Bradstreet*] Reports
DB Sound Eng Mag — DB. The Sound Engineering Magazine
Dbt — Downbeat
DBTEAD — Diabete [*Later, Diabete et Metabolisme*]
DBTGAJ — Diabetologia
DBW — Dresdner Bank Wirtschaftsbericht
DBWBD — Deutsche Bibliographie. Woechentliches Verzeichnis. Reihe B
DBWCD — Deutsche Bibliographie. Woechentliches Verzeichnis. Reihe C
DBWVA — Deutsche Bibliographie. Woechentliches Verzeichnis. Reihe A
DBZ — Deutsche Bauzeitung
DBZT-A — Deutsche Bauzeitung
DC — [*The*] Daily Chronicle
DC — Developments in Crop Science [*Elsevier Book Series*]
DC — Documentation Catholique
DCB — Developments in Cell Biology [*Elsevier Book Series*]
DCB — Dictionary of Christian Biography [*London*]
DCB J — DC Bar Journal
DCCN — Dimensions of Critical Care Nursing
DCD — Kredietwaardigheden
DCDI — Dairy Council Digest
DCE — Developments in Civil Engineering [*Elsevier Book Series*]
DCF — Direction Commerciale Francaise
D Ch — Deutsche Chirurgie
DCHTA — Doklady Chemical Technology [*English Translation*]
DCI — Developpement et Civilisation
DCIMDQ — Developmental and Comparative Immunology
DCINA — Drug and Cosmetic Industry
D & C Ind — Drug and Cosmetic Industry
DCKHDL — Denryoku Chuo Kenkyusho Hokoku
DC Lib — District of Columbia Libraries
DCMS — Deccan College. Monograph Series
DCN — Daily Commercial News and Shipping List
DCNAA — Dental Clinics of North America
DCNAAC — Dental Clinics of North America
DCNNAH — Decheniana
DCNQ — Devon and Cornwall. Notes and Queries
DC Nurs Action — District of Columbia Nursing Action
DCO — DnC Monthly Survey of Norwegian Trade, Industry, and Finance

DCR — Developments in Cancer Research [*Elsevier Book Series*]
DCR — District Court Reports
DCR (NSW) — District Court Reports (New South Wales)
DCS — Defects in Crystalline Solids [*Later, Defects in Solids*] [*Elsevier Book Series*]
DCSCDC — Developments in Crop Science
DD — Dance and Dancers
DD — Deutsche Dialektgeographie
DD — Development Digest
DD — Diskussion Deutsch
DDB — Der Deutsche Beamte
DdB — Distrito de Braga
D Dev Rd — Deutsche Devisen-Rundschau
DDG — Deutsche Dialektgeographie
DDH — Dialogo Dor Haemshej
DDI — Documenti Diplomatici Italiani
DDIAEW — Dialogue on Diarrhoea
DDJ — Deutsches Dante Jahrbuch
DDO — Der Deutsche Oekonomist
DDP — Die Deutsche Post
D Dr — Deutsche Drama
DDR — Developments in Diabetes Research [*Elsevier Book Series*]
DDRKA — Doshisha Daigaku Rikogaku Kenkyu Hokoku
DDR-Med-Rep — DDR-Medizin-Report
DDS — Digest of Dental Science
DDSB — Duke Divinity School. Bulletin [*Later, Duke Divinity School. Review*]
DDSCD — Digestive Diseases and Sciences
DDSCDJ — Digestive Diseases and Sciences
DDT — Darling Downs Times
DDZ — Dokumentation der Zeit
DDZZA — DDZ. Das Deutsche Zahnaerzteblatt
DE — Daily Express [*United Kingdom*]
DE — DE. Journal of Dental Engineering
DE — Dene Express. Fort Good Hope
DE — Deutsche Erde
DE — Developing Economies
DE — Diritto Ecclesiastico
DE — Dynamic Economics [*Elsevier Book Series*]
DE — Journal of Dental Engineering
DE — Journal of Drug Education
DEA — Daily Engineering Articles
Deaconess Hosp Med Bull — Deaconess Hospital. Medical Bulletin
Deafness Res & Train Cent — Deafness Research and Training Center
DEASA — Dental Assistant
Death Educ — Death Education
Death Pen Rep — Death Penalty Reporter
DEB — Department of State. Bulletin
DEB — Dictionnaire Encyclopedique de la Bible
DEBEAC — Decheniana Beihefte
DEBEDF — Deviant Behavior
DEBFDI — Developments in Environmental Biology of Fishes
DEBIAO — Developmental Biology
DEBIDR — Developments in Biochemistry
DEBl — Deutsch-Evangelische Blaetter
De Bow — De Bow's Commercial Review
Debrecceni Mezogazd Akad Tud Evk — Debrecceni Mezogazdasagi Akademia Tudomanyos Evkonyve
Debrecceni Sz — Debrecceni Szemle
DEBSAK — Developmental Biology. Supplement
DEBZA — Deutsche Bauzeitschrift. Fachblatt fuer Entwurf und Ausfuehrung
Dec — Decade of Short Stories
DEC — Decision Sciences
DEC — Deutscher Baustellen Informationsdienst
DECAA — Dental Cadmos
Decalogue J — Decalogue Journal
Decc Geogr — Deccan Geographer
DECHEMA Monogr — DECHEMA [*Deutsche Gesellschaft fuer Chemisches Apparatewesen*] Monographien
Decheniana Beih — Decheniana Beihefte
Decid Fruit Grow — Deciduous Fruit Grower
Decid Fruit Grow Sagtevrugteboer — Deciduous Fruit Grower. Die Sagtevrugteboer
Deciduous Fruit Grow — Deciduous Fruit Grower
Decimal Research Bul — Decimal Research Bulletin
Decorator — Decorator and Painter for Australia and New Zealand
Decs — Decision
Ded — Dedalo
DEDIA — Dental Digest
DE Dom Eng — DE. Domestic Engineering [*Formerly, DE Journal*]
DeEc — De Economist
DEECAL — Dental Echo
DEED — Death Education. Pedagogy, Counseling, Care
Deep Sea Drill Proj Initial Rep — Deep Sea Drilling Project. Initial Reports
Deep Sea Re — Deep-Sea Research [*Later, Deep-Sea Research with Oceanographic Literature Review*]

Deep Sea Res — Deep-Sea Research [*Later, Deep-Sea Research with Oceanographic Literature Review*]
Deep Sea Res Oceanogr Abstr — Deep Sea Research and Oceanographic Abstracts
Deep Sea Res & Oceanogr Abstr — Deep Sea Research and Oceanographic Abstracts
Deep-Sea Res Part A — Deep-Sea Research. Part A. Oceanographic Research Papers [*Later, Deep-Sea Research with Oceanographic Literature Review*]
Deep-Sea Res Part A Oceanogr Res Pap — Deep-Sea Research. Part A. Oceanographic Research Papers [*Later, Deep-Sea Research with Oceanographic Literature Review*]
Deep-Sea Res Pt A Oceanogr Res Pap — Deep-Sea Research. Part A. Oceanographic Research Papers [*Later, Deep-Sea Research with Oceanographic Literature Review*]
Deep-Sea Res Pt B Oceanogr Lit Rev — Deep-Sea Research. Part B. Oceanographic Literature Review
Def Aer — Defence Aerienne
DEFAZET Dtsche Farben Z — DEFAZET. Deutsche Farben Zeitschrift
DEFEDZ — Defenders
Defektol — Defektologija
Defektosk — Defektoskopiya
Defenders Wildl — Defenders of Wildlife Magazine [*Later, Defenders*]
Defenders Wildl Int — Defenders of Wildlife International
Defenders Wildl News — Defenders of Wildlife News
Defense L J — Defense Law Journal
Defense Sci J — Defense Science Journal
Defense Veg — Defense des Vegetaux
DEFGA — Deciduous Fruit Grower [*South Africa*]
Def J — Defence Journal
Def Law J — Defense Law Journal
Def L J — Defense Law Journal
Def Man J — Defense Management Journal
Def Nat — Defense Nationale
Def Natl — Defense Nationale
Def Occident — Defense de l'Occident
Deform Razrushenie Neravnomernykh Temp Polyakh — Deformatsiya i Razrushenie v Neravnomernykh Temperaturnykh Polyakh
Def Sci J — Defence Science Journal
Def Stand Lab DSL Rep — Australia. Defence Standards Laboratories. DSL Report
Def Stand Lab Rep — Australia. Defence Standards Laboratories. Report
Def Stand Lab Tech Memo — Australia. Defence Standards Laboratories. Technical Memorandum
Def Stand Lab Tech Note — Australia. Defence Standards Laboratories. Technical Note
Def Syst Man Rev — Defense Systems Management Review
Def Tech Inf Cent Dig — Defense Technical Information Center. Digest
Def Transp J — Defense Transportation Journal
Def Veg — Defense des Vegetaux
DEG — Design [*London*]
DEG — Developments in Economic Geology [*Elsevier Book Series*]
DeH — De Homine
DEHEA8 — Dental Health [*London*]
DEHYD3 — Developments in Hydrobiology
DEIMD6 — Developments in Immunology
DE/J — DE Journal [*Later, DE. Domestic Engineering*]
DE J Dent Eng — DE. Journal of Dental Engineering
DeKalb — DeKalb Literary Arts Journal
DeKalb Lit — DeKalb Literary Arts Journal
Dek Iskusstvo — Dekorativnoe Iskusstvo SSSR
Dekor Isk SSSR — Dekorativnoe Iskusstvo SSSR
Del Ag Exp — Delaware. Agricultural Experiment Station. Publications
Del Agric Exp Stn Bull — Delaware. Agricultural Experiment Station. Bulletin
Del Agric Exp Stn Circ — Delaware. Agricultural Experiment Station. Circular
Delaware Co Inst Sc Pr — Delaware County Institute of Science. Proceedings
Delaware Hist Soc Papers — Delaware Historical Society. Papers
Del-Chem Bull — Del-Chem Bulletin
Del Cty Farm Home News — Delaware County Farm and Home News
Delft Prog Rep — Delft Progress Report
Delft Prog Report — Delft Progress Report
Delft Prog Rep Ser A — Delft Progress Report. Series A. Chemistry and Physics, Chemical and Physical Engineering
Delft Prog Rep Ser B — Delft Progress Report. Series B. Electrical, Electronic, and Information Engineering
Delft Prog Rep Ser C — Delft Progress Report. Series C. Mechanical and Aeronautical Engineering and Shipbuilding
Delft Prog Rep Ser D — Delft Progress Report. Series D. Architecture, Industrial Design, Social Sciences
Delft Prog Rep Ser E — Delft Progress Report. Series E. Geosciences
Delft Prog Rep Ser F — Delft Progress Report. Series F. Mathematical Engineering, Mathematics, and Information Engineering
Delft Progress Rep Ser F — Delft Progress Report. Series F
Del Geol Surv Bull — Delaware. Geological Survey. Bulletin
Del Geol Survey Ann Rept Bull Rept Inv — Delaware. Geological Survey. Annual Report. Bulletin. Report of Investigations

Del Geol Surv Rep Invest — Delaware. Geological Survey. Report of Investigations
DelH — Delaware History
Delhi Alum Patrika — Delhi Aluminium Patrika
Delhi L R — Delhi Law Review
Delhi L Rev — Delhi Law Review
Delhi L Times — Delhi Law Times
Del Hist — Delaware History
Delin — Delineator
Delius — Delius Society. Journal
Del J Corp L — Delaware Journal of Corporate Law
Delkeletdunantuli Mezogazd Kiserl Intez Kozl — Delkeletdunantuli Mezogazdasagi Kiserleti Intezet Kozlemenye
Del L R — Delhi Law Review
Del Med J — Delaware Medical Journal
DelN — Delaware Notes
Del Note — Delaware Notes
Del Notes — Delaware Notes
Del Nurs — Delaware Nurse
Del State Med J — Delaware State Medical Journal
Delt Agrotikes Trapezes — Deltion Agrotikes Trapezes
Delta Kappa Gamma Bull — Delta Kappa Gamma Bulletin
Delta Pi Epsilon J — Delta Pi Epsilon Journal
Delt Hellen Mikrobiol Hyg Hetair — Deltion Hellenikes Mikrobiologikes kai Hygieinologikes Hetaireias [*Greece*]
Delt Hell Geol Hetair — Deltion tes Hellenikes Geolokne Hetaireias
Delt Hell Kteniatr Hetair — Deltion tes Hellenikes Kteniatrikes Hetaireias
Delt Hell Mikrobiol Hygieinol Hetair — Deltion Hellenikes Mikrobiologikes kai Hygieinologikes Hetaireias
Delt Inst Technol Phytikon Proionton — Deltion tou Institoutou Technologias Phytikon Proionton
Deltion — Archaiologikon Deltion
Del Univ Sea Grant Program Annu Rep — Delaware University. Sea Grant Program. Annual Report
Del Univ Water Resour Semin Proc — Delaware University. Water Resources Seminars. Proceedings
DEM — Developments in Environmental Modelling [*Elsevier Book Series*]
DEMAB — Dental Management
DEMAEP — Dental Materials
Demag Nachr — Demag Nachrichten
DEMO — Demography
Democratic R — Democratic Review
Democr e Dir — Democrazia e Diritto
Demografia y Econ — Demografia y Economia
Demogr Bull — Demographic Bulletin [*New Zealand*]
Demogr y Econ — Demografia y Economia
Demokr Recht — Demokratie und Recht
Demo Left — Democratic Left
Demo Left — Newsletter of the Democratic Left
Demonstratio Math — Demonstratio Mathematica
Dem R — Democratic Review
DemStud — Demotische Studien [*Leipzig*]
DEn — Delavska Enotnost
DENED7 — Developmental Neuroscience
DENFA7 — Dendroflora
Den'gi i Kred — Den'gi i Kredit
Deniliquin Hist Soc News — Deniliquin Historical Society. Newsletter
Denison Univ Sci Lab Jour — Denison University. Scientific Laboratories. Journal
Denison Univ Sc Lab B — Denison University. Scientific Laboratories. Bulletin
Den JILP — Denver Journal of International Law and Policy
Den J Int'l L & Pol'y — Denver Journal of International Law and Policy
Denki Kag — Denki Kagaku
Denkschr Schweiz Naturforsch Ges — Denkschriften. Schweizerische Naturforschende Gesellschaft
Den LCJ — Denver Law Center. Journal
Den L J — Denver Law Journal
Denmark Gronlands Geol Undersogelse Rapp — Denmark. Groenlands Geologiske Undersoegelse Rapport
DENN — Dene Nation Newsletter
DENPA3 — Dental Progress
Den Q — Denver Quarterly
Den Res Establ Risoe Rep — Denmark. Research Establishment Risoe. Report
Den Res Establ Risoe Risoe Rep — Denmark. Research Establishment Risoe. Risoe Report
DENS — Denosa. Department of Northern Saskatchewan
Dent Abstr — Dental Abstracts
Dent Anaesth Sedat — Dental Anaesthesia and Sedation
Dent Assist — Dental Assistant
Dent Cadmos — Dental Cadmos
Dent Clin N — Dental Clinics of North America
Dent Clin North Am — Dental Clinics of North America
Dent Dialogue — Dental Dialogue
Dent Dig — Dental Digest
Dent Dimens — Dental Dimensions
Dent Discourse — Dental Discourse

Dent Echo — Dental Echo
Den Tech Univ Struct Res Lab Rep — Denmark. Technical University. Structural Research Laboratory. Report
Dent Econ — Dental Economics
Dent Health (Lond) — Dental Health (London)
Dent Hyg — Dental Hygiene
Dent Images — Dental Images
Dent Ind — Dental Literature Index
Dent Items Interest — Dental Items of Interest
Dent J — Dental Journal
Dent J Aust — Dental Journal of Australia
Dent Jpn (Tokyo) — Dentistry in Japan (Tokyo)
Dent Labor (Munch) — Dental Labor (Munich)
Dent Lab Rev — Dental Laboratory Review
Dent Manage — Dental Management
Dento Maxillo Fac Radiol — Dento Maxillo Facial Radiology
Dent Outlook — Dental Outlook [Japan]
Dent Pract Dent Rec — Dental Practitioner and Dental Record [England]
Dent Press — Dental Press
Dent Prog — Dental Progress
Dent Radiogr Photogr — Dental Radiography and Photography
Dent Stud — Dental Student
Dent Surv — Dental Survey
Dent Tech — Dental Technician
Dent Update — Dental Update
Denver J Internat Law and Policy — Denver Journal of International Law and Policy
Denver J Int Law Policy — Denver Journal of International Law and Policy
Denver J Int L & Pol — Denver Journal of International Law and Policy
Denver Law — Denver Law Journal
Denver LCJ — Denver Law Center. Journal
Denver L J — Denver Law Journal
Denver Med Bull — Denver Medical Bulletin
Denver Med Times — Denver Medical Times
Denver Mus Nat History Mus Pictorial Pop Ser Proc — Denver Museum of Natural History. Museum Pictorial Popular Series. Proceedings
DenverQ — Denver Quarterly
Denver West Roundup — Denver Western Roundup
DEOPDB — Developments in Ophthalmology
DeP — DePaul Law Review
DEP — Division of Electronic Products [Series]
Dep Agric Straits Settlements Fed Malay States Econ Ser — Department of Agriculture. Straits Settlements and Federated Malay States. Economic Series
Dep Agric Straits Settlements Fed Malay States Gen Ser — Department of Agriculture. Straits Settlements and Federated Malay States. General Series
Dep Agric Straits Settlements Fed Malay States Sci Ser — Department of Agriculture. Straits Settlements and Federated Malay States. Scientific Series
Dep Agric (Victoria Aust) Tech Bull — Department of Agriculture (Victoria, Australia). Technical Bulletin
De Paul L Rev — De Paul Law Review
DEPBA — Developmental Psychobiology
DEPBA5 — Developmental Psychobiology
Dep Biol Coll Bourget Rigaud Bull — Departement de Biologie. College Bourget Rigaud. Bulletin.
Dep Bull US Dep Agric — Department Bulletin. United States Department of Agriculture
Dep Circ US Dep Agric — Department Circular. United States Department of Agriculture
Dep Def Aeronaut Res Lab Mech Eng Rep (Aust) — Department of Defence. Aeronautical Research Laboratories. Mechanical Engineering Report (Australia)
Dep Environ Fire Res St Fire Res Tech Pap (UK) — Department of the Environment. Fire Research Station. Fire Research Technical Paper (United Kingdom)
Dep Harbours Mar Queensl Fish Notes — Queensland Department of Harbours and Marine. Fisheries Notes
Dep Health Educ Welfare Natl Inst Health Publ — Department of Health, Education, and Welfare. National Institutes of Health. Publication
Dep Health Educ Welfare Natl Inst Occup Saf Health Publ (US) — Department of Health, Education, and Welfare. National Institute for Occupational Safety and Health. Publication (United States)
Dep Health Educ Welfare Publ (Health Serv Adm) (US) — Department of Health, Education, and Welfare. Publication (Health Services Administration) (United States)
De Phil — De Philosophia
Dep Ind (Bombay) Bull — Department of Industries (Bombay). Bulletin
DeP LR — DePaul Law Review
Dep Nac Agric (Costa Rica) Bol Tec — Departamento Nacional de Agricultura (Costa Rica). Boletin Tecnica
Dep Primary Ind Brisbane Fish Branch Fish Notes (New Ser) — Department of Primary Industries. Brisbane Fisheries Branch. Fisheries Notes (New Series)

Dept Bull US Dept Agric — Department Bulletin. United States Department of Agriculture
Dep Tech Rep Tex Agric Exp Stn — Departmental Technical Report. Texas Agricultural Experiment Station
Dept Econ et Sociol Rurales Bul Info — Departement d'Economie et de Sociologie Rurales. Bulletin d'Information
Dept of Ed and Science Repts — Department of Education and Science: Reports on Education [London]
Dept El Sch Prin B — Department of Elementary School Principals. Bulletin
Dept Employment Gaz (Gt Britain) — Department of Employment. Gazette (Great Britain)
Dept Sec Sch Prin B — Department of Secondary School Principals. Bulletin
Dept Sta Bul — Department of State. Bulletin
Dept Sta Nl — Department of State. Newsletter
Dept State Bul — Department of State. Bulletin
Dept State Bull — Department of State. Bulletin
Dept State Newsletter — Department of State. Newsletter
Dept St Bull — Department of State. Bulletin
DERAAC — Dermatologica [Basel]
Derbyshire Archaeol J — Derbyshire Archaeological Journal
Derbyshire Arch J — Derbyshire Archaeological Journal
Derecho Reforma Agrar Rev — Derecho y Reforma Agraria Revista
Derecho Vivo — Actas Procesales del Derecho Vivo
DEREES — Developmental Review
Derevoobrab Prom-st — Derevoobrabatyvaiushchaia Promyshlennost
Derevopererab Lesokhim Promst — Derevopererabatyvayushchaya i Lesokhimicheskaya Promyshlennost
Derev Prom — Derevoobrabatyvaiushchaia Promyslennost
Derg Rev Fac For Univ Istanbul Ser A — Dergisi. Review of the Faculty of Forestry. University of Istanbul. Series A
DERIA — Dermatologia Internationalis
DERIA2 — Dermatologia Internationalis
Deri Muz Ev — Deri Muzeum Evkoenyve
Der Integr — Derecho de la Integracion
DERMAE — Dermatologia [Mexico]
Dermatol Int — Dermatologia Internationalis
Dermatol Monatsschr — Dermatologische Monatsschrift
Dermatolog — Dermatologica
Dermatologica Suppl — Dermatologica Supplementum
Dermatol Trop Ecol Geogr — Dermatologia Tropica et Ecologia Geographica
Dermatol Venerol — Dermatologiya i Venerologiya
Dermatol Wochenschr — Dermatologische Wochenschrift
Dermatoses Prof — Dermatoses Professionnelles
Dermato-Vener — Dermato-Venerologie
Dermat Wochnschr — Dermatologische Wochenschrift
Derm Beruf Umwelt — Dermatosen in Beruf und Umwelt
Derm Venerol — Dermato-Venerologie
DERVA7 — Dermato-Venerologie [Bucharest]
Derwent Archaeol Soc Res Rep — Derwent Archaeological Society. Research Reports
Desalinatn — Desalination
Desarr Econ — Desarrollo Economico
Desarr Indoamer — Desarrollo Indoamericano
Desarrollo Econ — Desarrollo Economico
Desarrollo Indoam — Desarrollo Indoamericano
Desarrollo y Soc — Desarrollo y Sociedad
Desarr Rural Am — Desarrollo Rural en las Americas
Desarr Rur Amer — Desarrollo Rural en las Americas
Des Arts Educ — Design for Arts in Education
DESB — Delta Epsilon Sigma Bulletin
Des Compon Engn — Design and Components in Engineering
Descrip Appl Ling — Descriptive and Applied Linguistics
Des Electron — Design Electronics
Des Eng — Design Engineering
Des Engng (GB) — Design Engineering (Great Britain)
Des Engng (USA) — Design Engineering (United States of America)
Des Eng (Toronto) — Design Engineering (Toronto)
Desert Bot Gard (Phoenix) Sci Bull — Desert Botanical Garden (Phoenix). Science Bulletin
Desert Inst Bull — Desert Institute. Bulletin
Desert Inst Bull ARE — Desert Institute. Bulletin ARE
Desert Locust Control Organ E Afr Tech Rep — Desert Locust Control Organization for Eastern Africa. Technical Report
Desert Mag — Desert Magazine
Design — Design Magazine
Design Ind — Design for Industry
Design for Ind — Design for Industry
Design Q — Design Quarterly
Design Qly — Design Quarterly
Design Qly (Heery) — Design Quarterly (Heery)
Desinfekt Gesundheitswes — Desinfektion und Gesundheitswesen
Desinfekt Schaedlingsbekaempf — Desinfektion Schaedlingsbekaempfung
Des Manage Resour Recovery — Design and Management for Resource Recovery
Des News — Design News
Des Prod Appln — Design Products and Applications

DESRAY — Deep-Sea Research [*Later, Deep-Sea Research with Oceanographic Literature Review*]
Des Special Needs — Design for Special Needs
Des in Steel — Design in Steel
DESTA — Deutsche Stomatologie
Destill Lehrling — Destillateur Lehrling
Destill Likoerfabr — Destillateur Likoerfabrikant
DESUA9 — Dental Survey
Detali Mash Podemno Transp Mash — Detali Mashin i Pod'emno Transportnye Mashiny
Det CLR — Detroit College of Law. Review
Det CL Rev — Detroit College of Law. Review
Det Coll LR — Detroit College of Law. Review
Det Coll L Rev — Detroit College of Law. Review
Determ Org Struct Phys Methods — Determination of Organic Structures by Physical Methods
DETJA — Defense Transportation Journal
Det Law — Detroit Lawyer
Detr MJ — Detroit Medical Journal
Detroit Acad Nat Sci Occasional Paper — Detroit Academy of Natural Sciences. Occasional Papers
Detroit Inst Bul — Detroit Institute of Arts. Bulletin
Detroit Law — Detroit Lawyer
Detroit Med News — Detroit Medical News
Detroit Perspect — Detroit in Perspective
Detroit Rev Med and Pharm — Detroit Review of Medicine and Pharmacy
Detroit Sym — Detroit Symphony Orchestra. Program Notes
Deu E — Deutschlands Erneuerung
DEUPD7 — Dermatology Update
Deut Agrartech — Deutsche Agrartechnik
Deut Ausschuss Stahlbeton — Deutscher Ausschuss fuer Stahlbeton
Deutch Archaeol Inst Jahrb — Deutsches Archaeologisches Institut. Jahrbuch
Deut Entomol Z — Deutsche Entomologische Zeitschrift
Deut Geod Komm Veroeff Reihe E Gesch Entwickl Geod — Deutsche Geodaetische Kommission. Veroeffentlichungen. Reihe E. Geschichte und Entwicklung der Geodaesie
Deut Geog Blaetter — Deutsche Geographische Blaetter
Deut Landwirt — Deutsche Landwirtschaft
Deut Lebensm Rundsch — Deutsche Lebensmittel Rundschau
Deut Luft Raumfahrt Forschungsber — Deutsche Luft- und Raumfahrt. Forschungsbericht
Deut Med Wo — Deutsche Medizinische Wochenschrift
Deut Mueller Ztg — Deutsche Mueller Zeitung
Deut Oesterr Alpen-Ver Zs — Deutscher und Oesterreichischer Alpen-Verein. Zeitschrift
Deut Papierwirtsch — Deutsche Papierwirtschaft
DeutR — Deutsche Revue
Deut Rundschau — Deutsche Rundschau
Deutsch Archaeol Inst Roem Mitt — Deutsches Archaeologisches Institut. Mitteilungen. Roemische Abteilung
Deutsch Dante Jahrb — Deutsches Dante Jahrbuch
Deutsch-Dominikan Tropenforschungsinstitut Veroeff — Deutsch-Dominikanisches Tropenforschungsinstitut Veroeffentlichungen
Deutsche Aerzte-Ztg — Deutsche Aerztezeitung
Deutsche Akad Wissen Berlin Schr — Deutsche Akademie der Wissenschaften zu Berlin. Schriften der Sektion fuer Vor- und Fruehgeschichte
Deutsche Bundesbank — Monthly Report. Deutsche Bundesbank
Deutsche Entom Ztschr "Iris" — Deutsche Entomologische Zeitschrift "Iris"
Deutsche Geol Gesell Zeitschr — Deutsche Geologische Gesellschaft Zeitschrift
Deutsche Keramische Gesell Ber — Deutsche Keramische Gesellschaft. Berichte
Deutsche Med Wochenschr — Deutsche Medizinische Wochenschrift
Deutsche Med-Ztg — Deutsche Medizinal-Zeitung
Deutsche Mineralog Gesell Fortschr Mineralogie — Deutsche Mineralogische Gesellschaft. Fortschritte der Mineralogie
Deutsche Oper — Deutsche Oper am Rhein
Deutscher Geographentag Verh — Deutscher Geographentag Verhandlungen
Deutsches Arch Klin Med — Deutsches Archiv fuer Klinische Medizin
Deutsche Schlacht-u Viehhof-Ztg — Deutsche Schlacht-und Viehhof-Zeitung
Deutsche Tieraerztl Wochenschr — Deutsche Tieraerztliche Wochenschrift
Deutsche Ztschr Chir — Deutsche Zeitschrift fuer Chirurgie
Deutsche Ztschr Nervenh — Deutsche Zeitschrift fuer Nervenheilkunde
Deutsch Gesell Geol Wiss Ber — Deutschen Gesellschaft fuer Geologische Wissenschaften. Berichte
Deutsch Jahrb Musikw — Deutsches Jahrbuch fuer Musikwissenschaft
Deutsch Kam — Deutsche Kameramann
Deutschoesterr Spirit Ztg — Deutschoesterreichische Spirituisen-Zeitung
Deutschoesterr Tieraerztl Wchnschr — Deutschoesterreichische Tieraerztliche Wochenschrift
Deutsch Shakespeare Ges West Jahrb — Deutsch Shakespeare Gesellschaft West. Jahrbuch
Deutsch-Taschenb — Deutsch-Taschenbuecher
Deutsch Verein Kunstwis Z — Deutscher Verein fuer Kunstwissenschaft. Zeitschrift
Deutsch Zool Ges Verh — Deutsche Zoologische Gesellschaft. Verhandlungen

Deut Vier Lit — Deutsche Vierteljahrsschrift fuer Literaturwissenschaft und Geistesgeschichte
Deut Z Phil — Deutsche Zeitschrift fuer Philosophie
Deu Viertel — Deutsche Vierteljahrsschrift fuer Literaturwissenschaft und Geistesgeschichte
DEV — Development News
DEvA — Deutsch-Evangelisch im Auslande
Dev Appl Spectrosc — Developments in Applied Spectroscopy
DevB — Devil's Box
Dev Biochem — Developments in Biochemistry
Dev Biol — Developmental Biology
Dev Biol Stand — Developments in Biological Standardization
Dev Biol Suppl — Developmental Biology. Supplement
Dev Cell Biol — Developmental and Cell Biology
Dev Cell Biol (Amsterdam) — Developments in Cell Biology (Amsterdam)
Dev Change — Development and Change
Dev Comp Immunol — Developmental and Comparative Immunology
Dev Crop Sci — Developments in Crop Science
DEVEAA — Defense des Vegetaux
Dev Econ — Developing Economies
Dev Econ Geol — Developments in Economic Geology
Dev Educ — Developing Education
Devel Biol — Developmental Biology
Devel Civ — Developpement et Civilisation
Devel Dig — Development Digest
Devel Ind Microbiol — Developments in Industrial Microbiology
Develop Bio — Developmental Biology
Develop Biol — Developmental Biology
Develop Cha — Development and Change
Develop and Change — Development and Change
Develop et Civilis — Developpement et Civilisation
Develop Dialogue — Development Dialogue
Develop Eco — Developing Economies
Develop Econ — Developing Economies
Develop Gr — Development, Growth, and Differentiation
Develop in Mech — Developments in Mechanics
Develop Med — Developmental Medicine and Child Neurology
Development — Development Forum [*General Edition*]
Development & Materials Bull — Development and Materials Bulletin
Develop Psy — Developmental Psychobiology
Develop Psychol — Developmental Psychology
Develop in Statist — Developments in Statistics
Develop VIC — Develop Victoria
Develop VIC J — Develop Victoria Journal
Devel Psych — Developmental Psychology
Devel Psychobiol — Development Psychobiology
Dev Food Packag — Developments in Food Packaging
Dev Forum — Development Forum
Dev Genet — Developmental Genetics
Dev Genet (Amsterdam) — Developments in Genetics (Amsterdam)
Dev Geochem — Developments in Geochemistry
Dev Geotech Eng — Developments in Geotechnical Engineering
Dev Geotectonics — Developments in Geotectonics
Dev Growth Differ — Development, Growth, and Differentiation
Dev Growth Differ (Nagoya) — Development, Growth, and Differentiation (Nagoya)
Dev Ind Microbiol — Developments in Industrial Microbiology
Dev Ind Sci — Developpement Industriel et Scientifique
Dev Innovation Aust Process Ind Pap Aust Chem Eng Conf — Development and Innovation for Australian Process Industries. Papers of the Australian Chemical Engineering Conference [*Newcastle, 1972*]
Dev Mamm — Development in Mammals
Dev Mech — Developments in Mechanics
Dev Med Child Neurol — Developmental Medicine and Child Neurology
Dev Med Child Neurol Suppl — Developmental Medicine and Child Neurology. Supplement
Dev Neurosci — Developmental Neuroscience
Dev Nucl Med — Developments in Nuclear Medicine
Dev Nutr Metab — Developments in Nutrition and Metabolism
Devonshire Assoc — Devonshire Association
Dev Ophthalmol — Developments in Ophthalmology
DEVPA — Developmental Psychology
DEVPA9 — Developmental Psychology
Dev Pharmacol Ther — Developmental Pharmacology and Therapeutics
Dev Plant Biol — Developments in Plant Biology
Dev Plant Genet Breed — Developments in Plant Genetics and Breeding
Dev Psychobiol — Developmental Psychobiology
Dev Psychol — Developmental Psychology
Dev Psychol Monogr — Developmental Psychology. Monograph
Devs Biol Standardiz — Developments in Biological Standardization
Dev Sedimentol — Developments in Sedimentology
Dev Soil Sci — Developments in Soil Science
Dev Stud (Sthn Afr) — Development Studies (Southern Africa)
Dev Toxicol Environ Sci — Developments in Toxicology and Environmental Science
DEWTA — DEW [*Deutsche Edelstahlwerke*] Technische Berichte

DEW Tech Ber — DEW [*Deutsche Edelstahlwerke*] Technische Berichte
D Exp — Dairy Exporter
DEZB — Deutsche Entomologische Zeitschrift (Berlin)
DF — Dandke Folkemaal
DFA — Droguerie Francaise. La Couleur
DFBO Mitt — DFBO [*Deutsche Forschungsgesellschaft fuer Blechverarbeitung und Oberflaechenbehandlung*] Mitteilungen
DFFNAW — Differentiation
DFG Mitt — DFG Mitteilungen. Deutsche Forschungsgemeinschaft
DFIFAO — Documents de Fouilles. Institut Francais d'Archeologie Orientale du Caire [*Cairo*]
DFL Ber — DFL [*Deutsche Forschungsanstalt fuer Luftfahrt*] Bericht
DFM — Dansk Folkemal
DFMhe — Deutsch-Franzoesische Monatshefte
DFO — Danish Journal. A Magazine about Denmark
DFR — Deutsch-Franzoesische Rundschau
DFS — Developments in Food Science [*Elsevier Book Series*]
DFSCDX — Developments in Food Science
DG — Developments in Geotectonics [*Elsevier Book Series*]
Dg — Dialog [*Warsaw*]
DG — Dublin Gazette
DGB — Drogistenweekblad. Onafhankelijk Vakblad voor de Drogisterijbranche
DGBl — Deutsche Geographische Blaetter
DG Bl — Deutsche Geschichtsblaetter
DGC — Deutsche Gaststatte. Deutsche Hotelzeitung
DGC — Developments in Geochemistry [*Elsevier Book Series*]
DGDFA5 — Development, Growth, and Differentiation
DGE — Developments in Geotechnical Engineering [*Elsevier Book Series*]
D Gefl Ztg — Deutsche Gefluegel-Zeitung
DGEND — Developments in Geotechnical Engineering
D Geogr Bl — Deutsche Geographische Blaetter
DGF — Danmarks Gamle Folkeviser
DGKRA — Denki Gakkai Ronbunshi. A
DGM — Developments in Geomathematics [*Elsevier Book Series*]
DGNSAQ — Diagnostica
DGNTDW — Developmental Genetics
DGRBB — Denki Gakkai Ronbunshi. B
DGRCA — Denki Gakkai Ronbunshi. C
DGRHA — Doboku Gakkai Ronbun Hokokushu
DGTPA — Diesel and Gas Turbine Progress [*Later, Diesel Progress North American*]
DGUAB8 — Geological Survey of Denmark. Yearbook
DGUADA — Geological Survey of Denmark. Serie A
DGUBAA — Geological Survey of Denmark. II Series
DGUBDD — Geological Survey of Denmark. Serie B
DGUCAD — Geological Survey of Denmark. III Series
DGURBP — Geological Survey of Denmark. Report
DGZAA — Denki Gakkai Zasshi
DH — Delaware History
DH — Deutsches Handwerksblatt
DH — Documents d'Histoire
DHA — Dialogues d'Histoire Ancienne
DHBAA — Dock and Harbour Authority
DHC — Documents Relatifs a l'Histoire des Croisades
D H Lawrence R — D. H. Lawrence Review
DHLR — D. H. Lawrence Review
DHM — Developments in Halophilic Microorganisms [*Elsevier Book Series*]
DHR — Duquesne Hispanic Review
DHS — Deutsches Handwerksblatt
DHS — Dix-Huitieme Siecle
DHSTEV — Data Handling in Science and Technology
DHStL — Deutsch-Hebraeische Sterbeliste [*Berlin*]
DHT — Dvar Hashavua (Tel Aviv)
DHZ — Deutsche Hochschulzeitung
D Hz — Die Holzzucht
DI — Der Islam
DI — Developments in Immunology [*Elsevier Book Series*]
DI — Diagnostic Immunology
Di — Dial. A Magazine for Literature, Philosophy, and Religion
Di — Dialog
Di — Dialoghi
Di — Didaskaleion
DI — Dissertationes Inaugurales
DI — Drvna Industrija
DI — Educational Documentation and Information Bulletin [*UNESCO*]
Dia — Dialog
Dia — Dialoghi
Diab — Diabete [*Later, Diabete et Metabolisme*]
Diab Abstr — Diabetes Abstracts
Diabet — Diabetes
Diabet — Diabetologia
Diabet Dig — Diabetic Digest
Diabete Met — Diabete et Metabolisme
Diabete Metab — Diabete et Metabolisme
Diabetes Res — Diabetes Research

Diabetic J of Aust — Diabetic Journal of Australia
Diabet J — Diabetic Journal
Diabetolog — Diabetologia
Diab Lit Ind — Diabetes Literature Index
DIA Bol Divulg — DIA [*Division de Investigaciones Agropecuarias*] Boletin de Divulgacion
DIA Bol Tec — DIA [*Division de Investigaciones Agropecuarias*] Boletin Tecnico
DIAEAZ — Diabetes
Diagn — Diagnostica
Diagn Gynecol Obstet — Diagnostic Gynecology and Obstetrics
Diagn Histopathol — Diagnostic Histopathology
Diagn Imaging — Diagnostic Imaging
Diagn Intensivther — Diagnostik und Intensivtherapie
Diagn Lab — Diagnostyka Laboratoryjna
Diagn Lab Clin — Diagnosi Laboratorio e Clinica
Diagn Med — Diagnostic Medicine
Diagn Plazmy — Diagnostika Plazmy [*USSR*]
Diagn Tec Lab — Diagnostica e Tecnica di Laboratorio
Diagn Ther — Diagnosis and Therapy [*Japan*]
Diagn Trait — Diagnostics et Traitements
Diagn Treat — Diagnosis and Treatment [*Japan*]
Dial — Dialog [*Minneapolis*]
Dial — Dialoghi
Dial — Dialogos. Problemi della Scuola Italiana
Dial — Dialogues. Cahiers de Litterature et de Linguistique
Dial Anthro — Dialectical Anthropology
Dial Ar — Dialoghi di Archeologia
Dial Arch — Dialoghi di Archeologia
DialB — Dialektolohicnyi Bjuleten
Dial Belg-Rom — Dialectes Belgo-Romans
Dial (Ch) — Dial (Chicago)
Dialec — Dialectica
Dial Ec — Dialogo Ecumenico
Dialec Hum — Dialectics and Humanism
DialEcum — Dialogo Ecumenico [*Salamanca*]
Dialektika Ob'ekt Sub'ekt Poznanie Prakt Dejatel'nosti — Dialektika Ob'ektivnogo i Sub'ektivnogo v Poznanie i Prakticeskoj Dejatel'nosti
Dialog Fairleigh Dickinson Univ Sch Dent — Dialog. Fairleigh Dickinson University. School of Dentistry
Dialogue (Canada) — Dialogue: Canadian Philosophical Review
Dialogue (PST) — Dialogue (Phi Sigma Tau)
Dialog (W) — Dialog (Warsaw)
DialS — Dialog: Teatertidskrift (Stockholm)
Dial Transplant — Dialysis and Transplantation
Dial Transplant Nephrol Pro Congr Eur Dial Transplant Assoc — Dialysis, Transplantation, Nephrology. Proceedings. Congress of the European Dialysis and Transplant Association
DIA Med — DIA [*Division de Investigaciones Agropecuarias*] Medico
DIA Med Urug — DIA [*Division de Investigaciones Agropecuarias*] Medico Uruguayo
Diamond Res — Diamond Research
Diap — Diapason
Diario Of Minist Mar — Diario Oficial. Ministerio de Marina
DIATAC — DIA [*Division de Investigaciones Agropecuarias*] Boletin Tecnico
Diatomic Research Bull — Diatomic Research Bulletin
DIB — Defense Industry Bulletin [*DoD*]
DIB — Documentatie en Informatie over Toerisme
DIBLAR — Desert Institute. Bulletin ARE
DIBtn — Defense Industry Bulletin [*DoD*]
DICEA — Die Casting Engineer
DICHA — Diseases of the Chest
DICHAK — Diseases of the Chest
Dicht u Volkst — Dichtung und Volkstum
Dick — Dickensian
Dickens — Dickensian
Dickinson L Rev — Dickinson Law Review
DickinsonR — Dickinson Review
Dick L R — Dickinson Law Review
Dick L Rev — Dickinson Law Review
DICMD4 — Diagnostic Imaging in Clinical Medicine
DICPB — Drug Intelligence and Clinical Pharmacy
DICRA — Diseases of the Colon and Rectum
DICRAG — Diseases of the Colon and Rectum
Dic S — Dickinson Studies
Dict Apol — Dictionnaire Apologetique
Dict Class Hist Nat — Dictionnaire Classique d'Histoire Naturelle
Dict Limb Rom — Dictionarul Limbii Romane
Did — Didaskaleion
DID — Drug Induced Diseases [*Elsevier Book Series*]
Didasc — Didascalia
Didask — Didaskalos
DIDIEW — Digestive Diseases
Did S — Diderot Studies
DIE — Developments in Endocrinology [*Elsevier Book Series*]
Die Cast Eng — Die Casting Engineer

Diecasting Met Moulding — Diecasting and Metal Moulding
Diecast Met Mould — Diecasting and Metal Moulding
Diehlektr Poluprovodn — Diehlektriki i Poluprovodniki
Dielectr Opt Aspects Intermol Interact — Dielectric and Optical Aspects of Intermolecular Interactions
Dielectr Relat Mol Processes — Dielectric and Related Molecular Processes
DIEQA — Differential Equations
Diergeneesk Memo — Diergeneeskundig Memorandum
Diesel Eng — Diesel Engineering [*England*]
Diesel Eng Us Ass Report — Diesel Engineers and Users Association. Reports
Diesel Eng Users Ass Publ — Diesel Engineers and Users Association. Publication
Diesel Equip Supt — Diesel Equipment Superintendent
Diesel Gas Turbine Prog — Diesel and Gas Turbine Progress [*Later, Diesel Progress North American*]
Diesel Gas Turbine Progr — Diesel and Gas Turbine Progress [*Later, Diesel Progress North American*]
Diesel Gas Turbine Worldwide — Diesel and Gas Turbine Worldwide
Diesel Gas Turb Prog Worldwide — Diesel and Gas Turbine Progress Worldwide [*Later, Diesel and Gas Turbine Worldwide*]
Diesel Power Diesel Transp — Diesel Power and Diesel Transportation
Diesel Prog — Diesel Progress
Diesel Prog — Diesel Progress North American
Diesel Prog N Amer — Diesel Progress North American
Dies Rail Tract — Diesel Railway Traction
Diet Collect — Dietetique et Collectivites
Diet Currents — Dietetic Currents
Diet Hyg Gaz — Dietetic and Hygienic Gazette
Diet Nutr — Dietetique et Nutrition
Diet et Nutr — Dietetique et Nutrition
Dietol Dietoter — Dietologia e Dietoterapia
Dietsk Med — Dietskaia Meditsina
DIFDA — Diffusion Data
Differencial'nye Uravnenija i Vycisl Mat — Differencial'nye Uravnenija i Vycislitelnaja Matematika
Differentia — Differentiation
Differ Equations — Differential Equations
Differ Uravn — Differentsial'nye Uravneniya
Differ Uravn Primen — Differentsial'nye Uravneniya i Ikh Primenenie
Diffus Data — Diffusion Data [*Later, Diffusion and Defect Data*]
Diffus Defect Data — Diffusion and Defect Data [*Switzerland*]
Diffus Defect Monogr Ser — Diffusion and Defect Monograph Series
Diffuz Svarka Vak Met Splavov Nemet Mater — Diffuzionnaya Svarka v Vakuume Metallov. Splavov i Nemetallicheskikh Materialov [*USSR*]
Difusion Econ — Difusion Economica
DIG — Developments in Genetics [*Elsevier Book Series*]
Dig Agric Econ — Digest of Agricultural Economics
Dig Dis Sci — Digestive Diseases and Sciences
DIGEB — Digestion
DIGEBW — Digestion
Digeste Soc — Digeste Social
Digest Mod Teach — Digest of Modern Teaching
Dig Int Conf Med Biol Eng — Digest. International Conference on Medical and Biological Engineering [*Sweden*]
Digital Syst Ind Autom — Digital Systems for Industrial Automation
Digit Comp Newsl — Digital Computer Newsletter
Digit Process — Digital Processes
Dig Lit Dielec — Digest of Literature on Dielectrics
Dig Lit Dielect — Digest of Literature on Dielectrics
Dig Metab Ruminant Proc Int Symp — Digestion and Metabolism in the Ruminant. Proceedings of the International Symposium on Ruminant Physiology
Dig Neurol Psychiat — Digest of Neurology and Psychiatry
Dig Ophthal Otolaryng — Digest of Ophthalmology and Otolaryngology
Dig Pap IEEE Comput Soc Int Conf — Digest of Papers. IEEE Computer Society International Conference
Dig Pap Semicond Test Symp — Digest of Papers. Semiconductor Test Symposium
DIGRD — Discipline and Grievances
Dig Stat ICAO — Digest of Statistics. International Civil Aviation Organization
Dig Tech Pap IEEE Int Solid State Circuits Conf — Digest of Technical Papers. IEEE International Solid State Circuits Conference
Dig Tech Pap IEEE MTTS Int Microwave Symp — Digest of Technical Papers. IEEE MTTS International Microwave Symposium
Dig Treatm — Digest of Treatment
DIHEA — District Heating
DIHIDH — Diagnostic Histopathology
DIIMD — Diagnostic Imaging
DIIMDY — Diagnostic Imaging
DIIMEZ — Diagnostic Immunology
DiJ — Dzis i Jutro
DIKNAA — Annual Report. National Veterinary Assay Laboratory
Dikorastushchie Introd Polezn Rast Bashk — Dikorastushchie i Introdtsiruemye Poleznye Rasteniya v Bashkirii
DilR — Diliman Review

DIM — Diamant. Maandelijks Tijdschrift voor de Studie van het Diamantbedrijf
DIM — Direct Marketing
DIMCAL — Developments in Industrial Microbiology
DIME — Dialogue in Instrumental Music Education
DIMEAR — DIA [*Division de Investigaciones Agropecuarias*] Medico
Dim Econ Bourgogne — Dimensions Economiques de la Bourgogne
DIMEDU — Diabete et Metabolisme
Dimen NBS — Dimensions. [*US*] National Bureau of Standards
Dimens — Dimensioni. Revista Abruzzese di Cultura e d'Arte
Dimens Health Serv — Dimensions in Health Service
Dimension — Canadian Dimension
Dimensions NBS — Dimensions. [*US*] National Bureau of Standards
DIMIA — DIN [*Deutsches Institut fuer Normung*] Mitteilungen
D Imm — Deutsche Immobilien
DIMOA — DM/Disease-a-Month
DIMS — Dimensions. Ontario Metis and Non-Status Indian Association
DIN — Developments in Neurology [*Elsevier Book Series*]
DIN — Dialogue North
Dinamika Sploshn Sredy — Dinamika Sploshnoj Sredy. Institut Gidrodinamiki Sibirskogo Otdeleniya Akademii Nauk SSSR
DINC — Dialogue North. Combined Edition
DINE — Dialogue North. Eastern Arctic Edition
Dinglers Polytech J — Dinglers Polytechnisches Journal
DINM — Developments in Nutrition and Metabolism [*Elsevier Book Series*]
DIN Mitt — DIN [*Deutsches Institut fuer Normung*] Mitteilungen [*West Germany*]
Din Prochn Mashin — Dinamika i Prochnost Mashin
Din Sploshn Sredy — Dinamika Sploshnoj Sredy
DIN Taschenb — DIN [*Deutsches Institut fuer Normung*] Taschenbuch [*West Germany*]
DINW — Dialogue North. Western Arctic Edition
Diog — Diogene
Dion — Dioniso
DIP — Developments in Psychiatry [*Elsevier Book Series*]
Dipl Hist — Diplomatic History
DIPOA — Diesel Power
DIPRDG — Discourse Processes
DIR — Director
DIR — Florida Music Director
Dir Ancient Monum Hist Bldgs Occas Pap — Directorate of Ancient Monuments and Historic Buildings. Occasional Papers [*England*]
Dir Boards — Directors and Boards
Dir fr Cu — Direct from Cuba
Direc — Direction
Direct Curr — Direct Current
Direct Curr & Power Electron — Direct Current and Power Electronics
Direct Inf Nuklearmed — Direct Information. Nuklearmedizin
Direct Inf Strahlenschutz — Direct Information. Strahlenschutz
Direct Mark — Direct Marketing
Direct Midrex — Direct from Midrex
Direct Mkt — Magazine of Direct Marketing
Directors and Bds — Directors and Boards
Direito Nucl — Direito Nuclear
Dir Gen Agric (Peru) Divulg Inf — Direccion General de Agricultura (Peru). Divulgaciones e Informaciones
Dir Gen Bol — Direccion General de Archivos y Bibliotecas. Boletin
Dir Gen Inventario Nac For Publ — Direccion General del Inventario Nacional Forestal. Publicacion
Dir et Gestion — Direction et Gestion des Entreprises
Dir Gestion — Direction et Gestion
Dir Gestion Entr — Direction et Gestion des Entreprises
Dir e Giur — Diritto e Giurisprudenza
DIRH — Directions in Health, Physical Education, and Recreation. Monograph Series
Dir Indiana Crop Impr Ass Seed Certif Serv — Directory. Indiana Crop Improvement Association. Seed Certification Service
Diritto Lav — Diritto del Lavoro
Dir LR — Directors Law Reporter
Dir Nac Propiedad Ind (Argent) — Direccion Nacional de la Propiedad Industrial (Argentina)
Dir Online Databases — Directory of Online Databases [*United States*]
Dir Publ Proc — Directory of Published Proceedings [*United States*]
DiS — Dickens Studies
DIS — Dislocations in Solids [*Elsevier Book Series*]
Dis — Dissent
DIS — Distrifood. Weekblad voor de Betaillist en Groothandel in Food en Nonfood
DisA — Dissertation Abstracts [*Later, Dissertation Abstracts International*]
Dis Abst — Dissertation Abstracts [*Later, Dissertation Abstracts International*]
DISA Inf — DISA [*Danske Industri Syndikat A/S*] Information
Disarm — Disarmament
Disarm & Arms Control — Disarmament and Arms Control
Disaster Prev Res Inst Annu — Disaster Prevention Research Institute. Annual [*Japan*]

Disaster Prev Res Inst Kyoto Univ Bull — Disaster Prevention Research Institute. Kyoto University. Bulletin
Disc — Discovery
DISCA — Discovery [*England*]
DISCAH — Discovery [*New Haven*]
DISCBI — Discovery [*London*]
Disc Excav (Scot) — Discovery and Excavation (Scotland)
Dis Chest — Diseases of the Chest
Discip Grievances — Discipline and Grievances
Disc L and Proc Adv Sheets — Disciplinary Law and Procedure Advance Sheets
Discn Faraday Soc — Discussions. Faraday Society
Disco Forum — Discographical Forum
Dis Colon Rectum — Diseases of the Colon and Rectum
Dis Col Rec — Diseases of the Colon and Rectum
Discoteca — Discoteca alta Fedalta I
Discount M — Discount Merchandiser
Discoveries Pharmacol — Discoveries in Pharmacology
Discovery Excav (Scot) — Discovery and Excavation (Scotland)
Discovery Rep — Discovery Reports
Discrete Appl Math — Discrete Applied Mathematics
Discrete Math — Discrete Mathematics
Discr Math — Discrete Mathematics
Discuss Alphabet — Discussion sur l'Alphabetisation
Discuss Faraday Soc — Discussions. Faraday Society
Dishekim Derg — Dishekimligi Dergisi
Diskret Analiz — Diskretnyi Analiz. Sbornik Trudov
Dis Ner Sys — Diseases of the Nervous System
Dis Nerv Syst — Diseases of the Nervous System
DISOAJ — Difesa Sociale
Dispersnye Sist Ikh Povedenie Elektr Magn Polyakh — Dispersnye Sistemy i Ikh Povedenie v Elektricheskikh i Magnitnykh Polyakh
Dispos Intern — Disposables International and Nonwoven Fabric Review
Disp Technol and Appl — Displays. Technology and Applications
Disquis Math Hungar — Disquisitiones Mathematicae Hungaricae
Diss Abs — Dissertation Abstracts [*Later, Dissertation Abstracts International*]
Diss Abstr — Dissertation Abstracts [*Later, Dissertation Abstracts International*]
Diss Abstr Int B — Dissertation Abstracts International. Section B. Sciences and Engineering
Diss Abstr Int B Sci Eng — Dissertation Abstracts International. Section B. Sciences and Engineering
Diss Abstr Int Sec B — Dissertation Abstracts International. Section B. Sciences and Engineering
Diss Abstr Int Sect B — Dissertation Abstracts International. Section B. Sciences and Engineering
Diss Abstr Int Sect C — Dissertation Abstracts International. Section C. European Dissertations
Dissert Abs Internat — Dissertation Abstracts International
Dissert Abstr Int — Dissertation Abstracts International
Dissertationes Math (Rozprawy Mat) — Dissertationes Mathematicae (Rozprawy Matematyczny)
Diss Hohenheim Landwirt Hochsch — Dissertation. Hohenheim Landwirtschaftliche Hochschule
Diss Pan — Dissertationes Pannonicae
Diss Pharm — Dissertationes Pharmaceuticae
Diss Pharm Pharmacol — Dissertationes Pharmaceuticae et Pharmacologicae
DissUW — Dissertationen der Universitaet (Wien)
Distance Educ — Distance Education
Dist Drum — Distant Drummer
Dist Heat — District Heating
Distill Feed Res Counc Conf Proc — Distillers Feed Research Council. Conference Proceedings
Dist Proc — Distributed Processing Newsletter
Distr — Distribution
Distr Heat — District Heating
Distr Heat Ass J — District Heating Association. Journal
Distrib Age — Distribution Age
Distrib Mgr — Distribution Manager
Distributive Wkr — Distributive Worker
Distrib Worldwide — Distribution Worldwide
District Law — District Lawyer
District Law (DC) — District Lawyer (District of Columbia)
Distr Worldwide — Distribution Worldwide
DISUD6 — Digestive Surgery
Ditchley J — Ditchley Journal
Div — Divan
Div — Divinitas
DIV — Divisions
Div Appl Chem Tech Pap CSIRO Aust — Australia. Commonwealth Scientific and Industrial Research Organisation. Division of Applied Chemistry. Technical Paper
Div Appl Org Chem Tech Pap CSIRO Aust — Australia. Commonwealth Scientific and Industrial Research Organisation. Division of Applied Organic Chemistry. Technical Paper

Div Atmos Phys Tech Pap Aust CSIRO — Australia. Commonwealth Scientific and Industrial Research Organisation. Division of Atmospheric Physics. Technical Paper
Div Chem Technol Tech Pap CSIRO Aust — Australia. Commonwealth Scientific and Industrial Research Organisation. Division of Chemical Technology. Technical Paper
Div Fish Oceanogr Tech Pap Aust CSIRO — Division of Fisheries and Oceanography. Technical Paper. Australia Commonwealth Scientific and Industrial Research Organisation
DIVID — Divice
Div Land Resour Manage Tech Pap CSIRO Aust — Australia. Commonwealth Scientific and Industrial Research Organisation. Division of Land Resources Management. Technical Paper
Div Land Res Tech Pap CSIRO Aust — Australia. Commonwealth Scientific and Industrial Research Organisation. Division of Land Research. Technical Paper
Div Land Use Res Tech Pap Aust CSIRO — Australia. Commonwealth Scientific and Industrial Research Organisation. Division of Land Use Research. Technical Paper
Div Land Use Res Tech Pap Aust CSIRO — Division of Land Use Research. Technical Paper. Australia Commonwealth Scientific and Industrial Research Organisation
Div Land Use Res Tech Pap CSIRO Aust — Australia. Commonwealth Scientific and Industrial Research Organisation. Division of Land Use Research. Technical Paper
Divl Rep Dep Agric Br Guiana — Divisional Reports. Department of Agriculture. British Guiana
Div Rep Div Soils CSIRO — Divisional Report. Division of Soils. Commonwealth Scientific and Industrial Research Organisation
Div Soils Div Rep CSIRO Aust — Australia. Commonwealth Scientific and Industrial Research Organisation. Division of Soils. Divisional Report
Div Soils Tech Pap CSIRO Aust — Australia. Commonwealth Scientific and Industrial Research Organisation. Division of Soils. Technical Paper
Div Tech Conf Soc Plast Eng Tech Pap — Divisional Technical Conference. Society of Plastics Engineers. Technical Papers
Div Trop Agron Tech Pap CSIRO Aust — Australia. Commonwealth Scientific and Industrial Research Organisation. Division of Tropical Agronomy. Technical Paper
Div Trop Agron Tech Pap CSIRO (Aust) — Division of Tropical Agronomy. Technical Paper. Commonwealth Scientific and Industrial Research Organisation (Australia)
Div Trop Crops Pastures Tech Pap CSIRO Aust — Australia. Commonwealth Scientific and Industrial Research Organisation. Division of Tropical Crops and Pastures. Technical Paper
Div Trop Crops Pastures Tech Pap CSIRO (Aust) — Division of Tropical Crops and Pastures. Technical Paper. Commonwealth Scientific and Industrial Research Organisation (Australia)
Div Trop Pastures Tech Pap CSIRO Aust — Australia. Commonwealth Scientific and Industrial Research Organisation. Division of Tropical Pastures. Technical Paper
Divulg Pesq Dir Gen Pesca (Bogota) — Divulgacion Pesquera Direccion General de Pesca (Bogota)
DIW — Visual Merchandising
Dix-Huit Siecle — Dix-Huitieme Siecle
Dix-Sept S — Dix-Septieme Siecle
D-I-Y — Do-It-Yourselfer
DIZ — Deutsch-Israelitische Zeitung
Dizion Vet — Dizionario Veterinario
DJ — Denver Law Journal
DJ — Discipleship Journal
DJ — Dzis i Jutro
DJbN — Deutsches Jahrbuch fuer Numismatik
DJBR — Development of the James Bay Region/Societe de Developpement de la Baie James
DjbVk — Deutsches Jahrbuch fuer Volkskunde
DJGKN — Doshida Joshidaigaku Gakujutsu Kenkyu Nenpo
DJM — Dentsu Japan Marketing Advertising
DJS — Slagersambacht
DJT — Digest of Japanese Industry and Technology
DJV — Deutsches Jahrbuch fuer Volkskunde
D i K — Den'gi i Kredit
DK — Die Kultur
DK — Dukovna Kultura
DkA — Deutschkundliche Arbeiten
DKath — De Katholick
Dk of Bay — Dock of the Bay
DKBSA — Doklady Biological Sciences [*English Translation*]
DKBSB — Doklady Botanical Sciences [*English Translation*]
DKCHA — Doklady Chemistry [*English Translation*]
DKDP — Deutsche Kunst und Denkmalpflege
DKESA — Doklady. Earth Sciences Sections
DKHHD — Denryoku Chuo Kenkyusho Hokoku. Sogo Hokoku
DKKIB — Denpa Kenkyusho Kiho
DK Mitt — DK Mitteilungen
DKNHDO — Denryoku Chuo Kenkyusho Noden Kenkyusho Hokoku
DKPCA — Doklady Physical Chemistry [*English Translation*]

DKVS — Det Kongelige Videnskapers Selskap
DKZ — Deutsche Kolonialzeitung
DL — Detskaya Literatura
DL — Deus Loci
DL — Deutsche Literaturzeitung
DL — Die Literatur
DL — Douro Litoral
DL — Droit et Liberte, Contre le Racisme, l'Antisemitisme, pour la Paix [*Paris*]
DLAJ — DeKalb Literary Arts Journal
DLevZ — Deutsche Levante-Zeitung
DLG Mit Dtsch Landwirtsch Ges — DLG. Mitteilungen. Deutsch Landwirtschafts Gesellschaft
DLI — Diabetes Literature Index
DLit — Deutsche Literatur
DLJ — University of Detroit. Law Journal
DLJNAQ — Diagnostyka Laboratoryjna
DLL — Dictionnaire de la Langue Louvite [*Paris*]
DLMov — Doslidzennja z Literaturoznavstava ta Movoznavstva
DLN — Doris Lessing Newsletter
DLP — Douro Litoral (Portugal)
Dl Planet — Daily Planet
DLPNAM — Delpinoa
DLQ — Drexel Library Quarterly
DLR — Dominion Law Reports [*Database*]
DLRB — Digest of Decisions of the National Labor Relations Board
DLR (Can) — Dominion Law Reports (Canada)
DLR 2d — Dominion Law Reports. Second Series
DLR 3d — Dominion Law Reports. Third Series
DLR 2d (Can) — Dominion Law Reports. Second Series (Canada)
DLRED — Duquesne Law Review
DLS — Deutsche Literatur und Sprachstudien
DLTPAE — Dialysis and Transplantation
DLTRBL — Desert Locust Control Organization for Eastern Africa. Technical Report
DLtz — Deutsche Literaturzeitung
DLTZA — DLZ. Die Landtechnische Zeitschrift
DLZ — Deutsche Literaturzeitung
DLZ Die Landtech Z — DLZ. Die Landtechnische Zeitschrift
DM — Daily Mail
DM — Dance Magazine
DM — Danske Magazin
DM — Debater's Magazine
DM — Direct Marketing
DM — DM/Disease-a-Month
DM — Dublin Magazine
DMAMDM — Development in Mammals
DmB — Driemaandelijkse Bladen
DMBUA — Danish Medical Bulletin
DMC — Merkblaetter fuer den Aussenhandel
DMCBDX — Developments in Molecular and Cellular Biochemistry
DMCNA — Developmental Medicine and Child Neurology
DMCNAW — Developmental Medicine and Child Neurology
DMCSAD — Developmental Medicine and Child Neurology. Supplement
DMDGA — DECHEMA [*Deutsche Gesellschaft fuer Chemisches Apparatewesen*] Monographien
DMG — Data Management
DMG — De Maasgouw. Orgaan voor Limbrugsche Geschiedenis, Taal-en Letterkunde
DMG — Deutsche Morgenlaendische Gesellschaft
DMG — Deutsches Mozartfest der Deutschen Mozart-Gesellschaft
DMG-DRS J — DMG-DRS [*Design Methods Group - Design Research*] Journal
DMGYA — Demography
DMICP — Danish Meteorological Institute. Climatological Papers [*Danske Meteorologiske Institut Klimatologiske Meddelelser*]
DMID — Diagnostic Microbiology and Infectious Disease
DMIDDZ — Diagnostic Microbiology and Infectious Disease
DMIM — Danske Meteorologiske Institut. Meddelelser
DMJ — Defense Management Journal
DMJOB — Defense Management Journal
DMKK — Deutsche Monatsschrift fuer Kolonialpolitik und Kolonisation
DMMRB — Daily Missouri-Mississippi River Bulletin
DMNHA — Dimensions in Health Service
DMOA — Documenta et Monumenta Orientis Antiqui
DMONBP — Dermatologische Monatsschrift
DMov — Doslidzennja z Movoznavstva Zbirnyk Statej Aspirantiv i Dysertantiv
DMREEG — Diabetes Metabolism Reviews
DMRRDK — Design and Management for Resource Recovery
DMTRA — Drug Metabolism Reviews
DMUkrM — Doslidzennja i Materijaly z Ukrjins'koji Movy
DMW — Deutsche Medizinische Wochenschrift
DN — Dagens Nyheter
DN — Daily Nation
DN — [*The*] Daily News
DN — Dance News

DN — Detroit News
DN — Disraeli Newsletter
DN — Druzba Narodov
DNAL — Diario de Noticias (Lisbon, Portugal)
DNav — De Navorscher
DNB — Deutsche Nationalbibliographie
DNB — Dictionary of National Biography
DNBSB — Dimensions. [*US*] National Bureau of Standards
DNCPA — Dental Concepts
DND — Development News Digest [*Later, Development Dossier*]
DNDJA — Dainichi Nippon Densen Jiho
DNF — Denmark Review
DNFV — Dansk Naturhistorisk Forening. Videnskabelige Meddelelser
DNHYAT — Dental Hygiene
DNK — Doklady na Naucnych Konferencijach
DNKHAR — Deltion tes Hellenikes Kteniatrikes Hetaireias
DNL — Die Neue Literatur
Dn LJ — Denver Law Journal
DNRPAI — Dana-Report. Carlsberg Foundation
DNS — Daily News [*Tanzania*]
DNS — Die Neueren Sprachen
DNSYA — Diseases of the Nervous System
DNSYAG — Diseases of the Nervous System
DNT — De Nieuwe Taglalgids
DNUND — Dopovidi Akademii Nauk Ukrains'koi RSR. Seriia A. Fiziko-Matematichni ta Tekhnichni Nauki
DNVS — Det Norske Videnskapers Selskap
DNW — Der Neue Weg
DO — Dance Observer
D d O — Digest des Ostens
DOA — Abstracts on Tropical Agriculture
Dobycha Obogashch Rud Tsvetn Met — Dobycha i Obogashchenie Rud Tsvetnykh Metallov
Dobycha Pererab Goryuch Slantsev — Dobycha i Pererabotka Goryuchikh Slantsev [*USSR*]
Dobycha Pererab Nerudn Stroit Mater — Dobycha i Pererabotka Nerudnykh Stroitel'nykh Materialov
DOC — Dictionary of Organic Compounds
Doc Abstr — Documentation Abstracts
Doc Bibl — Documentacion Bibliotecologica
Doc et Bibl — Documentation et Bibliotheques
Doc Biol — Documents on Biology
Doc Biol Pract — Documentation du Biologiste Practicien
Doc Bull Natl Res Cent (Egypt) — Documentation Bulletin. National Research Centre (Egypt)
Doc Bull Nat Res Cent (UAR) — Documentation Bulletin. National Research Centre (United Arab Republic)
DocC — Documentation Catholique [*Paris*]
Doc Cartogr Ecol — Documents de Cartographie Ecologique
Doc Cath — Documentation Catholique
Doc Centre Et Revenus Couts — Documents du Centre d'Etude des Revenus et des Couts
Doc CEPESS — Documents CEPESS [*Centre d'Etudes Politiques, Economiques, et Sociales*]
Doc Chem Yugosl — Documenta Chemica Yugoslavica
Doc Combust Eng Assoc — Document. Combustion Engineering Association [*England*]
Doc Coop — Documenti Cooperativi
Doc d'Et Droit Const — Documents d'Etudes. Droit Constitutionnel et Institutions Politiques
Doc d'Et Droit Internat Publ — Documents d'Etudes. Droit International Public
Doc Geogr — Documentatio Geographica
Doc Haematol (Bucharest) — Documenta Haematologica (Bucharest)
Doc Inform Gestion — Documents d'Information et de Gestion
Doc Invest Hidrol — Documentos de Investigacion Hidrologica
Dock Harb Auth — Dock and Harbour Authority
Dock & Harbour — Dock and Harbour Authority [*London*]
Doc Lab Geol Fac Sci Lyon — Documents des Laboratoires de Geologie de la Faculte des Sciences de Lyon
Doc Med Geogr Trop — Documenta de Medicina Geographica et Tropica
Doc Neerl Indones Morb Trop — Documenta Neerlandica et Indonesica de Morbis Tropicis
Doc Ophthal — Documenta Ophthalmologica
Doc Ophthalmol — Documenta Ophthalmologica
Doc Ophthalmol Proc Ser — Documenta Ophthalmologica. Proceedings Series
Doc Polit — Documentos Politicos
Docs CEPESS — Documents. CEPESS [*Centre d'Etudes Politiques, Economiques, et Sociales*]
Doc Sci XVe Siecle — Documents Scientifiques du XVe Siecle [*Geneva*]
Doc Swed Counc Build Res — Document. Swedish Council for Building Research
DoctCom — Doctor Communis [*Rome*]
Doc Tech Charbon Fr — Documents Techniques. Charbonnages de France
Doc Tech Inst Natl Rech Agron Tunis — Documents Techniques Institut National de la Recherche Agronomique de Tunisie

Doc Tech SCPA (Soc Commer Potasses Azote) — Document Technique de la SCPA (Societe Commerciale des Potasses et de l'Azote)

Doc Travail — Document de Travail [*Besancon*]

DoctrLife — Doctrine and Life [*Dublin*]

Docum Adm — Documentacion Administrativa

Docum Admin — Documentacion Administrativa

Docum et Biblio — Documentation et Bibliotheques

Docum Cath — Documentation Catholique

Docum Centre Nat Rech For — Document. Centre National de Recherches Forestieres

Docum Econ — Documentacion Economica [*Madrid*]

Docum Econ Colombiana — Documentacion Economica Colombiana

Docum Econ (Paris) — Documentation Economique (Paris)

Documen — Documentation Etc.

Documents CEGM — Documents. Centre d'Etudes Geologiques et Minieres

Docum Europ — Documentation Europeenne

Docum Europe Centr — Documentation sur l'Europe Centrale

Docum Eur Ser Syndicale et Ouvriere — Documentation Europeenne Serie Syndicale et Ouvriere

Docum Franc Illustr — Documentation Francaise Illustree

Docum Inform Pedag — Documentation et Information Pedagogiques

Docum Jur — Documentacion Juridica

Docum Legis Afr — Documentation Legislative Africaine

Docum Paesi Est — Documentazione sui Paesi de l'Est

Doc Vet — Documenta Veterinaria

DOE Pat Available Licens — DOE [*US Department of Energy*] Patents Available for Licensing [*United States*]

DOE Transp Lib Bull — DOE [*US Department of Energy*] and Transport Library Bulletin

DOFTAB — Dansk Ornithologisk Forenings Tidsskrift

DOG — Documentation sur l'Europe Centrale

Doga Bilim Derg Seri A — Doga Bilim Dergisi. Seri A

Doga Bilim Derg Seri A1 — Doga Bilim Dergisi. Seri A1

Doga Bilim Derg Seri A2 — Doga Bilim Dergisi. Seri A2

Doga Bilim Derg Seri D — Doga Bilim Dergisi. Seri D

Doga Bilim Derg Seri D1 — Doga Bilim Dergisi. Seri D1

Doga Bilim Derg Seri D2 — Doga Bilim Dergisi. Seri D2

DOGYDY — Developments in Obstetrics and Gynecology

DOH — Dock and Harbour Authority [*London*]

DOHNA — Domestic Heating News

DOJb — Deutsches Orient-Jahrbuch

DOK — Oesterreich Nederland

Dok Arbeitsmed — Dokumentation Arbeitsmedizin

DOKBA — Doklady Biophysics [*English Translation*]

DOKEA — Dokumenteshon Kenkyu

Dok Fachbibl Werkbuech — Dokumentation Fachbibliothek Werkbuecherei

Dok/Inf — Dokumentation/Information

Dokl Acad Sci USSR Earth Sci Sect — Doklady Academy of Sciences of the USSR. Earth Science Sections

Dokl Akad Nauk Arm SSR — Doklady Akademii Nauk Armyanskoi SSR

Dokl Akad Nauk Azerb SSR — Doklady Akademii Nauk Azerbajdzanskoj SSR

Dokl Akad Nauk Az SSR — Doklady Akademii Nauk Azerbaidzanskoj SSR

Dokl Akad Nauk Beloruss SSR — Doklady Akademii Nauk Belorusskoi SSR

Dokl Akad Nauk B SSR — Doklady Akademii Nauk Belorusskoi SSR

Dokl Akad Nauk SSR Biochem Sect (Engl Transl) — Doklady Akademii Nauk SSSR. Biochemistry Section (English Translation)

Dokl Akad Nauk SSR Bot Sci Sect (Engl Transl) — Doklady Akademii Nauk SSSR. Botanical Sciences Section (English Translation)

Dokl Akad Nauk SSSR — Doklady Akademii Nauk SSSR

Dokl Akad Nauk SSSR Biochem Sect (Engl Transl) — Doklady Akademii Nauk SSSR. Biochemistry Section (English Translation)

Dokl Akad Nauk SSSR Biol Sci Sect (Engl Transl) — Doklady Akademii Nauk SSSR. Biological Science Section (English Translation)

Dokl Akad Nauk SSSR Bot Sci Sect (Engl Transl) — Doklady Akademii Nauk SSSR. Botanical Sciences Section (English Translation)

Dokl Akad Nauk SSSR Ser A — Doklady Akademii Nauk SSSR. Seriya A

Dokl Akad Nauk SSSR Ser Biol — Doklady Akademii Nauk SSSR. Seriya Biologiya

Dokl Akad Nauk SSSR Ser Geol — Doklady Akademii Nauk SSSR. Seriya Geologiya [*USSR*]

Dokl Akad Nauk SSSR Ser Khim — Doklady Akademii Nauk SSSR. Seriya Khimiya

Dokl Akad Nauk SSSR Ser Mat Fiz — Doklady Akademii Nauk SSSR. Seriya Matematika Fizika

Dokl Akad Nauk Tadzh SSR — Doklady Akademii Nauk Tadzhikskoi SSR

Dokl Akad Nauk Tadzik SSR — Doklady Akademii Nauk Tadzikskoi SSR

Dokl Akad Nauk Ukr SSR — Doklady Akademii Nauk Ukrainskoi SSR [*Ukrainian SSR*]

Dokl Akad Nauk Uzbek SSR — Doklady Akademii Nauk Uzbekskoi SSR

Dokl Akad Nauk Uzb SSR — Doklady Akademii Nauk Uzbekskoi SSR

Dokl Akad Nauk UzSSR — Doklady Akademii Nauk UzSSR

Dokl Akad Pedagog Nauk RSFSR — Doklady Akademii Pedagogicheskikh Nauk RSFSR

Dokl Akad Skh Nauk Bolg — Doklady Akademii Sel'skohozyaistvennykh Nauk v Bolgarii

Dokl Biochem (Engl Transl Dokl Akad Nauk SSSR Ser Biokhim) — Doklady Biochemistry (English Translation of Doklady Akademii Nauk SSSR. Seriya Biokhimiya)

Dokl Biol Sci (Engl Transl Dokl Akad Nauk SSSR Ser Biol) — Doklady Biological Sciences (English Translation of Doklady Akademii Nauk SSSR. Seriya Biologiya)

Dokl Biophys — Doklady Biophysics

Dokl Biophys (Engl Transl Dokl Akad Nauk SSSR Ser Biofiz) — Doklady Biophysics (English Translation of Doklady Akademii Nauk SSSR. Seriya Biofizika)

Dokl Bolg Akad Nauk — Doklady Bolgarskoi Akademii Nauk

Dokl Bot Sci — Doklady Botanical Sciences

Dokl Bot Sci (Engl Transl Dokl Akad Nauk SSSR Ser Bot) — Doklady Botanical Sciences (English Translation of Doklady Akademii Nauk SSSR. Seriya Botanika)

Dokl Chem — Doklady Chemistry

Dokl Chem Technol — Doklady Chemical Technology. Academy of Sciences of the USSR. Chemical Technology Section

Dokl Inst Geogr Sib Dal'nego Vostoka — Doklady Instituta Geografii Sibiri i Dal'nego Vostoka

Dokl Inst Geogr Sib Dal'n Vost — Doklady Instituta Geografii Sibiri i Dal'nego Vostoka

Dokl Irkutsk Protivochumn Inst — Doklady Irkutskogo Protivochumnogo Instituta

DoklIRuJa — Doklady i Soobscenija Instituta Russkogo Jazyka

Dokl Kom Aerosemki Fotogrametrii Geogr Obs SSR — Doklady Komissii Aeros'emki i Fotogrametrii Geograficheskogo Obshcheskogo SSR

Dokl Kom Aeros'emki Fotogr Geogr O-va SSR — Doklady Komissii Aeros'emki i Fotogrametrii Geograficheskogo Obshchestva SSR

Dokl Konf Vopr Tsito Gistokhim — Doklady Konferentsiya po Voprosam Tsito-i Gistokhimii

Dokl L'vov Politekh Inst — Doklady L'vovskogo Politekhnicheskogo Instituta

Dokl L'vov Politekh Inst Khim Khim Tekhnol — Doklady L'vovskogo Politekhnicheskogo Instituta Khimiya i Khimicheskaya Tekhnologiya

Dokl Mosk Inst Inzh Skh Proizvod — Doklady Moskovskogo Instituta Inzhenerov Sel'skohozyaistvennogo Proizvodstva

Dokl Mosk Ova Ispyt Prir Obshch Biol — Doklady Moskovskogo Obshchestva Ispytatelei Prirody Obshchaya Biologiya

Dokl Mosk Sel'Khoz Akad K A Timiryazeva — Doklady Moskovskoi Sel'skokhozyaistvennoi Akademii Imeni K. A. Timiryazeva

Dokl Mosk Skh Akad — Doklady Moskovskaya Sel'skokhozyaistvennaya Akademiya Imeni K. A. Timiryazeva

Dokl Mosk S-kh Akad Im K A Timiryazeva — Doklady Moskovskoi Sel'skokhozyaistvennoi Akademii Imeni K. A. Timiryazeva

DoklMU — Doklady i Soobscenija Filologoceskogo Fakul'teta Moskovskogo Universiteta

Dokl Nauchn Konf Yarosl Gos Pedagog Inst — Doklady na Nauchnykh Konferentsiyakh Yaroslavskii Gosudarstvennyi Pedagogicheskii Institut

Dokl Nauchn Konf Yarosl Gosud Pedagog Inst — Doklady na Nauchnykh Konferentsiyakh Yaroslavskii Gosudarstvennyi Pedagogicheskii Institut

Dokl Otd Kom Geogr O-va SSSR — Doklady Otdelov i Komissii Geograficheskogo Obshchestva SSSR

Dokl Otd Kom Geogr Ovo SSSR — Doklady Otdelenii i Komissii Geograficheskoe Obshchestvo SSSR

Dokl Ross S-kh Akad Im K A Timiryazeva — Doklady Rossiiskoi Sel'skokhozyaistvennoi Akademii Imeni K. A. Timiryazeva

Dokl Sochinskogo Otd Geogr Ova SSSR — Doklady Sochinskogo Otdela Geograficheskogo Obshchestva SSSR

Dokl Soil Sci (Engl Transl) — Doklady Soil Science (English Translation)

Dokl Soobshch Kormoproizvod — Doklady i Soobshcheniya po Kormoproizvodstvu

Dokl Soobshch Uzhgorod Gos Univ Ser Biol — Doklady i Soobshcheniya Uzhgorodskogo Gosudarstvennogo Universiteta. Seriya Biologicheskaya

Dokl Soobshch Uzhgorod Gos Univ Ser Fiz Mat Khim — Doklady i Soobshcheniya Uzhgorodskogo Gosudarstvennogo Universiteta. Seriya Fiziko. Matematicheskaya i Khimicheskaya

Dokl Soobshch Uzhgorod Gos Univ Ser Fiz Mat Nauk — Doklady i Soobshcheniya Uzhgorodskogo Gosudarstvennogo Universiteta. Seriya Fiziko. Matematicheskikh Nauk

Dokl Sooshch Uzhgorod Gos Univ Ser Khim — Doklady i Soobshcheniya Uzhgorodskogo Gosudarstvennogo Universiteta. Seriya Khimicheskaya

Dokl Sov Geol Mezhdunar Geol Kongr — Doklady Sovetskikh Geologov Mezhdunarodnyi Geologicheskii Kongress

Dokl Tbilis Nauchn O-va Anat Gistol Embriol — Doklady Tbilisskogo Nauchnogo Obshchestva Anatomii, Gistologii, i Embriologii

Dokl Timiryazevsk S-kh Akad — Doklady Timiryazevskaya Sel'Skokhozyaistvennaya Akademiya

Dokl TSKHA — Doklady Timiryazevskaya Sel'skokhozyaistvennaya Akademiya

Dokl Vses Akad Sel'khoz Nauk — Doklady Vsesoyuznoi Akademii Sel'skokhozyaistvennykh Nauk Imeni V. I. Lenina

Dokl Vses Akad S-kh Nauk Im V I Lenina — Doklady Vsesoyuznoi Akademii Sel'skokhozyaistvennykh Nauk Imeni V. I. Lenina [*USSR*]

Dokl Vses Konf "Fiz Khrupkogo Razrusheniya" — Doklady Vsesoyuznoi Konferentsii "Fizika Khrupkogo Razrusheniya"

Dokl Vses Konf Teplofiz Svoistvam Veshchestv — Doklady Vsesoyuznoi Konferentsii po Teplofizicheskim Svoistvam Veshchestv
Dokl Vses Ordena Lenina Akad S-kh Nauk Im V I Lenina — Doklady Vsesoyuznoi Ordena Lenina Akademii Sel'skokhozyaistvennykh Nauk Imeni V. I. Lenina
Dok Raum — Dokumentation zur Raumentwicklung
Dok Str — Dokumentation Strasse
Doktorsavh Chalmers Tek Hoegsk — Doktorsavhandlingar vid Chalmers Tekniska Hoegskola [*Sweden*]
Dokum As Mitt — Dokumentationsdienst Asien Mitteilungen
DOKWA — Dokumentation Wasser
Dok Wasser — Dokumentation Wasser [*West Germany*]
Dok Zemed Lesn — Dokumentace Zemedelska a Lesnicka
Dolciani Math Exp — [*The*] Dolciani Mathematical Expositions
Dollars — Dollars and Sense
Doll & Sen — Dollars and Sense
Dolmetsch B — Bulletin: The Dolmetsch Foundation
Dom Comm — Domestic Commerce
Dom Eng — Domestic Engineering
Dom Engr — Dominion Engineer
Domest Anim Endocrinol — Domestic Animal Endocrinology
Domest Eng Heat Vent — Domestic Engineering. Heat and Ventilation [*England*]
Domest Heat News — Domestic Heating News [*England*]
Domestic Heat Air Cond News — Domestic Heating and Air Conditioning News
Dominion Observatory (Ottawa) Contr — Dominion Observatory (Ottawa). Contributions
Dominion Observatory Seismol Ser — Dominion Observatory. Seismological Series
Dom LR — Dominion Law Reports
Dom Mus Bull — Dominion Museum Bulletin [*Wellington*]
Dom Mus Rec Entomol (Wellington) — Dominion Museum Records in Entomology (Wellington)
Dom Mus Rec Zool (Wellington) — Dominion Museum Records in Zoology (Wellington)
Donauraum — Zeitschrift fuer Donauraum-Forschung
Dong-A Ronchong Dong-A Univ — Dong-A Ronchong. Dong-A University
Dongguk J — Dongguk Journal
Donnees Statist Limousin — Donnees Statistiques du Limousin
DOOPA — Documenta Ophthalmologica
DOP — Dumbarton Oaks Papers
Dop Akad Nauk Ukr RSR — Dopovidi Akademii Nauk Ukrains'koi RSR
DOPapers — Dumbarton Oaks Papers
DOPOA — Dornier-Post [*English Edition*]
Dopov Akad Nauk Ukr RSR — Dopovidi Akademii Nauk Ukrains'koi RSR
Dopov Akad Nauk Ukr RSR Ser B Heol Heofiz Khim Biol — Dopovidi Akademiyi Nauk Ukrayins'koyi RSR. Seriya B. Heolohiya, Heofizyka, Khimiya, ta Biolohiya
Dopov Akad Nauk Ukr RSR Ser B Heol Khim Biol Nauky — Dopovidi Akademiyi Nauk Ukrayins'koyi RSR. Seriya B. Heolohichni, Khimichni, ta Biolohichni Nauky
Dopovidi Akad Nauk Ukrain RSR Ser B — Dopovidi Akademii Nauk Ukrains'koi RSR. Seriya B
Dopov Povidomlenniya L'viv Derzh Univ — Dopovidi ta Povidomlenniya L'vivs'koho Derzhavnoho Universytetu
Dopov Povidomlennya L'viv Derzh Pedagog Inst Sekts Biol Khim — Dopovidt ta Povidomlennya. L'vivs'kii Derzhvnii Institut. Sektsiya Biologii Khimii
Dopov Ukr Akad Sil's'kogospod Nauk — Dopovidt Ukrains'koi Akademii Sil's'kogospodars'kikh Nauk
Dop Ukr A — Dopovidi Akademii Nauk Ukrains'koi RSR. Seriya A
Dop Ukr B — Dopovidi Akademii Nauk Ukrains'koi RSR. Seriya B
DoR — Downside Review
DOR — Reproduktie
Doshisha L — Doshisha Literature
Dosl Tvarinnitstvi — Doslidzhennya v Tvarinnitstvi
Dosl Zootekh L'vivskoho Zootekh Vet Inst — Doslidzhennya Zootekhniki L'vivskoho Zootekhnicheskoho Veterinars'koho Instituta
Doss Archeol — Dossiers de l'Archeologie
Doss Bis Jeune Afr Econ — Dossiers Bis Jeune Afrique et Economia
Doss Econ Lorraine — Dossiers de l'Economie Lorraine
Dossiers Archeol — Dossiers Archeologiques
Doss Mundo — Dossier Mundo
Doss Polit Agric Commune — Dossiers de la Politique Agricole Commune
Dostizh Nauki Tekh Peredovoi Opyt Promsti Stroit — Dostizheniya Nauki i Tekhniki i Peredovoi Opyt v Promyshlennosti i Stroitel'stve
Dottore Sci Agrar For — Il Dottore in Scienze Agrarie Forestali
DOVEB — Documenta Veterinaria (Brno)
Down Bt — Down Beat
Down Earth — Down to Earth
DownR — Downside Review
DowR — Downside Review [*Downside Abbey, Bath, England*]
DP — Dance Perspectives
DP — Dawson Packet
DP — Delegation en Perse. Memoires
DP — Deutsche Philologie

DP — Developmental Psychology
DP — Developments in Petrology [*Elsevier Book Series*]
DP — Die Presse
DP — Discourse Processes
DPAA — Dissertazioni. Pontificia Accademia Roman di Archeologia
DPALD — DOE [*US Department of Energy*] Patents Available for Licensing
DPAS — Developments in Palaeontology and Stratigraphy [*Elsevier Book Series*]
DPB — Developments in Plant Biology [*Elsevier Book Series*]
DPC — Dredging and Port Construction
DPDroh — Dopovidi ta Povidomlennja. Materialy Konferencij Drohobyc'koho Derzvnoho Pedahohicnoho Instytutu Imeni I. Ja. Franka. Serija Filolohicnych Nauk. Drohobyc
DPfBl — Deutsches Pfarrerblatt [*Essen, Germany*]
DPG — Developments in Precambrian Geology [*Elsevier Book Series*]
DPGB — Digest of Public General Bills [*Library of Congress*]
DPHFA — Dissertationes Pharmaceuticae et Pharmacologicae
DPL — De Proprietatibus Litterarum
DPLR — De Paul Law Review
DPMAA — Data Processing Magazine
DPPSA — Directory of Published Proceedings [*United States*]
DPR — Economic Progress Report
DPRAC — Delft Progress Report. Series A. Chemistry and Physics, Chemical and Physical Engineering
DPRBA — Delft Progress Report. Series B. Electrical, Electronic, and Information Engineering
DPRCB — Delft Progress Report. Series C. Mechanical and Aeronautical Engineering and Shipbuilding
DPRED — Delft Progress Report
DPRPB — Delft Progress Report. Series A-F
DPS — Developments in Petroleum Science [*Elsevier Book Series*]
DPTHDL — Developmental Pharmacology and Therapeutics
DQ — Denver Quarterly
DQ — Design Quarterly
DQR — Dutch Quarterly Review of Anglo-American Letters
DR — Dalhousie Review
DR — Deutsche Rundschau
DR — Diliman Review
DR — Downside Review
DR — Drake Law Review
DR — Drama: The Quarterly Theatre Review
DR — Drum. Inuvik
DR — Dublin Review
DR — Dun's Review
DR — Duquesne Review
DRAE — Diccionario de la Real Academia Espanola
DRAEA — Draegerheft
Draegerh — Draegerheft. Mitteilungen der Draegerwerk AG Luebeck
Draeger Rev — Draeger Review [*West Germany*]
Drag — Dragonfly
Dragoco Ber (Engl Edn) — Dragoco Berichte (English Edition)
Dragoco Rep Engl Ed — Dragoco Report. English Edition
Dragoco Rep Ger Ed — Dragoco Report. German Edition
Drake Law R — Drake Law Review
Drake L Rev — Drake Law Review
Dram — Drammaturgia
Drama R — Drama Review
Drama Rev — Drama Review
Drama Surv — Drama Survey
DramC — Drama Critique
DramS — Drama Survey
Draper — Draper of Australasia
Draper Fund Rep — Draper Fund Report
Draper Fund Rept — Draper Fund Report
Draper World Population Fund Rept — Draper World Population Fund Report
DRB — Director. Journal of Business Leadership
DRBIA — Drill Bit
DRCPE9 — Diabetes Research and Clinical Practice
DRCWDT — Colorado. Division of Wildlife. Division Report
DRD — Deltawerken. Driemaandelijks Bericht
DRDCD — Drilling - DCW [*Drilling Completion, Well Servicing*]
Dr Dobb's J — Dr. Dobb's Journal
Dr Dobb's J Comput Calisthenics and Orthod — Dr. Dobb's Journal of Computer Calisthenics and Orthodontia
Dredged Mater Res — Dredged Material Research
Dredging & Port Constr — Dredging and Port Construction
DreiN — Dreiser Newsletter
DREOR — Defence Research Board of Canada. Defence Research Establishment Ottawa. Reports
DREPR — Defence Research Board of Canada. Defence Research Establishment Pacific. Reports
Dresdner Kunstbl — Dresdner Kunstblaetter. Monatsschrift. Staatliche Kunstsammlungen Dresden
DRETN — Defence Research Board of Canada. Defence Research Establishment Ottawa. Technical Note
DRev — Deutsche Revue

Drev Vysk — Drevarsky Vyskum
Drev Vyskum — Drevarsky Vyskum
Drexel Libr Q — Drexel Library Quarterly
Drexel Tech J — Drexel Technical Journal
Drex Lib Q — Drexel Library Quarterly
DrG — Drew Gateway
DRGBAH — Danish Review of Game Biology
DRILA — Drilling
Drilling Contract — Drilling Contractor
Drill News — Drilling News
Drill Prod Pract — Drilling and Production Practice
DRINA — Drvna Industrija
Dritte Welt Mag — Dritte Welt Magazin
Driver Ed Bul — Driver Education Bulletin
Drives and Controls Int — Drives and Controls International
Dr LR — Drake Law Review
Dr Marit — Droit Maritime
Dr Marit Franc — Droit Maritime Francais
DrN — Druzba Narodov
DRO — Drogist. Vakblad voor Schoonheid, Gezondheid, en Hygiene
DROAAK — Deep Sea Research and Oceanographic Abstracts
DROFAZ — Data Record of Oceanographic Observations and Exploratory Fishing [*Hokkaido*]
DROGA — Drogownictwo
Droit et Pratique Commer Internat — Droit et Pratique du Commerce International
Dr Ouvr — Droit Ouvrier
DRPPD5 — Deep-Sea Research. Part A. Oceanographic Research Papers [*Later, Deep-Sea Research with Oceanogaphic Literature Review*]
Dr Pratique Com Int — Droit et Pratique du Commerce International
DRPRB — Druck Print
DrR — Drama Review
DRS — Data Resources Series [*Elsevier Book Series*]
DRs — Deutsche Rundschau
DRS — Dominion Report Service
Dr Sanit Soc — Droit Sanitaire et Social
DRSEDL — Diagnostic Radiology Series
DRSN — Drug Survival News
Dr Soc — Droit Social
DRSPA — Druckspiegel
DRSPAAJC — Documents et Rapports de la Societe Paleontologique et Archeologique de l'Arrondissement Judiciaire de Charleroi
DRTBB — Drug and Therapeutics Bulletin
DRTRD — Director
DRu — Deutsche Rundschau
Drug Abu MS — Drug Abuse Council. Monograph Series
Drug Abu PPS — Drug Abuse Council. Public Policy Series
Drug Abuse Prev Rep — Drug Abuse Prevention Report
Drug Action Drug Resist Bact — Drug Action and Drug Resistance in Bacteria
Drug Alcohol Depend — Drug and Alcohol Dependence
Drug Alert — Nurse's Drug Alert
Drug Allied Ind — Drug and Allied Industries
Drug Chem Exports — Drug and Chemical Exports
Drug Chem Toxicol — Drug and Chemical Toxicology
Drug Circ — Druggists Circular
Drug Cosmet — Drug and Cosmetic Industry
Drug and Cosmetic Ind — Drug and Cosmetic Industry
Drug Cosmet Ind — Drug and Cosmetic Industry
Drug Dev C — Drug Development Communications
Drug Dev Commun — Drug Development Communications
Drug Dev Ind Pharm — Drug Development and Industrial Pharmacy
Drug Dig — Drug Digests
Drug Enf — Drug Enforcement
Drug Enforce — Drug Enforcement
Drug Inf Bull — Drug Information Bulletin
Drug Inf J — Drug Information Journal
Drug Intel — Drug Intelligence and Clinical Pharmacy [*Formerly, Drug Intelligence*]
Drug Intell — Drug Intelligence [*Later, Drug Intelligence and Clinical Pharmacy*]
Drug Intell Clin Pharm — Drug Intelligence and Clinical Pharmacy [*Formerly, Drug Intelligence*]
Drug Metab — Drug Metabolism Reviews
Drug Metab Dispos — Drug Metabolism and Disposition
Drug Metab Disposition — Drug Metabolism and Disposition
Drug Metab Rev — Drug Metabolism Reviews
Drug Meta D — Drug Metabolism and Disposition
Drug Res — Drug Research
Drugs Health Care — Drugs in Health Care
Drugs Made Ger — Drugs Made in Germany
Drugs Pharm Sci — Drugs and the Pharmaceutical Sciences
Drug Stand — Drug Standards
Drug Ther — Drug Therapy
Drug Ther Bull — Drug and Therapeutics Bulletin
Drug Ther Hosp Ed — Drug Therapy. Hospital Edition

Drug Ther Prescr Pract Probl — Drug Therapy. Prescribing Practices and Problems
Drug Ther Rev — Drug Therapy. Reviews
Drug Vitam Allied Ind — Drug, Vitamin, and Allied Industries
DRUIA — Drug Intelligence [*Later, Drug Intelligence and Clinical Pharmacy*]
D Rund — Deutsche Rundschau
Drury Coll Bradley G Field Sta B — Drury College. Bradley Geological Field Station. Bulletin
Drvna Ind — Drvna Industrija
DRVYA — Drevarsky Vyskum
DRW — Repro en Druk
DRWEA — Draht-Welt
Dry Valley Drill Proj Bull — Dry Valley Drilling Project. Bulletin. Northern Illinois University. Department of Geology
DS — Danske Studier
DS — Deutsche Studien
DS — Developments in Sedimentology [*Elsevier Book Series*]
DS — Diderot Studies
DS — Dominican Studies
DS — Drama Survey
DS — Dynamic Stories
DSA — Dickens Studies. Annual
DSARDS — Dante Studies with the Annual Report of the Dante Society
DSASDE — Alabama. Agricultural Experiment Station. Auburn University. Agronomy and Soils Departmental Series
DSECEL — DGU [*Geological Survey of Denmark*] Series C
DSEG — Developments in Solid Earth Geophysics [*Elsevier Book Series*]
DSF — Dynamic Science Fiction
DSFNS — Deutsche-Slawische Forschungen zur Namenkunde und Siedlungsgeschichte
DSFTA — Dansk Skovforenings Tidsskrift
DSFTA5 — Dansk Skovforenings Tidsskrift
DSG — Deutsche Studien zur Geistesgeschichte
DSGEAX — Desinfektion und Gesundheitswesen
Dsgn Eng — Design Engineering
DSGRD7 — Delaware Sea Grant. Technical Report Del-SG
DSH — DSH [*Deafness, Speech, and Hearing*] Abstracts
DSHA — DSH [*Deafness, Speech, and Hearing*] Abstracts
DSHIP — Digest of Selected Health and Insurance Plans
DSI Bull — DSI [*Dairy Society International*] Bulletin
DSIJa — Doklady i Soobscenija Instituta Jazykozanija Akademiji Nauk SSSR
DSJOA — Defence Science Journal [*New Delhi*]
DSJOAA — Defence Science Journal
DSKSAR — Denki Seirigaku Kenkyu
DSKSAR — Electrophysiology
DSL — Danske Sprog-og Literaturselskab
DSLL — Duquesne Studies in Language and Literature
DSMHA — Discrete Mathematics
DSMJA — Delaware Medical Journal
DSMJBB — Dar Es Salaam Medical Journal
DSN — Dickens Studies. Newsletter
DSNGA6 — Denkschriften. Schweizerische Naturforschende Gesellschaft
DSNJDI — Dirasat Natural Sciences [*Amman*]
DSNQ — Design Quarterly
DSOL — Defects in Solids [*Elsevier Book Series*]
DSp — Deutsche Sprache
DSpir — Dictionnaire de Spiritualite [*Paris*]
DSPP — Digest of Selected Pension Plans [*Bureau of Labor Statistics*]
DSPS — Duquesne Studies. Philological Series
DSRAB9 — Desarrollo Rural en las Americas
DSS — Developments in Soil Science [*Elsevier Book Series*]
DSS — Dynamic Science Stories
DSS — XVIIe Siecle
DSSCDM — Developments in Soil Science
DSSSS — Developments in Solar System and Space Science [*Elsevier Book Series*]
DSt — Danske Studier
DSt — Deutsche Studien
DSUzU — Doklady i Soobscenija Uzgorodskogo Universiteta
DT — Daily Telegraph
DT — Developments in Toxicology and Environmental Science [*Elsevier Book Series*]
DT — Divus Thomas
D & T — Drama and Theatre
DT — Duscepoleznie Tchtenie
Dt ApothZtg — Deutsche Apotheker-Zeitung
DTB — Distribution
Dt Bienenkal — Deutsche Bienenkalender
Dt Bienenztg — Deutsche Bienenzeitung
Dt Bienenzucht — Deutsche Bienenzucht
DTBSD — Database [*United States*]
DTC — Dictionnaire de Theologie Catholique [*Paris*]
DTCFA — Documents Techniques. Charbonnages de France
DTD — Documentatieblad. Nieuwe Reeks
DTDRA — Denki Tsushin Daigaku Gakuho
DTE — Database

DTEGA2 — Dermatologia Tropica et Ecologia Geographica
Dt Ent Z — Deutsche Entomologische Zeitschrift
Dteol T — Dansk Teologisk Tidsskrift
DTESD — Developments in Toxicology and Environmental Science
DTFAA — Dansk Tidsskrift foer Farmaci
DTFAAN — Dansk Tidsskrift foer Farmaci
DTGDA — Denshi Tsushin Gakkai Rombunshi. Part D
DTGHD — Denshi Tsushin Gakkai Gijutsu Kenkyu Hokoku
DTGZA — Denki Tsushin Gakkai Zasshi
DTh — Deutsche Theologie: Monatsschrift fuer die Deutsche Evangelische Kirche
DTh — Divus Thomas
Dt Ill Bienenztg — Deutsche Illustrierte Bienenzeitung
Dt Imkerfuehrer — Deutsche Imkerfuehrer
Dt Imkerkal — Deutscher Imkerkalender
Dt Imkerztg — Deutsche Imkerzeitung
Dt Indinst Ber Wirtpol — Berichte. Deutsches Industrieinstitut zur Wirtschaftspolitik
Dt Inst Wirtschaftsforsch Wochenber — Deutsches Institut fuer Wirtschaftsforschung. Wochenbericht
DtIsrZtg — Deutsche Israelitische Zeitung [*Regensburg*]
DTKTA — Dansk Teknisk Tidsskrift
Dt Landwirt — Deutsche Landwirtschaft
Dt Landwirt (Berlin) — Deutsche Landwirtschaft (Berlin)
Dtl Arch — Deutschland Archiv
Dt LebensmittRdsch — Deutsche Lebensmittel Rundschau
DTM — Deutsche Texte des Mittelalters
Dt Med J — Deutsches Medizinisches Journal
Dt Med Wschr — Deutsche Medizinische Wochenschrift
Dt Milchwirt — Deutsche Milchwirtschaft
DTMNA — Datamation
DT (Newspr)(Tas) — Daily Telegraph Reports (Newspaper) (Tasmania)
DTR — Drug Therapy. Reviews [*Elsevier Book Series*]
DTS — Diarium Terrae Sanctae [*Jerusalem*]
Dtsch Aerztebl — Deutsches Aerzteblatt. Aerztliche Mitteilungen
Dtsch Agrartech — Deutsche Agrartechnik [*West Germany*]
Dtsch Akad Landwirtschaftwiss Berl Tagungber — Deutsche Akademie der Landwirtschaftwissenschaften zu Berlin. Tagungsberichte
Dtsch Akad Wiss Berlin Vortr Schr — Deutsche Akademie der Wissenschaften zu Berlin. Vortraege und Schriften
Dtsch Akad Wiss Berlin Zentralinst Phys Erde Veroeff — Deutsche Akademie der Wissenschaften zu Berlin. Zentralinstituts Physik der Erde. Veroeffentlichungen
Dtsch Apoth — Deutsche Apotheker
Dtsch Apoth-Ztg — Deutsche Apotheker-Zeitung
Dtsch Apoth Ztg Beil Neue Arzneim Spez — Deutsche Apotheker-Zeitung. Beilage. Neue Arzneimittel und Spezialitaeten
Dtsch Archit — Deutsches Architektenblatt [*West Germany*]
Dtsch Arch Klin Med — Deutsches Archiv fuer Klinische Medizin
Dtsch Aussenpolitik — Deutsche Aussenpolitik [*East Germany*]
Dtsch Baumsch — Deutsche Baumschule
Dtsch Bauz — Deutsche Bauzeitschrift. Fachblatt fuer Entwurf und Ausfuehrung
Dtsch Bauz Fachbl Entwurf Ausfuhrung — Deutsche Bauzeitschrift. Fachblatt fuer Entwurf und Ausfuehrung [*West Germany*]
Dtsch Beitr Geotech — Deutsche Beitraege zur Geotechnik
Dtsch Bibliogr Halbjahres Verzeichnis — Deutsche Bibliographie. Halbjahres-Verzeichnis [*West Germany*]
Dtsch Bibliogr Woech Verzeichnis A — Deutsche Bibliographie. Woechentliches Verzeichnis. Reihe A [*West Germany*]
Dtsch Bibliogr Woech Verzeichnis B — Deutsche Bibliographie. Woechentliches Verzeichnis. Reihe B [*West Germany*]
Dtsch Bibliogr Woech Verzeichnis C — Deutsche Bibliographie. Woechentliches Verzeichnis. Reihe C [*West Germany*]
Dtsch Bienenwirtsch — Deutsche Bienenwirtschaft
Dtsch Chem Z — Deutsche Chemiker-Zeitschrift
Dtsch Dendrol Ges Kurzmitt — Deutsche Dendrologische Gesellschaft Kurzmitteilungen
Dtsch Destill Ztg — Deutsche Destillateur Zeitung
Dtsch Druckgewerbe — Deutsche Druckgewerbe
Dtsche A — Deutsche Annalen
Dtsch Aussenpolit — Deutsche Aussenpolitik
Dtsch Eisenbahntech — Deutsche Eisenbahntechnik
Dtsch Elektrotech — Deutsche Elektrotechnik [*East Germany*]
Dtsch Engl Med Rundsch — Deutsch-Englische Medizinische Rundschau
Dtsch Entomol Z — Deutsche Entomologische Zeitschrift
Dtsch Stud — Deutsche Studien. Vierteljahreshefte fuer Vergleichende Gegenwartskunde
Dtsch Z Philos — Deutsche Zeitschrift fuer Philosophie
Dtsch Farben Z — Deutsche Farben Zeitschrift
Dtsch Faserst Spinnpflanzen — Deutsche Faserstoffe und Spinnpflanzen
Dtsch Fischereirundsch — Deutsche Fischereirundschau
Dtsch Fisch Rundsch — Deutsche Fischerei-Rundschau
Dtsch Fischwirtsch — Deutsche Fischwirtschaft
Dtsch Fisch Ztg — Deutsche Fischerei Zeitung
Dtsch Flungtec — Deutsche Flungtechnik

Dtsch Forschungsdienst Sonderber Kernenerg — Deutscher Forschungsdienst. Sonderbericht Kernenergie [*West Germany*]
Dtsch Forschungsgem Farbst Komm Mitt — Deutsche Forschungsgemeinschaft Farbstoff Kommission Mitteilung
Dtsch Forschungsgem Komm Erforsch Luftverunreinigung Mitt — Deutsche Forschungsgemeinschaft Kommission zur Erforschung der Luftverunreinigung. Mitteilung [*West Germany*]
Dtsch Forschungsgem Komm Geowiss Gemeinschaftsforsch Mitt — Deutsche Forschungsgemeinschaft Kommission fuer Geowissenschaftliche Gemeinschaftsforschung Mitteilung [*West Germany*]
Dtsch Forschungsgem Mitt — Deutsche Forschungsgemeinschaft Mitteilungen [*West Germany*]
Dtsch Forsch Versuchsanst Luft Raumfahrt Nachr — Deutsche Forschungs- und Versuchsanstalt fuer Luft und Raumfahrt. Nachrichten [*West Germany*]
Dtsch Gaertnerboerse — Deutsche Gaertnerboerse
Dtsch Gartenbau — Deutsche Gartenbau
Dtsch Ges Arbeitsmed Jahrestag — Deutsche Gesellschaft fuer Arbeitsmedizin. Jahrestagung
Dtsch Ges Mineraloelwiss Kohlechem Compend — Deutsche Gesellschaft fuer Mineraloelwissenschaft und Kohlechemie. Compendium [*West Germany*]
Dtsch Gesundheitsw — Deutsche Gesundheitswesen
Dtsch Gesundheitswes — Deutsche Gesundheitswesen
Dtsch Gewaesserkd Mitt — Deutsche Gewaesserkundliche Mitteilungen
Dtsch Hebe Foerdertech — Deutsche Hebe und Foerdertechnik
Dtsch Hydrogr Inst Jahresber — Deutsches Hydrographisches Institut. Jahresbericht
Dtsch Hydrogr Z — Deutsche Hydrographische Zeitschrift
Dtsch Inst Wirtschaftsforsch Wochenber — Deutsches Institut fuer Wirtschaftsforschung. Wochenbericht
Dtsch Kaelte Klimatech Ver Abh — Deutscher Kaelte und Klimatechnischer Verein. Abhandlungen
Dtsch Kaeltetech Ver Abh — Deutscher Kaeltetechnischer Verein. Abhandlungen
Dtsch Kongr Perinat Med — Deutscher Kongress fuer Perinatale Medizin
Dtsch Kraftfahrtforsch Strassenverkehrstech — Deutsche Kraftfahrtforschung Strassenverkehrstechnik
Dtsch Krankenpflegez — Deutsche Krankenpflegezeitschrift
Dtsch Kunstseiden Ztg Spezialorgan Zellwolle — Deutsche Kunstseiden Zeitung und Spezialorgan fuer Zellwolle
Dtsch Landwirtsch — Deutsche Landwirtschaft
Dtsch Landwirtsch Ges Mitt — Deutsche Landwirtschafts-Gesellschaft Mitteilungen
Dtsch Landwirtsch Rundsch — Deutsche Landwirtschaftliche Rundschau
Dtsch Lebensm Rundsch — Deutsche Lebensmittel Rundschau
Dtsch Licht Wasserfach Ztg — Deutsche Licht- und Wasserfach Zeitung
Dtsch Luftfahrt Raumfahrt Forschungsber — Deutsche Luft- und Raumfahrt. Forschungsbericht
Dtsch Luftfahrt Raumfahrt Mitt — Deutsche Luft- und Raumfahrt. Mitteilung
Dtsch Luft Raumfahrt Mitt — Deutsche Luft- und Raumfahrt. Mitteilung
Dtschl-Union-Dienst — Deutschland-Union-Dienst [*West Germany*]
Dtsch Med Forsch — Deutsche Medizinische Forschung
Dtsch Med J — Deutsches Medizinisches Journal
Dtsch Med Wochenschr — Deutsche Medizinische Wochenschrift
Dtsch Med Wschr — Deutsche Medizinische Wochenschrift
Dtsch Metallwaren Ind — Deutsche Metallwaren Industrie
Dtsch Milchwirtsch (Gelsenkirchen) — Deutsche Milchwirtschaft (Gelsenkirchen) [*West Germany*]
Dtsch Milchwirtsch (Leipzig) — Deutsche Milchwirtschaft (Leipzig)
Dtsch Molkerei Ztg — Deutsche Molkerei-Zeitung
Dtsch Molk Fettwirtsch — Deutsche Molkerei- und Fettwirtschaft
Dtsch Mot Z — Deutsche Motor-Zeitschrift
Dtsch Muellerei — Deutsche Muellerei
Dtsch Mus Abh Ber — Deutsches Museum. Abhandlungen und Berichte
Dtsch Nahrungsm Rundsch — Deutsche Nahrungsmittel. Rundschau
Dtsch Ophthalmol Ges Ber — Deutsche Ophthalmologische Gesellschaft. Bericht
Dtsch Ophthalmol Ges Heidelberg Ber Zusammenkunft — Deutsche Ophthalmologische Gesellschaft in Heidelberg. Bericht ueber die Zusammenkunft
Dtsch Opt Wochenschr Cent Ztg Opt Mech — Deutsche Optische Wochenschrift und Central-Zeitung fuer Optik und Mechanik
Dtsch Opt Wochenschrift — Deutsche Optische Wochenschrift
Dtsch Pelztierz — Deutsche Pelztierzuchter
Dtsch Roheisen — Deutsches Roheisen
Dtsch Schiffahrtsarch — Deutsches Schiffahrtsarchiv
Dtsch Schwarzbunte — Deutsche Schwarzbunte
Dtsch Stomatol — Deutsche Stomatologie
Dtsch Tab Ztg — Deutsche Tabak Zeitung
Dtsch Tech — Deutsche Technik
Dtsch Textilgewerbe — Deutsche Textilgewerbe
Dtsch Textiltech — Deutsche Textiltechnik
Dtsch Textilwirtsch — Deutsche Textilwirtschaft
Dtsch Tieraerztl Wochenschr — Deutsche Tieraerztliche Wochenschrift

Dtsch Tieraerztl Wochenschr Tieraerztl Rundsch — Deutsche Tieraerztliche Wochenschrift Tieraerztliche Rundschau
Dtsch Tierarztebl — Deutsches Tierarzteblatt
Dtsch Toepfer Ziegler Ztg — Deutsche Toepfer und Ziegler Zeitung
Dtsch Tropenmed Z — Deutsche Tropenmedizinische Zeitschrift
Dtsch Tuberk Bl — Deutsches Tuberkulose Blatt
Dtsch Ver Gas Wasserfachmaennern Schriften Gas — Deutscher Verein von Gas- und Wasserfachmaennern. Schriftenreihe. Gas
Dtsch Versuchsanst Luft Raumfahrt Ber — Deutsche Versuchsanstalt fuer Luft- und Raumfahrt. Bericht
Dtsch Verwaltungsbl Verwaltungsarch — Deutsches Verwaltungsblatt und Verwaltungsarchiv
Dtsch Weinbau — Deutsche Weinbau
Dtsch Wein Ztg — Deutsche Wein-Zeitung
Dtsch Wirker Ztg — Deutsche Wirker Zeitung
Dtsch Wollen Gewerbe — Deutsche Wollen Gewerbe
Dtsch Zahnaerztl Wochenschr — Deutsche Zahnaerztliche Wochenschrift
Dtsch Zahnaerztl Z — Deutsche Zahnaerztliche Zeitschrift
Dtsch Zahn- Mund- Kieferheilkd — Deutsche Zahn- Mund- und Kieferheilkunde
Dtsch Z Gesamte Gerichtl Med — Deutsche Zeitschrift fuer die Gesamte Gerichtliche Medizin
Dtsch Z Nervenheilkd — Deutsche Zeitschrift fuer Nervenheilkunde
Dtsch Z Verdau Stoffwechselkr — Deutsche Zeitschrift fuer Verdauungs und Stoffwechselkrankheiten
DTSERD — Driver and Traffic Safety Education Research Digest
DTT — Dansk Teologisk Tidsskrift [*Copenhagen*]
DTTid — Dansk Teologisk Tidsskrift
DTTP — Documents to the People
DtVis — Deutsche Vierteljahrsschrift fuer Literaturwissenschaft und Geistesgeschichte
Dt Vischr — Deutsche Vierteljahrsschrift fuer Literaturwissenschaft und Geistesgeschichte
DTW — DTW. Deutsche Tierarztliche Wochenschrift
Dt Wirtinst Forschhft — Deutsches Wirtschaftsinstitut Forschungshefte
DU — Deutschunterricht
DUA — Deutschunterricht fuer Auslaender
DUABA8 — Delaware. Agricultural Experiment Station. Bulletin
Dublin J Med Sci — Dublin Journal of Medical Science
Dublin Med Press — Dublin Medical Press
Dublin Q J Med Sc — Dublin Quarterly Journal of Medical Science
Dublin Q J Sc — Dublin Quarterly Journal of Science
DublinRev — Dublin Review
Dublin ULJ — Dublin University. Law Journal
Dublin UL Rev — Dublin University. Law Review
Dub Mag — Dublin Magazine
DubR — Dublin Review
Dub Rev — Dublin Review
DUBSDX — Dhaka University Studies. Part B
Dub Univ — Dublin University Magazine
Dudley Ednl J — Dudley Educational Journal
DuE — Dichtung und Erkenntnis
DUEMEV — Directory of Unpublished Experimental Mental Measures
Duesseldorfer Jahrb — Duesseldorfer Jahrbuch
Duinen — De Duinen. Bulletin du Centre Scientifique et Culturel de l'Abbaye des Dunes et du Westhoek
DUJ — Durham University Journal
DUKAB — Dopovidi Akademii Nauk Ukrains'koi RSR. Seriya A. Fiziko-Tekhnichni ta Matematichni Nauki
Duke Bar J — Duke Bar Journal
Duke B J — Duke Bar Journal
Duke Div R — Duke Divinity School. Review
Duke Law J — Duke Law Journal
Duke L J — Duke Law Journal
Duke Math J — Duke Mathematical Journal
Duke Univ Mar Stn Bull — Duke University Marine Station Bulletin
Duke Univ Math Ser — Duke University Mathematics Series
DUKRA — Dopovidi Akademii Nauk Ukrains'koi RSR
Du Kunstz — Du Kunstzeitschrift
Du LJ — Duke Law Journal
DULN — Duke University Library Notes
DULR — Dublin University Law Review
DULR — Duquesne University. Law Review
Dumbarton OP — Dumbarton Oaks Papers
DumbOaksP — Dumbarton Oaks Papers [*Cambridge, MA*]
DUMJA — Duke Mathematical Journal
DUMP HEAP — Journal of Diverse Unsung Miracle Plants for Healthy Evolution among People
DUN — Dun's Business Month
DunR — [*The*] Dunwoodie Review
Dun's — Dun's Review
Dun's Int R — Dun's International Review
Dun's R — Dun's Review
Dun's Stat R — Dun's Statistical Review
DUODA — Duodecim

DUPMA — Du Pont Magazine
Du Pont Mag — Du Pont Magazine
Du Pont Mag Eur Edn — Du Pont Magazine. European Edition
Duq — Duquesne Law Review
Duq LR — Duquesne Law Review
Duq L Rev — Duquesne Law Review
Duquesne L Rev — Duquesne Law Review
Duquesne Sci Couns — Duquesne Science Counselor
Duquesne U L Rev — Duquesne University. Law Review
Durban Mus Art Gallery Annu Rep — Durban Museum and Art Gallery. Annual Report
Durban Mus Novit — Durban Museum Novitates
Durferrit Hausmitt — Durferrit Hausmitteilungen
Durham Res — Durham Research Review
Durham Univ — Durham University Journal
Durham Univ Biol Soc J — Durham University Biological Society. Journal
Durham Univ Dep Geogr Occas Publ New Ser — Durham University. Department of Geography. Occasional Publications. New Series
Durham Univ J — Durham University Journal
DurUJ — Durham University Journal
Durzh Vestn — Durzhaven Vestnik [*Bulgaria*]
DUS — Dacca University. Studies
Dusanbin Gos Ped Inst Ucen Zap — Dusanbinskii Gosudarstvennyi Pedagogiceskii Institut Imeni T. G. Sevcenko Ucenyi Zapiski
DuszpPZ — Duszpasterz Polski Zagranica [*Rome*]
Dutch Art & Archre Today — Dutch Art and Architecture Today
Dutch Q Rev — Dutch Quarterly Review of Anglo-American Letters
DutchS — Dutch Studies
DUULD5 — Annual Research Reviews. Duodenal Ulcer
DuV — Dichtung und Volkstum
DuW — Dichtung und Wirklichkeit
DUZ — Deutsche Universitaetszeitung
DV — Deutsche Vierteljahrsschrift
DV — Dichtung und Volkstum
DV — Dieu Vivant [*Paris*]
DVA — Development and Change
DVASA — Doklady Vsesoyuznoi Akademii Sel'skokhozyaistvennykh Nauk Imeni V. I. Lenina
DVBSA3 — Developments in Biological Standardization
DVCBAP — Developmental and Cell Biology
DVDSAD — Davidsonia
DVE — Developing Economies
DVENA3 — Dermatologiya i Venerologiya
DVI — Development Forum. Business Edition
Dvigateli Vnutr Sgoraniya (Kharkov) — Dvigateli Vnutrennego Sgoraniya (Kharkov) [*Ukrainian SSR*]
DVIOJ — Deutsche Vereinigung fuer die Interessen der Osteuropaeischen Juden
DVJS — Deutsche Vierteljahrsschrift fuer Literaturwissenschaft und Geistesgeschichte
DVLG — Deutsche Vierteljahrsschrift fuer Literaturwissenschaft und Geistesgeschichte
DVMMB7 — Data Processing in Medicine
DVMMB7 — Datenverarbeitung in der Medizin
DVPMAL — Developmental Psychology. Monograph
DVPSD8 — Developments in Plant and Soil Sciences
DVS — Development Forum
DVSB — Danske Videnskabernes Selskabs Biologiske. Skrifter
DVS Ber — DVS [*Deutscher Verband fuer Schweisstechnik*] Berichte [*West Germany*]
DVSM — Danske Videnskabernes Selskabs Historishfilologiske Meddelelser
DVSM — Det Kongelige Danske Videnskabernes Selskab. Historisk-Filologiske Meddelelser [*Copenhagen*]
DVSS — Danske Videnskabernes Selskabs Skrifter
DVT — Dejiny Ved a Techniky
DVZ Dtsch Verkehrs-Ztg — DVZ Deutsche Verkehrs-Zeitung [*West Germany*]
DW — Deutsche Woche
D d W — Dialectes de Wallonie
DW — Die Welt
DW — Die Weltliteratur
DWB — Deutsche Warande en Belfort
DWD — Deutsche Wissenschaftlicher Dienst
DWD — Dream World
DWEV — Deutsche Wissenschaft, Erziehung, und Volksbildung
DWINAU — Defenders of Wildlife News
DWLIAU — Defenders of Wildlife Magazine [*Later, Defenders*]
DW & RB — Daily Weather and River Bulletin
DWZP — Deutsche Wissenschaftliche Zeitschrift fuer Polen
Dyason H P — Dyaon House Papers
Dye Ind — Dyeing Industry [*Japan*]
Dyes Chem Tech Bull — Dyes and Chemicals Technical Bulletin. Paper Industry Issue
Dyn — Dynamite
Dynam Psych — Dynamische Psychiatrie
Dyn Atmos & Oceans — Dynamics of Atmospheres and Oceans

Dyn Mass Spectrom — Dynamic Mass Spectrometry
Dyn Psychiatr — Dynamische Psychiatrie
Dyn Solids Liq Neutron Scattering (1977) — Dynamics of Solids and Liquids by Neutron Scattering (1977)
Dyn Supervision — Dynamic Supervision
DYSUD — Dynamic Supervision
DYWIDAG Ber — DYWIDAG [*Dyckerhoff und Widmann AG*] Berichte [*West Germany*]
DzD — Dzejas Diena
DZI — Zuckerindustrie. Landwirtschaft, Technik, Chemie, Wirtschaft
DzKarSt — Dzveli Kartuli Enis K'atedris Stomebi
DZKR — Deutsche Zeitschrift fuer Kirchenrecht
Dz Lit — Dziennik Literacki
DZZEA — Deutsche Zahnaerztliche Zeitschrift

E

Earthqu Inf Bull — Earthquake Information Bulletin
Earthqu Notes — Earthquake Notes
Earth S — Earth Science
Earth Sci — Earth Science
Earth Sci Bull — Earth Science Bulletin
Earth Sci Digest — Earth Science Digest
Earth Sci Inst Special Pub — Earth Science Institute. Special Publication
Earth Sci J — Earth Science Journal
Earth Sci Jour — Earth Science Journal
Earth Sci R — Earth Science Reviews
Earth Sci Rev — Earth Science Reviews
Earth Shelter Dig Energy Rep — Earth Shelter Digest and Energy Report
Earth Surf Process — Earth Surface Processes
Earth Surf Processes — Earth Surface Processes
Earth Surf Processes and Landforms — Earth Surface Processes and Landforms
EAS — Essays in Arts and Sciences
EASCD — Earth Sciences
E Asian Executive Rep — East Asian Executive Reports
EASJ Th — East Asia Journal of Theology
EASMD — Engineering Aspects of Magnetohydrodynamics
East Afr Agric For J — East African Agricultural and Forestry Journal
East Afr Agric For Res Organ Annu Rep — East African Agricultural and Forestry Research Organization. Annual Report
East Afr Agric For Res Organ For Tech Note — East African Agriculture and Forestry Research Organization. Forestry Technical Note
East Afr Agric For Res Organ Rec Res Annu Rep — East African Agriculture and Forestry Research Organization. Record of Research. Annual Report
East Afr Agric J — East African Agricultural Journal
East Afr Agric J Kenya Tanganyika Uganda Zanzibar — East African Agricultural Journal of Kenya, Tanganyika, Uganda, and Zanzibar
East Afr Common Serv Organ East Afr Inst Med Res Annu Rep — East African Common Services Organization. East African Institute for Medical Research. Annual Report
East Afr Freshw Fish Res Org Annu Rep — East African Freshwater Fisheries Research Organization. Annual Report
East Afr Geogr R — East African Geographical Review
East Afr Inst Malaria Vector-Borne Dis Annu Rep — East African Institute of Malaria and Vector-Borne Diseases. Annual Report
East Afr Inst Med Res Annu Rep — East African Institute for Medical Research. Annual Report
East Afr J Med Res — East African Journal of Medical Research
East Afr J Rur Develop — Eastern Africa Journal of Rural Development
East Afr LR — Eastern Africa Law Review
East Afr L Rev — Eastern Africa Law Review
East Afr Med J — East African Medical Journal
East Afr Nat Resour Res Counc Annu Rep — East African Natural Resources Research Council. Annual Report
East Afr Trypanosomiasis Res Organ Annu Rep — East African Trypanosomiasis Research Organization. Annual Report
East Afr Trypanosomiasis Res Organ Rep — East African Trypanosomiasis Research Organization. Report
East Afr Tuberc Invest Cent Annu Rep — East African Tuberculosis Investigation Centre. Annual Report
East Afr Vet Res Organ Annu Rep — East African Veterinary Research Organization. Annual Report
East Afr Virus Res Inst Rep — East African Virus Research Institute. Report
East Afr Wildl J — East African Wildlife Journal
East Anthro — Eastern Anthropologist
East Anthropol — Eastern Anthropologist
East As Cult Stud — East Asian Cultural Studies
East Asian R — East Asian Review
East As R — East Asian Review
East Bay — East Bay Voice
East Buddhist — Eastern Buddhist
EastChQ — Eastern Churches Quarterly [*Ramsgate, London*]
East Ch R — Eastern Churches Review
East Econ — Eastern Economist
East End Environ — East End Environment
Eastern Africa J Rural Development — Eastern Africa Journal of Rural Development
Eastern Anthropol — Eastern Anthropologist
Eastern Eur Econ — Eastern European Economics
East Europ Quart — East European Quarterly
East Eur Q — East European Quarterly
East For Prod Lab (Can) Rep — Eastern Forest Products Laboratory (Canada). Report
East Fruit Grow — Eastern Fruit Grower
East Grape Grow Winery News — Eastern Grape Grower and Winery News
East Horiz — Eastern Horizon
East Librn — Eastern Librarian
East Malays Geol Surv Rep — East Malaysia Geological Survey. Report
East Malling Res Stn Annu Rep — East Malling Research Station. Annual Report

East Malling Res Stn (Maidstone England) Rep — East Malling Research Station (Maidstone, England). Report
Eastman Org Chem Bull — Eastman Organic Chemical Bulletin
East Met Rev — Eastern Metals Review
East Midl Geogr — East Midland Geographer
East Pharm — Eastern Pharmacist
East Tenn Hist Soc Publ — East Tennessee Historical Society. Publications
East Underw — Eastern Underwriter
East West — East West Journal
EAT — Economic Inquiry
Eau Ind — Eau et l'Industrie
Eau Que — Eau du Quebec
EAW — Environmental Policy and Law
EAZ — Ethnographisch-Archaeologische Zeitschrift
EB — Eastern Buddhist
EB — Educational Broadcasting
EB — Encyclopaedia Britannica
EB — Environment and Behavior
EB — Estudios Biblicos
EB — Etudes Balzaciennes
EB — Etudes Bibliques [*Paris*]
EB — Everybody's Magazine
EBADAS — Endocrine Bioassay Data
EBAFE — Economic Bulletin for Asia and the Far East [*Later, Economic Bulletin for Asia and the Pacific*]
EBALD — Energy at Booz-Allen
EBB — Economic Analysis and Workers' Management (Beograd)
EBB — Eibei Bungaku [*British and American Literature: The Rikkyo Review of Arts and Letters*]
EBB — Evangelische Blaetter aus Bethlehem
EBC — Economic Bulletin/Warta Cafi
EBE — Economic Outlook
EBEH — Environment and Behavior
EBEUA — Economic Bulletin for Europe
EBG — Economic Bulletin of Ghana
EBI — Educational Broadcasting International
EBI — Electronic Business
EBI — Energy Bibliography and Index [*Gulf Publishing Co.*] [*Houston, TX*]
EBI — Estudios Biblicos
EBIB — Encyclopaedia Biblica
EBib — Estudios Biblicos
EBIPA — Enka Biniiru To Porima
EBJ — Employee Benefits Journal
EBMOA — Elektronika Bol'shikh Moshchnostei
EBn — Enchiridion Biblicum. Editionis Napoli/Roma
EBN — Essobron
EBPR — Employee Benefit Plan Review
EBR — Educational Broadcasting Review
EBra — Estudos Brasileiros
EBS Bulletin — Bulletin. Experimental Building Station
EBSC — Eibungaku Shicho [*Current Thoughts in English Literature*]
Ebsco Bull Ser Changes — Ebsco Bulletin of Serials Changes
EBSK — Erlanger Beitrage zur Sprach- und Kunstwissenschaft
EBT — Etudes Balkaniques Tchecoslovaques
EBTA J — EBTA [*Eastern Business Teachers Association*] Journal
EBTA Y — EBTA [*Eastern Business Teachers Association*] Yearbook
E B Tch — Etudes Balkaniques Tchecoslovaques
EBU — Economic Bulletin for Europe
E Buddhist — Eastern Buddhist
EBU Rev — EBU [*European Broadcasting Union*] Review
EBU Rev A — EBU [*European Broadcasting Union*] Review. Part A
EBU Rev Part A — EBU [*European Broadcasting Union*] Review. Part A. Technical [*Switzerland*]
EBU Rev Tech — EBU [*European Broadcasting Union*] Review. Technical
EBYLA2 — Embryologia
EByz — Etudes Byzantines
EC — Ecology
EC — Economica
EC — Economist
EC — Education and Culture
EC — Egypte Contemporaine
EC — Essays in Criticism
EC — Etudes Celtiques
EC — Journal of Educational Computing Research
ECA — Economic Information on Argentina
Ec An — Economic Analysis
ECarm — Ephemerides Carmeliticae
ECB — Estudos de Castelo Branco
ECBOA — Economic Botany
ECBU — Economic Bulletin. Bank of Norway
Ec Bul Eur — Economic Bulletin for Europe
ECCND — Electric Comfort Conditioning News
ECEA — Exceptional Child Education Abstracts [*Later, ECER*]
ECelt — Etudes Celtiques
E Cent — Eighteenth Century
E Cent Eur — East Central Europe

ECG — Egyptian Cotton Gazette [*Alexandria*]
ECGEA — Economic Geography
ECGLA — Economic Geology and the Bulletin of the Society of Economic Geologists
ECGWAK — Empire Cotton Growing Corporation. Review
ECGYA — Ecology [*English Translation*]
ECh — Enseignement Chretien
Echanges Int Develop — Echanges Internationaux et Developpement
Echang Univ — Echangiste Universel. Revue Mensuelle des Collectionneurs de Timbres et des Numismates
ECHC — Etudes Carmelitaines Historiques et Critiques
ECHMB — Electrochemistry
EchO — Echos d'Orient
Echo Brass — Echo de la Brasserie
Echo Mines Metall — Echo des Mines et de la Metallurgie [*France*]
Echo Rech — Echo des Recherches
Echo Vet — Echo Veterinaire
EChr — Enseignement Chretien
ECI — Economist
ECIN — Economic Indicators
ECIND — Economic Inquiry
ECIWDSS — Environment Canada. Inland Waters Directorate. Scientific Series
ECJ — Economic Journal [*United Kingdom*]
ECJOA — Economic Journal
ECJPA — Endocrinologia Japonica
ECJPAE — Endocrinologia Japonica
Eck — Eckart [*Berlin*]
ECK — Economic and Commercial News
Eckart J — Eckart Jahrbuch [*Witten*]
E Cl — Etudes Classiques
ECLA — Etudes Classiques
EClas — Estudios Clasicos
EClass — Les Etudes Classiques [*Namur*]
ECLED — Economics Letters
Ecl Engin — Eclectic Engineering Magazine [*Van Nostrand's*]
Eclet Quim — Ecletica Quimica
E-C Life — Eighteenth-Century Life
Ecl M — Eclectic Magazine
Ecl Mus — Eclectic Museum
Eclogae Geol Helv — Eclogae Geologicae Helvetiae
Ecl R — Eclectic Review
ECM — Econometrica
ECM — Estudios de Cultura Maya
ECMAA — Economie et Medecine Animales [*France*]
ECMCC — Encyclopedie Medico-Chirurgicale
ECMM — Etudes Carmelitaines Mystiques et Missionnaires
ECMOA — Ecological Monographs
ECMTA — Econometrica
ECN — Economist
ECN — Estudios de Cultura Nahuatl
Ec N Bulg — Economic News of Bulgaria
ECNEA — Electroencephalography and Clinical Neurophysiology
ECNEAZ — Electroencephalography and Clinical Neurophysiology
EC Nebr Univ Coop Ext Serv — EC. Cooperative Extension Service. University of Nebraska
ECNSB — Electrical Consultant
ECO — Economica
ECO — Environment Centre Outlook
Eco Argent — Economic Information on Argentina
ECOBDY — Eisenhower Consortium. Bulletin
Eco Cient — Eco Cientifico
ECOGA — Ecologist
ECOL — Ecology
ECOLA — Ecology [*United States*]
Ecol Abstr — Ecological Abstracts
Ecol Action Newsl — Ecology Action Newsletter
Ecol Bull — Ecological Bulletin [*Sweden*]
Ecol Bull - NFR (Statens Naturvetensk Forskningsrad) — Ecological Bulletins - NFR (Statens Naturvetenskapliga Forskningsrad)
Ecol Conserv — Ecology and Conservation
Ecol Ent — Ecological Entomology
Ecol Entom — Ecological Entomology
Ecol Entomol — Ecological Entomology
Ecol Food Nutr — Ecology of Food and Nutrition
Ecol Law Q — Ecology Law Quarterly
Ecol LQ — Ecology Law Quarterly
Ecol L Quart — Ecology Law Quarterly
Ecol Model — Ecological Modelling
Ecol Monogr — Ecological Monographs
Ecology L Q — Ecology Law Quarterly
Ecol Q — Ecologist Quarterly [*Later, Ecologist*] [*England*]
Ecol Res Comm Bull — Ecological Research Committee. Bulletin
Ecol Rev — Ecological Review
Ecol Rev — Ecology Review
Ecol Soc Aust Mem — Ecological Society of Australia. Memoirs

Ecol Soc Aust Proc — Ecological Society of Australia. Proceedings
Ecol Stud — Ecological Studies
ECOMA — Electrical Construction and Maintenance
Econ — Economia
Econ — Economist
EconAb — Economic Abstracts
Econ Activity — Economic Activity in Western Australia
Econ Activity in WA — Economic Activity in Western Australia
Econ Activity WA — Economic Activity in Western Australia
Econ Act West Aust — Economic Activity in Western Australia
Econ Aff — Economic Affairs
Econ Afr — Economic Bulletin for Africa
Econ Agr (Paris) — Economie Agricole (Paris)
Econ Anal & Policy — Economic Analysis and Policy
Econ Analysis and Policy (NS) — Economic Analysis and Policy (New Series)
Econ Ann — Economic Annalist
Econ Appl — Economie Appliquee
Econ Appliq — Economie Appliquee
Econ Appliquee — Economie Appliquee
ECONB — Electrical Contracting [*United States*]
Econ B Afr — Economic Bulletin for Africa
Econ B Asia Far East — Economic Bulletin for Asia and the Far East [*Later, Economic Bulletin for Asia and the Pacific*]
Econ B Asia Pacific — Economic Bulletin for Asia and the Pacific
Econ B (Athens) — Economic Bulletin. Commercial Bank of Greece (Athens)
Econ B (Cairo) — Economic Bulletin. National Bank of Egypt (Cairo)
Econ B Europe — Economic Bulletin for Europe
Econ B Latin Amer — Economic Bulletin for Latin America
Econ B (Oslo) — Economic Bulletin (Oslo)
Econ Bot — Economic Botany
Econ Botan — Economic Botany
Econ Bul A — Economic Bulletin for Asia and the Pacific
Econ Bul Asia and Far East — Economic Bulletin for Asia and the Far East [*Later, Economic Bulletin for Asia and the Pacific*]
Econ Bul Asia and Pacific — Economic Bulletin for Asia and the Pacific
Econ Bul Europe — Economic Bulletin for Europe
Econ Bull Eur — Economic Bulletin for Europe
Econ Bull for Europe — Economic Bulletin for Europe
Econ Bus R — Economic and Business Review
Econ Cienc Soc — Economia y Ciencias Sociales
Econ Comput Econ Cybern Stud Res — Economic Computation and Economic Cybernetics Studies and Research
Econ Cont — Contents of Recent Economics Journals
ECOND — Energy Consumer
Econ y Desarrollo — Economia y Desarrollo
Econ Dev Cu — Economic Development and Cultural Change
Econ Dev & Cul Change — Economic Development and Cultural Change
Econ Dev Cult Change — Economic Development and Cultural Change
Econ Devel and Cult Change — Economic Development and Cultural Change
Econ Devel Cult Change — Economic Development and Cultural Change
Econ Develop Cult Change — Economic Development and Cultural Change
Econ Development and Cultural Change — Economic Development and Cultural Change
Econ EC — Economia EC
Econ Educ Bul — Economic Education Bulletin
Econ Eye — Economic Eye
Econ Financial Surv Aust — Economic and Financial Survey of Australia
Econ & Financial Survey Aust — Economic and Financial Survey of Australia
Econ Financ R Central Bank Nigeria — Economic and Financial Review. Central Bank of Nigeria
Econ Finan Surv Aust — Economic and Financial Survey of Australia
Econ y Fin Esp — Economia y Finanzas Espanolas
Econ et Fins Agrics — Economie et Finances Agricoles
Econ Forum — Economic Forum
Econ Geog — Economic Geography
Econ Geogr — Economic Geography
Econ-Geogr — Economie-Geographie
Econ Geography — Economic Geography
Econ Geol — Economic Geology
Econ Geol — Economic Geology and the Bulletin of the Society of Economic Geologists
Econ Geol Bull Soc Econ Geol — Economic Geology and the Bulletin of the Society of Economic Geologists
Econ Geology Mon — Economic Geology. Monograph
Econ Geol Rep Alberta Res Counc — Economic Geology Report. Alberta Research Council
Econ Geol VT Geol Surv — Economic Geology. Vermont Geological Survey
Econ e Gestao — Economia e Gestao
Econ Hist — Economic History
Econ Hist — Economy and History
Econ Hist R — Economic History Review
Econ Hist Rev — Economic History Review
Econ Hist Rev Second Ser — Economic History Review. Second Series
EconHR — Economic History Review
Econ et Human — Economie et Humanisme
Econ et Humanisme — Economie et Humanisme

Econ Ind — Economia Industrial
Econ & Ind Democ — Economic and Industrial Democracy
Econ Indic — Economic Indicators
Econ Indicators — Economic Indicators
Econ Inf Argentina — Economic Information on Argentina
Econ Info Argentina — Economic Information on Argentina
Econ Inf Rep Food Resour Econ Dep Univ Fla Agric Exp Stns — Economic Information Report. University of Florida. Food and Resource Economics Department. Agricultural Experiment Stations
Econ Inq — Economic Inquiry
Econ Inquiry — Economic Inquiry
Econ Internaz — Economia Internazionale
Econ Internaz Fonti Energia — Economia Internazionale delle Fonti di Energia
Econ Int Fonti Energia — Economia Internazionale delle Fonti di Energia
Econ Int (Genova) — Economia Internazionale (Genova)
Econ Issues Dep Agric Econ Coll Agric Life Sci Univ Wis — Economic Issues. Department of Agricultural Economics. College of Agricultural and Life Sciences. University of Wisconsin
Econ Istruzione e Formazione Professionale — Economia. Istruzione e Formazione Professionale
Econ Italy — Economic News from Italy
Econ J — Economic Journal
Econ e Lav — Economia e Lavoro
Econ Leaf — Economic Leaflets [*Florida*]
Econ Leaflets — Economic Leaflets
Econ Lett — Economics Letters [*Netherlands*]
Econ (Lisbon) — Economia (Lisbon)
Econ (London) — Economica (London)
Econ Marche — Economia Marche
Econ Med Anim — Economie et Medecine Animales
Econ Meridionale — Economie Meridionale
Econ Mex — Economista Mexicano
Econ Mex — Review of the Economic Situation of Mexico
Econ Microbiol — Economic Microbiology
Econ Monographs — Economic Monographs [*Sydney*]
Econ Monograph (Vic) — Economic Monograph (Melbourne, Victoria)
Econ News — Economic News
Econom Comp Econom Cybernet Stud Res — Economic Computation and Economic Cybernetics Studies and Research [*Bucharest*]
Econom Comput Econom Cybernet Stud Res — Economic Computation and Economic Cybernetics Studies and Research [*Bucharest*]
Econometrics Oper Res — Econometrics and Operations Research
Economic Activity in WA — Economic Activity in Western Australia
Econom Lett — Economics Letters [*Amsterdam*]
Econom Theory Econometrics Math Econom — Economic Theory, Econometrics, and Mathematical Economics
Econ Outlk — Economic Outlook
Econ Outlook — Economic Outlook USA
Econ Outlook (London) — Economic Outlook (London)
Econ Outlook USA — Economic Outlook USA
Econ Panorama Bancomer — Economic Panorama Bancomer
Econ Pap — Economic Papers
Econ Papers — Economic Papers
Econ Pas (Australia and NZ) — Economic Papers (Australia and New Zealand)
Econ Pas (Warsaw) — Economic Papers (Warsaw)
Econ Pays Arabes — Economie des Pays Arabes
Econ Perspectives — Economic Perspectives
Econ Planning — Economics of Planning
Econ Planning (Helsinki) — Economic Planning (Helsinki)
Econ et Polit — Economie et Politique
Econ Polit Wkly — Economic and Political Weekly
Econ Pol W — Economic and Political Weekly
Econ Priorities Rep — Economic Priorities Report
Econ Proc R Dublin Soc — Economic Proceedings. Royal Dublin Society
Econ Progress Rep — Economic Progress Report
Econ R — Economic Review
Econ R Bank Israel — Economic Review. Bank of Israel
Econ R (Colombo) — Economic Review (Colombo)
Econ Rec — Economic Record
Econ Rep Dep Agric Appl Econ Univ Minn — Economic Report. Department of Agricultural and Applied Economics. University of Minnesota
Econ Rep Edinburgh Sch Agr — Economic Report. Edinburgh School of Agriculture
Econ Rep Geol Surv Dep (Zambia) — Economic Report. Geological Survey Department (Zambia)
Econ Reporter — Economic Reporter
Econ Rep Univ Fla Agric Exp Stns — Economics Report. University of Florida. Agricultural Experiment Stations
Econ Res — Economic Research [*Nagoya, Japan*]
Econ Rev — Economic Review
Econ R Kansallis Osake-Pankki — Economic Review. Kansallis Osake-Pankki
Econ R (Karachi) — Economic Review (Karachi)
Econ Rur — Economie Rurale
Econ Rurale — Economie Rurale
Econ Salvad — Economia Salvadorena

Econ et Sante — Economie et Sante
Econ Situation Rep — Economic Situation Report
Econ and Soc — Economy and Society
Econ Soc Aust NZ NSW Br Econ Monog — Economic Society of Australia and New Zealand. New South Wales Branch. Economic Monograph
Econ Societ — Economy and Society
Econ Soc R — Economic and Social Review
Econ Soc Tijds — Economisch en Sociaal Tijdschrift/Vie Economique et Sociale
Econ-Sta Ber — Economisch-Statistische Berichten
Econ and Statis R (East Africa) — Economic and Statistical Review (East Africa)
Econ et Statist — Economie et Statistique
Econ-Statist Ber — Economisch-Statistische Berichten
Econ e Storia (2a Ser) — Economia e Storia (Seconda Serie)
Econ Stud — Economic Studies
Econ Tech Rev Rep EPS (Can) — Economic and Technical Review. Report EPS [*Environmental Protection Service*] (Canada)
Econ Tiers-Monde — Economiste du Tiers-Monde
Econ Trend — Tendances/Trends. Economie et Finances
Econ Trends — Economic Trends
Econ Trentina — Economia Trentina [*Italy*]
Econ W — Economic World
Eco Out (UK) — Economic Outlook (United Kingdom)
ECOPD — Engineering Conference. Proceedings [*United States*]
ECOQD — Electricity Conservation Quarterly [*India*]
Ecotoxicol Environ Qual — Ecotoxicology and Environmental Quality
Ecotoxicol Environ Saf — Ecotoxicology and Environmental Safety
Ecotoxicol Environ Safety — Ecotoxicology and Environmental Safety
ECPED — Engineering Costs and Production Economics
ECPRAG — Empire Cotton Growing Corporation. Progress Reports from Experiment Stations
Ec Prat Hautes Etud Inst Montp Mem Trav — Ecole Pratique des Hautes Etudes. Institut de Montpellier. Memoires et Travaux
ECP Rep — ECP [*Energy Conservation Project*] Report [*United States*]
ECQUA — Engineering. Cornell Quarterly
ECR — Eastern Churches Review
ECR — Economic Record
Ec R — Ecumenical Review
ECr — Esprit Createur
ECr — Essays in Criticism
ECRCA — Echo des Recherches
ECRDA — Economic Record (Australia)
Ec Rev — Ecumenical Review
ECRQDQ — Conseil de la Recherche et du Developpement Forestiers du Quebec. Etude
ECS — Eighteenth-Century Studies
ECS — Tijdschrift voor Economie en Management
ECSBA — Economisch-Statistische Berichten
ECSDA — Electromechanical Components and Systems Design
ECSMB — Environmental Control and Safety Management
ECSSD — Estuarine, Coastal, and Shelf Science
ECSTA — Economist [*London*]
ECSTC — Electrocomponent Science and Technology
Ec Stor — Economia e Storia; Rivista Italiana di Storia Economica e Sociale
Ec Super Agric Suede Ann — Ecole Superieure d'Agriculture de la Suede. Annales
ECT — Ecopress Italia
ECTAA — Electra [*Rijswijk*]
ECTTA — Economia Trentina
ECU — Economia Internazionale
Ecuador Dir Gen Geol Minas Publ — Ecuador. Direccion General de Geologia y Minas. Publication
Ecumenical R — Ecumenical Review
Ecumen Rev — Ecumenical Review
Ecum R — Ecumenical Review
EcuR — Ecumenical Review [*Geneva*]
Ec W — Economic Weekly
ECW — Essays on Canadian Writing
ECX — Echos. Le Quotidien de l'Economie
Eczacilik Bul — Eczacilik Bulteni
Ed — Edda. Revue de Litterature
Ed — Education
ED — Ephemeris Dacoromana
ED — Euntes Docete
EDA — Economic Development and Cultural Change
EdAb — Education Abstracts
EdAd — Educational Administration Abstracts
Ed Adm Q — Educational Administration Quarterly
Ed Adm & Sup — Educational Administration and Supervision
EDAH — Etudes Dahomeennes
Ed Arn — Editiones Arnamagnaeanae
EDB — Emily Dickinson Bulletin
EDBCA — Electricite de France. Direction des Etudes et Recherches. Bulletin. Serie C. Mathematiques-Informatique
Ed Bi-Mo — Educational Bi-Monthly

Ed Books and Equip — Educational Books and Equipment
Ed Can — Education Canada
Ed Cat — Ediciones Catedra
EDCC — Economic Development and Cultural Change
EDCCA — Economic Development and Cultural Change
EDCHA — Education in Chemistry
Ed in Chem — Education in Chemistry
Ed Circ (WA) — Education Circular (Education Department. Western Australia)
Ed for Dev — Education for Development
EDDID — Energy and Development Digest
Ed Digest — Education Digest
EDENA — Educator
EDESA — Ediciones Espanolas Sociedad Anonima
EDETD — Energy Detente
Ed Exec Overview — Educational Executive's Overview
Ed F — Educational Forum
Ed Forum — Educational Forum
Ed Gaz (NSW) — Education Gazette (New South Wales. Department of Education)
Ed Gaz (SA) — Education Gazette (South Australia. Department of Education)
Ed Gaz & Teach Aid (Vic) — Education Gazette and Teachers Aid (Victoria)
Edgerton Germeshausen & Grier Rept — Edgerton, Germeshausen, and Grier Report
EdH — Educational Horizons
EDH — Essays by Divers Hands
Ed Horiz — Educational Horizons
EdI — Education Index
EDI — Educational Documentation and Information
EDI — Endocrinology Index
EDICUDA — Editorial Cuadernos para el Dialogo
EDIGA — Engineering Digest
EDIGD — Energy Digest [*Colorado Springs, CO*]
Edinb Dent Hosp Gaz — Edinburgh Dental Hospital. Gazette
Edinb G Soc Tr — Edinburgh Geological Society. Transactions
Edinb Med J — Edinburgh Medical Journal
Edinb Med and S J — Edinburgh Medical and Surgical Journal
Edinb Sch Agric Annu Rep — Edinburgh School of Agriculture. Annual Report
Edinb Sch Agric Exp Work — Edinburgh School of Agriculture. Experimental Work
Edinburgh Bibliogr Soc Trans — Edinburgh Bibliographical Society. Transactions
Edinburgh Geol Soc Trans — Edinburgh Geological Society. Transactions
Edinburgh J Sci — Edinburgh Journal of Science
Edin Rev — Edinburgh Review
EDISD — EDIS. Environmental Data and Information Service
Edison Electr Inst Bull — Edison Electric Institute. Bulletin
Edison Electr Inst Stat Yearb Electr Util Ind — Edison Electric Institute. Statistical Yearbook. Electric Utility Industry
Editorial Research Repts — Editorial Research Reports
Edit Publ — Editor and Publisher
EDK — Handels Rundschau
EdL — Educational Leadership
EdL — Etudes de Lettres [*Universite de Lausanne*]
EDLA — Estudios de Linguistica Aplicada
Ed Lead — Educational Leadership
Ed Lib Bulletin — Education Libraries Bulletin
EdM — Education Media
Ed Mag — Educational Magazine
Ed Man — Education Manitoba
Ed Meth — Educational Method
ED MJ — Edinburgh Medical Journal
Ed Mo — Edinburgh Monthly Review
Edmonton Geol Soc Quart — Edmonton Geological Society. Quarterly
Edmonton P L News Notes — Edmonton Public Library. News Notes
Ed Mus — Educazione Musicale
Ed Mus Mag — Education Music Magazine
Ed New Philos J — Edinburgh New Philosophical Journal
Ed News — Education News
Ednl Administration Bull — Educational Administration Bulletin
Ednl Broadcasting International — Educational Broadcasting International
Ednl Change and Dev — Educational Change and Development
Ednl Dev — Educational Development
Ednl Dev Centre R — Educational Development Centre Review
Ednl Dev International — Educational Development International
Ednl Documentation and Information — Educational Documentation and Information
Ednl R — Educational Review
Ednl Research — Educational Research
Ednl Sciences — Educational Sciences
Ednl Studies — Educational Studies
Ednl Studies in Maths — Educational Studies in Mathematics
Ed in the North — Education in the North
Ed NS — Education Nova Scotia
Ed (NSW) — Education (New South Wales Teachers Federation)

Ed Off Gaz (Qld) — Education Office Gazette (Queensland Department of Education)
Ed Outl — Educational Outlook
EDP — EDP [*Electronic Data Processing*] Industry Report
EDPAA — EDP [*Electronic Data Processing*] Analyzer
EDP A C S — EDP [*Electronic Data Processing*] Audit, Control, and Security Newsletter
EDP Anal — EDP [*Electronic Data Processing*] Analyzer
EDP Aud — EDP [*Electronic Data Processing*] Auditor
EDP Europa — EDP [*Electronic Data Processing*] Europa Report
Ed Philos J — Edinburgh Philosophical Journal
EDP In-Depth Rep — EDP [*Electronic Data Processing*] In-Depth Reports
EDP Indus Rep — EDP [*Electronic Data Processing*] Industry Report
EDP Performance Rev — EDP [*Electronic Data Processing*] Performance Review
EDP Perf Rev — EDP [*Electronic Data Processing*] Performance Review
Ed Prod Rep — Educational Product Report
Ed & Psychol M — Educational and Psychological Measurement
Ed & Pub — Editor and Publisher
Ed R — Edinburgh Review
EdR — Educational Record
Ed R — Educational Review [*United Kingdom*]
EDR Anthrc — Energy Data Reports. Distribution of Pennsylvania Anthracite
EDRCAM — Endocrine Research Communications
Ed R (China) — Educational Review (China)
EDR Coal B & L — Energy Data Reports. Coal, Bituminous and Lignite
Ed Rec — Educational Record [*Tasmania Education Department*]
Ed Rec Bur Bul — Educational Records Bureau Bulletins [*Greenwich, Connecticut*]
Ed Res — Educational Research [*Oxford*]
Ed Res B — Educational Research Bulletin
Ed Res Record — Educational Research Record
Ed Res Rep (Wash DC) — Editorial Research Reports (Washington, DC)
EDR Ker — Energy Data Reports. Sales of Fuel Oil and Kerosene
EDR LPS — Energy Data Reports. Liquefied Petroleum Sales
EDRRA — Editorial Research Reports
EDRSA2 — Elma Dill Russell Spencer Foundation Series
EDS — Economic Digest
EdS — Ecrits des Saints
EDS — English Dance and Song
Ed Screen — Educational Screen
Ed Screen AV G — Educational Screen and Audiovisual Guide [*Later, AV Guide: The Learning Media Magazine*]
Ed Ser Fla Dep Nat Resour Mar Res Lab — Educational Series. Florida Department of Natural Resources. Marine Research Laboratory
Ed & Social Science — Education and Social Science
Ed Studies — Educational Studies
Ed Stud Math — Educational Studies in Mathematics [*Dordrecht*]
Ed Survey — Educational Survey
EdT — Educational Technology
ED T — Educational Times
E D Tch — Etudes et Documents Tchadiens
Ed for Teaching — Education for Teaching
Ed Tech — Educational Technology
Ed Theatre J — Educational Theatre Journal
Ed Theory — Educational Theory
Ed & Training — Education and Training
Ed & Train Men Retard — Education and Training of the Mentally Retarded
EDTRED — Endodontics and Dental Traumatology
Ed TV Int — Educational Television International
Educ — Education
Educa — Education
Educ Adm — Educational Administration
Educ Admin — Educational Administration Quarterly
Educ Admin Abstr — Educational Administration Abstracts
Educ Adm Q — Educational Administration Quarterly
Educ Adm & Sup — Educational Administration and Supervision
Educa R — Educational Review
Educational Bldg Digest — Educational Building Digest
Educ Brdcstng — Educational Broadcasting
Educ Broadcast Int — Educational Broadcasting International
Educ Broad Int — Educational Broadcasting International
Educ Bull — Education Bulletin
Educ Can — Education Canada
Educ Cap — Education Capital
Educ Chem — Education in Chemistry
Educ Comm & Tech J — Educational Communication and Technology Journal
Educ Comput — Educational Computing
Educ et Cult — Education et Culture
Educ Dent (Ica) — Educacion Dental (Ica, Peru)
Educ et Develop — Education et Developpement
Educ Dig — Education Digest
Educ Digest — Education Digest
Educ Dir Dent Aux — Educational Directions for Dental Auxiliaries
Educ Doc & Inf — Educational Documentation and Information
EducF — Educational Forum

Educ Film Guide — Educational Film Guide
Educ Focus — Educational Focus
Educ Forum — Educational Forum
Educ Found Am Soc Plast Reconstr Surg Proc Symp — Educational Foundation. American Society of Plastic and Reconstructive Surgeons. Proceedings of the Symposium
Educ Gaz — Education Gazette
Educ Gazette — Education Gazette [*Sydney*]
Educ Gaz (SA) — Education Gazette (South Australia. Department of Education)
Educ Gerontol — Educational Gerontology
Educ Horiz — Educational Horizons
Educ Ind — Education Index
Educ Ind Telev — Educational and Industrial Television
Educ Innovations — Educational Innovations
Educ J — Education Journal
Educ Lead — Educational Leadership
Educ Lg Cit — Education in Large Cities
Educ Libr Bull — Education Libraries Bulletin
Educ Libr Serv Bull — Education Library Service Bulletin
Educ Mag — Educational Magazine
Educ Media — Educational Media
Educ Media Int — Educational Media International
Educ and Medicine — Education and Medicine
Educ Med Salud — Educacion Medica y Salud
Educ Mus Mag — Educational Music Magazine
Educ N — Education News
Educ News — Education News
Educ (NSW) — Education (New South Wales Teachers Federation)
EDUCOM — EDUCOM [*Educational Communications*] Bulletin
EDUCOM Bull — EDUCOM [*Educational Communications*] Bulletin
Educ Ont — Education Ontario
Educ Outl — Educational Outlook
Educ Perm — Education Permanente
Educ Philos Theory — Educational Philosophy and Theory
Educ Phil Theor — Educational Philosophy and Theory
Educ Policy Bull — Education Policy Bulletin
Educ Prod Rept — Educational Product Report
Educ Psychol — Educational Psychologist
Educ & Psychol M — Educational and Psychological Measurement
Educ & Psychol Meas — Educational and Psychological Measurement
Educ Psychol Measure — Educational and Psychological Measurement
Educ Psyc M — Educational and Psychological Measurement
Educ Q — Education Quarterly
Educ Q Nepal — Education Quarterly. Katmandu Nepal College of Education
Educ R — Educational Review
Educ Rec — Educational Record
Educ Rec Bur Bull — Educational Records Bureau Bulletins [*Greenwich, Connecticut*]
Educ Recd — Educational Record
Educ Record — Educational Record
Educ Res — Educational Research [*Oxford*]
Educ Res Bul — Educational Research Bulletin
Educ Researcher — Educational Researcher
Educ Res Perspect — Education Research and Perspectives
Educ Res Q — Educational Research Quarterly
Educ Res Quart — Educational Research Quarterly
Educ Rev — Education Review
Educ Screen — Educational Screen
Educ Sordomuti — Educazione dei Sordomuti
Educ Stud — Educational Studies
Educ Stud Math — Educational Studies in Mathematics
Educ Tech — Educational Technology
Educ Technol — Educational Technology
Educ Theatre J — Educational Theatre Journal
Educ Theor — Educational Theory
Educ Theory — Educational Theory
Educ Through Technol — Education through Technology
Educ and Train — Education and Training
Educ & Train Men Retard — Education and Training of the Mentally Retarded
Educ & Train Mentally Retard — Education and Training of the Mentally Retarded
Educ TV — Educational and Industrial Television
Educ Urban — Education and Urban Society
Educ & Urban Soc — Education and Urban Society
Educ and Urban Society — Education and Urban Society
Educ Urb Soc — Education and Urban Society
Educ Vict — Education for Victory
Educ Visual — Education of the Visually Handicapped
Educ (WA) — Education (Perth, Western Australia)
Educ (WA) — Education (Western Australia)
Edu D — Educational Digest
Ed USA — Education USA
EDV — Economic Development Review
Ed Vis Hand — Education of the Visually Handicapped

EDV Med Biol — EDV [*Elektronische Datenverarbeitung*] in Medizin und Biologie
Ed (WA) — Education (Western Australia)
Ed World — Education Around the World
EE — East Europe
EE — Eastern Economist
EE — Elementary English
EE — Enlightenment Essays
EE — Erasmus in English
EE — Estudios Ecclesiasticos
EE — Estudios Eruditos en Memoriam de Bonilla y San Martin
EE — Journal of Environmental Engineering
EEA — Educational Administration Abstracts
EEA — Electrical and Electronic Abstracts [*United Kingdom*]
EEA — Electrical Engineering Abstracts
EEAVA — Elektroenergetika i Avtomatika
EEB — European Trends
EEC — Engineering Economist
EEC Bull — European Economic Community. Bulletin of the European Communities
EEC Bull S — European Economic Community. Bulletin of the European Communities. Supplement
EECIT — Estudios Escenicos. Cuadernos del Instituto del Teatro
EECSB3 — Electroencephalography and Clinical Neurophysiology. Supplement
EED — Eastern Economist
EEDID — Energy Executive Directory
EEDND — Energy Educator Newsletter
EEE — Eastern European Economics
EEF — Egypt Exploration Fund
EEG Cl Neur — Electroencephalography and Clinical Neurophysiology
EEGEA — EEG/EMG; Zeitschrift fuer Elektroenzephalographie, Elektromyographie, und Verwandte Gebiete [*West Germany*]
EEH — European Economic Review
EEH — Explorations in Economic History
EEI — Edison Electric Institute. Bulletin
EEIBA — EEI [*Edison Electric Institute*] Bulletin
EEI Bul — Edison Electric Institute. Bulletin
EEI Elec P — Edison Electric Institute. Electric Perspectives
EEIND — Energy and the Environment: Interactions
EEISD — EIS. Environmental Impact Statements
EEJ — Eastern Economic Journal
EEK — Economisch en Sociaal Instituut voor de Middenstand. Informatieblad
EEL — Energy Policy
EELMA — Electricite-Electronique Moderne
EEMA — Eglise et l'Etat au Moyen Age
EEMB — Emanu-El Men's Bulletin
EEMB — Estudios Eruditos en Memoriam de Bonilla y San Martin
EEMCA — Estudios de Edad Media de la Corona de Aragon
EEN — Environment
E End News — East End News
EENMA — Electrical Engineer and Merchandiser
EENTA — Eye, Ear, Nose, and Throat Journal
EEO Spotl — EEO [*Equal Employment Opportunity*] Spotlight
EEPMD — Energy Economics, Policy, and Management
EEPSAPT — Epistemonike Epeteris tes Philosophikes Scholes tou Aristoteleiou Panepistemiou Thessalonikes
EEPSPA — Epistemonike Epeteris tes Philosophikes Scholes tou Panepistemiou Athenon
EEQEA — Electronic Equipment Engineering
EEQNA — Electronic Equipment News
EER — European Economic Review
EERGD — Energy (Ottawa)
EEROA — Elektro
EESB — Expression. Journal of the English Society
EEsc — Estudis Escenics. Quaderns de l'Institut del Teatre de la Diputacio de Barcelona
EESGRM — Egypt Exploration Society. Graeco-Roman Memoirs
Eesti NSV Tead Akad — Eesti NSV Teaduste Akadeemia Toimetised [*USSR*]
Eesti NSV Tead Akad Fueues Astronoom Inst Uurim — Eesti NSV Teaduste Akadeemia Fueuesika ja Astronoomia Instituudi Uurimused
Eesti NSV Tead Akad Fueues Inst Uurim — Eesti NSV Teaduste Akadeemia Fueuesika Instituudi Uurimused
Eesti NSV Tead Akad Fuus Inst Uurim — Eesti NSV Teaduste Akadeemia Fueuesika Instituudi Uurimused
Eesti NSV Tead Akad Tartu Astronoom Observ Publ — Eesti NSV Teaduste Akadeemia Tartu Astronoomia Observatooriumi Publikatsioonik
Eesti NSV Tead Akad Toim Biol — Eesti NSV Teaduste Akadeemia Toimetised. Bioloogia
Eesti NSV Tead Akad Toim Biol Ser — Eesti NSV Teaduste Akadeemia Toimetised. Bioloogiline Seeria [*Estonian SSR*]
Eesti NSV Tead Akad Toim Fuus Mat — Eesti NSV Teaduste Akadeemia Toimetised. Fueuesika. Matemaatika
Eesti NSV Tead Akad Toim Fuus Mat — Eesti NSV Teaduste Akadeemia Toimetised. Fueuesikalis-Matemaatiliste ja Tehniliste Teaduste Seeria [*Estonian SSR*]

Eesti NSV Tead Akad Toim Fuus Mat Tehnikatead Seer — Eesti NSV Teaduste Akadeemia Toimetised. Fueuesika. Matemaatika ja Tehnikateaduste Seeria
Eesti NSV Tead Akad Toim Geol Izv Akad Nauk Est SSR Geol — Eesti NSV Teaduste Akadeemia Toimetised Geoloog Izvestiia Akademii Nauk Estonskoi SSR Geologiia
Eesti NSV Tead Akad Toim Izv Ser Geol — Eesti NSV Teaduste Akadeemia Toimetised Izvestiya. Seria Geoloogia [Estonian SSR]
Eesti NSV Tead Akad Toim Izv Ser Keem — Eesti NSV Teaduste Akadeemia Toimetised Izvestiya. Seria Keemia [Estonian SSR]
Eesti NSV Tead Akad Toim Keem Geol — Eesti NSV Teaduste Akadeemia Toimetised. Keemia. Geoloogia
Eesti NSV Tead Akad Toim Keem Izv Akad Nauk Est SSR Khim — Eesti NSV Teaduste Akadeemia Toimetised Keemia. Izvestiia Akademii Nauk Estonskoi SSR Khimiia
Eesti Vabariigi Tartu Ulik Toim A — Eesti Vabariigi Tartu Ulikooli Toimetised A. Mathematica, Physica, Medica
Eesti Vabariigi Tartu Ulik Toim C — Eesti Vabariigi Tartu Ulikooli Toimetised C. Annales
EE/Systems Eng — EE/Systems Engineering Today
E/E Syst Eng Today — E/E Systems Engineering Today
Ee T — Eglise et Theologie
EETAD — ETA. Elektrowaerme im Technischen Ausbau
EETED — Elektrische Energie-Technik
EEU — East European Markets
E Eur — East Europe
E Eur Econ — Eastern European Economics
E Europe Q — East European Quarterly
E Eur Q — East European Quarterly
EF — Estudis Franciscans
EF — Etudes Franciscaines
EF — Experiments in Fluids
EFAID — Energie Fluide, l'Air Industriel
EFAPA — Electronica y Fisica Aplicada
EFATD — Energia del Fuego al Atomo
EFBSA — Bulletin. Direction des Etudes et Recherches. Serie A. Supplement (France)
EFCPA — Electric Furnace Conference. Proceedings
EFD — European Energy Report
EFDBA — Bulletin. Direction des Etudes et Recherches. Serie B (France)
EFDNA — Bulletin. Direction des Etudes et Recherches. Serie A (France)
EFE — EFTA [European Free Trade Association] Bulletin
EFF — European Taxation
Eff Environ Cells Tissues Proc World Congr Anat Clin Pathol — Effects of Environment on Cells and Tissues. Proceedings. World Congress of Anatomic and Clinical Pathology
Effic Text — Efficience Textile
Effi Text — Efficience Textile
Effluent Water Treat J — Effluent and Water Treatment Journal
Eff Udobr — Effectivnost Udobrenii
Eff Wat Tre — Effluent and Water Treatment Journal
EFI — Enrico Fermi International Summer School of Physics [Elsevier Book Series]
EFI — Euromarkt Nieuws
EFil — Estudios Filologicos
EFL — Essays in French Literature [University of Western Australia]
EFMEA — Engineering Fracture Mechanics
EFNED — Energy Forum in New England
EFOC Fiber Opt Commun Proc — EFOC [European Fiber Optics and Communications] Fiber Optics and Communications. Proceedings
EFP — Economiste Arabe. L'Economie et les Finances des Pays Arabes
EFPOD — Electric Farm Power [United States]
EFPS — Elsevier Series in Forensic and Police Science [Elsevier Book Series]
EFPSD9 — Annual Research Reviews. Effects of Psychotherapy
EFR — Editeurs Francais Reunis
EFR — Empire Forestry Review
EFran — Etudes Franciscaines
EFSPA — L'Economie et la Finance de la Syrie et de Pays Arabes [Damascus]
EFT — English Fiction in Transition, 1880-1920 [Later, English Literature in Transition, 1880-1920]
EFTA Bull — EFTA [European Free Trade Association] Bulletin
EG — Economic Geography
EG — Employment Gazette
EG — English and Germanic Studies
EG — Estudios Geograficos
EG — Etudes Germaniques
EG — Evangelisches Gemeindeblatt fuer Galizien
EGAABL — Eley Game Advisory Station. Annual Review
EGASA6 — Eley Game Advisory Service. Booklet
EgC — Egypte Contemporaine
Eg Cont — Egypte Contemporaine
EGD — Economic News of Bulgaria
EGE Actual — EGE [Eau-Gaz-Electricite et Applications] Actualites
EGerm — Etudes Germaniques
E & Ger St — English and Germanic Studies
EGESA — Egeszsegtudomany

Egesz — Egeszsegtudomany
Ege Univ Fen Fak Ilmi Rap Ser — Ege Universitesi Fen Fakultesi Ilmi Raporlar Serisi
Ege Univ Ziraat Fak Derg Seri A — Ege Universitesi Ziraat. Fakultesi Dergisi. Seri A
Ege Univ Ziraat Fak Yayin — Ege Universitesi Ziraat. Fakultesi Yayinlari
Eg Fil Koez — Egyetemes Filologiai Koezloeny
EGGOA — Engineering Geology (Amsterdam)
Eg Gov School Med Rec — Egyptian Government School of Medicine. Records
Egg Prod — Egg Producer
EGGVG — Einfuehrungsgesetz zum Gerichtsverfassungsgesetz
EGHVA — Eclogae Geologicae Helvetiae
EGI — Industrial Egypt
EGIND — Energinfo
EGKAA — Energetika
EGKO — Einfuehrungsgesetz zur Konkursordnung
EGKZA — Engei Gakkai Zasshi
EGLI — Essay and General Literature Index
Eglise Th — Eglise et Theologie
Egl Th — Eglise et Theologie
Egl Viv — Eglise Vivante
EGN — Ellen Glasgow Newsletter
EGOPA — Engineering Optimization
EGP — Economic Geography
EgR — Egyptian Religion
Egri Muz Ev — Az Egri Muzeum Evkoenyve
EGRTA — Energy Report (Alton, England)
EGS — English and Germanic Studies
EGSMA — Energomashinostroenie
E and G Stud — English and Germanic Studies
EGTKA — Energetik
EGYAA — Energetyka
EGYDA — Energy Digest [Washington, DC]
Egypt Agric Organ Bahtim Exp Stn Tech Bull — Egyptian Agricultural Organization. Bahtim Experiment Station Technical Bulletin
Egypt Agric Rev — Egyptian Agricultural Review
Egypt Cott Gaz — Egyptian Cotton Gazette
Egypt Dent J — Egyptian Dental Journal
Egypte Contemp — Egypte Contemporaine
Egypt Geol Surv Ann — Egypt Geological Survey. Annals
Egypt Geol Surv Min Auth Pap — Egyptian Geological Survey and Mining Authority. Paper
Egypt Geol Surv Pap — Egypt Geological Survey. Paper
Egyptian Statist J — Egyptian Statistical Journal
Egypt J Agron — Egyptian Journal of Agronomy
Egypt J Anim Prod — Egyptian Journal of Animal Production
Egypt J Bilharz — Egyptian Journal of Bilharziasis
Egypt J Bilharziasis — Egyptian Journal of Bilharziasis
Egypt J Bot — Egyptian Journal of Botany
Egypt J Ch — Egyptian Journal of Chemistry
Egypt J Chem — Egyptian Journal of Chemistry
Egypt J Chest Dis Tuberc — Egyptian Journal of Chest Diseases and Tuberculosis
Egypt J Food Sci — Egyptian Journal of Food Science
Egypt J Genet Cytol — Egyptian Journal of Genetics and Cytology
Egypt J Geol — Egyptian Journal of Geology
Egypt J Hortic — Egyptian Journal of Horticulture
Egypt J Microbiol — Egyptian Journal of Microbiology
Egypt J Neurol Psychiat Neurosurg — Egyptian Journal of Neurology, Psychiatry, and Neurosurgery
Egypt J Pharm Sci — Egyptian Journal of Pharmaceutical Sciences
Egypt J Phyopathol — Egyptian Journal of Phytopathology
Egypt J Phys — Egyptian Journal of Physics
Egypt J Physiol Sci — Egyptian Journal of Physiological Sciences
Egypt J Psychiatry — Egyptian Journal of Psychiatry
Egypt J Psychol — Egyptian Journal of Psychology
Egypt J Soc Med — Egyptian Journal of Social Medicine
Egypt J Soil Sci — Egyptian Journal of Soil Science
Egypt J Vet Sci — Egyptian Journal of Veterinary Science
Egypt Pharm Bull — Egyptian Pharmaceutical Bulletin
Egypt Pharm J — Egyptian Pharmaceutical Journal
Egypt Pharm Rep — Egyptian Pharmaceutical Reports. Pharmaceutical Society of Egypt and the Syndicate of Pharmacists
Egypt Popul Fam Plann Rev — Egyptian Population and Family Planning Review
Egypt Revs Sci — Egyptian Reviews of Science
Egypt Sugar Distill Co Sugar Cane Dep Res Bull — Egyptian Sugar and Distillation Company. Sugar Cane Department. Research Bulletin
Egypt Sugar Distill Co Sugar Cane Dep Tech Bull — Egyptian Sugar and Distillation Company. Sugar Cane Department. Technical Bulletin
EGYSA — Energy Sources [New York]
Egyt Trav Mag — Egypt Travel Magazine
EH — Eastern Horizon [Hong Kong]
EH — Economic History
E & H — Economy and History
EH — Editiones Heidelbergenses

EH — Environmental Health
EH — Ethiopian Herald
EH — Europaeische Hochschulschriften
EHA — Einzelhandelsberater
EHAF — Employee Health and Fitness
E Handel — Elektro-Handel
EHB — Modern Power Systems
EHBS — Epeteris tes Hetaireias Byzantinon Spoudon
EHD — English Historical Documents
Ehe G — Ehegesetz
Ehe Ges G — Ehegesundheitsgesetz
EHHD — Epeteris tou Kentrou Ereunes tes Historias tou Hellenikou Dikaiou
Ehime Daigaku Nogaku Kiyo Mem Coll Agric Ehime Univ — Ehime Daigaku Nogaku-bu Kiyo. Memoirs of the College of Agriculture. Ehime University
EHJ — Economisch-Historisch Jaarboek
EHJIA — Ehara Jiho
E H K — Eine Heilige Kirche
EHK — Ermlaendischer Hauskalender
EHKM — Epeteris Hetaireias Kykladikon Meleton
Ehkon Neft Prom-st — Ehkonomika Neftyanoj Promyshlennosti
Ehksp Khir Anesteziol — Ehksperimental'naya Khirurgiya i Anesteziologiya
Ehksp Onkol — Ehksperimental'naya Onkologiya
Ehkspress-Inf Lab Tekhnol Issled Obogashch Miner Syr'ya — Ehkspress-Informatsiya. Laboratornye Tekhnologicheskie Issledovaniya i Obogashchenie Mineral'nogo Syr'ya
Ehkspress-Inf Montazh Oborudovaniya Tepl Ehlektrostn — Ehkspress-Informatsiya. Montazh Oborudovaniya na Teplovykh Ehlektrostantsiyakh
Ehkspress-Inf Neftegazov Geol Geofiz — Ehkspress-Informatsiya. Neftegazovaya Geologiya i Geofizika
Ehkspress-Inf Ser Reg Razved Promysl Geofiz — Ehkspress-Informatsiya. Seriya. Regional'naya. Razvedochnaya i Promyslovaya Geofizika
Ehkspress-Inf Stroit Tepl Ehlektrostn — Ehkspress-Informatsiya. Stroitel'stvo Teplovykh Ehlektrostantsij
Ehkspress-Inf Svar Rab — Ehkspress-Informatsiya. Svarochnye Raboty
EHLD — Etudes d'Histoire Litteraire et Doctrinale
Ehlektrofiz Appar — Ehlektrofizicheskaya Apparatura
Ehlektrokhim — Ehlektrokhimiya. Akademiya Nauk SSSR. Ezhemesyachnyj Zhurnal
Ehlektron Ionnye Protessy Tverd Telakh — Ehlektronnye i Ionnye Protessy v Tverdykh Telakh
Ehlektron Obrab Mater — Ehlektronnaya Obrabotka Materialov
Ehlektrosvyaz' Radiotekh — Ehlektrosvyaz' i Radiotekhnika
Ehlektr Stn — Ehlektricheskie Stantsii
Ehnerg Ehlektrif — Ehnergetika i Ehlektrifikatsiya
Ehnerg Stroit — Ehnergeticheskoe Stroitel'stvo
Ehnerg Stroit Rubezhom — Ehnergeticheskoe Stroitel'stvo za Rubezhom
Ehntomol Obozr — Ehntomologicheskoe Obozrenie
EHPh R — Etudes d'Histoire et de Philosophie Religieuses
EHPR — Etudes d'Histoire et de Philosophie Religieuses
EHPRUS — Etudes d'Histoire et de Philosophie Religieuses. Universite de Strausbourg
EHR — Economic History Review
EHR — English Historical Review
EHR — Europese Documentatie
EHRR — European Human Rights Reports
EHSE — Estudios de Historia Social de Espana
EHSM — Epeteris Hetaireias Stereoelladikon Meleton
EHSQ — Emergency Health Services Quarterly
EHSRE2 — Emergency Health Services Review
EHTED — Energie Alternative
EHU — Economie et Humanisme
E Hy — Weichardts Ergebnisse der Hygiene, Bakterien-, Immunitaetsforschung, und Experimentellen Therapie
EI — Economia Internazionale
EI — Education Index
EI — Elet es Irodalom
EI — Enciclopedia Italiana
EI — Encyclopaedia of Islam
EI — Encyclopedie de l'Islam
Ei — Engineering Index
EI — English Illustrated Magazine
EI — Epigraphia Indica
EI — Eretz - Israel
EI — Estudios Ibericos
EI — Estudios Italianos
EI — Etudes Irlandaises
EI — Etudes Italiennes
EI — Excerpta Indonesica
EI — Journal of Professional Issues in Engineering
EI — L'Educatore Israelita
EI — L'Egypte Industrielle [*Cairo*]
EIA — Environment Information Abstracts
EIA — Estudos Ibero-Americanos
EIAEA — Equipement Industriel. Achats et Entretien

EIA Publ New Releases — EIA [*Electronics Industries Association*] Publications. New Releases [*United States*]
EIB — Earthquake Information Bulletin
EIB — Educational/Instructional Broadcasting
EIB — Eigen Huis en Interieur
EIC — Ephemerides Iuris Canonici
EIC — Essays in Criticism
Eich O — Eichordnung
Eichsfelder Heimath — Eichsfelder Heimathefte
Eichstaedter Bienenztg — Eichstaedter Bienenzeitung
Eickhogg-Mitt — Eickhogg-Mitteilungen [*West Germany*]
EIC Ne — EIC [*Engineering Institute of Canada*] News
EIC Trans — EIC [*Engineering Institute of Canada*] Transactions
Eid — Eidos. A Journal of Painting, Sculpture, and Design
EID — Electronic Instrument Digest
EIDAA — Electrical India
Eidg Anst Forstl Versuchswes Mitt — Eidgenoessische Anstalt fuer das Forstliche Versuchswesen. Mitteilungen
Eidg Tech Hochsch Versuchsanst Wasserbau Erdbau Mitt — Eidgenoessische Technische Hochschule, Versuchsanstalt fuer Wasserbau und Erdbau. Mitteilungen (Zurich)
EIE — Economia Industrial
EIE — English Institute. Essays
EIEAD — Elektrowaerme International. Edition A. Elektrowaerme im Technischen Ausbau
EIEBD — Elektrowaerme International. Edition B. Industrielle Elektrowaerme
EIFAC Occas Pap — EIFAC [*European Inland Fisheries Advisory Commission*] Occasional Paper
EIFAC Tech Pap — EIFAC [*European Inland Fisheries Advisory Commission*] Technical Paper
EIFEB — Economia Internazionale delle Fonti di Energia
Eig — Eigse
Eight Ct — Eighteenth Century. Theory and Interpretation
Eight-Ct L — Eighteenth-Century Life
Eight-Ct St — Eighteenth-Century Studies
Eighteenth Cent Life — Eighteenth-Century Life
Eighteenth-Cent Stud — Eighteenth-Century Studies
Eigo S — Eigo Seinen
EIHC — Essex Institute. Historical Collections
Eih Pbl — Eichstaetter Pastoralblatt
EIJID — Ebara Infiruko Jiho
EIK — Elektronische Informationsverarbeitung und Kybernetik
EIL — Echo de l'Industrie. Revue Luxembourgeoise de la Vie Economique et Sociale
EiL — Ezik i Literatura
EIMKH — Ergebnisse der Inneren Medizin und Kinderheilkunde
EIMOB — Ekspress-Informatsiya. Montazh Oborudovaniya na Teplovykh Elektrostantsiyakh
EIN — Europa Informatie, Buitenlandse Betrekkingen
EINDA — Electrified Industry
Einfuehr Molekularbiol — Einfuehrungen zur Molekularbiologie
Einfuehrungen Molekularbiol — Einfuehrungen zur Molekularbiologie
Einfuehrungen Molekularbiol — Einfuehrungen zur Molekularbiologie
Einh — Einheit. Organ der Industriegewerkschaft Bergbau und Energie
Einh — Einheit. Theoretische Zeitschrift des Wissenschaftlichen Sozialismus
EINS — Etudes/Inuit/Studies
EINSD — Eau et l'Industrie
Einzelv — Einzelveroeffentlichungen des Seewetteramtes
EIP — Estudos Italianos em Portugal
EIPGA — Ekspress-Informatsiya. Seriya: Regional'naya, Razvedochnaya, i Promyslovaya Geofizika
Eir — Eirene. Studia Graeca et Latina
EIR-Ber — Eidgenaessische Institut fuer Reaktorforschung. Bericht
EIR-Ber (Wuerenlingen) — EIR-[*Eidgenoessisches Institut fuer Reaktorforschung*] Bericht (Wuerenlingen)
EIRC — Exploration in Renaissance Culture
Eire — Ireland. A Journal of Irish Studies
EIRJa — Etimologiceskie Issledovanija po Russkomu Jazyku
EIRR — European Industrial Relations Review
Eisenbahn-Ing — Eisenbahn-Ingenieur
Eisenbahntech Rundsch — Eisenbahntechnische Rundschau
Eisenhower Consortium Bull — Eisenhower Consortium. Bulletin
Eisenhower Consortium Bull Rocky Mt For Range Exp — Eisenhower Consortium. Bulletin. United States Rocky Mountain Forest and Range Experiment Station
EISOAU — Eiyo To Shokuryo
EISRA — Ekspress-Informatsiya. Svarochnye Raboty
Eiszeitalter Gegenw — Eiszeitalter und Gegenwart
EIT — Ezhegodnik Imperatorskikh Teatrov
EITBA — Engelhard Industries. Technical Bulletin
EITEA — Ekspress-Informatsiya. Stroitel'stvo Teplovykh Elektrostantsii
E & ITV — Education and Industrial Television
EIUES — English Institute of the University of Uppsala. Essays and Studies on English Language and Literature
EIVKA — Elektronische Informatsionsverarbeitung und Kybernetik
EIY — Economic Inquiry

Eiyogaku Zasshi Jap J Nutr — Eiyogaku Zasshi/Japanese Journal of Nutrition
EJ — Economic Journal
EJ — Edoth (Jerusalem)
EJ — English Journal
EJ — Estudios Josefinos
EJ — European Judaism
EJAMA — European Journal of Applied Microbiology
EJAPC — European Journal of Applied Physiology and Occupational Physiology
EJASA — Engineering Journal [New York]
EJB — Engineering Industries of Japan
EJb — Eranos-Jahrbuch [Zurich]
EJCOD — European Journal of Cancer and Clinical Oncology
EJCPA — European Journal of Clinical Pharmacology
EJDPD — European Journal of Drug Metabolism and Pharmacokinetics
EJEA — Empire Journal of Experimental Agriculture
EJEAAR — Empire Journal of Experimental Agriculture
EJEV — Eusko-Jakintza. Revista de Estudios Vascos
EJFPA — European Journal of Forest Pathology
EJM — European Journal of Marketing
EJMED — Eizo Joho. Medikaru
EJOR — European Journal of Operational Research
EJP — European Journal of Parapsychology
EK — Evangelische Kirchenzeitung [Berlin]
EKANA — Elektro-Anzeiger
EKBRD5 — Ekologia-CSSR
EKC — Economic Review. Federal Reserve Bank of Kansas City
EKD — Economic Titles/Abstracts
EKEEK — Epeteris tou Kentrou Epistemonikon Ereunon Kyprou
EKEHL — Epeteris tou Kentrou Ereunes tes Hellenikes Laographias
EKHAA — Eksperimental'naya Khirurgiya i Anesteziologiya
EKHAAF — Eksperimental'naya Khirurgiya i Anesteziologiya
EKI — Ekistic Index
EKI — Ekonomi dan Keuangan Indonesia
EKIAAK — Ekologiya
EKISA — Ekistics
Ekist Ind — Ekistic Index
EKMMA8 — Eksperimentalna Meditsina i Morfologiya
EKMZAD — Conference Europeenne sur la Microcirculation/Conferenza Europea di Microcircolazione
EKNPA — Ekonomika Neftianoi Promyshlennosti
EKNTB — Elektronika
EKOLDI — Ekologiya [Sofia]
Ekol Fiziol Osob Rast Yuzhn Urala Ikh Resur — Ekologicheskie i Fiziologicheskie Osobennosti Rastenii Yuzhnogo Urala i Ikh Resursy
Ekol Pol — Ekologia Polska
Ekol Pol Pol J Ecol — Ekologia Polska. Polish Journal of Ecology
Ekol Pol Ser A — Ekologia Polska. Seria A
Ekol Pol Ser B — Ekologia Polska. Seria B
Ekol Polska — Ekologia Polska
Ekon Cas — Ekonomicky Casopis
Ekon Forscknstift Skogsarb — Ekonomi. Forskningsstiftelsen Skogsarbeten
Ekon Gaz — Ekonomicheskaya Gazeta
Ekon Keuangan — Ekonomi dan Keuangan Indonesia
Ekon Matem Metody — Ekonomika i Matematiceskie Metody
Ekon-Mate O — Ekonomicko-Matematicky Obzor
Ekon-Mat Obz — Ekonomicko-Matematicky Obzor
Ekon Nauki — Ekonomiceskie Nauki
Ekon Neft Prom-sti — Ekonomika Neftianoi Promyshlennosti [USSR]
Ekonom i Mat Metody — Ekonomika i Matematiceskie Metody
Ekonom-Mat Obzor — Ceskoslovenska Akademie Ved. Ekonomicko-Matematicky Obzor
Ekon Org Promysl Proizvodstva — Ekonomika i Organizacija Promyslennogo Proizvodstva
Ekon Poljopr — Ekonomika Poljoprivrede
Ekon Poljopriv — Ekonomika Poljoprivrede
Ekon Probl Effekt — Ekonomiceskie Problemy Effektivnosti Proizvodstva
Ekon R (Ljubljana) — Ekonomska Revija (Ljubljana)
Ekon R (Stockholm) — Ekonomisk Revy (Stockholm)
Ekon Samf T — Ekonomiska Samfundets Tidskrift
Ekon Samfund Ts — Ekonomiska Samfundets Tidskrift
Ekon Sel' Khoz — Ekonomika Sel'skogo Khozyaistva
Ekon Sel'sk Hoz — Ekonomika Sel'skogo Hozjajstva
Ekon Sel'sk Khoz — Ekonomika Sel'skogo Khozyaistva
Ekon Sov Ukr — Ekonomika Sovetskoi Ukrainy
Ekon Stavebnictva — Ekonomika Stavebnictva [Czechoslovakia]
Ekon Zemed — Ekonomika Zemedelstvi
EKOSB — Ekonomika Stavebnictva
EKPOAT — Ekologia Polska. Seria A
EKRKA — Elektronik
EKSODD — Eksperimental'naya Onkologiya
Eksp Issled Fiziol Biofiz Farmakol — Eksperimental'nye Issledovaniya po Fiziologii, Biofizike, i Farmakologii
Eksp Khir — Eksperimental'naya Khirurgiya
Eksp Khir Anesteziol — Eksperimental'naya Khirurgiya i Anesteziologiya
Eksp Klin Farmakoter — Eksperimental'naya i Klinicheskaya Farmakoterapiya

Eksp Klin Radiol — Eksperimental'naya i Klinicheskaya a Radiologiya [Ukrainian SSR]
Eksp Klin Stomatol — Eksperimentalnaia Klinicheskaia Stomatologiia
Eksp Med — Eksperimentalna Meditsina
Eksp Med Morfol — Eksperimentalna Meditsina i Morfologiya
Ekspress-Inf Lab Tekhnol Issled Obogashch Miner Syr'ya — Ekspress-Informatsiya Laboratornye Tekhnologicheskie Issledovaniya i Obogashchenie Mineral'nogo Syr'ya [USSR]
Ekspress-Inf Montazh Oborudovaniya Teplovykh Elektrosn — Ekspress-Informatsiya. Montazh Oborudovaniya na Teplovykh Elektrostantsiyakh [USSR]
Ekspress Inf Morsk Gidrofiz Inst Akad Nauk Ukr SSR — Ekspress-Informatsiya. Morskoi Gidrofizicheskii Institut Akademiya Nauk Ukrainskoi SSR
Ekspress-Inf Nauchno-Issled Inst Sel Khoz Severn Zaural'ya — Ekspress-Informatsiya Nauchno-Issledovatel'skii Institut Sel'skogo Khozyaistva Severnogo Zaural'ya
Ekspress-Inf Neftegazov Geol Geofiz — Ekspress-Informatsiya. Neftegazovaya Geologiya i Geofizika [USSR]
Ekspress-Inf Ser Reg Razved Prom Geofiz — Ekspress-Informatsiya. Seriya Regional'naya, Razvedochnaya, i Promyslovaya Geofizika [USSR]
Ekspress-Inf Stroit Tepl Elektrostn — Ekspress-Informatsiya. Stroitel'stvo Teplovykh Elektrostantsii [USSR]
Ekspress-Inf Svar Rab — Ekspress-Informatsiya. Svarochnye Raboty [USSR]
Eksp Tekh Svoistva Primen Avtomob Top Smaz Mater Sperszhidk — Ekspluatatsionno Tekhnicheskie Svoistva i Primenenie Avtomobil'nykh Topliv. Smazochnykh Materialov i Sperszhidkostei
Eksp Vodn Toksikol — Eksperimental'naya Vodnaya Toksikologiya
EKSTA — Electricheskie Stantsii
EKSTB — Ekonomiska Samfundets Tidskrift
EKTCB — Elektrotechnik
EKTKA — Elektrotechnik
EKTMA — Elektroteknikeren
EKTRA — Elektrie
EKTRB — Elektrotechnik
EKZVA — Elektrizitaetsverwertung
EKZVA — Elktrosvyaz
EKZWA — Elektrizitaetswirtschaft
EL — Educational Leadership
EL — Elsevier Lexica [Elsevier Book Series]
EL — Ephemerides Liturgicae
EL — Etudes de Lettres
EL — Europa Letteraria
EL — Europaeische Literatur
EL — Ezik i Literatura
ELA — Etudes de Linguistique Appliquee
ELABB — Electroanalytical Abstracts
Elabuz Gos Ped Inst Ucen Zap — Elabuzskii Gosudarstvennyi Pedagogiceskii Institut. Ucenye Zapiski
E Lang T — English Language Teaching [Later, English Language Teaching Journal]
Elast — Elastomerics
ELB — Environmental Law Bulletin
ELBAA — Elektrische Bahnen
ELBUA — Electrical Business
ELCAA — Electrochimica Acta
ELCCA — Electronic Components
ELCFR — English Linguistics, 1500-1800: A Collection of Facsimile Reprints
ELCIA — Electronics and Instrumentation
ELCMA — Electrical Communication
ELCNC4 — Electron [Brussels]
ELCRD — Electro Conference Record
ELCTDN — Electrophoresis
ELCWA — Electronics World
ELDDA — Electricidade
Elders W — Elders Weekly
ELDNB — Elektrodienst
ELDO/ESRO Bull — ELDO/ESRO [European Launcher Development Organization/European Space Research Organization] Bulletin [France]
ELDO/ESRO Sci Tech Rev — ELDO/ESRO [European Launcher Development Organization/European Space Research Organization] Scientific and Technical Review [France]
ELE — European Electronics
Elec — [The] Electrician
ELEC — English Language Education Council. Bulletin
ELEC — Etudes de Litterature Etrangere et Comparee
ELECA — Electronics
ELECAD — Electronics
Elec Aust — Electronics Australia
Elec Austr — Electronic Australia
Elec Busns — Electronic Business
Elec Com — Electrical Communication
Elec Comft — Electric Comfort Conditioning News
Elec Commun — Electrical Communication
Elec Constr Maint — Electrical Construction and Maintenance

Elec Contractor — Electrical Contractor
Elec Des — Electronic Design
Elec Desgn — Electronic Design
Elec Ed — Electronic Education
Elec & Electron Abstr — Electrical and Electronic Abstracts
Elec Eng — Electrical Engineer
Elec Eng — Electrical Engineering
Elec Eng Abstr — Electrical Engineering Abstracts
Elec Eng Japan — Electrical Engineering in Japan
Elec Eng (Melbourne) — Electrical Engineer (Melbourne)
Elec Eng & Merchandiser — Electrical Engineer and Merchandiser
Elec Engr — Electrical Engineer
Elec Eng Rev — Electrical Engineering Review
Elec Engrg Electron — Electrical Engineering and Electronics
Elec Engrg and Electronics — Electrical Engineering and Electronics
Elec Eng T — Electronic Engineering Times
Elec En Jap — Electrical Engineering in Japan
Elec Farm Mag — Electricity on the Farm Magazine
Elec Fr Bull Dir Etud Rech Ser A Nucl Hydraul Therm — Electricite de France. Bulletin de la Direction des Etudes et Recherches. Serie A. Nucleaire, Hydraulique, Thermique
Elec Fr Bull Dir Etud Rech Ser B Reseaux Elec Mater Elec — Electricite de France. Bulletin de la Direction des Etudes et Recherches. Serie B. Reseaux Electriques, Materiels Electriques
Elec Furnace Conf Proc AIME — Electric Furnace Conference Proceedings. Metallurgical Society of AIME. Iron and Steel Division
Elec J — Electrical Journal
Elec Manuf — Electrical Manufacturing
Elec Merch — Electrical Merchandising
Elec Merch W — Electrical Merchandising Week
Elec Mkt T — Electronic Market Trends
Elec M & M Sys — Electronic Mail and Message Systems
Elec Mus R — Electronic Music Review
Elec News — Electronic News
Elec News Eng — Electrical News and Engineering
Elec Prod — Electronic Products
Elec Prog — Electronic Progress
Elec Publ Rev — Electronic Publishing Review
Elec R — Electrical Review
Elec Res Ass ERA Rep — Electrical Research Association. ERA Report
Elec Retail — Electronics Retailing
Elec Rev — Electrical Review
Elec Ry J — Electric Railway Journal
Elect Contractor — Electrical Contractor
Elec Technol (USSR) — Electric Technology (USSR)
Elect Electron Mfr — Electrical and Electronics Manufacturer
Elect Electron Trader — Electrical and Electronic Trader
Elect Engng Trans Instn Engrs Aust — Electrical Engineering Transactions. Institution of Engineers Australia
Elect Engr (Melb) — Electrical Engineer (Melbourne)
Elect Equip — Electrical Equipment
Elec Times — Electric Times
Elec T Intnl — Electronics Today International
Elect J — Electric Journal
Electl Engr — Electrical Engineer
Elect Mech Engng Trans — Institution of Engineers of Australia. Electrical and Mechanical Engineering Transactions
Elec Tod — Electronics Today International
Elect Pwr — Electrical Power Engineer
Elect Pwr Engr — Electrical Power Engineer
Electr Act — Electrochimica Acta
Elec Traction — Electric Traction
Electr App — Electrical Apparatus
Electr Automob — Electricite Automobile
Electr Calculation — Electrical Calculation [Japan]
Electr Co J — Electronics and Communications in Japan
Electr Comf Cond J — Electric Comfort Conditioning Journal
Electr Comf Cond News — Electric Comfort Conditioning News
Electr Commun — Electrical Communication
Electr Commun Lab Tech J — Electrical Communication Laboratories. Technical Journal
Electr Conserv Q — Electricity Conservation Quarterly [India]
Electr Consult — Electrical Consultant
Electr Contract — Electrical Contracting
Electr Dig — Electrical Digest [Canada]
Electr Distrib — Electrical Distribution [England]
Electr-Electron Mod — Electricite-Electronique Moderne
Electr Energ Electron — Electricidade, Energia, Electronica
Electr Eng — Electrical Engineer
Electr Eng — Electronic Engineering [London]
Electr Eng Jap — Electrical Engineering in Japan
Electr Eng (Johannesburg) — Electrical Engineer (Johannesburg)
Electr Eng Jpn — Electrical Engineering in Japan
Electr Eng (Melb) — Electrical Engineer (Melbourne)
Electr Eng Merch — Electrical Engineer and Merchandiser [Australia]
Electr Eng Rev — Electrical Engineering Review

Electr Eng Trans — Electrical Engineering Transactions [Australia]
Electr Eng Trans Inst Eng Aust — Electrical Engineering Tranactions. Institution of Engineers Australia
Electr Equip — Electrical Equipment
Elect Rev — Electrical Review
Electr Farm Power — Electric Farm Power
Electr Forum — Electric Forum
Electr Fr Bull Dir Etud Rech Ser A Nucl Hydraul Therm — Electricite de France. Bulletin de la Direction des Etudes et Recherches. Serie A. Nucleaire, Hydraulique, Thermique
Electr Fr Bull Dir Etud et Rech Ser A Nucl Hydraul Therm — Electricite de France. Bulletin de la Direction des Etudes et Recherches. Serie A. Nucleaire, Hydraulique, Thermique
Electr Furn Conf Proc — Electric Furnace Conference. Proceedings
Electr Furn Proc Metall Soc AIME — Electric Furnace Conference Proceedings. Metallurgical Society of AIME. Iron and Steel Division
Electr Furn Steel Proc — Electric Furnace. Steel Proceedings
Electr Heat J — Electric Heating Journal
Electric — Electrician and Electrical Engineer
Electric Comp — Electric Company Magazine
Electrified Ind — Electrified Industry
Electr Ind — Electricien Industriel
Electr India — Electrical India
Electr Inf — Electrical Information [Japan]
Electrique — Industries Electriques et Electroniques
Electr Lett — Electronics Letters
Electr Light & Power — Electric Light and Power
Electr Light Power (Boston) — Electric Light and Power (Boston)
Electr Light Power Energy/Gener — Electric Light and Power. Energy/Generation
Electr Light Power Transm/Distrib — Electric Light and Power. Transmission/Distribution
Electr Mach and Power Syst — Electric Machines and Power Systems
Electr Mach Electromech — Electric Machines and Electromechanics
Electr Mach and Electromech — Electric Machines and Electromechanics
Electr Mag Ohm — Electrical Magazine Ohm [Japan]
Electr Mech Eng Trans Inst Eng Aust — Electrical and Mechanical Engineering Transactions. Institution of Engineers Australia
Electr and Mech Executive Eng — Electrical and Mechanical Executive Engineer
Electr News Eng — Electrical News and Engineering
Electr Nucl Technol — Electrical and Nuclear Technology
Electroanal Abstr — Electroanalytical Abstracts
Electroanal Chem — Electroanalytical Chemistry
Electrochem Ind Phys Chem — Electrochemistry and Industrial Physical Chemistry [Japan]
Electrochem Ind Process and Biol — Electrochemistry in Industrial Processing and Biology
Electrochem Ind Process Biol (Engl Transl) — Electrochemistry in Industrial Processing and Biology (English Translation)
Electrochem Metall Ind — Electrochemical and Metallurgical Industry
Electrochem Molten and Solid Electrolytes — Electrochemistry of Molten and Solid Electrolytes
Electrochem Soc J — Electrochemical Society. Journal
Electrochem Tech — Electrochemical Technology
Electrochem Technol — Electrochemical Technology
Electrochim Acta — Electrochimica Acta
Electrochim Metal — Electrochimica Metallorum
Electrocomponent Sci Technol — Electrocomponent Science and Technology
Electrocompon Sci Technol — Electrocomponent Science and Technology
Electrodeposition & Surf Treat — Electrodeposition and Surface Treatment
Electroencephalogr Clin Neurophysiol — Electroencephalography and Clinical Neurophysiology
Electroencephalogr Clin Neurophysiol Suppl — Electroencephalography and Clinical Neurophysiology. Supplement
Electroenceph Clin Neurophysiol — Electroencephalography and Clinical Neurophysiology
Electromech Compon Syst Des — Electromechanical Components and Systems Design
Electromech Des — Electromechanical Design
Electromed — Electromedica
Electromet Met Alloys Rev — Electromet Metals and Alloys Review
Electromet Rev — Electromet Review
Electromyogr Clin Neurophysiol — Electromyography and Clinical Neurophysiology
Electron — Electronics
Electron Abstr J — Electronics Abstracts Journal
Electron Appl — Electronic Applications
Electron Appl Bull — Electronic Applications. Bulletin
Electron Appl Components Mater — Electronic Applications. Components and Materials [Netherlands]
Electron Appl Ind — Electronique et Applications Industrielles [France]
Electron Aust — Electronics Australia
Electron Bus — Electronic Business
Electron Comm Japan — Electronics and Communications in Japan
Electron Commun — Electronic Communicator

Electron & Communic Abstr J — Electronics and Communications Abstracts Journal
Electron Commun Japan — Electronics and Communications in Japan
Electron Commun Jpn — Electronics and Communications in Japan
Electron Compon — Electronic Components
Electron Components — Electronic Components
Electron Components Appl — Electronic Components and Applications [*Netherlands*]
Electron Components and Appl — Electronic Components and Applications
Electron Des — Electronic Design
Electron Device Lett — Electron Device Letters
Electron Electro-Opt Infrared Countermeas — Electronic, Electro-Optic, and Infrared Countermeasures
Electron Eng (Lond) — Electronic Engineering (London)
Electron Eng (Phila) — Electronic Engineering (Philadelphia)
Electron Equip Eng — Electronic Equipment Engineering
Electron Equip News — Electronic Equipment News
Electron Fis Apl — Electronica y Fisica Aplicada
Electronic Ind & Tele-Tech — Electronic Industries and Tele-Tech
Electronic N — Electronic News
Electronic & Radio Eng — Electronic and Radio Engineer
Electronics Aust — Electronics Australia
Electronics Today — Electronics Today International
Electron Ind — Electronic Industries
Electron Ind — Electronics Industry
Electron Ind — Electronique Industrielle
Electron Ind Electron Instrum — Electronic Industries and Electronic Instrumentation
Electron Inf and Plann — Electronics Information and Planning
Electron Inf Plann — Electronics Information and Planning
Electron Instrum — Electronics and Instrumentation
Electron Learn — Electronic Learning
Electron Lett — Electronics Letters
Electron Library — Electronic Library
Electron Mag — Electronics Magazine
Electron Meas — Electronic Measuring
Electron Med — Electronique Medicale
Electron Meten — Electronisch Meten
Electron Mfr — Electronics Manufacturer
Electron Microelectron Ind — Electronique et Microelectronique Industrielles
Electron et Microelectron Ind — Electronique et Microelectronique Industrielles
Electron Microsc Soc Am Annu Meet Proc — Electron Microscopy Society of America. Annual Meeting. Proceedings
Electron Micros Soc Southern Afr Proc — Electron Microscopy Society of Southern Africa. Proceedings
Electron Nouv — Electronique Nouvelle
Electron Packag Prod — Electronic Packaging and Production
Electron & Power — Electronics and Power
Electron Power — Electronics and Power
Electron and Power — Electronics and Power. Journal of the Institution of Electrical Engineers
Electron Prod — Electronic Products Magazine
Electron Prod Methods & Equip — Electronic Production Methods and Equipment
Electron Prog — Electronic Progress
Electron Publishing Rev — Electronic Publishing Review
Electron Pwr — Electronics and Power
Electron and Radio Tech — Electronic and Radio Technician
Electron Reliab Microminiaturization — Electronics Reliability and Microminiaturization [*England*]
Electron Rev (Tokyo) — Electronics Review (Tokyo)
Electron Sound and RTE — Electronic Sound and RTE
Electron Spectrosc Theory Tech Appl — Electron Spectroscopy Theory, Techniques, and Applications
Electron Struct Magnet Inorg Comp — Electronic Structure and Magnetism of Inorganic Compounds
Electron Surv Comput — Electronic Survey Computing
Electron Surv Computing — Electronic Survey Computing
Electron Technol — Electron Technology
Electron Technol Q — Electron Technology. Quarterly
Electron Technol Rep — Electronic Technology Reports [*South Korea*]
Electron Test — Electronics Test
Electron Times — Electronic Times
Electron Today — Electronics Today
Electron Today Int — Electronics Today International
Electron Warf Def Electron — Electronic Warfare Defense Electronics
Electron Wkly — Electronics Weekly
Electron World — Electronics World
Electro-Opt — Electro-Optics
Electro Opt Ser — Electro-Optics Series
Electro-Opt Syst Des — Electro-Optical Systems Design
Electro-Opt Systems — Electro-Optical Systems Design
Electrophotogr — Electrophotography
Electroplat Met Finish — Electroplating and Metal Finishing
Electroplat and Met Finish — Electroplating and Metal Finishing

Electroquim Corrasao — Electroquimica e Corrasao
Electro-Rev — Electro-Revue
Electro-Tech — Electro-Techniek
Electro-Tech — Electro-Technology
Electrotech J Jpn — Electrotechnical Journal of Japan
Electro-Technol — Electro-Technology
Electro-Technol (Bangalore India) — Electro-Technology (Bangalore, India)
Electro-Technol (NY) — Electro-Technology (New York)
Electroteh Electron Autom Electroteh — Electrotehnica, Electronica, si Automatica. Serie Electrotehnica [*Romania*]
Electrothermie Int Ed B — Electrothermie International. Edition B. Applications Industrielles de l'Electrothermie
Electr Perspect — Electric Perspectives
Electr Pow — Electronics and Power
Electr Power Commun — Electric Power Communicator [*Canada*]
Electr Power Energy Syst — Electrical Power and Energy Systems [*England*]
Electr Power Mon — Electric Power Monthly [*Japan*]
Electr Power Res Inst (Rep) EPRI AF — Electric Power Research Institute (Report) EPRI AF
Electr Power Res Inst (Rep) EPRI EA — Electric Power Research Institute (Report) EPRI EA
Electr Power Res Inst (Rep) EPRI EL — Electric Power Research Institute (Report) EPRI EL
Electr Power Res Inst (Rep) EPRI EM — Electric Power Research Institute (Report) EPRI EM
Electr Power Res Inst (Rep) EPRI ER — Electric Power Research Institute (Report) EPRI ER
Electr Power Res Inst (Rep) EPRI ER (Palo Alto Calif) — Electric Power Research Institute (Report) EPRI ER (Palo Alto, California)
Electr Power Res Inst (Rep) EPRI FP — Electric Power Research Institute (Report) EPRI FP
Electr Power Res Inst (Rep) EPRI FP (Palo Alto Calif) — Electric Power Research Institute (Report) EPRI FP (Palo Alto, California)
Electr Power Res Inst (Rep) EPRI NP — Electric Power Research Institute (Report) EPRI NP
Electr Power Res Inst (Rep) EPRI SR (Palo Alto Calif) — Electric Power Research Institute (Report) EPRI SR (Palo Alto, California)
Electr Power Syst Res — Electric Power Systems Research
Electr Prod — Electronic Products Magazine
Electr Rev — Electrical Review
Electr Rev Int — Electrical Review International
Electr Superv — Electrical Supervisor
Electr Technol (USSR) — Electric Technology (USSR)
Electr Times — Electrical Times
Electr Util & Energy Abs — Electrical Utilization and Energy Abstracts
Electr Veh — Electric Vehicles
Electr Veh Batteries — Electric Vehicles and Batteries [*England*]
Electr Veh Dev — Electric Vehicle Developments [*England*]
Electr Veh News — Electric Vehicle News
Electr Week — Electrical Week
Electr World — Electrical World
Elect Supervis — Electrical Supervisor
Elect Times — Electrical Times
Elect Tract — Electric Traction
Elect World — Electrical World
Elec Veh — Electric Vehicle News
Elec W — Electrical Weekly
Elec Week — Electronics Weekly
Elec West — Electrical West
Elec World — Electrical World
ELEGA — Electronic Engineering
ELEGC — Electric Light and Power. Energy/Generation
ELEKA — Elektrichestvo
Elek Bahnen — Elektrische Bahnen
Elektr Ausruestung — Elektrische Ausruestung
Elektr Bahnen — Elektrische Bahnen
Elektr Energ-Tech — Elektrische Energie-Technik
Elektr Masch — Elektrische Maschinen
Elektr Muhendisligi — Elektrik Muhendisligi
Elektr Nachrichtenwes — Elektrisches Nachrichtenwesen
Elektr Nachr Tech — Elektrische Nachrichten Technik
Elektro-Anz — Elektro-Anzeiger
Elektrochem Z — Elektrochemische Zeitschrift
Elektroenerget i Avtomat — Elektroenergetika i Avtomatika
Elektrofiz Appar — Elektrofizicheskaya Apparatura
Elektrofiz App Sb Statei — Electrofizicheskaya Apparatura Sbornik Statei [*USSR*]
Elektroizolacna Kablova Tech — Elektroizolacna a Kablova Technika [*Czechoslovakia*]
Elektro-Jahrb — Elektro-Jahrbuch [*Switzerland*]
Elektro Med Biomed und Tech — Elektro Medizin, Biomedizin, und Technik
Elektromeister & Dtsch Elektrohandwerk — Elektromeister und Deutsches Elektrohandwerk
Elektron Anz — Elektronik-Anzeiger
Elektron Appl — Elektronik Applikation
Elektron Bol'shikh Moshch — Elektronika Bol'shikh Moshchnostei [*USSR*]

Elektron Datenverarb — Elektronische Datenverarbeitung
Elektron Entwickl — Elektronik Entwicklung
Elektron Heute — Elektronik Heute
Elektronik — Elektronik-Zeitung
Elektron Ind — Elektronik Industrie
Elektron Inf — Elektronik Informationen
Elektron Informationsverarbeit Kybernetik — Elektronische
    Informationsverarbeitung und Kybernetik
Elektron Informationsverarb Kybern — Elektronische Informationsverarbeitung
    und Kybernetik
Elektron Informationsverarb Kybernet — Elektronische
    Informationsverarbeitung und Kybernetik [*Berlin*]
Elektron Int — Elektron International
Elektron Ionnye Protsessy Tverd Telakh — Elektronnye i Ionnye Protsessy v
    Tverdykh Telakh
Elektron J — Elektronik Journal
Elektron Khim Kardiol — Elektronika i Khimiya v Kardiologii
Elektronmikroskopiever Suidelike Afr Verrig — Elektronmikroskopievereniging
    van Suidelike Afrika. Verrigtings
Elektron Model — Elektronnoe Modelirovanie [*Ukrainian SSR*]
Elektron (Muenchen) — Elektronik (Muenchen)
Elektronnaya Obrab Mater — Elektronnaya Obrabotka Materialov
Elektron Obrab Mater — Elektronnaya Obrabotka Materialov
Elektron Prax — Elektronik Praxis
Elektron Radio Telev — Elektroniikka Radio Televisio [*Finland*]
Elektron Rechenanlagen — Elektronische Rechenanlagen
Elektron Rechenanlagen Comput Prax — Elektronische Rechenanlagen mit
    Computer Praxis
Elektron Rechnen und Regeln — Elektronisches Rechnen und Regeln
Elektron Rechnen und Regeln. Sonderband — Elektronisches Rechnen und
    Regeln. Sonderband
Elektron Rechnen Regeln Sonderband — Elektronisches Rechnen und Reveln.
    Sonderband
Elektron Rech Regeln — Elektronisches Rechnen und Regeln
Elektron Tekh Ser 12 — Elektronnaya Tekhnika. Seriya 12
Elektron Tekh Ser 1 Elektron — Elektronnaya Tekhnika. Seriya 1. Elektronika
    [*USSR*]
Elektron Wiss Tech — Elektron in Wissenschaft und Technik
Elektron-Ztg — Elektronik-Zeitung [*West Germany*]
Elektro-Prakt — Elektro-Praktiker [*East Germany*]
Elektroprom-st Priborostr — Elektropromishlenost i Priborostroene [*Bulgaria*]
Elektrotech Cas — Elektrotechniky Casopis
Elektrotech Maschinenbau — Elektrotechnik und Maschinenbau
Elektrotech Obz — Elektrotechnicky Obzor
Elektrotech Z A — Elektrotechnische Zeitschrift. A
Elektrotech Z Ausg A — Elektrotechnische Zeitschrift. Ausgabe A
Elektrotech Z Ausg B — Elektrotechnische Zeitschrift. Ausgabe B
Elektrotech Z B — Elektrotechnische Zeitschrift. B
Elektrotech Zeit — Elektrotechnische Zeitschrift
Elektrotech Z ETZ A — Elektrotechnische Zeitschrift. ETZ A
Elektrotech Z ETZ B — Elektrotechnische Zeitschrift. ETZ B
Elektroteh Ind Pogonu — Elektrotehnika u Industriji Pogonu
Elektroteh Vestn — Elektrotehniski Vestnik
Elektrotek Tidsskr — Elektroteknisk Tidsskrift
Elektrowaerme A — Elektrowaerme im Technischen-Ausbau
Elektrowaerme Int — Elektrowaerme International
Elektrowaerme Int A — Elektrowaerme International. A
Elektrowaerme Int A Elektrowaerme Tech Ausbau — Elektrowaerme
    International. A. Elektrowaerme im Technischen Ausbau
Elektrowaerme Int B — Elektrowaerme International. B
Elektrowaerme Int B Elektrowaerme — Elektrowaerme International. B.
    Industrielle Elektrowaerme
Elektrowaerme Int Ed A — Elektrowaerme International. Edition A.
    Elektrowaerme im Technischen Ausbau
Elektrowaerme Int Ed B — Elektrowaerme International. Edition B.
    Industrielle Elektrowaerme
Elektrowrm Tech-Ausbau — Elektrowaerme im Technischen-Ausbau
Elektr Stantsii — Elektricheskie Stantsii
Elektr Stn — Elektricheskie Stantsii
Elektr & Teplovoznaya Tyaga — Elektricheskaya i Teplovoznaya Tyaga
Elektr Teplovoz Tyaga — Elektricheskaya i Teplovoznaya Tyaga
Elektr Z B — Elektrotechnische Zeitschrift. Ausgabe B
Elelmez Ipar — Elelmezesi Ipar
Elelm Ipar — Elelmezesi Ipar
Elelmiszervizgalati Kozl — Elelmiszervizgalati Kozlemenyek
Elelmiszerv Koezl — Elelmiszervizgalati Koezlemenyek
ELEMA — Electrical Engineer (Melbourne, Australia)
Elem Chastitsy Kosm Luchi — Elementarnye Chastitsy i Kosmicheskie Luchi
ElemE — Elementary English
Elem Math — Elemente der Mathematik
Elem Math Suppl — Elemente der Mathematik. Supplement
Elem Sch J — Elementary School Journal
ELENA — Electrical Engineering (American Institute of Electrical Engineers)
ELEND — Electrical Engineer
El and Energi Elektrotek — El and Energi Elektroteknikeren
El Engl — Elementary English

El Engl R — Elementary English Review
ELEQB — Electric Equipment
ELet — Europa Letteraria
ELETB — Electrical Engineering Transactions
Elettron Oggi — Elettronica Oggi
Elettron & Telecomun — Elettronica e Telecomunicazioni
Elettrotecn — Elettrotecnica
Elettrotecnica Suppl — Elettrotecnica. Supplemento [*Italy*]
Elev Insemination — Elevage Insemination
Elev Kosmos — Elevtheros Kosmos
Elev Porcin — Elevage Porcin
ELEWA — Electrical West [*United States*]
Eley Game Advis Serv Annu Rep — Eley Game Advisory Service. Annual
    Report
Eley Game Advis Serv Bookl — Eley Game Advisory Service. Booklet
Eley Game Advis Stn Annu Rep — Eley Game Advisory Station. Annual Report
ELF — Etude de la Langue Francaise
ELFOD — Electric Forum [*United States*]
ELH — Journal of English Literary History
ELH Engl L — ELH. English Literary History
ELIDA — Electronic Industries
El Ind — Electrical Industry
ELIND — Electricien Industriel
ELing — Etudes Linguistiques
Elin-Z — Elin- Zeitschrift
Elisha Mitchell Sci Soc J — Elisha Mitchell Scientific Society. Journal
ELiT — English Literature in Transition, 1880-1920
ELit — Estafeta Literaria
ELit — Etudes Litteraires
ElizS — Elizabethan Studies
ELJAA — Elektro-Jahrbuch
ELKCA — Elektrotechnicky Casopis
ELKHA — Elektro-Handel
ELKOA — Elektronik
ELKRD — Elektronik-Centralen. Report. ECR
ELkT — Epitheorese Logou Kai Technes
ELKTA — Elektrotekhnika
ELKTD — Elektronikk
ELKWA — Elektrowirtschaft
ELKZ — Evangelisch-Lutherische Kirchenzeitung [*Berlin*]
ELL — English Language and Literature
ELLEA — Electronics Letters
ELLF — Etudes de Langue et de Litterature Francaises
Elliott Soc N H Charleston Pr — Elliott Society of Natural History of
    Charleston. Proceedings
Ellis Horwood Ser Comput Appl — Ellis Horwood Series. Computers and Their
    Applications
Ellis Horwood Ser Math Appl — Ellis Horwood Series. Mathematics and Its
    Applications
ELLPA — Electric Light and Power
ELLS — English Literature and Language [*Tokyo, Japan*]
Ellwanger Jb — Ellwanger Jahrbuch: Ein Volksbuch fuer Heimatpflege in
    Virngau und Ries
ELM — El Urogallo (Madrid)
ELMAA — Electrical Manufacturing
Elma Dill Russell Spencer Found Ser — Elma Dill Russell Spencer Foundation
    Series
ELMCBK — Electromedica [*English Edition*]
ELMMA — Elemente der Mathematik
ELMOD — Elektronnoe Modelirovanie
ELMYA — Electromyography [*Later, Electromyography and Clinical
    Neurophysiology*]
ELMYAH — Electromyography [*Later, Electromyography and Clinical
    Neurophysiology*]
ELMZA — Elelmiszertudomany
ELN — English Language Notes
ELN — Environmental Law Newsletter
ELODA — Electronic Design
ELOSA9 — Elsevier Oceanography Series
ELOWA — Electro-Technology [*New York*]
El Pal — El Palacio
El Paso Geol Soc Annu Field Trip (Guideb) — El Paso Geological Society.
    Annual Field Trip (Guidebook)
ELPBA — Elektropromishlenost i Priborostroene
ELPLBS — Ekologia Polska
ELPLD — Electronics Information and Planning
ELPOA — Electronic Products
ELPPA — Electronic Packaging and Production
ELPVA — Elektroprivreda
ELPWA — Electronics and Power
ELR — English Literary Renaissance
ELR — Environmental Law Reporter [*Environmental Law Institute*]
ELR — Environmental Law Reporter of New South Wales
ELR — European Law Review
ELRAA — Elektronische Rechenanlagen
ELREA — Electrical Review [*London*]

EL Rev — European Law Review
ELRMD — Electric Ratemaking
ELRPA — Environmental Law Reporter
ELRPD — ELCON [*Electricity Consumers Resource Council*] Report
Els — Elsinore
ELS — English Literary Studies
El Salvador Servicio Geol Nac Anales Bol Bol Sismol — El Salvador. Servicio Geologico Nacional. Anales. Boletin. Boletin Sismologico
El Salvador Univ Inst Tropical Inv Cient Anuario Comun — El Salvador Universidad. Instituto Tropical de Investigaciones Cientificas. Anuario Comunicaciones
El Salv Dir Gen Invest Agron Secc Agron Bol Tec — El Salvador. Direccion General de Investigaciones Agronomicas. Seccion de Agronomia. Boletin Tecnico
El Salv Dir Gen Invest Agron Secc Entomol Bol Tec — El Salvador. Direccion General de Investigaciones Agronomicas. Seccion de Entomologia. Boletin Tecnico
El Sch Guid & Counsel — Elementary School Guidance and Counseling
El Sch J — Elementary School Journal
El School T — Elementary School Teacher
Elsevier Oceanogr Ser — Elsevier Oceanography Series [*Elsevier Book Series*]
Elsevier Oceanogr Ser (Amsterdam) — Elsevier Oceanography Series (Amsterdam) [*Elsevier Book Series*]
ELSM — Els Marges [*Barcelona*]
ELSPA — Elektricheskie Seti i Sistemy
ELSRB — Electrotechnical Laboratory. Summaries of Reports [*Japan*]
ELSUA — Electrical Supervisor
ELT — Electra
ELT — English Language Teaching [*Later, English Language Teaching Journal*]
ELT — English Literature in Transition, 1880-1920
ELTCA — Electricite
ELTEA — Electro-Technology [*Bangalore, India*]
Eltek Aktuell Elektron — Elteknik Med Aktuell Elektronik
Eltek Aktuell Elektron A — Elteknik Med Aktuell Elektronik. Edition A
Elteknik Med Aktuel Elektron — Elteknik Med Aktuell Elektronik
ELTGA — Electric Technology (USSR) [*English Translation*]
ELTHB — Elektrotehnika
ELTIA — Electrical Times
ELTJ — English Language Teaching Journal
ELTKA — Elektrotechniek
ELTPA — Electronic Progress
ELTRD — Elektronikschau
ELTSA — Elettrotecnica. Supplemento
ELTTA — Electrotehnica
ELTZA — Elettrificazione
ELu — Estudios Lulianos
ELul — Estudios Lulianos
ELVEA — Elektrontehniski Vestnik
ELWIU — Essays in Literature. Western Illinois University
ELWLA — Elektrowelt
ELWOA — Electrical World
ELWYA — Electronics Weekly
EM — Ecological Monographs
EM — Econometrica
Em — Emerita
EM — Empirical Studies of the Arts
EM — Endocrinology and Metabolism
EM — English Miscellany
EM — Espana Misionera
EM — Ethnikon Mouseion
Em — Ethnomusicology
EM — Etudes Mauritaniennes
EM — Excavation Memoirs [*London*]
EM — Excerpta Medica [*Amsterdam*]
EM — Journal of Engineering Mechanics
EMA — Environmental Monitoring and Assessment
EMA — Europe in the Middle Ages. Selected Studies [*Elsevier Book Series*]
EMAAA — Epeteris Mesaionikou Archeiou Akademias Athenon
EmAb — Employment Relations Abstracts
Emailletech Mon Bl — Emailletechnische Monats Blaetter
EMASD — Environmental Monitoring and Assessment
EMB — Emballages Magazine
EMB — Engineering Manpower Bulletin [*Engineers' Joint Council*]
Emballage Dig — Emballage Digest
Em Benefit — Employee Benefit Plan Review
Emberiza Vogelschutz Vogelkd Rheinl Pfalz — Emberiza Vogelschutz und Vogelkunde in Rheinland Pfalz
Embouteillage Cond — Embouteillage Conditionnement
EMBRAPA Empresa Bras Pesqui Agropecu — EMBRAPA. Empresa Brasileira de Pesquisa Agropecuaria
EMBZA6 — Emberiza
EMC — El Monte Carmelo
EMC — El Museo Canario
EMCNA9 — Electromyography and Clinical Neurophysiology
EMD — English Miscellany. St. Stephen's College (Delhi)

Emder Jb — Emder Jahrbuch
EM & D J Eng Mater Compon Des — EM and D [*Engineering Materials and Design*] Journal of Engineering Materials, Components, and Design
EM D J Mater Components Des — EM and D [*Engineering Materials and Design*] Journal of Engineering Materials, Components, and Design
EM & D Prod Data — EM and D [*Engineering Materials and Design*] Product Data
EME — Euromoney
EMEA — Employment and Earnings
EM Econ Mocambique — EM. Economia de Mocambique
EMEED — Electrical and Mechanical Executive Engineer [*England*]
EMELD — Electric Machines and Electromechanics
Emer — Emerita
E Mercks Jahresber — E Merck's Jahresberichte
Emergency Lib — Emergency Librarian
Emerg Lib — Emergency Librarian
Emerg Med — Emergency Medicine
Emerg Med Annu — Emergency Medicine Annual
Emerg Med Serv — Emergency Medical Services
Emerg Med Tech Legal Bull — Emergency Medical Technician Legal Bulletin
Emerg Nurse Legal Bull — Emergency Nurse Legal Bulletin
Emerg Plann Dig — Emergency Planning Digest
Emerg Serv News — Emergency Services News
Emer Libr — Emergency Librarian
EMETD — Energy Meetings
EMFIA — Electroplating and Metal Finishing
EMFRA2 — Empire Forestry Review
EMIDD — Environment Midwest
EMIPA — Elelmezesi Ipar
EMJ — Engineering and Mining Journal
EMJODG — EMBO [*European Molecular Biology Organization*] Journal
E & M Jour — Engineering and Mining Journal
Em LJ — Emory Law Journal
EMM — Etudes de Metaphysique et de Morale
EMNED — Energy Management News
EMNGD — Environmental Management
EMODA — EMO [*Emergency Measures Organization*] Digest [*Canada*]
EMO (Emerg Meas Organ) Dig — EMO (Emergency Measures Organization) Digest (Canada)
E Mong — Etudes Mongoles
Emory L J — Emory Law Journal
Emory Univ Quart — Emory University Quarterly
EMPA — Etudes Mensuelles sur l'Economie et les Finances de la Syrie et des Pays Arabes [*Damascus*]
Emp Cotton Grow Corp Prog Rep Exp Stn — Empire Cotton Growing Corporation. Progress Reports from Experiment Stations
Emp Cotton Grow Rev — Empire Cotton Growing Corporation. Review
Emp For J — Empire Forestry Journal
Emp For Rev — Empire Forestry Review
Empire For J — Empire Forestry Journal
Empire Prod — Empire Producer
Empir Res T — Empirical Research in Theatre
Emp J Exp Ag — Empire Journal of Experimental Agriculture
Emp J Exp Agric — Empire Journal of Experimental Agriculture
Empl Benefit Plan Rev — Employee Benefit Plan Review
Empl Benefits J — Employee Benefits Journal
Empl News — Employment News
Employ Benefit Plan Rev — Employee Benefit Plan Review
Employ Benefits J — Employee Benefits Journal
Employee Rel — Employee Relations
Employers R — Employers' Review
Employ Gaz — Employment Gazette
Employment — Employment and Earnings
Employ Rel Abstr — Employment Relations Abstracts
Employ Relat Law J — Employee Relations Law Journal
Empl RA — Employment Relations Abstracts
Empl Rel LJ — Employee Relations Law Journal
Emporia St Res Stud — Emporia State Research Studies
Emp Prod — Empire Producer
Emp R — Empire Review
Emp Rel — Employee Relations
Emp Rel LJ — Employee Relations Law Journal
EMPSA — Experimental and Molecular Pathology. Supplement
EMQ — Evangelical Missions Quarterly
EMR — Employee Relations
EMRIWTB — Canada. Department of Energy. Mines and Resources. Inland Waters Branch. Technical Bulletin
EMROD — Ekspluatatsiya, Modernizatsiya i Remont Oborudovaniya v Neftepererabatyvayushchei i Neftekhimicheskoi Promyshlennosti
EmSA — Emakeele Seltsi Aastaraamat
EMSCD — English Miscellany. St. Stephen's College (Delhi)
EMSM — Employee Services Management
EMS Newsl — EMS [*Environmental Mutagen Society*] Newsletter
EMT — Econometrica
EMTDA — Engineering Materials and Design
EMT J — EMT [*Emergency Medical Technician*] Journal

EMT Legal Bull — Emergency Medical Technician Legal Bulletin
EMTRA — Eastern Metals Review
EMW — Enquetes du Musee de la Vie Wallonne
EM Wash State Univ Coop Ext Serv — EM. Washington State University. Cooperative Extension Service
EN — Economic News
EN — Education Nationale
EN — Electronic News
En — Encounter
EN — Etudes Numismatiques
EN — European Numismatics
EN — Experimental Neurology
ENAAD — Energetika (Alma-Ata)
ENACD — Environmental Action
ENAEA — Electrical News and Engineering
ENALD — Energy and Alternatives Magazine
ENATA — Energia es Atomtechnika
ENB — Energiebesparing in Bedrijf en Instelling
ENC — Els Nostres Classics
ENC — Encounter
Enc Brit — Encyclopaedia Britannica
Enc Buddh — Encylopaedia of Buddhism
Enc Catt — Enciclopedia Cattolica
ENCEA — Encephale
ENCEAN — Encephale
Enceph — Encephale
Ench B — Enchiridion Biblicum
Ench Symb — Enchiridion Symbolorum
EncI — Encounter (Indianapolis)
Enc I — Encyclopedie de l'Islam
EncL — Encounter (London)
ENCLD — Energy Clearinghouse
Enc Lik Umj — Enciklopedija Likovnik Umjetnosti
ENCMD — Energy Dollars and Sense of Conservation
Enc Mens O Mer — Encyclopedie Mensuelle d'Outre-Mer
Enc Mus — Encyclopedie de la Musique
ENCO — Environmental Conservation
En Conserv — Energy Conservation News
Encore — Encore American and Worldwide News
Encount — Encounter
Encounter (Chr Theol Sem) — Encounter (Christian Theological Seminary)
Enc Pamphl Ser — Encounter Pamphlet Series
Enc Psych — Encyclopedia of Psychology
ENCR — Environmental Carcinogenesis Reviews
Enc SEI — Enciclopedia SEI [*Societa Editrice Internazionale*]
Enc Spett — Enciclopedia dello Spettacolo
Enc Unif Sci — Encyclopedia of Unified Science
ENCYA — Engineering Cybernetics [*English Translation*]
Ency Amer — Encyclopaedia Americana
Ency Brit — Encyclopaedia Britannica
Encycl Biol (Paris) — Encyclopedie Biologique (Paris)
Encycl Chem Technol — Encyclopedia of Chemical Technology
Encycl Entomol — Encyclopedie Entomologique
Encycl Med-Chir — Encyclopedie Medico-Chirurgicale
Encycl Mycol — Encyclopedie Mycologique
Encyclopedia Math Appl — Encyclopedia of Mathematics and Its Applications
Encycl Ornithol (Paris) — Encyclopedie Ornithologique (Paris)
Encycl Plant Physiol New Ser — Encyclopedia of Plant Physiology. New Series
Encycl Urol — Encyclopedia of Urology
Encycl Vet Med Surg and Obst — Encyclopaedia of Veterinary Medicine, Surgery, and Obstetrics
ENCYDI — Encyclia
ENDCA — Endoscopy
ENDE — Endeavour
ENDEA — Endeavour
ENDEAS — Endeavour [*Oxford*]
Endeavour New Ser — Endeavour. New Series
ENDED — Energy Development
Endem Dis Bull Nagasaki Univ — Endemic Diseases Bulletin. Nagasaki University
ENDGA — Engineers' Digest
ENDGD — Energy Digest [*Bombay*]
ENDID — Energy Dialog
ENDKA — Endokrinologie
ENDKAC — Endokrinologie
ENDOA — Endocrinology
ENDOAO — Endocrinology
Endocr Bioassay Data — Endocrine Bioassay Data. United States Department of Health, Education, and Welfare
Endocr Exp — Endocrinologia Experimentalis
Endocrinol — Endocrinologie
Endocrinol Exp — Endocrinologia Experimentalis
Endocrinol Ind — Endocrinology Index
Endocrinol Jpn — Endocrinologia Japonica
Endocrinol Jpn Suppl — Endocrinologia Japonica. Supplement
Endocrinol Metab Ser — Endocrinology and Metabolism Series

Endocrinol Sci Cost — Endocrinologia e Scienza della Costituzione
Endocr Jap — Endocrinologia Japonica
Endocr Res — Endocrine Research Communications
Endocr Res Commun — Endocrine Research Communications
Endocr Rev — Endocrine Reviews
Endok Mekh Regul Prisposobleniya Org Myshechnoi Deyat — Endokrinnye Mekhanizmy Regulyatsii Prisposobleniya Organizma k Myshechnoi Deyatel'nosti
Endokr — Endokrinologie
Endokrinol — Endokrinologie
Endokr Pol — Endokrynologia Polska
Endokrynol Pol — Endokrynologia Polska
ENDRD — Energy Directory
ENE — Energy Economics
ENEAD — Energy in Agriculture
ENECA — Engineering Economist
ENEDD — Energy and Education
ENEGA — Energies
ENEIB — Energy International
ENELA — Energia Elettrica
ENERA — Energie
ENERB — Energy Conversion
ENERD — Energy
Energa Atom — Energia es Atomtechnika
Energ Alternative — Energie Alternative [*Italy*]
Energa Nu — Energia Nucleare [*Milan*]
Energa Nucl — Energia Nucleare [*Milan*]
Energ es Atomtech — Energia es Atomtechnika
Energ Atomtech — Energia es Atomtechnika
Energ Avtom — Energetika i Avtomatika [*USSR*]
Energ-Brief — Energie-Brief
Energ Bull — Energeticeskij Bjulleten
Energ Byull — Energeticheskii Byulleten
Energ Commun — Energy Communications
Energ El — Energia Elettrica
Energ Elektrif — Energetika i Elektrifikatsiya
Energ Elektrif (Kiev) — Energetika i Elektrifikatsiya (Kiev)
Energ Elet — Energia Elettrica
Energ Elettr — Energia Elettrica
Energ Elettr B — Energia Elettrica. B
Energeteknol Ispol'z Topl — Energetekhnologicheskow Ispol'zovanie Toplova [*USSR*]
Energ Fluide — Energie Fluide
Energ Fluide et Lubr Hydraul Pneum Asservissements — Energie Fluide et Lubrification et Hydraulique Pneumatique Asservissements
Energ Fontes Altern — Energia. Fontes Alternativas
Energ Fuego At — Energia del Fuego al Atomo
Energ Hidroteh — Energetica si Hidrotehnica
Energia — Publicacion sobre Energia
Energieonder Cent Ned Rep — Energieonderzoek Centrum Nederland Report
Energietech — Energietechnik
Energiewirtsch Tagesfragen — Energiewirtschaftliche Tagesfragen
Energ Ind — Energia e Industria
Energ Inst Im G M Krzhizhanovskogo Sb Tr — Energeticheskii Institut Imeni G. M. Krzhizhanovskogo. Sbornik Trudov
Energ Manage — Energy Management
Energ Nucl — Energia Nuclear
Energ Nucl Agric — Energia Nuclear e Agricultura
Energ Nucl (Lisbon) — Energia Nuclear. Boletim Informativo do Forum Atomico Portugues (Lisbon)
Energ Nucl (Madrid) — Energia Nuclear (Madrid)
Energ Nucl (Milan) — Energia Nucleare (Milan)
Energ Nucl (Paris) — Energie Nucleaire (Paris)
Energ Polic — Energy Policy
Energ Stroit — Energeticheskoe Stroitel'stvo [*USSR*]
Energ Stroit Rubezhom — Energeticheskoe Stroitel'stvo za Rubezhom [*USSR*]
Energ Tech — Energie und Technik
Energ Techn — Energie und Technik
Energ Techn — Energietechnik
Energ Technik — Energie und Technik
Energ Trans — Energetika i Transport
Energ Transp — Energetika i Transport [*USSR*]
Energy — Energy User News
Energy Abstr Policy Anal — Energy Abstracts for Policy Analysis
Energy Advis Bull Tex Manuf — Energy Advisory Bulletin for Texas Manufacturers
Energy Alternatives Mag — Energy and Alternatives Magazine
Energy Bldgs — Energy and Buildings
Energy Bldgs — Energy in Buildings
Energy in Bldgs — Energy in Buildings
Energy and Build — Energy and Buildings
Energy Build — Energy and Buildings
Energy Clgh — Energy Clearinghouse
Energy Cnvers & Manage — Energy Conversion and Management
Energy Commun — Energy Communications

Energy Conserv Dig — Energy Conservation Digest
Energy Conserv Rep — Energy Conservation Report [*Canada*]
Energy Conserv Update — Energy Conservation Update
Energy Consum — Energy Consumer
Energy Conv — Energy Conversion
Energy Convers — Energy Conversion
Energy Convers Intl J — Energy Conversion. An International Journal
Energy Convers and Manage — Energy Conversion and Management
Energy Convers Manage — Energy Conversion and Management
Energy Convers Tech Rep Aust Natl Univ Dep Eng Phys — Australian National
    University. Department of Engineering Physics. Energy Conversion
    Technical Report
Energy Dev — Energy and Development Journal
Energy Dev — Energy Developments
Energy Dev Jpn — Energy Developments in Japan
Energy Dev (New York) — Energy Development (New York). IEEE Power
    Engineering Society Papers
Energy Dig — Energy Digest
Energy Dig (Colo Spring Colo) — Energy Digest (Colorado Springs, Colorado)
Energy Dig (London) — Energy Digest (London)
Energy Dig (Wash DC) — Energy Digest (Washington, DC)
Energy Dly — Energy Daily
Energy Dollars Sense Conserv — Energy Dollars and Sense of Conservation
Energy Econ — Energy Economics
Energy Econ Policy Manage — Energy Economics, Policy, and Management
Energy Educ — Energy and Education
Energy Educ Newsl — Energy Educator Newsletter
Energy Eng — Energy Engineering
Energy Enging — Energy Engineering
Energy Environ — Energy and Environment [*South Africa*]
Energy Environ (NY) — Energy and the Environment (New York)
Energy Environ (Oak Ridge Tenn) — Energy and the Environment (Oak Ridge,
    Tennessee)
Energy Environ Proc Nat Conf — Energy and the Environment. Proceedings of
    the National Conference
Energy Exec Dir — Energy Executive Directory
Energy Forum N Engl — Energy Forum in New England
Energy Ind — Energy Index
Energy Ind Commerce Q Bull — Energy for Industry and Commerce. Quarterly
    Bulletin
Energy Int — Energy International
Energy J — Energy Journal [*New Zealand*]
Energy LJ — Energy Law Journal
Energy Manage — Energy Management
Energy Manage (Cleveland Ohio) — Energy Management (Cleveland, Ohio)
Energy Manage (India) — Energy Management (India)
Energy Manage News — Energy Management News
Energy Meet — Energy Meetings [*United States*]
Energy Newsl — Energy Newsletter [*United States*]
Energy Perspect — Energy Perspectives
Energy Pipelines Syst — Energy Pipelines and Systems
Energy Plann Network — Energy Planning Network [*United States*]
Energy Pol — Energy Policy
Energy Pollut Control — Energy and Pollution Control [*Japan*]
Energy Process (Can) — Energy Processing (Canada)
Energy Prog — Energy Progress
Energy Q — Energy Quarterly [*Taiwan*]
Energy Rep (Alton Engl) — Energy Report (Alton, England)
Energy Rep States — Energy Report to the States
Energy Res — Energy Research [*England*]
Energy Res Abstr — Energy Research Abstracts
Energy Res Dig — Energy Research Digest
Energy Resourc Technol — Energy Resources and Technology
Energy Resour (Osaka) — Energy and Resources (Osaka)
Energy Res Rep — Energy Research Reports
Energy Rev — Energy Review
Energy Systems Pol — Energy Systems and Policy
Energy Syst Policy — Energy Systems and Policy
Energy Technol Conf Proc — Energy Technology Conference. Proceedings
Energy Technol Rev — Energy Technology Review
Energy Technol (Wash DC) — Energy Technology (Washington, DC)
Energy Top — Energy Topics
Energy Wld — Energy World
ENETD — Environmental Ethics
ENEXA — Endocrinologia Experimentalis
ENEXAM — Endocrinologia Experimentalis
EnF — Encontro com o Folclore
ENFAD — Fusion Power Associates. Executive Newsletter
Enfant Milieu Trop — Enfant en Milieu Tropical
Enferm Torax — Enfermedades del Torax
Enferm Torax Tuberc — Enfermedades del Torax y Tuberculosis
ENFL — Energy File [*Vancouver, British Columbia*]
ENFLA — Energie Fluide
Eng — [*The*] Engineer
Eng — Engineering
Eng — English

Engage/Soc Act — Engage/Social Action
Eng Apprent — Engineer Apprentice
Eng Aspects Magnetohydrodyn — Engineering Aspects of
    Magnetohydrodynamics
Eng As South Tr — Engineering Association of the South. Transactions
Eng Aust — Engineers Australia
Eng in Aust — English in Australia
Eng Boilerhouse Rev — Engineering and Boilerhouse Review
Eng Boil H Rev — Engineering and Boiler House Review
Eng Build — Engineer and Builder
Eng Bull — Engineering Bulletin
Eng Bull Purdue Univ — Engineering Bulletin. Purdue University
Eng Bull Purdue Univ Eng Ext Ser — Engineering Bulletin. Purdue University.
    Engineering Extension Series
Eng & Bu Rec — Engineering and Building Record [*USA*]
Eng Buy Guide — Engineer Buyers Guide
Eng Cem World — Engineering and Cement World
Eng Chem Dig — Engineering and Chemical Digest
Eng Club Phila Pr — Engineers' Club of Philadelphia. Proceedings
Eng Comput — Engineering Computers
Eng Constr World — Engineering Construction World
Eng Contract Rec — Engineering and Contract Record
Eng Cornell Q — Engineering. Cornell Quarterly
Eng Costs Prod Econ — Engineering Costs and Production Economics
    [*Netherlands*]
Eng Cybern — Engineering Cybernetics
Eng Cyc — English Cyclopaedia
Eng Dance — English Dance and Song
Eng Dig — Engineers' Digest
Eng Dig (London) — Engineers' Digest (London)
Eng Dig (NY) — Engineering Digest (New York)
Eng Dig (Toronto) — Engineering Digest (Toronto)
Eng Dom M — Englishwoman's Domestic Magazine
Eng Econ — Engineering Economist
Eng Economist — Engineering Economist
Eng Educ — Engineering Education
Eng Educ — English Education
Eng Educ (Lancaster PA) — Engineering Education (Lancaster, Pennsylvania)
Engei Gakkai Zasshi J Jap Soc Hortic Sci — Engei Gakkai Zasshi/Journal of
    the Japanese Society for Horticultural Science
Engelhard Ind Tech Bull — Engelhard Industries. Technical Bulletin
Engenh Min Met — Engenharia, Mineracao, Metalurgia
Engenh Quim — Engenharia e Quimica
Eng Exp Stat News — Engineering Experiment Station News
Eng FD & S Soc Jl — English Folk Dance and Song Society. Journal
Eng Foundryman — Engineer and Foundryman
Eng Fract Mech — Engineering Fracture Mechanics
ENGGD — Ekspress-Informatsiya. Neftegazovaya Geologiya i Geofizika
Eng Geol — Engineering Geology
Eng Geol (Amsterdam) — Engineering Geology (Amsterdam)
Eng Geol Case Hist — Engineering Geology Case Histories
Eng Geol Soils Eng Symp Proc — Engineering Geology and Soils Engineering
    Symposium. Proceedings
Eng Graphics — Engineering Graphics
Eng His R — English Historical Review
Eng Hist Bul — English History Bulletin for Teachers in Secondary Schools
Eng Hist R — English Historical Review
Eng Hist Rev — English Historical Review
EngI — Engineering Index
ENGIA — [*The*] Engineer
Eng Illust — English Illustrated Magazine
Eng Ind — Engineering Index
Eng Index Energy Abstr — Engineering Index. Energy Abstracts
Eng Index Monthly Author Index — Engineering Index Monthly and Author
    Index
Eng Ind India — Engineering Index of India
Eng Ind (Iraq) — Engineering Industries (Iraq)
Engineers' Bull — Engineers' Bulletin
Engineers Gaz — Engineers' Gazette
Engin M — Engineering Magazine
Engin N — Engineering News-Record
Eng Insp — Engineering Inspection
Eng Inst Canada Trans — Engineering Institute of Canada. Transactions
Eng & Instrumentation — Engineering and Instrumentation
Eng Issues — Engineering Issues
Eng J — Engineering Journal
Eng J — Engineering Journal. American Institute of Steel Construction
Eng J — English Journal
Eng J Am Inst Steel Constr — Engineering Journal. American Institute of Steel
    Construction
Eng J (Montreal) — Engineering Journal (Montreal)
Eng J (NY) — Engineering Journal (New York)
Eng J Singapore — Engineering Journal of Singapore
Engl Abstr Sel Art Sov Bloc Mainland China Tech J Ser 1 — English Abstracts
    of Selected Articles from Soviet Bloc and Mainland China Technical
    Journals. Series 1. Physics and Mathematics

Engl Abstr Sel Art Sov Bloc Mainland China Tech J Ser 2 — English Abstracts of Selected Articles from Soviet Bloc and Mainland China Technical Journals. Series 2. Chemistry
Engl Abstr Sel Art Sov Bloc Mainland China Tech J Ser 3 — English Abstracts of Selected Articles from Soviet Bloc and Mainland China Technical Journals. Series 3. Metals
Engl Abstr Sel Art Sov Bloc Mainland China Tech J Ser 5 — English Abstracts of Selected Articles from Soviet Bloc and Mainland China Technical Journals. Series 5. Electronics and Electrical Engineering
Engl Abstr Sel Art Sov Bloc Mainland China Tech J Ser 6 — English Abstracts of Selected Articles from Soviet Bloc and Mainland China Technical Journals. Series 6. Bio-Sciences
Engl Afr — English in Africa
Engl Alive — English Alive
Eng Lang Notes — English Language Notes
Eng Lang Teach J — English Language Teaching Journal
Engl Aust — English in Australia
Engl Elec J — English Electric Journal
Engl El J — English Electric Journal
Engl Heritage Monit — English Heritage Monitor
Engl Hist R — English Historical Review
Engl Hist Rev — English Historical Review
Engl Hist Rev — English History Review
Engl Inst Ann — English Institute. Annual
Engl Inst N — English Institute. New Series
English Church M — English Church Music
English in Ed — English in Education
English His — English Historical Review
English History Bul — English History Bulletin for Teachers in Secondary Schools
English Language Teaching J — English Language Teaching Journal
English MJ — English Music Journal
English R — English Review
Eng Lit in Trans — English Literature in Transition, 1880-1920
Eng LJ — Energy Law Journal
Engl J — English Journal
Engl J (Col Ed) — English Journal (College Edition)
Engl J (HS Ed) — English Journal (High School Edition)
Engl Lang Lit — English Language and Literature
Engl Lang N — English Language Notes
Engl Lang Not — English Language Notes
Engl Lang Notes — English Language Notes
Engl Lang Teach — English Language Teaching [*Later, English Language Teaching Journal*]
Engl Lit Lang — English Literature and Language
Engl Lit Re — English Literary Renaissance
Engl Lit Renaissance — English Literary Renaissance
Engl Lit Tr — English Literature in Transition, 1880-1920
Engl Lit Transition — English Literature in Transition, 1880-1920
Engl Misc — English Miscellany. A Symposium of History
Engl NZ — English in New Zealand
Engl Place-Name Soc — English Place-Name Society. Annual Volume
Engl Q — English Quarterly
Engl Rec — English Record
Engl Rev — English Review
Engl St — English Studies. A Journal of English Letters and Philology
Engl St Afr — English Studies in Africa
Engl St Can — English Studies in Canada
Engl Stud — Englische Studien
Engl Stud — English Studies
Engl Stud Afr — English Studies in Africa
Eng L T — English Language Teaching [*Later, English Language Teaching Journal*]
Engl Teach Assoc NSW Newsl — English Teachers Association of New South Wales. Newsletter
Engl Teach For — English Teaching Forum
Engl Usage Sthn Afr — English Usage in Southern Africa
Eng M — Engineering Magazine
Eng Mag — Engineering Magazine
Eng Man — Engineering Management and Equipment Digest
Eng Mat — Engineering Materials
Eng Mat Des — Engineering Materials and Design
Eng Mater — Engineering Materials [*Japan*]
Eng Mater Des — Engineering Materials and Design
Eng Mater & Des — Engineering Materials and Design
Eng Mater Process Methods — Engineering Materials and Processing Methods
Eng Med — Engineering in Medicine
Eng Mineracao Met — Engenharia, Mineracao, Metalurgia
Eng Mining J — Engineering and Mining Journal
Eng & Min J — Engineering and Mining Journal
Eng Min J — Engineering and Mining Journal
Eng Min J Press — Engineering and Mining Journal Press
Eng Min Metal — Engenharia, Mineracao, Metalurgia
Eng Min World — Engineering and Mining World
Eng N — Engineering News-Record
ENGNA — Engineering

Eng New-Rc — Engineering News-Record
Eng News — Engineering News
Eng News (NY) — Engineering News (New York)
Eng News-Rec — Engineering News-Record
Eng News (Tokyo) — Engineering News (Tokyo)
Engng — Engineering
Engng Des — Engineering Designer
Engng Des Int — Engineering Design International
Engng Geol — Engineering Geology
Engng Index Mthlys — Engineering Index Monthlies
Engng J — Engineering Journal
Engng J (Can) — Engineering Journal (Canada)
Engng Mat Des — Engineering Materials and Design
Engng Mater Des — Engineering Materials and Design
Engng Med — Engineering in Medicine
Engng Min J — Engineering and Mining Journal
Engng Outlook — Engineering Outlook
Engng Prod — Engineering Production
Engng Struct — Engineering Structures
Engng Thermophys China — Engineering Thermophysics in China
Engng Today — Engineering Today
Eng Optim — Engineering Optimization
Eng Optimization — Engineering Optimization
Eng Outlook Univ Ill — Engineering Outlook. University of Illinois
Eng Process Econ — Engineering and Process Economics
Eng Prod — Engineering Production
Eng Progr Univ Fla Bull — Engineering Progress. University of Florida. Bulletin
Eng Progr Univ Fla Tech Progr Rep — Engineering Progress. University of Florida. Technical Progress Report
Eng Quim — Engenharia e Quimica
Engr — [*The*] Engineer
EngR — English Record
EngR — English Review
Eng Res Bull — Engineering Research Bulletin
Eng Res Bull Rutgers Univ Coll Eng — Engineering Research Bulletin. Rutgers University. College of Engineering
Eng Rev — English Review. Salem State College
Engrg Cybernetics — Engineering Cybernetics
Engrs Dig — Engineers' Digest
Engrs' Digest — Engineers' Digest [*London*]
EngS — English Studies [*Amsterdam*]
Eng Sci — Engineering and Science
Eng and Sci — Engineering and Science
Eng-Sci News — Engineering-Science News
Eng Soc Libr ESL Bibliogr — Engineering Societies Library. ESL Bibliography
Eng Soc W Pa — Engineers' Society of Western Pennsylvania. Proceedings
Eng Soc York Pr — Engineering Society of York. Proceedings
Eng St — English Studies
Eng Struct — Engineering Structures
Eng Stud — English Studies
Eng T — Engineering Times
ENGTB — Energetika (Sofia, Bulgaria)
Eng Teach — English Teacher
Eng Teach Assn NSW News — English Teachers Association of New South Wales. Newsletter
Eng Teach Assoc NSW Newsl — English Teachers Association of New South Wales. Newsletter
Eng and Technol — Engineering and Technology
Eng Technol (Osaka) — Engineering and Technology (Osaka) [*Japan*]
Eng Times — Engineering Times
Eng Times (Calcutta) — Engineering Times (Calcutta)
Eng Today — Engineering Today
Eng Week — Engineering Week
Eng WR — Englishwomen's Review
Engy Insidr — Energy Insider
ENH — Carrosserie
Enhanced Oil-Recovery Field Rep — Enhanced Oil-Recovery Field Reports
ENHEA — Environmental Health [*Nagpur*]
ENHID — Energy Highlights
ENI — Engineering Index
En Jnl — Energy Journal
ENJOA — Engineering Journal [*Montreal*]
ENJOD — Energy Journal
EnJuYB — Encyclopaedia Judaica Year Book
ENLB — Emergency Nurse Legal Bulletin
Enl E — Enlightenment Essays
ENM — Economie
ENMAA — Enseignement Mathematique
ENMGD — Energy Management
ENMJA — Engineering and Mining Journal
ENMS — Environments. Journal of Interdisciplinary Studies
ENN — Export News (New Zealand)
ENNCA — Energia Nuclear
ENNE — Environment News. Alberta Department of the Environment
ENNLA — Energia Nucleare

ENNOD — Energy News Notes. CERI [*Colorado Energy Research Institute*]
ENNSD — Energy News [*Pakistan*]
ENNUA — Energie Nucleaire
En Nucl — Energie Nucleaire
ENNWD — Energy News [*United States*]
ENO — Econotities
ENORAK — Encyclopedie Ornithologique [*Paris*]
ENP — Nouvel Economiste (Paris)
En Pas — En Passant
ENPBB — Environmental Physiology and Biochemistry
ENPED — Energy Perspectives
ENPGD — Energy Progress
Enquete Mens Conjonct — Enquete Mensuelle de Conjoncture
ENR — Engineering News-Record
ENRE — Energy Report. Community Information Center. Fairbanks North
      Star Borough
ENREA — Engineering News-Record
ENREB — Entomological Review [*English Translation*]
ENRGD — Energies
ENRPD — Energy Report (Denver, Colorado)
ENRSD — Energy Research
ENRSE8 — Endocrine Research
ENRYD — Energy
ENSABO — Anais. Escola Nacional de Saude Publica e de Medicina Tropical
Ensay Estud — Ensayos y Estudios
Ensayos Pol Econ — Ensayos sobre Politica Economica
Enseignement Math — Enseignement Mathematique
Enseign Techn — Enseignement Technique
Ensenanza Invest Psicol — Ensenanza e Investigacion en Psicologia
ENSOD — Energy Sources
ENT — Environmental Science and Technology
ENTAD — Energy News [*United States*]
Ent Ber (Amst) — Entomologische Berichten (Amsterdam)
Ent Ber (Berlin) — Entomologische Berichten (Berlin)
Ent Circ Dep Agric (Br Columb) — Entomological Circular. Department of
      Agriculture (British Columbia)
Ent Circ Div Pl Ind Fla Dep Agric Consumer Serv — Entomology Circular.
      Division of Plant Industry. Florida Department of Agriculture and
      Consumer Services
ENTEA — Energie und Technik
Enterp Western Aust — Enterprise Western Australia
Ent Exp App — Entomologia Experimentalis et Applicata
Ent Fact Sheet Univ Minn — Entomology Fact Sheet. University of Minnesota
Ent Germ — Entomologica Germanica
ENT J — Ear, Nose, and Throat Journal
Ent Leafl Univ MD — Entomology Leaflet. University of Maryland
Ent Meddr — Entomologiske Meddelelser
Ent Meded Ned Indiee — Entomologische Mededeelingen van Nederlandsch-
      Indiee
Ent Mitt — Entomologische Mitteilungen
Ent Mitt Zool Mus (Hamburg) — Entomologische Mitteilungen. Zoologischen
      Museum (Hamburg)
Ent Mon Mag — Entomologist's Monthly Magazine
Ent Nachr — Entomologische Nachrichten
ENTND2 — ISSCT [*International Society of Sugarcane Technologists*]
      Entomology Newsletter
Ent News — Entomological News
Ent Obozr — Entomologiceskoe Obozrenie
Entom Month Mag — Entomologist's Monthly Magazine
Entom N — Entomological News
Entom News — Entomological News
Entomol — Entomologist
Entomol Abh (Dres) — Entomologische Abhandlungen (Dresden)
Entomol Abstr — Entomology Abstracts
Entomol Am — Entomologica Americana
Entomol Arb Mus G Frey (Tutzing-bei Muench) — Entomologische Arbeiten.
      Museum G. Frey (Tutzing-bei Muenchen)
Entomol Arb Mus G Frey (Tutzing Muenchen) — Entomologische Arbeiten.
      Museum G. Frey (Tutzing-bei Muenchen)
Entomol Ber (Amst) — Entomologische Berichten (Amsterdam)
Entomol Ber (Berl) — Entomologische Berichten (Berlin)
Entomol Bl — Entomologische Blaetter
Entomol Bl Biol Syst Kaefer — Entomologische Blaetter fuer Biologie und
      Systematik der Kaefer
Entomol Bull Brit Mus (Natur Hist) — Entomology Bulletin. British Museum
      (Natural History)
Entomol Exp Appl — Entomologia Experimentalis et Applicata
Entomol Gaz — Entomologist's Gazette
Entomol Gen — Entomologia Generalis
Entomol Ger — Entomologica Germanica
Entomol Listy — Entomologicke Listy
Entomol Medd — Entomologiske Meddelelser
Entomol Mimeo Ser Utah State Univ Agr Ext Serv — Entomology Mimeo
      Series. Utah State University. Agricultural Extension Service
Entomol Mitt Zool Mus Hamb — Entomologische Mitteilungen. Zoologischen
      Museum Hamburg

Entomol Mitt Zool Staatsinst Zool Mus (Hamb) — Entomologische
      Mitteilungen. Zoologischen Staatsinstitut und Zoologischen Museum
      (Hamburg)
Entomol Mon Mag — Entomologist's Monthly Magazine
Entomol Nachr — Entomologische Nachrichten
Entomol News — Entomological News
Entomol Newsl — Entomologists' Newsletter
Entomol Obozr — Entomologicheskoe Obozrenie
Entomologia Exp Appl — Entomologia Experimentalis et Applicata
Entomologia Gen — Entomologia Generalis
Entomologie Phytopath Appl — Entomologie et Phytopathologie Appliquees
Entomologist's Gaz — Entomologist's Gazette
Entomologist's Mon Mag — Entomologist's Monthly Magazine
Entomologists Newsl — Entomologists' Newsletter
Entomologist's Rep Dep Agric Tanganyika — Entomologist's Report.
      Department of Agriculture. Tanganyika
Entomol Phytopathol Appl — Entomologie et Phytopathologie Appliquees
Entomol Probl — Entomologicke Problemy
Entomol Rec J Var — Entomologist's Record and Journal of Variation
Entomol Rev — Entomological Review
Entomol Rev (Engl Transl Entomol Obozr) — Entomological Review (English
      Translation of Entomologicheskoye Obozreniye)
Entomol Scand — Entomologica Scandinavica
Entomol Scand Suppl — Entomologica Scandinavica. Supplementum
Entomol Soc Amer N Cent State Br Proc — Entomological Society of America.
      North Central State Branch. Proceedings
Entomol Soc Nigeria Occas Publ — Entomological Society of Nigeria.
      Occasional Publication
Entomol Soc NZ Bull — Entomological Society of New Zealand. Bulletin
Entomol Soc Ont Annu Rep — Entomological Society of Ontario. Annual
      Report
Entomol Tidskr — Entomologisk Tidskrift
Entomol Z — Entomologische Zeitschrift
Entomophaga Mem Hors Ser — Entomophaga Memoire Hors Serie
Entom Soc Am Ann — Entomological Society of America. Annals
ENTPA — Entropie
Ent Problemy — Entomologicke Problemy
En Trends — Energy Trends
Entrep — Entrepreneur
Entrepteneur — Entrepreneur Magazine
Entretiens Bichat Chir Spec — Entretiens de Bichat Chirurgie Specialites
Entretiens Bichat Med Biol — Entretiens de Bichat Medecine et Biologie
Entretiens Bichat Stomatol — Entretiens de Bichat Stomatologie [*France*]
Entretiens Bichat Ther — Entretiens de Bichat Therapeutique
Entretiens Chize Ser Ecol Ethol — Entretiens de Chize. Serie Ecologie et
      Ethologie
Entretiens Chize Ser Physiol — Entretiens de Chize. Serie Physiologie
Ent Scand — Entomologica Scandinavica
ENTSD — Energy Times [*India*]
Entsikl Izmer Kontrolya Avtom — Entsiklopediya Izmerenii. Kontrolya i
      Avtomatizatsii
Ent Tidskr — Entomologisk Tidskrift
Entwicklungsber Siemens und Halske — Entwicklungsberichte der Siemens und
      Halske Aktiengesellschaft
Entwicklungsgesch Syst Pflanz — Entwicklungsgeschichte und Systematik der
      Pflanzen
Ent Z (Frankf A M) — Entomologische Zeitschrift (Frankfurt Am Main)
ENUP — Environment Update. Environment Canada
ENUSA — Experimental Neurology. Supplement
Env — Environment
Env — Environment/Ecology
Env — Environment Information Access
ENVA — Environmental Affairs
Env Action — Environment Action Bulletin
Env Aff — Environmental Affairs
Env Data Serv — Environmental Data Service
Env Entomol — Environmental Entomology
ENVG — Environment and Planning. A
ENVHA — Environmental Health [*London*]
Env Health Persp — Environmental Health Perspectives
EnvI — Environment Index
Envir Action — Environmental Action
Envir Behav — Environment and Behavior
Envir Conserv — Environmental Conservation
Envir Ent — Environmental Entomology
Envir & Exper Bot — Environmental and Experimental Botany
Envir Geol — Environmental Geology
Envir Lett — Environmental Letters
Envir L Rep — Environmental Law Reporter
Envirn Sci — Environmental Science and Technology
Environ Abstr — Environmental Abstracts
Environ Action — Environmental Action
Environ Aff — Environmental Affairs
Environ Behav — Environment and Behavior
Environ & Behavior — Environment and Behavior
Environ Biol — Environmental Biology

Environ Biol Fishes — Environmental Biology of Fishes
Environ Biol Med — Environmental Biology and Medicine
Environ Can Annu Rep — Environment Canada. Annual Report
Environ Can For Pest Manage Inst Rep FPM-X — Environment Canada. Forest Pest Management Institute. Report FPM-X
Environ Can Rapp Annu — Environnement Canada. Rapport Annuel
Environ Change — Environment and Change
Environ Chem — Environmental Chemistry
Environ Chem Hum Anim Health — Environmental Chemicals. Human and Animal Health. Proceedings of Annual Conference
Environ Comment — Environmental Comment
Environ Conser — Environmental Conservation
Environ Conserv — Environmental Conservation
Environ Conserv Eng — Environmental Conservation Engineering [*Japan*]
Environ Contr Manage — Environmental Control Management
Environ Control Biol — Environment Control in Biology [*Japan*]
Environ Contr Safety Manage — Environmental Control and Safety Management
Environ Creation — Environmental Creation [*Japan*]
Environ Data Serv — Environmental Data Service
Environ Data Serv Rep — Environmental Data Services Report
Environ Educ — Environmental Education
Environ Eng — Environmental Engineering
Environ Entomol — Environmental Entomology
Environ Ethics — Environmental Ethics
Environ Exp Bot — Environmental and Experimental Botany
Environ Geol — Environmental Geology
Environ Geol Notes Ill State Geol Surv — Environmental Geology Notes. Illinois State Geological Survey
Environ Health — Environmental Health [*London*]
Environ Health (Nagpur) — Environmental Health (Nagpur)
Environ Health Perspect — Environmental Health Perspectives
Environ Impact Assess Rev — Environmental Impact Assessment Review
Environ Impact News — Environmental Impact News
Environ Int — Environment International
Environ L — Environmental Law
Environ Law — Environmental Law
Environ Law Rep — Environmental Law Reporter
Environ Law Rev — Environment Law Review
Environ Lett — Environmental Letters
Environ L Rev — Environment Law Review
Environ Man — Environment and Man
Environ Manage — Environmental Management
Environ Meas Lab Environ Rep US Dep of Energy — Environmental Measurements Laboratory. Environmental Report. United States Department of Energy
Environ Med — Environmental Medicine. Annual Report of the Research Institute of Environmental Medicine. Nagoya University
Environ Midwest — Environment Midwest
Environm L — Environmental Law
Environ Monit Assess — Environmental Monitoring Assessment [*Netherlands*]
Environm Policy & L — Environmental Policy and Law
Environmt — Environmental Action
Environ Mutagen — Environmental Mutagenesis
Environ Mutagenesis — Environmental Mutagenesis
Environ Newsl — Environmental Newsletter
Environ Per Bibl — Environmental Periodicals Bibliography
Environ Physiol — Environmental Physiology
Environ Physiol Biochem — Environmental Physiology and Biochemistry
Environ Plann A — Environment and Planning. A
Environ and Planning — Environment and Planning
Environ Policy Law — Environmental Policy and Law
Environ Pol Law — Environmental Policy and Law
Environ Pollut — Environment and Pollution [*Republic of Korea*]
Environ Pollut — Environmental Pollution
Environ Pollut — Environnement et Pollution
Environ Pollut Manage — Environmental Pollution Management
Environ Pollut Mgmt — Environmental Pollution Management
Environ Pollut Ser A — Environmental Pollution. Series A. Ecological and Biological
Environ Pollut Ser B — Environmental Pollution. Series B. Chemical and Physical
Environ Prof — Environmental Professional
Environ Prog — Environmental Progress
Environ Prot Eng — Environment Protection Engineering
Environ Prot Surv — Environmental Protection Survey [*England*]
Environ Prot Technol Ser — Environmental Protection Technology Series
Environ Prot Technol Ser EPA — Environmental Protection Technology Series. EPA [*Environmental Protection Agency*]
Environ Psychol Nonverbal Behav — Environmental Psychology and Nonverbal Behavior
Environ Q — Environmental Quarterly
Environ Qual — Environmental Quality
Environ Qual Abstr — Environmental Quality Abstracts
Environ Qual Saf — Environmental Quality and Safety
Environ Qual Saf Suppl — Environmental Quality and Safety. Supplement

Environ Quart — Environmental Quarterly
Environ Radiat Bull — Environmental Radiation Bulletin
Environ Rep Environ Meas Lab US Dep Energy — Environmental Report. Environmental Measurements Laboratory. United States Department of Energy
Environ Res — Environmental Research
Environ Res Inst Mich Annu Rep — Environmental Research Institute of Michigan. Annual Report
Environ Resour — Environmental Resource
Environ Sci Res — Environmental Science Research
Environ Sci & Tech — Environmental Science and Technology
Environ Sci Technol — Environmental Science and Technology
Environ Sc Tech — Environmental Science and Technology
Environ Southwest — Environment Southwest
Environ Space Sci — Environmental Space Sciences
Environ Technol Lett — Environmental Technology Letters
Environ This Mon — Environment This Month
Envir Plann — Environment and Planning
Envir Poll Control — Environmental Pollution Control
Envir Pollu — Environmental Pollution
Envir Res — Environmental Research
Envir Sci & Tech — Environmental Science and Technology
Env L — Environmental Law
Env L Rev — Environmental Law Review
Env L Rptr — Environmental Law Reporter
ENVPA — Environmental Pollution
ENVPD — Environmental Progress
Env Phys Bi — Environmental Physiology and Biochemistry
Env Plann — Environment and Planning
ENVQA — Environmental Quarterly
ENVRA — Environmental Research
ENVRB — Environment Report
ENVS — Environment Views. Alberta Department of the Environment
Env Sci Tec — Environmental Science and Technology
ENVTA — Environment
Envtl L — Environmental Law
Envtl LQ Newsl — Environmental Law Quarterly Newsletter
Envtl L Rep — Environmental Law Reporter
ENW — Economic News
En Watch — Energy Watch
ENWSD — Energy Newsletter
ENY — Energy
ENZYA — Enzymologia
Enzyme Eng — Enzyme Engineering
Enzymes Med — Enzymes in Medicine
Enzyme Technol Rotenburg Ferment Symp — Enzyme Technology. Rotenburg Fermentation Symposium
Enzymol Biol Clin — Enzymologia Biologica et Clinica
Enzymologia — Enzymologia Acta Biocatalytica
EO — Echos d'Orient
E/O — Engineering Opportunities
EO — Europaeische Osten
EO — Europe and Oil
EO — Europe Orientale
EOATD — Earth-Oriented Applications of Space Technology [*Formerly, Advances in Earth-Oriented Applications of Space Technology*]
EOBMA — Elektronnaya Obrabotka Materialov
EOBMAF — Elektronnaya Obrabotka Materialov
EOMC — Estudios Orientales (Mexico City)
EON — Eugene O'Neill Newsletter
EONE — Eastern Offshore News. Eastcoast Petroleum Operators' Association
EOO — Erasmi Opera Omnia [*Elsevier Book Series*]
EOP — Economics of Planning
EOPPA — Ekonomika i Organizatsiya Promyshlennogo Proizvodstva
EOS — Elsevier Oceanography Series [*Elsevier Book Series*]
EOT — Economic Impact. A Quarterly Review of World Economics
EOUPD — Ekonomika, Organizatsiya i Upravlenie v Neftepererabatyvayushchei i Neftekhimicheskoi Promyshlennosti
EOUSD — Economic Outlook USA
EP — Economic Papers
EP — Economic Planning; Journal for Agriculture and Related Industries
EP — Editor and Publisher
E & P — Editor and Publisher
EP — El Pais [*Spain*]
EP — Estate Planning
EP — Etudes Papyrologiques
EP — Etudes Philosophiques
EPA Cit Bul — EPA [*Environmental Protection Agency*] Citizens' Bulletin
EPA J — EPA [*Environmental Protection Agency*] Journal
EPap — Etudes de Papyrologie
EPB — Electronic Publishing and Bookselling
EPB — Employee Benefit Plan Review
EPB — Environmental Periodicals Bibliography
EPBCA — Ergebnisse der Physiologie, Biologischen Chemie, und Experimentellen Pharmakologie
EPBGPN — Environment Protection Board. Gas Pipeline Newsletter

EPE — Export Direction

EPEOD — Energy People

EPESA — Ediciones y Publicaciones Espanolas Sociedad Anonima

Epet — Epeteris tes Hetaireias Byzantinon Spoudon

EPFBA — Florida. University. Engineering and Industrial Experiment Station. Bulletin Series

EPh — Ecclesiasticos Pharos

EpH — Epeirotike Hestia

EPh — Etudes Philosophiques

EphC — Ephemerides Carmeliticae

EphCarm — Ephemerides Carmeliticae. Cura Pontificiae Facultatis Theologicae S. Teresiae a Jesu et Ionnis a Cruce [Rome]

Eph Dac — Ephemeris Dacoromana

EPHE — Ecole Pratique des Hautes Etudes

Eph Ep — Ephemeris Epigraphica

EPHESHPhA — Ecole Pratique des Hautes Etudes IVe Section. Sciences Historiques et Philologiques. Annuaire

EPHESRA — Ecole Pratique des Hautes Etudes Ve Section. Sciences Religieuses. Annuaire

EPhK — Egyetemes Philologiai Koezloeny

EphL — Ephemerides Liturgicae

EphLitg — Ephemerides Liturgicae [Rome]

EphMar — Ephemerides Mariologicae [Madrid]

Eph Th L — Ephemerides Theologicae Lovanienses

Epidemiol Community Health — Epidemiology and Community Health

Epidemiol Mikrobiol Infekts Boles — Epidemiologiya Mikrobiologiya i Infektsiozni Bolesti

Epidemiol Rev (Engl Transl Przegl Epidemiol) — Epidemiological Review (English Translation of Przeglad Epidemiologiczny)

Epidem Mikrobiol — Epidemiologiya Mikrobiologiya i Infektsiozni Bolesti

Epig Indica — Epigraphia Indica

Epigraph Stud — Epigraphische Studies

Epigr Vostok — Epigrafika Vostoka. Sbornik Statei

EPILA — Epilepsia

Epistemon Epeteris Kteniatr Sch — Epistemonike Epeteris Kteniatrikes Scholes

EPJ — Essay-Proof Journal

EPK — Egyetemes Philologiai Koezloeny

EPK — Entwicklungspolitische Korrespondenz

EPKE — Epitheoresis Koinonikon Ereunon

EPM — Educational and Psychological Measurement

EPM — Environmental Pollution Management

EPM — Etudes de Philosophie Medievale

EPMEA — Educational and Psychological Measurement

EPMSR — Environment Canada. Pacific Marine Science Reports

EPN — European Plastics News

EPN — Expansion

EPNED — Energy Planning Network

EPo — Esperienza Poetica

EPPO Bull — EPPO [European and Mediterranean Plant Protection Organization] Bulletin

EPPO Plant Health Newsl Publ Ser B — EPPO [European and Mediterranean Plant Protection Organization] Plant Health Newsletter Publications. Series B

EPPO Publ Ser C — EPPO [European and Mediterranean Plant Protection Organization] Publications. Series C

EPR — Earthquake Prediction Research

EPR — Electronic Publishing Review

EPr — Etudes de Presse

EPRAD — Elektro-Praktiker

EPRCD — Electric Power Research Institute (Report) EPRI CS

EPRDB8 — Ekologia Polska. Seria B

EPRI J — EPRI [Electric Power Research Institute] Journal

EPRI Rep NP — EPRI [Electric Power Research Institute] Report. NP [United States]

EPRJD — EPRI [Electric Power Research Institute] Journal

EPROER — Etudes Preliminaires aux Religions Orientales dans l'Empire Romain

EPS — English Philological Studies

EPS3AP — Environment Protection Service. Air Pollution Report

EPSLA — Earth and Planetary Science Letters

EPsM — Educational and Psychological Measurement

EPSMD — Elektrotekhnicheskaya Promyshlennost. Seriya. Elektrotekhnicheskie Materialy

EPSNA — Sbornik Nauchnykh Trudov Estonskoi Sel'skokhozyaistvennoi Akademii

EPSnEC — Environment Protection Service. Environmental Impact Control Directorate. Surveillance Report

EPSnES — Environmental Protection Service. Environmental Strategies Directorate. Economic and Technical Review

EPSnNW — Environment Protection Service. Northwest Region. Department of the Environment. Reports

EPS4NW — Environment Protection Service. Northwest Region. Technology Development Report

EPSRD — Electric Power Systems Research

EPST — Electric Power Statistics

EPS3WP — Environment Protection Service. Water Pollution Report

EP & T — Electronic Products & Technology [Canada]

EPTDA — Electric Light and Power. Transmission/Distribution

EPTSB — Environmental Protection Technology Series

EPubl — Enseignement Public

EQ — Education Quarterly [New Delhi]

EQ — Evangelical Quarterly

EQA — Environmental Quality Abstracts

EQA — Eurodoc

EQL Memo Calif Inst Technol Environ Qual Lab — EQL Memorandum. California Institute of Technology. Environmental Quality Laboratory

EQM — Environmental Quality Magazine

EQMM — Ellery Queen's Mystery Magazine

EQNX — Equinox

Equal Opportunities Int — Equal Opportunities International

Equine Vet J — Equine Veterinary Journal

Equip Dev Test Rep US For Serv Equip Dev Ctr San Dimas Calif — Equipment Development and Test Report. United States Forest Service. Equipment Center (San Dimas, California)

Equipement — Equipement - Logement - Transports

Equip Ind Achats & Entretien — Equipement Industriel. Achats et Entretien

Equip Mec — Equipement Mecanique [France]

Equip Preview Chem Process Ind — Equipment Preview of Chemical Process Industries

Equip Tips US Dep Agric For Serv Equip Dev Cent — Equip Tips. United States Department of Agriculture. Forest Service Equipment Development Center

ER — Ecclesiastical Review

ER — Economic Record

ER — Ecumenical Review

ER — Edinburgh Review

ER — Educational Review

ER — Ekonomska Revija [Ljubljana]

ER — Energy Research [Elsevier Book Series]

ER — Energy Review

ER — English Review

ER — Episcopal Recorder

Er — Eranos

Er — Eriu

ER — Estudis Romanics

ER — Eternelle Revue

ER — Etudes Rabelaisiennes

ER — Etudes Rhodaniennes

ER — Evergreen Review

ERA — Economic Record (Australia)

ERA — Energy Research Abstracts

ERA — ERA. Education Research Abstracts

ERab — Etudes Rabelaisiennes

ERA Foeren Elektr Ration Anvaendning — ERA. Foerening foer Elektricitetens Rationella Anvaendning

EranJb — Eranos-Jahrbuch

Eranos-Jb — Eranos-Jahrbuch

Erasmus E — Erasmus in English

ErasmusR — Erasmus Review

Era Social — Era Socialista

ErasR — Erasmus Review

ERB — Educational Research Bulletin

ERB — Etudes Romanes de Brno

ERB — Key to Economic Science

ErbAuf — Erbe und Auftrag [Beuron]

Erbe der V — Erbe der Vergangenheit

ERBr — Etudes Romanes de Brno

ERCEW — Ethical and Religious Classics of East and West

ERCHD — Energy Report from Chase

ERD — Erdoel und Kohle, Erdgas, Petrochemie

Erdeszeti Faipari Egy Tud Kozl — Erdeszeti es Faipari Egyetem Tudomanyos Kozlemenyei

Erdeszeti Kut — Erdeszeti Kutatasok

Erdeszettud Kozl — Erdeszettudomanyi Kozlemenyek

Erdesz Faipari Egyetem Kiad — Erdeszeti es Faipari Egyetem Kiadvanyai

Erdesz Faipari Egyetem Tud Kozl — Erdeszeti es Faipari Egyetem Tudomanyos Kozlemenyei

Erdesz Kutat — Erdeszeti Kutatasok

Erdesz Kutatas — Erdeszeti Kutatasok

Erd Koh EPB — Erdoel und Kohle, Erdgas, Petrochemie Vereinigt mit Brennstoff-Chemie

Erdoel-Erdgas Z — Erdoel-Erdgas Zeitschrift

Erdoel Erdgas Z Int Ed — Erdoel-Erdgas Zeitschrift. International Edition

Erdoel Kohle — Erdoel und Kohle, Erdgas, Petrochemie

Erdoel Kohle Erdgas Petrochem — Erdoel und Kohle, Erdgas, Petrochemie [West Germany]

Erdoel Kohle Erdgas Petrochem Brennst-Chem — Erdoel und Kohle, Erdgas, Petrochemie Vereinigt mit Brennstoff-Chemie

Erdoel Kohle Erdgas Petrochem Ver Brennst Chem — Erdoel und Kohle, Erdgas, Petrochemie Vereinigt mit Brennstoff-Chemie

Erdoel Z Bohr Foerdertech — Erdoel-Zeitschrift fuer Bohr- und Foerdertechnik

ERec — English Record

EREND — Energy and the Environment
ERes — Education Research
Erevan Gos Univ Ucen Zap Estesv Nauki — Erevanskii Gosudarstvennyi Universitet. Ucenye Zapiski. Estestvennye Nauki
Erfahr Denk — Erfahrung und Denken
Erfahrungswiss Bl — Erfahrungswissenschaftliche Blaetter
Ergeb Allgem Pathol Pathol Anat — Ergebnisse der Allgemeinen Pathologie und Pathologischen Anatomie [*West Germany*]
Ergeb Anat Entwicklungsgesch — Ergebnisse der Anatomie und Entwicklungsgeschichte
Ergeb Angiol — Ergebnisse der Angiologie
Ergeb Biol — Ergebnisse der Biologie
Ergeb Exakten Naturwiss — Ergebnisse der Exakten Naturwissenschaften [*West Germany*]
Ergeb Exp Med — Ergebnisse der Experimentellen Medizin
Ergeb Inn Med Kinderheilkd — Ergebnisse der Inneren Medizin und Kinderheilkunde
Ergeb Limnol — Ergebnisse der Limnologie
Ergeb Math Grenzgeb — Ergebnisse der Mathematik und Ihrer Grenzgebiete
Ergeb Mikrobiol Immunitaetsforsch — Ergebnisse der Mikrobiologie und Immunitaetsforschung
Ergebn Allg Path u Path Anat — Ergebnisse der Allgemeinen Pathologie und Pathologischen Anatomie des Menschen und der Tiere
Ergebn Biol — Ergebnisse der Biologie
Ergebn Physiol — Ergebnisse der Physiologie, Biologischen Chemie, und Experimentellen Pharmakologie
Ergeb Pathol — Ergebnisse der Pathologie
Ergeb Physiol Biol Chem Exp Pharmakol — Ergebnisse der Physiologie, Biologischen Chemie, und Experimentellen Pharmakologie
Ergeb Plasmaphys Gaselektron — Ergebnisse der Plasmaphysik und der Gaselektronik
Ergeb Plasmaphysik Gaselektronik — Ergebnisse der Plasmaphysik und der Gaselektronik
Ergeb Tech Roentgenkd — Ergebnisse der Technischen Roentgenkunde
Ergeb Vitam Hormonforsch — Ergebnisse der Vitamin und Hormonforschung
Ergnzngsbde Ztschr Veterinaerk — Ergaenzungsbaende zur Zeitschrift fuer Veterinaerkunde
ERGOA — Ergonomics
Ergon Abstr — Ergonomics Abstracts
ERGS — ETC: A Review of General Semantics
ERGTB — Engineering Times
ERGWD — Energiewesen
ERGYA — Energy
ERGYD — Energyline
ERH — Euronet News
ERHAD — Elektro Radio Handel
ERIAD — Electric Power Research Institute (Report) EPRI AP
Ericsson Rev — Ericsson Review
Ericsson Te — Ericsson Technics
Ericsson Tech — Ericsson Technics
E Riding Archaeol — East Riding Archaeologist
ERIND — Electrical Review International
ERJ — Economic Research Journal
Erjedesipari Kut Intez Kozl — Erjedesipari Kutato Intezet Koslemenyei
ERK — Maandschrift Economie
ERL — Employee Relations Law Journal
ERL — Etudes Romanes de Liege
Erlanger Forsch Reihe B — Erlanger Forschungen. Reihe B. Naturwissenschaften
Erlanger Geol Abh — Erlanger Geologische Abhandlungen
Erlanger Jb Bienenk — Erlanger Jahrbuch fuer Bienenkunde
ERN — Installatie Journaal
Ernaehr Umsch — Ernaehrungs-Umschau
Ernaehrungsforsch Inst Ernaehr (Potsdam) — Ernaehrungsforschung. Institut fuer Ernaehrung (Potsdam)
Ernaehrungsl Prax — Ernaehrungslehre und- Praxis
Ernaehrungswirtsch Lebensmitteltech (Hamburg) — Ernaehrungswirtschaft. Lebensmitteltechnik (Hamburg)
Eroeterv Koezl — Eroeterv Koezlemenyek
ERS — En Route Supplement
ERS — English Reprint Series
ERS Staff Rep US Dep Agric Econ Res Serv — ERS Staff Report. United States Department of Agriculture. Economic Research Service
ERSTD — Energy Report to the States
ERT — Elektronikka Radio Television
ERT (Energy Resour Technol) — ERT (Energy Resources and Technology) [*Formerly, Energy Resources Report*]
ERTLA — Elektroniikka Radio Televisio
ERV — Electrical Review
ERW — European Research. Marketing, Opinion, Advertising
ES — Educational Studies
ES — Englische Studien
ES — Englisches Seminar
ES — English Studies
Es — Escorial
E & S — Essays and Studies [*London*]

ES — Essays and Studies [*London*]
ES — Estudios Segovianos
ES — Journal of Environmental Systems
ESA — Emakeele Seltsi Aastaraamat
ESA — English Studies in Africa
ESA — Eurasia Septentrionalis Antiqua
ESA Bull — ESA [*European Space Agency*] Bulletin [*France*]
ESAfr — English Studies in Africa
ESA J — ESA [*European Space Agency*] Journal
ESAJD — ESA [*European Space Agency*] Journal
Esakia Occas Pap Hikosan Biol Lab Entomol — Esakia Occasional Papers of the Hikosan Biological Laboratory in Entomology
ESAUAS — Endocrine Society of Australia. Proceedings
ESB — Economisch-Statistische Berichten
ESB — Eigen Schoon en de Brabander
ESBGA — Eisenbahn-Ingenieur
ESBP — Ezik i Stil na Balgarskite Pitsateli
ESC — Eastern Snow Conference Annual Meetings. Proceedings
ESC — English Studies in Canada
Esc — Escorial
EsC — Esprit Createur
Esc Agron Amazonia Bol — Escola de Agronomia da Amazonia. Boletim
ESCBA — Earth Science Bulletin
Esc Eng Univ Minas Gerais Inst Pesqui Radioat Publ — Escola de Engenharia. Universidade de Minas Gerais. Instituto de Pesquisas Radioativas. Publicacao
Esc Farm — Escuela de Farmacia
Esc Farm Guatem — Escuela de Farmacia Guatemala
EsCl — Estudios Clasicos
Esc Nac Agric (Chapingo) Monogr — Escuela Nacional de Agricultura (Chapingo). Monografias
Esc Nac Agric (Chapingo) Rev — Escuela Nacional de Agricultura (Chapingo). Revista
Esc Nac Agric (Chapingo) Ser Apuntes — Escuela Nacional de Agricultura (Chapingo). Serie de Apuntes
Esc Nac Agric (Chapingo) Ser Invest — Escuela Nacional de Agricultura (Chapingo). Serie de Investigaciones
Esc Super Agric Luiz De Queiroz (Sao Paulo) Bol — Escola Superior de Agricultura "Luiz De Queiroz" (Sao Paulo). Boletin
ESD — Energy Systems and Policy
ESDBAK — Japanese Journal of Sanitary Zoology
ESDCA — Endocrinologia e Scienze della Costituzione
ESDU Data Items — Engineering Sciences Data Unit. Data Items
ESE — Review of the Economic Situation of Mexico
E Sec — L'Enseignement Secondaire
E Sef — Estudios Sefardies
ESELL — Essays and Studies in English Language and Literature
ESGM — Eta Sigma Gamma
ESHG — Etudes Suisses d'Histoire Generale
ESI — Edizioni Scientifiche Italiane
Esic-Market Estud Gestion Com Empr — Esic-Market, Estudios de Gestion Comercial y Empresa
ESISD — ESIS Newsletter
ESKGA — Eisei Kagaku
ESKHA — Eisei Shikenjo Hokoku
ESKHA5 — Eisei Shikenjo Hokoku
ESKI — Eskimo
ESKTD — Elektrotekhnicheskaya Promyshlennost. Seriya. Khimicheskie i Fizicheskie Istochniki Toka
ESI — Etudes Slaves et Est-Europeennes
ESL — European Studies in Law [*Elsevier Book Series*]
ESLR — Etudes Slaves et Roumaines
ESMS — Eta Sigma Gamma. Monograph Series
ESMSLCC — Edward Sapir Monograph Series in Language, Culture, and Cognition
ESn — Englische Studien
ESOUA — Ekonomika Sovetskoi Ukrainy
ESov — Etudes Sovietiques
ESP — English Symposium Papers
EspA — Espanol Actual
Espace Geogr — Espace Geographique
Espaces et Soc — Espaces et Societes
Esper Ricer Ist Agr Gen Colt Erbacee Univ Pisa — Esperienze e Ricerche. Istituto di Agronomia Generale e Coltivazioni Erbacee. Universita di Pisa
Esp Ganad — Espana Ganadera
ESPSL — O Estado de Sao Paulo. Suplemento Literario
ESQ — Emerson Society Quarterly
Esq — Esquire
Esquisses Math — Esquisses Mathematiques
ESR — Economic and Social Review
ESR — Emory Sources and Reprints
ESR — Etudes Slaves et Roumaines
ESR — European Studies Review
ESR — Extension Service Review
ESRBB — Energeticheskoe Stroitel'stvo za Rubezhom

ESREA — Earth Science Reviews
ESRN — ESSO Resources News
ESRO/ELDO Bull — ESRO/ELDO [*European Space Research Organization/European Launcher Development Organization*] Bulletin
ESRS — Emporia State Research Studies
ESs — English Studies
ESS — Environmental Science Series [*Elsevier Book Series*]
Ess — Essence
Essays Biochem — Essays in Biochemistry
Essays Can Wri — Essays on Canadian Writing
Essays Crit — Essays in Criticism
Essays Fr L — Essays in French Literature
Essays Fundam Immunol — Essays in Fundamental Immunology
Essays Lit — Essays in Literature
Essays Neurochem Neuropharmacol — Essays in Neurochemistry and Neuropharmacology
Essays Pap — Essays and Papers. Soong Jun University [*Korea*]
Essays Pap Soong Jun Univ — Essays and Papers. Soong Jun University
Essays Phys — Essays in Physics
Essays Poet — Essays in Poetics
Essays Stud — Essays and Studies
Essays Stud Fac Hiroshima Jogakuin Coll — Essays and Studies by the Faculty of Hiroshima Jogakuin College
Essays Toxicol — Essays in Toxicology
Ess Crit — Essays in Criticism
Essenze Deriv Agrum — Essenze e Derivati Agrumari
Essex Archaeol Hist — Essex Archaeology and History
Essex Arch Hist — Essex Archaeology and History
Essex Co N H Soc J — Essex County Natural History Society. Journal
Essex I His — Essex Institute. Historical Collections
Essex Inst B — Essex Institute. Bulletin
Essex Inst Coll — Essex Institute. Historical Collections
Essex Inst Hist Coll — Essex Institute. Historical Collections
Essex Inst Hist Collect — Essex Institute. Historical Collections
Essex Inst Pr — Essex Institute. Proceedings
Essex J — Essex Journal
Essex Nat (Lond) — Essex Naturalist (London)
Essex Natur — Essex Naturalist
ESSN — ESSO North
ESSO Agr — ESSO Agricola
ESSO Mag — ESSO Magazine
ESSO Oilways Int — ESSO Oilways International
Essor Frigorif Fr — Essor Frigorifique Francais
Ess R — Essex Review
ESSSD — Ekonomicheskoe Sotrudnichestvo Stran-Chlenov SEV
ESt — English Studies
ES & T — Environmental Science and Technology
ESt — Erlanger Studien
Est — Estudios
Estac Cent Ecol Bol (Spain) — Estacion Central de Ecologia. Boletin (Spain)
Estac Exp Agric Tucuman Bol — Estacion Experimental Agricola de Tucuman. Boletin
Estac Exp Agric Tucuman Circ — Estacion Experimental Agricola de Tucuman. Circular
Estac Exp Agric Tucuman Publ Misc — Estacion Experimental Agricola de Tucuman. Publicacion Miscelanea
Estac Exp Agropecu Pergamino Bol Divulg — Estacion Experimental Agropecuaria Pergamino. Boletin de Divulgacion
Estac Exp Agropecu Pergamino Publ Tec — Estacion Experimental Agropecuaria Pergamino. Publicacion Tecnico
Estac Exp Aula dei Zaragoza Bol — Estacion Experimental de Aula dei Zaragoza. Boletin
Estac Exp Aula dei Zaragoza Dep Mejora Ens — Estacion Experimental de Aula dei Zaragoza. Departamento de Mejora Ensayos
Estadist Espanola — Estadistica Espanola
Estadistica Esp — Estadistica Espanola
Est Ag — Estudio Agustiniano
Estates Gaz — Estates Gazette
Estates Q — Estates and Trusts Quarterly
Estates Times Rev — Estates Times Review
EstB — Estudios Biblicos [*Madrid*]
EstBib — Estudios Biblicos [*Madrid*]
Est Coas M — Estuarine and Coastal Marine Science
Est Cult Maya — Estudios de Cultura Maya
EstD — Estudios. Duquesne University
EstdH — Estudios de Hispanofila
EstE — Estudios Eclesiasticos [*Madrid*]
EstE — Estudios Escenicos
EstEcl — Estudios Eclesiasticos [*Madrid*]
Estel-Ber Forsch Entwickl Unserer Werke — Estel-Berichte aus Forschung und Entwicklung Unserer Werke
Est Europ — Est Europeen
EstF — Estudios Franciscanos
EstFilRelOr — Estudios de Filosofia y Religion Orientales [*Buenos Aires*]
EstFr — Estudios Franciscanos [*Barcelona*]
EstFranc — Estudios Franciscanos [*Barcelona*]

Est Gaz — Estates Gazette
Est Gaz Dig — Estates Gazette Digest of Land and Property Cases
ESTHA — Environmental Science and Technology
EstHM — Estudios de Historia Moderna
EstLit — Estafeta Literaria
EstMar — Estudios Marianos [*Madrid*]
EStn — Englische Studien
Estomatol Cult — Estomatologia e Cultura
EstOr — Estudios Orientales
Est-Ouest — Est et Ouest. Bulletin de l'Association d'Etudes et d'Informations Politiques Internationales
Est Plan — Estate Planning
ESTS — Early Scottish Text Society
Est & Tr Q — Estates and Trusts Quarterly
Est & Tr Rep — Estates and Trusts Reports
Estuarine Bull — Estuarine Bulletin
Estuarine Coastal Mar Sci — Estuarine and Coastal Marine Science
Estuarine Coastal Shelf Sci — Estuarine, Coastal, and Shelf Science [*England*]
Estuarine Res — Estuarine Research
EStud — English Studies
Estud Agron — Estudos Agronomicos
Estud Agron Missao Estud Agron Ultramar — Estudos Agronomicos. Missao de Estudos Agronomicos do Ultramar
Estud Andin — Estudios Andinos
Estud As Afr — Estudios de Asia y Africa
Estud Clas — Estudios Clasicos
Estud Coop — Estudios Cooperativos
Estud Cult Nahuatl — Estudios de Cultura Nahuatl
Estud Econ — Estudios de Economia
Estud Econ Argentina — Estudios sobre la Economia Argentina
Estud Econs — Estudos Economicos
Estud Empresar — Estudios Empresariales
Estud Empresariales — Estudios Empresariales
Estud Ensaios Doc Junta Invest Cient Ultramar (Port) — Estudos, Ensaios, e Documentos. Junta de Investigacoes Cientificas do Ultramar (Portugal)
Estud Esteril — Estudios sobre Esterilidad
Estud Extremenos — Estudios Extremenos; Revista Historica, Literaria, y Artistica
Estud Fauna Port — Estudos sobre a Fauna Portuguesa
Estud Filosof — Estudios Filosoficos
Estud Geogr — Estudios Geograficos
Estud Geogr Inst Juan Sebastian Elcano — Estudios Geograficos. Instituto "Juan Sebastian Elcano"
Estud Geol (Inst Invest Geol "Lucas Mallada") — Estudios Geologicos (Instituto de Investigaciones Geologicas "Lucas Mallada")
Estud Geol (Madr) — Estudios Geologicos (Madrid)
E Studies — English Studies
Estud Inform Serv Flor Aquic (Portugal) — Estudos e Informacao. Servicos Florestais e Aquicolas (Portugal)
Estud Int — Estudios Internacionales
Estudios Geol — Estudios Geologicos
Estud Legis — Estudos Legislativos
Estud Leopold — Estudos Leopoldenses
Estud Notas Trab Serv Fom Min (Port) — Estudos. Notas e Trabalhos do Servico de Fomento Mineiro (Portugal)
Estudos Agron — Estudos Agronomicos
Estud Quim Inst Nac Invest Ind (Port) — Estudos de Quimica. Instituto Nacional de Investigacao Industrial (Portugal)
Estud Sindic — Estudios Sindicales
Estud Sindicales — Estudios Sindicales
Estud Sindicales y Coops — Estudios Sindicales y Cooperativos
Estud Soc — Estudios Sociales. Revista de Ciencias Sociales
Estud Soc C — Estudios Sociales Centroamericanos
Estud Soc Centroamer — Estudios Sociales Centroamericanos
ESU Bus Rev — Emporia State University. Business Review
ESY — Economisch en Sociaal Tijdschrift
ET — Educational Television
ET — Eildon Tree
ET — Ekonomisk Tidskrift
ET — Epitheorese Technes
Et — Ethics
ET — Ethnomusicology
Et — Etoiles
Et — Etudes
ET — Etudes Traditionnelles
ET — Etudes et Travaux. Travaux du Centre d'Archeologie Mediterraneenne. Academie Polonaise de Sciences [*Warsaw*]
ET — Evangelische Theologie
ET — Expository Times
ET — Journal of Educational Technology
EtA — Etudes Anglaises
ETAb — English Teaching Abstracts
ETA Elektrowaerme Tech Ausbau Ed A — ETA. Elektrowaerme im Technischen Ausbau. Edition A
Et Angl — Etudes Anglaises

ETANSW News — English Teachers Association of New South Wales. Newsletter
Et Ar — Etudes Arabes
ETAT — Eesti NSV Teaduste Akadeemia Toimetised. Uhiskonnateaduste Seeria
ETATA — Eesti NSV Teaduste Akadeemia Toimetised. Bioloogia
Etat San Animaux Belgique — Etat Sanitaire des Animaux de la Belgique
Et Balkan — Etudes Balkaniques
ETB TUG — ETB - TUG. Equipement Technique du Batiment - Technische Uitrusting van het Gebouw
EtByz — Etudes Byzantines
ETC — Environmental Toxicology and Chemistry
Et Celt — Etudes Celtiques
EtCl — Etudes Classiques
Et Class — Etudes Classiques
ETC Quart Index — European Translations Centre. Quarterly Index
ETC Rev Gen — ETC: A Review of General Semantics
Et et Doc (Educ Nat) — Etudes et Documents (Education Nationale)
ETEAA — Entomologia Experimentalis et Applicata
Et Econ (Mons) — Etudes Economiques (Mons, Belgium)
E Tenn Hist Soc Pub — East Tennessee Historical Society. Publications
Eter — Eternity Magazine
ETERD — Energy Technology Review
EtF — Etudes Franciscaines
EtFranc — Etudes Franciscaines [*Blois*]
Et Gaul — Etudes Gaulliennes
Et Germ — Etudes Germaniques
E & Th — Eglise et Theologie
EthF — Ethnologia Fennica [*Finnish Studies in Ethnology*]
Ethics Animals — Ethics and Animals
Ethics Sci Med — Ethics in Science and Medicine
Ethiop Geol Surv Annu Rep — Ethiopia Geological Survey. Annual Report
Ethiop Geol Surv Bull — Ethiopia Geological Survey. Bulletin
Ethiop Inst Agric Res Rep — Ethiopian Institute of Agricultural Research. Report
Ethiop Med J — Ethiopian Medical Journal
EThL — Ephemerides Theologicae Lovanienses
Ethmus — Ethnomusicology
Ethmus Sel Repts — Ethnomusicology. Selected Reports
Ethnic & Racial Stud — Ethnic and Racial Studies
Ethnic Stud — Ethnic Studies
Ethno — Ethnohistory
EthnoE — Ethnologia Europaea
EthnoF — Ethnologie Francaise
Ethnogr Mus Univ Oslo Yb — Ethnographic Museum. University of Oslo. Yearbook
Ethnohist — Ethnohistory
Ethnol Amer — Ethnologia Americana
Ethnol Anz — Ethnologischer Anzeiger
Ethnol Europ — Ethnologia Europaea
Ethnol Fennica — Ethnologia Fennica [*Finnish Studies in Ethnology*]
Ethnol Fr — Ethnologie Francaise
Ethnol Franc — Ethnologie Francaise
Ethnol Scand — Ethnologia Scandinavica
Ethnol Slavia — Ethnologia Slavia
Ethnol Z — Ethnologische Zeitschrift
Ethnomedizin — Ethnomedizin. Ethnomedicine Zeitschrift fuer Interdisziplinare Forschung
Ethnomusic — Ethnomusicology
Ethnomusicol — Ethnomusicology
Ethno-Psych — Ethno-Psychologie
Ethno-Psychol — Ethno-Psychologie
Ethn Racial Stud — Ethnic and Racial Studies
Ethn Stud — Ethnic Studies
EThR — Etudes Theologiques et Religieuses
Eth Rec — Ethical Record
Eth S — Ethnologia Slavica
Eth Sc — Ethnologia Scandinavica
ETI — Electronics Today International
ETI — En Terre d'Islam
ETI — Foreign Economic Trends and Their Implications for the United States
EtIE — Etudes Indo-Europeennes
ETiM — Echo Teatrolne i Muzyczne
ETINA — Electronique Industrielle
Et Int — Etudes Internationales
ETITA — Energetekhnologicheskow Ispol'zovanie Toplova
ETJ — Educational Theatre Journal
ET J — ET [*Enterostomal Therapy*] Journal
EtK — Epeteris tou Kalabryton
ETKKA — Elteknik
ETL — Ephemerides Theologicae Lovanienses
EtL — Etudes de Lettres
ETL — Explicacion de Textos Literarios
ETLA — Epeteris tou Laographikov Arkheiov
ETM — Export Turkey Magazine
Et Mal — Etudes Maliennes

EtMar — Etudes Mariales [*Paris*]
ETMNA — Entomological News
ETMSB — Ethnomusicology
ETN — Elektrotechniek. Technisch-Economisch Tijdschrift
ETNKA — Energietechnik
Etnogr Polska — Etnografia Polska
Etnol Antropol Cult — Etnologia Antropologia Culturale
Etnol Stud — Etnologiska Studier
Et Normandes — Etudes Normandes
Et Notes Inform Batiment — Etudes et Notes d'Information. Direction du Batiment et des Travaux Publics et de la Conjoncture
ETOPD — Energy Topics
EtP — Etnoloski Pregled
ETP — Excise Tariff Proposals
EtPapyr — Etudes de Papyrologie [*Cairo*]
Et Planning Familial — Etudes de Planning Familial
EtPol — Etnografia Polska
Et Polemol — Etudes Polemologiques
ETQ — Estates and Trusts Quarterly
ETR — East Timor Report
ETR — Employment Review
ETR — Estates and Trusts Reports
Etr — Eternity
ETR — ETR. Eisenbahntechnische Rundschau
ETR — Etudes Rurales: Revue Trimestrielle d'Histoire, Geographie, Sociologie, et Economie des Campagnes
ETR — Etudes Theologiques et Religieuses
Et Region Paris — Etudes de la Region Parisienne
E T Rel — Etudes Theologiques et Religieuses
ETRMD — Electromagnetics
ETRSD — Electronic Technology Reports
ETRTA — Elettrotecnica
ETRUA — Eisenbahntechnische Rundschau
Et Rur — Etudes Rurales
ETs — Etudes Tsiganes
ETS — Journal. Evangelical Theological Society
ETS — Scandinavian Journal of Economics
Et Soc (Paris) — Etudes Sociales (Paris)
ETSSD — Elektronnaya Tekhnika, Seriya 1. Elektronika
Et Statist Banque Etats Afr Centr — Etudes et Statistiques. Banque des Etats de l'Afrique Centrale. Bulletin Mensuel
ETTCA — Elektrotechniker
ETTCB — Elettronica e Telecomunicazioni
Ettore Majorana Internat Sci Ser Phys Sci — Ettore Majorana International Science Series. Physical Sciences
Ettore Majorana Int Sci Ser Phys Sci — Ettore Majorana International Science Series. Physical Sciences
ETU — Economie et Statistique
Etud Ang — Etudes Anglaises
Etud Angl — Etudes Anglaises
Etud Anglaises — Etudes Anglaises
Etud Balk — Etudes Balkaniques
Etud Cinema — Etudes Cinematographiques
Etud Class — Etudes Classiques
Etud Classiq — Etudes Classiques
Etude CEE Ser Agr — Etudes CEE [*Communaute Economique Europeenne*]. Serie Agriculture
Etude Cent Nat Etude Experim Machin Agr — Etude. Centre National d'Etudes et d'Experimentation de Machinisme Agricole
Etud Econs (Mons) — Etudes Economiques (Mons, Belgium)
Etud Econs (Paris) — Etudes Economiques (Paris)
Etudes Cin — Etudes Cinematographiques
Etude Spec Minist Richesses Nat Que — Etude Speciale Ministere des Richesses Naturelles du Quebec
Etude Stat Inst Nat Stat — Etudes Statistiques. Institute National de la Statistique et des Etudes Economiques
Etude Trav — Etude du Travail
Etud et Expansion — Etudes et Expansion
Etud Fran — Etudes Francaises
Etud Ger — Etudes Germaniques
Etud Germaniques — Etudes Germaniques
Etud Hist Droit Canon — Etudes Historiques de Droit Canonique
Etud Int — Etudes Internationales
Etud Internat — Etudes Internationales
Etud Irland — Etudes Irlandaises
Etud Ital — Etudes Italiennes
Etud Limousines — Etudes Limousines
Etud Lit — Etudes Litteraires
Etud Mar — Etudes Mariales
Etud Phil — Etudes Philosophiques
Etud Philos — Etudes Philosophiques
Etud Psychother — Etudes Psychotherapiques
Etud Rech Inst Meteorol Part 2 — Etudes et Recherches. Institut de Meteorologie. Part 2. Hydrologie
Etud Reg Paris — Etudes de la Region Parisienne
Etud Rur — Etudes Rurales

Etud Rurales — Etudes Rurales
Etud Slav E — Etudes Slaves et Est-Europeennes
Etud Socs — Etudes Sociales
Etud Statis (Brussels) — Etudes Statistiques (Brussels)
Etud Tech Econ Ser E (Inst Geol Geophys) — Etudes Techniques et
    Economiques. Seria E. Hydrogeologie (Institut de Geologie et
    Geophysique)
Etud Theol — Etudes Theologiques et Religieuses
Etud Trad — Etudes Traditionnelles
Etud Trav Ec Maroc Agric Publ — Etudes et Travaux. Ecole Marocaine
    d'Agriculture. Publication
Ety — Eternity
Et Zair — Etudes Zairoises
ETZ Arch — ETZ. Elektrotechnische Zeitschrift. Archiv
ETZ Elektrotech Z — ETZ. Elektrotechnische Zeitschrift
ETZ Elektrotech Z Ausg A — ETZ. Elektrotechnische Zeitschrift. Ausgabe A
    [*West Germany*]
Eu — East Europe
EU — Estudos Universitarios [*Recife*]
Eu — Euphorion
EU — Euromoney
EUC — Estudis Universitaris Catalans
EUCLB — Euroclay
EUDEBA — Editorial Universitaria de Buenos Aires
EUE — Europeen, Europaer. Magazine de l'Economie et de la Culture
EUFID — European File
EUG — European Industrial Relations Review
Eugen Lab Mem — Eugenics Laboratory. Memoirs
Eugen Q — Eugenics Quarterly
Eugen Rev — Eugenics Review
Eugen Soc Symp — Eugenics Society Symposia
Eug R — Eugenics Review
EUL — Europa van Morgen
EULEP Newsl — EULEP [*European Late Effects Project Group*] Newsletter
Eul J — Eulenspiegel-Jahrbuch
Eul Ji Med J — Eul Ji Medical Journal
EUN — European Plastics News
EuntDoc — Euntes Docete [*Rome*]
EUP — Extension [*O Intercambio*] Universitaria de la Plata
Euph — Euphorion
Euphoria Cacophoria (Int Ed) — Euphoria et Cacophoria (International
    Edition)
EUPJA — European Polymer Journal
EUPNA — Europhysics News
EUPNB — European Plastics News
EUQ — Emory University Quarterly
Eurafr Trib Tiers-Monde — Eurafrica et Tribune de Tiers-Monde
Eur Appl Res Rep — European Applied Research Reports
Eur Appl Res Rep-Nucl Sci Technol Sect — European Applied Research
    Reports. Nuclear Science and Technology Section
Eur Arch — Europa-Archiv
Eur Assoc Anim Prod Publ — European Association for Animal Production.
    Publication
EURATOM Bull — EURATOM [*European Atomic Energy Community*]
    Bulletin [*Belgium*]
EURATOM Bull Eur At Energy Community — EURATOM. Bulletin of the
    European Atomic Energy Community
EURATOM Rev Eur At Energy Community — EURATOM Review. European
    Atomic Energy Community [*Belgium*]
Eur Biophys J — European Biophysics Journal
Eur Brew Conv Proc Congr — European Brewery Convention. Proceedings of
    the Congress
Eur Chem N — European Chemical News
Eur Chem News — European Chemical News [*England*]
Eur Chir Forsch — Europaeische Chirurgische Forschung
Eur Community (Engl Ed) — European Community (English Edition)
Eur Conf Anim Blood Groups Biochem Polymorphism — European Conference
    on Animal Blood Groups and Biochemical Polymorphism
Eur Conf Microcirc — European Conference on Microcirculation
EURCUP — Estudos Universitarios: Revista de Cultura da Universidade de
    Pernambuco
Eur Demographic Info Bul (Hague) — European Demographic Information
    Bulletin (The Hague)
Eur Dial Transplant Assoc Eur Renal Assoc Proc — European Dialysis and
    Transplant Association - European Renal Association. Proceedings
Eur Dial Transplant Assoc Proc — European Dialysis and Transplant
    Association. Proceedings
Eur Domani — Europa Domani
EUREA — Eugenics Review
Eur Economy — European Economy
Eur Econ R — European Economic Review
Eur File — European File [*Luxembourg*]
Eur Geophys Soc Meet Abstr — European Geophysical Society. Meeting.
    Abstracts
Eur Grundrechte — Europaeische Grundrechte
EurH — Europaeische Hochschulschriften

Eur Heart J — European Heart Journal
Euriam Bul — Euriam Bulteni
Eur Intellectual Property Rev — European Intellectual Property Review
Eur Intell Prop R — European Intellectual Property Review
Euristop Off Inf Bookl — Eurisotop Office Information Booklet
EURJA — European Rubber Journal
Eur J Anaesthesiol — European Journal of Anaesthesiology
Eur J A Phy — European Journal of Applied Physiology and Occupational
    Physiology
Eur J Appl Microbiol — European Journal of Applied Microbiology
Eur J Appl Microbiol Biotechnol — European Journal of Applied Microbiology
    and Biotechnology
Eur J Appl Physiol Occup Physiol — European Journal of Applied Physiology
    and Occupational Physiology
Eur J App M — European Journal of Applied Microbiology
Eur J Bioch — European Journal of Biochemistry
Eur J Biochem — European Journal of Biochemistry
Eur J Canc — European Journal of Cancer
Eur J Cancer — European Journal of Cancer
Eur J Cancer Clin Oncol — European Journal of Cancer and Clinical Oncology
Eur J Cardiol — European Journal of Cardiology
Eur J Cell Biol — European Journal of Cell Biology
Eur J Cl In — European Journal of Clinical Investigation
Eur J Clin Biol Res — European Journal of Clinical and Biological Research
    [*France*]
Eur J Clin Invest — European Journal of Clinical Investigation
Eur J Clin Pharmacol — European Journal of Clinical Pharmacology
Eur J Cl Ph — European Journal of Clinical Pharmacology
Eur J Comb — European Journal of Combinatorics
Eur J Drug Metab Pharmacokinet — European Journal of Drug Metabolism
    and Pharmacokinetics
Eur J For Pathol — European Journal of Forest Pathology
Eur J I Car — European Journal of Intensive Care Medicine
Eur J Immun — European Journal of Immunology
Eur J Immunol — European Journal of Immunology
Eur J Intensive Care Med — European Journal of Intensive Care Medicine
Eur J Med Chem — European Journal of Medicinal Chemistry
Eur J Med Chem Chim Ther — European Journal of Medicinal Chemistry.
    Chimica Therapeutica
Eur J Mktg — European Journal of Marketing
Eur J Nucl Med — European Journal of Nuclear Medicine
Eur J Obstet Gynecol Reprod Biol — European Journal of Obstetrics,
    Gynecology, and Reproductive Biology
Eur J Oper Res — European Journal of Operational Research
Eur J Orthod — European Journal of Orthodontics
Eur J Ped — European Journal of Pediatrics
Eur J Pediatr — European Journal of Pediatrics
Eur J Pharm — European Journal of Pharmacology
Eur J Pharmacol — European Journal of Pharmacology
Eur J Phys — European Journal of Physics
Eur J Radiol — European Journal of Radiology
Eur J Respir Dis — European Journal of Respiratory Diseases
Eur J Respir Dis Suppl — European Journal of Respiratory Diseases.
    Supplement
Eur J Sci Educ — European Journal of Science Education
Eur J Sociol — European Journal of Sociology
Eur J Soc P — European Journal of Social Psychology
Eur J Steroids — European Journal of Steroids
Eur J Toxicol — European Journal of Toxicology
Eur J Toxicol Environ Hyg — European Journal of Toxicology and
    Environmental Hygiene
Eur Konf Mikrozirk — Europaeische Konferenz ueber Mikrozirkulation
Eur Mediterr Plant Prot Organ Publ Ser A — European and Mediterranean
    Plant Protection Organization. Publications. Series A
Eur Mediterr Plant Prot Organ Publ Ser D — European and Mediterranean
    Plant Protection Organization. Publications. Series D
Eur Meet Wildfowl Conserv Proc — European Meeting on Wildfowl
    Conservation. Proceedings
Eur Neurol — European Neurology
Eur Nouv — Europe Nouvelle
Euro Abstr Sec 1 — Euro Abstracts. Section 1. EURATOM [*European Atomic
    Energy Community*] and EEC [*European Economic Community*]
    Research [*Luxembourg*]
Euro Abstr Sect 2 — Euro Abstracts. Section 2. Coal and Steel [*Luxembourg*]
Euro Coop — Euro Cooperation
Eur Oil — Europe and Oil [*West Germany*]
Eur Oil Gas Mag — European Oil and Gas Magazine [*West Germany*]
Euromicro J — Euromicro Journal [*Netherlands*]
Euromicro Newsl — Euromicro Newsletters
Eurom Surveys Aust NZ Series — Euromarket Surveys. Australian/New
    Zealand Series
Europ Busin — European Business
Europ Chem — Europa Chemie
Europ Demogr Inform B — European Demographic Information Bulletin
European Assocn for Archtl Education Newsheet — European Association for
    Architectural Education. Newsheet

European Ind Relations Rev — European Industrial Relations Review
European Inf Serv — European Information Service
European J Ed — European Journal of Education
European J Engineering Ed — European Journal of Engineering Education
European J Oper Res — European Journal of Operational Research
European J of Science Ed — European Journal of Science Education
European L Rev — European Law Review
European Photogr — European Photography
European Rubber J — European Rubber Journal
European Sm Bus J — European Small Business Journal
Europe Com — European Community
Europ Econ and Pol Survey — European Economic and Political Survey
Europ Econ R — European Economic Review
Europe Daily Bull — Europe Daily Bulletin
Europe O Mer — Europe Outremer
Europhys Conf Abstr — Europhysics Conference Abstracts [*Switzerland*]
Europhys News — Europhysics News
Europ Intell Prop Rev — European Intellectual Property Review
Europ J Polit Res — European Journal of Political Research
Europ J Soc Psychol — European Journal of Social Psychology
Europlas Mon — Europlastics Monthly [*England*]
Europlast Mon — Europlastics Monthly
Europ R Agric Econ — European Review of Agricultural Economics
Europ Rdsch — Europaeische Rundschau
Europ Stud Newsl — European Studies Newsletter
Europ Stud R — European Studies Review
Europ Wehrkunde — Europaeische Wehrkunde
Europ YB — European Yearbook
Euro Res — European Research
Eur Organ Res Fluorine Dent Caries Prev Proc Congr — European Organization for Research on Fluorine and Dental Caries Prevention. Proceedings of the Congress
Eur Organ Res Treat Cancer Monog Ser — European Organization for Research on Treatment of Cancer. Monograph Series
Eur Organ Treat Cancer Monogr Ser — European Organization for Research on Treatment of Cancer. Monograph Series
Euro Space Agency (Spec Publ) ESA SP — European Space Agency (Special Publication). ESA SP [*France*]
Euro Spectr — Euro-Spectra
Eurotest Tech Bull — Eurotest Technical Bulletin
Eur Outremer — Europe Outremer
Eur Plast News — European Plastics News
Eur Polym J — European Polymer Journal
Eur Potato J — European Potato Journal
Eur Rdsch — Europaeische Rundschau
Eur Research — European Research
Eur Rev Agric Econ — European Review of Agricultural Economics
Eur Rev Endocrinol — European Review of Endocrinology
Eur Rev Endocrinol Suppl — European Review of Endocrinology. Supplement
Eur Rev Lit — Europe. Revue Litteraire Mensuelle
Eur Rubber J — European Rubber Journal
Eur Rubb J — European Rubber Journal
Eur Semicond Prod — European Semiconductor Production
Eur Shipbldg — European Shipbuilding
Eur Solid State Device Res Conf — European Solid State Device. Research Conference
Eur South Obs Bull — European Southern Observatory Bulletin [*West Germany*]
Eur Space Agency Sci Tech Rev — European Space Agency. Scientific and Technical Review
Eur Space Res Organ Contract Rep — European Space Research Organization. Contractor Report
Eur Stud R — European Studies Review
Eur Sud-Est 5e Ser — Europe Sud-Est. Cinquieme Serie
Eur Surg Re — European Surgical Research
Eur Surg Res — European Surgical Research
Eur Symp Calcif Tissues Proc — European Symposium on Calcified Tissues. Proceedings
Eur Symp Chem React Eng — European Symposium on Chemical Reaction Engineering
Eur Symp Horm Cell Regul — European Symposium on Hormones and Cell Regulation
Eur Symp Lindane — European Symposium on Lindane
Eur Symp Powder Metall Prepr — European Symposium for Powder Metallurgy. Preprints
Eur Symp Pulvermetall Vorabdrucke — Europaeisches Symposium fuer Pulvermetallurgie. Vorabdrucke
Eur Taxation — European Taxation
Eur Urol — European Urology
Eur Wehrkunde — Europaeische Wehrkunde
Eur Z Forstpathologie — Europaeische Zeitschrift fuer Forstpathologie
Eur Z Kartoffelforsch — Europaeische Zeitschrift fuer Kartoffelforschung
EUS — Economic Outlook USA
EUS — Market Research Europe
EUSND — Energy User News
EUV — Europa-Archiv

Eu W N — Eudora Welty Newsletter
EUZ — European Chemical News
EV — Ecos de Valvanera
EV — Elektrotehniski Vestnik
EV — Epegrafika Vostika
EV — Evergreen Review
EVA — European Review of Agricultural Economics
Eval Eng — Evaluation Engineering
Eval & Exper — Evaluation and Experiment. Some Critical Issues in Assessing Social Programs
Eval Health Prof — Evaluation and the Health Professions
Eval Program Plann — Evaluation and Program Planning
Evaluation Health Professions — Evaluation and the Health Professions
Evaluatn — Evaluation: A Forum for Human Services Decision-Makers
Evalu Stu — Evaluation Studies. Review Annual
Evang — Evangelical Quarterly
Evang Komment — Evangelische Kommentare [*West Germany*]
Evang Q — Evangelical Quarterly
Evang R — Evangelical Review
Evang Th — Evangelische Theologie
Evan Kirchor — Evangelische Kirchenchor
EVBAA — Electric Vehicles and Batteries
EVBHA — Environment and Behavior
EVBMA — Environmental Biology and Medicine
EVD — Exportmededelingen
Everday Sci — Everyday Science
Everglades Nat History — Everglades Natural History
Everyman's Sci — Everyman's Science
EVETB — Environmental Entomology
EVF — Tendance des Ventes du Vetement Masculin pour Hommes et Juniors
EVH — Wereldmarkt
EvK — Evangelische Kommentare [*Stuttgart*]
EVKOD — Evangelische Kommentare
EvKom — Evangelische Kommentare [*Stuttgart*]
EVLTA — Environmental Letters
EVLWA — Environmental Law
EVM — Evangelie en Maatschappij
Ev MQ — Evangelical Missions Quarterly
EVNSA — Electric Vehicle News
Evol — Evolution
Evol Biol — Evolutionary Biology
Evol Genet Res Rep — Evolutionary Genetics Research Reports
Evol Med — Evolution Medicale
Evol Psychiatr — Evolution Psychiatrique
Evol Theory — Evolutionary Theory
EVPHB — Environmental Physiology
EVPSA — Evolution Psychiatrique
EVPTD — Energy Viewpoint
EvQ — Evangelical Quarterly [*London*]
EVQMA — Environmental Quality
EvR — Evergreen Review
EVS — Economische Voorlichting Suriname
Ev Sat — Every Saturday
EVSCB — Everyman's Science
EvT — Evangelische Theologie [*Munich*]
EvTC — Evangelizing Today's Child
EvTh — Evangelische Theologie [*Munich*]
EvThB — Evangelische Theologie (Beiheft)
EvWelt — Evangelische Welt. Bethel bei Bielefeld [*Germany*]
E & W — East and West
EW — East and West
EW — Eastern World
EW — Eco/Log Week
EW — Economic Week
EW — Ecosystems of the World [*Elsevier Book Series*]
EWB — Ernaehrungswirtschaft
EWCR — East-West Center Review
EWD — Elseviers Weekblad
EWD — Europaeischer Wissenschaftsdienst
EWI — Ecologist
EWM — Elseviers Magazine
EWN — Evelyn Waugh Newsletter
E World — Eastern World
EWR — East-West Review
EWRSI Newsl — EWRSI [*East-West Resource Systems Institute*] Newsletter
EWTFA — Energiewirtschaftliche Tagesfragen
EWTJA — Effluent and Water Treatment Journal
Ex — Examiner [*Quezon City*]
Ex — Explicator
Exam Sit Econ Mexico — Examen de la Situacion Economica de Mexico
EXav — Ecclesiastica Xaveriana [*Bogota*]
EXBRA — Experimental Brain Research
EXCCA — Exceptional Children
Excep Child — Exceptional Children
Except Chil — Exceptional Children
Except Child — Exceptional Child

Except Parent — Exceptional Parent
Excerp Bot — Excerpta Botanica
Excerp Criminol — Excerpta Criminologica
Excerpta Med (Amst) — Excerpta Medica (Amsterdam)
Excerpta Med Int Congr Ser — Excerpta Medica. International Congress
    Series [*Amsterdam*]
Excerpta Med Sect 1 — Excerpta Medica. Section 1. Anatomy, Anthropology,
    Embryology, and Histology
Excerpta Med Sect 3 — Excerpta Medica. Section 3. Endocrinology
Excerpta Med Sect 4 — Excerpta Medica. Section 4. Medical Microbiology
    and Hygiene
Excerpta Med Sect 5 — Excerpta Medica. Section 5. General Pathology and
    Pathological Anatomy
Excerpta Med Sect 6 — Excerpta Medica. Section 6. Internal Medicine
Excerpta Med Sect 7 — Excerpta Medica. Section 7. Pediatrics
Excerpta Med Sect 8 — Excerpta Medica. Section 8. Neurology and Psychiatry
Excerpta Med Sect 9 — Excerpta Medica. Section 9. Surgery
Excerpta Med Sect 10 — Excerpta Medica. Section 10. Obstetrics and
    Gynecology
Excerpta Med Sect 11 — Excerpta Medica. Section 11. Oto-Rhino-
    Laryngology
Excerpta Med Sect 12 — Excerpta Medica. Section 12. Ophthalmology
Excerpta Med Sect 13 — Excerpta Medica. Section 13. Dermatology and
    Venereology
Excerpta Med Sect 14 — Excerpta Medica. Section 14. Radiology
Excerpta Med Sect 15 — Excerpta Medica. Section 15. Chest Diseases,
    Thoracic Surgery, and Tuberculosis
Excerpta Med Sect 16 — Excerpta Medica. Section 16. Cancer
Excerpta Med Sect 17 — Excerpta Medica. Section 17. Public Health, Social
    Medicine, and Hygiene
Excerpta Med Sect 23 — Excerpta Medica. Section 23. Nuclear Medicine
Excerpta Med Sect 30 — Excerpta Medica. Section 30. Pharmacology and
    Toxicology
Excerpta Med Sect 2B — Excerpta Medica. Section 2B. Biochemistry
Excerpta Med Sect 2C — Excerpta Medica. Section 2C. Pharmacology and
    Toxicology
Excerpta Med Sect 4 Med Microbiol Immunol Serol — Excerpta Medica.
    Section 4. Medical Microbiology, Immunology, and Serology
ExChAb — Exceptional Child Education Abstracts
Exch Flower Nursery Gard Cent Trade — Exchange for the Flower, Nursery,
    and Garden Center Trade
Excursions Rec Math Ser — Excursions in Recreational Mathematics Series
Exec — Executive
Exec Fit Newsl — Executive Fitness Newsletter
Exec Housekeeper — Executive Housekeeper
Exec Mem Jogger — Executive's Memory Jogger
Exec Sci Inst — Executive Sciences Institute
Exercise Sport Sci Rev — Exercise and Sport Sciences Reviews
Exerc Sport Sci Rev — Exercise and Sport Sciences Reviews
Exer Pat — Exercices de la Patience
EXG — Exhibition Bulletin
EXGEA — Experimental Gerontology
Exhaust Gas Air Pollut Abs — Exhaust Gas and Air Pollution Abstracts
EXHE — Executive Health
EXHEB — Experimental Hematology
Exhib & Conf Gaz — Exhibitions and Conferences Gazette
Exhibition Bull — Exhibition Bulletin
Ex H Lec — Exeter Hall Lectures
Exist Psychiat — Existential Psychiatry
EXJO — Explorers Journal
EXKTA — Exaktn
EXM — Export Markt
EX Mag — EX Magazine
EXMDA — International Congress Series. Excerpta Medica
EXNEA — Experimental Neurology
EXON — Exxon USA
Exp — Experiment
Exp — Explicator
EXP — Export
Exp — Expositor
Exp — Express
Exp Ag — Experimental Agriculture
Exp Aging Res — Experimental Aging Research
Exp Agric — Experimental Agriculture
Exp Anim — Experimentation Animale
Exp Anim (Tokyo) — Experimental Animals (Jikken Dobutsu) (Tokyo)
Expansion Reg — Expansion Regionale
Expans Region — Expansion Regionale
Expans Region (Paris) — Expansion Regionale (Paris)
Exp Biol — Experimental Biology
Exp Biol Med — Experimental Biology and Medicine
Exp Bot — Experimental Botany
Exp Bot Int Ser Monogr — Experimental Botany: An International Series of
    Monographs
Exp Brain R — Experimental Brain Research
Exp Brain Res — Experimental Brain Research

Exp Cell Biol — Experimental Cell Biology
Exp Cell Re — Experimental Cell Research
Exp Cell Res — Experimental Cell Research
Exp Cell Res Suppl — Experimental Cell Research. Supplement
Exp Cereb — Experimentation Cerebrale
Exp Chem Thermodyn — Experimental Chemical Thermodynamics
Exp Clin Endocrinol — Experimental and Clinical Endocrinology
Exp Clin Immunogenet — Experimental and Clinical Immunogenetics
EXPEA — Experientia
Exped — Expedition
Expedition — Expedition Bulletin. University Museum. University of
    Pennsylvania
Exp Embryol Teratol — Experimental Embryology and Teratology
Exper — Experientia
Exper Agric — Experimental Agriculture
Experiment Tech Phys — Experimentelle Technik der Physik
Exper Mech — Experimental Mechanics
Exper Suppl — Experientia Supplementum
Exper Suppl (Basel) — Experientia Supplementum (Basel)
Exp Eye Res — Experimental Eye Research
Exp Geront — Experimental Gerontology
Exp Gerontol — Experimental Gerontology
Exp Hematol — Experimental Hematology [*Lawrence, Kansas*]
Exp Hematol (Copenh) — Experimental Hematology (Copenhagen)
Exp Hematol (Oak Ridge Tenn) — Experimental Hematology (Oak Ridge,
    Tennessee)
Exp Hirnforsch — Experimentelle Hirnforschung
Exp Hort — Experimental Horticulture
Exp Hortic — Experimental Horticulture
Exp Husb — Experimental Husbandry
Expl — Explicator
EXPL — Explore. Alberta's Outdoor Magazine
Expl Agric — Experimental Agriculture
Explan Leafl Intervention Bd Agric Prod — Explanatory Leaflet. Intervention
    Board for Agricultural Produce
Expl Brain Res — Experimental Brain Research
Expl Cell Res — Experimental Cell Research
Expl Ec His — Explorations in Economic History
Expl Gerontol — Experimental Gerontology
Expl Hort — Experimental Horticulture
Expl Husb — Experimental Husbandry
Explo Econ Hist — Explorations in Economic History
Explor — Explorations
Explor Econ Hist — Explorations in Economic History
Explor Econ Petrol Ind — Exploration and Economics of the Petroleum
    Industry
Explor Econ Res — Explorations in Economic Research
Explor Entrep Hist — Explorations in Entrepreneurial History
Explor Geophys — Exploration Geophysics
Explor Geophys (USSR) — Exploration Geophysics (USSR)
Explor J — Explorers Journal
Explosives Eng — Explosives Engineer
Explosivst — Explosivstoffe
Expl Parasit — Experimental Parasitology
Expl Path — Experimental Pathology
Expl Rec Dep Agric S Aust — Experimental Record. Department of
    Agriculture. South Australia
Expl Text L — Explicacion de Textos Literarios
Exp Lung Res — Experimental Lung Research
Exp Mech — Experimental Mechanics
Exp Med Microbiol — Experimental Medicine and Microbiology
Exp Med Microbiol (Engl Transl Med Dosw Mikrobiol) — Experimental
    Medicine and Microbiology (English Translation of Medycyna
    Doswiadczalna i Mikrobiologia)
Exp Med Pathol Klin — Experimentelle Medizin, Pathologie, und Klinik
Exp Med Surg — Experimental Medicine and Surgery
Exp Molecul Pathol — Experimental and Molecular Pathology
Exp Mol Pat — Experimental and Molecular Pathology
Exp Mol Pathol — Experimental and Molecular Pathology
Exp Mol Pathol Suppl — Experimental and Molecular Pathology. Supplement
Exp Mycol — Experimental Mycology
Exp Neurol — Experimental Neurology
Exp Neurol Suppl — Experimental Neurology. Supplement
Expo Annu Biochim Med — Exposes Annuels de Biochimie Medicale
Export Rev Br Drug Chem Ind — Export Review of the British Drug and
    ´Chemical Industries
Exports of Aust — Exports of Australia
Exports of Aust & NZ — Exports of Australia and New Zealand
Expos — Expositor
Expos Ann Biochim Med — Exposes Annuels de Biochimie Medicale
Expos Annu Biochim Med — Exposes Annuels de Biochimie Medicale
Exposit Tim — Expository Times
Expos T — Expository Times
Exp Parasit — Experimental Parasitology
Exp Parasitol — Experimental Parasitology
Exp Path — Experimentelle Pathologie

Exp Pathol — Experimentelle Pathologie
Exp Pathol (Jena) — Experimental Pathology (Jena)
Exp Physiol Biochem — Experiments in Physiology and Biochemistry
Exp Progr Grassland Res Inst (Hurley) — Experiments in Progress. Grassland Research Institute (Hurley)
Exp R — Expatriate Review
Exp Rec Dep Agric S Aust — Experimental Record. Department of Agriculture. South Australia
Exp Rep Equine Health Lab — Experimental Reports of Equine Health Laboratory
Express Transl Serv List — Express Translation Service List
Exp Ship Guide — Export Shipping Guide
Exp Sta Record — Experiment Station Record
Exp Stn Rec — Experiment Station Record. United States Department of Agriculture
Exp St Rec — Experiment Station Record [*Washington, DC*]
ExpT — Expository Times
Exp Tech — Experimental Techniques
Exp Tech Phys — Experimentelle Technik der Physik [*East Germany*]
ExpTim — Expository Times [*Edinburgh*]
Exp Veterinaermed — Experimentelle Veterinaermedizin
EXS — Executive Skills
EXSP — Extracts from the Soviet Press on the Soviet North and Antarctic
Ex T — Expository Times
Ext — Extrapolation
Ext Abstr Conf Solid State Devices Mater — Extended Abstracts. Conference on Solid State Devices and Materials
Ext Affairs — External Affairs
Ext Amer — Extension en las Americas
Ext Bull Agric Ext Serv Univ Minn — Extension Bulletin. Agriculture Extension Service. University of Minnesota
Ext Bull Cornell Agric Exp Stn — Extension Bulletin. Cornell Agricultural Experiment Station
Ext Bull Del Univ Agr Ext Serv — Extension Bulletin. Delaware University. Agricultural Extension Service
Ext Bull Dep Agric S Aust — Extension Bulletin. Department of Agriculture. South Australia
Ext Bull Dept Agric South Aust — Extension Bulletin. Department of Agriculture and Fisheries. South Australia
Ext Bull E Coop Ext Serv Mich State Univ — Extension Bulletin E. Cooperative Extension Service. Michigan State University
Ext Bull Flor Agric Exp St — Extension Bulletin. Florida Agricultural Experiment Station
Ext Bull Ind Agric Exp Stn — Extension Bulletin. Indiana Agricultural Experiment Station
Ext Bull Iowa State Univ — Extension Bulletin. Iowa State University
Ext Bull MD Univ Coop Ext Serv — Extension Bulletin. Maryland University. Cooperative Extension Service
Ext Bull Mich State Univ Coop Ext Serv — Extension Bulletin. Michigan State University. Cooperative Extension Service
Ext Bull Mich St Coll — Extension Bulletin. Michigan State College
Ext Bull Ohio State Univ Coll Agr Coop Ext Serv — Extension Bulletin. Ohio State University. College of Agriculture. Cooperative Extension Service
Ext Bull Ohio St Univ — Extension Bulletin. Ohio State University
Ext Bull Oreg State Univ Coop Ext Serv — Extension Bulletin. Oregon State University. Cooperative Extension Service
Ext Bull Purdue Univ Dep Agric Ext — Extension Bulletin. Purdue University. Department of Agricultural Extension
Ext Bull Univ MD Coop Ext Serv — Extension Bulletin. University of Maryland. Cooperative Extension Service
Ext Bull Univ Minn Agr Ext Serv — Extension Bulletin. University of Minnesota. Agricultural Extension Service
Ext Bull Univ Minn Agric Ext Serv — Extension Bulletin. University of Minnesota. Agricultural Extension Service
Ext Bull US Dep Agric — Extension Bulletin. United States Department of Agriculture
Ext Bull Wash State Univ Coll Agr Ext Serv — Extension Bulletin. Washington State University. College of Agriculture. Extension Service
Ext Bull Wash St Coll — Extension Bulletin. Washington State College
Ext Circ Ark Coll Agric — Extension Circular. Arkansas College of Agriculture
Ext Circ Ill Univ — Extension Circular. Illinois University
Ext Circ N Carol Agric Exp Stn — Extension Circular. North Carolina Agricultural Experiment Station
Ext Circ NC State Univ Agr Ext Serv — Extension Circular. North Carolina State University. Agricultural Extension Service
Ext Circ Oreg State Univ Ext Serv — Extension Circular. Oregon State University. Extension Service
Ext Circ PA St Coll Agric — Extension Circular. Pennsylvania State College. School of Agriculture
Ext Circ P Auburn Univ Agr Ext Serv — Extension Circular P. Auburn University. Agricultural Extension Service
Ext Circ Purdue Univ Dept Agr Ext — Extension Circular. Purdue University. Department of Agricultural Extension
Ext Circ S Dak Coll Agric — Extension Circular. South Dakota College of Agriculture

Ext Circ S Dak State Univ Coop Ext Serv — Extension Circular. South Dakota State University. Cooperative Extension Service
Ext Circ Utah Agric Coll — Extension Circular. Utah Agricultural College
Ext Circ Wash State Univ Coll Agr Ext Serv — Extension Circular. Washington State University. College of Agriculture. Extension Service
Ext Circ Wash State Univ Coop Ext Serv — Extension Circular. Washington State University. Cooperative Extension Service
Ext Course Lect Ak Prim Assoc — Extension Course Lectures. Auckland Primary Principals Association
Ext Dev Unit Rep — Extension Development Unit Report
Extel Handbook Mark Leaders — Extel Handbook of Market Leaders
Extended Abstr Program Bienn Conf Carbon — Extended Abstracts and Program. Biennial Conference on Carbon
Extensn — Extension
Exterm Log — Exterminators' Log
External Stud Gaz — External Studies Gazette
External Studies Gaz — External Studies Gazette
Externer Ber Kernforschungszentr Karlsruhe — Externer Bericht. Kernforschungszentrum Karlsruhe
Externer Ber Kernforschungszentrum Karlsruhe — Externer Bericht. Kernforschungszentrum Karlsruhe
Ext Folder Mich State Univ Agr Appl Sci Coop Ext Serv — Extension Folder. Michigan State University of Agriculture and Applied Science. Cooperative Extension Service
Ext Folder Mich St Univ — Extension Folder. Michigan State University
Ext Folder NC Agric Ext Serv — Extension Folder. North Carolina Agricultural Extension Service
Ext Folder NC State Univ Agr Ext Serv — Extension Folder. North Carolina State University. Agricultural Extension Service
Ext Folder Univ Minn Agr Ext Serv — Extension Folder. University of Minnesota. Agricultural Extension Service
Ext Folder Univ NH Coll Agr Ext Serv — Extension Folder. University of New Hampshire. College of Agriculture. Extension Service
ExTL — Explicacion de Textos Literarios
Ext Leafl Ohio State Univ Coll Agr Coop Ext Serv — Extension Leaflet. Ohio State University. College of Agriculture. Cooperative Extension Service
Ext Leafl Utah State Univ Agr Ext Serv — Extension Leaflet. Utah State University. Agricultural Extension Service
Ext Leafl Utah St Univ — Extension Leaflet. Utah State University
Ext Mimeogr Circ S Dak State Univ Coop Ext Serv — Extension Mimeographed Circular. South Dakota State University. Cooperative Extension Service
Ext Mimeo Wash State Univ Coll Agr Ext Serv — Extension Mimeo. Washington State University. College of Agriculture. Extension Service
Ext Publ Ill Univ N Cent Reg — Extension Publication. Illinois University. North Central Region
Ext Publ LA State Univ Agr Ext Serv — Extension Publication. Louisiana State University. Agricultural Extension Service
Ext Publ Wash St Coll — Extension Publication. Washington State College
Extrapolat — Extrapolation
Extr Or Med — Extreme-Orient Medical
Ext Serv R — Extension Service Review
Ext Serv Rev — Extension Service Review
Ext Stud PA State Univ Ext Serv — Extension Studies. Pennsylvania State University. Extension Service
EXW — Europa Chemie
Ex W — Express Wieczorny
EXX — Expo Data
EXY — Excerpta Indonesica
EY — European Yearbook
EY — Journal of Energy Engineering
EYBIA5 — Encyclopedie Biologique [*Paris*]
Eye Ear Nos — Eye, Ear, Nose, and Throat Monthly
Eye Ear Nose Throat Mon — Eye, Ear, Nose, and Throat Monthly
EYENAZ — Encyclopedie Entomologique
EYETD — Energy Economist
Eyewit — Eyewitness
EYGZAD — Eiyogaku Zasshi
EYGZAD — Japanese Journal of Nutrition
EY Loc Hist Ser — East Yorkshire Local History Series
EYMYA6 — Encyclopedie Mycologique
EYPSB — Energy Pipelines and Systems
EZ — Elektronik-Zeitung fuer Industrie, Wirtschaft, Wissenschaft, und Verwaltung
Ezeg Muz Ist Rel At Ak N SSSR — Ezhegodnik Muzeja Istorii Religii i Ateizma Akademii Nauk SSSR
Ezheg Geol Mineral Ross — Ezhegodnik po Geologii i Mineralogii Rossii
Ezheg Inst Geokhim Sib Otd Akad Nauk SSSR — Ezhegodnik Instituta Geokhimii Sibirskogo Otdeleniya Akademii Nauk SSSR
Ezheg Nauchn Rab Alma-At Inst Usoversh Vrachei — Ezhegodnik Nauchnykh Rabot Alma-Atinskii Institut Usovershenstvovaniya Vrachei
Ezhegodnik GIM — Ezhegodnik Gosudarstvennyi Istoricheskii Muzei
Ezhegodnik Zool Muz Akad Nauk SSSR — Ezhegodnik Zoologicheskogo Muzeia Akademii Nauk Sofuza Sovetskikh Sotsialisticheskikh Respublik

Ezhegodnik Zool Muz Ross Akad Nauk — Ezhegodnik Zoologicheskogo
    Muzeia Rossiiskoi Akademii Nauk
Ezheg O-va Estestvoispyt Akad Nauk Est SSR — Ezhegodnik Obshchestva
    Estestvoispytatelei Akademiya Nauk. Estonskoi SSR
Ezheg Sib Inst Geokhim — Ezhegodnik Sibirskogo Instituta Geokhimii
Ez Lit — Ezik i Literatura
EZV — Erlanger Zeitschriften-Verzeichnis
EZZ — Ethnologische Zeitschrift (Zuerich)

F

FAIR Newsl — Fast Access Information Retrieval. Newsletter
FAJAAY — Folia Anatomica Japonica
Fak Mat Univ Kiril Metodij Skopje Godisen — Skopje Univezitetot Kiril i Metodij Fakultet na Matematicka Godisen Zbornik (Skopje)
Faktory Vneshn Sredy Ikh Znach Zdorov ya Naseleniya — Faktory Vneshnei Sredy i Ikh Znachenie dlya Zdorov ya Naseleniya
Fakt Vneshn Sred Znach Zdor Nasel Resp Mezhved Sb — Faktory Vneshnykh Sred Znachenie Zdorov'ya Naseleniya Respublikanskii Mezhvedomstvennyi Sbornik
FAL — Food and Agricultural Legislation
FALAA — Farbe und Lack
Falke Monatsschr Ornithol — Falke Monatsschrift fuer Ornithologie und Vivarienkunde
Falke Monatsschr Ornithol Vivarienkd Ausg A — Falke Monatsschrift fuer Ornithologie und Vivarienkunde. Ausgabe A
Falkl Isl Depend Surv Sci Rep — Falkland Islands Dependencies Survey. Scientific Reports
Falk Symp — Falk Symposium [*England*]
FAm — Folklore Americano
FAm — Folklore Americas
FAM — Fontes Artis Musicae
Fam Adv — Family Advocate
Fa Man — Farm Management
Fam Bibl — Familiengeschichtliche Bibliographie
Fam Community Health — Family and Community Health
Fam Coord — Family Coordinator
Fam Dev — Famille et Developpement
Fa Mechan — Farm Mechanization
Fam Ec Rev — Family Economics Review
Fam Health — Family Health
Family Hlth — Family Health
Family LQ — Family Law Quarterly
Family Plann Digest — Family Planning Digest
Fam L — Family Law
Fam Law — Family Law
Fam Law Q — Family Law Quarterly
Fam L Coord — Family Life Coordinator
FAMLI — Family Medicine Literature Index
Fam LN — Family Law Notes
Fam L Newsl — Family Law Newsletter
Fam LQ — Family Law Quarterly
Fam LR — Family Law Reports
Fam LR — Family Law Review
Fam L Rep — Family Law Reporter
Fam L Rev — Family Law Review
Fam Physician — Family Physician
Fam Plann (Lond) — Family Planning (London)
Fam Plann Perspect — Family Planning Perspectives
Fam Plann Resume — Family Planning Resume
Fam Plan Pe — Family Planning Perspectives
Fam Pract News — Family Practice News
Fam Pract Res J — Family Practice Research Journal
Fam Proc — Family Process
Fam Process — Family Process
FAMR — Family Relations
Fam Relat — Family Relations
FAN — Fantasy Fiction
Fa N — Francais au Nigeria
FANA — Fantasiae
F Anal Jrl — Financial Analysts Journal
FanF — Fantasy Fiction
FANO — Fauna Norrlandica. Department of Ecological Zoology. Umea University
Fans — Fantasy: The Magazine of Science Fiction
FanS — Fantasy Stories
Fant — Fantasy
Fant & Sci Fict — Fantasy and Science Fiction
FAO Agric Dev Pap — FAO [*Food and Agriculture Organization of the United Nations*] Agricultural Development Papers
FAO Agric Stud — FAO [*Food and Agriculture Organization of the United Nations*] Agricultural Studies
FAO At Energy Ser — FAO [*Food and Agriculture Organization of the United Nations*] Atomic Energy Series
FAO Atom En Ser — FAO [*Food and Agriculture Organization of the United Nations*] Atomic Energy Series
FAOBA — Farmaceuticky Obzor
FAO Dev Program — FAO [*Food and Agriculture Organization of the United Nations*] Development Program
FAO Doc — FAO [*Food and Agriculture Organization of the United Nations*] Documentation
FAO Econ Soc Dev Ser — FAO [*Food and Agriculture Organization of the United Nations*] Economic and Social Development Series
FAO Fish Biol Synop — FAO [*Food and Agriculture Organization of the United Nations*] Fisheries Biology Synopsis
FAO Fish Biol Tech Pap — FAO [*Food and Agriculture Organization of the United Nations*] Fisheries Biology Technical Paper

FAO Fish Bull — FAO [*Food and Agriculture Organization of the United Nations*] Fisheries Bulletin
FAO Fish Circ — FAO [*Food and Agriculture Organization of the United Nations*] Fisheries Circular
FAO Fish Rep — FAO [*Food and Agriculture Organization of the United Nations*] Fisheries Reports
FAO Fish Synop — FAO [*Food and Agriculture Organization of the United Nations*] Fisheries Synopsis
FAO Fish Tech Pap — FAO [*Food and Agriculture Organization of the United Nations*] Fisheries Technical Paper
FAO Food Nutr Pap — FAO [*Food and Agriculture Organization of the United Nations*] Food and Nutrition Paper
FAO Food Nutr Ser — FAO [*Food and Agriculture Organization of the United Nations*] Food and Nutrition Series
FAO For Developm Pap — FAO [*Food and Agriculture Organization of the United Nations*] Forestry Development Papers
FAO For & For Prod Stud — FAO [*Food and Agriculture Organization of the United Nations*] Forestry and Forest Products Studies
FAO Gen Fish Counc Mediterr Stud Rev — FAO [*Food and Agriculture Organization of the United Nations*] General Fisheries Council for the Mediterranean. Studies and Reviews
FAO Inf Serv Bull — FAO [*Food and Agriculture Organization of the United Nations*] Information Service Bulletin
FAO Irrig Drain Pap — Food and Agriculture Organization of the United Nations. Irrigation and Drainage Paper
FAO Man Fish Sci — FAO [*Food and Agriculture Organization of the United Nations*] Manuals in Fisheries Science
FAO Mo Bul Ag Econ & Stat — FAO [*Food and Agriculture Organization of the United Nations*] Monthly Bulletin of Agricultural Economics and Statistics [*Later, FAO Monthly Bulletin of Statistics*]
FAO Nutr Meet Rep Ser — FAO [*Food and Agriculture Organization of the United Nations*] Nutrition Meetings. Report Series
FAO Nutr Stud — FAO [*Food and Agriculture Organization of the United Nations*] Nutritional Studies
FAO Pasture Fodder Crop Stud — FAO [*Food and Agriculture Organization of the United Nations*] Pasture and Fodder Crop Studies
FAO Plant — FAO [*Food and Agriculture Organization of the United Nations*] Plant Protection Bulletin
FAO Plant Prod Prot Ser — FAO [*Food and Agriculture Organization of the United Nations*] Plant Production and Protection Series
FAO Plant Prot Bull — FAO [*Food and Agriculture Organization of the United Nations*] Plant Protection Bulletin
FAO Rep — FAO [*Food and Agriculture Organization of the United Nations*] Report
FAO Soils Bull — FAO [*Food and Agriculture Organization of the United Nations*] Soils Bulletin
FAP — Fiscale en Administratieve Praktijkvragen
FAPCES — Fundamental Aspects of Pollution Control and Environmental Science [*Elsevier Book Series*]
FA Peguy — Feuillets Mensuels d'Information de l'Amitie Charles Peguy
FAPOA — Farmacja Polska
FAR — French American Review
Faraday Dis — Faraday Discussions of the Chemical Society
Faraday Discuss — Faraday Discussions of the Chemical Society
Faraday Discuss Chem Soc — Faraday Discussions of the Chemical Society
Faraday Soc Trans — Faraday Society. Transactions
Faraday Spec Discuss Chem Soc — Faraday Special Discussions of the Chemical Society
Faraday Symp Chem Soc — Faraday Symposia of the Chemical Society
Farben Ztg — Farben Zeitung
FARCA — Farm Chemicals
Far East Ass Trop Med — Far Eastern Association of Tropical Medicine
Far East Ceram Bull — Far Eastern Ceramic Bulletin
Far East Econ R — Far Eastern Economic Review
Far Eastern Econ Rev — Far Eastern Economic Review
Far East J Anesth — Far East Journal of Anesthesia
Far East LR — Far Eastern Law Review
Far East Med J — Far East Medical Journal
Far East Q — Far Eastern Quarterly
Far East R — Far Eastern Review
Far East S — Far Eastern Survey
Far East Surv — Far Eastern Survey
Far East Univ Fac J — Far Eastern University. Faculty Journal
Far E Econ R — Far Eastern Economic Review
FAR Horiz — Foreign Area Research Horizons
Farm — Farmacia
Farm — Farmacija
Farm — Farmaco
Farmacihist Ars — Farmacihistoriska Saellskapets Arsskrift
Farmaco Ed Prat — Farmaco. Edizione Pratica
Farmaco Ed Sci — Farmaco. Edizione Scientifica [*Italy*]
Farmaco Ed Scient — Farmaco. Edizione Scientifica
Farmaco Pra — Farmaco. Edizione Pratica
Farmaco Sci — Farmaco. Edizione Scientifica
Farm Aikak — Farmaseuttinen Aikakauslehti
Farmakol T — Farmakologiya i Toksikologiya

Farmakol Toksikol — Farmakologiya i Toksikologiya
Farmakol Toksikol (Kiev) — Farmakologiya i Toksikologiya (Kiev) [*Ukrainian SSR*]
Farmakol Toksikol (Mosc) — Farmakologiya i Toksikologiya (Moscow)
Farmakol Toksikol Resp Mezhved Sb — Farmakologiya i Toksikologiya Respublikanskii Mezhvedomstvennyi Sbornik
Farmak Toks — Farmakologiya i Toksikologiya
Farm Bldg Progress — Farm Building Progress
Farm Bldg R & D Studies — Farm Building R and D Studies
Farm Bldgs Digest — Farm Buildings Digest
Farm Bras — Farmaceutico Brasileiro
Farm Chem — Farm Chemicals
Farm Clin — Farmacia Clinica
Farm Coop — Farmer Cooperatives
Farm Delt Ed Sci — Farmakeftikon Deltion. Edition Scientifique
Farm Econ — Farm Economics
Farm Econ — Farm Economist
Farm Ed Prat — Farmaco. Edizione Pratica
Farm Ed Sci — Farmaco. Edizione Scientifica
Farm Eng — Farm Engineering
Farm Eq — Farm Equipment News
Farm Equip Dealer — Farm Equipment Dealer
Farmer Coop US Dep Agric Econ Stat Coop Serv — Farmer Cooperatives. United States Department of Agriculture. Economics Statistics and Cooperatives Service
Farmer's Advocate Can Countryman — Farmer's Advocate and Canadian Countryman
Farmers' B — Farmers' Bulletin
Farmers Bull — Farmers' Bulletin
Farmers Bull USDA — Farmers' Bulletin. United States Department of Agriculture
Farmers Newsl — Farmers' Newsletter
Farmers Rep Leeds Univ Dept Agr Econ Sect — Farmers' Report. Leeds University. Department of Agriculture. Economics Section
Farmers' Sci Joint Conf — Farmers' and Scientists' Joint Conference
Farmer Stockbr — Farmer and Stockbreeder
Farmers Wkly — Farmers Weekly [*South Africa*]
Farmers Wkly (Bloemfontein S Afr) — Farmers Weekly (Bloemfontein, South Africa)
Farm Farmakol — Farmatsiya i Farmakologiya
Farm Food Res — Farm and Food Research
Farm For — Farm Forestry
Farm & Garden Ind — Farm and Garden Index
Farm Glas — Farmaceutski Glasnik
Farm & Home Sci — Farm and Home Science
Farm Home Sci — Farm and Home Science
Farm In — Farm Index
Farming Dig — Farming Digest
Farming Mech — Farming Mechanization
Farming Progr — Farming Progress
Farming Rev — Farming Review
Farming S Afr — Farming in South Africa
Farm J — Farm Journal
Farm J Brit Guiana — Farm Journal of British Guiana
Farm J (Calcutta) — Farm Journal (Calcutta)
Farm J (E Ed) — Farm Journal (Eastern Edition)
Farmkoter Zpr — Farmakoterapeuticke Zpravy
Farmkoter Zpr Suppl — Farmakoterapeuticke Zpravy. Supplementum
Farmline US Dep Agric Econ Stat Coop Serv — Farmline. United States Department of Agriculture. Economics Statistics and Cooperatives Service
Farm Manage Notes — Farm Management Notes
Farm Manage Rev — Farm Management Review
Farm Mech — Farm Mechanization
Farm Mech Stud — Farm Mechanization Studies
Farmnote West Aust Dep Agric — Farmnote. Western Australian Department of Agriculture
Farm Nueva — Farmacia Nueva
Farm Obz — Farmaceuticky Obzor
Farm Pol — Farm Policy
Farm Pol — Farmacja Polska
Farm Pol (1902-1914) — Farmaceuta Polski (1902-1914)
Farm Policy Rev Conf — Farm Policy Review Conference
Farm Power Equip — Farm and Power Equipment
Farm Q — Farm Quarterly
Farm Quart — Farm Quarterly
Farm Ranch Home Q — Farm, Ranch, and Home Quarterly
Farm Res — Farm Research
Farm Res News — Farm Research News
Farm Revy — Farmacevtisk Revy
Farm Safety Rev — Farm Safety Review
Farm Technol — Farm Technology
Farm Tid — Farmaceutisk Tidende
Farm Tijdschr Belg — Farmaceutisch Tijdschrift voor Belgie
Farm Vestn — Farmacevtski Vestnik
Farm Z — Farmatsevtychnyi Zhurnal

Farm Zh — Farmatsevtychnyi Zhurnal
Farm Zh (Kharkov) — Farmatsevticheskii Zhurnal (Kharkov)
Farm Zh (Kiev) — Farmatsevtychnyi Zhurnal (Kiev)
Farm Zh (Leningrad) — Farmatsevticheskii Zhurnal (Leningrad)
FARRA — Farm Research [*Switzerland*]
Far Seas Fish Res Lab S Ser — Far Seas Fisheries Research Laboratory. S Series
F Arts Q — Fine Arts Quarterly
FARUA — Farumashia
FAS — Fantastic Stories
FASBB — Soils Bulletin
Fasc Math — Fasciculi Mathematici
FASEB Monogr — FASEB [*Federation of American Societies for Experimental Biology*] Monographs
Faserforsch Textiltech — Faserforschung und Textiltechnik
Faserst Spinnpflanzen — Faserstoffe und Spinnpflanzen
FASF — Fantastic Science Fiction
FAST J — FAST Journal
Fataburen — Fataburen. Nordiska Museets och Skansens Arsbok
Fatigue Eng Mater Struct — Fatigue of Engineering Materials and Structures
Fatigue Eng Mater and Struct — Fatigue of Engineering Materials and Structures
Fatigue Eng Mat Struct — Fatigue of Engineering Materials and Structures
FATIS — FATIS [*Food and Agriculture Technical Information Service*] Publications
FATIS Rev — FATIS [*Food and Agriculture Technical Information Service*] Review
FATOA — Farmakologiya i Toksikologiya [*Moscow*]
FAU — Fantastic Universe Science Fiction
FAUCAR — Folia Anatomica Universitatis Conimbrigensis [*Coimbra*]
Faun Abh (Dres) — Faunistische Abhandlungen (Dresden)
Fauna Fenn — Fauna Fennica
Fauna Flora (Stockh) — Fauna och Flora (Stockholm)
Fauna Flora (Transvaal) — Fauna and Flora (Transvaal)
Fauna Hung — Fauna Hungariae
Fauna Ital — Fauna d'Italia
Fauna Pol — Fauna Polski
Faune Fr — Faune de France
Faune Que — Faune du Quebec
Faune Que Rapp Spec — Faune du Quebec. Rapport Special
Faun-Oekol Mitt — Faunistisch-Oekologische Mitteilungen
Faust B — Faust Blaetter
FAVUA — Fiziologicheski Aktivnye Veshchestva [*Ukrainian SSR*]
FAWEA — Farmers Weekly [*London*]
FAWEB — Farmers Weekly (Bloemfontein, South Africa)
FAY — Fantastic Adventures Yearbook
FB — Fabula
FB — Fantasy Book
FB — First Break
FB — Folklore Brabancon
FB — Fontane Blaetter
FB — Forschungen und Berichte [*Graz*]
FB — Franse Boek
FBAA — Frankfurter Beitraege zur Anglistik und Amerikanistik
FBB — Fabrimetal
FBBGAJ — Folia Biochimica e Biologica Graeca
FBCICSR — Fairbanks North Star Borough. Community Information Center. Special Report
FBCN — Federation of British Columbia Naturalists. Newsletter
FBG — Frankfurter Beitraege zur Germanistik
FBH — Fichero Bibliografico Hispano-Americano
FBIICR — Fairbanks North Star Borough. Impact Information Center. Report
FBIICSR — Fairbanks North Star Borough. Impact Information Center. Special Reports
FBI Law Enf Bul — FBI [*Federal Bureau of Investigation*] Law Enforcement Bulletin
FBILEB — FBI [*Federal Bureau of Investigation*] Law Enforcement Bulletin
FBK — Fantasy Book
FBKRA — Fiziologiya i Biokhimiya Kul'turnykh Rastenii
FBL — Farbe und Lack. Zentralblatt der Farbenindustrie und Lackindustrie und des Handels
FBMIDF — Folia Botanica Miscellanea
FBPG — Forschungen zur Brandenburgisch-Preussischen Geschichte
F Brab — Folklore Brabancon
FBSSD — Fushoku Boshoku Shinpojumu Shiryo
F Bul — Film Bulletin
FBVBA — Fortschritt-Berichte. VDI [*Verein Deutscher Ingenieure*] Zeitschriften. Reihe 4. Bauingenieurwesen
FC — Family Circle
FC — Fathers of the Church
FC — Film Comment
FCA — Feiten en Cijfers. Economisch, Financieel, Sociaal, Fiscaal, Juridisch
FCB — Fenedexpress
FCCADG — Focus on Critical Care
FCE — Fondo de Cultura Economica [*Mexico*]
FCEMN — 14th Century English Mystics Newsletter

FCHQ — Filson Club History Quarterly
FChrLDG — Forschungen zur Christlichen Literatur- und Dogmengeschichte
FCIQ — Fairbanks North Star Borough. Community Information Center. Quarterly
FCL — Federal Communications Law Journal
FCLBAR — Folia Clinica et Biologica
FCO — Federal Career Opportunities
F Com — Film Comment
F Comment — Film Comment
FCR — Federal Court Reporter
FCR — Filmcritica
FCR — Food and Cookery Review
FCR — Free China Review
F Criticism — Film Criticism
FCS — Fifteenth-Century Studies
FCTF — Flue-Cured Tobacco Farmer
FCTOD7 — Food and Chemical Toxicology
FCTXAV — Food and Cosmetics Toxicology
FCTYA — Factory
F CUL — Film Culture
F Cultura — Filme Cultura
F Culture — Film Culture
FD — Fanfulla della Domenica
F a D — Film a Divadio
FD — Filosofska Dumka
F and D — Finance and Development
FD — Financieel Dagblad
F & D — Fonetica si Dialectologie
FD — Fonetica si Dialectologie
FDA — Freiburger Diozesanarchiv
FDA — Fremdenverkehr + das Reiseburo. Tourismus und Kongress
FDACB — FDA [*Food and Drug Administration*] Consumer
FDA Consum — FDA [*Food and Drug Administration*] Consumer
FDADA — FDA [*Food and Drug Administration*] Drug Bulletin
FDA Drug Bull — FDA [*Food and Drug Administration*] Drug Bulletin
FDA Pap — FDA [*Food and Drug Administration*] Papers
Fd Can — Food in Canada
Fd Chem News Guide — Food Chemical News Guide
Fd Chem Toxic — Food and Chemical Toxicology
FDCOA — Fundicao
Fd Cosmet Toxicol — Food and Cosmetics Toxicology
FdD — Fouilles de Delphes
FDEC — Forum for Death Education and Counseling. Newsletter
FDEVDS — Food Development
FDG — Folk Dance Guide
FDGK — Fukui Daigaku Gakugeigakubu Kiyo
FDHRS — Freies Deutsches Hochstift: Reihe der Schriften
FDI — Food Engineering
FDIIA6 — Food Irradiation Information
Fd Inds — Food Industries
F Directions — Film Directions
FdL — Forum der Letteren
FDLJAO — Food, Drug, Cosmetic Law Journal
FDM — Furniture Design and Manufacturing
Fd Mf — Food Manufacture
Fd Nutr — Food and Nutrition
Fd Nutr Notes Rev — Food and Nutrition. Notes and Reviews
Fd Nutr Notes Revs — Food and Nutrition. Notes and Reviews
F & Doba — Film a Doba
F Doba — Film a Doba
F Dope — Film Dope
FDP — Foodpress, Economisch, en Technisch Weekblad voor de Voedingsmiddelenindustrie en Genotmiddelenindustrie en Groothandel in de Benelux
FDP — Four Decades of Poetry 1890-1930
F & D Pkg — Food and Drug Packaging
Fd Process — Food Processing
Fd Process Ind — Food Processing Industry
Fd Process Market — Food Processing and Marketing [*Chicago*]
Fd Process Packag — Food Processing and Packaging
Fd Prod Dev — Food Product Development
FDQ — Florida Designers Quarterly
FDQTA — Fields and Quanta
Fd Res — Food Research
FDS — Fountainwell Drama Series
FDSD — Forschungen zur Deutschen Sprache und Dichtung
FDSTA — Feedstuffs
FDSUDR — Folia Dendrologica. Supplementum
FDT — Fountainwell Drama Texts
Fd Technol — Food Technology
Fd Technol Aust — Food Technology in Australia
Fd Trade Rev — Food Trade Review
FDTSC — Folger Documents of Tudor and Stuart Civilization
FDU — Flying Dutchman
FE — France-Eurafrique
FE — Organo de Falange Espanola

FEA — Financieel Economisch Magazine (Amsterdam)
FEAKA — Fel'dsher i Akusherka
FEARTR — Federal Environmental Assessment Review Office. Technical Report
FEBJA — Federal Bar Journal
FEBS Lett — FEBS [*Federation of European Biochemical Societies*] Letters
FEBS Proc Meet — FEBS [*Federation of European Biochemical Societies*] Proceedings of the Meeting
FEC — Far Eastern Economic Review
FECMDW — Forest Ecology and Management
Fed Accountant — Federal Accountant
Fed Atlant — Federal Reserve Bank of Atlanta. Economic Review
Fed Aust Music Teach Assoc Q Mag — Federation of Australian Music Teachers' Associations Quarterly Magazine
Fed BAJ — Federal Bar Association. Journal
Fed BA Jo — Federal Bar Association. Journal
Fed B J — Federal Bar Journal
Fed BN — Federal Bar News
Fed Bull — Federation Bulletin
Fed Can M Inst J — Federated Canadian Mining Institute. Journal
Fed Com B J — Federal Communications Bar Journal [*Later, Federal Communications Law Journal*]
Fed Com LJ — Federal Communications Law Journal
Fed Comm BJ — Federal Communications Bar. Law Journal
Fed Dallas — Federal Reserve Bank of Dallas. Farm and Ranch Bulletin
Feddes Repert — Feddes Repertorium
Feddes Repert Specierum Nov Regni Veg — Feddes Repertorium. Specierum Novarum Regni Vegetabilis
Feddes Repert Specierum Nov Regni Veg Beih — Feddes Repertorium. Specierum Novarum Regni Vegetabilis Beihefte
Feddes Repert Z Bot Taxon Geobot — Feddes Repertorium. Zeitschrift fuer Botanische Taxonomie und Geobotanik
Feddes Reprium Z Bot Taxon Geobot — Feddes Repertorium. Zeitschrift fuer Botanische Taxonomie und Geobotanik
Federal Home Loan Bank Bd J — Federal Home Loan Bank Board. Journal
Federal Law Rev — Federal Law Review
Federal L Rev — Federal Law Review
Federal Reserve Mo Chart Bk — Federal Reserve Monthly Chart Book
Federation Ins Couns Q — Federation of Insurance Counsel. Quarterly
Fed Est & Gift Tax Rep — Federal Estate and Gift Tax Reports [*Commerce Clearing House*]
Fed Eur Biochem Soc Meet Proc — Federation of European Biochemical Societies. Meeting Proceedings [*England*]
Fed Fr Soc Sci Nat Bull Trimest — Federation Francaise des Societes de Sciences Naturelles. Bulletin Trimestriel
Fed Home Loan Bank Bd J — Federal Home Loan Bank Board. Journal
Fed Home Loan Bank Board J — Federal Home Loan Bank Board. Journal
Fed Home Loan Bk Bd J — Federal Home Loan Bank Board. Journal
Fed Inst M Eng Tr — Federated Institution of Mining Engineers. Transactions
Fed Int Lait Bull Annu — Federation Internationale de Laiterie. Bulletin Annuel
Fed KC — Federal Reserve Bank of Kansas City. Monthly Review
Fed LR — Federal Law Reports
Fedl Register — Federal Register
Fed L Rep — Federal Law Reports
Fed L Rev — Federal Law Review
Fed Malaya Dep Agric Bull — Federation of Malaya. Department of Agriculture. Bulletin
Fed Malaya Dep Agric Econ Ser — Federation of Malaya. Department of Agriculture. Economic Series
Fed Malaya Dep Agric Gen Ser — Federation of Malaya. Department of Agriculture. General Series
Fed Malaya Dep Agric Sci Ser — Federation of Malaya. Department of Agriculture. Scientific Series
Fed'n Ins Counsel Q — Federation of Insurance Counsel. Quarterly
Fedn Proc Fedn Am Socs Exp Biol — Federation Proceedings. Federation of American Societies for Experimental Biology
Fed P — Federation Proceedings
Fed Phila — Federal Reserve Bank of Philadelphia. Business Review
Fed Prob — Federal Probation
Fed Probat — Federal Probation
Fed Proc — Federation Proceedings
Fed Proc Fed Am Soc Exp Biol — Federation Proceedings. Federation of American Societies for Experimental Biology
Fed Proc Transl Suppl — Federation Proceedings. Translation Supplement [*United States*]
FED Publ Am Soc Mech Eng Fluids Eng Div — FED Publication. American Society of Mechanical Engineers. Fluids Engineering Division
Fed Pub Serv J — Federal Public Service Journal
Fed R D — Federal Rules Decisions
Fed Reg — Federal Register
Fed Regist — Federal Register
Fed Regist (Wash DC) — Federal Register (Washington, DC)
Fed Res Bank NY — Federal Reserve Bank of New York. Quarterly Review
Fed Res Bull — Federal Reserve Bulletin
Fed Reserve B — Federal Reserve Bulletin

Fed Reserve Bank NYQ Rev — Federal Reserve Bank of New York. Quarterly Review
Fed Reserve Bank St Louis Rev — Federal Reserve Bank of St. Louis. Review
Fed Reserve Bull — Federal Reserve Bulletin
Fed Rules Dec — Federal Rules Decisions
Fed Sci Prog — Federal Science Progress
Fed Ser Coat Technol — Federation Series on Coating Technology
Fed St L — Federal Reserve Bank of St. Louis. Monthly Review
Fed Times — Federal Times [*United States*]
Fed Yellow Book — Federal Yellow Book [*United States*]
Feed Addit Compend — Feed Additive Compendium
Feed Bag Mag — Feed Bag Magazine
Feed Feed Dig — Feed and Feeding Digest
Feed Illus — Feeds Illustrated
Feed Ind Rev — Feed Industry Review
Feed Manage E Ed — Feed Management. Eastern Edition
FEER — Far Eastern Economic Review
FEI — Foreign Investment Review
Feingeraete Tech — Feingeraete Technik
Feinwerktech Messtech — Feinwerktechnik und Messtechnik
Feinwerktech & Micronic — Feinwerktechnik und Micronic
FEJ — Far East Journal
FEKTA — Forum foer Ekonomi och Teknik
FeL — Filologia e Letteratura
Fel'dsher Akush — Fel'dsher i Akusherka
Feline Pract — Feline Practice
Fell — Fellowship
FELR — Far Eastern Law Review
Fel Rav — Felix Ravenna
Felsmech Ingenieurgeol — Felsmechanik und Ingenieurgeologie [*Austria*]
FEMAA — Feed Management
FEMED — Feinwerktechnik und Messtechnik
FEM (Fact Equip Mater) — FEM (Factory Equipment and Materials) [*South Africa*]
Feminist — Feminist Studies
Feminist Rev — Feminist Review
Feminist Stud — Feminist Studies
Femip Kut Intez Kozl — Femipari Kutato Intezet Kozlemenyei
Femip Kut Intez Kozlem — Femipari Kutato Intezet Kozlemenyei [*Hungary*]
Fem Rview — Feminist Review
FEMS Microbiol Lett — FEMS [*Federation of European Microbiological Societies*] Microbiology Letters
Fem Stud — Feminist Studies
FEMXAA — Folia Entomologica Mexicana
FEN — Antara Financial and Economic News [*Jakarta*]
FEN — FEN. Factory Equipment News
Fenarete — Fenarete-Letture d'Italia
FENEA — Fertiliser News
FEN Finite Elem News — FEN. Finite Element News [*England*]
FENN — Fennia
FENUD — Fusion Energy Update
Fenway C — Fenway Court
FEPNDW — Forest Environmental Protection. United States Forest Service. Northern Region
FEPRA — Federation Proceedings
FEPXA — Fernmelde-Praxis
FEQ — Far Eastern Quarterly
FER — Fear
FER — Federal Economic Review
Fermentn Spirt Prom-st' — Fermentnaya i Spirtovaya Promyshlennost'
Fermes Mod — Fermes Modernes
Fern Gaz — Fern Gazette
Fernmelde-Ing — Fernmelde-Ingenieur
Fernmelde-Prax — Fernmelde-Praxis
Fernmeldetech Z — Fernmeldetechnische Zeitschrift [*West Germany*]
Fernseh- & Kino- Tech — Fernseh- und Kino- Technik
Fernwaerme Int — Fernwaerme International
FEROA — Ferroelectrics
Ferodo Int Tech News — Ferodo International Technical News
Ferrara Univ Ann Sez 9 — Ferrara. Universita. Annali. Sezione 9. Scienze Geologiche e Paleontologiche
Ferroelectr — Ferroelectrics
Ferroelectr Lett — Ferroelectrics Letters [*United Kingdom*]
Ferroelectr Lett Sect — Ferroelectrics Letters Section
Ferroelectr Relat Phenom — Ferroelectricity and Related Phenomena
Fert Abstr — Fertilizer Abstracts
Fert Assoc India Proc — Fertiliser Association of India. Proceedings
Fert Contracept — Fertility and Contraception
Fert Embryog Ovulated Plants Proc Int Cytoembryol Symp — Fertilization and Embryogenesis in Ovulated Plants. Proceedings. International Cytoembryological Symposium
Fert Farming Food — Fertilizer, Farming, and Food
Fert Feed Stuffs J — Fertilizer and Feeding Stuffs Journal
Fert Green Bk — Fertilizer Green Book
Fertigungstech Betr — Fertigungstechnik und Betrieb
Fertil Feed Stuffs J — Fertilizer and Feeding Stuffs Journal

Fertil Orthogenie — Fertilite Orthogenie
Fertil Steril — Fertility and Sterility
Fertil Steril Proc World Congr — Fertility and Sterility. Proceedings. World Congress on Fertility and Sterility
Fert Inst (Delhi) Proc — Fertiliser Institute (Delhi). Proceedings
Fert Int — Fertiliser International
Fert Intnl — Fertiliser International
Fert Mark News — Fertilizer Marketing News
Fert News — Fertilizer News
Fert R — Fertilizer Review
Fert Res — Fertilizer Research
Fert Sci Technol Ser — Fertilizer Science and Technology Series
Fert Soc S Afr J — Fertilizer Society of South Africa. Journal
Fert Solutions — Fertilizer Solutions
Fert Steril — Fertility and Sterility
Fert Technol — Fertilizer Technology
FES — Asian Survey
FES — Far Eastern Survey
FESTA — Fertility and Sterility
Festkoerperprobl — Festkoerperprobleme
FET — Financieel Ekonomische Tijd
FET — Milling Feed and Fertilizer
FETID — Federal Times
Fet Sei Ans — Fette - Seifen - Anstrichmittel. Verbunden mit der Zeitschrift die Ernaehrungs Industrie
Fettchem Umsch — Fettchemische Umschau
Fette Seifen Anstrichm — Fette - Seifen - Anstrichmittel
Fette Seifen Anstrmittel — Fette - Seifen - Anstrichmittel
FEUFJ — Far Eastern University. Faculty Journal
Feuill Biol — Feuillets de Biologie
Feuill Prat — Feuillets du Praticien
FEX — Financial Executive
F on F — Facts on File
FF — Faith and Form
FF — Fanfare
FF — Fast Food
FF — Filmfacts
F & F — Films and Filming
FF — Films and Filming
FF — Folklore
FF — Folklore Forum
FF — Forgotten Fantasy
FF — Forschungen und Fortschritte
F & F — Forschungen und Fortschritte
FF — Fraenkische Forschungen
FF — France Franciscaine
FF — Frate Francesco
FFA — Frankfurter Allgemeine Zeitung fuer Deutschland
FFB — Fertilizer International
FFC — Folklore Fellows Communications
FFC Abstr — Forest Fire Control Abstracts
F F Commun — F F Communications
FFE — Blick durch die Wirtschaft
F & Fernsehen — Film und Fernsehen
FFF — Faith for the Family
FFHAET — Flora and Fauna Handbook
FFHC Basic Stud — FFHC [*Freedom from Hunger Campaign*] Basic Studies
FFI (Forsvarets Forskningsints) Mikrosk — FFI (Forsvarets Forskningsinstitutt) Mikroskopet [*Norway*]
FFI Mikrosk — FFI [*Forsvarets Forskningsinstitutt*] Mikroskopet [*Norway*]
FFKL — Freiburger Forschungen zur Kunst und Literaturgeschichte
FFLR — Florida Foreign Language Reporter
FFM — Famous Fantastic Mysteries
FFM — Fast Food Management
FFM — Film Fan Monthly
FFMA — Folklore and Folk Music Archivist
FFMDAP — Folia Facultatis Medicae Universitatis Comenianae Bratislaviensis
FFN — Fantasy Stories
F Form — Film Form
FForum — Folklore Forum
FForumB — Folklore Forum. Bibliographic and Special Series
FFP — Fouilles Franco-Polonaises [*Cairo*]
FFPBAY — Folia Forestalia Polonica. Seria B. Drzewnictwo
FFPOA5 — Folia Forestalia Polonica. Seria A. Lesnictwo
FFR — Film Forum Review
FFRED — Farm and Food Research
FFS — Fast Foodservice
FFSCDL — Folia Facultatis Scientiarum Naturalium Universitatis Purkynianae Brunensis: Chemia
FFTPAS — Forests Commission Victoria. Forestry Technical Papers
FFUBAP — Folia Facultatis Scientiarum Naturalium Universitatis Purkynianae Brunensis: Biologia
FG — Financial Gazette [*South Africa*]
FG — Form und Geist
FGADL — Forschungen zur Geschichte der Aelteren Deutschen Literatur

FGGHA — Fukushima Daigaku Gakugei Gakubu Rika Hokoku
FGGYA — Fortschritte der Geburtshilfe und Gynaekologie
FGLOA — Figyelo
FGLP — Forschungen zur Geschichte und Lehre des Protestantismus [*Munich*]
FGO — Forschungen zur Geschichte Oberoesterreichs
FGPBA7 — Folia Geobotanica et Phytotaxonomica
FGR — Filmograph
FGrHist — Fragmente der Griechischen Historiker
FGRNA — Fortschritte auf dem Gebiete der Roentgenstrahlen und der Nuklearmedizin
FGRTA — Feingeraetetechnik
F & G Rundsch — F und G [*Felten und Guilleaume*] Rundschau
FH — Feuilles d'Histoire
F et H — Fides et Historia
FH — Fides et Historia
FH — Foodservice and Hospitality
FH — Frankfurter Hefte
FHA — Fitzgerald-Hemingway Annual
FHCYAI — Folia Histochemica et Cytochemica
FHCYEM — Folia Histochemica et Cytobiologica
F Her — Film Heritage
FHG — Mueller. Fragmenta Historicorum Graecorum
FhG Ber — FhG [*Fraunhofer-Gesellschaft*] Berichte
FHist — Fides et Historia
FHL — Federal Home Loan Bank Board. Journal
FHLBA — Family Health Bulletin
FHLBB Jrl — Federal Home Loan Bank Board. Journal
FHP — Fort Hare Papers
FHPAD — Fort Hare Papers
FHQ — Florida Historical Quarterly
FHS — French Historical Studies
FI — Farm Index
Fi — Filologia
FI — Folklore Italiano
FI — Forum Italicum
FIA — Financial Analysts Journal
FIAS — Frontiers in Aging Series
FIB — Fish Industry Board. Bulletin [*New Zealand*]
FIBBD — F + I Bau
Fiber and Integrated Opt — Fiber and Integrated Optics
Fiber Integr Opt — Fiber and Integrated Optics
Fiber Laser — Fiber Laser News
Fiber Opt Commun — Fiber Optics and Communications
Fiberoptcs — Fiberoptics Report
Fiber Prod — Fiber Producer
Fibonacci Q — Fibonacci Quarterly
Fibonacci Quart — Fibonacci Quarterly
FIBQA — Fibonacci Quarterly
Fibre Chem — Fibre Chemistry
Fibre Containers — Fibre Containers and Paperboard Mills
Fibre Fabr — Fibre and Fabric
Fibre Sci Technol — Fibre Science and Technology
Fibres Fabr Cordage — Fibres, Fabrics, and Cordage
Fibres Fabr J — Fibres and Fabrics Journal
Fibres Plast — Fibres and Plastics
Fibres & Polym — Fibres and Polymers
FICAAL — Flore Illustree des Champignons d'Afrique Centrale
Fichero Med Ter Purissimus — Fichero Medico Terapeutico Purissimus
Fiches Identif Zooplancton — Fiches d'Identification du Zooplancton
Fiches Phytopathol Trop — Fiches de Phytopathologie Tropicale
Fichier Micropaleontol Gen — Fichier Micropaleontologique General
Fic Int — Fiction International
FICO — Fireweed Country. Magazine of the Yukon
FICQ — Federation of Insurance Counsel. Quarterly
FICU — Folklore. Boletin del Departamento de Folklore del Instituto de Cooperacion Universitaria
FID News Bull — Federation Internationale de Documentation. News Bulletin
FID R Doc — Federation Internationale de Documentation. Revue de la Documentation
Field Col Mus Pub G S Zool S — Field Columbian Museum. Publications. Geological Series. Zoological Series
Field Columbian Mus Publ Geol Ser — Field Columbian Museum. Publications. Geological Series
Field Conf Guideb NM Geol Soc — Field Conference Guidebook. New Mexico Geological Society
Field Crop Abstr — Field Crop Abstracts
Field Drain — Field Drainage
Field w Fie — Fields within Fields within Fields
Fieldiana Bot — Fieldiana Botany
Fieldiana Geol — Fieldiana Geology
Fieldiana Geol Mem — Fieldiana Geology. Memoirs
Fieldiana Geology Mem — Fieldiana Geology. Memoirs
Fieldiana Tech — Fieldiana. Technique
Fieldiana Zool — Fieldiana Zoology
Fieldiana Zool Mem — Fieldiana Zoology. Memoirs

Fieldiana Zoology Mem — Fieldiana Zoology. Memoirs
Field Il — Field Illustrated
Field Lab — Field and Laboratory
Field & Lab — Field and Laboratory
Field Mus Nat Hist Publ Bot Ser — Field Museum of Natural History Publications. Botanical Series
Field Mus Nat Hist Publ Geol Ser — Field Museum of Natural History Publications. Geological Series
Field Mus Nat Hist Publ Zool Ser — Field Museum of Natural History Publications. Zoological Series
Field Nat — Field Naturalist
Field Notes US For Serv — Field Notes. United States Forest Service
Field Res Proj Man Nat Ser — Field Research Projects. Man and Nature Series
Field Res Proj Nat Area Stud — Field Research Projects. Natural Area Studies
Field & S — Field and Stream
Field Seed Certif Guide Ill Crop Impr Ass — Field Seed Certification Guide. Illinois Crop Improvement Association
Field Stat Rec Div Plant Ind CSIRO — Field Station Record. Division of Plant Industry. Commonwealth Scientific and Industrial Research Organisation
Field Stn Rec — Field Station Record. Division of Plant Industry. Commonwealth Scientific and Industrial Research Organisation
Field Stn Rec Aust CSIRO Div Plant Ind — Australia. Commonwealth Scientific and Industrial Research Organisation. Division of Plant Industry. Field Station Record
Field Stn Rec Div Plant Ind CSIRO — Field Station Record. Division of Plant Industry. Commonwealth Scientific and Industrial Research Organisation
Field Stud — Field Studies
FIENA — Fire Engineering
FIEP Bull — FIEP [*Federation Internationale d'Education Physique*] Bulletin
Fie Sci Abs — Fire Science Abstracts
FIFAO — Fouilles de l'Institut Francais d'Archeologie Orientale
FI (For Ital) — FI (Forum Italicum)
Fifth Est — Fifth Estate
FIG — Figaro
FIGCAD — Flore Iconographique des Champignons du Congo
FIGWA — Forschung im Ingenieurwesen
FIHUL — Filmihullu
FII — Fussboden Zeitung
Fiji Agric J — Fiji Agricultural Journal
Fiji Archt — Fiji Architect
Fiji Dep Agric Bull — Fiji. Department of Agriculture. Bulletin
Fiji Geol Surv Dep Bull — Fiji. Geological Survey Department. Bulletin
Fiji Geol Surv Dep Econ Invest — Fiji. Geological Survey Department. Economic Investigation
Fiji Geol Surv Dep Econ Rep — Fiji. Geological Survey Department. Economic Report
Fiji Miner Resour Div Bull — Fiji. Mineral Resources Division. Bulletin
Fiji Timb — Fiji Timbers and Their Uses
FIK — Financiele Koerier
F II — Films Illustrated
Fil — Filosofia
Filam Fungi — Filamentous Fungi
Fil Ist — File de Istorie. Culegere de Studii, Articole si Comunicari
Film Appreciation News — Film Appreciation Newsletter
Film Comm — Film Comment
Film Crit — Film Criticism
Filmf — Filmfacts
Film J — Film Journal
Film Lib Q — Film Library Quarterly
Film Lit Ind — Film Literature Index
Film Mus — Film Music
Film Mus Notes — Film Music Notes
Film Q — Film Quarterly
Films & F — Films and Filming
Films in R — Films in Review
Filo — Filologica
Filol Vesti — Filologiceskie Vesti
Filos Nauc Kommunizm — Filosofija i Naucnyj Kommunizm
Filos Nauki — Filosofskie Nauki
Filosof Cas CSAV — Filosoficky Casopis CSAV [*Ceskoslovesnska Akademie Ved*]
Filos Probl Obsc Soznanija — Filosofskie Problemy Obscestvennogo Soznanija
Filos Probl Suchasnoho Pryrodozn — Filosofski Problemy Suchasnoho Pryrodoznavstva
Filos Probl Suchasnoho Przyr Mizhvid Nauk Zb — Filosofichnii Problemy Suchasnoho Przyrodoznavstva Mizhvidomchyi Naukovyi Zbirnyk
Filos Vopr Fiz Khim — Filosofskie Voprosy Fiziki i Khimii
Filos Vopr Medicin Biol — Filosofskie Voprosy Mediciny i Biologii
Filoz Cas — Filozoficky Casopis
FILS — Filologicke Studie
FilSbAlm — Filologiceskij Sbornik [*Stat'i Aspirantov i Soiskatelej*]. Alma-Ata
Filson Club Hist Q — Filson Club History Quarterly
Filson C Q — Filson Club Quarterly

FILSUA — Forest Industry Lecture Series. University of Alberta Forestry Program

Filtration — Filtration and Separation

Filtr Sep — Filtration and Separation

Filtr Tech Sep — Filtration et Techniques Separatives [*France*]

Filtr Tech Separatives — Filtration et Techniques Separatives

FilZ — Filologija (Zagreb)

FilM — Filologia Moderna

FIM — Financial Market Trends [*Paris*]

FIMR — Finnish Marine Research

FIMS — Folklore Institute. Monograph Series

FIN — Financieel Dagblad voor Handel, Industrie, Scheepvaart, en Cultures

Fin Agr — Financing Agriculture

Final Control Elem — Final Control Elements

Fin Anal J — Financial Analysts Journal

Fin Analyst — Financial Analysts Journal

Fin Analysts J — Financial Analysts Journal

Financ Analysts J — Financial Analysts Journal

Financ Dag — Financieel Dagblad

Finance Dev — Finance and Development

Finance & Dev — Finance and Development

Finance Trade R — Finance and Trade Review

Financ Exec — Financial Executive

Financ Executive — Financial Executive

Financial E — Financial Executive

Financ Mail — Financial Mail

Financ Times Europ Energy Rep — Financial Times. European Energy Report

Financ Trade Rev — Finance and Trade Review

Financ Week — Finance Week

Financ World — Financial World

Finan Manag — Financial Management

Finanstid — Finanstidende

Fincl Mail — Financial Mail

Fin Dev — Finance and Development

Fin & Devel — Finance and Development

Fine Arts J — Fine Arts Journal

Fine Pt — Fine Print

Fin Exec — Financial Executive

Fin Fisk — Finlands Fiskerier

FINGA — Fernmelde-Ingenieur

Finish Ind — Finishing Industries

Finishing Ind — Finishing Industries

Fin Kemistsamf Medd — Finska Kemistsamfundet. Meddelanden

Fin Lakaresallsk Handl — Finska Lakaresallskapets Handlingar

Finlande Comm Geol Bull — Finlande Commission Geologique. Bulletin

Finlay Rev Med-Hist Cubana — Finlay Revista Medico-Historica Cubana

Finl Geodeettinen Laitos Julk — Finland Geodeettinen Laitos. Julkaisuja

Finl Geol Tutkimuslaitos Opas — Finland Geologinen Tutkimuslaitos. Opas

Finl Geol Tutkimuslatos Bull — Finland Geologinen Tutkimuslaitos. Bulletin

Finl Vesitutkimuslaitos Julk — Finland Vesitutkimuslaitos. Julkaisuja

Fin Mail (South Africa) — Financial Mail (South Africa)

Fin Mgt — Financial Management

Fin Mosskulturforen Arsb — Finska Mosskulturforeningens Arsbok

Finn Chem L — Finnish Chemical Letters

Finn Chem Lett — Finnish Chemical Letters

Finn Fish Res — Finnish Fisheries Research

Finn Found Alcohol Stud — Finnish Foundation for Alcohol Studies

Finn Game Res — Finnish Game Research

Finnish Pap Timber — Finnish Paper and Timber Journal

Finn J Dairy Sci — Finnish Journal of Dairy Science

Finn Pap Timb — Finnish Paper and Timber Journal

Finn Pap Timber — Finnish Paper and Timber Journal

Finn Psychiatry — Finnish Psychiatry

Finommech-Mikrotech — Finommechanika-Mikrotechnika

Fin Paper — Finnish Paper and Timber Journal

Fin Planner — Financial Planner

Fin Planning Today — Financial Planning Today

Fin Plan Today — Financial Planning Today

Fin Post — Financial Post

Fin Post M — Financial Post Magazine

Fin Post Mag — Financial Post Magazine

Fin R — Financial Review

FINRA — Fishery Industrial Research [*United States*]

FINS — Fishing Industry News Science

Finshng Ind — Finishing Industries

Finskt Mus — Finskt Museum

Fin Times — Financial Times

Fin Trade — Finnish Trade Review

Fin and Trade R (South Africa) — Finance and Trade Review (South Africa)

Fin Wkly — Financial Weekly

Fin World — Financial World

FIO — Financieel Overheidsbeheer

FIPRD — Fiber Producer

FIR — Films in Review

FiR — Filologia Romanza

FIRA Bull — FIRA [*Furniture Industry Research Association*] Bulletin

FIRA Bull (Furn Ind Res Ass) — FIRA (Furniture Industry Research Association) Bulletin

FIRAD — Fiziologiya Rastenii [*Moscow*]

FIRA Tech Rep (Furn Ind Res Ass) — FIRA (Furniture Industry Research Association) Technical Report

FIRA Trans (Furn Ind Res Ass) — FIRA (Furniture Industry Research Association) Transaction

Fire Eng — Fire Engineering

Fire Eng J — Fire Engineers Journal

Fire Engnrs J — Fire Engineers Journal

Fire J — Fire Journal

Fire J (Boston) — Fire Journal (Boston)

Fire Manage Notes USDA For Serv — Fire Management Notes. United States Department of Agriculture. Forest Service

Fire Mater — Fire and Materials

Fire Prev — Fire Prevention [*England*]

Fire Prev Sci Tech — Fire Prevention Science and Technology

Fire Prev Sci Technol — Fire Prevention Science and Technology

Fire Prot — Fire Protection

Fire Protect — Fire Protection

Fire Prot Yearb — Fire Protection Yearbook

Fire Res Abstr & Rev — Fire Research Abstracts and Reviews

Fire Res (Lausanne) — Fire Research (Lausanne)

Fire Saf J — Fire Safety Journal [*Switzerland*]

Fire Sci Abs — Fire Science Abstracts

Fire Surv — Fire Surveyor

Fire Tech — Fire Technology

Fire Technol — Fire Technology

Fire Water Eng — Fire and Water Engineering

First Chi — First Chicago Report

First Internat Econ Hist — First International Conference of Economic History

First Nat City Bank — First National City Bank [*Later, Citibank*] of New York. Monthly Economic Letter

FISC — Fisheries of Canada

Fiscalite Eur — Fiscalite Europeenne

Fisc Europ — Fiscalite Europeenne

Fischereiforsch Inf Prax — Fischereiforschung. Informationen fuer der Praxis

Fischer Taschenb — Fischer Taschenbuecher

Fisch-Forsch — Fischerei-Forschung

Fischwaren Feinkost Ind — Fischwaren und Feinkost Industrie

Fischwirtsch Fischind Fischereiwelt — Fischwirtschaft mit die Fischindustrie und Fischereiwelt

Fish B — Fishery Bulletin

Fish Board Swed Inst Freshwater Res (Drottningholm) Rep — Fishery Board of Sweden. Institute of Freshwater Research (Drottningholm). Report

Fish Board Swed Inst Mar Res Rep — Fishery Board of Sweden. Institute of Marine Research. Report

Fish Board Swed Ser Hydrogr Rep — Fishery Board of Sweden. Series Hydrography. Report

Fish Bull — Fishery Bulletin

Fish Bull S Afr — Fisheries Bulletin. South Africa

Fish Contr Vict — Victoria. Fisheries and Wildlife Department. Fisheries Contribution

FISHD — Fisheries

Fisheries Nletter — Fisheries Newsletter

Fishery Ind Res — Fishery Industrial Research

Fish Farming Int — Fish Farming International

Fishg News Int — Fishing News International

Fish Ind Res — Fishery Industrial Research

Fish Invest Minist Agric Fish Food (GB) Ser — Fishery Investigations. Ministry of Agriculture, Fisheries, and Food (Great Britain). Series II. Salmon and Freshwater Fisheries

Fish Invest Minist Agric Fish Food (GB) Ser IV — Fishery Investigations. Ministry of Agriculture, Fisheries, and Food (Great Britain) Series IV

Fish Invest Ser II Mar Fish GB Minist Agric Fish Food — Fishery Investigations. Series II. Marine Fisheries. Great Britain Ministry of Agriculture, Fisheries, and Food

Fish Manage — Fisheries Management

Fish News — Fisheries Newsletter

Fish News Int — Fishing News International

Fish Newsl — Fisheries Newsletter

Fish Notes — Queensland. Department of Harbours and Marine. Fisheries Notes

Fish Notes Dep Prim Ind QD — Fisheries Notes. Department of Primary Industries. Queensland

Fish Notes Dep Prim Ind Queensl — Fisheries Notes. Department of Primary Industries. Queensland

Fish Pap Dep Prim Ind — Australia. Department of Primary Industry. Fisheries Paper

Fish Rep Dep Agric — Fisheries Report. Department of Agriculture

Fish Rep Dep Prim Ind — Australia. Department of Primary Industry. Fisheries Report

Fish Res Board Can Annu Rep — Fisheries Research Board of Canada. Annual Report

Fish Res Board Can ARO Circ — Fisheries Research Board of Canada. ARO [*Atlantic Regional Office*] Circular

Fish Res Board Can Bull — Fisheries Research Board of Canada. Bulletin
Fish Res Board Can Gen Ser Circ — Fisheries Research Board of Canada. General Series Circular
Fish Res Board Can Misc Spec Publ — Fisheries Research Board of Canada. Miscellaneous Special Publication
Fish Res Board Can Prog Rep Atl Coast Stn — Fisheries Research Board of Canada. Progress Reports of the Atlantic Coast Stations
Fish Res Board Can Prog Rep Pac Coast Stn — Fisheries Research Board of Canada. Progress Reports of the Pacific Coast Station
Fish Res Board Can Rev — Fisheries Research Board of Canada. Review
Fish Res Board Can Tech Pap — Fisheries Research Board of Canada. Technical Paper
Fish Res Bull — Fisheries Research Bulletin
Fish Res Bull (West Aust Mar Res Lab) — Fisheries Research Bulletin (Western Australia Marine Research Laboratories)
Fish Res Div Occas Publ (NZ) — Fisheries Research Division. Occasional Publication (New Zealand)
Fish Res Ves Kapala Cruise Rep — Cruise Report. Fisheries Research Vessel Kapala
Fish Synopsis Div Fish Oceanogr CSIRO — Fisheries Synopsis. Division of Fisheries and Oceanography. Commonwealth Scientific and Industrial Research Organisation
Fish Technol — Fishery Technology
Fish Wildl Serv (US) Res Rep — Fish and Wildlife Service (United States). Research Report
Fisiol Med (Rome) — Fisiologia e Medicina (Rome)
FISK — Fiskeridirektoratets Skrifter. Serie Havundersokelser
Fiskeridir Skr Ser Fisk — Fiskeridirektoratets Skrifter. Serie Fiskeri
Fiskeridir Skr Ser Havunders — Fiskeridirektoratets Skrifter. Serie Havundersokelser
Fiskeridir Skr Ser Teknol Unders — Fiskeridirektoratets Skrifter. Serie Teknologiske Undersokelser
FISTB — Field and Stream
FISZA — Fizikai Szemle
FITCA — Fire Technology
FITEA — Fishery Technology [India]
Fitopatol — Fitopatologia
Fitopatol Bras — Fitopatologia Brasileira
Fitopatol Mex — Fitopatologia Mexicana
Fitotec Latinoam — Fitotecnia Latinoamericana
Fitotecnia Latinoam — Fitotecnia Latinoamericana
FiTs — Finsk Tidskrift
FitzN — Fitzgerald Newsletter
FIWOA — Financial World
FIX — FID [Federation Internationale de Documentation] News Bulletin
FIZ — Farhang-E Iran-Zamin [Revue Trimestrielle des Etudes Iranologiques]
Fiz Aerodispersnykh Sist — Fizika Aerodispersnykh Sistem
Fiz Chastits Vys Energ — Fizika Chastits Vysokikh Energii
Fiz Chastits Vys Energ Akad Nauk Gruz SSR Inst Fiz — Fizika Chastits Vysokikh Energii. Akademiya Nauk Gruzinskoi SSR. Institut Fiziki [Georgian SSR]
Fiz Dielektr Radiospektrosk — Fizyka Dielektrykow i Radiospektroskopia
Fiz Ehlektron (L'vov) — Fizichna Ehlektronika (L'vov)
Fiz Ehlektron (Moskva) — Fizicheskaya Ehlektronika (Moskva)
Fiz Ehlem Chastits At Yad — Fizika Elementarnykh Chastits i Atomnogo Yadra
Fiz Elektron (Lvov) — Fizichna Elektronika (Lvov)
Fiz Elektron (Moscow) — Fizicheskaya Elektronika (Moscow)
Fiz Elem Chastits At Yadra — Fizika Elementarnykh Chastits i Atomnogo Yadra
Fiz Elementar Castic i Atom Jadra — Fizika Elementarnyh Castic i Atomnogo Jadra
Fiz Energ Inst Rap FEI — Fiziko-Energeticheskii Institut. Raport FEI [Fiziko-Energeticheskii Institut]
Fiz Fiz-Khim Zhidk — Fizika i Fiziko-Khimiya Zhidkostei
Fiz Gazorazryadnoi Plazmy — Fizika Gazorazryadnoi Plazmy
Fiz Geogr — Fizicheskaya Geografiya
Fiz Geogr Geomorfol — Fizichna Geografiya ta Geomorfologiya
Fiz Gidrodin Kinet Zhidk — Fizicheskaya Gidrodinamika i Kinetika Zhidkosti
Fiz Goreniya Metody Ed Issled — Fizika Goreniya i Metody. Ed. Issledovaniya [USSR]
Fiz Goreniya & Vzryva — Fizika Goreniya i Vzryva
Fiz Gorn Porod Protsessov — Fizika Gornykh Porod i Protsessov
FIZHD — Fiziologicheskii Zhurnal [Kiev]
Fiz Heohr Heomorfol Mizhvid Nauk Zb — Fizycheskaya Heohrafiya ta Heomorfolohiya Mizhvidomchyi Naukovyi Zbirnykh
Fizika (Zagreb) Suppl — Fizika (Zagreb). Supplement [Yugoslavia]
Fiziol Aktiv Veshchestva — Fiziologicheski Aktivnye Veshchestva [Ukrainian SSR]
Fiziol Akt Veshchestva — Fiziologicheski Aktivnye Veshchestva
Fiziol Biokhim Kul't Rast — Fiziologiya i Biokhimiya Kul'turnykh Rastenii
Fiziol Biokhim Osn Pitan Rast — Fiziologo-Biokhimicheskie Osnovy Pitaniya Rastenii
Fiziol Biokhim Patol Endokr Sist — Fiziologiya, Biokhimiya, i Patologiya Endokrinnoi Sistemy

Fiziol Biokhim Sil's'kogospod Tvarin — Fiziologiya i Biokhimiya Sil's'kogospodars'kikh Tvarin
Fiziol Chel — Fiziologiya Cheloveka
Fiziol Drev Rast — Fiziologiya Drevesnykh Rastenii
Fiziol Fiz-Khim Mekh Regul Obmennykh Protsessov Org — Fiziologicheskie i Fiziko-Khimicheskie Mekhanizmy Regulyatsii Obmennykh Protsessov Organizma [USSR]
Fiziol Norm Patol — Fiziologiya Normala si Patologica
Fiziologiya Rast — Fiziologiya Rastenii
Fiziol Patol Vyssh Nervn Deyat — Fiziologiya i Patologiya Vysshei Nervnoi Deyatel'nosti
Fiziol Rast — Fiziologiya Rastenii
Fiziol Rast (Engl Transl Plant Physiol) — Fiziologiya Rastenii (English Translation Plant Physiology) (Moscow)
Fiziol Rast (Mosc) — Fiziologiya Rastenii (Moscow)
Fiziol Rast (Sofia) — Fiziologiya na Rasteniyata (Sofia)
Fiziol Vodoobmena Ustoich Rast — Fiziologiya Vodoobmena i Ustoichivosti Rastenii
Fiziol Zh — Fiziologichnyi Zhurnal
Fiziol Zh Akad Nauk Ukr RSR — Fiziologichnij Zhurnal. Akademiya Nauk Ukrainskoj RSR
Fiziol Zh (Kiev) — Fiziolohichnyi Zhurnal (Kiev)
Fiziol Zh SSSR — Fiziologicheskii Zhurnal SSSR Imeni I. M. Sechenova
Fiziol Zh SSSR Im I M Sechenova — Fiziologicheskii Zhurnal SSSR Imeni I. M. Sechenova
Fiz Khim — Fizicheskaya Khimiya [USSR]
Fiz Khim Issled Prir Sorbentov Ryada Anal Sist — Fiziko-Khimicheskoe Issledovanie Prirodnykh Sorbentov i Ryada Analiticheskikh Sistem
Fiz-Khim Mekh Liofil' Dispers Sist — Fiziko-Khimicheskaya Mekhanika i Liofil'nost Dispersnykh Sistem
Fiz-Khim Mekh Mater — Fiziko-Khimicheskaya Mekhanika Materialov [Ukrainian SSR]
Fiz Khim (Moscow) — Fizicheskaya Khimiya (Moscow)
Fiz Khim Obrab Mater — Fizika i Khimiya Obrabotki Materialov
Fiz i Khim Obrab Mater — Fizika i Khimiya Obrabotki Materialov
Fiz Khim Prir Sint Polim — Fizika i Khimiya Prirodnykh i Sinteticheskikh Polimerov
Fiz Khim Probl Krist — Fiziko-Khimicheskie Problemy Kristallizatsii [Kazakh SSR]
Fiz i Khim Stekla — Fizika i Khimiya Stekla
Fiz Khim Stekla — Fizika i Khimiya Stekla
Fiz Khim Svoistva Individ Uglevodorodov — Fiziko Khimicheskie Svoistva Individual'nykh Uglevodorodov
Fiz Khim Tekhnol Silik Neorg Mater — Fizicheskaya Khimiya i Tekhnologiya Silikatnykh i Neorganicheskikh Materialov
Fiz Kondens Sostoyaniya — Fizika Kondensirovannogo Sostoyaniya
Fiz Kurortnye Faktory Ikh Lech Primen — Fizicheskie i Kurortnye Faktory i Ikh Lechebnow Primenenie
Fiz Magn Plenok — Fizika Magnitnykh Plenok
Fiz-Mat Spis — Fiziko-Matematichesko Spisanie [Bulgaria]
Fiz Mekh — Fizicheskaya Mekhanika [USSR]
Fiz Metallov Metalloved — Fizika Metallov i Metallovedenie
Fiz Metal M — Fizika Metallov i Metallovedenie
Fiz Met i Metalloved — Fizika Metallov i Metallovedenie
Fiz Met Metalloved Akad Nauk SSSR Ural Fil — Fizika Metallov i Metallovedenie Akademiia Nauk SSSR Ural'skii Filial [USSR]
Fiz Miner — Fizika Mineralov
Fiz Mnogochastichnykh Sist — Fizika Mnogochastichnykh Sistem
Fiz Mol — Fizika Molekul
Fiz Nizk Temp — Fizika Nizkikh Temperatur
Fiz Nizk Temp (Kiev) — Fizika Nizkikh Temperatur (Kiev) [Ukrainian SSR]
Fiz Plazmy (Moskva) — Fizika Plazmy (Moskva)
Fiz Plazmy Probl Upr Termoyad Sin — Fizika Plazmy i Problemy Upravlyaemogo Termoyadernogo Sinteza [Ukrainian SSR]
Fiz Plazmy (Tbilisi) — Fizika Plazmy (Tbilisi)
Fiz Poluprovodn Poluprovodn Elektron — Fizika Poluprovodnikov i Poluprovodnikovaya Elektronika
Fiz Prochn Plast Met Elektrodin Yavleniya Veshchestve — Fizika Prochnosti Plastichnosti Metallov i Elektrodinamicheskie Yavleniya v Veshchestve
Fiz Protsessy Gorn Proizvod — Fizicheskie Protsessy Gornogo Proizvodstva
Fiz Rezaniya Met — Fizika Rezaniya Metallov
Fiz Sb L'vov Gos Univ — Fizicheskii Sbornik. L'vovskii Gosudarstvennyi Universitet [Ukrainian SSR]
Fiz Sk — Fizika v Skole
Fiz Sz — Fizikai Szemle
Fiz Szk — Fizyka w Szkole [Poland]
Fiz Tekhnol Vopr Kibern Semin — Fiziko-Tekhnologicheskie Voprosy Kibernetiki. Seminar [Ukrainian SSR]
Fiz Tekhn Poluprov — Fizika i Tekhnika Poluprovodnikov
Fiz Tekh Poluprovo — Fizika i Tekhnika Poluprovodnikov
Fiz-Tekh Probl Razrab Polez Iskop — Fiziko-Tekhnicheskie Problemy Razrabotki Poleznykh Iskopaemykh
Fiz Tverd T — Fizika Tverdogo Tela
Fiz Tverd Tel — Fizika Tverdogo Tela
Fiz Tverd Tela — Fizika Tverdogo Tela
Fiz Yad Reakt — Fizika Yadernykh Reaktorov

iz Z — Fiziceskij Zurnal
iz Zap — Fizichni Zapiski
iz Zemli — Fizika Zemli
iz Zhidk Sostoyaniya — Fizika Zhidkogo Sostoyaniya
'J — Film Journal
J — Forst und Jagd
'J — Fort Smith Journal
'J — Friesisches Jahrbuch
JA — Furniture Manufacturer
JB — Frankfurter Judaistische Beitraege
JF — Forschungen zur Judenfrage
JMSA — Fukushima Journal of Medical Science
Journal — Film Journal
JS — Fu Jen Studies
K — Filologiai Koezloeny
o K — Folk og Kultur
KAMA — Finska Kemistsamfundet. Meddelanden
KD — Forschungen zur Kirchen- und Dogmengeschichte
KDG — Forschungen zur Kirchen- und Dogmengeschichte (Goettingen)
KDRA — Fukuoka Kyoiku Daigaku Kiyo, Dai-3-Bu, Rika-Hen
KGG — Forschungen zur Kirchen- und Geistesgeschichte
KG(NF) — Forschungen zur Kirchen- und Geistesgeschichte (Neue Folge)
KIZA — Fukuoka Igaku Zasshi [Japan]
KKAD — Funtai Kogaku Kaishi
KOMA — Fizika i Khimiya Obrabotki Materialov
'kr — Filmkritik
'KT — Fernseh- und Kino- Technik
Kultura — Film Kultura
Kunst — Filmkunst
'L — Fall
a L — Field and Laboratory. Contributions from the Science Departments
'L — Figaro Litteraire
'L — Filologia e Letteratura
'L — Folia Linguistica
'L — Folklore
'L — Forum der Letteren
'L — Foundations of Language
'L — France Libre
'L — Franciscaans Leven
'L — Franciscansch Leven
'LA — Foreign Language Annals
'la Acad Sci Q J — Florida Academy of Sciences. Quarterly Journal
'la Admin Weekly — Florida Administrative Weekly
'la Ag Dept Quar B — Florida. Department of Agriculture. Quarterly Bulletin
'la Ag Exp — Florida. Agricultural Experiment Stations. Publications
'la Agric Exp Stn Annu Rep — Florida. Agricultural Experiment Stations. Annual Report
'la Agric Exp Stn Bull — Florida. Agricultural Experiment Stations. Bulletin
'la Agric Exp Stn Circ — Florida. Agricultural Experiment Stations. Circular
'la Agric Exp Stn Monogr Ser — Florida. Agricultural Experiment Stations. Monograph Series
'la Agric Exp Stn Res Rep — Florida. Agricultural Experiment Stations. Research Report
'la Agric Ext Serv Bull — Florida. Agricultural Extension Service. Bulletin
'la Anthropol — Florida Anthropologist
'la Archit — Florida Architect
'la B J — Florida Bar Journal
'la Board Conserv Mar Lab Prof Pap Ser — Florida Board of Conservation. Marine Research Laboratory. Professional Papers Series
'la Board Conserv Mar Res Lab Leafl Ser — Florida Board of Conservation. Marine Research Laboratory. Leaflet Series
'la Board Conserv Mar Res Lab Spec Sci Rep — Florida Board of Conservation. Marine Research Laboratory. Special Scientific Report
'la Board Conserv Mar Res Lab Tech Ser — Florida Board of Conservation. Marine Research Laboratory. Technical Series
Fla Bur Geol Geol Bull — Florida Bureau of Geology. Geological Bulletin
Fla Bur Geol Inf Circ — Florida Bureau of Geology. Information Circular
Fla Bur Geol Rep Invest — Florida Bureau of Geology. Report of Investigation
Fla Cattlem Livest J — Florida Cattleman and Livestock Journal
Fla Conserv News — Florida Conservation News
Fla Dent J — Florida Dental Journal
Fla Dep Agric Consum Serv Div Plant Ind Bienn Rep — Florida. Department of Agriculture and Consumer Services. Division of Plant Industry. Biennial Report
Fla Dep Agric Consum Serv Div Plant Ind Bull — Florida. Department of Agriculture and Consumer Services. Division of Plant Industry. Bulletin
Fla Dep Agric Consum Serv Div Plant Ind Entomol Circ — Florida. Department of Agriculture and Consumer Services. Division of Plant Industry. Entomology Circular
Fla Dep Agric Consum Serv Div Plant Ind Nematol Circ — Florida. Department of Agriculture and Consumer Services. Division of Plant Industry. Nematology Circular
Fla Dep Agric Consum Serv Div Plant Ind Plant Pathol Circ — Florida. Department of Agriculture and Consumer Services. Division of Plant Industry. Plant Pathology Circular

Fla Dep Nat Resour Bienn Rep — Florida. Department of Natural Resources. Biennial Report
Fla Dep Nat Resour Bur Geol Bull — Florida. Department of Natural Resources. Bureau of Geology. Bulletin
Fla Dep Nat Resour Bur Geol Rep Invest — Florida. Department of Natural Resources. Bureau of Geology. Report of Investigations
Fla Dep Nat Resour Educ Ser — Florida. Department of Natural Resources. Educational Series
Fla Dep Nat Resour Mar Res Lab Leafl Ser — Florida. Department of Natural Resources. Marine Research Laboratory. Leaflet Series
Fla Dep Nat Resour Mar Res Lab Prof Pap Ser — Florida. Department of Natural Resources. Marine Research Laboratory. Professional Papers Series
Fla Dep Nat Resour Mar Res Lab Tech Ser — Florida. Department of Natural Resources. Marine Research Laboratory. Technical Series
Fla Dept Nat Resour Mar Res Lab Spec Sci Rep — Florida. Department of Natural Resources. Marine Research Laboratory. Special Scientific Report
Fla Ent — Florida Entomologist
Fla Entomol — Florida Entomologist
Fla Environmental and Urban Issues — Florida Environmental and Urban Issues
Fla Field Nat — Florida Field Naturalist
Fla Food Resour Econ Coop Ext Serv Univ Fla — Florida Food and Resource Economics. Cooperative Extension Service. University of Florida
Fla Geol Surv Geol Bull — Florida. Geological Survey. Geological Bulletin
Fla Geol Surv Inf Circ — Florida. Geological Survey. Information Circular
Fla Geol Surv Inform Circ — Florida. Geological Survey. Information Circular
Fla Geol Surv Rep Invest — Florida. Geological Survey. Report of Investigations
Fla Geol Surv Spec Publ — Florida. Geological Survey. Special Publication
Fla G S An Rp — Florida. Geological Survey. Annual Report
Fla His S — Florida Historical Society. Quarterly
Fla Hist Q — Florida Historical Quarterly
Fla Hist Quar — Florida Historical Quarterly
Fla Lib — Florida Libraries
Fla Libr — Florida Libraries
Fla Mar Res Publ — Florida Marine Research Publications
Flamb — Flambeau
Flame Retardancy Polym Mater — Flame Retardancy of Polymeric Materials
Flamme Therm — Flamme et Thermique [France]
Fla Nat — Florida Naturalist
F Lang — Foundations of Language
Fla Nurse — Florida Nurse
FLAPA9 — Flora do Parana. Instituto Paranaense de Botanica Curitiba
Fla Sci — Florida Scientist
FLASH — List of Australian Subject Headings. First Edition
Fla State Board Conserv Bien Rep — Florida. State Board of Conservation. Biennial Report
Fla State Board Conserv Div Water Survey and Research Paper — Florida. State Board of Conservation. Division of Water Survey and Research. Paper
Fla State Board Health Monogr Ser — Florida. State Board of Health. Monograph Series
Fla State L Rev — Florida State University. Law Review
Fla State Mus Biol Sci Bull — Florida State Museum. Biological Sciences Bulletin
Fla State Plant Bd — Florida State Plant Board. Publications
Fla State Univ Dep Geol Sedimentol Res Lab Contrib — Florida State University. Department of Geology. Sedimentological Research Laboratory. Contribution
Fla State Univ Studies — Florida State University. Studies
Fla St Hort Soc Q — Florida. State Horticultural Society. Quarterly
Fla St U L Rev — Florida State University. Law Review
Fla St Univ Slavic Papers — Florida State University. Slavic Papers
Fla Trend — Florida Trend
Fla Univ Agric Ext Serv Circ — Florida. University. Agricultural Extension Service. Circular
Fla Univ Eng Exp Sta Bull — Florida. University. Engineering and Industrial Experiment Station. Bulletin
Fla Univ Eng Ind Exp Stn Bull Ser — Florida. University. Engineering and Industrial Experiment Station. Bulletin Series
Fla Univ Eng Ind Exp Stn Leafl Ser — Florida. University. Engineering and Industrial Experiment Station. Leaflet Series
Fla Univ Eng Ind Exp Stn Tech Pap Ser — Florida. University. Engineering and Industrial Experiment Station. Technical Paper Series
Fla Univ Eng Ind Exp Stn Tech Prog Rep — Florida. University. Engineering and Industrial Experiment Station. Technical Progress Report
Flavour Ind — Flavour Industry
Flavours Fruit Juices Spices Rev — Flavours, Fruit Juices, and Spices Review
FL Bank — Florida Banker
FL Build — Florida Builder
FLBWA — Fries Landbouwblad
FLC — Australian Family Law Cases
FLC — Folklore (Calcutta)
FL Constr Ind — Florida Construction Industry

FL Cont and Build — Florida Contractor and Builder
Fld Crop Abstr — Field Crop Abstracts
FLDSD2 — Ireland. Department of Fisheries and Forestry. Trade and Information Section. Fishery Leaflet
Fld Stn Rec Div Plant Ind CSIRO — Field Station Record. Division of Plant Industry. Commonwealth Scientific and Industrial Research Organisation
Fld Stn Rec Div Pl Ind CSIRO — Field Station Record. Division of Plant Industry. Commonwealth Scientific and Industrial Research Organisation
Fld Stud — Field Studies
FLe — Fiera Letteraria
FLECDR — Flora of Ecuador
FL Econ Ind — Florida Economic Indicators
FLED — Family Life Educator
Fleet — Fleet, Cars, Vans, and Utilities
Fleischw — Fleischwirtschaft
FL Env Urb Iss — Florida Environmental and Urban Issues
Fletcher F — Fletcher Forum
Flet Mjeks Shquip — Fletorja Mjeksore Shquiptare
FLett — Fiera Letteraria
FLFAAN — Flora og Fauna
FLFE — Flora Fennica
FLFEAZ — Flour and Feed
FLFNAS — Flora Fennica
Fl Forum — Fletcher Forum
FLFRB7 — Flore de France
FLFSA9 — Folia Forestalia [*Helsinki*]
FLGRAB — Flower Grower
FLHAA — Finska Lakaresallskapets Handlingar
FLI — Film Literature Index
FLI — Foreign Language Index
F Lib Q — Film Library Quarterly [*New York*]
F Lib Quarterly — Film Library Quarterly
Flight Aircr Eng — Flight and Aircraft Engineer
Flight Int — Flight International
Flight Int (London) — Flight International (London)
FLin — Folia Linguistica
Flinders Inst Atmos Mar Sci Cruise Rep — Cruise Report. Flinders Institute for Atmospheric and Marine Science. Flinders University of South Australia
Flinders J Hist Polit — Flinders Journal of History and Politics
Flintshire Hist Soc Publ — Flintshire Historical Society. Publications
FLISAO — Folia Limnologica Scandinavica
FLiv — Folk-Liv
Fl J — Folklore Journal
FL LR — University of Florida. Law Review
FLMC — Federal Labor-Management Consultant
FL Monthly — Florida Monthly
FLMPB2 — Flora Malesiana. Series II. Pteridophyta
FL (Neb) — Foreign Languages (Nebraska)
FLNMAV — Flora Neotropica. Monograph
FloQ — Florida Quarterly
Flora Allg Bot Ztg Abt A Physiol Biochem (Jena) — Flora oder Allgemeine Botanische Zeitung. Abteilung A. Physiologie und Biochemie (Jena)
Flora Allg Bot Ztg Abt B Morphol Geobot (Jena) — Flora oder Allgemeine Botanische Zeitung. Abteilung B. Morphologie und Geobotanik (Jena)
Flora Allg Bot Ztg (Jena) — Flora oder Allgemeine Botanische Zeitung (Jena)
Flora Fenn — Flora Fennica
Flora (Jena) — Flora oder Allgemeine Botanische Zeitung (Jena)
Flora (Jena) Abt A — Flora (Jena). Abteilung A. Physiologie und Biochemie [*East Germany*]
Flora Malesiana Ser II Pteridophyta — Flora Malesiana. Series II. Pteridophyta
Flora Malesiana Ser I Spermatophyta — Flora Malesiana. Series I. Spermatophyta
Flora Ned — Flora van Nederland
Flora Neerl — Flora Neerlandica
Flora of NSW — Flora of New South Wales
Flora NSW — Flora of New South Wales
Flor Anthr — Florida Anthropologist
Flora Pak — Flora of Pakistan
Flora Parana Inst Parana Bot Curitiba — Flora do Parana. Instituto Paranaense de Botanica Curitiba
Flora Timarit Isl Grasafraedi — Flora Timarit um Islenzka Grasafraedi
Flore Iconogr Champignons Congo — Flore Iconographique des Champignons du Congo
Flore Illus Champignons Afr Cent — Flore Illustree des Champignons d'Afrique Centrale
Flor Exc — Florists' Exchange
Florida Anthropol — Florida Anthropologist
Florida BJ — Florida Bar Journal
Florida Bur Geology Geol Bull — Florida. Department of Natural Resources. Bureau of Geology. Geological Bulletin
Florida Bur Geology Inf Circ — Florida. Department of Natural Resources. Bureau of Geology. Information Circular

Florida Geol Surv Bull — Florida. Geological Survey. Bulletin
Florida State Mus Bull Biol Sci — Florida State Museum. Bulletin. Biological Sciences
Florida State Univ Sedimentol Research Lab Contr — Florida State University. Department of Geology. Sedimentological Research Laboratory. Contribution
Florida Univ Eng Progr Leafl — Florida University. Engineering Progress. Leaflet
Florida Univ Eng Progr Tech Pap — Florida University. Engineering Progress. Technical Paper
Florida Univ Eng Progr Tech Progr Rep — Florida University. Engineering Progress. Technical Progress Report
Florists Exch Hortic Trade World — Florists' Exchange and Horticultural Trade World
Flor Nat — Florida Naturalist
FlorQ — Florida Quarterly
Flor Rev — Florists' Review
Flower Grow — Flower Grower
Flowering Plants Afr — Flowering Plants of Africa
FLPOAD — Flora Polska; Rosliny Naczyniowe Polski i Ziem Osciennych
FLQ — Film Library Quarterly
FLQRAR — Fluoride Quarterly Reports
FLR — Federal Law Reports
FLR — Federal Law Review
Fl R — Folklore Record
FLR — University of Florida. Law Review
F L Rev — Federal Law Review
FLS — Foundations of Linguistics Series [*Elsevier Book Series*]
FLS — French Literature Series [*Columbia, South Carolina*]
FLSC — Folia Limnologica Scandinavica
FLTGA9 — Flora Timarit um Islenzka Grasafraedi
Flt Intnl — Flight International
FL Trend — Florida Trend
FLTXAQ — Flora of Texas
Flue Cured Tob Farmer — Flue-Cured Tobacco Farmer
Flue SG — Fluechtlingssiedlungsgesetz
Flug Rev — Flug Revue
Flug-Rev Int — Flug-Revue International [*West Germany*]
Fluid Apparecchiature Idraul & Pneum — Fluid Apparecchiature Idrauliche e Pneumatiche
Fluid Apparecch Idraul & Pneum — Fluid Apparecchiature Idrauliche e Pneumatiche
Fluid Contr Inst FCI Stand — Fluid Controls Institute. FCI Standards
Fluid Dyn — Fluid Dynamics
Fluid Dyn Trans — Fluid Dynamics. Transactions
Fluid Eng — Fluid Engineering [*Japan*]
Fluidics Q — Fluidics Quarterly
Fluid Mech Sov Res — Fluid Mechanics. Soviet Research
Fluidos Hidraul Neumatica Lubr — Fluidos Hidraulica Neumatica Lubricacion
Fluid Phase Equilib — Fluid Phase Equilibria
Fluid Phase Equilibria — Fluid Phase Equilibria [*Netherlands*]
Fluid Power Int — Fluid Power International
Fluid Pwr Int — Fluid Power International
Fluid Q — Fluidics Quarterly
Fluids Handl — Fluids Handling
Flui Handl — Fluid Handling
FLUOA4 — Fluoride
Fluoresc Miner Soc J — Fluorescent Mineral Society. Journal
Fluoride Q Rep — Fluoride Quarterly Reports
Flur BG — Flurbereinigungsgesetz
FLVER — Vermont Foreign Language Association. Bulletin
FL Vk — Forschungen zur Deutschen Landes- und Volkskunde
Fly — Flying
F-Lyd-Bild — Film-Lyd-Bilde
Flygtek Forsoksanst Medd — Flygtekniska Forsoksanstalten. Meddelande
F M — Film Making
FM — Filosofska Misul
FM — Francais Moderne
FM — Freight Management
FMA — Financial Management
FMA — Food Manufacture
FMAID — Financial Mail [*South Africa*]
FMAMA — Factory Management and Maintenance
FMAS — Fruehmittelalterliche Studien
FMBCAG — Folia Medica Bialostocensia
FMBMA — Fiziko-Matematichesko Spisanie (Bulgaria)
Fm Bull Indian Coun Agric Res — Farm Bulletin. Indian Council of Agricultural Research
FMC — Intertax
Fm Chem — Farm Chemicals
FMCRAW — Folia Medica Cracoviensia
FMDA Abt II Monographien — FMDA [*Forschungen und Materialien zur Deutschen Aufklarung*] Abteilung II. Monographien
FMDLAJ — Folia Mendeliana
FMDZA — Fortschritte der Medizin
Fm Economist — Farm Economist

'MF — Famous Science Fiction
' & M Feinwerktech Messtech — F und M, Feinwerktechnik und Messtechnik
' M-Feinw M — F und M, Feinwerktechnik und Messtechnik
'm Forest (Nigeria) — Farm and Forest (Nigeria)
'MG — Financial Management
'mg Forum — Farming Forum
'mg Rev — Farming Review
'mg S Afr — Farming in South Africa
'mg Zambia — Farming in Zambia
'MH — Focus on Mental Health [*Quezon City*]
'MICDK — Food Microstructure
'MJ — Federation Museums Journal
'MJ — Financial Mail (Johannesburg)
'MJ — Folk Music Journal
'MLS — Forum for Modern Language Studies
'MM — Filmmakers' Monthly
'MMEA — Fizika Metallov i Metallovedenie
'm Mgmt — Farm Management
'MMTA — Fizika Metallov i Metallovedenie
'MN — Federal Reserve Bank of Minneapolis. Quarterly Review
'MN — Filmmakers' Newsletter
'Mod — Filologia Moderna
'Monde — Francais dans le Monde
'MORAO — Folia Morphologica [*Prague*]
'm Policy — Farm Policy
'MQ — Federal Reserve Bank of Minneapolis. Quarterly Review
'MR — Franco Maria Ricci
'm Res News — Farm Research News
'mr Forester — Farmer and Forester
'MRLA — Fortschritte der Mineralogie
'mrs Bull Dep Agric (Can) — Farmer's Bulletin. Department of Agriculture (Canada)
'mr's Bull (Rhodesia) — Farmer's Bulletin (Rhodesia)
'mrs Bull US Dep Agric — Farmers' Bulletin. United States Department of Agriculture
'mrs Newsl — Farmers' Newsletter
'mr Stk Breed — Farmer and Stock Breeder
'MSp — Fiziko-Matematichesko Spisanie
'MSPA4 — Flora Malesiana. Series I. Spermatophyta
'MSt — Folkmalsstudier
'MSVA — Fluid Mechanics. Soviet Research
'm Technol — Farm Technology
' Music Ntbk — Film Music Notebook
'N — Fantastic Novels
'N — Film News
'N — Filologiceskie Nauki
'N — Folklore. Rivista di Tradizioni Popolari (Naples)
'N — Food and Nutrition
'N — Fort Smith News
'N — Fortid og Nutid
'n — Fortnightly
'NA — Finanzarchiv
'NAMA — Arizona. Bureau of Mines. Field Notes
'NDPA — Foundations of Physics
'NDV-A — Finance and Development
'NEEAA — Flora van Nederland/Flora Neerlandica
' Neur Psyc — Fortschritte der Neurologie, Psychiatrie, und Ihrer Grenzgebiete
' News — Film News
'NIB — Federation Nationale des Infirmieres Belges
'NIN — Fridtjof Nansen Institute. Newsletter
'NL — Fantasy Newsletter
'NL — Financial Mail
'NL — Fitzgerald Newsletter
'NLG — Forschungen zur Neueren Literaturgeschichte
'NM — Fantastic Novels Magazine
'NMKA — Finommechanika-Mikrotechnika
'NPGA — Fortschritte der Neurologie, Psychiatrie, und Ihrer Grenzgebiete
'NP Newsl Food Nutr Health — FNP [*Food & Nutrition Press, Inc.*] Newsletter. Food, Nutrition, and Health
'NPQAX — Folia Neuropsiquiatrica del Sur y Este de Espana
'NPTA — Finnish Paper and Timber Journal
'NRRDF — Focus on Renewable Natural Resources
'NS — Agriculture, Food, and Nutrition Service. Publications
'NSCA6 — Forensic Science [*Later, Forensic Science International*]
'NT — Foilseachain Naisiunta Tta
'NY — Federal Reserve Bank of New York. Quarterly Review
'NY — Food Policy
'NZ — Zuivelzicht
'O — Facultad de Odontologia
'O — Folia Orientalia
'o — Folklore
'o — Fornvaennen
'O — Fortune
'OA — Foreign Affairs

FOAGB4 — Foreign Agriculture
FOALAI — Folia Allergologica [*Later, Folia Allergologica et Immunologica Clinica*]
FOA Rep — FOA [*Foersvarets Forskningsanstalt*] Reports
FOB — Flannery O'Connor Bulletin
FOB — Frontiers of Biology [*Elsevier Book Series*]
FOBGA8 — Folia Biologica [*Cracow*]
FOBLAN — Folia Biologica [*Prague*]
Foc — Focus/Midwest
FOCAAT — Folia Cardiologica
Focale Mag — Focale Magazine
Foc Exc Chi — Focus on Exceptional Children
Foc F — Focus on Film
FOCHDJ — Food Chemistry
FOCIA — Folia Clinica Internacional
FOCNAY — Food in Canada
Focus — Focus on Indiana Libraries
Focus — Focus/Midwest
Focus Excep Child — Focus on Exceptional Children
Focus on F — Focus on Film
Focus Indiana Libr — Focus on Indiana Libraries
Focus Indo — Focus on Indonesia
Focus Jpn — Focus Japan
FODEDF — Folia Dendrologica
FODN — Foothills Dempster Newsletter
FOEG — Forschungen zur Ost Europaeischen Geschichte
FOEGAN — Food Engineering [*New York*]
Foeldmuevel Min Allami Gazd Foeigazgatosaga (Budapest) — Foeldmuevelesuegyi Miniszterium. Allami Gazdasagok Foeigazgatosaga (Budapest)
Foeldrajzi Ert — Foeldrajzi Ertesito
Foeldrajzi Ertes — Foeldrajzi Ertesito
Foeldrajzi Koezl — Foeldrajzi Koezlemenyek
Foeldt Koezl — Foeldtani Koezlony
Foeldt Kut — Foeldtani Kutatas
FOENAA — Folia Endocrinologica
FOFL — Fauna och Flora
FOFUA — Funtai Oyobi Funmatsuyakin
FOG — Forschungen zur Ost Europaeischen Geschichte
FOGGA — Fuel-, Orr-, Gegegyogyaszat
Fogg Mus Bul — Fogg Art Museum. Bulletin [*Harvard University*]
Fogorv Sz — Fogorvosi Szemle
FOGRA (Dtsche Forshungsges Druck Reproduktionstech) Mitt — FOGRA (Deutsche Forschungsgesellschaft fuer Druck und Reproduktionstechnik) Mitteilungen
FOH — Focus on Holland
FOHEAW — Folia Haematologica [*Leipzig*]
FOHPAV — Folia Hereditaria et Pathologica
FOHWA — Forst- und Holzwirt
FoI — Forum Italicum
FOIJA — Food Industries Journal
FOIRA — Food Irradiation
FOIRA8 — Irradiation des Aliments [*English Edition*]
FOKOA9 — Foldtani Kozlony
FoL — Folk Life [*Cardiff*]
FoL — Foundations of Language
Fol Biol — Folia Biologica
FolcL — Folclor Leterar
Folder Mont State Coll Coop Ext — Folder. Montana State College. Cooperative Extension Service
Folder Univ Ariz Agric Exp Stn — Folder. University of Arizona. Agricultural Experiment Station
Folder Univ MO Coll Agr Ext Serv — Folder. University of Missouri. College of Agriculture. Extension Service
Foldrajzi Ert — Foeldrajzi Ertesito
Foldrajzi Ertes — Foeldrajzi Ertesito
Foldt Kozl — Foldtani Kozlony
Folha Med — Folha Medica
Folha Med (Rio De Janeiro) — Folha Medica (Rio De Janeiro)
Folh Divulg Serv Flor Aquic (Portugal) — Folhetas de Divulgacao. Servicos Florestais e Aquicolas (Portugal)
Fol Hist Cy — Folia Histochemica et Cytochemica [*Later, Folio Histochemica et Cytobiologica*]
Fol Humanis — Folia Humanistica
Fo Li — Folia Linguistica
Folia Allergol — Folia Allergologica [*Later, Folia Allergologica et Immunologica Clinica*]
Folia Allergol Immunol Clin — Folia Allergologica et Immunologica Clinica
Folia Anat Jpn — Folia Anatomica Japonica
Folia Anat Univ Conimbrigensis (Coimbra) — Folia Anatomica Universitatis Conimbrigensis (Coimbra)
Folia Arch — Folia Archeologica [*Lodz*]
Folia Archaeol — Folia Archaeologica [*Budapest*]
Folia Biochim Biol Graeca — Folia Biochimica et Biologica Graeca
Folia Biol — Folia Biologica
Folia Biol (Cracow) — Folia Biologica (Cracow)

Folia Biol (Prague) — Folia Biologica (Prague)
Folia Biol (Praha) — Folia Biologica (Praha)
Folia Cardiol — Folia Cardiologica
Folia Clin Biol — Folia Clinica et Biologica
Folia Clin Biol Nova Ser — Folia Clinica et Biologica. Nova Serie
Folia Clin Chim Microsc — Folia Clinica. Chimica et Microscopica
Folia Clin Int — Folia Clinica Internacional
Folia Clin Int (Barc) — Folia Clinica Internacional (Barcelona)
Folia Endocrinol — Folia Endocrinologica
Folia Endocrinol Jpn — Folia Endocrinologica Japonica
Folia Endocrinol (Pisa) — Folia Endocrinologica (Pisa)
Folia Endocrinol (Rome) — Folia Endocrinologica (Rome)
Folia Ent Hung — Folia Entomologica Hungarica
Folia Ent Mex — Folia Entomologica Mexicana
Folia Entomol Hung — Folia Entomologica Hungarica
Folia Entomol Hung Rovartani Kozl — Folia Entomologica Hungarica. Rovartani Kozlemenyek
Folia Entomol Mex — Folia Entomologica Mexicana
Folia Fac Med — Folia Facultatis Medicae
Folia Fac Med Univ Comenianae Bratisl — Folia Facultatis Medicae Universitatis Comenianae Bratislaviensis
Folia Fac Sci Nat Univ Purkynianae Brun Biol — Folia Facultatis Scientiarum Naturalium Universitatis Purkynianae Brunensis: Biologia
Folia Fac Sci Nat Univ Purkynianae Brunensis Phys — Folia Facultatis Scientiarum Naturalium Universitatis Purkynianae Brunensis: Physica
Folia For — Folia Forestalia
Folia For (Helsinki) — Folia Forestalia (Helsinki)
Folia For Inst For Fenn — Folia Forestalia Instituti Forestalis Fenniae
Folia For Polon (Drzewn) — Folia Forestalia Polonica. Seria B (Drzewnictwo)
Folia For Polon (Lesn) — Folia Forestalia Polonica. Seria A (Lesnictwo)
Folia For Pol Ser A (Lesn) — Folia Forestalia Polonica. Seria A (Lesnictwo)
Folia For Pol Ser B (Drzewnictwo) — Folia Forestalia Polonica. Seria B (Drzewnictwo)
Folia Geobot Phytotaxon — Folia Geobotanica et Phytotaxonomica
Folia Geogr Ser Geogr Phys — Folia Geographica. Series Geographica-Physica
Folia Gynaec (Pavia) — Folia Gynaecologica (Pavia)
Folia Haematol (Frankfurt Am Main) — Folia Haematologica (Frankfurt Am Main)
Folia Haematol (Leipz) — Folia Haematologica (Leipzig)
Folia Haematol (Leipzig) Arch — Folia Haematologica (Leipzig). Archiv
Folia Haematol (Leipzig) Zentralorgan — Folia Haematologica (Leipzig). Zentralorgan
Folia Hered Pathol — Folia Hereditaria et Pathologica
Folia Histochem Cytobiol — Folia Histochemica et Cytobiologica
Folia Histochem Cytochem — Folia Histochemica et Cytochemica [*Later, Folia Histochemica et Cytobiologica*]
Folia Histochem Cytochem (Krakow) — Folia Histochemica et Cytochemica (Krakow) [*Later, Folia Histochemica et Cytobiologica*]
Folia Limnol Scand — Folia Limnologica Scandinavica
Folia Med Bialostocensia — Folia Medica Bialostocensia
Folia Med Cracov — Folia Medica Cracoviensia
Folia Med Fac Med Univ Saraev — Folia Medica Facultatis. Medicinae Universitatis Saraeviensis
Folia Med Lodz — Folia Medica Lodziensia
Folia Med (Naples) — Folia Medica (Naples)
Folia Med Neerl — Folia Medica Neerlandica
Folia Med (Plovdiv) — Folia Medica (Plovdiv)
Folia Microbiol — Folia Microbiologica
Folia Microbiol (Prague) — Folia Microbiologica (Prague)
Folia Morph — Folia Morphologica
Folia Morphol (Prague) — Folia Morphologica (Prague)
Folia Morphol (Praha) — Folia Morphologica (Praha)
Folia Morphol (Warsaw) — Folia Morphologica (Warsaw)
Folia Mus Rerum Nat Bohemiae Occident Geol — Folia Musei Rerum Naturalium Bohemiae Occidentalis. Geologica
Folia Neuropsiquiatr Sur Este Esp — Folia Neuropsiquiatrica del Sur y Este de Espana
Folia O — Folia Orientalia
Folia Ophthalmol Jpn — Folia Ophthalmologica Japonica
Folia Orient — Folia Orientalia
Folia Parasit — Folia Parasitologica
Folia Parasitol (Prague) — Folia Parasitologica (Prague)
Folia Pharm — Folia Pharmaceutica
Folia Pharmacol Jpn — Folia Pharmacologica Japonica
Folia Pharm (Istanbul) — Folia Pharmaceutica (Istanbul)
Folia Phoniatr — Folia Phoniatrica
Folia Phoniatr (Basel) — Folia Phoniatrica (Basel)
Folia Primat — Folia Primatologica
Folia Primatol — Folia Primatologica
Folia Psychiatr Neurol Jpn — Folia Psychiatrica et Neurologica Japonica
Folia Quat — Folia Quaternaria
Folia Sci Afr Cent — Folia Scientifica Africae Centralis [*Congo*]
Folia Serol — Folia Serologica
Folia Soc Sci Lublinensis — Folia Societatis Scientiarum Lublinensis
Folia Univ — Folia Universitaria
Folia Univ Cochabamba — Folia Universitaria Cochabamba

Folia Vet — Folia Veterinaria
Folia Vet Lat — Folia Veterinaria Latina
Folia Vet (Prague) — Folia Veterinaria (Prague)
Folia Zool — Folia Zoologica
FOLK — Folk. Dansk Ethnografisk Tidsskrift
Folk — Folklore
Folk Harp J — Folk Harp Journal
Folk Inst — Folklore Institute. Journal
Folkl Champagne — Folklore de Champagne
Folklore Am — Folklore Americano
Folklore C — Folklore (Calcutta)
Folk-Lore J — Folk-Lore Journal
Folkl Stud — Folklore Studies
Folkl Suisse — Folklore Suisse
Folk Mus Arch — Folklore and Folk Music Archivist
Folk Music — Folk Music Journal
Folk Mus J — Folk Music Journal
FolkS — Folklore Studies
Foll Divulg Inst For (Chile) — Folleto de Divulgacion. Instituto Forestal (Santiago De Chile)
Fol Ling — Folia Linguistica
Foll Tec For — Folletos Tecnicos Forestales
Foll Tec For Adm Nac Bosques (Argent) — Folletos Tecnicos Forestales. Administracion Nacional de Bosques (Argentina)
FOLMA8 — Folia Medica [*Plovdiv*]
Fol Microb — Folia Microbiologica
Fol Oecon Cracov — Folia Oeconomica Cracoviensia
Fol Or — Folia Orientalia
Fol Pharm J — Folia Pharmacologica Japonica
Fol Phoniat — Folia Phoniatrica
Fol Primat — Folia Primatologica
Fo LR — Fordham Law Review
Fol Tec Secr Agr Ganad Inst Nac Invest Agr (Mexico) — Folleto Tecnico. Secretaria de Agricultura y Ganaderia. Instituto Nacional de Investigaciones Agricolas (Mexico)
FOMAAB — Food Manufacture
FOMDA — Folia Medica
FOMDAK — Folia Medica [*Naples*]
FOMEAN — Folha Medica
FOMIAZ — Folia Microbiologica
FOMIE5 — Food Microbiology [*London*]
FOMNAG — Folia Medica Neerlandica
FOMOAJ — Folia Morphologica [*Warsaw*]
FoN — Fortid og Nutid
Fonderia Ital — Fonderia Italiana
Fondeur — Fondeur d'Aujourd'hui
Fondren Sci Ser — Fondren Science Series
Fonds Rech For Univ Laval Bull — Fonds de Recherches Forestieres. Universite Laval. Bulletin
Fonds Rech For Univ Laval Contrib — Fonds de Recherches Forestieres. Universite Laval. Contribution
Fond Univ Luxemb Ser Notes Rech — Fondation Universitaire Luxembourgeoise. Serie Notes de Recherche
FONN — Federation of Ontario Naturalists. Newsletter
FONOBP — Forest Notes. New Hampshire's Conservation Magazine
Font — Fontaine
Fontane Bl — Fontane Blaetter
Fontes — Fontes Artis Musicae
FontesArtisM — Fontes Artis Musicae
FONYA — Forskningsnytt
FOO — Food Processing
Food Addit Contam — Food Additives and Contaminants
Food Agric Leg — Food and Agricultural Legislation
Food Bus — Food Business
Food Canad — Food in Canada
Food Chem Microbiol Technol — Food Chemistry, Microbiology, Technology
Food Chem Toxicol — Food and Chemical Toxicology
Food Cosmet Toxicol — Food and Cosmetics Toxicology
Food Cosmetics Toxicol — Food and Cosmetics Toxicology
Food Cosmet Toxicol — Food and Cosmetics Toxicology
Food Devel — Food Development
Food Drug C — Food, Drug, Cosmetic Law Journal
Food Drug Cosmet Law Q — Food, Drug, Cosmetic Law Quarterly
Food Drug Cosm LJ — Food, Drug, Cosmetic Law Journal
Food Drug Cosm LQ — Food, Drug, Cosmetic Law Quarterly
Food Drugs Ind Bull — Food and Drugs Industry Bulletin
Food Eng — Food Engineering
Food Eng Int — Food Engineering International
Food Eng (NY) — Food Engineering (New York)
Food Eng (Philadelphia) — Food Engineering (Philadelphia)
Food Eng Syst — Food Engineering Systems
Food Farming Agric — Food Farming and Agriculture. Journal for the Development of Food and Agriculture [*India*]
Food Fish Mark Rev & Outl — Food Fish Market Review and Outlook
Food Flavour Ingredients Processing and Packaging — Food Flavouring Ingredients. Processing and Packaging

Food Hyg Stud — Food Hygiene Study [*Japan*]
Food Ind — Food Industry
Food Ind J — Food Industries Journal
Food Ind S Afr — Food Industries of South Africa
Food Ind (Tokyo) — Food Industry (Tokyo)
Food Irradiat — Food Irradiation [*France*]
Food Irradiat Inf — Food Irradiation Information
Food Irradiat (Jpn) — Food Irradiation (Japan)
Food Manage — Food Management
Food Manuf — Food Manufacture
Food Mater Equip — Food Materials and Equipment
Food Mon — Food Monitor
FoodMonit — Food Monitor
Food Nutr — Food and Nutrition
Food & Nutr — Food and Nutrition
Food Nutr Bull — Food and Nutrition Bulletin
Food Nutr Notes Rev — Food and Nutrition. Notes and Reviews
Food and Nutr Notes and Rev — Food and Nutrition. Notes and Reviews
Food & Nutr Notes Revs — Food and Nutrition. Notes and Reviews
Food Nutr (Rome) — Food and Nutrition (Rome)
Food Pol — Food from Poland
Food Pol — Food Policy
Food Preservation Q — Food Preservation Quarterly
Food Preserv Q — Food Preservation Quarterly
Food Proc — Food Processing Industry
Food Proc — Food Processing News
Food Process — Food Processing
Food Process (Chic) — Food Processing (Chicago)
Food Process Ind — Food Processing Industry
Food Processing Mktg — Food Processing and Marketing [*Chicago*]
Food Process Mark (Chic) — Food Processing and Marketing (Chicago)
Food Process Packag — Food Processing and Packaging
Food Prod — Food Product Development
Food Prod Devel — Food Product Development
Food Prod/Manage — Food Production/Management
Food Res — Food Research
Food Res Dep Div Food Res CSIRO — Food Research Report. Division of Food Research. Commonwealth Scientific and Industrial Research Organisation
Food Res Inst Stud — Food Research Institute. Studies
Food Res Inst Stud Agric Econ Trade Dev (Stanford) — Food Research Institute. Studies in Agricultural Economics, Trade, and Development (Stanford)
Food Res Inst Stud (Stanford) — Food Research Institute. Studies (Stanford)
Food Sci (NY) — Food Science (New York)
Food Sci & Tech Abstr — Food Science and Technology. Abstracts
Food Sci Technol — Food Science and Technology
Food Sci Technol Ser Monogr — Food Science and Technology. A Series of Monographs
Food Sci & Technol (Zur) — Food Science and Technology (Zurich)
Food Serv Mkt — Food Service Marketing
Food S Mkt — Food Service Marketing
Foods Nutr Dent Health — Foods, Nutrition, and Dental Health
Food Tech — Food Technology
Food Tech in Aust — Food Technology in Australia
Food Tech Aust — Food Technology in Australia
Food Technol — Food Technology
Food Technol Aust — Food Technology in Australia
Food Technol NZ — Food Technology in New Zealand
Food Technology in Aust — Food Technology in Australia
Food Technol Rev — Food Technology Review
Food Tech NZ — Food Technology in New Zealand
Food Trade R — Food Trade Review
FOOHA — Fueloil and Oil Heat
FOOPDZ — Folia Ophthalmologica [*Leipzig*]
FOPAAQ — Food Packer
FOPE — Forgotten People
FOPHA — Folia Phoniatrica
FOPHAD — Aktuelle Probleme der Phoniatrie und Logopaedie
FOPHAD — Folia Phoniatrica
FOPMAS — Folia Pharmaceutica [*Istanbul*]
FOPMBT — Food Processing and Marketing [*Chicago*]
FOPOD3 — Food Policy
FOPRA9 — Food Processing [*Chicago*]
FOPRB — Foret Privee
FOQUAN — Folia Quaternaria
FOR — Foreign Affairs
For Abstr — Forestry Abstracts
For Aff — Foreign Affairs
For Affairs — Foreign Affairs
For Aff Rep — Foreign Affairs Reports
Forage Res — Forage Research
For Agric — Foreign Agriculture
For and Bird — Forest and Bird [*New Zealand*]
For Bur Aust For Res Notes — Australia. Commonwealth Forestry and Timber Bureau. Forestry Research Notes

For Bur Aust Leaf — Australia. Commonwealth Forestry and Timber Bureau. Leaflet
For Bur Aust Timber Supp Rev — Australia. Commonwealth Forestry and Timber Bureau. Timber Supply Review
FORC — Forces. Hydro Quebec
For Chron — Forestry Chronicle
For Comm — Foreign Commerce Weekly
For Comm Victoria Bull — Forests Commission Victoria. Bulletin
For Comm Victoria For Tech Pap — Forests Commission Victoria. Forestry Technical Papers
For Def — For the Defense
For Dep Bull For Dep (Zambia) — Forest Department Bulletin. Forest Department (Zambia)
For Dep West Aust Res Pap — Forests Department of Western Australia. Research Paper
Fordham Int'l LJ — Fordham International Law Journal
Fordham L Rev — Fordham Law Review
Fordham Urban L J — Fordham Urban Law Journal
Fordham Urb LJ — Fordham Urban Law Journal
For Dig (Philippines) — Forestry Digest (Philippines)
For Div Tech Note For Div (Tanz) — Forest Division Technical Note. Forest Division. (Dar Es Salaam, Tanzania)
Ford L Rev — Fordham Law Review
Ford Urban LJ — Fordham Urban Law Journal
FOREAE — Food Research
Forecast Home Econ — Forecast for Home Economics
For Ecol Manage — Forest Ecology and Management
For Ecol & Mgt — Forest Ecology and Management
For Econ NY St Coll For — Forestry Economics. New York State University. College of Forestry at Syracuse University
For Econ Trd — Foreign Economic Trends and Their Implications for the United States
For of Educ — Forum of Education
Foreign Aff — Foreign Affairs
Foreign Aff Rep — Foreign Affairs Reports
Foreign Agric Canned Fruits FCAN US Foreign Agric Serv — Foreign Agriculture Circular. Canned Fruits. FCAN. United States Foreign Agricultural Service
Foreign Agric Circ Dried Fruit FDF USDA Foreign Agric Serv — Foreign Agriculture Circular. Dried Fruits. FDF. United States Department of Agriculture. Foreign Agricultural Service
Foreign Agric Circ Grains FG US Dep Agric Foreign Agric Serv — Foreign Agriculture Circular. Grains. FG. United States Department of Agriculture. Foreign Agricultural Service
Foreign Agric Circ US Dep Agric — Foreign Agriculture Circular. United States Department of Agriculture
Foreign Agric Circ US Dep Agric Serv Spices FTEA — Foreign Agricultural Circular. United States Department of Agriculture. Foreign Agricultural Services. Spices. FTEA
Foreign Agr Trade US — Foreign Agriculture Trade of the United States
Foreign Compd Metab Mamm — Foreign Compound Metabolism in Mammals
Foreign Econ Trends Their Implic US — Foreign Economic Trends and Their Implications for the United States
Foreign Lan — Foreign Language Annals
Foreign Leg Per — Foreign Legal Periodicals Index
Foreign Pet Technol — Foreign Petroleum Technology
Foreign Pol — Foreign Policy
Foreign Sci Publ Natn Cent Sci Tech Econ Inf (Warsaw) — Foreign Scientific Publication. National Center for Scientific, Technical, and Economic Information (Warsaw) [*Poland*]
Foreign Tr — Foreign Trade
Forensic Sci — Forensic Science [*Later, Forensic Science International*]
Forensic Sci Int — Forensic Science International
Forensic Sci Soc J — Forensic Science Society Journal
For Environ Prot US For Serv North Reg — Forest Environmental Protection. United States Forest Service. Northern Region
For Equipm Note FAO — Forestry Equipment Notes. FAO [*Food and Agriculture Organization of the United Nations*]
Forest Abstr — Forestry Abstracts
Forest Chro — Forestry Chronicle
Forester N Ire — Forester. Ministry of Agriculture of Northern Ireland
Forest Fire Losses Can — Forest Fire Losses in Canada
Forest Hist — Forest History
Forest Ind — Forest Industries
Forest Prod J — Forest Products Journal
Forest Res News Midsouth — Forest Research News for the Midsouth
Forestry Abstr — Forestry Abstracts
Forestry Chron — Forestry Chronicle
Forestry Res Newsl — Forestry Research Newsletter
Forestry Res Rept Agr Expt Sta Univ Ill — Forestry Research Report. Agricultural Experiment Station. University of Illinois
Forestry Tech Paper — Forestry Technical Paper
Forest Sci — Forest Science
Forest Sci Monogr — Forest Science Monographs
Forest Timb — Forest and Timber

Forest Tre Ser For Timb Bur — Forest Tree Series. Forestry and Timber
  Bureau
Foret-Conserv — Foret-Conservation
For Farmer — Forest Farmer
For Fire Control Abstr — Forest Fire Control Abstracts
For Focus — Forest Focus
FORGA — Forages
Forgn Agr — Foreign Agriculture
Forg Top — Forging Topics
FORIAQ — Forest Research in India
For Ind Rev — Forest Industries Equipment Review
For Insect Dis Cond US — Forest Insect and Disease Conditions in the United
  States
For Insect Dis Leafl USDA For Serv — Forest Insect and Disease Leaflet.
  United States Department of Agriculture. Forest Service
For Inst For GB — Forestry. Institute of Foresters of Great Britain
For Int LJ — Fordham International Law Journal
For Investment R — Foreign Investment Review
FOR KY Univ Coop Ext Serv — FOR. Kentucky University Cooperative
  Extension Service
For L — Forum Linguisticum
For Ling — Forum Linguisticum
For Log — Forestry Log
For LR — Fordham Law Review
Forma Functio — Forma et Function
Formage Trait Metaux — Formage et Traitements des Metaux
Format Continue — Formation Continue
Formation Agric Develop Rur — Formation pour l'Agriculture et le
  Developpement Rural
Formazione Dom — Formazione Domani
For Mgmt Note BC For Serv — Forest Management Note. British Columbia
  Forest Service
Formirov Celov Kom Obsc — Formirovanie Celovska Kommunisticeskogo
  Obscestva
Formosan Agr Rev — Formosan Agricultural Review
Formosan Sci — Formosan Science
Form Tech — Form und Technik
For Note Ill Agric Exp Sta — Forestry Note. University of Illinois. Agricultural
  Experiment Station
For Notes — Forest Notes. New Hampshire's Conservation Magazine
Fornv — Fornvaennen
For Occ Pap FAO — Forestry Occasional Paper. FAO [*Food and Agriculture
  Organization of the United Nations*]
Foro Int — Foro Internacional
Foro Internac — Foro Internacional
Foro It — Foro Italiano
Foro Pad — Foro Padano
Foro Pen — Foro Penale
For & Outdoors — Forest and Outdoors
FORP — Forestry Report. Northern Forest Research Centre. Canadian
  Forestry Service [*Edmonton*]
For Pest Leafl — Forest Pest Leaflet
For Pest Leafl US For Serv — Forest Pest Leaflet. United States Forest Service
For Pol — Foreign Policy
For Policy — Foreign Policy
For Policy Bul — Foreign Policy Bulletin
For Policy Rep — Foreign Policy Reports
FORPRIDE Dig — FORPRIDE [*Forest Products Research and Industries
  Development*] Digest
For Prod J — Forest Products Journal
For Prod Ne Lett — Forest Products News Letter
For Prod Newsl — Forest Products Newsletter. Commonwealth Scientific and
  Industrial Research Organisation. Division of Forest Products
For Prod Res — Forest Products Research
For Prod Res — Forest Products Research. Department of Scientific and
  Industrial Research [*London*]
For Prod Res Bull (GB) — Forest Products Research Bulletin (Great Britain)
For Prod Res Dev Inst J — Forest Products Research and Development
  Institute. Journal
For Prod Res Ind Dev Dig — Forest Products Research and Industries
  Development Digest
For Prod Res No — Forest Products Research Notes. Forest Research Institute
  [*New Zealand*]
For Prod Res Rec Div For Prod (Zambia) — Forest Products Research Record.
  Division of Forest Products (Zambia)
For Prod Res Rep Dep For Res (Nigeria) — Forest Products Research Reports.
  Department of Forest Research (Nigeria)
For Prod Util Tech Rep US For Serv Coop For Div — Forest Products
  Utilization Technical Report. United States Forest Service. Cooperative
  Forestry Division
For Q — Foreign Quarterly Review
FOR Q — Forestry Quarterly [*New York*]
For Quar — Forest Quarterly
For R — Foreign Review
FORRAJ — Forest Record [*London*]
For Rec For Comm (Lond) — Forest Record. Forestry Commission (London)

For Rec (Lond) — Forest Record (London)
For Res Bull For Dep (Zambia) — Forest Research Bulletin. Forest Department
  (Zambia)
For Res India — Forest Research in India
For Res Inf Pap Minist Natl Res (Ont) — Forest Research Information Paper.
  Ministry of Natural Resources (Ontario)
For Res Inst (Bogor) Commun — Forest Research Institute (Bogor).
  Communication
For Res Note Ont For Res Cent — Forest Research Note. Ontario Forest
  Research Centre
For Res Notes — Forestry Research Notes
For Res Notes Weyerhaeuser Timber Co — Forestry Research Notes.
  Weyerhaeuser Timber Company
For Res Note Wis Coll Agric — Forestry Research Notes. University of
  Wisconsin. College of Agriculture
For Resour Newslett — Forest Resources Newsletter
For Resour Rep US For Serv — Forest Resource Report. United States Forest
  Service
For Res Pamphl Div For Res (Zambia) — Forest Research Pamphlet. Division
  of Forest Research (Zambia)
For Res Rep — Forest Resource Report. United States Forest Service
For Res Rep Agric Exp Stn Univ Ill — Forestry Research Report. Agricultural
  Experiment Station. University of Illinois
For Res Rep Ont Minist Nat Resour — Forest Research Report. Ontario
  Ministry of Natural Resources
For Res Rev — Forest Research Review. British Columbia Forest Service
For Res Southeast US Southern For Exp Stn — Forest Research in the
  Southeast. United States Southeastern Forest Experiment Station
For Res West US For Serv — Forestry Research West. United States Forest
  Service
For Res What's New West — Forestry Research. What's New in the West
For the Riverina Teach — For the Riverina Teacher
For S Afr — Forestry in South Africa
Forsch u Berat — Forschung und Beratung. Forstwirtschaft
Forsch Berat Forstw — Forschung und Beratung. Forstwirtschaft
Forsch Ber Evangel Studiengemeinsch — Forschungen und Berichte.
  Evangelische Studiengemeinschaft
Forsch Ber Staatl Mus Berlin — Forschungen und Berichte. Staatliche Museen
  zu Berlin
Forsch D Ld u Volksk — Forschungen zur Deutschen Landes- und Volkskunde
Forsch Dt Landeskde — Forschungen zur Deutschen Landes- und Volkskunde
Forsch F — Forschungen und Fortschritte
Forsch u Fortschr — Forschungen und Fortschritte
Forsch Fortschr Dtsch Wiss — Forschungen und Fortschritte.
  Nachrichtenblatt der Deutschen Wissenschaft und Technik
Forsch Geb Ingenieurwes — Forschung auf dem Gebiete des Ingenieurwesens
Forsch Geogr Ges — Forschungen. Geographische Gesellschaft in Luebeck
Forsch Gesch Opt — Forschungen zur Geschichte der Optik
Forsch H Schiffst — Forschungshefte fuer Schiffstechnik, Schiffbau, und
  Schiffsmaschinenbau
Forsch H Stahlbau — Forschungshefte aus dem Gebiete des Stahlbaues
Forsch Ing — Forschung auf dem Gebiete des Ingenieurwesens
Forsch Ingenieurw — Forschung im Ingenieurwesen
Forsch Ingenieurwes — Forschung im Ingenieurwesen
Forsch Klin Lab — Forschung in der Klinik und im Labor
Forschn Fortschr — Forschungen und Fortschritte
Forsch Ost Eur G — Forschungen zur Ost Europaeischen Geschichte
Forsch Planen Bauen — Forschen, Planen, Bauen
Forschungsber Dtsch Forsch Versuchsant Luft-Raumfahrt —
  Forschungsbericht. Deutsche Forschungs- und Versuchsanstalt fuer
  Luft- und Raumfahrt [*West Germany*]
Forschungsber Fachbereich Bauwesen — Forschungsbericht aus dem
  Fachbereich Bauwesen
Forschungsber Landes Nordrhein-Westfalen — Forschungsberichte des Landes
  Nordrhein-Westfalen
Forschungsber Wirtsch Verkehrminist Nordrhein Westfalen —
  Forschungsberichte des Wirtschafts- und Verkehrsministeriums
  Nordrhein-Westfalen
Forschungsber Wirtsch Verkehrsminist Nordrhein-Westfalen —
  Forschungsberichte des Wirtschafts- und Verkehrsministeriums
  Nordrhein-Westfalen
Forschungsber Wirtsch Verkehrsminist Nordrh Westfalen —
  Forschungsberichte des Wirtschafts- und Verkehrsministeriums
  Nordrhein-Westfalen [*West Germany*]
Forschungsh Geb Stahlbaues — Forschungshefte aus dem Gebiete des
  Stahlbaues
Forschungsh Studienges Hoechstspannungsanlagen — Forschungshefte.
  Studiengesellschaft fuer Hoechstspannungsanlagen
Forsch Volks Land — Forschungen zur Volks- und Landeskunde
Forsch Vor und Fruehgesch — Forschungen zur Vor- und Fruehgeschichte
For Sci — Forest Science
For Sci Intl — Forensic Science International
For Sci Monogr — Forest Science Monographs

For Serv Res Note NE Northeast For Exp Stn US Dep Agric — Forest Service Research Note NE. Northeastern Forest Experiment Station. Forest Service. Department of Agriculture

For Serv Res Pap NE (US) — Forest Service Research Paper NE (United States)

Fors u Fort — Forschungen und Fortschritte

Forsk Fors Landbr — Forskning og Forsok i Landbruket

Forsk Fors Landbruket — Forskning og Forsok i Landbruket

Forsk Framsteg — Forskning och Framsteg

Forsk Groenl — Forskning i Groenland [*Denmark*]

Forsk Udvikling Uddannelse — Forskning Udvikling Uddannelse

For Social Agric Sci — For Socialist Agricultural Science

For Soils Jpn — Forest Soils of Japan

Forsokmeld Landbrukstek Inst — Forsoksmelding. Landbruksteknisk Institutt

Forst Forsokvaes Dan — Forstlige Forsoksvaesen i Danmark

Forst- u Holzw — Forst- und Holzwirt

Forstl Bundesversuchsanst — Forstliche Bundesversuchsanstalt

Forstl Bundesversuchsanst Wien Jahresber — Forstliche Bundesversuchsanstalt Wien. Jahresbericht

Forstl Forsogsv (Danm) — Forstlige Forsogvaesen (Danmark)

Forsttech Inform — Forsttechnische Informationen

Forstw Centbl — Forstwirtschaftliches Centralblatt

Forstwirtsch Holzwirtsch — Forstwirtschaft Holzwirtschaft

Forstwiss Cbl — Forstwissenschaftliches Centralblatt

Forstwiss Centralbl (Hamb) — Forstwissenschaftliches Centralblatt (Hamburg)

Forstwiss Forsch — Forstwissenschaftliche Forschungen

Forstwiss Forsch Beih Forstwiss Centralbl — Forstwissenschaftliche Forschungen. Beihefte zum Forstwissenschaftlichen Centralblatt

Forstwiss Zentbl — Forstwissenschaftliches Zentralblatt

For Surv Note BC For Serv — Forest Survey Notes. British Columbia Forest Service

FORTA — Fortune

Fortbildungskurse Rheumatol — Fortbildungskurse fuer Rheumatologie

Fortbildungskurse Schweiz Ges Psychiatr — Fortbildungskurse. Schweizerische Gesellschaft fuer Psychiatrie

Fort Dodge Bio-Chem Rev — Fort Dodge Bio-Chemic Review

For Tech Note NH Agric Exp Sta — Forestry Technical Notes. University of New Hampshire. Agricultural Experiment Station

For Tech Pap — Forest Technical Paper [*Australia*]

For Tech Pap — Forestry Technical Papers

For Tech Pap For Comm Vict — Forestry Technical Papers. Forests Commission of Victoria

Fort Hare Pap — Fort Hare Papers

Fort Hays Stud New Ser Sci Ser — Fort Hays Studies. New Series. Science Series

Forthcoming Int Sci & Tech Conf — Forthcoming International Scientific and Technical Conference

For Timb — Forest and Timber

For and Timb — Forest and Timber

For Timber — Forest and Timber

Fortn — Fortnightly Review

FortnR — Fortnightly Review

Fortn Rev Chic Dent Soc — Fortnightly Review of the Chicago Dental Society

Fortpflanz Besamung Aufzucht Haustiere — Fortpflanzung Besamung und Aufzucht der Haustiere

Fort Pierce ARC Res Rep R1 Univ Fla Agric Res Cent — Fort Pierce ARC Research Report R1. University of Florida. Agricultural Research Center

For Tree Improv — Forest Tree Improvement

For Tree Ser Div For Res CSIRO — Forest Tree Series. Division of Forest Research. Commonwealth Scientific and Industrial Research Organisation

Fort Rev — Fortnightly Review

Fortsch-Ber VDI Z Reihe — Fortschritt-Berichte. VDI [*Verein Deutscher Ingenieure*] Zeitschriften. Reihe [*West Germany*]

Fortschr Acker- Pflanzenbau — Fortschritte im Acker- und Pflanzenbau

Fortschr Allergiel — Fortschritte der Allergielehre

Fortschr Androl — Fortschritte der Andrologie

Fortschr Anorg Chem Ind — Fortschritte in der Anorganisch Chemischen Industrie

Fortschr Antimikrob Antineoplast Chemother — Fortschritte der Antimikrobiellen und Antineoplastischen Chemotherapie

Fortschr Arzneimittelforsch — Fortschritte der Arzneimittelforschung

Fortschr Augenheilkd — Fortschritte der Augenheilkunde

Fortschrber Landw — Fortschrittsberichte fuer die Landwirtschaft

Fortschr Ber VDI Z — Fortschritt-Berichte. VDI [*Verein Deutscher Ingenieure*] Zeitschrift

Fortschr Ber VDI Zeitschr Reihe II — Fortschritt-Berichte. VDI [*Verein Deutscher Ingenieure*] Zeitschriften. Reihe II

Fortschr-Ber VDI Z Reihe 4 — Fortschritt-Berichte. VDI [*Verein Deutscher Ingenieure*] Zeitschriften. Reihe 4. Bauingenieurwesen [*West Germany*]

Fortschr Bot — Fortschritte der Botanik

Fortschr Chem Forsch — Fortschritte der Chemischen Forschung

Fortschr Chem Org Natr — Fortschritte der Chemie Organischer Naturstoffe

Fortschr Chem Org Natstoffe — Fortschritte der Chemie Organischer Naturstoffe

Fortschr Chem Org Naturst — Fortschritte der Chemie Organischer Naturstoffe

Fortschr Evolutionsforsch — Fortschritte der Evolutionsforschung

Fortschr Exp Theor Biophys — Fortschritte der Experimentellen und Theoretischen Biophysik

Fortschr Exp Tumorforsch — Fortschritte der Experimentellen Tumorforschung

Fortschr Geb Roentgenstr Nuklearmed — Fortschritte auf dem Gebiete der Roentgenstrahlen und der Nuklearmedizin

Fortschr Geb Roentgenstr Ver Roentgenprax — Fortschritte auf dem Gebiete der Roentgenstrahlen Vereinigt mit Roentgenpraxis

Fortschr Geburtshilfe Gynaekol — Fortschritte der Geburtshilfe und Gynaekologie

Fortschr Geol Rheinland Westfalen — Fortschritte in der Geologie von Rheinland und Westfalen

Fortschr Geol Rheinl Westfalen — Fortschritte in der Geologie von Rheinland und Westfalen

Fortschr Hals- Nasen Ohrenheilkd — Fortschritte der Hals- Nasen- Ohrenheilkunde

Fortschr Hochpolym-Forsch — Fortschritte der Hochpolymeren-Forschung

Fortschr Immunitaetsforsch — Fortschritte der Immunitaetsforschung

Fortschritt Ber VDI Zeitschrift Reihe 11 — Fortschritt-Berichte. VDI [*Verein Deutscher Ingenieure*] Zeitschriften. Reihe 11

Fortschritt Ber VDI Zeitschr Reihe 8 — Fortschritt-Berichte. VDI [*Verein Deutscher Ingenieure*] Zeitschriften. Reihe 8

Fortschrittsber Chem Ztg — Fortschrittsberichte der Chemiker-Zeitung

Fortschrittsber Kolloide Polym — Fortschrittsberichte ueber Kolloide und Polymere

Fortschrittsber Landwirtsch — Fortschrittsberichte fuer die Landwirtschaft

Fortschr Kardiol — Fortschritte der Kardiologie

Fortschr Kiefer Gesichtschir — Fortschritte der Kiefer und Geschichts Chirurgie

Fortschr Kieferorthop — Fortschritte der Kieferorthopaedie

Fortschr Krebsforsch — Fortschritte der Krebsforschung

Fortschr Landwirtsch — Fortschritte der Landwirtschaft

Fortschr Med — Fortschritte der Medizin

Fortschr Med Mikrobiol — Fortschritte der Medizinischen Mikrobiologie

Fortschr Med Virusforsch — Fortschritte der Medizinischen Virusforschung

Fortschr Mineral — Fortschritte der Mineralogie

Fortschr Mineral Beihe — Fortschritte der Mineralogie. Beiheft

Fortschr Mineral Kristallogr Petrogr — Fortschritte der Mineralogie, Kristallographie, und Petrographie

Fortschr Miner Beih — Fortschritte der Mineralogie. Beiheft

Fortschr Neurol Psychiatr — Fortschritte der Neurologie, Psychiatrie, und Ihrer Grenzgebiete

Fortschr Neurol Psychiatr Grenzgeb — Fortschritte der Neurologie, Psychiatrie, und Ihrer Grenzgebiete

Fortschr Neurol Psychiatr Ihrer Grenzgeb — Fortschritte der Neurologie, Psychiatrie, und Ihrer Grenzgebiete

Fortschr Pflanzenzuecht — Fortschritte der Pflanzenzuechtung

Fortschr Ph — Fortschritte der Physik

Fortschr Phys — Fortschritte der Physik

Fortschr Phys Chem — Fortschritte der Physikalischen Chemie

Fortschr Phys Dtsche Phys Ges — Fortschritte der Physik. Deutsche Physikalische Gesellschaft

Fortschr Physik — Fortschritte der Physik

Fortschr Psychosom Med — Fortschritte der Psychosomatischen Medizin

Fortschr Ther — Fortschritte der Therapie

Fortschr Tierphysiol Tierernaehr — Fortschritte in der Tierphysiologie und Tierernaehrung

Fortschr Tuberkuloseforsch — Fortschritte der Tuberkuloseforschung

Fortschr Verfahrenstech — Fortschritte der Verfahrenstechnik

Fortschr Verhaltensforsch — Fortschritte der Verhaltensforschung

Fortschr Veterinaermed — Fortschritte der Veterinaermedizin

Fortschr Wasserchem Ihrer Grenzgeb — Fortschritte der Wasserchemie und Ihrer Grenzgebiete [*East Germany*]

Fortschr Wasserchem Ihrer Grenzgebie — Fortschritte der Wasserchemie und Ihrer Grenzgebiete

Fortschr Zool — Fortschritte der Zoologie

Fortuna Ital — Fortuna Italiana

Forum — Forum for the Discussion of New Trends in Education

Forum — International Trade Forum

Forum Ed — Forum of Education

Forum Educ — Forum of Education

Forum Ekon Tek — Forum foer Ekonomi och Teknik

ForumH — Forum (Houston)

Forum Med — Forum on Medicine

Forum Microbiol — Forum Microbiologicum

Forum Mikrobiol — Forum Microbiologie [*West Germany*]

Forum Mod L — Forum for Modern Language Studies

Forum Pub Aff — Forum on Public Affairs

Forum Rep Sci Ind Forum Aust Acad Sci — Australian Academy of Science. Science and Industry Forum. Forum Report

ForumS — Forum: A Ukrainian Review (Scranton, Pennsylvania)

Forum Sekolah Pasca Sarjana Inst Pertanian Bogor — Forum Sekolah Pasca Sarjana Institut Pertanian Bogor
Forum Staedte Hyg — Forum Staedte Hygiene
Forum Umwelt Hyg — Forum Umwelt Hygiene
Forum Umw Hyg — Forum Umwelt Hygiene
ForumZ — Forum (Zagreb)
FOSCAD — Forest Science
FOSCDG — Food Science [*New York*]
FOSMA9 — Forest Science Monographs
Foster Mo Ref — Foster's Monthly Reference Lists
FOSZAE — Fogorvosi Szemle
FOT — Fortune
FOTEAO — Food Technology
FOTIB3 — Forest and Timber
Fotokhim Prom — Fotokhimicheskaya Promyshlennost
FOU — Foundation
Foun — Foundations [*Baptist*]
FOUNA — Foundry
Found Control Eng — Foundations of Control Engineering [*Poland*]
Found Facts — Foundation Facts
Found Fundam Res Matter Yearb — Foundation for Fundamental Research on Matter. Yearbook
Found Inst Nucl Res Yearb — Foundation Institute for Nuclear Research. Yearbook
Found Lang — Foundations of Language
Found Language — International Journal of Language and Philosophy. Foundations of Language
Found News — Foundation News
Found Phys — Foundations of Physics
Foundry Manage Technol — Foundry Management and Technology
Foundry Pract — Foundry Practice
Found Sci Research Surinam and Netherlands Antilles Pub — Foundation for Scientific Research in Surinam and the Netherlands Antilles. Publication
Found Trade J — Foundry Trade Journal
Four Corners Geol Soc Bull — Four Corners Geological Society. Bulletin
Four Corners Geol Soc Field Conf Guideb — Four Corners Geological Society. Field Conference. Guidebook
Four Qt — Four Quarters
Four Quart — Four Quarters
FOUVAC — Folia Universitaria Cochabamba
FOV — Visserijnieuws
FOWJ — Foothills Wilderness Journal
FOX — Focus
Fox Breeders Gaz — Fox Breeders Gazette
FOYB — Foothills Yukon Bulletin
FOZODJ — Folia Zoologica
FP — Filoil Pipeline [*Manila*]
FP — Filoloski Pregled [*Belgrade*]
FP — Financial Post Magazine
FPARA9 — Folia Parasitologica [*Prague*]
F Phon — Folia Phoniatrica
FPJOAB — Forest Products Journal
FPK — Processed Prepared Food
FPLAAD — Flowering Plants of Africa
FPLY — Foothills Pipe Line (Yukon) Limited. News Releases
FPMMA — Fortschritte der Psychosomatischen Medizin
FPn — Fryske Plaknammen
FPNJAG — Folia Psychiatrica et Neurologica Japonica
FPO — Financial Post [*Toronto*]
FPORD — Fusion Power Report
FPR — Foreign Projects Newsletter
FPRDAI — Food Product Development
FPRDI J — FPRDI [*Forest Products Research and Development Institute*] Journal
FPRMAB — Folia Primatologica
FPSTB — Fire Prevention Science and Technology
FPt — Far Point
FPTED — Fuel Processing Technology
FPYKA — Fortschritte der Physik
FQ — Faerie Queene
FQ — Film Quarterly
FQ — Florida Quarterly
FQ — Four Quarters
FQ — French Quarterly
FQNZA — Frequenz
F Quarterly — Film Quarterly
FR — Australian Financial Review
F and R — Faith and Reason
FR — Felix Ravenna
FR — Fordham Law Review
FR — Fortnightly Review
FR — French Review
FR — Furtwaengler und Reichhold, Griechische Vasenmalerei
FRA — Fontes Rerum Austriacarum
FRA — Fra Randers Amt

Fr A — Fraenkische Alb
FrA — France-Asie
Frac — Fracastoro
FRACA — Fracastoro
Fr Actuelle — France Actuelle
Fra Fys Verden — Fra Fysikkens Verden
Fragm Balcan — Fragmenta Balcanica. Musei Macedonici Scientiarum Naturalium
Fragm Balc Mus Macedonici Sci Nat — Fragmenta Balcanica. Musei Macedonici Scientiarum Naturalium
Fragm Bot — Fragmenta Botanica
Fragm Coleopterol — Fragmenta Coleopterologica
Fragm Ent — Fragmenta Entomologica
Fragm Entomol — Fragmenta Entomologica
Fragm Faun — Fragmenta Faunistica
Fragm Faun Hung — Fragmenta Faunistica Hungarica
Fragm Faun (Warsaw) — Fragmenta Faunistica (Warsaw)
Fragm Flor Geobot — Fragmenta Floristica et Geobotanica
Fragm Florist Geobot (Cracow) — Fragmenta Floristica et Geobotanica (Cracow)
Fragm Herbol Jugosl — Fragmenta Herbologica Jugoslavica
Fragm Mineral Palaeontol — Fragmenta Mineralogica et Palaeontologica
Fr Agric — France Agricole
Fr Am Commer — French American Commerce
FRAME — Fund for the Replacement of Animals in Medical Experiments. Technical News
Fr Am Rev — French American Review
Franc — Franciscana
France Apic — La France Apicole
France As — France-Asie; Revue de Culture et de Synthese Franco-Asiatique
France Illus — France Illustration
France Illus Sup — France Illustration. Supplement
FrancLA — Studii Biblici Franciscani. Liber Annuus [*Jerusalem*]
Franc Lev — Franciscaans Leven
Franc Mod — Francais Moderne
Franc S — Franciscan Studies
FrancSt — Franciscan Studies. Annual [*St. Bonaventure, New York*]
FrankfAllg — Frankfurter Allgemeine
Frankf Hefte — Frankfurter Hefte. Zeitschrift fuer Kultur und Politik
Frankf Hist Forsch — Frankfurter Historische Forschungen
Frankfurter Ver Geog Jber — Frankfurter Verein fuer Geographie und Statistik. Jahresbericht
Frankfurt H — Frankfurter Hefte
Frankf Z Path — Frankfurter Zeitschrift fuer Pathologie
Frankf Z Pathol — Frankfurter Zeitschrift fuer Pathologie
Frankf Zt — Frankfurter Allgemeine Zeitung fuer Deutschland
Fran Mod — Francais Moderne
FranS — Franciscan Studies
Fran Stds — Franciscan Studies
Fran Stud — Franciscan Studies
Franz Forsch — Franziskanische Forschungen
FranzS — Franziskanische Studien [*Padeborn*]
Franz St — Franziskanische Studien
FRAR — Fire Research Abstracts and Reviews
FRARA — Fire Research Abstracts and Reviews
Fraser — Fraser's Magazine
Fraser of Allander Inst Q Econ Commentary — Fraser of Allander Institute. Quarterly Economic Commentary
Fra Sundhedsstyr (Copenhagen) — Fra Sundhedsstyrelsen (Copenhagen)
FRB — Federal Reserve Bulletin
FRBCB — Fisheries Research Board of Canada. Bulletin
FRBCTR — Fisheries Research Board of Canada. Technical Report
FRBMRS — Fisheries Research Board of Canada. Manuscript Report Series
Fr Br — Front og Bro
FRBRD — Federal Reserve Bank of St. Louis. Review
Fr Bur Rech Geol Minieres Bull Ser 2 Sect 1 — France. Bureau de Recherches Geologiques et Minieres. Bulletin. Serie 2. Section 1. Geologie de la France
Fr Bur Rech Geol Minieres Bull Ser 2 Sect 4 — France. Bureau de Recherches Geologiques et Minieres. Bulletin. Serie 2. Section 4
Fr Bur Rech Geol Minieres Mem — France. Bureau de Recherches Geologiques et Minieres. Memoires
Fr Bur Rech Geol Min Mem — France. Bureau de Recherches Geologiques et Minieres. Memoires
Fr Cent Natl Exploit Oceans Publ Result Compagnes Mer — France. Centre National pour l'Exploitation des Oceans. Publications. Resultats des Compagnes a la Mer Brest
FrChr — Freier Christentum
FRCRAX — Forestry Chronicle
FRD — Federal Rules Decisions
FRDCA — Fridericiana
F Reader — Film Reader
FREDA — Freddo
Free Assoc — Free Association
Free China R — Free China Review
Freedom Soc — Freedom Socialist

Free Inq — Free Inquiry
Free L — Free Lance
Free Lbr Wld — Free Labour World
Free News — Freedom News
Free Soc — Freedom Socialist
Free Spir — Freeing the Spirit
Freiberger Forsch H — Freiberger Forschungshefte
Freiberger Forsch Ser C — Freiberger Forschungshefte. Series C. Geologie. Geophysik. Mineralogie-Lagerstaettenlehre und Paleontologie
Freiberger Forschungsh B Metall — Freiberger Forschungshefte. Reihe B. Metallurgie
Freiberg Forschungsh B — Freiberger Forschungshefte. Reihe B [*East Germany*]
Freiberg Forschungsh C — Freiberger Forschungshefte. Reihe C
Freiberg Forschungsh D — Freiberger Forschungshefte. Reihe D [*East Germany*]
Freiberg Forschungsh Reihe A — Freiberger Forschungshefte. Reihe A
Freiberg Forschungsh Reihe C — Freiberger Forschungshefte. Reihe C
Freib FH — Freiberger Forschungshefte
FreibRu — Freiburger Rundbrief [*Freiburg Im Breisgau*]
Freib Symp Med Univ Klin — Freiburger Symposion an der Medizinischen Universitaets-Klinik
FreibThSt — Freiburger Theologische Studien
Freiburger Geog Mitt — Freiburger Geographische Mitteilungen
FreibZ — Freiburger Zeitschrift fuer Philosophie und Theologie
Freight & Container Transp — Freight and Container Transportation
Freight Mgmt — Freight Management
Frei Z Phil Theol — Freiburger Zeitschrift fuer Philosophie und Theologie
French Am Rev — French American Review
French Hist St — French Historical Studies
French R — French Review
French Tech Building Civ Engng & Town Planning — French Techniques. Building, Civil Engineering, and Town Planning
French Tech Electr Engn & Electron Ind — French Techniques. Electrical Engineering and Electronics Industries
French Tech Mech Hydraul & Consult Engng Ind — French Techniques. Mechanical, Hydraulic, and Consultant Engineering Industries
French Tech Metal Ind — French Techniques. Metal Industries
French Tech Misc Ind & Consum Goods — French Techniques. Miscellaneous Industries and Consumer Goods
French Tech Tranp Stud & Res — French Techniques. Transportation Studies and Research
Freq — Frequenz
FRERDC — Forest Recreation Research
F Res — Food Research
Fresenius Z Anal Chem — Fresenius' Zeitschrift fuer Analytische Chemie
Freshwater Fish Newsl — Freshwater Fisheries Newsletter
Freshwat Fish Newsl — Freshwat Fisheries Newsletter
Freshw Biol — Freshwater Biology
Freshw Biol Assoc Annu Rep — Freshwater Biological Association. Annual Report
Freshw Biol Assoc Sci Publ — Freshwater Biological Association. Scientific Publication
Freunde Naturw Ber (Haidinger) — Freunde der Naturwissenschaften in Wien. Berichte ueber die Mittheilungen (W. Haidinger)
Fr F — French Forum
Fr For NW Dt Zahn Ae — Freies Forum. Nordwestdeutscher Zahnaerzte
FRG — Revista de Filologia Romanica si Germanica [*Bucarest*]
Fr Graph — France Graphique
Fr H — Frankfurter Hefte
FrH — Franzoesisch Heute
FRHED — Frankfurter Hefte
Fr Hist Stu — French Historical Studies
Fr Hist Stud — French Historical Studies
Frict Wear Mach — Friction and Wear in Machinery
Fridericiana Z Univ Karlsruhe — Fridericiana. Zeitschrift der Universitaet Karlsruhe
Fried G Bl — Friedberger Geschichtsblaetter
Friends Hist Assoc Bull — Friends Historical Association. Bulletin
Friends PI Nixon Med Hist Libr — Friends of the P. I. Nixon Medical Historical Library
Fries Landbouwbl — Fries Landbouwblad [*Netherlands*]
FRIJ — Frost i Jord/Frost Action in Soils
FRILAB — Indian Forest Leaflet
FRIN — FRI [*Fuel Research Institute*] News
Fr Ind — France-Inde
Fr Ind — France-Indochine
FRINEL — Food Reviews International
Fr Inst Natl Propr Ind Bull Off Propr Ind Abr — France. Institut National de la Propriete Industrielle. Bulletin Officiel de la Propriete Industrielle. Abreges
Fris — Frigisinga
FRIS — Stanford University Food Research Institute Studies
Friuli Med — Friuli Medico
Friul Med — Friuli Medico

FRL — Forschungen zur Religion und Literatur des Alten und Neuen Testaments
FrL — France Latine
Fr L — Frank Leslie's Popular Monthly
FRLANT — Forschungen zur Religion und Literatur des Alten und Neuen Testaments
Frld — Frankenland
Fr LM — French Literature on Microfiche
Fr M — Francais Moderne
FRM — France Alimentaire
FRMBA — Farmacia (Bucharest)
FRM Bericht — Forschungsreaktor Muenchen. Bericht
Fr Med — France Medicale
Fr Minist Agric Bull Tech Inf — France. Ministere de l'Agriculture. Bulletin Technique d'Information
Fr Mo — Francais dans le Monde
FRNM Bull — FRNM [*Foundation for Research on the Nature of Man*] Bulletin
FRNTA — Frontiers
Froebel J — Froebel Journal
F Roent Nuk — Fortschritte auf dem Gebiete der Roentgenstrahlen und der Nuklearmedizin
Froid Clim — Froid et la Climatisation
FRom — Filologia Romanza
Fr O-Mer — France d'Outre-Mer
Frommanns Klassiker — Frommann's Klassiker der Philosophie
Fron Matrix Biol — Frontiers of Matrix Biology
Front — Frontier
Front Biol — Frontiers of Biology
Front Clin Neurosci — Frontiers of Clinical Neuroscience
Front Diabetes — Frontiers in Diabetes
Front Gastrointest Res — Frontiers of Gastrointestinal Research
Front Horm Res — Frontiers of Hormone Research
Frontiers Plant Sci — Frontiers of Plant Science
Front Nauki Tekh — Front Nauki i Tekhniki [*USSR*]
Front Nurs Serv Q Bull — Frontier Nursing Service. Quarterly Bulletin
Front Oral Physiol — Frontiers of Oral Physiology
Front Phys — Frontiers in Physics
Front Plant Sci — Frontiers of Plant Science
Front Plant Sci Conn Agric Exp Stn (New Haven) — Frontiers of Plant Science. Connecticut Agricultural Experiment Station (New Haven)
Front Radiat Ther Oncol — Frontiers of Radiation Therapy and Oncology
Front Sl — Front Slobode
Fr ORSTOM Cah Ser Geophys — France. Office de la Recherche Scientifique et Technique d'Outre-Mer. Cahiers. Serie Geophysique
Fr ORSTOM Cah Ser Hydrol — France. Office de la Recherche Scientifique et Technique d'Outre-Mer. Cahiers. Serie Hydrologie
Fr ORSTOM Cah Ser Pedol — France. Office de la Recherche Scientifique et Technique d'Outre-Mer. Cahiers. Serie Pedologie
Fr ORSTOM Monogr Hydrol — France. Office de la Recherche Scientifique et Technique d'Outre-Mer. Monographies Hydrologiques
Frozen Fds — Frozen Foods
FRP — Foreign Report
Fr P — France-Pologne
FR Ph — Forschungen zur Romanischen Philologie
Fr Pharm — France-Pharmacie
Fr Railw Tech — French Railway Techniques
Fr Rev — French Review
Fr Ru — Freiburger Rundbrief
FRS — Frozen Foods
FRSABT — Food Research Institute. Studies in Agricultural Economics, Trade, and Development [*Stanford*]
Fr Sci N — French Science News
Fr Ses Parfums — France et Ses Parfums
FrSM — Franziskanische Studien. Muenster
Fr St — Franciscan Studies
FrSt — Franziskanische Studien
Fr St — French Studies
Fr Stud — French Studies. A Quarterly Review
FRSUB — Fra Sundhedsstyrelsen
FRT — Fruitteelt
FRTAA — Forstarchiv
Fr Tech — French Techniques
Fru — Fruits
Fruchtsaft Ind — Fruchtsaft Industrie
Fruehma St — Fruehmittelalterliche Studien
FRUIA — Fruits
Fruit Grow — Fruit Grower
Fruit Notes Coop Ext Serv Univ Mass — Fruit Notes. Cooperative Extension Service. University of Massachusetts
Fruit Prod J Am Food Manuf — Fruit Products Journal and American Food Manufacturer
Fruit Prod J Am Vinegar Ind — Fruit Products Journal and American Vinegar Industry
Fruit Sci Rep (Skierniewice) — Fruit Science Reports (Skierniewice)

Fruit Situat US Dep Agric Econ Res Serv — Fruit Situation TFS. United States Department of Agriculture. Economic Research Service
Fruits Prim Afr Nord — Fruits et Primeurs de l'Afrique du Nord
Fruit Var Hortic Dig — Fruit Varieties and Horticultural Digest
Fruit Var J — Fruit Varieties Journal
Fruit Veg Honey Crop Mkt Rep — Fruit, Vegetable, and Honey Crop and Market Report
Fruit & Veg R — Fruit and Vegetable Review
Fruit World Ann — Fruit World Annual
Fruit World Annu Orchardists' Guide — Fruit World Annual and Orchardists' Guide
Fruit World Mark Grow — Fruit World and Market Grower
Fruit Yb — Fruit Yearbook
Fru O-Mer — Fruits d'Outre-Mer
FRUS — Foreign Relations of the United States
Frust Entomol Ist Entomol — Frustula Entomologica. Istituto di Entomologia
Frustula Entomol — Frustula Entomologica
F Rutan — Filmrutan
Fr Warte — Die Friedenswarte
FRWMA — Fernwaerme International
FRXZZ — Archivos. Fundacion Roux-Ocefa
FryskJb — Frysk Jierboek
FRZ — Zeitschrift fuer Familienrecht
Frz F — Franziskanische Forschungen
FS — Feminist Studies
FS — Folklore Studies
FS — Forest Science
FS — Fort Simpson Journal
FS — Franciscan Studies
FS — Franziskanische Studien
FS — French Studies
FS — Funbericht aus Schwaben
FS — Furman Studies
FSAFA — Farming in South Africa
FSASA — Fette - Seifen - Anstrichmittel
Fsch PG — Forschungen zur Neueren Philosophie und Ihrer Geschichte
F Sci Abstr — Food Science Abstracts
FSC Ne — FSC [*Friends Service Council*] News
FSCS — Fundamental Studies in Computer Science [*Elsevier Book Series*]
FsD — Fonetica si Dialectologie
FSE — Fundamental Studies in Engineering [*Elsevier Book Series*]
FSEPA — Filtration and Separation
FSF — Magazine of Fantasy and Science Fiction
FS Fact Sheet Oreg State Univ Ext Serv — FS. Fact Sheet. Oregon State University. Extension Service
FSFMA — Forskning och Framsteg
FSIND — Forensic Science International
FSINDR — Forensic Science International
FSIZA — Fukushima Igaku Zasshi
FSJOD — Fire Safety Journal
FSL — Fleet Street Letter
FSLPAB — Flora Slodkowodna Polski
FSM — Fantastic Story Magazine
FSMNA — Fishermen's News
FSO — Flying Saucers from Other Worlds
F Soc Rev — Film Society Review
FS Oe Th — Forschungen zur Systematischen und Oekumenischen Theologie
FSQ — Fantastic Story Quarterly
FSQS US Dep Agric Food Saf Qual Serve — FSQS. United States Department of Agriculture. Food Safety and Quality Service
FSRTS — Fyra Svenska Reformationsskrifter Tryckta i Stockholm Ar 1562
FSSA — French Studies in Southern Africa
FSt — Franciscan Studies
F St — Franziskanische Studien
F St — French Studies
FSTA — Food Science and Technology Abstracts [*International Food Information Service*] [*Bibliographic database*] [*Frankfurt, West Germany*]
FSTEB — Fibre Science and Technology
FS Th R — Forschungen zur Systematischen Theologie und Religionsphilosophie
F Stud — Franciscan Studies
F Stud — Franziskanische Studien
FSTXA — Faserforschung und Textiltechnik
F Supp — Federal Supplement
FSUS — Florida State University. Studies
FSUSP — Florida State University Slavic Papers
FT — Faserforschung und Textiltechnik
FT — Filipino Teacher
FT — Financial Times
FT — Finsk Tidskrift
FT — Fort McMurray Today
FT — Funk-Technik
FTA — Food Technology in Australia
FTA — Food Trade Review
FTAUAC — Food Technology in Australia

FTBR — Fort McMurray Today. Oil Sands Business Report
F & Televisie — Film et Televisie
FTF — Financial Times (Frankfurt)
FTGBA — Fertigungstechnik und Betrieb
FThL — Forum Theologiae Linguisticae
FThought — Faith and Thought. Journal of the Victoria Institute [*Croydon, Surrey*]
FTIPA3 — Forest Tree Improvement
FTMEA — Formage et Traitements des Metaux
F & Ton — Film und Ton
FTP — Fruit and Tropical Products
FTPP — Folklore. Tribuna del Pensamiento Peruano
FTPPA — Fizika i Tekhnika Poluprovodnikov [*Leningrad*]
FTR — Finnish Trade Review [*Helsinki*]
FTRIA — Fiziko-Tekhnicheskie Problemy Razrabotki Poleznykh Iskopaemykh
FTS — Financial Times
FTS — Financial Times. Supplements
FTSED — Filtration et Techniques Separatives
FTST — Futurist
FTT — Fanciful Tales of Time and Space
F & TV — Film et Televisie
F & TV Kam — Film und TV Kameramann
F & TV Tech — Film and Television Technician
FTW — Foreign Trade Review
Ftwr News — Footwear News
FTY — Fookien Times Yearbook [*Manila*]
FUB — Finance and Development
Fu B — Forschungen und Berichte
FUB — Furman University Bulletin
FUBA — Filologia. Instituto de Filologia Romancia Facultad de Filosofia y Letras. Universidad de Buenos Aires
Fudan J — Fudan Journal
Fuel Abstr Curr Titles — Fuel Abstracts and Current Titles
Fuel Combust — Fuel and Combustion [*Japan*]
Fuel Econ — Fuel Economy
Fuel Econ Rev — Fuel Economy Review
Fuel Effic — Fuel Efficiency
Fuel & Energy Abstr — Fuel and Energy Abstracts
Fuel Oil J — Fuel Oil Journal
Fueloil & Oil Heat — Fueloil and Oil Heat and Solar Systems
Fueloil Oil Heat Sol Syst — Fueloil and Oil Heat and Solar Systems
Fuel Oil Temp J — Fuel Oil and Temperature Journal
Fuel- Orr- Gegegyogy — Fuel-, Orr-, Gegegyogyaszat [*Hungary*]
Fuel Process Technol — Fuel Processing Technology [*Netherlands*]
Fuel Res Inst (Pretoria) Bull — Fuel Research Institute (Pretoria). Bulletin
Fuel Res Inst S Afr Bull — Fuel Research Institute of South Africa. Bulletin
Fuel Sci Prac — Fuel in Science and Practice
Fuel Sci Pract — Fuel in Science and Practice [*England*]
Fuels Furn — Fuels and Furnaces
Fuel Soc J — Fuel Society Journal [*England*]
FUF — Finnisch-Ugrische Forschungen
FuF — Forschungen und Fortschritte
FUFAB — Funk-Fachhaendler
FUFOD — Fusion Forefront
Fugg Magyar — Fuggetlen Magyarorszag
FUHYD — Forum Umwelt Hygiene
FUJ — Fuji Bank Bulletin [*Tokyo*]
Fuji Bank Bul — Fuji Bank Bulletin
Fuji Electr J — Fuji Electric Journal
Fuji Electr Rev — Fuji Electric Review
Fujikura Tech Rev — Fujikura Technical Review
Fujitsu Sci Tech J — Fujitsu Scientific and Technical Journal [*Japan*]
FUJTA — Fujitsu
Fukien Acad Res Bull — Fukien Academy. Research Bulletin
Fukien Agric J — Fukien Agricultural Journal
Fukien Christ Univ Sci J — Fukien Christian University. Science Journal
FUKOB — Funtai Kogaku
Fukuoka Acta Med — Fukuoka Acta Medica
Fukushima J Med Sci — Fukushima Journal of Medical Science
Fukushima Med J — Fukushima Medical Journal
Fulbright Educ Dev Program Grantee Rep — Fulbright Educational Development Program Grantee Reports
Fulbright Univ Adm Program Grantee Rep — Fulbright University Administrator Program Grantee Reports
Fulmer Res Inst Newsl — Fulmer Research Institute. Newsletter
FulN — Fulbright Newsletter
FUN — From Unknown Worlds
Funct Approximatio Comment Math — Functiones et Approximatio Commentarii Mathematici
Functional Anal Appl — Functional Analysis and Its Applications
Funct Photgr — Functional Photography
Fundam Aerosp Instrum — Fundamentals of Aerospace Instrumentation
Fundam Appl Toxicol — Fundamental and Applied Toxicology
Fundam Balneo Bioclimatol — Fundamenta Balneo Bioclimatologica
Fundam Cosmic Phys — Fundamentals of Cosmic Physics
Fundam Cosm Phys — Fundamentals of Cosmic Physics

Fundamental Stud in Comput Sci — Fundamental Studies in Computer Science
Fundam Phenom Mater Sci — Fundamental Phenomena in the Material Sciences
Fundam Radiol — Fundamental Radiologica
Fundam Sci — Fundamenta Scientiae
Fundber Hessen — Fundberichte aus Hessen
Fundber Oesterreich — Fundberichte aus Oesterreich
Fundber Schwaben — Fundberichte aus Schwaben
Fund Bras Conserv Nat Bol Inf — Fundacao Brasileira para a Conservacao da Natureza Boletim Informativo
Fund Inform — Fundamenta Informaticae
Fund Informat — Fundamenta Informaticae
Fund Math — Fundamenta Mathematicae
Fund Miguel Lillo Misc — Fundacion Miguel Lillo Miscelanea
Fund Raising Manage — Fund Raising Management
Fund Raising Mgt — Fund Raising Management
Fund Sci — Fundamenta Scientiae
Fungi Can — Fungi Canadenses
Funkcial Ekvac — Funkcialaj Ekvaciog
Funk-Tech — Funk-Technik
Funkt Morphol Organ Zelle — Funktionelle und Morphologische Organisation der Zelle
Funktsional Anal i Prilozhen — Akademiya Nauk SSSR. Funktsional'nyi Analiz i ego Prilozheniya
Funkts Org Usloviyakh Izmen Gazov Sredy — Funktsii Organizma v Usloviyakh Izmenennoi Gazovoi Sredy
FUQ — Free University Quarterly. A Quarterly for Christian Knowledge and Life [*Amsterdam*]
Fur — Furioso
FurmS — Furman Studies
Furnit Manuf — Furniture Manufacturer
Furniture Wkrs P — Furniture Workers Press
Fur Trade J Can — Fur Trade Journal of Canada
FURWA — Furrow
FUSHA — Funkschau
Fusion Energy Found Newsl — Fusion Energy Foundation. Newsletter
Fusion Power Assoc Exec Newsl — Fusion Power Associates. Executive Newsletter
Fusion Power Rep — Fusion Power Report
Fusion Technol — Fusion Technology
Fussboden Ztg — Fussboden Zeitung [*West Germany*]
FUSTA — Fujitsu Scientific and Technical Journal [*Japan*]
Fut — Future Fiction
Fut — Futures
Fut — Futurist
Fut Abstr — Future Abstracts
FUTEA — Funk-Technik
FUTF — Future Science Fiction
FUTJA — Foundry Trade Journal
FUTS — Futuristic Stories
FUTU — Futures
FUTUA — Futurist
FUTUB — Futures
FUTUD — Futuribles
FUZED — Fussboden Zeitung
Fuzzy Math — Fuzzy Mathematics
FVFSA — Fortschritte der Verfahrenstechnik
FVL — Forschungen zur Volks- und Landeskunde
FVMUDL — Flora et Vegetatio Mundi
FVTLAQ — Folia Veterinaria Latina
FW — Financial World
FW — Folktales of the World
FWBLA — Freshwater Biology
FWD — Furniture World and Furniture Buyer and Decorator
FWF — Far Western Forum
F Wiss Beit — Filmwissenschaftliche Beitraege
FWN — Footwear News
FWP J — FWP [*Founding, Welding, Production Engineering*] Journal [*South Africa*]
FWPJA — FWP [*Founding, Welding, Production Engineering*] Journal
FWSCA — Forstwissenschaftliches Centralblatt
FYCAB — Fyzikalny Casopis. Vydavatel'stvo Slovenskej Akademie Vied
Fyiz Tverd Tyila — Fyizika Tverdogo Tyila
FYJKA — Fysiokjemikeren
FyL — Filosofia y Letras
Fysiatr Reumatol Vestn — Fysiatricky a Reumatologicky Vestnik
Fysiatr Vestn — Fysiatricky Vestnik
Fys Tidsskr — Fysisk Tidsskrift
FYTIA — Fysisk Tidsskrift [*Denmark*]
FYVDA — Fra Fysikkens Verden
Fyz Cas — Fyzikalny Casopis
FzB — Forschung zur Bibel [*Wuerzburg*]
FzG — Forschungsberichte zur Germanistik [*Osaka-Kobe*]
FZKAA — Fizika [*Zagreb*]
FZKSA — Fizika [*Zagreb*]. Supplement
FZLZA — Fiziologicheskii Zhurnal SSSR Imeni I. M. Sechenova

FZNPA — Fiziologia Normala si Patologica
FZPT — Freiburger Zeitschrift fuer Philosophie und Theologie
FZRSA — Fiziologiya na Rasteniyata [*Sofia*]
FZUKA — Fiziologichnii Zhurnal (Kiev)

G

G — Germano-Slavica
G — Gids
G — Guardian
GA — Gazette Archeologique
GA — Geistige Arbeit
GA — Geografiska Annaler
GA — Geographical Abstracts
GA — Geographischer Anzeiger
GA — Geotechnical Abstracts
GA — Germanistische Abhandlungen
GA — Germanistische Arbeitshefte
GA — Glos Anglii
GA — Graphic Arts Monthly
GAA — Gene Amplification and Analysis Series [*Elsevier Book Series*]
GAA — Graphic Arts Abstracts
GAA — Skrifter Utgivna av Kungliga. Gustav Adolfs Akademien
GAABA — Gas Abstracts
GAAC — Gastroenterology. Abstracts and Citations
GAAGA — Gas Age
GA Ag Coll — Georgia State College of Agriculture. Publications
GA Ag Exp — Georgia. Agricultural Experiment Station. Publications
GA Agric Exp Stn Annu Rep — Georgia. Agricultural Experiment Station. Annual Report
GA Agric Exp Stn Bienn Rep — Georgia. Agricultural Experiment Stations. Biennial Report
GA Agric Exp Stn Bull — Georgia. Agricultural Experiment Station. Bulletin
GA Agric Exp Stn Circ — Georgia. Agricultural Experiment Station. Circular
GA Agric Exp Stn Field Crops Variety Trials — Georgia. Agricultural Experiment Stations. Field Crops Variety Trials
GA Agric Exp Stn Leafl — Georgia. Agricultural Experiment Station. Leaflet
GA Agric Exp Stn Mimeogr Ser — Georgia. Agricultural Experiment Station. Mimeograph Series
GA Agric Exp Stn Res Bull — Georgia. Agricultural Experiment Station. Research Bulletin
GA Agric Exp Stn Res Rep — Georgia. Agricultural Experiment Station. Research Report
GA Agric Exp Stn Tech Bull — Georgia. Agricultural Experiment Station. Technical Bulletin
GA Agric Res — Georgia Agricultural Research
GA Agric Res GA Exp Stn — Georgia Agricultural Research. Georgia Experiment Stations
GA Agr Res — Georgia Agricultural Research. University of Georgia
GAB — Geoppinger Akademische Beitraege
GAB — Gifts and Decorative Accessories
GA Bar J — Georgia Bar Journal
GA B J — Georgia Bar Journal
GA Bus — Georgia Business
GAC — Government Accountants Journal
Gac AVDA — Gaceta de AVDA
G Accad Med Torino — Giornale. Accademia di Medicina di Torino
Gac Colmen — Gaceta del Colmenar
Gaceta Mat I — Gaceta Matematica. Primera Serie [*Madrid*]
Gac Farm — Gaceta Farmaceutica
Gac Mat (Madrid) — Gaceta Matematica (Madrid)
Gac Med Caracas — Gaceta Medica de Caracas

Gac Med Catalana — Gaceta Medica Catalana
Gac Med (Guayaquil) — Gaceta Medica (Guayaquil) Ecuador
Gac Med Mex — Gaceta Medica de Mexico
Gac Med Norte Bilbao — Gaceta Medica del Norte Bilbao
Gac Med Urug — Gaceta Medica del Uruguay
Gac Med Zool — Gaceta de Medicina Zoologica
Gac Num — Gaceta Numismatica
GACOD — Graefe's Archive for Clinical and Experimental Ophthalmology
Gac San Mil — Gaceta de Sanidad Militar
GACTD2 — Glossary of Acarological Terminology/Glossaire de la Terminologie Acarologique
Gac Vet (B Aires) — Gaceta Veterinaria (Buenos Aires)
GA Dep Mines Min Geol Geol Surv Bull — Georgia. Department of Mines, Mining, and Geology. Geological Survey. Bulletin
GA Dep Mines Min Geol Geol Surv Circ — Georgia. Department of Mines, Mining, and Geology. Geological Survey. Circular
GA Dep Mines Mining Geol Geol Surv Bull — Georgia. Department of Mines, Mining, and Geology. Geological Survey. Bulletin
GA Dep Nat Resour Geol Water Resour Div Inf Circ — Georgia. Department of Natural Resources. Geologic and Water Resources Division. Information Circular
GAENA — Gas Engineer
GA Engineer — Georgia Engineer
GAf — Geneve-Afrique
GA For Res Counc Annu Rep — Georgia. Forest Research Council. Annual Report
GA For Res Counc Rep — Georgia. Forest Research Council. Report
GA For Res Pap — Georgia Forest Research. Paper
GAG — Goeppinger Arbeiten zur Germanistik
GAGE — Gerontology and Geriatrics Education
GAGEA — Gakujutsu Geppo
GA Geol Surv Bull — Georgia. Geological Survey. Bulletin
GA Geol Surv Circ — Georgia. Geological Survey. Circular
GA Geol Water Resour Div Inf Circ — Georgia. Geologic and Water Resources Division. Information Circular
G Agr — Giornale di Agricoltura
G Agr Domen — Giornale di Agricoltura Domenica
GA GSB — Georgia. Geological Survey. Bulletin
GAHAD — Genshiryoku Anzen Hakusho
GAHEDG — Geologische Abhandlungen Hessen
GAHGAJ — Geografiska Annaler. Series B. Human Geography
GA His Q — Georgia Historical Quarterly
GA His S — Georgia Historical Society
GA Hist Quart — Georgia Historical Quarterly
GA Hist Soc Coll — Georgia Historical Society. Collections
GAHQ — Georgia Historical Quarterly
GAI — Gli Archivi Italiani
GAIGD — Genshiryoku Anzen Iinkai Geppo
GA Inst Technol Eng Exp Sta Bull — Georgia Institute of Technology. Engineering Experiment Station. Bulletin
GA Inst Technol Eng Exp Stn Rep — Georgia Institute of Technology. Engineering Experiment Station. Report
GA Inst Technol Eng Exp Stn Repr — Georgia Institute of Technology. Engineering Experiment Station. Reprints

GA Inst Technol Eng Exp Stn Spec Rep — Georgia Institute of Technology. Engineering Experiment Station. Special Reports
GA Inst Technol Environ Resour Cent ERC (Rep) — Georgia Institute of Technology. Environmental Resources Center. ERC (Report)
GA Inst Technol Ser Nucl Eng — Georgia Institute of Technology. Series in Nuclear Engineering
GaiS — Lo Gai Saber [*Toulouse*]
GAJ — General-Anzeiger fuer die Gesamten Interessen des Judentums [*Berlin*]
GA J Int & Comp L — Georgia Journal of International and Comparative Law
GA J Internat and Comparative Law — Georgia Journal of International and Comparative Law
GA J Int'l & Comp L — Georgia Journal of International and Comparative Law
GA J Sci — Georgia Journal of Science
GAKS — Gesammelte Aufsaetze zur Kulturgeschichte Spaniens
Gakujutsu Hokoku Bull Fac Agric Kagoshima Univ — Gakujutsu Hokoku. Bulletin. Faculty of Agriculture. Kagoshima University
Gakujutsu Hokoku Bull Utsunomiya Univ — Gakujutsu Hokoku. Bulletin of the College of Agriculture. Utsunomiya University
Gakujutsu Hokoku Tokushu Spec Bull — Gakujutsu Hokoku Tokushu. Special Bulletin
Gakujutsu Kenkyu Hokoku Res Bull Obihiro Univ — Gakujutsu Kenkyu Hokoku. Research Bulletin. Obihiro University
Gakujutsu Kenkyu Hokoku Res Rep Kochi Univ Nogaku — Gakujutsu Kenkyu Hokoku. Research Reports. Kochi University Nogaku
GAL — Galaxy
GA L — Georgia Law Review
GA Law R — Georgia Law Review
GAlb — Gjurmime Albanologijike
Gali — Galileo
GA Libn — Georgia Librarian
GA Librn — Georgia Librarian
Galicia Clin — Galicia Clinica
Galleon — Galleon. Bulletin of the Society for Colonial History
Gallerie Grandi Opere Sotter — Gallerie e Grandi Opere Sotterranee
G Allevatori — Giornale degli Allevatori [*Italy*]
Gallup Rep — Gallup Report
Gallup Rept — Gallup Report
Gallup Rpt — Gallup Report
GALPBX — Geologie Alpine
Galpin S J — Galpin Society. Journal
Galpin Soc — Galpin Society. Journal
Galpin Soc J — Galpin Society. Journal
GA LR — Georgia Law Review
GA L Rev — Georgia Law Review
GALVA — Galvano [*France*]
Galvano Tec — Galvano Tecnica [*Later, Galvanotecnica & Processi al Plasma*]
Galvanotec Processi Plasma — Galvanotecnica e Processi al Plasma
Gam — Gambit
GAM — Gamma
Game Conservancy Annu Rev — Game Conservancy Annual Review
Game Res Assoc Annu Rep — Game Research Association. Annual Report
Gamete Res — Gamete Research [*United States*]
GA Mineral Newsletter — Georgia Mineral Newsletter
Gamma Field Symp — Gamma Field Symposia
Ganita — Ganita Bharat Ganita Parisad [*Lucknow*]
GANMA — Gann Monograph
Gann — Gann Japanese Journal of Cancer Research
Gann Monogr — Gann Monograph
Gannon Coll Chem J — Gannon College. Chemistry Journal
GA Nurse — Georgia Nursing
GAO (Gen Accounting Office) R — GAO (General Accounting Office) Review
GA Oper — Georgia Operator
GAO Rev — GAO [*General Accounting Office*] Review
GAP — GAP [*Group for the Advancement of Psychiatry*] Report
GAR — Galling Report on Italy
GA R — Georgia Review
GARAD — Gastrointestinal Radiology
GArb — Geistige Arbeit
Garcia de Orta (Lisb) — Garcia de Orta (Lisbon)
Garcia de Orta Ser Bot — Garcia de Orta. Serie de Botanica [*Lisbon*]
Garcia de Orta Ser Estud Agron — Garcia de Orta. Serie de Estudos Agronomicos [*Lisbon*]
Garcia de Orta Ser Zool — Garcia de Orta. Serie de Zoologia [*Lisbon*]
Gard Abstr — Gardener's Abstracts
Gard Bull (Singapore) — Gardens Bulletin (Singapore)
Gard Chron Am — Gardeners' Chronicle of America
Gard Chron (Lond) — Gardeners' Chronicle (London)
Gard Digest — Garden Digest
Garden & F — Garden and Forest
Garden Is — Garden Island
Gard & Home B — Garden and Home Builder
Gard J — Garden Journal
Gard J NY Bot Gard — Garden Journal. New York Botanical Garden
Gard M — Garden Magazine

GARIA7 — Ghana. Animal Research Institute. Annual Report
GARP Publ Ser — GARP [*Global Atmospheric Research Programme*] Publications Series
Gartenbauwiss — Gartenbauwissenschaft
Garten u Kleintierz C (Imker) — Garten und Kleintierzucht. C (Imker)
G Arteriosclr — Giornale della Arteriosclerosi
Gart Landschaft Landscape Archit Plann — Garten Landschaft. Landscape Architecture Planning
GAS — Gas. Maandblad voor de Gasindustrie
GAS — German-American Studies
GASAA — Gazzetta Sanitaria
Gas Abstr — Gas Abstracts
Gas Age Rec Nat Gas — Gas Age Record and Natural Gas
GA SBJ — Georgia State Bar Journal
Gas Chromat Abstr — Gas Chromatography Abstracts
Gas Chromatogr Int Sym — Gas Chromatography. International Symposium
Gas Chromatogr Proc Int Symp (Eur) — Gas Chromatography. Proceedings of the International Symposium (Europe)
GA Sch Technol State Eng Exp Stn Repr — Georgia. School of Technology. State Engineering Experiment Station. Reprint
Gas Counc (Gt Brit) Res Commun — Gas Council (Great Britain) Research Communications
Gas Dig — Gas Digest
Gas Eng — Gas Engineer [*England*]
Gas Engine Manage — Gas Engineering and Management
Gas Eng Manage — Gas Engineering and Management
Gas Engng Mgmt — Gas Engineering and Management
Gas Engng Mgmt — Gas Engineering and Management
Gaseous Air Pollut Plant Metab Proc Int Symp — Gaseous Air Pollutants and Plant Metabolism. Proceedings. International Symposium on Gaseous Air Pollutants and Plant Metabolism
Gaseous Dielectr Proc Int Symp — Gaseous Dielectrics. Proceedings. International Symposium on Gaseous Dielectrics
Gases Res Ind — Gases in Research and Industry
Gases Res Ind Gas Div CIG — Gases in Research and Industry. Commonwealth Industrial Gases Ltd.
GASGB — Gasgemeinschaft
GASHD — Gazo Shindan
Gas Ind — Gas Industries
Gas Ind (Leipzig) — Gas Industrie (Leipzig)
Gas Ind (London) — Gas Industry (London)
Gas Ind Manuf Gas Ed — Gas Industry. Manufactured Gas Edition
Gas Ind Nat Gas Ed — Gas Industry. Natural Gas Edition
Gas Inst News — Gas Institute News
Gas J — Gas Journal
G As (London) Pr — Geologists' Association (London). Proceedings
Gas Mag — Gas Magazine [*United States*]
Gas Oil Pwr — Gas and Oil Power
GASPBY — Geological Association of Canada. Special Paper
Gas (Phila) — Gas (Philadelphia)
Gas Process Assoc Proc — Gas Processors Association. Proceedings
Gas Res Inst Dig — Gas Research Institute Digest
Gas Supply Rev — Gas Supply Review
GA St BJ — Georgia State Bar Journal
Gastroenterol — Gastroenterologia
Gastroenterol Abstr & Cit — Gastroenterology. Abstracts and Citations
Gastroenterol Clin Biol — Gastroenterologie Clinique et Biologique
Gastroenterol Jpn — Gastroenterologia Japonica
Gastroenty — Gastroenterology
Gastroin En — Gastrointestinal Endoscopy
Gastrointest Endosc — Gastrointestinal Endoscopy
Gastrointest Radiol — Gastrointestinal Radiology
Gas Turbine Int — Gas Turbine International
Gas Waerme Int — Gas Waerme International
Gas Wld — Gas World
Gas World Gas J — Gas World and Gas Journal
Gas Z Ration Energieanwend — Gas. Zeitschrift fuer Rationelle Energieanwendung [*West Germany*]
GATF Bull — GATF [*Graphic Arts Technical Foundation*] Bulletin
GATF Envir Control Rept — GATF [*Graphic Arts Technical Foundation*] Environmental Control Report
GATF Res Progr — GATF [*Graphic Arts Technical Foundation*] Research Progress
GATF Res Prog Rep — GATF [*Graphic Arts Technical Foundation*] Research Progress Report
GATF Tech Serv Inform — GATF [*Graphic Arts Technical Foundation*] Technical Service Information
GATN (German-Am Trade News) — GATN (German-American Trade News)
Gatooma Res Stn Annu Rep — Gatooma Research Station. Annual Report
GAUSD — Gasohol USA
Gauss Ges (Goettingen) Mitt — Gauss Gesellschaft eV. (Goettingen). Mitteilungen
Gav — Gavroche
GAVEA — Galpin Society. Journal
Gavel — Milwaukee Bar Association. Gavel

GA Vet — Georgia Veterinarian
GA Water Qual Control Board Tech Rep — Georgia. Water Quality Control Board. Technical Report
Gay — Gay Liberation
Gayana Bot — Gayana Botanica
Gayana Bot Misc — Gayana Botanica Miscelanea
Gayana Misc — Gayana Miscelanea
Gayana Zool — Gayana Zoologia
Gay Insrg — Gay Insurgent
Gay L — Gay Literature
Gay News — Gay Community News
Gay Sun — Gay Sunshine
Gaz Agr (Angola) — Gazeta do Agricultor (Angola)
Gaz Apic — Gazette Apicole
Gaz Arch — Gazette Archeologique
Gaz Aujourd — Gaz d'Aujourd'hui
Gaz Bea-Art — Gazette des Beaux-Arts
Gaz Beaux-Arts — Gazette des Beaux-Arts
Gaz Chim It — Gazzetta Chimica Italiana
Gaz Chim Ital — Gazzetta Chimica Italiana
Gaz Clin — Gazeta Clinica
Gaz Clin (S Paulo) — Gazeta Clinica (Sao Paulo)
Gaz Com — Gazzetta Commerciale
Gaz Cukrow — Gazeta Cukrownicza
Gazdasag es Jogtud — Gazdasag es Jogtudomany
Gaz Egypt Paediatr Assoc — Gazette. Egyptian Paediatric Association
Gaz Egypt Soc Gynaecol Obstet — Gazette. Egyptian Society of Gynaecology and Obstetrics
Gazeta Agric Angola — Gazeta Agricola de Angola
Gazeta Cukrown — Gazeta Cukrownicza
Gazette — Law Society. Gazette
Gazette — Rhode Island Foreign Language Gazette
Gazette Univ WA — Gazette. University of Western Australia
Gaz Fis — Gazeta di Fisica
Gaz Hebd Sc Med Bordeaux — Gazette Hebdomadaire des Sciences Medicales de Bordeaux
Gaz Hop Civ Mil — Gazette des Hopitaux Civils et Militaires
Gaz India — Gazette India
Gaz Inst Med Lab Sci — Gazette. Institute of Medical Laboratory Science
Gaz Kasr El Aini Fac Med — Gazette. Kasr El Aini Faculty of Medicine
Gaz Mat — Gazeta de Matematica
Gaz Mat Mat Inform — Gazeta Matematica Perfectionare Metodica si Metodologica in Matematica si Informatica
Gaz Mat Publ Lunara pentru Tineret — Gazeta Matematica Publicatie Lunara pentru Tineret
Gaz Mat Ser A — Societatea de Stiinte Matematice din RPR. Gazeta Matematica Publicatie pentru Studiul si Raspindirea Stiintelor Matematice. Seria A
Gaz Med — Gazettes Medicales
Gaz Med Algerie — Gazette Medicale de l'Algerie
Gaz Med Bahia — Gazeta Medica da Bahia
Gaz Med Fr — Gazette Medicale de France
Gaz Med Nantes — Gazette Medicale de Nantes
Gaz Med Orient — Gazette Medicale d'Orient
Gaz Med Paris — Gazette Medicale de Paris
Gaz Med Picardie — Gazette Medicale de Picardie
Gaz Med Port — Gazeta Medica Portuguesa
Gaz Mus — Gazeta Musical e de Todas las Artes
Gaz Num — Gazzettino Numismatico
Gazov Delo — Gazovoe Delo [*USSR*]
Gazov Khromatogr — Gazovaya Khromatografiya [*USSR*]
Gazov Promst — Gazovaya Promyshlennost
Gaz Pharm — Gazeta da Pharmacia
Gaz Trav — Gazette du Travail
Gaz Univ Newcastle — Gazette. University of Newcastle
Gaz Univ Syd — Gazette. University of Sydney
Gaz Univ WA — Gazette. University of Western Australia
Gaz Univ Wits — Gazette. University of the Witwatersrand
Gaz WA Inst Tech — Gazette: Official Journal of the Western Australian Institute of Technology
Gaz Woda Tech Sanit — Gaz Woda i Technika Sanitarna
Gazz Chim Ital — Gazzetta Chimica Italiana
Gazz Clin Sped Civ Palermo — Gazzetta Clinica dello Spedale Civico di Palermo
Gazz Internaz Med — Gazzetta Internazionale di Medicina
Gazz Int Med Chir — Gazzetta Internazionale di Medicina e Chirurgia [*Italy*]
Gazz Med Ital — Gazzetta Medica Italiana
Gazz Med Ital Arch Sci Med — Gazzetta Medica Italiana. Archivio per le Scienze Mediche
Gazz Med Ital Prov Venete — Gazzetta Medica Italiana. Provincie Venete
Gazz Med Sicil — Gazzetta Medica Siciliana [*Italy*]
Gazz Osp Milano — Gazzetta degli Ospitali Milano
Gazz Sanit Edn Francaise — Gazzetta Sanitaria. Edition Francaise
Gazz Sanit (Engl Issue) — Gazzetta Sanitaria (English Issue)
Gazz Sicil Med e Chir — Gazzetta Siciliana di Medicina e Chirurgia d'Igiene e d'Interessi Professionali

Gazz Uff Repub Ital — Gazzetta Ufficiale della Repubblica Italiana
GB — Geschiedkundige Bladen
Gb — Gildeboek
GB — Grazer Beitraege
GBA — Gazette des Beaux-Arts
GB Aeronaut Res Counc Curr Pap — Great Britain. Aeronautical Research Council. Current Papers
G Batteriol Immunol — Giornale di Batteriologia e Immunologia
G Batteriol Virol Immunol — Giornale di Batteriologia, Virologia, ed Immunologia
G Batteriol Virol Immunol Ann Osp Maria Vittoria Torino — Giornale di Batteriologia, Virologia, ed Immunologia. Annali dell' Ospedale Maria Vittoria di Torino
GB Dep Health Soc Secur Rep Public Health Med Subj — Great Britain. Department of Health and Social Security. Reports on Public Health and Medical Subjects
GB Dep Sci Ind Res Chem Res Spec Rep — Great Britain. Department of Scientific and Industrial Research. Chemical Research. Special Report
GB Dep Sci Ind Res Food Invest Board Spec Rep — Great Britain. Department of Scientific and Industrial Research. Food Investigation Board. Special Report
GB Dep Sci Ind Res Food Invest Tech Pap — Great Britain. Department of Scientific and Industrial Research. Food Investigation Board. Technical Paper
GB Dep Sci Ind Res For Prod Res Bull — Great Britain. Department of Scientific and Industrial Research. Forest Products Research Bulletin
GB Dep Sci Ind Res For Prod Res Spec Rep — Great Britain. Department of Scientific and Industrial Research. Forest Products Research Special Report
GB Dep Sci Ind Res Fuel Res — Great Britain. Department of Scientific and Industrial Research. Fuel Research. Publication
GB Dep Sci Ind Res Fuel Res Surv Pap — Great Britain. Department of Scientific and Industrial Research. Fuel Research. Survey Paper
GB Dep Sci Ind Res Fuel Res Tech Pap — Great Britain. Department of Scientific and Industrial Research. Fuel Research. Technical Paper
GB Dep Sci Ind Res Natl Build Stud Res Pap — Great Britain. Department of Scientific and Industrial Research. National Building Studies Research Paper
GB Dep Sci Ind Res Overseas Tech Rep — Great Britain. Department of Scientific and Industrial Research. Overseas Technical Report
GB Dep Sci Ind Res Road Note — Great Britain. Department of Scientific and Industrial Research. Road Note
GB Dep Sci Ind Res Road Res Lab Rep RRL — Great Britain. Department of Scientific and Industrial Research. Road Research Laboratory. Report RRL
GB Dep Sci Ind Res Torry Res Stn Annu Rep — Great Britain. Department of Scientific and Industrial Research. Torry Research Station. Annual Report
GB Dep Sci Ind Res Torry Tech Pap — Great Britain. Department of Scientific and Industrial Research. Torry Technical Paper
GB Dep Trade Ind Warren Spring Lab Rev — Great Britain. Department of Trade and Industry. Warren Spring Laboratory. Review
GB Digest — GB Digest (Girls' Brigade)
GBDP — Giessener Beitraege zur Deutschen Philologie
GBE — Great Britain and the East
GB For Comm Annu Rep For Comm — Great Britain Forestry Commission. Annual Report of the Forestry Commissioners
GB For Comm Bookl — Great Britain Forestry Commission. Booklet
GB For Comm Bull — Great Britain Forestry Commission. Bulletin
GB For Comm For Rec — Great Britain Forestry Commission. Forest Record
GB For Comm Leafl — Great Britain Forestry Commission. Leaflet
GB For Comm Rep For Res — Great Britain Forestry Commission. Report on Forest Research
GB For Comm Res Dev Pap — Great Britain Forestry Commission. Research and Development Paper
GB For Prod Res Board Bull — Great Britain. Forest Products Research Board. Bulletin
GB For Prod Res Bull — Great Britain. Forest Products Research Bulletin
GB For Prod Res Spec Rep — Great Britain. Forest Products Research Special Report
GB Inst Geol Sci Annu Rep — Great Britain. Institute of Geological Sciences. Annual Report
GB Inst Geol Sci Geomagn Bull — Great Britain. Institute of Geological Sciences. Geomagnetic Bulletin
GB Inst Geol Sci Miner Assess Rep — Great Britain. Institute of Geological Sciences. Mineral Assessment Report
GB Inst Geol Sci Miner Resour Consult Comm Miner Dossier — Great Britain. Institute of Geological Sciences. Mineral Resources Consultative Committee. Mineral Dossier
GB Inst Geol Sci Overseas Mem — Great Britain. Institute of Geological Sciences. Overseas Memoir
GB Inst Geol Sci Rep — Great Britain. Institute of Geological Sciences. Report
G Biochim — Giornale de Biochimica
G Biol Ind Agrar Aliment — Giornale di Biologia Industriale Agraria ed Alimentare
G Biol Med Sper — Giornale di Biologia e Medicina Sperimentale

GBISAX — Godisnik Bioloskog Instituta Univerziteta u Sarajevu
GBJ — Georgia Bar Journal
GBKG — Gentsche Bijdragen tot de Kunstgeschiedenis
GBKMA — Gesellschaft zur Bekampfung der Krebskrankheiten im Nordrhein-Westfalen. Mitteilungsdienst
GBL — Brandstoffen Visie. Vakblad voor de Mandel in Aardolieprodukten en Vaste Brandstoffen
GB Land Resour Div Land Resour Study — Great Britain. Land Resources Division. Land Resource Study
GBM — Gelre. Bijdragen en Mededeelingen
GBM — Golden Book Magazine
GB Minist Agric Fish Food Bull — Great Britain. Ministry of Agriculture, Fisheries, and Food. Bulletin
GB Minist Agric Fish Food Dir Fish Res Lab Leafl — Great Britain. Ministry of Agriculture, Fisheries, and Food. Directorate of Fisheries Research. Laboratory Leaflet
GB Minist Agric Fish Food Tech Bull — Great Britain. Ministry of Agriculture, Fisheries, and Food. Technical Bulletin
GB Minist Aviat Aeronaut Res Counc Curr Pap — Great Britain. Ministry of Aviation. Aeronautic Research Council. Current Papers
GB Minist Overseas Dev Land Resour Div Land Resour Bibliogr — Great Britain. Ministry of Overseas Development. Land Resources Division. Land Resource Bibliography
GB Minist Overseas Dev Land Resour Div Prog Rep — Great Britain. Ministry of Overseas Development. Land Resources Division. Progress Report
GB Minist Power Saf Mines Res Establ Res Rep — Great Britain. Ministry of Power. Safety in Mines Research Establishment. Research Report
GB Ministry Agric Fish Food Fish Lab Leafl New Ser — Great Britain. Ministry of Agriculture, Fisheries, and Food. Fisheries Laboratory Leaflet. New Series
GB Minist Technol For Prod Res Bull — Great Britain. Ministry of Technology. Forest Products Research. Bulletin
GB Minist Technol For Prod Res Spec Rep — Great Britain. Ministry of Technology. Forest Products Research. Special Report
GB Nat Build Stud Res Pap — Great Britain. National Building Studies. Research Paper
GB Nat Build Stud Tech Pap — Great Britain. National Building Studies. Technical Paper
GB Nat Environ Res Counc News J — Great Britain. Natural Environment Research Council. News Journal
GB Nat Environ Res Counc Rep — Great Britain. Natural Environment Research Council. Report
GBNBA7 — Geologische Blaetter fuer Nordost-Bayern und Angrenzende Gebiete
GBOIA — Giornale Botanico Italiano
GBOSBU — Geobios [*Jodhpur*]
G Bot Ital — Giornale Botanico Italiano
GB Pest Infest Res Board Rep — Great Britain. Pest Infestation Research Board. Report
GBPUA6 — Geological Bulletin. Punjab University
GBQMAL — Genie Biologique et Medical
GBR — Gemengde Branche. Vakblad voor de Huishoudelijke en Luxe Artikelen, Glas, Porselein, Aardewerk, en Kunstnijverheid
GB R Aircr Establ Tech Rep — Great Britain. Royal Aircraft Establishment. Technical Report
GB Road Res Lab Road Note — Great Britain. Road Research Laboratory. Road Note
GB Road Res Lab Road Tech Pap — Great Britain. Road Research Laboratory. Road Research Technical Paper
GBRP — Giessener Beitraege zur Romanischen Philologie
GBS — Glasgow Bibliographical Society
G & BS — Greek and Byzantine Studies
GB Soil Surv Engl Wales Annu Rep — Great Britain. Soil Survey of England and Wales. Annual Report
GB Soil Surv Spec Surv — Great Britain. Soil Survey. Special Survey
GBVID — Giornale di Batteriologia, Virologia, ed Immunologia
GB Warren Spring Lab Rep — Great Britain. Warren Spring Laboratory. Report
GB Warren Spring Lab Rev — Great Britain. Warren Spring Laboratory. Review
GB Water Resour Board Publ — Great Britain Water Resource Board. Publication
GBZUA — Gidrobiologicheskii Zhurnal
GBZUAM — Gidrobiologicheskii Zhurnal
GC — Graphic Communications Weekly
GCACAK — Geochimica et Cosmochimica Acta
GCAJS — Gratz College. Annual of Jewish Studies
GCASD — Geochimica et Cosmochimica Acta. Supplement
GCB — Gas. Zeitschrift fuer Rationelle Energieanwendung
GCBI — Godisnjak Centra za Balkanoloska Ispitivanja
GCCA Newsletter — GCCA [*Graduate Careers Council of Australia*] Newsletter
GCFI — Giornale Critico della Filosofia Italiana
GCGGA — Gulf Coast Association of Geological Societies. Field Trip Guidebook
G Chim Appl — Giornale di Chimica Applicata

G Chim Ind — Giornale di Chimica Industriale
G Chim Ind Appl — Giornale di Chimica Industriale ed Applicata
G Clin Med — Giornale de Clinica Medica
G Clin Med (Bologna) — Giornale di Clinica Medica (Bologna)
GCN — Gay Community News
GCN — Government Computer News
GCNA — Guild of Carillonneurs in North America. Bulletin
GCNED — Government Computer News
GCOS — Great Canadian Sands News
GCQBD — Geo-Heat Center. Quarterly Bulletin
GCR — German Canadian Review
G Crit Filosof Ital — Giornale Critico della Filosofia Italiana
GCRRAE — Glasshouse Crops Research Institute. Annual Report
GCS — Die Griechische Christliche Schriftsteller der Ersten Drei Jahrhunderte
GCW — Graphic Communications Weekly
GCWOD — Graphic Communications World
GD — Giornale Dantesco
GD — Global Digest
GDAJA — Journal. Georgia Dental Association
Gdansk Tow Nauk Rozpr Wydz — Gdanskie Towarzystwo Naukowe Rozparawy Wydzialu [*Poland*]
GdB — Giornale di Bordo. Mensile di Storia, Letteratura, ed Arte
GdD — Gegenwart der Dichtung
GDDTD — Gesetzblatt der Deutschen Demokratischen Republik. Teil 1
GdG — Grundlagen der Germanistik
Gd House — Good Housekeeping
GdI — Giornale d'Italia
GDIKAN — Gifu Daigaku Igakubu Kiyo
GdiM — Giornale di Metafisica
GDKKD2 — Annual Report. Faculty of Education. Gunma University. Art, Technology, Health, and Physical Education and Science of Human Living Series
GDKTA — Genshi Doryoku Kenkyukai Teirei Kenkyukai Nenkai Hokokusho
GDKYA7 — Annual Report. Faculty of Education. Gunma University. Art and Technology Series
GDM — Gads Danske Magasin
GdM — Gazzetta del Mezzogiorno
Gdng Ill — Gardening Illustrated
Gdn J NY Bot Gdn — Garden Journal. New York Botanical Garden
Gdns Bull — Gardens Bulletin
Gdns Bull (Singapore) — Gardens Bulletin (Singapore)
GDROA — Gidroaeromekhanika
GDS — Going Down Swinging
GDS — Overheidsdocumentatie. Orgaan voor Documentatie en Administratieve Organisatie der Overheid
Gd Times — Good Times
GDVMA — Gidravlicheskie Mashiny
GDWDA — Glaciological Data. World Data Center A
GDWDCA — Glaciological Data. World Data Center A
Ge — Gegenwart
GE — Giornale degli Economisti e Annali di Economia
GEAEA — Geomagnetizm i Aeronomiya
GEARA — Georgia Agricultural Research
GEASA — Geofizika i Astronomiya Informatsionnyi Byulleten
GEB — Chefmagazin fuer Kleinbetriebe und Mittelbetriebe
GEBAAX — Geologica Bavarica
GEBAD2 — Geologica Balcanica
Gebrauchs — Gebrauchsgraphik
Gebrauchs Novum — Gebrauchsgraphik Novum
GEBSAJ — Geobios [*Lyon*]
Geburtsh Fr — Geburtshilfe und Frauenheilkunde
Geburtshilfe Frauenheilkd — Geburtshilfe und Frauenheilkunde
Geburtshilfe Fraunheilkd — Geburtshilfe und Frauenheilkunde
GEC At Energy Rev — GEC [*General Electric Company*] Atomic Energy Review
GECHB — Geochemistry [*Nagoya*]
GECHD — Geochronique
GEC J — GEC [*General Electric Company*] Journal
GEC J Sci & Technol — GEC [*General Electric Company*] Journal of Science and Technology
G Economisti — Giornale degli Economisti e Annali di Economia
GEC Telecommun — GEC [*General Electric Company*] Telecommunications
GEDEAL — Gesundheitswesen und Desinfektion
GEDED — General Dentistry
GEDID2 — Gerbil Digest
GEDMAB — Geoderma
Gedrag T P — Gedrag-Tijdschrift voor Psychologie
GEFO — Geoforum
GEFR — George Eliot Fellowship Review
GEG — Geluid en Omgeving
Gegenbaurs Morphol Jahrb — Gegenbaurs Morphologisches Jahrbuch
Geg G S Erz — Gegenwartskunde Gesellschaft Staat Erziehung
GEGIA — Geneeskundige Gids
GEHAD — Gekkan Haikibutsu
GEHEA7 — Gentes Herbarum
GEHIA — Gencho Hiroshima Igaku

GEINA — Gesundheits-Ingenieur
GEIRD — Gendai Iryo
GeistLeb — Geist und Leben [*Wuerzburg*]
GEJAA — Geologisches Jahrbuch
GEJAA5 — Geologisches Jahrbuch
GEJBA8 — Geologisches Jahrbuch. Beihefte
GEJO — Geographical Journal
GEJOBE — Geochemical Journal
GEJODG — Geomicrobiology Journal
GEKYA — Gensen-Kyo
Gel and Glue Res Assoc — Gelatin and Glue Research Association
GeM — Geographical Magazine
GEMA — Geographical Magazine
Gematol Pereliv Krovi — Gematologiya i Perelivanie Krovi
Gematol Pereliv Krovi Resp Mezhved Sb — Gematologiya i Perelivanie Krovi Respublikanskoi Mezhvedomstvennyi Sbornik
GEMBAN — Getreide Mehl und Brot
GEMEE2 — Genitourinary Medicine
Gemeinsames Amtsbl A — Gemeinsames Amtsblatt. Ausgabe A [*West Germany*]
Gemeinsames Amtsbl Landes Baden-Wuerttemb A — Gemeinsames Amtsblatt des Landes Baden-Wuerttemberg. Ausgabe A
Gemeinsames Ministerialbl A — Gemeinsames Ministerialblatt A
GEMGA4 — Geological Magazine
GEMIA — Geologie en Mijnbouw
GEMIAA — Geologie en Mijnbouw
Gemmol Soc Jap J — Gemmological Society of Japan Journal
Gems Gemol — Gems and Gemology. Gemological Institute of America
Gem State News Lett — Gem State News Letter
GEN — GEN. Government Equipment News
Gen — Genava
Gen Arm — Generals of the Army and the Air Force and Admirals of the Navy
Gen C Endoc — General and Comparative Endocrinology
Gen Comp Endocr — General and Comparative Endocrinology
Gen Comp Endocrinol — General and Comparative Endocrinology
Gen Comp Endocrinol Suppl — General and Comparative Endocrinology. Supplement
Gen Cytochem Methods — General Cytochemical Methods
Gen Dent — General Dentistry
GENEA3 — Genetica [*The Hague*]
GENEAL MAG — Genealogical Magazine
Genealog Mag — Genealogists' Magazine
Geneal Per Ind — Genealogical Periodical. Annual Index
Geneesk Courant — Geneeskundige Courant voor het Koningrijk der Nederlanden
Geneeskd — Geneeskunde
Geneeskd Gids — Geneeskundige Gids
Geneeskd Sport — Geneeskunde en Sport
Geneesk Tijdschr Nederl-Indiee — Geneeskundig Tijdschrift voor Nederlandsch-Indiee
Geneesk Tijdschr Ned Indie — Geneeskundig Tijdschrift voor Nederlandsch-Indie
Gen Elec R — General Electrical Review
Gen Electr Co Ltd J Sci Technol — General Electric Company Limited. Journal of Science and Technology
Gen Electr Rev — General Electric Review
Gen Eng — General Engineer [*United Kingdom*]
Gen Eng Trans — General Engineering Transactions [*Australia*]
General Ed — General Education
General Topology and Appl — General Topology and Its Applications
Genet — Genetics
Genet Abstr — Genetics Abstracts
Genet Agr — Genetica Agraria
Genet Agrar — Genetica Agraria
Genet Biokhim Immunokhim Osobo Opasnykh Infekts — Genetika Biokhimiya i Immunokhimiya Osobo Opasnykh Infektsii
Genet Biokhim Immunokhim Osobo Opasnykh Infektsii — Genetika Biokhimiya i Immunokhimiya Osobo Opasnykh Infektsii
Genet Biol Drosophila — Genetics and Biology of Drosophila
Genet Iber — Genetica Iberica
Genetics Suppl — Genetics. Supplement [*United States*]
Genet Lect — Genetics Lectures
Genet Physiol Note Inst Paper Chem — Genetics and Physiology Notes. Institute of Paper Chemistry
Genet Physiol Notes — Genetics and Physiology Notes
Genet Plant Breed — Genetics and Plant Breeding
Genet Pol — Genetica Polonica
Genet Psych — Genetic Psychology Monographs
Genet Psychol Monog — Genetic Psychology Monographs
Genet Psychol Monogr — Genetic Psychology Monographs
Genet Res — Genetical Research
Genet Sel — Genetika i Selektsiya
Genet Sel Azerb — Genetika i Selektsiia v Azerbaidzhan
Genet Selektsiya — Genetika i Selektsiya
Genet Sel Genet Plant Breed — Genetika i Selektsiia. Genetics and Plant Breeding

Genet Sinica — Genetica Sinica [*Peking*]
Genet Slechteni — Genetika a Slechteni
Geneve-Afr — Geneve-Afrique
Gen Fish Counc Mediterr Sess Rep — General Fisheries Council for the Mediterranean. Session Report
GENGA — Geologiya Nefti i Gaza
Gen Heterocycl Chem Ser — General Heterocyclic Chemistry Series
Gen Hosp Psychiatry — General Hospital Psychiatry
Genie Biol Med — Genie Biologique et Medical
Genie Chim — Genie Chimique [*France*]
Genie Civ — Genie Civil
Genie Ind — Genie Industrial [*France*]
Gen Linguis — General Linguistics
Gen M As Que J — General Mining Association of the Province of Quebec. Journal
Gen Mot Corp Res Lab Res Publ — General Motors Corporation. Research Laboratories. Research Publication
Gen Mot Eng J — General Motors Engineering Journal [*United States*]
Gen Newsl Natl Res Counc (Can) Div Mech Eng — General Newsletter. National Research Council (Canada). Division of Mechanical Engineering
Gen Pharm — General Pharmacology
Gen Pharmacol — General Pharmacology
Gen Pract Clin — General Practice Clinics
Gen Practnr (Lond) — General Practitioner (London)
GENRA8 — Genetical Research
GENRB — Genie Rural
Gen Relat G — General Relativity and Gravitation
Gen Relativ and Gravitation — General Relativity and Gravitation
Gen Relativ Gravitation — General Relativity and Gravitation
Gen Relativity Gravitation — General Relativity and Gravitation
Gen Rep Dep Archit Sci Syd Univ — General Report. Department of Architectural Science. University of Sydney
Gen Rep Minist Mines Prov Que — General Report. Minister of Mines. Province of Quebec
Gen Repos — General Repository
GENSA — Journal. Georgia Entomological Society
Gen Sci Q — General Science Quarterly
Gen Ser Colo State Agr Exp Sta — General Series. Colorado State University. Agricultural Experiment Station
Gen Syst — General Systems
Gen Syst — General Systems Bulletin
GENTAE — Genetics
Gen Tech Rep FPL US Dep Agric For Serv For Prod Lab — General Technical Report FPL. United States Department of Agriculture. Forest Service. Forest Products Laboratory
Gen Tech Rep FPL US For Prod Lab (Madison Wis) — General Technical Report FPL. United States. Forest Products Laboratory (Madison, Wisconsin)
Gen Tech Rep RM Rocky Mt For Range Exp Stn US For Serv — General Technical Report. RM. Rocky Mountain Forest and Range Experiment Station. United States Forest Service
Gentes Herb — Gentes Herbarum
Gent Herb — Gentes Herbarum
Gent M — Gentleman's Magazine
Gent M ns — Gentleman's Magazine. New Series
Geo — Georgetown Law Journal
Ge O — Graecolatina et Orientalia
GeoAb — Geographical Abstracts
Geo Abstr — Geographical Abstracts
Geo Abstr E Sedimentology — Geo Abstracts. E. Sedimentology
Geo Abstr G Remote Sensing Photogram Cartogr — Geo Abstracts. G. Remote Sensing, Photogrammetry, and Cartography
GEOBD2 — Geobotany
Geobot Inst Rubel Veroeff — Geobotanisches Institut Rubel Veroeffentlichungen
GEOCD — Geochimica [*English Translation*]
Geoch Cos A — Geochimica et Cosmochimica Acta
Geochem Int — Geochemistry International
Geochem J — Geochemical Journal
Geochem J (Geochem Soc Jap) — Geochemical Journal (Geochemical Society of Japan)
Geochem J (Nagoya) — Geochemical Journal (Nagoya)
Geochem J (Tokyo) — Geochemical Journal (Tokyo)
Geochem News — Geochemical News
Geochem Soc India Bull — Geochemical Society of India. Bulletin
Geochim Cosmochim Acta — Geochimica et Cosmochimica Acta
Geochim Cosmochim Acta Suppl — Geochimica et Cosmochimica Acta. Supplement
Geod Aerophotogr (USSR) — Geodesy and Aerophotography [*Later, Geodesy, Mapping, and Photogrammetry*] (USSR)
Geodaet Inst Medd — Geodaetisk Institut. Meddelelse
Geod Darb — Geodezijos Darbai [*Lithuanian SSR*]
Geodes Mapp Photogramm — Geodesy, Mapping, and Photogrammetry
Geod Inst (Den) Medd — Geodaetisk Institut (Denmark). Meddelelse
Geod Inst Medd — Geodaetisk Institut. Meddelelse

Geod Inst Skr — Geodaetisk Institut. Skrifter
Geod Kartogr — Geodezia es Kartografia
Geod Kartogr — Geodeziya i Kartografiya
Geod Kartogr Aerofotos — Geodeziia, Kartografiia, i Aerofotos'emka [*Ukrainian SSR*]
Geod Kartogr (Budap) — Geodezia es Kartografia (Budapest)
Geod Kartogr Obzor — Geodeticky a Kartograficky Obzor
Geod Mapp Photogramm — Geodesy, Mapping, and Photogrammetry
Geod Mapp Photogramm Engl Transl — Geodesy, Mapping, and Photogrammetry. English Translation
Geod Soc Jap J — Geodetic Society of Japan. Journal
Geoexplor — Geoexploration
Geoexplor Monogr — Geoexploration Monographs
GEOF — Geoforum
Geofis Int — Geofisica International
Geofis Meteorol — Geofisica e Meteorologia
Geofis Pura Appl — Geofisica Pura e Applicata [*Italy*]
Geofiz App — Geofizicheskaya Apparatura [*USSR*]
Geofiz Appar — Geofizicheskaya Apparatura
Geofiz Astron Inf Byull — Geofizika i Astronomiya Informatsionnyi Byulleten [*Ukrainian SSR*]
Geofiz Byull — Geofizicheskii Byulleten [*USSR*]
Geofiz Geol Naft — Geofizyka i Geologia Naftowa [*Poland*]
Geofiz Issled — Geofizicheskie Issledovaniya
Geofiz Issled Reshenii Geol Zadach Vost Sib — Geofizicheskie Issledovaniya pri Reshenii Geologicheskikh Zadach v Vostochnoi Sibri
Geofiz Koeslemenyek — Geofizikae Koslemenyek
Geofiz Kozl — Geofizikai Kozlemenyek
Geofiz Metody Razved Arkt — Geofizicheskie Metody Razvedki v Arktike
Geofiz Priborostr — Geofizicheskoe Priborostroenie
Geofiz Razved — Geofizicheskaya Razvedka
Geofiz Sb Akad Nauk Ukr SSR Inst Geofiz — Geofizicheskii Sbornik. Akademiya Nauk Ukrainskoi SSR. Institut Geofiziki [*Ukrainian SSR*]
Geofiz Sb (Kiev) — Geofizicheskii Sbornik (Kiev) [*Ukrainian SSR*]
Geofiz Sb (Sverdlovsk) — Geofizicheskii Sbornik (Sverdlovsk)
Geofiz Zh — Geofizicheskii Zhurnal [*Ukrainian SSR*]
Geof Publ — Geofysiske Publikasjoner
Geofys Publ — Geofysiske Publikasjoner
Geofys Sb — Geofysikalni Sbornik
Geog Annaler — Geografiska Annaler
Geog Bul — Geographical Bulletin
Geog Gesell Hamburg Mitt — Geographische Gesellschaft in Hamburg. Mitteilungen
Geog Ges Muenchen Jber — Geographische Gesellschaft in Muenchen. Jahresbericht
Geog J — Geographical Journal
Geog Jnl — Geographical Journal
Geog M — Geographical Magazine
Geog Mag — Geographical Magazine
Geog Map Div Bull — Geography and Map Division Bulletin [*Special Libraries Association*]
Geog Phys et Quat — Geographie Physique et Quaternaire
Geogr — Geographia
Geogr — Geographica
Geog R — Geographical Review
Geogr — Geography
Geogr A — Geografiska Annaler
Geogr Anal — Geographical Analysis
Geogr Ann — Geografiska Annaler
Geogr Ann B — Geografiska Annaler. Series B. Human Geography
Geogr Annlr — Geografiska Annaler
Geogr Ann Ser B Hum Geogr — Geografiska Annaler. Series B. Human Geography
Geogr B — Geographical Bulletin
Geogr Ber — Geographische Berichte
Geogr Can — Geographe Canadien
Geogr Cas — Geografiske Casopis
Geog Rdsch — Geographische Rundschau
Geogr Educ — Geographical Education
Geog Rev — Geographical Review
Geogr Ezheg Geogr Ova Lit SSR — Geografiya Ezhegodnogo Geograficheskogo Obshchestva Litovskoi SSR
Geogr Geol Meded Physiogr Geol Reeks Geogr Inst (Utrecht) — Geographische en Geologische Mededelingen, Physiographisch Geologische Reeks, Geographisch Instituut (Utrecht)
Geogr Ges Hamb Mitt — Geographische Gesellschaft in Hamburg. Mitteilungen
Geogr Glas — Geografski Glasnik
Geogr Glasn — Geografski Glasnik
Geogr Helv — Geographica Helvetica
Geog R Ind — Geographical Review of India
Geogr Inf — Geographische Informationen
Geogr J — Geographical Journal
Geogr Jb — Geographisches Jahrbuch
Geogr Jber Oesterr — Geographischer Jahresbericht aus Oesterreich
Geogr J (Lond) — Geographical Journal (London)

Geogr Journ — Geographical Journal
Geogr Knowl (Peking) — Geographical Knowledge (Peking)
Geogrl Abstr — Geographical Abstracts
Geogrl J — Geographical Journal
Geogrl Rev — Geographical Review
Geogr Mag (Lond) — Geographical Magazine (London)
Geogr Med — Geographia Medica
Geogr Metrastis — Geografinis Metrastis
Geogr Ovo SSSR Dokl — Geograficheskoe Obshchestvo SSSR Doklady
Geogr Pol — Geographia Polonica
Geogr Pregl — Geografski Pregled
Geogr R — Geographical Review
Geogr Raka Turkm — Geografiya Raka v Turkmenii
Geogr Rdsch — Geographische Rundschau
Geogr Rev — Geographical Review
Geogr Rev Jap — Geographical Review of Japan
Geogr Rev (New York) — Geographical Review (New York)
Geogr RI — Geographical Review of India
Geogr Rundsch — Geographische Rundschau
Geogr Sb — Geograficeskij Sbornik
Geogr Sb Penz Otd Geogr O-va SSSR — Geograficheskii Sbornik Penzenskogo Otdeleniya Geograficheskogo Obshchestva SSSR
Geogr Shk — Geografiya v Shkole [*USSR*]
Geogr Stud — Geographical Studies
Geogr TB — Geographisches Taschenbuch
Geogr Teach — Geography Teacher
Geogr Tjds — Geografisch Tijdschrift
Geog Rund — Geographische Rundschau
Geogr Vestn — Geografski Vestnik
Geogr Z — Geographische Zeitschrift
Geog Soc Chicago B — Geographic Society of Chicago. Bulletin
Geog Soc Phila — Geographical Society of Philadelphia. Bulletin
Geog Soc Phila B — Geographical Society of Philadelphia. Bulletin
Geog Tidsskr — Geografisk Tidsskrift
Geog Z — Geographische Zeitschrift
GEOHAH — Geologi [*Helsinki*]
Geo Heat Cent Q Bull — Geo-Heat Center. Quarterly Bulletin [*United States*]
Geo-Heat Util Center Q Bull — Geo-Heat Utilization Center. Quarterly Bulletin
Geo-Heat Util Cent Q Bull — Geo-Heat Utilization Center. Quarterly Bulletin [*United States*]
GEOIM — Geodaetisk Institut. Meddelelse
GEOIS — Geodaetisk Institut. Skrifter
Geo J — Geo Journal
GEOJA — Geophysical Journal. Royal Astronomical Society
GEOJDQ — Geojournal
Geokhim — Geokhimiya
Geokhim Akad Nauk SSSR — Geokhimiya Akademiya Nauk SSSR
Geokhim Issled — Geokhimicheskie Issledovaniya
Geokhim Metody Poiskakh Razved Rudn Mestorozhd — Geokhimicheskie Metody pri Poiskakh i Razvedke Rudnykh Mestorozhdenii
Geokhim Metody Poiskov Nefti Gaza — Geokhimicheskie Metody Poiskov. Nefti i Gaza
Geokhim Rudoobraz — Geokhimiya i Rudoobrazovanie
Geokhim Sb — Geokhimicheskii Sbornik
GeoL — Geographica (Lisbon)
Geol — Geologie
Geol — Geologija
Geol Alp — Geologie Alpine
Geol Anagoriseis Ekthesis — Geologikai Anagnoriseis Ekthesis
Geol An Balk Poluostrva — Geolshki Anali Balkanskoga Poluostrva
Geol Appl Idrogeol — Geologia Applicata e Idrogeologia
Geol Appl Prospect Miniere — Geologie Appliquee et Prospection Miniere
Geol Assoc Canada Proc — Geological Association of Canada. Proceedings
Geol Assoc Can Cordilleran Sect Programme Abstr — Geological Association of Canada. Cordilleran Section. Programme and Abstracts
Geol Assoc Can Spec Pap — Geological Association of Canada. Special Paper
Geol Assoc (Lond) Proc — Geologists' Association (London). Proceedings
Geol Atlas PA — Geologic Atlas of Pennsylvania
GEOLB — Geologues
Geol Balc — Geologica Balcanica
Geol Balc (Sofia) — Geologica Balcanica. Bulgarska Akademiya ne Naukite (Sofia)
Geol Bauwes — Geologie und Bauwesen
Geol Bav — Geologica Bavarica
Geol Bavarica — Geologica Bavarica
Geol Beih — Geologie. Beihefte
Geol Bl — Geologische Blaetter fuer Nordost-Bayern und Angrenzende Gebiete
Geol Bl Nordost-Bayern — Geologische Blaetter fuer Nordost-Bayern und Angrenzende Gebiete
Geol Bl Nordost-Bayern Angrenzende Geb — Geologische Blaetter fuer Nordost-Bayern und Angrenzende Gebiete
Geol Bull Natl Geol Surv China — Geological Bulletin. National Geological Survey of China [*People's Republic of China*]
Geol Bull Punjab Univ — Geological Bulletin. Punjab University

Geol Bull Soc Belge Geol — Geologie. Bulletin de la Societe Belge de Geologie
Geol Bull Univ Peshawar — Geological Bulletin. University of Peshawar
Geol Center Research Ser — Geological Center. Research Series
Geol Colomb — Geologia Colombiana
Geol Explor Min BC — Geology. Exploration and Mining in British Columbia
Geol Foeren St Foerh — Geologiska Foereningens i Stockholm. Foerhandlingar
Geol Foeren Stockh Foerh — Geologiska Foereningens i Stockholm. Foerhandlingar
Geol Foer Stockh Foerh — Geologiska Foereningens i Stockholm. Foerhandlingar
Geol Foren Stockh Forh — Geologiska Foereningens i Stockholm. Foerhandlingar
Geol Fr — Geologie de la France
Geol i Geofiz — Geologiya i Geofizika
Geol Geofiz — Geologiya i Geofizika
Geol Geokhim — Geologiya i Geokhimiya
Geol Geokhim Goryuch Iskop — Geologiya i Geokhimiya Goryuchikh Iskopaemykh [*Ukrainian SSR*]
Geol Geokhim Goryuch Iskop Akad Nauk Ukr SSR — Geologiya i Geokhimiya Goryuchikh Iskopaemykh Akademiya Nauk Ukrainskoy SSR
Geol Geokhim Goryuch Kopalin Akad Nauk Ukr RSR — Geologiya i Geokhimiya Goryuchikh Kopalin Akademiya Nauk Ukrain'skoi RSR
Geol Geokhim Mestorozhd Tverd Goryuch Iskop — Geologiya i Geokhimiya Mestorozhdenii Tverdykh Goryuchikh Iskopaemykh
Geol Geokhim Neft Gazov Mestorozhd — Geologiya i Geokhimiya Neftyanskh i Gazovykh Mestorozhdenii
Geol Glas — Geoloski Glasnik [*Yugoslavia*]
Geol Glas Posebna Izd — Geoloski Glasnik. Posebna Izdanja
Geol Glas (Titograd Yugosl) — Geoloski Glasnik (Titograd, Yugoslavia)
Geol Hung — Geologica Hungarica
Geol Hung Ser Palaeontol — Geologica Hungarica. Series Palaeontologica
Geol Invest Ser Geol Surv Pak Interim Geol Rep — Geological Investigation Series. Geological Survey of Pakistan. Interim Geological Report
Geol Izuch SSR — Geologicheskaya Izuchennost SSR
Geol J — Geological Journal
Geo LJ — Georgetown Law Journal
Geol Jahrb — Geologisches Jahrbuch
Geol Jahrb Beih — Geologisches Jahrbuch. Beihefte
Geol Jahrb Hessen — Geologisches Jahrbuch Hessen
Geol Jahrb Reihe A — Geologisches Jahrbuch. Reihe A. Allgemeine und Regionale Geologie BR Deutschland und Nachbargebiete, Tektonik, Stratigraphie, Palaeontologie
Geol Jahrb Reihe B — Geologisches Jahrbuch. Reihe B. Regionale Geologie Ausland
Geol Jahrb Reihe C — Geologisches Jahrbuch. Reihe C. Hydrogeologie, Ingenieurgeologie [*West Germany*]
Geol Jahrb Reihe D — Geologisches Jahrbuch. Reihe D. Mineralogie, Petrographie, Geochemie, Lagerstaettenkunde
Geol Jahrb Reihe E — Geologisches Jahrbuch. Reihe E. Geophysik [*West Germany*]
Geol Jahrb Reihe E Geophys — Geologisches Jahrbuch. Reihe E. Geophysik
Geol Jahrb Reihe F Bodenk — Geologisches Jahrbuch. Reihe F. Bodenkunde
Geol Jb — Geologisches Jahrbuch
Geol J (Liverpool) — Geological Journal (Liverpool)
Geol J Queen Mary Coll — Geological Journal of Queen Mary College
Geol Lit SSSR Bibliogr Yezhegodnik — Geologicheskaya Literatura SSSR Bibliograficheskiy Yezhegodnik
Geol M — Geological Magazine
Geol Mag — Geological Magazine
Geol Mediter — Geologie Mediterraneenne
Geol Mem Geol Surv China Ser A — Geological Memoirs. Geological Survey of China. Series A
Geol Mem Geol Surv China Ser B — Geological Memoirs. Geological Survey of China. Series B
Geol Mestorozhd Redk Elem — Geologiya Mestorozhdenii Redkikh Elementov
Geol Metal — Geologia y Metalurgia [*Bolivia*]
Geol Metal Bol — Geologia e Metalurgia. Boletim
Geol Metal (San Luis Potosi) — Geologia y Metalurgia (San Luis Potosi)
Geol Metal (Sao Paulo) — Geologia e Metalurgia (Sao Paulo)
Geol Met Bol — Geologia e Metalurgia. Boletim. Escola Politecnica. Universidade de Sao Paulo
Geol Metod Tekh Razved Lab Rab — Geologiya. Metodika i Tekhnika Razvedki. Laboratornye Raboty
Geol Mjnb — Geologie en Mijnbouw
Geol Mijnbouw — Geologie en Mijnbouw
Geol Mineral — Geologiya i Mineralogiya
Geol Min Metall Soc India Q J — Geological, Mining, and Metallurgical Society of India. Quarterly Journal
Geol Min Metall Soc Liberia Bull — Geological, Mining, and Metallurgical Society of Liberia. Bulletin
Geol Min Met Soc Liberia Bull — Geological, Mining, and Metallurgical Society of Liberia. Bulletin
Geol Mitt — Geologische Mitteilungen
Geol Morya — Geologiya Morya
Geol Nefti — Geologiya Nefti
Geol Nefti i Gaza — Geologiya Nefti i Gaza

Geol Nefti Gaza — Geologiya Nefti i Gaza
Geol Nefti Gaza Sev Vostoka Evr Chasti SSSR — Geologiya Nefti i Gaza Severo-Vostoka Evropeiskoi Chasti SSSR
Geologie Mijnb — Geologie en Mijnbouw
Geologists' Assoc (London) Proc — Geologists' Association (London). Proceedings
Geology Club Puerto Rico Bull — Geology Club of Puerto Rico. Bulletin
Geol Palaeontol — Geologica et Palaeontologica
Geol Palaeontol Southeast Asia — Geology and Palaeontology of Southeast Asia
Geol Pap Carleton Univ Dep Geol — Geological Paper. Carleton University. Department of Geology
Geol Poberezh'ya Dna Chern Azovskogo Morei Predelakh Ukr SSR — Geologiya Poberezh'ya i Dna Chernogo i Azovskogo Morei v Predelakh Ukrainskoi SSR
Geol Poiski Razved Nerudn Polezn Iskop — Geologiya, Poiski, i Razvedka Nerudnykh Poleznykh Iskopaemykh
Geol Polezn Iskop Urala — Geologiya i Poleznye Iskopaemye Urala
Geol Polezn Iskop Zapadn Kaz — Geologiya i Poleznye Iskopaemye Zapadnogo Kazakhstana
Geol Pr — Geologicke Prace
Geol Prace Zpr — Geologicke Prace. Zpravy
Geol Pr (Bratisl) — Geologicke Prace (Bratislava)
Geol Pr Spravy — Geologicke Prace. Spravy
Geol Pruzkum — Geologicky Pruzkum
Geol Razved Gazov Gazokondens Mestorozhd — Geologiya i Razvedka Gazovykh i Gazokondensatnykh Mestorozhdenii
Geol Rep Dep Nat Resour (Queb) — Geological Reports. Department of Natural Resources (Quebec)
Geol Rep Hiroshima Univ — Geological Report. Hiroshima University
Geol Rep Shimane Univ — Geological Reports. Shimane University
Geol Rom — Geologica Romana
Geol Roman — Geologica Romana
Geol Rud Mestorozhd — Geologiya Rudnykh Mestorozhdenii
Geol Rudn Mestorozhd — Geologiya Rudnykh Mestorozhdenii
Geol Rudonosn Yuga Ukr — Geologiya i Rudonosnost Yuga Ukrainy
Geol Rundsch — Geologische Rundschau
Geol Rundschau — Geologische Rundschau
Geol S Am B — Geological Society of America. Bulletin
Geol Sb (Lvov) — Geologicheskii Sbornik (Lvov)
Geol Sbornik — Geologicheskii Sbornik
Geol Sb (Tiflis) — Geologicheskii Sbornik (Tiflis)
Geol Sb Vses Inst Nauchno Tekhnol Inf — Geologicheskii Sbornik Vsesoyuznogo Instituta Nauchno Tekhnologicheskoi Informatsii
Geol Sect Bull Libya Minist Ind — Geological Section. Bulletin. Libya Ministry of Industry
Geol Soc Am Abstr Programs — Geological Society of America. Abstracts with Programs
Geol Soc Am Annu Meet Field Trip Guideb — Geological Society of America. Annual Meeting. Field Trip Guidebook
Geol Soc Am Bull — Geological Society of America. Bulletin
Geol Soc Am Cordilleran Sect Annu Meet Guideb — Geological Society of America. Cordilleran Section. Annual Meeting Guidebook
Geol Soc Amer Bull — Geological Society of America. Bulletin
Geol Soc Amer Eng Geol Case Hist — Geological Society of America. Engineering Geology Case Histories
Geol Soc America Abs with Programs — Geological Society of America. Abstracts with Programs
Geol Soc America Spec Paper — Geological Society of America. Special Papers
Geol Soc Amer Mem — Geological Society of America. Memoir
Geol Soc Amer Spec Pap — Geological Society of America. Special Paper
Geol Soc Am Map Chart Ser — Geological Society of America. Map and Chart Series
Geol Soc Am Mem — Geological Society of America. Memoir
Geol Soc Am Microform Publ — Geological Society of America. Microform Publication
Geol Soc Am Proc — Geological Society of America. Proceedings
Geol Soc Am Southeast Sect Guideb — Geological Society of America. Southeastern Section Guidebook
Geol Soc Am Spec Pap — Geological Society of America. Special Paper
Geol Soc Am Spec Pap (Reg Stud) — Geological Society of America. Special Paper (Regional Studies)
Geol Soc Australia J — Geological Society of Australia. Journal
Geol Soc Bull — Geological Society of America. Bulletin
Geol Soc China Proc — Geological Society of China. Proceedings
Geol Soc Egypt Annu Meet Abstr — Geological Society of Egypt. Annual Meeting. Abstracts
Geol Soc Finl Bull — Geological Society of Finland. Bulletin
Geol Soc Greece Bull — Geological Society of Greece. Bulletin
Geol Soc India Bull — Geological Society of India. Bulletin
Geol Soc India J — Geological Society of India. Journal
Geol Soc India Jour — Geological Society of India. Journal
Geol Soc India Mem — Geological Society of India. Memoir
Geol Soc Iraq J — Geological Society of Iraq. Journal
Geol Soc Jam J — Geological Society of Jamaica. Journal
Geol Soc Jap J — Geological Society of Japan. Journal

Geol Soc Korea J — Geological Society of Korea. Journal
Geol Soc Lond J — Geological Society of London. Journal
Geol Soc Lond Misc Pap — Geological Society of London. Miscellaneous Paper
Geol Soc London Mem — Geological Society of London. Memoirs
Geol Soc Lond Q J — Geological Society of London. Quarterly Journal
Geol Soc Lond Spec Rep — Geological Society of London. Special Report
Geol Soc Malays Bull — Geological Society of Malaysia. Bulletin
Geol Soc Malays Newsl — Geological Society of Malaysia. Newsletter
Geol Soc NJ Rept — Geological Society of New Jersey. Report
Geol Soc Norfolk Bull — Geological Society of Norfolk. Bulletin
Geol Soc Oregon Country News Letter — Geological Society of the Oregon Country. News Letter
Geol Soc Philipp J — Geological Society of the Philippines. Journal
Geol Soc Proc — Geological Society of America. Proceedings
Geol Soc S Afr Congr Abstr — Geological Society of South Africa. Congress Abstracts
Geol Soc S Afr Q News Bull — Geological Society of South Africa. Quarterly News Bulletin
Geol Soc S Afr Spec Publ — Geological Society of South Africa. Special Publication
Geol Soc So Africa Trans — Geological Society of South Africa. Transactions and Proceedings
Geol Soc Zimbabwe Spec Publ — Geological Society of Zimbabwe. Special Publication
Geol SSSR — Geologiya SSSR
Geol Str Poleznye Iskop Kalmytskoi ASSR — Geologicheskoe Stroenie i Poleznye Iskopaemye Kalmytskoi ASSR
Geol Sudetica (Warsaw) — Geologia Sudetica (Warsaw)
Geol Surv Br Guiana Bull — Geological Survey of British Guiana. Bulletin
Geol Surv Bull Tasmania — Tasmania. Geological Survey. Bulletin
Geol Surv Can Bull — Geological Survey of Canada. Bulletin
Geol Surv Can Econ Geol Rep — Geological Survey of Canada. Economic Geology Report
Geol Surv Can Mem — Geological Survey of Canada. Memoir
Geol Surv Can Pap — Geological Survey of Canada. Paper
Geol Surv Ceylon Mem — Geological Survey of Ceylon. Memoir
Geol Surv Den III Ser — Geological Survey of Denmark. III Series
Geol Surv Den II Ser — Geological Survey of Denmark. II Series
Geol Surv Den Rep — Geological Survey of Denmark. Report
Geol Surv Den Yearb — Geological Survey of Denmark. Yearbook
Geol Surv Dep (Jam) Bull — Geological Survey Department (Jamaica). Bulletin
Geol Surv Dep (Jam West Indies) Occas Pap — Geological Survey Department (Jamaica, West Indies). Occasional Paper
Geol Surv Finl Bull — Geological Survey of Finland. Bulletin
Geol Surv GA Bull — Geological Survey of Georgia. Bulletin
Geol Surv GB Mem Geol Surv (Scotl) — Geological Survey of Great Britain. Memoirs of the Geological Survey (Scotland)
Geol Surv Greenland Rep — Geological Survey of Greenland. Report
Geol Surv Guyana Bull — Geological Survey of Guyana. Bulletin
Geol Surv India Misc Publ — Geological Survey of India. Miscellaneous Publication
Geol Surv India News — Geological Survey of India. News
Geol Surv Iran Rep — Geological Survey of Iran. Report
Geol Surv Isr Bull — Geological Survey of Israel. Bulletin
Geol Surv Jap Hydrogeol Maps Jap — Geological Survey of Japan. Hydrogeological Maps of Japan
Geol Surv Jap Rep — Geological Survey of Japan. Report
Geol Surv Jpn Rep — Geological Survey of Japan. Report
Geol Surv Kenya Rep — Geological Survey of Kenya. Report
Geol Surv Korea Tech Pap — Geological Survey of Korea. Technical Paper
Geol Surv Malays Dist Mem — Geological Survey of Malaysia. District Memoir
Geol Surv Nigeria Bull — Geological Survey of Nigeria. Bulletin
Geol Surv NSW Bull — Geological Survey of New South Wales. Bulletin
Geol Surv NSW Bull — New South Wales. Geological Survey. Bulletin
Geol Surv NSW Geol Surv Rep — Geological Survey of New South Wales. Geological Survey Report
Geol Surv of NSW Miner Ind NSW — Geological Survey of New South Wales. Department of Mines. The Mineral Industry of New South Wales
Geol Surv NSW Miner Ind NSW — New South Wales. Geological Survey. Mineral Industry of New South Wales
Geol Surv NSW Rep — Geological Survey of New South Wales. Geological Survey Report
Geol Surv NSW Rep — New South Wales. Geological Survey. Report
Geol Surv Pap Tas Dep Mines — Geological Survey Paper. Department of Mines. Tasmania
Geol Surv Queensl Pub — Geological Survey of Queensland. Publication
Geol Surv Queensl Publ — Geological Survey of Queensland. Publication
Geol Surv Queensl Rep — Geological Survey of Queensland. Report
Geol Surv Uganda Rep — Geological Survey of Uganda. Report
Geol Surv Victoria Bull — Geological Survey of Victoria. Bulletin
Geol Surv Victoria Bull — Victoria. Geological Survey. Bulletin
Geol Surv Victoria Mem — Geological Survey of Victoria. Memoir
Geol Surv W Aust Bull — Geological Survey of Western Australia. Bulletin
Geol Surv West Aust Bull — Western Australia. Geological Survey. Bulletin

Geol Surv West Malaysia Dist Mem — Geological Survey of West Malaysia. District Memoir
Geol Surv Wyo Bull — Geological Survey of Wyoming. Bulletin
Geol Surv Wyo C Resour Ser — Geological Survey of Wyoming. County Resource Series
Geol Surv Wyo Mem — Geological Survey of Wyoming. Memoir
Geol Surv Wyo Prelim Rep — Geological Survey of Wyoming. Preliminary Report
Geol Surv Wyo Rep Invest — Geological Survey of Wyoming. Report of Investigations
Geol Tec — Geologia Tecnica
Geol Tutkimuslaitos Geotek Julk — Geologinen Tutkimuslaitos. Geoteknillisia Julkaisuja
Geol Ultriectina — Geologica Ultriectina
Geol Ver S-Afr Kwart Nuusbull — Geologiese Vereniging van Suid-Afrika. Kwartaallikse Nuusbulletin
Geol Vjesn (Zagreb) — Geoloski Vjesnik (Zagreb)
Geol Zakaspiya — Geologiya Zakaspiya
Geol Zb — Geologicky Zbornik
Geol Zb Geol Carpathica — Geologicky Zbornik - Geologica Carpathica
Geol Zb Slov Akad Vied — Geologicky Zbornik - Geologica Carpathica. Slovenska Akademia Vied
Geol Zh (Russ Ed) — Geologicheskii Zhurnal (Russian Edition)
Geol Zh (Ukr Ed) — Geologichnii Zhurnal (Ukrainian Edition)
GEOMA — Geophysical Magazine [*Tokyo*]
Geomag Aer — Geomagnetizm i Aeronomiya
Geomagn and Aeron — Geomagnetism and Aeronomy (English Translation)
Geomagn Aeron — Geomagnetizm i Aeronomiya
Geomagn Aeron (USSR) — Geomagnetism and Aeronomy (USSR)
Geomagn Bull Inst Geol Sci — Geomagnetic Bulletin. Institute of Geological Sciences
Geomagn Ser Earth Phys Branch — Geomagnetic Series. Earth Physics Branch
Geo Mason UL Rev — George Mason University. Law Review
GEOMD — Geomimet
Geom Dedicata — Geometriae Dedicata
Geomech Comput Progm — Geomechanics Computing Programme
Geomorph Abstr — Geomorphological Abstracts
GEOPA7 — Geologicke Prace [*Bratislava*]
Geophys — Geophysics
Geophys Abstr — Geophysical Abstracts
Geophys Arb Mitt Meteorol Astrophys — Geophysikalische Arbeiten sowie Mitteilungen aus Meteorologie und Astrophysik
Geophys and Astrophys Fluid Dyn — Geophysical and Astrophysical Fluid Dynamics
Geophys Astrophys Fluid Dyn — Geophysical and Astrophysical Fluid Dynamics
Geophys Astrophys Monogr — Geophysics and Astrophysics Monographs
Geophys Case Histories — Geophysical Case Histories
Geophys Fluid Dyn — Geophysical Fluid Dynamics
Geophys Geol — Geophysik und Geologie
Geophys Inst Fac Sci Tokyo Univ Geophys Notes Suppl — Geophysical Institute. Faculty of Science. Tokyo University. Geophysical Notes. Supplement
Geophys J — Geophysical Journal
Geophys Jour — Geophysical Journal
Geophys J R — Geophysical Journal. Royal Astronomical Society
Geophys J R Astronom Soc — Geophysical Journal. Royal Astronomical Society
Geophys J R Astron Soc — Geophysical Journal. Royal Astronomical Society
Geophys J R Astr Soc — Geophysical Journal. Royal Astronomical Society
Geophys Mag — Geophysical Magazine
Geophys Mag (Tokyo) — Geophysical Magazine (Tokyo)
Geophys Mem (Lond) — Geophysical Memoirs (London)
Geophys Monogr — Geophysical Monograph
Geophys Monogr Am Geophys Union — Geophysical Monograph. American Geophysical Union
Geophys Norv — Geophysica Norvegica
Geophys Note (Tokyo) — Geophysical Note (Tokyo)
Geophys Prospect — Geophysical Prospecting
Geophys Prospect — Geophysical Prospecting
Geophys Prospect (The Hague) — Geophysical Prospecting (The Hague)
Geophys R B — Geophysical Research Bulletin
Geophys Res Bull — Geophysical Research Bulletin
Geophys Res Lett — Geophysical Research Letters
Geophys Res Pap — Geophysical Research Papers
Geophys R L — Geophysical Research Letters
Geophys Soc Tulsa Proc — Geophysical Society of Tulsa. Proceedings
Geophys Space Data Bull — Geophysics and Space Data Bulletin
Geophys Surv — Geophysical Surveys
GEOQ — Geos. Canada Department of Energy, Mines, and Resources
GeoR — Geographical Review
Geo R — Georgia Review
GEORAD — Geographical Review
Geo Rev — Georgia Law Review
Georget Law — Georgetown Law Journal

Georget LJ — Georgetown Law Journal
Georgetown Dent J — Georgetown Dental Journal
Georgetown Law J — Georgetown Law Journal
Georgetown LJ — Georgetown Law Journal
Georgetown Med Bull — Georgetown Medical Bulletin
George Wash — George Washington Law Review
George Washington J Internat Law and Econ — George Washington Journal of International Law and Economics
George Washington Law R — George Washington Law Review
George Washington Univ Bull — George Washington University. Bulletin
George Wash L Rev — George Washington Law Review
Georgia BJ — Georgia Bar Journal
Georgia J Int Comp L — Georgia Journal of International and Comparative Law
Georgia L Rev — Georgia Law Review
Georgia R — Georgia Review
Georgia St BJ — Georgia State Bar Journal
Georgikon Delt — Georgikon Deltion
Georgr et Rech — Geographie et Recherche
GEOS — Geoscope
Geosci Can — Geoscience Canada
Geosci Doc — Geoscience Documentation
Geoscience Abs — Geoscience Abstracts
Geoscience Inf Soc Proc — Geoscience Information Society. Proceedings
Geosci Man — Geoscience and Man
Geosci Stud — Geoscience Studies [*Japan*]
Geostand Newsl — Geostandards Newsletter
GEOTA — Geotimes
GEOTAJ — Geotimes
Geotech Abstr — Geotechnical Abstracts
Geotech Eng — Geotechnical Engineering
Geotechniq — Geotechnique
Geotech Test J — Geotechnical Testing Journal
Geotecton — Geotectonics
Geotek Julk — Geoteknillisia Julkaisuja
Geoteknisk Inst Bull — Geoteknisk Institut. Bulletin
Geotekton — Geotektonika
Geotekton Forsch — Geotektonische Forschungen
Geotektonika Tektonofiz Geodinamika — Geotektonika, Tektonofizika, i Geodinamika
Geotektonische Forsch — Geotektonische Forschungen
Geotherm — Geothermics
Geotherm Energy — Geothermal Energy
Geotherm Energy Mag — Geothermal Energy Magazine
Geotherm Energy Update — Geothermal Energy Update
Geotherm Hot Line — Geothermal Hot Line
Geotherm Rep — Geothermal Report
Geotherm Resour Counc Spec Rep — Geothermal Resources Council. Special Report
Geotherm Resour Counc Trans — Geothermal Resources Council. Transactions [*People's Republic of China*]
Geotherm Technol — Geothermal Technology [*Japan*]
Geo Wash J Int L — George Washington Journal of International Law and Economics
Geo Wash J Intl L and Econ — George Washington Journal of International Law and Economics
Geo Wash L Rev — George Washington Law Review
GEP — Graduate English Papers
GEPACDE — Geographical Paper. Canada Department of Environment
GEPCA — GP. Journal of the American Academy of General Practice
GEPGA — Gepgyartastechnologia [*Hungary*]
GeR — Gengogaku Ronso
GER — German Economic Review
Ger — Germania
Ger — Germanistik
Gerbil Dig — Gerbil Digest
Ger Bundesanst Bodenforsch Geol Jahrb Beih — Germany. Bundesanstalt fuer Bodenforschung und Geologische Landesaemter. Geologisches Jahrbuch. Beiheft
Ger Chem Eng — German Chemical Engineering
Ger Chem Engng — German Chemical Engineering
Gercke Norden — Gercke und Norden. Einleitung in die Altertumswissenschaft
GEREA — General Electric Review
Ger Ec Bul — Economic Bulletin (Germany)
Ger Econ Re — German Economic Review
GERED — Geothermal Report
GerefTTS — Gereformeerd Theologisch Tijdschrift [*Kampen*]
Gerfaut Rev Sci Belge Ornithol — Gerfaut. Revue Scientifique Belge d'Ornithologie
GERIA — Geriatrics
Geriatric Nurs — Geriatric Nursing
Geriatr Nurs — Geriatric Nursing
GERIAZ — Geriatrics
Gerlands Beitr Geophys — Gerlands Beitraege zur Geophysik
Ger Life L — German Life and Letters
Ger Life Lett — German Life and Letters

Ger L & L — German Life and Letters
German Econ R — German Economic Review
German Int — German International
German Internat — German International
German Q — German Quarterly
German TN — German American Trade News
GERMD — German Mining
Ger Med — German Medicine
Ger Med Mon — German Medical Monthly
GermL — Germanistische Linguistik
Germ R — Germanic Review
Germ-Rom Monat — Germanisch-Romanische Monatsschrift
GERNDJ — Gerontology
Ger Note — Germanic Notes
GEROA — Gerontologia
GEROAJ — Gerontologia [*Basel*]
Gerontol — Gerontologist
Gerontol Clin — Gerontologia Clinica [*Later, Gerontology*]
Ger Plast — German Plastics [*West Germany*]
Ger Q — German Quarterly
Ger Quart — German Quarterly
GERR — Government Employee Relations Report
Ger Rev — Germanic Review
Ger Rom Mon — Germanisch-Romanische Monatsschrift
Ger Slav — Germano-Slavica
Ger S R — German Studies Review
Ger St Rev — German Studies Review
Ger Tekh — Germanskaya Tekhnika
GERUA — Geologische Rundschau
Ger Zent Geol Inst Abh — Germany. Zentrales Geologisches Institut. Abhandlungen
Ger Zent Geol Inst Jahrb Geol — Germany. Zentrales Geologisches Institut. Jahrbuch fuer Geologie
Ger Zentrales Geol Inst Wiss-Tech Informationsdienst — Germany. Zentrales Geologisches Institut. Wissenschaftlich-Technischer Informationsdienst
Gesammelte Abh Dtsch Lederinst (Freiberg) — Gesammelte Abhandlungen. Deutsches Lederinstitut (Freiberg)
Gesammelte Abh Kenn Kohle — Gesammelte Abhandlungen zur Kenntnis der Kohle
Gesammelte Ber Betr Forsch Ruhrgas Ag — Gesammelte Berichte aus Betrieb und Forschung der Ruhrgas Aktiengesellschaft [*West Germany*]
GESBA — Geologicky Zbornik [*Bratislava, Czechoslovakia*]
GESBAJ — Geologicky Zbornik
Ges Bekampf Krebskr Nordrhein-Westfalen Mitteilungdienst — Gesellschaft zur Bekampfung der Krebskrankheiten im Nordrhein-Westfalen. Mitteilungsdienst [*West Germany*]
Gesch Ges — Geschichte und Gesellschaft
Gesch Wiss Unterr — Geschichte in Wissenschaft und Unterricht
Ges Dtsch Metallhuetten- und Bergleute Schr — Gesellschaft Deutscher Metallhuetten- und Bergleute. Schriften
Ges Dtsch Naturforsch Aerzte Wiss Konf — Gesellschaft Deutscher Naturforscher und Aerzte. Wissenschaftliche Konferenz
Gesell Erdk Leipz Mitt — Gesellschaft fuer Erdkunde zu Leipzig. Mitteilungen
Gesell Kieler Stadtgesch Mitt — Gesellschaft fuer Kieler Stadtgeschichte. Mitteilungen
Gesell f Kieler Stadtgesch Mitt — Gesellschaft fuer Kieler Stadtgeschichte. Mitteilungen
Ges Erdk Berlin Verh Zs — Gesellschaft fuer Erdkunde zu Berlin. Verhandlungen. Zeitschrift
Gesetzbl Dtsch Demokr Repub — Gesetzblatt der Deutschen Demokratischen Republik [*East Germany*]
Gesetzbl Baden-Wuerttemb — Gesetzblatt fuer Baden-Wuerttemberg
Gesetzbl DDR Teil I — Gesetzblatt der Deutschen Demokratischen Republik. Teil I [*German Democratic Republic*]
Gesetz- Verordnungsbl Land Hessen Teil 1 — Gesetz- und Verordnungsblatt fuer das Land Hessen. Teil 1
Ges Geol Bergbaustud Oesterr Mitt — Gesellschaft der Geologie- und Bergbaustudenten in Oesterreich. Mitteilungen
Ges Geol Bergbaustud Wien Mitt — Gesellschaft der Geologie- und Bergbaustudenten in Wien. Mitteilungen
Ges Gesch & Bibliog Brauwes Jahrb — Gesellschaft fuer die Geschichte und Bibliographie des Brauwesens. Jahrbuch [*Berlin*]
GESHA — Genden Shiryo
GESKAC — Genetika i Selektsiya
GESLB — Genetika a Slechteni
GESLBG — Genetika a Slechteni
Ges Naturf Freund Berlin Szb — Gesellschaft Naturforschender Freunde zu Berlin. Sitzungsberichte
Ges Naturkd Wuerttemb Jahresh — Gesellschaft fuer Naturkunde in Wuerttemberg. Jahreshefte
Ges Naturw Marburg Schrift — Gesellschaft zur Befoerderung der Gesammten Naturwissenschaften zu Marburg. Schriften
Ges Reaktorsicherh Ber GRS-S — Gesellschaft fuer Reaktorsicherheit. Bericht GRS-S [*West Germany*]
Gesunde Pfl — Gesunde Pflanzen
Gesunde Pflanz — Gesunde Pflanzen

Gesundheitsfuehr Dtsch Volkes — Gesundheitsfuehrung des Deutschen Volkes
Gesundheits-Ing — Gesundheits-Ingenieur
Gesundheitswes Desinfekt — Gesundheitswesen und Desinfektion
Gesundh-Ing — Gesundheits-Ingenieur
Gesund-Ing — Gesundheits-Ingenieur
Gesund-Ing Haustech-Bauphys-Umwelttech — Gesundheits-Ingenieur. Haustechnik-Bauphysik-Umwelttechnik
Gesun Wohlfahrt — Gesundheit und Wohlfahrt
GET — Geografisch Tijdschrift. Nieuwe Reeks
GETD — Geografisk Tidsskrift
Geterog Katal — Geterogennyi Kataliz. Trudy Mezhdunarodnogo Simpoziuma po Geterogennomu Katalizu
GETMA — Getreide und Mehl
Getreide Mehl Brot — Getreide Mehl und Brot
Getriebe Mot Antriebselem — Getriebe Motoren Antriebselemente
GEVJA — Geoloski Vjesnik
GEVJAO — Geoloski Vjesnik [*Zagreb*]
GeW — Germanica Wratislaviensia
GEWAD5 — Gewasbescherming
GEWED — Gewerbearchiv
Gewerbl Rechtsschutz Urheberrecht — Gewerblicher Rechtsschutz und Urheberrecht
Gewerkschaftliche Mhefte — Gewerkschaftliche Monatshefte
Gewerkschaftl Mh — Gewerkschaftliche Monatshefte
Gewerksch Monatsh — Gewerkschaftliche Monatshefte
Gewerksch Rundsch — Gewerkschaftliche Rundschau
Geyer DT — Geyer's Dealer Topics
GEYPA — Geologicky Pruzkum
GEYSD — Geyser
GEZHD — Geofizicheskii Zhurnal
Gezira Res Stn Substn Annu Rep — Gezira Research Station and Substations. Annual Report
GF — Governmental Finance
GF — Grafiskt Forum
G Farm Chim — Giornale di Farmacia Chimica e Scienze Affini
G Farm Chim Sci Affini — Giornale di Farmacia Chimica e Scienze Affini
GFB — Gustav Freytag Blaetter
GFF — Geologiska Foereningens i Stockholm. Foerhandlingar
GFF — Grillparzer Forum Forchtenstein
GFF (Geol Foren Stockholm Forhandl) — GFF (Geologiska Foreningen i Stockholm Forhandlingar)
GFFNS — Godisnjak Filozofskog Fakulteta u Novom Sadu
GFI — Giornale Critico della Filosofia Italiana
G Fis Sanit — Giornale di Fisica Sanitaria e Protezione Contro le Radiazioni
G Fis Sanit Protez Contro Radiaz — Giornale di Fisica Sanitaria e Protezione Contro le Radiazioni
G Fis Sanit Prot Radiaz — Giornale di Fisica Sanitaria e Protezione Contro le Radiazioni
G Fis Soc Ital Fis — Giornale di Fisica. Societa Italiana di Fisica [*Italy*]
GFM — Marktforschung
G Foeren Stockholm Foerh — Geologiska Foereningens i Stockholm. Foerhandlingar
GFPIAW — Ghana. Council for Scientific and Industrial Research. Forest Products Research Institute. Annual Report
GFR — Groenten en Fruit
GFRRA — Georgia. Forest Research Council. Report
GFS — Government Finance Statistics Yearbook
GFSFA — Geologiska Foereningens i Stockholm. Foerhandlingar
GFSFA4 — Geologiska Foereningens i Stockholm. Foerhandlingar
GFSRA — Giornale di Fisica Sanitaria e Protezione Contro le Radiazioni
GFTNAX — Ghana. Council for Scientific and Industrial Research. Forest Products Research Institute. Technical Newsletter
GFW — Druk en Werk
GFWJ — Gesellschaft zur Foerderung der Wissenschaft des Judentums
GFZSA — Geofizicheskii Sbornik. Akademiya Nauk Ukrainskoi SSR. Institut Geofiziki
GG — Golden Goose
GGA — Goettingische Gelehrte Anzeiger
GGAB — Ghana Geographical Association. Bulletin
GGASA — Geologiya i Geofizika
G Genio Civ — Giornale del Genio Civile
G Geol (Bologna) — Giornale di Geologia (Bologna)
G Geol Mus Geol Bologna Ann — Giornale di Geologia. Museo Geologico di Bologna. Annali
G Gerontol — Giornale di Gerontologia
G Gerontol Suppl — Giornale di Gerontologia. Supplemento
GGFA — Geografiska Annaler. Series A
GGHVA4 — Geographica Helvetica
GGHY-A — Geography
GGHYAD — Geography
GGJO-A — Geographical Journal
GGK — Gaigokugo Gaigoku Bungaku Kenkyu
GGKGA — Godishnik na Sofiiskiya Universitet. Geologo-Geografski Fakultet. Kniga 1. Geologiya
GGI — Geografski Glasnik
GGMA-A — Geographical Magazine

GGNTAS — Glasgow Naturalist
GGPI — Pedagogical Institute in Gorki. Transactions
GGR — Geology and Geophysics. Academy of Sciences (USSR)
GGR — Goed Geraakt
GGTI-A — Geografisk Tidsskrift
GGUB — Groenlands Geologiske Undersoegelse. Bulletin
GGUMP — Groenlands Geologiske Undersoegelse. Miscellaneous Papers
GGUR — Groenlands Geologiske Undersoegelse. Reports
GH — Gelbe Hefte
GH — Glasgow Herald
GH — Good Housekeeping
GH — Gure Herria
GHA — Gas, Wasser, Abwasser. Schweizerische Monatszeitschrift fuer Gasfoerderung und Siedlungswasserwirtschaft
GHA — Goeteborgs Hogskolas Arsskrift
Ghana Anim Res Inst Annu Rep — Ghana. Animal Research Institute. Annual Report
Ghana B Theol — Ghana Bulletin of Theology
Ghana Counc Sci Ind Res For Prod Res Inst Tech Newsl — Ghana. Council for Scientific and Industrial Research. Forest Products Research Institute. Technical Newsletter
Ghana CSIR For Prod Res Inst Annu Rep — Ghana. Council for Scientific and Industrial Research. Forest Products Research Institute. Annual Report
Ghana CSIR For Prod Res Inst Tech Newsl — Ghana. Council for Scientific and Industrial Research. Forest Products Research Institute. Technical Newsletter
Ghana Fish Res Unit Inf Rep — Ghana. Fishery Research Unit. Information Report
Ghana Fish Res Unit Mar Fish Res Rep — Ghana. Fishery Research Unit. Marine Fishery Research Reports
Ghana Fmr — Ghana Farmer
Ghana For J — Ghana Forestry Journal
Ghana J Agric Sci — Ghana Journal of Agricultural Science
Ghana J Sci — Ghana Journal of Science
Ghana J Sociol — Ghana Journal of Sociology
Ghana Libr J — Ghana Library Journal
Ghana Med J — Ghana Medical Journal
Ghana Nurse — Ghanaian Nurse
Ghana Soc S — Ghana Social Science Journal
GHAT — Goettinger Handkommentar zum Alten Testament (1917-1922)
GHBUD — GI. Haustechnik, Bauphysik, Umwelttechnik
GHDBAX — Glasnik Khemijskog Drushtva [*Beograd*]
GHJ — George Herbert Journal
GHJSA — Ghana Journal of Science
GHJSAC — Ghana Journal of Science
GHLID — Geothermal Hot Line
GHMJA — Ghana Medical Journal
GHMJAY — Ghana Medical Journal
GHPADP — Geologica Hungarica. Series Palaeontologica
GHQ — Georgia Historical Quarterly
GHREA — Guy's Hospital Reports
GHRKA — Genshiryoku Heiwa Riyo Kenkyu Seika Hokokusho
GHT — Gas World
GHT — Goeteborgs Handelstidning
GI — Gazette d'Israel [*Tunis*]
GI — Glossaria Interpretum [*Elsevier Book Series*]
GIC — Gids
GICLDY — Ginecologia Clinica
GICQA — Gifted Child Quarterly
GIDAD — Gijutsu Daijesuto
Gidravl Gidrotekh — Gidravlika i Gidrotekhnika
Gidroaeromeh i Teor Uprogosti — Gidroaeromehanika i Teorija Uprugosti
Gidrobiol Zh — Gidrobiologicheskii Zhurnal
Gidrobiol Zh Akad Nauk Ukr SSR — Gidrobiologicheskij Zhurnal Akademiya Nauk Ukrainskoj SSR
Gidrobiol Zh Hydrobiol J — Gidrobiologicheskii Zhurnal Hydrobiological Journal
Gidrodin Bol'shikh Skorostei — Gidrodinamika Bol'shikh Skorostei
Gidrodin Teploobmen — Gidrodinamika i Teploobmen
Gidrogeol Gidrogeokhim — Gidrogeologiya i Gidrogeokhimiya
Gidrogeol Sb — Gidrogeologicheskii Sbornik
Gidrokhim Mater — Gidrokhimicheskiye Materialy
Gidroliz Lesokhim Promysh — Gidroliznaya i Lesokhimicheskaya Promyshlennost
Gidrol Lesohim Prom — Gidroliznaja i Lesohimiceskaja Promyshlennost
Gidroprivod Gidropnevmoavtomatika — Gidroprivod Gidropnevmoavtomatika
Gidrotekh Melior — Gidrotekhnika i Melioratsiya
Gidrotekh Stroit — Gidrotekhnicheskoe Stroitel'stvo
Gids — De Gids
GIE — Constructeur. Vaktijdschrift voor het Werktuigbouwkundig Construeren naar Functie, Vorm, en Kostprijs
GIERB — Giesserei-Rundschau
GIESA — Giesserei [*West Germany*]
Giessener Abh Agr WirtForsch Eur Ostens — Giessener Abhandlungen zur Agrar- und Wirtschaftsforschung des Europaeischen Ostens
Giessener Geol Schr — Giessener Geologische Schriften

Giessener Schriftenr Tierz Haustiergenet — Giessener Schriftenreihe Tierzucht und Haustiergenetik

Giesserei-Erfah — Giesserei-Erfahrungsaustausch

Giesserei Maschinenbau Ztg — Giesserei und Maschinenbau Zeitung

Giesserei-Rundsch — Giesserei-Rundschau [Austria]

GIF — Giornale Italiano di Filologia

Gift Child — Gifted Child Quarterly

Gifted Child Q — Gifted Child Quarterly

Gig i Epidemiol — Gigiena i Epidemiologiia

G Ig Med Prev — Giornale di Igiene e Medicina Preventiva

Gig Naselennykh Mest — Gigiena Naselennykh Mest [Ukrainian SSR]

Gig Nasel Mest Resp Mezhved Sb — Gigiena Naselennykh Mest Respublikanskoi Mezhvedomstvennyi Sbornik

Gig Primen Polim Mater Izdelii Nikh — Gigiena Primeneniya Polimernykh Materialov i Izdelii iz Nikh

Gig Sanit — Gigiena i Sanitariya

GIGTA7 — Gigiena Truda Respublikanskii Mezhvedomstvennyi Sbornik

Gig Toksikol Pestitsi Klin Otravlenii — Gigiena i Toksikologiya Pestitsidov i Klinika Otravlenii

Gig Tr — Gigiena Truda [Ukrainian SSR]

Gig Tr Prof Patol Est SSR — Gigiena Truda i Professional'naya Patologiya v Estonskoi SSR [Estonian SSR]

Gig Tr Prof Zabol — Gigiena Truda i Professional'nye Zabolevaniya

Gig Tr Resp Mezhved Sb — Gigiena Truda Respublikanskii Mezhvedomstvennyi Sbornik

Giho Res Dev Headquarters Jpn Defense Agency — Giho. Research and Development Headquarters. Japan Defense Agency

GIJUA — Gijutsu

Gillett Mem Lect — Gillett Memorial Lecture

GInd — Guide to Indian Periodical Literature

GINDB — Genie Industrial

G Indian Per Lit — Guide to Indian Periodical Literature

Ginecol Bras — Ginecologia Brasileira

Ginecol Obstet (Lima) — Ginecologia y Obstetricia (Lima)

Ginecol Obstet Mex — Ginecologia y Obstetricia de Mexico

Ginekol Pol — Ginekologia Polska

Ginekol Pol Supl — Ginekologia Polska. Suplement

GINGA — Gas Industry. Natural Gas Edition

Gior Clin Med — Giornale de Clinica Medica

Gior Geront — Giornale di Gerontologia

Gior Internaz Sc Med — Giornale Internazionale delle Scienze Mediche

Gior Ital Mal Esot e Trop ed Ig Colon — Giornale Italiano di Malattie Esotiche e Tropicali ed Iglene Coloniale

Gior Ital Mal Ven — Giornale Italiano delle Malattie Veneree e della Pelle

Gior Lett Italia — Giornale de Letterati d'Italia

Gior Med Prat — Giornale di Medicina Practica

Gior Med R Esercito — Giornale Medico del Regio Esercito e della Regia Marina

Gior Med Vet — Giornale di Medicina Veterinaria

Giornale Econ — Giornale Economico

Giornale Economisti e Ann Econ — Giornale degli Economisti e Annali di Economia

Giorn Econom Ann Econom — Giornale degli Economisti e Annali di Economia

Giorn Mat Battaglini — Giornale di Matematiche di Battaglini

Giorn Mat Battaglini 6 — Giornale di Matematiche di Battaglini. Serie 6 [Naples]

Gior R Accad Med Torino — Giornale della Reale Accademia di Medicina di Torino

Gior R Soc Ital Ig — Giornale della Reale Societa Italiana d'Igiene

Gior Sc Lett ed Arti Sicilia — Giornale di Scienze, Lettere, ed Arti per la Sicilia

Gior Storico — Giornale Storico della Letteratura Italiana

Giperton Bolezn Ateroskler Koron Nedostatochn — Gipertonicheskaya Bolezn Ateroskleroz i Koronarnaya Nedostatochnost

GIPLA — Giornale die Pollicoltori

GIPND — General Information Programme-UNISIST [Universal System for Information in Science and Technology] Newsletter

GIPOA — Ginekologia Polska

GIPOA3 — Ginekologia Polska

GIPSB — Giornale Italiano di Psicologia

GIPXA — Giessereipraxis

GIS — Gids op Maatschappelijk Gebied. Tijdschrift voor Syndicale, Culturele, en Sociale Problemen

GISAA — Gigiena i Sanitariya

GISAA — Gigiyena i Sanitariia

GISAAA — Gigiena i Sanitariya

GISPA — Geoscience Information Society. Proceedings

Gissing N — Gissing Newsletter

GIT — Glas- und Instrumenten Technik Fachzeitschrift fuer das Laboratorium

G Ital Anest Analg — Giornale Italiano di Anestesia e di Analgesia

G Ital Anestesiol — Giornale Italiano di Anestesiologia

G Ital Cardiol — Giornale Italiano di Cardiologia

G Ital Chemioter — Giornale Italiano di Chemioterapia

G Ital Chir — Giornale Italiano di Chirurgia

G Ital Dermatol — Giornale Italiano di Dermatologia [Later, Giornale Italiano di Dermatologia e Venereologia]

G Ital Dermatol Minerva Dermatol — Giornale Italiano di Dermatologia Minerva Dermatologica

G Ital Mal Torace — Giornale Italiano delle Malattie del Torace

G Ital Mal Torace Suppl — Giornale Italiano delle Malattie del Torace. Supplemento

G Ital Oftalmol — Giornale Italiano di Oftalmologia

G Ital Patol Sci Affini — Giornale Italiano di Patologia e di Scienze Affini

G Ital Tuberc — Giornale Italiano della Tubercolosi

G Ital Tuberc Mal Torace — Giornale Italiano della Tubercolosi e delle Malattie del Torace

GITEA — GIT [Glas- und Instrumenten-Technik] Fachzeitschrift fuer das Laboratorium [West Germany]

GIT Fachz Lab — Glas- und Instrumenten Technik Fachzeitschrift fuer das Laboratorium

GIT Fachz Lab Suppl — GIT [Glas- und Instrumenten-Technik] Fachzeitschrift fuer das Laboratorium. Supplement

GIT Labor Med — GIT [Glas- und Instrumenten-Technik] Labor-Medizin

GIT Suppl — GIT [Glas- und Instrumenten-Technik] Supplement

Gitut'yun Texnika — Gitut'yun ew Texnika

GIUAC — Geophysical Institute. University of Alaska. Contribution Series

GIUAG R — Geophysical Institute. University of Alaska. UAG Report Series

Giur Cost — Giurisprudenza Costituzionale

Giust Civ — Giustizia Civile

Givaudan Flavor — Givaudan Flavorist

GJ — Gas Journal

GJ — Geographical Journal

GJ — Gutenberg-Jahrbuch

GjA — Gjurmime Albanologijike [Prishtina]

GJASA — Ghana Journal of Agricultural Science

GJASAF — Ghana Journal of Agricultural Science

GJb — Geographisches Jahrbuch

G Jb — Gutenberg-Jahrbuch

GJCHD — Gesuido Jigyo Chosahi Hokoku

GJHEDB — Geologisches Jahrbuch Hessen

GJL — Geographical Journal (London)

GJOUD — Geophysical Journal

GJS — Ghana Journal of Sociology

GJSCD — Georgia Journal of Science

GK — Gazeta Krakowska

GK — Gengo Kenkyu

GK — Geodezija i Kartografija

GK — Goethe-Kalender

GK — Gottesdienst und Kirchenmusik

GKAEA — Geodeziia, Kartografiia, i Aerofotos'emka

GKAR — Gesetz ueber Kassenarztrecht

GKB Zt — GKB [Graz-Koeflacher Eisenbahn und Bergbaugesellschaft] Zeitung fuer Eisenbahn und Bergbau

GKF — Grope Kunstfuehrer

GKG — Grundlagenstudien aus Kybernetik und Geisteswissenschaft

GKG — Grundriss der Kirchengeschichte

GK Oe D — Gesamtkommentar Oeffentliches Dienstrecht

GKPSAT — Ginekologia Polska. Suplement

GKSBA — Geokhimicheskii Sbornik

GKSHA — Gijutsu Kenkyusho Shoho

GKT — Kaffee und Tee Markt

GKVVH — Goeteborgs Kungliga Vetenskaps-och Vitterhets-Samhaelles Handlingar

GKWW — Gespraechskreis Wissenschaft und Wirtschaft

GL — Gazette des Lettres

GL — Geist und Leben

GL — General Linguistics

GL — Giornale della Libreria

Gl — Glasnik

Gl — Globe

Gl — Glossa

Gl — Glotta

GL — Guitar and Lute

GLa — Gazette de Lausanne

Gla Bi — Glasul Bisericii

Glacier Nat History Assoc Special Bull — Glacier Natural History Association. Special Bulletin

GLAD — Greater London Association for the Disabled. Quarterly

GLADB — Gladiolus

GLAIU — Gledaliski List Akademije za Igralsko Umetnost

GLAL — German Life and Letters

Glamorgan Hist — Glamorgan Historian

Glas — Glasnik

Glas Appar — Glas und Apparat

Glas-Email-Keramo-Tech — Glas-Email-Keramo-Technik [West Germany]

Glas Em Ker — Glas-Email-Keramo-Technik

Glasers Ann — Glasers Annalen

Glasers Ann ZEV — Glasers Annalen ZEV [Zeitschrift fuer Eisenbahnwesen und Verkehrstechnik]

Glasg Dent J — Glasgow Dental Journal

Glasg Med J — Glasgow Medical Journal

Glasg Nat — Glasgow Naturalist
GlasgOrTrans — Glasgow University Oriental Society. Transactions [*Glasgow*]
Glasgow Archaeol J — Glasgow Archaeological Journal
Glasgow Arch J — Glasgow Archaeological Journal
Glasgow Art R — Glasgow Art Gallery and Museums Association. Review
Glasgow Med J — Glasgow Medical Journal
Glasgow Nat — Glasgow Naturalist
Glasg Univ Publ — Glasgow University. Publications
Glas Hem Drus (Beograd) — Glasnik Hemijskog Drustva (Beograd)
Glas Hem Drush — Glasnik Hemijskog Drushtva
Glas Hem Drus Kralj Jugosl — Glasnik Hemijskog Drustva Kraljevine Jugoslavije
Glas Hemicara Technol Bosne Hercegovine — Glasnik Hemicara i Technologa Bosne i Hercegovine [*Yugoslavia*]
Glas Hem Technol Bosne Hercegovine — Glasnik Hemicara i Technologa Bosne i Hercegovine
Glas Hochvak Tech — Glas- und Hochvakuum Technik
Glas Hochv Techn — Glas- und Hochvakuum Technik
Glas-Instrum-Tech — Glas-Instrument-Technik [*West Germany*]
Glas Khem Drush (Beogr) — Glasnik Khemijskog Drushtva (Beograd)
Glas Mat — Glasnik Matematicki
Glas Mat-Fiz Astron — Glasnik Matematicko-Fizicki i Astronomski [*Yugoslavia*]
Glas Math J — Glasgow Mathematical Journal
Glasn — Glasnik
Glasn Biol Sekc Hrv Prir Dr — Glasnik. Bioloske Sekcije. Hrvatsko Prirodoslovno Drustvo
Glasn Hem Drust (Beogr) — Glasnik Hemijskog Drustva (Beograd)
Glasnik Mat Ser III — Glasnik Matematicki. Serija III. Drustvo Matematicara i Fizicara SR Hrvatske.
Glasnik Sumar Fak Univ Beogradu — Glasnik Sumarskog Fakulteta Univerzitet u Beogradu
Glasnik Tsentral Khig Zavoda (Beograd) — Glasnik Tsentralnogo Khigiyenskog Zavoda (Beograd)
Glas Prir Muz Beogradu Ser A — Glasnik Prirodnjackog Muzeja u Beogradu. Serija A. Mineralogija, Geologija, Paleontologija
Glas Prir Muz Beogradu Serija A — Glasnik Prirodnjackog Muzeja u Beogradu. Serija A. Mineralogija, Geologija, Palentologija [*Yugoslavia*]
Glas Prir Muz Srp Zemlje Ser A — Glasnik Prirodnjackog Muzeja Srpske Zemlje. Serija A. Mineralogiya, Geologija, Paleontologija
Glas Repub Zavoda Zast Prir Prir Muz Titogradu — Glasnik Republickog Zavoda za Zastitu Prirode i Prirodnjackog Muzeja Titogradu
Glass — Glassworks
GlasSAN — Glas Srpska Akademija Nauka
Glass Aust — Glass in Australia
Glass Ceram — Glass and Ceramics
Glasshouse Crops Res Inst Annu Rep — Glasshouse Crops Research Institute. Annual Report
Glass Ind — Glass Industry
Glas Srp Akad Nauka Umet Od Prir Mat Nauka — Glas Srpska Akademija Nauka i Umetnosti Odeljenje Prirodno-Matematickikh Nauka
Glas Srp Akad Nauk Umet Od Med Nauk — Glas Srpska Akademija Nauka i Umetnosti Odeljenje Medicinskih Nauka
Glas Srpska Akad Nauka Umet Od Prir-Mat Nauka — Glas Srpska Akademija Nauka i Umetnosti Odeljenje Prirodno-Matematickikh Nauka
Glass Tech — Glass Technology
Glass Technol — Glass Technology
Glas Sumske Pokuse — Glasnik za Sumske Pokuse
Glass Wkrs News — Glass Workers News
Glastech Ber — Glastechnische Berichte
Glastek Tidskr — Glasteknisk Tidskrift [*Sweden*]
Glastek Tidskrift — Glasteknisk Tidskrift
GLAUD4 — Glaucoma
Glaxo Vol — Glaxo Volume
GLBCAK — Gleanings in Bee Culture
GLBO — Glenbow
GLC — Glossari di Lingua Contemporanea
Glean Bee Cult — Gleanings in Bee Culture
Gleanings — Gleanings in Bee Culture
Gleanings Bee Cult — Gleanings in Bee Culture
GLECS — Groupe Linguistique d'Etudes Chamito-Semitiques. Comptes Rendus
Glendale L Rev — Glendale Law Review
GLFM — Gulf Mirror
GLFT — Gulf Times
GLGSA — Geologist [*New York*]
GLGYB — Geology
GLGYBA — Geology [*Boulder*]
GlH — Glass Hill
GLI — Glass Industry
GLIJ — Greater London Intelligence Journal
GLit — Gazeta Literara
GLKPA — Gidroliznaya i Lesokhimicheskaya Promyshlennost
GL & L — German Life and Letters

GLL — German Life and Letters
GLLM — German Language and Literature Monographs
GLLNS — German Life and Letters. New Series
GLMDD — GIT [*Glas- und Instrumenten-Technik*] Labor-Medizin
GLO — Graecolatina et Orientalia
Global Anal Pure Appl Adv — Global Analysis Pure and Applied. Advanced
Global Atmos Res Programme Publ Ser — Global Atmospheric Research Programme. Publications Series
Global Commun — Global Communications
Globe Mail Rep Bus Globe Mail Ltd — Globe and Mail Report on Business. Globe and Mail Limited
Glow — Glow International
GLOXAC — Gloxinian
GLP — Gastrointestinal and Liver Physiology
GLPAAG — Glass Packer
GLPU — Gasline Planning Update. Northwest Alaska Pipeline Company. Manpower and Impact Planning Department
GLR — Garcia Lorca Review
GLR — Georgia Law Review
GLR — Ghana Law Reports
GLR — Gujarat Law Reporter
GlSAN — Glas Srpska Akademija Nauka
GLSDA6 — Geologia Sudetica [*Warsaw*]
GLSNG-L — Gledaliski List Slovenskega Narodnega Gledalisca v Ljubljane
GLSNG-M — Gledaliski List Slovenskega Narodnega Gledalisca v Mariboru
GLSPA8 — Glasnik za Sumske Pokuse
Glueckauf-Forschungsh — Glueckauf-Forschungshefte
GLVOAK — Glaxo Volume
Glyph Jon H — Glyph. Johns Hopkins Textual Studies
GM — Gandhi Marg
GM — Gazeta Musical
GM — Gentleman's Magazine
GM — Geographical Magazine
GM — Giornale di Metafisica
GM — Gopher Music Notes
G Mag — Geological Magazine
G Mal Infett Parassit — Giornale di Malattie Infettive e Parassitarie
GMAMA — Gemeinsames Amtsblatt. Ausgabe A
GMARA — Geomagnetism and Aeronomy [*English Translation*]
GMDCB4 — Geographia Medica
G Med Mil — Giornale di Medicina Militare
G Metaf — Giornale di Metafisica
GMFRBP — Ghana. Fishery Research Unit. Marine Fishery Research
GMGZA — Gas Magazine
G Microbiol — Giornale di Microbiologia
GMI Short Pap Oreg Dep Geol Miner Ind — GMI Short Paper. Oregon Department of Geology and Mineral Industries
GMit — Germanistische Mitteilungen. Zeitschrift des Belgischen Germanisten- und Deutschlehrerverbandes
GMMEA — Gaceta Medica de Mexico
GMOND — Gewerkschaftliche Monatshefte
GMP — Guide to Microforms in Print
GMRLA — Research Publication. General Motors Corporation. Research Laboratories
GMS — Gemeentestem; Weekblad, aan de Belangen van de Gemeente in Nederland Gewijd
GM Search — General Motors Research Laboratories. Search
GMSED — GBF Monograph Series
GMSLL — Georgetown University. Monograph Series on Languages and Linguistics
G M Soc Am Univ Y Bk — Geological and Mining Society of American Universities. Year Book and Directory
GMU LR — George Mason University. Law Review
GMU L Rev — George Mason University. Law Review
GN — Geldgeschichtliche Nachrichten
GN — Georgia Music News
GN — Germanic Notes
Gn — Gnomon
GNA — Genossenschafts Forum. Raiffeisenrundschau und Blaetter fuer Genossenschaftswesen
GNAMAP — Gigiena Naselennykh Mest Respublikanskoi Mezhvedomstvennyi Sbornik
GNCBA — Ginecologia Brasileira
GNCBA2 — Ginecologia Brasileira
G & N Coop — G & N Cooperator (Gippsland and Northern Cooperative)
GNDBiH — Godisnjak Naucnog Drustva Nr Bosne i Hercegovine
GNKAA5 — Genetika
GNKEAH — Gifu Daigaku Nogakubu Kenkyu Hokoku
GNKNA — Genshi Nenryo Kosha Nempo
GNNED — General Newsletter. National Research Council (Canada). Division of Mechanical Engineering
GNS — Gazette Numismatique Suisse
GNSHD — Gendai No Shinryo
GNTAA — Ganita [*India*]
GNTGD — Gensan Nenji Taikai Gijiroku
GNTKAC — Genetik

GNTSA — Genetics. Supplement
GNTUD — Geologiya i Neftegazonosnost Turkmenistana
GOC — Grafisch Orgaan
GOCA — Geoscience Canada
God — Godisnik na Sofijskiya Universitet. Istorikofilologiceski Fakultet
God Biol Inst Univ Sarajevu — Godisnjak Bioloskog Instituta Univerziteta u Sarajevu
God Durzh Politekh (Sofiya) — Godishnik na Durzhavna ta Politekhnika (Sofiya)
God Energoproekt — Godisnik na Energoproekt
Godey — Godey's Lady's Book
GodFFNS — Godisnjak Filozofskog Fakulteta u Novom Sadu
God Inzh Stroit Inst — Godishnik na Inzhenerno-Stroitelniya Institut
Godis Ekon Fak (Skopje) — Godisnik na Ekonomski ot Fakultet (Skopje)
Godisen Zb Zemjod-Fak Univ Skopje Ovostarstvo — Godisen Zbornik na Zemjodelsko-Sumarskiot. Fakultet na Univerzitetot Skopje Ovostarstvo
Godisen Zb Zemjod-Sum Fak Univ Skopje — Godisen Zbornik na Zemjodelsko-Sumarskiot. Fakultet na Univerzitetot Skopje
Godishnik Vissh Khimikotekhn Inst Burgas — Godishnik Visshiya Khimikotekhnologicheski Institut. Burgas
Godishnik Vissh Ped Inst Shumen Prirod-Mat Fak — Godishnik na Visshiya Pedagogiceski Institut v Shumen. Prirodo-Matematicheski Fakultet
Godishnik Vissh Uchebn Zaved Tekhn Mekh — Godishnik na Visshite Uchebni Zavedeniya. Tekhnicheski Mekhanika
Godisnik Viss Himikotehn Inst (Burgas) — Godisnik Vissija Himikotehnologiceski Institut (Burgas)
Godisnik Viss Inz-Stroitel Inst — Godisnik na Vissija Inzerno-Stroitelnija Institut
Godisnik Viss Ped Inst Sumen Prirod-Mat Fak — Godisnik na Vissija Pedagogiceski Institut v Sumen Prirodo-Matematiceski Fakultet
Godisnik Viss Tehn Ucebn Zaved Fiz — Godisnik na Vissite Tehniceski Ucebni Zavedenija. Fizika
Godisnik Viss Tehn Ucebn Zaved Mat — Godisnik na Vissite Tehniceski Ucebni Zavedenija. Matematika
Godisnik Viss Ucebn Zaved Prilozna Mat — Godisnik na Vissite Ucebni Zavedenija. Prilozna Matematika
Godisnik Viss Ucebn Zaved Tehn Fiz — Godisnik na Vissite Ucebni Zavedinija. Tehniceski Fizika
Godisnjak Pomorskog Muz Kotoru — Godisnjak Pomorskog Muzeja u Kotoru
God Khim Tekhnol Inst — Godishnik na Khimiko Tekhnologicheskiya Institut
God Mash Elektrotekh Inst — Godishnik na Mashino Elektrotekhnicheskiya Institut
God Med Akad (Sofia) — Godishnik na Meditsinkata Akademiya "Vulko Chervenkov" (Sofia)
God Minniya Nauchnoizsled Inst — Godishnik na Minniya Nauchnosledovatelski Institut
God Nauchnoizsled Inst Khim Prom — Godishnik na Nauchnoizsledovatelskiya Institut po Khimicheska Promishlennost
God Nauchnoizsled Inst Koksokhim Neftoprerab — Godishnik na Nauchnoizsledovatelskiya Institut po Koksokhimiya i Neftoprerabotvane
God Nauchnoizsled Inst Metal Obogat — Godishnik na Nauchnoizsledovatelskiya Institut po Metalurgiya i Obogatyatvane
God Nauchnoizsled Inst Neftoprerab Neftokhim — Godishnik na Nauchnoizsledovatelskiya Institut po Neftoprerabotvane i Neftokhimiya
God Nauchnoizsled Inst Tekhnol Izsled Gorivata — Godishnik na Nauchnoizsledovatelskiya Institut za Tekhnolozhki Izsledovaniya na Gorivata
God Nauchnoizsled Inst Tsvetna Metal (Plovdiv) — Godishnik na Nauchnoizsledovatelskiya Institut po Tsvetna Metalurgiya (Plovdiv) [*Bulgaria*]
God Nauchnoizsled Proekt Inst Rudodobiv Obogat — Godishnik na Nauchnoizsledovatelskiya i Proektantski Institut za Rudodobiv i Obogatyavane
GODORT DTTP — GODORT [*Government Documents Round Table*] Documents to the People
God Otchet Durzh Zemled Opitna Kontrolna Stn (Sofia) — Godishen Otchet. Durzhavna Zemledelska Opitna i Kontrolna Stantsiya (Sofia)
God Selskostop Akad George Dimitrov — Godishnik na Selsko-Stopanskata Akademiya Georgi Dimitrov Sofiya
God Sofii Univ Agron Lesovud Fak — Godishnik na Sofiiskiya Universitet. Agronomo Lesovudski Fakultet
God Sofii Univ Biol Fak — Godisnik na Sofiiskiya Universitet. Biologicheski Fakultet
God Sofii Univ Biol Fak Kn I Zool Fiziol Biokhim Zhivotn — Godishnik na Sofiiskiya Universitet. Biologicheski Fakultet. Kniga I. Zoologiya, Fiziologiya, i Biokhimiya na Zhivotnite
God Sofii Univ Biol-Geol-Geogr Fak Kn I Biol — Godishnik na Sofiiskiya Universitet. Biologo-Geologo-Geografski Fakultet. Kniga I. Biologiya
God Sofii Univ Biol-Geol-Geogr Fak Kn I Biol (Bot) — Godishnik na Sofiiskiya Universitet. Biologo-Geologo-Geografski Fakultet. Kniga I. Biologiya (Botanika)

God Sofii Univ Biol-Geol-Geogr Fak Kn I Biol (Zool) — Godishnik na Sofiiskiya Universitet. Biologo-Geologo-Geografski Fakultet. Kniga I. Biologiya (Zoologiya)
God Sofii Univ Fiz Fak — Godishnik na Sofiiskiya Universitet. Fizicheski Fakultet [*Bulgaria*]
God Sofii Univ Lesovud Fak — Godishnik na Sofiiskiya Universitet. Lesovuden Fakultet
God Sofii Univ Med Fak — Godishnik na Sofiiskiya Universitet. Meditsinski Fakultet
God Sofii Univ Prir Mat Fak — Godishnik na Sofiiskiya Universitet. Prirodo-Matematicheski Fakultet
GodSU — Godisnik na Sofijskiya Universitet. Fakultet po Slavjanski Filologii
God Vissh Inst Arkhit Stroit (Sofiya) — Godishnik na Visshiya Institut po Arkhitektura i Stroitelstvo (Sofiya)
God Vissh Inzh Stroit Inst — Godishnik na Visshiya Inzhenerno-Stroitelen Institut
God Vissh Khimikotekhnol Inst — Godishnik na Visshiya Khimikotekhnologicheski Institut [*Bulgaria*]
God Vissh Khimikotekhnol Inst Sofia — Godishnik na Visshiya Khimikotekhnologicheski Institut Sofia
God Vissh Khim-Tekhnol Inst (Burgas Bulg) — Godishnik na Visshiya Khimiko-Tekhnologicheski Institut (Burgas, Bulgaria)
God Vissh Mash Elektrotekh Inst — Godishnik na Visshiya Mashino-Elektrotekhnicheski Institut
God Vissh Minno-Geol Inst (Sofia) — Godishnik na Visshiya Minno-Geolozhki Institut (Sofia)
God Vissh Tekh Uchebni Zaved Mekh — Godishnik na Visshite Tekhnicheski Uchebni Zavedeniya. Prilozhna Mekhanika
God Vissh Tekh Uchebn Zaved Prilozh Mekh — Godishnik na Visshite Tekhnicheski Uchebni Zavedeniya. Prilozhna Mekhanika
God Vissh Uchebn Zaveden (Ser) Tekh Fiz — Godishnik na Visshite Uchebni Zavedeniya (Seriya). Tekhnicheska Fizika [*Bulgaria*]
God Vissh Uchebn Zaved Prilozh Mat — Godishnik na Visshite Uchebni Zavedeniya. Prilozhna Matematika
God Zb Annu Biol — Godishen Zbornik Annuaire. Biologie
God Zb Biol Prir-Mat Fak Univ Kiril Metodij Skopje — Godishen Zbornik Biologija Priridno-Matematichki. Fakultet na Univerzitetot Kiril i Metodij Skopje
God Zb Filoz Fak Univ Skopje Prir Mat Oddel — Godisen Zbornik. Filozofski. Fakultet na Univerzitetot Skopje. Prirodno-Matematicki Oddel
God Zb Med Fak Skopje — Godishen Zbornik na Meditsinskiot. Fakultet vo Skopje
God Zbor Zemjodel Sumar Fak Univ Skoplje — Godisen Zbornik ka Zemjodelsko-Sumarskoit. Fakultet na Univerzitetot Skoplje
God Zb Prir Mat Fak Univ Skopje — Godisen Zbornik. Prirodno-Matematicki. Fakultet na Univerzitetot Skopje
God Zb Prir Mat Fak Univ Skopje Mat Fiz Hem — Godisen Zbornik. Prirodno-Matematicki. Fakultet na Univerzitetot Skopje. Matematika, Fizika, i Hemija
God Zb Sumar Fak Univ (Skopje) — Godisen Zbornik na Sumarskiot. Fakultet na Univerzitetot (Skopje)
God Zb Zemjod Sumar Fak Univ Skopje Sumar — Godisen Zbornik na Zemjodelsko-Sumarskiot. Fakultet na Univerzitetot Skopje. Sumarstvo
God Zb Zemjod Sumar Fak Univ Skopje Zemjod — Godisen Zbornik na Zemjodelsko-Sumarskiot. Fakultet na Univerzitetot Skopje. Zemjodelstvo
Goe — Goethe. Vierteljahresschrift der Goethe-Gesellschaft
Goeteborgs K Vetensk-o Vitterhets Samh Handl — Goeteborgs Kungliga Vetenskaps-och Vitterhets-Samhaelles Handlingar
Goethe-Al — Goethe-Almanach
Goethe-Jahr — Goethe-Jahrbuch
Goethe-Jahrb — Goethe-Jahrbuch
Goett Arb Geol Palaeontol — Goettinger Arbeiten zur Geologie und Palaeontologie
Goett Florist Rundbriefe — Goettinger Floristische Rundbriefe
Goettinger Wirtsch Sozialwissensch Stud — Goettinger Wirtschafts- und Sozialwissenschaftliche Studien
Goetting J Naturw — Goettingisches Journal der Naturwissenschaften
Goett Jahrb — Goettinger Jahrbuch
Goett Nachr — Nachrichten. Gesellschaft der Wissenschaften zu Goettingen
GOF — Golden Fleece
GOF — Governmental Finance
GOL — Golden Gate University. Law Review
Gold Bull — Gold Bulletin
Gold Coast Geol Surv Bull — Gold Coast Geological Survey. Bulletin
Golden Bk — Golden Book Magazine
Golden Gate L Rev — Golden Gate Law Review
Golden Gate UL Rev — Golden Gate University. Law Review
Gold Fleece — Golden Fleece
Gold K — Goldene Keyt
Gold Placer Deposits Foot East Cordillera Bolivia — Gold Placer Deposits at the Foot of the Eastern Cordillera of Bolivia
Goldschmidt Inf — Goldschmidt Informiert
Goldsmiths J Gemm — Goldsmiths Journal and Gemmologist
Golf Course Rep — Golf Course Reporter
Golf Dig — Golf Digest

Golf Dig Mag — Golf Digest Magazine
Golf Mag — Golf Magazine
GOMAB — Goriva i Maziva
Gomal Univ J Res — Gomal University. Journal of Research
GONAAR — Forest Science [*Sofia*]
Gonzaga L Rev — Gonzaga Law Review
Gonz L Rev — Gonzaga Law Review
Good Farming Quart — Good Farming Quarterly
Goodfellow — Goodfellow Review of Crafts
Good H — Good Housekeeping
Good House — Good Housekeeping
Good Pkg — Good Packaging
Goodrich — BF Goodrich Co. Economic and Business Facts and Forecasts
GOP — Girls' Own Paper
GOPOA — Gas and Oil Power
GOR — Gordian. Internationale Zeitschrift fuer Lebensmittel und Lebensmitteltechnologie
GORABE — GO. Revista de Atualizacao em Ginecologia e Obstetricia
GO Rev Atualizacao Ginecol Obstet — GO. Revista de Atualizacao em Ginecologia e Obstetricia
Gor'k Gos Nauchno Issled Inst Gig Tr Profbolezn Tr — Gor'kovskii Gosudarstvennyi Nauchno-Issledovatel'skii Institut Gigieny Truda i Profboleznei. Trudy
Gor'kov Gos Univ Ucen Zap — Gor'kovskii Gosudarstvennyi Universitet. Ucenye Zapiski
Gor'k Skh Inst Tr — Gor'kovskii Sel'skokhozyaistvennyi Institut. Trudy
Gorn Mash Avtom — Gornye Mashiny i Avtomatika
Gorn Odkrywkowe — Gornictwo Odkrywkowe
Gorno-Obogat Delo — Gorno-Obogatitel'noe Delo
Gorno-Obogat Zh — Gorno-Obogatitel'nyi Zhurnal
Gorn Zh — Gornyi Zhurnal
Gorn Zh (Mos) — Gornyi Zhurnal (Moscow)
Gor R — Gordon Review
Gorsko Stop — Gorsko Stopanstvo [*Bulgaria*]
Gorskostop Nauka — Gorskostopanska Nauka
Gorskostop Nauka For Sci — Gorskostopanska Nauka. Forest Science
Gorskostop Nauka Izv Akad Selskostop Nauke — Gorskostopanska Nauka Izvestiya na Akademiiata na Selskostopankite Nauke
Goryuch Slantsy Khim Tekhnol — Goryuchie Slantsy. Khimiya i Tekhnologiya [*Estonian SSR*]
Goryuch Slantsy (Moscow) — Goryuchie Slantsy (Moscow)
Goryuch Slantsy (Tallinn) — Goryuchie Slantsy (Tallinn) [*Estonian SSR*]
GOS — Gaekwad's Oriental Series
GOS — Group and Organization Studies
GOSD — Goinsiday
Gos Inst Prikl Khim Tr — Gosudarstvennyi Institut Prikladnoi Khimii Trudy
Gos Nauchno Issled Energ Inst Im G M Krzhizhanovskogo Sb Tr — Gosudarstvennyi Nauchno-Issledovatel'skii Energeticheskii Institut Imeni G. M. Krzhizhanovskogo Sbornik Trudov
Gos Nauchno Issled Inst Keram Promsti Tr — Gosudarstvennyi Nauchno-Issledovatel'skii Institut Keramicheskoi Promyshlennosti Trudy
Gos Nauchno Issled Rentgeno Radiol Inst Tr — Gosudarstvennyi Nauchno-Issledovatel'skii Rentgeno-Radiologicheskii Institut Trudy
Gosp Delo — Gospital'noe Delo
Gospod Miesna — Gospodarka Miesna
Gospod Paliwami Energ — Gospodarka Paliwami i Energia
Gospod Wodna — Gospodarka Wodna
Gosp Planowa — Gospodarka Planowa
GOSTA — Gorsko Stopanstvo
G Ostet Ginecol — Giornale di Ostetricia e Ginecologia
Gos Vses Nauchno Issled Inst Tsem Promsti Nauchn Soobshch — Gosudarstvennyi Vsesoyuznyi Nauchno-Issledovatel'skii Institut Tsementnoi Promyshlennosti Nauchnye Soobshcheniya
Gos Vses Proektn Nauchno Issled Inst Tsem Promsti Tr — Gosudarstvennyi Vsesoyuznyi Proektnyi i Nauchno-Issledovatel'skii Institut Tsementnoi Promyshlennosti Trudy
Goteb Ethnogr Mus — Goteborgs Ethnographical Museum
Goteb Naturhist Mus Arstryck — Goteborgs Naturhistoriska Museum Arstryck
Goteborg Univ Naturgeogr Inst Rapp — Goteborg Universitet. Naturgeografiska Institutionen. Rapport
Gothenburg Stud Phys — Gothenburg Studies in Physics
Goth SE — Gothenburg Studies in English
Gotlaendskt Arkiv — Gotlaendskt Arkiv
Gott Abh — Abhandlungen der Kungliga. Gessellschaft der Wissenschaften zu Goettingen
Gottesdienst Km — Gottesdienst und Kirchenmusik
Gottesd u Kir — Gottesdienst und Kirchenmusik
Gouc Col Se — Goucher College Series
Goulcae J Educ — Goulcae Journal of Education (Goulburn College of Advanced Education)
Gould League NSW Notes — Gould League of Bird Lovers of New South Wales. Notes
GOV — Government Executive
GOVAD — Golden Fleece

Gov Agric Res Cent Ghent Act Rep — Government Agricultural Research Centre. Ghent. Activity Report
Gov Data Syst — Government Data Systems [*United States*]
Governmental Research Bul (Fla) — Governmental Research Bulletin (Florida)
Gov Finance — Governmental Finance
Gov Metall Lab Repub S Afr Rep — Government Metallurgical Laboratory. Republic of South Africa. Report
Gov Pest Infest Lab Annu Rep — Government Pest Infestation Laboratory. Annual Report
Gov Pub R — Government Publications Review
Gov Relat Note — Government Relations Note
Gov Rep Announce — Government Reports Announcements
Gov Rep Announce Index — Government Reports Announcements and Index
Gov Reports Announce & Index — Government Reports Announcements and Index
GOVT — Government [*Boston*]
Govt Col Econ J — Government College Economic Journal
Govt Data Sys — Government Data Systems
Gov't Empl Rel Rep — Government Employee Relations Report
Govt Fin — Governmental Finance
Govt Gaz W Aust — Government Gazette. Western Australia
Govt & Oppos — Government and Opposition
Govt Oppos — Government and Opposition
Govt and Opposition — Government and Opposition
Govt Publns — Government Publications [*England*]
Govt Pubns R — Government Publications Review
Govt Pubns Rev — Government Publications Review
Govt Pubns R (Pt A) — Government Publications Review (Part A)
Govt Pub R — Government Publications Review
Govt Pub Rev — Government Publications Review
Govt Union R — Government Union Review
Govt Union Rev — Government Union Review
Gozd Vestn — Gozdarski Vestnik
Goz Klin Bul — Goz Klinigi Bulteni
GP — General Practice
GP — Geuzenpenning Munt- en Penningkundig Nieuws
GP — Giornale dei Poeti
GP — Gregorios ho Palamas
GP — Growing Point
GP — Guitar Player
GP — Gulden Passer
G PA — Geology of Pennsylvania
GPA — Guide to the Performing Arts
G Pal Abh — Geologische und Paleontologische Abhandlungen
GPerfArts — Guide to the Performing Arts
GPHTAR — Geophytology
GPJ — Great Plains Journal
GP J Am Acad Gen Pract — GP. Journal of the American Academy of General Practice
GPLAD — German Plastics
GPM — Genetic Psychology Monographs
GPMGAD — Geophysical Monograph
GPMOA3 — Genetic Psychology Monographs
G Pneumol — Giornale di Pneumologia
GPNOA — Geophysica Norvegica
G Pollicolt — Giornale dei Pollicoltori
GPOND — GPO [*Government Printing Office*] Newsletter
GPO Newsl — GPO [*Government Printing Office*] Newsletter [*United States*]
GPPEDP — Genetics; Principles and Perspectives
GPPRA — Geophysical Prospecting
GPQ — Great Plains Quarterly
GPrag — Germanistica Pragensia
GPRID — Geologiya, Poiski, i Razvedka Nerudnykh Poleznykh Iskopaemykh
G Psichiatr Neuropatol — Giornale di Psichiatria e di Neuropatologia
GPSR — Glossaire des Patois de la Suisse Romande
GPSVA — Geophysical Surveys
GPTKS — Glasnik Pravoslavne Tzrkve u Kraljevini Srbiji
GPVJ — Gesellschaft pro Vindonissa. Jahresbericht
GPYSA — Geophysics
GQ — Gentlemen's Quarterly
GQ — German Quarterly
GR — Geographical Review
GR — Georgia Review
GR — Germanic Review
GR — Girl's Realm
GR — Gramophone
GR — Grande Revue
G & R — Greece and Rome
Gra — Gravida
Grace Th J — Grace Theological Journal
Gradbeni Vestn — Gradbeni Vestnik [*Yugoslavia*]
GRADD — Graduate [*Canada*]
Grade Teach — Grade Teacher
Gradevin Fak Rad (Sarajevo) — Gradevinski Fakultet Radovi (Sarajevo)
Gradevinski Fak Sarajevo Rad — Gradevinski Fakultet. Sarajevo. Radovi
Grad Fac Phil J — Graduate Faculty Philosophy Journal

Gradinar Lozar Nauk — Gradinarska i Lozarska Nauka
Gradinar Lozar Nauka — Gradinarska i Lozarska Nauka
Gradinar Lozar Nauka Hortic Vitic Sci — Gradinarska i Lozarska Nauka. Horticulture and Viticultural Science
Gradja — Gradja za Povijest Knjizevnosti Hrvatske
Grad Res Ed — Graduate Research in Education and Related Disciplines
Grad Sem J — Graduate Seminar Journal
Grad Texts Math — Graduate Texts in Mathematics
Graefes Arch Klin Exp Ophthalmol — Graefes Archiv fuer Klinische und Experimentelle Ophthalmologie
Grafische Tech — Grafische Technik Dokumentationsdienst
Grafiska Forskningslab Medd — Grafiska Forskningslaboratoriets. Meddelande
Grafiska Forskningslab Projektrapp — Grafiska Forskningslaboratoriet. Projektrapport
Grafiske Hojskoles Smaskr — Grafiske Hojskoles Smaskrifter
Grain — Grain de Sel
Grain Feed J Consol — Grain and Feed Journals Consolidated
Grain Feed Rev — Grain and Feed Review
Grainger J — Grainger Journal
Grain Prod News — Grain Producer News
Grains J — Grains Journal
Grain Trade Buyers Guide Manage Ref — Grain Trade Buyers Guide and Management Reference
Grana Palynol — Grana Palynologica
Grand Canyon Nat History Assoc Bull — Grand Canyon Natural History Association. Bulletin
Granite Mo — Granite Monthly
Gran Mo — Granite Monthly
Granos Semilla Selec — Granos Semilla Selecta
Gran St M — Granite State Magazine [Manchester, NH]
Grants Mag — Grants Magazine
Grantsmanship Cent News — Grantsmanship Center. News
Graph Arts Abstr — Graphic Arts Abstracts
Graph Arts Mon Print Ind — Graphic Arts Monthly and the Printing Industry
Graphic Arts Bul — Graphic Arts Bulletin
Graphic Arts Lit Abstr — Graphic Arts Literature Abstracts
Graphic Arts M — Graphic Arts Monthly
Graphic Arts Mon — Graphic Arts Monthly and the Printing Industry
Graphic Arts Prog — Graphic Arts Progress
Graphic Commun World — Graphic Communications World
Graphic Comm Wk — Graphic Communications Weekly
Graphic Sci — Graphic Science
Grasas Aceit — Grasas y Aceites
Grasas Aceites — Grasas y Aceites
Grass J Br Assoc Green Crop Driers — Grass: The Journal of the British Association of Green Crop Driers
Grassl Res Inst (Hurley) Annu Rep — Grassland Research Institute (Hurley). Annual Report
Grassl Res Inst (Hurley) Exp Prog — Grassland Research Institute (Hurley). Experiments in Progress
Grassl Res Inst (Hurley) Tech Rep — Grassland Research Institute (Hurley). Technical Report
Grassl Soc South Afr Proc — Grassland Society of Southern Africa. Proceedings
GratzCAJS — Gratz College. Annual of Jewish Studies
Graver Water Cond Co Tech Repr — Graver Water Conditioning Company. Technical Reprint
Gravitatsiya Teor Otnositel'nosti — Gravitatsiya i Teoriya Otnositel'nosti [USSR]
Graylands Ed News — Graylands Education News
Gray Pant — Gray Panther Network
Grazer Phil Stud — Grazer Philosophische Studien
Grazhdanskaya Aviats — Grazhdanskaya Aviatsiya
Graz Landesmus Joanneum Abt Geol Palaeontol Bergbau Mitt — Graz. Landesmuseum Joanneum. Abteilung fuer Geologie, Palaeontologie, und Bergbau. Mitteilungen
Graz Landesmus Joanneum Abt Mineral Mitteilungsbl — Graz Landesmuseum Joanneum. Abteilung fuer Mineralogie. Mitteilungsblatt
Graz Landesmus Joanneum Jahresber — Graz Landesmuseum Joanneum. Jahresbericht
Graz Landesmus Joanneum Mus Bergbau Geol Tech Mitt — Graz Landesmuseum Joanneum. Museum fuer Bergbau, Geologie, und Technik. Mitteilungen
GRBM — Greek, Roman, and Byzantine Monographs
GR & BS — Greek, Roman, and Byzantine Studies
GRBS — Greek, Roman, and Byzantine Studies
GRBSA — Greek, Roman, and Byzantine Scholarly Aids
GRBSC — Greenland Bioscience. Meddelelser om Gronland
GRBUD — Geophysical Research Bulletin
GRC — Growth and Change
Grc Bk Eco — Economic Bulletin. Commercial Bank of Greece
GRDND6 — Gerodontology
Great Basin Nat — Great Basin Naturalist
Great Basin Nat Mem — Great Basin Naturalist. Memoirs
Greater Milw Dent Bull — Greater Milwaukee Dental Bulletin

Great Lakes — Great Lakes Review
Great Lakes Entomol — Great Lakes Entomologist
Great Lakes Fish Comm Annu Rep — Great Lakes Fishery Commission. Annual Report
Great Lakes Fish Comm Tech Rep — Great Lakes Fishery Commission. Technical Report
Great Lakes Res Div Univ Mich Publ — Great Lakes Research Division. University of Michigan. Publication
Great Plains Agric Counc Publ — Great Plains Agricultural Council. Publication
Great Synag Cong J — Great Synagogue Congregational Journal
Greece Bk — National Bank of Greece. Bulletin
Greece & Rome New Surv Class — Greece and Rome. New Surveys in the Classics
Greek Rom B — Greek, Roman, and Byzantine Studies
Greek Rom & Byz Stud — Greek, Roman, and Byzantine Studies
Greek Stat — Monthly Statistical Bulletin (Greece)
Green Bull — Green Bulletin
Greenkeepers Rep — Greenkeepers Reporter
Greenland Geol Unders Bull — Greenland. Geologiske Undersoegelse. Bulletin
Greenland Geol Unders Rapp — Greenland. Geologiske Undersoegelse. Rapport
Greenl Geosci — Greenland Geoscience [Denmark]
Green R — Greenfield Review
Green Rev — Green Revolution
Greenwich Time Rep — Greenwich Time Report
Greg — Gregorianum
Gregor — Gregoriusblad
G Reichs-Mus Leiden Samm — Geologische Reichs-Museum in Leiden. Sammlungen
G Rel Per — Guide to Religious Periodicals
Grenada Agric Dep Rep — Grenada Agricultural Department. Report
Grenoble Fac Sci Lab Geol Mem — Grenoble. Faculte des Sciences. Laboratoire de Geologie. Memoires
Grenoble Univ Lett Ann — Universite de Grenoble. Lettres-Droit. Annales
Grenoble Univ Sci Ann — Universite de Grenoble. Sciences-Medecine. Annales
Grenzgeb Med — Grenzgebiete der Medizin
G Rep Sask Res Counc Geol Div — G Report. Saskatchewan Research Council. Geology Division
GRF — Graficus; Onafhankelijk Weekblad voor de Grafische Industrie [Rijswijk]
GRFIA — Grinding and Finishing
GRFTAV — Gerfaut
GRFTAV — Giervalk
GRG — Den Haag. Maandblad van de Gemeente ('S-Gravenhage)
GRGSC — Greenland Geoscience. Meddelelser om Gronland
GRGSD — Gesellschaft fuer Reaktorsicherheit. Bericht GRS-S
GRHKA — Grudnaya Khirurgiya
GRI — Geographical Review of India
Griffin's Statist Monograph Ser — Griffin's Statistical Monograph Series
GRIN-A — Geographical Review of India
Grinding Finish — Grinding and Finishing
Grindlays Bank R — Grindlays Bank Review
GRI Newsl — GRI [Gravure Research Institute] Newsletter
Gripp Respir Virusn Infektsii — Gripp i Respiratornye Virusnye Infektsii
G Risic — Giornale di Risicoltura
Grits Grinds (Worcester, Mass) — Grits and Grinds (Worcester, Massachusetts)
GRLH — Garland Reference Library of the Humanities
Gr LJ — Georgetown Law Journal
GrLR — Great Lakes Review. A Journal of Midwest Culture
GRM — Germanisch-Romanische Monatsschrift
GRM — Groene Amsterdammer
GRMAA — Geologiya Rudnykh Mestorozhdenii
GRMDA — German Medicine
GRMMA — German Medical Monthly
G-R Mon — Germanisch-Romanische Monatsschrift
GRMS — Germanisch-Romanische Monatsschrift
GRNCA — Gerontologia Clinica
GRNCAK — Gerontologia Clinica
GRNL — Greenland Newsletter. Greenland Home Rule Information Service (Tusarliivik)
GRNR — Greinar
GRNTA — Gerontologist
Groc & Storekeeping News — Grocery and Storekeeping News
Groenlands Geol Unders Bull — Groenlands Geologiske Undersoegelse. Bulletin
Groenlands Geol Unders Misc Pap — Groenlands Geologiske Undersoegelse. Miscellaneous Papers
Groenlands Geol Undersoegelse Bull — Groenlands Geologiske Undersoegelse. Bulletin
Groenl Geol Unders Rap — Groenlands Geologiske Undersoegelse. Rapport
GROKA — Gornictwo Odkrywkowe
GROMAL — Geologica Romana
Grondboor Hamer — Grondboor en Hamer [Nederlandse Geologische Vereniging Tijdschrift]
Gr Orth Th R — Greek Orthodox Theological Review
GrOrthTR — Greek Orthodox Theological Review [Brookline, MA]

Grosses Zool Prakt — Grosses Zoologisches Praktikum
Ground Eng — Ground Engineering
Ground Wat — Ground Water Age
Ground Water Heat Pump J — Ground Water Heat Pump Journal
Group Avan Mec Ind — Groupement pour l'Avancement de la Mecanique Industrielle
Group Health J — Group Health Journal
Group Org Stud — Group and Organization Studies
Group Pract — Group Practice
Group Pract J — Group Practice Journal
Group Psych — Group Psychotherapy and Psychodrama [*Later, Group Psychotherapy, Psychodrama, and Sociometry*]
Group Psychother Psychodrama Sociometry — Group Psychotherapy, Psychodrama, and Sociometry
Grower Annu — Grower Annual
Growers' Dir Ill Crop Impr Ass — Growers' Directory. Illinois Crop Improvement Association
Growers' Handb Annu Proc — Growers' Handbook and Annual Proceedings. Ohio Vegetable and Potato Growers' Association
Growth Chan — Growth and Change
Grozn Neft — Groznenskii Neftyznik
Grozn Neft Inst Tr — Groznenskii Neftyanoi Institut. Trudy
GRPCD — GraphiCommunicator
GRPHA — Graphis
GRPSB — Group Psychotherapy [*Later, Group Psychotherapy, Psychodrama, and Sociometry*]
GRR — Green River Review
GRS — Gereedschap
GRS (Ges Reaktorsicherheit) Kurz-Inf Reihe A — GRS (Gesellschaft fuer Reaktorsicherheit). Kurz-Information. Reihe A
GRS (Ges Reaktorsicherheit) Kurz-Inf Reihe B — GRS (Gesellschaft fuer Reaktorsicherheit). Kurz-Information. Reihe B
GRS (Ges Reaktorsicherheit) Kurz-Inf Reihe C — GRS (Gesellschaft fuer Reaktorsicherheit). Kurz-Information. Reihe C
GRS (Ges Reaktorsicherheit) Kurz-Inf Reihe D — GRS (Gesellschaft fuer Reaktorsicherheit). Kurz-Information. Reihe D
GRS (Ges Reaktorsicherheit) Kurz-Inf Reihe E — GRS (Gesellschaft fuer Reaktorsicherheit). Kurz-Information. Reihe E
GRS (Ges Reaktorsicherheit) Kurz-Inf Reihe F — GRS (Gesellschaft fuer Reaktorsicherheit). Kurz-Information. Reihe F
GRS (Ges Reaktorsicherheit) Kurz-Inf Reihe G — GRS (Gesellschaft fuer Reaktorsicherheit). Kurz-Information. Reihe G
GRS (Ges Reaktorsicherheit) Kurz-Inf Reihe H — GRS (Gesellschaft fuer Reaktorsicherheit). Kurz-Information. Reihe H
GRS Kurz-Inf Reihe J — GRS (Gesellschaft fuer Reaktorsicherheit). Kurz-Information. Reihe J [*West Germany*]
GrSt — Grundtvig Studier
Grt Barrier Reef Comm Pap — Great Barrier Reef Committee. Heron Island Research Station. Papers
Grt Bird — Great Speckled Bird
GRU — Geographische Rundschau; Zeitschrift fuer Schulgeographie
Grudn Khir — Grudnaya Khirurgiya
GRUND — Grundeigentum
Grundkurs Math — Grundkurs Mathematik
Grundkurs Phys — Grundkurs Physik
Grund Kyber Geist — Grundlagenstudien aus Kybernetik und Geisteswissenschaft
Grundlagen Math Inform — Grundlagen der Mathematik und Informatik
Grundlehren Math Wiss — Grundlehren der Mathematischen Wissenschaften
G Rundschau — Geologische Rundschau
Grundwissen Math — Grundwissen Mathematik
Gruppenpsyc — Gruppenpsychotherapie und Gruppendynamik
Gruzin Politehn Inst Trudy — Gruzinskii Politehniceskii Institut Imeni V. I. Lenina Trudy
Gruz Skh Inst Nauchn Tr — Gruzinskii Sel'skokhozyaistvennyi Institut Nauchnye Trudy
Gruz Skh Inst Tr — Gruzinskii Sel'skokhozyaistvennyi Institut Trudy
GRW — Griechischer Wirtschaftsdienst
GRZ — Growth and Change
GRZZAD — Glasnik Republickog Zavoda za Zastitu Prirode i Prirodnjackog Muzeja Titogradu
GS — Gengo Seikatsu
GS — Germanistische Studien
GS — Gesammelte Schriften
GS — Grai si Suflet
G & S — Grai si Suflet
GSA — German Studies in America
GSAI — Giornale della Societa Asiatica Italiana
GSAKAK — Glas Srpska Akademija Nauka i Umetnosti Odeljenje Prirodno-Matematickikh Nauka
GSAMAQ — Geological Society of America. Memoir
GSAPAZ — Geological Society of America. Special Paper (Regional Studies)
GSA Spec Pap (Reg Stud) — GSA [*Geological Society of America*] Special Paper (Regional Studies)
GSB — General Semantics Bulletin
GSB — Georgia State Bar Journal

GSBBAW — Godishnik na Sofiiskiya Universitet. Biologo-Geologo-Geografski Fakultet. Kniga I. Biologiya
GSBIAJ — Annuaire. Universite de Sofia. Faculte de Biologie
GSBIAJ — Godishnik na Sofiiskiya Universitet. Biologicheski Fakultet
GSBZA2 — Godishnik na Sofiiskiya Universitet. Biologicheski Fakultet. Kniga 1. Zoologiya, Fiziologiya, i Biokhimiya na Zhivotnite
G Sc B — Geological and Scientific Bulletin
GSCB — Geological Survey of Canada. Bulletin
G Sci Med — Giornale di Scienze Mediche
GSCM — Geological Survey of Canada. Memoir
GSCN — Grantsmanship Center. News
GSCP — Geological Survey of Canada. Paper
GSD — Geistes- und Sozialwissenschaftliche Dissertationen
GSDBA — Geophysics and Space Data Bulletin
GSDCB — Geoscience Documentation [*England*]
GSDMA — Gornye, Stroitel'nye i Dorozhnye Mashiny
GSE — Gothenburg Studies in English
GSE — Graduate Student of English
GSEVD8 — Genetique, Selection, Evolution
GSF — Galaxy Science Fiction
GSFB — Geological Survey of Finland. Bulletin
GSFGB — Giessereiforschung
GSFN — Galaxy Science Fiction Novels
GSFNAK — Geological Survey of Finland. Bulletin
GSFS — Great Science Fiction Stories
GSGMEQ — Genetic, Social, and General Psychology Monographs
GSIBAX — Geological Society of India. Bulletin
GSJ — Galpin Society. Journal
G & S J — Gilbert and Sullivan Journal
Gsl — Germano-Slavica
GSL — Medieval Studies in Memory of Gertrude Schoepperle Loomis
G Slav — Germano-Slavica
GSLI — Giornale Storico della Letteratura Italiana
GSLL — Giornale Storico e Letterario della Liguria
GSMBBK — Geological Society of Malaysia. Bulletin
GSMMBJ — Geological Survey of Malaysia. District Memoir
GSMNBM — Geological Society of Malaysia. Newsletter
GSMPAR — Geological Survey of Malaysia. Geological Papers
GS News Tech Rep — GS News Technical Report [*Japan*]
G Soc Am B — Geological Society of America. Bulletin
G Soc Dublin J — Geological Society of Dublin. Journal
G Soc Glas Tr — Geological Society of Glasgow. Transactions
G Soc PA Tr — Geological Society of Pennsylvania. Transactions
G Soc Tokyo J — Geological Society of Tokyo. Journal
GSORD — Geological Survey Open-File Report [*United States*]
GSP — Glasnik za Sumske Pokuse
GSP — Royal Geographical Society. Proceedings
GSPGAF — Geograficheskii Sbornik Penzenskogo Otdeleniya Geograficheskogo Obshchestva SSSR
GSQ — German Shepherd Quarterly
GSQNA — Geological Society of South Africa. Quarterly News Bulletin
GSRED — Gas Supply Review
GSRTA — Giessereitechnik
GSSRPL — Guide to Social Science and Religion in Periodical Literature
GSt — Germanische Studien
GST — Glass Science and Technology [*Elsevier Book Series*]
GSTHA4 — Giessener Schriftenreihe Tierzucht und Haustiergenetik
G Stor Let — Giornale Storico della Letteratura Italiana
GStud — Grudtvig Studier
GSU — Godisnik na Sofijskiya Universitet. Filologiceski Fakultet
GSUF — Godisnik na Sofijskiya Universitet. Filologiceski Fakultet
GSUFD6 — Annuaire. Universite de Sofia. Kliment Ochridski Faculte de Biologie
GSUFD6 — Godishnik na Sofiiskiya Universitet. Kliment Okhridski Biologicheski Fakultet
GSUFZF — Godisnik na Sofijskiya Universitet. Fakultet po Zapadni Filologii
GT — Geografisk Tidsskrift
GT — Ghanaian Times
GT — Journal of Geotechnical Engineering
GTA Dig — GTA [*Grain Terminal Association*] Digest
Gt Basin Nat — Great Basin Naturalist
Gt Brit & East — Great Britain and the East
GTBWA — Gartenbauwissenschaft
GTE Auto — GTE [*General Telephone and Electronics Corp.*] Automatic Electric Technical Journal [*Later, GTE Automatic Electric World-Wide Communications Journal*]
GTE Autom Electr J — GTE [*General Telephone and Electronics Corp.*] Automatic Electric Technical Journal [*Later, GTE Automatic Electric World-Wide Communications Journal*]
GTE Autom Electr Tech J — GTE [*General Telephone and Electronics Corp.*] Automatic Electric Technical Journal [*Later, GTE Automatic Electric World-Wide Communications Journal*]
GTE Autom Electr World-Wide Commun J — GTE [*General Telephone and Electronics Corp.*] Automatic Electric World-Wide Communications Journal
GThT — Gereformeerd Theologisch Tijdschrift [*Kampen*]

GTJ — Grace Theological Journal
GTKRD — Gan To Kagaku Ryoho
GTKTA — Geotektonika
Gt Lakes Ent — Great Lakes Entomologist
GTMBAQ — Georgetown Medical Bulletin
GTMCA — Geothermics
GTNEEA — Genetic Technology News
GTNQA — Geotechnique [England]
Gt Plains Jour — Great Plains Journal
GTPPA — Gigiena Truda i Professional'naya Patologiya v Estonskoi SSR
GTPZA — Gigiena Truda i Professional'nye Zabolevaniya
GTPZA — Gigiyena Truda i Professional'nyye Zabolevaniia
GTPZAB — Gigiena Truda i Professional'nye Zabolevaniya
GTR — Greek Orthodox Theological Review
GTR — Guitar Review
GTRWA — Gdanskie Towarzystwo Naukowe Rozparawy Wydzialu
GTS — Germanistische Texte und Studien
GTS — Gettysburg Theological Studies
GTSTA — Gidrotekhnicheskoe Stroitel'stvo
GTT — Gereformeerd Theologisch Tijdschrift
GTWOD — Gas Turbine World
GU — Guitar Review
GUA — Goeteborgs Universitets Arsskrift
Guam Ag Exp — Guam Agricultural Experiment Station. Publications
Guatem Indig — Guatemala Indigena
Guertler Bijout Metallwaren Ind — Guertler. Bijouterie und Metallwaren Industrie
Guetersloher Beitr — Guetersloher Beitraege zur Heimatund Landeskunde
GuG — Gestalt und Gedanke. Ein Jahrbuch
Guideb Annu Field Conf Mont Geol Soc — Guidebook. Annual Field Conference. Montana Geological Society
Guideb Geol Utah — Guidebook to the Geology of Utah
Guideb Ser Geol Inst (Bucharest) — Guidebook Series. Geological Institute (Bucharest)
Guidhall Stud London Hist — Guildhall Studies in London History
Guid Spec Educ Bull — Guidance and Special Education Bulletin
Guild C Psych — National Guild of Catholic Psychiatrists. Bulletin
Guildhall Misc — Guildhall Miscellany
Guildhall S — Guildhall Studies in London History
Guild Nts — Guild Notes
Guild Prac — Guild Practitioner
GUISA — Guide to Scientific Instruments
Guitar R — Guitar Review
Guitarra — Guitarra Magazine
Guitar Rev — Guitar Review
Gujarat Agric Univ Res J — Gujarat Agricultural University. Research Journal
Gujarat Statist Rev — Gujarat Statistical Review
Guj LT — Gujarat Law Times
GUJRD — Gomal University. Journal of Research
Gulf Caribb Fish Inst Univ Miami Proc — Gulf and Caribbean Fisheries Institute. University of Miami. Proceedings
Gulf Coast Assoc Geol Socs Trans — Gulf Coast Association of Geological Societies. Transactions
Gulf Coast Cattlem — Gulf Coast Cattleman
Gulf Res Rep — Gulf Research Reports
GUM — Gummi, Asbest, Kunststoffe. Internationale Unabhangige Fachzeitschrift
Gummi Asbest Kunstst — Gummi, Asbest, Kunststoffe [Later, Gummi, Fasern, Kunststoffe]
Gummi Fasern Kunstst — Gummi, Fasern, Kunststoffe
Gummi Kunst — Gummi, Asbest, Kunststoffe [Later, Gummi, Fasern, Kunststoffe]
GUMSL — Georgetown University. Monograph Series on Languages and Linguistics
Gunma J Libr Arts Sci — Gunma Journal of Liberal Arts and Science
Gunma J Med Sci — Gunma Journal of Medical Science
Gunma J Med Sci Suppl — Gunma Journal of Medical Sciences. Supplementum
Gunma Rep Med Sci — Gunma Reports of Medical Sciences
Gunma Symp Endocrinol — Gunma Symposia on Endocrinology
Gunton — Gunton's Magazine
GUP — Georgetown University. Papers on Languages and Linguistics
GUR — Government Union Review
GURID — Gazzetta Ufficiale della Repubblica Italiana
GURT — Georgetown University. Round Table on Languages and Linguistics
Gurukula Kangri Vishwavidyalaya J Sci Res — Gurukula Kangri Vishwavidyalaya. Journal of Scientific Research
GUSYA — Gunma Symposia on Endocrinology
GuT — Geist und Tat
Guthrie Bull — Guthrie Bulletin
GUXUD — Guangxue Xuebao
Guyana Geol Surv Dep Rep — Guyana. Geological Survey Department. Report
Guyana J Sci — Guyana Journal of Science
Guyana Minist Agric Nat Resour Agric Land Dev Ann Rep — Guyana. Ministry of Agriculture and Natural Resources. Agriculture and Land Developments. Annual Report

Guyana Minist Agric Nat Resour Geol Surv Dep Rep — Guyana. Ministry of Agriculture and Natural Resources. Geological Survey Department. Report
Guyana Mist Agric Nat Resourc Agric Land Dev Dep Annu Rep — Guyana. Ministry of Agriculture and Natural Resources. Agriculture and Land Development Departments. Annual Report
Guyana Sugar Exp Stn Bull — Guyana Sugar Experiment Station's Bulletin
Guy's Hosp Gaz — Guy's Hospital Gazette
Guy's Hosp Rep — Guy's Hospital Reports
GuZ — Geist und Zeit
GV — Gil Vicente
GVA — Groningsche Volksalmanach
GVDSB — Government Data Systems
G Veneto Sci Med — Giornale Veneto di Scienze Mediche
GVKIA — Godishnik na Visshiya Khimikotekhnologicheski Institut
GVMKD — Gibridnye Vychislitel'nye Mashiny i Kompleksy
GVRAA — Government Reports Announcements [United States]
GVTKA — Galvanotechnik
Gvt and Opposition — Government and Opposition
GW — Genesis West
GW — George Washington Law Review
GW — Germanica Wratislaviensia
GW — Guardian Weekly
GW — Gymnasium und Wissenschaft
GWA — Gewerbearchiv. Zeitschrift fuer Gewerbeverwaltungsrecht und Wirtschaftsverwaltungsrecht
GWASA — Gas, Wasser, Abwasser
GWF — Graphik Visuelles Marketing
GWHJD — Ground Water Heat Pump Journal
GW LR — George Washington Law Review
GWLRA — George Washington Law Review
GWM — Gewerkschaftliche Monatshefte
GWWAA — GWF. Gas- und Wasserfach: Wasser/Abwasser
GYDKA9 — Annual Proceedings. Gifu Pharmaceutical University
GYDKA9 — Gifu Yakka Daigaku Kiyo
Gym — Gymnasium
Gynaekol Rundsch — Gynaekologische Rundschau
Gynecol Inv — Gynecologic Investigation
Gynecol Invest — Gynecologic Investigation
Gynecol Obstet — Gynecologie et Obstetrique
Gynecol Obstet Invest — Gynecologic and Obstetric Investigation
Gynecol Oncol — Gynecologic Oncology
Gynecol Prat — Gynecologie Pratique
GYNOA — Gynecologic Oncology
GYOBA — Gynecologie et Obstetrique de Langue Francaise
Gy S — Gypsy Scholar
GZ — Gazeta Zydowska
GZ — Geographische Zeitschrift
GZH — Gdanskie Zeszyty Humanistyczne
GZINB — Bharat Ka Rajpatra
GZM — Glasnik Zemaljskog Muzeja [Subseries] Etnologija
GZMS — Glasnik Zemaljskog Muzeja u Sarajevu
GZSRAA — Gezira Research Station and Substations. Annual Report

H

H — Harper's Magazine
H — Hermes. Zeitschrift fuer Klassische Philologie
H — Hispania
H — History
HA — Handes Amsorya
Ha — Harpers
HA — Heidelberger Abhandlungen
HA — Helvetia Archaeologica
Ha — Hermathena
HA — Historical Abstracts [ABC-Clio] [Santa Barbara, CA]
HAA — Hitotsubashi University. Hitotsubashi Academy. Annals
HAA J — HAA [Herpetological Association of Africa] Journal
HAB — Humanities Association. Bulletin
Habana Mus y Biblioteca Malacologia Circ — Habana Museo y Biblioteca de
    Malacologia. Circulares
Habana Mus y Biblioteca Zoologia Circ — Habana Museo y Biblioteca de
    Zoologia. Circulares
HABI — Habitat
Habitat Aust — Habitat Australia
Habitat Int — Habitat International [England]
Habitat Vie Soc — Habitat et Vie Sociale
HABRA — Harvard Business Review
HABT-A — Habitat
HAC — Heating and Air Conditioning Journal
HACCA — Heating and Air Conditioning Contractor
Hacett B SS — Hacettepe Bulletin of Social Sciences and Humanities
Hacettepe Bull Med-Surg — Hacettepe Bulletin of Medicine-Surgery
Hacettepe Fen Muhendislik Bilimleri Derg — Hacettepe Fen ve Muhendislik
    Bilimleri Dergisi
Hacettepe Muhendislik Bilimleri Derg — Hacettepe Fen ve Muhendislik
    Bilimleri Dergisi [Turkey]
Hacienda Publica Esp — Hacienda Publica Espanola
Hadashot Arch — Hadashot Archaeologioth
Hadronic J — Hadronic Journal
HAEC — Holarctic Ecology
HAEK — Historische. Archiv fuer die Erzbistum Koeln
HAEMA — Haematologica
Haematol Bluttransfus — Haematologie und Bluttransfusion [Haematology
    and Blood Transfusion]
Haematol Lat — Haematologica Latina
Haerterei-Tech Mitt — Haerterei-Technische Mitteilungen
Haerterei-Tech Waermebehandl — Haerterei-Technik und Waermebehandlung
Haert-Tech Mitt — Haerterei-Technische Mitteilungen
HAFFB — Health Affairs
Haffkine Inst Annu Rep — Haffkine Institute. Annual Report
HAHGG — Historiche Avonden. Uitgegeven door het Historiche Genootschap
    te Groningen ter Gelegenheid van Zijn Twintigjarig Bestaan
Ha Hinnuk Ham M — Ha-Hinnuk Ham-Musiquali
Hahnemann Symp — Hahnemann Symposium
HAHR — Hispanic American Historical Review
Haile Selassie I Univ Dep Geol Annu Rep — Haile Selassie I University.
    Department of Geology. Annual Report
Hakone Symp Proc — Hakone Symposium. Proceedings
Halbmon Literaturverz Fortschr Phys — Halbmonatliches Literaturverzeichnis
    der Fortschrifte der Physik

HALEA — Harvey Lectures
Half-Yrly J Mysore Univ Sect B Sci Incl Med Eng — Half-Yearly Journal.
    Mysore University. Section B. Science Including Medicine and
    Engineering
(Halle) Beitr — Beitraege zur Geschichte der Deutschen Sprache und Literatur
    (Halle)
Haller Mb — Haller Muenzblaetter
Hallesches Jahrb Mitteldtsh Erdgesch — Hallesches Jahrbuch fuer
    Mitteldeutsche Erdgeschichte
Halle Univ Wiss Z Gesellsch & Sprachw Reihe — Halle Universitaet.
    Wissenschaftliche Zeitschrift Gesellschafts und Sprachwissenschaftliche
    Reihe
HALRA — Harvard Law Review
Halsbury — Halsbury's Law of England
Halsbury L Eng — Halsbury's Law of England
Halsbury's Laws — Halsbury's Law of England
HAMAA — Harper's Magazine
HAMAD — Harvard Magazine
Hamb Beitr Angew Mineral Kristallphys Petrog — Hamburger Beitraege zur
    Angewandten Mineralogie, Kristallphysik, und Petrogenese
Hamb Geophys Einzelschriften — Hamburger Geophysikalische Einzelschriften
Hamb St u Z Nachr — Hamburger Steuer und Zoll-Nachrichten
Hamburg Geol Staatsinstitut Mitt — Hamburg Geologischen Staatsinstitut.
    Mitteilungen
Hamburg Jb Wirtsch- u Ges-Polit — Hamburger Jahrbuch fuer Wirtschafts-
    und Gesellschaftspolitik
Hamb Wirtsch — Hamburger Wirtschaft [Mitteilungen der Handelskammer
    Hamburg]
Hamb Wschr Ae Zahn Ae — Hamburger Wochenschrift fuer Aerzte und
    Zahnaerzte
Hamb Zool Staatsinst u Zool Mus Mitt — Hamburg. Zoologisches
    Staatsinstitut und Zoologisches Museum. Mitteilungen
Hamdard Islam — Hamdard Islamicus
Hamdard Med Dig — Hamdard Medical Digest
HAMIA — Hasler-Mitteilungen
Hamilton As J Pr — Hamilton Association. Journal and Proceedings
Hamilton Sc As J Pr — Hamilton Scientific Association. Journal and
    Proceedings
Hamline LR — Hamline Law Review
Hamline L Rev — Hamline Law Review
Ham Mo Bul — Ham (Walter P.) and Company. Monthly Bulletin
Hamps Beekpr — Hampshire Beekeeper
Hampton — Hampton's Magazine
HAMSB — Heidelberger Akademie der Wissenschaften. Mathematisch-
    Naturwissenschaftliche Klasse. Sitzungsberichte
Hand — Hand Book
Handball Mag — Handball Magazine
Handb Exp Pharmak — Handbuch der Experimentellen
Handb Lebensmittelchemie — Handbuch der Lebensmittelchemie
Handb Med Radiol — Handbuch der Medizinschen Radiologie [West
    Germany]
Handb Mineral — Handbuch der Mineralogie
Handbook Appl Math Guidebook — Handbook of Applicable Mathematics
    Guidebook
Handbooks in Econom — Handbooks in Economics

Handb Pflernahr Dueng — Handbuch der Pflanzenernahrung und Duengung
Handb Phys — Handbuch der Physik
Handb Physiol — Handbook of Physiology
Handb Spez Path Anat Haustiere (Ernst Joest) — Handbuch der Speziellen Pathologischen Anatomie der Haustiere (Ernst Joest)
Handb Urol — Handbuch der Urologie
Handb US Natn Bur Stand — Handbook. United States National Bureau of Standards
Handb Zool — Handbuch der Zoologie
Handel Ind — Handel en Industrie
Handelingen Commissie Toponymie & Dialectologie — Handelingen. Koninklijke Commissie voor Toponymie en Dialectologie
Handelingen Ned Phonol Werkgemeenschap — Handelingen. Nederlandse Phonologische Werkgemeenschap
Handel Jb — Handel Jahrbuch
Handel Ned Nat Geneeskd Congr — Handelingen. Nederlands Natuur- en Geneeskundig Congres
Handel Oudheidkunde Mechelen — Handelingen. Koninklijke Kring voor Oudheidkunde. Letteren en Kunst van Mechelen Malines [*Belgium*]
Handelsblt — Handelsblatt
Handel Voeding Ver Suidel — Handelinge. Voedingvereeniging van Suidelike Afrika
Handel Wewn — Handel Wewnetrzny
Handel Zagran — Handel Zagraniczy
Handes Amsorya — Handes Amsorya. Monatschrift fuer Armenische Philologie
HandKonCommTop-Dial — Handelingen. Koninklijke Commissie voor Toponymie en Dialectologie
Handl Conveying Autom — Handling, Conveying, Automation [*West Germany*]
Handl & Shipp — Handling and Shipping [*Later, Handling and Shipping Management*]
Handl Shipp Manage — Handling and Shipping Management
Handl & Shipp Mgt — Handling and Shipping Management
Hand Ned Jur V — Handelingen. Nederlandse Juristen-Vereeniging
HandNFc — Handelingen. Nederlands Filologencongres
Hand Vl Fc — Handelingen. Vlaamse Filologiecongres
Handweaver — Handweaver and Craftsman
Hand Wewn — Handel Wewnetrzny
Handw O — Handwerksordnung
Handyman — Family Handyman
Hang L — Hanging Loose
Han'guk Sikp'un Kwhak Hoechi Korea J Food Sci Technol — Han'guk Sikp'un Kwahak Hoechi. Korean Journal of Food Science and Technology
Hannah Dairy Res Inst Rep — Hannah Dairy Research Institute. Report
Hannah Res Inst Rep — Hannah Research Institute. Report
Hann Rpfl — Hannoversche Rechtspflege
Hansard (C) — Hansard (Commons)
Hansard House Commons Off Rep — Hansard. House of Commons. Official Report [*Great Britain*]
Hansard (L) — Hansard (Lords)
HANSB — Hanseniase
Hanseniase Resumos Not — Hanseniase. Resumos e Noticias
Hansenol Int — Hansenologia Internationalis
Hans G Bl — Hansische Geschichtsblaetter
Hans JV Bl — Hanseatisches Justizverwaltungsblatt
HAnt — Hispania Antiqua
Hant Ams — Hantes Amsoriay
Hanzaigaku Zasshi (Acta Criminol Med Leg Jpn) — Hanzaigaku Zasshi (Acta Criminologiae et Medicinae Legalis Japonica)
HAPG — Heidelberger Abhandlungen zur Philosophie und Ihrer Geschichte
HAR — Hamburger Akademische Rundschau
HAR — Harvard Journal on Legislation
HAR — Hebrew Annual Review
HAR — Humanities Association. Review
Har Alum Bull — Harvard Alumni Bulletin
H Arb G — Heimarbeitsgesetz
Harbour — Australian Coal, Shipping, Steel, and the Harbour
Harbour & Shipp — Harbour and Shipping
Har Bus R — Harvard Business Review
Hardware J — Hardware Journal
Hardware R — Hardware Retailing
Hardware Trade J — Hardware Trade Journal
HAREA — Harefuah
Haref — Harefuah
Har Int LJ — Harvard International Law Journal
Har J Leg — Harvard Journal on Legislation
Harker Geol Soc J — Harker Geological Society. Journal
Harl Hosp Bull — Harlem Hospital Bulletin
Har LR — Harvard Law Review
Harmonika Jb — Harmonika-Jahrbuch
Harokeach Haivri Heb Pharm (Sci Ed) — Harokeach Haivri. The Hebrew Pharmacist (Science Edition)
Harold L Lyon Arbor Lect — Harold L. Lyon Arboretum. Lecture
Harp — Harper's Magazine

Harp Ad Util Poult J — Harper Adams Utility Poultry Journal
Harp B — Harper's Bazaar
Harp Baz — Harper's Bazaar
Harper — Harper's Magazine
Harper Hosp Bull — Harper Hospital. Bulletin
Harper's Mag — Harper's New Monthly Magazine
Harp MM — Harper's Monthly Magazine
Harp N — Harp News
Harp W — Harper's Weekly
Harris County Physician — Harris County Physician Newsletter
HarSemSer — Harvard Semitic Series [*Cambridge, MA*]
Hartf Hosp Bull — Hartford Hospital. Bulletin
Hartford Hosp Bull — Hartford Hospital. Bulletin
Hartf Sem Rec — Hartford Seminary Record
Hartf Stud Ling — Hartford Studies in Linguistics
Har Theol Rev — Harvard Theological Review
Hart Q — Hartford Quarterly
Hart R — Hartwick Review
Hart-Tech Mitt — Harterei-Technische Mitteilungen [*West Germany*]
Harv Ad — Harvard Advocate
Harvard A — Harvard Advocate
Harvard Archre Review — Harvard Architecture Review
Harvard BR — Harvard Business Review
Harvard Bsns R — Harvard Business Review
Harvard Bus R — Harvard Business Review
Harvard Bus Rev — Harvard Business Review
Harvard Civil Rights - Civil Liberties Law R — Harvard Civil Rights - Civil Liberties Law Review
Harvard Civil Rights L Rev — Harvard Civil Rights-Civil Liberties Law Review
Harvard Coll Mus Comp Zoology Bull — Harvard College. Museum of Comparative Zoology. Bulletin
Harvard Coll Mus CZ An Rp — Harvard College. Museum of Comparative Zoology. Annual Report
Harvard Coll Mus C Z B — Harvard College. Museum of Comparative Zoology. Bulletin
Harvard Coll Mus C Z Mem — Harvard College. Museum of Comparative Zoology. Memoirs
Harvard Ed R — Harvard Educational Review
Harvard Educ R — Harvard Educational Review
Harvard Engl Stud — Harvard English Studies
Harvard Environmental Law R — Harvard Environmental Law Review
Harvard Forest Bull — Harvard Forest. Bulletin
Harvard Internat Law J — Harvard International Law Journal
Harvard Int LJ — Harvard International Law Journal
Harvard J Asiat Stud — Harvard Journal of Asiatic Studies
Harvard J Law and Public Policy — Harvard Journal of Law and Public Policy
Harvard J on Legis — Harvard Journal on Legislation
Harvard J Legislation — Harvard Journal on Legislation
Harvard Law R — Harvard Law Review
Harvard Lib Bul — Harvard Library Bulletin
Harvard L Rev — Harvard Law Review
Harvard Med Alumni Bull — Harvard Medical Alumni Bulletin
Harvard Med Sch Health Let — Harvard Medical School. Health Letter
Harvard Mon Applied Sci — Harvard Monographs in Applied Science
Harvard Public Health Alumni Bull — Harvard Public Health Alumni Bulletin
Harvard Theol R — Harvard Theological Review
Harvard Univ B — Harvard University. Bulletin
Harvard Univ Bot Mus Leaflets — Harvard University. Botanical Museum Leaflets
Harvard Univ Dep Eng Publ — Harvard University. Department of Engineering. Publications
Harvard Univ Gray Herbarium Contr — Harvard University. Gray Herbarium. Contributions
Harvard Univ Harvard Soil Mech Ser — Harvard University. Harvard Soil Mechanics Series
Harvard Univ Mus Comp Zoology Bull — Harvard University. Museum of Comparative Zoology. Bulletin
Harvard Women's Law J — Harvard Women's Law Journal
Harv Asia — Harvard Journal of Asiatic Studies
Harv Bus Re — Harvard Business Review
Harv Bus Rev — Harvard Business Review
Harv Civil Rights L Rev — Harvard Civil Rights - Civil Liberties Law Review
Harv Civ Rights - Civ Liberties Law Rev — Harvard Civil Rights - Civil Liberties Law Review
Harv Class Phil — Harvard Studies in Classical Philology
Harv CR-CLL — Harvard Civil Rights - Civil Liberties Law Review
Harv CR-CLL Rev — Harvard Civil Rights - Civil Liberties Law Review
HarvDBull — Harvard Divinity School. Bulletin [*Cambridge, MA*]
Harv Div B — Harvard Divinity Bulletin
Harv East As Ser — Harvard East Asian Series
Harv Edu Re — Harvard Educational Review
Harv Environ Law Rev — Harvard Environmental Law Review
Harv Envtl L Rev — Harvard Environmental Law Review
Harvester in Aust — Harvester in Australia
Harvester Readings Hist Sci Philos — Harvester Readings in the History of Science and Philosophy [*Brighton*]

Harvest Q — Harvest Quarterly
Harvey Lect — Harvey Lectures
Harv For Annu Rep — Harvard Forest. Annual Report
Harv For Bull — Harvard Forest. Bulletin
Harv For Pap — Harvard Forest. Papers
Harv Grad M — Harvard Graduates' Magazine
Harv Int L J — Harvard International Law Journal
Harv Int'l LJ — Harvard International Law Journal
Harv J Asia — Harvard Journal of Asiatic Studies
Harv J Asiatic Stud — Harvard Journal of Asiatic Studies
Harv J Leg — Harvard Journal on Legislation
Harv J on Legis — Harvard Journal on Legislation
Harv J Legis — Harvard Journal on Legislation
Harv JL and Pub Poly — Harvard Journal of Law and Public Policy
Harv Law R — Harvard Law Review
Harv Law Rev — Harvard Law Review
Harv Lib Bull — Harvard Library Bulletin
Harv Libr B — Harvard Library Bulletin
Harv Libr Bull — Harvard Library Bulletin
Harv L Rev — Harvard Law Review
Harv LS Bull — Harvard Law School Bulletin
Harv Mag — Harvard Magazine
Harv Med Alumni Bull — Harvard Medical Alumni Bulletin
Harv Med Sch Health Lett — Harvard Medical School. Health Letter
Harv Mo — Harvard Monthly
Harv Pathophysiol Ser — Harvard Pathophysiology Series
Harv Public Health Alumni Bull — Harvard Public Health Alumni Bulletin
Harv R — Harvard Review
Harv St Cla — Harvard Studies in Classical Philology
Harv Stud Class Philol — Harvard Studies in Classical Philology
Harv Theol — Harvard Theological Review
Harv Theol R — Harvard Theological Review
Harv Theol Rev — Harvard Theological Review
Harv Th R — Harvard Theological Review
HarvTR — Harvard Theological Review [*Cambridge, MA*]
Harv Univ Mus Comp Zool Bull — Harvard University. Museum of Comparative Zoology. Bulletin
Harv Univ Mus Comp Zool Spec Occas Publ — Harvard University. Museum of Comparative Zoology. Special Occasional Publication
Harv Univ Sch Public Health Dean's Rep — Harvard University. School of Public Health. Dean's Report
Harv Women LJ — Harvard Women's Law Journal
Har Women LR — Harvard Women's Law Review
Haryana Agric Univ J Res — Haryana Agricultural University. Journal of Research
Haryana J Hort Sci — Haryana Journal of Horticulture Sciences
Harz Z — Harz Zeitschrift
Has Con LQ — Hastings Constitutional Law Quarterly
Has Int and Comp LR — Hastings International and Comparative Law Review
Hasler Mitt — Hasler-Mitteilungen
Hasler Rev — Hasler Review
Has LJ — Hastings Law Journal
HASSA — Hassadeh
Hast Cen St — Hastings Center. Studies
Hast Cent Rpt — Hastings Center. Report
Hast Cent St — Hastings Center. Studies
Hast Const LQ — Hastings Constitutional Law Quarterly
Hast Deering News — Hastings Deering News
Hastings Area Archaeol Pap — Hastings Area Archaeological Papers
Hastings Cent Rep — Hastings Center. Report
Hastings Cent Stud — Hastings Center. Studies
Hastings Const LQ — Hastings Constitutional Law Quarterly
Hastings Ctr Rept — Hastings Center. Report
Hastings E Suss Nat — Hastings and East Sussex Naturalist
Hastings Intl and Comp L Rev — Hastings International and Comparative Law Review
Hastings L J — Hastings Law Journal
Hast Law J — Hastings Law Journal
Hast LJ — Hastings Law Journal
HAT — Handelsblatt. Wirtschaftzeitung und Finanzzeitung
HATAA4 — Amino Acid and Nucleic Acid
HAUID — Hanguk Uikwahak
HAUND — Hannover Uni
HAURBR — Encyclopedia of Urology
Hausm — Hausmusik
Hausmitt Jos Schneider — Hausmitteilungen Jos Schneider
Hausmus — Hausmusik
Haus Tech — Haus Technik [*West Germany*]
Haustech Bauphys Umwelttech — Haustechnik, Bauphysik, Umwelttechnik
Haus Tech Essen Vortragsveroeff — Haus der Technik-Essen-Vortragsveroeffentlichungen
Haustech Rundsch — Haustechnische Rundschau [*West Germany*]
Haus Tech-Vortrag-Veroeff — Haus der Technik-Vortrags-Veroeffentlichungen
Hausz VAW Erftwerk AG Alum — Hauszeitschrift der VAW und der Erftwerk AG fuer Aluminium

HAUTA — Hautarzt [*Austria*]
Havana Bibl Nac R — Havana Biblioteca Nacional. Revista
Havana Univ Cienc Ser 4 Cienc Biol — Havana Universidad. Ciencias. Serie 4. Ciencias Biologicas
Havana Univ Cienc Ser 7 Geogr — Havana Universidad. Ciencias. Serie 7. Geografia
Havana Univ Cienc Ser 8 Invest Mar — Havana Universidad. Ciencias. Serie 8. Investigaciones Marinas
Havana Univ Tecnol Ser 10 Ing Hidraul — Havana Universidad. Tecnologia. Serie 10. Ingenieria Hidraulica
Havforskningsinst Skr — Havsforskningsinstituets Skrift
Hawaii Ag Exp — Hawaii. Agricultural Experiment Station. Publications
Hawaii Agric Exp Stn Agric Econ Bull — Hawaii. Agricultural Experiment Station. Agricultural Economics Bulletin
Hawaii Agric Exp Stn Bienn Rep — Hawaii. Agricultural Experiment Station. Biennial Report
Hawaii Agric Exp Stn Bull — Hawaii. Agricultural Experiment Station. Bulletin
Hawaii Agric Exp Stn Circ — Hawaii. Agricultural Experiment Station. Circular
Hawaii Agric Exp Stn Misc Pub — Hawaii. Agricultural Experiment Station. Miscellaneous Publication
Hawaii Agric Exp Stn Prog Notes — Hawaii. Agricultural Experiment Station. Progress Notes
Hawaii Agric Exp Stn Res Bull — Hawaii. Agricultural Experiment Station. Research Bulletin
Hawaii Agric Exp Stn Res Rep — Hawaii. Agricultural Experiment Station. Research Report
Hawaii Agric Exp Stn Spec Publ — Hawaii. Agricultural Experiment Station. Special Publication
Hawaii Agric Exp Stn Tech Bull — Hawaii. Agricultural Experiment Station. Technical Bulletin
Hawaii Agric Exp Stn Tech Prog Rep — Hawaii. Agricultural Experiment Station. Technical Progress Report
Hawaiian For — Hawaiian Forester and Agriculturist
Hawaiian Vol Obs — Hawaiian Volcano Observatory
Hawaii B J — Hawaii Bar Journal
Hawaii Bus — Hawaii Business
Hawaii Div Hydrogr Bull — Hawaii. Division of Hydrography. Bulletin
Hawaii Div Water Land Dev Circ — Hawaii. Division of Water and Land Development. Circular
Hawaii Div Water Land Dev Rep — Hawaii. Division of Water and Land Development. Report
Hawaii Farm Sci — Hawaii Farm Science
Hawaii Food Process Hawaii Univ Coop Ext Serv — Hawaii Food Processor. Hawaii University. Cooperative Extension Service
Hawaii Inst Geophys Bienn Rep — Hawaii Institute of Geophysics. Biennial Report
Hawaii Inst Geophys Publ — Hawaii Institute of Geophysics. Publication
Hawaii J Hist — Hawaii Journal of History
Hawaii Lib Assn J — Hawaii Library Association. Journal
Hawaii Med J — Hawaii Medical Journal
Hawaii Med J Inter Isl Nurses Bull — Hawaii Medical Journal and Inter-Island Nurses' Bulletin
Hawaii Orchid J — Hawaii Orchid Journal
Hawaii Plant Mon — Hawaiian Planters' Monthly
Hawaii Plant Rec — Hawaiian Planters' Record
Hawaii Plrs' Rec — Hawaiian Planters' Record
Hawaii Shell News (Honolulu) — Hawaiian Shell News (Honolulu)
Hawaii Sugar Plant Assoc Exp Stn Annu Rep — Hawaiian Sugar Planters' Association. Experiment Station. Annual Report
Hawaii Sugar Technol Rep — Hawaiian Sugar Technologists Reports
Hawaii Univ Coop Ext Serv Circ — Hawaii University. Cooperative Extension Service. Circular
Hawaii Univ Inst Geophys — Hawaii University. Institute of Geophysics. Report
Hawaii Univ Inst Geophys Contrib — Hawaii University. Institute of Geophysics. Contributions
Hawaii Univ Look Lab Oceanogr Eng Tech Rep — Hawaii University. Look Laboratory of Oceanographic Engineering. Technical Report
Hawaii Univ Sea Grant Prog Rep — Hawaii University. Sea Grant Program. Reports
Hawaii Univ Water Resour Res Cent Annu Rep — Hawaii University. Water Resources Research Center. Annual Report
Hawaii Univ Water Resour Res Cent Tech Rep — Hawaii University. Water Resources Research Center. Technical Report
Hawaii Uni Water Resour Cent Tech Rep — Hawaii University. Water Resources Research Center. Technical Report
HAWFA — Hawaii Farm Science
HAWIA — Hauswirtschaft und Wissenschaft
Hawker Siddeley Tech Rev — Hawker Siddeley Technical Review
Haydn-Stud — Haydn-Studien
Haydn Yb — Haydn Yearbook
Haygaz Hayag Handes — Haygazean Hayagitagan Handes
Hazard Cargo Bull — Hazardous Cargo Bulletin
Hazard Mater Manage J — Hazardous Materials Management Journal

Hazardous Cargo Bull — Hazardous Cargo Bulletin
Hazards Bull — Hazards Bulletin
Hazard Waste — Hazardous Waste
Haz Bull — Hazards Bulletin
Haz Rev — Hazards Review
HB — Handelsblatt
HB — Hebraeische Bibliographie [*Berlin*]
HB — Het Boek
HB — Historical Bulletin
HB — Horn Book
HB — Hub. Hay River
HB — Human Behavior
HBA — Historiografia y Bibliografia Americanistas
HBalt — Hispania (Baltimore)
HbAT — Handbuch zum Alten Testament [*Tuebingen*]
HBD — Detailhandel Magazine
HBd — Haarlemsch Bijdragen
HBL — Hofmannsthal Blaetter
HBM — Die Haghe. Bijdragen en Mededeelingen
HBMB — Holy Blossom Men's Bulletin
HBN — Hamburger Beitraege zur Numismatik
HBR — Harvard Business Review [*John Wiley & Sons, Inc.*] [*Bibliographic database*]
HBR — Heidelberger Beitraege zur Romanistik
HBSA — Hjalmar Bergman Samfundet Arsbok
HBTF-A — Habiter
HBV — Hessische Blaetter fuer Volkskunde
HBVk — Hessische Blaetter fuer Volkskunde
HbzAT — Handbuch zum Alten Testament [*Tuebingen*]
HC — Hessische Chronik
HC — Historicky Casopis
HC — Hollins Critic
HC — Horn Call
HC — Hristianskoe Ctenie
HCACA — Helvetica Chimica Acta
HCal — Hispania (Stanford, California)
HCATA — Helvetica Chirurgica Acta
HCAUA — Handling, Conveying, Automation
HCFA Rev — Health Care Financing Review
HCHY — Hovering Craft and Hydrofoil
HCI — Human Cancer Immunology [*Elsevier Book Series*]
4-H Circ Univ MO Coll Agr Ext Serv — 4-H Circular. University of Missouri. College of Agriculture. Extension Service
HCM — Health Care Management Review
HCMR — Health Care Management Review
HCN — Hart Crane Newsletter
HCompL — Hebrew Computational Linguistics
H and CP — Hospital and Community Psychiatry
HCR — Horeca Info
HCR — Hotel and Catering Review
HCRCA — Harvard Civil Rights - Civil Liberties Law Journal
HCRE — Human Communications Research
HCSTA — Hastings Center. Studies
HD — Harpsichord
HD — Hechos y Dichos
HD — Human Development
HDGHA — Hiroshima Daigaku Genbaku Hoshano Igaku Kenkyusho Nenpo
HDIZA — Medical Journal. Hiroshima University
HDKKA — Hokkaido Daigaku Kogakubu Kenkyu Hokoku
HDL — Handbuch der Deutschen Literaturgeschichte
HDLYDQ — Annual Research Reviews. Hodgkin's Disease and the Lymphomas
HDSB — Harvard Divinity School. Bulletin
HDTYA — Heredity [*England*]
HDW Werkztg — Howaldtswerke Deutsche Werft. Aktiengesellschaft. Hamburg und Kiel. Werkzeitung
HDZ — Hrvatski Dijalektoloski Zbornik
HDZb — Hrvatski Dijalektoloski Zbornik
HE — Handbooks in Economics [*Elsevier Book Series*]
HE — Hare Express. Fort Good Hope
He — Henceforth
HE — Human Events
HEADA — Headache
Headline Ser — Headline Series
Head Neck Surg — Head and Neck Surgery
Head Nec Surg — Head and Neck Surgery
Head Teachers' R — Head Teachers' Review
HEAHB — Health
Heal Ed Mon — Health Education Monographs
Health — Health Law in Canada
Health Aspects Chem Saf Interim Doc — Health Aspects of Chemical Safety. Interim Document
Health Bul — Health Bulletin
Health Bull — Health Bulletin
Health Bull (Edinb) — Health Bulletin (Edinburgh)
Health Care Can — Health Care in Canada

Health Care Dimen — Health Care Dimensions
Health Care Educ — Health Care Education
Health Care Financing R — Health Care Financing Review
Healthcare Financ Manage — Healthcare Financial Management
Health Care Financ Rev — Health Care Financing Review
Health Care Financ Trends — Health Care Financing Trends
Health Care Manage Rev — Health Care Management Review
Health Care Newsl — Health Care Newsletter
Health Care Plan & Mkt — Health Care Planning and Marketing
Health Care Plann Market — Health Care Planning and Marketing
Health Care Superv — Health Care Supervisor
Health Care Syst — Health Care Systems
Health Care Wk — Health Care Week
Health Care Women Int — Health Care for Women, International
Health Commun Informatics — Health Communications and Informatics
Health Ed — Health Education
Health Ed J — Health Education Journal
Health Educ — Health Education
Health Educ — Health Education Journal
Health Educ Assoc NSW Newsl — Health Education Association of New South Wales. Newsletter
Health Educ Bull — Health Education Bulletin
Health Educ J — Health Education Journal
Health Educ Monogr — Health Education Monographs
Health Educ Q — Health Education Quarterly
Health Foods Bus — Health Foods Business
Health Inspectors Conf — Annual Conference of Health Inspectors of New South Wales
Health Insur Stat — Health Insurance Statistics [*United States Health, Education, and Welfare Department*]
Health Lab — Health Laboratory Science
Health Lab Sci — Health Laboratory Science
Health L Can — Health Law in Canada
Health Libr Rev — Health Libraries Review
Health Manpow Lit — Health Manpower Literature
Health Manpow Rep — Health Manpower Report [*Later, Health Planning and Manpower Report*]
Health & Med — Health and Medicine
Health Med Care Serv Rev — Health and Medical Care Services Review
Health Mkt Q — Health Marketing Quarterly
Health NSW — Health in New South Wales
Health Officers J — Health Officers' Journal
Health-PAC Bull — Health-PAC [*Policy Advisory Center*] Bulletin
Health Perspect — Health Perspectives [*Later, Consumer Health Perspectives*]
Health Perspect Issues — Health Perspectives and Issues
Health Phys — Health Physics
Health Phys (Tokyo) — Health Physics (Tokyo)
Health Plann Manpower Rep — Health Planning and Manpower Report
Health Plann Manpow Rep — Health Planning and Manpower Report
Health Policy Educ — Health Policy and Education
Health Policy Q — Health Policy Quarterly
Health Pract Physician Assist — Health Practitioner. Physician Assistant
Health Prog — Health Progress
Health Saf Bull — Health and Safety Bulletin
Health Saf Work — Health and Safety at Work
Health Serv — Health Services Report
Health Serv Manager — Health Services Manager
Health Serv Manpow Rev — Health Services Manpower Review
Health Serv Rep — Health Service Reports
Health Serv Res — Health Services Research [*Chicago*]
Health Social Serv J — Health and Social Service Journal
Health Soc Serv J — Health and Social Service Journal
Health Soc Work — Health and Social Work
Health Visit — Health Visitor
Health Welfare Stat — Health and Welfare Statistics
Hear Aid J — Hearing Aid Journal
Hear Instrum — Hearing Instruments
Hear Rehab Quart — Hearing Rehabilitation Quarterly
Hear Res — Hearing Research
Hearst's M — Hearst's Magazine
Heart Bull — Heart Bulletin
Heart Cent Bull St Francis Hosp (Roslyn NY) — Heart Center Bulletin. St. Francis Hospital (Roslyn, New York)
Heart and Lung — Heart and Lung. Journal of Critical Care
HEAS — Harvard East Asian Series
Heat — Heating and Ventilating Engineer
Heat Air Cond Contr — Heating and Air Conditioning Contractor
Heat Air Condit J — Heating and Air Conditioning Journal
Heat Air Condit Refrig — Heating, Air Conditioning, and Refrigeration
Heat and Air Cond J — Heating and Air Conditioning Journal
Heat Air Cond J — Heating and Air Conditioning Journal
Heat Air Cond Refrig — Heating, Air Conditioning, and Refrigeration
Heat Combust Equip News — Heating/Combustion Equipment News
Heat Eng — Heat Engineering
Heating & Air Conditioning Jnl — Heating and Air Conditioning Journal
Heating Piping — Heating, Piping, and Air Conditioning

Heat Manage Pollut Control — Heat Management and Pollution Control [*Japan*]
Heat Pip Air Condit — Heating, Piping, and Air Conditioning
Heat Piping Air Cond — Heating, Piping, and Air Conditioning
Heat Technol — Heat Technology
Heat Transfer Eng — Heat Transfer Engineering
Heat Transfer Engng — Heat Transfer Engineering
Heat Transfer & Fluid Flow Dig — Heat Transfer and Fluid Flow Digest
Heat Transfer Fluid Mech Inst Prepr Pap — Heat Transfer and Fluid Mechanics Institute. Preprints of Papers
Heat Transfer - Japan Res — Heat Transfer. Japanese Research
Heat Transfer Jap Res — Heat Transfer. Japanese Research
Heat Transfer Jpn Res — Heat Transfer. Japanese Research
Heat Transfer Sov Res — Heat Transfer. Soviet Research
Heat Treat — Heat Treating
Heat Treat Forg — Heat Treating and Forging
Heat Treat Met — Heat Treatment of Metals
Heat Treat Met (China) — Heat Treatment of Metals (China)
Heat & Vent — Heating and Ventilating
Heat Vent Eng — Heating and Ventilating Engineer
Heat and Vent Eng — Heating and Ventilating Engineer
Heat Vent Eng J Air Cond — Heating and Ventilating Engineer and Journal of Air Conditioning
Heat Vent Engr — Heating and Ventilating Engineer
Heat & Vent Engr — Heating and Ventilating Engineer
Heat Vent News — Heating and Ventilating News
Heat Vent Rev — Heating and Ventilating Review
Heavy Met Environ Int Conf 4th — Heavy Metals in the Environment. International Conference. 4th
Hebbel-Jahrb — Hebbel-Jahrbuch
Heb Med J — Hebrew Medical Journal
Heb Pharm — Hebrew Pharmacist
Hebrew Univ (Jerusalem) — Hebrew University (Jerusalem)
Hebrew U St — Hebrew University. Studies in Literature
Hebridean Nat — Hebridean Naturalist
HebrUCA — Hebrew Union College. Annual
Heb Tech Coll (Haifa) Sci Publ — Hebrew Technical College (Haifa). Scientific Publications
HEBUA — Heart Bulletin
Hedeselsk Tidsskr — Hedeselskabets Tidsskrift
HEDJ — Health Education Journal [*London*]
HEDO — Health Education [*Ottawa*]
HEDQ — Health Education Quarterly
HEdR — Harvard Educational Review
HEDU — Health Educator. Newsletter
HEDW — Health Education (Washington)
HEEMA — Health Education Monographs
HEENA — Heat Engineering [*Livingston, NJ*]
HEFOA — Hebezeuge und Foerdermittel
Hefte Unfallheilkd — Hefte zur Unfallheilkunde
Heft Unfallheilk — Hefte zur Unfallheilkunde [*West Germany*]
HEG — Handbook of Exploration Geochemistry [*Elsevier Book Series*]
Hegel-Jrbh — Hegel-Jahrbuch
Hegel-Stud — Hegel-Studien
HEHUA — Herba Hungarica
HEI — Handelsreiziger
Heidelberg Akad Wiss Math Naturwiss Kl Sitzungsber — Heidelberger Akademie der Wissenschaften. Mathematisch-Naturwissenschaftliche Klasse. Sitzungsberichte [*West Germany*]
Heidelberger Beitr Mineralogie u Petrographie — Heidelberger Beitrage zur Mineralogie und Petrographie
Heidelb Jahrb — Heidelberger Jahrbuecher
Heidelb Sci Libr — Heidelberg Science Library
Heidelb Taschenb — Heidelberger Taschenbuecher
HeidJb — Heidelberger Jahrbuecher
Heid Sitzb — Heidelberger Akademie der Wissenschaften. Sitzungsberichte
HEIG — Handbook of Environmental Isotope Geochemistry [*Elsevier Book Series*]
Heil Gewuerz-Pflanz — Heil Gewuerz-Pflanzen
Heilpaedagog Forsch — Heilpaedagogische Forschung
Heilpaed For — Heilpaedagogische Forschung
HeineJ — Heine-Jahrbuch
Heine-Jahrb — Heine-Jahrbuch
Heiz Lueft Haustech — Heizung, Lueftung, Haustechnik [*Later, HLH. Zeitschrift fuer Heizung, Lueftung, Klimatechnik, Haustechnik*]
Heizung-Lueftung Haustech — Heizung, Lueftung, Haustechnik [*Later, HLH. Zeitschrift fuer Heizung, Lueftung, Klimatechnik, Haustechnik*] [*West Germany*]
HEKOD — Herder Korrespondenz
Hel — Helicon
Hel — Hellas-Jahrbuch
Helgolander Wiss Meeresunters Mar Invest — Helgolaender Wissenschaftliche Meeresuntersuchungen/Marine Investigations
Helgol Meeresunters — Helgolaender Meeresuntersuchungen
Helgol Wiss Meeresunters — Helgolaender Wissenschaftliche Meeresuntersuchungen

Helg W Meer — Helgolaender Wissenschaftliche Meeresuntersuchungen
Helicop Wld — Helicopter World
Helikon — Helikon. Revista di Tradizione e Cultura Classica dell'Universita di Messina
Helinium — Helinium. Revue Consacree a l'Archeologie des Pays-Bas de la Belgique et du Grand Duche de Luxembourg
Hell Adelphe — Hellenis Adelphe
HellasJB — Hellas-Jahrbuch
Hellen — Hellenika [*Salonika*]
Hellenika (S) — Hellenika (Salonika)
Hell Kteniatr — Hellenike Kteniatrike
Hell Mikrobiol Hygieinol Hetaireia Delt — Hellenike Mikrobiologike kai Hygieinologike Hetaireia Deltion
Hell Stomatol Chron — Hellenika Stomatologika Chronika
Hell Vet Med — Hellenic Veterinary Medicine
Helminth Abstr — Helminthological Abstracts
Helminthol — Helminthologia
HELOA — Helgolaender Wissenschaftliche Meeresuntersuchungen
Helsingin Tek Korkeakoulu Tiet Julk — Helsingin Teknillinen Korkeakoulu Tieteellisia Julkaisuja
Helsinki Univ Technol Lab Phys Res Rep — Helsinki University of Technology. Laboratory of Physics. Research Report
Helsinki Univ Technol Res Pap — Helsinki University of Technology. Research Papers
Helv Chim A — Helvetica Chimica Acta
Helv Chim Acta — Helvetica Chimica Acta
Helv Chir Acta — Helvetica Chirurgica Acta
Helv Chir Acta Suppl — Helvetica Chirurgica Acta. Supplementum
Helvet Arch — Helvetia Archaeologica
Helvetica Odontol Acta Suppl — Helvetica Odontologica Acta. Supplementum
Helv Med Acta — Helvetica Medica Acta
Helv Med Acta Suppl — Helvetica Medica Acta. Supplementum
Helv Odon A — Helvetica Odontologica Acta
Helv Odontol Acta — Helvetica Odontologica Acta
Helv Paed A — Helvetica Paediatrica Acta
Helv Paediat Acta — Helvetica Paediatrica Acta
Helv Paediatr Acta — Helvetica Paediatrica Acta
Helv Paediatr Acta Suppl — Helvetica Paediatrica Acta. Supplementum
Helv Phys A — Helvetica Physica Acta
Helv Phys Acta — Helvetica Physica Acta
Helv Phys Acta Suppl — Helvetica Physica Acta. Supplementum
Helv Physiol Pharmac Acta — Helvetica Physiologica et Pharmacologica Acta
Helv Physiol Pharmacol Acta — Helvetica Physiologica et Pharmacologica Acta
Helv Physiol Pharmacol Acta Suppl — Helvetica Physiologica et Pharmacologica Acta. Supplementum
Hem — Ons Hemecht
HEMEA — Hemel en Dampkring
Hem Ind — Hemijska Industrija
Hemis — Hemisphere
HEMOA — Hemostase
HEMOD — Hemoglobin
Hennepin Law — Hennepin Lawyer
Henry E Sigerist Suppl Bull Hist Med — Henry E. Sigerist Supplements. Bulletin of the History of Medicine
Henry Ford Hosp Med Bull — Henry Ford Hospital. Medical Bulletin
Henry Ford Hosp Med J — Henry Ford Hospital. Medical Journal
Heohr Zb Lviv Vida Heohr Tov Ukr SSR — Heohragicheskyi Zbirnyk L'vivs'koho Vida Heohraficheskoho Tovarystva Ukrains'koho SSR
HEP — HEP [*Higher Education Publications*] Higher Education Directory
HEP — Hong Kong Economic Papers
Hepato-Gastroenterol — Hepato-Gastroenterology
HEPIA — High Energy Physics Index
HER — Harvard Educational Review
Herald Lib Sci — Herald of Library Science
Herald Research Bul — Herald Research Bulletin
Herb Abstr — Herbage Abstracts
Herba Hung — Herba Hungarica
Herba Pol — Herba Polonica
HERCA — Hercynia
Hercynia Fachgeb Bot-Geogr-Geol Palaeontol-Zool — Hercynia fuer die Fachgebiete Botanik-Geographie-Geologie Palaeontologie-Zoologie
Herder Korresp — Herder Korrespondenz
HEREA — Hereditas
Hered — Hereditas
Hered — Heredity
Hereford J Sthn Afr — Hereford Journal of Southern Africa
Hereford Q — Hereford Quarterly
HERI — Heritage. Monthly Newsletter. Alaska Office of History and Archaeology
Herion Inf — Herion Informationen
HERJ — Home Economics Research Journal
Her Libr Sci — Herald of Library Science
Hermes Z Kl — Hermes. Zeitschrift fuer Klassische Philologie
Hermsdorfer Tech Mitt — Hermsdorfer Technische Mitteilungen

Herold — Der Herold. Vierteljahrsschrift fuer Heraldik, Genealogie, und Verwandte Wissenschaften
Heron (Engl Ed) — Heron (English Edition)
HERP — Health Education Reports
Herpetol Rev — Herpetological Review
Hertfordshire Arch — Hertfordshire Archaeology
Hertfordshire Archaeol — Hertfordshire Archaeology
Hertfordshire Archaeol Rev — Hertfordshire Archaeological Review
Herz Kreisl — Herz Kreislauf
HES — Harvard English Studies
Hesdoerffers Monatsh Blumen Gartenfreunde — Hesdoerffers Monatshefte fuer Blumen- und Gartenfreunde
HESEA — Health Services Research
HESOD — Heizen mit Sonne
Hesp — Hesperia
Hess Aerztebl — Hessisches Aerzteblatt
Hess Biene — Hessische Biene
Hesse Landesamt Bodenforsch Notizblatt — Hesse Landesamt fuer Bodenforschung Notizblatt
Hess Florist Briefe — Hessische Floristische Briefe
Hess Jb Landesgesch — Hessisches Jahrbuch fuer Landesgeschichte
Hess Lagerstaettenarch — Hessisches Lagerstaettenarchiv
Heterog Catal Proc Int Symp — Heterogeneous Catalysis. Proceedings. International Symposium
Het Voice — Heterodoxical Voice
Heubner Foundation Monograph Ser — Heubner Foundation Monograph Series
Heurtey Bull Inform — Heurtey Bulletin d'Informations. English Edition
HEVEA — Heating and Ventilating
HEW — Department of Health, Education, and Welfare. Publications
HEWE — Heritage West. British Columbia's Leading Heritage Magazine
Hewlett — Hewlett-Packard Journal
Hewlett-Packard J — Hewlett-Packard Journal
HeythJ — Heythrop Journal. A Quarterly Review of Philosophy and Theology [Oxford]
Heythrop — Heythrop Journal
Heythrop J — Heythrop Journal
HF — Hamburger Fremdenblatt
HF — Heidelberger Forschungen
HF — High Fidelity
HF — Hoosier Folklore
HF — Husky Fever (The Musher's Monthly News. Insert in Northern News Report)
HFB — Bouwhandel
HFB — Hoosier Folklore Bulletin
HFBT — Helps for Bible Translators
HFC — Hants Field Club and Archaeological Society
HFE — Housing Finance Review
HFF — Health Affairs
HFHJA — Henry Ford Hospital. Medical Journal
HFK — Holland Quarterly
HFM — Healthcare Financial Management
HFM — Historisk-Filosofiske Meddelelser Udgivet af det Kongelinge Danske Videnskabernes Selskab
HFMKDVS — Historisk-Filosofiske Meddelelser Udgivet af det Kongelinge Danske Videnskabernes Selskab
HFN — Hi-Fi News and Record Review
HG — Hannoversche Geschichtsblaetter
HG — Humanistisches Gymnasium
HGAMA — Hidrotehnica Gospodarirea Apelor. Meteorologia
HGB — Hansische Geschichtsblaetter
HGB — Het Gildeboek. Tijdschrift voor Kerkelijke Kunst en Oudheidkunde
HGG — Hotelgewerbe und Gastgewerbe Rundschau. Unabhangiges Fachorgan fuer Gastronomie, Betriebstechnische, und Kuhltechnische Praxis und Gemeinschaftsverpflegung
HGGSEB — Handelingen. Genootschap voor Geschiedenis Gesticht Onder de Benaming. Societe d'Emulation de Bruges
HGH — Hansische Geschichtsblaetter
HGKV — Hefte fuer Geschichte, Kunst, und Volkskunde
HGM — Harvard Graduates' Magazine
HGS — Harvard Germanic Studies
HGSD News — Harvard Graduate School of Design. News
H u H — Holzforschung und Holzverwertung
H & H — Hoofs and Horns
HHBLA — Harper Hospital. Bulletin
HHHCA — Journal. Oceanological Society of Korea [South Korea]
HHHHD — Heh Hua Hsueh Yu Fang She Hua Hsueh
HHHPA — Hua Hsueh Hsueh Pao
HHI Geophys Data — Heinrich Hertz Institut Geophysical Data
HHI Sol Data — Heinrich Hertz Institut Solar Data
HHN — Houthandel en Houtnijverheid. Algemeen Vakblad voor de Houthandel en de Houtnijverheid
H Hol — Herald of Holiness
H & Home — House and Home
HHRV — Holistic Health Review
HHS — Hospital and Health Services Administration

HHTPA — Hua Hsueh Tung Pao [China]
Hi — Hid
Hi — Hispania
HI — Historica Iberica
HI — Humanities Index
HIAR — Hamburger Ibero-Amerikanische Reihe
HIAS — Heritage of Indian Art Series
HibbJ — Hibbert Journal
Hibernation Torpor Mamm Birds — Hibernation and Torpor in Mammals and Birds
HibJ — Hibbert Journal
Hibridni Kukuruz Jugoslav — Hibridni Kukuruz Jugoslavie
HIC — Higher Education and Research in the Netherlands
Hickenia (Bol Darwinion) — Hickenia (Boletin del Darwinion)
Hickory Task Force Rep Stheast For Exp Sta — Hickory Task Force Report. Southeastern Forest Experiment Station
HICL — Histoire des Idees et Critique Litteraire
HICW — History of the Canadian West
HIDKA — Hiroshima Daigaku Kogakubu Kenkyu Hokoku
HIDRA — Hidrologiai Koezloeny
Hidrol Koezl — Hidrologiai Koezloeny
Hidroteh Gospod Apelor Meteorol — Hidrotehnica Gospodarirea Apelor. Meteorologia [Romania]
Hidroteh Melior Latv PSR — Hidrotehnika un Melioracija Latvijas PSR
HIE — Express. Daily Financial Newspaper [Athens]
HIECA — High Energy Chemistry [English Translation]
Hiero — Hierophant
Hi Fi — High Fidelity
Hi Fi — High Fidelity/Musical America
Hi Fi/Mus Am — High Fidelity/Musical America
Hi-Fi News Rec Rev — Hi-Fi News and Record Review
Higg J Poet — Higginson Journal of Poetry
High Educ — Higher Education
High Educ R — Higher Education Review
High Energy Chem — High Energy Chemistry
Higher Ed — Higher Education
Higher Ed J — Higher Education Journal
Higher Ed R — Higher Education Review
Highlights Agr Res — Highlights of Agricultural Research. Alabama Agricultural Experiment Station
HIG (Honolulu) HI — Hawaii Institute of Geophysics (Honolulu). University of Hawaii
High Polym — High Polymers
High Polym (Jpn) — High Polymers (Japan)
High Sch Chem Teach Mag — High School Chemistry Teachers' Magazine
High Sch J — High School Journal
High Speed Ground Transp J — High Speed Ground Transportation Journal
High Speed Gr Transpn J — High Speed Ground Transportation Journal
High-Speed Surf Craft — High-Speed Surface Craft
High Tech — High Technology
High Technol — High Technology [United States]
High Temp — High Temperature
High Temp High Pressures — High Temperatures - High Pressures
High Temp R — High Temperature USSR
High Temp S — High Temperature Science
High Temp Sci — High Temperature Science
High Temp Technol — High Temperature Technology
Highw — Highway
Highway Geol Symp Proc — Highway Geology Symposium Proceedings
Highway User Q — Highway User Quarterly
Highw Des Constr — Highways Design and Construction
Highw Eng — Highway Engineer
Highw Eng Aust — Highway Engineering in Australia
Highw Engng Aust — Highway Engineering in Australia
Highw Heavy Constr — Highway and Heavy Construction
Highw Public Wks — Highways and Public Works
Highw Publ Wks — Highways and Public Works
Highw Rd Constr — Highways and Road Construction
Highw Res Bd Nat Coop Highw Res Program Rep — Highway Research Board National Cooperative Highway Research Program. Report
Highw Res Board Bull — Highway Research Board. Bulletin
Highw Res Board Bull Spec Rep — Highway Research Board. Bulletin. Special Reports
Highw Res Board Natl Coop Highw Res Program — Highway Research Board. National Cooperative Highway Research Program. Report
Highw Res Board Spec Rep — Highway Research Board. Special Report
Highw Res Bull — Highway Research Bulletin [India]
Highw Res News — Highway Research News
Highw Res Rec — Highway Research Record
Highw Road Const — Highways and Road Construction
Highw Traff Engng — Highways of Traffic Engineering
Highw Transp — Highway Transport
Highw Urban Mass Transp — Highway and Urban Mass Transportation [United States]
HIHAD — Hanyang Idae Haksuljip
HIISAP — Industrija Secera

HIJMA — Hiroshima Journal of Medical Sciences
HIKAA — Hikaku Kagaku [*Japan*]
Hikobia J Hiroshima Bot Club — Hikobia Journal of the Hiroshima Botanical Club
HIKYA — Hinyokika Kiyo [*Japan*]
HILGA — Hilgardia
Hi Lo — High/Low Report
HiM — Hispania (Madrid)
Himachal J Agric Res — Himachal Journal of Agricultural Research
Himalayan Geol — Himalayan Geology
HINAA — Hindustan Antibiotics Bulletin
Hind Antibiot Bull — Hindustan Antibiotics Bulletin
Hindu Astronom Math Text Ser — Hindu Astronomical and Mathematical Text Series
HINL — History of Ideas Newsletter
HINTD — Habitat International
HIPOA — High Polymers
HIPPA — Hippokrates
HIR — Hispanic Review
HIRAA — Hiradastechnika [*Hungary*]
Hiradastech Ipari Kutatointez Kozl — Hiradastechnikai Ipari Kutatointezet Koezlemenyei
Hiradastech Ipari Kut Intez Koezl — Hiradastechnikai Ipari Kutato Intezet Koezlemenyei
Hiram Po R — Hiram Poetry Review
HIRDAP — Geological Report. Hiroshima University
HIRIA — Hirosaki Igaku [*Japan*]
HIRIB — Hifuka No Rinsho [*Japan*]
HIROA — Hirosaki Daigaku Nogakubu Gakujutsu Hokoku
HiroBK — Hiroshima Daigaku Bungakubu Kiyo
Hirosaki Med J — Hirosaki Medical Journal
Hiroshima J Med Sci — Hiroshima Journal of Medical Sciences
Hiroshima Math J — Hiroshima Mathematical Journal
Hiroshima Med J — Hiroshima Medical Journal [*Japan*]
Hiroshima Univ Geol Rep — Hiroshima University Geological Report
Hiroshima Univ J Sci Ser C — Hiroshima University Journal of Science. Series C. Geology and Mineralogy
Hiros J Med — Hiroshima Journal of Medical Sciences
HIRRA — Highway Research Record
His — Hispania
HIS — Humanities in Society
His Am Hist Rev — Hispanic American Historical Review
HisK — Hispania (University of Kansas. Lawrence)
HisL — Hispania (University of Kansas. Lawrence)
His Med Ser — History of Medicine Series
His Outlook — Historical Outlook
Hisp — Hispania [*Madrid*]
Hispam — Hispamerica. Revista de Literatura
Hisp Amer Hist Rev — Hispanic American Historical Review
Hispan Am H — Hispanic American Historical Review
Hispan Am Hist R — Hispanic American Historical Review
Hispan Am Rep — Hispanic American Report
Hispanic Am His R — Hispanic American Historical Review
Hispanic Bus — Hispanic Business
Hispano — Hispanofila [*Madrid*]
Hispan R — Hispanic Review
Hispan Rev — Hispanic Review
HispCal — Hispania (Stanford, California)
Hispl — Hispanofila [*Madrid and Illinois*]
HispM — Hispania (Madrid)
Hisp Press Ind — Hispanic Press Index
Hisp Rev — Hispanic Review
His Q — History Quarterly
HISS News-J — HISS [*Herpetological Information Search Systems*] News-Journal
Hist — Historian
Hist — Historica
Hist — History
HistAb — Historical Abstracts
Hist Abstr — Historical Abstracts
Hist Acad Roy Sc — Histoire de l'Academie Royale des Sciences
Hist Afr — History in Africa
Hist Africa — History in Africa
Hist Ag — Historia Agriculturae
Hist Arkisto — Historiallinen Arkisto
Hist Berwickshire Natur Club — History. Berwickshire Naturalists' Club
Hist Bull — Historical Bulletin
Hist Cas — Historicky Casopis
Hist Casopis — Historicky Casopis
Hist Child Q — History of Childhood Quarterly
His Teach M — History Teacher's Magazine
Hist Educ Jour — History of Education Journal
Hist Educ Q — History of Education Quarterly
Hist Eur Id — History of European Ideas
Hist Euro Ideas — History of European Ideas

Hist Hosp — Historia Hospitalium. Mitteilungen der Deutschen Gesellschaft fuer Kranken-Hausgeschichte
Hist J — Historical Journal
Hist Jahrb — Historisches Jahrbuch
HistJb — Historisches Jahrbuch der Goerresgesellschaft
Hist Jb Graz — Historisches Jahrbuch der Stadt Graz
Hist J Film — Historical Journal of Film, Radio, and Television
Hist J FR & TV — Historical Journal of Film, Radio, and Television
Hist Ju (Birmingham) — Historical Journal (Birmingham)
Hist J West Mass — Historical Journal of Western Massachusetts
HistL — Historiographia Linguistica
Hist Ling — Historiographia Linguistica
Hist M — Historical Magazine [*Dawson's*]
Hist Mag — Historical Magazine of the Protestant Episcopal Church
Hist Mag Protest Episc Church — Historical Magazine of the Protestant Episcopal Church
Hist Med — History of Medicine
Hist Med Vet — Historia Medicinae Veterinariae
Hist Metall — Historical Metallurgy
Hist Meth — Historical Methods
Hist Methods Newsl — Historical Methods Newsletter
Hist Mex — Historia Mexicana
Hist Nat — Histoire et Nature. Cahiers de l'Association pour l'Histoire des Sciences de la Nature
Hist NH — Historical New Hampshire
Histochemis — Histochemistry
Histochem J — Histochemical Journal
Historia Math — Historia Mathematica
Historia Z — Historia. Zeitschrift fuer Alte Geschichte
History — History Workshop
History of Ed Soc Bull — History of Education Society. Bulletin
Hist Outl — Historical Outlook
Hist Papers — Historical Papers
Hist Photo — History of Photography
Hist Photog — History of Photography
Hist of Photogr — History of Photography
Hist Pol Ec — History of Political Economy
Hist Pol Econ — History of Political Economy
Hist Pol Economy — History of Political Economy
Hist Polit — History of Political Economy
Hist Polit Econ — History of Political Economy
Hist Polit Thought — History of Political Thought
Hist Pol Th — History of Political Thought
Hist Pres — Historic Preservation
Hist Preser — Historic Preservation
Hist Preservation — Historic Preservation
Hist Refl D — Historical Reflections. Directions Series
Hist Reflec — Historical Reflections/Reflexions Historiques
Hist Rel — History of Religions
Hist Relig — History of Religions
Hist Rev — Historical Review (New Zealand)
Hist R New Bk — History. Review of New Books
Hist of Sci — History of Science
Hist Sci — History of Science
Hist Sci Med — Histoire des Sciences Medicales
Hist Sc Soc Manit Tr — Historical and Scientific Society of Manitoba. Transactions
Hist Ser Can Dep Agric — Historical Series. Canada Department of Agriculture
Hist Soc — Histoire Sociale/Social History
Hist Soc Mont Contr — Historical Society of Montana. Contributions
Hist Soc Q J — Historical Society of Queensland. Journal
Hist Soc Qld J — Historical Society of Queensland. Journal
Hist Soc Qld News — Historical Society of Queensland. News Bulletin
Hist Soc Sci Teach — History and Social Science Teacher
Hist St Prob — On the History of Statistics and Probability
Hist Stud — Historical Studies
Hist Stud — Historical Studies - Australia and New Zealand
Hist Stud Aust NZ — Historical Studies - Australia and New Zealand
Hist Stud Austral — Historical Studies - Australia and New Zealand
Hist Studies — Historical Studies - Australia and New Zealand
Hist Stud Phys Sci — Historical Studies in the Physical Sciences
Hist & T — History and Theory
Hist Tchr — History Teacher
Hist Teach — History Teacher
Hist Teach Assoc NSW Newsl — History Teachers Association of New South Wales. Newsletter
Hist Theor — History and Theory
Hist Theory — History and Theory
Hist and Theory — History and Theory
Hist Tidskr — Historisk Tidskrift
Hist Tidskr Finl — Historisk Tidskrift foer Finland
Hist Tidssk — Historisk Tidsskrift
Hist Today — History Today
Hist Univ — History of Universities

Hist Verein Oberpfalz & Regensburg Verh — Historischer Verein fuer Oberpfalz und Regensburg. Verhandlungen
Hist Ver f d Grafsch Ravensberg Jahresber — Historischer Verein fuer die Grafschaft Ravensberg zu Bielefeld. Jahresberichte
Hist Ver f Mittelfranken Jahresber — Historischer Verein fuer Mittelfranken. Jahresberichte
Hist Work S — History Workshop Series
Hist Worksh — History Workshop
Hist Workshop — History Workshop
Hist Z — Historische Zeitschrift
Hist Ztsch — Historische Zeitschrift
HIT — History of Political Economy
Hitachi Rev — Hitachi Review
Hitachi Zosen Tech Rev — Hitachi Zosen Technical Review
HITEA — High Temperature [*English Translation*]
HITK — Hungarologiai Intezet Tudomanyos Kozlemenyei
Hitots J Econ — Hitotsubashi Journal of Economics
Hitotsubashi J Arts Sc — Hitotsubashi Journal of Arts and Sciences
Hitotsubashi J Arts Sci — Hitotsubashi Journal of Arts and Sciences
Hitotsubashi J Com Manag — Hitotsubashi Journal of Commerce and Management
Hitotsubashi J Commer Manage — Hitotsubashi Journal of Commerce and Management
Hitotsubashi J Commer and Mgt — Hitotsubashi Journal of Commerce and Management
Hitotsubashi J Econ — Hitotsubashi Journal of Economics
Hitotsubashi J Law and Politics — Hitotsubashi Journal of Law and Politics
Hitotsubashi JL & Pol — Hitotsubashi Journal of Law and Politics
Hitotsubashi J Social Studies — Hitotsubashi Journal of Social Studies
Hitotsubashi J Soc Stud — Hitotsubashi Journal of Social Studies
HITSA — High Temperature Science
Hi Urb Mass Tran — Highway and Urban Mass Transportation
HiUS — Hispania (USA)
HJ — Hibbert Journal
HJ — Historia Judaica
HJ — Historisches Jahrbuch
HJAS — Harvard Journal of Asiatic Studies
HJAS — Hitotsubashi Journal of Arts and Sciences
H Jb — Handel Jahrbuch
HJb — Hebbel-Jahrbuch
HJC — Hitotsubashi Journal of Commerce and Management
HJE — Hitotsubashi Journal of Economics
Hj Kreis Hofgeismar — Heimatjahrbuch fuer den Kreis Hofgeismar
HJI — Hibbert Journal
HJMSA — Journal. Mysore University. Section B. Science
HJR — Henry James Review
HJSS — Hitotsubashi Journal of Social Studies
HJud — Historia Judaica
HK — Heritage of Kansas
HK — Hrvatsko Kolo
HKCSA — Hang K'ung Chih Shih
HKCTD — Handelingen. Koninklijke Commissie voor Toponymie en Dialectologie
HKDBK — Hokkaido Daigaku Bungakubu Kiyo
HK Econ Pap — Hong Kong Economic Papers
HK Law R — Hong Kong Law Review
HKN — Hogen Kenkyu Nenpo
HKOKD — Hakko Kogaku Kaishi
HKROD — Bulletin of Environmental Sciences [*South Korea*]
HKTSA — Haikan To Sochi
HKZM — Handelingen. Koninklijke Zuidnederlandse Maatschappij voor Taal en Letterkunde en Geschiedenis
HL — Hanging Loose
HL — Harvard Library Bulletin
HL — Historiographia Linguistica
Hl — Hochland
HL — Humanistica Lovaniensia
HLA J — Hawaii Library Association. Journal
HLB — Harvard Library Bulletin
HLB — Historisches Literaturblatt
HLB — Huntington Library. Bulletin
HLBFA — Heilberufe [*East Germany*]
HLEKT — Handbuch der Literaturgeschichte in Einzeldarstellungen. Kroeners Taschenausgabe
HLF — Histoire Litteraire de la France
H & L & H — HLH. Zeitschrift fuer Heizung, Lueftung, Klimatechnik, Haustechnik
HLH (Heiz Luftung Klimatech Haustech) — HLH. Zeitschrift fuer Heizung, Lueftung, Klimatechnik, Haustechnik
HLHZA — HLH. Heizung, Lueftung, Klimatechnik, Haustechnik
HLH Zeit Heizung Lueftung Klim Haustech — HLH. Zeitschrift fuer Heizung, Lueftung, Klimatechnik, Haustechnik
HLI — Hospital Literature Index
HLJ — Hastings Law Journal
HLK — Hanser Literatur-Kommentare
HLK — Hefte fuer Literatur und Kritik

HLPH — Holy Land Postal History
HLQ — Huntington Library. Quarterly
HLR — Haifa Law Reports
HLR — Harvard Law Review
HLS — Historiska och Litteraturhistoriska Studier
HLS — Leather and Shoes
HISAN — Helsingin Sanomat
HLSCA — Health Laboratory Science
Hlth Horiz — Health Horizon
Hlth Hyg Ho — Health and Hygiene in the Home
Hlth Inf Dig — Health Information Digest
Hlth Inf Dig Hot Count — Health Information Digest for Hot Countries
Hlth Instr Yb — Health Instruction Yearbook
Hlth Lab Sci — Health Laboratory Science
Hlth Ne — Health News
Hlth New — Health News
Hlth PAC — Health-PAC [*Policy Advisory Center*] Bulletin
Hlth Phys — Health Physics
Hlth Saf Exec Direct Inf and Advisory Services Transl — Health and Safety Executive Directorate of Information and Advisory Services. Translations [*England*]
Hlth Saf Monitor — Health and Safety Monitor
Hlth Saf at Work — Health and Safety at Work
Hlth Sch Ch — Health of the School Child
Hlth Serv — Health Services
Hlth Serv Res — Health Services Research
Hlth Soc Serv J — Health and Social Service Journal
Hlth Soc Wrk — Health and Social Work
Hlth Top — Health Topics
Hlth Yb — Health Yearbook
HLTPA — Health Physics
HLW — Landbode; Hollands Landbouwweekblad
HM — Harper's Magazine
HM — Hejnat Mariacki
Hm — Hermes
HM — Hommes et Mondes
H & M — Hommes et Mondes
HM — Hortus Musicus
HM — Hospitality Management
HMA — Helvetica Medica Acta
HMACA — Helvetica Medica Acta
HMad — Hispania (Madrid)
HMB — Hermannsburger Missionsblatt
HMD — Handbuch der Modernen Datenverarbeitung
HME — Historical Magazine of the Protestant Episcopal Church
HMENR — High Mountain Ecology Research Station (Finse, Norway) Reports
H Mex — Historia Mexicana
HMGOG — Handelingen. Maatschappij voor Geschiedenis en Oudheidkunde te Gent
HMK — Historiske Meddelelser om Staden Kobenhavn og dens Borgere
HMMNL — Handelingen en Mededeelingen. Maatschappij der Nederlandsche Letterkunde te Leiden
HMP — Homenaje a Menendez Pidal
HMPEC — Historical Magazine of the Protestant Episcopal Church
HMSO Daily Lists — Her Majesty's Stationery Office Daily Lists
HMT — Handwoerterbuch der Musikalischen Terminologie
HMW Jb — HMW [*Heilmittelwerke*] Jahrbuch
H M Y B — Hinrichsen's Musical Year Book
HMZ — Helvetische Muenzen-Zeitung
HMZA — Hamburg in Zahlen
HN — Hadassah Newsletter [*New York*]
HN — Hamann Newsletter
HN — Hemingway Notes
HN — Here and Now
H & N — Here and Now
Hn — Hochschulnachrichten
HND — Handwierk
HNDKB — Hyogo Noka Daigaku Kiyo
HNH — Historical New Hampshire
HNK — Ho Neos Koubaras
HNL — Hadassah Newsletter [*New York*]
HNL — HUD [*Housing and Urban Development*] Newsletter
HNO — HNO. Hals-, Nasen-, Ohren-Heilkunde
HNorv — Humaniora Norvegica
HNO Weg Fac — HNO: Wegweiser fuer die Fachaerztliche Praxis [*Later, HNO. Hals-, Nasen-, Ohren-Heilkunde*]
HNR — Hikone Ronso
HNSWA — Health in New South Wales
HO — Handbuch der Orientalistik
Ho — Hochland
HO — Human Organization
HOAGDS — Annual Research Reviews. Hormones and Aggression
Hoard's D — Hoard's Dairyman
Hob — Hobbies
Hobby Electron — Hobby Electronics

Hochfrequenztech Elektroakust — Hochfrequenztechnik und Elektroakustik [*East Germany*]
Hochl — Hochland
Hochschulb Math — Hochschulbuecher fuer Mathematik
Hochschulb Phys — Hochschulbuecher fuer Physik
Hochschulbuecher fuer Phys — Hochschulbuecher fuer Physik
Hochschullehrb Biol — Hochschullehrbuecher fuer Biologie
HochschulSammlung Ingenieurwiss Datenverarbeitung — HochschulSammlung Ingenieurwissenschaft Datenverarbeitung
HochschulSammlung Naturwiss Math — HochschulSammlung Naturwissenschaft Mathematik
HOD — Holz-Zentralblatt. Unabhangiges Organ fuer die Forstwirtschaft und Holzwirtschaft
Hodowla Rosl Aklim Nasienn — Hodowla Roslin Aklimatyzacja i Nasiennictwo
HoE — Ho Eranistes
Hoefchenbr Wiss Prax — Hoefchen-Briefe fuer Wissenschaft und Praxis
Hoehle Wiss Beih — Hoehlankunde Wissenschaftliche Beihefte
Hoe Jb — Hoelderlin-Jahrbuch
Hoesch Ber Forsch Entwickl Unserer Werke — Hoesch. Berichte aus Forschung und Entwicklung Unserer Werke
Hoesch Ber Forsch Entwickl Werke — Hoesch. Arbeitskreis Forschung und Entwicklung, Berichte aus Forschung und Entwicklung Unserer Werke
Ho & For R — Home and Foreign Review
Hofstra L Rev — Hofstra Law Review
Hofstra Univ Yrbk Bus — Hofstra University. Yearbook of Business
Hogarth Ess — Hogarth Essays
Hogg — Hogg's Instructor
Hog Kenk — Hogaku Kenkyu
Hog Prod — Hog Production
HOH — Haunt of Horror
HOH — Houtwereld Vakblad Gewijd aan de Belangen van de Houthändel en van de Houtverwerkende Industrie
HOI — Handbook of Inflammation [*Elsevier Book Series*]
Hoja Divulgativa Campo Agric Exp (Valle Fuerte) — Hoja Divulgativa. Campo Agricola Experimental (Valle del Fuerte)
Hoja Tisiol — Hoja Tisiologica
HoJb — Hoelderlin-Jahrbuch
Hoj Tisiol — Hoja Tisiologica
HOKBA — Hoken Butsuri
HOKDA — Hokkaido Daigaku Nogakubu Enshurin Kenkyu Hokoku
Hokkaido Forest Prod Res Inst Rept — Hokkaido Forest Products Research Institute. Reports
Hokkaido Geol Surv Rep — Hokkaido Geological Survey. Report
Hokkaido J Med Sci — Hokkaido Journal of Medical Science
Hokkaido Math J — Hokkaido Mathematical Journal
Hokkaido Natl Agric Exp Stn Data — Hokkaido National Agricultural Experiment Station. Data
Hokkaido Natl Agric Exp Stn Rep — Hokkaido National Agricultural Experiment Station. Report
Hokkaido Univ Fac Sci J Ser 4 — Hokkaido University. Faculty of Science. Journal. Series 4. Geology and Mineralogy
Hokkaido Univ Inst Low Temp Sci Low Temp Sci Ser A Phys Sci — Hokkaido University. Institute of Low Temperature Science. Low Temperature Science. Series A. Physical Sciences
Hokkaido Univ Med Libr Ser — Hokkaido University. Medical Library Series
Hokoku Aichi-ken Ringyo Shikenjo — Hokoku. Aichi-ken Ringyo Shikenjo
Hokoku Bull Chugoku Natl Agric Exp Stn Ser E Environ Div — Hokoku. Bulletin. Chugoku National Agricultural Experiment Station. Series E. Environment Division
Hokoku Bull Kagoshima Tob Exp Stn Kagoshima Tabako Shikenjo — Hokoku. Bulletin. Kagoshima Tobacco Experiment Station. Kagoshima Tabako Shikenjo
Hokoku Bull Tohoku Daigaku Nogaku Kenkyujo — Hokoku. Bulletin. Tohoku Daigaku Nogaku Kenkyujo
Hokoku Jap Tab Shikenjo Okayama/Bull Okayama Tob Exp Stn — Hokoku, Japan. Tabako Shikenjo Okayama/Bulletin. Okayama Tobacco Experiment Station
HOKSA — Hokkaido-Ritsu Kogyo Shikenjo Hokoku
Holarctic Ecol — Holarctic Ecology [*Denmark*]
Holb Rev — Holborn Review
Hol Crit — Hollins Critic
Holderlin-Jahrb — Hoelderlin-Jahrbuch
Holland Shipbuild — Holland Shipbuilding [*Netherlands*]
Holland Shipbuild — Holland Shipbuilding and Marine Engineering [*Later, Holland Shipbuilding*]
Hollands Maandbl — Hollands Maandblad
Holld Info — Holland Info
Holloman Symp Primate Immunol Mol Genet — Holloman Symposium on Primate Immunology and Molecular Genetics
Hollow Sec — Hollow Section [*United Kingdom*]
Hollywood Q — Hollywood Quarterly
Holstein World — Holstein-Friesian World
Holy Name Mo — Holy Name Monthly
Holzf Holzv — Holzforschung und Holzverwertung
Holzforsch — Holzforschung
Holzforsch Holzverwert — Holzforschung und Holzverwertung

Holz Roh We — Holz als Roh- und Werkstoff
Holz Roh- Werkst — Holz als Roh- und Werkstoff
Holztechnol — Holztechnologie
Holz Zbl — Holz-Zentralblatt
Hom — Homiletics
Hombre y Cult — Hombre y Cultura
Home Auto — Home and Auto Buyer Guide
Home Ec Bul — Home Economics Bulletin
Home Econ News — Home Economics News
Home Energy Dig Wood Burn Q — Home Energy Digest and Wood Burning Quarterly
Home Gard — Home Garden [*Later, Family Handyman*]
Home Gdn Bull — Home and Garden Bulletins
Home Geog Mo — Home Geographic Monthly
Home Health Care Serv Q — Home Health Care Services Quarterly
Home Health Rev — Home Health Review
Home Mag — Homemakers' Magazine
Home Off Res Bull — Home Office Research Bulletin
Home Prog — Home Progress
Home Sci — Home Science
Homme Oiseau — Homme et l'Oiseau
Hommes et Migr — Hommes et Migrations
Hommes et Migr Doc — Hommes et Migrations. Documents
Homme Soc — Homme et Societe
Homme et Soc — Homme et Societe
Hommes Tech — Hommes et Techniques
Hommes et Techn — Hommes et Techniques
Homoeopath — Homoeopathic Digest
Homogeneous Catal Org Inorg Chem — Homogeneous Catalysis in Organic and Inorganic Chemistry
Hom R — Homiletic Review
HOMS — Homme et Societe
HON — Revue Commerciale
HONAA — Helvetica Odontologica Acta
Honeywell Comput J — Honeywell Computer Journal
Hongik Univ J — Hongik University. Journal [*Republic of Korea*]
Hong Kong Eng — Hong Kong Engineer
Hong Kong Engr — Hong Kong Engineer
Hong Kong Nurs J — Hong Kong Nursing Journal
Hong Kong Univ Fish J — Hong Kong University. Fisheries Journal
Hoosier Sch Lib — Hoosier School Libraries
Hop Belge — Hopital Belge
Hoppe-Seyler's Z Physiol Chem — Hoppe-Seyler's Zeitschrift fuer Physiologische Chemie
Hoppe-Seyler's Ztschr Physiol Chem — Hoppe-Seyler's Zeitschrift fuer Physiologische Chemie
Hop R — Hopkins Review
HOPT — Handbook of Powder Technology [*Elsevier Book Series*]
HO Purdue Univ Coop Ext Serv — HO-Purdue University. Cooperative Extension Service
Hor — Horizon
HORI — Horizons
Horiz Biochem Biophys — Horizons in Biochemistry and Biophysics
Horm Behav — Hormones and Behavior
Horm Cell Regul — Hormones and Cell Regulation
Horm Metab Res — Hormone and Metabolic Research
Horm Metab Res (Suppl) — Hormone and Metabolic Research (Supplement)
Hormone Beh — Hormones and Behavior
Hormone Met — Hormone and Metabolic Research
Hormone Res — Hormone Research
Horm Res — Hormone Research
Horm Res (Basel) — Hormone Research (Basel)
Horn Afr — Horn of Africa
Horn Bk — Horn Book Magazine
Horol J — Horological Journal
HorsAb — Horseman's Abstracts
Hort — Horticulture
Hort Abstr — Horticultural Abstracts
Hortic Adv (Sahranpur) — Horticultural Advance (Sahranpur)
Hortic Bull — Horticultural Bulletin
Hortic Cent Loughgall Annu Rep — Horticultural Centre Loughgall. Annual Report
Hortic Dig Univ Hawaii Coop Ext Serv — Horticulture Digest. University of Hawaii. Cooperative Extension Service
Hortic Fr — Horticulture Francaise
Hortic News NJ State Hortic Soc — Horticultural News. New Jersey State Horticultural Society
Hortic NZ — Horticulture in New Zealand
Hortic Res — Horticultural Research
Hortic Res Inst Ont Rep — Horticultural Research Institute of Ontario. Report
Hortic Rev — Horticultural Reviews
Hortic Sci (Calcutta) — Horticultural Science (Calcutta)
Hortic Sci (Stuttg) — Horticultural Science (Stuttgart)
Horticulture Ind — Horticulture Industry
Hortic Vitic Sci (Sofia) — Horticultural and Viticultural Sciences (Sofia)
Hort N — Horticultural News

Hort Res — Horticultural Research
Hort Res (Edinb) — Horticultural Research (Edinburgh)
Hort Res Rec — Horticultural Research Record. New South Wales Department of Agriculture. Division of Horticulture
HortSci — HortScience
HOS — Holland Shipbuilding
Hos — Hospitality
Hoshasen Kagaku Append — Hoshasen Kagaku. Appendix [*Japan*]
HOSIA — Hospitals
Hosp — Hospitality
HospAb — Hospital Abstracts
Hosp Abstr Serv — Hospital Abstract Service
Hosp Adm Can — Hospital Administration in Canada
Hosp Adm (Chicago) — Hospital Administration (Chicago)
Hosp Admin Curr — Hospital Administration Currents
Hosp Adm (New Delhi) — Hospital Administration (New Delhi)
Hosp Assoc J — Hospitals' Association. Journal
Hosp Care — Hospital Care
Hosp Cent Mil (Lomas De Sotelo Mex) Publ Trimest — Hospital Central Militar (Lomas De Sotelo, Mexico). Publicacion Trimestral
Hosp Commun — Hospital and Community Psychiatry
Hosp Community Psychiatr — Hospital and Community Psychiatry
Hosp Community Psychiatry — Hospital and Community Psychiatry
Hosp Dev — Hospital Development
Hosp Develop — Hospital Development
Hosp Employee Health — Hospital Employee Health
Hosp Eng — Hospital Engineering
Hosp Equip Supplies — Hospital Equipment and Supplies
Hosp Financ Manage — Hospital Financial Management
Hosp Finan Manage — Hospital Financial Management
Hosp Fin Mgt — Hospital Financial Management
Hosp Formul — Hospital Formulary
Hosp Formul Manage — Hospital Formulary Management
Hosp Forum — Hospital Forum
Hosp Gen (Madr) — Hospital General (Madrid)
Hosp and Health — Hospital and Health Services Administration
Hosp Health Care Newsl — Hospital Health Care Newsletter
Hosp Health Serv Adm — Hospital and Health Services Administration
Hosp Health Serv Admin — Hospital and Health Services Administration
Hosp Health Serv Rev — Hospital and Health Services Review
Hosp-Hyg — Hospital-Hygiene
Hosp Infect Control — Hospital Infection Control
Hosp Int — Hospital International
Hospital Admin — Hospital Administration
Hospitality Educ — Hospitality Educator
Hospital Mag — Hospital Magazine
Hospital Mus News — Hospital Music Newsletter
Hospital (Rio De J) — Hospital (Rio De Janeiro)
Hosp Law Newsletter — Hospital Law Newsletter
Hosp Libr — Hospital Libraries
Hosp Lit Ind — Hospital Literature Index
Hosp Mater Manage Q — Hospital Materiel Management Quarterly
Hosp Med — Hospital Medicine
Hosp Med Staff — Hospital Medical Staff
Hosp Med Staff Advocate — Hospital Medical Staff Advocate
Hospos Zpr — Hospodarsky Zpravodaj
Hosp Peer Rev — Hospital Peer Review
Hosp Pharm — Hospital Pharmacy
Hosp Physician — Hospital Physician
Hosp Pract — Hospital Practice
Hosp Prog — Hospital Progress
Hosp Progr — Hospital Progress
Hosp Purch Manage — Hospital Purchasing Management
Hosp Servidores Estado Rev Med — Hospital dos Servidores do Estado. Revista Medica
Hosp Superv Bull — Hospital Supervisors Bulletin
Hosp Top — Hospital Topics
Hosp Trib — Hospital Tribune
Hosp Trustee — Hospital Trustee
Hosp Vina del Mar Bol Trimest — Hospital del Vina del Mar. Botetin Trimestral
Hosp Week — Hospital Week
Hotel Gaz SA — Hotel Gazette of South Australia
Hotel Motel Manage — Hotel and Motel Management
Hotel & Motel Mgt — Hotel and Motel Management
HOTOA — Hospital Topics
Houches Ec Ete Phys Theor — Houches. Ecole d'Ete de Physique Theoretique
Houil Blanc — Houille Blanche
Hou J Intl L — Houston Journal of International Law
Hou LR — Houston Law Review
HO Univ KY Coll Agr Coop Ext Serv — HO-University of Kentucky. College of Agriculture. Cooperative Extension Service
House B — House Beautiful
House Beautiful's Gard Outdoor Living — House Beautiful's Gardening and Outdoor Living [*United States*]
House Bldr — House Builder

House & G — House and Garden
House & Gard — House and Garden
House Garden Build Guide — House and Garden Building Guide [*United States*]
Household — Household and Personal Products Industry
House Words — Household Words
Housing Abs — Housing Abstracts
Housing & Constr Tech Bull — Housing and Construction Technical Bulletin
Housing Eur — Housing Europe
Housing Fin R — Housing Finance Review
Housing Mag — Housing Magazine
Housing Mo — Housing Monthly
Housing Mthly — Housing Monthly
Housing and Planning Refs — Housing and Planning References
Housing Plann Refs — Housing and Planning References
Housing Plann Rev — Housing and Planning Review
Housing Rev — Housing Review
Hous J Intl L — Houston Journal of International Law
Hous L Rev — Houston Law Review
HousP — Housing and Planning References
Houst L Rev — Houston Law Review
Houston Geol Soc Bull — Houston Geological Society. Bulletin
Houston J Int'l L — Houston Journal of International Law
Houston J Math — Houston Journal of Mathematics
Houston Law — Houston Law Review
Houston L Rev — Houston Law Review
Houston Sym — Houston Symphony. Program Notes
Hov Craft Hydrof — Hovering Craft and Hydrofoil
Hovercr Wld — Hovercraft World
HO Voice — Hartford's Other Voice [*Superseded by Wild Raspberry*]
Howard Journal — Howard Journal of Penology and Crime Prevention
Howard J Penology Crime Prev — Howard Journal of Penology and Crime Prevention
Howard Law J — Howard Law Journal
Howard L J — Howard Law Journal
How Eval Health Programs — How to Evaluate Health Programs
Howitt — Howitt's Journal
How J Pen — Howard Journal of Penology and Crime Prevention
How Law J — Howard Law Journal
How LJ — Howard Law Journal
HOY — Holland Schweiz
HOYU — Hospitality Yukon. Yukon Visitors Association
HPAAA — Helvetica Paediatrica Acta
HPA Bull — HPA [*Hospital Physicists Association*] Bulletin [*England*]
HPACA — Helvetica Physica Acta
HPANAJ — Encyclopedia of Plant Anatomy
HPAOA — Heating, Piping, and Air Conditioning
HPASA — Helvetica Physiologica et Pharmacologica Acta. Supplementum
HPB — Historisch-Politische Blaetter fuer das Katholische Deutschland
HPBKD — Historisch-Politische Blaetter fuer das Katholische Deutschland
HPBL — Historisch-Politische Blaetter fuer das Katholische Deutschland
HPCQA — Human Pathology
HPD — Harpsichord
HPE — History of Political Economy
HPEN — PEN Hongrois
HPHAD — Han'guk Pusik Hakhoechi
HPHBA — Harvard Public Health Alumni Bulletin
HPI — Holland in South East Asia
HPKYA — Harbin Gongye Daxue Xuebao
H Points — High Points
HPOQ — Health Policy Quarterly
HPPAA — Helvetica Physiologica et Pharmacologica Acta
HPPRA — Hydrocarbon Processing and Petroleum Refiner [*Later, Hydrocarbon Processing*]
HPR — Homiletic and Pastoral Review
HPRM — Health Promotion Monographs
HPS — Hamburger Philologische Studien
HPSO — Historical and Philosophical Society of Ohio. Bulletin
HPSY — Health Psychology
HPTGA — Herpetologica
HPWBA — Heilpaedagogische Werkblaetter
HQ — Hartford Quarterly
HQ — Hopkins Quarterly
HR — Hermes. Messager Scientifique et Populaire de l'Antiquite Classique en Russie
HR — Hispanic Review
HR — History of Religions
H R — Hudebni Revue
HR — Hudson Review
HR — Human Relations
HR — Humanisme et Renaissance
H & R — Humanisme et Renaissance
HRA — Historical Records of Australia
HRA — Human Resources Abstracts
HRB — Hopkins Research Bulletin
HRBC — Historical Review of Berks County

HRC — Horeca
HRC CC J High Resolut Chromatogr Chromatogr Commun — Journal of High Resolution Chromatography and Chromatography Communications [*West Germany*]
HRD — Hamburger Romanistische Dissertationen
H Rel — History of Religions
HRen — Humanisme et Renaissance
HRFADM — Annual Research Reviews. Hypothalamic Releasing Factors
HRH — TextielVisie
H & RI — Hotels and Restaurants International
HRIPA — Publications. Hungarian Mining Research Institute
HRISAK — Food and Nutrition
HRLSD J — HRLSD [*Health and Rehabilitative Library Services Division*] Journal
HRM — Human Reproductive Medicine [*Elsevier Book Series*]
HRM — Human Resource Management
HRNB — History. Review of New Books
HRNSW — Historical Records of New South Wales
HRO — Gastvrij
H Ro — Hudebni Rozhledy
HRP — Human Resource Planning
HRPV — Hermes. Revista del Pais Vasco
HRS — Historical Records and Studies
HRTG — Heritage. Alberta Department of Culture, Youth, and Recreation
HS — Handbook of Statistics [*Elsevier Book Series*]
H & S — Health and Safety
H & S — Health and Strength
HS — Hebrew Studies [*Louisville, KY*]
Hs — Hemisphere
HS — Hispania Sacra
HS — Historical Studies
HS — Humanities in the South
HS — International Journal of Health Services
HSA — Health Services Administration. Publications
HSan — Helsingin Sanomat
HSC — Histoire de la Spiritualite Chretienne
H Sch — High School
H Sch J — High School Journal
H Sch Q — High School Quarterly
H Sch Teach — High School Teacher
HSCL — Harvard Studies in Comparative Literature
HSCP — Harvard Studies in Classical Philology
HSCPA — Hospital and Community Psychiatry
HSCRA — Hastings Center. Report
HSE — Hungarian Studies in English
Hse Builder — House Builder
Hse and Garden — House and Garden
HSELL — Hiroshima Studies in English Language and Literature
Hse of Lords Select Commit Eur Commun Rep — House of Lords. Select Committee on the European Communities. Reports
HSGTA — High Speed Ground Transportation Journal
HSGTJ — High Speed Ground Transportation Journal
HSHCA — Han'guk Sikmul Poho Hakhoe Chi
HSHKA — Bulletin. Korean Fisheries Society [*South Korea*]
HSHRA — HSMHA [*Health Services and Mental Health Administration*] Health Report
HSJ — High School Journal
HSJ — Housman Society. Journal
HSKCA — Han'guk Sikp'um Kwahakhoe Chi
HSKEA — Hoshasen Seibutsu Kenkyu
HSL — Hartford Studies in Literature
HSL Abs — HSL [*Health and Safety Executive Library*] Abstract [*England*]
HSLS — Harvard Slavic Studies
HSM — Handbook of Soil Mechanics [*Elsevier Book Series*]
HSM — Handling and Shipping Management
HSM — Health Services and Mental Health Administration. Publications
HSM — Human Systems Management
H & S Mgmt — Handling and Shipping Management
HSN — Hawthorne Society. Newsletter
HSNPL — Harvard Studies and Notes in Philology and Literature
HSP — Hospitals
HSPh — Harvard Studies in Classical Philology
HSPhS — Historical Studies in the Physical Sciences
HSPL — Harvard Studies and Notes in Philology and Literature
HSR — Health Services Research
HSR — Hungarian Studies Review
HSRI (High Saf Res Inst) Res Rev — HSRI (Highway Safety Research Institute) Research Review
HSRI Rep — HSRI [*Highway Safety Research Institute*] Report
HSRI Res Rev — HSRI [*Highway Safety Research Institute*] Research Review
HSRL — Harvard Studies in Romance Languages
HSRPA — Health Services Report
HSS — Harvard Semitic Series
HSS — Harvard Slavic Studies

HSSC — High-Speed Surface Craft, Incorporating Hovering Craft and Hydrofoil
HSSC — Historical Society of Southern California. Quarterly
HSSCQ — Historical Society of Southern California. Quarterly
H St — Hamlet Studies
HST — Holland's Export Magazine. Holland Shipping and Trading [*Rotterdam*]
Hst Kreise Olpe — Heimatstimmen aus dem Kreise Olpe
H Studien — Hispanistische Studien
H-S Z Physl — Hoppe-Seyler's Zeitschrift fuer Physiologische Chemie
H-T — Hesperis-Tamuda
HT — High Times
HT — Historisk Tidskrift
H & T — History and Theory
HT — History Today
HT — Human Toxicology
HT — Humboldt-Taschenbuecher
HTB — Hoch- und Tiefbau
HTB — New York Herald Tribune Books
HTBHA — Han'guk T'oyang Bilyo Hakhoe Chi
HTD — Dansk Historisk Tidskrift
HTF — Historisk Tidskrift foer Finland
HTFFA — Heat and Fluid Flow
Htg — Holztechnologie
H Th G — Handbuch Theologischer Grundbegriffe
H Th K — Herders Theologischer Kommentar zum Neuen Testament
HTHPA — High Temperatures - High Pressures
HThR — Harvard Theological Review
HThSt — Harvard Theological Studies [*Cambridge, MA*]
HTI — Hindu Text Information
HTJ — Hardware Trade Journal
HTJPA — Heat Transfer. Japanese Research
HTK — Historisk Tidskrift
HTL — Hotel Revue. Beroepstijdschrift op Managementniveau
HTLStu — Historia i Teoria Literatury-Studia
HTM — History Teacher's Magazine
HTM Haerterei-Tech Mitt — Haerterei-Technische Mitteilungen (HTM) [*West Germany*]
HTO — Historisk Tidskrift (Oslo)
HTQ — Hsueh Tsung Quarterly
HTQ — Revue Francaise de Gestion. Hommes et Techniques
HTR — Harvard Theological Review
Ht R — Haustechnische Rundschau
HTRMB — Heat Treatment of Metals
HTS — Harvard Theological Studies [*Cambridge, MA*]
HTS — Hervormde Teologiese Studies
HTS — Historisk Tidskrift (Stockholm)
HTsFi — Historisk Tidskrift foer Finland
HTW — H2O. Tijdschrift voor Watervoorziening en Afvalwaterbehandeling
HUAKA — Hua Hsueh Shih Chieh
Hub Roz — Hudebni Rozhledy
HUCA — Hebrew Union College. Annual
HUD — Hungarian Digest
HUD Chal — HUD [*Housing and Urban Development*] Challenge
HUDEA — Human Development
Hudeiba Res Stn Annu Rep — Hudeiba Research Station. Annual Report
HUD Intl Bull — HUD [*Housing and Urban Development*] International Bulletin
HUD Intl Information Series — HUD [*Housing and Urban Development*] International Information Series
Hud R — Hudson Review
Hudrobiol Uurim — Hudrobioloogilised Uurimused
Hud Rozhl — Hudebni Rozhledy
Hudson R — Hudson Review
Hud Veda — Hudebni Veda
HUE — New Hungarian Exporter
Huenefeld Rep — Huenefeld Report [*United States*]
HUF — Hungarian Foreign Trade
HUFB — Hungarofilm Bulletin
HUG — Hungarian Economy
HUHEA — Human Heredity
Huisarts Wet — Huisarts en Wetenschap
HUL — Houston Law Review
Hule Mex Plast — Hule Mexicano y Plasticos
Hum — Humanidades
Hum — Humanist
Hum — Humanitas
Hum — Humus
Human Biol — Human Biology
Human Chr — Humanites Chretiennes
Human Comm Res — Human Communications Research
Human Cont — Human Context
Human Dev — Human Development
Human Ecol — Human Ecology
Human et Entr — Humanisme et Entreprise
Humane R — Humane Review

Human Fact — Human Factors
Humangenet — Humangenetik
Human Hered — Human Heredity
Humanidades Ser 4 Logica Mat — Humanidades. Serie 4. Logica Matematica
Human Org — Human Organization
Human Organ — Human Organization
Human Path — Human Pathology
Human Pracy — Humanizacja Pracy
Human Rel — Human Relations
Human Relat — Human Relations
Human Reprod Med — Human Reproductive Medicine
Human Resour Abstr — Human Resources Abstracts
Human Resource Mgt — Human Resource Management
Human S — Human Studies
Human Ser 4 Logica Mat — Humanidades. Serie 4. Logica Matematica [*Havana*]
Hum Ass Bull — Humanities Association of Canada. Bulletin
Hum Assoc R — Humanities Association. Review/Revue. Association des Humanites
HumB — Humanitas (Brescia)
Hum(BA) — Humanidades (Buenos Aires)
Hum Behav — Human Behavior
Hum Biol — Human Biology
Hum Biol Oceania — Human Biology in Oceania
Hum (Br) — Humanitas (Brescia)
Hum Chrom Newsl — Human Chromosome Newsletter
Hum Commun — Human Communications
Hum Contemp — Humanisme Contemporain
Hum Context — Human Context
Hum Dev — Human Development
Hum Ecol — Human Ecology
Hum Ecol Forum — Human Ecology Forum
Hum Environ Swed — Human Environment in Sweden [*United States*]
Hume Stud — Hume Studies
Hum Ev — Human Events
Hum Fact — Human Factors
Hum Factors — Human Factors
Hum Fertil — Human Fertility
Hum Genet — Human Genetics
Hum Genet Suppl — Human Genetics. Supplement
Hum Hered — Human Heredity
Hum Immunol — Human Immunology
Hum Ind — Humanities Index
Hum Lov — Humanistica Lovaniensia
Hum Needs — Human Needs
HumNL — Humanitas (Nuevo Leon)
Hum(NRH) — Humanitas: La Nouvelle Revue des Humanites
Hum Org — Human Organization
Hum Path — Human Pathology
Hum Pathol — Human Pathology
Hum Physiol — Human Physiology
Hum Potential — Human Potential
Humpty D — Humpty Dumpty's Magazine
Hum (Q) — Humanitas. Boletin Ecuatoriano de Antropologia (Quito)
Hum Rel — Human Relations
Hum Relat — Human Relations
Hum Relations — Human Relations
Hum (RES) — Humanites. Revue d'Enseignement Secondaire et d'Education
Hum Resource Mgt — Human Resource Management
Hum Resour Forum — Human Resources Forum [*United States*]
Hum Resour Manage — Human Resource Management
Hum Resour Manage (Aust) — Human Resource Management (Australia)
Hum Rev — Humanities Review
Hum Rights — Human Rights
Hum Rights J — Human Rights Journal
Hum (RIPh) — Humanitas. Revue Internationale de Philologie Classique et Humanites
Hum Sci — Human Science [*Inkan Kwahak*] [*Republic of Korea*]
Hum Settlements — Human Settlements
Hum Soc — Humanities in Society
Hum Stud — Humana Studia
HumT — Humanitas (Tucuman, Argentina)
Hum Toxicol — Human Toxicology
Hum Vetensk Samf i Lund Arsberatt — Humanistiska Vetenskaps-Samfundet i Lund Arsberattelse
Hum Wld — Human World
HUN — Hungaropress
Hung A Biol — Hungarica Acta Biologica
Hung Agric Rev — Hungarian Agricultural Review
Hung Agr Rev — Hungarian Agricultural Review
Hung Annu Meet Biochem Proc — Hungarian Annual Meeting for Biochemistry. Proceedings
Hungarofilm Bull — Hungarofilm Bulletin [*Budapest*]
Hung Econ — Hungarian Economy
Hung Foeldt Intez Evk — Hungary. Foeldtani Intezet. Evkoenyve
Hung For Sci Rev — Hungarian Forest Scientifical Review

Hung Heavy Ind — Hungarian Heavy Industries
Hung J Ind Chem — Hungarian Journal of Industrial Chemistry
Hung J Indus Chem — Hungarian Journal of Industrial Chemistry
Hung L Rev — Hungarian Law Review
Hung Mach — Hungarian Machinery
Hung Magy Allami Foeldt Intez Evk — Hungary. Magyar Allami Foeldtani Intezet. Evkoenyve
Hung Med Biblio — Hungarian Medical Bibliography
Hung Notes World Hung Educ Serv — Hunger Notes. World Hunger Education Service
Hung Press — Hungaropress
Hung R — Hungarian Review
Hung S — Hungarian Survey
Hung Sci Instrum — Hungarian Scientific Instruments
Hung Tech Abstr — Hungarian Technical Abstracts
HunQ — Hungarian Quarterly [*New York*]
Hunt — Hunt's Merchants' Magazine
Hunter Nat Hist — Hunter Natural History
Hunter Res Found J — Hunter Valley Research Foundation. Journal
Hunter Valley Res Fdn Monograph — Hunter Valley Research Foundation. Monograph
Hunter Valley Res Found Spec Rep — Hunter Valley Research Foundation. Special Report
Hunting Group Rev — Hunting Group Review
Huntington Libr Q — Huntington Library. Quarterly
Hunt Lib Bull — Huntington Library. Bulletin
Hunt Lib Q — Huntington Library. Quarterly
Hunt Libr Q — Huntington Library. Quarterly
HUPHD — Human Physiology [*English Translation*]
HUPPAE — Harvard University. Papers of the Peabody Museum of Archaeology and Ethnology
HuR — Hudson Review
HUR — Human Relations
HuR — Humanisme et Renaissance
HUS — Harvard Ukrainian Studies
HUSHA — Hua Hsueh [*Taiwan*]
HUSIA — Hungarian Scientific Instruments
HUSL — Hebrew University. Studies in Literature
HUSRA — Science Reports. Hirosaki University
HussR — Husson Review [*Bangor, ME*]
HUTMA — Houtim
Hutn Aktual — Hutnicke Aktuality [*Czechoslovakia*]
Hutn (Katowice) — Hutnik (Katowice)
Hutn Listy — Hutnicke Listy
Huyck Felt Bull — Huyck Felt Bulletin
HV — Historische Vierteljahrschrift
HV — Hudebni Veda
Hvalradets Skr — Hvalradets Skrifter
HVECA — Heating and Ventilating Engineer and Journal of Air Conditioning
HVHW — Health Values. Achieving High Level Wellness
HVJ — Historische Vierteljahrschrift
HVJS — Historische Vierteljahrschrift
HvM — Honar va Mardom
HVREA — Heating and Ventilating Review
HVV — Vrije Volk
HW — Historical Wyoming
Hware — Hardware Today
HWAY — Humble Way [*Exxon Corporation*]
HWMJA — Hawaii Medical Journal
HWRCB — Highways and Road Construction
HwyResAb — Highway Research Abstracts
Hy — Hymn
HY — Journal of Hydraulic Engineering
Hyacinth Control J — Hyacinth Control Journal
HYB — Herzl Year Book
HYCYD — Haksul Yonguchi - Chungnam Taehakkyo. Chayon Kwahak Yonguso
HYDCA — Hydrocarbure
Hydra Pneum — Hydraulics and Pneumatics
Hydraul & Air Engng — Hydraulic and Air Engineering
Hydraul & Pneum — Hydraulics and Pneumatics
Hydraul Pneum Mech Power — Hydraulic Pneumatic Mechanical Power
Hydraul Pneum Power — Hydraulic Pneumatic Power [*Later, Hydraulic Pneumatic Mechanical Power*]
Hydraul Pneum Pwr — Hydraulic Pneumatic Power [*Later, Hydraulic Pneumatic Mechanical Power*]
Hydrobiol — Hydrobiologia
Hydrobiol Bull — Hydrobiological Bulletin
Hydrobiol J — Hydrobiological Journal
Hydrobiol J (Engl Transl Gidrobiol Zh) — Hydrobiological Journal (English Translation of Gidrobiologicheskii Zhurnal)
Hydrobiol Stud — Hydrobiological Studies
Hydrocarbn — Hydrocarbon Processing
Hydrocarbon Process — Hydrocarbon Processing
Hydrocarbon Process Pet Refiner — Hydrocarbon Processing and Petroleum Refiner [*Later, Hydrocarbon Processing*]

Hydroc Proc — Hydrocarbon Processing
Hydro Electr Power — Hydro Electric Power [*Japan*]
Hydrogen Prog — Hydrogen Progress [*United States*]
Hydrogeol Inf (Czech) — Hydrogeologicke Informace (Czechoslovakia. Ustav Geologickeho Inzenyrstvi)
Hydro Lab J — Hydro-Lab Journal
Hydrol Rep St Bur Mines Miner Resour (New Mexico) — Hydrologic Reports. State Bureau of Mines and Mineral Resources (New Mexico)
Hydrol Sci Bull — Hydrological Sciences Bulletin [*England*]
Hydrol Sci Bull Int Assoc Hydrol Sci — Hydrological Sciences Bulletin. International Association of Hydrological Sciences
Hydrol Sci Bull Sci Hydrol — Hydrological Sciences. Bulletin des Sciences Hydrologiques
Hydrol Ser Aust Water Resour Counc — Hydrological Series. Australian Water Resources Council
Hydrol Ser Aust Wat Resour Coun — Hydrological Series. Australian Water Resources Council
Hydrol Symp Proc (Ottawa) — Hydrology Symposium. Proceedings (Ottawa)
Hydrol Water Resour Ariz Southwest — Hydrology and Water Resources in Arizona and the Southwest
Hydromech & Hydraul Engng Abstr — Hydromechanics and Hydraulic Engineering Abstracts
Hydrotech Constr — Hydrotechnical Construction
HYDWD — Hejubian Yu Dengliziti Wuli
Hyg Ment — Hygiene Mentale
Hyg Ment Suppl Encephale — Hygiene Mentale. Supplement de l'Encephale
HYGNA — Hyogo-Ken Gan Senta Nenpo
Hyg Rundschau — Hygienische Rundschau
Hyg Sanit — Hygiene and Sanitation
Hyg Viande Lait — Hygiene de la Viande et du Lait
HYHN — Hsin-Ya Shu-Yuan Hsueh-Shy Nien-K'an
HYKMA — Hyogo-Kenritsu Nogyo Shikenjo Kenkyu Hokoku
HYMEA — Hygiene Mentale
HYMNB — Hyomen
Hymn M — Hymnologiske Meddelelser. Vaerkstedsblad om Salmer
Hyperfine Interact — Hyperfine Interactions [*Netherlands*]
HYSAA — Hygiene and Sanitation
HZ — Historische Zeitschrift
HZBBA — Horizons in Biochemistry and Biophysics
HZKLA — Herz Kreislauf
HZKP — Hermes. Zeitschrift fuer Klassische Philologie
HZM — Handelingen. Zuidnederlandse Maatschappij voor Taal-En Letterkunde en Geschiedenis
HZMTLG — Handelingen. Zuidnederlandse Maatschappij voor Taal-En Letterkunde en Geschiedenis
HZnMTL — Handelingen. Zuidnederlandse Maatschappij voor Taal-En Letterkunde en Geschiedenis
HZOO — Hunick Zoo. Monthly Publication of Tanana Chiefs Conference

I

I — Idler
I — Isis
I — Italica
IA — Ibsen-Aarboken
IA — Insel-Almanach
IA — Insurance Advocate
IA — Insurance Asia [*Manila*]
IA — International Affairs
IA — Iranica Antiqua
IA — Italia Antichissima
IAA — Ibero-Amerikanisches Archiv
IAA — Inter-American Economic Affairs [*Washington*]
IAA — International Aerospace Abstracts
IAAAAM — International Archives of Allergy and Applied Immunology
IAAEJ — Institution of Automotive and Aeronautical Engineers, Australia and New Zealand. Journal
IAAE Journal — Institution of Automotive and Aeronautical Engineers, Australia and New Zealand. Journal
IA Ag Exp — Iowa State College of Agriculture and Mechanical Arts. Agricultural Experiment Station. Publications
IAAHA9 — Indian Council of Agricultural Research. Animal Husbandry Series
IAALD Q Bull — International Association of Agricultural Librarians and Documentalists. Quarterly Bulletin
IAANBS — International Archives of Occupational Health [*Later, International Archives of Occupational and Environmental Health*]
IAANBS — Internationales Archiv fuer Arbeitsmedizin
IAARA5 — Indian Council of Agricultural Research. Annual Technical Report
IAAROP — Institute of Arctic and Alpine Research. Occasional Papers
IAB — Institut fuer Auslandsbeziehungen
IABLA — Izvestiya Akademii Nauk Azerbaidzhanskoi SSR Seriya Biologicheskikh Nauk
IABNA — Izvestiya Akademii Nauk Armyanskoi SSR Biologicheskie Nauki
IABS — International Abstracts of Biological Sciences
IAC — Indo-Asian Culture
IACEAA — Indian Council of Agricultural Research. Cereal Crop Series
IACLAV — International Anesthesiology Clinics
IACPA — Proceedings. International Astronautical Congress
IADD — Index to American Doctoral Dissertations
IAE — India Economic Bulletin
IAE — Internationales Archiv fuer Ethnographie
IAEA Bibliogr Ser — International Atomic Energy Agency. Bibliographical Series
IAEA Bull — International Atomic Energy Agency. Bulletin
IAEA Proc Ser — International Atomic Energy Agency. Proceedings Series
IAEA Saf Ser — International Atomic Energy Agency. Safety Series
IAEA Tech Rep Ser — International Atomic Energy Agency. Technical Report Series
IAEHD — International Archives of Occupational and Environmental Health
IAEHDW — International Archives of Occupational and Environmental Health
IAEHDW — Internationales Archiv fuer Arbeits- und Umweltmedizin
IAEMAA — Indian Council of Agricultural Research. Entomological Monographs

IAEN — Department of Indian and Northern Affairs. Education Section. Northern Services Division. Newsletter
IAF — Internationales Afrikaforum
IAFBAG — International Commission for the Northwest Atlantic Fisheries. Research Bulletin
IAFPAO — International Commission for the Northwest Atlantic Fisheries. Special Publication
IAGFA — Izvestiya Akademii Nauk SSSR Seriya Geofizicheskaya
IAGGA — Izvestiya Akademii Nauk Armyanskoi SSR Geologicheskie i Geograficheskie Nauki
IAG J — IAG [*International Federation for Information Processing. Administrative Data Processing Group*] Journal
IAGPBU — Investigaciones Agropecuarias [*Lima, Peru*]
IAGRD4 — Investigacion Agricola [*Santiago*]
IAGYA — Izvestiya Akademii Nauk SSSR Seriya Geograficheskaya i Geofizicheskaya
IAHI — International Archives of the History of Ideas
IAIS — Indian and Inuit Supporter. A Newsletter of the Indian and Inuit Support Group of Newfoundland and Labrador
IA J — Iowa Journal of History and Politics
IAJRC — IAJRC [*International Association of Jazz Record Collectors*] Journal
IAJS — Index of Articles on Jewish Studies
IAK — Information Economique Africaine
IAKFA — Izvestiya Akademii Nauk Kazakhskoi SSR Seriya Fiziko-Matematicheskikh Nauk
IAKSA — Izvestiya Akademii Nauk SSSR
IAL — Industries Alimentaires et Agricoles
IALAA — Industries Alimentaires et Agricoles
IALAB — Lucrari Stiintifice. Institutul Agronomic "Dr. Petru Groza" (Cluj). Seria Agricultura
IA Law Rev — Iowa Law Review
IAL Bol Inst Adolfo Lutz — IAL Boletim. Instituto Adolfo Lutz
IALBull — Institut Archeologique Liegeois. Bulletin
IALR — International Anthropological and Linguistic Review
IA LR — Iowa Law Review
IALRB — Indian Journal of Animal Research
IALRBR — Indian Journal of Animal Research
IA L Rev — Iowa Law Review
IAM — International Affairs (Moscow)
IAM — Istanbul Asariatika Muzeleri Nesriyati
IAMI — Iron Age Metalworking International [*Later, Chilton's IAMI Iron Age Metalworking International*]
IAMNA — Izvestiya Akademii Nauk Armyanskoi SSR Seriya Fiziko-Matematicheskikh Nauk
IAMOAM — Indian Council of Agricultural Research. Monograph
IAN — Izvestiya Akademii Nauk SSSR Seriya Literatury i Jazyka [*Moscow*]
IANAB — Izvestiya Akademii Nauk Azerbaidzhanskoi SSR
IANFA — Izvestiya Akademii Nauk Seriya Fizicheskaya
IANMA — Izvestiya Akademii Nauk SSSR Otdelenie Tekhnicheskikh Nauk Metallurgiya i Toplivo
IAN-OGN — Izvestiya Akademii Nauk SSSR Otdeleniya Gumanitarnykh Nauk
IAN-OLJa — Izvestiya Akademii Nauk SSSR Otdeleniya Literatury i Jazyka

IAN OON — Izvestiya Akademii Nauk SSSR Otdeleniya Obscestvennykh Nauk
IAN ORJaSL — Izvestiya Akademii Nauk SSSR Otdeleniya Russkogo Jazyka i Slavesnosti Akademii Nauk
IANSA — Izvestiya Akademii Nauk SSSR Otdelenie Tekhnicheskikh Nauk Mekhanika i Mashinostroenie
IAN SSS Bio — Izvestiya Akademii Nauk SSSR Seriya Biologicheskaya
IAN SSS FAO — Izvestiya Akademii Nauk SSSR Seriya Fizika Atmosfery i Okeana
IAN SSS Fiz — Izvestiya Akademii Nauk SSSR Seriya Fizicheskaya
IANTA — Izvestiya Akademii Nauk SSSR Otdelenie Tekhnicheskikh Nauk
IANUz — Izvestiya Akademii Nauk Uzbekistanskoj SSSR
IANZA — Industrie-Anzeiger
IAOHD — International Archives of Allergy and Applied Immunology
IAOR — International Abstracts in Operations Research
IAPMA — Monographs in Pathology
IAPMAV — International Academy of Pathology. Monograph
IAPSB — Antennas and Propagation Society. International Symposium
IAPVA — Industria Alimentara. Produse Vegetale
IAPWA — International Journal of Air and Water Pollution
IAQ — Internationales Asienforum
IAQSB — Industries Atomiques et Spatiales
IAR — Indian Affairs Record
IAR — Ivor's Art Review
IARB — Inter-American Review of Bibliography
IARCC — IARC [*International Agency for Research on Cancer*] Scientific Publications
IARC Monogr — IARC [*International Agency for Research on Cancer*] Monographs
IARC Monogr Eval Carcinog Risk Chem Hum — IARC [*International Agency for Research on Cancer*] Monographs. Evaluation of the Carcinogenic Risk of Chemicals to Humans
IARC Monogr Eval Carcinog Risk Chem Hum Suppl — IARC [*International Agency for Research on Cancer*] Monographs. Evaluation of the Carcinogenic Risk of Chemicals to Humans. Supplement
IARC Sci Publ — IARC [*International Agency for Research on Cancer*] Scientific Publications
IARKA — Izvestiya Akademii Nauk Armyanskoi SSR Khimicheskie Nauki
IARTAS — Indian Council of Agricultural Research. Report Series
IAS — Industrial Arbitration Service
IAS — International Review of Administrative Sciences
IAS Annu Meet Conf Rec — Industry Applications Society. Annual Meeting. Conference Record [*United States*]
IAS Current Review — Industrial Arbitration Service. Current Review
IASF — Isaac Asimov's Science Fiction Magazine
IASFAP — International Atlantic Salmon Foundation. Special Publication Series
Iasi Univ An Stiint Sect 2 B Ser Noua — Iasi Universitatea. Analele Stiintifice. Sectiunea 2-B. Geologie. Serie Noua
IASL — Internationales Archiv fuer Sozialgeschichte der Deutschen Literatur
IASLIC Bull — IASLIC [*Indian Association of Special Libraries and Information Centres*] Bulletin
IASODL — International Advances in Surgical Oncology
IASOP — Institute of African Studies. Occasional Publications
IASUAB — Institute of Agricultural Sciences. University of Alaska. Bulletin
IASURR — Institute of Agricultural Sciences. University of Alaska. Research Reports
IAT — Izvestiya Akademii Nauk Turkmenskoi SSSR Seriya Obscestvennych Nauk
IATHA — Informations Aerauliques et Thermiques
IATUL Proc — International Association of Technological University Libraries. Proceedings
IAU Circ — International Astronomical Union. Circular
IAUSA — International Astronomical Union. Symposium
IAUTA — Ingenieurs de l'Automobile
IAWA Bull — IAWA [*International Association of Wood Anatomists*] Bulletin
IAWABV — International Association of Wood Anatomists. Bulletin
IAY — International Atomic Energy Agency. Bulletin
IAZ — Industrie-Anzeiger
Ib — Ibero-Romania
IB — Indogermanische Bibliothek
IB — Irish Book [*Bibliographical Society of Ireland*]
IBA of A — Investment Bankers Association of America. Bulletin
Ibadan — Ibadan Review
Ibadan Univ Dep For Bull — Ibadan University. Department of Forestry. Bulletin
IBASB — Izvestiya na Sektsiyata po Astronomiya. Bulgarska Akademiya na Naukite
IBA Tech Rev — IBA [*Independent Broadcasting Authority*] Technical Review
IBAZA — Proceedings of the Convention. Institute of Brewing (Australia and New Zealand Section)
IBB — International Bottler and Packer
IBBD Bol Inf — IBBD [*Instituto Brasileiro de Bibliografia e Documentacao*] Boletim Informativo

IBBD Not Diversas — IBBD [*Instituto Brasileiro de Bibliografia e Documentacao*] Noticias Diversas
IBBNA5 — International Bulletin of Bacteriological Nomenclature and Taxonomy
IBCOEH — Indian Botanical Contactor
IBCPAG — Atti. Istituto Botanico e Laboratorio Crittogamico. Universita di Pavia
IBD — Infant Behavior and Development
IBD — Internationaal Opereren
IBDBAD — International Biodeterioration Bulletin
IBEC Res Inst Bull — IBEC Research Institute. Bulletin
IBEJA8 — Indian Bee Journal
Ibero — Ibero-Romania
IBG — International Beverage News
IBHS — International Bibliography of Historical Sciences
IBi — Illustrazione Biellese
IBI — International Boat Industry
IBID — International Bibliography, Information, and Documentation
IBID — Izvestija na Balgarskoto Istoricesko Druzestvo
IBIGB — Information Bulletin on Isotopic Generators
IBIRDL — Irish Birds
IBJ — Illinois Bar Journal
IBk — Index to Book Reviews in the Humanities
IBK — Innsbrucker Beitraege zur Kulturwissenschaft
IBL — Instytut Badan Literackick Polskiej Akademii Nauk
IBLA — Institut Belles-Lettres Arabes. Revue [*Tunis*]
IBM J — IBM [*International Business Machines Corp.*] Journal of Research and Development
IBM J R D — IBM [*International Business Machines Corp.*] Journal of Research and Development
IBM J Res — IBM [*International Business Machines Corp.*] Journal of Research and Development
IBM J Res and Dev — IBM [*International Business Machines Corp.*] Journal of Research and Development
IBM J Res Dev — IBM [*International Business Machines Corp.*] Journal of Research and Development
IBM J Res Develop — IBM [*International Business Machines Corp.*] Journal of Research and Development
IBM Jrl — IBM [*International Business Machines Corp.*] Journal of Research and Development
IBM Nachr — IBM [*International Business Machines Corp.*] Nachrichten
IBMOEX — International Bioscience Monographs
IBM Systems J — IBM [*International Business Machines Corp.*] Systems Journal
IBM Syst J — IBM [*International Business Machines Corp.*] Systems Journal
IBM Tech Discl Bull — IBM [*International Business Machines Corp.*] Technical Disclosure Bulletin
IBM Tech Disclosure Bull — IBM [*International Business Machines Corp.*] Technical Disclosure Bulletin
IBM User — IBM [*International Business Machines Corp.*] System User
IBNS — International Bank Note Society. Quarterly Magazine
IbNY — Iberica (New York)
IBOJ — Informacni Bulletin pro Otazky Jazykovedne
IBOLB — Informatore Botanico Italiano
IBP — Italian Books and Periodicals
IBPRDM — International Biological Programme Series
IBREDR — Indian Botanical Reporter
IBRO Handb Ser — IBRO Handbook Series
IBRSDZ — International Brain Research Organization. Monograph Series
IBS — Informacion Comercial Espanola
IBS — Innsbrucker Beitraege zur Sprachwissenschaft
IBS — International Boundary Study
IBSA — Indian Behavioural Science Abstracts
Ibsen Yearb — Ibsen Yearbook
IBSS — International Bibliography of the Social Sciences
IBZ — Internationale Bibliographie der Zeitschriftenliteratur [*International Index to Periodicals*]
IC — Icelandic Canadian
IC — Iconclass [*Elsevier Book Series*]
I and C — Ideology and Consciousness
IC — Indian Culture
IC — Industrial Arbitration Cases [*Western Australia*]
IC — Instituto Coimbra
IC — Interfaces in Computing
IC — Islamic Culture
IC — Istoriski Casopis
ICA Inf — ICA [*Instituto Colombiano Agropecuario*] Informa
ICA Informa Inst Colomb Agropecu — ICA Informa. Instituto Colombiano Agropecuario
ICAMA — Industria della Carta
ICAM J — Institute of Corn and Agricultural Merchants. Journal
ICAO Bull — ICAO [*International Civil Aviation Organization*] Bulletin [*Canada*]
ICAPDG — Indian Journal of Comparative Animal Physiology
ICARAJ — Indian Council of Agricultural Research. Miscellaneous Bulletin
ICATAP — Indian Council of Agricultural Research. Technical Bulletin

ICBCBE — International Congress of Biochemistry. Abstracts
ICBEA — Industrie Chimique Belge
ICBRAO — India. Coffee Board. Annual Report
ICC — Information des Cours Complementaires
ICC — Instituto Caro y Cuervo
ICC — Intermediaire des Chercheurs et des Curieux
ICCPDQ — International Journal of Cancer Control and Prevention
ICC Pract J — ICC [*Interstate Commerce Commission*] Practitioners' Journal
ICD Sci Educ J — ICD [*International College of Dentists*] Scientific and Educational Journal
ICDSD6 — Indian Journal of Chest Diseases and Allied Sciences
ICE — Informacion Comercial Espanola
Ice Cream Field Ice Cream Trade J — Ice Cream Field and Ice Cream Trade Journal
Ice Cream R — Ice Cream Review
Ice Cream Rev — Ice Cream Review
Ice Cream Trade J — Ice Cream Trade Journal
ICEL — Ice (London)
Icel Fish Lab Annu Rep — Icelandic Fisheries Laboratories. Annual Report
ICEN — Ice News. Artec, Inc.
ICEN — ICEA [*International Childbirth Education Association*] News
ICEPAX — International Congress of Entomology. Proceedings
Ice Refrig — Ice and Refrigeration
ICEXBO — International Council for the Exploration of the Sea. Cooperative Research Report
ICFB — Integrative Control Functions of the Brain [*Elsevier Book Series*]
ICFTU Econ & Social Bul — ICFTU [*International Confederation of Free Trade Unions*] Economic and Social Bulletin
ICGAD — IEEE. Computer Graphics and Applications
ICGRAF — Indian Cotton Growing Review
ICHAA — Inorganica Chimica Acta
ICHCA J — ICHCA [*International Cargo Handling Coordination Association*] Journal
ICHCA Mon J — ICHCA [*International Cargo Handling Coordination Association*] Monthly Journal
ICHIA — Ingegneria Chimica
IChildMag — Subject Index to Children's Magazines
ICHR — Illinois Catholic Historical Review
Ichthyol Aquarium J — Ichthyologica: The Aquarium Journal
Ichthyol Ser Dep Biol Coll Sci Tunghai Univ — Ichthyological Series. Department of Biology. College of Science. Tunghai University
I Ch'uan Hsueh Pao Acta Genet Sin — I Ch'uan Hsueh Pao. Acta Genetica Sinica
ICI — Index to Current Information
ICI — Informations Catholiques Internationales
ICIA Inf Bull — ICIA [*International Center of Information on Antibiotics*] Information Bulletin
ICID Bull — ICID [*International Commission on Irrigation and Drainage*] Bulletin
ICIDCA Bol — ICIDCA [*Instituto Cubano de Investigaciones de los Derivados de la Cana de Azucar*] Boletin
ICI Engng Plast — ICI [*Imperial Chemical Industries Ltd.*] Engineering Plastics
ICITA — Instituto Cubano de Investigaciones Tecnologicas. Serie de Estudios sobre Trabajos de Investigacion
ICJ — Insurance Counsel Journal
ICJRAU — Indian Central Jute Committee. Annual Report of the Jute Agricultural Research Institute
ICJ Rev — Review. International Commission of Jurists
ICJYB — International Court of Justice. Yearbook
ICLIAD — Investigacion Clinica [*Maracaibo*]
ICLM — Index to Commonwealth Little Magazines
I & CLQ — International and Comparative Law Quarterly
ICL Tech J — ICL [*International Computers Limited*] Technical Journal
ICM — Imperial and Colonial Magazine
ICMFA — Indian Chemical Manufacturer
ICMJD — International Cast Metals Journal
ICN — Indonesian Commercial Newsletter
ICNABY — International Commission for the Northwest Atlantic Fisheries. Statistical Bulletin
ICNAF — International Commission for the Northwest Atlantic Fisheries. Research Bulletin
ICNAFSP — International Commission for the Northwest Atlantic Fisheries. Special Publication
ICNFAE — International Commission for the Northwest Atlantic Fisheries. Annual Proceedings
ICNS — Ice Cap News. American Society of Polar Philatelists
ICNSAJ — Iowa Conservationist
ICN-UCLA Symp Mol Cell Biol — ICN-UCLA [*International Chemical and Nuclear Corp. - University of California at Los Angeles*] Symposia on Molecular and Cellular Biology
ICNWAV — International Commission for the Northwest Atlantic Fisheries. Redbook. Part III
ICOAB5 — India. Coffee Board. Research Department. Annual Detailed Technical Report
ICOFAJ — Indian Coffee

ICOJAV — Indian Coconut Journal
ICONDC — Annual Research Reviews. Intrauterine Contraception
ICOPA — Industria Conserve
ICOPAF — Industria Conserve [*Parma*]
ICOTA — International Review of Connective Tissue Research
ICP — Index to Chinese Periodicals
ICP — Informacao Cultural Portugues
ICP — International Currency Review
ICPADC — Investigative and Cell Pathology
ICP Admin — ICP [*International Computer Programs, Inc.*] Interface Administrative and Accounting
ICP Bank Indus — ICP [*International Computer Programs, Inc.*] Interface Banking Industry
ICP DP Mgmt — ICP [*International Computer Programs, Inc.*] Interface Data Processing Management
ICP J Software Prod and Serv — ICP [*International Computer Programs, Inc.*] Journal of Software Products and Services
ICPR — International Clinical Products Review
ICr — Inscriptiones Creticae
ICR — International Currency Report
ICRE — Iceland Review
ICRISAT Annu Rep — ICRISAT [*International Crops Research Institute for the Semi-Arid Tropics*] Annual Report
ICRP Publ — ICRP [*International Commission on Radiological Protection*] Publication
ICRRA2 — Indian Council of Agricultural Research. Research Series
ICRS Med Rep Monogr Sov Med Sci — ICRS [*Institute of Contemporary Russian Studies*] Medical Reports. Monographs in Soviet Medical Science
ICRU Rep — ICRU [*International Commission on Radiological Units*] Report
ICS — Illinois Classical Studies
ICS — International Congress Series [*Elsevier Book Series*]
ICS — Italia Che Scrive
ICSMAQ — International Clearinghouse on Science and Mathematics. Curricular Developments Report
ICSP — Issues in Canadian Science Policy
ICSPD4 — Immunologia Clinica e Sperimentale
ICSU Rev World Sci — ICSU [*International Council of Scientific Unions*] Review of World Science
ICT — Industrial and Commercial Training
ICT — International Coal Trade [*Bureau of Mines*]
ICTPDF — Isozymes. Current Topics in Biological and Medical Research
ICTRA — Iron and Coal Trades Review
ICTSDI — IMLS [*Institute of Medical Laboratory Sciences*] Current Topics in Medical Laboratory Sciences
ICU — Hebdomadaire de la Production a la Distribution [*Paris*]
ICUIS Abstr Service — ICUIS [*Institute on the Church in Urban-Industrial Society*] Abstract Service
ICUNA5 — Improving College and University Teaching
ICUT — Improving College and University Teaching
ICWRBS — International Commission on Whaling. Report
ICYSB — International Review of Cytology. Supplement
ID — Institutional Distribution
ID — Ionospheric Data
ID — Irish Digest
ID — Italia Dialettale
IDABA — Annual Bulletin. International Dairy Federation
IDABAC — International Dairy Federation. Annual Bulletin
Idaho Ag Exp — Idaho. Agricultural Experiment Station. Publications
Idaho Agric Exp Stn Res Bull — Idaho. Agricultural Experiment Station. Research Bulletin
Idaho Agr Res Progr Rep — Idaho Agricultural Research Progress Report. University of Idaho. College of Agriculture
Idaho Agr Sci — Idaho Agricultural Science. University of Idaho. College of Agriculture
Idaho Bur Mines Geol Bull — Idaho. Bureau of Mines and Geology. Bulletin
Idaho Bur Mines Geol County Rep — Idaho. Bureau of Mines and Geology. County Report
Idaho Bur Mines Geol Inf Circ — Idaho. Bureau of Mines and Geology. Information Circular
Idaho Bur Mines Geol Miner Resour Rep — Idaho. Bureau of Mines and Geology. Mineral Resources Report
Idaho Bur Mines and Geology Earth Sci Ser — Idaho. Bureau of Mines and Geology. Earth Sciences Series
Idaho Bur Mines Geol Pam — Idaho. Bureau of Mines and Geology. Pamphlet
Idaho Dep Fish Game Wildl Bull — Idaho. Department of Fish and Game. Wildlife Bulletin
Idaho Dep Reclam Water Inf Bull — Idaho. Department of Reclamation. Water Information Bulletin
Idaho Dept Reclamation Water Inf Bull — Idaho. Department of Reclamation. Water Information Bulletin
Idaho Dep Water Adm Water Inf Bull — Idaho. Department of Water Administration. Water Information Bulletin
Idaho Dep Water Resour Basic Data Release — Idaho. Department of Water Resources. Basic Data Release

Idaho Dep Water Resour Water Inf Bull — Idaho. Department of Water Resources. Water Information Bulletin
Idaho For Wildl Range Exp Stn Bull — Idaho. Forest, Wildlife, and Range Experiment Station. Bulletin
Idaho For Wildl Range Exp Stn Inf Ser — Idaho. Forest, Wildlife, and Range Experiment Station. Information Series
Idaho For Wildl Range Exp Stn Note — Idaho. Forest, Wildlife, and Range Experiment Station. Note
Idaho For Wildl Range Exp Stn Pap — Idaho. Forest, Wildlife, and Range Experiment Station. Paper
Idaho For Wildl Range Exp Stn Tech Rep — Idaho. Forest, Wildlife, and Range Experiment Station. Technical Report
Idaho Libn — Idaho Librarian
Idaho Librn — Idaho Librarian
Idaho L Rev — Idaho Law Review
Idaho Min Industry Ann Rept — Idaho Mining Industry. Annual Report
Idaho Power Co Bull — Idaho Power Company. Bulletin
Idaho State Hortic Assoc Proc Annu Conv — Idaho. State Horticultural Association. Proceedings of the Annual Convention
Idaho Univ Agric Exp Stn Curr Inf Ser — Idaho University. Agricultural Experiment Station. Current Information Series
Idaho Univ Curr Inf Ser — Idaho University. Current Information Series
Idaho Univ Eng Exp Sta Bull — Idaho University. Engineering Experiment Station. Bulletin
Idaho Univ For Range Wildl Exp Stn Res Note — Idaho University. Forest, Range, and Wildlife Experiment Station. Research Note
Idaho Univ Water Resour Res Inst Res Tech Completion Rep — Idaho University. Water Resources Research Institute. Research Technical Completion Report
Idaho Yest — Idaho Yesterdays
IDCIDC — International Development Research Centre. Publication IDRC
IDCQA — Industrie Ceramique
IDD — Iowa State University of Science and Technology. Doctoral Dissertations. Abstracts and References
Idea — Idea: The Journal of Law and Technology
IDEA — Ideas/Idees. Department of Indian and Northern Affairs
Ideal Stud — Idealistic Studies
Ideas Manage — Ideas for Management
Ideas for Mgmt — Ideas for Management
Ideggyogy Sz — Ideggyogyaszati Szemle
Idemitsu Pet J — Idemitsu Petroleum Journal [*Japan*]
Idengaku Zasshi Suppl — Idengaku Zasshi. Supplement [*Japan*]
IDGEAH — Industrial Gerontology
Idg Forsch — Indogermanische Forschungen
IDHAA — Industrie und Handel
IDHLA9 — International Digest of Health Legislation
IDHOA — Proceedings. International District Heating Association
IDI — Management Today
IDIA — Informativo de Investigaciones Agricolas
IDIA Supl — IDIA [*Informativo de Investigaciones Agricolas*]. Suplemento
IDJOAS — International Dental Journal
IDKKB — Iwate Daigaku Kyoikugakubu Kenkyu Nenpo
IDKKBM — Annual Report. Faculty of Education. University of Iwate
IDKSA — Ibaraki Daigaku Kogakubu Kenkyu Shuho
IDL — Index to Dental Literature
IDLEB — Industrial Engineering
ID LR — Idaho Law Review
IDMA Bull — IDMA [*Indian Drug Manufacturers' Association*] Bulletin
IDMGB — Industrial Management
IDNGA — Ibaraki Daigaku Nogakubu Gakujutsu Hokoku
IDNHA — Iwate Daigaku Nogakubu Hokoku
IDOC Bul — IDOC [*International Documentation*] Bulletin
IDOJA — Idojaras
IDPGA — Industrial and Commercial Photography
IDP Rep — IDP [*Information and Data Base Publishing*] Report [*United States*]
IDR — Japan Letter
IDRCE2 — International Development Research Centre. Technical Studies IDRC-TS
IDRC Rep — IDRC [*International Development Research Centre*] Reports
IDRSA — Industrial Research
IDS — Izvestiya na Druzestvoto na Filolozite-Slavisti v Balgarija (Sofija)
IDSA J — IDSA [*Institute for Defense Studies and Analyses*] Journal [*India*]
IDSB — International Dostoevsky Society. Bulletin
IDS Bulletin — IDS [*Institute of Development Studies*] Bulletin
IDSFA — Institute for Defence Studies and Analyses. Journal [*India*]
IDS Report — Incomes Data Services Ltd. International Report
IDT — Integracion Latinoamericana
IDTAA — Industrie Agrarie
IDTKA — Industriell Teknik
IDUPA — Issledovaniya po Uprugosti i Plastichnosti
IDV — International Trade Documentation
IDW — Industriemagazin. Management, Marketing, Technologie
IE — Interdisciplinary Essays
IEBEA — IEEE. Transactions on Biomedical Engineering
IEBY — Iowa English Bulletin. Yearbook

IEc — Index of Economic Articles
I & EC — Industrial and Engineering Chemistry
IEC — Institut d'Estudis Catalans
IEC Bull — IEC [*International Electrotechnical Commission*] Bulletin
IECE — International Educational and Cultural Exchange [*Washington, DC*]
IECFA — Industrial and Engineering Chemistry. Fundamentals
IECHA — Industrial and Engineering Chemistry
IECI Annu Conf Proc — IECI [*Industrial Electronics and Control Instrumentation Group*] Annual Conference Proceedings [*United States*]
IECMB — IEEE. Transactions on Communications
I Econ J — Indian Economic Journal
IEC Prod Res Dev — Industrial and Engineering Chemistry. Product Research and Development
IEE — Indian Economic Journal
IEECA — IEEE. Transactions on Electronic Computers
IEE Conf Publ (Lond) — IEE [*Institution of Electrical Engineers*] Conference Publication (London)
IEE Control Engrg Ser — IEE [*Institution of Electrical Engineers*] Control Engineering Series
IEEE Acoust — IEEE. Transactions on Acoustics, Speech, and Signal Processing
IEEE Aer El — IEEE. Transactions on Aerospace and Electronic Systems
IEEE Annu Text Ind Tech Conf — IEEE. Annual Textile Industry Technical Conference
IEEE Annu Text Ind Tech Conf Proc — IEEE. Annual Textile Industry Technical Conference. Proceedings [*United States*]
IEEE Antenn — IEEE. Transactions on Antennas and Propagation
IEEE Auto C — IEEE. Transactions on Automatic Control
IEEE Biomed — IEEE. Transactions on Biomedical Engineering
IEEE Broadc — IEEE. Transactions on Broadcasting
IEEE Cem Ind Tech Conf Pap — IEEE. Cement Industry Technical Conference Paper
IEEE Circ S — IEEE. Transactions on Circuits and Systems
IEEE Circuits Syst Mag — IEEE. Circuits and Systems Magazine [*United States*]
IEEE Commun — IEEE. Transactions on Communications
IEEE Commun Mag — IEEE. Communications Magazine
IEEE Commun Soc Mag — IEEE. Communications Society. Magazine [*Later, IEEE. Communications Magazine*]
IEEE Comput — IEEE. Transactions on Computers
IEEE Comput Graphics and Appl — IEEE. Computer Graphics and Applications
IEEE Comput Group News — IEEE. Computer Group News
IEEE Conf Rec Annu Conf Electr Eng Probl Rubber Plast Ind — IEEE. Conference Record. Annual Conference of Electrical Engineering Problems in the Rubber and Plastics Industries
IEEE Conf Rec Ind Commer Power Syst Tech Conf — IEEE. Conference Record. Industrial and Commercial Power Systems. Technical Conference
IEEE Conf Rec Thermion Convers Spec Conf — IEEE. Conference Records. Thermionic Conversion Specialist Conference
IEEE Cons E — IEEE. Transactions on Consumer Electronics
IEEE Control Syst Mag — IEEE. Control Systems Magazine
IEEE Device — IEEE. Transactions on Electron Devices
IEEE Educat — IEEE. Transactions on Education
IEEE Electromagn Compat Symp — IEEE. Electromagnetic Compatibility Symposium. Record
IEEE Electron Aerosp Syst Conv Rec — IEEE. Electronics and Aerospace Systems. Convention Record [*United States*]
IEEE Electron Device Lett — IEEE. Electron Device Letters [*United States*]
IEEE El Ins — IEEE. Transactions on Electrical Insulation
IEEE Elmagn — IEEE. Transactions on Electromagnetic Compatibility
IEEE Eng Manage Rev — IEEE. Engineering Management Review
IEEE Eng Med and Biol Mag — IEEE. Engineering in Medicine and Biology Magazine
IEEE Geosci — IEEE. Transactions on Geoscience Electronics
IEEE Ind Ap — IEEE. Transactions on Industry Applications
IEEE Ind El — IEEE. Transactions on Industrial Electronics and Control Instrumentation [*Later, IEEE. Transactions on Industrial Electronics*]
IEEE Info T — IEEE. Transactions on Information Theory
IEEE Instr — IEEE. Transactions on Instrumentation and Measurement
IEEE Int Conv Dig — IEEE. International Convention. Digest
IEEE Int Conv Rec — IEEE. International Convention. Record
IEEE Intercon Tech Pap — IEEE. Intercon Technical Papers
IEEE J Ocean Eng — IEEE. Journal of Oceanic Engineering
IEEE J Oceanic Eng — IEEE. Journal of Oceanic Engineering
IEEE Journal of Oceanic Engineering — IEEE. Journal of Oceanic Engineering
IEEE J Q El — IEEE. Journal of Quantum Electronics
IEEE J Quantum Electron — IEEE. Journal of Quantum Electronics
IEEE J Sel Areas Commun — IEEE. Journal on Selected Areas in Communications
IEEE J Soli — IEEE. Journal of Solid-State Circuits
IEEE J Solid-State Circuits — IEEE. Journal of Solid-State Circuits
IEE Electromagn Waves Ser — IEE [*Institution of Electrical Engineers*] Electromagnetic Waves Series

IEEE Magnet — IEEE. Transactions on Magnetics

IEEE Manage — IEEE. Transactions on Engineering Management

IEEE Micr T — IEEE. Transactions on Microwave Theory and Techniques

IEEE Nucl S — IEEE. Transactions on Nuclear Science

IEEE Parts — IEEE. Transactions on Parts, Hybrids, and Packaging

IEEE Photovoltaic Spec Conf Conf Rec — IEEE. Photovoltaic Specialists Conference. Conference Record [*United States*]

IEEE Plas S — IEEE. Transactions on Plasma Science

IEEE Power — IEEE. Transactions on Power Apparatus and Systems

IEEE Power Eng Rev — IEEE. Power Engineering Review

IEEE Proc — IEEE. Proceedings

IEEE Proc Annu Symp Rel — IEEE. Proceedings. Annual Symposium on Reliability

IEEE Proc Conf Elec Appl Text Ind — IEEE. Proceedings. Conference on Electrical Applications for the Textile Industry

IEEE Proc Conf Eng Med Biol — IEEE. Proceedings. Conference on Engineering in Medicine and Biology

IEEE Proc Electron Components Conf — IEEE. Proceedings. Electronic Components Conference

IEEE Proc Intermag Conf — IEEE. International Conference on Magnetics. Proceedings of the Intermag Conference

IEEE Proc Nat Aerosp Electron Conf — IEEE. Proceedings. National Aerospace and Electronics Conference

IEEE Proc Natl Aerosp Electron Conf — IEEE. Proceedings. National Aerospace and Electronics Conference

IEEE Prof C — IEEE. Transactions on Professional Communications

IEEE Reg Six (West USA) Conf Rec — IEEE. Region Six (Western USA). Conference Record

IEEE Reliab — IEEE. Transactions on Reliability

IEEE S — IEEE. Spectrum

IEEE Son Ul — IEEE. Transactions on Sonics and Ultrasonics

IEEE Spectr — IEEE. Spectrum

IEEE Spectrum — IEEE. Spectrum

IEEE Stand Publ — IEEE. Standards Publications

IEEE Stud Pap — IEEE. Student Papers

IEEE Syst M — IEEE. Transactions on Systems, Man, and Cybernetics

IEEE Tech Act Guide — IEEE. Technical Activities Guide [*United States*]

IEEE T El Dev — IEEE. Transactions on Electron Devices

IEEE T Nucl Sci — IEEE. Transactions on Nuclear Science

IEEE T Pl Sci — IEEE. Transactions on Plasma Science

IEEE Trans — IEEE. Transactions on Computers

IEEE Trans Acoust Speech Signal Process — IEEE. Transactions on Acoustics, Speech, and Signal Processing

IEEE Trans Aerosp — IEEE. Transactions on Aerospace [*Later, IEEE. Transactions on Aerospace and Electronic Systems*]

IEEE Trans Aerospace Electron Systems — IEEE. Transactions on Aerospace and Electronic Systems

IEEE Trans Aerospace and Electron Systems — IEEE. Transactions on Aerospace and Electronic Systems

IEEE Trans Aerosp and Electron Syst — IEEE. Transactions on Aerospace and Electronic Systems

IEEE Trans Aerosp Electron Syst — IEEE. Transactions on Aerospace and Electronic Systems

IEEE Trans Aerosp Navig Electron — IEEE. Transactions on Aerospace and Navigational Electronics

IEEE Trans Antennas Propag — IEEE. Transactions on Antennas and Propagation

IEEE Trans Antennas Propagat — IEEE. Transactions on Antennas and Propagation

IEEE Trans Antennas and Propagation — IEEE. Transactions on Antennas and Propagation

IEEE Trans Appl Ind — IEEE. Transactions on Applications and Industry

IEEE Trans ASSP — IEEE. Transactions on Acoustics, Speech, and Signal Processing

IEEE Trans Audio — IEEE. Transactions on Audio

IEEE Trans Audio Electroacoust — IEEE. Transactions on Audio and Electroacoustics

IEEE Trans Audio and Electroacoust — IEEE. Transactions on Audio and Electroacoustics

IEEE Trans Automat Contr — IEEE. Transactions on Automatic Control

IEEE Trans Automat Control — IEEE. Transactions on Automatic Control

IEEE Trans Automatic Control — IEEE. Transactions on Automatic Control

IEEE Trans Autom Control — IEEE. Transactions on Automatic Control

IEEE Trans Bio Med Electron — IEEE. Transactions on Bio-Medical Electronics

IEEE Trans Biomed Eng — IEEE. Transactions on Biomedical Engineering

IEEE Trans Broadcast — IEEE. Transactions on Broadcasting

IEEE Trans Broadcast and Telev Receivers — IEEE. Transactions on Broadcast and Television Receivers

IEEE Trans Broadcast Telev Receivers — IEEE. Transactions on Broadcast and Television Receivers

IEEE Trans Cable Telev — IEEE. Transactions on Cable Television

IEEE Trans CAS — IEEE. Transactions on Circuits and Systems

IEEE Trans CATV — IEEE. Transactions on Cable Television

IEEE Trans CE — IEEE. Transactions on Consumer Electronics

IEEE Trans Circuits Syst — IEEE. Transactions on Circuits and Systems

IEEE Trans Circuits and Syst — IEEE. Transactions on Circuits and Systems

IEEE Trans Circuits and Systems — IEEE. Transactions on Circuits and Systems

IEEE Trans Circuit Theory — IEEE. Transactions on Circuit Theory

IEEE Trans Com — IEEE. Transactions on Communications

IEEE Trans Comm — IEEE. Transactions on Communications

IEEE Trans Commun — IEEE. Transactions on Communications

IEEE Trans Commun Electron — IEEE. Transactions on Communication and Electronics

IEEE Trans Commun Syst — IEEE. Transactions on Communications Systems

IEEE Trans Commun Technol — IEEE. Transactions on Communication Technology [*Later, IEEE. Transactions on Communications*]

IEEE Trans Component Parts — IEEE. Transactions on Component Parts

IEEE Trans Components Hybrids and Manuf Technol — IEEE. Transactions on Components, Hybrids, and Manufacturing Technology

IEEE Trans Components Hybrids Manuf Technol — IEEE. Transactions on Components, Hybrids, and Manufacturing Technology

IEEE Trans Comput — IEEE. Transactions on Computers

IEEE Trans Comput-Aided Des Integrated Circuits and Syst — IEEE. Transactions on Computer-Aided Design of Integrated Circuits and Systems

IEEE Trans Computers — IEEE. Transactions on Computers

IEEE Trans Com Tech — IEEE. Transactions on Communication Technology [*Later, IEEE. Transactions on Communications*]

IEEE Trans Consum Electron — IEEE. Transactions on Consumer Electronics

IEEE Trans Educ — IEEE. Transactions on Education

IEEE Trans Elec Insul — IEEE. Transactions on Electrical Insulation

IEEE Trans Electr Insul — IEEE. Transactions on Electrical Insulation

IEEE Trans Electromagn Compat — IEEE. Transactions on Electromagnetic Compatibility

IEEE Trans Electron Comput — IEEE. Transactions on Electronic Computers [*United States*]

IEEE Trans Electron Devices — IEEE. Transactions on Electron Devices

IEEE Trans Eng Manag — IEEE. Transactions on Engineering Management

IEEE Trans Eng Manage — IEEE. Transactions on Engineering Management

IEEE Trans Engng Man — IEEE. Engineering Management

IEEE Trans Engng Wrtg Speech — IEEE. Transactions on Engineering Writing and Speech

IEEE Trans Eng Writing Speech — IEEE. Transactions on Engineering Writing and Speech

IEEE Trans Eng Writ and Speech — IEEE. Transactions on Engineering Writing and Speech

IEEE Trans Geosci Electron — IEEE. Transactions on Geoscience Electronics

IEEE Trans Geosci Electronics — IEEE. Transactions on Geoscience Electronics

IEEE Trans Geosci Remote Sens — IEEE. Transactions on Geoscience and Remote Sensing [*United States*]

IEEE Trans Geosci Remote Sensing — IEEE. Transactions on Geoscience and Remote Sensing

IEEE Trans Geosci and Remote Sensing — IEEE. Transactions on Geoscience and Remote Sensing

IEEE Trans Hum Factors Electron — IEEE. Transactions on Human Factors in Electronics [*United States*]

IEEE Trans Ind Appl — IEEE. Transactions on Industry Applications

IEEE Trans Ind Electron — IEEE. Transactions on Industrial Electronics

IEEE Trans Ind Electron and Control Instrum — IEEE. Transactions on Industrial Electronics and Control Instrumentation [*Later, IEEE. Transactions on Industrial Electronics*]

IEEE Trans Ind Electron Control Instrum — IEEE. Transactions on Industrial Electronics and Control Instrumentation [*Later, IEEE. Transactions on Industrial Electronics*]

IEEE Trans Ind Gen Appl — IEEE. Transactions on Industry and General Applications [*Later, IEEE. Transactions on Industry Applications*]

IEEE Trans Ind and Gen Appl — IEEE. Transactions on Industry and General Applications [*Later, IEEE. Transactions on Industry Applications*]

IEEE Trans Information Theory — IEEE. Transactions on Information Theory

IEEE Trans Inform Theory — IEEE. Transactions on Information Theory

IEEE Trans Inf Theory — IEEE. Transactions on Information Theory

IEEE Trans Instrum Meas — IEEE. Transactions on Instrumentation and Measurement

IEEE Trans Instrum and Meas — IEEE. Transactions on Instrumentation and Measurement

IEEE Trans Magn — IEEE. Transactions on Magnetics

IEEE Trans Man-Mach Syst — IEEE. Transactions on Man-Machine Systems

IEEE Trans Manuf Technol — IEEE. Transactions on Manufacturing Technology

IEEE Trans Med Imaging — IEEE. Transactions on Medical Imaging

IEEE Trans Microwave Theory and Tech — IEEE. Transactions on Microwave Theory and Techniques

IEEE Trans Microwave Theory Tech — IEEE. Transactions on Microwave Theory and Techniques

IEEE Trans Mil Electron — IEEE. Transactions on Military Electronics

IEEE Trans Nucl Sci — IEEE. Transactions on Nuclear Science

IEEE Trans Parts Hybrids Packag — IEEE. Transactions on Parts, Hybrids, and Packaging

IEEE Trans Parts Hybrids and Packag — IEEE. Transactions on Parts, Hybrids, and Packaging

IEEE Trans Parts Mater and Packag — IEEE. Transactions on Parts, Materials, and Packaging

IEEE Trans Parts Mater Packag — IEEE. Transactions on Parts, Materials, and Packaging

IEEE Trans Pattern Anal and Mach Intell — IEEE. Transactions on Pattern Analysis and Machine Intelligence

IEEE Trans Plasma Sci — IEEE. Transactions on Plasma Science

IEEE Trans Power Appar and Syst — IEEE. Transactions on Power Apparatus and Systems

IEEE Trans Power App Syst — IEEE. Transactions on Power Apparatus and Systems

IEEE Trans Prod Eng Prod — IEEE. Transactions on Product Engineering and Production

IEEE Trans Prof Commun — IEEE. Transactions on Professional Communications

IEEE Trans PS — IEEE. Transactions on Plasma Science

IEEE Trans Rel — IEEE. Transactions on Reliability

IEEE Trans Reliab — IEEE. Transactions on Reliability

IEEE Trans Reliability — IEEE. Transactions on Reliability

IEEE Trans SE — IEEE. Transactions on Software Engineering

IEEE Trans Software Eng — IEEE. Transactions on Software Engineering

IEEE Trans Software Engrg — IEEE. Transactions on Software Engineering

IEEE Trans Sonics & Ultrason — IEEE. Transactions on Sonics and Ultrasonics

IEEE Trans Sonics Ultrason — IEEE. Transactions on Sonics and Ultrasonics

IEEE Trans Space Electron Telem — IEEE. Transactions on Space Electronics and Telemetry

IEEE Trans System — IEEE. Transactions on Systems, Man, and Cybernetics

IEEE Trans Systems Man Cybernet — IEEE. Transactions on Systems, Man, and Cybernetics

IEEE Trans Syst Man and Cybern — IEEE. Transactions on Systems, Man, and Cybernetics

IEEE Trans Syst Man Cybern — IEEE. Transactions on Systems, Man, and Cybernetics

IEEE Trans Syst Sci and Cybern — IEEE. Transactions on Systems, Science, and Cybernetics

IEEE Trans Syst Sci Cybern — IEEE. Transactions on Systems, Science, and Cybernetics

IEEE Trans Ultrasonics Eng — IEEE. Transactions on Ultrasonics Engineering

IEEE Trans Veh Commun — IEEE. Transactions on Vehicular Communications

IEEE Trans Veh Technol — IEEE. Transactions on Vehicular Technology

IEEE Veh T — IEEE. Transactions on Vehicular Technology

IEEE Wescon Conven Rec — IEEE. Wescon Convention Record

IEEE Wescon Tech Pap — IEEE. Wescon Technical Papers

IEE-IERE Proc (India) — IEE-IERE [*Institution of Electrical Engineers-Institution of Electronic and Radio Engineers*] Proceedings (India)

IEE J Comput Digital Tech — IEE [*Institution of Electrical Engineers*] Journal on Computers and Digital Techniques

IEE J Comput and Digital Tech — IEE [*Institution of Electrical Engineers*] Journal on Computers and Digital Techniques

IEE J Electron Circuits and Syst — IEE [*Institution of Electrical Engineers*] Journal on Electronic Circuits and Systems

IEE J Electron Circuits Syst — IEE [*Institution of Electrical Engineers*] Journal on Electronic Circuits and Systems

IEE J Electr Power Appl — IEE [*Institution of Electrical Engineers*] Journal on Electric Power Applications

IEE J Microwaves Opt Acoust — IEE [*Institution of Electrical Engineers*] Journal on Microwaves, Optics, and Acoustics

IEE J Solid-State Electron Devices — IEE [*Institution of Electrical Engineers*] Journal on Solid-State and Electron Devices

IEE J Solid-State and Electron Devices — IEE [*Institution of Electrical Engineers*] Journal on Solid-State and Electron Devices

IEE Monogr Ser — IEE [*Institution of Electrical Engineers*] Monograph Series

IEE Proc A — IEE [*Institution of Electrical Engineers*] Proceedings. Part A

IEE Proc B Elect Pwr Applics — IEE [*Institution of Electrical Engineers*] Proceedings. Part B. Electric Power Applications

IEE Proc B Electr Power Appl — IEE [*Institution of Electrical Engineers*] Proceedings. Part B. Electric Power Applications

IEE Proc C — IEE [*Institution of Electrical Engineers*] Proceedings. Part C. Generation, Transmission, and Distribution

IEE Proc C Gener Transm Distrib — IEE [*Institution of Electrical Engineers*] Proceedings. Part C. Generation, Transmission, and Distribution

IEE Proc D — IEE [*Institution of Electrical Engineers*] Proceedings. Part D. Control Theory and Applications

IEE Proc D Control Theory Applics — IEE [*Institution of Electrical Engineers*] Proceedings. Part D. Control Theory and Applications

IEE Proc E — IEE [*Institution of Electrical Engineers*] Proceedings. Part E. Computers and Digital Techniques

IEE Proc E Comput Digit Tech — IEE [*Institution of Electrical Engineers*] Proceedings. Part E. Computers and Digital Techniques

IEE Proc E Computers Digit Techniques — IEE [*Institution of Electrical Engineers*] Proceedings. Part E. Computers and Diigital Techniques

IEE Proc F — IEE [*Institution of Electrical Engineers*] Proceedings. Part F. Communications, Radar, and Signal Processing

IEE Proc F Commun Radar Signal Process — IEE [*Institution of Electrical Engineers*] Proceedings. Part F. Communications, Radar, and Signal Processing

IEE Proc G — IEE [*Institution of Electrical Engineers*] Proceedings. Part G. Electronic Circuits and Systems

IEE Proc G Electron Circuits Syst — IEE [*Institution of Electrical Engineers*] Proceedings. Part G. Electronic Circuits and Systems

IEE Proc Generation Transm Distrib — IEE [*Institution of Electrical Engineers*] Proceedings. Part C. Generation, Transmission, and Distribution

IEE Proc H — IEE [*Institution of Electrical Engineers*] Proceedings. Part H. Microwaves, Optics, and Antennas

IEE Proc H Microwaves Opt Antennas — IEE [*Institution of Electrical Engineers*] Proceedings. Part H. Microwaves, Optics, and Antennas

IEE Proc I — IEE [*Institution of Electrical Engineers*] Proceedings. Part I. Solid-State and Electron Devices

IEE Proc I Solid-State Electron Devices — IEE [*Institution of Electrical Engineers*] Proceedings. Part I. Solid-State and Electron Devices

IEE Proc Part C — IEE [*Institution of Electrical Engineers*] Proceedings. Part C. Generation, Transmission, and Distribution [*England*]

IEE Proc Part D — IEE [*Institution of Electrical Engineers*] Proceedings. Part D. Control Theory and Applications [*England*]

IEE Proc Part E — IEE [*Institution of Electrical Engineers*] Proceedings. Part E. Computers and Digital Techniques [*England*]

IEE Proc Part F — IEE [*Institution of Electrical Engineers*] Proceedings. Part F. Communications, Radar, and Signal Processing [*England*]

IEE Proc Part G — IEE [*Institution of Electrical Engineers*] Proceedings. Part G. Electronic Circuits and Systems [*England*]

IEE Proc Part H — IEE [*Institution of Electrical Engineers*] Proceedings. Part H. Microwaves, Optics, and Antennas [*England*]

IEE Proc Part I — IEE [*Institution of Electrical Engineers*] Proceedings. Part I. Solid-State and Electron Devices [*England*]

IEE Rev — IEE [*Institution of Electrical Engineers*] Reviews

IEEUA — IEEE. Transactions on Audio

IEFFA — Industrie-Elektronik in Forschung und Fertigung

IEGNA — Environmental Geology Notes. Illinois State Geological Survey

IEGRBU — Imperial Ethiopian Government Institute of Agricultural Research. Report

IEHFA — IEEE. Transactions on Human Factors in Electronics

IEIM — Izvestiya na Etnografskija Institut Muzej

IE Ind Eng — IE. Industrial Engineering

IEJ — Indian Economic Journal

IEJ — Indiana English Journal

IEJ — Israel Exploration Journal

IEJ — Nieuws uit Japan

IEKNA — Izvestiya Energeticheskogo Instituta Akademiya Nauk SSSR

IEKU — Institut foer Eskimologi. Kobenhavns Universitet

IEMSA — Izoliatsiya Elektricheskikh Mashin. Sbornik Sostavlen po Materialam Konferentsii Sozvannai Leningradskim Otdelenium Nauchno-Tekhnicheskogo Obshchestva Energetekii

IEN — Industrial Engineering

IEN — Industrial Equipment News

IEP — Informe Economico

IEPDA — Industrial and Engineering Chemistry. Process Design and Development

IEPRA — Industrial and Engineering Chemistry. Product Research and Development

IER — Indian Economic Review

IER — Irish Ecclesiastical Record

IER — Irish Ecclesiastical Review

IERBA2 — Iowa. Agricultural Experiment Station. Research Bulletin

IERE Conf Proc (Lond) — IERE [*Institution of Electronic and Radio Engineers*] Conference Proceedings (London)

IERWA — IEE [*Institution of Electrical Engineers*] Reviews

IESB — Bulletin of Indonesian Economic Studies [*Canberra*]

IESCDD — Irish Journal of Environmental Science

IESEB — Ion Exchange and Solvent Extraction

IESH — Indian Economic and Social History Review

IES Lighting Rev — IES [*Illuminating Engineering Societies of Australia*] Lighting Review

IES Light Rev — IES [*Illuminating Engineering Societies of Australia*] Lighting Review

IES Ltg Rev — IES [*Illuminating Engineering Societies of Australia*] Lighting Review

IESPA — Proceedings. Institute of Environmental Sciences

IET — Israel Economist

IETAB — IEEE. Transactions on Acoustics, Speech, and Signal Processing

IETMB — IEEE. Transactions on Manufacturing Technology

IET Z Elektr Inf Energietech — IET: Zeitschrift fuer Elektrische Informations- und Energietechnik

IEVCA — IEEE. Transactions on Vehicular Communications

IEX — Journal of Energy and Development

IEXMBW — Ion Exchange and Membranes

IEY — Iowa English Yearbook

IF — Indogermanische Forschungen
IF — Industrialization Forum [*Canada*]
IF — Insurance Forum
IFABA — Izvestiya na Fizicheskiya Instituta ANEB. Bulgarska Akademiya na Naukite
IFAOA — Izvestiya Akademii Nauk SSSR Fizika Atmosfery i Okeana
IFAOBE — Institut Francais d'Archeologie Orientale. Bibliotheque d'Etude
IFB — Industry of Free China
IFBQA8 — Industria Farmaceutica y Bioquimica
IFC — Industry of Free China [*Taipei*]
IFCNA — Information and Control
IFCPD — International Foundry Congress. Congress Papers
IFDAI — Istanbuler Forschungen. Deutsches Archaeologisches Institut
Ife Afr Stud — Ife African Studies
IFFBB — IFF [*Institut fuer Festkoerperforschung*] Bulletin
IFF Bull — IFF [*Institut fuer Festkoerperforschung*] Bulletin
IFFPAP — Indian Forest Records. Forest Pathology
IFIFAA — Irish Fisheries Investigations. Series A. Freshwater
IFIIA — Industrial Finishing (Wheaton, Illinois)
IFIMAV — Irish Fisheries Investigations. Series B. Marine
IFIPC — IFIP [*International Federation for Information Processing*] Congress Series [*Elsevier Book Series*]
IFIP (Int Fed Inf Process) Med Inf Monogr Ser — IFIP (International Federation for Information Processing) Medical Informatics Monograph Series
IFIP Med Inf Monogr Ser — IFIP [*International Federation for Information Processing*] Medical Informatics Monograph Series
IFIPW — IFIP [*International Federation for Information Processing*] World Conference Series on Medical Informatics [*Elsevier Book Series*]
IFiS — Instytut Filozofii i Socjologii Pan
IFJOD — IFLA [*International Federation of Library Associations and Institutions*] Journal
IFKKA — Izvestiya Sektora Fiziko-Khimicheskogo Analiza Institut Obshchei i Neorganicheskoi Khimii Imeni N. S. Kurnakova Akademiya Nauk SSSR
IFL — International Financial Law Review
IFLA News — International Federation of Library Associations. News
IFLB — Iowa Foreign Language Bulletin
IfL Mitt — IfL [*Institut fuer Leichtbau und Oekonomische Verwendung von Werkstoffen*] Mitteilung [*East Germany*]
IFLP — Index to Foreign Legal Periodicals
IFM — Information and Management [*Netherlands*]
IFMAA — Istanbul Universitesi Fen Fakultesi Mecmuasi. Seri A. Matematik-Fizik-Kimya
IFMBA — Istanbul Universitesi Fen Fakultesi Mecmuasi. Seri B
IFMCA — Istanbul Universitesi Fen Fakultesi Mecmuasi. Seri C. Astronomi-Fizik-Kimya
IFMCJ — International Folk Music Council. Journal
IFMCY — International Folk Music Council. Yearbook
IFMLL — International Federation for Modern Languages and Literatures
IFNS — International Financial News Survey
IFOBAS — Indian Forest Bulletin
IFOC — International Fiber Optics and Communications
IFOC Int Fiber Opt — IFOC. International Fiber Optics and Communications
IFORA8 — Indian Forester
IFP — Index to Free Periodicals
IFPAAU — Indian Food Packer
IFPLA — Information Processing Letters
IFQAA — Informacion de Quimica Analitica
I & FR — Indian and Foreign Review
IFR — International Fiction Review
IFr — Italia Francescana
IFRAA6 — Indian Forest Records. Wood Anatomy
IFRBA9 — Indian Forest Records. Botany
IFREAI — Indian Forest Records. Entomology
IFREDL — Indian Forest Records. Forest Management and Mensuration
IFRGA — Industriefeuerung
IFRMA8 — Indian Forest Records. Mycology
IFRPA — Izvestiya na Instituta po Fiziologiya na Rasteniyata. Bulgarska Akademiya na Naukite
IFRSAQ — Indian Forest Records. Silviculture
IFRSBR — Indian Forest Records. Statistical
IFRSDT — Indian Forest Records. Silvics
IFRTAT — Indian Forest Records. Timber Mechanics
IFS — International Financial Statistics
IFSRA — Information Storage and Retrieval
IFSRD — IF. Industrialization Forum
IFSSykt — Istoriko-Filologiceskij Sbornik Syktyvbar
IFSTD — Irish Journal of Food Science and Technology
IFSTD3 — Irish Journal of Food Science and Technology
IFT — Informations Economiques (Tunis)
IFU — IMF [*International Monetary Fund*] Survey
IFV — Informatie Bulletin
IFYGL Bull — International Field Year for the Great Lakes. Bulletin
IFZ — Istoriko-Filologiceskij Zurnal
IG — Inscriptiones Graecae

IG — Isotope Geoscience
IG — Istorijski Glasnik
IGA — International Journal of Government Auditing
IGAYA — Igaku No Ayumi [*Japan*]
IGB — International Trade Forum
IGBLBZ — Immergruene Blaetter
IGBMA — Izvestiya na Geofizichniya Institut. Bulgarska Akademiya na Naukite
IGC — Atlantica and Iceland Review
IGCS — International Guide to Classical Studies
IGDGA — Ingenieur-Digest
IGECB — Institution of Gas Engineers. Communications
Ig F — Indogermanische Forschungen
IGForsch — Indogermanische Forschungen
IGG — IGG [*Instituto Geografico e Geologico de Sao Paulo*] Revista
IGGEA — Ingegneria
IGGMA — Izvestiya na Geologicheskiya Institut. Bulgarska Akademiya na Naukite. Seriya Geokhimiya. Mineralogiya i Petrografiya
IGINA — Ingenieria e Industria (Argentina)
IG Inf Ser — IG [*Industrial Group, United Kingdom Atomic Energy Authority*] Information Series
IGJ — Indian Geographical Journal [*Madras*]
IGLQ — Igalaaq. Nortext [*Ottawa*]
IGLS — Inscriptions Grecques et Latines de la Syrie
IGLSyr — Inscriptions Grecques et Latines de la Syrie
IGMEA — Ingegneria Meccanica
Ig Microb Epidem — Igiena, Microbiologie, si Epidemiologie
Ig Microbiol Epidemiol — Igiena, Microbiologie, si Epidemiologie
Ig Mod — Igiene Moderna
IGMS — International Guide to Medieval Studies
IGNKB — Ispol'zovanie Gaza v Narodnom Khozyaistve
IGNTA — Ingenieurs et Techniciens
IGNTB — Ingenioer-Nytt
IGNVB — Izvestiya na Geologicheskiya Institut. Bulgarska Akademiya na Naukite. Seriya Neftena i Vuglishtna Geologiya [*Bulgaria*]
IGOPA — Izvestiya Glavnoi Astronomicheskoi Observatorii v Pulkove
IGPIA — Public Information Circular. Iowa Geological Survey
IGREB — Report. Institute of Geological Sciences
IGRR — Inscriptiones Graecae ad Res Romanas Pertinentes
Ig Sanita Pubblica — Igiene e Sanita Pubblica
Ig San Pubbl — Igiene e Sanita Pubblica
IGSKD — Izvestiya Akademii Nauk Gruzinskoi SSR Seriya Khimicheskaia
IGSSA — Illinois State Geological Survey. Guidebook Series
IGTJA — Indian Geotechnical Journal
IGT Nie — IGT [*Instituut voor Grafische Techniek*] Nieuws
IGU Newsl — IGU [*International Geographical Union*] Newsletter
IGUTP — Instituti Geographici Universitatis Turkuensis. Publications
IGW — Internationales Gewerbearchiv der Kleinbetrieb und Mittelbetrieb in der Modernen Wirtschaft
IGW Inf — IGW [*Institut fuer Gesellschaft und Wissenschaft*] Informationen zur Wissenschaftsentwicklung
IGY Bull — IGY [*International Geophysical Year*] Bulletin
IGY Gen Rep Ser — IGY [*International Geophysical Year*] General Report Series
IGY Sat Rep Ser — IGY [*International Geophysical Year*] Satellite Report Series
IGY World Data Center A Gen Rept Ser — International Geophysical Year. World Data Center. A. General Report Series
IGY World Data Center A Glaciol Rept Ser — International Geophysical Year. World Data Center. A. Glaciological Report Series
IH — Information Historique
IH — Information Hotline
IH — International Humanism Magazine [*Netherlands*]
IH — Internationaler Holzmarkt
IH — Ita Humanidades
IHA — Industrie Hoteliere
IHA — Information d'Histoire de l'Art
IHA — Islam d'Hier et Aujourd'hui
IHB — Indiana History Bulletin
IHB — International Journal of Social Economics (Bradford)
IHCTA2 — International Histological Classification of Tumors
IHE — Indice Historico Espanol
IHE — International Hospital Equipment
IHEJAG — Indian Heart Journal
Iheringia Ser Antropol — Iheringia. Serie Antropologia
Iheringia Ser Bot — Iheringia. Serie Botanica
Iheringia Ser Divulg — Iheringia. Serie Divulgacao
Iheringia Ser Geol — Iheringia. Serie Geologia
Iheringia Ser Zool — Iheringia. Serie Zoologia
IHG — Investitionshilfegesetz
IHG — Irish Banking Review
IHI Eng Rev — IHI [*Ishikawajima-Harima Heavy Industries*] Engineering Review
I Hist — Indian Historian
IHK — Industrie und Handelskammer
IHML — International Henry Miller Letter

I Horizons — Indian Horizons
IHPAB — Health Physics Research Abstracts
IHQ — Indian Historical Quarterly
IHR — International Hotel Review
IHRB — Institute of Historical Research. Bulletin
IHRC — Proceedings. Indian Historical Records Commission
IH Rev — IH Review [*New Zealand Society for the Intellectually Handicapped*]
IHS — Irish Historical Studies
IHT — International Herald Tribune
IHUOA9 — Institut de Recherches pour les Huiles et Oleagineux [*IRHO*]. Rapport Annuel
IHVE J — IHVE [*Institution of Heating and Ventilating Engineers*] Journal
IHYHA — Industrial Hygiene Highlights
IHYRB — Industrial Hygiene Review
II — Illustrazione Italiana
II — Institutional Investor
II — Irish Independent
II — Italia Intellettuale
IIASA Collab Publ — International Institute for Applied Systems Analysis. Collaborative Publications
IIASA Proc Ser — IIASA [*International Institute for Applied Systems Analysis*] Proceedings Series
IIASA Prof Pap — International Institute for Applied Systems Analysis. Professional Paper
IIASA Rep — IIASA [*International Institute for Applied Systems Analysis*] Reports
IIASA Research Reports — International Institute for Applied Systems Analysis. Research Reports
IIASA Res Memo — International Institute for Applied Systems Analysis. Research Memorandum
IIASA Res Rep — International Institute for Applied Systems Analysis. Research Report
IIBDA — Izvestiya Vuzov Mashinostroenie
IIBE — Izvestiya na Instituta za Belgarski Ezik
IIBL — Izvestiya na Instituta za Belgarska Literatura
IIC — International Review of Industrial Property and Copyright Law
IICC — Inuit. Inuit Circumpolar Conference [*Greenland*]
IICEA — Industria Italiana del Cemento
IICEW — Industria Italiana del Cemento
IID — Izvestiya na Istoriseskoto Druzestvo
IIDWA — Informatik
IIEBB — Izvestiya na Instituta po Elektronika. Bulgarska Akademiya na Naukite
IIENB — Institute of International Education. News Bulletin
IIE Trans — IIE [*Institute of Industrial Engineers, Inc.*] Transactions
IIFP — International Index to Film Periodicals
IIHR Rep — IIHR [*Iowa Institute of Hydraulic Research*] Report
IIHR Report — Iowa Institute of Hydraulic Research. Report
III — Industrial Marketing Digest
III — Institutional Investor. International Edition
IIJ — Indo-Iranian Journal
IIKMA — Izvestiya na Instituta po Khidrologiya i Meteorologiya. Bulgarska Akademiya na Naukite
IILSAH — Investigations of Indiana Lakes and Streams
IIM — International Insurance Monitor
IIM — Izvestiya na Instituta za Muzika
IIMMI — International Index to Multi-Media Information
IIn — Index India
IIN — Institutional Investor
IINCEH — Intercellular and Intracellular Communication
IIOOD — IO Management-Zeitschrift
IIP — Industrial and Intellectual Property in Australia
IIPA — Industrial and Intellectual Property in Australia
IIPTA — Izvestiya Nauchno-Issledovatel'skogo Instituta Postoyannogo Toka
IIRB Rev Inst Int Rech Better — IIRB. Revue de l'Institut International de Recherches Betteravieres
IISSA — Ionosfernye Issledovaniya
I Ist Kul't Narod Uzbek — Iz Istorii Kul'tury Narodov Uzbekistana
IIT — Information der Internationalen Treuhand AG
IJ — Indogermanische Jahrbuch
IJ — International Journal
IJ — Irish Jurist
IJA — International Journal of Andrology
IJACB — Indian Journal of Agricultural Chemistry
IJACBO — Indian Journal of Agricultural Chemistry
IJACDQ — Indian Journal of Acarology
IJAE — Indian Journal of Agricultural Economics
IJAGAZ — Indian Journal of Agronomy
IJAGC3 — Iranian Journal of Agricultural Research
I J Agr Sci — Indian Journal of Agricultural Science
IJAHA4 — Indian Journal of Animal Health
IJAHE8 — International Journal of Adolescent Medicine and Health
IJAHS — International Journal of African Historical Studies
IJAIDA — International Journal. Academy of Ichthyology
IJAL — International Journal of American Linguistics

IJALAG — Irish Journal of Agricultural Research
IJANBN — Indian Journal of Anaesthesia
IJANDP — International Journal of Andrology
IJAOD — International Journal of Artificial Organs
IJAODS — International Journal of Artificial Organs
IJAPA — International Journal of Air Pollution
IJAPBT — Indian Journal of Applied Psychology
IJAR — Israel Journal of Agricultural Research
IJARAY — International Journal of Applied Radiation and Isotopes
IJARC — Indian Journal of Agricultural Research
IJARC2 — Indian Journal of Agricultural Research
IJAS — Indian Journal of American Studies
IJaS — Inostrannye Jazyki v Skole
IJASA3 — Indian Journal of Agricultural Science
IJb — Indogermanische Jahrbuch
IJB — Israel Journal of Botany
IJBCAS — Indian Journal of Biochemistry [*Later, Indian Journal of Biochemistry and Biophysics*]
IJBCB — International Journal of Biomedical Computing
IJBCBT — International Journal of Bio-Medical Computing
IJBDDY — International Journal of Behavioral Development
IJBEAY — International Journal of Biomedical Engineering
I J Bioch B — Indian Journal of Biochemistry and Biophysics
IJBMAO — International Journal of Biometeorology
IJBMDR — International Journal of Biological Macromolecules
IJBOAU — Israel Journal of Botany
IJBOBV — International Journal of Biochemistry
IJBODX — Indian Journal of Botany
IJBPD2 — International Journal of Biological Research in Pregnancy
IJC — Indian Journal of Commerce [*Chandigarh*]
IJC — International Journal of Computer and Information Sciences
IJCAAR — Indian Journal of Cancer
IJCADU — Indian Journal of Chemistry. Section A. Inorganic, Physical, Theoretical, and Analytical
IJCBA — International Journal of Chronobiology
IJCBAU — International Journal of Chronobiology
IJCBD — International Journal of Clinical Pharmacology and Biopharmacy
IJCBDX — International Journal of Clinical Pharmacology and Biopharmacy
IJCCE3 — International Journal of Cell Cloning
IJCDA2 — Indian Journal of Chest Diseases [*Later, Indian Journal of Chest Diseases and Allied Sciences*]
IJCDD5 — International Journal of Cardiology
IJCEA — Indian Journal of Chemical Education
IJCGD — International Journal of Coal Geology
IJCHA — Indian Journal of Child Health
I J Chem — Indian Journal of Chemistry
IJCIS — International Journal of Computer and Information Sciences
IJCKBO — International Journal of Chemical Kinetics
IJCMDW — International Journal of Cosmetic Science
IJCNAW — International Journal of Cancer
IJCNF2 — International Journal of Clinical Neuropsychology
IJCPB5 — International Journal of Clinical Pharmacology, Therapy, and Toxicology
IJCRD — Indian Journal of Cryogenics
IJCREE — International Journal of Crude Drug Research
IJDEAA — Indian Journal of Dermatology [*Later, Indian Journal of Dermatology, Venereology, and Leprology*]
IJDEBB — International Journal of Dermatology
IJDLDY — Indian Journal of Dermatology, Venereology, and Leprology
IJDMAY — Israel Journal of Dental Medicine
IJDN — International Journal of Developmental Neuroscience
IJDND6 — International Journal of Developmental Neuroscience
IJDSAI — Indian Journal of Dairy Science
IJDVAR — Indian Journal of Dermatology and Venereology [*Later, Indian Journal of Dermatology, Venereology, and Leprology*]
IJE — Indian Journal of Economics
IJE — International Journal of Ethics
IJEAA3 — International Journal of Environmental Analytical Chemistry
IJEAB — Indian Journal of Earth Sciences
IJEAB4 — Indian Journal of Earth Sciences
IJEAD — Electric Power Applications. IEE Journal
IJEBA6 — Indian Journal of Experimental Biology
IJECDC — Indian Journal of Ecology
IJEHA — International Journal of Clinical and Experimental Hypnosis
IJEHAO — International Journal of Clinical and Experimental Hypnosis
IJEHB — Indian Journal of Environmental Health
IJEHBP — Indian Journal of Environmental Health
IJEMA5 — Israel Journal of Experimental Medicine
IJENA8 — Indian Journal of Entomology
IJENB9 — Israel Journal of Entomology
IJENEC — International Journal of Entomology
IJEPAE — Indian Journal of Experimental Psychology
IJEPBF — International Journal of Epidemiology
IJERAK — Israel Journal of Earth-Sciences
IJERD — International Journal of Energy Research
IJES — Indian Journal of English Studies [*Calcutta*]

IJES — International Journal of Environmental Studies
IJESDQ — International Journal of Ecology and Environmental Sciences
IJEVAW — International Journal of Environmental Studies
IJewAr — Index of Articles on Jewish Studies
IJewPer — Index to Jewish Periodicals
I J Ex Biol — Indian Journal of Experimental Biology
IJFIAW — Indian Journal of Fisheries
IJFMDD — International Journal of Food Microbiology
IJFODJ — Indian Journal of Forestry
IJFPDM — International Journal of Family Psychiatry
IJFSBT — Indian Journal of Farm Sciences
IJGBAG — Indian Journal of Genetics and Plant Breeding
I J Genet P — Indian Journal of Genetics and Plant Breeding
IJGOAL — International Journal of Gynaecology and Obstetrics
IJGPA — International Journal of Group Psychotherapy
IJGPAO — International Journal of Group Psychotherapy
IJGPDR — International Journal of Gynecological Pathology
IJGSAX — International Journal of General Systems
IJH — Iowa Journal of History
IJHE — International Journal of Health Education
IJHEAU — Indian Journal of Helminthology
IJHM — Indian Journal of the History of Medicine
IJHMA — International Journal of Heat and Mass Transfer
IJHOAQ — Indian Journal of Horticulture
IJHP — Iowa Journal of History and Politics
IJHPBU — Indian Journal of Hospital Pharmacy
IJHYEQ — International Journal of Hyperthermia
IJIAA — Indian Journal of Science and Industry. Section A. Agricultural Sciences [Later, Indian Journal of Agricultural Research]
IJIDAW — Indian Journal of Industrial Medicine
IJIDE2 — International Journal of Invertebrate Reproduction and Development
IJIL — Indian Journal of International Law
IJIMBQ — International Journal of Insect Morphology and Embryology
IJIMDS — International Journal of Immunopharmacology
IJIMET — International Journal of Immunotherapy
I J Ind Rel — Indian Journal of Industrial Relations
IJIRD9 — International Journal of Invertebrate Reproduction
IJLAA4 — Indian Journal of Animal Sciences
IJLEAG — International Journal of Leprosy [Later, International Journal of Leprosy and Other Mycobacterial Diseases]
IJLL — International Journal of Law Libraries
IJM — International Journal of Manpower
IJMAA9 — Indian Journal of Malariology
IJMBA — Indian Journal of Microbiology
IJMCEJ — International Journal of Clinical Monitoring and Computing
IJMDAI — Israel Journal of Medical Sciences
I J Med Res — Indian Journal of Medical Research
IJMES — International Journal of Middle East Studies
IJMNB — Indian Journal of Marine Sciences
IJMS — Israel Journal of Medical Sciences
IJMSAT — Irish Journal of Medical Science
IJN — International Journal of Neuroscience
IJNA — International Journal of Nautical Archaeology and Underwater Exploration
IJNGD — International Journal for Numerical and Analytical Methods in Geomechanics
IJNMC — International Journal of Nuclear Medicine and Biology
IJNUB — International Journal of Neuroscience
I J Nutr D — Indian Journal of Nutrition and Dietetics
IJO — International Journal of Operations and Production Management
IJOAAJ — Israel Journal of Agricultural Research
IJOADM — International Journal of Acarology
IJOAR — International Journal of Opinion and Attitude Research
IJOCAP — Indian Journal of Chemistry
IJOH — International Journal of Oral History [Canada]
IJP — International Journal of Parapsychology
IJP — International Journal of Public Administration
IJPA — Indian Journal of Public Administration
I J PA Phys — Indian Journal of Pure and Applied Physics
IJPHC — Iran Journal of Public Health
IJPHCD — Iranian Journal of Public Health
I J Physics — Indian Journal of Physics
IJPLBO — Iranian Journal of Plant Pathology
IJPPC — International Journal of Peptide and Protein Research
IJPS — Indian Journal of Political Science
IJPsa — International Journal of Psychoanalysis
I J Psychol — Indian Journal of Psychology
IJRE — International Journal of Religious Education
IJRED — International Journal of Radiation Engineering
IJRR — [The] International Journal of Robotics Research
IJRSA — Indian Journal of Radio and Space Physics
IJRSD — International Journal of Radiation Sterilization
IJS — Inostrannye Jazyki v Skole
IJS — International Journal of Sexology

IJSBDB — Indian Journal of Chemistry. Section B. Organic Chemistry, Including Medicinal Chemistry
IJSCC — International Journal of Sulfur Chemistry
IJSCDE — Islamabad Journal of Sciences
IJSE — International Journal of Social Economics
IJSEA — Indian Journal of Sericulture
IJSL — International Journal of the Sociology of Language
IJSLP — International Journal of Slavic Linguistics and Poetics
I J Soc Res — Indian Journal of Social Research
IJSPA — International Journal of Social Psychiatry
IJSPDJ — International Journal of Andrology. Supplement
IJS Rep R — IJS [Institut "Jozef Stefan"] Report R
IJSTBT — Iranian Journal of Science and Technology
IJSW — Indian Journal of Social Work
IJSym — International Journal of Symbology
IJT — Indian Journal of Theology
IJT — International Journal of Transport Economics
I J Techn — Indian Journal of Technology
I J Theor P — Indian Journal of Theoretical Physics
IJUSC3 — International Journal of Health Services
IJVEAW — Indian Journal of Agricultural and Veterinary Education
IJVMEQ — Israel Journal of Veterinary Medicine
IJWS — International Journal of Women's Studies
IJZ — Israel Journal of Zoology
IJZOAE — Israel Journal of Zoology
IK — Inukshuk. Frobisher Bay
IK — Irodalomtorteneti Kozlemenyek
IKAOA — Izvestiya Krymskoi Astrofizicheskoi Observatorii
IKBKA — Izvestiya na Khimicheskiya Institut. Bulgarska Akademiya na Naukite
IKE — Iberiul-K'avk'asiuri Enatmecniereba
IKEND — Iwate-Ken Eisei Kenkyusho Nenpo
IKMLA — Ikonomicheska Mis'l
Ikon Mekh Selsk Stop — Ikonomika i Mekhanizatsiya na Selskoto Stopanstvo
Ikon Selskoto Stop Rural Econ — Ikonomika na Selskoto Stopanstvo. Rural Economics
IKV — International Kongress der Volkserzaehlungsforscher
IKZ — Internationale Kirchliche Zeitschrift
IKZKA — Itogi Nauki i Tekhniki Korroziya i Zashchita ot Korrozii
I & L — Iazyk i Literatura
I & L — Ideologies and Literature
IL — Index Library
IL — Indian Linguistics
IL — Information Litteraire
IL — International Literature [USSR]
ILA — International Literary Annual [London]
ILABAY — Instruments et Laboratoires
ILA Rec — Illinois Library Association. Record
IlATos — Ilmij Asarlari. V. I. Lenin Monidagi Toskent Davlat Universiteti
ILBEA — Industrie Lackier-Betrieb
ILD — International Labour Documentation
Ile — Ilerda
ILENDP — Industrial Engineering
ILEUA — Izvestiya Leningradskogo Elektrotekhnicheskogo Instituta
ILF — Studii si Cercetari de Istorie Literara si Folclor
ILG — Indian Labour Gazette
ILGCA — Illinois State Geological Survey. Circular
ILGIA — Report of Investigations. Illinois State Geological Survey
ILGPA — Illinois State Geological Survey. Illinois Petroleum
ILGU — Izvestiya Leningradskogo Gosudarstvennogo Universiteta
I Lib — Indian Librarian
I L Ideol L — I and L. Ideologies and Literature
ILing — Incontri Linguistici
I Ling — Initiation a la Linguistique
I Lit — Iasul Literar
I Lit — Indian Literature
ILJ — Indiana Law Journal
ILJ — Insurance Law Journal
ILJM — Illinois Journal of Mathematics
Ill — Illiterati
ILL — Illustration
ILL — International Labour Documentation
Ill Ac Sc Tr — Illinois Academy of Science. Transactions
Ill Ag Exp — Illinois. Agricultural Experiment Station. Publications
Ill Agr Econ — Illinois Agricultural Economics
Ill Agric Econ Dep Agric Econ Ill Univ Agric Exp Stn — Illinois Agricultural Economics. Department of Agricultural Economics. Illinois University. Agricultural Experiment Station
Ill Agric Exp Stn Bull — Illinois. Agricultural Experiment Station. Bulletin
Ill Agric Exp Stn Circ — Illinois. Agricultural Experiment Station. Circular
Ill Agric Exp Stn Dep For For Res Rep — Illinois. Agricultural Experiment Station. Department of Forestry. Forestry Research Report
Ill Agric Exp Stn For Note — Illinois. Agricultural Experiment Station. Forestry Note
Illawarra Hist Soc Newsletter — Illawarra Historical Society. Newsletter
Illaw Hist Soc M Notice — Illawarra Historical Society. Monthly Notice

Ill Bar J — Illinois Bar Journal
Ill Biol Mon — Illinois Biological Monographs
Ill Biol Monogr — Illinois Biological Monographs
Ill B J — Illinois Bar Journal
Ill Bus R — Illinois Business Review
Ill Cath His R — Illinois Catholic Historical Review
Ill Class Stud — Illinois Classical Studies
Ill CLE — Illinois Continuing Legal Education
Ill Coal M Investigations B — Illinois Coal Mining Investigations. Cooperative Agreement. Bulletin
Ill Cont Legal Ed — Illinois Continuing Legal Education
Ill Dent J — Illinois Dental Journal
Ill Dep Conserv Tech Bull — Illinois. Department of Conservation. Technical Bulletin
Ill Div Fish Spec Fish Rep — Illinois. Division of Fisheries. Special Fisheries Report
Ill Div Indus Plan and Devel Atlas Ill Res — Illinois. Division of Industrial Planning and Development. Atlas of Illinois Resources
Ill Educ — Illinois Education
Ill Energy Notes — Illinois Energy Notes
Ill Geogr Soc Bull — Illinois Geographical Society. Bulletin
Ill Geol Surv Guide Leafl — Illinois State Geological Survey. Guide Leaflet
Ill Geol Surv Oil Gas Drill Ill Mon Rep — Illinois. Geological Survey. Oil and Gas Drilling in Illinois. Monthly Report
Ill Geol Surv Rev Act — Illinois State Geological Survey. Review of Activities
Ill G S B — Illinois State Geological Survey. Bulletin
Ill His Col — Illinois State Historical Library. Collections
Ill His J — Illinois State Historical Society. Journal
Ill His L — Illinois State Historical Library. Publications
Ill His S Trans — Illinois State Historical Society. Transactions
Ill Hist Coll — Illinois State Historical Library. Collections
Ill His Trans — Illinois State Historical Society. Transactions
Ill Horiz — Illinois Horizons
Illinois Acad Sci Trans — Illinois State Academy of Science. Transactions
Illinois F — Illinois Farmer
Illinois Geol Survey Circ — Illinois State Geological Survey. Circular
Illinois Med J — Illinois Medical Journal
Illinois Water Survey Rept Inv — Illinois State Water Survey. Reports of Investigations
Ill Issues — Illinois Issues
Ill J Math — Illinois Journal of Mathematics
Ill Law Rev — Illinois Law Review
Ill Lib — Illinois Libraries
Ill Libr — Illinois Libraries
Ill L Rev — Illinois Law Review
Ill Med J — Illinois Medical Journal
Ill Mo — Illinois Monthly Magazine
Ill Monogr Med Sci — Illinois Monographs in Medical Sciences
Ill Nat Hist Surv Biol Notes — Illinois Natural History Survey. Biological Notes
Ill Nat Hist Surv Bull — Illinois Natural History Survey. Bulletin
Ill Nat Hist Surv Circ — Illinois Natural History Survey. Circular
Illne Scient — Illustrazione Scientifica
Ill N H Soc Tr — Illinois Natural History Society. Transactions
Ill Pet — Illinois Petroleum
Ill Q — Illinois Quarterly
Ill Res — Illinois Research
Ill Sch J — Illinois Schools Journal
Ill Soc Eng — Illinois Society of Engineers and Surveyors
Ill St Ac Sc Tr — Illinois State Academy of Science. Transactions
Ill State Acad Sci Trans — Illinois State Academy of Science. Transactions
Ill State Florists Assoc Bull — Illinois State Florists Association. Bulletin
Ill State Geol Surv Bull — Illinois State Geological Survey. Bulletin
Ill State Geol Surv Circ — Illinois State Geological Survey. Circular
Ill State Geol Surv Guideb Ser — Illinois State Geological Survey. Guidebook Series
Ill State Geol Surv Ill Miner Note — Illinois State Geological Survey. Illinois Minerals Note
Ill State Geol Surv Ill Petrol — Illinois State Geological Survey. Illinois Petroleum
Ill State Geol Surv Ind Miner Notes — Illinois State Geological Survey. Industrial Minerals Notes
Ill State Hist Soc Jour — Illinois State Historical Society. Journal
Ill State Hort Soc N L — Illinois State Horticultural Society. Newsletter
Ill State Mus Pop Sci Ser Sci Paper Story Ill Ser — Illinois State Museum. Popular Science Series. Scientific Papers. Story of Illinois Series
Ill State Mus Rep Invest — Illinois State Museum. Reports of Investigations
Ill State Univ Jour — Illinois State University. Journal
Ill State Water Surv Bull — Illinois State Water Survey. Bulletin
Ill State Water Surv Circ — Illinois State Water Survey. Circular
Ill State Water Survey Cooperative Ground-Water Rept — Illinois State Water Survey. Cooperative Ground-Water Report
Ill State Water Survey Div Bull Circ Rept Inv — Illinois State Water Survey. Division Bulletin. Circular. Reports of Investigations
Ill State Water Surv Rep Invest — Illinois State Water Survey. Reports of Investigations

Ill State Water Surv State Geol Surv Coop Resour Rep — Illinois State Water Survey and State Geological Survey. Cooperative Resources Report
Ill St Lab N H B — Illinois State Laboratory of Natural History. Bulletin
Ill St Mus N H B — Illinois State Museum of Natural History. Bulletin
Ill Stud Anthropol — Illinois Studies in Anthropology
Ill Teach — Illinois Teacher
Ill U Eng Exp Sta Bul — Illinois University. Engineering Experiment Station. Bulletin
Ill U Eng Exp Sta Circ — Illinois University. Engineering Experiment Station. Circular
Illum Eng — Illuminating Engineering [*Later, Illuminating Engineering Society. Journal*]
Illum Eng Soc J — Illuminating Engineering Society. Journal
Illum Eng Soc Trans — Illuminating Engineering Society. Transactions
Ill Univ B Univ Studies — Illinois University. Bulletin. University Studies
Ill Univ (Chicago Circle) Dep Geol Sci Tech Rep — Illinois University (Chicago Circle). Department of Geological Sciences. Technical Report
Ill Univ Civ Eng Stud Constr Res Ser — Illinois University. Civil Engineering Studies. Construction Research Series
Ill Univ Civ Eng Stud Hydraul Eng Ser — Illinois University. Civil Engineering Studies. Hydraulic Engineering Series
Ill Univ Civ Eng Stud Soil Mech Ser — Illinois University. Civil Engineering Studies. Soil Mechnanics Series
Ill Univ Civ Eng Stud Struct Res Ser — Illinois University. Civil Engineering Studies. Structural Research Series
Ill Univ Coop Ext Serv Circ — Illinois University. Cooperative Extension Service. Circular
Ill Univ Dep Civ Eng Struct Res Ser — Illinois University. Department of Civil Engineering. Structural Research Series
Ill Univ Dep Electr Eng Aeron Lab Aeron Rep — Illinois University. Department of Electrical Engineering. Aeronomy Laboratory. Aeronomy Report
Ill Univ Dep Theor Appl Mech TAM Rep — Illinois University. Department of Theoretical and Applied Mechanics. TAM Report
Ill Univ Eng Exp Sta Bull — Illinois University. Engineering Experiment Station. Bulletin
Ill Univ Eng Exp Stn Tech Rep — Illinois University. Engineering Experiment Station. Technical Report
Ill Univ Eng Expt Sta Bull Circ — Illinois University. Engineering Experiment Station. Bulletin. Circulars
Ill Univ Proc Sanit Eng Conf — Illinois University. Proceedings of the Sanitary Engineering Conference
Ill Univ TAM Rep — Illinois University. Department of Theoretical and Applied Mechanics. TAM Report
Ill Univ Water Resour Cent Res Rep — Illinois University. Water Resources Center. Research Report
Illus Archaeol — Illustrated Archaeologist
Illus Landwirtsch Ztg — Illustrierte Landwirtschaftlichte Zeitung
Illus Lond N — Illustrated London News
Illus London News — Illustrated London News
Illus W Ind — Illustrated Weekly of India
Illus W Ind A — Illustrated Weekly of India. Annual
Ill Vet — Illinois Veterinarian
ILM — Industrial Minerals
ILM — International Legal Materials
Ilmenau Tech Hochsch Wiss Z — Ilmenau, Technische Hochschule, Wissenschaftliche Zeitschrift
ILML — Istituto Lombardo. Accademia di Scienze e Lettere. Memorie della Classe di Lettere
ILMN — Il Mondo
ILN — Illustrated London News
ILN — Indonesia Letter
Ilocos R — Ilocos Review
ILP — Il Ponte
ILP — Index to Legal Periodicals
ILPEAG — Agricultural Science [*Jogjakarta*]
ILPO — Il Polo. Istituto Geografico Polare
ILQ — International Law Quarterly
ILR — Indian Law Review
ILR — International Labour Review
ILR — International Language Reporter
ILR — Iowa Law Review
ILR — Israel Business and Investors' Report
ILR — Israel Law Review
ILRBBI — Istituto Lombardo. Accademia di Scienze e Lettere. Rendiconti. B. Scienze Biologiche e Mediche
ILRL — Istituto Lombardo. Accademia di Scienze e Lettere. Rendiconti. Classe de Lettere
ILRR — Industrial and Labor Relations Review
ILS — Inscriptiones Latinae Selectae
ILT — Il Tesaur
ILT — Irish Law Times
ILTSJ — Institute of Low Temperature Science. Contributions (Japan)
ILT & SJ — Irish Law Times and Solicitors' Journal
Im — Illuminare
Im — Imagination

Im — Imago
IM — Imago Mundi
IM — Incontri Musicali
IM — Index Medicus
IM — Industrial Management
IM — Industrial Minerals
IM — Insurance Magazine
IM — International Journal of Instructional Media
IMA — Instituts Mitteilungen
IMAC — International Marine and Air Catering
Image Dyn Sci Med — Image Dynamics in Science and Medicine
Image Technol — Image Technology
IMA J Appl Math — IMA [*Institute of Math and Applications*] Journal of Applied Mathematics
IMARD — Industrial Marketing [*Later, Business Marketing*]
IMB — International Medieval Bibliography
IMBMA — Izvestiya na Instituta po Morfologiya. Bulgarska Akademiya na Naukite
IMCHAZ — Immunochemistry
IMC Jrnl — IMC [*International Information Management Congress*] Journal
IMCVA9 — Investigaciones Marinas. Universidad Catolica de Valparaiso
IMD — Industrial Marketing Management
IMDJBD — Irish Medical Journal
IME — Insurance, Mathematics, and Economics
IME — Iparmueveszeti Muzeum Evkoenyvei
IMed — Index Medicus
IMEIDH — Investigacion Medica Internacional
IMF — Informatienieuws
IMF — International Monetary Fund. Staff Papers
IMF F & D — International Monetary Fund. Finance and Development
IMF Staff Pa — International Monetary Fund. Staff Papers
IMF Svy — IMF [*International Monetary Fund*] Survey
IMF Symp Publ — IMF [*Institute of Metal Finishing*] Symposium. Publication
IMG — Indian Medical Gazette
IMGIA — Itogi Nauki i Tekhniki Mestorozhdeniya Goryuchikh Poleznykh Iskopaemykh
IMH — Indiana Magazine of History
IMH — Itim Mizrah News Agency Hadashot. Current Comment
IMI — International Management Information
IMIDB — Instrumentation in the Mining and Metallurgy Industries
IMIND — Immunitaet und Infektion
IMINDI — Immunitaet und Infektion
IMINEJ — Immunological Investigations
IMIT — Izraelita Magyar Irodalmi Tarsulat Evkonyv
IMJ — Illinois Medical Journal
IMJ — Illustrierte Monatshefte fuer die Gesammten Interessen des Judentums
IMK — Industrial Marketing
IMKRA3 — Imkerfreund
IML — Information
IMLCA — Immunological Communications
IMLCAV — Immunological Communications
IMLED — Immunology Letters
IMLED6 — Immunology Letters
Immergrune Bl — Immergruene Blaetter
Imm J — Immigration Journal
IMMLC — Industrie Minerale. Serie Mineralurgie
IMMLDW — Immunologiya
IMMNB — Industrie Minerale. Serie Mine
IMMND4 — Immunobiology
IMMUAM — Immunology
IMMUDP — Immunopharmacology
Immun Infekt — Immunitaet und Infektion
Immunochem — Immunochemistry
Immunogenet — Immunogenetics
Immunol Com — Immunological Communications
Immunol Commun — Immunological Communications
Immunol Lett — Immunology Letters
Immunol Pol — Immunologia Polska
Immunol Rev — Immunological Reviews
IMN — Irisleabhar Mha Nuad
IMNGA — Immunologiya
IMNGBK — Immunogenetics
IMNSA — Izvestiya na Mikrobiologicheskiya Institut. Bulgarska Akademiya na Naukite
IMO — Itim Mizrah News Agency. Bulletin on Palestinian Organizations
Imono J Japan Foundrymen's Soc — Imono. Journal of the Japan Foundrymen's Society
IMOR — Imperial Oil Review
Impact Agric Res Tex Annu Rep — Impact Agricultural Research in Texas. Annual Report
Impact Sci — Impact of Science on Society
Impact Sci Soc — Impact of Science on Society
Imp Coll Sci Technol Appl Geochem Res Group Tech Commun — Imperial College of Science and Technology. Applied Geochemistry Research Group. Technical Communication

Imp Coll Sci Technol Geochem Prospect Res Cent Tech Commun — Imperial College of Science and Technology. Geochemical Prospecting Research Centre. Technical Communication
Imp Coll Sci Technol Rock Mech Res Rep — Imperial College of Science and Technology. Rock Mechanics Research Report
Imp Coll Trop Agric (Trinidad) Circ — Imperial College of Tropical Agriculture (Trinidad). Circular
Imp Coll Trop Agric (Trinidad) Low Temp Res Stn Mem — Imperial College of Tropical Agriculture (Trinidad). Low Temperature Research Station. Memoirs
Imp Coll Trop Agric (Trinidad) Mem Mycol Ser — Imperial College of Tropical Agriculture (Trinidad). Memoirs. Mycological Series
IMPE — Impetus. Magazine Supplement of the Financial Post
Imp Earthquake Investigation Com B — Imperial Earthquake Investigation Committee. Bulletin
Imperial Oil R — Imperial Oil Review
Imp Ethiop Gov Inst Agric Res Rep — Imperial Ethiopian Government Institute of Agricultural Research. Report
IMPID — Impianti
Imp Inst Agric Res (Pusa) Bull — Imperial Institute of Agricultural Research (Pusa). Bulletin
IMPODM — Immunologia Polska
Imp Oil R — Imperial Oil Review
Imp Rev — Imperial Review
Impr Hum P — Improving Human Performance
Imprim Ind Graphiques — Imprimerie et Industries Graphiques
Improv Coll Univ Teach — Improving College and University Teaching
Improv Coll & Univ Teach — Improving College and University Teaching
Improving Coll & Univ Teach — Improving College and University Teaching
Imp Sci Soc — Impact of Science on Society
Imp & Tractr — Implement and Tractor
Impul'snaya Fotom — Impul'snaya Fotometriya
Impulstech — Impulstechniken
Imp Univ Tokyo Fac Sci J — Tokyo. Imperial University. Faculty of Science. Journal
Imp Zootech Exp Stn Bull — Imperial Zootechnical Experiment Station. Bulletin
IMRED2 — Immunological Reviews
IMR Ind Manage Rev — IMR. Industrial Management Review
IMRSB8 — Indian Council of Medical Research. Technical Report Series
IMRSEB — Immunologic Research
IMRVB — International Metallurgical Reviews
IMS — Impact of Science on Society
IMS — International Marine Science [*IOC*]
IMS — International Musicological Society. Report of the Congress
IMS — Internationale Monatsschrift
IMSCE2 — IRCS [*International Research Communications System*] Medical Science
IMS Clin Proc — IMS [*Industrial Management Society*] Clinical Proceedings
IMSED7 — Immunology Series
IMSN — Institute of Marine Science. Notes. University of Alaska
IMSUA — Industrial Medicine and Surgery
IMSUAI — Industrial Medicine and Surgery
IMTCE7 — Immunoassay Technology
IMTOA — Itogi Nauki i Tekhniki Metallovedenie i Termicheskaya Obrabotka
IMTOD8 — Immunology Today
IMU — Italia Medioevale e Umanistica
IMW — Sloan Management Review
IN — Indiana Musicator
IN — Indiana Names [*Indiana State University*]
IN — Instrumentalist
In — Insula
IN — International NOTAMS [*Notices to Airmen*]
In — Interpretation
IN — Interpreter
IN — Italia Numismatica
INA — International Affairs
INA — International Nannoplankton Association. Newsletter
INAB — Indian and Northern Affairs Backgrounder
INAC — Indian and Northern Affairs Communique
INAGAT — Indian Agriculturist
INAJA4 — Irish Naturalists' Journal
INALA — Industria Alimentara
INALB — Industrie Alimentari
INAM — Indian America
INARA — Ingenieur-Archiv. Gesellschaft fuer Angewandte Mathematik und Mechanik
INATA — Industries Atomiques
INAUA — Instrumentenbau Musik International
INAUA3 — Instruments and Automation
INB — In Business
InB — International Bulletin of Missionary Research
INB — Israel Numismatic Bulletin
INBID9 — Indian Biologist
INBIEA — International Biodeterioration Bulletin
INBLA — Ingenieursblad

In Bus — In Business
INC — Indian Numismatic Chronicle
Inc Aust Insurance Inst J — Incorporated Australian Insurance Institute.
    Journal
IncL — Incorporated Linguist [*London*]
INCLD — International Classification
Inc Linguist — Incorporated Linguist
Income Tax Rep — Income Tax Reporter
Incompat Newsl — Incompatibility Newsletter
Incorp Bus — Incorporating Your Business
Inco Vitro — Inco Vitro v CSSR
INCPA — Instrumentation in the Chemical and Petroleum Industries
INCRA Res Rep — INCRA [*International Copper Research Association, Inc.*]
    Research Report
IND — Independent
Ind — Indice de Arte y Letras
IndA — Independent Agent
Ind Acad Sci Proc — Indiana Academy of Science. Proceedings
Ind Adv — Indian Advocate
Ind Ag Exp — Purdue University. Indiana Agricultural Experiment Station.
    Publications
Indag Math — Indagationes Mathematicae
Ind Agr — Industrie Agrarie [*Italy*]
Ind Agri Am Lat Caribe — Indice Agricole de America Latina y el Caribe
Ind Aliment — Industria Alimentaria
Ind Aliment Agr — Industries Alimentaires et Agricoles
Ind Aliment Agric (Paris) — Industries Alimentaires et Agricoles (Paris)
Ind Aliment Anim — Industries de l'Alimentation Animale
Ind Aliment (Bucharest) — Industria Alimentara (Bucharest)
Ind Aliment (Havana) — Industria Alimenticia (Havana)
Ind Aliment (Mexico City) — Industrias de la Alimentacion (Mexico City)
Ind Aliment (Pinerolo Italy) — Industrie Alimentari (Pinerolo, Italy)
Ind Aliment Prod Anim — Industria Alimentara. Produse Animale
Ind Aliment Prod Veg — Industria Alimentara. Produse Vegetale [*Romania*]
Ind Aliment Veget — Industria Alimentara. Produse Vegetale
Ind Amer Per Verse — Index of American Periodical Verse
Ind Anthro — Indian Anthropologist
Ind-Anz — Industrie-Anzeiger
Ind Archaeol — Industrial Archaeology
Ind Archaeol Rev — Industrial Archaeology Review
Ind-Arts M — Industrial-Arts Magazine
Ind Arts & Voc Ed — Industrial Arts and Vocational Education/Technical
    Education
Ind As Cult — Indo-Asian Culture
Ind At — Industries Atomiques
Ind At & Spat — Industries Atomiques et Spatiales
Ind At Spatiales — Industries Atomiques et Spatiales
Ind Aurel — Index Aureliensis
Ind Aust & Min Standard — Industrial Australian and Mining Standard
Ind Austr Min Stand — Industrial Australian and Mining Standard
Ind Azucar — Industria Azucarera
Ind Bevande — Industrie delle Bevande
Ind Bibl — Index Bibliographicus
Ind Bl — Industrieblatt
Ind Bldg — Industrialised Building
Ind Buk Kenk — Indogaku Bukkyogaku Kenkyu
Ind Bull — Industrial Bulletin
Ind Bull Arthur D Little Inc — Industrial Bulletin of Arthur D. Little,
    Incorporated
Ind Bull NY State Dep Labor — Industrial Bulletin. New York State
    Department of Labor
INDCA — Industrial Chemist
Ind Can — Industrial Canada
Ind Carta — Industria della Carta
Ind Carta Arti Grafiche — Industria della Carta e delle Arti Grafiche
Ind Ceram — Industrie Ceramique
Ind Ceram Silicat — Industria della Ceramica e Silicati
Ind Chem — Industrial Chemist
Ind Chem Bull — Industrial Chemistry Bulletin
Ind Ch HR — Indian Church History Review
Ind Child Mag — Subject Index to Children's Magazines
Ind Chim — Industrie Chimique
Ind Chim Belge — Industrie Chimique Belge
Ind Chim Min Metall — Industria Chimica, Mineraria, e Metallurgica
Ind Chim (Paris) — Industrie Chimique (Paris)
Ind Chim (Rome) — Industria Chimica (Rome)
Ind Chur Hist R — Indian Church History Review
Ind & Coml Training — Industrial and Commercial Training
Ind Commercial Photographer — Industrial and Commercial Photographer
Ind Commer Photogr — Industrial and Commercial Photographer
Ind Comm Gas — Industrial and Commercial Gas
Ind Conserve — Industria Conserve
Ind Conserve (Parma) — Industria Conserve (Parma)
Ind Constr Mater Constr — Industria Constructiilor si a Materialelor de
    Constructii
Ind Coop R — Indian Cooperative Review

Ind Corps Gras — Industries des Corps Gras
Ind Cott Grow Rev — Indian Cotton Growing Review
Ind Cott Text Ind — Indian Cotton Textile Industry
Ind Cult — Indian Culture
Ind Cult Esp — Indice Cultural Espanol
Ind Cult Q — India Cultures Quarterly
Ind Curr Urb Doc — Index to Current Urban Documents
Ind Datatek — Industriell Datateknik
Ind Dent Rev — Indian Dental Review
Ind Des — Industrial Design
Ind Design — Industrial Design
Ind Dev — Industrial Development
Ind Dev — Industrial Development and Manufacturers Record [*Later,
    Industrial Development*]
Ind Devel — Industrial Development
Ind Develop Abstr — Industrial Development Abstracts
Ind Development of WA — Industrial Development of Western Australia
Ind Dev Manuf Rec — Industrial Development and Manufacturers Record
    [*Later, Industrial Development*]
Ind Dev Officers — Industrial Development Officers
Ind Diamanten Rundsch — Industrie Diamanten Rundschau
Ind Diam Dev — Industrial Diamond Development
Ind Diamond Abstr — Industrial Diamond Abstracts
Ind Diam Re — Industrial Diamond Review
Ind Diam Rev — Industrial Diamond Review
Ind Distr — Industrial Distribution
Ind Distrib — Industrial Distribution
Ind Div Water Res Bull — Indiana. Division of Water Resources. Bulletin
INDEA — Information Dentaire
Ind Eccl St — Indian Ecclesiastical Studies
Ind Econ J — Index of Economic Journals
Ind Econ J — Indian Economic Journal
Ind Econ R — Indian Economic Review
Ind Econ Soc Hist R — Indian Economic and Social History Review
IndEcSt — Indian Ecclesiastical Studies [*Belgium*]
Ind Ed M — Industrial Education Magazine
Ind Educ — Industrial Education Magazine
Ind Educ M — Industrial Education Magazine
Ind Educ R — Indian Educational Review
Ind EJ — Indian Economic Journal
Ind Electr Electron — Industries Electriques et Electroniques
Ind Electron — Industrial Electronics [*England*]
Ind Electron — Industries Electroniques
Ind Electr (Osaka) — Industry and Electricity (Osaka) [*Japan*]
Ind-Elektr Elektron — Industrie-Elektrik und Elektronik
Ind-Elektron Forsch Fertigung — Industrie-Elektronik in Forschung und
    Fertigung [*West Germany*]
Ind Eng — Industrial Engineering
Ind & Eng Chem — Industrial and Engineering Chemistry
Ind Eng Chem — Industrial and Engineering Chemistry
Ind Eng Chem Anal Ed — Industrial and Engineering Chemistry. Analytical
    Edition [*United States*]
Ind Eng Chem Fundam — Industrial and Engineering Chemistry. Fundamentals
Ind Eng Chem Fundamentals — Industrial and Engineering Chemistry.
    Fundamentals
Ind & Eng Chem Fundamentals — Industrial and Engineering Chemistry.
    Fundamentals
Ind Eng Chem News Ed — Industrial and Engineering Chemistry. News
    Edition [*United States*]
Ind & Eng Chem Process Des Dev — Industrial and Engineering Chemistry.
    Process Design and Development
Ind & Eng Chem Process Design — Industrial and Engineering Chemistry.
    Process Design and Development
Ind Eng Chem Prod Res Dev — Industrial and Engineering Chemistry. Product
    Research and Development
Ind and Eng Chem Prod Res and Dev — Industrial and Engineering Chemistry.
    Product Research and Development
Ind Eng F — Industrial and Engineering Chemistry. Fundamentals
Ind Engng Chem Analyt Edn — Industrial and Engineering Chemistry.
    Analytical Edition
Ind & Engng Chem Fundam — Industrial and Engineering Chemistry.
    Fundamentals
Ind & Engng Chem Process Des & Dev — Industrial and Engineering
    Chemistry. Process Design and Development
Ind Eng PDD — Industrial and Engineering Chemistry. Process Design and
    Development
Ind Eng PRD — Industrial and Engineering Chemistry. Product Research and
    Development
Ind Environ — Industry and Environment [*Japan*]
INDEP — Independent
Indep Broadcast — Independent Broadcasting
Indep Coal Oper — Independent Coal Operator [*United States*]
Indep Ed — Independent Education
Indep Educ — Independent Education
Independent Petroleum Assoc America Monthly — Independent Petroleum
    Association of America. Monthly

Independ J Phil — Independent Journal of Philosophy
Indep F J — Independent Film Journal
Indep Pet Assoc Am Mon — Independent Petroleum Association of America. Monthly
Ind Equip Mater & Serv — Industrial Equipment Materials and Services
Ind Equip News — Industrial Equipment News
Ind Ethn — Index Ethnographicus
Index Anal Cancerol — Index Analyticus Cancerologiae
Index Cat Med Vet Zool — Index Catalog of Medical and Veterinary Zoology
Index Censor — Index on Censorship
Index Conf Proc Received by BLLD — Index of Conference Proceedings Received by the British Library Lending Division
Index Current Urban Docs — Index to Current Urban Documents
Index Legal Period — Index to Legal Periodicals [*United States*]
Index Lit Food Invest — Index to the Literature of Food Investigation
Index Period Artic Relat Law — Index to Periodical Articles Related to Law
Ind Explos — Industrial Explosives [*Japan*]
Ind F — Indian Farming
IndF — Indiana Folklore
Ind Farm — Indian Farming
Ind Farm Bioquim — Industria Farmaceutica y Bioquimica
Ind Fin — Industrial Finishing
Ind Finish — Industrial Finishing
Ind Finish Surf Coat — Industrial Finishing and Surface Coatings
Ind Finish & Surf Coatings — Industrial Finishing and Surface Coatings
Ind Finish (Wheaton Ill) — Industrial Finishing (Wheaton, Illinois)
Ind Finish Yearb — Industrial Finishing Yearbook
Ind Fr Equip — Industries Francaises d'Equipement [*France*]
Ind Gas — Industrial Gas
Ind Gas Acquedotti — Industria del Gas e degli Acquedotti
Ind Gas (Duluth) — Industrial Gas (Duluth)
Ind Gas Energy — Industrial Gas and Energy [*United States*]
Ind Geog J — Indian Geographical Journal
Ind Geogr — Indian Geographer
Ind Geogr J — Indian Geographical Journal
Ind Geront — Industrial Gerontology
Ind Gerontol — Industrial Gerontology
Ind d Gomma — Industria della Gomma [*Italy*]
Ind Handel — Industrie und Handel
Ind Health — Industrial Health
Ind Health (Kawasaki) — Industrial Health (Kawasaki)
Ind Health Rev — Industrial Health Review
Ind Heart J — Indian Heart Journal
Ind Heat — Industrial Heating
Ind Heat Eng — Industrial Heating Engineer
Ind Heat (Pittsburg) — Industrial Heating (Pittsburg)
Ind Heat (Tokyo) — Industrial Heating (Tokyo)
Ind His Col — Indiana Historical Commission. Collections
Ind His S — Indiana Historical Society. Publications
Ind Hist Bull — Indiana History Bulletin
Ind Hist Esp — Indice Historico Espanol
Ind Hist Q — Indian Historical Quarterly
Ind Hist Soc Publ — Indiana Historical Society. Publications
Ind Hor — Indian Horizons
Ind Horizons — Indian Horizons
Ind Hyg Dig — Industrial Hygiene Digest
Ind Hyg Found Am Leg Ser Bull — Industrial Hygiene Foundation of America. Legal Series. Bulletin
Ind Hyg Found Am Med Ser Bull — Industrial Hygiene Foundation of America. Medical Series. Bulletin
Ind Hyg Found Am Trans Bull — Industrial Hygiene Foundation of America. Transactions. Bulletin
Ind Hyg Highlights — Industrial Hygiene Highlights [*United States*]
Ind Hygiene — Industrial Hygiene [*Japan*]
Ind Hyg Rev — Industrial Hygiene Review [*United States*]
India AEC Bhabha At Res Cent Rep — India. Atomic Energy Commission. Bhabha Atomic Research Centre. Report
India Coffee Bd Res Dep Annu Detailed Tech Rep — India. Coffee Board. Research Department. Annual Detailed Technical Report
India Coffee Board Annu Rep — India. Coffee Board. Annual Report
India Coffee Board Res Dep Annu Detailed Tech Rep — India. Coffee Board. Research Department. Annual Detailed Technical Report
India Coffee Board Res Dep Annu Rep — India. Coffee Board. Research Department. Annual Report
India Coffee Board Res Dep Bull — India. Coffee Board. Research Department. Bulletin
India CSIR Zool Mem — India. CSIR [*Council of Scientific and Industrial Research*] Zoological Memoir
India Dir Plant Prot Quar Storage Plant Prot Bull — India. Directorate of Plant Protection, Quarantine, and Storage. Plant Protection Bulletin
India Econ Soc Hist R — Indian Economic and Social History Review
India Geol Surv Bull Ser A — India. Geological Survey. Bulletins. Series A. Economic Geology
India Geol Surv Bull Ser B — India. Geological Survey. Bulletins. Series B. Engineering Geology and Ground-Water
India Geol Surv Mem — India. Geological Survey. Memoirs

India Geol Surv Mem Palaeontol Indica New Ser — India. Geological Survey. Memoirs. Palaeontologia Indica. New Series
India Geol Surv Misc Publ — India. Geological Survey. Miscellaneous Publication
India Geol Surv News — India. Geological Survey. News
India J Pol Sci — Indian Journal of Political Science
Indiana Acad Sci Monogr — Indiana Academy of Science. Monograph
Indiana Agric Exp Stn Insp Rep — Indiana. Agricultural Experiment Station. Inspection Report
Indiana Agric Exp Stn Res Prog Rep — Indiana. Agricultural Experiment Station. Research Progress Report
Indiana Busin R — Indiana Business Review
Indian Acad Geosci J — Indian Academy of Geoscience. Journal
Indian Acad Med Sci Ann — Indian Academy of Medical Sciences. Annual
Indian Acad Sci Pro — Indian Academy of Sciences. Proceedings
Indiana Div Water Bull — Indiana. Division of Water. Bulletin
Indiana Geol Surv Bull — Indiana. Geological Survey. Bulletin
Indiana Geol Survey Mineral Economics Ser — Indiana. Geological Survey. Mineral Economics Series
Indiana Geol Surv Mineral Econ Ser — Indiana. Geological Survey. Mineral Economics Series
Indiana Geol Surv Miner Econ Ser — Indiana. Geological Survey. Mineral Economics Series
Indiana Geol Surv Misc Map — Indiana. Geological Survey. Miscellaneous Map
Indiana Geol Surv Occas Pap — Indiana. Geological Survey. Occasional Paper
Indiana Geol Surv Rep Prog — Indiana. Geological Survey. Report of Progress
Indiana Geol Surv Spec Rep — Indiana. Geological Survey. Special Report
Indian Agr — Indian Agriculturist
Indian Agric — Indian Agriculturist
Indian Agric Res Inst (New Delhi) Annu Rep — Indian Agricultural Research Institute (New Delhi). Annual Report
Indian Agric Res Inst (New Delhi) Annu Sci Rep — Indian Agricultural Research Institute (New Delhi). Annual Scientific Report
Indiana Law — Indiana Law Journal
Indiana Leg Forum — Indiana Legal Forum
Indiana LJ — Indiana Law Journal
Indiana L Rev — Indiana Law Review
Indian Ant — Indian Antiquary
Indian Archt — Indian Architect
Indian Assoc Cultiv Sci Proc — Indian Association for the Cultivation of Science. Proceedings
Indiana State Univ Dep Geogr Geol Prof Pap — Indiana State University. Department of Geography and Geology. Professional Paper
Indiana Theory R — Indiana Theory Review
India Natl Acad Sci Proc Sect B — India. National Academy of Science. Proceedings. Section B
Indiana Univ Ed Bul — Indiana University. School of Education. Bulletin
Indiana Univ Math J — Indiana University. Mathematics Journal
Indian Bee J — Indian Bee Journal
Indian Biol — Indian Biologist
Indian Bur Mines Miner Econ Div Mark Surv Ser — Indian Bureau of Mines. Mineral Economics Division. Market Survey Series
Indian Cent Jute Comm Annu Rep Jute Agric Res Inst — Indian Central Jute Committee. Annual Report of the Jute Agricultural Research Institute
Indian Ceram — Indian Ceramics [*India*]
Indian Ceramic Soc Trans — Indian Ceramic Society. Transactions
Indian Ceram Soc Trans — Indian Ceramic Society. Transactions
Indian Chem J — Indian Chemical Journal
Indian Chem J Ann Number — Indian Chemical Journal. Annual Number [*India*]
Indian Chem Manuf — Indian Chemical Manufacturer
Indian Church Hist R — Indian Church History Review
Indian Coconut J — Indian Coconut Journal
Indian Cof — Indian Coffee
Indian Concr J — Indian Concrete Journal
Indian Cott Grow Rev — Indian Cotton Growing Review
Indian Cott J — Indian Cotton Journal
Indian Cotton Grow Rev — Indian Cotton Growing Review
Indian Counc Agric Res Anim Husb Ser — Indian Council of Agricultural Research. Animal Husbandry Series
Indian Counc Agric Res Annu Tech Rep — Indian Council of Agricultural Research. Annual Technical Report
Indian Counc Agric Res Cereal Crop Ser — Indian Council of Agricultural Research. Cereal Crop Series
Indian Counc Agric Res Entomol Monogr — Indian Council of Agricultural Research. Entomological Monographs
Indian Counc Agric Res Misc Bull — Indian Council of Agricultural Research. Miscellaneous Bulletin
Indian Counc Agric Res Monogr — Indian Council of Agricultural Research. Monograph
Indian Counc Agric Res Rep Ser — Indian Council of Agricultural Research. Report Series
Indian Counc Agric Res Res Ser — Indian Council of Agricultural Research. Research Series

Indian Counc Agric Res Rev Ser — Indian Council of Agricultural Research. Review Series
Indian Counc Agric Res Tech Bull — Indian Council of Agricultural Research. Technical Bulletin
Indian Counc Med Res Annu Rep — Indian Council of Medical Research. Annual Report
Indian Counc Med Res Tech Rep Ser — Indian Council of Medical Research. Technical Report Series
Indian East Eng — Indian and Eastern Engineer
Indian Ecol — Indian Ecologist
Indian Econ Soc Hist Rev — Indian Economic and Social History Review
Indian Eng — Indian Engineer
Indian Export Trade J — Indian Export Trade Journal
Indian Farm Mech — Indian Farm Mechanization
Indian Fmg — Indian Farming
Indian Food Pack — Indian Food Packer
Indian For — Indian Forester
Indian For Bull — Indian Forest Bulletin
Indian For Leafl — Indian Forest Leaflet
Indian For Rec — Indian Forest Records
Indian For Rec Bot — Indian Forest Records. Botany
Indian For Rec Entomol — Indian Forest Records. Entomology
Indian For Rec For Pathol — Indian Forest Records. Forest Pathology
Indian For Rec Mycol — Indian Forest Records. Mycology
Indian For Rec Silvic — Indian Forest Records. Silviculture
Indian For Rec Stat — Indian Forest Records. Statistical
Indian For Rec Timber Mech — Indian Forest Records. Timber Mechanics
Indian For Rec Wild Life Recreation — Indian Forest Records. Wild Life and Recreation
Indian For Rec Wood Anat — Indian Forest Records. Wood Anatomy
Indian For Rec Wood Preserv — Indian Forest Records. Wood Preservation
Indian For Rec Wood Seas — Indian Forest Records. Wood Seasoning
Indian For Rec Wood Technol — Indian Forest Records. Wood Technology
Indian Foundry J — Indian Foundry Journal
Indian Geohydrol — Indian Geohydrology
Indian Geol Assoc Bull — Indian Geologists Association. Bulletin
Indian Geol Index — Indian Geological Index
Indian Geotech J — Indian Geotechnical Journal
Indian Heart J — Indian Heart Journal
Indian Heart J Teach Ser — Indian Heart Journal. Teaching Series
Indian Highw — Indian Highways
Indian Hist — Indian Historian
Indian Hist Q — Indian Historical Quarterly
Indian Hort — Indian Horticulture
Indian Hortic — Indian Horticulture
Indian Ind — Indian Industries
Indian Inst of Archts Jnl — Indian Institute of Architects. Journal
Indian Inst Bankers J — Journal. Indian Institute of Bankers
Indian J Agr Econ — Indian Journal of Agricultural Economics
Indian J Agric Chem — Indian Journal of Agricultural Chemistry
Indian J Agric Econ — Indian Journal of Agricultural Economics
Indian J Agric Res — Indian Journal of Agricultural Research
Indian J Agric Sci — Indian Journal of Agricultural Science
Indian J Agric Vet Educ — Indian Journal of Agricultural and Veterinary Education
Indian J Agron — Indian Journal of Agronomy
Indian J Agr Sci — Indian Journal of Agricultural Science
Indian J Air Pollut Control — Indian Journal of Air Pollution Control [*India*]
Indian J Anaesth — Indian Journal of Anaesthesia
Indian J Animal Health — Indian Journal of Animal Health
Indian J Anim Res — Indian Journal of Animal Research
Indian J Anim Sci — Indian Journal of Animal Sciences
Indian J Appl Chem — Indian Journal of Applied Chemistry
Indian J Appl Psychol — Indian Journal of Applied Psychology
Indian J Biochem — Indian Journal of Biochemistry [*Later, Indian Journal of Biochemistry and Biophysics*]
Indian J Biochem Biophys — Indian Journal of Biochemistry and Biophysics
Indian J Bot — Indian Journal of Botany [*India*]
Indian J Cancer — Indian Journal of Cancer
Indian J Cancer Chemother — Indian Journal of Cancer Chemotherapy
Indian J Chem — Indian Journal of Chemistry
Indian J Chem A — Indian Journal of Chemistry. Section A. Inorganic, Physical, Theoretical, and Analytical
Indian J Chem Educ — Indian Journal of Chemical Education
Indian J Chem Sect A — Indian Journal of Chemistry. Section A. Inorganic, Physical, Theoretical, and Analytical
Indian J Chem Sect A Inorg Phys Theor Anal — Indian Journal of Chemistry. Section A. Inorganic, Physical, Theoretical, and Analytical
Indian J Chem Sect B — Indian Journal of Chemistry. Section B
Indian J Chem Sect B Org Chem incl Med Chem — Indian Journal of Chemistry. Section B. Organic Chemistry, Including Medicinal Chemistry
Indian J Chest Dis — Indian Journal of Chest Diseases [*Later, Indian Journal of Chest Diseases and Allied Sciences*]
Indian J Chest Dis Allied Sci — Indian Journal of Chest Diseases and Allied Sciences

Indian J Child Health — Indian Journal of Child Health [*India*]
Indian J Criminol — Indian Journal of Criminology
Indian J Cryog — Indian Journal of Cryogenics
Indian J Dairy Sci — Indian Journal of Dairy Science
Indian J Dermatol — Indian Journal of Dermatology [*Later, Indian Journal of Dermatology, Venereology, and Leprology*]
Indian J Dermatol Venereol — Indian Journal of Dermatology and Venereology [*Later, Indian Journal of Dermatology, Venereology, and Leprology*]
Indian J Dermatol Venereol Leprol — Indian Journal of Dermatology, Venereology, and Leprology
Indian J Earth Sci — Indian Journal of Earth Sciences
Indian J Ecol — Indian Journal of Ecology
Indian J Engrg Math — Indian Journal of Engineering Mathematics
Indian J Ent — Indian Journal of Entomology
Indian J Entomol — Indian Journal of Entomology
Indian J Environ Health — Indian Journal of Environmental Health
Indian J Environ Prot — Indian Journal of Environmental Protection [*India*]
Indian J Exp Biol — Indian Journal of Experimental Biology
Indian J Exp Psychol — Indian Journal of Experimental Psychology
Indian J Ext Educ — Indian Journal of Extension Education
Indian J Farm Chem — Indian Journal of Farm Chemicals
Indian J Farm Sci — Indian Journal of Farm Sciences
Indian J Fish — Indian Journal of Fisheries
Indian J Genet Plant Breed — Indian Journal of Genetics and Plant Breeding
Indian J Genet Pl Breed — Indian Journal of Genetics and Plant Breeding
Indian J Helminthol — Indian Journal of Helminthology
Indian J Hered — Indian Journal of Heredity
Indian J History Sci — Indian Journal of History of Science. National Institute of Sciences of India [*New Delhi*]
Indian J Hist Sci — Indian Journal of History of Science
Indian J Hortic — Indian Journal of Horticulture
Indian J Hosp Pharm — Indian Journal of Hospital Pharmacy
Indian J Ind Med — Indian Journal of Industrial Medicine
Indian J of Internat L — Indian Journal of International Law
Indian J Int Law — Indian Journal of International Law
Indian J Int'l L — Indian Journal of International Law
Indian J Malariol — Indian Journal of Malariology
Indian J Mar Sci — Indian Journal of Marine Sciences
Indian J Math — Indian Journal of Mathematics
Indian J Mech Math — Indian Journal of Mechanics and Mathematics
Indian J Med Res — Indian Journal of Medical Research
Indian J Med Research — Indian Journal of Medical Research
Indian J Med Sci — Indian Journal of Medical Sciences
Indian J Med Surg — Indian Journal of Medicine and Surgery
Indian J Meteorol and Geophys — Indian Journal of Meteorology and Geophysics [*Later, Mausam*]
Indian J Meteorol Geophys — Indian Journal of Meteorology and Geophysics [*Later, Mausam*]
Indian J Meteorol Hydrol Geophys — Indian Journal of Meteorology, Hydrology, and Geophysics [*Later, Mausam*]
Indian J Microbiol — Indian Journal of Microbiology
Indian J Mycol Plant Pathol — Indian Journal of Mycology and Plant Pathology
Indian J Mycol Res — Indian Journal of Mycological Research
Indian J Nematol — Indian Journal of Nematology
Indian J Nutr Diet — Indian Journal of Nutrition and Dietetics
Indian J Occup Health — Indian Journal of Occupational Health
Indian J Ophthalmol — Indian Journal of Ophthalmology
Indian J Orthop — Indian Journal of Orthopaedics [*India*]
Indian J Otolaryngol — Indian Journal of Otolaryngology
Indian J Pathol Bacteriol — Indian Journal of Pathology and Bacteriology [*Later, Indian Journal of Pathology and Microbiology*]
Indian J Pathol Microbiol — Indian Journal of Pathology and Microbiology
Indian J Pediatr — Indian Journal of Pediatrics
Indian J Pharm — Indian Journal of Pharmacy
Indian J Pharmacol — Indian Journal of Pharmacology
Indian J Pharm Sci — Indian Journal of Pharmaceutical Sciences
Indian J Phys — Indian Journal of Physics
Indian J Phys — Indian Journal of Physics. Part A
Indian J Phys Anthropol Hum Genet — Indian Journal of Physical Anthropology and Human Genetics
Indian J Physiol Allied Sci — Indian Journal of Physiology and Allied Sciences
Indian J Physiol Pharmacol — Indian Journal of Physiology and Pharmacology
Indian J Phys Part B — Indian Journal of Physics. Part B
Indian J Plant Physiol — Indian Journal of Plant Physiology
Indian J Poult Sci — Indian Journal of Poultry Science
Indian J Power and River Val Dev — Indian Journal of Power and River Valley Development
Indian J Power River Val Dev — Indian Journal of Power and River Valley Development
Indian J Power River Val Develop — Indian Journal of Power and River Valley Development
Indian J Psychiatry — Indian Journal of Psychiatry
Indian J Psychol — Indian Journal of Psychology
Indian J Pub Admin — Indian Journal of Public Administration
Indian J of Publ Adm — Indian Journal of Public Administration

Indian J Publ Health — Indian Journal of Public Health
Indian J Public Health — Indian Journal of Public Health
Indian J Pure and Appl Math — Indian Journal of Pure and Applied Mathematics
Indian J Pure Appl Math — Indian Journal of Pure and Applied Mathematics
Indian J Pure and Appl Phys — Indian Journal of Pure and Applied Physics
Indian J Pure Appl Phys — Indian Journal of Pure and Applied Physics
Indian J Pure Appl Sci — Indian Journal of Pure and Applied Science
Indian J Radiol — Indian Journal of Radiology
Indian J Radio and Space Phys — Indian Journal of Radio and Space Physics
Indian J Radio Space Phys — Indian Journal of Radio and Space Physics
Indian J Reg Sci — Indian Journal of Regional Science
Indian J Sci Ind — Indian Journal of Science and Industry
Indian J Sci Ind Sect A — Indian Journal of Science and Industry. Section A. Agricultural Sciences [*Later, Indian Journal of Agricultural Research*]
Indian J Sci Ind Sect B Anim Sci — Indian Journal of Science and Industry. Section B. Animal Sciences [*Later, Indian Journal of Animal Research*]
Indian J Seric — Indian Journal of Sericulture
Indian J Social Work — Indian Journal of Social Work
Indian J Soil Conser — Indian Journal of Soil Conservation
Indian J Sugar Cane Res Dev — Indian Journal of Sugar Cane Research and Development
Indian J Surg — Indian Journal of Surgery
Indian J Technol — Indian Journal of Technology
Indian J Text Res — Indian Journal of Textile Research
Indian J Theor Phys — Indian Journal of Theoretical Physics
Indian J Tuberculosis — Indian Journal of Tuberculosis
Indian J Vet Pathol — Indian Journal of Veterinary Pathology
Indian J Vet Sci — Indian Journal of Veterinary Science and Animal Husbandry
Indian J Vet Sci Anim Husb — Indian Journal of Veterinary Science and Animal Husbandry
Indian J Weed Sci — Indian Journal of Weed Science
Indian J Zool — Indian Journal of Zoology
Indian J Zootomy — Indian Journal of Zootomy
Indian Lac Res Inst Annu Rep — Indian Lac Research Institute. Annual Report
Indian Lac Res Inst Bull — Indian Lac Research Institute. Bulletin
Indian Lac Res Inst Res Notes — Indian Lac Research Institute. Research Notes
Indian Lac Res Inst Tech Note — Indian Lac Research Institute. Technical Notes
Indian Lib Assn J — Indian Library Association. Journal
Indian Libr Ass Bull — Indian Library Association. Bulletin
Indian Librn — Indian Librarian
Indian Lib Sci Abstr — Indian Library Science Abstracts
Indian L Rev — Indian Law Review
Indian Med Forum — Indian Medical Forum
Indian Med Gaz — Indian Medical Gazette
Indian Med J (Calcutta) — Indian Medical Journal (Calcutta)
Indian Med Res Mem — Indian Medical Research Memoirs
Indian Min Engng J — Indian Mining and Engineering Journal
Indian Miner — Indian Minerals
Indian Mineral — Indian Mineralogist
Indian Miner Yearb — Indian Minerals Yearbook
Indian MJ — Indian Music Journal
Indian M S — Indian Musicological Society. Journal
Indian Mus Bull — Indian Museum. Bulletin
Indian Mus Q — Indian Music Quarterly
Indian Mus Rec — Indian Museum. Records
Indian Natl Sci Acad Proc Part A — Indian National Science Academy. Proceedings. Part A. Physical Sciences
Indian Nat Sci Acad Bull — Indian National Science Academy. Bulletin
Indian Paediatr — Indian Paediatrics
Indian Pediatr — Indian Pediatrics
Indian Perfum — Indian Perfumer
Indian Phil Cult — Indian Philosophy and Culture
Indian Phil Quart — Indian Philosophical Quarterly
Indian Phys Math J — Indian Physico-Mathematical Journal
Indian Phytopathol — Indian Phytopathology
Indian Potash J — Indian Potash Journal
Indian Potato J — Indian Potato Journal
Indian Poult Gaz — Indian Poultry Gazette [*India*]
Indian Poult Rev — Indian Poultry Review
Indian Pract — Indian Practitioner
Indian Psychol Abstr — Indian Psychological Abstracts
Indian Psychol R — Indian Psychological Review
Indian Pulp Pap — Indian Pulp and Paper
Indian Sci Abstr — Indian Science Abstracts
Indian Sci Abstracts — Indian Science Abstracts
Indian Sci Cong Assoc Proc — Indian Science Congress Association. Proceedings
Indian Sci Congr Assoc Proc — Indian Science Congress Association. Proceedings
Indian Sci Ind — Indian Science Index

Indian Soc Desert Technol Univ Cent Desert Stud Trans — Indian Society of Desert Technology and University Centre of Desert Studies. Transactions
Indian Soc Nuclear Tech Agric Biol Newsl — Indian Society for Nuclear Techniques in Agriculture and Biology. Newsletter
Indian Soc Soil Sci Bull — Indian Society of Soil Science. Bulletin
Indian Soc Soil Sci J — Indian Society of Soil Science. Journal
Indian Sug — Indian Sugar
Indian Tea Assoc Proc Annu Conf — Indian Tea Association. Proceedings of the Annual Conference
Indian Tea Assoc Sci Dep Tocklai Exp Stn Annu Rep — Indian Tea Association. Scientific Department. Tocklai Experimental Station. Annual Report
Indian Tea Assoc Sci Dep Tocklai Exp Stn Memo — Indian Tea Association. Scientific Department. Tocklai Experimental Station. Memorandum
Indian Tea Assoc Tocklai Exp Stn Annu Rep — Indian Tea Association. Tocklai Experimental Station. Annual Report
Indian Tea Assoc Tocklai Exp Stn Memo — Indian Tea Association. Tocklai Experimental Station. Memorandum
Indian Tea Assoc Tocklai Exp Stn Memor — Indian Tea Association. Tocklai Experimental Station. Memorandum
Indian Text J — Indian Textile Journal
Indian Tob J — Indian Tobacco Journal
Indian Vet J — Indian Veterinary Journal
Indian Vet Med J — Indian Veterinary Medical Journal
Indian Weld J — Indian Welding Journal
Indian Yb of Internat Aff — Indian Yearbook of International Affairs
Indian Zool — Indian Zoologist
Indian Zool Mem — Indian Zoological Memoirs
India Oil Nat Gas Comm Bull — India. Oil and Natural Gas Commission. Bulletin
India Pol Sci R — Indian Political Science Review
India Q — India Quarterly
India Quar — India Quarterly
Indicadores Econs (Mexico) — Indicadores Economicos (Mexico)
Indicadores Econs (RS) — Indicadores Economicos (Rio Grande Do Sul)
Indicateurs Econ Centre — Indicateurs de l'Economie du Centre
Indic Cartotec — Indicatore Cartotecnico
Indice Bibliogr Lepra — Indice Bibliografico de Lepra
Indic Grafico — Indicatore Grafico
INDIDJ — International Journal of Eating Disorders
Indi Math J — Indiana University. Mathematics Journal
Ind India — Index India
Ind India — Industrial India
Ind Information Bul — Industrial Information Bulletin
Ind & Int Prop Aus — Industrial and Intellectual Property in Australia
Indirect — Indirections [*Ontario Council of Teachers of English*]
Ind Islam — Index Islamicus
Ind Ital Cem — Industria Italiana del Cemento
Ind Ital Conserve — Industria Italiana delle Conserve
Ind Ital Conserve Aliment — Industria Italiana delle Conserve Alimentari
Ind Ital Elettrotec — Industria Italiana Elettrotecnica [*Italy*]
Ind Ital Elettrotec & Elettron — Industria Italiana Elettrotecnica ed Elettronica
Ind Ital Freddo — Industria Italiana del Freddo
Ind Ital Laterizi — Industria Italiana dei Laterizi
Individ Onsite Wastewater Syst — Individual Onsite Wastewater Systems
Indiv Inst — Individual Instruction
Indiv Psych — Individual Psychologist
Ind J Agr Econ — Indian Journal of Agricultural Economics
Ind J Agric Econ — Indian Journal of Agricultural Economics
Ind J Ag Sci — Indian Journal of Agricultural Science
Ind J Commer — Indian Journal of Commerce
Ind J Econ — Indian Journal of Economics
Ind Jew Per — Index to Jewish Periodicals
Ind J Forest — Indian Journal of Forestry
Ind J Indus Rel — Indian Journal of Industrial Relations
Ind J Industr Relat — Indian Journal of Industrial Relations
Ind J Int L — Indian Journal of International Law
Ind J Polit — Indian Journal of Politics
Ind J Polit Sci — Indian Journal of Political Science
Ind J Pol Sci — Indian Journal of Political Science
Ind J Publ Adm — Indian Journal of Public Administration
Ind J Soc Res — Indian Journal of Social Research
Ind J Soc Wk — Indian Journal of Social Work
IndJT — Indian Journal of Theology [*Serampore*]
Ind J Th — Indian Journal of Theology
Ind J Vet Sci — Indian Journal of Veterinary Science
Ind L — Indian Literature
INDLA — Industrial Laboratory [*English Translation*]
Ind Lab — Industrial Laboratories [*Chicago*]
Ind Lab J — Indian Labour Journal
Ind and Labor Relations Forum — Industrial and Labor Relations Forum
Ind and Labor Relations R — Industrial and Labor Relations Review
Ind and Labor Relations Rept — Industrial and Labor Relations Report
Ind Labor Relat Rev — Industrial and Labor Relations Review

Ind & Labor Rel R — Industrial and Labor Relations Review
Ind and Labor Rels Rev — Industrial and Labor Relations Review
Ind Lab Rel — Industrial and Labor Relations Review
Ind & Lab Rel Rev — Industrial and Labor Relations Review
Ind Lab (US) — Industrial Laboratory (United States)
Ind Lab (USSR) — Industrial Laboratory (USSR)
Ind-Lackier-Betr — Industrie-Lackier-Betrieb
Ind Lackier-Betrb — Industrie Lackier-Betrieb
Ind Latt Zootee — Industria Lattiera e Zooteenia
Ind Law J — Industrial Law Journal
Ind Law Jour — Indiana Law Journal
Ind & Lbr Rel R — Industrial and Labor Relations Review
Ind Legal F — Indiana Legal Forum
Ind Leg Per — Index to Legal Periodicals
Ind Lemnului — Industria Lemnului
Ind Lemnului Celul Hirtiei — Industria Lemnului Celulozei si Hirtiei
Ind Lib — Indian Librarian
Ind Ling — Indian Linguistics
Ind Linguist — Indian Linguistics
IndLit — Indian Literature
Ind Lit Amer Indian — Index to Literature on the American Indian
Ind Lit Dent — Indice de la Literatura Dental en Castellano
Ind Little Mag — Index to Little Magazines
Ind L J — Indiana Law Journal
Ind LR — Indian Law Review
Ind LR — Indiana Law Review
Ind & L Rel Rev — Industrial and Labor Relations Review
Ind L Rev — Indiana Law Review
Ind Lubric — Industrial Lubrication
Ind Lubric Tribology — Industrial Lubrication and Tribology
Ind Lubr & Technol — Industrial Lubrication and Technology
Ind Lubr Tribol — Industrial Lubrication and Tribology
Ind M — Indiana Magazine of History
Ind Mach — Industrial Machinery [*Japan*]
Ind Mag Hist — Indiana Magazine of History
Ind Manage — Industrial Management
Ind Manage and Data Syst — Industrial Management and Data Systems
Ind Management — Industrial Management [*New York*]
Ind Management (London) — Industrial Management (London)
Ind Management R — Industrial Management Review
Ind Mark — Industrial Marketing [*Later, Business Marketing*]
Ind Market — Industrial Marketing [*Later, Business Marketing*]
Ind Market Dig — Industrial Marketing Digest
Ind Mark Manage — Industrial Marketing Management
Ind Math — Industrial Mathematics
Ind Med — Index Medicus
Ind Med — Industrial Medicine and Surgery
Ind Med Esp — Indice Medico Espanol
Ind Med Surg — Industrial Medicine and Surgery
Ind Med & Surg — Industrial Medicine and Surgery
Ind Mgt — Industrial Management [*New York*]
Ind Mgt & Data Syst — Industrial Management and Data Systems
Ind Mgt R — Industrial Management Review
Ind Miljoe — Industri og Miljoe
Ind Min — Industrial Minerals
Ind Miner — Industrie Minerale
Ind Miner Mine — Industrie Minerale. Mine
Ind Miner Mineralurgie — Industrie Minerale. Mineralurgie
Ind Miner (Paris) — Industrie Minerale (Paris)
Ind Miner Rocks — Industrial Minerals and Rocks
Ind Miner Ser Mineralurgie — Industrie Minerale. Serie Mineralurgie
    [*France*] [*Later, Industrie Minerale. Serie Techniques*]
Ind Miner Ser Tech — Industrie Minerale. Serie Techniques [*St. Etienne, France*]
Ind Miner (St Etienne) — Industrie Minerale (St. Etienne) [*France*]
Ind Miner (St Etienne Fr) — Industrie Minerale (St. Etienne, France)
Ind Miner Suppl Techniques (St Etienne) — Industrie Minerale. Supplement. Les Techniques (St. Etienne) [*France*]
Ind Miner Tech — Industrie Minerale. Techniques
Ind Min (Madrid) — Industria Minera (Madrid)
Ind & Min R — Industrial and Mining Review
Ind Min (Rome) — Industria Mineraria (Rome)
Ind & Min S — Industrial and Mining Standard
Ind & Min Standard — Industrial and Mining Standard
Ind Mkt — Industrial Marketing [*Later, Business Marketing*]
Ind Mktg — Industrial Marketing [*Later, Business Marketing*]
Ind Mkt Man — Industrial Marketing Management
Ind Mkt Mgt — Industrial Marketing Management
INDN — Indian News
Ind Norte Port — Industria do Norte de Portugal
Ind NZ Per — Index to New Zealand Periodicals
Indo-As — Indo-Asia
Ind Obst- Gemueseverwert — Industrial Obst- und Gemueseverwertung
Indochina — Indochina Chronicle
Indo Iran J — Indo-Iranian Journal
Indo J Geog — Indonesian Journal of Geography

Indones Abstr — Indonesian Abstracts
Indones Dir Geol Publ Chusus — Indonesia. Direktorat Geologi. Publikasi Chusus
Indones Dir Geol Publ Tek Ser Geofis — Indonesia. Direktorat Geologi. Publikasi Teknik. Seri Geofisika
Indones Dir Geol Publ Tek Ser Geol Ekon — Indonesia. Direktorat Geologi. Publikasi Teknik. Serie Geologi Ekonomi
Indones Dir Geol Publ Tek Ser Paleontol — Indonesia. Direktorat Geologi. Publikasi Teknik. Seri Paleontologi
Indonesia New — Indonesia. News and Views
Indonesian J G — Indonesian Journal of Geography
Indones Inst Mar Res Oceanogr Cruise Rep — Indonesian Institute of Marine Research. Oceanographical Cruise Report
Indones J Geogr — Indonesian Journal of Geography
Indones Pet Assoc Annu Conv Proc — Indonesian Petroleum Association. Annual Convention. Proceedings
Indones Quart — Indonesian Quarterly
Indo-Pac Fish Counc Occas Pap — Indo-Pacific Fisheries Council. Occasional Papers
Indo-Pac Fish Counc Proc — Indo-Pacific Fisheries Council. Proceedings
Indo-Pac Fish Counc Reg Stud — Indo-Pacific Fisheries Council. Regional Studies
Indo-Pac Fish Counc Spec Publ — Indo-Pacific Fisheries Council. Special Publications
Indo-Pac Mollusca — Indo-Pacific Mollusca
Indo Q — Indonesian Quarterly
Ind Parfum Cosmet — Industries de la Parfumerie et de la Cosmetique
Ind Per Art Relat Law — Index to Periodical Articles Related to Law
Ind Per Blacks — Index to Periodical Articles by and about Blacks
Ind Per Negroes — Index to Periodical Articles by and about Negroes [*Later, Index to Periodical Articles by and about Blacks*]
Ind Pet — Industrie du Petrole [*France*]
Ind Pet Eur Gaz Chim — Industrie du Petrole en Europe. Gaz-Chimie
Ind Pet Monde Gaz-Chim — Industrie du Petrole dans le Monde. Gaz-Chimie [*France*]
Ind Petrol Gaz-Chim — Industrie du Petrole. Gaz-Chimie
Ind Phot — Industrial Photography
Ind Photogr — Industrial Photography
Ind Plann Dev — Industrial Planning and Development
Ind Plast (Paris) — Industries des Plastiques (Paris)
Ind Polit Sci R — Indian Political Science Review
Ind Pol Sci R — Indian Political Science Review
Ind Power — Industry and Power [*United States*]
Ind Power Mass Prod — Industrial Power and Mass Production
Ind Process Heat — Industrial and Process Heating
Ind Prod Eng — Industrial and Production Engineering
Ind Progress — Industrial Progress and Development
Ind Progress and Development — Industrial Progress and Development
Ind Prop Sem — Industrial Property Seminar (Monash University, 1972)
Ind Psych R — Indian Psychological Review
Ind Q — India Quarterly
Ind Quality Control — Industrial Quality Control
Ind Quim (Buenos Aires) — Industria y Quimica (Buenos Aires)
INDRA — Industrial Diamond Review
Ind Radiogr Non Destr Test — Industrial Radiography and Non-Destructive Testing
Ind Rare Met — Industrial Rare Metals [*Japan*]
INDRBA — Indian Drugs
Ind Rel — Industrial Relations
Ind Relations (Berkeley) — Industrial Relations (Berkeley)
Ind Relat J S Afr — Industrial Relations Journal of South Africa
Ind Relat Rev Rep — Industrial Relations Review and Report
Ind Rel Briefing — Industrial Relations Briefing
Ind Rel J — Industrial Relations Journal
Ind Rel Law J — Industrial Relations Law Journal
Ind Rel LJ — Industrial Relations Law Journal
Ind Rel News — Industrial Relations News
Ind Rel Soc Proc — Industrial Relations Society. Proceedings of Convention
Ind Rept Chemicals — Industry Report. Chemicals
Ind Rept Containers Pkg — Industry Report. Containers and Packaging
Ind Rept Pulp Pbd — Industry Report. Pulp, Paper, and Board
Ind Res — Industrial Research
Ind Res/Dev — Industrial Research/Development [*United States*]
Ind Res & Devel — Industrial Research and Development
Ind Res (Lond) — Industrial Research (London)
Ind Res News — Industrial Research News [*Australia*]
Ind Res News CSIRO — Industrial Research News. Commonwealth Scientific and Industrial Research Organisation
Ind R & Mining Yrbk — Industrial Review and Mining Year Book
Ind Robot — Industrial Robot
Ind S — Indian Studies: Past and Present
Ind Sacc Ital — Industria Saccarifera Italiana [*Italy*]
Ind Saf — Industrial Safety
Ind Saf Chron — Industrial Safety Chronicle
Ind Saf Data File — Industrial Safety Data File
Ind Saf Surv — Industrial Safety Survey

Ind SA Per — Index to South African Periodicals
Ind Sapon Olii Stearin Profum — Industria Saponiera e degli Olii. Steariniera. Profumiera
Ind Sch Bull — Independent School Bulletin
Ind Sci Eng — Industrial Science and Engineering
Ind Sci Instrum — Industrial and Scientific Instruments
Ind Sci Rev — Index to Scientific Reviews
Ind Sci Technol — Industrial Science and Technology [Japan]
Ind Secera — Industrija Secera
Ind Sel Per — Index to Selected Periodicals
Inds Habillement — Industries de l'Habillement
Ind Short-Term Trends — Industrial Short-Term Trends
Ind Spec — Industrial Specification
Ind Stand — Industrial Standardization
Ind Stand Commer Stand Mon — Industrial Standardization and Commercial Standards. Monthly
Ind Stud — Indian Studies
INDTA — Industries et Techniques
Ind Tech — Industries et Techniques
Ind Tek — Industriell Teknik [Sweden]
Ind Therm — Industries Thermiques
Ind Therm Aerauliques — Industries Thermiques et Aerauliques
Ind Today — Industry Today
Ind de Transformacao — Industrias de Transformacao
Ind Trav O-Mer — Industries et Travaux d'Outre-Mer
INDUA — Industria
Ind Univ Extension Division Bull — Indiana University. Extension Division Bulletin
Ind Univ Sch Ed B — Indiana University. School of Education. Bulletin
Indus Diamond Rev — Industrial Diamond Review
Indus Eng — Industrial Engineering
Indus and Eng Chemistry — Industrial and Engineering Chemistry
Indus Fish Prod Mark Rev & Outl — Industrial Fishery Products Market Review and Outlook
Indus Free China — Industry of Free China
Ind US Gov Per — Index to United States Government Periodicals
Indus & Lab Rel F — Industrial and Labor Relations Forum
Indus & Lab Rel Rev — Industrial and Labor Relations Review
Indus LJ — Industrial Law Journal
Indus Minerals — Industrial Minerals
Ind Usoara — Industria Usoara [Romania]
Ind Usoara Piel — Industria Usoara Pielarie
Indus Rel — Industrial Relations
Indus Rel LJ — Industrial Relations Law Journal
Indus Sit Ind — Industrial Situation in India
Indust Engineering — Industrial Engineering
Indust Engr — Industrial Engineer
Indust LJ — Industrial Law Journal
Indust & L Rel Rev — Industrial and Labor Relations Review
Indust L Rev Q — Industrial Law Review Quarterly
Indust Math — Industrial Mathematics
Indust Progress — Industrial Progress and Development
Industr Engng Chem (Int Ed) — Industrial and Engineering Chemistry (International Edition)
Industr Franc Coton Fibres Alliees — Industrie Francaise du Coton et des Fibres Alliees
Industr Gerontol — Industrial Gerontology
Industrial & Labor Rel Rev — Industrial and Labor Relations Review
Industrial L Rev Q — Industrial Law Review Quarterly
Industrial et Productiv — Industrialisation et Productivite
Industrie Agr — Industrie Agrarie
Industrie Aliment — Industrie Alimentari
Industr Lab Relat R — Industrial and Labor Relations Review
Industr Progr — Industrial Progress and Development
Industr Relat — Industrial Relations
Industr Res Study Timb Res Developm Ass — Industrial Research Study. Timber Research and Development Association
Industr Trav O-Mer — Industries et Travaux d'Outre-Mer
Indus Week — Industry Week
Ind Util Sugar Mill By-Prod — Industrial Utilisation of Sugar and Mill By-Products
Ind Vernice — Industria della Vernice
Ind Vet — Index Veterinarius
Ind Vic — Industrial Victoria
Ind W — Industry Week
Ind Waste Conf Proc — Industrial Waste Conference Proceedings
Ind Wastes — Industrial Wastes
Ind Wastes (Chicago) — Industrial Wastes (Chicago)
Ind Water Eng — Industrial Water Engineering
Ind Water Wastes — Industrial Water and Wastes
Ind Week — Industry Week
Ind Weld — Industry and Welding
Ind Woman — Independent Woman
Ind Wrkr — Industrial Worker
Ind YBIA — Indian Yearbook of International Affairs
Ind Yb Int Aff — Indian Yearbook of International Affairs

INE — Industriele Eigendom
INED — Indian-Ed. University of Alberta
INeg — Index to Periodical Articles by and about Negroes [Later, Index to Periodical Articles by and about Blacks]
INEN — Indian Education Newsletter [Vancouver, British Columbia]
INENE6 — Invertebrate Endocrinology
INEP — Index to New England Periodicals
Inequal Educ — Inequality in Education
INER — International Environment Reporter
INEUB — Izvestiya Nauchno-Issledovatel'skogo Instituta Nefte- i Uglekhimicheskogo Sinteza pri Irkutskom Universitete
Inf — Infinity Science Fiction
INF — Information Services and Use
Inf — Information ueber Steuer und Wirtschaft
InF — Inozemna Filologiya [L'vov]
INFAA2 — Indian Farming
INFAC — Interfaces
Inf Aerauliques Therm — Informations Aerauliques et Thermiques
Inf Age — Information Age
Inf Agric (Paris) — Information Agricole (Paris)
Inf Battelle Frankfurt — Information Battelle Frankfurt
Inf Bienenw — Information Bienenwirtschaft
Inf Bild Wiss — Informationen Bildung Wissenschaft
InfBl — Informationsblatt fuer die Gemeinden in den Niederdeutschen Lutherischen Landeskirchen [Hamburg]
Inf Bot Ital — Informatore Botanico Italiano
Inf Bull: Append Provis Nomencl Symb Terminol Conv (IUPAC) — Information Bulletin: Appendices on Provisional Nomenclature, Symbols, Terminology, and Convention (International Union of Pure and Applied Chemistry)
Inf Bull Append Provis Nomencl Symb Units Stand (IUPAC) — Information Bulletin: Appendices on Provisional Nomenclature, Symbols, Units, and Standards (International Union of Pure and Applied Chemistry)
Inf Bull Append Prov Nomencl Symb Terminol Conv (IUPAC) — Information Bulletin: Appendices on Provisional Nomenclature, Symbols, Terminology, and Conventions (International Union of Pure and Applied Chemistry)
Inf Bull Bitum Coal Res — Information Bulletin. Bituminous Coal Research
Inf Bull Coop Ext NY St Coll Agric Life Sci — Information Bulletin. Cooperative Extension. New York State College of Agriculture and Life Sciences
Inf Bull Div Anim Prodn CSIRO — Information Bulletin. Division of Animal Production. Commonwealth Scientific and Industrial Research Organisation
Inf Bull Int Cent Inf Antibiot — Information Bulletin. International Center of Information on Antibiotics
Inf Bull Int Scient Rad Un — Information Bulletin. International Scientific Radio Union
Inf Bull Isot Generators — Information Bulletin on Isotopic Generators [France]
Inf Bull ISWA (Int Solid Wastes Public Clean Assoc) — Information Bulletin. ISWA (International Solid Wastes Public Cleansing Association)
Inf Bull IUPAC Append Provis Nomencl Symb Units Stand — Information Bulletin. International Union of Pure and Applied Chemistry. Appendices on Provisional Nomenclature, Symbols, Units, and Standards
Inf Bull IUPAC Tech Rep — Information Bulletin. International Union of Pure and Applied Chemistry. Technical Reports
Inf Bull Libr Autom Syst Inf Exch — Information Bulletin. Library Automated Systems Information Exchange
Inf Bull NY St Coll Agric — Information Bulletin. New York State College of Agriculture
Inf Byull Inst Geol Arkt — Informatsionnyi Byulleten' Instituta Geologii Arktiki
Inf Byull Inst Geol Arktiki — Informatsionnyi Byulleten' Instituta Geologii Arktiki
Inf Byull Mezhved Geofiz Kom Prezidiume Akad Nauk Ukr SSR — Informatsionnyi Byulleten' Mezhvedomstvennyi Geofizicheskii Komitet pri Prezidiume Akademii Nauk Ukrainskoi SSR
Inf Byull Mikroelem Sib — Informatsionnyi Byulleten' Mikroelementy Sibirii
Inf Byull Mosk Nauchno Issled Inst Sanit Gig — Informatsionnyi Byulleten' Moskovskogo Nauchno Issledovatel'skogo Instituta Sanitarii i Gigieny
Inf Byull Nauchn Sov Probl Radiobiol Akad Nauk SSSR — Informatsionnyi Byulleten' Nauchnyi Sovet po Problemam Radiobiologii Akademiya Nauk SSSR
Inf Byull Sib Inst Fiziol Biokhim Rast — Informatsionnyi Byulleten' Sibirskii Institut Fiziologii i Biokhimii Rastenii
Inf Byull Sov Antarkt Eksped — Informatsionnyi Byulleten' Sovetskoi Antarkticheskoi Ekspeditsii
Inf Byull Vses Nauchno Issled Inst Mash Promsti Stroit Mater — Informatsionnyi Byulleten' Vsesoyuznyi Nauchno Issledovatel'skii Institut po Mashinam dlya Promyshlennosti Stroitel'nykh Materialov
Inf C — Information and Control
INFCA — Informations-Chimie
Inf Cath Int — Informations Catholiques Internationales

Inf Chil Nitrate Agric Serv — Information. Chilean Nitrate Agricultural Service
Inf-Chim — Informations-Chimie
Inf Cient — Informaciones Cientificas
Inf Circ Arkans Geol Comm — Information Circular. Arkansas Geological Commission
Inf Circ BHP Central Res Lab — Information Circular. BHP [*Broken Hill Proprietary Ltd.*] Central Research Laboratories
Inf Circ Div Fish Oceanogr CSIRO — Information Circular. Division of Fisheries and Oceanography. Commonwealth Scientific and Industrial Research Organisation
Inf Circ Econ Geol Res Unit Univ Witwaters — Information Circular. Economic Geology Research Unit. University of the Witwatersrand
Inf Circ GA Geol Water Resour Div — Information Circular. Georgia Geologic and Water Resources Division
Inf Circ Geol Physiogr Sect Nat Conserv Counc — Information Circular. Geology and Physiography Section. Nature Conservancy Council
Inf Circ Newfoundland Labrador Miner Resour Div — Information Circular. Newfoundland and Labrador Mineral Resources Division
Inf Circ Newfoundland Miner Resour Div — Information Circular. Newfoundland Mineral Resources Division
Inf Circ Philipp Bur Mines — Information Circular. Philippines Bureau of Mines
Inf Circ Tenn Div Geol — Information Circular. Tennessee Division of Geology
Inf Circ US Bur Mines — Information Circular. United States Bureau of Mines
Inf Constr — Informes de la Construccion
Inf Contr — Information and Control
Inf Control — Information and Control
Inf and Control — Information and Control
Inf Dent — Informacion Dental
Inf Dent — Information Dentaire
Inf Digest — Information Digest
Inf Disp — Information Display
Inf Display — Information Display
Inf & Doc — Information et Documentation
Inf Doc Sel Teh Nucl — Informare si Documentare Selectiva. Tehnica Nucleara
INFEA — Ingegneria Ferroviaria
Infec Immun — Infection and Immunity
Inf Econ Inst Econ Agric — Informacoes Economicas. Instituto de Economia Agricola
Infect Control — Infection Control
Infect Control Rounds — Infection Control Rounds
Infect Dis Rev — Infectious Disease Reviews
Infect Immun — Infection and Immunity
Infektionskr Ihre Erreger — Infektionskrankheiten und Ihre Erreger
Infekts Gepatit — Infektsionnyi Gepatit
Infekts Gepatit Resp Mezhved Sb — Infektsionnye Gepatit Respublikanskoi Mezhvedomstvennyi Sbornik
Inf-Elektron — Informacio-Elektronika
Inf Elettron — Informazione Elettronica
Inf-Fachber — Informatik-Fachberichte
Inf Fischwirtsch — Informationen fuer die Fischwirtschaft
Inf Fitopatol — Informatore Fitopatologico
Inf Geogr — Informaciones Geograficas
Inf Geogr — Information Geographique
Inf & Gestion — Informatique et Gestion
Inf Giovane Entomol — Informatore del Giovane Entomologo
Inf Hist — Information Historique
Inf Hotline — Information Hotline [*United States*]
INFIB — Infection and Immunity
INFID — Information fuer die Fischwirtschaft
INF Inf Tec — INF [*Inventario Nacional Forestal*] Informacion Tecnica
Inf INT — Informativo do INT [*Instituto Nacional de Tecnologia*] [*Brazil*]
Inf Intell Online Newsl — Information Intelligence Online Newsletter
Inf Invest Agric (Mexico) — Informe de Investigacion Agricola (Mexico)
Inf Invest Cent Invest Tecnol (Pando Urug) — Informe de Investigacion. Centro de Investigaciones Tecnologicas (Pando, Uruguay)
Infirm Can — Infirmiere Canadienne
Infirm Fr — Infirmiere Francaise
Inf Irradiat Denrees — Informations sur l'Irradiation des Denrees
Inf Kerntech Normung — Informationen Kerntechnische Normung
Inf Litt — Information Litteraire
Inf Manage — Information and Management
Inf and Manage — Information and Management
Inf Med — Informaciones Medicas
Inf Med — Informatore Medico
Inf Med (Genoa) — Informatore Medico (Genoa)
Inf Med (Havana) — Informaciones Medicas (Havana)
Inf Med Roum — Information Medicale Roumaine
Inf Mem Soc Ing Peru — Informaciones y Memorias. Sociedad de Ingenieros del Peru
Infmes Cient Tec Univ Nac Cuyo — Informes Cientificos y Tecnicos. Universidad Nacional de Cuyo
INFN — Information North. AINA [*Arctic Institute of North America*] Newsletter

Inf Nauchno Issled Rab Fil VIN i TI — Informatsiya o Nauchno-Issledovatel'skikh Rabotakh Filial Vsesoyuznogo Instituta Nauchnoi i Tekhnicheskoi Informatsii
Inf Nauchno Issled Rab Inst Tekh Ekon Inf — Informatsiya o Nauchno-Issledovatel'skikh Rabotakh Institut Tekhniko-Ekonomicheskoi Informatsii
Inf News & Sources — Information News and Sources
Inf Num — Information Numismatique
Info — Information
Info Age — Information Age
Infobrief Res Technol — Infobrief Research and Technology [*West Germany*]
Info Chimie — Information Chimie
Info Econ — Informe Economico
Info Econ Afr — Information Economique Africaine
Info & Mgmt — Information and Management
Info Mgr — Information Manager
INFOR Canad J Operational Res and Information Processing — INFOR. Canadian Journal of Operational Research and Information Processing
INFOR Canad J Oper Res Inform Process — INFOR. Canadian Journal of Operational Research and Information Processing
Info Rec Mgmt — Information and Records Management
Info and Referral — Information and Referral
Info Relaciones Mex-Estados Unidos — Informe Relaciones Mexico-Estados Unidos
INFOR J — INFOR. Canadian Journal of Operational Research and Information Processing
Informac-Elektron — Informacio-Elektronika
Informac Quim Analit — Informacion de Quimica Analitica
Inform Agr — Informatore Agrario
Inform Apic — Informador Apicola
Informat et Gestion — Informatique et Gestion
Informatik-Ber (Bonn) — Informatik-Berichte (Bonn)
Informatik-Fachber — Informatik-Fachberichte
Information Bulletin IGCP Project No 61 Sealevel — Information Bulletin. International Geological Correlation Programme. Project Number 61. Sealevel
Information Commun Europ — Information. Commission des Communautes Europeennes
Information Processing Lett — Information Processing Letters
Information Sci — Information Sciences
Informationsdienst Arbeitsgem Pharm Verfahrenstech — Informationsdienst. Arbeitsgemeinschaft fuer Pharmazeutische Verfahrenstechnik
Information Syst — Information Systems
Inform Bull Timb Res Developm Ass — Information Bulletin. Timber Research and Development Association
Inform Card Clemson Agr Coll Ext Serv — Information Card. Clemson Agricultural College. Extension Service
Inform Cathol Int — Informations Catholiques Internationales
Inform Com Esp — Informacion Comercial Espanola
Inform Constit Parl — Informations Constitutionnelles et Parlementaires
Inform Contr — Information and Control
Inform and Control — Information and Control
Inform Coop — Informations Cooperatives
Inform et Doc — Informations et Documents
Inform Doc Agr — Informations et Documentation Agricoles
Informe Anu Labores Costa Rica Min Agr Ganad — Informe Anual de Labores. Costa Rica. Ministerio de Agricultura y Ganaderia
Inform-Elektron — Informacio-Elektronika
Informe Mens Estac Exp Agr "La Molina" (Lima) — Informe Mensual. Estacion Experimental Agricola de "La Molina" (Lima)
Informe Tec — Informe Tecnico. Instituto Forestal [*Chile*]
Informe Tec Estac Exp Agropecuar (Pergamino) — Informe Tecnico. Estacion Experimental Agropecuaria (Pergamino)
Inform Fitopatol — Informatore Fitopatologico
Inform Geogr — Information Geographique
Inform Grasas Aceites — Informaciones sobre Grasas y Aceites
Inform Kybernet Rechentech — Informatik - Kybernetik - Rechentechnik
Inform Process Japan — Information Processing in Japan
Inform Process Lett — Information Processing Letters
Inform Process Mach — Information Processing Machines
Inform Raumentwicklung — Informationen zur Raumentwicklung
Inform Rep For Fire Res Inst (Ottawa) — Information Report. Forest Fire Research Institute (Ottawa)
Inform Rep For Mgmt Inst (Ottawa) — Information Report. Forest Management Institute (Ottawa)
Inform Rep For Prod Lab (Vancouver) — Information Report. Forest Products Laboratory (Vancouver)
Inform Rep For Res Lab (Calgary) — Information Report. Forest Research Laboratory (Calgary)
Inform Rep For Res Lab (Quebec) — Information Report. Forest Research Laboratory (Quebec)
Inform Rep For Res Lab (Victoria BC) — Information Report. Forest Research Laboratory (Victoria, British Columbia)
Inform Sci — Information Science Abstracts
Inform Sci — Information Sciences
Inform Sci Humaines — Informatique et Sciences Humaines

Inform Ser Agr Econ Univ Calif Agr Ext Serv — Information Series in Agricultural Economics. University of California. Agricultural Extension Service
Inform Ser NZ For Serv — Information Series. New Zealand Forest Service
Inform Sheet Miss Agr Exp Sta — Information Sheet. Mississippi Agricultural Experiment Station
Inform Soc (Paris) — Informations Sociales (Paris)
Inform Stor Retrieval — Information Storage and Retrieval
Inform (Swed) — Information (Swedish Pulp and Paper Association)
Inform Tech Ser — Information Technology Series
Inform Univ Profes Int — Informations Universitaires et Professionnelles Internationales
Inform Yugoslav — Informatologia Yugoslavica
Inform Zootec — Informatore Zootecnico
Inf Orthod Kieferorthop — Informationen aus Orthodontie und Kieferorthopaedie mit Beitraegen aus der Internationalen Literatur
Inf Ortoflorofruttic — Informatore di Ortoflorofrutticoltura
Infort Traum Lav — Infortunistica e Traumatologia del Lavoro
InfoS — Information Sciences
Info Serv Leafl Div Mech Eng CSIRO — Information Service Leaflet. Division of Mechanical Engineering. Commonwealth Scientific and Industrial Research Organisation
Info Soc — Informacao Social
Info Stud Vivaldiani — Informazioni e Studi Vivaldiani
Infosys — Infosystems [*Wheaton, IL*]
Info Sys New — Information Systems News
Info Systems — Information Systems [*Elmsford, NY*]
Info Tech — Information Technology and Libraries
InfP — Information Processing Journal
INFPA — Infrared Physics
Inf Pap Aust AEC — Australian Atomic Energy Commission. Information Paper
Inf Pap Aust AEC — Information Paper. Australian Atomic Energy Commission
Inf Privacy — Information Privacy
Inf Pr Man — Information Processing and Management
Inf Processing & Mgt — Information Processing and Management
Inf Process Lett — Information Processing Letters
Inf Process Mach — Information Processing Machines
Inf Process and Manage — Information Processing and Management
Inf Process Manage — Information Processing and Management
Inf Process Soc Jpn (Joho Shori) — Information Processing Society of Japan (Joho Shori)
Inf Proc Man — Information Processing and Management
Inf Prov Buenos Aires Com Invest Cient — Informes. Provincia de Buenos Aires. Comision de Investigaciones Cientificas
Inf Psiquiat — Informaciones Psiquiatricas
Inf Psychiat — Information Psychiatrique
Inf Psychiatr — Information Psychiatrique
Inf: Pt 1 — Information: Part 1: News/Sources/Profiles
Inf: Pt 2 — Information: Part 2: Reports/Bibliographies
Inf Publ Stredisko Tech Inf Potravin Prum — Informacni Publikace. Stredisko Technickych Informacni Potravinarskeho Prumyslu
Inf Quim Anal — Informacion de Quimica Analitica
Inf Quim Anal (Madrid) — Informacion de Quimica Analitica (Madrid)
Inf Quim Anal Pura Apl Ind — Informacion de Quimica Analitica, Pura, y Aplicada a la Industria
Inf Rade Koncar — Informacije Rade Koncar
Infrared Phys — Infrared Physics
Infrar Phys — Infrared Physics
Inf Raumentwickl — Informationen zur Raumentwicklung
Inf and Referral J Alliance Inf Referral Syst — Information and Referral. Journal of the Alliance of Information and Referral Systems
In Freight — International Freighting Weekly
Inf Rep Chem Control Res Inst (Can) — Information Report. Chemical Control Research Institute (Canada)
Inf Rep Chem Control Res Inst Envir Can For Serv — Information Report. Chemical Control Research Institute. Environment Canada Forestry Service
Inf Rep FMR-X For Manage Inst — Information Report FMR-X. Forest Management Institute
Inf Rep FPM-X For Pest Manage Inst — Information Report FPM-X. Forest Pest Management Institute
Inf Rep NOR-X North For Res Cent — Information Report NOR-X. Northern Forest Research Centre
Inf Rep Ser Fish — Information Report Series. Fisheries
Inf Rept Bibliog — Information. Reports and Bibliographies
Inf Rep Washington Res — Information Report. Washington Researches [*United States*]
Inf Retr Libr Automn — Information Retrieval and Library Automation Letter
Inf Sb Inst Zemnoi Kory Sib Otd Akad Nauk SSSR — Informatsionnyi Sbornik Institut Zemnoi Kory Sibirskoe Otdelenie Akademiya Nauk SSSR
Inf Sb Tr Vychisl Tsentra Irkutsk Gos Univ — Informatsionnyi Sbornik Trudov Vychislitel'nogo Tsentra Irkutskii Gosudarstvennyi Universitet
Inf Sb Vses Nauchno Issled Geol Inst — Informatsionnyi Sbornik Vsesoyuznyi Nauchno-Issledovatel'skii Geologicheskii Institut

Inf Sci — Information Sciences
Inf Sci — Informations Scientifiques
InfSciAb — Information Science Abstracts
Inf Sciences — Information Sciences
Inf Scient — Information Scientist
Inf Scientist — Information Scientist
Inf Ser Dep Scient Ind Res (NZ) — Information Series. New Zealand Department of Scientific and Industrial Research
Inf Ser NZ Dep Sci Ind Res — Information Series. New Zealand Department of Scientific and Industrial Research
Inf Ser NZ For Serv — Information Series. New Zealand Forest Service
Inf Serv — National Council of Churches of Christ in the USA. Information Service
Inf Serv Leafl CILES CSIRO — Information Service Leaflet. Central Information, Library, and Editorial Section. Commonwealth Scientific and Industrial Research Organisation
Inf Serv Sheet Div Build Res CSIRO — Information Service Sheet. Division of Building Research. Commonwealth Scientific and Industrial Research Organisation
Inf Serv Sheet Div Mech Eng CSIRO — Information Service Sheet. Division of Mechanical Engineering. Commonwealth Scientific and Industrial Research Organisation
Inf Serv Use — Information Services and Use [*Netherlands*]
Inf Sheet Miss State Univ Coop Ext Serv — Information Sheet. Mississippi State University. Cooperative Extension Service
Inf Sh Miss Agric Exp Stn — Information Sheet. Agricultural Experiment Station. Mississippi State University
Inf So — Informazioni Soimet
Inf Soc — Information Society
Inf Soc — Informations Sociales [*Paris*]
Inf Soc Franc Photogr — Informations. Societe Francaise de Photographie
Inf Soc (L) — Informaciones Sociales (Lima)
Inf Soc (P) — Informations Sociales (Paris)
Inf-Spektrum — Informatik-Spektrum
Infs Tech Serv Vet — Informations Techniques des Services Veterinaires
Inf Storage — Information Storage and Retrieval
Inf Storage Retr — Information Storage and Retrieval
Inf Storage & Retr — Information Storage and Retrieval
Inf Stor Retr — Information Storage and Retrieval
Inf Syst — Information Systems
INFTD — Informant
Inf Tec Argent Repub Estac Exp Agropecu Manfredi — Informacion Tecnica. Argentine Republic. Estacion Experimental Agropecuaria Manfredi
Inf Tec Estac Exp Reg Agropecu (Pergamino) — Informe Tecnico. Estacion Experimental Regional Agropecuaria (Pergamino)
Inf Tech Cent Tech Interprof Ol Metrop — Informations Techniques. Centre Technique Interprofessionnel des Oleagineux Metropolitains
Inf Techn CETIOM — Informations Techniques. Centre Technique Interprofessionnel des Oleagineux Metropolitains
Inf Technol and Libr — Information Technology and Libraries
Inf Technol Res and Dev — Information Technology. Research and Development
Inf Tech People — Information Technology and People
Inf Tec ICAITI — Informe Tecnico. Instituto Centroamericano de Investigacion y Tecnologia Industrial
Inf Tec Inst Centroam Invest Tecnol Ind — Informe Tecnico. Instituto Centroamericano de Investigacion y Tecnologia Industrial
Inf Tec Inst For (Santiago Chile) — Informe Tecnico. Instituto Forestal (Santiago, Chile)
Inftore Agr — Informatore Agrario
Inftore Fitopatol — Informatore Fitopatologico
Infusionsther Klin Ernaehr — Infusionstherapie und Klinische Ernaehrung
Infusionsther Klin Ernaehr Sonderh — Infusionstherapie und Klinische Ernaehrung. Sonderheft
Infusionsther Klin Ernaer Forsch Prax — Infusionstherapie und Klinische Ernaehrung. Forschung und Praxis
Inf World (Abingdon) — Information World (Abingdon) [*England*]
Inf World Rev — Information World Review
Inf World (Washington DC) — Information World (Washington, DC)
Inf Zootec — Informatore Zootecnico
Inf Zp VLIS — Informacni Zpravodaj VLIS [*Vojenska Lekarska Informacni Sluzba*]
Inf Zukunfts-Friedensforsch — Information Zukunfts- und Friedensforschung
Ing — Ingenieur
Ing Aeronaut Astronaut — Ingenieria Aeronautica y Astronautica [*Spain*]
Ing Agron — Ingenieria Agronomica
Ing Ambientale — Ingegneria Ambientale [*Italy*]
Ing-Arch — Ingenieur-Archiv
Ing-Arch — Ingenieur-Archiv. Gesellschaft fuer Angewandte Mathematik und Mechanik [*West Germany*]
Ing Arquit — Ingenieria y Arquitectura
Ing Arts Metiers — Ingenieurs. Arts et Metiers
Ing Auto — Ingenieurs de l'Automobile
Ing Bygningsvaes — Ingenioer- og Bygningsvaesen [*Denmark*]
Ing Bygningsv Ugeovers — Ingenioer- og Bygningsvaesen Ugeoversigt [*Denmark*]

Ing Chim (Brussels) — Ingenieur Chimiste (Brussels)
Ing Chim It — Quaderni dell' Ingegnere Chimico Italiano
Ing Chim (Milan) — Ingegneria Chimica (Milan)
Ing Civ (Havana) — Ingenieria Civil (Havana)
Ing Civil — Ingenieria Civil
Ing-Dig — Ingenieur-Digest
Ing Dt Bu Po — Ingenieur der Deutschen Bundespost
INGEA — Ingenioeren (1892-1966)
Ing Ec Super Phys Chim Ind — Ingenieurs de l'Ecole Superieure de Physique et
     de Chimie Industrielles
Ing Electr & Mec — Ingenieria Electrica y Mecanica
Ingen For — Ingenieria Forestal
Ingenieria Hidraul Mex — Ingenieria Hidraulica en Mexico
Ingenioersvetenskapsakad Handl — Ingenioersvetenskapsakademien.
     Handlingar
Ingenioervidensk Skr — Ingenioervidenskabelige Skrifter
Ingenioervidensk Skr Ser A — Ingenioervidenskabelige Skrifter. Series A
Ingenioervidensk Skr Ser B — Ingenioervidenskabelige Skrifter. Series B
Ingen Villes France — Ingenieurs des Villes de France
Ing EPCI — Ingenieurs de l'Ecole Superieure de Physique et de Chimie
     Industrielles
Ing Ferrov — Ingegneria Ferroviaria
Ing-Forsk — Ingenioeren-Forskning [*Denmark*]
Ing Hidraul Mexico — Ingenieria Hidraulica en Mexico
Ing-Mag — Ingenioer-Magasinet [*Denmark*]
Ing Mecc — Ingegneria Meccanica
Ing Mec y Electr — Ingenieria Mecanica y Electrica
INGNA — Industrial Gas
Ing Nav (Madrid) — Ingenieria Naval (Madrid)
Ing Ned Indie — Ingenieur in Nederlandsch Indie
Ing Nucl — Ingegneria Nucleare
Ing Pet — Ingenieria Petrolera [*Mexico*]
Ing Quim Ind — Ingenieria Quimica e Industrias
Ing Quim (Medellin Colombia) — Ingenieria Quimica (Medellin, Colombia)
Ing Quim (Mexico City) — Ingenieria Quimica (Mexico City)
INGRA — Ingenieur
Ing Sanit — Ingegneria Sanitaria
Ing & Tech — Ingenieurs et Techniciens
Ing Text (Barcelona) — Ingenieria Textil (Barcelona)
Ing Ugebl — Ingenioerens Ugeblad
Ing Vetenskaps Akad Medd — Ingeniors Vetenskaps Akademien. Meddelande
Inhaled Part — Inhaled Particles
Inha Univ IIR — Inha University IIR
INHBA — Bulletin. Illinois Natural History Survey
INHEA — Industrial Health
INHEAO — Industrial Health
INHEES — Index Hepaticarum
INHOAK — Indian Horticulture
INHP — Indiana Journal. Indiana Association for Health, Physical Education,
     and Recreation
INHTA — Industrial Heating
INI — International Nursing Index
ININA — Industrial India
INIREB Informa Inst Invest Recur Bioticos — INIREB Informa. Instituto de
     Investigaciones sobre Recursos Bioticos
INITB — Installatore Italiano
Initiative — Industrial Arts Initiative
Iniz — Iniziative
INJ — Internationales Verkehrswesen; Fachzeitschrift fuer Information und
     Kommunikation in Verkehr
INJ — Israel Numismatic Journal
INJABN — International Journal of the Addictions
INJFA3 — International Journal of Fertility
INJHA — Indian Journal of Heredity
INJHA9 — Indian Journal of Heredity
INJPA — Indian Journal of Psychology
INKYD — Rihaknonjip. Research Institute of Applied Science. Kon-Kuk
     University
InL — Indian Literature
InL — Inostrannaya Literatura [*Moscow*]
Inland Archt — Inland Architect
Inland Printer Am Lithogr — Inland Printer/American Lithographer
Inland Ptr — Inland Printer
Inland & Ptr & Lithog — Inland and American Printer and Lithographer
Inl Bird-Banding News — Inland Bird-Banding News
IN LF — Indiana Legal Forum
InLi — Incontri Linguistici
IN LJ — Indiana Law Journal
IN LR — Indiana Law Review
INLR-A — International Labour Review
INM — Industrial Management
INM — Industrie Textile. Revue Mensuelle Internationale Technique et
     Economique Textile
INMAD — Invention Management
Inmersion Cienc — Inmersion y Ciencia
INMI — International Migration

INMID — Industria Minera
INMOA — Ingenieur (Montreal)
INMRA — Industria Mineraria
INNDDK — Investigational New Drugs
Innere Med — Innere Medizin
Innes Rev — Innes Review
INNLA — INIS [*International Nuclear Information System*] Newsletter
INNO — Inter-Nord
INNS — International Nuclear News Service
INNUA — Ingegneria Nucleare
INO — Indonesia
INOCA — Inorganic Chemistry
INOGA — Industrielle Obst- und Gemueseverwertung
INOGAV — Industrielle Obst- und Gemueseverwertung
INOK — Inuit Okakheet. Kitikmeot Inuit Association
INOMA — Inorganic Materials [*English Translation*]
INOPA — Investigations in Ophthalmology and Visual Science
INOPAO — Investigative Ophthalmology [*Later, Investigative Ophthalmology
     and Visual Science*]
INOPD — International Ophthalmology
Inorg Chem — Inorganic Chemistry
Inorg Chem Main Group Elem — Inorganic Chemistry of the Main Group
     Elements
Inorg Chem Transition Elem — Inorganic Chemistry of the Transition Elements
Inorg Chim — Inorganica Chimica Acta
Inorg Chim Acta — Inorganica Chimica Acta
Inorg Chim Acta Rev — Inorganica Chimica Acta. Reviews
Inorg Macromol Rev — Inorganic Macromolecules Reviews
Inorg Mater — Inorganic Materials
Inorg Mater (USSR) — Inorganic Materials (USSR)
Inorg Nucl — Inorganic and Nuclear Chemistry Letters
Inorg Nucl Chem Lett — Inorganic and Nuclear Chemistry Letters
Inorg and Nucl Chem Lett — Inorganic and Nuclear Chemistry Letters
Inorg Perspect Biol Med — Inorganic Perspectives in Biology and Medicine
Inorg React Mech — Inorganic Reaction Mechanisms
InostrJazyki — Inostrannye Jazyki v Skole
InozF — Inozemna Filolohiji
INPAA — Instrument Practice
InPEN — Indian PEN
INPFCB — International North Pacific Fisheries Commission. Bulletin
INPHA — Industrial Photography
INPI — Information Pipeline. Norman Wells Project Review
In-Plant Reprod — In-Plant Reproductions [*United States*]
INPO Impact — INPO [*Institute of Nuclear Power Operations*] Impact
     [*United States*]
INPO Rev — INPO [*Institute of Nuclear Power Operations*] Review [*United
     States*]
In Pract — In Practice
INPS — Individual Psychology
INPXAJ — Internistische Praxis
INQ — Innovatie Informatiebulletin ter Bevordering van de Industriele
     Vernieuwing in Ons Land
Inq — Inquiry
INQB — Information North Quebec. Bulletin de Liaison des Centres de
     Recherches Nordique de Quebec
INQU — Indians of Quebec. Confederation of Indians of Quebec
Inqueritos Nac de Precos (Capitais) — Inqueritos Nacional de Precos (Capitais)
Inqueritos Nac de Precos (Unidades da Federacao) — Inqueritos Nacional de
     Precos (Unidades da Federacao)
Inquiry Mag — Inquiry Magazine
INQYA — Inquiry
INR — Industrial Relations [*Canada*]
INRE — Indian Record
In Rev — In Review. Canadian Books for Young People
INRFDC — Interferon
INRSDH — International Goat and Sheep Research
INS — Industrial Society
InS — Inland Seas
INS — Insight
Ins — Instrumentalist
Ins — Insula
INS — Insurance
INSAA — Ingegneria Sanitaria
INSA Bull — Indian National Science Academy. Bulletin
Ins Coun J — Insurance Counsel Journal
Ins Counsel J — Insurance Counsel Journal
In Search — In Search/En Quete [*Canada*]
Insecta Matsum — Insecta Matsumurana
Insecta Matsumurana Suppl — Insecta Matsumurana. Supplement
Insect Answers Coop Ext Serv Wash St Univ — Insect Answers. Cooperative
     Extension Service. Washington State University
Insect Bioc — Insect Biochemistry
Insect Biochem — Insect Biochemistry
Insect Dis Rep US For Serv North Reg — Insect Disease Report. United States
     Forest Service. Northern Region
Insect Ecol — Insect Ecology

Insectic Acaricide Tests — Insecticide and Acaricide Tests
Insect Sci Its Applica — Insect Science and Its Application
Insects Micronesia — Insects of Micronesia
Insect Soc — Insectes Sociaux
Insects Soc Soc Insects — Insectes Sociaux/Social Insects
Insect Wld Dig — Insect World Digest
INSERM Colloq — INSERM [*Institut National de la Sante et de la Recherche Medicale*] Colloque
INSERM Symp — INSERM [*Institut National de la Sante et de la Recherche Medicale*] Symposia
Ins Field (Fire Ed) — Insurance Field (Fire and Casualty Edition)
Ins Field (Life Ed) — Insurance Field (Life Edition)
Ins Geog Geol Estado Sao Paulo Bol — Instituto Geografico e Geologico. Estado de Sao Paulo. Boletim
INSI — Insight
INSIA — Industria Saccarifera Italiana
Inside Canb — Inside Canberra
Inside Educ — Inside Education
Insiders' Chr — Insiders' Chronicle
In Situ Oil Coal Shale Miner — In Situ. Oil-Coal-Shale-Minerals
Ins Law J — Insurance Law Journal
Ins L J — Insurance Law Journal
INSMD4 — Intersectum
INSPEL — INSPEL. International Journal of Special Libraries
INSRAG — Instrumentation
Insrg Soc — Insurgent Sociologist
Inst — Institutions
Inst — Instructor
Inst Aeronaut Sci Sherman M. Fairchild Publ Fund Prepr — Institute of the Aeronautical Sciences. Sherman M. Fairchild Publication Fund. Preprint
Inst Afr Stud — Institute of African Studies
Inst Agric Res Annu Rep (Addis Ababa) — Institute of Agricultural Research. Annual Report (Addis Ababa)
Inst Agric Res Annu Res Semin Proc (Addis Ababa) — Institute of Agricultural Research. Annual Research Seminar. Proceedings (Addis Ababa)
Inst Agric Res Prog Rep (Addis Ababa) — Institute of Agricultural Research. Progress Report (Addis Ababa)
Inst Agric Res Samaru Annu Rep — Institute of Agricultural Research. Samaru. Annual Report
Inst Agron Dr Petru Groza (Cluj) Lucr Stiint Ser Agric — Institutul Agronomic "Dr. Petru Groza" (Cluj). Lucrari Stiintifice. Seria Agricultura
Inst Agron "Dr Petru Groza" Cluj Lucr Stiint Ser Med Vet — Institutul Agronomic "Dr. Petru Groza" Cluj Lucrari Stiintifice. Seria Medicina Veterinara
Inst Agron Ion Ionescu de la Brad (Iasi) Lucr Stiint — Institutul Agronomic "Ion Ionescu de la Brad" (Iasi). Lucrari Stiintifice
Inst Agron Timisoara Lucr Stiint Ser Agron — Institutul Agronomic Timisoara Lucrari Stiintifice. Seria Agronomie
Inst Agron Timisoara Lucr Stiint Ser Med Vet — Institutul Agronomic Timisoara Lucrari Stiintifice. Seria Medicina Veterinara
Inst Alatne Masine Alate Monogr — Institut za Alatne Masine i Alate. Monografije
Inst Alatne Masine Alate Saopstenja — Institut za Alatne Masine i Alate. Saopstenja
Installatore Ital — Installatore Italiano
Install Ital — Installatore Italiano [*Italy*]
Inst Anim Physiol Rep — Institute of Animal Physiology. Report
Inst Antart Argent Contrib — Instituto Antartico Argentino. Contribuciones
Inst Antart Chileno Bol — Instituto Antartico Chileno. Boletin
Instant Res — Instant Research on Peace and Violence
Instant Res Peace Violence — Instant Research on Peace and Violence
Inst Appl Res Nat Resour (Abu Ghraib Iraq) Tech Rep — Institute for Applied Research on Natural Resources (Abu-Ghraib, Iraq). Technical Report
Inst Appl Res Nat Resour Tech Rep (Bull) — Institute for Applied Research on Natural Resources. Technical Report (Bulletin)
Inst Arch Ethnog — Internationales Archiv fuer Ethnographie
Inst At Energ I V Kurchatova Rap IAE — Institut Atomnoi Energii Imeni I. V. Kurchatova. Raport IAE
Inst Aust Foundrymen Annu Proc — Institute of Australian Foundrymen. Annual Proceedings
Inst Bankers J — Institute of Bankers. Journal
Inst Bauwissenschaftliche Forsch Publ — Institut fuer Bauwissenschaftliche Forschung. Publikation
Inst Bauwissensch Forsch Publ — Institut fuer Bauwissenschaftliche Forschung. Publikation [*Switzerland*]
Inst Belge Amelior Betterave Publ — Institut Belge pour l'Amelioration de la Betterave. Publication
Inst Belge Amelior Betterave Publ Trimest — Institut Belge pour l'Amelioration de la Betterave. Publication Trimestrielle
Inst Biol Apl Publ (Barcelona) — Instituto de Biologia Aplicada. Publicaciones (Barcelona)
Inst Biol Bahia Bol — Instituto Biologico da Bahia. Boletim
Inst Biol J — Institute of Biology [*London*]. Journal
Inst Biol (Lond) Symp — Institute of Biology (London). Symposium

Inst Biol Mar (Mar Del Plata) Contrib — Instituto de Biologia Marina (Mar Del Plata). Contribucion
Inst Biol Mar (Mar Del Plata) Mem Anu — Instituto de Biologia Marina (Mar Del Plata). Memoria Anual
Inst Biol Mar (Mar Del Plata) Ser Contrib — Instituto de Biologia Marina (Mar Del Plata). Serie Contribuciones
Inst Biol Pesqui Tecnol (Curitiba) Bol — Instituto de Biologia e Pesquisas Tecnologicas (Curitiba). Boletim
Inst Biol Scheikd Onderz Landbouwgewassen (Wageningen) Jaarb — Instituut voor Biologisch en Scheikundig Onderzoek van Landbouwgewassen (Wageningen). Jaarboek
Inst Biol Scheikd Onderz Landbouwgewassen (Wageningen) Meded — Instituut voor Biologisch en Scheikundig Onderzoek van Landbouwgewassen (Wageningen). Mededeling
Inst Biol Stud Biol — Institute of Biology's Studies in Biology
Inst Bodemvruchtbaarheid Haren-Gr Jaarversl — Instituut voor Bodemvruchtbaarheid Haren-Groningen. Jaarverslag
Inst Bodemvruchtbaarheid Haren-Gr Rapp — Instituut voor Bodemvruchtbaarheid Haren-Groningen. Rapport
Inst Bodemvruchtbaarheid Jaarversl — Instituut voor Bodemvruchtbaarheid Jaarverslag
Inst Bodemvruchtbaarheid Rapp — Instituut voor Bodemvruchtbaarheid. Rapport
Inst Bot Acad Sin Monogr Ser — Institute of Botany. Academia Sinica Monograph Series
Inst Bot "Dr Goncalo Sampaio" Fac Cien Univ Porto Publ — Instituto de Botanica "Dr. Goncalo Sampaio." Faculdade de Ciencias. Universidade do Porto. Publicacoes
Inst Brew (Aust NZ Sect) Proc Conv — Institute of Brewing (Australia and New Zealand Section). Proceedings of the Convention
Inst Br Geographers Trans — Institute of British Geographers. Transactions
Inst Br Geogr Trans — Institute of British Geographers. Transactions
Inst Cancer Res (Phila) Sci Rep — Institute for Cancer Research (Philadelphia). Scientific Report
Inst Cercet Ind Chim Aliment Lucr Cercet — Institutul de Cercetari pentru Industrie si Chimie Alimentara. Lucrari de Cercetare
Inst Certif Mech Electr Eng S Afr Arthur Hallet Mem Lect — Institution of Certificated Mechanical and Electrical Engineers. South Africa. Arthur Hallet Memorial Lectures
Inst Chem Eng Symp Ser — Institution of Chemical Engineers. Symposium Series
Inst Chem Eng Trans — Institution of Chemical Engineers. Transactions
Inst Chem Irel J — Institute of Chemistry of Ireland. Journal
Inst Chim Aliment Lucr Cercet — Institutul de Chimie Alimentara. Lucrari de Cercetare
Inst Ciencias Socs R — Revista. Instituto de Ciencias Sociales
Inst Cienc Nat Mat Univ El Salvador Comun — Instituto de Ciencias Naturales y Matematicas. Universidad de El Salvador. Comunicaciones
Inst Civ Engr Proc — Institution of Civil Engineers. Proceedings
Inst Civ Engrs Proc Part 1 — Institution of Civil Engineers. Proceedings. Part 1. Design and Construction
Inst Civ Engrs Proc Part 2 — Institution of Civil Engineers. Proceedings. Part 2. Research and Theory
Inst of Clerks of Works Jnl — Institute of Clerks of Works. Journal
Inst Colomb Agropecu Bol Tec — Instituto Colombiano Agropecuario. Boletin Tecnico
Inst Cubano Invest Tecnol Ser Estud Trab Invest — Instituto Cubano de Investigaciones Tecnologicas. Serie de Estudios sobre Trabajos de Investigacion [*Cuba*]
Inst Def Anal Pap — Institute for Defense Analyses. Paper
Inst Def Stud Anal J — Institute for Defence Studies and Analyses. Journal
Inst Dent Res Bienn Rep (Syd) — Institute of Dental Research. Biennial Report (Sydney)
Inst Dent Res United Dent Hosp Sydney Annu Rep — Institute of Dental Research. United Dental Hospital of Sydney. Annual Report
Inst Dev Stud Bull — Institute of Development Studies. Bulletin [*England*]
Inst E B — Instituto de Estudos Brasileiros
Inst Econ Prod Ganad Ebro Comun — Instituto de Economia y Producciones Ganaderas del Ebro. Comunicaciones
Inst Ecuat Cienc Nat Contrib — Instituto Ecuatoriano de Ciencias Naturales. Contribucion
Inst E E J — Institution of Electrical Engineers. Journal
Inst E E Proc — Institution of Electrical Engineers. Proceedings
Inst d'Egypte Bull — Institut d'Egypte Bulletin
Inst Elec Eng Conf Publ — Institution of Electrical Engineers. Conference Publication
Inst Elec Eng J — Institution of Electrical Engineers. Journal
Inst Elect & Electronics Eng Proc — Institute of Electrical and Electronics Engineers. Proceedings
Inst Elect & Electronics Eng Trans IA — Institute of Electrical and Electronics Engineers. Transactions on Industry Application
Inst Elect & Electronics Eng Trans PAS — Institute of Electrical and Electronics Engineers. Transactions on Power Apparatus and Systems
Inst Electron Radio Eng Conf Proc — Institution of Electronic and Radio Engineers. Conference Proceedings

Inst Electron Telecommun Eng J — Institution of Electronics and
    Telecommunication Engineers. Journal
Inst Elie Cartan — Institut Elie Cartan
Inst Energ Biul — Instytut Energetyki. Biuletyn
Inst Eng Aust Chem Eng Aust — Institution of Engineers of Australia.
    Chemical Engineering in Australia
Inst Eng Aust Chem Eng Trans — Institution of Engineers of Australia.
    Chemical Engineering Transactions
Inst Eng Aust Civ Eng Trans — Institution of Engineers of Australia. Civil
    Engineering Transactions
Inst Eng (Aust) Elec Eng Trans — Institution of Engineers of Australia.
    Electrical Engineering Transactions
Inst Eng Aust Electr Eng Trans — Institution of Engineers of Australia.
    Electrical Engineering Transactions
Inst Eng (Aust) Gen Eng Trans — Institution of Engineers of Australia. General
    Engineering Transactions
Inst Eng Aust J — Institution of Engineers of Australia. Journal
Inst Eng (Aust) Mech Chem Eng Trans — Institution of Engineers of Australia.
    Mechanical and Chemical Engineering Transactions
Inst Eng Aust Mech & Chem Trans — Institution of Engineers of Australia.
    Mechanical and Chemical Transactions
Inst Eng (Aust) Mech Eng Trans — Institution of Engineers of Australia.
    Mechanical Engineering Transactions
Inst Eng Aust Queensland Div Tech Pap — Institution of Engineers of
    Australia. Queensland Division. Technical Papers
Inst Eng Aust South Aust Div Bull — Institution of Engineers of Australia.
    South Australia Division. Bulletin
Inst Eng (Ceylon) Trans — Institution of Engineers (Ceylon). Transactions
Inst Engineers Aust J — Institution of Engineers of Australia. Journal
Inst Engrs Tas Bul — Institution of Engineers of Australia. Tasmanian
    Division. Bulletin
Inst Environ Sci Annu Tech Meet Proc — Institute of Environmental Sciences.
    Annual Technical Meeting. Proceedings
Inst Ernaehrungsforsch (Rueschlikon-Zuerich) Schriftenr — Institut fuer
    Ernaehrungsforschung (Rueschlikon-Zuerich). Schriftenreihe
Inst Esp Oceanogr Notas Resumenes — Instituto Espanol de Oceanografia.
    Notas y Resumenes
Inst Estate Plan — Institute on Estate Planning
Inst Ethmus Sel Repts — Institute of Ethnomusicology. Selected Reports
Inst Exp Invest Fom Agric Ganad (St Fe) Publ Tec — Instituto Experimental de
    Investigacion y Fomento Agricola-Ganadero (Santa Fe). Publicacion
    Tecnica
Inst Farb Lakierow Biul Inf — Instytut Farb i Lakierow. Biuletyn Informacyjny
Inst Fed Rech For Mem — Institut Federal de Recherches Forestieres.
    Memoires
Inst Ferment Res Commun (Osaka) — Institute for Fermentation Research
    Communications (Osaka)
Inst Fire Eng Q — Institution of Fire Engineers. Quarterly
Inst Fisico-Geog Nac Costa Rica An — Instituto Fisico-Geografico Nacional de
    Costa Rica. Anales
Inst Fiz At Rep (Rom) — Institutul de Fizica Atomica. Report (Romania)
Inst Fiz Ing Nucl Rep (Rom) — Institutul de Fizica si Inginerie Nucleara.
    Report (Romania)
Inst Florest Bol Tec (Sao Paulo) — Instituto Florestal. Boletim Tecnico (Sao
    Paulo)
Inst Florest Publ (Sao Paulo) — Instituto Florestal. Publicacao (Sao Paulo)
Inst Folk — Boletin. Instituto de Folklore
Inst Fom Algod (Bogota) — Instituto de Fomento Algodonero (Bogota)
Inst Fom Pesq Bol Cient — Instituto de Fomento Pesquero. Boletin Cientifico
Inst Fom Pesq Publ — Instituto de Fomento Pesquero. Publicacion
Inst Fondam Afr Noire Bull Ser A — Institut Fondamental d'Afrique Noire.
    Bulletin. Serie A. Sciences Naturelles [*Dakar*]
Inst For Aust Newslett — Institute of Foresters of Australia. Newsletter
Inst Foresters Aust Newsl — Institute of Foresters of Australia. Newsletter
Inst Foresters Aust Newslett — Institute of Foresters of Australia. Newsletter
Inst For Invest Exp Comun — Instituto Forestal de Investigaciones y
    Experiencias (Madrid). Comunicacion
Inst For Invest Exper (Madrid) An — Instituto Forestal de Investigaciones y
    Experiencias (Madrid). Anales
Inst For Invest Exper (Madrid) Bol — Instituto Forestal de Investigaciones y
    Experiencias (Madrid). Boletim
Inst For Invest Exper (Madrid) Comun — Instituto Forestal de Investigaciones y
    Experiencias (Madrid). Comunicacion
Inst For Invest Exper (Madrid) Trab — Instituto Forestal de Investigaciones y
    Experiencias (Madrid). Trabajos
Inst For Nac Foll Tec For — Instituto Forestal Nacional. Folleto Tecnico
    Forestal
Inst For Prod Colleg For Resour Univ Wash Contrib — Institute of Forest
    Products. College of Forest Resources. University of Washington.
    Contribution
Inst Forum — Institute Forum
Inst For Zool Res Notes — Institute of Forest Zoology. Research Notes
Inst Francais d'Haiti Mem — Institut Francais d'Haiti. Memoires
Inst Francais Petrole Rev — Institut Francais du Petrole. Revue et Annales des
    Combustible Liquides [*Later, Institut Francais du Petrole. Revue*]
Inst Fr Cafe Cacao Bull — Institut Francais du Cafe et du Cacao. Bulletin

Inst Freshwater Res (Drottningholm) Rep — Institute of Freshwater Research
    (Drottningholm). Report
Inst Freshw Res Drottningholm Rep — Institute of Freshwater Research
    (Drottningholm). Report
Inst Fr Etud Andines — Institut Francais d'Etudes Andines. Bulletin
Inst Fr Pet Rev — Institut Francais du Petrole. Revue et Annales des
    Combustible Liquides [*Later, Institut Francais du Petrole. Revue*]
Inst Fuel (London) Bull — Institute of Fuel (London). Bulletin
Inst Fuel (London) Wartime Bull — Institute of Fuel (London). Wartime
    Bulletin
Inst Fuel Symp Ser (London) — Institute of Fuel. Symposium Series (London)
Inst Gas Eng — Institution of Gas Engineers. Communications [*Finland*]
Inst Gas Eng Commun — Institution of Gas Engineers. Communications
Inst Gas Eng J — Institution of Gas Engineers. Journal
Inst Gas Technol (Chicago) Res Bull — Institute of Gas Technology (Chicago).
    Research Bulletin
Inst Gas Technol (Chicago) Tech Rep — Institute of Gas Technology (Chicago).
    Technical Report
Inst Gemol Esp Bol — Instituto Gemologico Espanol. Boletin
Inst Geofis Andes Colomb Publ Ser A — Instituto Geofisico de los Andes
    Colombianos. Publicacion. Serie A. Sismologia
Inst Geog Nac Bol Geol (Guatemala) — Instituto Geografico Nacional. Boletin
    Geologico (Guatemala)
Inst Geogr Geol Estado Sao Paulo Bol — Instituto Geografico e Geologico.
    Estado de Sao Paulo. Boletim
Inst Geogr Na (Guatem) Bol Geol — Instituto Geografico Nacional
    (Guatemala). Boletin Geologico
Inst Geol Bassin Aquitaine Bull — Institut de Geologie du Bassin d'Aquitaine.
    Bulletin
Inst Geol Bassin Aquitaine Mem — Institut de Geologie du Bassin d'Aquitaine.
    Memoires
Inst Geol Geofiz Stud Teh Econ Ser E — Institutul de Geologie si Geofizica.
    Studii Tehnice si Economice. Seria E. Hidrogeologie
Inst Geol Geofiz Stud Teh Econ Ser I — Institutul de Geologie si Geofizica.
    Studii Tehnice si Economice. Seria I. Mineralogie-Petrografie
Inst Geol Min Esp Mapa Geol Esp — Instituto Geologico y Minero de Espana.
    Mapa Geologico de Espana
Inst Geol Min Rev Univ Nac Tucuman — Instituto de Geologia y Mineria.
    Revista. Universidad Nacional de Tucuman
Inst Geol Sci Charles Univ Rep Res — Institute of Geological Science. Charles
    University. Report on Research
Inst Geol Sci (London) Rep — Institute of Geological Sciences (London).
    Report
Inst Geol Sci Rep — Institute of Geological Sciences. Report [*England*]
Inst Geol Stud Teh Econ Ser E — Institutul Geologic. Studii Tehnice si
    Economice. Seria E. Hidrogeologie
Inst Geol Stud Teh Econ Ser I — Institutul Geologic. Studii Tehnice si
    Economice. Seria I. Mineralogie-Petrografie
Inst Geol Urug Bol — Instituto Geologico del Uruguay. Boletin
Inst Geol (Warsaw) Pr — Instytut Geolgiczny (Warsaw). Prace
Inst Gerontol Ser — Institute of Gerontology Series
Inst Gezondheidstech TNO Rapp — Instituut voor Gezondheidstechniek TNO
    [*Toegepast-Natuurwetenschappelijk Onderzoek*]. Rapport
Inst Goryuch Iskop Tr — Institut Goryuchikh Iskopaemykh Trudy
Inst Grand Ducal Luxemb Sect Sci Nat Phys Math Arch — Institut Grand-
    Ducal de Luxembourg. Section des Sciences Naturelles. Physiques et
    Mathematiques. Archives
Inst Hautes Etudes Sci Publ Math — Institut des Hautes Etudes Scientifiques.
    Publications Mathematiques
Inst Hierro Acero (Madrid) Publ — Instituto del Hierro y del Acero (Madrid).
    Publicaciones
Inst Highw Engrs J — Institution of Highway Engineers. Journal
Inst Husdyrernaering Foringslaere Nor Landbrukshogsk Beret — Institutt foer
    Husdyrernaering og Foringslaere Norges Landbrukshogskole Beretning
Inst Hutn Pr — Instytutow Hutniczych. Prace
Inst Hydromech Wasserwirtsch Eidg Tech Hochsch Zuerich — Institut fuer
    Hydromechanik und Wasserwirtschaft. Eidgenoessische Technische
    Hochschule Zuerich
Inst Int Educ N Bul — Institute of International Education. News Bulletin
Inst Interam Nino Bol — Instituto Interamericano del Nino. Boletin
Inst Internat Admin Publique Bul — Bulletin. Institut International
    d'Administration Publique
Inst Interuniv Sci Nucl Monogr — Institut Interuniversitaire des Sciences
    Nucleaires. Monographie
Inst Interuniv Sci Nucl Rapp Annu — Institut Interuniversitaire des Sciences
    Nucleaires. Rapport Annuel
Inst Int Rech Better Congr Hiver CR — Institut International de Recherches
    Betteravieres. Congres d'Hiver. Compte Rendu
Inst Int Rech Better CR Definitif Assem — Institut International de Recherches
    Betteravieres. Compte Rendu Definitif de l'Assemblee
Inst Int Rech Better Rev — Institut International de Recherches Betteravieres.
    Revue
Inst Int Rel Proc — Institute of International Relations. Proceedings
Inst Int Stat R — Institut International de Statistique. Revue
Inst Invest — Institutional Investor

Inst Invest Agron (Angola) Ser Cient — Instituto de Investigacao Agronomica (Angola). Serie Cientifica

Inst Invest Agron (Angola) Ser Tec — Instituto de Investigacao Agronomica (Angola). Serie Tecnica

Inst Invest Agron (Mocambique) Ser Mem — Instituto de Investigacao Agronomica (Mocambique). Serie Memorias

Inst Invest Biomed Univ Nac Auton Mex Inf — Instituto de Investigaciones Biomedicas. Universidad Nacional Autonoma de Mexico. Informe

Inst Invest Cient (Angola) Relat Comun — Instituto de Investigacao Cientifica (Angola). Relatorios e Comunicacoes

Inst Investor — Institutional Investor

Inst Invest Recur Mar (Callao) Inf — Instituto de Investigacion de los Recursos Marinos (Callao). Informe

Inst Invst — Institutional Investor

Institutiones Math — Institutiones Mathematicae

Inst Jozef Stefan IJS Porocilo — Institut Jozef Stefan. IJS Porocilo

Inst Jozef Stefan IJS Rep — Institut Jozef Stefan. IJS Report

Inst Kerntech Tech Univ (Berlin) Ber — Institut fuer Kerntechnik der Technischen Universitaet (Berlin). Bericht

Inst Khim Akad Nauk Tadzh SSR Tr — Institut Khimii Akademiya Nauk Tadzhikskoi SSR Trudy

Inst Lake Super Geol Tech Sess Abstr Field Guides — Institute on Lake Superior Geology. Technical Sessions, Abstracts, and Field Guides

Inst Lekow Biul Inf — Instytut Lekow. Biuletyn Informacyjny

Inst Locomotive Eng J — Institution of Locomotive Engineers. Journal

Inst Mar Eng Annu Rep — Institute of Marine Engineers. Annual Report

Inst Mar Eng Annu Vol — Institute of Marine Engineers. Annual Volume

Inst Mar Eng Trans — Institute of Marine Engineers. Transactions

Inst Mar Eng Trans Ser C — Institute of Marine Engineers. Transactions. Series C

Inst Mar Environ Res Rep — Institute for Marine Environmental Research. Report

Inst Marine Sci Pub — Institute of Marine Science. Publications

Inst Mar Peru (Callao) Inf — Instituto del Mar del Peru (Callao). Informe

Inst Mar Res Lysekil Ser Biol Rep — Institute of Marine Research. Lysekil Series Biology Report

Inst Mar Sci Rep Univ Alaska — Institute of Marine Science. Report. University of Alaska

Inst Mater Modelos Estruct Bol Tec Univ Cent Venez — Instituto de Materiales y Modelos Estructurales. Boletin Tecnico. Universidad Central de Venezuela

Inst Mater Ogniotrwalych Biul Inf — Instytut Materialow Ogniotrwalych. Biuletyn Informacyjny

Inst Math Its Appl Bull — Institute of Mathematics and Its Applications. Bulletin

Inst Math Statist Bull — Institute of Mathematical Statistics. Bulletin

Inst Maurice Thorez Cah Hist — Cahiers d'Histoire. Institut Maurice Thorez

Inst Maurice Thorez Confs — Conferences. Institut Maurice Thorez

Inst Mech Eng J & Proc — Institution of Mechanical Engineers. Journal and Proceedings

Inst Mech Eng (Lond) Proc — Institution of Mechanical Engineers (London). Proceedings

Inst Mech Eng Proc — Institution of Mechanical Engineers. Proceedings

Inst Mech Eng Ry Div J — Institution of Mechanical Engineers. Railway Division. Journal [*London*]

Inst Mech Eng War Emerg Proc — Institution of Mechanical Engineers. War Emergency Proceedings

Inst Meh Moskov Gos Univ Naucn Trudy — Institut Mehaniki Moskovskogo Gosudarstvennogo Universiteta Naucnye Trudy

Inst M Eng Tr — Institution of Mining Engineers. Transactions

Inst Metall Autumn Rev Course Ser 3 (London) — Institution of Metallurgists. Autumn Review Course. Series 3 (London)

Inst Metall Course Vol Ser 3 (London) — Institution of Metallurgists. Course Volume. Series 3 (London)

Inst Metall Ser 3 (London) — Institution of Metallurgists. Series 3 (London)

Inst Metall Spring Resid Course Ser 3 (London) — Institution of Metallurgists. Spring Residential Course. Series 3 (London)

Inst Metall Tech Conf Pap (London) — Institute of Metallurgical Technicians. Conference Papers (London)

Inst Metals J — Institute of Metals. Journal

Inst Metal Zelaza Pr — Instytut Metalurgii Zelaza. Prace

Inst Meteorol Hidrol Culegere Lucr Meteorol — Institutul de Meteorologie si Hidrologie. Culegere de Lucrari de Meteorologie

Inst Meteorol Hidrol Stud Cercet Partea 1 — Institutul de Meteorologie si Hidrologie. Studii si Cercetari. Partea 1. Meteorologie

Inst Meteorol Hidrol Stud Cercet Partea 2 — Institutul de Meteorologie si Hidrologie. Studii si Cercetari. Partea 2. Hidrologie

Inst Met Monogr Rep Ser — Institute of Metals. Monograph and Report Series

Inst Met Niezelazn Biul — Instytut Metali Niezelaznych. Biuletyn

Inst Mex Minas Met Inf — Instituto Mexicano de Minas y Metalurgia. Informes y Memorias

Inst Mex Pet Publ — Instituto Mexicano del Petroleo. Publicacion

Inst Mex Petrol Rev — Institute Mexicano del Petroleo. Revista

Inst Mex Recur Nat Renov Ser Mesas Redondas — Instituto Mexicano de Recursos Naturales Renovables. Serie de Mesas Redondas

Inst Microbiol Rutgers Univ Annu Rep — Institute of Microbiology. Rutgers University. Annual Report

Inst Mine Petrosani Lucr Stiint — Institutul de Mine Petrosani. Lucrarile Stiintifice

Inst Mining Met Trans Sect B — Institution of Mining and Metallurgy. Transactions. Section B

Inst Min L — Institute on Mineral Law

Inst Min Metall Bull — Institution of Mining and Metallurgy. Bulletin

Inst Min Metall Trans Sect A — Institution of Mining and Metallurgy. Transactions. Section A. Mining Industry

Inst Min Metall Trans Sect A Min Ind — Institution of Mining and Metallurgy. Transactions. Section A. Mining Industry

Inst Min Metall Trans Sect B — Institution of Mining and Metallurgy. Transactions. Section B. Applied Earth Science

Inst Min Metall Trans Sect C — Institution of Mining and Metallurgy. Transactions. Section C. Mineral Processing and Extractive Metallurgy

Inst Min & Met Trans — Institution of Mining and Metallurgy. Transactions

Inst Min Miner Res Univ K Tech Rep — Institute for Mining and Mineral Research. University of Kentucky. Technical Report

Inst Munic Cienc Nat Misc Zool — Instituto Municipal de Ciencias Naturales Miscelanea. Zoologica

Inst Munic Engrs J — Institution of Municipal Engineers. Journal

Inst Munic Eng S Afr Dist Annu J — Institution of Municipal Engineers. South African District. Annual Journal

Inst Nac Carbon (Oviedo Spain) Bol Inf — Instituto Nacional del Carbon (Oviedo, Spain). Boletin Informativo

Inst Nac Carbon Sus Deriv "Francisco Pintado Fe" Publ INCAR — Instituto Nacional del Carbon y Sus Derivados "Francisco Pintado Fe." Publicacion INCAR

Inst Nac Conserv Nat Estac Cent Ecol Bol (Spain) — Instituto Nacional para la Conservacion de la Natureleza. Estacion Central de Ecologia. Boletin (Spain)

Inst Nac Invest Agrar Comun Ser Prot Veg (Spain) — Instituto Nacional de Investigaciones Agrarias. Comunicaciones. Serie: Proteccion Vegetal (Spain)

Inst Nac Invest Agric SAG (Mex) Foll Tec — Instituto Nacional de Investigaciones Agricolas. Secretaria de Agricultura y Ganaderia (Mexico). Folleto Tecnico

Inst Nac Invest Agric Secr Agric Ganad (Mex) Foll Tec — Instituto Nacional de Investigaciones Agricolas. Secretaria de Agricultura y Ganaderia (Mexico). Folleto Tecnico

Inst Nac Invest Agron Bol — Instituto Nacional de Investigaciones Agronomicas. Boletin [*Spain*]

Inst Nac Invest Agron (Madr) Conf — Instituto Nacional de Investigaciones Agronomicas (Madrid). Conferencias

Inst Nac Invest Agron (Spain) Cuad — Instituto Nacional de Investigaciones Agronomicas (Spain). Cuaderno

Inst Nac Invest Fom Min (Peru) Ser Memo — Instituto Nacional de Investigacion y Fomento Mineros (Peru). Serie Memorandum

Inst Nac Med Leg Colomb Rev — Instituto Nacional de Medicina Legal de Colombia. Revista

Inst Nac Nutr Caracas Publ — Instituto Nacional de Nutricion. Caracas. Publicacion

Inst Nac Pesca Bol Cient Tec — Instituto Nacional de Pesca. Boletin Cientifico y Tecnico

Inst Nac Pesca (Cuba) Cent Invest Pesq Bol Divulg Tec — Instituto Nacional de la Pesca (Cuba). Centro de Investigaciones Pesqueras. Boletin de Divulgacion Tecnica

Inst Nac Pesca Cuba Cent Invest Pesq Contrib — Instituto Nacional de la Pesca. Cuba. Centro de Investigaciones Pesqueras. Contribucion

Inst Nac Pesca (Ecuador) Bol Inf — Instituto Nacional de Pesca (Ecuador). Boletin Informativo

Inst Nac Pesqui Amazonia Publ Quim — Instituto Nacional de Pesqui Amazonia. Publicacao Quimica

Inst Nac Tecnol Agropecu Bol Inf — Instituto Nacional de Tecnologia Agropecuaria. Boletin Informativo

Inst Nac Tecnol Agropecu Suelos Publ — Instituto Nacional de Tecnologia Agropecuaria. Suelos Publicacion

Inst Napoleon R — Institut Napoleon. Revue

Inst Nat Amelior Conserves Legumes Bull Trimest (Belg) — Institut National pour l'Amelioration des Conserves de Legumes. Bulletin Trimestriel (Belgium)

Inst Nat Ind Charbonniere Bull Tech-Mines — Institut National de l'Industrie Charbonniere. Bulletin Technique - Mines

Inst Nat Ind Extr Bull Tech-Mines Carrieres — Institut National des Industries Extractives. Bulletin Technique. Mines et Carrieres [*Liege*]

Inst Natl Amelior Conserves Legumes Bull Bimest (Belg) — Institut National pour l'Amelioration des Conserves de Legumes. Bulletin Bimestriel (Belgium)

Inst Natl Genevois Bull — Institut National Genevois. Bulletin

Inst Natl Genevois Bull NS — Institut National Genevois. Bulletin. New Series

Inst Natl Ind Extr (Liege) Bull Tech Mines Carriere — Institut National des Industries Extractives (Liege). Bulletin Technique. Mines et Carrieres

Inst Natl Radioelem (Belg) Rapp — Institut National des Radioelements (Belgium). Rapport

Inst Natl Rech Agron Serv Ind Agric Aliment — Institut National de la Recherche Agronomique au Service des Industries Agricoles et Alimentaires

Inst Natl Rech Agron Tunisie Doc Tech — Institut National de la Recherche Agronomique de Tunisie. Documents Techniques

Inst Natl Rech Agron Tunisie Lab Arboric Fruit Rapp Act — Institut National de la Recherche Agronomique de Tunisie. Laboratoire d'Arboriculture Fruitiere. Rapport d'Activite

Inst Natl Rech Agron Tunis Lab Aboriculture Fruit Rapp Act — Institut National de la Recherche Agronomique de Tunisie. Laboratoire d'Arboriculture Fruitiere. Rapport d'Activite

Inst Nat Rech Agron (Paris) — Institut National de la Recherche Agronomique (Paris)

Inst Nat Rech Agron Tunisie — Institut National de la Recherche Agronomique de Tunisie

Inst Nat Sci Nanyang Univ Tech Rep — Institute of Natural Sciences. Nanyang University. Technical Report

Inst Neorg Khim Elektrokhim Akad Nauk Gruz SSR Sb — Institut Neorganicheskoi Khimii i Elektrokhimii Akademiya Nauk Gruzinskoi SSR Sbornik

Inst Nisk Temp Badan Strukt PAN Pr Ser Pr Kom Krystalogr — Instytut Niskich Temperatur i Badan Strukturalnych PAN Prace. Seria. Prace Komitetu Krystalografii

Inst N L — Instituto Nacional do Livro

Inst Nucl Phys (Cracow) Rep — Institute of Nuclear Physics (Cracow). Report

Inst Nucl Res (Warsaw) Rep — Institute of Nuclear Research (Warsaw). Report

Inst Nucl Study Univ Tokyo Rep — Institute for Nuclear Study. University of Tokyo. Reports

Inst Oceanogr Ann — Institut Oceanographique. Annales

Inst Oceanogr Nha Trang — Institut Oceanographique de Nha Trang

Inst Oceanogr Ribar Split Biljeske — Institut za Oceanografiju i Ribarstvo Split Biljeske

Inst Oil & Gas L & Taxation — Institute on Oil and Gas Law and Taxation

Inst Orientac Asist Tec Oeste Anu — Instituto de Orientacion y Asistencia Tecnica del Oeste. Anuario

Inst Parcs Nationaux Congo Belge Explor Parc Natl Albert — Institut des Parcs Nationaux du Congo Belge. Exploration du Parc National Albert

Inst Parcs Nationaux Congo Explor Parc Natl Albert — Institut des Parcs Nationaux du Congo Belge. Exploration du Parc National Albert

Inst Pasteur Bangui Rapp Annu — Institut Pasteur Bangui. Rapport Annuel

Inst Pasteur Repub Unie Cameroun Rapp Fonct Tech — Institut Pasteur de la Republique Unie du Cameroun. Rapport sur le Fonctionnement Technique

Inst Pathol Ig Anim Colect Indrumari (Buchar) — Institutul de Pathologie si Igiena Animala. Colectia Indrumari (Bucharest)

Inst Pathol Ig Anim Probl Epizootol Vet (Buchar) — Institutul de Pathologie si Igiena Animala. Probleme de Epizootologie Veterinara (Bucharest)

Inst Personnel Mgmt Dig — Institute of Personnel Management. Digest

Inst Pesqui Agron Pernambuco Bol Tec — Instituto de Pesquisas Agronomicas de Pernambuco. Boletim Tecnico

Inst Pesqui Agron Pernambuco Circ — Instituto de Pesquisas Agronomicas de Pernambuco. Circular

Inst Pesqui Agron Pernambuco Publ — Instituto de Pesquisas Agronomicas de Pernambuco. Publicacao

Inst Pesqui Agron (Recife) Bol Tec — Instituto de Pesquisas Agronimicas (Recife). Boletim Tecnico

Inst Pesqui Agropecu Norte Bol Tec — Instituto de Pesquisas Agropecuarias do Norte. Boletim Tecnico

Inst Pesqui Agropecu Norte (IPEAN) Ser Fitotec — Instituto de Pesquisas e Experimentacao Agropecuarias do Norte (IPEAN). Serie Fitotecnia

Inst Pesqui Agropecu Sul Bol Tec — Instituto de Pesquisas Agropecuarias do Sul. Boletim Tecnico

Inst Pesqui Exp Agropecu Norte (Belem) Bol Tec — Instituto de Pesquisas e Experimentacao Agropecuarias do Norte (Belem). Boletim Tecnico

Inst Pesqui Exp Agropecu Norte (IPEAN) (Belem) Bol Tec — Instituto de Pesquisas e Experimentacao Agropecuarias do Norte (IPEAN) (Belem). Boletim Tecnico

Inst Pesqui Exp Agropecu Norte (IPEAN) Ser Bot Fisiol Veg — Instituto de Pesquisas e Experimentacao Agropecuarias do Norte (IPEAN). Serie Botanica e Fisiologia Vegetal

Inst Pesqui Exp Agropecu Norte (IPEAN) Ser Cult Amazonia — Instituto de Pesquisas e Experimentacao Agropecuarias do Norte (IPEAN). Serie Culturas da Amazonia

Inst Pesqui Exp Agropecu Norte (IPEAN) Ser Estud Bovinos — Instituto de Pesquisas e Experimentacao Agropecuarias do Norte (IPEAN). Serie Estudos sobre Bovinos

Inst Pesqui Exp Agropecu Norte (IPEAN) Ser Estud Bubalinos — Instituto de Pesquisas e Experimentacao Agropecuarias do Norte (IPEAN). Serie Estudos sobre Bubalinos

Inst Pesqui Exp Agropecu Norte (IPEAN) Ser Estud Ens — Instituto de Pesquisas e Experimentacao Agropecuarias do Norte (IPEAN). Serie Estudos e Ensaios

Inst Pesqui Exp Agropecu Norte (IPEAN) Ser Estud Ensaios — Instituto de Pesquisas e Experimentacao Agropecuarias do Norte (IPEAN). Serie Estudos e Ensaios

Inst Pesqui Exp Agropecu Norte (IPEAN) Ser Fertil Solos — Instituto de Pesquisas e Experimentacao Agropecuarias do Norte (IPEAN). Serie Fertilidade de Solos

Inst Pesqui Exp Agropecu Norte (IPEAN) Ser Fitotec — Instituto de Pesquisas e Experimentacao Agropecuarias do Norte (IPEAN). Serie Fitotecnia

Inst Pesqui Exp Agropecu Norte (IPEAN) Ser Quim Solos — Instituto de Pesquisas e Experimentacao Agropecuarias do Norte (IPEAN). Serie Quimica de Solos

Inst Pesqui Exp Agropecu Norte (IPEAN) Ser Solos Amazonia — Instituto de Pesquisas e Experimentacao Agropecuarias do Norte (IPEAN). Serie Solos da Amazonia

Inst Pesqui Exp Agropecu Norte (IPEAN) Ser Tecnol — Instituto de Pesquisas e Experimentacao Agropecuarias do Norte (IPEAN). Serie Tecnologia

Inst Pesqui Exp Agropecu Norte Ser Bot Fisiol Veg — Instituto de Pesquisas e Experimentacao Agropecuarias do Norte. Serie Botanica e Fisiologia Vegetal

Inst Pesqui Exp Agropecu Norte Ser Cult Amazonia — Instituto de Pesquisas e Experimentacao Agropecuarias do Norte. Serie Culturas da Amazonia

Inst Pesqui Exp Agropecu Norte Ser Estud Bovinos — Instituto de Pesquisas e Experimentacao Agropecuarias do Norte. Serie Estudos sobre Bovinos

Inst Pesqui Exp Agropecu Norte Ser Estud Bubalinos — Instituto de Pesquisas e Experimentacao Agropecuarias do Norte. Serie Estudos sobre Bubalinos

Inst Pesqui Exp Agropecu Norte Ser Estud Ens — Instituto de Pesquisas e Experimentacao Agropecuarias do Norte. Serie Estudos e Ensaios

Inst Pesqui Exp Agropecu Norte Ser Fertil Solos — Instituto de Pesquisas e Experimentacao Agropecuarias do Norte. Serie Fertilidade do Solos

Inst Pesqui Exp Agropecu Norte Ser Fitotec — Instituto de Pesquisas e Experimentacao Agropecuarias do Norte. Serie Fitotecnia

Inst Pesqui Exp Agropecu Norte Ser Quim Solos — Instituto de Pesquisas e Experimentacao Agropecuarias do Norte. Serie Quimica de Solos

Inst Pesqui Exp Agropecu Norte Ser Solos Amazonia — Instituto de Pesquisas e Experimentacao Agropecuarias do Norte. Serie Solos da Amazonia

Inst Pesqui Exp Agropecu Norte Ser Tecnol — Instituto de Pesquisas e Experimentacao Agropecuarias do Norte. Serie Tecnologia

Inst Pesqui Exp Agropecu Sul Circ — Instituto de Pesquisas e Experimentacao Agropecuarias do Sul. Circular

Inst Pesqui Tecnol (Sao Paulo) Boletim — Instituto de Pesquisas Tecnologicas (Sao Paulo). Boletim

Inst Pesqui Tecnol (Sao Paulo) Publ — Instituto de Pesquisas Tecnologicas (Sao Paulo). Publicacao

Inst Pet Abstr — Institute of Petroleum. Abstracts

Inst Pet Gaze Bucuresti Stud — Institutul de Petrol si Gaze din Bucuresti. Studii

Inst Pet J — Institute of Petroleum. Journal

Inst Pet (Lond) Pap — Institute of Petroleum (London). Papers

Inst Petroleum Rev — Institute of Petroleum. Review

Inst Petroleum Tech J — Institution of Petroleum Technologists. Journal

Inst Petrol Tech Pap — Institute of Petroleum. Technical Papers

Inst Pet Tech Pap IP — Institute of Petroleum. Technical Paper. IP

Inst Phonet Rep — Institute of Phonetics. Report

Inst Phys Chem Res Rikagaku Kenkyusho Sci Pap — Institute of Physical and Chemical Research. Rikagaku Kenkyusho. Scientific Papers

Inst Phys Conf Dig — Institute of Physics. Conference Digest

Inst Phys Conf Ser — Institute of Physics. Conference Series

Inst Phys Nucl Eng Rep (Rom) — Institute for Physics and Nuclear Engineering Report (Romania)

Inst Phytopathol Res Annu Rep — Institute of Phytopathology Research. Annual Report

Inst Plant Eng J — Institution of Plant Engineers. Journal [*England*]

Inst on Plan Zon and Eminent Domain Proc — Institute on Planning, Zoning, and Eminent Domain. Proceedings

Inst Pluimveeonderz "Het Spelderholt" Jaarversl — Instituut voor Pluimveeonderzoek "Het Spelderholt". Jaarverslag

Inst Pluimveeonderz "Het Spelderholt" Meded — Instituut voor Pluimveeonderzoek "Het Spelderholt". Mededeling

Inst Politeh Gheorghe Gheorghiu Dej Bucuresti Bul Ser Chim — Institutul Politehnic "Gheorghe Gheorghiu-Dej" Bucuresti. Buletinul. Seria Chimie

Inst Politeh Gheorghe Gheorghiu Dej Bucuresti Bul Ser Mec — Institutul Politehnic "Gheorghe Gheorghiu-Dej" Bucuresti. Buletinul. Seria Mecanica

Inst Politeh Iasi Bul Sect 1 — Institutul Politehnic din Iasi. Buletinul. Sectia 1. Matematica, Mecanica Teoretica, Fizica [*Romania*]

Inst Politeh Iasi Bul Sect 5 — Institutul Politehnic din Iasi. Buletinul. Sectia 5. Constructii-Arhitectura

Inst Politeh Traian Vuia Semin Mat Fiz Lucr — Institutul Politehnic "Traian Vuia". Seminarul di Matematica si Fizica. Lucrarile

Inst Post Office Elec Eng Paper — Institution of Post Office Electrical Engineers. Paper

Inst Printed Circuits Tech Rep — Institute of Printed Circuits. Technical Report

Inst Private Investments — Institute on Private Investments Abroad and Foreign Trade

Inst on Priv Invest and Investors Abroad Proc — Institute on Private Investments and Investors Abroad. Proceedings

Inst Prof Librn Ont Newsl — Institute of Professional Librarians of Ontario. Newsletter

Inst Prov Agropecuar (Mendoza) Bol Tec — Instituto Provincial Agropecuario (Mendoza). Boletin Tecnica

Inst Prov Paleontol Sabadell Bol Inf — Instituto Provincial de Paleontologia de Sabadell. Boletin Informativo

Inst Przem Org Pr — Instytut Przemyslu Organicznego. Prace

Inst Przem Tworzyw Farb Biul Inf — Instytut Przemyslu Tworzyw i Farb. Biuletyn Informacyjny

Inst Przem Wiazacych Mater Budow Krakow Biul Inf — Instytut Przemyslu Wiazacych Materialow Budowlanych. Krakow. Biuletyn Informacyjny

Inst Psychiatry Maudsley Monogr — Institute of Psychiatry. Maudsley Monographs

Inst Public Serv Vocat Train Bull — Institute for Public Service and Vocational Training. Bulletin

Inst Quim Agric (Rio De Janeiro) Mem — Instituto de Quimica Agricola (Rio De Janeiro). Memoria

Inst Quim Apl Farm (Lima) Bol Inf — Instituto de Quimica Aplicada a la Farmacia (Lima). Boletim Informativo

Instr — Instructor

Inst Radio Electron Eng (Aust) Proc — Institution of Radio and Electronics Engineers of Australia. Proceedings

Inst Radio & Electron Engrs Aust Proc — Institution of Radio and Electronics Engineers of Australia. Proceedings

Inst Radio Eng Proc — Institute of Radio Engineers. Proceedings

Instr & Autom — Instruments and Automation

Inst R Colon Belge Bull Seances — Institut Royal Colonial Belge. Bulletin des Seances

Inst R Colon Belge Sect Sci Nat Med Mem Collect 4o — Institut Royal Colonial Belge. Section des Sciences Naturelles et Medicales. Memoires. Collection in Quarto

Instr Contr — Instruments and Control Systems

Instr Course Lect — Instructional Course Lectures

Inst Rech Caoutch Viet Nam Arch — Institut des Recherches sur le Caoutchouc au Viet-Nam. Archive

Inst Rech Caoutch Viet Nam Laikhe Rapp Annu — Institut des Recherches sur le Caoutchouc au Viet-Nam Laikhe. Rapports Annuels

Inst Rech Entomol Phytopathol Evine Dep Bot — Institut de Recherches Entomologiques et Phytopathologiques d'Evine. Departement de Botanique

Inst Rech Huiles Oleagineux (IRHO) Rapp Annu — Institut de Recherches pour les Huiles et Oleagineux (IRHO). Rapport Annuel

Inst Rech Huiles Ol Rapp Annu — Institut de Recherches pour les Huiles et Oleagineux [*IRHO*]. Rapport Annuel

Inst Rech Ressour Hydraul (Budapest) Commun Lang Etrang — Institut de Recherches des Ressources Hydrauliques (Budapest). Communications en Langues Etrangeres

Inst Res Ment Retard Monogr (Oxford) — Institute for Research into Mental Retardation. Monograph (Oxford)

Inst Res Ment Retard (Oxford) Symp — Institute for Research into Mental Retardation (Oxford). Symposium

Instr Exp Techn — Instruments and Experimental Techniques

Inst Ribni Resur (Varna) Izv — Institut po Ribni Resursi (Varna). Izvestiya

Instr Innov — Instructional Innovator

Instr Innovator — Instructional Innovator

Inst R Meteorol Belg Bull Trimest Obs Ozone — Institut Royal Meteorologique de Belgique. Bulletin Trimestriel. Observations d'Ozone

Instrn Technol — Instrumentation Technology

Inst Roy Sci Natur Belgique Bul — Institut Royal des Sciences Naturelles de Belgique. Bulletin

Instr Sci — Instructional Science

Inst R Sci Nat Belg Bull — Institut Royal des Sciences Naturelles de Belgique. Bulletin

Inst R Sci Nat Belg Bull Sci Terre — Institut Royal des Sciences Naturelles de Belgique. Bulletin. Sciences de la Terre

Inst R Sci Nat Belg Doc Trav — Institut Royal des Sciences Naturelles de Belgique. Documents de Travail

Inst R Sci Nat Belg Mem — Institut Royal des Sciences Naturelles de Belgique. Memoires

Inst R Sci Nat Belg Mem Deuxieme Ser — Institut Royal des Sciences Naturelles de Belgique. Memoires. Deuxieme Serie

Instr Sh Cent Exp Fm (Ottawa) — Instruction Sheet. Central Experimental Farm (Ottawa)

Instr Tech — Instrumentation Technology

Instrum Abstr — Instrument Abstracts

Instrum Aerosp Ind — Instrumentation in the Aerospace Industry

Instrum Autom — Instrumentation and Automation

Instrum Automat — Instruments and Automation

Instrum Bull — Instrumentation Bulletin

Instrum Chem Pet Ind — Instrumentation in the Chemical and Petroleum Industries

Instrum Constr (USSR) — Instrument Construction (USSR)

Instrum Control Engng — Instrument and Control Engineering

Instrum and Control Syst — Instruments and Control Systems

Instrum Control Syst — Instruments and Control Systems

Instrum Contr Syst — Instruments and Control Systems

Instrum Cryog Ind — Instrumentation in the Cryogenic Industry

Instrum Electr Dev — Instruments and Electronics Developments

Instrum Eng — Instrument Engineer

Instrument — Instrumentalist

Instrumentation Tech — Instrumentation Technology

Instrumentenbau Z — Instrumentenbau-Zeitschrift

Instrum Exp Tech — Instruments and Experimental Techniques

Instrum and Exp Tech — Instruments and Experimental Techniques

Instrum Food Beverage Ind — Instrumentation in the Food and Beverage Industry

Instrum Forsch — Instrument und Forschung

Instrum India — Instruments India

Instrum Iron Steel Ind — Instrumentation in the Iron and Steel Industry

Instrum Lab — Instruments et Laboratoires

Instrum Maint Manage — Instrument Maintenance Management

Instrum Maker — Instrument Maker

Instrum Manuf — Instrument Manufacturing

Instrum Med — Instrumentation in Medicine [*England*]

Instrum Met Ind — Instrumentation in the Metals Industries

Instrum Min Metall Ind — Instrumentation in the Mining and Metallurgy Industries

Instrum News — Instrument News

Instrum Nucl — Instrumentation Nucleaire [*France*]

Instrum Power Ind — Instrumentation in the Power Industry

Instrum Pract — Instrument Practice

Instrum Pulp Pap Ind — Instrumentation in the Pulp and Paper Industry [*United States*]

Instrum Rev — Instrument Review [*England*]

Instrum Rev (Leiden) — Instrument Revue (Leiden)

Instrum Soc Amer Conf Preprint — Instrument Society of America. Conference Preprint

Instrum Soc Am Instrum Index — Instrument Society of America. Instrumentation Index

Instrum Soc India J — Instrument Society of India. Journal

Instrum Tech — Instrumentation Technology

Instrum Technol — Instrumentation Technology

Instrum Test Rep Bur Meteor — Instrumentation Test Report. Bureau of Meteorology

Inst Sci Agron Burundi (ISABU) Rapp Annu Notes Annexes — Institut des Sciences Agronomiques du Burundi (ISABU). Rapport Annuel et Notes Annexes

Inst Sci Cherifien Trav Ser Gen — Institut Scientifique Cherifien. Travaux. Serie Generale

Inst Sci Cherifien Trav Ser Sci Phys — Institut Scientifique Cherifien. Travaux. Serie Sciences Physiques

Inst Sci Mag — Institute of Science Magazine

Inst on Sec Reg — Institute on Securities Regulation

Inst Securities Reg — Institute on Securities Regulation

Inst Skoglig Mat Stat Rapp Uppsatser — Institutionen foer Skoglig Matematisk Statistik Rapporter och Uppsatser

Inst Skogsforyngring Rapp Uppsatser — Institutionen foer Skogsforyngring Rapporter och Uppsatser

Inst Skogszool Rapp Uppsatser — Institutionen foer Skogszoologi Rapporter och Uppsatser

Inst Social Science (Tokyo) Annals — Annals. Institute of Social Sciences (Tokyo)

Inst Sociol R — Revue. Institut de Sociologie

Inst Sound Vib — Institute of Sound and Vibration

Inst Space Aeronaut Sci Univ Tokyo Rep — Institute of Space and Aeronautical Science. University of Tokyo. Report

Inst Stud Proiect Energ Bul — Institutul de Studii si Proiectari Energetice. Buletinul [*Romania*]

Inst Suisse Rech For Mem — Institut Suisse de Recherches Forestieres. Memoires

Inst Tech Batim Trav Pub Ann — Institut Technique du Batiment et des Travaux Publics. Annales

Inst Technol Mater Elektron Pr — Instytut Technologii Materialow Elektronicznych. Prace

Inst Tec Monterrey Div Cienc Agropecu Marit Inf Invest — Instituto Tecnologico de Monterrey. Division de Ciencias Agropecuarias y Maritimas. Informe de Investigacion

Inst Tecnol Estud Super Monterrey Dep Quim Bol — Instituto Tecnologico y de Estudios Superiores de Monterrey. Departamento de Quimica. Boletin

Inst Tecnol Ind Estado Minas Gerais Avulso — Instituto de Tecnologia Industrial. Estado de Minas Gerais. Avulso

Inst Tecnol Ind Estado Minas Gerais Boletim — Instituto de Tecnologia Industrial. Estado de Minas Gerais. Boletim

Inst Tecnol Monterrey Div Cien Agropecu Marit Inf Invest — Instituto Tecnologico de Monterrey. Division de Ciencias Agropecuarias y Maritimas. Informe de Investigacion

Inst Tecnol Rio Grande Sul Bol — Instituto Tecnologico do Rio Grande Do Sul. Boletim

Inst Text Faserforsch Stuttgart Ber — Institut fuer Textil- und Faserforschung. Stuttgart. Berichte

Inst Text Fr Nord Bull Inf — Institut Textile de France-Nord. Bulletin d'Information

Inst Toegepast Biol Onderzoek Meded — Instituut voor Toegepast Biologisch Onderzoek in de Natuur [*Institute for Biological Field Research*]. Mededeling

Inst Tsvetna Metal Plovdiv God — Institut po Tsvetna Metalurgiya. Plovdiv. Godishnik

Inst Verkstadstek Forsk IVF Resultat — Institutet fuer Verkstadsteknisk Forskning. IVF Resultat

Inst Vitreous Enamellers Bull — Institute of Vitreous Enamellers. Bulletin

Inst Vol Feed — Institutions/Volume Feeding

Inst/Vol Feeding Mgt — Institutions/Volume Feeding Management [*Later, Institutions/Volume Feeding*]

Inst Water Eng J — Institution of Water Engineers. Journal [*Later, Institution of Water Engineers and Scientists. Journal*]

Inst Water Eng Sci J — Institution of Water Engineers and Scientists. Journal [*Formerly, Institution of Water Engineers. Journal*]

Inst World Affairs Proc — Institute of World Affairs. Proceedings

Inst Zast Bilja Posebna Izd — Institut za Zastitu Bilja. Posebna Izdanja

Inst Zool Parazitol Akad Nauk Tadzh SSR Tr — Institut Zoologii i Parazitologii Akademiya Nauk Tadzhikskoi SSR Trudy

Inst Zootec (Sao Paulo) Bol Tec — Instituto de Zootecnia (Sao Paulo). Boletim Tecnico

Insul — Insulana

Insul — Insulation

Insulation J — Insulation Journal

Insulatn — Insulation

Insul/Circuits — Insulation/Circuits

Insurance D — Insurance Decisions

Insur Couns J — Insurance Counsel Journal

Insur Law J — Insurance Law Journal

Insur Lines — Insurance Lines

Insur LJ — Insurance Law Journal

INT — International Science Fiction

INT — International Textiles

Int — Interpretation. A Journal of Bible and Theology [*Richmond, VA*]

Int — Interpreter

Int A Aller — International Archives of Allergy and Applied Immunology

Int Abstr Biol Sci — International Abstracts of Biological Sciences

Int Abstr Oper Res — International Abstracts in Operations Research

Int Abstr Surg — International Abstracts of Surgery

Int Acad Pathol Monogr — International Academy of Pathology. Monograph

Int Advertiser — International Advertiser

Int Adv Nondestr Test — International Advances in Nondestructive Testing

Int Adv Surg Oncol — International Advances in Surgical Oncology

IntAe — International Aerospace Abstracts

INTA Estac Exp Manfredi Inf Tec — INTA [*Instituto Nacional de Tecnologia Agropecuaria*]. Estacion Experimental Manfredi. Informacion Tecnica

INTA Estac Exp Reg Agropecu (Parana) Ser Tec — INTA [*Instituto Nacional de Tecnologia Agropecuaria*]. Estacion Experimental Regional Agropecuaria (Parana). Serie Tecnica

INTA Estac Exp Reg Agropecu Pergamino Inf Tec — INTA [*Instituto Nacional de Tecnologia Agropecuaria*]. Estacion Experimental Regional Agropecuaria (Pergamino). Informe Tecnico

INTA Estac Exp Reg Agropecu Pergamino Publ Tec — INTA [*Instituto Nacional de Tecnologia Agropecuaria*]. Estacion Experimental Regional Agropecuaria (Pergamino). Publicacion Tecnica

Int Aff — International Affairs

Int Affairs — International Affairs [*England*]

Int Aff Bull — International Affairs. Bulletin

Int Aff (London) — International Affairs (London)

Int Aff Stud — International Affairs. Studies

Int Afr Forum — Internationales Afrikaforum

Int Agency Res Cancer Monogr Eval Carcinog Risk Chem Man — International Agency for Research on Cancer. Monographs on the Evaluation of Carcinogenic Risk of Chemicals to Man

INTA (Inst Nac Tecnol Agropecu) Ser Tec — INTA (Instituto Nacional de Tecnologia Agropecuaria). Serie Tecnia

Intam Inst Mus Res — Inter-American Institute for Musical Research. Yearbook

Int-Am L Rev — Inter-American Law Review

Intam Mus B — Boletin Interamericano de Musica/Inter-American Music Bulletin

Intam Mus B (Eng Ed) — Inter-American Music Bulletin (English Edition)

Intam Mus R — Inter-American Music Review

Intam Mus Res Yrbk — Inter-American Musical Research. Yearbook

Int Anesthesiol Clin — International Anesthesiology Clinics

Int A Occup — International Archives of Occupational and Environmental Health

Int Arch Allergy Appl Immunol — International Archives of Allergy and Applied Immunology

Int Arch Arbeitsmed — Internationales Archiv fuer Arbeitsmedizin

Int Arch Arbeits-Umweltmed — Internationales Archiv fuer Arbeits- und Umweltmedizin

Int Arch Gewerbepathol Gewerbehyg — Internationales Archiv fuer Gewerbepathologie und Gewerbehygiene

Int Archit — International Architect

Int Archiv Ethnog — Internationales Archiv fuer Ethnographie

Int Arch Occup Environ Health — International Archives of Occupational and Environmental Health

Int Arch Occup Health — International Archives of Occupational Health [*Later, International Archives of Occupational and Environmental Health*]

Int Arch Photogramm — International Archives of Photogrammetry

Int Archs Allergy Appl Immun — International Archives of Allergy and Applied Immunology

Int As For — Internationales Asienforum

Int Asienf — Internationales Asienforum

Int Asien Forum — Internationales Asienforum

Int Ass — International Association

Int Ass Bridge Struct Eng Publ — International Association for Bridge and Structural Engineering. Publications

Int Assoc/Assoc Int — International Associations/Associations Internationales

Int Assoc Dairy Milk Insp Annu Rep — International Association of Dairy and Milk Inspectors. Annual Report

Int Assoc Dent Child J — International Association of Dentistry for Children. Journal

Int Assoc Eng Geol Bull — International Association of Engineering Geology. Bulletin

Int Assoc Hydraul Res Congr Proc — International Association for Hydraulic Research. Congress. Proceedings

Int Assoc Hydrogeol Mem — International Association of Hydrogeologists. Memoirs

Int Assoc Hydrol Sci Assoc Int Sci Hydrol Publ — International Association of Hydrological Sciences - Association Internationale des Sciences Hydrologiques. Publication

Int Assoc Hydrol Sci Hydrol Sci Bull — International Association of Hydrological Sciences. Hydrological Sciences Bulletin

Int Assoc Hydrol Sci Publ — International Association of Hydrological Sciences. Publication

Int Assoc Math Geol J — International Association for Mathematical Geology. Journal

Int Assoc Sci Hydrol Bull — International Association of Scientific Hydrology. Bulletin

Int Assoc Theor Appl Limnol Commun — International Association of Theoretical and Applied Limnology. Communication [*West Germany*]

Int Assoc Theor Appl Limnol Proc — International Association of Theoretical and Applied Limnology. Proceedings

Int Assoc Volcanol Chem Earth's Inter Spe Ser — International Association of Volcanology and Chemistry of the Earth's Interior. Special Series

Int Assoc Wood Anat Bull — International Association of Wood Anatomists. Bulletin

Int Astronaut Congr Proc — International Astronautical Congress. Proceedings

Int Astron Union Symp — International Astronomical Union. Symposium

Int At Energy Ag Bibliogr Ser — International Atomic Energy Agency. Bibliographical Series

Int At Energy Agency Bull — International Atomic Energy Agency. Bulletin

Int At Energy Agency Saf Ser — International Atomic Energy Agency. Safety Series

Int At Energy Agency Tech Rep Ser — International Atomic Energy Agency. Technical Report Series

Int At Energy Ag Proc Ser — International Atomic Energy Agency. Proceedings Series

Int Atl Salmon Found Spec Publ Ser — International Atlantic Salmon Foundation. Special Publication Series

Int Aud — Internal Auditor

Int Auditor — Internal Auditor

Int Bauxite Assoc Q Rev — International Bauxite Association. Quarterly Review

INTBEB — Interferon y Biotecnologia

Int Beekeep Congr Prelim Sci Meet — International Beekeeping Congress. Preliminary Scientific Meeting

Int Beekeep Congr Summ Suppl — International Beekeeping Congress. Summaries Supplement

Int Behav Scientist — International Behavioural Scientist

Int Bergwirtsch Bergtech — Internationale Bergwirtschaft und Bergtechnik

Int Bibl Soc Sci — International Bibliography of the Social Sciences

Int Biod B — International Biodeterioration Bulletin

Int Biodeterior Bull — International Biodeterioration Bulletin

Int Biol Programme — International Biological Programme Series

Int Biol Programme Handb — International Biological Programme. Handbook

Int B Miss R — International Bulletin of Missionary Research

Int Bot Congr Recent Advan Bot — International Botanical Congress. Recent Advances in Botany

Int Brain Res Organ Monogr Ser — International Brain Research Organization. Monograph Series

Int Broadcast Eng — International Broadcast Engineer

Int Broadcast Syst and Oper — International Broadcasting Systems and Operation

Int Broadc Engr — International Broadcast Engineer

Int Build Serv Abstr — International Building Services Abstracts

Int Bull Bacteriol Nomencl Taxon — International Bulletin of Bacteriological Nomenclature and Taxonomy

Int Bull Res E Eur — International Bulletin for Research on Law in Eastern Europe
Int Bur Ed B — International Bureau of Education. Bulletin
Int Bus Equip — International Business Equipment
Int Cancer Res Found Rep Act — International Cancer Research Foundation. Report of Activities
Int Cast Met J — International Cast Metals Journal
Int Cataloguing — International Cataloguing
Int Cent Arid Semi-Arid Land Stud Publ — International Center for Arid and Semi-Arid Land Studies. Publication
Int Cent Mech Sci Courses Lect — International Centre for Mechanical Sciences. Courses and Lectures
Int Chem En — International Chemical Engineering
Int Chem Eng — International Chemical Engineering
Int Chem Engng — International Chemical Engineering
Int Chem Eng Process Ind — International Chemical Engineering and Processing Industries
Int Chem Export Ind — International Chemical and Export Industry
Int Civ Eng Mon — International Civil Engineering Monthly
Int Classif — International Classification
Int Classification — International Classification
Int Clgh Sci Math Curricular Dev Rep — International Clearinghouse on Science and Mathematics. Curricular Developments Report
Int Coal Rep — International Coal Report [England]
Int Comet Q — International Comet Quarterly
Int Comm — International Commerce
Int Comm Bird Preserv Pan Am Sect Res Rep — International Committee for Bird Preservation. Pan American Section. Research Report
Int Commer — International Commerce
Int Comm Hist Geol Sci Newsl — International Committee on the History of Geological Sciences. Newsletter
Int Comm Illum Proc — International Commission on Illumination. Proceedings
Int Comm Northwest Atl Fish Annu Proc — International Commission for the Northwest Atlantic Fisheries. Annual Proceedings
Int Comm Northwest Atl Fish Annu Rep — International Commission for the Northwest Atlantic Fisheries. Annual Report
Int Comm Northwest Atl Fish Redb Part III — International Commission for the Northwest Atlantic Fisheries. Redbook. Part III
Int Comm Northwest Atl Fish Res Bull — International Commission for the Northwest Atlantic Fisheries. Research Bulletin
Int Comm Northwest Atl Fish Spec Publ — International Commission for the Northwest Atlantic Fisheries. Special Publication
Int Comm Northwest Atl Fish Stat Bull — International Commission for the Northwest Atlantic Fisheries. Statistical Bulletin
Int Comm Radiol Prot Ann — International Commission on Radiological Protection. Annals
Int Comm Radiol Prot Publ — International Commission on Radiological Protection. Publication
Int Comm Whaling Rep — International Commission on Whaling. Report
Int Comp — Interactive Computing
Int & Comp — International and Comparative Law Quarterly
Int Comp Law Q — International and Comparative Law Quarterly
Int Comp Law Quart — International and Comparative Law Quarterly
Int & Comp L Q — International and Comparative Law Quarterly
Int Concil — International Conciliation
Int Conf Cent High Energy Form Proc — International Conference. Center for High Energy Forming. Proceedings
Int Conf Fire Saf Proc — International Conference on Fire Safety. Proceedings
Int Conf Fluid Sealing Proc — International Conference on Fluid Sealing. Proceedings
Int Conf Food Sci Refrig Air Cond — International Conference on Food Science. Refrigeration and Air Conditioning
Int Conf Genet — International Conference on Genetics
Int Conf High Energy Phys Proc — International Conference on High Energy Physics. Proceedings
Int Conf High Energy Rate Fabr Proc — International Conference on High Energy Rate Fabrication. Proceedings
Int Conf Hyperbaric Med Proc — International Conference on Hyperbaric Medicine. Proceedings
Int Conf Insect Path Biol Control — International Conference on Insect Pathology and Biological Control
Int Conf Large Electr Syst Proc — International Conference on Large Electric Systems. Proceedings [France]
Int Conf Noise Control Eng Proc — International Conference on Noise Control Engineering. Proceedings
Int Conf Org Coat Sci Technol Proc (Technomic Publ) — International Conference in Organic Coatings Science and Technology. Proceedings (Technomic Publication)
Int Conf Soil Mech Found Eng Proc — International Conference on Soil Mechanics and Foundation Engineering. Proceedings
Int Conf Therm Anal Proc — International Conference on Thermal Analysis. Proceedings
Int Conf Transfer Water Resour Knowl Proc — International Conference on Transfer of Water Resources Knowledge. Proceedings

Int Conf Water Pollut Res — International Conference on Water Pollution Research. Proceedings
Int Congr Anim Reprod Artif Insemin — International Congress on Animal Reproduction and Artificial Insemination
Int Congr Appl Lasers Electro-Opt Proc — International Congress of Applications of Lasers and Electro-Optics. Proceedings
Int Congr Astronaut Proc — International Congress on Astronautics. Proceedings
Int Congr Biochem Abstr — International Congress of Biochemistry. Abstracts
Int Congr Biogenet — International Congress of Biogenetics
Int Congr Catal Prepr — International Congress on Catalysis. Preprints
Int Congr Electron Micros Proc — International Congress on Electron Microscopy. Proceedings
Int Congr Entomol Proc — International Congress of Entomology. Proceedings
Int Congr Hematol Lect — International Congress of Hematology. Lectures
Int Congr Industr Chem — International Congress of Industrial Chemistry
Int Congr Large Dams — International Congress on Large Dams
Int Congr Microbiol Symp — International Congress for Microbiology. Symposia
Int Congr Ophthalmol — International Congress of Ophthalmology
Int Congr Pl Prot — International Congress of Plant Protection
Int Congr Pteridines Handb — International Congress on Pteridines. Handbook
Int Congr Ser Excerpta Med — International Congress Series. Excerpta Medica [Netherlands]
Int Congr Soc Advanc Breed Res Asia Oceania — International Congress of the Society for the Advancement of Breeding Researches in Asia and Oceania
Int Congr Speleol Abh — International Congress of Speleology. Abhandlungen
Int Cong Zool Pr — International Congress of Zoology. Proceedings
Int Constr — International Construction
Int Copper Inf Bull — International Copper Information Bulletin
Int Counc Explor Sea Coop Res Rep — International Council for the Exploration of the Sea. Cooperative Research Report
Int Counc Explor Sea Coop Res Rep Ser A — International Council for the Exploration of the Sea. Cooperative Research Report. Series A
Int Counc Explor Sea Coop Res Rep Ser B — International Council for the Exploration of the Sea. Cooperative Research Report. Series B
Int Counc Sci Unions Inter-Union Comm Geodynamics Rep — International Council of Scientific Unions. Inter-Union Commission on Geodynamics. Report
Int Crim Police Rev — International Criminal Police Review
Int Cryog Eng Conf — International Cryogenic Engineering Conferences
Int Currency R — International Currency Review
Int Curr Meter Group Rep — International Current Meter Group. Report
Int Curr Rev — International Currency Review
Int Dairy Fed Annu Bull — International Dairy Federation. Annual Bulletin
Int Dent J — International Dental Journal
Int Des — Interior Design
Int Develop R — International Development Review
Int Dev Rev — International Development Review
Int Dialog Z — Internationale Dialog Zeitschrift
Int Dig — International Digest
Int Dig Health Legis — International Digest of Health Legislation
Int Dist Heat Assoc Off Proc — International District Heating Association. Official Proceedings
Int Dredg Abstr — International Dredging Abstracts
Int Dredging Rev — International Dredging Review
Int Drug Regul Monit — International Drug Regulatory Monitor
Int Dyer — International Dyer, Textile Printer, Bleacher, and Finisher
Int Dyer Text Printer Bleacher Finish — International Dyer, Textile Printer, Bleacher, and Finisher
INTEAG — Internist
InTech (Instrum Technol) — InTech (Instrumentation Technology)
Int Econ R — International Economic Review
Int Ec R — International Economic Review
Int Ed & Cul Exch — International Educational and Cultural Exchange
Integ Ed — Integrated Education: Race and Schools
Integ Educ — Integrated Education
Integrated Circuits Int — Integrated Circuits International
Integrated Educ — Integrated Education
Integr Ind — Integral Industrial [Colombia]
Int El Dep Conf — International Electrodeposition Conference
Int Electrotech Comm Publ — International Electrotechnical Commission. Publications
Int Elektr — Internationale Elektronische Rundschau
Int Elektron Rundsch — Internationale Elektronische Rundschau
Intell Dig — Intelligence Digest
Intell Prop L Rev — Intellectual Property Law Review
Intel Obs — Intellectual Observer
Inten Agric — Intensive Agriculture
Int Energie Forum — Internationales Energie-Forum
Intensive Agr — Intensive Agriculture
Intensive Care Med — Intensive Care Medicine
Intensivmed Diagn — Intensivmedizin und Diagnostik
Intensivmed Notfallmed Anaesthesiol — Intensivmedizin, Notfallmedizin, Anaesthesiologie

Intensivmed Prax — Intensivmedizinische Praxis
Int Environ Saf — International Environment and Safety
Int Env Saf — International Environment and Safety
Inter — Interiors
IntER — International Economic Review
Inter-Am — Inter-American
Inter-Am Econ Affairs — Inter-American Economic Affairs
Inter-Amer Econ Aff — Inter-American Economic Affairs
Inter Amer M Bul — Inter-American Music Bulletin
Inter-Amer M R — Inter-American Music Review
Interam J P — Interamerican Journal of Psychology
Inter-Am L Rev — Inter-American Law Review
Inter Am M — Inter-American Music Review
Inter-Am Q — Inter-American Quarterly
Interam Rev Bibliogr — Inter-American Review of Bibliography
Inter-Am Trop Tuna Comm Bull — Inter-American Tropical Tuna
    Commission. Bulletin
Inter-Am Trop Tuna Comm Spec Rep — Inter-American Tropical Tuna
    Commission. Special Report
Interavia (Engl Ed) — Interavia (English Edition)
Inter B C — Interracial Books for Children. Bulletin
Interchurch N — Interchurch News
Intercolon Med J Australas — Intercolonial Medical Journal of Australasia
Intercont — Intercontinental Press
Intercontinental Pr — Intercontinental Press
Interdep Comm Atmos Sci Rep US — Interdepartmental Committee for
    Atmospheric Sciences. Report. United States
Inter Depend — Inter Dependent
Inter Des — Interior Design
Interdisciplinary Math — Interdisciplinary Mathematics
Interdisciplinary Sci Rev — Interdisciplinary Science Reviews
Interdisciplinary Systems Res — Interdisciplinary Systems Research
Interdiscip Sci Rev — Interdisciplinary Science Reviews
Interdiscip Top Gerontol — Interdisciplinary Topics in Gerontology
Interecon — Intereconomics
Inter Econ Indic & Comp Tr — International Economic Indicators and
    Competitive Trends
Inter Ed & Cul Ex — International Educational and Cultural Exchange
Inter Electron — Inter Electronique [*France*]
Interface Comput Educ Q — Interface. The Computer Education Quarterly
Interfaces Comput — Interfaces in Computing
Intergov Oceanogr Comm Tech Ser — Intergovernmental Oceanographic
    Commission. Technical Series
Intergov Oceanogr Comm Workshop Rep — Intergovernmental Oceanographic
    Commission. Workshop Report
Intergov Persp — Intergovernmental Perspective
Interior Des — Interior Design
Interior Landscape Intl — Interior Landscape International
Interlend and Doc Supply — Interlending and Document Supply
Interlending Rev — Interlending Review
Inter M — International Monthly
Intermed Sci Curric Study Newsl — Intermediate Science Curriculum Study.
    Newsletter
Intermountain Econ R — Intermountain Economic Review
Intermt Assoc Geol Annu Field Conf (Guideb) — Intermountain Association of
    Geologists. Annual Field Conference (Guidebook)
Intermt Assoc Pet Geol Annu Field Conf Guideb — Intermountain Association
    of Petroleum Geologists. Annual Field Conference. Guidebook
Intermt Econ Rev — Intermountain Economic Review
Internasjonal Polit — Internasjonal Politikk [*Norway*]
Internat — International Quarterly
Internat Affairs (London) — International Affairs (London)
Internat Affairs (Moscow) — International Affairs (Moscow)
Internat Afrikaforum — Internationales Afrikaforum
Internat Annals Criminology — International Annals of Criminology
Internat Archiv f Ethno — Internationales Archiv fuer Ethnologie
Internat Asienforum — Internationales Asienforum
Internat Ass Med Mus Bull — International Association of Medical Museums.
    Bulletin and Journal of Technical Methods
Internat Assoc Sci Hydrology Bull — International Association of Scientific
    Hydrology. Bulletin
Internat Assoc Sci Hydrology Bull Pub — International Association of
    Scientific Hydrology. Bulletin. Publication
Internat Assoc Sci Hydrology Pub — International Association of Scientific
    Hydrology. Publications
Internat Betriebswirt Zeitschriftenreport — Internationaler
    Betriebswirtschaftlicher Zeitschriftenreport
Internat Bus — International Business
Internat Clin — International Clinics
Internat Comm Coal Petrology Proc — International Committee for Coal
    Petrology. Proceedings
Internat Commer Bank China Econ R — International Commercial Bank of
    China. Economic Review
Internat Comm Jurists R — International Commission of Jurists. Review
Internat and Comparative Law Q 4th Ser — International and Comparative
    Law Quarterly. Fourth Series

Internat Comp LQ — International and Comparative Law Quarterly
Internat Contract — International Contract
Internat Correspondence Schools Serial — International Correspondence
    Schools. Serial
Internat Currency R — International Currency Review
Internat Development R — International Development Review
Internat Econ Indicators — International Economic Indicators
Internat Econom Rev — International Economic Review
Internat Econ R — International Economic Review
Internat Entwicklung — Internationale Entwicklung
Internat Family Planning Perspectives — International Family Planning
    Perspectives
Internat Family Planning Perspectives and Dig — International Family
    Planning Perspectives and Digest
Internat Fin Chase — International Finance. Chase Manhattan Bank
Internat Geology Rev — International Geology Review
International R Ed — International Review of Education
Internat J Accounting — International Journal of Accounting
Internat J Bio-Med Comput — International Journal of Bio-Medical
    Computing
Internat J Circuit Theory Appl — International Journal of Circuit Theory and
    Applications
Internat J Comput and Fluids — International Journal. Computers and Fluids
Internat J Comput Information Sci — International Journal of Computer and
    Information Sciences
Internat J Comput Inform Sci — International Journal of Computer and
    Information Sciences
Internat J Comput Math — International Journal of Computer Mathematics.
    Section A
Internat J Control — International Journal of Control
Internat J Electron — International Journal of Electronics
Internat J Engrg Sci — International Journal of Engineering Science
Internat J Environmental Studies — International Journal of Environmental
    Studies
Internat J Fracture — International Journal of Fracture
Internat J Game Theory — International Journal of Game Theory
Internat J Gen Syst — International Journal of General Systems
Internat J Gen Systems — International Journal of General Systems
Internat J Man-Machine Studies — International Journal of Man-Machine
    Studies
Internat J Man-Mach Stud — International Journal of Man-Machine Studies
Internat J Math Ed Sci Tech — International Journal of Mathematical
    Education in Science and Technology
Internat J Math Math Sci — International Journal of Mathematics and
    Mathematical Sciences
Internat J Middle East Studies — International Journal of Middle East Studies
Internat J Numer Analyt Methods Geomech — International Journal for
    Numerical and Analytical Methods in Geomechanics
Internat J Numer Methods Fluids — International Journal for Numerical
    Methods in Fluids
Internat Jour Rock Mechanics and Mining Sci — International Journal of Rock
    Mechanics and Mining Sciences [*Later, International Journal of Rock
    Mechanics and Mining Sciences and Geomechanics Abstracts*]
Internat J Policy Anal Inform Systems — International Journal of Policy
    Analysis and Information Systems
Internat J Social Econ — International Journal of Social Economics
Internat J Systems Sci — International Journal of Systems Science
Internat J Urban and Regional Research — International Journal of Urban and
    Regional Research
Internat Lawyer — International Lawyer. Quarterly Publication of the Section
    of International and Comparative Law of the American Bar Association
Internatl Cong Hist Sci Proc — International Congress of Historical Sciences.
    Proceedings
Internat Legal Materials — International Legal Materials
Internatl Jour — International Journal
Internat Logic Rev — International Logic Review
Internatl Organ — International Organization
Internat LQ — International Law Quarterly
Internat M — International Magazine
Internat Math News — International Mathematical News
Internat Mgt — International Management
Internat Migration — International Migration
Internat Migration R — International Migration Review
Internat Mo — International Monthly
Internat Monetary Fund Staff Pas — International Monetary Fund. Staff
    Papers
Internat Oceanog Found Bull — International Oceanographic Foundation.
    Bulletin
Internat Perspectives (Can) — International Perspectives (Canada)
Internat Problems (Tel Aviv) — International Problems (Tel Aviv)
Internat R — International Review
Internat R Admin Science (Brussels) — International Review of Administrative
    Sciences (Brussels)
Internat Recht und Diplomatie — Internationales Recht und Diplomatie
Internat Schriftenreihe Numer Math — Internationale Schriftenreihe zur
    Numerischen Mathematik

Internat Security R — International Security Review
Internat Ser Mod Appl Math Comput Sci — International Series in Modern Applied Mathematics and Computer Science
Internat Ser Monographs in Natural Philos — International Series of Monographs in Natural Philosophy
Internat Ser Monographs Pure Appl Math — International Series of Monographs in Pure and Applied Mathematics
Internat Ser Natural Philos — International Series in Natural Philosophy
Internat Ser Nonlinear Math Theory Methods Appl — International Series in Nonlinear Mathematics. Theory, Methods, and Application
Internat Ser Pure Appl Math — International Series in Pure and Applied Mathematics
Internat Spectator — Internationale Spectator
Internat Statist Rev — International Statistical Review
Internat Tax J — International Tax Journal
Internat Trade Law and Practice — International Trade Law and Practice
Intern Audit — Internal Auditor
Intern Biodet Bull — International Biodeterioration Bulletin. Reference Index
Intern Combust Eng — Internal Combustion Engine [*Japan*]
Internist Welt — Internistische Welt
Intern J System Bacteriol — International Journal of Systematic Bacteriology
Internl Photogr — International Photographer
Intern Med News — Internal Medicine News
Intern Med (Tokyo) — Internal Medicine (Tokyo)
Intern Pbd Ind — International Paper Board Industry [*European Edition*]
Intern Phot — International Photography
Intern Phot Tech — International Photography Techniques
Intern Sci Technol — International Science and Technology
Interntl F G — International Film Guide
Interp — Interpretation
Inter-Parliamentary Bul — Inter-Parliamentary Bulletin
Interpers D — Interpersonal Development
Interpr — Interpretation. A Journal of Bible and Theology [*Richmond, VA*]
Interpretat — Interpretation
Interracial Bks Child Bull — Interracial Books for Children. Bulletin
Interracial Rev — Interracial Review
Inter Reg — Inter Regions
Inter Rev for Bus Ed — International Review for Business Education
Intersch Ath Adm — Interscholastic Athletic Administration
Intersch Athl Adm — Interscholastic Athletic Administration
Intersci Conf Antimicrob Agents Chemother Proc — Interscience Conference on Antimicrobial Agents and Chemotherapy. Proceedings
Interscience Libr Chem Eng Process — Interscience Library of Chemical Engineering and Processing
Intersci Monogr Texts Phys Astron — Interscience Monographs and Texts in Physics and Astronomy
Inter Sci Techn — International Science and Technology
Intersoc Energy Convers Eng Conf Proc — Intersociety Energy Conversion Engineering Conference. Proceedings
Interstate Conf of Headmistresses — Interstate Conference of Headmistresses of Australian Girls' Schools. Report
Interstate Oil Compact Comm Comm Bull — Interstate Oil Compact Commission. Committee Bulletin
Interstate Oil Compact Quart Bull — Interstate Oil Compact. Quarterly Bulletin
Inter-Union Comm Geodyn Sci Rep — Inter-Union Commission on Geodynamics. Scientific Report
Inter-Univ Electron Ser — Inter-University Electronics Series
Interv — Interview
Intervirolo — Intervirology
Int Export Chem — International Export Chemist
Int Fam Plann Dig — International Family Planning Digest
Int Fict R — International Fiction Review
Int Field Year Great Lakes Tech Man Ser — International Field Year for the Great Lakes. Technical Manual Series
Int Fire Fighter — International Fire Fighter
Int Folk Mus Council Jl — International Folk Music Council. Journal
Int Forum Inf and Doc — International Forum on Information and Documentation
Int Forum Inf Docum — International Forum on Information and Documentation
Int Foundry Cong (Congr Pap) — International Foundry Congress (Congress Papers) [*Switzerland*]
Int Freight — International Freighting Weekly
Int Fruchtsaftunion Wiss-Tech Komm Ber — Internationale Fruchtsaftunion. Wissenschaftlich-Technische Kommission. Berichte
Int Fruit World — International Fruit World
Int Fund Res Symp — International Fundamental Research Symposium
INTGA — In Theory Only
Int Gas Technol Highlights — International Gas Technology Highlights
Int G Class Stud — International Guide to Classical Studies
Int Geochem Explor Symp Proc — International Geochemical Exploration Symposium. Proceedings
Int Geog Cong Rp Verh — International Geographical Congress. Report. Verhandlungen
Int Geogr Congr — International Geographical Congress

Int Geogr Congr Pap - Congr Int Geogr Commun — International Geographical Congress. Papers - Congres International de Geographie. Communications
Int Geol Congr — International Geological Congress
Int Geol Congr Abstr Congr Geol Int Resumes — International Geological Congress. Abstracts. Congres Geologique International. Resumes
Int Geol Rev — International Geology Review
Int Geophys Ser — International Geophysics Series: A Series of Monographs
Int Glaciospeleological Surv Bull — International Glaciospeleological Survey. Bulletin
Int Gstaad Symp Proc — International Gstaad Symposium. Proceedings
IntGuC — International Guide to Classical Studies
Int Gym — International Gymnast
Int Health News — International Health News
Int Hist R — International History Review
Int Holzmarkt — Internationaler Holzmarkt
Int Hort Congr — International Horticulture Congress
Int Hyd Rev — International Hydrographic Review
Int Hydrocarbon Process — International Hydrocarbon Processing
Int Hydrogr Conf — International Hydrographic Conference
Int Hydrogr Rev — International Hydrographic Review
Int Hydrol Decade Newsl — International Hydrological Decade. Newsletter
Int Ind — International Index
Int Ind — International Industry
Int Ind Film — International Index to Film Periodicals
Int Inst Appl Syst Anal Collab Proc Ser — International Institute for Applied Systems Analysis. Collaborative Proceedings Series
Int Inst Appl Syst Anal Res Mem — International Institute for Applied Systems Analysis. Research Memorandum
Int Inst Land Reclam Impr (Netherlands) Bibliogr — International Institute for Land Reclamation and Improvement (Netherlands). Bibliography
Int Inst Land Reclam Impr (Netherlands) Bull — International Institute for Land Reclamation and Improvement (Netherlands). Bulletin
Int Inst Land Reclam Impr (Netherlands) Publ — International Institute for Land Reclamation and Improvement (Netherlands). Publication
Int Inst Land Reclam Improv Annu Rep — International Institute for Land Reclamation and Improvement. Annual Report
Int Inst Land Reclam Improv Bull — International Institute for Land Reclamation and Improvement. Bulletin
Int Inst Land Reclam Improv (Neth) Pub — International Institute for Land Reclamation and Improvement (Netherlands). Publication
Int Inst Land Reclam Improv Publ — International Institute for Land Reclamation and Improvement. Publication
Int Inst Ld Reclam Improv — International Institute for Land Reclamation and Improvement. Publication
Int Inst Ph — International Institute of Philosophy. Symposia
Int Inst Seismol Earthquake Eng Bull — International Institute of Seismology and Earthquake Engineering. Bulletin
Int Inst Seismol Earthquake Eng Individ Stud — International Institute of Seismology and Earthquake Engineering. Individual Studies by Participants
Int Inst Sugar Beet Res J — International Institute for Sugar Beet Research. Journal
Int J — International Journal
Int J A Aff — International Journal of Agrarian Affairs
Int J Addic — International Journal of the Addictions
Int J Addict — International Journal of the Addictions
Int J Adhes Adhes — International Journal of Adhesion and Adhesives [*England*]
Int J Adhesion & Adhesives — International Journal of Adhesion and Adhesives
Int J Adult Youth Ed — International Journal of Adult and Youth Education
Int J Afr H — International Journal of African Historical Studies
Int J Afric Hist Stud — International Journal of African Historical Studies
Int J Afr Stud — International Journal of African Historical Studies
Int J Ag Affairs — International Journal of Agrarian Affairs
Int J Aging — International Journal of Aging and Human Development
Int J Aging Hum Dev — International Journal of Aging and Human Development
Int J Agr Aff — International Journal of Agrarian Affairs
Int J Air Pollut — International Journal of Air Pollution
Int J Air Water Pollut — International Journal of Air and Water Pollution [*England*]
Int J Amb Energy — International Journal of Ambient Energy
Int J Ambient Energy — International Journal of Ambient Energy [*England*]
Int J Amer — International Journal of American Linguistics
Int J Am Ling — International Journal of American Linguistics
Int J Androl — International Journal of Andrology
Int J Andrology — International Journal of Andrology
Int J Anesth — International Journal of Anesthesia
Int J Appl Radiat — International Journal of Applied Radiation and Isotopes
Int J Appl Radiat Isot — International Journal of Applied Radiation and Isotopes
Int J Appl Radiat and Isot — International Journal of Applied Radiation and Isotopes

Int J Appl Radiat Isotopes — International Journal of Applied Radiation and Isotopes
Int J A Rad — International Journal of Applied Radiation and Isotopes
Int J Artif Organs — International Journal of Artificial Organs
Int J Behav Dev — International Journal of Behavioral Development
Int J Behav Geriatrics — International Journal of Behavioral Geriatrics
Int J Bioch — International Journal of Biochemistry
Int J Biochem — International Journal of Biochemistry
Int J Bioclim — International Journal of Bioclimatology and Biometeorology
Int J Bioclimatol Biometeorol — International Journal of Bioclimatology and Biometeorology
Int J Bioclim Biomet — International Journal of Bioclimatology and Biometeorology
Int J Bio-M — International Journal of Bio-Medical Computing
Int J Biom — International Journal of Biometeorology
Int J Biomed Comp — International Journal of Biomedical Computing
Int J Bio-Med Comput — International Journal of Bio-Medical Computing
Int J Biomed Eng — International Journal of Biomedical Engineering
Int J Biometeorol — International Journal of Biometeorology
Int Jb Pol — Internationales Jahrbuch der Politik
Int Jb Relig Soziol — Internationales Jahrbuch fuer Religionssoziologie
Int J Canc — International Journal of Cancer
Int J Cancer — International Journal of Cancer
Int J C E Hy — International Journal of Clinical and Experimental Hypnosis
Int J Cement Composites — International Journal of Cement Composites
Int J Chem Kinet — International Journal of Chemical Kinetics
Int J Child — International Journal of Child Psychotherapy
Int J Ch K — International Journal of Chemical Kinetics
Int J Chronobiol — International Journal of Chronobiology
Int J C Inf — International Journal of Computer and Information Sciences
Int J Circuit Theory Appl — International Journal of Circuit Theory and Applications
Int J Circuit Theory and Appl — International Journal of Circuit Theory and Applications
Int J Clin — International Journal of Clinical Pharmacology and Biopharmacy
Int J Clin Exp Hypn — International Journal of Clinical and Experimental Hypnosis
Int J Clin Exp Hypnos — International Journal of Clinical and Experimental Hypnosis
Int J Clin & Exp Hypnosis — International Journal of Clinical and Experimental Hypnosis
Int J Clin Pharm — International Journal of Clinical Pharmacology, Therapy, and Toxicology
Int J Clin Pharmacol Biopharm — International Journal of Clinical Pharmacology and Biopharmacy
Int J Clin Pharmacol Ther Toxicol — International Journal of Clinical Pharmacology, Therapy, and Toxicology
Int J Coal Geol — International Journal of Coal Geology [*Netherlands*]
Int J Com M — International Journal of Computer Mathematics
Int J Com P — International Journal of Community Psychiatry and Experimental Psychotherapy
Int J Comp — International Journal of Comparative Sociology
Int J Compar Sociol — International Journal of Comparative Sociology
Int J Comp Soc — International Journal of Comparative Sociology
Int J Comp Sociol — International Journal of Comparative Sociology
Int J Comput & Inf Sci — International Journal of Computer and Information Sciences
Int J Comput Math — International Journal of Computer Mathematics
Int J Comput Math Sect A — International Journal of Computer Mathematics. Section A. Programming Languages. Theory and Methods
Int J Comput Math Sect B — International Journal of Computer Mathematics. Section B. Computational Methods
Int J Con S — International Journal of Contemporary Sociology
Int J Contemp Sociol — International Journal of Contemporary Sociology
Int J Contr — International Journal of Control
Int J Control — International Journal of Control
Int J Dermatol — International Journal of Dermatology
Int J Dravid Ling — International Journal of Dravidian Linguistics
Int J Earthquake Eng Struct Dyn — International Journal of Earthquake Engineering and Structural Dynamics
Int J Ecol Environ Sci — International Journal of Ecology and Environmental Sciences
Int J Elec Eng Educ — International Journal of Electrical Engineering Education
Int J Elect — International Journal of Electronics
Int J Electr Eng Educ — International Journal of Electrical Engineering Education
Int J Electron — International Journal of Electronics
Int J Electr Power Energy Syst — International Journal of Electrical Power Amp Energy Systems [*England*]
Int J El En — International Journal of Electrical Engineering Education
Int J Energy Res — International Journal of Energy Research
Int J Engng Sci — International Journal of Engineering Science
Int J Eng S — International Journal of Engineering Science
Int J Eng Sci — International Journal of Engineering Science

Int J Environ Anal Chem — International Journal of Environmental Analytical Chemistry
Int J Environ Stud — International Journal of Environmental Studies
Int J Environ Studies — International Journal of Environmental Studies
Int J Env S — International Journal of Environmental Studies
Int J Epid — International Journal of Epidemiology
Int J Epidemiol — International Journal of Epidemiology
Int J Equilib Res — International Journal of Equilibrium Research
Int J Ethics — International Journal of Ethics
Int J Fatigue — International Journal of Fatigue
Int J Fert — International Journal of Fertility
Int J Fertil — International Journal of Fertility
Int J Food Microbiol — International Journal of Food Microbiology
Int J Forensic Dent — International Journal of Forensic Dentistry
Int J Fract — International Journal of Fracture
Int J Fract Mech — International Journal of Fracture Mechanics
Int J Fusion Energy — International Journal of Fusion Energy
Int J Game Theory — International Journal of Game Theory
Int J Gen S — International Journal of General Systems
Int J Gen Syst — International Journal of General Systems
Int J Group Psychother — International Journal of Group Psychotherapy
Int J Group Tensions — International Journal of Group Tensions
Int J Grp P — International Journal of Group Psychotherapy
Int J Grp T — International Journal of Group Tensions
Int J Gynaecol Obstet — International Journal of Gynaecology and Obstetrics
Int J Healt — International Journal of Health Education
Int J Health Educ — International Journal of Health Education
Int J Health Serv — International Journal of Health Services
Int J Heat — International Journal of Heat and Mass Transfer
Int J Heat Fluid Flow — International Journal of Heat and Fluid Flow [*England*]
Int J Heat Mass Transfer — International Journal of Heat and Mass Transfer
Int J Heat & Mass Transfer — International Journal of Heat and Mass Transfer
Int J He Se — International Journal of Health Services
Int J Housing Sc Applications — International Journal for Housing Science and Its Applications
Int J Hous Sci Appl — International Journal for Housing Science and Its Applications
Int J Hybrid Microelectron — International Journal for Hybrid Microelectronics
Int J Hydrogen Energy — International Journal of Hydrogen Energy
Int J Immunochem — International Journal of Immunochemistry [*England*]
Int J Immunopharmacol — International Journal of Immunopharmacology
Int J Infrared Millim Waves — International Journal of Infrared and Millimeter Waves [*United States*]
Int J Insect Morph Embryol — International Journal of Insect Morphology and Embryology
Int J Insect Morphol Embryol — International Journal of Insect Morphology and Embryology
Int J Instr Media — International Journal of Instructional Media
Int J Invertebr Reprod — International Journal of Invertebrate Reproduction
Int J Invertebr Reprod Dev — International Journal of Invertebrate Reproduction and Development
Int J Law Lib — International Journal of Law Libraries
Int J Law Libr — International Journal of Law Libraries
Int J Law Psychiatry — International Journal of Law and Psychiatry
Int J Law Sci — International Journal of Law and Science
Int J Lepr — International Journal of Leprosy [*Later, International Journal of Leprosy and Other Mycobacterial Diseases*]
Int J Lepr Other Mycobact Dis — International Journal of Leprosy and Other Mycobacterial Diseases
Int J Mach — International Journal of Machine Tool Design and Research
Int J Mach Tool Des Res — International Journal of Machine Tool Design and Research
Int J Magn — International Journal of Magnetism
Int J Mamm Biol — International Journal of Mammalian Biology
Int J Man-M — International Journal of Man-Machine Studies
Int J Man-Mach Stud — International Journal of Man-Machine Studies
Int J Manpower — International Journal of Manpower
Int J Masonry Constr — International Journal of Masonry Construction
Int J Mass — International Journal of Mass Spectrometry and Ion Physics [*Later, International Journal of Mass Spectrometry and Ion Processes*]
Int J Mass Spectrom Ion Phys — International Journal of Mass Spectrometry and Ion Physics [*Later, International Journal of Mass Spectrometry and Ion Processes*]
Int J Mass Spectrom and Ion Phys — International Journal of Mass Spectrometry and Ion Physics [*Later, International Journal of Mass Spectrometry and Ion Processes*]
Int J Mass Spectrom Ion Processes — International Journal of Mass Spectrometry and Ion Processes
Int J Mater Eng Appl — International Journal of Materials in Engineering Applications
Int J Mater Eng Res — International Journal of Materials Engineering Research

Int J Math Educ Sci and Technol — International Journal of Mathematical Education in Science and Technology

Int J Math Educ Sci Technol — International Journal of Mathematical Education in Science and Technology

Int J Mech — International Journal of Mechanical Sciences

Int J Mech Sci — International Journal of Mechanical Sciences

Int J Ment — International Journal of Mental Health

Int J Ment Health — International Journal of Mental Health

Int J M E St — International Journal of Middle East Studies

Int J Microbiol Hyg Ser A — International Journal of Microbiology and Hygiene. Series A. Medical Microbiology, Infectious Diseases, Virology, Parasitology

Int J Microgr and Video Technol — International Journal of Micrographics and Video Technology

Int J Middle East Stud — International Journal of Middle East Studies

Int J Mid East Stud — International Journal of Middle East Studies

Int J Mid E Stud — International Journal of Middle East Studies

Int J Miner Process — International Journal of Mineral Processing

Int J Mine Water — International Journal of Mine Water

Int J Mini and Microcomput — International Journal of Mini and Microcomputers

Int J Multiphase Flow — International Journal of Multiphase Flow

Int J Multiph Flow — International Journal of Multiphase Flow

Int J Naut — International Journal of Nautical Archaeology and Underwater Exploration

Int J Naut Archaeol Underwater Explor — International Journal of Nautical Archaeology and Underwater Exploration

Int J Neuro — International Journal of Neurology

Int J Neurol — International Journal of Neurology

Int J Neuropharmacol — International Journal of Neuropharmacology

Int J Neuropsychiatr — International Journal of Neuropsychiatry

Int J Neuropsychiatry Suppl — International Journal of Neuropsychiatry. Supplement

Int J Neurosci — International Journal of Neuroscience

Int J Neurs — International Journal of Neuroscience

Int J Nondestr Test — International Journal of Nondestructive Testing

Int J Nondestruct Test — International Journal of Nondestructive Testing

Int J Non-Linear Mech — International Journal of Non-Linear Mechanics

Int J Nucl Med & Biol — International Journal of Nuclear Medicine and Biology

Int J Nucl Med Biol — International Journal of Nuclear Medicine and Biology

Int J Nuc M — International Journal of Nuclear Medicine and Biology

Int J Num Anal Meth Geomech — International Journal for Numerical and Analytical Methods in Geomechanics

Int J Numer and Anal Methods Geomech — International Journal for Numerical and Analytical Methods in Geomechanics

Int J Numer Anal Methods Geomech — International Journal for Numerical and Analytical Methods in Geomechanics

Int J Numer Methods Eng — International Journal for Numerical Methods in Engineering

Int J Numer Methods Engng — International Journal for Numerical Methods in Engineering

Int J Numer Methods Fluids — International Journal for Numerical Methods in Fluids

Int J Num Meth Engng — International Journal for Numerical Methods in Engineering

Int J Nurs — International Journal of Nursing Studies

Int J Nurs Stud — International Journal of Nursing Studies

Int J Obes — International Journal of Obesity

Int J Occ H — International Journal of Occupational Health and Safety

Int J Occup Health Saf — International Journal of Occupational Health and Safety

Int J Occup Health and Saf — International Journal of Occupational Health and Safety

Int J Oceanol Limnol — International Journal of Oceanology and Limnology

Int J Offen — International Journal of Offender Therapy [*Later, International Journal of Offender Therapy and Comparative Criminology*]

Int J Offend Therapy — International Journal of Offender Therapy and Comparative Criminology

Int J Oper and Prod Manage — International Journal of Operations and Production Management

Int J Oral — International Journal of Oral History

Int J Oral Myol — International Journal of Oral Myology

Int J Oral Surg — International Journal of Oral Surgery

Int J Or Su — International Journal of Oral Surgery

Int J Orthod — International Journal of Orthodontics

Int J Orthod Dent Child — International Journal of Orthodontia and Dentistry for Children

Int J Orthodont — International Journal of Orthodontics

Int J Paras — International Journal for Parasitology

Int J Parasitol — International Journal for Parasitology

Int J Partial Hosp — International Journal of Partial Hospitalization

Int J PE — International Journal of Physical Education

Int J Pediatr Otorhinolaryngol — International Journal of Pediatric Otorhinolaryngology

Int J Pept — International Journal of Peptide and Protein Research

Int J Peptide Protein Res — International Journal of Peptide and Protein Research

Int J Peptide Prot Res — International Journal of Peptide and Protein Research

Int J Pept Protein Res — International Journal of Peptide and Protein Research

Int J Pharm — International Journal of Pharmaceutics

Int J Phil — International Journal for Philosophy of Religion

Int J Philos Relig — International Journal for Philosophy of Religion

IntJPhilRel — International Journal for Philosophy of Religion [*The Hague*]

Int J Phil Relig — International Journal for Philosophy of Religion

Int J Ph Rel — International Journal for Philosophy of Religion

Int J Phys Distrib J Ser — International Journal of Physical Distribution. Journal Series

Int J Phys Distrib Monogr Ser — International Journal of Physical Distribution. Monograph Series

Int J Phys Educ — International Journal of Physical Education

Int J Plant Physiol (Stuttgart) — International Journal of Plant Physiology (Stuttgart)

Int J Policy Anal Inf Syst — International Journal of Policy Analysis and Information Systems [*United States*]

Int J Policy and Inf — International Journal on Policy and Information

Int J Polit — International Journal of Politics

Int J Polym Mat — International Journal of Polymeric Materials

Int J Polym Mater — International Journal of Polymeric Materials

Int J Powd — International Journal of Powder Metallurgy

Int J Powder Metall — International Journal of Powder Metallurgy

Int J Powder Metall & Powder Tech — International Journal of Powder Metallurgy and Powder Technology

Int J Powder Metall Powder Technol — International Journal of Powder Metallurgy and Powder Technology

Int J Powder Metall Technol — International Journal of Powder Metallurgy and Powder Technology

Int J Pressure Vessels Piping — International Journal of Pressure Vessels and Piping

Int J Prod Res — International Journal of Production Research

Int J Prophyl Med Sozialhyg — Internationales Journal fuer Prophylaktische Medizin und Sozialhygiene

Int J Protein Res — International Journal of Protein Research

Int J Ps Ps — International Journal of Psychoanalytic Psychotherapy

Int J Psych — International Journal of Psychoanalysis

Int J Psychiat — International Journal of Psychiatry

Int J Psychiatry — International Journal of Psychiatry

Int J Psychiatry Med — International Journal of Psychiatry in Medicine

Int J Psychoanal — International Journal of Psychoanalysis

Int J Psychoanal Psychother — International Journal of Psychoanalytic Psychotherapy

Int J Psychobiol — International Journal of Psychobiology

Int J Psyci — International Journal of Psychiatry

Int J Psyco — International Journal of Psychology

Int J Psy M — International Journal of Psychiatry in Medicine

Int J Quant — International Journal of Quantum Chemistry

Int J Quant Chem — International Journal of Quantum Chemistry

Int J Quant Chem Quant Biol Symp — International Journal of Quantum Chemistry. Quantum Biology Symposium [*United States*]

Int J Quant Chem Symp — International Journal of Quantum Chemistry. Symposium

Int J Quantum Chem — International Journal of Quantum Chemistry

Int J Quantum Chem Quantum Biol Symp — International Journal of Quantum Chemistry. Quantum Biology Symposium

Int J Quantum Chem Quantum Chem Symp — International Journal of Quantum Chemistry. Quantum Chemistry Symposia

Int J Quantum Chem Sym — International Journal of Quantum Chemistry. Symposium

Int J Rad B — International Journal of Radiation Biology

Int J Radiat Biol — International Journal of Radiation Biology and Related Studies in Physics, Chemistry, and Medicine

Int J Radiat Biol Relat Stud Phys Chem Med — International Journal of Radiation Biology and Related Studies in Physics, Chemistry, and Medicine

Int J Radiat Eng — International Journal of Radiation Engineering [*Israel*]

Int J Radiat Oncol-Biol-Phys — International Journal of Radiation: Oncology-Biology-Physics

Int J Radiat Oncology Biol Phys — International Journal of Radiation: Oncology-Biology-Physics

Int J Radiat Phys Chem — International Journal for Radiation Physics and Chemistry [*Later, Radiation Physics and Chemistry*]

Int J Radiat Phys and Chem — International Journal for Radiation Physics and Chemistry

Int J Radiat Steril — International Journal of Radiation Sterilization [*Israel*]

Int J Rad O — International Journal of Radiation: Oncology-Biology-Physics

Int J Rad P — International Journal for Radiation Physics and Chemistry [*Later, Radiation Physics and Chemistry*]

Int J Refract and Hard Met — International Journal of Refractory and Hard Metals

Int J Refract Hard Met — International Journal of Refractory and Hard Metals

Int J Refrig — International Journal of Refrigeration

Int J Rehabil Res — International Journal of Rehabilitation Research
Int J Relig Ed — International Journal of Religious Education
Int J Res Manage — International Journal of Research Management [*United States*]
Int J Rock — International Journal of Rock Mechanics
Int J Rock Mech Mining Sci — International Journal of Rock Mechanics and Mining Sciences [*Later, International Journal of Rock Mechanics and Mining Sciences and Geomechanics Abstracts*]
Int J Rock Mech Mining Sci Geomech Abstr — International Journal of Rock Mechanics and Mining Sciences and Geomechanics Abstracts
Int J Rock Mech Min Sci — International Journal of Rock Mechanics and Mining Sciences [*Later, International Journal of Rock Mechanics and Mining Sciences and Geomechanics Abstracts*]
Int J Rock Mech Min Sci Geomech Abstr — International Journal of Rock Mechanics and Mining Sciences and Geomechanics Abstracts
Int J Rock Mech and Min Sci and Geomech Abstr — International Journal of Rock Mechanics and Mining Sciences and Geomechanics Abstracts
Int J Soc Econ — International Journal of Social Economics
Int J Soc F — International Journal of Sociology of the Family
Int J Social Psychiat — International Journal of Social Psychiatry
Int J Sociol — International Journal of Sociology
Int J Sociol Family — International Journal of Sociology of the Family
Int J Sociol Lang — International Journal of the Sociology of Language
Int J Sociol Law — International Journal of the Sociology of Law
Int J Sociol Soc Policy — International Journal of Sociology and Social Policy
Int J Soc L — International Journal of the Sociology of Law
Int J Soc Lang — International Journal of the Sociology of Language
Int J Soc P — International Journal of Social Psychiatry
Int J Soc Psych — International Journal of Social Psychiatry
Int J Soc Psychiatry — International Journal of Social Psychiatry
Int J Soil Dyn and Earthquake Eng — International Journal of Soil Dynamics and Earthquake Engineering
Int J Sol Energy — International Journal of Solar Energy
Int J Solids Struct — International Journal of Solids and Structures
Int J Speleol — International Journal of Speleology
Int J Sport Psychol — International Journal of Sport Psychology
Int J Sp Ps — International Journal of Sport Psychology
Int J Sulfur Chem Part A — International Journal of Sulfur Chemistry. Part A. Original Experimental
Int J Sulfur Chem Part B — International Journal of Sulfur Chemistry. Part B. Quarterly Reports on Sulfur Chemistry
Int J Sulfur Chem Part C — International Journal of Sulfur Chemistry. Part C. Mechanisms of Reactions of Sulfur Compounds
Int J Sy B — International Journal of Systematic Bacteriology
Int J Symb — International Journal of Symbology
Int J Syst — International Journal of Systems Science
Int J Syst Bacteriol — International Journal of Systematic Bacteriology
Int J Syst Sci — International Journal of Systems Science
Int J Theor — International Journal of Theoretical Physics
Int J Theor Phys — International Journal of Theoretical Physics
Int J Thermophys — International Journal of Thermophysics
Int J Tissue React — International Journal on Tissue Reactions
Int J Transp Econ — International Journal of Transport Economics
Int J Urban Reg Res — International Journal of Urban and Regional Research
Int J Veh Des — International Journal of Vehicle Design
Int J Vitam Nutr Res — International Journal for Vitamin and Nutrition Research
Int J Vit N — International Journal for Vitamin and Nutrition Research
Int J Womens Stud — International Journal of Women's Studies
Int J Zoonoses — International Journal of Zoonoses
IntKiZ — Internationale Kirchliche Zeitschrift [*Bern*]
Int Kongr Tier Fortpflanz Kuenstliche Besamung — Internationaler Kongress ueber die Tierische Fortpflanzung und die Kuenstliche Besamung
Int Lab — International Laboratory
Int Labmate — International Labmate
Int Labor Organ Occup Saf Health Ser — International Labor Organization. Occupational Safety and Health Series
Int Labor W — International Labor and Working Class History
Int Labour Off Occup Saf Health Ser — International Labour Office. Occupational Safety and Health Series
Int Labour R — International Labour Review
Int Labour Rev — International Labour Review
Int Labour R Stat Sup — International Labour Review. Statistical Supplement
Int Lab R — International Labour Review
Int Lab Rev — International Labour Review
Intl Archt — International Architect
Intl Asbestos Cement Review — International Asbestos-Cement Review
Int Law — International Lawyer
Int Lawyer — International Lawyer
Int Lbr R — International Labour Review
Int'l Bull Research E Eur — International Bulletin for Research on Law in Eastern Europe
Int'l Comm Jurists Rev — International Commission of Jurists. Review
Int'l & Comp LQ — International and Comparative Law Quarterly
Intl Comp Symp — International Computer Symposium Proceedings
Int'l Dig — International Digest

Int Lib Ph — International Library of Philosophy
Int Lib R — International Library Review
Int Libr Re — International Library Review
Int Libr Rev — International Library Review
Int Lighting Rev — International Lighting Review
Int'l J — International Journal
Int'l J Envir Stud — International Journal of Environmental Studies
Int'l J Legal Info — International Journal of Legal Information
Int'l J Legal Infor — International Journal of Legal Information
Int'l JL Lib — International Journal of Law Libraries
Intl J L and Psych — International Journal of Law and Psychiatry
Intl Jnl of Ambient Energy — International Journal of Ambient Energy
Intl Jnl Rel Ed — International Journal of Religious Education
Intl J Offend Ther and Comp Criminology — International Journal of Offender Therapy and Comparative Criminology
Int'l J Pol — International Journal of Politics
Int'l J of PRD — International Journal of Periodontics and Restorative Dentistry
Int'l J Soc L — International Journal of the Sociology of Law
Int'l Lab Off Leg S — International Labour Office. Legislative Series [*London, England*]
Int'l Lab Rev — International Labour Review
Int'l Lawyer — International Lawyer
Int'l Legal Mat — International Legal Materials
Int'l Legal Materials — International Legal Materials
Intl Lighting Review — International Lighting Review
Int'l LQ — International Law Quarterly
Int L News — International Law News
Int Log Rev — International Logic Review
Int LQ — International Law Quarterly
Int'l Rev Ind Prop & C'right L — International Review of Industrial Property and Copyright Law
Int'l Rev Ind Prop'y & Copyr — International Review of Industrial Property and Copyright Law
Int'l Rev L & Econ — International Review of Law and Economics
Int'l Tax J — International Tax Journal
Int Ltg Rev — International Lighting Review
Int'l Trade L & Prac — International Trade Law and Practice
Int Manag — International Management
Int Manage — International Management
Int M Cong — International Mining Congress
Int Med Abstr Rev — International Medical Abstracts and Reviews
Int Med Dig — International Medical Digest
Int Medieval Bibliogr — International Medieval Bibliography
Int Metall Rev — International Metallurgical Reviews
Int Metall Revs — International Metallurgical Reviews
Int Met Rev — International Metals Reviews
Int Mgt — International Management
Int Microelectron Symp Proc — International Microelectronic Symposium. Proceedings
Int Migration R — International Migration Review
Int Migr Re — International Migration Review
Int Min Equip — International Mining Equipment
Int Mitt Bodenkd — Internationale Mitteilungen fuer Bodenkunde
Int Mod Foundry — International Modern Foundry
Int Monetar — International Monetary Fund. Staff Papers
Int Monetary Fund Staff Pa — International Monetary Fund. Staff Papers
Int Monet Fund Staff Pap — International Monetary Fund. Staff Papers
Int Mus — International Musician
Int Mus Ed — International Music Educator
INTN — Inuit Today Newsletter. Inuit Ublumi Tusagatsangit
Int Nickel — International Nickel
Intnl Advt — International Advertiser
Int North Pac Fish Comm Annu Rep — International North Pacific Fisheries Commission. Annual Report
Int North Pac Fish Comm Bull — International North Pacific Fisheries Commission. Bulletin
IntNurI — International Nursing Index
Int Nurs Re — International Nursing Review
Int Nurs Rev — International Nursing Review
Int Off Cocoa Choc Period Bull — International Office of Cocoa and Chocolate. Periodic Bulletin
Int Oil Scouts Assoc Yearb — International Oil Scouts Association. Yearbook
Int Ophthalmol — International Ophthalmology
Int Ophthalmol Clin — International Ophthalmology Clinics
Int Org — International Organization
Int Organ — International Organization
Int Orthop — International Orthopaedics
Int Pac Halibut Comm Annu Rep — International Pacific Halibut Commission. Annual Report
Int Pac Halibut Comm Sci Rep — International Pacific Halibut Commission. Scientific Report
Int Pac Halibut Comm Tech Rep — International Pacific Halibut Commission. Technical Report
Int Packag Abs — International Packaging Abstracts

nt Pac Salmon Fish Comm Annu Rep — International Pacific Salmon Fisheries Commission. Annual Report
nt Pac Salmon Fish Comm Bull — International Pacific Salmon Fisheries Commission. Bulletin
nt Pac Salmon Fish Comm Prog Rep — International Pacific Salmon Fisheries Commission. Progress Report
nt Peat Congr Proc — International Peat Congress. Proceedings
nt Peat Soc Bull — International Peat Society. Bulletin
nt Perspect — International Perspectives
nt Pest Contr — International Pest Control
nt Pest Control — International Pest Control
nt Pet Abstr — International Petroleum Abstracts
nt Petrol Annu — International Petroleum Annual
nt Petrol Times — International Petroleum Times
nt Petr Tms — International Petroleum Times
nt Pet Technol — International Petroleum Technology
nt Pet Times — International Petroleum Times
nt Pharmac — International Pharmacopsychiatry
nt Pharmacopsychiatry — International Pharmacopsychiatry
nt Philo Q — International Philosophical Quarterly
nt Philos Q — International Philosophical Quarterly
nt Phil Q — International Philosophical Quarterly
nt Phil Quart — International Philosophical Quarterly
nt Photobiol Congr — International Photobiological Congress
nt Photogr — International Photographer
nt Photo Tech — International Photo-Technik
nt Phys Workshop Ser — International Physics Workshop Series
nt Pipe Ln — International Pipe Line Industry
nt Pipes Pipelines — International Pipes and Pipelines
nt Plann Parent Fed Med Bull — International Planned Parenthood Federation. Medical Bulletin
nt Polit (Bergen) — Internasjonal Politikk (Bergen)
nt Polit (O) — Internasjonal Politikk (Oslo)
ntPolSc — International Political Science Abstracts
nt Polym Sci & Technol — International Polymer Science and Technology
nt Potash Inst Bull — International Potash Institute. Bulletin
nt Potash Inst Colloq Proc — International Potash Institute. Colloquium. Proceedings
nt Potash Inst Res Top — International Potash Institute. Research Topics
nt Power Generation — International Power Generation [England]
ntpr — Interpretation. A Journal of Bible and Theology
nt Presidents Bul — International President's Bulletin
nt Probl (Belgrade) — International Problems (Belgrade)
nt Probl (Tel-Aviv) — International Problems (Tel-Aviv)
nt Prog Urethanes — International Progress in Urethanes
nt Proj — International Projectionist [United States]
nt Psychiatry Clin — International Psychiatry Clinics
nt Q — International Quarterly
INTQ — International Tourism Quarterly
INTR — Interpreter
Int R Admin Sci — International Review of Administrative Sciences
Int R Adm Sci — International Review of Administrative Sciences
Int R Aesthestics Sociology M — International Review of the Aesthetics and Sociology of Music
Int R Aesthetics & Soc — International Review of the Aesthetics and Sociology of Music
Int R Aesthetics & Soc Mus — International Review of the Aesthetics and Sociology of Music
Int R Ag — International Review of Agriculture
Int R Ag Econ — International Review of Agricultural Economics
Int Railw Gaz — International Railway Gazette
Int Railw J — International Railway Journal
Intra L Rev (Am U) — Intramural Law Review of American University
Intra L Rev (NYU) — Intramural Law Review of New York University
Intra L Rev (UCLA) — Intramural Law Review of University of California at Los Angeles
Intra-Sci Chem Rep — Intra-Science Chemistry Reports
Int R Com Dev — International Review of Community Development
Int R Community Develop — International Review of Community Development
Int Read Assn Conf Pa — International Reading Association Conference. Papers
Int Read Assn Conv Pa — International Reading Association Convention. Papers
Int Recht u Diplom — Internationales Recht und Diplomatie
Int Rec Med — International Record of Medicine
Int Rec Med Gen Pract Clin — International Record. Medicine and General Practice Clinics
Int R Ed — International Review of Education
Int R Ed Cinemat — International Review of Educational Cinematography
Int R Educ — International Review of Education
Int Reg Sci Rev — International Regional Science Review [United States]
Int Rehabil Med — International Rehabilitation Medicine
Int Rehab Rev — International Rehabilitation Review
Int Rel — International Relations
Int Relat (London) — International Relations (London)
Int Relat (Prague) — International Relations (Prague)

Int Relat (Teheran) — International Relations (Teheran)
Int Rep Div Mech Eng CSIRO — Internal Report. Division of Mechanical Engineering. Commonwealth Scientific and Industrial Research Organisation
Int Res Commun Syst Med Sci Libr Compend — International Research Communications System Medical Science. Library Compendium
Int Rescuer — International Rescuer
Int Res Group Refuse Disposal Inf Bull — International Research Group on Refuse Disposal Information. Bulletin
Int Rev Aerosol Phys Chem — International Reviews in Aerosol Physics and Chemistry
Int Rev Aes — International Review of the Aesthetics and Sociology of Music
Int Rev Army Navy Air Force Med Serv — International Review of the Army, Navy, and Air Force Medical Services
Int Rev Biochem — International Review of Biochemistry
Int Rev Connect Tissue Res — International Review of Connective Tissue Research
Int Rev Cyt — International Review of Cytology
Int Rev Cytol — International Review of Cytology
Int Rev Cytol Suppl — International Review of Cytology. Supplement
Int Rev Edu — International Review of Education
Int Rev Exp Pathol — International Review of Experimental Pathology
Int Rev For Res — International Review of Forestry Research
Int Rev Gen Exp Zool — International Review of General and Experimental Zoology
Int Rev Gesamten Hydrobiol — Internationale Revue der Gesamten Hydrobiologie
Int Rev Gesamten Hydrobiol Hydrogr — Internationale Revue der Gesamten Hydrobiologie und Hydrographie
Int Rev Gesamten Hydrobiol Syst Beih — Internationale Revue der Gesamten Hydrobiologie. Systematische Beihefte
Int Rev His — International Review of History and Political Science
Int Rev Mod — International Review of Modern Sociology
Int Rev Neurobiol — International Review of Neurobiology
Int Rev Neurobiol Suppl — International Review of Neurobiology. Supplement
Int Rev Phys Chem — International Reviews in Physical Chemistry [England]
Int Rev Physiol — International Review of Physiology
Int Rev Serv — International Review Service [United States]
Int Rev S H — International Review of Social History
Int Rev Soc Hist — International Review of Social History
Int Rev Trach — International Review of Trachoma
Int Rev Trop Med — International Review of Tropical Medicine
Int R Hist Polit Sci — International Review of History and Political Science
Int R Hist Pol Sci — International Review of History and Political Science
Int Rice Comm Newsl — International Rice Commission. Newsletter
Int Rice Res Inst (Los Banos) Annu Rep — International Rice Research Institute (Los Banos). Annual Report
Int Rice Res Inst (Los Banos) Tech Bull — International Rice Research Institute (Los Banos). Technical Bulletin
Int Rice Res Inst Res Pap Ser — International Rice Research Institute. Research Paper Series
Int R Miss — International Review of Missions
Int R Missions — International Review of Missions
Int R Mod Sociol — International Review of Modern Sociology
Introd Aklim Rosl Ukr — Introduktsiya ta Aklimatizatsiya Roslin na Ukraini
Introd Eksp Ekol Rosl — Introduktsiya ta Eksperimental'na Ekologiya Roslin
Int Roehrenind — Internationale Roehrenindustrie
Int Ropeway Rev — International Ropeway Review
Int R Sci & Prac Ag — International Review of the Science and Practice of Agriculture
Int R Scl Hist — International Review of Social History
Int R Soc Hist — International Review of Social History
Int R Sport Sociol — International Review of Sport Sociology
Int Rubb Dig — International Rubber Digest
Int Rv — International Review
Int Salzburg Conf — International Salzburg Conference
Int Sci Counc Trypanosomiasis Res Publ — International Scientific Council for Trypanosomiasis. Research Publication
Int Sci Res News — International Science Research News
Int Sci Rev Ser — International Science Review Series
Int Sci Technol — International Science and Technology
Int Sec — International Security
Int Secur — International Security
Int Secur Rev — International Security Review
Int Seismol Cent Bull — International Seismological Centre. Bulletin
Int Semin Reprod Physiol Sex Endocrinol — International Seminar on Reproductive Physiology and Sexual Endocrinology
Int Ser Mater Sci Technol — International Series on Materials Science and Technology
Int Ser Monogr Anal Chem — International Series of Monographs in Analytical Chemistry
Int Ser Monogr Exp Psychol — International Series of Monographs in Experimental Psychology
Int Ser Monogr Nat Philos — International Series of Monographs in Natural Philosophy

Int Ser Monogr Nucl Energy — International Series of Monographs on Nuclear Energy

Int Ser Monogr Nucl Energy Div 7 — International Series of Monographs on Nuclear Energy. Division 7. Reactor Engineering

Int Ser Monogr Oral Biol — International Series of Monographs in Oral Biology

Int Ser Monogr Pure Appl Biol Div Biochem — International Series of Monographs on Pure and Applied Biology. Division Biochemistry

Int Ser Monogr Pure Appl Biol Div Bot — International Series of Monographs on Pure and Applied Biology. Division Botany

Int Ser Monogr Pure Appl Biol Mod Trends Physiol Sci — International Series of Monographs on Pure and Applied Biology. Modern Trends in Physiological Sciences

Int Ser Monogr Sci Solid State — International Series of Monographs in the Science of the Solid State

Int Ser Pure Appl Biol Zool Div — International Series of Monographs on Pure and Applied Biology. Zoology Division

Int Ser Sci Solid State — International Series of Monographs in the Science of the Solid State

Int Ser Sport Sci — International Series on Sport Sciences

Int Shade Tree Conf Proc — International Shade Tree Conference. Proceedings

Int Shipbldg Progr — International Shipbuilding Progress

Int Shipbuild Prog — International Shipbuilding Progress

Int Shipbuild Progress — International Shipbuilding Progress

Int Ship Painting Corros Conf Proc — International Ship Painting and Corrosion Conference. Proceedings

Int Soc Dev — International Social Development Review

Int Social R — International Socialist Review

Int Social Sci J — International Social Science Journal [*UNESCO*]

Int Soc Rock Mech Congr Proc — International Society for Rock Mechanics. Congress Proceedings

Int Soc Sci — International Social Science Journal [*UNESCO*]

Int Soc Sci J — International Social Science Journal [*UNESCO*]

Int Soc Secur R — International Social Security Review

Int Soc Secur Rev — International Social Security Review

Int Soc Work — International Social Work

Int Sol Energy Soc Am Sect Proc Annu Meet — International Solar Energy Society. American Section. Proceedings of the Annual Meeting

Int Solid Wastes Public Clean Assoc Inf Bull — International Solid Wastes and Public Cleansing Association. Information Bulletin

Int Sourceb Corros Mar Environ — International Sourcebook. Corrosion in Marine Environment

Int Spectator — International Spectator

Int Stat R — International Statistical Review

Int Stat Rev — International Statistical Review

Int St E As — International Studies. East Asian Series Research Publication

Int St Rvw — International Statistical Review

Int Stud — International Studies [*New Delhi*]

Int Studio — International Studio

Int Stud Manage Org — International Studies of Management and Organization

Int Stud (New Delhi) — International Studies (New Delhi)

Int Stud Phil — International Studies in Philosophy

Int Stud Q — International Studies Quarterly

Int Stud Quart — International Studies Quarterly

Int Stud Sparrows — International Studies on Sparrows

Int Stud (Stockholm) — Internationelle Studier (Stockholm)

Int Sugar Confect Manuf Assoc Period Bull — International Sugar Confectionery Manufacturers' Association. Periodic Bulletin

Int Sugar J — International Sugar Journal

Int Sug J — International Sugar Journal

Int Surg — International Surgery

Int Symp Can Soc Immunol — International Symposium. Canadian Society for Immunology

Int Symp Carotenoids Other than Vitam A Abstr Commun — International Symposium on Carotenoids Other than Vitamin A. Abstracts of Communications

Int Symp Chemother — International Symposium on Chemotherapy

Int Symp Combust Pap — International Symposium on Combustion. Papers

Int Symp Corals Coral Reefs Proc — International Symposium on Corals and Coral Reefs. Proceedings

Int Symp Crop Prot Pap — International Symposium on Crop Protection. Papers

Int Symp Flammability Fire Retard Proc — International Symposium on Flammability and Fire Retardants. Proceedings

Int Symp Heterog Catal Proc — International Symposium on Heterogeneous Catalysis. Proceedings

Int Symp Humidity and Moisture — International Symposium on Humidity and Moisture

Int Symp Landslide Control Proc — International Symposium on Landslide Control. Proceedings

Int Symp Microb Drug Resist — International Symposium on Microbial Drug Resistance

Int Symp Radiosensitizers Radioprot Drugs — International Symposium on Radiosensitizers and Radioprotective Drugs

Int Symp Remote Sensing Environ Proc — International Symposium on Remote Sensing of Environment. Proceedings

Int Tax J — International Tax Journal

Int Teach — Intermediate Teacher

Int Teamster — International Teamster

Int Telemetering Conf (Proc) — International Telemetering Conference (Proceedings) [*United States*]

Int Thyroid Conf Proc — International Thyroid Conference. Proceedings

Int Tijdschr Brouw Mout — Internationaal Tijdschrift voor Brouwertj en Mouterij

Int Tin Res Counc Rep — International Tin Research Council. Reports

Int Tracts Comput Sci Technol Their Appl — International Tracts in Computer Science and Technology and Their Application

Int Trade Forum — International Trade Forum

Int Tug Conv (Proc) — International Tug Convention (Proceedings)

Int Turtle Tortoise Soc J — International Turtle and Tortoise Society. Journal

INTU — Indian Truth

Int Union Air Pollut Prev Assoc Int Clean Air Congr Pap — International Union of Air Pollution Prevention Associations. International Clean Air Congress. Papers

Int Union Biol Sci Ser B — International Union of Biological Sciences. Series B

Int Union Biol Sci Ser D Newsl — International Union of Biological Sciences. Series D. Newsletter

Int Union Cancer Monogr Ser — International Union Against Cancer. Monograph Series

Int Union Cancer Tech Rep Ser — International Union Against Cancer. Technical Report Series

Int Union Conserv Nat Nat Resour Annu Rep — International Union for Conservation of Nature and Natural Resources. Annual Report

Int Union Crystallogr Comm Crystallogr Appar Bibliogr — International Union of Crystallography. Commission on Crystallographic Apparatus. Bibliography

Int Union Geol Sci Int Subcomm Stratigr Cl Circ — International Union of Geological Sciences. International Subcommission on Stratigraphic Classification. Circular

Int Union Geol Sci Ser A — International Union of Geological Sciences. Series A

Int Urol Nephrol — International Urology and Nephrology

Int Ver Theor Angew Limnol Mitt — International Vereinigung fuer Theoretische und Angewandte Limnologie. Mitteilungen [*West Germany*]

Int Ver Theor Angew Limnol Verh — Internationale Vereinigung fuer Theoretische und Angewandte Limnologie und Verhandlungen

Int Vet Bull — International Veterinary Bulletin

Int Vet News — International Veterinary News

Int Virol — International Virology

Int Water Pollut Res Conf Pap — International Water Pollution Research Conference. Papers

Int Water Power Dam — International Water Power and Dam Construction

Int Water Power & Dam Constr — International Water Power and Dam Construction

Int Water Supply Assoc Congr — International Water Supply Association. Congress

Int Whaling Comm Rep — International Whaling Commission. Reports

Int Wildl — International Wildlife

Int Wildlife — International Wildlife

Int Wire Cable Symp Proc — International Wire and Cable Symposium. Proceedings

Int Wiss Kolloq Tech Hochsch Ilmenau — Internationales Wissenschaftliches Kolloquium der Technischen Hochschule Ilmenau

Int Wiss Korresp Gesch Dtsch Arb-Bew — Internazional Wissenschaftliche Korrespondenz zur Geschichte der Deutschen Arbeiterbewegung

Int Woodworker — International Woodworker

Int Workshop Nude Mice Proc — International Workshop on Nude Mice. Proceedings

Int Yearbook Ag Leg — International Yearbook of Agricultural Legislation

Int Yearbook of Ed — International Yearbook of Education

Int Yrbk Ed — International Yearbook of Education

Int Z Angew Phsyiol Einschl Arbeitsphysiol — Internationale Zeitschrift fuer Angewandte Physiologie Einschliesslich Arbeitsphysiologie

Int Z Angew Physiol — Internationale Zeitschrift fuer Angewandte Physiologie Einschliesslich Arbeitsphysiologie [*West Germany*]

Int Z Bibelwiss — Internationale Zeitschriftenschall fuer Bibelwissenschaft und Grenzgebiete

Int Z Bohrtech Erdoelbergbau Geol — Internationale Zeitschrift fuer Bohrtechnik, Erdoelbergbau, und Geologie

Int Z Elektrowaerme — Internationale Zeitschrift fuer Elektrowaerme

Int Z Erzieh — Internationale Zeitschrift fuer Erziehungswissenschaft

Int Z Klin Pharmakol Ther Toxicol — Internationale Zeitschrift fuer Klinische Pharmakologie Therapie und Toxicologie

Int Z Landwirtsch — Internationale Zeitschrift der Landwirtschaft

Int Z Metallogr — Internationale Zeitschrift fuer Metallographie

Int Zool Cong — International Zoological Congress

Int Zoo Yearb — International Zoo Yearbook

Int Z Phys Chem Biol — Internationale Zeitschrift fuer Physikalisch Chemische Biologie

Int Z Theor Angew Genet — Internationale Zeitschrift fuer Theoretische und Angewandte Genetik

Int Z Vitam-Ernaehrungsforsch — Internationale Zeitschrift fuer Vitamin und Ernaehrungsforschung

Int Z Vitamforsch — Internationale Zeitschrift fuer Vitaminforschung

Int Z Vitaminforsch — Internationale Zeitschrift fuer Vitaminforschung

Int Z Vitaminforsch Beih — Internationale Zeitschrift fuer Vitaminforschung. Beiheft

INUCA — Inorganic and Nuclear Chemistry Letters

INUI — Inuit Today

INUL — Inulirijut. Department of Indian and Northern Affairs. Education Section. Social Development Division [Canada]

INUM — Inummarit

INUN — Inuit North [Nortext, Ottawa]

In Univ Fol — Indiana University. Folklore Institute. Monograph Series

INURAQ — Investigative Urology

INUSA — Industria Usoara

INUT — Inuttitut

INUV — Inuvialuit

Inv — Inventario

INV — Investment Review

Inv Banking — Investment Banking

Inv Chron — Investors Chronicle and Stock Exchange Gazette

Inv DD — Investment Dealers' Digest

Inventaire Mineral Fr — Inventaire Mineralogique de la France

Invent Intell — Invention Intelligence [India]

Invention — Invention Intelligence

Invent Manage — Invention Management [United States]

Invent Math — Inventiones Mathematicae

Invest Agric (Santiago) — Investigacion Agricola (Santiago)

Invest Agropecu (Lima) — Investigaciones Agropecuarias (Lima, Peru)

Invest Agropecu (Peru) — Investigaciones Agropecuarias (Lima, Peru)

Invest Anal J — Investment Analysts Journal

Invest Cell Pathol — Investigative and Cell Pathology

Invest Clin Lab — Investigacion en la Clinica y en el Laboratorio

Invest Clin (Maracaibo) — Investigacion Clinica (Maracaibo)

Invest Econ — Investigacion Economica

Invest Fish Control — Investigations in Fish Control

Investigacion Agric — Investigacion Agricola

Investigacion Econ — Investigacion Economica

Investigacion Oper — Investigacion Operacional [Havana]

Investigacion Pesq — Investigacion Pesquera

Investigation Air Pollut-Deposit Gauge Lead Diox Candle — Investigation of Air Pollution - Deposit Gauge and Lead Dioxide Candle

Investigation Air Pollut Smoke Sulph Diox Surv — Investigation of Air Pollution - Smoke and Sulphur Dioxide Survey

Investigation Report-CSIRO Institute of Earth Resources — Investigation Report. Commonwealth Scientific and Industrial Research Organization. Institute of Earth Resources

Invest Indiana Lakes Streams — Investigations of Indiana Lakes and Streams

Invest Inf Text — Investigacion e Informacion Textil

Invest Inf Text Tens — Investigacion e Informacion Textil y de Tensioactivos

Invest Lab Quim Biol Univ Nac Cordoba — Investigaciones. Laboratorio de Quimica Biologica. Universidad Nacional de Cordoba

Invest Mar Univ Catol Valparaiso — Investigaciones Marinas. Universidad Catolica de Valparaiso

Investment Dealers Dig — Investment Dealers' Digest

Invest Microtech Med Biol — Investigative Microtechniques in Medicine and Biology

Invest Ophthalmol — Investigative Ophthalmology [Later, Investigative Ophthalmology and Visual Science]

Invest Ophthalmol Vis Sci — Investigative Ophthalmology and Visual Science

Invest Ophthalmol Visual Sci — Investigative Ophthalmology and Visual Science

Invest Ophthal Visual Sci — Investigative Ophthalmology and Visual Science

Investor Owned Hosp Rev — Investor-Owned Hospital Review

Investors Chron — Investors Chronicle

Investors Chronicle — Investors Chronicle and Financial World

Invest Pediatr — Investigacion Pediatrica

Invest Pesq — Investigacion Pesquera

Invest Prog Agric — Investigacion y Progreso Agricola

Invest Radiol — Investigative Radiology

Invest Rep CSIRO (Aust) — Investigation Reports. Commonwealth Scientific and Industrial Research Organisation (Australia)

Invest Rep CSIRO Inst Earth Resour — CSIRO [Commonwealth Scientific and Industrial Research Organisation] Institute of Earth Resources. Investigation Report

Invest Rep CSIRO Miner Res Lab — CSIRO [Commonwealth Scientific and Industrial Research Organisation] Minerals Research Laboratories. Investigation Report

Invest Rep Div Miner Chem CSIRO — Investigation Report. Division of Mineral Chemistry. Commonwealth Scientific and Industrial Research Organisation

Invest Rep Div Miner CSIRO — Investigation Report. Division of Mineralogy. Commonwealth Scientific and Industrial Research Organisation

Invest Rep Div Miner Phys CSIRO — Investigation Report. Division of Mineral Physics. Commonwealth Scientific and Industrial Research Organisation

Invest Rep Miner Res Lab CSIRO — Investigation Report. Minerals Research Laboratories. Commonwealth Scientific and Industrial Research Organisation

Invest Tec Papel — Investigacion y Tecnica del Papel

Invest Urol — Investigative Urology

Invest Zool Chil — Investigaciones Zoologicas Chilenas

Inv Ind Lakes and Streams — Investigations of Indiana Lakes and Streams

In Vitro J Tissue Cult Assoc — In Vitro. Journal of the Tissue Culture Association

In Vitro Monogr — In Vitro Monograph

INVL — Inuvialuit

INVMDJ — Invasion and Metastasis

INVO — Indian Voice

Inv Ophth — Investigative Ophthalmology [Later, Investigative Ophthalmology and Visual Science]

Inv Pesq — Investigacion Pesquera

Inv Radiol — Investigative Radiology

INVRAV — Investigative Radiology

Inv Urol — Investigative Urology

Inv Zool Chilenas — Investigaciones Zoologicas Chilenas

INWAB — Industrial Wastes

Inwest i Budown — Inwestycje i Budownictwo

INWI — International Wildlife

INWO — Indian World

INWWAH — Industrial Water and Wastes

INX — Eigen Vervoer. Magazine voor Eigen Vervoerders en Verladers

INZAA — Insatsu Zasshi

Inz Apar Chem — Inzynieria i Aparatura Chemiczna [Poland]

Inz Budownictwo — Inzynieria i Budownictwo

Inz Chem — Inzynieria Chemiczna

Inz-Fiz Z — Inzenerno-Fiziceskii Zurnal

Inzh-Fiz Zh — Inzhenerno-Fizicheskii Zhurnal

Inzh-Fiz Zh Akad Nauk Belorus SSR — Inzhenerno-Fizicheskii Zhurnal Akademiya Nauk Beloruskoi SSR

Inzh Sb — Inzhenernyi Sbornik [USSR]

Inzh Zh — Inzhenernyi Zhurnal [USSR]

Inzh Zh Mekh Tverd Tela — Inzhenernyi Zhurnal, Mekhanika Tverdogo Tela

Inz Materialowa — Inzynieria Materialowa

INZSA — Inzhenernyi Sbornik

Inz Stavby — Inzenyrske Stavby

Inz-Stroitel Inst Kuibysev Sb Trudov — Moskovskii Ordena Trudovogo Krasnogo Znameni Inzenerno-Stroitel'nyi Institut Imeni V. V. Kuibyseva Sbornik Trudov

Inz Z Meh Tverd Tela — Inzenernyi Zurnal Mehanika Tverdogo Tela

IO — Iowa Music Educator

IOBKA — Izvestiya na Instituta po Obshta i Neorganichna Khimiya. Bulgarska Akademiya na Naukite

IOBLAM — Iowa Bird Life

IOC — Isotopes in Organic Chemistry [Elsevier Book Series]

IOCTAH — Intergovernmental Oceanographic Commission. Technical Series

IOE — Industry and Development

IOG — International Organization

IOHSA — International Journal of Occupational Health and Safety

IOKKA — Izvestiya na Instituta po Organichna Khimiya. Bulgarska Akademiya na Naukite [Bulgaria]

IOKNA — Izvestiya na Otdelenieto za Khimicheski Nauki. Bulgarska Akademiya na Naukite

IOLRAM — Israel Oceanographic and Limnological Research. Annual Report

Ion Exch — Ion Exchange and Membranes

Ion Exch Membr — Ion Exchange and Membranes

Ion Exch Prog — Ion Exchange Progress

Ion Exch Solvent Extr — Ion Exchange and Solvent Extraction

Ionos Issled — Ionosfernye Issledovaniya [USSR]

Ion-Selective Electrode Rev — Ion-Selective Electrode Reviews

IOPCA — International Ophthalmology Clinics

IOPIA — Itogi Nauki i Tekhniki Obogashchenie Poleznykh Iskopaemykh

IOR — Management Zeitschrift

IOSCR — Institute of Ocean Sciences. Patricia Bay. Contractor Report

IOS Report — Institute of Oceanographic Sciences. Report

IOVSDA — Investigative Ophthalmology and Visual Science

Iowa Acad Sci Proc — Iowa Academy of Science. Proceedings

Iowa Ac Sc Pr — Iowa Academy of Science. Proceedings

Iowa Agric Exp Stn Res Bull — Iowa. Agricultural Experiment Station. Research Bulletin

Iowa Agric Home Econ Exp Stn Res Bull — Iowa. Agriculture and Home Economics Experiment Station. Research Bulletin

Iowa Agric Home Econ Exp Stn Spec Rep — Iowa. Agriculture and Home Economics Experiment Station. Special Report

Iowa Conserv — Iowa Conservationist

Iowa Dent Bull — Iowa Dental Bulletin

Iowa Dent J — Iowa Dental Journal

Iowa Farm Sci — Iowa Farm Science

Iowa Geol Survey Water Atlas — Iowa. Geological Survey. Water Atlas

Iowa Geol Survey Water-Supply Bull — Iowa. Geological Survey. Water-Supply Bulletin
Iowa Geol Surv Rep Invest — Iowa. Geological Survey. Report of Investigations
Iowa Geol Surv Tech Pap — Iowa. Geological Survey. Technical Paper
Iowa Hist Rec — Iowa Historical Record
Iowa Institutions B — Iowa State Institutions. Bulletin
Iowa Jour Hist and Pol — Iowa Journal of History and Politics
Iowa Lib Q — Iowa Library Quarterly
Iowa L Rev — Iowa Law Review
Iowa Med J — Iowa Medical Journal
Iowa Nat — Iowa Naturalist
IowaR — Iowa Review
Iowa State Coll Agric Mech Arts Eng Exp Stn Bull — Iowa State College of Agriculture and Mechanical Arts. Engineering Experiment Station. Bulletin
Iowa State Coll Agric Mech Arts Eng Exp Stn Eng Rep — Iowa State College of Agriculture and Mechanical Arts. Engineering Experiment Station. Engineering Report
Iowa State Coll Eng Expt Sta Eng Rept Proj — Iowa State College. Engineering Experiment Station. Engineering Report. Project
Iowa State Coll Vet — Iowa State College Veterinarian
Iowa State J Res — Iowa State Journal of Research
Iowa State J Sci — Iowa State Journal of Science
Iowa State Univ (Ames) Eng Res Inst Rep — Iowa State University (Ames). Engineering Research Institute. Report
Iowa State Univ Dept Earth Sci Pub — Iowa State University. Department of Earth Sciences. Publication
Iowa State Univ Eng Exp Sta Bull — Iowa State University of Science and Technology. Engineering Experiment Station. Bulletin [*Ames, IA*]
Iowa State Univ Sci Technol Eng Exp Stn Bull — Iowa State University of Science and Technology. Engineering Experiment Station. Bulletin
Iowa State Univ Sci Technol Eng Exp Stn Eng Rep — Iowa State University of Science and Technology. Engineering Experiment Station. Engineering Report
Iowa State Univ Sci and Technology Eng Expt Sta Bull — Iowa State University of Science and Technology. Engineering Experiment Station. Bulletin
Iowa State Univ Stat Lab Annu Rep — Iowa State University. Statistical Laboratory. Annual Report
Iowa State Water Resour Res Inst Annu Rep — Iowa State Water Resources Research Institute. Annual Report
Iowa St BA News Bull — Iowa State Bar Association. News Bulletin
Iowa St J Sci — Iowa State Journal of Science
Iowa Univ Lab N H B — Iowa State University. Laboratories of Natural History. Bulletin
IP — Inuit Nipingat. Baker Lane. Northwest Territory
IP — Investigacion y Progreso
IPA — International Pharmaceutical Abstracts [*American Society of Hospital Pharmacists*] [*Bibliographic database*]
IPAGBA — Investigacion y Progreso Agricola
IPAJ — International Phonetic Association Journal
IPAR — IPA [*Institute of Public Affairs*] Review
IPA Rev — IPA [*Institute of Public Affairs*] Review
IPA Rev — IPA [*International Pharmaceutical Abstracts*] Review
Ipargazd Szle — Ipargazdasagi Szemle
Ipari Energiagazd — Ipari Energiagazdalkodas
Iparmuveszeti Muz Ev — Iparmueveszeti Muzeum Evkoenyvei
IPA (VIC) R — Institute of Public Affairs (Victoria). Review
IPBKA — Izvestiya Sektora Platiny i Drugikh Blagorodnykh Metallov Institut Obshchei i Neorganicheskoi Khimii, Akademiya Nauk SSSR
IPC — Indian Philosophy and Culture. Quarterly
IPCBA — Bibliographic Series. Institute of Paper Chemistry
IPC Mg — IPC [*Institute of Philippine Culture*] Monographs
IPC Pap — IPC [*Institute of Philippine Culture*] Papers
IPCTAO — Impact Agricultural Research in Texas. Annual Report
IPD — International Journal of Physical Distribution and Materials Management
IPE — International Paper Board Industry. Corrugated Manufacture and Conversion
IPEF Publ Semest — IPEF [*Instituto de Pesquisas e Estudos Florestais*] Publicacao Semestral
IPE Ind Prod Eng — IPE. Industrial and Production Engineering
IPE Int Ind Prod Eng — IPE International Industrial and Production Engineering
IPEN — Indian PEN
IPESAV — Investigacion Pesquera
I Pest Cntrl — International Pest Control
IPETA — Industrie du Petrole
IPEUB — Industrie du Petrole en Europe. Gaz-Chimie
IPF — Japan Pulp and Paper
IPG — International Planning Glossaries [*Elsevier Book Series*]
IPHCSR — International Pacific Halibut Commission. Scientific Report
IPHCTR — International Pacific Halibut Commission. Technical Report
IPHJAJ — Israel Pharmaceutical Journal
IPHSA — Institute of Physics. Conference Series
IPHYA — Indian Phytopathology

IPIBD3 — IPI [*International Potash Institute*] Bulletin
IPI Bull — IPI [*International Potash Institute*] Bulletin
IPI Res Top — IPI [*International Potash Institute*] Research Topics
IPK — Petroleum Economist
IPLL — Illinois Publications in Language and Literature
IPLO Q — IPLO [*Institute of Professional Librarians of Ontario*] Quarterly
IPLRB — Revue. Institut Pasteur de Lyon
IPM — Industrial Products Magazine
IPMCD — Industrie du Petrole dans le Monde. Gaz-Chimie
IPMPC — International Journal of Powder Metallurgy and Powder Technology
IPNA — Instituto Peruano-Norte Americano
IPOGA — Indian Musician
I Polit Sci — Indian Political Science Review
IPOTA — Izobreteniya Promyshlennye Obraztsy Tovarnye Znaki
IPPF Med Bull — IPPF [*International Planned Parenthood Federation*] Medical Bulletin
IPPIC — Instrumentation in the Pulp and Paper Industry
IPP Presseinf — IPP [*Max Planck Institut fuer Plasmaphysik*] Presseinformationen
IPPTA — Indian Pulp and Paper Technical Association. Journal
IPQ — International Petroleum Quarterly
IPQ — International Philosophical Quarterly
IPR — Internacia Pedagogia Recuo
IPRAA — Indian Practitioner
IPRADB — Intensivmedizinische Praxis
IPRCDH — In Practice
IPRDA — Israeli Annals of Psychiatry
IPRDAH — Israel Annals of Psychiatry and Related Disciplines
IPREA — Institute of Petroleum. Review
IPRHA — Industrial and Process Heating
IPRSDV — Israel Journal of Psychiatry and Related Sciences
IPSFCPR — International Pacific Salmon Fisheries Commission. Progress Reports
IPSOCS — Institute of Polar Studies (Ohio). Contribution Series
IPSYA — Individual Psychologist
I Psychol R — Indian Psychological Review
IPTCB — Collection. Colloques et Seminaires. Institut Francais du Petrole
IPTHA5 — International Congress on Pteridines. Handbook
IPW Ber — IPW [*Institut fuer Politik und Wirtschaft*] Berichte
IPW Forsch-H — IPW [*Institut fuer Politik und Wirtschaft*] Forschungshefte
IPWIA — Instrumentation in the Power Industry
IQ — India Quarterly
IQ — International Quarterly of Community Health Education
IQ — Investment Quality Trends
IQ — Islamic Quarterly
IQ — Italian Quarterly
IQAPA — Informacion de Quimica Analitica, Pura, y Aplicada a la Industria
Iqbal R — Iqbal Review
IQE — Israel Quarterly of Economics
IqR — Iqbal Review
IQT — International Tourism Quarterly
IR — Iliff Review
IR — Industrial Relations
IR — Innere Reich
IR — International Relations
IR — Israelitische Rundschau [*Berlin*]
IR — Iton Rishmi [*Official Gazette*]
IR — Journal of Irrigation and Drainage
IR — South Australian Industrial Reports
IRA — Iron Age
Ir Age Int — Iron Age Metalworking International [*Later, Chilton's IAMI Iron Age Metalworking International*]
IRAL — International Review of Applied Linguistics in Language Teaching
IRAMD — International Review of the Aesthetics and Sociology of Music
Iran — Iran Journal. British Institute of Persian Studies
IRAN — Izvestiia Rossiiskoi Akademii Nauk
Iran Antiq — Iranica Antiqua
Iran Geol Surv Rep — Iran Geological Survey. Report
Iranica Ant — Iranica Antiqua
Iran J Agric Res — Iranian Journal of Agricultural Research
Iran J Plant Pathol — Iranian Journal of Plant Pathology
Iran J Public Health — Iranian Journal of Public Health
Iran J Sci and Technol — Iranian Journal of Science and Technology
Iran J Sci Technol — Iranian Journal of Science and Technology
Iran R Int Relat — Iranian Review of International Relations
IranS — Iranian Studies
Iran Stud — Iranian Studies
IrAnt — Iranica Antiqua [*Leiden*]
Iraqi Chem Soc J — Iraqi Chemical Society. Journal
Iraqi Dent J — Iraqi Dental Journal
Iraqi J Sci — Iraqi Journal of Science
Iraq Nat Hist Mus Publ — Iraq Natural History Museum. Publication
Iraq Nat Hist Mus Rep — Iraq Natural History Museum. Report
IRAS — Iranica Antiqua. Supplements
IRASM — International Review of the Aesthetics and Sociology of Music

Ira Stud — Iranian Studies
IRBAA — Bulletin. Institut International du Froid. Annexe
IRBB — Institut Royal Colonial Belge. Bulletin des Seances
IRC — Steel Times (Redhill)
IRCD-A — International Review of Community Development
IRCD Bul — Yeshiva University. Information Retrieval Center on the
    Disadvantaged. Bulletin
Ir Comput — Irish Computer
IRCPA — IRE [*Institute of Radio Engineers*] Transactions on Component
    Parts
IRCS Med Sci-Libr Compend — IRCS [*International Research
    Communications System*] Medical Science. Library Compendium
IRCTD — IRCS [*International Research Communications System*] Research
    on Clinical Pharmacology and Therapeutics
IRCYA — International Review of Cytology
IREBI — Indices de Revista de Bibliotecologia
IrEccRec — Irish Ecclesiastical Record
Ir Econ Soc Hist — Irish Economic and Social History
IRE Int Conv Rec — IRE [*Institute of Radio Engineers*] International
    Convention Record
Irel Geol Surv Bull — Ireland. Geological Survey. Bulletin
Irel Natl Soil Surv Soil Surv Bull — Ireland National Soil Survey. Soil Survey
    Bulletin
Iren — Irenikon
IrERec — Irish Ecclesiastical Record [*Dublin*]
IRE Trans Component Parts — IRE [*Institute of Radio Engineers*]
    Transactions on Component Parts
IRE Trans Electron Comput — IRE [*Institute of Radio Engineers*]
    Transactions on Electronic Computers
IRE Trans Inform Theory — Institute of Radio Engineers. Transactions on
    Information Theory
IRE Trans Instrum — IRE [*Institute of Radio Engineers*] Transactions on
    Instrumentation
IRE Trans Microwave Theory Tech — IRE [*Institute of Radio Engineers*]
    Transactions on Microwave Theory and Techniques
IRE Trans Mil Electron — IRE [*Institute of Radio Engineers*] Transactions on
    Military Electronics
IRE Trans Nucl Sci — IRE [*Institute of Radio Engineers*] Transactions on
    Nuclear Science
IRE Trans Prod Tech — IRE [*Institute of Radio Engineers*] Transactions on
    Production Techniques
IRE Trans Reliab Qual Control — IRE [*Institute of Radio Engineers*]
    Transactions on Reliability and Quality Control
Ir Fish Invest Ser A Freshwater — Irish Fisheries Investigations. Series A.
    Freshwater
Ir Fish Invest Ser B Mar — Irish Fisheries Investigations. Series B. Marine
IRFOA4 — Irish Forestry
Ir For — Irish Forestry
IRG — Issues in Bank Regulation
IRGGA — Internationales Archiv fuer Gewerbepathologie und
    Gewerbehygiene
IRGGAJ — Internationales Archiv fuer Gewerbepathologie und
    Gewerbehygiene
Ir Hist Stud — Irish Historical Studies
IRIABC — Indian Agricultural Research Institute [*New Delhi*]. Annual
    Report
IRISAV — Indian Agricultural Research Institute [*New Delhi*]. Annual
    Scientific Report
Irish Agr Creamery Rev — Irish Agricultural and Creamery Review
Irish Astr — Irish Astronomical Journal
Irish Astron J — Irish Astronomical Journal
Irish Banking R — Irish Banking Review
Irish Bcasting R — Irish Broadcasting Review [*Republic of Ireland*]
Irish Beekpr — Irish Beekeeper
Irish Bldr & Engineer — Irish Builder and Engineer
Irish Bus — Business and Finance (Ireland)
Irish Econ — Irish Economist
Irish Folk M Stud — Irish Folk Music Studies
Irish For — Irish Forestry
Irish Georgian Soc Bull — Irish Georgian Society. Bulletin
Irish Georgian Soc Qly Bull — Irish Georgian Society. Quarterly Bulletin
Irish Hist — Irish Historical Studies
Irish Hist Stud — Irish Historical Studies
Irish J Agr — Irish Journal of Agricultural Research
Irish J Agric Econ and Rural Sociol — Irish Journal of Agricultural Economics
    and Rural Sociology
Irish J Agr Res — Irish Journal of Agricultural Research
Irish J Ed — Irish Journal of Education
Irish J Food Sci Technol — Irish Journal of Food Science and Technology
Irish J Med — Irish Journal of Medical Science
Irish J Psy — Irish Journal of Psychology
Irish Jur — Irish Jurist
Irish Lib Bul — Irish Library Bulletin
Irish Lit S — Irish Literary Studies
Irish LT — Irish Law Times
Irish Med J — Irish Medical Journal

Irish Med Times — Irish Medical Times
Irish Mo — Irish Monthly
Irish Num — Irish Numismatics
Irish Q — Irish Quarterly Review
Irish S — Irish Sword
Irish Stat — Irish Statistical Bulletin
Irish Statis Bul — Irish Statistical Bulletin
IrishThQ — Irish Theological Quarterly [*Maynooth*]
Irish U Rev — Irish University Review
Irish Wildfowl Comm Publ — Irish Wildfowl Committee. Publication [*Ireland*]
IRJ — European Rubber Journal
IRJ — Industrial Relations Journal
IRJ — Industrial Relations Law Journal
IRJADJ — Iranian Journal of Agricultural Sciences
Ir J Agric Res — Irish Journal of Agricultural Research
IRJaSl — Institut Russkogo Jazyka i Slovesnosti pri Akademii Nauk SSSR
Ir J Food Sci Technol — Irish Journal of Food Science and Technology
Ir J Med Sci — Irish Journal of Medical Science
IRJPAR — Irish Journal of Psychology
IRJPDU — Irish Journal of Psychotherapy
Ir J Psychol — Irish Journal of Psychology
IRJSD5 — Iraqi Journal of Science
Ir Jur — Irish Jurist
Ir Jur NS — Irish Jurist. New Series [*1856-67*]
Irkutsk Politehn Inst Trudy — Irkutskii Politehniceskii Institut Trudy
IRL — Industrial Relations Law Journal
IRLA — Information Retrieval and Library Automation
Ir Law T — Irish Law Times
IRLCAW — IRCS [*International Research Communications System*] Medical
    Science. Library Compendium
IRLCD — IRCS [*International Research Communications System*] Medical
    Science. Library Compendium
IRLI — Italianistica. Revista di Letteratura Italiana
IRLIB — Industrial Relations Legal Information Bulletin
Ir L T — Irish Law Times
Ir L Times and Solicitors' J — Irish Law Times and Solicitors' Journal. A
    Weekly Gazette of Legal News and Information
Ir LTJ — Irish Law Times and Solicitors' Journal
Ir LT Journal — Irish Law Times and Solicitors' Journal
IRM — Information Management
IRM — Information and Records Management
IRM — International Review of Missions
IrM — Irish Monthly
IRMA J — IRMA [*Indian Refractory Makers Association*] Journal
IRMAS — International Review of Music Aesthetics and Sociology [*Later,
    International Review of the Aesthetics and Sociology of Music*]
Ir Med J — Irish Medical Journal
I & R Mgmt — Information and Records Management
IRMLA — IRE [*Institute of Radio Engineers*] Transactions on Military
    Electronics
IRMMD2 — IRMMH [*Institute for Research into Mental and Multiple
    Handicap*] Monograph
IRMMH Monogr — IRMMH [*Institute for Research into Mental and
    Multiple Handicap*] Monograph
IRMNA2 — Institute for Research into Mental Retardation. Monograph
    [*Oxford*]
Ir Nat J — Irish Naturalists' Journal
IRNGA — Itogi Nauki i Tekhniki Razrabotka Neftyanykh i Gazovykh
    Mestorozhdenii
IRNRAJ — Iraq Natural History Museum. Report
IRNSA — IRE [*Institute of Radio Engineers*] Transactions on Nuclear
    Science
Ir Nurs News — Irish Nursing News
Irodal F — Irodalomtorteneti Fuzetek
Irod Szle — Irodalmi Szemle
Iron — Ironwood
Iron Age Metalwork Int — Iron Age Metalworking International [*Later,
    Chilton's IAMI Iron Age Metalworking International*]
Iron Coal Trades Rev — Iron and Coal Trades Review [*England*]
Ironmaking Conf Proc — Ironmaking Conference Proceedings
Ironmaking Proc AIME — Ironmaking Proceedings. Metallurgical Society of
    AIME. Iron and Steel Division
Ironmkg Steelmkg — Ironmaking and Steelmaking
Iron St — Iron and Steel
Iron Steel — Iron and Steel
Iron Steel Eng — Iron and Steel Engineer
Iron and Steel Eng — Iron and Steel Engineer
Iron Steel Inst Carnegie Scholarship Mem — Iron and Steel Institute. Carnegie
    Scholarship Memoirs
Iron Steel Inst (London) Bibliogr Ser — Iron and Steel Institute (London).
    Bibliographical Series
Iron Steel Inst (London) Publ — Iron and Steel Institute (London). Publication
Iron Steel Inst (London) Spec Rep — Iron and Steel Institute (London). Special
    Report
Iron Steel Int — Iron and Steel International
Iron and Steel Int — Iron and Steel International

Iron St Int — Iron and Steel International
Iron Tr R — Iron Trade Review
IRPHD — International Review of Physiology
IRPRD — In-Plant Reproductions
IRPSDZ — IRRI [*International Rice Research Institute*] Research
IRPWA — Irrigation and Power
IRR — Industrial Relations Research Association. Proceedings
IRRA — Industrial Relations Research Association. Proceedings
Irradiat Aliments — Irradiation des Aliments
Irradiat Aliments (Engl Ed) — Irradiation des Aliments (English Edition)
Irr Age — Irrigation Age
IR Research Repts — IR Research Reports
Irrig Age — Irrigation Age
Irrig Drain Pap — Irrigation and Drainage Paper
Irrig Drain Pap (FAO) — Irrigation and Drainage Paper (Food and Agriculture
    Organization of the United Nations)
Irrig Eng Maint — Irrigation Engineering and Maintenance
Irrig Farmer — Irrigation Farmer
Irrig Fmr — Irrigation Farmer
Irrig J — Irrigation Journal
Irrig Power — Irrigation and Power
Irrig & Power Abstr — Irrigation and Power Abstracts
Irrig Sci — Irrigation Science
Irrig Winter Wheat Tech Publ — Irrigated Winter Wheat. Technical
    Publication
IRRI Res Pap Ser — IRRI [*International Rice Research Institute*] Research
    Paper Series
IRRI Res Pap Ser Int Rice Res Inst — IRRI Research Paper Series.
    International Rice Research Institute
IRRSA8 — Indian Council of Agricultural Research. Review Series
IRS — Iran Service
IRSCD2 — Irrigation Science
IRSH — International Review of Social History
IRS Kurz-Inf Reihe A — IRS [*Institut fuer Reaktorischerheit der Technischen
    Ueberwachungs-Vereine*] Kurz-Information. Reihe A [*West Germany*]
IRS Kurz-Inf Reihe B — IRS [*Institut fuer Reaktorischerheit der Technischen
    Ueberwachungs-Vereine*] Kurz-Information. Reihe B [*West Germany*]
IRS Kurz-Inf Reihe C — IRS [*Institut fuer Reaktorischerheit der Technischen
    Ueberwachungs-Vereine*] Kurz-Information. Reihe C [*West Germany*]
IRS Kurz-Inf Reihe D — IRS [*Institut fuer Reaktorischerheit der Technischen
    Ueberwachungs-Vereine*] Kurz-Information. Reihe D [*West Germany*]
IRSL — International Review of Slavic Linguistics
IRS Mitt — IRS [*Institut fuer Reaktorischerheit der Technischen
    Ueberwachungs-Vereine*] Mitteilungen [*West Germany*]
IRSNAW — Koninklijk Belgisch Instituut voor Natuurwetenschappen.
    Studiedocumenten
Ir Spelaeol — Irish Spelaeology
Ir Sword — Irish Sword
IRT — Irish Times
IRTCA4 — Instrumentation Technology
Ir Text J — Irish Textile Journal
IRT Nucl J — IR and T Nuclear Journal [*United States*]
IRTOD9 — IPI [*International Potash Institute*] Research Topics
IrTQ — Irish Theological Quarterly [*Maynooth*]
IRV — Istituto Tecnico Statale Commerciale e per Geometri Roberto Valturio
    [*Rimini*]
Ir Vet J — Irish Veterinary Journal
Irving View — Irving Trust Company. Economic View from One Wall Street
IRW — Rubber World
IS — Industrial Society
IS — INSERM [*Institut National de la Sante et de la Recherche Medicale*]
    Symposia [*Elsevier Book Series*]
IS — Insurance Salesman
IS — International Socialist
IS — International Studies
IS — Irish Statesman
Is — Isis
IS — Italian Studies
IS — Italienische Studien
ISA — Illinois Studies in Anthropology
ISA — Information Science Abstracts
ISAC — Issues and Commentary [*Alaska*]
ISAFA — Industrial Safety
ISA J — ISA [*Instrument Society of America*] Journal
ISAJA — ISA [*Instrument Society of America*] Journal
ISA Prepr — ISA [*Instrument Society of America*] Conference Preprint
ISA Proc Int Power Instrum Symp — ISA [*Instrument Society of America*]
    Proceedings. International Power Instrumentation Symposium
ISA Proc Natl Aerosp Instrum Symp — ISA [*Instrument Society of America*]
    Proceedings. National Aerospace Instrumentation Symposium [*United
    States*]
ISA Proc Natl Power Instrum Symp — ISA [*Instrument Society of America*]
    Proceedings. National Power Instrumentation Symposium [*United
    States*]
ISATA — ISA [*Instrument Society of America*] Transactions
ISATAZ — ISA [*Instrument Society of America*] Transactions

ISA Trans — ISA [*Instrument Society of America*] Transactions
ISB — Independent School Bulletin
ISB — International Society of Bassists. Newsletter
ISB — Internationale Spectator
ISCC Newsl — Inter-Society Color Council Newsletter
ISE — Ibadan Studies in English
ISE — International Journal of Social Economics
ISEGRN — Institute of Social, Economic, and Government Research.
    University of Alaska. Research Notes
ISEGROP — Institute of Social, Economic, and Government Research.
    University of Alaska. Occasional Papers
ISEGRR — Institute of Social, Economic, and Government Research.
    University of Alaska. Report
ISEGRS — Institute of Social, Economic, and Government Research.
    University of Alaska. Research Summary
ISF — Imagination Science Fiction
ISFAM — Israelitisches Familienblatt [*Hamburg*]
ISGBBC — Geological Survey of Israel. Bulletin
ISGBBC — Israel. Geological Survey. Bulletin
ISGEA — Issledovaniya po Genetike
Is Geol Univ Milano Pubbl Ser G — Istituto di Geologia. Universita di Milano.
    Pubblicazione. Serie G
ISGE Trans Geotherm J — ISGE [*International Society for Geothermal
    Engineering*] Transactions and the Geothermal Journal [*United States*]
ISGE Trans Geotherm World J — ISGE [*International Society for Geothermal
    Engineering*] Transactions and Geothermal World Journal [*United
    States*]
I Sh — Independent Shavian
I Shaw — Independent Shavian
ISHGA — Ishikawajima-Harima Giho
Ishikawajima-Harima Eng Rev — Ishikawajima-Harima Engineering Review
ISHM J — ISHM [*International Society for Hybrid Microelectronics*] Journal
ISHM Proc — ISHM [*International Society for Hybrid Microelectronics*]
    Proceedings
ISHS — Illinois State Historical Society. Journal
ISHSJ — Illinois State Historical Society. Journal
ISI Bull — ISI [*Indian Standards Institution*] Bulletin
ISIDB — Instruments India
ISIP — Iron and Steel Industry Profiles
ISJ — Israel Export and Trade Journal
ISJCAT — Israel Journal of Chemistry
ISJM — Israeli Journal of Mathematics
ISJRA — Iowa State Journal of Research
ISJRA6 — Iowa State Journal of Research
ISJSA9 — Iowa State Journal of Science
ISJTAC — Israel Journal of Technology
ISKHDI — Ishikawa-Ken Nogyo Shikenjo Kenkyu Hokoku
Iskus K — Iskusstvo Kino
Iskusstvo K — Iskusstvo Kino
Iskusstv Sputniki Zemli — Iskusstvennye Sputniki Zemli
Iskusstv Sputniki Zemli Akad Nauk SSSR — Iskusstvennye Sputniki Zemli
    Akademiya Nauk SSSR [*USSR*]
Iskusstv Volokno — Iskusstvennoe Volokno
ISL — Industrie Lackier-Betrieb. Zentralblatt fuer Lackiertechnik und
    Beschichtungstechnik
Islam — Der Islam. Zeitschrift fuer Geschichte und Kultur des Islamischen
    Orients
Islamabad J Sci — Islamabad Journal of Sciences. Journal of Mathematics and
    Sciences
Islam Cult — Islamic Culture
Islam Mod Age — Islam and the Modern Age
Islam Stud — Islamic Studies
ISLIC Bull — Israel Society of Special Libraries and Information Centers.
    Bulletin
Is Lit — Islamic Literature
ISLL — Illinois Studies in Language and Literature
Isl Landbunadarrannsoknir — Islenzkar Landbunadarrannsoknir
IslQ — Islamic Quarterly [*London*]
Is LR — Israel Law Review
ISLRBH — Islenzkar Landbunadarrannsoknir
ISLRBH — Journal of Agricultural Research in Iceland
ISLS — Information System Language Studies
Isl St — Islamic Studies
ISM — International Studies of Management and Organization
ISM — Mitteilungen. Internationale Stiftung Mozarteum
ISMCEE — International Series of Monographs on Chemistry
ISME Yb — ISME [*International Society for Music Education*] Yearbook
ISMJAV — Israel Medical Journal
ISMTB — Instrumentalist
ISO — International Society of Organbuilders
ISO — Oxford Bulletin of Economics and Statistics
ISOBA — Izotopy v SSSR
ISOKD — Izvestiya Sibirskogo Otdeleniya Geologicheskogo Komiteta
ISOOA — Izvestiya Sibirskogo Otdeleniya Akademii Nauk SSSR Seriya
    Obshchestvennykh Nauk

Isot Generator Inf Cent (Gif Sur Yvettte) Newsl — Isotopic Generator Information Centre (Gif-Sur-Yvette). Newsletter
Isot Ind Landwirtsch — Isotope in Industrie und Landwirtschaft
Isot News — Isotope News [*Japan*]
Isotopenprax — Isotopenpraxis
Isotopes Radiat — Isotopes Radiation
Isotop Radiat Technol — Isotopes and Radiation Technology
Isot Radiat — Isotopes and Radiation [*Japan*]
Isot Radiat Res — Isotope and Radiation Research [*Egypt*]
Isot Radiat Res Anim Dis Vec — Isotope and Radiation Research on Animal Diseases and Their Vectors. Proceedings
Isot Radiat Technol — Isotopes and Radiation Technology
Isozymes Curr Top Biol Med Res — Isozymes. Current Topics in Biological and Medical Research
ISPBA — Buletinul. Institutului de Studii si Projectari Energetice
Ispol'z Gaza Nar Khoz — Ispol'zovanie Gaza v Narodnom Khozyaistve [*USSR*]
Ispolz Mikroorg Nar Khoz — Ispol'zovanie Mikroorganizmov v Narodnom Khozyaistve
Ispol'z Neorg Resur Okeanicheskoi Vody — Ispol'zovanie Neorganicheskikh Resursov Okeanicheskoi Vody
Ispol'z Tverd Topl Sernistykh Mazutov Gaza — Ispol'zovanie Tverdykh Topliv Sernistykh Mazutov i Gaza [*USSR*]
ISPOR — Institute of Polar Studies (Ohio). Reports
ISQ — Informatie. Maandblad voor Informatieverwerking
IsQ — Islamic Quarterly
ISR — Index to Scientific Reviews
ISR — Information Processing and Management
ISR — Interdisciplinary Science Reviews
Isr AEC IA Rep — Israel. Atomic Energy Commission. IA Report
Isr AEC LS Rep — Israel. Atomic Energy Commission. LS Report
Israel Ann Psychiat — Israel Annals of Psychiatry
Israel E — Israel Economist
Israel Inv — Israel Business and Investors' Report
Israel J Agric Res — Israel Journal of Agricultural Research
Israel J Agr Res — Israel Journal of Agricultural Research
Israel J Bot — Israel Journal of Botany
Israel J Chem — Israel Journal of Chemistry
Israel J Earth Sci — Israel Journal of Earth-Sciences
Israel J Ent — Israel Journal of Entomology
Israel J Math — Israel Journal of Mathematics
Israel J Tech — Israel Journal of Technology
Israel J Technol — Israel Journal of Technology
Israel J Zool — Israel Journal of Zoology
Israel Law R — Israel Law Review
Israel L Rev — Israel Law Review
Israel Yb on Human Rights — Israel Yearbook on Human Rights
Isr Agric Res Org Div For Trienn Rep Res — Israel. Agricultural Research Organization. Division of Forestry. Triennial Report of Research
Isr Ann Psy — Israel Annals of Psychiatry and Related Disciplines
Isr Ann Psychiatry — Israel Annals of Psychiatry and Related Disciplines
Isr Ann Psychiatry Relat Discip — Israel Annals of Psychiatry and Related Disciplines
IsrEJ — Israel Exploration Journal [*Jerusalem*]
I S Revw — International Socialist Review
Isr Expl J — Israel Exploration Journal
Isr Geol Surv Bull — Israel. Geological Survey. Bulletin
Isr Geol Surv Geol Data Process Unit Rep — Israel. Geological Survey. Geological Data Processing Unit. Report
Isr Geol Surv Rep — Israel. Geological Survey. Report
Isr Hydrol Serv Rep — Israel. Hydrological Service. Report
Isr Inst Agric Eng Sci Act — Israel. Institute of Agricultural Engineering. Scientific Activities
Isr Inst Anim Sci Sci Act — Israel. Institute of Animal Science. Scientific Activities
Isr Inst Field Gard Crops Sci Act — Israel. Institute of Field and Garden Crops. Scientific Activities
Isr Inst Hortic Sci Act — Israel. Institute of Horticulture. Scientific Activities
Isr Inst Plant Prot Sci Act — Israel. Institute of Plant Protection. Scientific Activities
Isr Inst Soils Water Sci Act — Israel. Institute of Soils and Water. Scientific Activities
Isr Inst Technol Storage Agric Prod Sci Act — Israel. Institute for Technology and Storage of Agricultural Products. Scientific Activities
Isr J Agric Res — Israel Journal of Agricultural Research
Isr J Bot — Israel Journal of Botany
Isr J Chem — Israel Journal of Chemistry
Isr J Dent Med — Israel Journal of Dental Medicine
Isr J Earth — Israel Journal of Earth-Sciences
Isr J Earth-Sci — Israel Journal of Earth-Sciences
Isr J Entomol — Israel Journal of Entomology
Isr J Exp Med — Israel Journal of Experimental Medicine
Isr J Math — Israel Journal of Mathematics
Isr J Med S — Israel Journal of Medical Sciences
Isr J Med Sci — Israel Journal of Medical Sciences
Isr J Psychiatr Relat Sci — Israel Journal of Psychiatry and Related Sciences

Isr J Tech — Israel Journal of Technology
Isr J Technol — Israel Journal of Technology
Isr J Zool — Israel Journal of Zoology
Isr Law Rev — Israel Law Review
IsrLLetters — Israel Life and Letters [*New York*]
Isr Med J — Israel Medical Journal
Isr Min Agr Water Comm Hydrol Serv Hydrol Paper — Israel. Ministry of Agriculture. Water Commission. Hydrological Service. Hydrological Paper
Isr Natl Counc Res Dev Rep — Israel. National Council for Research and Development. Report
Isr Natl Counc Res Dev Rep NCRD — Israel. National Council for Research and Development. Report NCRD
Isr Oceanogr Limnol Res Annu Rep — Israel Oceanographic and Limnological Research. Annual Report
Isr Orient Stud — Israel Oriental Studies
Isr Pharm J — Israel Pharmaceutical Journal
ISRRT Newsl — ISRRT [*International Society of Radiographers and Radiological Technicians*] Newsletter [*England*]
Isr Soc Spec Libr Inf Cent Bull — Israel Society of Special Libraries and Information Centers. Bulletin
ISRTAI — Isotopes and Radiation Technology
ISS — Indiana Slavic Studies
ISSJ — International Social Science Journal [*UNESCO*]
Issled Betonu Zhelezobetonu — Issledovaniya po Betonu i Zhelezobetonu
Issled Dalnevost Morei SSSR — Issledovaniya Dal'nevostochnykh Morei SSSR
Issled Elektrokhim Magnetokhim Elektrokhim Metodam Anal — Issledovaniya po Elektrokhimii Magnetokhimii i Elektrokhimicheskim Metodam Analiza
Issled Fauny Morei — Issledovaniya Fauny Morei
Issled Fiz Atmos Akad Nauk Est SSR — Issledovaniya po Fizike Atmosfery Akademiya Nauk Estonskoi SSR [*Estonian SSR*]
Issled Fiz Kipeniya — Issledovaniya po Fizike Kipeniya [*USSR*]
Issled Genet — Issledovaniya po Genetike
Issled Geomagn Aeron Fiz Solntsa — Issledovaniya po Geomagnetizmii, Aeronomii, i Fizike Solntsa
Issled Ispolz Soln Energ — Issledovaniya po Ispol'zovaniyu Solnechnoi Energii
Issled Kosm Prostranstva — Issledovanie Kosmicheskogo Prostranstva
Issled Mikrobiol — Issledovaniya po Mikrobiologii
Issled Nekotoryh Voprosov Mat Kibernet — Issledovanija Nekotoryh Voprosov Matematiceskoi Kibernetiki
Issled Obl Fiz Khim Kauch Rezin — Issledovaniya v Oblasti Fiziki i Khimii Kauchukov i Rezin
Issled Obl Khim Tekhnol Prod Pererab Goryuch Iskop — Issledovaniya v Oblasti Khimii i Tekhnologii Produktov Pererabotki Goryuchikh Iskopaemykh
Issled Obl Kinet Model Optim Khim Protsessov — Issledovaniya v Oblasti Kinetiki Modelirovaniya i Optimizatsii Khimicheskikh Protsessov
Issled Obl Kompleksn Ispol'z Topl — Issledovaniya v Oblasti Kompleksnogo Ispol'zovaniya Topliv [*USSR*]
Issled Operacii i Statist — Issledovanie Operacii i Statisticeskoe Modelirovanie
Issled Plazmennykh Sgustkov — Issledovanie Plazmennykh Sgustkov
Issled Prikl Mat — Kazanskii Universitet Issledovanija po Prikladnoi Matematike
Issled Protsessov Obrab Met Davleniem — Issledovanie Protsessov Obrabotki Metallov Davleniem
Issled Sist — Issledovanie Sistem
Issled Splavov Tsvetn Met — Issledovanie Splavov Tsvetnykh Metallov
Issled Stroit — Issledovaniya po Stroitel'stvu [*Estonian SSR*]
Issled Strukt Sostoyaniya Neorg Veshchestv — Issledovaniya Strukturnogo Sostoyaniya Neorganicheskikh Veshchestv
Issled Tekhnol Stroit Mater — Issledovaniya po Tekhnologii Stroitel'nykh Materialov
Issled Teor Plastin Obolochek — Issledovaniya po Teorii Plastin i Obolochek
Issled Teor Plastin i Obolochek — Kazanskii Universitet Issledovaniya po Teorii Plastin i Obolochek
Issled Tsentr Am Morei — Issledovaniya Tsentral'no-Amerikanskikh Morei
Issled Uprug Plast — Issledovaniya po Uprugosti i Plastichnosti
Issled Vodopodgot — Issledovaniya po Vodopodgotovke
Issled Vyazhushchikh Veshchestv Izdelii Ikh Osn — Issledovaniya Vyazhushchikh Veshchestv i Izdelii na Ikh Osnove
Issled Zharoproch Splavam — Issledovaniya po Zharoprochnym Splavam [*USSR*]
ISSOA8 — Impact of Science on Society [*English Edition*]
Iss Stud — Issues and Studies
Issue Briefing Pap USDA Off Gov Pub Aff — Issue Briefing Paper. United States Department of Agriculture. Office of Governmental and Public Affairs
Issues Bank Regul — Issues in Bank Regulation
Issues Compr Pediatr Nurs — Issues in Comprehensive Pediatric Nursing
Issues Crim — Issues in Criminology
Issues Eng — Issues in Engineering [*United States*]
Issues Engng J Prof Activities Proc ASCE — Issues in Engineering. Journal of Professional Activities. Proceedings of the American Society of Civil Engineers
Issues Health Care Women — Issues in Health Care of Women

Issues Ment Health Nurs — Issues in Mental Health Nursing
Issues Policy Summ — Issues and Policy Summaries [*United States*]
Issues Stud — Issues and Studies
Issues and Stud — Issues and Studies
ISt — Insemnari Stiintifice
ISt — Italian Studies
Istanbul Ark Muz Yilligi — Istanbul Arkeologi Muzeleri Yilligi
Istanbul Contrib Clin Sci — Istanbul Contribution to Clinical Science
Istanbuler Beitr Klin Wiss — Istanbuler Beitrage zur Klinischen Wissenschaft
Istanbul Med Fac Med Bull Istanbul Univ — Istanbul Medical Faculty Medical Bulletin. Istanbul University
Istanbul Tek Univ Bul — Istanbul Teknik Universitesi Bulteni
Istanbul Tek Univ Derg — Istanbul Teknik Universitesi Dergisi
Istanbul Tek Univ Nukl Enerji Enst Bul — Istanbul Teknik Universitesi Nukleer Enerji Enstitusu. Bulten
Istanbul Tip Fak Mecm — Istanbul Tip Fakultesi Mecmuasi
Istanbul Univ Dishekim Fak Derg — Istanbul Universitesi Dishekimligi Fakultesi Dergisi
Istanbul Univ Eczacilik Fak Mecm — Istanbul Universitesi Eczacilik Fakultesi Mecmuasi
Istanbul Univ Edebiyat Fak Turk ve Edebiyat Dergisi — Istanbul Universitesi Edebiyat Fakultesi Turk ve Edebiyat Dergisi
Istanbul Univ Fen Fak Hidrobiol Arastirma Enst Yayin — Istanbul Universitesi Fen Fakultesi Hidrobiologi Arastirma Enstitusu Yayinlari
Istanbul Univ Fen Fak Mecm Ser A — Istanbul Universitesi Fen Fakultesi Mecmuasi. Seri A. Sirfi ve Tatbiki Matematik
Istanbul Univ Fen Fak Mecm Ser B — Istanbul Universitesi Fen Fakultesi Mecmuasi. Seri B. Tabii Ilimler
Istanbul Univ Fen Fak Mecm Ser C — Istanbul Universitesi Fen Fakultesi Mecmuasi. Seri C. Astronomi-Fizik-Kimya
Istanbul Univ Fen Fak Mecm Seri B Tabii Ilimler — Istanbul Universitesi Fen Fakultesi Mecmuasi. Seri B. Tabii Ilimler
Istanbul Univ Med Bull — Istanbul University. Medical Bulletin
Istanbul Univ Med Fac Med Bull — Istanbul University. Medical Faculty. Medical Bulletin
Istanbul Univ Obs Yazilari — Istanbul Universitesi Observatuari Yazilari
Istanbul Univ Rev Geog Inst Internat Ed — Istanbul University. Review of the Geographical Institute. International Edition
Istanbul Univ Vet Fak Derg — Istanbul Universitesi Veteriner Fakultesi Dergisi
Istanbul Univ Vet Fak Derg J Fac Vet Med Univ Istanbul — Istanbul Universitesi Veteriner Fakultesi Dergisi/Journal of the Faculty of Veterinary Medicine. University of Istanbul
Istanbul Univ Yay (Orm Fak) — Istanbul Universitesi. Yaymlam (Orman Fakultesi)
Istanb Univ fen Fak Mecm — Istanbul Universitesi fen Fakueltesi Mecmuasi
Istanb Univ Orman Fak Derg — Istanbul Universitesi Orman Fakultesi Dergisi
Ist Ark Etnog Sred Azii — Istoriia, Arkheologiia, i Etnografiia Srednei Azii
Ist Autom Univ Roma Not — Istituto di Automatica. Universita di Roma Notiziario
Ist Bologna R Ac Sc Cl Sc Fis Mem — Istituto de Bologna. Reale Accademia delle Scienze. Classe di Scienze Fisiche. Memorie
Ist Chim Agrar Sper Gorizia Nuovi Ann Pubbl — Istituto Chimico Agrario Sperimentale di Gorizia. Nuovi Annali. Pubblicazione
Ist Dzerela Vykorystannja — Istoryeni Dzerela ta ich Vykorystannja
Ist Fed Ric For Mem — Istituto Federale di Ricerche Forestali. Memorie
Ist-Filol Z — Istoriko-Filologiceskij Zurnal
Ist Filol Zh — Istoriko-Filologiceskii Zhurnal
Ist Geof (Trieste) Pubbl — Istituto Geofisico (Trieste). Pubblicazione
Istit Veneto Sci Lett Arti Atti Cl Sci Mat Natur — Istituto Veneto di Scienze, Lettere, ed Arti. Venezia. Atti. Classe di Scienze Matematiche e Naturali
Ist Lomb Accad Sci Lett Rend A Sci Mat Fis Chim Geol — Istituto Lombardo. Accademia di Scienze e Lettere. Rendiconti. A. Scienze Matematiche, Fisiche, Chimiche, e Geologiche
Ist Lombardo Accad Sci e Lettere Rend — Istituto Lombardo. Accademia di Scienze e Lettere. Rendiconti
Ist Lombardo Accad Sci Lett Rend A — Istituto Lombardo. Accademia di Scienze e Lettere. Rendiconti. Scienze Matematiche, Fisiche, Chimiche, e Geologiche. A
Ist Lombardo Accad Sci Lett Rend Sci Biol Med B — Istituto Lombardo. Accademia di Scienze e Lettere. Rendiconti. Scienze Biologiche e Mediche. B
Ist Mat Kul't Uzbek — Istoriia Material-noj Kul'tury Uzbekistana
Ist Mit — Istanbuler Mitteilungen
Ist Mitt — Mitteilungen. Deutsches Archaeologische Institut. Abteilung Istanbul
Ist Mitt Bh — Istanbuler Mitteilungen. Beiheft
Ist Naz Genet Cerealicolt Nazareno Strampelli — Istituto Nazionale di Genetica per la Cerealicoltura Nazareno Strampelli
Istochniki Rudn Veshchestva Endog Mestorozhd — Istochniki Rudnogo Veshchestva Endogonnykh Mestorozhdenii
Istor-Astronom Issled — Istoriko-Astronomiceskie Issledovanija
Istoria Artei — Studii si Cercetari de Istoria Artei
Istor-Mat Issled — Istoriko-Matematiceskie Issledovanija
Istor Metodol Estestv Nauk — Istoriya i Metodologiya Estestvennykh Nauk
IS & TP — Index to Scientific and Technical Proceedings

Ist Patologia Libro Boll — Istituto di Patologia del Libro. Bollettino
Ist Sb Inst Ist Arheol Etnogr — Istoriceskij Sbornik Instituta Istorii, Arheologii, i Etnografii
Ist Sper Met Leggeri Mem Rapp — Istituto Sperimentale dei Metalli Leggeri. Memorie e Rapport
Ist SSSR — Istorija SSSR
Ist Super Sanita Lab Fis Rapp — Istituto Superiore di Sanita. Laboritori di Fisica. Rapporti
Ist Svizz Ric For Mem — Istituto Svizzero di Ricerche Forestali. Memorie
Ist Tec Agr Stat (Macerata) — Istituto Tecnico Agrario Statale (Macerata)
Ist Veneto Sci Lett Arti Atti Cl Sci Mat Natur — Istituto Veneto di Scienze, Lettere, ed Arti. Venezia. Atti. Classe di Scienze Matematiche e Naturali
IstZap — Istoriceskii Zapiski
ISU — International Sugar Journal
ISUDX — Information Services and Use
ISU Mitt — Interdisziplinarer Sonderbereich Umweltschutz. Mitteilungen
ISV — Informations-Chimie
ISWA Inf Bull — ISWA [*International Solid Wastes and Public Cleansing Association*] Information Bulletin
ISWOS — Israelitische Wochenschrift [*Breslau/Magdeburg*]
ISY — IBM [*International Business Machines Corp.*] Systems Journal
I Sz — Irodalmi Szemle
IT — Information Today
IT — Iraq Times
IT — Islenzk Tunga
It — Italia Che Scrive
It — Italica
ITA — Interavia. Revue Internationale Aeronautique, Astronautique, Electronique
It Agr — Italia Agricola
ITA J — International Trombone Association. Journal
Ital — Italianistica. Revista di Letteratura Italiana
Ital — Italica
Ital A — Italian Americana
Ital Agr — Italia Agricola
Ital Agric — Italia Agricola
Ital Am — Italian Americana
Italamer — Italamerican
Ital Aust Bul Commerce — Italian-Australian Bulletin of Commerce
Ital Cereali — Italia e i Cereali
Ital Exped Karakorum Hindu Kush Sci Rep — Italian Expeditions to the Karakorum [*K²*] and Hindu Kush. Scientific Reports
Ital For Mont — Italia Forestale e Montana
Ital Gen Rev Derm — Italian General Review of Dermatology
Ital Gen Rev Dermatol — Italian General Review of Dermatology
Ital Gen Rev Oto-Rhino-Laryng — Italian General Review of Oto-Rhino-Laryngology
Italian Am Bus — Italian American Business
Italia R Comitato G B — Italia Real Comitato Geologico. Bollettino
Ital J Bioc — Italian Journal of Biochemistry
Ital J Biochem — Italian Journal of Biochemistry
Ital J Biochem (Engl Ed) — Italian Journal of Biochemistry (English Edition)
Ital J Orthop Traumatol — Italian Journal of Orthopaedics and Traumatology
Ital J Orthop Traumatol Suppl — Italian Journal of Orthopaedics and Traumatology. Supplementum
Ital J Zool — Italian Journal of Zoology
Ital L — Italian Linguistics
Ital Med — Italia Medica
Ital Q — Italian Quarterly
Ital Quart — Italian Quarterly
Ital Vinic Agrar — Italia Vinicola ed Agraria
Italy Docs and Notes — Italy. Documents and Notes
Italy Ist Super Poste Telecomun Note Recens Not — Italy. Istituto Superiore delle Poste e delle Telecomunicazioni. Note Recensioni e Notizie
Italy Minist Agric For Collana Verde — Italy. Ministero dell'Agricoltura e delle Foreste Collana Verde
Italy Serv Geol Boll — Italy. Servizio Geologico. Bollettino
Italy Serv Geol Mem — Italy. Servizio Geologico. Memorie per Servire alla Descrizione della Carta Geologica d'Italia
ITA N — International Trombone Association. Newsletter
ItB — It Beaken
ITC — International Travel Catering
ITCCC — ITCC [*International Technical Cooperation Centre*] Review
ITCC Rev — ITCC [*International Technical Cooperation Centre*] Review [*Israel*]
ITCSA — In Vitro. Journal of the Tissue Culture Association
ITCSAF — In Vitro [*Rockville*]
ITDA — Income Tax Decisions of Australasia
ITEAA5 — INTA [*Instituto Nacional de Tecnologia Agropecuaria*]. Estacion Experimental Regional Agropecuaria [*Parana*]. Serie Tecnica
ITE J — ITE [*Institute of Transportation Engineers*] Journal [*United States*]
ITF — International Trade Forum
ITF — Italy. Documents and Notes
ItF — Italyan Filolojisi
It For Montan — Italia Forestale e Montana

ITG — International Trumpet Guild. Journal
ITGEA — Interdisciplinary Topics in Gerontology
ITGEAR — Interdisciplinary Topics in Gerontology
ITG J — International Trumpet Guild. Journal
ITG N — International Trumpet Guild. Newsletter
ITH — Internationaler Holzmarkt
I Th Q — Irish Theological Quarterly
ITI — Intermediair. Informatie voor Leidinggevende Functionarissen
Itin — Itinerari
ITJ — International Tax Journal
ITKBA — Izvestiya na Tsentralnata Khelmintologichna Laboratoriya. Bulgarska Akademiya na Naukite
ITMIB2 — Instituto Tecnologico de Monterrey. Division de Ciencias Agropecuarias y Maritimas. Informe de Investigacion
ITMZBJ — Intensivmedizin
ITO — In Theory Only
ITOBAO — Akhboroti Akademiyai Fankhoi RSS Tochikiston Shu-Bai Fankhoi Biologi
Itogi Nauki Astron — Itogi Nauki Astronomiya
Itogi Nauki Biol Khim — Itogi Nauki Biologicheskaya Khimiya
Itogi Nauki Biol Nauki — Itogi Nauki Biologicheskie Nauki
Itogi Nauki Biol Osn Rastenievod — Itogi Nauki Biologicheski Osnovy Rastenievodstva
Itogi Nauki Elektrokhim — Itogi Nauki Elektrokhimiya
Itogi Nauki Embriol — Itogi Nauki Embriologiya
Itogi Nauki Farmakol Toksikol — Itogi Nauki Farmakologiya. Toksikologiya
Itogi Nauki Fiz Khim — Itogi Nauki Fizicheskaya Khimiya
Itogi Nauki Geofiz — Itogi Nauki Geofizika
Itogi Nauki Geokhim Mineral Petrogr — Itogi Nauki Geokhimiya Mineralogiya Petrografiya
Itogi Nauki Khim Nauki — Itogi Nauki Khimicheskie Nauki
Itogi Nauki Korroz Zashch Korroz — Itogi Nauki Korroziya i Zashchita ot Korrozii
Itogi Nauki Nemet Posezn Iskop — Itogi Nauki Nemetallicheskie Poseznye Iskopaemye
Itogi Nauki Obshch Genet — Itogi Nauki Obshchaya Genetika
Itogi Nauki Obshch Vopr Patol — Itogi Nauki Obshchie Voprosy Patologii
Itogi Nauki Rudn Mestorozhd — Itogi Nauki Rudnye Mestorozhdeniya
Itogi Nauki Tekh At Energ — Itogi Nauki i Tekhniki Atomnaya Energetika
Itogi Nauki i Tekh Farmakol Khimioter Sredstva — Itogi Nauki i Tekhniki Farmakologiya, Khimioterapevticheskie Sredstva
Itogi Nauki Tekh Farmakol Khimioter Sredstva Toksikol — Itogi Nauki i Tekhniki Farmakologiya Khimioterapevtcheski Sredstva Toksikolog iya
Itogi Nauki Tekh Fiziol Rast — Itogi Nauki i Tekhniki Fiziologiya Rastenii
Itogi Nauki Tekh Fiz Khim Kinet — Itogi Nauki i Tekhniki Fizicheskaya Khimiya Kinetika
Itogi Nauki Tekh Geokhim Mineral Petrogr — Itogi Nauki i Tekhniki Geokhimiya Mineralogiya Petrografiya
Itogi Nauki Tekh Gidrogeol Inzh Geol — Itogi Nauki i Tekhniki Gidrogeologiya, Inzhenernaya Geologiya
Itogi Nauki Tekh Issled Kosm Prostranstva — Itogi Nauki i Tekhniki Issledovanie Kosmicheskogo Prostranstva
Itogi Nauki Tekh Khim Tekhn Vysokimol Soedin — Itogi Nauki i Tekhniki Khimiya i Tekhnologiya Vysokimolekulyarnykh Soedininii
Itogi Nauki Tekh Khim Termodin Ravnovesiya — Itogi Nauki i Tekhniki Khimicheskaya Termodinamika i Ravnovesiya
Itogi Nauki Tekh Korroz Zashch Korroz — Itogi Nauki i Tekhniki Korroziya i Zashchita ot Korrozii [*USSR*]
Itogi Nauki Tekh Kristallokhim — Itogi Nauki i Tekhniki Kristallokhimiya
Itogi Nauki Tekh Mestorozhd Goryuch Polezn Iskop — Itogi Nauki i Tekhniki Mestorozhdeniya Goryuchikh Poleznykh Iskopaemykh [*USSR*]
Itogi Nauki Tekh Metalloved Term Obrab — Itogi Nauki i Tekhniki Metallovedenie i Termicheskaya Obrabotka
Itogi Nauki Tekh Metall Tsvetn Redk Met — Itogi Nauki i Tekhniki Metallurgiya Tsvetnykh i Redkikh Metallov
Itogi Nauki Tekh Mikrobiol — Itogi Nauki i Tekhniki Mikrobiologiya
Itogi Nauki Tekh Mol Biol — Itogi Nauki i Tekhniki Molekulyarnaya Biologiya
Itogi Nauki Tekh Nauki — Itogi Nauki Tekhnicheskie Nauki
Itogi Nauki Tekh Nemet Polezn Iskop — Itogi Nauki i Tekhniki Nemetallicheskie Poleznye Iskopaemye
Itogi Nauki Tekh Neorg Khim — Itogi Nauki i Tekhniki Neorganicheskaya Khimiya
Itogi Nauki Tekhnol Org Veshchestv — Itogi Nauki Tekhnologiya Organicheskikh Veshchestv
Itogi Nauki Tekh Obogashch Polezn Iskop — Itogi Nauki i Tekhniki Obogashchenie Poleznykh Iskopaemykh
Itogi Nauki Tekh Obshch Ekol Biotsenol — Itogi Nauki i Tekhniki Obshchaya Ekologiya, Biotsenologiya
Itogi Nauki Tekh Obshch Geol — Itogi Nauki i Tekhniki Obshchaya Geologiya
Itogi Nauki Tekh Onkol — Itogi Nauki i Tekhniki Onkologiya
Itogi Nauki Tekh Pozharnaya Okhr — Itogi Nauki i Tekhniki Pozharnaya Okhrana

Itogi Nauki Tekh Proizvod Chuguna Stali — Itogi Nauki i Tekhniki Proizvodstvo Chuguna i Stali
Itogi Nauki Tekh Rudn Mestorozhd — Itogi Nauki i Tekhniki Rudnye Mestorozhdeniya
Itogi Nauki Tekh Ser Biotekhnol — Itogi Nauki i Tekhniki Seriya Biotekhnologiya
Itogi Nauki Tekh Ser Tekhnol Mashinostr — Itogi Nauki i Tekhniki Seriya Tekhnologiya Mashinostroeniya
Itogi Nauki Tekh Svarka — Itogi Nauki i Tekhniki Svarka
Itogi Nauki Tekh Svetotekh Infrakrasnaya Tekh — Itogi Nauki i Tekhniki Svetotekhnika i Infrakrasnaya Tekhniki
Itogi Nauki Tekh Tekhnol Mashinostr — Itogi Nauki i Tekhniki Tekhnologiya Mashinostroeniya
Itogi Nauki Tekh Teor Metall Protsessov — Itogi Nauki i Tekhniki Teoriya Metallurgicheskikh Protsessov
Itogi Nauki Tekh Toksikol — Itogi Nauki i Tekhniki Toksikologiya
Itogi Nauki Tekh Virusol — Itogi Nauki i Tekhniki Virusologiya
Itogi Nauki Tekh Zhivotnovod Vet — Itogi Nauki i Tekhniki Zhivotnovodstvo i Veterinariya
Itogi Nauki Tsitol Obshch Genet Genet Chel — Itogi Nauki Tsitologiya Obshchaya Genetika. Genetika Cheloveka
Itogi Nauki Vet — Itogi Nauki Veterinariya
Itogi Nauki Virusol Mikrobiol — Itogi Nauki Virusologiya i Mikrobiologiya
Itogi Nauki Vysokomol Soedin — Itogi Nauki Vysokomolekulyarnye Soedineniya
Itogi Nauki Zashch Rast — Itogi Nauki Zashchita Rastenii
Itogi Nauk & Tekh Ser Issled Kosm Prostranstva — Itogi Nauki i Tekhniki Seriya Issledovanie Kosmicheskogo Prostranstva
Itogi Polev Rabot Inst Etnogr — Itogi Polevyh Rabot Instituta Etnografii
ITOIAE — Izvestija Tavreiceskogo Obscestva Istorii, Archeologii, Etnografii
ITOMA — Industries et Travaux d'Outre-Mer
ITORGO — Izvestija Turkestanskogo Otdela Russkogo Geograficeskogo Obscestva
ITPR — Inuit Tapirisat of Canada. Press Release
ITPSB — IEEE. Transactions on Plasma Science
ITPTBG — Interpretation
ITQ — Irish Theological Quarterly
ItQ — Italian Quarterly
ITR — International Trade Reporter
ITRCDB — Interciencia
ITRID — Itogi Nauki i Tekhniki Razrabotka Mestorozhdenii Tverdykh Poleznykh Iskopaemyk h
ITRMB5 — Conseil Scientifique International de Recherches sur les Trypanosomiases
ITSMA — Ispol'zovanie Tverdykh Topliv Sernistykh Mazutov i Gaza
ITSOD — Itogi Nauki i Tekhniki Seriya Okeanologiya
ITT — In These Times
ITUFA — Izvestiya Akademii Nauk Turkmenskoi SSR Seriya Fiziko-Tekhnicheskikh Khimicheskikh, i Geologicheskikh Nauk
ITXPA9 — INTA [*Instituto Nacional de Tecnologia Agropecuaria*]. Estacion Experimental Regional Agropecuaria [*Pergamino*]. Publicacion Tecnica
IUB — Indiana University Bookman
IUB (Int Union Biochem) Symp Ser — IUB (International Union of Biochemistry) Symposium Series
IUCC Bull — IUCC [*Inter-University Committee on Computing*] Bulletin
IUCC Newsl — IUCC [*Inter-University Committee on Computing*] Newsletter
IUCN — International Union for Conservation of Nature and Natural Resources. Technical Meeting
IUCN Bull — IUCN [*International Union for Conservation of Nature and Natural Resources*] Bulletin
IUCN Publ New Ser — IUCN [*International Union for Conservation of Nature and Natural Resources*] Publications. New Series
IUCN Yearb — IUCN [*International Union for Conservation of Nature and Natural Resources*] Yearbook
IUFS — Indiana University. Folklore Series
IUGG Chron — IUGG [*International Union of Geodesy and Geophysics*] Chronicle
IUGG Newsl — International Union of Geodesy and Geophysics. Newsletter
Iugosl Physiol Pharmacol Acta — Iugoslavica Physiologica Pharmacologica Acta
IUH — In Touch with the Dutch
IUHS — Indiana University. Humanities Series
IUPAC Inf Bull — International Union of Pure and Applied Chemistry. Information Bulletin
IUPAC Inf Bull Append Provis Nomencl Symb Terminol Conv — International Union of Pure and Applied Chemistry. Information Bulletin. Appendices on Provisional Nomenclature, Symbols, Terminology, and Conventions
IUPAC Inf Bull Append Tentative Nomencl Symb Units Stand — International Union of Pure and Applied Chemistry. Information Bulletin. Appendices on Tentative Nomenclature, Symbols, Units, and Standards
IUPAL — Indiana University Publications. Anthropology and Linguistics
IUPFS — Indiana University Publications. Folklore Series
IUPHS — Indiana University Publications. Humanistic Series
IUPLSM — Indiana University Publications. Language Science Monographs
IUPSEES — Indiana University Publications. Slavic and East European Series

IUPUAS — Indiana University Publications. Uralic and Altaic Series
IUR — International UFO Reporter [*Center for Unidentified Flying Object Studies*]
IUR — Irish University Review
IURCAFL — Indiana University. Research Center in Anthropology, Folklore, and Linguistics
IUS — Industrie
IUSHTL — Indiana University Studies in the History and Theory of Linguistics
IUSRAV — Iowa State University. Statistical Laboratory. Annual Report
IUTFAY — Istanbul Tip Fakultesi Mecmuasi
IV — Der Israelitische Volkslehrer
I & V — Ideas y Valores
IV — Illustrazione Vaticana
IV — Istoritcheskii Viestnik
IVA — IVA [*Ingenjoersvetenskapsakademien*] och des Laboratorien
IVA — IVA [*Ingenjoersvetenskapsakademien*] Tidskrift foer Teknisk-Vetenskaplig Forskning
IVA — Jugobanka. Economic News
IVAAA — IVA [*Ingenjoersvetenskapsakademien*] Tidskrift foer Teknisk-Vetenskaplig Forskning
IVAD — Izvestija na Varnenskoto Archeologicesko Druzestvo
IVA (Ingenjoersvetenskapsakad) Medd — IVA (Ingenjoersvetenskapsakademien) Meddelande
Ivano Frankivs'kii Derzh Med Inst Nauk Zap — Ivano-Frankivs'kii Derzhavnii Medichnii Institut Naukovi Zapiski
Ivanov Gos Ped Inst Ucen Zap — Ivanovskii Gosudarstvennyi Pedagogiceskii Institut Imeni D. A. Furmanova Ivanovskoe Matematiceskoe Obscestvo Ucenye Zapiski
Ivanov Gos Univ Ucen Zap — Ivanovskii Gosudarstvennyi Universitet Ucenye Zapiski
IVat — Illustrazione Vaticana
IVA Tidskr Tek-Vetenskaplig Forsk — IVA [*Ingenjoersvetenskapsakademien*] Tidskrift foer Teknisk-Vetenskaplig Forskning
IVA Tidskr Tek Vetensk Forsk — IVA [*Ingenjoersvetenskapsakademien*] Tidskrift foer Teknisk-Vetenskaplig Forskning [*Sweden*]
IVGO — Izvestija Vsesojuznogo Geograficeskogo Obscestva
IVGOA — Izvestiya Vsesoyuznogo Geograficheskogo Obshchestva
IVGPI — Izvestiya Voronezskogo Gosudarstvennogo Pedagogiceskogo Instituta
IVI — Ikuska. Instituto Vasco de Investigaciones
IVL — Internationale Wirtschaft mit den Mitteilungen der Bundeswirtschaftskammer
IVL Bull — IVL [*Instituet foer Vatten och Luftvardsforskning*] Bulletin
IVM — Incentive Marketing
IVMOD2 — In Vitro Monograph
IVNCDN — Investigations on Cetacea
Ivor's Art R — Ivor's Art Review
Ivory Coast Dir Mines Geol Bull — Ivory Coast. Direction des Mines et de la Geologie. Bulletin
IVR — International Journal of Physical Distribution and Materials Management
IVRYA — Intervirology
IVRYAK — Intervirology
IVS — Index of Veterinary Specialities
IVSOIRGO — Izvestija Vostocno-Sibirskogo Otdela Imperatorskogo Russkogo Geograficeskogo Obscestva
IVSORGO — Izvestija Vostocno-Sibirskogo Otdela Russkogo Geograficeskogo Obscestva
IVT Jaarversl — IVT [*Instituut voor de Veredeling van Tuinbouwgewassen*] Jaarverslag
IVTLAP — International Association of Theoretical and Applied Limnology. Proceedings
IVTMAS — Communications. Association Internationale de Limnologie Theorique et Appliquee
IVTMAS — Communications. International Association of Theoretical and Applied Limnology
IVT Mededel — IVT [*Instituut voor de Veredeling van Tuinbouwgewassen*] Mededeling
IVTRBA — In Vitro v CSSR
IVUAA — Izvestiya Vysshikh Uchebnykh Zavedenii Aviatsionnaya Tekhnika
IVUGA — Izvestiya Vysshikh Uchebnykh Zavedenii Geologiya i Razvedka
IVUKA — Izvestiya Vysshikh Uchebnykh Zavedenii Khimiya i Khimicheskaya Tekhnologiya
IVUMA — Izvestiya Vysshikh Uchebnykh Zavedenii Chernaya Metallurgiya
IVUNA — Izvestiya Vysshikh Uchebnykh Zavedenii Neft' i Gaz
IVUPA — Izvestiya Vysshikh Uchebnykh Zavedenii Pishchevaya Tekhnologiya
IVUPA8 — Izvestiya Vysshikh Uchebnykh Zavedenii Pishchevaya Tekhnologiya
IVUZ Fiz — Izvestiya Vysshikh Uchebnykh Zavedenii Fizika
IVZEA — Izvestiya Vysshikh Uchebnykh Zavedenii Energetika
IW — Israelitisches Wochenblatt
Iwata Tob Shikenjo Hokoku Bull Iwata Tob Exp Stn — Iwata Tob Shikenjo Hokoku/Bulletin. Iwata Tobacco Experimental Station

Iwate Univ Technol Rep — Iwate University. Faculty of Engineering. Technology Reports
IWB — Israelitisches Wochenblatt (Berlin)
IWB — Literatuurinformatie Wetenschapsbeleid
IWCR — International Whaling Commission. Reports
IWCRSI — International Whaling Commission. Reports. Special Issue
IWEEA — Industry Week
IWEGA — Industrial Water Engineering
IWEGAA — Industrial Water Engineering
IWGIAD — IWGIA [*International Work Group for Indigenous Affairs*] Document
IWGIAN — IWGIA [*International Work Group for Indigenous Affairs*] Newsletter
IWK — Internationale Wissenschaftliche Korrespondenz zur Geschichte der Deutschen Arbeiterbewegung
IWK — Israelitische Wochenschrift (Klausner)
IWLRAA — Indian Forest Records. Wild Life and Recreation
IWO — Informationsdienst West-Ost
IWPCD — International Water Power and Dam Construction
IWRBBR — Iowa. Agriculture and Home Economics Experiment Station. Research Bulletin
IWRUAR — Institute for Water Resources. University of Alaska. Report
IWSRBC — Iowa. Agriculture and Home Economics Experiment Station. Special Report
IWT — Indiana Writing Today
IWWDD — Information World
IWX — Aspekten van Internationale Samenwerking
IXS — International Social Science Journal
IXSAAZ — International Council for the Exploration of the Sea. Cooperative Research Report. Series A
IXSBB5 — International Council for the Exploration of the Sea. Cooperative Research Report. Series B
IY — Idaho Yesterdays
IYaSh — Inostrannye Jazyki v Skole
IYB — [*The*] Israel Year Book
IYH — Israel Youth Horizon [*Jerusalem*]
IYHR — Israel Yearbook on Human Rights
IYIA — Indian Yearbook of International Affairs
IYYYA8 — Immok Yukchong Yonku-So Yongu Pogo
IZ — Instrumentenbau-Zeitschrift
IZ — Istoriceskii Zapiski Akademii Nauk SSSR
IZ — Istoriceskij Zurnal
Iz — Izvestiya [*Moscow*]
IZAPA — Internationale Zeitschrift fuer Angewandte Physiologie
Iz Balg Muz — Izvestiia na Balgarskite Muzei
IZBG — Internationale Zeitschriftenschau fuer Bibelwissenschaft und Grenzgebiete [*Stuttgart/Duesseldorf*]
IzBID — Izvestiia na B'lgarskoto Istorichesko Druzestvo
IZBTBM — Instituto de Zootecnia [*Sao Paulo*]. Boletim Tecnico
Izd Zavod Hidroteh Gradevinskog Fak Sarajevu — Izdanja Zavod za Hidrotehniku Gradevinskog Fakulteta u Sarajevu
IZFMB — Izvestiya Akademii Nauk Moldavskoi SSR Seriya Fiziko-Tekhnicheskikh i Matemati cheskikh Nauk
Izhevsk Med Inst Tr — Izhevskii Meditsinskii Institut Trudy
Iz Istor Biol — Iz Istorii Biologii
Izk — Izkustvo
Izmen Pochv Okyl't Klassif Diagnostika "Kolos" — Izmenenie Pochvy pri Okyl'turivanii Ikh Klassifikatsiya i Diagnostika "Kolos"
Izmer Techn — Izmerital'naja Tehnika
Izmer Tekh — Izmeritel'naya Tehnika
Izmer Tekh Proverochn Delo — Izmeritel'naya Tekhnika i Proverochnoe Delo
Iz Narod Muz (Rousse) — Izvestiia na Narodniia Muzei (Rousse)
Iz Narod Muz Sumen — Izvestiia Narodni Muzefa Sumen Bulgaria
Iz Narod Muz (Varna) — Izvestiia na Narodniia Muzei (Varna)
Iznos Zashch Konstr Prom Zdanii — Iznos i Zashchita Konstruktsu Promyshlennykh Zdanii
Izobret Prom Obraztsy Tovarnye Znaki — Izobreteniya Promyshlennye Obraztsy Tovarnye Znaki
Izobret Ratsion — Izobretatel i Ratsionalizator [*USSR*]
IZOCAZ — Investigaciones Zoologicas Chilenas
Izol Elektr Mash — Izolyatsiya Elektricheskikh Mashin
IZSch — Internationale Zeitschriftenschau fuer Bibelwissenschaft und Grenzgebiete [*Stuttgart/Duesseldorf*]
IZSEA — Izvestiya Akademii Nauk SSSR Seriya Ekonomicheskaia
IZSORGO — Izvestija Zapadno-Sibirskogo Otdela Russkogo Geograficeskogo Obscestva
Izv Abhaz Inst Jaz Lit Ist — Izvestija Abhazskogo Instituta Jazyka, Literatury, i Istorii
Izv Acad Sci USSR Atmos and Oceanic Phys — Izvestiya. Academy of Sciences USSR. Atmospheric and Oceanic Physics
Izv Acad Sci USSR Atmos Oceanic Phys — Izvestiya. Academy of Sciences USSR. Atmospheric and Oceanic Physics
Izv Acad Sci USSR Atmospher Ocean Phys — Izvestiya. Academy of Sciences USSR. Atmospheric and Oceanic Physics
Izv Acad Sci USSR Geol Ser — Izvestiya. Academy of Sciences USSR. Geologic Series

Izv Acad Sci USSR Phys Solid Earth — Izvestiya. Academy of Sciences USSR. Physics of the Solid Earth

Izv Akad Krupnogo Sots Selsk Khoz — Izvestiya Akademii Krupnogo Sotsialisticheskogo Sel'skogo Khozyaistva

Izv Akad Latv SSR Ser Fiz Tekh Nauk — Izvestiya Akademii Latviiskoi SSR Seriya Fizicheskikh i Tekhnicheskikh Nauk [*L atvian SSR*]

Izv Akad Nauk — Izvestiya Akademii Nauk

Izv Akad Nauk Armjan SSR Ser Fiz — Izvestija Akademii Nauk Armjanskoi SSR Serija Fizika

Izv Akad Nauk Armjan SSR Ser Mat — Izvestija Akademii Nauk Armjanskoi SSR Serija Matematika

Izv Akad Nauk Armjan SSR Ser Meh — Izvestija Akademii Nauk Armjanskoi SSR Serija Mehanika

Izv Akad Nauk Armjan SSR Ser Tehn Nauk — Izvestija Akademii Nauk Armjanskoi SSR Serija Tehniceskih Nauk

Izv Akad Nauk Arm SSR — Izvestiya Akademii Nauk Armyanskoi SSR

Izv Akad Nauk Arm SSR Biol Nauki — Izvestiya Akademii Nauk Armyanskoi SSR Biologicheskie Nauki

Izv Akad Nauk Arm SSR Biol S-kh Nauki — Izvestiya Akademii Nauk Armyanskoi SSR Biologicheskie i Sel'skokhozyaistvennye Nauki

Izv Akad Nauk Arm SSR Estestv Nauki — Izvestiya Akademii Nauk Armyanskoi SSR Estestvennye Nauki

Izv Akad Nauk Arm SSR Fiz — Izvestiya Akademia Nauk Armyanskoi SSR Fizika

Izv Akad Nauk Arm SSR Fiz Mat Estest Tekh Nauki — Izvestiya Akademii Nauk Armyanskoi SSR Fiziko Matematicheskie Estestvennye i T ekhnicheskie Nauki

Izv Akad Nauk Arm SSR Geol Geogr Nauki — Izvestiya Akademii Nauk Armyanskoi SSR Geologicheskie i Geograficheskie Nauki [*Armenian SSR*]

Izv Akad Nauk Arm SSR Khim Nauki — Izvestiya Akademii Nauk Armyanskoi SSR Khimicheskie Nauki [*Armenian SSR*]

Izv Akad Nauk Arm SSR Med Nauki — Izvestiya Akademii Nauk Armyanskoi SSR Meditsinskie Nauki

Izv Akad Nauk Arm SSR Mekh — Izvestiya Akademii Nauk Armyanskoi SSR Mekhanika

Izv Akad Nauk Arm SSR Nauki Zemle — Izvestiya Akademii Nauk Armyanskoi SSR Nauki po Zemle [*Armenian SSR*]

Izv Akad Nauk Arm SSR Ser Fiz-Mat Nauk — Izvestiya Akademii Nauk Armyanskoi SSR Seriya Fiziko-Matematicheskikh Nauk [*Armenian SSR*]

Izv Akad Nauk Arm SSR Ser Mat — Izvestiya Akademii Nauk Armyanskoi SSR Seriya Matematika [*Armenian SSR*]

Izv Akad Nauk Arm SSR Ser Mekh — Izvestiya Akademii Nauk Armyanskoi SSR Seriya Mekhanika [*Armenian SSR*]

Izv Akad Nauk Arm SSR Ser Tekh Nauk — Izvestiya Akademii Nauk Armyanskoi SSR Seriya Tekhnicheskikh Nauk [*Armenian SSR*]

Izv Akad Nauk Armyan SSR Biol Nauk — Izvestiya Akademiya Nauk Armyanskoi SSR Biologicheskie Nauk

Izv Akad Nauk Armyan SSR Ser Mekh — Izvestiya Akademii Nauk Armyanskoi SSR Seriya Mekhanika

Izv Akad Nauk Azerbaidzan SSR Ser Fiz Tehn Mat Nauk — Izvestija Akademii Nauk Azerbaidzanskoi SSR Serija Fiziko-Tehniceskih i Matematiceskih Nauk

Izv Akad Nauk Azerb SSR Ser Biol Nauk — Izvestiya Akademii Nauk Azerbaidzhanskoi SSR Seriya Biologicheskikh Nauk

Izv Akad Nauk Azerb SSR Ser Lit Jaz Isk — Izvestija Akademii Nauk Azerbajdzanskogo SSR Serija Literatury, Jazyka, i Iskusstva

Izv Akad Nauk Azerb SSR Ser Nauk Zemle — Izvestiya Akademii Nauk Azerbajdzhanskoj SSR Seriya Nauk i Zemle

Izv Akad Nauk Az SSR — Izvestiya Akademii Nauk Azerbaidzhanskoi SSR

Izv Akad Nauk Az SSR Ser Biol Med Nauk — Izvestiya Akademii Nauk Azerbaidzhanskoi SSR Seriya Biologicheskikh i Meditsinskikh Nauk

Izv Akad Nauk Az SSR Ser Biol Nauk — Izvestiya. Akademii Nauk Azerbaidzhanskoi SSR Seriya Biologicheskikh Nauk

Izv Akad Nauk Az SSR Ser Fiz-Tekh Mat Nauk — Izvestiya Akademii Nauk Azerbaidzhanskoi SSR Seriya Fiziko-Tekhnicheskikh i Matematicheskikh Nauk [*Azerbaidzhan SSR*]

Izv Akad Nauk B SSR — Izvestiya Akademii Nauk Belorusskoi SSR

Izv Akad Nauk B SSR Ser Biol Nauk — Izvestiya Akademii Nauk Belorusskoi SSR Seriya Biologicheskikh Nauk

Izv Akad Nauk BSSR Ser Fiz-Mat Nauk — Izvestiya Akademii Nauk BSSR Seriya Fiziko-Matematicheskikh Nauk [*Belorussian S SR*]

Izv Akad Nauk B SSR Ser S Kh Nauk — Izvestiya Akademii Nauk Belorusskoi SSR Seriya Sel'skokhozyaistvennykh Nauk

Izv Akad Nauk Ehst SSR Geol — Izvestiya Akademii Nauk Ehstonskoj SSR Geologiya

Izv Akad Nauk Ehst SSR Khim Geol — Izvestiya Akademii Nauk Ehstonskoj SSR Khimiya i Geologiya

Izv Akad Nauk Estonskoi SSR Fiz Mat — Izvestiya Akademii Nauk Estonskoi SSR Seriya Fizichesko. Matematicheskaya

Izv Akad Nauk Eston SSR Obsc Nauki — Izvestija Akademii Nauk Estonskoj SSR Obscestvennye Nauki

Izv Akad Nauk Eston SSR Ser Biol — Izvestiya Akademii Nauk Estonskoi SSR Seriya Biologicheskaya

Izv Akad Nauk Est SSR Fiz Mat — Izvestiya Akademii Nauk Estonskoi SSR Fizika Matematika [*Estonian SSR*]

Izv Akad Nauk Est SSR Khim Eesti NSV Tead Akad Toim Keem — Izvestiia Akademii Nauk Estonski SSR Khimiia Eesti NSV Teaduste Akadeemia Toimetised Keemia

Izv Akad Nauk Est SSR Ser Biol — Izvestiya Akademii Nauk Estonskoi SSR Seriya Biologicheskaya

Izv Akad Nauk Est SSR Ser Fiz Mat Tekh Nauk — Izvestiia Akademii Nauk Estonskoi SSR Seriia Fiziko-Matematicheskikh i Tekhnicheskikh Nauk [*Estonian SSR*]

Izv Akad Nauk Est SSR Ser Tekh Fiz-Mat Nauk — Izvestiya Akademii Nauk Estonskoi SSR Seriya Tekhnicheskikh i Fiziko-Matematicheskikh Nauk [*Estonian SSR*]

Izv Akad Nauk Gruz SSR Ser Biol — Izvestiya Akademii Nauk Gruzinskoi SSR Seriya Biologicheskaya [*Georgian SSR*]

Izv Akad Nauk Gruz SSR Ser Khim — Izvestiya Akademii Nauk Gruzinskoj SSR Seriya Khimicheskaya

Izv Akad Nauk Kazah SSR Ser Fiz-Mat — Izvestija Akademii Nauk Kazahskoj SSR Serija Fiziko-Matematiceskaja

Izv Akad Nauk Kazah SSR Ser Obsc Nauk — Izvestija Akademii Nauk Kazahskoj SSR Serija Obscestvennyh Nauk

Izv Akad Nauk Kazakh SSR Ser Biol — Izvestiya Akademii Nauk Kazakhskoi SSR Seriya Biologicheskaya

Izv Akad Nauk Kazakh SSR Ser Bot Pochvoved — Izvestiya Akademii Nauk Kazakhskoi SSR Seriya Botaniki i Pochvovedeniya

Izv Akad Nauk Kaz SSR Ser Astron Fiz — Izvestiya Akademii Nauk Kazakhskoi SSR Seriya Astronomicheskaya i Fizicheskaya

Izv Akad Nauk Kaz SSR Ser Astron Fiz Mat Mekh — Izvestiya Akademii Nauk Kazakaskhkoi SSR Seriya Astronomii, Fiziki, Matematiki, Mekhaniki

Izv Akad Nauk Kaz SSR Ser Biol — Izvestiya Akademii Nauk Kazakhskoi SSR Seriya Biologicheskaya

Izv Akad Nauk Kaz SSR Ser Biol Nauk — Izvestiya Akademii Nauk Kazakhskoi SSR Seriya Biologicheskikh Nauk

Izv Akad Nauk Kaz SSR Ser Bot Pochvoved — Izvestiya Akademii Nauk Kazakhskoi SSR Seriya Botaniki i Pochvovedeniya

Izv Akad Nauk Kaz SSR Ser Energ — Izvestiya Akademii Nauk Kazakhskoi SSR Seriya Energeticheskaya

Izv Akad Nauk Kaz SSR Ser Fiziol — Izvestiya Akademii Nauk Kazakhskoi SSR Seriya Fiziologicheskaya

Izv Akad Nauk Kaz SSR Ser Fiziol Biokhim Rast — Izvestiya Akademii Nauk Kazakhskoi SSR Seriya Fiziologii i Biokhimii Rastenii

Izv Akad Nauk Kaz SSR Ser Fiz-Mat — Izvestiya Akademii Nauk Kazakhskoi SSR Seriya Fiziko-Matematicheskaya

Izv Akad Nauk Kaz SSR Ser Fiz-Mat Nauk — Izvestiya Akademii Nauk Kazakhskoi SSR Seriya Fiziko-Matematicheskikh Nauk [*Kaz akh SSR*]

Izv Akad Nauk Kaz SSR Ser Geol — Izvestiya Akademii Nauk Kazakhskoi SSR Seriya Geologicheskaya

Izv Akad Nauk Kaz SSR Ser Gorn Dela — Izvestiya Akademii Nauk Kazakhskoi SSR Seriya Gornogo Dela

Izv Akad Nauk Kaz SSR Ser Gorn Dela Metall Stroit Stroimat — Izvestiya Akademii Nauk Kazakhskoi SSR Seriya Gornogo Dela Metallurgii Stroitel'stva i Stroimaterialov

Izv Akad Nauk Kaz SSR Ser Khim — Izvestiya Akademii Nauk Kazakhskoi SSR Seriya Khimicheskaya

Izv Akad Nauk Kaz SSR Ser Mat Mekh — Izvestiya Akademii Nauk Kazakhskoi SSR Seriya Matematiki i Mekhaniki

Izv Akad Nauk Kaz SSR Ser Med Fiziol — Izvestiya Akademii Nauk Kazakhskoi SSR Seriya Meditsiny i Fiziologii

Izv Akad Nauk Kaz SSR Ser Med Nauk — Izvestiya Akademii Nauk Kazakhskoi SSR Seriya Meditsinskikh Nauk

Izv Akad Nauk Kaz SSR Ser Mikrobiol — Izvestiya Akademii Nauk Kazakhskoi SSR Seriya Mikrobiologicheskaya

Izv Akad Nauk Kaz SSR Ser Zool — Izvestiya Akademii Nauk Kazakhskoi SSR Seriya Zoologicheskaya

Izv Akad Nauk Kirgiz SSR — Izvestija Akademija Nauk Kirgizskoi SSR

Izv Akad Nauk Kirgiz SSR Ser Biol Nauk — Izvestiya Akademii Nauk Kirgizkoi SSR Seriya Biologicheskikh Nauk

Izv Akad Nauk Kirg SSR — Izvestiya Akademii Nauk Kirgizskoi SSR

Izv Akad Nauk Kirg SSR Ser Biol Nauk — Izvestiya Akademii Nauk Kirgizskoi SSR Seriya Biologicheskikh Nauk

Izv Akad Nauk Kirg SSR Ser Estestv Tekh Nauk — Izvestiya Akademii Nauk Kirgizskoi SSR Seriya Estestvennykh i Tekhnicheskikh Nauk [*Kirgiz SSR*]

Izv Akad Nauk Latvii SSR — Izvestiya Akademii Nauk Latviiskoi SSR

Izv Akad Nauk Latv SSR — Izvestiya Akademii Nauk Latviiskoi SSR

Izv Akad Nauk Latv SSR Khim — Izvestiya Akademii Nauk Latviiskoi SSR Seriya Khimicheskikh Nauk

Izv Akad Nauk Latv SSR Ser Fiz Tekh Nauk — Izvestiya Akademii Nauk Latviiskoi SSR Seriya Fizicheskikh i Tekhnicheskikh Nauk

Izv Akad Nauk Latv SSR Ser Khim — Izvestiya Akademii Nauk Latviiskoi SSR Seriya Khimicheskaya

Izv Akad Nauk Moldav SSR — Izvestiya Akademii Nauk Moldavskoi SSR

Izv Akad Nauk Mold SSR — Izvestiya Akademii Nauk Moldavskoi SSR

Izv Akad Nauk Mold SSR Ser Biol — Izvestiya Akademii Nauk Moldavskoi SSR Seriya Biologicheskaya

Izv Akad Nauk Mold SSR Ser Biol Khim Nauk — Izvestiya Akademii Nauk Moldavskoi SSR Seriya Biologicheskikh i Khimicheskikh Nauk

Izv Akad Nauk Mold SSR Ser Biol S-Kh Nauk — Izvestiya Akademii Nauk Moldavskoi SSR Seriya Biologicheskikh i Sel'skokhozya istvennykh Nauk

Izv Akad Nauk Mold SSR Ser Fiz-Tekh Mat Nauk — Izvestiya Akademii Nauk Moldavskoi SSR Seriya Fiziko-Tekhnicheskikh i Matemat icheskikh Nauk

Izv Akad Nauk Mold SSR Ser Obsc Nauk — Izvestija Akademii Nauk Moldavskoj SSR Serija Obscestvennyh Nauk

Izv Akad Nauk SSR Mekh Zhidc Gaza — Izvestiya Akademii Nauk SSSR Mekhanika Zhidkosti i Gaza

Izv Akad Nauk SSSR — Izvestiya Akademii Nauk SSSR

Izv Akad Nauk SSSR Biol — Izvestiya Akademii Nauk SSSR Seriia Biologicheskaya

Izv Akad Nauk SSSR Energ Transp — Izvestiya Akademii Nauk SSSR Energetika i Transport

Izv Akad Nauk SSSR Fiz — Izvestiya Akademii Nauk SSSR Seriya Fizicheskaya

Izv Akad Nauk SSSR Fiz Atmos Okeana — Izvestiya Akademii Nauk SSSR Fizika Atmosfery i Okeana

Izv Akad Nauk SSSR Fiz Atmos i Okeana — Izvestiya Akademii Nauk SSSR Fizika Atmosfery i Okeana

Izv Akad Nauk SSSR Fiz Zemli — Izvestiya Akademii Nauk SSSR Fizika Zemli

Izv Akad Nauk SSSR Khim — Izvestiya Akademii Nauk SSSR Seriya Khimicheskaya

Izv Akad Nauk SSSR Meh Tverd Tela — Izvestija Akademii Nauk SSSR Mehanika Tverdogo Tela

Izv Akad Nauk SSSR Meh Zidk Gaza — Izvestija Akademii Nauk SSSR Mehanika Zidkosti i Gaza

Izv Akad Nauk SSSR Mekh — Izvestiya Akademii Nauk SSSR Mekhanika

Izv Akad Nauk SSSR Mekh Mashinostr — Izvestiya Akademii Nauk SSSR Mekhanika i Mashinostroenie

Izv Akad Nauk SSSR Mekh Tverd Tela — Izvestiya Akademii Nauk SSSR Mekhanika Tverdogo Tela

Izv Akad Nauk SSSR Mekh Zhidk Gaza — Izvestiya Akademii Nauk SSSR Mekhanika Zhidkosti i Gaza

Izv Akad Nauk SSSR Mekh Zhidk i Gaza — Izvestiya Akademii Nauk SSSR Mekhanika Zhidkosti i Gaza

Izv Akad Nauk SSSR Mekh Zhidkosti Gaza — Izvestiya Akademii Nauk SSSR Mekhanika Zhidkosti i Gaza

Izv Akad Nauk SSSR Met — Izvestiya Akademii Nauk SSSR Metally

Izv Akad Nauk SSSR Metally — Izvestiya Akademii Nauk SSSR Metally

Izv Akad Nauk SSSR Neorg Mater — Izvestiya Akademii Nauk SSSR Neorganicheskie Materialy

Izv Akad Nauk SSSR Otd Mat Estestv Nauk — Izvestiya Akademii Nauk SSSR Otdelenie Matematicheskikh i Estestvennykh Nauk

Izv Akad Nauk SSSR Otd Tekh Nauk — Izvestiya Akademii Nauk SSSR Otdelenie Tekhnicheskikh Nauk [*USSR*]

Izv Akad Nauk SSSR Otd Tekh Nauk Energ Avtom — Izvestiya Akademii Nauk SSSR Otdelenie Tekhnicheskikh Nauk Energetika i Avtomatika [*USSR*]

Izv Akad Nauk SSSR Otd Tekh Nauk Energ Transp — Izvestiya Akademii Nauk SSSR Otdelenie Tekhnicheskikh Nauk Energetika i Transport

Izv Akad Nauk SSSR Otd Tekh Nauk Mekh Mashinstr — Izvestiya Akademii Nauk SSSR Otdelenie Tekhnicheskikh Nauk Mekhanika i Mashinostroenie [*USSR*]

Izv Akad Nauk SSSR Otd Tekh Nauk Metall Topl — Izvestiya Akademii Nauk SSSR Otdelenie Tekhnicheskikh Nauk Metallurgiya i Toplivo [*USSR*]

Izv Akad Nauk SSSR Ser Biol — Izvestiya Akademii Nauk SSSR Seriya Biologicheskaya

Izv Akad Nauk SSSR Ser Ekon — Izvestija Akademii Nauk SSSR Serija Ekonomiceskaja

Izv Akad Nauk SSSR Ser Fiz — Izvestiya Akademii Nauk SSSR Seriya Fizicheskaya

Izv Akad Nauk SSSR Ser Fiz Zemli — Izvestiya Akademii Nauk SSSR Serija Fizika Zemli

Izv Akad Nauk SSSR Ser Geofiz — Izvestiya Akademii Nauk SSSR Seriya Geofizicheskaya [*USSR*]

Izv Akad Nauk SSSR Ser Geogr — Izvestija Akademii Nauk SSSR Serija Geografii

Izv Akad Nauk SSSR Ser Geogr — Izvestiya Akademii Nauk SSSR Seriya Geograficheskaya

Izv Akad Nauk SSSR Ser Geogr Geofiz — Izvestiya Akademii Nauk SSSR Seriya Geograficheskaya i Geofizicheskaya

Izv Akad Nauk SSSR Ser Geol — Izvestiya Akademii Nauk SSSR Seriya Geologicheskaya

Izv Akad Nauk SSSR Ser Geol (Transl Abstr) — Izvestiya Akademii Nauk SSSR Seriya Geologicheskaya (Translated Abstracts)

Izv Akad Nauk SSSR Ser Khim — Izvestiya Akademii Nauk SSSR Seriya Khimicheskaya

Izv Akad Nauk SSSR Ser Mat — Izvestiya Akademii Nauk SSSR Seriya Matematicheskaya

Izv Akad Nauk SSSR Tehn Kibernet — Izvestija Akademii Nauk SSSR Tekhniceskaja Kibernetika

Izv Akad Nauk SSSR Tekh Kibern — Izvestiya Akademii Nauk SSSR Tekhnicheskaja Kibernetika

Izv Akad Nauk Tadzhik SSR Otd Biol Nauk — Izvestiya Akademii Nauk Tadzhikskoi SSR Otdelenie Biologicheskikh Nauk

Izv Akad Nauk Tadzhik SSR Otdel Fiz-Mat Khim i Geol Nauk — Izvestiya Akademii Nauk Tadzhikskoi SSR Otdelenie Fiziko-Matematicheskikh, Khimicheskikh, i Geologicheskikh Nauk

Izv Akad Nauk Tadzhik SSR Otd Fiz-Tekh Khim Nauk — Izvestiya Akademii Nauk Tadzhikskoi SSR Otdelenie Fizichesko-Tekhnicheskikh Kh imicheskikh Nauk

Izv Akad Nauk Tadzh SSR Otd Biol Nauk — Izvestiya Akademii Nauk Tadzhikskoi SSR Otdelenie Biologicheskikh Nauk

Izv Akad Nauk Tadzh SSR Otd Estestv Nauk — Izvestiya Akademii Nauk Tadzhikskoi SSR Otdelenie Estestvennykh Nauk

Izv Akad Nauk Tadzh SSR Otd Fiz-Mat Geol-Khim Nauk — Izvestiya Akademii Nauk Tadzhikskoi SSR Otdelenie Fiziko-Matematicheskikh i Geologo-Khimicheskikh Nauk [*Later, Izvestiya Akademi Nauk Tadzhikskoi SSR Otdelenie Fiziko-Matematicheskikh, Khimicheskikh, i Geologicheskikh Nauk*]

Izv Akad Nauk Tadzh SSR Otd Fiz Mat Khim Geol Nauk — Izvestiya Akademii Nauk Tadzhikskoi SSR Otdelenie Fiziko-Matematicheskikh, Khimicheskikh, i Geologicheskikh Nauk

Izv Akad Nauk Tadzh SSR Otd Fiz-Tekh Khim Nauk — Izvestiya Akademii Nauk Tadzhikskoi SSR Otdelenie Fiziko-Tekhnicheskikh i Khimicheskikh Nauk [*Tadzhik SSR*]

Izv Akad Nauk Tadzh SSR Otd S-Kh Biol Nauk — Izvestiya Akademii Nauk Tadzhikskoi SSR Otdelenie Sel'skokhozyaistvennykh i Biologicheskikh Nauk

Izv Akad Nauk Tadzik SSR Otdel Fiz-Mat i Geolog-Him Nauk — Izvestija Akademii Nauk Tadzikskoi SSR Otdelenie Fiziko-Matematiceskih i Geologo-Himiceskih Nauk

Izv Akad Nauk Tadz SSR Otdelenie Obsc Nauk — Izvestija Akademii Nauk Tadzikiskoj SSR Otdelenie Obscestvennyh Nauk

Izv Akad Nauk Turkmen SSR Ser Biol Nauk — Izvestiya Akademii Nauk Turkmenskoi SSR Seriya Biologicheskikh Nauk

Izv Akad Nauk Turkmen SSR Ser Fiz-Tehn Him Geol Nauk — Izvestija Akademii Nauk Turkmenskoi SSR Serija Fiziko-Tehniceskih Himiceskih i Geologiceskih Nauk

Izv Akad Nauk Turkm SSR — Izvestiya Akademii Nauk Turkmenskoi SSR

Izv Akad Nauk Turkm SSR Ser Biol Nauk — Izvestiya Akademii Nauk Turkmenskoi SSR Seriya Biologicheskikh Nauk

Izv Akad Nauk Turkm SSR Ser Fiz-Tekh Khim Geol Nauk — Izvestiya Akademii Nauk Turkmenskoi SSR Seriya Fiziko-Tekhnicheskikh Khimicheskikh i Geologicheskikh Nauk

Izv Akad Nauk Turkm SSR Ser Obsc Nauk — Izvestija Akademii Nauk Turkmenskoj SSR Serija Obscestvennyh Nauk

Izv Akad Nauk Turkm SSR Ser Obshchestv Nauk — Izvestiya Akademii Nauk Turkmenskoi SSR Seriya Obshchestvennykh Nauk

Izv Akad Nauk Uzb SSR Ser Biol — Izvestiya Akademii Nauk Uzbekskoi SSR Seriya Biologicheskaya

Izv Akad Nauk Uzb SSR Ser Fiz-Mat Nauk — Izvestiya Akademii Nauk Uzbekskoi SSR Seriya Fiziko-Matematicheskikh Nauk

Izv Akad Nauk Uzb SSR Ser Geol — Izvestiya Akademii Nauk Uzbekskoi SSR Seriya Geologicheskaya

Izv Akad Nauk Uzb SSR Ser Med — Izvestiya Akademii Nauk Uzbekskoi SSR Seriya Meditsinskaya

Izv Akad Nauk Uzb SSR Ser Tekh Nauk — Izvestiya Akademii Nauk Uzbekskoi SSR Seriya Tekhnicheskikh Nauk

Izv Akad Nauk UzSSR Ser Fiz-Mat Nauk — Izvestija Akademii Nauk UzSSR. Serija Fiziko-Matematiceskih Nauk

Izv Akad Nauk UzSSR Ser Tekh Nauk — Izvestiya Akademii Nauk UzSSR Seriya Tekhnicheskikh Nauk

Izv Akad Pedagog Nauk RSFSR — Izvestiya Akademii Pedagogicheskikh Nauk RSFSR

Izv Akad Uzb SSR — Izvestiya Akademii Nauk Uzbekskoi SSR

Izv Ak N Armj SSR — Izvestija Akademii Nauk Armjanskoj SSR

Izv Ak N Kaz — Izvestija Akademii Nauk Kazahskoj SSR

Izv Ak N Mold SSR — Izvestija Akademii Nauk Moldavskoj SSR

Izv Ak N SSSR — Izvestija Akademii Nauk SSSR

Izv Ak N SSSR Ser Geogr — Izvestija Akademii Nauk SSSR Serija Geograficeskaja I Geofiziceskaja

Izv Altai Otd Geogr O-va SSSR — Izvestiya Altaiskogo Otdela Geograficheskogo Obshcestva SSSR

IzvAN — Izvestija Akademii Nauk SSSR Otdelenie Literatury i Jazyka

IzvANArm — Izvestiya Akademii Nauk Armjanskoj SSR Obscestvennyh Nauk

IzvANAzerb — Izvestija Akademii Nauk Azerbajdzhanskoj SSR Seriya Obscestvennych Nauk

IzvANKaz — Izvestiya Akademii Nauk Kazakhskoj SSR Seriya Filologii i Iskusstvovedeniya

Izv ANO Ch N — Izvestija Akademii Nauk Otdelenie Chimicheskich Nauk

Izvanredna Izd Farmakol Inst Zagrebu — Izvanredna Izdanja Farmakoloskog Instituta Zagrebu

IzvANTadz — Izvestiya Akademii Nauk Tadzhickoi SSR Otdelenie Obscestvennych Nauk

IzvANTurkm — Izvestiya Akademii Nauk Turkmenskoi SSSR Seriya
   Obscestvennych Nauk
Izv Arch Inst — Izvestija na Archeologiceskija Institut
Izv Arm Fil Akad Nauk SSSR Estestv Nauki — Izvestiya Armyanskogo Filiala
   Akademii Nauk SSSR Estestvennye Nauki
IzvArmZPI — Izvestiya Armyanskogo Gosudarstvennogo Zaocnogo
   Pedagogiceskogo Instituta
IZVBA — Internationale Zeitschrift fuer Vitaminforschung. Beiheft
IzvBAI — Izvestiya na Balgarskiya Archeologiceski Institut
Izv Batum Bot Sada — Izvestiya Batumskogo Botanicheskogo Sada
Izv Batum Bot Sada Akad Nauk Gruz SSR — Izvestiya Batumskogo
   Botanicheskogo Sada Akademii Nauk Gruzinskoi SSR
Izv Biol Geogr Nauchno Issled Inst Irkutsk Gos Univ — Izvestiya Biologo-
   Geograficheskogo Nauchno-Issledovatel'skogo Instituta pri Irkutskom
   Gosudarstvennom Universitete
Izv Biol Nauchno-Issled Inst Biol Stn Permsk Gos Univ — Izvestiya
   Biologicheskogo Nauchno-Issledovatel'skogo Instituta i Biologicheskoi
   Stantsii pri Permskom Gosudarstvennom Universitete
Izv Bot Inst — Izvestija na Botaniceskija Institut
Izv Bot Inst B Akad Nauk Otd Biol Nauki — Izvestiya na Botanicheskiya
   Institut B'lgarska Akademiya Naukite Otdelenie za Biologichni Nauki
Izv Bot Inst B'lg Akad Nauk — Izvestiya na Botanicheskiya Instituta B'lgarska
   Akademiya na Naukite
Izv Cent Chelmint Lab — Izvestija na Centralnata Chelmintologicna
   Laboratorija
IzvCIngNII — Izvestiya Ceceno-Ingusskogo Naucno-Issledovatel-Skogo
   Instituta Istorii, Jazyka, i Literatury
Izv Dnepropetr Gorn Inst — Izvestiya Dnepropetrovskogo Gornogo Instituta
Izv Dobruzhan Selskostop Nauchnoizsled Inst Tolbukhin — Izvestiya na
   Dobrudzhanskiya Selskostopanski Nauchnoizsledovatelski Institut
   Tolbukhin
IzvDS — Izvestiya na Druzestovoto na Filolozite-Slavisti v Balgarija (Sofija)
Izv Ekaterinosl Vyssh Gorn Uchil — Izvestiya Ekaterinoslavskogo Vysshago
   Gornago Uchilishcha
Izv Energ Inst Akad Nauk SSSR — Izvestiya Energeticheskogo Instituta
   Akademiya Nauk SSSR
Izv Estestvennonauchn Inst Permsk Gos Univ — Izvestiya
   Estestvennonauchnogo Instituta pri Permskom Gosudarstvennom
   Universitet [*USSR*]
Izv Estestv Nauchn Inst Im P S Lesgafta — Izvestiya Estestvenno-Nauchnogo
   Instituta Imeni P. S. Lesgafta
Izv Estestv-Nauchn Inst Molotov Gos Univ Im M Gor'kogo — Izvestiya
   Estestvenno-Nauchnogo Instituta pri Molotovskom Gosudarstvennom
   Universiteta Imeni M. Gor'kogo
Izvest Imp Akad Nauk S Petersburg — Izvestiya Imperatorskoi Akademii Nauk
   St. Petersburg
Izvestiya Akad Nauk SSSR — Izvestiya Akademii Nauk SSSR Otdelenie
   Literatury i Jazyka
Izvestiya Jugo-Oset Nauc-Issl Inst — Izvestiya Jugo-Osetinskogo Naucno-
   Issledovatel'skogo Instituta Akademii Nauk-Gruzinskoj SSR
Izvestiya Kirgiz Filiala Akad Nauk SSSR — Izvestiya Kirgizskogo Filiala
   Akademii Nauk SSSR
Izvestiya Turkm Filiala Akad Nauk SSSR — Izvestiya Turkmenskogo Filiala
   Akademii Nauk SSSR
Izvestiya Voronezskogo Gos Ped Inst — Izvestiya Voronezskogo
   Gosudarstvennego Pedagogiceskogo Instituta
Izvest Ross Akad Nauk — Izvestiia Rossiiskoi Akademii Nauk
Izv Fak S kh Nauk Moshonmad'yarovar Vengriya — Izvestiya Fakul'teta
   Sel'skokhozyaistvennykh Nauk Moshonmad'yarovar Vengriya
Izv Fiz Inst ANEB Bylg Akad Nauk — Izvestiya na Fizicheskiya Instituta
   ANEB. Bylgarska Akademiya na Naukite
Izv Fiz-Khim Nauchno-Issled Inst Irkutsk Gos Univ — Izvestiya Fiziko-
   Khimicheskogo Nauchno-Issledovatel'skogo Instituta pri Irkutskom
   Gosudarstvennom Universitete
Izv Geofiz Inst — Izvestiya na Geofizichniya Institut
Izv Geofiz Inst Bulg Akad Nauk — Izvestiya na Geofizichniya Institut.
   Bulgarska Akademiya na Naukite [*Bulgaria*]
Izv Geol Inst Bulg Akad Nauk — Izvestiya na Geologicheskiya Institut.
   Bulgarska Akademiya na Naukite
Izv Geol Inst Bulg Akad Nauk Ser Geokhim Mineral Petrogr — Izvestiya na
   Geologicheskiya Institut. Bulgarska Akademiya na Naukite. Seriya
   Geokhimiya, Mineralogiya, i Petrografiya [*Bulgaria*]
Izv Geol Inst Bulg Akad Nauk Ser Geotekton — Izvestiya na Geologicheskiya
   Institut. Bulgarska Akademiya na Naukite. Seria Geotektonika
Izv Geol Inst Bulg Akad Nauk Ser Geotektonika Stratigr Litol — Izvestiya na
   Geologicheskiya Institut. Bulgarska Akademiya na Naukite. Seriya
   Geotektonika. Stratigrafiya i Litologiya
Izv Geol Inst Bulg Akad Nauk Ser Neftena Vuglishtna Geol — Izvestiya na
   Geologicheskiya Institut. Bulgarska Akademiya na Naukite. Seriya
   Neftena i Vuglishtna Geologiya
Izv Geol Inst Bulg Akad Nauk Ser Prilozhna Geof — Izvestiya na
   Geologicheskiya Institut. Bulgarska Akademiya na Naukite. Seriya
   Prilozhna Geofizika
Izv Geol Inst Bulg Akad Nauk Ser Stratigr Litol — Izvestiya na
   Geologicheskiya Institut. Bulgarska Akademiya na Naukite. Seriya
   Stratigrafiya i Litologiya

Izv Geol Inst Ser Paleontol (Sofia) — Izvestiya na Geologicheskiya Institut.
   Seriya Paleontologiya (Sofia)
Izv Geol Inst Ser Prilozh Geofiz — Izvestiya na Geologicheskiya Institut. Seriya
   Prilozhna Geofizika
Izv Gl Astron Obs Pulkove — Izvestiya Glavnoi Astronomicheskoi Observatorii
   v Pulkove
Izv Gorskogo S'kh Inst — Izvestiya Gorskogo Sel'skokhozyaistvennogo
   Instituta
Izv Gos Nauchno-Issled Inst Kolloidn Khim — Izvestiya Gosudarstvennogo
   Nauchno-Issledovatel'skogo Instituta Kolloidnoi Khimii
Izv Gos Nauchno-Issled Inst Ozern Rechn Rybn Khoz — Izvestiya
   Gosudarstvennogo Nauchno-Issledovatel'skogo Instituta Ozernogo i
   Rechnogo Rybnogo Khozyaistva
IzvIBE — Izvestiya na Instituta za Belgarski Ezik
Izv Inst Biol Bulg Akad Nauk — Izvestiya na Instituta po Biologiya. Bulgarska
   Akademiya na Naukite
Izv Inst Biol "Metod Popov" Bulg Akad Nauk — Izvestiya na Instituta po
   Biologiya "Metodii Popov." Bulgarskoi Akademii Nauk
Izv Inst Chist Khim Reakt — Izvestiya Instituta Chistykh Khimicheskikh
   Reaktivov
Izv Inst Eksp Med Bulg Akad Nauk — Izvestiya na Instituta po
   Eksperimentalna Meditsina. Bulgarska Akademiya na Naukite
Izv Inst Eksp Vet Med Bulg Akad Nauk — Izvestiya na Instituta po
   Eksperimentalna Veterinarna Meditsina. Bulgarska Akademiya na
   Naukite
Izv Inst Elektron — Izvestiya na Instituta po Elektronika
Izv Inst Elektron Bulg Akad Nauk — Izvestiya na Instituta po Elektronika.
   Bulgarska Akademiya na Naukite
Izv Inst Energ Bulg Akad Nauk — Izvestiya na Instituta po Energetika.
   Bulgarska Akademiya na Naukite
Izv Inst Fiziol B'lg Akad Nauk — Izvestiya na Instituta po Fiziologiya.
   B'lgarska Akademiya na Naukite
Izv Inst Fiziol Rast Bulg Akad Nauk — Izvestiya na Instituta po Fiziologiya na
   Rasteniyata. Bulgarska Akademiya na Naukite [*Bulgaria*]
Izv Inst Fiziol Rast "Metodii Popov" Bulg Akad Nauk — Izvestiya na Instituta
   po Fiziologiya na Rasteniyata "Metodii Popov." Bulgarska Akademiya
   na Naukite
Izv Inst Fiziol Rast "Metod Popov" Bulg Akad Nauk — Izvestiya na Instituta
   po Fiziologiya na Rasteniyata "Metodii Popov." Bulgarskoi Akademii
   Nauk
Izv Inst Furazhite Pleven — Izvestiya. Institut po Furazhite. Pleven
Izv Inst Gorata Akad Selskostop Nauki Bulg — Izvestiya na Instituta za
   Gorata. Akademiya na Selskostopanskite Nauki v Bulgariya
Izv Inst Khidrol Meteor — Izvestiya na Instituta po Khidrologiya i
   Meteorologiya. Bylgarska Akademiya na Naukite
Izv Inst Khidrol Meteorol Bulg Akad Nauk — Izvestiya na Instituta po
   Khidrologiya i Meteorologiya. Bulgarska Akademiya na Naukite
   [*Bulgaria*]
Izv Inst Khidrotekh Melior Akad Selskostop Nauki Bulg — Izvestiya na
   Instituta Khidrotekhnika i Melioratsii. Akademiya Selskostopanskite
   Nauki v Bulgariya
Izv Inst Khranene Bulg Akad Nauk — Izvestiya na Instituta po Khranene.
   Bulgarska Akademiya na Naukite
Izv Inst Klin Obshchest Med Bulg Akad Nauk — Izvestiya na Instituta za
   Klinichna i Obshchestvena Meditsina. Bulgarska Akademiya na
   Naukite
Izv Inst Morfol B'lg Akad Nauk Med Nauki — Izvestiya na Instituta po
   Morfologiya Bulgarska Akademiya na Naukite za Meditsinski Nauki
Izv Inst Morfol Bulg Akad Nauk — Izvestiya na Instituta po Morfologiya.
   Bulgarska Akademiya na Naukite [*Bulgaria*]
Izv Inst Nauk Iskusstv SSR Arm — Izvestiya Instituta Nauk i Iskusstv SSR
   Armenii
Izv Inst Obshcha Sravn Patol B'lg Akad Nauk — Izvestiya na Instituta po
   Obshcha i Sravnitelna Patologiya. Bulgarska Akademiya na Naukite
Izv Inst Obshch Sravn Patol Bulg Akad Nauk — Izvestiya na Instituta po
   Obshcha i Sravnitelna Patologiya. Bulgarska Akademiya na Naukite
   [*Bulgaria*]
Izv Inst Obshta Neorg Khim Bulg Akad Nauk — Izvestiya na Instituta po
   Obshta i Neorganichna Khimiya. Bulgarska Akademiya na Naukite
Izv Inst Okeanogr Ribno Stop Bulg Akad Nauk — Izvestiya na Instituta po
   Okeanografiya i Ribno Stopanstvo. Bulgarska Akademiya na Naukite
Izv Inst Org Khim Bulg Akad Nauk — Izvestiya na Instituta po Organichna
   Khimiya. Bulgarska Akademiya na Naukite
Izv Inst Ovoshcharstvo — Izvestiya na Instituta po Ovoshcharstvo. Gara
   Kostinbrod
Izv Inst Pamuka (Chirpan) — Izvestiya na Instituta po Pamuka (Chirpan)
Izv Inst Pshenitsata Slunchogleda (Tolbukhin) — Izvestiya. Institut po
   Pshenitsata i Slunchogleda (Tolbukhin)
Izv Inst Rast Bulg Akad Nauk — Izvestiya na Instituta po Rastenievudstvo.
   Bulgarska Akademiya na Naukite
Izv Inst Rastenievud Akad Selskostop Nauki Bulg — Izvestiya na Instituta po
   Rastenievudstvo. Akademiya na Selskostopanskite Nauki v Bulgariya
Izv Inst Ribni Resur (Varna) — Izvestiya. Institut Ribni Resursov (Varna)
Izv Inst Rybn Resur — Izvestiya Institut Rybnykh Resursov (Varna)
Izv Inst Sravn Patol Zhitvotnykh — Izvestiya na Instituta po Sravnitelna
   Patologiya na Zhitvotnykh

Izv Inst Sravn Patol Zhivotn — Izvestiya na Instituta po Sravnitelna Patologiya na Zhivotnite

Izv Inst Sravn Patol Zhivotn B'lg Akad Nauk Otd Biol Nauki — Izvestiya na Instituta po Sravnitelna Patologiya na Zhivotnite. Bulgarska Akademiya na Naukite Otdelenie za Biologichni Nauki

Izv Inst Sravn Patol Zhivotn Bulg Akad Nauk — Izvestiya na Instituta po Sravnitelna Patologiya na Zhivotnite. Bulgarska Akademiya na Naukite

Izv Inst Srav Patol Zhivotn Bulg Akad Nauk — Izvestiya na Instituta po Sravnitelna Patologiya na Zhivotnite. Bulgarska Akademiya na Naukite [*Bulgaria*]

Izv Inst Tekh Kibern — Izvestiya na Instituta po Tekhnicheska Kibernetika

Izv Inst Tekh Mekh Bulg Akad Nauk — Izvestiya na Instituta po Tekhnicheska Mekhanika. Bulgarska Akademiya na Naukite

Izv Inst Tsarevitsata-Knezha — Izvestiya na Instituta po Tsarevitsata-Knezha

Izv Inst Vodni Probl Bulg Akad Nauk — Izvestiya na Instituta po Vodni Problemi. Bulgarska Akademiya na Naukite

Izv Inst Vodn Probl Bylg Akad Nauk — Izvestiya na Instituta po Vodni Problemi. Bulgarska Akademiya na Naukite. Otdelenie za Tekhnicheskij Nauki

Izv Inst Zhivotn Bulg Akad Nauk — Izvestiia. Institut za Zhivotnovudstvo Bulgarska Akademiia na Naukite

IzvIRGruz — Izvestiya. Institut Rukopisej Akademii Nauk Gruzinskoj SSR

Izv Irkutsk Nauchno-Issled Protivochumn Inst Sib Dal'n Vost — Izvestiya Irkutskogo Nauchno-Issledovatel'skogo Protivochumnogo Instituta Sibiri i Dal'nego Vostoka

Izv Irkutsk Skh Inst — Izvestiya Irkutskogo Sel'skokhozyaistvennogo Instituta

Izv Ivanovo Voznesensk Politekh Inst — Izvestiya Ivanovo-Voznesenskogo Politekhnicheskogo Instituta

Izv Ivanov Skh Inst — Izvestiya Ivanovskogo Sel'skokhozyaistvennogo Instituta

IzvJOsNII — Izvestiya Jugo-Osetinskogo Naucno-Issledovatel'skogo Instituta

Izv Jugo Oset Nauc-Issled Inst Akad Nauk Gruz SSR — Izvestija Jugo-Osetinskogo Naucno-Issledovatelskogo Instituta Akademii Nauk Gruzinskoj SSR

IzvJuOsI — Izvestiya Jugo-Osetinskogo Naucno-Issledovatel'skogo Instituta Akademii Nauk-Gruzinskoj SSR

Izv Kamarata Nar Kult Ser Biol Zemed Lesovud — Izvestiya na Kamarata na Narodnata Kultura. Seriya Biologiya Zemedelie i Les ovudstvo

Izv Kazan Fil Akad Nauk SSR — Izvestiya Kazanskogo Filiala Akademii Nauk SSR

Izv Kazan Fil Akad Nauk SSSR Ser Biol Nauk — Izvestiya Kazanskogo Filiala Akademii Nauk SSSR Seriya Biologicheskikh Nauk

Izv Kazan Fil Akad Nauk SSSR Ser Biol Skh Nauk — Izvestiya Kazanskogo Filiala Akademii Nauk SSSR Seriya Biologicheskikh i Sel's kokhozyaistvennykh Nauk

Izv Kazan Fil Akad Nauk SSSR Ser Fiz-Mat i Tehn Nauk — Izvestija Kazanskogo Filiala Akademii Nauk SSSR Serija Fiziko-Matematiceskih i Tehniceskih Nauk

Izv Kazan Fil Akad Nauk SSSR Ser Geol Nauk — Izvestiya Kazanskogo Filiala Akademii Nauk SSSR Seriya Geologicheskikh Nauk

Izv Kazan Lesotekh Inst — Izvestiya Kazanskogo Lesotekhnicheskogo Instituta

Izv Khidravl Lab Vissh Inzh Stroit Inst — Izvestiya na Khidravlicheskata Laboratoriya Vissh Inzhenerno-Stroitelen Instit ut

Izv Khim Inst Bulg Akad Nauk — Izvestiya na Khimicheskiya Institut. Bulgarska Akademiya na Naukite [*Bulgaria*]

Izv Khlopchatobum Prom — Izvestiya Khlopchatobumazhnoi Promyshlennosti

Izv Kiev Politekh Inst — Izvestiya Kievskogo Politekhnicheskogo Instituta

Izv Kirg Fil Akad Nauk SSSR — Izvestiya Kirgizskogo Filiala Akademii Nauk SSSR

Izv Kirg Fil Vses Ova Pochvovedov — Izvestiya Kirgizskogo Filiala Vsesoyuznogo Obshchestva Pochvovedov

Izv Kirg Geogr Ova — Izvestiya Kirgizskogo Geograficheskogo Obshchestva

Izv Kom Fiz Planet Akad Nauk SSSR — Izvestiya Komissii po Fizike Planet Akademiya Nauk SSSR

Izv Komi Fil Geogr Obsc SSSR — Izvestija Komi Filiala Geograficeskogo Obscestva SSSR

Izv Komi Fil Vses Geogr Obshch — Izvestiya Komi Filiala Vsesoyuznogo Geograficheskogo Obshchestva

Izv Komi Fil Vses Geogr O-va SSSR — Izvestiya Komi Filiala Vsesoyuznogo Geograficheskogo Obshchestva SSSR

Izv Kompleks Selskostop Nauchnoizsled Inst (Karnobat) — Izvestiya na Kompleksniya Selskostopanski Nauchnoizsledvatelski Institut (Karnobat)

Izv Krym Astrofiz Obs — Izvestiya Krymskoi Astrofizicheskoi Observatorii

Izv Krym Otd Geogr Ova SSSR — Izvestiya Krymskogo Otdela Geograficheskogo Obshchestva SSSR

Izv Krym Pedagog Inst — Izvestiya Krymskogo Pedagogicheskogo Instituta

Izv Krymsk Otd Geog Obshch Soyuza SSR — Izvestiya Krymskogo Otdela Geograficheskogo Obshchestva SSSR

Izv Kuibyshev Inzh Melior Inst — Izvestiya Kuibyshevskogo Inzhenerno-Meliorativnogo Instituta

Izv Kuibyshev Sel'khoz Inst — Izvestiya Kuibyshevskogo Sel'skokhozyaistvennogo Instituta

Izv Kuibyshev S-kh Inst — Izvestiya Kuibyshevskogo Sel'skokhozyaistvennogo Instituta

Izv Leningr Elektrotekh Inst — Izvestiya Leningradskogo Elektrotekhnicheskogo Instituta

Izv Lesotekh Akad — Izvestiya Lesotekhnicheskoi Akademii

Izv Med Inst Bulg Akad Nauk — Izvestiya na Meditsinskite Institut. Bulgarska Akademiya na Naukite

Izv Mikrobiol Inst Bulg Akad Nauk — Izvestiya na Mikrobiologicheskiya Institut. Bulgarska Akademiya na Naukite

Izv Mikrobiol Inst Sof — Izvestiya na Mikrobiologicheskiya Institut Sofiya

Izv Minist Proizvod Zagotovok S-kh Prod Arm SSR — Izvestiya Ministerstvo Proizvodstva i Zagotovok Sel'skokhozyaistvennykh Productov Armyanskoi SSR

Izv Minist Selsk Khoz Arm SSR — Izvestiya Ministerstvo Sel'skogo Khozyaistva Armyanskoi SSR

Izv Minist Sel'sk Khoz Arm SSR S-Kh Nauki — Izvestiya Ministerstvo Sel'skogo Khozyaistva Armyanskoi SSR Sel'skokhozyaistvennye Nauki

Izv Minist Skh Arm SSR — Izvestiya Ministerstvo Sel'skokhozyaistva Armyanskoi SSR

Izv Mold Fil Akad Nauk SSSR — Izvestiya Moldavskogo Filiala Akademii Nauk SSSR

Izv Mosk Skh Inst — Izvestiya Moskovskogo Selskokhozyaistvennogo Instituta

Izv Mosk Tekst Inst — Izvestiya Moskovskii Tekstil'nyi Institut

Izv Nachnoizsled Inst Okeanogr Ribno Stop (Varna) — Izvestiya na Nauchnoizsledovatelskiya Institut po Okeanografiya i Ribno Stopanstvo (Varna)

Izv Nauchno-Issled Inst Nefte Uglekhim Sint Irkutsk Univ — Izvestiya Nauchno-Issledovatel'skogo Instituta Nefte- i Uglekhimicheskogo Sinteza pri Irkutskom Universitete

Izv Nauchno Issled Inst Ozern Rechn Rybn Khoz — Izvestiya Nauchno-Issledovatel'skogo Instituta Ozernogo i Rechnogo Rybnogo Khozyaistva

Izv Nauchno-Issled Inst Postoyan Toka — Izvestiya Nauchno-Issledovatel'skogo Instituta Postoyannogo Toka [*USSR*]

Izv Nauchnoizsled Geol Inst (Sofia) — Izvestiya na Nauchnoizsledovatelskiya Geolozhki Institut (Sofia)

Izv Nauchnoizsled Inst Kinematogr Radio — Izvestiya na Nauchnoizsledovatelskiya Institut po Kinematografiya i Radio

Izv Omsk Otd Geogr O-va SSR — Izvestiya Omskogo Otdeleniya Geograficheskogo Obshchestva SSR

Izv Otd Biol Med Nauki Bulg Akad Nauk — Izvestiya na Otdelenieto za Biologicheski i Meditsinski Nauki. Bulgarska Akademiya na Naukite

Izv Otdel Obshchest Nauk A N Tadzh — Izvestiia Otdeleniia Obshchestvennykh Nauk Akademiia Nauk Tadzhikskoi SSR

Izv Otd Estestv Nauk Akad Nauk Tadzh SSR — Izvestiya Otdeleniya Estestvennykh Nauk. Akademiya Nauk Tadzhikskoi SSR

Izv Otd Khim Nauki Bulg Akad — Izvestiya na Otdelenieto za Khimicheski Nauki. Bulgarska Akademiya na Naukite

Izv Otd Khim Nauki Bulg Akad Nauk — Izvestiya na Otdelenieto za Khimicheski Nauki. Bulgarska Akademiya na Naukite

Izv Permsk Biol Nauchno-Issled Inst — Izvestiya Permskogo Biologicheskogo Nauchno-Issledovatel'skogo Instituta

Izv Petrovsk Skh Akad — Izvestiya Petrovskoi Sel'skokhozyaistvennoi Akademii

Izv Petrovsk Zemled Lesn Akad — Izvestiya Petrovskoi Zemledel'cheskoi i Lesnoi Akademii

Izv Phys Solid Earth — Izvestiya. Physics of the Solid Earth

Izv Pochv Inst Bulg Akad Nauk — Izvestiya na Pochveniya Institut. Bulgarska Akademiya na Naukite

Izv Povolzh Lesotekh Inst — Izvestiya Povolzhskogo Lesotekhnicheskogo Instituta

Izv Ross Inst Prikl Khim — Izvestiya Rossiiskogo Instituta Prikladnoi Khimii

Izv Rostov Donu Nauchno-Issled Inst Epidemiol Mikrobiol Gig — Izvestiya Rostovskog na Donu Nauchno-Issledovatel'skogo Instituta Epidemiologii Mikrobiologii i Gigieny

Izv Sakhalin Otd Geogr Ova SSSR — Izvestiya Sakhalinskogo Otdela Geograficheskogo Obshchestva SSSR

Izv Samar Skh Inst — Izvestiya Samarskogo Sel'skokhozyaistvennogo Instituta

Izv Sarat Ova Estestvoispyt — Izvestiya Saratovskogo Obshchestva Estestvoispytatelei

Izv Sekt Fiz-Khim Anal Inst Obshch Neorg Khim Akad Nauk SSSR — Izvestiya Sektora Fiziko-Khimicheskogo Analiza Institut Obshchei i Neorganicheskoi Khimii Akademiya Nauk SSSR

Izv Sekt Platiny Drugikh Obshch Neorg Khim Akad Nauk SSSR — Izvestiya Sektora Platiny i Drugikh Blagorodnykh Metallov Institut Obshchei i Neorganicheskoi Khimii Akademiya Nauk SSSR [*USSR*]

Izv Sekts Astron Bulg Akad Nauk — Izvestiya na Sektsiyata po Astronomiya. Bulgarska Akademiya na Naukite

Izv Sel'khoz Nauk — Izvestiya Sel'skokhozyaistvennykh Nauk

Izv Sel'-khoz Nauki Minist Sel' Khoz Armyan SSR — Izvestiya Sel'skokhozyaistvennoi Nauki Ministerstvo Sel'skogo Khozyaistva Armya nskoi SSR

Izv Severo-Kavkaz Nauchn Tsentra Vyssh Shkoly Ser Tekhn Nauk — Izvestiya Severo-Kavkazskogo Nauchnogo Tsentra Vysshei Shkoly Seriya Tekhnicheskie Nauki

Izv Severo-Kavkaz Naucn Centra Vyss Skoly Ser Estestv Nauk — Izvestija Severo-Kavkazskogo Naucnogo Centra Vyssei Skoly Serija Estestvennye Nauki

Izv Severo-Kavkaz Naucn Centra Vyss Skoly Ser Tehn Nauk — Izvestija Severo-Kavkazskogo Naucnogo Centra Vyssei Skoly Serija Tehniceskie Nauki

Izv Sev-Kavk Nauc Centra Vyss Skoly Ser Obsc Nauk — Izvestija Severo-Kavkazskogo Naucnogo Centra Vyssej Skoly Serija Obscestvennyh Nauk

Izv Sev-Kavk Nauchn Tsentra Vyssh Shk Estestv Nauki — Izvestiya Severo-Kavkazskogo Nauchnogo Tsentra Vysshei Shkoly Estestvennye Nauki

Izv Sev-Kavk Nauchn Tsentra Vyssh Shk Ser Estestv Nauk — Izvestiya Severo-Kavkazskogo Nauchnogo Tsentra Vysshei Shkoly Seriya Estestvennykh Nauk [USSR]

Izv Sibir Otd Akad Nauk SSSR — Izvestiya Sibirskogo Otdeleniya Akademii Nauk SSSR

Izv Sibir Otd Akad Nauk SSSR Khim — Izvestiya Sibirskogo Otdeleniya Akademii Nauk SSSR Seriya Khimicheskikh Nauk

Izv Sibir Otd Akad Nauk SSSR Ser Khim Nauk — Izvestiya Sibirskogo Otdeleniya Akademii Nauk SSSR Seriya Khimicheskikh Nauk

Izv Sibir Otd Akad Nauk SSSR Ser Tekh Nauk — Izvestiya Sibirskogo Otdeleniya Akademii Nauk SSSR Seriya Tekhnicheskikh Nauk

Izv Sibir Otd Akad Nauk SSSR Tekh — Izvestiya Sibirskogo Otdeleniya Akademii Nauk SSSR Seriya Tekhnicheskikh Nauk

Izv Sibir Otdel Akad Nauk SSSR Ser Biol Nauk — Izvestiya Sibirskogo Otdelenija Akademii Nauk SSSR Serija Biologiceskih Nauk

Izv Sibirsk Otdel Akad Nauk SSSR — Izvestija Sibirskogo Otdelenija Akademija Nauk SSSR

Izv Sibirsk Otdel Akad Nauk SSSR Ser Tehn Nauk — Izvestija Sibirskogo Otdelenija Akademija Nauk SSSR Serija Tehniceskih Nauk

Izv Sib Mekh-Mashinostroit Inst — Izvestiya Sibirskogo Mekhaniko-Mashinostroitel'nogo Instituta

Izv Sib Otd Akad Nauk SSSR — Izvestiya Sibirskogo Otdeleniya Akademii Nauk SSSR

Izv Sib Otd Akad Nauk SSSR Geol Geofiz — Izvestiya Sibirskogo Otdeleniya Akademii Nauk SSSR Geologiya i Geofizika

Izv Sib Otd Akad Nauk SSSR Ser Biol-Med Nauk — Izvestiya Sibirskogo Otdeleniya Akademii Nauk SSSR Seriya Biologo-Meditsinskikh Nauk

Izv Sib Otd Akad Nauk SSSR Ser Biol Nauk — Izvestiya Sibirskogo Otdeleniya Akademii Nauk SSSR Seriya Biologicheskikh Nauk

Izv Sib Otd Akad Nauk SSSR Ser Khim Nauk — Izvestiya Sibirskogo Otdeleniya Akademii Nauk SSSR Seriya Khimicheskikh Nauk

Izv Sib Otd Akad Nauk SSSR Ser Obshchestv Nauk — Izvestiya Sibirskogo Otdeleniya Akademii Nauk SSSR Seriya Obshchestvennykh Nauk [USSR]

Izv Sib Otd Akad Nauk SSSR Ser Tekh Nauk — Izvestiya Sibirskogo Otdeleniya Akademii Nauk SSSR Seriya Tekhnicheskikh Nauk

Izv Sib Otdel Akad Nauk SSSR Ser Biol-Med Nauk — Izvestiya Sibirskogo Otdeleniya Akademii Nauk SSSR Seriya Biologo-Meditsinskikh Nauk

Izv Sib Otdel Akad Nauk SSSR Ser Biol Nauk — Izvestiya Sibirskogo Otdeleniya Akademii Nauk SSSR Seriya Biologicheskikh Nauk

Izv Sib Otdel Akad Nauk SSSR Ser Obsc Nauk — Izvestija Sibirskogo Otdelenija Akademii Nauk SSSR Serija Obscestvennyh Nauk

Izv Sib Otd Geol Kom — Izvestiya Sibirskogo Otdeleniya Geologicheskogo Komiteta [USSR]

Izv Sib Tekhnol Inst — Izvestiya Sibirskogo Tekhnologicheskogo Instituta

Izv Skh Akad Im KA Timiryazeva — Izvestiya Sel'skokhozyaistvennoi Akademii Imeni K. A. Timiryazeva

Izv S-kh Nauk — Izvestiya Sel'skokhozyaistvennykh Nauk

IzvSLF — Izvestiya Seminara po Slavjanske Filologija

IzvSOsNII — Izvestiya Severo-Osetinskogo Naucno-Issledovatel'skogo Instituta

IzvTadzikAN — Izvestiya Tadzikskogo Filiala Akademii Nauk

Izv Tbilis Nauchno Issled Inst Sooruzh Gidroenerg — Izvestiya Tbilisskogo Nauchno-Issledovatel'skogo Instituta Sooruzhenii i Gidroenergetiki

Izv Tekst Promsti Torg — Izvestiya Tekstil'noi Promyshlennosti i Torgovli

Izv Tikhookean Nauchno-Issled Inst Rybn Khoz Okeanogr — Izvestiya Tikhookeanskogo Nauchno-Issledovatel'skogo Instituta Rybnogo Khozyaistva i Okeanografii

Izv Tikhookean Nauchno-Issled Ist Rybn Khoz Okeanogr — Izvestiya Tikhookeanskog Nauchno-Issledovatel'Skogo Instituta Rybnogo Khozyaistva i Okeanografii

Izv Timiryazev Sel'-khoz Akad — Izvestiya Timiryazevskoi Sel'skokhozyaistvennoi Akademii

Izv Timiryazev S-kh Akad — Izvestiya Timiryazevskoi Sel'skokhozyaistvennoi Akademii

Izv Tomsk Ind Inst — Izvestiya Tomskogo Industrial'nogo Instituta

Izv Tomsk Otd Vses Bot Ova — Izvestiya Tomskogo Otdeleniya Vsesoyuznogo Botanicheskogo Obshchestva

Izv Tomsk Politehn Inst — Izvestiya Tomskogo Ordena Trudovogo Krasnogo Znameni Politehniceskogo Instituta Imeni S. M. Kirova

Izv Tomsk Politekh Inst — Izvestiya Tomskogo Politekhnicheskogo Instituta Imeni S. M. Kirova

Izv Tomsk Politekh Inst Mekh Mashinostr — Izvestiya Tomskogo Politekhnicheskogo Instituta Mekhanika i Mashinostroenia

Izv Tr Kharb Politekh Inst — Izvestiya i Trudy Kharbinskogo Politekhnicheskogo Instituta

Izv Tsent Nauchnoizsled Inst Zasht Rast — Izvestiya na Tsentralniya. Nauchnoizsledovatelski Institut za Zashnita na Rasteniyata

Izv Tsent Nauchnoizsled Inst Zhivotnovud "Georgi Dimitrov" — Izvestiya na Tsentralniya. Nauchnoizsledovatelski Institut po Zhivotnovudstvo "Georgi Dimitrov"

Izv Tsentr Khelmintol Lab B'lg Akad Nauk — Izvestiya na Tsentralnata Khelmintologichna Laboratoriya. Bulgarska Akademiya na Naukite

Izv Tsentr Lab Biokhim Bulg Akad Nauk — Izvestiya na Tsentralnata Laboratoriya po Biokhimiya. Bulgarska Akademiya na Naukite

Izv Tsentr Lab Energ Bulg Akad Nauk — Izvestiya na Tsentralnata Laboratoriya po Energetika. Bulgarska Akademiya na Naukite

Izv Tsentr Nauchno Issled Inst Kozh Promsti — Izvestiya Tsentral'nogo Nauchno-Issledovatel'skogo Instituta Kozhevennoi Promyshlennosti

Izv Turkm Fil Akad Nauk SSR — Izvestiya Turkmenskogo Filiala Akademii Nauk SSR

Izv Ural Gorn Inst Ekaterinburge — Izvestiya Ural'skogo Gornogo Instituta v Ekaterinburge

Izv Ural Politekh Inst — Izvestiya Ural'skogo Politekhnicheskogo Instituta

Izv Uzb Fil Geogr Ova SSSR — Izvestiya Uzbekistanskogo Filiala Geograficheskogo Obshchestva SSSR

Izv Uzb Geogr Ova — Izvestiya Uzbekskogo Geograficheskogo Obshchestva

Izv Veng S'kh Nauchno-Issled Inst A — Izvestiya Vengerskikh Sel'skokhozyaistvennykh Nauchno-Issledovatel'skikh Institutow A. Rastenievodstvo

Izv Veng S kh Nauchno-Issled Inst C — Izvestiya Vengerskikh Sel'skokhozyaistvennykh Nauchno-Issledovatel'skikh Institutow C. Sadovodstvo

Izv Vet Inst Virusol Akad Selskostop Nauki Bulg — Izvestiya na Veterinarniya Institut po Virusologiya. Akademiya na Selskostopanskite Nauki v Bulgaria

Izv Vissh Mash-Elektrotekh Inst Lenin — Izvestiya na Visshiya Mashinno-Elektrotekhnicheski Institut Lenin [*Bulgaria*]

Izv Vmei "Lenin" — Izvestiya na Vmei "Lenin"

Izv Voronez Gos Ped Inst — Izvestija Voronezskogo Gosudarstvennogo Pedagogiceskogo Instituta

Izv Voronezh Gos Ped Inst — Izvestiya Voronezhskogo Gosudarstvennogo Pedagogiceskogo Instituta

Izv Voronez Pedag Inst — Izvestija Voronezskogo Pedagogiceskogo Instituta

IzvVorPI — Izvestiya Voronezskogo Gosudarstvennogo Pedagogiceskogo Instituta

Izv Vost Fil Akad Nauk SSSR — Izvestiya Vostochnykh Filialov Akademii Nauk SSSR

Izv Vost Filial Akad Nauk SSSR — Izvestiya Vostochnykh Filialov Akademii Nauk SSSR [USSR]

Izv Vostochnosib Skh Inst — Izvestiya Vostochnosibirskogo Sel'skokhozyaistvennogo Instituta

Izv Vost Sib Otd Geogr Ova SSSR — Izvestiya Vostochno-Sibirskogo Otdela Geograficheskogo Obshchestva SSSR

Izv Vses Geogr Obshch — Izvestiya Vsesoyuznogo Geograficheskogo Obshchestva

Izv Vses Geogr O-va — Izvestiya Vsesoyuznogo Geograficheskogo Obshchestva

Izv Vses Nauchno-Issled Inst Gidrotekh — Izvestiya Vsesoyuznogo Nauchnogo-Issledovatel'skogo Instituta Gidrotekhniki [USSR]

Izv Vses Nauchno Issled Inst Ozern Rechn Rybn Khoz — Izvestiya Vsesoyuznogo Nauchno-Issledovatel'skogo Instituta Ozernogo i Rechnogo Rybnogo Khozyaistva

Izv Vsesojuz Geogr Obsc — Izvestiya Vsesojuznogo Geograficeskogo Obscestva

Izv Vses Teplotekh Inst — Izvestiya Vsesoyuznogo Teplotekhnicheskogo Instituta

Izv VUZ Aviats Tekh — Izvestiya Vysshikh Uchebnykh Zavedenii Aviatsionnaya Tekhnika

Izv VUZ Chernaya Metall — Izvestiya Vysshikh Uchebnykh Zavedenii Chernaya Metallurgiya

Izv VUZ Elektromekh — Izvestiya Vysshikh Uchebnykh Zavedenii Elektromekhanika

Izv VUZ Energ — Izvestiya Vysshikh Uchebnykh Zavedenii Energetika

Izv VUZ Fiz — Izvestiya Vysshikh Uchebnykh Zavedenii Fizika

Izv VUZ Gornyi Zh — Izvestiya Vysshikh Uchebnykh Zavedenii Gornyi Zhurnal

Izv VUZ Khim i Khim Tekhnol — Izvestiya Vysshikh Uchebnykh Zavedenii Khimiya i Khimicheskaya Tekhnologiya

Izv VUZ Kh i Kh Tekh — Izvestiya Vyssikh Uchebnykh Zavedenii Khimiya i Khimicheskaya Tekhnologiya

Izv VUZ Lesnoi Zh — Izvestiya Vysshikh Uchebnykh Zavedenii Lesnoi Zhurnal

Izv VUZ Mashinostr — Izvestiya Vysshikh Uchebnykh Zavedenii Mashinostroenie

Izv VUZ Mat — Izvestiya Vysshikh Uchebnykh Zavedenii Matematika

Izv Vuzov Mashinostr — Izvestiya Vuzov Mashinostroenie [USSR]

Izv VUZ Pishch Tekhnol — Izvestiya Vysshikh Uchebnykh Zavedenii Pishchevaya Tekhnologiya

Izv VUZ Priborostr — Izvestiya Vysshikh Uchebnykh Zavedenii Priborostroenie

Izv VUZ Radioelektron — Izvestiya Vysshikh Uchebnykh Zavedenii Radioelektronika

Izv VUZ Radiofiz — Izvestiya Vysshikh Uchebnykh Zavedenii Radiofizika

Izv VUZ Tekh Leg Prom — Izvestiya Vysshikh Uchebnykh Zavedenii Tekhnologiya Legkoi Promyshlennosti

Izv VUZ Tekhnol Legkoi Prom-st — Izvestiya Vysshikh Uchebnykh Zavedenii Tekhnologiya Legkoi Promyshlennosti

Izv VUZ Tekhnol Tekstil Prom — Izvestiya Vysshikh Uchebnykh Zavedenii Tekhnologiya Tekstil'noi Promyshlennosti
Izv VUZ Tsvetn Metall — Izvestiya Vysshikh Uchebnykh Zavedenii Tsvetnaya Metallurgiya
Izv Vyssh Uchebn Zaved Aviats Tekh — Izvestiya Vysshikh Uchebnykh Zavedenii Aviatsionnaya Tekhnika
Izv Vyssh Uchebn Zaved Chern Metall — Izvestiya Vysshikh Uchebnykh Zavedenii Chernaya Metallurgiya
Izv Vyssh Uchebn Zaved Ehlektromekh — Izvestiya Vysshikh Uchebnykh Zavedenii Ehlektromekhanika
Izv Vyssh Uchebn Zaved Ehnerg — Izvestiya Vysshikh Uchebnykh Zavedenii Ehnergetika
Izv Vyssh Uchebn Zaved Fiz — Izvestiya Vysshikh Uchebnykh Zavedenij Fizika
Izv Vyssh Uchebn Zaved Geod Aerofotos'emka — Izvestiya Vysshikh Uchebnykh Zavedenii Geodeziya i Aerofotos'emka [*USSR*]
Izv Vyssh Uchebn Zaved Geol Razved — Izvestiya Vysshikh Uchebnykh Zavedenii Geologiya i Razvedka
Izv Vyssh Uchebn Zaved Gorn Zh — Izvestiya Vysshikh Uchebnykh Zavedenij Gornyj Zhurnal
Izv Vyssh Uchebn Zaved Khim Khim Tekhnol — Izvestiya Vysshikh Uchebnykh Zavedenii Khimiya i Khimicheskaya Tekhnologiya
Izv Vyssh Uchebn Zaved Lesn Zh — Izvestiya Vysshikh Uchebnykh Zavedenii Lesnoi Zhurnal
Izv Vyssh Uchebn Zaved Mashinostr — Izvestiya Vysshikh Uchebnykh Zavedenii Mashinostroenie
Izv Vyssh Uchebn Zaved Neft' Gaz — Izvestiya Vysshikh Uchebnykh Zavedenii Neft' i Gaz
Izv Vyssh Uchebn Zaved Pishch Tekhnol — Izvestiya Vysshikh Uchebnykh Zavedenii Pishchevaya Tekhnologiya
Izv Vyssh Uchebn Zaved Priborostr — Izvestiya Vysshikh Uchebnykh Zavedenii Priborostroenie
Izv Vyssh Uchebn Zaved Radioelektron — Izvestiya Vysshikh Uchebnykh Zavedenii Radioelektronika
Izv Vyssh Uchebn Zaved Radiofiz — Izvestiya Vysshikh Uchebnykh Zavedenij Radiofizika
Izv Vyssh Uchebn Zaved Radiotekh — Izvestiya Vysshikh Uchebnykh Zavedenii Radiotekhnika
Izv Vyssh Uchebn Zaved Stroit Arkhit — Izvestiya Vysshikh Uchebnykh Zavedenii Stroitel'stvo i Arkhitektura
Izv Vyssh Uchebn Zaved Tekhnol Legk Promsti — Izvestiya Vysshikh Uchebnykh Zavedenii Tekhnologiya Legkoi Promyshlennosti
Izv Vyssh Uchebn Zaved Tekhnol Tekst Prom-sti — Izvestiia Vysshikh Uchebnykh Zavedenii Tekhnologiia Tekstil'noi Promyshlennosti
Izv Vyssh Uchebn Zaved Tekhnol Tekst Promsti — Izvestiya Vysshikh Uchebnykh Zavedenii Tekhnologiya Tekstil'noi Promyshlennosti
Izv Vyssh Uchebn Zaved Tsvetn Metall — Izvestiya Vysshikh Uchebnykh Zavedenii Tsvetnaya Metallurgiya
Izv Vyssh Ucheb Zaved Chern Met — Izvestiya Vysshikh Uchebnykh Zavedenii Chernaya Metallurgiya
Izv Vyssh Ucheb Zaved Elektromekh — Izvestiya Vysshikh Uchebnykh Zavedenii Elektromekhanika
Izv Vyssh Ucheb Zaved Energ — Izvestiya Vysshikh Uchebnykh Zavedenii Energetika
Izv Vyssh Ucheb Zavedenii Geol Razvedka — Izvestiya Vysshikh Uchebnykh Zavedenii Geologiya i Razvedka
Izv Vyssh Ucheb Zaved Geol i Razved — Izvestiya Vysshikh Uchebnykh Zavedenii Geologiya i Razvedka
Izv Vyssh Ucheb Zaved Gorn Zh — Izvestiya Vysshikh Uchebnykh Zavedenii Gornyi Zhurnal
Izv Vyssh Ucheb Zaved Khim i Khim — Izvestiya Vysshikh Uchebnykh Zavedenii Khimiya i Khimicheskaya
Izv Vyssh Ucheb Zaved Neft i Gaz — Izvestiya Vysshikh Uchebnykh Zavedenii Neft' i Gaz
Izv Vyssh Ucheb Zaved Ser Pishch Tekhnol — Izvestiya Vysshikh Uchebnykh Zavedenii Seriya Pishchevaya Tekhnologiya
Izv Vyssh Ucheb Zaved Tekh Legk — Izvestiya Vysshikh Uchebnykh Zavedenii Tekhnologiya Legkoi Promyshlennosti
Izv Vyssh Ucheb Zaved Tsvet Met — Izvestiya Vysshikh Uchebnykh Zavedenii Tsvetnaya Metallurgiya
Izv Vyss Ucebn Zaved Aviacion Tehn — Izvestija Vyssih Ucebnyh Zavedenii Aviacionnaja Tehnika
Izv Vyss Ucebn Zaved Elektromehanika — Izvestija Vyssih Ucebnyh Zavedenii Elektromehanika
Izv Vyss Ucebn Zaved Fizika — Izvestija Vyssih Ucebnyh Zavedenii Fizika
Izv Vyss Ucebn Zaved Geod i Aerofot — Izvestija Vyssih Ucebnyh Zavedenii Geodezija i Aerofotos Emka
Izv Vyss Ucebn Zaved Matematika — Izvestija Vyssih Ucebnyh Zavedenii Matematika
Izv Vyss Ucebn Zaved Radiofizika — Izvestija Vyssih Ucebnyh Zavedenii Radiofizika
Izv Zabaik Fil Geogr O-va SSSR — Izvestiya Zabaikal'skogo Filiala Geograficheskogo Obshchestva SSSR [*USSR*]
IZWWAX — Instytut Zootechniki w Polsce Wydawnictwa Wlasne

J

J — Jeunesse
J — Jezik
J — Judiciary
JA — Jahrbuch fuer Amerikastudien
JA — January
JA — Japan Architect
JA — Jeune Afrique
JA — Jewish Advocate [*Bombay*]
J A — Journal A. Presses Academiques Europeennes
JA — Journal of Aesthetics and Art Criticism
JA — Journal of Andrology
JA — Journal of Apocrypha
JA — Journal Asiatique
JAA — Journal of Accounting Auditing and Finance
JAA — Journal of African Administration
JAA — Journal of Anthropological Archaeology
JAA — Journal of Astrophysics and Astronomy
JAA — Journal. British Archaeological Association
JAAC — Journal of Aesthetics and Art Criticism
JAACP — Journal. American Chamber of Commerce of the Philippines
JAADDB — Journal. American Academy of Dermatology
JAAHBL — Journal. American Animal Hospital Association
JAAK — Jahrbuch fuer Aesthetik und Allgemeine Kunstwissenschaft
Ja Ann Int Law — Japanese Annual of International Law
Ja Ann Law Pol — Japan Annual of Law and Politics
J AANNT — Journal. American Association of Nephrology Nurses and Technicians
JAAPCC — Journal. American Academy of Psychoanalysis
JAAPD — Journal of Analytical and Applied Pyrolysis
JAAPDD — Journal of Analytical and Applied Pyrolysis
JAAR — Journal. American Academy of Religion
Jaarb Ak Amst — Jaarboek. Akademie te Amsterdam
Jaarb Inst Biol Scheik Onderz LandbGewass — Jaarboek. Instituut voor Biologisch en Scheikundig Onderzoek van Landbouwgewassen
Jaarb K Acad Overzeese Wet (Brussels) — Jaarboek. Koninklijke Academie voor Overzeese Wetenschappen (Brussels)
Jaarb Kankeronderz Kankerbestrijding Ned — Jaarboek van Kankeronderzoek en Kankerbestrijding in Nederland [*Netherlands*]
Jaarb Karakul Breeders Soc S Afr — Jaarboek. Karakul Breeders Society of South Africa
Jaarbl Bot Ver S-Afr — Jaarblad. Botaniese Vereniging van Suid-Afrika
Jaarb Ned Natuurk Ver — Jaarboek. Nederlandse Natuurkundige Vereniging [*Netherlands*]
Jaarb Proefstat Boomkwekerij Boskoop — Jaarboek. Proefstation voor de Boomkwekerij te Boskoop
Jaarb Rijksuniv Utrecht — Jaarboek. Rijksuniversiteit te Utrecht
Jaarb Sticht Fundam Onderz Mater Sticht Inst Kernphys Onderz — Jaarboek. Stichting voor Fundamenteel Onderzoek der Materie en Stichting Instituut voor Kernphysisch Onderzoek
Jaarversl Inst Graan Meel Brood (Wageningen) — Jaarverslag. Institut voor Graan, Meel, en Brood (Wageningen)
Jaarversl Lab Bloembollenonderz Lisse — Jaarverslag. Laboratorium voor Bloembollenonderzoek Lisse
Jaarversl TNO — Jaarverslag. TNO [*Toegepast Natuurwetenschappelijk Onderzoek*]

JAAS — Journal of Asian and African Studies
JAASAJ — Journal. Alabama Academy of Science
JAASD — Journal. American Audiology Society
JAB — Journal of Applied Behavioral Science
JAB — Journal of Applied Biochemistry
JABAA4 — Journal of Applied Bacteriology
JABAE8 — Journal of Animal Breeding and Genetics
JABCAA — Journal of Abnormal Child Psychology
J Abdom Surg — Journal of Abdominal Surgery
JABGDP — Journal. Adelaide Botanic Gardens
JABIDV — Journal of Applied Biochemistry
J Abnorm Child Psychol — Journal of Abnormal Child Psychology
J Abnorm Psychol — Journal of Abnormal Psychology
J Abnorm Psychol Monogr — Journal of Abnormal Psychology. Monograph
J Abnorm Soc Psychol — Journal of Abnormal and Social Psychology
J Abn Psych — Journal of Abnormal Psychology
JAbP — Journal of Abnormal Psychology
JABPAF — Journal of Abnormal Psychology. Monograph
JABS — Journal of Applied Behavioral Science
JABSBP — Journal of Abdominal Surgery
J Abstr Br Ship — Journal of Abstracts. British Ship Research Association
JAC — Jahrbuch fuer Antike und Christentum
JAC — Journal of Accountancy
J Acad Libnship — Journal of Academic Librarianship
J Acad Librarianship — Journal of Academic Librarianship
J Acad Nat Sci Phila — Journal. Academy of Natural Sciences of Philadelphia
JACBB — Journal of Applied Chemistry and Biotechnology
JACCDI — Journal. American College of Cardiology
J Accidental Med — Journal of Accidental Medicine [*Japan*]
J Account — Journal of Accountancy
J Accountancy — Journal of Accountancy
J Account Audit Finance — Journal of Accounting Auditing and Finance
J Accountin — Journal of Accounting Research
J Accounting Res — Journal of Accounting Research
J Account Res — Journal of Accounting Research
J Acctcy — Journal of Accountancy
J Acct Res — Journal of Accounting Research
J Accy — Journal of Accountancy
JACDA — Journal. American College of Dentists
JACEB — JACEP. Journal of the American College of Emergency Physicians
JACEP — Journal. American College of Emergency Physicians and the University Association for Emergency Medical Services
JACh — Jahrbuch fuer Antike und Christentum
JACH — Journal of American College Health
JACHD — Journal of Antimicrobial Chemotherapy
JACHDX — Journal of Antimicrobial Chemotherapy
JACHEY — Journal of American College Health
Ja Christ Q — Japan Christian Quarterly
JACHS — Australian Catholic Historical Society. Journal
JACIA — Journal. American Concrete Institute
JACIBY — Journal of Allergy and Clinical Immunology
JACM — Journal. Association for Computing Machinery
JACODK — Journal of Altered States of Consciousness
J Acoust Emiss — Journal of Acoustic Emission
J Acoustical Soc Am — Journal. Acoustical Society of America

J Acoust So — Journal. Acoustical Society of America
J Acoust Soc Am — Journal. Acoustical Society of America
J Acoust Soc Amer — Journal. Acoustical Society of America
J Acoust Soc Am Suppl — Journal. Acoustical Society of America. Supplement
J Acoust Soc India — Journal. Acoustical Society of India
J Acoust Soc Jap — Journal. Acoustical Society of Japan
J Acoust Soc Jpn — Journal. Acoustical Society of Japan
JACPA — Journal. American Academy of Child Psychiatry
JACRAQ — Journal of Apicultural Research
JAcS — Journal. Acoustical Society of America
JACS — Journal. American Chemical Society
JACSA — Journal. American Chemical Society
JACSAT — Journal. American Chemical Society
JACT — Journal. American College of Toxicology
JACTA — Journal. American Ceramic Society
JACTA — Journal. Australasian Commercial Teachers' Association
JACTDZ — Journal. American College of Toxicology
JAD — Journal of Advertising Research
JADAA — Journal. American Dietetic Association
JADAAE — Journal. American Dietetic Association
Jadav J Comp Lit — Jadavpur Journal of Comparative Literature
J Addict Res Found — Journal. Addiction Research Foundation
JADE — Journal of Alcohol and Drug Education
JADEA — Jaderna Energie
J Adelaide Bot Gard — Journal. Adelaide Botanic Gardens
Jad Energ — Jaderna Energie
Jadernaja Fiz — Jadernaja Fizika
J Adhes — Journal of Adhesion
J Adhesion — Journal of Adhesion
J Adhes Sealant Counc — Journal. Adhesive and Sealant Council [*United States*]
J Adhes Soc Jpn — Journal. Adhesion Society of Japan
JADID7 — Journal of Affective Disorders
J Admin Overseas — Journal of Administration Overseas
J Adm Overs — Journal of Administration Overseas
J Adm Overseas — Journal of Administration Overseas
JADO — Journal of Administration Overseas
J Adolesc — Journal of Adolescence
J Adolescence — Journal of Adolescence
J Adolesc Health Care — Journal of Adolescent Health Care
JADPDS — Journal of Applied Developmental Psychology
JADSA — Journal. American Dental Association
JADSAY — Journal. American Dental Association
J Adult Ed — Journal of Adult Education
J Adv — Journal of Advertising
J Advanced Transp — Journal of Advanced Transportation
J Adv Educ — Journal of Advanced Education
J Advert — Journal of Advertising
J Advertising — Journal of Advertising
J Advert Res — Journal of Advertising Research
J Adv Nurs — Journal of Advanced Nursing
J Adv Res — Journal of Advertising Research
J Adv Transp — Journal of Advanced Transportation [*United States*]
JAe — Jahrbuch fuer Aesthetik und Allgemeine Kunstwissenschaft
JAE — Jeune Afrique Economie
JAE — Journal of Accounting and Economics [*Netherlands*]
JAE — Journal of Aesthetic Education
JAE — Journal of Agricultural Economics
JAE — Training and Development Journal
JAECAP — Journal of Animal Ecology
Ja Echo — Japan Echo
Ja Econ Stud — Japanese Economic Studies
JAEDB — Journal of Aesthetic Education
JAEMA — Journal. Albert Einstein Medical Center
JAEMAL — Journal. Albert Einstein Medical Center [*Philadelphia*]
JAENES — Journal of Agricultural Entomology
JAERA2 — Journal of Agricultural Engineering Research
J Aero Med Soc India — Journal. Aero Medical Society of India
J Aeronaut Soc India — Journal. Aeronautical Society of India
J Aeronaut Soc S Afr — Journal. Aeronautical Society of South Africa
J Aero Sci — Journal of the Aeronautical Sciences
J Aerosol Sci — Journal of Aerosol Science
J Aero/Space Sci — Journal of the Aero/Space Sciences [*Later, American Institute of Aeronautics and Astronautics. Journal*]
J Aerosp Transp Div Am Soc Civ Eng — Journal. Aerospace Transport Division. American Society of Civil Engineers
JAERT — Journal. Association for Education by Radio-Television
JAES — Journal of African Earth Sciences
JAES — Journal. Audio Engineering Society
J Aes Art C — Journal of Aesthetics and Art Criticism
J Aes Art Crit — Journal of Aesthetics and Art Criticism
J Aes Ed — Journal of Aesthetic Education
J Aes Educ — Journal of Aesthetic Education
J Aesth — Journal of Aesthetics and Art Criticism
J Aesth & Art C — Journal of Aesthetics and Art Criticism
J Aesth Educ — Journal of Aesthetic Education

J Aesthet E — Journal of Aesthetic Education
J Aesthetic Educ — Journal of Aesthetic Education
J Aesthetics — Journal of Aesthetics and Art Criticism
JAf — Jewish Affairs
JAF — Journal of American Folklore
JA & FC — Journal of Agricultural and Food Chemistry
JAFCAU — Journal of Agricultural and Food Chemistry
JAff — Jewish Affairs
J Affective Disord — Journal of Affective Disorders
JAFL — Journal of American Folklore
Ja Found Newsl — Japan Foundation Newsletter
JAfrH — Journal of African History
J Afr Hist — Journal of African History
J Afric Hist — Journal of African History
JAfrL — Journal of African Languages
J Afr L — Journal of African Law
J Afr Law — Journal of African Law
J Afr S — Journal of the African Society
J Afr Stud — Journal of African Studies
JAG — JAG [*Judge Advocate General, US Air Force*] Bulletin
JAG — Journal. Alaska Geological Society
J Ag Econ — Journal of Agricultural Economics
J Ag & Food Chem — Journal of Agricultural and Food Chemistry
JAGGAD — Journal des Agreges
Jagger J — Jagger Journal
JAG J — JAG [*Judge Advocate General, US Navy*] Journal
J Ag New Zealand — New Zealand Journal of Agriculture
J Ag Pratique — Journal d'Agriculture Pratique
JAGRA — Journal of Agricultural Research
J Agr Ass China — Journal. Agricultural Association of China
J Agr Che J — Journal. Agricultural Chemical Society of Japan
J Agr Chem Soc Jap — Journal. Agricultural Chemical Society of Japan
J Agr Econ — Journal of Agricultural Economics
J Agr Econ Dev — Journal of Agricultural Economics and Development
J Agr Eng R — Journal of Agricultural Engineering Research
J Agr Eng Res — Journal of Agricultural Engineering Research
J Agr Eng Soc Jap — Journal. Agricultural Engineering Society of Japan
J Ag Res — Journal of Agricultural Research
J Agr Exp Sta Chosen — Journal. Agricultural Experiment Station of Chosen
J Agr Food — Journal of Agricultural and Food Chemistry
J Agr Food Chem — Journal of Agricultural and Food Chemistry
J Agric — Journal of Agriculture
J Agric Ass China — Journal. Agricultural Association of China
J Agric Chem Soc Japan — Journal. Agricultural Chemical Society of Japan
J Agric Chem Soc Jpn — Journal. Agricultural Chemical Society of Japan
J Agric Econ — Journal of Agricultural Economics
J Agric Econ Dev — Journal of Agricultural Economics and Development
J Agric Eng — Journal of Agricultural Engineering
J Agric Engin Res — Journal of Agricultural Engineering Research
J Agric Engng Res — Journal of Agricultural Engineering Research
J Agric Eng Res — Journal of Agricultural Engineering Research
J Agric Entomol — Journal of Agricultural Entomology
J Agric Fd Chem — Journal of Agricultural and Food Chemistry
J Agric Food Chem — Journal of Agricultural and Food Chemistry
J Agric For — Journal of Agriculture and Forestry
J Agric Lab (Chiba) — Journal. Agricultural Laboratory (Chiba)
J Agric Meteorol — Journal of Agricultural Meteorology [*Tokyo*]
J Agric Met (Tokyo) — Journal of Agricultural Meteorology (Tokyo)
J Agric Res — Journal of Agricultural Research
J Agric Res (Alexandria) — Journal of Agricultural Research (Alexandria)
J Agric Res China — Journal of Agricultural Research of China
J Agric Res Icel — Journal of Agricultural Research in Iceland
J Agric (S Aust) — Journal of Agriculture (South Australia)
J Agric Sci — Journal of Agricultural Science
J Agric Sci (Camb) — Journal of Agricultural Science (Cambridge)
J Agric Sci Tokyo Nogyo Daigaku — Journal of Agricultural Science. Tokyo Nogyo Daigaku
J Agric Soc Jpn — Journal. Agricultural Society of Japan
J Agric Soc Trin — Journal. Agricultural Society of Trinidad and Tobago
J Agric Soc Trinidad Tobago — Journal. Agricultural Society of Trinidad and Tobago
J Agric Soc Trin & Tobago — Journal. Agricultural Society of Trinidad and Tobago
J Agric Soc Univ Coll Wales — Journal. Agricultural Society. University College of Wales
J Agric Soc Univ Coll Wales (Aberyst) — Journal. Agricultural Society. University College of Wales (Aberystwyth)
J Agric (South Aust) — Journal of Agriculture (South Australia)
J Agric Trop — Journal d'Agriculture Tropicale
J Agric Trop Botan Appl — Journal d'Agriculture Tropicale et de Botanique Appliquee [*Later, Journal d'Agriculture Traditionnelle et de Botanique Appliquee*]
J Agric Trop Bot Appl — Journal d'Agriculture Tropicale et de Botanique Appliquee [*Later, Journal d'Agriculture Traditionnelle et de Botanique Appliquee*]
J Agric Univ PR — Journal of Agriculture. University of Puerto Rico

J Agric Univ Puerto Rico — Journal of Agriculture. University of Puerto Rico
J Agric (VIC) — Journal of Agriculture (Department of Agriculture. Victoria)
J Agric (Vict) — Journal of Agriculture (Victoria)
J Agric Vict Dep Agric — Journal of Agriculture. Victoria Department of Agriculture
J Agric (Victoria) — Journal of Agriculture (Victoria)
J Agric (West Aust) — Journal of Agriculture (Department of Agriculture. Western Australia)
J Agr Lab — Journal. Agricultural Laboratory
J Agr (Melbourne) — Journal of Agriculture (Melbourne)
J Agr Meteorol (Japan) — Journal of Agricultural Meteorology (Japan)
J Agron Crop Sci — Journal of Agronomy and Crop Science
J Agr Prat — Journal d'Agriculture Pratique
J Agr Res — Journal of Agricultural Research
J Agr Res Tokai-Kinki Reg — Journal of the Agricultural Research in the Tokai-Kinki Region
J Agr (S Aust) — Journal of Agriculture (South Australia)
J Agr Sci — Journal of Agricultural Science
J Agr Sci Tokyo Nogyo Daigaku — Journal of Agricultural Science. Tokyo Nogyo Daigaku
J Agr Soc Trinidad Tobago — Journal. Agricultural Society of Trinidad and Tobago
J Agr Soc Wales — Journal. Agricultural Society. University College of Wales
J Agr Trad Bot Appl — Journal d'Agriculture Traditionnelle et de Botanique Appliquee
J Agr Trop Bot Appl — Journal d'Agriculture Tropicale et de Botanique Appliquee [Later, Journal d'Agriculture Traditionnelle et de Botanique Appliquee]
J Agr Univ PR — Journal of Agriculture. University of Puerto Rico
J Agr W Aust — Journal of Agriculture of Western Australia
J Ag (SA) — Journal of Agriculture (South Australia)
JAGSA — Journal. American Geriatrics Society
JAGSAF — Journal. American Geriatrics Society
J Ag T and L — Journal of Agricultural Taxation and Law
J Ag Univ Puerto Rico — Journal of Agriculture. University of Puerto Rico
JAGVAO — Journal of Agriculture [Victoria]
J Ag (VIC) — Journal of Agriculture (Department of Agriculture. Victoria)
J Ag (WA) — Journal of Agriculture (Department of Agriculture. Western Australia)
JAH — Journal of African History
JAH — Journal of American History
JAHAA — Journal. American College Health Association
JAHAAY — Journal. American College Health Association
JahAs — Jahrbuch fuer Amerikastudien
JAHCD9 — Journal of Adolescent Health Care
JAHEDF — Journal of Allied Health
Jahrb Akad Wiss Gottingen — Jahrbuch. Akademie der Wissenschaften in Goettingen
Jahrb Akad Wiss Lit (Mainz) — Jahrbuch. Akademie der Wissenschaften und der Literatur (Mainz)
Jahrb Amerikastud — Jahrbuch fuer Amerikastudien
Jahrb Arbeitsgemein Futterungsberat — Jahrbuch. Arbeitsgemeinschaft fuer Fuetterungsberatung
Jahrb Arbeitsgem Fuetterungsberat — Jahrbuch. Arbeitsgemeinschaft fuer Fuetterungsberatung
Jahrb Bayer Akad Wiss — Jahrbuch. Bayerische Akademie der Wissenschaften
Jahrb Bergbau Energ Mineraloel Chem — Jahrbuch fuer Bergbau Energie Mineraloel und Chemie
Jahrb Ber M — Jahrbuch. Berliner Museen
Jahrb Brandenburg Landesgesch — Jahrbuch fuer Brandenburgische Landesgeschichte
Jahrb Bundesanst Pflanzebau Samenpruef (Wien) — Jahrbuch. Bundesanstalt fuer Pflanzenbau und Samenpruefung (Wien)
Jahrb Bundesanst Pflanzenbau Samenpruf — Jahrbuch. Bundesanstalt fuer Pflanzenbau und Samenpruefung
Jahrb Coburg Landesstift — Jahrbuch. Coburger Landesstiftung
Jahrb Deut Akad Landwirt Wiss (Berlin) — Jahrbuch. Deutsche Akademie der Landwirtschaftswissenschaften (Berlin)
Jahrb Dtsch Ges Chronom — Jahrbuch. Deutsche Gesellschaft fuer Chronometrie
Jahrb Eisenbahnwes — Jahrbuch des Eisenbahnwesens [West Germany]
Jahr Berliner Mus — Jahrbuch. Berliner Museen
Jahrb Geol Bundesanst — Jahrbuch. Geologische Bundesanstalt
Jahrb Geol Bundesanst Sonderb — Jahrbuch. Geologische Bundesanstalt. Sonderband
Jahrb Gesch — Jahrbuecher fuer Geschichte Osteuropas
Jahrb Gesch & Kunst Mittelrheins & Nachbargeb — Jahrbuch fuer Geschichte und Kunst des Mittelrheins und Seiner Nachbargebiete
Jahrb Gesch Mittel Ostdtschl — Jahrbuch fuer die Geschichte Mittel- und Ostdeutschlands
Jahrb Gesch Osteur — Jahrbuecher fuer Geschichte Osteuropas
Jahrb Gesch Osteurop — Jahrbuecher fuer Geschichte Osteuropas
Jahrb Hafenbautech Ges — Jahrbuch. Hafenbautechnische Gesellschaft [West Germany]
Jahrb Kinderh — Jahrbuch fuer Kinderheilkunde und Physische Erziehung

Jahrb Kinderheilkd Phys Erzieh — Jahrbuch fuer Kinderheilkunde und Physische Erziehung
Jahrb d Kunsthist Samml d Kaiserhauses — Jahrbuch. Kunsthistorische Sammlungen des Allerhochsten Kaiserhauses
Jahrb Kunsth Samml Kaiserh — Jahrbuch. Kunsthistorische Sammlungen des Allerhoechsten Kaiserhauses
Jahrb Lederwirtsch Oesterr — Jahrbuch. Lederwirtschaft Oesterreich
Jahrb Liturg & Hymnol — Jahrbuch fuer Liturgik und Hymnologie
Jahrb Nassau Ver Naturkd — Jahrbuecher. Nassauischer Verein fuer Naturkunde
Jahrb Nordrh Westfal Landesamt Forsch — Jahrbuch. Nordrhein Westfalen Landesamt fuer Forschung
Jahrb N St — Jahrbuecher fuer National-Oekonomie und Statistik
Jahrb Oberflaechentech — Jahrbuch Oberflaechentechnik [West Germany]
Jahrb Oberoesterr Musealver — Jahrbuch. Oberoesterreichische Musealverein
Jahrb Oesterr Byzantinistik — Jahrbuch der Oesterreichischen Byzantinistik
Jahrb Opt Feinmech — Jahrbuch fuer Optik und Feinmechanik
Jahrb Org Chem — Jahrbuch der Organischen Chemie
Jahrb Philos Fak 2 Univ Bern — Jahrbuch der Philosophischen. Fakultaet 2. Universitaet Bern
Jahrb Photogr Reproduktionstech — Jahrbuch fuer Photographie und Reproduktionstechnik
Jahrb Preuss Geol Landesanst — Jahrbuch. Preussische Geologische Landesanstalt
Jahrb Preuss Kunstsamml — Jahrbuch. Preussische Kunstsammlungen
Jahrb d Preuss Kunstsamml — Jahrbuch. Preussische Kunstsammlungen
Jahrb Radioakt Elektron — Jahrbuch der Radioaktivitaet und Elektronik
Jahrb Reichsstelle Bodenforsch (Ger) — Jahrbuch der Reichsstelle fuer Bodenforschung (Germany)
Jahrb Schiffbautech Ges — Jahrbuch. Schiffbautechnische Gesellschaft
Jahrb Sozia — Jahrbuch fuer Sozialwissenschaft
Jahrb Staatl Mus Mineral Geol Dresden — Jahrbuch. Staatliches Museum fuer Mineralogie und Geologie zu Dresden
Jahrb Tech Univ Muenchen — Jahrbuch. Technische Universitaet Muenchen
Jahrbuch Hamburger Kunstsam — Jahrbuch. Hamburger Kunstsammlungen
Jahrbuch Niederdonau — Jahrbuch fuer Landeskunde von Niederdonau
Jahrb Vers Lehranst Brau Berlin — Jahrbuch. Versuch und Lehranstalt fuer Brauerei in Berlin
Jahrb Volks — Jahrbuch fuer Volksliedforschung
Jahrb Wiss Bot — Jahrbuecher fuer Wissenschaftliche Botanik
Jahrb Wiss Forschungsinst Buntmetall Plovdiv — Jahrbuch. Wissenschaftliches Forschungsinstitut fuer Buntmetallurgie. Plovdiv
Jahr Deutsch Archaeol Inst — Jahrbuch. Deutsches Archaeologische Institut
Jahresber Chem Tech Reichsanst — Jahresbericht. Chemisch Technische Reichsanstalt
Jahresber Dtsch Hydrogr Inst (Hamburg) — Jahresbericht. Deutsches Hydrographische Institut (Hamburg)
Jahresber Dtsch Pflanzenschutzdienstes — Jahresberichte des Deutschen Pflanzenschutzdienstes
Jahresber Fortschr Chem Verw Theile Andrer Wiss — Jahresbericht ueber die Fortschritte der Chemie und Verwandter Theile Anderer Wissenschaften
Jahresber Fortschr Gesamtgeb Agrikulturchem — Jahresbericht ueber die Fortschritte auf dem Gesamtgebiete der Agrikulturchemie
Jahresber Fortschr Physiol — Jahresbericht ueber die Fortschritte der Physiologie
Jahresber Fortschr Tierchm — Jahresbericht ueber die Fortschritte der Tierchemie
Jahresbericht Grabunden — Jahresbericht. Historisch-Antiquarische Gesellschaft von Grabunden
Jahresber Inst Strahlenphys Kernphys Univ Bonn — Jahresbericht. Institut fuer Strahlen- und Kernphysik. Universitaet Bonn
Jahresber Kernforschungsanlage Juelich — Jahresbericht. Kernforschungsanlage Juelich
Jahresber Kurashiki-Zentralhosp — Jahresbericht. Kurashiki-Zentralhospital
Jahresber Mitt Oberrheinischen Geol Ver — Jahresberichte und Mitteilungen. Oberrheinischer Geologische Verein
Jahresber Schweiz Ges Vererbungsforsch — Jahresbericht. Schweizerische Gesellschaft fuer Vererbungsforschung
Jahresber Univ Wuerzb — Jahresbericht. Universitaet Wuerzburg
Jahresb Schles Gesellsch Vaterl Kult — Jahresberichte. Schlesische Gesellschaft fuer Vaterlaendische Kultur
Jahresb Vet Med — Jahresbericht Veterinaer-Medizin
Jahresh Geol Landesamtes Baden Wuerttemb — Jahresheft. Geologisches Landesamt in Baden Wuerttemberg
Jahresh Ges Naturkd Wuerttemb — Jahreshefte. Gesellschaft fuer Naturkunde in Wuerttemberg
Jahresh Ver Vaterl Naturkd Wuerttemb — Jahreshefte. Verein fuer Vaterlaendische Naturkunde in Wuerttemberg
Jahreskurse Aerztl Fortbild — Jahreskurse fuer Aerztliche Fortbildung
Jahr Hamburger Kunstsam — Jahrbuch. Hamburger Kunstsammlungen
Jahr Kunsthist Sam (Wien) — Jahrbuch. Kunsthistorische Sammlungen (Wien)
JAHum — Journal of American Humor
JAHYA4 — Journal. American Dental Hygienists' Association
JAI — Journal of Advertising Research
JAI — Journal of American Insurance

JAI — Journal. Royal Anthropological Institute of Great Britain and Ireland
JAIA — Journal. Archaeological Institute of America
JAIAS — Journal. Australian Institute of Agricultural Science
JAIB — Journal. Royal Anthropological Institute of Great Britain and Ireland
JAIH — Journal of Ancient Indian History
JAIHA — Journal. American Institute of Homeopathy
JAIHAQ — Journal. American Institute of Homeopathy
JaiL — Jazyk i Literatura
JAINAA — Journal. Anatomical Society of India
J Aircr — Journal of Aircraft
J Aircraft — Journal of Aircraft
J Air L — Journal of Air Law and Commerce
J Air L and Com — Journal of Air Law and Commerce
J of Air L & Commerce — Journal of Air Law and Commerce
J Air Pollu — Journal. Air Pollution Control Association
J Air Pollut Contr Ass — Journal. Air Pollution Control Association
J Air Pollut Control Assoc — Journal. Air Pollution Control Association
J Air Transp Div Am Soc Civ Eng — Journal. Air Transport Division. American Society of Civil Engineers
JAISDS — Journal. All India Institute of Medical Sciences
JAJ — Jewish Affairs (Johannesburg)
Ja J — Judge Advocate Journal
JAJAAA — Journal of Antibiotics. Series A [*Tokyo*]
JaJGL — Jahrbuecher fuer Juedische Geschichte und Literatur
JAK — Jahrbuch der Asiatischen Kunst
JAk — Jazykovedny Aktuality
JAL — Japan (London)
JAL — Jewish Affairs (London)
JAL — Journal of Academic Librarianship
JAL — Journal of African Languages
JAL — Journal of African Law
J Ala Acad Sci — Journal. Alabama Academy of Science
J Ala Dent Assoc — Journal. Alabama Dental Association
J Alberta Soc Pet Geol — Journal. Alberta Society of Petroleum Geologists
J Albert Einstein Med Cent — Journal. Albert Einstein Medical Center
J Albert Einstein Med Cent (Phila) — Journal. Albert Einstein Medical Center (Philadelphia)
J Alc — Journal of Alcoholism
JALCA — Journal. American Leather Chemists' Association
JALCAQ — Journal. American Leather Chemists' Association
JALCBR — Journal of Alcoholism
J Alc Drug — Journal of Alcohol and Drug Education
J Alcohol — Journal of Alcoholism
J Alcohol & Drug Educ — Journal of Alcohol and Drug Education
J Algebra — Journal of Algebra
J Algorithms — Journal of Algorithms
Ja Lit Today — Japanese Literature Today
JALL — Journal of African Languages and Linguistics
J Allerg Cl — Journal of Allergy and Clinical Immunology
J Allergy — Journal of Allergy [*Later, Journal of Allergy and Clinical Immunology*]
J Allergy Clin Immun — Journal of Allergy and Clinical Immunology
J Allergy Clin Immunol — Journal of Allergy and Clinical Immunology
J Allied Dent Soc — Journal. Allied Dental Societies
J Allied Health — Journal of Allied Health
J All India Inst Ment Health — Journal. All India Institute of Mental Health
J All India Ophthalmol Soc — Journal. All India Ophthalmological Society
JALP — Japan Annual of Law and Politics
J ALS — Journal. American Liszt Society
J Altered States Conscious — Journal of Altered States of Consciousness
J Alumni Ass Coll Phys and Surg (Baltimore) — Journal. Alumni Association. College of Physicians and Surgeons (Baltimore)
JAM — Jamaica Exports. Complimentary Guide to Trade and Investment Opportunities
JAM — Journal of American Musicology
JAM — Journal. American Planning Association
JAM — Journal d'Analyse Mathematique [*Jerusalem*]
JAM — Journal of Applied Management
JAMA — Journal. American Medical Association
JAMAA — Journal. American Medical Association
JAMAAP — Journal. American Medical Association
J Am Acad Appl Nutr — Journal. American Academy of Applied Nutrition
J Am Acad Child Psych — Journal. American Academy of Child Psychiatry
J Am Acad Child Psychiatry — Journal. American Academy of Child Psychiatry
J Am Acad Dermatol — Journal. American Academy of Dermatology
J Am Academy Child Psychiatry — Journal. American Academy of Child Psychiatry
J Am Acad P — Journal. American Academy of Psychoanalysis
J Am Acad Psychoanal — Journal. American Academy of Psychoanalysis
J Am Acad Rel — Journal. American Academy of Religion
J Am Acad Relig — Journal. American Academy of Religion
J Am Acad Religion — Journal. American Academy of Religion
J Am A Chil — Journal. American Academy of Child Psychiatry
JAmAcRel — Journal. American Academy of Religion [*Brattleboro, VT*]
JAMAET — Journal. American Mosquito Control Association

Jamaica Ag Soc J — Jamaica Agricultural Society. Journal
Jamaica Arclt — Jamaica Architect
Jamaica Geol Survey Dept Ann Rept — Jamaica. Geological Survey Department. Annual Report
Jamaica Geol Survey Dept Bull — Jamaica. Geological Survey Department. Bulletin
Jamaica Geol Survey Dept Occ Pap — Jamaica. Geological Survey Department. Occasional Paper
Jamaica Geol Survey Dept Short Pap — Jamaica. Geological Survey Department. Short Paper
Jamaica Geol Survey Pub — Jamaica. Geological Survey Department. Publication
Jamaica Handb — Jamaica Handbook
J Am Analg Soc — Journal. American Analgesia Society
J Am Anim Hosp Assoc — Journal. American Animal Hospital Association
J Am A Rel — Journal. American Academy of Religion
J Am Assoc — Journal. American Association for Hygiene and Baths
J Am Assoc Cereal Chem — Journal. American Association of Cereal Chemists
J Am Assoc Nephrol Nurses Tech — Journal. American Association of Nephrology Nurses and Technicians
J Am Assoc Nurse Anesth — Journal. American Association of Nurse Anesthetists
J Am Assoc Promot Hyg Public Baths — Journal. American Association for Promoting Hygiene and Public Baths
J Am Assoc Teach Educ Agric — Journal. American Association of Teacher Educators in Agriculture
J Am Assoc Variable Star Obs — Journal. American Association of Variable Star Observers
J Am Audiol Soc — Journal. American Audiology Society
J Am Bakers Assoc Am Inst Baking — Journal. American Bakers Association and American Institute of Baking
J Ambulatory Care Manage — Journal of Ambulatory Care Management
J Ambul Care Manage — Journal of Ambulatory Care Management
J Am Ceram — Journal. American Ceramic Society
J Am Ceram Soc — Journal. American Ceramic Society
J Am Chem S — Journal. American Chemical Society
J Am Chem Soc — Journal. American Chemical Society
J Am Coll Cardiol — Journal. American College of Cardiology
J Am Coll Dent — Journal. American College of Dentists
J Am Coll H — Journal. American College Health Association
J Am Coll Health — Journal of American College Health
J Am Coll Health Assn — Journal. American College Health Association
J Am Coll Health Assoc — Journal. American College Health Association
J Am Concr Inst — Journal. American Concrete Institute
J Am Cult — Journal of American Culture
JAMDAY — Journal. American Medical Technologists
J Am Dent A — Journal. American Dental Association
J Am Dent Assoc — Journal. American Dental Association
J Am Dent Assoc Dent Cosmos — Journal. American Dental Association and the Dental Cosmos
J Am Dent Hyg Assoc — Journal. American Dental Hygienists' Association
Jam Dep Agric Bull — Jamaica. Department of Agriculture. Bulletin
J Am Diet A — Journal. American Dietetic Association
J Am Diet Assoc — Journal. American Dietetic Association
J Amer Ceram Soc — Journal. American Ceramic Society
J Amer Chem Soc — Journal. American Chemical Society
J Amer Coll Dent — Journal. American College of Dentists
J Amer Diet Ass — Journal. American Dietetic Association
J Amer Inst Planners — Journal. American Institute of Planners
J Amer Leather Chem Ass — Journal. American Leather Chemists' Association
J Amer Musicol Soc — Journal. American Musicological Society
J Amer Oil — Journal. American Oil Chemists' Society
J Amer Oil Chem Soc — Journal. American Oil Chemists' Society
J Amer Pharm Ass Sci Ed — Journal. American Pharmaceutical Association. Scientific Edition
J Amer Plann Assoc — Journal. American Planning Association
J Amer Soc Agron — Journal. American Society of Agronomy
J Amer Soc Farm Manage Rural Appraisers — Journal. American Society of Farm Managers and Rural Appraisers
J Amer Soc Hort Sci — Journal. American Society for Horticultural Science
J Amer Soc Inform Sci — Journal. American Society for Information Science
J Amer Soc Safety Eng — Journal. American Society of Safety Engineers
J Amer Soc Sugar Beet Tech — Journal. American Society of Sugar Beet Technologists
J Amer Statist Assoc — Journal. American Statistical Association
J Amer Stud — Journal of American Studies
J Amer Vet Med Ass — Journal. American Veterinary Medical Association
J Amer Water Works Ass — Journal. American Water Works Association
James Arthur Lect Evol Hum Brain — James Arthur Lecture on the Evolution of the Human Brain
James Joyce Q — James Joyce Quarterly
James Joy Q — James Joyce Quarterly
James Madison J — James Madison Journal
James Sprunt Hist Publ — James Sprunt Historical Publications
James Sprunt Hist Stud — James Sprunt Historical Studies
J Am F-lore — Journal of American Folklore

J Am Folk — Journal of American Folklore
J Am Folkl — Journal of American Folklore
J Am Folklo — Journal of American Folklore
J Am Folklore — Journal of American Folklore
Jam Geol Surv Dep Econ Geol Rep — Jamaica. Geological Survey Department. Economic Geology Report
J Am Geriatr Soc — Journal. American Geriatrics Society
J Am Ger So — Journal. American Geriatrics Society
J Am Health Care Assoc — Journal. American Health Care Association
J Am Helicopter Soc — Journal. American Helicopter Society
J Am His — Journal of American History
J Am Hist — Journal of American History
Jam Hist Rev — Jamaican Historical Review
J Am Ind Hyg Assoc — Journal. American Industrial Hygiene Association
J Am Indian Ed — Journal of American Indian Education
J Am Ins — Journal of American Insurance
J Am Inst Electr Eng — Journal. American Institute of Electrical Engineers
J Am Inst Homeop — Journal. American Institute of Homeopathy
J Am Inst Homeopath — Journal. American Institute of Homeopathy
J Am Inst P — Journal. American Institute of Planners
J Am Inst Plann — Journal. American Institute of Planners
J Am Insur — Journal of American Insurance
J Am Intraocul Implant Soc — Journal. American Intraocular Implant Society
Ja Mission B — Japan Missionary Bulletin
J Am Jud Soc — Journal. American Judicature Society
J Am Killifish Assoc — Journal. American Killifish Association
JAMLD — Journal of Applied Metalworking
J Am Leath — Journal. American Leather Chemists' Association
J Am Leather Chem Assoc — Journal. American Leather Chemists' Association
J Am Leather Chem Assoc Suppl — Journal. American Leather Chemists' Association. Supplement
JAMM — JAMM. Journal for Australian Music and Musicians
JAMMD — Journal. Australian Mathematical Society. Series B. Applied Mathematics
J Am Med A — Journal. American Medical Association
J Am Med Ass — Journal. American Medical Association
J Am Med Assoc — Journal. American Medical Association
J Am Med Rec Assoc — Journal. American Medical Record Association
J Am Med Technol — Journal. American Medical Technologists
J Am Med Wom Ass — Journal. American Medical Women's Association
J Am Med Wom Assoc — Journal. American Medical Women's Association
J Am Med Women Assoc — Journal. American Medical Women's Association
J Am Med Women's Assoc — Journal. American Medical Women's Association
Jam Mines Geol Div Spec Publ — Jamaica. Mines and Geology Division. Special Publication
Jam Minist Agric Fish Bull — Jamaica. Ministry of Agriculture and Fisheries. Bulletin
Jam Minist Agric Lands Annu Rep — Jamaica. Ministry of Agriculture and Lands. Annual Report
Jam Minist Agric Lands Bull — Jamaica. Ministry of Agriculture and Lands. Bulletin
J Am Music — Journal. American Musicological Society
J Am Mus In — Journal. American Musical Instrument Society
J Am Oil Ch — Journal. American Oil Chemists' Society
J Am Oil Chem Soc — Journal. American Oil Chemists' Society
J Am Optom Assoc — Journal. American Optometric Association
J Am Orient — Journal. American Oriental Society
J Am Orient Soc — Journal. American Oriental Society
J Am Or Soc — Journal. American Oriental Society
J Am Osteopath Assoc — Journal. American Osteopathic Association
JAMPA2 — Journal of Animal Morphology and Physiology
JAMPB3 — Journal. American Peanut Research and Education Association
J Am Peanut Res Educ Assoc — Journal. American Peanut Research and Education Association
J Am Peat Soc — Journal. American Peat Society
J Am Phar — Journal. American Pharmaceutical Association. Practical Pharmacy Edition
J Am Pharm — Journal. American Pharmaceutical Association
J Am Pharm Ass — Journal. American Pharmaceutical Association
J Am Pharm Assoc — Journal. American Pharmaceutical Association
J Am Pharm Assoc Pract Pharm Ed — Journal. American Pharmaceutical Association. Practical Pharmacy Edition
J Am Pharm Assoc Sci Ed — Journal. American Pharmaceutical Association. Scientific Edition
J Am Plann Assoc — Journal. American Planning Association
J Am Podiatry Assoc — Journal. American Podiatry Association
J Am Psycho — Journal. American Psychoanalytic Association
J Am Psychonal Assoc — Journal. American Psychoanalytic Association
J Am Real Estate Urban Econ Assoc — Journal. American Real Estate and Urban Economics Association
J Am Rocket Soc — Journal. American Rocket Society
JAMS — Journal. American Musicological Society
JAmS — Journal of American Studies
JAMSA — Journal. Arkansas Medical Society
J Am S Hort — Journal. American Society for Horticultural Science

J Am S Infor — Journal. American Society for Information Science
J Am Soc Agron — Journal. American Society of Agronomy
J Am Soc Brew Chem — Journal. American Society of Brewing Chemists
J Am Soc CLU — Journal. American Society of Chartered Life Underwriters
J Am Soc Heat Vent Eng — Journal. American Society of Heating and Ventilating Engineers
J Am Soc Hortic Sci — Journal. American Society for Horticultural Science
J Am Soc Hort Sci — Journal. American Society for Horticultural Science
J Am Soc Inf Sci — Journal. American Society for Information Science
J Am Soc Mech Eng — Journal. American Society of Mechanical Engineers
J Am Soc Nav Eng — Journal. American Society of Naval Engineers
J Am Soc Prev Dent — Journal. American Society for Preventive Dentistry
J Am Soc Psychosom Dent — Journal. American Society of Psychosomatic Dentistry and Medicine
J Am Soc Psychosom Dent Med — Journal. American Society of Psychosomatic Dentistry and Medicine
J Am Soc Saf Eng — Journal. American Society of Safety Engineers
J Am Soc Sugar Beet Technol — Journal. American Society of Sugar Beet Technologists
J Am Soc Sug Beet Technol — Journal. American Society of Sugar Beet Technologists
J Am S Psyc — Journal. American Society for Psychical Research
J Am St — Journal of American Studies
J Am Stat A — Journal. American Statistical Association
J Am Stat Assoc — Journal. American Statistical Association
J Am Steel Treaters' Soc — Journal. American Steel Treaters' Society
J Am Stud — Journal of American Studies
J Am Studies — Journal of American Studies
JAMTD — Journal. Canadian Association for Music Therapy
J Am Vener Dis Assoc — Journal. American Venereal Disease Association
J Am Vet Me — Journal. American Veterinary Medical Association
J Am Vet Med Assoc — Journal. American Veterinary Medical Association
J Am Vet Ra — Journal. American Veterinary Radiology Society
J Am Vet Radiol Soc — Journal. American Veterinary Radiology Society
JAMWA — Journal. American Medical Women's Association
JAMWAN — Journal. American Medical Women's Association
J Am Water — Journal. American Water Works Association
J Am Water Works Assoc — Journal. American Water Works Association
J Am Zinc Inst — Journal. American Zinc Institute
Jan — Janus. Archives Internationales pour l'Histoire de la Medecine
JAN — Japan. The Economic and Trade Picture [London]
JAN — Jewish Affairs (New York)
JAN — Journal International d'Archeologie Numismatique
J Anal Chem — Journal of Analytical Chemistry of the USSR
J Anal Math — Journal d'Analyse Mathematique
J Anal Psych — Journal of Analytical Psychology
J Anal Psychol — Journal of Analytical Psychology
J Anal Toxicol — Journal of Analytical Toxicology
J Analyse Math — Journal d'Analyse Mathematique [Jerusalem]
J Anat — Journal of Anatomy
J Anat Phys — Journal of Anatomy and Physiology
J Anat Physiol Norm Pathol Homme Anim — Journal de l'Anatomie et de la Physiologie Normales et Pathologiques de l'Homme et des Animaux
J Anat Soc India — Journal. Anatomical Society of India
J Anc Ind Hist — Journal of Ancient Indian History
J Anc Near East Soc Columbia Univ — Journal. Ancient Near Eastern Society. Columbia University
J Andhra Hist Res Soc — Journal. Andhra Historical Research Society
JANES — Journal. Ancient Near Eastern Society
J Anglo-Mongol Soc — Journal. Anglo-Mongolian Society
J Animal Ecol — Journal of Animal Ecology
J Animal Ecology — Journal of Animal Ecology
J Animal Sci — Journal of Animal Science
J Anim Breed Genet — Journal of Animal Breeding and Genetics
J Anim Ecol — Journal of Animal Ecology
J Anim Morphol Physiol — Journal of Animal Morphology and Physiology
J Anim Morph Physiol — Journal of Animal Morphology and Physiology
J Anim Physiol Anim Nutr — Journal of Animal Physiology and Animal Nutrition
J Anim Prod UAR — Journal of Animal Production of the United Arab Republic
J Anim Prod Un Arab Repub — Journal of Animal Production of the United Arab Republic
J Anim Sci — Journal of Animal Science
J Anim Tech Ass — Journal. Animal Technicians Association
J Anim Tech Assoc — Journal. Animal Technicians Association
JanL — Janua Linguarum
JANMA — Japanese Nuclear Medicine
J Annamalai Univ — Journal. Annamalai University
J Annamalai Univ Part B — Journal. Annamalai University. Part B
JANPA7 — Journal of Analytical Psychology
JANSA — Journal of Animal Science
JANSAG — Journal of Animal Science
JANTAJ — Journal of Antibiotics [Tokyo]
JAnthrI — Journal. Royal Anthropological Institute of Great Britain and Ireland

J Anthropol Res — Journal of Anthropological Research
J Anthropol Soc Nippon — Journal. Anthropological Society of Nippon
J Anthropol Soc Oxford — Journal. Anthropological Society of Oxford
J Anthrop Res — Journal of Anthropological Research
J Anthro Res — Journal of Anthropological Research
J Anthr Res — Journal of Anthropological Research
J Anthr S N — Journal. Anthropological Society of Nippon
J Antibiot — Journal of Antibiotics [*Tokyo*]
J Antibiot Ser B (Japan) — Journal of Antibiotics. Series B (Japan)
J Antibiot (Tokyo) — Journal of Antibiotics (Tokyo)
J Antibiot (Tokyo) Ser A — Journal of Antibiotics (Tokyo). Series A
J Antimicrob Chemother — Journal of Antimicrobial Chemotherapy
J Antro Sos — Jernal Antropoloji dan Sosioloji
JAOA — Journal. American Osteopathic Association
JAOAA — Journal. American Osteopathic Association
JAOAAZ — Journal. American Osteopathic Association
J AOAC — Journal. Association of Official Analytical Chemists
JAOCA — Journal. American Oil Chemists' Society
JAOCA7 — Journal. American Oil Chemists' Society
JAOCS — Journal. American Oil Chemists' Society
JAOPB — Journal. American Optometric Association
JAOPBD — Journal. American Optometric Association
JAOS — Journal. American Oriental Society
J Aoyama Gakuin Woman's Jr Coll — Journal. Aoyama Gakuin Woman's Junior College
JAP — Journal of Abnormal Psychology
JAP — Journal of Applied Physics
JAP — Journal of Applied Psychology
Jap Acad Proc — Japan Academy. Proceedings
JAPAEA — Journal. American Podiatric Medical Association
Jap Agric Res Q — Japanese Agricultural Research Quarterly
Japan Annu Int Law — Japanese Annual of International Law
Japan Arch — Japan Architect
Japan Archt — Japan Architect
Japan A Soc Psychol — Japanese Annals of Social Psychology
Japan Chem — Japan Chemical Week
Japan Econ Stud — Japanese Economic Studies
Japanese An Internat Law — Japanese Annual of International Law
Japanese Econ Studies — Japanese Economic Studies
Japanese Fin and Industry — Japanese Finance and Industry
Japanese Jour Geology and Geography — Japanese Journal of Geology and Geography
Japan Inter — Japan Interpreter
Japan J Geol & Geog — Japanese Journal of Geology and Geography
Japan J Math — Japanese Journal of Mathematics
Japan J Math NS — Japanese Journal of Mathematics. New Series
Japan J Med Sc Pt IV Pharmacol — Japanese Journal of Medical Sciences. Part IV. Pharmacology
Japan J Nurs Art — Japanese Journal of Nursing Art
Japan Lbr Bul — Japan Labor Bulletin
Japan Med Gaz — Japan Medical Gazette
Japan Med World — Japan Medical World
Jap Ann of Law & Pol — Japan Annual of Law and Politics
Japan Pestic Inf — Japan Pesticide Information
Japan Q — Japan Quarterly
Japan Quart — Japan Quarterly
Japan Soc B — Japan Society Bulletin
Japan Stud — Japanese Studies
Japan Stud Hist Sci — Japanese Studies in the History of Science
Jap Assoc Mineral Petrol Econ Geol J — Japanese Association of Mineralogists, Petrologists, and Economic Geologists. Journal
Jap Assoc Pet Technol J — Japanese Association of Petroleum Technologists. Journal
Jap Bee J — Japanese Bee Journal
J Ap Behav Sci — Journal of Applied Behavioral Science
JAPCA — Journal of Abnormal Psychology
JAPCA — Journal. Air Pollution Control Association
JAPCAC — Journal of Abnormal Psychology
Jap Chem Week — Japan Chemical Week
Jap Chr Q — Japan Christian Quarterly
Jap Circ J — Japanese Circulation Journal
JAPE — Journal of Australian Political Economy
JAPEAI — Journal of Applied Ecology
J Ap Ecol — Journal of Applied Ecology
Jap Econ St — Japanese Economic Studies
Jap Geol Surv Bull — Japan Geological Survey. Bulletin
Jap Geol Surv Rep — Japan Geological Survey. Report
Jap Geotherm Energy Assoc J — Japan Geothermal Energy Association. Journal
Jap Heart J — Japanese Heart Journal
J Apic Res — Journal of Apicultural Research
Jap Inst Nav J — Japan. Institute of Navigation. Journal
Jap Inter — Japan Interpreter
Jap J A Phy — Japanese Journal of Applied Physics
Jap J Appl Entomol Zool — Japanese Journal of Applied Entomology and Zoology

Jap J Appl Ent Zool — Japanese Journal of Applied Entomology and Zoology
Jap J Appl Phys — Japanese Journal of Applied Physics
Jap J Appl Phys Suppl — Japanese Journal of Applied Physics. Supplement
Jap J Bot — Japanese Journal of Botany
Jap J Botan — Japanese Journal of Botany
Jap J Breed — Japanese Journal of Breeding
Jap J Child — Japanese Journal of Child Psychiatry
Jap J Ecol — Japanese Journal of Ecology
Jap J Edu P — Japanese Journal of Educational Psychology
Jap J Exp M — Japanese Journal of Experimental Medicine
Jap J Exp Med — Japanese Journal of Experimental Medicine
Jap J Genet — Japanese Journal of Genetics
Jap J Geol Geogr — Japanese Journal of Geology and Geography
Jap J Hum G — Japanese Journal of Human Genetics
Jap J Limnol — Japanese Journal of Limnology
Jap J Med — Japanese Journal of Medicine
Jap J Med Electron & Biol Eng — Japanese Journal of Medical Electronics and Biological Engineering
Jap J Med S — Japanese Journal of Medical Science and Biology
Jap J Med Sci Biol — Japanese Journal of Medical Science and Biology
Jap J Micro — Japanese Journal of Microbiology
Jap J Midwife — Japanese Journal for the Midwife
Jap J Nurs — Japanese Journal of Nursing
Jap J Nurses Educ — Japan Journal of Nurses' Education
Jap J Nurs Res — Japanese Journal of Nursing Research
Jap J Nutr — Japanese Journal of Nutrition
Jap J Palynol — Japanese Journal of Palynology
Jap J Pharm — Japanese Journal of Pharmacology
Jap J Pharmac — Japanese Journal of Pharmacology
Jap J Pharmacogn — Japanese Journal of Pharmacognosy
Jap J Physi — Japanese Journal of Physiology
Jap J Physiol — Japanese Journal of Physiology
Jap J Psych — Japanese Journal of Psychology
Jap J Sanit Zool — Japanese Journal of Sanitary Zoology
Jap J Trop Agr — Japanese Journal of Tropical Agriculture
Jap J Vet R — Japanese Journal of Veterinary Research
Jap J Vet Res — Japanese Journal of Veterinary Research
Jap J Vet S — Japanese Journal of Veterinary Science
Jap J Vet Sci — Japanese Journal of Veterinary Science
Jap J Vet Sci Nigon Juigaku Zasshi — Japanese Journal of Veterinary Science/ Nigon Juigaku Zasshi
Jap J Zool — Japanese Journal of Zoology
Jap J Zootech Sci — Japanese Journal of Zootechnical Science
JAPLA — Journal. Atlantic Provinces Linguistic Association/Revue. Association de Linguistique des Provinces Atlantiques
JAPLD — Japanese Journal of Applied Physics. Part 2. Letters
JAPMA8 — Journal. American Pharmaceutical Association. Scientific Edition
Jap Meteorol Agency Volcanol Bull — Japan Meteorological Agency. Volcanological Bulletin
J Ap Meterol — Journal of Applied Meteorology
Jap Nat Ry Ry Tech Res — Japanese National Railways. Railway Technical Research
JAPND — Japanese Journal of Applied Physics. Part 1. Regular Papers and Short Notes
JAPNEF — Journal of Animal Physiology and Animal Nutrition
J Ap Nutrition — Journal of Applied Nutrition
JAPOA — Journal. American Psychoanalytic Association
JAPOAE — Journal. American Psychoanalytic Association
J App Bact — Journal of Applied Bacteriology
J App Bacteriol — Journal of Applied Bacteriology
J App Behav Anal — Journal of Applied Behavior Analysis
J App Behavioral Sci — Journal of Applied Behavioral Science
J App Behavior Anal — Journal of Applied Behavior Analysis
J App Behav Sci — Journal of Applied Behavioral Science
J App Ecol — Journal of Applied Ecology
Jap Per Ind — Japanese Periodicals Index
Jap Pestic Inf — Japan Pesticide Information
Jap Plast Age — Japan Plastics Age
J Appl Bact — Journal of Applied Bacteriology
J Appl Bacteriol — Journal of Applied Bacteriology
J Appl Be A — Journal of Applied Behavior Analysis
J Appl Beh — Journal of Applied Behavioral Science
J Appl Behav Anal — Journal of Applied Behavior Analysis
J Appl Behav Sci — Journal of Applied Behavioral Science
J Appl Biochem — Journal of Applied Biochemistry
J Appl Biol — Journal of Applied Biology
J Appl Ch B — Journal of Applied Chemistry and Biotechnology
J Appl Chem — Journal of Applied Chemistry
J Appl Chem — Journal of Applied Chemistry of the USSR
J Appl Chem Abstr — Journal of Applied Chemistry. Abstracts
J Appl Chem and Biotechnol — Journal of Applied Chemistry and Biotechnology
J Appl Chem Biotechnol — Journal of Applied Chemistry and Biotechnology
J Appl Chem Biotechnol Abstr — Journal of Applied Chemistry and Biotechnology. Abstracts
J Appl Chem (London) — Journal of Applied Chemistry (London)

J Appl Chem USSR — Journal of Applied Chemistry of the USSR
J Appl Cosmetol — Journal of Applied Cosmetology
J Appl Crys — Journal of Applied Crystallography
J Appl Crystallogr — Journal of Applied Crystallography
J Appl Ecol — Journal of Applied Ecology
J Appl Elec — Journal of Applied Electrochemistry
J Appl Electrochem — Journal of Applied Electrochemistry
J Appl Entomol — Journal of Applied Entomology
J Applied Ecology — Journal of Applied Ecology
J Applied Ednl Studies — Journal of Applied Educational Studies
J Applied Micr (Rochester NY) — Journal of Applied Microscopy (Rochester, New York)
J Applied Physics — Journal of Applied Physics
J Appl Manage — Journal of Applied Management
J Appl Math Mech — Journal of Applied Mathematics and Mechanics
J Appl Mech — Journal of Applied Mechanics. Transactions. ASME [*American Society of Mechanical Engineers*]
J Appl Mech and Tech Phys — Journal of Applied Mechanics and Technical Physics
J Appl Mech Tech Phys — Journal of Applied Mechanics and Technical Physics
J Appl Mech Trans ASME — Journal of Applied Mechanics. Transactions. ASME [*American Society of Mechanical Engineers*]
J Appl Med — Journal of Applied Medicine
J Appl Met — Journal of Applied Meteorology
J Appl Metalwork — Journal of Applied Metalworking
J Appl Meteorol — Journal of Applied Meteorology
J Appl Nutr — Journal of Applied Nutrition
J Appl Photogr Eng — Journal of Applied Photographic Engineering
J Appl Phys — Journal of Applied Physics
J Appl Physiol — Journal of Applied Physiology [*Later, Journal of Applied Physiology: Respiratory, Environmental, and Exercise Physiology*]
J Appl Physiol Respir Environ Exercise Physiol — Journal of Applied Physiology: Respiratory, Environmental, and Exercise Physiology
J Appl Physiol Respir Environ Exerc Physiol — Journal of Applied Physiology: Respiratory, Environmental, and Exercise Physiology
J Appl Pneum — Journal of Applied Pneumatics
J Appl Poly — Journal of Applied Polymer Science
J Appl Polym Sci — Journal of Applied Polymer Science
J Appl Polym Sci Appl Polym Symp — Journal of Applied Polymer Science. Applied Polymer Symposium
J Appl Probab — Journal of Applied Probability
J Appl Probability — Journal of Applied Probability
J Appl Psyc — Journal of Applied Psychology
J Appl Psychol — Journal of Applied Psychology
J Appl Sci — Journal of Applied Sciences
J Appl Sci Eng A — Journal of Applied Science and Engineering. Section A. Electrical Power and Information Systems
J Appl So P — Journal of Applied Social Psychology
J Appl Spectrosc — Journal of Applied Spectroscopy
J Appl Spectrosc (USSR) — Journal of Applied Spectroscopy (USSR)
J Appl Syst Anal — Journal of Applied Systems Analysis
J Appl Systems Analysis — Journal of Applied Systems Analysis
J App Mech — Journal of Applied Mechanics
J App Meteor — Journal of Applied Meteorology
J App Nutr — Journal of Applied Nutrition
Jap Poultry Sci — Japanese Poultry Science
Jap Poult Sci — Japanese Poultry Science
J App Physiol — Journal of Applied Physiology [*Later, Journal of Applied Physiology: Respiratory, Environmental, and Exercise Physiology*]
J App Prob — Journal of Applied Probability
J App Psy — Journal of Applied Psychology
J App Psychol — Journal of Applied Psychology
Jap Prog Climatol — Japanese Progress in Climatology
J Approximation Theory — Journal of Approximation Theory
J Approx Th — Journal of Approximation Theory
J Approx Theory — Journal of Approximation Theory
J App Soc Psychol — Journal of Applied Social Psychology
J Ap Psychol — Journal of Applied Psychology
Jap Psy Res — Japanese Psychological Research
Jap Public Works Res Inst Rep (Minist Constr) — Japan Public Works Research Institute. Report. Ministry of Construction
Jap Pulp Pap — Japan Pulp and Paper
Jap Q — Japan Quarterly
Jap Quart — Japan Quarterly
Jap R — Japanese Religions
JAPRCP — Journal of Anthropological Research
JAPRDQ — Journal of Animal Production Research
JAPS — Journal. American Portuguese Society
JAPs — Journal of Applied Psychology
JAPSA — Journal of Applied Psychology
Jap Shipbldg Mar Eng — Japan Shipbuilding and Marine Engineering
Jap Shipbuild & Mar Engng — Japan Shipbuilding and Marine Engineering
J Ap Sociol — Journal of Applied Sociology

Jap Soc Promot Sci Sub-Comm Phys Chem Steelmaking Spec Rep — Japan Society for the Promotion of Science. Sub-Committee for Physical Chemistry of Steelmaking. Special Report
JAPT — Journal of Approximation Theory
JAPTB — Journal. American Physical Therapy Association
JAPTB — Physical Therapy
Jap Telecom — Japan Telecommunications Review
Jap Weld Soc Trans — Japan Welding Society. Transactions
JAPYA — Journal of Applied Physiology [*Later, Journal of Applied Physiology: Respiratory, Environmental, and Exercise Physiology*]
Ja Q — Japan Quarterly
JAQ — Journal of Buyouts and Acquisitions
JA Quart J Automat Control — Journal. A Quarterly Journal of Automatic Control
J Aquatic Pl Management — Journal of Aquatic Plant Management
J Aquat Plant Manage — Journal of Aquatic Plant Management
JAR — Journal of Accounting Research
JAR — Journal of Anthropological Research
JAR — Juedischer Altestenrat
J Arab Affairs — Journal of Arab Affairs
JArabL — Journal of Arabic Literature
J Arab Lit — Journal of Arabic Literature
J Arab Vet Med Assoc — Journal. Arab Veterinary Medical Association
J Arachnol — Journal of Arachnology
J Arboric — Journal of Arboriculture
JARCA — Journal of Aesthetics and Art Criticism
JARCE — Journal. American Research Center in Egypt
J Archaeol Chem — Journal of Archaeological Chemistry
J Archaeol Sci — Journal of Archaeological Science
J Arch Sci — Journal of Archaeological Science
JAREB — Japanese Railway Engineering
JARED — JASCO [*Japan Spectroscopic Co.*] Report
Ja Rel — Japanese Religions
JARE Sci Rep Ser E Biol — JARE [*Japanese Antarctic Research Expedition*] Scientific Reports. Series E. Biology
JARF — Journal. Addiction Research Foundation
JARGV — Jahrbuch. Arbeitsgemeinschaft der Rheinischen Geschichtsvereine
JARI — Journal of Agricultural Research in Iceland [*Islenzkar Landbunadar Rannsoknir*]
J Arid Environ — Journal of Arid Environments
J Ariz Acad Sci — Journal. Arizona Academy of Science
JArizH — Journal of Arizona History
J Ariz Hist — Journal of Arizona History
J Arkansas Med Soc — Journal. Arkansas Medical Society
J Arms Armour Soc — Journal. Arms and Armour Society
Jarmuevek Mezoegazd Gepek — Jarmuevek, Mezoegazdasagi Gepek [*Hungary*]
J Arn Arbor — Journal. Arnold Arboretum
J Arnold Arbor — Journal. Arnold Arboretum. Harvard University
J Arnold Arbor Harv Univ — Journal. Arnold Arboretum. Harvard University
J Arnold Schoenberg Inst — Journal. Arnold Schoenberg Institute
Jaroslav Gos Ped Inst Dokl Naucn Konfer — Jaroslavskii Gosudarstvennyi Pedagogiceskii Institut Doklady na Naucnyh Konferencijah
Jaroslav Gos Ped Inst Ucen Zap — Jaroslavskii Gosudarstvennyi Pedagogiceskii Institut Imeni K. D. Usinskogo Ucenye Zapiski
Jaroslav Tehn Inst Fiz-Mat Nauk Sb Naucn Trudov — Jaroslavskii Tehnologiceskii Institut Fiziko-Matematiceskie Nauki Sbornik Naucnyh Trudov
JARQ Jap Agric Res Q — JARQ. Japan Agricultural Research Quarterly
JARR — Journal of Architectural Research
JARS — Journal. Assam Research Society
J Art Mgmt L — Journal of Arts Management and Law
J Arts Mgt and L — Journal of Arts Management and Law
JAS — Jahrbuch fuer Amerikastudien
JAS — Journal. Acoustical Society of America
JAS — Journal of Aerospace Science
JAS — Journal. American Society for Information Science
JAS — Journal of American Studies
JAS — Journal of Archaeological Science
JAS — Journal of Asian Studies
JAS — Journal. Asiatic Society of Great Britain and Ireland
JAs — Journal Asiatique [*Paris*]
JAS — Journal des Associations Patronales
JAS — Journal of Australian Studies
JAS — Journal of Austronesian Studies
JASA — Journal. Acoustical Society of America
JASA — Journal. American Scientific Affiliation
JASA — Journal. American Statistical Association
J As Aff — Journal of Asian Affairs
J As Afr Stud (T) — Journal of Asian and African Studies (Tokyo)
J Asahikawa Tech Coll — Journal. Asahikawa Technical College
J Asahikawa Tech College — Journal. Asahikawa Technical College
JASAT — Journal. American Studies Association of Texas
JASB — Journal. Asiatic Society of Bengal
JAS B — Journal. Asiatic Society of Bombay
JASBA — Journal. American Society of Sugar Beet Technologists

JASBAO — Journal. American Society of Sugar Beet Technologists
JASC — Journal. Asiatic Society of Calcutta
JAS Calcutta — Journal. Asiatic Society of Calcutta
JASCEV — Journal of Agronomy and Crop Science
J A Schoenb — Journal. Arnold Schoenberg Institute
JASCO Appl Notes — Japan Spectroscopic Company. Application Notes
JASCO Rep — JASCO [*Japan Spectroscopic Co.*] Report
J As Cult — Journal of Asian Culture
JASFE6 — Journal of Agricultural Science in Finland
J As Hist — Journal of Asian History
JASIAB — Journal of Agricultural Science
J Asian Afr — Journal of Asian and African Studies
J Asian & Afric Stud — Journal of Asian and African Studies
J Asian Afr Stud — Journal of Asian and African Studies
J Asian His — Journal of Asian History
J Asian Hist — Journal of Asian History
J Asian St — Journal of Asian Studies
J Asian Stud — Journal of Asian Studies
J Asia Stud — Journal of Asian Studies
J Asiat — Journal Asiatique
J Asiat Soc — Journal. Asiatic Society
J Asiat Soc Bangla — Journal. Asiatic Society of Bangladesh
J Asiat Soc Bengal Lett — Journal. Asiatic Society of Bengal. Letters
J Asiat Soc Bengal Sci — Journal. Asiatic Society of Bengal. Science
J Asiat Soc Bombay — Journal. Asiatic Society of Bombay
J Asiat Soc Sci — Journal. Asiatic Society. Science
J Asiat Stud — Journal of Asiatic Studies
JASIS — Journal. American Society for Information Science
JASL — Journal. Asiatic Society. Letters
JASMA — Journal. Acoustical Society of America
JASMAN — Journal. Acoustical Society of America
Ja Socialist R — Japan Socialist Review
Ja Soc Lond B — Japan Society of London. Bulletin
JASP — Journal of Abnormal and Social Psychology
JASP — Journal of Applied Social Psychology
JASP — Journal. Asiatic Society of Pakistan
J As Pac World — Journal of Asian-Pacific and World Perspectives
JASPAW — Journal of Abnormal and Social Psychology
JASPR — Journal. American Society for Psychical Research
JASRE8 — Journal of Agricultural and Scientific Research
JASSA — JASSA. Journal of the Australian Society of Security Analysts
J Ass Advan Med Instrum — Journal. Association for the Advancement of Medical Instrumentation
J Assam Res Soc — Journal. Assam Research Society
J Assam Sci Soc — Journal. Assam Science Society
J Ass Comput Mach — Journal. Association for Computing Machinery
J Assoc Adv Med Instrum — Journal. Association for the Advancement of Medical Instrumentation
J Assoc Am Med Coll — Journal. Association of American Medical Colleges
J Assoc Can Radiol — Journal. Association Canadienne des Radiologistes
J Assoc Care Child Health — Journal. Association for the Care of Children's Health
J Assoc Care Child Hosp — Journal. Association for the Care of Children in Hospitals
J Assoc Comput Mach — Journal. Association for Computing Machinery
J Assoc Eng Archit Isr — Journal. Association of Engineers and Architects in Israel
J Assoc Eng Archit Palest — Journal. Association of Engineers and Architects in Palestine
J Assoc Eng (Calcutta) — Journal. Association of Engineers (Calcutta)
J Assoc Eng (India) — Journal. Association of Engineers (India)
J Assoc Eng Soc — Journal. Association of Engineering Societies
J Assoc Hosp Med Educ — Journal. Association for Hospital Medical Education
J Assoc Lunar and Planet Obs Strolling Astron — Journal. Association of Lunar and Planetary Observers. Strolling Astronomer
J Assoc Med Can — Journal. Association Medicale Canadienne
J Assoc Off Agric Chem — Journal. Association of Official Agricultural Chemists
J Assoc Off Anal Chem — Journal. Association of Official Analytical Chemists
J Assoc Offic Anal Chem — Journal. Association of Official Analytical Chemists
J Assoc Pediatr Oncol Nurses — Journal. Association of Pediatric Oncology Nurses
J Assoc Pers Comput Chem — Journal. Association of Personal Computers for Chemists
J Assoc Physicians India — Journal. Association of Physicians of India
J Assoc Phys Ment Rehabil — Journal. Association for Physical and Mental Rehabilitation [*United States*]
J Assoc Public Anal — Journal. Association of Public Analysts
J Assoc Sci Ouest Afr — Journal. Association Scientifique de l'Ouest Africain
J Assoc Study Percept — Journal. Association for the Study of Perception
J Ass Off Agric Chem — Journal. Association of Official Agricultural Chemists
J Ass Off Analyt Chem — Journal. Association of Official Analytical Chemists
J Ass Offic Anal Chem — Journal. Association of Official Analytical Chemists
J Asso Teach Ja — Journal. Association of Teachers of Japanese

J Ass Public Analysts — Journal. Association of Public Analysts
J As Stud P — Journal. Association for the Study of Perception
JASt — Journal of Asian Studies
JASTAA — Journal. Agricultural Society of Trinidad and Tobago
J Asthma — Journal of Asthma
J Asthma Res — Journal of Asthma Research [*Later, Journal of Asthma*]
J Astronaut — Journal of the Astronautical Sciences
J Astronaut Sci — Journal of the Astronautical Sciences
J Astronomical Soc VIC — Journal. Astronomical Society of Victoria
J Astron (Peiping) — Journal of Astronomy (Peiping)
J Astrophys Astron — Journal of Astrophysics and Astronomy
J Astrophys and Astron — Journal of Astrophysics and Astronomy
JAStud — Journal of American Studies
Ja Stud Hist Sci — Japanese Studies in the History of Science
JAT — Jaarboekje van J. A. Alberdingk-Thym
JAT — Journal of Applied Toxicology
JATAAQ — Journal. Animal Technicians Association
JATADT — Journal d'Agriculture Traditionnelle et de Botanique Appliquee. Travaux d'Ethnobotanique et d'Ethnozoologie
JATBAT — Journal d'Agriculture Tropicale et de Botanique Appliquee [*Later, Journal d'Agriculture Traditionnelle et de Botanique Appliquee*]
JATC — Journal of Air Traffic Control
J At Energy Comm (Jpn) — Journal. Atomic Energy Commission (Japan)
J At Energy Soc Jap — Journal. Atomic Energy Society of Japan
J At Energy Soc Jpn — Journal. Atomic Energy Society of Japan
J Atheroscler Res — Journal of Atherosclerosis Research
JATI — Journal. Association of Teachers of Italian
JATJ — Journal-Newsletter. Association of Teachers of Japanese
J Atmos Chem — Journal of Atmospheric Chemistry
J Atmospheric Sci — Journal of the Atmospheric Sciences
J Atmos Sci — Journal of the Atmospheric Sciences
J Atmos Terr Phys — Journal of Atmospheric and Terrestrial Physics
J Atmos and Terr Phys — Journal of Atmospheric and Terrestrial Physics
J Atm Ter P — Journal of Atmospheric and Terrestrial Physics
JATOD3 — Journal of Analytical Toxicology
JAUCB — Journal of Autism and Childhood Schizophrenia
J Aud Eng S — Journal. Audio Engineering Society
J Aud Eng Soc — Journal. Audio Engineering Society
J Audio Eng Soc — Journal. Audio Engineering Society
J Audiov Media Med — Journal of Audiovisual Media in Medicine
J Aud Res — Journal of Auditory Research
J Aud Res Suppl — Journal of Auditory Research. Supplement
JAUEA — Journal of Automotive Engineering
JAUK — Jahrbuch. Albertus Universitaet zu Koenigsberg
JAUMA — Journal. Australian Mathematical Society
JAUMLA — Journal. Australasian Universities Modern Language Association
JAUPA — Journal of Agriculture. University of Puerto Rico
JAUPA8 — Journal of Agriculture. University of Puerto Rico
JAURA — Journal of Auditory Research
J Aus I Agr — Journal. Australian Institute of Agricultural Science
J Aus I Met — Journal. Australian Institute of Metals
J Aust Cath Hist Soc — Journal. Australian Catholic Historical Society
J Aust Ceramic Soc — Journal. Australian Ceramic Society
J Aust Ceram Soc — Journal. Australian Ceramic Society
J Aust Coll Speech Ther — Journal. Australian College of Speech Therapists
J Aust Entomol Soc — Australian Entomological Society. Journal
J Aust Entomol Soc — Journal. Australian Entomological Society
J Aust Ent Soc — Australian Entomological Society. Journal
J Aust Ent Soc — Journal. Australian Entomological Society
J Aust Inst Agric Sci — Journal. Australian Institute of Agricultural Science
J Aust Inst Agr Sci — Journal. Australian Institute of Agricultural Science
J Aust Inst Ag Science — Journal. Australian Institute of Agricultural Science
J Aust Inst Hort — Journal. Australian Institute of Horticulture
J Aust Inst Hortic — Journal. Australian Institute of Horticulture
J Aust Inst Met — Journal. Australian Institute of Metals
J Aust Inst Metals — Journal. Australian Institute of Metals
J Aust Inst Surg Dent Tech — Journal. Australian Institute of Surgical and Dental Technicians
J Aust Math Soc — Journal. Australian Mathematical Society
J Aust Planning Inst — Journal. Australian Planning Institute
J Aust Polit Econ — Journal of Australian Political Economy
J Australas Inst Met — Australasian Institute of Metals. Journal
J Australas Inst Met — Journal. Australasian Institute of Metals
J Australas Inst Metals — Australasian Institute of Metals. Journal
J Austral Math Soc Ser A — Journal. Australian Mathematical Society. Series A
J Austral Math Soc Ser B — Journal. Australian Mathematical Society. Series B
J Austronesian Stud — Journal of Austronesian Studies
J Autism Ch — Journal of Autism and Childhood Schizophrenia
J Autism & Child Schizo — Journal of Autism and Childhood Schizophrenia
J Autism Child Schizophrenia — Journal of Autism and Childhood Schizophrenia
J Autism Dev Disord — Journal of Autism and Developmental Disorders
J Autism Dev Disorders — Journal of Autism and Development Disorders
J Autism & Devel Dis — Journal of Autism and Developmental Disorders

J Autom Chem — Journal of Automatic Chemistry [England]
J Automot Eng — Journal of Automotive Engineering
J Auton Nerv Syst — Journal of the Autonomic Nervous System
JAVAD5 — Journal. American Venereal Disease Association
J Aviat Hist Soc Aust — Aviation Historical Society of Australia. Journal
JAVMA — Journal. American Veterinary Medical Association
JAVMA4 — Journal. American Veterinary Medical Association
JAVR — Jewish Audio-Visual Review
JAVRAJ — Journal. American Veterinary Radiology Society
JAVTA — Journal. South African Veterinary Association
JAW — Jahresberichte ueber die Fortschritte der Klassischen Altertumswissenschaft
JAWAA7 — Journal of Agriculture of Western Australia
JAWRES — Journal of Agriculture and Water Resources Research
JAWWA — Journal. American Water Works Association
JAWWA5 — American Water Works Association. Journal
JAY — Journal of Applied Psychology
JAZ — Jahrbuch fuer Sozialwissenschaft. Zeitschrift fuer Wirtschaftswissenschaften
JazA — Jazykovedny Aktuality. Zpravodaj Jazykovedneho Sdruzeni pri Ceskoslovenske Akademii Ved
JAZODX — Journal of Advanced Zoology
JazS — Jazykovedny Studie
JazSb — Jazykovedny Sbornik
JAZU — Jugoslavenske Akademije Znanosti i Umjetnosti
Jazz Ed J — Jazz Educators Journal
Jazzf — Jazzforschung
Jazz Ieri — Jazz di Ieri e di Oggi
Jazz J — Jazz Journal [Later, Jazz Journal International]
Jazz J Int — Jazz Journal International
Jazz Jl — Jazz Journal [Later, Jazz Journal International]
Jazz Mag — Jazz Magazine
Jazz Mag (US) — Jazz Magazine (United States)
Jazz Mo — Jazz Monthly
Jazz R — Jazz Review
Jazz Rept — Jazz Report
Jazz Res — Jazz Research
Jazz Rytm — Jazz Rytm i Piosenka
Jazz T — Jazz Times
JB — Journal of Band Research
JB — Journal of Broadcasting
JB — Journal of Business
JB — Judaica Bohemiae
JB — Junior Bookshelf
JBA — Jewish Book Annual [New York]
JBA — Journal of Banking and Finance [Netherlands]
JBA — Journal. Board of Agriculture
JBA — Journal of Business Administration
JBAA — Journal. British Archaeological Association
Jb Absatz und Verbrauchsforsch — Jahrbuch der Absatz- und Verbrauchsforschung
JbAC — Jahrbuch fuer Antike und Christentum
J BAC — Journal. International Union of Bricklayers and Allied Craftsmen
JbAChr — Jahrbuch fuer Antike und Christentum
J Bact — Journal of Bacteriology
J Bacteriol — Journal of Bacteriology
J BADC — Journal. Bar Association of the District of Columbia
JBA Dist Colum — Journal. Bar Association of the District of Columbia
J BA Kan — Journal. Bar Association of the State of Kansas
J Ballist — Journal of Ballistics
JBalS — Journal of Baltic Studies
J Bal Stud — Journal of Baltic Studies
J Baltic St — Journal of Baltic Studies
J Baltimore Coll Dent Surg — Journal. Baltimore College of Dental Surgery
J Band Res — Journal of Band Research
J Bangladesh Acad Sci — Journal. Bangladesh Academy of Sciences
J Bankers Inst Australas — Bankers' Institute of Australasia. Journal
J Bank Finance — Journal of Banking and Finance
J Banking and Fin — Journal of Banking and Finance
J Bank Res — Journal of Bank Research
Jb AS — Jahrbuch fuer Amerikastudien
JBASB — Journal of Band Research
J Basic Eng — Journal of Basic Engineering
J Basic Eng Trans ASME — Journal of Basic Engineering. Transactions. ASME [American Society of Mechanical Engineers]
J Basic Eng Trans ASME Ser D — Journal of Basic Engineering. Transactions. ASME [American Society of Mechanical Engineers] Series D
JB Assn St Kan — Journal. Bar Association of the State of Kansas
JBAW — Jahrbuch. Bayerische Akademie der Wissenschaften
JbAWG — Jahrbuch. Akademie der Wissenschaften in Goettingen
JbAWL — Jahrbuch. Akademie der Wissenschaften und der Literatur [Mainz]
JbBAW — Jahrbuch. Bayerische Akademie der Wissenschaften
JB Bern Hist Mus — Jahrbuch. Bernisches Historische Museum
Jb Bischof Gymnas Kolleg Petrinum — Jahresbericht. Bischoefliches Gymnasium und Dioezesanseminar. Kollegium Petrinum in Urfar

JBBMD — Journal of Biochemical and Biophysical Methods
JBC — Journal of Business Communication
J of Bcasting — Journal of Broadcasting
Jb Coburg Landesst — Jahrbuch. Coburger Landesstiftung
JBCSA — Journal. British Ceramic Society
J Bd Ag — Journal. Board of Agriculture [Great Britain]
J Bd Agric (London) — Journal. Board of Agriculture (London)
JbDAI — Jahrbuch. Deutsches Archaeologische Institut [Berlin]
JbDAI ArAnz — Jahrbuch. Deutsches Archaeologische Institut. Archaeologischer Anzeiger [Berlin]
JbDAW — Jahrbuch. Deutsche Akademie der Wissenschaften zu Berlin
JbDG — Jahrbuch. Dante Gesellschaft
Jb Diplom Akad (Wien) — Jahrbuch. Diplomatische Akademie (Wien)
JBE — Journal of Business Education
J Beckett S — Journal of Beckett Studies
J Behav Exp — Journal of Behavior Therapy and Experimental Psychiatry
J Behav Med — Journal of Behavioral Medicine
J Behav Sci — Journal of Behavioural Science
J Behav Ther Exp Psychiatry — Journal of Behavior Therapy and Experimental Psychiatry
J Belge Med Phys Rehabil — Journal Belge de Medecine Physique et de Rehabilitation
J Belge Radiol — Journal Belge de Radiologie
J Belge Radiol Monogr — Journal Belge de Radiologie. Monographie [Belgium]
J Belge Rhumatol Med Phys — Journal Belge de Rhumatologie et de Medecine Physique
J Belg Rad — Journal Belge de Radiologie
JbEOL — Jaarbericht. Vooraziatische-Egyptisch Genootschap "Ex Oriente Lux"
Jber Deutsch Math-Verein — Jahresbericht. Deutsche Mathematiker-Vereinigung
J Bergen Cty Dent Soc — Journal. Bergen County Dental Society
J Berl M — Jahrbuch. Berliner Museen
Jber Naturf Ges Fraubuendens — Jahresbericht. Naturforschende Gesellschaft Fraubuendens
Jber Naturw Ver Wuppertal — Jahresbericht. Naturwissenschaftlicher Verein zu Wuppertal
Jb u Ersch Ger Lit — Jahresberichte ueber die Erscheinungem auf dem Gebiete der Germanischen Literaturgeschichte
J Beverly Hills Ba — Journal. Beverly Hills Bar Association
J Bev Hills BA — Journal. Beverly Hills Bar Association
JBF — Journal of Business Finance and Accounting
JbFL — Jahrbuch fuer Fraenkische Landesforschung
Jb Friedens- u Konfliktforsch — Jahrbuch fuer Friedens- und Konfliktforschung
JBG — Brazil Journal
JBG — Jahrbuch. Barlach-Gesellschaft
JBG — Jinbungaku [Studies in Humanities]
JBG — Journal of Business Logistics
Jb Ges Wiener Theater F — Jahrbuch. Gesellschaft fuer Wiener Theater-Forschung
JBGH — Jinbun Gakuho [Journal of Social Science and Humanities]
JBHVMF — Jahresbericht. Historischer Verein fuer Mittelfranken
J Bib Lit — Journal of Biblical Literature
J Bibl Lit — Journal of Biblical Literature
JBIC — Journal of Biocommunication
J Bihar Agric Coll — Journal. Bihar Agricultural College
Jb Imkers — Jahrbuch der Imkers
Jb Int Recht — Jahrbuch fuer Internationales Recht
J Biochem — Journal of Biochemistry
J Biochem Microbiol Tech Eng — Journal of Biochemical and Microbiological Technology and Engineering
J Biochem (Tokyo) — Journal of Biochemistry (Tokyo)
J Biocommun — Journal of Biocommunication
J Bioelectr — Journal of Bioelectricity
J Bioenerg — Journal of Bioenergetics [Later, Journal of Bioenergetics and Biomembranes]
J Bioenerg Biomembr — Journal of Bioenergetics and Biomembranes
J Bioeng — Journal of Bioengineering
J Biogeogr — Journal of Biogeography
J Biol Board Can — Journal. Biological Board of Canada
J Biol (Bronx NY) — Journal of Biology (Bronx, NY)
J Biol Bucc — Journal de Biologie Buccale
J Biol Buccale — Journal de Biologie Buccale
J Biol Chem — Journal of Biological Chemistry
J Biol Educ — Journal of Biological Education
J Biological Ed — Journal of Biological Education
J Biol Osaka City Univ — Journal of Biology. Osaka City University
J Biol Phot — Journal. Biological Photographic Association
J Biol Photogr Ass — Journal. Biological Photographic Association
J Biol Photogr Assoc — Journal. Biological Photographic Association
J Biol Phys — Journal of Biological Physics
J Biol Psychol — Journal of Biological Psychology
J Biol Sci — Journal of Biological Sciences
J Biol Stan — Journal of Biological Standardization

J Biol Stand — Journal of Biological Standardization
J Biomech — Journal of Biomechanics
J Biomechan — Journal of Biomechanics
J Biomed Eng — Journal of Biomedical Engineering
J Biomed Mater Res — Journal of Biomedical Materials Research
J Biomed Mater Res Biomed Mater Symp — Journal of Biomedical Materials Research. Biomedical Materials Symposium
J Biomed Mat Res — Journal of Biomedical Materials Research
J Biomed MR — Journal of Biomedical Materials Research
J Biomed Syst — Journal of Biomedical Systems
J Biomol Struct Dyn — Journal of Biomolecular Structure and Dynamics
J Biophys Biochem Cytol — Journal of Biophysical and Biochemical Cytology
J Biophys Med Nucl — Journal de Biophysique et Medecine Nucleaire
J Biophys Soc Jpn — Journal. Biophysical Society of Japan
J Biophys (Tokyo) — Journal of Biophysics (Tokyo)
J Biosoc — Journal of Biosocial Science
J Biosoc Sc — Journal of Biosocial Science
J Biosoc Sci — Journal of Biosocial Science
J Biotechnol — Journal of Biotechnology
J Birla Inst Technol and Sci — Journal. Birla Institute of Technology and Science
J Birla Inst Technol Sci — Journal. Birla Institute of Technology and Science
JBIRS — Journal. Bihar Research Society
JBIS — Journal. British Interplanetary Society
JbJTS — Jahresberichte. Juedisch-Theologisches Seminar "Frankelsche Stiftung"
JBK — Journal. Bar Association of the State of Kansas
JbKAF — Jahrbuch fuer Kleinasiatische Forschung
JBKG — Jahrbuch fuer Brandenburgische Kirchengeschichte
JBKK — Jinbun Kenkyu [*Studies in Humanities*]
Jb K Mus Schon Kunst Antwerp — Jaarboek. Koninklijke Museum voor Schone Kunsten Antwerpen
JbKNA — Jaarboek. Koninklijke Nederlandsche Academie van Wetenschappen
Jb Kunsthist Samml (Wien) — Jahrbuch. Kunsthistorische Sammlungen (Wien)
JbKVA — Jaarboek. Koninklijke Vlaamse Academie voor Taal-en Letterkunde
JbKVAW — Jaarboek. Koninklijke Vlaamse Academie voor Wetenschappen
JBL — Journal of Biblical Literature
JBL — Journal of Business Law [*British*]
JBl — Juristische Blaetter
J Black Poetry — Journal of Black Poetry
J Black St — Journal of Black Studies
J Black Stud — Journal of Black Studies
J of Black Stud — Journal of Black Studies
J Black Studies — Journal of Black Studies
Jb Leipzig Bienenztg — Jahrbuch. Leipziger Bienenzeitung
JBLG — Jahresberichte. Berliner Literatur Gesellschaft
JbLitHymn — Jahrbuch fuer Liturgik und Hymnologie [*Kassel*]
Jb Liturgik Hymnologie — Jahrbuch fuer Liturgik und Hymnologie
JBLMS — Journal of Biblical Literature. Monograph Series
JBM — Jahrbuch. Berliner Museen
JBM — Jahrbuch. Bernisches Historische Museum
JBM — Jahrbuch fuer das Bistum (Mainz)
JBM — Journal of Organizational Behavior Management
Jb Max Planck Ges Foerd Wiss — Jahrbuch. Max-Planck-Gesellschaft zur Foerderung der Wissenschaften
JBM J Bras Med — JBM. Jornal Brasileiro de Medicina
JBMNA — Journal de Biologie et de Medecine Nucleaires
JbMNL — Jaarboek. Maatschappij der Nederlandsche Letterkunde te Leiden
JbMu — Jahrbuch. Marburger Universitaetsbund
Jb Musik Volks-u Voelkerk — Jahrbuch fuer Musikalische Volks- und Voelkerkunde
Jb M Volks Volkerkunde — Jahrbuch fuer Musikalische Volks- und Voelkerkunde
JBN — Judaica Book News
Jb Nationaloekon und Statis — Jahrbuecher fuer Nationaloekonomie und Statistik
Jb f Niederdeut Spr — Jahrbuch fuer Niederdeutsche Sprachforschung
Jb f Niederdt Spr — Jahrbuch fuer Niederdeutsche Sprachforschung
JbNo — Jahrbuch fuer Landeskunde von Niederoesterreich
JBNSA — Journal. British Nuclear Energy Society
JBO — Journal of Economic Behavior and Organization
J Board Agric (GB) — Journal. Board of Agriculture (Great Britain)
J Board Dir Am Soc Civ Eng — Journal. Board of Direction. American Society of Civil Engineers
J Board Greenkeeping Res — Journal. Board of Greenkeeping Research
Jb Oeff Rechts — Jahrbuch des Oeffentlichen Rechts der Gegenwart
Jb Oldenburger Muensterland — Jahrbuch fuer das Oldenburger Muensterland
J Bombay Nat Hist Soc — Journal. Bombay Natural History Society
J Bone-Am V — Journal of Bone and Joint Surgery (American Volume)
J Bone-Br V — Journal of Bone and Joint Surgery (British Volume)
J Bone Joint Surg — Journal of Bone and Joint Surgery
J Bone Joint Surg (Am) — Journal of Bone and Joint Surgery (American Volume)
J Bone Joint Surg (Br) — Journal of Bone and Joint Surgery (British Volume)

J Bone Jt Surg (Am Vol) — Journal of Bone and Joint Surgery (American Volume)
J Bone Jt Surg (Br Vol) — Journal of Bone and Joint Surgery (British Volume)
JBORS — Journal. Bihar and Orissa Research Society [*Later, Journal. Bihar Research Society*]
Jb Osterreich Kultur Gesch — Jahrbuch fuer Oesterreichische Kulturgeschichte
J Boston Soc Civ Eng — Journal. Boston Society of Civil Engineers
Jb Ostrecht — Jahrbuch fuer Ostrecht
J Bot Br Foreign — Journal of Botany. British and Foreign
J Bot Soc S Afr — Journal. Botanical Society of South Africa
J Bot UAR — Journal of Botany. United Arab Republic
J Bowman Gray Sch Med Wake For Coll — Journal. Bowman Gray School of Medicine. Wake Forest College
JBPAA — Journal. Biological Photographic Association
Jb Peters — Jahrbuch Peters
JBPHB — Journal of Biological Physics
JBPSA — Jornal Brasileiro de Psiquiatria
JBR — Journal of Bank Research
JBR — Journal of Bible and Religion
JBRAS — Journal. Bombay Branch. Royal Asiatic Society
J Bras Ginecol — Jornal Brasileiro de Ginecologia
J Bras Med — Jornal Brasileiro de Medicina
J Bras Neurol — Jornal Brasileiro de Neurologia
J Bras Psiquiatr — Jornal Brasileiro de Psiquiatria
J Br Astron Assoc — Journal. British Astronomical Association
J Bras Urol — Jornal Brasileiro de Urologia
J Br Boot Shoe Instn — Journal. British Boot and Shoe Institution
J Br Dent Assoc — Journal. British Dental Association
Jb Rechnung Hist Mus (Basel) — Jahresberichte und Rechnungen. Historisches Museum (Basel) [*Switzerland*]
J Br Endod Soc — Journal. British Endodontic Society
J Br Grassl — Journal. British Grassland Society
J Br Grassld Soc — Journal. British Grassland Society
J Br Grassl Soc — Journal. British Grassland Society
J Br Inst Radio Eng — Journal. British Institution of Radio Engineers
J Brit Archaeol Ass 3 Ser — Journal. British Archaeological Association. Series 3
J Brit Ceram Soc — Journal. British Ceramic Society
J Brit Interplanet Soc — Journal. British Interplanetary Society
J Brit Nucl Energy Soc — Journal. British Nuclear Energy Society
J Brit Ship Res Ass — Journal. British Ship Research Association
J Brit Soc Master Glass Paint — Journal. British Society of Master Glass Painters
J Brit Soc Phenomenol — Journal. British Society for Phenomenology
J Brit Stud — Journal of British Studies
JBRM — Journal of Biological Response Modifiers
JBRMA — Jornal Brasileiro de Medicina
JBRNA — Jornal Brasileiro de Neurologia
Jb-r Nat-Oekon Statist — Jahrbuecher fuer National-Oekonomie und Statistik
J Br Nucl E — Journal. British Nuclear Energy Society
J Br Nucl Energy Soc — Journal. British Nuclear Energy Society
J Broadcast — Journal of Broadcasting
J Broadcasting — Journal of Broadcasting
J Bromeliad Soc — Journal. Bromeliad Society
JBRS — Journal. Bihar Research Society
JBRS — Journal. Burma Research Society
J Br Soc Ph — Journal. British Society for Phenomenology
J Br Stud — Journal of British Studies
J Br Waterworks Assoc — Journal. British Waterworks Association
J Br Wood Preserv Assoc — Journal. British Wood Preserving Association
J Bryol — Journal of Bryology
JBS — Journal of Applied Behavioral Science
JBS — Journal of British Studies
JBS — Journal of Business Research
JBS — Journal of Byelorussian Studies
JbSAW — Jahrbuch. Saechsische Akademie der Wissenschaften zu Leipzig
Jb Schweiz Ges Ur Fruehgesch — Jahrbuch. Schweizerische Gesellschaft fuer Ur- und Fruehgeschichte
JbShG — Jahrbuch. Shakespeare Gesellschaft
J Bsns — Journal of Business
J Bsns Ed — Journal of Business Education
J Bsns Educ — Journal of Business Education
Jb Sozialwiss — Jahrbuch fuer Sozialwissenschaft
Jb Soz -Wiss — Jahrbuch fuer Sozialwissenschaft
JBSTB — Journal of Biological Standardization
Jb St Kunstsamml Dresden — Jahrbuch. Staatliche Kunstsammlungen Dresden
JBT — Journal of Business Ethics
JBU — Journal of Business
JBU — Journal of Business Research
JBUA — Journal. Bombay University. Arts
Jbuch — Jahrbuch ueber die Fortschritte der Mathematik
Jbuch Heidelberger Akad Wiss — Jahrbuch. Heidelberger Akademie der Wissenschaften
J Burn Care Rehabil — Journal of Burn Care and Rehabilitation
J Bus — Journal of Business
J Busan Med Coll — Journal. Busan Medical College

J Bus Commun — Journal of Business Communication
J Bus Communic — Journal of Business Communication
J Bus Ed — Journal of Business Education
J Bus Ethics — Journal of Business Ethics
J Busin — Journal of Business
J Bus L — Journal of Business Law [*British*]
J Bus Res — Journal of Business Research
J Bus Research — Journal of Business Research
J Bus Strategy — Journal of Business Strategy
JBV — Juedische Buch Vereinigung [*Berlin*]
JbVH — Jahrbuch fuer Volkskunde der Heimatvertriebenen
Jb Volksk Kulturgesch — Jahrbuch fuer Volkskunde und Kulturgeschichte
Jb Volksliedf — Jahrbuch fuer Volksliedforschung
JbWerkKaTNed — Jaarboek. Werkgenootschap van Katholieke Theologen in Nederland [*Hilversum*]
Jb Wirtschaftsgesch — Jahrbuch fuer Wirtschaftsgeschichte
Jb Wirtsch -Gesch — Jahrbuch fuer Wirtschaftsgeschichte
Jb Wirtsch Osteuropas — Jahrbuch der Wirtschaft Osteuropas
Jb Wiss Prakt Tierzucht — Jahrbuch fuer Wissenschaftliche und Praktische Tierzucht
JByelS — Journal of Byelorussian Studies
JC — Jazykovedny Casopis
JC — Jewish Chronicle [*London*]
JC — Journal of Church Music
JC — Journal of Communication
JCA — Journal of Color and Appearance
JCA — Journal of Consumer Affairs
J Caisses Epargne — Journal des Caisses d'Epargne
J Calif Dent Assoc — Journal. California Dental Association
J Calif Hortic Soc — Journal. California Horticultural Society
J Calif State Dent Assoc — Journal. California State Dental Association
J Camera Club (London) — Journal. Camera Club (London)
J Can Art Hist — Journal of Canadian Art History
J Can Assoc Radiol — Journal. Canadian Association of Radiologists
J Can Ath Ther Assoc — Journal. Canadian Athletic Therapists Association
J Can Ba — Journal. Canadian Bar Association
J Can B Ass'n — Journal. Canadian Bar Association
J Can Biochim — Journal Canadien de Biochimie
J Can Bot — Journal Canadien de Botanique
J Can Ceram Soc — Journal. Canadian Ceramic Society
J Cancer Cent Niigata Hosp — Journal. Cancer Center. Niigata Hospital [*Japan*]
J Cancer Res Clin Oncol — Journal of Cancer Research and Clinical Oncology
J Can Chir — Journal Canadien de Chirurgie
J Can Dent Assoc — Journal. Canadian Dental Association
J Can Diet Ass — Journal. Canadian Dietetic Association
J Can Diet Assoc — Journal. Canadian Dietetic Association
J Can Fic — Journal of Canadian Fiction
J Can Genet Cytol — Journal Canadien de Genetique et de Cytologie
J Can Microbiol — Journal Canadien de Microbiologie
J Can Ophtalmol — Journal Canadien d'Ophtalmologie
J Can Otolaryngol — Journal Canadien d'Otolaryngologie
J Can Petrol Technol — Journal of Canadian Petroleum Technology
J Can Pet T — Journal of Canadian Petroleum Technology
J Can Pet Technol — Journal of Canadian Petroleum Technology
J Can Physiol Pharmacol — Journal Canadien de Physiologie et Pharmacologie
J Can Rech For — Journal Canadien de la Recherche Forestiere
J Can Sci Appl Sport — Journal Canadien des Sciences Appliquees au Sport
J Can Sci Neurol — Journal Canadien des Sciences Neurologiques
J Can Sci Terre — Journal Canadien des Sciences de la Terre
J Can Soc Forensic Sci — Journal. Canadian Society of Forensic Science
J Can Stud — Journal of Canadian Studies
J Can Zool — Journal Canadien de Zoologie
JCARA — Journal. Canadian Association of Radiologists
J Carb-Nucl — Journal of Carbohydrates-Nucleosides-Nucleotides
J Carbohyd-Nucl-Nucl — Journal of Carbohydrates-Nucleosides-Nucleotides
J Carbohydr-Nucleosides-Nucleotides — Journal of Carbohydrates-Nucleosides-Nucleotides
J Cardiogr — Journal of Cardiography
J Cardiovasc Pharmacol — Journal of Cardiovascular Pharmacology
J Cardiovasc Surg — Journal of Cardiovascular Surgery
J Cardiovasc Surg (Torino) — Journal of Cardiovascular Surgery (Torino)
J Card Surg — Journal of Cardiovascular Surgery
J Car Ed — Journal of Career Education
J Catal — Journal of Catalysis
J Catalysis — Journal of Catalysis
J Cat & Class — Journal of Cataloging and Classification
JCATD — Journal of Computer Assisted Tomography
J Cathol Med Coll — Journal. Catholic Medical College
JCB — Journal of Creative Behavior
JCB — Kansas Judicial Council. Bulletin
JCBF — Journal of Cerebral Blood Flow and Metabolism
JCC — Journal of Carbohydrate Chemistry
JCC — Journal of Computational Chemistry
JCCBD — Journal of Clinical Chemistry and Clinical Biochemistry
JCCMB — Journal of Coordination Chemistry

JCCS — Journal. Canadian Ceramic Society
JCCSA — Journal. Canadian Ceramic Society
JCDAA — Journal. Canadian Dental Association
JCDEA — Journal. California State Dental Association
JCDIA — Journal of Communication Disorders
JCDVA — Journal of Child Development
JCE — Journal of Christian Education
JCEA — Journal of Central European Affairs
JCEBD — Journal of Cellular Biochemistry
JC & ED — Journal of Chemical and Engineering Data
J Cell Biochem — Journal of Cellular Biochemistry
J Cell Biol — Journal of Cell Biology
J Cell Comp Physiol — Journal of Cellular and Comparative Physiology [*Later, Journal of Cellular Physiology*]
J Cell Phys — Journal of Cellular Physiology
J Cell Physiol — Journal of Cellular Physiology
J Cell Physiol Suppl — Journal of Cellular Physiology. Supplement
J Cell Plast — Journal of Cellular Plastics
J Cell Sci — Journal of Cell Science
J Cellular Plastics — Journal of Cellular Plastics
JCeltS — Journal of Celtic Studies
JCEM — Journal of Clinical Endocrinology and Metabolism
JCEN — Journal of Continuing Education in Nursing
JCEND — Journal of Clinical Engineering
J Cent Agr Exp Sta — Journal. Central Agricultural Experiment Station
J Cent Agric Exp Stn — Journal. Central Agricultural Experiment Station
J Cent Bur Anim Husb Dairy India — Journal. Central Bureau for Animal Husbandry and Dairying in India
J Cent Eur Aff — Journal of Central European Affairs
J Cent Eur Affairs — Journal of Central European Affairs
J Ceram Soc Jpn — Journal. Ceramic Society of Japan
J Cereb Blood Flow Metab — Journal of Cerebral Blood Flow and Metabolism
J Cer Soc Jap — Journal. Ceramic Society of Japan
J Ceylon Br Brit Med Ass — Journal. Ceylon Branch. British Medical Association
JCF — Journal of Canadian Fiction
JCFRB — Journal of Coffee Research
JCFS — Journal of Comparative Family Studies
JCG — Journal of Commerce. European Edition
J Changchun Geol Inst — Journal. Changchun Geological Institute [*People's Republic of China*]
J Chart Inst Bld Serv — Journal. Chartered Institution of Building Services
J Chart Inst Build Serv — Journal. Chartered Institution of Building Services [*England*]
J Chart Inst Transp — Journal. Chartered Institute of Transport
JCHAS — Journal. Cork Historical and Archaeological Society
J Chem Doc — Journal of Chemical Documentation
J Chem Docum — Journal of Chemical Documentation
J Chem Ecol — Journal of Chemical Ecology
J Chem Ed — Journal of Chemical Education
J Chem Educ — Journal of Chemical Education
J Chem En D — Journal of Chemical and Engineering Data
J Chem Eng Data — Journal of Chemical and Engineering Data
J Chem Eng Educ — Journal of Chemical Engineering Education
J Chem Eng Jap — Journal of Chemical Engineering of Japan
J Chem Eng Jpn — Journal of Chemical Engineering of Japan
J Chem Engng Data — Journal of Chemical Engineering Data
J Chem Engng Japan — Journal of Chemical Engineering of Japan
J Chem Ind Eng — Journal of Chemical Industry and Engineering
J Chem Inf — Journal of Chemical Information and Computer Sciences
J Chem Inf Comp Sci — Journal of Chemical Information and Computer Sciences
J Chem Inf Comput Sci — Journal of Chemical Information and Computer Sciences
J Chem Inf and Comput Sci — Journal of Chemical Information and Computer Sciences
J Chem Metall Min Soc S Afr — Journal. Chemical, Metallurgical, and Mining Society of South Africa
J Chem Metall Soc S Afr — Journal. Chemical and Metallurgical Society of South Africa
J Chemother Adv Ther — Journal of Chemotherapy and Advanced Therapeutics
J Chem Phys — Journal of Chemical Physics
J Chem Phys — Journal fuer Chemie und Physik
J Chem Res M — Journal of Chemical Research. Part M
J Chem Res Part S — Journal of Chemical Research. Part S (Synopses)
J Chem Res S — Journal of Chemical Research. Part S
J Chem Res Synop — Journal of Chemical Research. Synopses [*England*]
J Chem S Ch — Journal. Chemical Society. Chemical Communications
J Chem S Da — Journal. Chemical Society. Dalton Transactions
J Chem S F1 — Journal. Chemical Society. Faraday Transactions 1
J Chem S F2 — Journal. Chemical Society. Faraday Transactions 2
J Chem Soc — Journal. Chemical Society
J Chem Soc Abstr — Journal. Chemical Society. Abstracts
J Chem Soc Chem Commun — Journal. Chemical Society. Chemical Communications

J Chem Soc D Chem Commun — Journal. Chemical Society. D. Chemical Communications
J Chem Soc Faraday Trans I — Journal. Chemical Society. Faraday Transactions. I
J Chem Soc Faraday Trans II — Journal. Chemical Society. Faraday Transactions. II
J Chem Soc Jap Ind Chem Sect — Journal. Chemical Society of Japan. Industrial Chemistry Section
J Chem Soc Jpn Chem Ind Chem — Journal. Chemical Society of Japan. Chemistry and Industrial Chemistry
J Chem Soc Jpn Pure Chem Sect — Journal. Chemical Society of Japan. Pure Chemistry Section
J Chem Soc (London) — Journal. Chemical Society (London)
J Chem Soc (London) A Inorg Phys Theor — Journal. Chemical Society (London). A. Inorganic, Physical, Theoretical
J Chem Soc (London) B Phys Org — Journal. Chemical Society (London). B. Physical, Organic
J Chem Soc (London) Chem Commun — Journal. Chemical Society (London). Chemical Communications
J Chem Soc (London) C Org — Journal. Chemical Society (London). C. Organic
J Chem Soc (London) Dalton Trans — Journal. Chemical Society (London). Dalton Transactions
J Chem Soc (London) D Chem Commun — Journal. Chemical Society (London). D. Chemical Communications
J Chem Soc (London) Faraday Trans I — Journal. Chemical Society (London). Faraday Transactions. I
J Chem Soc (London) Faraday Trans II — Journal. Chemical Society (London). Faraday Transactions. II
J Chem Soc (London) Perkin Trans I — Journal. Chemical Society (London). Perkin Transactions. I
J Chem Soc (London) Perkin Trans II — Journal. Chemical Society (London). Perkin Transactions. II
J Chem Soc Perkin Trans — Journal. Chemical Society. Perkin Transactions. 1
J Chem Soc Perkin Trans I — Journal. Chemical Society. Perkin Transactions. I
J Chem Soc Perkin Trans II — Journal. Chemical Society. Perkin Transactions. II
J Chem S P1 — Journal. Chemical Society. Perkin Transactions. 1
J Chem S P2 — Journal. Chemical Society. Perkin Transactions. 2
J Chem Tech Biotech — Journal of Chemical Technology and Biotechnology
J Chem Technol and Biotechnol — Journal of Chemical Technology and Biotechnology
J Chem Technol Biotechnol — Journal of Chemical Technology and Biotechnology
J Chem Ther — Journal of Chemical Thermodynamics
J Chem Thermodyn — Journal of Chemical Thermodynamics
J Chem UAR — Journal of Chemistry. United Arab Republic
J Che Soc Sect C Org Chem — Journal. Chemical Society. Section C. Organic Chemistry
J Chester Archaeol Soc — Journal. Chester Archaeological Society
J Chester Arch Soc — Journal. Chester Archaeological Society
J Chiba Med Soc — Journal. Chiba Medical Society
J Child Contemp Soc — Journal of Children in Contemporary Society
J Child Lang — Journal of Child Language
J Child Language — Journal of Child Language
J Child Psy — Journal of Child Psychology and Psychiatry
J Child Psychol — Journal of Child Psychology and Psychiatry
J Child Psychol & Psych — Journal of Child Psychology and Psychiatry and Allied Disciplines [*Later, Journal of Child Psychology and Psychiatry*]
J Child Psychol Psychiat — Journal of Child Psychology and Psychiatry
J Child Psychol Psychiatry — Journal of Child Psychology and Psychiatry and Allied Disciplines [*Later, Journal of Child Psychology and Psychiatry*]
J Child Psychol Psychiatry Allied Discipl — Journal of Child Psychology and Psychiatry and Allied Disciplines [*Later, Journal of Child Psychology and Psychiatry*]
J Child Psychol Psychiatry Book Suppl — Journal of Child Psychology and Psychiatry. Book Supplement
J Child Psychotherapy — Journal of Child Psychotherapy
J Child Psych & Psychiatry — Journal of Child Psychology and Psychiatry
J Chim Med Pharm Toxicol — Journal de Chimie Medicale, de Pharmacie, et de Toxicologie
J Chim Phys — Journal de Chimie Physique [*France*]
J Chim Phys — Journal de Chimie Physique et de Physico-Chimie Biologique
J Chim Phys Phys-Chim Biol — Journal de Chimie Physique et de Physico-Chimie Biologique
J Chim Phys et Phys-Chim Biol — Journal de Chimie Physique et de Physico-Chimie Biologique
J Chim Phys Rev Gen Colloides — Journal de Chimie Physique et Revue Generale des Colloides [*France*]
J China Coal Soc — Journal. China Coal Society [*People's Republic of China*]
J Chin Biochem Soc — Journal. Chinese Biochemical Society
J Chin Chem — Journal. Chinese Chemical Society
J Chin Chem Soc — Journal. Chinese Chemical Society
J Chinese Inst Engrs — Journal. Chinese Institute of Engineers [*Taipei*]
J Chinese Ling — Journal of Chinese Linguistics

J Ching Hua Univ — Journal. Ching Hua University [*People's Republic of China*]
J Chin Inst Eng — Journal. Chinese Institute of Engineers
JChinL — Journal of Chinese Linguistics
J Chin Lang Teach Asso — Journal. Chinese Language Teachers Association
J Chin Ling — Journal of Chinese Linguistics
JChinP — Journal of Chinese Philosophy
J Chin Phil — Journal of Chinese Philosophy
J Chin Philo — Journal of Chinese Philosophy
J Chin Rare Earth Soc — Journal. Chinese Rare Earth Society
J Chin Silicates Soc — Journal. Chinese Silicates Society
J Chin U HK — Journal. Chinese University of Hong Kong
J Chin Univ Hong Kong — Journal. Chinese University of Hong Kong
J Chir — Journal de Chirurgie
J Chiro — Journal of Chiropractic
J Ch L — Journal of Child Language
JCHOD — Journal of Clinical Hematology and Oncology
JCHQA — Japan Chemical Quarterly
JChr — Jewish Chronicle [*London*]
J Christ Educ — Journal of Christian Education
J Christian Ed — Journal of Christian Education
J Christian Educ — Journal of Christian Education
J Christian Juris — Journal of Christian Jurisprudence
J Christ Juris — Journal of Christian Jurisprudence
J Christ Med Assoc India — Journal. Christian Medical Association of India
J Christ Nurse — Journal of Christian Nursing
J Chromat — Journal of Chromatography
J Chromat Biomed Appl — Journal of Chromatography. Biomedical Applications
J Chromat Chromat Rev — Journal of Chromatography. Chromatographic Reviews
J Chromatogr — Journal of Chromatography
J Chromatogr Biomed Appl — Journal of Chromatography. Biomedical Applications
J Chromatogr Sci — Journal of Chromatographic Science
J Chromatogr Suppl Vol — Journal of Chromatography. Supplementary Volume
J Chromat Sci — Journal of Chromatographic Science
J Chrom Sci — Journal of Chromatographic Science
J Chron Dis — Journal of Chronic Diseases
J Chronic Dis — Journal of Chronic Diseases
J Chr Philos — Journal of Christian Philosophy
J Ch St — Journal of Church and State
J Church M — Journal of Church Music
J Church Mus — Journal of Church Music
J Church St — Journal of Church and State
J Church & State — Journal of Church and State
J Church State — Journal of Church and State
JCICS — Journal of Chemical Information and Computer Sciences
JCIMD — Journal of Clinical Immunology
JCIRA — Japanese Circulation Journal [*English edition*]
JCISD — Journal of Chemical Information and Computer Sciences
J City Plann Div Am Soc Civ Eng — Journal. City Planning Division. American Society of Civil Engineers
J Civ Eng Des — Journal of Civil Engineering Design [*United States*]
J Civ Eng (Taipei) — Journal of Civil Engineering (Taipei)
JCL — Journal of Chromatography Library [*Elsevier Book Series*]
JCL — Journal of Commonwealth Literature
JCL — Journal of Corporation Law
JCL — Journal of Criminal Law
JCLA — Journal. Canadian Linguistic Association [*Edmonton*]
JCLa — Journal of Child Language
JCLA — Journal of Comparative Literature and Aesthetics
J Clay Sci Soc Jpn — Journal. Clay Science Society of Japan
JCLCPS — Journal of Criminal Law, Criminology, and Police Science [*Later, Journal of Criminal Law and Criminology*]
JCLIA — Jornal dos Clinicos
JCL & IL — Journal of Comparative Legislation and International Law
JCLIL — Journal of Comparative Legislation and International Law
J Clim and Appl Meteorol — Journal of Climate and Applied Meteorology
J Climatol — Journal of Climatology
J Clin Chem Clin Biochem — Journal of Clinical Chemistry and Clinical Biochemistry
J Clin Chil — Journal of Clinical Child Psychology
J Clin Comput — Journal of Clinical Computing
J Clin Dermatol — Journal of Clinical Dermatology [*Japan*]
J Clin Electron Microsc — Journal of Clinical Electron Microscopy
J Clin Electron Microsc Soc Jpn — Journal. Clinical Electron Microscopy Society of Japan
J Clin Endocr — Journal of Clinical Endocrinology
J Clin Endocrinol Metab — Journal of Clinical Endocrinology and Metabolism
J Clin Eng — Journal of Clinical Engineering
J Clin Exp Hypn — Journal of Clinical and Experimental Hypnosis
J Clin Exp Psychopathol Q Rev Psychiatry Neurol — Journal of Clinical and Experimental Psychopathology and Quarterly Review of Psychiatry and Neurology

J Clin Gastroenterol — Journal of Clinical Gastroenterology

J Clin Hematol Oncol — Journal of Clinical Hematology and Oncology

J Clin Hosp Pharm — Journal of Clinical and Hospital Pharmacy

J Clin Immunol — Journal of Clinical Immunology

J Clin Inv — Journal of Clinical Investigation

J Clin Invest — Journal of Clinical Investigation

J Clin Lab Autom — Journal of Clinical Laboratory Automation

J Clin Lab Immunol — Journal of Clinical and Laboratory Immunology

J Clin Med — Journal of Clinical Medicine

J Clin Micr — Journal of Clinical Microbiology

J Clin Microbiol — Journal of Clinical Microbiology

J Clin Neuro-Ophthalmol — Journal of Clinical Neuro-Ophthalmology

J Clin Neuropsychol — Journal of Clinical Neuropsychology

J Clin Nutr — Journal of Clinical Nutrition

J Clin Orthod — Journal of Clinical Orthodontics

J Clin Path — Journal of Clinical Pathology [*London*]

J Clin Pathol (Lond) — Journal of Clinical Pathology (London)

J Clin Pathol (Suppl) — Journal of Clinical Pathology (Supplement)

J Clin Periodontol — Journal of Clinical Periodontology

J Clin Phar — Journal of Clinical Pharmacology

J Clin Pharmacol — Journal of Clinical Pharmacology

J Clin Pharmacol J New Drugs — Journal of Clinical Pharmacology and the
    Journal of New Drugs [*United States*]

J Clin Pharmacol New Drugs — Journal of Clinical Pharmacology and New
    Drugs [*Later, Journal of Clinical Pharmacology*]

J Clin Psyc — Journal of Clinical Psychology

J Clin Psychiatry — Journal of Clinical Psychiatry

J Clin Psychol — Journal of Clinical Psychology

J Clin Psychopharmacol — Journal of Clinical Psychopharmacology

J Clin Surg — Journal of Clinical Surgery

J Clin Ultrasound — Journal of Clinical Ultrasound [*United States*]

JCLPB — Journal of Consulting and Clinical Psychology

JCLTA — Journal. Chinese Language Teachers Association

JCLTB — Journal of Clinical Ultrasound

J Clube Mineral — Jornal. Clube de Mineralogia

JCM — Journal of Country Music

JCMID — Journal of Clinical Microbiology

JCMNA — Journal of Communication

JCMS — Journal of Crystal and Molecular Structure

JCMVASA — Journal. Central Mississippi Valley American Studies
    Association

JCN — Journal of Collective Negotiations in the Public Sector

JCNEA — Journal of Comparative Neurology

JCNOD — Journal of Clinical Neuro-Ophthalmology

JCNPS — Journal of Collective Negotiations in the Public Sector

JCNRD — Journal of Cyclic Nucleotide Research

J Coated Fabr — Journal of Coated Fabrics

J Coated Fabrics — Journal of Coated Fabrics

J Coated Fibrous Mater — Journal of Coated Fibrous Materials

J Coatings Technol — Journal of Coatings Technology

J Coat Technol — Journal of Coatings Technology

J Coconut Ind — Journal of Coconut Industries

J Coffee Res — Journal of Coffee Research

JCOI — Journal. Cama Oriental Institute

J Co Kildare Archaeol Soc — Journal. County Kildare Archaeological Society

J Coll Ag Tokyo — Journal. College of Agriculture. Tokyo Imperial University

J Coll Arts Sci Chiba Univ — Journal. College of Arts and Sciences. Chiba
    University

J Coll Arts Sci Chiba Univ Nat Sci — Journal. College of Arts and Sciences.
    Chiba University. Natural Science [*Japan*]

J Coll Dairy Agr — Journal. College of Dairy Agriculture

J Coll Dairy Agric — Journal. College of Dairy Agriculture

J Coll Dairy Agric (Nopporo) — Journal. College of Dairy Agriculture
    (Nopporo)

J Coll Dairy Agri (Ebetsu Japan) — Journal. College of Dairy Agriculture
    (Ebetsu, Japan)

J Coll Dairy (Ebetsu Japan) — Journal. College of Dairying (Ebetsu, Japan)

J Coll Dairy (Nopporo) — Journal. College of Dairying (Nopporo)

J Collect Negotiations Public Sect — Journal of Collective Negotiations in the
    Public Sector

J Coll Educ Seoul Natl Univ — Journal. College of Education. Seoul National
    University

J College Place — Journal of College Placement

J College Sci Univ Riyadh — Journal. College of Science. University of Riyadh

J Coll Eng Technol Jadavpur Univ — Journal. College of Engineering and
    Technology. Jadavpur University

J Coll Ind Technol Nihon Univ — Journal. College of Industrial Technology.
    Nihon University [*Japan*]

J Coll Ind Technol Nihon Univ A — Journal. College of Industrial Technology.
    Nihon University. Series A

J Coll Ind Technol Nihon Univ B — Journal. College of Industrial Technology.
    Nihon University. Series B

J Coll I Sc — Journal of Colloid and Interface Science

J Coll Mar Sci Technol Tokai Univ — Journal. College of Marine Science and
    Technology. Tokai University

J Colloid and Interface Sci — Journal of Colloid and Interface Science

J Colloid Interface Sci — Journal of Colloid and Interface Science

J Colloid Sci — Journal of Colloid Science [*Later, Journal of Colloid and
    Interface Science*]

J Coll Placement — Journal of College Placement

J Coll Radiol Australas — Journal. College of Radiologists of Australasia

J Coll Radiol Australasia — Journal. College of Radiologists of Australasia

J Coll Sci Teach — Journal of College Science Teaching

J Coll Stud — Journal of College Student Personnel

J Coll Student Personnel — Journal of College Student Personnel

J Coll Stud Personnel — Journal of College Student Personnel

J Coll Surgeons Australasia — Journal. College of Surgeons of Australasia

J Coll and U L — Journal of College and University Law

J Coll Univ — Journal. College and University Personnel Association

J Coll & Univ L — Journal of College and University Law

J Coll & Univ Personnel Assn — Journal. College and University Personnel
    Association

J Col Negot — Journal of Collective Negotiations in the Public Sector

J Colo Dent Assoc — Journal. Colorado Dental Association

J Color — Journal of Color and Appearance

J Color Appearance — Journal of Color and Appearance

J Colo-Wyo Acad Sci — Journal. Colorado-Wyoming Academy of Science

J Col Placement — Journal of College Placement

J Col Stud Personnel — Journal of College Student Personnel

J Combinatorial Theory Ser A — Journal of Combinatorial Theory. Series A

J Combinatorial Theory Ser B — Journal of Combinatorial Theory. Series B

J Combinatorics Information Syst Sci — Journal of Combinatorics,
    Information, and System Sciences

J Combin Inform System Sci — Journal of Combinatorics, Information, and
    System Sciences [*Delhi*]

J Combin Theory Ser A — Journal of Combinatorial Theory. Series A

J Combin Theory Ser B — Journal of Combinatorial Theory. Series B

J Comb Th A — Journal of Combinatorial Theory. Series A

J Comb Th B — Journal of Combinatorial Theory. Series B

J Comb Theory — Journal of Combinatorial Theory

J Comb Theory Ser A — Journal of Combinatorial Theory. Series A

J Comb Theory Ser B — Journal of Combinatorial Theory. Series B

J Combustion Toxicol — Journal of Combustion Toxicology

J Combust Toxic — Journal of Combustion Toxicology

J Combust Toxicol — Journal of Combustion Toxicology

JComLit — Journal of Commonwealth Literature

J Comm — Journal of Communication

J Comm Bank Lending — Journal of Commercial Bank Lending

J Comm Dis — Journal of Communication Disorders

J Commer Bank Lending — Journal of Commercial Bank Lending

J Commercio — Jornal do Commercio

J Com Mkt S — Journal of Common Market Studies

J Comm Mkt Stud — Journal of Common Market Studies

J Common Market Stud — Journal of Common Market Studies

J Common Market Studies — Journal of Common Market Studies

J Common Mark Stud — Journal of Common Market Studies

J Commonw Mkt Stud — Journal of Common Market Studies

J Commonw Comp Pol — Journal of Commonwealth and Comparative Politics

J Commonwealth Comp Polit — Journal of Commonwealth and Comparative
    Politics

J Commonwealth Lit — Journal of Commonwealth Literature

J Comm Rural Reconstr China (US Repub China) Plant Ind Ser — Joint
    Commission on Rural Reconstruction in China (United States and
    Republic of China). Plant Industry Series

J Commun Dis — Journal of Communicable Diseases

J Commun Disord — Journal of Communication Disorders

J Commun Health — Journal of Community Health

J Communication — Journal of Communication

J Community Action — Journal of Community Action

J Community Health — Journal of Community Health

J Community Health Nurs — Journal of Community Health Nursing

J Community Psychol — Journal of Community Psychology

J Comp Adm — Journal of Comparative Administration

J Company Master Mar Aust — Company of Master Mariners of Australia.
    Journal

J Comparative Econ — Journal of Comparative Economics

J Comp Corp L and Sec — Journal of Comparative Corporate Law and
    Securities Regulation

J Comp Corp L and Sec Reg — Journal of Comparative Corporate Law and
    Securities Regulation

J Comp Econ — Journal of Comparative Economics

J Comp Ethol — Journal of Comparative Ethology

J Comp Family Stud — Journal of Comparative Family Studies

J Comp Fam Stud — Journal of Comparative Family Studies

J Com Physl — Journal of Comparative and Physiological Psychology [*1947-
    1982*]

J Comp Leg & Int Law — Journal of Comparative Legislation and
    International Law

J Comp Legis — Journal of Comparative Legislation and International Law

J Comp Med and Vet Arch — Journal of Comparative Medicine and Veterinary
    Archives

J Comp Neur — Journal of Comparative Neurology

J Comp Neurol — Journal of Comparative Neurology
J Composite Mat — Journal of Composite Materials
J Compos Ma — Journal of Composite Materials
J Compos Mater — Journal of Composite Materials
J Comp Path — Journal of Comparative Pathology
J Comp Pathol — Journal of Comparative Pathology
J Comp Pathol Ther — Journal of Comparative Pathology and Therapeutics
J Comp Path and Therap — Journal of Comparative Pathology and Therapeutics
J Comp Phys — Journal of Comparative Physiology
J Comp Physiol — Journal of Comparative Physiology
J Comp Physiol A — Journal of Comparative Physiology. A. Sensory, Neural, and Behavioral Physiology
J Comp Physiol A Sens Neural Behav Physiol — Journal of Comparative Physiology. A. Sensory, Neural, and Behavioral Physiology
J Comp Physiol B — Journal of Comparative Physiology. B. Biochemical, Systemic, and Environmental Physiology
J Comp Physiol B Metab Transp Funct — Journal of Comparative Physiology. B. Metabolic and Transport Functions
J Comp & Physiol Psychol — Journal of Comparative and Physiological Psychology [*1947-1982*]
J Comp Physiol Psychol — Journal of Comparative and Physiological Psychology [*1947-1982*]
J Comp Psychol — Journal of Comparative Psychology
J Comput Appl Math — Journal of Computational and Applied Mathematics
J Comput Assisted Tomogr — Journal of Computer Assisted Tomography
J Comput Assist Tomogr — Journal of Computer Assisted Tomography
J Computational Phys — Journal of Computational Physics
J Comput Based Instr — Journal of Computer-Based Instruction
J Comput Chem — Journal of Computational Chemistry
J Comput Math and Sci Teach — Journal of Computers in Mathematics and Science Teaching
J Comput Ph — Journal of Computational Physics
J Comput Phys — Journal of Computational Physics
J Comput Soc India — Journal. Computer Society of India
J Comput Sy — Journal of Computer and System Sciences
J Comput System Sci — Journal of Computer and System Sciences
J Comput and Syst Sci — Journal of Computer and System Sciences
J Comput Syst Sci — Journal of Computer and System Sciences
J Con A — Journal of Consumer Affairs
J Conchol — Journal of Conchology
J Conchyl — Journal de Conchyliologie
J Conf Chem Inst Can Am Chem Soc Abstr Pap — Joint Conference. Chemical Institute of Canada/American Chemical Society. Abstracts of Papers
J Conf CIC/ACS Abstr Pap — Joint Conference. Chemical Institute of Canada/American Chemical Society. Abstracts of Papers
J Conflict Resol — Journal of Conflict Resolution
J Conflict Resolu — Journal of Conflict Resolution
J Conflict Resolution — Journal of Conflict Resolution
J Confl Res — Journal of Conflict Resolution
J Conn Med Chir — Journal des Connaissances Medico-Chirurgicales
J Conn State Dent Assoc — Journal. Connecticut State Dental Association
J Cons Affairs — Journal of Consumer Affairs
J Cons ASCE — Journal. Construction Division. American Society of Civil Engineers
J Cons Clin — Journal of Consulting and Clinical Psychology
J Cons Cons Int Explor Mer — Journal du Conseil. Conseil International pour l'Exploration de la Mer
J Conseil — Journal du Conseil
J Cons Int Explor Mer — Journal du Conseil. Conseil International pour l'Exploration de la Mer
J Const Div Proc ASCE — Journal. Construction Division. Proceedings. American Society of Civil Engineers
J Const Parl Stud — Journal of Constitutional and Parliamentary Studies
J Constr Div Amer Soc Civil Eng Proc — Journal. Construction Division. Proceedings. American Society of Civil Engineers.
J Constr Div Am Soc Civ Eng — Journal. Construction Division. Proceedings. American Society of Civil Engineers
J Constr Steel Res — Journal of Constructional Steel Research
J Consult Clin Psychol — Journal of Consulting and Clinical Psychology
J Consult & Clin Psychol — Journal of Consulting and Clinical Psychology
J Consult Psychol — Journal of Consulting Psychology
J Consum Af — Journal of Consumer Affairs
J Consum Aff — Journal of Consumer Affairs
J Consumer Aff — Journal of Consumer Affairs
J Consumer Affairs — Journal of Consumer Affairs
J Consumer Policy — Journal of Consumer Policy
J Consumer Prod Flamm — Journal of Consumer Product Flammability
J Consumer Prod Flammability — Journal of Consumer Product Flammability
J Consumer Res — Journal of Consumer Research
J Consumer Studies and Home Econ — Journal of Consumer Studies and Home Economics
J Consum Prod Flamm — Journal of Consumer Product Flammability
J Consum Prod Flammability — Journal of Consumer Product Flammability
J Consum Res — Journal of Consumer Research
J Cont Bus — Journal of Contemporary Business

J Cont Ed Nurs — Journal of Continuing Education in Nursing
J Contemp — Journal of Contemporary Asia
J Contemp Afr Stud — Journal of Contemporary African Studies
J Contemp Asia — Journal of Contemporary Asia
J Contemp Bus — Journal of Contemporary Business
J Contemp Busin — Journal of Contemporary Business
J Contemp Hist — Journal of Contemporary History
J Contemp L — Journal of Contemporary Law
J Contemporary Bus — Journal of Contemporary Business
J Contemporary Studies — Journal of Contemporary Studies
J Contemp Stud — Journal of Contemporary Studies
J Cont Hist — Journal of Contemporary History
J Contin Educ Nurs — Journal of Continuing Education in Nursing
J Cont L — Journal of Contemporary Law
J Cont Psyt — Journal of Contemporary Psychotherapy
J Controlled Release — Journal of Controlled Release
J Cooling Tower Inst — Journal. Cooling Tower Institute
J Coop Educ — Journal of Cooperative Education
J Coord Ch — Journal of Coordination Chemistry
J Coord Chem — Journal of Coordination Chemistry
J Copyright Socy USA — Journal. Copyright Society of the USA
J Cork Hist Archaeol Soc — Journal. Cork Historical and Archaeological Society
J Corp L — Journal of Corporation Law
J Corp Law — Journal of Corporation Law
J Corpn L — Journal of Corporation Law
J Corporate Taxation — Journal of Corporate Taxation
J Corp Tax — Journal of Corporate Taxation
J Corros Sci Soc Korea — Journal. Corrosion Science Society of Korea
J Counc Sci Ind Res (Australia) — Journal. Council for Scientific and Industrial Research (Australia)
J Coun Psyc — Journal of Counseling Psychology
J Coun Scient Ind Res (Aust) — Journal. Council for Scientific and Industrial Research (Australia)
J Counsel Ply — Journal of Counseling Psychology
J Counsel Psychol — Journal of Counseling Psychology
J Country M — Journal of Country Music
JCP — Journal of Clinical Psychology
JCP — Journal of Comparative Psychology
JCP — Journal of Counseling Psychology
JCPFD — Journal of Consumer Product Flammability
JCPGB — Journal of Cross-Cultural Psychology
JCPHA — Journal of Consulting Psychology
JCPP — Journal of Comparative and Physiological Psychology [*1947-1982*]
JCPPA — Journal of Comparative and Physiological Psychology [*1947-1982*]
JCPQA — Journal de Chimie Physique
JCPs — Journal of Clinical Psychology
JCPS — Journal of Constitutional and Parliamentary Studies [*India*]
JCPSA — Journal of Chemical Physics
JCPSB — Journal of Cellular Physiology. Supplement
JCPSD — Journal of Community Psychology
JCPT — Journal of Canadian Petroleum Technology
JCPYA — Journal of Clinical Psychology
JCQ — Japan Christian Quarterly
JCR — Journal of Christian Reconstruction
JCR — Journal Citation Reports
JCR — Journal of Conflict Resolution
JCR — Journal of Consumer Research
J Craniofacial Genet Dev Biol — Journal of Craniofacial Genetics and Developmental Biology
JCRAS — Journal. Ceylon Branch. Royal Asiatic Society
JCRDA — Proceedings. Japan Conference on Radioisotopes
J Creat Beh — Journal of Creative Behavior
J Creative Behavior — Journal of Creative Behavior
J Criminal Justice — Journal of Criminal Justice
J Criminal Law and Criminology — Journal of Criminal Law and Criminology
J Crim Jus — Journal of Criminal Justice
J Crim Just — Journal of Criminal Justice
J Crim L — Journal of Criminal Law
J Crim L — Journal of Criminal Law and Criminology
J Crim Law — Journal of Criminal Law and Criminology
J Crim Law & Criminol — Journal of Criminal Law and Criminology
J Crim Law Criminol Police Sci — Journal of Criminal Law, Criminology, and Police Science [*Later, Journal of Criminal Law and Criminology*]
J Crim LC & PS — Journal of Criminal Law, Criminology, and Police Science [*Later, Journal of Criminal Law and Criminology*]
J Crim L and Criminology — Journal of Criminal Law and Criminology
J Crim L (Eng) — Journal of Criminal Law (English)
J Crit Anal — Journal of Critical Analysis
J Croatian Studies — Journal of Croatian Studies
J Cross-Cul — Journal of Cross-Cultural Psychology
J Cross-Cult Psych — Journal of Cross-Cultural Psychology
J Cross-Cult Psychol — Journal of Cross-Cultural Psychology
J Crystallogr Soc Jap — Journal. Crystallographic Society of Japan
J Crystallogr and Spectrosc Res — Journal of Crystallographic and Spectroscopal Research

J Cryst Gr — Journal of Crystal Growth
J Cryst Growth — Journal of Crystal Growth
J Cryst Mol — Journal of Crystal and Molecular Structure
J Cryst and Mol Struct — Journal of Crystal and Molecular Structure
J Cryst Mol Struct — Journal of Crystal and Molecular Structure
JCS — Journal of Celtic Studies
JCS — Journal of Cereal Science
JCS — Journal. Chemical Society
JCS — Journal of Church and State
JCS — Journal of Classical Studies [*Kyoto University*]
JCS — Journal of Common Market Studies
JCS — Journal of Croatian Studies
JCS — Journal of Cuneiform Studies
JCS — Journal of Curriculum Studies
JCSA — Journal. Catch Society of America
JCSA — Journal. Chemical Society. Abstracts
JCSCA — Journal of Colloid Science [*Later, Journal of Colloid and Interface Science*]
JCS Chem Comm — Journal. Chemical Society. Chemical Communications
JCS Dalton — Journal. Chemical Society. Dalton Transactions. Inorganic Chemistry
JCS Faraday I — Journal. Chemical Society. Faraday Transactions. I. Physical Chemistry
JCS Faraday II — Journal. Chemical Society. Faraday Transactions. II. Chemical Physics
JcSH — Jihocesky Sbornik Historicky
JCS Perkin I — Journal. Chemical Society. Perkin Transactions. I. Organic and Bioorganic Chemistry
JCS Perkin II — Journal. Chemical Society. Perkin Transactions. II. Physical Organic Chemistry
JCSS — Journal of Computer and System Sciences
JC St — Journal of Caribbean Studies
JCST — Journal of Chemical Society Transactions
J C St — Journal of Church and State
JCSTD — Journal of Contemporary Studies
JCT — Journal of Common Market Studies
JCT — Journal of Corporate Taxation
JCTED — Journal of Coatings Technology
JCTOD — Journal of Combustion Toxicology
J Ctry Mus — Journal of Country Music
JCU — Journal of Clinical Ultrasound
JCU J Clin Ultrasound — JCU. Journal of Clinical Ultrasound
JC and UL — Journal of College and University Law
J Cuneiform Stud — Journal of Cuneiform Studies
J Cun S — Journal of Cuneiform Studies
J Current Social Issues — Journal of Current Social Issues
J Curric St — Journal of Curriculum Studies
J Curr Laser Abstr — Journal of Current Laser Abstracts
J Curr Soc Issues — Journal of Current Social Issues [*United States*]
J Cur Soc Issues — Journal of Current Social Issues
J Cutaneous Pathol — Journal of Cutaneous Pathology
J Cutan Pathol — Journal of Cutaneous Pathology
J Cut Path — Journal of Cutaneous Pathology
JCW — Japan Chemical Week
JCW — Journal of Comparative Business and Capital Market Law
JCWTS — Journal. Civil War Token Society
J Cybern — Journal of Cybernetics
J Cybernet — Journal of Cybernetics
J Cybern Inf Sci — Journal of Cybernetics and Information Science
J Cybern and Inf Sci — Journal of Cybernetics and Information Science
J Cycle Res — Journal of Cycle Research
J Cyclic Nucleotide Res — Journal of Cyclic Nucleotide Research
J Cycl Nucl — Journal of Cyclic Nucleotide Research
JD — Journal of Documentation
JD — Juris Doctor
JDA — Journal of Developing Areas
JDAI — Jahrbuch. Deutsches Archaeologische Institut
J Dairy Res — Journal of Dairy Research
J Dairy Sci — Journal of Dairy Science
J Dalian Eng Inst — Journal. Dalian Engineering Institute
J Dalian Inst Technol — Journal. Dalian Institute of Technology
JdAM — Journal d'Analyse Mathematique [*Jerusalem*]
JDASD — Jahrbuch. Deutsche Akademie fuer Sprache und Dichtung in Darmstadt
J Data Ed — Journal of Data Education
J Data Manage — Journal of Data Management
J Data Mgt — Journal of Data Management
JDB — Jewish Daily Bulletin
JDBP — Journal of Developmental and Behavioral Pediatrics
J DC Dent Soc — Journal. District of Columbia Dental Society
JDCHA — Journal of Dentistry for Children
Jd Co — Journal des Communautes
JDD — Journal of Developing Areas
JDE — Journal of Development Economics
J Debats — Journal des Debats
JDECU — Journal Department of English. Calcutta University

J Dendrol — Journal of Dendrology
J Dent — Journal of Dentistry
J Dent Assoc S Afr — Journal. Dental Association of South Africa
J Dent Assoc Thai — Journal. Dental Association of Thailand
J Dent Chil — Journal of Dentistry for Children
J Dent Child — Journal of Dentistry for Children
J Dent Educ — Journal of Dental Education
J Dent Eng — Journal of Dental Engineering
J Dent Guid Counc Handicap — Journal. Dental Guidance Council on the Handicapped
J Dent Handicap — Journal of Dentistry for the Handicapped
J Dent Health (Tokyo) — Journal of Dental Health (Tokyo)
J Dent Med — Journal of Dental Medicine
J Dent Que — Journal Dentaire du Quebec
J Dent Res — Journal of Dental Research
J Dent Tech — Journal of Dental Technics
J Dep Agric Fish Irel — Journal. Department of Agriculture and Fisheries. Republic of Ireland
J Dep Agric Repub Irel — Journal. Department of Agriculture. Republic of Ireland
J Dep Agric S Aust — Journal. Department of Agriculture. South Australia
J Dep Agric Un S Afr — Journal. Department of Agriculture. Union of South Africa
J Dep Agric Vict — Journal. Department of Agriculture. Victoria [*Australia*]
J Dep Agric W Aust — Journal. Department of Agriculture. Western Australia
J Dep Agric West Aust — Journal. Department of Agriculture. Western Australia
J Dep Geogr Natl Univ Malaysia — Journal. Department of Geography. National University of Malaysia
J Dept Ag Ireland — Journal. Irish Free State Department of Agriculture
J Dept Ag Puerto Rico — Journal. Department of Agriculture. Puerto Rico
J Dept Agr Fish (Dublin) — Journal. Department of Agriculture and Fisheries (Dublin)
J Dept Agric W Aust — Journal. Department of Agriculture. Western Australia
J Dept Agr S Aust — Journal. Department of Agriculture. South Australia
J Dept Agr Victoria — Journal. Department of Agriculture. Victoria
J Dept Agr W Aust — Journal. Department of Agriculture. Western Australia
J Dept Ag SA — Journal. Department of Agriculture. South Australia
J Dept Ag S Africa — Journal. Department of Agriculture. South Africa
J Dept Ag S Australia — Journal. Department of Agriculture. South Australia
J Dept Ag VIC — Journal. Department of Agriculture. Victoria
J Dept Ag Victoria — Journal. Department of Agriculture. Victoria
J Dermatol Surg — Journal of Dermatologic Surgery
J Dermatol Surg Oncol — Journal of Dermatologic Surgery and Oncology
J Dermatol (Tokyo) — Journal of Dermatology (Tokyo)
J Des Autom and Fault-Tolerant Comput — Journal of Design Automation and Fault-Tolerant Computing
J Des Autom Fault Tolerant Comput — Journal of Design Automation and Fault-Tolerant Computing
J Design Automat Fault-Tolerant Comput — Journal of Design Automation and Fault-Tolerant Computing
J Deterg Collect Chem — Journal of Detergents and Collective Chemistry
J Dev Areas — Journal of Developing Areas
J Devel Areas — Journal of Developing Areas
J Devel Econ — Journal of Development Economics
J Develop Areas — Journal of Developing Areas
J Developing Areas — Journal of Developing Areas
J Development Econ — Journal of Development Economics
J Development Planning — Journal of Development Planning
J Development Studies — Journal of Development Studies
J Develop Plan — Journal of Development Planning
J Develop Read — Journal of Developmental Reading
J Develop Stud — Journal of Development Studies
J Devel Stud — Journal of Development Studies
J Devon Trust Nat Conserv — Journal. Devon Trust for Nature Conservation
J Dev Physiol — Journal of Developmental Physiology
J Dev Planning — Journal of Development Planning
J Dev Stud — Journal of Development Studies
J Dev Studies — Journal of Development Studies
JDF — Jewish Daily Forward
JDG — Jahrbuch. Droste-Gesellschaft
J Dharma — Journal of Dharma
JdI — Jahrbuch. Deutsches Archaeologische Institut
J Diabetic Assoc India — Journal. Diabetic Association of India
JDIAD — Journal of Dialysis
J Dial — Journal of Dialysis
JDI-EH — Jahrbuch. Deutsches Archaeologische Institut. Ergaenzungsheft
J Diet Assoc (Victoria) — Journal. Dietetic Association (Victoria)
J Diet Home Econ — Journal of Dietetics and Home Economics [*South Africa*]
J Diff Equa — Journal of Differential Equations
J Differential Equations — Journal of Differential Equations
J Differential Geom — Journal of Differential Geometry
J Differential Geometry — Journal of Differential Geometry
J Differ Equations — Journal of Differential Equations
J Digital Syst — Journal of Digital Systems

J Digital Systems — Journal of Digital Systems
J Dispersion Sci Technol — Journal of Dispersion Science and Technology
J Distrib — Journal of Distribution [*Japan*]
JDJ — John Donne Journal. Studies in the Age of Donne
JdL — Jornal de Letras
JDM — Jahrbuch der Musikwelt
JDM — Journal of Data Management
JDNB — Jewish Telegraphic Agency. Daily News Bulletin
J Doc — Journal of Documentation
J Doc Reprod — Journal of Documentary Reproduction
J Docum — Journal of Documentation
J Documentation — Journal of Documentation
JdOI — Jahreshefte. Oesterreichisches Archaeologische Institut in Wien
JDP — Journal of Development Studies
JDPL — Journal des Debats Politiques et Litteraires
JDR — Journal of Defense Research
J Dr Int — Journal du Droit International
JDR J Drug Res — JDR. Journal of Drug Research
JDR J Drugther Res — JDR. Journal for Drugtherapy and Research
J Droit Afr — Journal de Droit Africain
J Droit Internat — Journal du Droit International
J du Droit Int'l — Journal du Droit International
J Drug Educ — Journal of Drug Education
J Drug Iss — Journal of Drug Issues
J Drug Issues — Journal of Drug Issues
J Drug Res (Cairo) — Journal of Drug Research (Cairo)
J Drug Res JDR — Journal of Drug Research. JDR
J Drugther Res — Journal for Drugtherapy and Research
JDS — Jacobean Drama Studies
JDS — Journal of Development Studies
JdS — Journal des Savants
JDSEA — Jido Seigyo
JDSG — Jahrbuch. Deutsche Schiller-Gesellschaft
JDSh — Jahrbuch. Deutsche Shakespeare-Gesellschaft
JDT — Jahrbuecher fuer Deutsche Theologie [*Stuttgart/Gotha*]
JDTh — Jahrbuecher fuer Deutsche Theologie [*Stuttgart/Gotha*]
JDU — Journal. Durham University
J Durham Sch Agr — Journal. Durham School of Agriculture
J Dyn Syst Meas Control — Journal of Dynamic Systems, Measurement, and Control
JE — Journal of Education
JE — Juedisches Echo [*Munich*]
JE — June
JEA — Journal of Egyptian Archaeology
JEA — Journal des Etudes Anciennes
JEAB — Journal of the Experimental Analysis of Behavior
JEAfrSC — Journal. East African Swahili Committee
Jealott's Hill Bull — Jealott's Hill Bulletin
Jean-Paul-Gesellsch Jahrb — Jean-Paul-Gesellschaft. Jahrbuch
JEARD — Journal of Eastern African Research and Development
J Earth Sci — Journal of Earth Sciences
J Earth Sci Nagoya Univ — Journal of Earth Sciences. Nagoya University
J Earth Space Phys (Tehran) — Journal of the Earth and Space Physics (Tehran)
JEAS — Journal of East Asiatic Studies
JEASC — Journal. East African Swahili Committee
J East Afr Nat Hist Soc Natl Mus — Journal. East Africa Natural History Society and National Museum
J East Afr Res Develop — Journal of Eastern African Research and Development
J East Asian Affairs — Journal of East Asian Affairs
J East China Inst Text Sci Technol — Journal. East China Institute of Textile Science and Technology
J East China Petrol Inst — Journal. East China Petroleum Institute
J East West Stud — Journal of East and West Studies
JEB — Journal of Economic Behavior
JEB — Journal of Economic Literature
JEB — Journal of Economics and Business
JEB — Journal of Education (Boston University School of Education)
JEBH — Journal of Economic and Business History
Je C — Jewish Currents
JEC — Journal of Econometrics
JECAB — Journal of Electrocardiology
J Ecclesiast Hist — Journal of Ecclesiastical History
J Eccl H — Journal of Ecclesiastical History
J Eccl Hist — Journal of Ecclesiastical History
JECEA — Journal. Institution of Engineers (India). Part CH. Chemical Engineering Division
Je Ci — Jewish Civilization
JECMA — Journal of Electronic Materials
JECMB — Journal of Econometrics
J Ecol — Journal of Ecology
J Econ — Journal de Economistes
J Econ Abstr — Journal of Economic Abstracts
J Econ Aff — Journal of Economic Affairs
J Econ Biol — Journal of Economic Biology

J Econ Bus — Journal of Economics and Business
J Econ and Bus — Journal of Economics and Business
J Econ Bus Hist — Journal of Economic and Business History
J Econ Dyn and Control — Journal of Economic Dynamics and Control
J Econ Ed — Journal of Economic Education
J Econ Educ — Journal of Economic Education
J Econ Ent — Journal of Economic Entomology
J Econ Entom — Journal of Economic Entomology
J Econ Entomol — Journal of Economic Entomology
J Econ H — Journal of Economic History
J Econ Hist — Journal of Economic History
J Econ Iss — Journal of Economic Issues
J Econ Issues — Journal of Economics Issues
JEconLit — Journal of Economic Literature
J Econ Liter — Journal of Economic Literature
J Econom — Journal of Econometrics
J Econom Behavior Organization — Journal of Economic Behavior and Organization
J Econom Dynamics Control — Journal of Economic Dynamics and Control
J Economet — Journal of Econometrics
J Econometrics — Journal of Econometrics
J Economistes — Journal de Economistes
J Econom Theory — Journal of Economic Theory
J Econ Soc Hist Or — Journal of the Economic and Social History of the Orient
J Econ Soc Hist Orient — Journal of the Economic and Social History of the Orient
J Econ Studies — Journal of Economic Studies
J Econ Theo — Journal of Economic Theory
JECPA — Journal of Experimental Child Psychology
J Ec Polytech — Journal. Ecole Polytechnique
J Ec St — Journal of Ecumenical Studies
J Ecumen Stud — Journal of Ecumenical Studies
J Ecum Stud — Journal of Ecumenical Studies
JECVA — Journal. Institution of Engineers (India). Civil Engineering Division
J Ed — Jewish Education
JED — Journal of Economic Dynamics and Control
J Ed — Journal of Education
J Ed Admin — Journal of Educational Administration
J Ed Data Process — Journal of Educational Data Processing
J Ed (London) — Journal of Education (London)
J Ed M — Journal of Educational Measurement
J Ednl Admin and History — Journal of Educational Administration and History
J Ednl Technology — Journal of Educational Technology
J of Ed (NS) — Journal of Education. Department of Education (Nova Scotia)
J Ed Psychol — Journal of Educational Psychology
J Ed Res — Journal of Educational Research
J Ed Soc — Journal of Educational Sociology
J Ed Stat — Journal of Educational Statisics
J Ed Thought — Journal of Educational Thought
J Educ — Journal of Education
J Educ Adm — Journal of Educational Administration
J Educ Adm Hist — Journal of Educational Administration and History
J Educ Data Proc — Journal of Educational Data Processing
J Educ Dept Niigata Univ — Journal. Education Department. Niigata University
J Educ D P — Journal of Educational Data Processing
J Educ Fin — Journal of Education Finance
J Educ Libr — Journal of Education for Librarianship
J Educ Librarianship — Journal of Education for Librarianship
J Educ (Lond) — Journal of Education (London)
J Educ M — Journal of Educational Measurement
J Educ Media Science — Journal of Educational Media Science
J Educ Method — Journal of Educational Method
J Educ Psyc — Journal of Educational Psychology
J Educ Psych — Journal of Education and Psychology
J Educ Res — Journal of Educational Research
J Educ Soc — Journal of Education for Social Work
J Educ Social — Journal of Educational Sociology
J Educ Soc Work — Journal of Education for Social Work
J Educ Technol Syst — Journal of Educational Technology Systems
J Educ Tech Syst — Journal of Educational Technology Systems
J Educ Th — Journal of Educational Thought
J Educ Univ Natal — Journal of Education. Faculty of Education. University of Natal
JEE — Japan Electronic Engineering
JEE — JEE. Journal of Electronic Engineering
JEE — Journal of Engineering Education
JEE — Journal of Environmental Economics and Management
JEE — Journal of Experimental Education
JEED — Journal. Environmental Engineering Division. Proceedings. American Society of Civil Engineers
JEEGA — Journal. Environmental Engineering Division. American Society of Civil Engineers
JEE J Electron Eng — JEE. Journal of Electronic Engineering [*Japan*]

JEELA — Journal. Institution of Engineers (India). Electrical Engineering Division
JEEMD — Journal of Environmental Economics and Management
JEEND — JEE. Journal of Electronic Engineering
JEF — Japan Economic Journal
JEFDS — Journal. English Folk Dance and Song Society
JEFDSS — Journal. English Folk Dance and Song Society
JEFS — Journal. English Folk Dance and Song Society
JEGP — Journal of English and Germanic Philology
JEGPA — Journal. Egyptian Public Health Association
JEG Ph — Journal of English and Germanic Philology
JEG Phil — Journal of English and Germanic Philology
J Egypt Archaeol — Journal of Egyptian Archaeology
J Egypt Med Ass — Journal. Egyptian Medical Association
J Egypt Med Assoc — Journal. Egyptian Medical Association
J Egypt Pharm — Journal of Egyptian Pharmacy
J Egypt Public Health Assoc — Journal. Egyptian Public Health Association
J Egypt Soc Parasitol — Journal. Egyptian Society of Parasitology
J Egypt Vet Med Ass — Journal. Egyptian Veterinary Medical Association
JEH — Journal of Ecclesiastical History
JEH — Journal of Economic History
JEH/S — Journal of Economic History (Supplement)
JEI — Japan Electronics Industry
JEI — Journal of Economic Issues
JEI — Journal. English Institute
JEI J Electron Ind — JEI. Journal of the Electronics Industry
JEI Jpn Electron Ind — JEI. Japan Electronic Industry
JEIND — Journal of Endocrinological Investigation
JEJ — Japan Economic Journal
JEL — Journal of Economic Literature [*Pittsburgh, PA*]
JEL — Journal of English Linguistics
J Elast — Journal of Elasticity
J Elasticity — Journal of Elasticity
J Elastomers Plast — Journal of Elastomers and Plastics
J Elastoplast — Journal of Elastoplastics [*Later, Journal of Elastomers and Plastics*]
J Elcardiol — Journal of Electrocardiology [*San Diego*]
J Elchem So — Journal. Electrochemical Society
J Elec — Journal of Electricity
J Elec Chem — Journal of Electroanalytical Chemistry and Interfacial Electrochemistry
J Elec Def — Journal of Electronic Defense
J Elec E — Journal of Electronic Engineering
J Elec Mat — Journal of Electronic Materials
J Elec Micr — Journal of Electron Microscopy
J Elec Spec — Journal of Electron Spectroscopy and Related Phenomena
J Electr Electron Eng (Aust) — Journal of Electrical and Electronics Engineering (Australia)
J Electroanal Chem — Journal of Electroanalytical Chemistry [*Netherlands*]
J Electroanal Chem Abstr Sect — Journal of Electroanalytical Chemistry. Abstract Section
J Electroanal Chem Interfacial Electrochem — Journal of Electroanalytical Chemistry and Interfacial Electrochemistry
J Electrocardiol — Journal of Electrocardiology
J Electrocardiol (San Diego) — Journal of Electrocardiology (San Diego)
J Electrochem Soc — Journal. Electrochemical Society
J Electrochem Soc India — Journal. Electrochemical Society of India
J Electrochem Soc Japan — Journal. Electrochemical Society of Japan
J Electron (Beijing) — Journal of Electronics (Beijing)
J Electron Control — Journal of Electronics and Control [*England*]
J Electron Eng — Journal of Electronic Engineering
J Electron Mater — Journal of Electronic Materials
J Electron Microsc — Journal of Electron Microscopy
J Electron Microsc Tech — Journal of Electron Microscopy Technique
J Electron Microsc (Tokyo) — Journal of Electron Microscopy (Tokyo)
J Electron Micry — Journal of Electron Microscopy
J Electron Spectrosc and Relat Phenom — Journal of Electron Spectroscopy and Related Phenomena
J Electron Spectrosc Relat Phenom — Journal of Electron Spectroscopy and Related Phenomena
J Electrostat — Journal of Electrostatics
J Electr Spectr — Journal of Electron Spectroscopy and Related Phenomena
J Elisha Mitchell Scient Soc — Journal. Elisha Mitchell Scientific Society
J Elisha Mitchell Sci Soc — Journal. Elisha Mitchell Scientific Society
JEM — Journal of Enterprise Management
JEM — Journal of Environmental Economics and Management
JEMAA — Journal. Egyptian Medical Association
J Emb Exp M — Journal of Embryology and Experimental Morphology
J Embryol Exp Morphol — Journal of Embryology and Experimental Morphology
J Emergency Nurs — Journal of Emergency Nursing
J Emerg Med — Journal of Emergency Medicine
J Emerg Nurs — Journal of Emergency Nursing
J Emerg Services — Journal of Emergency Services
JEMFA — JEMF [*John Edwards Memorial Foundation*] Quarterly
JEMFQ — JEMF [*John Edwards Memorial Foundation*] Quarterly

JEMIC Tech Rep — JEMIC [*Japan Electric Meters Inspection Corporation*] Technical Report
Jemna Mech Opt — Jemna Mechanika a Optika
J Empl Coun — Journal of Employment Counseling
J Employ Counsel — Journal of Employment Counseling
JEMSA — Journal. Elisha Mitchell Scientific Society
JEN — Journal of Emergency Nursing
J En — Journal of English
Jenaische Ztschr Med u Naturw — Jenaische Zeitschrift fuer Medizin und Naturwissenschaft
Jenaische Ztschr Naturw — Jenaische Zeitschrift fuer Naturwissenschaft
Jena Rev — Jena Review
Jena Rev Suppl — Jena Review. Supplement [*East Germany*]
Jena Rundsch — Jenaer Rundschau
Jena Z Med Naturwiss — Jenaische Zeitschrift fuer Medizin und Naturwissenschaft [*East Germany*]
Jena Z Naturw — Jenaische Zeitschrift fuer Naturwissenschaft
Jena Z Naturwiss — Jenaische Zeitschrift fuer Naturwissenschaft
JENDD — Journal of Energy and Development
J Endocr — Journal of Endocrinology
J Endocrinol — Journal of Endocrinology
J Endocrinol Invest — Journal of Endocrinological Investigation
J Endod — Journal of Endodontics
J Energy — Journal of Energy
J Energy Dev — Journal of Energy and Development
J Energy Develop — Journal of Energy and Development
J Energy and Development — Journal of Energy and Development
J Energy Div Am Soc Civ Eng — Journal. Energy Division. American Society of Civil Engineers
J Energy Div ASCE — Journal. Energy Division. American Society of Civil Engineers
J Energy Div Proc ASCE — Journal. Energy Division. American Society of Civil Engineers. Proceedings
J Energy Eng — Journal of Energy Engineering
J Energy Law and Policy — Journal of Energy Law and Policy
J Energy L P — Journal of Energy Law and Policy
J Energy L & Pol'y — Journal of Energy Law and Policy
J Energy Resources Technol — Journal of Energy Resources Technology
J Energy Resour Technol — Journal of Energy Resources Technology
J Energy Resour Technol Trans ASME — Journal of Energy Resources Technology. Transactions of the American Society of Mechanical Engineers
J Eng Ed — Journal of Engineering Education
J Eng Educ — Journal of Engineering Education
J Eng Gas Turbines Power — Journal of Engineering for Gas Turbines and Power
J Eng and Germ Philol — Journal of English and Germanic Philology
J Eng Ger Philol — Journal of English and Germanic Philology
J Eng Ind — Journal of Engineering for Industry
J Eng Ind Tran ASME — Journal of Engineering for Industry. Transactions of the American Society of Mechanical Engineers
J Eng Ind Trans ASME — Journal of Engineering for Industry. Transactions of the American Society of Mechanical Engineers
J Eng L — Journal of English Linguistics
J Engl Ger — Journal of English and Germanic Philology
J Engl & Germ Philol — Journal of English and Germanic Philology
J Engl Place-Name Soc — Journal. English Place-Name Society
J Eng Mater — Journal of Engineering Materials and Technology
J Eng Materials & Tech — Journal of Engineering Materials and Technology
J Eng Mater Technol — Journal of Engineering Materials and Technology
J Eng Mater Technol Trans ASME — Journal of Engineering Materials and Technology. Transactions of the American Society of Mechanical Engineers
J Eng Math — Journal of Engineering Mathematics
J Eng Mat & Tech — Journal of Engineering Materials and Technology
J Eng Mech — Journal of Engineering Mechanics
J Eng Mech Div Amer Soc Civil Eng Proc — Journal. Engineering Mechanics Division. American Society of Civil Engineers. Proceedings
J Eng Mech Div Am Soc Civ Eng — Journal. Engineering Mechanics Division. Proceedings. American Society of Civil Engineers
J Engng Math — Journal of Engineering Mathematics
J Engng Mech Div Proc ASCE — Journal. Engineering Mechanics Division. Proceedings. American Society of Civil Engineers
J Engn Phys — Journal of Engineering Physics
J Eng Phys — Journal of Engineering Physics
J Eng Phys (Belgrade) — Journal of Engineering Physics (Belgrade)
J Eng Phys (Engl Transl) — Journal of Engineering Physics (English Translation of Inzhenerno-Fizicheskii Zhurnal) [*Belorussian SSR*]
J Eng Power — Journal of Engineering for Power
J Eng Power Trans ASME — Journal of Engineering for Power. Transactions of the American Society of Mechanical Engineers
J Eng Psychol — Journal of Engineering Psychology
J Engrg Math — Journal of Engineering Mathematics
J Engrg Phys — Journal of Engineering Physics
J Eng S — Journal of English Studies
J Eng Sci — Journal of Engineering Sciences

J Eng Sci (Saudi Arabia) — Journal of Engineering Sciences (Saudi Arabia)
JENS — Journal. Eighteen Nineties Society
Jen-Sal J — Jen-Sal Journal
J Ent — Journal of Entomology
J Enterostom Ther — Journal of Enterostomal Therapy
J Entomol A — Journal of Entomology. Series A. General Entomology
J Entomol B — Journal of Entomology. Series B. Taxonomy
J Entomol Res — Journal of Entomological Research
J Entomol Ser A — Journal of Entomology. Series A. General Entomology
J Entomol Ser A Gen Entomol — Journal of Entomology. Series A. General Entomology
J Entomol Ser A Physiol Behav — Journal of Entomology. Series A. Physiology and Behaviour
J Entomol Ser B Taxon — Journal of Entomology. Series B. Taxonomy
J Entomol Ser B Taxon Syst — Journal of Entomology. Series B. Taxonomy and Systematics
J Entomol Soc Aust — Journal. Entomological Society of Australia
J Entomol Soc Aust (NSW) — Journal. Entomological Society of Australia (New South Wales)
J Entomol Soc BC — Journal. Entomological Society of British Columbia
J Entomol Soc S Afr — Journal. Entomological Society of Southern Africa
J Entomol Soc South Afr — Journal. Entomological Society of Southern Africa
J Entomol Soc Sthn Afr — Journal. Entomological Society of Southern Africa
J Entomol Zool — Journal of Entomology and Zoology
J Ent Soc Aust — Journal. Entomological Society of Australia
J Ent Soc Aust (NSW) — Journal. Entomological Society of Australia (New South Wales Branch)
J Ent Soc BC — Journal. Entomological Society of British Columbia
J Ent Soc Qd — Entomological Society of Queensland. Journal
J Ent Soc Qd — Journal. Entomological Society of Queensland
J Ent Soc Sth Afr — Journal. Entomological Society of Southern Africa
J Env Educ — Journal of Environmental Education
J Envir Eng — Journal. Environmental Engineering Division. American Society of Civil Engineers
J Envir Mgm — Journal of Environmental Management
J Environ Econ Manage — Journal of Environmental Economics and Management
J Environ Educ — Journal of Environmental Education
J Environ Eng Div Am Soc Civ Eng — Journal. Environmental Engineering Division. American Society of Civil Engineers
J Environ Eng Div ASCE — Journal. Environmental Engineering Division. American Society of Civil Engineers
J Environ Engng Div Proc ASCE — Journal. Environmental Engineering Division. Proceedings. American Society of Civil Engineers
J Environ Health — Journal of Environmental Health
J Environ Hortic — Journal of Environmental Horticulture
J Environ Manage — Journal of Environmental Management
J Environmental Econ and Mgt — Journal of Environmental Economics and Management
J Environ Pathol Toxicol — Journal of Environmental Pathology and Toxicology
J Environ Plann Pollut Control — Journal of Environmental Planning and Pollution Control
J Environ Pollut Control (Tokyo) — Journal of Environmental Pollution Control (Tokyo)
J Environ Qual — Journal of Environmental Quality
J Environ Radioact — Journal of Environmental Radioactivity
J Environ Sci — Journal of Environmental Sciences
J Environ Sci Health B — Journal of Environmental Science and Health. Part B. Pesticides, Food Contaminants, and Agricultural Wastes
J Environ Sci Health (C) — Journal of Environmental Science and Health. Part C. Environmental Health Sciences
J Environ Sci Health Part A — Journal of Environmental Science and Health. Part A. Environmental Science and Engineering
J Environ Sci Health Part A Environ Sci Eng — Journal of Environmental Science and Health. Part A. Environmental Science and Engineering
J Environ Sci Health Part B — Journal of Environmental Science and Health. Part B. Pesticides, Food Contaminants, and Agricultural Wastes
J Environ Sci Health Part B Pestic Food Contam Agric Wastes — Journal of Environmental Science and Health. Part B. Pesticides, Food Contaminants, and Agricultural Wastes
J Environ Sci Health Part C — Journal of Environmental Science and Health. Part C
J Environ Syst — Journal of Environmental Systems
J Environ Systems — Journal of Environmental Systems
J Envir Q — Journal of Environmental Quality
J Envir Qual — Journal of Environmental Quality
J Envir Quality — Journal of Environmental Quality
J Envir Sci — Journal of Environmental Sciences
J Envir Sci Hlth — Journal of Environmental Science and Health
JEOFD — Jeofizik
JEOL — Jaarbericht. Vooraziatische-Egyptisch Genootschap "Ex Oriente Lux"
JEP — Journal of Economic Psychology
JEP — Journal of Educational Psychology
JEP — Journal of General Management

J Epidemiol Community Health — Journal of Epidemiology and Community Health
JEPLA — Journal of Elastomers and Plastics
JEPs — Journal of Educational Psychology
JEPSA — Journal of Experimental Psychology
JEPSB — Journal Europeen des Steroides
Je Q — Jerusalem Quarterly
J Equine Med Surg — Journal of Equine Medicine and Surgery
J Equip Electr et Electron — Journal de l'Equipement Electrique et Electronique
JER — Journal of Educational Research
Jernkon Ann — Jernkontorets Annaler
Jernkontorets Ann — Jernkontorets Annaler
Jernkontorets Ann Ed A — Jernkontorets Annaler. Edition A
Jernkontorets Ann Ed B — Jernkontorets Annaler. Edition B
Jersey B — Jersey Bulletin and Dairy World
Jersey Bul — Jersey Bulletin
Jersey J — Jersey Journal
JERTD — Journal of Energy Resources Techology
Jerusalem J Int Relat — Jerusalem Journal of International Relations
Jerusalem Q — Jerusalem Quarterly
Jerus J Int Rel — Jerusalem Journal of International Relations
Jerus Symp Quantum Chem Biochem — Jerusalem Symposia on Quantum Chemistry and Biochemistry
JES — Japanese Economic Studies. A Journal of Translations
JES — Journal of Economic Studies
JES — Journal of Ecumenical Studies
JES — Journal of European Studies
JESHO — Journal of the Economic and Social History of the Orient
JESIA — Journal. Electrochemical Society of India
JESOA — Journal. Electrochemical Society [*United States*]
JESt — Journal of Ethiopian Studies [*Addis Ababa/London*]
JET — Journal of Economic Theory
JET — Journal of Environmental Systems
JET — Journal of Real Estate Taxation
JETAA — Journal. Faculty of Engineering. University of Tokyo. Series A. Annual Report
JETBA — Journal. Faculty of Engineering. University of Tokyo. Series B
JETCA — Journal of Ethnic Studies
JEthiopSt — Journal of Ethiopian Studies [*Addis Ababa/London*]
J Ethiop Stud — Journal of Ethiopian Studies
J Ethnic Stud — Journal of Ethnic Studies
J Ethnopharmacol — Journal of Ethnopharmacology
JEthS — Journal of Ethiopian Studies
J Eth S — Journal of Ethnic Studies
JETI — JETI. Japan Energy and Technology Intelligence
JETP — Journal of Experimental and Theoretical Physics
JETPA — Jet Propulsion
JETP Lett — JETP Letters [*English Translation of JETP Pis'ma v Redaktsiyu*]
Jet Propul — Jet Propulsion [*United States*]
Jet Propul Lab Tech Memo — Jet Propulsion Laboratory. Technical Memorandum
JETS — Journal. Evangelical Theological Society
JETXA — Journal of Existentialism
JEU — Jeune Afrique [*Paris*]
JEU — Journal of European Industrial Training
JeuneA — Jeune Afrique
Jeune C — Jeune Cinema
Jeune Sci — Jeune Scientifique [*Canada*]
Jeunesse — Jeunesse et Orgue
Jeunes Trav — Jeunes Travailleurs
J Eur Econ Hist — Journal of European Economic History
J Eur Ind Training — Journal of European Industrial Training
J Europ Training — Journal of European Training
J Eur Pathol For — Journal Europeen de Pathologie Forestiere
J Eur Steroides — Journal Europeen des Steroides [*France*]
J Eur Stud — Journal of European Studies
J Eur Toxicol — Journal Europeen de Toxicologie
J Eur Toxicol Suppl — Journal Europeen de Toxicologie. Supplement
J Evang Th S — Journal. Evangelical Theological Society
JEVEB — Journal of Environmental Education
J Evol Biochem Physiol (Engl Transl Zh Evol Biokhim Fiziol) — Journal of Evolutionary Biochemistry and Physiology (English Translation of Zhurnal Evolyutsionnoi Biokhimii i Fiziologii)
J Evol Biochem Physiol (USSR) — Journal of Evolutionary Biochemistry and Physiology (USSR)
J Evolut Biochem Physiol — Journal of Evolutionary Biochemistry and Physiology
JEVQA — Journal of Environmental Quality
JEVSB — Journal of Environmental Systems
JEVWK — Jahrbuch. Evangelischer Verein fuer Westfaelische Kirchengeschichte
Jew Aff — Jewish Affairs
JewChron — Jewish Chronicle [*London*]
Jew Hist Soc Engl Trans — Jewish Historical Society of England. Transactions

Jewish Cu — Jewish Currents
Jewish Ed — Jewish Education
Jewish Educ — Jewish Education
Jewish Hist Soc of England Trans — Jewish Historical Society of England. Transactions
Jewish Soc Stud — Jewish Social Studies
JewJSoc — Jewish Journal of Sociology [London]
Jew J Socio — Jewish Journal of Sociology
JewL — Jewish Life [New York]
JewQ — Jewish Quarterly Review
Jew Q R — Jewish Quarterly Review
Jew Q Rev — Jewish Quarterly Review
Jew Quart R — Jewish Quarterly Review
JewRev — Jewish Review [London]
JewSocSt — Jewish Social Studies [New York]
Jew Soc Stu — Jewish Social Studies
J An Beh — Journal of the Experimental Analysis of Behavior
J Excep Child — Journal of Exceptional Children
JExP — Journal of Experimental Psychology
J Exp Anal Behav — Journal of the Experimental Analysis of Behavior
J Exp Analysis Behav — Journal of the Experimental Analysis of Behavior
J Exp Anim Sci — Journal of Experimental Animal Science
J Exp Biol — Journal of Experimental Biology
J Exp Bot — Journal of Experimental Botany
J Exp Child Psy — Journal of Experimental Child Psychology
J Exp Child Psychol — Journal of Experimental Child Psychology
J Exp Clin Cancer Res — Journal of Experimental and Clinical Cancer Research
J Exp C Psy — Journal of Experimental Child Psychology
J Exp Ed — Journal of Experimental Education
J Exper Anal Behav — Journal of the Experimental Analysis of Behavior
J Exper Biol — Journal of Experimental Biology
J Exper Bot — Journal of Experimental Botany
J Exper Child Psychol — Journal of Experimental Child Psychology
J Exper Educ — Journal of Experimental Education
J Exper Marine Biol & Ecol — Journal of Experimental Marine Biology and Ecology
J Exper Med — Journal of Experimental Medicine
J Exper Psychol Human Learn Mem — Journal of Experimental Psychology: Human Learning and Memory
J Exper Psychol Human Percept & Perf — Journal of Experimental Psychology: Human Perception and Performance
J Exper Social Psychol — Journal of Experimental Social Psychology
J Exper Soc Psychol — Journal of Experimental Social Psychology
J Exper Zool — Journal of Experimental Zoology
J Ex P H P — Journal of Experimental Psychology: Human Perception and Performance
J Ex P L — Journal of Experimental Psychology: Human Learning and Memory
J Exp Mar B — Journal of Experimental Marine Biology and Ecology
J Exp Mar Biol Ecol — Journal of Experimental Marine Biology and Ecology
J Exp Med — Journal of Experimental Medicine
J Exp Med Sci — Journal of Experimental Medical Sciences
J Exp Psy A — Journal of Experimental Psychology: Animal Behavior Processes
J Exp Psych — Journal of Experimental Psychology
J Exp Psychol — Journal of Experimental Psychology
J Exp Psychol (Animal Behav Proc) — Journal of Experimental Psychology: Animal Behavior Processes
J Exp Psychol Gen — Journal of Experimental Psychology: General
J Exp Psychol Hum Learn Mem — Journal of Experimental Psychology: Human Learning and Memory
J Exp Psychol Hum Percept Perform — Journal of Experimental Psychology: Human Perception and Performance
J Exp Psychol Hum Perc Perf — Journal of Experimental Psychology: Human Perception and Performance
J Exp Psychol Monogr — Journal of Experimental Psychology: Monograph
J Exp Psy G — Journal of Experimental Psychology: General
J Exp Psy H — Journal of Experimental Psychology: Human Learning and Memory
J Exp Psy P — Journal of Experimental Psychology: Human Perception and Performance
J Exp Res Pers — Journal of Experimental Research in Personality
J Exp Soc Psychol — Journal of Experimental Social Psychology
J Exp S Psy — Journal of Experimental Social Psychology
J Exp Zool — Journal of Experimental Zoology
J Ext — Journal of Extension
J Extra Corporeal Technol — Journal of Extra-Corporeal Technology
JEY — Journal of Employment Counseling
J Eye — Journal of the Eye
JF — Jewish Frontier
JF — Jornal de Filologia
JF — Journal of Finance
JF — Juznoslovenski Filolog
JFA — Jahresbericht ueber die Fortschritte der Klassischen Altertumswissenschaft

JFA — Journal of Field Archaeology
JfAaK — Jahrbuch fuer Aesthetik und Allgemeine Kunstwissenschaft
J Fabr Sucre — Journal des Fabricants de Sucre
J Fac Agric Hokkaido Univ — Journal. Faculty of Agriculture. Hokkaido University
J Fac Agric Hokkaido Univ Ser Entomol — Journal. Faculty of Agriculture. Hokkaido University. Series Entomology
J Fac Agric Iwate Univ — Journal. Faculty of Agriculture. Iwate University
J Fac Agric Kyushu Univ — Journal. Faculty of Agriculture. Kyushu University
J Fac Agric Shinshu Univ — Journal. Faculty of Agriculture. Shinshu University
J Fac Agric Tottori Univ — Journal. Faculty of Agriculture. Tottori University
J Fac Agr Iwate Univ — Journal. Faculty of Agriculture. Iwate University
J Fac Agr Kyushu Univ — Journal. Faculty of Agriculture. Kyushu University
J Fac Agr Shinshu Univ — Journal. Faculty of Agriculture. Shinshu University
J Fac Agr Tottori Univ — Journal. Faculty of Agriculture. Tottori University
J Fac Ed Saga Univ — Journal. Faculty of Education. Saga University
J Fac Ed Saga Univ Part 1 — Saga University. Faculty of Education. Journal. Part 1
J Fac Educ Nat Sci Tottori Univ — Journal. Faculty of Education. Natural Sciences. Tottori University [Japan]
J Fac Educ Tottori Univ Nat Sci — Journal. Faculty of Education. Tottori University. Natural Science
J Fac Eng Chiba Univ — Journal. Faculty of Engineering. Chiba University
J Fac Eng Ibaraki Univ — Journal. Faculty of Engineering. Ibaraki University [Japan]
J Fac Engng Univ Tokyo — Journal. Faculty of Engineering. University of Tokyo
J Fac Engrg Chiba Univ — Journal. Faculty of Engineering. Chiba University
J Fac Engrg Univ Tokyo Ser B — Journal. Faculty of Engineering. University of Tokyo. Series B
J Fac Eng Shinshu Univ — Journal. Faculty of Engineering. Shinshu University
J Fac Eng Univ Tokyo — Journal. Faculty of Engineering. University of Tokyo
J Fac Eng Univ Tokyo Ser A — Journal. Faculty of Engineering. University of Tokyo. Series A. Annual Report
J Fac Eng Univ Tokyo Ser B — Journal. Faculty of Engineering. University of Tokyo. Series B
J Fac Fish Anim Husb Hiroshima Univ — Journal. Faculty of Fisheries and Animal Husbandry. Hiroshima University
J Fac Fish Anim Husb Hir Univ — Journal. Faculty of Fisheries and Animal Husbandry. Hiroshima University
J Fac Fish Prefect Univ Mie — Journal. Faculty of Fisheries. Prefectural University of Mie
J Fac Lib Arts Shinshu Univ Part II Nat Sci — Journal. Faculty of Liberal Arts. Shinshu University. Part II. Natural Sciences
J Fac Liberal Arts Yamaguchi Univ Natur Sci — Journal. Faculty of Liberal Arts. Yamaguchi University. Natural Sciences
J Fac Mar Sci Technol Tokai Univ — Journal. Faculty of Marine Science and Technology. Tokai University
J Fac Med (Baghdad) — Journal. Faculty of Medicine (Baghdad)
J Fac Med Univ Ankara — Journal. Faculty of Medicine. University of Ankara
J Fac Med Univ Ankara Suppl — Journal. Faculty of Medicine. University of Ankara. Supplement
J Fac Oceanogr Tokai Univ — Journal. Faculty of Oceanography. Tokai University
J Fac Pharm Istanbul Univ — Journal. Faculty of Pharmacy. Istanbul University
J Fac Polit Sci Econ Tokai Univ — Journal. Faculty of Political Science and Economics. Tokai University
J Fac Radiol (Lond) — Journal. Faculty of Radiologists (London)
J Fac Sci Hokkaido Univ — Journal. Faculty of Science. Hokkaido University
J Fac Sci Hokkaido Univ Ser IV Geol Mineral — Journal. Faculty of Science. Hokkaido University. Series IV. Geology and Mineralogy
J Fac Sci Hokkaido Univ Ser V Bot — Journal. Faculty of Science. Hokkaido University. Series V. Botany
J Fac Sci Hokkaido Univ Ser VII — Journal. Faculty of Science. Hokkaido University. Series VII. Geophysics
J Fac Sci Hokkaido Univ Ser VI Zool — Journal. Faculty of Science. Hokkaido University. Series VI. Zoology
J Fac Sci Imp Univ Tokyo Sect IV Zool — Journal. Faculty of Science. Imperial University of Tokyo. Section IV. Zoology
J Fac Sci Niigata Univ Ser II Biol Geol Mineral — Journal. Faculty of Science. Niigata University. Series II. Biology, Geology, and Mineralogy
J Fac Sci Shinshu Univ — Journal. Faculty of Science. Shinshu University
J Fac Sci Tokyo Univ — Journal. Faculty of Science. Tokyo University
J Fac Sci Univ Tokyo Sect IA Math — Journal. Faculty of Science. University of Tokyo. Section IA. Mathematics
J Fac Sci Univ Tokyo Sect II Geol Mineral Geogr Geophys — Journal. Faculty of Science. University of Tokyo. Section II. Geology, Mineralogy, Geography, Geophysics
J Fac Sci Univ Tokyo Sect III Bot — Journal. Faculty of Science. University of Tokyo. Section III. Botany
J Fac Sci Univ Tokyo Sect IV — Journal. Faculty of Science. University of Tokyo. Section IV [Japan]
J Fac Sci Univ Tokyo Sect IV Zool — Journal. Faculty of Science. University of Tokyo. Section IV. Zoology

J Fac Sci Univ Tokyo Sect V — Journal. Faculty of Science. University of Tokyo. Section V. Anthropology
J Fac Sci Univ Tokyo Sect V Anthropol — Journal. Faculty of Science. University of Tokyo. Section V. Anthropology
J Fac Text Sci Technol Shinshu Univ Ser A Biol — Journal. Faculty of Textile Science and Technology. Shinshu University. Series A. Biology
J Fac Text Sci Technol Shinshu Univ Ser B — Journal. Faculty of Textile Science and Technology. Shinshu University. Series B. Textile Engineering
J Fac Text Sci Technol Shinshu Univ Ser D — Journal. Faculty of Textile Science and Technology. Shinshu University. Series D. Arts
J Fac Text Sci Technol Shinshu Univ Ser E Agric Seric — Journal. Faculty of Textile Science and Technology. Shinshu University. Series E. Agriculture and Sericulture
J Fac Text Seric Shinshu Ser E Seric — Journal. Faculty of Textile and Sericulture. Shinshu University. Series E. Sericulture
J Fac Text Seric Shinshu Univ Ser A — Journal. Faculty of Textile and Sericulture. Shinshu University. Series A. Biology
J Fac Text Seric Shinshu Univ Ser B — Journal. Faculty of Textile and Sericulture. Shinshu University. Series B. Textile Engineering
J Fac Text Seric Shinshu Univ Ser C — Journal. Faculty of Textile and Sericulture. Shinshu University. Series C. Chemistry
J Fac Text Seric Shinshu Univ Ser D — Journal. Faculty of Textile and Sericulture. Shinshu University. Series D. Arts and Sciences
J Fac Text Seric Shinshu Univ Ser E — Journal. Faculty of Textile and Sericulture. Shinshu University. Series E. Sericulture
J Fac Text Sericu Shinshu Univ Ser A Biol — Journal. Faculty of Textile and Sericulture. Shinshu University. Series A. Biology
J Fac Tok I — Journal. Faculty of Science. University of Tokyo. Section I. Mathematics, Astronomy, Physics, Chemistry
J Faculty Arts Roy Univ Malta — Journal. Faculty of Arts. Royal University of Malta
J Fac Vet Med Univ Ankara — Journal. Faculty of Veterinary Medicine. University of Ankara
JFAKA — Journal. Faculty of Agriculture. Kyushu University
J Fam Couns — Journal of Family Counseling
J Fam Hist — Journal of Family History
J Family L — Journal of Family Law
J Fam L — Journal of Family Law
J Fam Law — Journal of Family Law
J Fam Pract — Journal of Family Practice
J Fam Wel — Journal of Family Welfare
J Fam Welf — Journal of Family Welfare
J Farm — Jornal dos Farmaceuticos
J Farm Econ — Journal of Farm Economics
J Farmers' Club — Journal. Farmers' Club
J Farnham Mus Soc — Journal. Farnham Museum Society
JFBND — Journal Francais de Biophysique et Medecine Nucleaire
JFDH — Jahrbuch. Freies Deutsche Hochstift
J Fd Hyg Soc Jap — Journal. Food Hygienic Society of Japan
J Fd Sci — Journal of Food Science
J Fd Sci Technol — Journal of Food Science and Technology
JFE — Journal of Farm Economics
JFE — Journal of Financial Economics
JFE — Journal of Fusion Energy
JFEND — Journal of Fusion Energy
J Ferment Assoc Jpn — Journal. Fermentation Association of Japan
J Ferment Ind — Journal of Fermentation Industries
J Ferment Technol — Journal of Fermentation Technology
J Ferment Technol (Osaka) — Journal of Fermentation Technology (Osaka) [*Japan*]
J Ferm Tech — Journal of Fermentation Technology
J Ferrocem — Journal of Ferrocement
J Ferrocement — Journal of Ferrocement [*New Zealand*]
JFF — Juedische Familien Forschung
JFF — Jugend Film Fernsehen
JFFJ — Japanese Fantasy Film Journal
JFG — Jahrbuch der Philosophischen. Fakultaet der Universitaet zu Goettingen
JFHLA — Federal Home Loan Bank Board. Journal
JFI — Journal of Finance
JFI — Journal. Folklore Institute
JFI — Journal. Franklin Institute
J Field Arch — Journal of Field Archaeology
J Fin — Journal of Finance
JFINA — Journal. Franklin Institute
J Finance — Journal of Finance
J Financ Quant Anal — Journal of Financial and Quantitative Analysis
J Fin Qu An — Journal of Financial and Quantitative Analysis
J Fire Flamm — Journal of Fire and Flammability
J Fire Flammability — Journal of Fire and Flammability
J Fire Retardant Chem — Journal of Fire Retardant Chemistry
J Fire Retard Chem — Journal of Fire Retardant Chemistry
J Fire Sc — Journal of Fire Sciences
J Fish Biol — Journal of Fish Biology
J Fish Dis — Journal of Fish Diseases [*England*]

J Fisheries Res Board Can — Journal. Fisheries Research Board of Canada
J Fish Res — Journal. Fisheries Research Board of Canada
J Fish Res Board Can — Journal. Fisheries Research Board of Canada
J Fiz Malays — Jurnal Fizik Malaysia
JFKAW — Jahresberichte ueber die Fortschritte der Klassischen Altertumswissenschaft
JFL — Jahrbuch fuer Fraenkische Landesforschung
JFL — Jewish Family Living
J Fla Acad Gen Pract — Journal. Florida Academy of General Practice
J Fla Med Assoc — Journal. Florida Medical Association
J FL Eng Soc — Journal. Florida Engineering Society
JFLF — Jahrbuch fuer Fraenkische Landesforschung
J Floresc Miner Soc — Journal. Fluorescent Mineral Society
J Flour Anim Feed Milling — Journal of Flour and Animal Feed Milling
J Fluency Dis — Journal of Fluency Disorders
J Fluid Eng Trans ASME — Journal of Fluids Engineering. Transactions of the American Society of Mechanical Engineers
J Fluid Mec — Journal of Fluid Mechanics
J Fluid Mech — Journal of Fluid Mechanics
J Fluids Eng — Journal of Fluids Engineering. Transactions of the American Society of Mechanical Engineers
J Fluorine — Journal of Fluorine Chemistry
J Fluorine Chem — Journal of Fluorine Chemistry
JFMA — Journal. Florida Medical Association
JfNG — Jahrbuch fuer Numismatik und Geldgeschichte
JFOAB — Journal Francais d'Oto-Rhino-Laryngologie, Audiophonologie, et Chirurgie Maxillo-Faciale
J Folk Inst — Journal. Folklore Institute
J Folkl Inst — Journal. Folklore Institute
J Food Biochem — Journal of Food Biochemistry
J Food Hyg Soc Jap — Journal. Food Hygienic Society of Japan
J Food Hyg Soc Jpn — Journal. Food Hygienic Society of Japan
J Food Process Eng — Journal of Food Process Engineering
J Food Process Preserv — Journal of Food Processing and Preservation
J Food Prot — Journal of Food Protection
J Food Protect — Journal of Food Protection
J Food Qual — Journal of Food Quality
J Food Resour Dev — Journal of Food Resources Development
J Food Sci — Journal of Food Science
J Food Sci Kyoto Women's Univ — Journal of Food Science. Kyoto Women's University
J Food Sci Tech — Journal of Food Science and Technology
J Food Sci Technol — Journal of Food Science and Technology
J Food Sci Technol (Mysore) — Journal of Food Science and Technology (Mysore)
J Food Technol — Journal of Food Technology
J Foot Surg — Journal of Foot Surgery
J For — Journal of Forestry
J Foraminiferal Res — Journal of Foraminiferal Research
J For Comm — Journal. Forestry Commission
J Forecasting — Journal of Forecasting
J Forensic Med — Journal of Forensic Medicine
J Forensic Sci — Journal of Forensic Sciences
J Forensic Sci Soc — Journal. Forensic Science Society
J Forest — Journal of Forestry
J For Hist — Journal of Forest History
JFORL — Journal Francais d'Oto-Rhino-Laryngologie
J For Med — Journal of Forensic Medicine
J Formosan Med Assoc — Journal. Formosan Medical Association
J For Prod Res Soc — Journal. Forest Products Research Society
J For Sci — Journal of Forensic Sciences
J For Sci Socy — Journal. Forensic Science Society
J For Suisse — Journal Forestier Suisse
J For Suisse Schweiz Z Forstwes — Journal Forestier Suisse/Schweizerische Zeitschrift fuer Forstwesen
J Four Elec — Journal du Four Electrique
JFP — Journal of Financial Planning Today
JFPRD — Journal of Food Protection
JFQ — Journal of Financial and Quantitative Analysis
JFQA — Journal of Financial and Quantitative Analysis
JFR — Journal of Folklore Research
J Fr Agric — Journal de la France Agricole
J Frankl I — Journal. Franklin Institute
J Franklin Inst — Journal. Franklin Institute
JFRB — Journal. Fisheries Research Board of Canada
JFRBA — Journal. Fisheries Research Board of Canada
J Fr Biophys Med Nucl — Journal Francais de Biophysique et Medecine Nucleaire
JFRCD — Journal of Fire Retardant Chemistry
JFRDD — Journal of Food Resources Development
J Freshwater — Journal of Freshwater
J Fr Med Chir Thorac — Journal Francais de Medecine et Chirurgie Thoraciques
J Fron — Jewish Frontier
J Fr Ophtalmol — Journal Francais d'Ophtalmologie

J Fr Oto-Rhino-Laryngol — Journal Francais d'Oto-Rhino-Laryngologie et Chirurgie Maxillo-Faciale [*Later, Journal Francais d'Oto-Rhino-Laryngologie*]

J Fr Rhino Laryngol Audio Phonol Chir Maxillo Fac — Journal Francais d'Oto-Rhino-Laryngologie, Audio Phonologie, et Chirurgie Maxillo-Faciale

J Fr Oto Rhino Laryngol Chir Maxillo Fac — Journal Francais d'Oto-Rhino-Laryngologie et Chirurgie Maxillo-Faciale [*Later, Journal Francias d'Oto-Rhino-Laryngologie*]

J Frottement Ind — Journal du Frottement Industriel [*France*]

JFS — Jane's Fighting Ships

JFSGW — Journal. Folklore Society of Greater Washington

JFSS — Journal. Folk Song Society

JFSUB — Journal of Foot Surgery

JFTED — Journal of Fermentation Technology

JFU — Journal of Futures Markets

J Fuel Heat Technol — Journal of Fuel and Heat Technology

J Fuel Soc Jap — Journal. Fuel Society of Japan [*Nenryo Kyokai-Shi*]

J Fujian Agric Coll — Journal. Fujian Agricultural College

J Funct Ana — Journal of Functional Analysis

J Funct Anal — Journal of Functional Analysis

J Functional Analysis — Journal of Functional Analysis

JFUS — Journal of Forestry (United States)

J Fusion Energy — Journal of Fusion Energy

J Futures Markets — Journal of Futures Markets

JG — Journal de Geneve

JG — Journal of Geography

JG — Juedisches Gemeinde

J Ga — Jauna Gaita

J GA Dent Assoc — Journal. Georgia Dental Association

J GA Entomol Soc — Journal. Georgia Entomological Society

J GA Ent Soc — Journal. Georgia Entomological Society

J Gakugei Tokushima Univ Nat Sci — Journal. Gakugei Tokushima University. Natural Science

J Galway Archaeol Hist Soc — Journal. Galway Archaeological and Historical Society

J Gan Jha Kend Sans Vid — Journal. Ganganatha Jha Kendriya Sanskrit Vidyapeetha

J Garden Hist — Journal of Garden History

J Gard Hist — Journal of Garden History

J Gas Chromatogr — Journal of Gas Chromatography

J Gas Light Water Supply Sanit Improv — Journal of Gas Lighting, Water Supply, and Sanitary Improvement

JGC — Journal of General Chemistry

JGCEA — Journal of Geochemical Exploration

JGCRA — Journal of Gas Chromatography

JGE — Journal of General Education

J Gemmol — Journal of Gemmology

J Gen A Mic — Journal of General and Applied Microbiology

J Gen Appl Microbiol — Journal of General and Applied Microbiology

J Gen Chem USSR — Journal of General Chemistry of the USSR

J Gen Ed — Journal of General Education

J Gen Educ — Journal of General Education

J Genet — Journal of Genetics

J Genet Hum — Journal de Genetique Humaine

J Genet Psy — Journal of Genetic Psychology

J Genet Psychol — Journal of Genetic Psychology

J Gen Manag — Journal of General Management

J Gen Med Chir et Pharm — Journal General de Medecine, de Chirurgie, et de Pharmacie

J Gen Mgt — Journal of General Management

J Gen Micro — Journal of General Microbiology

J Gen Microbiol — Journal of General Microbiology

J Gen Physiol — Journal of General Physiology

J Gen Physl — Journal of General Physiology

J Gen Ps — Journal of Genetic Psychology

J Gen Psych — Journal of General Psychology

J Gen Psychol — Journal of General Psychology

J Gen Virol — Journal of General Virology

J Geo — Journal of Geology

J Geobot — Journal of Geobotany

J Geochem E — Journal of Geochemical Exploration

J Geochem Explor — Journal of Geochemical Exploration

J Geochem Soc India — Journal. Geochemical Society of India

JGEOD — Journal of Geophysics

J Geog — Journal Geographica

J Geog — Journal of Geography

J Geogr (Tokyo) — Journal of Geography (Tokyo)

J Geol — Journal of Geology

J Geol Educ — Journal of Geological Education

J Geol S In — Journal. Geological Society of India

J Geol Soc Aust — Journal. Geological Society of Australia

J Geol Soc Australia — Journal. Geological Society of Australia

J Geol Soc India — Journal. Geological Society of India

J Geol Soc Iraq — Journal. Geological Society of Iraq

J Geol Soc Jam — Journal. Geological Society of Jamaica

J Geol Soc Jpn — Journal. Geological Society of Japan

J Geol Soc London — Journal. Geological Society of London

J Geol Soc Philipp — Journal. Geological Society of the Philippines

J Geol Soc (Seoul) — Journal. Geological Society (Seoul)

J Geol Soc Thailand — Journal. Geological Society of Thailand

J Geol Soc Tokyo — Journal. Geological Society of Tokyo

J Geol UAR — Journal of Geology. United Arab Republic

J Geom — Journal of Geometry

J Geomagn G — Journal of Geomagnetism and Geoelectricity

J Geomagn Geoelec — Journal of Geomagnetism and Geoelectricity

J Geomagn & Geoelectr — Journal of Geomagnetism and Geoelectricity

J Geometry — Journal of Geometry

J Geoph Res — Journal of Geophysical Research

J Geophys — Journal of Geophysics

J Geophys Res — Journal of Geophysical Research

J Geophys Res B — Journal of Geophysical Research. Series B

J Geophys Res C Oceans — Journal of Geophysical Research. Series C. Oceans

J Geophys Res C Oceans Atmos — Journal of Geophysical Research. Series C. Oceans and Atmospheres

J Geophys Res D Atmos — Journal of Geophysical Research. Series D. Atmospheres

J Geo R-O A — Journal of Geophysical Research. Oceans and Atmosphere

J Geo R-S P — Journal of Geophysical Research. Space Physics

J Geosci Osaka City Univ — Journal of Geosciences. Osaka City University

J Geotech Eng Div Amer Soc Civil Eng Proc — Journal. Geotechnical Engineering Division. Proceedings of the American Society of Civil Engineers

J Geotech Eng Div Am Soc Civ Eng — Journal. Geotechnical Engineering Division. Proceedings of the American Society of Civil Engineers

J Geotech Engng Div ASCE — Journal. Geotechnical Engineering Division. American Society of Civil Engineers

J Geotech Engng Div Proc ASCE — Journal. Geotechnical Engineering Division. Proceedings of the American Society of Civil Engineers

JGEPs — Journal of Genetic Psychology

J Geriat Ps — Journal of Geriatric Psychiatry

J Geriatr Psychiatry — Journal of Geriatric Psychiatry

J Geront — Journal of Gerontology

J Gerontol — Journal of Gerontology

J Gerontol Nurs — Journal of Gerontological Nursing

J Gerontology — Journal of Gerontology

J Gerontol Soc Work — Journal of Gerontological Social Work

J Gesamte Oberflaechentech — Journal of Gesamte Oberflaechentechnik

JGF — Jenaer Germanistische Forschungen

JGG — Jahrbuch. Goethe-Gesellschaft

JGG — Jahrbuch. Grillparzer-Gesellschaft

JGGAS — Journal. Hongkong University. Geographical, Geological, and Archaeological Society

JGGJC — Jahrbuch. Gesellschaft fuer Geschichte der Juden in der Cechoslovakischen Republik [*Prague*]

JGGPO — Jahrbuch. Gesellschaft fuer die Geschichte des Protestantismus in Oesterreich

JGGPOes — Jahrbuch. Gesellschaft fuer die Geschichte des Protestantismus in Oesterreich

JGJ — Jahrbuch fuer die Geschichte der Juden

JGJC — Jahrbuch. Gesellschaft fuer Geschichte der Juden in der Cechoslovakischen Republik [*Prague*]

JGJJ — Jahrbuch fuer die Geschichte der Juden und des Judentums

JGJRI — Journal. Ganganatha Jha Research Institute

JGL — Jahrbuch fuer Juedische Geschichte und Literatur

JGL — Juedische Gemeinde Luzern

J Glaciol — Journal of Glaciology

J Glass Stud — Journal of Glass Studies

JGLGA — Jahrbuch. Gesellschaft fuer Lothringische Geschichte und Altertumskunde

JGLGAK — Jahrbuch. Gesellschaft fuer Lothringische Geschichte und Altertumskunde

JGLRD — Journal of Great Lakes Research

JGLS — Journal. Gypsy Lore Society

JGM — Journal of General Management [*United Kingdom*]

JGMAA — Journal of General Management

JGMOD — Jahrbuch fuer die Geschichte Mittel- und Ostdeutschlands

J GMS OSU — Journal. Graduate Music Students. Ohio State University

JGNOAC — Jugoslovenska Ginekologija i Opstetricija

JGNSKG — Jahrbuch. Gesellschaft fuer Niedersaechsische Kirchengeschichte

JGO — Jahrbuecher fuer Geschichte Osteuropas

JGOBA — Journal de Gynecologie, Obstetrique, et Biologie de la Reproduction [*Paris*]

JGOE — Jahrbuecher fuer Geschichte Osteuropas

JGOLR — Jaarboekje voor Geschiedenis en Oudheidkunde van Leiden en Rijnland

JGP — Journal of General Psychology

JGP — Journal of Genetic Psychology

JGPs — Journal of General Psychology

JGPSA — Journal of General Psychology

JGPYA — Journal of Genetic Psychology

JGR — Journal of Geophysical Research

J Grad Res Cent — Journal. Graduate Research Center.
J Grad Res Cent South Methodist Univ — Journal. Graduate Research Center. Southern Methodist University
J Graph Theory — Journal of Graph Theory
JGR C — Journal of Geophysical Research. Series C. Oceans and Atmospheres
J Great Lakes Res — Journal of Great Lakes Research
JGrG — Jahrbuch. Grillparzer-Gesellschaft
JGRI — Journal. Ganganatha Jha Research Institute
JGR J Geophys Res C Oceans Atmos — JGR. Journal of Geophysical Research. Series C. Oceans and Atmospheres
JGR J Geophys Res D Atmos — JGR. Journal of Geophysical Research. Series D. Atmospheres
J Group Experts Sci Aspects Mar Pollut — Joint Group of Experts on the Scientific Aspects of Marine Pollution
J Growth — Journal of Growth
JGRS — Journal. Gujarat Research Society [*India*]
JGS — Journal of Glass Studies
JGSLA — Journal. Geological Society of London
JGSTD — Journal. Gyeongsang National University. Science and Technology
JGSW — Journal of Gerontological Social Work
J Guidance & Control — Journal of Guidance and Control
J Guidance Control — Journal of Guidance and Control
J Guid Control — Journal of Guidance and Control [*United States*]
J Guid and Control — Journal of Guidance and Control
J Guid Control and Dyn — Journal of Guidance, Control, and Dynamics
J Gujarat Res Soc — Journal. Gujarat Research Society [*India*]
J Guj Res Soc — Journal. Gujarat Research Society [*India*]
JGW — Jahresbericht fuer Geschichtswissenschaft
JGWT — Jahrbuch. Gesellschaft fuer Wiener Theater-Forschung
J Gyeongsang Natl Univ Nat Sci — Journal. Gyeongsang National University. Natural Sciences [*Republic of Korea*]
J Gyeongsang Natl Univ Sci Technol — Journal. Gyeongsang National University. Science and Technology
JGyLS — Journal. Gypsy Lore Society
J Gynecol Obstet Biol Reprod — Journal de Gynecologie, Obstetrique, et Biologie de la Reproduction [*Paris*]
J Gynecol Pract — Journal of Gynecological Practice [*Japan*]
JH — Journal of History
J Hand Surg — Journal of Hand Surgery
J Hanyang Med Coll — Journal. Hanyang Medical College [*South Korea*]
J Haryana Stud — Journal of Haryana Studies
J Hattori Bot Lab — Journal. Hattori Botanical Laboratory
JHAW — Jahrbuch. Heidelberger Akademie der Wissenschaften
J Hawaii Dent Assoc — Journal. Hawaii Dental Association
J Hazard Mater — Journal of Hazardous Materials
J Hazard Materials — Journal of Hazardous Materials
J Hazardous Mat — Journal of Hazardous Materials
JHBSA — Journal of the History of the Behavioral Sciences
JhBW — Jahrbuch. Biblische Wissenschaften
J H Clearing House — Junior High Clearing House
JHD — Journal of the Hellenic Diaspora
JHE — Journal of Home Economics
J Health Care Market — Journal of Health Care Marketing
J Health Care Mkt — Journal of Health Care Marketing
J Health Econ — Journal of Health Economics
J Health Hum Behav — Journal of Health and Human Behavior
J Health Hum Resour Adm — Journal of Health and Human Resources Administration
J Health Hum Resources Admin — Journal of Health and Human Resources Administration
J Health Phys Ed Rec — Journal of Health, Physical Education, Recreation
J Health Phys Radiat Prot — Journal of Health Physics and Radiation Protection
J Health Pol — Journal of Health Politics, Policy, and Law
J Health Polit Policy Law — Journal of Health Politics, Policy, and Law
J Health Pol Poly and L — Journal of Health Politics, Policy, and Law
J Health So — Journal of Health and Social Behavior
J Health Soc Behav — Journal of Health and Social Behavior
J Health & Soc Behav — Journal of Health and Social Behavior
J Health & Social Behavior — Journal of Health and Social Behavior
J Heat Recovery Syst — Journal of Heat Recovery Systems [*England*]
J Heat Tran — Journal of Heat Transfer. Transactions of the American Society of Mechanical Engineers
J Heat Transfer — Journal of Heat Transfer. Transactions of the American Society of Mechanical Engineers. Series C
J Heat Transfer Trans ASME — Journal of Heat Transfer. Transactions of the American Society of Mechanical Engineers
J Heat Treat — Journal of Heat Treating [*United States*]
J Hebd Med — Journal Hebdomadaire de Medecine
J Hebei Univ Nat Sci Ed — Journal. Hebei University. Natural Science Edition
JHebrSt — Journal of Hebraic Studies [*New York*]
JHEL — Journal of Hellenic Studies
J Hellenic Stud — Journal of Hellenic Studies
J Hellen St — Journal of Hellenic Studies
J Hellen Stud — Journal of Hellenic Studies
J Hell Stud — Journal of Hellenic Studies

J Helminth — Journal of Helminthology
J Helminthol — Journal of Helminthology
J Hel Stud — Journal of Hellenic Studies
J Hered — Journal of Heredity
J Heredity — Journal of Heredity
J Herpetol — Journal of Herpetology
J Herpetol Assoc Afr — Journal. Herpetological Association of Africa
J Hetero Ch — Journal of Heterocyclic Chemistry
J Heterocycl Chem — Journal of Heterocyclic Chemistry
JHGA — Jahrbuch. K. K. Heraldische Gesellschaft, "Adler"
JHH — Journal of Health and Human Resources Administration
JHI — Journal of the History of Ideas
J Hi E — Journal of Higher Education
J High Educ — Journal of Higher Education
J Higher Educ — Journal of Higher Education
J High Polym (Shanghai) — Journal of High Polymers (Shanghai)
J High Resolut Chromatogr Chromatogr Commun — Journal of High Resolution Chromatography and Chromatography Communications [*West Germany*]
J High Temp Soc — Journal. High Temperature Society [*Japan*]
J High Temp Soc (Jpn) — Journal. High Temperature Society (Japan)
J Highw Div Am Soc Civ Eng — Journal. Highway Division. American Society of Civil Engineers
J Hirnforsch — Journal fuer Hirnforschung
J Hiroshima Med Assoc — Journal. Hiroshima Medical Association [*Japan*]
J Hiroshima Univ Dent Soc — Journal. Hiroshima University. Dental Society
J Hispan Ph — Journal of Hispanic Philology
J Hist Arabic Sci — Journal for the History of Arabic Science
J Hist Astron — Journal for the History of Astronomy
J Hist Astronom — Journal for the History of Astronomy
J Hist Beh — Journal of the History of the Behavioral Sciences
J Hist Behav Sci — Journal of the History of the Behavioral Sciences
J Hist Beh Sci — Journal of the History of the Behavioral Sciences
J Hist Biol — Journal of the History of Biology
J Hist Cyto — Journal of Histochemistry and Cytochemistry
J Hist Firearms Soc S Afr — Journal. Historical Firearms Society of South Africa
J Hist G — Journal of Historical Geography
J Hist Geog — Journal of Historical Geography
J Hist Geogr — Journal of Historical Geography
J Hist Idea — Journal of the History of Ideas
J Hist Ideas — Journal of the History of Ideas
J Hist Med — Journal of the History of Medicine and Allied Sciences
J Hist Med Allied Sci — Journal of the History of Medicine and Allied Sciences
J Histochem Cytochem — Journal of Histochemistry and Cytochemistry
J Histotechnol — Journal of Histotechnology [*United States*]
J Hist Phil — Journal of the History of Philosophy
J Hist Philos — Journal of the History of Philosophy
J Hist Res — Journal of Historical Research
J Hist Soc Church Wales — Journal. Historical Society of the Church in Wales
J Hist Soc Nigeria — Journal. Historical Society of Nigeria
J Hist Soc QD — Historical Society of Queensland. Journal
J Hist Soc Qld — Historical Society of Queensland. Journal
J Hist Stud — Journal of Historical Studies
J HK Br Roy Asiat Soc — Journal. Hong Kong Branch. Royal Asiatic Society
JHLB — Journal. Federal Home Loan Bank Board
JHM — Journal of the History of Medicine
JHMa — Johns Hopkins Magazine
JHO — Journal of Housing
JhOAI — Jahreshefte. Oesterreichisches Archaeologische Institut in Wien
J Ho E — Journal of Home Economics
J Hokkaido Dent Assoc — Journal. Hokkaido Dental Association
J Hokkaido Forest Prod Res Inst — Journal. Hokkaido Forest Products Research Institute
J Hokkaido Gakugei Univ — Journal. Hokkaido Gakugei University
J Hokkaido Gakugei Univ Sect B — Journal. Hokkaido Gakugei University. Section B [*Japan*]
J Hokkaido Univ Ed Sect IIA — Journal. Hokkaido University of Education. Section II-A
J Hokkaido Univ Educ — Journal. Hokkaido University of Education
J Hokkaido Univ Educ IIB — Journal. Hokkaido University of Education. Section II-B
J Hokkaido Univ Educ Sect II A — Journal. Hokkaido University of Education. Section II-A [*Japan*]
J Hokkaido Univ Educ Sect II-B — Journal. Hokkaido University of Education. Section II-B
J Hokkaido Univ Educ Sect II C — Journal. Hokkaido University of Education. Section II-C [*Japan*]
J of Home Ec Ed — Journal of Home Economics Education
J Home Econ — Journal of Home Economics
J Homosex — Journal of Homosexuality
J Homosexuality — Journal of Homosexuality
J Hong Kong Branch Roy Asiatic Soc — Journal. Hong Kong Branch. Royal Asiatic Society
J Hopeh Univ Nat Sci — Journal. Hopeh University. Natural Science [*People's Republic of China*]

J Horol Inst Jpn — Journal. Horological Institute of Japan
J Hortic Sci — Journal of Horticultural Science
J Hort Sci — Journal of Horticultural Science
J Hosp Dent Pract — Journal of Hospital Dental Practice
J Hospitality Educ — Journal of Hospitality Education
J Hotel Dieu de Montreal — Journal. Hotel Dieu de Montreal
J Housing — Journal of Housing
JHP — Journal of Hispanic Philology
JHP — Journal of the History of Philosophy
JHPh — Journal of the History of Philosophy
JHPLD — Journal of Health Politics, Policy, and Law
JHPP — Journal of Health Politics, Policy, and Law
JHR — Journal of Human Resources
JHS — Jewish History Series
JHS — Journal of Hellenic Studies
JHS — Journal of Historical Studies
JHS-AR — Journal of Hellenic Studies. Archaeological Reports
JHSB — Journal of Health and Social Behavior
JHSch — Jahresberichte ueber das Hoehre Schulwesen
JHSCW — Journal. Historical Society of the Church in Wales
JHSEM — Jewish Historical Society of England. Miscellanies
JHSET — Jewish Historical Society of England. Transactions
JHSN — Journal. Historical Society of Nigeria
JHSRLL — Johns Hopkins Studies in Romance Language and Literature
JHSS — Journal of History for Senior Students
JHSSA — Journal. Historical Society of South Australia
JHStud — Journal of Historical Studies
JHSUD — Journal of Hand Surgery
J Huazhong Inst Tech — Journal. Huazhong Institute of Technology. English Edition
J Huazhong Inst Technol — Journal. Huazhong Institute of Technology [*People's Republic of China*]
J Huazhong Inst Technol Engl Ed — Journal. Huazhong Institute of Technology. English Edition
J Huazhong Univ Sci Tech — Journal. Huazhong [*Central China*] University of Science and Technology. English Edition
JHUC — Journal. Hebrew Union College [*Cincinnati*]
J Humanistic Psychol — Journal of Humanistic Psychology
J of Human Rela — Journal of Human Relations
J Human Resources — Journal of Human Resources
J Human Stress — Journal of Human Stress
J Hum Ergol — Journal of Human Ergology
J Hum Ergol (Tokyo) — Journal of Human Ergology (Tokyo)
J Hum Evol — Journal of Human Evolution
J Hum Nutr — Journal of Human Nutrition
J Hu Move Stud — Journal of Human Movement Studies
J Hum Psy — Journal of Humanistic Psychology
J Hum Relat — Journal of Human Relations
J Hum Resources — Journal of Human Resources
J Hum Stress — Journal of Human Stress
J Hunan Univ — Journal. Hunan University
J Hunter Valley Research Foundation — Journal. Hunter Valley Research Foundation
J H U Studies — Johns Hopkins University. Studies in Historical and Political Science
JHVD — Jahrbuch. Historischer Verein Dillingen
JHVFB — Jahrbuch. Historischer Verein fuer das Fuerstbistum Bamberg
J Hyderabad Geol Surv — Journal. Hyderabad Geological Survey
J Hydr-ASCE — Journal. Hydraulics Division. American Society of Civil Engineers
J Hydraul Div Amer Soc Civil Eng Proc — Journal. Hydraulics Division. American Society of Civil Engineers. Proceedings
J Hydraul Div Am Soc Civ Eng — Journal. Hydraulics Division. American Society of Civil Engineers
J Hydraul Div Proc ASCE — Journal. Hydraulic Division. Proceedings of the American Society of Civil Engineers
J Hydraul Eng (Peking) — Journal of Hydraulic Engineering (Peking)
J Hydraul Res — Journal of Hydraulic Research
J Hydraul Res J Rech Hydraul — Journal of Hydraulic Research/Journal de Recherches Hydrauliques
J Hydrol — Journal of Hydrology [*New Zealand*]
J Hydrol (Neth) — Journal of Hydrology (Netherlands)
J Hydrol Sci — Journal of Hydrological Sciences [*Poland*]
J Hydronaut — Journal of Hydronautics
J Hyg — Journal of Hygiene
J Hyg (Camb) — Journal of Hygiene (Cambridge)
J Hyg Chem — Journal of Hygienic Chemistry
J Hyg Chem Soc Japan — Journal. Hygienic Chemical Society of Japan
J Hyg Epidemiol Microbiol Immunol — Journal of Hygiene, Epidemiology, Microbiology, and Immunology
J Hyg Epidemiol Microbiol Immunol (Prague) — Journal of Hygiene, Epidemiology, Microbiology, and Immunology (Prague)
J Hyg Ep Mi — Journal of Hygiene, Epidemiology, Microbiology, and Immunology
J Hygiene — Journal of Hygiene
J Hyg (Lond) — Journal of Hygiene (London)

J Hyg (Paris) — Journal d'Hygiene Clintologie (Paris)
JI — Japan Interpreter
JI — Journal. American Musical Instrument Society
JI — Journal of Insurance
JIA — Journal of Industrial Archaeology
JIA — Journal of International Affairs
JIAN — Journal International d'Archeologie Numismatique
JIAP — Journal. Indian Academy of Philosophy
J IARI Post-Grad Sch — Journal. IARI [*Indian Agricultural Research Institute*]. Post-Graduate School
JIAS — Journal. Indian Anthropological Society
JIAS — Journal of Interamerican Studies
JIASRA — Journal. International Arthur Schnitzler Research Association
JIB — Journal. Institute of Bankers
JIB — Journal of International Business Studies
J I Brewing — Journal. Institute of Brewing
JIBS — Journal of Indian and Buddhist Studies
J Ichthyol (Engl Trans Vopr Ikhtiol) — Journal of Ichthyology (English Translation of Voprosy Ikhtiologii)
J Ichthyol (USSR) — Journal of Ichthyology (USSR)
JICJ — International Commission of Jurists. Journal
JIDXA — Journal. Indiana State Medical Association
JIE — Journal of Industrial Economics
JIE — Journal of International Economics
JIECA — Journal of Industrial and Engineering Chemistry
JIEND — Jinetsu Enerugi
JIES — Journal of Indo-European Studies
JIFC — Journal. International Folk Music Council
JIFM — Journal. International Folk Music Council
JIFMC — Journal. International Folk Music Council
JIFSA — Journal. Indian Academy of Forensic Sciences
JIFUA — Journal. Institute of Fuel
J I Fuel — Journal. Institute of Fuel
JIG — Jahrbuch fuer Internationale Germanistik
JIG — Journal of Irish Genealogy
JIH — Journal of Indian History
JIHS — Journal. Illinois State Historical Society
JIHTA — Journal of Industrial Hygiene and Toxicology
JIHVE — Journal. Institution of Heating and Ventilating Engineers
JIIB — Journal. Indian Institute of Bankers
JIIM — Journal of Information and Image Management
JIKEA — Jikken Keitaigakushi
Jikeikai Med J — Jikeikai Medical Journal
JIL — George Washington Journal of International Law and Economics
JIL — Journal of Irish Literature
JILA Inf Cent Rep — Joint Institute for Laboratory Astrophysics. Information Center. Report
JILA Rep — Joint Institute for Laboratory Astrophysics. Report
JILEA — Journal. Institution of Locomotive Engineers
JILI — Journal. Indian Law Institute
J Ill Hist Soc — Journal. Illinois State Historical Society
JILLHS — Journal. Illinois State Historical Society
J Ill State Hist Soc — Journal. Illinois State Historical Society
J Illum Eng Inst Jap — Journal. Illuminating Engineering Institute of Japan
J Illum Engng Soc — Journal. Illuminating Engineering Society
J Illum Eng Soc — Journal. Illuminating Engineering Society
JIM — Journal of Information Management
J IMA — Journal. Islamic Medical Association of the United States and Canada
J Imaging Technol — Journal of Imaging Technology
J I Math Ap — Journal. Institute of Mathematics and Its Applications
JIMEA — Journal. Institute of Metals
JIMGA — Journal of Immunogenetics
J Immun — Journal of Immunology
J Immunoassay — Journal of Immunoassay
J Immunogen — Journal of Immunogenetics
J Immunogenet — Journal of Immunogenetics
J Immunol — Journal of Immunology
J Immunol M — Journal of Immunological Methods
J Immunol Methods — Journal of Immunological Methods
J Immunopharmacol — Journal of Immunopharmacology
J Imp Agr Exp Sta (Tokyo) — Journal. Imperial Agricultural Experiment Station (Tokyo)
J Imp Coll Chem Eng Soc — Journal. Imperial College. Chemical Engineering Society
J Imp Coll Chem Soc — Journal. Imperial College. Chemical Society
J Imp Com H — Journal of Imperial and Commonwealth History
J Imp Commonw Hist — Journal of Imperial and Commonwealth History
J Imp Fish Inst (Jpn) — Journal. Imperial Fisheries Institute (Japan)
JIMS — Journal. Indian Mathematical Society
JIMSA — Journal. Irish Medical Association
JIN — Journal of International Economics
JIN — Journal of Israel Numismatics
JINBA — Journal. Institute of Brewing
J Inc Aust Insurance Inst — Journal. Incorporated Australian Insurance Institute

J Inc Brew Guild — Journal. Incorporated Brewers' Guild
J Inc Clerks Works Assoc GB — Journal. Incorporated Clerks of Works Association of Great Britain
J Ind — Journal of Industry
J Ind Acad Philo — Journal. Indian Academy of Philosophy
J Ind Aero — Journal of Industrial Aerodynamics
J Ind Aerodyn — Journal of Industrial Aerodynamics
J Ind Anthropol Soc — Journal. Indian Anthropological Society
J Ind Arts Ed — Journal of Industrial Arts Education
J Ind Bot Soc — Journal. Indian Botanical Society
J Ind Ch S — Journal. Indian Chemical Society
J Ind Econ — Journal of Industrial Economics
J Ind Eng — Journal of Industrial Engineering
J Ind Eng Chem — Journal of Industrial and Engineering Chemistry [*United States*]
J Ind Engng Chem — Journal of Industrial and Engineering Chemistry
J Ind Explos Soc (Jap) — Journal. Industrial Explosives Society. Explosion and Explosives (Japan)
J Ind Gaz — Journal des Industries du Gaz
J Ind Hist — Journal of Indian History
J Ind Hyg — Journal of Industrial Hygiene
J Ind Hyg — Journal of Industrial Hygiene and Toxicology
J Ind Hyg Toxicol — Journal of Industrial Hygiene and Toxicology
J Indian Acad Forensic Sci — Journal. Indian Academy of Forensic Sciences
J Indian Acad Geosci — Journal. Indian Academy of Geoscience
J Indian Acad Phil — Journal. Indian Academy of Philosophy
J Indian Acad Sci — Journal. Indian Academy of Sciences
J Indian Acad Wood Sci — Journal. Indian Academy of Wood Science
J Indiana Dent Assoc — Journal. Indiana Dental Association
J Indian Anthropol Soc — Journal. Indian Anthropological Society
J Indianap Dist Dent Soc — Journal. Indianapolis District Dental Society
J Indiana State Med Assoc — Journal. Indiana State Medical Association
J Indian Bot Soc — Journal. Indian Botanical Society
J Indian Ceram Soc — Journal. Indian Ceramic Society
J Indian Chem Soc — Journal. Indian Chemical Society
J Indian Chem Soc Ind News Ed — Journal. Indian Chemical Society. Industrial and News Edition [*India*]
J Indian Dent Assoc — Journal. Indian Dental Association
J Indian Geophys Union — Journal. Indian Geophysical Union
J Indian Hist — Journal of Indian History
J Indian I — Journal. Indian Institute of Science
J Indian Ind Labour — Journal of Indian Industries and Labour
J Indian Inst Sci — Journal. Indian Institute of Science
J Indian Inst Sci Sect A — Journal. Indian Institute of Science. Section A
J Indian Inst Sci Sect B — Journal. Indian Institute of Science. Section B
J Indian Inst Sci Sect C — Journal. Indian Institute of Science. Section C
J Indian Leather Technol Assoc — Journal. Indian Leather Technologists Association
J Indian Math Soc — Journal. Indian Mathematical Society
J Indian Med Ass — Journal. Indian Medical Association
J Indian Med Assoc — Journal. Indian Medical Association
J Indian Med Prof — Journal of the Indian Medical Profession
J Indian Musicol Soc — Journal. Indian Musicological Society
J Indian Nat Soc Soil Mech Found Eng — Journal. Indian National Society of Soil Mechanics and Foundation Engineering
J Indian P — Journal of Indian Philosophy
J Indian Pediatr Soc — Journal. Indian Pediatric Society
J Indian Phil — Journal of Indian Philosophy
J Indian Refract Makers Assoc — Journal. Indian Refractory Makers Association
J Indian Roads Congr — Journal. Indian Roads Congress
J Indian Soc Agric Stat — Journal. Indian Society of Agricultural Statistics
J Indian Soc Agr Statist — Journal. Indian Society of Agricultural Statistics
J Indian Soc Soil Sci — Journal. Indian Society of Soil Science
J Indian Soc Statist Oper Res — Journal. Indian Society of Statistics and Operations Research
J Indian Statist Assoc — Journal. Indian Statistical Association
J India Soc Eng — Journal. India Society of Engineers
J Individ Psychol — Journal of Individual Psychology
J Indiv Psy — Journal of Individual Psychology
J Ind Musicol Soc — Journal. Indian Musicological Society
J Indn Acad Math — Indian Academy of Mathematics. Journal
J Indn St A — Journal. Indian Statistical Association
J Indo-Eur — Journal of Indo-European Studies
J Indo-European Stud — Journal of Indo-European Studies
J Ind Philo — Journal of Indian Philosophy
J Ind Rel — Journal of Industrial Relations
J Ind Relations — Journal of Industrial Relations
J Ind Teach Educ — Journal of Industrial Teacher Education
J Ind Technol — Journal of Industrial Technology [*South Korea*]
J Ind Technol Myong-Ji Univ — Journal of Industrial Technology. Myong-Ji University [*Republic of Korea*]
J Ind Trade — Journal of Industry and Trade
J Indus Rel — Journal of Industrial Relations
J Indust — Journal of Industry
J Indust Hyg — Journal of Industrial Hygiene

J Industr Econ — Journal of Industrial Economics
J Indust Relations — Journal of Industrial Relations
J Industr Relat — Journal of Industrial Relations
J Industr Teacher Educ — Journal of Industrial Teacher Education
J Industry — Journal of Industry
JINEA — Journal. Indian Chemical Society. Industrial and News Edition
J Infect Dis — Journal of Infectious Diseases
J Info Mgmt — Journal of Information Management
J Inf and Optimiz Sci — Journal of Information and Optimization Sciences
J Information Processing — Journal of Information Processing
J Inform Optim Sci — Journal of Information and Optimization Sciences
J Inform Process — Journal of Information Processing
J Info Sci — Journal of Information Science. Principles and Practice
J Info Sys Mgmt — Journal of Information Systems Management
J Inf Process Soc Jap — Journal. Information Processing Society of Japan
J Inf Process Soc Jpn — Journal. Information Processing Society of Japan
J Inf Sci — Journal of Information Science [*Netherlands*]
J Inf Sci Princ and Pract — Journal of Information Science. Principles and Practice
J Inf Tech Ind Fonderie — Journal d'Informations Techniques des Industries de la Fonderie
J Ing — Journal des Ingenieurs
J Inherited Metab Dis — Journal of Inherited Metabolic Disease
J Inl Fish Soc India — Journal. Inland Fisheries Society of India
J Inorg Biochem — Journal of Inorganic Biochemistry
J Inorg Chem (USSR) — Journal of Inorganic Chemistry (USSR)
J Inorg Nuc — Journal of Inorganic and Nuclear Chemistry
J Inorg Nucl Chem — Journal of Inorganic and Nuclear Chemistry
J Inorg and Nucl Chem — Journal of Inorganic and Nuclear Chemistry
J Ins — Journal of Insurance
J Insect Path — Journal of Insect Pathology
J Insect Pathol — Journal of Insect Pathology
J Insect Ph — Journal of Insect Physiology
J Insect Physiol — Journal of Insect Physiology
Jinsen Med J — Jinsen Medical Journal
J Insp Sch — Journal of Inspectors of Schools of Australia and New Zealand
J Inst Agric Resour Utiliz Chinju Agric Coll — Journal. Institute for Agricultural Resources Utilization. Chinju Agricultural College
J Inst Anim Tech — Journal. Institute of Animal Technicians
J Inst Auto & Aero Engrs — Journal. Institution of Automotive and Aeronautical Engineers
J Inst Automob Eng (London) — Journal. Institution of Automobile Engineers (London)
J Inst Automot Aeronaut Eng — Journal. Institution of Automotive and Aeronautical Engineers
J Inst Automotive & Aeronautical Eng — Journal. Institution of Automotive and Aeronautical Engineers
J Inst Automotive & Aeronautical Engrs — Journal. Institution of Automotive and Aeronautical Engineers
J Inst Brew — Journal. Institute of Brewing
J Inst Br Foundrymen — Journal. Institute of British Foundrymen
J Inst Can Sci Technol Aliment — Journal. Institut Canadien de Science et Technologie Alimentaire
J Inst Can Technol Aliment — Journal. Institut Canadien de Technologie Alimentaire
J Inst Certif Eng (S Afr) — Journal. Institution of Certificated Engineers (South Africa)
J Inst Chem (India) — Journal. Institute of Chemistry (India)
J Inst Chem (India) — Journal. Institution of Chemists (India)
J Inst Civ Eng — Journal. Institution of Civil Engineers
J Inst Clerks Works GB — Journal. Institute of Clerks of Works of Great Britain
J Inst Clerks Works G Bt — Journal. Institute of Clerks of Works of Great Britain
J Inst Comput Sci — Journal. Institution of Computer Sciences
J Inst Def Stud Anal — Journal. Institute for Defence Studies and Analyses
J Inst Draftsmen — Journal. Institute of Draftsmen
J Inst Electr Commun Eng Jap — Journal. Institute of Electrical Communication Engineers of Japan [*Later, Journal. Institute of Electronics and Communication Engineers of Japan*]
J Inst Electr Eng — Journal. Institute of Electrical Engineers [*South Korea*]
J Inst Electr Eng — Journal. Institution of Electrical Engineers [*England*]
J Inst Electr Eng Jpn — Journal. Institution of Electrical Engineers of Japan
J Inst Electr Eng Part 1 — Journal. Institution of Electrical Engineers. Part 1. General
J Inst Electr Eng Part 2 — Journal. Institution of Electrical Engineers. Part 2. Power Engineering
J Inst Electr Eng Part 3 — Journal. Institution of Electrical Engineers. Part 3. Radio and Communication Engineering
J Inst Electron Commun Eng Jap — Journal. Institute of Electronics and Communication Engineers of Japan
J Inst Electron and Commun Eng Jpn — Journal. Institute of Electronics and Communication Engineers of Japan
J Inst Electron Telecommun Eng — Journal. Institution of Electronics and Telecommunication Engineers
J Inst Energy — Journal. Institute of Energy [*United Kingdom*]

J Inst Eng (Aust) — Journal. Institution of Engineers (Australia)
J Inst Eng (India) — Journal. Institution of Engineers (India)
J Inst Eng (India) Chem Eng Div — Journal. Institution of Engineers (India). Chemical Engineering Division
J Inst Eng (India) Civ Eng Div — Journal. Institution of Engineers (India). Civil Engineering Division
J Inst Eng (India) Elec Eng Div — Journal. Institution of Engineers (India). Electrical Engineering Division
J Inst Eng (India) Electron Telecommun Eng Div — Journal. Institution of Engineers (India). Electronics and Telecommunication Engineering Division
J Inst Eng (India) Electron and Telecommun Eng Div — Journal. Institution of Engineers (India). Electronics and Telecommunication Engineering Division
J Inst Eng (India) Gen Eng Div — Journal. Institution of Engineers (India). General Engineering Division
J Inst Eng (India) Ind Dev Gen Eng Div — Journal. Institution of Engineers (India). Industrial Development and General Engineering Division
J Inst Eng (India) Interdisciplinary and Gen Eng — Journal. Institution of Engineers (India). Interdisciplinary and General Engineering
J Inst Eng (India) Mech Eng Div — Journal. Institution of Engineers (India). Mechanical Engineering Division
J Inst Eng (India) Mining Met Div — Journal. Institution of Engineers (India). Mining and Metallurgy Division
J Inst Eng (India) Min Metall Div — Journal. Institution of Engineers (India). Mining and Metallurgy Division
J Inst Eng (India) Min and Metall Div — Journal. Institution of Engineers (India). Mining and Metallurgy Division
J Inst Eng (India) Part IDGE — Journal. Institution of Engineers (India). Part IDGE [*Industrial Development and General Engineering*]
J Inst Eng (India) Pub Health Eng Div — Journal. Institution of Engineers (India). Public Health Engineering Division
J Inst Eng (India) Public Health Eng Div — Journal. Institution of Engineers (India). Public Health Engineering Division
J Inst Eng (Malaysia) — Journal. Institution of Engineers (Malaysia)
J Inst Engrs (Aust) — Journal. Institution of Engineers (Australia)
J Inst Engrs (Australia) — Journal. Institution of Engineers (Australia)
J Inst Engrs (India) Part CI — Journal. Institution of Engineers (India). Part CI
J Inst Engrs (India) Part ME — Journal. Institution of Engineers (India). Part ME
J Inst Fuel — Journal. Institute of Fuel
J Inst Geol Vikram Univ — Journal. Institute of Geology. Vikram University
J Inst Highw Eng — Journal. Institute of Highway Engineers
J Inst (India) Electron Telecommun Eng Div — Journal. Institution of Engineers (India). Electronics and Telecommunication Engineering Division
J Institute Socioecon Stud — Journal. Institute for Socioeconomic Studies
J Inst Math and Appl — Journal. Institute of Mathematics and Its Applications
J Inst Math Appl — Journal. Institute of Mathematics and Its Applications
J Inst Math Applic — Journal. Institute of Mathematics and Its Applications
J Inst Math Its Appl — Journal. Institute of Mathematics and Its Applications
J Inst Met (Lond) — Journal. Institute of Metals (London)
J Inst Mine Surv S Afr — Journal. Institute of Mine Surveyors of South Africa
J Inst Min Surv S Afr — Journal. Institute of Mine Surveyors of South Africa
J Inst Munic Eng — Journal. Institution of Municipal Engineers
J Inst Navig — Journal. Institute of Navigation
J Instn Engrs (Aust) — Journal. Institution of Engineers (Australia)
J Instn Gas Engrs — Journal. Institution of Gas Engineers
J Instn Heat Vent Engrs — Journal. Institution of Heating and Ventilating Engineers
J Instn Highw Engrs — Journal. Institution of Highway Engineers
J Instn Loco Engrs — Journal. Institution of Locomotive Engineers
J Instn Munic Engrs — Journal. Institution of Municipal Engineers
J Instn Nucl Engrs — Journal. Institution of Nuclear Engineers
J Instn Rubb Ind — Journal. Institution of the Rubber Industry
J Inst Nucl Eng — Journal. Institution of Nuclear Engineers
J Inst Nucl Mater Manage — Journal. Institute of Nuclear Materials Management
J Instn Wat Engrs — Journal. Institution of Water Engineers
J Instn Wat Engrs Scientists — Journal. Institution of Water Engineers and Scientists
J Inst Pet — Journal. Institute of Petroleum
J Inst Pet Abstr — Journal. Institute of Petroleum. Abstracts
J Inst Pet Technol — Journal. Institution of Petroleum Technologists [*England*]
J Inst Polytech Osaka City Univ Ser C — Journal. Institute of Polytechnics. Osaka City University. Series C. Chemistry
J Inst Polytech Osaka City Univ Ser D — Journal. Institute of Polytechnics. Osaka City University. Series D. Biology
J Inst Polytech Osaka City Univ Ser E — Journal. Institute of Polytechnics. Osaka City University. Series E. Engineering
J Inst Polytech Osaka City Univ Ser G — Journal. Institute of Polytechnics. Osaka City University. Series G. Geoscience
J Inst Polytech Osaka Cy Univ — Journal. Institute of Polytechnics. Osaka City University
J Inst Prod Eng — Journal. Institution of Production Engineers
J Inst Public Health Eng — Journal. Institution of Public Health Engineers

J Instr Psychol — Journal of Instructional Psychology
J Inst Rubber Ind — Journal. Institution of the Rubber Industry
J Instrum Soc Am — Journal. Instrument Society of America
J Inst Saf High Pressure Gas Eng — Journal. Institute of Safety of High Pressure Gas Engineering [*Japan*]
J Inst Sanit Eng — Journal. Institution of Sanitary Engineers
J Inst Sci Technol — Journal. Institute of Science Technology
J Inst Socioecon Stud — Journal. Institute for Socioeconomic Studies [*United States*]
J Inst Telecommun Eng — Journal. Institution of Telecommunication Engineers
J Inst Telecommun Eng (New Delhi) — Journal. Institution of Telecommunication Engineers (New Delhi)
J Inst Telev Eng Jpn — Journal. Institute of Television Engineers of Japan
J Inst Transp — Journal. Institute of Transport
J Inst Transport — Journal. Institute of Transport (Australian Section)
J Inst Water Eng — Journal. Institution of Water Engineers
J Inst Water Engrs & Sci — Journal. Institution of Water Engineers and Scientists
J Inst Wood Sci — Journal. Institute of Wood Science
J Int Aff — Journal of International Affairs
J Int A Mat — Journal. International Association for Mathematical Geology
J Intam St — Journal of Interamerican Studies and World Affairs
J Int Ass Math Geol — Journal. International Association for Mathematical Geology
J Int Assoc Artif Prolongation Hum Specific Lifespan — Journal. International Association on the Artificial Prolongation of the Human Specific Lifespan
J Int Assoc Math Geol — Journal. International Association for Mathematical Geology
J Int Bus Stud — Journal of International Business Studies
J Int Cancer — Journal International du Cancer
J Int Coll Surg — Journal. International College of Surgeons [*United States*]
JINTD — Journal of Industrial Technology. Myong-Ji University
J Int Econ — Journal of International Economics
J Integral Equations — Journal of Integral Equations
J Interamer Stud — Journal of Interamerican Studies and World Affairs
J Interam Stud — Journal of Interamerican Studies and World Affairs
J Interam Stud World Aff — Journal of Interamerican Studies and World Affairs
J Intercultural Stud — Journal of Intercultural Studies
J Interd Cy — Journal of Interdisciplinary Cycle Research
J Interd H — Journal of Interdisciplinary History
J Interdiscip Cycle Res — Journal of Interdisciplinary Cycle Research
J Interdiscip Hist — Journal of Interdisciplinary History
J Interdiscipl Cycle Res — Journal of Interdisciplinary Cycle Research
J Interdisciplinary Modeling Simulation — Journal of Interdisciplinary Modeling and Simulation
J Interdis H — Journal of Interdisciplinary History
J Interdis Hist — Journal of Interdisciplinary History
J Intergroup Rel — Journal of Intergroup Relations
J of Intergroup Rela — Journal of Intergroup Relations
J Internat Affairs — Journal of International Affairs
J Internat Assoc Mathematical Geol — Journal. International Association for Mathematical Geology
J Internat Assoc Math Geol — Journal. International Association for Mathematical Geology
J Internat Bus Studies — Journal of International Business Studies
J Internat Econ — Journal of International Economics
J Internat Law and Econ — Journal of International Law and Economics
J of Internat L and Econ — Journal of International Law and Economics
J Internat Rel — Journal of International Relations
J Intern Rel — Journal of International Relations
J Int Fed Gynaecol Obstet — Journal. International Federation of Gynaecology and Obstetrics
J Int Inst Sugar Beet Res — Journal. International Institute for Sugar Beet Research
J Intl Aff — Journal of International Affairs
J Int Law E — Journal of International Law and Economics
J Int Law & Econ — Journal of International Law and Economics
J Int L and Ec — Journal of International Law and Economics
J Intl L and Econ — Journal of International Law and Economics
J Int Med R — Journal of International Medical Research
J Int Med Res — Journal of International Medical Research
J Int Num — Journal of International Numismatics
J Int Phonetic Assoc — Journal. International Phonetic Association
J Int Psychol — Journal International de Psychologie
J Int Relations — Journal of International Relations
J Int Th C — Journal. Interdenominational Theological Center
J Int Vitaminol Nutr — Journal International de Vitaminologie et de Nutrition
J I Nucl En — Journal. Institution of Nuclear Engineers
J Inver Pat — Journal of Invertebrate Pathology
J Invertebr Pathol — Journal of Invertebrate Pathology
J Invert Path — Journal of Invertebrate Pathology
J Inves Der — Journal of Investigative Dermatology
J Invest Dermatol — Journal of Investigative Dermatology
JIO — Journal of Industrial Economics (Oxford)

JIOS — Journal of Information and Optimization Sciences
J Iowa Med Soc — Journal. Iowa Medical Society
J Iowa State Med Soc — Journal. Iowa State Medical Society
JIP — Journal of Indian Philosophy
JIPA — Journal. Indian Potato Association
JIPA — Journal. International Phonetic Association
JIPEA — Journal. Institute of Petroleum
JIPHA — Journal of Insect Physiology
JIR — Journal of Industrial Relations
J Iraqi Chem Soc — Journal. Iraqi Chemical Society
J Iraqi Med Prof — Journal of the Iraqi Medical Professions
J Ir Coll Physicians Surg — Journal. Irish Colleges of Physicians and Surgeons
J Ir Dent Assoc — Journal. Irish Dental Association
JIRIA — Jibi To Rinsho
J Irish C P — Journal. Irish Colleges of Physicians and Surgeons
J Irish Lit — Journal of Irish Literature
J Ir Med Assoc — Journal. Irish Medical Association
J Iron & Steel Eng — Journal of Iron and Steel Engineering
J Iron Steel Inst Jpn — Journal. Iron and Steel Institute of Japan
J Iron Steel Inst (London) — Journal. Iron and Steel Institute (London)
J Iron St Inst — Journal. Iron and Steel Institute
J Irrig Drain Div Am Soc Civ Eng — Journal. Irrigation and Drainage Division. Proceedings of the American Society of Civil Engineers
J Irrig Drain Div ASCE — Journal. Irrigation and Drainage Division. American Society of Civil Engineers
J Irrig & Drain Div Proc ASCE — Journal. Irrigation and Drainage Division. Proceedings of the American Society of Civil Engineers
JiS — Jezik in Slovstvo
JIS — Journal. Institute for Socioeconomic Studies
JIS — Journal of Insurance
JISCD — Journal of Information Science
JISGA — Journal. Institution of Engineers (Australia)
JISHS — Journal. Illinois State Historical Society
J-ism Quart — Journalism Quarterly
J Isr Med Assoc — Journal. Israel Medical Association
JISS — Journal. Indian Sociological Society
JISSD — Journal. Institute for Socioeconomic Studies
JITE — Journal. Institution of Telecommunication Engineers
JITH — Journal of Indian Textile History
JITHA — Journal of Ichthyology [*English Translation*]
JITUD — Journal of Industrial Technology. Daegu University
JIUEAV — Junta de Investigacoes do Ultramar. Estudos, Ensaios, e Documentos
J Iwate Daigaku Nogaku — Journal. Iwate Daigaku Nogaku-Bu
J Iwate Med Assoc — Journal. Iwate Medical Association
JIWE — Journal of Indian Writing in English
J I Wood Sc — Journal. Institute of Wood Science
JIWSA — Journal. Institute of Wood Science
JIZAAA — Journal. Anthropological Society of Nippon
JJ — Journal of Jazz Studies
J Japanese Trade and Industry — Journal of Japanese Trade and Industry
J Japan Hydraul & Pneum Soc — Journal. Japan Hydraulic and Pneumatic Society
J Japan Soc Lubr Engrs — Journal. Japan Society of Lubrication Engineers
J Japan Soc Lubr Enrs Int Edn — Journal. Japan Society of Lubrication Engineers. International Edition
J Japan Soc Precis Engng — Journal. Japan Society of Precision Engineering
J Japan Soc Vet Sc — Journal. Japanese Society of Veterinary Science
J Japan Statist Soc — Journal. Japan Statistical Society
J Japan Wood Res Soc — Journal. Japan Wood Research Society
J Jap Assoc Autom Control Eng — Journal. Japan Association of Automatic Control Engineers
J Jap Assoc Infect Dis — Journal. Japanese Association for Infectious Diseases
J Jap Assoc Philos Sci — Journal. Japan Association for Philosophy of Science
J Jap Biochem Soc — Journal. Japanese Biochemical Society
J Jap Bot — Journal of Japanese Botany
J Jap Chem — Journal of Japanese Chemistry
J Jap For Soc — Journal. Japanese Forestry Society
J Jap Inst Light Metals — Journal. Japan Institute of Light Metals
J Jap Inst Met — Journal. Japan Institute of Light Metals
J Jap S Lub — Journal. Japan Society of Lubrication Engineers
J Jap Soc Air Pol — Journal. Japan Society of Air Pollution
J Jap Soc Civ Eng — Journal. Japan Society of Civil Engineers
J Jap Soc Fd Nutr — Journal. Japanese Society of Food and Nutrition
J Jap Soc Food Nutr — Journal. Japanese Society of Food and Nutrition
J Jap Soc Grassland Sci — Journal. Japanese Society of Grassland Science
J Jap Soc Grassld Sci — Journal. Japanese Society of Grassland Science
J Jap Soc Mech Eng — Journal. Japan Society of Mechanical Engineers
J Jap Soc Powder Met — Journal. Japan Society of Powder and Powder Metallurgy
J Jap Soc Precis Eng — Journal. Japan Society of Precision Engineering
J Jap Soc Technol Plast — Journal. Japan Society for Technology of Plasticity
J Jap Turfgrass Res Assoc — Journal. Japan Turfgrass Research Association
J Jap Vet Med Ass — Journal. Japan Veterinary Medical Association
J Jap Wood Res Soc — Journal. Japan Wood Research Society
J Ja Stud — Journal of Japanese Studies

J Jazz Stud — Journal of Jazz Studies
J Jazz Studies — Journal of Jazz Studies
JJCL — Jadavpur Journal of Comparative Literature
JJCRA — Japanese Journal of Clinical Radiology
JJCS — Journal of Jewish Communal Service
JJE — Japanese Journal of Ethnology
JJeCoS — Journal of Jewish Communal Service
J Jew Commun Serv — Journal of Jewish Communal Service
J Jewish Communal Service — Journal of Jewish Communal Service
J Jewish St — Journal of Jewish Studies
JJewLorePh — Journal of Jewish Lore and Philosophy [*New York*]
JJewS — Journal of Jewish Studies
JJFED — JFE. Journal du Four Electrique and des Industries Electrochimiques
JJGL — Jahrbuch fuer Juedische Geschichte und Literatur [*Berlin*]
JJIND — JNCI. Journal of the National Cancer Institute
J Jinsen Med Sci — Journal of Jinsen Medical Sciences
J Jiwaji Univ — Journal. Jiwaji University
J JJ Group Hosp Grant Med Coll — Journal. JJ Group of Hospitals and Grant Medical College
JJK — Josai Jinbun Kenkyu [*Studies in the Humanities*]
JJLG — Jahrbuch. Juedisch-Literarische Gesellschaft [*Frankfurt Am Main*]
JJOGA — Journal. Japanese Obstetrical and Gynecological Society
J Johannesburg Hist Found — Journal. Johannesburg Historical Foundation
J Joint Panel Nucl Mar Propul — Journal. Joint Panel on Nuclear Marine Propulsion
JJOMD — JOM. Journal of Occupational Medicine
JJOPA7 — Japanese Journal of Ophthalmology
JJP — Journal of Juristic Papyrology
JJPAA — Japanese Journal of Pharmacology
JJPAAZ — Japanese Journal of Pharmacology
JJPES — Journal. Jewish Palestine Exploration Society [*Jerusalem*]
JJPG — Jahrbuch. Jean-Paul-Gesellschaft
JJPHA — Japanese Journal of Physiology
JJPHAM — Japanese Journal of Physiology
JJPHDP — Japanese Journal of Phycology
J Jpn Accident Med Assoc — Journal. Japan Accident Medical Association
J Jpn Anodizing Assoc — Journal. Japanese Anodizing Association
J Jpn Assoc Automat Control Eng — Journal. Japan Association of Automatic Control Engineers
J Jpn Assoc Infect Dis — Journal. Japanese Association for Infectious Diseases
J Jpn Assoc Mineral Pet Econ Geol — Journal. Japanese Association of Mineralogists, Petrologists, and Economic Geologists
J Jpn Assoc Periodontol — Journal. Japanese Association of Periodontology
J Jpn Assoc Pet Technol — Journal. Japanese Association of Petroleum Technologists
J Jpn Assoc Phys Med Balneol Climatol — Journal. Japanese Association of Physical Medicine, Balneology, and Climatology
J Jpn Assoc Thorac Surg — Journal. Japanese Association for Thoracic Surgery
J Jpn Biochem Soc — Journal. Japanese Biochemical Society
J Jpn Boiler Assoc — Journal. Japan Boiler Association
J Jpn Bot — Journal of Japanese Botany
J Jpn Broncho-Esophagol Soc — Journal. Japan Broncho-Esophagological Society
J Jpn Chem — Journal of Japanese Chemistry
J Jpn Chem Suppl — Journal of Japanese Chemistry. Supplement
J Jpn Coll Angiol — Journal. Japanese College of Angiology
J Jpn Contact Lens Soc — Journal. Japan Contact Lens Society
J Jpn Crystallogr Soc — Journal. Japanese Crystallographical Society
J Jpn Dent Anesth Soc — Journal. Japanese Dental Anesthesia Society
J Jpn Dermatol Assoc — Journal. Japanese Dermatological Association
J Jpn Diabetic Soc — Journal. Japan Diabetic Society
J Jpn Electr Assoc — Journal. Japan Electric Association
J Jpn For Soc — Journal. Japanese Forestry Society
J Jpn Gas Assoc — Journal. Japan Gas Association
J Jpn Geotherm Energy Assoc — Journal. Japan Geothermal Energy Association
J Jpn Health Phys Soc — Journal. Japan Health Physics Society
J Jpn Hosp Assoc — Journal. Japan Hospital Association
J Jpn Inst Landscape Archit — Journal. Japanese Institute of Landscape Architects
J Jpn Inst Light Met — Journal. Japan Institute of Light Metals
J Jpn Inst Met — Journal. Japan Institute of Metals
J Jpn Inst Met (Sendai) — Journal. Japan Institute of Metals (Sendai)
J Jpn Inst Navig — Journal. Japan Institute of Navigation
J Jpn Med Assoc — Journal. Japan Medical Association
J Jpn Med Coll — Journal. Japan Medical College
J Jpn Obstet Gynecol Soc (Engl Ed) — Journal. Japanese Obstetrical and Gynecological Society (English Edition)
J Jpn Obstet Gynecol Soc (Jpn Ed) — Journal. Japanese Obstetrical and Gynecological Society (Japanese Edition)
J Jpn Oil Chem Soc — Journal. Japan Oil Chemists Society
J Jpn Orthop Assoc — Journal. Japanese Orthopaedic Association
J Jpn Pet Inst — Journal. Japan Petroleum Institute
J Jpn Psychosom Soc — Journal. Japanese Psychosomatic Society

J Jpn Res Assoc Text End-Uses — Journal. Japan Research Association for Textile End-Uses

J Jpn Soc Aeronaut and Space Sci — Journal. Japan Society for Aeronautical and Space Sciences

J Jpn Soc Air Pollut — Journal. Japan Society of Air Pollution

J Jpn Soc Blood Transfus — Journal. Japan Society of Blood Transfusion

J Jpn Soc Cancer Ther — Journal. Japan Society for Cancer Therapy

J Jpn Soc Compos Mater — Journal. Japan Society of Composite Materials

J Jpn Soc Dent Appar Mater — Journal. Japan Society for Dental Apparatus and Materials

J Jpn Soc Food Nutr — Journal. Japanese Society of Food and Nutrition

J Jpn Soc Grassl Sci — Journal. Japanese Society of Grassland Science

J Jpn Soc Herb Crops Grassl Farming — Journal. Japanese Society of Herbage Crops and Grassland Farming

J Jpn Soc Hortic Sci — Journal. Japanese Society for Horticultural Science

J Jpn Soc Lubr Eng — Journal. Japan Society of Lubrication Engineers

J Jpn Soc Powder Metall — Journal. Japan Society of Powder and Powder Metallurgy

J Jpn Soc Powder Powder Metall — Journal. Japan Society of Powder and Powder Metallurgy

J Jpn Soc Precis Eng — Journal. Japan Society of Precision Engineering

J Jpn Soc Reticuloendothel Syst — Journal. Japan Society of the Reticuloendothelial System

J Jpn Soc Simulation Technol — Journal. Japan Society for Simulation Technology

J Jpn Soc Strength Fract Mater — Journal. Japanese Society for Strength and Fracture of Materials

J Jpn Soc Technol Plast — Journal. Japan Society for Technology of Plasticity

J Jpn Stud — Journal of Japanese Studies

J Jpn Surg Soc — Journal. Japanese Surgical Society

J Jpn Tech Assoc Pulp Pap Ind — Journal. Japanese Technical Association of the Pulp and Paper Industry

J Jpn Turfgrass Res Assoc — Journal. Japan Turfgrass Research Association

J Jpn Vet Med Assoc — Journal. Japan Veterinary Medical Association

J Jpn Water Works Assoc — Journal. Japan Water Works Association

J Jpn Weld Soc — Journal. Japan Welding Society

J Jpn Wood Res Soc — Journal. Japan Wood Research Society

JJQ — James Joyce Quarterly

JJR — James Joyce Review

J Jr Inst Eng (London) — Journal. Junior Institution of Engineers (London)

JJS — Jewish Journal of Sociology

JJS — Journal of Japanese Studies

JJS — Journal of Jewish Studies

JJSAAG — Japanese Journal of Studies on Alcohol

JJSGA — Japanese Journal of Surgery

JJSGAY — Japanese Journal of Surgery

J JSLE (Jpn Soc Lubr Eng) Int Ed — Journal. JSLE (Japan Society of Lubrication Engineers). International Edition

JJSO — Jewish Journal of Sociology

JJSt — Journal of Jewish Studies [*London*]

JJTCAR — Japanese Journal of Tuberculosis and Chest Diseases

J Jt Panel Nucl Mar Propul — Journal. Joint Panel on Nuclear Marine Propulsion [*England*]

J Jur Pap — Journal of Juristic Papyrology

J Juvenile Res — Journal of Juvenile Research

J Juv L — Journal of Juvenile Law

J Juzen Med Soc — Journal. Juzen Medical Society

JJV — Jahrbuch fuer Juedische Volkskunde

JJVRA — Japanese Journal of Veterinary Research

JJVRAE — Japanese Journal of Veterinary Research

JJWUA — Journal. Jiwaji University

JJZOAP — Japanese Journal of Zoology

JKAF — Jahrbuch fuer Kleinasiatische Forschung. Internationale Orientalistische Zeitschrift

J Kagawa Nutr Coll — Journal. Kagawa Nutrition College

JKAHS — Journal. Kerry Archaeological and Historical Society

J Kanagawa Prefect J Coll Nutr — Journal. Kanagawa Prefectural Junior College of Nutrition

J Kan BA — Journal. Kansas Bar Association

J Kan Med Soc — Journal. Kansas Medical Society

J Kansai Med Sch — Journal. Kansai Medical School [*Japan*]

J Kansai Med Univ — Journal. Kansai Medical University

J Kansas Med Soc — Journal. Kansas Medical Society

J Kans Entomol Soc — Journal. Kansas Entomological Society

J Kans Ent Soc — Journal. Kansas Entomological Society

J Kans Med Soc — Journal. Kansas Medical Society

J Kans State Dent Assoc — Journal. Kansas State Dental Association

J Kanto-Tosan Agr Exp Sta — Journal. Kanto-Tosan Agricultural Experiment Station

J Karnatak U Hum — Journal. Karnatak University. Humanities

J Karnatak Univ — Journal. Karnatak University

J Karnatak Univ Sci — Journal. Karnatak University. Science

J Karnatak U Soc Sci — Journal. Karnatak University. Social Sciences

J Karyopathol Tumor Tumorvirus — Journal of Karyopathology; Especially Tumor and Tumorvirus

JKAUA — Journal. Karnatak University

JKAWA — Jaarboek. Koninklijke Academie van Wetenschappen (Amsterdam)

JKE — Journal of Post Keynesian Economics

J Keio Med Soc — Journal. Keio Medical Society [*Japan*]

J Kerala Acad Biol — Journal. Kerala Academy of Biology

J Kerry Archaeol Hist Soc — Journal. Kerry Archaeological and Historical Society

JKF — Jahrbuch fuer Kleinasiatische Forschung

JKFSD — Journal. Korean Forestry Society

JKG — Jahrbuch. Kleist-Gesellschaft

JKG — Jidische Kultur Gezelschaft [*Argentina*]

JKG — Juedische Kulturgemeinschaft

JKGKA — Joho Kagaku Gijutsu Kenkyu Shukai Happyo Ronbunshu

JKGS — Jahrbuecher fuer Kultur und Geschichte der Slaven

JKGV — Jahrbuch. Koelnischer Geschichtsverein

JKHHA — Journal. Korea Institute of Electronics Engineers

JKIEA — Journal. Korean Institute of Electrical Engineers [*Republic of Korea*]

JKKNA — Jaarboek van Kankeronderzoek en Kankerbestrijding in Nederland

JKMAD — Journal. Korea Military Academy

JKMG — Jahrbuch. Karl-May-Gesellschaft

JKMSA — Journal. Kansas Medical Society

JKMSD — Journal. Korean Mathematical Society

JKNA — Jaarboek. Koninklijke Nederlandsche Academie

JKNCD — Journal. Kongju National Teacher's College

J Kongju Natl Teach Coll — Journal. Kongju National Teacher's College [*Republic of Korea*]

J Korea Electr Assoc — Journal. Korea Electric Association [*Republic of Korea*]

J Korea Inf Sci Soc — Journal. Korea Information Science Society

J Korea Inst Electron Eng — Journal. Korea Institute of Electronics Engineers

J Korea Merch Mar Coll Nat Sci Ser — Journal. Korea Merchant Marine College. Natural Sciences Series [*Republic of Korea*]

J Korea Mil Acad — Journal. Korea Military Academy [*Republic of Korea*]

J Korean Acad Maxillofac Radiol — Journal. Korean Academy of Maxillofacial Radiology [*Republic of Korea*]

J Korean Agric Chem Soc — Journal. Korean Agricultural Chemical Society [*Republic of Korea*]

J Korean Cancer Res Assoc — Journal. Korean Cancer Research Association

J Korean Ceram Soc — Journal. Korean Ceramic Society [*Republic of Korea*]

J Korean Chem Soc — Journal. Korean Chemical Society

J Korean Dent Assoc — Journal. Korean Dental Association [*Republic of Korea*]

J Korean For Soc — Journal. Korean Forestry Society [*Republic of Korea*]

J Korean Inst Chem Eng — Journal. Korean Institute of Chemical Engineers [*Republic of Korea*]

J Korean Inst Electr Eng — Journal. Korean Institute of Electrical Engineers [*Republic of Korea*]

J Korean Inst Electron Eng — Journal. Korean Institute of Electronics Engineers

J Korean Inst Met — Journal. Korean Institute of Metals [*Republic of Korea*]

J Korean Inst Min — Journal. Korean Institute of Mining [*Republic of Korea*]

J Korean Inst Miner Mining Eng — Journal. Korean Institute of Mineral and Mining Engineers [*Republic of Korea*]

J Korean Inst Min Geol — Journal. Korean Institute of Mining Geology [*Republic of Korea*]

J Korean Math Soc — Journal. Korean Mathematical Society

J Korean Med Assoc — Journal. Korean Medical Association [*Republic of Korea*]

J Korean Meteorol Soc — Journal. Korean Meteorological Society [*Republic of Korea*]

J Korean Nucl Soc — Journal. Korean Nuclear Society [*Republic of Korea*]

J Korean Ophthalmol Soc — Journal. Korean Ophthalmological Society

J Korean Phys Soc — Journal. Korean Physical Society

J Korean Radiol Soc — Journal. Korean Radiological Society [*Republic of Korea*]

J Korean Res Soc Radiol Technol — Journal. Korean Research Society of Radiological Technology [*Republic of Korea*]

J Korean Soc Agric Mach — Journal. Korean Society of Agricultural Machinery

J Korean Soc Civ Eng — Journal. Korean Society of Civil Engineers [*Republic of Korea*]

J Korean Soc Crop Sci — Journal. Korean Society of Crop Science [*Republic of Korea*]

J Korean Soc Hort Sci — Journal. Korean Society for Horticultural Science

J Korean Soc Mech Eng — Journal. Korean Society of Mechanical Engineers [*Republic of Korea*]

J Korean Soc Soil Sci Fert — Journal. Korean Society of Soil Science and Fertilizer

J Korean Soc Text Eng Chem — Journal. Korean Society of Textile Engineers and Chemists [*Republic of Korea*]

J Korean Statist Soc — Journal. Korean Statistical Society

J Korean Surg Soc — Journal. Korean Surgical Society

JKORS — Journal. Korean Operations Research Society

J Koyasan Univ — Journal. Koyasan University

JKS — Jahrbuch. Kunsthistorische Sammlungen

JKSW — Jahrbuch. Kunsthistorische Sammlungen (Wien)
JKU — Journal. Karnatak University [*Dharwar*]
J Kumamoto Women's Univ — Journal. Kumamoto Women's University
J Kumasi Univ Sci Technol — Journal. Kumasi University of Science and Technology
JKUR — Jammu and Kashmir University Review
J Kurume Med Assoc — Journal. Kurume Medical Association
J Kuwait Med Assoc — Journal. Kuwait Medical Association
JKVA — Jaarboek. Koninklijke Vlaamse Academie voor Wetenschappen. Letteren en Schone Kunsten van Belgie
JKW — Jahrbuch fuer Kunstwissenschaft
J KY Med Assoc — Journal. Kentucky Medical Association
JKYND — Journal. Materials Science Research Institute. Dongguk University
J Kyorin Med Soc — Journal. Kyorin Medical Society
J Kyoto Prefect Med Univ — Journal. Kyoto Prefectural Medical University [*Japan*]
J Kyoto Prefect Univ Med — Journal. Kyoto Prefectural University of Medicine
J Kyungpook Eng — Journal. Kyungpook Engineering [*Republic of Korea*]
J Kyungpook Eng Kyungpook Natl Univ — Journal. Kyungpook Engineering. Kyungpook National University
J Kyushu Dent Soc — Journal. Kyushu Dental Society [*Japan*]
J Kyushu Hematol Soc — Journal. Kyushu Hematological Society
JL — Jornal de Letras
JL — Journal. American Liszt Society
JL — Journal of Linguistics
JL — Juedisches Lexikon
JL — July
JLA — Jornal de Letras e Artes
J Lab Clin Med — Journal of Laboratory and Clinical Medicine
J Label Com — Journal of Labelled Compounds [*Later, Journal of Labelled Compounds and Radiopharmaceuticals*]
J Label Compound Radiopharm — Journal of Labelled Compounds and Radiopharmaceuticals
J Labelled Compd — Journal of Labelled Compounds [*Later, Journal of Labelled Compounds and Radiopharmaceuticals*]
J Labelled Compd Radiopharm — Journal of Labelled Compounds and Radiopharmaceuticals
J Labor Research — Journal of Labor Research
J Labour Hyg Iron Steel Ind — Journal of Labour Hygiene in Iron and Steel Industry
JLACBF — Justus Liebigs Annalen der Chemie
J La Cl Med — Journal of Laboratory and Clinical Medicine
JLAEA — Journal. Language Association of Eastern Africa
Jl Aesthetics — Journal of Aesthetics and Art Criticism
JLAL — Journal of Latin American Lore
J-Lancet — Journal-Lancet
J Land & Pub Util Econ — Journal of Land and Public Utility Economics
J Land & PU Econ — Journal of Land and Public Utility Economics
J Landwirtsch — Journal fuer Landwirtschaft
J Lang Teach — Journal for Language Teaching
Jl Appl Photogr Engin — Journal of Applied Photographic Engineering
J Laryngol Otol — Journal of Laryngology and Otology
J Laryngol Otol Suppl — Journal of Laryngology and Otology. Supplement
J Laryng Ot — Journal of Laryngology and Otology
JLAS — Journal. Linguistic Association of the Southwest
J LA State Med Soc — Journal. Louisiana State Medical Society
J Lat Am L — Journal of Latin American Lore
J Lat Am St — Journal of Latin American Studies
J Lat Am Stud — Journal of Latin American Studies
J Latin Amer Stud — Journal of Latin American Studies
J Law & Econ — Journal of Law and Economics
J Law Econ — Journal of Law and Economics
J Law & Econ Dev — Journal of Law and Economic Development
J Law & Educ — Journal of Law and Education
J Law Soc — Journal of Law and Society
J Law Soc Sc — Journal. Law Society of Scotland
J Law Soc Scot — Journal. Law Society of Scotland
JLB — Journal of Labor Economics
JLB — Juedisches Litteratur-Blatt
Jl Belge Radiol — Journal Belge de Radiologie
J Lbr Res — Journal of Labor Research
Jl Bus Fin — Journal of Business Finance and Accounting
Jl Bus Strat — Journal of Business Strategy
J L and Com — Journal of Law and Commerce
Jl Cont B — Journal of Contemporary Business
JLCPA — Journal of Counseling Psychology
JLCRD — Journal of Labelled Compounds and Radiopharmaceuticals
JLCSA4 — Journal. American Leather Chemists' Association. Supplement
JLD — Journal of Learning Disabilities
JLDIA — Journal of Learning Disabilities
JLDS — Journal. Lancashire Dialect Society
JLE — Journal of Law and Economics
J Lear Disabil — Journal of Learning Disabilities
J Learn Di — Journal of Learning Disabilities
J Learn Dis — Journal of Learning Disabilities

J Learn Disabil — Journal of Learning Disabilities
Jl E Asiat Stud — Journal of East Asiatic Studies
J L and Ec — Journal of Law and Economics
J L & Econ — Journal of Law and Economics
JL & Econ Dev — Journal of Law and Economic Development
J L & Econ Develop — Journal of Law and Economic Development
J L and Ed — Journal of Law and Education
J L & Educ — Journal of Law and Education
J Leeds Univ Text Stud Assoc — Journal. Leeds University Textile Students' Association
J Leeds Univ Union Chem Soc — Journal. Leeds University Union Chemical Society
J Legal Ed — Journal of Legal Education
J Legal Educ — Journal of Legal Education
J Legal Med — Journal of Legal Medicine
J Legal Prof — Journal of the Legal Profession
J Legal Stud — Journal of Legal Studies
J Leg Ed — Journal of Legal Education
J Leg Educ — Journal of Legal Education
J Leg Hist — Journal of Legal History
J Legis — Journal of Legislation [*United States*]
J Legislation — Journal of Legislation
J Leg Med — Journal of Legal Medicine
J Leg Plur — Journal of Legal Pluralism and Unofficial Law
J Leg Stud — Journal of Legal Studies
J Leis Res — Journal of Leisure Research
J Leisur — Journal of Leisurability
J Leisurability — Journal of Leisurability
J Leisure — Journal of Leisure Research
J Leisure Res — Journal of Leisure Research
JLEMA — Journal of Engineering Mathematics
J Lepid Soc — Journal. Lepidopterists' Society
JLER — Journal of Leisure Research
J Less-C Met — Journal of the Less-Common Metals
J Less Common Met — Journal of the Less-Common Metals
J Leukocyte Biol — Journal of Leukocyte Biology
JLFAA — Journal de la France Agricole
JLG — Jahrbuch. Juedisch Literarische Gesellschaft [*Frankfurt Am Main*]
JLH — Jahrbuch fuer Liturgik und Hymnologie
JLH — Journal of Library History [*Later, Journal of Library History, Philosophy, and Comparative Librarianship*]
JLH — Journal of Library History, Philosophy, and Comparative Librarianship
JLHPA — Jan Liao Hsueh Pao
JLi — Jewish Life
J Lib Admin — Journal of Library Administration
J Lib Arts Sci Kitasato Univ — Journal of Liberal Arts and Sciences. Kitasato University
J Lib Automation — Journal of Library Automation
J Liber Stud — Journal of Libertarian Studies
J Lib Hist — Journal of Library History [*Later, Journal of Library History, Philosophy, and Comparative Librarianship*]
J Lib Hist — Journal of Library History, Philosophy, and Comparative Librarianship
J Lib and Info Science — Journal of Library and Information Science
J Lib Inf Sci — Journal of Library and Information Science
J Libnship — Journal of Librarianship
J Libr — Journal of Librarianship
J Librarianship — Journal of Librarianship
J Libr Aut — Journal of Library Automation
J Libr Auto — Journal of Library Automation
J Libr Autom — Journal of Library Automation
J Libr Automn — Journal of Library Automation
J Libr Hist — Journal of Library History [*Later, Journal of Library History, Philosophy, and Comparative Librarianship*]
J Libr Hist — Journal of Library History, Philosophy, and Comparative Librarianship
J Libr Inf Sci — Journal of Library and Information Science
JLIEA — Journal of Industrial Engineering
J Limnol Soc South Afr — Journal. Limnological Society of South Africa
J Ling — Journal of Linguistics
J Linguist — Journal of Linguistics
J Linguistics — Journal of Linguistics
J Linn Soc Lond Bot — Journal. Linnean Society of London. Botany
J Linn Soc Lond Zool — Journal. Linnean Society of London. Zoology
J Lipid Res — Journal of Lipid Research
J Liq Chromatogr — Journal of Liquid Chromatography
J Liquid Chromatogr — Journal of Liquid Chromatography
JLIS — Journal of Law and Information Science
J Lit Sem — Journal of Literary Semantics
JLKNO — Jahrbuch fuer Landeskunde von Niederoesterreich
J L Med — Journal of Legal Medicine
JLMPA — Journal of Microwave Power
JLMS — Journal. London Mathematical Society
Jl Musicology — Journal of Musicology
JLN — Jack London Newsletter

Jl NY Ent Soc — Journal. New York Entomological Society
Jl NZ Diet Ass — Journal. New Zealand Dietetic Association
J Lond Math — Journal. London Mathematical Society
J London Math Soc — Journal. London Mathematical Society
J London Math Soc (2) — Journal. London Mathematical Society. Second Series
J London School Trop Med — Journal. London School of Tropical Medicine
J Long Term Care — Journal of Long Term Care Administration
J Long Term Care Admin — Journal of Long Term Care Administration
JLOTA — Journal of Laryngology and Otology
J Low Freq Noise Vib — Journal of Low Frequency Noise and Vibration
J Low Temp Phys — Journal of Low Temperature Physics
JLR — Jewish Language Review
JLR — Journal of Labor Research
JLR — Journal of Linguistic Research
Jl R Agric Soc — Journal. Royal Agricultural Society of England
Jl R Anthrop Inst — Journal. Royal Anthropological Institute of Great Britain and Ireland
Jl R Aust Hist Soc — Royal Australian Historical Society. Journal
Jl of Research — Journal of Research in Music Education
Jl R Hist Soc Qd — Royal Historical Society of Queensland. Journal
Jl R Hort Soc — Journal. Royal Horticulture Society
Jl R Microsc Soc — Journal. Royal Microscopical Society
Jl R Soc Arts — Journal. Royal Society of Arts
Jl R Soc NZ — Journal. Royal Society of New Zealand
JLRU — Journal. Library of Rutgers University
JLS — Journal. Law Society of Scotland
JLS — Journal of Literary Semantics
Jl S Afr Bot — Journal of South African Botany
Jl S-East Agric Coll (Wye) — Journal. South-Eastern Agricultural College (Wye) [Kent]
JLSMA — Journal. Louisiana State Medical Society
Jl Small Bus — American Journal of Small Business
Jl Soc Mot Pict Telev Engin — Journal. Society of Motion Picture and Television Engineers
Jl Soc Photogr Sci — Journal. Society of Photographic Science and Technology of Japan
Jl Soc Photogr Sci Technol Japan — Journal. Society of Photographic Science and Technology of Japan
J of the L Soc of Scotl — Journal. Law Society of Scotland
JL Soc Scotland — Journal. Law Society of Scotland
JL Soc'y — Journal. Law Society of Scotland
J L Socy Scot — Journal. Law Society of Scotland
J L Studies — Journal of Legal Studies
JLT — Journal du Textile [Paris]
J L Temp Ph — Journal of Low Temperature Physics
J Lubric Technol Trans ASME — Journal of Lubrication Technology. Transactions of the American Society of Mechanical Engineers
J Lubr Tech — Journal of Lubrication Technology
J Lubr Technol — Journal of Lubrication Technology
J Lubr Technol Trans ASME — Journal of Lubrication Technology. Transactions of the American Society of Mechanical Engineers
J Lub Tech — Journal of Lubrication Technology. Transactions of the American Society of Mechanical Engineers
J Lumin — Journal of Luminescence
J Luminesc — Journal of Luminescence
J Lute — Journal. Lute Society of America
J Lute Soc Amer — Journal. Lute Society of America
JLW — Jahrbuch fuer Liturgiewissenschaft
JLZ — Jahresberichte des Literarischen Zentralblattes
JM — Journal of Marketing
JM — Journal of Music Theory
JMA — Journal of Macroeconomics
J Macomb Dent Soc — Journal. Macomb Dental Society
J Macromol Chem — Journal of Macromolecular Chemistry
J Macromol Sci A — Journal of Macromolecular Science. Part A
J Macromol Sci B — Journal of Macromolecular Science. Part B
J Macromol Sci C — Journal of Macromolecular Science. Part C
J Macromol Sci Chem A — Journal of Macromolecular Science. Part A. Chemistry
J Macromol Sci Part A — Journal of Macromolecular Science. Part A. Chemistry
J Macromol Sci Part B — Journal of Macromolecular Science. Part B. Physics
J Macromol Sci Phys — Journal of Macromolecular Science. Part B. Physics
J Macromol Sci Rev Macromol Chem — Journal of Macromolecular Science. Part C. Reviews in Macromolecular Chemistry
J Macromol Sci Rev Polym Technol — Journal of Macromolecular Science. Part D. Reviews in Polymer Technology
J Macr S Ch — Journal of Macromolecular Science. Part A. Chemistry
J Macr S Ph — Journal of Macromolecular Science. Part B. Physics
J Macr S Rm — Journal of Macromolecular Science. Part C. Reviews in Macromolecular Chemistry
J of MACT — Journal. Maulana Azad College of Technology
J MACT — Journal. Maulana Azad College of Technology [India]
J Madras Agric Stud Union — Journal. Madras Agricultural Students' Union
J Madras Inst Technol — Journal. Madras Institute of Technology

J Madras Univ — Journal. Madras University
J Madras Univ B — Journal. Madras University. Section B. Contributions in Mathematics, Physical and Biological Science
J Madras Univ Sect B — Journal. Madras University. Section B
J Madurai Univ — Madurai University. Journal
JMAG — Journal of Molecular and Applied Genetics
J Magn and Magn Mater — Journal of Magnetism and Magnetic Materials
J Magn Magn Mater — Journal of Magnetism and Magnetic Materials
J Magn Res — Journal of Magnetic Resonance
J Magn Resonance — Journal of Magnetic Resonance
J Maharaja Sayajirao Univ Baroda — Journal. Maharaja Sayajirao University of Baroda
J Maharashtra Agric Univ — Journal. Maharashtra Agricultural Universities
J Mahar Sayayira Univ Baroda — Journal. Maharaja Sayayira University of Baroda
J Maine Med Assoc — Journal. Maine Medical Association
J Makromol Chem — Journal fuer Makromolekulare Chemie
J Malacol Soc Aust — Journal. Malacological Society of Australia
J Malac Soc Aust — Journal. Malacological Society of Australia
J Malar Inst India — Journal. Malaria Institute of India
J Malay Branch Roy Asiatic Soc — Journal. Malaysian Branch. Royal Asiatic Society
J Malays Branch R Asiat Soc — Journal. Malaysian Branch. Royal Asiatic Society
J Mal Br Roy Asiat Soc — Journal. Malaysian Branch. Royal Asiatic Society
J Mal & Comp L — Journal of Malaysian and Comparative Law
J Mal Vasc — Journal des Maladies Vasculaires
JMAM — Journal of Mammalogy
JMAM — Journal. Music Academy (Madras)
J Mammal — Journal of Mammalogy
J Mammal Soc Jpn — Journal. Mammalogical Society of Japan
J Manag Stu — Journal of Management Studies
J Manip Physiol Ther — Journal of Manipulative and Physiological Therapeutics
J Manipulative Physiol Ther — Journal of Manipulative and Physiological Therapeutics
JMAPD — Journal de Mecanique Appliquee
J Mar Biol Assoc (India) — Journal. Marine Biological Association (India)
J Mar Biol Assoc (UK) — Journal. Marine Biological Association (United Kingdom)
J Mar Fam — Journal of Marriage and the Family
J Marine Bi — Journal. Marine Biological Association [United Kingdom]
J Marine Biol Ass (United Kingdom) — Journal. Marine Biological Association (United Kingdom)
J Marine Re — Journal of Marine Research
J Marine Res — Journal of Marine Research
J Maritime L — Journal of Maritime Law and Commerce
J Maritime Law and Commer — Journal of Maritime Law and Commerce
J Marit Law — Journal of Maritime Law and Commerce
J of Marit L and Commerce — Journal of Maritime Law and Commerce
J Marit Saf Acad Part 2 — Journal. Maritime Safety Academy. Part 2 [Japan]
J Mar J Prac & Proc — John Marshall Journal of Practice and Procedure
J Market — Journal of Marketing
J Marketing — Journal of Marketing
J Marketing Res — Journal of Marketing Research
J Market (L) — Journal. Market Research Society (London)
J Market R — Journal of Marketing Research
J Market Research Society Vic — Journal. Market Research Society of Victoria
J Market Res Soc — Journal. Market Research Society
J Marktforsch — Journal fuer Marktforschung
J Mar Law & Com — Journal of Maritime Law and Commerce
J Mar L and Com — Journal of Maritime Law and Commerce
J Mar LR — John Marshall Law Review
J Mar L Rev — John Marshall Law Review
J Mar March — Journal de la Marine Marchande
J Mar Res — Journal of Marine Research
J Marr & Fam — Journal of Marriage and the Family
J Marriage — Journal of Marriage and the Family
J Marriage & Fam — Journal of Marriage and the Family
J Marriage Family — Journal of Marriage and the Family
J Marshall J — John Marshall Journal of Practice and Procedure
J Mar Technol Soc — Journal. Marine Technology Society
JMAS — Journal of Modern African Studies
J Mass Dent Soc — Journal. Massachussetts Dental Society
J Mass Spectrom Ion Phys — Journal of Mass Spectrometry and Ion Physics
J Mass Sp Ion P — Journal of Mass Spectrometry and Ion Physics
J Mater — Journal of Materials
J Mater Energy Syst — Journal of Materials for Energy Systems
J Materials Sci — Journal of Materials Science
J Mater Sci — Journal of Materials Science
J Mater Sci Lett — Journal of Materials Science. Letters
J Mater Sci Res Inst Dongguk Univ — Journal. Materials Science Research Institute. Dongguk University
J Mater Sci Soc Jpn — Journal. Materials Science Society of Japan

J Mater Test Res Assoc — Journal. Material Testing Research Association [*Japan*]
J Math Anal — Journal of Mathematical Analysis and Applications
J Math Anal Appl — Journal of Mathematical Analysis and Applications
J Math Anal and Appl — Journal of Mathematical Analysis and Applications
J Math Biol — Journal of Mathematical Biology
J Math Econom — Journal of Mathematical Economics
J Mathematical Phys — Journal of Mathematical Physics
J Mathematical and Physical Sci — Journal of Mathematical and Physical Sciences
J Mathematical Psychology — Journal of Mathematical Psychology
J Mathematical Sociology — Journal of Mathematical Sociology
J Math (Jabalpur) — Journal of Mathematics (Jabalpur)
J Math Jap — Journal. Mathematical Society of Japan
J Math Kyoto Univ — Journal of Mathematics. Kyoto University
J Math Mech — Journal of Mathematics and Mechanics
J Math Modelling Teach — Journal of Mathematical Modelling for Teachers
J Math NS — Journal of Mathematics. New Series
J Math P A — Journal de Mathematiques Pures et Appliquees
J Math Phys — Journal of Mathematics and Physics
J Math & Phys — Journal of Mathematics and Physics
J Math Phys (Cambridge Mass) — Journal of Mathematics and Physics (Cambridge, Massachusetts)
J Math Phys (NY) — Journal of Mathematical Physics (New York)
J Math Phys Sci — Journal of Mathematical and Physical Sciences
J Math and Phys Sci — Journal of Mathematical and Physical Sciences
J Math Psyc — Journal of Mathematical Psychology
J Math Psych — Journal of Mathematical Psychology
J Math Psychol — Journal of Mathematical Psychology
J Math Pures Appl — Journal de Mathematiques Pures et Appliquees
J Math Pures Appl 9 — Journal de Mathematiques Pures et Appliquees. Neuvieme Serie
J Math Res Exposition — Journal of Mathematical Research and Exposition
J Math & Sci — Journal of Mathematics and Sciences
J Math Sci — Journal of Mathematics and Sciences
J Math Soci — Journal of Mathematical Sociology
J Math Sociol — Journal of Mathematical Sociology
J Math Soc Japan — Journal. Mathematical Society of Japan
J Math Soc Jpn — Journal. Mathematical Society of Japan
J Math Tokushima Univ — Journal of Mathematics. Tokushima University
J Mat Sci — Journal of Materials Science
J Mat Sci Lett — Journal of Materials Science. Letters
J Maulana Azad College Tech — Journal. Maulana Azad College of Technology
J Maxillofac Surg — Journal of Maxillofacial Surgery
JMB — Japan Missionary Bulletin [*Tokyo*]
JMB — Journal of Money, Credit, and Banking
JMBCD — Journal de Microscopie et de Biologie Cellulaire
JMBRAS — Journal. Malayan Branch. Royal Asiatic Society
JMBXA — Journal de Medecine de Bordeaux
JMC — Journal of Medicinal Chemistry
JMCAD — Journal of Molecular Catalysis
JMCI — Journal of Molecular and Cellular Immunology
JMD — Journal of Management Development
J MD Acad Sci — Journal. Maryland Academy of Sciences
JMDR — Journal of Missile Defense Research
J MD State Dent Assoc — Journal. Maryland State Dental Association
JME — Journal of Mathematical Economics
JME — Journal of Monetary Economics
J Mec — Journal de Mecanique
J Mecanique — Journal de Mecanique
J Mec Appl — Journal de Mecanique Appliquee
J Mech — Journal of Mechanisms
J Mechanochem Cell Motility — Journal of Mechanochemistry and Cell Motility
J Mechanochem & Cell Motility — Journal of Mechanochemistry and Cell Motility
J Mech Des — Journal of Mechanical Design [*United States*]
J Mech Des Trans ASME — Journal of Mechanical Design. Transactions of the American Society of Mechanical Engineers
J Mech E — Journal of Mechanical Engineering Science
J Mech Eng — Journal of Mechanical Engineering Science
J Mech Eng Lab — Journal. Mechanical Engineering Laboratory [*Japan*]
J Mech Eng Lab (Tokyo) — Journal. Mechanical Engineering Laboratory (Tokyo)
J Mech Engng Lab — Journal. Mechanical Engineering Laboratory
J Mech Engng Sci — Journal of Mechanical Engineering Science
J Mech Eng Sci — Journal of Mechanical Engineering Science
J Mech Lab Jap — Journal. Mechanical Laboratory of Japan
J Mech Lab (Tokyo) — Journal. Mechanical Laboratory (Tokyo)
J Mech Phys — Journal of the Mechanics and Physics of Solids
J Mech Phys Solids — Journal of the Mechanics and Physics of Solids
J Mech Working Technol — Journal of Mechanical Working Technology
J Mech Work Technol — Journal of Mechanical Working Technology
J Mec Phys Atmos — Journal de Mecanique et Physique de l'Atmosphere [*France*]

J Mec Theor Appl — Journal de Mecanique Theorique et Appliquee [*Journal of Theoretical and Applied Mechanics*]
J Mec Theor et Appl — Journal de Mecanique Theorique et Appliquee [*Journal of Theoretical and Applied Mechanics*]
J Med — Journal of Medicine
JMEDA — Journal of Medical Education
J Med Assn GA — Journal. Medical Association of Georgia
J Med Assoc Eire — Journal. Medical Association of Eire
J Med Assoc GA — Journal. Medical Association of Georgia
J Med Assoc Iwate Prefect Hosp — Journal. Medical Association of Iwate Prefectural Hospital [*Japan*]
J Med Assoc Jam — Journal. Medical Association of Jamaica
J Med Assoc State Ala — Journal. Medical Association of the State of Alabama
J Med Assoc State Alabama — Journal. Medical Association of the State of Alabama
J Med Assoc Thail — Journal. Medical Association of Thailand
J Med Ass South Africa — Journal. Medical Association of South Africa
J Med (Basel) — Journal of Medicine. Experimental and Clinical (Basel)
J Med Besancon — Journal de Medecine de Besancon
J Med Bordeaux — Journal de Medecine de Bordeaux
J Med Bord Sud-Ouest — Journal de Medecine de Bordeaux et du Sud-Ouest
J Med Caen — Journal de Medecine de Caen
J Med Chem — Journal of Medicinal Chemistry
J Med Chir Pharm (Paris) — Journal de Medecine, Chirurgie, Pharmacie (Paris)
J Med Chir Prat — Journal de Medecine et de Chirurgie Pratiques
J Med et Chir Prat — Journal de Medecine et de Chirurgie Pratiques
J Med (Cincinnati) — Journal of Medicine (Cincinnati)
J Med Coll Keijo — Journal. Medical College in Keijo
J Med Ed — Journal of Medical Education
J Med Educ — Journal of Medical Education
J Med Electron — Journal of Medical Electronics
J Med Eng Technol — Journal of Medical Engineering and Technology
J Med Ent — Journal of Medical Entomology
J Med Entomol — Journal of Medical Entomology
J Med Entomol Suppl — Journal of Medical Entomology. Supplement
J Med Ethics — Journal of Medical Ethics
J Med Franc — Journal Medical Francais
J Med Genet — Journal of Medical Genetics
J Medicaid Manage — Journal for Medicaid Management
J Mediev Hi — Journal of Medieval History
J Mediev R — Journal of Medieval and Renaissance Studies
J Mediev Renaissance Stud — Journal of Medieval and Renaissance Studies
J Med Lab Technol — Journal of Medical Laboratory Technology
J Med Liban — Journal Medical Libanais
J Med Lyon — Journal de Medecine de Lyon
J Med Micro — Journal of Medical Microbiology
J Med Microbiol — Journal of Medical Microbiology
J Med Montp — Journal de Medecine de Montpellier
J Med Pernambuco — Jornal de Medicina de Pernambuco
J Med Pharm Chem — Journal of Medicinal and Pharmaceutical Chemistry
J Med Phil — Journal of Medicine and Philosophy
J Med Philos — Journal of Medicine and Philosophy
J Med Poitiers — Journal de Medecine de Poitiers
J Med (Porto) — Jornal do Medico (Porto)
J Med Prim — Journal of Medical Primatology
J Med Primatol — Journal of Medical Primatology
J Med Sci — Journal of Medical Sciences
J Med Sci Banaras Hindu Univ — Journal of Medical Sciences. Banaras Hindu University
J Med Soc New Jers — Journal. Medical Society of New Jersey
J Med Soc NJ — Journal. Medical Society of New Jersey
J Med Soc Toho Univ — Journal. Medical Society of Toho University
J Med Strasb — Journal de Medecine de Strasbourg
J Med Strasbourg — Journal de Medecine de Strasbourg [*France*]
J Med Syst — Journal of Medical Systems
J Med Technol — Journal of Medical Technology
J Med Vet et Comp — Journal de Medecine Veterinaire et Comparee
J Med Vet (Lyon) — Journal de Medecine Veterinaire (Lyon)
J Med Vet Mil — Journal de Medecine Veterinaire Militaire
J Med Vet et Zootech (Lyon) — Journal de Medecine Veterinaire et de Zootechnie (Lyon)
J Med Virol — Journal of Medical Virology
J Med (Westbury NY) — Journal of Medicine (Westbury, New York)
J Membrane Biol — Journal of Membrane Biology
J Membrane Sci — Journal of Membrane Science
J Membr Bio — Journal of Membrane Biology
J Membr Biol — Journal of Membrane Biology
J Membr Sci — Journal of Membrane Science
J Mental Def Research — Journal of Mental Deficiency Research
J Ment Def — Journal of Mental Deficiency Research
J Ment Defic Res — Journal of Mental Deficiency Research
J Ment Health — Journal of Mental Health
J Ment Health Adm — Journal. Mental Health Administration
J Ment Sci — Journal of Mental Science

J Ment Subnorm — Journal of Mental Subnormality
J Merioneth Hist Rec Soc — Journal. Merioneth Historical Record Society
JMES — Journal. Middle East Society [*Jerusalem*]
J Met — Journal of Metals
J Metal Finish Soc Korea — Journal. Metal Finishing Society of Korea
J Metall Club R Coll Sci Technol — Journal. Metallurgical Club. Royal College of Science and Technology
J Metall Club Univ Strathclyde — Journal. Metallurgical Club. University of Strathclyde
J Metals — Journal of Metals
J Metamorph Geol — Journal of Metamorphic Geology
J Meteorol — Journal of Meteorology [*United States*]
J Meteorol Res — Journal of Meteorological Research [*Japan*]
J Meteorol Soc Jpn — Journal. Meteorological Society of Japan
J Met Finish Soc Jap — Journal. Metal Finishing Society of Japan
J Met Finish Soc Jpn — Journal. Metal Finishing Society of Japan
J Mex Am Hist — Journal of Mexican American History
JMF — Journal of Marriage and the Family
JMFT — Journal of Milk and Food Technology [*Later, Journal of Food Protection*]
JMG — Journal of Management Consulting
JMG — Journal of Metamorphic Geology
JMG — Journal of Micrographics
JMG — Journal of Molecular Graphics
JMGS — Journal of Modern Greek Studies
J Mgt — Journal of Management
J Mgt Stud — Journal of Management Studies
J Mgt Studies — Journal of Management Studies
JMH — Journal of Medieval History
JMH — Journal of Mississippi History
JMH — Journal of Modern History
J Mich Dent Assoc — Journal. Michigan Dental Association
J Mich State Dent Assoc — Journal. Michigan State Dental Association
J Mich State Dent Soc — Journal. Michigan State Dental Society
J Mich State Med Soc — Journal. Michigan State Medical Society
J Micr and Nat Sc — Journal of Microscopy and Natural Science
J Microbiol Epidemiol Immunobiol (USSR) — Journal of Microbiology, Epidemiology, and Immunobiology (USSR)
J Microbiol UAR — Journal of Microbiology of the United Arab Republic
J Microcomput Appl — Journal of Microcomputer Applications
J Microencapsulation — Journal of Microencapsulation
J Microg — Journal de Micrographie
J Microgr — Journal of Micrographics
J Micrographics — Journal of Micrographics
J Microphotogr — Journal of Microphotography
J Microsc — Journal de Microscopie [*France*]
J Microsc — Journal of Microscopy
J Microsc B — Journal de Microscopie et de Biologie Cellulaire
J Microsc Biol Cell — Journal de Microscopie et de Biologie Cellulaire
J Microsc (O) — Journal of Microscopy (Oxford)
J Microscopie — Journal de Microscopie
J Microscopy — Journal of Microscopy
J Microsc (Oxf) — Journal of Microscopy (Oxford)
J Microsc (Paris) — Journal de Microscopie (Paris)
J Microsc Spectrosc Electron — Journal de Microscopie et de Spectroscopie Electroniques
J Microsc et Spectrosc Electron — Journal de Microscopie et de Spectroscopie Electroniques
J Microsc Spectrosc Electron (France) — Journal de Microscopie et de Spectroscopie Electroniques (France)
J Microsurg — Journal of Microsurgery
J Microwave Power — Journal of Microwave Power
J Microwave Pwr — Journal of Microwave Power
J Mie Med Coll — Journal. Mie Medical College
JMiH — Journal of Mississippi History
J Milk Food — Journal of Milk and Food Technology [*Later, Journal of Food Protection*]
J Milk & Food Tech — Journal of Milk and Food Technology [*Later, Journal of Food Protection*]
J Milk Food Technol — Journal of Milk and Food Technology [*Later, Journal of Food Protection*]
J Milk Tech — Journal of Milk Technology
J Mil Serv Inst — Journal. Military Service Institution
J Min Coll Akita Univ Ser A — Journal. Mining College. Akita University. Series A. Mining Geology
J Mineral Soc Jpn — Journal. Mineralogical Society of Japan
J Mines Met Fuels — Journal of Mines, Metals, and Fuels
J Mines Met Fuels (Calcutta) — Journal of Mines, Metals, and Fuels (Calcutta)
J Mine Vent Soc S Afr — Journal. Mine Ventilation Society of South Africa
J Min Geol — Journal of Mining and Geology [*Nigeria*]
J Mining Met Inst Jap — Journal. Mining and Metallurgical Institute of Japan
J Min Inst Kyushu — Journal. Mining Institute of Kyushu [*Japan*]
J Minist Agric (GB) — Journal. Ministry of Agriculture (Great Britain)
J Ministry Ag — Agriculture (Journal of the Ministry of Agriculture)
J Min Metall Inst Jap — Journal. Mining and Metallurgical Institute of Japan
J Minn Acad Sci — Journal. Minnesota Academy of Science

JMIR — Journal. Ministere de l'Instruction Publique en Russie
J Miss Acad Sci — Journal. Mississippi Academy of Sciences
JMissH — Journal of Mississippi History
J Miss Hist — Journal of Mississippi History
J Mississippi Med Ass — Journal. Mississippi State Medical Association
J Miss State Med Assoc — Journal. Mississippi State Medical Association
JMJ — John Marshall Journal of Practice and Procedure
JMK — Journal of Marketing
JMKNA2 — Annual Reports. Institute of Population Problems
JMKOA — Jemna Mechanika a Optika
J Mkt — Journal of Marketing
J Mktg — Journal of Marketing
J Mktg Res — Journal of Marketing Research
J Mkting — Journal of Marketing
J Mkting Res — Journal of Marketing Research
J Mkt Res — Journal of Marketing Research
JMKU — Journal of Mathematics. Kyoto University
JML — Journal of Modern Literature
JM Ling — Journal of Mayan Linguistics
JMLR — John Marshall Law Review
JMM — Journal of Macromarketing
JMM — Journal. Manx Museum
JMM — Journal de la Marine Marchande et de la Navigation Aerienne
JMM — Journal of Microbiological Methods
JMMAA — Journal. Maine Medical Association
JMMMD — Journal of Magnetism and Magnetic Materials
JMMNA — Journal de la Marine Marchande et de la Navigation Aerienne
JMMSD — Journal. Korea Merchant Marine College. Natural Sciences Series
JMN — Journal of Management Studies
J MO B — Journal. Missouri Bar
J MO Bar — Journal. Missouri Bar
J Mod Afric Stud — Journal of Modern African Studies
J Mod Afr S — Journal of Modern African Studies
J Mod Afr Stud — Journal of Modern African Studies
J MO Dent Assoc — Journal. Missouri Dental Association
J Mod Hist — Journal of Modern History
J Mod Lit — Journal of Modern Literature
J Mol Biol — Journal of Molecular Biology
J Mol Catal — Journal of Molecular Catalysis
J Mol Cel C — Journal of Molecular and Cellular Cardiology
J Mol Cell Cardiol — Journal of Molecular and Cellular Cardiology
J Molec Biol — Journal of Molecular Biology
J Mol Evol — Journal of Molecular Evolution
J Mol Liq — Journal of Molecular Liquids
J Molluscan Stud — Journal of Molluscan Studies
J Molluscan Stud Suppl — Journal of Molluscan Studies. Supplement
J Mol Med — Journal of Molecular Medicine
J Mol Spect — Journal of Molecular Spectroscopy
J Mol Spectrosc — Journal of Molecular Spectroscopy
J Mol Struct — Journal of Molecular Structure
J Mond Pharm — Journal Mondial de Pharmacie
J Monetary Econ — Journal of Monetary Economics
J Money Cred Bank — Journal of Money, Credit, and Banking
J Money Cred & Bank — Journal of Money, Credit, and Banking
J Money Credit Bank — Journal of Money, Credit, and Banking
J Money Credit & Banking — Journal of Money, Credit, and Banking
J Moral Ed — Journal of Moral Education
J Moral Educ — Journal of Moral Education
J Mormon Hist — Journal of Mormon History
J Morph — Journal of Morphology
J Morphol — Journal of Morphology
J Morphol Physiol — Journal of Morphology and Physiology
J Morph and Physiol — Journal of Morphology and Physiology
J Moscow Patr — Journal of the Moscow Patriarchate
J Mot Behav — Journal of Motor Behavior
J Motion Pict Soc India — Journal. Motion Picture Society of India
J Motor Beh — Journal of Motor Behavior
J MO Water Sewage Conf — Journal. Missouri Water and Sewage Conference
JMPMA — Journal of Medical Primatology
JMPO — Journal of Microwave Power
JMPPD — Journal of Marketing and Public Policy
JMPSB — Journal of Mathematical and Physical Sciences
JMR — Journal of Marketing Research
JMRAS — Journal. Malayan Branch. Royal Asiatic Society
JMRPDC — Japan Medical Research Foundation. Publication
JMRS — Journal. Market Research Society
JMRS — Journal of Medieval and Renaissance Studies
JMS — Journal of Maltese Studies
JMS — Journal of Management Studies
JMSBA — Journal of Mental Subnormality
JMSCA — Journal of Mental Science
JMSED — Journal de Microscopie et de Spectroscopie Electroniques
JMSJ — Journal. Mathematical Society of Japan
JMSMD — Journal of Materials for Energy Systems
JMSNA — Journal. Medical Society of New Jersey
JMSUB — Journal. Maharaja Sayajirao University of Baroda

JMT — Journal of Music Therapy
JMTAA — Journal. Institute of Mathematics and Its Applications
J Mt Sinai Hosp — Journal. Mount Sinai Hospital
JMUEOS — Journal. Manchester University Egyptian and Oriental Society
JMultiAn — Journal of Multivariate Analysis
J Multivar Anal — Journal of Multivariate Analysis
JMUSA — Journal. American Musicological Society
J Muscle Res Cell Motil — Journal of Muscle Research and Cell Motility
J Mus Francais — Journal Musical Francais
J Music Res — Journal of Musicological Research
J Music Ther — Journal of Music Therapy
J Music Thr — Journal of Music Theory
J Mus Theory — Journal of Music Theory
J Mus Ther — Journal of Music Therapy
J Mus Therapy — Journal of Music Therapy
JMUTA — Journal of Music Therapy
JMUTB — Journal of Music Theory
JMV — Jahresschrift fuer Mitteldeutsche Vorgeschichte
JMVL — Jahrbuch. Museum fuer Voelkerkunde zu Leipzig
J Mysore Agr Exp Union — Journal. Mysore Agricultural and Experimental Union
J Mysore Med Assoc — Journal. Mysore Medical Association
J Mysore U Arts — Journal. Mysore University. Section A. Arts
J Mysore Univ Sect B Sci — Journal. Mysore University. Section B. Science [*India*]
JN — Jewish Newsletter
JN — Journal of Neuroscience
JN — Journal Numismatique
JN — Juilliard News Bulletin
JNAA — Journal. National Academy of Administration [*India*]
JNABD — Journal of Nuclear Agriculture and Biology
JNAFS — Journal of Northwest Atlantic Fishery Science
J Nagoya City Univ Med Assoc — Journal. Nagoya City University Medical Association [*Japan*]
J Nagoya Med Assoc — Journal. Nagoya Medical Association
JNALA — Journal of the New African Literature and the Arts
J Nanjing Inst For — Journal. Nanjing Institute of Forestry
J Nanjing Inst Technol — Journal. Nanjing Institute of Technology
J Nanjing Technol Coll For Prod — Journal. Nanjing Technological College of Forest Products
J Nara Gakugei Univ — Journal. Nara Gakugei University [*Japan*]
J Nara Med Ass — Journal. Nara Medical Association
J Nara Med Assoc — Journal. Nara Medical Association
J Narr Tech — Journal of Narrative Technique
J Nat Assn Col Adm Counsel — Journal. National Association of College Admissions Counselors
J Nat Canc — Journal. National Cancer Institute
J Nat Cancer Inst — Journal. National Cancer Institute
J Nat Hist — Journal of Natural History
J Nat Inst Hospital Adm — Journal. National Institute of Hospital Administration
J Nat Inst Soc Sci — Journal. National Institute of Social Sciences
J Natl Acad Sci — Journal. National Academy of Sciences [*Republic of Korea*]
J Natl Acad Sci (Repub Korea) Nat Sci Ser — Journal. National Academy of Sciences (Republic of Korea). Natural Sciences Series
J Natl Agric Soc Ceylon — Journal. National Agricultural Society of Ceylon
J Natl Assn Coll Adm Counsel — Journal. National Association of College Admissions Counselors
J Natl Assn Women Deans Adm & Counsel — Journal. National Association for Women Deans, Administrators, and Counselors
J Natl Cancer Inst — Journal. National Cancer Institute
J Natl Chem Lab Ind — Journal. National Chemical Laboratory for Industry [*Japan*]
J Natl Chiao Tung Univ — Journal. National Chiao Tung University
J Natl Inst Agric Bot — Journal. National Institute of Agricultural Botany
J Natl Inst Pers Res S Afr CSIR — Journal. National Institute for Personnel Research. South African Council for Scientific and Industrial Research
J Natl Med Assoc — Journal. [*US*] National Medical Association
J Natl Res Counc Thail — Journal. National Research Council of Thailand
J Natl Res Counc Thailand — Journal. National Research Council of Thailand
J Natl Sci Counc Sri Lanka — Journal. National Science Council of Sri Lanka
J Natl Tech Assoc — Journal. National Technical Association [*United States*]
J Natn Cancer Inst — Journal. National Cancer Institute
J Natn Inst Agric Bot — Journal. National Institute of Agricultural Botany
J Nat Prod — Journal of Natural Products
J Nat Res Coun Thai — Journal. National Research Council of Thailand
J Nat Sci — Journal of Natural Sciences [*Malaysia*]
J Nat Sci Chonnam Natl Univ — Journal of Natural Science. Chonnam National University
J Nat Sci Math (Lahore) — Journal of Natural Sciences and Mathematics (Lahore)
J Nat Sci Res Inst — Journal. Natural Science Research Institute. Yonsei University [*Republic of Korea*]
J Nat Sci Soc Ichimura Gakuen J Coll — Journal. Natural Scientific Society. Ichimura Gakuen Junior College

J Nat Sci Soc Ichimura Gakuen Univ Ichimura Gakuen J Coll — Journal. Natural Scientific Society. Ichimura Gakuen University and Ichimura Gakuen Junior College
J Natural Hist — Journal of Natural History
J Natur Sci and Math — Journal of Natural Sciences and Mathematics
J Naut Arch — International Journal of Nautical Archaeology and Underwater Exploration
J Naut Soc Jpn — Journal. Nautical Society of Japan
J Navig — Journal of Navigation
J Navigation — Royal Institute of Navigation. Journal of Navigation [*London*]
J NAWDAC — Journal. National Association for Women Deans, Administrators, and Counselors
JNBIA — Journal. Newark Beth Israel Hospital
JNC — Journal. National Cancer Institute
J N Ch R A S — Journal. North China Branch. Royal Asiatic Society
JNCLA — Journal. National Chemical Laboratory for Industry
J NC Sect Am Water Works Assoc NC Water Pollut Control Assoc — Journal. North Carolina Section of the American Water Works Association and North Carolina Water Pollution Control Association
JNCUD — Journal of Natural Science. Chonnam National University
JNCYA — Journal of Neurocytology
J NDI — Journal of NDI [*Japan*]
JNDRA — Journal of New Drugs
JNE — Journal of Near Eastern Studies
JNE — Journal of Negro Education
JNE — Journal of Nursing Education
JNE — Journal of Nutrition Education
J Near East — Journal of Near Eastern Studies
J Near Eastern Stud — Journal of Near Eastern Studies
J Near East Stud — Journal of Near Eastern Studies
J Near E St — Journal of Near Eastern Studies
J Near E Stud — Journal of Near Eastern Studies
JNEEA — Journal of Negro Education
J Ne Exp Ne — Journal of Neuropathology and Experimental Neurology
J of Neg Ed — Journal of Negro Education
J Neg Hist — Journal of Negro History
J Negro Ed — Journal of Negro Education
J of Negro Educ — Journal of Negro Education
J Negro Educ — Journal of Negro Education
J Negro His — Journal of Negro History
J Negro Hist — Journal of Negro History
J Nematol — Journal of Nematology
J Ne Ne Psy — Journal of Neurology, Neurosurgery, and Psychiatry
J N Engl Water Pollut Control Assoc — Journal. New England Water Pollution Control Association
J N Engl Water Works Assoc — Journal. New England Water Works Association
J Nerv Ment — Journal of Nervous and Mental Disease
J Nerv Ment Dis — Journal of Nervous and Mental Disease
JNES — Journal of Near Eastern Studies
JNETD — Journal of Non-Equilibrium Thermodynamics
J Neural Tr — Journal of Neural Transmission
J Neural Transm — Journal of Neural Transmission
J Neural Transm Suppl — Journal of Neural Transmission. Supplementum
J Neurobiol — Journal of Neurobiology
J Neurochem — Journal of Neurochemistry
J Neurocyt — Journal of Neurocytology
J Neurocytol — Journal of Neurocytology
J Neurol — Journal of Neurology
J Neurol (Berlin) — Journal of Neurology (Berlin)
J Neurol Neurosurg Psychiatry — Journal of Neurology, Neurosurgery, and Psychiatry
J Neurol Sci — Journal of the Neurological Sciences
J Neuropath Exp Neurol — Journal of Neuropathology and Experimental Neurology
J Neuropathol Exp Neurol — Journal of Neuropathology and Experimental Neurology
J Neurophysiol — Journal of Neurophysiology
J Neuropsychiatr Suppl — Journal of Neuropsychiatry. Supplement
J Neuropsychiatry — Journal of Neuropsychiatry
J Neuroradiol — Journal of Neuroradiology
J Neurosci — Journal of Neuroscience
J Neurosci Methods — Journal of Neuroscience Methods
J Neurosci Res — Journal of Neuroscience Research
J Neurosurg — Journal of Neurosurgery
J Neurosurg Nurs — Journal of Neurosurgical Nursing
J Neurosurg Sci — Journal of Neurosurgical Sciences
J Neuro-Visc Relat — Journal of Neuro-Visceral Relations
J Neurphysl — Journal of Neurophysiology
J Neur Sci — Journal of the Neurological Sciences
J Newark Beth Israel Hosp — Journal. Newark Beth Israel Hospital [*United States*]
J Newark Beth Isr Hosp — Journal. Newark Beth Israel Hospital
J Newark Beth Isr Med Cent — Journal. Newark Beth Israel Medical Center
J Newcastle Sch Arts — Newcastle School of Arts. Journal
J New Drugs — Journal of New Drugs

J New Engl Water Works Ass — Journal. New England Water Works Association

JNFA — Journal of Numismatic Fine Arts

JNFS — Journal of Northwest Atlantic Fishery Science

JNG — Jahrbuch fuer Numismatik und Geldgeschichte

JNGG — Jahrbuch fuer Numismatik und Geldgeschichte

JNH — Journal of Negro History

JNI — Jahrbuch. Nordfriesisches Institut

J Nigerian Inst Oil Palm Res — Journal. Nigerian Institute for Oil Palm Research

J Nihon Univ Sch Dent — Journal. Nihon University School of Dentistry

JNIPRMSI — Japan. National Institute of Polar Research. Memoirs. Special Issue

J Nissei Hosp — Journal. Nissei Hospital [*Japan*]

J NJ State Dent Soc — Journal. New Jersey State Dental Society

JNKVV Res J — JNKVV [*Jawaharlal Nehru Krishi Vishwa Vidyalaya*] Research Journal

JNL — Johnsonian News Letter

JNL — Journal of Northern Luzon

JNL — Journalist. Orgaan van de Nederlandse Vereniging van Journalisten

Jnl Aesthetics — Journal of Aesthetics and Art Criticism

Jnl Aesthetics & Art Crit — Journal of Aesthetics and Art Criticism

Jnl Am Folklore — Journal of American Folklore

Jnl Am Hist — Journal of American History

Jnl of Archtl Education — Journal of Architectural Education

Jnl of Archtl Research — Journal of Architectural Research

Jnl Asian Stu — Journal of Asian Studies

Jnl Business Ed — Journal of Business Education

Jnl of Canadian Art History — Journal of Canadian Art History

Jnl Counsel Psych — Journal of Counseling Psychology

Jnl Econ Hist — Journal of Economic History

Jnl Engl Ger Philol — Journal of English and Germanic Philology

Jnl of Environmental Psychology — Journal of Environmental Psychology

Jnl of Garden History — Journal of Garden History

Jnl Gen Ed — Journal of General Education

Jnl Higher Ed — Journal of Higher Education

Jnl Hist Ideas — Journal of the History of Ideas

Jnl Home Econ — Journal of Home Economics

Jnl Lib Hist — Journal of Library History [*Later, Journal of Library History, Philosophy, and Comparative Librarianship*]

Jnl Marketing — Journal of Marketing

Jnl Marr & Fam — Journal of Marriage and the Family

Jnl Mod Hist — Journal of Modern History

Jnl Negro Ed — Journal of Negro Education

Jnl Negro Hist — Journal of Negro History

JnlOBP — Journal of Black Poetry

JnlONJP — Journal of New Jersey Poets

JnlOPC — Journal of Popular Culture

Jnl Philos — Journal of Philosophy

Jnl of Planning & Environment Law — Journal of Planning and Environment Law

Jnl Polit Econ — Journal of Political Economy

Jnl Politics — Journal of Politics

Jnl Relig — Journal of Religion

JNM — JNM. Journal of Nuclear Medicine

JNMD — Journal of Nervous and Mental Disease

JNMDA — Journal of Nervous and Mental Disease

JNMED — Journal of Neuroscience Methods

JNMSD — Journal of Nuclear Medicine and Allied Sciences

JNMTA — Journal of Nonmetals [*Later, Semiconductors and Insulators*] [*England*]

JNNPA — Journal of Neurology, Neurosurgery, and Psychiatry

JNNVA — Jaarboek. Nederlandse Natuurkundige Vereniging

J No Luzon — Journal of Northern Luzon

J Non-Cryst — Journal of Non-Crystalline Solids

J Non-Cryst Solids — Journal of Non-Crystalline Solids

J Nondestr Eval — Journal of Nondestructive Evaluation [*United States*]

J Non-Destr Insp — Journal of Non-Destructive Inspection

J Non-Equilib Thermodyn — Journal of Non-Equilibrium Thermodynamics

J Nonmet — Journal of Nonmetals [*Later, Semiconductors and Insulators*]

J Nonmet and Semicond — Journal of Nonmetals and Semiconductors [*Later, Semiconductors and Insulators*]

J Nonmet Semicond — Journal of Nonmetals and Semiconductors [*Later, Semiconductors and Insulators*]

J Non-Newtonian Fluid Mech — Journal of Non-Newtonian Fluid Mechanics

J Northampton Mus — Journal. Northampton Museum and Art Gallery

J Northamptonshire Natur Hist Soc Fld Club — Journal. Northamptonshire Natural History Society and Field Club

J Northeast Asian Studies — Journal of Northeast Asian Studies

J Northwest Univ Nat Sci Ed — Journal. Northwest University. Natural Science Edition

J Norw Med Assoc — Journal. Norwegian Medical Association

JNPAB — Journal of Personality Assessment

JNPRD — Journal of Natural Products

JNPS — Journal. Nagari Pracarini Sabha

JNRM — Journal of Natural Resources Management and Interdisciplinary Studies

JNS — Jahrbuecher fuer National-Oekonomie und Statistik

JNSCA — Journal of the Neurological Sciences

JNSEL — Journal of the Northwest Semitic Languages [*Leiden*]

JNSI — Journal. Numismatic Society of India

JNSL — Journal of the Northwest Semitic Languages [*Leiden*]

JNSMP — Journal. Numismatic Society of Madhya Pradesh

JNSNA — Journal of Neurosurgical Nursing

JNSSB — Journal of Neurosurgical Sciences

J NSW Council for Mentally Handicapped — Journal. New South Wales Council for the Mentally Handicapped

JNT — Journal of Narrative Technique

JNTAD — Journal. National Technical Association

JNUCA — Journal of Nuclear Energy [*New York*] [*1954-59*]

J Nucl Agric Biol — Journal of Nuclear Agriculture and Biology

J Nucl Biol — Journal of Nuclear Biology and Medicine

J Nucl Biol Med — Journal of Nuclear Biology and Medicine

J Nucl Energy — Journal of Nuclear Energy

J Nucl Energy Part A — Journal of Nuclear Energy. Part A. Reactor Science

J Nucl Energy Part B — Journal of Nuclear Energy. Part B. Reactor Technology

J Nucl Energy Part C — Journal of Nuclear Energy. Part C. Plasma Physics, Accelerators, Thermonuclear Research

J Nucl Energy Parts A/B — Journal of Nuclear Energy. Parts A/B. Reactor Science and Technology

J Nucl Mat — Journal of Nuclear Materials

J Nucl Mater — Journal of Nuclear Materials

J Nucl Med — Journal of Nuclear Medicine

J Nucl Med Allied Sci — Journal of Nuclear Medicine and Allied Sciences

J Nucl Med Pam — Journal of Nuclear Medicine. Pamphlet

J Nucl Med Suppl — Journal of Nuclear Medicine. Supplement

J Nucl Med Technol — Journal of Nuclear Medicine Technology

J Nucl Radiochem (Peking) — Journal of Nuclear and Radiochemistry (Peking)

J Nucl Sci (Seoul) — Journal of Nuclear Sciences (Seoul)

J Nucl Sci and Technol — Journal of Nuclear Science and Technology

J Nucl Sci Technol — Journal of Nuclear Science and Technology

J Nuc Sci T — Journal of Nuclear Science and Technology

J Number Th — Journal of Number Theory

J Number Theory — Journal of Number Theory

J Nurs Adm — Journal of Nursing Administration

J Nurs Admin — Journal of Nursing Administration

J Nurs Care — Journal of Nursing Care

J Nurs Ed — Journal of Nursery Education

J Nurs Ed — Journal of Nursing Education

J Nurse Midwife — Journal of Nurse Midwifery

J Nurs Midwife — Journal of Nurse Midwifery

J Nurs (Taipei) — Journal of Nursing (Taipei)

J Nutr — Journal of Nutrition

J Nutr Diet — Journal of Nutrition and Dietetics

J Nutr Educ — Journal of Nutrition Education

J Nutr Sci — Journal of Nutritional Sciences

J Nutr Sci Vitaminol — Journal of Nutritional Science and Vitaminology

J Nutr Sc V — Journal of Nutritional Science and Vitaminology

J Nutr Suppl — Journal of Nutrition. Supplement [*United States*]

J NVCA — Journal. National Volleyball Coaches Association

JNWSemL — Journal of the Northwest Semitic Languages [*Leiden*]

J Nw SL — Journal of the Northwest Semitic Languages

J NY Entomol Soc — Journal. New York Entomological Society

J NY Ent So — Journal. New York Entomological Society

J NY Med Coll Flower and Fifth Ave Hosp — Journal. New York Medical College. Flower and Fifth Avenue Hospitals

J NY Med Coll Flower Fifth Ave Hosp — Journal. New York Medical College. Flower and Fifth Avenue Hospitals

J NY State Nurses Assoc — Journal. New York State Nurses Association

J NZ Assoc Bacteriol — Journal. New Zealand Association of Bacteriologists

J NZ Diet Assoc — Journal. New Zealand Dietetic Association

J NZ Fed Hist Soc — Journal. New Zealand Federation of Historical Societies

J NZ Inst Chem — Journal. New Zealand Institute of Chemistry

J NZ Inst Med Lab Technol — Journal. New Zealand Institute of Medical Laboratory Technology

JNZKA — Jinko Zoki

JO — Jewish Observer and Middle East Review [*London*]

JoA — Jewel of Africa [*Zambia*]

JOA — Journal of Advertising

JOABAW — Journal of Applied Behavior Analysis

JOAD — Journal. American Dietetic Association

JOADE8 — Journal of Adolescence

JOAEEB — Journal of Applied Entomology

JOALAS — Journal of Allergy [*Later, Journal of Allergy and Clinical Immunology*]

JOAN — Journal of Applied Nutrition

JOANAY — Journal of Anatomy

JOAND3 — Journal of Andrology

JOAP — Journal of Applied Psychology

JOB — Journal of Business

JOB — Journal of Business Administration [*Canada*]
JOBG — Jahrbuch. Oesterreichische Byzantinische Gesellschaft
JOBM — Journal of Behavioral Medicine
Job Safe & H — Job Safety and Health
Jobsons Invest Dig — Jobson's Investment Digest
Jobsons Investment D — Jobson's Investment Digest
J Obstet Gynaec Br Commonw — Journal of Obstetrics and Gynaecology of the British Commonwealth
J Obstet Gynaec Brit Cmwlth — Journal of Obstetrics and Gynaecology of the British Commonwealth
J Obstet Gynaec Brit Emp — Journal of Obstetrics and Gynaecology of the British Empire
J Obstet Gynaecol Br Commonw — Journal of Obstetrics and Gynaecology of the British Commonwealth
J Obstet Gynaecol Br Emp — Journal of Obstetrics and Gynaecology of the British Empire
J Obstet Gynaecol India — Journal of Obstetrics and Gynaecology of India
JOC — Journal of Communication Management
J OCCA — Journal. Oil and Colour Chemists' Association
J Occ Bhvr — Journal of Occupational Behaviour
J Occup Accid — Journal of Occupational Accidents
J Occupa Med — Journal of Occupational Medicine
J Occupa Psychol — Journal of Occupational Psychology
J Occupational Accidents — Journal of Occupational Accidents
J Occupat Med — Journal of Occupational Medicine
J Occup Med — Journal of Occupational Medicine
J Oceanogr Soc Jpn — Journal. Oceanographical Society of Japan
J Oceanol Soc Korea — Journal. Oceanological Society of Korea
J Ocean Technol — Journal of Ocean Technology
JOCH — Journal of Community Health
JOCMA — Journal of Occupational Medicine
JOCS — Journal of Offender Counseling, Services, and Rehabilitation
JOD — Journal of Development
JOD — Journal of Documentation [*London*]
JOD — Juedischer Ordnungsdienst
JODC — Journal of Dentistry for Children
JODE — Journal of Drug Education
JODI — Journal of Drug Issues
J Odor Control — Journal of Odor Control
JODV — Journal of Divorce
JOEAI — Jahreshefte. Oesterreichisches Archaeologische Institut in Wien
JOEByz — Jahrbuch der Oesterreichischen Byzantinistik
JOEEA — Journal of Emotional Education
JOENA — Journal of Endocrinology
Joenkoepings Laens Hushallningssaellsk Tidskr — Joenkoepings Laens Hushallningssaellskaps. Tidskrift
Joensuun Korkeakoulun Julk Sar Bii — Joensuun Korkeakoulun Julkaisuja. Sarja Bii
JOERA — Journal of Educational Research
JoES — Journal of European Studies
JOET — Journal of Education for Teaching
JOF — Journal of Forecasting
J Off Rech Pech Can — Journal. Office des Recherches sur les Pecheries du Canada
J Off Repub Fr — Journal Officiel de la Republique Francaise
JOFH — Journal of Family History. Studies in Family, Kinship, and Demography
JOGEA — Journal of Gerontology
JOGL — Journal of Glaciology
JOGM — Jord og Myr. Tidsskrift foer det Norske Jord-og Myselskap
JOGNB — JOGN [*Journal of Obstetric, Gynecologic, and Neonatal Nursing*] Nursing
JOGN Nurs — JOGN [*Journal of Obstetric, Gynecologic, and Neonatal Nursing*] Nursing
Jogtud Koezl — Jogtudomanyi Koezloeny
JOH — Journal of Housing
JOHE — Journal of Health Economics
JOHEA — Journal of Heredity
JOHH — Journal of Holistic Health
J Ohio Herpetol Soc — Journal. Ohio Herpetological Society
JOHJ — John O'Hara Journal
John Alexander Monogr Ser Var Phases Thorac Surg — John Alexander Monograph Series on Various Phases of Thoracic Surgery
John Dewey Soc Yrbk — John Dewey Society. Yearbook
John Herron Art Inst Bul — John Herron Art Institute. Bulletin [*Indianapolis*]
John Innes Bull — John Innes Bulletin
John Innes Hortic Inst Annu Rep — John Innes Horticultural Institution. Annual Report
John Innes Inst Annu Rep — John Innes Institute. Annual Report
John Mar J Prac & Proc — John Marshall Journal of Practice and Procedure
John Marshall J — John Marshall Journal of Practice and Procedure
John Marshall Jr — John Marshall Journal of Practice and Procedure
John Marsh L Rev — John Marshall Law Review
John Rylands Lib Bul — John Rylands Library. Bulletin
Johns H Med — Johns Hopkins Medical Journal

Johns Hopkins APL Tech Dig — Johns Hopkins University. Applied Physics Laboratory. Technical Digest [*United States*]
Johns Hopkins APL Technical Digest — Johns Hopkins University. Applied Physics Laboratory. Technical Digest
Johns Hopkins M — Johns Hopkins Magazine
Johns Hopkins Med J — Johns Hopkins Medical Journal
Johns Hopkins Med J Suppl — Johns Hopkins Medical Journal. Supplement
Johns Hopkins Oceanogr Stud — Johns Hopkins Oceanographic Studies
Johns Hopkins Ser in Math Sci — Johns Hopkins Series in the Mathematical Sciences
Johns Hopkins Univ Appl Phys Lab Spec Rep — Johns Hopkins University. Applied Physics Laboratory. Special Report
Johns Hopkins Univ Cir — Johns Hopkins University. Circular
Johns Hopkins Univ McCollum Pratt Inst Contrib — Johns Hopkins University McCollum Pratt Institute. Contribution
Johns Hopkins Univ Stud — Johns Hopkins University. Studies in Historical and Political Science
Johns H U Stud — Johns Hopkins University. Studies in Historical and Political Science
JOHOA — Journal of Housing
JOHPER — Journal of Health, Physical Education, Recreation
JoHS — Journal of Hellenic Studies
JOHX — Journal of Homosexuality
JOIB — Journal. Oriental Institute (Baroda)
JOICA — Journal. Institution of Chemists
JOIDES Journal — Joint Oceanographic Institutions for Deep Earth Sampling. Journal
J Oil Col C — Journal. Oil and Colour Chemists' Association
J Oil Colour Chem Ass — Journal. Oil and Colour Chemists' Association
J Oil Colour Chem Assoc — Journal. Oil and Colour Chemists' Association
J Oil Fat Ind — Journal of Oil and Fat Industries
J Oil Technol Assoc India — Journal. Oil Technologists' Association of India
J Oil Technol Assoc India (Bombay) — Journal. Oil Technologists' Association of India (Bombay)
J Oil Technol Assoc India (Kanpur India) — Journal. Oil Technologists' Association of India (Kanpur, India)
Joint Automat Contr Conf Prepr Tech Pap — Joint Automatic Control Conference. Preprints of Technical Papers
JOJAA — Journal of Otolaryngology of Japan
Jo Je S — Journal of Jewish Studies
J Okayama Med Soc — Journal. Okayama Medical Society [*Japan*]
J Okayama Med Soc Suppl — Journal. Okayama Medical Society. Supplement [*Japan*]
J Okla State Dent Assoc — Journal. Oklahoma State Dental Association
J Okla State Med Assoc — Journal. Oklahoma State Medical Association
JOKU — Jokull
JOKUA — Joekull (Reykjavik)
JOL — Journal of Oriental Literature
JOLA — Journal of Library Automation
JOLAB — Journal-Lancet
J Old Wexford Soc — Journal. Old Wexford Society
JOM — Journal of Metals
JOM — Journal of Occupational Medicine
JOMA — Journal of Military Assistance
JOMER — Jewish Observer and Middle East Review
JOM J Occup Med — JOM. Journal of Occupational Medicine [*United States*]
JOMMA — Journal of Mathematics and Mechanics
JOMS — Journal of Oral and Maxillofacial Surgery
JOMSD — Journal of Oral and Maxillofacial Surgery
JOMV — Jahrbuch. Oberoesterreichischer Musealverein
JOMYA — Journal of Meteorology
J Oncol Tianjin Med J Suppl — Journal of Oncology. Tianjin Medical Journal. Supplement
JONE — Journal of Nutrition Education
JONEA — Journal of Neurophysiology
J Ont Dent Assoc — Journal. Ontario Dental Association [*Canada*]
JONUDL — Journal. American College of Nutrition
JOOM — Journal of Occupational Medicine
JOP — Journal of Occupational Psychology
JOPD — Journal of Psychoactive Drugs
JOPDA — Journal of Pediatrics
J Open Educ Assoc Qld — Journal. Open Education Association of Queensland
J Operational Psychiatr — Journal of Operational Psychiatry
J Operations Res Soc Japan — Journal. Operations Research Society of Japan
J Operator Theory — Journal of Operator Theory
J Oper Res Soc — Journal. Operational Research Society
J Oper Res Soc Am — Journal. Operation Research Society of America
J Oper Res Soc Jap — Journal. Operations Research Society of Japan
JOPHA — Journal de Physiologie
JOPID — Journal of Pipelines
JOPP — Journal of Primary Prevention
JOPPA — Journal de Physiologie (Paris). Supplement
J Op Res So — Journal. Operations Research Society of Japan
J Op Res Soc — Journal. Operational Research Society
JOPSA — Journal of Psychology

J Opt — Journal of Optics
J Opt Commun — Journal of Optical Communications
J Optimization Theory Appl — Journal of Optimization Theory and Applications
J Optimiz Theory and Appl — Journal of Optimization Theory and Applications
J Optim Th — Journal of Optimization Theory and Applications
J Optim Theory Appl — Journal of Optimization Theory and Applications
J Opt Soc — Journal. Optical Society of America
J Opt Soc Am — Journal. Optical Society of America
J Opt Soc Am A — Journal. Optical Society of America. A. Optics and Image Science
J Opt Soc Am B Opt Phys — Journal. Optical Society of America. B. Optical Physics
J Opt Soc Amer — Journal. Optical Society of America
J Opt Soc Am Rev Sci Instrum — Journal. Optical Society of America and Review of Scientific Instruments
JOR — Journal of Organizational Behavior Management
JOR — Journal of Oriental Research
J Oral Implantol — Journal of Oral Implantology
J Oral Implant Transplant Surg — Journal of Oral Implant and Transplant Surgery
J Oral Maxillofac Surg — Journal of Oral and Maxillofacial Surgery
J Oral Med — Journal of Oral Medicine
J Oral Pathol — Journal of Oral Pathology
J Oral Rehabil — Journal of Oral Rehabilitation
J Oral Surg — Journal of Oral Surgery
J Oral Surg Anesth Hosp Dent Serv — Journal of Oral Surgery, Anesthesia, and Hospital Dental Service
J Oral Ther Pharmacol — Journal of Oral Therapeutics and Pharmacology
Jordan Med J — Jordan Medical Journal
Jordan Minist Agric Annu Rep (Eng Ed) — Jordan. Ministry of Agriculture. Annual Report (English Edition)
Jordbruksekon Medd Statens Jordbruksnamned — Jordbruksekonomiska Meddelanden. Statens Jordbruksnamned
Jordbrukstek Inst Cirk — Jordbrukstekniska Institutet. Cirkulaer
Jord-ekon Medd — Jordbruksekonomiska Meddelanden
JORDM — Journal Officiel. Republique Democratique de Madagascar
JOREA — Journal of Rehabilitation
JORF — Journal Officiel de la Republique Francaise
J Organometal Chem — Journal of Organometallic Chemistry
J Organometallic Chem — Journal of Organometallic Chemistry
J Organomet Chem — Journal of Organometallic Chemistry
J Organomet Chem Libr — Journal. Organometallic Chemistry Library
J Org Chem — Journal of Organic Chemistry
J Org Chem USSR — Journal of Organic Chemistry of the USSR
J Orgl Bhvr Mgt — Journal of Organizational Behavior Management
J Orgl Com — Journal of Organizational Communication
J Orgmet Ch — Journal of Organometallic Chemistry
J Oriental Soc Aust — Journal. Oriental Society of Australia
J Orient Inst (Baroda) — Journal. Oriental Institute (Baroda)
J Orissa Math Soc — Journal of Orissa Mathematical Society
Jornadas Agron Trab — Jornadas Agronomicas. Trabajos
Jornadas Agron Vet Univ Buenos Aires Fac Agron Vet — Jornadas Agronomicas y Veterinarias. Universidad de Buenos Aires. Facultad de Agronomia y Veterinaria
Jorn Bras Psicol — Jornal Brasileiro de Psicologia
J Ornithol — Journal fuer Ornithologie
JORS — Journal. Operational Research Society
JORSJ — Journal. Operations Research Society of Japan
J Or Soc Aust — Journal. Oriental Society of Australia
J Or Stud — Journal of Oriental Studies
J Orthomol Psychiatry — Journal of Orthomolecular Psychiatry
J Orthop Sports Phys Ther — Journal of Orthopaedic and Sports Physical Therapy
J Ortho and Sports Phys Ther — Journal of Orthopaedic and Sports Physical Therapy
JOS — Jezyki Obce w Szkole
JOS — Journal of Oriental Studies
JOSA — Journal. Optical Society of America
JOSAA — Journal. Optical Society of America
Josa Andras Muz Ev — Josa Andras Muzeum Evkoenyve
J Osaka City Med Cent — Journal. Osaka City Medical Center
J Osaka Dent Univ — Journal. Osaka Dental University
J Osaka Inst Sci Technol Part 1 — Journal. Osaka Institute of Science and Technology. Part 1
J Osaka Med Coll — Journal. Osaka Medical College [Japan]
J Osaka Odontol Soc — Journal. Osaka Odontological Society
J Osaka Univ Dent Sch — Journal. Osaka University Dental School
J Osaka Univ Dent Soc — Journal. Osaka University Dental Society [Japan]
JOSH — Journal of School Health
JOSHA — Joho Shori
JOSHB — Journal. American Society for Horticultural Science
JOSHB5 — Journal. American Society for Horticultural Science
J Oslo City Hosp — Journal. Oslo City Hospital
J Osmania Univ — Journal. Osmania University

JOstByzGes — Jahrbuch. Oesterreichische Byzantinische Gesellschaft [Vienna]
JOT — Journal of Coatings Technology
JOT — Journal of Taxation
JOT J Oberflaechentech — JOT. Journal fuer Oberflaechentechnik
JOTOD — Journal of Otolaryngology
J Otolaryngol — Journal of Otolaryngology
J Oto-Laryngol Soc Aust — Journal. Oto-Laryngological Society of Australia
J Otolaryngol Suppl — Journal of Otolaryngology. Supplement
J Oto-Rhino-Laryngol Soc Jpn — Journal. Oto-Rhino-Laryngological Society of Japan
JOTPA — Journal of Oral Therapeutics and Pharmacology
J Otto Rank — Journal. Otto Rank Association
Jour Acoust Soc — Journal. Acoustical Society of America
Jour Aesthetics and Art Crit — Journal of Aesthetics and Art Criticism
Jour Am Folklore — Journal of American Folklore
Jour Am Inst Archit — Journal. American Institute of Architecture
Jour Am Jud Soc — Journal. American Judicature Society
Jour Am Studies — Journal of American Studies
Jour Brit Studies — Journal of British Studies
Jour Chem Physics — Journal of Chemical Physics
Jour Church and State — Journal of Church and State
Jour Conchyliologie — Journal de Conchyliologie
Jour Conflict Resolution — Journal of Conflict Resolution
Jour Conseil — Journal du Conseil
Jour Contemp Hist — Journal of Contemporary History
Jour Crim L — Journal of Criminal Law and Criminology
Jour Crim Law — Journal of Criminal Law, Criminology, and Police Science [Later, Journal of Criminal Law and Criminology]
Jour Devel Areas — Journal of Developmental Areas
Jour Eccl Hist — Journal of Ecclesiastical History
Jour Ecology — Journal of Ecology
Jour Econ and Bus Hist — Journal of Economic and Business History
Jour Econ Hist — Journal of Economic History
Jour Farm Hist — Journal of Farm History
Jour Folklore Inst — Journal. Folklore Institute
Jour Gemmology — Journal of Gemmology and Proceedings of the Gemmological Association of Great Britain
Jour Geol Education — Journal of Geological Education
Jour Glaciology — Journal of Glaciology
Jour Hist Ideas — Journal of the History of Ideas
Jour Hist Med — Journal of the History of Medicine
Jour Hist Phil — Journal of the History of Philosophy
Jour Human Rel — Journal of Human Relations
Jour of Indian Art and Ind — Journal of Indian Art and Industry
Jour Inorganic and Nuclear Chemistry — Journal of Inorganic and Nuclear Chemistry
Jour of Int Affairs — Journal of International Affairs
Jour Interam Studies — Journal of Interamerican Studies and World Affairs
Jour Land Public Utility Econ — Journal of Land and Public Utility Economics
Jour Law and Econ — Journal of Law and Economic Development
Jour Legal Ed — Journal of Legal Education
Jour Lib Hist — Journal of Library History [Later, Journal of Library History, Philosophy, and Comparative Librarianship]
Jour Miss Hist — Journal of Mississippi History
Jour Mod Hist — Journal of Modern History
Journal Cork Hist Soc — Journal. Cork Historical and Archaeological Society
Journal Greater India Soc — Journal. Greater India Society
Journal Gujarat Research Soc — Journal. Gujarat Research Society [India]
Journalism Conf Workshop ADA — Journalism Conference and Workshop. American Dental Association Council on Journalism and American Association of Dental Editors
Journalism Educ — Journalism Educator
Journalism Q — Journalism Quarterly
Journal of RPS — Journal. Royal Photographic Society
Journal Sadul Rajasthani Research Inst — Journal. Sadul Rajasthani Research Institute
Journal Soc Antiq — Journal. Royal Society of Antiquaries of Ireland
Journal Soc Finno-Ougr — Journal. Societe Finno-Ougrienne
Journ Annu Diabetol Hotel-Dieu — Journees Annuelles de Diabetologie Hotel-Dieu
Journ Calorim Anal Therm Prepr — Journees de Calorimetrie et d'Analyse Thermique. Preprints
Journ Hist Behavioral Sci — Journal of the History of the Behavioral Sciences
Journ Pharm Fr — Journees Pharmaceutiques Francaises
Journ Q — Journalism Quarterly
Journ Rech Ovine Caprine — Journees de la Recherche Ovine et Caprine
Journ Sci Cent Natl Coord Etud Rech Nutr Aliment — Journees Scientifiques. Centre National de Coordination des Etudes et Recherches sur la Nutrition et l'Alimentation
Journ Vinic Export — Journee Vinicole Export
Jour Pac Hist — Journal of Pacific History
Jour Palynology — Journal of Palynology
Jour Philos — Journal of Philosophy
Jour Pol Econ — Journal of Political Economy
Jour Politics — Journal of Politics

Jour Presby Hist — Journal of Presbyterian History
Jour f Psychol u Neurol — Journal fuer Psychologie und Neurologie
Jour Pub Law — Journal of Public Law
Jour of Relig — Journal of Religion
Jour Relig Hist — Journal of Religious History
Jour Soc Hist — Journal of Social History
Jour Society Archit Historians — Journal. Society of Architectural Historians
Jour of Soc Issues — Journal of Social Issues
Jour Soc Philos — Journal of Social Philosophy
Jour Soc Sci — Journal of Social Sciences
Jour Speech Disorders — Journal of Speech Disorders
Jour of West — Journal of the West
JOUSD — Journal of Science. Busan National University
JOV — Jahrbuch des Oesterreichischen Volksliedwerkes
JOV — Jahrbuch fuer Ostdeutsche Volkskunde
JP — Jahrbuch fuer Philologie
JP — Jerusalem Post
JP — Jezyk Polski
JP — Journal of Parapsychology
JP — Journal of Philology
JP — Journal of Philosophy
JP — Journal of Politics
JP — Journal de Psychologie Normale et Pathologique
JP — Journal of Psychology
JPA — Jurisprudences du Port D'Anvers [*Belgium*]
J Pac Hist — Journal of Pacific History
J Pacif Hist — Journal of Pacific History
J Pacific Hist — Journal of Pacific History
J Paint Tec — Journal of Paint Technology
J Paix — Journal de la Paix
J Pak Hist Soc — Journal. Pakistan Historical Society
J Pak Med Assoc — Journal. Pakistan Medical Association
J Paleont — Journal of Paleontology
J Paleontol — Journal of Paleontology
J Pales Stu — Journal of Palestine Studies
J Palestine Stud — Journal of Palestine Studies
J Palynol — Journal of Palynology
JPAMD — Journal of Policy Analysis and Management
JPaOrS — Journal. Palestine Oriental Society
JPAPD — Journal of Experimental Psychology: Animal Behavior Processes
J Papua NG Society — Journal. Papua and New Guinea Society
J Parapsych — Journal of Parapsychology
J Parapsychol — Journal of Parapsychology
J Parasit — Journal of Parasitology
J Parasitol — Journal of Parasitology
J Parasitology — Journal of Parasitology
J Parlia Info — Journal of Parliamentary Information
J Past Care — Journal of Pastoral Care
J Past Coun — Journal of Pastoral Counseling
J Pastoral Care — Journal of Pastoral Care
J Path Bact — Journal of Pathology and Bacteriology
J Path and Bacteriol — Journal of Pathology and Bacteriology
J Pathol — Journal of Pathology
J Pathol Bacteriol — Journal of Pathology and Bacteriology
J Pathology — Journal of Pathology
J Patient Acc Manage — Journal of Patient Account Management
J Pat Off Soc'y — Journal. Patent Office Society
J Pat Of So — Journal. Patent Office Society
J PA Water Works Oper Assoc — Journal. Pennsylvania Water Works Operators' Association
JPB — Journal des Poetes (Brussels)
JPBEA — Journal de Pharmacie de Belgique
JPBPB — Journal of Pharmacokinetics and Biopharmaceutics
JPC — Journal of Pastoral Care
JPC — Journal of Popular Culture
JPCAAC — Journal. Air Pollution Control Association
JPCCA — Journal of Physical and Colloid Chemistry
JPCMA — Journal of Photochemistry
JPCRB — Journal of Physical and Chemical Reference Data
JPCRD — Journal of Physical and Chemical Reference Data
JPCSB — Journal of Physics and Chemistry of Solids. Supplement
JPCSC — Journal of Physical and Chemical Reference Data. Supplement
JPDAAH — Journal. American Podiatry Association
JPDEA — Journal of Prosthetic Dentistry
JPDMB — American Society of Psychosomatic Dentistry and Medicine. Journal
JPDMBK — Journal. American Society of Psychosomatic Dentistry and Medicine
JPDPA — Journal of Periodontology - Periodontics
JPE — Journal of Political Economy
J Peace Res — Journal of Peace Research
J Peace Research — Journal of Peace Research
J Peace Sci — Journal of Peace Science
J Peasant Stud — Journal of Peasant Studies
J Peasant Studies — Journal of Peasant Studies
J Peas Stud — Journal of Peasant Studies

J Ped — Journal of Pediatrics
JPEDD — Journal of Physics Education
J Pediat — Journal of Pediatrics
J Pediat Psychol — Journal of Pediatric Psychology
J Pediatr — Journal of Pediatrics
J Pediatr Ophthalmol — Journal of Pediatric Ophthalmology
J Pediatr Ophthalmol Strabismus — Journal of Pediatric Ophthalmology and Strabismus
J Pediatr Surg — Journal of Pediatric Surgery
J Pedod — Journal of Pedodontics
J Ped Surg — Journal of Pediatric Surgery
JPEL — Journal of Planning and Environment Law
JPEN — Journal of Parenteral and Enteral Nutrition
JPEN J Parent Enteral Nutr — JPEN. Journal of Parenteral and Enteral Nutrition
J Pen Pl and Comp — Journal of Pension Planning and Compliance
J Pension Plan and Compliance — Journal of Pension Planning and Compliance
J Pension Planning and Compliance — Journal of Pension Planning and Compliance
JPer — Journal of Personality
J PERD — Journal of Physical Education, Recreation, and Dance
J Perinat Med — Journal of Perinatal Medicine
J Periodont — Journal of Periodontology
J Periodontal Res — Journal of Periodontal Research
J Periodontal Res Suppl — Journal of Periodontal Research. Supplement
J Periodontol — Journal of Periodontology
J Periodontol-Periodontics — Journal of Periodontology - Periodontics
J Period Re — Journal of Periodontal Research
J Perm Way Instn — Permanent Way Institution. Journal
JPers — Journal of Personality
J Pers Asse — Journal of Personality Assessment
J Pers Assess — Journal of Personality Assessment
J Personal — Journal of Personality
J Pers Soc — Journal of Personality and Social Psychology
J Pers Soc Psychol — Journal of Personality and Social Psychology
J Perth Hosp — Journal. Perth Hospital
JPESB — Jewish Palestine Exploration Society. Bulletin
J Pestic Sci (Nihon Noyakugaku Kaishi) — Journal of Pesticide Science (Nihon Noyakugaku Kaishi)
JPET — Journal of Petroleum Technology
J Pet Geol — Journal of Petroleum Geology [*England*]
J Petrol — Journal of Petrology
J Petrol Geol — Journal of Petroleum Geology
J Petrol Technol — Journal of Petroleum Technology
J Petro Tec — Journal of Petroleum Technology
J Pet Tech — Journal of Petroleum Technology
J Pet Technol — Journal of Petroleum Technology
JPF — Journal of Popular Film [*Later, Journal of Popular Film and Television*]
JPFMA — Journal of Physics. F: Metal Physics
JPGED — Journal of Experimental Psychology: General
JPGR — Journal of Plant Growth Regulation
JPH — Journal of Pacific History
JPh — Journal of Philosophy
JPh — Journal of Phonetics
JPH — Journal of Presbyterian History
JPHAA — Journal. American Pharmaceutical Association
JPHAA3 — Journal. American Pharmaceutical Association
JPHAC — Journal of Physics. A: Mathematical and General
J Phar Biop — Journal of Pharmacokinetics and Biopharmaceutics
J Pharm — Journal de Pharmacie
J Pharmacokinet Biopharm — Journal of Pharmacokinetics and Biopharmaceutics
J Pharmacol — Journal de Pharmacologie
J Pharmacol Clin — Journal de Pharmacologie Clinique
J Pharmacol Exp Ther — Journal of Pharmacology and Experimental Therapeutics
J Pharmacol Methods — Journal of Pharmacological Methods
J Pharm Assoc Thailand — Journal. Pharmaceutical Association of Thailand
J Pharm Belg — Journal de Pharmacie de Belgique
J Pharm Exp — Journal of Pharmacology and Experimental Therapeutics
J Pharm (Paris) — Journal de Pharmacie et des Sciences Accessoires (Paris)
J Pharm Pha — Journal of Pharmacy and Pharmacology
J Pharm Pharmac — Journal of Pharmacy and Pharmacology
J Pharm Pharmacol — Journal of Pharmacy and Pharmacology
J Pharm Sci — Journal of Pharmaceutical Sciences
J Pharm Sci Accessoires — Journal de Pharmacie et des Sciences Accessoires
J Pharm Sci UAR — Journal of Pharmaceutical Sciences of the United Arab Republic
J Pharm Soc Japan — Journal. Pharmaceutical Society of Japan
J Pharm Soc Jpn — Journal. Pharmaceutical Society of Japan
J Pharm Soc Korea — Journal. Pharmaceutical Society of Korea
J Ph Ch Ref Data — Journal of Physical and Chemical Reference Data
JPHD — Journal of Public Health Dentistry
J Phenomen — Journal of Phenomenological Psychology
JPHGB — Journal of Physics. G: Nuclear Physics

J Phil — Journal of Philosophy
J Philadelphia Coll Pharm — Journal. Philadelphia College of Pharmacy
J Philadelphia Gen Hosp — Journal. Philadelphia General Hospital
J Phil Educ — Journal of Philosophy of Education
J Philippine Development — Journal of Philippine Development
J Philippine Statis — Journal of Philippine Statistics
J Philipp Isl Med Assoc — Journal. Philippine Islands Medical Association
J Philipp Med Assoc — Journal. Philippine Medical Association
J Philipp Pharm Assoc — Journal. Philippine Pharmaceutical Association
J Philipp Vet Med Assoc — Journal. Philippine Veterinary Medical Association
J Phil Log — Journal of Philosophical Logic
J Philos — Journal of Philosophy
J Philos Lo — Journal of Philosophical Logic
J Philos Logic — Journal of Philosophical Logic
J Phil Sport — Journal of the Philosophy of Sport
JPHMD — Journal of Experimental Psychology: Human Learning and Memory
JPhon — Journal of Phonetics
J Photochem — Journal of Photochemistry
J Photogr Sci — Journal of Photographic Science
J Photomicrogr Soc — Journal. Photomicrographic Society
J Phot Sci — Journal of Photographic Science
JPHP — Journal of Public Health Policy
JPHPD — Journal of Experimental Psychology: Human Perception and Performance
JPHS — Journal. Presbyterian Historical Society
JPhV — Jahresbericht. Philologischer Verein
JPHYA — Journal of Physiology
J Phycol — Journal of Phycology
J Phycology — Journal of Phycology
J Phys — Journal de Physique
J Phys A — Journal of Physics. A: Mathematical and General [Bristol]
J Phys A Gen Phys — Journal of Physics. A: General Physics
J Phys A (London) — Journal of Physics. A: General Physics (London)
J Phys A (London) Proc Phys Soc Gen — Journal of Physics. A: Proceedings. Physical Society. General (London)
J Phys A Math Nucl Gen — Journal of Physics. A: Mathematical, Nuclear, and General
J Phys B — Journal of Physics. B: Atomic and Molecular Physics
J of Phys B At Mol Phys — Journal of Physics. B: Atomic and Molecular Physics
J Phys B (London) — Journal of Physics. B: Atomic and Molecular Physics (London)
J Phys C — Journal of Physics. C: Solid State Physics
J Phys Chem — Journal of Physical Chemistry
J Phys & Chem Ref Data — Journal of Physical and Chemical Reference Data
J Phys Chem Ref Data — Journal of Physical and Chemical Reference Data
J Phys Chem Ref Data Suppl — Journal of Physical and Chemical Reference Data. Supplement
J Phys Chem Sol — Journal of Physics and Chemistry of Solids
J Phys and Chem Solids — Journal of Physics and Chemistry of Solids
J Phys Chem Solids — Journal of Physics and Chemistry of Solids
J Phys Chem Solids Suppl — Journal of Physics and Chemistry of Solids. Supplement [England]
J Phys Chem (Wash) — Journal of Physical Chemistry (Washington, DC)
J Phys Ch S — Journal of Physics and Chemistry of Solids
J Phys C (London) — Journal of Physics. C: Solid State Physics (London)
J Phys & Colloid Chem — Journal of Physical and Colloid Chemistry
J Phys D Appl Phys — Journal of Physics. D: Applied Physics
J Phys D (London) — Journal of Physics. D: Applied Physics (London)
J Phys E — Journal of Physics. E: Scientific Instruments
J Phys Earth — Journal of Physics of the Earth
J Phys Ed — Journal of Physical Education
J Phys Educ — Journal of Physical Education
J Phys Educ & Rec — Journal of Physical Education and Recreation [Later, Journal of Physical Education, Recreation, and Dance]
J Phys Educ Rec & Dance — Journal of Physical Education, Recreation, and Dance
J Phys Educ Recr — Journal of Physical Education and Recreation [Later, Journal of Physical Education, Recreation, and Dance]
J Phys E (London) Sci Instrum — Journal of Physics. E: Scientific Instruments (London)
J Phys E Sci Instrum — Journal of Physics. E: Scientific Instruments
J Phys F — Journal of Physics. F: Metal Physics
J Phys F Met Phys — Journal of Physics. F: Metal Physics
J Phys G — Journal of Physics. G: Nuclear Physics
J Phys G Nu — Journal of Physics. G: Nuclear Physics
J Physiol — Journal of Physiology
J Physiol Exper — Journal de Physiologie Experimentale et Pathologique
J Physiol (Lond) — Journal of Physiology (London)
J Physiol (Paris) — Journal de Physiologie (Paris)
J Physiol (Paris) Suppl — Journal de Physiologie (Paris). Supplement [France]
J Physiol et Path Gen — Journal de Physiologie et de Pathologie Generale
J Physiol Soc Jpn — Journal. Physiological Society of Japan
J Physique — Journal de Physique
J Phys Jap — Journal. Physical Society of Japan

J Phys Lett — Journal de Physique. Lettres
J Physl (Lon) — Journal of Physiology (London)
J Physl (Par) — Journal de Physiologie (Paris)
J Phys (Moscow) — Journal of Physics (Moscow) [USSR]
J Phys Ocea — Journal of Physical Oceanography
J Phys Oceanogr — Journal of Physical Oceanography
J Phys (Orsay Fr) — Journal de Physique (Orsay, France)
J Phys (Paris) — Journal de Physique (Paris)
J Phys (Paris) Colloq — Journal de Physique (Paris). Colloque
J Phys (Paris) Lett — Journal de Physique. Lettres (Paris)
J Phys (Paris) Suppl — Journal de Physique (Paris). Supplement
J Phys Radium — Journal de Physique et le Radium [France]
J Phys (Soc Fr Phys) Colloq — Journal de Physique (Societe Francaise de Physique). Colloque
J Phys Soc Jap — Journal. Physical Society of Japan
J Phys Soc Jpn Suppl — Journal. Physical Society of Japan. Supplement
J Phys Theor Appl — Journal de Physique Theorique et Appliquee
J Phytopathol (Berl) — Journal of Phytopathology (Berlin)
J Phytopathol (UAR) — Journal of Phytopathology (UAR)
JPIFAN — Japan Pesticide Information
J Pineal Res — Journal of Pineal Research
J Pipeline Div Am Soc Civ Eng — Journal. Pipeline Division. American Society of Civil Engineers
J Pipelines — Journal of Pipelines
JPJu — Journal of Psychology and Judaism
JPKS — Jahrbuch. Preussische Kunstsammlungen
JPL — Journal of Philosophical Logic
J P L — Journal of Planning Law
JPL — Journal of Products Liability
J P and L — Journal of Psychiatry and Law
J Plan Envir Law — Journal of Planning and Environment Law
J Plan & Environ L — Journal of Planning and Environment Law
J Planif Develop — Journal de la Planification du Developpement
J Plankton Res — Journal of Plankton Research [England]
J Plann Environ Law — Journal of Planning and Environment Law
J Planning and Environment Law — Journal of Planning and Environment Law
J Plann Property Law — Journal of Planning and Property Law
J Plan & Prop L — Journal of Planning and Property Law
J Plant Breed — Journal of Plant Breeding
J Plant Crops — Journal of Plantation Crops
J Plant Dis Prot — Journal of Plant Diseases and Protection
J Plantn Crops — Journal of Plantation Crops
J Plant Nutr Soil Sci — Journal of Plant Nutrition and Soil Science
J Plant Physiol — Journal of Plant Physiology
J Plant Prot — Journal of Plant Protection
J Plas Age — Japan Plastics Age
J Plasma Ph — Journal of Plasma Physics
J Plasma Phys — Journal of Plasma Physics
J Plast Reconstr Surg Nurs — Journal of Plastic and Reconstructive Surgical Nursing
J Platn Crops — Journal of Plantation Crops
J Pl L — Journal of Planning Law
JPL Publ 78 — Jet Propulsion Laboratory. Publication 78
JPL Q Tech Rev — JPL [Jet Propulsion Laboratory] Quarterly Technical Review
JPLSA — Journal. Polarographic Society
JPL Space Programs Summ — Jet Propulsion Laboratory. Space Programs Summary
JPL Tech Memo — JPL [Jet Propulsion Laboratory] Technical Memorandum
JPL Tech Rep — JPL [Jet Propulsion Laboratory] Technical Report
JPM — Jerusalem Post Magazine
JPM — Journal of Property Management
JPM — Personnel Management
JPMEA — Journal. Philippine Medical Association
JPMSA — Journal of Pharmaceutical Sciences
Jpn Agric Res Q — Japan Agricultural Research. Quarterly
Jpn Analyst — Japan Analyst
Jpn Annu Rev Electron Comput Telecommun — Japan Annual Reviews in Electronics, Computers, and Telecommunications
Jpn Arch Histol — Japanese Archives of Histology
Jpn Arch Intern Med — Japanese Archives of Internal Medicine
Jpn Archit — Japan Architect
Jpn At Energy Res Inst Annu Rep Acc — Japan. Atomic Energy Research Institute. Annual Report and Account
Jpn At Energy Res Inst Rep Res Rep — Japan. Atomic Energy Research Institute. Report. Research Report
Jpn Chem Ind — Japan Chemical Industry
Jpn Chem Q — Japan Chemical Quarterly
Jpn Chem Rev — Japan Chemical Review
Jpn Circ J — Japanese Circulation Journal
Jpn Dtsch Med Ber — Japanisch-Deutsche Medizinische Berichte
Jpn Econ J — Japan Economic Journal
Jpn Electron Eng — Japan Electronic Engineering
Jpn Energy Technol Intell — Japan Energy and Technology Intelligence
Jpn Gas Assoc J — Japan Gas Association. Journal
Jpn-Ger Med Rep — Japan-Germany Medical Reports

Jpn Heart J — Japanese Heart Journal
Jpn Ind Technol Bull — Japan Industrial and Technological Bulletin
Jpn J Aerosp Med Psychol — Japanese Journal of Aerospace Medicine and Psychology
Jpn J Allergol — Japanese Journal of Allergology
Jpn J Allergy — Japanese Journal of Allergy
Jpn J Anesthesiol — Japanese Journal of Anesthesiology
Jpn J Antibiot — Japanese Journal of Antibiotics
Jpn J Appl Entomol Zool — Japanese Journal of Applied Entomology and Zoology
Jpn J Appl Phys — Japanese Journal of Applied Physics
Jpn J Appl Phys 1 — Japanese Journal of Applied Physics. Part 1
Jpn J Appl Phys 2 Lett — Japanese Journal of Applied Physics. Part 2. Letters
Jpn J Appl Phys Part 1 — Japanese Journal of Applied Physics. Part 1. Regular Papers and Short Notes
Jpn J Appl Phys Part 2 — Japanese Journal of Applied Physics. Part 2. Letters
Jpn J Astron — Japanese Journal of Astronomy
Jpn J Astron Geophys — Japanese Journal of Astronomy and Geophysics
Jpn J Bacteriol — Japanese Journal of Bacteriology
Jpn J Bot — Japanese Journal of Botany
Jpn J Breed — Japanese Journal of Breeding
Jpn J Cancer Clin — Japanese Journal of Cancer Clinics
Jpn J Cancer Res — Japanese Journal of Cancer Research
Jpn J Chem — Japanese Journal of Chemistry
Jpn J Chest Dis — Japanese Journal of Chest Diseases
Jpn J Clin Electron Microsc — Japanese Journal of Clinical Electron Microscopy
Jpn J Clin Exp Med — Japanese Journal of Clinical and Experimental Medicine
Jpn J Clin Hematol — Japanese Journal of Clinical Hematology
Jpn J Clin Med — Japanese Journal of Clinical Medicine
Jpn J Clin Oncol — Japanese Journal of Clinical Oncology
Jpn J Clin Ophthalmol — Japanese Journal of Clinical Ophthalmology
Jpn J Clin Pathol — Japanese Journal of Clinical Pathology
Jpn J Clin Pathol Suppl — Japanese Journal of Clinical Pathology. Supplement
Jpn J Clin Pharmacol — Japanese Journal of Clinical Pharmacology
Jpn J Clin Radiol — Japanese Journal of Clinical Radiology
Jpn J Const Med — Japanese Journal of Constitutional Medicine
Jpn J Crop Sci — Japanese Journal of Crop Science
Jpn J Dairy Food Sci — Japanese Journal of Dairy and Food Science
Jpn J Dairy Sci — Japanese Journal of Dairy Science
Jpn J Dermatol — Japanese Journal of Dermatology
Jpn J Dermatol Ser B (Engl Ed) — Japanese Journal of Dermatology. Series B (English Edition)
Jpn J Ecol — Japanese Journal of Ecology
Jpn J Eng Abstr — Japanese Journal of Engineering. Abstracts
Jpn J Ergonomics — Japanese Journal of Ergonomics
Jpn J Ethnol — Japanese Journal of Ethnology
Jpn J Exp Med — Japanese Journal of Experimental Medicine
Jpn J Exp Morphol — Japanese Journal of Experimental Morphology
Jpn J Fertil Steril — Japanese Journal of Fertility and Sterility
Jpn J Gastroenterol — Japanese Journal of Gastroenterology
Jpn J Genet — Japanese Journal of Genetics
Jpn J Genet Suppl — Japanese Journal of Genetics. Supplement
Jpn J Geol Geogr — Japanese Journal of Geology and Geography
Jpn J Geriatr — Japanese Journal of Geriatrics
Jpn J Herpetol — Japanese Journal of Herpetology
Jpn J Hum Genet — Japanese Journal of Human Genetics
Jpn J Hyg — Japanese Journal of Hygiene
Jpn J Ichthyol — Japanese Journal of Ichthyology
Jpn J Ind Health — Japanese Journal of Industrial Health
Jpn J Lepr — Japanese Journal of Leprosy
Jpn J Limnol — Japanese Journal of Limnology
Jpn J Malacol — Japanese Journal of Malacology
Jpn J Math — Japanese Journal of Mathematics
Jpn J Med — Japanese Journal of Medicine
Jpn J Med Electron Biol Eng — Japanese Journal of Medical Electronics and Biological Engineering
Jpn J Med Mycol — Japanese Journal of Medical Mycology
Jpn J Med Sci 1 — Japanese Journal of Medical Sciences. Part 1. Anatomy
Jpn J Med Sci 2 — Japanese Journal of Medical Sciences. Part 2. Biochemistry
Jpn J Med Sci 3 — Japanese Journal of Medical Sciences. Part 3. Biophysics
Jpn J Med Sci 4 — Japanese Journal of Medical Sciences. Part 4. Pharmacology
Jpn J Med Sci 5 — Japanese Journal of Medical Sciences. Part 5. Pathology
Jpn J Med Sci 6 — Japanese Journal of Medical Sciences. Part 6. Bacteriology and Parasitology
Jpn J Med Sci 7 — Japanese Journal of Medical Sciences. Part 7. Social Medicine and Hygiene
Jpn J Med Sci 8 — Japanese Journal of Medical Sciences. Part 8. Internal Medicine, Pediatry, and Psychiatry
Jpn J Med Sci 9 — Japanese Journal of Medical Sciences. Part 9. Surgery, Orthopedy, and Odontology
Jpn J Med Sci 10 — Japanese Journal of Medical Sciences. Part 10. Ophthalmology

Jpn J Med Sci 11 — Japanese Journal of Medical Sciences. Part 11. Gynecology and Tocology
Jpn J Med Sci 12 — Japanese Journal of Medical Sciences. Part 12. Oto-Rhino-Laryngology
Jpn J Med Sci 13 — Japanese Journal of Medical Sciences. Part 13. Dermatology and Urology
Jpn J Med Sci Biol — Japanese Journal of Medical Science and Biology
Jpn J Microbiol — Japanese Journal of Microbiology
Jpn J Midwife — Japanese Journal for the Midwife
Jpn J Nephrol — Japanese Journal of Nephrology
Jpn J Neurol Psychiatry — Japanese Journal of Neurology and Psychiatry
Jpn J Nucl Med — Japanese Journal of Nuclear Medicine
Jpn J Nurs — Japanese Journal of Nursing
Jpn J Nurs Res — Japanese Journal of Nursing Research
Jpn J Nutr — Japanese Journal of Nutrition
Jpn J Obstet Gynecol — Japanese Journal of Obstetrics and Gynecology
Jpn J Ophthalmol — Japanese Journal of Ophthalmology
Jpn J Oral Biol — Japanese Journal of Oral Biology
Jpn J Palynol — Japanese Journal of Palynology
Jpn J Parasitol — Japanese Journal of Parasitology
Jpn J Pediat — Japanese Journal of Pediatrics
Jpn J Pediat Surg Med — Japanese Journal of Pediatric Surgery and Medicine
Jpn J Pharm — Japanese Journal of Pharmacognosy
Jpn J Pharmacognosy — Japanese Journal of Pharmacognosy
Jpn J Pharmacol — Japanese Journal of Pharmacology
Jpn J Pharm Chem — Japanese Journal of Pharmacy and Chemistry
Jpn J Phys — Japanese Journal of Physics
Jpn J Phys Fitness Sports Med — Japanese Journal of Physical Fitness and Sports Medicine
Jpn J Physiol — Japanese Journal of Physiology
Jpn J Plast Reconstr Surg — Japanese Journal of Plastic and Reconstructive Surgery
Jpn J Psychol — Japanese Journal of Psychology
Jpn J Psychosom Med — Japanese Journal of Psychosomatic Medicine
Jpn J Public Health — Japanese Journal of Public Health
Jpn J Radiol Technol — Japanese Journal of Radiological Technology
Jpn J Relig — Japanese Journal of Religious Studies
Jpn J Sanit Zool — Japanese Journal of Sanitary Zoology
Jpn J Smooth Muscle Res — Japanese Journal of Smooth Muscle Research
Jpn J Surg — Japanese Journal of Surgery
Jpn J Thorac Dis — Japanese Journal of Thoracic Diseases
Jpn J Trop Agric — Japanese Journal of Tropical Agriculture
Jpn J Trop Med Hyg — Japanese Journal of Tropical Medicine and Hygiene
Jpn J Tuberc — Japanese Journal of Tuberculosis
Jpn J Tuberc Chest Dis — Japanese Journal of Tuberculosis and Chest Diseases
Jpn J Urol — Japanese Journal of Urology
Jpn J Vet Res — Japanese Journal of Veterinary Research
Jpn J Vet Sci — Japanese Journal of Veterinary Science
Jpn J Zool — Japanese Journal of Zoology
Jpn J Zootech Sci — Japanese Journal of Zootechnical Science
Jpn Light Met Weld — Japan Light Metal Welding
Jpn Med J — Japanese Medical Journal
JPNNB — Journal of Psychiatric Nursing and Mental Health Services
Jpn Nucl Med — Japanese Nuclear Medicine
JPNP — Journal de Psychologie Normale et Pathologique
JPNPA — Journal de Psychologie Normale et Pathologique
Jpn Pestic Inf — Japan Pesticide Information
Jpn Plast — Japan Plastics
Jpn Poult Sci — Japanese Poultry Science
Jpn Printer — Japan Printer
Jpn Psychol Res — Japanese Psychological Research
Jpn Quart — Japan Quarterly
Jpn Railw Eng — Japanese Railway Engineering
Jpn Rev Clin Ophthalmol — Japanese Review of Clinical Ophthalmology
Jpn Sci Mon — Japanese Scientific Monthly
Jpn Sci Rev Med Sci — Japan Science Review. Medical Sciences
Jpn Sci Rev Min Metall — Japanese Science Review. Mining and Metallurgy
Jpn Soc Aeronaut Space Sci Trans — Japan Society for Aeronautical and Space Sciences. Transactions
Jpn Soc Tuberc Annu Rep — Japanese Society for Tuberculosis. Annual Report
Jpn Spectros Co Appl Notes — Japan Spectroscopic Company. Application Notes
Jpn Steel Bull — Japan Steel Bulletin
Jpn Steel Tube Tech Rev — Japan Steel and Tube Technical Review
Jpn Steel Works Tech News — Japan Steel Works. Technical News
Jpn Steel Works Tech Rev — Japan Steel Works. Technical Review
Jpn Steel Works Tech Rev (Engl Ed) — Japan Steel Works. Technical Review (English Edition)
Jpn Stud Hist Sci — Japanese Studies in the History of Science
JP (NSW) — Justice of the Peace (New South Wales)
Jpn Tappi — Japan Tappi
Jpn Telecommun Rev — Japan Telecommunications Review
JPOCB — Journal of Popular Culture
JPol — Jezyk Polski
JPol — Journal of Politics
J Polarogr Soc — Journal. Polarographic Society [*England*]

J Pol Econ — Journal of Political Economy
J Pol Economy — Journal of Political Economy
J Police Sci & Ad — Journal of Police Science and Administration
J Police Sci & Adm — Journal of Police Science and Administration
J Police Sci Adm — Journal of Police Science and Administration
J Polic Sci — Journal of Police Science and Administration
J Policy Anal Manage — Journal of Policy Analysis and Management
J Policy Analysis Manage — Journal of Policy Analysis and Management
J Policy Analysis and Mgt — Journal of Policy Analysis and Management
J Policy Model — Journal of Policy Modeling
J Polit — Journal of Politics
J Polit Ec — Journal of Political Economy
J Polit Econ — Journal of Political Economy
J Politics — Journal of Politics
J Polit Mil — Journal of Political and Military Sociology
J Polit Milit Sociol — Journal of Political and Military Sociology
J Polit Stud — Journal of Political Studies
J Pol Mil Sociol — Journal of Political and Military Sociology
J Pol Sci C — Journal of Polymer Science. Part C: Polymer Symposia [Later, Journal of Polymer Science. Polymer Symposia Edition]
J Pol Sc PC — Journal of Polymer Science. Polymer Chemistry Edition
J Pol Sc PL — Journal of Polymer Science. Polymer Letters Edition
J Pol Sc PP — Journal of Polymer Science. Polymer Physics Edition
J Pol Stud — Journal of Political Studies
J Polym Mater — Journal of Polymer Materials
J Polym Sci — Journal of Polymer Science
J Polym Sci A-1 — Journal of Polymer Science. Part A-1: Polymer Chemistry
J Polym Sci A-2 — Journal of Polymer Science. Part A-2: Polymer Physics
J Polym Sci B — Journal of Polymer Science. Part B: Polymer Letters
J Polym Sci Macromol Rev — Journal of Polymer Science. Macromolecular Reviews
J Polym Sci Part A-1: Polym Chem — Journal of Polymer Science. Part A-1: Polymer Chemistry
J Polym Sci Part A-2: Polym Phys — Journal of Polymer Science. Part A-2: Polymer Physics
J Polym Sci Part B: Polym Lett — Journal of Polymer Science. Part B: Polymer Letters
J Polym Sci Part C — Journal of Polymer Science. Part C: Polymer Symposia [Later, Journal of Polymer Science. Polymer Symposia Edition]
J Polym Sci Part C: Polym Symp — Journal of Polymer Science. Part C: Polymer Symposia [Later, Journal of Polymer Science. Polymer Symposia Edition]
J Polym Sci Part D — Journal of Polymer Science. Part D: Macromolecular Reviews
J Polym Sci Part D: Macromol Rev — Journal of Polymer Science. Part D: Macromolecular Reviews
J Polym Sci Polym Chem — Journal of Polymer Science. Polymer Chemistry Edition
J Polym Sci Polym Chem Ed — Journal of Polymer Science. Polymer Chemistry Edition
J Polym Sci Polym Lett — Journal of Polymer Science. Polymer Letters Edition
J Polym Sci Polym Lett Ed — Journal of Polymer Science. Polymer Letters Edition
J Polym Sci Polym Phys — Journal of Polymer Science. Polymer Physics Edition
J Polym Sci Polym Phys Ed — Journal of Polymer Science. Polymer Physics Edition
J Polym Sci Polym Symp — Journal of Polymer Science. Polymer Symposia
J Polynesia — Journal. Polynesian Society
J Polynes Soc — Journal. Polynesian Society
J Polyn Soc — Journal. Polynesian Society
J Pomol — Journal of Pomology
J Pomology — Journal of Pomology and Horticultural Science
J Pop Cul — Journal of Popular Culture
J Pop Cult — Journal of Popular Culture
J Pop Culture — Journal of Popular Culture
J Pop Film & TV — Journal of Popular Film and Television
J Pop Fi TV — Journal of Popular Film and Television
J Pop F & TV — Journal of Popular Film and Television
J Pop Res — Journal of Population Research
J Popular F — Journal of Popular Film and Television
J Port Econ e Fins — Jornal Portugues de Economia e Financas
J Portf Manage — Journal of Portfolio Management
J Portfolio Mgt — Journal of Portfolio Management
JPOS — Journal. Palestine Oriental Society
J POS — Journal. Patent Office Society
J Postgrad Med (Bombay) — Journal of Postgraduate Medicine (Bombay)
J Post Grad Sch Indian Agric Res Inst — Journal. Post Graduate School. Indian Agricultural Research Institute
J Post Keynes Econ — Journal of Post Keynesian Economics
J Powder Bulk Solids Technol — Journal of Powder and Bulk Solids Technology
J Power Div Am Soc Civ Eng — Journal. Power Division. American Society of Civil Engineers
J Power Sources — Journal of Power Sources

JPP — Journal of Pastoral Practice
JPPDA — Journal of Child Psychology and Psychiatry and Allied Disciplines [Later, Journal of Child Psychology and Psychiatry]
JPPIAX — Jugoslovenska Pediajatrija
JPPL — Journal of Planning and Property Law
JPPMB — Jahrbuch fuer Psychologie, Psychotherapie, und Medizinische Anthropologie
JPPSA — Journal of Pharmacy and Pharmacology. Supplement
JPQCA — Journal de Physique Colloque
JPQSA — Journal de Physique. Supplement
JPr — Die Juedische Presse [Berlin]
JPR — Journal of Psycholinguistic Research
JPR — Journal of Purchasing and Materials Management
J of Prac App — Journal of Practical Approaches to Developmental Handicap
J Pract Heilk — Journal der Practischen Heilkunde
J Pract Nurs — Journal of Practical Nursing
J Prag — Journal of Pragmatics
J Prak Chem — Journal fuer Praktische Chemie
J Prakt Chem — Journal fuer Praktische Chemie
J Prat de Droit Fiscal — Journal Pratique de Droit Fiscal et Financier
JPREA — Japanese Psychological Research
JPREAV — Japanese Psychological Research
J Pre Concr — Journal. Prestressed Concrete Institute
J Pre-Med Course Sapporo Med Coll — Journal of Pre-Medical Course. Sapporo Medical College
J Pre-Raph — Journal of Pre-Raphaelite Studies
J Presby H — Journal of Presbyterian History
J Presby Hist Soc — Journal. Presbyterian Historical Society
J Pres H — Journal of Presbyterian History
J Pressure Vessel Technol — Journal of Pressure Vessel Technology
J Pressure Vessel Technol Trans ASME — Journal of Pressure Vessel Technology. Transaction. ASME [American Society of Mechanical Engineers]
J Prestressed Concr Inst — Journal. Prestressed Concrete Institute
J Prev Dent — Journal of Preventive Dentistry
JPRGA — Journal de Chimie Physique et Revue Generale des Colloides
JPRH — Journal of Prison Health
J Print Hist Soc — Journal. Printing Historical Society
J Prison Jail Health — Journal of Prison and Jail Health
JPrKS — Jahrbuch. Preussische Kunstsammlungen
JPRLB — Journal of Psycholinguistic Research
J Proc Am Hort Soc — Journal of Proceedings. American Horticultural Society
J & Proc A'sian Methodist Historical Soc — Australasian Methodist Historical Society. Journal and Proceedings
J Proc Asiat Soc Bengal — Journal and Proceedings. Asiatic Society of Bengal
J Proc Aust Hist Soc — Australian Historical Society. Journal and Proceedings
J Proc Aust Jewish Hist Soc — Australian Jewish Historical Society. Journal and Proceedings
J & Proc Aust Methodist Hist Soc — Australasian Methodist Historical Society. Journal and Proceedings
J Proc Australas Meth Hist Soc — Australasian Methodist Historical Society. Journal and Proceedings
J Proc Broken Hill Hist Soc — Broken Hill Historical Society. Journal and Proceedings
J Proc Inst Chem (India) — Journal and Proceedings. Institution of Chemists (India)
J Proc Instn Chem (India) — Journal and Proceedings. Institution of Chemists (India)
J Proc Inst Rd Transp Engrs — Journal and Proceedings. Institute of Road Transport Engineers
J Proc Inst Sewage Purif — Journal and Proceedings. Institute of Sewage Purification
J Proc Newcastle Hunter Dist Hist Soc — Newcastle and Hunter District Historical Society. Journal and Proceedings
J Proc Oil Technol Assoc — Journal and Proceedings. Oil Technologists' Association
J Proc Parramatta Dist Hist Soc — Parramatta and District Historical Society. Journal and Proceedings
J Proc R Aust Hist Soc — Royal Australian Historical Society. Journal and Proceedings
J Proc Roy Soc NSW — Journal and Proceedings. Royal Society of New South Wales
J Proc R Soc NSW — Journal and Proceedings. Royal Society of New South Wales
J Proc R Soc West Aust — Journal and Proceedings. Royal Society of Western Australia
J Proc Sydney Tech Coll Chem Soc — Journal and Proceedings. Sydney Technical College. Chemical Society
J Proc W Aust Hist Soc — Western Australian Historical Society. Journal and Proceedings
J Prod Liab — Journal of Products Liability
J Prod Liability — Journal of Products Liability
J Project Techniques — Journal of Projective Techniques and Personality Assessment [Later, Journal of Personality Assessment]
J Property Mgt — Journal of Property Management
J Prop Manage — Journal of Property Management

J Prop Mgt — Journal of Property Management
J Pros Dent — Journal of Prosthetic Dentistry
J Prosthet Dent — Journal of Prosthetic Dentistry
J Protozool — Journal of Protozoology
JPRSA — Journal and Proceedings. Royal Society of New South Wales
J Prsbyt Hist — Journal of Presbyterian History
JPS — Journal of Collective Negotiations in the Public Sector
JPS — Journal of Palestine Studies
JPS — Journal of Personal Selling and Sales Management
JPS — Journal of Polymer Science
JPS — Journal. Polynesian Society
JPs — Journal of Psychology
JPSA — Journal. Photographic Society of America
JPSBA — Journal of Psychology of the Blind
JPSCD — Journal of Polymer Science. Part C. Polymer Symposia [*Later, Journal of Polymer Science. Polymer Symposia Edition*]
JPsNP — Journal de Psychologie Normale et Pathologique
JPSP — Journal of Personality and Social Psychology
JPSPB — Journal of Personality and Social Psychology
JPSRB — Journal of Psychological Researches
JPSS — Journal of Personality and Social Systems
JPST — Jahrbuch fuer Philosophie und Spekulative Theologie
JPsy — Journal of Psychology
JPsych — Journal de Psychologie Normale et Pathologique
J Psychedel Drugs — Journal of Psychedelic Drugs
J Psychedelic Drugs — Journal of Psychedelic Drugs
J Psychiatr Nurs — Journal of Psychiatric Nursing and Mental Health Services
J Psychiatr Res — Journal of Psychiatric Research
J Psychiatry & L — Journal of Psychiatry and Law
J Psych & L — Journal of Psychiatry and Law
J Psych & Law — Journal of Psychiatry and Law
J Psych Law — Journal of Psychiatry and Law
J Psychohist — Journal of Psychohistory
J Psychol — Journal of Psychology
J Psycholin — Journal of Psycholinguistic Research
J Psycholing Res — Journal of Psycholinguistic Research
J Psycholinguist Res — Journal of Psycholinguistic Research
J Psychol u Neurol — Journal fuer Psychologie und Neurologie
J Psychol Res — Journal of Psychological Researches
J Psychosocial Nurs — Journal of Psychosocial Nursing and Mental Health Services
J Psychosoc Nurs — Journal of Psychosocial Nursing and Mental Health Services
J Psychosom — Journal of Psychosomatic Research
J Psychosom Res — Journal of Psychosomatic Research
J Psych Res — Journal of Psychiatric Research
J Psych Th — Journal of Psychology and Theology
JPsyR — Journal of Psycholinguistic Research
JPT — Jahrbuch fuer Philosophie und Spekulative Theologie
JPT — Jahrbuecher fuer Protestantische Theologie [*Leipzig/Braunschweig*]
JPT — Journal of Petroleum Technology
JPT — Journal of Psychology and Theology
JPTEA — Journal of Projective Techniques [*Later, Journal of Personality Assessment*]
JPT J Pet Technol — JPT. Journal of Petroleum Technology
JPTUAL — Japanese Journal of Tuberculosis
JPU — Journal. Poona University
JPU — Journal of Public Economics
J Pub L — Journal of Public Law
J Publ Econ — Journal of Public Economics
J Public Econ — Journal of Public Economics
J Public Health Dent — Journal of Public Health Dentistry
J Public Health Med Technol Korea Univ — Journal of Public Health and Medical Technology. Korea University
J Public Health Policy — Journal of Public Health Policy
J Public Health Pract — Journal of Public Health Practice [*Japan*]
J Public and Internat Affairs — Journal of Public and International Affairs
J Public Policy — Journal of Public Policy
J Public Service Papua & NG — Journal. Public Service of Papua and New Guinea
J Purch — Journal of Purchasing [*Later, Journal of Purchasing and Materials Management*]
J Purchasing & Materials Mgt — Journal of Purchasing and Materials Management
J Purch Mater Manage — Journal of Purchasing and Materials Management
J Pure Appl Algebra — Journal of Pure and Applied Algebra
J Pure Appl Sci — Journal of Pure and Applied Sciences
J Pure Appl Sci (Ankara) — Journal of Pure and Applied Sciences (Ankara)
J Pusan Med Coll — Journal. Pusan Medical College
JPVDA — Journal of Preventive Dentistry
JPVTA — Journal of Pressure Vessel Technology
JPW — Jerusalem Post Weekly
JP (WA) — Justice of the Peace (Western Australia)
JPY — Journal of Political Economy
JPYBA — Journal of Polymer Science. Polymer Letters Edition

JPYCA — Journal of Polymer Science. Polymer Symposia Edition [*Formerly, Journal of Polymer Science. Part C. Polymer Symposia*]
JQ — Japan Quarterly
JQ — Jewish Quarterly
JQ — Journalism Quarterly
JQE — Journal of Quantum Electronics
J Qing Hua Univ — Journal. Qing Hua University
JQR — Jewish Quarterly Review
JQT — Journal of Quality Technology
J Quality Tech — Journal of Quality Technology
J Qual Tech — Journal of Quality Technology
J Qual Technol — Journal of Quality Technology
J Quan Spec — Journal of Quantitative Spectroscopy and Radiative Transfer
J Quant Spectrosc Radiat Transfer — Journal of Quantitative Spectroscopy and Radiative Transfer
J Quant Spectrosc and Radiat Transfer — Journal of Quantitative Spectroscopy and Radiative Transfer
J Quekett Microsc Club — Journal. Quekett Microscopical Club
J e R — Jeta e Re
JR — Jezyk Rosyjski
JR — Journal of Religion
JR — Juedische Rundschau [*Berlin*]
JR — Juridical Review
Jr A — Journal of Arizona History
JRA — Journal. Society of Research Administrators
J Race Dev — Journal of Race Development
J Racial Aff — Journal of Racial Affairs
JRADA — Journal of Radiology
J Rad Chem — Journal of Radioanalytical Chemistry [*Later, Journal of Radioanalytical and Nuclear Chemistry*]
J Radiat Curing — Journal of Radiation Curing
J Radiat Res — Journal of Radiation Research
J Radiat Res Radiat Process — Journal of Radiation Research and Radiation Processing
J Radiat Res (Tokyo) — Journal of Radiation Research (Tokyo)
J Radioanal Chem — Journal of Radioanalytical Chemistry [*Later, Journal of Radioanalytical and Nuclear Chemistry*]
J Radioanal Nucl Chem — Journal of Radioanalytical and Nuclear Chemistry
J Radiol — Journal de Radiologie
J Radiol Electrol — Journal de Radiologie et d'Electrologie
J Radiol Electrol Med Nucl — Journal de Radiologie, d'Electrologie, et de Medecine Nucleaire [*Later, Journal de Radiologie*]
J Radiol Phys Ther Univ Kanazawa — Journal of Radiology and Physical Therapy. University of Kanazawa
J Radio Res Lab — Journal. Radio Research Laboratories [*Japan*]
J Rad Res L — Journal. Radio Research Laboratories [*Japan*]
J R Aeronaut Soc — Journal. Royal Aeronautical Society [*England*]
J R Afr Soc — Journal. Royal African Society
JRAfS — Journal. Royal African Society
J R Agric Soc — Journal. Royal Agricultural Society
JRAHS — Journal. Royal Australian Historical Society
JRAI — Journal. Royal Anthropological Institute of Great Britain and Ireland
J Raj Inst Hist Res — Journal. Rajasthan Institute of Historical Research
JRAMA — Journal. Royal Army Medical Corps
J Raman Sp — Journal of Raman Spectroscopy
J Raman Spectrosc — Journal of Raman Spectroscopy
J Range Man — Journal of Range Management
J Range Manage — Journal of Range Management
J Range Mgt — Journal of Range Management
J R Anthropol Inst GB Irel — Journal. Royal Anthropological Institute of Great Britain and Ireland
JRARA — Journal of Radiation Research
J R Army Med Corps — Journal. Royal Army Medical Corps
J R Army Vet Corps — Journal. Royal Army Veterinary Corps
JRAS — Journal. Royal Asiatic Society of Great Britain and Ireland
JRASA — Journal. Royal Astronomical Society of Canada
JRASBB — Journal. Royal Asiatic Society. Bombay Branch
JRASBengal — Journal. Royal Asiatic Society of Bengal
JRAS Bombay — Journal. Bombay Branch. Royal Asiatic Society
JRASCB — Journal. Royal Asiatic Society. Ceylon Branch
JRASHKB — Journal. Royal Asiatic Society. Hong Kong Branch
JR Asiat Soc GB Irel — Journal. Royal Asiatic Society of Great Britain and Ireland
JRASM — Journal. Royal Asiatic Society. Malayan Branch
JRASMB — Journal. Royal Asiatic Society. Malayan Branch
J R Astron Soc Can — Journal. Royal Astronomical Society of Canada
J R Aust Hist Soc — Journal. Royal Australian Historical Society
JRB — Journal of Retail Banking
JRBA-A — Journal. Royal Institute of British Architects
Jr Bkshelf — Junior Bookshelf
JRBM — Journal of Renaissance and Baroque Music
JRCAS — Journal. Royal Central Asian Society
JRCE-A — Journal. Irrigation and Drainage Division. Proceedings. American Society of Civil Engineers
JRCI — Journal. Regional Cultural Institute
J R Coll Gen Pract — Journal. Royal College of General Practitioners

J R Coll Gen Pract Occas Pap — Journal. Royal College of General Practitioners. Occasional Paper
Jr Coll J — Junior College Journal
Jr Coll Jnl — Junior College Journal
J R Coll Physicians — Journal. Royal College of Physicians of London
J R Coll Physicians Lond — Journal. Royal College of Physicians of London
J R Coll Surg Edinb — Journal. Royal College of Surgeons of Edinburgh
J R Coll Surg Irel — Journal. Royal College of Surgeons in Ireland
JRCSA — Journal. Royal College of Surgeons of Edinburgh
JRD — Jahrbuch der Rheinischen Denkmalpflege
JRd — Juedische Rundschau [*Berlin*]
JRDCA — Journal of Radiation Curing
JRDP — Jahrbuch der Rheinischen Denkmalpflege
JRE — Journal of Econometrics
JRE — Journal of Real Estate Taxation
JRe — Journal of Religion
JRE — Journal of Religious Ethics
J Read — Journal of Reading
J Read Beh — Journal of Reading Behavior
J Read Behav — Journal of Reading Behavior
J Real Est Tax — Journal of Real Estate Taxation
J Rech Atmos — Journal de Recherches Atmospheriques
J Rech Cent Natl Rech Sci Lab Bellevue (Paris) — Journal des Recherches. Centre National de la Recherche Scientifique. Laboratoires de Bellevue (Paris)
J Rech CNRS — Journal des Recherches. Centre National de la Recherche Scientifique [*France*]
J Rech Oceanogr — Journal de Recherche Oceanographique
J Recreational Math — Journal of Recreational Mathematics
J Refrig — Journal of Refrigeration
J Region Sci — Journal of Regional Science
J Reg Sc — Journal of Regional Science
J Reg Sci — Journal of Regional Science
J Rehab — Journal of Rehabilitation
J Rehabil — Journal of Rehabilitation
J Rehabil Asia — Journal of Rehabilitation in Asia
J Rehabil D — Journal of Rehabilitation of the Deaf
J Reine Angew Math — Journal fuer die Reine und Angewandte Mathematik
J Reinf Plast Comp — Journal of Reinforced Plastics and Composites
J Reinf Plast Compos — Journal of Reinforced Plastics and Composites
J Rein Math — Journal fuer die Reine und Angewandte Mathematik
J Rel — Journal of Religion
J Rel Africa — Journal of Religion in Africa
JR Electr and Mech Eng — Journal. Royal Electrical and Mechanical Engineers
J R Electr Mech Eng — Journal. Royal Electrical and Mechanical Engineers [*England*]
J Rel Ethics — Journal of Religious Ethics
J Rel H — Journal of Religious History
J Rel Health — Journal of Religion and Health
J Rel Hist — Journal of Religious History
J Relig — Journal of Religion
J Relig Afr — Journal of Religion in Africa
J Relig Ethics — Journal of Religious Ethics
J Relig H — Journal of Religion and Health
J Relig His — Journal of Religious History
J Relig Hist — Journal of Religious History
J Religious History — Journal of Religious History
J Rel Thot — Journal of Religious Thought
J of Rel Thought — Journal of Religious Thought
JRelThought — Journal of Religious Thought [*New York*]
J Remote Sensing — Journal of Remote Sensing
Remount Vet Corps — Journal of the Remount and Veterinary Corps
J Ren & Bar Mus — Journal of Renaissance and Baroque Music
J Reprd & Fert — Journal of Reproduction and Fertility
J Repr Fert — Journal of Reproduction and Fertility
J Reprod Fertil — Journal of Reproduction and Fertility
J Reprod Fertil Suppl — Journal of Reproduction and Fertility. Supplement
J Reprod Med — Journal of Reproductive Medicine
J Reprod Med Lying-In — Journal of Reproductive Medicine. Lying-In
J Re S — Journal of Religious Studies
J Res Crime — Journal of Research in Crime and Delinquency
J Res Crime & Del — Journal of Research in Crime and Delinquency
J Res Dev E — Journal of Research and Development in Education
J Res & Devel Educ — Journal of Research and Development in Education
J Res Develop Educ — Journal of Research and Development in Education
J Res Dev Lab Portland Cem Assoc — Journal. Research and Development Laboratories. Portland Cement Association
J Research M Education — Journal of Research in Music Education
J Res Haryana Agric Univ — Haryana Agricultural University. Journal of Research
J Res Indian Med — Journal of Research in Indian Medicine
J Res Inst Catal Hokkaido Univ — Journal. Research Institute for Catalysis. Hokkaido University
J Res Inst Catalysis Hokkaido Univ — Journal. Research Institute for Catalysis. Hokkaido University

J Res Inst Sci Technol Nihon Univ — Journal. Research Institute of Science and Technology. Nihon University [*Japan*]
J Res Inst Sci and Technol Nihon Univ — Journal. Research Institute of Science and Technology. Nihon University
J Res (Jpn) — Journal of Research (Japan)
J Res Lepid — Journal of Research on the Lepidoptera
J Res (Ludhiana) — Journal of Research (Ludhiana) [*India*]
J Res Math Educ — Journal for Research in Mathematics Education
J Res Mus Ed — Journal of Research in Music Education
J Res Mus Educ — Journal of Research in Music Education
J Res Music — Journal of Research in Music Education
J Res Music Educ — Journal of Research in Music Education
J Res Nat Bur Stand — Journal of Research. [*US*] National Bureau of Standards
J Res Nat Bur Standards — Journal of Research. [*US*] National Bureau of Standards
J Res Nat Bur Stand Sect A Phys Chem — Journal of Research. [*US*] National Bureau of Standards. Section A. Physics and Chemistry
J Res Nat Bur Stand Sect B Math Sci — Journal of Research. [*US*] National Bureau of Standards. Section B. Mathematical Sciences
J Res Nat Bur Stand Sect C — Journal of Research. [*US*] National Bureau of Standards. Section C. Engineering and Instrumentation
J Res Nat Bur Stand Sect C Eng Instrum — Journal of Research. [*US*] National Bureau of Standards. Section C. Engineering and Instrumentation
J Res Nat Bur Stand Sect D — Journal of Research. [*US*] National Bureau of Standards. Section D. Radio Science
J Res Natl Bur Stand A — Journal of Research. [*US*] National Bureau of Standards. A. Physics and Chemistry
J Res Natl Bur Stand B — Journal of Research. [*US*] National Bureau of Standards. B. Mathematics and Mathematical Physics
J Res Natl Bur Stand C — Journal of Research. [*US*] National Bureau of Standards. C. Engineering and Instrumentation
J Res Natl Bur Stand (US) — Journal of Research. National Bureau of Standards (United States)
J Res NBS — Journal of Research. [*US*] National Bureau of Standards
J Res NBS A — Journal of Research. [*US*] National Bureau of Standards. A. Physics and Chemistry
J Res NBS B — Journal of Research. [*US*] National Bureau of Standards. B. Mathematical Sciences
J Res Pers — Journal of Research in Personality
J Res Punjab Agric Univ — Journal of Research. Punjab Agricultural University
J Res Punjab Agr Univ — Journal of Research. Punjab Agricultural University
J Res Sci Agra Univ — Journal of Research. Science. Agra University
J Res Sci Teach — Journal of Research in Science Teaching
J Res Singing — Journal of Research in Singing
J Res US Geol Surv — Journal of Research. United States Geological Survey
J Res US G S — Journal of Research. United States Geological Survey
J Retail — Journal of Retailing
J Retail Bank — Journal of Retail Banking
J Retail Banking — Journal of Retail Banking
J Retailing — Journal of Retailing
J Retail Traders Assn NSW — Journal of the Retail Traders' Association of New South Wales
J Retail Traders Assoc NSW — Journal of the Retail Traders' Association of New South Wales
J Retic Soc — Journal. Reticuloendothelial Society
J Reticuloendothel Soc — Journal. Reticuloendothelial Society
JRG — Jahrbuch. Raabe-Gesellschaft
JRGZ — Jahrbuch. Roemisch-Germanisches Zentralmuseum [*Mainz*]
JRGZMainz — Jahrbuch. Roemisch-Germanisches Zentralmuseum (Mainz)
JRH — Journal of Religious History
J Rheol — Journal of Rheology
J Rheumatol — Journal of Rheumatology
J R Hortic Soc — Journal. Royal Horticulture Society
JRI — Journal of Risk and Insurance
JRIMD — Journal of Reproductive Immunology
JRINA — Journal. Research Institute for Catalysis. Hokkaido University
J R Inst Br Archit — Journal. Royal Institute of British Architects
J R Inst Chem — Journal. Royal Institute of Chemistry
J R Inst Public Health — Journal. Royal Institute of Public Health [*England*]
J R Inst Public Health Hyg — Journal. Royal Institute of Public Health and Hygiene
J Rio Grande Val Hortic Soc — Journal. Rio Grande Valley Horticulture Society
J Risk Ins — Journal of Risk and Insurance
J Risk & Insur — Journal of Risk and Insurance
J Risk Insur — Journal of Risk and Insurance
JRJ — Journal of Reform Judaism
JRL — Journal of Retailing
Jrl Ad Res — Journal of Advertising Research
Jrl Audit — Journal of Accounting Auditing and Finance
JRLB — John Rylands Library. Bulletin
Jrl Bus — Journal of Business
Jrl Coatng — Journal of Coatings Technology

Jrl Comm — Journal of Commerce
Jrl Elec I — Journal of the Electronics Industry
Jrl Eng Pwr — Journal of Engineering for Power
Jr Lib — Junior Libraries
Jrl Int B — Journal of International Business Studies
Jrl Market — Journal of Marketing
Jrl Metals — Journal of Metals
Jrl Mkt R — Journal of Marketing Research
Jrl P — Journal. Patent Office Society
Jrl Petro — Journal of Petroleum Technology
Jrl P Mgmt — Journal of Portfolio Management
Jrl RE Tax — Journal of Real Estate Taxation
Jrl Solar — Journal of Solar Energy Engineering
J Rly Div Instn Mech Engrs — Institution of Mechanical Engineers. Railway
　　Division. Journal
JRM — Journal of Research in Music Education
JRME — Journal of Research in Music Education
JRMEA — Journal of Research in Music Education
J R Microsc Soc — Journal. Royal Microscopical Society
JRMMRA — Journal. Rocky Mountain Medieval and Renaissance Association
JRMS — Journal. Royal Meteorological Society
J R Nav Med Serv — Journal. Royal Naval Medical Service
JRNBA — Journal of Research. [*US*] National Bureau of Standards
Jr N H — Journal of Negro History
JRNMA — Journal. Royal Naval Medical Service
J Roman Stud — Journal of Roman Studies
J Rom S — Journal of Roman Studies
J Rom Stud — Journal of Roman Studies
J Root Crops — Journal of Root Crops
J Rossica Soc — Journal. Rossica Society of Russian Philately
J Roy Agr S — Journal. Royal Agricultural Society of England
J Royal Aust Hist Soc — Journal. Royal Australian Historical Society
J Royal Military College Aust — Journal. Royal Military College of Australia
J Royal Soc New Zeal — Journal. Royal Society of New Zealand
J Royal Soc WA — Journal. Royal Society of Western Australia
J Roy Artil — Journal of the Royal Artillery
J Roy Asia — Journal. Royal Asiatic Society of Great Britain and Ireland
J Roy Asiatic Soc — Journal. Royal Asiatic Society
J Roy Asiat Soc — Journal. Royal Asiatic Society
J Roy Astro — Journal. Royal Astronomical Society of Canada
J Roy Aust — Journal. Royal Australian Historical Society
J Roy Inst Cornwall N Ser — Journal. Royal Institution of Cornwall. New
　　Series
J Roy Microscop Soc — Journal. Royal Microscopical Society
J Roy Micr Soc — Journal. Royal Microscopical Society
J Roy Soc Antiq Ir — Journal. Royal Society of Antiquaries of Ireland
J Roy Soc Arts — Journal. Royal Society of Arts
J Roy Soc NSW — Royal Society of New South Wales. Journal and
　　Proceedings
J Roy Soc W Aust — Royal Society of Western Australia. Journal
J Roy Sta A — Journal. Royal Statistical Society. Series A. General
J Roy Sta B — Journal. Royal Statistical Society. Series B. Methodological
J Roy Sta C — Journal. Royal Statistical Society. Series C. Applied Statistics
J Roy Statis — Journal. Royal Statistical Society
J Roy Statist Soc Ser A — Journal. Royal Statistical Society. Series A
J Roy Statist Soc Ser B — Journal. Royal Statistical Society. Series B
J Roy Statist Soc Ser C — Journal. Royal Statistical Society. Series C
J Roy Statist Soc Ser C Appl Statist — Journal. Royal Statistical Society.
　　Series C. Applied Statistics
JRPFA — Journal of Reproduction and Fertility
JRPUA — Journal of Research. Punjab Agricultural University
J RRI Malaysia — Journal. Rubber Research Institute of Malaysia
J RRI Sri Lanka — Journal. Rubber Research Institute of Sri Lanka
JRRLA — Journal. Radio Research Laboratories [*Tokyo*]
JRS — Journal. Market Research Society
JRS — Journal of Regional Science
JRS — Journal of Research in Singing
JRS — Journal of Roman Studies
JRS — Journal of Russian Studies
JRSAA — Journal. Royal Society of Arts
JRSAI — Journal. Royal Society of Antiquaries of Ireland
J R Sanit Inst — Journal. Royal Sanitary Institute [*England*]
JRSAntl — Journal. Royal Society of Antiquaries of Ireland
Jr Schol — Junior Scholastic
JR Signals Inst — Journal. Royal Signals Institution
J RSNZ — Journal. Royal Society of New Zealand
J R Soc Arts — Journal. Royal Society of Arts [*England*]
J R Soc Encour Arts Manuf Commer — Journal. Royal Society for the
　　Encouragement of Arts, Manufactures, and Commerce
J R Soc Hlth — Journal. Royal Society of Health
J R Soc Med — Journal. Royal Society of Medicine
J R Soc NZ — Journal. Royal Society of New Zealand
J R Soc W Aust — Royal Society of Western Australia. Journal
J R Soc West Aust — Journal. Royal Society of Western Australia
JRSOD — Journal. Reticuloendothelial Society
JRSS — Journal. Royal Statistical Society

J R Stat Soc — Journal. Royal Statistical Society [*England*]
JRSUA — Journal. Royal Society of Western Australia
JRT — Journal of Religious Thought
JRT — Journal of Retailing
JR Telev Soc — Journal. Royal Television Society
J R Th — Journal of Religious Thought
J Rubber Res Inst Malays — Journal. Rubber Research Institute of Malaysia
J Rubber Res Inst Sri Lanka — Journal. Rubber Research Institute of Sri
　　Lanka
J Rubb Res Inst Malaya — Journal. Rubber Research Institute of Malaya
JRUL — Journal. Rutgers University Library
J R United Serv Inst — Journal. Royal United Service Institution
J Rural Coop Int Res Cent Rural Coop Communities — Journal of Rural
　　Cooperation. International Research Center on Rural Cooperative
　　Communities
J Rural Dev — Journal of Rural Development
J Rural Econ and Development — Journal of Rural Economics and
　　Development
J Rural Educ — Journal of Rural Education
J Rur Coop — Journal of Rural Cooperation
JRuS — Journal of Russian Studies
J Rutgers Univ Libr — Journal. Rutgers University Library
JRVSB — Jena Review. Supplement
JS — Janus. Supplements
JS — Jazykovedny Sbornik
JS — Jazykovedny Studie
JS — Journal. Arnold Schoenberg Institute
JS — Journal des Savants
JS — Judaic Studies
JS — Junior Scholastic
JSA — Journal. Societe des Africanistes
JSA — Journal. Societe des Americanistes
JSACA — Journal. South African Chemical Institute
J SA Chem I — Journal. South African Chemical Institute
JSAED — Journal of Strain Analysis for Engineering Design
JSAf — Journal. Societe des Africanistes
JSAFE — Journal of South-East Asia and the Far East
J Safe Res — Journal of Safety Research
J SA For Assoc — Journal. South African Forestry Association
JSAfr — Journal. Societe des Africanistes
J S Afr Assoc Anal Chem — Journal. South African Association of Analytical
　　Chemists
J S Afr Biol Soc — Journal. South African Biological Society
J S Afr Bot — Journal of South African Botany
J S Afr Bot Suppl Vol — Journal of South African Botany. Supplementary
　　Volume
J Saf Res — Journal of Safety Research
J S Afr Inst Eng — Journal. South African Institution of Engineers
J S Afr Inst Mining Met — Journal. South African Institute of Mining and
　　Metallurgy
J S Afr Inst Min Metall — Journal. South African Institute of Mining and
　　Metallurgy
J S Afr Vet Assoc — Journal. South African Veterinary Association
J S Afr Vet Med Assoc — Journal. South African Veterinary Medical
　　Association
JSAH — Journal. Society of Architectural Historians
JSAH — Journal of Southeast Asian History
J SA I Min — Journal. South African Institute of Mining and Metallurgy
J Sains Nukl — Jernal Sains Nuklear
J Saitama Univ Fac Ed Math Natur Sci — Journal. Saitama University.
　　Faculty of Education. Mathematics and Natural Science
J Saitama Univ Nat Sci — Journal. Saitama University. Natural Science
　　[*Japan*]
JSALO — Journal of Studies on Alcohol
JSAm — Journal. Societe des Americanistes de Paris
JSAMA — Journal. South African Institute of Mining and Metallurgy
JSAmP — Journal. Societe des Americanistes de Paris
J Sanit Eng Div Proc Am Soc Civ Eng — Journal. Sanitary Engineering
　　Division. Proceedings. American Society of Civil Engineers
J San'yo Assoc Adv Sci Technol — Journal. San'yo Association for
　　Advancement of Science and Technology [*Japan*]
JSAP — Journal. Societe des Americanistes de Paris
J Sapporo Munic Gen Hosp — Journal. Sapporo Municipal General Hospital
　　[*Japan*]
J S Archit — Journal. Society of Architectural Historians
JSAS — Journal of Southeast Asian Studies
J S Asia L — Journal of South Asian Literature
JSav — Journal des Savants
J Savants — Journal des Savants
JSB — Journal of Small Business Management
JSBCD3 — Journal. American Society of Brewing Chemists
JSC — Journal. Institute for Socioeconomic Studies
JSC — Journal of Structural Chemistry
J Sch Healt — Journal of School Health
J Sch Health — Journal of School Health
J Sch Hlth — Journal of School Health

J Sc Hiroshima Univ S B Div 1 Zool — Journal of Science. Hiroshima University. Series B. Division 1. Zoology
J Sch Lib Assoc Qld — Journal. School Library Association of Queensland
J Sch Lib Ass Q — Journal. School Library Association of Queensland
J Sch Libr Assoc Qld — Journal. School Library Association of Queensland
J Sch Pharm Univ Tehran — Journal. School of Pharmacy. University of Tehran
J Sch Psych — Journal of School Psychology
J Sch Psychol — Journal of School Psychology
Jschr Mitteldtsch Vorgesch — Jahresschrift fuer Mitteldeutsche Vorgeschichte
J Sci — Journal of Science
J Sci Agric Soc Finl — Journal. Scientific Agricultural Society of Finland
J Sci Agr Res — Journal for Scientific Agricultural Research
J Sci Assoc Maharajah's Coll — Journal. Science Association. Maharajah's College
J Sci Busan Natl Univ — Journal of Science. Busan National University
J Sci Club — Journal of the Science Club
J Sci Coll Gen Educ Univ Tokushima — Journal of Science. College of General Education. University of Tokushima
J Sci Educ Chonnam Natl Univ — Journal of Science Education. Chonnam National University
J Sci Educ Chungbuk Natl Univ — Journal of Science Education. Chungbuk National University
J Sci Educ Jeonbug Natl Univ — Journal of Science Education. Jeonbug National University
J Sci Educ (Jeonju) — Journal of Science Education (Jeonju)
J Sci Educ Sci Educ Res Inst Teach Coll Kyungpook Univ — Journal of Science Education. Science Education Research Institute Teacher's College. Kyungpook University
J Sci Eng Res — Journal of Science and Engineering Research [India]
J Sci Engrg Res — Journal of Science and Engineering Research
J Scient Agric Soc Finl — Journal. Scientific Agricultural Society of Finland
J Scient Ind Res — Journal of Scientific and Industrial Research
J Scient Instrum — Journal of Scientific Instruments
J Scient Stud Relig — Journal for the Scientific Study of Religion
J Sci Fd Agric — Journal of the Science of Food and Agriculture
J Sci Food — Journal of the Science of Food and Agriculture
J Sci Food Agr — Journal of the Science of Food and Agriculture
J Sci Food Agric — Journal of the Science of Food and Agriculture
J Sci Food Agric Abstr — Journal of the Science of Food and Agriculture. Abstracts
J Sci Hiroshima Univ — Journal of Science. Hiroshima University
J Sci Hiroshima Univ A — Journal of Science. Hiroshima University. Series A. Physics and Chemistry
J Sci Hiroshima Univ Ser A — Journal of Science. Hiroshima University. Series A. Physics and Chemistry
J Sci Hiroshima Univ Ser A-II — Journal of Science. Hiroshima University. Series A-II
J Sci Hiroshima Univ Ser A Math Phys Chem — Journal of Science. Hiroshima University. Series A. Mathematics, Physics, Chemistry
J Sci Hiroshima Univ Ser A Phys Chem — Journal of Science. Hiroshima University. Series A. Physics and Chemistry
J Sci Hiroshima Univ Ser B Div 2 Bot — Journal of Science. Hiroshima University. Series B. Division 2. Botany
J Sci Hiroshima Univ Ser B Div 1 Zool — Journal of Science. Hiroshima University. Series B. Division 1. Zoology
J Sci Hiroshima Univ Ser C — Journal of Science. Hiroshima University. Series C. Geology and Mineralogy
J Sci Hiroshima Univ Ser C (Geol Mineral) — Journal of Science. Hiroshima University. Series C. Geology and Mineralogy
J Sci Ind R — Journal of Scientific and Industrial Research
J Sci and Ind Res — Journal of Scientific and Industrial Research
J Sci Ind Res — Journal of Scientific and Industrial Research
J Sci Ind Res (India) — Journal of Scientific and Industrial Research (India)
J Sci Ind Res Sect A — Journal of Scientific and Industrial Research. Section A. General
J Sci Ind Res Sect B — Journal of Scientific and Industrial Research. Section B
J Sci Ind Res Sect C — Journal of Scientific and Industrial Research. Section C. Biological Sciences
J Sci Ind Res Sect D — Journal of Scientific and Industrial Research. Section D. Technology
J Sci Instr — Journal of Scientific Instruments
J Sci Instrum — Journal of Scientific Instruments
J Sci Instrum Phys Ind — Journal of Scientific Instruments and Physics in Industry
J Sci Instrum Suppl — Journal of Scientific Instruments. Supplement
J Sci (Karachi) — Journal of Science (Karachi)
J Sci Lab D — Journal. Scientific Laboratories. Denison University
J Sci Lab Denison Univ — Journal. Scientific Laboratories. Denison University
J Sci Labor — Journal of Science of Labor [Japan]
J Sci Labour Part 2 — Journal of Science of Labour. Part 2
J Sci Med Lille — Journal des Sciences Medicales de Lille
J Sci Meteorol — Journal Scientifique de la Meteorologie
J Sci Nutr — Journal des Sciences de la Nutrition
J Sci Res — Journal of Scientific Research

J Sci Res Banaras Hindu Univ — Journal of Scientific Research. Banaras Hindu University
J Sci Res (Bhopal) — Journal of Scientific Research (Bhopal)
J Sci Res Counc Jam — Journal. Scientific Research Council of Jamaica
J Sci Res (Hardwar) — Journal of Scientific Research (Hardwar)
J Sci Res (Hardwar India) — Journal of Scientific Research (Hardwar, India)
J Sci Res (Indones) — Journal of Scientific Research (Indonesia)
J Sci Res Inst (Tokyo) — Journal. Scientific Research Institute (Tokyo)
J Sci Res (Lahore) — Journal of Scientific Research (Lahore)
J Sci Soc Thailand — Journal. Science Society of Thailand
J Sci Soil Manure (Jap) — Journal of the Science of Soil and Manure (Japan)
J Sci St Re — Journal for the Scientific Study of Religion
J Sci Stud Rel — Journal for the Scientific Study of Religion
J Sci Stud Relig — Journal for the Scientific Study of Religion
J Sci Tech — Journal of Science and Technology
J Sci and Technol — Journal of Science and Technology
J Sci Technol — Journal of Science and Technology
J Sci Technol (Aberdeen Scotl) — Journal of Science Technology (Aberdeen, Scotland)
J Sci Technol (London) — Journal of Science and Technology (London)
JSCJA — Journal. Society of Chemical Industry (Japan)
JSCMA — Journal. South Carolina Medical Association
J SC Med Assoc — Journal. South Carolina Medical Association
JSCOD — Job Safety Consultant
J S Cosm Ch — Journal. Society of Cosmetic Chemists
J Scott Assoc Geogr Teach — Journal. Scottish Association of Geography Teachers
JSCPB — Proceedings. Japan Society of Civil Engineers
JSCSA — Journal of Statistical Computation and Simulation
JScStRel — Journal for the Scientific Study of Religion [New Haven, CT]
JSCUD — Journal of Science Education. Chungbuk National University
J Scunthorpe Mus Soc — Journal. Scunthorpe Museum Society
J S Dye Col — Journal. Society of Dyers and Colourists
J SE Asian Hist — Journal of Southeast Asian History
J SE Asian Stud — Journal of Southeast Asian Studies
J SE Asia S — Journal of Southeast Asian Studies
J Se As Stud — Journal of Southeast Asian Studies
J Sec Ed — Journal of Secondary Education
J Sediment Petrol — Journal of Sedimentary Petrology
J Sediment Petrology — Journal of Sedimentary Petrology
J Sed Petrol — Journal of Sedimentary Petrology
J Seed Technol — Journal of Seed Technology
J Sej — Jernal Sejarah
J Semitic S — Journal of Semitic Studies
JSemS — Journal of Semitic Studies [Manchester]
J Sem St — Journal of Semitic Studies
J Seoul Woman's Coll — Journal. Seoul Woman's College
J Seric Sci Jpn — Journal of Sericultural Science of Japan
JSeS — Journal of Semitic Studies [Manchester]
JSET — Journal of Sex Education and Therapy
J Severance Union Med Coll — Journal. Severance Union Medical College
J Sex Marital Ther — Journal of Sex and Marital Therapy
J Sex Res — Journal of Sex Research
JSFA — Journal of the Science of Food and Agriculture
JSFOu — Journal. Societe Finno-Ougrienne
JSFWUB — Jahrbuch. Schlesische Friedrich-Wilhelm Universitaet zu Breslau
JSG — Jahrbuch. Schiller-Gesellschaft
JSGLL — Japanese Studies in German Language and Literature
JSGU — Jahrbuch. Schweizerische Gesellschaft fuer Urgeschichte
JSH — Jihocesky Sbornik Historicky
JSH — Journal of Southern History
J Shanghai Coll Text Technol — Journal. Shanghai College of Textile Technology
J Shanghai Jiaotong Univ — Journal of Shanghai Jiaotong University/ Shanghai Jiaotong Daxue Xuebao
J Shanghai Sci Inst — Journal. Shanghai Science Institute
J Shanghai Sci Inst Sect 1 — Journal. Shanghai Science Institute. Section 1. Experimental Biology and Medicine
J Shanghai Sci Inst Sect 1 — Journal. Shanghai Science Institute. Section 1. Mathematics, Astronomy, Physics, Geophysics, Chemistry, and Allied Sciences
J Shanghai Sci Inst Sect 2 — Journal. Shanghai Science Institute. Section 2. Geology, Palaeontology, Mineralogy, and Petrology
J Shanghai Sci Inst Sect 3 — Journal. Shanghai Science Institute. Section 3. Systematic and Morphological Biology
J Shanghai Sci Inst Sect 5 — Journal. Shanghai Science Institute. Section 5. General
J SHASE — Journal. Society of Heating, Air Conditioning, and Sanitary Engineers of Japan
JSHD — Journal of Speech and Hearing Disorders
JSHDA — Journal of Speech and Hearing Disorders
JSHEA — Journal of School Health
J Sheffield Univ Met Soc — Journal. Sheffield University Metallurgical Society
J Shimane Med Assoc — Journal. Shimane Medical Association [Japan]
J Shimonoseki Coll Fish — Journal. Shimonoseki College of Fisheries
J Shimonoseki Univ Fish — Journal. Shimonoseki University of Fisheries

J Ship Res — Journal of Ship Research
J S Hist — Journal of Southern History
J Shivaji Univ — Journal. Shivaji University
J Shivaji Univ Sci — Journal. Shivaji University (Science)
J Showa Med Assoc — Journal. Showa Medical Association [*Japan*]
JSHR — Journal of Speech and Hearing Research
J-S H Sch Clearing House — Junior-Senior High School Clearing House
JSI — Journal. American Society for Information Science
JSI — Journal of Social Issues
JSIAM — Journal. Society of Industrial and Applied Mathematics
J Siam Soc — Journal. Siam Society
J Signalaufzeichnungsmater — Journal fuer Signalaufzeichnungsmaterialien
J Signalaufzeichnungsmaterialien — Journal fuer Signalaufzeichnungsmaterialien
JSIN — Journal. Society for International Numismatics
J Singapore Nat Acad Sci — Journal. Singapore National Academy of Science
J Singapore Natl Acad Sci — Journal. Singapore National Academy of Science
JSISD — Journal of Current Social Issues
JSJ — Journal for the Study of Judaism
JSJ — Journal for the Study of Judaism in the Persian, Hellenistic, and Roman Periods [*Leiden*]
JSK — Jahrbuch. Sammlung Kippenberg Duesseldorf
JSL — Journal. School of Languages
JSL — Journal of Symbolic Logic
JSLCA — Journal of Solution Chemistry
JslF — Juznoslovenski Filolog
JSLQ — Journal of Symbolic Logic. Quarterly
JSM — Journal of Synagogue Music
JSM — Journal of Systems Management
J Small Anim Pract — Journal of Small Animal Practice
J Small Bus Manage — Journal of Small Business Management
J Small Bus Mgt — Journal of Small Business Management
J Sm Anim P — Journal of Small Animal Practice
JSMMART — Journal. Society for Mass Media and Resource Technology
JSMPE — Journal. Society of Motion Picture Engineers
J SMPTE — Journal. SMPTE [*Society of Motion Picture and Television Engineers*]
JSNT — Journal for the Study of the New Testament
JSNTDC — Annuaire. Societe Helvetique des Sciences Naturelles. Partie Scientifique
JSO — Journal. Societe des Oceanistes
J So AL — Journal of South Asian Literature
JSOc — Journal. Societe des Oceanistes
J Soc African — Journal. Societe des Africanistes
J Soc Amer — Journal. Societe des Americanistes
J Soc Arch — Journal. Society of Archivists
J Soc Archer-Antiq — Journal. Society of Archer-Antiquaries
J Soc Arch Hist — Journal. Society of Architectural Historians
J Soc Army Hist Res — Journal. Society for Army Historical Research
J Soc Arts — Journal. Society of Arts
J Soc Automot Eng — Journal. Society of Automotive Engineers
J Soc Automot Eng Jpn Inc — Journal. Society of Automotive Engineers of Japan, Incorporated
J Soc Automot Engrs Australas — Society of Automotive Engineers of Australasia. Journal
J Soc Bibliogr Nat Hist — Journal. Society for the Bibliography of Natural History
J Soc Brew (Japan) — Journal. Society of Brewing (Japan)
J Soc Brew (Tokyo) — Journal. Society of Brewing (Tokyo)
J Soc Can Anesth — Journal. Societe Canadienne des Anesthesistes
J Soc Can Sci Judiciaires — Journal. Societe Canadienne des Sciences Judiciaires
J Soc Chem Ind (Jpn) — Journal. Society of Chemical Industry (Japan)
J Soc Chem Ind (Lond) — Journal. Society of Chemical Industry (London)
J Soc Chem Ind (London) — Journal. Society of Chemical Industry (London)
J Soc Chem Ind (London) Abstr — Journal. Society of Chemical Industry (London). Abstracts
J Soc Chem Ind (London) Rev Sect — Journal. Society of Chemical Industry (London). Review Section
J Soc Chem Ind (London) Trans Commun — Journal. Society of Chemical Industry (London). Transactions and Communications
J Soc Chem Ind Vic — Journal. Society of Chemical Industry of Victoria
J Soc Cosmet Chem — Journal. Society of Cosmetic Chemists
J Soc Dairy Technol — Journal. Society of Dairy Technology
J Soc Dy Colour — Journal. Society of Dyers and Colourists
J Soc Dyers Colourists — Journal. Society of Dyers and Colourists
J Soc Eng (Lond) — Journal. Society of Engineers (London)
J Soc Eng Miner Springs — Journal. Society of Engineers for Mineral Springs [*Japan*]
J Soc Env Engrs — Journal. Society of Environmental Engineers
J Soc Environ Eng — Journal. Society of Environmental Engineers
J Soc Environ Engrs — Journal. Society of Environmental Engineers
J Soc Exp Agric — Journal. Society of Experimental Agriculturists
J Soc Glass Technol — Journal. Society of Glass Technology
J Soc Hist — Journal of Social History
J Soc Hygiene — Journal of Social Hygiene

J Social Casework — Journal of Social Casework
J Social and Econ Studies — Journal of Social and Economic Studies
J Social Forces — Journal of Social Forces
J Social Hyg — Journal of Social Hygiene
J Social Issues — Journal of Social Issues
J Social Pol and Econ Studies — Journal of Social, Political, and Economic Studies
J Social Policy — Journal of Social Policy
J Social and Pol Studies — Journal of Social and Political Studies
J Social Psychol — Journal of Social Psychology
J Soc Ind Appl Math — Journal. Society of Industrial and Applied Mathematics [*United States*]
J Soc Instrum and Control — Journal. Society of Instrument and Control Engineers
J Soc Iss — Journal of Social Issues
J Soc Issue — Journal of Social Issues
J Soc Issues — Journal of Societal Issues
J Soc Leath Technol Chem — Journal. Society of Leather Technologists and Chemists
J Soc Leath Trades Chem — Journal. Society of Leather Trades Chemists
J Soc Mater Sci (Jpn) — Journal. Society of Materials Science (Japan)
J Soc Motion Pict Eng — Journal. Society of Motion Picture Engineers
J Soc Motion Pict and Telev Eng — Journal. Society of Motion Picture and Television Engineers
J Soc Motion Pict Telev Eng — Journal. Society of Motion Picture and Television Engineers
J Soc Nav Archit Jpn — Journal. Society of Naval Architects of Japan
J Soc Nav Arch Japan — Journal. Society of Naval Architects of Japan
J Soc Non-Destr Test — Journal. Society for Non-Destructive Testing
J Soc Occup Med — Journal. Society of Occupational Medicine
J Soc Ocean — Journal. Societe des Oceanistes
J Soc Oceanistes — Journal. Societe des Oceanistes
J Soc Org Syn Chem (Jpn) — Journal. Society of Organic Synthetic Chemistry (Japan)
J Soc Org Synth Chem — Journal. Society of Organic Synthetic Chemistry (Japan)
J Soc Phil — Journal of Social Philosophy
J Soc Photogr Sci and Technol Jpn — Journal. Society of Photographic Science and Technology of Japan
J Soc Photo Opt Instrum Eng — Journal. Society of Photo-Optical Instrumentation Engineers
J Soc Pol — Journal of Social Policy
J Soc Polic — Journal of Social Policy
J Soc Policy — Journal of Social Policy
J Soc Psych — Journal of Social Psychology
J Soc Psychol — Journal of Social Psychology
J Soc Pub Teach Law N S — Journal. Society of Public Teachers of Law. New Series
J Soc Pub T L — Journal. Society of Public Teachers of Law
J Soc Radiol Prot — Journal. Society for Radiological Protection
J Soc Res — Journal of Social Research
J Soc Rubber Ind (Jpn) — Journal. Society of Rubber Industry (Japan)
J Soc Sci — Journal of Social Sciences
J Soc Sci Hum — Journal of Social Sciences and Humanities
J Soc Sci Photogr Jpn — Journal. Society of Scientific Photography of Japan
J Soc Statist Paris — Journal. Societe Statistique de Paris
J Soc Underwater Technol — Journal. Society for Underwater Technology
J Soc Welfare L — Journal of Social Welfare Law
J Socy Pub Tchrs L — Journal. Society of Public Teachers of Law
J So Hist — Journal of Southern History
J Soil Conservation Serv NSW — Journal. Soil Conservation Service of New South Wales
J Soil Conserv NSW — Journal. Soil Conservation Service of New South Wales
J Soil Conserv Service NSW — Journal. Soil Conservation Service of New South Wales
J Soil Conserv Serv NSW — Journal. Soil Conservation Service of New South Wales
J Soil Mech Found Div Am Soc Civ Eng — Journal. Soil Mechanics and Foundations Division. American Society of Civil Engineers
J Soil Sci — Journal of Soil Science
J Soil Sci Soc Philipp — Journal. Soil Science Society of the Philippines
J Soil Sci UAR — Journal of Soil Science of the United Arab Republic
J Soil Sci Un Arab Repub — Journal of Soil Science of the United Arab Republic
J Soil Wat — Journal of Soil and Water Conservation [*US*]
J Soil & Water Conser — Journal of Soil and Water Conservation
J Soil Water Conserv — Journal of Soil and Water Conservation [*US*]
J Soil Water Conserv India — Journal of Soil and Water Conservation in India
J Sol Chem — Journal of Solution Chemistry
J Sol Energy Eng — Journal of Solar Energy Engineering [*United States*]
J Sol Energy Res — Journal of Solar Energy Research
J Sol Energy Sci Eng — Journal of Solar Energy Science and Engineering [*United States*]
J Sol Energy Soc Korea — Journal. Solar Energy Society of Korea [*Republic of Korea*]
J Solid Lubr — Journal of Solid Lubrication
J Solid-Phase Biochem — Journal of Solid-Phase Biochemistry

J Solid State Chem — Journal of Solid State Chemistry
J Solid Wastes — Journal of Solid Wastes
J Solid Wastes Manage — Journal of Solid Wastes Management [*Japan*]
J Soln Chem — Journal of Solution Chemistry
J Sol St Ch — Journal of Solid State Chemistry
J Solut Chem — Journal of Solution Chemistry
J Solution Chem — Journal of Solution Chemistry
J Soonchunhyang Coll — Journal. Soonchunhyang College
JSOR — Journal. Society of Oriental Research
JSOT — Journal for the Study of the Old Testament
J Sound and Vib — Journal of Sound and Vibration
J Sound Vib — Journal of Sound and Vibration
J South Afr Stud — Journal of Southern African Studies
J South Afr Vet Assoc — Journal. South African Veterinary Association
J South Afr Wildl Manage Assoc — Journal. Southern African Wildlife
    Management Association
J South Asian Lit — Journal of South Asian Literature
J South As Lit — Journal of South Asian Literature
J South Calif Dent Assoc — Journal. Southern California Dental Association
J South Calif State Dent Assoc — Journal. Southern California State Dental
    Association
J Southeast Agric Coll (Wye England) — Journal. Southeastern Agricultural
    College (Wye, England)
J Southeast Asian Stud — Journal of Southeast Asian Studies
J Southeast Sect Am Water Works Assoc — Journal. Southeastern Section.
    American Water Works Association
J Southern Hist — Journal of Southern History
J South His — Journal of Southern History
J South Hist — Journal of Southern History
J Soviet Math — Journal of Soviet Mathematics
JSP — Journal of Social Psychology
J Spacecr Rockets — Journal of Spacecraft and Rockets
J Space L — Journal of Space Law
J Space Law — Journal of Space Law
J Spac Rock — Journal of Spacecraft and Rockets
JSPDA5 — Journal. American Society of Psychosomatic Dentistry
J Sp Disorders — Journal of Speech and Hearing Disorders
JSPEB — Journal of Special Education
J Spec — Jewish Spectator
J Spec Ed — Journal of Special Education
J Spec Ed Men Retard — Journal for Special Educators of the Mentally
    Retarded [*Later, Journal for Special Educators*]
J Spec Educ — Journal of Special Education
J Spec Philos — Journal of the Speculative Philosophy
J Spectros Soc Jpn — Journal. Spectroscopical Society of Japan
J Sp Educ — Journal of Special Education
J Sp Educators — Journal for Special Educators
J Sp Educ Men Retard — Journal for Special Educators of the Mentally
    Retarded [*Later, Journal for Special Educators*]
J Speech D — Journal of Speech and Hearing Disorders
J Speech He — Journal of Speech and Hearing Research
J Speech & Hear Dis — Journal of Speech and Hearing Disorders
J Speech & Hear Disord — Journal of Speech and Hearing Disorders
J Speech Hear Disord — Journal of Speech and Hearing Disorders
J Speech & Hear Res — Journal of Speech and Hearing Research
J Speech Hear Res — Journal of Speech and Hearing Research
JSPHA — Journal of Speech and Hearing Research
JSPIJ — Journal of Social and Political Ideas in Japan
JSPMA — Journal of Supramolecular Structure
J Sport Behav — Journal of Sport Behavior
J Sport Hist — Journal of Sport History
J Sports Med Phys Fit — Journal of Sports Medicine and Physical Fitness
J Sports Med Phys Fitness — Journal of Sports Medicine and Physical Fitness
J Sport Soc Iss — Journal of Sport and Social Issues
J Sports Turf Res Inst — Journal of the Sports Turf Research Institute
JSPR — Journal. Society for Psychical Research
JSPs — Journal of Social Psychology
JSPSA — Journal of Social Psychology
JSPTL — Journal. Society of Public Teachers of Law
JSR — Japan Socialist Review
JSR — Japanese Sociological Review
JSR — Jewish Student Review
JSR — Journal of Social Research
JSR — Journal of Spacecraft and Rockets
JSRBA — Journal of Scientific Research. Banaras Hindu University
JSRHS — Japan Science Review. Humanistic Studies
JSR LPH — Japan Science Review. Literature, Philosophy, and History
JSRS — Jewish Social Research Series
JSRSA — JARE [*Japanese Antarctic Research Expedition*] Scientific Reports.
    Special Issue
JSS — Jewish Social Studies
JSS — Journal of Semitic Studies
JSS — Journal. Siam Society [*Bangkok*]
JSS — Journal of Spanish Studies. Twentieth Century
JSS — Journal of Sports Sciences
JSSB — Journal. Siam Society (Bangkok)

JSSC — Journal of Solid-State Circuits (IEEE)
JSSEA — Journal. American Society of Safety Engineers
JSSP News — JSSP [*Junior Secondary Science Project*] Newsletter
JSSQ — Jewish Social Service Quarterly
JSSR — Journal for the Scientific Study of Religion
JSSRel — Journal for the Scientific Study of Religion
JSSSG — Journal. Society for the Study of State Governments [*Varanasi*]
JSSTC — Journal of Spanish Studies. Twentieth Century
JSTAA — Journal. Royal Statistical Society. Series A. General
J Starch Technol Res Soc Jpn — Journal of Starch Technology. Research
    Society of Japan
J Stat Comput Simul — Journal of Statistical Computation and Simulation
J Statis Soc — Journal. Statistical Society
J Statist Comp and Simulation — Journal of Statistical Computation and
    Simulation
J Statist Comput Simulation — Journal of Statistical Computation and
    Simulation
J Statist Phys — Journal of Statistical Physics
J Statist Plann Inference — Journal of Statistical Planning and Inference
J Statist Res — Journal of Statistical Research
J Stat Phys — Journal of Statistical Physics
J Stat Plann and Inference — Journal of Statistical Planning and Inference
J Stat Plann Inference — Journal of Statistical Planning and Inference
J Stat Rsr — Journal of Statistical Research
JSTBA — Journal. Royal Statistical Society. Series B. Methodological
J Steroid B — Journal of Steroid Biochemistry
J Steroid Biochem — Journal of Steroid Biochemistry
J Steward Anthropol Soc — Journal. Steward Anthropological Society
J Steward Anthro Soc — Journal. Steward Anthropological Society
JStJu — Journal for the Study of Judaism in the Persian, Hellenistic, and
    Roman Periods [*Leiden*]
J St Jud — Journal for the Study of Judaism [*Later, Journal for the Study of
    Judaism in the Persian, Hellenistic, and Roman Periods*]
J St Med — Journal of State Medicine
JSTNA — Journal. American Statistical Association
J Stored Pr — Journal of Stored Products Research
J Stored Prod Res — Journal of Stored Products Research
JSTPD — Journal of Science and Technology (Peshawar, Pakistan)
J Strain Anal — Journal of Strain Analysis
J Strain Anal Eng Des — Journal of Strain Analysis for Engineering Design
J Strain Anal Engng Des — Journal of Strain Analysis for Engineering Design
J Strain Analysis — Journal of Strain Analysis
J Struc Mec — Journal of Structural Mechanics
J Struct Ch — Journal of Structural Chemistry
J Struct Chem — Journal of Structural Chemistry
J Struct Di — Journal. Structural Division. American Society of Civil
    Engineers
J Struct Div Amer Soc Civil Eng Proc — Journal. Structural Division.
    American Society of Civil Engineers. Proceedings
J Struct Div Proc ASCE — Journal. Structural Division. American Society of
    Civil Engineers. Proceedings.
J Struct Geol — Journal of Structural Geology
J Struct Le — Journal of Structural Learning
J Struct Mech — Journal of Structural Mechanics
J Structural Learning — Journal of Structural Learning
J Structural Mech — Journal of Structural Mechanics
J Stud Alc — Journal of Studies on Alcohol
J Stud Alcohol — Journal of Studies on Alcohol
J Stud Alcohol (Suppl) — Journal of Studies on Alcohol (Supplement)
J Stud Econ Economet — Journal for Studies in Economics and Econometrics
J Studies Alcohol — Journal of Studies on Alcohol
J Studies Econ and Econometrics — Journal for Studies in Economics and
    Econometrics
JSUB — Jahrbuch. Schlesische Friedrich-Wilhelm Universitaet zu Breslau
J Submic Cy — Journal of Submicroscopic Cytology
J Submicrosc Cytol — Journal of Submicroscopic Cytology
J Suffolk Acad L — Journal. Suffolk Academy of Law
J Suisse Apic — Journal Suisse d'Apiculture
J Suisse Horlog — Journal Suisse d'Horlogerie
J Suisse Horlog Bijout — Journal Suisse d'Horlogerie et de Bijouterie
J Suisse Med — Journal Suisse de Medecine
J Supervision Tr Min — Journal of Supervision and Training in Ministry
J Supramolecular Struct — Journal of Supramolecular Structure [*Later,
    Journal of Cellular Biochemistry*]
J Supramol Struct — Journal of Supramolecular Structure [*Later, Journal of
    Cellular Biochemistry*]
J Supramol Struct Cell Biochem — Journal of Supramolecular Structure and
    Cellular Biochemistry [*Later, Journal of Cellular Biochemistry*]
J Supramol Struct (Suppl) — Journal of Supramolecular Structure
    (Supplement)
J Supram St — Journal of Supramolecular Structure [*Later, Journal of
    Cellular Biochemistry*]
J Surg Oncol — Journal of Surgical Oncology
J Surg Res — Journal of Surgical Research
J Surv Mapp — Journal. Surveying and Mapping Division. American Society of
    Civil Engineers

J Surv & Mapp Div Proc ASCE — Journal. Surveying and Mapping Division. American Society of Civil Engineers. Proceedings
J Surv Mapping Div Amer Soc Civil Eng Proc — Journal. Surveying and Mapping Division. American Society of Civil Engineers. Proceedings
JSVIA — Journal of Sound and Vibration
J SWA Sci Soc — Journal. South West African Scientific Society
JSWC — Journal of Soil and Water Conservation
JSWL — Journal of Social Welfare Law
JSWS — Journal of Social Work and Human Sexuality
JSW Tech Rev — JSW [*Japan Steel Works*] Technical Review
J Symb Anthropol — Journal of Symbolic Anthropology
J Symb Log — Journal of Symbolic Logic
J Symb Logic — Journal of Symbolic Logic
J Symbolic Logic — Journal of Symbolic Logic
J Symbol Logic — Journal of Symbolic Logic
J Sym Log — Journal of Symbolic Logic
J Syn Org J — Journal of Synthetic Organic Chemistry (Japan)
J Synth Lubr — Journal of Synthetic Lubrication
J Synth Org Chem (Jpn) — Journal of Synthetic Organic Chemistry (Japan)
J Synth Rubber Ind (Lanzhou People's Repub China) — Journal of Synthetic Rubber Industry (Lanzhou, People's Republic of China)
J Sys Mgmt — Journal of Systems Management
J Sys Mgt — Journal of Systems Management
J Sys and Soft — Journal of Systems and Software
J Systems Mgt — Journal of Systems Management
J Systems Software — Journal of Systems and Software
J Syst Eng — Journal of Systems Engineering
J Syst Engng — Journal of Systems Engineering
J Syst Man — Journal of Systems Management
J Syst Manage — Journal of Systems Management
J Syst Mgt — Journal of Systems Management
J Syst and Software — Journal of Systems and Software
JT — Jewish Tribune [*Bombay*]
JT — Journal of Music Therapy
JT — Journal des Tribunaux
JTA — Journal of Thermal Analysis
J Taiwan Agric Res — Journal of Taiwan Agricultural Research
J Taiwan Agr Res — Journal of Taiwan Agricultural Research
J Takeda Res Lab — Journal. Takeda Research Laboratories
J Takeda Res Labs — Journal. Takeda Research Laboratories [*Japan*]
J Tamil Stud — Journal of Tamil Studies
J Tam S — Journal of Tamil Studies
JTASA — Journal. Tennessee Academy of Science
J Tax — Journal of Taxation
J Taxation — Journal of Taxation
J Tax'n — Journal of Taxation
JTB — Journal of Theoretical Biology
JTC — Journal for Theology and the Church
JTCh — Journal for Theology and the Church
JTCMD — Journal of Tissue Culture Methods
JTDAA — Journal. Tennessee Dental Association
JTE — Journal of Teacher Education
JTE — Journal of Transport Economics and Policy
J Teach Ed — Journal of Teacher Education
J Teach Educ — Journal of Teacher Education
J Teaching PE — Journal of Teaching in Physical Education
J Tech Assoc Fur Ind — Journal. Technical Association of the Fur Industry
J Tech Bengal Engrg College — Journal of Technology. Bengal Engineering College
J Tech Councils ASCE Proc ASCE — Journal. Technical Councils of ASCE. Proceedings. American Society of Civil Engineers
J Tech Lab (Tokyo) — Journal. Technical Laboratory (Tokyo)
J Technol — Journal of Technology
J Technol Eng — Journal of Technology and Engineering
J Tech Writ Commun — Journal of Technical Writing and Communication
J Teflon — Journal of Teflon
J Telecommun Networks — Journal of Telecommunication Networks
J Telecom Net — Journal of Telecommunication Networks
J Tenn Acad Sci — Journal. Tennessee Academy of Science
J Tenn Dent Assoc — Journal. Tennessee Dental Association
J Tenn Med Assoc — Journal. Tennessee Medical Association
J Terramech — Journal of Terramechanics
J Terramechanics — Journal of Terramechanics
J Tertiary Educ Adm — Journal of Tertiary Educational Administration
J Test Eval — Journal of Testing and Evaluation
J Test and Eval — Journal of Testing and Evaluation
JTEVA — Journal of Testing and Evaluation
J Textile Inst — Journal. Textile Institute
J Text Inst — Journal. Textile Institute
J Text Inst Abstr — Journal. Textile Institute. Abstracts
J Text Mach Soc Jap — Journal. Textile Machinery Society of Japan
J Texture Stud — Journal of Texture Studies
J Thanatol — Journal of Thanatology
J Theol St — Journal of Theological Studies
J Theol Sthn Afr — Journal of Theology for Southern Africa
J Theor Bio — Journal of Theoretical Biology

J Theor Biol — Journal of Theoretical Biology
J Theoret Biol — Journal of Theoretical Biology
J Theor Soc Behav — Journal for the Theory of Social Behavior
J Thermal Anal — Journal of Thermal Analysis
J Thermal Insulation — Journal of Thermal Insulation
J Therm Ana — Journal of Thermal Analysis
J Therm Bio — Journal of Thermal Biology
J Therm Eng — Journal of Thermal Engineering
J Therm Engng — Journal of Thermal Engineering
J Therm Stresses — Journal of Thermal Stresses
J Thora Cardiovasc Surg — Journal of Thoracic and Cardiovascular Surgery
J Thorac Cardiovasc Surg — Journal of Thoracic and Cardiovascular Surgery
J Thorac Surg — Journal of Thoracic Surgery
J Thor Surg — Journal of Thoracic and Cardiovascular Surgery
J Thought — Journal of Thought
JThS — Journal of Theological Studies
J Th St — Journal of Theological Studies
J Timber Dev Assoc India — Journal. Timber Development Association of India
J Timber Dryers Preserv Assoc India — Journal. Timber Dryers' and Preservers' Association of India
J Time Ser Anal — Journal of Time Series Analysis
Jt Inst Lab Astrophy Rep — Joint Institute for Laboratory Astrophysics. Report
JTMMA — Journal. Tennessee Medical Association
J Tohoku Min Soc — Journal. Tohoku Mining Society [*Japan*]
J Tokyo Coll Fish — Journal. Tokyo College of Fisheries
J Tokyo Dent Coll Soc — Journal. Tokyo Dental College Society
J Tokyo Med Assoc — Journal. Tokyo Medical Association
J Tokyo Med Coll — Journal. Tokyo Medical College
J Tokyo Univ Fish — Journal. Tokyo University of Fisheries
J Tokyo Women's Med Coll — Journal. Tokyo Women's Medical College
J Tottori Daigaku Nogaku — Journal. Tottori Daigaku Nogaku-Buo
J Town Pl I — Journal of Town Planning Institute
J Town Reg Plann — Journal for Town and Regional Planning
J Tox Env H — Journal of Toxicology and Environmental Health
J Toxicol Environ Health — Journal of Toxicology and Environmental Health
J Toxicol Sci — Journal of Toxicological Sciences
JTP — Journal of Transport Economics and Policy
JTR — Journal of European Industrial Training
JTR — Journal of Typographic Research
J Transp Ec — Journal of Transport Economics and Policy
J Transp Econ Policy — Journal of Transport Economics and Policy
J Transp Eng Div Amer Soc Civil Eng Proc — Journal. Transportation Engineering Division. American Society of Civil Engineers. Proceedings
J Transp Hist — Journal of Transport History
J Transp Med — Journal of Transportation Medicine [*Japan*]
J Transport Econ Pol — Journal of Transport Economics and Policy
J Transport Econ and Policy — Journal of Transport Economics and Policy
J Trans Soc Eng (London) — Journal and Transactions. Society of Engineers (London)
J Trauma — Journal of Trauma
J Travis County Med Soc — Journal. Travis County Medical Society [*Michigan*]
J Tribol — Journal of Tribology
J Trop Geog — Journal of Tropical Geography
J Tropical Geography — Journal of Tropical Geography
J Trop Med — Journal of Tropical Medicine and Hygiene
J Trop Med Hyg — Journal of Tropical Medicine and Hygiene
J Trop Med and Hyg (London) — Journal of Tropical Medicine and Hygiene (London)
J Trop Med (London) — Journal of Tropical Medicine (London)
J Trop Pediatr — Journal of Tropical Pediatrics
J Trop Pediatr — Journal of Tropical Pediatrics and Environmental Child Health
J Trop Pediatr Afr Child Health — Journal of Tropical Pediatrics and African Child Health
J Trop Pediatr Environ Child Health — Journal of Tropical Pediatrics and Environmental Child Health
J Trop Pediatr Environ Child Health Monogr — Journal of Tropical Pediatrics and Environmental Child Health. Monograph
J Trop Vet Sc — Journal of Tropical Veterinary Science
JTRS — Journal. Thailand Research Society
JTS — Journal of Theological Studies
J T S Behav — Journal for the Theory of Social Behavior
J Tsing Hua Univ — Journal. Tsing Hua University
J Tsuda College — Journal. Tsuda College
J Tuberc Lepr — Journal of Tuberculosis and Leprosy [*Japan*]
JTUFA — Journal. Tokyo University of Fisheries
J Tung-Chi Univ — Journal. Tung-Chi University
J Turk Phytopathol — Journal of Turkish Phytopathology
JTVI — Journal of Transactions. Victoria Institute
JTX — Journal of Taxation
J Typogr Res — Journal of Typographic Research
Ju — Judaism
JU — Juilliard Review. Annual
JUAG — Jahrbuch. Ungarische Archaeologische Gesellschaft

JUARA — Journal of Chemistry. United Arab Republic
JUCO Rev — JUCO [*National Junior College Athletic Association*] Review
JUD — Jahrbuch. Universitaet Duesseldorf
Jud — Judaica [*Zurich*]
Jud — Judaism
Judge Advo J — Judge Advocate Journal
Judges J — Judges' Journal
Judic — Judicature
Judicature — Journal. American Judicature Society
Judicature J Am Jud Soc'y — Judicature. Journal of the American Judicature
Society
Jud J — Judges' Journal
JUE — Journal of Urban Economics
J U Film As — Journal. University Film Association
Jugosl Drus Prouc Zemljista Posebne Publ — Jugoslovensko Drustvo za
Proucavanje Zemljista. Posebne Publikacije
Jugosl Ginekol Opstet — Jugoslovenska Ginekologija i Opstetricija
Jugosl Med Biokem — Jugoslavenska Medicinska Biokemija
Jugosl Pcelarstvo — Jugoslovensko Pcelarstvo
Jugosl Pedijatr — Jugoslovenska Pediajatrija
Jugosl Pregl — Jugoslovenski Pregled
Jugosl Pronalazastvo — Jugoslovensko Pronalazastvo
Jugosl Vinograd Vinar — Jugoslovensko Vinogradarstvo i Vinarstvo
Jugosl Vocarstvo — Jugoslovensko Vocarstvo
Juilliard R — Juilliard Review
J Ukr Stud — Journal of Ukrainian Studies
JUL — Journal of Urban Law
Julk Oulu Yliopisto Ydintek Laitos — Julkaisuja-Oulu Yliopisto.
Ydintekniikkan Laitos
J Ultra Res — Journal of Ultrastructure Research
J Ultrastruct Res — Journal of Ultrastructure Research
J Ultrastruct Res Suppl — Journal of Ultrastructure Research. Supplement
JUM — Judaism
JUNA — Juedische Nachrichten
Jun Col J — Junior College Journal
Junior Coll J — Junior College Journal
Junior Inst Eng London J Rec Trans — Junior Institution of Engineers. London.
Journal and Record of Transactions
J United Serv Inst India — Journal. United Service Institution of India
J Univ Bombay — Journal. University of Bombay
J Univ Bombay NS — Journal. University of Bombay. New Series
J Univ Durban-Westville — Journal. University of Durban-Westville
J Univ F Assoc — Journal. University Film Association [*Carbondale*]
J Univ Gauhati — Journal. University of Gauhati
J Univ Geol Soc (Nagpur) — Journal. University Geological Society (Nagpur)
J Univ Kuwait (Sci) — Journal. University of Kuwait (Science)
J Univ Peshawar — Journal. University of Peshawar
J Univ Poona — Journal. University of Poona
J Univ Poona Sci Technol — Journal. University of Poona. Science and
Technology
J Univ Saugar — Journal. University of Saugar
J Univ Saugar Part 2 Sect A — Journal. University of Saugar. Part 2. Section
A. Physical Sciences
J Univ Sheffield Geol Soc — Journal. University of Sheffield. Geological
Society
J Univ Stud — Journal of University Studies
JUNKA — Junkatsu
Junta Energ Nucl Rep (Spain) — Junta de Energia Nuclear. Report (Spain)
Junta Invest Cient Ultramar Estud Ensaios Doc (Port) — Junta de Investigacoes
Cientificas do Ultramar. Estudos, Ensaios, e Documentos (Portugal)
Junta Invest Ultramar Estud Ens Doc — Junta de Investigacoes do Ultramar.
Estudos, Ensaios, e Documentos
J UOEH — Journal of UOEH [*University of Occupational and Environmental
Health*] [*Japan*]
JUPOA — Journal of Undergraduate Psychological Research
JUPOA — Journal. University of Poona. Science and Technology
JUPSA — Journal. Physical Society of Japan
JUr — Journal of Urology
Jur — Jurist. Quarterly Journal of Jurisprudence
J Urban — Journal of Urban Law
J Urban Affairs — Journal of Urban Affairs
J Urban Anal — Journal of Urban Analysis
J Urban Analysis — Journal of Urban Analysis
J Urban Ec — Journal of Urban Economics
J Urban Econ — Journal of Urban Economics
J Urban H — Journal of Urban History
J Urban His — Journal of Urban History
J Urban Hist — Journal of Urban History
J Urban L — Journal of Urban Law
J Urban Law — Journal of Urban Law
J Urban Living Health Assoc — Journal. Urban Living and Health Association
[*Japan*]
J Urban Pla — Journal. Urban Planning and Development Division. American
Society of Civil Engineers

J Urban Planning & Dev Div Proc ASCE — Journal. Urban Planning and
Development Division. Proceedings. American Society of Civil
Engineers
Juridical Rev — Juridical Review
Jurid R — Juridical Review
Jurid Rev — Juridical Review
Juri J — Jurimetrics Journal
Jurimetrics — Jurimetrics Journal
Jurimetrics J — Jurimetrics Journal
J Urol — Journal of Urology
J Urol Med Chir — Journal d'Urologie Medicale et Chirurgicale
J Urol Neph — Journal d'Urologie et de Nephrologie
J Urol Nephrol — Journal d'Urologie et de Nephrologie
JUR R — Juridical Review
Jur Rev — Juridical Review
JURT — Juneau Report
J Urusvati Himalayan Res Inst Roerich Mus — Journal. Urusvati Himalayan
Research Institute of Roerich Museum
Jus — Jus; Rivista di Scienze Giuridiche
J US Artillery — Journal. United States Artillery
Jus Eccl — Jus Ecclesiasticum
JUSII — Journal. United Service Institution of India
J Usines Gaz — Journal des Usines a Gaz [*France*]
JUSNC — Journal. United States National Committee
Just Econ — Just Economics
Just P — Justice of the Peace
Just Sys J — Justice System Journal
Just Syst J — Justice System Journal
Justus Liebigs Ann Chem — Justus Liebigs Annalen der Chemie
Jute Bull — Jute Bulletin
Jute Jute Fabr Bangladesh Newsl — Jute and Jute Fabrics. Bangladesh
Newsletter
Jutendo Med — Jutendo Medicine [*Japan*]
J Utiliz Agr Prod — Journal of Utilization of Agricultural Products
Juv Ct JJ — Juvenile Court Judges Journal
Juv Ct Judges J — Juvenile Court Judges Journal
Juven Just — Juvenile Justice
Juv and Fam Courts J — Juvenile and Family Court Journal
Juv & Fam Ct J — Juvenile and Family Court Journal
JUZIAG — Juzen Igakkai Zasshi
JV — Jahrbuch fuer Volksliedforschung
JV — Journal. Violin Society of America
JVA — Jaarboek. Vereeniging Amstelodanum
JVA — Jahrbuch. Verein von Altertumsfreunden im Rheinland
JVA — Journal of Volunteer Administration
J Vac Sci T — Journal of Vacuum Science and Technology
J Vac Sci Tech — Journal of Vacuum Science and Technology
J Vac Sci and Technol — Journal of Vacuum Science and Technology
J Vac Sci Technol — Journal of Vacuum Science and Technology
J Vac Sci and Technol A — Journal of Vacuum Science and Technology. A.
Vacuum, Surfaces, and Films
J Vac Sci and Technol B — Journal of Vacuum Science and Technology. B.
Micro-Electronics Processing and Phenomena
J Vac Soc Jpn — Journal. Vacuum Society of Japan
J Value Eng — Journal of Value Engineering
J Value Inq — Journal of Value Inquiry
JVARh — Jahrbuch. Verein von Altertumsfreunden im Rheinland
JVB — Juedisches Volksblatt (Breslau)
JVEG — Jaarbericht. Vooraziatische-Egyptisch Genootschap "Ex Oriente
Lux"
J Vener Dis Inf — Journal of Venereal Disease Information
J Verbal Learn — Journal of Verbal Learning and Verbal Behavior
J Verb Learn — Journal of Verbal Learning and Verbal Behavior
J Verb Learn Verb Behav — Journal of Verbal Learning and Verbal Behavior
J Ver Vaterl Naturk Wuertt — Jahresheft. Verein fuer Vaterlaendische
Naturkunde in Wuerttemberg
J Vet Anim Husb Res (India) — Journal of Veterinary and Animal Husbandry
Research (India)
J Vet Fac Univ Tehran — Journal. Veterinary Faculty. University of Tehran
J Vet Med — Journal of Veterinary Medicine [*Japan*]
J Vet Med Educ — Journal of Veterinary Medical Education
J Vet Midi — Journal des Veterinaires du Midi
J Vet Pharmacol Ther — Journal of Veterinary Pharmacology and
Therapeutics
J Vet Sci UAR — Journal of Veterinary Science of the United Arab Republic
JVF — Jahrbuch fuer Volksliedforschung
JVH — Jahrbuch fuer Volkskunde der Heimatvertriebenen
J Vic Teachers Union — Journal of the Victorian Teachers' Union
J Vinyl Technol — Journal of Vinyl Technology
J Viola da Gamba Soc Amer — Journal. Viola da Gamba Society of America
J Violin S — Journal. Violin Society of America
J Violin Soc Amer — Journal. Violin Society of America
J Virol — Journal of Virology
J Virol Methods — Journal of Virological Methods
J Virology — Journal of Virology
J Vitaminol — Journal of Vitaminology

J Vitaminol (Kyoto) — Journal of Vitaminology (Kyoto)
JVJE — Jahrbuch. Vereinigung Juedischer Exportakademiker
JVJGL — Jahrbuch. Verein fuer Juedische Geschichte und Literatur
JVLBA — Journal of Verbal Learning and Verbal Behavior
JVLHOD — Jahrbuch. Verein fuer Landeskunde und Heimatpflege im Gau Oberdonau
JVLVB — Journal of Verbal Learning and Verbal Behavior
JVMED — Journal of Virological Methods
J V N M — Jaarboek. Vereeniging voor Nederlandsche Muziekgeschiedenis
JVNS — Jahrbuch. Verein fuer Niederdeutsche Sprachforschung
J Vocat Beh — Journal of Vocational Behavior
J Voc Behav — Journal of Vocational Behavior
J Volcanol Geotherm Res — Journal of Volcanology and Geothermal Research
J Volun Act — Journal of Voluntary Action Research
JVP — Journal of Vertebrate Paleontology
JVSch — Jahrbuch. Verein Schweizerischer Gymnasial-Lehrer
JVWK — Jahrbuch. Verein fuer Westfaelische Kirchengeschichte
JVZ — Juedische Volkszeitung [*Oberingelheim/Leipzig*]
JW — [*The*] Jewish Week
JW — Journal of the West
JWAfrL — Journal of West African Languages
JWAG — Journal. Walters Art Gallery
J Wagga Wagga Dist Hist Soc — Wagga Wagga and District Historical Society. Journal
J Wakayama Med Soc — Journal. Wakayama Medical Society
JWAL — Journal of West African Languages
JWalt — Journal. Walters Art Gallery
J WA Nurses — Journal. Western Australian Nurses Association
JWarb — Journal. Warburg and Courtauld Institute
J Warburg C — Journal. Warburg and Courtauld Institute
J Warburg Courtauld Inst — Journal. Warburg and Courtauld Institute
J Warburg and Courtauld Inst — Journal. Warburg and Courtauld Institute
JWASA — Journal. Washington Academy of Sciences
J Wash Acad Sci — Journal. Washington Academy of Sciences
J Washington Acad Sci — Journal. Washington Academy of Sciences
J Water P C — Journal. Water Pollution Control Federation
J Water Pollut Contr Fed — Journal. Water Pollution Control Federation
J Water Pollut Control Fed — Journal. Water Pollution Control Federation
J Water Pollut Control Fed — Water Pollution Control Federation. Journal
J Water Resour Planning & Manage Div Proc ASCE — Journal. Water Resources Planning and Management Division. Proceedings. American Society of Civil Engineers
J Water Resour Plann Manage Div Am Soc Civ Eng — Journal. Water Resources Planning and Management Division. Proceedings. American Society of Civil Engineers
J Water Resour Plann Manage Div ASCE — Journal. Water Resources Planning and Management Division. American Society of Civil Engineers
J Water Waste — Journal of Water and Waste [*Japan*]
J Waterway — Journal. Waterways, Harbors, and Coastal Engineering Division. American Society of Civil Engineers
J Waterway Port Coastal Ocean Div Amer Soc Civil Eng Proc — Journal. Waterways, Port, Coastal, and Ocean Division. American Society of Civil Engineers. Proceedings
J Waterway Port Coastal & Ocean Div Proc ASCE — Journal. Waterways, Port, Coastal, and Ocean Division. Proceedings. American Society of Civil Engineers
J Waterw Harbors Div Am Soc Civ Eng — Journal. Waterways and Harbors Division. American Society of Civil Engineers
J Water Works Assoc — Journal. Water Works Association [*Japan*]
J Waterw Port Coastal Ocean Div ASCE — Journal. Waterways, Port, Coastal, and Ocean Division. American Society of Civil Engineers
JWB — Jahrbuch der Wittheit zu Bremen
JWBS — Journal. Welsh Bibliographic Society
JWCBRS — Journal. West China Border Research Society
JWCI — Journal. Warburg and Courtauld Institute
JWCTD — Journal of Wood Chemistry and Technology
J West — Journal of the West
J West Afr Inst Oil Palm Res — Journal. West African Institute for Oil Palm Research
J West Afr Sci Assoc — Journal. West African Science Association
J West Scot Iron Steel Inst — Journal. West of Scotland Iron and Steel Institute
J West Soc Eng — Journal. Western Society of Engineers
J West Soc Periodontol — Journal. Western Society of Periodontology
JWG — Jahrbuch fuer Wirtschaftsgeschichte
JWGV — Jahrbuch. Wiener Goethe-Verein
JWH — Journal of World History
JWI — Journal. Warburg and Courtauld Institute [*London*]
JWIDA — Journal of Wildlife Diseases
J Wildl Dis — Journal of Wildlife Diseases
J Wildlife Mgt — Journal of Wildlife Management
J Wildl Man — Journal of Wildlife Management
J Wildl Manage — Journal of Wildlife Management
JWIM — Journal of Wildlife Management

J Wind Eng and Ind — Journal of Wind Engineering and Industrial Aerodynamics
J Wind Engng & Ind Aerodyn — Journal of Wind Engineering and Industrial Aerodynamics
J Wind Engng Ind Aerodynam — Journal of Wind Engineering and Industrial Aerodynamics
J Wld Trade Law — Journal of World Trade Law
JWMS — Journal. William Morris Society
J Won Kwang Public Health Jr Coll — Journal. Won Kwang Public Health Junior College
J World Hist — Journal of World History
J World Tr — Journal of World Trade Law
J World Trade L — Journal of World Trade Law
J World Trade Law — Journal of World Trade Law
J World Tr L — Journal of World Trade Law
JWPCF — Journal. Water Pollution Control Federation
JWPFA — Journal. Water Pollution Control Federation
JWS — Journal of Western Speech
JWSL — Journal of Women's Studies in Literature
JWT — Journal of World Trade Law
JWTL — Journal of World Trade Law
J W Vir Phil Soc — Journal. West Virginia Philosophical Society
JWWJA — Journal. Japan Water Works Association
JWZ — Juedische Wochenzeitung
J X-Ray Technol — Journal of X-Ray Technology
J Yamagata Agric For Soc — Journal. Yamagata Agriculture and Forestry Society
JYB — Jewish Year Book
JYCE-A — Journal. Hydraulics Division. American Society of Civil Engineers. Proceedings
JYM — Journal of Property Management
J Yokohama Munic Univ — Journal. Yokohama Municipal University
J Yonago Med Assoc — Journal. Yonago Medical Association
J Youth Ado — Journal of Youth and Adolescence
J Youth & Adolescence — Journal of Youth and Adolescence
JZ — Jazykovedny Zbornik
Jz — Jazz Magazine
Jz — Jezykoznawca
JZ — Jinruigaku Zasshi [*Anthropological Journal*]
JZ — Juedische Zeitung
JZ — Juristenzeitung
J Zhejiang Med Univ — Journal. Zhejiang Medical University
JZO — Juedische Zeitung fuer Ostdeutschland [*Breslau*]
J Zoo Anim Med — Journal of Zoo Animal Medicine
J Zool — Journal of Zoology
J Zool Res — Journal of Zoological Research
J Zool Soc India — Journal. Zoological Society of India
JZWL — Juedische Zeitschrift fuer Wissenschaft und Leben

K

K — Klio. Beitraege zur Alten Geschichte
K — Knjizevnost
K — Knowledge
K — Kultur
KA — Kansas Music Review
KA — Korean Affairs
KA — Kultura
KA — Kunstmuseets Arsskrift
KA — Kyrkohistorisk Arsskrift
Kabard Balkar Gos Univ Sb Nauchn Rab Aspir — Kabardino-Balkarskii
    Gosudarstvennyi Universitet. Sbornik Nauchnykh Rabot Aspirantov
Kabardino-Balkarsk Gos Univ Ucen Zap — Kabardino-Balkarskii
    Gosudarstvennyi Universitet. Ucenyi Zapiski
Kabel Tekh — Kabel'naya Tekhnika
K d Abg Sten Ber — Verhandlungen. Kammer der Abgeordneten des
    Bayerischen Landtags. Stenographische Berichte
Kab Seb — Kabar Sebarang. Sulating Maphilindo
Kabul Univ Fac Agric Res Note — Kabul University. Faculty of Agriculture.
    Research Notes
Kabul Univ Fac Agric Tech Bull — Kabul University. Faculty of Agriculture.
    Technical Bulletin
KAC — Kapper
K Acad Belg Jaarb — Koninklijk Academie van Belgie. Jaarboek
Kadel R — Kadelpian Review
Kadry Selsk Khoz — Kadry Sel'sko Khoziaistva
Kaelte-Klima-Prakt — Kaelte-Klima-Praktiker
Kaelte Klimatech — Kaelte und Klimatechnik
Kaeltetech-Klim — Kaeltetechnik-Klimatisierung
KAF — Kleinasiatische Forschungen
KAFPAC — Catalogus Faunae Poloniae
KagoBH — Kagoshima Daigaku Bunka Hokoku [*Cultural Science Reports.*
    Kagoshima University]
KAIGBZ — Japanese Journal of Nuclear Medicine
Kais Akad d Wiss Denksch Philos-Hist Kl — Kaiserliche Akademie der
    Wissenschaften in Wien. Philosophisch-Historische Klasse.
    Denkschriften
Kais Akad d Wissensch Sitzungsb Philos-Hist Klasse — Kaiserliche Akademie
    der Wissenschaften in Wien. Philosophisch-Historische Klasse.
    Sitzungsberichte
Kais-Deutsch Archaol Inst Jahrb — Kaiserlich-Deutsches Archaeologisches
    Institut. Jahrbuch
Kaiser Found Med Bull — Kaiser Foundation Medical Bulletin
Kaiser Found Med Bull Abstr Issue — Kaiser Foundation Medical Bulletin.
    Abstract Issue
Kaj Ekon Mal — Kajian Ekonomi Malaysia
Kajian Vet — Kajian Veterinaire
KAJKA — Kagaku Kojo
Kaju Shikenjo Hokoku Bull Fruit Tree Res Stn Ser A Yatabe — Kaju Shikenjo
    Hokoku. Bulletin of the Fruit Tree Research Station. Series A. Yatabe
Kakao Zuck — Kakao und Zucker
Kakatiya J Eng Stud — Kakatiya Journal of English Studies
KAKEA — Kakuyugo Kenkyu
KAKOA — Kagaku Kogyo
Kakteen Sukkulenten — Kakteen und Andere Sukkulenten

Kakuriken Kenkyu Hokoku Suppl — Kakuriken Kenkyu Hokoku. Supplement
    [*Japan*]
K Ak Wiss Mat-Nat Cl Szb — Kaiserliche Akademie der Wissenschaften.
    Mathematische-Naturwissenschaftliche Klasse. Sitzungsberichte
KAKYA — Kagaku (Kyoto)
KAKZA — Kagaku Keizai
KAL — Kyushu American Literature [*Fukuoka, Japan*]
Kalamazoo Med — Kalamazoo Medicine
Kalinin Gos Ped Inst Ucen Zap — Kalininskii Gosudarstvennyi Pedagogiceskii
    Institut Imeni M. I. Kalinina Ucenye Zapiski
Kaliningrad Gos Ped Inst Ucen Zap — Kaliningradskii Gosudarstvennyi
    Pedagogiceskii Institut Ucenye Zapiski
Kaliningrad Gos Univ Differencial'naja Geom Mnogoobraz Figur —
    Kaliningradskogo Gosudarstvennogo Universitet Differencial'naja
    Geometrija Mnogoobrazii Figur
Kaliningrad Gos Univ Trudy Kaf Teoret i Eksper Fiz — Kaliningradskii
    Gosudarstvennyi Universitet Trudy Kafedry Teoreticeskoi i
    Eksperimental'noi Fiziki
Kaliningrad Gos Univ Ucen Zap — Kaliningradskii Gosudarstvennyi
    Universitet Ucenye Zapiski
Kal Inser — Kaleidoscope Insert
Kal Mad — Kaleidoscope-Madison
Kal Mil — Kaleidoscope-Milwaukee
Kal Schweiz Imkers — Kalender des Schweizer Imkers
Kam — Kamena
KAMJD — Kawasaki Medical Journal
Kan Acad Sci Trans — Kansas Academy of Science. Transactions
Kanagawa Prefect Mus Bull — Kanagawa Prefectural Museum. Bulletin
Kan Ag Exp — Kansas State Agricultural College. Agricultural Experiment
    Station. Publications
Kanazawa Univ Res Inst Tuberc Annu Rep — Kanazawa University. Research
    Institute of Tuberculosis. Annual Report
KanazHB — Kanazawa Daigaku Hobungakubu Ronshu. Bungakuhen [*Studies*
    and Essays. Faculty of Law and Literature. Kanazawa University.
    Literature]
KanazJK — Kanazawa Daigaku Kyoyobu Ronshu. Jinbunkagakuhen [*Studies*
    in Humanities. College of Liberal Arts. Kanazawa University]
Kan BAJ — Kansas Bar Association. Journal
Kan B Ass'n J — Kansas Bar Association. Journal
Kan Hist Quar — Kansas Historical Quarterly
Kan Jud Council Bull — Kansas Judicial Council. Bulletin
Kan Law Rev — Kansas Law Review
Kan Lib Bull — Kansas Library Bulletin
Kan Libr Bull — Kansas Library Bulletin
Kan L Rev — Kansas Law Review
Kano S — Kano Studies [*Nigeria*]
KanQ — Kansas Quarterly
Kans Acad Sci Trans — Kansas Academy of Science. Transactions
Kans Ac Sc Tr — Kansas Academy of Science. Transactions
Kans Agric Exp Stn Bienn Rep Dir — Kansas Agricultural Experiment Station.
    Biennial Report of the Director
Kans Agric Exp Stn Bull — Kansas Agricultural Experiment Station. Bulletin
Kans Agric Exp Stn Circ — Kansas Agricultural Experiment Station. Circular
Kans Agric Exp Stn Res Publ — Kansas Agricultural Experiment Station.
    Research Publication

Kans Agric Exp Stn Tech Bull — Kansas Agricultural Experiment Station. Technical Bulletin
Kans Agr Situation — Kansas Agricultural Situation. Kansas State University of Agriculture and Applied Science. Extension Service
Kansai Soc NA Jnl — Kansai Society of Naval Architects. Journal
Kansallis-Osake-Pankki Econ R — Kansallis-Osake-Pankki. Economic Review
Kansantal Aikakausk — Kansantaloudellinen Aikakauskirja
Kansas Acad Sci Trans — Kansas Academy of Science. Transactions
Kansas Bus Tchr — Kansas Business Teacher
Kansas City L Rev — University of Kansas City. Law Review
Kansas City Rv Sc — Kansas City Review of Science and Industry
Kansas Geol Survey Map — Kansas Geological Survey. Map
Kansas J Sociol — Kansas Journal of Sociology
Kansas Lib Bul — Kansas Library Bulletin
Kansas R — Kansas City Review
Kansas Univ Mus Nat History Misc Pub — Kansas University. Museum of Natural History. Miscellaneous Publication
Kansas Univ Paleont Contr — Kansas University. Paleontological Contributions
Kansas Water Resources Board Bull — Kansas State Water Resources Board. Bulletin
Kans Eng Exp Stn Bull — Kansas Engineering Experiment Station. Bulletin
Kans Eng Exp Stn (Manhattan Kans) Spec Rep — Kansas. Engineering Experiment Station (Manhattan, Kansas). Special Report
Kans Environ Health Serv Bull — Kansas Environmental Health Services Bulletin
Kans Geol Surv Bull — Kansas Geological Survey. Bulletin
Kans Geol Surv Ser Spat Anal — Kansas Geological Survey. Series on Spatial Analysis
Kans Ground Water Basic-Data Release — Kansas Ground Water. Basic-Data Release
Kans Hist Q — Kansas Historical Quarterly
Kans Nurse — Kansas Nurse
Kans Sch Nat — Kansas School Naturalist
Kans State Board Agric Div Entomol Act — Kansas State Board of Agriculture. Division of Entomology. Activities
Kans State Geol Surv Bull — Kansas State Geological Survey. Bulletin
Kans State Geol Surv Comput Contrib — Kansas State Geological Survey. Computer Contribution
Kans State Geol Surv Computer Contrib — Kansas State Geological Survey. Computer Contribution
Kans State Geol Surv Spec Distrib Publ — Kansas State Geological Survey. Special Distribution Publication
Kans State Geol Surv Spec Distribution Publication — Kansas State Geological Survey. Special Distribution Publication
Kans State Hortic Soc Trans — Kansas State Horticultural Society. Transactions
Kans State Univ Bull Kans Eng Exp Sta Bull — Kansas State University Bulletin. Kansas Engineering Experiment Station. Bulletin
Kans State Univ Eng Exp Stn Bull — Kansas State University. Engineering Experiment Station. Bulletin
Kans State Univ Eng Exp Stn Repr — Kansas State University. Engineering Experiment Station. Reprint
Kans State Univ Inst Syst Des Optim Rep — Kansas State University. Institute for Systems Design and Optimization. Report
Kans St Bd Agr Tr An Rp Bien Rp — Kansas State Board of Agriculture. Transactions. Annual Report. Biennial Report
Kans Stockman — Kansas Stockman
Kan State Hist Soc Coll — Kansas State Historical Society. Collections
Kan State Univ Inst Syst Des Optim Rep — Kansas State University. Institute for Systems Design and Optimization. Report
Kans Teach — Kansas Teacher and Western School Journal
Kans Univ B Ed — Kansas University. Bulletin of Education
Kans Univ Mus Nat History Pub Paleont Contr Sci Bull — Kansas University. Museum of Natural History Publications. Paleontological Contributions. Science Bulletin
Kans Univ Paleontol Contrib Pap — Kansas University. Paleontology Contribution Paper
Kans Univ Q — Kansas University Quarterly
Kans Univ Sc B — Kansas University. Science Bulletin
Kans Univ Sci Bull — Kansas University. Science Bulletin
Kans Water Res Board Bull — Kansas Water Resources Board. Bulletin
Kans Wheat Qual Kans State Board Agr — Kansas Wheat Quality. Kansas State Board of Agriculture [*Kansas Wheat Commission*]
Kanto J Orthop Traumatol — Kanto Journal of Orthopedics and Traumatology [*Japan*]
Kant-Stud — Kant-Studien
Kan Univ Kan Studies Ed — Kansas University. Kansas Studies in Education
KAnz — Kunstgeschichtliche Anzeigen
KAP — Kampioen
Kapitalis — Kapitalistate
K Ar — Kansatieteellinen Arkisto
Karachi Univ J Sci — Karachi University. Journal of Science
Kardiol Pol — Kardiologia Polska
Kardiol Pol Tow Internistow Pol Sek Kardiol — Kardiologia Polska. Towarzystwo Internistow Polskich. Sekeja Kardiologiczna

Kariba Stud — Kariba Studies
KARJA — Karjantuote
KARKA — Karada No Kagaku
Karl-August-Forster-Lect — Karl-August-Forster-Lectures
Kar LJ — Karachi Law Journal
Karlov Laz Cas — Karlovarsky Lazensky Casopis
Karlsruher Beitr Entwicklungsphysiol Pflanz — Karlsruher Beitraege zur Entwicklungsphysiologie der Pflanzen
Karlsruher Geogr Hefte — Karlsruher Geographische Hefte
Karnataka Med J — Karnataka Medical Journal
Karnatak Univ J Sci — Karnatak University. Journal of Science
Karolinska Symp Res Methods Reprod Endocrinol — Karolinska Symposia on Research Methods in Reproductive Endocrinology
Karpato Balk Geol Assots Mater Kom Mineral Geokhim — Karpato-Balkanskaya Geologicheskaya Assotsiatsiya. Materialy Komissii Mineralogii i Geokhimii
Kartogr Let — Kartograficeskaja Letopis
Kartogr Nachr (Stuttg) — Kartographische Nachrichten (Stuttgart)
Kartogr Pr — Kartograficky Prehled
Kartonagen Papierwaren Ztg — Kartonagen und Papierwaren-Zeitung
KASEA — Kagaku To Seibutsu
Kaseigaku Zasshi J Home Econ Jap — Kaseigaku Zasshi. Journal of Home Economics of Japan
Kasetsart J — Kasetsart Journal
Kasetsart Univ Fish Res Bull — Kasetsart University. Fishery Research Bulletin
Kas His S — Kansas State Historical Society. Collections
Kashmir Sci — Kashmir Science
Kashmir Univ Fac Sci Res J — Kashmir University. Faculty of Science. Research Journal
Kasr El-Aini J Surg — Kasr El-Aini Journal of Surgery
Kat — Katholiek
Katal — Katallagete
Katal Katal — Kataliz i Katalizatory [*USSR*]
Katal Pererab Uglevodorodnogo Syr'ya — Kataliticheskaya Pererabotka Uglevodorodnogo Syr'ya
Kat Bl — Katechetische Blaetter
Kat Fauny Pol — Katalog Fauny Polski
Kath — Katholiek
Kath MJS — Katholisches Missionsjahrbuch der Schweiz
Katilolehti — Katilolehti. Tidskrift foer Barnmorskor
Katl Prevrashch Uglevodorodov — Kataliticheskie Prevrascheniya Uglevodorodov
Kauno Politech Inst Darb — Kauno Politechnikos Instituto Darbai
Kauno Valstybinio Med Inst Darb — Kauno Valstybinio Medicinos Instituto Darbai
Kautch Gummi Kunstst Asbest — Kautschuk und Gummi. Kunststoffe. Asbest
Kaut Gum Ku — Kautschuk und Gummi. Kunststoffe
Kaut u Gummi Kunst — Kautschuk und Gummi. Kunststoffe
Kautsch Gummi Kunstst — Kautschuk und Gummi. Kunststoffe
Kautsch Gummi Kunstst Plastomere Elastomere Duromere — Kautschuk und Gummi. Kunststoffe. Plastomere, Elastomere, Duromere
Kavk Etnogr Sb — Kavkazskij Etnograficeskij Sbornik
Kawasaki Med J — Kawasaki Medical Journal
Kawasaki Rozai Tech Rep — Kawasaki Rozai Technical Report
Kawasaki Steelmaking Tech Rep — Kawasaki Steelmaking Technical Report [*Japan*]
Kawasaki Steel Tech Bull — Kawasaki Steel Technical Bulletin
Kawasaki Steel Tech Rep — Kawasaki Steel Technical Report [*Japan*]
Kawasaki Tech Rev — Kawasaki Technical Review [*Japan*]
KAZ — Konsument. Test Magazine der Konsumenteninformation
Kazah Gos Ped Inst Ucen Zap — Kazakhskii Gosudarstvennyi Pedagogiceskii Institut Imeni Abaja Ucenye Zapiski
Kazan Gos Univ Ucen Zap — Kazanskii Ordena Trudovogo Krasnogo Znameni Gosudarstvennyi Universitet Imeni V. I. Ul'janova-Lenina Ucenye Zapiski
Kazan Med Z — Kazanskii Meditsinskii Zhurnal
Kazan Med Zh — Kazanskii Meditsinskii Zhurnal
Kazan Med Zhurnal — Kazanskii Meditsinskii Zhurnal
Kaz Nauchno-Issled Inst Lesn Khoz Agrolesomelio Tr — Kazakhskii Nauchno-Issledovatel'skii Institut Lesnogo Khozyaistva i Agrolesomelioratsii Trudy
Kaz Nauchno-Issled Inst Lesn Khoz Tr — Kazakhskii Nauchno-Issledovatel'skii Institut Lesnogo Khozyaistva Trudy
KB — Kew Bulletin
KB — Komunist (Belgrade)
KB — Kulturos Barai
KBA — Korte Berichten voor de Machinebranche en Apparatenbranche
KBAA — Kieler Beitraege zur Anglistik und Amerikanistik
KBAMA — Kosmicheskaya Biologiya i Aviakosmicheskaya Meditsina
K-Bayer Ak Wiss Muenchen Mat-Phys Kl Szb Abh — Koeniglich-Bayerische Akademie der Wissenschaften zu Muenchen. Mathematisch-Physikalische Klasse. Sitzungsberichte. Abhandlungen
KBB — Kentucky Bench and Bar
KBB — Kulturas Biroja Biletins [*Bulletin. Cultural Bureau of the American Latvian Association in the US*]

KBCJ — Koninklijke Belgische Commissie voor Volkskunde, Vlaamse Afdeling Jaarboek

KBDA — Korrespondenzblatt. Gesamtverein der Deutschen Geschichte und Altertumsvereine

KBDF — Kleine Beitraege zur Droste-Forschung [*Munster*]

KBE — Korean Business Review

KBE — Kratka Bulgarska Enciklopedija

KBEA J — Kentucky Business Education Association. Journal

KBEBD — Kvartalsskrift. Bergen Bank

K Belg Inst Natuurwet Studiedoc — Koninklijk Belgisch Instituut voor Natuurwetenschappen. Studiedocumenten

K Belg Inst Natuurwet Verh — Koninklijk Belgisch Instituut voor Natuurwetenschappen. Verhandelingen

KBEMD — Kultuurpatronen. Bulletin Etnografisch Museum (Delft)

KBGL — Kopenhagener Beitraege zur Germanistischen Linguistik

KBGWAB — Koninklijk Museum voor Midden-Afrika [*Tervuren, Belgie*]. Annalen. Reeks in Octavo. Geologische Wetenschappen

KBJ — Kentucky Bar Journal

KBK — Korte Berichten voor de Kledingbranche

KBKL — Kritische Berichte zur Kunstgeschichtlichen Literatur

KBKOD — Steinkohlenbergbauverein Kurznachrichten

Kbl — Korrespondenzblatt. Verein fuer Niederdeutsche Sprachforschung

K Bl BE — Koelner Blaetter fuer Berufserziehung

KBLG — Kritische Blaetter zur Literatur der Gegenwart

KBl Ref — Kirchenblatt fuer die Reformierte Schweiz [*Basel*]

Kbl RS — Kirchenblatt fuer die Reformierte Schweiz

KBM — Korte Berichten voor de Meubelbranche en Stofferingsbranche

KBMEA — Kosmicheskaya Biologiya i Meditsina

KBO — Berichten uit het Buitenland

K-Boehm Ges Wiss Mat-Nat Cl Szb — Koeniglich-Boehmische Gesellschaft der Wissenschaften in Prag. Mathematisch-Naturwissenschaftliche Klasse. Sitzungsberichte

KBP — Korte Berichten voor de Verpakkingsbranche

KBP Q — Kappa Beta Pi Quarterly

KBR — Keio Business Review

KBR — Rheinisch-Westfaelisches Institut fuer Wirtschaftsforschung. Konjunkturberichte

KBSEA — Bulletin. Kyoto Educational University. Series B. Mathematics and Natural Science

KBV — Korte Berichten voor de Verfbranche

KBW — Korrespondenzblatt fuer die Hoeheren Schulen Wuerttembergs

KC — Keyboard Classics

KC — Kritika Chronika

K & C — Kunst en Cultuur

KC — Kunstchronik

KCH — Korte Berichten voor de Chemiebranche

K Ch — Kritika Chronika

KC Phil — Kansas City Philharmonic Program Notes

KCR — University of Kansas City. Law Review

KCR — University of Missouri at Kansas City. Law Review

KCRAB8 — Annual Report. Cancer Research Institute. Kanazawa University

KCSN — Kralovska Ceska Spolecnost Nauk

KCT — Katholiek Cultureel Tijdschrift

K D — Kerygma und Dogma

KD — Kirchliche Dogmatik

KD — Kristeligt Dagblad

K Danske Vidensk Selsk Skr — Kongelige Danske Videnskabernes Selskab. Skrifter

K Dan Vidensk Selsk Biol Skr — Kongelige Danske Videnskabernes Selskab. Biologiske Skrifter

K Dan Vidensk Selsk Mat Fys Medd — Kongelige Danske Videnskabernes Selskab. Matematisk-Fysisk Meddelelser [*Denmark*]

K Dan Vidensk Selsk Mat Fys Skr — Kongelige Danske Videnskabernes Selskab. Matematisk-Fysisk Skrifter [*Denmark*]

K Dan Vidensk Selsk Over Selsk Virksomhed — Kongelige Danske Videnskabernes Selskab. Oversigt Selskabets Virksomhed

K Dan Vidensk Selsk Skr Naturvidensk Mat Afd — Kongelige Danske Videnskabernes Selskab. Skrifter. Naturvidenskabelig og Mathematisk Afdeling

KDD Tech J — KDD Technical Journal

KDF — Koenigsberger Deutsche Forschungen

KDGNB — Kinki Daigaku Genshiryoku Kenkyusho Nenpo

KDGNBX — Annual Report. Kinki University. Atomic Energy Research Institute

KDKHB — Kyoto Daigaku Kogyo Kyoin Yoseijo Kenkyu Hokoku

KDKIA — Kyoto Daigaku Kogaku Kenkyusho Iho

KDKKB — Kagoshima Daigaku Kogakubu Kenkyu Hokoku

KDKSB — Kyushu Daigaku Kogaku Shuho

KDPM — Kleine Deutsche Prosadenkmaeler des Mittelalters

KDRNBK — Annual Report. Noto Marine Laboratory

KDSGA — Kagoshima Daigaku Suisangakubu Kiyo

KDSL — Konzepte der Sprack- und Literaturwissenschaft

KDTIA — Kumamoto Daigaku Taishitsu Igaku Kenkyusho Hokoku

KDV — Kalender der Detuschen Volksgemeinschaft fuer Rumaenien

KDVS — Kongelige Danske Videnskabernes Selskab. Historisk-Filosofiske Meddelelser [*Copenhagen*]

KDVSA — Kongelige Danske Videnskabernes Selskab. Matematisk-Fysisk Meddelelser

KE — Keewatin Echo

Keats-Shell — Keats-Shelley Journal

Keats-Shelley J — Keats-Shelley Journal

Keats-Shelley J Ann Bibl — Keats-Shelley Journal. Annual Bibliography

Keats Sh M — Keats-Shelley Memorial Association. Bulletin

KEBR — Kobe Economic and Business Review

Ke Do — Kerygma und Dogma

KEE — Kantoor en Efficiency

Keep Abreast J — Keeping Abreast Journal of Human Nurturing

Keep Abreast J Hum Nurt — Keeping Abreast Journal of Human Nurturing

KEGEAC — Japanese Journal of Plastic and Reconstructive Surgery

Kehutanan Indones — Kehutanan Indonesia

KEI — Keidanren Review of Japanese Economy

KEIKA — Keikinzoku

Keio Bus R — Keio Business Review [*Tokyo*]

Keio Econ S — Keio Economic Studies

Keio Econ Stud — Keio Economic Studies [*Tokyo*]

Keio Eng Rep — Keio Engineering Reports

Keio Engrg Rep — Keio Engineering Reports

Keio J Med — Keio Journal of Medicine

Keio J Polit — Keio Journal of Politics

Keio Math Sem Rep — Keio Mathematical Seminar. Reports

Keio Sci Tech Rep — Keio Science and Technology Reports

Keith Shipton Dev Spec Study — Keith Shipton Developments. Special Study

Ke K — Keiryo Kokugogaku [*Mathematical Linguistics*]

KEK Annu Rep (Natl Lab High Energy Phys) — KEK Annual Report (National Laboratory for High Energy Physics)

KEKHA — Koshu Eiseiin Kenkyu Hokoku

KEMA Publ — KEMA [*Keuring van Electrotechnische Materialen Arnhem*] Publikaties

KEMA Sci Tech Rep — KEMA [*Keuring van Elektrotechnische Materialen Arnhem*] Scientific and Technical Reports

Kemerov Gos Ped Inst Ucen Zap — Kemerovskii Gosudarstvennyi Pedagogiceskii Institut Ucenye Zapiski

Kem Ind — Kemija u Industriji [*Yugoslavia*]

Kem-Kemi — Kemia-Kemi

Kem Kozl — Kemiai Kozlemenyek

Kem Kozlem — Kemiai Kozlemenyek

Kem Maandesbl Nord Handelsbl Kem Ind — Kemisk Maandesblad. Nordisk Handelsblad foer Kemisk Industri

Kem-Talajt — Kemia-Talajtani Tanszek

Kem Teollisuus — Kemian Teollisuus [*Finland*]

Kem Tidskr — Kemisk Tidskrift

Kenana Res Stn Annu Rep — Kenana Research Station. Annual Report

Kenkyu Hokoku Bull Fac Agric Tamagawa Univ — Kenkyu Hokoku. Bulletin. Faculty of Agriculture. Tamagawa University

Kenkyu Hokoku J Niigata Agricultural Experiment Station — Kenkyu Hokoku. Journal. Niigata Agricultural Experiment Station

Kenkyu Hokoku J Tottori Univ Nat Sci — Kenkyu Hokoku. Journal. Faculty of Education. Tottori University. Natural Science

Kenkyu Hokoku Res Bull Hokkaido Natl Agric Exp Stn — Kenkyu Hokoku. Research Bulletin. Hokkaido National Agricultural Experiment Station

Kenkyu Hokoku Sci Pap Cent Res Inst Jap Tob Salt Public Corp — Kenkyu Hokoku. Scientific Papers. Central Research Institute. Japan Tobacco and Salt Public Corporation

Kenley Abstr — Kenley Abstracts

Kent Archaeol Rev — Kent Archaeological Review

Kent Rev — Kent Review

Kent Tech Rev — Kent Technical Review

Kentucky Acad Sci Trans — Kentucky Academy of Science. Transactions

Kentucky Geol Surv Bull — Kentucky. Geological Survey. Bulletin

Kentucky Geol Survey Bull — Kentucky. Geological Survey. Bulletin

Kentucky Geol Survey County Rept — Kentucky Geological Survey. County Report

Kentucky Geol Survey Inf Circ — Kentucky Geological Survey. Information Circular

Kentucky Geol Survey Rept Inv — Kentucky Geological Survey. Report of Investigations

Kentucky Geol Survey Spec Pub — Kentucky Geological Survey. Special Publication

Kentucky LJ — Kentucky Law Journal

Kentucky Med J — Kentucky Medical Journal

Kenya Colony Prot Geol Surv Mem — Kenya. Colony and Protectorate. Geological Survey. Memoir

Kenya Dep Agric Annu Rep — Kenya. Department of Agriculture. Annual Report

Kenya and East African Med J — Kenya and East African Medical Journal

Kenya Fmr — Kenya Farmer

Kenya Inform Serv Bull — Kenya Information Services. Bulletin

Kenya Med J — Kenya Medical Journal

Kenya Nurs J — Kenya Nursing Journal

Kenya R — Kenya Review

Kenyon R — Kenyon Review

Kenyon Rev — Kenyon Review

Kep es Hangtech — Kep- es Hangtechnika
KER — Kern
Kerala J Vet Sci — Kerala Journal of Veterinary Science
Keram Rundsch Kunst-Keram — Keramische Rundschau und Kunst-Keramik
Keram Sb — Keramicheskii Sbornik
Keram Z — Keramische Zeitschrift
KerC — Kerkyraika Chronika
KerDo — Kerygma und Dogma
Ker LT — Kerala Law Times
Kernenerg — Kernenergie
Kernenerg Beil — Kernenergie. Beilage [*East Germany*]
Kernforschungsz Karlsruhe Ber — Kernforschungszentrum Karlsruhe. Bericht
Kerntechnik Isotpentech Chem — Kerntechnik, Isotopentechnik, und Chemie
Kerntech Normung Inf — Kerntechnische Normung Informationen [*West Germany*]
Kert Egy Kozl — Kerteszeti Egyetem Kozlemenyei
Kertesz Egyet Kozl — Kerteszeti Egyetem Kozlemenyei
Kertesz Szolesz Foisk — Kerteszeti es Szoleszeti Foiskola Evkoryve
Kertesz Szolesz Foisk Kozl — Kerteszeti es Szoleszeti Foiskola Kozlemenyei
Kert Szolesz Foiskola Evk — Kerteszeti es Szoleszeti Foiskola Evkoryve
Kert Szolesz Foiskola Kozl — Kerteszeti es Szoleszeti Foiskola Kozlemenyei
KES — Keio Economic Studies
KESS — Kartvelur Enata St'rukt'uris Sak'itzebi
Keston News — Keston News Service
Keszthelyi Mezogazd Akad Kiad — Keszthelyi Mezogazdasagi Akademia Kiadvanyai
Keszthelyi Mezogazdasagtud Kar Kozl — Keszthelyi Mezogazdasagtudomanyi Kar Kozlemenyei
Keuring Elektrotech Mater Sci Tech Rep — Keuring van Elektrotechnische Materialen. Scientific and Technical Reports
KEVN — Kevo Notes
Kew Bull — Kew Bulletin
Kew Bull Addit Ser — Kew Bulletin. Additional Series
Key — Key to Christian Education
Keybd Mag — Keyboard Magazine
Key Notes — Key Notes Donemus
KEYRA — Keyboard
Keystone News Bull — Keystone News Bulletin [*United States*]
KF — Kleinasiatische Forschungen
KFFMA — Klepzig Fachberichte fuer die Fuehrungskraefte aus Maschinenbau und Huettenwesen
KFFUA — Kraftfutter
KFIZA — Kyoto Furitsu Ika Daigaku Zasshi
KFK Hausmitt — KFK [*Kernforschungszentrum Karlsruhe*] Hausmitteilungen
KFKI Kozl — KFKI [*Kozponti Fizikai Kutato Intezet*] Kozlemenvek
KFK Nachr — KFK [*Kernforschungszentrum Karlsruhe*] Nachrichten
KFLQ — Kentucky Foreign Language Quarterly
K & F (NSW) — Knox and Fitzharding's Reports (New South Wales)
KFQ — Keystone Folklore Quarterly
KFR — Kentucky Folklore Record
KFS — Kentucky Folklore Series
KFSAAX — Kungliga Fysiografiska Sallskapets i Lund. Arsbok
KFSLAW — Kungliga Fysiografiska Sallskapets i Lund. Foerhandlingar
KFT — KFT. Kraftfahrzeugtechnik
KFTTA — Kao Fen Tzu T'ung Hsun
K Fysiogr Sallsk Lund Arsb — Kungliga Fysiografiska Sallskapets i Lund. Arsbok
K Fysiogr Sallsk Lund Forh — Kungliga Fysiografiska Sallskapets i Lund. Foerhandlingar
KFZTA — Kraftfahrzeugtechnik
KG — Katholische Gedanken
KGA — Kunstgeschichtliche Anzeigen
KGAAM — Kungliga Gustav Adolfs Akademiens. Minnesbok
K Gad — Kritikas Gadagramata
K Ges Wiss Goettingen Abh — Koenigliche Gesellschaft der Wissenschaften zu Goettingen. Abhandlungen
KGGJ — Klaus-Groth-Gesellschaft. Jahresgabe
KGH — Kanbum Gakkai Kaiho [*Journal. Sinological Society*]
KGHKA — Kogyo Gijutsuin. Hakko Kenkyusho Kenkyu Hokoku
KGI — Komeet
KGKK — Kangaku Kenkyu [*Sinological Studies*]
KGKR — Kansai Gaidai Kenkyu Ronshu [*Journal. Kansai University of Foreign Studies*]
KGKZA — Kogyo Kagaku Zasshi
Kgl Danske Vidensk Selsk Oversigt — Kongelige Danske Videnskabernes Selskab. Oversigt Selskabets Virksomhed
KGNBA — Kenritsu Gan Senta Niigata Byoin Ishi
KGR — Kobe Gaidai Ronso [*Kobe City University Journal*]
KGS — Koelner Germanistische Studien
KGUAS — Kwansei Gakuin University. Annual Studies
KH — Kwartalnik Historyczny
Khadi Gram — Khadi Gramodyong [*India*]
Kharchova Promst — Kharchova Promyslovist
Khar'k Inst Mekh Elektrif Sel'sk Khoz Nauchn Zap — Khar'kovskii Institut Mekhanizatsii i Elektrifikatsii Sel'skogo Khozyaistva Nauchnye Zapiski
Khar'k Med Inst Tr — Khar'kovskii Meditsinskii Institut Trudy

KHCLA — K'o Hsueh Chi Lu
Kheberleri Izv — Kheberleri Izvestiya [*USSR*]
Khematol Kruvoprelivane — Khematologiya i Kruvoprelivane
Khidrol Met — Khidrologiya i Meteorologiya
Khidrol Meteorol — Khidrologiya i Meteorologiya
KHIGA — Khirurgiya
Khig Epidemiol Mikrobiol — Khigiena. Epidemiologiya i Mikrobiologiya
Khig Zdraveopaz — Khigiena i Zdraveopazvane
Khig Zdraveopazvane — Khigiena i Zdraveopazvane
Khim Belka — Khimiya Belka
Khim Drev — Khimiya Drevesiny
Khim Elementoorg Soedin — Khimiya Elementoorganicheskikh Soedinenii
Khim Farm Promst — Khimiko Farmatsevticheskaya Promyshlennost
Khim-Farm Zh — Khimiko-Farmatsevticheskii Zhurnal
Khim-Far Zh — Khimiko-Farmatsevticheskii Zhurnal
Khim Fiz-Khim Prir Sint Polim — Khimiya i Fiziko-Khimiya Prirodnykh i Sinteticheskikh Polimerov
Khim Geogr Gidrogeokhim — Khimicheskaya Geografiya i Gidrogeokhimiya
Khim Getero — Khimiya Geterotsiklicheskikh Soedineniya
Khim Geterotsiklich Soedin — Khimiya Geterotsiklicheskikh Soedinenii
Khim Geterotsikl Soedin Akad Nauk Latv SSR — Khimiya Geterotsiklicheskikh Soedinenii Akademiya Nauk Latviiskoi SSR [*Latvian SSR*]
Khim Geterotsikl Soedin Sb — Khimiya Geterotsiklicheskikh Soedinenii Sbornik
Khim Ind — Khimiya i Industriya
Khim Khim Tekhnol (Alma-Ata) — Khimiya i Khimicheskaya Tekhnologiya (Alma-Ata)
Khim Khim Tekhnol Drev — Khimiya i Khimicheskaya Tekhnologiya Drevesiny [*USSR*]
Khim Khim Tekhnol (Lvov) — Khimiya i Khimicheskaya Tekhnologiya (Lvov)
Khim Khim Teknol (Cheboksary USSR) — Khimiya i Khimicheskaya Tekhnologiya (Cheboksary, USSR)
Khim Mashinostr Mosk Inst Khim Mashinostr — Khimicheskoe Mashinostroenie Moskovskii Institut Khimicheskogo Mashinostroeniya
Khim Med — Khimiya i Meditsina
Khim Nauka Prom-st — Khimicheskaya Nauka i Promyshlennost
Khim i Neft Mashinostr — Khimicheskoe i Neftyanoe Mashinostroenie
Khim Neft Mashinostr — Khimicheskoe i Neftyanoe Mashinostroenie
Khim Pererab Drev — Khimicheskaya Pererabotka Drevesiny
Khim Pererab Drev Nauchno-Tekh Sb — Khimicheskaya Pererabotka Drevesiny Nauchno-Tekhnicheskii Sbornik [*USSR*]
Khim Plazmy — Khimiya Plazmy Sbornik Statej
Khim Prirod Soed — Khimiya Prirodnykh Soedinenii
Khim Prir S — Khimiya Prirodnykh Soedinenii
Khim Prir Soedin (Tashk) — Khimiya Prirodnykh Soedinenii (Tashkent)
Khim Prod Koksovaniya Uglei Vostoka SSSR — Khimicheskie Produkty Koksovaniya Uglei Vostoka SSSR
Khim Prom — Khimicheskaya Promyshlennost
Khim Promst (Moscow) — Khimicheskaya Promyshlennost (Moscow)
Khim Promst Ser Fosfornaya Promst — Khimicheskaya Promyshlennost Seriya Fosfornaya Promyshlennost
Khim Promst Ser Okhr Okruzh Sredy Ratsion Ispol'z Prir Resur — Khimicheskaya Promyshlennost Seriya Okhrana Okruzhayushchei Sredy i Ratsional'noe Ispol'zovanie Prirodnykh Resursov
Khim Prom-st' Ukr — Khimicheskaya Promyshlennost' Ukrainy
Khim Reakt Prep — Khimicheskie Reaktivy i Preparaty
Khim Redk Elem — Khimiya Redkikh Elementov
Khim Sel'Khoz — Khimiya v Sel'skom Khozyaistve
Khim Sel'sk Khoz — Khimiya v Sel'skom Khozyaistve
Khim Sel'sk Khoz Bashk — Khimizatsiya Sel'skogo Khozyaistva Bashkirii
Khim Sera Azotorg Soedin Soderzh Neftyakh Nefteprod — Khimiya Sera- i Azotorganicheskikh Soedinenii Soderzhashchikhsiya v Neftyakh i Nefteproduktakh
Khim Seraorg Soedin Soderzh Neftyakh Nefteprod — Khimiya Seraorganicheskikh Soedinenii, Soderzhashchikhsya v Neftyakh i Nefteproduktakh [*USSR*]
Khim Signal Zhivotn — Khimicheskie Signaly Zhivotnykh
Khim Sots Zemled — Khimizatsiya Sotsialisticheskogo Zemledeliya
Khim Svyaz' Krist Fiz Svoj — Khimicheskaya Svyaz' v Kristallakh i Ikh Fizicheskie Svojstva
Khim Tekhnol — Khimicheskaia Tekhnologiia
Khim Tekhnol Drev Tsellyul Bum — Khimiya i Tekhnologiya Drevesiny Tsellyulozy i Bumagi
Khim Tekhnol Goryuch Slantsev Prod Ikh Pererab — Khimiya i Tekhnologiya Goryuchikh Slantsev i Produktov Ikh Pererabotki [*USSR*]
Khim Tekhnol (Kharkov) — Khimicheskaya Tekhnologiya (Kharkov) [*Ukrainian SSR*]
Khim Tekhnol (Kiev) — Khimicheskaya Tekhnologiya (Kiev) [*Ukrainian SSR*]
Khim Tekhnol Molbdena Vol'frama — Khimiya i Tekhnologiya Molibdena i Vol'frama
Khim Tekhnol Neorg Proizvod — Khimiya i Tekhnologiya Neorganicheskikh Proizvodstv
Khim Tekhnol Svoistva Primen Plastmass — Khimicheskaya Tekhnologiya Svoistva i Primenenie Plastmass
Khim i Tekhnol Topliv i Masel — Khimiya i Tekhnologiya Topliv i Masel
Khim Tekhnol Topl Masel — Khimiya i Tekhnologiya Topliv i Masel

Khim Tekhnol Topl Prod Ego Pererab — Khimiya i Tekhnologiya Topliva i Produktov Ego Pererabotki
Khim Tekhnol Top Masel — Khimiya i Tekhnologiya Topliv i Masel [*USSR*]
Khim Termodin Rastvorov — Khimiya i Termodinamika Rastvorov
Khim Tverd Topl (Leningrad) — Khimiya Tverdogo Topliva (Leningrad)
Khim Tverd Topl (Moscow) — Khimiya Tverdogo Topliva (Moscow)
Khim Volokna — Khimicheskie Volokna
Khim Vys Ehnerg — Khimiya Vysokikh Ehnergij
Khir Lietop — Khirurgicheskaia Lietopis
Khir Zhelchevyvodyashchikh Putei — Khirurgiya Zhelchevyvodyashchikh Putei
KHI Tech Rev — KHI [*Kawasaki Heavy Industries*] Technical Review [*Japan*]
Khlebopekar Konditer Prom — Khlebopekarnaya i Konditerskaya Promyshlennost
Khlebopek Kondter Promst — Khlebopekarnaya i Konditerskaya Promyshlennost
Khlebopek Promst — Khlebopekarnaya Promyshlennost
Khlopehatobuma Promst — Khlopehatobumazhnaya Promyshlennost
Khlopkovod — Khlopkovodstvo
KHMEA — Khidrologiya i Meteorologiya
Kholod Tekh — Kholodil'naya Tekhnika [*USSR*]
Kholod Tekhn — Kholodil'naya Tekhnika
Kholod Tekh Tekhnol — Kholodil'naya Tekhnika i Tekhnologiya [*Ukrainian SSR*]
KHQ — Kansas Historical Quarterly
Khranitelna Prom-st — Khranitelna Promishlenost
Khranit Prom — Khranitelna Promishlenost
Khranit Prom-st — Khranitelna Promishlenost
Khron VOZ — Khronika VOZ [*Vsemirnoj Organisatsij Zdravookhraneniya*]
KHS — Kentucky Historical Society. Register
KHSR — Kentucky Historical Society. Register
KHSYA — Kexue Shiyan
KHVSU — Kungliga Humanistiska Vetenskapssamfundet i Uppsala
KHZAD — Kachiku Hanshokugaku Zasshi
Ki — Kierunki
KI — Kinatuinamot Illengajuk
KIBBA — Konstruktiver Ingenieurbau Berichte
Kibern Avtom — Kibernetika i Avtomatika
Kibernet i Vychisl Tekhn — Kibernetika i Vychislitelnaya Tekhnika
Kibernet i Vycisl Tehn — Kibernetika i Vycislitel'naya Tehnika
Kibern Vychisl Tekh — Kibernetika i Vychislitel'naya Tekhnika [*Ukrainian SSR*]
Kibern i Vychisl Tekh — Kibernetika i Vychislitel'naya Tekhnika
Kidma Isr J Dev — Kidma. Israel Journal of Development
Kidney Int — Kidney International
Kidney Int Suppl — Kidney International. Supplement
KIDZD — Kanazawa Ika Daigaku Zasshi
Kie — Kierkegaardiana
Kiel Meeresforsch — Kieler Meeresforschungen
Kiel Milchwirtsch Forschungsber — Kieler Milchwirtschaftliche Forschungsberichte
Kiel Not Pflanzenkd Schleswig Holstein — Kieler Notizen zur Pflanzenkunde in Schleswig Holstein
KIER Bulletin — Korea. Institute of Energy and Resources. Bulletin
Kiev Univ Visn Ser Geogr — Kiev Universitet Visnik Seriya Geografi
KIGAM Bull — KIGAM [*Korea Research Institute of Geoscience and Mineral Resources*] Bulletin
KII — Kwartaalreeks over Informatie en Informatie Beleid
KIIGD — Kitasato Igaku
Kiito Kensajo Kenkyu Hokoku Res Rep Silk Cond — Kiito Kensajo Kenkyu Hokoku. Research Reports of the Silk Conditioning Houses
Kiiv Derzh Univ Im T G Shevchenka Nauk Shchorichnik — Kiivs'kii Derzhavnii Universitet Imeni T. G. Shevchenka Naukovii Shchorichnik
Kiiv Derzh Univ Stud Nauk Pr — Kiivs'kii Derzhavnii Universitet Students'ki Naukovi Pratsi
KiJ — Knjizevnost i Jezik
Kilobaud Microcomput — Kilobaud Microcomputing
Kimball's D F — Kimball's Dairy Farmer
Kim Muhendisligi — Kimya Muhendisligi [*Turkey*]
Kim Sanayi — Kimya ve Sanayi [*Turkey*]
Kinderaerztl Prax — Kinderaerztliche Praxis
Kind and First Grade — Kindergarten and First Grade
Kind M — Kindergarten Primary Magazine
Kinesither Sci — Kinesitherapie Scientifique
Kinet Catal — Kinetics and Catalysis
Kinet Goreniya Iskop Topl — Kinetika Goreniya Iskopaemykh Topliv
Kinet Katal — Kinetika i Kataliz
Kinet Mech Polym — Kinetics and Mechanisms of Polymerization
King Abdulaziz Med J — King Abdulaziz Medical Journal
Kingston LR — Kingston Law Review
Kingston L Rev — Kingston Law Review
Kingston-On-Hull Mus Bull — Kingston-On-Hull Museums. Bulletin
Kino Photo Ind — Kino-Photo Industry
Kinotech — Kinotechnik
Kinotech Filmtech Ausg A — Kinotechnik und Filmtechnik. Ausgabe A
Kinotech Filmtech Ausg B — Kinotechnik und Filmtechnik. Ausgabe B

K Inst Tropen Meded Afd Tropische Producten — Koninklijk Instituut voor de Tropen. Mededeling. Afdeling Tropische Producten
Kintyre Antiqu Nat Hist Soc Mag — Kintyre Antiquarian and Natural History Society. Magazine
KIPOB — Kompleksnye Issledovaniya Prirody Okeana
KIPR — Kwartalnik Instituta Polsko-Radzieckiego
KiR — Kniga i Revoljucija
KI Rapp — Korrosionsinstitutet. Rapport
Kirchor — Kirchenchor
Kirch PA — Kirchner, Prosopographia Attica
Kirin Univ J Nat Sci — Kirin University Journal. Natural Sciences [*People's Republic of China*]
Kirkus — Virginia Kirkus' Service. Bulletin
Kirkus R — Kirkus Reviews
Kirmus — Kirchenmusiker
Kirov Gos Pedagog Inst Uch Zap — Kirovskii Gosudarstvennyi Pedagogicheskii Institut. Uchenye Zapiski
KiS — Kultura i Spoleczenstwo
KISDA — Report. Institute for Systems Design and Optimization. Kansas State University
Kiserletugyi Koezlem — Kiserletugyi Koezlemenyek
Kiserletugyi Kozl A — Kiserletugyi Koezlemenyek. A Kotet. Novenytermesztes
Kiserletugyi Kozl B — Kiserletugyi Koezlemenyek. B Kotet. Allattenyesztes
Kiserletugyi Kozl C — Kiserletugyi Koezlemenyek. C Kotet. Kerteszet
Kiserl Koezl Erdogazdasag — Kiserletugyi Koezlemenyek. Erdogazdasag
Kiserl Kozl — Kiserletugyi Koezlemenyek
Kiserl Orvostud — Kiserletes Orvostudomany
Kisinev Gos Univ Ucen Zap — Kisinevskii Gosudarstvennyi Universitet. Ucenye Zapiski
KISZAR — Japanese Journal of Parasitology
KIT — Koninklijk Instituut voor de Tropen. Centrale Bibliotheek. Aanwinstenlijst
Kitakanto Med J — Kitakanto Medical Journal
Kitano Hosp J Med — Kitano Hospital Journal of Medicine
Kitasato Arch Exp Med — Kitasato Archives of Experimental Medicine
Kitasato Med — Kitasato Medicine
Kitto — Kitto's Journal of Sacred Literature
KiW — Ksiazka i Wiedza
Kiyo J Fac Sci Hokkaido Univ Ser VI Zool — Kiyo. Journal of the Faculty of Science. Hokkaido University. Series VI. Zoology
KIZRA — Kinzoku Zairyo
KJ — Kipling Journal
KJ — Knjizevnost i Jezik
K Jb — Kirchenmusikalisches Jahrbuch
KJG — Kunstwissenschaftliches Jahrbuch der Gorresgesellschaft
KjK — Keel ja Kirjandus
KJMDA — Kobe Journal of Medical Sciences
KJNNA — Koku Igaku Jikkentai Hokoku
KJS — Knjizevnost i Jezik u Skoli
KJSAA — Kumamoto Journal of Science. Series A. Mathematics, Physics, and Chemistry
KJSBA — Kumamoto Journal of Science. Series B. Section 2. Biology
KJVSA — Kerala Journal of Veterinary Science
KK — Kirke og Kultur
KK — Kokugo To Kokubungaku
K & K — Kunst und Kuenstler
KK — Kwartalnik Klasyczny
KKA — Kamer van Koophandel en Fabrieken te Paramaribo. Bulletin
KKATD — Klima-Kaelte-Technik
KKEHA — Kobayashi Rigaku Kenkyusho Hokoku
K-K Geog Ges Wien Mitt — Kaiserlich-Koenigliche Geographische Gesellschaft in Wien. Mitteilungen
KKH — Kunst und Kultur der Hethiter
KKHKA — Kagaku Keisatsu Kenkyusho Hokoku, Hokagaku Hen
KKIU — Keele ja Kirjanduse Instituudi Uurimused
KKJHD — Koseisho Gan Kenkyu Joseikin Ni Yoru Kenkyu Hokoku
KKK — Kokugo Kokubun No Kenkyu [*Studies in Japanese Language and Literature*]
KKKDB — Kyushu Ketsueki Kenkyu Dokokaishi
K-K Naturh Hofmus An — Kaiserlich-Koenigliche Naturhistorische Hofmuseum. Annalen
KKOSB — Kagaku Kogyo. Supplement
K Krigsvetenskapad Handlingar Tidskr — Kungliga Krigsvetenskapsakademiens. Handlingar och Tidskrift
KKRTD — KFT. Kraftfahrzeugtechnik
KKSKA — Kanagawa-Ken Kogyo Shikenjo Kenkyu Hokoku
KKYHB — Kakuriken Kenkyu Hokoku
Kl — Klio. Beitraege zur Alten Geschichte
KL — Kultur in Literatur
Kl — Kunstliteratur
KL — Kypriakos Logos
Klank — Klank en Weerklank
K Lantbrhogsk Annlr — Kungliga Lantbrukshoegskolans. Annaler
K Lantbruksakad Tidskr — Kungliga Lantbruksakademiens. Tidskrift

K Lantbrukshoegsk Statens Lantbruksfoers Jordbruksfoers Medd — Kungliga Lantbrukshoegskolan och Statens Lantbruksfoersoek. Statens Jordbruksfoersoek Meddelande
K Lantbrukshogsk Ann — Kungliga Lantbrukshoegskolans. Annaler
Klasicni Naucn Spisi Mat Inst (Beograd) — Klasicni Naucn. Spisi. Matematicki Institut (Beograd)
KLATA8 — Kungliga Lantbruksakademiens. Tidskrift
Klei Keram — Klei en Keramiek [*Netherlands*]
Kleine Ergaenzungsreihe Hochschulbuechern Math — Kleine Ergaenzungsreihe zu den Hochschulbuechern fuer Mathematik
Kleine Naturwiss Bibliothek — Kleine Naturwissenschaftliche Bibliothek
Kleinheubacher Ber — Kleinheubacher Berichte [*East Germany*]
Kleintier Prax — Kleintier-Praxis
KLEPA — Kleintier-Praxis
Klepzig Fachber — Klepzig Fachberichte fuer die Fuehrungskraefte aus Maschinenbau und Huettenwesen
Klepzig Fachber Fuehrungskraefte Ind Tech — Klepzig Fachberichte fuer die Fuehrungskraefte aus Industrie und Technik
KLF — Kleinasiatische Forschungen [*Weimar*]
KLFO — Kleinasiatische Forschungen [*Weimar*]
KlForsch — Kleinasiatische Forschungen [*Weimar*]
KLHAAK — Kungliga Lantbrukshoegskolans. Annaler
KLI — Herrenjournal International. Fachzeitschrift fuer Herrenmode
Kliatt — Kliatt Paperback Book Guide
Klima Kaelte Heiz — Klima, Kaelte, Heizung
Klima Kaelteing — Klima und Kaelteingenieur
Klima-Kaelte-Tech — Klima-Kaelte-Technik
Klima-Tech — Klima-Technik
Klim Grej Hlad — Klimatisacija Grejanje Hladenje
Klim Kaelte Ing — Klima und Kaelte Ingenieur
Klin — Klinikus
Klin Anaesthesiol Intensivther — Klinische Anaesthesiologie und Intensivtherapie
Klin Eksp Med — Kliniska un Eksperimentala Medicina
Klin Jahrb — Klinisches Jahrbuch
Klin Khir — Klinicheskaya Khirurgiya [*Kiev*]
Klin Lech Zlokach Novoobraz — Klinika i Lechenie Zlokachestvennykh Novoobrazovanii
Klin Med (Mosc) — Klinicheskaya Meditsina (Moscow)
Klin Med (Vienna) — Klinische Medizin (Vienna)
Klin Monats — Klinische Monatsblaetter fuer Augenheilkunde
Klin Monatsbl Augenheilkd — Klinische Monatsblaetter fuer Augenheilkunde
Klin Oczna — Klinika Oczna
Klin Paediat — Klinische Paediatrie
Klin Paediatr — Klinische Paediatrie
Klin Rentgenol Resp Mezhved Sb — Klinicheskoi Rentgenologii Respublikanskoi Mezhvedomstvennyi Sbornik
Klin Therap Wchnschr — Klinisch-Therapeutische Wochenschrift
Klin Wchnschr — Klinische Wochenschrift
Klin Woch — Klinische Wochenschrift
Klin Wochenschr — Klinische Wochenschrift
Klin Wschr — Klinische Wochenschrift
Klio — Klio. Beitraege zur Alten Geschichte
KLJ — Kentucky Law Journal
KLKHA — Klinicheskaya Khirurgiya
KLKIA — Ki, Klima + Kaelte-Ingenieur
KLMIA — Klinicheskaya Meditsina
KLSSAR — Kungliga Lantbrukshoegskolan och Statens Lantbruksfoersoek. Statens Husdjursforsok Meddelande
KLT — Kerala Law Times
Klueze Oznaczania Owadow Pol — Klueze do Oznaczania Owadow Polski
KLWOA — Klinische Wochenschrift
KLY — Klei en Keramiek
KM — Kansas Magazine
Km — Kirchenmusiker
KM — Kwartalnik Muzyczny
KMA — Koopman
KMAGA — Konstruktion im Maschinen-, Apparate-, und Geraetebau
KMAUA — Klinische Monatsblaetter fuer Augenheilkunde
KMHP — K'ung Meng Msueh-Pao [*Journal. Confucius Mencius Society*]
KMI — Commercium. Maandblad voor Economisch, Administratief, en Ondernemersonderwijs
Km J — Kirchenmusikalisches Jahrbuch
Km Jb — Kirchenmusikalisches Jahrbuch
KMLWA — Kommunalwirtschaft
KMMRA — Khimicheskoe Mashinostroenie
Km Nachrichten — Kirchenmusikalische Nachrichten
K Mus Midden-Afr (Tervuren Belg) Ann Reeks Octavo Geol Wet — Koninklijk Museum voor Midden-Afrika (Tervuren, Belgie). Annalen. Reeks in Octavo Geologische Wetenschappen
K Mus Midden-Afr (Tervuren Belg) Ann Reeks Octavo Zool Wet — Koninklijk Museum voor Midden-Afrika (Tervuren, Belgie). Annalen. Reeks in Octavo Zoologische Wetenschappen
K Mus Midden Afr (Tervuren Belg) Ann Reeks 8o Geol Wet — Koninklijk Museum voor Midden-Afrika (Tervuren, Belgie). Annalen. Reeks in Octavo. Geologische Wetenschappen

K Mus Midden-Afr (Tervuren Belg) Rapp Annu Dep Geol Mineral — Koninklijk Museum voor Midden-Afrika (Tervuren, Belgie). Rapport Annuel. Departement de Geologie et de Mineralogie
K Mus Midden-Afr (Tervuren Belg) Zool Doc — Koninklijk Museum voor Midden-Afrika (Tervuren, Belgie). Zoologische Documentatie
KN — Kainai News
Kn — Knox's Supreme Court Reports
KN — Krasnaja Nov'
KN — Kunst der Nederlanden
KN — Kwartalnik Neofilologiczny
K Ned Akad Wet Proc Ser A — Koninklijke Nederlandse Akademie van Wetenschappen. Proceedings. Series A [*Netherlands*]
K Ned Akad Wet Proc Ser B Palaeontol Geol Phys Chem — Koninklijke Nederlandse Akademie van Wetenschappen. Proceedings. Series B. Palaeontology, Geology, Physics, and Chemistry
K Ned Akad Wet Proc Ser B Phys Sci — Koninklijke Nederlandse Akademie van Wetenschappen. Proceedings. Series B. Physical Sciences [*Later, Koninklijke Nederlandse Akademie van Wetenschappen. Proceedings. Series B. Palaeontology, Geology, Physics, and Chemistry*] [*Netherlands*]
K Ned Akad Wet Proc Ser C — Koninklijke Nederlandse Akademie van Wetenschappen. Proceedings. Series C [*Netherlands*]
K Ned Akad Wet Versl Gewone Vergad Afd Natuurkd — Koninklijke Nederlandse Akademie van Wetenschappen. Verslag van de Gewone Vergadering van de Afdeling Natuurkunde
K Nederlandsch Aardrijkskundig Genootschap Tijdschrift — Koninklijk Nederlandsch Aardrijkskundig Genootschap. Tijdschrift
K Nederlandsch Geol-Mijn Genootschap Verh Geol Ser — Koninklijk Nederlandsch Geologisch-Mijnbouwkundig Genootschap Verhandelingen. Geologische Serie
K Nederlandse Akad Wetensch Afd Natuurk Verh Proc — Koninklijke Nederlandse Akademie van Wetenschappen. Afdeling Natuurkunde. Verhandelingen. Proceedings
K Ned Natuurhist Ver Uitg — Koninklijke Nederlandse Natuurhistorische Vereniging. Uitgave
KNf — Kwartalnik Neofilologiczny
KNGYA — K'uang Yeh
Knick — Knickerbocker Magazine
Knih Ustred Ustavu Geol — Knihovna Ustredniho Ustavu Geologickeho
Knit Times — Knitting Times
Knitting Int — Knitting International
Knizhnaya Letopis Dopl Vyp — Knizhnaya Letopis. Dopolnitel'nyi Vypusk
Knizhnaya Letopis Ukazatel Ser Izdanii — Knizhnaya Letopis Ukazatel Seriinykh Izdanii
Kniznaja Letopis Dopl Vyp — Kniznaja Letopis Dopolnitelnyi Vypusk
Kniznice Odborn Ved Spisu Vysoke Uceni Tech v Brne — Kniznice Odbornych a Vedeckych Spisu Vysokeho Uceni Technickeho v Brne
Kniznice Odb Ved Spisu Vys Uceni Tech Brne — Kniznice Odbornych a Vedeckych Spisu Vysokeho Uceni Technickeho v Brne [*Czechoslovakia*]
Kniznice Odb Ved Spisu Vys Uceni Tech Brne B — Kniznice Odbornych a Vedeckych Spisu Vysokeho Uceni Technickeho v Brne. Rada B [*Czechoslovakia*]
Kniznice & Ved Inf — Kniznice a Vedecke Informacie
Knji — Knjizevnost
KnjiK — Knjizevna Kritika. Casopis za Estetiku Knjizevnosti
KnjiNov — Knjizevne Novine
KnjIst — Knjizevna Istorija
Knjiz Sigma — Knjizica Sigma
Kn Letopis Dop Vyp — Knizhnaya Letopis. Dopolnitel'nyi Vypusk [*USSR*]
KNM — Ondernemersvisie
KnN — Knjizevne Novine
Kn (NSW) — Knox's Supreme Court Reports (New South Wales)
KNNUDP — Koninklijke Nederlandse Natuurhistorische Vereniging. Uitgave
KNO — Kwartalnik Naucyciela Opolskiego
K Nor Vidensk Selsk Foerhandl — Kongelige Norske Videnskabers Selskabs. Foerhandlinger
K Nor Vidensk Selsk Forh — Kongelige Norske Videnskabers Selskabs. Foerhandlinger
K Nor Vidensk Selsk Mus Misc — Kongelige Norske Videnskabers Selskabs. Museet Miscellanea
K Nor Vidensk Selsk Skr — Kongelige Norske Videnskabers Selskabs. Skrifter
Knowl — Knowledge
Knowledge Practice Math — Knowledge and Practice of Mathematics
Knox & Fitz — Knox and Fitzharding's Reports [*New South Wales*]
Knox (NSW) — Knox's Supreme Court Reports (New South Wales)
KNPJB — Konepajamies
KNSFA2 — Kongelige Norske Videnskabers Selskabs. Foerhandlinger
KNSJA — Journal. Korean Nuclear Society
KNVS — Kongelige Norske Videnskapers Selskap
KNWAA — Koninklijke Nederlandse Akademie van Wetenschappen. Proceedings. Series A
KNWBA — Proceedings. Koninklijke Nederlandse Akademie van Wetenschappen. Series B. Physical Sciences
KNWCA — Koninklijke Nederlandse Akademie van Wetenschappen. Proceedings. Series C. Biological and Medical Sciences

KO — Kongo-Overzee. Tijdschrift voor en Over Belgisch-Kongo en Andere Overzeese Gewesten
Ko — Kovcezic
KOAOA — Klinika Oczna
Kobe J Med Sci — Kobe Journal of Medical Sciences
Kobe Kogyo Tech Rep — Kobe Kogyo Technical Report [*Japan*]
Kobelco Tech Bull — Kobelco Technical Bulletin
Kobe Res Dev — Kobe Research Development
Kobe Steel Rep — Kobe Steel Report
Kobe Univ Econ R — Kobe University. Economic Review
Kobe Univ L Rev — Kobe University. Law Review
Kobunshi Ronbun — Kobunshi Ronbunshu
Kobunsh Ron — Kobunshi Ronbunshu
KOCMA — Koroze a Ochrana Materialu
Kodaikanal Obs Bull A — Kodaikanal Observatory Bulletin. Series A
Kodaikanal Obs Bull B — Kodaikanal Observatory Bulletin. Series B
Kodaikanal Obs Bull Ser A — Kodaikanal Observatory Bulletin. Series A [*India*]
Kodai Math J — Kodai Mathematical Journal
Kodai Math Sem Rep — Kodai Mathematical Seminar Reports
Kodak Data Book of Applied Phot — Kodak Data Book of Applied Photography
Kodak Internat Fotogr — Kodak International Fotografie
Kodak Publ G 47 — Kodak Publication. G-47
Kodak Publ G 49 — Kodak Publication. G-49
Kodak Publ G 102 — Kodak Publication. G-102
Kodak Res Lab Mon Abstr Bull — Kodak Research Laboratories. Monthly Abstract Bulletin
Koedoe Monogr — Koedoe Monograph
K d Oe L — Kritik des Oeffentlichen Lebens
Koeln — Koeln. Vierteljahreschrift fuer Freunde der Stadt
Koelner Z Soz — Koelner Zeitschrift fuer Soziologie und Sozial-Psychologie
Koelner Z Soziol u Soz-Psychol — Koelner Zeitschrift fuer Soziologie und Sozial-Psychologie
Koeln Geogr Arb — Koelner Geographische Arbeiten
KOERA — Kolorisztikai Ertesito
Koezgazd Szle — Koezgazdasagi Szemle
Koezlekedes Tud Sz — Koezlekedes Tudomanyi Szemle
Koezlemenyek-MTA Szamitastechn Automat Kutato Int Budapest — Koezlemenyek-MTA Szamitastechnikai es Automatizalasi Kutato Intezet Budapest
Koezl Magy Tud Akad Musz Fiz Kut Intez — Koezlemenyei Magyar Tudomanyos Akademia Muszaki Fizikai Kutato Intezetenek
Koezl-MTA Szamitastech Automat Kutato Int Budapest — Koezlemenyek-MTA Szamitastechnikai es Automatizalasi Kutato Intezet Budapest
KOF — Kultur og Folkeminder
KOGAA — Koatsu Gasu
KOGJA — Kogyo Gijutsu
KOH — Konjunkturpolitik. Zeitschrift fuer Angewandte Konjunkturforschung. Beihefte
Kohasz Lapok — Kohaszati Lapok [*Hungary*]
KOHED — Kohle und Heizoel
Koinonike Epitheor — Koinonike Epitheoresis
KOISA — Kosmicheskie Issledovaniya
KOJ — Konjunkturpolitik. Zeitschrift fuer Angewandte Konjunkturforschung
KoJ — Korea Journal
KOJAA — Konkurito Janaru
KOJUA — Kokyu To Junkan
KOK — Keukenkompas. Vakblad voor Inbouwkeukens, Inbouwapparatuur, en Accessoires
KoK — Kirke og Kultur
KOKAA — Kobunshi Kagaku
KOKAB — Kobunshi Kako
Kokalos — Kokalos Studi Pubblicati. Istituto di Storia Antica. Universita di Palermo
Kok Gak Zas — Kokka Gakkai Zassi [*Journal. Association of Political and Social Science*]
KOKKA — Koks i Khimiya
Koks Khim — Koks i Khimiya [*USSR*]
Koleopterol Rundsch — Koleopterologische Rundschau
Kolhospnyk Ukr — Kolhospnyk Ukrainy
Kolkhozno-Sovkhoznoe Proizod Turkm — Kolkhozno-Sovkhoznoe Proizvodstvo Turkmenistana
Kolkhoz Proizvod — Kolkhoznoe Proizvodstvo
Kolkhoz-Sovkhoz Proizvod — Kolkhozno-Sovkhoznoe Proizvodstvo
Kolkhoz-Sovkhoz Proizvod Kirgizii — Kolkhozno-Sovkhoznoe Proizvodstvo Kirgizii
Kolkhoz-Sovkhoz Proizvod Mold — Kolkhozno-Sovkhoznoe Proizvodstvo Moldavil
Kolkhoz-Sovkhoz Proizvod RSFSR — Kolkhozno-Sovkhoznoe Proizvodstvo RSFSR
Koll Azerb — Kollektsioner Azerbaidzhana
Kolloidnyi Zh — Kolloidnyi Zhurnal
Kolloid-Z — Kolloid-Zeitschrift [*West Germany*]
Kolloid-Z — Kolloid-Zeitschrift und Zeitschrift fuer Polymere
Kolloid Zh — Kolloidnyi Zhurnal

Kolloid-Z & Z Polym — Kolloid-Zeitschrift und Zeitschrift fuer Polymere
Koll Zh — Kolloidnyi Zhurnal
Koln Jb Vor Fruh Gesch — Koelner Jahrbuch fuer Vor- und Fruehgeschichte
Kolomen Ped Inst Ucen Zap — Kolomenskii Pedagogiceskii Institut Ucenye Zapiski
Kolor Ert — Kolorisztikai Ertesitoe
KOM — Tijdschrift voor Effectief Directiebeleid
KOMAA — Kovove Materialy
KOMAB — Korean Medical Abstracts
Komarom Meg Muz Koz — Komarom Megyei Muzeumok Koezlemenei
Komarovskie Chteniya Bot Inst Akad Nauk SSSR — Komarovskie Chteniya Botanicheskogo Instituta Academii Nauk SSSR
Kombin Anal — Kombinatornyi Analiz
Kombinatornyi Anal — Kombinatornyi Analiz
Kom Krystalogr PAN Biul Inf — Komisja Krystalografii PAN [*Polska Akademia Nauk*]. Biuletyn Informacyjny
Kom Mazur-Warmin — Komunikaty Mazursko-Warminskie
Kommunist Azerbajd — Kommunist Azerbajdzana
Kommunist Sov Latvii — Kommunist Sovetskoj Latvii
Kommun u Klassenkampf — Kommunismus und Klassenkampf
Kompleksn Ispol'z Miner Syr'ya — Kompleksnoe Ispol'zovanie Mineral'nogo Syr'ya
Kompleksn Issled Kasp Morya — Kompleksnye Issledovaniya Kaspiiskogo Morya
Kompleksn Issled Vodokhran — Kompleksnye Issledovaniya Vodokhranilishch
Konan Women's Coll Res — Konan Women's College. Researches
Kong Zentralbl Ges Innere Med — Kongresszentralblatt fuer die Gesamte Innere Medizin und Ihre Grenzgebiete
Konigsberg Univ Jahrb — Koenigsberg Universitaet. Jahrbuch
Koninkl Nederlandse Akad Wetensch Proc — Koninklijke Nederlandse Akademie van Wetenschappen. Proceedings
Koninkl Nederlandse Akad Wetensch Verh Afd Natuurk — Koninklijke Nederlandse Akademie van Wetenschappen. Verhandelingen Afdeling Natuurkunde
KONJD — Konjunkturberichte
Konjunkturpol — Konjunkturpolitik
KONPA — Konzerv- es Paprikaipar
Konservn Ovoshchesush Prom-st — Konservnaya i Ovoshchesushil'naya Promyshlennost'
Konserv Ovoshchesush Prom — Konservnaya i Ovoshchesushil'naya Promyshlennost'
Konsthist T — Konsthistorisk Tidskrift
Konsthist Tid — Konsthistorisk Tidskrift
Konsthist Tidskrift — Konsthistorisk Tidskrift
Konstr Elem Methoden — Konstruktion, Elemente, Methoden
Konstr Giessen — Konstruieren und Giessen [*West Germany*]
Konstr Ingenieurbau Ber — Konstruktiver Ingenieurbau Berichte
Konstr Masch-Appar- Geraetebau — Konstruktion im Maschinen-, Apparate-, und Geraetebau
Konstr Masch App Geraetebau — Konstruktion im Maschinen-, Apparate-, und Geraetebau
Konstr Mater Osn Grafita — Konstruktsionnye Materialy na Osnove Grafita
Konstr Mater Osn Ugleroda — Konstruktsionnye Materialy na Osnove Ugleroda
Konstr Uglegrafitovye Mater Sb Tr — Konstruktsionnye Uglegrafitovye Materialy Sbornik Trudov
Konst Svoistva Miner — Konstitutsiya i Svoistva Mineralov
Konst Svoj Miner — Konstitutsiya i Svoistva Mineralov
Konsult Mater Ukr Gos Inst Eksp Farm — Konsultatsionnye Materialy Ukrainskii Gosudarstvennyi Institut Eksperimental'noi Farmatsii
Kontrol'no Izmer Tekh — Kontrol'no Izmeritel'naya Tekhnika
Kontrol Tekhnol Protsessov Obogashch Polezn Iskop — Kontrol i Tekhnologiya Protsessov Obogashcheniya Poleznykh Iskopaemykh
Konyvtari Figy — Konyvtari Figyelo
Konzepte Zeitgemaess Physikunterrichts — Konzepte eines Zeitgemaessen Physikunterrichts
Konzerv-Paprikaip — Konzerv- es Paprikaipar
KOOPA — Kozhevenno-Obuvanaya Promyshlennost
Kooper Zemed — Kooperativno Zemedelie
Koord Khim — Koordinatsionnaya Khimiya
KopGS — Kopenhagener Germanistische Studien
KOPRA — Konservnaya i Ovoshchesushil'naya Promyshlennost'
Koranyi Sandor Tarsasag Tud Ulesei — Koranyi Sandor Tarsasag Tudomanyos Ulesei
Korea Geol and Miner Inst Rep of Geol Miner Explor — Korea. Geological and Mineral Institute. Report of Geological and Mineral Exploration
Korea Inst Forest Genet Res Rept — Korea. Institute of Forest Genetics. Research Reports
Korea J — Korea Journal
Korea Med J — Korea Medical Journal
Koreana Quart — Koreana Quarterly
Korean Bee J — Korean Bee Journal
Korean Biochem J — Korean Biochemical Journal
Korean Cent J Med — Korean Central Journal of Medicine
Korean Inst Miner Min Eng J — Korean Institute of Mineral and Mining Engineers. Journal [*Republic of Korea*]

Korean J Agric Econ — Korean Journal of Agricultural Economics
Korean J Anim Sci — Korean Journal of Animal Sciences
Korean J Appl Microbiol Bioeng — Korean Journal of Applied Microbiology and Bioengineering [*Republic of Korea*]
Korean J Biochem — Korean Journal of Biochemistry
Korean J Bot — Korean Journal of Botany
Korean J Breed — Korean Journal of Breeding [*Republic of Korea*]
Korean J Chem Eng — Korean Journal of Chemical Engineering
Korean J Dermatol — Korean Journal of Dermatology
Korean J Entomol — Korean Journal of Entomology
Korean J Environ Health Soc — Korean Journal of Environmental Health Society [*Republic of Korea*]
Korean J Fd Sci Technol — Korean Journal of Food Science and Technology
Korean J Food Sci Technol — Korean Journal of Food Science and Technology
Korean J Hortic Sci — Korean Journal of Horticultural Science
Korean J Hort Sci — Korean Journal of Horticultural Science [*South Korea*]
Korean J Intern Med — Korean Journal of Internal Medicine
Korean J Microbiol — Korean Journal of Microbiology
Korean J Nucl Med — Korean Journal of Nuclear Medicine
Korean J Obstet Gynecol — Korean Journal of Obstetrics and Gynecology
Korean J Parasitol — Korean Journal of Parasitology
Korean J Pharmacogn — Korean Journal of Pharmacognosy
Korean J Pharmacol — Korean Journal of Pharmacology
Korean J Physiol — Korean Journal of Physiology [*South Korea*]
Korean J Plant Prot — Korean Journal of Plant Protection [*South Korea*]
Korean J Public Health — Korean Journal of Public Health
Korean J Urol — Korean Journal of Urology [*Republic of Korea*]
Korean J Vet Res — Korean Journal of Veterinary Research [*Republic of Korea*]
Korean J Zool — Korean Journal of Zoology
Korean Sci Abstr — Korean Scientific Abstracts [*South Korea*]
Korean Sci Abstracts — Korean Scientific Abstracts
Korean Stud For — Korean Studies Forum [*Republic of Korea*]
Korea Res Inst Geosci Miner Resour KIGAM Bull — Korea Research Institute of Geoscience and Mineral Resources. KIGAM Bulletin
Korea Univ Med J — Korea University. Medical Journal
Korh Orvostech — Korhaz- es Orvostechnika [*Hungary*]
Kor J — Korea Journal [*Republic of Korea*]
Kor J Comp Law — Korea Journal of Comparative Law [*Republic of Korea*]
Kor J Int Stud — Korea Journal of International Studies [*Republic of Korea*]
Korma Korml Skh Zhivotn — Korma i Kormlenie Sel'skokhozyaitvennykh Zhivotnykh
Kormi Godivlya Sil's'kogospod Tvarin — Kormi ta Godivlya Sil's'kogospodars'kikh Tvarin
Korml Skh Zhivotn — Kormlenie Sel'skokhozyaistvennykh Zhivotnykh
Kormoproizvod Sb Nauchn Rab — Kormoproizvodstvo Sbornik Nauchnykh Rabot
Korn Mag — Korn Magasinet
Kor Obs — Korea Observer [*Republic of Korea*]
Koroze Ochr Mater — Koroze a Ochrana Materialu
Koroz Zast — Korozija i Zastita
Korresp Abwasser — Korrespondenz Abwasser
Korrespondenzbriefe Zuckerfabr — Korrespondenzbriefe fuer Zuckerfabriken
Korrosionsinst Rapp — Korrosionsinstitutet. Rapport
Korroz Khim Proizvod Sposoby Zashch — Korroziya v Khimicheskikh Proizvodstvakh i Sposoby Zashchity
Korroz Met Splavov — Korroziya Metallov i Splavov [*USSR*]
Korroz Zashch — Korroziya i Zashchita v Neftegazovoi Promyshlennosti Nauchno-Tekhnicheskii Sbornik
Korroz Zashch Neftegazov Prom-st — Korroziya i Zashchita v Neftegazovoi Promyshlennosti [*USSR*]
Korte Meded Bosbouwproefsta — Korte Mededeling Stichting Bosbouwproefstation "De Dorschkamp"
KOS — Kansallis-Osake-Pankki. Economic Review
KOSAB — Korean Scientific Abstracts
KOSBA — Kosmos. Seria A. Biologia (Warsaw)
Kosm B Av M — Kosmicheskaya Biologiya i Aviakosmicheskaya Meditsina
Kosm Biol Aviakosm Med — Kosmicheskaya Biologiya i Aviakosmicheskaya Meditsina
Kosm Biol Med — Kosmicheskaya Biologiya i Meditsina
Kosmet J — Kosmetik Journal
Kosmet Parfum Drogen Rundsch — Kosmetik-Parfum-Drogen Rundschau
Kosmices Issled — Kosmiceskie Issledovanija
Kosm Issled — Kosmicheskie Issledovaniya
Kosm Issled Ukr — Kosmicheskie Issledovaniya na Ukraine [*Ukrainian SSR*]
Kosm Issled Zemnykh Resur — Kosmicheskie Issledovaniya Zemnykh Resursov Metody i Sredstva Izmerenii i ObrAabotki Informatsii
Kosmos Bibl — Kosmos Bibliothek
Kosmos Ser A Biol (Warsaw) — Kosmos. Seria A. Biologia (Warsaw)
Kosmos Ser A (Warsaw) — Kosmos. Seria A. Biologia (Warsaw)
Kosmos (Warsaw) Ser B — Kosmos. Seria B. Przyroda Nieozywiona (Warsaw)
Kostrom Gos Ped Inst Ucen Zap — Kostromskoi Gosudarstvennyi Pedagogiceskii Institut Imeni N. A. Nekrasova UcenyEe Zapiski
Kov — Kovcezic
Kovove Mater — Kovove Materialy

KOZAA — Kozarstvi
KOZHA — Kolloidnyi Zhurnal
Kozh-Obuvn Prom-st — Kozhevenno-Obuvanaya Promyshlennost [*USSR*]
Kozlem Agrartud Oszt Magy Tud Akad — Koezlemenyei. Agrartudomanyok Osztalyanak. Magyar Tudomanyos Akademia
Kozlemenyek-MTA Szamitastechn Automat Kutato Int Budapest — Koezlemenyek-MTA Szamitastechnikai es Automatizalasi Kutato Intezet Budapest
Kozlem Mosonmagyoarovari Agrartud Foiskola — Koezlemenyei. Mosonmagyoarovari Agrartudomanyi Foiskola
KP — Kritika Phylla
KP — Kulturni Politika
KP — Kwartalnik Prasoznawczy
KPAB — Kentucky Philological Association. Bulletin
KPG — Kliatt Paperback Book Guide
KPK — Kampeer + Caravan Kampioen
KPR — Kniga i Proletarskaya Revolyutsiya
KPSJA — Journal. Korean Physical Society [*Republic of Korea*]
KPT — Keeping Posted for Teachers [*New York*]
KQ — Kansas Quarterly
KQ — Koreana Quarterly
KQYK — Kalikaq Yugnek. Bethel Regional High School
KR — Kenyon Review
KR — Kirkus Reviews
KRA — Koelner Romanistische Arbeiten
KRA — Kroniek van het Ambacht/Kleinbedrijf en Middenbedrijf
Kraeved Zap Kamc Obl Kraeved Muzeja — Kraevedceskie Zapiski Kamcatskaja Oblastnajakraevedceskaja Muzeja
Kraeved Zap Obl Kraeved Muz Upr Magadan Oblispolkoma — Kraevedcheskie Zapiski Oblastnoi Kraevedcheskoi Muzei Upravleniya Magadanskogo Oblispolkoma
Kraev Zadachi Differ Uravn — Kraevye Zadachi dlya Differentsial'nykh Uravnenij
Kraftfahrtech Forschungsarb — Kraftfahrtechnische Forschungsarbeiten
Kratkije Soobscenija Inst Eth — Kratkije Soobscenija Instituta Ethnografiji Akademiji Nauk SSSR
Kratk Soobshch Buryat Kompleksn Nauchno-Issled Inst — Kratkie Soobshcheniya Buryatskogo Kompleksnogo Nauchno-Issledovatel'skogo Instituta
Kratk Soobshch Fiz — Kratkie Soobshcheniya po Fizike
Krat Soob Inst Ark A N SSSR — Kratkie Soobshcheniia Instituta Arkheologii Akademii Nauk SSSR
Krat Soob Inst Etnogr — Kratkie Soobshcheniia Institut Etnografii Akademiia Nauk SSSR
Krat Soob Inst Ist Mater Kul't — Kratkie Soobshcheniia Institut Istorii Material'noi Kul'tury Akademiia Nauk SSSR
Krat Soob OGAM — Kratkie Soobshcheniia o Polevykh Arkheologicheskikh Issledovaniiakh Odesskogo Gosudarstvennogo Arkheologicheskogo Muzeia
KRB — Kredietbank. Weekberichten
Kr Chron — Kritika Chronika
KRE — Korea Exchange Bank. Monthly Review
Krebsforsch — Krebsforschung
Krebsforsch Krebsbekaempf — Krebsforschung und Krebsbekaempfung [*West Germany*]
Kredietbank W Bul — Kredietbank Weekly. Bulletin
Kresge Art Bull — Kresge Art Center. Bulletin
KrestR — Krestanska Revue [*Prague*]
KrestRTPril — Krestanska Revue. Theologicka Priloha [*Prague*]
Krim Forensische Wiss — Kriminalistik und Forensische Wissenschaften
Kriog Vak Tekh — Kriogennaya i Vakuumnaya Tekhnika [*Ukrainian SSR*]
KRISA — Kristallografiya
Kris Study Group NY Psychoanal Inst Monogr — Kris Study Group of the New York Psychoanalytic Institute. Monograph
Kristallogr — Kristallografiya
Kristallogr Grundl Anwend — Kristallographie. Grundlagen und Anwendung
Krist Tech — Kristall und Technik
Krit — Kriterion
KritC — Kritik (Copenhagen)
Krit Justiz — Kritische Justiz
KRJUD — Kritische Justiz
KrK — Krestanska Revue [*Prague*]
KRKHB — Krankenhaus-Umschau
KRMJA — Kurme Medical Journal
KRMNA — Kriminalistik
KRN — Food Magazine
Kroc Found Ser — Kroc Foundation Series
Kroc Found Symp — Kroc Foundation Symposia
Kroeber Anthro Soc Pap — Kroeber Anthropological Society Papers
Krolikovod Zverovod — Krolikovodstvo i Zverovodstvo
Kron — Kronika
Kronobergsboken — Kronobergsboken Arsbok foer Hylten-Cavallius Foereningen
KRQ — Kentucky Romance Quarterly
KrRThPr — Krestanska Revue. Theologicka Priloha [*Prague*]

KrSoob(Kiev) — Kratkije Soobscenija Breves Communications de l'Institute d'Archeologie (Kiev)

Kr Soobsc Inst Arheol — Kratkie Soobscenija Instituta Arheologii

KRTEA — Kristall und Technik

KRTRA — Krupp Technical Review [*English Translation*]

Krupp Tech Rev (Engl Transl) — Krupp Technical Review (English Translation) [*West Germany*]

Krym Gos Med Inst Tr — Krymskii Gosudarstvennyi Meditsinskii Institut Trudy

KS — Akademiia Nauk SSSR. Institut Narodov Azii. Kratkie Soobshcheniia [*Moscow*]

KS — Kant-Studien

KS — Korean Survey

KS — Kultura Slova

K & S — Kunst und Sprache

KSABD — Korean Scientific Abstracts

K-Saechs Ges Wiss Leipzig Mat-Phys Cl Ber — Koeniglich-Saechsische Gesellschaft der Wissenschaften zu Leipzig. Mathematisch-Physische Klasse. Berichte ueber die Verhandlungen

KSB Tech Ber — KSB [*Klein, Schanzlin, Becker*] Technische Berichte [*West Germany*]

KSBurNII — Kratkir Soobscenija Burjatskogo Kompleksnogo Naucnoissledovatel'skogo Instituta Serija Storiko-Filologiceskaja

KSCGH — Kyushu Chugokugakkaiho [*Journal of the Sinological Society of Kyushu*]

KSDKA — Kobe Shosen Daigaku Kiyo. Dai-2-Rui. Kokai, Kikan, Rigaku-Hen

KSDL — Kieler Studien zur Deutschen Literaturgeschichte

KSGT — Kleine Schriften. Gesellschaft fuer Theatergeschichte

KSHSR — Kentucky State Historical Society. Register

KSINA — Kratkije Soobscenija Instituta Narodov Azii

KSISL — Kratkije Soobscenija Instituta Slajanovednija Akademija Nauk SSSR

KSIV — Kratkije Soobscenija Instituta Vostokovedenija Akademija Nauk SSSR

KSJ — Keats-Shelley Journal

K Skogs o Lantbr Akad Tidskr — Kungliga Skogs- och Lantbruksakademiens. Tidskrift

KSl — Kultura Slova

KS LR — Kansas Law Review

KSLTA — Kungl Skogs- och Lantbruksakademiens Tidskrift

KSMB — Keats-Shelley Memorial Bulletin [*Rome*]

KSMBR — Keats-Shelley Memorial Bulletin (Rome)

KSMGA — Koks, Smola, Gaz

KSMSA — Kosmos [*Stuttgart*]

KSPRA — Kuznechno-Shtampovochnoe Proizvodstvo

KSRNA — Kiso To Rinsho

KSRS — Kevo Subarctic Research Station. Reports

KSt — Kant-Studien

KSU (Kyoto Sangyo Univ) Econ and Bus R — KSU (Kyoto Sangyo University). Economic and Business Review

KSV — Kirjallisuudentutkijain Seuran Vuosikirja

K Svenska Vet-Ak Hdl Oefv — Kungliga Svenska Vetenskaps-Akademiens. Handlingar. Oefversigt til Handlingar

K Sven Vetenskapsakad Avh Naturskyddsarenden — Kungliga Svenska Vetenskapsakademiens. Avhandlingar i Naturskyddsarenden

K Sven Vetenskapsakad Handl — Kungliga Svenska Vetenskapsakademiens. Handlingar

K Sven Vetenskapsakad Skr Naturskyddsarenden — Kungliga Svenska Vetenskapsakademiens. Skrifter i Naturskyddsarenden

KSVK — Kalevalaseuran Vuosikirja

KT — Khristianskoe Tchtenie

Ktavim Rec Agric Res Stn — Ktavim Records of the Agricultural Research Station

K Tek Hoegsk Handl — Kungliga Tekniska Hoegskolans. Handlingar [*Sweden*]

KTF — Kwartaalfacetten. Informatie over Krediet en Financiering

KTh — Kerk en Theologie [*Wageningen*]

KTheol — Kerk en Theologie [*Wageningen*]

KTL Ber Landtech — Kuratorium fuer Technik in der Landwirtschaft. Berichte ueber Landtechnik

KTMK — Katimavik. Faculty of Physical Education. University of Alberta

KtoK — Kokugo To Kokubungaku [*Japanese Language and Literature*]

KTR — Korea Trade Report

KTVU — Kleine Texte fuer Vorlesungen und Uebungen

KUA — Kobe University. Economic Review

Kuban Gos Univ Naucn Trudy — Kubanskii Gosudarstvennyi Universitet Naucnyi Trudy

KUBEA — Kunststoff-Berater

KuD — Kerygma und Dogma [*Goettingen*]

KUDKA — Kumamoto Daigaku Kogakubu Kenkyu Hokoku

Kuehn-Arch — Kuehn-Archiv

Kuelfoeldi Mehesz Szemle — Kuelfoeldi Meheszeti Szemle

KUER — Kobe University. Economic Review

Kugellager-Z — Kugellager-Zeitschrift

KUHCA — Journal. Korean Institute of Metals [*Republic of Korea*]

Kuibysev Gos Ped Inst Ucen Zap — Ministerstvo Prosvescenija RSFSR Kuibysevskii Gosudarstvennyi Pedagogiceskii Institut Imeni V. V. Kuibyseva Ucenyi Zapiski [*Kuybyshev*]

Kuibyshev Inzh Stroit Inst Tr — Kuibyshevskii Inzhenerno-Stroitel'nyi Institut Trudy

KUISA — Japanese Journal of Aerospace Medicine and Psychology

KUK — Temperatur Technik. Zeitschrift fuer das Gesamte Temperaturgebiet Kaltetechnik, Klimatechnik und Heizungstechnik Einschliesslich Isolierung Lueftung, Kuehltransport und Tiefkuehltransport

Ku Kl — Kultur og Klasse

KUKUA — Kukuruza

KuKv — Klassizismus und Kulturverfall

KuL — Kunst und Literatur

Kult i Spolecz — Kultura i Spoleczenstwo

KulturaW — Kultura (Warsaw)

Kulturen — Kulturen Arsbok till Medlemmerna av Kulturhistoriska Foerening foer Soedra Sverige

Kulturpflanze Beih — Kulturpflanze Beiheft

Kumamoto Jour Sci Ser A Mathematics Physics and Chemistry — Kumamoto Journal of Science. Series A. Mathematics, Physics, and Chemistry

Kumamoto J Sci — Kumamoto Journal of Science

Kumamoto J Sci Biol — Kumamoto Journal of Science. Biology

Kumamoto J Sci Geol — Kumamoto Journal of Science. Geology

Kumamoto J Sci Math — Kumamoto Journal of Science. Mathematics

Kumamoto J Sci Ser A — Kumamoto Journal of Science. Series A. Mathematics, Physics, and Chemistry

Kumamoto J Sci Ser B Sect 1 — Kumamoto Journal of Science. Series B. Section 1. Geology

Kumamoto J Sci Ser B Sect 2 Biol — Kumamoto Journal of Science. Series B. Section 2. Biology

Kumamoto Med J — Kumamoto Medical Journal

Kumamoto Pharm Bull — Kumamoto Pharmaceutical Bulletin

KUMJA — Kumamoto Medical Journal

KUMJB — Kyungpook University Medical Journal

KUN — Kunststoffe

Kun Chung Hseuh Pao Acta Entomol Sin — Kun Chung Hseuh Pao. Acta Entomologica Sinica

KUNSA — Kunststoffe. Organ der Deutschen Kunststoff-Fachverbaende

Kunst-Ber — Kunststoff-Berater

Kunst u Lit — Kunst und Literatur

Kunst u Lit — Kunst und Literatur. Sowjetwissenschaft Zeitschrift zur Verbreitung Sowjetischer Erfahrungen

Kunstst — Kunststoffe

Kunstst Bau — Kunststoffe im Bau

Kunstst-Berat — Kunststoff-Berater

Kunstst-Berat Rundsch Tech — Kunststoff-Berater Vereinigt mit Kunststoff-Rundschau und Kunststoff-Technik

Kunstst Ger Plast — Kunststoffe - German Plastics

Kunstst J — Kunststoff Journal

Kunststoffberat Rundsch Tech — Kunststoffberater, Rundschau, und Technik

Kunstst-Plast — Kunststoffe-Plastics

Kunstst-Rundsch — Kunststoff-Rundschau

Kunstst Tech Kunstst Anwend — Kunststoff-Technik und Kunststoff-Anwendung

KUP — Kunststoffe-Plastics; Schweizerische Fachzeitschrift fuer Herstellung, Verarbeitung, und Anwendung von Kunststoffen

KUPLA — Kunststoffe-Plastics

KURAAV — Annual Reports. Research Reactor Institute. Kyoto University

Kurator Tech Landwirt Flugschr — Kuratorium fuer Technik in der Landwirtschaft. Flugschrift

Kurme Med J — Kurme Medical Journal

Kurortol Fizioter — Kurortologiia i Fizioterapiia [*USSR*]

Kurortol Fizioter — Kurortologiya i Fizioterapiya [*Bulgaria*]

Kurortol Uurim — Kurortoloogilised Uurimused

Kursk Gos Med Inst Sb Tr — Kurskii Gosudarstvennyi Meditsinskii Institut. Sbornik Trudov

Kursk Gos Ped Inst Ucen Zap — Kurskii Gosudarstvennyi Pedagogiceskii Institut. Ucenye Zapiski

KURUA — Kunststoff-Rundschau

Kurznachr Akad Wiss Goettingen — Kurznachrichten der Akademie der Wissenschaften in Goettingen [*West Germany*]

Kurznachr Akad Wiss Goettingen Sammelh — Kurznachrichten der Akademie der Wissenschaften in Goettingen. Sammelheft

KUSEB — Kuki Seijo

Kuz — Kuznica

Kuznechno-Shtampov — Kuznechno-Shtampovochnoe Proizvodstvo

KV — Kalevalaseuran Vuosikirja

KV — Kirkens Verden

KV — Korte Verklaring der Heilige Schrift [*Kampen*]

Kvan Elektr — Kvantovia Elektronika

Kvant — Akademija Nauk SSSR i Akademija Pedagogiceskih Nauk SSSR. Kvant

Kvantovaya Ehlektron — Kvantovaya Ehlektronika

Kvantovaya Elektron (Kiev) — Kvantovaya Elektronika (Kiev)

Kvantovaya Elektron (Moskva) — Kvantovaya Elektronika (Moskva)

Kvasny Prum — Kvasny Prumysl [*Czechoslovakia*]

KVATL — Koninklijke Vlaamse Academie voor Taal- en Letterkunde
K Vetensk Acad Handl — Kungliga Vetenskaps-Academiens. Handlingar
K Vetensk Acad N Handl (Stockholm) — Kungliga Vetenskaps-Academiens. Nya Handlingar (Stockholm)
K Vetenskapssamh Uppsala Arsb — Kungliga Vetenskapssamhaellets i Uppsala. Arsbok
K Vetensk-Soc Arsb — Kungliga Vetenskaps-Societetens. Arsbok
K Vet-Landbohojsk Arsskr — Kongelige Veterinaer-og Landbohojskole Arsskrift
KVG — Kritische Vierteljahresschrift fuer Gesetzgebung
KVHAAH — Kungliga Vitterhets Historie och Antikvitets Akademiens. Handlingar
KVJS — Kritische Vierteljahresschrift
KVKEK — Kroniek van Kunst en Kultur
KVMFA — Kongelige Danske Videnskabernes Selskab. Matematisk-Fysisk Skrifter
KVNS — Korrespondenzblatt. Verein fuer Niederdeutsche Sprachforschung
KVPRA — Kvasny Prumysl
KVS — Kabelvisie Onafhankelijk Tijdschrift voor Kabel en Lokale Televisie
Kwangju Teach Coll Sci Educ Cent Rev — Kwangju Teachers College. Science Education Center. Review
Kwansei Gakuin Sociol Dept Stud — Kwansei Gakuin University. Sociology Department Studies
Kwansei Gakuin U Ann Stud — Kwansei Gakuin University. Annual Studies
Kwansei Gakuin Univ Annual Stud — Kwansei Gakuin University. Annual Studies
Kwartalnik Geol — Kwartalnik Geologiczny
Kwart Geol — Kwartalnik Geologiczny
Kwart Geol (Pol Inst Geol) — Kwartalnik Geologiczny (Poland. Instytut Geologiczny)
Kwart Hist Kult — Kwartalnik Historii Kultury
Kwart Hist Kult Mater — Kwartalnik Historii Kultury Materialnej
Kwart Hist Nauki Tech — Kwartalnik Historii Nauki i Techniki
Kwart Hist Nauki i Tech — Kwartalnik Historii Nauki i Techniki
Kwart Opolski — Kwartalnik Opolski
KWDR — Kwandur Newsletter. Council for Yukon Indians
KWGEA — Kwartalnik Geologiczny
KWHCA — Kwangsan Hakhoe Chi
KwO — Kwartalnik Opolski
KWT — Kuwait Times
KWURA — KWU [*Kraftwerk Union AG, Muehlheim*] Report
KWU Rep — KWU [*Kraftwerk Union AG, Muehlheim*] Report
KY Ag Exp — Kentucky. Agricultural Experiment Station. Publications
KY Agri-Bus Q — Kentucky Agri-Business Quarterly
KY AgriBus Spotlight — Kentucky Agri-Business Spotlight
KY Agric Exp Stn Annu Rep — Kentucky. Agricultural Experiment Station. Annual Report
KY Agric Exp Stn Bull — Kentucky. Agricultural Experiment Station. Bulletin
KY Agric Exp Stn Misc Pubs — Kentucky. Agricultural Experiment Station. Miscellaneous Publications
KY Agric Exp Stn Prog Rep — Kentucky. Agricultural Experiment Station. Progress Report
KY Agric Exp Stn Regul Bull — Kentucky. Agricultural Experiment Station. Regulatory Bulletin
KY Agric Exp Stn Results Res — Kentucky. Agricultural Experiment Station. Results of Research
Kyb — Kybernetika
KY Bench and B — Kentucky Bench and Bar
Kybernetika Suppl — Kybernetika Supplement
KY B J — Kentucky Bar Journal
KYBNA — Kybernetika
KyC — Kypriaka Chronika
Ky Coal J — Kentucky Coal Journal
KYCSA — K'uang Yeh Chi Shu
KY Dep Fish Wildl Resour Fish Bull — Kentucky. Department of Fish and Wildlife Resources. Fisheries Bulletin
KY Dep Mines Miner Geol Div Ser 8 Bull — Kentucky. Department of Mines and Minerals. Geological Division. Series 8. Bulletin
KYDKAJ — Annual Report. Kyoritsu College of Pharmacy
KY Economy — Kentucky Economy
KY Farm Home Sci — Kentucky Farm and Home Science
KY Folkl Rec — Kentucky Folklore Record
KY Folk Rec — Kentucky Folklore Record
KY Geol Survey Bull Inf Circ Rept Inv Special Pub — Kentucky. Geological Survey. Bulletin. Information Circular. Report of Investigations. Special Publication
KY Geol Surv Rep Invest — Kentucky Geological Survey. Report of Investigations
KY Geol Surv Ser 9 Bull — Kentucky. Geological Survey. Series 9. Bulletin
KY Geol Surv Ser 10 Cty Rep — Kentucky. Geological Survey. Series 10. County Report
KY Geol Surv Ser 9 Rep Invest — Kentucky. Geological Survey. Series 9. Report of Investigation
KY Geol Surv Ser 10 Rep Invest — Kentucky. Geological Survey. Series 10. Report of Investigation

KY Geol Surv Ser 9 Spec Publ — Kentucky. Geological Survey. Series 9. Special Publication
Ky Geol Surv Spec Publ — Kentucky. Geological Survey. Special Publication
KY Geol Surv Thesis Ser — Kentucky. Geological Survey. Thesis Series
KY G S Rp Prog B — Kentucky Geological Survey. Report of Progress. Bulletin
KY Hist Soc Reg — Kentucky Historical Society. Register
KYHS — Kentucky Historical Society. Register
Kyk — Kyklos
Kyklos Int Z Sozialwiss Int Rev Soc Sci — Kyklos. Internationale Zeitschrift fuer Sozialwissenschaften. Revue International des Sciences Sociales. International Review for Social Sciences
KY Law J — Kentucky Law Journal
KY Lib Assn Bull — Kentucky Library Association. Bulletin
KY Libr Ass Bull — Kentucky Library Association. Bulletin
KY L J — Kentucky Law Journal
KY Nurse — Kentucky Nurse
KY Nurses Assoc Newsl — Kentucky Nurses' Association. Newsletter
Kyo — Kyoto University. Economic Review
Kyorin J Med Med Technol — Kyorin Journal of Medicine and Medical Technology
Kyoto Daigaku Nogaku-Bu Enshurin Hokoku Bull Kyoto Univ For — Kyoto Daigaku Nogaku-Bu Enshurin Hokoku/Bulletin. Kyoto University Forests
Kyoto Univ Afr Stud — Kyoto University. African Studies
Kyoto Univ Econ R — Kyoto University. Economic Review
Kyoto Univ Fac Sci Mem Ser Geol Mineral — Kyoto University. Faculty of Science. Memoirs. Series of Geology and Mineralogy
Kyoto Univ Geophys Res Stn Rep — Kyoto University. Geophysical Research Station. Reports
KYR — Kentucky Review
KY Reg — Kentucky State Historical Society. Register
Kyrkohist Arsskr — Kyrkohistorisk Arsskrift
KY Roman Q — Kentucky Romance Quarterly
KyS — Kypriakai Spoudai
KY Sch J — Kentucky School Journal
Kyungpook Educ Forum — Kyungpook Education Forum
Kyungpook Math J — Kyungpook Mathematical Journal
Kyungpook Univ Med J — Kyungpook University Medical Journal
KY Univ Office Res Eng Services Bull — Kentucky University. Office of Research and Engineering Services. Bulletin
KY Univ Off Res Eng Serv Bull — Kentucky University. Office of Research and Engineering Services. Bulletin
Kyushu Agr Res — Kyushu Agricultural Research
Kyushu J Med Sci — Kyushu Journal of Medical Science
Kyushu Univ Coll Gen Educ Rep Earth Sci — Kyushu University. College of General Education. Reports on Earth Science
Kyushu Univ Dep Geol Sci Rep — Kyushu University. Department of Geology. Science Reports
Kyushu Univ Fac Agr Sci Bull — Kyushu University. Faculty of Agriculture. Science Bulletin
Kyushu Univ Fac Sci Mem Ser D — Kyushu University. Faculty of Science. Memoirs. Series D. Geology
Kyushu Univ Faculty Sci Mem — Kyushu University. Faculty of Science. Memoirs
KY Warbler — Kentucky Warbler
KZ — Kirchliche Zeitschrift
KZ — Kulturny Zivot [*Bratislava*]
KZAIA — Kogyo Zairyo
KZGKA — Kinzoku Zairyo Gijutsu Kenkyusho Kenkyu Hokoku
KZMTLG — Koninklijke Zuidnederlandse Maatschappij voor Taal- en Letterkunde en Geschiedenis
KZSS — Koelner Zeitschrift fuer Soziologie und Sozial-Psychologie
KZZPA — Kolloid-Zeitschrift und Zeitschrift fuer Polymere

L

L — Lancet [*London*]
L — Language
L — Latomus
L — Leodium
LA — Language Arts
LA — Le Arti
La — Letteratura
LA — Lincoln Annex
LA — Linguistica Antverpiensia
LA — Linguistische Arbeiten
LA — Lisan Al-'Arabi
LA — Literarische Anzeiger
LA — Living Age
LAAA — Liverpool Annuals of Archaeology and Anthropology
LAACB — Langenbecks Archiv fuer Chirurgie
LA Ag Exp — Louisiana. Agricultural Experiment Station. Publications
LA Agr — Louisiana Agriculture
LA Agric — Louisiana Agriculture
LA Agric Exp Stn Bull — Louisiana. Agricultural Experiment Station. Bulletin
L A of Alta Bul — Library Association of Alberta. Bulletin
LAA Univ & Coll Lib Sec News — Library Association of Australia. University and College Libraries Section. News Sheet
LAA Univ Lib Sec News — Library Association of Australia. University Libraries Section. News Sheet
LAA Univ Lib Sec News Sheet — Library Association of Australia. University Libraries Section. News Sheet
LAAW — Lotus. Afro-Asian Writings
La B — La Bas
LAB — Los Angeles Bar Bulletin
Lab Anim — Laboratory Animals
Lab Anim Care — Laboratory Animal Care
Lab Anim Handb — Laboratory Animal Handbooks
Lab Anim Sc — Laboratory Animal Science
Lab Anim Sci — Laboratory Animal Science
Lab Anim Symp — Laboratory Animal Symposia
LA Bar J — Louisiana Bar Journal
LABB — Los Angeles Bar Bulletin
Lab Biochim Nutr Publ Univ Cathol Louvain Fac Sci Agron — Laboratoire de Biochimie de la Nutrition. Publication. Universite Catholique de Louvain. Faculte des Sciences Agronomiques
Lab-Bl — Laboratoriums-Blaetter
LAB Bull — Los Angeles Bar Bulletin
Lab Cent Ponts Chaussees Bull Liaison Lab Ponts Chaussees — Laboratoire Central des Ponts et Chaussees. Bulletin de Liaison des Laboratoires des Ponts et Chaussees
Lab Cent Ponts Chaussees Note Inf Tech — Laboratoire Central des Ponts et Chaussees. Note d'Information Technique
Lab Cent Ponts Chaussees Rapp Rech — Laboratoire Central des Ponts et Chaussees. Rapport de Recherche
Lab Central Ensayo Mater Constr Madrid Publ — Laboratorio Central de Ensayo de Materiales de Construccion. Madrid. Publicacion
Lab Clin Stress Res Karolinska Sjukhuset Rep — Laboratory for Clinical Stress Research. Karolinska Sjukhuset. Reports
LABDA — Laboratornoe Delo
Lab Delo — Laboratornoe Delo

Labdev J Sci Technol — Labdev Journal of Science and Technology
Labdev J Sci & Technol A — Labdev Journal of Science and Technology. Part A
Labdev J Sci & Technol B — Labdev Journal of Science and Technology. Part B
Labdev J Sci Technol Part B Life Sci — Labdev Journal of Science and Technology. Part B. Life Sciences
Labdev J Sci Tech Part A — Labdev Journal of Science and Technology. Part A. Physical Sciences
Labdev Part A — Labdev Journal of Science and Technology. Part A. Physical Sciences
Labdev Part B — Labdev Journal of Science and Technology. Part B. Life Sciences
Lab Diagn — Laboratoriumi Diagnosztika
Lab Dig — Laboratory Digest
Lab and Emp — Labour and Employment Gazette
Lab and Empl — Labour and Employment Gazette
Lab and Empl L — Labor and Employment Law
Lab Ensayo Mater Invest Tecnol An — Laboratorio de Ensayo de Materiales e Investigaciones Tecnologicas. Anales
Lab Equip Dig — Laboratory Equipment Digest
Lab Gaz — Labour Gazette
Lab Gov Chem (GB) Misc Rep — Laboratory of the Government Chemist (Great Britain). Miscellaneous Report
Lab Gov Chem (GB) Occas Pap — Laboratory of the Government Chemist (Great Britain). Occasional Paper
Lab Hist — Labor History
Lab Hist — Labour History
Lab Instrum Tech Ser — Laboratory Instrumentation and Techniques Series
Lab Inv — Laboratory Investigation
Lab Invest — Laboratory Investigation
LABJ — Los Angeles Bar Journal
LA B J — Louisiana Bar Journal
Lab J Australas — Laboratory Journal of Australasia
LABLD — Laboratoriums-Blaetter
Lab L J — Labor Law Journal
LABMA — Laboratory Management
Lab Manage — Laboratory Management
Lab Med — Laboratory Medicine
Lab Microcomput — Laboratory Microcomputer
Lab Mo — Labour Monthly
Lab Nac Eng Civ (Port) Mem — Laboratorio Nacional de Engenharia Civil (Portugal). Memoria
Laboratoriumsbl Med Diagn E Behring — Laboratoriumsblaetter fuer die Medizinische Diagnostik E. V. Behring
Labor His — Labor History
Labor Hist — Labor History
Labor Hyg Occup Dis (Engl Transl) — Labor Hygiene and Occupational Diseases (English Translation)
Labor Hyg Occup Dis (USSR) — Labor Hygiene and Occupational Diseases (USSR)
Labor Law J — Labor Law Journal
Labor L J — Labor Law Journal
Labor Med — Labor-Medizin
Labor Nts — Labor Notes

LaborPraxis Med — LaborPraxis in der Medizin
Labor Tdy — Labor Today
Labour — Labour/Le Travailleur
Labour and Employment Gaz — Labour and Employment Gazette
Labour Gaz — Labour Gazette
Labour Hist — Labour History
Labour Mo — Labour Monthly
Labour Res — Labour Research
Labour Research Bul — Labour Research Bulletin
Labour Wkly — Labour Weekly
LABPA — Laboratory Practice
Lab Ponts Chaussees Bull Liaison — Laboratoire des Ponts et Chaussees. Bulletin de Liaison
Lab Ponts Chaussees Rapp Rech — Laboratoire des Ponts et Chaussees. Rapport de Recherche
Lab Pract — Laboratory Practice
Lab Practice — Laboratory Practice
Lab Prod For Est (Can) Rapp — Laboratoire des Produits Forestiers de l'Est (Canada). Rapport
Lab Radiol Dozim Cesk Akad Ved Report — Laborator Radiologicke Dozimetrie. Ceskoslovenska Akademie Ved. Report
Lab Rel and Empl News — Labor Relations and Employment News
Lab Rel Rep — Labor Relations Reporter
Lab Rep Franklin Inst — Laboratory Report. Franklin Institute
Lab Res Methods Biol Med — Laboratory and Research Methods in Biology and Medicine
Labr Hist — Labour History
Lab Tech Rep Div Mech Eng Natl Res Counc Can — Laboratory Technical Report. Division of Mechanical Engineering. National Research Council of Canada
Lab Tuinbouwplantenteelt Landbouwhogesch Wageningen Publ — Laboratorium voor Tuinbouwplantenteelt Landbouwhogeschool Wageningen Publikatie
LA Bus R — Louisiana Business Review
LA Bus Survey — Louisiana Business Survey
LA Bus Svy — Louisiana Business Survey
LAC — Letteratura ed Arte Contemporanea
LACB — Legal Aid Clearinghouse. Bulletin
LACHD — Liebigs Annalen der Chemie
Lac Jur — Lackawanna Jurist
Lackawanna Inst Pr — Lackawanna Institute of History and Science. Proceedings and Collections
Lack Farben Chem — Lack- und Farben-Chemie
Lack Farben Z — Lack- und Farben-Zeitschrift
Lack Jur — Lackawanna Jurist
Lack Jurist — Lackawanna Jurist
LACR — Latin America Commodities Report
LACSD — Los Angeles Council of Engineers and Scientists. Proceedings Series
Lactation Rev — Lactation Review
LACUNY J — LACUNY [*Library Association. City University of New York*] Journal
LA Daily J — Los Angeles Daily Journal
LA Dep Conserv Geol Surv Miner Resour Bull — Louisiana. Department of Conservation. Geological Survey. Mineral Resources Bulletin
LA Dep Public Works Basic Rec Rep — Louisiana. Department of Public Works. Basic Records Report
LA Dep Public Works Tech Rep — Louisiana. Department of Public Works. Technical Report
LA Dept Conserv Bienn Rept — Louisiana. Department of Conservation. Biennial Report
LA Dept Public Works Water Res Pamph — Louisiana. Department of Public Works. Water Resources Pamphlet
Lad HJ — Ladies' Home Journal
Ladies' H J — Ladies' Home Journal
Ladies Home J — Ladies' Home Journal
LAEADA — Alabama. Agricultural Experiment Station. Leaflet (Auburn University)
LAECA — Land Economics
LA Economy — Louisiana Economy
LA Eng — Louisiana Engineer
LAER — Latin America Economic Report
LaF — Langue Francaise
LAFacTLima — Libro Anual. Facultad de Teologia. Universidad Pontificia y Civil [*Lima, Peru*]
Lafayette Clin Stud Schizophr — Lafayette Clinic. Studies on Schizophrenia
LAFOA — Laser Focus
LA Free P — Los Angeles Free Press
LaG — La Giustizia
Lag Bull — Lag Bulletin
La Geog — La Geographie
LA Geol Surv Clay Resour Bull — Louisiana. Geological Survey. Clay Resources Bulletin
LA Geol Surv Geol Bull — Louisiana. Geological Survey. Geological Bulletin
LA Geol Surv Miner Resour Bull — Louisiana. Geological Survey. Mineral Resources Bulletin

LA Geol Surv Water Resour Bull — Louisiana. Geological Survey and Department of Public Works. Water Resources Bulletin
LA Geol Surv Water Resour Pam — Louisiana. Geological Survey and Department of Public Works. Water Resources Pamphlet
Lagos Notes Rec — Lagos Notes and Records
La H — Labor History
LaH — Louisiana History
Lahey Clin Found Bull — Lahey Clinic Foundation. Bulletin
LA His Q — Louisiana Historical Quarterly
LA His S — Louisiana Historical Society. Publications
LA Hist — Louisiana History
LA Hist Quar — Louisiana Historical Quarterly
LAIL — Latin American Indian Literatures
LAINA — Laboratory Investigation
LaK — Literatur als Kunst
LAKAA — Laekartidningen
Lakeside — Lakeside Monthly
Lakes Lett — Lakes Letter [*United States*]
Lakokras Mater Ikh Primen — Lakokrasochnye Materialy i Ikh Primenenie
L Akt — Linguistik Aktuell
LA Law — Los Angeles Lawyer
LA Law Rev — Louisiana Law Review
LA Lib Assn Bull — Louisiana Library Association. Bulletin
LA Lib Bul — Louisiana Library Association. Bulletin
LALR — Latin American Literary Review
LA LR — Louisiana Law Review
LA L Rev — Louisiana Law Review
LaM — Langues Modernes
LAMAA — Lakokrasochnye Materialy i Ikh Primenenie
LAMEA — Laval Medical
La Molina Peru Estac Exp Agric Inf — La Molina Peru Estacion Experimental Agricola. Informe
LAMR — Latin American Music Review/Revista de Musica Latinoamericana
LAN — Life Association News
Lanbau Vol — Lanbauforschung Volkenrode
LANC — Land. Newsletter. Lands Directorate. Environment Canada
LANCA — Lancet
Lanchow Univ J Nat Sci — Lanchow University Journal. Natural Sciences [*People's Republic of China*]
Land — Land. Bureau of Land Management [*Alaska*]
Land — Land and Land News
Land App Ct Cas — Land Appeal Court Cases [*New South Wales*]
Landarb — Landarbeit
Landarb Tech — Landarbeit und Technik
Land Arch — Landscape Architecture
Landbauforsch Voelkenrode — Landbauforschung Voelkenrode
Landbauforsch Voelkenrode Sonderh — Landbauforschung Voelkenrode. Sonderheft
Landbouwkd Tijdschr — Landbouwkundig Tijdschrift
Landbouwmechan — Landbouwmechanisatie
Landbouwproefstn Suriname Bull — Landbouwproefstation Suriname. Bulletin
Landbouwproefstn Suriname Meded — Landbouwproefstation Suriname. Mededeling
Landbouwvoorl — Landbouwvoorlichting
Landbouwvoorlichting — Rijkslandbouwvoorlichtingsdienst
Landbrugsokonomiske Stud Copenh Vet Landbohojsk Okon Inst — Landbrugsokonomiske. Studier. Copenhagen Veterinaer. Og Landbohojskole. Okonomisk Institut
Land Conserv Ser Dep NT — Land Conservation Series. Department of the Northern Territory
Land Econ — Land Economics
Landerbank — Landerbank Economic Bulletin
Landis & Gyr Rev — Landis and Gyr Review
Land Issues Probl VA Polytech Inst State Univ Coop Ext Serv — Land Issues and Problems. Virginia Polytechnic Institute and State University. Cooperative Extension Service
Land L Serv — Land Laws Service
Landmasch-Markt — Landmaschinen-Markt
Landmasch Rundsch — Landmaschinen-Rundschau
Landmasch-Rundschau — Landmaschinen-Rundschau [*West Germany*]
Landoekonom Forsoglab Aarbog (Copenhagen) — Landoekonomisk Forsogslaboratorium Aarbog (Copenhagen)
Landokon Forsogslab Efterars — Landoekonomisk Forsogslaboratoriums Efterarsmode
Landowning in Scot — Landowning in Scotland
Land Reform — Land Reform, Land Settlement, and Cooperatives
Land Resour Div Dir Overseas Surv Land Resour Study — Land Resources Division. Directorate of Overseas Surveys. Land Resource Study
Land Resour Div Dir Overseas Surv Tech Bull — Land Resources Division. Directorate of Overseas Surveys. Technical Bulletin
Land Resour Manage Ser Div Land Resour Manage CSIRO — Land Resources Management Series. Division of Land Resources Management. Commonwealth Scientific and Industrial Research Organisation
Land Resour Mgmt Ser Div Land Resour Mgmt CSIRO — Land Resources Management Series. Division of Land Resources Management. Commonwealth Scientific and Industrial Research Organisation

Land Resour Stud Land Resour Div Dir Overseas Surv — Land Resource Study. Land Resources Division. Directorate of Overseas Surveys

Land Res Ser Commonw Sci Industr Res Organ (Aust) — Land Research Series. Commonwealth Scientific and Industrial Research Organisation (Melbourne, Australia)

Land Res Ser CSIRO — Land Research Series. Commonwealth Scientific and Industrial Research Organisation

Land Res Ser CSIRO (Aust) — Land Research Series. Commonwealth Scientific and Industrial Research Organisation (Australia)

Landscape Arch — Landscape Architecture

Landscape Archre — Landscape Architecture

Landscape Des — Landscape Design

Landscape Intl — Landscape International

Landscape Plann — Landscape Planning

Landsc Arch — Landscape Architecture

Land of Sun — Land of Sunshine

Landtech — Landtechnik

Land-Tuinbouw Jaarb — Land en Tuinbouw Jaarboek

Land Use Built Form Stud Inf Notes — Land Use Built Form Studies. Information Notes

Land Use Built Form Stud Reps — Land Use Built Form Studies. Reports

Land Use Built Form Stud Wking Paps — Land Use Built Form Studies. Working Papers

Land Use Built Form Tech Notes — Land Use Built Form Studies. Technical Notes

Land Use and Env L Rev — Land Use and Environment Law Review

Land Use Law and Zoning Dig — Land Use Law and Zoning Digest

Land & Water LR — Land and Water Law Review

Land & Water L Rev — Land and Water Law Review

Landw Forsch — Landwirtschaftliche Forschung

Landwirt — Landwirtschaft

Landwirt-Angew Wiss Bundesmin Ernahr Landwirt Forsten — Landwirtschaft-Angewandte Wissenschaft. Bundesministerium fuer Ernaehrung, Landwirtschaft, und Forsten

Landwirt Forsch Sonderh — Landwirtschaftliche Forschung. Sonderheft

Landwirtsch Angew Wiss — Landwirtschaft-Angewandte Wissenschaft

Landwirtsch Chem Bundesversuchsanst (Linz) Veroeff — Landwirtschaftlich-Chemische Bundesversuchsanstalt (Linz). Veroeffentlichungen

Landwirtsch Forsch — Landwirtschaftliche Forschung

Landwirtsch Jahrb — Landwirtschaftliche Jahrbuecher

Landwirtsch Jahrb Schweiz — Landwirtschaftliches Jahrbuch der Schweiz

Landwirt Schriftenr Boden Pflanze — Landwirtschaftliche Schriftenreihe Boden und Pflanze

Landwirtsch Ver Stn — Landwirtschaftlichen Versuchs-Stationen

Landwirt Zentralbl — Landwirtschaftliches Zentralblatt

Landw Jb Schweiz — Landwirtschaftliches Jahrbuch der Schweiz

Landw Mh — Landwirtschaftliche-Monatshefte

Landw Wbl Kurhessen-Waldeck — Landwirtschaftliches Wochenblatt fuer Kurhessen-Waldeck

Landw Wbl (Muenchen) — Landwirtschaftliches Wochenblatt (Muenchen)

LANE — Labrador Nor-Eastern

Lang — Language

LangA — Language and Automation

LangAb — Language and Language Behavior Abstracts

Lang Arts — Language Arts

Lang and C — Language and Culture [*Hokkaido University*]

Lang and Commun — Language and Communication

Langenbeck — Langenbecks Archiv fuer Chirurgie

Langenbecks Arch Chir — Langenbecks Archiv fuer Chirurgie

LangL — Language Learning

Lang & L — Language and Literature

Lang Learn — Language Learning

Lang Mod — Langues Modernes

LangMono — Language Monographs

LangQ — Language Quarterly

Lang R — Language Research

LangS — Language Sciences

LangS — Language and Style

Lang & S — Language and Style

Lang Soc — Language in Society [*London*]

Lang & Speech — Language and Speech

Lang Speech — Language and Speech

Lang Speech & Hearing Serv Sch — Language, Speech, and Hearing Services in Schools

Lang Speech Hear Serv Sch — Language, Speech, and Hearing Services in Schools

Lang Style — Language and Style

LangTAb — Language Teaching Abstracts [*Later, Language Teaching and Linguistics Abstracts*]

Lang Teach & Ling Abstr — Language Teaching and Linguistics Abstracts

LanM — Langues Modernes

Lantbrhogsk Annlr — Lantbrukshogskolans Annaler

Lantbrhogsk Meddn — Lantbrukshogskolans Meddelanden

Lantbruks-Hoegsk Ann — Lantbruks-Hoegskolans Annaler

Lantbrukshogsk Ann — Lantbrukshogskolans Annaler

Lantbrukshogsk Husdjursforsoksanst Medd — Lantbrukshogskolan Husdjursforsoksanstalten Meddelande

Lantbrukshogsk Meddel — Lantbrukshogskolans Meddelanden

Lantbrukshogsk Medd Ser A — Lantbrukshogskolans Meddelanden. Series A

Lantbrukshogsk Medd Ser B — Lantbrukshogskolans Meddelanden. Series B

Lantbrukstidskr Stockholms Lan Stad — Lantbrukstidskrift foer Stockholms Lan och Stad

Lanterne Med — Lanterne Medicale

Lantm Andelsfolk — Lantman och Andelsfolk

LANZA — Landarzt

LA Off Public Works Water Resour Basic Rec Rep — Louisiana. Office of Public Works. Water Resources. Basic Records Report

LaPar — La Parisienne

LA Phil — Los Angeles Philharmonic. Program Notes

LA Phil Sym Mag — Los Angeles Philharmonic Orchestra. Symphony Magazine

Lapidary Jour — Lapidary Journal

LA Plant Sugar Manuf — Louisiana. Planter and Sugar Manufacturer

LAPLD — Landscape Planning

Lap Lemb Penelit Kehutanan — Laporan. Lembaga Penelitian Kehutanan

LAPR — Latin America Political Report

LAQ — Livres et Auteurs Quebecois

LaR — La Rassegna

LAR — Library Association. Record

L Arb — Linguistische Arbeiten

LARC Rep — LARC Reports

LARFEN — Agricultural Research Organization. Department of Forestry. Ilanot Leaflet

LARR — Latin American Research Review

LA Rural Econ — Louisiana Rural Economist. Louisiana State University. Department of Agriculture and Agribusiness

LARYA — Laryngoscope

Laryngol Rhinol Otol — Laryngologie, Rhinologie, Otologie

Laryngol Rhinol Otol Ihre Grenzeb — Laryngologie, Rhinologie, Otologie, und Ihre Grenzebiete

Laryngol Rhinol Otol (Stuttg) — Laryngologie, Rhinologie, Otologie (Stuttgart)

Laryngoscop — Laryngoscope

LaS — Louisiana Studies

Laser und Angew Strahlentech — Laser und Angewandte Strahlentechnik

Laser Appl Med Biol — Laser Applications in Medicine and Biology

Laser & Elektro-Opt — Laser und Elektro-Optik

Laser Elektro-Opt — Laser und Elektro-Optik

Laser Foc — Laser Focus Buyers Guide

Laser Focus Fiberoptic Commun — Laser Focus with Fiberoptic Communications

Laser Focus Fiberoptic Technol — Laser Focus with Fiberoptic Technology

Laser Opt Non Conv — Lasers et Optique Non Conventionelle [*France*]

Laser Optoelektron — Laser und Optoelektronik

Laser und Optoelektron — Laser und Optoelektronik

Laser Rep — Laser Report

Laser Rev — Laser Review

Laser & Unconv Opt J — Laser and Unconventional Optics Journal

LASH — List of Australian Subject Headings

LASIE — Information Bulletin. Library Automated Systems Information Exchange

LASORS — Literature Analysis System. Office of Road Safety

LASRB — Laser Review

LA State Dep Conserv Geol Bull — Louisiana State Department of Conservation. Geological Bulletin

LA State Med Soc J — Louisiana State Medical Society. Journal

LA State Univ Agric Mech Coll Eng Exp Stn Repr Ser — Louisiana State University and Agricultural and Mechanical College. Engineering Experiment Station. Reprint Series

LA State Univ and Agr Mech Coll Tech Rept — Louisiana State University and Agricultural and Mechanical College. Technical Reports

LA State Univ Div Eng Res Bull — Louisiana State University. Division of Engineering Research. Bulletin

LA State Univ Div Eng Res Eng — Louisiana State University. Division of Engineering Research. Engineering Research Bulletin

LA State Univ Div Eng Res Eng Res Bull — Louisiana State University. Division of Engineering Research. Engineering Research Bulletin.

LA State Univ Eng Expt Sta Bull Studies Phys Sci Ser — Louisiana State University. Engineering Experiment Station. Bulletin. Studies. Physical Science Series

LA State Univ Proc Annu For Symp — Louisiana State University. Proceedings. Annual Forestry Symposium

LA State Univ Stud Biol Sci Ser — Louisiana State University. Studies. Biological Science Series

LA State Univ Stud Coastal Stud Ser — Louisiana State University. Studies. Coastal Studies Series

LA St Exp Sta G Agr LA — Louisiana State Experiment Stations. Geology and Agriculture of Louisiana

LA Stud — Louisiana Studies

LA St Univ An Rp Sup — Louisiana State University. Annual Report of the Superintendent

Las Vegas Rev J — Las Vegas Review. Journal
LaT — La Torre
LAT — Latin America Regional Reports
Lat — Latomus
LatAm — Index to Latin American Periodicals
Lat Am — Latin America
Lat Amer — Latin American Perspectives
Lat Amer Mg — Latin American Monographs
Lat Am Ind — Latin American Indian Literatures
Lat Am Lit — Latin American Literary Review
Lat Am Mus — Latin American Music Review/Revista de Musica
　　Latinoamericana
Lat Am Res — Latin American Research Review
Lat Am Res R — Latin American Research Review
Lat Am Thea — Latin American Theater Review
LATBR — Los Angeles Times Book Review
Lateinam Anders — Lateinamerika Anders
Lateinam-Studien — Lateinamerika-Studien
LATIA — Landbouwkundig Tijdschrift
Latin Am and Empire Rept — NACLA's [*North American Congress on Latin
　　America*] Latin America and Empire Report
Latin Amer — Latinskaja Amerika
Latin Amer P — Latin American Perspectives
Latin Amer Perspect — Latin American Perspectives
Latin Amer Res R — Latin American Research Review
Latin Am Perspectives — Latin American Perspectives
Latin Am Research R — Latin American Research Review
Latin Am Res R — Latin American Research Review
Latin Am Times — Latin American Times
Latinsk Amer — Latinskaja Amerika
Latomus — Latomus; Revue d'Etudes Latines
LATR — Latin American Theater Review
La Trobe Library J — La Trobe Library Journal
LatT — Latin Teaching
Latv Ent — Latvijas Entomologs
Latv Fil Vses Ova Pochvovedov Sb Tr — Latviiskii Filial Vsesoyuznogo
　　Obshchestva Pochvovedov Sbornik Trudov
Latviisk Gos Univ Ucen Zap — Latviiskii Gosudarstvennyi Universitet Imeni
　　Petra Stucki Ucenyi Zapiski
Latviisk Mat Ezegodnik — Latviiskii Matematiceskii Ezegodnik
Latvijas PSR Zinatn Akad Vestis — Latvijas PSR Zinatnu Akademijas. Vestis
Latvijas PSR Zinatn Akad Vestis Fiz Tehn Zinatn Ser — Latvijas PSR Zinatnu
　　Akademijas. Vestis. Fizikas un Tehnisko Zinatnu Serija
Latvijas Valsts Univ Zinatn Raksti — PSRS Augstakas Izglitibas Ministrija.
　　Petera Stuckas Latvijas Valsts Universitate. Zinatniskie Raksti
Latv Lauksaimn Akad Raktsi — Latvijas Lauksaimniecibas Akademijas Raktsi
Latv Lopkopibas Vet Inst Raksti — Latvijas Lopkopibas un Veterinarijas
　　Zinatniski Petnieciska Instituta Raksti
Latv Lopkopibas Vet Zinat Petnieciska Inst Raksti — Latvijas Lopkopibas un
　　Veterinarijas Zinatniski Petnieciska Instituta Raksti
Latv Mat Ezheg — Latvijskij Matematicheskij Ezhegodnik
Latv Mat Ezhegodnik — Latviiskii Gosudarstvennyi Universitet Imeni Petra
　　Stucki Latviiskii Matematiceskii Ezhegodnik
Latv PSR Zinat Akad Biol Inst Dzivnieku Fiziol Sekt Raksti — Latvijas PSR
　　Zinatnu Akademija. Biologijas Instituts. Dzivnieku Fiziologijas Sektora
　　Raksti
Latv PSR Zinat Akad Biol Inst Raksti — Latvijas PSR Zinatnu Akademija
　　Biologijas Instituta Raksti
Latv PSR Zinat Akad Kim Inst Zinat Raksti — Latvijas PSR Zinatnu
　　Akademija Kimijas Instituta Zinatniskie Raksti
Latv PSR Zinat Akad Mezsaimn Probl Koksnes Kim Inst Raksti — Latvijas
　　PSR Zinatnu Akademija Mezsaimniecibas Problemu un Koksnes
　　Kimijas Instituta Raksti
Latv PSR Zinat Akad Vestis — Latvijas PSR Zinatnu Akademijas. Vestis
　　[*Riga*]
Latv PSR Zinat Akad Vestis Fiz Teh Ser — Latvijas PSR Zinatnu Akademijas.
　　Vestis. Fizikas un Tehnisko Zinatnu Serija
Latv PSR Zinat Akad Vestis Fiz Teh Zinat Ser — Latvijas PSR Zinatnu
　　Akademijas. Vestis. Fizikas un Tehnisko Zinatnu Serija
Latv PSR Zinat Akad Vestis Kim Ser — Latvijas PSR Zinatnu Akademijas.
　　Vestis. Kimijas Serija
Latv Univ Raksti Kim Fak Ser — Latvijas Universitates Raksti. Kimijas
　　Fakultates Serijas
Latv Univ Raksti Lauksaimn Fak Ser — Latvijas Universitates Raksti.
　　Lauksaimniecibas Fakultates Serija
Latv Univ Raksti Mat Dabas Zinat Fak Ser — Latvijas Universitates Raksti.
　　Matematikas un Dabas Zinatnu. Fakultates Serija
Latv Univ Raksti Med Fak Ser — Latvijas Universitates Raksti. Medicinas
　　Fakultates Serija
Latv Valsts Univ Bot Darza Raksti — Latvijas Valsts Universitates Botaniska
　　Darza Raksti
Laund News — Laundry News
Laundry Dry Clean J Can — Laundry and Dry Cleaning Journal of Canada
Lau R — Laurel Review
Laval Med — Laval Medical
Laval Theol — Laval Theologique et Philosophique

Laval Theol Phil — Laval Theologique et Philosophique
Laval Univ For Res Found Contrib — Laval University Forest Research
　　Foundation. Contributions
Lav Arroz — Lavoura Arrozeira
Lav Ist Anat Istol Patol Perugia — Lavori. Istituto di Anatomia e Istologia
　　Patologica. Universita degli Studi di Perugia
Lav Ist Anat Istol Patol Univ Studi (Perugia) — Lavori. Istituto di Anatomia e
　　Istologia Patologica. Universita degli Studi (Perugia)
Lav Ist Bot Giardino Colon Palermo — Lavori. Istituto Botanico Giardino
　　Coloniale di Palermo
LAVMA — Lavoro e Medicina
Lav Med — Lavoro e Medicina
Lav Neuropsichiatr — Lavoro Neuropsichiatrico
Lavori Ist Anat Istol Patol Univ Studi (Perugia) — Lavori. Istituto di Anatomia
　　e Istologia Patologica. Universita degli Studi (Perugia) [*Italy*]
LavTP — Laval Theologique et Philosophique
Lav Um — Lavoro Umano
Lav Um Suppl — Lavoro Umano. Supplemento [*Italy*]
Law — Alabama Lawyer
Law — London Law Magazine
Law Am — Lawyer of the Americas
Law Amer — Lawyer of the Americas
Law Americas — Lawyer of the Americas
Lawasia CLB — Lawasia Commercial Law Bulletin
Lawasia (NS) — Lawasia (New Series)
LA Water Resour Res Inst Bull — Louisiana Water Resources Research
　　Institute. Bulletin
Law Bul — Law Bulletin
Law & Comp Tech — Law and Computer Technology
Law & Comput Tech — Law and Computer Technology
Law & Comput Technol — Law and Computer Technology
Law and Con Pr — Law and Contemporary Problems
Law & Contemp Prob — Law and Contemporary Problems
Law Contemp Probl Ser — Law and Contemporary Problems Series
Law Cont Pr — Law and Contemporary Problems
Law Council Newsl — Law Council Newsletter
Law Dig — Law Digest
LAWFA — Landwirtschaftliche Forschung
Law Guild Rev — Lawyers Guild Review
Law and Housing J — Law and Housing Journal
Law and Hum Behav — Law and Human Behavior
Law Inst J — Law Institute Journal
Law & Int Aff — Law and International Affairs
Law J — Lawyers Journal
Law Ja — Law in Japan
Law Jour — Law Journal
Law and Just — Law and Justice
Law Lib — Law Librarian
Law Lib J — Law Library Journal
Law Libn — Law Librarian
Law Libr J — Law Library Journal
Law Librn — Law Librarian
Law & L N — Lawyer and Law Notes
Law Med Health Care — Law, Medicine, and Health Care
Law Med & Health Care — Law, Medicine, and Health Care
Law Med J — Lawyer's Medical Journal
Law N — Law Notes
Lawn Gard Mark — Lawn and Garden Marketing
Lawn Gardn — Lawn and Garden Marketing
Law Off Econ & Management — Law Office Economics and Management
Law Off Econ and Mgt — Law Office Economics and Management
Law Off Information Service — Law Office Information Service
Law Phil — Law and Philosophy
Law and Policy Internat Bus — Law and Policy in International Business
Law and Pol Int Bus — Law and Policy in International Business
Law & Pol Int'l Bus — Law and Policy in International Business
Law and Poly Intl Bus — Law and Policy in International Business
Law and Poly Q — Law and Policy Quarterly
Law and Psych Rev — Law and Psychology Review
Law Q — Law Quarterly Review
Law Q R — Law Quarterly Review
Law Q Rev — Law Quarterly Review
Law Quar Rev — Law Quarterly Review
Law Quart — Law Quarterly Review
Law Quart R — Law Quarterly Review
Law Quart Rev — Law Quarterly Review
Law R — Law Review
LAWR — Weekly Report (Latin American)
Lawrence Livermore Lab Rep — Lawrence Livermore Laboratory. Report
Law Rev — Law Review
Law Soc Bull — Law Society. Bulletin [*South Australia*]
Law Soc Gaz — Law Society's Gazette
Law and Society R — Law and Society Review
Law Soc J — Law Society. Journal
Law & Soc Ord — Law and the Social Order
Law & Soc Order — Law and the Social Order

Law Soc Prob — Law and Social Problems [*Pondicherry*]
Law Soc R — Law and Society Review
Law & Soc R — Law and Society Review
Law & Soc Rev — Law and Society Review
Law Socy Gaz — Law Society. Gazette
Law Socy J — Law Society. Journal
Law and Socy Rev — Law and Society Review
Law State — Law and State
Law Tcher — Law Teacher
Law Tech — Law/Technology
Law/Technol — Law/Technology
Law Title Guar Funds News — Lawyers Title Guaranty Funds News
Lawyers Med J — Lawyer's Medical Journal
Lawy & LN — Lawyer and Law Notes
Lawy Med J — Lawyer's Medical Journal
La-Yaaran For Israel For Assoc — La-Ya'aran/The Forester. Israel Forestry
 Association
LB — Leuvense Bijdragen [*Bijblad*]
LB — Levende Billeder
LB — Linguistica Biblica
LBANA — Laboratory Animals
LBASA — Laboratory Animal Science
LBB — Leuvense Bijdragen (Bijblad)
LBC News — Law Book Company Ltd. Newsletter
LB Cos Indust Arb Serv — Law Book Company's Industrial Arbitration Service
LB Cos Practical Forms — Law Book Company's Practical Forms and
 Precedents
LB Cos Tax Serv — Law Book Company's Taxation Service
L Bella — Lingua Bella
LBer — Linguistische Berichte
LB Free P — Long Beach Free Press
LBIB — Linguistica Biblica
LBj — Leksykohraficny j Bjuleten
LBL — Literaturblatt fuer Germanische und Romanische Philologie
L Bl — Living Blues
LBL Comput Cent Newsl — LBL [*Lawrence Berkeley Laboratory*] Computer
 Center Newsletter
LBLJA — Labor Law Journal
LBL Newsmag — LBL [*Lawrence Berkeley Laboratory*] Newsmagazine
 [*United States*]
LbR — Limba Romana [*Bucuresti*]
LBR — Lloyd's Bank Review
LBR — Luso-Brazilian Review
Lbr Hist (Australia) — Labour History (Australia)
Lbr Hist (US) — Labor History (United States)
Lbr Studies J — Labor Studies Journal
LBT — Landbouwkundig Tijdschrift
LBWTAP — Food Science and Technology [*Zurich*]
LC — Letterature Contemporanea
LC — Library Chronicle
LCB — Centraal Bureau voor de Statistiek. Bibliotheek en
 Documentatiedienst. Lijst van Aanwinsten
LCC (NSW) — Land Appeal Court Cases (New South Wales)
LCCP — Linguistic Circle of Canberra. Publications
LCD — Litterarisches Centralblatt fuer Deutschland
LCFBA — Lahey Clinic Foundation. Bulletin
LCh — Liberte Chretienne
LCHP — Lancaster County Historical Society. Papers
LChQ — Lutheran Church Quarterly
LChr — Logotechnika Chronika
LChR — [*The*] Lutheran Church Review
LCHS — Lancaster County Historical Society. Papers
LC Inf Bul — United States. Library of Congress. Information Bulletin
LC Listy Cukrov — LC. Listy Cukrovarnicke
LCM — Literary Criterion (Mysore)
LCMF — Lettre aux Communautes de la Mission de France
LCN — Law Council Newsletter
L & Comp Technol — Law and Computer Technology
L & Contemp Prob — Law and Contemporary Problems
L and Contemp Probl — Law and Contemporary Problems
LCP — Latinitas Christianorum Primaeva
LCP — Law and Contemporary Problems
LCPC Note Inf Tech — Laboratoire Central des Ponts et Chaussees. Note
 d'Information Technique
LC Pract — LC [*Liquid Chromatography*] in Practice
LCQ — Lutheran Church Quarterly
LCQJCA — Library of Congress. Quarterly Journal of Current Acquisitions
LCrit — Literary Criterion [*Mysore*]
LCSCF — Libera Cattedra di Storia della Civilta Fiorentina
LCUP — Library Chronicle. University of Pennsylvania
LCUT — Library Chronicle. University of Texas
LD — Language Dissertations
LD — Legislative Digest. Forecast and Review [*Anchorage, AK*]
LD — Literary Digest
LD — Lithuanian Days
LD — Lituanistikos Darbai [*Chicago*]

LD — Livres Disponibles
LDAA — Lexikographikon Deltion Akademias Athenon
LDA J — Louisiana Dental Association. Journal
LDBMA — Landbouwmechanisatie
LdD — Letras de Deusto
LDG — Korte Berichten over Handel, Ambacht, Dienstverlening, Toerisme,
 Middenbedrijf, en Kleinbedrijf
LDL — Letopis Doma Literatorov
LdM — Lautbibliothek der Deutschen Mundarten
LDM — Lingue del Mondo
LDO — Documentatiecentrum voor Overheidspersoneel. Literatuuroverzicht
LdP — Livros de Portugal
LdProv — Lettore di Provincia
Le — Asia-Philippines Leader
LE — Lagina Ephemeris Aegyptiaca et Universa
LE — Land Economics
LE — Learning Exchange
LE — Liberal Education
LE — Literarisches Echo
Lea — Leadership
LEA — Leathergoods
Lead Abstr — Lead Abstracts
Lead Res Dig — Lead Research Digest
Leafl Amat Ent Soc — Leaflet. Amateur Entomologist's Society
Leafl Anim Prod Div Kenya Minist Agric — Leaflet. Animal Production
 Division. Kenya Ministry of Agriculture
Leafl Br Isles Bee Breeders Ass — Leaflet. British Isles Bee Breeders'
 Association
Leafl Calif Agric Exp Stn — Leaflet. California Agricultural Experiment
 Station
Leafl Calif Agric Exp Stn Ext Serv — Leaflet. California Agricultural
 Experiment Station. Extension Service
Leafl Coop Ext Serv Univ GA — Leaflet. Cooperative Extension Service.
 University of Georgia
Leafl Coop Ext Univ Calif — Leaflet. Cooperative Extension. University of
 California
Leafl Dep Agric Tech Instruct Ire — Leaflet. Department of Agriculture and
 Technical Instruction for Ireland
Leaflet US Dep Agric — Leaflet. United States Department of Agriculture
Leafl Ext Serv Utah St Univ — Leaflet. Extension Service. Utah State
 University
Leafl Forests Dep West Aust — Leaflet. Forests Department. Western
 Australia
Leafl For Timb Bur — Leaflet. Forestry and Timber Bureau
Leafl Israel Agric Res Organ Div For (Ilanot) — Leaflet. Israel Agricultural
 Research Organization. Division of Forestry (Ilanot)
Leafl L Tex Agric Ext Serv Tex AM Univ Syst — Leaflet L. Texas Agricultural
 Extension Service. Texas A & M University System
Leafl Minist Agric (Nth Ire) — Leaflet. Ministry of Agriculture (Northern
 Ireland)
Leafl Montreal Bot Gdn — Leaflet. Montreal Botanical Garden
Leafl Okla State Univ Agr Appl Sci Agr Ext Serv — Leaflet. Oklahoma State
 University of Agriculture and Applied Science. Agricultural Extension
 Service
Leafl PA State Univ Ext Serv — Leaflet. Cooperative Extension Service.
 Pennsylvania State University
Leafl Rutgers State Univ Coll Agr Environ Sci Ext Serv — Leaflet. Rutgers
 State University. College of Agriculture and Environmental Science.
 Extension Service
Leafl Univ Calif Coop Ext Serv — Leaflet. University of California.
 Cooperative Extension Service
Leafl Univ Hawaii Coop Ext Serv — Leaflet. University of Hawaii. Cooperative
 Extension Service
Leafl US Dep Agric — Leaflet. United States Department of Agriculture
Leafl VBBA — Leaflet. Village Bee Breeders Association
Leafl West Bot — Leaflets of Western Botany
League Exch — League Exchange
League Int Food Educ Newsl — League for International Food Education.
 Newsletter
League Nations Bull Health Org — League of Nations. Bulletin of the Health
 Organization
Learn — Learning
Learn Exch — Learning Exchange
Learn & Motiv — Learning and Motivation
Learn Motiv — Learning and Motivation
Learn Today — Learning Today
LEAT — Lea Transit Compendium
Leather Chem — Leather Chemistry [*Japan*]
Leather Sci (Madras) — Leather Science (Madras)
Leath Sci — Leather Science
Leath Shoe — Leather and Shoes
Leaves Paint Res Noteb — Leaves from a Paint Research Notebook
Leban Med J — Lebanese Medical Journal
Leban Pharm J — Lebanese Pharmaceutical Journal
Leben Erde — Lebendige Erde
Lebensm Ernaehrung — Lebensmittel und Ernaehrung

Lebensm Ind — Lebensmittel-Industrie
Lebensmittelchem Gerichtl Chem — Lebensmittelchemie und Gerichtliche Chemie
Lebensmittelchemie u Gerichtl Chemie — Lebensmittelchemie und Gerichtliche Chemie
Lebensmittelchem Lebensmittelqual — Lebensmittelchemie, Lebensmittelqualitaet
Lebensmittel-Ind — Lebensmittel-Industrie
Lebensm-Wiss Technol — Lebensmittel-Wissenschaft Technologie
Lebensversicher Med — Lebensversicherungs Medizin
Leben Umwelt (Aarau) — Leben und Umwelt (Aarau)
Leben Umwelt (Wiesb) — Leben und Umwelt (Wiesbaden)
Leber Mag D — Leber Magen Darm
Leb Pharm J — Lebanese Pharmaceutical Journal
LEC — Land Economics
LEC — Les Etudes Classiques
LeC — Lingua e Cultura
Lech Kurortakh Zabaik — Lechenie na Kurortakh Zabaikal'ya
Lech Kurortakh Zabaikalya — Lechenie na Kurortakh Zabaikal'ya
Lec Ser Div Appl Geomech CSIRO — Lecture Series. Division of Applied Geomechanics. Commonwealth Scientific and Industrial Research Organisation
Lect — Lecturas
Lect Biblioth — Lecture et Bibliotheques
Lect Cent Ass Beekrps — Lecture to Central Association of Bee-Keepers
Lect Coral Gables Conf Fundam Interact High Energy — Lectures from the Coral Gables Conference on Fundamental Interactions at High Energy
Lect Hall Chem Pharmacol — Lecture Hall for Chemistry and Pharmacology [*Japan*]
Lect Int Symp Migr — Lectures. International Symposium on Migration
Lect Math Life Sci — Lectures on Mathematics in the Life Sciences
Lect Monogr Rep R Inst Chem — Lectures, Monographs, and Reports. Royal Institute of Chemistry
Lect Notes Biomath — Lecture Notes in Biomathematics
Lect Notes Chem — Lecture Notes in Chemistry
Lect Notes Comput Sci — Lecture Notes in Computer Science
Lect Notes Div Tech Conf Soc Plast Eng Vinyl Plast Div — Lecture Notes Division. Technical Conference. Society of Plastics Engineers. Vinyl Plastics Divisions
Lect Notes Math — Lecture Notes in Mathematics
Lect Notes Phys — Lecture Notes in Physics
Lect Notes Suppl Phys — Lecture Notes and Supplements in Physics
Lect Sci Basis Med — Lectures on the Scientific Basis of Medicine
Lect Theor Phys — Lectures in Theoretical Physics
Lecturas Econ — Lecturas de Economia
Lecture Notes in Biomath — Lecture Notes in Biomathematics
Lecture Notes in Chem — Lecture Notes in Chemistry [*Berlin*]
Lecture Notes in Comput Sci — Lecture Notes in Computer Science
Lecture Notes in Control and Information Sci — Lecture Notes in Control and Information Sciences
Lecture Notes in Econom and Math Systems — Lecture Notes in Economics and Mathematical Systems
Lecture Notes in Math — Lecture Notes in Mathematics
Lecture Notes in Med Inform — Lecture Notes in Medical Informatics
Lecture Notes in Phys — Lecture Notes in Physics
Lecture Notes in Pure and Appl Math — Lecture Notes in Pure and Applied Mathematics
Lecture Notes in Statist — Lecture Notes in Statistics
Lecture Notes and Suppl in Phys — Lecture Notes and Supplements in Physics
Lectures in Appl Math — Lectures in Applied Mathematics
Lectures LSUC — Special Lectures. Law Society of Upper Canada
Lectures in Math — Lectures in Mathematics [*Tokyo*]
Lectures Math Life Sci — Lectures on Mathematics in the Life Sciences
LED — Literatuuroverzicht Medezeggenschap
LEE — Leefmilieu
Leeds G As Tr — Leeds Geological Association. Transactions
Leeds Northr Tech J — Leeds and Northrup Technical Journal
LeedsSE — Leeds Studies in English
Lee Found Nutr Res Rep — Lee Foundation for Nutritional Research. Report
Leeuwenhoek Ned Tijdschr — Leeuwenhoek Nederlandsch Tijdschrift
Leg Aid Rev — Legal Aid Review
Legal Aid Rev — Legal Aid Review
Legal Aspects Med Prac — Legal Aspects of Medical Practice
Legal Econ — Legal Economics
Legal Educ Newsl — Legal Education Newsletter
Legal Med Ann — Legal Medicine Annual
Legal Med Q — Legal Medical Quarterly
Legal Res J — Legal Research Journal
Legal Serv Bull — Legal Service Bulletin
Legal Service Bul — Legal Service Bulletin
Legal Stud — Legal Studies
Legal Times Wash — Legal Times of Washington
Leg Aspects Med Pract — Legal Aspects of Medical Practice
Leg Ec — Legal Economics
Leg Econ — Legal Economics
Leg Exec — Legal Executive

Legge — Legge's Supreme Court Cases
Legisl Stud Quart — Legislative Studies Quarterly
Legis Roundup — Legislative Roundup
Legka Tekst Promst — Legka i Tekstilna Promislovist
Legk Pishch Promst Podmoskov'ya — Legkaya i Pishchevaya Promyshlennost Podmoskov'ya
Legk Promst (Kaz) — Legkaya Promyshlennost (Kazakhstana)
Legk Promst (Kiev) — Legkaya Promyshlennost (Kiev)
Legk Promst (Moscow) — Legkaya Promyshlennost (Moscow)
Leg Med — Legal Medicine
Leg Med Annu — Legal Medicine Annual [*Later, Legal Medicine*]
Leg Med Annual — Legal Medicine Annual
Leg Med Q — Legal Medicine Quarterly
Leg Notes and View Q — Legal Notes and Viewpoints Quarterly
LegPer — Index to Legal Periodicals
Leg Ref Serv Q — Legal Reference Services Quarterly
Leg Res J — Legal Research Journal
Leg Ser B — Legal Service Bulletin
Leg Serv Bull — Legal Service Bulletin
Leg Stud Q — Legislative Studies Quarterly
Lehigh Alumni Bull — Lehigh Alumni Bulletin
Lehrb Allg Geogr — Lehrbuch der Allgemeinen Geographie
Lehrb Anthropol — Lehrbuch der Anthropologie
Lehrb Handb Ingenieurwiss — Lehr- und Handbuecher der Ingenieurwissenschaften
Lehrbuecher Monograph Geb Exakten Wissensch Math Reihe — Lehrbuecher und Monographien aus dem Gebiete der Exakten Wissenschaften [*LMW*]. Mathematische Reihe
Lei — Leitura
Leica Fotogr (Engl Ed) — Leica Fotografie (English Edition)
Leichhardt Hist J — Leichhardt Historical Journal
Leidsche Geol Meded — Leidsche Geologische Mededeelingen [*Later, Leidse Geologische Mededelingen*]
Leidse Geol Meded — Leidse Geologische Mededelingen
Leiegouw — Verslagen en Mededeelingen van de Leiegouw
Leipz Monatsschr Text Ind — Leipziger Monatsschrifter fuer Textil-Industrie
Leis Hour — Leisure Hour
Leis Stud — Leisure Studies
Leitfaden Elektrotech — Leitfaeden der Elektrotechnik
Leitfaeden Angew Math Mech — Leitfaeden der Angewandten Mathematik und Mechanik
Leitz-Mitt Wissen Technik — Leitz-Mitteilungen fuer Wissenschaft und Technik
Leitz-Mitt Wiss & Tech — Leitz-Mitteilungen fuer Wissenschaft und Technik
Leitz Sci and Tech Inf — Leitz Scientific and Technical Information
Lek Obz — Lekarsky Obzor
Lek Pr — Lekarske Prace
Lek Sredstva Dal'nego Vostoka — Lekarstvennye Sredstva Dal'nego Vostoka
Lek Syrevye Resur Irkutsk Obl — Lekarstvennye i Syrevye Resursy Irkutskoi Oblasti
Lek Veda Zahr — Lekarska Veda v Zahranici
Lek Wojsk — Lekarz Wojskowy [*Poland*]
Lek Zpr — Lekarsky Zpravy
Lek Zpr Lek Fak Karlovy Univ Hradci Kralove — Lekarske Zpravy Lekarske Fakulty Karlovy University v Hradci Kralove
Leland Stanford Jr Univ Pub — Leland Stanford Junior University. Publications
LEM — Le Matin [*Morocco*]
LEMIT An — LEMIT [*Laboratorio de Ensayo de Materiales e Investigaciones Tecnologicas*] Anales
LEMIT An Ser 2 — LEMIT [*Laboratorio de Ensayo de Materiales e Investigaciones Tecnologicas*] Anales. Serie 2
LeMo — Letterature Moderne
LEN — Land and Environment Notes
LenauA — Lenau Almanach
Lenauf — Lenau Forum
LenC — Lenguaje y Ciencias
Lend a H — Lend a Hand
Lending LF — Lending Law Forum
Lend LF — Lending Law Forum
LengM — Lenguas Modernas
Leninabad Gos Ped Inst Ucen Zap — Leninabadskii Gosudarstvennyi Pedagogiceskii Institut Ucenye Zapiski
Leningrad Gorn Inst Zap — Leningrad Gornyy Institut Zapiski
Leningrad Gos Ped Inst Ucen Zap — Leningradskii Gosudarstvennyi Pedagogiceskii Institut Imeni A. I. Gercena Ucenye Zapiski
Leningrad Gos Univ Ucen Zap Ser Mat Nauk — Leningradskii Gosudarstvennyi Ordena Lenina Universitet Imeni A. A. Zdanova Ucenye Zapiski Serija Matematiceskih Nauk
Leningrad Inz-Ekonom Inst Trudy — Leningradskii Inzenerno-Ekonomiceskii Institut Imeni Pal'miro Tol'jatti Trudy
Leningrad Inz-Stroitel Inst Sb Trudov — Leningradskii Inzhenerno-Stroitel'skii Institut Sbornik Trudov

Leningrad Meh Inst Sb Trudov (LMI) — Leningradskii Mekhaniceskii Institut Sbornik Trudov (LMI)
Leningrad Politehn Inst Trudy — Leningradskii Politehniceskii Institut Imeni M. I. Kalinina Trudy LPI
Leningrad Univ Vestn Geol Geogr — Leningradskii Universitet Vestnik Geologiya i Geografiya
Leningr Inst Sov Torg Sb Tr — Leningradskii Institut Sovetskoi Torgovli Sbornik Trudov
Leningr Inst Tochn Mekh Opt Tr — Leningradskii Institut Tochnoi Mekhaniki i Optiki Trudy
Leningr Inzh Mezhvuz Temat Sb Tr — Leningradskii Inzhenerno-Stroitel'nyi Institut Mezhvuzovskii Tematicheskii Sbornik Trudov
Leningr Inzh Stroit Inst Mezhvuz Temat Sb — Leningradskii Inzhenerno-Stroitel'nyi Institut Mezhvuzovskii Tematicheskii Sbornik
Leningr Inzh Stroit Inst Sb Tr — Leningradskii Inzhenerno-Stroitel'nyi Institut Sbornik Trudov
Leningr Mekh Inst Sb Tr — Leningradskii Mekhanicheskii Institut Sbornik Trudov
Leningr Met Zavod Tr — Leningradskii Metallicheskii Zavod Trudy
Leningr Nauchno Issled Inst Gematol Pereliv Krovi Sb Tr — Leningradskii Nauchno-Issledovatel'skii Institut Gematologii i Perelivaniya Krovi Sbornik Trudov
Leningr Nauchno Issled Inst Lesn Khoz Sb Nauchn Tr — Leningradskii Nauchno-Issledovatel'skii Institut Lesnogo Khozyaistva Sbornik Nauchnykh Trudov
Leningr Nauchno Issled Konstr Inst Khim Mashinostr Tr — Leningradskii Nauchno-Issledovatel'skii i Konstruktorskii Institut Khimicheskogo Mashinostroeniya Trudy
Leningr Tekhnol Inst Tsellyul Bum Promsti Tr — Leningradskii Tekhnologicheskii Institut Tsellyulozno-Bumazhnoi Promyshlennosti Trudy
Len Konop — Len i Konopliya
Lenzinger Ber — Lenzinger Berichte
Leo — Leonardo
Leo Baeck Inst Jews Germ Yrbk — Leo Baeck Institute of Jews from Germany. Yearbook
Leon — Leonardo
LEP — Latin America Weekly Report
Lep Rev — Leprosy Review
Lepr India — Leprosy in India
Leprosy Rev — Leprosy Review
Lepr Rev — Leprosy Review
LEREA — Leprosy Review
Les — Lesonenu. Quarterly of Hebrew
LeS — Lingua e Stile [Bologna]
Les Khoz — Lesnoe Khozyaistvo
Lesnaya Prom — Lesnaya Promyshlennost
Lesn Bum Derevoobrab Promst (Kiev) — Lesnaya Bumazhnaya i Derevoobrabatyvayushchaya Promyshlennost (Kiev)
Lesn Cas — Lesnicky Casopis
Lesn Hoz — Lesnoe Hozjajstvo
Lesnoe Khoz — Lesnoe Khozyaistvo
Lesn Pr — Lesnicka Prace
Lesn Prace — Lesnicka Prace
Lesn Prom — Lesnaja Promyslennost
Lesn Prom-st — Lesnaya Promyshlennost [USSR]
Lesn Zh (Archangel USSR) — Lesnoi Zhurnal (Archangel, USSR)
Lesokhim Promst — Lesokhimicheskaya Promyshlennost
Lesoved — Lesovedenie
Lesovod Agrolesomelior — Lesovodstvo i Agrolesomelioratsiia
Lesovod Agrolesomelior Resp Mezhved Temat Sb — Lesovodstvo i Agrolesomelioratsiya Respublikanskii Mezhvedomstvennyi Tematicheskii Sbornik
L'Esprit — L'Esprit Createur
Les Prom — Lesnaya Promyshlennost
LEst — Le Lingue Estere
Les Zh — Lesnoi Zhurnal
Let — Letteratura
LetD — Letras de Deusto
Let It — Lettere Italiane
LetM — Lettres Modernes
LetMs — Letopis Matice Srpske
LetN — Lettres Nouvelles
Letopisi Khig-Epidemiol Inst — Letopisi na Khigienno-Epidemiologichnite Instituti
Letopisi Khig-Epidemiol Sluzhba — Letopisi na Khigienno-Epidemiologichnata Sluzhba [Bulgaria]
Letopis Jschr Serb Volksforsch — Letopis Jahresschrift des Instituts fuer Serbische Volksforschung
Letop Nauc Rad Poljopriv Fak Novi Sad — Letopis Naucnih Radova. Poljoprivredni Fakultet. Novi Sad
Let Rom — Lettres Romanes
Lett — Letteratura
Lett Appl and Eng Sci — Letters in Applied and Engineering Sciences
Lett Appl Eng Sci — Letters in Applied and Engineering Sciences
Lett Heat Mass Transf — Letters in Heat and Mass Transfer

Lett Heat Mass Transfer — Letters in Heat and Mass Transfer
Lett Ital — Lettere Italiane
Lett Math Phys — Letters in Mathematical Physics
Lett Mod — Letterature Moderne
Lett Nuov C — Lettere al Nuovo Cimento
Lett Nuovo Cim — Lettere al Nuovo Cimento
Lett Nuovo Cimento — Lettere al Nuovo Cimento
Lett Nuovo Cimento Soc Ital Fis — Lettere al Nuovo Cimento. Societa Italiana di Fisica [Italy]
Lett Roman — Lettres Romanes
Lettura Oft — Lettura Oftalmologica
Leu Bij — Leuvense Bijdragen
Leuk Res — Leukemia Research
Leuk Soc Am Res Inc Annu Scholar Fellow Meet — Leukemia Society of America Research, Inc. Annual Scholar Fellow Meeting
Leuv Bijdr — Leuvense Bijdragen
Levant Recursos Nat Proj Radam (Bras) — Levantamento de Recursos Naturais. Projecto Radam (Brasil)
Leveltari Kozlem — Leveltari Kozlemenyei
Levende Nat — Levende Natuur
LEVID — Leviathan
LevT — Levende Talen
LE & W — Literature East and West
LEW Nachr — LEW [Lokomotivbau-Elektrotechnische Werke] Nachrichten
Lex — Lexis
L Exr — Launceston Examiner
L Exr (Newspr) (Tas) — Launceston Examiner (Newspaper) (Tasmania)
Lex Sci — Lex et Scientia
Lex Th Q — Lexington Theological Quarterly
Leyte-Samar Stud — Leyte-Samar Studies
LF — Lettres Francaises
LF — Lia Fail
LF — Listy Filologicke
LF — Literaturen Front [Sofia]
LF — University of Illinois. Law Forum
L Fem — Letras Femeninas
LFFTD — Laser Focus with Fiberoptic Technology
LFil — Listy Filologicke
LFQ — Literature/Film Quarterly
LFr — Langue Francaise
LF(RA) — Listy Filologicke. Supplement. Revue Archeologique
L Front — Literaturen Front
LFS — Lettres Francaises
LfSC — Librarians for Social Change. Journal
LG — La Geographie
Lg — Language
L & G — Latina et Graeca
LG — Literary Guide
LG — Literaturnaya Gazeta
LG — London Gazette
LGATR — Local Government Appeals Tribunal Reports
LGATR (NSW) — Local Government Appeals Tribunal Reports (New South Wales)
LGB — Local Government Bulletin
LGE — Food and Nonfood. Fachzeitschrift fuer Unternehmer und Fuhrungskrafte Moderner Grossformen in Lebensmittelhandel
LGF — Lunder Germanistische Forschungen
LGJ — Lost Generation Journal
LGL & P — Local Government Law and Practice [Gifford]
LGO — Local Government Officer
LGO — Local Government Ordinances
Lgoru Inf Bull — Lgoru Information Bulletin
LGPIT — Leningrad Pedagogical Institute of Foreign Languages. Transactions
LGr — Literaturnaya Gruziya [Tbilisi]
LGR — New South Wales Local Government Reports
LGRA — Local Government Reports of Australia
LGRED — Local Government Review
LG Rev — Local Government Review
LGR (NSW) — Local Government Law Reports (New South Wales)
LGRP — Literaturblatt fuer Germanische und Romanische Philologie
LGRPh — Literaturblatt fuer Germanische und Romanische Philologie
LGSHA — Language, Speech, and Hearing Services in Schools
LGTRA — Logistics and Transportation Review
LGU — Leningrad State University. Philology Series. Transactions
LH — Labour History
LH — Lincoln Herald
LH — Literarischer Handweiser
L & H — Literature and History
LH — Livres Hebdomadaires
LH — Lodging Hospitality
LH — Lone Hand
LHB — Lock Haven Bulletin
LHJ — Ladies' Home Journal
LHQ — Louisiana Historical Quarterly
LHR — Lock Haven Review
LHSb — Literarnohistoricky Sbornik

LHSl — Litteraria Historica Slovaca
LHSSP — Les Houches Summer School Proceedings [*Elsevier Book Series*]
L & Human Behav — Law and Human Behavior
LHW — Literarischer Handweiser
LHY — Literary Half-Yearly
LI — Lettere Italiane
LI — Libro Italiano
Li — Lingua
Li — Listener
LI — Literature and Art [*Russia*]
L & I — Literature and Ideology
LI — Luce Intellettuale
Liaison Rep Commonw Geol Liaison Off — Liaison Report. Commonwealth Geological Liaison Office
Liaisons Soc — Liaisons Sociales
Liais Serv Note For Res Lab (Winnipeg) — Liaison and Services Note. Forest Research Laboratory (Winnipeg)
LIB — Library
Lib — Libya
LibAnt — Libya Antiqua
Lib Assn Alta Bull — Library Association of Alberta. Bulletin
Lib Assn R — Library Association. Record
Lib Assn Rec — Library Association. Record
Lib Assn Yrbk — Library Association. Yearbook
Lib Assoc Rec — Library Association. Record
Lib Binder — Library Binder
Lib Brow — Librarians' Browser
LibC — Library Chronicle
Lib Chron — Library Chronicle
Lib Coll J — Library College Journal
Lib Cong Inf Bull — Library of Congress. Information Bulletin
Lib Cong Q J — Library of Congress. Quarterly Journal
Lib Cong Q J Cur Acq — Library of Congress. Quarterly Journal of Current Acquisitions
Liber — Liberation
Liberal Ed — Liberal Education
Liberal Educ — Liberal Education
Liberal Geol Soc Cross Sec Type Log — Liberal Geological Society. Cross Sections. Type Log
LIBER Bull — Ligue des Bibliotheques Europeennes de Recherche. Bulletin
Liberian LJ — Liberian Law Journal
LiberianSJ — Liberian Studies Journal
Liber Stud J — Liberian Studies Journal
Libertas Math — Libertas Mathematica
Lib Hist — Library History
Lib Inf Bull — Library Information Bulletin
Lib Inf Sci — Library and Information Science
LibJ — Library Journal
Lib Leaves — Library Leaves from the Library of Long Island University
LibLit — Library Literature
Lib (London) — Library (London)
Libn & Bk W — Librarian and Book World
Lib News Bul — Library News Bulletin
Lib Occurrent — Library Occurrent
Lib Op — Library Opinion
Lib Opinion — Liberal Opinion
Lib Opinion — Library Opinion
Lib Period Round Table Newsletter — Library Periodicals Round Table. Newsletter
Lib Pty Aust NSW Div Res Bull — Liberal Party of Australia. New South Wales Division. Research Bulletin
Lib Q — Library Quarterly
Lib R — Library Review
Libr AR — Library Association. Record
Library Op — Library Opinion
Library Sci (Japan) — Library Science (Japan)
Libr Ass Aust Univ Coll Libr Sect News Sh — Library Association of Australia. University and College Libraries Section. News Sheet
Libr Assoc Rec — Library Association. Record
Libr Binder — Library Binder
Libr Bull Univ Lond — Library Bulletin. University of London
Libr Chron — Library Chronicle
Libr Coll J — Library College Journal
Libr Congr Inf Bull — Library of Congress. Information Bulletin
Lib Res — Library Research
Lib Resources & Tech Serv — Library Resources and Technical Services
Lib Resources and Tech Services — Library Resources and Technical Services
Lib Res Tec — Library Resources and Technical Services
Lib Rev — Library Review
Libr Her — Library Herald
Libr Hist — Library History
Libr Inf Bull — Library and Information Bulletin
Libr and Inf Sci — Library and Information Science
Libri Oncol — Libri Oncologici [*Yugoslavia*]
Libr J — Library Journal
Libr Mater Afr — Library Materials on Africa

Libr News Bull — Library News Bulletin
Libr Newsl — Librarians' Newsletter [*United States*]
Libr Q — Library Quarterly
Libr Resources Tech Serv — Library Resources and Technical Services
Libr Resour Tech Serv — Library Resources and Technical Services
Libr Resour and Tech Serv — Library Resources and Technical Services
Libr Rev — Library Review
Libr Rev For Comm (Lond) — Library Review. Forestry Commission (London)
Libr Sci Slant Docum — Library Science with a Slant to Documentation
Libr Technol Rep — Library Technology Reports
Libr Trends — Library Trends
Libr W — Library World
Libr Wld — Library World
Lib Scene — Library Scene
LibSciAb — Library and Information Science Abstracts
Lib Sci Slant Doc — Library Science with a Slant to Documentation
Lib Tech Rep — Library Technology Reports
Lib Trends — Library Trends
Lib W — Library World
Libya Ant — Libya Antiqua
Libya Minist Ind Geol Sec Bull — Libya. Ministry of Industry. Geological Section. Bulletin
Libya Minist Ind Geol Sect Bull — Libya. Ministry of Industry. Geological Section. Bulletin
Libyan J Agric — Libyan Journal of Agriculture
Libyan J Earth Sci — Libyan Journal of Earth Science
Libyan J Sci — Libyan Journal of Science
LIC — Life Insurance in Canada
Licensing L and Bus Rep — Licensing Law and Business Report
Licentiate All-India Mon J Med Surg — Licentiate All-India Monthly Journal of Medicine and Surgery
LICH — Lichenologist
Lichttech — Lichttechnik
LicP — Liceus de Portugal
LiD — Literatur im Dialog
LIE — Lectures in Economics. Theory, Institutions, Policy [*Elsevier Book Series*]
LIE — Legal Issues of European Integration
Liebigs Ann Chem — Liebigs Annalen der Chemie
Lie Groups Hist Frontiers and Appl — Lie Groups. History. Frontiers and Applications
Liet Fiz Rink — Lietuvos Fizikos Rinkinys
Liet Fiz Rinkinys — Lietuvos Fizikos Rinkinys [*Lithuanian SSR*]
Liet Gyvulinink Mokslinio Tyrimo Inst Darb — Lietuvos Gyvulininkystes Mokslinio Tyrimo Instituto Darbai
Liet Gyvulinink Vet Mokslinio Tyrimo Inst Darb — Lietuvos Gyvulininkystes ir Veterinarijos Mokslinio Tyrimo Instituto Darbai
Liet Hidrotech Melior Mokslinio Tyrimo Inst Darb — Lietuvos Hidrotechnikas ir Melioracijos Mokslinio Tyrimo Instituto Darbai
Liet Mat Rink — Lietuvos Matematikos Rinkinys
Liet Misku Ukio Mokslinio Tyrimo Inst Darb — Lietuvos Misku Ukio Mokslinio Tyrimo Instituto Darbai
Liet TSR Aukst Mokslo Darb Chem Chem Technol — Lietuvos TSR Aukstuju Mokyklu Mokslo Darbai. Chemija ir Chemine Technologija [*Lithuanian SSR*]
Liet TSR Aukst Mokyklu Moksl Darb Ultragarsas — Lietuvos TSR Aukstuju Mokyklu Mokslo Darbai. Ultragarsas
Liet TSR Aukst Mokyklu Mokslo Darb Biol — Lietuvos TSR Aukstuju Mokyklu Mokslo Darbai. Biologija
Liet TSR Aukst Mokyklu Mokslo Darb Chem Chem Technol — Lietuvos TSR Aukstuju Mokyklu Mokslo Darbai. Chemija ir Chemine Technologija
Liet TSR Aukst Mokyklu Mokslo Darb Elektrotech Autom — Lietuvos TSR Aukstuju Mokyklu Mokslo Darbai. Elektrotechnika ir Automatika
Liet TSR Aukst Mokyklu Mokslo Darb Elektrotech Mech — Lietuvos TSR Aukstuju Mokyklu Mokslo Darbai. Elektrotechnika ir Mechanika
Liet TSR Aukst Mokyklu Mokslo Darb Geogr Geol — Lietuvos TSR Aukstuju Mokyklu Mokslo Darbai. Geografija ir Geologija
Liet TSR Aukst Mokyklu Mokslo Darb Mech — Lietuvos TSR Aukstuju Mokyklu Mokslo Darbai. Mechanika
Liet TSR Aukst Mokyklu Mokslo Darb Mech Technol — Lietuvos TSR Aukstuju Mokyklu Mokslo Darbai. Mechanine Technologija
Liet TSR Aukst Mokyklu Mokslo Darb Med — Lietuvos TSR Aukstuju Mokyklu Mokslo Darbai. Medicina
Liet TSR Aukst Mokyklu Mokslo Darb Statyba Archit — Lietuvos TSR Aukstuju Mokyklu Mokslo Darbai. Statyba ir Architektura
Liet TSR Aukst Mokyklu Mokslo Darb Tekst Odos Technol — Lietuvos TSR Aukstuju Mokyklu Mokslo Darbai. Tekstiles ir Odos Technologija
Liet TSR Mokslu Akad Bot Inst Bot Klausimai — Lietuvos TSR Mokslu Akademiya Botanikos Institutas. Botanikos Klausimai
Liet TSR Mokslu Akad Bot Inst Straipsniu Rinkinys — Lietuvos TSR Mokslu Akademija Botanikos Institutas Straipsniu Rinkinys
Liet TSR Mokslu Akad Darb — Lietuvos TSR Mokslu Akademijos Darbai
Liet TSR Mokslu Akad Darbai B — Lietuvos TSR Mokslu Akademijos Darbai. Serija B
Liet TSR Mokslu Akad Darb Ser B — Lietuvos TSR Mokslu Akademijos Darbai. Serija B

Liet TSR Mokslu Akad Darb Ser C — Lietuvos TSR Mokslu Akademijos Darbai. Serija C

Liet TSR Mokslu Akad Darb Ser C Biol Mokslai — Lietuvos TSR Mokslu Akademijos Darbai. Serija C. Biologijos Mokslai

Liet TSR Mokslu Akad Eksp Med Inst Darb — Lietuvos TSR Mokslu Akademijos Eksperimentines Medicinos Instituto Darbai

Liet TSR Mokslu Akad Geogr Skyrius Moksliniai Pranesimai — Lietuvos TSR Mokslu Akademija Geografijos Skyrius Moksliniai Pranesimai

Liet TSR Mokslu Akad Geol Geogr Inst Moksliniai Pranesimai — Lietuvos TSR Mokslu Akademija Geologijos Geografijos Instituta Moksliniai Pranesimai

Liet TSR Mokslu Akad Zinynas — Lietuvos TSR Mokslu Akademijas Zinynas

Lietuvos Mok Akad Darbai — Lietuvos TSR Mokslu Akademijos Darbai

Liet Vet Akad Darb — Lietuvos Veterinarijos Akademijos Darbai

Liet Zemdir Moks Tyrimo Inst Darb — Lietuvos Zemdirbystes Mokslinio Tyrimo Instituto Darbai

Liet Zemes Ukio Akad Mokslo Darb — Lietuvos Zemes Ukio Akademija Mokslo Darbai

Life Aust — Life Australia

Life Chem Rep Suppl Ser — Life Chemistry Reports. Supplement Series

Life D — Life Digest

Life Dig — Life Digest

Life Environ — Life and Environment [*Japan*]

Life Ins Courant — Life Insurance Courant

Life & Lett — Life and Letters

Lifelong Learn — Lifelong Learning

Lifelong Learn Adult Years — Lifelong Learning: The Adult Years

Life with Mus — Life with Music

Life Sci — Life Sciences

Life Sci Agric Exp Stn Tech Bull (Maine) — Life Sciences and Agriculture Experiment Station. Technical Bulletin (Maine)

Life Sci Inst Kivo Jochi Daigaku Seimei Kagaku Kenkyusho — Life Science Institute Kivo/Jochi Daigaku Seimei Kagaku Kenkyusho

Life Sci Monogr — Life Sciences Monographs

Life Sci Part I — Life Sciences. Part I. Physiology and Pharmacology

Life Sci Part II — Life Sciences. Part II. Biochemistry. General and Molecular Biology

Life Sci Part II Biochem Gen Mol Biol — Life Sciences. Part II. Biochemistry. General and Molecular Biology

Life Sci Part I Physiol Pharmacol — Life Sciences. Part I. Physiology and Pharmacology

Life Sci Res Rep — Life Sciences Research Reports

Life Sci Space Res — Life Sciences and Space Research [*Netherlands*]

Life-Threat — Life-Threatening Behavior

LIFSA — Life Sciences

Lift Elevator Lift Ropeway Eng — Lift, Elevator Lift, and Ropeway Engineering

LiG — Literatur in der Gesellschaft

Light Aust — Lighting in Australia

Light Des Appl — Lighting Design and Application

Light Equip News — Lighting Equipment News

Lighting Des Applic — Lighting Design and Application

Lighting Design & Appl — Lighting Design and Application

Lighting Equip News — Lighting Equipment News

Lighting Res Tech — Lighting Research and Technology

Light and Light — Light and Lighting

Light Light — Light and Lighting

Light and Light and Environ Des — Light and Lighting and Environmental Design

Light Light Environ Des — Light and Lighting and Environmental Design

Light Met Age — Light Metal Age

Light Met (London) — Light Metals (London)

Light Met Met Ind — Light Metals and Metal Industry [*England*]

Light Met (New York) — Light Metals: Proceedings of Sessions. American Institute of Mining, Metallurgical, and Petroleum Engineers. Annual Meeting (New York)

Light Met (Tokyo) — Light Metals (Tokyo)

Light Mtl — Light Metal Age

Light Res Technol — Lighting Research and Technology

Light Res and Technol — Lighting Research and Technology

LI Hist Soc Memoirs — Long Island Historical Society. Memoirs

LII — Nieuwe Linie

Liiketal Aikakausk — Liiketaloudellinen Aikakauskirja [*Journal of Business Economics*]

LIJ — Law Institute Journal

Lijec Vjesn — Lijecnicki Vjesnik

LiK — Liaudies Kuryba

LiK — Literatura ir Kalba

LiL — Limba si Literatura

LiLi — Zeitschrift fuer Literaturwissenschaft und Linguistik

Lilla — Lillabulero

Lille Chir — Lille Chirurgical

Lille Med — Lille Medical

Lille Med Actual — Lille Medical. Actualites

Lily Yearb North Am Lily Soc — Lily Yearbook. North American Lily Society

LiM — Lingue del Mondo

LiM — Literatura i Marksizm

LiM — Literatura i Mastatsva

LIMC — Lexicon Iconographicum Mythologiae Classicae

Li Men — Literatura ir Menas

Limn Ocean — Limnology and Oceanography

Limnol Donau — Limnologie der Donau

Limnol & Oceanog — Limnology and Oceanography

Limnol & Oceanogr — Limnology and Oceanography

Limnol Oceanogr — Limnology and Oceanography

Limnol Oceanogr Suppl — Limnology and Oceanography. Supplement

LimR — Limba Romana [*Bucuresti*]

Linacre — Linacre Quarterly

Linacre Q — Linacre Quarterly

Lin Alg App — Linear Algebra and Its Applications

Linc Farm Conf Proc — Lincoln College. Farmers' Conference. Proceedings

Linc LR — Lincoln Law Review

Lincoln L Rev — Lincoln Law Review

Lincoln Rec Soc — Lincoln Record Society

Lincolnshire Hist Arch — Lincolnshire History and Archaeology

Lindbergia J Bryol — Lindbergia. A Journal of Bryology

Linde-Ber Tech Wiss — Linde-Berichte aus Technik und Wissenschaft

Linde Reports Sci & Technol — Linde Reports on Science and Technology

Linde Rep Sci and Technol — Linde Reports on Science and Technology

Linde Rep Sci Technol — Linde Reports on Science and Technology

L'Ind Ital del Cemento — L'Industria Italiana del Cemento

Linear Algebra and Appl — Linear Algebra and Its Applications

Linear Algebra Appl — Linear Algebra and Its Applications

Linear Algebra Its Appl — Linear Algebra and Its Applications

Linen News — Linen Supply News

Lines Rev — Lines Review

Ling — Linguistica

Ling A — Linguistic Analysis

LingB — Linguistische Berichte

LingBib — Linguistica Biblica [*Bonn*]

Ling Bibl — Linguistica Biblica

LingC — Linguistic Communications

Ling Cal — Linguistic Calculation

Ling Est — Lingue Estere

LingH — Linguistics (The Hague)

LingI — Linguistic Inquiry

Ling Inq — Linguistic Inquiry

Ling Inquiry — Linguistic Inquiry

Ling Inv — Linguisticae Investigationes

Ling e L — Lingua e Literatura

Lingnan Sci J — Lingnan Science Journal

Ling & P — Linguistics and Philosophy

LingP — Linguistique (Paris)

Ling Phil — Linguistics and Philosophy

Ling Philos — Linguistics and Philosophy

Ling R — Linguistic Reporter

Ling Stile — Lingua e Stile

Linguist An — Linguistic Analysis

Linguist Ber — Linguistische Berichte

Linguistic Circle Manitoba and N Dak Proc — Linguistic Circle of Manitoba and North Dakota. Proceedings

Linguist In — Linguistic Inquiry

Lin Invest — Linguisticae Investigationes. Supplementa. Studies in French and General Linguistics

Lin Lit S — Linguistic and Literary Studies in Eastern Europe

Linn Belg — Linneana Belgica

Linneana Belg — Linneana Belgica

Linnean Soc Biol J — Linnean Society. Biological Journal

Linnean Soc NSW Proc — Proceedings. Linnean Society of New South Wales

Linn Soc J Zool — Linnean Society. Journal. Zoology

Linn Soc Lond Biol J — Linnean Society of London. Biological Journal

Linn Soc Lond Zool J — Linnean Society of London. Zoological Journal

Linn Soc NSW Proc — Linnean Society of New South Wales. Proceedings

Linn Soc Symp Ser — Linnean Society. Symposium Series

L Inst J — Law Institute Journal

L Inst J Vict — Law Institute Journal of Victoria

Linzer Biol Beitr — Linzer Biologische Beitraege

Liofilizzazione Criobiol Appl Criog — Liofilizzazione Criobiologia Applicazioni Criogeniche

Lion Unicor — Lion and the Unicorn

LIPL — Living Places

LIPP — Lippincott's Monthly

Lippay Janos Tud Ulesszak Eloadasai — Lippay Janos Tudomanyos Ulesszak Eloadasai

Lippinc — Lippincott's Magazine

Lippincott's Med Sci — Lippincott's Medical Science

Liq Cryst Ordered Fluids — Liquid Crystals and Ordered Fluids

Liq Scintill Count — Liquid Scintillation Counting

Liq Scintill Counting — Liquid Scintillation Counting

Liquefied Nat Gas — Liquefied Natural Gas

LiR — Limba Romana [*Bucuresti*]

LIS — Life Insurance Selling

LIs — Lingua Islandica
LIS — Linguisticae Investigationes. Supplementa. Studies in French and General Linguistics
Lis — Listener
LISA — Library and Information Science Abstracts [*Library Association Publishing Ltd.*] [*Bibliographic database*] [*England*]
Li Sa — Litteratur og Samfund
LISL — Amsterdam Studies in the Theory and History of Linguistic Science. Series V. Library and Information Sources in Linguistics
LISL — Letopis Instituta za Serbski Iudospyt w Budysinje pri Nemskej Akademiji Wedo-Moscow w Berlinje Rjad A Rec A Literatura
LISR — Legal Information Service. Reports. Native Law Centre. University of Saskatchewan
List — List Sdruzeni Moravskych Spisovatelu
List — Listener
Liste Abbrev Mots Titres — Liste d'Abbreviations de Mots des Titres de Periodiques
Listprokatnoe Proizvod — Listoprokatnoe Proizvodstvo
List of Stat Instr — List of Statutory Instruments
Listy Cukrov — Listy Cukrovarnicke
Listy Fil — Listy Filologicke
LIt — Lettere Italiane
LIt — Libro Italiano
Lit — Literarisches
Lit — Literatur
Lit — Litigation
Lit — Litterature [*University of Paris*]
Lit — Litteris
LitA — Literaturnaya Armeniya [*Erevan*]
LITA ITAL — LITA [*Library and Information Technology Association*] Information Technology and Libraries
LItal — Lettere Italiane
LitAP — Literarni Archiv Pamatniku Narodniho Pisemnictvi
Lit Arts — Liturgical Arts
Lit AS — Literatur als Sprache. Literaturtheorie-Interpretation-Sprachkritik
Lit Automat — New Literature on Automation
Lit Criterion — Literary Criterion
Lit D — Literary Digest
Lit Dig — Literary Digest
Lit E — Literary Endeavour
Liteinoe Proizvod — Liteinoe Proizvodstvo [*USSR*]
Liteinoe Prozvod — Liteinoe Proizvodstvo
Literature — Literature East and West
Liter Discussion — Literacy Discussion
LitEW — Literature East and West
Lit/F Q — Literature/Film Quarterly
Lit/F Quarterly — Literature/Film Quarterly
Lit Half — Literary Half-Yearly
Lit Hist — Literature and History
Lit Hist Soc Quebec Tr — Literary and Historical Society of Quebec. Transactions
Lithol Issled Kaz — Litologicheskie Issledovanniya v Kazakhstane [*USSR*]
Lithol Miner Resour — Lithology and Mineral Resources
Lithuanian Math J — Lithuanian Mathematical Journal
Lithuanian Math Trans — Lithuanian Mathematical Transactions
Lit Jb — Liturgisches Jahrbuch
Lit Krit — Literatur und Kritik
LItL — Letteratura Italiana Laterza
LitL — Literarni Listy
LitL — Literatura Ludowa
Lit Letter — Literary Letter
LitM — Literarni Mesicnik
LitM — Literaturnaya Mysl
Lit Mus Fin — Literature, Music, Fine Arts
Lit Mys — Literatura i Mystectvo
LitN — Literarni Noviny [*Praha*]
Litol Geokhim Paleogeogr Neftegazonosn Osad Form Uzb — Litologiya, Geokhimiya, i Paleogeografiya Neftegazonosn Osadochnykh Formatsii Uzbekistana
Litol i Polez Iskop — Litologiya i Poleznye Iskopaemye
Litov Fiz Sb — Litovskii Fizicheskii Sbornik
Litov Mekh Sb — Litovskii Mekhanicheskii Sbornik
Litovsk Mat Sb — Litovskii Matematiceskii Sbornik
LitP — Literature in Perspective
LitP — Literature and Psychology
Lit Per — Literary Perspectives
Lit Ph Soc NY Tr — Literary and Philosophical Society of New York. Transactions
Lit Psychol — Literature and Psychology
Lit & Psychol — Literature and Psychology
Lit R — Literary Review
Lit Res New — Literary Research Newsletter
Lit Rev — Literary Review
Lit Rev Oils Fats — Literature Review on Oils and Fats
LitS — Literatura i Sucanist
Lit Steam Pwr — Light Steam Power

Litt — Litteraria
Litt — Litteris
Lit & Theo R — Literary and Theological Review
LittK — Litterae (Kuemmerle)
Little M — Little Magazine
LittleR — Little Review
Lit U — Literaturna Ukrajina
Liturg Arts — Liturgical Arts
Lit W (Bost) — Library World (Boston)
Lit ZentB — Literarisches Zentralblatt
Liv Age — Littell's Living Age
Liv Blues — Living Blues
Liverp Manch Geol J — Liverpool and Manchester Geological Journal
Liverpool G As Tr J — Liverpool Geological Association. Transactions. Journal
Liverpool Geog Soc Tr An Rp — Liverpool Geographical Society. Transactions and Annual Report of the Council
Liverpool G Soc Pr — Liverpool Geological Society. Proceedings
Liverpool L Rev — Liverpool Law Review
Liverpool and Manchester Geol Jour — Liverpool and Manchester Geological Journal
Liverpool School Trop Med Mem — Liverpool School of Tropical Medicine. Memoirs
Liver Quant Aspects Struct Func — Liver: Quantitative Aspects of Structure and Function. Proceedings of the International Gstaad Symposium
Livest Int — Livestock International
Live Stock Bul — Live Stock Bulletin
Live Stock J and Fancier's Gaz — Live Stock Journal and Fancier's Gazette
Livest Prod Sci — Livestock Production Science
Living Mus — Living Museum
Liv Wild — Living Wilderness
Liv Wildn — Living Wilderness
Liv for Young Home — Living for Young Homemakers
LJ — Law Journal. New Series
LJ — Library Journal
LJ — Limburg's Jaarboek
LJ — Liturgisches Jahrbuch
LJ — New York Law Journal
LJ — Ohio State Law Journal
LJA — Ljetopis Jugoslavenske Akademije
L in Japan — Law in Japan
LJb — Literaturwissenschaftliches Jahrbuch der Goerres-Gesellschaft
L-Jb — Luther-Jahrbuch
LJGG — Literaturwissenschaftliches Jahrbuch der Goerres-Gesellschaft
LJH — Legon Journal of the Humanities
L J Hum — Lamar Journal of the Humanities
LJOS — Law Journal. Old Series
LJR — Low Jet Routes
LJ/SLJ — Library Journal/School Library Journal
L & Just — Law and Justice
LK — Literatur und Kritik. Oesterreichische Monatsschrift
LK — Literatura ir Kalba
LK — Literaturnyj Kritik
LKAAAN — Annual Report. Laboratory of Algology [*Trebon*]
LKI — Is Lietuviu Kulturos Istorijos
LKK — Lietuviu Kalbotyros Klausimai
LKTRD — Elektro-Tehniek
LL — Lakeside Leader [*Slave Lake, Alberta*]
LL — Language Learning
L & L — Lehrproben und Lehrgaenge
LL — Letras (Lima)
LL — Library Literature
LL — Life and Letters
LL — Lifelong Learning: The Adult Years
L si L — Limba si Literatura
L & L — Lingua e Literatura
L & L — Linguistica et Litteraria
LL — Literatur und Leben
LL — Lloyd's List
LLA — Leshonenu La'am
LLB — Lawyers Liberation Bulletin
LLBA — Linguistics and Language Behavior Abstracts [*Sociological Abstracts, Inc.*] [*San Diego, CA*] [*Bibliographic database*]
LL and C — Language Learning and Communication
LlC — Llen Cymru
LLG — Luggage and Travelware
L Lib — Law Librarian
L Lib J — Law Library Journal
L Libr J — Law Library Journal
L and Lin M — Language and Linguistics in Melanesia
LLJ — Labor Law Journal
LLJ — Law Library Journal
LLM — Langues et Lettres Modernes
LLM — Limba si Literatura Moldoveneasca Chisinau
Lloydia — Lloydia. Lloyd Library and Museum
Lloydia J Nat Prod — Lloydia. Journal of Natural Products
Lloyd's Bank R — Lloyd's Bank Review

Lloyds Mar and Com LQ — Lloyd's Maritime and Commercial Law Quarterly
Lloyds Mex — Lloyd's Mexican Economic Report
LLR — Luzerne Legal Register
LLSEE — Linguistic and Literary Studies in Eastern Europe
LLud — Literatura Ludowa
LM — Lady's Magazine
LM — Language Monographs
LM — Langues Modernes
LM — Le Monde
LM — Letterature Moderne
L and M — Literature and Medicine
LM — London Law Magazine
LM — London Magazine
LM — London Mercury
LM — Ludus Magistralis
LM — Luna Monthly
LMA — Le Moyen Age
LMAD — Lietuvos TSR Mokslu Akademijos Darbai. Serija A [*Vilnius*]
L Mag — London Law Magazine
L Mag — London Magazine
LMags — Index to Little Magazines
LMAOS — Liverpool Monographs in Archaeology and Oriental Studies
LMC — Literature, Meaning, Culture
LMD — Australian Legal Monthly Digest
LMD — La Maison-Dieu
L Med and Health — Law, Medicine, and Health Care
L Med Q — Legal Medical Quarterly
L Mer — London Mercury
LMG Rep Data and Word Process Libr — LMG [*Library Management Group*] Report on Data and Word Processing for Libraries
LMH — Lebensmittelzeitung
LMi — Literaturna Misel [*Sofia*]
LMLG — Luther. Mitteilungen der Luthergesellschaft
LMLP — La Monda Lingvo-Problemo
LMLSA — Language Monographs. Linguistic Society of America
LMNTD — Elements
L Mod — Langues Modernes
LMod — Lettres Modernes
LMold — Limba si Literatura Moldoveneasca
LMQ — Legal Medical Quarterly
LMS — Letopis Matice Srpske. Novi Sad
LMS — London Mediaeval Studies
LMSLA — Lantmannen (Sweden)
LMT — Library Management
L de Muz — Lucrari de Muzicologie
LN — Law Notes
LN — Library Notes
LN — Lingua Nostra
LN — Literaturnoe Nasledstvo
LnA — London Aphrodite
LNB — Leipziger Namenkundliche Beitraege
LNI — La Nuova Italia
LNL — Langues Neo-Latines
LNLJ — Linguistic Notes from La Jolla
LnM — London Mercury
LNMVA — Learning and Motivation
LNN — Leipziger Neueste Nachrichten
LNo — Lingua Nostra
Lno Penko-Dzhutovaya Promst — Lno Penko-Dzhutovaya Promyshlennost
LNos — Lingua Nostra
L Notes (NY) — Law Notes (New York)
LNouv — Lettres Nouvelles
LNQ — Lincolnshire Notes and Queries
LNR — Lagos Notes and Records
LNS — Lundastudier i Nordisk Sprakvetenskap
LNU — Negentien Nu
LO — Limnology and Oceanography
LO — Literaturnoe Obozrenie
Lo — Lochlann
LO — Louisiana Musician
LOAF — Look at Finland
Loc — Locus
Local Fin — Local Finance
Local Fin (The Hague) — Local Finance (The Hague)
Local Gov Adm — Local Government Administration
Local Gov J of Western Aust — Local Government Journal of Western Australia
Local Gov in South Aust — Local Government in South Australia
Local Gov South Aust — Local Government in South Australia
Local Gov in Sthn Afr — Local Government in Southern Africa
Local Gov Stud — Local Government Studies
Local Govt — Local Government
Local Govt Adm — Local Government Administration
Local Govt Admin — Local Government Administration
Local Govt Chron — Local Government Chronicle
Local Govt Eng — Local Government Engineer

Local Govt Forum — Local Government Forum
Local Govt IULA Newsl — Local Government - IULA [*International Union of Local Authorities*] Newsletter
Local Govt Manpower — Local Government Manpower
Local Govt News — Local Government News
Local Govt Policy Making — Local Government Policy Making
Local Govt R Austl — Local Government Reports of Australia
Local Govt Rev — Local Government Review
Local Govt R Japan — Local Government Review in Japan
Local Govt Stud — Local Government Studies
Local Hist — Local Historian
Local Popul Stud — Local Population Studies Magazine and Newsletter
Locat Rep Div Miner Chem CSIRO — Location Report. Division of Mineral Chemistry. Commonwealth Scientific and Industrial Research Organisation
Loc Finance — Local Finance
Locgov Dig — Locgov Digest
Loc Gov Rev — Local Government Review
Loc Govt Rev — Local Government Review
Locke News — Locke Newsletter
Lockheed GA Q — Lockheed Georgia Quarterly
Lockheed Horiz — Lockheed Horizons
Lockheed Symp Magnetohydrodyn — Lockheed Symposia on Magnetohydrodynamics
Lockwood Dir — Lockwood's Directory of the Paper and Allied Trades
Loco J — Locomotive Journal
Lodzki Num — Lodzki Numizmatyk
Lodz Stud Etnogr — Lodzkie Studia Etnograficzne
Lodz Tow Nauk Pr Wydz 3 — Lodzkie Towarzystwo Naukowe Prace Wydzialu 3. Nauk Matematyczno-Przyrodniczych
Lodz Tow Nauk Pr Wydz 4 — Lodzkie Towarzystwo Naukowe Prace Wydzialu 4. Nauk Lekarskich
Lodz Tow Nauk Pr Wydz 3 Nauk Mat-Przyr — Lodzkie Towarzystwo Naukowe Prace Wydzialu 3. Nauk Matematyczno-Przyrodniczych
L Off Ec and Mgmt — Law Office Economics and Management
L Off Econ & Man — Law Office Economics and Management
Log — Logos. Internationale Zeitschrift fuer Philosophie und Kultur
Log Anal — Log Analyst
Log Anal — Logique et Analyse
Loggers Handb Pac Logging Congr — Loggers Handbook. Pacific Logging Congress
Logik Grundlagen Math — Logik und Grundlagen der Mathematik
Logique et Anal NS — Logique et Analyse. Nouvelle Serie
Logist Spectrum — Logistics Spectrum
Logist & Transp Rev — Logistics and Transportation Review
Logos — Logos Journal
Lohnuntern Land-Forstwirt — Lohnunternehmen in Land- und Forstwirtschaft
Lollipops — Lollipops, Ladybugs, and Lucky Stars
Lo LR — Loyola Law Review
Lond Clin Med J — London Clinic Medical Journal
L'Ondes Electr — L'Ondes Electronique
Lond Gaz — London Gazette
Lond J — London Journal
Lond M — London Magazine
Lond Mag — London Magazine
Lond Math Soc Lect Note Ser — London Mathematical Society. Lecture Note Series
Lond Math Soc Monogr — London Mathematical Society. Monographs
Lond Med Gaz — London Medical Gazette
Lond Med St — London Mediaeval Studies
Lond Mercury — London Mercury
Lond Nat — London Naturalist
London Archaeol — London Archaeologist
London Archit — London Architect
London Archt — London Architect
London Bus Mag — London Bus Magazine
London Bus School J — London Business School. Journal
London Commun Wk Serv Newsl — London Community Work Service Newsletter
London Docklands Dev Newsl — London Docklands Development Newsletter
London Ednl R — London Educational Review
London Hlth News — London Health News
London Ind Centre News — London Industrial Centre News
London J — London Journal
London Jnl — London Journal
London Labour Brief — London Labour Briefing
London Lesbian Newsl — London Lesbian Newsletter
London Mag — London Magazine
London Math Soc Lecture Note Ser — London Mathematical Society. Lecture Note Series
London Meas Rates Mat Prices — London Measured Rates and Materials Prices
London Natur — London Naturalist
London Rev Public Admin — London Review of Public Administration
London Shellac Res Bur Bull — London Shellac Research Bureau. Bulletin
London Soc Jnl — London Society. Journal

London Volunt News — London Voluntary News
Lond Q — London Quarterly Review
LondQHolbR — London Quarterly and Holborn Review
Lond QHR — London Quarterly and Holborn Review
Lond Q R — London Quarterly and Holborn Review
Lond School Trop Med Research Mem Ser — London School of Tropical Medicine. Research Memoir Series
Lond Soc — London Society
Lond Studio — London Studio
Lond Topog Rec — London Topographical Record
Long Ashton Res Stn Rep — Long Ashton Research Station. Report
Longest R — Longest Revolution
Long Isl Forum — Long Island Forum
Longm — Longman's Magazine
Long Point Bird Obs Annu Rep — Long Point Bird Observatory. Annual Report
Long Range Plan — Long-Range Planning
Long Range Plann — Long-Range Planning
Long-Rang P — Long-Range Planning
Long Term Care Health Serv Adm Q — Long Term Care and Health Services Administration. Quarterly
LonM — London Magazine
Lon Mag — London Magazine
Lon R Bks — London Review of Books
Loodusuurijate Selts Tappistead Sekts Toim — Loodusuurijate Selts Tappisteaduste Sektsiooni Toimetised
Loodusuur Seltsi Aastar — Loodusuurijate. Seltsi Aastaraaman
Look Ahead Proj Highlights — Looking Ahead and Projection Highlights
Look Jpn — Look Japan
Look Lab (Hawaii) — Look Laboratory (Hawaii)
Loonb Land-Tuinbouw — Loonbedrijf in Land- en Tuinbouw
Lopatochnye Mash Struinye Appar — Lopatochnye Mashiny i Struinye Apparaty
LOR — Long-Range Planning
Lore & L — Lore and Language
LOS — Literary Onomastics Studies
Los Ang Cty Mus Contrib Sci — Los Angeles County Museum. Contributions in Science
Los Angeles B Bull — Los Angeles Bar Bulletin
Los Angeles Bus and Econ — Los Angeles Business and Economics
Los Angeles Counc Eng Sci Proc Ser — Los Angeles Council of Engineers and Scientists. Proceedings Series
Los Angeles County Mus Contr Sci — Los Angeles County Museum. Contributions in Science
Los Angeles County Mus Nat History Quart — Los Angeles County Museum of Natural History. Quarterly
Los Angeles Ed Res B — Los Angeles Educational Research Bulletin
Los Angeles Mus Art Bull — Los Angeles County Museum. Bulletin of the Art Division
Los Angeles Mus Bul — Los Angeles County Museum. Bulletin of the Art Division
Los Angeles Mus Q — Los Angeles County Museum of History, Science, and Art. Quarterly
Loss Pre — Loss Prevention
Loss Prev — Loss Prevention: A CEP Technical Manual
Lotta Antiparass — Lotta Antiparassitaria
Lotta Tuberc — Lotta Contro la Tubercolosi
Lotta Tuberc Mal Polm Soc — Lotta Contro la Tubercolosi e le Malattie Polmonari Sociali
Lotus Int — Lotus International
Loughborough Univ Technol Chem Eng J — Loughborough University of Technology. Chemical Engineering Journal
Loughborough Univ Technol Chem Eng Soc J — Loughborough University of Technology. Chemical Engineering Society. Journal
Loughborough Univ Technol Dep Transp Technol TT Rep — Loughborough University of Technology. Department of Transport Technology. TT Report
Louisiana Geol Surv Bull — Louisiana. Geological Survey. Bulletin
Louisiana L Rev — Louisiana Law Review
Louisiana Water Resources Research Inst Bull — Louisiana Water Resources Research Institute. Bulletin
Louisville Lawyer — Louisville Lawyer
Louisville Med News — Louisville Medical News
Lou L Rev — Louisiana Law Review
Louvain Stds — Louvain Studies
Louvain Univ Inst Geol Mem — Louvain Universite. Institut Geologique. Memoires
Louv Med — Louvain Medical
LouvSt — Louvain Studies [*Leuven*]
Louv Univ Inst Geol Mem — Louvain Universite. Institut Geologique. Memoires
Low Count H — Low Countries History. Yearbook [*Acta Historiae Neerlandicae*]
Low-Level Radioact Waste Technol Newsl — Low-Level Radioactive Waste Technology Newsletter
Low Pay Bull — Low Pay Bulletin
Low Pay Rev — Low Pay Review

Low Temp Phys (Kiev) — Low Temperature Physics (Kiev)
Low Temp Res Stn (Camb) Annu Rep — Low Temperature Research Station (Cambridge). Annual Report
Low Temp Sci Ser A — Low Temperature Science. Series A. Physical Sciences
Low Temp Sci Ser B Biol Sci — Low Temperature Science. Series B. Biological Sciences
Loy Chi LJ — Loyola University of Chicago. Law Journal
Loy LA Int'l and Comp L Ann — Loyola of Los Angeles. International and Comparative Law Annual
Loy LA Int'l & Comp LJ — Loyola of Los Angeles. International and Comparative Law Journal
Loy LA L Rev — Loyola University of Los Angeles [*later, Loyola Marymount University*]. Law Review
Loy L Rev — Loyola Law Review
Loyola Los AL Rev — Loyola of Los Angeles. Law Review
Loyola of Los Angeles L Rev — Loyola of Los Angeles. Law Review
Loyola Los Ang Int'l & Comp L Ann — Loyola of Los Angeles. International and Comparative Law Annual
Loyola L Rev — Loyola Law Review
Loyola U Chi LJ — Loyola University of Chicago. Law Journal
Loyola ULA L Rev — Loyola University of Los Angeles [*later, Loyola Marymount University*]. Law Review
Loyola ULJ (Chicago) — Loyola University Law Journal (Chicago)
Loyola UL Rev (LA) — Loyola University of Los Angeles [*later, Loyola Marymount University*]. Law Review
Loyola Univ of Chicago LJ — Loyola University of Chicago. Law Journal
Loy R — Loyola Law Review
Loy U Chi LJ — Loyola University of Chicago. Law Journal
Lozar Vinar — Lozarstvo Vinarstvo
LP — Lingua Portuguesa
LP — Lingua Posnaniensis
L & P — Literature and Psychology
LP — Literature and Psychology
LP — Litho-Printer Magazine [*British*]
LPB — Laser and Particle Beams
LPer — Literature in Performance
LPFMRD — Lingvisticheskie Problemy Funktsional'nogo Modelirovaniia Rechevoi Deiatel'nosti
LPHLA — Laporan Lembaga Penelitian Hasil Hutan
LPI — Law and Policy in International Business
LPI Contribution — Lunar and Planetary Institute. Contribution
LPI Technical Report — Lunar and Planetary Institute. Technical Report
LPLP — Language Problems and Language Planning
LPM — Leipziger Messe Journal
L & Pol Int'l Bus — Law and Policy in International Business
LPosn — Lingua Posnaniensis
LPP — La Parola del Passato
L Psy R — Law and Psychology Review
LPTV — Lapin Tutkimusseura Vuosikirja [*Research Society of Lapland. Yearbook*]
LPW — [*The*] Age. Large Print Weekly
LQ — International and Comparative Law Quarterly
LQ — Library Quarterly
LQ — London Quarterly
LQ — Lutheran Quarterly
LQF — Liturgiegeschichtliche Quellen und Forschungen [*Muenster*]
LQHR — London Quarterly and Holborn Review
LQR — Law Quarterly Review
LQR — London Quarterly Review
L Q Rev — Law Quarterly Review
LR — Alabama Law Review
LR — Law Reports
LR — Law Review
LR — Les Lettres Romanes
LR — Library Review
LR — Literary Review
LR — Literaturnaya Rossiya
LR — Lutherische Rundschau
LRA — Library Record of Australasia
Lrab Hasarakakan Gitutyun — Lraber Hasarakakan Gitutyunneri
LRAC — Labrador. Resources Advisory Council. Newsletter
LRB — La Revue Bibliographique
L Rb — Lutherischer Rundblick
LRE — La Recherche
LRe — Linguistische Reihe
L Rev — Law Review
LRI — Libri e Riviste d'Italia
LRIF — Logos. Rivista Internazionale di Filosofia
LRKD — Literarische Rundschau fuer das Katholische Deutschland
LRN — Literary Research Newsletter
LR (NSW) — Law Reports (New South Wales)
LR (NSW) B & P — Law Reports (New South Wales). Bankruptcy and Probate
LR (NSW) D — Law Reports (New South Wales). Divorce
LR (NSW) Eq — Law Reports (New South Wales). Equity
LR (NSW) Vice-Adm — Law Reports (New South Wales). Vice-Admiralty

L Rom — Limba Romana
LROTD — Laryngologie, Rhinologie, Otologie
LROTD — Laryngologie, Rhinologie, Otologie Vereinigt mit Monatsschrift fuer Ohrenheilkunde
LRP — Long-Range Planning
LRR — Labor Relations Reporter [*Bureau of National Affairs*]
LRS — Leipziger Rechtswissenschaftliche Studien
LRS — Leipziger Romanistischer Studien
LRS — Lincoln Record Society
LRS — Ljudska Republika Slovenije
LRSA — South Australian Law Reports
LRsch — Lutherische Rundschau [*Stuttgart*]
LRTS — Library Resources and Technical Services
LRVSA — Landmaschinen-Rundschau
LS — Language and Speech
L & S — Language and Speech
LS — Le Soir
LS — Le Soleil [*Dakar*]
LS — Lebendige Schule
LS — Lebendige Seelsorge
LS — Leksikograficeskij Sbornik
L & S — Lingua e Stile
LS — Lingua e Stile
LS — Lingue Straniere
LS — Linguistica Slovaca
LS — Literatura v Shkole
LS — Literaturny Sovremennik
LS — Lusitania Sacra
LS — Lute Society of America. Journal
LS — Spectator (London)
LSA — Lebende Sprachen. Zeitschrift fuer Fremde Sprachen in Wissenschaft und Praxis
LSA — Libre Service Actualites
LSa — Lusitania Sacra
LSAB — Linguistic Society of America. Bulletin
LSA Exp Stn Tech Bull (Maine) — LSA [*Life Sciences and Agricultural*] Experiment Station. Technical Bulletin (Maine)
LSARA — Landscape Architecture
LSB — La Sainte Bible
LSB — Legal Service Bulletin
LSb — Leksikograficeskij Sbornik
LSB — Linguistic Survey Bulletin
LSB — Sitzungsberichte. Saechsische Akademie der Wissenschaften zu Leipzig
LSBCA — Lucrari Stiintifice ale Institutului Agronomic "Nicolae Balcescu" (Bucuresti). Seria C
LSB (SA) — Law Society. Bulletin (South Australia)
LSC — Libre Service Actualites
L'scape — Landscape
LSci — Language Sciences
LSD — Litteraria; Studie a Dokumenty
LSE — Leeds Studies in English and Kindred Languages
LSE — Lexikon Strassenverkehrsrechtlicher Entscheidungen
LSE — Lund Studies in English
LSEBA — LSE [*Laurence, Scott, & Electromotors Ltd.*] Engineering Bulletin
LSE Eng Bull — LSE [*Laurence, Scott, & Electromotors Ltd.*] Engineering Bulletin
LSEMSA — London School of Economics. Monographs on Social Anthropology
LSG — Law Society. Gazette
LS Gaz — Law Society's Gazette
LSh — Literatura v Shkole [*Moscow*]
LSI — Lexique Stratigraphique International
LSI Contrib — LSI [*Lunar Science Institute*] Contribution
LSJ — Labor Studies Journal
LSJ — Law Society. Journal
LSJ — Lute Society. Journal
LSJS — Law Society Judgement Scheme [*South Australia*]
LS Judg Sch — Law Society Judgement Scheme [*South Australia*]
LsL — Limba si Literatura
LSl — Linguistica Slovaca
LSlov — Livre Slovene [*Yugoslavia*]
LSLT — Li-Shih Lun-Ts'ung [*Collection of Articles on History*]
LSM News — Liberation Support Movement News
LSNS — Lundastudier i Nordisk Sprakvetenskap
LSoc — Language in Society
L Soc Gaz — Law Society's Gazette
L Soc J — Law Society. Journal
L & Soc Order — Law and the Social Order
L and Soc Rev — Law and Society Review
L Soc'y Gaz — Law Society. Gazette
LSp — Language and Speech
LSp — Lebende Sprachen
LSP — Leitsaetze fuer die Preisermittlung
LSP — Lingvisticeskij Sbornik. Petrozavodsk
LSPPA — Life Sciences. Part I. Physiology and Pharmacology

L Spr — Lebende Sprachen
LSR — Lettera di Sociologia Religiosa
LSR — Lone Star Review
LSR — Luttrell Society. Reprints
Ls S — Letopis' Zurnal'nych Statej
LSS — Leyte-Samar Studies
LST — Listener
L St VG — Bayerisches Landesstraf- und Verordnungsgesetz
LSty — Language and Style
LSU For Note LA Sch For — LSU Forestry Notes. Louisiana State University. School of Forestry and Wildlife Management
LSU For Notes LA Agric Exp Stn — LSU [*Louisiana State University*] Forestry Notes. Louisiana Agricultural Experiment Station
LSUHS — Louisiana State University. Humanistic Series
L Sup M Inst Pr — Lake Superior Mining Institute. Proceedings
LSUSHS — Louisiana State University. Studies. Humanities Series
LSU Wood Util Note LA Sch For — LSU Wood Utilization Notes. Louisiana State University. School of Forestry and Wildlife Management
Lsvl Orch — Louisville Orchestra Program Notes
LSW — Ludowa Spoldzielnia Wydawnicza
LT — La Torre
L T — Law Times
LT — Levende Talen
LTB — Laboratory Techniques in Biochemistry and Molecular Biology [*Elsevier Book Series*]
LTBA — Lexikalischen Tafelserien der Babylonier und Assyrer
LTBA — Linguistics of the Tibeto-Burman Area
LTCO — London Transactions. International Congress of Orientalists
LTE — Tunisie Economique
L Teach — Law Teacher
L Teacher — Law Teacher. Journal of the Association of Law Teachers, London
LTECA — Landtechnik
LTF Res Progr — LTF [*Lithographic Technical Foundation*] Research Progress
Ltg Des Appl — Lighting Design and Application
Ltg Equip News — Lighting Equipment News
Ltg J (Thorn) — Lighting Journal (Thorn)
Ltg Res Tech — Lighting Research and Technology
L Th K — Lexikon fuer Theologie und Kirche
LTHPA — Lectures in Theoretical Physics
LThPh — Laval Theologique et Philosophique
LTHS — La Trobe Historical Studies
LTIED — Ekspress-Informatsiya Laboratornye Tekhnologicheskie Issledovaniya i Obogashchenie Mineral'nogo Syr'ya
LTimesLS — Times Literary Supplement (London)
LT Jo — Law Times
LT Jour — Law Times
LTK — Lexikon fuer Theologie und Kirche
Lt L — Leksykolohiia ta Leksykohrafiia Mizhvidomchyi Zbirnyk
LTLA — Language Teaching and Linguistics Abstracts
LTLJ — La Trobe Library Journal
LTLS — (London) Times Literary Supplement
Lt Ltg — Light and Lighting
LTM — Leeds Texts and Monographs
LTP — Laval Theologique et Philosophique
Lt Prod Engng — Light Production Engineering
LTQ — Lexington Theological Quarterly
LTR — Leather. International Journal of the Industry
LTR — Levant Trade Review
LTR — Library Technology Reports
LTR — Logistics and Transportation Review
L in Trans — Law in Transition
LTS — (London) Times Literary Supplement
LTSB — Low Temperature Science. Series B. Biological Sciences
LTW — List Taschenbuecher der Wissenschaft
L & U — Lion and the Unicorn
Lu — Lusiada
LUA — Lunds Universitet. Arsskrift
Lubr Eng — Lubrication Engineering
Lubric Eng — Lubrication Engineering
Lubric Engng — Lubrication Engineering
Luc — Luceafarul
Lucas Engng Rev — Lucas Engineering Review
Lucas Eng Rev — Lucas Engineering Review
Lucrari Muzicol — Lucrari de Muzicologie
Lucrari Sti Inst Ped Galati — Lucrari Stiintifice. Institutul Pedagogic Galati
Lucr Cercet Inst Cercet Ind Chim Aliment — Lucrari de Cercetare. Institutul de Cercetari pentru Industrie si Chimie Alimentara
Lucr Cercet Inst Cercet Project Aliment — Lucrari de Cercetare. Institutul de Cercetari si Projectari Alimentare
Lucr Cercet Inst Chim Aliment — Lucrari de Cercetare. Institutul de Chimie Alimentara
Lucr Grad Bot (Bucuresti) — Lucrarile Gradinii Botanice (Bucuresti)
Lucr Gradinii Bot (Bucur) — Lucrarile Gradinii Botanice (Bucuresti)

Lucr ICPE — Lucrarile ICPE [*Institutul de Cercetare si Proiectare pentru Industria Electrotehnica*] [*Romania*]

Lucr Inst Cercet Alim — Lucrarile Institutului de Cercetari Alimentare

Lucr Inst Cercet Aliment — Lucrarile Institutului de Cercetari Alimentare

Lucr Inst Cercet Vet Bioprep Pasteur — Lucrarile Institutului de Cercetari Veterinare si Biopreparate Pasteur

Lucr Inst Pet Gaze Bucuresti — Lucrarile Institutului de Petrol si Gaze din Bucuresti

Lucr Inst Pet Gaz Geol Bucuresti — Lucrarile Institutului de Petrol, Gaze, si Geologie din Bucuresti

Lucr Semin Mat Fiz Inst Politeh "Traian Vuia" (Timisoara) — Lucrarile Seminarului de Matematica si Fizica. Institutului Politehnic "Traian Vuia" (Timisoara)

Lucr Ses Stiint Inst Agron Nicolae Balcescu — Lucrarile Sesiunii Stiintifice. Institutul Agronomic "Nicolae Balcescu"

Lucr Ses Stiint Inst Agron Nicolae Balcescu Ser C — Lucrarile Sesiunii Stiintifice. Institutul Agronomic "Nicolae Balcescu" (Bucuresti). Seria C. Zootehnie si Medicina Veterinara

Lucr Simp Biodeterior Clim — Lucrarile. Simpozion de Biodeteriorare si Climatizare

Lucr Sti Inst Agron Dr Petru Groza (Cluj) — Lucrari Stiintifice. Institutul Agronomic "Dr. Petru Groza" (Cluj)

Lucr Sti Inst Agron Dr Petru Groza (Cluj) Ser Agr — Lucrari Stiintifice. Institutul Agronomic "Dr. Petru Groza" (Cluj). Seria Agricultura

Lucr Sti Inst Agron Ion Ionescu de la Brad (Iasi) — Lucrari Stiintifice. Institutul Agronomic "Ion Ionescu de la Brad" (Iasi)

Lucr Sti Inst Agron N Balcescu (Bucuresti) Ser A B C — Lucrari Stiintifice. Institutul Agronomic "Nicolae Balcescu" (Bucuresti). Seria A, B, C

Lucr Sti Inst Agron Professor Ion Ionescu de la Brad — Lucrari Stiintifice. Institutul Agronomic "Professor Ion Ionescu de la Brad"

Lucr Sti Inst Agron Timisoara (Bucuresti) — Lucrari Stiintifice. Institutul Agronomic Timisoara (Bucuresti)

Lucr Sti Inst Agron "T Vladimirescu" (Craiova) — Lucrari Stiintifice. Institutul Agronomic "T. Vladimirescu" (Craiova)

Lucr Sti Inst Cercet Zooteh — Lucrarile Stiintifice. Institutului de Cercetari Zootehnice

Lucr Stiint Cent Exp Ingrasaminte Bact (Bucharest) — Lucrari Stiintifice. Centrul Experimental de Ingrasaminte Bacteriene (Bucharest)

Lucr Stiint Inst Agron (Bucuresti) Ser A — Lucrari Stiintifice. Institutul Agronomic "Nicolae Balcescu" (Bucuresti). Seria A. Agronomie [*Romania*]

Lucr Stiint Inst Agron (Bucuresti) Ser B — Lucrari Stiintifice. Institutul Agronomic "Nicolae Balcescu" (Bucuresti). Seria B. Horticultura

Lucr Stiint Inst Agron (Bucuresti) Ser C — Lucrari Stiintifice. Institutul Agronomic "Nicolae Balcescu" (Bucuresti). Seria C. Zootehnie si Medicina Veterinara

Lucr Stiint Inst Agron (Bucuresti) Ser D Zooteh — Lucrari Stiintifice. Institutul Agronomic "Nicolae Balcescu" (Bucuresti). Seria D. Zootehnie

Lucr Stiint Inst Agron (Cluj) — Lucrari Stiintifice. Institutul Agronomic "Dr. Petru Groza" (Cluj)

Lucr Stiint Inst Agron (Cluj) Ser Agric — Lucrari Stiintifice. Institutul Agronomic "Dr. Petru Groza" (Cluj). Seria Agricultura

Lucr Stiint Inst Agron (Cluj) Ser Med Vet — Lucrari Stiintifice. Institutul Agronomic "Dr. Petru Groza" (Cluj). Seria Medicina Veterinari

Lucr Stiint Inst Agron (Cluj) Ser Med Vet Zooteh — Lucrari Stiintifice. Institutul Agronomic "Dr. Petru Groza" (Cluj). Seria Medicina Veterinara si Zootehnie

Lucr Stiint Inst Agron (Cluj) Ser Zooteh — Lucrari Stiintifice. Institutul Agronomic "Dr. Petru Groza" (Cluj). Seria Zootehnie

Lucr Stiint Inst Agron (Iasi) — Lucrarile Stiintifice. Institutul Agronomic "Professor Ion Ionescu de la Brad" (Iasi)

Lucr Stiint Inst Agron Ion Ionescu de la Brad (Iasi) — Lucrarile Stiintifice. Institutul Agronomic "Professor Ion Ionescu de la Brad" (Iasi) [*Romania*]

Lucr Stiint Inst Agron N Balcescu (Bucuresti) Ser C — Lucrari Stiintifice ale Institutului Agronomic "Nicolae Balcescu" (Bucuresti). Seria C [*Romania*]

Lucr Stiint Inst Agron N Balcescu (Bucur) Ser C — Lucrari Stiintifice ale Institutului Agronomic "Nicolae Balcescu" (Bucuresti). Seria C

Lucr Stiint Inst Agron "Nicolae Balcescu" Agron — Lucrari Stiintifice. Institutul Agronomic "Nicolae Balcescu." Agronomie

Lucr Stiint Inst Agron "Nicolae Balcescu" Hortic — Lucrari Stiintifice. Institutul Agronomic "Nicolae Balcescu." Horticultura

Lucr Stiint Inst Agron "Nicolae Balcescu" Imbunatatiri Fun — Lucrari Stiintifice. Institutul Agronomic "Nicolae Balcescu." Imbunatatiri Funciare

Lucr Stiint Inst Agron "Nicolae Balcescu" Med Vet — Lucrari Stiintifice. Institutul Agronomic "Nicolae Balcescu." Medicina Veterinara

Lucr Stiint Inst Agron "Nicolae Balcescu" Zooteh — Lucrari Stiintifice. Institutul Agronomic "Nicolae Balcescu." Zootehnie

Lucr Stiint Inst Agron (Timisoara) Seri Medna Vet — Lucrari Stiintifice. Institutul Agronomic (Timisoara). Seria Medicina Veterinara

Lucr Stiint Inst Agron (Timisoara) Ser Med Vet — Lucrari Stiintifice. Institutul Agronomic (Timisoara). Seria Medicina Veterinara

Lucr Stiint Inst Agron (Timisoara) Ser Zooteh — Lucrari Stiintifice. Institutul Agronomic (Timisoara). Seria Zootehnie

Lucr Stiint Inst Cercet Zooteh — Lucrarile Stiintifice. Institutului de Cercetari Zootehnice

Lucr Stiint Inst Cerc Zooteh — Lucrarile Stiintifice. Institutului de Cercetari Zootehnice

Lucr Stiint Inst Mine Petrosani — Lucrarile Stiintifice. Institutului de Mine Petrosani

Lucr Stiint Inst Mine Petrosani Ser 4 — Lucrarile Stiintifice. Institutului de Mine Petrosani. Seria 4. Stiinte de Cultura Tehnica Generala

Lucr Stiint Inst Mine Petrosani Ser 5 — Lucrarile Stiintifice. Institutului de Mine Petrosani. Seria 5. Geologie

Lucr Stiint Inst Mine Petrosani Ser 6 — Lucrarile Stiintifice. Institutului de Mine Petrosani. Seria 6. Stiinte Sociale

Lucr Stiint Inst Patol Ig Anim — Lucrarile Stiintifice. Institutului de Patologie si Igiena Animala

Lucr Stiint Inst Pedagog Oradea Ser Mat Fiz Chim — Lucrari Stiintifice. Institutul Pedagogic din Oradea. Seria Matematica, Fizica, Chimie

Lucr Stiint Inst Politeh (Cluj) — Lucrarile Stiintifice. Institutul Politehnic (Cluj)

Lucr Stiint Inst Politeh (Galati) — Lucrari Stiintifice. Institutul Politehnic (Galati)

Lucr Stiint Inst Seruri Vacc Pasteur (Bucur) — Lucrarile Stiintifice. Institutului de Seruri si Vaccinuri Pasteur (Bucuresti)

Lucr Stiint Ser C VII — Lucrari Stiintifice. Seria C VII. Zootehnie si Medicina Veterinara [*Bucuresti*]

Lucr Stiint Ser Zooteh Med Vet — Lucrari Stiintifice. Seria Zootehnie si Medicina Veterinara

Lucr Stint Inst Agron (Timisoara) Ser Agron — Lucrari Stiintifice. Institutul Agronomic (Timisoara). Seria Agronomie

LuD — Linguistik und Didaktik

Lueneburger B — Lueneburger Blaetter

LUF — Librarie Universelle de France

LUFBBK — Fonds de Recherches Forestieres. Universite Laval. Bulletin

Luftfahrttech Raumfahrttech — Luftfahrttechnik, Raumfahrttechnik

Luft- Kaeltetech — Luft- und Kaeltetechnik

LuG — Literatur und Geschichte. Eine Schriftenreihe

LUH — Ledermarkt und Hautemarkt mit Gerbereiwissenschaft und Praxis. Das Wochenjournal fuer die Lederindustrie, den Hautegrosshandel und Ledergrosshandel

LUK — Literatur und Kritik [*Wien*]

LuL — Literatur und Leben

LuM — Literatura un Maksla

Lum — Lumiere

Lumen — Lumen Vitae

Lumiere — Lumiere et Vie

LumVie — Lumiere et Vie [*Lyons*]

LumViSup — Lumiere et Vie. Supplement Biblique

LumVit — Lumen Vitae [*Brussels*]

Lunar and Planetary Explor Colloquium Proc — Lunar and Planetary Exploration Colloquium. Proceedings

Lunar Sci Inst Contrib — Lunar Science Institute. Contribution

Lun Ger For — Lunder Germanistische Forschungen

Luonnon Tutk — Luonnon Tutkija

LuQ — Lutheran Quarterly

LuR — Literature und Reflexion

LUR — Petera Stuckas Latvijas Valsts Universitate Zinatniskie Raksti. Filologijas Zinatnes. A Serija (Riga)

LURB — List of Unlocated Research Books

Luso J Sci Tech — Luso Journal of Science and Technology

Luth — Lutheran

LuthChQ — Lutheran Church Quarterly

Luth Educ — Lutheran Education

Luther-Jahrb — Luther-Jahrbuch

LuthJB — Luther-Jahrbuch [*Hamburg*]

LuthMonh — Lutherische Monatshefte [*Hamburg*]

LuthQ — Lutheran Quarterly

LuthRu — Lutherische Rundschau [*Geneva*]

Luth S — Lutheran Standard

Luth W — Lutheran Witness

LuthW — Lutheran World

Lutte Cancer — Lutte Contre le Cancer [*France*]

LuW — Literatur und Wirklichkeit

Luxemb Bienenztg — Luxemburgische Bienen-Zeitung

Luzerne Leg Reg (PA) — Luzerne Legal Register [*Pennsylvania*]

Luz Leg Reg — Luzerne Legal Register

Luz LR — Luzerne Legal Register

LUZR — Petera Stuckas Latvijas Valsts Universitate Zinatniskie Raksti

LV — Leningradskij Universitet Vestnik Serija Istorii, Literatury, i Jazyka

LV — Lumen Vitae

LV — Lumiere et Vie [*Lyons*]

L'viv Zootekh Vet Inst Nauk Pr — L'vivskii Zootekhnichno-Veterinarnii Institut. Naukovi Pratsi

LVKJ — Latviesu Valodas Kulturas Jautajumi

LVLG — Luther. Vierteljahresschrift der Luthergesellschaft

L'vov Politehn Inst Naucn Zap Ser Fiz-Mat — L'vovskii Politehniceskii Institut. Naucnye Zapiski. Serija Fiziko-Matematiceskaja

L'vov Torg Ekon Inst Nauchn Zap — L'vovskii Torgovo-Ekonomicheskii Institut. Nauchnye Zapiski
LVR — Land and Valuation Court Reports [*New South Wales*]
LvS — Literatura v Shkole
LvSK — Literatura v Shkole
LW — Literarische Wochenschrift
LW — Living Wilderness
LWK — Leerblad. Vakblad voor de Lederwarenbranche en Reisartikelenbranche in de Beneluxlanden
LWLR — Land and Water Law Review
LWLRD — Land and Water Law Review
LWN — Landbouwwereldnieuws
LWorld — Lutheran World
LWR — Land and Water Law Review
LWU — Literatur in Wissenschaft und Unterricht
LWZ — Lederwaren Zeitung
LXAAAC — Annual Report. Laboratory of Experimental Algology and Department of Applied Algology [*Trebon*]
LY — Lessing Yearbook
Ly — Lychnos
LyC — Lenguaje y Ciencias
Lychnos Lardomshist Samf Arsb — Lychnos Lardomshistoriska Samfundets Arsbok
Lyc N H NY An Pr — Lyceum of Natural History of New York. Annals. Proceedings
LydgN — Lydgate Newsletter
Lying-In J Reprod Med — Lying-In Journal of Reproductive Medicine
Lynx Suppl (Prague) — Lynx Supplementum (Prague)
Lyon Chir — Lyon Chirurgical
Lyon Med — Lyon Medical
Lyon Pharm — Lyon Pharmaceutique
Lyons Fac Sci Lab Geol Doc — Lyons. Faculte des Sciences. Laboratoires de Geologie. Documents
LyP — Libro y Pueblo
Lysosomes Biol Pathol — Lysosomes in Biology and Pathology
Lyumin Mater Osobo Chist Veshchestva — Lyuminestsentnye Materialy i Osobo Chistye Veshchestva. Sbornik Nauchnykh Trudov
LZ — Literarisches Zentralblatt fuer Deutschland
LZ — Literaturen Zbor
LZ — Literaturnye Zapiski
LZAV — Latvijas PSR Zinatnu Akademijas. Vestis [*Riga*]
LZB — Literarisches Zentralblatt fuer Deutschland
LZD — Literarisches Zentralblatt fuer Deutschland
LzT — Listy z Teatru

M

M — M. Gentle Men for Gender Justice
M — Manuscripts
M — Marketing
M — Merkur
M — Missiology
M — Mnemosyne
M — Monde
M — Museon. Revue d'Etudes Orientales
M — Musica
M — Musicology
MA — Mackenzie News
MA — Madison Avenue
MA — Magazine of Art
MA — Management Abstracts
Ma — Maryland Music Educator
MA — Masters Abstracts
MA — Medical Annual
MA — Medium Aevum
MA — Microfilm Abstracts
M-A — Mid-America: An Historical Review
MA — Military Affairs
MA — Modern Age
MA — Monographs in Anaesthesiology [Elsevier Book Series]
MA — Moyen Age
MA — Musical Antiquary
MAA — Maatschappijbelangen
MAA — Management Accounting
MAA — Mededeelingen. Koninklijke Nederlandse Akademie van
Wetenschappen te Amsterdam
MAAA — Memoirs. American Anthropological Association
MAAL — Monumenti Antichi. Reale Accademia Nazionale dei Lincei
MAAN — Memorie. Reale Accademia di Archeologia, Lettere, e Belle Arti di
Napoli
Maandbl Landbouwvoorlichtingsdienst (Neth) — Maandblad voor de
Landbouwvoorlichtingsdienst (Netherlands)
Maandbl Pieper — Maandblad de Pieper
Maandbl Vlaam Bieenb — Maandblad van de Vlaamse Bieenbond
Maandbl Vlaam Imkersb — Maandblad van de Vlaamse Imkersbond
Maandschr Bijent — Maandschrift voor Bijenteelt
Maandschr Kindergeneeskd — Maandschrift voor Kindergeneeskunde
MAAR — Memoirs. American Academy at Rome
MAA Stud Math — MAA [Mathematical Association of America] Studies in
Mathematics
Maatalouden Tutkimuskeskus Maantutkimuslaitos Agrogeol Julk —
Maatalouden Tutkimuskeskus. Maantutkimuslaitos. Agrogeologisia
Julkaisuja
Maatalouden Tutkimuskeskus Maantutkimuslaitos Agrogeol Kart —
Maatalouden Tutkimuskeskus. Maantutkimuslaitos. Agrogeologisia
Karttoja
Maataloushal Aikakausk — Maataloushallinnon Aikakauskirja
Maatalous Koetoim — Maatalous ja Koetoiminta
Maataloust Aikakausk — Maataloustieteelinen Aikakauskirja
Maatalousstiet Aikak — Maataloustieteelinen Aikakauskirja
Maataloustieteelinen Aikak — Maataloustieteelinen Aikakauskirja
MAB — Maandblad voor Accountancy en Bedrijfshuishoudkunde

MAB — Magazine of Bank Administration
MAb — Masters Abstracts
MAB — Memoires. Academie Royale de Belgique
MABFAI — Muenchener Beitraege zur Abwasser-, Fischerei-, und
Flussbiologie
MAC — Commercial Courier
MAC — MAC [Media Agencies Clients]/Western Advertising
MAC — Macabre
Mac — Maclean's
Mac — Macmillan's Magazine
Mac — Media, Agencies, Clients [Later, Adweek]
MAC — Memorias. Academia das Ciencias de Lisboa. Classe de Letras
MAC — Mergers and Acquisitions
MAC — Motor Accidents Cases
Macaroni J — Macaroni Journal
Macaulay Inst Soil Res Annu Rep — Macaulay Institute for Soil Research.
Annual Report
Macaulay Inst Soil Res Collect Pap — Macaulay Institute for Soil Research.
Collected Papers
Macch Motori Agr — Macchine e Motori Agricoli
MACD — Metabolic Aspects of Cardiovascular Disease [Elsevier Book Series]
MACDA — Michigan Academician
MACEJ — Manitoba Association of Confluent Education. Journal
Mach — Machinery [Later, Machinery and Production Engineering]
Mach Agric Equip Rural — Machinisme Agricole et Equipement Rural
[France]
Mach Agric Trop — Machinisme Agricole Tropical
Mach Agr Trop — Machinisme Agricole Tropical
Mach Build Ind — Machine Building Industry [India]
Mach Des — Machine Design
Mach Design — Machine Design
Mach Equip Food Ind — Machinery and Equipment for Food Industry
Machine D — Machine Design
Machinery Prod Engng — Machinery and Production Engineering
Mach Korea — Machinery Korea
Mach Lloyd Int Rev Eng Equip — Machinery Lloyd. International Review of
Engineering Equipment
Mach Market — Machinery Market
Mach Mod — Machine Moderne
Mach Outil Fr — Machine Outil Francaise
Mach Prod E — Machinery and Production Engineering
Mach and Prod Eng — Machinery and Production Engineering
Mach Prod Eng — Machinery and Production Engineering
Mach & Prod Engng — Machinery and Production Engineering
Mach Shop — Machine Shop
Mach Shop Eng Manuf — Machine Shop and Engineering Manufacture
[England]
Mach Tool — Machines and Tooling [English Translation of Stanki i
Instrument]
Mach and Tool — Machines and Tooling
Mach Tool Blue Book — Machine and Tool Blue Book
Mach Tool Eng — Machine Tool Engineering
Mach Tool Engl Transl — Machines and Tooling. English Translation
Mach Tool R — Machine Tool Review
MACL — Memoires. Academie d'Histoire de la Culture de Leningrad

MACL — Memorias. Academia das Ciencias de Lisboa. Classe de Letras
MACLCL — Memorias. Academia das Ciencias de Lisboa. Classe de Letras
MACLL — Memorias. Academia das Ciencias de Lisboa. Classe de Letras
Macl Mag — Maclean's Magazine
Maclurean Lyc Contr — Maclurean Lyceum. Contributions
Macmil — Macmillan's Magazine
Mac R — Macedonian Review
MACR — Molecular Aspects of Cell Regulation [*Elsevier Book Series*]
Macromolec — Macromolecules
Macromol Phys — Macromolecular Physics
Macromol R — Macromolecular Reviews. Part D. Journal of Polymer Science
Macromol Rev — Macromolecular Reviews
Macromols — Macromolecules
MAC/WA — MAC [*Media Agencies Clients*]/Western Advertising
MAD — Memoires. Academie des Sciences, des Arts, et des Belles-Lettres de Dijon
Madagascar Dir Ind Mines Rapp Act Geol — Madagascar. Direction de l'Industrie et des Mines. Rapports d'Activite. Geologie
Madagascar Rev Geogr — Madagascar. Revue de Geographie
Madem — Mademoiselle
Made in Mex — Made in Mexico
Maden Tetkik Arama Enst Mecm — Maden Tetkik ve Arama Enstitusu Mecmuasi
Maden Tetkik Arama Enst Yayin — Maden Tetkik ve Arama Enstitusu Yayinlarindan
Maden Tetkik Arama Enst Yayinlarindan — Maden Tetkik ve Arama Enstitusu Yayinlarindan [*Turkey*]
Maden Tetkik Arama Enst Yayin Seri A — Maden Tetkik ve Arama Enstitusu Yayinlarindan. Seri A. Bildirigler
Maden Tetkik Arama Enst Yayin Seri B — Maden Tetkik ve Arama Enstitusu Yayinlarindan. Seri B. Irdeller
Maden Tetkik Arama Enst Yayin Seri C — Maden Tetkik ve Arama Enstitusu Yayinlarindan. Seri C. Monografiler
Maden Tetkik Arama Enst Yayin Seri D — Maden Tetkik ve Arama Enstitusu Yayinlarindan. Seri D. Jeolojik Harta Materye-Leri
Madhya Bharati J Univ Saugar Part 2 Sect B Nat Sci — Madhya Bharati. Journal of the University of Saugar. Part 2. Section B. Natural Sciences
Madhya Bharati Pt 2 Sect A — Madhya Bharati. Part 2. Section A. Physical Sciences
Madison Ave — Madison Avenue
Madjalah Inst Tek Bandung Proc — Madjalah Institut Teknologi Bandung Proceedings [*Indonesia*]
Madjelis Ilmu Pengetahuan Indones Penerbitan — Madjelis Ilmu Pengetahuan Indonesia Penerbitan
Mad LJ — Madras Law Journal
Madness — Madness Network News
MADNV — Mitteilungsblatt des Allgemeiner Deutscher Neuphilologenverband
Madoqua Ser I — Madoqua. Series I
Madoqua Ser II — Modoqua. Series II
Mad Q — Madison Quarterly
Mad R — Madras Review
Madras Agric J — Madras Agricultural Journal
Madras Agr J — Madras Agricultural Journal
Madras LJ — Madras Law Journal
Madras Med J — Madras Medical Journal
Madras Vet Coll Annu — Madras Veterinary College. Annual
Madras Vet J — Madras Veterinary Journal
Madrid Univ Fac Med Arch — Madrid Universidad. Facultad de Medicina. Archivos
Madr Mitt — Mitteilungen. Deutsches Archaeologische Institut. Abteilung Madrid
MADZAK — Koninklijk Museum voor Midden-Afrika [*Tervuren, Belgie*]. Zoologische Documentatie
MAE — Medium Aevum
MAECA — Modern Aspects of Electrochemistry
MAECDR — Marine Ecology. Pubblicazioni della Stazione Zoologica di Napoli. I
MAEQA — Meetings on Atomic Energy
Maerisch-Schlesische Heimat — Maerisch-Schlesische Heimat. Vierteljahresschrift fuer Kultur und Wirtschaft
MAev — Medium Aevum
MAFES Res Highlights Miss Agric For Exp Stn — MAFES Research Highlights. Mississippi Agricultural and Forestry Experiment Station
MAFR — Marine Fisheries Review
MAFR — Marriage and Family Review
MAG — Magazine Article Guide
Mag Antiq — Magazine of Antiques
Mag Art — Magazine of Art
Mag of Art — Magazine of Art
Mag Asvanyolaj Foldgaz Kiserl Intez Kozl — Magyar Asvanyolaj-es Foldgaz Kiserleti Intezet Koezlemenyei
Mag Bank Adm — Magazine of Bank Administration
Mag Belorv Arch Ideggyogy Sz — Magyar Belorvosi Archivum es Ideggyogyaszati Szemle
Mag Bihar Agr Coll — Magazine. Bihar Agricultural College

Mag Biol Kutatointez Munkai — Magyar Biologiai Kutatointezet Munkai
Mag Bldg — Magazine of Building
Mag Build Equip — Magazine of Building Equipment [*Japan*]
Mag of Business — Magazine of Business
Mag Concrete Res — Magazine of Concrete Research
Mag Concr R — Magazine of Concrete Research
MAGDA — Mechanisms of Ageing and Development
Mag Datenverarb — Magazin fuer Datenverarbeitung
Mag Fantasy & Sci Fict — Magazine of Fantasy and Science Fiction
Mag of Hist — Magazine of History
Maghreb — Maghreb-Machrek
Mag I — Magazine Index
Mag Istor — Magazin Istoric
MAGJB — Magyar Allami Eoetvoes Lorand Geofizikai Intezet. Evi Jelentese
Mag Kir Szolo Borgazd Kozp Kiserl Allomas Ampelol Intez Evk — Magyar Kir. Szolo es Borgazdasagi Kozponti Kiserleti Allomas (Ampelologiai Intezet) Evkonyve
Mag Kozlekedes Mely Vizepites — Magyar Kozlekedes. Mely es Vizepites
Mag Lond (Roy Free Hosp) School Med Women — Magazine. London (Royal Free Hospital) School of Medicine for Women
Mag Macl — Magazine Maclean
Mag Mern Epitesz Egylet Kozl — Magyar Mernok es Epitesz Egylet Koezloenye
Mag Min Health Saf MESA — Magazine of Mining Health and Safety. MESA [*Mining Enforcement and Safety Administration*] [*United States*]
MagN — Magyar Nyelvor
Mag Nagpur Agr Coll — Magazine. Nagpur Agricultural College
Mag Nat Hist — Magazine of Natural History
Mag N Entdeck Ges Naturk — Magazin fuer die Neuesten Entdeckungen in der Gesammten Naturkunde
Magnetohydrodyn — Magnetohydrodynamics
Magn Gidrodin — Magnitnaya Gidrodinamika
Mag N H — Magazine of Natural History [*London*]
Magnitogidrodin Metod Poluch Elektroenergii — Magnitogidrodinamicheskii Metod Polucheniya Elektroenergii
Magnitogidrodin Metod Preobraz Energ — Magnitogidrodinamicheskii Metod Preobrazovaniya Energii [*USSR*]
Magn Lett — Magnetism Letters
Magn Lovushki — Magnitnye Lovushki
Magn Magn Mater Dig — Magnetism and Magnetic Materials Digest
Magn Resonance Rev — Magnetic Resonance Review
Magn Reson Rev — Magnetic Resonance Review
Magn Soc India Newsl — Magnetics Society of India. Newsletter
Magon Inst Rech Agron Publ Ser Sci — Magon Institut de Recherches Agronomiques. Publication. Serie Scientifique
Magon Inst Rech Agron Publ Ser Tech — Magon Institut de Recherches Agronomiques. Publication. Serie Technique
Mag of Stand — Magazine of Standards
Mag Stand — Magazine of Standards
Mag Std — Magazine of Standards
Mag Traumatol Orthop Helyreallito Sebesz — Magyar Traumatologia, Orthopaedia, es Helyreallito-Sebeszet
Mag Tud Akad Agrartud Oszt Kozl — Magyar Tudomanyos Akademia. Agrartudomanyok Osztalyanak Koezlemenyei
Mag Tud Akad Biol Tud Oszt Kozl — Magyar Tudomanyos Akademia. Biologiai Tudomanyok Osztalyanak Koezlemenyei
Mag Tud Akad Kem Tud Oszt Kozl — Magyar Tudomanyos Akademia. Kemiai Tudomanyok Osztalyanak Koezlemenyei
Mag Tud Akad Kozp Fiz Kut Intez Kozl — Magyar Tudomanyos Akademia. Kozponti Fizikai Kutato Intezetenek Koezlemenyei
Mag Tud Akad Kozp Kem Intez Kozl — Magyar Tudomanyos Akademia. Kozponti Kemiai Kutato Intezetenek Koezlemenyei
Mag Tud Akad Mat Fiz Tud Oszt Kozl — Magyar Tudomanyos Akademia. Matematikai es Fizikai Tudomanyok Osztalyanak Koezlemenyei
Mag Tud Akad Musz Tud Oszt Kozl — Magyar Tudomanyos Akademia. Mueszaki Tudomanyok Osztalyanak Koezlemenyei
Mag Tud Akad 5 Otodik Orv Tud Oszt Kozl — Magyar Tudomanyos Akademia. 5 Otodik Orvosi Tudomanyok Osztalyanak Koezlemenyei
MAGW — Mitteilungen. Anthropologische Gesellschaft in Wien
Mag of Wall St — Magazine of Wall Street
Mag Wall St — Magazine of Wall Street
Mag Wall Street — Magazine of Wall Street
MagWJ — Magazin fuer die Wissenschaft des Judentums
Magy Allami Eoetvoes Lorand Geofiz Intez Evi Jelentese — Magyar Allami Eoetvoes Lorand Geofizikai Intezet. Evi Jelentese
Magy Allatorv Lap — Magyar Allatorvosok Lapja
Magy Allatorv Lapja — Magyar Allatorvosok Lapja
Magy Allatorv Lap Kueloenszama — Magyar Allatorvosok Lapja Kueloenszama
Magy All Eotvos Lorand Geofiz Intez Evi Jel — Magyar Allami Eoetvoes Lorand Geofizikai Intezet. Evi Jelentese
Magy All Foldt Intez Evi Jel — Magyar Allami Foldtani Intezet. Evi Jelentese
Magy All Foldt Intez Evk — Magyar Allami Foldtani Intezet. Evkoenyve
Magy All Foldt Intez Modszertani Kozl — Magyar Allami Foldtani Intezet. Modszertani Koezlemenyek

Magy Alum — Magyar Aluminium
Magyar Filoz Szle — Magyar Filozofiai Szemle
Magyar Num Tars Ev — Magyar Numizmatikai Tarsulat Evkoenyve
Magyarorsz Allatvilaga — Magyarorszag Allatvilaga
Magyar Pszichol Szle — Magyar Pszichologiai Szemle
Magyar Textiltech — Magyar Textiltechnika
Magyar Tud Akad Filoz-Tort Oszt Kozlem — Magyar Tudomanyos Akademia. Filozofiai-Torteneti Osztalyanak Koezlemenyei
Magyar Tud Akad Mat Fiz Oszt Koezl — Magyar Tudomanyos Akademia. Matematikai es Fizikai Tudomanyok Osztalyanak Koezlemenyei
Magy Asvanyolaj-Foeldgazkiserl Intez Koezl — Magyar Asvanyolaj-es Foeldgazkiserleti Intezet Koezlemenyei
Magy Asvanyolaj Foldgaz Kiserl Intez Kiadv — Magyar Asvanyolaj-es Foldgaz Kiserleti Intezet Kiadvanyai [Hungary]
Magy Asvanyolaj Foldgaz Kiserl Intez Kozl — Magyar Asvanyolaj-es Foldgaz Kiserleti Intezet Koezlemenyei [Hungary]
Magy Belorv Arch — Magyar Belorvosi Archivum
Magy Biol Kutato Intezet Munkai — Magyar Biologiai Kutato Intezet Munkai
Magy Chem Folyoirat — Magyar Chemiai Folyoirat [Hungary]
Magy Epitoeipar — Magyar Epitoeipar
Magy Fiz Foly — Magyar Fizikai Folyoirat
Magy Geofiz — Magyar Geofizika
Magy Kem Fo — Magyar Kemiai Folyoirat
Magy Kem Foly — Magyar Kemiai Folyoirat
Magy Kem Folyoirat — Magyar Kemiai Folyoirat
Magy Kem Lapja — Magyar Kemikusok Lapja
Magy Koenyvszle — Magyar Koenyvszemle
Magy Koezl — Magyar Koezloeny
Magy Kult — Magyarorszag Kulturfloraja
Magy Kulturfloraja — Magyarorszag Kulturfloraja
Magy Mezoegazd — Magyar Mezoegazdasag
Magy Mezogazd — Magyar Mezoegazdasag
Magy Noeorv Lapja — Magyar Noeorvosok Lapja
Magy Onkol — Magyar Onkologia
Magy Radiol — Magyar Radiologia
Magy Reumatol — Magyar Reumatologia
Magy Sebesz — Magyar Sebeszet
Magy Textiltech — Magyar Textiltechnika [Hungary]
Magy Traumatol Orthop — Magyar Traumatologia, Orthopaedia, es Helyreallito-Sebeszet
Magy Traumatol Orthop Helyreallito Sebesz — Magyar Traumatologia, Orthopaedia, es Helyreallito-Sebeszet
Magy Tud — Magyar Tudomany
Magy Tud Akad Agrartud Osztal Kozl — Magyar Tudomanyos Akademia. Agrartudomanyok Osztalyanak Koezlemenyei
Magy Tud Akad Biol Csoportjanak Kozlem (Budapest) — Magyar Tudomanyos Akademia. Biologiai Csoportjanak Koezlemenyei (Budapest)
Magy Tud Akad Biol Orv Tud Oszt Kozl — Magyar Tudomanyos Akademia. Biologiai es Orvosi Tudomanyok Osztalyanak Koezlemenyei
Magy Tud Akad Biol Tud Oszt Koezl — Magyar Tudomanyos Akademia. Biologiai Tudomanyok Osztalyanak Koezlemenyei
Magy Tud Akad Kem Tud Oszt Kozlem — Magyar Tudomanyos Akademia. Kemiai Tudomanyok Osztalyanak Koezlemenyei [Hungary]
Magy Tud Akad Mat Fiz Tud Oszt Kozlem — Magyar Tudomanyos Akademia. Matematikai es Fizikai Tudomanyok Osztalyanak Koezlemenyei [Hungary]
Magy Tud Akad Mat Kut Intez Kozlem — Magyar Tudomanyos Akademia. Matematikai Kutato Intezetenek Koezlemenyei [Hungary]
Magy Tud Akad Muesz Fiz Kut Intez Koezl — Magyar Tudomanyos Akademia. Mueszaki Fizikai Kutato Intezetenek Koezlemenyei [Hungary]
Magy Tud Akad Muszaki Tud Oszt Kozlem — Magyar Tudomanyos Akademia. Mueszaki Tudomanyok Osztalyanak Koezlemenyei [Hungary]
Magy Tud Akad Tihanyi Biol Kutatointez Evk — Magyar Tudomanyos Akademia. Tihanyi Biologiai Kutatointezet Evkoenyve
Magy Tud Akad Veszpremi Akad Bizottsaganak Ert — Magyar Tudomanyos Akademia. Veszpremi Akademiai Bizottsaganak Ertesitoje [Hungary]
Magy Tudom Akad Biol Osztal Kozl — Magyar Tudomanyos Akademia. Biologiai Osztalyanak Koezlemenyei
Magy Villamos Muevek Troeszt Koezl — Magyar Villamos Muevek Troeszt Koezlemenyei
MAGZ — Mitteilungen. Antiquarische Gesellschaft in Zurich
MAH — Medical Abbreviations Handbook
MAH — Melanges d'Archeologie et d'Histoire
MAH — Metaal en Techniek. Vakblad voor de Metaalnijverheid
Maharaja Sayajirao Mem Lect — Maharaja Sayajirao Memorial Lectures
Maharashtra Coop Q — Maharashtra Cooperative Quarterly
Maharastra Coop Quart — Maharashtra Cooperative Quarterly
Mahatma Phule Agric Univ Res J — Mahatma Phule Agricultural University. Research Journal
MAHR — Mid-America: An Historical Review
MAI — Memoires. Institut National de France. Academie des Inscriptions et Belles-Lettres
Main Curr M — Main Currents in Modern Thought
Maine Ag Dept B — Maine. Department of Agriculture. Quarterly Bulletin
Maine Ag Exp — Maine. Agricultural Experiment Station. Publications

Maine Agric Exp Stn Bull — Maine. Agricultural Experiment Station. Bulletin
Maine Agric Exp Stn Misc Publ — Maine. Agricultural Experiment Station. Miscellaneous Publication
Maine Agric Exp Stn Misc Rep — Maine. Agricultural Experiment Station. Miscellaneous Report
Maine Agric Exp Stn Official Inspect — Maine. Agricultural Experiment Station. Official Inspections
Maine Agric Exp Stn Tech Bull — Maine. Agricultural Experiment Station. Technical Bulletin
Maine Farm Res — Maine Farm Research
Maine Field Nat — Maine Field Naturalist
Maine Geol Surv Spec Econ Stud Ser Bull — Maine. Geological Survey. Special Economic Studies Series. Bulletin
Maine Hist Soc Coll — Maine Historical Society. Collections
Maine Lib Assn Bul — Maine Library Association. Bulletin
Maine Life Agric Exp Stn Tech Bull — Maine. Life Sciences and Agricultural Experiment Station. Technical Bulletin
Maine Life Sci Agric Exp Stn Bull — Maine. Life Sciences and Agricultural Experiment Station. Bulletin
Maine Life Sci Agric Exp Stn Off Inspect — Maine. Life Sciences and Agricultural Experiment Station. Official Inspections
Maine Life Sci Agric Exp Stn Tech Bull — Maine. Life Sciences and Agricultural Experiment Station. Technical Bulletin
Maine L R — Maine Law Review
Maine L Rev — Maine Law Review
Maine Technol Exp Stn Univ Maine Pap — Maine. Technology Experiment Station. University of Maine. Paper
Maine Technology Expt Sta Bull Paper — Maine. Technology Experiment Station. Bulletin. Papers
Mainfraenk Jahrb — Mainfraenkisches Jahrbuch fuer Geschichte und Kunst
Mainfraenk Jb Gesch Kunst — Mainfraenkisches Jahrbuch fuer Geschichte und Kunst
Main Rds — Main Roads
Maint Eng — Maintenance Engineering
Maint Eng (London) — Maintenance Engineering (London)
Maint Mgmt Internat — Maintenance Management International
Mainzer Geowiss Mitt — Mainzer Geowissenschaftliche Mitteilungen
Maipu Chile Estac Exp Agron Bol Tec — Maipu, Chile. Estacion Experimental Agronomica. Boletin Tecnico
MAIR — Memorie. Classe di Scienze Morali, Storiche, e Filologiche. Accademia d'Italia (Roma)
MAISBP — Marine Invertebrates of Scandinavia
MaitrePhon — Maitre Phonetique
Maize Genet Coop News Lett — Maize Genetics Cooperation. News Letter
Majalah Kedokt Surabaya — Majalah Kedokteran Surabaya
MAJBAC — Muelleria
Maj Daneshgah e Tehran Daneshkade ye Darusazi — Majallah. Daneshgah- e Tehran. Daneshkade- ye Darusazi
Maj Demog Indo — Majalah Demografi Indonesia
Majority — Majority Report
Major Probl Clin Pediatr — Major Problems in Clinical Pediatrics
Major Probl Clin Surg — Major Problems in Clinical Surgery
Major Probl Intern Med — Major Problems in Internal Medicine
Major Probl Obstet Gynecol — Major Problems in Obstetrics and Gynecology
Major Probl Pathol — Major Problems in Pathology
Maked Folkl — Makedonski Folklor
Makedon Akad Nauk Umet Oddel Mat-Tehn Nauk Prilozi — Makedonska Akademija na Naukite i Umetnostite Oddelenie za Matematichki-Tehnichki Nauki. Prilozi
Makedon Akad Nauk Umet Oddel Prirod-Mat Nauk Prilozi — Makedonska Akademija na Naukite i Umetnostite Oddelenie za Prirodo-Matematicki Nauki Prilozi
Makedon Med Pregl — Makedonski Medicinski Pregled
Makerere LJ — Makerere Law Journal
Makerere Med J — Makerere Medical Journal
Mak F NY — Making Films in New York
MAKIA — Maandschrift voor Kindergeneeskunde
Making Mus — Making Music
Mak LJ — Makerere Law Journal
Makrom Chem — Makromolekulare Chemie
Makromol Chem — Makromolekulare Chemie
Makromol Chem Rapid Commun — Makromolekulare Chemie. Rapid Communications
MAKW — Mitteilungen. Altertumskommission fuer Westphalen
MAL — Atti. Accademia Nazionale dei Lincei. Memorie. Classe di Scienze Morali, Storiche, e Filologiche
MAL — Markenartikel. Zeitschrift fuer die Markenartikelindustrie
MAL — Modern Austrian Literature
MAL — Monumenti Antichi. Accademia Nazionale dei Lincei
Malacol Int J Malacol — Malacologia. International Journal of Malacology
Malacolog Soc London Proc — Malacological Society of London. Proceedings
Malacol Rev — Malacological Review
Malacol Soc Aust J — Malacological Society of Australia. Journal
Malacol Soc L Pr — Malacological Society of London. Proceedings
Mala Econ R — Malayan Economic Review

Malagasy Rapp Annu Serv Geol — Malagasy. Rapport Annuel du Service Geologique
Malahat Rev — Malahat Review
Malakol Abh (Dres) — Malakologische Abhandlungen (Dresden)
MalaR — Malahat Review
Malaria Internat Arch (Leipzig) — Malaria. International Archives (Leipzig)
Malaria (Roma) — Malaria e Malattie dei Paesi Caldi (Roma)
Malawian Geogr — Malawian Geographer
Malawi Annu Rep Dep Agric — Malawi. Annual Report of the Department of Agriculture
Malawi Dep Agric Fish Annu Rep Fish Part 2 — Malawi. Department of Agriculture and Fisheries. Annual Report. Fisheries Research. Part 2
Malawi For Res Inst Res Rec — Malawi Forest Research Institute. Research Record
Malawi Geol Surv Dep Bull — Malawi. Geological Survey Department. Bulletin
Malawi Geol Surv Dep Mem — Malawi. Geological Survey Department. Memoir
Malaya Dep Agric Bull — Malaya. Department of Agriculture. Bulletin
Malaya For Res Inst Res Pam — Malaya. Forest Research Institute. Research Pamphlet
Malaya Geol Surv Dep Mem — Malaya. Geological Survey Department. Memoir
Malay Agric J — Malayan Agricultural Journal
Malaya Law R — Malaya Law Review
Malaya LR — Malaya Law Review
Malaya L Rev — Malaya Law Review
Malayan Ag J — Malayan Agricultural Journal
Malayan Agric J — Malayan Agricultural Journal
Malayan Agr J — Malayan Agricultural Journal
Malayan Econ R — Malayan Economic Review
Malayan Lib J — Malayan Library Journal
Malayan LJ — Malayan Law Journal
Malay For Rec — Malayan Forest Records
Malay Nat J — Malayan Nature Journal
Malay Rep For Admin — Malay Report on Forest Administration
Malays Agric J — Malaysian Agricultural Journal
Malays Annu Rep Inst Med Res — Malaysia. Annual Report. Institute for Medical Research
Malays Appl Bio — Malaysian Applied Biology
Malays Borneo Reg Annu Rep Geol Surv — Malaysia. Borneo Region. Annual Report of the Geological Survey
Malays Div Agric Bull — Malaysia. Division of Agriculture. Bulletin
Malays For — Malaysian Forester
Malays For Res Inst Kepong Res Pam — Malaysia Forest Research Institute. Kepong Research Pamphlet
Malays Geol Surv Annu Rep — Malaysia. Geological Survey. Annual Report
Malays Geol Surv Borneo Reg Bull — Malaysia. Geological Survey. Borneo Region. Bulletin
Malays Geol Surv Borneo Reg Mem — Malaysia. Geological Survey. Borneo Region. Memoir
Malays Geol Surv Borneo Reg Rep — Malaysia. Geological Survey. Borneo Region. Report
Malays Geol Surv Dist Mem — Malaysia. Geological Survey. District Memoir
Malays Geol Surv Map Bull — Malaysia. Geological Survey. Map Bulletin
Malays Geol Surv Rep — Malaysia. Geological Survey. Report
Malaysian Agric Res — Malaysian Agricultural Research
Malaysian Rubb Rev — Malaysian Rubber Review
Malays Inst Med Res Annu Rep — Malaysia Institute for Medical Research. Annual Report
Malays J Pathol — Malaysian Journal of Pathology
Malays J Sci — Malaysian Journal of Science
Malays Minist Agric Co-Op Bull — Malaysia. Ministry of Agriculture and Co-Operatives. Bulletin
Malays Minist Agric Fish Bull — Malaysia. Ministry of Agriculture and Fisheries. Bulletin
Malays Minist Agric Lands Bull — Malaysia. Ministry of Agriculture and Lands. Bulletin
Malays Minist Agric Lands Tech Leafl — Malaysia. Ministry of Agriculture and Lands. Technical Leaflet
Malays Minist Agric Rural Dev Bull — Malaysia. Ministry of Agriculture and Rural Development. Bulletin
Malays Minist Agric Rural Dev Fish Bull — Malaysia. Ministry of Agriculture and Rural Development. Fisheries Bulletin
Malays Minist Lands Mines Annu Rep Geol Surv Malays — Malaysia. Ministry of Lands and Mines. Annual Report of the Geological Survey of Malaysia
Malays Rep For Admin West Malaysia — Malaysia. Report on Forest Administration in West Malaysia
Malays Vet J — Malaysian Veterinary Journal
Malay Tin Rubber J — Malayan Tin and Rubber Journal
Mal Cardiovasc — Malattie Cardiovascolari
Mal Econ R — Malayan Economic Review
Malgache Repub Ann Geol Madagascar — Malgache Republique. Annales Geologiques de Madagascar
Malgache Repub Rapp Annu Serv Geol — Malgache Republique. Rapport Annuel. Service Geologique

MALHC — Mensuario de Arte, Literatura, Historia, y Ciencia
Mal Hist — Malaysia in History
MALinc — Atti. Accademia Nazionale dei Lincei. Memorie. Classe di Scienze Morali, Storiche, e Filologiche
MALincei — Atti. Accademia Nazionale dei Lincei. Memorie. Classe di Scienze Morali, Storiche, e Filologiche
Mal Law R — Malaya Law Review
Mallee Hort Dig — Mallee Horticulture Digest
Mallee Hortic Dig — Mallee Horticulture Digest
Mal LJ — Malayan Law Journal
Malmohus Lans Hushallningssallsk Kvartallsskr — Malmoehus Laens Hushallningssaellskaps Kvartallsskrift
Malpract Dig — Malpractice Digest
Mal R — Malahat Review
M Altar — Musik und Altar
MALT Bulletin — Montana. Association of Language Teachers. Bulletin
Malting Brew Allied Processes — Malting, Brewing, and Allied Processes
Malt Res Inst Publ — Malt Research Institute. Publication
MAM — Machinery Market
MAM — Memoires. Academie Malgache
MAMA — Monumenta Asiae Minoris Antiqua [*Manchester*]
MAMAD — Manager Magazin [*West Germany*]
MAME — Mawdsley Memoirs
M Am Hist — Magazine of American History
MAMIDH — Marine Micropaleontology
MAMLAN — Mammalia
Mammal Rev — Mammal Review
Mamm Depicta — Mammalia Depicta
Mamm Depicta Beih Z Saeugetierkd — Mammalia Depicta. Beihefte zur Zeitschrift fuer Saeugetierkunde
Mamm Species — Mammalian Species
MAN — Management Focus
Man — Mankind
Man — Mannus. Zeitschrift fuer Vorgeschichte
Man — Manuscripta
MAN — Men's Association News
MANAAT — Man: A Monthly Record of Anthropological Science
MANADW — Manitoba Nature
Manag — Management
Manage Abstr — Management Abstracts
Manage Account — Management Accounting
Manage Advis — Management Adviser
Manage Controls — Management Controls
Manage Datamatics — Management Datamatics
Manage Decis — Management Decision
Manage Focus — Management Focus
Manage Gov — Management in Government
Manage e Inf — Management e Informatica
Manage Inf — Management Informatics
Manage Inf Syst Q — Management Information Systems Quarterly
Manage Int Rev — Management International Review
Management D — Management Digest
Management Inf Serv — Management Information Services
Management NZ — Management. New Zealand Institute of Management
Management's Bibliog Data — Management's Bibliographic Data
Management Sci — Management Science
Management Servs — Management Services
Manage Objectives — Management by Objectives
Manage Plann — Managerial Planning
Manage Plng — Managerial Planning
Manage Rev — Management Review
Managerial Decis Econ — Managerial and Decision Economics [*England*]
Managerial and Decision Econ — Managerial and Decision Economics
Managerial Fin — Managerial Finance
Managerial Plan — Managerial Planning
Manage Sci — Management Science
Manage Serv — Management Services
Manage Serv Gov — Management Services in Government
Manage Today — Management Today
Manage World — Management World
Manag Int R — Management International Review
Manag Japan — Management Japan
Manag Objectives — Management by Objectives
Manag Sci — Management Science
Manag Sci A — Management Science. Series A. Theory
Manag Sci B — Management Science. Series B. Application
Manag Today — Management Today
Man Bar News — Manitoba Bar News
Man B New — Manitoba Bar News
Manch — Manchester Literary Club. Papers
Manchester — Manchester School of Economic and Social Studies
Manchester Assoc Eng Trans — Manchester Association of Engineers. Transactions
Manchester G Soc Tr — Manchester Geological Society. Transactions
Manchester Lit Ph Soc Mem — Manchester Literary and Philosophical Society. Memoirs and Proceedings

Manchester Med Gaz — Manchester Medical Gazette [*England*]
Manchester M Soc Tr — Manchester Mining Society. Transactions
Manchester Sch Econ Soc Stud — Manchester School of Economic and Social Studies
Manchester Sch Ed Gazette — University of Manchester. School of Education. Gazette
Manchester School — Manchester School of Economic and Social Studies
Manch Guard — Manchester Guardian Weekly
Manch Lit Phil Soc Mem Proc — Manchester Literary and Philosophical Society. Memoirs and Proceedings
Manch Med Gaz — Manchester Medical Gazette
Manch Q — Manchester Quarterly
Manchr Rev — Manchester Review
Man Couns — Manitoba Counsellor
Mandschr Kindergeneeskd — Mandschrift voor Kindergeneeskunde
Man Ed Res C Res B — Manitoba Educational Research Council. Research Bulletins
Man Farm — Manual Farmaceutico
Manf Eng Trans — Manufacturing Engineering Transactions
MAN Forsch Planen Bauen — MAN [*Maschinenfabrik Augsburg Nuernberg*] Forschen, Planen, Bauen
Manganese Dioxide Symp Proc — Manganese Dioxide Symposium. Proceedings
Manhat — Manhattan
Man His Environ — Man and His Environment
MANIAJ — Man in India
Mani LJ — Manitoba Law Journal
Man Ind — Man in India
Manit CoOp — Manitoba Co-Operator
Manit Dep Mines Nat Resour Mines Branch Publ — Manitoba. Department of Mines and Natural Resources. Mines Branch. Publication
Manit Entomol — Manitoba Entomologist
Manit Nat — Manitoba Nature
Manitoba Dep Mines Natur Resour Mines Br Publ — Manitoba. Department of Mines and Natural Resources. Mines Branch. Publication
Manitoba Ent — Manitoba Entomologist
Manitoba LJ — Manitoba Law Journal
Man J R Anthropol Inst — Man. Journal of the Royal Anthropological Institute
Mankind Monogr — Mankind Monographs
Mankind Q — Mankind Quarterly
MANL — Memorie. Accademia Nazionale dei Lincei
Man L J — Manitoba Law Journal
Man LSJ — Manitoba Law School. Journal
Man-Made T — Man-Made Textiles in India
Man-Math T — Manitoba Math Teacher
Man Med — Man and Medicine
Man MLJ — Manitoba Modern Language Journal
Man Mon Rec Anthropol Sci — Man: A Monthly Record of Anthropological Science
Man Mus Ed — Manitoba Music Educator
Man Nat — Man and Nature
Mannesmann Forschungsber — Mannesmann Forschungsberichte
Manpower J — Manpower Journal
Manpower Unempl Res Afr — Manpower and Unemployment Research in Africa: A Newsletter
Man Q — Manchester Quarterly
ManR — Manchester Review
MAN Res Eng Manuf — MAN [*Maschinenfabrik Augsburg-Nuernberg*] Research, Engineering, Manufacturing
Man Sci — Management Science
Man/Soc/Tech — Man/Society/Technology
Man Text Ind Can — Manual of the Textile Industry of Canada
M Ant Fr — Memoires. Societe Nationale des Antiquaires de France
Man Tr — Manual Training Magazine [*Peoria, IL*]
Manual Arts Bul — Manual Arts Bulletin for Teachers in Secondary Schools
Manual Calif Agr Exp Sta — Manual. California Agricultural Experiment Station
Manual Inst For (Chile) — Manual. Instituto Forestal (Santiago De Chile)
Manual Train — Manual Training Magazine
Manufacturing Ind — Manufacturing Industries
Manuf Bul — Manufacturers' Bulletin
Manuf Ch Ae — Manufacturing Chemist and Aerosol News
Manuf Chem — Manufacturing Chemist [*England*]
Manuf Chem — Manufacturing Chemist and Aerosol News
Manuf Chem Assoc Chem Saf Data Sheet — Manufacturing Chemists' Association. Chemical Safety Data Sheet
Manuf Chemist — Manufacturing Chemist
Manuf Confect — Manufacturing Confectioner
Manuf Eng — Manufacturing Engineering
Manuf Eng Manage — Manufacturing Engineering and Management [*Later, Manufacturing Engineering*]
Manuf Eng & Mgt — Manufacturing Engineering and Management [*Later, Manufacturing Engineering*]
Manuf Ind — Manufacturing Industries
Manuf & Management — Manufacturing and Management
Manuf Milk Prod J — Manufactured Milk Products Journal

Manuf Mo — Manufacturers' Monthly
Manuf Mon — Manufacturers' Monthly
Manuf Perfum — Manufacturing Perfumer
Manuf Rec — Manufacturers' Record
Manuf Technol Horiz — Manufacturing Technology Horizons
Man Univ Calif Agric Ext Serv — Manual. University of California. Agricultural Extension Service
Manusc Math — Manuscripta Mathematica
Manuscr Geod — Manuscripta Geodaetica
Manuscripta Math — Manuscripta Mathematica
Manuscr Rep McGill Univ (Montreal) Mar Sci Cent — Manuscript Report. McGill University (Montreal). Marine Sciences Centre
Manx J Agr — Manx Journal of Agriculture
Manx J Agric — Manx Journal of Agriculture
MaNy — Magyar Nyelvor
MAOB — Marine Observer
MAoG — Mitteilungen. Altorientalische Gesellschaft [*Leipzig*]
Ma Opf & St — Mathematische Operationsforschung und Statistik
MAP — Mediaeval Academy Publications
Maple Syrup Dig — Maple Syrup Digest
Map Read — Map Reader
MAPS — Medium Aevum. Philologische Studien
MAPS — Memoirs. American Philosophical Society
MAQ — Maandnotities Betreffende de Economische Toestand
MAQR — Michigan Alumni Quarterly Review
Maquinas — Maquinas & Metais
Mar — Mar del Sur
Mar — Marianum
MAR — Markeur. Marketing Magazine voor Universiteit en Bedrijfsleven
MAR — Monumenta Artis Romanae
MAR — Municipal Association Reports
Marathwada Univ J Sci — Marathwada University. Journal of Science
Marathwada Univ J Sci Sect A Phys Sci — Marathwada University. Journal of Science. Section A. Physical Sciences
Marathwada Univ J Sci Sect B Biol Sci — Marathwada University. Journal of Science. Section B. Biological Sciences
MARBAI — Morris Arboretum. Bulletin
Mar Behav Physiol — Marine Behaviour and Physiology
Mar Behav and Physiol — Marine Behaviour and Physiology
Marb Geogr Schr — Marburger Geographische Schriften
Mar Biol — Marine Biology. International Journal of Life in Oceans and Coastal Waters
Mar Biol Assoc India J — Marine Biological Association of India. Journal
Mar Biol (Berl) — Marine Biology (Berlin)
Mar Biol Lett — Marine Biology Letters
Mar Biol (NY) — Marine Biology (New York)
Mar Biol (Vladivostok) — Marine Biology (Vladivostok)
Mar BJ — Maryland Bar Journal
Marb Winck Prog — Marburger Winckelmann Programm
MArch — Medieval Archaeology
M3 Archaeol — M3 Archaeology [*England*]
Mar Chem — Marine Chemistry
Mar Coat Conf Proc — Marine Coatings Conference. Proceedings
Marconi Instrum — Marconi Instrumentation
Marconi Rev — Marconi Review
Mar Eng — Marine Engineering [*Japan*]
Mar Eng/Log — Marine Engineering/Log
Mar Eng Nav Architect — Marine Engineer and Naval Architect
Mar Eng Rev — Marine Engineers Review
Mar Engrs J — Marine Engineers Journal
Mar Engrs Rev — Marine Engineers Review
Mar Environ Res — Marine Environmental Research
Mar Fish Re — Marine Fisheries Review
Mar Geol — Marine Geology
Mar Geophys Res — Marine Geophysical Researches
Mar Geotech — Marine Geotechnology
Mar Geotechnol — Marine Geotechnology
Mar I — March of India
Marian Libr Stud — Marian Library Studies
Marian Stds — Marian Studies
Mari Gos Ped Inst Ucen Zap — Mariiskii Gosudarstvennyi Pedagogiceskii Institut. Ucenye Zapiski
Marine Bio — Marine Biology
Marine Biol Assn UK J — Marine Biological Association of the United Kingdom. Journal
Marine Eng — Marine Engineering
Marine Eng/Log — Marine Engineering/Log
Marine Fisheries R — Marine Fisheries Review
Marine Geotech — Marine Geotechnology
Marine Geotechnol — Marine Geotechnology
Marine March — Marine Marchande
Mariner Mir — Mariner's Mirror
Mariners Mir — Mariner's Mirror
Marine Tech Soc J — Marine Technology Society. Journal
Mar Invertebr Scand — Marine Invertebrates of Scandinavia
Mariol St — Mariologische Studien

Marion County Med Soc Bull — Marion County Medical Society. Bulletin [*Indiana*]
Marisia — Marisia Studii si Materiale Arheologice. Istorie. Etnografie
Maritime Sediments Atlantic Geol — Maritime Sediments and Atlantic Geology
Marit Policy & Manage — Maritime Policy and Management
Marit Sediments — Maritime Sediments [*Later, Maritime Sediments and Atlantic Geology*]
Marit Sediments & Atl Geol — Maritime Sediments and Atlantic Geology
Mark — Mark Twain Journal
Mark Commun — Marketing Communications
Market Com — Marketing Communications
Marketing — Marketing Magazine
Marketing Res Rep USDA — Marketing Research Report. United States Department of Agriculture
Marketing Ser Agr Marketing Adv (India) — Marketing Series. Agricultural Marketing Adviser (India)
Market J — Marketing Journal
Market Research Soc J — Journal. Market Research Society
Markgr Jb — Markgraefler Jahrbuch
Mark Grow J — Market Grower's Journal
Markham R — Markham Review
Markham Rev — Markham Review
Mark Hung — Marketing in Hungary
Mark Media Decis — Marketing and Media Decisions
Mark Mix — Marketing Mix
Mark News — Marketing News
MarkR — Markham Review
Mark Res Abstr — Market Research Abstracts
Mark Res Rep US Dep Agric — Marketing Research Report. United States Department of Agriculture
Mark Twain — Mark Twain Journal
Mar Law — Maritime Lawyer
Mar L and Com — Journal of Maritime Law and Commerce
Mar L Rev — Maryland Law Review
Mar M — Marbacher Magazin
MARMDK — Marine Mining
Mar Med — Maroc Medical
Mar Micropaleontol — Marine Micropaleontology
Mar Min — Marine Mining
Mar Mining — Marine Mining
Mar Mirror — Mariner's Mirror
Mar Moore N — Marianne Moore Newsletter
Mar Obs — Marine Observer
Maroc Med — Maroc Medical
Maroc Serv Geol Notes Mem Serv Geol — Maroc. Service Geologique. Notes et Memoires du Service Geologique
MArOr — Monographs. Archiv Orientalni
Mar Pet Geol — Marine and Petroleum Geology
Mar Policy — Marine Policy [*England*]
Mar Policy Manage — Marine Policy and Management [*England*]
Mar Pollut Bull — Marine Pollution Bulletin
Mar Psyiat Q — Maryland Psychiatric Quarterly
Marq LR — Marquette Law Review
Marq L Rev — Marquette Law Review
Marquette Busin R — Marquette Business Review
Marquette Geologists Assoc Bull — Marquette Geologists Association. Bulletin
Marquette L Rev — Marquette Law Review
Mar Rd — Marine-Rundschau
MARRDZ — Marine Research. Department of Agriculture and Fisheries for Scotland
Mar Res Dep Agric Fish Scotl — Marine Research. Department of Agriculture and Fisheries for Scotland
Mar Res Indones — Marine Research in Indonesia
Mar Res Lab Educ Ser (St Petersburg FL) — Marine Research Laboratory. Educational Series (St. Petersburg, Florida)
Mar Res Lab Invest Rep (S-W Afr) — Marine Research Laboratory. Investigational Report (South-West Africa)
Mar Res Lab Spec Sci Rep (St Petersburg FL) — Marine Research Laboratory. Special Scientific Report (St. Petersburg, Florida)
Mar Res Lab Tech Ser (St Petersburg FL) — Marine Research Laboratory. Technical Series (St. Petersburg, Florida)
Mar Res Ser Scott Home Dep — Marine Research Series. Scottish Home Department
Marriage — Marriage and Family Living
MarS — Marian Studies [*New York*]
MARSB2 — Maritime Sediments [*Later, Maritime Sediments and Atlantic Geology*]
Mars Chir — Marseille Chirurgical
Mar Sci Cent Manuscr Rep McGill Univ (Montreal) — Marine Sciences Centre. Manuscript Report. McGill University (Montreal)
Mar Sci Commun — Marine Science Communications
Mar Sci Cont Tab — Marine Science Contents Tables
Mar Sci Instrum — Marine Sciences Instrumentation
Mar Sci (NY) — Marine Science (New York)

Mar Sci Res Cent (Stony Brook) Tech Rep — Marine Sciences Research Center (Stony Brook). Technical Report
MARSD4 — Marine Science [*New York*]
Marseille Med — Marseille Medical
M of Art — Magazine of Art [*Cassell's*]
MArt — Magazine of Art
Mart — Mart Magazine
MART — Meaning and Art [*Elsevier Book Series*]
MArt — Mundus Artium
Mar Technol — Marine Technology
Mar Technol Soc Annu Conf Prepr — Marine Technology Society. Annual Conference. Preprints
Mar Technol Soc Annu Conf Proc — Marine Technology Society. Annual Conference. Proceedings
Mar Technol Soc J — Marine Technology Society. Journal
Mar Tech S J — Marine Technology Society. Journal
Martin Ctr Archit Urban Stud — Martin Centre for Architectural and Urban Studies. Transactions
MarTropMed — Marches Tropicaux et Mediterraneens
Mar Week — Marine Week
Marx Bl — Marxistische Blaetter
Marxist Quar — Marxist Quarterly
Marx Td — Marxism Today
Maryland Geol Survey County Geol Map — Maryland. Geological Survey. County Geologic Map
Maryland Geol Survey Rept Inv — Maryland. Geological Survey. Report of Investigations
Maryland L Rev — Maryland Law Review
Mary L Rev — Maryland Law Review
Maryl St Med J — Maryland State Medical Journal
Maryl St MJ — Maryland State Medical Journal
Mar Zool — Marine Zoologist
MAS — Muenchener Aegyptologische Studien [*Berlin*]
MAS — Survey of Economic Conditions in Japan
MASCA Journal — Museum Applied Science Center for Archaeology. Journal
MASCAP — Museum Applied Science Center for Archaeology. Pamphlet
MASCAR — Museum Applied Science Center for Archaeology. Report
Masch Elektrotech — Maschinenwelt Elektrotechnik
Maschinenbau Betr — Maschinenbau der Betrich
Maschintec — Maschinenbautechnik
Masch Werkzeung — Maschine und Werkzeung [*West Germany*]
Mash Tekhnol Pererab Polim — Mashiny i Tekhnologiya Pererabotki Polimerov
MASJ — Midcontinent American Studies. Journal
Maskin J — Maskinjournalen
Mask Koth — Maske und Kothurn
Maslob Zhir Delo — Masloboino Zhirovoe Delo
Maslob Zhirov Prom — Masloboino Zhirovaya Promyshlennost' [*Later, Maslozhirovaya Promyshlennost*]
Maslob Zhir Promst — Masloboino Zhirovaya Promyshlennost [*Later, Maslozhirovaya Promyshlennost*]
Maslob Zir Prom — Masloboino Zirovaya Promyshlennost
Maslo Sapunena Promst — Maslo Sapunena Promyshlennost
Maslo Zhir Promst — Maslozhirovaya Promyshlennost [*Formerly, Masloboino Zhirovaya Promyshlennost*]
Masl Zhir Prom — Masloboino Zhirovaya Promyshlennost [*Later, Maslozhirovaya Promyshlennost*]
MASO — Meijerbergs Arkiv foer Svensk Ordforskning
MASP — Materialy po Arkheologii Severnogo Prichernomor'ia
Massachusetts Stud Engl — Massachusetts Studies in English
Mass Ag Exp — Massachusetts Agricultural Experiment Station. Publications
Mass Agric Exp Stn Bull — Massachusetts Agricultural Experiment Station. Bulletin
Mass Agric Exp Stn Control Ser Bull — Massachusetts Agricultural Experiment Station. Control Series. Bulletin
Mass Agric Exp Stn Ext Serv Publ — Massachusetts Agricultural Experiment Station. Extension Service Publication
Mass Agric Exp Stn Monogr Ser — Massachusetts Agricultural Experiment Station. Monograph Series
Mass Basic Data Rep Ground Water Ser — Massachusetts Basic Data Report. Ground Water Series
Mass Dent Soc J — Massachusetts Dental Society. Journal
Mass Dep Nat Resour Div Mar Fish Monogr Ser — Massachusetts Department of Natural Resources. Division of Marine Fisheries. Monographs Series
Mass Div Mar Fish Tech Ser — Massachusetts. Division of Marine Fisheries. Technical Series
Masses Ouvr — Masses Ouvrieres
Massey Agric Coll Dairyfarm Annu — Massey Agricultural College. Dairyfarming Annual
Massey Agric Coll Sheepfarm Annu — Massey Agricultural College. Sheepfarming Annual
Massey-Ferguson R — Massey-Ferguson Review
Mass Fruit Grow Assoc Rep Annu Meet — Massachusetts Fruit Growers' Association. Report of the Annual Meeting
Mass Hist Soc Coll — Massachusetts Historical Society. Collections
Mass Hist Soc Proc — Massachusetts Historical Society. Proceedings

Mass Hlth J — Massachusetts Health Journal

Mass H R — Massachusetts House of Representatives

Mass Hydrol Data Rep — Massachusetts Hydrologic Data Report

Mass Inst Tech Dep Civ Eng Hydrodyn Lab Rep — Massachusetts Institute of Technology. School of Engineering. Department of Civil Engineering. Hydrodynamics Laboratory. Report

Mass Inst Tech Dep Civ Eng Res Earth Phys Res Rep — Massachusetts Institute of Technology. School of Engineering. Department of Civil Engineering. Research in Earth Physics. Research Report

Mass Inst Tech Dep Civ Eng Soils Publ — Massachusetts Institute of Technology. School of Engineering. Department of Civil Engineering. Soils Publication

Mass Inst Tech Dep Nav Architect Mar Eng Rep — Massachusetts Institute of Technology. Department of Naval Architecture and Marine Engineering. Report

Mass Inst Tech Fluid Mech Lab Publ — Massachusetts Institute of Technology. Fluid Mechanics Laboratory. Publication

Mass Inst Technology Abs Theses — Massachusetts Institute of Technology. Abstracts of Theses

Mass Inst Technology and Woods Hole Oceanog Inst Paper — Massachusetts Institute of Technology and Woods Hole Oceanographic Institution. Papers

Mass Inst Technol Res Lab Electron Tech Rep — Massachusetts Institute of Technology. Research Laboratory of Electronics. Technical Report

Mass Inst Tech Res Lab Electron Tech Rep — Massachusetts Institute of Technology. Research Laboratory of Electronics. Technical Report

Mass Lib Assn Bul — Massachusetts Library Association. Bulletin

Mass L Q — Massachusetts Law Quarterly

Mass LR — Massachusetts Law Review

Mass L Rev — Massachusetts Law Review

Mass M — Massachusetts Magazine

Mass Med J — Massachusetts Medical Journal

Mass Nurse — Massachusetts Nurse

Massoobmennye Protsessy Khim Tekhnol — Massoobmennye Protsessy Khimicheskoi Tekhnologii [*USSR*]

Mass Ouvr — Masses Ouvrieres

Mass Prod — Mass Production

Mass Q — Massachusetts Quarterly Review

Mass R — Massachusetts Review

Mass Rev — Massachusetts Review

Mass Spect Bull — Mass Spectrometry Bulletin

Mass Spectrom Bull — Mass Spectrometry Bulletin [*England*]

Mass Spectrom New Instrum Tech — Mass Spectrometry New Instruments and Techniques

Mass Spectrosc — Mass Spectroscopy

Mass St Bd Educ — Massachusetts State Board of Education

Mass Transp — Mass Transportation

Mass Tribut — Massimario Tributario

Mass Univ Coll Food Nat Resour Agric Exp Stn Res Bull — Massachusetts University. College of Food and Natural Resources. Agricultural Experiment Station. Research Bulletin

Mass Univ Dep Geol Contrib — Massachusetts University. Department of Geology. Contribution

Mass Univ Dept Geology and Mineralogy Special Dept Pub — Massachusetts University. Department of Geology and Mineralogy. Special Department Publication

MAST — Memorie. Reale Accademia delle Scienze di Torino

Mast in Art — Masters in Art

Mast Draw — Master Drawings

Mas Teh Glas — Masinsko-Tehnicki Glasnik

Master Bldr — Master Builder

Master Carriers NSW — Master Carriers of New South Wales

Master Draw — Master Drawings

Master Painter Aust — Master Painter of Australia

Master Plumber of SA — Master Plumber of South Australia

MAST J — Manitoba Association of School Trustees. Journal

Mast in Music — Masters in Music

Mas Trakt St — Masino-Traktornaja Stancija

Masya Indo — Masyarakat Indonesia

MASYDR — MRC [*Medical Research Council*] [*Great Britain*]. Laboratory Animals Centre. Symposia

Ma T — Marxism Today

Mat — Matrix

MAT — Memorie. Reale Accademia delle Scienze di Torino

Mat AB — Materialien aus der Arbeitsmarkt und Berufsforschung

Mat Apl Comput — Matematica Aplicada e Computacional

Mat Bilten — Matematicki Bilten

Mat Cas — Matematicky Casopis

Mat Casopis Sloven Akad Vied — Matematicky Casopis Slovenskej Akademie Vied

Mat-Child Nurs J — Maternal-Child Nursing Journal

Mat Des — Material and Design

Matematika Period Sb Perevodov Inostran Statei — Matematika. Periodiceskii Sbornik Perevodov Inostrannyh Statei

Mat Engng — Materials Engineering

Mat Ensenanza — Matematicas y Ensenanza

Mat Ensenanza Univ — Matematica Ensenanza Universitaria [*Bogota*]

Mater Badaq Inst Gospod Wodnej — Materialy Badaqcze Instytut Gospodarki Wodnej

Mater Badaw Ser Gospod Wodna Ochr Wod — Materialy Badawcze. Seria. Gospodarka Wodna i Ochrona Wod

Mater Budow — Materialy Budowlane

Mater Chem — Materials Chemistry

Mater Chem and Phys — Materials Chemistry and Physics

Mater Compon Fossil Energy Appl — Materials and Components in Fossil Energy Applications

Mater Compon Newsl — Materials and Components Newsletter

Mater Constr (Bucharest) — Materiale de Constructs (Bucharest)

Mater Constr (Madrid) — Materiales de Construccion (Madrid)

Mater Constr Mater Struct — Materiaux et Constructions/Materials and Structures

Mater Constr (Paris) — Materiaux et Constructions (Paris)

Mater Des Eng — Materials in Design Engineering

Mater Eng — Materials Engineering

Mater Eng (Cleveland) — Materials Engineering (Cleveland)

Mater Eval — Materials Evaluation

Mater Evaluation — Materials Evaluation

Mater Evol Fiziol — Materialy po Evolyutsionnoi Fiziologii

Mater Floryst Geobot — Materialy Florystyczne i Geobotaniczne

Mater Flow — Material Flow

Mater Genet Eksp Miner — Materialy po Geneticheskoi i Eksperimental'noi Mineralogii

Mater Geol Metallog Kol'sk Poluostrova — Materialy po Geologii i Metallogenii Kol'skogo Poluostrova

Mater Geol Polezn Iskop Buryat ASSR — Materialy po Geologii i Poleznym Iskopaemym Buryatskoi ASSR

Mater Geol Polezn Iskop Chit Obl — Materialy po Geologii i Poleznym Iskopaemym Chitinskoi Oblasti

Mater Geol Polezn Iskop Dal'nevost Kraya — Materialy po Geologii i Poleznym Iskopaemym Dal'nevostochnogo Kraya

Mater Geol Polezn Iskop Irkutsk Obl — Materialy po Geologii i Poleznym Iskopaemym Irkutskoi Oblasti

Mater Geol Polezn Iskop Krasnoyarsk Kraya — Materialy po Geologii i Poleznym Iskopaemym Krasnoyarskogo Kraya

Mater Geol Polezn Iskop Sev Vostoka Evr Chasti SSSR — Materialy po Geologii i Poleznym Iskopaemym Severo Vostoka Evropeiskoi Chasti SSSR

Mater Geol Polezn Iskop Sev Zapada RSFSR — Materialy po Geologii i Poleznym Iskopaemym Severo-Zapada RSFSR

Mater Geol Polezn Iskop Sev Zapada SSSR — Materialy po Geologii i Poleznym Iskopaemym Severo-Zapada SSSR

Mater Geol Polezn Iskop Tsentr Raionov Evr Chasti SSSR — Materialy po Geologii i Poleznym Iskopaemym Tsentral'nykh Raionov Evropeiskoi Chasti SSSR

Mater Geol Polezn Iskop Urala — Materialy po Geologii i Poleznym Iskopaemym Urala

Mater Geol Polezn Iskop Vost Sib — Materialy po Geologii i Poleznym Iskopaemym Vostochnoi Sibiri

Mater Geol Polezn Iskop Yakutsk ASSR — Materialy po Geologii i Poleznym Iskopaemym Yakutskoi ASSR

Mater Geol Polezn Iskop Yuzhn Kaz — Materialy po Geologii i Poleznym Iskopaemym Yuzhnogo Kazakhstana

Mater Geol Polezn Iskop Yuzhn Urala — Materialy po Geologii i Poleznym Iskopaemym Yuzhnogo Urala

Mater Geol Polezy Iskop Kaz — Materialy po Geologii i Poleznym Iskopaemym Kazakhstana

Mater Geol Suisse Geophys — Materiaux pour la Geologie de la Suisse. Geophysique

Mater Geol Tsentr Kaz — Materialy po Geologii Tsentral'nogo Kazakhstana

Mater Geol Tuvinskoi ASSR — Materialy po Geologii Tuvinskoi ASSR

Mater Geol Tyan Shanya — Materialy po Geologii Tyan-Shanya

Mater Geol Zapadno Sib Nizmennosti — Materialy po Geologii Zapadno Sibirskoi Nizmennosti

Mater Geol Zapadn Sib — Materialy po Geologii Zapadnoi Sibiri

Mater Handl Eng — Material Handling Engineering

Mater Handl Mgmt — Materials Handling and Management

Mater Handl News — Materials Handling News

Mater Handl & Storage — Materials Handling and Storage

Materiale — Materiale si Cercetari Arheologice

Materialkd-Tech Reihe — Materialkundliche-Technische Reihe

Materialpruef — Materialpruefung

Materials Eng — Materials Engineering

Materials Eval — Materials Evaluation

Materialy Arch — Materialy Archeologiczne

Materialy Sem Kibernet — Materialy Seminara po Kibernetike

Mater Issled Pomoshch Proekt Stroit Karakum Kanala — Materialy Issledovanii v Pomoshch Proektirovaniyu i Stroitelstvu Karakumskogo Kanala

Mater Istor Zemled SSSR — Materialy po Istorii Zemledeliya SSSR

Mater Izuch Stavrop Kraya — Materialy po Izucheniyu Stavropol'skogo Kraya

Mater Izuch Zhen'shenya Drugikh Lek Sredstv Dal'nego Vostoka — Materialy k Izucheniyu Zhen'shenya i Drugikh Lekarstvennykh Sredstv Dal'nego Vostoka

Mater J SAMPE Quart — Materials Journal. SAMPE [*Society for the Advancement of Material and Process Engineering*] Quarterly

Mater Khar'k Otd Geogr Ova Ukr — Materialy Khar'kovskogo Otdela Geograficheskogo Obshchestva Ukrainy

Mater Kom Mineral Geochem Karpato Balk Geol Assoz — Materialien der Komission fuer Mineralogie und Geochemie. Karpato-Balkanische Geologische Assoziation

Mater Kom Mineral Geokhim Karpato Balk Geol Assots — Materialy Komissii Mineralogii i Geokhimii Karpato-Balkanskaya Geologicheskaya Assotsiatsiya

Mater Kompleksn Izuch Belogo Morya — Materialy po Kompleksnomu Izucheniyu Belogo Morya

Mater Konf Molodykh Biol Kirg — Materialy Konferentsii Molodykh Biologov Kirgizii

Mater Lett — Materials Letters

Mater Leve Geobot Suisse — Materiaux pour le Leve Geobotanique de la Suisse

Mater Manage J Rev — Material Management Journal and Review

Mater Maquinaria Metodos Constr — Materiales Maquinaria y Metodos para la Construccion

Mater Med Nordmark — Materia Medica Nordmark

Mater Med Pol — Material Medica Polona

Mater Met Konstr — Materialy po Metallicheskim Konstruktsiyam

Mater Metod Tekh Geologorazved Rab — Materialy po Metodike i Tekhnike Geologorazved Rabot

Mater Mineral Geokhim Petrogr Zabaik — Materialy po Mineralogii, Geokhimii, i Petrografii Zabaikal'ya

Mater Mineral Geokhim Petrogr Zabaikal'ya — Materialy po Mineralogii, Geokhimii, i Petrografii Zabaikal'ya

Mater Mineral Kol'sk Poluostrova — Materialy po Mineralogii Kol'skogo Poluostrova

Mater Mineral Petrogr Polezn Iskop Zapadn Sib — Materialy po Mineralogii, Petrografii, i Poleznym Iskopaemym Zapadnoi Sibiri

Mater Mol Res Div Newsl — Materials and Molecular Research Division. Newsletter [*United States*]

Maternal-Child Nurs J — Maternal-Child Nursing Journal

Mater Nauchn Konf Voronezh Skh Inst — Materialy Nauchnoi Konferentsii Voronezhskogo Sel'skokhozyaistvennyi Institut

Mater Nauchno Tekh Konf Leningr Elektrotekh Inst Svyazi — Materialy Nauchno-Tekhnicheskoi Konferentsii Leningradskogo Elektrotekhnicheskogo Instituta Svyazi

Mater Nauc Konfer Aspir Azerb Pedag Inst Im Lenina — Materialy Naucnoi Konferencii Aspirantov Posvjascennoj Poluvekovomu Jubileju Azerbajdzanskogo Pedagoceskogo Instituta Imeni V. I. Lenina

Matern Child Nurs J — Maternal-Child Nursing Journal

Matern Inf — Maternita e Infanzia

Matern Infanc — Maternidade e Infancia

Mater Note Aust Aeronaut Res Lab — Australia. Aeronautical Research Laboratories. Materials Note

Mater Nouv Tech Mond — Materiels Nouveaux et Techniques Mondiales

Mater Obmenu Opytom Nauchn Dostizh Med Promsti — Materialy po Obmenu Opytom i Nauchnymi Dostizheniyami v Meditsinskoi Promyshlennosti

Mater Ogniotrwale — Materialy Ogniotrwale [*Poland*]

Mater Org — Material und Organismen

Mater u Organ — Material und Organismen

Mater Org Beih — Materials und Organismen Beihefte

Mater Org (Berl) — Material und Organismen (Berlin)

Mater Perf — Materials Performance

Mater Perform — Materials Performance

Mater Performance — Materials Performance

Mater Plast (Bucharest) — Materiale Plastice (Bucharest)

Mater Plast Elastomeri — Materiale Plastice ed Elastomeri

Mater Plast Elastomeri Fibre Sint — Materiale Plastice, Elastomeri, Fibre Sintetice

Mater Polit Bildung — Materialien zur Politischen Bildung

Mater Poznaniyu Fauny Flory SSSR Otd Bot — Materialy k Poznaniyu Fauny i Flory SSSR Otdel Botanicheskii

Mater Poznaniyu Fauny Flory SSSR Otd Zool — Materialy k Poznaniyu Fauny i Flory SSSR Otdel Zoologicheskii

Mater Pr Antropol — Materialy i Prace Antropologiczne

Mater Process Technol — Materials and Process Technology

Mater Proizvod Silam Uzb — Materialy po Proizvoditel'nym Silam Uzbekistana

Mater Prot — Materials Protection [*Later, Materials Performance*]

Mater Prot Perform — Materials Protection and Performance [*Later, Materials Performance*]

Mater Prot Performance — Materials Protection and Performance [*Later, Materials Performance*]

Mater Pr Pol Akad Nauk Inst Geofiz — Materialy i Prace. Polska Akademia Nauk. Instytut Geofizyki

Materpruefengsamt Bauw Tech Hochsch Muenchen Ber — Materialpruefungsamt fuer das Bauwesen der Technischen Hochschule Muenchen. Bericht

Mater Pr Zakl Geofiz Pol Akad Nauk — Materialy i Prace. Zaklad Geofizyki Polska Akademia Nauk

Mater Rep Aust Aeronaut Res Lab — Australia. Aeronautical Research Laboratories. Materials Report

Mater Rep Univ Mus Univ Tokyo — Material Reports. University Museum. University of Tokyo

Mater Res AECL — Materials Research in AECL [*Atomic Energy of Canada Limited*]

Mater Res Bull — Materials Research Bulletin

Mater Res Soc Symp Proc — Materials Research Society. Symposia. Proceedings

Mater Res and Stand — Materials Research and Standards

Mater Res Stand — Materials Research and Standards

Mater Sb Statni Vyzk Ustav Mater — Materialovy Sbornik Statni Vyzkumny Ustav Materialu

Mater Sci — Materials Science [*Poland*]

Mater Sci E — Materials Science and Engineering

Mater Sci and Eng — Material Science and Engineering

Mater Sci Eng — Materials Science and Engineering

Mater Sci Res — Materials Science Research

Mater Semin Kibern — Materialy Seminara po Kibernetike

Mater Soc — Materials and Society

Mater Stud Nauchn Ova Khar'k Politekh Inst — Materialy Studencheskogo Nauchnogo Obshchestva. Khar'kovskii Politekhnicheskii Institut

Mater Tech — Materiaux et Techniques

Mater Tech (Paris) — Materiaux et Techniques (Paris)

Mater Tekh Snabzhenie — Material'no Tekhnicheskoe Snabzhenie [*USSR*]

Mater Teknol (Sofia) — Materialoznavie i Tekhnologiya (Sofia) [*Bulgaria*]

Mater Teor Klin Med — Materialy Teoreticheskoi i Klinicheskoi Meditsiny

Mater Test — Materials Testing

Mater Tezisy VI Konf Khim Sel' Khoz — Materialy i Tezisy VI Konferentsii po Khimizatsii Sel'skogo Khozyaistva

Mater Ther — Materia Therapeutica

Mater Toksikol Radioakt Veshchestv — Materialy po Toksikologii Radioaktivnykh Veshchestv

Mater Tsentr Nauchno Issled Inst Bum Promsti — Materialy Tsentral'nogo Nauchno-Issledovatel'skogo Instituta Bumazhnoi Promyshlennosti

Mater Tsentr Nauchno Issled Inst Tekst Promsti — Materialy Tsentral'nogo Nauchno-Issledovatel'skogo Instituta Tekstil'noi Promyshlennosti

Mater Uch Merzlykh Zonakh Zemnoi Kory — Materialy k Ucheniyu o Merzlykh Zonakh Zemnoi Kory

Mater Vopr Prom Toksikol Klin Prof Bolezn — Materialy po Voprosam Promyshlennoi Toksikologii i Kliniki Professional'nykh Boleznei

Mater Vses Nauchno Issled Geol Inst — Materialy Vsesoyuznogo Nauchno-Issledovatel'skogo Geologicheskogo Instituta

Mater Vses Nauchno Issled Inst Bum Tsellyul Promsti — Materialy Vsesoyuznogo Nauchno-Issledovatel'skogo Instituta Bumazhnoi i Tsellyuloznoi Promyshlennosti

Mater Zachodniopomorskie Muz Pomorza Zachodniego — Materialy Zachodniopomorskie. Muzeum Pomorza Zachodniego

Mat Eval — Materials Evaluation

Mat Fak Univ Kiril Metodij (Skopje) Godisen Zb — Matematicki Fakultet Univerzitetot Kiril i Metodij (Skopje). Godisen Zbornik

Mat Fiz — Akademiya Nauk Ukrainskoi SSR. Institut Matematiki. Matematicheskaya Fizika

Mat Fiz — Matematicheskaya Fizika

Mat Fiz i Funkcional Anal — Matematiceskaja Fizika i Funkcional'nyi Analiz

Mat Fiz List Ucenike Srednjih Sk — Matematicko Fizicki List za Ucenike Srednjih Skola

Mat-Fys Med — Matematisk-Fysiske Meddelelser Kongelige Danske Videnskabernes Selskab

Mat-Fys Medd Danske Vid Selsk — Matematisk-Fysiske Meddelelser Udgivet af det Kongelige Danske Videnskabernes Selskab

Mat-Fys Medd Dan Vidensk Selsk — Matematisk-Fysiske Meddelelser Kongelige Danske Videnskabernes Selskab

Mat Fyz Cas — Matematicko-Fyzikalny Casopis

Mat-Fyz Cas Slov Akad Vied — Matematicko-Fyzikalny Casopis. Slovenskej Akademie Vied [*Czechoslovakia*]

Math Agoge — Mathematike Agoge

Math Algorithms — Mathematical Algorithms

Math Ann — Mathematische Annalen

Math Annal — Mathematische Annalen

Math Anwendungen Phys Tech — Mathematik und Ihre Anwendungen in Physik und Technik

Math Appl — Mathematics and Its Applications

Math Appl Polit Sci — Mathematical Applications in Political Science

Math-Arbeitspapiere — Mathematik-Arbeitspapiere

Math Balk — Mathematica Balkanica

Math Biosci — Mathematical Biosciences

Math Chronicle — Mathematical Chronicle

Math Colloq Univ Cape Town — Mathematics Colloquium. University of Cape Town

Math and Comp in Simulation — Mathematics and Computers in Simulation

Math of Comput — Mathematics of Computation

Math Comput — Mathematics of Computation

Math Comput Simul — Mathematics and Computers in Simulation

Math Comput Simulation — Mathematics and Computers in Simulation
Math Concepts and Methods in Sci and Engrg — Mathematical Concepts and Methods in Science and Engineering
Math Dept Rep — Mathematics Department Report
Math Didaktik Unterrichtspraxis — Mathematik. Didaktik und Unterrichtspraxis
Math Ed for Teaching — Mathematical Education for Teaching
Math Education — Mathematics Education
Math Forschungsber — Mathematische Forschungsberichte
Math Forum — Mathematical Forum
Math Gazette — Mathematical Gazette
Math Ingen Naturwiss Oekonom Landwirte — Mathematik fuer Ingenieure, Naturwissenschaftler, Oekonomen, und Landwirte
Math Ing Naturwiss Okon Landwirte — Mathematik fuer Ingenieure, Naturwissenschaftler, Oekonomen, und Landwirte
Math Japon — Mathematica Japonicae
Math J Okayama Univ — Mathematical Journal. Okayama University
Math Kibernet Zogierth Sakith Gamokw — Mathematikuri Kibernetikis Zogierthi Sakithxis Gamokwewa
Math Lehrb Monogr I — Mathematische Lehrbuecher und Monographien. I
Math Lehrbuecher Monogr I Abt Math Lehrbuecher — Mathematische Lehrbuecher und Monographien. I. Abteilung. Mathematische Lehrbuecher
Math Lehrbuecher Monogr II Abt Math Monogr — Mathematische Lehrbuecher und Monographien. II. Abteilung. Mathematische Monographien
Math Lehrer — Mathematik fuer Lehrer
Math Mag — Mathematics Magazine
Math Math Phys (Washington DC) — Mathematics and Mathematical Physics (Washington, DC)
Math Medley — Mathematical Medley
Math Methods Appl Sci — Mathematical Methods in the Applied Sciences
Math Methods Oper Res — Mathematical Methods of Operations Research
Math Miniaturen — Mathematische Miniaturen
Math Mo — Mathematical Monthly
Math Modelling — Mathematical Modelling
Math Monograph — Mathematische Monographien
Math Nachr — Mathematische Nachrichten
Math-Naturwiss Bibliothek — Mathematisch-Naturwissenschaftliche Bibliothek
Math-Naturwiss Taschenb — Mathematisch-Naturwissenschaftliche Taschenbuecher
Math Naturwiss Tech — Mathematik fuer Naturwissenschaft und Technik
Math Naturwiss Unterr — Mathematische und Naturwissenschaftliche Unterricht
Math Naturw Unterr — Mathematische und Naturwissenschaftliche Unterricht
Math Notae — Mathematicae Notae
Math Notes — Mathematical Notes
Math Notes Acad Sci (USSR) — Mathematical Notes. Academy of Sciences (USSR)
Math Numer Sin — Mathematica Numerica Sinica
Math Numer Sinica — Mathematica Numerica Sinica
Math Operationsforsch Stat — Mathematische Operationsforschung und Statistik
Math Operationsforsch und Stat — Mathematische Operationsforschung und Statistik
Math Operationsforsch Statist — Mathematische Operationsforschung und Statistik
Math Operationsforsch Statist Ser Optim — Mathematische Operationsforschung und Statistik. Series Optimization
Math Operationsforsch Statist Ser Optimization — Mathematische Operationsforschung und Statistik. Series Optimization
Math Operationsforsch Statist Ser Statist — Mathematische Operationsforschung und Statistik. Series Statistik
Math Operationsforsch und Stat Ser Optimiz — Mathematische Operationsforschung und Statistik. Series Optimization
Math Operationsforsch und Stat Ser Stat — Mathematische Operationsforschung und Statistik. Series Statistik
Math Oper Res — Mathematics of Operations Research
Math Phys — Mathematik fuer Physiker
Math Phys Appl Math — Mathematical Physics and Applied Mathematics
Math Physiker — Mathematik fuer Physiker
Math Phys Monograph Ser — Mathematical Physics Monograph Series
Math Phys Monogr Ser — Mathematical Physics Monograph Series
Math-Phys Semesterber — Mathematisch-Physikalische Semesterberichte
Math Phys Stud — Mathematical Physics Studies
Math Proc C — Mathematical Proceedings. Cambridge Philosophical Society
Math Proc Camb Philos Soc — Mathematical Proceedings. Cambridge Philosophical Society
Math Proc Cambridge Philos Soc — Mathematical Proceedings. Cambridge Philosophical Society
Math Proc Cambridge Phil Soc — Mathematical Proceedings. Cambridge Philosophical Society
Math Prog — Mathematical Programming
Math Progr — Mathematical Programming

Math Program — Mathematical Programming
Math Programming — Mathematical Programming
Math Programming Stud — Mathematical Programming Study
Math Program Stud — Mathematical Programming Studies
MathR — Mathematical Reviews
Math Reihe — Mathematische Reihe
Math Rep College General Ed Kyushu Univ — Mathematical Reports. College of General Education. Kyushu University
Math Rep Kyushu Univ — Mathematical Reports. College of General Education. Kyushu University
Math Rep Toyama Univ — Toyama University. Mathematics Reports
Math Res — Mathematical Research
Math Research — Mathematical Research
Math Rev — Mathematical Reviews
Math Rev Sect — Mathematical Reviews Sections
Maths Bul — Mathematics Bulletin for Teachers in Secondary Schools
Math Scand — Mathematica Scandinavica
Math in School — Mathematics in School
Math Schuelerbuecherei — Mathematische Schuelerbuecherei
Math Sci — Mathematical Sciences
Math Sci — Mathematical Scientist
Math Sci Eng — Mathematics in Science and Engineering
Math Sci Engrg — Mathematics in Science and Engineering
Math Scientist — Mathematical Scientist
Math Sci Hum — Mathematiques et Sciences Humaines
Math Sci Humaines — Centre de Mathematique Sociale. Ecole Pratique des Hautes Etudes. Mathematiques et Sciences Humaines
Math Sem — Mathematics Seminar [Delhi]
Math Semesterber — Mathematische Semesterberichte
Math Seminar — Mathematics Seminar
Math Sem Notes Kobe Univ — Mathematics Seminar. Notes. Kobe University
Math Sem Notes Kobe Univ Second Ed — Kobe University. Mathematics Seminar Notes. Second Edition
Math Ser — Mathematics Series
Math Slovaca — Mathematica Slovaca
Math Social Sci — Mathematical Social Sciences
Math Soc Sci — Mathematical Social Sciences
Math Spectrum — Mathematical Spectrum
Math Student — Mathematics Student
Math Surveys — Mathematical Surveys
Math Systems in Econom — Mathematical Systems in Economics
Math Systems Theory — Mathematical Systems Theory
Math Syst T — Mathematical Systems Theory
Math Teach — Mathematics Teacher
Math Teaching — Mathematics Teaching
Math Trans (Engl Transl) — Mathematical Transactions (English Translation of Matematicheskii Sbornik)
Math USSR Izv — Mathematics of the USSR. Izvestiya
Math USSR Sb — Mathematics of the USSR. Sbornik
Math Wirtschaftswiss — Mathematik fuer Wirtschaftswissenschaftler
Math Z — Mathematische Zeitschrift
MatIRJa — Materialy i Issledovanija po Istorii Russkogo Jazyka
Mat Issled — Matematicheskie Issledovaniya
Mat Ist Muz (Bucuresti) — Materiale de Istorie si Muzeografie (Bucuresti)
Mat Kul't Tadzh — Material'naia Kul'tura Tadzhikistana
Mat Lapok — Matematikai Lapok
Matls Sci — Materials Science
Mat Metody Din Kosm App Akad Nauk SSSR Vychisl Tsentr — Matematicheskie Metody v Dinamike Kosmicheskikh Apparatov Akademiya Nauk SSSR Vychisislitel'nyi Tsentr [USSR]
Mat Metody i Fiz-Meh Polja — Akademija Nauk Ukrainskoi SSR L'vovskii Filial Matematiceskoi Fiziki Instituta Matematiki. Matematiceskie Metody i Fiziko-Mehaniceskie Polja
Mat Metody i Fiz-Mekh Polya — Matematicheskie Metody i Fiziko-Mekhanicheskie Polya
Mat Model Teor Elektr Tsepei — Matematicheskoe Modelirovanie i Teoriya Elektricheskikh Tsepei [USSR]
Mat News Int — Materials News International
Mat-Phys Semesterber — Mathematisch-Physikalische Semesterberichte
Mat Plast — Materiale Plastice
Mat Plast Elast — Materie Plastiche ed Elastomeri
Mat Probl Geofiz — Matematicheskie Problemy Geofiziki [USSR]
MatRD — Materialy i Issledovanija po Russkoj Dialektologii
Matrix and Tensor Q — Matrix and Tensor Quarterly
Matrix Tensor Quart — Matrix and Tensor Quarterly [London]
Matrl Eng — Materials Engineering
Matrl Hand — Material Handling Engineering
Matr Tens Q — Matrix and Tensor Quarterly
Mat Sb — Matematicheskie Sbornik
Mat Sb (NS) — Matematiceskii Sbornik (Novaja Serija)
Mat Sb (Tomsk) — Matematiceskii Sbornik (Tomsk)
Matscience Rep — Matscience Report [Madras]
Mat v Skole — Ministerstvo Prosvescenija RSSR Matematika v Skole
MatSl — Matica Slovenska
Mats Perf — Materials Performance
Mats Reclam Wkly — Materials Reclamation Weekly

Mats Struct — Materials and Structures
Mat Stos — Matematyka Stosowana
Mat Stos 3 — Roczniki Polskiego Towarzystwa Matematycznego. Seria III. Matematyka Stosowana
Matsushita Electr Works Tech Rep — Matsushita Electric Works. Technical Report
Mat Vesnik — Matematicki Vesnik
Mat Vesn Nova Ser — Matematichki Vesnik. Nova Seriya [*Yugoslavia*]
Mat Voprosy Upravlen Proizvodstvom — Moskovskii Gosudarstvennyi Universitet. Mehaniko-Matematiceskii Fakul'tet. Matematiceskii Voprosy Upravlenija Proizvodstvom
MATYC J — MATYC [*Mathematics Association of Two-Year Colleges*] Journal
Mat Zachodnio-Pomorskie — Materialy Zachodnio-Pomorskie
Mat Zametki — Matematicheskie Zametki
MAUOA — Music. American Guild of Organists
Maur — Mauretania
Mauritius Dep Agric Annu Rep — Mauritius. Department of Agriculture. Annual Report
Mauritius Dep Agric Bull — Mauritius. Department of Agriculture. Bulletin
Mauritius Inst Bull — Mauritius Institute. Bulletin
Mauritius Sugar Cane Res Stn Annu Rep — Mauritius. Sugar Cane Research Station. Annual Report
Mauritius Sugar Ind Res Inst Annu Rep — Mauritius Sugar Industry Research Institute. Annual Report
Mauritius Sugar Ind Res Inst Bull — Mauritius Sugar Industry Research Institute. Bulletins
Mauritius Sugar Ind Res Inst Leafl — Mauritius Sugar Industry Research Institute. Leaflet
Mauritius Sugar Ind Res Inst Occas Pap — Mauritius Sugar Industry Research Institute. Occasional Paper
Mauritius Sugar Ind Res Inst Tech Circ — Mauritius Sugar Industry Research Institute. Technical Circular
MAUSB — Metals Australia [*Later, Metals Australasia*]
MAV — Madison Avenue
MAW — Mededeelingen. Akademie van Wetenschappen
MAW — Mythologies in the Ancient World
Mawdsley Mem — Mawdsley Memoirs
MAX — Maschinenmarkt
Max-Planck-Ges Ber Mitt — Max-Planck-Gesellschaft. Berichte und Mitteilungen
Max-Planck-Ges Jahrb — Max-Planck-Gesellschaft. Jahrbuch
Max Planck Inst Kernphys Rep MPI H — Max-Planck-Institut fuer Kernphysik. Report MPI H
Max-Planck-Inst Plasmaphys Presseinf — Max-Planck-Institut fuer Plasmaphysik. Presseinformation
Max Von Pettenkofer Inst Ber — Max-Von-Pettenkofer-Institut. Berichte
Maxwell R — Maxwell Review
Mayo Clin P — Mayo Clinic. Proceedings
Mayo Clin Proc — Mayo Clinic. Proceedings
MAZ — Manager's Magazine
Maz — Mazungumzo
MAZ — Personal. Mensch und Arbeit in Betrieb
MAZOAT — Marine Zoologist
MB — Magazine of Building
MB — Mare Balticum
MB — Mediaevalia Bohemica
MB — Melanges Baldensperger
MB — Mission Bulletin
MB — Mitteilungsblatt. Irgun Olej Merkas Europa [*Tel-Aviv*]
MB — More Books
MB — Musee Belge
MBA — Europees Parlement. EP Nieuws
MBA — MBA/Masters in Business Administration
MBANA — Methods of Biochemical Analysis
M Bank Admin — Magazine of Bank Administration
MBAS (Calcutta) — Monthly Bulletin. Asiatic Society (Calcutta)
MBB — Deutsche Bundesbank. Monatsberichte mit Statistischen Beiheften
MbBAW — Monatsbericht. Berliner Akademie der Wissenschaft
MBBull — Bulletin Bibliographique. Musee Belge
MBB WF-Inf — MBB [*Messerschmitt-Boelkow-Blohm*] WF-Information [*German Federal Republic*]
MBDL — Muenstersche Beitraege zur Deutschen Literatur
MBEA J — Mississippi Business Education Association. Journal
MBEA Today — Michigan Business Education Association Today
MBENA — Medical and Biological Engineering [*Later, Medical and Biological Engineering and Computing*]
MBFLD — Mitteilungsblatt. Bundesanstalt fuer Fleischforschung
MBG — Marburger Beitraege zur Germanistik
MBGBA — Montana. Bureau of Mines and Geology. Bulletin
MBGSA — Montana. Bureau of Mines and Geology. Special Publication
MBI — MBI. Medico-Biologic Information
M Bildung — Musik und Bildung
MBIOAJ — Marine Biology [*Berlin*]
MBJ — Michigan State Bar Journal
MbJb — Mecklenburger Jahrbuch Schwerin

MBK — Schouw Vakblad voor Verwarming, Sanitair, en Keukenapparatuur
MBL — Modern British Literature
MBLED — Marine Biology Letters
MBLED7 — Marine Biology Letters
Mbl Freiheitliche Wirtschaftspol — Monatsblaetter fuer Freiheitliche Wirtschaftspolitik
MBM — Malaysian Business
MBM — Metal Bulletin Monthly
MBM — Molecular Biology and Medicine
MBMRF — Muenchener Beitraege zur Mediavistik und Renaissance-Forschung
MBO — Maandblad voor Bedrijfsadministratie en Organisatie
MBOP — Moniteur Bibliographique. Bulletin Officiel des Imprimes Publies en Pologne
MBP — Muenchener Beitraege zur Papyrusforschung
MB Pharm Bull — M and B Pharmaceutical Bulletin
MBPHAX — Marine Behaviour and Physiology
MBQ — Montana Business Quarterly
MBR — Belastingbeschouwingen. Onafhankelijk Maandblad voor Belastingrecht en Belastingpraktijk
MBR — Multivariate Behavioral Research
MBRMAO — Multivariate Behavioral Research Monograph
MBRWA — Monthly Bulletin. International Railway Congress Association
MBS — Monthly Bulletin of Statistics [*Israel*]
MBU — FAO [*Food and Agriculture Organization of the United Nations*] Monthly Bulletin of Statistics
Mbuehne — Musikbuehne
MBV — Maandstatistiek van de Binnenlandse Handel en Dienstverlening
MBW — Metaalbewerking Werkplaatstechnisch Vakblad voor Nederland en Belgie
MC — American Maritime Cases
MC — Marketing Communications
MC — McMurray Courier
MC — Medal Collector
M & C — Media and Consumer
MC — Medical Chronicle [*Manchester*]
M & C — Memory and Cognition
MC — Mondo Classico
MC — Monte Carmelo
MC — Monthly Criterion
MC — United States. Government Printing Office. Monthly Catalog of United States Government Publications
MCACO — Memoires. Commission des Antiquites de la Cote d'Or
MCar — Monte Carmelo
MCASDZ — Instituto Universitario Pedagogico de Caracas. Monografias Cientificas "Augusto Pi Suner"
MCB — Maandschrift van het Centraal Bureau voor de Statistiek
MCB — Melanges Chinois et Bouddhiques
MCB — Molecular and Cellular Biology
MCBEB — Microbial Ecology
McBride's — McBride's Magazine
McCl — McClure's Magazine [*New York*]
McClure — McClure's Magazine [*New York*]
McClure's — McClure's Magazine
McCQ — McCormick Quarterly
MCDW — Monthly Climatic Data for the World
MCERA — Mining and Chemical Engineering Review (Australia)
MCG — Marche. L'Hebdomadaire du Dirigeant
MCG — Monatshefte der Comenius-Gesellschaft
McGill J Educ — McGill Journal of Education
McGill L J — McGill Law Journal
McGill Univ Axel Heiberg Isl Res Rep Glaciol — McGill University. Axel Heiberg Island Research Reports. Glaciology
McGill Univ (Montreal) Mar Sci Cent Manuscr Rep — McGill University (Montreal). Marine Sciences Centre. Manuscript Report
McGill Univ Peter Redpath Mus — McGill University [*Montreal*]. Peter Redpath Museum
McG LJ — McGill Law Journal
McGraw ST — McGraw-Hill Publications. US Business Outlook. Short Term
MCh — Mikrasiatiki Chronika
MCHAC — Memoires. Cercle Historique et Archeologique de Courtrai
MCHEB — Mechanical and Chemical Engineering Transactions
MCHMDI — Manufacturing Chemist
M Chr Lit — Magazine of Christian Literature
MCIC Rep — MCIC [*Metals and Ceramics Information Center*] Report
MCJ — Mensajero del Corazon de Jesus
MCJ News — Milton Centre of Japan. News
MCKBA — Memoirs. College of Science. University of Kyoto. Series B
McKinsey Q — McKinsey Quarterly
McKinsey Quart — McKinsey Quarterly
MCL — Cebecoskoop
MCL — Martin Classical Lectures
M Cl — Mondo Classico
MCLB — Modern and Classical Language Bulletin
McLean Foram Lab Rept — McLean Foraminiferal Laboratory. Reports
McLean Paleont Lab Rept — McLean Paleontological Laboratory. Reports

MCM — Magic Carpet Magazine
MCM — Marketing Communications
MCM — Music Clubs Magazine
McMaster Symp Iron Steelmaking Proc — McMaster University. Symposium on Iron and Steelmaking. Proceedings
MCMJ — Michigan Mathematical Journal
MCMSM — Modern Analytical and Computational Methods in Science and Mathematics [Elsevier Book Series]
MCMT — Main Currents in Modern Thought
MCN — American Journal of Maternal Child Nursing
MCN — Motor Cycle News
MCNJA — Maternal-Child Nursing Journal
McN R — McNeese Review
MCNYA — Machinery [Later, Machinery and Production Engineering]
MCO — Marches Tropicaux et Mediterraneens
MCOFA — Machine Outil Francaise
MCOM — Medical Communications
MCom — Miscelanea Comillas
MCOPB — Methods in Computational Physics
MCP — Massachusetts CPA [Certified Public Accountant] Review
MCP — Materials Chemistry and Physics
MCP — Mineral Commodity Profiles. US Bureau of Mines
MCR — Melbourne Critical Review [University of Melbourne]
MCr — Museum Criticum
MCREDA — Multivariate Experimental Clinical Research
MCRFA — Microscope and Crystal Front
MCRHAC — Memoires. Cercle Royal Historique et Archeologique de Courtrai
MCS — Manchester Cuneiform Studies
MCS — Monumenta Christiana Selecta
MCV — Melanges de la Casa de Velazquez
MCVQ Med Coll VA Q — MCVQ. Medical College of Virginia. Quarterly
MCZAAZ — Museum of Comparative Zoology [Harvard University]. Annual Report
MD — Mackenzie Drift [Canada]
MD — MD: Medical Newsmagazine
MD — Media Decisions
MD — Modern Drama
MD — Modern Drummer
MD — Musica Disciplina
MDA — Dagbladpers
MDA — Marketing and Distribution Abstracts
MdA — Melanges d'Archeologie Egyptienne et Assyrienne [Paris]
MDAC — Mystery and Detection Annual
MD Acad Sci Bull — Maryland Academy of Sciences. Bulletin
MD Ac Sc Tr — Maryland Academy of Sciences. Transactions
MD Ag Exp — Maryland. Agricultural Experiment Station. Publications
MD Agric Exp Stn Bull — Maryland. Agricultural Experiment Station. Bulletin
MD Agric Exp Stn MP — Maryland. Agricultural Experiment Station. MP
MDAI — Mitteilungen. Deutsches Archaeologische Institut
MDAIA — Mitteilungen. Deutsches Archaeologische Institut. Abteilung Athens
MDAIK — Mitteilungen. Deutsches Archaeologische Institut. Abteilung Kairo
MDAIM — Mitteilungen. Deutsches Archaeologische Institut. Abteilung Madrid
MDAIR — Mitteilungen. Deutsches Archaeologische Institut. Abteilung Rome
MDAM — Majalle(H)-Ye Daneshkade(H)-Ye Adabiyyat-E Mashhad
MDan — Meddelelser fra Dansklaererforeningen
MDAP — Memoirs. Department of Archaeology in Pakistan
MDARC — Medecine et Armees
MDA (Tehran) — Majalle(H)-Ye Daneshkade(H)-Ye Adabiyyat Va Olun-E Ensanie-Ye (Tehran)
MD BJ — Maryland Bar Journal
MD Bur Mines Ann Rept — Maryland. Bureau of Mines. Annual Report
MDC — Medisch Contact
MD Conserv — Maryland Conservationist
MDD — Middenstand
MD Dep Geol Mines Water Resour Bull — Maryland. Department of Geology. Mines and Water Resources Bulletin
MD Dept Geology Mines and Water Res Bull County Rept — Maryland. Department of Geology. Mines and Water Resources Bulletin. County Reports
MDE — Management Decision
MDE Digest — Marketing and Distributive Educators' Digest
MD Energy Saver — Maryland Energy Saver
MDERD — Monatsschrift fuer Deutsches Recht
MdF — Mercure de France
MDF — Mitteldeutsche Forschungen
MdF — Musees de France
MDG — Monatsschrift fuer das Deutsche Geistesleben
MD Geol Surv Basic Data Rep — Maryland. Geological Survey. Basic Data Report
MD Geol Surv Bull — Maryland. Geological Survey. Bulletin
MD Geol Surv Guideb — Maryland. Geological Survey. Guidebook
MD Geol Surv Inf Circ — Maryland. Geological Survey. Information Circular

MD Geol Surv Quadrangle Atlas — Maryland. Geological Survey. Quadrangle Atlas
MD Geol Surv Rep Invest — Maryland. Geological Survey. Report of Investigations
MDGFA — Bulletin. Geological Society of Denmark
MDGNVO — Mitteilungen. Deutsche Gesellschaft fuer Natur- und Voelkerkunde Ostasiens
MD G S Sp Pub — Maryland. Geological Survey. Special Publication
MD His M — Maryland Historical Magazine
MD Hist — Maryland Historian
MD Hist M — Maryland Historical Magazine
MD Hist Mag — Maryland Historical Magazine
MD Hist Soc Fund-Publ — Maryland Historical Society. Fund-Publications
MdHM — Maryland Historical Magazine
MDI — Mitteilungen. Deutsches Archaeologische Institut
MDIA — Mitteilungen. Deutsches Institut fuer Aegyptische Altertumskunde (Kairo)
MDIGB — Mitteilungen. Deutsch-Israelitischer Gemeindebund
MDIK — Mitteilungen. Deutsches Institut fuer Aegyptische Altertumskunde (Kairo)
MDIOME — Mitteilungsblatt. Irgun Olej Merkas Europa
M Disciplina — Musica Disciplina
MDJ — Middle East Journal
MdJb — Mitteldeutsches Jahrbuch
MDKHD — Mukogawa Joshi Daigaku Kiyo. Yakugaku Hen
MDL — Landbouwdocumentatie
MDL — Materialien zur Deutschen Literatur
MD Law R — Maryland Law Review
MD LF — Maryland Law Forum
MD Libr — Maryland Libraries
MD LR — Maryland Law Review
MD L Rev — Maryland Law Review
MDM — Mededelingenblad Bedrijfsorganisatie
MD Mag — Maryland Magazine
MD Nat — Maryland Naturalist
MD Naturalist — Maryland Naturalist
MDNKA — Miyazaki Daigaku Nogakubu. Kenkyu Hokoku
MDNPAR — Direccion General del Inventario Nacional Forestal. Publicacion
MD Nurse — Maryland Nurse
MDO — Mitteilungen. Deutsche Orient-Gesellschaft zu Berlin
MDOG — Mitteilungen. Deutsche Orient-Gesellschaft zu Berlin
MDP — Memoires. Delegation en Perse [Paris]
MDP — Memoires. Mission Archeologique en Iran/Perse
MD Pharm — Maryland Pharmacist
MD Poultryman — Maryland Poultryman
MDPTB — Medical Progress through Technology
MDPV — Mitteilungen und Nachrichten. Deutscher Palaestina-Verein
MDRP — Mackenzie Delta Research Project [Canada]
MDS — Memoires Presentes par Divers Savants a l'Academie des Inscriptions et Belles-Lettres [Paris]
MDSAI — Memoires Presentes par Divers Savants a l'Academie des Inscriptions et Belles-Lettres [Paris]
MDSC — Medical Self-Care
MDSJA — Medical Service Journal [Canada]
MD State Med J — Maryland State Medical Journal
MDTHA — Medicina Thoracalis
MDtShG — Mitteilungen. Deutsche Shakespeare-Gesellschaft
MDU — Monatshefte fuer Deutschen Unterricht
MDY — Milieudefensie
ME — Marketing in Europe
Me — Meander
Me — Meaning
ME — Medical Economics
ME — Metis Newsletter. Metis Association of the Northwest Territories [Canada]
ME — Middle East Series [Elsevier Book Series]
ME — Musikerziehung
MEA — Accountantadviseur
Mea — Meander
MEA — Middle Eastern Affairs
Mead Johnson Symp Perinat Dev Med — Mead Johnson Symposium on Perinatal and Developmental Medicine
MEAH — Miscelanea de Estudios Arabes y Hebraicos
Meanjin — Meanjin Quarterly [University of Melbourne]
Meanjin Q — Meanjin Quarterly
Meas — Measure
Meas & Autom News — Measurement and Automation News
Meas Contr — Measurement and Control
Meas and Control — Measurement and Control
Meas Eval G — Measurement and Evaluation in Guidance
Meas Focus — Measurement Focus
Meas and Insp Technol — Measurement and Inspection Technology
Meas Insp Technol — Measurement and Inspection Technology
Meas Instrum Rev — Measurement and Instrument Review [England]
Measmt Control — Measurement and Control
Measmt & Eval in Guid — Measurement and Evaluation in Guidance

Meas Tech — Measurement Techniques [*USSR*]
Meas Tech R — Measurement Techniques (USSR)
Meat Ind — Meat Industry
Meat Ind Bul — Meat Industry Bulletin
Meat Ind J — Meat Industry Journal
Meat Ind J Q — Meat Industry Journal of Queensland
Meat Marketing in Aust — Meat Marketing in Australia
Meat Proc — Meat Processing
Meat Process — Meat Processing
Meat Prod & Exp — Meat Producer and Exporter
Meat Res News Lett — Meat Research News Letter
Meat Sci — Meat Science
Meat Sci Inst Proc — Meat Science Institute. Proceedings
Meat Situat Outlook — Meat. Situation and Outlook
Meat Trades J Aust — Meat Trades Journal of Australia
MEAVDO — Istituto Federale di Ricerche Forestali. Memorie
MEB — Missouri English Bulletin
ME Bd Agr An Rp — Maine. Board of Agriculture. Annual Report
MEBEA — Medical Electronics and Biological Engineering
MEC — Ministerio de Educacao e Cultura
Mecan Electrif Agr — Mecanizarea si Electrificarea Agriculturii
Mecc Agr — Meccanizzazione Agricola
Mecc Ital — Meccanica Italiana
Mec Elec — Mecanique Electricite
Mec Electr — Mecanique Electricite
Mech Age D — Mechanisms of Ageing and Development
Mech Ageing Dev — Mechanisms of Ageing and Development
Mechanik — Mechanik Miesiecznik Naukowo-Techniczny
Mech Autom Adm — Mechanizace Automatizace Administrativy
Mech Chem Engng Trans Instn Engrs (Aust) — Mechanical and Chemical
    Engineering Transactions. Institution of Engineers (Australia)
Mech Chem Eng Trans — Mechanical and Chemical Engineering Transactions
    [*Australia*]
Mech Chem Eng Trans Inst Eng (Aust) — Mechanical and Chemical
    Engineering Transactions. Institution of Engineers (Australia)
Mech Compos Mater — Mechanics of Composite Materials
Mech Contract — Mechanical Contractor
Mech Corros Prop A Key Eng Mater — Mechanical and Corrosion Properties
    A. Key Engineering Materials
Mech Corros Prop B Single Cryst Prop — Mechanical and Corrosion Properties
    B. Single Crystal Properties
Mech Des — Mechanical Design [*Japan*]
Mech Eng — Mechanical Engineering
Mech Eng Bull — Mechanical Engineering Bulletin
Mech Eng News (Washington DC) — Mechanical Engineering News
    (Washington, DC)
Mech Engng — Mechanical Engineering
Mech Engng Bull — Mechanical Engineering Bulletin
Mech Engng J — Mechanical Engineering Journal
Mech Engng News — Mechanical Engineering News
Mech Eng Rep Aust Aeronaut Res Lab — Mechanical Engineering Report.
    Australia. Aeronautical Research Laboratories
Mech Eng Rep MP Natl Res Counc Can Div Mech Eng — Mechanical
    Engineering Report MP. National Research Council of Canada.
    Division of Mechanical Engineering
Mech Eng Sci Monogr — Mechanical Engineering Science Monograph.
    Institution of Mechanical Engineers [*London*]
Mech Eng Technol — Mechanical Engineering Technology [*England*]
Mech Eng Trans Inst Eng (Aust) — Mechanical Engineering Transactions.
    Institution of Engineers (Australia)
Mechenye Biol Atk Veshchestva — Mechenye Biologicheski Atkivnye
    Veshchestva
Mech Handl — Mechanical Handling
Mech Illus — Mechanix Illustrated
Mech Leafl GB Min Agr Fish Food — Mechanisation Leaflet. Great Britain
    Ministry of Agriculture, Fisheries, and Food
Mech Mach T — Mechanism and Machine Theory
Mech Mater — Mechanics of Materials
Mech Miesiecznik Nauk-Tech — Mechanik Miesiecznik Naukowo-Techniczny
Mech Mies Nauk Tech — Mechanik Miesiecznik Naukowo-Techniczny
Mech Mol Migr — Mechanisms of Molecular Migrations
Mech Polim — Mechanika Polimerov
Mech Practice — Mechanics and Practice. Lixue Yu Shijian
Mech React Sulfur Comp — Mechanisms of Reactions of Sulfur Compounds
Mech React Sulfur Compd — Mechanisms of Reactions of Sulfur Compounds
Mech Res Comm — Mechanics Research Communications
Mech Res Commun — Mechanics Research Communications
Mech Roln — Mechanizacja Rolnictwa
Mech Sci — Mechanical Sciences. Mashinovdeniye
Mech Solids — Mechanics of Solids
Mech Technol Budowy Masz (Bydgoszcz Pol) — Mechanika, Technologia
    Budowy Maszyn (Bydgoszcz, Poland)
Mech Teor i Stoso — Mechanika Teoretyczna i Stosowana
Mech Teor i Stosow — Mechanika Teoretyczna i Stosowana
Mech World Eng Rec — Mechanical World and Engineering Record
    [*England*]

Mec-Mat-Elec — Mecanique- Materiaux- Electricite
Mec Mater Electr — Mecanique- Materiaux- Electricite
Mecmuasi Univ Fen Fak (Istanbul) — Mecmuasi Universite. Fen Fakulte
    (Istanbul)
Mecon J — Mecon Journal
Mec Roches — Mecanique des Roches
Med — Medica
Med — Medico
Med — Mediterraneo
MED — Middle English Dictionary
M Ed — Monde de l'Education
Med Abstr — Medical Abstract Service
Med Actuelle — Medecine Actuelle
MedAe — Medium Aevum
Med Aero — Medecine Aeronautique
Med Aeronaut — Medecine Aeronautique
Med Aeronaut Spat Med Subaquat Hyperbare — Medecine Aeronautique et
    Spatiale, Medecine Subaquatique et Hyperbare
MedAev — Medium Aevum
Med Afr Noire — Medecine d'Afrique Noire
Med Aktuell — Medizin Aktuell
Med Ann (DC) — Medical Annals (District of Columbia)
Med Annu — Medical Annual [*England*]
Med Anthro — Medical Anthropology
Med Arb — Medicinsk Arbog
Med Arch — Medicinskij Archiv
Med Arch — Medieval Archaeology
Med Arh — Medicinski Arhiv
Med Arhiv — Medicinski Arhiv
Med Arkh — Meditsinski Arkhiv [*Bulgaria*]
Med Armees — Medecine et Armees
Med Arts Sci — Medical Arts and Sciences
Med Aspects Hum Sex — Medical Aspects of Human Sexuality
Med Ass — Zeitschrift fuer Medizinstudenten und Assistenten
Med Assoc State Ala J — Medical Association of the State of Alabama.
    Journal
Med Audiovision — Medecine et Audiovision [*France*]
Med Avh Univ Bergen — Medisinske Avhandlinger. Universitet i Bergen
Med (B) — Medicina (Bogota)
Med Bio Eng — Medical and Biological Engineering [*Later, Medical and*
    Biological Engineering and Computing]
Med Bio Ill — Medical and Biological Illustration
Med Biol — Medecine et Biologie
Med Biol — Medical Biology
Med Biol Eng — Medical and Biological Engineering [*Later, Medical and*
    Biological Engineering and Computing]
Med and Biol Eng — Medical and Biological Engineering [*Later, Medical and*
    Biological Engineering and Computing]
Med Biol Eng Comput — Medical and Biological Engineering and Computing
Med and Biol Eng and Comput — Medical and Biological Engineering and
    Computing
Med Biol Engng — Medical and Biological Engineering [*Later, Medical and*
    Biological Engineering and Computing]
Med Biol (Helsinki) — Medical Biology (Helsinki)
Med Biol Illus — Medical and Biological Illustration
Med Biol Illustr — Medical Biology Illustrations
Med Biol (Tokyo) — Medicine and Biology (Tokyo)
Med Bl — Medizinische Blaetter
Med Bull Exxon Corp Affil Co — Medical Bulletin. Exxon Corporation and
    Affiliated Companies
Med Bull Fukuoka Univ — Medical Bulletin. Fukuoka University
Med Bull Istanbul Fac Med Istanbul Univ — Medical Bulletin. Istanbul Faculty
    of Medicine. Istanbul University
Med Bull Istanbul Med Fac Istanbul Univ — Medical Bulletin. Istanbul
    Medical Faculty. Istanbul University
Med Bull Istanbul Univ — Medical Bulletin. Istanbul University
Med Bull Natl Med Cent (Seoul) — Medical Bulletin. National Medical Center
    (Seoul)
Med Bull No Virginia — Medical Bulletin of Northern Virginia
Med Bull Providence Hosp (Southfield Mich) — Medical Bulletin. Providence
    Hospital (Southfield, Michigan)
Med Bull Stand Oil Co (NJ) Affil Co — Medical Bulletin. Standard Oil
    Company (New Jersey) and Affiliated Companies
Med Bull Univ Cincinnati — Medical Bulletin. University of Cincinnati
Med Bull (US Army) — Medical Bulletin (United States Army)
Med Bull US Army (Eur) — Medical Bulletin. US Army (Europe)
Med Bydr — Mediese Bydraes
Med Bydraes — Mediese Bydraes
Med Care — Medical Care
Med Care Rev — Medical Care Review
Med Cent J Univ Mich — Medical Center Journal. University of Michigan
Med Chem (Leverkusen Ger) — Medizin und Chemie (Leverkusen, Germany)
Med Chem Ser Monogr — Medicinal Chemistry: A Series of Monographs
Med Chem Ser Rev — Medicinal Chemistry: A Series of Reviews
Med Chir Dig — Medecine et Chirurgie Digestives
Med Cir — Medicina y Cirugia

Med Cir Farm — Medicina, Cirurgia, Farmacia

Med Cir Gu — Medicina y Cirugia de Guerra

Med Clin — Medicina Clinica

Med Clin NA — Medical Clinics of North America

Med Clin N Am — Medical Clinics of North America

Med Clin North Am — Medical Clinics of North America

Med Clin Sper — Medicina Clinica e Sperimentale

Med Colon (Madr) — Medicina Colonial (Madrid)

Med Commun — Medical Communications

Med and Comp — Medicine and Computer

Med Cond — Medico Condotto

Med Condotto — Medico Condotto

Med Consult New Remedies — Medical Consultation and New Remedies

Med Cont — Medicina Contemporanea

Med Contact — Medisch Contact [*Netherlands*]

Med Contemp — Medicina Contemporanea

Med Contemp (Lisbon) — Medicina Contemporanea (Lisbon)

Med Convers Bl — Medizinisches Conversationsblatt

Med Cor-Bl Bayer Aerzte — Medizinisches Correspondenz-Blatt Bayerischer Aerzte

Med Cor-Bl Rhein u Westfael Aerzte — Medizinisches Correspondenzblatt Rheinischer und Westfaelischer Aerzte

Med Cor-Bl Wuerttemb Aerztl Landesver — Medizinisches Correspondenzblatt. Wuerttembergischer Aerztliche Landesverein

Med Cor-Bl Wuerttemb Aerztl Ver — Medizinisches Correspondenzblatt. Wuerttembergischer Aerztliche Verein

Med Cult — Medicina e Cultura

Med Cut — Medicina Cutanea [*Later, Medicina Cutanea Ibero-Latino-Americana*]

Med Cutanea — Medicina Cutanea [*Later, Medicina Cutanea Ibero-Latino-Americana*]

Med Cutan Iber Lat Am — Medicina Cutanea Ibero-Latino-Americana

Med C Virg — Medical College of Virginia. Quarterly

Medd Abo Akad Geol Mineral Inst — Meddelanden fran Abo Akademis Geologisk-Mineralogiska Institut

Medd Alnarpsinst Mejeriavd Statens Mejerifoers — Meddelande fran Alnarpsinstitutets Mejeriavdelning och Statens Mejerifoersoek

Medd Carlsberg Lab — Meddelelser fra Carlsberg Laboratorium

Medd Centralstyr Malmohus Lans Forsoks-Vaxtskyddsringar — Meddelande fran Centralstyrelsen foer Malmoehus Laens Foersoeksoch Vaxtskyddsringar

Medd Dan Fisk Havunders — Meddelelser fra Danmarks Fiskfri-og Havundersogelser

Medd Dan Geol Foren — Meddelelser fra Dansk Geologisk Forening

Medd Dansk Geol Forend — Meddelanden fra Dansk Geologiske Forendlingen

Med Decision Making — Medical Decision Making

Meddel om Gronland — Meddelelser om Groenland

Meddel Komm Byggn — Meddelanden fran Statens Kommitte foer Byggnadsforskning

Meddel Lund U Hist Mus — Meddelanden fran Lunds Universitets Historika Museum

Meddel Skogsfoers Anst — Meddelanden fran Statens Skogsfoersoeksanstalt

Med Dent J — Medical/Dental Journal

Medd Grafiska Forskningslab — Meddelande. Grafiska Forskningslaboratoriet

Medd Groenl — Meddelelser om Groenland

Medd Groenland — Meddelelser om Groenland

Medd Groenl Geosci — Meddelelser om Groenland. Geoscience

Medd Gronl — Meddelelser om Groenland

Medd Havsfiskelab Lysekil — Meddelande fran Havsfiskelaboratoriet Lysekil

Med Dimensions — Medical Dimensions

Medd Inst Maltdrycksforsk — Meddelande fran Institutet foer Maltdrycksforskning

Med Dir Tuinb — Mededelingen. Directeur van de Tuinbouw

Medd Jordbrukste Inst — Meddelande-Jordbruksteknisk Institutet

Medd Kvismare Fagelstn — Meddelande fran Kvismare Fagelstation

Medd Lunds Geol Mineral Inst — Meddelanden fran Lunds Geologisk-Mineralogiska Institut

Medd Lunds Univ Hist Mus — Meddelanden fran Lunds Universitets Historika Museum

Meddn K Lantbrhogsk Lantbrfors Jordbrfors — Meddelanden fran Kungliga Lantbrukshogskolan och [*Statens*] Lantbruksforsok [*Statens*] Jordbruksforsok

Medd Nor Farm Selsk — Meddelelser fra Norsk Farmaceutisk Selskap

Medd Nor Inst Skogforsk — Meddelelser fra Norsk Institute foer Skogforskning

Medd Nor Myrselsk — Meddelelser fra det Norske Myrselskap

Medd Nor Sk — Meddelelser fra det Norske Skogforsoeksvesen

Medd Nor Skogforsoksves — Meddelelser fra det Norske Skogforsoeksvesen

Meddn St Skogsforskinst (Stockholm) — Meddelanden fran Statens Skogsforskningsinstitut (Stockholm)

Meddn Sverig FroeodlFoerb — Meddelanden fran Sveriges Froeodlarefoerbund

Med Dosw Mikrobiol — Medycyna Doswiadczalna i Mikrobiologia

Med Dosw Mikrobiol (Transl) — Medycyna Doswiadczalna i Mikrobiologia (Translation)

Med Dosw Spoleczna — Medycyna Doswiadczalna i Spoleczna

Medd Papirind Forskningsinst — Meddelelse fra Papirindustriens Forskningsinstitutt

Meddr Norske Myrselsk — Meddelelser fra det Norske Myrselskap

Medd Statens Mejerifoers (Swed) — Meddelande fran Statens Mejerifoersoek (Sweden)

Medd Statens Planteavsforsog — Meddelesse Statens Planteavlsforsog

Medd Statens Skeppsprovningsanst — Meddelanden fran Statens Skeppsprovningsanstalt

Medd Statens Skogsforskningsinst — Meddelanden fran Statens Skogsforskningsinstitut

Medd Statens Skogsforskningsinst (Swed) — Meddelanden fran Statens Skogsforskningsinstitut (Sweden)

Medd Statens Viltunders — Meddelelser fra Statens Viltundersokelser [*Papers. Norwegian State Game Research Institute*]

Medd Statens Viltunders (Pap Norw State Game Res Inst) — Meddelelser fra Statens Viltundersokelser (Papers. Norwegian State Game Research Institute)

Medd Stat Forskningsanst Lantmannabyggnader — Meddelande fran Statens Forskningsanst Lantmannabyggnader

Medd Stift Rasforadl Skogstrad — Meddelanden fran Stiftelsen foer Rasforadling av Skogstrad

Medd Sven Mejeriernas Riksfoeren Produkttek Avd — Meddelande. Svenska Mejeriernas Riksfoerening. Produkttekniska Avdelningen

Medd Svenska Traforskn Inst (Trakem PappTekn) — Meddelanden fran Svenska Traforskningsinstitutet (Trakemi och Pappersteknik)

Medd Sven Textilforskningsinst — Meddelanden fran Svenska Textilforskningsinstitutet

Medd Sven Traskyddsinst — Meddelanden fran Svenska Traskyddsinstitutet

Medd Sver Kem Industrikontor — Meddelanden fran Sveriges Kemiska Industrikontor

Medd Vestland Forstl Forsokssta — Meddelelser fra Vestlandets Forstlige Forsoeksstasjon

Medd Vestl Forstl Forsoeksstn — Meddelelser fra Vestlandets Forstlige Forsoeksstasjon

MEDEA — Medecine

Med Econ — Medical Economics

Med Econ Surgeons — Medical Economics for Surgeons

Meded Alg Proefstn AVROS — Mededeelingen. Algemeen Proefstation der AVROS [*Algemeene Vereniging van Rubberplanters ter Oostkust van Sumatra*]

Meded Dir Tuinb — Mededelingen. Directeur van de Tuinbouw

Meded Fac Diergeneeskd Rijksuniv (Gent) — Mededelingen. Faculteit Diergeneeskunde Rijksuniversiteit (Gent)

Meded Fac Landbouwwet Rijksuniv (Gent) — Mededelingen. Faculteit Landbouwwetenschappen. Rijksuniversiteit (Gent)

Meded Fac LandWet (Gent) — Mededelingen. Faculteit Landbouwwetenschappen. Rijksuniversiteit (Gent)

Meded Geol Sticht — Mededelingen. Geologische Stichting

Meded Geol Sticht Nieuwe Ser (Neth) — Mededelingen. Geologische Stichting. Nieuwe Serie (Netherlands)

Meded Indones Inst Rubberonderz — Mededeelingen. Indonesisch Instituut voor Rubberonderzoek

Meded Ins Ratio Suikerprod — Mededelingen. Instituut voor Rationele Suikerproductie

Meded Inst Biol Scheik Onderz LandbGewass — Mededelingen. Instituut voor Biologisch en Scheikundig Onderzoek van Landbouwgewassen

Meded Inst Biol Scheik Onderz Landbougewassen (Wageningen) — Mededelingen. Instituut voor Biologisch en Scheikundig Onderzoek van Landbouwgewassen (Wageningen)

Meded Inst Graan Meel Brood TNO (Wageningen) — Mededeling. Instituut voor Graan. Meel en Brood TNO [*Toegepast Natuurwetenschappelijk Onderzoek*] (Wageningen)

Meded Inst Mod Veevoeding De Schothorst Hoogland Amersfoorst — Mededeling. Instituut voor Moderne Veevoeding "De Schothorst" te Hoogland bij Amersfoorst

Meded Inst Ration Suikerprod — Mededelingen. Instituut voor Rationele Suikerproductie

Meded Inst Rat Suik Prod — Mededelingen. Instituut voor Rationele Suikerproductie

Meded Inst Toegep Biol Onderz Nat — Mededelingen. Instituut voor Toegepast Biologisch Onderzoek in der Natuur

Meded K Acad Wet Lett en Schone Kunsten Belg — Mededelingen. Koninklijke Academie voor Wetenschappen. Letteren en Schone Kunsten van Belgie

Meded K Acad Wet Lett Schone Kunsten Belg Kl Wet — Mededelingen. Koninklijke Academie voor Wetenschappen. Letteren en Schone Kunsten van Belgie. Klasse der Wetenschappen

Meded Kon Nederl Ak Wetensch — Mededeelingen. Koninklijke Nederlandsche Akademie van Wetenschappen

Meded Kon Vl Ak Wetensch — Mededelingen. Koninklijke Vlaamse Akademie van Wetenschappen

Meded K Vlaam Acad Wet Lett Schone Kunsten Belg Kl Wet — Mededelingen. Koninklijke Vlaamse Academie voor Wetenschappen. Letteren en Schone Kunsten van Belgie. Klasse der Wetenschappen

Meded Lab Houttechnol Rijkslandbouwhogesch (Gent) — Mededelingen. Laboratorium voor Houttechnologie. Rijkslandbouwhogeschool (Gent)

Meded Lab Physiol Chem Univ Amsterdam — Mededelingen. Laboratorium voor Physiologische Chemie der Universiteit van Amsterdam

Meded Lab Physiol Chem Univ Amsterdam Ned Inst Volksvoed — Mededelingen. Laboratorium voor Physiologische Chemie. Universiteit van Amsterdam et Nederlands Instituut voor Volksvoeding

Meded Lab Scheikd Onderz Buitenzorg — Mededeeling. Laboratorium voor Scheikundig Onderzoek te Buitenzorg

Meded LandbHogesch OpzoekStns Gent — Mededelingen. Landbouwhogeschool en Opzoekingsstations van de Staat te Gent

Meded Landbhogesch Wageningen — Mededelingen. Landbouwhogeschool te Wageningen

Meded Landbouwhogesch (Ghent) — Mededelingen. Landbouwhogeschool (Ghent)

Meded Landbouwhogesch Opzoekingssta (Ghent) — Mededelingen. Landbouwhogeschool en Opzoekingsstations (Ghent)

Meded Landbouwhogesch Opzoekingsstn Staat Gent — Mededelingen. Landbouwhogeschool en Opzoekingsstations van de Staat te Gent

Meded Landbouwhogesch Wageningen — Mededelingen. Landbouwhogeschool te Wageningen

Meded LandProefstn Suriname — Mededelingen. Landbouwproefstation in Suriname

Meded Lederinst TNO — Mededelingen. Lederinstituut TNO [*Toegepast Natuurwetenschappelijk Onderzoek*]

Meded L Vlaam Acad Wet Belg Kl Wet — Mededelingen. Koninklijke Vlaamse Academie voor Wetenschappen. Letteren on Schone Kunsten van Belgie. Klasse der Wetenschappen

Meded Nat Coop Aan- Verkoopver Landbouw Cen Bur — Mededelingen. Nationale Cooperatieve Aan- en Verkoopvereniging voor de Landbouw Central Bureau

Meded Ned Vacuumver — Mededelingenblad. Nederlandse Vacuumvereiniging

Meded Ned Ver Koeltech — Mededelingen. Nederlande Vereniging voor Koeltechniek

Meded Proefstn Akker- en Weideb — Mededelingen. Proefstation voor de Akker- en Weidebouw

Meded Proefstn Groenteteelt Vollegrond Ned — Mededeling. Proefstation voor de Groenteteelt in de Vollegrond in Nederland

Meded Rijksfac Landbouwwet Gent — Mededelingen. Rijksfaculteit Landbouwwetenschappen te Gent

Meded Rijks Geol Dienst — Mededelingen. Rijks Geologische Dienst

Meded Rijks Geol Dienst Nieuwe Ser (Neth) — Mededelingen. Rijks Geologische Dienst. Nieuwe Serie (Netherlands)

Meded Rijks Inst Pharm Ther Onderz — Mededelingen. Rijks Instituut voor Pharmaco-Therapeutisch Onderzoek

Meded Rijksproefstat Zaadcontr (Wageningen) — Mededeling. Rijksproefstation voor Zaadcontrole (Wageningen)

Meded Rubber-Sticht (Delft) — Mededelingen. Rubber-Stichting (Delft)

Meded Stichting Nederl Graan-Cent — Mededeling. Stichting Nederlands Graan-Centrum

Meded Stichting Plantenveredeling (Wageningen) — Mededelingen. Stichting voor Plantenveredeling (Wageningen)

Med Educ — Medical Education

Meded Veeartsenijsch Rijksuniv Gent — Mededelingen. Veeartsenijschool. Rijksuniversiteit te Gent

Meded Vezelinst TNO — Mededeling. Vezelinstituut TNO [*Toegepast Natuurwetenschappelijk Onderzoek*]

Meded Vlaam Chem Ver — Mededelingen. Vlaamse Chemische Vereniging

Meded Vl Topon Ver — Mededeelingen Uitgegeven. Vlaamse Toponymische Vereniging

Meded Zittingen K Acad Overzeese Wet (Brussels) — Mededelingen der Zittingen. Koninklijke Academie voor Overzeese Wetenschappen (Brussels)

Meded Zuid-Nederl Dial Centr — Mededeelingen. Zuid-Nederlandsche Dialect Centrale

Med Elec — Medical Electronics and Data

Med Electron — Medical Electronics

Med Electron Biol Eng — Medical Electronics and Biological Engineering

Med Electron Data — Medical Electronics and Data

Med Era (St Louis) — Medical Era (St. Louis)

Med Ernaehr — Medizin und Ernaehrung

Med Esp — Medicina Espanola

Med Esporte — Medicina do Esporte

Med Essays and Obs (Edinb) — Medical Essays and Observations (Edinburgh)

Med Exp — Medicina Experimentalis

Med Fis Rehabil — Medicina Fisica y Rehabilitacion

Med Fr — Medecin de France

Med Ges — Medizin und Gesellschaft

Med Glas — Medicinski Glasnik

Med Group Manage — Medical Group Management

Med Group News — Medical Group News

Med Grundlagenforsch — Medizinische Grundlagenforschung

Med Gynaecol Androl Sociol — Medical Gynaecology, Andrology, and Sociology

Med Gynaecol Sociol — Medical Gynaecology and Sociology

Med Hist — Medical History

Med Hoje — Medicina de Hoje

Med et Hum — Mediaevalia et Humanistica

MedHum — Mediaevalia et Humanistica

Med Hyg — Medecine et Hygiene

Med Hyg (Geneve) — Medecine et Hygiene (Geneve)

Med Hypotheses — Medical Hypotheses

Media — Mediafile

Media, C & S — Media, Culture, and Society [*United Kingdom*]

Media Culture Soc — Media, Culture, and Society

Media Eco — Media Ecology Review

Media Educ and Dev — Media in Education and Development

Media in Educ Dev — Media in Education and Development

Mediaev Philos Pol — Mediaevalia Philosophica Polonorum

Mediaev St — Mediaeval Studies

Mediaev Stud — Mediaeval Studies

Media Inf Aust — Media Information Australia

Media L Notes — Media Law Notes

Media Per — Media Perspektiven

Media Rep — Media Reporter [*United Kingdom*]

Media Rev Dig — Media Review Digest

Media Rpt — Media Report to Women

Medical — Medical Self-Care

Medical J Aust — Medical Journal of Australia

Medicamenta (Ed Farm) — Medicamenta (Edicion para el Farmaceutico)

Medico-Legal J — Medical Legal Journal

Medico Legal J — Medico-Legal Journal

Medico-Legal Soc Proc — Medico-Legal Society. Proceedings

Medico-Legal Soc VIC Proc — Medico-Legal Society of Victoria. Proceedings

Medicoleg News — Medicolegal News

Medico Vet (Torino) — Il Medico Veterinario (Torino)

Medien — Medien und Erziehung

Medieval Arch — Medieval Archaeology

Medieval Archaeol — Medieval Archaeology

Medieval Ceram — Medieval Ceramics

Mediev et Hum — Mediaevalia et Humanistica

Med Imaging — Medical Imaging

Med Infant — Medecine Infantile

Med Inf (Lond) — Medecine et Informatique (London)

Med Inform Statist — Medizinische Informatik und Statistik

Med Instrum — Medical Instrumentation

Med Instrum (Arlington) — Medical Instrumentation (Arlington)

Med Int — Medicine International [*Great Britain*]

Med Interna — Medicina Interna

Med Interna (Buchar) — Medicina Interna (Bucharest)

Med Interne — Medecine Interne

Med Istraz — Medicinska Istrazivanja

Med Istraz Suppl — Medicinska Istrazivanja. Supplementum

Medit — Mediterraneo

Mediterr Med — Mediterranee Medicale

Meditsin Referat Zh — Meditsinskii Referatinynyi Zhurnal

Medium Aev — Medium Aevum

Medizinhist J — Medizinhistorisches Journal

M Ed J — Music Educators Journal

MEDJA — Music Educators Journal

Med J Armed Forces (India) — Medical Journal. Armed Forces (India)

Med J Aust — Medical Journal of Australia

Med J Aust Supp — Medical Journal of Australia. Supplement

Med J Chulalongkorn Hosp Med Sch (Bangkok) — Medical Journal. Chulalongkorn Hospital Medical School (Bangkok)

Med J Commun — Medical Journal for Communication

Med J (Engl Transl Lijec Vjesn) — Medical Journal (English Translation of Lijecnicki Vjesnik)

Med J Fraternity Mem Hosp — Medical Journal. Fraternity Memorial Hospital

Med J Han-il Hosp — Medical Journal. Han-il Hospital

Med J Hiroshima Prefect Hosp — Medical Journal. Hiroshima Prefectural Hospital

Med J Hiroshima Univ — Medical Journal. Hiroshima University [*Japan*]

Med J Kagoshima Univ — Medical Journal. Kagoshima University

Med J Kobe Univ — Medical Journal. Kobe University

Med J Malaya — Medical Journal of Malaya [*Later, Medical Journal of Malaysia*]

Med J Malaysia — Medical Journal of Malaysia

Med J Minami Osaka Hosp — Medical Journal. Minami Osaka Hospital [*Japan*]

Med J Mutual Aid Assoc — Medical Journal. Mutual Aid Association [*Japan*]

Med J Osaka Univ — Medical Journal. Osaka University

Med J Osaka Univ (Engl Ed) — Medical Journal. Osaka University (English Edition)

Med J Osaka Univ (Jpn Ed) — Medical Journal. Osaka University (Japanese Edition)

Med J Shinshu Univ — Medical Journal. Shinshu University

Med J South West — Medical Journal. South West

Med J Zambia — Medical Journal of Zambia

Med Klin — Medizinische Klinik

Med Klin (Berlin) — Medizinische Klinik (Berlin)

Med Klin (Muenchen) — Medizinische Klinik (Muenchen)

Med (L) — Medicina (Lisbon)

Med Lab — Medizinische Laboratorium [*West Germany*]
Med Lab Observer — Medical Laboratory Observer
Med Laboratory Advisory — Medical Laboratory Advisory Service
Med Lab Sci — Medical Laboratory Sciences
Med Lab (Stuttg) — Medizinische Laboratorium/Laboratoire Medical (Stuttgart)
Med Lab Tec — Medical Laboratory Technology
Med Lab Technol — Medical Laboratory Technology
Med Lab World — Medical Laboratory World
Med Lav — Medicina del Lavoro
Med Leg Assicur — Medicina Legale e delle Assicurazioni
Med Leg Bull — Medico-Legal Bulletin
Med-Leg Criminol Rev — Medico-Legal and Criminological Review
Med Leg & Crim Rev — Medico-Legal and Criminological Review
Med Leg Dommage Corpor — Medecine Legale et Dommage Corporel
Med Leg J — Medico-Legal Journal
Med-Leg J (London) — Medico-Legal Journal (London)
Med-Leg J (NY) — Medico-Legal Journal (New York)
Med Leg N — Medico-Legal News
Medlemsbl Dan Dyrlaegeforen — Medlemsblad foer den Danske Dyrlaegeforening
Medlemsbl Nor Veterinaerforen — Medlemsblad den Norske Veterinaerforening
Med Lett Drugs Ther — Medical Letter on Drugs and Therapeutics
Med Liability Advisory — Medical Liability Advisory Service
Med Lib Assn Bul — Medical Library Association. Bulletin
Med Lib Assn Bull — Medical Library Association. Bulletin
Med Libr — Medical Libraries
Med LJ — Medico-Legal Journal
Med Market/Acta Medicotech — Medizinal-Market/Acta Medicotechnica [*West Germany*]
Med Mark Media — Medical Marketing and Media
Med Microbi — Medical Microbiology and Immunology
Med Microbiol Immunol — Medical Microbiology and Immunology
Med Mkt — Medical Marketing and Media
Med Mod — Medicina Moderna
Med Mod Can — Medecine Moderne du Canada
Med Mod (Paris) — Medecine Moderne (Paris)
Med Monatsschr — Medizinische Monatsschrift
Med Monatsschr Pharm — Medizinische Monatsschrift fuer Pharmazeuten
Med Monatssp — Medizinischer Monatsspiegel
Med Monde — Medecine dans le Monde
Med Morale — Medicina e Morale
Med Mysl Uzbekistana — Meditsinskaia Mysl Uzbekistana
Medna Esp — Medicina Espanola
Med Naturwiss Arch — Medizinisch-Naturwissenschaftliches Archiv
Med News — Medical News
Med Nucl Radiobiol Lat — Medicina Nucleare. Radiobiologica Latina
Med Nucl Radiobiol Lat Suppl — Medicina Nucleare. Radiobiologica Latina. Supplement [*Italy*]
Med Nutr — Medecine et Nutrition
Med Obozr — Meditsinskoe Obozrienio Sprimona
Med Officer — Medical Officer [*England*]
Med Oncol Tumor Pharmacother — Medical Oncology and Tumor Pharmacotherapy
Med (P) — Medicina (Parma)
Med Paedagog Jugendkd — Medizinische und Paedagogische Jugendkunde
Med Paises Calidos — Medicina de los Paises Calidos
Med Parazitol — Meditsinskaia Parazitologiia i Parazitarnye Bolezni
Med Parazitol Parazit Bolezni — Meditsinskaya Parazitologiya i Parazitarnye Bolezni
Med Pediatr Oncol — Medical and Pediatric Oncology
Med Pharmacol Exp — Medicina et Pharmacologia Experimentalis
Med and Phil Comment — Medical and Philosophical Commentaries
Med Phys — Medical Physics
Med Phys J — Medical and Physical Journal
Med Podmladak — Medicinski Podmladak
Med Post — Medical Post [*Canada*]
Med Pr — Medycyna Pracy
Med Prat — Medecine Praticienne
Med Prat (Napoli) — Medicina Pratica (Napoli)
Med Pregl — Medicinski Pregled
Med Press — Medical Press
Med Press and Circ — Medical Press and Circular
Med Prisma — Medizinische Prisma
Med Probl — Medicinski Problemi [*Bulgaria*]
Med Proc — Medical Proceedings
Med Prod Salesman — Medical Products Salesman
Med Prog Technol — Medical Progress through Technology
Med Prom-st SSSR — Meditsinskaya Promyshlennost SSSR
Med Pr Tech — Medical Progress through Technology
Med Psicosom — Medicina Psicosomatica
Med Q Indiana Univ Sch Med — Medical Quarterly. Indiana University. School of Medicine
Med R — Medioevo Romanzo
MedR — Mediterranean Review

Med Radiogr Photogr — Medical Radiography and Photography
Med Radiol — Meditsinskaya Radiologiya
Med Radiol (Mosk) — Meditsinskaia Radiologiia (Moskva)
Med Radiol (USSR) — Medical Radiology (USSR)
Med Razgledi — Medicinski Razgledi
Med Rec — Medical Record
Med Rec Ann — Medical Record and Annals
Med Rec Mississippi — Medical Record of Mississippi
Med Rec News — Medical Record News
Med Rec (NY) — Medical Record (New York)
Med Ren — Mediaeval and Renaissance Studies
Med Rep Charles Univ Med Fac Hradec Kralove — Medical Reports. Charles University Medical Faculty at Hradec Kralove
Med Reposit — Medical Repository
Med Res Bull Repat Dept — Repatriation Department. Medical Research Bulletin [*Australia*]
Med Res Cent (Nairobi) Annu Rep — Medical Research Centre (Nairobi). Annual Report
Med Res Counc (GB) Annu Rep — Medical Research Council (Great Britain). Annual Report
Med Res Counc (GB) Ind Health Res Board Rep — Medical Research Council (Great Britain). Industrial Health Research Board Report
Med Res Counc (GB) Memo — Medical Research Council (Great Britain). Memorandum
Med Res Counc (GB) Monit Rep — Medical Research Council (Great Britain). Monitoring Report
Med Res Counc (GB) Spec Rep Ser — Medical Research Council (Great Britain). Special Report Series
Med Res Eng — Medical Research Engineering
Med Res Inst Tokyo Med Dent Univ Annu Rep — Medical Research Institute. Tokyo Medical and Dental University. Annual Report
Med Res Photosensit Dyes — Medical Researches for Photosensitizing Dyes
Med Res Ser Monogr — Medicinal Research: A Series of Monographs
Med Rev (Belgr) — Medicinska Revija (Belgrade)
Med Rev CARL — Medicina Revista do CARL [*Centro Academico Rocha Lima*]
Med Rev Cent Acad Rocha Lima (Sao Paulo) — Medicina Revista do Centro Academico Rocha Lima (Sao Paulo)
Med Rev Mex — Medicina Revista Mexicana
MedRom — Medioevo Romanzo
MedS — Mediaeval Studies
MedS — Medical Socioeconomic Research Sources. American Medical Association
Med (S) — Medizinische (Stuttgart)
Med Schl — Medical School Rounds
Med Sci — Medical Science
Med Sci & L — Medicine, Science, and the Law
Med Sci Law — Medicine, Science, and the Law
Med Sci Sports — Medicine and Science in Sports
Med Sci Spt — Medicine and Science in Sports
Med Segur Trab (Madr) — Medicina y Seguridad del Trabajo (Madrid)
Med Serv — Medical Service
Med Serv J (Can) — Medical Service Journal (Canada)
Med Sestra — Meditsinskaya Sestra
MEDSOC — Medical Socioeconomic Research Sources. American Medical Association
Med Soc PA Tr — Medical Society of the State of Pennsylvania. Transactions
Med Soc (Turin) — Medicina Sociale (Turin)
Med Sper — Medicina Sperimentale
Med Sper Arch Ital — Medicina Sperimentale. Archivio Italiano
Med Sport — Medecine du Sport
Med Sport (Basel) — Medicine and Sport (Basel)
Med Sport (Berlin) — Medizin und Sport (Berlin)
Med Sport (Turin) — Medicina dello Sport (Turin)
Med St — Mediaeval Studies
Med Strucni Cas Zlh Podruznica Rijeka — Medicina Strucni Casopis Zlh Podruznica Rijeka
Med Surg — Medicine and Surgery
Med and Surg Monit — Medical and Surgical Monitor
Med Tech — Medizinische Technik [*West Germany*]
Med Tech Bull — Medical Technicians Bulletin
Med Technol Aust — Medical Technology in Australasia
Med Technol Aust — Medical Technology in Australia
Med Technol Ser — Medical Technology Series
Med Tech Publ Co Int Rev Sci Biochem — Medical and Technical Publishing Company. International Review of Science. Biochemistry
Med Tekh — Meditsinskaya Tekhnika
Med Thorac — Medicina Thoracalis
Med Times — Medical Times
Med Times and Gaz (London) — Medical Times and Gazette (London)
Med Times (London) — Medical Times (London)
Med Times (NY) — Medical Times (New York)
Med Tradic — Medicina Tradicionale
Med Treat (Tokyo) — Medical Treatment (Tokyo)
Med Trial Technique Q — Medical Trial Technique Quarterly
Med Trial Tech Q — Medical Trial Technique Quarterly

Med Trib — Medical Tribune
Med Trop — Medecine Tropicale
Med Trop (Madr) — Medicina Tropical (Madrid)
Med Trop (Mars) — Medecine Tropicale (Marseilles)
Med Tr TQ — Medical Trial Technique Quarterly
M Educators J — Music Educators Journal
Med Ultrasound — Medical Ultrasound
Med Univers — Medicina Universal
Medun Probl — Medunarodni Problemi
Med Unserer Zeit — Medizin in Unserer Zeit
Med Utilization Rev — Medical Utilization Review
Med Versuche u Bemerk (Edinb) — Medizinischen Versuche und Bemerkungen
   (Edinburgh)
Med Vet Hell — Medecine Veterinaire Hellenique
Med Vjesnik — Medicinski Vjesnik
Med Welt — Medizinische Welt
Med Weter — Medycyna Weterynaryjna
Med World — Medical World News
Med World News — Medical World News
Medycyna Wet — Medycyna Weterynaryjna
Med Zh Uzb — Meditsinskii Zhurnal Uzbekistana
Med Ztg — Medizinische Zeitung
Med Ztg Russlands — Medizinische Zeitung. Russlands
MEE — Middle East Economist [*Cairo*]
MEE — Middle East Executive Reports
MEED — Middle East Economic Digest [*London*]
MEEP — Middle East Economic Papers
MEEPA — Methods of Experimental Physics
Meerestech Mar Tech — Meerestechnik/Marine Technology
Meerestechnik Mar Technol — Meerestechnik/Marine Technology
MEES — Middle East Economic Survey
Meeting Nw — Meeting News
Meet Place J R Ont Mus — Meeting Place Journal. Royal Ontario Museum
ME Fm Res — Maine Farm Research
MEFo — Middle East Focus
MEFO — Miscelanea de Estudios Dedicados a Fernando Ortiz por Sus
   Discipulos
MEFR — Melanges d'Archeologie et d'Histoire. Ecole Francaise de Rome
MEFRA — Melanges. Ecole Francaise de Rome. Antiquite
MEFRM — Melanges. Ecole Francaise de Rome. Moyen Age. Temps
   Modernes
MEH — Materials Handling News
Mehanika Period Sb Perevodov Inostran Statei — Mehanika. Periodiceskii
   Sbornik Perevodov Inostrannyh Statei
Mehanika Polimerov — Akademija Nauk Latviiskoi SSR. Institut Mehaniki
   Polimerov. Mehanika Polimerov
Meh Autom — Mehanizacija i Automatizacija
MEHBA — Meteorology and Hydrology
ME His S — Maine Historical Society. Collections
Meh Tverd Tela — Mehanika Tverdogo Tela
MEHUA — Memoirs. Faculty of Engineering. Hokkaido University
MEHYA — Mental Hygiene
MEI — Media Info
Meiden Rev (Int Ed) — Meiden Review (International Edition)
Meidensha Rev (Int Ed) — Meidensha Review [*later, Meiden Review*]
   (International Edition)
MEIFD — Minerva Ecologica, Idroclimatologica, Fisicosanitaria
Meijeritiet Aikak — Meijeritieteellinen Aikakauskirja
MEINA — Metal Industry
MEISA — Minzoku Eisei
MEJ — Middle East Journal
MEJ — Music Educators Journal
Mejeritek Medd — Mejeritekniska Meddelanden
MEK — Melk
MEKEA — Memoirs. Faculty of Science. Kyushu University. Series E. Biology
Mekhan Elektrif Sots Sel'Khoz — Mekhanizatsiya Elektrifikatsiya
   Sotsialisticheskogo Sel'skogo Khozyaistva
Mekh & Avtom Proiz — Mekhanizatsiya i Avtomatizatsiya Proizvodstva
Mekh and Avtom Proizvod — Mekhanizatsiya i Avtomatizatsiya Proizvodstva
Mekh Avtom Proizvod — Mekhanizatsiya i Avtomatizatsiya Proizvodstva
Mekh i Avtom Upr — Mekhanizahriya i Avtomahzatsiya Upravleniya
Mekh Avtom Upr — Mekhanizatsiya i Avtomatizatsiya Upravleniya
Mekh Deform Tverd Tel — Mekhanika Deformiruemykh Tverdykh Tel
   [*USSR*]
Mekh Elektrif Sel'sk Khoz — Mekhanizatsiia i Elektrifikatsiia Sel'skogo
   Khoziaistva
Mekh Khlopkovod — Mekhanizatsiya Khlopkovodstva
Mekh Kompozitnykh Mater — Mekhanika Kompozitnykh Materialov
Mekh Kompoz Mater — Mekhanika Kompozitnykh Materialov [*Latvian SSR*]
Mekh Nek Patol Protsessov — Mekhanizmy Nekotorykh Patologicheskikh
   Protsessov
Mekh Obrab Drev — Mekhanicheskaya Obrabotka. Drevesiny
Mekh Patol Protsessov — Mekhanizmy Patologicheskikh Protsessov
Mekh Polim — Mekhanika Polimerov

Mekh Razrusheniya Metal Nauk Ukr SSR Repub Mezhvedom Sb —
   Mekhanizm Razrusheniya Metallov Akademiya Nauk Ukrainskoi SSR
   Republikanskii Mezhvedomstvennyi Sbornik
Mekh Tverd Tela — Mekhanika Tverdogo Tela
Mekh Zhidk Gaza — Mekhanika Zhidkosti i Gaza [*USSR*]
MEKLA — Medizinische Klinik
MEKMA — Memoirs. Faculty of Engineering. Kumamoto University
MEKOA — Metallurgiya i Koksokhimiya
MEKSA — Memoirs. Faculty of Engineering. Kyushu University
MEKYA — Memoirs. Faculty of Engineering. Kyoto University
Mel — Melanges
MEL — Metal Bulletin
MELAA — Medicina del Lavoro
Melanesian Law J — Melanesian Law Journal
Melanesian LJ — Melanesian Law Journal
Melanges Chamard — Melanges d'Histoire Litteraire de la Renaissance Offerts
   a Henri Chamard
Melanges Hoepffner — Melanges de Philologie Romane et de Litterature
   Medievale Offerts a Ernest Hoepffner
Melanges Roques — Melanges de Linguistique et de Litterature Romanes
   Offerts a Mario Roques
Melb Chamber of Commerce Yrbk — Melbourne Chamber of Commerce.
   Yearbook
Melb City Mission Rec — Melbourne City Mission Record
Melb Critical R — Melbourne Critical Review
Melb Crit R — Melbourne Critical Review
Melb Grad — Melbourne Graduate
Melb Graduate — Melbourne Graduate
Melb Hist J — Melbourne Historical Journal
Melb Legacy Week Bul — Melbourne Legacy Week. Bulletin
Melb Metro Board Works Monograph — Monograph. Melbourne and
   Metropolitan Board of Works
Melb Mon Mag — Melbourne Monthly Magazine
Melbourne Critical Rev — Melbourne Critical Review
Melbourne Hist J — Melbourne Historical Journal
Melbourne Stud in Educ — Melbourne Studies in Education
Melbourne ULR — Melbourne University. Law Review
Melbourne Univ Dep Civ Eng Transp Sect Bull — University of Melbourne.
   Department of Civil Engineering. Transport Section. Bulletin
Melbourne Univ Dep Civ Eng Transp Sect Spec Rep — University of
   Melbourne. Department of Civil Engineering. Transport Section.
   Special Report
Melbourne Univ Dep Mech Eng Hum Factors Group HF Rep — University of
   Melbourne. Department of Mechanical Engineering. Human Factors
   Group. HF Report
Melbourne Univ Law Rev — Melbourne University. Law Review
Melbourne Univ L Rev — Melbourne University. Law Review
Melb Rev — Melbourne Review
MelbSS — Melbourne Slavonic Studies
Melb Stud Educ — Melbourne Studies in Education
Melb Studies in Educ — Melbourne Studies in Education
Melb UL Rev — Melbourne University. Law Review
Melb Univ Circ to Sch — Melbourne University. Circular to Schools
Melb Univ Elect Engng Dep Rep — University of Melbourne. Department of
   Electrical Engineering. Report
Melb Univ Gaz — Melbourne University. Gazette
Melb Univ Law R — Melbourne University. Law Review
Melb Univ Law Rev — Melbourne University. Law Review
Melb Univ LR — Melbourne University. Law Review
Melb Univ L Rev — Melbourne University. Law Review
Melb Univ Mag — Melbourne University. Magazine
Melb Univ Sch For Bull — University of Melbourne. School of Forestry.
   Bulletin
Melb Walker — Melbourne Walker
Meld Norg Landbrukshogsk — Meldinger fra Norges Landbrukshogskole
Meld Nor Landbrukshogsk — Meldinger fra Norges Landbrukshogskole
Meld Nor Landbrukshogsk Inst Blomsterdyrk Veksthusforsok — Melding-
   Norges Landbrukshogskole. Institutt foer Blomsterdyrking og
   Veksthusforsok
Meld St ForsGard Kvithamar — Melding Statens Forsoksgard Kvithamar
Melekess Gos Ped Inst Ucen Zap — Melekesskii Gosudarstvennyi
   Pedagogiceskii Institut. Ucenye Zapiski
Meliorace Prehl Lit Zemed Lesn Melior — Meliorace. Prehled Literatury
   Zemedelskych a Lesnickych Melioraci
Meliorat Acker- Pflanzenbau — Melioration Acker- und Pflanzenbau
Melior Ispol'z Osushennykh Zemel — Melioratsiya i Ispol'zovaniya
   Osushennykh Zemel
Melior Vodn Khoz — Melioratsiya Vodnoe Khozyaistva
Meliss Ellas — Melissokomike Ellas
MeliT — Melita Theologica. The Reviews of the Royal University Students'
   Theological Association [*La Valetta, Malta*]
MelitaT — Melita Theologica. The Reviews of the Royal University Students'
   Theological Association [*La Valetta, Malta*]
Melittologists' Bull — Melittologists' Bulletin
Melliand Textilber — Melliand Textilberichte International
Melliand Textilber Int — Melliand Textilberichte International

Mel Maker — Melody Maker

MelPHLJ — Melanges de Philosophie et de Litterature Juives [*Paris*]

ME L Rev — Maine Law Review

Mel Rom — Melanges d'Archeologie et d'Histoire. Ecole Francaise de Rome

MelScR — Melanges de Science Religieuse

Melsheimer Entomol Ser — Melsheimer Entomological Series

Melsunger Med Pharm Mitt Wiss Prax — Melsunger Medizinisch Pharmazeutische Mitteilungen aus Wissenschaft und Praxis

Melsunger Med Pharm Mitt Wiss Prax Suppl — Melsunger Medizinisch Pharmazeutische Mitteilungen aus Wissenschaft und Praxis. Supplement

Mel Univ St Joseph — Melanges. Universite Saint Joseph

MelUSJ — Melanges. Universite Saint Joseph

MeM — Materiales en Marcha

MEM — Mens en Maatschappij. Tijdschrift voor Sociale Wetenschappen

MeM — Mens en Muziek

MEM — Middle Eastern Monographs

Mem Acad Chir — Memoires. Academie de Chirurgie [*France*]

Mem Acad Cienc Lisb Cl Cienc — Memorias. Academia das Ciencias de Lisboa. Classe de Ciencias

Mem Acad Cienc Zaragoza — Memorias. Academia de Ciencias de Zaragoza

Mem Acad Malgache — Memoires. Academie Malgache

Mem Acad Med (Paris) — Memoires. Academie de Medecine (Paris)

Mem Acad Mex Estud Num — Memorias. Academia Mexicana de Estudios Numismaticos

Mem Acad R Belg Cl Sci Collect 4o — Memoires. Academie Royale de Belgique. Classe des Sciences. Collection in Quarto

Mem Acad R Med Belg — Memoires. Academie Royale de Medecine de Belgique

Mem Acad Roy Sci Lett Belg — Memoires. Academie Royale des Sciences, des Lettres, et des Beaux-Arts de Belgique

Mem Acad Roy Sci Outre-Mer (Brussels) — Memoires. Academie Royale des Sciences d'Outre-Mer (Brussels)

Mem Acad Sci — Memoires. Academie des Sciences. Institut de France

Mem Acad Sci Inscr B-Lett Toulouse — Memoires. Academie des Sciences, Inscriptions, et Belles-Lettres de Toulouse

Mem Acad Sci Inscriptions B L Toulouse — Memoires. Academie des Sciences, Inscriptions, et Belles-Lettres de Toulouse

Mem Acad Sci Inst Fr — Memoires. Academie des Sciences. Institut de France

Mem Acad Sci Toulouse — Memoires. Academie des Sciences, Inscriptions, et Belles-Lettres de Toulouse [*France*]

Mem Accad Sci Ist Bologna Cl Sci Fis — Memorie. Accademia delle Scienze. Istituto di Bologna. Classe di Scienze Fisiche

Mem Accad Sci Med Chir (Naples) — Memorie. Accademia di Scienze Mediche e Chirurgiche (Naples)

Mem Accad Sci Torino Cl Sci Fis Mat Nat — Memorie. Accademia delle Scienze di Torino. Classe di Scienze Fisiche, Matematiche, e Naturali

Mem Accad Sci Torino Cl Sci Fis Mat Nat Ser 4A — Memorie. Accademia delle Scienze di Torino. Classe di Scienze Fisiche, Matematiche, e Naturali. Serie 4A

Mem Accad Sci Torino Cl Sci Fis Mat Natur — Memorie. Accademia delle Scienze di Torino. Classe di Scienze Fisiche, Matematiche, e Naturali [*Turin*]

Mem Accad Sci Torino Cl Sci Fis Mat Natur 4 — Memorie. Accademia delle Scienze di Torino. Classe di Scienze Fisiche, Matematiche, e Naturali. Serie 4 [*Turin*]

Mem Ac Inscr — Memoires Presentes par Divers Savants a l'Academie des Inscriptions et Belles Lettres

Mem Akita Univ — Memoirs. Akita University

Mem Am Acad Arts Sci — Memoirs. American Academy of Arts and Sciences

Mem Am Assoc Pet Geol — Memoir. American Association of Petroleum Geologists

Mem Am Entomol Inst (Ann Arbor) — Memoirs. American Entomological Institute (Ann Arbor)

Mem Am Entomol Soc — Memoirs. American Entomological Society

Mem Am Math — Memoirs. American Mathematical Society

Mem Am Philos Soc — Memoirs. American Philosophical Society

Mem Antiq — Memoria Antiquitatis

Mem Artillerie Fr — Memorial de l'Artillerie Francaise

Mem Artillerie Fr Sci Tech Armement — Memorial de l'Artillerie Francaise. Sciences et Techniques de l'Armement

Mem Asoc Latinoam Prod Anim — Memoria. Asociacion Latinoamericana de Produccion Animal

Mem Assoc Int Hydrogeol — Memoires. Association Internationale des Hydrogeologues

Mem Assoc Int Hydrogeol Reunion Istanbul — Memoires. Association Internationale des Hydrogeologues. Reunion d'Istanbul

Mem Astron Soc India — Memoirs. Astronomical Society of India

Mem Atti Cent Studi Ing Agrar — Memorie ed Atti. Centro di Studi per l'Ingegneria Agraria

Mem Aust Mus — Memoirs. Australian Museum

Mem Biol Mar Oceanogr — Memorie di Biologia Marina e di Oceanografia

Mem Boston Soc Nat Hist — Memoirs. Boston Society of Natural History

Mem Botan Surv S Afr — Memoirs. Botanical Survey of South Africa

Mem Bot Opname S-Afr — Memoirs. Botaniese Opname van Suid-Afrika

Mem Bot Surv S Afr — Memoir. Botanical Survey of South Africa

Membrane Biochem — Membrane Biochemistry

Membr Biochem — Membrane Biochemistry

Mem BRGM — Memoires. Bureau de Recherches Geologiques et Minieres [*France*]

Membr Proteins — Membrane Proteins

Mem Bur Rech Geol Minieres — Memoires. Bureau de Recherches Geologiques et Minieres [*France*]

Mem Can Soc Pet Geol — Memoir. Canadian Society of Petroleum Geologists

Mem Cent Natl Rech Metall Sect Hainaut — Memoires. Centre National de Recherches Metallurgiques. Section du Hainaut

Mem Cent Nat Rech Metall Sect Hainaut — Memoires. Centre National de Recherches Metallurgiques. Section du Hainaut

Mem Chubu Electr Power Co Ltd — Memoirs. Chubu Electric Power Company Limited [*Japan*]

Mem Chubu Inst Technol — Memoirs. Chubu Institute of Technology

Mem Chubu Inst Technol A — Memoirs. Chubu Institute of Technology. Series A

Mem Chukyo Women's Coll Chukyo Women's J Coll — Memoirs. Chukyo Women's College. Chukyo Women's Junior College

Mem Cl Sci Acad R Belg Collect 8o — Memoires. Classe des Sciences. Academie Royale de Belgique. Collection in Octavo

Mem Cognit — Memory and Cognition

Mem Cognition — Memory and Cognition

Mem Coll Agric Ehime Univ — Memoirs. College of Agriculture. Ehime University

Mem Coll Agric Kyoto Univ — Memoirs. College of Agriculture. Kyoto University

Mem Coll Agric Kyoto Univ Agric Econ Ser — Memoirs. College of Agriculture. Kyoto University. Agricultural Economy Series

Mem Coll Agric Kyoto Univ Anim Sci Ser — Memoirs. College of Agriculture. Kyoto University. Animal Science Series

Mem Coll Agric Kyoto Univ Bot Ser — Memoirs. College of Agriculture. Kyoto University. Botanical Series

Mem Coll Agric Kyoto Univ Chem Ser — Memoirs. College of Agriculture. Kyoto University. Chemical Series

Mem Coll Agric Kyoto Univ Entomol Ser — Memoirs. College of Agriculture. Kyoto University. Entomological Series

Mem Coll Agric Kyoto Univ Fish Ser — Memoirs. College of Agriculture. Kyoto University. Fisheries Series

Mem Coll Agric Kyoto Univ Food Sci Technol Ser — Memoirs. College of Agriculture. Kyoto University. Food Science and Technology Series

Mem Coll Agric Kyoto Univ Genet Ser — Memoirs. College of Agriculture. Kyoto University. Genetical Series

Mem Coll Agric Kyoto Univ Hortic Ser — Memoirs. College of Agriculture. Kyoto University. Horticultural Series

Mem Coll Agric Kyoto Univ Phytopathol Ser — Memoirs. College of Agriculture. Kyoto University. Phytopathological Series

Mem Coll Agric Kyoto Univ Plant Breed Ser — Memoirs. College of Agriculture. Kyoto University. Plant Breeding Series

Mem Coll Agric Kyoto Univ Wood Sci Technol Ser — Memoirs. College of Agriculture. Kyoto University. Wood Science and Technology Series

Mem Coll Agric Natl Taiwan Univ — Memoirs. College of Agriculture. National Taiwan University

Mem Coll Agr Kyoto Univ — Memoirs. College of Agriculture. Kyoto University

Mem Coll Eng Kyoto Imp Univ — Memoirs. College of Engineering. Kyoto Imperial University

Mem Coll Eng Kyushu Imp Univ — Memoirs. College of Engineering. Kyushu Imperial University

Mem Coll Sci Kyoto Imp Univ — Memoirs. College of Science. Kyoto Imperial University

Mem Coll Sci Univ Kyoto Ser A — Memoirs. College of Science. University of Kyoto. Series A

Mem Coll Sci Univ Kyoto Ser A Math — Memoirs. College of Science. University of Kyoto. Series A. Mathematics

Mem Coll Sci Univ Kyoto Ser B — Memoirs. College of Science. University of Kyoto. Series B [*Japan*]

Mem Coll Sci Univ Kyoto Ser B Geol Biol — Memoirs. College of Science. University of Kyoto. Series B. Geology and Biology

Mem Comun Inst Geol (Barcelona) — Memorias y Comunicaciones. Instituto Geologico (Barcelona)

Mem Conf Anu ATAC — Memoria. Conferencia Anual de la ATAC

Mem Cong Med Latino-Am (Buenos Aires) — Memoria. Congreso Medico Latino-Americano (Buenos Aires)

Mem Congr Nac Med Vet Zootec — Memorias. Congreso Nacional de Medicina Veterinaria y Zootecnia

Mem Conn Acad Arts Sci — Memoirs. Connecticut Academy of Arts and Sciences

Mem Cons Oceanogr Ibero Am — Memorias. Consejo Oceanografico Ibero-Americano

Mem Cornell Univ Agric Exper Station — Memoirs. Cornell University. Agricultural Experiment Station

Mem Cornell Univ Agric Exp Stn — Memoirs. Cornell University. Agricultural Experiment Station

Mem C R Soc R Can — Memoires et Comptes Rendus. Societe Royale du Canada

Mem Def Acad — Memoirs. Defense Academy
Mem Def Acad (Jap) — Memoirs. Defense Academy (Japan)
Mem Def Acad Math Phys Chem Eng — Memoirs. Defense Academy. Mathematics, Physics, Chemistry, and Engineering
Mem Def Acad Math Phys Chem Eng (Yokosuka Jpn) — Memoirs. Defense Academy. Mathematics, Physics, Chemistry, and Engineering (Yokosuka, Japan)
Mem Defense Acad — Memoirs. Defense Academy. Mathematics, Physics, Chemistry, and Engineering [*Yokosuka*]
Mem Dep Agric India Bacteriol Ser — Memoirs. Department of Agriculture in India. Bacteriological Series
Mem Dep Agric India Bot Ser — Memoirs. Department of Agriculture in India. Botanical Series
Mem Dep Agric India Chem Ser — Memoirs. Department of Agriculture in India. Chemical Series
Mem Dep Agric India Entomol Ser — Memoirs. Department of Agriculture in India. Entomological Series
Mem Dep Mineral Univ Geneve — Memoire. Departement de Mineralogie. Universite de Geneve
Mem Ecol Soc Aust — Memoirs. Ecological Society of Australia
Mem Ehime Univ — Memoirs. Ehime University
Mem Ehime Univ Nat Sci Ser B (Biol) — Memoirs. Ehime University. Natural Science. Series B (Biology)
Mem Ehime Univ Nat Sci Ser C — Memoirs. Ehime University. Natural Science. Series C
Mem Ehime Univ Natur Sci Ser A — Memoirs. Ehime University. Natural Science. Series A
Mem Ehime Univ Sect 6 (Agric) — Memoirs. Ehime University. Section 6 (Agriculture)
Mem Ehime Univ Sect 3 Eng — Memoirs. Ehime University. Section 3. Engineering [*Japan*]
Mem Ehime Univ Sect III Engrg — Memoirs. Ehime University. Section III. Engineering
Mem Ehime Univ Sect II Nat Sci — Memoirs. Ehime University. Section II. Natural Science
Mem Ehime Univ Sect 2 Ser C — Memoirs. Ehime University. Section 2. Natural Science. Series C. Chemistry
Mem Ehime Univ Sect VI Agr — Memoirs. Ehime University. Section VI. Agriculture
Mem Entomol Soc Can — Memoirs. Entomological Society of Canada
Mem Entomol Soc Que — Memoirs. Entomological Society of Quebec
Mem Entomol Soc South Afr — Memoirs. Entomological Society of Southern Africa
Mem Entomol Soc Wash — Memoirs. Entomological Society of Washington
Mem Ent S C — Memoirs. Entomological Society of Canada
Mem Estud Mus Zool Univ Coimbra — Memorias e Estudos. Museu Zoologico. Universidade de Coimbra
MeMeth — Media and Methods
Mem Etud Sci Rev Metall — Memoires et Etudes Scientifiques de la Revue de Metallurgie
Mem Explic Cartes Geol Min Belg — Memoires pour Servir a l'Explication des Cartes Geologiques et Minieres de la Belgique
MEMFA — Metallurgia and Metal Forming
Mem Fac Agr Hokkaido U — Memoirs. Faculty of Agriculture. Hokkaido University
Mem Fac Agr Hokkaido Univ — Memoirs. Faculty of Agriculture. Hokkaido University
Mem Fac Agric Hokkaido Univ — Memoirs. Faculty of Agriculture. Hokkaido University
Mem Fac Agric Kagawa Univ — Memoirs. Faculty of Agriculture. Kagawa University
Mem Fac Agric Kagoshima Univ — Memoirs. Faculty of Agriculture. Kagoshima University
Mem Fac Agric Kinki Univ — Memoirs. Faculty of Agriculture. Kinki University
Mem Fac Agric Kochi Univ — Memoirs. Faculty of Agriculture. Kochi University
Mem Fac Agric Niigata Univ — Memoirs. Faculty of Agriculture. Niigata University
Mem Fac Agric Univ Miyazaki — Memoirs. Faculty of Agriculture. University of Miyazaki
Mem Fac Agr Kagawa Univ — Memoirs. Faculty of Agriculture. Kagawa University
Mem Fac Agr Kinki Univ — Memoirs. Faculty of Agriculture. Kinki University
Mem Fac Agr Univ Miyazaki — Memoirs. Faculty of Agriculture. University of Miyazaki
Mem Fac Ed Kumamoto Univ Natur Sci — Kumamoto University. Faculty of Education. Memoirs. Natural Science
Mem Fac Ed Kumamoto Univ Sect 1 — Memoirs. Faculty of Education. Kumamoto University. Section 1 (Natural Science)
Mem Fac Ed Miyazaki Univ — Memoirs. Faculty of Education. Miyazaki University
Mem Fac Ed Shiga Univ Natur Sci — Shiga University. Faculty of Education. Memoirs. Natural Science
Mem Fac Educ Akita Univ — Memoirs. Faculty of Education. Akita University

Mem Fac Educ Akita Univ Nat Sci — Memoirs. Faculty of Education. Akita University. Natural Science
Mem Fac Educ Kumamoto Univ — Memoirs. Faculty of Education. Kumamoto University
Mem Fac Educ Kumamoto Univ Sect 1 (Nat Sci) — Memoirs. Faculty of Education. Kumamoto University. Section 1 (Natural Science)
Mem Fac Educ Mie Univ — Memoirs. Faculty of Education. Mie University
Mem Fac Educ Niigata Univ — Memoirs. Faculty of Education. Niigata University
Mem Fac Educ Shiga Univ Nat Sci — Memoirs. Faculty of Education. Shiga University. Natural Science
Mem Fac Educ Toyama Univ — Memoirs. Faculty of Education. Toyama University
Mem Fac Educ Yamanashi Univ — Memoirs. Faculty of Education. Yamanashi University [*Japan*]
Mem Fac Eng Fukui Univ — Memoirs. Faculty of Engineering. Fukui University [*Japan*]
Mem Fac Eng Hiroshima Univ — Memoirs. Faculty of Engineering. Hiroshima University
Mem Fac Eng Hokkaido Imp Univ — Memoirs. Faculty of Engineering. Hokkaido Imperial University
Mem Fac Eng Hokkaido Univ — Memoirs. Faculty of Engineering. Hokkaido University
Mem Fac Eng Hokkaido Univ (Sapporo Jpn) — Memoirs. Faculty of Engineering. Hokkaido University (Sapporo, Japan)
Mem Fac Eng Kobe Univ — Memoirs. Faculty of Engineering. Kobe University
Mem Fac Eng Kumamoto Univ — Memoirs. Faculty of Engineering. Kumamoto University
Mem Fac Eng Kyoto Univ — Memoirs. Faculty of Engineering. Kyoto University
Mem Fac Eng Kyushu Univ — Memoirs. Faculty of Engineering. Kyushu University
Mem Fac Eng Miyazaki Univ — Memoirs. Faculty of Engineering. Miyazaki University
Mem Fac Eng Nagoya Univ — Memoirs. Faculty of Engineering. Nagoya University
Mem Fac Engng Kyoto Univ — Memoirs. Faculty of Engineering. Kyoto University
Mem Fac Engng Nagoya Univ — Memoirs. Faculty of Engineering. Nagoya University
Mem Fac Eng Osaka City Univ — Memoirs. Faculty of Engineering. Osaka City University
Mem Fac Engrg Hiroshima Univ — Memoirs. Faculty of Engineering. Hiroshima University
Mem Fac Engrg Kyoto Univ — Memoirs. Faculty of Engineering. Kyoto University
Mem Fac Engrg Miyazaki Univ — Memoirs. Faculty of Engineering. Miyazaki University
Mem Fac Eng Tamagawa Univ — Memoirs. Faculty of Engineering. Tamagawa University
Mem Fac Eng Tehran Univ — Memoirs. Faculty of Engineering. Tehran University
Mem Fac Eng Yamaguchi Univ — Memoirs. Faculty of Engineering. Yamaguchi University [*Japan*]
Mem Fac Fish Hokkaido Univ — Memoirs. Faculty of Fisheries. Hokkaido University
Mem Fac Fish Kagoshima Univ — Memoirs. Faculty of Fisheries. Kagoshima University
Mem Fac Gen Ed Kumamoto Univ Natur Sci — Memoirs. Kumamoto University. Faculty of General Education. Natural Sciences
Mem Fac Gen Educ Hiroshima Univ — Memoirs. Faculty of General Education. Hiroshima University
Mem Fac Ind Arts Kyoto Tech Univ — Memoirs. Faculty of Industrial Arts. Kyoto Technical University. Science and Technology
Mem Fac Ind Arts Kyoto Tech Univ Sci and Technol — Memoirs. Faculty of Industrial Arts. Kyoto Technical University. Science and Technology
Mem Fac Indust Arts Kyoto Tech Univ Sci and Tech — Memoirs. Faculty of Industrial Arts. Kyoto Technical University. Science and Technology
Mem Fac Lib Arts Educ Miyazaki Univ — Memoirs. Faculty of Liberal Arts Education. Miyazaki University
Mem Fac Lib Arts Fukui Univ — Memoirs. Faculty of Liberal Arts. Fukui University
Mem Fac Liberal Arts Educ Yamanashi Univ — Memoirs. Faculty of Liberal Arts and Education. Yamanashi University [*Japan*]
Mem Fac Lit Sci Shimane Univ Nat Sci — Memoirs. Faculty of Literature and Science. Shimane University. Natural Sciences
Mem Fac Lit Sci Shimane Univ Natur Sci — Memoirs. Faculty of Literature and Science. Shimane University. Natural Sciences [*Matsue*]
Mem Fac Sci Eng Waseda Univ — Memoirs. Faculty of Science and Engineering. Waseda University
Mem Fac Sci Kochi Univ Ser A Math — Kochi University. Faculty of Science. Memoirs. Series A. Mathematics
Mem Fac Sci Kyoto Univ Ser Biol — Memoirs. Faculty of Science. Kyoto University. Series of Biology
Mem Fac Sci Kyoto Univ Ser Geol Mineral — Memoirs. Faculty of Science. Kyoto University. Series of Geology and Mineralogy

Mem Fac Sci Kyoto Univ Ser Phys Astrophys Geophys Chem — Memoirs. Faculty of Science. Kyoto University. Series of Physics, Astrophysics, Geophysics, and Chemistry

Mem Fac Sci Kyushu Univ B — Memoirs. Faculty of Science. Kyushu University. Series B

Mem Fac Sci Kyushu Univ C — Memoirs. Faculty of Science. Kyushu University. Series C

Mem Fac Sci Kyushu Univ Ser A — Memoirs. Faculty of Science. Kyushu University. Series A. Mathematics

Mem Fac Sci Kyushu Univ Ser B — Memoirs. Faculty of Science. Kyushu University. Series B. Physics

Mem Fac Sci Kyushu Univ Ser C — Memoirs. Faculty of Science. Kyushu University. Series C. Chemistry

Mem Fac Sci Kyushu Univ Ser D — Memoirs. Faculty of Science. Kyushu University. Series D. Geology

Mem Fac Sci Kyushu Univ Ser D Geol — Memoirs. Faculty of Science. Kyushu University. Series D. Geology

Mem Fac Sci Kyushu Univ Ser E — Memoirs. Faculty of Science. Kyushu University. Series E. Biology

Mem Fac Sci Kyushu Univ Ser E Biol — Memoirs. Faculty of Science. Kyushu University. Series E. Biology

Mem Fac Sci Shimane Univ — Shimane University. Faculty of Science. Memoirs

Mem Fac Technol Kanazawa Univ — Memoirs. Faculty of Technology. Kanazawa University

Mem Fac Technol Tokyo Metrop Univ — Memoirs. Faculty of Technology. Tokyo Metropolitan University

Mem Fac Tech Tokyo Metropolitan Univ — Memoirs. Faculty of Technology. Tokyo Metropolitan University

Mem Gen Inst Geol Min Esp — Memoria General. Instituto Geologico y Minero de Espana

Mem Geol Surv Can — Memoirs. Geological Survey of Canada

Mem Geol Surv GB Engl Wales Explan Sheet — Memoirs. Geological Survey of Great Britain. England and Wales Explanation Sheet

Mem Geol Surv GB (Scotl) — Memoirs. Geological Survey of Great Britain (Scotland)

Mem Geol Surv Gt Br — Memoirs. Geological Survey of Great Britain

Mem Geol Surv India — Memoirs. Geological Survey of India

Mem Geol Surv NSW — Memoirs. Geological Survey of New South Wales

Mem Geol Surv of NSW — Memoirs. Geological Survey of New South Wales

Mem Geol Surv of NSW Geol — Memoirs. Geological Survey of New South Wales. Department of Mines. Geology

Mem Geol Surv NSW Geol — New South Wales. Geological Survey. Memoirs. Geology

Mem Geol Surv NSW Palaeontol — Memoirs. Geological Survey of New South Wales. Palaeontology

Mem Geol Surv Papua New Guinea — Memoirs. Geological Survey of Papua New Guinea

Mem Geol Surv S Afr — Memoirs. Geological Survey of South Africa

Mem Geol Surv VIC — Memoirs. Geological Survey of Victoria

Mem Geol Surv Vict — Memoirs. Geological Survey of Victoria

Mem Geol Surv West Aust — Memoirs. Geological Survey of Western Australia

Mem Geopaleontol Univ Ferrara — Memorie Geopaleontologiche. Universita di Ferrara

Mem Gifu Tech Coll — Memoirs. Gifu Technical College

Mem Hokkaido Inst Technol — Memoirs. Hokkaido Institute of Technology

Mem Hourglass Cruises — Memoirs. Hourglass Cruises

Mem Hyogo Univ Agric — Memoirs. Hyogo University of Agriculture

Mem Indian Bot Soc — Memoirs. Indian Botanical Society

Mem Indian Mus — Memoirs. Indian Museum

Mem Inst — Memoires. Institut Francais d'Archeologie Orientale

Mem Inst Butantan — Memorias. Instituto Butantan

Mem Inst Butantan (Sao Paulo) — Memorias. Instituto Butantan (Sao Paulo)

Mem Inst Egypt — Memoires. Institut d'Egypte

Mem Inst Esp Oceanogr — Memorias. Instituto Espanol de Oceanografia

Mem Inst Geol Min Esp — Memorias. Instituto Geologico y Minero de Espana

Mem Inst Geol (Rom) — Memorii. Institutul Geologie (Romania)

Mem Inst Geol Univ Louv — Memoires. Institut Geologique. Universite de Louvain

Mem Inst High Speed Mech Tohoku Univ — Memoirs. Institute of High Speed Mechanics. Tohoku University [Japan]

Mem Inst Invest Cient Mocambique Ser A Cienc Biol — Memorias. Instituto de Investigacao Cientifica de Mocambique. Serie A. Ciencias Biologicas

Mem Inst Oceanogr (Monaco) — Memoires. Institut Oceanographique (Monaco)

Mem Inst Oswaldo Cruz — Memorias. Instituto Oswaldo Cruz

Mem Inst Oswaldo Cruz (Rio De J) — Memorias. Instituto Oswaldo Cruz (Rio De Janeiro)

Mem Inst Protein Res Osaka Univ — Memoirs. Institute of Protein Research. Osaka University

Mem Inst Rech Sci Madagascar Ser A Biol Anim — Memoires. Institut de Recherche Scientifique de Madagascar. Serie A. Biologie Animale

Mem Inst Rech Sci Madagascar Ser B Biol Veg — Memoires. Institut de Recherche Scientifique de Madagascar. Serie B. Biologie Vegetale

Mem Inst Rech Sci Madagascar Ser F Oceanogr — Memoires. Institut de Recherche Scientifique de Madagascar. Serie F. Oceanographie

Mem Inst Sci Ind Res Osaka Univ — Memoirs. Institute of Scientific and Industrial Research. Osaka University

Mem Inst Sci Madagascar Ser B — Memoires. Institut de Recherche Scientifique de Madagascar. Serie B. Biologie

Mem Inst Sci Madagascar Ser D — Memoires. Institut de Recherche Scientifique de Madagascar. Serie D. Sciences de la Terre

Mem Int Assoc Hydrogeol — Memoirs. International Association of Hydrogeologists

Mem Int Soc Sugar Cane Technol — Memoirs. International Society of Sugar Cane Technologists

Mem Ist Geol Mineral Univ Padova — Memorie. Istituti di Geologia e Mineralogia. Universita di Padova

Mem Ist Ital Idrobiol — Memorie. Istituto Italiano di Idrobiologia

Mem Ist Ital Idrobiol Dott Marco De Marchi — Memorie. Istituto Italiano di Idrobiologia Dottore Marco De Marchi [Italy]

Mem Ist Ital Idrobiol Dott Marco De Marchi (Pallanza Italy) — Memorie. Istituto Italiano di Idrobiologia Dottore Marco De Marchi (Pallanza, Italy)

Mem Ist Ital Idrobiol Dott Marco Marchi — Memorie. Istituto Italiano di Idrobiologia Dottore Marco De Marchi

Mem Jornadas Agron — Memoria Jornadas Agronomicas

Mem Junta Invest Ultramar (Port) — Memorias. Junta de Investigacoes do Ultramar (Portugal)

Mem Junta Invest Ultramar Ser II — Memorias. Junta de Investigacoes do Ultramar. Serie II

Mem Junta Missoes Geogr Invest Ultramar (Port) — Memorias. Junta das Missoes Geograficas e de Investigacoes do Ultramar (Portugal)

Mem Kakioka Magn Obs — Memoirs. Kakioka Magnetic Observatory [Japan]

Mem Kanazawa Inst Technol — Memoirs. Kanazawa Institute of Technology

Mem Kitami Inst Tech — Memoirs. Kitami Institute of Technology

Mem Kobe Mar Obs (Kobe Jpn) — Memoirs. Kobe Marine Observatory (Kobe, Japan)

Mem Konan Univ Sci Ser — Memoirs. Konan University. Science Series

Mem Kyoto Tech Univ Sci Tech — Memoirs. Faculty of Industrial Arts. Kyoto Technical University. Science and Technology

Mem Kyushu Inst Technol Eng — Memoirs. Kyushu Institute of Technology. Engineering

Meml Meteorol Natl — Memorial de la Meteorologie Nationale

Mem Mat Inst Jorge Juan — Memorias de Matematica. Instituto Jorge Juan [Madrid]

Mem Meteorol Natl — Memorial de la Meteorologie Nationale

Mem Miner Resour Div (Tanzania) — Memoirs. Mineral Resources Division (Tanzania)

Mem Miner Resour Geol Surv Szechuan — Memoirs of Mineral Resources. Geological Survey of Szechuan

Mem Miyakonojo Tech Coll — Memoirs. Miyakonojo Technical College

Mem Muroran Inst Tech — Memoirs. Muroran Institute of Technology

Mem Muroran Inst Technol — Memoirs. Muroran Institute of Technology [Japan]

Mem Mus Civ Stor Nat Verona — Memorie. Museo Civico di Storia Naturale di Verona

Mem Mus Dr Alvaro De Castro — Memorias. Museu Dr. Alvaro De Castro

Mem Mus Hist Nat "Javier Prado" — Memorias. Museo de Historia Natural "Javier Prado"

Mem Mus Hist Nat (Paris) Ser C — Memoires. Museum National d'Histoire Naturelle (Paris). Serie C. Sciences de la Terre

Mem Mus Natl His Nat Ser C Sci Terre — Memoires. Museum National d'Histoire Naturelle. Serie C. Sciences de la Terre

Mem Mus Natl Hist Nat — Memoires. Museum National d'Histoire Naturelle

Mem Mus Natl Hist Nat Ser A (Paris) — Memoires. Museum National d'Histoire Naturelle. Serie A. Zoologie (Paris)

Mem Mus Natl Hist Nat Ser A Zool — Memoires. Museum National d'Histoire Naturelle. Serie A. Zoologie

Mem Mus Natl Hist Nat Ser B Bot — Memoires. Museum National d'Histoire Naturelle. Serie B. Botanique

Mem Mus Natl Hist Nat Ser C (Paris) — Memoires. Museum National d'Histoire Naturelle. Serie C. Sciences de la Terre (Paris)

Mem Mus Natl Hist Nat Ser D (Paris) — Memoires. Museum National d'Histoire Naturelle. Serie D. Sciences Physico-Chimiques (Paris)

Mem Mus Tridentino Sci Nat — Memorie. Museo Tridentino di Scienze Naturali

Mem Nas Mus Bloemfontein — Memoirs. Nasionale Museum Bloemfontein

Mem Nat Cult Res San-In Reg — Memoirs of Natural and Cultural Researches of the San-In Region

Mem Natl Def Acad — Memoirs. National Defense Academy

Mem Natl Inst Polar Res Ser E Biol Med Sci — Memoirs. National Institute of Polar Research. Series E. Biology and Medical Science

Mem Natl Mus Vict — Memoirs. National Museum of Victoria

Mem Natl Mus Victoria — Memoirs. National Museum of Victoria

Mem Natl Sci Mus (Tokyo) — Memoirs. National Science Museum (Tokyo)

Mem Nat Mus VIC — Memoirs. National Museum of Victoria

Mem Natn Mus (Melb) — Memoirs. National Museum (Melbourne)

Mem Niihama Tech Coll — Memoirs. Niihama Technical College [Japan]

Mem Niihama Tech Coll Nat Sci — Memoirs. Niihama Technical College. Natural Sciences
Mem NM Bur Mines Miner Resour — Memoir. New Mexico Bureau of Mines and Mineral Resources
Mem Note Ist Geol Appl Univ Napoli — Memorie e Note. Istituto di Geologia Applicata. Universita di Napoli
Mem Notic Mus Miner Geol Univ Coimbra — Memorias e Noticias. Museu e Laboratorio Mineralogico e Geologico. Universidade de Coimbra
Mem NS Dep Mines — Memoirs. Nova Scotia Department of Mines
Mem Numer Math — Memoirs of Numerical Mathematics
Mem NY Agr Exp Sta — Memoir. New York Agricultural Experiment Station
Mem NY Bot Gard — Memoirs. New York Botanical Gardens
MEMOA — Medizinische Monatsschrift
Memo Div Chem Eng CSIRO — Memorandum. Division of Chemical Engineering. Commonwealth Scientific and Industrial Research Organisation
Memo Div Chem Engng CSIRO — Memorandum. Division of Chemical Engineering. Commonwealth Scientific and Industrial Research Organisation
Memo Fed Dept Agr Res (Nigeria) — Memorandum. Federal Department of Agricultural Research (Nigeria)
Mem Off Rech Sci Tech Outre-Mer — Memoires. Office de la Recherche Scientifique et Technique d'Outre-Mer
Mem Ofic Estud Espec Min Agr Dir Agr Pesca (Chile) — Memoria. Oficina de Estudios Especiales. Ministerio de Agricultura. Direccion de Agricultura y Pesca (Chile)
Memo Indian Tea Assoc Tocklai Exp Stn — Memorandum. Indian Tea Association. Tocklai Experimental Station
Memo Meat Res Inst — Memorandum. Meat Research Institute
Memo Nor Landbrukshogsk Inst Landbrukskom — Memorandum. Norges Landbrukshogskole Institutt foer Landbruksokonomi
Memorabilia Zool — Memorabilia Zoologica
Memorie Soc Ent Ital — Memorie. Societa Entomologica Italiana
Mem ORSTOM — Memoires. Office de la Recherche Scientifique et Technique d'Outre-Mer
Mem Osaka Inst Technol Ser A Sci Technol — Memoirs. Osaka Institute of Technology. Series A. Science and Technology
Mem Osaka Inst Tech Ser A — Memoirs. Osaka Institute of Technology. Series A. Science and Technology
Mem Osaka Kyoiku Univ — Memoires. Osaka Kyoiku University
Mem Osaka Kyoiku Univ III Nat Sci Appl Sci — Memoirs. Osaka Kyoiku University. III. Natural Science and Applied Science
Mem Osaka Kyoiku Univ III Natur Sci Appl Sci — Memoirs. Osaka Kyoiku University. III. Natural Science and Applied Science
Mem Osaka Univ Lib Arts Educ B Natur Sci — Memoirs. Osaka University of Liberal Arts and Education. B. Natural Science
Memo Soc Fauna Flora Fenn — Memoranda Societatis pro Fauna et Flora Fennica
Memo Univ Coll Wales Dept Geogr — Memorandum. University College of Wales. Department of Geography
Mem Pac Coast Entomol Soc — Memoirs. Pacific Coast Entomological Society
Mem Palaeontol Ser Geol Surv (NSW) — Memoirs. Palaeontology Series. Geological Survey (New South Wales)
MEMPB — Moessbauer Effect Methodology. Proceedings of the Symposium
Memphis J Med Sc — Memphis Journal of the Medical Sciences
Memphis Med Month — Memphis Medical Monthly
Memphis Mid-South Med J — Memphis and Mid-South Medical Journal
Memphis State UL Rev — Memphis State University. Law Review
Memphis State Univ L Rev — Memphis State University. Law Review
Memphis St U L Rev — Memphis State University. Law Review
Mem Pont Acc — Atti. Pontificia Accademia Romana di Archeologia. Memorie
Mem Poudres — Memorial des Poudres [*France*]
Mem Proc Manchester Lit Philos Soc — Memoirs and Proceedings. Manchester Literary and Philosophical Society
Mem Publ Soc Sci Arts Lett Hainaut — Memoires et Publications. Societe des Sciences, des Arts, et des Lettres du Hainaut
Mem QD Mus — Memoirs. Queensland Museum
Mem Queensl Mus — Memoirs. Queensland Museum
Mem R Acad Cienc Artes Barc — Memorias. Real Academia de Ciencias y Artes de Barcelona
Mem R Acad Cienc Exactas Fis Nat Madrid — Memorias. Real Academia de Ciencias Exactas, Fisicas, y Naturales de Madrid
Mem R Acad Cienc Exactas Fis Nat Madrid Ser Cienc Exactas — Memorias. Real Academia de Ciencias Exactas, Fisicas, y Naturales de Madrid. Serie de Ciencias Exactas
Mem R Acad Cienc Exactas Fis Nat Madrid Ser Cienc Fis-Quim — Memorias. Real Academia de Ciencias Exactas, Fisicas, y Naturales de Madrid. Serie de Ciencias Fisico-Quimicas
Mem R Acad Cienc Exactas Fis Nat Madrid Ser Cienc Nat — Memorias. Real Academia de Ciencias Exactas, Fisicas, y Naturales de Madrid. Serie de Ciencias Naturales
Mem R Acad Cienc Exactas Fis Nat Madr Ser Cienc Nat — Memorias. Real Academia de Ciencias Exactas, Fisicas, y Naturales de Madrid. Serie de Ciencias Naturales

Mem R Accad Ital Cl Sci Fis Mat Nat — Memorie. Reale Accademia d'Italia. Classe di Scienze Fisiche, Matematiche, e Naturali
Mem R Accad Ital Cl Sci Fis Mat Nat Biol — Memorie. Reale Accademia d'Italia. Classe di Scienze Fisiche, Matematiche, e Naturali. Biologia
Mem R Accad Ital Cl Sci Fis Mat Nat Chim — Memorie. Reale Accademia d'Italia. Classe di Scienze Fisiche, Matematiche, e Naturali. Chimica
Mem R Accad Ital Cl Sci Fis Mat Nat Fis — Memorie. Reale Accademia d'Italia. Classe di Scienze Fisiche, Matematiche, e Naturali. Fisica
Mem R Accad Ital Cl Sci Fis Mat Nat Ing — Memorie. Reale Accademia d'Italia. Classe di Scienze Fisiche, Matematiche, e Naturali. Ingegneria
Mem R Accad Ital Cl Sci Fis Mat Nat Mat — Memorie. Reale Accademia d'Italia. Classe di Scienze Fisiche, Matematiche, e Naturali. Matematica
Mem R Accad Sci Ist Bologna Cl Sci Fis — Memorie. Reale Accademia delle Scienze. Istituto di Bologna. Classe di Scienze Fisiche
Mem R Accad Sci Lett Arti (Modena) — Memorie. Reale Accademia di Scienze, Lettere, ed Arti (Modena)
Mem Raman Res Inst — Memoirs. Raman Research Institute
Mem R Asiat Soc Bengal — Memoirs. Royal Asiatic Society of Bengal
Mem R Astron Soc — Memoirs. Royal Astronomical Society
Mem Real Acad Ci Art Barcelona — Memorias. Real Academia de Ciencias y Artes de Barcelona
Mem Real Acad Cienc Artes Barcelona — Memorias. Real Academia de Ciencias y Artes de Barcelona
Mem Real Acad Ci Exact Fis Natur Madrid — Memorias. Real Academia de Ciencias Exactas, Fisicas, y Naturales de Madrid. Serie de Ciencias Exactas
Mem Rend Accad Zel Acireale — Memorie e Rendiconti. Accademia di Scienze, Lettere, e Belle Arti degli Zelanti e dei Dafnici di Acireale
Mem Res Depart Toyo Bunko — Memoirs. Research Department. Toyo Bunko
Mem Res Inst Acoust Sci Osaka Univ — Memoirs. Research Institute of Acoustical Science. Osaka University
Mem Res Inst Food Sci Kyoto Univ — Memoirs. Research Institute for Food Science. Kyoto University
Mem Res Inst Sci and Eng Ritsumeikan Univ — Memoirs. Research Institute of Science and Engineering. Ritsumeikan University
Mem Res Inst Sci Eng Ritsumeikan Univ — Memoirs. Research Institute of Science and Engineering. Ritsumeikan University [*Kyoto, Japan*]
Mem Reun Tec Nac Mania — Memoria. Reunion Tecnica Nacional de Mania
Mem Rev Acad Nac Cienc — Memorias y Revista. Academia Nacional de Ciencias
Mem Rev Acad Nac Cienc "Antonio Alzate" — Memorias y Revista. Academia Nacional de Ciencias "Antonio Alzate"
Mem Sagami Inst Technol — Memoirs. Sagami Institute of Technology
Mem Sch Eng Okayama Univ — Memoirs. School of Engineering. Okayama University
Mem School Engrg Okayama Univ — Memoirs. School of Engineering. Okayama University
Mem School Sci Engrg Waseda Univ — Memoirs. School of Science and Engineering. Waseda University
Mem School Sci Eng Waseda Univ — Memoirs. School of Science and Engineering. Waseda University
Mem Sch Sci Eng Waseda Univ — Memoirs. School of Science and Engineering. Waseda University
Mem Sch Sci and Eng Waseda Univ — Memoirs. School of Science and Engineering. Waseda University
Mem Sci Rev Met — Memoires Scientifiques de la Revue de Metallurgie
Mem Sci Rev Metall — Memoires Scientifiques de la Revue de Metallurgie
Mems Comn Invest Paleont Prehist (Madr) — Memorias. Comision de Investigaciones Paleontologicas y Prehistoricas. Instituto Nacional de Ciencias Fisico-Naturales (Madrid)
Mem Semin Latino-Amer Irrig — Memoria. Seminario Latino-Americano de Irrigacion
Mem Ser Calcutta Math Soc — Memoir Series. Calcutta Mathematical Society
Mem Serv Carte Geol Alsace Lorraine — Memoires. Service de la Carte Geologique d'Alsace et de Lorraine
Mem Serv Chim Etat — Memorial des Services Chimiques de l'Etat
Mem Serv Geol Belg — Memoire. Service Geologique de Belgique
Mem Serv Geol Port — Memorias. Servicos Geologicos de Portugal
Mem Servir Explication Carte Geol Detaill Fr — Memoires pour Servir a l'Explication de la Carte Geologique Detaillee de la France
Mems Estud Mus Zool Univ Coimbra — Memorias e Estudos. Museu Zoologico. Universidade de Coimbra
Mems Inst Oswaldo Cruz — Memorias. Instituto Oswaldo Cruz
Mems Jta Invest Ultramar — Memorias. Junta de Investigacoes do Ultramar
Mem Soc Agric Commer Sci Arts (Marne) — Memoires. Societe d'Agriculture, Commerce, Sciences, et Arts du Departement de la Marne (Chalons Sur Marne)
Mem Soc Ant Picardie — Memoires. Societe des Antiquaires de Picardie
Mem Soc Astron Ital — Memorie. Societa Astronomica Italiana
Mem Soc Astronom Ital NS — Memorie. Societa Astronomica Italiana. Nuova Serie
Mem Soc Belge Geol Paleontol Hydrol Ser 8 — Memoires. Societe Belge de Geologie, de Paleontologie, et d'Hydrologie. Serie in Octavo
Mem Soc Bot Fr — Memoires. Societe Botanique de France
Mem Soc Broteriana — Memorias. Sociedade Broteriana

Mem Soc Centr Med Vet — Memoires. Societe Centrale de Medecine Veterinaire

Mem Soc Cienc Nat (La Salle) — Memoria. Sociedad de Ciencias Naturales (La Salle)

Mem Soc Cient "Antonio Alzate" — Memorias. Sociedad Cientifica "Antonio Alzate"

Mem Soc Cubana Hist Nat "Felipe Poey" — Memorias. Sociedad Cubana de Historia Natural "Felipe Poey"

Mem Soc Endocrinol — Memoirs. Society for Endocrinology

Mem Soc Entomol Ital — Memorie. Societa Entomologica Italiana

Mem Soc Entomol Que — Memoires. Societe Entomologique du Quebec

Mem Soc Frib Sci Nat Bot — Memoires. Societe Fribourgeoise des Sciences Naturelles. Botanique

Mem Soc Frib Sci Nat Chim — Memoires. Societe Fribourgeoise des Sciences Naturelles. Chimie

Mem Soc Frib Sci Nat Geol Geogr — Memoires. Societe Fribourgeoise des Sciences Naturelles. Geologie et Geographie

Mem Soc Frib Sci Nat Math Phys — Memoires. Societe Fribourgeoise des Sciences Naturelles. Mathematique et Physique

Mem Soc Frib Sci Nat Physiol Hyg Bacteriol — Memoires. Societe Fribourgeoise des Sciences Naturelles. Physiologie, Hygiene, Bacteriologie

Mem Soc Frib Sci Nat Zool — Memoires. Societe Fribourgeoise des Sciences Naturelles. Zoologie

Mem Soc Geol Fr — Memoires. Societe Geologique de France

Mem Soc Geol Ital — Memorie. Societa Geologica Italiana

Mem Soc Geol Mineral Bretagne — Memoires. Societe Geologique et Mineralogique de Bretagne

Mem Soc Helv Sci Nat — Memoires. Societe Helvetique des Sciences Naturelles

Mem Soc Hist Nat Afr Nord — Memoires. Societe d'Histoire Naturelle de l'Afrique du Nord

Mem Soc Hist Natur Afr Nord — Memoires. Societe d'Histoire Naturelle de l'Afrique du Nord

Mem Soc Ital Sci Nat Mus Civ Stor Nat Milano — Memorie. Societa Italiana di Scienze Naturali e Museo Civico di Storia Naturale di Milano

Mem Soc Math France NS — Memoire. Societe Mathematique de France. Nouvelle Serie

Mem Soc Natl Sci Nat Math Cherbg — Memoires. Societe Nationale des Sciences Naturelles et Mathematiques de Cherbourg

Mem Soc Neuchatel Sci Nat — Memoires. Societe Neuchateloise des Sciences Naturelles

Mem Soc R Belge Entomol — Memoires. Societe Royale Belge d'Entomologie

Mem Soc R Bot Belg — Memoires. Societe Royale de Botanique de Belgique

Mem Soc R Can — Memoires. Societe Royale du Canada

Mem Soc R Ent Belg — Memoires. Societe Royale Entomologique de Belgique

Mem Soc Roy Liege — Memorandum. Societe Royale de Liege

Mem Soc Roy Sci Liege Coll in-8o — Memoires. Societe Royale des Sciences de Liege. Collection in Octavo

Mem Soc R Sci Liege — Memoires. Societe Royale des Sciences de Liege

Mem Soc R Sci Liege 4o — Memoires. Societe Royale des Sciences de Liege. Collection in Quarto

Mem Soc R Sci Liege 8o — Memoires. Societe Royale des Sciences de Liege. Collection in Octavo

Mem Soc R Sci Liege Vol Hors Ser — Memoires. Societe Royale des Sciences de Liege. Volume Hors Serie [*Belgium*]

Mem Soc Sci Nancy — Memoires. Societe des Sciences de Nancy

Mem Soc Sci Nat Phys Maroc Bot — Memoires. Societe des Sciences Naturelles et Physiques du Maroc. Botanique

Mem Soc Sci Nat Phys Maroc Zool — Memoires. Societe des Sciences Naturelles et Physiques du Maroc. Zoologie

Mem Soc Sci Phys Nat Bordeaux — Memoires. Societe des Sciences Physiques et Naturelles de Bordeaux

Mem Soc Vaudoise Sci Nat — Memoires. Societe Vaudoise des Sciences Naturelles

Mem Soc Zool Fr — Memoires. Societe Zoologique de France

Mem Soil Res Inst (Kumasi Ghana) — Memoir. Soil Research Institute (Kumasi, Ghana)

Mem South Calif Acad Sci — Memoirs. Southern California Academy of Sciences

Mem S R Met — Memoires Scientifiques de la Revue de Metallurgie

Mem St Bur Mines Miner Resour (New Mex) — Memoirs. State Bureau of Mines and Mineral Resources (New Mexico)

Mem St ULR — Memphis State University. Law Review

Mem Suzuka Coll Technol — Memoirs. Suzuka College of Technology

Mem Tec Congr Latinoam Sider — Memoria Tecnica. Congreso Latinoamericano de Siderurgia

Mem Tokyo Univ Agr — Memoirs. Tokyo University of Agriculture

Mem Tokyo Univ Agric — Memoirs. Tokyo University of Agriculture

Mem Torrey Bot Club — Memoirs. Torrey Botanical Club

Mem Tottori Agric Coll — Memoirs. Tottori Agricultural College

Mem Trav Fac Cath — Memoires et Travaux. Facultes Catholiques de Lille

Mem Trav Soc Hydrot France — Memoires et Travaux. Societe Hydrotechnique de France

Mem Univ Calif — Memoirs. University of California

Mem Univ Lab Phys Chem Med Public Health Har Univ — Memoirs. University Laboratory of Physical Chemistry Related to Medicine and Public Health. Harvard University

MEN — Meatworks Extension News

Menabo — Menabo di Letteratura

Mendel Chem J — Mendeleev Chemistry Journal

Mendeleev Chem J — Mendeleev Chemistry Journal

Mendel Newsl — Mendel Newsletter

Men Dis LR — Mental Disability Law Reporter

Me Ne — Meroitic Newsletter

Menemui Mat — Menemui Matematik [*Kuala Lumpur*]

M Engy Rev — Monthly Energy Review

MenJ — Menorah Journal

Menn — Mennonite

Menn L — Mennonite Life

Mennonite Q R — Mennonite Quarterly Review

Menn Q R — Mennonite Quarterly Review

MENOA — Metano, Petrolio, e Nuove Energie

Menorah J — Menorah Journal

Men Retard — Mental Retardation

MENS — Man-Environment Systems

Mensaje Bol Inf Fed Iberoam Parques — Mensaje Boletin Informativo. Federacion Iberoamericana de Parques Zoologicos

Mensajero For — Mensajero Forestal

Mens Maatschap — Mens en Maatschappij

Mens en Mel — Mens en Melodie

Mens en Mij — Mens en Maatschappij

Mens Ond — Mens en Onderneming

Mental Disab L Rep — Mental Disability Law Reporter

Mental Health in Aust — Mental Health in Australia

Mental Hyg — Mental Hygiene

Mental Reta — Mental Retardation

Ment Health Aust — Mental Health in Australia

Ment Health Program Rep — Mental Health Program Reports

Ment Health Res Inst Univ Mich Annu Rep — Mental Health Research Institute. University of Michigan. Annual Report

Ment Health Soc — Mental Health and Society

Ment Health Stat Note — Mental Health Statistical Note

Ment Hlth Stat — Mental Health Statistics

Ment Hyg — Mental Hygiene

Ment Ret — Mental Retardation

Ment Retard — Mental Retardation

Ment Retard Absts — Mental Retardation Abstracts

Ment Ret Bul — Mental Retardation Bulletin

MENZA — Methods in Enzymology

MEOC — Methods of Elemento-Organic Chemistry [*Elsevier Book Series*]

MEOL — Mededeelingen Ex Oriente Lux

MeP — Mekedonski Pregled. Spisanie za Nauka. Literatura i Obsteostven Zivot

MEP — MEP: Multicultural Education Papers

MEQ — Metal Bulletin Monthly

MER — Malayan Economic Review

MER — MER (Marine Engineers Review) [*United States*]

Mer — Mercer Law Review

Mer — Merian

MER — Middle East Record

MER — Midwest English Review

Merc — London Mercury

Merc — Mercury [*Hobart*]

Mercer Dent Soc Newsl — Mercer Dental Society. Newsletter

Mercer Law — Mercer Law Review

Mercer Law Rev — Mercer Law Review

Mercer L Rev — Mercer Law Review

Mercersb — Mercersburg Review

Merc France — Mercure de France

Merch — Merchandising

Merchand Vision — Merchandising Vision

Merch W — Merchandising Week [*Later, Merchandising*]

Mercian Geol — Mercian Geologist

Merck Agr Memo — Merck Agricultural Memo

Merck Sharp Dohme Semin Rep — Merck, Sharp, and Dohme. Seminar Report

Merc LR — Mercer Law Review

Merc (Newspr) (Tas) — Mercury Reports (Newspaper) (Tasmania)

Merc S Arch — Mercury Series. Archaeological Survey of Canada. Papers

Merc S Ethn — Mercury Series. Ethnology Division. Papers

Mercure — Mercure de France

Mercy Med — Mercy Medicine

MERDD — Monthly Energy Review

Merentutkimuslaitoksen Julk — Merentutkimuslaitoksen Julkaisu

Meres Autom — Meres es Automatika

Meres es Autom — Meres es Automatika

Meresuegyi Koezl — Meresuegyi Koezlemenyek

MERF — Melanges. Ecole Roumaine en France

Merg and Acq — Mergers and Acquisitions

Mergers — Mergers and Acquisitions

Mergers & Acquis — Mergers and Acquisitions

Mergers Acquis — Mergers and Acquisitions
Merino Breed J — Merino Breeders' Journal
MERIP — MERIP [*Middle East Research and Information Project*] Reports
MERJD — Moessbauer Effect Reference and Data Journal
Merkbl Angew Parasitenkd Schaedlingsbekaempf — Merkblaetter ueber Angewandte Parasitenkunde und Schaedlingsbekaempfung
Merkblatt Imker Verb Kleingaertner Siedler Kleintierz — Merkblatt. Imker des Verbandes der Kleingaertner, Siedler, und Kleintierzuechter
Merkbl Biol Bundesanst Land Forstwirtsch — Merkblatt. Biologische Bundesanstalt fuer Land und Forstwirtschaft
Merkbl Biol Bundesanst Land Forstwirtsch (Braunschweig) — Merkblatt. Biologische Bundesanstalt fuer Land und Forstwirtschaft (Braunschweig)
Merkbl Deutsch Landwirtsch Ges — Merkblatt. Deutsche Landwirtschafts-Gesellschaft
Merkbl Ver Zellst Chem — Merkblatt. Verein der Zellstoff- und Papier-Chemiker und -Ingenieure
Mernoekgeol Sz — Mernoekgeologiai Szemle
Mer O-Mer — Mer-Outre-Mer
Merova Tech — Merova Technika
MerP — Mercurio Peruano
Merrill ML — Merrill Lynch Market Letter
Merrill-Palmer Q — Merrill-Palmer Quarterly
Merril-Pal — Merrill-Palmer Quarterly
MERSDW — Marine Environmental Research
Mersey Quart — Mersey Quarterly
MERTB — Mental Retardation
Mer (Tokyo) Bull Soc Fr Jpn Oceanogr — Mer (Tokyo). Bulletin de la Societe Franco-Japonaise d'Oceanographie
M Erz — Musikerziehung
MES — Medical Economics
MES — Middle Eastern Studies
MESA Mag Min Health Saf — MESA [*Mining Enforcement and Safety Administration*] Magazine of Mining Health and Safety [*United States*]
MESA NY Bight Atlas Monogr — MESA [*Marine Ecosystems Analysis*] New York. Bight Atlas Monograph
Mes Controle Ind — Mesures et Controle Industriel
Mes Cope St — Mesopotamia. Copenhagen Studies in Assyriology
MESEDT — Marine Ecology - Progress Series
Mesic Prehl Met Pozor — Mesicni Prehled Meteorologickych Pozorovani
Mesopot Agric — Mesopotamia Agriculture
Mesopotamia J Agric — Mesopotamia Journal of Agriculture
Mes Reg Aut — Mesures, Regulation, Automatisme
Mes Regul Autom — Mesures, Regulation, Automatisme
Mes Regul Automat — Mesures, Regulation, Automatisme
Mess — Messenger
Mess und Pruef — Messen und Pruefen
Mess Pruef — Messen und Pruefen
Mess Pruef Autom — Messen und Pruefen/Automatik
Mess Pruef Ver Autom — Messen und Pruefen Vereinigt mit Automatik
Mess-Steuern-Regeln — Messen-Steuern-Regeln
Mess Steuern Regeln mit Automatisierungsprax — Messen, Steuern, Regeln mit Automatisierungspraxis
Mes-Steuern-Regeln — Messen-Steuern-Regeln
MESTARABH — Miscelanea de Estudios Arabes y Hebraicos [*Granada*]
Mestn Promysl Chud Prom — Mestnaja Promyslennost' i Chudozestvennye Promysly
ME St Water Storage Comm An Rp — Maine State Water Storage Commission. Annual Report
Met — Metall
Met — Metals Abstracts
Met — Metroeconomica
MET — Monthly Energy Review
Met A — Meteorologiske Annaler
Metaalinst TNO Circ — Metaalinstituut TNO [*Nederlands Centrale Organisatie voor Toegepast-Natuurwetenschappelijk Onderzoek*]. Circulaire
Metaalinst TNO Publ — Metaalinstituut TNO [*Nederlands Centrale Organisatie voor Toegepast-Natuurwetenschappelijk Onderzoek*]. Publikatie
Metaal Tech — Metaal en Techniek
MetAb — Metals Abstracts
METAB — Metalurgija [*Sisak, Yugoslavia*]
Metab Bone Dis Relat Res — Metabolic Bone Disease and Related Research
Metab Clin Exp — Metabolism - Clinical and Experimental
Metab Dis — Metabolism and Disease [*Japan*]
Met ABM — Metalurgia. ABM [*Associacao Brasileira de Metais*]
Metabolism — Metabolism - Clinical and Experimental
Metab Ophthalmol — Metabolic Ophthalmology
Metab Pediatr Ophthalmol — Metabolic and Pediatric Ophthalmology
Met Abstr — Metallurgical Abstracts
META J — Manitoba Elementary Teachers' Association. Journal
Metal ABM — Metalurgia. ABM [*Associacao Brasileira de Metais*]
Metal Bul — Metal Bulletin
Metal Bull Mon — Metal Bulletin Monthly

Metal Cons — Metal Construction
Metal Constr Br Weld J — Metal Construction and British Welding Journal [*Later, Metal Construction*]
Metal & Electr — Metalurgia y Electricidad
Metal Electr — Metalurgia y Electricidad
Metal Eng Q — Metals Engineering Quarterly
Metal Fin — Metal Finishing
Metal Finish — Metal Finishing
Metal Form — Metal Forming
Metal Ind — Metal Industry
Metall — Metallurgist
Metall Abstr — Metallurgical Abstracts
Metall Constr Mec — Metallurgie et la Construction Mecanique
Metall Eng IIT (Bombay) — Metallurgical Engineer. Indian Institute of Technology (Bombay)
Metallges Mitt Arbeitsbereich — Metallgesellschaft. Mitteilungen aus dem Arbeitsbereich
Metallges Period Rev — Metallgesellschaft. Periodic Review
Metallges Rev Act — Metallgesellschaft. Review of the Activities
Metallges Rev Activ — Metallgesellschaft AG [*Frankfurt/Main*]. Review of the Activities
Metall Gornorudn Promst — Metallurgicheskaya i Gornorudnaya Promyshlennost
Metall Ital — Metallurgia Italiana
Metall J — Metallurgical Journal
Metall Khim Prom Kaz — Metallurgicheskaya i Khimicheskaya Promyshlennost Kazakhstana
Metall Koksokhim — Metallurgiya i Koksokhimiya
Metall Mater Technol — Metallurgist and Materials Technologist
Metall Met — Metallurgia and Metal Forming
Metall & Metal Form — Metallurgia and Metal Forming
Metall Metalloved Chist Met — Metallurgiya i Metallovedenie Chistykh Metallov
Metall Metalloved Chist Met Sb Nauchn Rab — Metallurgiya i Metallovedenie Chistykh Metallov Moskovskij Inzhenerno-Fizicheskij Institut Sbornik Nauchnykh Rabot
Metall Met Form — Metallurgia and Metal Forming
Metalloberfl — Metalloberflaeche-Angewandte Elektrochemie
Metalloberflaeche-Angew Elektrochem — Metalloberflaeche-Angewandte Elektrochemie
Metallofiz — Metallofizika
Metallog Geol Issled — Metallogenicheskie i Geologicheskie Issledovaniya
Metallogr Rev — Metallographic Review
Metalloved Sb Statei — Metallovedenie. Sbornik Statei
Metalloved Term Obrab — Metallovedenie i Termicheskaya Obrabotka
Metalloved Term Obrab Met — Metallovedenie i Termicheskaya Obrabotka Metallov
Metalloved i Term Obrab Met — Metallovedenie i Termicheskaya Obrabotka Metallov
Metallov i Term Obrab Metal — Metallovedenie i Termicheskaya Obrabotka Metallov
Metall Plant Technol — Metallurgical Plant and Technology [*West Germany*]
Metall-Reinig Vorbehandl — Metall-Reinigung und Vorbehandlung [*West Germany*]
Metall Rep Aeronaut Res Lab Aust — Australia. Aeronautical Research Laboratories. Metallurgy Report
Metall Rep CRM — Metallurgical Reports. CRM [*Centre de Recherches Metallurgiques*]
Metall Rev — Metallurgical Reviews (Supplement to Metals and Materials)
Metall Rev MMIJ — Metallurgical Review. MMIJ [*Mining and Metallurgical Institute of Japan*]
Metall Soc Conf — Metallurgical Society. Conferences
Metall Soc Conf Proc — Metallurgical Society. Conferences. Proceedings
Metall Spec (Paris) — Metallurgie Speciale (Paris)
Metall T-A — Metallurgical Transactions. A. Physical Metallurgy and Materials Science
Metall T-B — Metallurgical Transactions. B. Process Metallurgy
Metall Tech Memo Aust Aeronaut Res Lab — Australia. Aeronautical Research Laboratories. Metallurgy Technical Memorandum
Metall Topl — Mettallurgija i Toplivo
Metall Trans — Metallurgical Transactions
Metall Trans A — Metallurgical Transactions. A
Metall Trans B — Metallurgical Transactions. B
Metallwaren Ind Galvanotech — Metallwaren-Industrie und Galvanotechnik
Metallwirtsch — Metallwirtschaft, Metallwissenschaft, Metalltechnik
Metallwirtsch Metallwiss Metalltech — Metallwirtschaft, Metallwissenschaft, Metalltechnik
Metallwirtsch Wiss Tech — Metallwirtschaft, Metallwissenschaft, Metalltechnik [*East Germany*]
Metal Mod — Metalurgia Moderna
Metal Odlew — Metalurgia i Odlewnictwo
Metal Powder Ind Fed Stand — Metal Powder Industries Federation. MPIF Standard
33 Metal Prod — 33 Metal Producing
Metal Prog — Metal Progress
Metal Proszkow — Metalurgia Proszkow

Metals Abstr Index — Metals Abstracts Index
Metals Aust — Metals Australia [*Later, Metals Australasia*]
Metal Sci H — Metal Science and Heat Treatment
Metal Sci J — Metal Science Journal [*Later, Metal Science*]
Metals Eng Quart — Metals Engineering Quarterly
Metals Mater — Metals and Materials
Metals Mats — Metals and Materials
Metal Stamp — Metal Stamping
Metals Tech — Metals Technology
Metal Trades J — Metal Trades Journal
Metal Treat — Metal Treating
Metalwork Econ — Metalworking Economics
Metalwork Interfaces — Metalworking Interfaces
Metalwork Manag — Metalworking Management
Metalwork Prod — Metalworking Production
Metalwrkg Prod — Metalworking Production
Met Anal Outlook — Metals Analysis and Outlook
Met Ann — Meteorologiske Annaler
Met Annu Conf Australas Inst Met — Metals. Annual Conference. Australasian Institute of Metals
Metano Pet Nuove Energ — Metano, Petrolio, e Nuove Energie
Metaphilos — Metaphilosophy
Met Aust — Metals Australasia
Met Aust — Metals Australia [*Later, Metals Australasia*]
Met Australas — Metals Australasia
Metaux (Corros-Ind) — Metaux (Corrosion-Industries)
Metaux Deform — Metaux Deformation
Met Bull — Metal Bulletin
Met Bull (Loosdrecht Netherlands) — Metallic Bulletin (Loosdrecht, Netherlands)
Met Bull Mon — Metal Bulletin Monthly
Met Bur Bull — Bureau of Meteorology. Bulletin [*Australia*]
Met Bur Met Study — Bureau of Meteorology. Meteorological Study [*Australia*]
Met Bur Met Summ — Bureau of Meteorology. Meteorological Summary [*Australia*]
Met Bur Proj Rep — Bureau of Meteorology. Project Report [*Australia*]
Met Bur Working Paper — Bureau of Meteorology. Working Paper [*Australia*]
Met Constr — Metal Construction
Met Constr Br Weld J — Metal Construction and British Welding Journal [*Later, Metal Construction*]
Met Constr Mec — Metallurgie et la Construction Mecanique
Met (Corros-Ind) — Metaux (Corrosion-Industries)
Met Deform — Metaux Deformation
Met Electr (Madrid) — Metalurgia y Electricidad (Madrid)
Met & Eng — Metal and Engineering
Met Eng — Metals in Engineering [*Japan*]
Met Eng Q — Metals Engineering Quarterly
Meteor Forschungsergeb Reihe C — Meteor Forschungsergebnisse. Reihe C. Geologie und Geophysik
Meteor Forschungsergeb Reihe D Biol — Meteor Forschungsergebnisse. Reihe D. Biologie
Meteor Forschungsergen Reihe B — Meteor Forschungsergebnisse. Reihe B. Meteorologie und Aeronomie
Meteor & Geoastrophys Abstr — Meteorological and Geoastrophysical Abstracts
Meteor Gidrol Inf Byull — Meteorologiya i Gidrologiya. Informatsionnyi Byulleten
Meteorit Soc Contr — Meteoritical Society. Contributions
Meteor Klimat Gidrol — Meteorologija, Klimatologija, i Gidrologija
Meteor Mag — Meteorological Magazine
Meteorol Abh Inst Meteorol Geophys Freie Univ (Berl) — Meteorologische Abhandlungen. Institut fuer Meteorologie und Geophysik. Freie Universitaet (Berlin)
Meteorol Abst and Biblio — Meteorological Abstracts and Bibliography
Meteorol Ann — Meteorologiske Annaler
Meteorol Dienst DDR Veroeff — Meteorologischer Dienst der Deutschen Demokratischen Republik. Veroeffentlichungen
Meteorol Geoastrophys Abstr — Meteorological and Geoastrophysical Abstracts
Meteorol i Gidrol — Meteorologiya i Gidrologiya
Meteorol Gidrol — Meteorologiya i Gidrologiya
Meteorol Gidrolog — Meteorologiya i Gidrologiya
Meteorol Hydrol — Meteorology and Hydrology [*United States*]
Meteorol Mag — Meteorological Magazine
Meteorol Monogr — Meteorological Monographs
Meteorol Rundsch — Meteorologische Rundschau
Meteorol Stud — Meteorological Study
Meteorol Stud Meteorol Bur — Bureau of Meteorology. Meteorological Study [*Australia*]
Meteorol Zpr — Meteorologicke Zpravy
Meteor Rund — Meteorologische Rundschau
Met Fabr News — Metal Fabricating News
Met Finish — Metal Finishing
Met Finish Abstr — Metal Finishing Abstracts

Met Finish J — Metal Finishing Journal
Met Form — Metal Forming [*England*]
Met Form Drop Forger — Metal Forming, Incorporating the Drop Forger
Met Forum — Metals Forum [*Australia*]
Met & GeoAb — Meteorological and Geoastrophysical Abstracts
Met Geoastrophys Abstr — Meteorological and Geoastrophysical Abstracts
MetH — Mediaevalia et Humanistica
Meth Cancer Res — Methods in Cancer Research
MethH — Methodist History
Meth Inf Med — Methods of Information in Medicine
Meth M — Methodist Magazine
Meth Membrane Biol — Methods in Membrane Biology
Meth Mol Biol — Methods in Molecular Biology
Method Appraisal Phys Sci — Method and Appraisal in the Physical Sciences
Methoden Verfahren Math Phys — Methoden und Verfahren der Mathematischen Physik
Methodes Math Inform — Methodes Mathematiques de l'Informatique [*Paris*]
Methodes Phys Anal — Methodes Physiques d'Analyse [*Revue de Groupement pour l'Avancement des Methodes Spectrographiques*]
Method Inf Med — Methodik der Information in der Medizin
Methodist Hosp Dallas Med Staff Bull — Methodist Hospital of Dallas. Medical Staff. Bulletin
Methodol Dev Biochem — Methodological Developments in Biochemistry
Method Phys Anal — Methodes Physiques d'Analyse [*Revue de Groupement pour l'Avancement des Methodes Spectrographiques*]
Methods Achiev Exp Pathol — Methods and Achievements in Experimental Pathology
Methods Anim Exp — Methods of Animal Experimentation
Methods Biochem Anal — Methods of Biochemical Analysis
Methods Cancer Res — Methods in Cancer Research
Methods Carbohydr Chem — Methods in Carbohydrate Chemistry
Methods Cell Biol — Methods in Cell Biology
Method Sci — Methodology and Science
Methods Clin Pharmacol — Methods in Clinical Pharmacology
Methods Comput Phys — Methods in Computational Physics. Advances in Research and Applications
Methods Enzymol — Methods in Enzymology
Methods Exp Phys — Methods of Experimental Physics
Methods Find Exp Clin Pharmacol — Methods and Findings in Experimental and Clinical Pharmacology
Methods Free Radical Chem — Methods in Free Radical Chemistry
Methods Immunol Immunochem — Methods in Immunology and Immunochemistry
Methods Inf Med — Methods of Information in Medicine
Methods Inf Med (Suppl) — Methods of Information in Medicine (Supplement)
Methods Invest Diagn Endocrinol — Methods in Investigative and Diagnostic Endocrinology
Methods Med Res — Methods in Medical Research
Methods Mod Math Phys — Methods of Modern Mathematical Physics
Methods Oper Res — Methods of Operations Research
Methods Pharmacol — Methods in Pharmacology
Methods Stereochem Anal — Methods in Stereochemical Analysis
Methods Subnucl Phys — Methods in Subnuclear Physics
Methods Virol — Methods in Virology
Meth Per Ind — Methodist Periodical Index
Meth Q — Methodist Quarterly
Meth Q R — Methodist Quarterly Review
Meth R — Methodist Review
METI — Metis
METIA — Medical Times
Met Ind (Johannesburg) — Metal Industries (Johannesburg)
Met Ind (London) — Metal Industry (London)
Met Inf Med — Methods of Information in Medicine
Met Ital — Metallurgia Italiana
Met Izv Akad Nauk SSSR — Metally Izvestiya Akademi Nauk SSSR
Met J Univ Strathclyde Glasgow — Metallurgical Journal. University of Strathclyde, Glasgow
Metl Bul M — Metal Bulletin Monthly
MET M — Metropolitan Magazine [*New York*]
Met Mag (Lond) — Meteorological Magazine (London)
Met Mark Place Met Congr — Metals in the Market Place. Metals Congress
Met Mark Rev — Metal Market Review
Met Mater — Metals and Materials
Met/Mater Today — Metals/Materials Today
METMD — Metamedicine
Met Miner Process — Metals and Minerals Processing [*South Africa*]
Met Miner Rev — Metals and Minerals Review [*India*]
Met Mus Bul — Metropolitan Museum of Art. Bulletin
Met Mus J — Metropolitan Museum. Journal
Met News (India) — Metal News (India)
Met Note Aust Aeronaut Res Lab — Australia. Aeronautical Research Laboratories. Metallurgy Note
Metod Mater Nauchn Soobshch — Metodicheskie Materialy i Nauchnye Soobshcheniya
Metodol Probl Nauki — Metodologiceskie Problemy Nauki

Metod Prepod Inostr Yazykov Vuze — Metodika Prepodavaniya Inostrannykh Yazykov v Vuze
Metod Prepod Khim — Metodika Prepodavaniya Khimii
Metod Prirucky Exp Bot — Metodicke Prirucky Experimentalni Botaniky
Metod Tekh Razved — Metodika i Tekhnika Razvedki
Metod Ukazaniya Geol S'emke Masshtaba 1:50000 — Metodicheskie Ukazaniya po Geologicheskoi S'emke Masshtaba 1:50,000
Metod Vopr Nauki — Metodologiceskie Voprosy Nauki
Metody Anal Khim Reakt Prep — Metody Analiza Khimicheskikh Reaktivov i Preparatov
Metody Anal Org Soedin Nefti Ikh Smesei Proizvodnykh — Metody Analiza Organicheskikh Soedinenii Nefti Ikh Smesei i Proizvodnykh
Metody Anal Org Soedin Neft Ikh Smesei Proizvodnykh — Metody Analiza Organicheskikh Soedinenii Nefti Ikh Smesei i Proizvodnykh [*USSR*]
Metody Anal Redkomet Miner Rud Gorn Porod — Metody Analiza Redkometal'nykh Mineralov Rud i Gornykh Porod
Metody Issled Katal Katal Reakts — Metody Issledovaniya Katalizatorov i Kataliticheskikh Reaktsii [*USSR*]
Metody Izuch Veshchestv Sostava i Ikh Primen — Metody Izucheniya Veshchestvennogo Sostava i Ikh Primenenie
Metody Khim Anal Miner Syr'ya — Metody Khimicheskogo Analiza Mineral'nogo Syr'ya
Metody Opred Pestits Vode — Metody Opredeleniya Pestitsidov v Vode
Metody Paleogeogr Issled — Metody Paleogeograficheskikh Issledovanii
Metody Pochody Chem Technol — Metody a Pochody Chemicke Technologie
Metody Razved Geofiz — Metody Razvedochnoi Geofiziki
Metody Rudn Geofiz — Metody Rudnoi Geofiziki
Metody Vychisl — Leningradskii Ordena Lenina Gosudarstvennyi Imeni A. A. Zhdanova Metody Vychislenii
Metody Vycisl — Metody Vycislenii
Metod Zavadeni Vysledku Vyzk Praxe — Metodiky pro Zavadeni Vysledku Vyzkumu do Praxe
Metod Zavad Vysled Vyzk Praxe — Metodiky pro Zavadeni Vysledku Vyzkumu do Praxe
Met Phys — Metal Physics
Met Phys Semin — Metal Physics Seminar
Met Powder Rep — Metal Powder Report
33 Met Prod — 33 Metal Producing
Met Prog — Metal Progress
Met Prog Datab — Metal Progress Databook
Met Prop Counc Publ — Metal Properties Council. Publication
Metr — Metropolis
Met Rdsch — Meteorologische Rundschau
Met Rec Electroplat — Metal Records and Electroplater
Met Reinig Vorbehandl Oberflaechentech Form — Metall-Reinigung, Vorbehandlung, Oberflaechentechnik, Formung
Met Rev (Suppl Metals Mater) — Metallurgical Reviews (Supplement to Metals and Materials)
Metr Mus J — Metropolitan Museum. Journal
Metro — Metronome
Metroecon — Metroeconomica
Metrol — Metrologia
Metrol Apl — Metrologia Aplicata
Metrol Insp — Metrology and Inspection
Metrop — Metropolitan
Metrop Detroit Sci Rev — Metropolitan Detroit Science Review
Metrop Mus — Metropolitan Museum of Art. Bulletin
Metropolitan Life Stat Bul — Metropolitan Life Insurance Company. Statistical Bulletin
Metropolitan Life Statis Bul — Metropolitan Life Insurance Company. Statistical Bulletin
Metropolitan Toronto Bd Trade J — Metropolitan Toronto Board of Trade. Journal
Metropolitan Toronto Bus J — Metropolitan Toronto Business Journal
Metsanduse Tead Uurim Lab Metsandusl Uurim — Metsanduse Teadusliku Uurimise Laboratoorium. Metsanduslikud Uurimused
Metsatal Aikakausl — Metsataloudellinen Aikakauslehti
METSC — Metal Science
Met Sci — Metal Science
Met Sci Heat Treat — Metal Science and Heat Treatment
Met Sci and Heat Treat — Metal Science and Heat Treatment
Met Sci Heat Treat Met — Metal Science and Heat Treatment of Metals [*United States*]
Met Sci Heat Treat Met (Engl Transl) — Metal Science and Heat Treatment of Metals (English Translation) [*United States*]
Met Sci Heat Treat Met (USSR) — Metal Science and Heat Treatment of Metals (USSR)
Met Sci Heat Treat (USSR) — Metal Science and Heat Treatment (USSR)
Met Sci J — Metal Science Journal [*Later, Metal Science*]
Met Soc AIME Conf — Metallurgical Society. American Institute of Mining, Metallurgical, and Petroleum Engineers. Conferences
Met Soc AIME Inst Metals Div Spec Rep — Metallurgical Society. American Institute of Mining, Metallurgical, and Petroleum Engineers. Institute of Metals Division. Special Report
Met Soc AIME TMS Pap — Metallurgical Society. American Institute of Mining, Metallurgical, and Petroleum Engineers. TMS Papers

Met Soc World — Metals Society World
Met Stamp — Metal Stamping
Met Study Bur Met — Bureau of Meteorology. Meteorological Study [*Australia*]
Met Study Met Bur — Bureau of Meteorology. Meteorological Study [*Australia*]
Met Summary Met Bur — Bureau of Meteorology. Meteorological Summary [*Australia*]
Met Tech Inf — Metokika a Technika Informaci
Met Technol — Metals Technology
Met Technol (London) — Metals Technology. Institute of Metals (London)
Met Trans — Metallurgical Transactions
Met Treat — Metal Treating
Met Treat Drop Forg — Metal Treatment and Drop Forging [*England*]
METU Faculty of Archre Occasional Paper Series — METU [*Middle East Technical University*] Faculty of Architecture. Occasional Paper Series
METU J Pure Appl Sci — Middle East Technical University. Journal of Pure and Applied Sciences
METU Studies Develop — Middle East Technical University. Studies in Development
Metwork Prod — Metalworking Production
Meunerie Franc — La Meunerie Francaise
M & Eval Guid — Measurement and Evaluation in Guidance
MEWEA — Medizinische Welt
MEWOA — Medical World
MEX — Marketing in Europe
Mex Agr — Mexico Agricola
Mex Am R — Mexican-American Review [*Later, Mex Am Review*]
Mex Bosques — Mexico y Sus Bosques
Mex Com Dir Invest Recur Miner Bol — Mexico. Comite Directivo para la Investigacion de los Recursos Minerales. Boletin
Mex Cons Rec Nat No Ren Sem Int Anu Expl Geol Min Mem — Mexico. Consejo de Recursos Naturales No Renovables. Seminario Interno Anual sobre Exploracion Geologico-Minera. Memoria
Mex Cons Recur Nat No Renov Bol — Mexico. Consejo de Recursos Naturales No Renovables. Boletin
Mex Cons Recur Nat No Renov Publ — Mexico. Consejo de Recursos Naturales No Renovables. Publicacion
Mex Folkways — Mexican Folkways
Mex For — Mexico Forestal
Mexicn Rev — Mexican-American Review [*Later, Mex Am Review*]
Mexico Anales Inst Biologia — Mexico. Anales del Instituto de Biologia
Mexico Com Fomento Min Bol — Mexico. Comision de Fomento Minero. Boletin
Mexico Consejo Rec Naturales No Renovables Bol Pub — Mexico. Consejo de Recursos Naturales No Renovables. Boletin. Publicaciones
Mexico Escuela Nac Cienc Biol Anales — Mexico. Escuela Nacional de Ciencias Biologicas. Anales
Mexico Inst Nac Inv Rec Minerales Bol — Mexico. Instituto Nacional para la Investigacion de Recursos Minerales. Boletin
Mexico Univ Nac Autonoma Inst Geografia Bol — Mexico. Universidad Nacional Autonoma. Instituto de Geografia. Boletin
Mexico Univ Nac Autonoma Inst Geologia Bol — Mexico. Universidad Nacional Autonoma. Instituto de Geologia. Boletin
Mex I G — Mexico. Instituto Geologico
Mex Inst Nac Invest Recur Miner Bol — Mexico. Instituto Nacional para la Investigacion de Recursos Minerales. Boletin
Mex Min Fomento An — Mexico. Ministerio de Fomento. Anales
Mex M J — Mexican Mining Journal
Mex Sec Fomento Bol — Mexico. Secretaria de Fomento. Boletin
Mex Secr Agric Ganad Of Estud Espec Foll Divul — Mexico. Secretaria de Agricultura y Ganaderia. Oficina de Estudios Especiales. Folleto de Divulgacion
Mex Secr Agric Ganad Of Estud Espec Foll Misc — Mexico. Secretaria de Agricultura y Ganaderia. Oficina de Estudios Especiales. Folleto Miscelaneo
Mex Secr Agric Ganad Of Estud Espec Foll Tec — Mexico. Secretaria de Agricultura y Ganaderia. Oficina de Estudios Especiales. Folleto Tecnico
Mex Univ Nac Auton Inst Geol Paleontol Mex — Mexico. Universidad Nacional Autonoma. Instituto de Geologia Paleontologia Mexicana
Mex Univ Nac Auton Inst Geol Rev — Mexico. Universidad Nacional Autonoma. Instituto de Geologia. Revista
Mex Univ Nac Auton Inst Geol Ser Divulg — Mexico. Universidad Nacional Autonoma. Instituto de Geologia. Serie Divulgacion
MEYNA — Meyniana
Mezdun Ezeg Polit Ekon — Mezdunarodnyj Ezegodnik. Politika i Ekonomika
Mezdun Zizn — Mezdunarodnaja Zizn
Mezhdunar Konf Fiz Vys Energ — Mezhdunarodnaya Konferentsiya po Fizike Vysokikh Energii
Mezhdunar Kongr Astronavt Dokl — Mezhdunarodnaya Kongress po Astronavtike Doklady
Mezhdunar Nauch Suvesh Kheterozisa — Mezhdunarodno Nauchno Suveshtanie po Kheterozisa
Mezhdunar Sel-Khoz Zh — Mezhdunarodnyi Sel'skokhozyaistvennyi Zhurnal

Mezhdunar Sel'skokhoz Zh — Mezhdunarodnyi Sel'skokhozyaistvennyi Zhurnal
Mezhdunar Selskostop Spis — Mezhdunarodno Selskostopansko Spisanie
Mezhdunar Simp Geterog Katal Tr — Mezhdunarodnyi Simpozium po Geterogennomu Katalizu Trudy
Mezhdunar S-kh Zh — Mezhdunarodnyi Sel'skokhozyaistvennyi Zhurnal
Mezhduved Geofiz Kom — Mezhduvedomstvennyi Geofizicheskikh Komitet [USSR]
Mezhved Geofiz Kom Prezidiume Akad Nauk Ukr SSR Inf Byull — Mezhvedomstvennyi Geofizicheskii Komitet pri Prezidiume Akademii Nauk Ukrainskoi SSR Informatsionnyi Byulleten
Mezhvuzovskii Tematicheskii Sb-Yaroslavskii Gos Univ — Mezhvuzovskii Tematicheskii Sbornik-Yaroslavskii Gosudarstvennyi Universitet
Mezhvuz Sb Nauchn Tr Erevan Politekh Inst Ser 19 — Mezhvuzovskii Sbornik Nauchnykh Trudov Erevanskii Politekhnicheskii Institut Seriya 19 Khimicheskaya Tekhnologiya
Mezhvuz Sb Tr Biol Kafedry Kirg Univ Ser Bot — Mezhvuzovskii Sbornik Trudov Biologicheskoi Kafedry Kirgizskogo Universiteta Seriya Botanicheskaya
Mezhvuz Temat Sb Leningr Inzh Stroit Inst — Mezhvuzovskii Tematicheskii Sbornik Leningradskii Inzhenerno Stroitel'nyi Institut
Mezhvuz Temat Sb Nauchn Tr Leningr Inzh Stroit Inst — Mezhvuzovskii Tematicheskii Sbornik Nauchnykh Trudov Leningradskii Inzhenerno Stroitel'nyi Institut
Mezhvuz Temat Sb Tr Leningr Inzh Stroit Inst — Mezhvuzovskii Tematicheskii Sbornik Trudov Leningradskii Inzhenerno Stroitel'nyi Institut
Mezhvuz Temat Sb Yarosl Gos Univ — Mezhvuzovskii Tematicheskii Sbornik Yaroslavskii Gosudarstvennyi Universitet
Mezin Vztahy — Mezinaradni Vztahy
Mezoegazd Kutat — Mezoegazdasagi Kutatasok
Mezogazd Gepesitesi Tanulmanyok Mezogazd Gepkiserl Intez — Mezogazdasagi Gepesitesi Tanulmanyok A. Mezogazdasag Gepkiserleti Intezet
Mezogazd Tech — Mezogazdasagi Technika
Mezogazd Tud Kozl — Mezogazdasagi Tudomanyos Koezlemenyek
Mezogazd Vilagirod — Mezogazdasagi Vilagirodalom
Mezogazd Vilagirodalom — Mezogazdasagi Vilagirodalom
Mezzogiorno d'Europa Q R — Mezzogiorno d'Europa. Quarterly Review
MF — Makedonski Folklor
MF — Mercure de France
MF — Midwest Folklore
MF — Miscellanea Francescana
MF — Misiones Franciscanos
MF — Musikforschung
MfAb — Microfilm Abstracts
MFA Bull — MFA Bulletin. Museum of Fine Arts [Boston]
MFB — Europese Investeringsbank. Mededelingen
M F B — Monthly Film Bulletin
MFBMA — Mitteilungen. Forstliche Bundes-Versuchsanstalt (Mariabrunn)
MFC — Manufacturing Chemist, Incorporating Chemical Age
MFCBAC — Montana. Forest and Conservation Experiment Station. Bulletin
MFCG — Mitteilungen und Forschungsbeitraege. Cusanus-Gesellschaft
MFCL — Memoire et Travaux Publies par les Facultes Catholiques de Lille
MFCNAE — Montana. Forest and Conservation Experiment Station. Note
MFCSAT — Montana. Forest and Conservation Experiment Station. Special Publication
MFCusanusG — Mitteilungen und Forschungsbeitraege. Cusanus-Gesellschaft
MFDGAW — Communications. Faculte de Medecine Veterinaire. Universite de l'Etat Gand
MFDGAW — Communications. Faculty of Veterinary Medicine. State University [Ghent]
MFDU — Monatshefte fuer Deutschen Unterricht
MFE — Mazingira. The World Forum for Environment and Development
MFEHA — Memoirs. Faculty of Engineering. Hiroshima University
MFEKA — Memoirs. Faculty of Engineering. Kobe University
MFEMA — Manufacturing Engineering and Management [Later, Manufacturing Engineering]
MFENAO — Montana. Forest and Conservation Experiment Station. Research Note
MFG — Middle East Observer
Mfg Chem — Manufacturing Chemist
Mfg Chem Aerosol News — Manufacturing Chemist and Aerosol News
MFGEB — Manufacturing Engineering
Mfg Eng — Manufacturing Engineering
Mfg Eng Manage — Manufacturing Engineering and Management [Later, Manufacturing Engineering]
MFH — Mitteilungen. Institut fuer Handelsforschung. Universitaet zu Koeln
MFI — Managerial Finance
MFI — Midwest Folklore (Indiana University)
MFITD — Fukui Kogyo Daigaku Kenkyu Kiyo
MFIZA — Metallofizika
MFJ — Municipal Finance Journal
MFKCA — Memoirs. Faculty of Science. Kyushu University. Series C [Japan]
MFKDA — Memoirs. Faculty of Science. Kyushu University. Series D. Geology

MFKPA — Memoirs. Faculty of Science. Kyoto University. Series of Physics, Astrophysics, Geophysics, and Chemistry
MFLB — Massachusetts Foreign Language Bulletin
MFLRA — Mededelingen. Faculteit Landbouwwetenschappen. Rijksuniversiteit (Gent)
MFM Mod Fototech — MFM. Moderne Fototechnik
MFN — Mitteilungen fuer Namenskunde [Aachen]
MFNV — Meddelelser fra Norsk Viltforskning
M Forskning — Musik und Forskning
M Forum — Music Forum
MFP — Monographs in Fetal Physiology [Elsevier Book Series]
MFP Prepnt — Mineral Facts and Problems. Preprints
MFPSA — Monographies Francaises de Psychologie
MFR — Maltese Folklore Review [Balzan]
MFr — Mercure de France
MFr — Miscellanea Francescana
M Fra — Moyen Francais
MfrChemAer — Manufacturing Chemist and Aerosol News
MFRVA — Microform Review
MFS — Meddelanden fran Strindbergssaellskapet
MFS — Modern Fiction Studies
MFSF — Magazine of Fantasy and Science Fiction
MFSV — Meddelelser fra Statens Viltundersokelser [Papers. Norwegian State Game Research Institute]
MFVFF — Meddelelser fra Vestlandets Forstlige Forsoeksstasjon
MG — Manchester Guardian
MG — Mandaeische Grammatik
MG — Massorah Magna
MG — Methods in Geomathematics [Elsevier Book Series]
MG — Migne Series. Graeca
MG — Molodaya Gvardiya [Moscow]
M & GA — Meteorological and Geoastrophysical Abstracts [American Meteorological Society] [Bibliographic database]
MGA — Meteorological and Geoastrophysical Abstracts [American Meteorological Society] [Boston, MA] [Bibliographic database]
MGA — Mitteilungen. Gesamtarchiv der Deutschen Juden
MGADJ — Mitteilungen. Gesamtarchiv der Deutschen Juden
MGAGB — Montana Geological Society. Annual Field Conference. Guidebook
MGAJA — Magyar Allami Foldtani Intezet. Evi Jelentese
MGATC — Modern German Authors. Texts and Contexts
MGB — Muenchener Germanistische Beitraege
MGbl — Muehlhauser Geschichtsblaetter
Mg C Pop Cr — Monographs. Carolina Population Center
MGD — Guardian
MGEK — Mitteilungen. Gesellschaft zur Erforschung Judischer Kunstdenkmaeler
MGESA — Mededelingen. Geologische Stichting. Nieuwe Serie
MGF — Men's Guide to Fashion
MGFIB — Morskie Gidrofizicheskie Issledovaniya
MGG — Methods in Geochemistry and Geophysics [Elsevier Book Series]
MGG — MGG. Molecular and General Genetics
MGGH — Mitteilungen. Geographische Gesellschaft in Hamburg
MGG Mol Gen Genet — MGG. Molecular and General Genetics
MGGW — Mitteilungen. Geographische Gesellschaft in Wien
MGH — International Management
MGH — Monumenta Germaniae Historica
MGH News — Montreal General Hospital. News
MGJ — Monatsschrift fuer die Geschichte und Wissenschaft des Judentums
MGJF — Mitteilungen. Gesellschaft fuer Juedische Familienforschung [Berlin]
MGJFF — Mitteilungen. Gesellschaft fuer Juedische Familienforschung [Berlin]
MGJOAP — Market Grower's Journal
MGJV — Mitteilungen. Gesellschaft fuer Juedische Volkskunde
MGkK — Monatsschrift fuer Gottesdienst und Kirchliche Kunst [Goettingen]
MGM — Miscellanea Giovanni Mercati [Vatican City]
MGMPA — Memorie. Istituti di Geologia e Mineralogia. Universita di Padova
Mgmt Acct — Management Accounting
Mgmt Focus — Management Focus
Mgmt in Govt — Management in Government
Mgmt Printing — Management in Printing
Mgmt Res News — Management Research News
Mgmt Rev — Management Review
Mgmt Rev Dig — Management Review and Digest
Mgmt Sci — Management Science
Mgmt Serv Govt — Management Services in Government
Mgmt Today — Management Today
MGN — Finish [Amsterdam]
MGNM — Mitteilungen. Germanisches Nationalmuseum
MGNVO — Mitteilungen. Gesellschaft fuer Natur- und Voelkerkunde Ostasiens
MGOKL — Mededeelingen. Geschied- en Oudheidkundige Kring voor Leuven en Omgeving
MGOKLeuven — Mededeelingen. Geschied- en Oudheidkundige Kring voor Leuven en Omgeving
MGottesdienst — Musik und Gottesdienst

MGPGA — Monatsblaetter. Gesellschaft fuer Pommersche Geschichte und Altertumskunde
MGPNA — Metallurgicheskaya i Gornorudnaya Promyshlennost
MGQ — Management Science
MGR — Miscellanea Greca e Romana
Mgrl Plan — Managerial Planning
MGS — Michigan Germanic Studies
MGSACU — Geological Survey of Malaysia. Annual Report
MGSDA — Annual Statistical Summary. Michigan Geological Survey Division
MGSL — Minas Gerais. Suplemento Literario
MGSLK — Mitteilungen. Gesellschaft fuer Salzburger Landeskunde
MGSMC — Michigan. Geological Survey Division. Miscellany
Mg Soc Anth — Monographs on Social Anthropology
MGSVAN — Geological Survey of Victoria. Memoir
Mg S Wld — Monograph Series in World Affairs. University of Denver
Mgt Accounting — Management Accounting
Mgt Acct — Management Accounting
Mgt Adviser — Management Adviser
Mgt Controls — Management Controls
Mgt Educ & Dev — Management, Education, and Development
Mgt Focus — Management Focus
Mgt in Govt — Management in Government
Mgt Info Service Rept — Management Information Service Report
Mgt Int R — Management International Review
Mgt Methods — Management Methods
MGTOA — Magyar Tudomanyos Akademia. Kemiai Tudomanyok Osztalyanak Koezlemenyei
Mgt Q — Management Quarterly
Mgt R — Management Review
Mgt Rec — Management Record
Mgt Sci — Management Science
Mgt Ser — Management Services
Mgt Services — Management Services
Mgt Today — Management Today
Mgt World — Management World
MGv — Molodaia Gvardiia. Ezhemesiachnyi Literaturno-Khudozhestvennyi i Obshchestvenn-Politicheskii Zhurnal
MGW — Manchester Guardian Weekly
MGWJ — Monatsschrift fuer die Geschichte und Wissenschaft des Judentums
MGZ — Edelmetaal, Uurwerken, Edelstenen. Maandblad voor de Edelmetaalbranche, Uurwerkenbranche, Edelstenenbranche, en Diamantbranche
M & H — Mediaevalia et Humanistica
MH — Mediaevalia et Humanistica
MH — Mental Hygiene
MH — Methodist History
MH — Michigan History Magazine
MH — Minnesota History
MH — Missionalia Hispanica
MH — Monde Hebdomadaire
MH — Museum Helveticum
MH — Musichandel
MHAR — Memoires. Section Historique. Academie Roumaine
MHB — Mennonite Historical Bulletin
MHB — Museum Ha'aretz Bulletin [*Tel Aviv*]
MHBRI — Mental Health Book Review Index
MHC — Modern Healthcare
Mh Chem — Monatshefte fuer Chemie und Verwandte Teile Anderer Wissenschaften
MHD — Maandstatistiek van de Buitenlandse Handel per Land
MHE — Middle East Economic Survey
MHETA J — Manitoba Home Economics Teachers' Association. Journal
MHF — Materialy do Historii Filozofii Stredniowiecznej w Polsce
MHF — Monuments Historiques de la France
MHG — Mitteilungen. E. T. A. Hoffman-Gesellschaft
MHis — Mundo Hispanico
M of Hist — Magazine of History
MHJ — Malayan Historical Journal
MHJ — Medizin-Historisches Journal
MHJ — Melbourne Historical Journal
MHJ — Monumenta Hungariae Judaica
MHL — Mitteilungen. Bundesstelle fuer Aussenhandelsinformation
MHL — Mitteilungen aus der Historischen Literatur
MHL — Modern Hebrew Literature
MHM — Maryland Historical Magazine
MHM — Michigan History Magazine
MHOSA — Mental Hospitals
MHP — Bedrijfskunde Tijdschrift voor Management
MHP — Materials Handling and Packaging
MHR — Missouri Historical Review
MHRA Bull — Modern Humanities Research Association. Bulletin
MHRADS — Modern Humanities Research Association. Dissertation Series
MHRev — Malahat Review
MHRKg — Monatshefte fuer Rheinische Kirchengeschichte
MHS — Melanges d'Histoire Sociale
MHS — Moravian Historical Society. Transactions

MHSB — Missouri Historical Society. Bulletin
MHSch — Monatsschrift fuer Hoehere Schulen
MHSJ — Monumenta Historica Societatis Jesu
MHT — Metalworking Production
MHT Financ — Manufacturers' Hanover Trust Co. Financial Digest
MHTRA — Metal Science and Heat Treatment of Metals [*English Translation*]
MHU — Marketing in Hungary
MHum — Mediaevalia et Humanistica
Mh VetMed — Monatshefte fuer Veterinaermedizin
MHVP — Mitteilungen. Historischer Verein fuer die Pfalz
MI — Man in India
MI — Management Index
MI — Marketing Insights
Mi — Mind
Mi — Missiology
MI — Missouri School Music Magazine
MIA — Materialy i Issledovanija po Arkheologii SSSR
MIA — Media Information Australia
MIA — Middle East Economic Digest
MIA — Mitteilungen. Institut fuer Auslandsbeziehungen [*Stuttgart*]
MIAH — Hamburg. Institut fuer Asienkunde. Mitteilungen
MIAKB — Myakkangaku
Miami Geol Soc Annu Field Trip (Guideb) — Miami Geological Society. Annual Field Trip (Guidebook)
Miami Med — Miami Medicine
Miami Univ Sch Marine Atmos Sci Annu Rep — Miami University. School of Marine and Atmospheric Science. Annual Report
Miami Winter Symp — Miami Winter Symposium
MIASA — Mineralogical Magazine and Journal of the Mineralogical Society (1876-1968) [*England*]
Miasn Ind SSSR — Miasnaia Industriia SSSR
MIB Miner Ind Bull — MIB. Mineral Industries Bulletin [*United States*]
MIBNAU — Instituut voor Toegepast Biologisch Onderzoek in de Natuur. Mededeling
MIBUB — Mikrobiyoloji Bulteni
Mic — Michigan Music Educator
MIC — Modeling Identification and Control
MICCC — Monograph Series. International Council for Computer Communications [*Elsevier Book Series*]
MichA — Michigan Academician
Mich Acad — Michigan Academician
Mich Acad Sci Papers — Michigan Academy of Science, Arts, and Letters. Papers
Mich Ac Sc Rp An Rp — Michigan Academy of Science. Report. Annual Report
Mich Ag Exp — Michigan. Agricultural Experiment Station. Publications
Mich Agric Exp Stn Annu Rep — Michigan. Agricultural Experiment Station. Annual Report
Mich Agric Exp Stn Mem — Michigan. Agricultural Experiment Station. Memoir
Mich Agric Exp Stn Q Bull — Michigan. Agricultural Experiment Station. Quarterly Bulletin
Mich Alumni Quar Rev — Michigan Alumni Quarterly Review
Mich Audubon Newsl — Michigan Audubon Newsletter
Mich BJ — Michigan Bar Journal
Mich Bot — Michigan Botanist
Mich Bus R — Michigan Business Review
Mich Corp Finance and Bus LJ — Michigan Corporate Finance and Business Law Journal
Mich Dent Assoc J — Michigan Dental Association. Journal
Mich Dep Conserv Game Div Rep — Michigan. Department of Conservation. Game Division Report
Mich Dep Conserv Geol Surv Div Water Invest — Michigan. Department of Conservation. Geological Survey Division. Water Investigation
Mich Ed J — Michigan Education Journal
Mich Energy — Michigan Energy
Mich Ent — Michigan Entomologist
Mich Entomol — Michigan Entomologist
Mich Farm Econ — Michigan Farm Economics. Michigan State University. Cooperative Extension Service
Mich Geol Surv Bull — Michigan. Geological Survey. Bulletin
Mich Geol Surv Circ — Michigan. Geological Survey. Circular
Mich Geol Surv Div Misc — Michigan. Geological Survey Division. Miscellany
Mich Geol Surv Div Prog Rep — Michigan. Geological Survey Division. Progress Report
Mich Geol Surv Div Publ — Michigan. Geological Survey Division. Publication
Mich Geol Surv Div Water Invest — Michigan. Geological Survey Division. Water Investigation
Mich Geol Surv Rep Invest — Michigan. Geological Survey. Report of Investigation
Mich G S Rp — Michigan. Geological Survey. Michigan State Board of Geological Survey. Report
MichH — Michigan History Magazine
Mich His Col — Michigan Historical Commission. Collections
Mich His M — Michigan History Magazine

Mich Hist — Michigan History
Mich Hist Soc Coll — Michigan Pioneer and Historical Society Collections
Mich Hosp — Michigan Hospitals
Michigan Geol Survey Ann Statistical Summ — Michigan. Geological Survey. Annual Statistical Summary
Michigan Geol Survey Rept Inv — Michigan. Geological Survey. Report of Investigation
Michigan Geol Survey Water Inv — Michigan. Geological Survey. Water Investigation
Michigan Univ Mus Paleontology Contr — Michigan University. Museum of Paleontology. Contributions
Michigan Univ Mus Zoology Occasional Paper — Michigan University. Museum of Zoology. Occasional Papers
Mich Law R — Michigan Law Review
Mich Law Rev — Michigan Law Review
Mich Libn — Michigan Librarian
Mich Lib News — Michigan Library News
Mich Librn — Michigan Librarian
Mich LR — Michigan Law Review
Mich L Rev — Michigan Law Review
Mich Math J — Michigan Mathematical Journal
Mich Med — Michigan Medicine
Mich Miner — Michigan Miner
Mich Munic R — Michigan Municipal Review
Mich Nat Resour Mag — Michigan Natural Resources Magazine
Mich Nurse — Michigan Nurse
Mich Nurse Newsl — Michigan Nurse Newsletter
Michoacan Mex Com For Bol Ser Tec — Michoacan, Mexico. Comision Forestal. Boletin. Serie Tecnica
MichQR — Michigan Quarterly Review
Mich Q Rev — Michigan Quarterly Review
Mich S B J — Michigan State Bar Journal
Mich Sci Action Mich Agric Exp Stn — Michigan Science in Action. Michigan Agricultural Experiment Station
Mich State Coll Vet — Michigan State College Veterinarian
Mich State Dent Assoc J — Michigan State Dental Association. Journal
Mich State Dent Soc Bull — Michigan State Dental Society. Bulletin
Mich State Dent Soc J — Michigan State Dental Society. Journal
Mich State Econ Rec — Michigan State Economic Record
Mich State Univ Agric Exp Stn Annu Rep — Michigan State University. Agricultural Experiment Station. Annual Report
Mich St BJ — Michigan State Bar Journal
Mich Technol Univ Ford For Cent Res Notes — Michigan Technological University. Ford Forestry Center. Research Notes
Mich Univ Eng Res Inst Eng Res Bull — Michigan University. Engineering Research Institute. Engineering Research Bulletin
Mich Univ Inst Sci Technol Rep — Michigan University. Institute of Science and Technology. Report
Mich Univ Mus Zool Oc P — Michigan University. Museum of Zoology. Occasional Papers
Mich Water Res Comm Rept — Michigan Water Resources Commission. Report
Mich YB Int'l Legal Stud — Michigan Yearbook of International Legal Studies
MIC Model Identif Control — MIC. Modeling, Identification, and Control [Norway]
MICOB — Micron
Micol Ital — Micologia Italiana
Micro — Microprocessing and Microprogramming
Microb Drug Resist — Microbial Drug Resistance
Microbeam Anal Soc Annu Conf Proc — Microbeam Analysis Society. Annual Conference. Proceedings
Microb Ecol — Microbial Ecology
Microb Genet Bull — Microbial Genetics Bulletin
Microbiol Abstr — Microbiological Abstracts
Microbiol Aliments Nutr — Microbiologie, Aliments, Nutrition
Microbiol Esp — Microbiologia Espanola
Microbiol Immunol — Microbiology and Immunology [Japan]
Microbiolog — Microbiology
Microbiol Parazitol Epidemiol — Microbiologia, Parazitologia, Epidemiologia
Microbiol Parazitol Epidemiol (Buchar) — Microbiologia, Parazitologia, Epidemiologia (Bucharest)
Microbiol Rev — Microbiological Reviews
Microbios L — Microbios Letters
Microbios Lett — Microbios Letters
Microchem J — Microchemical Journal
Microchem J Symp Ser — Microchemical Journal. Symposium Series
Microcirc Endothelium Lymphatics — Microcirculation, Endothelium, and Lymphatics
Microcomput Printout — Microcomputer Printout
Micro Decis — Micro Decision
Microelectron Eng — Microelectronic Engineering
Microelectron J — Microelectronics Journal
Microelectron and Reliab — Microelectronics and Reliability
Microelectron Reliab — Microelectronics and Reliability
Microel Rel — Microelectronics and Reliability
Microfiche Fdn Newsl — Microfiche Foundation. Newsletter

Microform R — Microform Review
Microform Rev — Microform Review
Microgr Newsl — Micrographics Newsletter
Micro-6502/6809 J — Micro - The 6502/6809 Journal
Micro Jrl — Microwave Journal
Microlepid Palearct — Microlepidoptera Palaearctica
Micronesica J Coll Guam — Micronesica. Journal of the College of Guam
Micronesica J Univ Guam — Micronesica. Journal of the University of Guam
Micron Microsc Acta — Micron and Microscopica Acta
Microorg Infect Dis — Microorganisms and Infectious Diseases
Micropaleontolog Spec Publ — Micropaleontology. Special Publication
Micro Proc Annu Workshop Microprogram — Micro Proceedings. Annual Workshop on Microprogramming
Microprocess and Microprogram — Microprocessing and Microprogramming
Microprocess and Microsyst — Microprocessors and Microsystems
Microprocessors Microsysts — Microprocessors and Microsystems
Microprocess Software Q — Microprocessor Software Quarterly
Microprocess Work — Microprocessors at Work
Microsc — Microscope
Microsc Act — Microscopica Acta
Microsc Acta — Microscopica Acta
Microsc Acta Suppl — Microscopica Acta. Supplement
Microsc Cryst Front — Microscope and Crystal Front [England]
Microsc Electron Biol Cel — Microscopia Electronica y Biologia Celular
Microsc J Quekett Microsc Club — Microscopy. Journal of the Quekett Microscopical Club
Microsc Soc Can Bull — Microscopical Society of Canada. Bulletin
Microstruct Sci — Microstructural Science
Micro Syst — Micro Systems
Microtec — Microtecnic
Microvasc R — Microvascular Research
Microvasc Res — Microvascular Research
Microwave Energy Appl Newsl — Microwave Energy Applications Newsletter
Microwave J — Microwave Journal
Microwave Syst News — Microwave Systems News
Microw Syst News — Microwave Systems News
MID — Midland Bank Review
Mid — Midstream
MidA — Mid-America: An Historical Review
MIDAD — NIDA Research Monograph
MiDAIK — Mitteilungen. Deutsches Archaeologische Institut. Abteilung Kairo
Mid-Am — Mid-America: An Historical Review
Mid-Am Hist — Mid-America: An Historical Review
Mid-Am Oil Gas Rep — Mid-America Oil and Gas Reporter
Mid Am Outlk — Mid-American Outlook
Mid-Am Spectrosc Symp Proc — Mid-America Spectroscopy Symposium. Proceedings
Mid-Atl Ind Waste Conf Proc — Mid-Atlantic Industrial Waste Conference. Proceedings [United States]
MIDCD — Modeling Identification and Control
Midcon Conf Rec — Midcon Conference Record
Mid-Cont — Mid-Continent
Midcontinent Am Stud Jour — Midcontinent American Studies. Journal
Mid-Cont Lepid Ser — Mid-Continent Lepidoptera Series
Middlebury Hist Soc Papers and Pr — Middlebury [Vermont] Historical Society. Papers and Proceedings
Middle East Archtl Design — Middle East Architectural Design
Middle East Econ Dig — Middle East Economic Digest
Middle East Electron — Middle East Electronics
Middle East Exec Repts — Middle East Executive Reports
Middle East J — Middle East Journal
Middle East J Anaesthesiol — Middle East Journal of Anaesthesiology
Middle East R — Middle East Review
Middle East Tech Univ J Pure Appl Sci — Middle East Technical University. Journal of Pure and Applied Sciences
Middle E Executive Rep — Middle East Executive Reports
Middle E J — Middle East Journal
Middle E Mg — Middle Eastern Monographs
Middle E St — Middle Eastern Studies
Middle States Assn Col & Sec Sch Proc — Middle States Association of Colleges and Secondary Schools. Proceedings
Middle States Council for Social Studies Proc — Middle States Council for the Social Studies. Proceedings
MIDE — Methods in Investigative and Diagnostic Endocrinology [Elsevier Book Series]
MidEast — Middle East
Mid East E — Middle East and African Economist
Mid East Elect — Middle East Electricity
Mid East J — Middle East Journal
Mid East J Anaesthesiol — Middle East Journal of Anaesthesiology
Mid East Stud — Middle Eastern Studies
Mid E J — Middle East Journal
MIDEO — Melanges. Institut Dominicain d'Etudes Orientales
Mid E Stud — Middle Eastern Studies
Mid E Studies — Middle Eastern Studies

MIDGA — Mitsubishi Denki Giho
Midland — Midland Monthly
Midland Bank R — Midland Bank Review
Midland Bank Rev — Midland Bank Review
Midland Hist — Midland History
Midland Sch — Midland Schools
Midl Drug Pharm Rev — Midland Druggist and Pharmaceutical Review
Midl Macromol Monogr — Midland Macromolecular Monographs
Midl Med Rev — Midland Medical Review
MidM — Midwest Monographs
MidQ — Midwest Quarterly
MidR — Midwest Review
Mid-S F — Mid-South Folklore
Mid-South Q Bus R — Mid-South Quarterly Business Review
Mid-West Bnk — Mid-Western Banker
Midwest Dent — Midwestern Dentist
Midwest Eng — Midwest Engineer
Midwest J — Midwest Journal
Midwest J Phil — Midwest Journal of Philosophy
Midwest Mus Conf Am Assoc Mus Q — Midwest Museums Conference. American Association of Museums. Quarterly
Midwest Q — Midwest Quarterly
Midwest R Publ Adm — Midwest Review of Public Administration
Midwest Stud Phil — Midwest Studies in Philosophy
Midwife Health Visit — Midwife and Health Visitor [*Later, Midwife, Health Visitor, and Community Nurse*]
Midwife Health Visit Community Nurse — Midwife, Health Visitor, and Community Nurse
Midwives Chron — Midwives Chronicle
Midw Jour Pol Sci — Midwest Journal of Political Science
Midw Q — Midwest Quarterly
Midw Quar — Midwest Quarterly
Midw Stud P — Midwest Studies in Philosophy
MIE — Memoires. Institut d'Egypte
MIE — Middle East and African Economist
Miel Fr — Miel de France
Mie Med J — Mie Medical Journal
Mie Med J Suppl — Mie Medical Journal. Supplement
Mie Med Sci — Mie Medical Science [*Japan*]
MiER — Middle East Review
MIFAO — Memoires Publies par les Membres de l'Institut Francais d'Archeologie Orientale du Caire
MIFAOC — Memoires Publies par les Membres de l'Institut Francais d'Archeologie Orientale du Caire
MIGFW — Mitteilungen. Institut fuer Geschichtsforschung und Archivwissenschaft in Wien
MIGKA — Mineralogiya i Geokhimiya
Migne P G — Patrologia Graeca (Migne)
Migne P L — Patrologia Latina (Migne)
Migraine Symp — Migraine Symposium
Migr Int — Migrations Internationales
Migr dans le Monde — Migrations dans le Monde
MIIGA — Mie Igaku
MIIMA — Memorie. Istituto Italiano di Idrobiologia Dottore Marco De Marchi
MIIMD — Microbiology and Immunology
MIKKA — Metody Issledovaniya Katalizatorov i Kataliticheskikh Reaktsii
Mikol Fitopat — Mikologia i Fitopatologiya
Mikol Fitopatol — Mikologiya i Fitopatologiya
Mikrobiol — Mikrobiologiya
Mikrobiol Prom Ref Sb — Mikrobiologicheskaya Promyshlennost Referativnyi Sbornik
Mikrobiol Protsessy Pochvakh Mold — Mikrobiologicheskie Protsessy v Pochvakh Moldavii
Mikrobiol Sint Sb Inf Mater — Mikrobiologicheskii Sintez Sbornik Informatsii Materialov
Mikrobiol Zh — Mikrobiologichnyi Zhurnal
Mikrobiol Zh (Kiev) — Mikrobiolohichnyi Zhurnal (Kiev)
Mikrobiyol Bul — Mikrobiyoloji Bulteni
Mikrobiyol Bul Suppl — Mikrobiyoloji Bulteni. Supplement
Mikroch Act — Mikrochimica Acta
Mikrochem Ver Mikrochim Acta — Mikrochemie Vereinigt mit Mikrochimica Acta
Mikrochim Acta — Mikrochimica Acta
Mikrochim Acta Suppl — Mikrochimica Acta. Supplement
Mikrochim Ichnoanal Acta — Mikrochimica et Ichnoanalytica Acta
Mikroehlektron — Mikroehlektronika
Mikroelektronika Akad Nauk SSSR — Mikroelektronika Akademiya Nauk SSSR [*USSR*]
Mikroelem Med — Mikroelementy v Meditsine [*Ukrainian SSR*]
Mikroelem Pochvakh Sov Soyuza — Mikroelementy v Pochvakh Sovetskogo Soyuza
Mikroelem Prod Rast — Mikroelementy i Produktivnost' Rastenii
Mikroelem Sel'sk Khoz Med — Mikroelementy v Sel'skom Khozyaistve i Meditsine
Mikroelem Sib — Mikroelementy v Sibiri

Mikroelem Sib Inf Byull — Mikroelementy Sibiri Informatsionnyi Byulleten
Mikroelem Vost Sib Dal'nem Vostoke — Mikroelementy v Vostochnoi Sibiri i na Dal'nem Vostoke
Mikroelem Zhivotnovod Rastenievod — Mikroelementy v Zhivotnovodstve i Rastenievodstve
Mikro-Klein Comput — Mikro-Klein Computer
Mikroorg Rast Trudy Inst Mikrobiol Akad Nauk Latvii SSR — Mikroorganizmy i Rasteniya Trudy Instituta Mikrobiologii Akademii Nauk Latviiskoi SSR
Mikrowellen Mag — Mikrowellen Magazin
MIL — Memorie. Istituto Lombardo
Mi L — Michigan Law Review
MIL — Middle East
Mi L — University of Miami. Law Review
Mil Aff — Military Affairs
Mil Affairs — Military Affairs
Milbank Mem — Milbank Memorial Fund. Quarterly
Milbank Mem Fund Annu Rep — Milbank Memorial Fund. Annual Report
Milbank Mem Fund Q — Milbank Memorial Fund. Quarterly
Milbank Meml Fund Q Health Soc — Milbank Memorial Fund. Quarterly. Health and Society
Milbank Memor Fund Quart — Milbank Memorial Fund. Quarterly
Milb Mem Fund Q — Milbank Memorial Fund. Quarterly
Mil Chapl Rev — Military Chaplains' Review
Milchforsch-Milchprax — Milchforschung-Milchpraxis
Milch Prax Rindermast — Milch Praxis und Rindermast
Milchwirtsch Ber Bundesanst Wolfpassing Rotholz — Milchwirtschaftliche Berichte aus dem Bundesanstalten Wolfpassing und Rotholz
Milchwiss — Milchwissenschaft
Milchwissenschaft Milk Sci Int — Milchwissenschaft. Milk Science International
Mil Electron/Countermeas — Military Electronics/Countermeasures
Mil Eng — Military Engineer
Miles Int Symp Ser — Miles International Symposium Series
Milestones Conn Agr Home Econ — Milestones in Connecticut Agricultural and Home Economics
Mil Hist J — Military History Journal
Militaergesch — Militaergeschichte
Militaerpol Dok — Militaerpolitik Dokumentation
Milit Aff — Military Affairs
Military Law R — Military Law Review
Military M — Military Market Annual
Military R — Military Review
Milit Hist Tex Southwest — Military History of Texas and the Southwest
Milit LR — Military Law Review
Milit Med — Military Medicine
Milk Board J — Milk Board Journal
Milk Dlr — Milk Dealer
Milk Ind Found Conv Proc Lab Sect — Milk Industry Foundation. Convention Proceedings. Laboratory Section
Milk Ind Found Conv Proc Milk Supplies Sect — Milk Industry Foundation. Convention Proceedings. Milk Supplies Section
Milk Plant Mo — Milk Plant Monthly
Milk Plant Mon — Milk Plant Monthly
Milk Prod J — Milk Products Journal
Milk Sci Int — Milk Science International
Mill Fact — Mill and Factory
Milling — Milling and Baking News
Milling Feed Fert — Milling Feed and Fertiliser
Milling F & F — Milling Feed and Fertilizer
Mill News — Mill Newsletter
Mil LR — Military Law Review
Mil L Rep — Military Law Reporter
Mil L Rev — Military Law Review
Mil Med — Military Medicine
Mil Rev — Military Review
Mil Sci Tech — Military Science and Technology
Mil Surgeon — Military Surgeon
MILT — Minister's Letter. Letter to Indian People on Current Issues. Minister of Indian Affairs and Northern Development
MILTA — Militaertechnik
Milt Law R — Military Law Review
Milton Keynes J Archaeol Hist — Milton Keynes Journal of Archaeology and History
Milton N — Milton Newsletter
Milton Q — Milton Quarterly
Milton S — Milton Studies
Milton Stud — Milton Studies
Milw BAG — Milwaukee Bar Association. Gavel
Milw Public Mus Contrib Biol Geol — Milwaukee Public Museum. Contributions in Biology and Geology
Milw Public Mus Occas Pap Nat Hist — Milwaukee Public Museum. Occasional Papers. Natural History
Milw Public Mus Spec Publ Biol Geol — Milwaukee Public Museum. Special Publications in Biology and Geology
MIM — Mining and Industrial Magazine [*Manila*]

MIM — Mining Magazine

MIMBD — Montanaro d'Italia - Monti e Boschi

MIMEA — Minerva Medica

Mimeo AS Indiana Agr Exp Sta — Mimeo AS. Indiana Agricultural Experiment Station

Mimeo AY Indiana Agr Exp Sta — Mimeo AY. Indiana Agricultural Experiment Station

Mimeo Circ NS Dep Agric — Mimeographed Circular Service. Nova Scotia Department of Agriculture and Marketing

Mimeo Circ Wyo Agric Exp Stn — Mimeograph Circular. Wyoming Agricultural Experiment Station

Mimeo Co-Op Ext Serv Purdue Univ — Mimeo. Co-Operative Extension Service. Purdue University

Mimeo EC Purdue Univ Coop Ext Serv — Mimeo EC. Purdue University. Cooperative Extension Service

Mimeogr Bull A-E Ohio State Univ Dept Agr Econ Rural Sociol — Mimeograph Bulletin A-E. Ohio State University. Department of Agricultural Economics and Rural Sociology

Mimeogr Circ Okla Agric Exp Stn — Mimeograph Circular. Oklahoma Agricultural Experiment Station

Mimeogr Circ Univ RI Ext Serv Agr Home Econ — Mimeograph Circular. University of Rhode Island. Extension Service in Agriculture and Home Economics

Mimeogr Circ Wyo Agr Exp Sta — Mimeograph Circular. Wyoming Agricultural Experiment Station

Mimeogrd Publ Commonw Bur Past Fld Crops — Mimeographed Publications. Commonwealth Bureau of Pastures and Field Crops

Mimeogr Publ Commonwealth Bur Pastures Field Crops — Mimeographed Publications. Commonwealth Bureau of Pastures and Field Crops

Mimeogr Publ Hawaii Univ Dept Hort — Mimeographed Publication. Hawaii University. Department of Horticulture

Mimeogr Rep Cambridge Univ Sch Agr Farm Econ Br — Mimeographed Report. Cambridge University. School of Agriculture. Farm Economics Branch

Mimeogr Ser Ark Agr Exp Sta — Mimeograph Series. Arkansas Agricultural Experiment Station

Mimeogr Ser Ark Agric Exp Stn — Mimeograph Series. Arkansas Agricultural Experiment Station

Mimeogr Ser GA Agr Exp Sta — Mimeograph Series. Georgia Agricultural Experiment Station

Mimeogr Ser GA Agric Exp Stn — Mimeograph Series. Georgia Agricultural Experiment Station

Mimeogr Ser Univ Arkansas Agric Exp Stn — Mimeograph Series. University of Arkansas. Agricultural Experiment Station

Mimeogr Ser Utah Agr Exp Sta — Mimeograph Series. Utah Agricultural Experiment Station

Mimeo ID Purdue Univ Dept Agr Ext — Mimeo ID. Purdue University. Department of Agricultural Extension

Mimeo Rep Fla Dep Agric Econ — Mimeo Report. Department of Agricultural Economics. Florida Agricultural Experiment Stations

Mimeo Rep Fla Everglades Exp Sta — Mimeo Report. Florida Everglades Experiment Station

MIMN — Micmac News

MIMS — Monthly Index of Medical Specialities

MIMSA — Minerva Medica. Supplemento

MIN — Korte Berichten voor Milieu

Min — Minerva

Minamata Dis — Minamata Disease

Min Annu Rev — Mining Annual Review [England]

Minas Gerais Braz Inst Agron Circ — Minas Gerais, Brazil. Instituto Agronomicao. Circular

Min B — Mining Bulletin

Min Can — Mining in Canada

Min Chem Engng Rev — Mining and Chemical Engineering Review

Min Chem Eng Rev — Mining and Chemical Engineering Review [Australia]

Min Cong J — Mining Congress Journal

Min Congr J — Mining Congress Journal

MInd — Metting Index

Min Deposit — Mineralium Deposita

Mind Your Own Bus — Mind Your Own Business

Mine Inj Worktime Q — Mine Injuries and Worktime Quarterly

Min Electr Mech Eng — Mining, Electrical, and Mechanical Engineer [England]

Min Eng — Mining Engineering

Min Eng (Colorado) — Mining Engineering (Colorado)

Min Eng (Littleton Colo) — Mining Engineering (Littleton, Colorado)

Min Eng (Lond) — Mining Engineer (London)

Min Engng — Mining Engineering

Min Eng (NY) — Mining Engineering (New York)

Min Engr — Mining Engineer

Mine Pet Gaze — Mine, Petrol, si Gaze [Romania]

Mine Pet & Gaze (Bucharest) — Mine, Petrol, si Gaze (Bucharest)

Mine Pet Gaze (Bucharest) — Mine, Petrol, si Gaze (Bucharest)

Mine & Quarry Eng — Mine and Quarry Engineering

Mine Quarry Mech — Mine and Quarry Mechanisation

Min Equip Int — Mining Equipment International

Mineral Abstr — Mineralogical Abstracts

Mineral Geokhim — Mineralogiya i Geokhimiya [USSR]

Mineral Industries Jour — Mineral Industries Journal

Mineral Issled — Mineralogicheskie Issledovaniya

Mineral J (Tokyo) — Mineralogical Journal (Tokyo)

Mineral Mag — Mineralogical Magazine

Mineral Mag J Mineral Soc (1876-1968) — Mineralogical Magazine and Journal of the Mineralogical Society (1876-1968) [England]

Mineralog Abstr — Mineralogical Abstracts

Mineralog Mag — Mineralogical Magazine

Mineralog et Petrog Acta — Mineralogica et Petrographica Acta

Mineralog Soc America Spec Paper — Mineralogical Society of America. Special Paper

Mineralog Soc Utah Bull — Mineralogical Society of Utah. Bulletin

Mineral Petrogr Acta — Mineralogica et Petrographica Acta

Mineral Petrogr Mitt — Mineralogische und Petrographische Mitteilungen

Mineral Petrogr Mitt Tschermaks — Mineralogische und Petrographische Mitteilungen Tschermaks [Austria]

Mineral Plann — Mineral Planning

Mineral Rec — Mineralogical Record

Mineral Sb (Lvov) — Mineralogicheskii Sbornik (Lvov)

Mineral Sb (L'vov Gos Univ) — Mineralogicheskiy Sbornik (L'vovskiy Gosudarstvennyy Universitet)

Mineral Sb (Sverdlovsk) — Mineralogicheskii Sbornik (Sverdlovsk)

Mineral Slovaca — Mineralia Slovaca

Mineral Soc Am Short Course Notes — Mineralogical Society of America. Short Course Notes

Mineral Soc Am Spec Pap — Mineralogical Society of America. Special Paper

Mineral Soc Bull — Mineralogical Society. Bulletin

Minerals Res CSIRO — Minerals Research in Commonwealth Scientific and Industrial Research Organisation

Mineral T N — Mineral Trade Notes

Mineral Zh — Mineralogicheskiy Zhurnal

Miner Assess Rep Inst Geol Sci — Mineral Assessment Report. Institute of Geological Sciences

Miner Bull — Mineral Bulletin [Canada]

Miner Deposita — Mineralium Deposita

Miner Dressing Notes — Mineral Dressing Notes

Miner Econ Ser (Indiana Geol Surv) — Mineral Economics Series (Indiana Geological Survey)

Miner Electrolyte Metab — Mineral and Electrolyte Metabolism [Switzerland]

Miner Energy Bull — Minerals and Energy Bulletin [Australia]

Miner Energy Resour — Mineral and Energy Resources [United States]

Miner Environ — Minerals and the Environment

Miner Fossiles Guide Collect — Mineraux et Fossiles. Guide du Collectionneur

Mineria Metal (Madrid) — Mineria y Metalurgia (Madrid)

Mineria Met (Mexico City) — Mineria y Metalurgia (Mexico City)

Miner Ind — Mineral Industries [United States]

Miner Ind Bull — Mineral Industries Bulletin

Miner Ind NSW — Mineral Industry of New South Wales

Miner Ind Res Lab Univ Alaska Rep — Mineral Industries Research Laboratory. University of Alaska. Report

Miner Ind Surv Sodium Compd — Mineral Industry Surveys. Sodium Compounds

Miner Ind (University Park PA) — Mineral Industries (University Park, Pennsylvania)

Miner Mag — Mineral Magazine and Journal. Mineralogical Society

Miner Metal — Mineracao, Metalurgia

Miner Metall Process — Minerals and Metallurgical Processing

Miner Met Rev — Minerals and Metals Review

Miner News Serv (Philipp) — Minerals News Service. Bureau of Mines (Philippines)

Miner Process — Minerals Processing

Miner Process Inf Note Warren Spring Lab — Mineral Processing Information Note. Warren Spring Laboratory

Miner Process Technol Rev — Mineral Processing and Technology Review

Miner Rec — Mineralogical Record

Miner Res CSIRO — Minerals Research in Commonwealth Scientific and Industrial Research Organisation

Miner Res CSIRO (Aust) — Minerals Research in Commonwealth Scientific and Industrial Research Organisation (Australia)

Miner Res (Nagpur) — Mineral Research (Nagpur)

Miner Resour Bull (Geol Surv West Aust) — Mineral Resources Bulletin (Geological Survey of Western Australia)

Miner Resour Bull Geol Surv West Aust — Western Australia. Geological Survey. Mineral Resources Bulletin

Miner Resour Bull LA Geol Surv — Mineral Resources Bulletin. Louisiana Geological Survey

Miner Resour Bull (Saudi Arabia) — Mineral Resources Bulletin. Directorate General of Mineral Resources (Saudi Arabia)

Miner Resour Circ (Univ Tex Austin Bur Econ Geol) — Mineral Resource Circular (University of Texas at Austin. Bureau of Economic Geology)

Miner Resour Consult Comm Miner Dossier (GB) — Mineral Resources Consultative Committee. Mineral Dossier (Great Britain)

Miner Resour Geol Geophys Bur 1:250000 Geol Ser — Mineral Resources. Geology and Geophysics. Bureau of 1:250,000 Geological Series

Miner Resour Geol Surv NSW — New South Wales. Geological Survey. Mineral Resources
Miner Resour Pam Geol Surv Guyana — Mineral Resources Pamphlet. Geological Survey of Guyana
Miner Resour Rep — Mineral Resources Report. Bureau of Mineral Resources. Geology and Geophysics
Miner Resour Rep Invest Saudi Arabia Dir Gen Miner Resour — Mineral Resources Report of Investigation. Saudi Arabia Directorate General of Mineral Resources
Miner Resour Rep PA Topogr Geol Surv — Mineral Resource Report. Pennsylvania Topographic and Geologic Survey
Miner Resour Res Dir Gen Miner Resour (Saudi Arabia) — Mineral Resources Research. Directorate General of Mineral Resources (Saudi Arabia)
Miner Resour Rev — Mineral Resources Review. Department of Mines. South Australia
Miner Resour Rev Dep Mines S Aust — Mineral Resources Review. Department of Mines. South Australia
Miner Resour Rev South Aust Dep Mines — Mineral Resources Review. Department of Mines. South Australia
Miner Resour Ser Rhod Geol Surv — Mineral Resources Series. Rhodesia Geological Survey
Miner Resour Ser WV Geol Econ Surv — Mineral Resources Series. West Virginia Geological and Economic Survey
Miner Resour Surv (NH Div Econ Dev) — Mineral Resources Survey (New Hampshire Division of Economic Development)
Miner Sci Eng — Minerals Science and Engineering
Miner Sci Eng (Johannesburg) — Minerals Science and Engineering (Johannesburg)
Miner Syr'e — Mineral'noe Syr'e
Miner Syr'e Ego Pererab — Mineral'noe Syr'e i Ego Pererabotka
Miner Syr'e Tsvetn Met — Mineral'noe Syr'e i Tsvetnye Metally
Miner Syr'e Vses Inst Miner Syr'ya — Mineral'noe Syr'e. Vsesoyuznyi Institut Mineral'nogo Syr'ya
Miner Syr'e Vses Nauchno Issled Inst Miner Syr'ya — Mineral'noe Syr'e. Vsesoyuznyi Nauchno-Issledovatel'skii Institut Mineral'nogo Syr'ya
Miner Udobr Insektofungis — Mineral'nye Udobreniya i Insektofungisidy
Minerva Aerosp — Minerva Aerospaziale
Minerva Anestesiol — Minerva Anestesiologica
Minerva Bioepistemol — Minerva Bioepistemologica
Minerva Biol — Minerva Biologica
Minerva Cardioangiol — Minerva Cardioangiologica
Minerva Chir — Minerva Chirurgica
Minerva Dermatol — Minerva Dermatologica [*Italy*]
Minerva Diet — Minerva Dietologica
Minerva Dietol — Minerva Dietologica [*Later, Minerva Dietologica e Gastroenterologica*]
Minerva Dietol Gastroenterol — Minerva Dietologica e Gastroenterologica
Minerva Ecol Idroclimatol Fisicosanit — Minerva Ecologica, Idroclimatologica, Fisicosanitaria
Minerva Ecol Idroclimatol Fis Sanit — Minerva Ecologica, Idroclimatologica, Fisicosanitaria
Minerva Farm — Minerva Farmaceutica
Minerva Fisiconucl — Minerva Fisiconucleare
Minerva Fisiconucl G Fis Sanit Prot Radiaz — Minerva Fisiconucleare. Giornale di Fisica, Sanitaria, e Protezione Contro le Radiazioni
Minerva Gastroenterol — Minerva Gastroenterologica
Minerva Ginecol — Minerva Ginecologica
Minerva Idroclimatol — Minerva Idroclimatologica [*Italy*]
Minerva Med — Minerva Medica
Minerva Med Eur Med — Minerva Medica. Europa Medica
Minerva Med Guiliana — Minerva Medica. Guiliana
Minerva Med Rass Ipnosi Med Psicosom — Minerva Medica. Rassegna Ipnosi e Medicina Psicosomatica
Minerva Med Roma — Minerva Medica Roma
Minerva Med Sicil — Minerva Medica. Siciliana
Minerva Med Suppl — Minerva Medica. Supplemento [*Italy*]
Minerva Nefrol — Minerva Nefrologica
Minerva Neurochir — Minerva Neurochirurgica
Minerva Nipiol — Minerva Nipiologica
Minerva Nucl — Minerva Nucleare [*Italy*]
Minerva Oftalmol — Minerva Oftalmologica [*Italy*]
Minerva ORL — Minerva Otorinolaringologica
Minerva Otorinolaringol — Minerva Otorinolaringologica
Minerva Ped — Minerva Pediatrica
Minerva Pediatr — Minerva Pediatrica
Minerva Pneumol — Minerva Pneumologica
Minerva Psichiatr — Minerva Psichiatrica
Minerva Psichiatr Psicol — Minerva Psichiatrica e Psicologica [*Later, Minerva Psichiatrica*]
Minerva Radiol — Minerva Radiologica
Minerva Radiol Fisioter Radio-Biol — Minerva Radiologica. Fisioterapica e Radio-Biologica [*Italy*]
Minerva Stomatol — Minerva Stomatologica
Minerva Urol — Minerva Urologica
Miner Waste Util Symp Proc — Mineral Waste Utilization Symposium. Proceedings

Miner Yearb — Minerals Yearbook [*United States*]
Mine Saf Health — Mine Safety and Health [*United States*]
Mines Dep Victoria Groundwater Invest Program Rep — Mines Department. Victoria Groundwater Investigation Program Report
Mines Mag — Mines Magazine
Mines Met — Mines et Metallurgie
Mines Metall — Mines et Metallurgie
Mines Miner (Scranton PA) — Mines and Minerals (Scranton, Pennsylvania)
Mingays Electrical W — Mingay's Electrical Weekly
Min Geol — Mining Geology [*Japan*]
Min & Geol J — Mining and Geological Journal
Min Geol J — Mining and Geological Journal
Min Geol (Soc Min Geol Jap) — Mining Geology (Society of Mining Geologists of Japan) Journal
Min Geol Spec Issue (Tokyo) — Mining Geology (Society of Mining Geologists of Japan) Special Issue (Tokyo)
Ming Stud — Ming Studies
Mini Applic — Minicomputer Applications Analyzer
Minicomput Rev — Minicomputer Review
Mini-Micro — Mini-Micro Systems
Mini-Micro Syst — Mini-Micro Systems
Min Ind Q — Mineral Industry Quarterly
Min Ind Quebec — Mining Industry in Quebec
Min Ind Technol — Mining Industry Technology [*Taiwan*]
Mining & Chem Eng R — Mining and Chemical Engineering Review
Mining Congr J — Mining Congress Journal
Mining Elec Mech Eng — Mining, Electrical, and Mechanical Engineer
Mining Eng (London) — Mining Engineer (London)
Mining Eng (NY) — Mining Engineering (New York)
Mining Jrl — Mining Journal
Mining Mag — Mining Magazine
Mining Met Quart — Mining and Metallurgy. Quarterly
Mining Miner Eng — Mining and Minerals Engineering
Mining R — Mining Review
Mining Technol — Mining Technology
Minist Agric Aliment Ont Bull (Ed Fr) — Ministere de l'Agriculture et de l'Alimentation de l'Ontario. Bulletin (Edition Francaise)
Minist Agric Inst Colomb Agropecu Programa Nac Entomol — Ministerio de Agricultura. Instituto Colombiano Agropecuario. Programa Nacional de Entomologia
Minist Agric Mktg Guide — Marketing Guide. Ministry of Agriculture [*United Kingdom*]
Minist Agric Nat Resour Cent Agric Stn Res Rep (Guyana) — Ministry of Agriculture and Natural Resources. Central Agricultural Station. Research Report (Guyana)
Minist Cult Educ Fund Miguel Lillo Misc — Ministerio de Cultura y Educacion. Fundacion Miguel Lillo. Miscelanea
Minist Ganad Agric Cent Invest Agric Alberto Boerger Bol Tec — Ministerio de Ganaderia y Agricultura. Centro de Investigaciones Agricolas "Alberto Boerger." Boletim Tecnico
Minist Ind Commer Que Rapp Annu — Ministere de l'Industrie et du Commerce du Quebec. Rapport Annuel
Minist Mar Merc Mem — Ministero della Marina Mercantile. Memoria
Mini Sys — Mini-Micro Systems
Miniwatt Dig — Miniwatt Digest
Miniwatt Tech Bull — Miniwatt Technical Bulletin
Min J — Mining Journal
Min J (Lond) — Mining Journal (London)
Min J (London) — Mining Journal (London)
Min Mag — Mining Magazine
Min & Met — Mining and Metallurgy
Min Metal — Mineracao, Metalurgia [*Brazil*]
Min Metal — Mineria y Metalurgia
Min Metall Q — Mining and Metallurgy. Quarterly
Min Metall Soc America Bull — Mining and Metallurgical Society of America. Bulletin
Min Metal Plast Electr — Mineria y Metalurgia, Plasticos y Electricidad
Min Metal (Taipei) — Mining and Metallurgy (Taipei)
Min Met Rev — Minerals and Metals Review
Min Mex — Minero Mexicano
Min Miner Engng — Mining and Minerals Engineering
Min Mirror — Mining Mirror
Min & Mtrl — Minerals and Materials: A Monthly Survey
Minn Acad Sci J — Minnesota Academy of Science. Journal
Minn Acad Sci Proc — Minnesota Academy of Science. Proceedings
Minn Ac N Sc B — Minnesota Academy of Natural Sciences. Bulletin
Minn Ag Exp — Minnesota. Agricultural Experiment Station. Publications
Minn Agric Exp Stn Bull — Minnesota. Agricultural Experiment Station. Bulletin
Minn Agric Exp Stn Misc Rep — Minnesota. Agricultural Experiment Station. Miscellaneous Report
Minn Agric Exp Stn Stn Bull — Minnesota. Agricultural Experiment Station. Station Bulletin
Minn Agric Exp Stn Tech Bull — Minnesota. Agricultural Experiment Station. Technical Bulletin
Minn Beekpr — Minnesota Beekeeper

Minn Dep Agric Annu Feed Bull — Minnesota. Department of Agriculture. Annual Feed Bulletin

Minn Dep Conserv Div Game Fish Sect Res Plann Invest Rep — Minnesota. Department of Conservation. Division of Game and Fish. Section on Research and Planning. Investigational Report

Minn Dep Conserv Tech Bull — Minnesota. Department of Conservation. Technical Bulletin

Minn Dep Nat Resour Div Fish Wildl Sect Wildl Wildl Res Q — Minnesota. Department of Natural Resources. Division of Fish and Wildlife. Section of Wildlife. Wildlife Research Quarterly

Minn Dep Nat Resour Div Game Fish Sect Tech Serv Invest Rep — Minnesota. Department of Natural Resources. Division of Game and Fish. Section of Technical Services. Investigational Report

Minn Dep Nat Resour Game Res Proj Q Prog Rep — Minnesota. Department of Natural Resources. Game Research Project. Quarterly Progress Report

Minn Dep Nat Resour Sect Fish Invest Rep — Minnesota. Department of Natural Resources. Section of Fisheries. Investigational Report

Minn Dept Conserv Div Waters Bull Tech Paper — Minnesota. Department of Conservation. Division of Waters. Bulletin. Technical Paper

Minneap Dist Dent J — Minneapolis District Dental Journal

Minneapolis Inst Bul — Minneapolis Institute of Arts. Bulletin

Minnesota Geol Survey Misc Map — Minnesota. Geological Survey. Miscellaneous Map

Minnesota Geol Survey Rept Inv — Minnesota. Geological Survey. Report of Investigations

Minnesota Geol Survey Spec Pub Ser — Minnesota. Geological Survey. Special Publication Series

Minnesota L Rev — Minnesota Law Review

Minnesota Univ Water Resources Research Center Bull — University of Minnesota. Graduate School. Water Resources Research Center. Bulletin

Min Neurochir — Minerva Neurochirurgica

Min Newsletter — Mining Newsletter

Minn Farm & Home Sci — Minnesota Farm and Home Science

Minn Farm Home Sci — Minnesota Farm and Home Science

Minn Fish Game Invest Fish Ser — Minnesota Fish and Game Investigations. Fish Series

Minn Fish Invest — Minnesota Fisheries Investigations

Minn Forestry Res Note — Minnesota Forestry Research Notes

Minn For Notes — Minnesota Forestry Notes

Minn For Res Notes — Minnesota Forestry Research Notes

Minn Geol Surv Bull — Minnesota. Geological Survey. Bulletin

Minn Geol Surv Rep Invest — Minnesota. Geological Survey. Report of Investigations

Minn Geol Surv Spec Publ Ser — Minnesota. Geological Survey. Special Publication Series

Minn G S — Minnesota. Geological and Natural History Survey

Minn H — Minnesota History

Minn His — Minnesota History

Minn His B — Minnesota History. Bulletin

Minn His S — Minnesota Historical Society. Collections

Minn Hist — Minnesota History

Minn Hist B — Minnesota History. Bulletin

Minn History — Minnesota History

Minn Hist Soc Educ Bull — Minnesota Historical Society. Educational Bulletin

Minn Hort — Minnesota Horticulturist

Minn Hortic — Minnesota Horticulturist

Minn Inst Arts Bul — Minneapolis Institute of Arts. Bulletin

Minn Inst Bul — Minneapolis Institute of Arts. Bulletin

Minn J of Ed — Minnesota Journal of Education

Minn J Ed — Minnesota Journal of Education

Minn Jour Sci — Minnesota Journal of Science

Minn J Sci — Minnesota Journal of Science

Minn Lib — Minnesota Libraries

Minn Libr — Minnesota Libraries

Minn L R — Minnesota Language Review

Minn LR — Minnesota Law Review

Minn L Rev — Minnesota Law Review

Minn Med — Minnesota Medicine

Minn Munic — Minnesota Municipalities

Minn Nurs Accent — Minnesota Nursing Accent

Minn Off Iron Range Resour Rehabil Rep Inventory — Minnesota. Office of Iron Range Resources and Rehabilitation. Report of Inventory

MinnR — Minnesota Review

Minn Rev — Minnesota Review

Minn Sch Mines Exp Sta B — Minnesota School of Mines. Experiment Station. Bulletin

Minn Sci — Minnesota Science

Minn Sci Minn Agric Exp Stn — Minnesota Science. Minnesota Agricultural Experiment Station

Minn Stat — Minnesota Statutes

Minn Symp Child Psychol — Minnesota Symposia on Child Psychology

Minn Univ Min Symp — Minnesota University. Mining Symposium

Minn Univ Q B — Minnesota University. Quarterly Bulletin

Minn Univ St Anthony Falls Hydraul Lab Proj Rep — Minnesota University. St. Anthony Falls Hydraulic Laboratory. Project Report

Minn Univ St Anthony Falls Hydraul Lab Tech Pap — Minnesota University. St. Anthony Falls Hydraulic Laboratory. Technical Paper

Minn Univ Water Resour Res Cent Bull — Minnesota University. Water Resources Research Center. Bulletin

Minoes Megbizh — Minoeseg es Megbizhatosag [*Hungary*]

Min Pediat — Minerva Pediatrica

Min R — Mining Review

Min Record — Mining Record

Min Res Bur Bull — Bureau of Mineral Resources. Bulletin [*Australia*]

Min Res Bur Geol Map — Bureau of Mineral Resources. Geological Map [*Australia*]

Min Res Bur 1:250000 Geol Ser — Bureau of Mineral Resources. 1:250,000 Geological Series [*Australia*]

Min Res Bur Geophys Obs Rep — Bureau of Mineral Resources. Geophysical Observatory Report [*Australia*]

Min Res Bur 1 Mile Geol Ser — Bureau of Mineral Resources. 1 Mile Geological Series [*Australia*]

Min Res Bur Pamph — Bureau of Mineral Resources. Pamphlet [*Australia*]

Min Res Bur Petrol Search Pub — Bureau of Mineral Resources. Petroleum Search Subsidy Acts. Publication [*Australia*]

Min Res Bur Petrol Search Publ — Bureau of Mineral Resources. Petroleum Search Subsidy Acts. Publication [*Australia*]

Min Res Bur Petrol Search Public — Bureau of Mineral Resources. Petroleum Search Subsidy Acts. Publication [*Australia*]

Min Res Bur Rep — Bureau of Mineral Resources. Report [*Australia*]

Min Res Bur Sum Rep — Bureau of Mineral Resources. Summary Report [*Australia*]

Min Rev — Mining Review

Min Rev Adelaide — Mining Review. Adelaide (South Australia Department of Mines)

Minsk Gos Med Inst Sb Nauchn Rab — Minskii Gosudarstvennyi Meditsinskii Institut Sbornik Nauchnykh Rabot

Min St — Ministry Studies

M Inst Rech Sci Mad — Memoires. Institut de Recherche Scientifique de Madagascar

Min Surv — Mining Survey [*Johannesburg*]

Min Surv (Johannesb) — Mining Survey (Johannesburg)

Min Techn — Mineraloel-Technik

Min Technol — Mining Technology

MINUA — Minerva Nucleare

Minufiya J Agric Res — Minufiya Journal of Agricultural Research

Minutes — Minutes. Seminar in Ukrainian Studies

Minutes Annu Meet Natl Plant Board — Minutes. Annual Meeting. National Plant Board

Minutes Meet PA Electr Assoc Eng Sect — Minutes. Meeting. Pennsylvania Electric Association. Engineering Section

Min Week — Mining Week [*South Africa*]

Min World — Mining World

Min Yearb (Denver) — Mining Yearbook (Denver)

Min Year Book — Mining Year Book [*United States*]

Minzokugaku — Minzokugaku-Kenkyu [*Japanese Journal of Ethnology*]

MIO — Mitteilungen. Institut fuer Orientforschung. Deutsche Akademie der Wissenschaften zu Berlin

MIO — Mitteilungen. Institut fuer Orientforschung. Geschichtsforschung

MIO — Musee Imperial Ottoman [*Istanbul*]

MIODAWB — Deutsche Akademie der Wissenschaften zu Berlin. Institut fuer Orientforschung. Mitteilungen

MIOEA — Mineraloel

MI Oe G — Mitteilungen. Institut fuer Oesterreichische Geschichtsforschung

MIOF — Mitteilungen. Institut fuer Orientforschung

MIOF — Mitteilungen. Institut fuer Orientforschung. Deutsche Akademie der Wissenschaften zu Berlin

MIOG — Mitteilungen. Institut fuer Oesterreichische Geschichtsforschung

MIOGF — Mitteilungen. Institut fuer Oesterreichische Geschichtsforschung

MI Or — Mitteilungen. Institut fuer Orientforschung

MIOTA — Minerva Otorinolaringologica

MIPEA — Minerva Pediatrica

MIR — Middle East Executive Reports

Mi R — Minnesota Review

Mir — Miracle Science and Fantasy Stories

MIRD — Materialy i Issledovanija po Russkoj Dialektologii

Mir Ek Mezd Otnos — Mirovaja Ekonomika i Mezdunarodnye Otnosenija

Mir Ekon Mezdun Otnos — Mirovaja Ekonomika i Mezdunarodnye Otnosenija

MIRNA8 — Koninklijk Belgisch Instituut voor Natuurwetenschappen. Verhandelingen

Mirovaya Ekon Mezhdunar Otnosheniya — Mirovaya Ekonomikai i Mezhdunarodnye Otnosheniya [*USSR*]

Mir Rybolovstvo — Mirovoe Rybolovstvo

MIRSDQ — MTP [*Medical & Technical Publishing Co.*] International Review of Science. Series One. Physiology

MIRV — Mining Review

MIS — Management Information Systems Quarterly

MIS — Misset's Pakblad

MIS — Mississippi Music Educator

Misaki Mar Biol Inst Kyoto Univ Spec Rep — Misaki Marine Biological Institute. Kyoto University. Special Report
MIS Alum — Mineral Industry Surveys. Aluminum
MIS Antim — Mineral Industry Surveys. Antimony
MIS Barite — Mineral Industry Surveys. Barite
MIS Baux — Mineral Industry Surveys. Bauxite
MIS Bromin — Mineral Industry Surveys. Bromine
MiscAgost — Miscellanea Agostiniana [*Rome*]
MIS Calcm — Mineral Industry Surveys. Calcium and Calcium Compounds
MiscBarc — Miscellanea Barcinonensia
Misc Bav Mon — Miscellanea Bavarica Monacensia
MiscBibl — Miscellanea Biblica Edita a Pontificio Instituto Biblico ad Celebrandum Annum XXV ex quo Conditum est Institutum [*Rome*]
Misc Bryol Lichenol — Miscellanea Bryologica et Lichenologica
Misc Bull Botanic Gdn (Adelaide) — Botanic Gardens (Adelaide). Miscellaneous Bulletin
Misc Bull Div Market Econ Dep Agric NSW — Miscellaneous Bulletin. Division of Marketing and Economics. Department of Agriculture. New South Wales
Misc Byz Mon — Miscellanea Byzantina Monacensia
Miscelanea Mat — Miscelanea Matematica
Misc Ext Publ NC Univ Ext Serv — Miscellaneous Extension Publication. North Carolina University. Extension Service
Misc For Adm Nac Bosques (Argent) — Miscelaneas Forestales. Administracion Nacional de Bosques (Buenos Aires, Argentina)
Misc Fr — Miscellanea Francescana
Misc Franc — Miscellanea Francescana
MIS Chrom — Mineral Industry Surveys. Chromium
Misc Inf Tokyo Univ For — Miscellaneous Information. Tokyo University Forests
Misc Invest Appl Sci Res Corp Thailand — Miscellaneous Investigation. Applied Scientific Research Corporation of Thailand
Misc Med — Miscellanea Mediaevalia
Misc Mon — Miscellanea Bavarica Monacensia
Misc Mus — Miscellanea Musicologica
MIS Cobalt — Mineral Industry Surveys. Cobalt
MIS Copper — Mineral Industry Surveys. Copper
Misc Pap Exp For Taiwan Univ — Miscellaneous Papers. Experimental Forest. National Taiwan University
Misc Pap Landbouwhogesch Wageningen — Miscellaneous Papers. Landbouwhogeschool Wageningen
Misc Pap Ont Div Mines — Miscellaneous Paper. Ontario Division of Mines
Misc Pap Ont Geol Surv — Miscellaneous Paper. Ontario Geological Survey
Misc Pap Oreg Dep Geol Miner Ind — Miscellaneous Paper. Oregon Department of Geology and Mineral Industries
Misc Pap Oreg State Coll Agr Exp Sta — Miscellaneous Paper. Oregon State College. Agricultural Experiment Station
Misc Pap Pac Southwest Forest Range Exp Sta US Forest Serv — Miscellaneous Paper. Pacific Southwest Forest and Range Experiment Station. US Forest Service
Misc Pap US Army Eng Waterw Exp Stn — Miscellaneous Paper. US Army Engineers. Waterways Experiment Station
Misc Publ Agric Exp Stn Okla State Univ — Miscellaneous Publication. Agricultural Experiment Station. Oklahoma State University
Misc Publ Aust Entomol Soc — Miscellaneous Publication. Australian Entomological Society
Misc Publ Aust Ent Soc — Miscellaneous Publication. Australian Entomological Society
Misc Publ Entomol Soc Am — Miscellaneous Publications. Entomological Society of America
Misc Publ Genet Soc Can — Miscellaneous Publications. Genetics Society of Canada
Misc Publ Geol Surv India — Miscellaneous Publications. Geological Survey of India
Misc Publ Hawaii Univ Coop Ext Serv — Miscellaneous Publication. Hawaii University. Cooperative Extension Service
Misc Publ Hokkaido Natl Agric Exp Stn — Miscellaneous Publication. Hokkaido National Agricultural Experimentation Station
Misc Publ Land Resour Div Dir Overseas Surv — Miscellaneous Publication. Land Resources Division. Directorate of Overseas Surveys
Misc Publ Mus Zool Univ Mich — Miscellaneous Publications. Museum of Zoology. University of Michigan
Misc Publ Okla State Univ Agr Exp Sta — Miscellaneous Publication. Oklahoma State University. Agricultural Experiment Station
Misc Publ S Carol Ext Serv — Miscellaneous Publications. South Carolina Extension Service
Misc Publs Ent Soc Am — Miscellaneous Publications. Entomological Society of America
Misc Publs Forest Dep West Aust — Miscellaneous Publications. Forests Department. Western Australia
Misc Publs Mus Zool Univ Mich — Miscellaneous Publications. Museum of Zoology. University of Michigan
Misc Publs Univ ME — Miscellaneous Publications. University of Maine
Misc Publs US Dep Agric — Miscellaneous Publications. United States Department of Agriculture

Misc Publs US Dep Agric Soil Conserv Serv — Miscellaneous Publications. United States Department of Agriculture. Soil Conservation Service
Misc Publ Tex Agr Exp Sta — Miscellaneous Publications. Texas Agricultural Experiment Station
Misc Publ Univ KY Co-Op Ext Serv Agr Home Econ HE — Miscellaneous Publication. University of Kentucky. Cooperative Extension Service. Agriculture and Home Economics. HE
Misc Publ Univ MD Agr Exp Sta — Miscellaneous Publication. University of Maryland. Agricultural Experiment Station
Misc Publ Univ NC State Coll Agr Eng Dept Agr Econ — Miscellaneous Publication. University of North Carolina. State College of Agriculture and Engineering. Department of Agricultural Economics
Misc Publ USDA — Miscellaneous Publication. United States Department of Agriculture
Misc Publ US Dep Agric — Miscellaneous Publication. United States Department of Agriculture
Misc Publ Wash State Univ Coll Agr Ext Serv — Miscellaneous Publication. Washington State University. College of Agriculture. Extension Service
Misc Publ W Va Univ Coll Agr Agr Ext Serv — Miscellaneous Publication. West Virginia University. College of Agriculture. Agricultural Extension Service
Misc Pub US Dep Agric — Miscellaneous Publication. United States Department of Agriculture
Misc Rep Agric Exp Stn Univ Minn — Miscellaneous Report. Agricultural Experiment Station. University of Minnesota
Misc Rep (Arusha) Trop Pestic Res Inst — Miscellaneous Report (Arusha). Tropical Pesticides Research Institute
Misc Rep Lab Gov Chem (GB) — Miscellaneous Report. Laboratory of the Government Chemist (Great Britain)
Misc Rep Maine Agr Exp Sta — Miscellaneous Report. Maine Agricultural Experiment Station
Misc Rep Minn Agric Exp Stn — Miscellaneous Report. Minnesota Agricultural Experiment Station
Misc Rep Nebr Agr Exp Sta — Miscellaneous Report. Nebraska Agricultural Experiment Station
Misc Rep Ohio Div Geol Surv — Miscellaneous Report. Ohio Division of Geological Survey
Misc Rep Res Inst Nat Resourc (Tokyo) — Miscellaneous Reports. Research Institute for Natural Resources (Tokyo)
Misc Rep Univ Minn Agr Exp Sta — Miscellaneous Report. University of Minnesota. Agricultural Experiment Station
Misc Rep Univ Minn Agric Exp Stn — Miscellaneous Report. University of Minnesota Agricultural Experiment Station
Misc Rep Yamashina Inst Ornithol — Miscellaneous Reports. Yamashina Institute for Ornithology
Misc Ser ND Geol Surv — Miscellaneous Series. North Dakota Geological Survey
Misc Stor Lig — Miscellanea di Storia Ligure
Misc Zool — Miscelanea Zoologica
MIS Diato — Mineral Industry Surveys. Diatomite
Mises Jour Cardiol — Mises a Jour Cardiologiques
Mises Jour Sci — Mises a Jour Scientifiques [*France*]
Mises Point Chim Anal Pure Appl Anal Bromatol — Mises au Point de Chimie Analytique, Pure, et Appliquee et d'Analyse Bromatologique
MIS Explsv — Mineral Industry Surveys. Explosives
MIS Feldsp — Mineral Industry Surveys. Feldspar and Related Minerals
MIS Fluor — Mineral Industry Surveys. Fluorspar in 1975
Mis Fra — Miscellanea Francescana
MIS Gold — Mineral Industry Surveys. Gold and Silver
MIS Graph — Mineral Industry Surveys. Natural Graphite
MIS Gypsum — Mineral Industry Surveys. Gypsum
MISIA — Memoirs. Institute of Scientific and Industrial Research. Osaka University
MIS Iodine — Mineral Industry Surveys. Iodine. Annual Advance Summary
MIS Iron O — Mineral Industry Surveys. Iron Ore
MIS Ir Ox — Mineral Industry Surveys. Iron Oxide Pigments
MIS I & S — Mineral Industry Surveys. Iron and Steel Scrap
MIS Lead — Mineral Industry Surveys. Lead Industry
MIS Lith — Mineral Industry Surveys. Lithium
MIS Mercury — Mineral Industry Surveys. Mercury
MIS Moly — Mineral Industry Surveys. Molybdenum
MIS Nickel — Mineral Industry Surveys. Nickel
MIS Nitro — Mineral Industry Surveys. Nitrogen
MISO — Materialy i Issledovanija Smolenskoj Oblasti
MisP — Miscellanea Phonetica
MIS Peat — Mineral Industry Surveys. Advance Data on Peat
MIS Perlit — Mineral Industry Surveys. Perlite
MIS Phos R — Mineral Industry Surveys. Phosphate Rock
MIS Plat — Mineral Industry Surveys. Platinum
MIS P Magn — Mineral Industry Surveys. Primary Magnesium
MIS Potash — Mineral Industry Surveys. Potash. Annual Advance Summary
MIS Pumice — Mineral Industry Surveys. Pumice and Volcanic Cinder
MIS Qtly — Mineral Industry Surveys. Quarterly
Mis R — Missionary Review of the World
Miss — Missiology
Miss Acad Sci J — Mississippi Academy of Sciences. Journal

Miss Acad Sci Jour — Mississippi Academy of Sciences. Journal
Miss Ag Exp — Mississippi. Agricultural Experiment Station. Publications
Miss Agr Exp Sta B — Mississippi. Agricultural Experiment Station. Bulletin
Miss Agric Exp Stn Annu Rep — Mississippi. Agricultural Experiment Station. Annual Report
Miss Agric Exp Stn Circ — Mississippi. Agricultural Experiment Station. Circular
Miss Agric Exp Stn Tech Bull — Mississippi. Agricultural Experiment Station. Technical Bulletin
Miss Agric For Exp Stn Annu Rep — Mississippi. Agricultural and Forestry Experiment Station. Annual Report
Miss Agric For Exp Stn Res Rep — Mississippi. Agricultural and Forestry Experiment Station. Research Report
MIS Salt — Mineral Industry Surveys. Salt
MIS Sand — Mineral Industry Surveys. Sand and Gravel
Miss Board Water Comm Bull — Mississippi. Board of Water Commissioners. Bulletin
Miss CL Rev — Mississippi College. Law Review
Miss Col LR — Mississippi College. Law Review
Miss Dent Assoc J — Mississippi Dental Association. Journal
MIS Sel — Mineral Industry Surveys. Selenium
Miss Farm Res — Mississippi Farm Research. Mississippi Agricultural Experiment Station
MissFR — Mississippi Folklore Register
Miss Geol — Mississippi Geology
Miss Geol Econ Topogr Surv Inf Ser MGS — Mississippi. Geological, Economic, and Topographical Survey. Information Series MGS
Miss Geol Surv Bull — Mississippi. Geological, Economic, and Topographical Survey. Bulletin
Miss G S B — Mississippi. Geological Survey. Bulletin
MissHisp — Missionalia Hispanica
Miss His S — Mississippi Historical Society. Publications
Miss Hist Soc Publ — Mississippi Historical Society. Publications
Missio — Missiology
MissionArchFrMem — Memoire. Mission Archeologique Francaise au Caire
Missionary R — Missionary Review
Mission Hisp — Missionalia Hispanica [*Madrid*]
Mission Rev — Missionary Review
Mississippi Geol Econ and Topog Survey Bull — Mississippi. Geological, Economic, and Topographical Survey. Bulletin
Mississippi Med Rec — Mississippi Medical Record
Mississippi Val J Busin Econ — Mississippi Valley Journal of Business and Economics
Miss Law J — Mississippi Law Journal
Miss Lib News — Mississippi Library News
Miss L J — Mississippi Law Journal
Miss Med — Missouri Medicine
MIS Sod C — Mineral Industry Surveys. Sodium Compounds Annual
Missouri Bot Garden Annals — Missouri Botanical Garden. Annals
Missouri Geol Survey and Water Resources Educ Ser — Missouri. Geological Survey and Water Resources. Educational Series
Missouri Geol Survey and Water Resources Inf Circ — Missouri. Geological Survey and Water Resources. Information Circular
Missouri Geol Survey and Water Resources Report — Missouri. Geological Survey and Water Resources. Report
Missouri Geol Survey and Water Resources Rept Inv — Missouri. Geological Survey and Water Resources. Report of Investigations
Missouri Geol Survey and Water Resources Spec Pub — Missouri. Geological Survey and Water Resources. Special Publication
Missouri Law R — Missouri Law Review
MissQ — Mississippi Quarterly
Miss Quart — Mississippi Quarterly
Miss R — Mississippi Review
Miss RN — Mississippi RN
Miss & Roc — Missiles and Rockets
Miss Rom — Missale Romanum
Miss State Geol Surv Bull — Mississippi State Geological Survey. Bulletin
Miss State Geol Survey Bull Circ — Mississippi State Geological Survey. Bulletin. Circular
Miss State Univ Agr Expt Sta Tech Bull — Mississippi State University. Agricultural Experiment Station. Technical Bulletin
MIS Sulfur — Mineral Industry Surveys. Sulfur
Miss Val Hist R — Mississippi Valley Historical Review
Miss Val Hist Rev — Mississippi Valley Historical Review. A Journal of American History
Miss V His R — Mississippi Valley Historical Review
MIS Talc — Mineral Industry Surveys. Talc, Soapstone, and Pyrophyllite
MISTB — Transactions. Missouri Academy of Science
MIS Tin — Mineral Industry Surveys. Tin
MIS Titanm — Mineral Industry Surveys. Titanium
MIS Tungst — Mineral Industry Surveys. Tungsten
Mita J Econ — Mita Journal of Economics
Mitchurin Beweg — Mitchurin Bewegung
MIT Fluid Mech Lab Publ — Massachusetts Institute of Technology. Fluid Mechanics Laboratory. Publication

MIT Hydrodyn Lab Tech Rep — MIT [*Massachusetts Institute of Technology*] Hydrodynamics Laboratory. Technical Report
Mit J — Mittellateinisches Jahrbuch
MIT (Mass Inst Technol) Press Res Monogr — MIT (Massachusetts Institute of Technology) Press. Research Monograph
MIT Press Res Monogr — MIT [*Massachusetts Institute of Technology*] Press. Research Monograph
MIT Press Ser Comput Sci — MIT [*Massachusetts Institute of Technology*] Press. Series in Computer Science
MIT Press Ser Signal Process Optim Control — MIT [*Massachusetts Institute of Technology*] Press. Series in Signal Processing. Optimization and Control
MIT Ralph M Parsons Lab Water Resour Hydrodyn Rep — Massachusetts Institute of Technology. School of Engineering. Ralph M. Parsons Laboratory for Water Resources and Hydrodynamics. Report
MitrOlt — Mitropolia Olteniei
Mitrop Olteniei — Mitropolia Olteniei
Mitsubishi Denki Lab Rep — Mitsubishi Denki Laboratory Reports
Mitsubishi Electr Adv — Mitsubishi Electric Advance
Mitsubishi Electr Eng — Mitsubishi Electric Engineer
Mitsubishi Heavy Ind Mitsubishi Tech Bull — Mitsubishi Heavy Industries. Mitsubishi Technical Bulletin
Mitsubishi Heavy Ind Tech Rev — Mitsubishi Heavy Industries Technical Review
Mitsubishi Plast Technol — Mitsubishi Plastics Technology [*Japan*]
Mitsubishi Steel Manuf Tech Rev — Mitsubishi Steel Manufacturing Technical Review
Mitsubishi Tech Bull — Mitsubishi Technical Bulletin
Mitsubishi Tech Rev — Mitsubishi Heavy Industries Technical Review
Mitsubishi Tech Rev — Mitsubishi Technical Review
Mitsui Tech Rev — Mitsui Technical Review
Mitsui Zosen Tech Rev — Mitsui Zosen Technical Review
Mitt (Agen) — Mitteilungen (Agen)
Mitt Agrarwiss Fak Mosonmagyarovar (Ung) — Mitteilungen. Agrarwissenschaftliche Fakultaet zu Mosonmagyarovar (Ungarn)
Mitt Agrarwiss Hochsch Mosonmagyarovar (Ung) — Mitteilungen. Agrarwissenschaftliche Hochschule zu Mosonmagyarovar (Ungarn)
Mitt Akad Wiss UdSSR — Mitteilungen. Akademie der Wissenschaften der UdSSR
Mitt Allg Pathol Pathol Anat — Mitteilungen ueber Allgemeine Pathologie und Pathologische Anatomie
Mitt Alpenl Geol Ver — Mitteilungen. Alpenlaendischer Geologische Verein
Mitt Anthropol Ges Wien — Mitteilungen. Anthropologische Gesellschaft in Wien
Mitt Arbeitsgem Florist Kartierung Bayerns — Mitteilungen. Arbeitsgemeinschaft zur Floristischen Kartierung Bayerns
Mitt Arbeitsgem Florist Schleswig-Holstein Hamburg — Mitteilungen. Arbeitsgemeinschaft fuer Floristik in Schleswig-Holstein und Hamburg
Mitt Arbeitsgem Geobot Schleswig-Holstein Hamburg — Mitteilungen. Arbeitsgemeinschaft Geobotanik in Schleswig-Holstein und Hamburg
Mitt Archaeol Inst Ung Akad Wiss — Mitteilungen. Archaeologisches Institut der Ungarischen Akademie der Wissenschaften
Mitt Astron Ges — Mitteilungen. Astronomische Gesellschaft [*German Federal Republic*]
Mitt Bad Geol Landesanst — Mitteilungen. Badische Geologische Landesanstalt
Mitt Bayer Landesanst Tier Grub Muenchen — Mitteilungen. Bayerische Landesanstalt fuer Tierzucht in Grub bei Muenchen
Mitt Bayer Landesanst Tierz Grub — Mitteilungen. Bayerische Landesanstalt fuer Tierzucht in Grub bei Muenchen
Mitt Bayer Staatssamml Palaeontol Hist Geol — Mitteilungen. Bayerische Staatssammlung fuer Palaeontologie und Historische Geologie
Mitt Berl Ges Anthropol — Mitteilungen. Berliner Gesellschaft fuer Anthropologie, Ethnologie, und Urgeschichte
Mitt B Fors — Mitteilungen. Bundesforschungsanstalt fuer Forst- und Holzwirtschaft
Mitt Biol Bund Anst Ld- u Forstw — Mitteilungen. Biologische Bundesanstalt fuer Land- und Forstwirtschaft
Mitt Biol Bundesanst Land- u Forstw — Mitteilungen. Biologische Bundesanstalt fuer Land- und Forstwirtschaft
Mitt Biol Bundesanst Land-Forstwirt (Berlin-Dahlem) — Mitteilungen. Biologische Bundesanstalt fuer Land- und Forstwirtschaft (Berlin-Dahlem)
Mitt Biol Bundesanst Land-Forstwirtsch (Berl-Dahlem) — Mitteilungen. Biologische Bundesanstalt fuer Land- und Forstwirtschaft (Berlin-Dahlem)
MittBl Chem Ges DDR — Mitteilungsblatt. Chemische Gesellschaft der Deutschen Demokratischen Republik
Mitt Bot Gart Mus Berl-Dahlem — Mitteilungen. Botanischer Garten und Museum Berlin-Dahlem
Mitt Bot Staatssamml Muench — Mitteilungen. Botanische Staatssammlung Muenchen
Mitt Brennstoffinst (Freiberg) — Mitteilungen. Brennstoffinstitut (Freiberg)
Mitt Bundesforschanst Forst- u Holzw — Mitteilungen. Bundesforschungsanstalt fuer Forst- und Holzwirtschaft

Mitt Bundesforsch (Reinbek/Hamburg) — Mitteilungen. Bundesforschungsanstalt fuer Forst- und Holzwirtschaft (Reinbek bei Hamburg)
Mitt Bundesforschungsanst Forst Holzwirtsch — Mitteilungen. Bundesforschungsanstalt fuer Forst- und Holzwirtschaft
Mitt Chem Forschungsinst Wirtsch Oesterr — Mitteilungen. Chemisches Forschungsinstitut der Wirtschaft Oesterreichs
Mitt Dachpappen Ind — Mitteilungen aus der Dachpappen-Industrie
Mitt DDR — Mitteilungen. Wissenschaftlichen Bibliothekswesen der Deutschen Demokratischen Republik
Mitt Deut Landwirt Ges — Mitteilungen. Deutsche Landwirtschafts Gesellschaft
Mitt Deutschen Ges M Orients — Mitteilungen. Deutsche Gesellschaft fuer Musik des Orients
Mitt Direktor Osterr Nat Bank — Mitteilungen. Direktorium der Oesterreichischen National Bank
Mitt DLG — Mitteilungen. Deutsche Landwirtschafts-Gesellschaft [West Germany]
Mitt Dt Ent Ges — Mitteilungen. Deutsche Entomologische Gesellschaft
Mitt Dt LandsGes (Frankfurt/Main) — Mitteilungen. Deutsche Landwirtschafts-Gesellschaft (Frankfurt/Main)
Mitt Dt Landw Ges — Mitteilungen. Deutsche Landwirtschafts Gesellschaft
Mitt Dt Pharm Ges — Mitteilungen. Deutsche Pharmazeutische Gesellschaft
Mitt Dtsch Archaeol Inst Abt Kairo — Mitteilungen. Deutsches Archaeologisches Institut. Abteilung Kairo
Mitt Dtsch Dendrol Ges — Mitteilungen. Deutsche Dendrologische Gesellschaft
Mitt Dtsche Ges Musik Orients — Mitteilungen. Deutsche Gesellschaft fuer Musik des Orients
Mitt Dtsch Entomol Ges — Mitteilungen. Deutsche Entomologische Gesellschaft
Mitt Dtsch Forschungsges Blechverarb Oberflaechenbehandl — Mitteilungen. Deutsche Forschungsgesellschaft fuer Blechverarbeitung und Oberflaechenbehandlung
Mitt Dtsch Forschungsinst Textilind Dresden — Mitteilungen. Deutsches Forschungsinstitut fuer Textilindustrie in Dresden
Mitt Dtsch Ges Holzforsch — Mitteilungen. Deutsche Gesellschaft fuer Holzforschung
Mitt Dtsch Landwirtsch Ges — Mitteilungen. Deutsche Landwirtschafts Gesellschaft
Mitt Dtsch Pharm Ges — Mitteilungen. Deutsche Pharmazeutische Gesellschaft
Mitteilungsbl Abt Mineral Landesmus Joanneum — Mitteilungsblatt. Abteilung fuer Mineralogie am Landesmuseum Joanneum [Austria]
Mitteilungsbl Bundesanst Fleischforsch — Mitteilungsblatt. Bundesanstalt fuer Fleischforschung
Mitteilungsbl Chem Ges DDR — Mitteilungsblatt. Chemische Gesellschaft der Deutschen Demokratischen Republik [East Germany]
Mitteilungsbl Chem Ges Dtsch Demokr Repub Beih — Mitteilungsblatt. Chemische Gesellschaft der Deutschen Demokratischen Republik. Beiheft
Mitteilungsbl Dtsch Ges Sonnenenergie — Mitteilungsblatt. Deutsche Gesellschaft fuer Sonnenenergie [West Germany]
Mitteilungsbl Dtsch Keram Ges — Mitteilungsblatt. Deutsche Keramische Gesellschaft
Mitteilungsbl Fraunhofer-Ges — Mitteilungsblatt. Fraunhofer-Gesellschaft zur Foerderung der Angewandten Forschung EV
Mitteilungsbl Fraunhofer-Ges Foerd Angew Forsch — Mitteilungsblatt. Fraunhofer-Gesellschaft zur Foerderung der Angewandten Forschung
Mitteilungsbl GDCh Fachgruppe Lebensmittelchem Gerichtl Chem — Mitteilungsblatt. GDCh [Gesellschaft Deutscher Chemiker] Fachgruppe Lebensmittelchemie und Gerichtliche Chemie
Mitteilungsbl Jungen Gerberei Tech — Mitteilungsblaetter fuer den Jungen Gerberei-Techniker
Mitteilungsbl Strahlungsmessgeraete — Mitteilungsblaetter Strahlungsmessgeraete [West Germany]
Mitt Eisenhuettenmaenn Inst Tech Hochsch (Aachen) — Mitteilungen. Eisenhuettenmaennisches Institut der Technischen Hochschule (Aachen)
Mitt Ent Ges (Basel) — Mitteilungen. Entomologische Gesellschaft (Basel)
Mitt Entomol Ges (Basel) — Mitteilungen. Entomologische Gesellschaft (Basel)
Mitt Entomol Ges BRD — Mitteilungen. Entomologische Gesellschaft in der Bundesrepublik Deutschland
Mitt Florist-Soziol Arbeitsgem — Mitteilungen. Floristische-Soziologische Arbeitsgemeinschaft
Mitt Forsch Konstr Stahlbau — Mitteilungen ueber Forschung und Konstruktion in Stahlbau
Mitt Forschungsanst Gutehoffnungshuette Konzerns — Mitteilungen. Forschungsanstalten von Gutehoffnungshuette-Konzerns
Mitt Forschungsinst Ver Stahlwerke Ag (Dortmund) — Mitteilungen. Forschungsinstitut der Vereinigten Stahlwerke Aktiengesellschaft (Dortmund)
Mitt Forschungslab AGFA Gevaert AG (Leverkusen Muenchen) — Mitteilungen. Forschungslaboratorien der AGFA-Gevaert AG (Leverkusen-Muenchen)

Mitt Forschungslab AGFA (Leverkusen) — Mitteilungen. Forschungslaboratorium AGFA (Leverkusen)
Mitt Forstl Bundesversuchsanstalt (Mariabrunn) — Mitteilungen. Forstliche Bundes-Versuchsanstalt (Mariabrunn) [Austria]
Mitt Forstl Bundes-Versuchsanst (Mariabrunn) — Mitteilungen. Forstliche Bundes-Versuchsanstalt (Mariabrunn)
Mitt Forstl Bundes-Versuchsanst (Wien) — Mitteilungen. Forstliche Bundes-Versuchsanstalt (Wien)
Mitt Forstl VersAnst — Mitteilungen. Forstliche Bundes-Versuchsanstalt
Mitt Geb Lebensmittelunters Hyg — Mitteilungen aus dem Gebiete der Lebensmitteluntersuchung und Hygiene
Mitt Geb Lebensmittelunters Hyg Trav Chim Aliment Hyg — Mitteilungen aus den Gebiete der Lebensmitteluntersuchung und Hygiene. Travaux de Chimie Alimentaire et d'Hygiene
Mitt Geb Naturwiss Tech — Mitteilungen aus den Gebieten der Naturwissenschaft und Technik
Mitt Geodaet Inst Tech Univ Graz — Mitteilungen. Geodaetische Institut der Technischen Universitaet Graz
Mitt Geogr Ges Hamb — Mitteilungen. Geographische Gesellschaft in Hamburg
Mitt Geol Ges Wien — Mitteilungen. Geologische Gesellschaft in Wien
Mitt Geol Inst Eidg Tech Hochsch Univ Zurich — Mitteilungen. Geologisches Institut der Eidgenoessischen Technischen Hochschule und der Universitaet Zuerich
Mitt Geol Palaeontol Inst Univ Hamburg — Mitteilungen. Geologisch-Palaeontologische Institut. Universitaet Hamburg
Mitt Geol Staatsinst Hamb — Mitteilungen. Geologisches Staatsinstitut in Hamburg
Mitt Ges Bayerische Mg — Mitteilungsblatt. Gesellschaft fuer Bayerische Musikgeschichte
Mitt Gesch Med Naturwiss Tech — Mitteilungen zur Geschichte der Medizin der Naturwissenschaften und Technik
Mitt Ges Geol Bergbaustud Oesterr — Mitteilungen. Gesellschaft der Geologie- und Bergbaustudenten in Oesterreich
Mitt Ges Geol Bergbaustud Wien — Mitteilungen. Gesellschaft der Geologie- und Bergbaustudenten in Wien
Mitt Grenzgeb Med u Chir — Mitteilungen aus den Grenzgebieten der Medizin und Chirurgie
Mitt Grossforschungszentrum Chemieanlagen — Mitteilungen. Grossforschungszentrum Chemieanlagen
Mitt Hamb Staatskrankenanst — Mitteilungen. Hamburgische Staatskrankenanstalten
Mitt Hamb Zool Mus Inst — Mitteilungen. Hamburgisches Zoologische Museum und Institut
Mitt Hans Pfitzner Ges — Mitteilungen. Hans-Pfitzner-Gesellschaft
Mitt Hess Landesforstverw — Mitteilungen. Hessische Landesforstverwaltung
Mitt Hoh Bundeslehr- u VersAnst Wein- Obst- u Gartenb — Mitteilungen. Hohere Bundeslehr- und Versuchsanstalten fuer Wein-, Obst-, und Gartenbau, Wien-Klosterneuburg und fuer Bienenkunde. Wien-Grinzing. A. Rebe und Wein. B. Obst und Garten
Mitt Ind Forschungszent Chemieanlagen — Mitteilungen. Industrie-Forschungszentrum Chemieanlagen
Mitt Inst Aerodyn — Mitteilungen. Institut fuer Aerodynamik an der Eidgenoessischen Technischen Hochschule in Zuerich
Mitt Inst Allgemeine Bot (Hamb) — Mitteilungen. Institut fuer Allgemeine Botanik (Hamburg)
Mitt Inst Baustatik — Mitteilungen. Institut fuer Baustatik. Eidgenoessische Technische Hochschule in Zuerich
Mitt Inst Bautech — Mitteilungen. Institut fuer Bautechnik
Mitt Inst Colombo-Aleman Invest Cient "Punta De Betin" — Mitteilungen. Instituto Colombo-Aleman de Investigaciones Cientificas "Punta De Betin"
Mitt Inst Grundbau Bodenmech Eidg Tech Hochsch (Zurich) — Mitteilungen. Institut fuer Grundbau und Bodenmechanik. Eidgenoessische Technische Hochschule (Zuerich)
Mitt Inst Hydraul Gewaesserkd — Mitteilungen. Institut fuer Hydraulik und Gewaesserkunde. Technische Hochschule [Muenchen]
Mitt Inst Orientforsch Dtsch Akad Wiss Berl — Mitteilungen. Institut fuer Orientforschung. Deutsche Akademie der Wissenschaften zu Berlin
Mitt Inst Textiltechnol Chemiefasern Rudolstadt — Mitteilungen. Institut fuer Textiltechnologie der Chemiefasern Rudolstadt
Mitt Inst Therm Turbomasch — Mitteilungen. Institut fuer Thermische Turbomaschinen. Eidgenoessische Technische Hochschule [Zuerich]
Mitt Int Moor-Torf-Ges — Mitteilungen. Internationale Moor- und Torf-Gesellschaft
Mitt Int Stiftung Mozarteum — Mitteilungen. Internationale Stiftung Mozarteum
Mitt Int Ver Saatgutpruefung — Mitteilungen. Internationale Vereinigung fuer Saatgutpruefung
Mitt Int Ver Theor Angew Limnol — Mitteilungen. Internationale Vereinigung fuer Theoretische und Angewandte Limnologie
Mitt Josef Haas Ges — Mitteilungsblatt. Josef-Haas-Gesellschaft
Mitt (Kairo) — Mitteilungen. Deutsches Institut fuer Aegyptische Altertumskunde (Kairo)
Mitt Kaiser Wilhelm Inst Eisenforsch Duesseldorf — Mitteilungen. Kaiser-Wilhelm-Institut fuer Eisenforschung zu Duesseldorf

Mitt Kali Forsch Anst — Mitteilungen. Kali-Forschungs-Anstalt

Mitt K Anst Land-u Forstw — Mitteilungen. Kaiserliche Anstalt fuer Land- und Forstwirtschaft

Mitt Klosterneuburg — Mitteilungen. Klosterneuburg

Mitt Kohle Eisenforsch GmbH — Mitteilungen. Kohle- und Eisenforschung GmbH

Mitt Kraftwerksanlagenbau (DDR) — Mitteilungen. Kraftwerksanlagenbau (DDR)

Mitt Kunst — Mitteilungen. Kunsthistorische Institut in Florenz

Mitt Lab Geol Dienstes (DDR) — Mitteilungen. Laboratorien des Geologischen Dienstes (DDR)

Mitt Lab Preuss Geol Landesanst — Mitteilungen. Laboratorien der Preusseschen Geologischen Landesanstalt

Mitt Landbau Agric Bull — Mitteilungen fuer den Landbau. Agricultural Bulletin

Mitt Landesanst Tierz Grub — Mitteilungen. Landesanstalt fuer Tierzucht in Grub

Mitt Landw (Berl) — Mitteilungen fuer die Landwirtschaft (Berlin)

Mitt Landwirtsch — Mitteilungen fuer die Landwirtschaft

Mitt Landwirtsch Versuchsstellen (Ung) A — Mitteilungen. Landwirtschaftliche Versuchsstellen (Ungarn). A. Pflanzenbau

Mitt Landwirtsch Versuchsstellen (Ung) C — Mitteilungen. Landwirtschaftliche Versuchsstellen (Ungarn). C. Gartenbau

Mitt Markscheidewes — Mitteilungen aus dem Markscheidewesen [*West Germany*]

Mitt Materialpruefungsanst Tech Hochsch (Darmstadt) — Mitteilungen. Materialpruefungsanstalt. Technische Hochschule (Darmstadt)

Mitt Math Ges DDR — Mitteilungen. Mathematische Gesellschaft. Deutsche Demokratische Republik

Mitt Math Gesellsch (Hamburg) — Mitteilungen. Mathematische Gesellschaft (Hamburg)

Mitt Math Sem (Giessen) — Mitteilungen. Mathematisches Seminar (Giessen)

Mitt Max-Planck-Ges — Mitteilungen. Max-Planck-Gesellschaft

Mitt Max-Planck-Ges Foerd Wiss — Mitteilungen. Max-Planck-Gesellschaft zur Foerderung der Wissenschaften

Mitt Max-Planck-Inst Stroemungsforsch Aerodyn Versuchsanst — Mitteilungen. Max-Planck-Institut fuer Stroemungsforschung und der Aerodynamischen Versuchsanstalt

Mitt Max Reger Inst — Mitteilungen. Max Reger Institut

Mitt Med Gesellsch Tokyo — Mitteilungen. Medizinische Gesellschaft zu Tokyo

Mitt Med Ges Tokyo — Mitteilungen. Medizinische Gesellschaft zu Tokyo

Mitt Mitglieder Tech Ueberwach-Ver (Bayern) — Mitteilungen fuer die Mitglieder des Technischen Ueberwachungs-Vereins (Bayern)

Mitt MPI Aeron — Mitteilungen. Max-Planck-Institut fuer Aeronomie

Mitt MPI Stroemungsforsch Aerodyn Versuchsanst — Mitteilungen. Max-Planck-Institut fuer Stroemungsforschung und der Aerodynamischen Versuchsanstalt

Mitt Muench Ent Ges — Mitteilungen. Muenchener Entomologische Gesellschaft

Mitt Muench Entomol Ges — Mitteilungen. Muenchener Entomologische Gesellschaft

Mitt Mus Voelkerk Hamburg — Mitteilungen. Museum fuer Voelkerkunde in Hamburg

Mitt Mus Voelkerk Leipzig — Mitteilungen. Museum fuer Voelkerkunde zu Leipzig

Mitt Naturforsch Ges Bern — Mitteilungen. Naturforschende Gesellschaft in Bern

Mitt Naturwiss Ges Winterthur — Mitteilungen. Naturwissenschaftliche Gesellschaft in Winterthur

Mitt Naturwiss Mus Stadt Aschaffenburg — Mitteilungen. Naturwissenschaftliches Museum der Stadt Aschaffenburg

Mitt Naturwiss Ver Steiermark — Mitteilungen. Naturwissenschaftlicher Verein fuer Steiermark

Mitt Num Ges — Mitteilungen. Numismatische Gesellschaft

Mitt Obstbauversuchsring Alten Landes — Mitteilungen. Obstbauversuchsring des Alten Landes

Mitt ObstbVersAnst — Mitteilungen der Obstbauversuchsanstalt

Mitt ObstbVersuchsr Alten Landes — Mitteilungen. Obstbauversuchsringes des Alten Landes

Mitt Obst Garten — Mitteilungen Obst und Garten

Mitt Oesterreich Ges Mw — Mitteilungen. Oesterreichische Gesellschaft fuer Musikwissenschaft

Mitt Oesterr Geol Ges — Mitteilungen. Oesterreichische Geologische Gesellschaft

Mitt Oesterr Ges Holzforsch — Mitteilungen. Oesterreichische Gesellschaft fuer Holzforschung

Mitt Oesterr Ges (Vienna) — Institut fuer Oesterreichische Geschichtsforschung. Mitteilungen (Vienna)

Mitt Oesterr Mineral Ges — Mitteilungen. Oesterreichische Mineralogische Gesellschaft

Mitt Oesterr Sanitaetsverwalt (Vienna) — Mitteilungen. Oesterreichische Sanitaetsverwaltung (Vienna)

Mitt O Geog — Mitteilungen. Oesterreichische Geographische Gesellschaft

Mitt Ost Bodenk Ges — Mitteilungen. Oesterreichische Bodenkundliche Gesellschaft

Mitt Pollichia Pfaelz Ver Naturkd Naturschutz — Mitteilungen. Pollichia des Pfaelzischen Vereins fuer Naturkunde und Naturschutz

Mitt Reichsamts Bodenforsch Zweigstelle Wien — Mitteilungen. Reichsamt Bodenforschung. Zweigstelle Wien

Mitt Rheinische Mg — Mitteilungen. Arbeitsgemeinschaft fuer Rheinische Musikgeschichte

Mitt Schweiz Anst Forstl Versuchsw — Mitteilungen. Schweizerische Anstalt fuer das Forstliche Versuchswesen

Mitt Schweiz Anst Forstl Versuchswes — Mitteilungen. Schweizerische Anstalt fuer das Forstliche Versuchswesen

Mitt Schweiz Apoth Ver — Mitteilungen. Schweizerischer Apotheker-Verein

Mitt Schweiz Ent Ges — Mitteilungen. Schweizerische Entomologische Gesellschaft

Mitt Schweiz Entomol Ges — Mitteilungen. Schweizerische Entomologische Gesellschaft

Mitt Schweiz Entomol Ges Bull Soc Entomol Suisse — Mitteilungen. Schweizerische Entomologische Gesellschaft. Bulletin de la Societe Entomologique Suisse

Mitt Schweiz Fleckviehzuchtverb — Mitteilungen. Schweizerischer Fleckviehzuchtverband

Mitt Schweiz Landw — Mitteilungen fuer die Schweizerische Landwirtschaft

Mitt Schweiz Landwirt — Mitteilungen fuer die Schweizerische Landwirtschaft

Mitt Schweiz Landwirtsch — Mitteilungen fuer die Schweizerische Landwirtschaft

Mitt Schweiz Mf Ges — Mitteilungsblatt. Schweizerische Musikforschende Gesellschaft

Mitt Staatl Heimat Schlossmus Burgk/Saale — Mitteilungen. Staatliches Heimat und Schlossmuseum Burgk/Saale

Mitt Staatsinst Allg Bot Hamb — Mitteilungen. Staatsinstitut fuer Allgemeine Botanik Hamburg

Mitt Staatsinst Allg Bot Hamburg — Mitteilungen. Staatsinstitut fuer Allgemeine Botanik Hamburg

Mitt Steiermarkisches Landesmus (Graz) Mus Bergbau Geol Tec — Mitteilung- Steiermarkisches Landesmuseum (Graz). Museum fuer Bergbau, Geologie, und Technik

Mitt Stforstverw Bayerns — Mitteilungen. Staatsforstverwaltung Bayern

Mitt Tech Univ Braunschweig — Mitteilungen. Technische Universitaet Carolo-Wilhelmina zu Braunschweig

Mitt Tech Univ Carolo-Wilheimina — Mitteilungen. Technische Universitaet Carolo-Wilheimina [*West Germany*]

Mitt Textilforsch Anst Krefeld — Mitteilungen. Textilforschungs-Anstalt Krefeld

Mitt Tieraerztl Fak Reichsuniv Gent — Mitteilungen. Tieraerztliche Fakultaet der Reichsuniversitaet Gent

Mitt Tieraerztl Praxis Preuss Staate — Mitteilungen. Tieraerztliche Praxis im Preussischen Staate

Mitt Vaterl Gesch St Gall — Mitteilungen zur Vaterlaendischen Geschichte. Hrsg. Vom Historischen Verein in St. Gallen

Mitt Ver Dtsch Emailfachl — Mitteilungen. Verein Deutscher Emailfachleute [*West Germany*]

Mitt Ver Dtsch Emailfachleute — Mitteilungen. Verein Deutscher Emailfachleute

Mitt Verein Schweiz Versicherungsmath — Vereinigung Schweizerischer Versicherungsmathematiker. Mitteilungen

Mitt Ver Forstl Standortskunde ForstpflZucht — Mitteilungen. Verein fuer Forstliche Standortskunde und Forstpflanzenzuechtung

Mitt Ver Grosskesselbesitzer — Mitteilungen. Vereinigung der Grosskesselbesitzer

Mitt Ver Grosskesselbetr — Mitteilungen. Vereinigung der Grosskesselbetreiber

Mitt Ver Metallwerke Ranshofen Berndorf — Mitteilungen. Vereinigte Metallwerke Ranshofen-Berndorf

Mitt Versuchsergeb Bundesanst Pflanzenbau Samenpruf Wien — Mitteilungen. Versuchsergebnissen der Bundesanstalt fuer Pflanzenbau und Samenpruefung in Wien

Mitt Versuchsstn Gaerungsgewerbe Wein — Mitteilungen. Versuchsstation fuer das Gaerungsgewerbe in Wein

Mitt Vers Wasserbau Hydrol Glaziologie — Mitteilungen. Versuchsanstalt fuer Wasserbau, Hydrologie, und Glaziologie

Mitt VGB (Tech Ver Grosskraftwerksbetr) — Mitteilungen. VGB (Technische Vereinigung der Grosskraftwerksbetreiber) [*German Federal Republic*]

Mitt VOB — Mitteilungen. Vereinigung Oesterreichischer Bibliothek

Mitt Zentr Soz Arbeitsgemeinsch — Mitteilungsblatt. Zentrale Sozialistische Arbeitsgemeinschaft

Mitt Zool Mus Berl — Mitteilungen. Zoologisches Museum in Berlin

MIWPD — Mid-Atlantic Industrial Waste Conference. Proceedings

Miyagi Prefect Inst Public Health. Annu Rep — Miyagi Prefectural Institute of Public Health. Annual Report

MIZ — Journal. Arab Maritime Transport Academy

MJ — Le Monde Juif

MJ — Makedonski Jazik

MJ — Menorah Journal

MJ — Midwest Journal

MJ — Mining Journal

MJ — Mittellateinisches Jahrbuch

MJ — Moudjahik

MJ — Municipal Journal
MJ — Museum Journal
MJ — Music Journal
MJA — Medical Journal of Australia
MJASA — Mysore Journal of Agricultural Sciences
MJAUA — Medical Journal of Australia
MJB — Mindener Jahrbuch
MJB — Muenchener Jahrbuch der Bildenden Kunst
MJBK — Muenchener Jahrbuch der Bildenden Kunst
MJDSA — Mukogawa Joshi Daigaku Kiyo. Shizenkagakuhen
M Jeu — Musique en Jeu
MJH — Michigan Jewish History
MJIMB — Major Problems in Internal Medicine
MJL — Marketing Journal
MJLF — Midwestern Journal of Language and Folklore
MJN — Muenchener Juedische Nachrichten
MJP — Management Japan
MJPS — Midwest Journal of Political Science
MJR — Missouri Journal of Research in Music Education
MJSFA — Mises a Jour Scientifiques
MJTG — Malayan Journal of Tropical Geography
MJTOA — Mineralogical Journal (Tokyo)
MJudaica — Musica Judaica
MJugend — Musikalische Jugend
MJULAO — Communications. Instituti Forestalis Fenniae
MJV — Mitteilungen zur Juedischen Volkskunde
MK — Magyar Koenyvszemle
MK — Miesiecznik Koscielny
MK — Minzokugaku-Kenkyu [*Japanese Journal of Ethnology*]
MK — Mysl Karaimska
MKAI — Majallat Kulliyat al-Adab, al-Iskandariyyah
MKASA — Mikrochimica Acta. Supplement
MKAW — Mededeelingen. Koninklijke Nederlandsche Akademie van Wetenschappen. Afdeling Letterkunde
MKAWA — Mededelingen. Koninklijke Academie voor Wetenschappen. Letteren en Schone Kunsten van Belgie. Klasse der Wetenschappen
MKD — Handelspartner. Nederlands Duitse Handelscourant
MKDKA — Muroran Kogyo Daigaku Kenkyu Hokoku
MKE — Market Research Europe
MKEMA — Mikroelementy v Meditsine
MKIMP — Mirovoe Khoziaistvo i Mirovaia Politika
M Kirche — Musik und Kirche
MKK — Mal Kwa Kul [*Speech and Language*]
MKK — Mobelkultur. Fachzeitschrift fuer die Mobelwirtschaft
MKL — Mededelingen. Koninklijke Nederlandse Academie van Wetenschappen. Afdeling Letterkunde [*Elsevier Book Series*]
MKNA — Mededelingen. Koninklijke Nederlandsche Akademie van Wetenschappen. Afdeling Letterkunde
MKNAL — Mededelingen. Koninklijke Nederlandsche Akademie van Wetenschappen. Afdeling Letterkunde
MKNAWL — Mededelingen. Koninklijke Nederlandsche Akademie van Wetenschappen. Afdeling Letterkunde
MKO — Machinery Korea
MKOH — Mededeelingen. Kunst- en Oudheidkundigen Kring van Herenthals
MKOUA — Memoirs. Konan University. Science Series
MKQUA4 — Mankind Quarterly
MKS — Mon-Khmer Studies
MKT — Marketing Times
MKTG — Marketing
Mktg Dec — Marketing and Media Decisions
Mktg Demonst Leafl Minist Agric — Marketing Demonstration Leaflet. Ministry of Agriculture and Fisheries [*United Kingdom*]
Mktg and DE Today — Marketing and Distributive Education Today
Mktg Eur — Marketing in Europe
Mktg Hung — Marketing in Hungary
Mktg Leafl Minist Agric — Marketing Leaflet. Ministry of Agriculture and Fisheries [*United Kingdom*]
Mktg News — Marketing News
Mktg Times — Marketing Times
Mktg Ungarn — Marketing in Ungarn
Mkt Inform Guide — [*The*] Marketing Information Guide
Mkt & Media Decisions — Marketing and Media Decisions
MKTW — Marketing Week
MKUBA — Memoirs. College of Agriculture. Kyoto University
MKVAB — Mededeelingen. Koninklijke Vlaamse Akademie van Wetenschappen, Letteren en Schone Kunsten v Belgie
ML — Mennonite Life
Ml — Mladost
ML — Modern Languages
ML — Modern Liturgy
ML — Monthly Letter EMG
ML — Music and Letters
M & L — Music and Letters
MLA — MLA [*Modern Language Association of America*] International Bibliography of Books and Articles on the Modern Languages and Literature [*Database*]

MLA — Modern Language Abstracts
MLAANZ Newsletter — Maritime Law Association of Australia and New Zealand. Newsletter
M Labor R — Monthly Labor Review
M Lab R — Monthly Labor Review
MLA Int Bibl — Modern Language Association of America. International Bibliography
MLAN — Music Library Association. Notes
M Lang — Modern Languages
MLA Q — Missouri Library Association. Quarterly
MlatJb — Mittellateinisches Jahrbuch
MLB — Suesswarenmarkt. Fachzeitschrift fuer Markt, Marketing, und Merchandising von Suesswaren
MLD — Maandstatistiek van de Landbouw
MLDMA — Melody Maker
MLEGB — Metallurgical Engineer. Indian Institute of Technology (Bombay)
Mlek Listy — Mlekarske Listy [*Supplement of Prumysl Potravin*] [*Czechoslovakia*]
Mlek Listy (1975-) — Mlekatske Listy (1975-) [*Czechoslovakia*]
MLetters — Music and Letters
MLF — Microlog Fiche Service from Micromedia
MLF — Modern Language Forum
MLF — Modersmalslararnas Forening. Arsskrift
MLFA — Modersmalslararnas Forening. Arsskrift
MLG — Mitteilungen aus der Livlandischen Geschichte
MLI — Metropolitan Life Insurance Company. Statistical Bulletin
M Ling — Modeles Linguistiques
MLISB — Medical Instrumentation [*Arlington, VA*]
MLit — Miesiecznik Literacki
MLJ — Madras Law Journal
MLJ — Makerere Law Journal
MLJ — Malayan Law Journal
MLJ — Manitoba Law Journal
MLJ — Mississippi Law Journal
MLJ — Modern Language Journal
MLJ Supp — Malayan Law Journal. Supplement
Mlle — Mademoiselle
MLN — Modern Language Notes
MLN Bull — MLN [*Minnesota League for Nursing*] Bulletin
M L New — Malcolm Lowry Newsletter
MLNSBP — Mammalian Species
MLO — Medical Laboratory Observer
Mlody Tech — Mlody Technik [*Poland*]
MLOSA — Mededelingen. Landbouwhogeschool en Opzoekingsstations van de Staat te Gent
MLP — Monthly List of Publications
MLPSA — Monthly List of Publications of South Australian Interest Received in the State Library of South Australia
MLQ — Modern Language Quarterly
MIR — Mladinska Revija
MLR — Modern Language Review
MLR — Modern Law Review
MLR — Monthly Labor Review
MLS — Modern Language Studies
MLS — Multinational Business
MLT — Malaysia Industrial Digest
MLV — Bedrijfsontwikkeling; Maandblad voor Agrarische Produktie, Verwerking, en Afzet
MLVBA — Metallverarbeitung
MLVS — Mededelingen mit de Leidse Verzameling van Spijkerschrift Inscripties
MLW — Mountain Life and Work
Mlyn L — Mlynarske Listy
Mlyn Pek Prum Tech Skladovani Obili — Mlynsko-Pekarensky Prumysl a Technika Skladovani Obili
Mlyn Pol — Mlynarz Polski
Mlynsko-Pekar Prum Tech Sklad Obili — Mlynsko-Pekarensky Prumysl a Technika Skladovani Obili
MM — Maal og Minne
MM — Maclean's Magazine
MM — Madrider Mitteilungen
MM — Maitland Mercury
MM — Manufacturers' Monthly
MM — Mariner's Mirror
MM — Massachusetts Music News
MM — Masses and Mainstream
MM — Melody Maker
MM — Mining Magazine
MM — Miscellaneous Man
MM — Mitteilungen. Internationale Stiftung Mozarteum
MM — Modern Music
MM — Monuments et Memoires Publies par l'Academie des Inscriptions et Belles-Lettres
MM — Moody Monthly
MM — Muenchener Museum
MM — Music and Musicians

MMA — Management Accounting
MMA — Miscellanea Musicologica
MMA — Monographs on Mediterranean Antiquity
MMAD — Macallat al-Macma al-Limi al-Arabi Dimasq
MMADA — Modern Materials. Advances in Development and Applications
MMAF — Memoires. Mission Archeologique Francaise au Caire [Paris]
MMAFC — Memoires. Mission Archeologique Francaise au Caire [Paris]
MMAI — Monuments et Memoires Publies par l'Academie des Inscriptions et Belles-Lettres
MMAP — Memorias. Museos Arqueologicos Provinciales [Madrid]
MMASA — Modern Machine Shop
MMB — Monumenta Musicae Belgicae
MMB — Muenzen- und Medaillensammler Berichte aus allen Gebieten der Geld-, Muenzen-, und Medaillenkunde
MMC — Miscellanea Musicologica
MMDPB7 — Mammalia Depicta
MMEDA — Military Medicine
MMEDDC — Man and Medicine
M Medii Aevi — Musica Medii Aevi
MMERD — MER (Marine Engineers Review)
MMER Rep Dep Mech Eng Monash Univ — MMER Report. Department of Mechanical Engineering. Monash University
M Met Soc Am B — Mining and Metallurgical Society of America. Bulletin
MMFN — Manitoba Metis Federation News [Canada]
MMFQ — Milbank Memorial Fund. Quarterly. Health and Society
MMFSBQ — Museo Civico di Storia Naturale di Verona. Memorie. Fuori Serie
M Mg — Monatshefte fuer Musikgeschichte
MMGS — Melbourne Monographs in Germanic Studies
MMH — Montana: The Magazine of Western History
MMI — Maintenance Management International
MMI — Medical Microbiology and Immunology
M Misc — Midwestern Miscellany
MMK — Materialy Mongol'skoj Kommissii
MMK — Mideast Markets
MMLA — Majallat Majma al-Lughah al-Arabiyah [Cairo]
MMLI — Majallat al-Majma al-Limi al-Iraqi
MMLMP — Materialy po Matematiceskoj Lingvistike i Masinnomu Perevodu
MMLRAI — Mammal Review
MMM — Melanges Malraux Miscellany
MMMSM — Millenaire Monastique du Mont Saint-Michel
MMN — Marianne Moore Newsletter
MMN — Mitteilungen zur Geschichte der Medizin und der Naturwissenschaft
MMNPAM — Manitoba. Department of Mines and Natural Resources. Mines Branch. Publication
MMNRW — Manitoba. Department of Mines, Natural Resources, and Environment. Wildlife Research MS Reports [Canada]
MMOSD — Molybdenum Mosaic
MMP — Microform Market Place
MMPJAE — Manufactured Milk Products Journal
MMQ — Management Quarterly
MMQ — Metalectrovisie
MMQUB — Mining and Metallurgy. Quarterly [English Translation]
MMR — Monthly Musical Record
MMRI — Multi-Media Reviews Index
MMR Miner Met Rev — MMR. Minerals and Metals Review [India]
MMRSA — Methods in Medical Research
M Ms — Medizinische Monatsschrift
MMS — Metropolitan Museum. Studies
MMS — Muenstersche Mittelalter-Schriften
MMSCEC — Marine Mammal Science
M Msch W — Mitteilungen aus dem Markscheidewesen
MM St — Mitteilungsblatt fuer Mathematische Statistik und Ihre Anwendungsgebiete
M Mus Lauriacum — Mitteilungen. Museumsverein "Lauriacum" [Enns]
MMW — Muenchener Medizinische Wochenschrift
MMWOA — Muenchener Medizinische Wochenschrift
MMWOAU — Muenchener Medizinische Wochenschrift
MMWR — Morbidity and Mortality Weekly Report [Centers for Disease Control]
MM Zt — Militaer-Musikerzeitung
MN — Malawi News
MN — Manchester Evening News
MN — Miscellanea Numismatica
Mn — Mnemosyne
MN — Monumenta Nipponica
MN — Moscow News
MN — Museum News
MNA — Medizinisch-Naturwissenschaftliches Archiv
MNAWL — Mededeelingen. Koninklijke Nederlandsche Akademie van Wetenschappen. Afdeling Letterkunde
MN Bl — Mathematisch-Naturwissenschaftliche Blaetter
MNC — Nederlands College voor Belastingconsulenten. Nationale Associatie van Accountantsadministratieconsulenten, Nederlandse Vereniging van Boekhoudbureaux en Administratiekantoren. Mededelingenblad

MNCBAY — Comunicaciones Botanicas. Museo de Historia Natural de Montevideo
MNCDN — Mededeelingen. Nijmeegse Centrale voor Dialecten Naamkunde
MND — Monde
MNDPV — Mitteilungen und Nachrichten. Deutscher Palaestina-Verein
MNEMA9 — Manitoba Entomologist
MNF — Textilia
M Nfr VH — Mitteilungen. Nordfriesischer Verein fuer Heimatkunde
MNFS — Meddelelser fra Norsk Forening foer Sprog-Videnskap
MNFSA — Meddelelser fra Norsk Farmaceutisk Selskap
MNGBA — Mitteilungen. Naturforschende Gesellschaft in Bern
MNGMD — Management
MNGS — Manitoba Geographical Series [Canada]
MnH — Minnesota History
MNHIR — Mededeelingen. Nederlandsch-Historisch Instituut le Rome
MNI — Modern Asia
MNI Microcomput News Int — MNI. Microcomputer News International
MNip — Monumenta Nipponica
MNIR — Mededeelingen. Nederlandsch-Historisch Instituut le Rome
MNJ — Mining Journal
MNKMA5 — Mankind Monographs
MNKP — Materialy po Nacional'no - Kolonial'nym Problemam
MN LR — Minnesota Law Review
MNMCA — Memoires. Societe Nationale des Sciences Naturelles et Mathematiques de Cherbourg
MNN — Muenchener Neueste Nachrichten
MNNA — Manitoba Nature [Canada]
MNNMBL — Museo Nacional de Historia Natural. Noticiario Mensual [Santiago]
MNNTB8 — Man and Nature
MNO — Meubelecho
M Not R Ast — Monthly Notices. Royal Astronomical Society
MNP — Monde Nouveau-Paru
MNPAAS — Morfologia Normala si Patologica [Bucharest]
MNRAA — Monthly Notices. Royal Astronomical Society
MNRLD — Mineraloel
MNRLSM — Manitoba. Department of Natural Resources. Library Service Manuscripts [Canada]
MNRTA — Mental Retardation
MNSKA — Meddelelser fra det Norske Skogforsoeksvesen
MNSV — Meddelelser fra Norsk Forening foer Sprog-Videnskap
Mntl Pt — Mental Patients Liberation/Therapy
Mntn Life — Mountain Life and Work
Mnu — Mundo Nuevo
MNVAD — Mededelingenblad. Nederlandse Vacuumvereniging
MNy — Magyar Nyelvjarasok
MNY — Messager de New York
MNyj — Magyar Nyelvjarasok
MO — Miscellanea Orientalia
MO — Missionerskoe Obozrienie
Mo — Monat
MO — Monatshefte
MO — Monde Oriental
Mo — Money
Mo — Moskva
MO — Movimento Operaio
MO — Musical Opinion
MO Acad Sci Occas Pap — Missouri Academy of Science. Occasional Paper
MO Ag Bd — Missouri State Board of Agriculture. Publications
MO Ag Exp — Missouri. Agricultural Experiment Station. Publications
MO Agric Exp Stn Res Bull — Missouri. Agricultural Experiment Station. Research Bulletin
MO Agric Exp Stn Spec Rep — Missouri. Agricultural Experiment Station. Special Report
Mo Aust Dem R — Monthly Australian Demographic Review
MO Bar J — Missouri Bar. Journal
MO B G — Missouri Bureau of Geology and Mines
Mobil Country J — Mobil Country Journal
Mobil Rev — Mobil Review
MO B J — Missouri Bar. Journal
MO Bot Gard Ann — Missouri Botanical Garden. Annals
MO Bot Gard Bull — Missouri Botanical Garden. Bulletin
MOC — Bedrijfshuishouding. Magazine voor Interne en Civiele Diensten
Mocambique Missao Combate Tripanossomiases Annu Rep — Mocambique Missao de Combate as Tripanossomiases. Annual Report
Moccasin Tel — Moccasin Telegraph
MOCI — MOCI. Moniteur du Commerce International
MOCI — Moniteur Officiel du Commerce International
MO Conserv — Missouri Conservationist
MOCRA — Molecular Crystals
MOCT — Moccasin Telegraph
Mod A — Modern Age
Mod Age — Modern Age
Mod Arts News — Modern Arts News
Mod Asian S — Modern Asian Studies
Mod Asian Stud — Modern Asian Studies

Mod Aspects Electrochem — Modern Aspects of Electrochemistry
Mod Aspects Neurosurg — Modern Aspects of Neurosurgery
Mod Aspects Vitreous State — Modern Aspects of the Vitreous State
Mod As Stud — Modern Asian Studies [*London*]
Mod Ath and Coach — Modern Athlete and Coach
Mod Athl Coach — Modern Athlete and Coach
Mod Aust L — Modern Austrian Literature
Mod Austrian Lit — Modern Austrian Literature
Mod B — Modern Boating
Mod Beekeep — Modern Beekeeping
Mod Biol — Modern Biology
Mod Brew — Modern Brewer
Mod Brew Age — Modern Brewery Age
Mod Brew M — Modern Brewery Age. Magazine Section
Mod Bus Law — Modern Business Law
Mod Camera Mag — Modern Camera Magazine
Mod Cast — Modern Castings
Mod Cast Am Foundryman — Modern Casting and American Foundryman
Mod C Cardi — Modern Concepts of Cardiovascular Disease
Mod Ch — Modern Churchman
Mod Chem — Modern Chemistry [*Japan*]
Mod China — Modern China
Mod Chin Lit Newsl — Modern Chinese Literature Newsletter [*Berkeley*]
ModChm — Modern Churchman
Mod Clin — Modern Clinics [*Japan*]
Mod Concepts Cardiovasc Dis — Modern Concepts of Cardiovascular Disease
Mod Concr — Modern Concrete
ModD — Modern Drama
Mod Dairy — Modern Dairy
Mod Data — Modern Data
Mod Dev Powder Metall — Modern Development in Powder Metallurgy
ModDr — Modern Drama
Mod Drama — Modern Drama
Mod Drugs — Modern Drugs
Mode — Modern Office and Data Equipment
Mod Ed — Modern Education
Model Biol Med Resp Mezhved Sb — Modelirovanie v Biologii i Meditsine Respublikanskii Mezhvedomstvennyi Sbornik
Model Eng — Model Engineer
Model Identif Control — Modeling Identification and Control [*Norway*]
Modelirovanie Ekonom Processov — Otdelenie Ekonomiceskoi Kivernetiki Ekonomiceskogo Fakul'teta Moskovogo Gosudarstvennogo Universiteta Imeni M. V. Lomonosova. Modelirovanie Ekonomiceskih Processov
Model Simul Proc Annu Pittsburgh Conf — Modeling and Simulation. Proceedings. Annual Pittsburgh Conference
Models Lab Rep Dep Archit Sci Syd Univ — Models Laboratory Reports. Department of Architectural Science. University of Sydney
Mod Eng — Modern Engineer
MO Dep Conserv Terr Ser — Missouri. Department of Conservation. Terrestrial Series
Modern Boating — Modern Boating and Seacraft
Modern Drum — Modern Drummer
Modern Lit — Modern Liturgy
Modern LR — Modern Law Review
Modern L Rev — Modern Law Review
Modern O — Modern Occasions
Modern P S — Modern Poetry Studies
Modern Vocational Trends Career Mon — Modern Vocational Trends. Career Monographs
Mod Farmer — Modern Farmer
Mod Farming Cent Afr — Modern Farming in Central Africa
Mod Fict St — Modern Fiction Studies
Mod Fict Stud — Modern Fiction Studies
Mod Geol — Modern Geology
Mod Health — Modern Healthcare
Mod Healthcare — Modern Healthcare
Mod Heb Lit — Modern Hebrew Literature
Mod Holzverarb — Moderne Holzverarbeitung
Mod Hosp — Modern Hospital
Modif Polim Mater — Modifikatsiya Polimernykh Materialov [*Latvian SSR*]
Mod Ind — Modern Industry
Mod Ind Energy — Modern Industrial Energy [*United States*]
Mod Int Dr — Modern International Drama
Mod Judaism — Modern Judaism
Mod Kemi — Modern Kemi
Mod Knit — Modern Knitting Management
Mod Lan — Modern Language Notes
Mod Lang — Modern Languages
Mod Lang Assn Pub — Modern Language Association of America. Publications
Mod Lang Forum — Modern Language Forum
Mod Lang J — Modern Language Journal
Mod Lang N — Modern Language Notes
Mod Lang Q — Modern Language Quarterly
Mod Lang R — Modern Language Review
Mod Lang Rev — Modern Language Review

Mod Lang St — Modern Language Studies
Mod Law R — Modern Law Review
Mod Law Soc — Modern Law and Society
Mod Libn — Modern Librarian
Mod Lit — Modern Liturgy
Mod Lithography — Modern Lithography
Mod L Rev — Modern Law Review
Mod M — Modern Motor
Mod Mach Shop — Modern Machine Shop
Mod Mater — Modern Materials
Mod Mater Adv Dev Appl — Modern Materials. Advances in Development and Applications
Mod Mater Handl — Modern Materials Handling
Mod Mat H — Modern Materials Handling
Mod Med Asia — Modern Medicine of Asia
Mod Med (Chicago) — Modern Medicine (Chicago)
Mod Med (Jpn) — Modern Medicine (Japan)
Mod Med (Minneapolis) — Modern Medicine (Minneapolis)
Mod Met — Modern Metals
Mod Metals — Modern Metals
Mod Met Finish — Modern Metal Finishing
Mod Mfg — Modern Manufacturing
Mod Miller — Modern Miller
Mod Miller Bakers News — Modern Miller and Bakers News
Mod Min — Modern Mining
Mod Motor — Modern Motor
Mod Mus — Modern Music
Mod Music — Modern Music
Mod Nurs Home — Modern Nursing Home
Mod Nutr — Modern Nutrition
Mod Off — Modern Office Procedures
Mod Off — Modern Office Technology
Mod Off and Data Manage — Modern Office and Data Management
Mod Off Proc — Modern Office Procedures
Mod Off Proced — Modern Office Procedures
Mod Off Procedures — Modern Office Procedures
Mod Packag — Modern Packaging
Mod Paint — Modern Paint and Coatings
Mod Perspect Psychiatry — Modern Perspectives in Psychiatry
Mod Pharm — Modern Pharmacology
Mod Phil — Modern Philology
Mod Philol — Modern Philology
Mod Phot — Modern Photography
Mod Photogr — Modern Photography
Mod Phys Monogr Ser — Modern Physics Monograph Series
Mod Pkg — Modern Packaging
Mod Pkg En — Modern Packaging Encyclopedia and Buyer's Guide Issue
Mod Plas — Modern Plastics
Mod Plast — Modern Plastics
Mod Plastics — Modern Plastics
Mod Plast Int — Modern Plastics International
Mod Plst Int — Modern Plastics International
Mod Poetry Stud — Modern Poetry Studies
Mod Poet St — Modern Poetry Studies
Mod Power Eng — Modern Power and Engineering
Mod Power and Eng — Modern Power and Engineering
Mod Power Syst — Modern Power Systems
Mod Probl Ophthalmol — Modern Problems in Ophthalmology
Mod Probl Paediatr — Modern Problems in Paediatrics
Mod Probl Paediatr — Moderne Probleme der Paediatrie [*Switzerland*]
Mod Probl Pharmacopsychiatry — Modern Problems of Pharmacopsychiatry
Mod Quart Misc — Modern Quarterly Miscellany
Mod Quart Res SE A — Modern Quarterly Research in Southeast Asia [*Rotterdam*]
Mod R — Modern Review
Mod Railw — Modern Railways
Mod R (Calcutta) — Modern Review (Calcutta)
Mod Refrig — Modern Refrigeration
Mod Refrig Air Cond — Modern Refrigeration and Air Conditioning
Mod Refrig Air Control News — Modern Refrigeration and Air Control News
ModRev — Modern Review
Mod Roentgen-Fotogr — Moderne Roentgen-Fotografie
Mod Rr — Modern Railroads
Mod Sch — Modern Schoolman
Mod Schoolm — Modern Schoolman
Mod Solid State Phys Simon Fraser Univ Lect — Modern Solid State Physics. Simon Fraser University. Lectures
Mod Sp — Moderne Sprachen
Mod St Lit — Modernist Studies. Literature and Culture, 1920-1940
Mod Stud — Modernist Studies
Mod Stud Assoc Yearb — Modern Studies Association Yearbook
Mod Sugar Plant — Modern Sugar Planter
Modszertani Kozl Mag All Foldt Intez — Modszertani Kozlemenyek. Magyar Allami Foldtani Intezet
Mod Teach — Modern Teaching
Mod Tex B — Modern Textile Business

Mod Text — Modern Textiles Magazine
Mod Text Mag — Modern Textiles Magazine
Mod Theor Chem — Modern Theoretical Chemistry
Mod Tire Dealer — Modern Tire Dealer
Mod Tramway — Modern Tramway
Mod Treat — Modern Treatment
Mod Trends Anaesth — Modern Trends in Anaesthesia
Mod Trends Cardiol — Modern Trends in Cardiology
Mod Trends Dermatol — Modern Trends in Dermatology
Mod Trends Drug Depend Alcohol — Modern Trends in Drug Dependence and Alcoholism
Mod Trends Endocrinol — Modern Trends in Endocrinology
Mod Trends Gastroenterol — Modern Trends in Gastroenterology
Mod Trends Hum Reprod Physiol — Modern Trends in Human Reproductive Physiology
Mod Trends Immunol — Modern Trends in Immunology
Mod Trends Med Virol — Modern Trends in Medical Virology
Mod Trends Neurol — Modern Trends in Neurology
Mod Trends Orthop — Modern Trends in Orthopaedics
Mod Trends Pharmacol Ther — Modern Trends in Pharmacology and Therapeutics
Mod Trends Psychosom Med — Modern Trends in Psychosomatic Medicine
Mod Trends Radiother — Modern Trends in Radiotherapy
Mod Trends Rheumatol — Modern Trends in Rheumatology
Mod Trends Ser Psychosom Med — Modern Trends Series. Psychosomatic Medicine
Mod Trends Surg — Modern Trends in Surgery
Modular I St — Modular Instruction in Statistics
Mod Unfallverhuet — Moderne Unfallverhuetung
Mod Vet Pract — Modern Veterinary Practice
Mod World — Modern World
Mod Ytbehandling — Modern Ytbehandling
MOE — Molecular Endocrinology [*Elsevier Book Series*]
MOEIG — Mitteilungen. Oesterreichisches Institut fuer Geschichtsforschung
MOEMDJ — Motivation and Emotion
Moessbauer Eff Methodol — Moessbauer Effect Methodology
Moessbauer Eff Methodol Proc Symp — Moessbauer Effect Methodology. Proceedings of the Symposium
MOGA — Mitteilungen. Oesterreichische Gesellschaft fuer Anthropologie, Ethnologie, und Praehistorie
MO Geol Surv Rep Invest — Missouri. Geological Survey. Report of Investigations
MO Geol Surv Water Resour Inf Circ — Missouri. Geological Survey and Water Resources. Information Circular
MO Geol Surv Water Resour Inform Circ — Missouri. Geological Survey and Water Resources. Information Circular
MO Geol Surv Water Resour Misc Publ — Missouri. Geological Survey and Water Resources. Miscellaneous Publication
MO Geol Surv Water Resour Rep — Missouri. Geological Survey and Water Resources. Report
MO Geol Surv Water Resour Rep Invest — Missouri. Geological Survey and Water Resources. Report of Investigations
MO Geol Surv Water Resour Spec Publ — Missouri. Geological Survey and Water Resources. Special Publication
MO Geol Surv Water Resour Water Resour Rep — Missouri. Geological Survey and Water Resources. Water Resources Report
MOGMS — Meddelelser om Groenland. Man and Society
MOGR — Meddelelser om Groenland
MO G S MO Bur G Mines — Missouri. Geological Survey. Missouri Bureau of Geology and Mines
MOH — Magazine of Horror
MoH — Monatshefte
MO His Col — Missouri Historical Society. Collections
MO His R — Missouri Historical Review
MO Hist Rev — Missouri Historical Review
MO Hist Soc Bull — Missouri Historical Society. Bulletin
MOHOA — Modern Hospital
MOI — Moniteur du Commerce International
MOIED — Modern Industrial Energy
MOIG — Mitteilungen. Oesterreichisches Institut fuer Geschichtsforschung
MOIGF — Mitteilungen. Oesterreichisches Institut fuer Geschichtsforschung
Mo Illust — Monthly Illustrator
Moirs Aust Investments — Moir's Australian Investments
Mois Chim Electrochim — Mois Chimique et Electrochimique
Mois Minier Metall — Mois Minier et Metallurgique
Mois Sci Ind — Mois Scientifique et Industriel
Moist Fert — Moisture and Fertility. American Potash Institute
Mo J Australian-American Assoc — Australian-American Association. Monthly Journal [*Sydney*]
MOJOD — Mother Jones
MO J Res Mus Ed — Missouri Journal of Research in Music Education
MOK — Oesterreichisches Institut fuer Wirtschaft Forschung. Monatsberichte
MOKIA — Monatsschrift fuer Kinderheilkunde
MOKOAI — Moskovskii Kolkhoznik
Mokslas Tech — Mokslas ir Technika

Mokslo Darb Vilniaus Valstybinis Pedagog Inst — Mokslo Darbai. Vilniaus Valstybinis Pedagoginis Institutas
MO L — Missouri Law Review
MOL — Molenaar Weekblad voor de Graanverwerkende Industrie en Veevoederindustrie
MOLAA — Monatsschrift fuer Ohrenheilkunde und Laryngo-Rhinologie
Mo Labor R — Monthly Labor Review
Mo Labor Rev — Monthly Labor Review
Mo Lab Rev — Monthly Labor Review
Mol Aspects Med — Molecular Aspects of Medicine
Mol Biochem Parasitol — Molecular and Biochemical Parasitology
Mol Biol — Molecular Biology
Mol Biol — Molekulyarnaya Biologiya
Mol Biol Biochem Biophys — Molecular Biology, Biochemistry, and Biophysics
Mol Biol Evol — Molecular Biology and Evolution
Mol Biol (Kiev) — Molekulyarnaya Biologiya (Kiev)
Mol Biol Mamm Gene Appar — Molecular Biology of the Mammalian Genetic Apparatus
Mol Biol (Mosc) — Molekulyarnaya Biologiya (Moscow)
Mol Biol Rep — Molecular Biology Reports
Mol Biol Rp — Molecular Biology Reports
Mo Lbr R — Monthly Labor Review
Mol C Bioch — Molecular and Cellular Biochemistry
Mol Cell Biochem — Molecular and Cellular Biochemistry
Mol Cell Biol — Molecular and Cellular Biology
Mol Cell Endocr — Molecular and Cellular Endocrinology
Mol Cell Endocrinol — Molecular and Cellular Endocrinology
Mol C Endoc — Molecular and Cellular Endocrinology
Mol Cryst — Molecular Crystals
Mol Cryst and Liq Cryst — Molecular Crystals and Liquid Crystals
Mol Cryst Liq Cryst — Molecular Crystals and Liquid Crystals
Mol Cryst Liq Cryst Lett — Molecular Crystals and Liquid Crystals. Letters
Molec Biol — Molecular Biology
Molec Cryst — Molecular Crystals and Liquid Crystals
Molec Pharm — Molecular Pharmacology
Molec Phys — Molecular Physics
Molecular Phys — Molecular Physics
Mol Fiz Biofiz Vodn Sist — Molekulyarnaya Fizika i Biofizika Vodnykh Sistem
Mol Fiz Biofiz Vod Sis — Molekulyarnaya Fizika i Biofizika Vodnykh Sistem
Mol Genet Mikrobiol Virusol — Molekulyarnaya Genetika, Mikrobiologiya, i Virusologiya
Mol Gen Genet — Molecular and General Genetics
Mol G Genet — Molecular and General Genetics
MO Lib Assn Newsl — Missouri Library Association. Newsletter
MO Lib Assn Q — Missouri Library Association. Quarterly
MO Libr Ass Q — Missouri Library Association. Quarterly
Mol Immunol — Molecular Immunology
Molini Ital — Molini d'Italia
MOLJA — Modern Language Journal
Molk Kaeserei Ztg — Molkerei- und Kaeserei- Zeitung
Molk Ztg (Berlin) — Molkerei-Zeitung (Berlin)
Molk Ztg (Hildesheim Ger) — Molkerei-Zeitung (Hildesheim, Germany)
Molk Ztg Welt Milch — Molkerei-Zeitung Welt der Milch [*West Germany*]
Moloch Myas Zhivotnovod — Molochnoe i Myasnoe Zhivotnovodstvo
Molochn Myasn Skotovod (Moscow) — Molochnoe i Myasnoe Skotovodstvo (Moscow)
Molochno Masloden Promst — Molochno-Maslodel'naya Promyshlennost
Molochno Myasn Skotovod (Kiev) — Molochnoe i Myasnoe Skotovodstvo (Kiev)
Molochn Prom-st — Molochnaya Promyshlennost
Molod Naucn Rabotnik — Molodoi Naucnyi Rabotnik
Molodoi Nauchn Rab Estestv Nauki — Molodoi Nauchnyi Rabotnik. Estestvennye Nauki
Mol Pharmacol — Molecular Pharmacology
Mol Photoch — Molecular Photochemistry
Mol Photochem — Molecular Photochemistry
Mol Phys — Molecular Physics
MO LR — Missouri Law Review
MO L Rev — Missouri Law Review
Mol Spectros — Molecular Spectroscopy
Mol Spectrosc Mod Res — Molecular Spectroscopy. Modern Research
Mol Spektrosk — Molekulyarnaya Spektroskopiya
Mol Struct Diffr Methods — Molecular Structure by Diffraction Methods
Mol Struct Dimensions Ser A — Molecular Structures and Dimensions. Series A
Molten Met — Molten Metal
Molysulfide Newslett — Molysulfide Newsletter [*United States*]
MOM — Mobelmarkt. Fachzeitschrift fuer die Mobelwirtschaft
MOMEA — Montpellier Medical
MO Med — Missouri Medicine
Mo Micro J — Monthly Microscopical Journal
Mo Mus Rec — Monthly Musical Record
MON — Ministerstvo Oborony Narodowej
Mon — [*The*] Monist
MonAeg — Monumenta Aegyptiaca [*Brussels*]

Mon Analyt Bull Inter-Afr Bur Soils — Monthly Analytical Bulletin. Inter-African Bureau for Soils
Mon Ant — Monumenti Antichi
Monash LR — Monash University. Law Review
Monash UL Rev — Monash University. Law Review
Monash Univ Gaz — Monash University. Gazette
Monash Univ L Rev — Monash University. Law Review
Monat f Deut Unt — Monatshefte fuer Deutschen Unterricht
Monatsber Deut Akad Wiss Berlin — Monatsberichte. Deutsche Akademie der Wissenschaften zu Berlin
Monatsber Dtsch Akad Wiss Berl — Monatsberichte. Deutsche Akademie der Wissenschaften zu Berlin
Monatsber Dtschen Bundesbank — Monatsberichte. Deutsche Bundesbank
Monatsber Int Altersforsch Altersbekaempf — Monatsberichte fuer Internationale Altersforschung und Altersbekaempfung
Monatsber Oesterr Inst Wirtsch-Forsch — Monatsberichte. Oesterreichisches Institut fuer Wirtschaftsforschung
Monats Chem — Monatshefte fuer Chemie
Monatschr Geburtsh u Gynak — Monatsschrift fuer Geburtshilfe und Gynaekologie
Monatschr Ornithol Vivarienkd Ausg B — Monatsschrift fuer Ornithologie und Vivarienkunde. Ausgabe B. Aquarien und Terrarien [East Germany]
Monatschr Psychiat u Neurol — Monatsschrift fuer Psychiatrie und Neurologie
Monatsh Chem — Monatshefte fuer Chemie
Monatsh Chem Verw Teile Anderer Wiss — Monatshefte fuer Chemie und Verwandte Teile Anderer Wissenschaften
Monatshefte — Monatshefte fuer Deutschen Unterricht. Deutsche Sprache und Literatur
Monatsh Math — Monatshefte fuer Mathematik [Vienna]
Monatsh Math Phys — Monatshefte fuer Mathematik und Physik [Austria]
Monatsh Naturwiss Unterr Aller Schulgattungen Natur Sch — Monatshefte fuer den Naturwissenschaftlichen Unterricht Aller Schulgattungen und Natur und Schule
Monatsh Prakt Dermat — Monatshefte fuer Praktische Dermatologie
Monatsh Prakt Tierh — Monatshefte fuer Praktische Tierheilkunde
Monatsh Seide Kunstseide Zellwolle — Monatshefte fuer Seide und Kunstseide. Zellwolle
Monatsh Tierheilkd — Monatshefte fuer Tierheilkunde
Monatsh Vet — Monatshefte fuer Veterinaermedizin
Monatsh Veterinaermed — Monatshefte fuer Veterinaermedizin
Monatsh Veterinarmed — Monatshefte fuer Veterinaermedizin
Monats Kind — Monatsschrift fuer Kinderheilkunde
Monatskurse Aerztl Fortbild — Monatskurse fuer die Aerztliche Fortbildung
Monats Math — Monatshefte fuer Mathematik
Monatsschr Brau — Monatsschrift fuer Brauerei
Monatsschr Brauerei — Monatsschrift fuer Brauerei
Monatsschr Dtsch Recht — Monatsschrift fuer Deutsches Recht
Monatsschr Geburshilfe Gynaekol — Monatsschrift fuer Geburtshilfe und Gynaekologie
Monatsschr Kinderheilkd — Monatsschrift fuer Kinderheilkunde
Monatsschr Krebsbekaempf — Monatsschrift fuer Krebsbekaempfung
Monatsschr Lungenkr Tuberk-Bekaempf — Monatsschrift fuer Lungenkrankheiten und Tuberkulose-Bekaempfung
Monatsschr Ohrenheilkd Laryngo-Rhinol — Monatsschrift fuer Ohrenheilkunde und Laryngo-Rhinologie
Monatsschr Ornithol Vivarienkd Ausg B Aquarien Terrarien — Monatsschrift fuer Ornithologie und Vivarienkunde. Ausgabe B. Aquarien und Terrarien
Monatsschr Psychiatr Neurol — Monatsschrift fuer Psychiatrie und Neurologie
Monatsschr Text Ind — Monatsschrift fuer Textil-Industrie
Monatsschr Unfallheikd Versicher-Versorg Verkehrsmed — Monatsschrift fuer Unfallheilkunde. Versicherungs-, Versorgungs-, und Verkehrsmedizin
Monatsschr Unfallheilkd — Monatsschrift fuer Unfallheilkunde
Monatsschr Unfallheilkd Versicher Versorg Verkehrsmed — Monatsschrift fuer Unfallheilkunde. Versicherungs-, Versorgungs-, und Verkehrsmedizin
Monats Unfa — Monatsschrift fuer Unfallheilkunde
MONBA — Monatsschrift fuer Brauerei
Mon Bull Agric Intell Plant Dis — Monthly Bulletin of Agricultural Intelligence and Plant Disease
Mon Bull Agric Sci Pract — Monthly Bulletin of Agricultural Science and Practice
Mon Bull Am Bakers Assoc — Monthly Bulletin. American Bakers Association
Mon Bull Can Inst Min Metall — Monthly Bulletin. Canadian Institute of Mining and Metallurgy
Mon Bull Can Min Inst — Monthly Bulletin. Canadian Mining Institute
Mon Bull Coffee Board Kenya — Monthly Bulletin. Coffee Board of Kenya
Mon Bull Int Railw Congr Assoc — Monthly Bulletin. International Railway Congress Association
Mon Bull Int Railw Congr Assoc (Engl Ed) — Monthly Bulletin. International Railway Congress Association (English Edition)
Mon Bull Int Ry Congr Ass Cybern Electron Ry — Monthly Bulletin. International Railway Congress Association. Cybernetics and Electronics of the Railways
Mon Bull Minist Health Public Health Lab — Monthly Bulletin. Ministry of Health and the Public Health Laboratory

Mon Bull Minist Health Public Health Lab Serv — Monthly Bulletin. Ministry of Health and the Public Health Laboratory Service [England]
Mon Bull Minst Mines Hydrocarbons (Caracas) — Monthly Bulletin. Ministry of Mines and Hydrocarbons (Caracas)
Mon Cat US Gov Publications — Monthly Catalog of United States Government Publications
Mon Checkl State Publ — Monthly Checklist of State Publications [United States]
Mon Corresp Befoerd Erd Himmelskunde — Monatliche Correspondenz zur Befoerderung der Erd und Himmelskunde [East Germany]
Monda Ling-Prob — Monda Lingvo-Problemo
Monde Alpin Rhod — Monde Alpin et Rhodanien
Monde Apic — Monde Apicole
Monde Med (Paris) — Monde Medical (Paris)
Monde Miner — Monde et les Mineraux
Monde Mod — Monde Moderne
Monde Plant — Monde des Plantes
Mondes Asiat — Mondes Asiatiques
Mondes Dev — Mondes en Developpement [Paris]
Mondes en Develop — Mondes en Developpement
Mond Nickel Bull — Mond Nickel Bulletin
Mondo Agric — Mondo Agricolo
Mondo Econ — Mondo Economico
Mondo Fin — Mondo Finanziario
Mondo Odontostomatol — Mondo Odontostomatologico
Mondo Ortod — Mondo Ortodontico
Mondo Tess — Mondo Tessile
Mon Econ Lett — Monthly Economic Letter [United States]
Moneda y Cred — Moneda y Credito
Mon Energy Rev — Monthly Energy Review
Moneta e Cred — Moneta e Credito
MonF — Monde Francais
MONG — Mitteilungen. Oesterreichische Numismatische Gesellschaft
Mongrafias Inst Eduardo Torroja Constr Cem — Monografias. Instituto Eduardo Torroja de la Construccion y del Cemento
Mong Stud — Mongolian Studies
Mon Inst — Monumenti Inediti Pubblicati dall'Instituto di Corrispondenza Archeologica
Monit Belge — Moniteur Belge
Monit Ceram Verrerie J Ceram Chaufournier Reunis — Moniteur de la Ceramique et de la Verrerie et Journal du Ceramiste et de Chaufournier Reunis
Monit Farm Ter — Monitor de la Farmacia y de la Terapeutica
Monit Hop — Moniteur des Hopitaux
Monit Hyg Salubr Publique — Moniteur d'Hygiene et de Salubrite Publique
Monit Maille — Moniteur de la Maille
Monitor Proc Inst Radio Electron Eng (Aust) — Monitor. Proceedings. Institution of Radio and Electronics Engineers (Australia)
Monit Ostet-Ginecol — Monitore Ostetrico-Ginecologico
Monit Ostet-Ginecol Endocrinol Metab — Monitore Ostetrico-Ginecologico di Endocrinologia e del Metabolismo
Monit Papet Belge — Moniteur de la Papeterie Belge
Monit Papet Fr — Moniteur de la Papeterie Francaise
Monit Peint — Moniteur de la Peinture
Monit Pet Roman — Monitorul Petrolului Roman
Monit Photogr — Moniteur de la Photographie
Monit Prod Chim — Moniteur des Produits Chimiques
Monit Prof Electr Electron — Moniteur Professionnel de l'Electricite et Electronique [France]
Monit Tec — Monitore Tecnico
Monit Tein Apprets Impress Tissus — Moniteur de la Teinture des Apprets et de l'Impression des Tissus
Monit Trav Publics Batim — Moniteur des Travaux Publics et du Batiment [France]
Monit Zool Ital — Monitore Zoologico Italiano
Monit Zool Ital Monogr — Monitore Zoologico Italiano. Monografia
Monit Zool Ital Suppl — Monitore Zoologico Italiano. Supplemento
Mon J Inst Ind Sci Univ Tokyo — Monthly Journal. Institute of Industrial Science. University of Tokyo
Mon Labor Rev — Monthly Labor Review
Mon Lab Re — Monthly Labor Review
Mon L R — Monash University. Law Review
Mon L Rev — Monash University. Law Review
Mon L Rev — Montana Law Review
Monmouth County Med Soc Newsletter — Monmouth County Medical Society. Newsletter
Monmouthshire Ant — Monmouthshire Antiquary. Proceedings. Monmouthshire and Caerleon Antiquarian Society
Monmouthshire Antiq — Monmouthshire Antiquary
Mon Nipp — Monumenta Nipponica
Mon Not Astron Soc S Afr — Monthly Notes. Astronomical Society of Southern Africa
Mon Notes Astron Soc South Afr — Monthly Notes. Astronomical Society of Southern Africa
Mon Not R Astron Soc — Monthly Notices. Royal Astronomical Society [England]

Monogr Acad Nat Sci Phila — Monographs. Academy of Natural Sciences of Philadelphia
Monograf Inst Mat — Monografias. Instituto de Matematicas [*Mexico City*]
Monograf Mat — Monografie Matematyczne
Monograf Math — Monografias de Matematica [*Rio De Janeiro*]
Monograf Mat Pura Apl — Monografias de Matematicas Pura e Aplicada [*Campinas*]
Monograf Psych — Monografie Psychologiczne
Monogr Allergy — Monographs in Allergy
Monogr Am Assoc Ment Defic — Monographs. American Association on Mental Deficiency
Monogr Amer Phytopathol Soc — Monograph. American Phytopathological Society
Monogr Am Soc Agron — Monographs. American Society of Agronomy
Monogr Anaesthesiol — Monographs in Anaesthesiology
Monogr Angew Entomol — Monographien zur Angewandten Entomologie
Monogr Ann Radiol — Monographies des Annales de Radiologie
Monogr Annu Soc Fr Biol Clin — Monographie Annuelle. Societe Francaise de Biologie Clinique
Monograph Enseign Math — Monographies de l'Enseignement Mathematique [*Geneva*]
Monographiae Biol — Monographiae Biologicae
Monographs Population Biol — Monographs in Population Biology
Monographs Stud Math — Monographs and Studies in Mathematics
Monographs Surveys Water Res Engrg — Monographs and Surveys in Water Resource Engineering
Monographs Textbooks Mech Solids Fluids Mech Continua — Monographs and Textbooks on Mechanics of Solids and Fluids. Mechanics of Continua
Monographs Textbooks Mech Solids Fluids Mech Dynam Systems — Monographs and Textbooks on Mechanics of Solids and Fluids. Mechanics of Dynamical Systems
Monographs Textbooks Mech Solids Fluids Mech Genesis Method — Monographs and Textbooks on Mechanics of Solids and Fluids. Mechanics of Genesis and Method
Monographs Textbooks Mech Solids Fluids Mech Plastic Solids — Monographs and Textbooks on Mechanics of Solids and Fluids. Mechanics of Plastic Solids
Monogr Atheroscler — Monographs on Atherosclerosis
Monogr Biol — Monographiae Biologicae
Monogr BIPM — Monographie. BIPM [*Bureau International des Poids et Mesures*]
Monogr Bot — Monographiae Botanicae
Monogr Clin Cytol — Monographs in Clinical Cytology
Monogr Dev Biol — Monographs in Developmental Biology
Monogr Dev Pediatr — Monographs in Developmental Pediatrics
Monogr Drugs — Monographs on Drugs
Monogr Endocrinol — Monographs on Endocrinology
Monogr Fauny Pol — Monografie Fauny Polski
Monogr Gesamtgeb Neurol Psychiatr — Monographien. Gesamtgebiete der Neurologie und Psychiatrie
Monogr Gesamtgeb Psychiatr (Berlin) — Monographien. Gesamtgebiete der Psychiatrie. Psychiatry Series (Berlin)
Monogr Giovanni Lorenzini Found — Monographs. Giovanni Lorenzini Foundation
Monogr Groupe Etude Main — Monographies. Groupe d'Etude de la Main
Monogr Hum Genet — Monographs in Human Genetics
Monogr Hunter Valley Res Fdn — Monograph. Hunter Valley Research Foundation
Monogr Hunter Valley Res Found — Monograph. Hunter Valley Research Foundation
Monogr INIA — Monografias. INIA [*Instituto Nacional de Investigaciones Agrarias*]
Monogr Inst Butantan (Sao Paulo) — Monografias. Instituto Butantan (Sao Paulo)
Monogr Inst Oswaldo Cruz (Rio De J) — Monografias. Instituto Oswaldo Cruz (Rio De Janeiro)
Monogr Mat — Monografie Matematyczne
Monogr Memo Natl Res Inst Mach Des (Bechovice Czech) — Monographs and Memoranda. National Research Institute for Machine Design (Bechovice, Czechoslovakia)
Monogr Mod Chem — Monographs in Modern Chemistry
Monogr Ned Entomol Ver — Monografieen van de Nederlandse Entomologische Vereniging
Monogr Neoplast Dis Various Sites — Monographs on Neoplastic Disease at Various Sites [*Scotland*]
Monogr Neural Sci — Monographs in Neural Sciences
Monogr Nucl Med Biol — Monographs on Nuclear Medicine and Biology
Monogr Nucl Med Biol Ser — Monographs on Nuclear Medicine and Biology Series
Monogr Oceanogr Methodol — Monographs on Oceanographic Methodology
Monogr Oral Sci — Monographs in Oral Science
Monogr Paediatr — Monographs in Paediatrics
Monogr Parazytol — Monografie Parazytologiczne
Monogr Pathol — Monographs in Pathology
Monogr Percy Fitzpatrick Inst Afr Ornithol — Monographs. Percy Fitzpatrick Institute of African Ornithology

Monogr Pharmacol Physiol — Monographs in Pharmacology and Physiology
Monogr Physiol Causale — Monographie de Physiologie Causale
Monogr Physiol Soc — Monographs. Physiological Society
Monogr Physiol Soc Phila — Monographs. Physiological Society of Philadelphia
Monogr Physiol Soc Philadelphia — Monographs. Physiological Society of Philadelphia
Monogr Physiol Veg — Monographies de Physiologie Vegetale
Monogr Plast — Monographs on Plastics
Monogr Popul Biol — Monographs in Population Biology
Monogr Psychiatr Clin Helsinki Univ Cent Hosp — Monographs. Psychiatric Clinic. Helsinki University Central Hospital
Monogr Quekett Microsc Club — Monographs. Quekett Microscopical Club
Monogr Rutgers Cent Alcohol Stud — Monographs. Rutgers Center of Alcohol Studies
Monogr Semicond Phys — Monographs in Semiconductor Physics
Monogr Ser Australas Inst Min Metall — Australasian Institute of Mining and Metallurgy. Monograph Series
Monogr Ser Australas Inst Min Metall — Monograph Series. Australasian Institute of Mining and Metallurgy
Monogr Ser Inst Bot Acad Sin — Monograph Series. Institute of Botany. Academia Sinica
Monogr Ser Res Inst Appl Electr Hokkaido Univ — Monograph Series. Research Institute of Applied Electricity. Hokkaido University
Monogr Soc Res Child Dev — Monographs. Society for Research in Child Development
Monogr Srpska Akad Nauka — Monografii Srpska Akademija Nauka
Monogr Surg Sci — Monographs in the Surgical Sciences [*United States*]
Monogr Tea Prod Ceylon — Monographs on Tea Production in Ceylon
Monogr Textb Mater Sci — Monographs and Textbooks in Material Science
Monogr Textb Mech Solids Fluids Mech Anal — Monographs and Textbooks on Mechanics of Solids and Fluids. Mechanics Analysis
Monogr Textb Mech Solids Fluids Mech Elast Stab — Monographs and Textbooks on Mechanics of Solids and Fluids. Mechanics of Elastic Stability
Monogr Textb Mech Solids Fluids Mech Surf Struct — Monographs and Textbooks on Mechanics of Solids and Fluids. Mechanics of Surface Structures
Monogr Theor Appl Genet — Monographs on Theoretical and Applied Genetics
Monogr Virol — Monographs in Virology
Monogr West Found Vertebr Zool — Monographs. Western Foundation of Vertebrate Zoology
Monokrist Stsintill Org Lyuminofory — Monokristally. Stsintillyatory i Organicheskie Lyuminofory
Monokrist Tekh — Monokristally i Tekhnika
Mo Notes — Monthly Notes. Australian School of Pacific Administration
Mon Paediat — Monographs in Paediatrics
Mon Piot — Monuments et Memoires Publies par l'Academie des Inscriptions et Belles-Lettres. Fondation Piot
Mon Rep Civ Eng Res Inst Hokkaido Dev Bur — Monthly Report. Civil Engineering Research Institute of Hokkaido. Development Bureau [*Japan*]
Mon Rev — Monthly Review
Mon Rev Am Electroplat Soc — Monthly Review. American Electroplaters' Society
Mon Rev Fed Reserve Bank Kans City — Monthly Review. Federal Reserve Bank of Kansas City
Monsanto R — Monsanto Review
Monsanto Tech Rev — Monsanto Technical Review
Mon S Res C — Monographs. Society for Research in Child Development
Mon Stud — Monastic Studies
Mont — Montana: The Magazine of Western History
Mont Acad Sci Proc — Montana Academy of Sciences. Proceedings
Mont Ag Exp — Montana. Agricultural Experiment Station. Publications
Mont Agric Exp Stn Bull — Montana. Agricultural Experiment Station. Bulletin
Mont Agric Exp Stn Circ — Montana. Agricultural Experiment Station. Circular
Montana Acad Sci Proc — Montana Academy of Sciences. Proceedings
Montana Bur Mines and Geology Bull — Montana. Bureau of Mines and Geology. Bulletin
Montana Bur Mines and Geology Spec Pub — Montana. Bureau of Mines and Geology. Special Publication
Montana Lib — Montana Libraries
Montana Lib Q — Montana Library Quarterly
Montana L Rev — Montana Law Review
Montanaro Ital-Monti Boschi — Montanaro d'Italia - Monti e Boschi [*Italy*]
Montan-Rundsch — Montan-Rundschau [*Austria*]
Montan-Ztg — Montan-Zeitung [*Austria*]
Mont Bur Mines Geol Bull — Montana. Bureau of Mines and Geology. Bulletin
Mont Bur Mines Geol Mem — Montana. Bureau of Mines and Geology. Memoir
Mont Bur Mines Geol Spec Publ — Montana. Bureau of Mines and Geology. Special Publication
Mont Co LR — Montgomery County Law Reporter
Mont Co L Rep — Montgomery County Law Reporter

Mon Tech Rev — Monthly Technical Review
Mont Ed — Montana Education
Mont For Conserv Exp Stn Bull — Montana. Forest and Conservation
    Experiment Station. Bulletin
Mont For Conserv Exp Stn Lubrecht Ser — Montana. Forest and Conservation
    Experiment Station. Lubrecht Series
Mont For Conserv Exp Stn Note — Montana. Forest and Conservation
    Experiment Station. Note
Mont For Conserv Exp Stn Res Note — Montana. Forest and Conservation
    Experiment Station. Research Note
Mont For Conserv Exp Stn Spec Publ — Montana. Forest and Conservation
    Experiment Station. Special Publication
Mont For Conserv Exp Stn Study Rep — Montana. Forest and Conservation
    Experiment Station. Study Report
Mont Forest Ind News — Montana Forest Industry News
Montfort — Montfort. Vierteljahresschrift fuer Geschichte und
    Gegenwartskunde Vorarlbergs
Mont G — Montana Gothic
Montg — Montgomery County Law Reporter
Montg Co — Montgomery County Law Reporter
Montg Co Law Rep'r — Montgomery County Law Reporter
Montg Co LR — Montgomery County Law Reporter
Mont'g Co L Rep — Montgomery County Law Reporter
Montg Co L Rep'r — Montgomery County Law Reporter
Montg Co LR (PA) — Montgomery County Law Reporter (Pennsylvania)
Mont Geol Soc Annu Field Conf Guideb — Montana Geological Society.
    Annual Field Conference. Guidebook
Mont'g L Rep — Montgomery County Law Reporter
Montgomeryshire Collect — Montgomeryshire Collections
Montg (PA) — Montgomery County Law Reporter (Pennsylvania)
Mont His S — Montana Historical Society. Contributions
Month Lab Rev — Monthly Labor Review
Monthly Am J G — Monthly American Journal of Geology and Natural
    Science
Monthly Catalog US Govt Publ — Monthly Catalog of United States
    Government Publications
Monthly Cat US Govt Pub — Monthly Catalog of United States Government
    Publications
Monthly Crop Rep — Monthly Crop Report
Monthly F Bull — Monthly Film Bulletin [*London*]
Monthly Labor R — Monthly Labor Review
Monthly Labor Rev — Monthly Labor Review
Monthly Notices Roy Astronom Soc — Monthly Notices. Royal Astronomical
    Society
Monthly R — Monthly Review
Monthly Statist Rev — Monthly Statistical Review [*England*]
Monthly Vital Stat Rep — Monthly Vital Statistics Report [*United States*]
Monthly Weather Rev — Monthly Weather Review
Month Pub Op Surv — Monthly Publication Opinion Surveys [*New Delhi*]
Mon Times — Monetary Times
Mont Instal — Montajes e Instalaciones
Mont Law Re — Montana Law Review
Mont LR — Montana Law Review
Mont L Rev — Montana Law Review
Mont Mag Hist — Montana: The Magazine of Western History
Montpellier Med — Montpellier Medical [*France*]
Montpel Med — Montpellier Medical
Montr — Montemora
Montreal Med J — Montreal Medical Journal
Montreal Pharm J — Montreal Pharmaceutical Journal
Montreal Univ Service Biogeographie Bull — Montreal Universite. Service de
    Biogeographie. Bulletin
Mont Rural Electr News — Montana Rural Electric News
Mont State Coll Eng Exp Stn Bull — Montana State College. Engineering
    Experiment Station. Bulletin
Mont Univ B — Montana University. Bulletin
Mont Wool Grow — Montana Wool Grower
MONU — Monumentum. International Council of Monuments and Sites
Monumenta Nip — Monumenta Nipponica
Monuments Piot — Academie des Inscriptions et Belles-Lettres. Fondation
    Eugene Piot. Monuments et Memoires [*Paris*]
Monum Nippon — Monumenta Nipponica
MO Nurse — Missouri Nurse
Mon Weather Rev — Monthly Weather Review
Moody — Moody's Magazine
Moody M — Moody Monthly
Moody's Inv Serv — Moody's Investors Service
Moon — 13th Moon
Moons L T — Moons and Lion Tailes
Moorg Wal S — Moorgate and Wall Street
MOP — Mary's Own Paper
MOP — Modern Office Procedures
MOP — Modern Plastics International
M Opinion — Musical Opinion
MOPLD — Moon and the Planets
MOR — Mathematics of Operations Research

MOR — Mining and Oil Review
Mo R — Monthly Review
Mora Ferenc Muz Ev — Mora Ferenc Muzeum Evkoenyve
Moral Ed — Moral Education
Moravian Mus — Moravian Music Foundation. Bulletin
Moravian Mus — Moravian Music Journal
Moravske Num Zpravy — Moravske Numismaticke Zpravy
Morav Th S Bul — Moravian Theological Seminary. Bulletin
Morbidity Mortality Wkly Rep US Dep Hlth Educ Welf — Morbidity and
    Mortality Weekly Report. United States Department of Health,
    Education, and Welfare
Morbid Mortal Weekly Rep — Morbidity and Mortality Weekly Report
Mo Rel M — Monthly Religious Magazine
Mo Rev — Monthly Review
Mo Review — Monthly Review
MORFA — Morskoi Flot
Morfog Regener — Morfogenez i Regeneratsiya
Morfol Norm Patol (Buchar) — Morfologia Normala si Patologica (Bucharest)
Morfol Osn Mikrotsirk (Moscow) — Morfologicheskie Osnovy
    Mikrotsirkulyatsii (Moscow)
Morfol Reakt Izmen Perifer Nervn Sist Usloviyakh Eksp — Morfologiya
    Reaktivnykh Izmenenii Perifericheskoi Nervnoi Sistemy v Usloviyakh
    Eksperimenta
Morgan Gty — Morgan Guaranty Survey
Morn Watch — Morning Watch
Morocco Serv Geol Notes Mem — Morocco. Service Geologique. Notes et
    Memoires
Morph Jb — Morphologisches Jahrbuch
Morphol Embryol — Morphologie et Embryologie [*Romania*]
Morphol Igazsagugyi Orv Sz — Morphologiai es Igazsagugyi Orvosi Szemle
Morphol Jahrb — Morphologisches Jahrbuch
Morris Arbor Bull — Morris Arboretum. Bulletin
Morsk Flot — Morskoi Flot
Morsk Gidrofiz Issled — Morskie Gidrofizicheskie Issledovaniya
Morski Inst Rybacki Pr Ser A — Morski Instytut Rybacki. Prace. Seria A.
    Oceanografia i Biologia Rybacka
Morsk Sb — Morskoj Sbornik
Mort Banker — Mortgage Banker
Mort Banking — Mortgage Banking
Mortg Bank — Mortgage Banking
Mortg Bnkr — Mortgage Banker
MOSA — Mitteilungen. Oesterreichisches Staatsarchiv
Mosaic J Molybdenum Metall — Mosaic. Journal of Molybdenum Metallurgy
MOSCEQ — Moscosoa
MO Sch Mines Metall Bull Tech Ser — Missouri School of Mines and
    Metallurgy. Bulletin. Technical Series
Moscow Nar — Press Bulletin. Moscow Narodny Bank Ltd.
Moscow Narodny Bank Q R — Moscow Narodny Bank. Quarterly Review
Moscow Univ Biol Sci Bull (Engl Transl) — Moscow University. Biological
    Sciences Bulletin (English Translation)
Moscow Univ Bull Ser 3 — Moscow University. Bulletin. Series 3. Physics and
    Astronomy
Moscow Univ Comput Math and Cybern — Moscow University. Computational
    Mathematics and Cybernetics
Moscow Univ Geol Bull (Engl Transl) — Moscow University. Geology Bulletin
    (English Translation)
Moscow Univ Math Bull — Moscow University. Mathematics Bulletin
Moscow Univ Math Bull (Engl Transl) — Moscow University. Mathematics
    Bulletin (English Translation)
Moscow Univ Mech Bull — Moscow University. Mechanics Bulletin [*English
    Translation of Vestnik Moskovskogo Universiteta. Mekhanika*]
Moscow Univ Mech Bull (Engl Transl) — Moscow University. Mechanics
    Bulletin (English Translation of Vestnik Moskovskogo Universiteta.
    Mekhanika)
Moscow Univ Phys Bull — Moscow University. Physics Bulletin
Moscow Univ Soil Sci Bull (Engl Transl) — Moscow University. Soil Science
    Bulletin (English Translation)
Mosc Univ Biol Sci Bull — Moscow University. Biological Sciences Bulletin
Mosc Univ Chem Bull — Moscow University. Chemistry Bulletin
Mosc Univ Comput Math Cybern — Moscow University. Computational
    Mathematics and Cybernetics
Mosc Univ Geol Bull — Moscow University. Geology Bulletin
Mosc Univ Math Bull — Moscow University. Mathematics Bulletin
Mosc Univ Mech Bull — Moscow University. Mechanics Bulletin
Mosc Univ Phys Bull — Moscow University. Physics Bulletin
Mosc Univ Soil Sci Bull — Moscow University. Soil Science Bulletin
Mosk Fiz Tekh Inst Tr Ser Obshch Mol Fiz — Moskovskii Fiziko-Tekhnicheskii
    Institut. Trudy. Seriya "Obshchaya i Molekulyarnaya Fizika"
Mosk Inst Nar Khoz Sverdl Fil Sb Nauchn Tr — Moskovskii Institut
    Narodnogo Khozyaistva. Sverdlovskii Filial. Sbornik Nauchnykh
    Trudov
Mosk Inst Stali Sb — Moskovskii Institut Stali. Sbornik
Mosk Inst Tonkoi Khim Tekhnol Tr — Moskovskii Institut Tonkoi
    Khimicheskoi Tekhnologii. Trudy
Mosk Kolkhozn — Moskovskii Kolkhoznik

Mosk Nauchno Issled Inst Gig Im F F Erismana Sb Nauchn Tr — Moskovskii Nauchno-Issledovatel'skii Institut Gigieny Imeni F. F. Erismana. Sbornik Nauchnykh Trudov

Moskov Aviacion Inst Ordzonikidze Trudy — Moskovskii Ordena Lenina Aviacionnyi Institut Imeni Sergo Ordzonikidze. Trudy

Moskov Gos Ped Inst Ucen Zap — Moskovskii Gosudarstvennyi Pedagogiceskii Institut Imeni V. I. Lenina. Ucenye Zapiski

Moskov Gos Univ Soobsc Gos Astronom Inst Sternberg — Moskovskii Gosudarstvennyi Universitet Imeni M. V. Lomonosova. Soobscenija Gosudarstvennogo Astronomiceskogo Instituta Imeni P. K. Sternberga

Moskov Gos Univ Soobshch Gos Astronom Inst Sternberga — Moskovskii Gosudarstvennyi Universitet Imeni M. V. Lomonosova. Soobshcheniya Gosudarstvennogo Astronomicheskogo Instituta Imeni P. K. Sternberga

Moskov Gos Univ Trudy Gos Astronom Inst Sternberg — Moskovskii Gosudarstvennyi Universitet Imeni M. V. Lomonosova. Trudy Gosudarstvennogo Astronomiceskogo Instituta Imeni P. K. Sternberga

Moskov Gos Zaocn Ped Inst Sb Naucn Trudov — Moskovskii Gosudarstvennyi Zaocnyi Pedagogiceskii Institut. Sbornik Naucnyh Trudov

Moskov Inst Elektron Masinostroenija-Trudy MIEM — Moskovskii Institut Elektronnogo Masinostroenija. Trudy MIEM

Moskov Inst Inzh Zheleznodorozh Transporta Trudy — Moskovskii Institut Inzhenerov Zheleznodorozhnogo Transporta. Trudy

Moskov Inst Inz Zeleznodoroz Transporta Trudy — Moskovskii Institut Inzenerov Zeleznodoroznogo Transporta. Trudy

Moskov Inz-Stroitel Inst Sb Trudov — Moskovskii Inzenerno-Stroitelskii Institut Imeni V. V. Kuibyseva. Sbornik Trudov

Moskov Lesotehn Inst Naucn Trudy — Moskovskii Lesotehniceskii Institut. Naucnye Trudy

Moskov Oblast Ped Inst Ucen Zap — Moskovskii Oblastnoi Pedagogiceskii Institut. Ucenye Zapiski

Moskov Obshch Ispytateley Prirody Byull Otdel Geol — Byulleten' Moskovskogo Obshchestva Ispytateley Prirody Otdel Geologicheskiy

Mosk O-vo Ispyt Prir Byull Otd Geol — Moskovskoye Obshchestvo Ispytateley Prirody. Byulleten. Otdel Geologicheskiy

Mosk Univ Vestn Ser 6 Biol Pochvoved — Moskovskiy Universitet. Vestnik. Seriya 6. Biologiya. Pochvovedeniye

Mosk Univ Vestn Ser Geogr — Moskovskiy Universitet. Vestnik. Seriya Geografii

Moslem W — Moslem World

Mosonmagy Agrartud Foisk Kozl — Mosonmagyarovari Agrartudomanyi Foiskola Kozlemenyei

Mosonmagyarovari Agrartud Foiskola Kozl — Mosonmagyarovari Agrartudomanyi Foiskola Kozlemenyei

Mosonmagyarovari Mezogazdasagtud Kar Kozl — Mosonmagyarovari Mezogazdasagtudomanyi Kar Kozlemenyei

MO Speleology — Missouri Speleology

MOSQAU — Mosquito News

Mosq Control Res Annu Rep — Mosquito Control Research. Annual Report

Mosq News — Mosquito News

Mosq Syst — Mosquito Systematics

Mosq Syst News Lett — Mosquito Systematics News Letter

Mosquito Ne — Mosquito News

M Ostens — Musik des Ostens

MOstf — Marburger Ostforschungen

Mostra Int Ind Conserve Aliment Congr — Mostra Internazionale delle Industrie per le Conserve Alimentari. Congressi

Mo Summary Aust Cond — Monthly Summary of Australian Conditions

MOSVA — Mitteilungen. Oesterreichische Sanitaetsverwaltung

Mo Tax Features — Monthly Tax Features

Mot Boat — Motor Boat

Mot Boat Yacht — Motor Boat and Yachting

Mot Cycle — Motor Cycle

Moth Earth — Mother Earth News

Mother J — Mother Jones

Moth Jones — Mother Jones

Moths Am North Mex — Moths of America, North of Mexico

Motion Pict Tech Bull — Motion Picture Technical Bulletin

Motn Life — Mountain Life and Work

Motor B — Motor Boating

Motor B & S — Motor Boating and Sailing

Motor Bus — Motor Business

MotorIntnl — Motor Report International

Motoris Agr — Motorisation Agricole

Motor M — Motor Manual

Motorola Tech Dev — Motorola Technical Developments

Motorola Tech Disclosure Bull — Motorola Technical Disclosure Bulletin

Motor Serv (Chicago) — Motor Service (Chicago)

Motor T — Motor Trend

Motortech Z — Motortechnische Zeitschrift

Motor Trade J — Motor Trade Journal

Motor Transp — Motor Transport

Mo Trade & Shipping R — Monthly Trade and Shipping Review

Mot Ship — Motor Ship

Mot Sk — Motor Skills. Theory into Practice

Mot Trader — Motor Trader

MOU — Motor Business

MO Univ Eng Exp Stn Eng Repr Ser — Missouri University. Engineering Experiment Station. Engineering Reprint Series

MO Univ Sch Mines Metall Bull Gen Ser — Missouri University. School of Mines and Metallurgy. Bulletin. General Series

Mountain Geol — Mountain Geologist

Mount Plains Libr Q — Mountain Plains Library Association. Quarterly

MO U Sch Mines & Met Bul Tech Ser — University of Missouri. School of Mines and Metallurgy. Bulletin. Technical Series

Mouth — Mouth of the Dragon

Mo Utopia — Modern Utopia

Mouvement Soc — Mouvement Social

Mouvement Synd Mond — Mouvement Syndical Mondial

Mov — Movoznavstvo

MOVB — Mitteilungen. Oesterreichischer Verein fuer Bibliothekwesen

MOVBW — Mitteilungen. Oesterreichischer Verein fuer Bibliothekwesen

Movietone — Movietone News

Movietone N — Movietone News

Mov Im — Moving Image

Mov M — Movie Maker

Mov Operaio Soc — Movimento Operaio e Socialista

Mozambique Serv Geol Minas Ser Geol Minas Mem Commun Bol — Mozambique. Servicos de Geologia e Minas. Serie de Geologia e Minas. Memorias e Communicacoes. Boletim

MozartJb — Mozart-Jahrbuch

MP — Mackenzie Pilot [*Canada*]

MP — Masinnyj Perevod Trudy Instituta Tocnoj Mechaniki i Vycislitel Hoj Techniki Akademiy Nauk SSR

MP — Medical Press and Circular

MP — Methods and Phenomena [*Elsevier Book Series*]

MP — Modern Packaging

MP — Modern Philology

MPA — Michigan CPA [*Certified Public Accountant*]

M Pad — Memorie. Reale Accademia di Scienze, Lettere, ed Arti di Padova

MP Arkansas Univ Coop Ext — MP - University of Arkansas. Cooperative Extension Service

MPC — Medical Press and Circular

MPC — Metal Pi Complexes [*Elsevier Book Series*]

MPCPC — Mathematical Proceedings. Cambridge Philosophical Society

MPD — Monographs in Psychobiology and Disease [*Elsevier Book Series*]

MPEEA — Moniteur Professionnel de l'Electricite et Electronique

MPESA7 — Mar y Pesca

MPETA J — Manitoba Physical Education Teachers' Association. Journal

MPG (Max-Planck-Ges) Spiegel Aktuel Inf — MPG (Max-Planck-Gesellschaft) Spiegel. Aktuelle Informationen [*West Germany*]

MPG Presseinf — MPG [*Max-Planck-Gesellschaft*] Presseinformation

MPG Spiegel Aktuelle Inf — MPG [*Max-Planck-Gesellschaft*] Spiegel. Aktuelle Informationen

MPh — Maitre Phonetique

MPh — Modern Philology

MPh — Museum. Maanblad voor Philologie en Geschiedenis

M Phil — Modern Philology

MPhL — Museum Philologum Londiniense

MPhon — Maitre Phonetique

M Photo — Modern Photography

MPhP — Mediaevalia Philosophica Polonorum

MPI — Militaerpsykologiska Institutet

MPiKL — Masinnyj Perevod i Prikladnaja Lingvistika

MPI (McKee Pedersen Instrum) Appl Notes — MPI (McKee-Pedersen Instruments) Applications Notes

MPL — Managerial Planning

MPL — Musician, Player, and Listener

MPLMB — Modifikatsiya Polimernykh Materialov

MPLR — Municipal and Planning Law Reports

MP MD Agric Exp Stn — MP. Maryland Agricultural Experiment Station

MPMTA — Tschermaks Mineralogische und Petrographische Mitteilungen

MPNBAZ — Marine Pollution Bulletin

MPO — Marine Policy. The International Journal of Ocean Affairs

MPOBA — Monographs in Population Biology

MPologne — Musique en Pologne

MPOTB — Modern Problems in Ophthalmology

MPOUA — Memorial des Poudres

MPP — Mediaevalia Philosophica Polonorum

MPPAA — Moderne Probleme der Paediatrie

MPR — Mervyn Peake Review

MPR Met Powder Rep — MPR. Metal Powder Report

MPS — Mathematical Programming Studies [*Elsevier Book Series*]

MPS — Modern Poetry Studies

MPSOA — Preprint Series. Institute of Mathematics. University of Oslo

MPSSA — Meditsinskaya Promyshlennost SSSR

MPSSP — Modern Problems in Solid State Physics [*Elsevier Book Series*]

MPSZA — Magyar Pszichologiai Szemle

MPTh — Monatsschrift fuer Pastoraltheologie [*Goettingen*]

MPTP — Materials Processing. Theory and Practices [*Elsevier Book Series*]

MQ — Massachusetts Law Quarterly

MQ — Midwest Quarterly

MQ — Milton Quarterly

MQ — Modern Quarterly
MQ — Musical Quarterly
MQELA — Mecanique Electricite
MQG — Mitteilungen. Rheinisch-Westfaelisches Institut fuer
    Wirtschaftsforschung
Mq L — Marquette Law Review
Mq LR — Marquette Law Review
MQR — Mennonite Quarterly Review
MQR — Michigan Quarterly Review
MQRYA — Mine and Quarry
MQU — Multinational Business
MR — March
MR — Marche Romane
MR — Massachusetts Review
Mr — Mathematical Reviews
Mr — Meander
M & R — Mediaeval and Renaissance Studies
MR — Microform Review
M & R — Milton and the Romantics
MR — Minnesota Review
MR — Missionswissenschaft und Religionswissenschaft
MR — Mladinska Revija
MR — Modern Review
MR — Montana Law Review
MR — Music Review
Mr — Musikrevy
MRA — Mental Retardation Abstracts
MRATCAB — Murray River and Tributaries - Current Awareness Bulletin
MRAZBN — Koninklijk Museum voor Midden-Afrika [Tervuren, Belgie].
    Annalen. Reeks in Octavo. Zoologische Wetenschappen
MRBOAS — Marine Biology [New York]
MRCHB — Marine Chemistry
MRCHBD — Marine Chemistry
MRCLBP — Marcellia
MRCOD — Mechanics Research Communications
MRCSA — Medical Research Council. Special Report Series
MRCYA — Mercury
MR & D — Management Review and Digest
MRD — Media Review Digest
MRD — Memoirs. Research Department. Toyo Bunko
MRDTB — Memoirs. Research Department. Toyo Bunko
MRE — Management Review
MRE — Monographies Reine Elisabeth [Brussels]
MRED — Mountain Research and Development
Mr Eng/Log — Marine Engineering/Log
M Reporter — Mining Reporter
MRERB — Marine Engineers Review
MRev — Mediterranean Review
MRF — Manager Magazin
MRFWA4 — Malaysia. Penyata Tahunan Perhutanan Di-Malaysia Barat
    Tahun
MRFWA4 — Malaysia. Report on Forest Administration in West Malaysia
MRG — Mitteilungen. Raabe-Gesellschaft
MRGB — Mittelrheinische Geschichtsblaetter
MRGGAT — Morgagni
MRGRAS — Koninklijk Museum voor Midden-Afrika [Tervuren, Belgie].
    Rapport Annuel. Departemente de Geologie et de Mineralogie
MRGTAY — Marine Geotechnology
MRI — Maandstatistiek van de Brijzen
MRINAQ — Marine Research in Indonesia
MRINCS — Multidisciplinary Research
MRI Technical Report Series — Mineral Resources Institute. Technical Report
    Series
MRKTD — Marktforschung
MRL — Monthly Retail Trade. Current Business Report
MRL — Mutation Research Letters
MRLAA2 — Marine Research Laboratory. Investigational Report [South-
    West Africa]
MRLAB — Mededelingen. Rijksfaculteit Landbouwwetenschappen te Gent
    (Belgium)
MRLTAP — Murrelet
MR Miss Agr Exp Sta — MR. Mississippi Agricultural Experiment Station
MRo — Marche Romane
MRom — Marche Romane
MRP — American Review of Public Administration
MRR — Mad River Review
MRR — Market Research Great Britain
MRRTS — Manitoba. Department of Renewable Resources and
    Transportation Services. Research Branch. Reports [Canada]
MRRVB — Meteornoe Rasprostranenie Radiovoln
MRS — Materials Research Society. Symposia. Proceedings [Elsevier Book
    Series]
M & RS — Mediaeval and Renaissance Studies
MRS — Mediaeval and Renaissance Studies
MRS — Michigan Romance Studies
MRSHAO — Marine Research Series. Scottish Home Department

MRSPD — Materials Research Society. Symposia. Proceedings
MRSQ — Medical Reference Services. Quarterly
MRTMBB — Maritimes
MRV — Mex-Am Review
MRWKA — Marine Week
MRX — National Bank of Ethiopia. Quarterly Bulletin. New Series
MRYAA — Memoirs. Royal Astronomical Society
MRZGA — Metody Razvedochnoi Geofiziki
MS — Manchester School of Economic and Social Studies
MS — Mar del Sur
M/S — Media/Scope
MS — Mediaeval Studies
MS — Melanges Syriens Offerts a Monsieur Rene Dussaud
MS — Memorias Succintas. Kahal Kados [Amsterdam]
MS — Microstructural Science [Elsevier Book Series]
MS — Midnight Sun. Igloolik
MS — Moderna Sprak
MS — Monde Slave
MS — Monumenta Serica
MS — Mouvement Sociologique
Ms — Ms Magazine
MS — MS. Manuscript [Los Angeles]
MS — Music Survey
M S — Muzikal'niy Sovremennik
MSA — Vakblad voor de Handel in Aardappelen, Groenten, en Fruit
MSAF — Memoires. Societe Nationale des Antiquaires de France
MSAGD9 — Maritime Sediments and Atlantic Geology
MSAM — Memoires. Societe des Antiquaires de la Morinie
MSAO — Memoires. Societe des Antiquaires de l'Ouest
MSAP — Memoires. Societe des Antiquaires de Picardie
MSARLRP — McGill Sub-Arctic Research Laboratory. Research Paper
MSATA — Societa Astronomica Italiana. Memorie
MSAVAH — Institut Suisse de Recherches Forestieres. Memoires
MSAVAH — Istituto Svizzero di Ricerche Forestali. Memorie
MSB — Mongolia Society. Bulletin
MSBCD2 — Marine Studies of San Pedro Bay, California
MSBG-A — Masalah Bangunan
MSBMRS — Marine Sciences Branch. Manuscript Report Series. Canada
    Department of Energy, Mines, and Resources
MSBTA — Memoires. Academie des Sciences, Inscriptions, et Belles-Lettres
    de Toulouse
MScan — Mediaeval Scandinavia
MSCDA — Monographs. Society for Research in Child Development
MSch — Modern Schoolman
Mschr Wien Tieraerztl — Monatsschrift Wiener Tieraerztliche
M Science — Mining Science
M Sci Rel — Melanges de Science Religieuse
MSCOA — Metallurgical Society. Conferences
M Sc Press — Mining and Scientific Press
MScRel — Melanges de Science Religieuse [Lille]
MSCS — Mankato State College [later Mankato State University] Studies
MSCT — Marine Science Contents Tables
MS Diss — Manuscript Dissertation
MSE — Massachusetts Studies in English
MSE — Mathematical Studies in Economics and Statistics in the USSR and
    Eastern Europe
MSEC — Memoires. Societe d'Emulation de Cambrai
MSER — Memoires. Societe d'Emulation de Roubaix
MSer — Monumenta Serica
MSEWA — Memoirs. School of Science and Engineering. Waseda University
M S Ex — Melville Society. Extracts
MSF — Marvel Science Fiction
MSF — Memorie Storiche Forogiuliesi
MSFFF — Memoranda Societatis pro Fauna et Flora Fennica
MSFL — Metodologia delle Scienze e Filosofia del Linguaggio
MSFO — Memoires. Societe Finno-Ougrienne
MSForogiuliesi — Memorie Storiche Forogiuliesi
MSFOu — Memoires. Societe Finno-Ougrienne
MSG — Mitteilungen. Sonzino-Gesellschaft
MSGFOK — Mitteilungen. Schweizerische Gesellschaft der Freunde
    Ostasiatischer Kultur
MSGSB — Gijutsu Shiryo. Mitsubishi Sekiyu Kabushiki Kaisha
MSGV — Mitteilungen. Schlesische Gesellschaft fuer Volkskunde
MSHDI — Memoires. Societe pour l'Histoire du Droit et des Institutions des
    Anciens Pays Bourguignons, Comtois, et Romands
MSJMAZ — Mount Sinai Journal of Medicine
MSK — Mitteilungen. Stadtarchiv von Koeln
MSL — Manchester School of Economic and Social Studies
MSL — Memoires. Societe Linguistique de Paris
MSL — Miscellanea di Storia Ligure
MSLBA — Muscle Biology
MSLC — Miscellanea di Studi Letteratura Cristiana Antica
MS LJ — Mississippi Law Journal
MSLL — Monograph Series on Languages and Linguistics. Georgetown
    University
MSLOB — Mineralia Slovaca

MSLP — Memoires. Societe Linguistique de Paris
MSLund — Meddelanden fran Seminarierna foer Slaviska Sprak, Jamforande Sprakforskning och Finsk-Ugriska Sprak vis Lunds Universitet
MSM — Materials Science Monographs [*Elsevier Book Series*]
MSM — Memoires. Societe d'Agriculture, Commerce, Sciences, et Arts du Departement de la Marne
MsM — Ms Magazine
MSMarne — Memoires. Societe d'Agriculture, Commerce, Sciences, et Arts du Departement de la Marne
MSMC — Masterkey. Southwest Museum (Los Angeles, California)
MSMHD — Medecine Aeronautique et Spatiale, Medecine Subaquatique et Hyperbare
MSMND — South African Medical Equipment News
MSMSD — Mechanics of Materials
MSN — Microwave Systems News
MSN — Monthly Science News
MSNAF — Memoires. Societe Nationale des Antiquaires de France
MSNH — Memoires. Societe Neophilologique de Helsinki
M Soc NS J — Mining Society of Nova Scotia. Journal
MSOS — Mitteilungen. Seminar fuer Orientalische Sprachen zu Berlin
MSOSD — Mathematical Social Sciences
MSp — Muttersprache
MSPA — Missinipe Achimowin. Churchill River Information
MSPAIRS — Missinipe Achimowin. Interim Report Supplement
MSPP — Maharastra Sahitya Parisad Patrika
MSpr — Moderna Sprak
MSprak — Moderna Sprak
MSQSAK — Mosquito Systematics
MSR — Industrie- und Handelsrevue
MSR — Malone Society. Reprints
MSR — Melanges de Science Religieuse
MSRC — Memoires. Societe Royale du Canada
MSRN — Mountain Safety Research Newsletter
MSRT J — MSRT [*Michigan Society for Respiratory Therapy*] Journal
MSS — Manuscripts
MSS — Marvel Science Stories
MSS — Muenchener Studien zur Sprachwissenschaft
MSSCD — Microstructural Science
MSSLA — Missili
MST — Middle East Transport
MSt — Mitteldeutsche Studien
MSt — Monastic Studies
MStud — Milton Studies
MSU — Mitteilungen. Septuaginta Unternehmen [*Berlin/Goettingen*]
MSU — MSU [*Michigan State University*] Business Topics
MSU Bus To — MSU [*Michigan State University*] Business Topics
MSU Bus Top — MSU [*Michigan State University*] Business Topics
MSU Bus Topics — MSU [*Michigan State University*] Business Topics
MSU (Mich State Univ) Bus Topics — MSU (Michigan State University) Business Topics
MSV — Maandstatistiek Verkeer en Vervoer
MSV — Miscellanea Storica della Valdelsa
MSWFA — Messwerte
MSYNAB — Mosquito Systematics News Letter
MSzA — Mainzer Studien zur Amerikanistik
MSZS — Muenchener Studien zur Sprachwissenschaft
MT — Machine Translation
MT — Management Today
MT — Marvel Tales
MT — Matematisk Tidsskrift
MT — Mechanical Translation
MT — Medical Times and Gazette [*London*]
mt — Meerestechnik
MT — Moccasin Telegraph. Fort Chipewyan
MT — Museum Tusculanum
MT — Music Theory Spectrum
MT — Musical Times
MTA — Magyar Tudomanyos Akademia. Nyelv-es Irodalomtudomanyi Osztalyanak. Koezlemenyei
MTA — Materials Engineering
MTAJ — MTA [*Motor Traders Association of New South Wales*] Official Journal
MTAK — Magyar Tudomanyos Akademia. Nyelv-es Irodalomtudomanyi Osztalyanak. Koezlemenyei
MTatD — Materialy po Tatarskoj Dialektologii
MTB — Tokyo. Toyo Bunko [*Oriental Library*]. Research Department. Memoirs
MTCA — Magazine. Texas Commission on Alcoholism
MTCPCI — Marine Technology Society. Annual Conference. Preprints
MTD — Management Decision
MTDFA — Metal Treatment and Drop Forging
MTDYA — Modern Trends in Dermatology
MTG — Medical Times and Gazette [*London*]
Mt Geol — Mountain Geologist
MTGRB — Metallographic Review
Mt Grow — Mountaineer Grower

MTGSA — Mitteilungen aus dem Arbeitsbereich. Metallgesellschaft AG
Mtherapie — Musiktherapie
Mthly Bull Constr Indices (Bldg Civil Engng) — Monthly Bulletin of Construction Indices (Building and Civil Engineering)
Mthly Dig Transp News — Monthly Digest of Transport News
Mthly Lab R — Monthly Labor Review
Mthly Publ Opin Surv — Monthly Public Opinion Surveys
Mthly R — Monthly Review
MThS — Muenchener Theologische Studien
M Th Z — Muenchener Theologische Zeitschrift
MTIAA — Metalurgiya [*Sofia, Bulgaria*]
M Times — Musical Times
MTJ — Mark Twain Journal
MTLGA — Metallurgie
MTM — Journal of Methods-Time Measurement
MTM — Management Team
MTM — Marches Tropicaux et Mediterraneens
MTO — Management Today
Mtone News — Movietone News
MTP Int Rev Sci Biochem — MTP [*Medical & Technical Publishing Co.*] International Review of Science. Biochemistry
Mt Plains Lib Assn Q — Mountain Plains Library Association. Quarterly
MTQ — Mark Twain Quarterly
MTS — Marine Technology Series [*Elsevier Book Series*]
MTS — Most Thrilling Science Ever Told
MTSHB5 — Morioka Tabako Shikenjo Hokoku
Mt Sinai J — Mount Sinai Journal of Medicine
Mt Sinai J Med — Mount Sinai Journal of Medicine
MTSJBB — Marine Technology Society. Journal
Mt States Miner Age — Mountain States Mineral Age
MTTKA — Meteoritika
MTTMA — Memoirs. Faculty of Technology. Tokyo Metropolitan University
MTTQ — Medical Trial Technique Quarterly
MTU — Muenchener Texte und Untersuchungen zur Deutschen Literatur des Mittelalters
MTUDLM — Muenchener Texte und Untersuchungen zur Deutschen Literatur des Mittelalters
MTWOA — Metalworking
MTY — MTM. Journal of Methods Time Measurement
MTZ — Motortechnische Zeitschrift [*Stuttgart*]
MTZ — Muenchener Theologische Zeitschrift
MTZ Motortech Z — MTZ. Motortechnische Zeitschrift
Mu — Mulino
Mu — Muttersprache. Zeitschrift zur Pflege und Erforschung der Deutschen Sprache
MUB — Melanges. Universite Saint Joseph (Beyrouth)
MUBBDD — Moscow University. Biological Sciences Bulletin
MUEHA — Muehle
Muehle Mischfuttertech — Muehle und Mischfuttertechnik
MUELC — Mundo Electronico
Muench Beit Abwasser-Fisch- Flussbiol — Muenchener Beitraege zur Abwasser-, Fischerei-, und Flussbiologie
Muench Beitr — Muenchener Beitraege zur Romanischen und Englischen Philologie
Muench Beitr Abwasser Fisch Flussbiol — Muenchener Beitraege zur Abwasser-, Fischerei-, und Flussbiologie [*West Germany*]
Muenchen Med Wchnschr — Muenchener Medizinische Wochenschrift
Muench Geogr Abh — Muenchener Geographische Abhandlungen
Muench Jahr Bild Kunst — Muenchener Jahrbuch der Bildenden Kunst
Muench Med Wochenschr — Muenchener Medizinische Wochenschrift
Muench Med Wschr — Muenchener Medizinische Wochenschrift
Muenchner Beitr Abwasser Fisch Flussbiol — Muenchener Beitraege zur Abwasser-, Fischerei-, und Flussbiologie
Muench Tieraerztl Wochenschr — Muenchener Tieraerztliche Wochenschrift
Muenster Forsch Geol Palaeontol — Muenstersche Forschungen zur Geologie und Palaeontologie
Muenstersche Forsch Geol Palaeontol — Muenstersche Forschungen zur Geologie und Palaeontologie
Muenstersche N Z — Muenstersche Numismatische Zeitung
Mueszaki Terv — Mueszaki Tervezes
Mueszeruegyi Merestech Koezl — Mueszeruegyi es Merestechnikai Koezlemenyek [*Hungary*]
Muesz Koezl Lang Gepgyar Muesz Gazd Tajek — Mueszaki Koezlemenyek. Lang Gepgyar Mueszaki es Gazdasagi Tajekoztatoja [*Hungary*]
Muesz Tud — Mueszaki Tudomany [*Hungary*]
MUFOB — Metempirical UFO [*Unidentified Flying Object*] Bulletin
MU Gazette — Melbourne University. Gazette
MUHLA2 — Muehlenzeitung
Muhle Mischfuttertech — Muehle und Mischfuttertechnik
MuI — Music Index
Muirhead Tech — Muirhead Technique
Muirh Lib P — Muirhead Library of Philosophy
MUJSAX — Marathwada University. Journal of Science. Section A. Physical Sciences
MUJSBY — Marathwada University. Journal of Science. Section B. Biological Sciences

MuK — Maske und Kothurn
MUK — Wirtschaftlichkeit
Mukomol' -Elevator Prom — Mukomol'no-Elevatornaya Promyshlennost'
Mukomolno Elevat Kombikormovaya Promst — Mukomol'no Elevatornaya i Kombikormovaya Promyshlennost
Mukomolno Elevat Promst — Mukomol'no-Elevatornaya Promyshlennost'
MuL — Music and Letters
MU Law R — Melbourne University. Law Review
Mullard Tech Commun — Mullard Technical Communications
MULR — Melbourne University. Law Review
MULRA6 — Muellerei
MULS — Minnesota Union List of Serials
Multicult — Multiculturalism
Multicult Ed — Multicultural Education
Multicult Ed J — Multicultural Education Journal
Multidisciplinary Res — Multidisciplinary Research
Multidiscip Res — Multidisciplinary Research
Multinational Bus — Multinational Business
Multinatl — Multinational Monitor
Multinatl Monit — Multinational Monitor
Multi Scler Abstr — Multiple Sclerosis Abstracts
Multivar Behav Res — Multivariate Behavioral Research
Multivar Behav Res Monogr — Multivariate Behavioral Research Monograph
Multiv Be R — Multivariate Behavioral Research
Mult Mon — Multinational Monitor
MUM — Melbourne University. Magazine
MUM — Music Ministry
MUMEB — Music Clubs Magazine
MUMED9 — Museum Memoir [*Salisbury*]
MUMEEA — Mundo Medico
MUMSCMR — McGill University. Marine Sciences Centre. Manuscript Report
MUMUA — Music and Musicians
MUN — Musical Newsletter
Mun Att'y — Municipal Attorney
Munca Sanit — Munca Sanitara
MunchThZ — Muenchener Theologische Zeitschrift [*Munich*]
Mund — Mundus Artium
Mundo Apic — Mundo Apicola
Mundo Electron — Mundo Electronico
MundusA — Mundus Artium
Mundus Art — Mundus Artium
MUNFA — Moderne Unfallverhuetung
Munger Africana Lib Notes — Munger Africana Library Notes
Munic Adm Eng — Municipal Administration and Engineering
Munic Aff — Municipal Affairs
Munic Bldg Mgmt — Municipal Building Management
Munic & Co Eng — Municipal and County Engineering
Munic Cty Eng — Municipal and County Engineering
Munic Eng — Municipal Engineer
Munic Eng in Aust — Municipal Engineering in Australia
Munic Eng Aust — Municipal Engineering in Australia
Munic Eng (Indianapolis) — Municipal Engineering (Indianapolis)
Munic Eng J — Municipal Engineers Journal
Munic Engng — Municipal Engineering
Munic J — Municipal Journal
Munic Mirror — Municipal Mirror and Queensland Shire Record
Munic News — Municipal News
Munic News Water Works — Municipal News and Water Works
Munic Ref Lib Notes — New York City Public Library. Municipal Reference Library. Notes
Munic Ref & Res Center Notes — New York City Municipal Reference and Research Center. Notes
Munic Rev — Municipal Review
Munic & Road Board Gaz — Municipal and Road Board Gazette
Munic & Road Board Gazette — Municipal and Road Board Gazette
Munic Sanit — Municipal Sanitation
Munic Util — Municipal Utilities
Munic Util Mag — Municipal Utilities Magazine
Munkaved Munka Uezemeue — Munkavedelem. Munka-es Uezemegeszseguegy
Mun L Ct Dec — Municipal Law Court Decisions
MUNOPB — Memorial University of Newfoundland. Occasional Papers in Biology
Mun Ord Rev — Municipal Ordinance Review
Mun Plan L Rep — Municipal and Planning Law Reports
MUNSDM — Marathwada University. Journal of Science
Munsey — Munsey's Magazine
MU Oddfellows Mag — Manchester Unity Oddfellows' Magazine
MUOX — Musk-Ox
MUOXD — Musk-Ox
MUR — Al-Mustansiriya University. Review [*Baghdad*]
Mur — Murray's Reports [*New South Wales*]
Murm Olenevodcheskaya Opytn Stn Sb Nauchn Rab — Murmanskaya Olenevodcheskaya Opytnaya Stantsiya. Sbornik Nauchnykh Rabot

Muromsk Gos Ped Inst Ucen Zap — Muromskii Gosudarstvennyi Pedagogiceskii Institut. Ucenye Zapiski
Murr — Murray's Reports [*New South Wales*]
Murray — Murray's Magazine
Murray VA — Murray Valley Annual
MURT — Murrelet
MUS — Multinational Services
Mus — Museon. Revue d'Etudes Orientales
Mus — Museum of Foreign Literature [*Littell's*]
Mus — Museum. Maanblad voor Philologie en Geschiedenis
Mus Academy Jl — Music Academy. Journal
Mus Afr — Museum Africum
Mus Am — Musical America
Mus Anal — Musical Analysis
Mus y Artes — Boletin de Musica y Artes Visuales
Mus & Artists — Music and Artists
MusB — Musee Belge
MUSBDU — Moscow University. Soil Science Bulletin
Mus u Bild — Musik und Bildung
Muscan — Musicanada [*English Edition*]
MU Sci R — Melbourne University. Science Review
Mus Civ Stor Nat Verona Mem Fuori Ser — Museo Civico di Storia Naturale di Verona. Memorie. Fuori Serie
Muscle Biol — Muscle Biology
Mus Clubs Mag — Music Clubs Magazine
Mus Comp Zool (Harv Univ) Annu Rep — Museum of Comparative Zoology (Harvard University). Annual Report
Mus Comp Zool Mem — Museum of Comparative Zoology [*Harvard University*]. Memoirs
Mus Cour — Musical Courier
Mus & Dance — Music and Dance
Mus Dealer — Music Dealer
Mus Denmark — Musical Denmark
Mus Dev — Muscular Development
Mus Disc — Musica Disciplina
Mus in Ed — Music in Education
Mus Ed J — Music Educators Journal
Mus Educ J — Music Educators Journal
Musee Guimet Annales Bibl d'Etud — Musee Guimet. Annales. Bibliotheque d'Etudes
Musee Guimet Annales Bibl de Vulg — Musee Guimet. Annales. Bibliotheque de Vulgarisation
Musee Nat Homme Centre Canad Et Culture Trad — Musee National de l'Homme. Centre Canadien d'Etudes sur la Culture Traditionnelle
Museo Nac de Hist Nat de Buenos Aires Anales — Museo Nacional de Historia Natural de Buenos Aires. Anales
Museum Comp Zool Memoirs — Harvard University. Museum of Comparative Zoology. Memoirs
Museum d'Hist Nat de Lyon Archives — Museum d'Histoire Naturelle de Lyon. Archives
Museums Jnl — Museums Journal
Museum Stud — Museum Studies
Mus Events — Musical Events
Mus Felipe Poey Acad Cienc Cuba Trab Divulg — Museo "Felipe Poey." Academia de Ciencias de Cuba. Trabajos de Divulgacion
Mus Forum — Music Forum
Mus Geneve — Musees de Geneve
Mus u Ges — Musik und Gesellschaft
Mus u Gottesd — Musik und Gottesdienst
Mus Guimet Ann Bibl Etudes — Musee Guimet. Annales. Bibliotheque d'Etudes
Mus Guimet Ann Bibl Vulg — Musee Guimet. Annales. Bibliotheque de Vulgarisation
MUSHA — Music Trades
Mus Ha'aretz Bull — Museum Ha'aretz Bulletin [*Tel Aviv*]
Mus Helv — Museum Helveticum
Mus Hist Nat Grigore Antipa Trav — Museum d'Histoire Naturelle Grigore Antipa. Travaux
Mus Hist Nat Lyon Nouv Arch — Museum d'Histoire Naturelle de Lyon. Nouvelles Archives
Mus Hist Nat Lyon Nouv Arch Suppl — Museum d'Histoire Naturelle de Lyon. Nouvelles Archives. Supplement
Mus Hist Nat Mars Bull — Museum d'Histoire Naturelle de Marseille. Bulletin
Mus at Home — Music at Home
Mushroom Sci — Mushroom Science
Mus I — Music Index
Music Am — Music America
Music Artic Guide — Music Article Guide
Music Disci — Musica Disciplina
Music in Ed — Music in Education
Music Ed Jnl — Music Educators Journal
Music Educ — Music Educators Journal
MusicI — Music Index
Music Ind — Music Index
Music J — Music Journal

Music Lett — Music and Letters
Music Lib Assn Notes — Music Library Association. Notes
Music Libr Ass Notes — Music Library Association. Notes
Music Man — Music and Man
Musicol — Musicology
Musicol Slovaca — Musicologica Slovaca
Music Quart — Musical Quarterly
Music R — Music Review
Music Rev — Music Review
Music (SMA) — Music (Schools of Music Association)
Music Teach — Music and the Teacher
Music Time — Musical Times
Music Trad — Music Trades
Musikforsch — Musikforschung
Musil S — Musil Studien
Mus Industry — Music Industry
Mus Int — Musik International - Instrumentenbau-Zeitschrift
MUSIP — Marquette University. Slavic Institute. Papers
MUSJ — Melanges. Universite Saint Joseph
Mus J — Museums Journal
Mus J — Music Journal
Mus Jazz — Musica Jazz
Mus Jeu — Musique en Jeu
Mus Jl — Music Journal
Mus Judaica — Musica Judaica
MUSKA — Music in Education
Mus u Kir — Musik und Kirche
MusL — Music and Letters
Mus Leader — Musical Leader
Mus and Let — Music and Letters
Mus & Lett — Music and Letters
Mus Lib Assn Notes — Music Library Association. Notes
Muslim W — Muslim World
Muslim Wld — Muslim World
Muslim Wrld — Muslim World
Mus et Lit — Musique et Liturgie
MuslW — Muslim World
Mus Mag — Music Magazine
Mus Mak — Music Maker
Mus Mem (Salisbury) — Museum Memoir (Salisbury)
Mus Midden-Afr Ann Reeks in 8O Geol Wet — Museum voor Midden-Afrika. Annalen. Reeks in Octavo. Geologische Wetenschappen
Mus Min — Music Ministry
Mus Mod Art Bul — New York City Museum of Modern Art. Bulletin
Mus & Mus — Music and Musicians
Mus N — Museum News
Mus Nac Hist Nat Bol (Santiago) — Museo Nacional de Historia Natural. Boletin (Santiago)
Mus Nac Hist Nat Bol (Santiago De Chile) — Museo Nacional de Historia Natural. Boletin (Santiago De Chile)
Mus Nac Hist Nat Notic Mens (Santiago) — Museo Nacional de Historia Natural. Noticiario Mensual (Santiago) [*Chile*]
Mus Nac Hist Nat Not Mens (Santiago) — Museo Nacional de Historia Natural. Noticiario Mensual (Santiago)
Mus Nac Hist Nat (Santiago De Chile) Publ Ocas — Museo Nacional de Historia Natural (Santiago De Chile). Publicacion Ocasional
Mus Nac Hist Natur Buenos Aires An — Museo Nacional de Historia Natural de Buenos Aires. Anales
Mus Nac Mex An — Museo Nacional de Mexico. Anales
Mus Nac Pubs Avulas — Museu Nacional. Publicacoes Avulsas
Mus Nat Homme Publ Ethnol — Musee National de l'Homme. Publications d'Ethnologie
Mus Nat Homme Public Archeol — Musee National de l'Homme. Publications d'Archeologie
Mus Natl Hist Nat Bull — Museum National d'Histoire Naturelle. Bulletin
Mus Natl Hist Nat Mem Ser A (Paris) — Museum National d'Histoire Naturelle. Memoires. Serie A. Zoologie (Paris)
Mus Natl Hist Nat Not Syst — Museum National d'Histoire Naturelle. Notulae Systematicae
Mus Natl Hist Nat (Paris) Mem Ser C — Museum National d'Histoire Naturelle. Memoires. Serie C. Sciences de la Terre (Paris)
Mus Natl Histoire Nat Bull — Museum National d'Histoire Naturelle. Bulletin
Mus Natl Hung Ann Hist-Nat — Museum Nationale Hungaricum. Annales Historico-Naturales
Mus Natnl Hist Nat (Paris) Mem Ser C — Museum National d'Histoire Naturelle. Memoires. Serie C (Paris)
Mus News — Music News
Mus News — Musical Newsletter
Mus News Prague — Music News from Prague
Mus North Ariz Bull — Museum of Northern Arizona. Bulletin
Mus North Ariz Res Cent (Flagstaff) Annu Rep — Museum of Northern Arizona and Research Center (Flagstaff). Annual Report
Mus d'Oggi — Musica d'Oggi. Rassegna di Vita e di Cultura Musicale
Mus Oggi — Musica d'Oggi. Rassegna di Vita e di Cultura Musicale

Mus Op — Musical Opinion
Mus Parade — Music Parade
Mus Para Emilio Goeldi Publ Avulsas — Museu Paraense Emilio Goeldi. Publicacoes Avulsas
Mus Par E Goeldi Pub Avulsas — Museu Paraense Emilio Goeldi. Publicacoes Avulsas
Mus P & L — Musician, Player, and Listener
Mus Q — Musical Quarterly
Mus Qu — Musical Quarterly
Mus R — Music Review
Mus R Afr Centr (Tervuren Belg) Rapp Annu Dep Geol Mineral — Musee Royal de l'Afrique Centrale (Tervuren, Belgique). Rapport Annuel du Departement de Geologie et de Mineralogie
Mus R Afr Cent (Tervuren Belg) Ann Ser Octavo Sci Geol — Musee Royal de l'Afrique Centrale (Tervuren, Belgique). Annales. Serie in Octavo. Sciences Geologiques
Mus R Afr Cent (Tervuren Belg) Ann Ser Octavo Sci Zool — Musee Royal de l'Afrique Centrale (Tervuren, Belgique). Annales. Serie in Octavo. Sciences Zoologiques
Mus R Afr Cent (Tervuren Belg) Doc Zool — Musee Royal de l'Afrique Centrale (Tervuren, Belgique). Documentation Zoologique
Mus R Afr Cent (Tervuren Belg) Do Zool — Musee Royal de l'Afrique Centrale (Tervuren, Belgique). Documentation Zoologique
Mus Rev — Music Review
Mus R d'Hist Nat Belgique B — Musee Royal d'Histoire Naturelle de Belgique. Bulletin
Mus Roy Afr Cent Dep Geol Mineral Rap Ann — Musee Royal de l'Afrique Centrale. Departement de Geologie et de Mineralogie. Rapport Annuel
MusS — Musees Suisses
Mus Sacra — Musica Sacra
Mus Scene — Music Scene
Mus Schall — Musica Schallplatte. Zeitschrift fuer Schallplattenfreunde
Mus in Schule — Musik in der Schule
Mus Slovaca — Musicologica Slovaca
Mus Stor Nat Ven Tridentia Studi Trentini Sci Nat — Museo di Storia Naturale della Venezia Tridentina. Studi Trentini di Scienze Naturali [*Italy*]
Mus Stud — Museum Studies. Art Institute of Chicago
Mus Superv J — Music Supervisors Journal
Mus Survey — Music Survey
Mus T — Musical Times
Mus Tcr — Music Teacher and Piano Student
Mus Teach Nat Assn Proc — Music Teachers National Association. Proceedings
Mus Teyler Archiv — Musee Teyler. Archives
Mus Theory Spectrum — Music Theory Spectrum
Mus Times — Musical Times
Mus Today Nl — Music Today Newsletter
Mus Trade Rev — Music Trade Review
Mus Trades — Music Trades
Mus West — Music of the West Magazine
Musz Elet — Muszaki Elet
Muszerugyi Merestech Kozl — Muszerugyi es Merestechnikai Kozlemenyek [*Hungary*]
Musz Tud — Muszaki Tudomany
Mut — Muttersprache
Mutat Res — Mutation Research
Mutat Res Genet Toxicol Test — Mutation Research; Genetic Toxicology Testing
Mutat Res Sect Environ Mutagenesis Relat Subj — Mutation Research. Section on Environmental Mutagenesis and Related Subjects
Mutech Chem Eng J — Mutech Chemical Engineering Journal
MUTED — Muszaki Tervezes
Mutisia Acta Bot Colomb — Mutisia. Acta Botanica Colombiana
MUTSA — Music Teacher
MUUJA — Musart
Muves Ertes — Mueveszettoerteneti Ertesitoe
MUY — Management International Review
Muz — Muzeon
Muz F — Muzykal'naya Fol'kloristika
Muz Istor Munic Bucur — Muzeul de Istorie al Municipiului Bucuresti
Muz Nat — Muzeul National
Muz Pam Kult — Muzei i Pametnizi na Kulturata
Muz Pitesti — Muzeul din Pitesti. Studii si Comunicari. Istorie-Stiintele Naturii
Muz Stiint Naturii Bacau Stud Comun — Muzeul de Stiintele Naturii Bacau Studii si Comunicari
Muz Vlastivedna Prace — Muzejni a Vlastivedna Prace
Muz Zbornik — Muzikoloski Zbornik - Musicological Annual
MV — Minority Voices
MVAA — Mitteilungen. Verein zur Abwehr des Antisemitismus
MVAeG — Mitteilungen. Vorderasiatisch-Aegyptische Gesellschaft
MVAG — Mitteilungen. Vorderasiatisch-Aegyptische Gesellschaft
MVB — Jahrbuch der Absatz- und Verbrauchsforschung
MVBI — Mitteilungen. Verband Ehemaliger Breslauer und Schlesier in Israel [*Tel Aviv*]

MVBRAV — Multivariate Behavioral Research
MVEJDP — Malaysian Veterinary Journal
MVEOL — Mededeelingen en Verhandelingen Ex Oriente Lux
MVGAFr — Mitteilungen. Verein fuer Geschichte und Altertumskunde in
    Frankfurt-Am-Main
MVGDB — Mitteilungen. Verein fuer Geschichte der Deutschen in Boehmen
MVGGA — Mitteilungen. Versuchsstation fuer das Gaerungsgewerbe in Wien
    (Austria)
MVGKA — Mitteilungen. Vereinigung der Grosskesselbesitzer
MVGKB — Mitteilungen. VGB [*Technische Vereinigung der
    Grosskraftwerksbetreiber*]
MVGOW — Mitteilungen. Verein fuer Geschichte von Ost- und West Preussen
MVGSN — Mitteilungen. Verein fuer Geschichte der Stadt Nuernberg
MVH — Munzautomat Mainz
MVHG — Mitteilungen. Verein der Freunde des Humanistischen Gymnasiums
MVHR — Mississippi Valley Historical Review
MVKAUO — Mitteilungen. Verein fuer Kunst und Altertum in Ulm und
    Oberschwaben Ulm
MVL — Maandschrift voor Liturgie
MVL — Monografieen over Vlaamse Letterkunde
MVLCA — Mededelingen. Vlaamse Chemische Vereniging
MVN — Mededeelingen Uitgegeven. Vereniging voor Naamkunde te Leuven
MVN — Mededeelingen. Vereniging Naamkunde te Leuven en Commissie
    Naamkunde te Amsterdam
MVNAG — Mitteilungen. Verein fuer Nassauische Altertumskunde und
    Geschichts-Forschung
MVNLA — Mededeelingen. Vereniging Naamkunde te Leuven en Commissie
    Naamkunde te Amsterdam
MVP Ber — MVP [*Max-Von-Pettenkofer-Institut*] Berichte
MVPhW — Mitteilungen. Verein Klassischer Philologen in Wien
MVV — Dibevo
MVW — Uitvaartwezen
MVZADA — Mitteilungen. Verein zur Abwehr des Antisemitismus
MW — Middle Way. Buddhist Society
MW — Muslim World
MWA — Men's Wear
MWBWA — Mededelingen. Koninklijke Vlaamse Academie voor
    Wetenschappen. Letteren en Schone Kunsten van Belgie. Klasse der
    Wetenschappen
MWD — Metalworking Digest
M Weather R — Monthly Weather Review
M Weath Rev — Monthly Weather Review
MWERA — Mechanical World and Engineering Record
M West Hist — Magazine of Western History
MWJ — Magazin fuer die Wissenschaft des Judentums
MWN — Medical World News
MWOGA2 — Montana Wool Grower
M World — Mining World
MWPL — Montreal Working Papers in Linguistics
MWQ — Midwest Quarterly
MWR — Monthly Wholesale Trade
MWW — Metall. Internationale Zeitschrift fuer Technik und Wirtschaft
Myasn Ind SSSR — Myasnaya Industriya SSSR
MYCGA — Memory and Cognition
Mycol — Mycologia
Mycol Abstr — Mycological Abstracts
Mycol Mem — Mycologia Memoir
Mycol Pap Commonw Mycol Inst — Mycological Papers. Commonwealth
    Mycological Institute
Mycopath Mycol Appl — Mycopathologia et Mycologia Applicata
Mycopathol Mycol Appl — Mycopathologia et Mycologia Applicata
Mycopathol Mycol Appl Suppl Iconogr Mycol — Mycopathologia et Mycologia
    Applicata. Supplementum Iconographia Mycologica
Mycopatholo — Mycopathologia
MYEAA — Minerals Yearbook
MYG — Food Analysis
MYH — Milieuhygiene
MYK — Metrovisie
Mykol Sb — Mykologicky Sbornik
Mykrobiol Zh — Mykrobiolchichniyi Zhurnal
MYL — Monthly Labor Review
MYOGA — Materialy Ogniotrwale
Myotis Mitteilungsbl Fledermauskundler — Myotis Mitteilungsblatt fuer
    Fledermauskundler
MYP Prod — Minerals Yearbook Preprint. Products
Mysore Agric J — Mysore Agricultural Journal
Mysore Agr J — Mysore Agricultural Journal
Mysore Dep Mines Geol Geol Stud — Mysore. Department of Mines and
    Geology. Geological Studies
Mysore J Agric Sci — Mysore Journal of Agricultural Sciences
MYT — Mysterious Traveler Mystery Reader
MYV — Maandstatistiek van de Industrie
MYZ — Mix. Ijzerwaren, Doe het Zelf
MZ — Mainzer Zeitschrift
MZ — Muzikoloski Zbornik - Musicological Annual
MZISA — Monitore Zoologico Italiano. Supplemento

MZWMA — Molkerei-Zeitung Welt der Milch

N

N — Nation
N — Neophilologus
N — November
NA — Names
NA — Nation and Athenaeum
N & A — Nation and Athenaeum
Na — Nature [*London*]
NA — Nederlandsch Archievenblad
NA — Neues Archiv der Gesellschaft fuer Aeltere Deutsche Geschichtskunde
NA — Neutestamentliche Abhandlungen
NA — New Adelphi
NA — News Agencies
NA — North American Archaeologist
NA — Note d'Archivio per la Storia Musicale
NA — Notes Africaines
NA — Nuova Antologia
NA — Nuovi Argomenti
NAA — Narody Azii i Afriki
NAA — Notices d'Archeologie Armoricaine
NAA Bul — National Association of Accountants. Bulletin
NA Anarch — North American Anarchist
NAAS — Newsletter. Association for Asian Studies
NAAS Advis Pap — National Agricultural Advisory Service. Advisory Papers [*England*]
NAAS Prog Rep — National Agricultural Advisory Service. Progress Report [*England*]
NAAS Q Rev — NAAS [*National Agricultural Advisory Service*] Quarterly Review [*England*]
NAAS Quart Rev — NAAS [*National Agricultural Advisory Service*] Quarterly Review [*England*]
NAB — Nation's Business
NAB — Nederlandsch Archievenblad
NAb — Neues Abendland
NABTE Rev — NABTE [*National Association for Business Teacher Education*] Review
NAC — Management Accounting
Nac — Nacion
NAC — National Association of College Wind and Percussion Instructors. Journal
NAC — Numismatica e Antichita Classiche
NacC — Nacional (Caracas)
Nachr Akad Wiss Goettingen — Nachrichten. Akademie der Wissenschaften zu Goettingen
Nachr Akad Wiss Goettingen Math-Phys Kl II — Nachrichten. Akademie der Wissenschaften zu Goettingen. II. Mathematisch-Physikalische Klasse
Nachr Akad Wiss Goett Philologisch-Hist Kl — Nachrichten. Akademie der Wissenschaften zu Goettingen. Philologisch-Historische Klasse
Nachr Akad Wiss UdSSR — Nachrichten. Akademie der Wissenschaften der UdSSR
NachrBl Bayer Ent — Nachrichtenblatt der Bayerischen Entomologen
Nachrbl Dt Pflschutzdienst (Berl) — Nachrichtenblatt. Deutscher Pflanzenschutzdienst (Berlin)
NachrBl Dt PflSchutzdienst (Berlin) — Nachrichtenblatt. Deutschen Pflanzenschutzdienst (Berlin)

Nachrbl Dt Pflschutzdienst (Stuttg) — Nachrichtenblatt. Deutschen Pflanzenschutzdienst (Stuttgart)
NachrBl Dt PflSchutzdienst (Stuttgart) — Nachrichtenblatt. Deutschen Pflanzenschutzdienst (Stuttgart)
Nachrbl Dtsch Pflschdienst (Berlin) — Nachrichtenblatt. Deutschen Pflanzenschutzdienst (Berlin)
Nachrbl Dtsch Pflschdienst (Braunschweig) — Nachrichtenblatt. Deutschen Pflanzenschutzdienst (Braunschweig)
NachrBl PflSchutzdienst DDR — Nachrichtenblatt fuer den Pflanzenschutzdienst in der DDR
Nachr Chem Tech — Nachrichten aus Chemie und Technik [*Later, Nachrichten aus Chemie, Technik, und Laboratorium*]
Nachr Chem Tech Lab — Nachrichten aus Chemie, Technik, und Laboratorium [*Formerly, Nachrichten aus Chemie und Technik*]
Nachr Dok — Nachrichten fuer Dokumentation
Nachr fuer Dok — Nachrichten fuer Dokumentation
Nachr Dokum — Nachrichten fuer Dokumentation
Nachr Elektron — Nachrichten Elektronik
Nachr Elektron and Telematik — Nachrichten Elektronik and Telematik
Nachr Ges Wiss Goettingen Math Phys Kl — Nachrichten. Gesellschaft der Wissenschaften zu Goettingen. Mathematisch-Physikalische Klasse
Nachr Ges Wiss Goettingen Math-Phys Kl Fachgruppe 2 — Nachrichten. Gesellschaft der Wissenschaften zu Goettingen. Mathematisch-Physikalische Klasse. Fachgruppe 2. Physik, Astronomie, Geophysik, Technik [*West Germany*]
Nachr Ges Wiss Goettingen Math Phys Kl Fachgruppe 3 — Nachrichten. Gesellschaft der Wissenschaften zu Goettingen. Mathematisch-Physikalische Klasse. Fachgruppe 3. Chemie, Einschliesslich Physikalische Chemie
Nachr Ges Wiss Goettingen Math Phys Kl Fachgruppe 4 — Nachrichten. Gesellschaft der Wissenschaften zu Goettingen. Mathematisch-Physikalische Klasse. Fachgruppe 4. Geologie und Mineralogie
Nachr Ges Wiss Goettingen Math Phys Kl Fachgruppe 6 — Nachrichten. Gesellschaft der Wissenschaften zu Goettingen. Mathematisch-Physikalische Klasse. Fachgruppe 6. Biologie
Nachr Ges Wiss Goetting Math Phys Kl Fachgruppe 1 — Nachrichten. Gesellschaft der Wissenschaften zu Goettingen. Mathematisch-Physikalische Klasse. Fachgruppe 1. Mathematik
Nachrichtenbl Deut Pflanzenschutzdienst (Stuttgart) — Nachrichtenblatt. Deutschen Pflanzenschutzdienst (Stuttgart)
Nachrichtenbl Dtsch Ges Gesch Med Naturwiss Tech — Nachrichtenblatt. Deutsche Gesellschaft fuer Geschichte der Medizin. Naturwissenschaft und Technik
Nachrichtenbl Dtsch Pflanzenschutzdienst (Berlin) — Nachrichtenblatt. Deutschen Pflanzenschutzdienst (Berlin)
Nachrichtenbl Dtsch Pflanzenschutzdienstes (Braunschweig) — Nachrichtenblatt. Deutschen Pflanzenschutzdienst (Braunschweig)
Nachrichtenbl Pflanzenschutz DDR — Nachrichtenblatt fuer den Pflanzenschutzdienst in der DDR
Nachrichtenbl Pflanzenschutzdienst DDR — Nachrichtenblatt fuer den Pflanzenschutzdienst in der DDR
Nachrichtenbl Photogr Handwerk — Nachrichtenblatt fuer das Photographen Handwerk
Nachrichtentech-Elektron — Nachrichtentechnik-Elektronik
Nachrichtentech Elektronik — Nachrichtentechnik-Elektronik

Nachrichtentech Fachber — Nachrichtentechnische Fachberichte [*West Germany*]
Nachrichtentech Fachber Beih NTZ — Nachrichtentechnische Fachberichte. Beihefte der Nachrichtentechnische Zeitschrift
Nachrichtentech Z — Nachrichtentechnische Zeitung
Nachr Naturwiss Mus Stadt (Aschaffenburg) — Nachrichten. Naturwissenschaftliches Museum der Stadt (Aschaffenburg)
Nachr Naturw Mus (Aschaffenb) — Nachrichten. Naturwissenschaftliches Museum der Stadt (Aschaffenburg)
Nachr Niedersachs Urgesch — Nachrichten aus Niedersachsens Urgeschichte
Nachr/Nouv/Notiz — Nachrichten/Nouvelles/Notizie
Nachrtech Z — Nachrichtentechnische Zeitschrift
Nachr Telefonbau & Normalzeit — Nachrichten der Telefonbau und Normalzeit
Nachr Trop Med (Tiflis) — Nachrichten der Tropischen Medizin (Tiflis)
Nachr Verein Schweizer Bibl — Nachrichten. Vereinigung Schweizerischer Bibliothekare
NACN — Native Canadian
NAC News Pestic Rev — NAC [*National Agriculture Chemicals Association*] News and Pesticide Review [*United States*]
NACTA J Natl Assoc Coll Teach Agric — NACTA Journal. National Association of Colleges and Teachers of Agriculture
NACWPI — NACWPI [*National Association of College Wind and Percussion Instructors*] Journal
NADA — Native Affairs Department. Annual
NADGA — Nagoya Kogyo Daigaku Gakuho
NADKA — Nagasaki Daigaku Suisan-Gakubu Kenkyu Hokoku
NADL J — NADL [*National Association of Dental Laboratories*] Journal
NADS — Newsletter. American Dialect Society
NAEBJ — National Association of Educational Broadcasters. Journal
Naehr — Naehrung. Chemie, Biochemie, Mikrobiologie, Technologie
NAERI — National Agricultural Economic Research Inventory
Naeringsforskning Suppl — Naeringsforskning. Supplement
NAF — National Forum. Phi Kappa Phi Journal
NAF — New African
NAfr — Notes Africaines
NAGADGK — Neues Archiv der Gesellschaft fuer Aeltere Deutsche Geschichtskunde
Nagasaki Igakkai Zasshi Suppl — Nagasaki Igakkai Zasshi. Supplement [*Japan*]
Nagasaki Med J — Nagasaki Medical Journal
NAGBA — National Gas Bulletin
NAGDA — Nara Gakugei Daigaku Kiyo
NAGMA — College of Agriculture (Nagpur). Magazine
Nag Math J — Nagoya Mathematical Journal
NagoKR — Nagoya Daigaku Bungakubu Kenkyu Ronshu [*Journal of the Faculty of Literature. Nagoya University*]
Nagoya J Med Sci — Nagoya Journal of Medical Science
Nagoya Math J — Nagoya Mathematical Journal
Nagoya Med J — Nagoya Medical Journal
Nagoya Univ Dep Earth Sci Collect Pap Earth Sci — Nagoya University. Department of Earth Sciences. Collected Papers on Earth Sciences
Nagoya Univ Inst Plasma Phys Annu Rev — Nagoya University. Institute of Plasma Physics. Annual Review
Nagoya Univ Jour Earth Sci — Nagoya University. Journal of Earth Sciences
Nagpur Agric Coll Mag — Nagpur Agricultural College. Magazine
Nagpur Coll Agric Mag — Nagpur College of Agriculture. Magazine
Nagpur Univ J — Nagpur University. Journal
NAGR — National Geographic Research
NAGSHKP — Neues Archiv fuer die Geschichte der Stadt Heidelberg und der Kurpfalz
NAGSHRP — Neues Archiv fuer die Geschichte der Stadt Heidelberg und der Rheinischen Pfalz
NAGZA — Nagasaki Igakkai Zasshi
NAIGA — Nagoya Igaku
NAIKAB — Internal Medicine
Nairobi J Med — Nairobi Journal of Medicine
NA Jl Expl Agric — New Zealand Journal of Experimental Agriculture
NAJN — North American Journal of Numismatics
NAk — Narodopisne Aktuality
NAkG — Nachrichten. Akademie der Wissenschaften zu Goettingen
NAKG — Nederlandsch Archief voor Kerkgeschiedenis
NAL — Newspapers in Australian Libraries
NALA — Native Library Advocate [*Ottawa, Canada*]
NALF — Negro American Literature Forum
NALLDJ — National Association of Language Laboratory Directors. Journal
N Am Bird Bander — North American Bird Bander
NAMC — Notiziario Archeologico del Ministero delle Colonie
NAmerR — North American Review
N Am Fauna — North American Fauna
N Am Flora — North American Flora
N Am Flora Ser II — North American Flora. Series II
NA Monthly — North Australian Monthly
N Am R — North American Review
N Am Rev — North American Review
N Am Vet — North American Veterinarian

NAN — Nachrichten fuer Dokumentation. Zeitschrift fuer Information und Dokumentation
NAN — Nassauische Annalen
NANED — Neuropathology and Applied Neurobiology
Nankai Univ Res Lab Appl Chem Rep — Nankai University. Research Laboratory of Applied Chemistry. Reports
N Ann Sc Nat (Bologna) — Nuovi Annali delle Scienze Naturali (Bologna)
Nansei Reg Fish Res Lab Bull — Nansei Regional Fisheries Research Laboratory. Bulletin [*Japan*]
NAnt — Nuova Antologia di Scienze, Lettere, ed Arti
Nanta Math — Nanta Mathematica
Nanyang Univ J Part III — Nanyang University. Journal. Part III. Natural Sciences
Na Okika O Hawaii Hawaii Orchid J — Na Okika O Hawaii/Hawaii Orchid Journal
NaR — Nasa Rec [*Paris*]
NAR — New American Review [*Later, American Review*]
NAR — North American Review
NAr — Nuovi Argomenti
NAREB — Nature and Resources [*France*]
N Arg — Nuovi Argomenti
NARHA — Nucleic Acids Research
Narisi Istor Prirodoznav i Tekhn — Narisi z Istorii Prirodoznavstva i Tekhniki
Narisi Istor Prirodozn Tekh — Narisi z Istorii Prirodoznavstva i Tekhniki [*USSR*]
Nar Khoz Sov Latv — Narodnoe Khozyaistvo Sovetskoi Latvii
Nar Khoz Uzb — Narodnoe Khozyaistvo Uzbekistana
Nar Muz (Prague) Cas Oddil Prirodoved — Narodni Muzeum. Casopis. Oddil Prirodovedny (Prague)
Narod Azii Afriki — Narody Azii i Afriki
Narod Khoz Uzbek — Narodnoe Khozyaistvo Uzbekistana
Narody AA — Narody Azii i Afriki [*Moscow*]
Narody Azii Afr — Narody Azii i Afriki
Narrag Reg — Narragansett Historical Register
Nar Tvor ta Etnogr — Narodna Tvorcist' ta Etnografija
Nar Zdravlje — Narodno Zdravlje [*Yugoslavia*]
NAS — Natuursteen
NAS — Norwegian-American Studies
NAS — Notizie degli Archivi di Stato
NASA Conf Publ — NASA [*National Aeronautics and Space Administration*] Conference Publication
NASA Contract Rep — NASA [*National Aeronautics and Space Administration*] Contractor Report
NASA Memo — NASA [*National Aeronautics and Space Administration*] Memorandum
NASA Ref Publ — NASA [*National Aeronautics and Space Administration*] Reference Publication
NASA Rep Ed — NASA [*National Aeronautics and Space Administration*] Report to Educators
NASA Spec Publ — NASA [*National Aeronautics and Space Administration*] Special Publications
NASA Tech Brief — NASA [*National Aeronautics and Space Administration*] Technical Briefs
NASA Tech Briefs — NASA [*National Aeronautics and Space Administration*] Technical Briefs
NASA Tech Memo — NASA [*National Aeronautics and Space Administration*] Technical Memorandum
NASA Tech Note — NASA [*National Aeronautics and Space Administration*] Technical Note
NASA Tech Pap — NASA [*National Aeronautics and Space Administration*] Technical Paper
NASA Tech Rep — NASA [*National Aeronautics and Space Administration*] Technical Report
NASA Tech Transl — NASA [*National Aeronautics and Space Administration*] Technical Translation
NASCA — NASA [*National Aeronautics and Space Administration*] Technical Note
NASGA — Neues Archiv fuer Saechsische Geschichte und Altertumskunde
NASGAK — Neues Archiv fuer Saechsische Geschichte und Altertumskunde
NASM — National Association of Schools of Music. Proceedings
Nas Mus Bloemfontein Jaarversl — Nasionale Museum Bloemfontein Jaarverslag
NAS-NRC D Chem Chem Technol Annu Rep — National Academy of Sciences - National Research Council. Division of Chemistry and Chemical Technology. Annual Report
NAS-NRC Div Chem Chem Technol Annu Rep — National Academy of Sciences - National Research Council. Division of Chemistry and Chemical Technology. Annual Report
NAS-NRC Nucl Sci Ser Rep — National Academy of Sciences - National Research Council. Nuclear Sciences Series. Report
NAS-NRC Publ — National Academy of Sciences - National Research Council. Publication
NASPA J — NASPA [*National Association of Student Personnel Administrators*] Journal
NASPSPA Newsl — NASPSPA [*North American Society for Psychology of Sport and Physical Activity*] Newsletter

NASR — Norwegian-American Studies and Records
NASRA — National Academy of Sciences - National Research Council. Publication [*United States*]
Nassauischer Ver Naturk Jb — Nassauischer Verein fuer Naturkunde. Jahrbuecher
Nassau L — Nassau Lawyer
NASSP-B — National Association of Secondary-School Principals. Bulletin
NASSP Bull — NASSP [*National Association of Secondary School Principals*] Bulletin
Na Stroikakh Ross — Na Stroikakh Rossii
Nas Versnellersentrum Nuus — Nasionale Versnellersentrum Nuus
Nat — Nation
NAT — National Association of Teachers of Singing. Bulletin
Nat — Naturalist
Nat A — Nationalmuseets Arbeidsmark
Nat Acad Sci Biog Mem — National Academy of Sciences. Biographical Memoirs
Nat Acad Sci Nat Res Counc Publ — National Academy of Sciences - National Research Council. Publication
Nat Acad Sci Proc — National Academy of Sciences. Proceedings
Nat Agr — Nation's Agriculture
Natal Inst Eng J — Natal Institute of Engineers. Journal
Natal Mus Ann — Natal Museum. Annals
Natal UL Rev — Natal University. Law Review
Natal Univ Law Rev — Natal University. Law Review
Nat Appl Sci Bull — Natural and Applied Science Bulletin
Nat Art Ed Assn Yrbk — National Art Education Association. Yearbook
Nat Assn Deans Women J — National Association of Deans of Women. Journal
Nat Assn Sec-Sch Prin Bul — National Association of Secondary-School Principals. Bulletin
Nat Assn State Univs Trans & Proc — National Association of State Universities. Transactions and Proceedings
Nat Assn Stud Council Yrbk — National Association of Student Councils. Yearbook
Nat Assoc of Inspectors and Ednl Advisers J — National Association of Inspectors and Educational Advisers. Journal
Nat Bank Austsia M Summ — National Bank of Australasia. Monthly Summary of Australian Conditions
Nat Bank Egypt Econ Bul — National Bank of Egypt. Economic Bulletin
Nat Bank Ethiopia Q Bul ns — National Bank of Ethiopia. Quarterly Bulletin. New Series
Nat Banking R — National Banking Review
Nat Bank Yugoslavia Q Bul — National Bank of Yugoslavia. Quarterly Bulletin
Nat Bar Bull — National Bar Bulletin
Nat Bee Krs Dig — National Bee Keepers Digest
Nat Belg — Naturalistes Belges
Nat Biol — Natura. Seria Biologie
Nat Bk (Aus) — National Bank. Monthly Summary (Australia)
Nat Bldgs Organisation Jnl — National Buildings Organisation. Journal
Nat Bldr — National Builder
Nat Bottlers' Gaz — National Bottlers' Gazette
Nat Bsns Ed Q — National Business Education Association. Quarterly
Nat Bsns Ed Yrbk — National Business Education Association. Yearbook
Nat Bsns Woman — National Business Woman
Nat Builder — National Builder
Nat Bur Stand Appl Math Ser — National Bureau of Standards. Applied Mathematics Series
Nat Bur Standards TNB — National Bureau of Standards. Technical News Bulletin
Nat Bur Stand Bldg Sci Ser — National Bureau of Standards. Building Science Series
Nat Bur Stand Handb — National Bureau of Standards. Handbook
Nat Bur Stand Misc Pubs — National Bureau of Standards. Miscellaneous Publications
Nat Bur Stand Monogr — National Bureau of Standards. Monographs
Nat Bur Stand Spec Publ — National Bureau of Standards. Special Publication
Nat Bur Stand Tech News Bull — National Bureau of Standards. Technical News Bulletin
Nat Bur Stand Tech Note — National Bureau of Standards. Technical Note
Nat Bus Educ Yrbk — National Business Education Association. Yearbook
Nat Butter & Cheese J — National Butter and Cheese Journal
Nat Butter J — National Butter Journal
Nat Cambs — Nature in Cambridgeshire
Nat Can — Nature Canada
Nat Canada — Nature Canada
Nat Can I M — National Cancer Institute. Monographs
Nat Can (Quebec) — Naturaliste Canadien (Quebec)
Nat Cath Ed Assn Bul — National Catholic Educational Association. Bulletin
Nat Cath Ed Assn Proc — National Catholic Educational Association. Proceedings
Nat Cath Rep — National Catholic Reporter
Nat Cheese J — National Cheese Journal
Nat Child Labor Com Proc — National Child Labor Committee. Proceedings
Nat Christ Coun R — National Christian Council. Review [*Mysore City*]
Nat Cities — Nation's Cities
Nat Civic R — National Civic Review

Nat Civic Rev — National Civic Review
Nat Civ Rev — National Civic Review
Nat Comm Teach Ed & Prof Stand Off Rep — National Commission on Teacher Education and Professional Standards. Official Report
Nat Conf City Govt — National Conference for Good City Government. Proceedings
Nat Conf Publ Inst Eng Aust — National Conference Publication. Institution of Engineers of Australia
Nat Conf Publs Instn Engrs Aust — National Conference Publications. Institution of Engineers of Australia
Nat Conf Soc Work — National Conference of Social Work. Proceedings
Nat Conserv Branch Transvaal Bull — Nature Conservation Branch. Transvaal Bulletin
Nat Conserv News — Nature Conservancy News [*United States*]
Nat Corp Rep — National Corporation Reporter
Nat Council O — National Council Outlook
Nat Council Social Stud Yrbk — National Council for the Social Studies. Yearbook
Nat Council Teach Math Yrbk — National Council of Teachers of Mathematics. Yearbook
Nat Development — National Development
Nat Dev Q — National Development Quarterly
Nat Ed Assn Proc — National Education Association. Addresses and Proceedings
Nat Ed Assn Res Bul — National Education Association. Research Bulletin
Nat Educ Assn J — National Education Association. Journal
Nat Elec Mfr Ass Stand Publ — National Electrical Manufacturers Association. Standards Publication
Nat El Prin — National Elementary Principal
NAtenea — Nueva Atenea [*Chile*]
Nat Eng — National Engineer
Nat Eng Lab Rep — National Engineering Laboratory. Report
Nat Environ Res Counc Inst Terr Ecol Annu Rep — Natural Environment Research Council. Institute of Terrestrial Ecology. Annual Report
Nat Environ Res Counc News J — Natural Environment Research Council. News Journal
Nat F — National Forum
Nat Fmrs Un Annu Conf — National Farmers' Union. Annual Conference
Nat Forum — National Forum
NATGA — Natuurwetenschappelijk Tijdschrift (Ghent)
Nat Gall SA Bull — National Gallery of South Australia. Bulletin
Nat Gall VIC A Bull — National Gallery of Victoria. Annual Bulletin
Nat Gal Rep — National Gallery of Art. Report
Nat Gas — Natural Gas
Nat Gas As Am Pr — Natural Gas Association of America. Proceedings
Nat Gas Bul — National Gas Bulletin
Nat Gas Bull — National Gas Bulletin
Nat Gas/Fuel Forecast Ser A — Natural Gas/Fuel Forecast. Series A. Geographic [*United States*]
Nat Gas/Fuel Forecast Ser B — Natural Gas/Fuel Forecast. Series B. Industrial [*United States*]
Nat Gas Gasoline J — Natural Gas and Gasoline Journal
Nat Gas Ind — Natural Gas Industry
Nat Gas Mag — Natural Gas Magazine
Nat Geog — National Geographic Magazine
Nat Geog J Ind — National Geographical Journal of India [*Varanasi*]
Nat Geog M — National Geographic Magazine
Nat Geog Soc Nat Geog Mon — National Geographic Society. National Geographic Monographs
Nat Geog World — National Geographic World
Nat Health Serv Inf Bul — National Health Services Information Bulletin
Nat Heimat — Natur und Heimat
Nat Herb NSW Contrib — National Herbarium of New South Wales. Contributions
Nat Hist — Natural History
Nat Hist Bull Siam Soc — Natural History Bulletin. Siam Society
Nat Hist Mag — Natural History Magazine
Nat Hist Misc (Chic) — Natural History Miscellanae (Chicago)
Nat Hist Mus Los Ang Cty Contrib Sci — Natural History Museum of Los Angeles County. Contributions in Science
Nat Hist Mus Los Ang Cty Sci Ser — Natural History Museum of Los Angeles County. Science Series
Nat Hist Mus Los Angeles Cty Sci Bull — Natural History Museum of Los Angeles County. Science Bulletin
Nat Hist (NY) — Natural History (New York)
Nat Hist Rennell Isl Br Solomon Isl — Natural History of Rennell Island, British Solomon Islands
Nat Hort M — National Horticultural Magazine
Nat Hosp — National Hospital
Nat Hospital — National Hospital
Nat I Anim — National Institute of Animal Health. Quarterly
Nat Immun Cell Growth Regul — Natural Immunity and Cell Growth Regulation
Nat Inst Arch Ed Bul — National Institute for Architectural Education. Bulletin

Nat Inst B Pr Pr N S — National Institution for the Promotion of Science. Bulletin of the Proceedings. Proceedings. New Series

Nat Inst Econ R — National Institute Economic Review

Nat Inst Econ Rev — National Institute Economic Review

Nat Inst Educ Res B — National Institute for Educational Research. Bulletin [*Tokyo*]

Nat Inst Soc Sci — National Institute of Social Sciences. Proceedings

National Inst Health Bull US Pub Health Serv — National Institute of Health. Bulletin. United States Public Health Service

Nation and Ath — Nation and Athenaeum

Nation Athen — Nation and Athenaeum

Nation (Lond) — Nation and Athenaeum (London)

Nation Rev — Nation Review

Nation's Ag — Nation's Agriculture

Nation's Agric — Nation's Agriculture

Nation's Bus — Nation's Business

Nation's Sch — Nation's Schools

Native Sch Bul — Native School Bulletin

Nat J — National Journal

Nat J Crim Def — National Journal of Criminal Defense

Nat J Criminal Defense — National Journal of Criminal Defense

Nat Jutl — Natura Jutlandica

Nat Jutlandica — Natur Jutlandica

NATLA — Nauchnye Trudy Leningradskaya Lesotekhnicheskaya Akademiya Imeni S. M. Kirova

Natl Acad Med Sci (India) Ann — National Academy of Medical Sciences (India). Annals

Natl Acad Sci Biog Mem Proc — National Academy of Sciences. Biographical Memoirs. Proceedings

Natl Acad Sci Comm Polar Res Rep US Antarc Res Act Rep SCAR — National Academy of Sciences. Committee on Polar Research. Report of United States Antarctic Research Activities. Report to SCAR [*Scientific Committee on Antarctic Research*]

Natl Acad Sci (India) Annu Number — National Academy of Sciences (India). Annual Number

Natl Acad Sci Lett — National Academy of Science and Letters [*India*]

Natl Acad Sci Natl Research Council Pub — National Academy of Sciences - National Research Council. Publication

Natl Acad Sci Proc — National Academy of Sciences. Proceedings

Natl Acad Sci Pub — National Academy of Sciences. Publication

Natl Acad Sci USA Biogr Mem — National Academy of Sciences of the United States of America. Biographical Memoirs

Natl Advis Comm Aeronaut Annu Rep — National Advisory Committee for Aeronautics. Annual Report

Natl Advis Comm Aeronaut Rep — National Advisory Committee for Aeronautics. Reports

Natl Advis Comm Aeronaut Tech Notes — National Advisory Committee for Aeronautics. Technical Notes

Natl Advisory Comm Research Geol Sci — National Advisory Committee on Research in the Geological Sciences

Natl Aeronaut Establ Mech Eng Rep MS (Can) — National Aeronautical Establishment. Mechanical Engineering Report MS (Canada)

Natl Aerosp Electron Conf Proc — National Aerospace Electronics Conference. Proceedings [*United States*]

Natl Air Pollut Control Adm (US) Publ AP Ser — National Air Pollution Control Administration (United States). Publication. AP Series

Natl Air Pollut Control Adm (US) Publ APTD Ser — National Air Pollution Control Administration (United States). Publication. APTD [*Air Pollution Technical Data*] Series

Natl Am Miller — National and American Miller

Nat Lamp — National Lampoon

Nat Land — Natur und Land

Nat Landschaft — Natur und Landschaft

Nat Landschap — Natuur en Landschap Tijdschrift van de Contact Commissie voor Natuur- en Landschapsebescherming

Natl Assn Sec-Schl Princ — National Association of Secondary-School Principals. Bulletin

Natl Assoc Corros Eng Meet Pap — National Association of Corrosion Engineers. Meeting Papers

Natl Assoc Margarine Manuf Bull — National Association of Margarine Manufacturers. Bulletin

Natl Bitum Concr Assoc Qual Improv Program Publ — National Bituminous Concrete Association. Quality Improvement Program. Publication

Natl Board Examiner — National Board Examiner [*United States*]

Natl Board Fire Underwrit Res Rep — National Board of Fire Underwriters. Research Report

Natl Board Fire Underwrit Tech Surv — National Board of Fire Underwriters. Technical Survey

Natl Bot Gard (Lucknow) Annu Rep — National Botanic Gardens (Lucknow). Annual Report

Natl Bur Stand (US) Circ — National Bureau of Standards (United States). Circular

Natl Bur Stand (US) Handb — National Bureau of Standards (United States). Handbook

Natl Bur Stand (US) Monogr — National Bureau of Standards (United States). Monograph

Natl Bur Stand (US) Spec Publ — National Bureau of Standards (United States). Special Publication

Natl Bur Stand (US) Tech News Bull — National Bureau of Standards (United States). Technical News Bulletin

Natl Bur Stand (US) Tech Note — National Bureau of Standards (United States). Technical Note

Natl Bus Educ Yrbk — National Business Education Association. Yearbook

Natl Bus Woman — National Business Woman

Natl Butter Cheese J — National Butter and Cheese Journal

Natl Butter J — National Butter Journal

Natl Cactus Succulent J — National Cactus and Succulent Journal

Natl Cancer Conf Proc — National Cancer Conference. Proceedings

Natl Cancer Inst Carcinog Tech Rep Ser (US) — National Cancer Institute. Carcinogenesis Technical Report Series (United States)

Natl Cancer Inst Monogr — National Cancer Institute. Monographs

Natl Canners' Assoc Res Lab Bull — National Canners' Association. Research Laboratory. Bulletin

Natl Canners' Assoc Res Lab Circ — National Canners' Association. Research Laboratory. Circular [*United States*]

Natl Cheese J — National Cheese Journal [*United States*]

Natl Chem Pet Instrum Symp — National Chemical and Petroleum Instrumentation Symposium

Natl Civic Rev — National Civic Review

Natl Clay Prod Quarrying — National Clay Products and Quarrying

Natl Cleaner Dyer — National Cleaner and Dyer [*United States*]

Natl Clgh Poison Control Cent Bull — National Clearinghouse for Poison Control Centers. Bulletin

Natl Comput Conf — National Computer Conference [*United States*]

Natl Conf Earth Sci Pap (Alberta Univ) — National Conference on Earth Science. Papers (Alberta University)

Natl Conf Individ Onsite Wastewater Syst Proc — National Conference for Individual Onsite Wastewater Systems. Proceedings

Natl Conf Publ Inst Eng Aust — National Conference Publications. Institution of Engineers of Australia

Natl Council Social Stud Yrbk — National Council for the Social Studies. Yearbook

Natl Council Teach Math Yrbk — National Council of Teachers of Mathematics. Yearbook

Natl Counc Radiat Prot Meas Annu Meet — National Council on Radiation Protection and Measurements. Annual Meeting

Natl Counc Res Dev Rep NCRD (Isr) — National Council for Research and Development. Report NCRD (Israel)

Natl Cycling — National Cycling

Natl Dairy Res Inst (Karnal) Annu Rep — National Dairy Research Institute (Karnal). Annual Report

Natl Def Med J (Tokyo) — National Defense Medical Journal (Tokyo)

Natl Dev — National Development [*Australia*]

Natl Dist Heat Assoc Off Proc — National District Heating Association. Official Proceedings

Natl Drug — National Druggist

Natl Eclectic Med Q — National Eclectic Medical Quarterly

Natl Eco — National Institute Economic Review

Natl Educ — National Education

Natl Electron Rev — National Electronics Review

Natl El Prin — National Elementary Principal

Natl Eng — National Engineer

Natl Eng Lab Rep (GB) — National Engineering Laboratory. Report (Great Britain)

Nat LF — Natural Law Forum

Natl Fert Rev — National Fertilizer Review

Natl Fire Codes — National Fire Codes [*United States*]

Natl Fisherman — National Fisherman

Natl Food Rev — National Food Review

Natl Found Cancer Res Cancer Res Assoc Symp — National Foundation for Cancer Research. Cancer Research Association Symposia

Natl Found March Dimes Birth Defects Orig Artic Ser — National Foundation. March of Dimes. Birth Defects Original Article Series

Natl Gas Bull — National Gas Bulletin

Natl Gas Bull (Melbourne) — National Gas Bulletin (Melbourne)

Natl Geographic Mag — National Geographic Magazine

Natl Geogr Soc Res Rep — National Geographic Society. Research Reports

Natl Geol Surv China Spec Rep — National Geological Survey of China. Special Report

Natl Glass Budget — National Glass Budget [*United States*]

Natl Ground Water Qual Symp Proc — National Ground Water Quality Symposium. Proceedings

Natl Health Insur Jt Comm Med Res Comm (GB) Spec Rep Ser — National Health Insurance Joint Committee. Medical Research Committee (Great Britain). Special Report Series

Natl Health Insur Rep — National Health Insurance Reports [*United States*]

Natl Health Med Res Counc (Canberra) Med Res Proj — National Health and Medical Research Council (Canberra). Medical Research Projects

Natl Health Med Res Counc (Canberra) Rep — National Health and Medical Research Council (Canberra). Report

Natl Hortic Mag — National Horticultural Magazine

Natl Hosp Health Care — National Hospital Health Care

Natl I Eco — National Institute Economic Review
Nat Life Southeast Asia — Nature and Life in Southeast Asia
Nat Lime Ass Bull — National Lime Association. Bulletin
Natl Ind Res Inst (Seoul) Rev — National Industrial Research Institute (Seoul). Review
Natl Inst Agric Bot (Camb) Rep Acc — National Institute of Agricultural Botany (Cambridge). Report and Accounts
Natl Inst Anim Health Q — National Institute of Animal Health. Quarterly
Natl Inst Drug Abuse Res Monogr Ser — National Institute on Drug Abuse. Research Monograph Series
Natl Inst Econ R — National Institute Economic Review
Natl Inst Econ Rev — National Institute Economic Review
Natl Inst Genet (Mishima) Annu Rep — National Institute of Genetics (Mishima). Annual Report
Natl Inst Metall Repub S Afr Rep — National Institute for Metallurgy. Republic of South Africa. Report
Natl Inst Nutr Annu Rep — National Institute of Nutrition. Annual Report
Natl Inst Polar Res Mem Ser C Earth Sci — National Institute of Polar Research. Memoirs. Series C. Earth Sciences
Natl Inst Polar Res Mem Spec Issue — National Institute of Polar Research. Memoirs. Special Issue
Natl Inst Polar Res (Tokyo) Antarct Geol Map Ser — National Institute of Polar Research (Tokyo). Antarctic Geological Map Series
Natl Inst Res Dairy Rep (Engl) — National Institute for Research in Dairying. Report (England)
Natl Inst Res Nucl Sci (GB) Rep — National Institute for Research in Nuclear Science (Great Britain). Report
Natl Inst Water Supply (Neth) Q Rep — National Institute for Water Supply (Netherlands). Quarterly Report
Natl J — National Journal [*United States*]
Nat'l J Crim Def — National Journal of Criminal Defense
Natl Jt Comm Fert Appl Proc Annu Meet — National Joint Committee on Fertilizer Application. Proceedings of the Annual Meeting
Nat'l Law Guild Prac — National Lawyers Guild. Practitioner
Natl Libr Wales J — National Library of Wales. Journal
Natl Lithogr — National Lithographer
Nat'l LJ — National Law Journal
Natl Lucht Ruimtevaartlab Rapp — Nationaal Lucht- en Ruimtevaartlaboratorium. Rapport
Natl Lucht Ruimtevaartlab Versl Verh — Nationaal Lucht- en Ruimtevaartlaboratorium. Verslagen en Verhandelingen
Nat'l M (Bost) — National Magazine (Boston)
Natl Meas Lab Tech Pap (Aust) — National Measurement Laboratory. Technical Paper (Australia)
Natl Meas Lab Tech Pap CSIRO Aust — Australia. Commonwealth Scientific and Industrial Research Organisation. National Measurement Laboratory. Technical Paper
Natl Med J China (Peking) — National Medical Journal of China (Peking)
Natl Miller — National Miller [*United States*]
Natl Miller Am Miller — National Miller and American Miller
Nat'l Mun Rev — National Municipal Review
Natl Mus Bloemfontein Annu Rep — National Museum Bloemfontein. Annual Report
Natl Mus Bloemfontein Res Mem — National Museum Bloemfontein. Researches Memoir
Natl Mus Can Bull — National Museum of Canada. Bulletin
Natl Mus Can Nat Hist Pap — National Museum of Canada. Natural History Papers
Natl Mus Korea Art Mag — National Museum of Korea. Art Magazine [*Republic of Korea*]
Natl Mus Nat Sci (Ottawa) Publ Biol Oceanogr — National Museum of Natural Sciences (Ottawa). Publications in Biological Oceanography
Natl Mus Nat Sci (Ottawa) Publ Bot — National Museum of Natural Sciences (Ottawa). Publications in Botany
Natl Mus Nat Sci (Ottawa) Publ Palaeontol — National Museum of Natural Sciences (Ottawa). Publications in Palaeontology
Natl Mus Nat Sci (Ottawa) Publ Zool — National Museum of Natural Sciences (Ottawa). Publications in Zoology
Natl Mus NZ Misc Ser — National Museum of New Zealand. Miscellaneous Series
Natl Mus NZ Rec — National Museum of New Zealand. Records
Natl Mus Victoria Mem — National Museum of Victoria. Memoirs
Natl Nosocomial Infect Study — National Nosocomial Infections Study
Natl Observer — National Observer
Natl Oceanic Atmos Adm (US) Circ — National Oceanic and Atmospheric Administration (United States). Circular
Natl Oceanic Atmos Adm (US) Fish Bull — National Oceanic and Atmospheric Administration (United States). Fishery Bulletin
Natl Oceanic Atmos Adm (US) Spec Sci Rep Fish — National Oceanic and Atmospheric Administration (United States). Special Scientific Report. Fisheries
Natl Paint Bull — National Paint Bulletin
Natl Painters Mag — National Painters Magazine
Natl Paint Varn Lacquer Assoc Abstr Rev — National Paint, Varnish, and Lacquer Association. Abstract Review

Natl Parks — National Parks Magazine [*Formerly, National Parks and Conservation Magazine*]
Natl Parks Conserv Mag — National Parks and Conservation Magazine [*Later, National Parks Magazine*]
Natl Parks Mag — National Parks Magazine [*Formerly, National Parks and Conservation Magazine*]
Natl Pet News — National Petroleum News [*United States*]
Natl Pet Refin Assoc Tech Publ — National Petroleum Refiners Association. Technical Publication [*United States*]
Natl Pet Refiners Assoc Pap — National Petroleum Refiners Association. Papers
Natl Pet Refiners Assoc Tech Publ — National Petroleum Refiners Association. Technical Publication
Natl Petroleum Bibliography — National Petroleum Bibliography
Natl Phys Lab Notes Appl Sci (UK) — National Physical Laboratory. Notes on Applied Science (United Kingdom)
Natl Phys Lab Rep — National Physical Laboratory. Reports [*United Kingdom*]
Natl Phys Lab (UK) Div Chem Stand Rep — National Physical Laboratory (United Kingdom). Division of Chemical Standards. Report
Natl Phys Lab (UK) Proc Symp — National Physical Laboratory (United Kingdom). Proceedings of a Symposium
Natl Phys Lab (UK) Rep — National Physical Laboratory (United Kingdom). Report
Natl Phys Lab (UK) Symp — National Physical Laboratory (United Kingdom). Symposium
Natl Prov — National Provisioner
Natl Racq — National Racquetball [*United States*]
Natl Ready Mixed Concr Assoc Publ — National Ready Mixed Concrete Association. Publication
Natl Real Estate Investor — National Real Estate Investor
Natl Res Cent Disaster Prev Rep — National Research Center for Disaster Prevention. Report
Natl Res Counc Build Res Advis Board Tech Rep — National Research Council. Building Research Advisory Board. Technical Report
Natl Res Counc Can Aeronaut Rep — National Research Council of Canada. Aeronautical Report
Natl Res Counc Can Bull — National Research Council of Canada. Bulletin
Natl Res Counc Can Div Build Res Tech Pap — National Research Council of Canada. Division of Building Research. Technical Paper
Natl Res Counc Can Div Mech Eng Energy — National Research Council of Canada. Division of Mechanical Engineering. Energy
Natl Res Counc Can Div Mech Eng Energy Newsl — National Research Council of Canada. Division of Mechanical Engineering. Energy Newsletter
Natl Res Counc Can Div Mech Eng Lab Tech Rep — National Research Council of Canada. Division of Mechanical Engineering. Laboratory Technical Report
Natl Res Counc Can Div Mech Eng Mech Eng Rep MP — National Research Council of Canada. Division of Mechanical Engineering. Mechanical Engineering Report. Series MP
Natl Res Counc Can Div Mech Eng Q Bull — National Research Council of Canada. Division of Mechanical Engineering. Quarterly Bulletin
Natl Res Counc Can Div Mech Gen Newsl — National Research Council of Canada. Division of Mechanical Engineering. General Newsletter
Natl Res Counc Can Environ Secr Publ — National Research Council of Canada. Environmental Secretariat. Publication
Natl Res Counc Can Mech Eng Rep MP — National Research Council of Canada. Mechanical Engineering Report. Series MP
Natl Res Counc Can Rep — National Research Council of Canada. Report
Natl Res Counc Philipp Bull — National Research Council of the Philippines. Bulletin
Natl Res Counc Rev — National Research Council. Review
Natl Res Inst Occup Dis S Afr Med Res Counc Annu Rep — National Research Institute for Occupational Diseases. South African Medical Research Council. Annual Report
Natl Rev — National Review
Natl Rural Letter Carrier — National Rural Letter Carrier
Natl Saf — National Safety
Natl Saf Congr Trans — National Safety Congress. Occupational Health Nursing Section. Transactions
Natl Saf News — National Safety News
Natl SAMPE Symp Exhib Proc — National SAMPE [*Society for the Advancement of Material and Process Engineering*] Symposium and Exhibition. Proceedings
Natl Sand Gravel Assoc NSGA Circ — National Sand and Gravel Association. NSGA Circular
Natl Sci Counc Mon — National Science Council. Monthly [*Taiwan*]
Natl Sci Found Annu Rep — National Science Foundation. Annual Report
Natl Sci Found Sci Manpower Bull — National Science Foundation. Scientific Manpower Bulletin
Natl Sci Mus Bull Ser C (Tokyo) — National Science Museum. Bulletin. Series C. Geology (Tokyo)
Natl Sci Mus (Tokyo) Bull Ser C Geol Paleontol — National Science Museum (Tokyo). Bulletin. Series C. Geology and Paleontology
Natl Sci Mus (Tokyo) Mem — National Science Museum (Tokyo). Memoirs

Natl Sfty News — National Safety News [*United States*]
Natl Shade Tree Conf Proc — National Shade Tree Conference. Proceedings
Natl Soc Clean Air Annu Conf Proc — National Society for Clean Air. Annual Conference. Proceedings
Natl Soc Stud Educ Yrbk — National Society for the Study of Education. Yearbook
Natl Speleol Soc Bull — National Speleological Society. Bulletin
Natl Speleol Soc Occasional Paper — National Speleological Society. Occasional Paper
Natl Stand Lab Tech Pap CSIRO Aust — Australia. Commonwealth Scientific and Industrial Research Organisation. National Standards Laboratory. Technical Paper
Natl Stand Ref Data Ser Natl Bur Stand — National Standard Reference Data Series. National Bureau of Standards
Natl Stand Ref Data Ser US Natl Bur Stand — National Standard Reference Data Series. United States National Bureau of Standards
Natl Swed Build Res Doc — National Swedish Building Research. Document [*Statens Institut foer Byggnadsforskning*]
Natl Sym — National Symphony Program Notes
Natl Tax J — National Tax Journal [*United States*]
Natl Tech Inf Serv Search — National Technical Information Service Search [*United States*]
Natl Tech Rep — National Technical Report
Natl Tech Rep (Matsushita Electr Ind C Osaka) — National Technical Report (Matsushita Electric Industrial Company, Osaka)
Natl Toxicol Program Tech Rep Ser — National Toxicology Program. Technical Report Series
Nat Lucht Ruimtevaartlab — National Lucht- en Ruimtevaartlaboratorium
Nat Lucht-Ruimtevaartlab Verslagen en Verhandel — Nationaal Lucht- en Ruimtevaartlaboratorium. Verslagen en Verhandelingen
Natl Underwrit (Life Health) — National Underwriter (Life and Health Insurance Edition)
Natl Underwrit (Life Health Insur Ed) — National Underwriter (Life and Health Insurance Edition)
Natl Univ Peiping Coll Agric Res Bull — National University of Peiping. College of Agriculture. Research Bulletin
Natl Veg Res Stn Annu Rep (Wellsbourne) — National Vegetable Research Station. Annual Report (Wellsbourne)
Natl Vitam Found Nutr Symp Ser — National Vitamin Foundation. Nutrition Symposium Series [*United States*]
Natl Vitamin Found Annu Rep — National Vitamin Foundation. Annual Report
Natl Waste News — National Waste News [*United States*]
Natl Westminster Bank Q Rev — National Westminster Bank. Quarterly Review [*England*]
Natl Wildl — National Wildlife
Natl Wool Grow — National Wool Grower
Nat M — National Magazine
NATMA — NASA [*National Aeronautics and Space Administration*] Technical Memorandum
Nat Mag — National Magazine
Nat Malays — Nature Malaysiana
Nat Malgache — Naturaliste Malgache
Nat Map Bull — National Mapping Bulletin
Nat Mensch — Natuur en Mensch
Nat Monspel — Naturalia Monspeliensia
Nat Monspeliensia Ser Bot — Naturalia Monspeliensia. Serie Botanique
Nat Monspel Ser Bot — Naturalia Monspeliensia. Serie Botanique
Nat Mosana — Natura Mosana
Nat Mosana Suppl B Bot — Natura Mosana. Supplement B. Botanique
Nat Mosana Suppl CD Zool — Natura Mosana. Supplement CD. Zoologie
Nat Munic R — National Municipal Review
Nat Munic Rev — National Municipal Review
Nat Mun Rev — National Municipal Review
Nat Mus — Natur und Museum
Nat Mus Council Bul — National Music Council. Bulletin
Nat Mus Senckenb Naturforsch Ges — Natur und Museum. Senckenbergische Naturforschende Gesellschaft
Nat Mus VIC Mem — National Museum of Victoria. Memoirs
Natn Bldr — National Builder
Nat New Biol — Nature: New Biology
NATNews — NATNews. National Association of Theatre Nurses
Natn Geogr Mag — National Geographic Magazine
Natn Jewish Mon — National Jewish Monthly
Natn Res Progm Agric Res Serv — National Research Program. Agricultural Research Service
Natns Bus — Nation's Business
Natn Symp Hydrol — National Symposium on Hydrology
Natn Times — National Times
NATO Adv Study Inst Ser B — NATO [*North Atlantic Treaty Organization*] Advanced Study Institutes. Series B. Physics
NATO Adv Study Inst Ser B Physics — NATO [*North Atlantic Treaty Organization*] Advanced Study Institutes. Series B. Physics
NATO Adv Study Inst Ser C — NATO [*North Atlantic Treaty Organization*] Advanced Study Institutes. Series C. Mathematical and Physical Sciences

NATO Adv Study Inst Ser D — NATO [*North Atlantic Treaty Organization*] Advanced Study Institutes. Series D. Behavioural and Social Sciences
NATO Adv Study Inst Ser E — NATO [*North Atlantic Treaty Organization*] Advanced Study Institutes. Series E. Applied Sciences
NATO/CCMS Air Pollut — NATO/CCMS [*North Atlantic Treaty Organization/Committee on the Challenges of Modern Society*] Air Pollution
NATO Comm Challenges Mod Soc Air Pollut — NATO [*North Atlantic Treaty Organization*]/Committee on the Challenges of Modern Society. Air Pollution
Nat -Okon Tss — Nationalokonomisk Tidsskrift
NATO's Fift Nations — NATO's [*North Atlantic Treaty Organization*] Fifteen Nations
Nat P — Nationalities Papers
Nat Pal Mus B — National Palace Museum. Bulletin [*Taipai*]
Nat Parent-Teach — National Parent-Teacher
Nat Parks — National Parks Magazine [*Formerly, National Parks and Conservation Magazine*]
Nat Parks & Con Mag — National Parks and Conservation Magazine [*Later, National Parks Magazine*]
Nat Pet N — National Petroleum News
Nat Petrol Refiners Ass Tech Papers — National Petroleum Refiners Association. Technical Papers
Nat Phys Lab (Gt Brit) Notes Appl Sci — National Physical Laboratory (Great Britain). Department of Scientific and Industrial Research. Notes on Applied Science
Nat Probation Assn Yrbk — National Probation and Parole Association. Yearbook
Nat Prod Rep — Natural Product Reports
Nat Q — National Quarterly Review
Nat Q Rev — National Quarterly Review
Nat R — Nation Review
Nat R — National Review
NATRA — Nature
Nat Racq — National Racquetball
Nat Real Estate Invest — National Real Estate Investor
Nat Real Estate Investor — National Real Estate Investor
Nat Rep — National Republic
Nat Res Counc Bldg Res Adv Bd Tech Rep — National Research Council. Building Research Advisory Board. Technical Report
Nat Res Counc Can Aeronaut Rep — National Research Council of Canada. Aeronautical Report
Nat Res Counc Can Annu Rep — National Research Council of Canada. Annual Report
Nat Res Counc Can Ass Comm Geod Geophys Proc Hydrol Symp — National Research Council of Canada. Associate Committee on Geodesy and Geophysics. Proceedings of Hydrology Symposium
Nat Res Counc Can Ass Comm Geotech Res Tech Memo — National Research Council of Canada. Associate Committee on Geotechnical Research. Technical Memorandum
Nat Res Counc Can Div Bldg Res Bibliogr — National Research Council of Canada. Division of Building Research. Bibliography
Nat Res Counc Can Div Mech Eng Mech Eng Rep — National Research Council of Canada. Division of Mechanical Engineering. Mechanical Engineering Report
Nat Res Counc Can Mech Eng Rep ME — National Research Council of Canada. Mechanical Engineering Report. ME
Nat Res Counc Can Unsteady Aerodyn Lab Lab Tech Rep — National Research Council of Canada. Unsteady Aerodynamics Laboratory. Laboratory Technical Report
Nat Res Counc Comm Probl Drug Depend Proc Annu Sci Meet (US) — National Research Council. Committee of Problems of Drug Dependence. Proceedings. Annual Scientific Meeting (United States)
Nat Res Counc Conf Elec Insul Annu Rep — National Research Council. Conference on Electrical Insulation. Annual Report
Nat Res Council Can Div Mech Engng Gen — National Research Council of Canada. Division of Mechanical Engineering. General
Nat Res Counc Nat Acad Sci Rep — [*US*] Research Council. National Academy of Sciences. Reports
Nat Res J — Natural Resources Journal
Nat Res Lawyer — Natural Resources Lawyer
Nat Resour — Nature and Resources
Nat Resources J — Natural Resources Journal
Nat Resources Jour — Natural Resources Journal
Nat Resources Law — Natural Resources Lawyer
Nat Resources L Newsl — Natural Resources Law Newsletter
Nat Resour Forum — Natural Resources Forum
Nat Resour Forum Libr — Natural Resources Forum Library
Nat Resour Lawyer — Natural Resources Lawyer
Nat Resour Res (Paris) — Natural Resources Research (Paris)
Nat Rev — Nation Review
Nat Rev — National Review
Nat Rubber — Natural Rubber News
Nat Rubb News — Natural Rubber News
NATS — National Association of Teachers of Singing. Bulletin
Nat Safety News — National Safety News

Nat Saf News — National Safety News

Nat Sand Gravel Ass NSGA Circ — National Sand and Gravel Association. NSGA Circular

NATS Bull — National Association of Teachers of Singing. Bulletin

Nat Sc As Staten Island Pr — Natural Science Association of Staten Island. Proceedings

Nat Sch — Nation's Schools

Nat Sci — Natural Science

Nat Sci Prog — Nature. Science Progress

Nat Sci Rep Ochanomizu Univ — Natural Science Report. Ochanomizu University

Nat Sculp R — National Sculpture Review

Nat Sculpt — National Sculpture Review

Nat Seedsman — National Seedsman

Nat Soc Study Ed Yrbk — National Society for the Study of Education. Yearbook

Nat Stock & F — National Stockman and Farmer

Nat Study — Nature Study

Nat T — National Times

Nat Tax J — National Tax Journal

Nat Tech Rep — National Technical Report [*Matsushita Electric Industrial Co., Osaka*]

Nat Times — National Times

Nat T Mag — National Times Magazine

Nat Trust — National Trust

Nat Trust Aust Bull — National Trust of Australia. Bulletin

Nat Trust Bul — National Trust Bulletin

Nat Trust Studies — National Trust Studies

NATUA — Nature

Nat UL Rev — Natal University. Law Review

Nat Underw — National Underwriter

Nat Underw (Fire Ed) — National Underwriter (Fire and Casualty Insurance Edition)

Nat Underw (Life) — National Underwriter (Life and Health Insurance Edition)

Nat Underw (Life Ed) — National Underwriter (Life and Health Insurance Edition)

Nat Underw (Prop Ed) — National Underwriter (Property and Casualty Insurance Edition)

Nat Underw (Property Ed) — National Underwriter (Property and Casualty Insurance Edition)

Natural Food Fmg — Natural Food and Farming

Natural Gard — Natural Gardening

Natural Gas Ind — Natural Gas for Industry

Natural Hi — Natural History

Naturalia Monspel Ser Bot — Naturalia Monspeliensia. Serie Botanique

Naturaliste Can — Naturaliste Canadien

Natural L F — Natural Law Forum

Natural Resources J — Natural Resources Journal

Natural Resources Jnl — Natural Resources Journal

Natural Resources Law — Natural Resources Lawyer

Natural Resources Lawy — Natural Resources Lawyer

Naturegp Ocean Guide Books — Naturegraph Ocean Guide Books

Nature and Life SE Asia — Nature and Life in Southeast Asia

Nature (London) Phys Sci — Nature (London). Physical Science

Nature Mag — Nature Magazine

Nature New Biol — Nature: New Biology

Nature: Phys Sci — Nature: Physical Science

Nature and Sci Ed R — Nature and Science Education Review

Naturf Gesell Basel Verh — Naturforschende Gesellschaft in Basel. Verhandlungen

Naturf Gesell Bern Mitt Neue Folge — Naturforschende Gesellschaft in Bern. Mitteilungen. Neue Folge

Naturf Gesell Zurich Vierteljahrsschr — Naturforschende Gesellschaft in Zuerich. Vierteljahresschrift

Naturforsch Ges Freib im Breisgau Ber — Naturforschende Gesellschaft zu Freiburg im Breisgau. Berichte

Natur Hist — Natural History

Naturhist Ges Hannover Ber — Naturhistorische Gesellschaft zu Hannover. Bericht

Naturhist Mus Stadt Bern Jahrb — Naturhistorisches Museum der Stadt Bern. Jahrbuch

Naturhist Mus Wien Ann — Naturhistorisches Museum in Wien. Annalen

Naturh-Med Ver Heidelberg Verh — Naturhistorisch-Medicinischer Verein zu Heidelberg. Verhandlungen

Naturh Ver Preus Rheinl Verh — Naturhistorischer Verein der Preussischen Rheinland und Westphalens. Verhandlungen

Naturh Ver Preus Rheinl Verh (Niederrhein Ges Bonn) Szb — Naturhistorischer Verein der Preussischen Rheinlande. Verhandlungen (Niederrheinische Gesellschaft fuer Naturund Heilkunde in Bonn). Sitzungsberichte

Natur Landsch — Natur und Landschaft

Natur u Mus — Natur und Museum

Natur Mus (Arhus) — Natur og Museum (Arhus)

Natur Mus (Frankf) — Natur und Museum (Frankfurt)

Natur Res J — Natural Resources Journal

Natur Res L — Natural Resources Lawyer

Natur Resou — Natural Resources Lawyer

Natur Resources Forum — Natural Resources Forum

Natur Resources J — Natural Resources Journal

Natursch Naturp — Naturschutz- und Naturparke

Natur Sci Rep Ochanomizu Univ — Natural Science Report. Ochanomizu University

Natur u Volk — Natur und Volk

Naturw Abh — Naturwissenschaftliche Abhandlungen

Naturwiss — Naturwissenschaften

Naturwissen — Naturwissenschaften

Naturwissenschaft Med — Naturwissenschaft und Medizin

Naturwiss Med — Naturwissenschaft und Medizin

Naturwiss Monatsh Biol Chem Geogr Geol Unterr — Naturwissenschaftliche Monatshefte fuer den Biologischen, Chemischen, Geographischen, und Geologischen Unterricht

Naturwiss Rundsch — Naturwissenschaftliche Rundschau

Naturwiss Umsch Chem Ztg — Naturwissenschaftliche Umschau der Chemiker-Zeitung

Naturwiss Unterr Phys/Chem — Naturwissenschaften im Unterricht (Teil) Physik/Chemie [*West Germany*]

Naturwiss Ver Schleswig-Holstein Schr — Naturwissenschaftlicher Verein fuer Schleswig-Holstein. Schriften

Naturwiss Z Forst Landwirtsch — Naturwissenschaftliche Zeitschrift fuer Forst- und Landwirtschaft

Naturw Rdsch — Naturwissenschaftliche Rundschau

Naturw Rdsch (Stuttg) — Naturwissenschaftliche Rundschau (Stuttgart)

Naturw Ver Neuvorpommern und Ruegen in Greifswald Mitt — Naturwissenschaftlicher Verein fuer Neuvorpommern und Ruegen in Greifswald. Mitteilungen

Naturw Ver Steiermark Mitt — Naturwissenschaftlicher Verein fuer Steiermark. Mitteilungen

Naturw Wchnschr — Naturwissenschaftliche Wochenschrift

Naturw Wochensch — Naturwissenschaftliche Wochenschrift

Naturw Z Forst u Landw — Naturwissenschaftliche Zeitschrift fuer Forst- und Landwirtschaft

Naturw Z Land-u Forstw — Naturwissenschaftliche Zeitschrift fuer Land- und Forstwirtschaft

Natuurhist Maandbl — Natuurhistorisch Maandblad

Natuurh Maandbl — Natuurhistorisch Maandblad

Natuurk Voordr — Natuurkundige Voordrachten

Natuurk Tijdschr Ned-Indie — Natuurkundig Tijdschrift voor Nederlandsch-Indie

Natuurwet Studiekring Suriname Ned Antillen Uitg — Natuurwetenschappelijke Studiekring voor Suriname en de Nederlandse Antillen. Uitgaven

Natuurwet Tijdschr — Natuurwetenschappelijk Tijdschrift

Natuurwet Tijdschr Ned Indie — Natuurwetenschappelijk Tijdschrift voor Nederlandsch-Indie

Natuurwet Werkgroep Nederlandse Antillen Uitgaven — Natuurwetenschappelijke Werkgroep Nederlandse Antillen Uitgaven

Nat Verden — Naturens Verden

Nat Vivante — Nature Vivante

Nat Volk (Frankf) — Natur und Volk (Frankfurt)

Nat Wales — Nature in Wales

Nat W Bank — National Westminster Bank. Quarterly Review

Nat West Bank Q Rev — National Westminster Bank. Quarterly Review

Nat Westminster Bank Q R — National Westminster Bank. Quarterly Review

Nat Wetlands Newsletter — National Wetlands Newsletter

Nat Wildlife — National Wildlife

Nauc Bjulletin Leningrad — Naucnyj Bjulletin Leningradskogo Gosud. Universiteta

Nauc Dokl Vyss Skoly Filos Nauki — Naucnye Doklady Vyssej Skoly Filosofskie Nauki

Nauc Dokl Vyss Skoly Nauc Kommunizma — Naucnye Doklady Vyssej Skoly Naucnyj Kommunizma

Nauch Dokl Vysshei Shkoly Biol Nauk — Nauchnye Doklady Vysshei Shkoly Biologicheskie Nauki

Nauchn Byull Leningr Gos Univ — Nauchnye Byulleten Leningradskogo Gosudarstvennogo Universiteta

Nauchn Byull Vses Nauchno Issled Inst Khlopku — Nauchni Byulleten Vsesoyuznogo Nauchno Issledovatel'skogo Instituta po Khlopku

Nauchn Dokl Vyssh Shk Biol Nauki — Nauchnye Doklady Vysshei Shkoly Biologicheskie Nauki

Nauchn Dokl Vyssh Shk Elektromekh Avtom — Nauchnye Doklady Vysshei Shkoly Elektromekhanika i Avtomatika

Nauchn Dokl Vyssh Shk Energ — Nauchnye Doklady Vysshei Shkoly Energetika

Nauchn Dokl Vyssh Shk Fiz Mat Nauki — Nauchnye Doklady Vysshei Shkoly Fiziko-Matematicheskie Nauki

Nauchn Dokl Vyssh Shk Geol Geogr Nauki — Nauchnye Doklady Vysshei Shkoly Geologo-Geograficheskie Nauki

Nauchn Dokl Vyssh Shk Gorn Delo — Nauchnye Doklady Vysshei Shkoly Gornoe Delo

Nauchn Dokl Vyssh Shk Khim Khim Tekhnol — Nauchnye Doklady Vysshei Shkoly Khimiya i Khimicheskaya Tekhnologiya [*USSR*]

Nauchn Dokl Vyssh Shk Lesoinzh Delo — Nauchnye Doklady Vysshei Shkoly Lesoinzhenernoe Delo

Nauchn Dokl Vyssh Shk Mashinostr Priborostr — Nauchnye Doklady Vysshei Shkoly Mashinostroenie i Priborostroenie

Nauchn Dokl Vyssh Shk Metall — Nauchnye Doklady Vysshei Shkoly Metallurgiya

Nauchn Dokl Vyssh Shk Radiotekh Elektron — Nauchnye Doklady Vysshei Shkoly Radiotekhnika i Elektronika

Nauchn Dokl Vyssh Shk Stroit — Nauchnye Doklady Vysshei Shkoly Stroitel'stvo

Nauchn Ezheg Chernovits Univ — Nauchnyi Ezhegodnik Chernovitskogo Universiteta

Nauchn Ezheg Chernovits Univ Biol Fak Chernovtsy — Nauchnye Ezhegodnik Chernovitskogo Universiteta Biologicheskii Fakul'tet Chernovtsy

Nauchn Ezheg Odess Gos Univ Biol Fak — Nauchnyi Ezhegodnik Odesskii Gosudarstvennyi Universitet Biologicheskii Fakul'tet

Nauchn Ezheg Odess Gos Univ Khim Fak — Nauchnyi Ezhegodnik Odesskii Gosudarstvennyi Universitet Khimicheskii Fakul'tet

Nauchn Ezheg Odess Univ — Nauchnyi Ezhegodnik Odesskogo Universiteta

Nauchn Issled Klin Lab — Nauchnye Issledovaniya v Klinikakh I V Laboratoriyakh

Nauchni Tr Inst Pochv Izsled — Nauchni Trudove. Instituta za Pochveni Izsledvaniya

Nauchni Tr Inst Spets Usuvursh Lek — Nauchni Trudove. Institut za Spetsializatsiya i Usuvurshenstvuvane na Lekarite

Nauchni Tr Nauchnoizsled Inst Durzh Kontrol Lek Sredstva — Nauchni Trudove. Nauchnoizsledovatelski Institut za Durzhaven Kontrol na Lekarstvenite Sredstva

Nauchni Tr Nauchnoizsled Inst Konservna Promst (Plovdiv) — Nauchni Trudove. Nauchnoizsledovatelski Institut po Konservna Promishlenost (Plovdiv)

Nauchni Tr Nauchnoizsled Inst Okhr Tr Prof Zabol — Nauchni Trudove. Nauchnoizsledovatelskiya Instituta po Okhrana na Truda i Profesionalnite Zabolyavaniya

Nauchni Tr Nauchnoizsled Inst Pediatr — Nauchni Trudove. Nauchnoizsledovatelskiya Instituta po Pediatriya

Nauchni Tr Nauchnoizsled Inst Radiobiol Radiats Khig — Nauchni Trudove. Nauchnoizsledovatelski Institut po Radiobiologiya i Radiatsionna Khigiena

Nauchni Tr Nauchnoizsled Inst Vinar Pivovar Promst (Sofia) — Nauchni Trudove. Nauchnoizsledovatelski Institut po Vinarska i Pivovarna Promishlenost (Sofia)

Nauchni Tr Plovdivski Univ Mat Fiz Khim Biol — Nauchni Trudove. Plovdivski Universitet. Matematika, Fizika, Khimiya, Biologiya [*Bulgaria*]

Nauchni Tr Selskostop Akad (Sofia) Ser Rastenievud — Nauchni Trudove. Selskostopanska Akademiya "Georgi Dimitrov" (Sofia) Seriya. Rastenievudstvo

Nauchni Tr Tsentr Nauchnoizsled Inst Tekhnol Mashinostr — Nauchni Trudove. Tsentralniya Nauchnoizsledovatelski Institut po Tekhnologiya na Mashinostroineto

Nauchni Trud Minist Zemed Gorite — Nauchni Trudove. Ministerstvo na Zemedelieto i Gorite

Nauchni Trudove Ser Gorsko Stop — Nauchni Trudove. Seriia Gorsko Stopanstvo

Nauchni Trud Vissh Lesotekh Inst — Nauchni Trudove. Vissh Lesotekhnicheski Institut

Nauchni Trud Vissh Selskostop Inst "Vasil Kolarov" — Nauchni Trudove. Vissh Selskostopanski Institut "Vasil Kolarov"

Nauchni Tr Vissh Inst Khranit Vkusova Promst (Plovdiv) — Nauchni Trudove. Vissh Institut po Khranitelna i Vkusova Promishlenost (Plovdiv)

Nauchni Tr Vissh Lesotekh Inst (Sofia) — Nauchni Trudove. Vissh Lesotekhnicheski Institut (Sofia) [*Bulgaria*]

Nauchni Tr Vissh Lesotekh Inst (Sofia) Ser Gorsko Stop — Nauchni Trudove. Vissh Lesotekhnicheski Institut (Sofia). Seriya Gorsko Stopanstvo

Nauchni Tr Vissh Lesotekh Inst (Sofia) Ser Mekh Tekhnol Durv — Nauchni Trudove. Vissh Lesotekhnicheski Institut (Sofia). Seriya Mekhanichna Tekhnologiya na Durvesinata [*Bulgaria*]

Nauchni Tr Vissh Lesotekh Inst (Sofia) Ser Ozelenyavane — Nauchni Trudove. Vissh Lesotekhnicheski Institut (Sofia). Seriya Ozelenyavane

Nauchni Tr Vissh Med Inst (Sofia) — Nauchni Trudove. Visshiya Meditsinski Institut (Sofia)

Nauchni Tr Vissh Med Inst (Varna) — Nauchni Trudove na Visshiya Meditsinski Institut (Varna)

Nauchni Tr Vissh Pedagog Inst (Plovdiv) Mat Fiz Khim Biol — Nauchni Trudove. Vissh Pedagogicheski Institut (Plovdiv). Matematika, Fizika, Khimiya, Biologiya

Nauchni Tr Vissh Selskostop Inst (Plovdiv) — Nauchni Trudove. Vissh Selskostopanski Institut "Vasil Kolarov" (Plovdiv)

Nauchni Tr Vissh Selskostop Inst (Sofia) Agron Fak — Nauchni Trudove. Vissh Selskostopanski Institut "Georgi Dimitrov" (Sofia). Agronomicheski Fakultet

Nauchni Tr Vissh Selskostop Inst Sofia Agron Fak Rastenievyd — Nauchni Trudove. Vissh Selskostopanski Institut (Sofia). Agronomicheski Fakultet. Seriya Rastenievydstvo

Nauchni Tr Vissh Selskostop Inst (Sofia) Zootekh Fak — Nauchni Trudove. Vissh Selskostopanski Institut "Georgi Dimitrov" (Sofia). Zootekhnicheski Fakultet

Nauchni Tr Vissh Veterinarnomed Inst (Sofia) — Nauchni Trudove. Vissh Veterinarnomeditsinski Institut "Prof. Dr. G. Pavlov" (Sofia)

Nauchno Agron Zh — Nauchno Agronomicheskii Zhurnal

Nauchno Inf Byull Nauchno Issled Otd Kiev Ind Inst — Nauchno-Informatsionnyi Byulleten Nauchno-Issledovatel'skogo Otdeleniya Kievskogo Industrial'nogo Instituta

Nauchno-Issled Inst Epidemio Mikrobiol Tr (Sofia) — Nauchno-Issledovatel'skii Institut Epidemiologii i Mikrobiologii Trudy (Sofia)

Nauchno Issled Inst Geol Arktiki Tr — Nauchno-Issledovatel'skiy Institut Geologii Arktiki Trudy

Nauchno Issled Kozhno Venerol Inst Sb Nauchn Tr (Minsk) — Nauchno-Issledovatel'skii Kozhno-Venerologicheskii Institut. Sbornik Nauchnykh Trudov (Minsk)

Nauchno-Issled Lab Geol Zarubezh Stran Tr — Nauchno-Issledovatel'skaya Laboratoriya Geologii Zarubezhnykh Stran Trudy

Nauchno-Issled Rab Vses Nauchno Issled Inst Torf Promsti — Nauchno-Issledovatel'skie Raboty Vsesoyuznogo Nauchno-Issledovatel'skogo Instituta Torfyanoi Promyshlennosti

Nauchno-Issled Tr Ivanov Tekst Inst — Nauchno-Issledovatel'skie Trudy Ivanovskii Tekstil'nye Institut

Nauchno-Issled Tr Kalinin Nauchno-Issled Inst Tekst Promsti — Nauchno-Issledovatel'skie Trudy Kalininskii Nauchno-Issledovatel'skii Institut Tekstil'noi Promyshlennosti

Nauchno-Issled Tr Latv Nauchno-Issled Inst Legk Promsti — Nauchno-Issledovatel'skie Trudy Latviiskii Nauchno-Issledovatel'skii Institut Legkoi Promyshlennosti

Nauchno-Issled Tr Litov Nauchno-Issled Inst Tekst Promsti — Nauchno-Issledovatel'skie Trudy Litovskii Nauchno-Issledovatel'skii Institut Tekstil'noi Promyshlennosti

Nauchno-Issled Tr Mosk Tekst Inst — Nauchno-Issledovatel'skie Trudy Moskovskii Tekstil'nyi Institut

Nauchno-Issled Tr Tsentr Nauchno-Tekh Inf Legk Promsti — Nauchno-Issledovatel'skie Trudy Tsentral'nyi Institut Nauchno-Tekhnicheskoi Informatsii Legkoi Promyshlennosti

Nauchno-Issled Tr Tsentr Nauchno-Issled Inst Sherst Promsti — Nauchno-Issledovatel'skie Trudy Tsentral'nyi Nauchno-Issledovatel'skii Institut Sherstyanoi Promyshlennosti

Nauchno-Issled Tr Vses Nauchno-Issled Inst Mekhovoi Promsti — Nauchno-Issledovatel'skie Trudy Vsesoyuznyi Nauchno-Issledovatel'skii Institut Mekhovoi Promyshlennosti

Nauchnoizsled Inst Epidemiol Mikrobiol Tr — Nauchnoizsledovatelski Institut po Epidemiologiya i Mikrobiologiya. Trudove

Nauchnoizsled Inst Okeanogr Ribno Stop Varna Izv — Nauchnoizsledovatelski Institut po Okeanografiya i Ribno Stopanstvo. Varna. Izvestiya

Nauchnoizsled Inst Okhr Tr Prof Zabol Tr — Nauchnoizsledovatelski Institut po Okhrana na Truda i Profesionalnite Zabolyavaniya. Trudove

Nauchnoizsled Inst Stroit Mater Tr (Sofia) — Nauchnoizsledovatelski Institut po Stroitelni Materiali Trudove (Sofia)

Nauchnoizsled Tr Inst Tekst Promost (Sofia) — Nauchnoizsledovatelski Trudove na Instituta po Tekstilna Promishlenost (Sofia)

Nauchno-Prakt Inf Tsentr Aptechn Nauchno-Issled Inst — Nauchno-Prakticheskaya Informatsiya. Tsentral'nyi Aptechnyi Nauchno-Issledovatel'skii Institut

Nauchno Tekh Biul Vses Nauchno Issled Inst Mekh Sel'sk Khoz — Nauchno-Tekhnicheskii Biulleten. Vsesoiuznyi Nauchno-Issledovatel'skii Institut Mekhanizatsii Sel'skogo Khoziaistva

Nauchno-Tekh Byull Agron Fiz — Nauchno-Tekhnicheskii Byulleten' po Agronomicheskoi Fizike

Nauchno-Tekh Byull Nauchno-Issled Inst Mekh Rybn Promsti — Nauchno-Tekhnicheskii Byulleten Nauchno-Issledovatel'skogo Instituta Mekhanizatsii Rybnoi Promyshlennosti

Nauchno-Tekh Byull Nauchno-Issled Inst Teploenerg Priborostr — Nauchno-Tekhnicheskii Byulleten Nauchno-Issledovatel'skii Institut Teploenergeticheskogo Priborostroeniya

Nauchno-Tekh Byull Tsentr Genet Lab — Nauchno-Tekhnicheskii Byulleten' Tsentral'noi Geneticheskoi Laboratorii

Nauchno-Tekh Byull Vses Nauchno-Issled Inst Khlopkovod — Nauchno-Tekhnicheskii Byulleten. Vsesoyuznyi Nauchno-Issledovatel'skii Institut Khlopkovodstva

Nauchno-Tekh Byull Vses Sel-Genet Inst — Nauchno-Tekhnicheskii Byulleten' Vsesoyuznogo Selektsionno-Geneticheskogo Instituta

Nauchno-Tekh Inf — Nauchno-Tekhnicheskaya Informatsiya

Nauchno-Tekh Inf Byull Leningr Politekh Inst — Nauchno-Tekhnicheskii Informatsionnyi Byulleten Leningradskogo Politekhnicheskogo Instituta [*USSR*]

Nauchno-Tekh Inf Byull Nauchn Inst Udobr Insektofungits — Nauchno-Tekhnicheskii Informatsionnyi Byulleten Nauchnogo Instituta po Udobreniyam i Insektofungitsidam

Nauchno-Tekh Inf Litov Nauchno-Issled Vet Inst — Nauchno-Tekhnicheskaya Informatsiya Litovskii Nauchno-Issledovatel'skii Veterinarnyi Institut

Nauchno-Tekh Inf Ser 1 — Nauchno-Tekhnicheskaya Informatsiya. Seriya 1. Organizatsiya i Metodika Informatsionnoi Raboty

Nauchno-Tekh Inf Ser 2 — Nauchno-Tekhnicheskaya Informatsiya. Seriya 2. Informatsionnye Protsessy i Sistemy

Nauchno-Tekh Inf (Sofia) — Nauchno-Tekhnicheskaya Informatsiya (Sofia)

Nauchno-Tekh Obz Ser Geol Razved Gaz Gazokondens Mestorozhd — Nauchno-Tekhnicheskii Obzor. Seriya. Geologiya, Razvedka Gazovykh, i Bazokondensatnykh Mestorozhdenii

Nauchno-Tekh Obz Ser Pererab Gaza Gazov Kondens — Nauchno-Tekhnicheskii Obzor. Seriya. Pererabotka Gaza i Gazovogo Kondensata

Nauchno-Tekh O-va SSSR — Nauchno-Tekhnicheskie Obshchestva SSSR [*USSR*]

Nauchno-Tekh Probl Goreniya Vzryva — Nauchno-Tekhnicheskie Problemy Goreniya i Vzryva

Nauchno Tekh Ref Sb Ser Fosfornaya Promst — Nauchno-Tekhnicheskii Referativnyi Sbornik. Seriya Fosfornaya Promyshlennost

Nauchno-Tekh Sb Dobyche Nefti — Nauchno-Tekhnicheskii Sbornik po Dobyche Nefti

Nauchno-Tekh Sb Geol Razrab Transp Ispolz Prir Gaza — Nauchno-Tekhnicheskii Sbornik po Geologii, Razrabotke, Transportu, i Ispol'zovaniyu Prirodnogo Gaza

Nauchno-Temat Sb Ufim Neft Inst — Nauchno-Tematicheskii Sbornik. Ufimskii Neftyanoi Institut

Nauchn i Prikl Fotogr i Kinematogr — Zhurnal Nauchnoi i Prikladnoi Fotografii i Kinematografii

Nauchn Rab Inst Okhr Tr Vses Tsentr Sov Prof Soyuz — Nauchnye Raboty Institutov Okhrany Truda Vsesoyuznogo Tsentral'nogo Soveta Professional'nykh Soyuzov

Nauchn Rab Inst Okhr Tr Vses Tsentr Sov Prof Soyuzov — Nauchnye Raboty Institutov Okhrany Truda Vsesoyuznogo Tsentral'nogo Soveta Professional'nykh Soyuzov

Nauchn Rab Stud Mosk Farm Inst — Nauchnye Raboty Studentov Moskovskogo Farmatsevticheskogo Instituta

Nauchn Rab Stud Mosk Gorn Inst — Nauchnye Raboty Studentov Moskovskogo Gornogo Instituta

Nauchn Rab Stud Mosk Med Stomatol Inst — Nauchnye Raboty Studentov Moskovskogo Meditsinskogo Stomatologicheskogo Instituta

Nauchn Rab Stud Novocherk Politekh Inst — Nauchnye Raboty Studentov Novocherkasskii Politekhnicheskii Institut

Nauchn Rab Stud Sverdl Gorn Inst — Nauchnye Raboty Studentov Sverdlovskii Gornyi Institut

Nauchn Rab Vrach Mord SSSR — Nauchnye Raboty Vrachei Mordovskoi SSSR

Nauchn Soobshch Arm Nauchno Issled Inst Stroit Mater Sooruzh — Nauchnye Soobshcheniya Armyanskii Nauchno-Issledovatel'skii Institut Stroitel'nykh Materialov i Sooruzhenii

Nauchn Soobshch Gos Vses Nauchno Issled Inst Tsem Prom-sti — Nauchnye Soobshcheniya Gosudarstvennyi Vsesoyuznyi Nauchno-Issledovatel'skii Institut Tsementnoi Promyshlennosti [*USSR*]

Nauchn Soobshch Inst Fiziol Akad Nauk SSSR — Nauchnye Soobshchiya Instituta Fiziologii Akademii Nauk SSSR

Nauchn Soobshch Inst Gorn Dela Im A A Skochinskogo — Nauchnye Soobshcheniya Institut Gornogo Dela Imeni A. A. Skochinskogo [*USSR*]

Nauchn Soobshch Inst Gorn Dela (Moscow) — Nauchnye Soobshcheniya Institut Gornogo Dela (Moscow)

Nauchn Soobshch Vses Nauchno Issled Inst Tsem Promsti — Nauchnye Soobshcheniya Vsesoyuznyi Nauchno-Issledovatel'skii Institut Tsementnoi Promyshlennosti

Nauchn Tr Akad Kommunal'n Khoz — Nauchnye Trudy Akademii Kommunal'nogo Khozyaistva

Nauchn Tr Aspir Odess Skh Inst — Nauchnye Trudy Aspirantov Odesskii Sel'skokhozyaistvennyi Institut

Nauchn Tr Aspir Odess Skh Inst — Nauchnye Trudy Odesskii Sel'skokhozyaistvennyi Institut

Nauchn Tr Aspir Ordinatorov Pervogo Mosk Med Inst — Nauchnye Trudy Aspirantov i Ordinatorov Pervogo Moskovskogo Meditsinskogo Instituta

Nauchn Tr Bashk Gos Med Inst — Nauchnye Trudy Bashkirskogo Gosudarstvennogo Meditsinskogo Instituta

Nauchn Tr Bashk Med Inst — Nauchnye Trudy Bashkirskogo Meditsinskogo Instituta

Nauchn Tr Bukhar Gos Pedagog Inst — Nauchnye Trudy Bukharskii Gosudarstvennyi Pedagogicheskii Institut

Nauchn Tr Bykovskoi Bakhchevoi Opytn Stn — Nauchnye Trudy Bykovskoi Bakhchevoi Opytnai Stantsii

Nauchn Tr Chelyab Obl Klin Bol'n — Nauchnye Trudy Chelyabinskoi Oblastnoi Klinicheskoi Bol'nitsy

Nauchn Tr Dnepropetr Metall Inst — Nauchnye Trudy Dnepropetrovskii Metallorgicheskii Institut

Nauchn Tr Donskoi Zon Nauchno Issled Inst Sel'sk Khoz — Nauchnye Trudy Donskoi Zonal'nyi Nauchno-Issledovatel'skii Institut Sel'skogo Khozyaistva

Nauchn Tr Erevan Gos Univ Ser Geol Nauk — Nauchnye Trudy Erevanskii Gosudarstvennyi Universitet Seriya Geologicheskikh Nauk

Nauchn Tr Erevan Gos Univ Ser Khim Nauk — Nauchnye Trudy Erevanskii Gosudarstvennyi Universitet Seriya Khimicheskikh Nauk

Nauchn Tr Gos Nauchno-Issled Proektn Inst Redkomet Prom-sti — Nauchnye Trudy Gosudarstvennyi Nauchno-Issledovatel'skii i Proektnyi Institut Redkometallicheskoi Promyshlennosti [*USSR*]

Nauchn Tr Gruz Skh Inst — Nauchnye Trudy Gruzinskii Sel'skokhozyaistvennyi Institut

Nauchn Tr Inst Avtom — Nauchnye Trudy Instituta Avtomatiki [*Ukrainian SSR*]

Nauchn Tr Inst Chern Metall (Dnepropetrovsk) — Nauchnye Trudy Institut Chernoi Metallurgii (Dnepropetrovsk)

Nauchn Tr Inst Entomol Fitopatol — Nauchnye Trudy Instituta Entomologii i Fitopatologii

Nauchn Tr Inst Entomol Fitopatol Akad Nauk Ukr SSR — Nauchnye Trudy Instituta Entomologii i Fitopatologii Akademii Nauk Ukrainskoi SSR

Nauchn Tr Inst Fiziol Rast Agrokhim Akad Nauk Ukr SSR — Nauchnye Trudy Institut Fiziologii Rastenii i Agrokhimii. Akademiya Nauk Ukrainskoi SSR

Nauchn Tr Inst Mineral Resur (Ukrainian SSR) — Nauchnye Trudy Instituta Mineral'nykh Resursov (Ukrainian SSR)

Nauchn Tr Irkutsk Gos Med Inst — Nauchnye Trudy Irkutskii Gosudarstvennyi Meditsinskii Institut

Nauchn Tr Irkutsk Gos Nauchno Issled Inst Redk Met — Nauchnye Trudy Irkutskii Gosudarstvennyi Nauchno-Issledovatel'skii Institut Redkikh Metallov

Nauchn Tr Irkutsk Gos Nauchno Issled Inst Redk Tsvetn Met — Nauchnye Trudy Irkutskii Gosudarstvennyi Nauchno-Issledovatel'skii Institut Redkikh i Tsvetnykh Metallov

Nauchn Tr Irkutsk Med Inst — Nauchnye Trudy Irkutskii Meditsinskii Institut

Nauchn Tr Kamenets Podol'sk Skh Inst — Nauchnye Trudy Kamenets Podol'skii Sel'skokhozyaistvennyi Institut

Nauchn Tr Karagand Fil Inst Obogashch Tverd Goryuch Iskop — Nauchnye Trudy Karagandinskii Filial Instituta Obogashcheniya Tverdykh Goryuchikh Iskopaemykh [*USSR*]

Nauchn Tr Karagand Nauchno Issled Ugol'n Inst — Nauchnye Trudy Karagandinskii Nauchno-Issledovatel'skii Ugol'nyi Institut

Nauchn Tr Kazan Med Inst — Nauchnye Trudy Kazanskogo Meditsinskogo Instituta

Nauchn Tr Khark Gorn Inst — Nauchnye Trudy Khar'kovskii Gornyi Institut

Nauchn Tr Khar'k Inst Inzh Kommunal'n Stroit — Nauchnye Trudy Khar'kovskii Institut Inzhenerov Kommunal'nogo Stroitel'stva

Nauchn Tr Khar'k S-kh Inst — Nauchnye Trudy Khar'kovskogo Sel'skokhozyaistvennogo Instituta

Nauchn Tr Kirg Med Inst — Nauchnye Trudy Kirgizskogo Meditsinskogo Instituta

Nauchn Tr Krasnodar God Pedagog Inst — Nauchnye Trudy Krasnodarskogo Gosudarstvennogo Pedagogicheskogo Instituta

Nauchn Tr Krasnodar Nauchno Issled Inst Sel'sk Khoz — Nauchnye Trudy Krasnodarskogo Nauchno-Issledovatel'skogo Instituta Sel'skogo Khozyaistva

Nauchn Tr Krasnodar Nauchno Issled Vet Stn — Nauchnye Trudy Krasnodarskoi Nauchno-Issledovat'skoi Veterinarnoi Stantsii

Nauchn Tr Krym Gos Med Inst — Nauchnye Trudy Krymskii Gosudarstvennyi Meditsinskii Institut

Nauchn Tr Kuban Gos Med Inst — Nauchnye Trudy Kubanskogo Gosudarstvennogo Meditsinskogo Instituta

Nauchn Tr Kuban Gos Univ — Nauchnye Trudy Kubanskii Gosudarstvennyi Universitet

Nauchn Tr Kurgan S-kh Inst — Nauchnye Trudy Kurganskogo Sel'skokhozyaistvennogo Instituta

Nauchn Tr Kursk Gos Pedagog Inst — Nauchnye Trudy Kurskij Gosudarstvennyj Pedagogicheskij Institut

Nauchn Tr Kursk Gos Skh Optn Stn — Nauchnye Trudy Kurskoi Gosudarstvennoi Sel'skokhozyaistvennoi Opytnoi Stantsii

Nauchn Tr Kursk Gos Skh Opytn Stn — Nauchnye Trudy Kurskoi Gosudarstvennoi Sel'skokhozyaistvennoi Opytnoi Stantsii

Nauchn Tr Kursk Politekh Inst — Nauchnye Trudy Kurskii Politekhnicheskii Institut [*USSR*]

Nauchn Tr Kursk Selkh Inst — Nauchnye Trudy Kurskogo Sel'skokhozyaistvennogo Instituta

Nauchn Tr Leningr Gorn Inst Nov Issled Khim Metall Obogashch — Nauchnye Trudy Leningradskii Gornyi Institut Novye Issledovaniya v Khimii, Metallurgii, i Obogashchenii

Nauchn Tr Leningr Gos Inst Usoversh Vrachei — Nauchnye Trudy Leningradskogo Gosudarstvennogo Instituta Usovershenstvovaniya Vrachei

Nauchn Tr Leningr Inst Tochn Mekh Opt — Nauchnye Trudy Leningradskii Institut Tochnoi Mekhaniki i Optiki

Nauchn Tr Leningr Inst Usoversh Vrachei Im S M Kirova — Nauchnye Trudy Leningradskogo Instituta Usovershenstvovaniya Vrachei Imeni S. M. Kirova

Nauchn Tr Leningr Inzh Stroit Inst — Nauchnye Trudy Leningradskii Inzhenerno-Stroitel'nyi Institut

Nauchn Tr Leningr Lesotekh Akad — Nauchnye Trudy Leningradskoi Lesotekhnicheskoi Akademii

Nauchn Tr Leningr Nauchno Issled Inst Pereliv Krovi — Nauchnye Trudy Leningradskii Nauchno-Issledovatel'skii Institut Perelivaniya Krovi

Nauchn Tr Leningr Tekhnol Inst Im Lensoveta — Nauchnye Trudy Leningradskogo Tekhnologicheskogo Instituta Imeni Lensoveta

Nauchn Tr Lesokhoz Fak Ukr Skh Akad — Nauchnye Trudy Lesokhoziastevennogo Fakul'teka Ukrainskoi Sel'skokhozyaistvennoi Akademii

Nauchn Tr Litov S-kh Akad — Nauchnye Trudy Litovskoi Sel'skokhozyaistvennoi Akademii

Nauchn Tr L'vov Lesotekh Inst — Nauchnye Trudy L'vovskogo Lesotekhnicheskogo Instituta

Nauchn Tr L'vov Zoovet Inst — Nauchnye Trudy L'vovskii Zooveterinarnyi Institut

Nauchn Tr Melitopol'skoi Opytn Stn Sadovod — Nauchnye Trudy Melitopol'skoi Opytnoi Stantsii Sadovodstva

Nauchn Tr Melitop Opytn Stn Sadovod — Nauchnye Trudy Melitopol'skoi Opytnoi Stantsii Sadovodstva

Nauchn Tr Mosk Gor Klin Bol'n N 52 — Nauchnye Trudy Moskovskoi Gorodskoi Kliniceskci Bol'nitsy N 52

Nauchn Tr Mosk Gorn Inst — Nauchnye Trudy Moskovskogo Gornogo Instituta [*USSR*]

Nauchn Tr Mosk Inst Radioelektron Gorn Elektromekh — Nauchnye Trudy Moskovskii Institut Radioelektroniki i Gornoi Elektromekhaniki

Nauchn Tr Mosk Inzh Ekon Inst — Nauchnye Trudy Moskovskogo Inzhenerno-Ekonomicheskogo Instituta [*USSR*]

Nauchn Tr Mosk Lesotekh Inst — Nauchnye Trudy Moskovskogo Lesotekhnicheskogo Instituta

Nauchn Tr Mosk Nauchno-Issled Inst Vaktsin Syvorot — Nauchnye Trudy Moskovskogo Nauchno-Issledovatel'skogo Instituta Vaktsin i Syvorotok

Nauchn Tr Mosk Poligr Inst — Nauchnye Trudy Moskovskii Poligraficheskii Institut

Nauchn Tr Mosk Tekhnol Inst Legk Promsti — Nauchnye Trudy Moskovskogo Tekhnologicheskogo Instituta Legkoi Promyshlennosti

Nauchn Tr Nauchno Issled Gornometall Inst Yerevan — Nauchnye Trudy Nauchno-Issledovatelskii Gornometallurgicheskii Instituta Yerevan

Nauchn Tr Nauchno-Issled Inst Gorn Sadovod Tsvetovod — Nauchnye Trudy Nauchno-Issledovatel'skogo Instituta Gornogo Sadovodstva i Tsvetovodstva

Nauchn Tr Nauchno-Issled Inst Kartofel'n Khoz — Nauchnye Trudy Nauchno-Issledovatel'skii Institut Kartofel'nogo Khoziaistva

Nauchn Tr Nauchno-Issled Inst Pediatr — Nauchnye Trudy Nauchno-Issledovatel'skogo Instituta po Pediatrii

Nauchn Tr Nauchno-Issled Inst Pushnogo Zverovod Krolikovod — Nauchnye Trudy Nauchno-Issledovatel'skii Institut Pushnogo Zverovodstva i Krolikovodstva

Nauchn Tr Nauchno-Issled Inst Radiol Radiats Gig — Nauchnye Trudy Nauchno-Issledovatel'skii Institut Radiologii i Radiatsionnoi Gigieny [*Bulgaria*]

Nauchn Tr Nauchno Issled Inst Sel'sk Khoz Yugo Vostoka — Nauchnye Trudy Nauchno-Issledovatel'skii Institut Sel'skogo Khozyaistva Yugo-Vostoka

Nauchn Tr Nauchno-Issled Inst S-Kh Yugo-Vost — Nauchnye Trudy Nauchno-Issledovatel'skogo Instituta Sel'skokhozyaistva Yugo-Vostoka

Nauchn Tr Nauchno Issled Vet Inst (Minsk) — Nauchnye Trudy Nauchno-Issledovatel'skogo Veterinarnogo Instituta (Minsk)

Nauchn Tr Novosib Med Inst — Nauchnye Trudy Novosibirskogo Meditsinskogo Instituta

Nauchn Tr Novosib Nauchno Issled Vet Stn — Nauchnye Trudy Novosibirskoi Nauchno-Issledovatel'skoi Veterinarnoi Stantsii

Nauchn Tr Obninskii Otd Geogr Ova SSSR — Nauchnye Trudy Obninskii Otdel Geograficheskogo Obshchestva SSSR

Nauchn Tr Obogashch Briket Uglei — Nauchnye Trudy po Obogashcheniyu i Briketirovaniyu Uglei [*USSR*]

Nauchn Tr Omsk Med Inst — Nauchnye Trudy Omskii Meditsinskii Institut

Nauchn Tr Omsk S-kh Inst — Nauchnye Trudy Omskogo Sel'skokhozyaistvennogo Instituta

Nauchn Tr Omsk Vet Inst — Nauchnye Trudy Omskogo Veterinarnogo Instituta

Nauchn Tr Orlov Ob Skh Opytn Stn — Nauchnye Trudy Orlovskaya Oblastnaya Sel'skohozyaistvennaya Opytnaya Stantsiya

Nauchn Tr Permsk Farm Inst — Nauchnye Trudy Permskogo Farmatsevticheskogo Instituta

Nauchn Tr Permsk Nauchno Issled Ugoln Inst — Nauchnye Trudy Permskii Nauchno Issledovatel'skii Ugol'nye Institut

Nauchn Tr Permsk Politekh Inst — Nauchnye Trudy Permskii Politekhnicheskii Institut [*USSR*]

Nauchn Tr Poltav Skh Inst — Nauchnye Trudy Poltavskii Sel'skokhozyaistvennyi Institut

Nauchn Tr Primorsk S-kh Inst — Nauchnye Trudy Primorskogo Sel'skokhozyaistvennogo Instituta

Nauchn Tr Rizh Nauchno Issled Inst Travmatol Ortop — Nauchnye Trudy Rizhskii Nauchno-Issledovatel'skii Institut Travmatologii i Ortopedii

Nauchn Tr Rostov Na Donu Inzh Stroit Inst — Nauchnye Trudy Rostovskii-Na-Donu Inzhenerno-Stroitel'nyi Institut

Nauchn Tr Ryazan Med Inst — Nauchnye Trudy Ryazanskii Meditsinskii Institut

Nauchn Tr Samark Gos Univ — Nauchnye Trudy Samarkandskogo Gosudarstvennogo Universiteta

Nauchn Tr Samark Koop Inst Tsentrosoyuza — Nauchnye Trudy Samarkandskogo Kooperativnogo Instituta Tsentrosoyuza

Nauchn Tr Samark Med Inst — Nauchnye Trudy Samarkandskogo Meditsinskogo Instituta

Nauchn Tr Samark Skh Inst — Nauchnye Trudy Samarkandskii Sel'skokhozyaistvennyi Institut

Nauchn Tr Samark Univ — Nauchnye Trudy Samarkandskogo Universiteta

Nauchn Tr Sarat Politekh Inst — Nauchnye Trudy Saratovskii Politekhnicheskii Institut

Nauchn Tr Sev-Zapadn Nauchno-Issled Inst Sel'sk Khoz — Nauchnye Trudy Severo-Zapadnogo Nauchno-Issledovatel'skogo Instituta Sel'skogo Khozyaistva

Nauchn Tr Sev Zapadn Nauchno Issled Inst Sel'sk Khoz — Nauchnye Trudy Severo-Zapadnyi Nauchno-Issledovatel'skii Institut Sel'skogo Khozyaistva

Nauchn Tr Sib Gos Nauchno Issled Proekt Inst Tsvet Metall — Nauchnye Trudy Sibirskii Gosudarstvennyi Nauchno-Issledovatel'skii i Proektnyi Institut Tsvetnoi Metallurgii [*USSR*]

Nauchn Tr Sib Gos Nauchno Issled Proektn Inst Tsvetn Metall — Nauchnye Trudy Sibirskii Gosudarstvennyi Nauchno-Issledovatel'skii i Proektnyi Institut Tsvetnoi Metallurgii

Nauchn Tr Sib Nauchno Issled Inst Selsk Khoz — Nauchnye Trudy Sibirskii Nauchno Issledovatel'skii Institut Sel'skogo Khozyaistva

Nauchn Tr S'kh Inst (Sofia) Agron Fak Ser Obshch Zemled — Nauchnye Trudy. Sel'skokhozyaistvennyi Institut (Sofia). Agronomicheskii Fakul'tet. Seriya Obshchee Zemledelie

Nauchn Tr Stavrop S-kh Inst — Nauchnye Trudy Stavropol'skogo Sel'skokhozyaistvennogo Instituta

Nauchn Tr Stud Gruz Skh Inst — Nauchnye Trudy Studentov Gruzinskii Sel'skokhozyaistvennyi Institut

Nauchn Tr Stud Gruz Ssk Inst — Nauchnye Trudy Studentov Gruzinskogo Sel'skokhozyaistvennogo Instituta

Nauchn Tr Sverdl Gos Pedagog Inst — Nauchnye Trudy Sverdlovskii Gosudarstvennyi Pedagogicheskii Institut

Nauchn Tr Tashk Gos Univ Im V I Lenina — Nauchnye Trudy Tashkentskii Gosudarstvennyi Universitet Imeni V. I. Lenina [*USSR*]

Nauchn Tr Tashk Tekst Inst — Nauchnye Trudy Tashkentskogo Tekstil'nogo Instituta

Nauchn Tr Tsentr Inst Usoversh Vrachei — Nauchnye Trudy Tsentral'nogo Instituta Usovershenstovaniya Vrachei

Nauchn Tr Tsentr Nauchno Issled Inst Mekh Obrab Drev — Nauchnye Trudy Tsentral'nyi Nauchno Issledovatel'skii Institut Mekhanicheskoi Obrabotki Drevesiny

Nauchn Tr Tsentr Nauchno-Issled Inst Olovyannoi Promsti — Nauchnye Trudy Tsentral'nyi Nauchno-Issledovatel'skii Institut Olovyannoi Promyshlennosti

Nauchn Tr Tsentr Nauchno Issled Inst Tsellyul Bum Promsti — Nauchnye Trudy Tsentral'nyi Nauchno-Issledovatel'skii Institut Tsellyuloznoi i Bumazhnoi Promyshlennosti

Nauchn Tr Tul Gorn Inst — Nauchnye Trudy Tul'skogo Gornogo Instituta

Nauchn Tr Tul Gos Pedagog Inst — Nauchnye Trudy Tulskogo Gosudarstvennogo Pedagogicheskogo Instituta

Nauchn Tr Tyumen Skh Inst — Nauchnye Trudy Tyumenskogo Sel'skokhozyaistvennogo Instituta

Nauchn Tr Uch Prakt Vrachei Uzb — Nauchnye Trudy Uchenykh i Prakticheskikh Vrachei Uzbekistana

Nauchn Tr Ukr Inst Eksp Vet — Nauchnye Trudy Ukrainskii Instituta Eksperimental'noi Veterinarii

Nauchn Tr Ukr Inst Gidrotekh Melior — Nauchnye Trudy Ukrainskogo Instituta Gidrotekhniki i Melioratsii

Nauchn Tr Ukr Nauchno Issled Inst Eksp Vet — Nauchnye Trudy Ukrainskii Nauchno-Issledovatel'skii Institut Eksperimental'noi Veterinarii

Nauchn Tr Ukr Nauchno Issled Inst Fiziol Rast — Nauchnye Trudy Ukrainskii Nauchno-Issledovatel'skii Institut Fiziologii Rastenii

Nauchn Tr Ukr Nauchno Issled Inst Gig Tr Profzabol — Nauchnye Trudy Ukrainskii Nauchno-Issledovatel'skii Institut Gigieny Truda i Profzabolevanii

Nauchn Tr Ukr Nauchno-Issled Inst Rastenievod Sel Genet — Nauchnye Trudy Ukrainskogo Nauchno-Issledovatel'skogo Instituta Rastenievodstva Selestsii i Genetiki

Nauchn Tr Ukr Nauchno Issled Inst Sadovod — Nauchnye Trudy Ukrainskii Nauchno-Issledovatel'skii Institut Sadovodstva

Nauchn Tr Ukr Nauchno Issled Inst Vinograd Vinodel — Nauchnye Trudy Ukrainskogo Nauchno-Issledovatel'skogo Instituta Vinogradarstva i Vinodeliya

Nauchn Tr Ukr Nauchno Issled Inst Zashch Rast — Nauchnye Trudy Ukrainskii Nauchno-Issledovatel'skii Institut Zashchity Rastenii

Nauchn Tr Ukr Nauchno-Issled Stn Vinograd Osvo Peskov — Nauchnye Trudy Ukrainskoi Nauchno-Issledovatel'skoi Stantsii Vinogradarstva i Osvoeniya Peskov

Nauchn Tr Ukr Skh Akad — Nauchnye Trudy Ukrainskaya Sel'skokhozyaistvennaya Akademiya

Nauchn Tr Uzb Skh Inst — Nauchnye Trudy Uzbekskogo Sel'skokhozyaistvennogo Instituta

Nauchn Tr Vopr Pererab Kach Uglei — Nauchnye Trudy Voprosam
Pererabotki i Kachestva Uglei

Nauchn Tr Voronezh Inzh Stroit Inst — Nauchnye Trudy Voronezhskii
Inzhenerno-Stroitel'nyi Institut

Nauchn Tr Voronezh Lesotekh Inst — Nauchnye Trudy Voronezhskogo
Lesotekhnicheskogo Instituta

Nauchn Tr Vses Nauchno Issled Inst Podzemn Gazif Uglei — Nauchnye Trudy
Vsesoyuznyi Nauchno-Issledovatel'skii Institut Podzemnoi Gazifikatsii
Uglei

Nauchn Tr Vses Sel Genet Inst — Nauchnye Trudy Vsesoyuznogo Selektsionno
Geneticheskogo Instituta

Nauchn Tr Vses Zaochn Mashinostroit Inst — Nauchnye Trudy Vsesoyuznyi
Zaochnyi Mashinostroitel'nyi Institut [USSR]

Nauchn Tr Vyssh Uchebn Zaved Lit SSR Med (Vilnius) — Nauchnye Trudy
Vysshykh Uchebnykh Zavedenii Litovskoi SSR Meditsina (Vilnius)

Nauchn Tr Vyssh Uchebn Zaved Lit SSR Ultrazvuk — Nauchnye Trudy
Vysshikh Uchebnykh Zavedenii Litovskoi SSR Ultrazvuk

Nauchn Tr Vyssh Uchebn Zaved Lit SSR Vibrotekh — Nauchnye Trudy
Vysshikh Uchebnykh Zavedenii Litovskoi SSR Vibrotekhnika

Nauchn Tr Zhitomir Skh Inst — Nauchnye Trudy Zhitomirskii
Sel'skokhozyaistvennyi Institut

Nauchn Tr Zootekhnol Fak Zoovet Inst — Nauchnye Trudy
Zootekhnologicheskogo Fakulteta Zooveterinarnogo Instituta

Nauchn Tr Zootekhnologicheskogo Inst — Nauchnye Trudy
Zootekhnologicheskogo Instituta

Nauchnye Zap Dnepropetr Gos Univ — Nauchnye Zapiski Dnepropetrovskogo
Gosudarstvennogo Universiteta

Nauchn Zap Belotserk Skh Inst — Nauchnye Zapiski Belotserkovskogo
Sel'skokhozyaistvennogo Instituta

Nauchn Zap Chernovits Gos Med Inst — Nauchnye Zapiski Chernovitskii
Gosudarstvennyi Meditsinskii Institut

Nauchn Zap Dnepropetr Gos Univ — Nauchnye Zapiski Dnepropetrovskogo
Gosudarstvennogo Universiteta

Nauchn Zap Donetsk Inst Sov Torg — Nauchnye Zapiski Donetskogo Instituta
Sovetskoi Torgovli

Nauchn Zap Gos Eksp Inst Sakh Promsti — Nauchnye Zapiski
Gosudarstvennogo Eksperimentnogo Instituta Sakharnoi
Promyshlennosti

Nauchn Zap Gos Nauchno-Issled Proektn Inst Ugol'n Prom-sti — Nauchnye
Zapiski Gosudarstvennyi Nauchno-Issledovatel'skii i Proektnyi Institut
Ugol'noi Promyshlennosti [USSR]

Nauchn Zap Khar'k Aviats Inst — Nauchnye Zapiski Khar'kovskogo
Aviatsionnogo Instituta

Nauchn Zap Khar'k Inst Mekh Elektrif Sel'sk Khoz — Nauchnye Zapiski
Khar'kovskii Institut Mekhanizatsii i Elektrifikatsii Sel'skogo
Khozyaistva

Nauchn Zap Khar'k Inst Mekh Sel'sk Khoz — Nauchnye Zapiski Khar'kovski
Institut Mekhanizatsii Sel'skogo Khozyaistva

Nauchn Zap Khar'k Inst Mekh Sots Sel'sk Khoz — Nauchnye Zapiski
Khar'kovskii Institut Mekhanizatsii Sotsialisticheskogo Sel'skogo
Khozyaistva

Nauchn Zap Khar'k Poligr Inst — Nauchnye Zapiski Khar'kovski
Poligraficheskii Institut

Nauchn Zap Kherson Skh Inst Im A D Tsiurupy — Nauchnye Zapiski
Khersonskogo Sel'skokhozyaistvennogo Instituta Imeni A. D. Tsiurupy

Nauchn Zap Lugansk Skh Inst — Nauchnye Zapiski Luganskogo
Sel'skokhozyaistvennogo Instituta

Nauchn Zap Lvov Politekh Inst — Nauchnye Zapiski L'vovskogo
Politekhnicheskogo Instituta

Nauchn Zap L'vov Skh Inst — Nauchnye Zapiski L'vovskogo
Sel'skokhozyaistvennogo Instituta

Nauchn Zap L'vov Torg Ekon Inst — Nauchnye Zapiski L'vovskogo Torgovo
Ekonomicheskogo Instituta

Nauchn Zap Mosk Gidromelior Inst — Nauchnye Zapiski Moskovskii
Gidromeliorativnyi Institut

Nauchn Zap Odess Politekh Inst — Nauchnye Zapiski Odesskii
Politekhnicheskii Institut

Nauchn Zap Sakh Promsti — Nauchnye Zapiski po Sakharnoi
Promyshlennosti

Nauchn Zap Sakh Promsti Agron Vyp — Nauchnye Zapiski po Sakharnoi
Promyshlennost Agronomicheskii Vypusk

Nauchn Zap Sakh Promsti Tekhnol Vyp — Nauchnye Zapiski po Sakharnoi
Promyshlennosti Tekhnologicheskii Vypusk

Nauchn Zap Ukr Poligr Inst — Nauchnye Zapiski Ukrainskii Poligraficheskii
Institut

Nauchn Zap Uzhgorod Gos Univ — Nauchnye Zapiski Uzhgorodskogo
Gosudarstvennogo Universiteta

Nauchn Zap Voronezh Lesokhim Inst — Nauchnye Zapiski Voronezhskogo
Lesokhimicheskogo Instituta

Nauchn Zap Voronezh Lesotekh Inst — Nauchnye Zapiski Voronezhskogo
Lesotekhnicheskogo Instituta

Nauchn Zap Voronezh Otd Geogr Ova SSSR — Nauchnye Zapiski
Voronezhskogo Otdela Geograficheskogo Obshchestva SSSR

Nauchn Zap Voronezh Otd Vses Bot Ova — Nauchnye Zapiski Voronezhskogo
Otdeleniya Vsesoyuznogo Botanicheskogo Obshchestva

Nauchn Zap Voroshilovgr Skh Inst — Nauchnye Zapiski Voroshilovgradskogo
Sel'skokhozyaistvennogo Instituta

Nauch Soobshch Inst Fiziol Pavlov — Nauchnye Sooobshcheniya Institut
Fiziologii Imeni I. P. Pavlova

Nauch-Tekh Inf — Nauchno-Tekhnicheskaya Informatsiya

Nauch Tr Dobrudzhan Selskostop Nauchnoizsled Inst — Nauchni Trudove na
Dobrudzhanskiya Selskostopanski Nauchnoizsledovatelski Institut

Nauch Tr Poltav Nauch-Issled Inst Svinovod — Nauchnye Trudy Poltavskii
Nauchno-Issledovatel'skii Institut Svinovodstva

Nauch Trudy — Nauchnye Trudy

Nauch Trudy Altaisk Nauchno-Issled Inst Sel Khoz — Nauchnye Trudy
Altaiskogo Nauchno-Issledovatel'skogo Instituta Sel'skogo Khozyaistva

Nauch Trudy Kuibyshev Gos Pedagog Inst Zhivot Povolzh'ya — Nauchnye
Trudy Kuibyshevskii Gosudarstvennyi Pedagogicheskii Institut
Zhivotnye Povolzh'ya

Nauch Trudy Kuibyshevskii Gos Ped Inst — Nauchnye Trudy Kuibyshevskii
Gosudarstvennyi Pedagogicheskii Institut Imeni V. V. Kuibysheva

Nauch Trudy Nauchno-Issled Inst Pchel — Nauchnye Trudy Nauchno-
Issledovatel'skii Institut Pchelovodstva

Nauch Trudy Stavropol Sek'Khoz Inst — Nauchnye Trudy Stavropol'skogo
Sel'Skokhozyaistvennogo Instituta

Nauch Trudy Ukr Nauchno-Issled Inst Les Khoz Agrolesomelior — Nauchnye
Trudy Ukrainskogo Nauchno-Issledovatel'skogo Instituta Lesnogo
Khozyaistva i Agrolesomelioratsii

Nauch Trudy Ukr Nauchno-Issled Inst Pochv — Nauchnye Trudy Ukrainskogo
Nauchno-Issledovatel'skogo Instituta Pochvovedeniya

Nauch Trudy Ukr Sel'Khoz Akad — Nauchnye Trudy Ukrainskoi
Sel'Skokhozyaistvennoi Akademii

Nauch Trudy Voronezh Sel'Khoz Inst — Nauchnye Trudy Voronezhskii
Sel'skokhozyaistvennyi

Nauch Tr Veselopodol Opyt-Selek Sta — Nauchnye Trudy Veselopodolyanskoi
Opytno-Selektsionnoi Stantsii

Nauch Tr Vissh Selskostop Inst "Georgi Dimitrov" Agron Fak — Nauchni
Trudove. Vissh Selskostopanski Institut "Georgi Dimitrov."
Agronomicheski Fakultet

Nauch Tr Vissh Selskostop Inst "Georgi Dimitrov" Zootekh Fak — Nauchni
Trudove. Vissh Selskostopanski Institut "Georgi Dimitrov" (Sofia).
Zootekhnicheski Fakultet

Nauch Tr Vissh Selskostop Inst "Vasil Kolarov" — Nauchni Trudove. Vissh
Selskostopanski Institut "Vasil Kolarov"

Naucno-Teh Pregl — Naucno-Tehnicki Pregled

Naucn Tr Mosk Nauchno-Issled Inst Vaktsin Syvorotok — Nauchnye Trudy
Moskovskogo Nauchno-Issledovatel'skogo Instituta Vaktsin i Syvorotok

Nauc Trud Lesoteh Inst (Ser Gorsko Stop) — Naucni Trudove Vissh
Lesotehniceski Institut (Serija Gorsko Stopanstvo)

Nauc Trud Lesoteh Inst (Ser Meh Tehn Darv) — Naucnye Trudove Vissh
Lesotehniceski Institut (Serija Mehanicna Tehnologija na Darvesinata)

Nauc Trudy Kursk Pedag Inst — Naucnye Trudy Kurskogo Pedagogiceskogo
Instituta

Nauc Trudy Leningr Lesoteh Akad — Naucnye Trudy Leningradskaja Ordena
Lenina Lesotehniceskja Akademija Imeni S. M. Kirova

Nauc Trudy (Novosib Gos Pedag Inst) — Naucnye Trudy (Novosibirskij
Gosudarstvennyj Pedagogiceskij Institut)

Nauc Trudy Novosib Pedag Inst — Naucnye Trudy Novosibirskogo
Pedagogiceskogo Instituta

Nauc Trudy Saratov Politehn Inst — Naucnye Trudy Saratovskogo
Politehniceskogo Instituta

Nauc Trudy Sverdlovsk Pedag Inst — Naucnye Trudy Sverdlovskogo
Pedagogiceskogo Instituta

Nauc Trudy Sverdlovsk Pedag Inst Sociol Probl — Naucnye Trudy
Sverdlovskogo Pedagogiceskogo Instituta. Sociologiceskogo Problemi

Nauc Trudy (Taskent Pedag Inst) — Naucnye Trudy (Taskentskij
Pedagogiceskij Institut)

Nauc Trudy Taskent Univ — Naucnye Trudy Taskentskogo Universiteta

Nauc Trudy Tjumensk Univ — Naucnye Trudy Tjumenskogo Universiteta

Nauc Trudy Vyss Uceb Zaved Litov SSR — Naucnye Trudy Vyssyh Ucebnyh
Zavedennij Litovskoj SSR

Nauc Upravl Obsc — Naucnye Upravlenie Obscestva

Nauheimer Fortbild-Lehrgaenge — Nauheimer Fortbildungs-Lehrgaenge

NAUJA — Nagpur University. Journal

Nauka Pered Opyt Sel'Khoz — Nauka i Peredovoi Opyt v Sel'skom
Khozyaistve

Nauka Peredovoi Opyt Sel'sk Khoz — Nauka i Peredovoi Opyt v Sel'skom
Khozyaistve

Nauka Pol — Nauka Polska

Nauka Skh Proizvod — Nauka Sel'skokhozyaistvennomu Proizvodstvu

Nauka Tekh Gor Khoz — Nauka i Tekhnika v Gorodskom Khozyaistve

Nauka Tekh (Leningrad) — Nauka i Tekhnika (Leningrad)

Nauka Zhivotnovod — Nauka Zhivotnovodstvu

Nauk & Inf — Naukovedenie i Informatika

Nauk Pr Aspir Ukr Akad Sil's'kogospod Nauk — Naukovi Pratsi Aspirantiv
Ukrains'ka Akademiya Sil's'kogospodars'kikh Nauk

Nauk Pratsi Ukr Sil-Hospod Akad — Naukovi Pratsi Ukrayins'ka
Sil's'kohospodars'ka Akademiya

Nauk Pr Inst Entomol Fitopatol Akad Nauk Ukr RSR — Naukovi Pratsi
Institut Entomologii ta Fitopatologii Akademii Nauk Ukrains'koi RSR

Nauk Pr Inst Livarnogo Virobnitstva Akad Nauk Ukr RSR — Naukovi Pratsi Institutu Livarnogo Virobnitstva Akademiya Nauk Ukrains'koi RSR

Nauk Pr Kamenets Podol'sk Sil's'kogospod Inst — Naukovi Pratsi Kamenets-Podol'skii Sil's'kogospodars'kii Institut

Nauk Pr Khark Sil's'kogospod Inst — Naukovi Pratsi Kharkivs'kii Sil's'kogospodars'kii Institut

Nauk Pr L'viv Sil's'kogospod Inst — Naukovi Pratsi L'vivs'kii Sil's'kogospodars'kii Institut

Nauk Pr L'viv Zootekh Vet Inst — Naukovi Pratsi L'vivs'kii Zootekhnichno-Veterinarnii Institut

Nauk Pr L'viv Zoovet Inst — Naukovi Pratsi L'vivs'kii Zooveterinarnii Institut

Nauk Pr Nauchn Tr Derzh Sil's'kohospod Dosl Stn — Naukovi Pratsi Nauchnye Trudy Derzhavna Sil's'kohospodars'ka Doslidna Stantsiya

Nauk Pr Poltav Sil's'kogospod Inst — Naukovi Pratsi Poltavs'kogo Sil's'kogospodars'kogo Institutu

Nauk Pr Ukr Inst Eksp Vet — Naukovi Pratsi Ukrains'kii Institut Eksperimental'noi Veterinarii

Nauk Pr Ukr Nauk Dosl Inst Eksp Vet — Naukovi Pratsi Ukrains'kii Naukovo-Doslidnii Institut Eksperimental'noi Veterinarii

Nauk Pr Ukr Nauk Dosl Inst Fiziol Rosl — Naukovi Pratsi Ukrains'kii Naukovo-Doslidnii Institut Fiziologii Roslin

Nauk Pr Ukr Nauk Dosl Inst Sadivn — Naukovi Pratsi Ukrains'kii Naukovo-Doslidnii Institut Sadivnitstva

Nauk Pr Ukr Nauk Dosl Inst Zakhistu Rosl — Naukovi Pratsi Ukrains'kii Naukovo-Doslidnii Institut Zakhistu Roslin

Nauk Pr Ukr Nauk Dosl Inst Zemlerob — Naukovi Pratsi Ukrainskii Naukovo-Doslidnoi Institut Zemlerobstva

Nauk Pr Ukr Sil'kohospod Akad — Naukovi Pratse Ukrayins'ka Sil's'kohospodars'ka Akademiya

Nauk Pr Vet Fak L'viv Zoovet Inst — Naukovi Pratsi Veterinarnogo Fakul'tetu L'vivs'kii Zooveterinarnii Institut

Nauk Pr Vet Fak L'viv Zoovet Inst — Naukovi Pratsi Veterynarnoho Fakul'tetu L'vivs'koho Zooveterynarnoho Instytutu

Nauk Pr Vet Fak Ukr Sil's'kohospod Akad — Naukovi Pratsi Veterynarnoho Fakul'tetu Ukrayins'koyi Sil's'kohospodars'koyi Akademii

Nauk Pr Volyn Derzh Sil's'kohospod Doslid Sta — Naukovi Pratsi Volyns'ka Derzhavna Sil's'kohospodars'ka Doslidna Stantsiya

Nauk Pr Zootekh Fak Kamenets Podol'sk Sil's'kogospod Inst — Naukovi Pratsi Zootekhnichnogo Fakul'tetu Kamenets-Podol'skii Sil's'kogospodars'kii Institut

Nauk Shchorichnik Kiiv Derzh Univ Im T G Shevchenka — Naukovii Shchorichnik. Kiivs'kii Derzhavnii Universitet Imeni T. G. Shevchenka

Nauk-Tekh Visn — Naukovo-Tekhnichnii Visnik

Nauk Zap Cherk Derzh Pedagog Inst — Naukovi Zapysky Cherkas'koho Derzhavnoho Pedagogichnoho Instytutu

Nauk Zap Dnepropetr Derzh Univ — Naukovi Zapiski Dnepropetrovs'kii Derzhavnii Universitet

Nauk Zap Ivano Frankivs'kii Derzh Med Inst — Naukovi Zapiski Ivano-Frankivs'kii Derzhavnii Medichnii Institut

Nauk Zap Kherson Derzh Pedagog Inst — Naukovi Zapiski Khersons'kogo Derzhavnogo Pedagogichnogo Instituta

Nauk Zap Kiiv Derzh Univ — Naukovi Zapiski Kiivs'kii Derzhavnii Universitet

Nauk Zap Kiiv Derzh Univ Pr Bot Sadu — Naukovi Zapiski Kiivs'kii Derzhavnii Universitet Pratsi Botanichnogo Sadu

Nauk Zap Krivoriz Derzh Pedagog Inst — Naukovi Zapiski Krivoriz'kogo Derzhavnogo Pedagogichnogo Instituta

Nauk Zap L'viv Derzh Pedagog Inst — Naukovi Zapysky L'vivs'koho Derzhavnoho Pedagogichnoho Instytutu

Nauk Zap L'viv Derzh Univ Ser Biol — Naukovi Zapiski L'vivs'kii Derzhavnii Universitet Seriya Biologichna

Nauk Zap L'viv Derzh Univ Ser Fiz Mat — Naukovi Zapiski L'vivs'kii Derzhavnii Universitet Seriya Fiziko-Matematichna

Nauk Zap L'viv Derzh Univ Ser Geol — Naukovi Zapiski L'vivs'kii Derzhavnii Universitet Seriya Geologichna

Nauk Zap L'viv Torg Ekon Inst — Naukovi Zapiski L'vivs'kogo Torgovo-Ekonomichnogo Instituta

Nauk Zap Nizhin Derzh Pedagog Inst — Naukovi Zapiski Nizhins'kii Derzhavnii Pedagogichni Institut

Nauk Zap Nizhyns'koho Derzh Pedagog Inst — Naukovi Zapysky Nizhyns'koho Derzhavnoho Pedagogichnoho Instytutu

Nauk Zap Odes Biol Stn Akad Nauk Ukr RSR — Naukovi Zapiski Odes'koi Biologichnoi Stantsii Akademiya Nauk Ukrains'koi RSR

Nauk Zap Odes Derzh Pedagog Inst — Naukovi Zapiski Odes'kii Derzhavnii Pedagogichnii Institut

Nauk Zap Odes Politekh Inst — Naukovi Zapiski Odes'kii Politekhnichnii Institut

Nauk Zap Stanisl Derzh Med Inst — Naukovi Zapiski Stanislavs'kii Derzhavnii Medichnii Institut

Nauk Zap Sumskogo Derzh Pedagog Inst — Naukovi Zapiski Sumskogo Derzhavnogo Pedagogicheskogo Instituta

Nauk Zap Ukr Biokhem Inst — Naukovi Zapiski Ukrains'kogo Biokhemichnogo Instituta

Nauk Zap Ukr Poligr Inst — Naukovi Zapiski Ukrains'kii Poligrafichnii Institut

Nauk Zap Ukr Tekh Gospod Inst (Munich) — Naukovi Zapiski Ukrains'kii Tekhnichno-Gospodars'kii Institut (Munich)

Nauk Zap Uzhgorod Derzh Univ — Naukovi Zapiski Uzhgorods'kogo Derzhavnogo Universitetu

Nauk Zap Uzhorod Derzh Univ — Naukovi Zapysky Uzhorods'koho Derzhavnoho Universytetu

Naunyn-Schmiedebergs Arch Exp Pathol Pharmakol — Naunyn-Schmiedebergs Archiv fuer Experimentelle Pathologie und Pharmakologie

Naunyn-Schmiedebergs Arch Exp Path Pharmak — Naunyn-Schmiedebergs Archiv fuer Experimentelle Pathologie und Pharmakologie

Naunyn-Schmiedebergs Arch Pharmacol — Naunyn-Schmiedeberg's Archives of Pharmacology

Naunyn-Schmiedebergs Arch Pharmakol — Naunyn-Schmiedebergs Archiv fuer Pharmakologie [*Formerly, Naunyn-Schmiedebergs Archiv fuer Pharmakologie und Experimentelle Pathologie*]

Naunyn-Schmiedebergs Arch Pharmakol Exp Pathol — Naunyn-Schmiedebergs Archiv fuer Pharmakologie und Experimentelle Pathologie [*Later, Naunyn-Schmiedebergs Archiv fuer Pharmakologie*]

N Aust M — North Australian Monthly

Nau Tekh Inf Ser 1 — Nauchno-Tekhnicheskaya Informatsiya. Seriya 1. Organizatsiya i Metodika Informatsionnoi Raboty

Nau-T Inf 1 — Nauchno-Tekhnicheskaya Informatsiya. Seriya 1. Organizatsiya i Metodika Informatsionnye Raboty

Nau-T Inf 2 — Nauchno-Tekhnicheskaya Informatsiya. Seriya 2. Informatsionnye Protessy i Sistemy

Naut M — Nautical Magazine

Nav — Navorscher

NAV — Nuovo Archivio Veneto

Naval Eng J — Naval Engineers' Journal

Naval Engrs J — American Society of Naval Engineers. Journal

Naval Res Logist Quart — Naval Research Logistics. Quarterly

Naval Res Log Quart — Naval Research Logistics. Quarterly

Naval Stores R — Naval Stores Review

Naval Stores Rev — Naval Stores Review

Naval War College R — Naval War College. Review

Nav Archit — Naval Architect

Nav Eng J — Naval Engineers' Journal

Navig — Navigation

Nav M — Naval Magazine

NAVMAG — Naval Magazine

Navorsinge Nas Mus (Bloemfontein) — Navorsinge van die Nasionale Museum (Bloemfontein)

Nav Reserv — Naval Reservist

Nav Res Log — Naval Research Logistics. Quarterly

Nav Res Logist Q — Naval Research Logistics. Quarterly

Nav Res Rev — Naval Research Reviews

NAVTRADEVCEN — Naval Training Device Center. Technical Report

Nav War Col Rev — Naval War College. Review

Navy Dep RAN Rep — Department of the Navy. RAN [*Royal Australian Navy*] Reports

Navy League J — Navy League Journal

Navy Rec Soc Publ — Navy Records Society. Publications

Navy Tech F S — Navy Technology Transfer Fact Sheet

NAWG — Nachrichten. Akademie der Wissenschaften zu Goettingen. Philologisch-Historische Klasse

NAWGott — Nachrichten. Akademie der Wissenschaften zu Goettingen

NB — Nachrichtenblatt. Deutscher Verein vom Heiligen Lande

NB — Namm och Bygd

NBA — National Bank. Monthly Summary [*Melbourne*]

NBAC — Nuovo Bulletino di Archeologia Cristiana

NBB — Central Bank of Libya. Economic Bulletin

NBB — Norsk Bibliografisk Bibliotek

NB Dep Nat Resour Miner Resour Branch Top Rep — New Brunswick. Department of Natural Resources. Mineral Resources Branch. Topical Report

NBE — National Bank of Egypt. Economic Bulletin

NBEA Y — National Business Education Association. Yearbook

NBER Gen S — National Bureau of Economic Research. General Studies

NBER Oc P — National Bureau of Economic Research. Occasional Papers

NBGPL — Nederlandsche Bijdragen op het Gebied van Germaansche Philologie en Linguistiek

NBGSA — Nippon Butsuri Gakkaishi

NB His S — New Brunswick Historical Society. Collections

NBHPB — Neuroscience and Behavioral Physiology

NBIC — News from Behind the Iron Curtain

NBJ — Noord Brabant

NB Jb — Neues Beethoven Jahrbuch

Nb L — Nebraska Law Review

NBL — Neue Beitraege zur Literaturwissenschaft

Nb LR — Nebraska Law Review

NBLU — Naucnyj Bjulleten Leningradskogo Universiteta

NB Miner Resour Branch Inf Circ — New Brunswick. Mineral Resources Branch. Information Circular

NB Miner Resour Branch Rep Invest — New Brunswick. Mineral Resources Branch. Report of Investigations

NB Miner Resour Branch Top Rep — New Brunswick. Mineral Resources Branch. Topical Report

NB Mus Monogr Ser — New Brunswick Museum. Monographic Series
NBNA Newsl — National Black Nurses Association. Newsletter
NBO — Boekblad
NBP — Wonen. Vakblad voor de Woninginrichting
NBR — Nederlandsche Bank NV. Kwartaalbericht
NBR — New Boston Review
NBS — National Australia Bank. Monthly Summary
NBS Build Sci Ser — National Bureau of Standards. Building Science Series [*United States*]
NBSMA — National Bureau of Standards. Monographs
NBS Monogr — National Bureau of Standards. Monographs
NBS Spec Publ — National Bureau of Standards. Special Publication
NBS Tech News Bull — National Bureau of Standards. Technical News Bulletin
NBT — Nederlands Bosbouw Tijdschrift Orgaan voor Bosbouw en Landschapsbouw
NBW — NABW [*National Association of Bank Women*] Journal
NC — New Criterion
NC — Nineteenth Century and After
NC — Nineteenth Century Music
NC — Numismatic Chronicle
NC — Numismatic Chronicle and Journal. Numismatic Society
NC — Nuova Corrente
NCAB — National Cyclopaedia of American Biography
NC Ag Exp — North Carolina. Agricultural Experiment Station. Publications
NC Agric Exp Stn Bull — North Carolina. Agricultural Experiment Station. Bulletin
NC Agric Exp Stn Tech Bull — North Carolina. Agricultural Experiment Station. Technical Bulletin
NC Agric Ext Serv Ext Circ — North Carolina. Agricultural Extension Service. Extension Circular
NC Agric Ext Serv Ext Folder — North Carolina. Agricultural Extension Service. Extension Folder
NC Agric Ext Serv Leafl — North Carolina. Agricultural Extension Service. Leaflet
NC Agr Statist — North Carolina Agricultural Statistics
N Car Central LJ — North Carolina Central Law Journal
NCarF — North Carolina Folklore
N Carolina Lib — North Carolina Libraries
NCAR Q — National Center for Atmospheric Research. Quarterly
NCASI Atm Poll Tech Bull — National Council of the Paper Industry for Air and Stream Improvement. Atmospheric Pollution Technical Bulletin
NCASI Monthly Bull — National Council of the Paper Industry for Air and Stream Improvement. Monthly Bulletin
NCASI Regul Rev — National Council of the Paper Industry for Air and Stream Improvement. Regulatory Review
NCASI Tech Bull — National Council of the Paper Industry for Air and Stream Improvement. Technical Bulletin
NCASI Tech Bull Atmos Qual Improv Tech Bull — National Council of the Paper Industry for Air and Stream Improvement. Technical Bulletin. Atmospheric Quality Improvement. Technical Bulletin
NCASI Tech Rev — National Council of the Paper Industry for Air and Stream Improvement. Technical Review
NCathW — New Catholic World
NCB — New Comprehensive Biochemistry [*Elsevier Book Series*]
NC Cave Surv — North Carolina Cave Survey
NC Cent LJ — North Carolina Central Law Journal
NC Central L J — North Carolina Central Law Journal
NCC Proc — National Computer Conference. Proceedings
NCC Res Rep Dig — Nature Conservancy Council. Research Reports Digest
NC Dent J — North Carolina Dental Journal
NC Dep Conserv Dev Div Miner Resour Bull — North Carolina. Department of Conservation and Development. Division of Mineral Resources. Bulletin
NC Dep Conserv Dev Econ Pap — North Carolina. Department of Conservation and Development. Economic Paper
NC Dep Nat Econ Resour Groundwater Sect Rep Invest — North Carolina. Department of Natural and Economic Resources. Groundwater Section. Report of Investigation
NC Dep Nat Econ Resour Reg Geol Ser — North Carolina. Department of Natural and Economic Resources. Regional Geology Series
NC Div Ground Water Ground Water Bull — North Carolina. Division of Ground Water. Ground Water Bulletin
NC Div Ground Water Ground Water Circ — North Carolina. Division of Ground Water. Ground Water Circular
NC Div Miner Resour Bull — North Carolina. Department of Conservation and Development. Division of Mineral Resources. Bulletin
NC Div Miner Resour Bull — North Carolina. Division of Mineral Resources. Bulletin
NC Div Miner Resour Inf Circ — North Carolina. Division of Mineral Resources. Information Circular
NC Div Resour Plann Eval Miner Resour Sect Bull — North Carolina. Division of Resource Planning and Evaluation. Mineral Resources Section. Bulletin
NC Div Resour Plann Eval Miner Resour Sect Educ Ser — North Carolina. Division of Resource Planning and Evaluation. Mineral Resources Section. Educational Series

NC Div Resour Plann Eval Miner Resour Sect Reg Geol Ser — North Carolina. Division of Resource Planning and Evaluation. Mineral Resources Section. Regional Geology Series
NC Div Resour Plann Eval Reg Geol Ser — North Carolina. Division of Resource Planning and Evaluation. Regional Geology Series
NC Div Water Resour Div Stream Sanit Hydrol Bull — North Carolina. Department of Water Resources. Division of Stream Sanitation and Hydrology. Bulletin
NCE — North Carolina Music Educator
NCEGA — Noise Control Engineering
N Cen Assn Q — North Central Association. Quarterly
N Cent — Nineteenth Century
N Cent Corn Breed Res Comm Minutes Meet — North Central Corn Breeding Research Committee. Minutes of Meeting
NCF — Nineteenth-Century Fiction
NCF — North Carolina Folklore
NCFLN — Northern California Foreign Language Newsletter
NC Folk — North Carolina Folklore
NCFR — National Council on Family Relations. Newsletter
NCFS — Nineteenth-Century French Studies
NCGH — Nippon Chugoku Gakkaiho [*Bulletin of the Sinological Society of Japan*]
NCGS — Fra Ny-Carlsberg Glyptoteks Sammlingen
NCGS B — North Carolina Geological Survey. Bulletin
NCHE — National Center for Health Education. Newsletter
NC His R — North Carolina Historical Review
NC Hist R — North Carolina Historical Review
NC Hist Rev — North Carolina Historical Review
NChn — Numismatic Chronicle [*London*]
NCHR — North Carolina Historical Review
NChr — Numismatic Chronicle [*London*]
NChrIsr — Nouvelles Chretiennes d'Israel [*Jerusalem*]
NCHRP Prog Rep — National Cooperative Highway Research Program. Report
NCHRP Rep — National Cooperative Highway Research Program. Report
NCHRP Synthesis Highw Prac — National Cooperative Highway Research Program. Synthesis of Highway Practice
N Church R — New Church Review
NCI — Notiziario Culturale Italiano
NCI — Nouvelles Chretiennes d'Israel [*Jerusalem*]
NCIAA — Nuovo Cimento. Sezione A
NCIBA — Nuovo Cimento. Sezione B
NCIMA — National Cancer Institute. Monographs [*United States*]
NCirc — Numismatic Circular
NCL — North Carolina Law Review
NCL — Nossos Classicos
NCL — Notes on Contemporary Literature
NC Law R — North Carolina Law Review
NC Lib — North Carolina Libraries
NClio — La Nouvelle Clio [*Brussels*]
NCLR — North Carolina Law Review
NC L Rev — North Carolina Law Review
NC Med J — North Carolina Medical Journal
NC Miner Resour Sect Reg Geol Ser — North Carolina. Mineral Resources Section. Regional Geology Series
NCN — Netherlands American Trade
NCoHS — Northumberland County Historical Society. Proceedings
NCoHSP — Northumberland County Historical Society. Proceedings
N Col — New Colophon
NConL — Notes on Contemporary Literature
NC Pestic Manual — North Carolina Pesticide Manual
NCR — Cooperatie
NCR — National Catholic Reporter
NCR — National Civic Review
NCR Bus and Econ — North Carolina Review of Business and Economics
NCRMM — Nouvelle Critique. Revue du Marxisme Militant
NCRP Rep — National Council on Radiation Protection and Measurements. Reports
NCRR Bull — NCRR [*National Center for Resource Recovery*] Bulletin [*United States*]
NCSA — Newsletter. Copyright Society of Australia
NCSC Manual — National Companies and Securities Commission. Manual
NCSS B — National Council for the Social Studies. Bulletin
NCSS Read — National Council for the Social Studies. Readings
NCSS Res B — National Council for the Social Studies. Research Bulletin
NCSS Yearb — National Council for the Social Studies. Yearbook
NC State Coll Agric Eng Eng Exp Stn Bull — North Carolina State College of Agriculture and Engineering. Engineering Experiment Station. Bulletin
NC State Coll Dep Eng Res Bull — North Carolina State College. Department of Engineering Research. Bulletin
NC State Coll Dept Eng Research Bull — North Carolina State College. Department of Engineering Research. Bulletin
NC State Coll Sch Agric Annu Rep — North Carolina State College. School of Agriculture. Annual Report
NC State Univ Dep Eng Res Bull — North Carolina State University. Department of Engineering. Research Bulletin

NC State Univ Eng Sch Bull — North Carolina State University. Engineering School Bulletin
NC State Univ Miner Res Lab Lab Notes — North Carolina State University. Minerals Research Laboratory. Laboratory Notes
NC State Univ Miner Res Lab Rep — North Carolina State University. Minerals Research Laboratory. Report
NC State Univ Sch Agric Life Sci Annu Rep — North Carolina State University. School of Agriculture and Life Sciences. Annual Report
NC St BQ — North Carolina State Bar Quarterly
NCTR — Nineteenth-Century Theatre Research
NCUA Q — National Credit Union Administration. Quarterly
NCult — Nuova Cultura
NCW — New Catholic World
NCW News — NCW News (National Council of Women of New South Wales)
NCYBD — Nuclear Canada Yearbook
ND — La Nueva Democracia [*New York*]
N f D — Nachrichten fuer Dokumentation
ND — Neues Deutschland
ND — New Directions
ND — Nowe Drogi
ND — Nuovo Didaskaleion
ND Acad Sci Proc — North Dakota Academy of Science. Proceedings
ND Ag Exp — North Dakota. Agricultural Experiment Station. Publications
N Dak Acad Sci Proc — North Dakota Academy of Science. Proceedings
N Dak Agr Coll Exp Sta Bien Rep — North Dakota Agricultural College. Experiment Station. Biennial Report
N Dak Farm Res Bimon Bull — North Dakota Farm Research. Bimonthly Bulletin. North Dakota Agricultural College. Agricultural Experiment Station
N Dak Geol Surv Bull — North Dakota. Geological Survey. Bulletin
N Dak Geol Surv Circ — North Dakota. Geological Survey. Circular
N Dak Geol Surv Misc Ser — North Dakota. Geological Survey. Miscellaneous Series
N Dak Geol Surv Rep Invest — North Dakota. Geological Survey. Report of Investigations
N Dak G S Bien Rp — North Dakota. Geological Survey. Biennial Report
N Dak His S — North Dakota State Historical Society. Collections
N Dak History — North Dakota History
N Dak Lib Notes — North Dakota Library Notes
N Dak M — North Dakota Magazine
N Dak Outdoors — North Dakota Outdoors
N Dak Research Found Bull Circ — North Dakota Research Foundation Bulletin. Circular
N Dame J Ed — Notre Dame Journal of Education
NDAT — Nashriyye(H)-Ye Daneshkade(H)-Ye Adabiyyat va Olum-E Ensani-Ye Tabriz
NDB — Neue Deutsche Biographie
NDBSB — Nogyo Doboku Shikenjo Hokoku
NDBZ — Neue Deutsche Beamtenzeitung
Nd B Zt — Neudeutsche Bauzeitung
NDCAB — Nippon Dental College. Annual Publications
Ndd Jb — Niederdeutsches Jahrbuch
NDEJ — Notre Dame English Journal
NDF — Nederlands-Duitse Kamer van Koophandel. Mededelingen
NDF — Neue Deutsche Forschung
ND Farm Res — North Dakota Farm Research
NDFKAH — Endemic Diseases Bulletin. Nagasaki University
NDFN — Nauchnye Doklady Vysshei Shkoly Filologicheskie Nauki [*Moscow*]
NDFW — New Directions for Women
ND Geol Surv Bull — North Dakota. Geological Survey. Bulletin
ND Geol Surv Circ — North Dakota. Geological Survey. Circular
ND Geol Surv Educ Ser — North Dakota. Geological Survey. Educational Series
ND Geol Surv Misc Map — North Dakota. Geological Survey. Miscellaneous Map
ND Geol Surv Misc Ser — North Dakota. Geological Survey. Miscellaneous Series
NDGI — Nachrichten. Deutsche Gesellschaft fuer Islamkunde
NDGKA — Nogyo Doboku Gakkai Ronbunshu
NDGXA — Miscellaneous Series. North Dakota Geological Survey
NDH — Neue Deutsche Hefte
NDH — Nordic Economic Outlook
NDH — North Dakota History
NDHi — North Dakota History
ND His Q — North Dakota Historical Quarterly
ND Hist — North Dakota History
NDHR — NDH-Rapport. Norland Distrikshogskole
NDim — Nuove Dimensioni
Nd Jb — Niederdeutsches Jahrbuch
Nd Jb — Niederdeutsches Jahrbuch fuer Volkskunde
Nd Kbl — Korrespondenzblatt. Verein fuer Niederdeutsche Sprachforschung
NDKGA — Nippon Daicho Komonbyo Gakkai Zasshi
NDKIA — Nagoya Daigaku Kankyo Igaku Kenkyusho Nenpo
Nd Ko Bl — Korrespondenzblatt. Verein fuer Niederdeutsche Sprachforschung
NDKSBX — Journal. Agricultural Laboratory [*Chiba*]

NDL — Neudrucke Deutscher Literaturwerke
NDL — Neue Deutsche Literatur
NDL — Notre Dame Lawyer
NDLR — North Dakota Law Review
NDL Rev — North Dakota Law Review
ND L Review — North Dakota Law Review
NdM — Niederdeutsche Mitteilungen
NDMG — Norddeutsche Missionsgesellschaft
Nd Mitt — Niederdeutsche Mitteilungen
NDP — Neue Deutsche Presse
NDQ — North Dakota Quarterly
ND Quar J — North Dakota University. Quarterly Journal
NDR — Neue Deutsche Rundschau
NDR — North Dakota Law Review
NDR — Revue de la Navigation Fluviale Europeenne. Ports et Industries
NDRCAJ — Contributions. Department of Geology and Mineralogy. Niigata University
ND REC Mag — North Dakota REC [*Rural Electric Cooperatives*] Magazine
Nd Rhein Jb — Niederrheinisches Jahrbuch
NdS — Niederdeutsche Studien
NDSAA — Nuclear Data. Section A
NDSFB — Nogyo Doboku Shikenjo Giho, F. Sogo
Nds GV Bl — Niedersaechsisches Gesetz- und Verordnungsblatt
NDSK — Nydanske Studier og Almen Kommunikationsteori
Nds Rpfl — Niedersaechsische Rechtspflege
ND State Lab Dep Bull — North Dakota. State Laboratories Department. Bulletin
Ndt F — Norddeutsche Familienkunde
NDTI — National Disease and Therapeutic Index
NDT Int — Non-Destructive Testing International
NDTI Rev — NDTI [*National Disease and Therapeutic Index*] Review [*United States*]
NDT News — Non-Destructive Testing News
NDTSB — Nuclear Data Sheets
NDV — Nachrichtendienst. Deutscher Verein fuer Oeffentliche und Private Fuersorge
NDV — Notes et Documents Voltaiques
NDVS — Naucnye Doklady Vyssej Skoly
NDVS-F — Naucnye Doklady Vyssej Skoly Filologiceskie Nauki
NDVTB — Nederlands Tijdschrift voor Vacuumtechniek
NDW — Niederdeutsches Wort
NDZKA — Noodzaak
Nd Z Vk — Niederdeutsche Zeitschrift fuer Volkskunde und Blaetter fuer Niedersaechsische Heimatpflege
Ne — Neva
NE — Numismatica i Epigrafica
NeaH — Nea Hestia
NEA J — National Education Association. Journal
Neap — Neapolis
Near East — Near East and India
NEA Res Bul — National Education Association. Research Bulletin
NEA Res Div Rept — National Education Association. Research Division. Reports
NE Asia J Th — Northeast Asia Journal of Theology
Neb — Nebula Science Fiction
Neb Ag Exp — Nebraska. Agricultural Experiment Station. Publications
Neb Agric Exp Stn Circ — Nebraska. Agricultural Experiment Station. Circular
NEBBA — Neue Bergbautechnik
Neb Ed J — Nebraska Educational Journal
NebH — Nebraska History
Neb His — Nebraska History
Neb His M — Nebraska History. Magazine
Neb His S — Nebraska State Historical Society. Collections
Neb Hist — Nebraska History
Neb J Econ and Bus — Nebraska Journal of Economics and Business
Neb Lib Assn Q — Nebraska Library Association. Quarterly
Neb L Rev — Nebraska Law Review
Nebr Ac Sc Pub Pr — Nebraska Academy of Sciences. Publications. Proceedings
Nebr Agric Exp Stn Annu Rep — Nebraska. Agricultural Experiment Station. Annual Report
Nebr Agric Exp Stn Bull — Nebraska. Agricultural Experiment Station. Bulletin
Nebr Agric Exp Stn Res Bull — Nebraska. Agricultural Experiment Station. Research Bulletin
Nebraska Acad Sci Proc — Nebraska Academy of Sciences and Affiliated Societies. Proceedings
Nebraska Geol Survey Paper — Nebraska Geological Survey. Paper
Nebraska L Rev — Nebraska Law Review
Nebraska Univ State Mus Bull — Nebraska University. State Museum. Bulletin
Nebr BA — Nebraska State Bar Journal
Nebr Bird Rev — Nebraska Bird Review
Nebr Conserv Bull — Nebraska Conservation Bulletin
Nebr Energy News — Nebraska Energy News
Nebr Exp Stn Q — Nebraska Experiment Station Quarterly

Nebr Farm Ranch Econ — Nebraska Farm Ranch Economics
Nebr Geol Surv Bull — Nebraska Geological Survey. Bulletin
Nebr L Rev — Nebraska Law Review
Nebr Med J — Nebraska Medical Journal
Nebr Nurse — Nebraska Nurse
Nebr State Med J — Nebraska State Medical Journal
Nebr State Mus Bull — Nebraska State Museum. Bulletin
Nebr St Bd Agr An Rp — Nebraska State Board of Agriculture. Annual Report
Nebr St Hist Soc Pr — Nebraska State Historical Society. Proceedings and
    Collections
Nebr Symp Motiv — Nebraska Symposium on Motivation
Nebr Univ Agric Exp Stn Annu Rep — Nebraska University. Agricultural
    Experiment Station. Annual Report
Nebr Univ Studies — Nebraska University. Studies
Nebr Water Surv Pap — Nebraska Water Survey Paper
Nebr Wheat Variety Estimate Nebr Grain Impr Ass — Nebraska Wheat
    Variety Estimate. Nebraska Grain Improvement Association
Neb SBJ — Nebraska State Bar Journal
Neb St BJ — Nebraska State Bar Journal
NEBTA — Nederlands Bosbouw Tijdschrift
NEC — Nippon Electric Company News [Japan]
NECG — New Ecologist
N Ecl — New Eclectic
NEC Res Dev — NEC [Nippon Electric Company] Research and Development
NEC Res and Dev — NEC [Nippon Electric Company] Research and
    Development
NEC Rev — NEC [Nippon Electric Company] Review
NedA — Nederlandsch Archievenblad
Ned Akad Wet Afd Natuurkd Verh Eerste Reeks — Nederlandse Akademie van
    Wetenschappen, Afdeling Natuurkunde. Verhandelingen. Eerste Reeks
Ned Akad Wet Proc Ser B — Nederlandse Akademie van Wetenschappen
    [Koninklijke]. Proceedings. Series B. Physical Sciences
Ned Bosb Tijdschr — Nederlands Bosbouw Tijdschrift
Ned Chem Ind — Nederlandse Chemische Industrie
Ned Dendrol Ver Jaarb — Nederlandse Dendrologische Vereniging. Jaarboek
Ned Entomol Ver Jaarb — Nederlandse Entomologische Vereniging. Jaarboek
Nederl Akad Wetensch Indag Math — Koninklijke Nederlandse Akademie van
    Wetenschappen. Indagationes Mathematicae ex Actis Quibus Titulus
Nederl Akad Wetensch Proc Ser A — Koninklijke Nederlandse Akademie van
    Wetenschappen. Proceedings. Series A. Mathematical Sciences
Nederl Akad Wetensch Proc Ser B — Koninklijke Nederlandse Akademie van
    Wetenschappen. Proceedings. Series B. Physical Sciences [Later,
    Koninklijke Nederlandse Akademie van Wetenschappen. Proceedings.
    Series B. Palaeontology, Geology, Physics, and Chemistry]
Nederl Akad Wetensch Verslag Afd Natuurk — Koninklijke Nederlandse
    Akademie van Wetenschappen. Verslag van de Gewone Vergadering van
    de Afdeling Natuurkunde
Nederlandsch Hist Inst Rome Med — Nederlandsch Historisch Instituut te
    Rome. Mededeelingen
Nederlands Kunsthist Jaar — Nederlands Kunsthistorisch Jaarboek
Nederl-Ind Blad Diergeneesk — Nederlandsch-Indische Bladen voor
    Diergeneeskunde
Nederl Lancet — Nederlandsch Lancet
Ned Geol Mijnbouwkd Genoot Verh — Nederlands Geologisch
    Mijnbouwkundig Genootschap [Koninklijk]. Verhandelingen
NedGerefTTs — Nederduitse Gereformeerde Teologiese Tydskrif [Kaapstad]
NE Dialog — Northeast Dialog
Ned Ind Eigendom — Nederland Industriele Eigendom
Ned Kruidkd Arch — Nederlandsch Kruidkundig Archief
NedL — Nederlandse Leeuw
Ned Maandschr Geneeskd — Nederlandsch Maandschrift voor Geneeskunde
Ned Melk Zuiveltijdschr — Nederlands Melk-en Zuiveltijdschrift
Ned Mil Geneeskd Tijdschr — Nederlands Militair Geneeskundig Tijdschrift
Ned Rubberind — Nederlandse Rubberindustrie
Ned Scheepsstudiecent TNO Rep — Nederlands Scheepsstudiecentrum TNO.
    Report
Ned Staatscourant — Nederlandse Staatscourant
NedThT — Nederlands Theologisch Tijdschrift [Wageningen]
Ned Tijdschr Geneeskd — Nederlands Tijdschrift voor Geneeskunde
Ned Tijdschr Gerontol — Nederlands Tijdschrift voor Gerontologie
Ned Tijdschr Hyg Microbiol Serol — Nederlandsch Tijdschrift voor Hygiene,
    Microbiologie, en Serologie
Ned Tijdschr Natuurk A — Nederlands Tijdschrift voor Natuurkunde. Series A
Ned Tijdschr Natuurkd — Nederlands Tijdschrift voor Natuurkunde
Ned Tijdschr Natuurkd A — Nederlands Tijdschrift voor Natuurkunde. Series
    A
Ned Tijdschr Tandheelkd — Nederlands Tijdschrift voor Tandheelkunde
Ned Tijdschr Vacuumtech — Nederlands Tijdschrift voor Vacuumtechniek
Ned Tijdschr Verloskd Gynaecol — Nederlandsch Tijdschrift voor Verloskunde
    en Gynaecologie
NedTT — Nederlands Theologisch Tijdschrift [Wageningen]
NedTTs — Nederlands Theologisch Tijdschrift [Wageningen]
Ned Ver Klin Chem Tijdschr — Nederlandse Vereniging voor Klinische
    Chemie. Tijdschrift
Needlework Bul — Needlework Bulletin for Teachers in Secondary Schools
Nef — Nef: Cahier Trimestriel

NEF — Northeast Folklore
NEF — Notas y Estudios de Filosofia
NEFNB — Neftepererabotka i Neftekhimiya
Neftegazovaya Geol Geofiz — Neftegazovaya Geologiya i Geofizika
Neftegazov Geol Geofiz — Neftegazovaya Geologiya i Geofizika
Neftepererab Neftekhim (Kiev) — Neftepererabotka i Neftekhimiya (Kiev)
Neftepererab Neftekhim (Moscow) — Neftepererabotka i Neftekhimiya
    (Moscow)
Neftepromysl Delo — Neftepromyslovoe Delo
Neftepromysl Delo (Moscow) — Neftepromyslovoe Delo (Moscow)
Neft Gazova Promst Sredn Azii — Neftyanaya i Gazovaya Promyshlennost
    Srednei Azii
Neft Gazov Prom-st' — Neftyanaya i Gazovaya Promyshlennost'
Neft Gazov Promst Sredn Azii — Neftyanaya i Gazovaya Promyshlennost
    Srednei Azii
Neft Khim — Neft i Khimiya
Neft Khoz — Neftyanoe Khozyaistvo
Neft Slants Khoz — Neftyanoe i Slantsevoe Khozyaistvo
Neft Vuglishtna Geol — Neftena i Vuglishtna Geologiya [Bulgaria]
NEFZB — Neirofiziologila
NEG — Nederlandse Gemeente
Neg Ed Rev — Negro Educational Review
Neg His Bull — Negro History Bulletin
Negro D — Negro Digest
Negro Ed R — Negro Educational Review
Negro Educ R — Negro Educational Review
Negro H B — Negro History Bulletin
Negro His B — Negro History Bulletin
Negro Hist B — Negro History Bulletin
Negro Hist Bul — Negro History Bulletin
Negro Hist Bull — Negro History Bulletin
Nehezip Muesz Egy Koezl — Nehezipari Mueszaki Egyetem Koezlemenyei
Nehezip Musz Egy Miskolc Idegennyelvu Kozl — Nehezipari Mueszaki
    Egyetem, Miskolc, Idegennyelvu Koezlemenyei
Nehezip Musz Egy Miskolc Kozl — Nehezipari Mueszaki Egyetem, Miskolc,
    Koezlemenyei
Nehezvegyip Kut Intez Kozl — Nehezvegyipari Kutato Intezet Kozlemenyei
    [Hungary]
NEHGR — New England Historical and Genealogical Register
NEI — Nuclear Engineering International
NEIC — News from Iceland
NEIN — News Inuit. News Releases from Inuit Tapirisat of Canada
NEI Rev — NEI [Northern Engineering Industries] Review [England]
Neirokhim Fiziol Sinapticheskikh Protsessov — Neirokhimiya i Fiziologiya
    Sinapticheskikh Protsessov
NEJ Crim and Civ Con — New England Journal on Criminal and Civil
    Confinement
NEJM — New England Journal of Medicine
NEJMA — New England Journal of Medicine
NEJPA — Neues Jahrbuch fuer Geologie und Palaeontologie. Abhandlungen
Nek Aktual Vopr Biol Med — Nekotorye Aktual'nye Voprosy Biologii i
    Meditsiny
Nek Filos Probl Gos Prava — Nekotorye Filosofskie Problemy Gosudarstva i
    Prava
Nekot Probl Biokibern Primen Elektron Biol Med — Nekotorye Problemy
    Biokibernetiki Primenenie Elektroniki v Biologii i Meditsine [Ukrainian
    SSR]
Nek Vopr Eksp Fiz — Nekotorye Voposry Eksperimental'noi Fiziki [USSR]
Nek Vopr Inzh Fiz — Nekotorye Voprosy Inzhenernoi Fiziki
Nek Vopr Stroit Skvazhin Oslozhnennykh Usloviyakh Uzb — Nekotorye
    Voprosy Stroitel'stva Skvazhin v Oslozhnennykh Usloviyakh
    Uzbekistana
NELA Bul — National Electric Light Association. Bulletin
NELA Newsl — NELA [New England Library Association] Newsletter
N Elec Telesis — Northern Electric Telesis
NELED — Neuroscience Letters
Nelson Loose-Leaf Med — Nelson Loose-Leaf Medicine
Nem — Neman [Moscow]
NEM — New England Magazine
NEM — New Mexico Musician
Nematol — Nematologica
Nematol Mediterr — Nematologia Mediterranea
NEMSB — Newsletter. Environmental Mutagen Society
Nemzetkozi Mezogazd Sz — Nemzetkozi Mezogazdasagi Szemle
NENA — New Nation. Manitoba Native Newspaper
NENBD — New England Business
N Eng — New Englander
N Eng Hist Geneal Reg — New England Historical and Genealogical Register
N Eng J Med — New England Journal of Medicine
N England J Med — New England Journal of Medicine
N Engl Bus — New England Business
N Engl Dairyman — New England Dairyman
N Engl Econ Rev — New England Economic Review
N Engl Eng — New England Engineer

N Engl Fruit Meet Proc Annu Meet Mass Fruit Grow Assoc — New England Fruit Meetings. Proceedings. Annual Meeting. Massachusetts Fruit Growers' Association
N Engl Galaxy — New England Galaxy
N Engl J Med — New England Journal of Medicine
N Engl J Med Med Prog Ser — New England Journal of Medicine. Medical Progress Series
N Engl L Rev — New England Law Review
N Eng LR — New England Law Review
N Eng L Rev — New England Law Review
N Eng Mag — New England Magazine
N Eng Q — New England Quarterly. An Historical Review of the New England Life and Letters
N Eng Rev — New England Review
N Eng Soc Stud Bull — New England Social Studies Bulletin
NENJA — NERC [*National Electronics Research Council*] News Journal
NENKA — Nenryo Kyokai-Shi
NENO — News of Norway
NENOA8 — Japanese Journal of Tropical Agriculture
Neo — Neophilologus
NEONA — Nenryo Oyobi Nensho
Neophil — Neophilologus
Neophilolog — Neophilologus
Neorg Lyuminofory Prikl Naznacheniya — Neorganicheskie Lyuminofory Prikladnogo Naznacheniya
Neorg Mater — Neorganicheskie Materialy [*USSR*]
Neosan Avic — Neosan Avicola
NEPAB — Neuropaediatrie
Nepalese J Agric — Nepalese Journal of Agriculture
Nepal Gaz — Nepal Gazette
Nepali Math Sci Rep — Nepali Mathematical Sciences Report
NEPEA — Nepegeszsegugy
Nephrol Nurse — Nephrology Nurse
Nephro Nurse — Nephrology Nurse
Nepr Ertes — Neprajzi Ertesito
NEQ — Nederlands Economisch Persbureau en Adviesbureau [*NEPAB*]. Nieuwsbrief
NEQ — New England Quarterly
NE Quar — New England Quarterly
NER — National and English Review
NER — National Institute Economic Review
NER — New England Review
NER — New England Review and Bread Loaf Quarterly
NERC News J — NERC [*National Electronics Research Council*] News Journal [*England*]
N Ercolani — Nuovo Ercolani
N E Reg — New England Historical and Genealogical Register
NEREM Rec — NEREM [*Northeast Electronics Research and Engineering Meeting*] Record
NERIC Bull — NERIC [*Nuclear Engineering Research in Cambridge*] Bulletin
Nerudn Stroit Mater — Nerudnye Stroitel'nye Materialy
NERVA — Nervenarzt
Nerv Child — Nervous Child
Nervn Sist — Nervnaya Sistema
Nerv Sist — Nervnaia Sistema
Nerv Sist Leningr Gos Univ Fiziol Inst — Nervnaya Sistema Leningradskij Gosudarstvennyj Universitet Imeni A. A. Zhdanova Fiziologicheskij Institut
Nerv Syst Electr Curr — Nervous System and Electric Currents
N60ES — North of 60. Environmental Studies [*Canada*]
NESI — Nesika
NESP Rep — NESP [*National Environmental Studies Project*] Report [*United States*]
Nestle Nutr Workshop Ser — Nestle Nutrition Workshop Series
NETHA — Nederlandsch Tijdschrift voor Hygiene, Microbiologie, en Serologie
Neth Energy Res Found ECN Rep — Netherlands Energy Research Foundation. ECN [*Energieonderzoek Centrum Nederland*] Report
Neth Geol Dienst Toelichting Geol Kaart Ned 1:50,000 — Netherlands. Geologische Dienst. Toelichting bij de Geologische Kaart van Nederland 1:50,000
Neth Geol Sticht Meded Nieuwe Ser — Netherlands. Geologische Stichting. Mededelingen. Nieuwe Serie
Neth J Agric Sci — Netherlands Journal of Agricultural Science
Neth J Agr Sci — Netherlands Journal of Agricultural Science
Neth J Med — Netherlands Journal of Medicine
Neth J Plant Pathol — Netherlands Journal of Plant Pathology
Neth J Sea Res — Netherlands Journal of Sea Research
Neth J Surg — Netherlands Journal of Surgery
Neth J Vet Sci — Netherlands Journal of Veterinary Science
Neth J Zool — Netherlands Journal of Zoology
Neth Milk D — Netherlands Milk and Dairy Journal
Neth Milk Dairy J — Netherlands Milk and Dairy Journal
Neth Nitrogen Tech Bull — Netherlands Nitrogen Technical Bulletin

Neth Rijks Geol Dienst Jaarversl — Netherlands. Rijks Geologische Dienst. Jaarverslag
Neth Rijks Geol Dienst Meded Nieuwe Ser — Netherlands. Rijks Geologische Dienst. Mededelingen. Nieuwe Serie
Neth Sticht Bodemkartering Bodemkund Stud — Netherlands. Stichting voor Bodemkartering. Bodemkundige Studies
NETJA — Nederlands Tijdschrift voor Geneeskunde
Ne T T — Nederlands Theologisch Tijdschrift
NEUDA — Neue Deliwa-Zeitschrift
Neue Arzneim Spez — Neue Arzneimittel und Spezialitaeten
Neue Arzneim Spez Geheimm — Neue Arzneimittel. Spezialitaeten und Geheimmittel
Neue Aspekte Trasylol-Ther — Neue Aspekte der Trasylol-Therapie
Neue Beitr Gesch Deutsch Altert — Neue Beitraege zur Geschichte des Deutschen Altertums
Neue Bergbautech — Neue Bergbautechnik [*Wissenschaftliche Zeitschrift fuer Bergbau, Geowissenschaften und Aufbereitung*]
Neue Deliwa-Z — Neue Deliwa-Zeitschrift
Neue Denkschr Naturhist Mus Wien — Neue Denkschriften des Naturhistorischen Museums in Wien
Neue Dtsch Pap Ztg — Neue Deutsche Papier-Zeitung
Neue Entwicklungspol — Neue Entwicklungspolitik
Neue Ges — Neue Gesellschaft
Neue Gesellsch — Neue Gesellschaft
Neue Jurist Wochenschr — Neue Juristische Wochenschrift
Neue Mitt Landwirtsch — Neue Mitteilungen fuer die Landwirtschaft
Neue Muench Beitr Gesch Med Medizinhist — Neue Muenchner Beitraege zur Geschichte der Medizin und Naturwissenschaften. Medizinhistorische Reihe
Neue Muench Beitr Gesch Med Naturwiss Medizinhist Reihe — Neue Muenchner Beitraege zur Geschichte der Medizin und Naturwissenschaften. Medizinhistorische Reihe
Neue Mz — Neue Musikzeitung
Neue Oesterr Z Kinderheilkd — Neue Oesterreichische Zeitschrift fuer Kinderheilkunde
Neue Oest Z Kinderheilk — Neue Oesterreichische Zeitschrift fuer Kinderheilkunde
Neue Ordnung — Neue Ordnung in Kirche, Staat, Gesellschaft, Kultur
Neue Phys — Neue Physik
Neue Pol Lit — Neue Politische Literatur
Neue Rund — Neue Rundschau
Neue Rundsch — Neue Rundschau
Neues Arch Niedersachs — Neues Archiv fuer Niedersachsen
Neues Jahrb Geologie u Palaeontologie Monatsh — Neues Jahrbuch fuer Geologie und Palaeontologie. Monatshefte
Neues Jahrb Geol Palaeontol Abh — Neues Jahrbuch fuer Geologie und Palaeontologie. Abhandlungen
Neues Jahrb Geol Palaeontol Abh B — Neues Jahrbuch fuer Geologie und Palaeontologie. Abhandlungen B
Neues Jahrb Geol Palaeontol Monatsh — Neues Jahrbuch fuer Geologie und Palaeontologie. Monatshefte
Neues Jahrb Mineral Abh — Neues Jahrbuch fuer Mineralogie. Abhandlungen
Neues Jahrb Mineral Geol Palaeontol Abh Abt A — Neues Jahrbuch fuer Mineralogie, Geologie, und Palaeontologie. Abhandlungen. Abteilung A. Mineralogie, Petrographie
Neues Jahrb Mineral Geol Palaeontol Abh Abt B — Neues Jahrbuch fuer Mineralogie, Geologie, und Palaeontologie. Abhandlungen. Abteilung B. Geologie, Palaeontologie
Neues Jahrb Mineral Geol Palaeontol Monatsh Abt 1 — Neues Jahrbuch fuer Mineralogie, Geologie, und Palaeontologie. Monatshefte. Abteilung 1. Mineralogie, Gesteinskunde
Neues Jahrb Mineral Geol Palaeontol Monatsh Abt 2 — Neues Jahrbuch fuer Mineralogie, Geologie, und Palaeontologie. Monatshefte. Abteilung 2. Geologie, Palaeontologie
Neues Jahrb Mineral Geol Palaeontol Ref — Neues Jahrbuch fuer Mineralogie, Geologie, und Palaeontologie. Referate
Neues Jahrb Mineral Monatsh — Neues Jahrbuch fuer Mineralogie. Monatshefte
Neues Jahrb Mineralogie Abh — Neues Jahrbuch fuer Mineralogie. Abhandlungen
Neues Jahrb Mineralogie Monatsh — Neues Jahrbuch fuer Mineralogie. Monatshefte
Neues Jahrbuch Geologie u Palaeontologie Abh Monatsh — Neues Jahrbuch fuer Geologie und Palaeontologie. Abhandlungen. Monatshefte
Neues Jahrbuch Geol Palaeontol Abhandl — Neues Jahrbuch fuer Geologie und Palaeontologie. Abhandlungen
Neues Jahrbuch Geol Palaeontol Monatsh — Neues Jahrbuch fuer Geologie und Palaeontologie. Monatshefte
Neues Jahrbuch Mineralogie Abh Monatsh — Neues Jahrbuch fuer Mineralogie. Abhandlungen. Monatshefte
Neues Jb Miner Geol Palaeont Mh — Neues Jahrbuch fuer Mineralogie, Geologie, und Palaeontologie. Monatshefte
Neues J Pharm — Neues Journal der Pharmacie
Neues J Phys — Neues Journal der Physik
Neues Optiker Jl — Neues Optiker Journal
Neuesten Entdeckungen Chem — Neuesten Entdeckungen in der Chemie

Neuestes Chem Arch — Neuestes Chemisches Archiv
Neue Tech — Neue Technik
Neue Tech A — Neue Technik. Abteilung A. Automatik und Industrielle Elektronik [*Switzerland*]
Neue Tech B — Neue Technik. Abteilung B. Kerntechnik [*Switzerland*]
Neue Tech Buero — Neue Technik im Buero
Neue Verpack — Neue Verpackung [*West Germany*]
Neue Wirtsch — Neue Wirtschaft
Neue ZFM — Neue Zeitschrift fuer Musik
Neue Z Mission — Neue Zeitschrift fuer Missionswissenschaft/Nouvelle Revue de Science Missionaire
Neue Z Miss Wiss — Neue Zeitschrift fuer Missionswissenschaft
Neue Z Ruebenzucker Ind — Neue Zeitschrift fuer Ruebenzucker-Industrie
Neue Z Sys Th — Neue Zeitschrift fuer Systematische Theologie und Religionsphilosophie
Neue Zuer Ztg — Neue Zuericher Zeitung [*Switzerland*]
Neue Z Verwaltungsr — Neue Zeitschrift fuer Verwaltungsrecht
Neujahrsblatt Naturforsch Ges Zur — Neujahrsblatt. Naturforschende Gesellschaft in Zuerich
Neujahrsbl Sachs — Neujahrsblaetter Herausgegeben von der Historischen Kommission fuer die Provinz Sachsen
Neumol Cir Torax — Neumologia y Cirugia de Torax
NE Univ Bul — New England University. Bulletin
NE Univ External Stud Gaz — University of New England. External Studies Gazette
NE Univ Union Rec — University of New England. Union Record
NeuP — Neuphilologische Monatsschrift
Neuphil Mit — Neuphilologische Mitteilungen
Neuphilol M — Neuphilologische Mitteilungen
Neuphilol Mitt — Neuphilologische Mitteilungen
NEURA — Neurology
Neurobehav Toxicol — Neurobehavioral Toxicology
Neurobiol Biochem Morphol — Neurobiology, Biochemistry, and Morphology
Neurochem Res — Neurochemical Research
Neuro Chir — Neuro-Chirurgie
Neurochira — Neurochirurgia
Neuro-Chire — Neuro-Chirurgie
Neuroendocr — Neuroendocrinology
Neurol Centralbl — Neurologisches Centralblatt
Neurol India — Neurology India
Neurol Med-Chir — Neurologia Medico-Chirurgica
Neurol Neurochir Pol — Neurologia i Neurochirurgia Polska
Neurol Neurochir Psychiatr Pol — Neurologia, Neurochirurgia, i Psychiatria Polska [*Poland*]
Neurol Neurocir Psiquiatr — Neurologia, Neurocirurgia, Psiquiatria
Neurol Psihiatr Neurochir (Buchar) — Neurologia Psihiatria Neurochirurgia (Bucharest)
Neurol Res — Neurological Research
Neurol Surg — Neurological Surgery
Neuropadiat — Neuropaediatrie
Neurop Ap N — Neuropathology and Applied Neurobiology
Neuropathol Appl Neurobiol — Neuropathology and Applied Neurobiology
Neuropatol Pol — Neuropatologia Polska
Neuropharm — Neuropharmacology
Neuropsichiatr Infant — Neuropsichiatria Infantile
Neuropsycho — Neuropsychologia
Neuroradiol — Neuroradiology
Neurosci Behav Physiol — Neuroscience and Behavioral Physiology
Neurosci Biobehav Rev — Neuroscience and Biobehavioral Reviews
Neurosci L — Neuroscience Letters
Neurosci Lett — Neuroscience Letters
Neurosci Lett Suppl — Neuroscience Letters. Supplement
Neurosci Res — Neurosciences Research
Neurosci Res Program Bull — Neurosciences Research. Program Bulletin
Neurosci Res (Shannon Irel) — Neuroscience Research (Shannon, Ireland)
Neurosci Res Symp Summ — Neurosciences Research. Symposium Summaries
Neurosci Ser — Neuroscience Series
Neurosci Symp — Neuroscience Symposia
Neurosci Transl — Neuroscience Translations
Neurospora Newsl — Neurospora Newsletter
NeuS — Neuere Sprachen
Neu Spr — Neuere Sprachen
Nevada Bur Mines Map — Nevada. Bureau of Mines. Map
Nevada Univ Center Water Resources Research Proj Rept — Nevada University. Desert Research Institute. Center for Water Resources Research. Project Report
Nev Ag Exp — Nevada. Agricultural Experiment Station. Publications
Nev Agric Exp Stn B — Nevada. Agricultural Experiment Station. B
Nev Agric Exp Stn Circ — Nevada. Agricultural Experiment Station. Circular
Nev Agric Exp Stn R — Nevada. Agricultural Experiment Station. R
Nev Agric Exp Stn Ser B — Nevada. Agricultural Experiment Station. Series B
Nev Agric Exp Stn T — Nevada. Agricultural Experiment Station. T
Nev Agric Exp Stn Tech Bull — Nevada. Agricultural Experiment Station. Technical Bulletin
Nev Bur Mines Bull — Nevada. Bureau of Mines. Bulletin
Nev Bur Mines Geol Bull — Nevada. Bureau of Mines and Geology. Bulletin

Nev Bur Mines Geol Rep — Nevada. Bureau of Mines and Geology. Report
Nev Bur Mines Rep — Nevada. Bureau of Mines. Report
Nev Dep Conserv Nat Resour Water Resour Bull — Nevada. Department of Conservation and Natural Resources. Water Resources Bulletin
Nev Dep Conserv Nat Resour Water Resour Inf Ser — Nevada. Department of Conservation and Natural Resources. Water Resources Information Series
Nev Dep Conserv Nat Resour Water Resour Reconnaissance Ser — Nevada. Department of Conservation and Natural Resources. Water Resources Rec onnaissance Series
Nev Div Water Resour Water Resour Bull — Nevada. Division of Water Resources. Water Resources Bulletin
Nev Div Water Resour Water Resour Reconnaissance Ser — Nevada. Division of Water Resources. Water Resources Reconnaissance Series
Nevelestud Kozlem — Nevelestudomanyi Koezlemenyek
Nev Highways and Parks — Nevada Highways and Parks
Nev Nurses Assoc Q Newslett — Nevada Nurses' Association. Quarterly Newsletter
Nev Off State Eng Water Resour Bull — Nevada. Office of the State Engineer. Water Resources Bulletin
Nev R Bus and Econ — Nevada Review of Business and Economics
Nev RNformation — Nevada RNformation
Nevrol Psikhiatr — Nevrologiya i Psikhiatriya
Nevrol Psikhiatr Nevrokhir — Nevrologiya, Psikhiatriya, i Nevrokhirurgiya
Nevropatol Psikhiat — Nevropatologiya i Psikhiatriya
Nev State Engineer's Office Water Res Bull — Nevada. State Engineer's Office. Water Resources Bulletin
Nev State Eng Water Resour Bull — Nevada. State Engineer. Water Resources Bulletin
Nev State Mus Anthropol Pap — Nevada State Museum. Anthropological Papers
Nev Univ Dp G M B — Nevada University. Department of Geology and Mining. Bulletin
Nev Univ Max C Fleischmann Coll Agric B — Nevada University. Max C. Fleischmann College of Agriculture. Series B
Nev Univ Max C Fleischmann Coll Agric R — Nevada University. Max C. Fleischmann College of Agriculture. Series R
Nev Wildl — Nevada Wildlife
New — New Age
NEW — Onderneming
NewA — New African
New A C P — New American and Canadian Poetry
New Am — New America
New Am Mercury — New American Mercury
New Argent — Newsletter Argentina
Newark Eng Notes — Newark Engineering Notes
New A'sian Post — New Australasian Post
N E Water Works Assn J — New England Water Works Association. Journal
Newberry Lib Bul — Newberry Library. Bulletin
New Biol — New Biology
New Blckfrs — New Blackfriars
New Bldg Projects — New Building Projects
New Bot — New Botanist
New Brunswick Dept Lands and Mines Ann Rept — New Brunswick. Department of Lands and Mines. Annual Report
New C — New Collage
New Caledonia Bull Geol — New Caledonia. Bulletin Geologique
New Can F — New Canadian Film
Newcastle Chamber of Commerce J — Newcastle Chamber of Commerce Journal
Newcastle Ch Comm J — Newcastle Chamber of Commerce Journal
Newcastle Inst Ed J — Institutes of Education of the Universities of Newcastle Upon Tyne and Durham. Journal
Newcastle Teach Coll Bul — Newcastle Teachers College. Bulletin
Newcastle Teach Coll Bull — Newcastle Teachers College. Bulletin
Newcastle Univ Gaz — Gazette. University of Newcastle
Newcastle Univ Phys Dep Res Pub — University of Newcastle. Department of Physics. Research Publication
New Cent Res Inst Electr Power Ind — News. Central Research Institute of Electrical Power Industry [*Japan*]
New Church R — New Church Review
New Civ Eng — New Civil Engineer [*United Kingdom*]
New Civ Engr — New Civil Engineer
New Civil Engr — New Civil Engineer
Newcomen Soc Trans — Newcomen Society. Transactions
New Commun — New Community
New Cov — New Covenant
New Dir Com — New Directions for Community Colleges
New Direct — New Directions
New Direct Com Coll — New Directions for Community Colleges
New Direct Higher Educ — New Directions for Higher Education
New Direct Inst Res — New Directions for Institutional Research
New Dir Hig — New Directions for Higher Education
New Dom — New Dominion Monthly
New Ecol — New Ecologist [*United Kingdom*]
New Educ — New Education

New Electron — New Electronics
New Eng — New Engineer [*United States*]
New Eng — New Englander
New Eng Hist — New England Historical and Genealogical Register
New Eng Hist Geneal Reg — New England Historical and Genealogical Register
New Eng J Crim & Civil Confinement — New England Journal on Criminal and Civil Confinement
New Eng J Prison — New England Journal of Prison Law
New Eng J Prison L — New England Journal of Prison Law
New England J Bus and Econ — New England Journal of Business and Economics
New England J Human Services — New England Journal of Human Services
New England J Prison L — New England Journal of Prison Law
New England L Rev — New England Law Review
New England Water Works Assoc Jour — New England Water Works Association. Journal
New Engl J Med — New England Journal of Medicine
New Eng L Rev — New England Law Review
New Engl Univ Explor Soc Rep — University of New England. Exploration Society. Report
New Eng Mag — New England Magazine
New Eng M ns — New England Magazine (New Series)
New Eng Q — New England Quarterly
New Entomol — New Entomologist
New Equip News — New Equipment News [*South Africa*]
New Era — New Era in Home and School
Newer Methods Nutr Biochem — Newer Methods of Nutritional Biochemistry
Newer Methods Nutr Biochem Appl Interpret — Newer Methods of Nutritional Biochemistry with Applications and Interpretations
Newer Met Ind — Newer Metal Industry [*Japan*]
New Food Ind — New Food Industry [*Japan*]
Newfoundland Dep Mines Energy Miner Dev Div Rep Act — Newfoundland. Department of Mines and Energy. Mineral Development Division. Report of Activities
Newfoundland Geol Survey Inf Circ Rept — Newfoundland. Geological Survey. Information Circular. Report
Newfoundland Geol Surv Inf Circ — Newfoundland. Geological Survey. Information Circular
Newfoundland and Labrador Mineral Resources Div Bull — Newfoundland and Labrador. Department of Mines, Agriculture, and Resources. Mineral Resources Division. Bulletin
Newfoundland Labrador Miner Dev Div Rep — Newfoundland and Labrador. Mineral Development Division. Report
Newfoundland Labrador Miner Resour Div Inf Circ — Newfoundland and Labrador. Mineral Resources Division. Information Circular
Newfoundland Labrador Miner Resour Div Miner Resour Rep — Newfoundland and Labrador. Mineral Resources Division. Mineral Resources Report
New Germ — New German Critique
New Germ Crit — New German Critique
New Guinea Austral Pacific SE Asia — New Guinea and Australia, the Pacific, and South East Asia
New Guinea Res B — New Guinea Research Bulletin
New Hamp BJ — New Hampshire Bar Journal
New Haven Sym — New Haven Symphony Orchestra. Program Notes
New Hebrides Annu Rep Geol Surv — New Hebrides. Annual Report of the Geological Survey
New Hebrides Geol Surv Annu Rep — New Hebrides. Geological Survey. Annual Report
New Hebrides Geol Surv Rep — New Hebrides. Geological Survey. Report
New Hor Educ — New Horizons in Education
New Horiz Educ — New Horizons in Education
New Horizons in Educ — New Horizons in Education
New Hungarian Q — New Hungarian Quarterly
New Hungar Quart — New Hungarian Quarterly
New Hung Q — New Hungarian Quarterly
New Inf Syst Serv — New Information Systems and Services [*United States*]
New Int — New Internationalist [*England*]
New Int Clin — New International Clinics
New Inter — New Internationalist
New Int Realities — New International Realities [*United States*]
New Istanbul Contrib Clin Sci — New Istanbul Contribution to Clinical Science
New Jers Beekprs Ass News — New Jersey Beekeepers Association. News
New Jersey Div Water Policy and Supply Spec Rept — State of New Jersey. Department of Conservation and Economic Development. Division of Water Policy and Supply. Special Report
New Jersey Div Water Policy and Supply Water Resources Circ — State of New Jersey. Department of Conservation and Economic Development. Division of Water Policy and Supply. Water Resources Circular
New Jersey LJ — New Jersey Law Journal
New Jers St Hort Soc News — New Jersey State Horticultural Society. News
New J Stat & Oper Res — New Journal of Statistics and Operational Research
NewL — New Leader
New L — New Letters
New Law J — New Law Journal
New Left — New Left Review

New Left R — New Left Review
New Lib — New Liberal Review
New Libr Wld — New Library World
New Lib W — New Library World
New Lib World — New Library World
New Lit His — New Literary History
New Lit Hist — New Literary History
New L J — New Law Journal
New Math Library — New Mathematical Library
New Med J — New Medical Journal
New Met Tech — New Metals and Technics [*Japan*]
New Mex Hist Rev — New Mexico Historical Review
New Mexico Bur Mines and Mineral Resources Bull — New Mexico. Bureau of Mines and Mineral Resources. Bulletin. New Mexico Institute of Mining and Technology
New Mexico Bur Mines and Mineral Resources Geol Map — New Mexico. Bureau of Mines and Mineral Resources. Geologic Map. New Mexico Institute of Mining and Technology
New Mexico Geol Soc Spec Pub — New Mexico Geological Society. Special Publication
New Mexico L Rev — New Mexico Law Review
New Mexico State Engineer Tech Rept — New Mexico State Engineer. Technical Report
New Mexico Univ Pubs Meteoritics — New Mexico University. Publications in Meteoritics
New Mex L Rev — New Mexico Law Review
New Nippon Electr Tech Rev — New Nippon Electric Technical Review
New O R — New Orleans Review
New Orleans Ac Sc Papers — New Orleans Academy of Sciences. Papers
New Orleans Med Surg J — New Orleans Medical and Surgical Journal
New Orleans Port Rec — New Orleans Port Record
New Orl Rev — New Orleans Review
New Per Ind — New Periodicals Index
New Phys — New Physics
New Phys (Korean Phys Soc) — New Physics (Korean Physical Society)
New Phys Suppl — New Physics. Supplement
New Phytol — New Phytologist
New Polit — New Political Science
New Polit — New Politics
New Pol Sci — New Political Science
Newport N H Soc Pr — Newport Natural History Society. Proceedings
New Princ — New Princeton Review
New Q — New Quarterly Review
New R — [*The*] New Republic
New R — New Review
New Real — New Realities
New Rena — New Renaissance
New Rep — [*The*] New Republic
New Repub — [*The*] New Republic
New Res Plant Anat — New Research in Plant Anatomy
New Rev — New Review
New Riv R — New River Review
NEWS — New England Weekly Survey
New S — New Scholar
NewS — New Statesman
News — News from Nowhere
News Bull Indian Dent Assoc — News Bulletin. Indian Dental Association
News Bull Soc Vertebr Paleontol — News Bulletin. Society of Vertebrate Paleontology
Newscast Reg 4 Amer Iris Soc — Newscast Region 4. American Iris Society
New Sch Ex — New Schools Exchange. Newsletter
New Schl — New Schools Exchange. Newsletter
New Schol — New Scholasticism
New Scholas — New Scholasticism
New Sci — New Scientist
New Scient — New Scientist
New Sci (London) — New Scientist (London)
News CIMMYT — News. Centro Internacional de Mejoramiento de Maiz y Trigo
New Sci Sci J — New Scientist and Science Journal
News Comment — News and Comments [*American Academy of Pediatrics*]
News Ed Am Chem Soc — News Edition. American Chemical Society
News Eng — News in Engineering
News Farmer Coop — News for Farmer Cooperatives
News Farmer Coops — News for Farmer Cooperatives
Newsfront — Newsfront International
News Geotherm Energy Convers Technol — News of Geothermal Energy Conversion Technology [*United States*]
Newsl Am Acad Health Adm — Newsletter. American Academy of Health Administration
Newsl Am Assoc Equine Pract — Newsletter. American Association of Equine Practitioners
Newsl Appl Nucl Methods Biol Agric — Newsletter on the Application of Nuclear Methods in Biology and Agriculture [*Netherlands*]
Newsl Aust Conserv Fdn — Australian Conservation Foundation. Newsletter
Newsl Aust Conserv Found — Australian Conservation Foundation. Newsletter

Newsl Aust NZ Soc Nucl Med — Newsletter. Australian and New Zealand Society of Nuclear Medicine
Newsl Biomed Saf Stand — Newsletter of Biomedical Safety and Standards
Newsl Commw Geol Liaison Off — Newsletter. Commonwealth Geological Liaison Office
Newsl Coop Invest Mediterr — Newsletter of the Cooperative Investigations in the Mediterranean
Newsl Environ Mutagen Soc — Newsletter. Environmental Mutagen Society
News Lepid Soc — News. Lepidopterists' Society
Newslet — Newsletter. American Symphony Orchestra League, Inc.
News Lett Assoc Off Seed Anal — News Letter. Association of Official Seed Analysts
Newsletter Comp Stud Communism — Newsletter on Comparative Studies of Communism
Newsletter R Aust Hist Soc — Royal Australian Historical Society. Newsletter
Newsletter WSEO — Newsletter. Washington State Energy Office
News Lett Florence Nightingale Int Nurs Assoc — News Letter. Florence Nightingale International Nurses Association
News Lett India Popul Proj UP — News Letter. India Population Project UP
Newslett Int Rice Comm — Newsletter. International Rice Commission
News Lett Popul Cent (Bangalore) — News Letter. Population Centre (Bangalore)
Newslett Stratigr — Newsletter on Stratigraphy
Newslett Tree Impr Introd — Newsletter of Tree Improvement and Introduction
Newsl Fusion Energy Found — Newsletter. Fusion Energy Foundation
Newsl Geol Soc NZ — Newsletter. Geological Society of New Zealand
Newsl-IGCP Proj 167 — Newsletter. International Geological Correlation Programme. Project 167
Newsl Indones Min Assoc — Newsletter. Indonesian Mining Association
Newsl Inst Foresters Aust — Institute of Foresters of Australia. Newsletter
Newsl Int Coll Dent India Sect — Newsletter. International College of Dentists. India Section
Newsl Intellectual Freedom — Newsletter on Intellectual Freedom
Newsl Int Rice Comm — Newsletter. International Rice Commission
Newsl Int Soc Radiogr Radiol Tech — Newsletter. International Society of Radiographers and Radiological Technicians
Newsl Int Union Biol Sci — Newsletter. International Union of Biological Sciences
Newsl Isot Generator Inf Cent — Newsletter. Isotopic Generator Information Centre [*France*]
Newsl League Int Fd Educ — Newsletter. League for International Food Education
Newsl NEA Comput Program Libr — Newsletter. NEA [*National Education Association*] Computer Program Library [*United States*]
Newsl NEA Data Bank — Newsletter. NEA [*Nuclear Energy Agency*] Data Bank
Newsl New Zealand Archaeol Assoc — Newsletter. New Zealand Archaeological Association
Newsl NZ Archaeol Assoc — Newsletter. New Zealand Archaeological Association
Newsl NZ Map Circle — Newsletter. New Zealand Mapkeepers Circle
Newsl Springfield Dent Soc — Newsletter. Springfield Dental Society
Newsl Stat Soc Aust — Statistical Society of Australia. Newsletter
Newsl Stratigr — Newsletters on Stratigraphy
Newsl Wildl Dis Assoc — Newsletter. Wildlife Disease Association
Newsl Wis League Nurs — Newsletter. Wisconsin League for Nursing
News Media and L — News Media and the Law
News Notes Calif Libr — News Notes of California Libraries
News Notes Calif Libs — News Notes of California Libraries
New Soc — New Society
New Soc (London) — New Society (London)
New South Wales Mag — New South Wales Magazine
New South Wales Soil Conserv Serv J — New South Wales. Soil Conservation Service. Journal
New South Wales Univ Sch Civ Eng UNICIV Rep — University of New South Wales. School of Civil Engineering. UNICIV Report
New So WL — New South Wales Law Reports
New So W St — New South Wales State Reports
New So WWN — New South Wales Weekly Notes
News Pestic Rev Nat Agr Chem Ass — News and Pesticide Review. National Agricultural Chemicals Association
NewSt — New Statesman
New Statesm — New Statesman
News Views Ohio League Nurs — News and Views. Ohio League for Nursing
News W — News Weekly
Newswk — Newsweek
New Tech Biophys Cell Biol — New Techniques in Biophysics and Cell Biology
New Tech Books — New Technical Books
New Test Abstr — New Testament Abstracts
New Test St — New Testament Studies
New Test Stud — New Testament Studies
New Times — New Womens Times
New Towns Bull — New Towns Bulletin
New Trends Chem Teach — New Trends in Chemistry Teaching
New University — New University and New Education

New Univ Q — New Universities. Quarterly
New Univ Quart — New Universities. Quarterly
New World A — New World Archaeological Record
New World R — New World Review
New W R — New World Review
New York — New York Magazine
New York Acad Sci Trans — New York Academy of Sciences. Transactions
New York City Board Education Curriculum Bull — New York City Board of Education. Curriculum Bulletins
New York Law School Law R — New York Law School. Law Review
New York State Mus and Sci Service Map and Chart Ser — New York State Museum and Science Service. Map and Chart Series
New York State Mus and Sci Service Mem — New York State Museum and Science Service. Memoir
New York Univ J Internat Law and Politics — New York University. Journal of International Law and Politics
New York Univ Law R — New York University. Law Review
New York Water Resources Comm Bull — New York Conservation Department. Water Resources Commission. Bulletin
New York Water Resources Comm Rept Inv — New York Conservation Department. Water Resources Commission. Report of Investigation
New Y Q — New York Quarterly
New Y R B — New York Review of Books
New Zealand Archt — New Zealand Architect
New Zealand Econ Pap — New Zealand Economic Papers
New Zealand Jour Geology and Geophysics — New Zealand Journal of Geology and Geophysics
New Zealand J Publ Adm — New Zealand Journal of Public Administration
New Zealand J Sci Tech — New Zealand Journal of Science and Technology
New Zealand Math Mag — New Zealand Mathematics Magazine
New Zealand Oper Res — New Zealand Operational Research
New Zealand Soc Wker — New Zealand Social Worker
New Zeal Dep Sci Ind Res Bull — New Zealand. Department of Scientific and Industrial Research. Bulletin
New Zeal Geol Surv Bull — New Zealand Geological Survey. Bulletin
New Zeal J Geol Geophys — New Zealand Journal of Geology and Geophysics
New Zeal LJ — New Zealand Law Journal
Next Year — Next Year Country
Nezelezne Kovy Technickoekon Zpravodaj — Nezelezne Kovy. Technickoekonomicky Zpravodaj [*Czechoslovakia*]
NEZSA — Bulletin. New Zealand Department of Scientific and Industrial Research
NEZTA — New Zealand Veterinary Journal
NF — Neerlandia Franciskana
NF — Neue Forschungen
NF — New York Folklore. Quarterly
NF — Nigerian Field
NF — Northeast Folklore
NF — Northland Free Press [*Slave Lake, Alberta*]
NFA — Nachrichten fuer Aussenhandel
NFAIS Newsl — NFAIS [*National Federation of Abstracting and Indexing Services*] Newsletter [*United States*]
NFAOD — Numerical Functional Analysis and Optimization
NFEFD — Newsletter. Fusion Energy Foundation
NFF — NATO [*North Atlantic Treaty Organization*] Review
NFI — NFIB [*National Federation of Independent Business*] Quarterly Economic Report
Nf J — Nordfriesisches Jahrbuch
NFJGG — Neue Folge des Jahrbuchs der Goethe Gesellschaft
NFL — New Found Land
Nfld & PEIR — Newfoundland and Prince Edward Island Reports
Nfld Q — Newfoundland Quarterly
NFNLA — NFAIS [*National Federation of Abstracting and Indexing Services*] Newsletter
NFS — Nottingham French Studies
NFSGWS — Newsletter. Folklore Society of Greater Washington. Supplement
NFU — Unitas. Economic Quarterly Review
NFULDA — Fondation Universitaire Luxembourgeoise. Serie Notes de Recherche
NFV — New Zealand Foreign Affairs Review
NG — Neue Germanistik
NG — Neue Gesellschaft
NG — New Guard
NG — Nieuwe Gids
NG — Nota Genitiva
NGC — New Generation Computing
NGC — New German Critique
NGET — Norsk Geografisk Tidsskrift
NGF — Nomina Geographica Flandrica
NGG — Nachrichten. Gesellschaft der Wissenschaften zu Goettingen
NGGW — Nachrichten. Gesellschaft der Wissenschaften zu Goettingen
NGJ — Nigerian Geographical Journal
NGKBA — Nogyo Gijutsu Kenkyusho Hokoku. B. Dojo Hiryo
NGKCA — Nogyo Gijutsu Kenkyusho Hokoku. C. Byori Konchu
NGKDA — Nogyo Gijutsu Kenkyusho Hokoku. D. Seiri, Iden, Sakumotsu Ippan

NGKJB — Nippon Genshiryokusen Kaihatsu Jigyodan Nenpo
NGKNA — Nippon Genshiryoku Kenkyusho Nenpo
NGKYA3 — Folia Ophthalmologica Japonica
NGM — National Geographic Magazine
NGMSA — Nauchnye Trudy Nauchno-Issledovatel'skii
    Gornometallurgicheskii Institut (Yerevan)
NGN — Nomina Geographica Neerlandica
NGNVO — Nachrichten. Gesellschaft fuer Natur- und Voelkerkunde Ostasiens
NGPI — New Guinea Periodicals Index
NGPSA — Neftyanaya i Gazovaya Promyshlennost'
NGQ — Numismatic Gazette Quarterly
NG Research Bul — New Guinea Research Bulletin
NGRPD — GREMP [*Geothermal Reservoir Engineering Management
    Program*] News
NGS — Neue Geisteswissenschaftliche Studien
NGS — New German Studies
NGS — Nieuw-Guinea Studien
NGSQ — National Genealogical Society. Quarterly
NGWG — Nachrichten. Gesellschaft der Wissenschaften zu Goettingen
NGWG — Nachrichten. Gesellschaft der Wissenschaften zu Goettingen.
    Philologisch-Historische Klasse
NGWGott — Nachrichten. Gesellschaft der Wissenschaften zu Goettingen
NH — Natural History
NH — Nebraska History
NH — New Hampshire Quarter Notes
NH — Northern History
NH Ag Exp — New Hampshire Agricultural Experiment Station. Publications
NHAM — North-Holland Series in Applied Mathematics and Mechanics
    [*Elsevier Book Series*]
NHB — Nederlandsche Historiebladen
NHB — Negro History Bulletin
NHB J — New Hampshire Bar Journal
NHBl — Nassauische Heimatblaetter
NHCG — North-Holland Series in Crystal Growth [*Elsevier Book Series*]
NH Dep Resour Econ Dev Bull — New Hampshire Department of Resources
    and Economic Development. Bulletin
NH Div Econ Dev Miner Resour Surv — New Hampshire Division of Economic
    Development. Mineral Resources Survey
NHE — Nederlandse Energiehuishouding. Witkomsten van Maandtellingen en
    Kwartaaltellingen
NHEIAY — Japanese Journal of Smooth Muscle Research
NHGZA — Nippon Igaku Hoshasen Gakkai Zasshi
NH His S — New Hampshire Historical Society. Proceedings
NHJ — Nathaniel Hawthorne Journal
NHJ — Neue Heidelberger Jahrbuecher
NHJ — New Hampshire Bar Journal
NHJB — Neue Heidelberger Jahrbuecher
NHK Lab Note — NHK [*Nippon Hoso Kyokai*] Laboratories Note
NHKNA — Nippon Hoshasen Kobunshi Kenkyu Kyokai Nempo
NHK Tech J — NHK [*Nippon Hoso Kyokai*] Technical Journal
NHK Tech Monogr — NHK [*Nippon Hoso Kyokai*] Technical Monograph
NHLS — North-Holland Linguistic Series [*Elsevier Book Series*]
NHML — North-Holland Mathematical Library [*Elsevier Book Series*]
NHMS — North-Holland Mathematics Studies [*Elsevier Book Series*]
NHMT — North-Holland Medieval Translations [*Elsevier Book Series*]
NHochland — Neues Hochland
NHOKA — NHK (Nippon Hoso Kyokai) Technical Monograph
NH Progr Rep — New Hampshire Progress Report
NHQ — New Hungarian Quarterly
NHRI Paper — National Hydrology Research Institute. Paper
N H Rv — Natural History Review
NHSC — North-Holland Systems and Control Series [*Elsevier Book Series*]
N H Soc NB B — Natural History Society of New Brunswick. Bulletin
NHSQ — Nevada Historical Society Quarterly
NHSS — North-Holland Studies in Silver [*Elsevier Book Series*]
NHSSD — North-Holland Series in Systems and Software Development
    [*Elsevier Book Series*]
NH State Plan Devel Comm Mineral Res Survey — New Hampshire State
    Planning and Development Commission. Mineral Resources Survey
NH State Plann Dev Comm Miner Resour Surv — New Hampshire State
    Planning and Development Commission. Mineral Resources Survey
NHT — International Herald Tribune
NHV — Nea Helliniki Vivliothiki
NHVKSG — Neujahrsblatt. Historischer Verein des Kantons St. Gallen
NI — Nuova Italia
NIBS Bull Biol Res — Nippon Institute for Biological Science. Bulletin.
    Biological Research
Nicaragua Servicio Geol Nac Bol — Nicaragua Servicio Geologico Nacional.
    Boletin
Nicar Inst Invest Sism Bol — Nicaragua Instituto de Investigaciones Sismicas.
    Boletin
Nicar Med — Nicaragua Medica
Nice Hist — Nice Historique
Nice Med — Nice Medical
NICKA3 — Japanese Journal of Zootechnical Science
Nickel Ber — Nickel Berichte

Nickel Bull — Nickel Bulletin
Nickel Steel Top — Nickel Steel Topics
Nickel Top — Nickel Topics
NID — National Intelligence Daily [*CIA*]
NIDA Res Monogr — National Institute on Drug Abuse. Research Monograph
NIDZA — Nippon Ika Daigaku Zasshi
Niederdeu Mit — Niederdeutsche Mitteilungen
Niederoest Imker — Niederoesterreichesche Imker
Niederrhein Ges Bonn Szb — Niederrheinische Gesellschaft fuer Natur und
    Heilkunde zu Bonn. Sitzungsberichte
Niederrhein Jahrb — Niederrheinisches Jahrbuch
Niedersaechs Ministerialbl — Niedersaechsisches Ministerialblatt
Nielson Rs — Nielson Researcher
Nien San Ann Univ Cantho — Nien San. Annals. University of Cantho
Nieren- Hochdruckkr — Nieren- und Hochdruckkrankheiten
NietzscheS — Nietzsche Studien
Nieuw Arch Wisk — Nieuw Archief voor Wiskunde
Nieuwe Verh Bataafsch Genoot Proefonderv Wijsbegeerte — Nieuwe
    Verhandelingen van het Bataafsch Genootschap der
    Proefondervindelijke Wijsbegeerte
Nieuw Tijdschr Wisk — Nieuw Tijdschrift voor Wiskunde
NIF — Newsletter on Intellectual Freedom
NIF — Nippon Facts
NIFAA — Nuovo Cimento. Societa Italiana di Fisica. Sezione A
NIFBA — Nuovo Cimento. Societa Italiana di Fisica. Sezione B
NIFCA — Nuovo Cimento. Societa Italiana di Fisica. Sezione C
NIGAB — Annual Report. National Institute of Genetics [*English Edition*]
    [*Japan*]
Niger Annu Rep Fed Dep Agric Res — Nigeria. Annual Report. Federal
    Department of Agricultural Research
Niger Annu Rep Geol Surv Dep — Nigeria. Annual Report. Geological Survey
    Department
Niger Dep For Res Programme Work — Nigeria. Department of Forest
    Research. Programme of Work
Niger Dep For Res Tech Note — Nigeria. Department of Forest Research.
    Technical Note
Niger Entomol Mag — Nigerian Entomologists' Magazine
Niger Fed Annu Rep Geol Surv — Nigeria Federation. Annual Report.
    Geological Survey
Niger Fed Dep Agric Res Memor — Nigeria Federal Department of
    Agricultural Research. Memorandum
Niger Field — Nigerian Field
Niger Fld — Nigerian Field
Niger For Inform Bull — Nigerian Forestry Information. Bulletin
Niger Geol Surv Div Annu Rep — Nigeria Geological Survey Division. Annual
    Report
Nigeria Annu Rep Fed Dep Agric Res — Nigeria. Annual Report. Federal
    Department of Agricultural Research
Nigeria Cocoa Res Inst Annu Rep — Nigeria Cocoa Research Institute. Annual
    Report
Nigeria Fed Dep Agric Res Memo — Nigeria Federal Department of
    Agricultural Research. Memorandum
Nigeria Fed Dep Fish Annu Rep — Nigeria Federal Department of Fisheries.
    Annual Report
Nigeria Fed Dep Fish Fed Fish Occas Pap — Nigeria Federal Department of
    Fisheries. Federal Fisheries. Occasional Paper
Nigeria Fed Dep For Res Annu Rep — Nigeria Federal Department of Forest
    Research. Annual Report
Nigeria Fed Dep For Res Res Pap (For Ser) — Nigeria Federal Department of
    Forest Research. Research Paper (Forest Series)
Nigeria Fed Dep For Res Res Pap (Savanna Ser) — Nigeria. Federal
    Department of Forest Research. Research Paper (Savanna Series)
Nigeria For Inf Bull — Nigeria Forestry Information Bulletin
Nigeria Geogr J — Nigerian Geographical Journal
Nigerian Agric J — Nigerian Agricultural Journal
Nigerian Agr J — Nigerian Agricultural Journal
Nigerian Entomol Mag — Nigerian Entomologists' Magazine
Nigerian Inst Oil Palm Res Annu Rep — Nigerian Institute for Oil Palm
    Research. Annual Report
Nigerian J Entomol — Nigerian Journal of Entomology
Nigerian J For — Nigerian Journal of Forestry
Nigerian J Paediatr — Nigerian Journal of Paediatrics
Nigerian J Sci — Nigerian Journal of Science
Nigerian Lib — Nigerian Libraries
Nigerian Libr — Nigerian Libraries
Nigerian Med J — Nigerian Medical Journal
Nigerian Stored Prod Res Inst Annu Rep — Nigerian Stored Products Research
    Institute. Annual Report
Nigeria Savanna For Res Stn Samaru Zaria Annu Rep — Nigeria Savanna
    Forestry Research Station. Samaru Zaria Annual Report
Nigeria Savanna For Res Stn Ser Res Pap — Nigeria Savanna Forestry
    Research Station. Series Research Paper
Niger J Anim Prod — Nigerian Journal of Animal Production
Niger J Entomol — Nigerian Journal of Entomology
Niger J For — Nigerian Journal of Forestry
Niger J Sci — Nigerian Journal of Science

Niger Mag — Nigeria Magazine
Niger Med J — Nigerian Medical Journal
Niger Nurse — Nigerian Nurse
Nig J Contemp L — Nigerian Journal of Contemporary Law
NIGLA — Nauchno-Tekhnicheskaya Informatsiya. Tsentral'nyi Institut Nauchno-Tekhnicheskoi Informatsii Bumazhnoi i Drevoobrabatyvayushchei Promyshlennosti, Tsellyulozno-Baumazhnaya, Gidroliznaya i Lesokhimicheskaya Promyshlennost
NigM — Nigeria Magazine
NIH — National Institutes of Health. Publications
NIHAE Bull — NIHAE [*National Institute of Health Administration and Education*] Bulletin
NIH Consensus Dev Conf Summ — NIH [*National Institutes of Health*] Consensus Development. Conference Summary
NIHOD — Nieren- und Hochdruckkrankheiten
Nihon Chikusan Gakkai Ho Jap J Zootech — Nihon Chikusan Gakkai Ho/ Japanese Journal of Zootechnical Science
Nihon Juishikai Zasshi J Jap Vet Med Assoc — Nihon Juishikai Zasshi/ Journal. Japan Veterinary Medical Association
Nihon Oyo Dobutsu Konchu Gakkai Shi Jap J Appl Entomol Zool — Nihon Oyo Dobutsu Konchu Gakkai Shi/Japanese Journal of Applied Entomology and Zoology
Nihon Ringakkai Shi J Jap For Soc — Nihon Ringakukai Shi. Journal. Japanese Forestry Society
Nihon Sanshigaku Zasshi J Seric Sci Jap — Nihon Sanshigaku Zasshi. Journal of Sericultural Science of Japan
Nihon Seirigaku Zasshi Jap — Nihon Seirigaku Zasshi/Journal. Physiological Society of Japan
Nihon Senchu Kenkyukai Shi Jap J Nematol — Nihon Senchu Kenkyukai Shi/ Japanese Journal of Nematology
Nihon Shokubutsu Byori Gakkaiho Ann Phytopathol Soc Jap — Nihon Shokubutsu Byori Gakkaiho/Annals. Phytopathological Society of Japan
Nihon Univ Dent J — Nihon University. Dental Journal [*Japan*]
Nihon Univ J Med — Nihon University. Journal of Medicine
Nihon Univ J Radiat Med Biol — Nihon University. Journal of Radiation Medicine and Biology [*Japan*]
Nihon Univ Med J — Nihon University. Medical Journal [*Japan*]
Nihon Univ Mishima Coll Humanit Sci Annu Rep Res — Nihon University. Mishima College of Humanities and Sciences. Annual Report of the Researches
Nihon Univ Mishima Coll Humanit Sci Annu Rep Res Nat Sci — Nihon University. Mishima College of Humanities and Sciences. Annual Report of the Researches. Natural Sciences
Niigata Agric For Res — Niigata Agriculture and Forestry Research
Niigata Agric Sci — Niigata Agricultural Science
Niigata Agr Sci — Niigata Agricultural Science
Niigata Med J — Niigata Medical Journal [*Japan*]
Niigata Univ Sci Rep Ser E — Niigata University. Science Reports. Series E (Geology and Mineralogy)
Nijhoff Internat Philos Ser — Nijhoff International Philosophy Series
NIJKA — Nippon Jozo Kyokai Zasshi
NIK — Nyelv-Es Irodalomtudomanyi Koezlemenyek
NIKGA — Nippon Kinzoku Gakkaishi
NIKHD — Niigata-Ken Kogai Kenkyusho Kenkyu Hokoku
NIKKA — Nippon Kogyo Kaishi
Nikko Mater — Nikko Materials
NIL — Nederland Israel
Niles' Reg — Niles' Register
NI Libr — Northern Ireland Libraries
N Ill LR — Northern Illinois University. Law Review
N Ill UL Rev — Northern Illinois University. Law Review
NILQ — Northern Ireland Legal Quarterly
NILR — Netherlands International Law Review
NIL Rev — Netherlands International Law Review
NIMRD — Nuclear Instruments and Methods in Physics Research
NIM Res Dig — NIM [*National Institute for Metallurgy*] Research Digest [*United States*]
NIN — New Products International
Nine Cen Mus — Nineteenth Century Music
Nine Ct — Nineteenth Century
Nine-Ct Fic — Nineteenth-Century Fiction
Nine-Ct Fr — Nineteenth-Century French Studies
Nine Ct Mus — Nineteenth Century Music
Nine Ct The — Nineteenth-Century Theatre Research
NINF Informasjon Nor Inst Naeringsmidforsk — NINF Informasjon. Norsk Institutt for Naeringsmiddelforskning
N Instr Meth — Nuclear Instruments and Methods [*Later, Nuclear Instruments and Methods in Physics Research*]
NINTD — New Internationalist
Ninth District Q — Ninth District Quarterly
NIOGA — Nippon Onkyo Gakkaishi
NIOSH/OSHA Current Intell Bull — NIOSH/OSHA Current Intelligence Bulletin
NIOSH Tech Inf — NIOSH [*National Institute for Occupational Safety and Health*] Technical Information

NIP — New Ideas in Psychology
NIPAA — Nippon Shokakibyo Gakkai Zasshi
NIPDA — Nihon Daigaku Nojuigakubu Gakujutsu Kenkyu Hokoku
NIPEA — Nippon Genshiryoku Kenkyusho Kenkyu Hokoku
NIPHA — Nippon Hoshasen Gijutsu Gakkai Zasshi
Nip Kag Kai — Nippon Kagaku Kaishi
Nippon Acta Radiol — Nippon Acta Radiologica [*Japan*]
Nippon Dent Coll Annu Publ — Nippon Dental College. Annual Publications
Nippon Dojo Hiryogaku Zasshi J Sci Soil Manure — Nippon Dojo Hiryogaku Zasshi/Journal of the Science of Soil and Manure [*Japan*]
Nippon Kagaku Kaishi J Chem Soc Jap Chem — Nippon Kagaku Kaishi/ Journal. Chemical Society of Japan. Chemistry and Industrial Chemistry
Nippon Kokan Tech Bull — Nippon Kokan Technical Bulletin
Nippon Kokan Tech Rep — Nippon Kokan Technical Reports
Nippon Kokan Tech Rep Overseas — Nippon Kokan Technical Reports Overseas
Nippon Nogei Kagakukai Shi J Agric Chem Soc Jap — Nippon Nogei Kagakukai-Shi/Journal. Agricultural Chemical Society of Japan
Nippon Noyaku Gakkaishi/J Pestic Sci — Nippon Noyaku Gakkaishi/Journal of Pesticide Science
Nippon-Orient — Nippon-Orient-Gakkai-Geppo
Nippon Sochi Gakkai Shi J Jap Soc Grassl Sci — Nippon Sochi Gakkai Shi/ Journal. Japanese Society of Grassland Science
Nippon Stainless Tech Rep — Nippon Stainless Technical Report
Nippon Steel Tech Rep — Nippon Steel Technical Report
Nippon Steel Tech Rep (Jpn Ed) — Nippon Steel Technical Report (Japanese Edition)
Nippon Steel Tech Rep (Overseas) — Nippon Steel Technical Reports (Overseas)
NIPRORUDA Sb Nauchni Tr Ser Obogat — NIPRORUDA [*Nauchnoizsledovatelski i Proektantski Institut za Rudodobiv i Obogatyavane*] Sbornik Nauchni Trudove. Seriya. Obogatyavanne
NIPRSMS — National Institute of Polar Research. Special Map Series
NIQ — National Institute Economic Review [*London*]
NIR — Netherlands International Law Review
NIRED — New International Realities
N Ireland Rec Agr Res — Northern Ireland Record of Agricultural Research
N Ire LQ — Northern Ireland Legal Quarterly
N Ir Legal Q — Northern Ireland Legal Quarterly
N Ir LQ — Northern Ireland Legal Quarterly
NIRSA — NIRSA. Journal of the National Intramural-Recreational Sports Association
NISAA — Nippon Sakumotsu Gakkai Kiji
NISEA — Nippon Seirigaku Zasshi
NISGA — Nisshin Seiko Giho
NISHB — Nichidai Shigaku
Nishinihon J Dermatol — Nishinihon Journal of Dermatology
Nishinihon J Urol — Nishinihon Journal of Urology
Nissan Diesel Rev — Nissan Diesel Review [*Japan*]
Nisseki Tech Rev — Nisseki Technical Review [*Japan*]
Nisshin Steel Tech Rep — Nisshin Steel Technical Report
NIt — Nuova Italia
NITTA — Nauchno-Issledovatel'skie Trudy Tsentral'nogo Nauchno-Issledovatel'skogo Instituta Kozhevenno-Obuvnoi Promyshlennosti
NIW — Nieuw Israelitisch Weekblad
NIYB — New International Year Book
Nizkotemp Vak Materialoved — Nizkotemperaturnoe i Vakuumnoe Materialovedenie [*Ukrainian SSR*]
NIZO Nieuws — Nederlands Instituut voor Zuivelonderzoek Nieuws
NJ — Nas Jezik
NJ — New Judaea [*London*]
NJ — Niederdeutsches Jahrbuch
NJ — Northern Journal [*Atlin, British Columbia*]
NJA — Neue Jahrbuecher fuer das Klassische Altertum
NJAB — Neue Jahrbuecher fuer Antike und Deutsche Bildung
NJADB — Neue Jahrbuecher fuer Antike und Deutsche Bildung
NJAF — Northern Journal of Applied Forestry
NJ Ag — New Jersey Agriculture
NJ Ag Dept — New Jersey. Department of Agriculture. Publications
NJ Ag Exp — New Jersey. Agricultural Experiment Station. Publications
NJ Agr — New Jersey Agriculture
NJ Agr Expt Sta Bull — New Jersey. Agricultural Experiment Station. Bulletin
NJ Agric — New Jersey Agriculture
NJ Agric Exp Stn Bull — New Jersey. Agricultural Experiment Station. Bulletin
NJ Agric Exp Stn Circ — New Jersey. Agricultural Experiment Station. Circular
NJB — Nederlands Juristenblad
NJb — Neue Jahrbuecher fuer Wissenschaft und Jugendbildung
NJb — Niederdeutsches Jahrbuch
N Jb Beil Bd — Neues Jahrbuch fuer Mineralogie, Geologie, und Palaeontologie. Beilage Band
NJBEA Newsletter — New Jersey Business Education Association. Newsletter
NJBO — Nordic Journal of Botany

NJ Bur Geol Topogr Bull — New Jersey. Bureau of Geology and Topography. Bulletin
NJ Bus — New Jersey Business
NjbWJB — Neue Jahrbuecher fuer Wissenschaft und Jugendbildung
NJCHD — Nouveau Journal de Chimie
NJ Dep Conserv Econ Develop Geol Rep Ser — New Jersey. Department of Conservation and Economic Development. Geologic Report Series
NJ Dep Environ Prot Div Nat Resour Bur Geol Topogr Bull — New Jersey. Department of Environmental Protection. Division of Natural Resources. Bureau of Geology and Topography. Bulletin
NJ Div Water Policy Supply Spec Rep — New Jersey. Division of Water Policy and Supply. Special Report
NJ Div Water Policy Supply Water Resour Cir — New Jersey. Division of Water Policy and Supply. Water Resources Circular
NJ Dp Conservation An Rp — New Jersey. Department of Conservation and Development. Annual Report
NJDW — Neue Jahrbuecher fuer Deutsche Wissenschaft
NJe — Nas Jezik
NJE — Nebraska Journal of Economics and Business
NJE — Nigerian Journal of Economic and Social Studies
NJESS — Nigerian Journal of Economic and Social Studies
NJ Geol Topogr Bull — New Jersey. Bureau of Geology and Topography. Bulletin
NJGKA — Nippon Jinzo Gakkaishi
NJ G S — New Jersey. Geological Survey
NJH — New Jersey History
NJ His S — New Jersey Historical Society. Proceedings
NJ His S Col — New Jersey Historical Society. Collections
NJ Hist — New Jersey History
NJHistS — New Jersey Historical Society. Proceedings
NJHS — New Jersey Historical Society. Proceedings
NJHSP — New Jersey Historical Society. Proceedings
NJIGA — Nippon Jibi-Inko-Ka Gakkai Kaiho Kaiho
NJ J Pharm — New Jersey. Journal of Pharmacy
NJK — Nastava Jezika i Knjizevnosti u Srednoj Skoli
NJKA — Neue Jahrbuecher fuer das Klassische Altertum
NJKAGDL — Neue Jahrbuecher fuer das Klassische Altertum, Geschichte, und Deutsche Literatur
NJL — Nordic Journal of Linguistics
NJ Law — New Jersey Lawyer
NJ Law J — New Jersey Law Journal
NJ Lawy — New Jersey Lawyer
NJ League Nurs News — New Jersey League for Nursing. News
NJ Lib — New Jersey Libraries
NJ Libr — New Jersey Libraries
NJLJ — New Jersey Law Journal
NJM — National Jewish Monthly
NJM — Neue Juedische Monatshefte
NJM — Nouvelles Juives Mondiales [*Paris*]
NJMIA — Neues Jahrbuch fuer Mineralogie. Abhandlungen
NJN — Neue Juedische Nachrichten
NJ Nurse — New Jersey Nurse
NJOG — Northern Offshore. Norwegian Journal of Oil and Gas
N Jour Med Chir Pharm (Paris) — Nouveau Journal de Medecine, Chirurgie, et Pharmacie (Paris)
N Jour Pharm (Leipzig) — Neues Journal der Pharmacie fuer Aerzte Apotheker und Chemiker (Leipzig)
NJP — Nederlandse Jurisprudentie. Uitspraken in Burgerlijke en Strafzaken
NJP — Neue Jahrbuecher fuer Paedogogik
NJS — Norwegian Bankers Association. Financial Review
NJ Sch Libn — New Jersey School Librarian
NJSNA News — NJSNA [*New Jersey State Nurses Association*] Newsletter [*Later, New Jersey Nurse*]
NJSNA Newsl — NJSNA [*New Jersey State Nurses Association*] Newsletter [*Later, New Jersey Nurse*]
NJSRB — Netherlands Journal of Sea Research
NJSUD — Netherlands Journal of Surgery
NJUGA — Nippon Junkanki Gakushi
NJUZA9 — Japanese Journal of Veterinary Science
NJW — Neue Jahrbuecher fuer Wissenschaft und Jugendbildung
NJW — Neue Juristische Wochenschrift
NJ Water Resour Spec Rep — New Jersey. Division of Water Resources. Special Report
NJWJ — Neue Jahrbuecher fuer Wissenschaft und Jugendbildung
NK — Narodna Kultura [*Sofia*]
NK — Nasza Ksiegarnia
NK — New Korea
NK — Nowe Kultura
NK — Numizmatikai Koezloeny
NK — Nyelvtudomanyi Koezlemenyek
NKAKB — Nippon Kagaku Kaishi
NKCHD — Nippon Kikai Gakkai Ronbunshu. C Hen
NKEZA — Nippon Koshu Eisei Zasshi
NKEZA4 — Japanese Journal of Public Health
NKGAD — Nippon Kikai Gakkai Ronbunshu. A Hen
NKGBD — Nippon Kikai Gakkai Ronbunshu. B Hen

NKGRB — Nippon Kenchiku Gakkai Ronbun Hokoku-shu
NKGWG — Nachrichten. Koeniglich Gesellschaft der Wissenschaften zu Goettingen
NKHJ — Nederlandsch Kunsthistorisch Jaarboek
NKHOAK — Bulletin. Agricultural Chemicals Inspection Station [*Tokyo*]
NKKGAB — Japanese Poultry Science
NKKOB — Nara Kogyo Koto Senmon Gakko Kenkyu Kiyo
NKOGA — Nippon Kokoka Gakkai Zasshi
NKOKD — Nichidai Koko Kagaku
NKRA — Neue Keilschriftliche Rechtsurkunden aus der el-Amarna-Zeit [*Koschaker*]
NKS — Nederlandsche Katholieke Stemmen
NKs — Nowe Ksiazki
NKSA — Newsletter. Kafka Society of America
NKSHB — Naikai-Ku Suisan Kenkyusho Kenkyu Hokoku
NKSKA — Nippon Kagaku Seni Kenkyusho Koenshu
NKT — Norske Klassiker-Tekster
NKT — Nursery and Kindergarten Teachers
NKTAD — Journal. Gyeongsang National University. Natural Sciences
NKTRA — Nippon Kokan Technical Reports Overseas
Nku — Naamkunde
NKYLR — Northern Kentucky Law Review
N KY L Rev — Northern Kentucky Law Review
NKYRA — Nippon Kyobu Rinsho
NKyrKTs — Ny Kyrklig Tidsskrift [*Uppsala*]
NKYZA2 — Japanese Journal of Thoracic Diseases
NKZ — Neue Kirchliche Zeitschrift
NKZAA — Nippon Kyobu Geka Gakkai Zasshi
NKZKA — Nippon Kinzoku Gakkai Kaiho
NL — New Law Journal
NL — New Leader
NL — Norwiny Literackie
NL — Nouvelles Litteraires
NL — Numismatic Literature
NLA — Norsk Litteraer Aarbok
NLauR — New Laurel Review
NLB — Newberry Library. Bulletin
NLB — Numismatisches Literatur-Blatt
NLC — New London Commentary
NLCHAIBS — Newberry Library. Center for the History of the American Indian. Bibliographical Series
NLE — Nuclear Engineering International
NLGI Spokesman — NLGI [*National Lubricating Grease Institute*] Spokesman
NLH — New Literary History
NLing — Notes on Linguistics
NListy — Numismaticke Listy
NLit — Neue Literatur
NLiW — Nowiny Literackie i Wydawnicze
NLJMA — Netherlands Journal of Medicine
NLL Rev — NLL Review
NLM — Neues Lausitzisches Magazin
NLMC — National Library of Medicine. Current Catalog
NLN — Neo-Latin News [*Queens College*]
NLN Publ — National League for Nursing. Publications
NLPGA Times — National LP-Gas Association Times [*United States*]
NLR — Dine Bizaad Nanil' Iih/Navajo Language Review
NLR — National Review (London)
Nl Res Men Health & Behav Sc — Newsletter for Research in Mental Health and Behavioral Sciences
N L Rev — New Literature Review
NLS — Natuur en Milieu
NLTSD — National Times
NLWJ — National Library of Wales. Journal
NLW Journ — National Library of Wales. Journal
NLZ — Numismatische Literatur-Zeitung
NM — National Music Council. Bulletin
NM — Naval Magazine
NM — Neuphilologische Mitteilungen
NM — Niederdeutsche Mitteilungen
NM — Northern Miner
NM — Northern Miscellany
NM — Numismatiska Meddelanden
NMAA Newsletter — Nursing Mothers' Association of Australia. Newsletter
NM Acad Sci Bull — New Mexico Academy of Science. Bulletin
NMAG — Naval Magazine
NM Ag Exp — New Mexico. Agricultural Experiment Station. Publications
NM Agric Exp Stn Bull — New Mexico. Agricultural Experiment Station. Bulletin
NM Agric Exp Stn Res Rep — New Mexico. Agricultural Experiment Station. Research Report
NMA Journal — National Microfilm Association. Journal
NMAL — Notes on Modern American Literature
NMBJD — New Mexico Business Journal
NM Bur Mines Miner Resour Bull — New Mexico. Bureau of Mines and Mineral Resources. Bulletin

NM Bur Mines Miner Resour Cir — New Mexico. Bureau of Mines and Mineral Resources. Circular
NM Bur Mines Miner Resour Circ — New Mexico. Bureau of Mines and Mineral Resources. Circular
NM Bur Mines Miner Resour Hydrol Rep — New Mexico. Bureau of Mines and Mineral Resources. Hydrologic Report
NM Bur Mines Miner Resour Mem — New Mexico. Bureau of Mines and Mineral Resources. Memoir
NM Bur Mines Miner Resour Miner Resour Rep — New Mexico. Bureau of Mines and Mineral Resources. Mineral Resources Report
NM Bur Mines Miner Resour Prog Rep — New Mexico. Bureau of Mines and Mineral Resources. Progress Report
NM Bur Mines Miner Resour Target Explor Rep — New Mexico. Bureau of Mines and Mineral Resources. Target Exploration Report
NM Bur Mines Miner Rsour Ground Water Rep — New Mexico. Bureau of Mines and Mineral Resources. Ground Water Report
NM Bus J — New Mexico Business Journal
NMC — Nuclear Medicine Communications
NMC Bul — National Music Council. Bulletin
NMCCFCS — National Museum of Man. Mercury Series. Canadian Centre for Folk Culture Studies. Papers
NMCMASC — National Museums of Canada. Mercury Series. Archaeological Survey of Canada. Papers
NMCMCES — National Museums of Canada. National Museum of Man. Mercury Series. Canadian Ethnology Service. Papers
NMCMED — National Museums of Canada. Mercury Series. Ethnology Division. Papers
NMCPA — National Museums of Canada. Publications in Archaeology
NMCPB — National Museums of Canada. Publications in Botany
NMCPBO — National Museums of Canada. Publications in Biological Oceanography
NMCPE — National Museums of Canada. Publications in Ethnology
NMCPFC — National Museums of Canada. Publications in Folk Culture
NMCPZ — National Museums of Canada. Publications in Zoology
NMD — Nahost und Mittelostverein eV. Rundschreiben
NM Dent J — New Mexico Dental Journal
NMDJA — Netherlands Milk and Dairy Journal
NMDTA — Novosti Meditsinskoi Tekhniki
NME — New Middle East [London]
NMEIA — Nauchnye Trudy Moskovskogo Inzhenerno-Ekonomicheskogo Instituta
NMessenger — Numismatic Messenger
N Mex Bur Mines Mineral Resources Bull — New Mexico State Bureau of Mines and Mineral Resources. Bulletin
N Mex Bur Mines Mineral Resources Mem — New Mexico State Bureau of Mines and Mineral Resources. Memoir
N Mex Bus — New Mexico Business
N Mex Ext N — New Mexico Extension News
N Mex Ext News N Mex State Univ Agr Ext Serv — New Mexico Extension News. New Mexico State University. Agricultural Extension Service
N Mex Geol — New Mexico Geology
N Mex Lib — New Mexico Libraries
N Mex L Rev — New Mexico Law Review
N Mex Miner — New Mexico Miner
N Mex State Engineer Office Tech Rept — New Mexico State Engineer Office. Technical Report
NM Ext News — New Mexico Extension News
N Mex Univ B G S — New Mexico University. Bulletin. Geological Series
N Mex Univ Pubs Geology Pubs Meteoritics — New Mexico University. Publications in Geology. Publications in Meteoritics
NMFR — New Mexico Folklore Record
NMG — New Management
NM Geol — New Mexico Geology
NM Geol Soc Annu Field Conf Guideb — New Mexico Geological Society. Annual Field Conference Guidebook
NM Geol Soc Field Conf Guideb — New Mexico Geological Society. Field Conference Guidebook
NM Geol Soc Guideb Annu Field Conf — New Mexico Geological Society. Guidebook of Annual Field Conference
NM Geol Soc Spec Publ — New Mexico Geological Society. Special Publication
NMGGA — Field Conference Guidebook. New Mexico Geological Society
NMGTA — Nederlands Militair Geneeskundig Tijdschrift
NMH — Newcastle Morning Herald
NM His R — New Mexico Historical Review
NMHQ — New Mexico Historical Quarterly
NMHR — New Mexico Historical Review
NMHUJ — New Mexico Highlands University. Journal
NMi — Neuphilologische Mitteilungen
NMIA — Norske Meteorologiske Institutt. Meteorologiske Annaler
NMIMA — Norske Meteorologiske Institutt. Meteorologiske Annaler
NMIRA — Nursing Mirror
NMis — Nova Misao
N Mitt — Neuphilologische Mitteilungen
NML — New Mexico Law Review
NM Lib Newsl — New Mexico Libraries. Newsletter

NMLR — New Mexico Law Review
NML Rev — New Mexico Law Review
NML Tech J — NML [National Metallurgical Laboratory] Technical Journal
NMM — Nuclear Methods Monographs [Elsevier Book Series]
NMMMA — Memoir. New Mexico Bureau of Mines and Mineral Resources
NM Nurse — New Mexico Nurse
NMo — Neuphilologische Monatsschrift
N Mon — Neuphilologische Monatsschrift
NMQ — New Mexico Quarterly
NMQR — New Mexico Quarterly. Review
NMR — New Magazine Review
NMR — New Mexico Review
NMRNB — Nuclear Magnetic Resonance
NMS — Nottingham Medieval Studies
NMSCS — Northwest Missouri State College Studies
NM Sol Energy Assoc Southwest Bull — New Mexico Solar Energy Association. Southwest Bulletin
NM State Bur Mines Miner Resour Annu Rep — New Mexico State Bureau of Mines and Mineral Resources. Annual Report
NM State Bur Mines Miner Resour Bull — New Mexico State Bureau of Mines and Mineral Resources. Bulletin
NM State Bur Mines Miner Resour Circ — New Mexico State Bureau of Mines and Mineral Resources. Circular
NM State Bur Mines Miner Resour Geol Map — New Mexico State Bureau of Mines and Mineral Resources. Geologic Map
NM State Bur Mines Miner Resour Mem — New Mexico State Bureau of Mines and Mineral Resources. Memoir
NM State Eng Basic Data Rep — New Mexico State Engineer. Basic Data Report
N Munster Antiq J — North Munster Antiquarian Journal
N Music R — New Music Review
NMW — Notes on Mississippi Writers
NM Wildl — New Mexico Wildlife
NN — New Nigerian
NN — News of the North
NN — Nucleosides and Nucleotides
NN — Numismatic News Weekly
NNA — Nordisk Numismatisk Arsskrift
NNAP — New Native People
NNb — Numismatisches Nachrichtenblatt. Organ des Verbandes der Deutschen Muenzvereine
NNBYA — Nature: New Biology
NNF Nytt — NNF. Nytt Meddelelser fra Norsk Numismatisk Forening
NNGNA — Novosti Neftyanoi i Gazovoi Tekhniki, Neftepererabotka, i Neftekhimiya
NNGZAZ — Folia Endocrinologica Japonica
NNGZB — Neujahrsblatt. Naturforschende Gesellschaft in Zuerich
NNH — Neuva Narrativa Hispanoamericana
NNKKAA — Journal. Agricultural Chemical Society of Japan
NNKKB — Nainen Kikan
NNM — Neueste Nachrichten aus dem Morgenlande
NNM — Numismatic Notes and Monographs
NNNE — Nigiqpaq Northwind News [Barrow, Alaska]
NNPPA — Neurologia, Neurochirurgia, i Psychiatria Polska
NNRF — Nouvelle Nouvelle Revue Francaise
NNUM — Nordisk Numismatisk Unions Medlemsblad
NNVPA — Nauchni Trudove. Nauchnoizsledovatelski Institut po Vinarska i Pivovarna Promishlenost
NO — Narodnoe Obrazovanie [Moscow]
NO — National Observer
NO — Neurooncology [Elsevier Book Series]
NO — New Orient [Prague]
NO — New Outlook [Tel Aviv]
No — Notes
N O — Nouvel Observateur
NO — Nova Obzorija
N O — Novy Orient. Casopis Orientalniho Ustava v Praze
NOAA Tech Rep NMFS Circ — NOAA [National Oceanic and Atmospheric Administration] Technical Report. NMFS [National Marine Fisheries Service] Circular
NOAA Tech Rep NMFS SSRF — NOAA [National Oceanic and Atmospheric Administration] Technical Report. NMFS [National Marine Fisheries Service] SSRF [Special Scientific Report Fisheries]
NOAF — Northern Affairs. Ontario Ministry of Northern Affairs
Noah's Ark Toy Libr Handicapped Child Newsletter — Noah's Ark Toy Library for Handicapped Children. Newsletter
NOALA — Nova Acta Leopoldina
No Am — North American Review
No Am R — North American Review
No Am Rev — North American Review
NOAR — Norwegian Archaeological Review
NoB — Namn och Bygd
NOB — New Orient Bimonthly
NOB — Norges Bank. Economic Bulletin
Nobel Symp — Nobel Symposium
NOBKSS — Norges Bank. Skrifter Series

No Brit — North British Review
NoC — Nouveaux Cahiers
No Ca Fo — North Carolina Folklore
No Cages — No More Cages
No Car Hist Rev — North Carolina Historical Review
No Car Law Rev — North Carolina Law Review
NOCOA — Noise Control
No Cordilleran — Northern Cordilleran
NOD — News of the Day
No Dak Hist — North Dakota History
No Dak Hist Quar — North Dakota Historical Quarterly
No Dak Quar — North Dakota Quarterly
NODE — Northern Development, Incorporating Arctic Digest
No D Law — Notre Dame Law Review
No East As J Theo — Northeast Asia Journal of Theology
NoEF — Northeast Folklore
NOEN — Northern Engineer
Noerdlinger Bienenztg — Noerdlinger Bienenzeitung
Noevenyved Kutato Intez Evkoen (Budapest) — Noevenyvedelmi Kutato Intezet Evkoenyve (Budapest)
Noevenyved Tud Tanacskozas Koezlem — Noevenyved Tudomanyos Tanacskozas Koezlemenyei
NOG — Northern Offshore. Norwegian Journal of Oil and Gas
Nogaku Iho Agric Bull Saga Univ Nogaku-Bu — Nogaku Iho. Agricultural Bulletin of Saga University. Saga Daigaku. Nogaku-Bu
Nogaku Shusho J Agric Sci (Setagoya) — Nogaku Shuho. Journal of Agricultural Science (Setagoya)
NOGDA — Nogyo Doboku Gakkai-Shi
NOGS Log — New Orleans Geographical Society. Log
NOGT — Norsk Geologisk Tidsskrift
NOGU — Norges Geologiske Undersoekelse
NOGUA — Noguchi Kenkyusho Jiho
Nogyo Doboku Shikenjo Hokoku Bull Natl Res Inst Agric Eng — Nogyo Doboku Shikenjo Hokoku/Bulletin. National Research Institute of Agricultural Engineering
Nogyo Gijutsu J Agric — Nogyo Gijutsu/Journal of Agricultural Science
Nogyo Kikai Gakkai Shi J Soc Agric Mach — Nogyo Kikai Gakkai Shi/Journal. Society of Agricultural Machinery [Japan]
Nogyo Oyobi Engei/Agric Hortic — Nogyo Oyobi Engei/Agriculture and Horticulture
N Ohio Bus — Northern Ohio Business Journal
NOHO — Northern Housing
NOHY — Nordic Hydrology
NOIRB — Non-Ionizing Radiation
No Ire L Q — Northern Ireland Legal Quarterly
Noise Control Eng — Noise Control Engineering
Noise Control Eng J — Noise Control Engineering Journal
Noise Control Engrg — Noise Control Engineering
Noise Control Vib — Noise Control, Vibration Isolation [Later, Noise and Vibration Control Worldwide]
Noise Control Vib Isol — Noise Control, Vibration Isolation [Later, Noise and Vibration Control Worldwide]
Noise Control and Vib Reduct — Noise Control and Vibration Reduction
Noise Control Vibr Reduct — Noise Control and Vibration Reduction [Later, Noise and Vibration Control Worldwide]
Noise Vib Bull — Noise and Vibration Bulletin
Noise Vib Control — Noise and Vibration Control
Noise & Vib Control Worldwide — Noise and Vibration Control Worldwide
Noise Vibr Contr Worldwide — Noise and Vibration Control Worldwide
NOJB — Norwegian Journal of Botany
NOJOA — Nordisk Jordbrugsforskning
NOJZ — Norwegian Journal of Zoology
NOKIAB — Journal of Agricultural Meteorology
NOLD — Northland
NOLI — Northern Lights. Diocese of Yukon
Nom — Nomisma. Untersuchungen auf dem Gebiete der Antiken Munskunde
NoM — Novyj Mir
Nomencl Chim — Nomenclatura Chimica
No Miner — Northern Miner
Nom Khron — Nomismatika Khronika
Nomograficheskii Sb — Nomograficheskii Sbornik
Nomos — Nomos. Yearbook of the American Society of Political and Legal Philosophy
Non-Destr T — Non-Destructive Testing
Non-Destr Test — Non-Destructive Testing
Non-Destr Test (Aust) — Non-Destructive Testing (Australia)
Nondestr Test (Chicago) — Non-Destructive Testing (Chicago)
Non-Destr Test (Guilford Eng) — Non-Destructive Testing (Guilford, England)
Non-Destr Test Int — Non-Destructive Testing International
Non-Dest Test — Non-Destructive Testing
Non-Ferrous Met (China) — Non-Ferrous Metals (China)
NonFMerch — Non-Foods Merchandising
Non-Ioniz Radiat — Non-Ionizing Radiation
Nonlinear Anal — Nonlinear Analysis
Nonlinear Anal Theory Methods and Appl — Nonlinear Analysis Theory. Methods and Applications

Nonlinear Vibr Probl — Nonlinear Vibration Problems
Nonmet Miner Process — Nonmetallic Minerals Processing
Nonmunjip Inha Tech Jr Coll — Nonmunjip. Inha Technical Junior College
Nonwoven Pat Dig — Nonwoven Patents Digest
Nonwovn In — Nonwovens Industry
NOP — New Orleans Poetry Journal
NOPA — Norsk Polar Institutt. Aarbok
NOPE — Northern Perspectives. Canadian Arctic Resources Committee
NOPH — Norsk Polar Institutt. Polarhandbok
NOPM — Norsk Polar Institutt. Meddelelser
NOPS — Norsk Polarinstitutt. Skrifter
NOPSA — Nordisk Psykologi
NOQ — Northwest Ohio Quarterly
NOR — New Orleans Review
NOR — Normalisatie
Nor — Norseman [London]
NoR — Northern Review
NORA — Northern Raven
Nor Apotekerforen Tidsskr — Norges Apotekerforenings Tidsskrift
Nor Arch Rev — Norwegian Archaeological Review
Nord — Nordia
Nord Adm Tss — Nordisk Administrativt Tidsskrift
Nord Betong — Nordisk Betong
Nord Bitidskr — Nordisk Bitidskr
Nord Bl Chem — Nordische Blaetter fuer die Chemie
Nord Datanytt Data — Nordisk Datanytt Med Data
Nordd J Mv G — Norddeutsches Jahrbuch fuer Muenzkunde und Verwandte Gebiete
Norddtsch Farben Ztg — Norddeutsche Farben Zeitung
Nordeuropaeisk Mejeri-Tidsskr — Nordeuropaeisk Mejeri-Tidsskrift
Nord Fotohist Jl — Nordisk Fotohistorisk Journal
Nord Hydrol — Nordic Hydrology
Nord Hyg Tidskr — Nordisk Hygienisk Tidskrift
Nord Hyg Tidskr Suppl — Nordisk Hygienisk Tidskrift. Supplementum
Nordic Hydrol — Nordic Hydrology
Nordisk Mat Tidskr — Nordisk Matematisk Tidskrift
Nordisk Tid — Nordisk Tidskrift foer Bok- och Biblioteksvaesen
Nordisk Tids Bok & Bibl — Nordisk Tidskrift foer Bok- och Biblioteksvaesen
Nord Jordbrforsk — Nordisk Jordbrugsforskning
Nord Jordbrugsforsk — Nordisk Jordbrugsforskning
Nord Jordbrugsforsk Suppl — Nordisk Jordbrugsforskning. Supplement
Nord Med — Nordisk Medicin
Nord Med Ark — Nordiskt Medicinskt Arkiv
Nord Med Ark Afd 2 Med — Nordiskt Medicinskt Arkiv Afdeling 2. Inre Medicine Arkiv foer Inre Medicin
Nord Medicinhist Arsb — Nordisk Medicinhistorisk Aarsbok
Nord Med Tidskr — Nordisk Medicinsk Tidskrift
Nord Mejeri Tidsskr — Nordisk Mejeri Tidsskrift
Nord Mus — Nordisk Musikkultur
Nord Psykiatr Tidsskr — Nordisk Psykiatrisk Tidsskrift
Nord Psykol — Nordisk Psykologi
Nord Tid — Nordisk Tidskrift foer Bok- och Biblioteksvaesen
Nord Tidskr — Nordisk Tidskrift foer Bok- och Biblioteksvaesen
Nord Tidskr Dov — Nordisk Tidskrift foer Dovundervisningen
Nord Tidskr Fotogr — Nordisk Tidskrift foer Fotografi
Nord Tidskr f Filol — Nordisk Tidsskrift foer Filologi
Nord Tidskr Medicotek — Nordisk Tidskrift foer Medicoteknik
Nord Tidskr f Vetensk — Nordisk Tidskrift foer Vetenskap, Konst, och Industri
Nord Tidsskr Kriminalvidensk — Nordisk Tidsskrift foer Kriminalvidenskab
Nord Tidsskr Logop Foniat — Nordisk Tidsskrift foer Logopedi og Foniatri
Nord Utredningsser — Nordisk Utredningsserie
Nord Veterinaermed — Nordisk Veterinaermedicin
Nord Veterinaermed Suppl — Nordisk Veterinaermedicin. Supplementum
Nord Vetmed — Nordisk Veterinaermedicin
Nordwestdt Imkerztg — Nordwestdeutsche Imkerzeitung
NORED — Norsk Olje Revy
Norelco Rep — Norelco Reporter
Nor Entomol Tidsskr — Norsk Entomologisk Tidsskrift
Nor Fag Foto — Norsk Fag Foto
Nor Farm Tidsskr — Norsk Farmaceutisk Tidsskrift
Nor Fisk — Norges Fiskerier
Nor Fiskeritid — Norsk Fiskeritidende
Norfolk Arch — Norfolk Archaeology
Norfolk Archaeol — Norfolk Archaeology
Nor Fotogr Tidsskr — Norsk Fotografisk Tidsskrift
Nor Geol Tidsskr — Norsk Geologisk Tidsskrift
Nor Geol Unders — Norges Geologiske Undersoekelse
Nor Geol Unders Bull — Norges Geologiske Undersoekelse. Bulletin
Nor Geol Unders Skr — Norges Geologiske Undersoekelse. Skrifter
Norges Bank Econ Bul — Norges Bank. Economic Bulletin
Norg Geol Unders (Publ) — Norges Geologiske Undersoekelse (Publikasjoner)
Norg Geotek Inst Publ — Norges Geotekniske Institut. Publikasjon [Oslo]
Nor Hvalfanst Tid — Norsk-Hvalfangst-Tidende
Nor Inst Tang- Tareforsk Rep — Norsk Institutt for Tang- og Tareforskning. Report
NORJ — Northward Journal

NORL — Northian Newsletter
Nor Landbrukshogsk Foringsforsok Beret — Norges Landbrukshogskole Foringsforsokene Beretning
N Orl Med and S J — New Orleans Medical and Surgical Journal
Nor Lovtid — Norsk Lovtidend
Nor Lovtid Avd I — Norsk Lovtidend Avdeling I [*Norway*]
Nor Mag Laegevidensk — Norsk Magasin foer Laegevidenskapen
Norm Instr and Prim Plans — Normal Instructor and Primary Plans
Norm Pathol Anat (Stuttg) — Normale und Pathologische Anatomie (Stuttgart)
Nor Myrselsk Medd — Norske Myrselskap. Meddelelser
Nor Nat — Norsk Natur
NOROD — Noroil
Nor Olje Revy — Norsk Olje Revy
Noro-Psikiyatri Ars — Noro-Psikiyatri Arsivi
NORP — Norpic
Nor Pelsdyrbl — Norsk Pelsdyrblad
Nor Polarinst Aarbok — Norsk Polarinstitutt. Aarbok
Nor Polarinst Medd — Norsk Polarinstitutt. Meddelelser
Nor Polarinst Polarhandb — Norsk Polarinstitutt. Polarhandbok
Nor Polarinst Skr — Norsk Polarinstitutt. Skrifter
Nor Prin — Northern Principal
Norrlands Skogsvforb Tidskr (Stockh) — Norrlands Skogsvardsforbunds Tidskrift (Stockholm)
NORS — Norseman
Norsk Entomol Tidsskr — Norsk Entomologisk Tidsskrift
Norsk Ent Tidsskr — Norsk Entomologisk Tidsskrift
Norske Vid-Akad Oslo Mat-Natur Kl Skr — Norske Videnskaps-Akademi i Oslo. Matematisk-Naturvidenskapelig Klasse. Skrifter
Norske Vid Selsk Forh (Trondheim) — Kongelige Norske Videnskabers Selskabs. Foerhandlinger (Trondheim)
Norske Vid Selsk Skr (Trondheim) — Kongelige Norske Videnskabers Selskabs. Skrifter (Trondheim)
Norsk Geogr Tidsskr — Norsk Geografisk Tidsskrift
Norsk Geog Tid — Norsk Geografisk Tidsskrift
Norsk Geol — Norsk Geologisk Tidsskrift
Norsk Geol Tids — Norsk Geologisk Tidsskrift
Norsk Geol Tidsskr — Norsk Geologisk Tidsskrift
Norsk Hagetid — Norsk Hagetidend
Norskind — Norsk Skogindustri
Norsk Mag Laegevidensk — Norsk Magazin foer Laegevidenskaben
Norsk Mus — Norsk Musikerblad
Nor Skogbruk — Norsk Skogbruk
Nor Skogind — Norsk Skogindustri
Norsk Polarinst Aarbok — Norsk Polarinstitutt. Aarbok
Norsk Skog — Norsk Skogindustri
Norsk Skogbr — Norsk Skogbruk
Norsk Vet-Tidsskr — Norsk Veterinaer-Tidsskrift
NORT — North
Nor Tannlaegeforen Tid — Norske Tannlaegeforenings Tidende
Nor Tek Naturvitensk Forskningsrad Metall Kom Medd — Norges Teknisk Naturvitenskapelige Forskningsrad. Metallurgisk Komite. Meddelelse
Nor Tek Vitenskapsakad Medd — Norges Tekniske Vitenskapsakademi. Meddelelse
North Amer Fauna — North American Fauna
North Am Flora — North American Flora
North Am Flora Ser II — North American Flora. Series II
North Am Gladiolus Counc Bull — North American Gladiolus Council. Bulletin
North Am Pomona — North American Pomona
North Am Pract — North American Practitioner
Northamptonshire Archaeol — Northamptonshire Archaeology
North Am R — North American Review
North Am Vet — North American Veterinarian
North Carolina Cent LJ — North Carolina Central Law Journal
North Carolina Div Ground Water Ground Water Bull — North Carolina. Department of Water and Air Resources. Division of Ground Water. Ground Water Bulletin
North Carolina Div Mineral Resources Geol Map Ser — North Carolina. Department of Conservation and Development. Division of Mineral Resources. Geologic Map Series
North Carolina Div Mineral Resources Inf Circ — North Carolina. Department of Conservation and Development. Division of Mineral Resources. Information Circular
North Carolina Div Mineral Resources Spec Pub — North Carolina. Department of Conservation and Development. Division of Mineral Resources. Special Publication
North Carolina Lib — North Carolina Libraries
North Cavern Mine Res Soc Occas Publ — Northern Cavern and Mine Research Society. Occasional Publication
North Cent Assn Q — North Central Association. Quarterly
North Cent Reg Ext Publ — North Central Regional Extension Publication
North Co — North Country Anvil
North Country Lib — North Country Libraries
North Dakota Acad Sci Proc — North Dakota Academy of Science. Proceedings
North Dakota Geol Survey Bull — North Dakota. Geological Survey. Bulletin

North Dakota Geol Survey Misc Map — North Dakota. Geological Survey. Miscellaneous Map
North Dakota Geol Survey Misc Ser — North Dakota. Geological Survey. Miscellaneous Series
North Dakota Geol Survey Rept Inv — North Dakota. Geological Survey. Report of Investigations
North Dakota L Rev — North Dakota Law Review
North East Coast Inst Eng Shipbuild Trans — North East Coast Institution of Engineers and Shipbuilders. Transactions
Northeast Electron Res Eng Meet Rec — Northeast Electronics Research and Engineering Meeting Record
Northeastern Ind World — Northeastern Industrial World
Northeast Geol — Northeastern Geology
Northeast Gulf Sci — Northeast Gulf Science
Northeast Wood Util Counc Inc Bull — Northeastern Wood Utilization Council, Incorporated. Bulletin
North Eng (Fairbanks) — Northern Engineer (Fairbanks)
Northern Archt — Northern Architect
Northern Cal R Bus and Econ — Northern California Review of Business and Economics
Northern Hist — Northern History [*England*]
Northern Ireland Lib — Northern Ireland Libraries
Northern KY Law R — Northern Kentucky Law Review
Northern L — Northern Lights
Northern Logger — Northern Logger and Timber Processor
Northern Scot — Northern Scotland
Northern Stud — Northern Studies [*England*]
North Fur Trade — Northern Fur Trade
North Hist — Northern History
North-Holland Math Library — North-Holland Mathematical Library
North-Holland Math Stud — North-Holland Mathematics Studies [*Elsevier Book Series*]
North-Holland Math Studies — North-Holland Mathematics Studies
North Holland Ser in Appl Math and Mech — North-Holland Series in Applied Mathematics and Mechanics
North-Holland Ser Appl Math Mech — North-Holland Series in Applied Mathematics and Mechanics [*Elsevier Book Series*]
North Holland Ser Gen Systems Res — North-Holland Series in General Systems Research
North Holland Ser System Sci Engrg — North-Holland Series in Systems Science and Engineering
North Holland Syst Control Ser — North-Holland Systems and Control Series
North Ireland LQ — Northern Ireland Legal Quarterly
North Irel Mem Geol Surv — Northern Ireland. Memoirs. Geological Survey
North Irel Minist Agric Annu Rep Res Tech Work — North Ireland Ministry of Agriculture. Annual Report on Research and Technical Work
North Irel Minist Agric Rec Agric Res — North Ireland Ministry of Agriculture. Record of Agricultural Research
North Irel Minist Agric Rec Agricultural Res — Northern Ireland. Ministry of Agriculture. Record of Agricultural Research
North KY LR — Northern Kentucky Law Review
North Log Timber Process — Northern Logger and Timber Processer
North Miner — Northern Miner
North Nigeria Reg Res Stn Tech Rep — Northern Nigeria. Regional Research Station. Technical Report
North Nut Grow Assoc Annu Rep — Northern Nut Growers Association. Annual Report
North Offshore — Northern Offshore
North Pac Fur Seal Comm Proc Annu Meet — North Pacific Fur Seal Commission. Proceedings of the Annual Meeting
North Queensl Conf Australas Inst Min Metall — North Queensland Conference. Australasian Institute of Mining and Metallurgy
North Queensl Nat — North Queensland Naturalist
North R — Northern Review
North Rhod Geol Surv Bull — Northern Rhodesia. Geological Survey. Bulletin
North Rhod Geol Surv Rep — Northern Rhodesia. Geological Survey. Report
Northrop ULJ Aero Energy and Envt — Northrop University. Law Journal of Aerospace, Energy, and the Environment
North Scot — Northern Scotland
North Staffordshire J Field Stud — North Staffordshire Journal of Field Studies
North Stud — Northern Studies
North UL Rev — Northwestern University. Law Review
Northwest Anthropol Res Notes — Northwest Anthropological Research Notes
Northwest Dent — Northwest Dentistry
Northwestern J Internat Law and Bus — Northwestern Journal of International Law and Business
Northwestern UL Rev — Northwestern University. Law Review
Northwestern Univ Dept Geography Studies Geography — Northwestern University. Department of Geography. Studies in Geography
Northwestern Univ Law R — Northwestern University. Law Review
Northwestern Univ L Rev — Northwestern University. Law Review
Northwest Geol — Northwest Geology
Northwest J Int'l L & Bus — Northwestern Journal of International Law and Business
Northwest Lancet — Northwestern Lancet

Northwest Livestock Dir — Northwest Livestock Directory
Northwest Lumberman — Northwestern Lumberman
Northwest Med — Northwest Medicine
Northwest Miller — Northwestern Miller
North West Newsl — North Western Newsletter
Northwest Ohio Q — Northwest Ohio Quarterly
Northwest Sci — Northwest Science
Northwest Univ Dent Res Grad Study Bull — Northwestern University. Dental Research and Graduate Study Bulletin
Northw L Rev — Northwestern University. Law Review
Northw Ohio Quar — Northwest Ohio Quarterly
Northw U La — Northwestern University. Law Review
Northw Univ Law Rev — Northwestern University. Law Review
Norton — Norton's Literary Letter
Nor Tr Bul — Norwegian Trade Bulletin
NorTTs — Norsk Teologisk Tidsskrift [*Oslo*]
NORV — Norveg. Journal of Norwegian Ethnology
Nor Vel — Norges Vel
Nor Veritas Publ — Norske Veritas. Publication
Nor Veterinaertidsskr — Norsk Veterinaertidsskrift
Nor Vet-Tidsskr — Norsk Veterinaer-Tidsskrift
Nor Vidensk-Akad Oslo Arbok — Norske Videnskaps-Akademi i Oslo. Aarbok
Nor Vidensk-Akad Oslo Mat Natur Kl N Ser — Norske Videnskaps-Akademi i Oslo. Matematisk-Naturvidenskapelig Klasse. Skrifter. Ny Serie
Nor Vidensk-Akad Skr — Norske Videnskaps-Akademi. Skrifter
Nor Vidensk Selsk Mus Misc — Norske Videnskabers Selskab. Museet. Miscellanea
Nor VVS — Norsk VVS [*Norsk Forening foer Varme-, Ventilasjon-, og Sanitaerteknikk*] [*Norway*]
Norw Archaeol Rev — Norwegian Archaeological Review
Norway Geol Undersoekelse Bull — Norway. Geologiske Undersoekelse. Bulletin
Norwegian — Norwegian American Commerce
Norwegian-Am Stud and Rec — Norwegian-American Studies and Records
Norwegian Commer Banks Fin R — Norwegian Commercial Banks. Financial Review
Nor'-West F — Nor'-West Farmer
Norw Geotech Inst Publ — Norwegian Geotechnical Institute. Publication
Norw J Bot — Norwegian Journal of Botany
Norw J Entomol — Norwegian Journal of Entomology
Norw J Zool — Norwegian Journal of Zoology
Norw Marit Res — Norwegian Maritime Research
Norw Oil Rev — Norwegian Oil Review
Norw Petrol Dir Pap — Norwegian Petroleum Directorate Paper
Norw Shipp News — Norwegian Shipping News
NOSK — Norsk Skogindustri
NOSKA — Norsk Skogindustri
Nos Oiseaux Bull Romande Etude Prot Oiseaux — Nos Oiseaux. Bulletin de la Societe Romande pour l'Etude et la Protection des Oiseaux
Nosokomeiaka Chron — Nosokomeiaka Chronika
NOSTA — Norges Offisielle Statistikk
NOSYAV — Museum National d'Histoire Naturelle. Notulae Systematicae
NOT — Notes on Translation
Not Af — Notes Africaines
Not Agric Serv Shell Agric — Noticias Agricolas. Servicio Shell para el Agricultor
Nota Inf Inst Nac Invest Forest (Mex) — Nota Informativa. Instituto Nacional de Investigaciones Forestales (Mexico)
Nota Invest Cent Invest Pesq (Bauta Cuba) — Nota sobre Investigaciones. Centro de Investigaciones Pesqueras (Bauta, Cuba)
Not Am Math — Notices. American Mathematical Society
NOTAMS — Notice to Airmen
Notas Agron — Notas Agronomicas
Notas Algebra Anal — Notas de Algebra y Analisis [*Bahia Blanca*]
Notas Cent Biol Aquat Trop (Lisb) — Notas. Centro de Biologia Aquatica Tropical (Lisbon)
Notas Cient Ser M Mat — Notas Cientificas. Serie M. Matematica [*Lima*]
Notas Ci Ser M Mat — Notas Cientificas. Serie M. Matematica
Notas Comun Inst Geol Min Esp — Notas y Comunicaciones. Instituto Geologico y Minero de Espana
Notas Divulg Inst Munic Bot (Buenos Aires) — Notas de Divulgacion del Instituto Municipal de Botanica (Buenos Aires)
Notas Estud Inst Biol Marit (Lisb) — Notas e Estudos. Instituto de Biologia Maritima (Lisbon)
Notas Fis — Notas de Fisica
Notas Fis Cent Bras Pesqui Fis — Notas de Fisica. Centro Brasileiro de Pesquisas Fisicas
Notas Geom Topol — Notas de Geometria y Topologia [*Bahia Blanca*]
Nota Silvic Adm Nac Bosques (Argent) — Notas Silvicolas. Administracion Nacional de Bosques (Buenos Aires, Argentina)
Notas Inst Mat Estatist Univ Sao Paulo Ser Mat — Notas. Instituto de Matematica e Estatistica da Universidade de Sao Paulo. Serie Matematica
Notas Mat — Notas de Matematica [*Amsterdam*]
Notas Mat Discreta — Notas de Matematica Discreta

Notas Mimeogr Cent Biol Aquat Trop (Lisb) — Notas Mimeografadas. Centro de Biologia Aquatica Tropical (Lisbon)
Notas Mus La Plata Antropol — Notas del Museo de La Plata. Antropologia
Notas Mus La Plata Bot — Notas del Museo de La Plata. Botanica
Notas Mus La Plata Paleontol — Notas del Museo de La Plata. Paleontologia
Notas Mus La Plata Zool — Notas del Museo de La Plata. Zoologia
Notas Pobl — Notas de Poblacion
Notas Prelim Estud Serv Geol Mineral Braz — Notas Preliminares e Estudos. Servico Geologico e Mineralogico do Brazil
Notas Quir Sanat Deschamps — Notas Quirurgicas. Sanatorio Deschamps
Notas Tec Inst Pesqui Mar (Rio De J) — Notas Tecnicas. Instituto de Pesquisas da Marinha (Rio De Janeiro)
Notas Tec Inst Pesqui Mar (Rio De Janeiro) — Notas Tecnicas. Instituto de Pesquisas da Marinha (Rio De Janeiro)
Nota Tec For Esc Ingen For Univ Chile — Notas Tecnico Forestales. Escuela de Ingenieria Forestal. Universidad de Chile
Nota Tec Inst For (Chile) — Nota Tecnica. Instituto Forestal (Santiago De Chile)
Nota Tec Inst Nac Invest For (Mex) — Nota Tecnica. Instituto Nacional de Investigaciones Forestales (Mexico)
Nota Tecnol For Adm Nac Bosques (Argent) — Notas Tecnologicas Forestales. Administracion Nacional de Bosques (Buenos Aires, Argentina)
Notatki Ornitol — Notatki Ornitologiczne
Not Chim Ind — Notiziario Chimico-Industriale
Not Chiostro Mon Magg — Notizie dal Chiostro del Monastero Maggiore
Not Com Naz Energ Nucl — Notiziario. Comitato Nazionale per l'Energia Nucleare
NOTEA — Novosti Tekhniki
Note Apunti Sper Ent Agr — Note ed Apunti Sperimentale di Entomologia Agraria
Noteb Empirical Petrol — Notebook of Empirical Petrology
Note Econ — Note Economiche
Note Fruttic — Note de Frutticultura
Note Inf Tech Lab Cent Ponts Chaussees — Note d'Information Technique. Laboratoire Central des Ponts et Chaussees
Note Lab Biol Mar Pesca-Fano — Note. Laboratorio di Biologia Marina e Pesca-Fano
Note Mat — Note di Matematica
Not Enol Aliment — Notiziario Enologico ed Alimentare
Not Entomol — Notulae Entomologicae
Note Recens & Not — Note Recensioni e Notizie
Note Rech Dep Exploit Util Bois Univ Laval — Note de Recherches. Departement d'Exploitation et Utilisation des Bois. Universite Laval
Note Rec Roy Soc London — Notes and Records. Royal Society of London
Note Riv Psichiatr — Note e Riviste di Psichiatria
No Tes — Novum Testamentum
Notes Afr — Notes Africaines
Notes Agric Res Cent Herb (Egypt) — Notes. Agricultural Research Centre Herbarium (Egypt)
Notes Appl Sci NPL — Notes on Applied Science. National Physical Laboratory
Notes Appl Sci UK Natl Phys Lab — Notes on Applied Science. United Kingdom National Physical Laboratory
Notes Bot Sch Trinity Coll (Dublin) — Notes. Botanical School of Trinity College (Dublin)
Notes Docum UN Unit Apartheid — Notes and Documents. United Nations Unit on Apartheid
Notes Ent Chin — Notes d'Entomologie Chinoise
Notes Etud Doc — Notes et Etudes Documentaires
Notes et Etud Docum — Notes et Etudes Documentaires
Notes et Etud Docum Ser Problemes Am Latine — Notes et Etudes Documentaires. Serie Problemes d'Amerique Latine
Notes on Higher Educ — Notes on Higher Education
Notes Inf CEA — Notes d'Information CEA [*Comissariat a l'Energie Atomique*]
Notes Inform Statist Banque Centr Afr Ouest — Notes d'Information et Statistiques. Banque Centrale des Etats de l'Afrique de l'Ouest
Notes Maroc — Notes Marocaines
Notes et Mem Moyen-Orient — Notes et Memoires sur le Moyen-Orient
Notes Mem Moyen-Orient — Notes et Memoires sur le Moyen-Orient
Notes Mem Serv Geol (Rabat) — Notes et Memoires du Service Geologique (Rabat)
Notes Mem UAR Hydrobiol Dep — Notes and Memoirs. United Arab Republic. Hydrobiological Department
Notes Met Natn (Fr) — Notes Meteorologie Nationale (France)
Notes Pure Math — Notes on Pure Mathematics
Notes on Pure Math — Notes on Pure Mathematics
Notes Quer — Notes and Queries
Notes & Quer — Notes and Queries
Notes Queries Soc West Highl Isl Hist Res — Notes and Queries. Society of West Highland and Island Historical Research
Notes R Bot Gard (Edinb) — Notes. Royal Botanic Garden (Edinburgh)
Notes R Bot Gdn (Edinb) — Notes. Royal Botanic Garden (Edinburgh)
Notes and Records Roy Soc London — Notes and Records. Royal Society of London
Notes Rec R — Notes and Records. Royal Society of London

Notes Rec Roy London — Notes and Records. Royal Society of London

Notes Rec R Soc Lond — Notes and Records. Royal Society of London

Notes on Sc Build — Notes on the Science of Building [*Australia Commonwealth Experimental Building Station*]

Notes Sci Bldg — Notes on the Science of Building [*Australia Commonwealth Experimental Building Station*]

Notes Sci Build — Notes on the Science of Building [*Australia Commonwealth Experimental Building Station*]

Notes on the Science of Bldg — Notes on the Science of Building [*Australia Commonwealth Experimental Building Station*]

Notes Serv Geol Maroc — Notes du Service Geologique du Maroc

Notes Soil Tech — Notes on Soil Technique [*Australia Commonwealth Scientific and Industrial Research Organisation. Division of Soils*]

Notes Tech Hydrol — Notes Techniques en Hydrologie

Notes on Univ Ed — Notes on University Education

Notes Water Pollut (Stevenage) — Notes on Water Pollution (Stevenage)

Notes Water Res — Notes on Water Research

Note Tech Centre Tech For Trop — Note Technique. Centre Technique Forestier Tropicale

Note Tech Cent Tech For Trop (Nogent Sur Marne Fr) — Note Technique. Centre Technique Forestier Tropical (Nogent-Sur-Marne, France)

Note Tech Dep Exploit Util Bois Univ Laval — Note Technique. Departement d'Exploitation et Utilisation des Bois. Universite Laval

Note Tech Inst Rebois Tunis — Note Technique. Institut de Reboisement de Tunis

Not Farm — Noticias Farmaceuticas

Not Farm (Coimbra) — Noticias Farmaceuticas (Coimbra)

Not Galapagos — Noticias de Galapagos

Notic Agr Serv Shell Agr — Noticias Agricolas. Servicio Shell para el Agricultor

Notic Arqueol Hispan Prehist — Noticiario Arqueologico Hispanico Prehistoria

Notices Amer Math Soc — Notices. American Mathematical Society

Notic Geomorfol — Noticia Geomorfologica

Noticiario Inst Forestal — Noticiario Instituto Forestal

Noticias — Brasil. Instituto Brasileiro de Bibliographia e Documentacao. Noticias

Not Ist Autom Univ Roma — Notiziario. Istituto di Automatica. Universita di Roma

Not Ist Vaccinogeno Antituberc — Notiziario. Istituto Vaccinogeno Antitubercolare

Notizbl Hess Landesamtes Bodenforsch Wiesb — Notizblatt. Hessisches Landesamt fuer Bodenforschung zu Wiesbaden

Notiz Cam Cam Commer Ind Agr Cuneo — Notiziario Camerale. Camera di Commercio. Industria e Agricoltura di Cuneo

Notiz IRI — Notizie IRI [*Istituto per la Ricostruzione Industriale*]

Notiz Malatt Piante — Notiziario sulle Malattie delle Piante

Notiz Mal Piante — Notiziario sulle Malattie delle Piante

NOTL — Northline Association of Canadian Universities for Northern Studies

Not Mal Piante — Notiziario sulle Malattie delle Piante

Not Man A — Not Man Apart

Not Mens Mus Nac Hist Nat — Noticiario Mensual. Museo Nacional de Historia Natural

Not Mineral Sicil Calabrese — Notizie di Mineralogia Siciliana e Calabrese

Not Nat Acad Nat Sci Philadelphia — Notulae Naturae. Academy of Natural Sciences of Philadelphia

Not Nat (Phila) — Notulae Naturae (Philadelphia)

NOTOA6 — Brain and Nerve [*Tokyo*]

NOTP — New Orleans Times-Picayune

Notr Dame E — Notre Dame English Journal

Notre Dame Eng J — Notre Dame English Journal

Notre Dame Est Plan Inst Proc — Notre Dame Estate Planning Institute. Proceedings

Notre Dame Inst on Char Giving Found and Tr — Notre Dame Institute on Charitable Giving. Foundations and Trusts

Notre Dame J Formal Logic — Notre Dame Journal of Formal Logic

Notre Dame J Form Log — Notre Dame Journal of Formal Logic

Notre Dame L — Notre Dame Lawyer

Notre Dame Law — Notre Dame Lawyer

Notre Dame Law R — Notre Dame Law Review

Notre Dame L Rev — Notre Dame Law Review

Notre Dame Sci Q — Notre Dame Science Quarterly [*United States*]

Not Ric Sci — Notiziario de "La Ricerca Scientifica"

Not Soc Ital Fitosoc — Notiziario. Societa Italiana di Fitosociologia

Not Syst — Notulae Systematicae

No TT — Norsk Teologisk Tidsskrift

Nott Fr St — Nottingham French Studies

Nottingham Medieval Stud — Nottingham Medieval Studies

Nottingham Univ Min Dep Mag — Nottingham University. Mining Department Magazine [*England*]

Notulae Entomol — Notulae Entomologicae

Notul Ent — Notulae Entomologicae

NOUTD — Nordisk Utredningsserie

Nouv Arch — Nouvelles Archives des Missions Scientifiques

Nouv Arch Hosp — Nouvelles Archives Hospitalieres

Nouv Autom — Nouvel Automatisme

Nouv Avic — Nouvelles de l'Aviculture

Nouv Cah — Nouveaux Cahiers

Nouv Caledoniennes — Nouvelles Caledoniennes

Nouv Chine — Nouvelle Chine

Nouv Clio — La Nouvelle Clio

Nouv Crit — Nouvelle Critique

Nouv Critique — Nouvelle Critique

Nouveau Cours de Math — Nouveau Cours de Mathematiques

Nouvel Autom — Nouvel Automatisme

Nouv Etud Hongroises — Nouvelles Etudes Hongroises

Nouv Hongrie — Nouvelles de Hongrie

Nouv J Chim — Nouveau Journal de Chimie

NouvLitt — Nouvelles Litteraires [*Paris*]

Nouv Med — Nouveautes Medicales

Nouv Polit Agric Commune — Nouvelles de la Politique Agricole Commune

Nouv Presse — Nouvelle Presse Medicale

Nouv Presse Med — Nouvelle Presse Medicale

Nouv R Deux Mondes — Nouvelle Revue des Deux Mondes

Nouv Rev Entomol — Nouvelle Revue d'Entomologie

Nouv Rev Fr — Nouvelle Revue Francaise

Nouv Rev Fr Hematol — Nouvelle Revue Francaise d'Hematologie. Blood Cells

Nouv Rev Fr Hematol Blood Cells — Nouvelle Revue Francaise d'Hematologie. Blood Cells

Nouv Rev Opt — Nouvelle Revue d'Optique

Nouv Rev Opt Appl — Nouvelle Revue d'Optique Appliquee

Nouv Rev Son — Nouvelle Revue du Son

Nouv Rev Theo — Nouvelle Revue Theologique

Nouv R F Hem — Nouvelle Revue Francaise d'Hematologie. Blood Cells

Nouv R Francaise — Nouvelle Revue Francaise

Nouv R Int — Nouvelle Revue Internationale

Nouv R Opt — Nouvelle Revue d'Optique

Nouv R Social — Nouvelle Revue Socialiste

Nouv Rythmes Monde — Nouveaux Rythmes du Monde

Nov — Noverim

Nova Acta Leopold — Nova Acta Leopoldina

Nova Acta Leopold Suppl — Nova Acta Leopoldina. Supplementum

Nova Acta Regiae Soc Sci Ups — Nova Acta Regiae Societatis Scientiarum Upsaliensis

Nova Acta Regiae Soc Sci Ups C — Nova Acta Regiae Societatis Scientiarum Upsaliensis. Seria C

Nova Acta R Soc Sc Upsaliensis — Nova Acta Regiae Societatis Scientiarum Upsaliensis

Nova Guinea Geol — Nova Guinea. Geology

Nova Hedwigia Z Kryptogamenkd — Nova Hedwigia Zeitschrift fuer Kryptogamenkunde

Nova LJ — Nova Law Journal

Nova Proizv — Nova Proizvodnja

Nova Proizvod — Nova Proizvodnya

Nova Scotia Dept Mines Ann Rept Mem — Nova Scotia. Department of Mines. Annual Report. Memoir

Nova Scotia Hist Rev — Nova Scotia Historical Review

Nova Scotia Med Bull — Nova Scotia Medical Bulletin

Nova Scotian Inst Sci Proc — Nova Scotian Institute of Science. Proceedings

Nov Comm Acad Sci Imp Petrop — Novi Commentarii Academiae Scientiarum Imperalis Petropolitanae

NOVDA — Norsk Veterinaer-Tidsskrift

Nov Dannye Geol Polezn Iskop Zapadn Sib — Novye Dannye po Geologii i Poleznym Iskopaemym Zapadnoi Sibiri

No Ve — Nova et Vetera

NOVEA — Noveny termeles

Noveishaya Tektonika Noveishie Otlozh Chel — Noveishaya Tektonika. Noveishie Otlozheniya i Chelovek

Novenynemes Novenytermesz Kutato Intez Koezl Sopronhorpacs — Novenynemesitesi es Novenytermesztesi Kutato Intezet. Sopronhorpacs Koezlemenyei

Novenytermeles Crop Prod — Novenytermeles/Crop Production

Novenyved Idoszeru Kerdesei — Novenyvedelem Idoszeru Kerdesei

Nove Virobnitstvi Budiv Mater — Nove u Virobnitstvi Budivel'nikh Materialiv

Nov Fiz Metody Obrab Pishch Prod — Novye Fizicheskie Metody Obrabotki Pishchevykh Produktov

Novgorod Golovn Gos Pedagog Inst Uch Zap — Novgorodskii Golovnoi Gosudarstvennyi Pedagogicheskii Institut. Uchenye Zapiski

Novgorod Golovn Gos Ped Inst Ucen Zap — Novgorodskii Golovnoi Gosudarstvennyi Pedagogiceskii Institut. Ucenye Zapiski

NoVidSF — Det Kongelige Norske Videnskabers Selskabs Forhandlinger

Novinky Poligr Prum — Novinky v Poligrafichem Prumyslu

Novi Probl Pediatr — Novi Problemi v Pediatriyata

Nov Issled Khim Metall Obogashch — Novye Issledovaniya v Khimii, Metallurgii, i Ogobashchenii

Nov Issled Metall Khim Obogashch — Novye Issledovaniya v Metallurgii, Khimii, i Obogashchenii

Nov Issled Pedagog Naukakh — Novye Issledovaniya v Pedagogicheskikh Naukakh

Nov Issled Psikhol Vozrastn Fiziol — Novye Issledovaniya v Psikhologii i Vozrastnoi Fiziologii

Novi Zb Mat Prob — Novi Zbornik Matematickih Problema

Nov Khir Arkh — Novyi Khirurgicheskii Arkhiv

Nov Lek Rast Sib Ikh Lech Prep Primen — Novye Lekarstvennye Rasteniya Sibiri Ikh Lechebnye Preparaty i Primenenie
Nov Lek Sredstva — Novye Lekarstvennye Sredstva
NovM — Novyj Mir
Nov Maloizvestnye Vidy Fauny Sib — Novye i Maloizvestnye Vidy Fauny Sibiri
Nov Mashinostr — Novoe v Mashinostroenii
Nov Med — Novosti Meditsiny
Nov Med Priborostr — Novosti Meditsinskogo Priborostroeniya [*USSR*]
Nov Med Tek — Novosti Meditsinskoi Tekhniki
Nov Med Tekh — Novosti Meditsinskoi Tekhniki
Nov Neftepererab — Novosti Neftepererabotki
Nov Neft Gazov Tekh Gazov Delo — Novosti Neftyanoi i Gazovoi Tekhniki Gazovoe Delo
Nov Neft Gazov Tekh Geol — Novosti Neftyanoi i Gazovoi Tekhniki. Geologiya
Nov Neft Gazov Tekh Neftepererab Neftekhim — Novosti Neftyanoi i Gazovoi Tekhniki, Neftepererabotka, i Neftekhimiya [*USSR*]
Nov Neft Gazov Tekh Neftepromysl Delo — Novosti Neftyanoi i Gazovoi Tekhniki Neftepromyslovoe Delo
Nov Neft Gazov Tekh Transp Khranenie Nefti Nefteprod — Novosti Neftyanoi i Gazovoi Tekhniki Transport i Khranenie Nefti i Nefteproduktov
Nov Neft Gaz Tekh Neft Oborudovanie Sredstva Avtom — Novosti Neftyanoi i Gazovoi Tekhniki Neftyanoe Oborudovanie i Sredstva Avtomatizatsii
Nov Neft Tekh — Novosti Neftyanoi Tekhniki
Nov Neft Tekh Geol — Novosti Neftyanoi Tekhniki. Geologiya
Nov Neft Tekh Neftepererab — Novosti Neftyanoi Tekhniki Neftepererabotka
Nov Neft Tekh Neftepromysl Delo — Novosti Neftyanoi Tekhniki Neftepromyslovoe Delo
Nov Neft Tekh Stroit Montazh — Novosti Neftyanoi Tekhniki Stroitel'stvo i Montazh
Nov Novejs Ist — Novaja i Novejsaga Istorija
Novosibirsk Gos Ped Inst Naucn Trudy — Novosibirskii Gosudarstvennyi Pedagogiceskii Institut Naucnye Trudy
Novos Taxa Ent — Novos Taxa Entomologicos
Novos Taxa Entomol — Novos Taxa Entomologicos
Nov Pishch Promsti — Novosti Pishchevoi Promyshlennosti
Nov Proizvod Khim Istochnikov Toka — Novoe v Proizvodstve Khimicheskikh Istochnikov Toka [*USSR*]
Nov Razrab Elem Radiotekh Ustroistv — Novye Razrabotki Elementov Radiotekhnicheskikh Ustroistv
Nov Sorbenty Khromatogr — Novye Sorbenty dlya Khromatografii
Nov Tekh — Novosti Tekhniki [*USSR*]
Nov Tekh Astron — Novaya Tekhnika v Astronomii
Nov Tekh Buren — Novosti Tekhniki Bureniya
Nov Neftedobychi — Novosti Tekhniki Neftedobychi
Nov Termoyad Issled SSSR Inf Byull — Novosti Termoyadernykh Issledovanii v SSSR Informatsionnyi Byulleten [*USSR*]
NovTest — Novum Testamentum
Novum Gebrauchs — Novum Gebrauchsgraphik
Novum Test — Novum Testamentum
NovZ — Novyj Zurnal
Nov Zhizni Nauke Tekh Khim — Novoe v Zhizni, Nauke, Tekhnike. Khimiya
Nov Zhizni Nauke Tekh Ser Biol — Novoe v Zhizni, Nauke, Tekhnike. Seriya Biologiia
Nov Zhizni Nauke Tekh Ser Fiz — Novoe v Zhizni, Nauke, Tekhnike. Seriya Fizika [*USSR*]
Nov Zhizni Nauke Tekh Ser IX Fiz Mat Astron — Novoe v Zhizni, Nauke, Tekhnike. Seriya IX. Fizika, Matematika, Astronomiya [*USSR*]
Nov Zhizni Nauke Tekh Ser Khim — Novoe v Zhizni, Nauke, Tekhnike. Seriya Khimiya
Nov Zhizni Nauke Tekh Ser Kosmonavt Astron — Novoe v Zhizni, Nauke, Tekhnike. Seriya Kosmonavtika Astronomiya [*USSR*]
Nov Zhizni Nauke Tekh Ser Tekh — Novoe v Zhizni, Nauke, Tekhnike. Seriya Tekhnika [*USSR*]
Nowa Tech Inz Sanit — Nowa Technika w Inzynierii Sanitarnej
Nowe Roln — Nowe Rolnictwo
Nowest R — Northwest Review
Now Lek — Nowiny Lekarskie
NOWR — Northwater. Institute of Water Resources. University of Alaska
Noyes — Catalog of New Publications. Noyes Data Corp.
NoZ — Novy Zivot
NP — Nasza Przeszlosc
NP — National Parks
NP — Native Press
NP — Nauka Polska
NP — Nea Poreia
Np — Neophilologus
NP — Neupunische Inschriften
NP — Neuroendocrine Perspectives [*Elsevier Book Series*]
NP — New Philosophy
NPA — National Public Accountant
NPAC — Northern Pipeline Agency News Releases and Communiques
NPCM — National Parks and Conservation Magazine [*Later, National Parks Magazine*]
NPD — New Products and Processes Highlights
NPfG — Nordpfalzer Geschichtsverein
NPh — Neophilologus

NphM — Neuphilologische Mitteilungen
NPHR — Notice Papers - House of Representatives
NphZ — Neuphilologische Zeitschrift
NPI — New Periodicals Index
NPI — Newsletter. Portuguese Industrial Association
NPJO — Northern Projects Journal. British Columbia Hydro
NPKZA — Nippon Kagaku Zasshi
NPlockie — Notatki Plockie
NPM — Neuphilologische Mitteilungen
NPM — Neuphilologische Monatsschrift
NPN — National Petroleum News
NPNMA — Nevrologiya, Psikhiatriya, i Nevrokhirurgiya
NPPA — National and Provincial Parks Association. Newsletter
NPR — National Productivity Review
N Princ — New Princeton Review
NPS — Nature: Physical Science
NPS — New Palaeographical Society
NPS — Notice Papers - Senate
NPU — Neue Verpackung. Zeitschrift fuer die Gesamte Verpackungswirtschaft des Inlandes und Auslandes
NQ — Notes and Queries
N & Q — Notes and Queries
N QD Nat — North Queensland Naturalist
N Qld Nat — North Queensland Naturalist
NQM — Nuovi Quaderni del Meridione
NQNS — Notes and Queries. New Series
NQ Register — North Queensland Register
N Queensl Nat — North Queensland Naturalist
NR — Nase Rec [*Prague*]
NR — Nassau Review
NR — Nation Review
NR — National Review
NR — Neue Rundschau
NR — Neues Reich in Aegypten
NR — New Records
NR — [*The*] New Republic
NR — News Release
NR — Northern News Report
NR — Northwest Review
NR — Nova Revija
NR — Numismatic Review
NRA — Nouvelle Revue Apologetique
NRam — New Rambler
NRA Report — NRA [*National Restaurant Association*] Washington Report
NRB — Nouvelle Revue de Bretagne
NRC — Nouvelle Revue Canadienne
NRC — Nouvelle Revue Critique
NRCAGTM — National Research Council of Canada. Associate Committee on Geotechnical Research. Technical Memorandum
NRCBRN — National Research Council. Building Research Note
NRCBRRP — National Research Council of Canada. Division of Building Research. Resesarch Paper
NRCBRTP — National Research Council of Canada. Division of Building Research. Technical Paper
NRCC Bull — NRCC [*National Research Council Canada*] Bulletin
NRCCTT — National Research Council of Canada. Technical Translation
NRCDBP — National Research Council of Canada. Division of Building Research. DBR Paper
NRCD Bull — National Reprographic Centre for Documentation. Bulletin
NRCE — National Research Council of Canada. Associate Committee on Ecological Reserves. Newsletter
NRCG — Numismatic Review and Coin Galleries [*Fixed Price List*]
NRCMET — National Research Council of Canada. Division of Mechanical Engineering. Transportation Newsletter
NRCN — NRC [*Northern Regions Centre*] Newsletter [*Hokkaido, Japan*]
NRC (Natl Res Counc Can) Bull — NRC (National Research Council of Canada) Bulletin
NRC (Natl Res Counc Can) Tech Transl — NRC (National Research Council of Canada) Technical Translation
NRC Res News — National Research Council. Research News
NRC Rev — NRC [*National Research Council of Canada*] Review
NR(Cyprus) — Numismatic Report (Cyprus)
NRD — National Bank of Pakistan. Monthly Economic Letter
NRE — Eco 3. Energies, Environnement, Matieres Premieres
NRE — National Real Estate Investor
NRE — Northern Reporter. Capital Communications Ltd.
NREL — Nouvelle Releve
NRep — [*The*] New Republic
NRF — Nouvelle Revue Francaise [*French periodical; initials also used on books published by Gallimard*]
NRFH — Nueva Revista de Filologia Hispanica
NRFOD — Natural Resources Forum
NRGID — Energia
NRGSD — Energiespectrum
NRGXD — Energoexport
NRH — Nouvelle Revue de Hongrie

NRH — Tweewieler
NRHD — Nouvelle Revue Historique de Droit Francais et Etranger
NRHDFE — Nouvelle Revue Historique de Droit Francais et Etranger
N Riding Sch Libr Guild Bull — North Riding School Library. Guild Bulletin
NRINA — Nippon Rinsho
NRJ — Natural Resources Journal
NRL — Nouvelles de la Republique des Lettres
NRLQ — Naval Research Logistics. Quarterly
NRM — Nuova Rivista Musicale Italiana
NRMI — Nuova Rivista Musicale Italiana
NRMS — Nottingham Renaissance and Modern Studies
NRP — Nouvelle Revue Pedagogique
NRP — Nueva Revista del Pacifico
NRPBA — Neurosciences Research. Program Bulletin
NRRBA — Bulletin. Radio and Electrical Engineering Division. National Research Council of Canada
NRS — Naucnye Raboty is Oobscenija Akademii Nauk Uzbekskoj SSR, Otdelenie Obscestvennych Nauk
NRs — Neue Rundschau
NRS — North-Holland Research Series in Early Detection and Prevention of Behaviour Disorders [Elsevier Book Series]
NRS — Nuova Rivista Storica
NRSDA — Science Dimension
NRSHB2 — Annual Report. Hokkaido Branch. Government Forest Experiment Station
NRSZD — Nippon Rinsho Saibo Gakkai Zasshi
NRT — Nouvelle Revue Theologique
N R Technol — Natural Rubber Technology
NRTh — Nouvelle Revue Theologique
NRTP — Nouvelle Revue des Traditions Populaires
NRu — Neue Rundschau
N Rund — Neue Rundschau
NRVN — Northern Raven. New Series
NRVU — Nuova Rivista di Varia Umanita
NS — Nederlandsche Spectator
NS — Neuere Sprachen
NS — New Scholasticism
NS — New Scientist
NS — New Statesman
NS — Noble Savage
NS — Nova Scotia Reports
NS — Novi Svet
NS — Nuclear Safety
NS — Numen Supplements
NS — Numismatic Studies
NS — Numismatica et Sphragistica
NSA — Notizie degli Scavi di Antichita
NSA — Nuclear Science Abstracts [Later, INIS Atomindex] [Bibliographic database] [Technical Information Center]
NSA — Numen Supplements. Altera Series
NSAA — Neue Studien zur Anglistik und Amerikanistik
NSAAB — Nuclear Science and Applications. Series A. Biological Science [Pakistan]
NSAC — Notices et Memoires. Societe Archeologique de Constantine
NSammlung — Neue Sammlung
NSAPA — Nuclear Science and Applications
NSAR — Nationalmusei Skriftserie. Analecta Reginensia
N-S Arch Ph — Naunyn-Schmiedeberg's Archives of Pharmacology
NSB — National Socialist Bulletin
NSB — Notes on the Science of Building [Australia Commonwealth Experimental Building Station]
NSBGA — Nippon Shokubutsu Byori Gakkaiho
NSC — Names in South Carolina
NSC — Nederlandse Staatscourant Officiele Uitgaven van het Koninkrijk der Nederlanden
NSc — Notizie degli Scavi di Antichita
NSCAA — National Society for Clean Air. Annual Conference. Proceedings [England]
NSCA J — National Strength and Conditioning Association. Journal
N Scav Ant — Notizie degli Scavi di Antichita
NSch — New Scholasticism
NSchwRundschau — Neue Schweizer Rundschau
N Scientist — New Scientist
N Sci R — New Science Review
NSCRA — NASA [National Aeronautics and Space Administration] Contractor Report. CR
NSC Rev 1977-8 — NSC [National Science Council] Review 1977-8 [Taiwan]
NSC Special Publication — National Science Council. Special Publication
NS(Czech) — Numismaticky Sbornik (Czechoslovakia)
NS Dep Lands For Annu Rep — Nova Scotia. Department of Lands and Forests. Annual Report
NS Dep Mines Annu Rep Mines — Nova Scotia. Department of Mines. Annual Report on Mines
NS Dep Mines Mem — Nova Scotia. Department of Mines. Memoir
NS Dp Mines Rp — Nova Scotia. Department of Mines. Report

NSDYA — Nagoya Shiritsu Daigaku Yakugakubu Kenkyu Nempo
NSDYAI — Annual Report. Faculty of Pharmaceutical Sciences. Nagoya City University
NSE — Norwegian Studies in English
NSEGA — Nippon Seikosho Giho
NSEN — Northern Science Education News Service. Scavengers College, Alaska
NSEQ — Nankai Social and Economic Quarterly
NSF Inform — NSF [Namnden foer Skoglig Flygbildteknik] Information
NSFNB — NSFI [Norges Skipaforsknings Institutt] Nytt
NSFZD — Nippon Sanka Fujinka Gakkai Chugoku Shikoku Godo Chihobukai Zasshi
NSGKA — Nippon Shashin Gakkai Kaishi
NSGSR — North-Holland Series in General Systems Research [Elsevier Book Series]
NSGZD — Nippon Shokaki Geka Gakkai Zasshi
NSH — Norwegian Shipping News [Oslo]
NSHIA — Nankyoku Shiryo [Antarctic Record] [Japan]
NS His S — Nova Scotia Historical Society. Collections
NS Hist — Nova Scotia History
NSHKA — Nippon Shika Ishikai Zasshi
NSHT — Norsk Slektshistorisk Tidsskrift
NSi — Nea Sion
NS Inst N Sc Pr Tr — Nova Scotia Institute of Natural Science. Proceedings and Transactions
NSJB — Niedersaechsisches Jahrbuch
NSJBH — Niedersaechsisches Jahrbuch. Hildesheim
NSJFS — North Staffordshire Journal of Field Studies
NSJLG — Niedersaechsisches Jahrbuch fuer Landesgeschichte
NSKIA — Nippon Soshikigaku Kiroku
NSKSA — Nippon Setchaku Kyokaishi
NSL — Det Norske Sprak-og Litteraturselskap
NSLFA — Nervnaia Sistema Leningradskii Gosudarstvennii Universitet Imeni A. A. Zhdanova Fiziologicheskii Institut
NS Lit Sc Soc Tr — Nova Scotia Literary and Scientific Society. Transactions
NSL News — Nova Scotia Law News
NSM — Nationalsozialistische Monatshefte
NSM — Neusprachliche Mitteilungen aus Wissenschaft und Praxis
NSM — Numismatic Scrapbook Magazine
NS Med Bull — Nova Scotia Medical Bulletin
NSMPA — Nauchnye Trudy Samarkandskii Meditsinskii Institut Imeni Akademika I. P. Pavlova
NSN — Akten Betreffende Naamloze Vennootschappen
NSN — New Statesman and Nation
NS & N — New Statesman and Nation
NSNN — Northern Science Network Newsletter. UNESCO-MAB Northern Science Network Secretariat [Edmonton]
NSO — National School Orchestra Association. Bulletin
NSOA — National School Orchestra Association. Bulletin
N Sov — Nas Sovremennik
NSp — Neuere Sprachen
NS Prov Dep Mines Annu Rep — Nova Scotia Province. Department of Mines. Annual Report
NSR — National Sculpture Review
NSR — National Shorthand Reporter
NSR — Neue Schweizer Rundschau
NSR — North Sea Observer
NSR — Nova Scotia Reports
NSR 2d — Nova Scotia Reports. Second Series
NSRDA — National Standard Reference Data Series. United States National Bureau of Standards
NSRDS Ref Data Rep — NSRDS [National Standards Reference Data System] Reference Data Report [United States]
NSREA — Neurosciences Research
NS Rep — Nova Scotia Reports
NSRPDU — Annual Report. Netherlands Institute for Sea Research
NSS — Nysvenska Studier
NSS — Statuten der Vereinigingen
NSS Bull — NSS [National Speleological Society] Bulletin
NSS Bulletin — National Speleological Society. Bulletin
NS Sch Bd Assn N — Nova Scotia School Boards Association. Newsletter
NSSJ — New Scientist and Science Journal
NSSJB — New Scientist and Science Journal
NSSPA — NASA [National Aeronautics and Space Administration] Special Publications
NSSVD — Naucni Sastanak Slavista u Vulove Dane
NST — New Scientist
N St — New Statesman
NSt — Nordische Studien
NST — Nouvelle Serie Theologique
N Staffordshire J Fld Stud — North Staffordshire Journal of Field Studies
NStat — New Statesman
NSTEA — Nuclear Structural Engineering
NS Tech Coll Dep Civ Eng Essays Timber Struct — Nova Scotia Technical College (Halifax). Department of Civil Engineering. Essays on Timber Structures

NStem — Nieuwe Stem
NSTGThK — Neue Studien zur Geschichte der Theologie und der Kirche
NStN — New Statesman and Nation
NStv — Narodno Stvaralastvo. Folklor
NSU — Uitspraken van de Raad voor de Luchtvaart en Scheepvaart
Nsukka Stud — Nsukka Studies in African Literature
NS (USSR) — Numizmaticheskii Sbornik Materialy k Katalogu
  Numizmaticheskogo Sobraniia Gosudarstvennyi Istoricheskii Muzei
  (USSR)
NSV — Akten Betreffende Cooperatieve Verenigingen
NsvS — Nysvenska Studier
NSW Ad — Law Reports (New South Wales). Vice-Admiralty
NSW Adm — Law Reports (New South Wales). Vice-Admiralty
NSW AR — Industrial Arbitration Reports (New South Wales)
NSW Art Gallery Q — New South Wales Art Gallery Quarterly
NSWB — New South Wales Bankruptcy Cases
NSW Bkptcy Cas — New South Wales Bankruptcy Cases
NSW Carpenters J — New South Wales Carpenters' Journal
NSWCMHJ — New South Wales Council for the Mentally Handicapped.
  Journal
NSW Contract Reporter — New South Wales Contract Reporter and Prices
  Current List
NSW Conv R — New South Wales Conveyancing Reports
NSW Country Trader — New South Wales Country Trader and Storekeeper
NSW CRD — New South Wales Court of Review Decisions
NSW Dep Agric Annu Rep — New South Wales. Department of Agriculture.
  Annual Report
NSW Dep Agric Biol Chem Res Inst Annu Plant Dis Surv — New South Wales.
  Department of Agriculture. Biological and Chemical Research Institute.
  Annual Plant Disease Survey
NSW Dep Agric Bull S — New South Wales. Department of Agriculture.
  Bulletin S
NSW Dep Agric Chem Branch — New South Wales. Department of
  Agriculture. Chemistry Branch. Bulletin S
NSW Dep Agric Div Sci Serv Entomol Branch Annu Rep — New South Wales.
  Department of Agriculture. Division of Science Services. Entomology
  Branch. Annual Report
NSW Dep Agric Div Sci Serv Entomol Branch Insect Pest Leafl — New South
  Wales. Department of Agriculture. Division of Science Services.
  Entomology Branch. Insect Pest Leaflet
NSW Dep Agric Rep — New South Wales. Department of Agriculture. Report
NSW Dep Agric Sci Bull — New South Wales. Department of Agriculture.
  Science Bulletin
NSW Dep Agric Tech Bull — New South Wales. Department of Agriculture.
  Technical Bulletin
NSW Dep Mines Chem Lab Rep — New South Wales. Department of Mines.
  Chemical Laboratory Report
NSW Dep Mines Coalfields Branch Tech Rep — New South Wales.
  Department of Mines. Coalfields Branch. Technical Report
NSW Dep Mines Geol Surv Bull — New South Wales. Department of Mines.
  Geological Survey. Bulletin
NSW Dep Mines Geol Surv Miner Ind NSW — New South Wales. Department
  of Mines. Geological Survey. Mineral Industry of New South Wales
NSW Dep Mines Geol Surv Rep — New South Wales. Department of Mines.
  Geological Survey. Report
NSW Dep Mines Mem Geol Surv NSW Geol — New South Wales. Department
  of Mines. Memoirs of the Geological Survey of New South Wales.
  Geology
NSW Dep Mines Mem Geol Surv NSW Palaeontol — New South Wales.
  Department of Mines. Memoirs of the Geological Survey of New South
  Wales. Palaeontology
NSW Dep Mines Tech Rep — New South Wales. Department of Mines.
  Technical Report
NSW Dep Mines Tech Rep CF — New South Wales. Department of Mines.
  Coalfields Branch. Technical Report CF
NSW Dept Mines Chem Lab Rep — New South Wales. Department of Mines.
  Chemical Laboratory. Report
NSW Ed Gaz — Education Gazette (New South Wales)
NSW Eq — Law Reports (New South Wales).Equity
NSW Fed INS Clubs Gen Newsletter — New South Wales. Federation of
  Infants and Nursery School Clubs. General Newsletter
NSW Fed INSC News — New South Wales Federation of Infants and Nursery
  School Clubs. News
NSW For Comm Dir For Mgmt Res Note — New South Wales. Forestry
  Commission. Division of Forest Management. Research Note
NSW For Comm Div Wood Technol Bull — New South Wales. Forestry
  Commission. Division of Wood Technology. Bulletin
NSW For Comm Div Wood Technol Leafl — New South Wales. Forestry
  Commission. Division of Wood Technology. Leaflet
NSW For Comm Div Wood Technol Pamph — New South Wales. Forestry
  Commission. Division of Wood Technology. Pamphlet
NSW For Comm Div Wood Technol Proj Rep — New South Wales. Forestry
  Commission. Division of Wood Technology. Project Reports
NSW For Comm Div Wood Technol Tech — New South Wales. Forestry
  Commission. Division of Wood Technology. Technical Notes

NSW For Comm Div Wood Technol Tech Notes — New South Wales. Forestry
  Commission. Division of Wood Technology. Technical Notes
NSW For Comm Res Note — New South Wales. Forestry Commission.
  Research Notes
NSW For Rec — New South Wales Forestry Recorder
NSW Freemason — New South Wales Freemason
NSW Geol Surv Bull — New South Wales. Geological Survey. Bulletin
NSW Geol Surv 1:250 000 Geol Ser — New South Wales. Geological Survey.
  1:250,000 Geological Series
NSW Geol Surv Mem Geol — New South Wales. Geological Survey. Memoirs.
  Geology
NSW Geol Surv Mem Palaeontol — New South Wales. Geological Survey.
  Memoirs. Palaeontology
NSW Geol Surv 4-Mile Geol Ser — New South Wales. Geological Survey. 4-
  Mile Geological Series
NSW Geol Surv Mineral Industry of NSW — New South Wales. Geological
  Survey. Mineral Industry of New South Wales
NSW Geol Surv Miner Resour — New South Wales. Geological Survey.
  Mineral Resources
NSW Geol Surv Min Res — New South Wales. Geological Survey. Mineral
  Resources
NSW Geol Surv Q Notes — New South Wales. Geological Survey. Quarterly
  Notes
NSW Geol Surv Rec — New South Wales. Geological Survey. Records
NSW Geol Surv Rep — New South Wales. Geological Survey. Report
NSWGG — New South Wales Government Gazette
NSW Herb Contr — New South Wales. National Herbarium. Contributions
NSW Herb Contr Flora Ser — New South Wales. National Herbarium.
  Contributions. Flora Series
NSWIER Bul — New South Wales Institute for Educational Research.
  Bulletin
NSW Ind Gaz — New South Wales Industrial Gazette
NSW Inst Ed Res Bul — New South Wales Institute for Educational Research.
  Bulletin
NSW Land App Cas — Land Appeal Court Cases (New South Wales)
NSW Lib Bul — New South Wales Library Bulletin
NSWLR — New South Wales Law Reports
NSWLR — New South Wales Letters of Registration
NSWLVR — New South Wales Land and Valuation Court Reports
NSWOP — New South Wales Official Publications
NSW Parl Deb — New South Wales Parliamentary Debates
NSW Parl Parl Deb — New South Wales. Parliament. Parliamentary Debates
NSWPD — New South Wales Parliamentary Debates
NSW Philatelic Ann — New South Wales Philatelic Annual
NSW Police News — New South Wales Police News
NSW Potato — New South Wales Potato
NSW Presbyterian — New South Wales Presbyterian
NSWR — Industrial Arbitration Reports (New South Wales). New South
  Wales Reports
(NSW) SCR (Eq) — Supreme Court Reports (Equity) (New South Wales)
(NSW) SCR (L) — Supreme Court Reports (Law) (New South Wales)
(NSW) SCR (NS) — Supreme Court Reports (New Series) (New South Wales)
NSWSR — New South Wales State Reports
NSW State Fish Cruise Rep — New South Wales. State Fisheries Cruise
  Report
NSW Statist Summ — New South Wales Statistical Summary
NSW Stat Reg — New South Wales Statistical Register
NSW St R — New South Wales State Reports
NSW Timber Worker — New South Wales Timber Worker
NSW Univ Engineering Yrbk — University of New South Wales. Faculty of
  Engineering. Yearbook
NSW Univ Inst Highw Traff Res Res Note — University of New South Wales.
  Institute of Highway and Traffic Research. Research Note
NSW Univ Sch Civ Eng UNICIV Rep Ser R — New South Wales University.
  School of Civil Engineering. UNICIV Report. Series R
NSW Univ UNICIV Rep — University of New South Wales. School of Civil
  Engineering. UNICIV Report
NSW Univ Wat Res Lab Rep — University of New South Wales. Water
  Research Laboratory. Report
NSW Vet Proc — Proceedings. Australian Veterinary Association. New South
  Wales Division
NSW Wat Conserv Irrig Comm Surv Thirty NSW River Valleys Rep — New
  South Wales. Water Conservation and Irrigation Commission. Survey of
  Thirty New South Wales River Valleys. Report
NSW WCR — Workers' Compensation Reports (New South Wales)
NSW Weath Rep — New South Wales Weather Report
NSWWN — New South Wales Weekly Notes
NSZ — Nederlands-Spaanse Kamer van Koophandel. Spaanse Aanvragen voor
  Handelskontakten met Nederland
NSZKA — Nauchnye Trudy Severo-Zapadnyi Nauchno-Issledovatel'skii
  Institut Sel'skogo Khozyaistva
NT — National Times
N T — New Testament
NT — New Times
NT — Nieuwe Taalgids
NT — Nordisk Tidskrift

NT — Nordisk Tidskrift foer Vetenskap, Konst, och Industri
NT — Northern Times [*Whitehorse, Canada*]
NT — Novum Testamentum
NT — Nuclear Theory [*Elsevier Book Series*]
NtA — Neutestamentliche Abhandlungen [*Muenster*]
NTA — New Testament Abstracts
NTAbstr — New Testament Abstracts [*Weston, MA*]
NTA Bul — Newfoundland Teachers' Association. Bulletin
NTAJ — Newfoundland Teachers' Association. Journal
NTAZA — Nippon Taishitsugaku Zasshi
NTB — New Technical Books
NTBB — Nordisk Tidskrift foer Bok- och Biblioteksvaesen
NTBBV — Nordisk Tidskrift foer Bok- och Biblioteksvaesen
NTC — Economisch Dagblad. Dagblad voor het Management
NTCNB — Nature Canada
NTCS — Newsletter for Targumic and Cognate Studies [*Toronto*]
NTD — Netherlands Trade and News Bulletin
NTE — Narodna Tvorcist' ta Etnografija
NTELA — Nachrichtentechnik-Elektronik
NTemp — Nostro Tempo
NTF — Neutestamentliche Forschungen
NTF — Nuclear Technology/Fusion
NTFDA — Natturufraedingurinn
NTFLDX — Fonds de Recherches Forestieres. Universite Laval. Note
　　Technique
NTFUD — Nuclear Technology/Fusion
NTG — Nieuwe Taalgids
NTg — Nieuwe Taalgids. Tijdschrift voor Neerlandici
NTGLA — Nauchnye Trudy Tashkentskii Gosudarstvennyi Universitet Imeni
　　V. I. Lenina
NTGNA — Nauchnye Trudy Gosudarstvennyi Nauchno-Issledovatel'skii i
　　Proektnyi Institut Redkometallicheskoi Promyshlennosti
NTHAA7 — Brain and Development
Nth Apiar — Northern Apiarist
Nth Forest Ranger Coll A — Northern Forest Ranger College Annual
Nth Gdnr — Northern Gardener
Nth Logger — Northern Logger
NThM — New Theatre Magazine
Nth Miner — Northern Miner
NThS — Nieuwe Theologische Studien
NThSt — Nieuwe Theologische Studien
NThT — Nieuwe Theologisch Tijdschrift
NThTs — Nederlands Theologisch Tijdschrift
NTI — Futuribles
NTIAA — Nauchnye Trudy Instituta Avtomatiki
NTIPI — Nauchnye Trudy Industrial'no-Pedagogicheskogo Instituta
NTIS Announc — NTIS [*National Technical Information Service*] Trade
　　Announcements
NTIS Mater Sci — NTIS [*National Technical Information Service*] Materials
　　Science
NTJ — National Tax Journal
NTJ — Nigeria Trade Journal
NTJ — Northern Territory Judgements
NTK — Nauchnye Trudy Krasnodarskogo Pedagogicheskogo Instituta
NTKAA — Neue Technik. Abteilung A. Automatik und Industrielle Elektronik
NTKBA — Neue Technik. Abteilung B. Kerntechnik
NTKPB — Nauchnye Trudy Kurskii Politekhnicheskii Institut
NTLLDT — Intelligence
NTLTL — Newsletter. Teaching Language through Literature
NTM — New Theatre Magazine
NTM — NTM. Schriftenreihe fuer Geschichte der Naturwissenschaften,
　　Technik, und Medizin
NTM — Nuestro Tiempo (Madrid)
NTMLB — Nauchni Trudove. Vissh Lesotekhnicheski Institut (Sofia). Seriya
　　Mekhanichna Tekhnologiya na Durvesinata (Bulgaria)
NTMSB — NTM. Schriftenreihe fuer Geschichte der Naturwissenschaften,
　　Technik, und Medizin
NTM Schr Geschichte Natur Tech Medizin — NTM. Schriftenreihe fuer
　　Geschichte der Naturwissenschaften, Technik, und Medizin
NTM Schr Geschichte Naturwiss Tech Medizin — NTM. Schriftenreihe fuer
　　Geschichte der Naturwissenschaften, Technik, und Medizin
NTM Schriftenr Gesch Naturwiss Tech Med — NTM. Schriftenreihe fuer
　　Geschichte der Naturwissenschaften, Technik, und Medizin
NTMTA — Nauchnye Trudy Moskovskogo Teknologicheskogo Instituta
　　Legkoi Promyshlennosti
NTN — Nederland Taiwan Nieuws
NTN — NTIS [*National Technical Information Service*] Energy Tech Notes
　　[*United States*]
NT Neue Tech — NT. Neue Technik [*Switzerland*]
NTNKA — Nederlands Tijdschrift voor Natuurkunde
NTNSDQ — Intensivbehandlung
NTOTD — Neurobehavioral Toxicology and Teratology
NTPGB — Nederlands Tijdschrift voor de Psychologie en Haar Grensgebieden
NTPPA — Nauchnye Trudy Permskii Politechnicheskii Institut
NTPUB — Nauchni Trudove. Plovdivski Universitet. Matematika, Fizika,
　　Khimiya, Biologiya

NTR — Northern Territory Reports
NTS — New Testament Studies
NTS — Nieuwe Theologische Studien
NTS — Norsk Tidsskrift foer Sprogvidenskap
NTS — Novum Testamentum. Supplements [*Leiden*]
NTsPsych — Nederlandsch Tijdschrift voor de Psychologie en Haar
　　Grensgebieden
NTSt — New Testament Studies
NTStud — New Testament Studies
NTSuppl — Novum Testamentum. Supplements [*Leiden*]
NT Suppls — Novum Testamentum. Supplements [*Leiden*]
NTSV — Nordisk Tidsskrift foer Sprogvidenskap
NTsV — Nordisk Tidskrift foer Vetenskap, Konst, och Industri
NTT — Nederlands Theologisch Tijdschrift
NTT — Nieuw Theologisch Tijdschrift
NTT — Norsk Teologisk Tidsskrift
NTTid — Norsk Teologisk Tidsskrift
NTTij — Nederlands Theologisch Tijdschrift
NTTO — Nordisk Tidsskrift foer Teknisk Okonomi
NTTS — New Testament Texts and Studies
NTTS — New Testament Tools and Studies
NTTS — Nordisk Tidsskrift foer Tale og Stemme
NTTSt — New Testament Texts and Studies
NTTSt — New Testament Tools and Studies [*Leiden*]
NTU — Nordiska Texter och Undersokningar
NTU Phytopathol Entomol — NTU [*National Taiwan University*]
　　Phytopathologist and Entomologist
NTURB — Natura (Plovdiv, Bulgaria)
NTVGA — Nederlandsch Tijdschrift voor Verloskunde en Gynaecologie
NTVK — Nederlandsch Tijdschrift voor Volkskunde
NTVMA — Nauchni Trudove na Visshiya Meditsinski Institut
NTZ-Commun J — NTZ-Communications Journal
NTZ Nachr Z NTZ-Commun J — NTZ. Nachrichtentechnische Zeitschrift/
　　NTZ-Communications Journal
NTZ Rep — NTZ. Nachrichtentechnische Zeitschrift. Report
NU — Nunatsiaq News
NuA — Nuova Antologia
NUAH — Nutrition and Health. A Journal of Preventive Medicine
NUAPA — Nuclear Applications
NUATA — Nuclear Applications and Technology
NUC — National Union Catalogue
NUCAD — Nutrition and Cancer
NUCAV — National Union Catalogue of Audio-Visual Materials
Nuc Compact Compact News Nucl Med — Nuc Compact. Compact News in
　　Nuclear Medicine [*West Germany*]
Nuc Energy — Nuclear Energy
NUC:H — National Union Catalogue of Library Materials for the
　　Handicapped
Nucl — Nucleus
Nucl Acid R — Nucleic Acids Research
Nucl Act — Nuclear Active
Nucl Active — Nuclear Active
Nucl Appl — Nuclear Applications
Nucl Appl and Technol — Nuclear Applications and Technology
Nucl Appl Technol — Nuclear Applications and Technology
Nucl Can/Can Nucl — Nuclear Canada/Canada Nucleaire
Nucl Can Yearb — Nuclear Canada Yearbook
Nucl Chem Waste Manage — Nuclear and Chemical Waste Management
Nucl-Chicago Tech Bull — Nuclear-Chicago Technical Bulletin
Nucl Data A — Nuclear Data. Section A
Nucl Data Sect A — Nuclear Data. Section A
Nucl Data Sect B — Nuclear Data. Section B
Nucl Data Sheets — Nuclear Data Sheets
Nucl Data Tables — Nuclear Data Tables
Nucl Data Tables US AEC — Nuclear Data Tables. United States Atomic
　　Energy Commission
Nuclear Eng — Nuclear Engineering International
Nuclear Law Bul — Nuclear Law Bulletin
Nuclear Phys A — Nuclear Physics. A
Nuclear Phys B — Nuclear Physics. B
Nuclear Sci Abstr — Nuclear Science Abstracts [*Later, INIS Atomindex*]
Nuclear Science Abstr — Nuclear Science Abstracts [*Later, INIS Atomindex*]
Nucleic Acids Res — Nucleic Acids Research
Nucleic Acids Symp Ser — Nucleic Acids Symposium Series
Nucl Electron Detect Technol — Nuclear Electronics and Detection
　　Technology
Nucl Energy — Nuclear Energy
Nucl Energy Br Nucl Energy Soc — Nuclear Energy. British Nuclear Energy
　　Society
Nucl Energy Dig — Nuclear Energy Digest
Nucl Eng — Nuclear Engineer. Institution of Nuclear Engineers
Nucl Eng Bull — Nuclear Engineering Bulletin
Nucl Eng Des — Nuclear Engineering and Design
Nucl Eng and Des — Nuclear Engineering and Design
Nucl Eng Des Fusion — Nuclear Engineering and Design/Fusion
Nucl Eng In — Nuclear Engineering International

Nucl Eng Inst Nucl Eng — Nuclear Engineer. Institution of Nuclear Engineers [*England*]
Nucl Eng Int — Nuclear Engineering International
Nucl Engng & Des — Nuclear Engineering and Design
Nucl Engng Int — Nuclear Engineering International
Nucl Engr — Nuclear Engineer
Nucl Eng (Tokyo) — Nuclear Engineering (Tokyo)
Nucl F Supplm — Nuclear Fusion. Supplement
Nucl Fuel Cycle Revis Ed — Nuclear Fuel Cycle. Revised Edition
Nucl Fusion — Nuclear Fusion
Nucl Fusion Res Rep — Nuclear Fusion Research Report [*Japan*]
Nucl Fusion Spec Publ — Nuclear Fusion. Special Publication
Nucl Geneeskd Bull — Nucleair Geneeskundig Bulletin
Nucl Hematol — Nuclear Hematology [*England*]
Nucl Ind — Nuclear Industry
Nucl India — Nuclear India
Nucl Inf — Nuclear Information
Nucl Instr — Nuclear Instruments and Methods [*Later, Nuclear Instruments and Methods in Physics Research*]
Nucl Instrum — Nuclear Instruments
Nucl Instrum and Methods — Nuclear Instruments and Methods [*Later, Nuclear Instruments and Methods in Physics Research*]
Nucl Instrum Methods — Nuclear Instruments and Methods [*Later, Nuclear Instruments and Methods in Physics Research*]
Nucl Instrum Methods Phys Res — Nuclear Instruments and Methods in Physics Research [*Netherlands*]
Nucl Instrum Methods Phys Res Sect A — Nuclear Instruments and Methods in Physics Research. Section A. Accelerators, Spectrometers, Detectors, and Associated Equipment
Nucl Instrum Methods Phys Res Sect B — Nuclear Instruments and Methods in Physics Research. Section B. Beam Interactions with Materials and Atoms
Nucl Issues — Nuclear Issues
Nucl Law Bull — Nuclear Law Bulletin
Nucl Law Bull Suppl — Nuclear Law Bulletin. Supplement
Nucl Magn Reson — Nuclear Magnetic Resonance
Nucl Mater Manage — Nuclear Materials Management. Journal of the Institute of Nuclear Materials Management
Nucl-Med — Nuclear-Medizin
Nucl Med Commun — Nuclear Medicine Communications
Nucl-Med (Stuttgart) — Nuclear-Medizin (Stuttgart)
Nucl Med Suppl — Nuclear-Medizin. Supplementum
Nucl-Med Suppl (Stuttgart) — Nuclear-Medizin. Supplementum (Stuttgart)
Nucl Metall — Nuclear Metallurgy
Nucl N — Nuclear News
Nucl News — Nuclear News
Nucl News (Colombo Sri Lanka) — Nuclear News (Colombo, Sri Lanka)
Nucl News (Hinsdale Ill) — Nuclear News (Hinsdale, Illinois)
Nucl News (La Grange Park Ill) — Nuclear News (La Grange Park, Illinois)
Nucl Newsl Switz — Nuclear Newsletter from Switzerland
Nucl Part Phys Annu — Nuclear and Particle Physics. Annual
Nucl Phys — Nuclear Physics
Nucl Phys A — Nuclear Physics. A
Nucl Phys B — Nuclear Physics. B
Nucl Phys B Field Theory and Stat Syst — Nuclear Physics. B. Field Theory and Statistical Systems
Nucl Power — Nuclear Power
Nucl Power Eng — Nuclear Power Engineering
Nucl React Built Being Built Planned — Nuclear Reactors Built, Being Built, or Planned
Nucl Res — Nuclear Research
Nucl Res Cent "Democritus" (Rep) — Nuclear Research Center "Democritus" (Report)
Nucl Saf — Nuclear Safety
Nucl Safety — Nuclear Safety
Nucl Sci Abstr — Nuclear Science Abstracts [*Later, INIS Atomindex*]
Nucl Sci Appl — Nuclear Science and Applications [*Pakistan*]
Nucl Sci Appl Sect A — Nuclear Science and Applications. Section A
Nucl Sci Appl Ser A — Nuclear Science and Applications. Series A
Nucl Sci Appl Ser B — Nuclear Science and Applications. Series B
Nucl Sci En — Nuclear Science and Engineering
Nucl Sci and Eng — Nuclear Science and Engineering
Nucl Sci Eng — Nuclear Science and Engineering
Nucl Sci Inf Jpn — Nuclear Science Information of Japan
Nucl Sci J — Nuclear Science Journal
Nucl Sci J (Bandar Baru Bangi Malays) — Nuclear Science Journal (Bandar Baru Bangi, Malaysia)
Nucl Sci J (Taiwan) — Nuclear Science Journal (Taiwan)
Nucl Sci (Taiwan) — Nuclear Science (Taiwan)
Nucl Sci Technol — Nuclear Science and Technology
Nucl Ships — Nuclear Ships [*Japan*]
Nucl Struct Eng — Nuclear Structural Engineering [*Netherlands*]
Nucl Study — Nuclear Study [*Japan*]
Nucl Tech — Nuclear Technology
Nucl Technol — Nuclear Technology
Nucl Technol/Fusion — Nuclear Technology/Fusion

Nucl Technol Suppl — Nuclear Technology. Supplement
Nucl Track Detect — Nuclear Track Detection
Nucl Tracks — Nuclear Tracks
NUCOM — National Union Catalogue of Monographs
NUCOMUSIC — National Union Catalogue of Music
NUCOS — National Union Catalogue of Serials
NUCSA — Nucleus [*Paris*]
NucSciAb — Nuclear Science Abstracts [*Later, INIS Atomindex*]
NUCUA — Nuovo Cimento. Supplemento
NUDIA — Nutritio et Dieta
NUENA — Nuclear Engineering
Nuestra Tierra — Nuestra Tierra. Paz y Progreso
Nueva Estaf — Nueva Estafeta
Nueva Pol — Nueva Politica
NUH — National Underwriter (Life and Health Insurance Edition)
NUHEA — Nuclear Hematology
Nuisances et Environ — Nuisances et Environnement
Nuisances Environ — Nuisances et Environnement
NUKKA — Nukleonik
Nukl Energ — Nuklearna Energija
Nukleonika Suppl — Nukleonika. Supplement [*Poland*]
NUKOA — Nauchno-Issledovatel'skii Trudy Ukrainskii Nauchno-Issledovatel'skii Institut Kozhevenno-Obuvnoi Promyshlennosti
NUL — Northwestern University. Law Review
NULAB — Nuclear Active
NULH — National Underwriter (Life and Health Insurance Edition)
NULR — Northwestern University. Law Review
NUm — Narodna Umjetnost
Num — Numismatist
Num Ant Clas — Quaderni Ticinesi. Numismatica e Antichita Classiche
Num Beitr — Numismatische Beitraege
Num Change — Numismatique et Change
Num Chron — Numismatic Chronicle and Journal [*London*]
NumCirc — Numismatic Circular
Num Circ — Spink and Son. Numismatic Circular
NUMDA — Nihon University. Journal of Medicine
Num Digest — Numismatic Digest
Numer Control Soc Proc Annu Meet Tech Conf — Numerical Control Society Proceedings. Annual Meeting and Technical Conference
Numer Eng — Numerical Engineering
Numer Funct Anal Optim — Numerical Functional Analysis and Optimization
Numer Funct Anal Optimiz — Numerical Functional Analysis and Optimization
Numer Heat Transfer — Numerical Heat Transfer
Numer Math — Numerische Mathematik
Numer Math Ingenieure Physiker — Numerische Mathematik fuer Ingenieure und Physiker
Numer Math J Chinese Univ — Numerical Mathematics. A Journal of Chinese Universities [*Nanjing*]
Num Hisp — Numario Hispanico
Numis — Numismatist
Numis Chron 7 Ser — Numismatic Chronicle. Series 7
Numis Circ — Numismatic Circular [*England*]
Numisma (Austral) — Numisma: An Occasional Numismatic Magazine (Australia)
Num Israel — Numismatics in Israel
Num J — Numismatic Journal
NUMMB — Nuclear Materials Management
Num Moravica — Numismatica Moravica
Num Sfrag — Numizmatika i Sfragistika
Num Stockholm — Numismatica Stockholmiensia. Annual Reports and Acquisitions of the Royal Coin Cabinet. National Museum of Monetary History
Nunt Radiol — Nuntius Radiologicus
Nuo Ant — Nuova Antologia
Nuo Ital — Nuova Italia
NUOL — Nursing Outlook
NUON — Nunavut Onipkaat. Kitikmeot Inuit Association
Nuo Riv Stor — Nuova Rivista Storica
Nuova Agr Lucana — Nuova Agricoltura Lucana
Nuova Antol — Nuova Antologia
Nuova Chim — Nuova Chimica
Nuova Econ — Nuova Economia
Nuova Riv Olii Veg Saponi — Nuova Rivista Olii Vegetali e Saponi
Nuova Riv Stor — Nuova Rivista Storica
Nuova RM Italiana — Nuova Rivista Musicale Italiana
Nuova Vet — Nuova Veterinaria
Nuov Bull — Nuovo Bulletino di Archeologia Cristiana
Nuov Cim A — Nuovo Cimento. A
Nuov Cim B — Nuovo Cimento. B
Nuovi Allevam — Nuovi Allevamenti
Nuovi Ann Agric — Nuovi Annali dell'Agricoltura
Nuovi Annali Ig Microbiol — Nuovi Annali d'Igiene e Microbiologia
Nuovi Ann Ig Microbiol — Nuovi Annali d'Igiene e Microbiologia
Nuovi Ann Ist Chim-Agr Sper Gorizia. Ser 2 — Nuovi Annali. Istituto Chimico-Agrario Sperimentale di Gorizia. Serie 2

Nuovi Studi Sta Chim-Agr Sper Udine — Nuovi Studi. Stazione Chimico-Agraria Sperimentale di Udine
Nuovo Arch Ital ORL — Nuovo Archivio Italiano di Otologia, Rinologia, e Laringologia
Nuovo Arch Ital Otol Rinol Laringol — Nuovo Archivio Italiano di Otologia, Rinologia, e Laringologia
Nuovo Cim — Nuovo Cimento
Nuovo Cim A — Nuovo Cimento. A
Nuovo Cim B — Nuovo Cimento. B
Nuovo Cim C — Nuovo Cimento. C
Nuovo Cimento C 1 — Nuovo Cimento. C. Serie 1
Nuovo Cimento Lett — Nuovo Cimento. Lettere [*Italy*]
Nuovo Cimento Soc Ital Fis A — Nuovo Cimento. Societa Italiana di Fisica. Sezione A
Nuovo Cimento Soc Ital Fis B — Nuovo Cimento. Societa Italiana di Fisica. Sezione B
Nuovo Cimento Suppl — Nuovo Cimento. Supplemento [*Italy*]
Nuovo G Bot Ital — Nuovo Giornale Botanico Italiano
Nuovo G Bot Ital (Nuovo Ser) — Nuovo Giornale Botanico Italiano (Nuovo Serie)
Nuov Riv M — Nuova Rivista Musicale Italiana
Nuov Riv St — Nuova Rivista Storica
NUP — National Underwriter (Property and Casualty Insurance Edition)
NUPBB — Nuclear Physics. B
NUPC — National Underwriter (Property and Casualty Insurance Edition)
NUPSA — Neuropsychologia
Nurs '78 — Nursing '78
Nurs '82 — Nursing '82
Nurs '80/'81 — Nursing '80/'81
Nurs 83/84 — Nursing '83/'84
Nurs Abstr — Nursing Abstracts
Nurs Admin Q — Nursing Administration. Quarterly
Nurs Adm Q — Nursing Administration. Quarterly
Nurs Care — Nursing Care
Nurs Careers — Nursing Careers
Nurs Clin N Am — Nursing Clinics of North America
Nurs Clin North Am — Nursing Clinics of North America
Nurs Digest — Nursing Digest
Nurs Dimens — Nursing Dimensions
Nurs Econ — Nursing Economics
Nurse Educ — Nurse Educator
Nurse Educ Today — Nurse Education Today
Nurse Isr — Nurse in Israel
Nurse Pract — Nurse Practitioner
Nurse Practit — Nurse Practitioner
Nursery Bus — Nursery Business
Nurserym Gdn Cent — Nurseryman and Garden Center
Nurs Focus — Nursing Focus
Nurs Forum — Nursing Forum
Nurs Forum (Auckl) — Nursing Forum (Auckland)
Nurs Health Care — Nursing and Health Care
Nurs Hlth Care — Nursing and Health Care
Nurs Homes — Nursing Homes
Nurs J — Nursing Journal
Nurs J India — Nursing Journal of India
Nurs J Singapore — Nursing Journal of Singapore
Nurs J (S Toms) — Nursing Journal (Santo Tomas, Manila)
Nurs Law Ethics — Nursing Law and Ethics
Nurs Leader — Nurse Leadership
Nurs Leadersh — Nursing Leadership
Nurs Leadership — Nursing Leadership
Nurs Life — Nursing Life
Nurs M — Nursing Management
Nurs Manage — Nursing Management
Nurs Mirror — Nursing Mirror and Midwives Journal [*Later, Nursing Mirror*]
Nurs (Montreal) — Nursing (Montreal)
Nurs News (Concord) — Nursing News (Concord)
Nurs News (Conn) — Nursing News (Connecticut)
Nurs News Conn — Nursing News. Connecticut Nurses' Association
Nurs News (Hartford) — Nursing News (Hartford)
Nurs News (Meriden) — Nursing News (Meriden)
Nurs News (New Hamp) — Nursing News (New Hampshire)
Nurs News New Hamp — Nursing News. New Hampshire Nurses' Association
Nurs News (So Africa) — Nursing News (South Africa)
Nurs Outlook — Nursing Outlook
Nurs Pap — Nursing Papers
Nurs Papers — Nursing Papers
Nurs Pulse New Engl — Nursing Pulse of New England
Nurs (Que) — Nursing (Quebec)
Nurs Res — Nursing Research
Nurs Res Conf — Nursing Research Conference
Nurs Res Rep — Nursing Research Report
Nurs Success Today — Nursing Success Today
Nurs Times — Nursing Times
Nurs Update — Nursing Update

NURVA — Nursing Research
NUSBA — Nuclear Science and Applications. Series B. Physical Sciences
NUSH — Northwestern University. Studies in the Humanities
NuSup — Numen Supplements [*Leiden*]
NUT — Norges Utenrikshandel
NUTIA — Nursing Times
Nutida M — Nutida Musik
Nutida Mus — Nutida Musik
NUTN — Nutrition News
NutrAb — Nutrition Abstracts
Nutr Abstr Rev — Nutrition Abstracts and Reviews
Nutr Action — Nutrition Action
Nutr Brain — Nutrition and the Brain
Nutr Bromatol Toxicol — Nutricion Bromatologia Toxicologia
Nutr Cancer — Nutrition and Cancer
Nutr Clin Nutr — Nutrition and Clinical Nutrition
Nutr Dent Health — Nutrition and Dental Health
Nutr Dieta — Nutritio et Dieta
Nutr Food Sci — Nutrition and Food Science
Nutr Food Sci Pres Knowl Util — Nutrition and Food Science. Present Knowledge and Utilization
Nutr Found Inc Rep — Nutrition Foundation, Incorporated. Report
Nutr Health Dis — Nutrition in Health and Disease
Nutr and MD — Nutrition and the MD
Nutr Metab — Nutrition and Metabolism
Nutr Monogr Ser — Nutrition Monograph Series
Nutr News — Nutrition News
Nutr Notes — Nutrition Notes
Nutr R — Nutrition Reviews
Nutr Rep In — Nutrition Reports International
Nutr Rep Int — Nutrition Reports International
Nutr Requir Domest Anim — Nutrient Requirements of Domestic Animals
Nutr Res — Nutrition Research
Nutr Res Bull — Nutrition Research Bulletin
Nutr Rev — Nutrition Reviews
Nutr Soc Proc — Nutrition Society Proceedings [*British*]
Nutr Support Serv — Nutritional Support Services
Nutr Today — Nutrition Today
Nutr Update — Nutrition Update
NUVN — Nuvuk News
NV — Nase Veda
NV — Nastavni Vjesnik
NV — Neerlands Volksleven
N & V — Nova et Vetera
NV — Nova et Vetera
NV — Numizmaticke Vijesti
NVA — Norske Videnskaps-Akademi. Aarbok
NVARA — Naval Architect
NVB — Noise and Vibration Bulletin
NVC — Narodopisny Vestnik Ceskoslovensky
NVE — Naamloze Vennootschap
NVet — Nova et Vetera [*Fribourg*]
NVHS — Norske Videnskaps-Akademi i Oslo. Hvalradets Skrifter
NVK — Koeltechniek/Klimaatregeling
NVLSA — Nauchni Trudove. Vissh Lesotekhnicheski Institut (Sofia)
NVROB — Nouvelle Revue d'Optique
NVS Nuus — Nasionale Versnellersentrum Nuus
NVT — Nieuw Vlaams Tijdschrift
NvT — Novum Testamentum [*Leiden*]
NVV — Recreatie
NW — Neue Weg
NW — Neue Welt
NW — New Worlds
Nw — Newsweek
NW — Nucleonics Week
NWA — New Worlds Science Fiction
NWA — Nieuw Europa. Tijdschrift van de Europese Beweging in Nederland
NWAC — Native Women's Association of Canada. Newsletter
NWAY — Norway
NWB — New Books and Periodicals
NWB — New Worlds (British)
NWELA — New Electronics
NWEX — Northwest Explorer. Northwest Territorial Airways [*Yellowknife, NT*]
NWGB — New Writers Group Bulletin
NWGPA — Nachrichten. Gesellschaft der Wissenschaften zu Goettingen. Mathematisch-Physikalische Klasse. Fachgruppe 2. Physik, Astronomie, Geophysik, Technik
NWH — Lebensmittel Praxis. Unabhangiges Fachmagazin fuer Unternehmensfuehrung, Werbung, und Verkauf im Lebensmittelhandel
NWI — Nieuws uit Zweden
NWIG — Nieuwe West-Indische Gids
NWJ — New Scientist
Nw J Intl L and Bus — Northwestern Journal of International Law and Business
NWK — Levensmiddelenmarkt

NWK — Newsweek
NWL — Northwestern University. Law Review
Nw LS — Northwestern University. Law Review. Supplement
NwMSCS — Northwest Missouri State College Studies
NW Newsl — North Western Newsletter
NW Ohio Q — Northwest Ohio Quarterly
NWOQ — Northwest Ohio Quarterly
NW Paper News — Northwest Pulp and Paper News
NW Passage — Northwest Passage
NWPYA — Sae Mulli
NWQ — New Worlds. Quarterly
NWR — Northwest Review
Nw School — New Schools Exchange. Newsletter
NW Sci — Northwest Science
NWSIA J — NWSIA [*National Water Supply Improvement Association*]
   Journal
Nws Lettr — News and Letters
NWT — Northwest Territories Reports
NW Terr (Can) — Northwest Territories Reports (Canada)
NWTG3 — NWT [*Northwest Territories, Canada*] Gazette. Part III
NWTGII — NWT [*Northwest Territories, Canada*] Gazette. Part II
NWT Rep — Northwest Territories Reports
NWTWN — NWT [*Northwest Territories, Canada*] Wildlife Notes
NWTWSCR — NWT [*Northwest Territories, Canada*] Wildlife Service.
   Completion Reports
NWTWSCT — NWT [*Northwest Territories, Canada*] Wildlife Service.
   Contact Reports
NWTWSFR — NWT [*Northwest Territories, Canada*] Wildlife Service. File
   Reports
NWTWSPR — NWT [*Northwest Territories, Canada*] Wildlife Service.
   Progress Reports
NWU — Viewpoint
NWULR — Northwestern University. Law Review
NW U L Rev — Northwestern University. Law Review
NW Univ Law R — Northwestern University. Law Review
NWW — New World Writing
NWZam — New Writing from Zambia
NY — New York
NY — New York Magazine
NY — New Yorker
NY — School Music News [*New York*]
NyA — Nya Argus
NY Acad Sci Ann — New York Academy of Sciences. Annals
NY Acad Sci Trans — New York Academy of Sciences. Transactions
NY Aff — New York Affairs
NY Ag Dept — New York Department of Agriculture. Publications
NY Agric Exp Stn (Geneva) Annu Rep — New York. Agricultural Experiment
   Station (Geneva). Annual Report
NY Agric Exp Stn (Geneva) Bull — New York. Agricultural Experiment Station
   (Geneva). Bulletin
NY Agric Exp Stn (Geneva) Res Circ — New York. Agricultural Experiment
   Station (Geneva). Research Circular
NY Agric Exp Stn (Geneva) Tech Bull — New York. Agricultural Experiment
   Station (Geneva). Technical Bulletin
NY Agric Exp Stn (Ithaca) Bull — New York. Agricultural Experiment Station
   (Ithaca). Bulletin
NY Agric Exp Stn (Ithaca) Mem — New York. Agricultural Experiment
   Station (Ithaca). Memoir
Nya Perspekt — Nya Perspektiv
NY Appl For Res Inst AFRI Misc Rep — New York Applied Forestry Research
   Institute. AFRI Miscellaneous Report
NY Appl For Res Inst AFRI Res Note — New York Applied Forestry Research
   Institute. AFRI Research Note
NY Appl For Res Inst AFRI Res Rep — New York Applied Forestry Research
   Institute. AFRI Research Report
NY Arts J — New York Arts Journal
Nyasaland Farmer Forest — Nyasaland Farmer and Forester
Nyasal Farmer For — Nyasaland Farmer and Forester
Nyasal Geol Surv Dep Mem — Nyasaland Protectorate. Geological Survey
   Department. Memoir
NY Bd Agr Mem — New York Board of Agriculture. Memoirs
NY Bot Gard Annu Rep — New York Botanical Garden. Annual Report
NY Bot Garden B — New York Botanical Garden. Bulletin
NYC Bd Ed Curric Bul — New York City Board of Education. Curriculum
   Bulletins
NY Cert Pub Acct — New York Certified Public Accountant
NYCKA — Neng Yuan Chi Kan
NY Comm St Res Niagara An Rp — New York Commissioners of the State
   Reservation at Niagara. Annual Report
NY County B Bull — New York County Lawyers Association. Bar Bulletin
NY County Law Ass'n B Bull — New York County Lawyers Association. Bar
   Bulletin
NY Dep Agric Mark Annu Rep — New York Department of Agriculture and
   Markets. Annual Report
NY Dep Agric Mark Circ — New York Department of Agriculture and
   Markets. Circular

NY Dep Transp Res Rep — New York State Department of Transport.
   Research Report
Nyelvtudomanyi Dolg Eotvos Lorand TudomEgy — Nyelvtudomanyi
   Dolgozatok. Eotvos Lorand Tudomanyegyetum
NYEP — New York Evening Post
NYEPLR — New York Evening Post Literary Review
NYF — New York Law Forum
NY Farms & Markets Dept — New York State Department of Farms and
   Markets. Publications
NY Fd Life Sci Q — New York's Food and Life Sciences Quarterly
NY Fish Game J — New York Fish and Game Journal
NY Folkl — New York Folklore
NY Folklore — New York Folklore
NY Folk Q — New York Folklore. Quarterly
NY Food Life Sci Bull — New York's Food and Life Sciences Bulletin
NY Food Life Sci Q — New York's Food and Life Sciences Quarterly
NYFQ — New York Folklore. Quarterly
NY G S — New York Geological Survey
NYGZA — Nippon Yuketsu Gakkai Zasshi
NYH — New York History
NY Herald Tribune Bk R — New York Herald Tribune. Book Review
NY Herald Tribune W Bk R — New York Herald Tribune. Weekly Book
   Review
NY Her Trib Lively Arts — New York Herald Tribune. Lively Arts Section
NY His — New York History
NY Hist — New York History
NY Hist Soc Coll — New York Historical Society. Collections
NY Hist Soc Q — New York Historical Society. Quarterly
NY Hist Soc Quar — New York Historical Society. Quarterly
NYHS — New York Historical Society. Quarterly
NYHSQ — New York Historical Society. Quarterly
NYHSQB — New York Historical Society. Quarterly Bulletin
NYHTB — New York Herald Tribune. Weekly Book Review
NyIK — Nyelvtudomanyi Intezet Koezlemenyek
NY J Dent — New York Journal of Dentistry
NYJ Int'l & Comp L — New York Law School. Journal of International and
   Comparative Law
NY J Med — New York State Journal of Medicine
NyK — Nyelvtudomanyi Koezlemenyek
NYKZAU — Folia Pharmacologica Japonica
NYL — New York University. Law Review
NYLAB — New York Language Association. Bulletin
NY Law Forum — New York Law Forum
NY Law J — New York Law Journal
NY Law R — New York Law Review
NY Law Rev — New York Law Review
NY L F — New York Law Forum
NY Lib Assn Bul — New York Library Association. Bulletin
NY Lit For — New York Literary Forum
NYLJ — New York Law Journal
NYL Rev — New York Law Review
NylroK — Nyelv-Es Irodalomtudomanyi Koezlemenyek
NY L Sch Intl L Socy J — New York Law School. International Law Society.
   Journal
NY L Sch J Intl and Comp L — New York Law School. Journal of
   International and Comparative Law
NY L Sch L Rev — New York Law School. Law Review
NYL School Rev — New York Law School. Law Review
NYLSLR — New York Law School. Law Review
NY L S L Rev — New York Law School. Law Review
NY Med — New York Medicine
NY Med J — New York Medical Journal
NY Med Phys J — New York Medical and Physical Journal
NY Micro Soc J — New York Microscopical Society. Journal
NY Miner Club B — New York Mineralogical Club. Bulletin
NYMZ — Nytt Magasin foer Zoologi
NY New Tech Bks — New York Public Library. New Technical Books
NYO — New York Observer
N York J Med — New York Journal of Medicine
N York Med J — New York Medical Journal
NYP — New York Post
NY Phil — New York Philharmonic Program Notes
NYPL Bull — New York Public Library. Bulletin
NY Prod R — New York Produce Review and American Creamery
NY Prod Rev Am Creamery — New York Produce Review and American
   Creamery
NY Pub Lib Br Lib Bk News — New York Public Library. Branch Library
   Book News
NY Public Lib Bull — New York City Public Library. Bulletin
NYQ — New York Quarterly
Nyr — Magyar Nyelvor
NYR — New York Reports [*New York*]
NYR — New York Review of Books
NYRB — New York Review of Books
NYR of Bk — New York Review of Books
NYR Bks — New York Review of Books

NY Rev Bks — New York Review of Books
NY Rev Book — New York Review of Books
NY Review — New York Review of Books
NYS — New York Sun
NYSB J — New York State Bar Journal
NY Sea Grant L and Pol'y J — New York Sea Grant Law and Policy Journal
NYSERDA Rev — NYSERDA [*New York State Energy Research and Development Authority*] Review
NY Soc Exp Study Ed Yrbk — New York Society for the Experimental Study of Education. Yearbook
Nys S — Nysvenska Studier
NYSSNTA J — NYSSNTA [*New York State School Nurse-Teachers Association*] Journal
NY St Agr Soc Tr — New York State Agricultural Society. Transactions
NY State Ag Exp — New York State Agricultural Experiment Station. Publications
NY State Agric Exp Stn Seed Res Circ — New York State Agricultural Experiment Station. Seed Research Circular
NY State Agric Exp Stn Spec Rep — New York State Agricultural Experiment Station. Special Report
NY State Assoc Milk Food Sanit Annu Rep — New York State Association of Milk and Food Sanitarians. Annual Report
NY State Assoc Milk Sanit Annu Rep — New York State Association of Milk Sanitarians. Annual Report
NY State Bar J — New York State Bar Journal
NY State Coll Ceramics Ceramic Expt Sta Bull — New York State College of Ceramics. Ceramic Experiment Station. Bulletin
NY State Coll For Syracuse Univ Bull — New York State College of Forestry. Syracuse University. Bulletin
NY State Conserv — New York State Conservationist
NY State Dent J — New York State Dental Journal
NY State Dep Environ Conserv Bull — New York State Department of Environmental Conservation. Bulletin
NY State Dep Health Div Lab Res Annu Rep — New York State Department of Health. Division of Laboratories and Research. Annual Report
NY State Dep Health Lab Res Oper Data — New York State Department of Health. Division of Laboratories and Research. Operations Data
NY State Dep Labor Div Ind Hyg Mon Rev — New York State Department of Labor. Division of Industrial Hygiene. Monthly Review
NY State Ed — New York State Education
NY State Flower Growers Bull — New York State Flower Growers. Bulletin
NY State Horti Soc Proc — New York State Horticultural Society. Proceedings
NY State J Med — New York State Journal of Medicine
NY State Mus Bull — New York State Museum. Bulletin
NY State Mus Circ Handb — New York State Museum Circular. Handbook
NY State Mus Sci Serv Bull — New York State Museum and Science Service. Bulletin
NY State Mus Sci Serv Circ — New York State Museum and Science Service. Circular
NY State Mus Sci Serv Educ Leafl — New York State Museum and Science Service. Educational Leaflet
NY State Mus and Sci Service Bull Circ — New York State Museum and Science Service. Bulletin. Circular
NY State Mus Sci Serv Map Chart Ser — New York State Museum and Science Service. Map and Chart Series
NY State Mus Sci Serv Mem — New York State Museum and Science Service. Memoir
NY State Sci Service Rept Inv — New York State Science Service. Report of Investigation
NY State Sci Serv Univ State NY Report Invest — New York State Science Service. University of the State of New York. Report of Investigation
NY State Water Resour Comm Basin Plann Rep — New York State Water Resources Commission. Basin Planning Report
NY St BJ — New York State Bar Journal
NY St Cab An Rp — New York State Cabinet of Natural History. Annual Report. Regents University
NYSTDL — Agricultural Research. Seoul National University
NY St G An Rp — New York State Geologist. Annual Report
NY St His As — New York State Historical Association. Proceedings
NY St His As Q J — New York State Historical Association. Quarterly Journal
NY St Hist Assn J — New York State Historical Association. Quarterly Journal
NY St J Med — New York State Journal of Medicine
NY St Mus — New York State Museum
NY St Mus An Rp — New York State Museum of Natural History. Annual Report
NYT — New York Times
NYT — New York Times Book Review
NYTB — New York Times Book Review
NYTBR — New York Times Book Review
Ny Tek — Ny Teknik
NY Theat Cr — New York Theatre Critics. Reviews
NYTIA — New York Times
NY Times — New York Times
NY Times — New York Times Book Review

NY Times Biog Service — New York Times Biographical Service
NY Times Bk R — New York Times Book Review
NY Times Book Rev — New York Times Book Review
NY Times M — New York Times Magazine
NY Times Mag — New York Times Magazine
NY Times R — New York Times Book Review
NYTKB — Ny Teknik
NYTLS — New York Times Literary Supplement
NYTM — New York Times Magazine
NYTMag — New York Times Magazine
NYTMS — New York Times Magazine Section
NYTRAH — Marine Sciences Research Center [*Stony Brook*]. Technical Report
Nytt Mag Bot (Oslo) — Nytt Magasin foer Botanikk (Oslo)
Nytt Mag Naturvid — Nytt Magasin foer Naturvidenskapene
Nytt Mag Naturvidensk — Nytt Magasin foer Naturvidenskapene
Nytt Mag Zool (Oslo) — Nytt Magasin foer Zoology (Oslo)
NYU Conf Lab — New York University. Conference on Labor
NYU Educ Q — New York University. Education Quarterly
NYU Eng Res Rev — NYU Engineering Research Review
NYUEQ — New York University. Education Quarterly
NYU Inst on Fed Tax — New York University. Institute on Federal Taxation
NYU Inst Fed Tax — New York University. Institute on Federal Taxation
NYU Inst Fed Taxation — New York University. Institute on Federal Taxation
NYU Intra L Rev — New York University. Intramural Law Review
NYU Intramur L Rev — New York University. Intramural Law Review
NYUJ Int'l Law & Pol — New York University. Journal of International Law and Politics
NYU J Int'l L & Pol — New York University. Journal of International Law and Politics
NYU J Int L & Pol — New York University. Journal of International Law and Politics
NYU J Int L & Politics — New York University. Journal of International Law and Politics
NYU Law Q Rev — New York University. Law Quarterly Review
NYULQ Rev — New York University. Law Quarterly Review
NYUL Qu Rev — New York University. Law Quarterly Review
NYULR — New York University. Law Review
NYU L Rev — New York University. Law Review
NY Univ J of Internat L and Polit — New York University. Journal of International Law and Politics
NY Univ L Rev — New York University. Law Review
NY Univ Res B — New York University. Research Bulletin in Commercial Education
NYU Rev Law & Soc C — New York University. Review of Law and Social Change
NYU Rev L & Soc — New York University. Review of Law and Social Change
NYU Rev L and Soc Ch — New York University. Review of Law and Social Change
NYU Rev L & Soc Change — New York University. Review of Law and Social Change
NYU Slav P — New York University. Slavic Papers
NYW — New York World
NY Water Power Control Comm Bull — New York State Water Power and Control Commission. Bulletin
NY Water Power and Control Comm Bull — New York Water Power and Control Commission. Bulletin
NY Water Resour Comm Bull — New York State Water Resources Commission. Bulletin
NYWJT — New York World Journal Tribune
NZ — Nasa Zena
NZ — Neue Zeitschrift fuer Musik
NZ — Neuphilologische Zeitschrift
NZ — Novyj Zurnal
NZ — Numismatische Zeitschrift
NZ Agi Sci — New Zealand Institution of Agricultural Science. Bulletin
NZ Agric Sci — New Zealand Agricultural Science
NZ Agricst — New Zealand Agriculturist
NZ Agr Sci — New Zealand Agricultural Science
NZ Arch — New Zealand Architect
NZ Archit — New Zealand Architect
NZ Beekeep — New Zealand Beekeeper
NZ Beekpr — New Zealand Beekeeper
NZ Beekprs J — New Zealand Beekeepers' Journal
NZ Bird Banding Scheme Annu Rep — New Zealand Bird Banding Scheme. Annual Report
NZ Bu Econ — New Zealand Building Economist
NZ Bu Insp — New Zealand Building Inspector
NZ Bus Con — New Zealand Business Conditions
NZC — New Zealand Commerce
NZ Cartogr J — New Zealand Cartographic Journal
NZCernU — Naukovi Zapyski Cernivec'koho Derzavnoho Universyteta
NZCerPI — Naukovi Zapyski Cerkas'koho Derzavnoho Pedahohicnoho Instytutu
NZ Chiro J — New Zealand Chiropractic Journal
NZ Coal — New Zealand Coal

NZ Com — New Zealand Commerce
NZ Com Grow — New Zealand Commercial Grower
NZ Commer Grow — New Zealand Commercial Grower
NZ Conc Constr — New Zealand Concrete Construction
NZ Concr Constr — NZ [*New Zealand*] Concrete Construction
NZ Dent J — New Zealand Dental Journal
NZ Dep Agric Rep — New Zealand. Department of Agriculture. Report
NZ Dep Health Spec Rep Ser — New Zealand. Department of Health. Special Report Series
NZ Dep Intern Aff Wildl Publ — New Zealand. Department of Internal Affairs. Wildlife Publication
NZ Dep Sci Ind Res Bull — New Zealand. Department of Scientific and Industrial Research. Bulletin
NZ Dep Sci Ind Res Chem Div Rep — New Zealand. Department of Scientific and Industrial Research. Chemistry Division. Report
NZ Dep Sci Ind Res Crop Res News — New Zealand. Department of Scientific and Industrial Research. Crop Research News
NZ Dep Sci Ind Res Geol Surv Paleontol Bull — New Zealand. Department of Scientific and Industrial Research. Geological Survey. Paleontological Bulletin
NZ Dep Sci Ind Res Geophys Div Rep — New Zealand. Department of Scientific and Industrial Research. Geophysics Division. Report
NZ Dep Sci Ind Res Geophys Div Tech Note — New Zealand. Department of Scientific and Industrial Research. Geophysics Division. Technical Note
NZ Dep Sci Ind Res Inf Ser — New Zealand. Department of Scientific and Industrial Research. Information Series
NZDnepU — Naucnye Zapyski Dnepropetrovskogo Gosudarstvennogo Universiteta
NZDonPI — Naukovi Zapyski Donec'koho Derzavnoho Pedahohicnoho Instytutu
NZ Draughtsman — New Zealand Draughtsman
NZDrohPI — Naukovi Zapyski Drohobyc'koho Derzavnoho Pedahohicnoho Instytutu
N Zealand Lib — New Zealand Libraries
NZ Ecol Soc Proc — New Zealand Ecological Society. Proceedings
NZ Elect Rev — New Zealand Electronics Review
NZ Electr J — New Zealand Electrical Journal
NZ Electronics — New Zealand Electronics. Supplement to Electrical Industry
NZ Electron Rev — New Zealand Electronics Review
NZ Energ J — New Zealand Energy Journal
NZ Energy J — New Zealand Energy Journal
NZ Energy Res Dev Comm Newsl — New Zealand Energy Research and Development Committee. Newsletter
NZ Eng — New Zealand Engineering
NZ Eng News — New Zealand Engineering News
NZ Engng — New Zealand Engineering
NZ Ent — New Zealand Entomologist
NZ Entomol — New Zealand Entomologist
NZ Environ — New Zealand Environment
NZEP — New Zealand Economic Papers
NZ Fam Phys — New Zealand Family Physician
NZ Farmer — New Zealand Farmer
NZ Fert — New Zealand Fertiliser Journal
NZ Fert J — New Zealand Fertiliser Journal
NZ Financ Rev — New Zealand Financial Review
NZ Fin Rev — New Zealand Financial Review
NZ Fish Res Div Fish Res Bull — New Zealand Fisheries. Research Division. Fisheries Research Bulletin
NZfM — Neue Zeitschrift fuer Musik
NZ For Affairs R — New Zealand Foreign Affairs Review
NZ Foreign Aff Rev — New Zealand Foreign Affairs Review
NZ For Res Inst For Serv Mapp Ser 6 — New Zealand Forest Research Institute. Forest Service Mapping. Series 6
NZ For Res Notes — New Zealand Forestry Research Notes
NZ For Serv For Res Inst FRI Symp — New Zealand. Forest Service. Forest Research Institute. FRI Symposium
NZ For Serv For Res Inst Tech Pap — New Zealand. Forest Service. Forest Research Institute. Technical Paper
NZ For Serv Inf Ser — New Zealand. Forest Service. Information Series
NZ For Serv Rep Dir-Gen For — New Zealand. Forest Service. Report of the Director-General of Forests
NZ For Serv Rep For Res Inst — New Zealand. Forest Service. Report of the Forest Research Institute
NZ For Serv Res Leafl — New Zealand. Forest Service. Research Leaflet
NZ For Serv Tech Pap — New Zealand. Forest Service. Technical Paper
NZ Fruit and Prod — New Zealand Fruit and Product Journal
NZFSA — New Zealand Journal of Forestry Science
NZ Furn — New Zealand Furniture
NZ Gard — New Zealand Gardener
NZ Geneal — New Zealand Genealogist
NZ Geochem Group Newsl — New Zealand Geochemical Group. Newsletter
NZ Geogr — New Zealand Geographer
NZ Geol Surv Bull — New Zealand. Geological Survey. Bulletin
NZ Geol Surv Ind Miner Rocks — New Zealand. Geological Survey. Industrial Minerals and Rocks

NZ Geol Surv Misc Ser Map — New Zealand. Geological Survey. Miscellaneous Series. Map
NZ Geol Surv Rep — New Zealand. Geological Survey. Report
NZGG-A — New Zealand Geographer
NZ He — New Zealand Herald
NZhi — Nauka i Zhizn' [*Moscow*]
NZ Home and Bu — New Zealand Home and Building
NZ Home and Build — New Zealand Home and Building
NZ Hosp — New Zealand Hospital
NZIE Proc Tech Groups — NZIE [*New Zealand Institution of Engineers*] Proceedings of Technical Groups
NZ Inst Eng Proc Tech Groups — New Zealand Institution of Engineers. Proceedings of Technical Groups
NZ Inst Eng Trans — New Zealand Institution of Engineers. Transactions
NZ Inter — New Zealand Interface
NZ Int Rev — New Zealand International Review
NZIR — Niemeyers Zeitschrift fuer Internationales Recht
NZIzmPI — Naukovi Zapyski Izmail's'koho Derzavnoho Pedahohicnoho Instytutu
NZ J Agr — New Zealand Journal of Agriculture
NZ J Agric — New Zealand Journal of Agriculture
NZ J Agric Res — New Zealand Journal of Agricultural Research
NZ J Agr Re — New Zealand Journal of Agricultural Research
NZ J Agr Res — New Zealand Journal of Agricultural Research
NZ J Archaeol — New Zealand Journal of Archaeology
NZ J Bot — New Zealand Journal of Botany
NZ J Bus — New Zealand Journal of Business
NZ J Dairy Sci — New Zealand Journal of Dairy Science and Technology
NZJ Dairy Sci Technol — New Zealand Journal of Dairy Science and Technology
NZ J Dairy Technol — New Zealand Journal of Dairy Technology
NZ J Educ — New Zealand Journal of Educational Studies
NZ J Educ Stud — New Zealand Journal of Educational Studies
NZ J Exp Agric — New Zealand Journal of Experimental Agriculture
NZ J Fam Plann — New Zealand Journal of Family Planning
NZ J For — New Zealand Journal of Forestry
NZ J For Sci — New Zealand Journal of Forestry Science
NZ J Fr Stud — New Zealand Journal of French Studies
NZ J Geogr — New Zealand Journal of Geography
NZ J Geol — New Zealand Journal of Geology and Geophysics
NZ J Geol Geophys — New Zealand Journal of Geology and Geophysics
NZ J Hist — New Zealand Journal of History
NZJHPER — New Zealand Journal of Health, Physical Education, and Recreation
NZ J Ind Relat — New Zealand Journal of Industrial Relations
NZ J Ind Relations — New Zealand Journal of Industrial Relations
NZ Jl Agric — New Zealand Journal of Agriculture
NZ Jl Bot — New Zealand Journal of Botany
NZ J Mar Freshwater Res — New Zealand Journal of Marine and Freshwater Research
NZ J Mar Freshw Res — New Zealand Journal of Marine and Freshwater Research
NZ J Mar Res — New Zealand Journal of Marine and Freshwater Research
NZ J Med Lab Technol — New Zealand Journal of Medical Laboratory Technology
NZ Jnl Bus — New Zealand Journal of Business
NZ J Phys Educ — New Zealand Journal of Health, Physical Education, and Recreation
NZ J Physiother — New Zealand Journal of Physiotherapy
NZ J Physiotherapy — New Zealand Journal of Physiotherapy
NZ J Pub Admin — New Zealand Journal of Public Administration
NZJ Publ Adm — New Zealand Journal of Public Administration
NZ J Public Admin — New Zealand Journal of Public Administration
NZ J Sci — New Zealand Journal of Science
NZ J Sci Technol — New Zealand Journal of Science and Technology
NZ J Sci Technol Sect A — New Zealand Journal of Science and Technology. Section A
NZ J Sci Technol Sect B — New Zealand Journal of Science and Technology. Section B
NZ J Sports Med — New Zealand Journal of Sports Medicine
NZ J Zool — New Zealand Journal of Zoology
NZKamPI — Naukovi Zapyski Kam'jancja-Polil's'koho Derzavnoho Pedahohicnoho Instytutu
NZKievPIIn — Naucnye Zapyski Kievskogo Pedagogiceskogo Instytutu Inostrannych Jazykov
NZKyiPI — Naukovi Zapyski Kyjivs'koho Derzavnoho Pedahohicnoho Instytutu
NZ Law J — New Zealand Law Journal
NZ Lib — New Zealand Libraries
NZ Libr — New Zealand Libraries
NZ Lincoln Coll Tech Publ — New Zealand Lincoln College. Technical Publication
NZ List — New Zealand Listener
NZ L J — New Zealand Law Journal
NZ Local Gov — New Zealand Local Government
NZ Loc Govt — New Zealand Local Government

NZM — Neue Zeitschrift fuer Missionswissenschaft
NZM — Neue Zeitschrift fuer Musik
NZ Mar Dep Fish Res Div Bull New Ser — New Zealand Marine Department. Fisheries Research Division. Bulletin. New Series
NZ Mar Dep Fish Tech Rep — New Zealand Marine Department. Fisheries Technical Report
NZ Mar Dep Rep — New Zealand Marine Department. Report
NZ Mar News — New Zealand Marine News
NZ Meat Prod — New Zealand Meat Producer
NZ Med J — New Zealand Medical Journal
NZ Med J Suppl — New Zealand Medical Journal. Supplement
NZ Minist Agric Fish Fish Tech Rep — New Zealand Ministry of Agriculture and Fisheries. Fisheries Technical Report
NZ Minist Agric Fish Rep Fish — New Zealand Ministry of Agriculture and Fisheries. Report on Fisheries
NZMiss — Neue Zeitschrift fuer Missionswissenschaft
NZMissWiss — Neue Zeitschrift fuer Missionswissenschaft [*Beckenried, Switzerland*]
NZMJA — New Zealand Medical Journal
NZMUKS — Naukovyj Zbirnik Museju Ukranjinskoji Kultury v Sydynku
N Z Musik — Neue Zeitschrift fuer Musik
NZMW — Neue Zeitschrift fuer Missionswissenschaft
NZNJ — New Zealand Numismatic Journal
NZ Num J — New Zealand Numismatic Journal
NZ Nurs Forum — New Zealand Nursing Forum
NZ Nurs J — New Zealand Nursing Journal
NZ Oceanogr Inst Collect Repr — New Zealand Oceanographic Institute. Collected Reprints
NZ Oceanogr Inst Mem — New Zealand Oceanographic Institute. Memoir
NZOI Oceanographic Field Report — New Zealand Oceanographic Institute. Oceanographic Field Report
NZOI Rec — NZOI [*New Zealand Oceanographic Institute*] Records
NZ Oper Res — New Zealand Operational Research
NZOR — New Zealand Operational Research
NZ Paint — New Zealand Painter and Decorator
NZ Pharm — New Zealand Pharmacy
NZ Plumb — New Zealand Plumbers Journal
NZ Pop — New Zealand Population Review
NZ Pot — New Zealand Potato Bulletin
NZ Potter — New Zealand Potter
NZ Psychol — New Zealand Psychologist
NZ Purch — New Zealand Purchasing and Materials Management Journal
NZ Railw Obs — New Zealand Railway Observer
NZ Real — New Zealand Real Estate
NZ Sch Dent Ser Gaz — New Zealand School Dental Service. Gazette
NZ Sci Rev — New Zealand Science Review
NZ Sci Teach — New Zealand Science Teacher
NZ Ship — New Zealand Shipping Gazette
NZSJ — New Zealand Slavonic Journal
NZ Slav J — New Zealand Slavonic Journal
NZ Soc Earthquake Eng Bull — New Zealand Society for Earthquake Engineering. Bulletin
NZ Soc Soil Sci Proc — New Zealand Society of Soil Science. Proceedings
NZ Soil Bur Bull — New Zealand. Soil Bureau. Bulletin
NZ Soil Bur Sci Rep — New Zealand. Soil Bureau. Scientific Report
NZ Soil News — New Zealand Soil News
NZ Soil Surv Rep — New Zealand. Soil Survey Report
NZ Speech Therapist J — New Zealand Speech Therapists' Journal
NZ Speech Ther J — New Zealand Speech Therapists' Journal
NZ Speleol Bull — New Zealand Speleological Bulletin
NZST — Neue Zeitschrift fuer Systematische Theologie
NZSThR — Neue Zeitschrift fuer Systematische Theologie und Religionsphilosophie
NZ Surv — New Zealand Surveyor
NZ Sys Th — Neue Zeitschrift fuer Systematische Theologie und Religionsphilosophie
NZT — Neue Zurcher Zeitung und Schweizerisches Handelsblatt
NZTBA — New Zealand Journal of Science and Technology. Section B. General Research
NZ Timb — New Zealand Timber Worker
NZ Timber J Wood Prod Rev — New Zealand Timber Journal and Wood Products Review
NZ Timb J — New Zealand Timber Journal
NZ Tob Grow J — New Zealand's Tobacco Growers' Journal
NZ Tour — New Zealand Tourism
NZ Tour Res — New Zealand Tourism Research Newsletter
NZu — Novyj Zurnal
NZU — Voedingsmiddelen Technologie
NZULR — New Zealand Universities Law Review
NZ U L Rev — New Zealand Universities Law Review
NZ Univ Law Rev — New Zealand Universities Law Review
NZ Univ LR — New Zealand Universities Law Review
NZ Univ L Rev — New Zealand Universities Law Review
NZ Univs Law R — New Zealand Universities Law Review
NZURA — Nauchnye Zapiski Gosudarstvennyi Nauchno-Issledovatel'skii i Proektnyi Institut Ugol'noi Promyshlennosti

NZ Val — New Zealand Valuer
NZ Vet J — New Zealand Veterinary Journal
NZW — Neue Zeitschrift fuer Wehrrecht
NZ Wehrr — Neue Zeitschrift fuer Wehrrecht
NZ Wheat Rev — New Zealand Wheat Review
NZ Wings — New Zealand Wings
NZZ — Neue Zuericher Zeitung
NZZytPI — Naukovi Zapyski Zytomyrs'koho Derzavnoho Pedahohicnoho Instytutu

O

O — October
O — Oktjabr
O — Orbis
O — Osteuropa
OA — Oceanic Abstracts
OA — Oesterbotten: Aarsbok
OA — Opuscula Archaeologica
OA — Oriental Art
OA — Oroems Antiquus
OAA — Oesterreichisches Bank-Archiv. Zeitschrift fuer das Gesamte Bankwesen und Sparkassenwesen, Borsenwesen, und Kreditwesen
OAA — Oeuvres Afro-Asiatiques
OAG — Official Airline Guide
OAG — Oil and Gas Journal
OAHQ — Ohio Archaeological and Historical Quarterly
OAKR — Oesterreichisches Archiv fuer Kirchenrecht
Oak Ridge Nat Lab Radiat Shielding Inf Cent Rep — Oak Ridge National Laboratory. Radiation Shielding Information Center. Report
Oak Ridge Natl Lab Heavy Sect Steel Technol Program Tech Rep — Oak Ridge National Laboratory. Heavy Section Steel Technology Program. Technical Report
Oak Ridge Natl Lab Rev — Oak Ridge National Laboratory. Review
OALS Bulletin — Office of Arid Lands Studies. Bulletin
OAM — OPEC [Organization of Petroleum Exporting Countries] Bulletin
OANAD — Online-ADL Nachrichten
OAP — OAPEC [Organization of Arab Petroleum Exporting Countries] News Bulletin
OAPEC News Bull — OAPEC [Organization of Arab Petroleum Exporting Countries] News Bulletin [Kuwait]
OAr — Orientalisches Archiv
O Arch Q — Ohio Archaeological and Historical Quarterly
OARID — Oesterreichische Abwasser Rundschau. OAR International
OAS — Oesterreich in Amerikanischer Sicht. Das Oesterreichbild im Amerikanischen Schulunterricht
OAth — Opuscula Atheniensia
OAW PHKD — Denkschriften der Oesterreichischen Akademie der Wissenschaften. Philosophisch-Historische Klasse
OAW PHKS — Oesterreichische Akademie der Wissenschaften. Philosophisch-Historische Klasse. Sitzungsberichte
OB — Observer [United Kingdom]
OB — Ord och Bild
OBA — Oberbayerisches Archiv fuer Vaterlaendische Geschichte
O Bar — Ohio State Bar Association. Report
Obd Vcelar Prekl — Obdorne Vcelarske Preklady
Obecna Chem Technol — Obecna Chemicka Technologie
Obedin Inst Yad Issled (Dubna USSR) Prepr — Ob'edinennyi Institut Yadernykh Issledovanii (Dubna, USSR). Preprint
Oberflaechentech/Metallprax — Oberflaechentechnik/Metallpraxis [West Germany]
Oberflaeche Surf — Oberflaeche Surface
Oberlin Coll Mus Bull — Oberlin College. Allen Memorial Art Museum. Bulletin
Oberoest Imker — Oberoesterreichische Imker
Oberrheinische Geol Abh — Oberrheinische Geologische Abhandlungen
Obesity & Bariatric Med — Obesity and Bariatric Medicine

OBGNA — Obstetrics and Gynecology
OB Hi-Tension News — Ohio Brass Hi-Tension News
OBI — Film [Amsterdam]
OBIMD — Oncodevelopmental Biology and Medicine
Obit — Obituary
OBL — Orientalia et Biblica Lovaniensia
OBMR — Occasional Bulletin of Missionary Research
Obogashch Briket Uglei — Obogashchenie i Briketirovanie Uglei
Obogashchenie Briket Uglei — Obogashchenie i Briketirovanie Uglei [USSR]
Obogashch Polezn Iskop — Obogashchenie Poleznykh Iskopaemykh
Obogashch Rud — Obogashchenie Rud
Obogashch Rud (Irkutsk) — Obogashchenie Rud (Irkutsk)
OBP — Organizational Behavior and Human Performance
Obrab Metal Davleniem Mashinostr — Obrabotka Metallov Davleniem v Mashinostroenii [Ukrainian SSR]
Obrab Met Davleniem Mashinostr — Obrabotka Metallov Davleniem v Mashinostroenii
Obrab Met Davleniem (Rostov-On-Don) — Obrabotka Metallov Davleniem (Rostov-On-Don)
Obrobka Plast — Obrobka Plastyczna
Obs — Observer
Obs — Obsidian
Obs Astronom Univ Nac La Plata Ser Astronom — Observatorio Astronomico de la Universidad Nacional de La Plata. Serie Astronomica
Obsc Nauki v Uzbek — Obscestvennye Nauki v Uzbekistane
Observer Des Brief — Observer Design Brief
Obshcha Sravn Patol — Obshcha i Sravnitelna Patologiya
Obshch Ekol Biotsenol Gidrobiol — Obshchaya Ekologiya, Biotsenologiya, Gidrobiologiya
Obshch Energ — Obshchaya Energetika
Obshchest Nauk Uzbek — Obshchestvennye Nauki v Uzbekistane
Obshchestv Pitan — Obshchestvennoe Pitanie
Obshch Mashinostr — Obshchee Mashinostroenie
Obshch Prikl Khim — Obshchaya i Prikladnaya Khimiya
Obshch Zakonomern Morfog Regener — Obshchie Zakonomernosti Morfogeneza i Regeneratsii
Obshta Sravnitelna Patol — Obshta i Sravnitelna Patologiia
OBSP — Oxford Bibliographical Society. Proceedings
OBSP — Oxford Bibliographical Society. Publications
Obs sur Phys — Observations sur la Physique, sur l'Histoire Naturelle, et sur les Arts
Obstet Ginecol — Obstetrica si Ginecologia
Obstet Ginecol (Buchar) — Obstetrica si Ginecologia (Bucharest)
Obstet Ginecol Lat-Am — Obstetrica y Ginecologia Latino-Americanas
Obstet Gyn — Obstetrics and Gynecology
Obstet Gynecol — Obstetrics and Gynecology
Obstet Gynecol Annu — Obstetrics and Gynecology. Annual
Obstet Gynecol Surv — Obstetrical and Gynecological Survey
Obstet Gynecol Ther — Obstetrical and Gynecological Therapy [Japan]
Obstet Gynecol (Tokyo) — Obstetrics and Gynecology (Tokyo)
Obstet Gynec Surv — Obstetrical and Gynecological Survey
Obst Gemuese Verwert Ind — Obst- und Gemuese-Verwertungs Industrie
OBSUA — Oberflaeche Surface
OBU — Ombudsman. Tijdschrift voor Klachtrecht Tegen Overheidsoptreden
OBW — Journal fuer Betriebswirtschaft

Obz Mat Fiz — Obzornik za Matematiko in Fiziko
Obzornik Mat Fiz — Obzornik za Matematiko in Fiziko
Obz Otd Proizvod Khim Promsti — Obzory po Otdel'nym Proizvodstvam Khimicheskoi Promyshlennosti
Obz Veng Lesovod Nauki — Obzor Vengerskoi Lesovodstvennoi Nauki
Oc — Occidente
O et C — Oeuvres et Critiques
OC — Old Cornwall
OC — Open Court
OC — Opera Canada
OC — Oracle Series. National Museums of Canada and Department of Indian and Northern Affairs
OC — Oriens Christianus
OCA — Orientalia Christiana Analecta
OCACD — Oceanologica Acta
OcBul — Occasional Bulletin of Missionary Research
Occ — Occidental
OCC — Open Court (Chicago)
Occasional Publ in Math — Occasional Publications in Mathematics
Occas Pap BC Prov Mus — Occasional Papers. British Columbia Provincial Museum
Occas Pap Bell Mus Nat Hist Univ Minn — Occasional Papers. Bell Museum of Natural History. University of Minnesota
Occas Pap Bernice Pauahi Bishop Mus — Occasional Papers. Bernice Pauahi Bishop Museum
Occas Pap Calif Acad Sci — Occasional Papers. California Academy of Sciences
Occas Pap C C Adams Cent Ecol Stud West Mich Univ — Occasional Papers. C. C. Adams Center for Ecological Studies. Western Michigan University
Occas Pap Dep Biochem Makerere Univ — Occasional Paper. Department of Biochemistry. Makerere University
Occas Pap Dep Biol Univ Puget Sound — Occasional Papers. Department of Biology. University of Puget Sound
Occas Pap Entomol (Sacramento) — Occasional Papers in Entomology (Sacramento)
Occas Pap Farlow Herb Cryptogam Bot Harv Univ — Occasional Papers. Farlow Herbarium of Cryptogamic Botany. Harvard University
Occas Pap Geol Surv (New Hebrides) — Occasional Paper. Geological Survey (New Hebrides)
Occas Pap Mauritius Sugar Ind Res Inst — Occasional Paper. Mauritius Sugar Industry Research Institute
Occas Pap Minn Mus Nat Hist — Occasional Papers. Minnesota Museum of Natural History
Occas Pap Mollusks Mus Comp Zool Harv Univ — Occasional Papers on Mollusks. Museum of Comparative Zoology. Harvard University
Occas Pap Mus Nat Hist Univ Kans — Occasional Papers. Museum of Natural History. University of Kansas
Occas Pap Mus Nat Hist Univ Puget Sound — Occasional Papers. Museum of Natural History. University of Puget Sound
Occas Pap Mus Zool LA State Univ — Occasional Papers. Museum of Zoology. Louisiana State University
Occas Pap Mus Zool Univ Mich — Occasional Papers. Museum of Zoology. University of Michigan
Occas Pap Natl Coll Agric Eng — Occasional Paper. National College of Agricultural Engineering
Occas Pap Natl Mus Monum Rhod Ser B Nat Sci — Occasional Papers. National Museums and Monuments of Rhodesia. Series B. Natural Sciences
Occas Pap Natl Speleol Soc — Occasional Papers. National Speleological Society
Occas Pap R Ont Mus Zool — Occasional Papers. Royal Ontario Museum of Zoology
Occas Pap San Diego Soc Nat Hist — Occasional Papers. San Diego Society of Natural History
Occas Pap S Forest Exp Sta US Forest Serv — Occasional Papers. Southern Forest Experiment Station. United States Forest Service
Occas Pap Trop Sci Cent (San Jose Costa Rica) — Occasional Paper. Tropical Science Center (San Jose, Costa Rica)
Occas Pap Veg Surv West Aust — Occasional Papers. Vegetation Survey of Western Australia. Department of Agriculture
Occas Publ Rowett Res Inst — Occasional Publication. Rowett Research Institute
Occas Rep VA Div For Dep Conserv Econ Dev — Occasional Report. Virginia Division of Forestry. Department of Conservation and Economic Development
Occ Bul Miss R — Occasional Bulletin of Missionary Research
Occ Hazards — Occupational Hazards
Occ Health Nurs — Occupational Health Nursing
Occ Health & Sfty — Occupational Health and Safety
Occid — Occidente
Occident Entomol — Occidental Entomologist
Occ Outlook Q — Occupational Outlook Quarterly
Occ Pap Bur For (Philippines) — Occasional Paper. Bureau of Forestry (Manila, Philippines)

Occ Pap Bur Trans Eco — Occasional Paper. Department of Transport (Bureau of Transport Economics)
Occ Pap Calif Acad Sci — Occasional Papers. California Academy of Sciences
Occ Pap Dep Biol Univ Guyana — Occasional Papers. Department of Biology. University of Guyana
Occ Pap Maurit Sug Ind Res Inst — Occasional Paper. Mauritius Sugar Industry Research Institute
Occ Pap Vegn Surv West Aust — Occasional Paper. Vegetation Survey of Western Australia
Occ Publs Aust Conserv Fdn — Occasional Publications. Australian Conservation Foundation
Occupational Outlook Q — Occupational Outlook Quarterly
Occup Dermatoses — Occupational Dermatoses
Occup Hazards — Occupational Hazards
Occup Health Bull (Ottawa) — Occupational Health Bulletin (Ottawa)
Occup Health (Lond) — Occupational Health (London)
Occup Health Nurs — Occupational Health Nursing
Occup Health Nurs (NY) — Occupational Health Nursing (New York)
Occup Health Rev — Occupational Health Review
Occup Health and Saf — Occupational Health and Safety
Occup Health Saf — Occupational Health and Safety
Occup Hlth — Occupational Health
Occup Hlth Nurs — Occupational Health Nursing
Occup Hzrd — Occupational Hazards
Occup Med — Occupational Medicine
Occup Outl Q — Occupational Outlook Quarterly
Occup Psych — Occupational Psychology
Occup Saf Health — Occupational Safety and Health
Occup Saf Health Ser Int Labour Off — Occupational Safety and Health Series. International Labour Office
Occup Saf Hlth — Occupational Safety and Health
Occup Saf Hlth Admin Sub Service Vols 1 & 4 — Occupational Safety and Health Administration. Subscription Service. Volumes 1 and 4
Occup Ther Ment Health — Occupational Therapy in Mental Health
OCD — Office of Child Development. Publications
OCD — Oxford Classical Dictionary
Oc Dev and Int L — Ocean Development and International Law
OceanAb — Oceanic Abstracts
Ocean Devel & Int L — Ocean Development and International Law
Ocean Develop Int Law — Ocean Development and International Law
Ocean Development and Internat Law — Ocean Development and International Law
Ocean Dev I — Ocean Development and International Law
Ocean Dev & Int L — Ocean Development and International Law
Ocean Dev and Intl LJ — Ocean Development and International Law Journal
Ocean Eng — Ocean Engineering
Ocean Eng Inf Ser — Ocean Engineering. Information Series
Ocean Engng — Ocean Engineering
Ocean Ind — Ocean Industry
Ocean Ling — Oceanic Linguistics
Ocean Manage — Ocean Management
Ocean Mgt — Ocean Management
Oceanogr Cruise Rep Inst Mar Res (Djakarta) — Oceanographical Cruise Report. Institute of Marine Research (Djakarta)
Oceanogrl Cruise Rep Div Fish Oceanogr CSIRO — Oceanographical Cruise Report. Division of Fisheries and Oceanography. Commonwealth Scientific and Industrial Research Organisation
Oceanogrl Stn List Div Fish Oceanogr CSIRO — Oceanographical Station List. Division of Fisheries and Oceanography. Commonwealth Scientific and Industrial Research Organisation
Oceanogr Mag (Tokyo) — Oceanographical Magazine (Tokyo)
Oceanogr Mar Biol — Oceanography and Marine Biology
Oceanogr Mar Biol Annu Rev — Oceanography and Marine Biology: An Annual Review
Oceanogr Res Inst (Durban) Invest Rep — Oceanographic Research Institute (Durban). Investigational Report
Oceanogr Soc Jap J — Oceanographical Society of Japan. Journal
Oceanol — Oceanology
Oceanol Acta — Oceanologica Acta
Oceanol Int — Oceanology International
Oceanol Limnol Sin — Oceanologica et Limnologia Sinica
Ocean Sci Eng — Ocean Science and Engineering
Oceans Mag — Oceans Magazine
O Ch A — Orientalia Christiana Analecta
Ochanomizu Med J — Ochanomizu Medical Journal [*Japan*]
Ocherki Fiz-Khim Petrol — Ocherki Fiziko-Khimicheskoi Petrologii
Ocherki Geol Sov Karpat — Ocherki po Geologii Sovetskikh Karpat
Ochistka Povtorn Ispol'z Stochnykh Vod Urale — Ochistka i Povtornoe Ispol'zovanie Stochnykh Vod na Urale
Ochistka Vodn Vozdushn Basseinov Predpr Chern Metall — Ochistka Vodnogo i Vozdushnogo Basseinov na Predpriyatiyakh Chernoi Metallurgii
O Chr — One in Christ
Ochr Koroz — Ochrona Przed Korozja
Ochr Ovzdusi — Ochrana Ovzdusi. Supplement to Vodni Hospodarstvi. Rada B
OChrP — Orientalia Christiana Periodica
Ochr Powietrza — Ochrona Powietrza

Ochr Pr — Ochrona Pracy
Ochr Przeciwpozarowa Przem Chem — Ochrona Przeciwpozarowa w Przemysle Chemicznym
Ochr Przed Koroz — Ochrona Przed Korozja
Ochr Przyr — Ochrona Przyrody
Ochr Rosl — Ochrona Roslin
Ochr Rostl — Ochrana Rostlin
OCHZA — Oesterreichische Chemiker-Zeitung
OCI — Ocean Industry. Engineering, Construction, and Operations
OcL — Oceanic Linguistics
OCM — Ocean Management
OCMAA — Oceanographical Magazine
OCMEA — Occupational Medicine
OCNA — Ouvrages sur la Culture Nord-Africaine
OCOC — Oceans of Canada
OCP — Ohio CPA [*Certified Public Accountant*] Journal
OCP — Orientalia Christiana Periodica
Oc P Anth P — Occasional Papers in Anthropology. Pennsylvania State University
Oc P Dev-A — Occasional Papers. Centre for Developing-Area Studies
Oc P Econ H — Occasional Papers in Economic and Social History
Oc P Geog — Occasional Papers in Geography
Oc P Int Af — Occasional Papers in International Affairs
Oc P Rur De — Occasional Papers. Rural Development Committee
Ocrotirea Nat — Ocrotirea Naturii
Ocrotirea Nat Med Inconjurator — Ocrotirea Naturii si a Mediului Inconjurator
OCSAPB — Outer Continental Shelf. Environmental Assessment Program. Arctic Project Bulletin
OCSAPSB — Outer Continental Shelf. Environmental Assessment Program. Arctic Project Special Bulletin [*United States*]
OCSB — Outer Continental Shelf. Environmental Assessment Program. Bering Sea - Gulf of Alaska Newsletter
Octagon Pap — Octagon Papers
Ocul Ther Complications Manage — Ocular Therapy. Complications and Management
Od — Odrodzenie
ODGKA — Oita Daigaku Gakugeigakubu Kenkyu Kiyo. Shizenkagaku
ODI (Overseas Development Inst) R — ODI (Overseas Development Institute). Review
ODIZA — Osaka Daigaku Igaku Zasshi
Odjel Teh Nauka — Odjeljenje Tehnickih Nauka [*Sarajevo*]
ODOKA — Okayama Daigaku Onsen Kenkyusho Hokoku
ODONA — Odontoiatria
Odontoiatr Prat — Odontoiatria Pratica
Odontol Bull — Odontological Bulletin
Odontol Chil — Odontologia Chilena
Odontol Conserv — Odontologie Conservatrice
Odontol Foren Tidskr — Odontologiska Foreningens Tidskrift
Odontol Peru — Odontologia Peruana
Odontol Revy — Odontologisk Revy
Odontol Samf Finl Arsb — Odontologiska Samfundft i Finland Arsbok
Odontol Tidskr — Odontologisk Tidskrift
Odontostomatol Implantoprotesi — Odontostomatologia e Implantoprotesi
Odontostomatol Proodos — Odontostomatologike Proodos
ODOPA — Publications. Dominion Observatory (Ottawa)
Odor Control Assoc J — Odor Control Association. Journal
Odor Res — Odor Research
Ody — Odyssey
Odyssey — Odyssey Review
OE — Onze Eeuw
OE — Oriens Extremus
OE — Oriental Economist
OEA Communique — Office Education Association. Communique
OEC — OECD [*Organization for Economic Cooperation and Development*] Economic Outlook
OeC — Oeuvres et Critiques
OEC — Oriental Economist
OECD Ber Dtsch Landwirtsch Ges Prufungsabt Landmasch — OCED Bericht-Deutsche Landwirtschafts-Gesellschaft Prufungsabteilung fuer Landmaschinen
OECD Inform — OECD [*Organization for Economic Cooperation and Development*] Informatics Studies
OECD Observer — OECD [*Organization for Economic Cooperation and Development*] Observer
OECD Outlk — OECD [*Organization for Economic Cooperation and Development*] Economic Outlook
OECD Svys — Organization for Economic Cooperation and Development. Economic Surveys of Member Countries
Oecol Plant — Oecologia Plantarum
Oecon Polon — Oeconomica Polona
Oeco Planta — Oecologia Plantarum
OEF — Management Totaal
Oeff Gesundheitsdienst — Oeffentliche Gesundheitsdienst [*West Germany*]
Oeff Gesundheitswes — Oeffentliche Gesundheitswesen

Oeff Verw — Oeffentliche Verwaltung [*Zeitschrift fuer Verwaltungsrecht und Verwaltungspolitik*]
Oeff Verwalt — Oeffentliche Verwaltung [*Zeitschrift fuer Verwaltungsrecht und Verwaltungspolitik*]
OEGWA — Oeffentliche Gesundheitswesen
OeJh — Jahreshefte. Oesterreichisches Archaeologische Institut
Oe Jh Beibl — Jahreshefte. Oesterreichisches Archaeologische Institut. Beiblatt
OEKOA — Oel und Kohle
Oekonom Unternehmensforsch — Oekonometrie und Unternehmensforschung
Oek S — Oekumenische Studien
Oel & Gas Feuerungstech — Oel und Gas und Feuerungstechnik [*West Germany*]
Oelhydraul Pneum — Oelhydraulik und Pneumatik
OEM — Oxford English Monographs
OEMA — Obras Escohidas de Machado de Assis
OEMZ — Oesterreichische Musikzeitschrift
OEN — Old English Newsletter
OEN — Oxford English Novels
OEO — OECD [*Organization for Economic Cooperation and Development*] Observer
OEP — Oxford Economic Papers
Oerlikon Schweissmitt — Oerlikon Schweissmitteilungen
OES — Oxford English Studies
Oest Bank-Arch — Oesterreichisches Bank-Archiv
Oest Bot Z — Oesterreichische Botanische Zeitschrift
Oesterr Abwasser Rundsch — Oesterreichische Abwasser Rundschau
Oesterr Aerztegtg — Oesterreichische Aerztezeitung
Oesterr Akad Wiss Erdwissenschaftliche Komm Schriftenr — Oesterreichische Akademie der Wissenschaften. Erdwissenschaftliche Kommission Schriftenreihe
Oesterr Akad Wiss Math Naturwiss Kl Sitzungsber — Oesterreichische Akademie der Wissenschaften. Mathematisch-Naturwissenschaftliche Klasse. Sitzungsberichte [*Austria*]
Oesterr Akad Wiss Math-Naturwiss Kl Sitzungsber Abt 1 — Oesterreichische Akademie der Wissenschaften. Mathematisch-Naturwissenschaftliche Klasse. Sitzungsberichte. Abteilung 1. Biologie, Mineralogie, Erdkunde, und Verwandte Wissenschaften
Oesterr Akad Wiss Math-Naturwiss Kl Sitzungsber Abt 2 — Oesterreichische Akademie der Wissenschaften. Mathematisch-Naturwissenschaftliche Klasse. Sitzungsberichte. Abteilung 2. Mathematik, Astronomie, Physik, Meteorologie, und Technik
Oesterr Akad Wiss Math Naturwiss Kl Sitzungsber Abt 2A — Oesterreichische Akademie der Wissenschaften. Mathematisch-Naturwissenschaftliche Klasse. Sitzungsberichte. Abteilung 2A. Mathematik, Astronomie, Physik, Meteorologie, und Technik
Oesterr Akad Wiss Math Naturwiss Kl Sitzungsber Abt 2B — Oesterreichische Akademie der Wissenschaften. Mathematisch-Naturwissenschaftliche Klasse. Sitzungsberichte. Abteilung 2B. Chemie
Oesterr Akad Wiss Math-Naturwiss Kl Sitzungsber Abt I — Oesterreichische Akademie der Wissenschaften. Mathematisch-Naturwissenschaftliche Klasse. Sitzungsberichte. Abteilung I
Oesterr Akad Wiss Math-Naturwiss Kl Sitzungsber Abt II — Oesterreichische Akademie der Wissenschaften. Mathematisch-Naturwissenschaftliche Klasse. Sitzungsberichte. Abteilung II
Oesterr Akad Wiss Philos-Hist Kl — Oesterreichische Akademie der Wissenschaften. Philosophisch-Historische Klasse
Oesterr Apoth Ztg — Oesterreichische Apotheker Zeitung
Oesterr Bot Z — Oesterreichische Botanische Zeitschrift
OeJh Chem-Z — Oesterreichische Chemie-Zeitschrift
Oesterr Chem-Ztg — Oesterreichische Chemiker-Zeitung
Oesterreich Akad Wiss Math-Natur Kl Denkschr — Oesterreichische Akademie der Wissenschaften. Mathematisch-Naturwissenschaftliche Klasse. Denkschriften
Oesterreich Akad Wiss Math-Natur Kl S-B II — Oesterreichische Akademie der Wissenschaften. Mathematisch-Naturwissenschaftliche Klasse. Sitzungsberichte. Abteilung II. Mathematik, Astronomie, Physik, Meteorologie, und Technik
Oesterreich Akad Wiss Math-Natur Kl Sitzungsber II — Oesterreichische Akademie der Wissenschaften. Mathematisch-Naturwissenschaftliche Klasse. Sitzungsberichte. Abteilung II. Mathematik, Astronomie, Physik, Meteorologie, und Technik [*Vienna*]
Oesterreich Akad Wiss Math Naturwiss Kl Denkschr — Oesterreichische Akademie der Wissenschaften. Mathematisch-Naturwissenschaftliche Klasse. Denkschriften
Oesterreich Akad Wiss Math-Naturwiss Kl SB II — Oesterreichische Akademie der Wissenschaften. Mathematisch-Naturwissenschaftliche Klasse. Sitzungsberichte. Abteilung II. Mathematik, Astronomie, Physik, Meteorologie, und Technik
Oesterreich Blasm — Oesterreichische Blasmusik
Oesterreich Geogr Ges Mitt — Oesterreichische Geographische Gesellschaft. Mitteilungen
Oesterreichische Zs Berg- u Huettenw — Oesterreichische Zeitschrift fuer Berg- und Huettenwesen
Oesterr Forst-Holzwirtsch — Oesterreichs Forst- und Holzwirtschaft
Oesterr Glaserztg — Oesterreichische Glaserzeitung
Oesterr Ing Arch — Oesterreichisches Ingenieur Archiv

Oesterr Ing & Archit Z — Oesterreichische Ingenieur und Architekten. Zeitschrift
Oesterr Ing-Z — Oesterreichische Ingenieur-Zeitschrift
Oesterr Jb Soziol — Oesterreichische Jahrbuch fuer Soziologie
Oesterr Krankenpflegez — Oesterreichische Krankenpflegezeitschrift
Oesterr Kunstst Rundsch — Oesterreichische Kunststoff-Rundschau
Oesterr Kunstst-Z — Oesterreichische Kunststoff-Zeitschrift [*Austria*]
Oesterr Landtech — Oesterreichische Landtechnik [*Austria*]
Oesterr Leder Haeutewirtsch — Oesterreichische Leder und Haeuterwirtschaft
Oesterr Leder Ztg — Oesterreichische Leder-Zeitung
Oesterr Mh — Oesterreichische Monatshefte
Oesterr Milchwirtsch — Oesterreichische Milchwirtschaft
Oesterr Milchwirtsch Ztg — Oesterreichische Milchwirtschaftliche Zeitung
Oesterr Mineral Ges Mitt — Oesterreichische Mineralogische Gesellschaft. Mitteilungen
Oesterr Molk Ztg — Oesterreichische Molkerei Zeitung
Oesterr Osth — Oesterreichische Osthefte
Oesterr Papier — Oesterreichische Papier
Oesterr Papier-Ztg — Oesterreichische Papier-Zeitung
Oesterr Pap Ztg — Oesterreichische Papier-Zeitung
Oesterr Schwesternztg — Oesterreichische Schwesternzeitung [*Austria*]
Oesterr Seifenfachbl — Oesterreichisches Seifenfachblatt
Oesterr Spirit Ztg — Oesterreichische Spirituosen Zeitung
Oesterr Studienges Atomenerg — Oesterreichische Studiengesellschaft fuer Atomenergie
Oesterr Textilz — Oesterreichische Textilzeitschrift
Oesterr Tierarzt — Oesterreichische Tieraerzt
Oesterr Tieraerzte Ztg — Oesterreichische Tieraerzte Zeitung
Oesterr Vierteljahresschr Forstwes — Oesterreichische Vierteljahresschrift fuer Forstwesen
Oesterr Vrtljschr Wissensch Veterinaerk — Oesterreichische Vierteljahresschrift fuer Wissenschaftliche Veterinaerkunde
Oesterr Wasserwirtsch — Oesterreichische Wasserwirtschaft
Oesterr Weidwerk — Oesterreichische Weidwerk
Oesterr Zahnaerzteztg — Oesterreichische Zahnaerzte-Zeitung
Oesterr Zahnprothet — Oesterreichische Zahnprothetik
Oesterr Zahntechnik — Oesterreichische Zahntechniker
Oesterr Z Aussenpol — Oesterreichische Zeitschrift fuer Aussenpolitik
Oesterr Z Berg Huettenwes — Oesterreichische Zeitschrift fuer Berg- und Huettenwesen
Oesterr Zeits Volksk — Oesterreichische Zeitschrift fuer Volkskunde
Oesterr Z Elektrizitaetswirtsch — Oesterreichische Zeitschrift fuer Elektrizitaetswirtschaft
Oesterr Z Erforsch Bekaempf Krebskr — Oesterreichische Zeitschrift fuer Erforschung und Bekaempfung der Krebskrankheit
Oesterr Z Erforsch Bekaempf Krebskrankheit — Oesterreichische Zeitschrift fuer Erforschung und Bekaempfung der Krebskrankheit [*Austria*]
Oesterr Z Kinderheilkd Kinderfuersorge — Oesterreichische Zeitschrift fuer Kinderheilkunde und Kinderfuersorge
Oesterr Z Oeff Recht — Oesterreichische Zeitschrift fuer Oeffentliches Recht
Oesterr Z Onkol — Oesterreichische Zeitschrift fuer Onkologie
Oesterr Zool Z — Oesterreichische Zoologische Zeitschrift
Oesterr Z Polit -Wiss — Oesterreichische Zeitschrift fuer Politikwissenschaft
Oesterr Z Stomatol — Oesterreichische Zeitschrift fuer Stomatologie
Oesterr Ztschr Kinderh — Oesterreichische Zeitschrift fuer Kinderheilkunde
Oesterr Z Volkskd — Oesterreichische Zeitschrift fuer Volkskunde
Oester Z Pol — Oesterreichische Zeitschrift fuer Politikwissenschaft
Oest Forschinst Wirt und Pol Ber — Oesterreichisches Forschungsinstitut fuer Wirtschaft und Politik. Berichte und Informationen
Oest Forschungsinst Sparkassenwesen VJ-Schriftenreihe — Oesterreichisches Forschungsinstitut fuer Sparkassenwesen Viertel Jahres-Schriftenreihe
Oest Ges Statis und Informatik Mitteilungsbl — Oesterreichische Gesellschaft fuer Statistik und Informatik. Mitteilungsblatt
Oest Imker — Oesterreichische Imker
Oest Imkerkal — Oester Imkerkalender
Oest Mhefte — Oesterreichische Monatshefte
Oest Osthefte — Oesterreichische Osthefte
Oest Volkswirt — Oesterreichische Volkswirt
Oest Z Aussenpol — Oesterreichische Zeitschrift fuer Aussenpolitik
Oest Zool Z — Oesterreichische Zoologische Zeitschrift
Oest Z Politikwiss — Oesterreichische Zeitschrift fuer Politikwissenschaft
OET — Oxford English Texts
OeTV Mag — OeTV [*Oeffentliche Dienste. Transport und Verkehr*] Magazin
Oeuvre Crit — Oeuvres et Critiques
OEV — Oesterreichische Volkswirt
Oevers Fin Vetensk Soc Foerh — Oeversigt af Finska Vetenskaps-Societetens Foerhandlingar
OEW — Osteuropa Wirtschaft
Oe Z E Oesterr Z Elek — Oe Z E/Oesterreichische Zeitschrift fuer Elektrizitaetswirtschaft
OF — Offshore Oil International [*Formerly, Offshore Oil Weekly*]
OFA — Old Farmer's Almanac
OFB — Oregon Folklore Bulletin
OFC — Offshore Research Focus
OFCA — Offshore Canada. Supplement of Offshore Oil Weekly
OFEN — Offshore Engineer. Incorporating Northern Offshore

OFEND — Offshore Engineer
Off — Office
OFF — Offshore Engineer
Off Adm Autom — Office Administration and Automation
Off Air Programs (US) Publ AP Ser — Office of Air Programs (United States). Publication. AP Series
Off Amer Horseman — Official American Horseman
Off Archit Plann — Official Architecture and Planning
Off Dig Fed Paint Varn Prod Clubs — Official Digest. Federation of Paint and Varnish Production Clubs
Off Dig Fed Soc Paint Technol — Official Digest. Federation of Societies for Paint Technology
Off Eng — Offshore Engineer
Off Gaz — Official Gazette
Off Gaz Pat Off — Official Gazette. United States Patent Office
Off Gaz US Pat Off — Official Gazette. United States Patent Office
Off Gaz US Pat Off Pat — Official Gazette. United States Patent Office. Patents
Off Gaz US Pat Trademark Off Pat — Official Gazette. United States Patent and Trademark Office. Patents
Off Gaz US Pat Trademks Off Pat — Official Gazette. United States Patent and Trademark Office. Patents
Off Gaz US Pat Trademks Off Trademks — Official Gazette. United States Patent and Trademark Office. Trademarks
Offic Board Markets — Official Board Markets
Office Adm & Automation — Office Administration and Automation
Office Admin — Office Administration
Office Archit Plann — Official Architecture and Planning
Office Eqp — Office Equipment and Products
Office Exec — Office Executive
Office Int Epizoot Bull — Office International des Epizooties. Bulletin [*France*]
Office Mgt — Office Management
Office Nat Etud Rech Aerosp (Fr) Publ — Office National d'Etudes et de Recherches Aerospatiales (France). Publication
Office Natl Etud Rech Aerosp Rep — Office National d'Etudes et de Recherches Aerospatiales. Reports
Office Tech People — Office: Technology and People
Offic Gaz US — Official Gazette. United States Patent and Trademark Office
Official Gazette USPO — United States. Patent Office. Official Gazette
Offic J (Pat) (Gr Brit) — Official Journal (Patents) (Great Britain)
Off Int Epizoot Bull — Office International des Epizooties. Bulletin
Off J Eur Communities — Official Journal of the European Communities
Off J Eur Communities Inf Not — Official Journal of the European Communities. Information and Notices. English Edition
Off J Inst Art Educ — Official Journal. Institute of Art Education
Off J Jpn Rheum Assoc — Official Journal. Japan Rheumatism Association
Off Jl (Pat) — Official Journal (Patents)
Off J (Pat) — Official Journal (Patents)
Off J Res Inst Med Sci Korea — Official Journal. Research Institute of Medical Science of Korea
Off Mach Guide — Office Machine Guide
Off Manage — Office Management
Off Meth Mach — Office Methods and Machines
Off Nat Etud Rech Aeronaut Note Tech — Office National d'Etudes et de Recherches Aeronautiques. Note Technique
Off Nat Etud Rech Aeronaut Publ — Office National d'Etudes et de Recherches Aeronautiques. Publication
Off Nat Etud Rech Aerosp (Fr) Note Tech — Office National d'Etudes et de Recherches Aerospatiales (France). Note Technique
Off Natl Etud Rech Aerosp (Fr) Tire Part — Office National d'Etudes et de Recherches Aerospatiales (France). Tire a Part
Off Nav Res (US) Res Rev — Office of Naval Research (United States). Research Review
Off Plast Caout — Officiel des Plastiques et du Caoutchouc
Off Plast Caoutch — Officiel des Plastiques et du Caoutchouc
Off Print Ink Maker — Official Printing Ink Maker
Off Proc Amer Ass Feed Micros — Official Proceedings. American Association of Feed Microscopists
Off Proc Annu Meet Am Assoc Feed Microsc — Official Proceedings. Annual Meeting. American Association of Feed Microscopists
Off Proc Annu Meet Int Dist Heat Assoc — Official Proceedings. Annual Meeting. International District Heating Association
Off Proc Natl Dist Heat Assoc — Official Proceedings. National District Heating Association
Off Publ Assoc Am Plant Food Control Off — Official Publication. Association of American Plant Food Control Officials
Off Rech Sci Tech Outre-Mer Trav Doc ORSTOM — Office de la Recherche Scientifique et Technique d'Outre-Mer. Travaux et Documents de l'ORSTOM
Off Rec WHO — Official Records. World Health Organization
Offshore Eng — Offshore Engineer
Offshore Engr — Offshore Engineer
Offshore Res Focus — Offshore Research Focus
Offshore Serv — Offshore Services
Offshore Serv Technol — Offshore Services and Technology

Offshore Technol Conf — Offshore Technology Conference
Offshore Technol Conf Proc — Offshore Technology Conference. Proceedings
Off Yrbk Cwealth Aust — Official Year Book. Commonwealth of Australia
Off Yrbk NSW — Official Yearbook. New South Wales
Off Yrbk Queensland — Official Yearbook. Queensland
Off Yrbk WA — Official Yearbook. Western Australia
OFIV — Our Family. Ilavut. Family Newspaper. Diocese of the Arctic
OFKSA — Osaka Furitsu Kogyo Shoreikan Hokoku
OFS — Offshore. The Journal of Ocean Business
OFSR — Offshore Resources
OFSVA — Offshore Services
Oftalmol Zh — Oftal'mologicheskii Zhurnal
OFZHA — Oftal'mologicheskii Zhurnal
OG — Official Gazette. United States Patent and Trademark Office
OG — Orientalia Gandensia [*Ghent*]
OGA — Oesterreichische Gastgewerbe und Hotel Zeitung
OGE — Ons Geestelijk Erf
OGF — Organic Gardening and Farming
OGIS — Orientis Graeci Inscriptiones Selectae
OGJ — Oil and Gas Journal
O & G Jour — Oil and Gas Journal. Forecast/Review
OGK — Onsei Gakkai Kaiho [*Bulletin of the Phonetic Society of Japan*]
OGL — Oesterreich in Geschichte und Literatur [*Wien*]
OGNPA — Ogneupory
OG Pat Off — Official Gazette. United States Patent Office
OGR — Official Guide of the Railways
OGS — Oxford German Studies
OH — Ohio History
OH — Ontario History
OH — Osteopathic Hospitals
OH — Oud-Holland
OHA — Occupational Hazards
OHEL — Oxford History of English Literature
Ohio Ag Dept — Ohio. Department of Agriculture. Bulletins
Ohio Ag Exp — Ohio. Agricultural Experiment Station. Publications
Ohio Agric Exp Stn Res Bull — Ohio. Agricultural Experiment Station. Research Bulletin
Ohio Agric Exp Stn Res Circ — Ohio. Agricultural Experiment Station. Research Circular
Ohio Agric Exp Stn Spec Circ — Ohio. Agricultural Experiment Station. Special Circular
Ohio Agric Res Dev Cent Res Bull — Ohio. Agricultural Research and Development Center. Research Bulletin
Ohio Agric Res Dev Cent Res Circ — Ohio. Agricultural Research and Development Center. Research Circular
Ohio Agric Res Dev Cent Res Summ — Ohio. Agricultural Research and Development Center. Research Summary
Ohio Agric Res Dev Cent Spec Circ — Ohio. Agricultural Research and Development Center. Special Circular
Ohio Agr Res Develop Cent Res Circ — Ohio. Agricultural Research and Development Center. Research Circular
OhioanaQ — Ohioana Quarterly
Ohio Archael — Ohio Archaeologist
Ohio Assn Sch Libn Bull — Ohio Association of School Librarians. Bulletin
Ohio Bar — Ohio State Bar Association. Report
Ohio Biol Surv Biol Notes — Ohio Biological Survey. Biological Notes
Ohio Biol Surv Bull — Ohio Biological Survey. Bulletin
Ohio Bus Tchr — Ohio Business Teacher
Ohio Conf Sewage Treat Annu Rep — Ohio Conference on Sewage Treatment. Annual Report
Ohio Conf Water Purif Annu Rep — Ohio Conference on Water Purification. Annual Report
Ohio Dent J — Ohio Dental Journal
Ohio Dep Nat Resour Div Geol Surv Misc Rep — Ohio. Department of Natural Resources. Division of Geological Survey. Miscellaneous Report
Ohio Div Geol Surv Bull — Ohio. Division of Geological Survey. Bulletin
Ohio Div Geol Surv Inform Circ — Ohio. Division of Geological Survey. Information Circular
Ohio Div Geol Surv Misc Rep — Ohio. Division of Geological Survey. Miscellaneous Report
Ohio Div Geol Surv Rep Invest — Ohio. Division of Geological Survey. Report of Investigations
Ohio Div Water Bull — Ohio. Division of Water. Bulletin
Ohio Div Water Inform Circ — Ohio. Division of Water. Information Circular
Ohio Div Water Ohio Water Plan Inventory Rep — Ohio. Division of Water. Ohio Water Plan Inventory. Report
Ohio Div Water Ohio Water Plan Invent Rep — Ohio. Division of Water. Ohio Water Plan Inventory. Report
Ohio Div Water Rep Ohio Water Table Surv — Ohio. Division of Water. Report on Ohio Water Table Survey
Ohio Div Water Tech Rep — Ohio. Division of Water. Technical Report
Ohio F — Ohio Farmer
Ohio Farm Home Res — Ohio Farm and Home Research
Ohio Fish Monogr — Ohio Fish Monographs
Ohio Fish Wildl Rep — Ohio Fish and Wildlife Report
Ohio Fm Home Res — Ohio Farm and Home Research

Ohio Game Monogr — Ohio Game Monographs
Ohio G S B — Ohio. Geological Survey. Bulletin
OhioH — Ohio History
Ohio Herpetol Soc Spec Publ — Ohio Herpetological Society. Special Publication
Ohio Hist — Ohio History
Ohio HQ — Ohio Historical Quarterly
Ohio Jour Sci — Ohio Journal of Science
Ohio J Rel St — Ohio Journal of Religious Studies
Ohio J Sci — Ohio Journal of Science
Ohio Lib Assn Bul — Ohio Library Association. Bulletin
Ohio Libr Ass Bull — Ohio Library Association. Bulletin
Ohio M J — Ohio Mining Journal
Ohio Nat — Ohio Naturalist. Ohio State University
Ohio Northern UL Rev — Ohio Northern University. Law Review
Ohio North L Rev — Ohio Northern University. Law Review
Ohio North Univ L Rev — Ohio Northern University. Law Review
Ohio NUL Rev — Ohio Northern University. Law Review
Ohio N Univ Law R — Ohio Northern University. Law Review
Ohio Nurses Rev — Ohio Nurses Review
OhioR — Ohio Review
Ohio Rep — Ohio Report
Ohio Rep Res Develop — Ohio Report on Research and Development (Biology, Agriculture, Home Economics). Ohio Agricultural Experiment Station
Ohio Rev — Ohio Review
Ohio Sch — Ohio Schools
Ohio S L J — Ohio State Law Journal
Ohio St Ac Sc An Rp — Ohio State Academy of Science. Annual Report
Ohio St Ac Sc Pr — Ohio State Academy of Science. Proceedings
Ohio St Ac Sc Sp P — Ohio State Academy of Science. Special Papers
Ohio State Archaeol and Hist Quar — Ohio State Archaeological and Historical Quarterly
Ohio State Law J — Ohio State Law Journal
Ohio State LJ — Ohio State Law Journal
Ohio State Med J — Ohio State Medical Journal
Ohio State Univ Biosci Colloq — Ohio State University. Biosciences Colloquia
Ohio State Univ Eng Exp Sta Bull — Ohio State University. Engineering Experiment Station. Bulletin
Ohio State Univ Eng Exp Stn Circ — Ohio State University. Engineering Experiment Station. Circular
Ohio State Univ Eng Exp Stn News — Ohio State University. Engineering Experiment Station. News
Ohio State Univ Inst Polar Studies Rept — Ohio State University. Institute of Polar Studies. Report
Ohio State Univ Inst Polar Stud Rep — Ohio State University. Institute of Polar Studies. Report
Ohio St BA Rep — Ohio State Bar Association. Report
Ohio St Law — Ohio State Law Journal
Ohio St LJ — Ohio State Law Journal
Ohio St Univ B — Ohio State University. Bulletin
Ohio St Univ Coop Ext Serv — Ohio State University. Cooperative Extension Service
O His — Ottawa Hispanica
OHLJ — Osgoode Hall. Law Journal
Oh NULR — Ohio Northern University. Law Review
OHQ — Ohio Historical Quarterly
OHQ — Oregon Historical Quarterly
OhR — Ohio Review
OHRJ — Orissa Historical Research Journal
OHRNA — Ontario Hydro-Research News
OHSAD — Occupational Health and Safety
Oh SLJ — Ohio State Law Journal
OI — O Instituto
OI — Old Irish
OIC — Oriental Institute. Communications
OIC — Polymers, Paint, and Colour Journal
OIEFA — Oil Engineering and Finance
OIF — Online Review
OIKO — Oikos
Oikos Suppl — Oikos. Supplementum
OILBA — Oil Bulletin
Oil Bull — Oil Bulletin [*Canada*]
Oil Can — Oil in Canada
Oil Colour Chem Assoc (Aust) Proc News — Oil and Colour Chemists' Association (Australia). Proceedings and News
Oil Colour Chemist Assoc J — Oil and Colour Chemists' Association. Journal
Oil Colour Trades J — Oil and Colour Trades Journal
Oil Eng Finance — Oil Engineering and Finance [*England*]
Oil Eng Technol — Oil Engineering and Technology
Oil Fat Ind — Oil and Fat Industry
Oil Field Eng — Oil Field Engineering
Oil Gas — Oil and Gas Bulletin
Oil and Gas Compact Bull — Oil and Gas Compact Bulletin
Oil Gas Compact Bull — Oil and Gas Compact Bulletin
Oil Gas Eur Mag — Oil Gas European Magazine [*Later, Oil Gas*]
Oil Gas Europ Mag — Oil Gas European Magazine

Oil Gas Int — Oil and Gas International [*England*]
Oil & Gas J — Oil and Gas Journal
Oil Gas J — Oil and Gas Journal
Oil Gas Mag (Hamburg) — Oil and Gas Magazine (Hamburg)
Oil Gas Petrochem Equip — Oil, Gas, and Petrochem Equipment
Oil & Gas Tax Q — Oil and Gas Tax Quarterly
Oil Gas Tax Q — Oil and Gas Tax Quarterly [*United States*]
Oil Mill Gazet — Oil Mill Gazetteer
Oil Paint Drug Rep — Oil, Paint, and Drug Reporter
Oil Prog — Oil Progress
OILS — Oilsander. Suncor Incorporated Resources Group. Oil Sands Division
Oil Shale Relat Fuels — Oil Shale and Related Fuels
Oil Shale Symp Proc — Oil Shale Symposium Proceedings
Oils Oilseeds J — Oils and Oilseeds Journal
Oil Spill Intell Rep — Oil Spill Intelligence Report
Oil Stat (Paris) — Oil Statistics (Paris)
Oil Technol — Oil Technologist
Oil Trade J — Oil Trade Journal
OILWA — Oil Weekly
Oil Wkly — Oil Weekly
OINOD — Energy [*South Korea*]
OIP — Oriental Institute. Publications [*The Oriental Institute of the University of Chicago*]
OIPOB — Otkrytiya, Izobreteniya, Promyshlennye Obraztsy, Tovarnye Znaki
OIS — Oxford University. Institute of Economics and Statistics. Bulletin
Oiseau Rev Fr Ornithol — Oiseau et la Revue Francaise d'Ornithologie
OIUC SAOC — Oriental Institute. University of Chicago. Studies in Ancient Oriental Civilization
OJ — Official Journal of the European Communities
OJ — Opera Journal
OJ — Oudheidkundig Jaarboek. Bulletijn Uitgegeven door den Nederlandschen Oudkundigen Bond
Ojb — Oldenburger Jahrbuch
OJBNOB — Oudheidkundig Jaarboek. Bulletijn Uitgegeven door den Nederlandschen Oudkundigen Bond
OJCH — Overijssel Jaarboek voor Cultuur en Historie
OJES — Osmania Journal of English Studies
OJ Eur Comm — Official Journal of the European Communities
O Judd Farmer — Orange Judd Farmer
O Judd Ill F — Orange Judd Illinois Farmer
OK — Oklahoma School Music News
OK — Onze Kongo
Okajimas Folia Anat Jpn — Okajimas Folia Anatomica Japonica
Okayama Igakkai Zasshi Suppl — Okayama Igakkai Zasshi. Supplement [*Japan*]
Okayama Univ Inst Therm Spring Res Pap — Okayama University. Institute for Thermal Spring Research. Papers
OKDIA — Osaka Kogyo Daigaku Kiyo. Riko-Hen
Okeanol — Okeanologiya
Okeanol Issled — Okeanologicheskie Issledovaniya
Okhota Okhot Khoz — Okhota i Okhotnich'e Khozyaistvo
Okhr Okruzh Sredy Zagryaz Prom Vybrosami — Okhrana Okruzhayushchei Sredy ot Zagryazneniya Promyshlennymi Vybrosami
Okhr Okruzh Sredy Zagryaz Prom Vybrosami TsBP — Okhrana Okruzhayushchei Sredy ot Zagryazneniya Promyshlennymi Vybrosami Tsellyulozno-Bumazhnaya Promyshlennost
Okhr Prir — Okhrana Prirody
Okhr Prir Dal'nem Vostoke — Okhrana Prirody na Dal'nem Vostoke
Okhr Prir Tsent-Chernozem Polosy — Okhrana Prirody Tsentral'no-Chernozemnoi Polosy
Okhr Prir Tsentr Chernozemn Polosy — Okhrana Prirody Tsentral'no-Chernozemnoi Polosy
Okhr Prir Urale — Okhrana Prirody na Urale
Okhr Prir Vod Urala — Okhrana Prirodnykh Vod Urala [*USSR*]
Okhr Tr Tekh Bezop Chern Metall — Okhrana Truda i Tekhnika Bezopasnosti v Chernoi Metallurgii
Okhr Zdor Detei Podrostkov (Kiev) — Okhrana Zdorov'ya Detei i Podrostkov (Kiev)
Oki Tech Rev — Oki Technical Review
Okla Acad Sci Proc — Oklahoma Academy of Science. Proceedings
Okla Ag Exp — Oklahoma. Agricultural Experiment Station. Publications
Okla Agric Exp Stn Annu Rep — Oklahoma. Agricultural Experiment Station. Annual Report
Okla Agric Exp Stn Bull — Oklahoma. Agricultural Experiment Station. Bulletin
Okla Agric Exp Stn Mimeogr Circ — Oklahoma. Agricultural Experiment Station. Mimeographed Circular
Okla Agric Exp Stn Misc Publ — Oklahoma. Agricultural Experiment Station. Miscellaneous Publication
Okla Agric Exp Stn M P — Oklahoma. Agricultural Experiment Station. Miscellaneous Publication
Okla Agric Exp Stn Processed Ser — Oklahoma. Agricultural Experiment Station. Processed Series
Okla Agric Exp Stn Process Ser — Oklahoma. Agricultural Experiment Station. Processed Series

Okla Agric Exp Stn Prog Rep — Oklahoma. Agricultural Experiment Station. Progress Report
Okla Agric Exp Stn Res Rep — Oklahoma. Agricultural Experiment Station. Research Report
Okla Agric Exp Stn Tech Bull — Oklahoma. Agricultural Experiment Station. Technical Bulletin
Okla BA J — Oklahoma Bar Association. Journal
Okla B Ass'n J — Oklahoma Bar Association. Journal
Okla BJ — Oklahoma Bar Journal
Okla Bus — Oklahoma Business
Okla Chronicles — Chronicles of Oklahoma
Okla City UL Rev — Oklahoma City University. Law Review
Okla Curr Farm Econ — Oklahoma Current Farm Economics
Okla Div Water Resour Bull — Oklahoma. Division of Water Resources. Bulletin
Okla Dp G N H Bien Rp — Oklahoma. Department of Geology and Natural History. Biennial Report
Okla Geol Notes — Oklahoma Geology Notes
Okla Geology Notes — Oklahoma Geology Notes
Okla Geol Surv Bull — Oklahoma. Geological Survey. Bulletin
Okla Geol Surv Circ — Oklahoma. Geological Survey. Circular
Okla Geol Surv Map — Oklahoma. Geological Survey. Map
Okla Geol Surv Miner Rep — Oklahoma. Geological Survey. Mineral Report
Okla G S — Oklahoma. Geological Survey
Oklahoma Acad Sci Proc — Oklahoma Academy of Science. Proceedings
Oklahoma Geology Notes — Oklahoma Geology Notes. Oklahoma Geological Survey
Oklahoma Geol Survey Guidebook — Oklahoma. Geological Survey. Guidebook
Oklahoma Geol Survey Map — Oklahoma. Geological Survey. Map
Oklahoma L Rev — Oklahoma Law Review
Oklahoma Univ Inf Sci Ser Mon — Oklahoma University. Information Science Series. Monograph
Okla Law R — Oklahoma Law Review
Okla Libn — Oklahoma Librarian
Okla Librn — Oklahoma Librarian
Okla LR — Oklahoma Law Review
Okla L Rev — Oklahoma Law Review
Okla Nurse — Oklahoma Nurse
OKL Arb Osterreichisches Kuratorium Landtech — OKL-Arbeit-Oesterreichisches Kuratorium fuer Landtechnik
Okla State Univ Agric Appl Sci Eng Exp Stn Publ — Oklahoma State University of Agriculture and Applied Science. Engineering Experiment Station. Publication
Okla Univ Research B — Oklahoma State University. Research Bulletin
Okla Water Res Board Bull — Oklahoma. Water Resources Board. Bulletin
OK LR — Oklahoma Law Review
OKMD — Oudheidkundige Mededelingen
Okon og Polit — Okonomi og Politik
OKRK — Okuruk
Okr Tr — Okhrana Truda
OKS — Ostkirchliche Studien
Okt — Oktjabr
OL — Oceanic Linguistics
OL — Orbis Litterarum
Olaj Szappan Kozmet — Olaj, Szappan, Kozmetika
Ol Ber — Bericht ueber die Ausgrabungen in Olympia [*1936-*]
Old Dominion J Med and S — Old Dominion Journal of Medicine and Surgery
Oldelft Sci Eng Q — Oldelft Scientific Engineering Quarterly
Oldenburg Landwirtschaftsbl — Oldenburgisches Landwirtschaftsblatt
Old House Jnl — Old-House Journal
Old Kilkenny Rev — Old Kilkenny Review
Old NW — Old Northwest Genealogical Quarterly
Old Test Abstr — Old Testament Abstracts
Old-Time N — Old-Time New England
Old-Time N E — Old-Time New England
Old-Time N Eng — Old-Time New England
Oleagineux Rev Int Corps Gras — Oleagineux. Revue Internationale des Corps Gras
Oleodin Pneum — Oleodinamica Pneumatica
Olfaction Taste Proc Int Symp — Olfaction and Taste. Proceedings of the International Symposium
Ol Forsch — Olympische Forschungen
Oli Grassi Deriv — Oli, Grassi, Derivati
Olii Miner Grassi Saponi Colori Vernici — Olii Minerali. Grassi e Saponi. Colori e Vernici
Olii Miner Olii Grassi Colori Vernici — Olii Minerali. Olii e Grassi. Colori e Vernici
OLP — Orientalia Lovaniensia Periodica
OLR — Ontario Library Review
OLR — Oregon Law Review
OLR — Oxford Literary Review
OLSP — Oceanic Linguistics. Special Publications
Oltenia — Oltenia Studii si Comunicari Istorie
OLV — Oil and Gas Journal
OLWE — Oilweek
Olym Rev — Olympic Review/Revue Olympique

Oly Rev — Olympic Review
OLZ — Orientalistische Literaturzeitung
OM — Objets et Monde
OM — Oduma Magazine
OM — Omega. The Journal of Death and Dying
OM — Only Music
OM — Opus Musicum
OM — Orientalische Miszellen
OM — Oriente Moderno
OM — Ostdeutsche Monatshefte
OM — Oudheidkundige Mededeelingen Uit's Rijksmuseum van Oudheden te Leiden
OM — Oxford Magazine
OMB — Management in Government
OME — Omega
OMEG — Omega. The Journal of Death and Dying
Omega-Int J — Omega - The International Journal of Management Science
OMF — Obzornik za Matematiko in Fiziko
OMIKE — Orszagos Magyar Izraelita Koezmueveloedesi Egyesuelet
OMKDK Modsz Kiad — Orszagos Mueszaki Koenyvtar es Dokumentacios Kozpoent. Modszertani Kiadvanyok
OMLLM — Oxford Modern Languages and Literature Monographs
OMM — Nouvel Officiel de l'Ameublement
OMMI Kiad Sorozat 1 — OMMI [*Orszagos Mezogazdasagi Minosegvizsgalo Intezet*] Kiadvanyai. Sorozat 1. Genetikus Talajterkepek
OMMI (Orsz Mezogazd Minosegvizsgalo Intez) Kiad Sorozat I — OMMI (Orszagos Mezogazdasagi Minosegvizsgalo Intezet) Kiadvanyai. Sorozat I. Genetikus Talajterkepek
OMML — Oudheidkundige Mededeelingen Uit's Rijksmuseum van Oudheden te Leiden
OMNAN — Ontario. Ministry of Northern Affairs. News Release
Omnia Med — Omnia Medica
Omnia Med Suppl — Omnia Medica. Supplemento
Omnia Med Ther — Omnia Medica et Therapeutica
Omnia Med Ther Arch — Omnia Medica et Therapeutica. Archivio
Omnia Ther — Omnia Therapeutica
Omnibus Mag — Omnibus Magazine
OMo — Oriente Moderno
OMorD — Ocerki Mordovskich Dialektov
OMRL — Oudheidkundige Mededeelingen Uit's Rijksmuseum van Oudheden te Leiden
Omron Tech — Omron Technics
OMR-Org Mag — Organic Magnetic Resonance
OMSGM — Ottendorfer Memorial Series of Germanic Monographs
Omsk Inst Inz Zeleznodoroz Transporta Naucn Trudy — Omskii Institut Inzenerov Zeleznodoroznogo Transporta. Naucnye Trudy
Omsk Med Zhurnal — Omskii Meditsinskii Zhurnal
O Mz — Oesterreichische Musikzeitschrift
OMZSA — Orszagos Magyar Zsido Segitoe Akcio
O & N — Old and New
ON — Old Northwest
On — Onomastica
ON — Opera News
ON — Orchestra News
ON — Orientalia Neerlandica [*Leiden, 1948*]
ONA J — Orthopedic Nurses' Association. Journal
ONCOA — Oncologia
Oncodev Biol Med — Oncodevelopmental Biology and Medicine [*Netherlands*]
Oncol Nurs Forum — Oncology Nursing Forum
Oncol Radiol — Oncologia si Radiologia
ONCR — On Campus Review
Onde Elec — Onde Electrique
Onde Electr — Onde Electrique
Onde Electr Suppl — Onde Electrique. Supplement [*France*]
Onderstepoort J Vet Res — Onderstepoort Journal of Veterinary Research
Onderstepoort J Vet Sci — Onderstepoort Journal of Veterinary Science and Animal Industry
ONERA Note Tech — Office National d'Etudes et de Recherches Aerospatiales. Note Technique
ONERA Publ — Office National d'Etudes et de Recherches Aerospatiales. Publication
ONESJ — Orient. Report of the Society for Near Eastern Studies in Japan
ONEX — Ontario Native Experience
ONIN — Ontario Indian
ONKAA — Onsen Kagaku
ONKIA — Onken Kiyo
ONKLA — Onkologiya
ONKOB — Onsen Kogakkaishi
ONLA — Our Native Land
On-Land Drill News — On-Land Drilling News
Online — Online Review
Online Database Rep — Online Database Report
Online Rev — Online Review
On-Line Rv — On-Line Review
ONN — Enkabe Contact
ONNA — Ontario Naturalist

ONO — Oculus
Ono — Onomastica
Onom — Onomastica
OnomJug — Onomastica Jugoslavica
Onondaga Ac Sc Pr — Onondaga Academy of Science. Proceedings
Onondaga Hist As Sc S — Onondaga Historical Association. Science Series
Onore Angelo Celli 25o An Insegnamento — Onore del Professore Angelo Celli nel 25o Anno di Insegnamento
OnsE — Ons Erfdeel
ONSN — Oriental Numismatic Society. Newsletter
ONSOP — Oriental Numismatic Society. Occasional Paper
Ontario Ag Dept — Ontario. Department of Agriculture. Publication
Ontario Dept Mines Geol Rept — Ontario. Department of Mines. Geological Report
Ontario Dept Mines Indus Mineral Rept — Ontario. Department of Mines. Industrial Mineral Report
Ontario Dept Mines Map — Ontario. Department of Mines. Map
Ontario Dept Mines Mineral Resources Circ — Ontario. Department of Mines. Mineral Resources Circular
Ontario Dept Mines Misc Paper — Ontario. Department of Mines. Miscellaneous Paper
Ontario Dept Mines Prelim Geochem Map — Ontario. Department of Mines. Preliminary Geochemical Map
Ontario Dept Mines Prelim Geol Map — Ontario. Department of Mines. Preliminary Geological Map
Ontario Dept Mines Prelim Map — Ontario. Department of Mines. Preliminary Map
Ontario Fuel Board Ann Rept — Ontario Fuel Board. Annual Report
Ontario Hist Soc Papers — Ontario Historical Society. Papers and Records
Ontario Med Rev — Ontario Medical Review
Ontario R — Ontario Review
Ontario Research Council Rept — Ontario Research Council. Report
Ont Bird Banding — Ontario Bird Banding
Ont Bur Mines An Rp — Ontario. Bureau of Mines. Annual Report
Ont Bur Mines B — Ontario. Bureau of Mines. Bulletin
Ont Dent — Ontario Dentist
Ont Dep Agric Food Publ — Ontario. Department of Agriculture and Food. Publication
Ont Dep Agric Publ — Ontario. Department of Agriculture. Publication
Ont Dep Mines Annu Rep — Ontario. Department of Mines. Annual Report
Ont Dep Mines Bull — Ontario. Department of Mines. Mines Inspection Branch. Bulletin
Ont Dep Mines Geol Circ — Ontario. Department of Mines. Geological Circular
Ont Dep Mines Geol Rep — Ontario. Department of Mines. Geological Report
Ont Dep Mines Ind Miner Rep — Ontario. Department of Mines. Industrial Mineral Report
Ont Dep Mines Miner Resour Circ — Ontario. Department of Mines. Mineral Resources Circular
Ont Dep Mines Misc Pap — Ontario. Department of Mines. Miscellaneous Paper
Ont Dep Mines North Aff Geol Rep — Ontario. Department of Mines and Northern Affairs. Geological Report
Ont Dep Mines North Aff Ind Miner Rep — Ontario. Department of Mines and Northern Affairs. Industrial Mineral Report
Ont Dep Mines North Aff Misc Pap — Ontario. Department of Mines and Northern Affairs. Miscellaneous Paper
Ont Dep Mines Rep — Ontario. Department of Mines. Report
Ont Div Mines Geol Rep — Ontario. Division of Mines. Geological Report
Ont Div Mines Geosci Rep — Ontario. Division of Mines. Geoscience Report
Ont Div Mines Ind Miner Rep — Ontario. Division of Mines. Industrial Mineral Report
Ont Div Mines Misc Pap — Ontario. Division of Mines. Miscellaneous Paper
Ont Div Mines Prelim Map Geol Ser — Ontario. Division of Mines. Preliminary Map. Geological Series
Ont Div Mines Prelim Map Geophys Ser — Ontario. Division of Mines. Preliminary Map. Geophysical Series
Ont Ed — Ontario Education
ONTED — Ontario Technologist
Ont Field Biol — Ontario Field Biologist
Ont Fish Wildl Rev — Ontario Fish and Wildlife Review
Ont Fld Biol — Ontario Field Biologist
Ont For — Ontario Forests
Ont Geography — Ontario Geography
Ont Geol Surv Misc Pap — Ontario. Geological Survey. Miscellaneous Paper
Ont His S — Ontario Historical Society. Papers and Records
Ont Hist — Ontario History
Ont Hortic Exp Stn Prod Lab Rep — Ontario. Horticulture Experiment Stations and Products Laboratory. Report
Ont Hydro-Res News — Ontario Hydro-Research News
Ont Hydro-Res Q — Ontario Hydro-Research Quarterly
Ont Hydro Res Rev — Ontario Hydro-Research News. Review
Ont Ind Arts Bul — Ontario Industrial Arts Association. Bulletin
Ont Ind Waste Conf Proc — Ontario Industrial Waste Conference. Proceedings
Ont Lib R — Ontario Library Review
Ont Libr Rev — Ontario Library Review

Ont Math G — Ontario Mathematics Gazette
Ont Med Rev — Ontario Medical Review
Ontog Razvit Zhivotn — Ontogeneticheskoe Razvitie Zhivotnykh
Ont Pet Inst Annu Conf Proc — Ontario Petroleum Institute. Annual Conference. Proceedings [*Canada*]
Ont Technol — Ontario Technologist
Ont Vet Coll Rep — Ontario Veterinary College. Report
ONU LR — Ohio Northern University. Law Review
ONWI — Battelle Memorial Institute. Office of Nuclear Waste-Isolation
OOB — OECD [*Organization for Economic Cooperation and Development*] Observer
O O B — Off Our Backs
OoB — Ord och Bild
OOH — Oesterreichische Osthefte
Oologists' Rec — Oologists' Record
OOPK — Ookpik
OOQ — Occupational Outlook Quarterly
Oostvlaam Zanten — Oostvlaamse Zanten. Tijdschrift van de Koninklijke Bond der Oostvlaamse Volkskundigen
OostvlZanten — Oostvlaamse Zanten
O P — Open Places
OP — Opera
OP — Opera News
Op — Opyty
OPA — Onze Pius-Almanak
OPAAER — Archaeological Survey of Alberta. Occasional Papers
OPACA — Optica Acta
OPARI — Occasional Publications. African and Afro-American Research Institute. University of Texas, Austin
OPBIA — Occasional Publications. British Institute of Archaeology at Ankara
OPCOCM Symposium — Symposium on the Occurrence, Prediction, and Control of Outbursts in Coal Mines
OPD — Chemical Marketing Reporter
OPEC (Org Petroleum Exporting Countries) Bul — OPEC (Organization of Petroleum Exporting Countries) Bulletin
Open Hearth Basic Oxygen Steel Conf Proc — Open Hearth and Basic Oxygen Steel Conference. Proceedings [*United States*]
Open Hearth Proc AIME — Open Hearth Proceedings. Metallurgical Society of AIME [*American Institute of Mining, Metallurgical, and Petroleum Engineers*]. Iron and Steel Division
Opera — Opera and Concert
Opera — Opera News
Opera Bot — Opera Botanica
Opera Can — Opera Canada
Opera Collecta Cent Bosbiol Onderz Bokrijk-Genk — Opera Collecta. Centrum voor Bosbiologisch Onderzoek. Bokrijk-Genk
Opera J — Opera Journal
Opera N — Opera News
Operational Res Quart — Operational Research Quarterly
Operation Res — Operations Research
Operator Theory Advances and Appl — Operator Theory. Advances and Applications
Operat Res — Operations Research
Operat Res Q — Operational Research Quarterly
Operat R Q — Operational Research Quarterly
Oper Dent — Operative Dentistry
Oper Miller — Operative Miller
Oper Program Systems Ser — Operating and Programming Systems Series
Oper Res — Operations Research
Oper Res Q — Operational Research Quarterly
Oper Res Quart — Operational Research Quarterly
Oper Syst Rev — Operating Systems Review
OPF — Public Finance. International Quarterly Journal
Ophthal Lit — Ophthalmic Literature
Ophthalmic Physiol Opt — Ophthalmic and Physiological Optics
Ophthalmic Res — Ophthalmic Research
Ophthalmic Semin — Ophthalmic Seminars
Ophthalmic Surg — Ophthalmic Surgery
Ophthalmola — Ophthalmologica
Ophthalmol Ibero Am — Ophthalmologia Ibero-Americana
Ophthalmol Times — Ophthalmology Times
Ophthalmol War Years — Ophthalmology in the War Years
Ophthal Res — Ophthalmic Research
Ophth Soc Aust Trans — Ophthalmological Society of Australia. Transactions
OPhW — Opuscula Philologa [*Katholisch-Akademischer Philologenverein*] (Wien)
OPI — Bibliotheek en Samenleving
Opin Int Commn Zool Nom — Opinions Rendered by the International Commission on Zoological Nomenclature
OPL — Osservatore Politico Letterario
OPL — Our Public Lands
OPLA — Our Public Lands
OPLiLL — Occasional Papers in Linguistics and Language Learning
OPLing — Occasional Papers on Linguistics
OPLLL — Occasional Papers in Language, Literature, and Linguistics
OPML — Occasional Papers in Modern Languages

Op News — Opera News
Opns Res — Operations Research
OPO — OPEC [*Organization of Petroleum Exporting Countries*] Review
OPO — Ophthalmic and Physiological Optics
Opolsk Roczn Ekon — Opolskie Roczniki Ekonomiczne
OPPI — Organic Preparations and Procedures International
Op Res — Operations Research
Op Res Q — Operational Research Quarterly
OPSED — Ophthalmic Seminars
Ops Research — Operations Research
OPSS — Operating and Programming Systems Series [*Elsevier Book Series*]
OPT — Optima [*Johannesburg*]
Opt Acta — Optica Acta
Opt Appl — Optica Applicata
Opt Commun — Optics Communications
Opt-Electron — Opto-Electronique
Opt Eng — Optical Engineering
Opteolektorn and Poluprovodn Tekh — Opteolektronika i Poluprovodnikovaya Tekhnika
Optik — Optik. Zeitschrift fuer Licht- und Elektronenoptik
Optimal Control Appl Methods — Optimal Control Applications and Methods
Optimal Planirovanie — Optimal'noe Planirovanie
Optimizacija — Akademija Nauk SSSR. Sibirskoe Otdelenie. Institut Matematiki. Optimizacija
Optimization — Mathematische Operationsforschung und Statistik. Series Optimization
Options Mediterr — Options Mediterraneennes
Opt Laser Technol — Optics and Laser Technology
Opt and Laser Technol — Optics and Laser Technology
Opt Laser Technol Spec Suppl — Optics and Laser Technology. Special Supplement
Opt Lett — Optics Letters
Opt-Mekh Prom — Optiko-Mekhanicheskaya Promyshlennost'
Opt-Mekh Prom-st' — Optiko-Mekhanicheskaya Promyshlennost'
Opt News — Optics News
Opto-Electron — Opto-Electronics
Optoelektron Poluprovodn Tekh — Optoelektronika i Poluprovodnikovaya Tekhnika
Optoelektron Spektrosk — Optoelektronika i Spektroskopiya
Opt Pura y Apl — Optica Pura y Aplicada
Opt Pura Apl — Optica Pura y Aplicada
Opt Quant E — Optical and Quantum Electronics
Opt and Quantum Electron — Optical and Quantum Electronics
Opt Quantum Electron — Optical and Quantum Electronics
Opt Soc Am J — Optical Society of America. Journal
Opt Spectra — Optical Spectra
Opt and Spectrosc — Optics and Spectroscopy
Opt Spectrosc (Engl Transl) — Optics and Spectroscopy (English Translation of Optika i Spektroskopiya) [*USSR*]
Opt Spectrosc (USSR) — Optics and Spectroscopy (USSR)
Opt Spectry — Optics and Spectroscopy
Opt Spektro — Optika i Spektroskopiya
Opt Spektrosk — Optika i Spektroskopiya
Opt & Spektrosk — Optika i Spektroskopiya
Opt Spektrosk Akad Nauk SSSR Otd Fiz-Mat Nauk — Optika i Spektroskopiya. Akademiya Nauk SSSR. Otdelenie Fiziko-Matematicheskikh Nauk [*USSR*]
Opt Technol — Optics Technology
Opus Arch — Opuscula Archaeologica
Opus Ath — Opuscula Atheniensia
Opusc Athen — Opuscula Atheniensia. Skrifter Utgivna av Svenska Institutet i Athen - Acta Instituti Atheniensis Regni Sueciae
Opusc Ent — Opuscula Entomologica
Opusc Entomol — Opuscula Entomologica
Opusc Med — Opuscula Medica
Opusc Med Suppl — Opuscula Medica. Supplementum
Opusc Zool (Bpest) — Opuscula Zoologica (Budapest)
Opusc Zool (Budap) — Opuscula Zoologica (Budapest)
Opusc Zool (Munich) — Opuscula Zoologica (Munich)
Opus M — Opus Musicum
Opus Mus — Opus Musicum
Opus Ph — Opuscula Philologica
Opus Rom — Opuscula Romana
Opus Zool (Muenchen) — Opuscula Zoologica (Muenchen)
OPWA — Official Publications of Western Australia
Opyt Izuch Regul Fiziol Funkts — Opyt Izucheniya Regulyatsii Fiziologicheskikh Funktsii
Opyt Paseka — Opytnaya Paseka
Opyt Primen Radioakt Metodov Poiskakh Razved Neradioakt Rud — Opyt Primeneniya Radioaktivnykh Metodov pri Poiskakh i Razvedke Neradioaktivnykh Rud
Opyt Rab Pchel — Opytnaya Rabota Pchelovodov
Opyt Rab Peredovogo Sovkhoznogo Proizvod — Opyt Raboty Peredovogo Sovkhoznogo Proizvodstva
OR — Odrodzenie i Reformacja w Polsce

OR — Oil and Resource Development Supplement. Fairbanks Daily News Miner
OR — Oklahoma Law Review
OR — Operational Research Quarterly
OR — Operations Research
OR — Oregon Music Educator
OR — Orient Review
Or — Orientalia. Commentari Periodici Pontificii Instituti Biblici
Or — Orizont
Or — Orpheus. Revista pentru Cultura Clasica
OR — Oxford Review
ORA — OR. Journal of the Operational Research Society
ORA — Outdoor Recreation Action
ORA — Overseas Reports Announcements
Orale Implantol — Orale Implantologie
Oral H — Oral History
Oral Implantol — Oral Implantology
Oral Res Abstr — Oral Research Abstracts
Oral Sci Rev — Oral Sciences Reviews
Oral Surgery — Oral Surgery, Oral Medicine, and Oral Pathology
Oral Surg O — Oral Surgery, Oral Medicine, and Oral Pathology
Oral Surg Oral Med Oral Pathol — Oral Surgery, Oral Medicine, and Oral Pathology
Or An — Oriens Antiquus
Orange County BJ — Orange County Bar Association. Journal
Orange County Bus — Orange County Business
Orange Cty Dent Soc Bull — Orange County [California] Dental Society. Bulletin
OrAnt — Oriens Antiquus [Rome]
OrAntBud — Oriens Antiquus [Budapest]
Or Art — Oriental Art [United Kingdom]
OrBiblLov — Orientalia et Biblica Lovaniensia [Louvain]
OrBibLov — Orientalia et Biblica Lovaniensia [Louvain]
Orbis Lit — Orbis Litterarum
Orbis Mus — Orbis Musicae
Orch — Orchardist
Orchardist NZ — Orchardist of New Zealand
Orchard NZ — Orchardist of New Zealand
Orchid Dig — Orchid Digest
OrChr — Oriens Christianus
OrChrA — Orientalia Christiana Analecta
OrChrPer — Orientalia Christiana Periodica [Rome]
ORCODO — Annual Research Reviews. Oral Contraceptives
ORD — Organizational Dynamics
Ord Dept Doc — Ordinance Department Document
Ordenskunde — Ordenskunde Beitraege zur Geschichte der Auszeichnungen
Ordre des Architectes du Quebec Bull Technique — Ordre des Architectes du Quebec. Bulletin Technique
ORE — Rekreaksie. Vakblad voor Recreatie Ondernemers
Ore Ag Exp — Oregon. Agricultural Experiment Station. Publications
Ore Agric Progr — Oregon's Agricultural Progress
OrEcon — Oriental Economist
Oreg Agric Exp Stn Bull — Oregon. Agricultural Experiment Station. Bulletin
Oreg Agric Exp Stn Misc Pap — Oregon. Agricultural Experiment Station. Miscellaneous Paper
Oreg Agric Exp Stn Spec Rep — Oregon. Agricultural Experiment Station. Special Report
Oreg Agric Exp Stn Stn Bull — Oregon. Agricultural Experiment Station. Station Bulletin
Oreg Agric Exp Stn Tech Bull — Oregon. Agricultural Experiment Station. Technical Bulletin
Oreg Agr Progr — Oregon's Agricultural Progress
Oreg Bur Mines Min Res Oreg — Oregon. Bureau of Mines and Geology. Mineral Resources of Oregon
Oreg Dep Geol Miner Ind Bull — Oregon. Department of Geology and Mineral Industries. Bulletin
Oreg Dep Geol Miner Ind GMI Short Pap — Oregon. Department of Geology and Mineral Industries. GMI Short Paper
Oreg Dep Geol Miner Ind Misc Pap — Oregon. Department of Geology and Mineral Industries. Miscellaneous Paper
Oreg Dep Geol Miner Ind Misc Paper — Oregon. Department of Geology and Mineral Industries. Miscellaneous Paper
Oregelkunst Vier T — Orgelkunst. Viermaandelijks Tijdschrift
Oreg Fish Comm Contrib — Oregon. Fish Commission. Contributions
Oreg Fish Comm Res Briefs — Oregon. Fish Commission. Research Briefs
Oreg For Prod Lab (Corvallis) Prog Rep — Oregon. Forest Products Laboratory (Corvallis). Progress Report
Oreg For Prod Res Cent Prog Rep — Oregon. Forest Products Research Center. Progress Report
Oreg Hist Q — Oregon Historical Quarterly
Oreg Insect Contr Handb — Oregon Insect Control Handbook
Oreg L Rev — Oregon Law Review
Oreg Nurs — Oregon Nurse
Oreg Nurse — Oregon Nurse
Oregon Dep Geol Mineral Ind Oil Gas Invest — Oregon. Department of Geology and Mineral Industries. Oil and Gas Investigation

Oregon Dept Geology and Mineral Industries Bull — Oregon. Department of Geology and Mineral Industries. Bulletin
Oregon Dept Geology and Mineral Industries Geol Map Ser — Oregon. Department of Geology and Mineral Industries. Geological Map Series
Oregon Geol — Oregon Geology
Oregon Hist Q — Oregon Historical Quarterly
Oreg State Agric Coll Eng Exp Stn — Oregon State Agricultural College. Engineering Experiment Station
Oreg State Coll Eng Exp Stn Circ — Oregon State College. Engineering Experiment Station. Circular
Oreg State Eng Ground Water Rep — Oregon State Engineer. Ground Water Report
Oreg State Monogr Stud Bacteriol — Oregon State Monographs. Studies in Bacteriology
Oreg State Monogr Stud Bot — Oregon State Monographs. Studies in Botany
Oreg State Monogr Stud Entomol — Oregon State Monographs. Studies in Entomology
Oreg State Monogr Stud Geol — Oregon State Monographs. Studies in Geology
Oreg State Monogr Stud Zool — Oregon State Monographs. Studies in Zoology
Oreg State Univ Biol Colloq — Oregon State University. Biology Colloquium
Oreg State Univ Eng Exp Sta Circ — Oregon State University (Corvallis). Engineering Experiment Station. Circular
Oreg State Univ Eng Exp Stn Circ — Oregon State University. Engineering Experiment Station. Circular
Oreg State Univ For Res Lab Annu Rep — Oregon State University. Forest Research Laboratory. Annual Report
Oreg State Univ For Res Lab Bull — Oregon State University. Forest Research Laboratory. Bulletin
Oreg State Univ For Res Lab Prog Rep — Oregon State University. Forest Research Laboratory. Progress Report
Oreg State Univ For Res Lab Res Bull — Oregon State University. Forest Research Laboratory. Research Bulletin
Oreg State Univ For Res Lab Res Pap — Oregon State University. Forest Research Laboratory. Research Paper
Oreg State Univ Sch For For Res Lab Res Note — Oregon State University. School of Forestry. Forest Research Laboratory. Research Notes
Oreg State Univ Water Resour Res Inst Semin Proc SEMIN WR — Oregon State University. Water Resources Research Institute. Seminar Proceedings. SEMIN WR
ORE HIS Q — Oregon Historical Society. Quarterly
Ore Hist Q — Oregon Historical Quarterly
Ore Hist Soc Quar — Oregon Historical Society. Quarterly
Orehovo-Zuev Ped Inst Ucen Zap Kaf Mat — Orehovo-Zuevskii Pedagogiceskii Institut. Ucenye Zapiski Kafedry Matematiki
OreHQ — Oregon Historical Quarterly
Ore LR — Oregon Law Review
Ore L Rev — Oregon Law Review
Orenburg Gos Ped Inst Ucen Zap — Orenburgskii Gosudarstvennyi Pedagogiceskii Institut Imeni V. P. Ckalova. Ucenye Zapiski
O R (English) — Osservatore Romano (English)
Ores Met — Ores and Metals
O Rev — Occasional Review
ORFE — Ornis Fennica
Organ Afr Unity Sci Tech Res Comm Publ — Organization of African Unity. Scientific and Technical Research Commission. Publication
Organ Am States Ann — Organization of American States. Annals
Organ Behav Hum Perform — Organizational Behavior and Human Performance
Organ Behavior & Human Perf — Organizational Behavior and Human Performance
Organ Beh H — Organizational Behavior and Human Performance
OrGand — Orientalia Gandensia
Organ Dyn — Organizational Dynamics
Organ Dynam — Organizational Dynamics
Organ Eur Mediterr Prot Plant Publ Ser A — Organisation Europeenne et Mediterraneenne pour la Protection des Plants. Publications. Serie A
Organ Eur Mediterr Prot Plant Publ Ser D — Organisation Europeenne et Mediterraneenne pour la Protection des Plants. Publications. Serie D
Organ Eur Rech Spat Contract Rep — Organisation Europeenne de Recherches Spatiales. Contractor Report
Organ Fortschr Eisenbahnwes — Organ fuer die Fortschritte des Eisenbahnwesens
Organic Gard — Organic Gardening
Organic Gard & F — Organic Gardening and Farming
Organic Geochem — Organic Geochemistry
Organists R — Organists Review
Organomet Chem — Organometallic Chemistry
Organomet Chem Rev — Organometallic Chemistry Reviews
Organomet Chem Rev Sect A — Organometallic Chemistry Reviews. Section A. Subject Reviews [Netherlands]
Organomet Chem Rev Sect B — Organometallic Chemistry Reviews. Section B. Annual Surveys
Organomet Chem Synth — Organometallics in Chemical Synthesis
Organomet React — Organometallic Reactions
Organomet React Synth — Organometallic Reactions and Syntheses
Organon — Textile Organon

Organophosphorus Chem — Organophosphorus Chemistry
Organ Stud — Organization Studies
Organ Yb — Organ Yearbook
Organzr — Organizer
Org Behav and Hum Perform — Organizational Behavior and Human Performance
Org Chem Bull — Organic Chemical Bulletin
Org Chem (New York) — Organic Chemistry (New York)
Org Chem Ser Monogr — Organic Chemistry: A Series of Monographs
Org Coat — Organic Coatings. Science and Technology
Org Coatings Appl Polym Sci Proc — Organic Coatings and Applied Polymer Science Proceedings
Org Coat Plast Chem — Organic Coatings and Plastics Chemistry
Org Compd Sulphu Selenium Tellurium — Organic Compounds of Sulphur, Selenium, and Tellurium
Org Dyn — Organizational Dynamics
Org Dynamics — Organizational Dynamics
Org Farmer — Organic Farmer
Org Finish — Organic Finishing
ORGG-A — Oriental Geographer
Org Gard — Organic Gardening
Org Gdng Fmg — Organic Gardening and Farming
Org Geochem — Organic Geochemistry [*England*]
Org Inst — Organ Institute. Quarterly
Org Inst Q — Organ Institute. Quarterly
Org Magn Resonance — Organic Magnetic Resonance
Org Mass Sp — Organic Mass Spectrometry
Org Mass Spectrom — Organic Mass Spectrometry
ORGND — Organometallics
Org Photochem — Organic Photochemistry
Org Photochem Synth — Organic Photochemical Syntheses
Org Poluprod Krasiteli — Organicheskie Poluprodukty i Krasiteli
Org Prep Proced — Organic Preparations and Procedures
Org Prep Proced Int — Organic Preparations and Procedures International
Org React — Organic Reactions
Org React — Organic Reactivity
Org React (Eng Transl) — Organic Reactivity (English Translation) [*New York*]
Org React Mech — Organic Reaction Mechanisms
Org React (Tartu) — Organic Reactivity (Tartu)
Org React (USSR) — Organic Reactivity (USSR)
ORGREB-Inst Kraftwerke Inf — ORGREB [*Organisation fuer Abnahme, Betriebsfuehrung, und Rationalisierung von Energieanlagen*]-Institut fuer Kraftwerke. Informationen [*German Democratic Republic*]
Org Sci — Organizational Science
Org Scientifique — Organisation Scientifique
Org Sulfur Compd — Organic Sulfur Compounds
Org Synt — Organic Syntheses
Org Techint Bol Informativo — Organizacion Techint. Boletin Informativo
ORHEA — Orvosi Hetilap
ORHPB — Orthopaede [*West Germany*]
OrHQ — Oregon Historical Quarterly
Orient — Orientalia. Commentarii de Rebus Assyro-Babylonicis, Arabicis, Aegyptiacis [*Rome*]
Orientacion Econ — Orientacion Economica
Oriental Soc Aust J — Oriental Society of Australia. Journal
Orientam Soc — Orientamenti Sociali
Orient Art — Oriental Art
Orientat Sc — Orientation Scolaire et Professionnelle
Orientat Scol Profes — Orientation Scolaire et Professionnelle
Orient Chr Per — Orientalia Christiana Periodica
Orient Cult — Orientamenti Culturali
Oriente Agropecu — Oriente Agropecuario
Orient Economist — Oriental Economist
Oriente Crist — Oriente Cristiano
Oriente Mod — Oriente Moderno
Orient Geogr — Orthographical Geographer
Orient Insects — Oriental Insects
Orient Insects Suppl — Oriental Insects. Supplementum
Orient Lit Ztg — Orientalistische Literaturzeitung
Orient Lovan — Orientalia Lovaniensia Periodica
Orient Prof/Voc Guid — Orientation Professionelle/Vocational Guidance
Orient Suecana — Orientalia Suecana
Origin Tech J — Origin Technical Journal
Orig Life — Origins of Life
ORIMB — Oral Implantology
Orissa Vet J — Orissa Veterinary Journal
Orizz Ortop Odie Riabil — Orizzonti della Ortopedia Odierna e della Riabilitazione [*Italy*]
Orizz Profess — Orizzonti Professionali
ORK — Orbis. A Journal of World Affairs
Orkester JL — Orkester Journalen
Ork J — Orkester Journalen
ORL — Orient. Deutsche Zeitschrift fuer Politik und Wirtschaft des Orients
ORL — ORL - Journal for Oto-Rhino-Laryngology and Its Borderlands
ORLA — Orthodox Alaska

ORLD — Oriental Review and Literary Digest
ORLIA — Oto-Rino-Laringologia Italiana
Or Lit — Orientalistische Literaturzeitung
ORL-J Oto R — ORL - Journal for Oto-Rhino-Laryngology and Its Borderlands
Orlov Gos Ped Inst Ucen Zap — Orlovskii Gosudarstvennyi Pedagogiceskii Institut. Ucenye Zapiski
OrLovPer — Orientalia Lovaniensia Periodica
Or LR — Oregon Law Review
Or L Rev — Oregon Law Review
OrLz — Orientalistische Literaturzeitung
Orm Arast Enst Derg — Ormancilik Arastirma Enstituesue Dergisi
Orm Arast Enst Muht Yay — Ormancilik Arastirma Enstituesue Muhtelif Yayinlar Serisi
Orm Arast Enst Tek Buelt — Ormancilik Arastirma Enstituesue Teknik Buelten
OrMod — Oriente Moderno [*Rome*]
Orm Vitam — Ormoni e Vitamine
Ornamentals Northwest Newsl Coop Ext Serv Oreg State Univ — Ornamentals Northwest. Newsletter. Cooperative Extension Service. Oregon State University
Ornis Fenn — Ornis Fennica
Ornis Scand — Ornis Scandinavica
Ornithol Abh — Ornithologische Abhandlungen
Ornithol Appl — Ornithologie Applique
Ornithol Beob — Ornithologische Beobachter
Ornithol Ber — Ornithologische Berichte
Ornithol Mitt — Ornithologische Mitteilungen
Ornithol Monatsber — Ornithologische Monatsberichte
ORNL TM — Oak Ridge National Laboratory. TM
ORNRA — Oak Ridge National Laboratory. Review
OrNS — Orientalia. Nova Series
ORom — Opuscula Romana
ORom — Osservatore Romano
ORP — Odrodzenie i Reformacja w Polsce
OrP — Orientamenti Pedagogici [*Torino*]
Orph — Orpheus. Revista pentru Cultura Clasica
ORS — Organization Studies
ORSA/TIMS Bull — ORSA [*Operations Research Society of America*]/TIMS [*The Institute of Management Sciences*] Bulletin
ORSC — Ornis Scandinavica
Orsk Gos Ped Inst Ucen Zap — Orskii Gosudarstvennyi Pedagogiceskii Institut Imeni T. G. Sevcenko. Ucenye Zapiski
OR Spektrum — Operations Research Spektrum
OrSuec — Orientalia Suecana [*Uppsala*]
OrSyr — Orient Syrien [*Vernon, France*]
Orszagos Mezoegazd Minoesegvizsgalo Intez Evkoen — Orszagos Mezoegazdasagi Minoesegvizsgalo Intezet Evkoenyve
Orsz Husipari Kut Intez Kozl — Orszagos Husipari Kutato Intezet Kozlemenyei
Orsz Met Intez Hivat Kiad — Orszagos Meteorologiai Intezet Hivatalos Kiadvanyai
Orsz Mezogazd Minosegv Intez Evk — Orszagos Mezogazdasagi Minoesegvizsgalo Intezet Evkoenyve
Orsz Mezogazd Minosegvizsgalo Intez Kiad Sorozat 1 — Orszagos Mezogazdasagi Minoesegvizsgalo Intezet Kiadvanyai. Sorozat 1. Genetikus Talajterkepek
ORT — Orientalia Rheno-Traiectina
OR Tech — OR Tech: Official Publication of the Association of Operating Room Technicians
Orthod Fr — Orthodontie Francaise
Orthomol Ps — Orthomolecular Psychiatry
Orthop Clin North Am — Orthopedic Clinics of North America
Orthoped Cl — Orthopedic Clinics of North America
Orthop Lect — Orthopaedic Lectures
Orthop Nurs — Orthopedic Nursing
Orthop Prax — Orthopaedische Praxis
Orthop Surg — Orthopedic Surgery [*Japan*]
Orthop Traumatol — Orthopedics and Traumatology [*Japan*]
Orthop Traumatol — Orthopedie Traumatologie
Orthotics Prosthet — Orthotics and Prosthetics
Orthot Pros — Orthotics and Prosthetics
Ortop Resp Mezhved Sb — Ortopediya Respublikanskii Mezhvedomstvennyi Sbornik
Ortop Traumatol Appar Mot — Ortopedia e Traumatologia dell'Apparato Motore
Ortop Travmatol — Ortopedia y Travmatologiya [*Japan*]
Ortop Travmatol Prot — Ortopediya, Travmatologiya, i Protezirovanie
Ortop Travmatol Protez — Ortopediya, Travmatologiya, i Protezirovanie
Ortop Travmatol (Sofia) — Ortopediya i Travmatologiya (Sofia)
Ortung Navig — Ortung und Navigation [*West Germany*]
ORV — Operations Research Verfahren
Orv Hetil — Orvosi Hetilap
Orv Lapja — Orvosok Lapja
Orvostort Kozl — Orvostorteneti Koezlemeneyek. Communications de Historia Artis Medicinae

Orv Sz — Orvosi Szemle
Orv Szle — Orvosi Szemle
Orv Tech — Orvos es Technika
Oryx — Oryx Journal. Fauna Preservation Society
Oryx J Fauna Preserv Soc — Oryx Journal. Fauna Preservation Society
Oryza J Assoc Rice Res Work — Oryza. Journal of the Association of Rice
    Research Workers
OS — Oekumenische Studien
OS — Orient Syrien
OS — Orientalia Suecana [Uppsala]
Os — Osiris
Os — Osvit
OS — Other Side
OS — Oudtestamentische Studien [Leiden]
OSA Coop Ext Univ Calif — One-Sheet Answers. Cooperative Extension.
    University of California
OSAHQ — Ohio State Archaeological and Historical Quarterly
Osaka City Med J — Osaka City Medical Journal
Osaka City U Econ R — Osaka City University. Economic Review
Osaka Econ Pap — Osaka Economic Papers
Osaka J Math — Osaka Journal of Mathematics
Osaka Mus Nat Hist Bull — Osaka Museum of Natural History. Bulletin
Osaka Prefect Univ Bull Ser A Eng Nat Sci — Osaka Prefecture. University.
    Bulletin. Series A. Engineering and Natural Sciences
Osaka Univ J Geosci — Osaka University. Journal of Geosciences
Osawatom — Osawatomie
OSD — OSD. Overseas Standards Digest
OSE — Oslo Studies in English
OSEND — Ocean Science and Engineering
OsEP — Osaka Economic Papers
OSEQD — Oldelft Scientific Engineering Quarterly
OSF — Orbit Science Fiction
OSFMA — Optika i Spektroskopiya. Akademiya Nauk SSSR. Otdelenie
    Fiziko-Matematicheskikh Nauk
OSFS — Original Science Fiction Stories
Osgoode Hall L J — Osgoode Hall. Law Journal
Osgoode Hall LSJ — Osgoode Hall Law School. Journal
Os Hall LJ — Osgoode Hall. Law Journal
OSHR — Occupational Safety and Health Reporter
OSH Rep (BNA) — Occupational Safety and Health Reporter (Bureau of
    National Affairs)
OSIA — On Site in Alberta
OSJ — Ordnance Survey of Jerusalem
Osjeckii Zbor — Osjeckii Zbornik
OSKR — One Sky Report
OSLP — Oxford Slavonic Papers
Osmania J Social Sciences — Osmania Journal of Social Sciences
OSN — Ocean Science News
Osnabrueck Mitt — Osnabruecker Mitteilungen
Osnabrueck Schrift Math — Osnabruecker Schriften zur Mathematik
Osn Fundam — Osnovaniya i Fundamenty
Osn Fundam Mekh Gruntov — Osnovaniya, Fundamenty, i Mekhanika Gruntov
    [USSR]
OSP — Oxford Slavonic Papers
Osp Ital Chir — Ospedali d'Italia-Chirurgia
Osp Magg — Ospedale Maggiore [Italy]
Osp Magg Novara — Ospedale Maggiore di Novara
Osp Psichiatr — Ospedale Psichiatrico
Osr Nauk Prod Mater Polprzewodn Pr — Osrodek Naukowo-Produkcyjny
    Materialow Polprzewodnikowych. Prace
Osrodek Badaw Rozwojowy Elektron Prozniowej (Pr) — Osrodek Badawczo-
    Rozwojowy Elektroniki Prozniowej (Prace)
Osrodek Inf Energ Jad Rev Rep — Osrodek Informacji o Energii Jadrowej.
    Review Report
OsRom — Osservatore Romano [Vatican City]
Osserv — Osservatore
Oss & Mem Oss Astrofis Arcetri — Osservazioni e Memorie. Osservatorio
    Astrofisico di Arcetri
OssRom — Osservatore Romano [Vatican City]
OSSTF For — OSSTF [Ontario Secondary School Teachers' Federation]
    Forum
OST — Osteuropa. Zeitschrift fuer Gegenwartsfragen des Ostens
Osteopath Ann — Osteopathic Annals
Osteopath Prof — Osteopathic Profession
Oster Musik — Oesterreichische Musikzeitschrift
Osterr Bot Z — Oesterreichische Botanische Zeitschrift
Osterr Dent Z — Oesterreichische Dentisten Zeitschrift
Osterr Hebammenztg — Oesterreichische Hebammenzeitung
Osterr Krankenpflegez — Oesterreichische Krankenpflegezeitschrift
Osterr Osth — Oesterreichische Osthefte
Osterr Z Aussenpolit — Oesterreichische Zeitschrift fuer Aussenpolitik
Osterr Z Off Recht — Oesterreichische Zeitschrift fuer Oeffentliches Recht
Osterr Z Polit-Wiss — Oesterreichische Zeitschrift fuer Politikwissenschaft
Osteur — Osteuropa
Osteur Naturwiss — Osteuropa Naturwissenschaft
Osteuropa Wirtsch — Osteuropa Wirtschaft

Osteur Wirt — Osteuropa Wirtschaft
OSTGU — Oriental Society. Transactions. Glasgow University
OSTI Newsl — Office for Scientific and Technical Information. Newsletter
Ostjydsk Hjemstavn — Ostjydsk Hjemstavnforenings Aarsskrift
Ostkirch St — Ostkirchliche Studien
OstM — Ostdeutsche Monatshefte
Ostmaerk Milchwirtsch Ztg — Ostmaerkische Milchwirtschaftliche Zeitung
Ostmaerk Spirit Ztg — Ostmaerkische Spirituosen-Zeitung
OSTO — Oesterreichische Osthefte
Ostrava Vys Ak Banska Sb Rada Hornicko-Geol — Ostrava. Vysoka Skola
    Banska. Sbornik. Rada Hornicko-Geologicka
Ostrich Suppl — Ostrich. Supplement
Ostwalds Klassiker Exakt Wiss — Ostwalds Klassiker der Exakten
    Wissenschaften
OSu — Orientalia Suecana
OsUA — Ortnamnssaellskapets i Uppsala Aarsskrift
OSUCLL — Ohio State University. Contributions in Language and Literature
OSU Ext Facts Coop Ext Serv Okla State Univ — OSU Extension Facts.
    Cooperative Extension Service. Oklahoma State University
OSUTCB — Ohio State University. Theatre Collection Bulletin
OSV — Our Sunday Visitor
OSVM — Our Sunday Visitor Magazine
OT — Old Testament
OT — Onze Taaltuin
OT — Onze Tijd
OTA — Onze Taal
Otago Acclim Soc Annu Rep — Otago Acclimatisation Society. Annual Report
Otago Law Rev — Otago Law Review
Otago LR — Otago Law Review
Otago L Rev — Otago Law Review
Otago Mus Zool Bull — Otago Museum of Zoology. Bulletin
OTAM — Ozbek Tili va Adabiet Masalalari
OTAN Newsl — OTAN [Organization of Tropical American Nematologists]
    Newsletter
Otbor i Peredaca Informacii — Otbor i Peredaca Informacii. Akademija Nauk
    Ukrainskoi SSR. Fiziko-Mehaniceskii Institut
Otbor i Peredacha Inf — Otbor i Peredacha Informatsii
Otbor Pereda Inf — Otbor i Peredacha Informatsii
OTC — Office: Technology and People
Otchery Mezhdunar O-va Khim Serna — Otchery Mezhdunarodnogo
    Obshchestva po Khimii Serna
Otd Tekh — Otdelochnaya Tekhnika
Otemon Econ Stud — Otemon Economic Studies
Othr Womn — Other Woman
Oth Sce — Other Scenes
OTI — Trend. Das Oesterreichische Wirtschaftsmagazin
Otkrytiya Izobret Prom Obraztsy Tovarnye Znaki — Otkrytiya, Izobreteniya,
    Promyshlennye Obraztsy, Tovarnye Znaki [Bulletin for Inventions,
    Designs, and Trademarks] [USSR]
Otkryt Izobret — Otkrytiya, Izobreteniya, Promyshlennye Obraztsy, Tovarnye
    Znaki [Bulletin for Inventions, Designs, and Trademarks] [USSR]
OTLR — Otago Law Review
OTLV — Onza, Tigra, y Leon. Revista para la Infancia Venezolana
OTM — Old Time Music
OTMPA — Oberflaechentechnik/Metallpraxis
Otolar Clin — Otolaryngologic Clinics of North America
Otolaryngol Clin N Am — Otolaryngologic Clinics of North America
Otolaryngol Clin North Am — Otolaryngologic Clinics of North America
Otolaryngol Head Neck Surg — Otolaryngology and Head and Neck Surgery
Otolaryngol Pol — Otolaryngologia Polska
Otol Fukuoka — Otologia Fukuoka
Otol Fukuoka Jibi To Rinsho — Otologia Fukuoka Jibi To Rinsho
Oto Noro Oftalmol — Oto-Noro Oftalmoloji
Otoplenie Vent Stroit Teplofiz — Otoplenie. Ventilyatsiya i Stroitel'naya
    Teplofizika
Oto-Rhino-Laryngol — Oto-Rhino-Laryngology
Oto-Rino-Laringol Ital — Oto-Rino-Laringologia Italiana
Oto-Rino-Laringol Oftalmol — Oto-Rino-Laringologie si Oftalmologie
OTPOA — Otolaryngologia Polska
OTRE — Ottawa Report. Canadian Wildlife Federation
OTS — Oudtestamentische Studien
Otsenka Mestorozhd Poiskakh Razved — Otsenka Mestorozhdenii pri Poiskakh
    i Razvedkakh
OTSt — Oudtestamentische Studien [Leiden]
OTT — Technieuws Ottawa. Korte Berichten op Technisch Wetenschappelijk
    Gebied
Ottawa Field Nat Club Tr — Ottawa Field Naturalists' Club. Transactions
Ottawa Law R — Ottawa Law Review
Ottawa Lit Sc Soc Tr — Ottawa Literary and Scientific Society. Transactions
Ottawa LR — Ottawa Law Review
Ottawa L Rev — Ottawa Law Review
Ottawa Nat — Ottawa Naturalist
Ott LR — Ottawa Law Review
Otto Graf Inst (Stuttgart) Tech Hochsch Schriftenr — Otto-Graf-Institut
    (Stuttgart). Technische Hochschule. Schriftenreihe

Otto-Graf-Inst (Stutt) Tech Hochsch Schriftenr — Otto-Graf-Institut (Stuttgart). Technische Hochschule. Schriftenreihe
OTW — Out of this World
OTWA — Out of this World Adventures
OTWerkSuidA — Die Ou Testamentiese Werkgemeenskap in Suid-Afrika [*Pretoria*]
OTWSA — Die Ou Testamentiese Werkgemeenskap in Suid-Afrika [*Pretoria*]
OTZ — Oesterreichische Textil Zeitung. Zentralblatt fuer die Gesamte Textilwirtschaft
OUA — Ortnamnssaellskapets i Uppsala Aarsskrift
OUB — Parfums, Cosmetiques, Aromes. L'Unique Journal Francais de Son Secteur
Oudh Med — Oudheidkundige Mededeelingen
OudSt — Oudtestamentische Studien [*Leiden*]
Ouest Apic — L'Ouest Apicole
Ouest Med — Ouest Medical
Oulun Yliopiston Ydintek Laitoksen Julk — Oulun Yliopiston Ydintekniikkan Laitoksen Julkaisuja
OUR — Ohio University Review
Our Gener — Our Generation
Ouro Preto Esc Minas Rev — Ouro Preto. Escola de Minas. Revista
Our Q Mag — Our Quarterly Magazine
OURS — Organ of Unemployed, Relief, and Sustenance Workers
Our World W — Our World Weekly
OuS — Oudtestamentische Studien [*Leiden*]
OUSE — Odense University Studies in English
Out — Outlands
Out — Outsider
Outdoor Am — Outdoor America
Outdoor Ind — Outdoor Indiana
Outdoor Okla — Outdoor Oklahoma
Outd Rec Act — Outdoor Recreation Action
Outl — Outlook
Outl Agric — Outlook on Agriculture
Outlook Agr — Outlook on Agriculture
Outlook Agric — Outlook on Agriculture
Outok News — Outokumpu News
Outstate Test Circ Univ Nebr Coll Agr Home Econ Agr Exp Sta — Outstate Testing Circular. University of Nebraska. College of Agriculture and Home Economics. Agricultural Experiment Station
OuTWP — Die Ou Testamentiese Werkgemeenskap in Suid-Afrika (Pretoria)
OUV — Openbare Uitgaven
OuW — Ost und West
OV — Ovation
OVC — Verwarming en Ventilatie. Maandblad voor Verwarming, Ventilatie, Airconditioning, en Koeling
Overland — Overland Monthly
Overland ns — Overland Monthly. New Series
Oversea Ed — Overseas Education
Overseas Bldg Notes — Overseas Building Notes
Overseas Geol Miner Resour — Overseas Geology and Mineral Resources [*Great Britain*]
Overseas Geol Miner Resour Suppl Ser Bull Suppl — Overseas Geology and Mineral Resources. Supplement Series. Bulletin Supplement
Overseas Mem Inst Geol Sci — Overseas Memoir. Institute of Geological Sciences
Overseas Trade Descrip Export & Import Stat — Overseas Trade Decriptions. Export and Import Statistics
Overseas Trade Stat UK — Overseas Trade Statistics of the United Kingdom
Overs K Danske Vidensk Selsk Forh — Oversigt over det Kongelige Danske Videnskabernes Selskabs. Forhandlinger
Overs K Dan Vidensk Selsk — Oversigt over Selskabets Virksomhed. Kongelige Danske Videnskabernes Selskab
Overs K Dan Vidensk Selsk Forh — Oversigt over det Kongelige Danske Videnskabernes Selskabs. Forhandlinger
OVIR — Otdel Viz i Registratsii
OVT — Overseas Trading
OW — Offshore Oil Weekly [*Later, Offshore Oil International*]
OW — Orient/West
OW — Ost und West
OW — Ostatnie Wiadomosci
OW — Other Worlds
OWB — Civis Mundi
OWN — Office World News
OWN — Oudtestamentisch Werkgezelschap in Nederland
OxAbs — Oxford Abstracts
Ox B Econ S — Oxford Bulletin of Economics and Statistics
Ox Econ Pap — Oxford Economic Papers
OXF — Oxford Bulletin of Economics and Statistics
Oxf Ger Stud — Oxford German Studies
Oxf Mag — Oxford Magazine
Oxford B Econ Statis — Oxford Bulletin of Economics and Statistics
Oxford Biol Readers — Oxford Biology Readers
Oxford/Carol Biol Readers — Oxford/Carolina Biology Readers
Oxford Econ Pa — Oxford Economic Papers
Oxford Econ Pas — Oxford Economic Papers

Oxford J Legal Stud — Oxford Journal of Legal Studies
Oxford R Educ — Oxford Review of Education
Oxford Slavonic Pa — Oxford Slavonic Papers
Oxf Phys Ser — Oxford Physics Series
Oxf Univ Pitt Rivers Mus Occas Pap Technol — Oxford University. Pitt Rivers Museum. Occasional Papers on Technology
Oxid Combust Rev — Oxidation and Combustion Reviews
Oxid Met — Oxidation of Metals
Ox Lit Rev — Oxford Literary Review
Ox Prize Ess — Oxford Prize Essays
OYBSA — Oyo Butsuri
OYGK — Okayama Daigaku Hobungakubu Gakujutsu Kiyo
OZDP — Oesterreichische Zeitschrift fuer Kunst und Denkmalpflege
Ozean Tech — Ozean und Technik [*West Germany*]
OZEBA — Oesterreichische Zeitschrift fuer Erforschung und Bekaempfung der Krebskrankheit
OZE Oesterr Z Elektr — Oe Z E/Oesterreichische Zeitschrift fuer Elektrizitaetswirtschaft
OZET — Obshchestvo Remeslennovo i Zemledel'cheskovo Truda
OZET — Obshchestvo Zemleistroistva Evreiskikh Trudiashchchikhsia v SSSR
OZKDP — Oesterreichische Zeitschrift fuer Kunst und Denkmalpflege
OZV — Oesterreichische Zeitschrift fuer Volkskunde

P

P — Palacio
P — Palaestra
P — Pazmaveb
P — Perspectives
P — Philologus. Zeitschrift fuer Klassische Altertum
P — Philosophy
P — Poetry
P — Polonystyka
P — Ponte
PA — Onze Pius-Almanak
PA — Pacific Affairs
Pa — Paideia
PA — Parliamentary Affairs
Pa — Paru
PA — Pastoral Music
PA — Petroleum Abstracts
PA — Pollution Abstracts
Pa — Polonystyka
PA — Presence Africaine
PA — Pro Arte
PA — Professional Administration
PA — Psychological Abstracts
PA — Public Administration
PAAAS — Proceedings. American Academy of Arts and Sciences
PAAAS — Publication. American Association for the Advancement of Science
PAABS Rev — PAABS [*Pan-American Association of Biochemical Societies*] Revista [*United States*]
PAABS Symp — PAABS [*Pan-American Association of Biochemical Societies*] Symposium
PA Acad Sci Proc — Pennsylvania Academy of Science. Proceedings
PA Ag Exp — Pennsylvania. Agricultural Experiment Station. Publications
PA Agric Exp Stn Bull — Pennsylvania. Agricultural Experiment Station. Bulletin
PA Agric Exp Stn Prog Rep — Pennsylvania. Agricultural Experiment Station. Progress Report
PAAJR — Proceedings. American Academy for Jewish Research
PAANA — Proceedings. Australian Society of Animal Production
PAAP — Panjabi Adabi Academy. Publication
PAAR — American Academy in Rome. Papers and Monographs
PA Arch — Pennsylvania Archaeologist
PA Archaeol — Pennsylvania Archaeologist
PAAS — Proceedings. American Antiquarian Society
PAATA — Praktika tes Akademias Athenon
PAAZA — Progressive Agriculture in Arizona
PABAQ — Pennsylvania Bar Association. Quarterly
PA Bar Asso Q — Pennsylvania Bar Association. Quarterly
PA B Ass'n Q — Pennsylvania Bar Association. Quarterly
PABIA — Pathologie et Biologie
PA Bsns Survey — Pennsylvania Business Survey
PA Bur Topogr Geol Surv Miner Resour Rep — Pennsylvania. Bureau of Topographic and Geologic Survey. Mineral Resource Report
PABVA — Pesquisa Agropecuaria Brasileira. Serie Veterinaria
PAC — Canada. Fisheries and Marine Service. Northern Operations Branch. Pacific Region. Data Report Series
Pac — Packaging

Pac A — Pacific Affairs
PACA — Proceedings. African Classical Association
PACAB — Pacific Affairs. Current Awareness Bulletin
Pac Aff — Pacific Affairs
Pac Affairs — Pacific Affairs
Pac Arts Newsl — Pacific Arts Newsletter
Pac Bird Obs — Pacific Bird Observer
Pac Builder Eng — Pacific Builder and Engineer
Pac Chem Eng Cong Proc — Pacific Chemical Engineering Congress. Proceedings [*United States*]
Pac Chem Metall Ind — Pacific Chemical and Metallurgical Industries
Pac Coast Gas Assoc Proc — Pacific Coast Gas Association. Proceedings
Pac Coast Med — Pacific Coast Medicine
Pac Com — Pacific Community [*Tokyo*]
Pac Commun — Pacific Community
Pac Discov — Pacific Discovery
Pac Discovery — Pacific Discovery
PACE — PACE. Pacing and Clinical Electrophysiology
PACE — PACE. Process and Chemical Engineering
PACE — Process and Chemical Engineering
Pace LR — Pace Law Review
Pace L Rev — Pace Law Review
PACE Process Chem Eng — PACE. Process and Chemical Engineering
Pac Fisherman — Pacific Fisherman
Pac Geol — Pacific Geology
PacH — Pacific Historian
Pac Hist R — Pacific Historical Review
Pac Hist Rev — Pacific Historical Review
Pac Hist Rev — Pacific History Review
Pac Hortic — Pacific Horticulture
PacHR — Pacific Historical Review
Pacif Aff — Pacific Affairs
Pacific Bus — Pacific Business
Pacific His R — Pacific Historical Review
Pacific Islands M — Pacific Islands Monthly
Pacific Islands Yrbk — Pacific Islands Year Book
Pacific J Math — Pacific Journal of Mathematics
Pacific L J — Pacific Law Journal
Pacific Northw Q — Pacific Northwest Quarterly
Pacific Perspect — Pacific Perspective
Pacific Sci — Pacific Science
Pacific Sociol R — Pacific Sociological Review
Pacif Imp — Pacific Imperialism Notebook
Pacif Insects — Pacific Insects
Pac Insects — Pacific Insects
Pac Insects Mongr — Pacific Insects Monograph
Pac Insects Monogr — Pacific Insects Monograph
Pac J Math — Pacific Journal of Mathematics
Pack — Packaging
Packag Abstr — Packaging Abstracts
Package Dev — Package Development
Package Dev Syst — Package Development and Systems
Package Eng — Package Engineering
Package Engng — Package Engineering
Packag (India) — Packaging (India)

Packag Inst Spec Rep — Packaging Institute. Special Report
Packag Rev — Packaging Review
Packag Rev (S Afr) — Packaging Review (South Africa)
Packa Rev — Packaging Review
Packer Process — Packer, Processor
Pack Print and Dyecutting — Package Printing and Dyecutting
Pac LJ — Pacific Law Journal
Pac Mar Fish Comm Annu Rep — Pacific Marine Fisheries Commission. Annual Report
Pac Mar Fish Comm Bull — Pacific Marine Fisheries Commission. Bulletin
Pac Med Surg — Pacific Medicine and Surgery
Pac Mo — Pacific Monthly [*Portland, Oregon*]
P Ac Nat S — Proceedings. Academy of Natural Sciences of Philadelphia
Pac Neighbours — Pacific Neighbours
Pac Northw — Pacific Northwest Quarterly
Pac Northwest — Pacific Northwesterner
Pac Northwesterner — Pacific Northwesterner
Pac Northwest For Range Exp Stn Res Note PNW — Pacific Northwest Forest and Range Experiment Station. Research Note PNW
Pac Northwest For Range Exp Stn Res Pap PNW — Pacific Northwest Forest and Range Experiment Station. Research Paper PNW
Pac Northwest Q — Pacific Northwest Quarterly
Pac Northwest Sea — Pacific Northwest Sea
PacNQ — Pacific Northwest Quarterly
Pac NWQ — Pacific Northwest Quarterly
PACPhA — Proceedings. American Catholic Philosophical Association
Pac Pharm — Pacific Pharmacist
Pac Philos Q — Pacific Philosophical Quarterly
Pac Phil Q — Pacific Philosophical Quarterly
Pac Phil Quart — Pacific Philosophical Quarterly
Pac Plast — Pacific Plastics
P Ac Poli S — Proceedings. Academy of Political Science
Pac Pulp Pap Ind — Pacific Pulp and Paper Industry
Pac Q — Pacific Quarterly
Pac Res — Pacific Research [*Formerly, Pacific Research and World Empire Telegram*]
Pac Rockets — Pacific Rockets
Pac Rocket Soc Bull — Pacific Rocket Society. Bulletin
Pac Sci — Pacific Science
Pac Sci Congr Proc — Pacific Science Congress. Proceedings
Pac Sci Congr Rec Proc — Pacific Science Congress. Record of Proceedings
Pac Search — Pacific Search [*United States*]
Pac Sociol R — Pacific Sociological Review
Pac Soc Rev — Pacific Sociological Review
PacSp — Pacific Spectator
Pac View — Pacific Viewpoint [*New Zealand*]
Pac Viewp — Pacific Viewpoint
Pac Wine Spirit Rev — Pacific Wine Spirit Review
PAD — Personnel Administrator
PA Dent J — Pennsylvania Dental Journal
PA Dep Environ Resour Water Resour Bull — Pennsylvania. Department of Environmental Resources. Water Resources Bulletin
PA Dep For Waters Water Resour Bull — Pennsylvania. Department of Forests and Waters. Water Resources Bulletin
PA Dept Int Affairs Monthly Bull — Pennsylvania. Department of Internal Affairs. Monthly Bulletin
Padiatr Pad — Paediatrie und Paedologie
PA Dp Agr An Rp — Pennsylvania. Department of Agriculture. Annual Report
PADS — Publications. American Dialect Society
PADSD — Proceedings. Analytical Division. Chemical Society
Paedag Hist — Paedagogica Historica
Paedagog Hist — Paedagogica Historica
Paedagogica Hist — Paedagogica Historica
Paedagog Run — Paedagogische Rundschau
Paediatr Fortbildungskurse Prax — Paediatrische Fortbildungskurse fuer die Praxis
Paediatr Grenzgeb — Paediatrie und Grenzgebiete
Paediatr Indones — Paediatrica Indonesiana
Paediatr Paedol — Paediatrie und Paedologie
Paediatr Paedol (Suppl) — Paediatrie und Paedologie (Supplementum)
PA Elec Ass Eng Sect Transm Distrib — Pennsylvania Electric Association. Engineering Section. Transmission and Distribution Committee. Minutes
PA Electr Assoc Annu Rep — Pennsylvania Electric Association. Annual Report
PA Electr Assoc Eng Sect Minutes Meet — Pennsylvania Electric Association. Engineering Section. Minutes of the Meeting
PA Energy Ext Serv News — Pennsylvania Energy Extension Service. News
PAES — Publications. Princeton University Archaeological Expeditions to Syria
PAF — Pacific Affairs
PA F — Pennsylvania Folklife
PA Farm Econ — Pennsylvania Farm Economics
PAFEA — Patologicheskaya Fiziologiya i Eksperimental'naya Terapiya
PA Folklife — Pennsylvania Folklife
PA For — Pennsylvania Forests

PA Fruit News — Pennsylvania Fruit News
PAFS — Publications. American Folklore Society
PAG — Packaging
PaGa — Printing and Graphic Arts
PAGAA — Pesquisa Agropecuaria Brasileira. Serie Agronomia
PA Gen As — Pennsylvania General Assembly
PA Geol — Pennsylvania Geology
PA Geol Surv Atlas — Pennsylvania. Geological Survey. Atlas
PA Geol Surv Gen Geol Rep — Pennsylvania. Geological Survey. General Geology Report
PA Geol Surv Inf Circ — Pennsylvania. Geological Survey. Information Circular
PA Geol Surv Miner Resour Rep — Pennsylvania. Geological Survey. Mineral Resource Report
PA Geol Surv Prog Rep — Pennsylvania. Geological Survey. Progress Report
PA Geol Surv Water Resour Rep — Pennsylvania. Geological Survey. Water Resource Report
PA-Ger — Pennsylvania-German
PA Ger Folk Soc Yr Bk — Pennsylvania German Folklore Society. Year Book
PA G S — Pennsylvania. Geological Survey
PAGS — Proceedings. Australian Goethe Society
PAGVA — Progres Agricole et Viticole
PAGYB — Pennsylvania Geology
Pahasapa Q — Pahasapa Quarterly
PAHEA — Pharmaceutica Acta Helvetiae
PA His — Pennsylvania History
PA Hist — Pennsylvania History
Pahlavi Med J — Pahlavi Medical Journal
PAIAA — Proceedings. National Academy of Sciences (India). Section A
Paid Dues — Paid My Dues
Paideia Studies in Nature of Modern Math — Paideia Studies in the Nature of Modern Mathematics
PAIDOL — Paidologist
PAIGS — Performing Arts Information Guide Series
Paine Webb — Paine, Webber, Jackson & Curtis, Inc. Research Notes
Pain Fr — Pain Francais
Pain Suppl — Pain. Supplement
Paint — Paintbrush
Paint Colour Rec — Paint and Colour Record
Paint Decor — Painting and Decorating
Painters J — Painters and Allied Trades Journal
Paint Ind — Paint Industry
Paint Ind Mag — Paint Industry Magazine
Painting Technol (Tokyo) — Painting Technology (Tokyo)
Paint J — Paint Journal
Paint J — Paint Journal of Australia and New Zealand
Paint J Aust NZ — Paint Journal of Australia and New Zealand
Paint Manuf — Paint Manufacture [*England*]
Paint Oil Chem Rev — Paint Oil and Chemical Review
Paint Oil Colour J — Paint Oil and Colour Journal
Paints Pak — Paints in Pakistan
Paint Technol — Paint Technology
Paint Varn Prod — Paint and Varnish Production
Paint Varn Prod Manager — Paint and Varnish Production Manager
PAIS — Public Affairs Information Service [*New York, NY*] [*Bibliographic database*]
PA J — American Academy of Physicians' Assistants. Journal
PA J — PA Journal [*Formerly, Physician's Associate*]
PAJ — Pan-African Journal
PAJHS — Publication. American Jewish Historical Society
Pak Agric — Pakistan Agriculture
Pak Assoc Adv Sci Annu Rep — Pakistan Association for the Advancement of Science. Annual Report
PAKBA — Promyshlennost Armenii
Pak Cottons — Pakistan Cottons
Pak CSIR Bull Monogr — Pakistan Council of Scientific and Industrial Research. Bulletin. Monograph
Pak Dent Rev — Pakistan Dental Review
Pak Dev R — Pakistan Development Review
Pak Dev Rev — Pakistan Development Review
Pak DR — Pakistan Development Review
Pak Eng — Pakistan Engineer
Pak Geogr Rev — Pakistan Geographical Review
Pak Geol Surv Inf Release — Pakistan Geological Survey. Information Release
Pak Geol Surv Rec — Pakistan Geological Survey. Records
Pakistan Develop R — Pakistan Development Review
Pakistan Econ and Social R — Pakistan Economic and Social Review
Pakistan Eng — Pakistan Engineer
Pakistan J Biol Agr Sci — Pakistan Journal of Biological and Agricultural Sciences
Pakistan J For — Pakistan Journal of Forestry
Pakistan J Med Res — Pakistan Journal of Medical Research
Pakistan J Sci — Pakistan Journal of Science
Pakistan J Sci Ind Res — Pakistan Journal of Scientific and Industrial Research
Pakistan J Sci Res — Pakistan Journal of Scientific Research

Pakistan J Soil Sci — Pakistan Journal of Soil Sciences
Pakistan Lib Bull — Pakistan Library Bulletin
Pakistan Lib R — Pakistan Library Review
Pakistan Phil J — Pakistan Philosophical Journal
Pakist J Agric Sci — Pakistan Journal of Agricultural Sciences
Pakist J Bot — Pakistan Journal of Botany
Pakist J Scient Res — Pakistan Journal of Scientific Research
Pakist J Zool — Pakistan Journal of Zoology
Pak J Agric Sci — Pakistan Journal of Agricultural Sciences
Pak J Agri Res — Pakistan Journal of Agricultural Research
Pak J Biochem — Pakistan Journal of Biochemistry
Pak J Biol Agric Sci — Pakistan Journal of Biological and Agricultural
  Sciences
Pak J Bot — Pakistan Journal of Botany
Pak J Fam Plann — Pakistan Journal of Family Planning
Pak J For — Pakistan Journal of Forestry
Pak J Geriatr — Pakistan Journal of Geriatrics
Pak J Health — Pakistan Journal of Health
Pak J Med Res — Pakistan Journal of Medical Research
Pak J Pharm — Pakistan Journal of Pharmacy
Pak J Pharmacol — Pakistan Journal of Pharmacology
Pak J Sci — Pakistan Journal of Science
Pak J Sci Ind Res — Pakistan Journal of Scientific and Industrial Research
Pak J Sci and Ind Res — Pakistan Journal of Scientific and Industrial Research
Pak J Sci Res — Pakistan Journal of Scientific Research
Pak J Zool — Pakistan Journal of Zoology
Pak Libr Ass Q J — Pakistan Library Association. Quarterly Journal
Pak Libr Rev — Pakistan Library Review
Pak Med Forum — Pakistan Medical Forum
Pak Med J — Pakistan Medical Journal
Pak Med Rev — Pakistan Medical Review
Pak Nurs Health Rev — Pakistan Nursing and Health Review
Pak Philos Congr Proc — Pakistan Philosophical Congress. Proceedings
PakQ — Pakistan Quarterly
PakR — Pakistan Review
Pak Sci Conf Proc — Pakistan Science Conference. Proceedings
Pak Text J — Pakistan Textile Journal
PAL — Pro Alesia
PA L — University of Pennsylvania. Law Review
Palabra Hom — Palabra y el Hombre
Palaeoecol Afr Surround Isl — Palaeoecology of Africa and the Surrounding
  Islands
Palaeogeogr Palaeoclimatol Palaeoecol — Palaeogeography,
  Palaeoclimatology, Palaeoecology
Palaeogeo P — Palaeogeography, Palaeoclimatology, Palaeoecology
Palaeont — Palaeontographica
Palaeont Abh (Dames u Kayser) — Palaeontologische Abhandlungen (Dames
  und Kayser)
Palaeontogr Abt A — Palaeontographica. Abteilung A. Palaeozoologie-
  Stratigraphie
Palaeontogr Abt A Palaeozool-Stratigr — Palaeontographica. Abteilung A.
  Palaeozoologie-Stratigraphie
Palaeontogr Abt B — Palaeontographica. Abteilung B. Palaeophytologie
Palaeontogr Am — Palaeontographica Americana
Palaeontogr Ital — Palaeontographia Italia
Palaeontogr Soc Monogr — Palaeontographical Society. Monographs
Palaeontogr Soc Monogr (Lond) — Palaeontographical Society. Monographs
  (London)
Palaeontol Afr — Palaeontologia Africana
Palaeontol Jugosl — Palaeontologia Jugoslavica
Palaeontol Jugoslav — Palaeontologia Jugoslavica
Palaeontol Mex Inst Geol (Mex) — Palaeontologia Mexicana. Instituto de
  Geologia (Mexico)
Palaeontol Pap Publ Geol Surv Queensl — Palaeontology Papers. Geological
  Survey of Queensland
Palaeontol Pol — Palaeontologia Polonica
Palaeontol Sin Ser B — Palaeontologia Sinica. Series B
Palaeontol Sin Ser C — Palaeontologia Sinica. Series C
Palaeontol Sin Ser D — Palaeontologia Sinica. Series D
Palaeontol Soc Japan Trans Proc NS — Palaeontological Society of Japan.
  Transactions and Proceedings. New Series
Palaeontol Soc Jpn Spec Pap — Palaeontological Society of Japan. Special
  Papers
Palaeontol Z — Palaeontologische Zeitschrift
Palaeont Soc Japan Trans and Proc — Palaeontological Society of Japan.
  Transactions and Proceedings
Palaeont Zeitschr — Palaeontologische Zeitschrift
Palaeont Zs — Palaeontologische Zeitschrift
Palaeovertebrata. Mem Extraordinaire — Palaeovertebrata. Memoire
  Extraordinaire
Palaeovertebr (Montp) — Palaeovertebrata (Montpellier)
Pa Lang & Lit — Papers on Language and Literature
Pal B — Paleontological Bulletins
PalCl — Palestra del Clero [Rovigo, Italy]
PALCOR — Palestine Correspondence
Paleobiol Cont — Paleobiologie Continentale

Paleontol Evol-Barc Inst Prov Paleontol — Paleontologia y Evolucion-
  Barcelona. Instituto Provincial de Paleontologia
Paleontol J — Paleontological Journal
Paleontol Mex — Paleontologia Mexicana
Paleontol Sb — Paleontologicheskiy Sbornik
Paleontol Soc Mem — Paleontological Society. Memoir
Paleontol Stratigr Litol — Paleontologiya Stratigrafiya i Litologiya
Paleontol Zh — Paleontologicheskii Zhurnal
Paleont Pap Publs Geol Suv QD — Paleontology Papers. Publications.
  Geological Survey of Queensland
Paleont Research Lab Special Inv Rept — Paleontological Research
  Laboratories. Special Investigation. Report
Paleopathol Newsl — Paleopathological Newsletter
PalEQ — Palestine Exploration Quarterly
Palest Board Sci Ind Res Rep — Palestine Board for Scientific and Industrial
  Research. Reports
Palest Citrogr — Palestine Citrograph
Palestine Explor Q — Palestine Exploration Quarterly
Palestine Explor Quart — Palestine Exploration Quarterly
Palest J Bot Hortic Sci — Palestine Journal of Botany and Horticultural
  Science
Palest J Bot Jerusalem Ser — Palestine Journal of Botany. Jerusalem Series
Palest J Bot Jerus Ser — Palestine Journal of Botany. Jerusalem Series
Palest J Bot Rehovot Ser — Palestine Journal of Botany. Rehovot Series
Palest Trib — Palestine Tribune
Pal Ex Q — Palestine Exploration Quarterly
PA Lib Assn Bull — Pennsylvania Library Association. Bulletin
PalJ — Palaestina-Jahrbuch
PalJb — Palaestina-Jahrbuch
PA LJ Rep — Pennsylvania Law Journal-Reporter
Palladio — Palladio. Rivista di Storia dell'Architettura
Pall Mall M — Pall Mall Magazine
PA L Rev — University of Pennsylvania. Law Review
PalSb — Palestinskii Sbornik [Moscow/Leningrad]
Pal Sbor — Palestinskii Sbornik
PALSD — Program: Automated Library and Information Systems
PALSGR — Palsgrave Dictionary
PALTREU — Palaestina Treuhandstelle zur Beratung Deutscher Juden
Palyaval Tanacs — Palyavalasztasi Tanacsadas
Palynol Bull — Palynological Bulletin
PA M — Pennsylvania Magazine of History and Biography
P Am Ac Ins — Proceedings. American Academy and Institute of Arts and
  Letters
PA Mag Hist — Pennsylvania Magazine of History and Biography
PA Mag Hist Biogr — Pennsylvania Magazine of History and Biography
P Am Antiq — Proceedings. American Antiquarian Society
P Am Ass Ca — Proceedings. American Association for Cancer Research
Pamatky Prir — Pamatky a Priroda
P Am Cath P — Proceedings. American Catholic Philosophical Association
PAMDA — Progress in Atomic Medicine
Pam Div Wood Technol For Comm NSW — Pamphlet. Division of Wood
  Technology. Forestry Commission. New South Wales
PA Med — Pennsylvania Medicine
PA Med J — Pennsylvania Medical Journal
Pamiet Konf Nauk Otolaryngol Dzieciecej Zakopane — Pamietnik Konferencji
  Naukowej Otolaryngologii Dzieciecej Zakopane
Pamietnik L — Pamietnik Literacki
Pamiet Pulawski — Pamietnik Pulawski
Pamiet Zjazdu Otolaryngol Pol Katowicach — Pamietnik Zjazdu
  Otolaryngologow Polskich w Katowicach
Pam Iowa State Univ Sci Tech Coop Ext Serv — Pamphlet. Iowa State
  University of Science and Technology. Cooperative Extension Service
PamL — Pamietnik Literacki
P Am Math S — Proceedings. American Mathematical Society
Pamph — Pamphleteer
Pamph Amat Ent Soc — Pamphlet. Amateur Entomologists' Society
Pamph Dep Agric (Qd) — Pamphlet. Department of Agriculture (Queensland)
Pamph Dep Agric (Tanganyika) — Pamphlet. Department of Agriculture
  (Tanganyika Territory)
Pamph Dep Agric Un S Afr — Pamphlet. Department of Agriculture. Union of
  South Africa
Pamph Div Sci Publs Volcani Cent Agric Res Orgn — Pamphlet. Division of
  Scientific Publications. Volcani Center. Agricultural Research
  Organisation
Pamph Div Wood Technol For Comm NSW — Pamphlet. Division of Wood
  Technology. Forestry Commission. New South Wales
Pamph Idaho Bur Mines Geol — Pamphlet. Idaho Bureau of Mines and
  Geology
P Am Phil S — Proceedings. American Philosophical Society
Pamphlet Archre — Pamphlet Architecture
Pamphl For Res Educ Proj For Dep (Sudan) — Pamphlet. Forestry Research
  and Education Project. Forests Department (Khartoum, Sudan)
Pamph Volcani Inst Agric Res — Pamphlet. Volcani Institute of Agricultural
  Research
Pam Pulaw — Pamietnik Pulawski
Pam Pulawski — Pamietnik Pulawski

PAMS — North-Holland Series in Probability and Applied Mathematics [*Elsevier Book Series*]
PAMS — Papers. American Musicological Society
PAMS — Proceedings. American Mathematical Society
PAMSB — Pharos of Alpha Omega Alpha Honor Medical Society
P Am S Info — Proceedings. American Society for Information Science
PamSL — Pamietnik Slowianski Czasopismo Naukowe Posiecone Slowianoznawstwu
PAMWS — Proceedings. Annual Meeting. Western Society for French History
PAMYA — Proceedings. American Mathematical Society
PAN — Packaging News
Pan — Panache
Pan — Panorama
PAN — Pastoral Music Notebook
PAN — Polska Akademia Nauk [*Polish Academy of Sciences*] [*Warsaw*]
PanA — Pan-Africanist
Panama Admin Recursos Minerales Mapa — Republica de Panama. Administracion de Recursos Minerales. Mapa
Panama Univ Dept Geografia Pub — Panama Universidad. Departamento de Geografia. Publicacion
Pan Am Fisherman — Pan American Fisherman
Pan Am Health Organ Off Doc — Pan American Health Organization. Official Document
Pan Am Health Organ Res Prog — Pan American Health Organization. Research in Progress
Pan Am Health Organ Sci Publ — Pan American Health Organization. Scientific Publication
Pan-Am Inst Geography and History Pub — Pan-American Institute of Geography and History. Publication
Pan Am Inst Min Eng Geol US Sect Tech Pap — Pan American Institute of Mining Engineering and Geology. United States Section. Technical Paper
Pan Am M — Pan American Magazine
Pan Am Union Bol Ciencia y Tecnologia — Pan American Union. Boletin de Ciencia y Tecnologia
Pan Am Union Bul — Pan American Union. Bulletin
PanAR — Pan American Review
PANE — Park News
Panhandle Geol Soc Strat Cross Sec — Panhandle Geological Society. Stratigraphic Cross Section
Pan Indian Ocean Sci Congr Proc Sect D Agr Sci — Pan Indian Ocean Science Congress. Proceedings. Section D. Agricultural Sciences
Panjab Univ (Chandigarh) Cent Adv Stu Geol Publ — Panjab University (Chandigarh). Centre of Advanced Study in Geology. Publication
Panminerva Med — Panminerva Medica
Panorama Democr Chr — Panorama Democrate Chretien
Panorama Econ (Chile) 2a Epoca — Panorama Economico (Chile). Segunda Epoca
Panorama Econ (Mexico) — Panorama Economico (Mexico)
Panorama M Instruments — Panorama de la Musique et des Instruments
Pan-Pac Ent — Pan-Pacific Entomologist
Pan-Pac Entomol — Pan-Pacific Entomologist
Pan-Pacif Ent — Pan-Pacific Entomologist
Pan Pipes — Pan Pipes of Sigma Alpha Iota
PANPJ — Polska Akademia Nauk. Komitet Jezykoznawstwa. Prace Jezykoznawcze
PANPKHL — Polska Akademia Nauk. Oddzial w Krakowie. Prace Komisji Historycznoliterackiej
PANPKS — Polska Akademia Nauk. Oddzial w Krakowie. Prace Komisji Slowianoznawstwa
Pan i Prawo — Panstwo i Prawo
P An Rel M — Proceedings. Annual Reliability and Maintainability Symposium
Panstw Sluzba Geol Panstw Inst Geol Biul — Panstwowa Sluzba Geologiczna. Pantswowy Instytut. Geologiczny Biuletyn
Panta J Med — Panta Journal of Medicine
PA Nurse — Pennsylvania Nurse
Panz Ann — Panzer Annales
PAORB — Problemes Actuels d'Oto-Rhino-Laryngologie
PAOS — Proceedings. American Oriental Society
PAOTA — Problemes Actuels d'Ophtalmologie
PAP — Papyrologica
PaP — Past and Present
PaP — Patterns of Prejudice
PAP — Psychobiology and Psychopathology [*Elsevier Book Series*]
PAPA — Proceedings. American Philological Association
PAPA — Publications. Arkansas Philological Association
PAPAA4 — American Psychopathological Association. Proceedings
Pap Am Chem Soc Div Paint Plast Print Ink — Papers. American Chemical Society. Division of Paint, Plastics, and Printing Ink
Pap Amer Soc Agr Eng — Paper. American Society of Agricultural Engineers
Pap Am Soc Ch Hist — Papers. American Society of Church History
Pap Annu Conv West Can Water Sewage Conf — Papers Presented at the Annual Convention. Western Canada Water and Sewage Conference
Pap Anthro — Papers in Anthropology [*Oklahoma*]

Pap Archit Sci Unit Univ Queensl — Paper. Architectural Science Unit. University of Queensland
Pap ASAE — Paper. American Society of Agricultural Engineers
Pap Avulsos Dep Zool (Sao Paulo) — Papeis Avulsos. Departmento de Zoologia (Sao Paulo)
Pap Avulsos Dep Zool Secr Agric Ind Comer (Sao Paulo) — Papeis Avulsos. Departmento de Zoologia. Secretaria de Agricultura Industria e Comercio (Sao Paulo)
Pap Avul Zool — Papeis Avulsos de Zoologia
Pap Bibliog — Papers. Bibliographical Society of America
Pap Bibliogr Soc Am — Papers. Bibliographical Society of America
Pap Bibliog Soc Am — Papers. Bibliographical Society of America
Pap Bibl Soc Am — Papers. Bibliographical Society of America
Papbrd Pkg — Paperboard Packaging
Pap Brit Sch Rome — Papers. British School at Rome
PAPC — Philological Association of the Pacific Coast
Pap Carton Cellul — Papier. Carton et Cellulose
Pap Celul — Papir a Celuloza
Pap Coal Util Symp Focus SO₂ Emiss Control — Papers. Coal Utilization Symposium. Focus on SO_2 Emission Control
Pap Commonw For Conf — Paper. Commonwealth Forestry Conference
Pap Congr Aust NZ Assoc Adv Sci — Australian and New Zealand Association for the Advancement of Science. Congress. Papers
Pap Congr Fed Int Precontrainte — Papers. Congress of the Federation Internationale de la Precontrainte
Pap Conv Am Nurs Assoc — Papers from the Convention. American Nurses' Association
Pap Converting — Paper Converting
Pap Czech Soil Sci Conf — Papers. Czechoslovak Soil Science Conference
Pap Dep Agric QD Univ — Papers. Department of Agriculture. University of Queensland
Pap Dep Geol QD Univ — Papers. Department of Geology. University of Queensland
Pap Dep Geol Queensl Univ — Papers. Department of Geology. University of Queensland
Pap Dep Geol Univ QD — Papers. Department of Geology. University of Queensland
Pap Dep Zool QD Univ — Papers. Department of Zoology. University of Queensland
Paper & Board Abs — Paper and Board Abstracts
Paperboard Packag — Paperboard Packaging
Paperboard Pkg — Paperboard Packaging
Paper Bul — Paper and Packaging Bulletin
Paper Film Foil Conv — Paper, Film, and Foil Converter
Paper Jour — Paper Trade Journal
Paper Makers Merch Dir — Paper Makers and Merchants. Directory of All Nations
Paper Mkr — Paper Maker
Paper Pulp Mill Catalogue — Paper and Pulp Mill Catalogue/Engineering Handbook
Papers Biblio Soc Am — Papers. Bibliographical Society of America
Papers in Ed (Anstey Coll) — Papers in Education (Anstey College of Physical Education)
Papers Far East Hist — Papers on Far Eastern History
Papers & Proc Roy Soc Tas — Papers and Proceedings. Royal Society of Tasmania
Papers and Proc Roy Soc Tasmania — Papers and Proceedings. Royal Society of Tasmania
Papers Proc Roy Soc Tasmania — Papers and Proceedings. Royal Society of Tasmania
Papers & Proc Tas Hist Res Assn — Papers and Proceedings. Tasmanian Historical Research Association
Paper Technol — Paper Technology
Paper Technol Ind — Paper Technology and Industry
Paper Tr J — Paper Trade Journal
Paper Twine J — Paper and Twine Journal
Paper Yrb — Paper Year Book
Papeterie Numero Spec — Papeterie. Numero Special
Pap FAO/IUFRO World Consult For Tree Breed — Paper. FAO [*Food and Agriculture Organization of the United Nations*]/IUFRO [*International Union of Forestry Research Organization*] World Consultation on Forest Tree Breeding
Pap Far Eas — Papers on Far Eastern History
Pap Far East Hist — Papers on Far Eastern History [*Australia*]
Pap Film Foil Converter — Paper, Film, and Foil Converter
Pap Geol Surv Can — Papers. Geological Survey of Canada
Pap Gifu Univ Sch Med — Papers. Gifu University. School of Medicine [*Japan*]
Pap Grt Barrier Reef Comm — Papers. Great Barrier Reef Committee
PAPhilosS — Proceedings. American Philosophical Society
PAPhS — Proceedings. American Philosophical Society
Pap IAALD World Congr — Papers. International Association of Agricultural Librarians and Documentalists. World Congress
Papier (Darmstadt) Beil — Papier (Darmstadt). Beilage
Papierfabr Wochenbl Papierfabr — Papierfabrikant - Wochenblatt fuer Papierfabrikation

Papiergesch — Papier Geschichte
Papierverarb — Papier- und Kunststoffverarbeiter
Pap Ind — Paper Industry
Pap Ind Pap World — Paper Industry and Paper World
Pap Inst Def Anal — Paper. Institute for Defense Analyses
Pap Inst Post Off Electr Eng — Printed Papers. Institution of Post Office
    Electrical Engineers
Pap Inst Therm Spring Res Okayama Univ — Papers. Institute for Thermal
    Spring Research. Okayama University
Pap Int Conf Fluid Sealing — Paper. International Conference on Fluid Sealing
Papirip Magy Grafika — Papiripar es Magyar Grafika
Pap Is Afr — Papers in International Studies. Africa Series. Ohio University
Pap Is Se A — Papers in International Studies. Southeast Asia Series. Ohio
    University
Pap J — Papir-Journalen
Pap Lab Tree-Ring Res Univ Ariz — Papers. Laboratory of Tree-Ring
    Research. University of Arizona
Pap Lanc Co Hist Soc — Historical Papers. Lancaster County Historical
    Society [Pennsylvania]
Pap Lang L — Papers on Language and Literature
Pap Lang Lit — Papers on Language and Literature
Pap Ling — Papers in Linguistics
Pap Maker (London) — Paper Maker and British Paper Trade Journal
    (London)
Pap Makers Assoc (GB Irel) Proc Tech Sect — Paper Makers' Association
    (Great Britain and Ireland). Proceedings of the Technical Section
Pap Makers Mon J — Paper Makers' Monthly Journal
Pap Maker (Wilmington Del) — Paper Maker (Wilmington, Delaware)
Pap Meteorol Geophys (Tokyo) — Papers in Meteorology and Geophysics
    (Tokyo)
Pap Met Geo — Papers in Meteorology and Geophysics
Pap Mich Acad — Papers. Michigan Academy of Science, Arts, and Letters
Pap Mich Acad Sci — Papers. Michigan Academy of Science, Arts, and Letters
Pap Mich Acad Sci Arts Lett — Papers. Michigan Academy of Science, Arts,
    and Letters
Pap Mill News — Paper Mill News
Pap Mill Wood Pulp News — Paper Mill and Wood Pulp News
Pap N Haven Col Hist Soc — Papers. New Haven Colony Historical Society
Pap Norw State Game Res Inst — Papers. Norwegian State Game Research
    Institute
Pap Nyomdatech — Papir es Nyomdatechnika
PapOxy — Oxyrhynchus Papyri
Pap Peabody Mus Archaeol Ethnol Harv Univ — Papers. Peabody Museum of
    Archaeology and Ethnology. Harvard University
Pap Phil Ling — Papers in Philippine Linguistics. Pacific Linguistics. Series A
    [Canberra]
Pap Presentations Proc Digital Equip Comput Users Soc — Papers and
    Presentations-Proceedings. Digital Equipment Computer Users Society
Pap Print Dig — Paper and Printing Digest
Pap Proc R Soc Tas — Papers and Proceedings. Royal Society of Tasmania
Pap Proc R Soc Tasm — Papers and Proceedings. Royal Society of Tasmania
Pap Proc R Soc Tasmania — Papers and Proceedings. Royal Society of
    Tasmania
Pap Proc Tas Hist Res Assoc — Tasmanian Historical Research Association.
    Papers and Proceedings
Pap ja Puu — Paperi ja Puu
Pap Puu — Paperi ja Puu - Papper och Tra
Pap Puu B Painos — Paperi ja Puu. B Painos
Pap Puu Painos — Paperi ja Puu. A Painos
Pap Roy Soc Tasm — Royal Society of Tasmania. Papers and Proceedings
Pap R Sociol — Papers. Revista de Sociologia
PAPS — Proceedings. American Philosophical Society
Pap Sci Ser — Papers in Science Series
Pap SE As Ling — Papers in South East Asian Linguistics. Pacific Linguistics.
    Series A [Canberra]
Pap SESA — Paper. SESA [Society for Experimental Stress Analysis]
Pap Ship Res Inst (Tokyo) — Papers. Ship Research Institute (Tokyo)
Pap S Shields Archaeol Hist Soc — Papers. South Shields Archaeological and
    Historical Society
P Ap St Dalho — Applied Statistics. Proceedings of Conference at Dalhousie
    University
Pap Sthn Afr — Paper Southern Africa
PA Psychiatr Q — Pennsylvania Psychiatric Quarterly
Pap Symp Coal Manage Tech — Papers Presented before the Symposium on
    Coal Management Techniques
Pap Symp Coal Mine Drainage Res — Papers Presented before the Symposium
    on Coal Mine Drainage Research
Pap Symp Coal Prep Util — Papers Presented before the Symposium on Coal
    Preparation and Utilization
Pap Symp Manage — Papers Presented before the Symposium on Management
Pap Symp Surf Min Reclam — Papers Presented before the Symposium on
    Surface Mining and Reclamation
Pap Symp Underground Min — Papers Presented before the Symposium on
    Underground Mining
Pap Synth Conf Proc — Paper Synthetics Conference. Proceedings [United
    States]

PAPTC — Practical Approach to Patents, Trademarks, and Copyrights
Pap Tech Mtg Int Union Conserv Nature — Paper. Technical Meeting.
    International Union for the Conservation of Nature and Natural
    Resources
Pap Technol — Paper Technology [England]
Pap Technol — Paper Technology and Industry
Pap Technol Ind — Paper Technology and Industry
Pap Trade J — Paper Trade Journal
Papua New Guin Agric J — Papua and New Guinea Agricultural Journal
Papua New Guinea Agric J — Papua and New Guinea Agricultural Journal
Papua New Guinea Agr J — Papua and New Guinea Agricultural Journal
Papua New Guinea Dep Agric Stock Fish Annu Rep — Papua New Guinea.
    Department of Agriculture, Stock, and Fisheries. Annual Report
Papua New Guinea Dep Agric Stock Fish Res Bull — Papua New Guinea.
    Department of Agriculture, Stock, and Fisheries. Research Bulletin
Papua New Guinea Geol Surv Mem — Papua New Guinea. Geological Survey.
    Memoir
Papua New Guinea Med J — Papua New Guinea Medical Journal
Papua & NG — Papua and New Guinea Law Reports
Pap Univ Maine Technol Exp Stn — Paper. University of Maine. Technology
    Experiment Station
Pap Univ MO-Columbia Dep Agric Econ — Paper. University of Missouri-
    Columbia. Department of Agricultural Economics
Pap US Geol Surv Wat Supply — Paper. United States Geological Survey.
    Water Supply
Pap Ztg — Papier-Zeitung
PAQ — Public Administration Quarterly
PAR — Kosmetiek
Par — Paragone
Par — Parents' Magazine and Better Family Living [Later, Parents'
    Magazine]
PAR — Performing Arts Resources
PAR — Performing Arts Review
PAR — Public Administration Review
Paramagn Rezon — Paramagnitnyj Rezonans
Para-Med — Para-Medico
Paramed Int — Paramedics International
Par Arter — Paroi Arterielle-Arterial Wall
Parasit — Parasitica
Parasite Immunol — Parasite Immunology
Parasit Hung — Parasitologia Hungarica
Parasitol — Parasitology
Parasitol Hung — Parasitologia Hungarica
Parasitol Schriftenr — Parasitologische Schriftenreihe
Parasit Res — Parasitology Research
Parazitol Sb — Parazitologicheskii Sbornik
Parazity Zhivotn Rast — Parazity Zhivotnykh i Rastenii
Parbhani Agric Coll Mag — Parbhani Agricultural College. Magazine
PAREA — Pharmacological Reviews
Parent Aust — Parent Australia
Parent & Cit — Parent and Citizen
Parents — Parents' Magazine
Parents' Mag — Parents' Magazine and Better Family Living [Later, Parents'
    Magazine]
Parfuem Kosmet — Parfuemerie und Kosmetik [West Germany]
Parfum Cosmet Savons — Parfums, Cosmetiques, Savons
Parfum Mod — Parfumerie Moderne
Parfums Cos — Parfums, Cosmetiques, Aromes
Parfums Cosmet Savons — Parfums, Cosmetiques, Savons
Parfums Cosmet Savons Fr — Parfums, Cosmetiques, Savons de France
Parfums Fr — Parfums de France
Paris Med — Paris Medical
ParisR — Paris Review
Paris Rev — Paris Review
Paris Univ Lab Micropaleontol Trav — Paris. Universite. Laboratoire de
    Micropaleontologie. Travaux
Paris Univ Lab Paleontol Trav — Paris. Universite. Laboratoire de
    Paleontologie. Travaux
PARK — Parks. International Journal for Managers of National Parks,
    Historic Sites, and Other Protected Areas
Park Adm — Park Administration
Parks and R — Parks and Recreation
Parks & Rec — Parks and Recreation
Parks & Wild — Parks and Wildlife
Parks Wildl — Parks and Wildlife
Parl Aff — Parliamentary Affairs
Parlam Beil Polit Zeitgesch — Parlament Beilage aus Politik und
    Zeitgeschichte
Parl Deb — Parliamentary Debates
PAR Legis Bul — PAR [Public Affairs Research] Legislative Bulletin
Parliam Af: — Parliamentary Affairs
Parliamentary Aff — Parliamentary Affairs
Parliam Liaison Group Altern Energy Strategies Bull — Parliamentary Liaison
    Group for Alternative Energy Strategies. Bulletin
Parlim Aff — Parliamentary Affairs
Par M — Parents' Magazine

Par Nucl — Particles and Nuclei
Parodontal Acad Rev — Parodontologie and Academy Review
Parola Passato — Parola del Passato. Rivista di Studi Antichi [*Naples*]
Parole et Soc — Parole et Societe
Par Pass — Parola del Passato
PAR Pseudo-Allerg React — PAR. Pseudo-Allergic Reactions
Parques Jard — Parques y Jardines
ParR — Paris Review
ParR — Partisan Review
Parsons J — Parsons Journal
Part Accel — Particle Accelerators
Part Charact — Particle Characterization
Particleboard/Compos Mater Ser — Particleboard/Composite Materials Series
Partisan R — Partisan Review
Partisan Rev — Partisan Review
Part and Nucl — Particles and Nuclei
Part Nucl — Particles and Nuclei
Part R — Partisan Review
Party — Party Newspapers
PARWAC — Archivum Veterinarium Polonicum
PaS — Pamietnik Slowianski
PAS — Papers. American School of Classical Studies [*Athens*]
PASC — Parkscan. Parks Canada
PA Sch J — Pennsylvania School Journal
PASED — Proceedings. Annual Symposium. Society of Flight Test Engineers
PASJD — Passive Solar Journal
Pa Slow — Pamietnik Slowianski
PASMB — Proceedings. Australian Society of Medical Research
Pas Mus — Pastoral Music
Passenger Transp — Passenger Transport
Passeng Transp J — Passenger Transport Journal [*England*]
PA State Coll Miner Ind Exp Stn Bull — Pennsylvania State College. Mineral Industries Experiment Station. Bulletin
PA State Coll Miner Ind Exp Stn Circ — Pennsylvania State College. Mineral Industries Experiment Station. Circular
PA State Coll Stud — Pennsylvania State College. Studies
PA State Univ Coll Agric Agric Exp Stn Prog Rep — Pennsylvania State University. College of Agriculture. Agricultural Experiment Station. Progress Report
PA State Univ Coll Agric Ext Serv Spec Circ — Pennsylvania State University. College of Agriculture. Agricultural Extension Service. Special Circular
PA State Univ Coll Earth Miner Sci Exp Stn Circ — Pennsylvania State University. College of Earth and Mineral Sciences. Experiment Station. Circular
PA State Univ Coll Earth Miner Sci Spec Publ — Pennsylvania State University. College of Earth and Mineral Sciences. Special Publication
PA State Univ Coll Eng Eng Proc — Pennsylvania State University. College of Engineering. Engineering Proceedings
PA State Univ Coll Eng Eng Res Bull — Pennsylvania State University. College of Engineering. Engineering Research Bulletin
PA State Univ Earth Miner Sci Exp Stn Circ — Pennsylvania State University. Earth and Mineral Sciences Experiment Station. Circular
PA State Univ Miner Ind Exp Stn Bull — Pennsylvania State University. Mineral Industries Experiment Station. Bulletin
PA State Univ Miner Ind Exp Stn Circ — Pennsylvania State University. Mineral Industries Experiment Station. Circular
PA State Univ Sch For Resour Res Briefs — Pennsylvania State University. School of Forest Resources. Research Briefs
PA State Univ Stud — Pennsylvania State University. Studies
PastBl — Pastoralblaetter [*Stuttgart*]
Past Care & Couns Abstr — Pastoral Care and Counseling Abstracts
PA St Coll An Rp — Pennsylvania State College. Annual Report
Pasteur Inst South India (Coonoor) Annu Rep Dir Sci Rep — Pasteur Institute of Southern India (Coonoor). Annual Report of the Director and Scientific Report
Past Mus — Pastoral Music
Pastoralist — Pastoralist and Grazier
Pastoral Rev — Pastoral Review
Pastoral Rev Graz Rec — Pastoral Review and Graziers' Record
Past & Pres — Past and Present
Past Pres — Past and Present. Studies in the History of Civilization
Past Presen — Past and Present
Past Psych — Pastoral Psychology
Past R — Pastoral Review and Graziers' Record
Past Rev — Pastoral Review and Graziers' Record
PASYD — Policy Analysis and Information Systems
PAT — Paper Trade Journal
PAT — Public Administration and Development
Patentbl — Patentblatt
Patentbl Ausg A — Patentblatt. Ausgabe A
Patentbl Ausg B — Patentblatt. Ausgabe B
Patenti Insluitende Handels-Merke Modelle — Patentioernaal Insluitende Handels-Merke en Modelle
Patentjoernaal (S Afr) — Patentjoernaal (South Africa)
Patent Off Soc Jour — Patent Office Society. Journal
Path Biol — Pathologie et Biologie [*Paris*]

Path Europ — Pathologia Europaea
Path Microb — Pathologia et Microbiologia
Pathobiol Annu — Pathobiology Annual
Pathol — Pathology
Pathol Annu — Pathology Annual
Pathol Biol — Pathologie et Biologie [*Paris*]
Pathol Biol (Paris) — Pathologie et Biologie (Paris)
Pathol Clin Med (Tokyo) — Pathology and Clinical Medicine (Tokyo)
Pathol Eur — Pathologia Europaea
Pathol Eur Suppl — Pathologia Europaea. Supplement
Pathol Gen — Pathologie Generale
Pathol Microbiol — Pathologia et Microbiologia
Pathol Microbiol Suppl — Pathologia et Microbiologia. Supplementum [*Switzerland*]
Pathol Res Pract — Pathology. Research and Practice
Pathol Vet — Pathologia Veterinaria
Path Res Pract — Pathology. Research and Practice
Patient Couns Health Educ — Patient Counselling and Health Education
Patient Educ Couns — Patient Education and Counseling
Pat J Incl Trade Marks Des — Patent Journal, Including Trade Marks and Designs
Pat J Incl Trade Marks Des Copyright Cinematogr Films — Patent Journal, Including Trade Marks, Designs, and Copyright in Cinematograph Films
Pat L Ann — Patent Law Annual
Patma-Banasirakan Handes Ist-Filol Zh — Patma-Banasirakan Handes. Istoriko-Filologicheskii Zhurnal
Patna J Med — Patna Journal of Medicine
Pat Off Gaz — Official Gazette. United States Patent Office
Pat Off Soc J — Patent Office Society. Journal
Patog Ter Dermatozov — Patogenez i Terapiya Dermatozov
Patol Clin Ostet Ginecol — Patologia e Clinica Ostetrica e Ginecologica
Patol Fiziol Eksp Ter — Patologicheskaya Fiziologiya i Eksperimental'naya Terapiya
Patol-Mex — Patologia-Mexico City
Patol Pol — Patologia Polska
Patol Sper — Patologia Sperimentale
PA Top G S Com — Pennsylvania Topographic and Geologic Survey Commission
PA Topogr Geol Surv Bull A — Pennsylvania Topographic and Geologic Survey. Bulletin A. Atlas Series
PA Topogr Geol Surv Bull C — Pennsylvania. Bureau of Topographic and Geologic Survey. Bulletin C [*County Report*]
PA Topogr Geol Surv Bull G — Pennsylvania. Bureau of Topographic and Geologic Survey. Bulletin G [*General Geology Report*]
PA Topogr Geol Surv Bull M — Pennsylvania Topographic and Geologic Survey. Bulletin M
PA Topogr Geol Surv Bull W — Pennsylvania Topographic and Geologic Survey. Bulletin W
PA Topogr Geol Surv Geol Atlas PA — Pennsylvania. Bureau of Topographic and Geologic Survey. Geologic Atlas of Pennsylvania
PA Topogr Geol Surv Inform Circ — Pennsylvania. Bureau of Topographic and Geologic Survey. Information Circular
PA Topogr Geol Surv Miner Resour Rep — Pennsylvania Topographic and Geologic Survey. Mineral Resources Report
PA Topogr Geol Surv Progr Rep — Pennsylvania. Bureau of Topographic and Geologic Survey. Progress Report
PA Topogr Geol Surv Spec Bull — Pennsylvania. Bureau of Topographic and Geologic Survey. Special Bulletin
Pa Trade J — Paper Trade Journal
PATREU — Palaestina Treuhandstelle zur Beratung Deutscher Juden
Pa Tr J — Paper Trade Journal
Patronato Biol Anim Rev — Patronato de Biologia Animal. Revista
Patronato Invest Cient Tec "Juan De La Cierva" Mem — Patronato de Investigacion Cientifica y Tecnica "Juan De La Cierva." Memoria
Patronato Invest Cient Tec "Juan De La Cierva" Publ Tec — Patronato de Investigacion Cientifica y Tecnica "Juan De La Cierva." Publicaciones Tecnicas
Pattern Recognition — Journal. Pattern Recognition Society
Pattern Recognition Lett — Pattern Recognition Letters
Pat TM & Copy J — Patent, Trademark, and Copyright Journal
Pat and TM Rev — Patent and Trade Mark Review
Patt Recog — Pattern Recognition
Pat & Tr Mk Rev — Patent and Trade Mark Review
PATUA — Proceedings. Research Institute of Atmospherics. Nagoya University
PAU — Polska Akademia Umiejetnosci
PAU-AN — Polska Akademia Umiejetnosci. Archivum Neophilologicum
PAUCA — Proceedings. Royal Australian Chemical Institute
PA Univ Lab Contr — Pennsylvania University. Laboratory Contributions
PA Univ Mus Bul — Pennsylvania University. University Museum. Bulletin
PA Univ Schoolmen's Week Proc — Pennsylvania University. Schoolmen's Week. Proceedings
PAus — Poetry Australia
PAusL — Papers in Australian Linguistics
P Aust Bioc — Proceedings. Australian Biochemical Society

PAV — Packaging Review
Pavia Univ Ist Geol Atti — Pavia Universita. Istituto Geologico. Atti
Pav J Biol — Pavlovian Journal of Biological Science
Pavlovian J Biol Sci — Pavlovian Journal of Biological Science
Pavlov J Biol Sci — Pavlovian Journal of Biological Science
Pavlov J Higher Nerv Act — Pavlov Journal of Higher Nervous Activity
PAZ — Paper and Packaging Bulletin
PB — Paedagogische Blaetter
PB — Pantheon Babylonicum: Nomina Deorum
PB — Pastor Bonus
Pb — Playboy
PB — Poetry Bag
PB — Prabuddha Bharata [Calcutta]
P and B — Pragmatics and Beyond
PB — Przeglad Biblioteczny
PB — Push from the Bush
PBA — Proceedings. British Academy
PBA — Schoenvisie. Maandblad voor de Schoenhandel en Schoenindustrie
PBANB — Pathobiology Annual
PBASA — Proceedings. Bihar Academy of Agricultural Sciences
P Bat Conf — Proceedings. Battle Conference on Anglo-Norman Studies
PBBCD — Promoclim B. Bulletin du Genie Climatique
PBBHA — Pharmacology, Biochemistry, and Behavior
Pbd Abstr — Paper and Board Abstracts
Pbd Pkg — Paperboard Packaging
PBE — Problemes Economiques. Selection de Textes Francais et Etrangers
PBEA Newsletter — Pennsylvania Business Education Association. Newsletter
PBELB — Promyshlennost Belorussii
PBF — Public Budgeting and Finance
PBFPA — Protides of the Biological Fluids. Proceedings of the Colloquium
PBH — Patma-Banasirakan Handes. Istoriko-Filologicheskii Zhurnal
PBIBA — Pochvy Bashkirii i Puti Ratsional'nogo Ikh Ispol'zovaniya
PBJOD — Plant Biochemical Journal
PBK — Pamietnik Biblioteki Kornickiej
PBL — Papers in Borneo Linguistics
PBLSA — Publius
PBM — Poetry Book Magazine
PBMAA — Publications. Research Institute for Mathematical Sciences. Series A [Japan]
PBMEA — Perspectives in Biology and Medicine
PBML — Prague Bulletin of Mathematical Linguistics
PBO — Polski Biuletyn Orientalistyczny
PBP — Paperbound Books in Print
PBP — Pinkas Bractwa Pogrzebowego
P and BR — Patristic and Byzantine Review
PBR — Progress in Brain Research [Elsevier Book Series]
PBRA — Polska Bibliografja Biblijna Adnotowana
PBRCA — Proceedings. British Ceramic Society
PBS — Publications. Babylonian Section. University Museum. University of Pennsylvania [Philadelphia]
PBSA — Papers. Bibliographical Society of America
PBSA — Publications. Bibliographical Society of America
PBSC — Papers. Bibliographical Society of Canada
PBSED — Proceedings. Bioenergy R and D Seminar
PBSR — Papers. British School at Rome
PBSUV — Papers. Bibliographical Society. University of Virginia
PBSWA — Proceedings. Biological Society of Washington
PC — Paraula Cristiana
PC — Peake's Commentary on the Bible
PC — Pensiero Critico
PC — People's China
PC — Presence Chretienne
PC — Problems of Communism
PCA — Proceedings. Classical Association
PCAABC — Centre for Agricultural Publications and Documentation [Wageningen]. Annual Report
PCAAS — Proceedings. Connecticut Academy of Arts and Sciences
P Camb Ph S — Proceedings. Cambridge Philological Society
PCAS — Proceedings. Cambridge Antiquarian Society
PCAS — Proceedings. Classical Association of Scotland
PCB — Poetry Chapbook
PCB — Pollution. Environmental News Bulletin
PCBPB — Pesticide Biochemistry and Physiology
PCBR — Progress in Clinical and Biological Research [Elsevier Book Series]
PCBRD — Progress in Clinical and Biological Research
PCCCD — Proceedings. Annual Allerton Conference on Communication, Control, and Computing
PCCOA — Professional Contributions. Colorado School of Mines
PCCSD — Proceedings. International Conference on Cybernetics and Society
PCEA Bol Trimest Exp Agropecu — PCEA [Programa Cooperativo de Experimentacion Agropecuaria] Boletin Trimestral de Experimentacion Agropecuaria
PCG — Package Engineering
PCGLA — Physics and Chemistry of Glasses
PCHEA — Petro/Chem Engineer
Pchela Sof — Pchela Sofiya

Pchel Mir — Pchelovodnyi Mir
Pchel Zhizn — Pchelovodnaya Zhizn'
PCH PhysicoChem Hydrodyn — PCH: PhysicoChemical Hydrodynamics [Later, Physicochemical Hydrodynamics] [England]
PCI — Pacific Viewpoint
PCIYA — Progress in Clinical Immunology
PCJ — Bangladesh Development Studies
Pckgng Eng — Packaging Engineering
Pckgng Rev — Packaging Review
PCL — Perspectives on Contemporary Literature
PCLAC — Proceedings. California Linguistics Association Conference
PCLQA — Physics and Chemistry of Liquids
PCLS — Proceedings. Comparative Literature Symposium
P Cmp Sc St — Proceedings. Computer Science and Statistics
PCN — Players Chess News
PCN — [The] Print Collector's Newsletter
PCNDP — Publication. Centre National de Documentation Pedagogique
PCO — Proceedings. Congress of Orientalists
PCOAD — Powder Coatings
PCOG — Press Clippings of Greenland
PCOMB — Physics of Condensed Matter
P Comp Lit — Proceedings. Comparative Literature Symposium
PCONA — Pest Control
PCP — Pacific Coast Philology
PCPHA — Plant and Cell Physiology
PCPhS — Proceedings. Cambridge Philological Society
PCPMDN — Annual Research Reviews. Proteins of Animal Cell Plasma Membranes
PCPP — Plasma Chemistry and Plasma Processing
PCPPD — Plasma Chemistry and Plasma Processing
PCPSA — Proceedings. Cambridge Philosophical Society [England]
PCPSD — Progress in Colloid and Polymer Science
PCPT — Perception. Canadian Magazine of Social Comment
PCRB — Parks Canada. Research Bulletin
PCRSAE — Colston Research Society. Proceedings of the Symposium
PCRSB — Proceedings. Canadian Rock Mechanics Symposium
PCSIB — Protection Civile et Securite Industrielle
PCSNA — Processing [England]
PCTCA — Protection [London]
PCTEB — Pennsylvania Council of Teachers of English. Bulletin
PCTE Bulletin — Pennsylvania Council of Teachers of English. Bulletin
PCTNB — Perception
PCVDA — Progress in Cardiovascular Diseases
PD — Paix et Droit [Paris]
PD — Papier und Druck
PD — Parliamentary Debates
PD — Pennsylvania Dutchman
PD — Poetic Drama
PD — Presidential Documents
PDA — Planning and Development in the Netherlands (Assen)
PDAGA — Pediatriia, Akusherstvo, i Ginekologiia
PDANB — Pediatric Annals
PDB — Pakistan Development Review
PDBIA — Periodicum Biologorum
PdD — Probleme der Dichtung
PDE — Preliminary Determination of Epicenters [National Oceanic and Atmospheric Administration]
PDENA — Production Engineer [London]
PDF — Packaging Technology
PDHMUA — Publication. Department of History. Muslim University (Aligarh)
PCJ
PDI — Planned Innovation
PDial — Poetry Dial
PDIS — Proceedings. National Symposia
PdL — Provincia di Lucca
PDM — Physicians Drug Manual
PDM — Poetry and Drama Magazine
PDMLA — PDM. Physicians' Drug Manual
PDNPD — Physica D. Nonlinear Phenomena
PdP — Parola del Popolo
PDPRA — Plastics Design and Processing
PDR — Pakistan Development Review
PDR — Peter De Ridder Press Publications
PDR — Plant Disease Reporter
PDRI — Publications. Diaspora Research Institute
PDT — Proceedings. European Society of Drug Toxicity [Elsevier Book Series]
PDZI — Przeglad Zachodni
PDZRA — Prace Dzialu Zywenia Roslin i Nawozenia
PE — Packaging Engineering
PE — Pennsylvania English
PE — Percussionist
PE — Personnel Executive
PE — Philippine Educator
PE — Poesia Espanola
PE — Politique Etrangere

PE — Problems of Economics
PEABA — Petroleum Abstracts
Peabody J E — Peabody Journal of Education
Peabody J Ed — Peabody Journal of Education
Peabody J Educ — Peabody Journal of Education
Peabody Mus Nat Hist Yale Univ Bull — Peabody Museum of Natural History. Yale University. Bulletin
PEACA — Progress in Nuclear Energy. Series 9
Peace — Peace Newsletter
Peace — Peace/Non-Violence
Peacemak — Peacemaker
Peace Nws — Peace News
PeaceResAb — Peace Research Abstracts
Peace Res Ja — Peace Research in Japan
Peace Res Rev — Peace Research Reviews
Peace and Sci — Peace and the Sciences
Peace Science Soc Internat Pas — Peace Science Society. International Papers
PEAL — Publishing, Entertainment, Advertising, and Allied Fields Law Quarterly
PEALQ — Publishing, Entertainment, Advertising, and Allied Fields Law Quarterly
PEANA — Proceedings. Easter School in Agricultural Science. University of Nottingham
Peanut J Nut World — Peanut Journal and Nut World
Peanut Sci — Peanut Science
Pearce-Sellards Ser Tex Mem Mus — Pearce-Sellards Series. Texas Memorial Museum
Peasant Stud Newsl — Peasant Studies Newsletter
Peat Plant Yearb — Peat and Plant Yearbook
Peb — Pebble
PEB — Philippine Economy Bulletin
PeC — Poesia e Critica
PEC — Polish Economic News
Pecan Q — Pecan Quarterly
PECHA — Petroleum Chemistry USSR [*English Translation*]
Peche Marit — Peche Maritime
PECO — Peace Country [*Grande Prairie, Alberta*]
PECS — Princeton Encyclopedia of Classical Sites
Pecsi Muesz Sz — Pecsi Mueszaki Szemle [*Hungary*]
Ped — Pedagogia
Pedagog Fak Plzni Sb Ser Chem — Pedagogicka Fakulta v Plzni. Sbornik. Serie Chemie
Pedagog Sem — Pedagogical Seminary
Pedag i Psihol — Pedagogika i Psihologija
Pedag Szle — Pedagogiai Szemle
Pedag Tidskr — Pedagogisk Tidskrift
Ped Clin NA — Pediatric Clinics of North America
Pedia — Pediatrics
Pediat Akush Ginek — Pediatriya, Akusherstvo, i Ginekologiya
Pediat Clins N Am — Pediatric Clinics of North America
Pediat Nurs — Pediatric Nursing
Pediatr Adolesc Endocrinol — Pediatric and Adolescent Endocrinology
Pediatr Akush Ginekol — Pediatriia, Akusherstvo, i Ginekologiia
Pediatr Ann — Pediatric Annals
Pediatr Cardiol — Pediatric Cardiology
Pediatr Clin N Am — Pediatric Clinics of North America
Pediatr Clin North Am — Pediatric Clinics of North America
Pediatr Dent — Pediatric Dentistry
Pediat Res — Pediatric Research
Pediatr Esp — Pediatria Espanola
Pediatria Arch — Pediatria. Archivio di Patologia e Clinica Pediatrica
Pediatrics Suppl — Pediatrics Supplement
Pediatr Int — Pediatria Internazionale
Pediatr Listy — Pediatricke Listy
Pediatr Med Chir — Pediatria Medica e Chirurgica
Pediatr Mod — Pediatria Moderna
Pediatr Nephrol — Pediatric Nephrology
Pediatr News — Pediatric News
Pediatr Nurs — Pediatric Nursing
Pediatr Nurse Pract — Pediatric Nurse Practitioner
Pediatr Pharmacol — Pediatric Pharmacology
Pediatr Pol — Pediatria Polska
Pediatr Prat — Pediatria Pratica
Pediatr Radiol — Pediatric Radiology
Pediatr Res — Pediatric Research
P Edin Math — Proceedings. Edinburgh Mathematical Society
Pedobiolog — Pedobiologia
Pedod Fr — Pedodontie Francaise
Pedology (Leningr) — Pedology (Leningrad)
Ped Sem — Pedagogical Seminary
P Educator — Physical Educator
PEEAD — Promoclim E
PEECD — Petroleum Economist
PEEID — Petroleum Engineer International
Peel Valley Hist Soc J — Peel Valley Historical Society. Journal
PEFA — Palestine Exploration Fund. Annual

PEFQ — Palestine Exploration Fund. Quarterly Statement
Peg — Pegaso
PEGEA — Petroleum Geology [*English Translation*]
Pegmatitovye Redkomet Mestorozhd — Pegmatitovye Redkometal'nye Mestorozhdeniya
PEGR — Press Extracts on Greenland
PEGS — Publications. English Goethe Society
PEGTA — Problemy Endokrinologii i Gormonoterapii
PEHPA — Progress in Nuclear Energy. Series 12
PEHYA — Petroleum and Hydrocarbons
PeI — Parole e le Idee
Peine Salzgitter Ber — Peine und Salzgitter Berichte
Peint Pigm Vernis — Peintures, Pigments, Vernis
PEJ — Pakistan Economic Journal
PEJ — Personnel Journal
PEJOA — Personnel Journal
Peking R — Peking Review
PEL — Penguin English Library
PELAA — Progress in Nuclear Energy. Series 10
PELL — Publications in English Language and Literature
PeM — Parole e Metodi
PEMJ — Pemmican Journal
PEMJA — Pesticides Monitoring Journal
PEM Process Eng Mag — PEM Process Engineering Magazine
Pen — Pensamiento [*Madrid*]
PEN — Petroleum News. Asia's Energy Journal
PENDA — Polish Endocrinology
Penelitian Indones — Penelitian Laut di Indonesia
Penelitian Laut Indones (Mar Res Indones) — Penelitian Laut in Indonesia (Marine Research in Indonesia)
Pengum Lemb Penelit Kehutanan — Pengumuman. Lembaga Penelitian Kehutanan
Penjelidikan Indones — Penjelidikan Laut di Indonesia
Penn Ba Q — Pennsylvania Bar Association. Quarterly
Penn Beekpr — Pennsylvania Beekeeper
Penn Dent J — Penn Dental Journal
Penn Geol Surv Atlas — Pennsylvania. Geological Survey. Atlas
Penn Geol Surv Bull — Pennsylvania. Geological Survey. Bulletin
Penn Geol Surv Gen Geol Rep — Pennsylvania. Geological Survey. General Geology Report
Penn Geol Surv Ground Water Rep — Pennsylvania. Geological Survey. Ground Water Report
Penn Geol Surv Inform Circ — Pennsylvania. Geological Survey. Information Circular
Penn Geol Surv Progr Rep — Pennsylvania. Geological Survey. Progress Report
Penn German Soc Proc — Pennsylvania German Society. Proceedings
Penn Hist — Pennsylvania History
Penn Lib Assn Bull — Pennsylvania Library Association. Bulletin
Penn Mag H — Pennsylvania Magazine of History and Biography
Penn Mag Hist Biog — Pennsylvania Magazine of History and Biography
Penn Mo — Penn Monthly
Penn Nurse — Pennsylvania Nurse
PennsF — Pennsylvania Folklife
Penn State F — Penn State Farmer
Penn State Univ Exp Sta Bull — Pennsylvania State University. Experiment Station. Bulletin
Penn State Univ Exp Sta Circ — Pennsylvania State University. Experiment Station. Circular
Penn St M Q — Penn State Mining Quarterly
Penn Stock & F — Pennsylvania Stockman and Farmer
Pennsyl M — Pennsylvania Magazine of History and Biography
Pennsylvania Acad Sci Newsletter — Pennsylvania Academy of Science. Newsletter
Pennsylvania Acad Sci Proc — Pennsylvania Academy of Science. Proceedings
Pennsylvania Bus Survey — Pennsylvania Business Survey
Pennsylvania Geol Survey Bull — Pennsylvania. Geological Survey. Bulletin
Pennsylvania Geol Survey Inf Circ — Pennsylvania. Geological Survey. Information Circular
Pennsylvania Geol Survey Prog Rept — Pennsylvania. Geological Survey. Progress Report
Penn Univ Mus Bul — Pennsylvania University. University Museum. Bulletin
Penny M — Penny Magazine
Penny Mech Chem — Penny Mechanic and the Chemist
PENRB — Professional Engineer [*Washington, DC*]
Penrose Ann — Penrose Annual
Pensamiento Polit — Pensamiento Politico
Pensee Nat — Pensee Nationale
Pensez Plast — Pensez Plastiques
Pensiero Med — Pensiero Medico
Pensiero Polit — Pensiero Politico
Pension FA — Pension Fund Sponsors Ranked by Assets
Pensions — Pensions and Investments [*Later, Pension & Investment Age*]
Pension Wld — Pension World
P Ent S Ont — Proceedings. Entomological Society of Ontario
P Ent S Was — Proceedings. Entomological Society of Washington
Pen Wld — Pension World

Penz Ped Inst Ucen Zap — Penzenskii Pedagogiceskii Institut Imeni V. G. Belinskogo. Ucenye Zapiski

Penz Politehn Inst Ucen Zap Mat Meh — Penzenskii Politehniceskii Institut. Matematika i Mehanika. Ucenye Zapiski

Penzuegyi Szemle — Penzuegyi Szemle

Penzugyi Szle — Penzuegyi Szemle

PEOED — Proceedings. European Offshore Petroleum Conference and Exhibition

Peop J — People's Journal

People — People Weekly

People and Plann — People and Planning

Peopl Tax — People and Taxes

Peoria Med Month — Peoria Medical Monthly

PEOUD — Petroleum Outlook

Peo World — People's World

PEPIA — Physics of the Earth and Planetary Interiors

Pepinier Hortic Maraichers — Pepinieristes, Horticulteurs, Maraichers [*France*]

Pepperdine LR — Pepperdine Law Review

Pepperdine L Rev — Pepperdine Law Review

Pepp LR — Pepperdine Law Review

PEPSB — Perception and Psychophysics

PEQ — Palestine Exploration Quarterly

PER — Personnel

Per — Perspective

Per — Perspectives

Per AJ — Performing Arts Journal

Per A R — Performing Arts Review

Per Biol — Periodicum Biologorum

Percept Cognit Devel — Perceptual Cognitive Development

Percept & Motor Skills — Perceptual and Motor Skills

Percept and Mot Sk — Perceptual and Motor Skills

Percept Mot Skills — Perceptual and Motor Skills

Percept Psychophys — Perception and Psychophysics

Perc Mot Sk — Perceptual and Motor Skills

Perc Notes — Percussive Notes

Perc Psych — Perception and Psychophysics

Peredovoi Opyt Stroit Ekspl Shakht — Peredovoi Opyt v Stroitel'stve i Ekspluatatsii Shakht

Peredovoi Opyt Stroit Eksp Shakht — Peredovoi Opyt v Stroitel'stve i Ekspluatatsii Shakht [*USSR*]

Pererab Gaza Gazov Kondens Nauchno-Tekh Obz — Pererabotka Gaza i Gazovogo Kondensata. Nauchno-Tekhnicheskii Obzor

Pererab Tverd Topl — Pererabotka Tverdogo Topliva [*USSR*]

PE Rev — Physical Education Review

Perf Art C — Performing Arts in Canada

Perf Art J — Performing Arts Journal

Perf Art R — Performing Arts Review

Perf Arts — Performing Arts in Canada

Perf Arts Can — Performing Arts in Canada

Perf Arts R — Performing Arts Review

Perf Eval — Performance Evaluation

Perf Eval Rev — Performance Evaluation Review

Performance Eval — Performance Evaluation

Performance Eval Rev — Performance Evaluation Review

Performing Arts Rev — Performing Arts Review

Perf Right — Performing Right

Perfumer — Perfumer and Flavorist

Perfum Essent Oil Rec — Perfumery and Essential Oil Record

Perfum Flavorist — Perfumer and Flavorist

Perfum Flavour — Perfumery and Flavouring [*Japan*]

Perfum J — Perfumers' Journal

Perfum Kosmet — Perfumerie und Kosmetik

Pergamon Ser Environ Sci — Pergamon Series on Environmental Science

Pergamon Ser Monogr Lab Tech — Pergamon Series of Monographs in Laboratory Techniques

Pergamon Texts Inorg Chem — Pergamon Texts in Inorganic Chemistry

Perg I S Da — Pergamon International Series on Dance and Related Disciplines

Perinat Med — Perinatal Medicine

Perinat Neonat — Perinatology/Neonatology

Period Anim Prod — Periodical on Animal Production

Period Biol — Periodicum Biologorum

Period Bull Int Sugar Confect Manuf Assoc Int Off Cocoa Choc — Periodic Bulletin. International Sugar Confectionery Manufacturers' Association and International Office of Cocoa and Chocolate

Period Mat — Periodico di Matematiche

Period Mat 5 — Periodico di Matematiche. Serie V

Period Math Hung — Periodica Mathematica Hungarica

Period Math Hungar — Periodica Mathematica Hungarica

Period Mineral — Periodico di Mineralogia [*Italy*]

Periodont Abstr — Periodontal Abstracts. Journal of the Western Society of Periodontology

Period Polytech — Periodica Polytechnica

Period Polytech Chem Eng — Periodica Polytechnica. Chemical Engineering

Period Polytech Civ Eng — Periodica Polytechnica. Civil Engineering [*Hungary*]

Period Polytech Civ Engng — Periodica Polytechnica. Civil Engineering

Period Polytech Electr Eng — Periodica Polytechnica. Electrical Engineering

Period Polytech Eng — Periodica Polytechnica. Engineering

Period Polytech Mech Eng — Periodica Polytechnica. Mechanical Engineering [*Hungary*]

Period Polytech Mech Engng — Periodica Polytechnica. Mechanical Engineering

Period Polytech Trans Engng — Periodica Polytechnica. Transportation Engineering

Period Speaking — Periodically Speaking

Perk — Perkins Journal

Perkin-Elmer Tech News — Perkin-Elmer Technical News

Perkins J — Perkins School of Theology. Journal

Perkins Obs Contrib Ser 2 — Perkins Observatory. Contributions. Series 2

PerManAb — Personal Management Abstracts

Permbledhje Stud — Permbledhje Studimesh

Permbledhje Stud Inst Kerkimeve Gjeol Miner — Permbledhje Studimesh. Instituti i Kerkimeve Gjeologijke dhe Minerale

Permbledhje Stud Inst Stud Kerkimeve Ind Miner — Permbledhje Studimesh. Instituti i Studimeve dhe Kerkimeve Industirale e Minerale

Perm Found Med Bull — Permanente Foundation Medical Bulletin

Perm Gos Ped Inst Ucen Zap — Permskii Gosudarstvennyi Pedagogiceskii Institut. Ucenye Zapiski

Perm Gos Univ Ucen Zap — Permskii Gosudarstvennyi Universitet Imeni A. M. Gor'kogo. Ucenye Zapiski

Perm Politehn Inst Sb Naucn Trudov — Permskii Politehniceskii Institut. Sbornik Naucnyh Trudov

Perm Way — Permanent Way

Per Poly CE — Periodica Polytechnica. Chemical Engineering

Per Poly EE — Periodica Polytechnica. Electrical Engineering

Per Poly ME — Periodica Polytechnica. Mechanical Engineering

Per Pract B — Personnel Practice Bulletin

Per Psy — Personnel Psychology

Per Rel St — Perspectives in Religious Studies

Pers — Personalist

Pers — Personnel

Pers — Perspektiv

Pers Adm — Personnel Administration

Pers Adm — Personnel Administrator

Pers Am Hist — Perspectives in American History

Pers Comput World — Personal Computer World

Pers Finance LQ — Personal Finance Law Quarterly Report

Pers Finance LQ Rep — Personal Finance Law Quarterly Report

Pers Guid J — Personnel and Guidance Journal

Pers Inj Ann — Personal Injury Annual

Pers Inj Deskbook — Personal Injury Deskbook

Pers J — Personnel Journal

Pers Manage — Personnel Management

Pers Manage Abstr — Personnel Management Abstracts

Pers Mgt — Personnel Management

Pers New Mus — Perspectives of New Music

Person — Personalist

Personal & Soc Psychol Bull — Personality and Social Psychology Bulletin

Personnel Exec — Personnel Executive

Personnel Guidance J — Personnel and Guidance Journal

Personnel & Guid J — Personnel and Guidance Journal

Personnel J — Personnel Journal

Personnel Manag (London) — Personnel Management (London)

Personnel Mgmt — Personnel Management

Personnel Mgt Abstracts — Personnel Management Abstracts

Personnel Practice B — Personnel Practice Bulletin

Personnel Practice Bul — Personnel Practice Bulletin

Personnel Psych — Personnel Psychology

Personnel Psychol — Personnel Psychology

Personn Pract Bull — Personnel Practice Bulletin

Persp Biol — Perspectives in Biology and Medicine

Perspec — Perspective

Perspec Biol & Med — Perspectives in Biology and Medicine

Perspec Ed — Perspectives on Education

Perspect Accredit — Perspectives on Accreditation

Perspect Am Hist — Perspectives in American History

Perspect Biol Med — Perspectives in Biology and Medicine

Perspect Brain Sci — Perspectives in the Brain Sciences

Perspect Cardiovasc Res — Perspectives in Cardiovascular Research

Perspect Comput — Perspectives in Computing

Perspect in Educ — Perspectives in Education

Perspect Hum Reprod — Perspectives in Human Reproduction

Perspect Ind Psychol — Perspectives in Industrial Psychology

Perspect Int — Perspectives Internationales

Perspective K — Perspective (Karachi)

Perspectives Civ Rights Q — Perspectives. The Civil Rights Quarterly

Perspectives Euro-Afr — Perspectives Euro-Africaines

Perspectives Latino-Am — Perspectives Latino-Americaines

Perspectives New M — Perspectives of New Music

Perspect Med — Perspectives in Medicine
Perspect Medicaid Medicare Manage — Perspectives on Medicaid and Medicare Management
Perspect Nephrol Hypertens — Perspectives in Nephrology and Hypertension
Perspect Pediatr Pathol — Perspectives in Pediatric Pathology
Perspect Polon — Perspectives Polonaises
Perspect Powder Metall — Perspectives in Powder Metallurgy
Perspect Psychiatr — Perspectives Psychiatriques
Perspect Psychiatr Care — Perspectives in Psychiatric Care
Perspect Virol — Perspectives in Virology
Perspekt Phil — Perspektiven der Philosophie
Persp N Mus — Perspectives of New Music
Pers Prac Bul — Personnel Practice Bulletin
Pers Pract Bull — Personnel Practice Bulletin
Pers Psych — Personnel Psychology
Pers Psych C — Perspectives in Psychiatric Care
Pers Psychol — Personnel Psychology
Pers Rep Exec — Personal Report for the Executive
Peru Dir Gen Mineria Bol — Peru Ministerio de Fomento y Obras Publicas. Direccion General de Mineria. Boletin
Peru Minist Agric Dir Gen Invest Agropecu Bol Tec — Peru. Ministerio de Agricultura. Direccion General de Investigaciones Agropecuarias. Boletin Tecnico
Peru Minist Agric Serv Invest Promoc Agrar Bol Tec — Peru. Ministerio de Agricultura. Servicio de Investigacion y Promocion Agraria. Boletin Tecnico
Peru Serv Geol Min Bol — Peru. Servicio de Geologia y Mineria. Boletin
Peru Serv Geol Min Estud Espec — Peru. Servicio de Geologia y Mineria. Estudios Especiales
Peru Serv Geol Min Geodinamica Ing Geol — Peru. Servicio de Geologia y Mineria. Geodinamica e Ingenieria Geologica
PES — Polish Economic Survey
Pesca Mar — Pesca y Marina
Pesca Pesqui — Pesca y Pesquisa
PESC Rec IEEE Power Electron Spec Conf — PESC Record. IEEE [*Institute of Electrical and Electronics Engineers*] Power Electronics Specialists Conference
Peshawar Univ Dep Geol Geol Bull — Peshawar. University. Department of Geology. Geological Bulletin
PESOD — Proceedings. Electrochemical Society
PESPD — Periodically Speaking
Pesqui Agropecuar Brasil Ser Agron — Pesquisa Agropecuaria Brasileira. Serie Agronomia
Pesqui Agropecuar Brasil Ser Vet — Pesquisa Agropecuaria Brasileira. Serie Veterinaria
Pesqui Agropecu Bras — Pesquisa Agropecuaria Brasileira
Pesqui Agropecu Bras Ser Agron — Pesquisa Agropecuaria Brasileira. Serie Agronomia
Pesqui Agropecu Bras Ser Vet — Pesquisa Agropecuaria Brasileira. Serie Veterinaria
Pesqui Agropecu Bras Ser Zootec — Pesquisa Agropecuaria Brasileira. Serie Zootecnia
Pesqui Agropecu Nordeste Recife — Pesquisas Agropecuarias do Nordeste Recife
Pesqui Bot (Porto Alegre) — Pesquisas Botanica (Porto Alegre)
Pesqui Commun (Porto Alegre) — Pesquisas Communications (Porto Alegre)
Pesqui Med — Pesquisa Medica
Pesquisa e Planejamento Econ — Pesquisa e Planejamento Economico
Pesquisas Antropol — Pesquisas Antropologia
Pesqui Secc B Cienc Nat (Porto Alegre) — Pesquisas. Seccao B. Ciencias Naturais (Porto Alegre)
Pesqui Zool (Porto Alegre) — Pesquisas Zoologia (Porto Alegre)
Pest Bioch — Pesticide Biochemistry and Physiology
Pest Contr — Pest Control
Pest Contro — Pest Control
Pest Control Circ — Pest Control Circular
PESTD — Proceedings. European Society of Toxicology
Pestic Abstr — Pesticides Abstracts and News Summary
Pestic Abstr News Sum Sect C Herbic — Pesticides Abstracts and News Summary. Section C. Herbicides
Pestic Biochem Physiol — Pesticide Biochemistry and Physiology
Pestic Monit J — Pesticides Monitoring Journal
Pestic Progr — Pesticide Progress
Pestic Res Rep Agric Can — Pesticide Research Report. Agriculture Canada
Pestic Sci — Pesticide Science
Pestic Tech — Pesticide and Technique
Pest Infest Control Lab Rep (Lond) — Pest Infestation Control. Laboratory Report (London)
Pest Infest Control (Lond) — Pest Infestation Control. Laboratory Report (London)
Pest Infest Res Rep Pest Infest Lab Agric Res Counc — Pest Infestation Research Report. Pest Infestation Laboratory. Agricultural Research Council
Pest Leafl Pac For Res Cent — Pest Leaflet. Pacific Forest Research Centre
Pest Mon J — Pesticides Monitoring Journal
Pest Sci — Pesticide Science

PESY — People Say. Bimonthly Newsletter [*Canada*]
Pet — Peters Notes
Pet Age — Petroleum Age
Pet Chem Ind Conf Rec Conf Pap — Petroleum and Chemical Industry Conference. Record of Conference Papers [*United States*]
Pet Chem Ind Dev — Petroleum and Chemical Industry Developments [*India*]
Pet Chem (USSR) — Petroleum Chemistry (USSR)
Pet Econ — Petroleum Economist
Pet Eng — Petroleum Engineer
Pet Eng Int — Petroleum Engineer International
Pet Equip — Petroleum Equipment
Pet Equip Serv — Petroleum Equipment and Services
Petermanns Geog Mitt — Petermanns Geographische Mitteilungen
Petermanns Geogr Mitt — Petermanns Geographische Mitteilungen
Petermanns Mitt — Petermanns. A. Mitteilungen aus J. Perthes Geographischer Anstalt
Petermanns Mitt Erg — Petermanns Mitteilungen. Ergaenzungsheft [*Gotha*]
Peterm Geog — Petermanns Geographische Mitteilungen
Peter Phot Mag — Petersen's Photographic Magazine
Pet Explor Dev — Petroleum Exploration and Development
Pet Gaz — Petroleum Gazette
Pet & Gaze — Petrol si Gaze [*Romania*]
Pet Gaze Supl — Petrol si Gaze. Supliment [*Romania*]
Pet Geol — Petroleum Geology
Pet Geol Taiwan — Petroleum Geology of Taiwan
Pet Hydrocarbons — Petroleum and Hydrocarbons [*India*]
Pet Indep — Petroleum Independent
Pet Inf — Petrole Informations
Pet Int — Petroleo Internacional
Pet Interam — Petroleo Interamericano
Pet Int (London) — Petroleum International (London)
Petit J Brass — Petit Journal du Brasseur
Pet Manage — Petroleum Management
Pet Mitt — Petermanns Mitteilungen
Pet News — Petroleum News [*Taiwan*]
Pet Newsl — Petroleum Newsletter
PETOA — Petrotecnica
Pet Outlook — Petroleum Outlook
Pet Petrochem — Petroleum and Petrochemicals [*Japan*]
Pet Petrochem Int — Petroleum and Petrochemical International [*England*]
Pet Petrochem (Tokyo) — Petroleum and Petrochemicals (Tokyo) [*Japan*]
Pet P M — Petersen's Photographic Magazine
Pet Press Serv — Petroleum Press Service [*England*]
Pet Process — Petroleum Processing
PETRASAFE — Petroleum Transport Scheme for Assistance in Freight Emergencies
PETRB — Petroleum Review
PETRD — Petrologie
Pet Refiner — Petroleum Refiner
Pet Refin Petrochem Lit Abstr — Petroleum Refining and Petrochemicals Literature Abstracts
Pet Rev — Petrocorp Review
Pet Rev — Petroleum Review
Petr Inde — Petroleum Independent
Petro/Chem Eng — Petro/Chem Engineer
Petrol Abstr — Petroleum Abstracts
Petrol Eng — Petroleum Engineer
Petrol Eng Int — Petroleum Engineer International
Petroleo — Petroleo Internacional
Petroleos Mexicanos Servicio Inf — Petroleos Mexicanos Servicio de Informacion
Petroleum — Petroleum Economist
Petroleum Gaz — Petroleum Gazette
Petrol Gaz — Petroleum Gazette
Petrol Geol — Petroleum Geology
Petrolieri Int — Petrolieri International
Petrol Independ — Petroleum Independent
Petrol Inform — Petrole Informations
Petrol Int — Petroleo Internacional
Petrol News — Petroleum News
Petrol Rev — Petroleum Review
Petrol Tech — Petrole et Techniques
Petrol Tecnol — Petroleo y Tecnologia
Petrozavodsk Gos Univ Ucen Zap — Petrozavodskii Gosudarstvennyi Universitet. Ucenye Zapiski
Petr Sit — Petroleum Situation
Pet Substitutes — Petroleum Substitutes
PETTA — Petroleum Times
Pet Tech — Petrole et Techniques
Pet Technol — Petroleum Technology
Pet Tech Rev — Petroleum Technical Review
Pet Times — Petroleum Times
Pet Today — Petroleum Today
Petty SR — Petty Sessions Review
Pet W — Petroleum Week
Pet World — Petroleum World [*London*]

Pet World (London) — Petroleum World (London)
Pet World (Los Angeles) — Petroleum World (Los Angeles)
Pet World Oil — Petroleum World and Oil
Pet World Oil Age — Petroleum World and Oil Age
PEUBA — Publikacije Elektrotehnickog Fakulteta Univerziteta u Beogradu. Serija Matematika i Fizika
P Evang — Pentecostal Evangel
PEW — Philosophy East and West
PE & W — Philosophy East and West
PF — Pennsylvania Folklife
PF — Pensee Francaise
PF — Philosophy Forum
P & F — Photography and Focus
PF — Poesie Francaise
PF — Polish Folklore
PF — Popular Foodservice
PF — Prace Filologiczne
PF — Public Finance
PFA — Korte Berichten over Buitenlandse Projecten
PFA — Public Finance and Accountancy
Pfaelzer H — Pfaelzer Heimat
PFATA — Problemy Fiziki Atmosfery
PFBFA — Power Farming and Better Farming Digest (Australia)
PFC — Progressive Fish-Culturist
PFCUA — Progressive Fish-Culturist
PFE — Paper, Film, and Foil Converter
PFF Convrt — Paper, Film, and Foil Converter
PFF Convt — Paper, Film, and Foil Converter
PFGGA — Professional Geographer
PfH — Pfaelzische Heimatblaetter
PFI — Profile Index. Micromedia Ltd.
PFil — Prace Filologiczne
PFil — Przeglad Filozoficzny
Pfitzner — Hans Pfitzner-Gesellschaft. Mitteilungen
Pfizer Med Monogr — Pfizer Medical Monographs
PFL — Pennsylvania Folklife
PFLAB — Pfluegers Archiv
PFLAB — Pfluegers Archiv. European Journal of Physiology
Pflanzenschutzber — Pflanzenschutzberichte
Pflanzenschutz-Nachr — Pflanzenschutz-Nachrichten
Pflanzenschutz-Nachr (Am Ed) — Pflanzenschutz-Nachrichten (American Edition)
PflBau PflSchutz PflZucht — Pflanzenbau, Pflanzenschutz, Pflanzenzucht
PFLDA — Physics of Fluids
PFLFT — Pubblicazioni. Facolta di Lettere e Filosofia. Universita di Torino
PFLSA — Physics of Fluids. Supplement
Pflueg Arch — Pfluegers Archiv. European Journal of Physiology
Pfluegers Arch Eur J Physiol — Pfluegers Archiv. European Journal of Physiology
Pfluegers Arch Ges Physiol — Pfluegers Archiv fuer die Gesamte Physiologie
Pfluegers Archiv Gesamte Physiol Menschen Tiere — Pfluegers Archiv fuer die Gesamte Physiologie des Menschen und der Tiere
PFLUS — Publications. Faculte des Lettres. Universite de Strasbourg
PFQ — Public Finance Quarterly
PFr — Presence Francophone
PFS — Progress in Filtration and Separation [Elsevier Book Series]
PFSCL — Papers on French Seventeenth Century Literature
PG — Palestine Gazette
PG — Patrologia Graeca
PG — Przeglad Geograficzny
PGA — Printing and Graphic Arts
PGAEA — Proceedings. Geologists' Association (England)
PGAZA — Petrol si Gaze
PGC — Pelican Gospel Commentaries [Harmondsworth]
PGD — Personnel and Guidance Journal
PGFS — Pennsylvania German Folklore Society. Bulletin
PGGJ-A — Philippine Geographical Journal
PGGUDU — Annual Research Reviews. Prostaglandins and the Gut
PGHTA — Progress in Hemostasis and Thrombosis
PGJ — Personnel and Guidance Journal
P & G Jour — Pipeline and Gas Journal
PGM — Petermanns Geographische Mitteilungen
PGM — Postgraduate Medicine
PGM — Program Manager
PGNGD — Prace Instytutu Gornictwa Naftowego i Gazownictwa
PGNMA — Progress in Nuclear Medicine
PGNS — Polar Gas News
PGO — Progressive Grocer
PGPKA — Problemy Gematologii i Perelivaniya Krovi
PGR — Pakistan Geographical Review
PGR — Plant Growth Regulation
PGRAA — Progressive Architecture
PGS — Pennsylvania German Society. Proceedings and Addresses
PGSP — Pennsylvania German Society. Proceedings and Addresses
PGTAA — Prager Tieraerztliches Archiv
PGTWA — Petroleum Geology of Taiwan

PH — Paedigogica Historica
PH — Pakistan Horizon
PH — Palabra y el Hombre. Revista de la Universidad Veracruzana
PH — Pennsylvania History
Ph — Philologus. Zeitschrift fuer Klassische Altertum
Ph — Philosophisches Jahrbuch
Ph — Philosophy
Ph — Phoenix
PH — Provence Historique
PH — Przeglad Historyczny
PHA — Pharmaceutisch Weekblad
Pha — Philologica
PHA — Philosophia Antiqua
PhAb — Photographic Abstracts
PHAGA — Philippine Agriculturist
PHARA — Pharmazie
Pharm Abstr — Pharmaceutical Abstracts
Pharmaceutical J — Pharmaceutical Journal and Transactions
Pharmacog Tit — Pharmacognosy Titles
Pharmacol — Pharmacology
Pharmacol Biochem Behav — Pharmacology, Biochemistry, and Behavior
Pharmacol Clin — Pharmacologia Clinica
Pharmacolog — Pharmacologist
Pharmacol Physicians — Pharmacology for Physicians
Pharmacol R — Pharmacological Research Communications
Pharmacol Res Commun — Pharmacological Research Communications
Pharmacol Rev — Pharmacological Reviews
Pharmacol Sleep — Pharmacology of Sleep
Pharmacol Ther — Pharmacology and Therapeutics
Pharmacol Ther (B) — Pharmacology and Therapeutics. Part B. General and Systematic Pharmacology
Pharmacol Ther Dent — Pharmacology and Therapeutics in Dentistry
Pharmacol Ther Part A Chemother Toxicol Metab Inhibitors — Pharmacology and Therapeutics. Part A. Chemotherapy, Toxicology, and Metabolic Inhibitors
Pharmacol Ther Part B Gen Syst Pharmacol — Pharmacology and Therapeutics. Part B. General and Systematic Pharmacology
Pharmacol Ther Part C — Pharmacology and Therapeutics. Part C. Clinical Pharmacology and Therapeutics
Pharmacol Toxicol (Engl Transl) — Pharmacology and Toxicology (English Translation of Farmakologiya Toksikologiya) [Moscow]
Pharmacol Toxicol (USSR) — Pharmacology and Toxicology (USSR)
Pharm Acta Helv — Pharmaceutica Acta Helvetiae
Pharm Act H — Pharmaceutica Acta Helvetiae
Pharma Int Engl Ed — Pharma International (English Edition)
Pharmakeutickon Delt Epistem Ekodosis — Pharmakeutikon Deltion. Epistemonike Ekodosis
Pharmakopsy — Pharmakopsychiatrie Neuro-Psychopharmakologie
Pharmakopsychiatr Neuro-Psychopharmakol — Pharmakopsychiatrie Neuro-Psychopharmakologie
Pharm Aquitaine — Pharmacien d'Aquitaine
Pharm Arch — Pharmaceutical Archives
Pharmazie Beih — Pharmazie. Beihefte
Pharm Bio B — Pharmacology, Biochemistry, and Behavior
Pharm Biol — Pharmacien Biologiste
Pharm Bull Nihon Univ — Pharmaceutical Bulletin. Nihon University
Pharm Chem J — Pharmaceutical Chemistry Journal
Pharm Cosmet — Pharmaceuticals and Cosmetics
Pharm Cosmet Rev — Pharmaceutical and Cosmetics Review [South Africa]
Pharm Delt Epistem Ekdosis — Pharmkeutikon Deltion Epistemonike Ekdosis
Pharm Era — Pharmaceutical Era
Pharm Hist — Pharmacy in History
Pharm Hosp Fr — Pharmacie Hospitaliere Francaise
Pharm Ind — Pharmazeutische Industrie
Pharm Ind Yugosl — Pharmaceutical Industry of Yugoslavia
Pharm Int — Pharmacy International [Netherlands]
Pharm J — Pharmaceutical Journal
Pharm J NZ — Pharmaceutical Journal of New Zealand
Pharm J Pharm — Pharmaceutical Journal and Pharmacist
Pharm Manage — Pharmacy Management
Pharm Manuf Assoc Yearb — Pharmaceutical Manufacturers Association. Yearbook
Pharm Monatsbl — Pharmazeutische Monatsblaetter
Pharm Monatsh — Pharmazeutische Monatshefte
Pharm Monogr — Pharmaceutical Monographs
Pharm Post — Pharmazeutische Post
Pharm Prax — Pharmazeutische Praxis
Pharm Presse — Pharmazeutische Presse
Pharm Presse Wiss Prakt Hefte — Pharmazeutische Presse. Wissenschaftlich-Praktische Hefte
Pharm Prod Pharm — Pharmacie-Produits Pharmaceutiques
Pharm Res — Pharmaceutical Research
Pharm Rev — Pharmaceutical Review
Pharm Rev — Pharmacological Reviews
Pharm Rundsch — Pharmazeutische Rundschau
Pharm Rural — Pharmacien Rural

Pharm Soc Jpn J — Pharmaceutical Society of Japan. Journal
Pharm Tijdschr Belg — Pharmaceutische Tijdschrift voor Belgie
Pharm Times — Pharmacy Times
Pharm Unserer Zeit — Pharmazie in Unserer Zeit
Pharm Weekbl — Pharmaceutisch Weekblad
Pharm Weekbl Ned — Pharmeceutish Weekblad voor Nederland
Pharm Weekbl Sci — Pharmaceutisch Weekblad. Scientific Edition
Pharm Zentralhalle — Pharmazeutische Zentralhalle
Pharm Zentralhalle Dtl — Pharmazeutische Zentralhalle fuer Deutschland
Pharm Zentralhalle Dtschl — Pharmazeutische Zentralhalle fuer Deutschland
Pharm Z Russl — Pharmaceutische Zeitschrift fuer Russland
Pharm Ztg — Pharmazeutische Zeitung
Pharm Ztg (Berl) — Pharmazeutische Zeitung (Berlin)
Pharm Ztg Nachr — Pharmazeutische Zeitung Nachrichten
Pharm Ztg Ver Apotheker-Ztg — Pharmazeutische Zeitung. Vereinigt mit Apotheker-Zeitung [West Germany]
Pharos — Pharos of Alpha Omega Alpha Honor Medical Society
P Hawaii En — Proceedings. Hawaiian Entomological Society
PhB — Philobiblon
PhB — Philosophische Bibliothek [Meiner]
PHBCD — Physica B + C
PHBHA — Physiology and Behavior
PHBIA — Pharmacien Biologiste
PHBLA — Physikalische Blaetter
PHBOA — Physiologia Bohemoslovenica [Later, Physiologia Bohemoslovaca]
PHCAA — Physics in Canada
PHCBA — Photochemistry and Photobiology
PHCCA — Progress in Histochemistry and Cytochemistry
PhCL — Pharmacochemistry Library [Elsevier Book Series]
PHCTB — Photophysiology
PHDK — Phi Delta Kappan
PHEDA — Physics Education
PhEJ — Philippine Economic Journal
P Helm Soc — Proceedings. Helminthological Society of Washington
PHESA — Proceedings. Hawaiian Entomological Society
P-H Est Plan — Estate Planning (Prentice-Hall, Inc.)
Ph E W — Philosophy East and West
PHFEA — Physica Fennica
Phi — Philosophy
Phi Del Kap — Phi Delta Kappan
Phi D K — Phi Delta Kappan
Phil — Philologus. Zeitschrift fuer Klassische Altertum
Philadelphia Med — Philadelphia Medicine
Phil Ag — Philippine Agriculturist
Phila Geog Soc Bull — Philadelphia Geographical Society. Bulletin
Phil Ag R — Philippine Agricultural Review
Phila Med — Philadelphia Medicine
Phila Med J — Philadelphia Medical Journal
Phila Med Phys J — Philadelphia Medical and Physical Journal
Phila Mus Bull — Philadelphia Museum of Art. Bulletin
Philanthrop — Philanthropist
Phila Orch — Philadelphia Orchestra. Program Notes
Phila Phot — Philadelphia Photographer
Philat Aust — Philately from Australia
Philat Bul — Philatelic Bulletin
Philately from Aust — Philately from Australia
Philat Pregl — Philatelen Pregled
Phil Books — Philosophical Books
Phil Bull — Philatelic Bulletin
Phil Bus R — Philippine Business Review
Phil Context — Philosophy in Context
Phil Dev — Philippine Development
Phil East West — Philosophy East and West
Phil Educ Proc — Proceedings. Far Western Philosophy of Education Society
Phil Exch — Philosophic Exchange
Phil Forum (Boston) — Philosophical Forum (Boston)
Phil Forum (De Kalb) — Philosophy Forum (De Kalb)
Phil Geog J — Philippine Geographical Journal
Philhar — Philharmonic
Phil Ind — Philosopher's Index
Phil Inq — Philosophical Inquiry
Phil Invest — Philosophical Investigators
Philip Abstr — Philippine Abstracts
Philipp AEC — Philippine Atomic Energy Commission. Publications
Philipp AEC Annu Rep — Philippine Atomic Energy Commission. Annual Report
Philipp AEC Rep — Philippine Atomic Energy Commission. Reports
Philipp Agric — Philippine Agriculturist
Philipp Agric Eng J — Philippine Agricultural Engineering Journal
Philipp Agric Rev — Philippine Agricultural Review
Philipp At Bull — Philippine Atomic Bulletin
Philipp Bur Mines Inf Circ — Philippines. Bureau of Mines. Information Circular
Philipp Bur Mines Rep Invest — Philippines. Bureau of Mines. Report of Investigations

Philipp Bur Mines Spec Proj Ser Publ — Philippines. Bureau of Mines. Special Projects Series. Publication
Philipp Dep Agric Nat Resour Bur Mines Inf Circ — Philippines. Department of Agriculture and Natural Resources. Bureau of Mines. Information Circular
Philipp Ent — Philippine Entomologist
Philipp Entomol — Philippine Entomologist
Philipp For — Philippine Forests
Philipp For Prod Res Ind Dev Comm FORPRIDE Dig — Philippines. Forest Products Research and Industries Development Commission. FORPRIDE Digest
Philipp Geogr J — Philippine Geographical Journal
Philipp Geol — Philippine Geologist
Philippine Ag R — Philippine Agricultural Review
Philippine Agr — Philippine Agriculturist
Philippine Agr Situation — Philippine Agricultural Situation
Philippine Econ J — Philippine Economic Journal
Philippine Economy and Ind J — Philippine Economy and Industrial Journal
Philippine Farm Gard — Philippine Farms and Gardens
Philippine J Nutr — Philippine Journal of Nutrition
Philippine J Plant Ind — Philippine Journal of Plant Industry
Philippine J Pub Adm — Philippine Journal of Public Administration
Philippine J Pub Admin — Philippine Journal of Public Administration
Philippine J Public Admin — Philippine Journal of Public Administration
Philippine J Sci — Philippine Journal of Science
Philippine Planning J — Philippine Planning Journal
Philippine Rice Corn Progr — Philippines Rice and Corn Progress
Philippines Bur Mines Geo-Sci Rep Invest — Philippines. Bureau of Mines and Geo-Sciences. Report of Investigation
Philippine Sociol R — Philippine Sociological Review
Philippine Stud — Philippine Studies
Philipp J Agric — Philippine Journal of Agriculture
Philipp J Anim Ind — Philippine Journal of Animal Industry
Philipp J Cardiol — Philippine Journal of Cardiology
Philipp J Coconut Stud — Philippine Journal of Coconut Studies
Philipp J Crop Sci — Philippine Journal of Crop Science
Philipp J Food Sci Technol — Philippine Journal of Food Science and Technology
Philipp J For — Philippine Journal of Forestry
Philipp J Intern Med — Philippine Journal of Internal Medicine
Philipp J Nurs — Philippine Journal of Nursing
Philipp J Nutr — Philippine Journal of Nutrition
Philipp J Ophthal — Philippine Journal of Ophthalmology
Philipp J Ophthalmol — Philippine Journal of Ophthalmology
Philipp J Pediatr — Philippine Journal of Pediatrics
Philipp J Plant Ind — Philippine Journal of Plant Industry
Philipp J Pub Admin — Philippine Journal of Public Administration
Philipp J Sci — Philippine Journal of Science
Philipp J Sci Sect A — Philippine Journal of Science. Section A. Chemical Sciences
Philipp J Sci Sect B — Philippine Journal of Science. Section B. Medical Sciences
Philipp J Sci Sect C — Philippine Journal of Science. Section C. Botany
Philipp J Surg Obstet Gynecol — Philippine Journal of Surgery, Obstetrics, and Gynecology
Philipp J Surg Surg Spec — Philippine Journal of Surgery and Surgical Specialties
Philipp J Vet Med — Philippine Journal of Veterinary Medicine
Philipp Lumberm — Philippine Lumberman
Philipp Med World (1946-1951) — Philippine Medical World (1946-1951)
Philipp Med World (1952-1962) — Philippine Medical World (1952-1962)
Philipp Min J — Philippine Mining Journal
Philipp Nucl J — Philippines Nuclear Journal
Philipp Phytopathol — Philippine Phytopathology
Philipp Q Cult Soc — Philippine Quarterly of Culture and Society
Philipp Quart Cult Soc — Philippine Quarterly of Culture and Society
Philipp Sci — Philippine Scientist
Philipp Sugar Inst Q — Philippine Sugar Institute. Quarterly
Philipp Text Inf Dig — Philippine Textile Information Digest
Philips — Philips Music Herald
PhilipSa — Philippiana Sacra [Manila]
Philips Ind Eng Bul — Philips Industrial Engineering Bulletin
Philips J Res — Philips Journal of Research
Philips Res Rep — Philips Research Reports
Philips Res Rep Suppl — Philips Research Reports. Supplements
Philips Serv Sci Ind — Philips Serving Science and Industry
PhilipSt — Philippine Studies [Manila]
Philips Tech Rev — Philips Technical Review
Philips Tech Rundsch — Philips Technische Rundschau
Philips Tech Rundschau — Philips Technische Rundschau [Netherlands]
Philips Telecommun Rev — Philips Telecommunication Review
Philips Weld Rep — Philips Welding Reporter
Phili S Rev — Philippine Sociological Review
Phil J Ag — Philippine Journal of Agriculture
Phil Jahr — Philosophisches Jahrbuch
Phil J Ling — Philippine Journal of Linguistics

Phil J Pub Admin — Philippine Journal of Public Administration
Phil Jrl — Business Journal (Philippines)
Phil J Sci — Philippine Journal of Science
Phil Lab R — Philippine Labor Review
Phil Ling — Philosophical Linguistics
Phillip J Sci — Phillippine Journal of Science
Phil Lit — Philosophy and Literature
Phil Log — Philosophie et Logique
Phil Mag — Philosophical Magazine
Phil Math — Philosophia Mathematica
Phil Natur — Philosophia Naturalis
Philologus ZKA — Philologus. Zeitschrift fuer Klassische Altertum
Philol Q — Philological Quarterly
Philos — Philosophy
Philos Abhandlungen — Philosophische Abhandlungen
Philos Bibliothek — Philosophische Bibliothek [*Hamburg*]
Philos Book — Philosophical Books
Philos Collect R Soc London — Philosophical Collections. Royal Society of London
Philos Curr — Philosophical Currents
Philos East & West — Philosophy East and West
Philos EW — Philosophy East and West
Philos Foru — Philosophy Forum
Philos Forum — Philosophical Forum
Philos Forum — Philosophy Forum
Philos Forum Quart — Philosophical Forum. A Quarterly
Philos His — Philosophy and History
Philos Hist — Philosophy and History. German Studies Section I
Philosl — Philosopher's Index
Philos J — Philosophical Journal
Philos Jahr — Philosophisches Jahrbuch
Philos Lit — Philosophy and Literature
Philos M — Philosophical Magazine
Philos Mag — Philosophical Magazine
Philos Mag A — Philosophical Magazine A. Physics of Condensed Matter, Defects, and Mechanical Properties
Philos Mag B — Philosophical Magazine B. Physics of Condensed Matter, Electronic, Optical, and Magnetic Properties
Philos Math — Philosophia Mathematica
Philos Nat — Philosophia Naturalis
Philos Natur — Philosophia Naturalis
Philosophy of Ed Soc Proc — Philosophy of Education Society of Great Britain. Proceedings
Philos Pap — Philosophical Papers
Philos Phen — Philosophy and Phenomenological Research
Philos Phenomenol Res — Philosophy and Phenomenological Research
Philos & Phenom Res — Philosophy and Phenomenological Research
Philos Pub — Philosophy and Public Affairs
Philos & Pub Affairs — Philosophy and Public Affairs
Philos Publ Aff — Philosophy and Public Affairs
PhilosQ — Philosophical Quarterly
Philos Quart — Philosophical Quarterly
Philos R — Philosophical Review
PhilosRdschau — Philosophische Rundschau
Philos Rev — Philosophical Review
Philos Rhet — Philosophy and Rhetoric
Philos Rund — Philosophische Rundschau
Philos Sci — Philosophy of Science
Philos Soc Sci — Philosophy of the Social Sciences
Philos S Sc — Philosophy of the Social Sciences
Philos Stud — Philosophical Studies
Philos Studies — Philosophical Studies [*Dordrecht*]
Philos Stud Ser Philos — Philosophical Studies Series in Philosophy
Philo Stds — Philosophical Studies
Philos Tod — Philosophy Today
Philos Top — Philosophical Topics
Philos Trans Roy Soc London Ser A — Philosophical Transactions. Royal Society of London. Series A. Mathematical and Physical Sciences
Philos Trans R Soc A — Philosophical Transactions. Royal Society of London. Series A
Philos Trans R Soc Lond A Math Phys Sci — Philosophical Transactions. Royal Society of London. Series A. Mathematical and Physical Sciences
Philos Trans R Soc Lond Biol — Philosophical Transactions. Royal Society of London. Series B. Biological Sciences
Philos Trans R Soc London — Philosophical Transactions. Royal Society of London
Philos Trans R Soc London A — Philosophical Transactions. Royal Society of London. Series A. Mathematical and Physical Sciences
Philos Trans R Soc London Ser A — Philosophical Transactions. Royal Society of London. Series A
Philos Trans R Soc London Ser B — Philosophical Transactions. Royal Society of London. Series B. Biological Sciences
Phil Papers — Philosophical Papers
Phil Perspekt — Philosophische Perspektiven
Phil Phenomenol Res — Philosophy and Phenomenological Research
Phil Plan J — Philippine Planning Journal

Phil Pol Sci J — Philippine Political Science Journal
Phil Post — Philharmonic Post
Phil Pub Affairs — Philosophy and Public Affairs
Phil Q — Philippines Quarterly
Phil Q — Philosophical Quarterly
Phil Q Cult Soc — Philippine Quarterly of Culture and Society
Phil Qy — Philological Quarterly
Phil R — Philosophical Review
PhilR — Philosophy and Rhetoric
Phil R Bus Econ — Philippine Review of Business and Economics
Phil Reform — Philosophia Reformata
Phil Res Arch — Philosophy Research Archives
Phil Res R — Philips Research Reports
Phil Rev — Philosophical Review
Phil Rev (Taiwan) — Philosophical Review (Taiwan)
Phil Rhet — Philosophy and Rhetoric
Phil Rundsch — Philosophische Rundschau
PhilS — Philosophical Studies
Phil Sacra — Philippine Sacra
Phil Sci — Philosophy of Science
Phil Soc — Philological Society. Transactions
Phil Soc Act — Philosophy and Social Action
Phil Soc Cr — Philosophy and Social Criticism
Phil Soc Crit — Philosophy and Social Criticism
Phil Sociol R — Philippine Sociological Review
Phil Soc Sci — Philosophy of the Social Sciences
Phil Soc Sci Hum R — Philippine Social Sciences and Humanities Review
Phil Stud — Philippine Studies
Phil Stud — Philosophical Studies
Phil Stud Educ — Philosophical Studies in Education
Phil Stud (Ireland) — Philosophical Studies (Ireland)
PhilT — Philosophy Today
Phil Tech R — Philips Technical Review
Phil Today — Philosophy Today
Phil Topics — Philosophical Topics
Phil Trans — Philosophical Transactions
Phil Trans Roy Soc Lond — Philosophical Transactions. Royal Society of London
Phil Trans Roy Soc Lond B — Philosophical Transactions. Royal Society of London. Series B. Biological Sciences
Phil Trans Roy Soc London Ser A Math Phys Sci — Philosophical Transactions. Royal Society of London. Series A. Mathematical and Physical Sciences
Phil Trans R Soc — Philosophical Transactions. Royal Society
Phil Woch — Philologische Wochenschrift
PHINA — Pharmazeutische Industrie
PHIND — Pharmacy International
Phi T Roy A — Philosophical Transactions. Royal Society of London. Series A. Mathematical and Physical Sciences
Phi T Roy B — Philosophical Transactions. Royal Society of London. Series B. Biological Sciences
PhJ — Philosophisches Jahrbuch
Ph Jb — Philosophisches Jahrbuch
PHJRD — Philips Journal of Research
PHK — Pootaardappelwereld
PHKOA — Photographische Korrespondenz (Austria)
PHLBA — Phlebologie
Phl Freep — Philadelphia Free Press
PHLTA — Physics Letters
PHMAA — Philosophical Magazine
Ph Mag — Philosophical Magazine
PHMBA — Physics in Medicine and Biology
PHMGB — Pharmacology
PHMMA — Physics of Metals and Metallography [*English Translation*]
PHMTD — Previews of Heat and Mass Transfer
PHNOA — Physica Norvegica
PHNTA — Phonetica
PhO — Philologia Orientalis
PhoenixC — Phoenix: The Classical Association of Canada
PhoenixK — Phoenix (Korea)
Phoenix Q — Phoenix Quarterly
Phon — Phonetica
PhonPr — Phonetica Pragensia
PHOPD — Photobiochemistry and Photobiophysics
Phospho Potas — Phosphorus and Potassium
Phosphore Agric — Phosphore et Agriculture [*France*]
Phosphor Sulfur Relat Elem — Phosphorus and Sulfur and the Related Elements
Phosphorus — Phosphorus and Potassium
Phosphorus Agric — Phosphorus in Agriculture
Phot — Photon
Phot Abstr — Photographic Abstracts
Phot Appln Sci — Photographic Applications in Science, Technology, and Medicine
Phot Appl Sci Tech Med — Photographic Applications in Science, Technology, and Medicine

Phot Arch — Photographisches Archiv
Phot Industrie — Photographische Industrie
Phot J — Photographic Journal
Phot J Amer — Photographic Journal of America
Phot Korr — Photographische Korrespondenz
Photo Abstr — Photographic Abstracts
Photo Art Mon — Photo Art Monthly
Photobiochem Photobiophys — Photobiochemistry and Photobiophysics
Photobiochem and Photobiophys — Photobiochemistry and Photobiophysics
Photobl — Photoblaetter
Photo Can — Photo Canada
Photo Chem Mach Photo Chem Etching — Photo Chemical Machining - Photo Chemical Etching
Photochem P — Photochemistry and Photobiology
Photochem Photobiol — Photochemistry and Photobiology
Photochem Photobiol Rev — Photochemical and Photobiological Reviews
Photo Cine Rev — Photo-Cine-Review
Photoelastic Soil Mech J — Photoelastic and Soil Mechanics Journal
Photoelectr Spectrom Group Bull — Photoelectric Spectrometry Group Bulletin
Photo Engravers Bull — Photo-Engravers' Bulletin
Photo Era Mag — Photo-Era Magazine
Photog Abstr — Photographic Abstracts
Photogr Alle — Photographie fuer Alle
Photogram Eng Remote Sensing — Photogrammetric Engineering and Remote Sensing
Photogramma — Photogrammetria
Photogramm Eng — Photogrammetric Engineering [*Later, Photogrammetric Engineering and Remote Sensing*]
Photogramm Eng Remote Sensing — Photogrammetric Engineering and Remote Sensing
Photogramm Eng and Remote Sensing — Photogrammetric Engineering and Remote Sensing
Photogrammetric Eng — Photogrammetric Engineering [*Later, Photogrammetric Engineering and Remote Sensing*]
Photogramm Rec — Photogrammetric Record
Photographie Forsch — Photographie und Forschung
Photogr Appl Sci Technol and Med — Photographic Applications in Science, Technology, and Medicine
Photogr Appl Sci Technol Med — Photographic Applications in Science, Technology, and Medicine
Photogr Canadiana — Photographic Canadiana
Photogr Chron — Photographische Chronik
Photogr Chron Allg Photogr Ztg — Photographische Chronik und Allgemeine Photographische Zeitung
Photogr Collector — Photographic Collector
Photogr Eng — Photographic Engineering
Photogr E R — Photogrammetric Engineering and Remote Sensing
Photogr Forsch — Photographie und Forschung
Photogr Ind — Photographische Industrie
Photogr J — Photographic Journal
Photogr J Sect A — Photographic Journal. Section A. Pictorial and General Photography
Photogr J Sect B — Photographic Journal. Section B. Scientific and Technical Photography
Photogr Korresp — Photographische Korrespondenz
Photogr Sci Eng — Photographic Science and Engineering
Photogr Sci and Eng — Photographic Science and Engineering
Photogr Sci Tech — Photographic Science and Technique
Photogr Sensitivity — Photographic Sensitivity
Photogr Welt — Photographische Welt
Photogr Wiss — Photographie und Wissenschaft
Photo Ind — Photo-Industrie und -Handel
Photo Ind — Photographische Industrie
Photo Lab Manag — Photo Lab Management
Photo-M — Photo-Miniature
Photo-Mag — Photo-Magazin
Photo Methods Ind — Photo Methods for Industry
Photo Min — Photo-Miniature
Photo Mkt — Photo Marketing
Photophysiol Curr Top — Photophysiology. Current Topics
Photoplay — Photoplay, Movies, and Video
Photo-Rev — Photo-Revue
Photosynthe — Photosynthetica
Photo Tech — Photo Technique
Phot Sci En — Photographic Science and Engineering
Phot Sci Eng — Photographic Science and Engineering
Phot Sci Tech — Photographic Society of America. Journal. Section B. Photographic Science and Technique
Phot Tech — Photo Technique
Phot Tech Wirt — Photo-Technik und -Wirtschaft
PHP — Peace, Happiness, Prosperity for All
PhP — Philologica Pragensia
PhP — Philologike Protochronia
Ph & Phen R — Philosophy and Phenomenological Research
PHPLA — Physiologia Plantarum
PHPXA — Pharmazeutische Praxis

PhQ — Philosophical Quarterly
PHR — Pacific Historical Review
PHR — Pharmazeutische Industrie
PHR — Philippine Historical Review
PhR — Philosophical Review
PHRA — Poverty and Human Resources Abstracts
Ph Rdschau — Philosophische Rundschau
PHRE — Public Health Reports
PHREA — Physiological Reviews
Ph Res — Philosophy and Phenomenological Research
Ph Rev — Philosophical Phenomenological Review
Ph & Rh — Philosophy and Rhetoric
PHRV — Public Health Reviews
PHRVA — Physical Review
PhS — Philologische Studien
PhS — Philosophical Studies
PHS — Public Health Service. Publications
PHS — Schippersweekblad
PHSBB — Physics Bulletin
PHSCA — Philippine Journal of Science
PHSIA — Physiotherapy
PHSNA — Philosophia Naturalis
PHSNB — Physics of Sintering
Ph Soc — Philosophy/Social Theory/Sociology
Ph Soc Glasgow Pr — Philosophical Society of Glasgow. Proceedings
Ph Soc Wash B — Philosophical Society of Washington. Bulletin
PhSR — Philippine Sociological Review
PHSSA — Physica Status Solidi
PhSt — Philosophical Studies
PHSTB — Physica Scripta
PHSWA — Proceedings. Helminthological Society of Washington
PHSYB — Photosynthetica
PHT — Personhistorisk Tidskrift
PHTEA — Physics Teacher
PHTED — Physiology Teacher
PHTOA — Physics Today
PHTTA — Philips Technische Tijdschrift
PHum — Przeglad Humanistyczny
PHUZA — Physik in Unserer Zeit
PhW — Philologische Wochenschrift
PHWEA — Pharmaceutisch Weekblad
PHXQA — Phoenix Quarterly
Phy — Phylon
PHYBA — Phyton (Buenos Aires)
PHYCA — Physics
Phyl — Phylon
PHYMA — Phytomorphology
Phys A — Physica A. Europhysics Journal
PHYSA — Physica (Amsterdam)
Phys Abstr — Physics Abstracts
Phys Acoust — Physical Acoustics. Principles and Methods
Phys Act Rep — Physical Activities Report
Phys Appl — Physics and Applications
Phys Atoms and Molecules — Physics of Atoms and Molecules
Phys B — Physica B. Europhysics Journal. Low Temperature and Solid State Physics
Phys Belustigungen — Physikalische Belustigungen
Phys Ber — Physikalische Berichte
Phys Bl — Physikalische Blaetter
Phys Briefs — Physics Briefs [*West Germany*]
Phys Bull — Physics Bulletin
Phys Bull (Peking) — Physics Bulletin (Peking)
Phys C — Physica C. Europhysics Journal. Atomic, Molecular, and Plasma Physics Optics
Phys Can — Physics in Canada
Phys C Glas — Physics and Chemistry of Glasses
Phys Chem — Physical Chemistry
Phys & Chem — Physics and Chemistry
Phys Chem — Physik und Chemie
Phys-Chem Biol (Chiba) — Physico-Chemical Biology (Chiba)
Phys Chem Centralbl — Physikalisch-Chemisches Centralblatt
Phys Chem Earth — Physics and Chemistry of the Earth
Phys and Chem Earth — Physics and Chemistry of the Earth
Phys Chem Fast React — Physical Chemistry of Fast Reactions
Phys Chem Glasses — Physics and Chemistry of Glasses
Phys and Chem Glasses — Physics and Chemistry of Glasses. Section B. Journal. Society of Glass Technology
Phys Chem Liq — Physics and Chemistry of Liquids
Phys and Chem Liq — Physics and Chemistry of Liquids
Phys Chem Mater Layered Struct — Physics and Chemistry of Materials with Layered Structures
Phys and Chem Miner — Physics and Chemistry of Minerals
Phys Chem Miner — Physics and Chemistry of Minerals
Phys Chem (NY) — Physical Chemistry (New York)
Phys Chem Ser Monogr — Physical Chemistry. Series of Monographs
Phys Chem Solids — Physics and Chemistry of Solids

Phys Chem Space — Physics and Chemistry in Space
Phys Condens Matter — Physics of Condensed Matter
Phys Con Matt — Physics of Condensed Matter
Phys D — Physica D
Phys Daten — Physik Daten [*Physics Data*]
Phys-Diaet Ther — Physikalisch-Diaetetische Therapie [*West Germany*]
Phys Didakt — Physik und Didaktik
Phys Earth Planetary Interiors — Physics of the Earth and Planetary Interiors
Phys Earth Planet Inter — Physics of the Earth and Planetary Interiors
Phys Earth and Planet Inter — Physics of the Earth and Planetary Interiors
Phys Ed — Physical Educator
Phys Ed Bul — Physical Education Bulletin for Teachers in Secondary Schools
Phys Ed J — Physical Education Journal
Phys Ed News — Physical Education News
Phys Educ — Physical Education
Phys Educ — Physical Educator
Phys Educ Newsl — Physical Education Newsletter
Phys Energ Fortis Phys Nucl — Physica Energiae Fortis et Physica Nuclearis [*People's Republic of China*]
Phys Energi Fort Phys Nuclear — Physica Energiae Fortis et Physica Nuclearis [*People's Republic of China*]
Phys Environ Rep Dep Archit Sci Syd Univ — Physical Environment Report. Department of Architectural Science. University of Sydney
Phys E Plan — Physics of the Earth and Planetary Interiors
Phys Failure Electron — Physics of Failure in Electronics
Phys Fenn — Physica Fennica
Phys Fit Newsl — Physical Fitness Newsletter
Phys Fit Res Dig — Physical Fitness Research Digest
Phys Fluids — Physics of Fluids
Phys Fluids Suppl — Physics of Fluids. Supplement
Phys Grundlagen Med Abh Biophys — Physikalische Grundlagen der Medizin. Abhandlungen aus der Biophysik
Physica A — Physica A. Theoretical and Statistical Physics
Physica B — Physica B. Europhysics Journal. Low Temperature and Solid State Physics
Physica C — Physica C. Europhysics Journal. Atomic, Molecular, and Plasma Physics Optics
Physical Educ J — Physical Education Journal
Physica Status Solidi A — Physica Status Solidi. Sectio A
Physica Status Solidi B — Physica Status Solidi. Sectio B
Physician Assist — Physician Assistant [*Later, Physician Assistant/Health Practitioner*]
Physician Assist Health — Physician Assistant/Health Practitioner
Physician Assist Health Pract — Physician Assistant/Health Practitioner
Physician Comput Monthly — Physician Computer Monthly
Physicians Manage — Physicians Management
Physician Sportsmed — Physician and Sports Medicine
Physician and Surg — Physician and Surgeon
Physicochem Hydrodyn — Physicochemical Hydrodynamics [*England*]
Physics & Chem — Physics and Chemistry
Physics Ed — Physics Education
Physics Teach — Physics Teacher
Physikertag Hauptvortr Jahrestag Verb Dtsch Phys Ges — Physikertagung. Hauptvortraege der Jahrestagung des Verbandes Deutscher Physikalischer Gesellschaften
Physikunterr — Physikunterricht
Physiol Behav — Physiology and Behavior
Physiol Biochem Cultiv Plants — Physiology and Biochemistry of Cultivated Plants
Physiol Biochem Cult Plants (USSR) — Physiology and Biochemistry of Cultivated Plants (USSR)
Physiol Bohemoslov — Physiologia Bohemoslovaca
Physiol Can — Physiology Canada
Physiol Chem Phys — Physiological Chemistry and Physics [*Later, Physiological Chemistry and Physics and Medical NMR*]
Physiol Chem Phys Med NMR — Physiological Chemistry and Physics and Medical NMR
Physiol Ecol — Physiology and Ecology
Physiol Ent — Physiological Entomology
Physiol Menschen — Physiologie des Menschen
Physiologia Comp Oecol — Physiologia Comparata et Oecologia
Physiol Pathophysiol Skin — Physiology and Pathophysiology of the Skin
Physiol Pharmacol Physicians — Physiology and Pharmacology for Physicians
Physiol Physicians — Physiology for Physicians
Physiol Plant — Physiologia Plantarum
Physiol Plant Pathol — Physiological Plant Pathology
Physiol Plant Suppl — Physiologia Plantarum. Supplementum
Physiol Psychol — Physiological Psychology
Physiol Rev — Physiological Reviews
Physiol Soc Philadelphia Monogr — Physiological Society of Philadelphia. Monographs
Physiol Teach — Physiology Teacher
Physiol Veg — Physiologie Vegetale
Physiol Zool — Physiological Zoology
Physiother Can — Physiotherapy Canada

Physis - Riv Internaz Storia Sci — Physis. Rivista Internazionale di Storia della Scienza
Physis Secc A Oceanos Org — Physis. Seccion A: Oceanos y Sus Organismos
Physis Secc A Oceanos Sus Org — Physis. Seccion A: Oceanos y Sus Organismos
Physis Secc B Aguas Cont Org — Physis. Seccion B: Aguas Continentales y Sus Organismos
Physis Secc B Aguas Cont Sus Org — Physis. Seccion B: Aguas Continentales y Sus Organismos
Physis Secc C Cont Org Terr — Physis. Seccion C: Continentes y Organismos Terrestres
Phys Kondens Mater — Physik der Kondensierten Materie
Physl Behav — Physiology and Behavior
Physl Bohem — Physiologia Bohemoslovaca
Physl Chem — Physiological Chemistry and Physics [*Later, Physiological Chemistry and Physics and Medical NMR*]
Phys Lett — Physics Letters [*Netherlands*]
Phys Lett A — Physics Letters. A
Phys Lett B — Physics Letters. B
Phys Lett C — Physics Letters. Section C [*Netherlands*]
Phys Letters — Physics Letters
Physl Plant — Physiologia Plantarum
Physl Pl P — Physiological Plant Pathology
Physl Psych — Physiological Psychology
Physl Veget — Physiologie Vegetale
Physl Zool — Physiological Zoology
Phys Med Bi — Physics in Medicine and Biology
Phys Med Biol — Physics in Medicine and Biology
Phys Med and Biol — Physics in Medicine and Biology
Phys Met — Physics of Metals
Phys Methods Chem Anal — Physical Methods in Chemical Analysis
Phys Met Metallogr — Physics of Metals and Metallography
Phys News — Physics News Bulletin. Indian Physics Association
Phys Norv — Physica Norvegica
Phys Norveg — Physica Norvegica
Phys Pap — Physics Papers
Phys Pap Silesian Univ Katowice — Physics Papers. Silesian University in Katowice [*Poland*]
Phys Quantum Electron — Physics of Quantum Electronics
Phys R — Physical Review
Phys Regelm Ber — Physik in Regelmaessigen Berichten
Phys Rep — Physics Reports. Review Section of Physics Letters. Section C [*Netherlands*]
Phys Rep Kumamoto Univ — Physics Reports. Kumamoto University
Phys Rep Phys Lett Sect C — Physics Reports. Physics Letters. Section C
Phys Rev — Physical Review
Phys Rev — Physiological Reviews
Phys Rev A — Physical Review. Section A. General Physics
Phys Rev A 3 — Physical Review. Section A. General Physics. Third Series
Phys Rev A Gen Phys — Physical Review. Section A. General Physics
Phys Rev B 3 — Physical Review. Section B. Condensed Matter. Third Series
Phys Rev B Conden Matt — Physical Review. Section B. Condensed Matter
Phys Rev B Condens Matter — Physical Review. Section B. Condensed Matter
Phys Rev C — Physical Review. Section C. Nuclear Physics
Phys Rev C 3 — Physical Review. Section C. Nuclear Physics. Third Series
Phys Rev D — Physical Review. Section D. Particles and Fields
Phys Rev D 3 — Physical Review. Section D. Particles and Fields. Third Series
Phys Rev L — Physical Review. Letters
Phys Rev Lett — Physical Review. Letters
Phys Rev Sect A — Physical Review. Section A
Phys Rev Sect B — Physical Review. Section B
Phys Rev Suppl — Physical Review. Supplement
Phys Sci Data — Physical Sciences Data [*Amsterdam*]
Phys Scr — Physica Scripta
Phys Scripta — Physica Scripta [*Stockholm*]
Phys Sintering — Physics of Sintering [*Yugoslavia*]
Phys Soc Lond Proc — Physical Society of London. Proceedings
Phys Solariterr — Physica Solariterrestris
Phys Solid Earth (Engl Ed) — Physics of the Solid Earth (English Edition)
Phys Stat Sol A — Physica Status Solidi. Sectio A
Phys Stat Sol B — Physica Status Solidi. Sectio B
Phys Status Solidi — Physica Status Solidi
Phys Status Solidi A — Physica Status Solidi. Sectio A
Phys Status Solidi B — Physica Status Solidi. Sectio B. Basic Research
Phys St S-A — Physica Status Solidi. Sectio A. Applied Research
Phys St S-B — Physica Status Solidi. Sectio B. Basic Research
Phys Teach — Physics Teacher
Phys Tech Biol Res — Physical Techniques in Biological Research
Phys Technol — Physics in Technology
Phys Ther — Physical Therapy
Phys Thin Films — Physics of Thin Films. Advances in Research and Development
Phys Today — Physics Today
Phys Unserer Zeit — Physik in Unserer Zeit
Phys Verh — Physikalische Verhandlungen
Phys Z — Physikalische Zeitschrift [*East Germany*]

Phys Zeit — Physikalische Zeitschrift
Phys Zool — Physiological Zoology
Phys Z Sowjetunion — Physikalische Zeitschrift der Sowjetunion
Phyt — Phytopathology
PHYTA — Phytopathology
PHYTB — Physics in Technology
Phytiat Phytopharm — Phytiatrie-Phytopharmacie
Phytiatr-Phytopharm Rev Fr Med Pharm Veg — Phytiatrie-Phytopharmacie. Revue Francaise de Medicine et de Pharmacie des Vegetaux
Phytochem — Phytochemistry [*Oxford*]
Phytochemistr (Oxf) — Phytochemistry (Oxford)
Phytoma Def Cult — Phytoma. Defense des Cultures [*France*]
Phytomorph — Phytomorphology
Phytomorphol — Phytomorphology
Phyton Ann Rei Bot — Phyton. Annales Rei Botanicae
Phyton Aust — Phyton. Annales Rei Botanicae Austria
Phyton Int J Exp Bot — Phyton. International Journal of Experimental Botany
Phyton Rev Int Bot Exp — Phyton. Revista Internacional de Botanica Experimental
Phytopathol — Phytopathology
Phytopathol Mediterr — Phytopathologie Mediterranea
Phytopathol News — Phytopathology News
Phytopathol Z — Phytopathologische Zeitschrift
Phytopathol ZJ Phytopathol — Phytopathologische Zeitschrift/Journal of Phytopathology
Phytopath Z — Phytopathologische Zeitschrift
Phytoprot — Phytoprotection
Phytotronic Newsl — Phytotronic Newsletter
PHYVA — Physiologie Vegetale
PHYZA — Phytopathologische Zeitschrift
PHZAA — Pharmazeutische Zeitung. Vereinigt mit Apotheker-Zeitung
PHZIA — Pharamazeutische Zeitung
PHZOA — Physiological Zoology
PI — Pagine Istriane
P & I — Parole e le Idee
PI — Peru Indigena
PI — Philosopher's Index
PI — Pilot. Fort Smith and Simpson [*Northwest Territory, Canada*]
PI — Printers' Ink
PIA — Pensions and Investment Age
PIA — Proceedings. Irish Academy
PIAAD — Proceedings. Indian Academy of Sciences. Series. Chemical Sciences
PIACA — Proceedings. Indiana Academy of Science
Piaget Theor Help Prof — Piagetian Theory and the Helping Professions
PIAMD — Proceedings. Indian Academy of Sciences. Series. Mathematical Sciences
PIAND — Proceedings. Indian Academy of Sciences. Series. Animal Sciences
Piano Q — Piano Quarterly
Piano Quart — Piano Quarterly
Piano Tech — Piano Technician
P I A Sci A — Proceedings. Indian Academy of Sciences. Section A
P I A Sci B — Proceedings. Indian Academy of Sciences. Section B
PIASH — Proceedings. Israel Academy of Sciences and Humanities [*Jerusalem*]
PIB — Public Information Bulletin [*Australian Taxation Office*]
PIB — Publishing Information Bulletin
PIBSB — Proceedings. Indian National Science Academy. Part B. Biological Sciences
PIC — Perspectives in Computing
PIC — Physical Inorganic Chemistry [*Elsevier Book Series*]
PICAM — Proceedings. International Congress of Americanists
Picardie Inform — Picardie Information
PICED — Proceedings. International Conference on Noise Control Engineering
PICI — Publications. Institut de Civilisation Indienne
P I Civ E 1 — Proceedings. Institution of Civil Engineers. Part 1. Design and Construction
P I Civ E 2 — Proceedings. Institution of Civil Engineers. Part 2. Research and Theory
Picker Clin Scintil — Picker Clinical Scintillator
Pickle Pak Sci — Pickle Pak Science
PICL — Proceedings. International Congress of Linguists
PICO — International Congress of Orientalists. Proceedings
PICO — Proceedings. International Congress of Orientalists
PICP — Proceedings. International Congress of Philosophy
PICPS — Proceedings. International Congress of Phonetic Sciences
PictR — Pictorial Review
PId — Parole e le Idee
PIEEA — Proceedings. Institution of Electrical Engineers
P IEEE — Proceedings. Institute of Electrical and Electronics Engineers
P IEE (Lond) — Proceedings. Institution of Electrical Engineers (London)
Pieleg Polozna — Pielegniarka i Polozna
Pienpuu Toimikun Julk — Pienpuualan Toimikunnan Julkaisu
PIESD — Proceedings. Indian Academy of Sciences. Series. Earth and Planetary Sciences

PIEWD — Prace Naukowe Instytutu Energoelektryki Politechniki Wroclawskiej
PIF — Paris et Ile-De-France. Memoires
P & IF — Paris et Ile-De-France. Memoires
PIFAO — Publications. Institut Francais d'Archeologie Orientale du Caire
PIFAO BEC — Publications. Institut Francais d'Archeologie Orientale. Bibliotheque d'Etudes Coptes
PIFAS — Publicaciones. Instituto de Filologia. Anejo de Sphinx
PIFLD — Problemy Yadernoi Fiziki i Kosmicheskikh Luchei
PIFMLL — Proceedings. International Federation for Modern Languages and Literatures
PIFWD — Prace Naukowe Instytutu Fizyki Politechniki Wroclawskiej
Pig — Pig Iron
PIG — Pork Industry Gazette
PIGBA — Proceedings. Royal Institution of Great Britain
Pigm Cell — Pigment Cell
Pigment Resin Tech — Pigment and Resin Technology
Pigment Resin Technol — Pigment and Resin Technology
Pig News Inf — Pig News and Information
PIGWA — Prace Instytutu Gospodarki Wodnej
PIHANS — Publications. Institut Historique et Archeologique Neerlandais de Stamboul [*Leiden*]
PIHUA — Prace Instytutow Hutniczych
PIIAA — Proceedings. National Institute of Sciences (India). Part A. Physical Sciences
PIKM — PIK. Northern Magazine for Children [*Northwest Territory, Canada*]
PIL — Papers in Linguistics
PILOA — Prace Instytutu Lotnictwa
PILSA — Progress in Immunobiological Standardization
PIM — Pacific Islands Monthly
PIM — Politica Internacional (Madrid)
PIM — Progress in Industrial Microbiology [*Elsevier Book Series*]
PIMA Mag — PIMA [*Paper Industry Management Association*] Magazine [*United States*]
PIMA Yrb — PIMA [*Paper Industry Management Association*] Yearbook
PIMBel — Pracy Instytuta Movaznaustva Akademii Nauk Belaruskaj SSR
PIME — Petrofi Irodalmi Muzeum Evkonyve
PIMGA — Production and Inventory Management
PIMRA — Progress in Industrial Microbiology
PIMSST — Pontifical Institute of Mediaeval Studies. Studies and Texts
PIMST — Pontifical Institute of Mediaeval Studies. Studies and Texts
PIMTB — Proceedings. Annual Technical Meeting. International Metallographic Society, Inc.
Pi Mu Epsilon J — Pi Mu Epsilon Journal
PIN — Policy Review
PIN — Public Interest
Pineal Res Rev — Pineal Research Reviews
Pineapple Q — Pineapple Quarterly
PINEDV — Annual Research Reviews. Pineal
Pine Inst Am Abstr Chem Sect — Pine Institute of America. Abstracts. Chemical Section
Pine Inst Am Tech Bull — Pine Institute of America. Technical Bulletin
PINHA3 — Iraq Natural History Museum. Publication
Pint Acabados Ind — Pinturas y Acabados Industriales
PIOCA — Progress in Inorganic Chemistry
Pioneering Concepts Mod Sci — Pioneering Concepts in Modern Science
Pioneers' Assoc of SA Pubs — Pioneers' Association of South Australia. Publications
PIP — Penny Illustrated Paper
PIP — Product Improvement Program
PIPE — Pipeline. Report of the Northern Pipeline Agency
Pipeline Eng — Pipeline Engineer
Pipeline Gas J — Pipeline and Gas Journal
Pipeline & Gas J — Pipeline and Gas Journal
Pipe Line Ind — Pipe Line Industry
Pipeline Manage Oper Eng Gas Distrib News — Pipeline Management, Operations, Engineering, and Gas Distribution News
Pipeline Underground Util Constr — Pipeline and Underground Utilities Construction
Pipeln Ind — International Pipe Line Industry
Pipes & Pipelines Int — Pipes and Pipelines International
Pipes Pipelines Int — Pipes and Pipelines International
Piping Eng — Piping Engineering
Piping Process Mach (Tokyo) — Piping and Process Machinery (Tokyo)
PIPLD — Proceedings. Indian Academy of Sciences. Series. Plant Sciences
PIPSD — Preprint. Institut Prikladnoi Matematiki Akademii Nauk SSSR
PIPWA — Paper Industry and Paper World
PIQUA — Pit and Quarry
PiR — Pecat' i Revoljucija
PIR — Prosopographia Imperii Romani
PIRED — Power Industry Research
PIRS — Perspectives in Religious Studies
PiS — Puskin i Ego Sovremenniki
PISAA7 — Indian Academy of Sciences. Proceedings. Section A

PISAD — Proceedings. International Symposium on Automotive Technology and Automation

PISBAA — Indian Academy of Sciences. Proceedings. Section B

Pishch Prom Kaz — Pishchevaya Promyshlennost Kazakhstana

Pishch Promst Kaz Mezhved Resp Nauchno Tekh Sb — Pishchevaya Promyshlennost Kazakhstana Mezhvedomstvennyi Respublikanskii Nauchno Tekhnicheskii Sbornik

Pishch Prom-st (Kiev 1965) — Pishchevaya Promyshlennost (Kiev, 1965)

Pishch Promst (Moscow) — Pishchevaya Promyshlennost (Moscow)

Pishch Prom-st' Nauchno-Proizvod Sb — Pishchevaya Promyshlennost' Nauchno-Proizvodstvennyi Sbornik

Pishch Promst Ser 6 Obz Inf — Pishchevaya Promyshlennost. Seriya 6. Maslo-Zhirovaya Promyshlennost. Obzornaya Informatsiya

Pishch Promst Ser 20 Obz Inf — Pishchevaya Promyshlennost. Seriya 20. Maslo-Zhirovaya Promyshlennost. Obzornaya Informatsiya

Pishch Promst SSSR — Pishchevaya Promyshlennost SSSR

Pis'ma Astron Zh — Pis'ma v Astronomicheskii Zhurnal

Pis'ma v Astron Zh — Pis'ma v Astronomicheskii Zhurnal

Pis'ma Zh Ehksp Teor Fiz — Pis'ma v Zhurnal Ehksperimental'noi i Teoreticheskoi Fiziki

Pis'ma v Zh Eksp i Teor Fiz — Pis'ma v Zhurnal Eksperimental'noi i Teoreticheskoi Fiziki

Pis'ma Zh Eksp Teor Fiz — Pis'ma v Zhurnal Eksperimental'noi i Teoreticheskoi Fiziki

Pis'ma v Zh Tekh Fiz — Pis'ma v Zhurnal Tekhnicheskoi Fiziki

Pis'ma Zh Tekh Fiz — Pis'ma v Zhurnal Tekhnicheskoi Fiziki

Pism Pam Vostoka — Pis'mennye Pamiatniki Vostoka

Pitanie Udobr Rast — Pitanie i Udobrenie Rastenii

PITBB — Piano Teachers Journal

Pitblado Lect — Isaac Pitblado Lectures on Continuing Legal Education

PITKA — Proceedings. Institut Teknologi Bandung. Supplement

Pit L — University of Pittsburgh. Law Review

Pit & Quar — Pit and Quarry

Pit Quarry — Pit and Quarry

Pitt Rivers Mus Univ Oxford Occas Pap Technol — Pitt Rivers Museum. University of Oxford. Occasional Papers on Technology

Pittsbg Bs — Pittsburgh Business Review

Pittsburgh Bus R — Pittsburgh Business Review

Pittsburgh Sch — Pittsburgh Schools

Pittsburgh Univ Bull — Pittsburgh University. Bulletin

Pittsburgh Univ Sch Ed J — Pittsburgh University. School of Education Journal

Pitts L Rev — University of Pittsburgh. Law Review

Pitt Sym — Pittsburgh Symphony Orchestra. Program Notes

Pitture Vern — Pitture e Vernici

PivS — Pivnicne Sjajvo

PIW — Petroleum Intelligence Weekly

PIW — Polski Instytut Wydawniczy

PIWCA — Proceedings. International Waste Conference

PIWSD — Proceedings. International Wire and Cable Symposium

PJ — ICC [*Interstate Commerce Commission*] Practitioners' Journal

PJ — Palastinajahrbuch. Deutsches Evangelische Institut fuer Altertumswissenschaft des Heiligen Landes zu Jerusalem [*Berlin*]

PJ — Personnel Journal

PJ — Pharmaceutical Journal

PJ — Philosophisches Jahrbuch

PJ — Poradnik Jezykowy

PJ — Preussische Jahrbuecher

PJ — Privacy Journal

PJ — Prudhoe Bay Journal

PJa — Papers on Japan

PJACA — Proceedings. Japan Academy

PJAIA — Philippine Journal of Animal Industry

P Jap Acad — Proceedings. Japan Academy

PJB — Palastinajahrbuch. Deutsches Evangelische Institut fuer Altertumswissenschaft des Heiligen Landes zu Jerusalem [*Berlin*]

PJb — Preussische Jahrbuecher

PJBSA — Pavlovian Journal of Biological Science

PJE — Peabody Journal of Education

PJez — Prace Jezykoznawcze Polskiej Akademii Nauk

PJGG — Philosophisches Jahrbuch der Gorres-Gesellschaft

PJJ — Provincial Judges Journal

PJL — Philippine Journal of Linguistics

PJLT — Philippine Journal of Language Teaching

PJN — Philippine Journal of Nursing

PJNu — Philippine Journal of Nutrition

PJOPA — Pakistan Journal of Psychology

PJP — Philippine Journal of Pediatrics

PJPA — Philippine Journal of Public Administration

PJPI — Philippine Journal of Plant Industry

PJRCM — Philippine Junior Red Cross Magazine

PJS — Philippine Journal of Science

PJSRA — Pakistan Journal of Scientific Research

PJSS — Philippine Journal of Surgical Specialties

PK — Philologike Kypros

PK — Pinkas ha-Kehilot [*Encyclopedia of Jewish Communities*]

PK — Prawo Kanoniczne

PK — Problemy Kibernetiki

PK — Przeglad Klasyczny

PK — Przeglad Koscielny

PKC — Beijing Review

PKCVA — Promyshlennost Khimicheskikh Reaktivov i Osobo Chistykh Veshchestv

PKDR-B — Pakistan Development Review

PKE — Pakistan and Gulf Economist

Pkg Abstr — Packaging Abstracts

Pkg Eng — Package Engineering

Pkg (India) — Packaging (India)

Pkg (London) — Packaging (London)

Pkg News — Packaging News

Pkg Technol — Packaging Technology and Management

PKH — Publikatieblad van de Europese Gemeenschappen. Handelingen van het Europese Parlement

PKIKA — Praxis der Kinderpsychologie und Kinderpsychiatrie

PKJ — Pitanja Knjizevnosti a Jezika

PKMKA — Prikladnaya Mekhanika

PKO — Parfuemerie und Kosmetik. Internationale Zeitschrift fuer Wissenschaftliche und Technische Grundlagen der Parfuem- und Kosmetika Industrie

PKOM — Publicationen. Kaiserlich Osmanische Museen [*Constantinople*]

PKOMA — Physik der Kondensierten Materie

P Kon Ned A — Proceedings. Koninklijke Nederlandse Akademie van Wetenschappen. Series A. Mathematical Sciences

P Kon Ned B — Proceedings. Koninklijke Nederlandse Akademie van Wetenschappen. Series B. Physical Sciences

P Kon Ned C — Proceedings. Koninklijke Nederlandse Akademie van Wetenschappen. Series C. Biological and Medical Sciences

PKS — Publikatieblad van de Europese Gemeenschappen. Serie C. Mededelingen en Bekendmakingen

PKS — Publikatieblad van de Europese Gemeenschappen. Supplement

Pks & Rec — Parks and Recreation

PKTDA — Prace Komisji Technologii Drewna. Poznanskie Towarzystwo Przyjaciol Nauk

PKVJA — PKV [*Punjabrao Krishi Vidyapeeth*] Research Journal

PKVOA — Produktivnost

PKV Res J — PKV [*Punjabrao Krishi Vidyapeeth*] Research Journal

PKy — Pneumatike Kypros

PKZZD — Problemy Kontrolya i Zashchita Atmosfery ot Zagryazneniya

PL — Palaeographia Latina

PL — Pamietnik Literacki

PL — Papers in Linguistics

PL — Patrologia Latina

P and L — Philosophy and Literature

PL — Poet Lore

P & L — Politics and Letters

PL — Programming Languages Series [*Elsevier Book Series*]

PLAB — Philadelphia Library Association. Bulletin

PLAB — Philippine Library Association. Bulletin

PLA Bull — PLA [*Pennsylvania Library Association*] Bulletin

Plain Ra — Plain Rapper

Plains Anthropol — Plains Anthropologist

PLAKA — Planovoe Khozyaistvo

PLAN — Polska Ludowa Akcja Niepodleglosci

PLANA — Planta

Plan Can — Plan Canada

Planen Pruef Investieren PPI — Planen-Pruefen-Investieren. PPI [*West Germany*]

Planet Assoc Clean Energy Newsl — Planetary Association for Clean Energy. Newsletter [*Canada*]

Planet Spac — Planetary and Space Science

Planet Space Sci — Planetary and Space Science

Plan Higher Educ — Planning for Higher Education

Plan Hospod — Planovane Hospodarstvi

Plan Hoz — Planovoe Hozjajstvo

Planif Habitat Inform — Planification, Habitat, Information

Plan Inovtn — Planned Innovation

Plan Khoz — Planovoe Khozyaistvo

Plann Admin — Planning and Administration

Plann Build Dev — Planning and Building Developments

Planned Innov — Planned Innovation [*England*]

Planning and Adm — Planning and Administration

Planning Bul — Planning Bulletin

Planning Develop Netherl — Planning and Development in the Netherlands

Planning History Bull — Planning History Bulletin

Plann News — Planning News

Plan Pam Nat Plann Ass — Planning Pamphlets. National Planning Association

Plan Rev — Planning Review

Planseeber Pulvermet — Planseeberichte fuer Pulvermetallurgie

Plant — Plant Maintenance and Engineering

Planta Med — Planta Medica

Plant Bibliogr — Plant Bibliography

Plant Biochem J — Plant Biochemical Journal
Plant Breed Abstr — Plant Breeding Abstracts
Plant Breed Rev — Plant Breeding Reviews
Plant Bull Rubber Res Inst Malays — Planters' Bulletin. Rubber Research Institute of Malaysia
Plant Cell Physiol — Plant and Cell Physiology
Plant Cell Physiol (Kyoto) — Plant and Cell Physiology (Kyoto)
Plant Cell Physiol (Tokyo) — Plant and Cell Physiology (Tokyo)
Plant Cel P — Plant and Cell Physiology
Plant Cultiv Repub Argent Inst Bot Agric (B Aires) — Plantas Cultivadas en la Republica Argentina. Instituto de Botanica Agricola (Buenos Aires)
Plant Dis Leafl Dept Agr Biol Br (NSW) — Plant Disease Leaflet. Department of Agriculture. Biological Branch (New South Wales)
Plant Dis R — Plant Disease Reporter
Plant Dis Rep — Plant Disease Reporter
Plant Dis Rep Suppl — Plant Disease Reporter. Supplement
Plant Energy Manage — Plant Energy Management
Plant Eng — Plant Engineer
Plant Eng — Plant Engineering
Plant & Eng Applications — Plant and Engineering Applications
Plant Eng (Lond) — Plant Engineer (London)
Plant Engng — Plant Engineering
Plant Engng & Maint — Plant Engineering and Maintenance
Plant Eng (Tokyo) — Plant Engineer (Tokyo)
Planter — Planter and Sugar Manufacturer
Plant Field Lab Mimeo Rep Fla Univ — Plantation Field Laboratory Mimeo Report. Florida University
Plant Food Rev — Plant Food Review
Plant Foods Hum Nutr — Plant Foods for Human Nutrition
Plant Gard — Plants and Gardens
Pl Anth — Plains Anthropologist
Plant Ind Dig (Manila) — Plant Industry Digest (Manila)
Plant Ind Ser Chin-Amer Joint Comm Rural Reconstr — Plant Industry Series. Chinese-American Joint Commission on Rural Reconstruction
Plant Ind Ser J Comm Rural Reconstr China (US Repub China) — Plant Industry Series. Joint Commission on Rural Reconstruction in China (United States and Republic of China)
Plant Maint — Plant Maintenance
Plant Maint Import Substitution — Plant Maintenance and Import Substitution
Plant Manage Eng — Plant Management and Engineering
Plant Med Phytother — Plantes Medicinales et Phytotherapie
Plant Operations Prog — Plant/Operations Progress
Plant Oper Manage — Plant Operating Management
Plant Path — Plant Pathology [*London*]
Plant Pathol — Plant Pathology
Plant Pathol (Lond) — Plant Pathology (London)
Plant Physiol — Plant Physiology
Plant Physiol (Bethesda) — Plant Physiology (Bethesda)
Plant Physiol Commun (Shanghai) — Plant Physiology Communications (Shanghai)
Plant Physiol Suppl — Plant Physiology. Supplement
Plant Physl — Plant Physiology
Plant & Power Services Eng — Plant and Power Services Engineer
Plant Propagat — Plant Propagator
Plant Prot — Plant Protection
Plant Prot Bull — Plant Protection Bulletin
Plant Prot Bull (Ankara) — Plant Protection Bulletin (Ankara)
Plant Prot Bull (New Delhi) — Plant Protection Bulletin (New Delhi)
Plant Sci Bull — Plant Science Bulletin
Plant Sci L — Plant Science Letters
Plant Sci Lett — Plant Science Letters
Plant Sci (Lucknow) — Plant Science (Lucknow)
Plant Sci (Lucknow India) — Plant Science (Lucknow, India)
Plant Sci (Sofia) — Plant Science (Sofia)
Plants Gard — Plants and Gardens
Plant Sys E — Plant Systematics and Evolution
Plant Syst Evol — Plant Systematics and Evolution
PLARA — Plastverarbeiter
Plas Desgn — Plastics Design Forum
Plas Eng — Plastics Engineering
Plas Ind Eur — Plastics Industry Europe
Plasma Phys — Plasma Physics
Plasma Phys Contr Nucl Fusion Res Conf Proc — Plasma Physics and Controlled Nuclear Fusion Research. Conference Proceedings
Plasma Phys Controlled Fusion — Plasma Physics and Controlled Fusion
Plasma Phys Index — Plasma Physics Index [*West Germany*]
Plas Massy — Plasticheskie Massy
Plas R Surg — Plastic and Reconstructive Surgery
Plas Rubbers Text — Plastics, Rubbers, Textiles
Plas Rub Int — Plastics and Rubber International
Plas Rubr — Plastics and Rubber Weekly
Plast Abstr — Plastic Abstracts
Plast Age — Plastics Age
Plast Aust — Plastics in Australia
Plast Bldg Constr — Plastics in Building Construction
Plast Build Constr — Plastics in Building Construction

Plast Bull (London) — Plastics Bulletin (London)
Plast Busin — Plastics Business
Plast Compd — Plastics Compounding
Plast Compounding — Plastics Compounding
Plast Des Process — Plastics Design and Processing
Plast Dig — Plastics Digest
PLASTEC Note — PLASTEC [*Plastics Technical Evaluation Center*] Note
PLASTEC Rep — PLASTEC [*Plastics Technical Evaluation Center*] Report
Plaste u Kaut — Plaste und Kautschuk
Plaste Kaut — Plaste und Kautschuk
Plast Eng — Plastics Engineering
Plast Engng — Plastics Engineering
Plast Flash — Plastiques Flash
Plast Hmoty Kauc — Plasticke Hmoty a Kaucuk
Plastiche — Materie Plastiche ed Elastomeri
Plastic IN — Plastics Industry News
Plastico — Noticiero del Plastico
Plastic Prod — Plastic Products
Plastics in Aust — Plastics in Australia
Plastics Engng — Plastics Engineering
Plast Ind — Plastic Industry [*India*]
Plast Ind News — Plastics Industry News
Plast Ind News (Jap) — Plastics Industry News (Japan)
Plast Ind (NY) — Plastics Industry (New York)
Plast Ind (Paris) — Plastiques et Industrie (Paris)
Plast Inst Trans — Plastics Institute. Transactions
Plast Inst Trans J — Plastics Institute. Transactions and Journal
Plast Inst Trans J Conf Suppl — Plastics Institute. Transactions and Journal. Conference Supplement
Plast Kauc — Plasty a Kaucuk
Plast Massen Wiss Tech — Plastische Massen in Wissenschaft und Technik
Plast Massy — Plasticheskie Massy
Plast Mater (Tokyo) — Plastics Materials (Tokyo)
Plast M & E — Plastics Machinery and Equipment
Plast Mod — Plasticos Modernos
Plast Mod Elast — Plastiques Modernes et Elastomeres
Plast Mod Elastomeres — Plastiques Modernes et Elastomeres
Plast Molded Prod — Plastics and Molded Products
Plast News — Plastics News
Plast News (Aust) — Plastics News (Australia)
Plast News Briefs — Plastics News. Briefs
Plast Paint Rubber — Plastics, Paint, and Rubber
Plast Panorama — Plast Panorama Scandinavia
Plast and Polym — Plastics and Polymers
Plast Polym — Plastics and Polymers
Plast Polym Conf Suppl — Plastics and Polymers. Conference Supplement
Plast Prod — Plastic Products
Plast Prog India — Plastics Progress in India
Plast Reconstr Surg — Plastic and Reconstructive Surgery
Plast Reconstr Surg Transplant Bull — Plastic and Reconstructive Surgery and the Transplantation Bulletin
Plast Renf Fibres Verre Text — Plastiques Renforces Fibres de Verre Textile
Plast Resinas — Plasticos y Resinas [*Mexico*]
Plast Resins — Plastics and Resins
Plast Retail Packag Bull — Plastics in Retail Packaging Bulletin
Plast em Rev — Plasticos em Revista
Plast Rubber — Plastics and Rubber [*Later, Plastics and Rubber International*]
Plast and Rubber — Plastics and Rubber [*Later, Plastics and Rubber International*]
Plast and Rubber Int — Plastics and Rubber International
Plast Rubber Int — Plastics and Rubber International
Plast Rubber Mater Appl — Plastics and Rubber. Material and Applications
Plast Rubber News — Plastics and Rubber News [*South Africa*]
Plast Rubber Proc Appl — Plastics and Rubber Processing and Applications
Plast Rubber Process — Plastics and Rubber Processing and Applications
Plast & Rubber Process & Appl — Plastics and Rubber Processing and Applications
Plast Rubbers Text — Plastics, Rubbers, Textiles
Plast Rubber Wkly — Plastics and Rubber Weekly [*England*]
Plast Rubb Int — Plastics and Rubber International
Plast Rubb News — Plastics and Rubber News [*South Africa*]
Plast Rubb Process Appln — Plastics and Rubber Processing and Applications
Plast Rub Wkly — Plastics and Rubber Weekly
Plast (S Afr) — Plastics (Southern Africa)
Plast (S Africa) — Plastics (Southern Africa)
Plast (Sthn Afr) — Plastics (Southern Africa)
Plast Surg Nurs — Plastic Surgical Nursing
Plast Technol — Plastics Technology
Plast Today — Plastics Today
Plast Trends — Plastics Trends
Plast Univers — Plasticos Universales
Plast World — Plastics World
PLATA — Plating
Plateau Q Mus North Ariz — Plateau. Quarterly of the Museum of Northern Arizona

Plating & Surface Finish — Plating and Surface Finishing
Platinum Met Rev — Platinum Metals Review
Platoon Sch — Platoon School
Plat and Surf Finish — Plating and Surface Finishing
Plat Surf Finish — Plating and Surface Finishing
PLAWA — Plastics World
PLAY — [The] Playgoer
Playb — Playboy
Players Mag — Players Magazine
Playmate — Children's Playmate Magazine
PLB — Papyrologica Lugduno-Batava
Pl Biochem J — Plant Biochemical Journal
Pl Breed Abstr — Plant Breeding Abstracts
PLBYD — Plan og Bygg
PLC — Princeton University Library Chronicle
PLCHB — Physiological Chemistry and Physics [Later, Physiological
    Chemistry and Physics and Medical NMR]
PLCM & ND — Proceedings. Linguistic Circle of Manitoba and North
    Dakota
PLCN-A — Plan Canada
PLCNY — Publications. Linguistic Circle of New York
PLCPB — Plant and Cell Physiology
PLCS — Proceedings. London Classical Society
PLD — Public Libraries Division. Reporter
PLDRA — Plant Disease Reporter
PLEGA — Plant Engineering
PLEGB — Plastics Engineering
PLENA — Plant Engineering
PLEND — Plumbing Engineer
PLF — Public Administration
Plf Adv — Plaintiff's Advocate
PLFS — Polarforschung
PLG — Plant Management and Engineering
PLG — Probleme de Lingvistica Genarala
PLGAA — Plants and Gardens
PLGFA — Poligrafiya
PLGJA — Pipeline and Gas Journal
PLHID — Plant Hire
PLHJA — Plumbing and Heating Journal
PLINA — Pipe Line Industry
Pling — Papers in Linguistics
PLJ — Philippine Library Journal
PLKAA — Plaste und Kautschuk
PLL — Papers on Language and Literature
PLLAA — Royal Society. Proceedings. Series A. Mathematical and Physical
    Sciences
PLLP — Polish Literature/Litterature Polonaise
PLLSA — Plzensky Lekarsky Sbornik
PLM — Papers in Linguistics of Melanesia
PLMEA — Planta Medica
PLMSA — Plasticheskie Massy
Pln Dealr — Cleveland Plain Dealer
PLNN-A — Plan
PLNSW Staff News — Public Library of New South Wales. Staff News
PLO — Pensiero e Linguaggio in Operazioni/Thought and Language in
    Operations
Plodorodie Pochv Karelii Akad Nauk SSSR Karel'sk Filial — Plodorodie Pochv
    Karelii. Akademiya Nauk SSSR. Karel'skii Filial
Pl Lond Math — Proceedings. London Mathematical Society
PLOP — Policy Options/Options Politiques
Ploughs — Ploughshares
Plovdiv Univ Naucn Trud — Plovdivski Universitet. Naucni Trudove
Pl Path — Plant Pathology
PLPHA — Plant Physiology
PLPHB — Plasma Physics
Pl Physics — Plasma Physics
Pl Physiol (Lancaster) — Plant Physiology (Lancaster)
Pl Physiol (Wash) — Plant Physiology (Washington)
PLPLS — Proceedings. Leeds Philosophical and Literary Society
PLPLS-LHS — Proceedings. Leeds Philosophical and Literary Society.
    Literary and Historical Section
PLPLS-SS — Proceedings. Leeds Philosophical and Literary Society.
    Scientific Section
Pl Prot (Tokyo) — Plant Protection (Tokyo)
PLPSA — Physiological Psychology
PLPUA — Planseeberichte fuer Pulvermetallurgie (Austria)
PLR — Palestine Law Reports
PLR — Plan. Zeitschrift fuer Planen, Bauen, und Umwelt
PLR — Planning Review
PLR — University of Pittsburgh. Law Review
PLRCA — Pharmacological Research Communications
PLRSA — Plasticos y Resinas
Plrs' Bull Rubb Res Inst Malaya — Planters' Bulletin. Rubber Research
    Institute of Malaya
PLSCB — Policy Sciences
Pls Gds — Plants and Gardens

PLSOA — Plant and Soil
PLSSA — Planetary and Space Science
PLT — Progress in Low Temperature Physics [Elsevier Book Series]
PLTEA — Plastics Technology
PLTPA — Progress in Low Temperature Physics
PLTVA — Plastvaerlden
Plucne Bolesti Tuberk — Plucne Bolesti i Tuberkuloza
Plucne Boles Tuberk — Plucne Bolesti i Tuberkuloza
PLUDA — Plutonium-Dokumentation
Plumb Heat J — Plumbing and Heating Journal
Plumbing Eng — Plumbing Engineer
Plumbing Engr — Plumbing Engineer
Plumbing Heat Equip News — Plumbing and Heating Equipment News
Plural Soc — Plural Societies [The Hague]
PLUTA — Pollution
Plutonium-Dok — Plutonium-Dokumentation [West Germany]
PLVDA — Progress in Liver Diseases
PLYGA — Psychologia: An International Journal of Psychology in the Orient
PLYHD — Polyhedron
Plyn Voda Zdra Tech — Plyn Voda a Zdravotni Technika
Plyw Plyw Prod — Plywood and Plywood Products
Plyw and Plyw Prod — Plywood and Plywood Products
PLZ — Plastics World
Plzen Lek Sb — Plzensky Lekarsky Sbornik
Plzen Lek Sb Suppl — Plzensky Lekarsky Sbornik. Supplementum
PM — International Journal of Psychiatry in Medicine
PM — Palace of Minos
PM — Paleographie Musicale
PM — Paper Maker
PM — Paper Money
P M — Paris Match
PM — Parole et Mission
PM — Petermanns Geographische Mitteilungen
PM — Peuples Mediterraneens
PM — Philippine Manager
PM — Placer Mining Times [Whitehorse]
PM — PM. Pharmacy Management
PM — Popular Mechanics
PM — Post Magazine and Insurance Monitor
PM — Pravna Misul
PM — Presse Medicale
PM — Process Metallurgy [Elsevier Book Series]
PM — Province du Maine
PM — Public Management
PMA — Personnel Management Abstracts
P M A — Proceedings. Musical Association
PMA — Publications. Mediaeval Academy
PMAHD3 — Annual Research Reviews. Peripheral Metabolism and Action of
    Thyroid Hormones
PMaine — Province du Maine
PMAI News Lett — PMAI [Powder Metallurgy Association of India] News
    Letter
PMAMA — Prikladnaya Matematika i Mekhanika
PMA News — PMA [Pharmaceutical Manufacturers Association] Newsletter
PMASAL — Publications. Michigan Academy of Science, Arts, and Letters
PMB — Polish Maritime News
PMBAA — Publications. Institut Royal Meteorologique de Belgique. Serie A
    ue
PMC — Pollution Engineering
PMC — Progress in Medicinal Chemistry [Elsevier Book Series]
PMCL — Periodica de Re Morali Canonica Liturgica
PMDA — Peace Messenger. Diocese of Athabasca. Peace River
PMDCA — Progress in Medicinal Chemistry
PME — Prace i Materialy Etnograficzne
PMELA — Plastiques Modernes et Elastomeres
PMF — Paint and Resin News
PMFAA — Pokroky Matematiky, Fyziky, a Astronomie
PMHB — Pennsylvania Magazine of History and Biography
PMHBA — Polish Medical Science and History Bulletin
PMHS — Proceedings. Massachusetts Historical Society
PMI — Photo Methods for Industry
PMICA — Proceedings. Institute of Medicine of Chicago
PM Iowa State Univ Sci Technol Coop Ext Serv — PM. Iowa State University
    of Science and Technology. Cooperative Extension Service
PMLA — Proceedings of the Modern Language Association
PMLA — Publications. Modern Language Association of America [Database]
PMLAAm — Publications. Modern Language Association of America
PMM — Pall Mall Magazine
PMMA — Publications. Metropolitan Museum of Art. Egyptian Expedition
    [New York]
PMMEA — Prensa Medica Mexicana
PMMF — Presbyterian Medical Mission Fund
PMMLA — Papers. Midwest Modern Language Association
PMNWA — Pressemitteilung Nordrhein-Westfalen
PMOGA — Progress in Medical Genetics
PMOJ — Pesticides Monitoring Journal

PMOSA — Perceptual and Motor Skills
PMPA — Publications. Missouri Philological Association
PMR — Philippine Mining Record
PMR — Proceedings. Patristic, Mediaeval, and Renaissance Conference
PMR — Progress in Mutation Research [*Elsevier Book Series*]
PMRGA — Prace Morski Instytut Rybacki w Gdyni
PMRS — Progress of Medieval and Renaissance Studies in the United States and Canada
PMS — Perceptual and Motor Skills
PMS — Popular Music and Society
PMSCD — Proceedings. Microscopical Society of Canada
PMSS — Progress in Mathematical and Social Sciences [*Elsevier Book Series*]
PMSTA — Promyshlennoe Stroitel'stvo
PMTF Zh Prikl Mekh Tekh Fiz — PMTF. Zhurnal Prikladnoi Mekhaniki Tekhnickeskio Fiziki
PMU — Progress in Medical Ultrasound [*Elsevier Book Series*]
PMVIA — Progress in Medical Virology
PN — Percussive Notes
PN — Poe Newsletter
PN — Poesia Nuova
PN — Poetry Northwest
PN — Portsmouth News [*United Kingdom*]
Pn — Poznan
PN — Pro Nervia
PNAS — Proceedings. National Academy of Sciences
P NAS (Ind) A — Proceedings. National Academy of Sciences (India). Section A. Physical Sciences
P NAS (Ind) B — Proceedings. National Academy of Sciences (India). Section B. Biological Sciences
P NAS US — Proceedings. National Academy of Sciences. United States of America
PNC — Personal Names from Cuneiform Inscriptions of Cappadocia
PNCCA — Proceedings. National Cancer Conference [*United States*]
PNCH — Proceedings. National Conference on Health Education Goals
PNCTD — Proceedings. National Conference on Power Transmission
PNEC — Proceedings. National Electronics Conference
PNECA — Proceedings. National Electronics Conference [*United States*]
PNEND — Progress in Nuclear Energy
Pneum Dig & Druckluft Prax — Pneumatic Digest and Druckluft Praxis
Pneumolog Hung — Pneumologia Hungarica [*Hungary*]
Pneumol/Pneumol — Pneumonologie/Pneumonology
Pneumonol-P — Pneumonologie/Pneumonology
Pneumonol Pol — Pneumonologia Polska
PNGL — Papers in New Guinea Linguistics
P & NGLR — Papua and New Guinea Law Reports
PNGUA8 — Forest Research Institute [*Bogor*]. Communication
PNHYD — Perspectives in Nephrology and Hypertension
PNI — Publications. Netherlands Institute of Archaeology and Arabic Studies [*Cairo*]
PNIIA — Prace Naukowe Instytutu Inzynierii Ochrony Srodowiska Politechniki Wroclawskiej
PNJHS — Proceedings. New Jersey Historical Society
PNL — Przewodnik Naukowy i Literacki
PNLA Q — Pacific Northwest Library Association. Quarterly
PNM — Perspectives of New Music
Pnm — Phantom
PNMBA — Progress in Nucleic Acid Research and Molecular Biology
PNMPA — Psychiatrie, Neurologie, und Medizinische Psychologie
PNMRA — Progress in Nuclear Magnetic Resonance Spectroscopy
PNMUB — Perspectives of New Music
PNMUD — PNM Update
PNotes — Pynchon Notes
PNOU-A — Planning Outlook
PNPRA — Progress in Nuclear Energy. Series 3
PNPSA — Progress in Neurology and Psychiatry
PNPSD — Prace Naukowe Politechniki Szczecinskiej
PNQ — Pacific Northwest Quarterly
PNSFA — Proceedings. National Shellfisheries Association [*United States*]
PNTEA — Progress in Nuclear Energy. Series 4
PNUED — Preprint. Akademiya Nauk Ukrainskoi SSR Institut Elektrodinamiki
PNUPA — Progress in Nuclear Physics
PNUS — Prace Naukowe Uniwersytetu Slaskiego
P Nutr Soc — Proceedings. Nutrition Society
PNW Pac Northwest Ext Publ Oreg State Univ Coop Ext Serv — PNW. Pacific Northwest Extension Publication. Oregon State University. Cooperative Extension Service
PNY — Poetry New York
PNYMD — Polytechnic Institute of New York. Department of Mechanical and Aerospace Engineering. Report POLY M/AE
PO — Patrologia Orientalis
Po — Poesie
Po — Polet
PO — Poona Orientalist
PO — Prairie Overcomer
PO — Przeglad Orientalistyczny

POAA — Problems of the Arctic and the Antarctic
POA Chronicle — Professional Officers' Association Chronicle
POAS — Poems on Affairs of State
POB — Polarboken
POBI — Polar Biology
POBUD — Polymer Bulletin
PoC — Problems of Communism
POC — Proche-Orient Chretien
P-O Chr — Proche-Orient Chretien
Poch Urozhai Latv Nauch-Issled Inst Zemled — Pochva i Urozhai. Latviiskii Nauchno-Issledovatel'skii Institut Zemledeliya
Pochv Issled Primen Udobr — Pochvennye Issledovaniya i Primenenie Udobrenii
Pochvoved — Pochvovedenie
Pochvozn Agrokhim — Pochvoznanie i Agrokhimiya
Pochv Usloviya Eff Udobr — Pochvennye Usloviya i Effektivnost Udobrenii
Pochvy Baskh Puti Ratsion Ikh Ispol'z — Pochvy Baskhirii i Puti Ratsional'nogo Ikh Ispol'zovaniya [*USSR*]
Pochvy Yuzhn Urala Povolzhya — Pochvy Yuzhnogo Urala i Povolzh'ya
Podgot Koksovanie Uglei — Podgotovka i Koksovanie Uglei
Podgot Vosstanov Rud — Podgotovka i Vosstanovlenie Rud
Podstawowe Probl Wspolczesnej Tech — Podstawowe Problemy Wspolczesnej Techniki
Podst Sterow — Podstawy Sterowania
PODU — Praci Odes'koho Derzavnoho Universytetu
Podzemn Gazif Uglei — Podzemnaya Gazifikatsiya Uglei [*USSR*]
Podzemn Gazif Uglei (1934-35) — Podzemnaya Gazifikatsiya Uglei (1934-35)
Podzemn Gazif Uglei (1957-59) — Podzemnaya Gazifikatsiya Uglei (1957-59)
Podzemn Vody SSSR — Podzemnye Vody SSSR
Poe — Poetik
Poe Chpbk — Poetry Chapbook
P O Elect Engrs J — Post Office Electrical Engineers. Journal
P O Electr Eng J — Post Office Electrical Engineers. Journal
Poe Pal — Poetry Palisade
POERD — Power Engineer
PoeS — Poe Studies
Poe Stud — Poe Studies
Poet — Poetica
Poet — Poetry
PoetC — Poet and Critic
Poet Crit — Poet and Critic
Poetics Tod — Poetics Today
Poet L — Poet Lore
Poetry Aust — Poetry Australia
Poetry Mag — Poetry Magazine
Poetry NW — Poetry Northwest
Poetry R — Poetry Review [*London*]
Poetry Wale — Poetry Wales
Poets — Poets in the South
Poeyana Inst Biol La Habana Ser A — Poeyana Instituto de Biologia. La Habana. Serie A
Poeyana Inst Biol La Habana Ser B — Poeyana Instituto de Biologia. La Habana. Serie B
Poeyana Inst Zool Acad Cienc Cuba — Poeyana Instituto de Zoologia. Academia de Ciencias de Cuba
POF — Prilozi za Orijentalnu Filologiju
POG — Official Gazette. United States Patent Office
Pog — Pogledi
POG — Tableware International
POGCA — Progress in Organic Coatings
POGE — Polar Geography and Geology
Poggendorffs Ann — Poggendorffs Annalen
POI — Politique Etrangere
Poimennye Pochvy Russ Ravniny — Poimennye Pochvy Russkoi Ravniny
Point Point Commun — Point-to-Point Communication [*Later, Communication and Broadcasting*]
Point Point Telecommun — Point-to-Point Telecommunications
Points Appui Econ Rhone-Alpes — Points d'Appui pour l'Economie Rhone-Alpes
Point Vet — Point Veterinaire
Pokroky Mat Fyz Astron — Pokroky Matematiky, Fyziky, a Astronomie
Pokroky Praskove Metal — Pokroky Praskove Metalurgie
Pokroky Praskove Metal VUPM — Pokroky Praskove Metalurgie VUPM [*Vyzkumny Ustav pro Praskovou Metalurgii*]
Pokroky Vinohrad Vina- Vysk — Pokroky vo Vinohradnickom a Vinarskom Vyskume
Pol — FS. Political Risk Letter
Pol — Politics
Pol — Polonystyka [*Warsaw*]
PolAb — Pollution Abstracts
Pol Acad Sci Bull Biol — Polish Academy of Sciences. Bulletin. Biology
Pol Acad Sci Bull Chem — Polish Academy of Sciences. Bulletin. Chemistry
Pol Acad Sci Bull Earth Sci — Polish Academy of Sciences. Bulletin. Earth Sciences
Pol Acad Sci Inst Ecol Rep Sci Act — Polish Academy of Sciences. Institute of Ecology. Report on Scientific Activities

Pol Acad Sci Inst Fundam Tech Res Nonlinear Vib Probl — Polish Academy of Sciences. Institute of Fundamental Technical Research. Nonlinear Vibration Problems

Pol Acad Sci Inst Fundam Tech Res Proc Vib Probl — Polish Academy of Sciences. Institute of Fundamental Technical Research. Proceedings of Vibration Problems

Pol Acad Sci Inst Geophys Publ Ser D — Polish Academy of Sciences. Institute of Geophysics. Publications. Series D. Atmosphere Physics

Pol Acad Sci Med Sect Ann — Polish Academy of Sciences. Medical Section. Annals

Pol Acad Sci Rev — Polish Academy of Sciences. Review

Pol Affairs — Political Affairs

Pol Akad Nauk Inst Geofiz Mater Pr — Polska Akademia Nauk. Instytut Geofizyki. Materialy i Prace

Pol Akad Nauk Kom Ceram Pr Ser Ceram — Polska Akademia Nauk. Komisja Ceramiczna. Prace. Serja Ceramika

Pol Akad Nauk Kom Krystalogr Biul Inf — Polska Akademia Nauk. Komisja Krystalografii. Biuletyn Informacyjny

Pol Akad Nauk Muz Ziemi Pr — Polska Akademia Nauk. Muzeum Ziemi. Prace

Pol Akad Nauk Oddzial Krakowie Kom Nauk Geol Pr Geol — Polska Akademia Nauk. Oddzial w Krakowie. Komisja Nauk Geologicznych. Prace Geologicane

Pol Akad Nauk Oddzial Krakowie Kom Nauk Mineral Pr Mineral — Polska Akademia Nauk. Oddzial w Krakowie. Komisja Nauk Mineralogicznych. Prace Mineralogiczne

Pol Akad Nauk Oddzial Krakowie Nauk Mineral Pr Mineral — Polska Akademia Nauk. Oddzial w Krakowie. Komisja Nauk Mineralogicznych. Prace Mineralogiczne

Pol Akad Nauk Oddzial Krakowie Pr Kom Ceram Ceram — Polska Akademia Nauk. Oddzial w Krakowie. Prace Komisji Ceramicznej. Ceramika

Pol Akad Nauk Oddzial Krakowie Pr Kom Ceram Ser Ceram — Polska Akademia Nauk. Oddzial w Krakowie. Prace Komisji Ceramicznej. Serja Ceramika

Pol Akad Nauk Oddzial Krakowie Pr Kom Metal Odlew Metal — Polska Akademia Nauk. Oddzial w Krakowie. Prace Komisji Metalurgiczno-Odlewniczej. Metalurgia

Pol Akad Nauk Oddzial Krakowie Pr Kom Metal-Odlew Metalurg — Polska Akademia Nauk. Oddzial w Krakowie. Prace Komisji Metalurgiczno-Odlewniczej. Metalurgia

Pol Akad Nauk Oddzial Krakowie Pr Kom Nauk Tech Ser Ceram — Polska Akademia Nauk. Oddzial w Krakowie. Prace Komisji Nauk Technicznych. Serja. Ceramika

Pol Akad Nauk Pr Inst Masz Przeplyw — Polska Akademia Nauk. Prace Instytutu Maszyn Przeplywowych

Pol Akad Nauk Pr Kom Nauk Tech Metal Fiz Met Stopow — Polska Akademia Nauk. Prace Komisji Nauk Technicznych Metalurgia Fizyka Metali i Stopow

Pol Akad Nauk Pr Kom Nauk Tech Ser Ceram — Polska Akademia Nauk. Prace Komisji Nauk Technicznych. Serja Ceramika

Pol Akad Nauk Rozpr Wydz Nauk Med — Polska Akademia Nauk. Rozprawy Wydzialu Nauk Medycznych

Pol Akad Umiejet Pr Muz Przyr — Polska Akademia Umiejetnosci. Prace Muzeum Przyrodniczego

Pol Akad Umiejet Pr Roln Lesne — Polska Akademia Umiejetnosci. Prace Rolniczo-Lesne

Pol Am Stds — Polish American Studies

Poland China — Poland China World

Poland Inst Geol Biul — Poland. Instytut Geologiczny. Biuletyn

Pol Arch Hydrobiol — Polskie Archiwum Hydrobiologii/Polish Archives of Hydrobiology

Pol Arch Med Wewn — Polskie Archiwum Medycyny Wewnetrznej

Pol Arch Wet — Polskie Archiwum Weterynaryjne

Pol Arch Weter — Polskie Archiwum Weterynaryjne

Polarogr Ber — Polarographische Berichte

Polar Rec — Polar Record

Pol Bildung — Politische Bildung

Pol Communication and Persuasion — Political Communication and Persuasion

POLEA — Polski Tygodnik Lekarski

Pol Ecol Bibliogr — Polish Ecological Bibliography

Pol Ecol Stud — Polish Ecological Studies

Pol Endocrinol — Polish Endocrinology

Pol Eng — Polish Engineering

Pol Eng Rev — Polish Engineering Review

Pol Etrang — Politique Etrangere [*Paris*]

POLFA — Polarforschung

POLI — Postal Life

POLIA — Polimery

Police J — Police Journal

Police Mag — Police Magazine

Police Mag (Syria) — Police Magazine (Syria)

Police Res Bull — Police Research Bulletin

Police Rev — Police Review

Police Sc Abs — Police Science Abstracts

Policlinico Sez Chir — Policlinico. Sezione Chirurgica

Policlinico Sez Med — Policlinico. Sezione Medica

Policlinico Sez Prat — Policlinico. Sezione Practica

Policy Anal — Policy Analysis [*Later, Journal of Policy Analysis and Management*]

Policy Pol — Policy and Politics

Policy Publ Rev — Policy Publication Review [*England*]

Policy R — Policy Review

Policy Rev — Policy Review

Policy Sci — Policy Sciences

Policy Stud — Policy Studies

Policy Studies J — Policy Studies Journal

Policy Studies R — Policy Studies Review

Policy Stud J — Policy Studies Journal

Policy Stud Rev — Policy Studies Review

POLID — Power Line

Poligr Promst Obz Inf — Poligraficheskaya Promyshlennost. Obzornaya Informatsiya

Polim Mashinostr — Polimery v Mashinostroenii [*Ukrainian SSR*]

Polim Mater Ikh Issled — Polimernye Materialy i Ikh Issledovanie

Polim Med — Polimery w Medycynie

Polim Medziagos Ju Tyrimas — Polimerines Medziagos ir Ju Tyrimas

Polim Medziagu Panaudojimas Liaudies Ukyje — Polimeriniu Medziagu Panaudojimas Liaudies Ukyje

Polim Sb Tr Nauchnoizsled Inst Kauch Plastmasova Promst — Polimeri Sbornik ot Trudove na Nauchnoizsledovatelskiya Institut po Kauchukova i Plastmasova Promishlenost

Polim Sb Tr Nauchnoizsled Inst Prerabotka Plastmasi — Polimeri Sbornik ot Trudove na Nauchnoizsledovatelskiya Institut po Prerabotkka na Plastmasi

Polim Tworzwa — Polimery Tworzywa [*Poland*]

Polim Tworz Wielk — Polimery-Tworzywa Wielkoczasteczkowe [*Poland*]

Polim Tworz Wielkoczast — Polimery-Tworzywa Wielkoczasteczkowe

Polim Vehomarim Plast — Polimerim Vehomarim Plastiim

Pol Inst Geol Bibliogr Geol Pol — Poland. Instytut Geologiczny. Bibliografia Geologiczna Polski

Pol Inst Meteorol Gospod Wodnej Pr — Poland. Instytut Meteorologii i Gospodarki Wodnej. Prace

Poliplasti Mater Rinf — Poliplasti e Materiali Rinforzati

Poliplasti Plast Rinf — Poliplasti e Plastici Rinforzati

Poli Q — Political Quarterly

Poli Sci — Political Science

Poli Sci Q — Political Science Quarterly

Polish Acad Sci Fluid Flow — Polish Academy of Sciences. Transactions. Institute of Fluid Flow Machinery [*Warsaw*]

Polish Am Stud — Polish American Studies

Polish F — Polish Film

Polish J Chem — Polish Journal of Chemistry

Polish J Pharmacol Pharmacy — Polish Journal of Pharmacology and Pharmacy

Polish Mus — Polish Music

Polish Perspect — Polish Perspectives

Polish R — Polish Review

Polish Sociol B — Polish Sociological Bulletin

Polish Tech & Econ Abstr — Polish Technical and Economic Abstracts

Poli Societ — Politics and Society

Polit Aff — Political Affairs

Polit Aujourd — Politique d'Aujourd'hui

Polit Belge — Politique Belge

Polit Dir — Politica del Diritto

Politech Rzeszowska Im Ignacego Lukasiewicza Rozpr — Politechnika Rzeszowska Imienia Ignacego Lukasiewicza. Rozprawy

Politech Rzeszowska Zesz Nauk — Politechnika Rzeszowska. Zeszyty Naukowe

Politech Warsz Pr Inst Podstaw Konstr Masz — Politechnika Warszawska. Prace Instytutu Podstaw Konstrukcji Maszyn

Politech Warsz Pr Nauk Mech — Politechnika Warszawska. Prace Naukowe. Mechanika

Polit Eco — Review of Radical Political Economics

Polit ed Econ — Politica ed Economia

Polit Econ — Politica ed Economia

Polit Ekon — Politicka Ekonomie

Polit Etr — Politique Etrangere

Polit Foisk Kozlem — Politikai Foiskola Kozlemenyei

Polit Gazdasag Tanulmany — Politikai Gazdasagtan Tanulmanyok

Politic St — Political Studies - London

Polit Int (Roma) — Politica Internazionale (Roma)

Polit Meinung — Politische Meinung

Polit Methodol — Political Methodology

Polit Perspect — Politiek Perspectief

Polit Q — Political Quarterly

Polit Quart — Political Quarterly

Polit Rdsch — Politische Rundschau

Polit Sci — Political Science

Polit Sci Ann — Political Science Annual

Polit Scientist — Political Scientist

Polit Sci Q — Political Science Quarterly

Polit Sci R — Political Science Review

Polit Sci R-er — Political Science Reviewer
Polit Sci (Wellington) — Political Science (Wellington)
Polit and Soc — Politics and Society
Polit Soc Econ Rev — Political, Social, Economic Review
Polit Spolecz — Polityka Spoleczna
Polit Stud — Politische Studien [*Muenchen*]
Polit Theor — Political Theory
Polit Today — Politics Today
Polit Vjschr — Politische Vierteljahresschrift
Polit Vjschr Sonderh — Politische Vierteljahresschrift. Sonderheft
Polit u Zeitgesch — Politik und Zeitgeschichte
Pol J Chem — Polish Journal of Chemistry
Pol J Ecol — Polish Journal of Ecology
Poljopriv Pregl — Poljoprivredni Pregled
Poljopriv Sumar — Poljoprivredna i Sumarstvo
Poljopriv Znan Smotra — Poljoprivredna Znanstvena Smotra
Poljopr Sumar — Poljoprivredna i Sumarstvo
Poljopr Znan Smotra — Poljoprivredna Znanstvena Smotra
Poljopr Znanst Smotra — Poljoprivredna Znanstvena Smotra
Pol J Phar — Polish Journal of Pharmacology and Pharmacy
Pol J Pharmacol Pharm — Polish Journal of Pharmacology and Pharmacy
Pol J Soil Sci — Polish Journal of Soil Science
PolL — Polonista (Lublin)
Poll Abstr — Pollution Abstracts
Pollack Mihaly Muesz Foeisk Tud Koezl — Pollack Mihaly Mueszaki Foeiskola Tudomanyos Koezlemenyei
POLLD — Pollimo
Pollen Grain US For Serv Southeast Area — Pollen Grain. United States Forest Service. Southeastern Area
Pollut Abstr — Pollution Abstracts
Pollut Atmos — Pollution Atmospherique
Pollut Control — Pollution Control [*Japan*]
Pollut Eng — Pollution Engineering
Pollut Eng Technol — Pollution Engineering and Technology
Pollution — Pollution Equipment News
Pollut Monitor — Pollution Monitor
Pollut Tech — Pollution Technology
Pol Mach Ind — Polish Machine Industry
Pol Med J — Polish Medical Journal
Pol Med Sci Hist Bull — Polish Medical Science and History Bulletin
Pol Methodol — Political Methodology
POLNA — Polnohospodarstvo
Polnohospod — Polnohospodarstvo
Pologne Aff Occid — Pologne et les Affaires Occidentales
Pologne Contemp — Pologne Contemporaine
Pol'ovnicky Zb — Pol'ovnicky Zbornik
PolP — Polish Perspectives
Pol Perspect — Polish Perspectives
Pol Pismo Entomol — Polskie Pismo Entomologiczne
Pol Pismo Entomol Ser B Entomol Stosow — Polskie Pismo Entomologiczne. Seria B. Entomologia Stosowana
Pol and Polit — Policy and Politics
Pol Przegl Chir — Polski Przeglad Chirurgiczny
Pol Przegl Radiol — Polski Przeglad Radiologii i Medycyny Nuklearnej
Pol Przegl Radiol Med Nukl — Polski Przeglad Radiologii i Medycyny Nuklearnej
Pol Psych B — Polish Psychological Bulletin
Pol Q — Political Quarterly
Pol Quar — Political Quarterly
Pol R — Policy Review
PolR — Polish Review [*New York*]
POLRA — Polar Record
Pol Rev Radiol Nucl Med — Polish Review of Radiology and Nuclear Medicine
Pol Sci — Policy Sciences
Pol Sci — Political Science
Pol Science Q — Political Science Quarterly
Pol Sci Q — Political Science Quarterly
Pol Sci R — Political Science Review [*Jaipur*]
Polska Akad Nauk Met — Polska Akademia Nauk. Metalurgia
Polska Akad Nauk Oddzial Krakowie Pr Kom Nauk Tech Ceram — Polska Akademia Nauk. Oddzial w Krakowie. Prace Komisji Nauk Technicznych. Ceramika
Polska Biblio Analit Mech — Polska Bibliografia Analityczna. Mechanika
Polska Gaz Lekar — Polska Gazeta Lekarska
Polskie Arch Med Wewnetrznej — Polskie Archiwum Medycyny Wewnetrznej
Polskie Archwm Wet — Polskie Archiwum Weterynaryjne
Polskie Pismo Entomol — Polskie Pismo Entomologiczne
Polskie Pismo Entomol Ser B Entomol Stosow — Polskie Pismo Entomologiczne. Seria B. Entomologia Stosowana
Polskie Tow Ent Klucze Oznaczania Owadow Pol — Polskie Towarzystwo Entomologiczne. Klucze do Oznaczania Owadow Polski
Polski Tygod Lek — Polski Tygodnik Lekarski
Pol & Soc — Politics and Society
Pol Soc — Politics and Society
Pol Soc B — Polish Sociological Bulletin
Pol Stud — Political Studies

Pol Studien — Politische Studien [*Muenchen*]
Pol Studies — Political Studies
Pol Stud J — Policy Studies Journal
Pol Szt Lud — Polska Sztuka Ludowa
Pol Tech Abstr — Polish Technical Abstracts
Pol Tech Econ Abstr — Polish Technical and Economic Abstracts
Pol Technol News — Polish Technological News
Pol Tech Rev — Polish Technical Review
Pol Theory — Political Theory
Pol Today — Politics Today
Pol Tow Entomol Klucze Oznaczania Owadow Pol — Polskie Towarzystwo Entomologiczne. Klucze do Oznaczania Owadow Polski
Pol Tow Geol Rocz — Polskie Towarzystwo Geologiczne. Rocznik
Pol Trasporti — Politica dei Trasporti
Pol Tyg Lek — Polski Tygodnik Lekarski
Pol Tyg Lek Wiad Lek — Polski Tygodnik Lekarski i Wiadomosci Lekarskie
Poluch Strukt Svoistva Sorbentov — Poluchenie, Struktura, i Svoistva Sorbentov
Poluch Svoistva Tonkikh Plenok — Poluchenie i Svoistva Tonkikh Plenok [*Ukrainian SSR*]
Poluprovdn Prib Tekh Elektrosvyazi — Poluprovodnikovye Pribory v Tekhnike Elektrosvyazi
Poluprovodn Elektron — Poluprovodnikovaya Elektronika
Poluprovodn Ikh Primen Elektrotekh — Poluprovodniki i Ikh Primenenie v Elektrotekhnike
Poluprovodn Prib Ikh Primen — Poluprovodnikovye Pribory i Ikh Primenenie
Poluprovodn Prib Primen — Poluprovodnikovye Pribory i Ikh Primenenie
Poluprovodn Tekh i Mikroelektron — Poluprovodnikovaya Tekhnika i Mikroelektronika
Poluprov Prib Ikh Primen Sb Statei — Poluprovodnikovye Pribory i Ikh Primenenie Sbornik Statei [*USSR*]
Poluprov Tekh Mikroelektron — Poluprovodnikovaya Tekhnika i Mikroelektronika [*Ukrainian SSR*]
Pol Vjschr — Politische Vierteljahresschrift
POLY-AE/AM Rep (Polytech Inst NY Dep Aerosp Eng Appl Mech) — POLY-AE/AM Report (Polytechnic Institute of New York. Department of Aerospace Engineering and Applied Mechanics)
Polyarn Siyaniya Svechenie Nochnogo Neba — Polyarnye Siyaniya i Svechenie Nochnogo Neba
Polyar Siyaniya — Polyarnye Siyaniya [*USSR*]
Poly L Rev — Poly Law Review
Polym Age — Polymer Age
Polym Appl — Polymer Application [*Japan*]
Polym Bull — Polymer Bulletin
Polym Bull (Berlin) — Polymer Bulletin (Berlin)
Polym Commun — Polymer Communications
Polym Compos — Polymer Composites
Polym Composites — Polymer Composites
Polym Degradat Stabil — Polymer Degradation and Stability
Polym Engng News — Polymer Engineering News
Polym Engng Rev — Polymer Engineering Reviews
Polym Engng Sci — Polymer Engineering and Science
Polym Eng S — Polymer Engineering and Science
Polym Eng and Sci — Polymer Engineering and Science
Polym Eng Sci — Polymer Engineering and Science
Polymer J — Polymer Journal
Polym J — Polymer Journal
Polym J (Jap) — Polymer Journal (Japan)
Polym Mech — Polymer Mechanics
Polym Monogr — Polymer Monographs
Polym News — Polymer News
Polym Paint Col J — Polymers, Paint, and Colour Journal
Polym Paint Colour J — Polymers, Paint, and Colour Journal
Polym Photochem — Polymer Photochemistry
Polym-Plast — Polymer-Plastics Technology and Engineering
Polym Plast Mater — Polymers and Plastic Materials
Polym-Plast Technol Eng — Polymer-Plastics Technology and Engineering
Polym Prepr Am Chem Soc Div Polym Chem — Polymer Preprints. American Chemical Society. Division of Polymer Chemistry
Polym Preprints — Polymer Preprints
Polym Rep — Polymer Report
Polym Rev — Polymer Reviews
Polym Sci Technol — Polymer Science and Technology
Polym Sci USSR — Polymer Science. USSR [*English Translation of Vysokomolekulyarnye Soyedineniya. Series A*]
Polym Test — Polymer Testing
Polyn Soc J — Polynesian Society Journal
Polysaccharides Biol Trans Conf — Polysaccharides in Biology. Transactions of the Conference
Polysar Prog — Polysar Progress
Polyscope Autom und Elektron — Polyscope. Automatik und Elektronik
Polyscope Comput und Elektron — Polyscope. Computer und Elektronik
Polytech Inst Brooklyn Microwave Res Inst Symp Ser — Polytechnic Institute of Brooklyn. Microwave Research Institute. Symposia Series
Polytech Tijdschr Bouwk Wegen- & Waterbouw — Polytechnisch Tijdschrift Bouwkune Wegen- en Waterbouw

Polytech Tijdschr Ed A — Polytechnisch Tijdschrift. Editie A. Werktuigbouwkunde en Elektrotechniek
Polytech Tijdschr Ed B — Polytechnisch Tijdschrift. Editie B
Polytech Tijdschr Elektrotech Elektron — Polytechnisch Tijdschrift. Elektrotechniek. Elektronica
Polytech Tijdschr Procestech — Polytechnisch Tijdschrift. Procestechniek
Polytech Tijdschr Werktuigbouw — Polytechnisch Tijdschrift. Werktuigbouw
Polytech Weekbl — Polytechnisch Weekblad
Polytek Revy — Polyteknisk Revy [*Norway*]
Polyt Rv — Polytechnic Review
POMDA — Postgraduate Medicine
POMDD — Poznanskie Roczniki Medyczne
Pomiary Autom Kontrola — Pomiary Automatyka Kontrola
POMJA — Polish Medical Journal
Pomme Terre Fr — Pomme de Terre Francaise
POMNDR — Museo Nacional de Historia Natural. Publicacion Ocasional [*Santiago*]
Pomol Fr — Pomologie Francaise
Pomol Fruit Grow Soc Annu Rep — Pomological and Fruit Growing Society. Annual Report
POMPA — Publications. Mississippi Philological Association
Pompebl — Pompebledon
Pon — Ponte
PON — Public Opinion
PONE — Polar News. Japan Polar Research Association
Po Now — Poetry Now
PONS — Polar Notes
PONSA — Platt's Oilgram News Service
Ponte Riv M — Ponte. Rivista Mensile di Politica e Letteratura
Pontif Acad Sci Acta — Pontificia Academia Scientiarum. Acta
Pontif Acad Sci Comment — Pontificia Academia Scientiarum. Commentarii
Pontif Acad Sci Scr Varia — Pontificia Academia Scientiarum. Scripta Varia
Poona Agr Col Mag — Poona Agricultural College Magazine
Poona Agric Coll Mag — Poona Agricultural College Magazine
PoP — Political Psychology
Pop Astron — Popular Astronomy
Pop Astronomy — Popular Astronomy
Pop B — Population Bulletin
Pop Bul — Population Bulletin
Pop Bull Colo State Univ Agr Exp Sta — Popular Bulletin. Colorado State University. Agricultural Experiment Station
Pop Comput — Popular Computing
POPDA — Polish Psychological Bulletin
Pop Dev R — Population and Development Review [*New York*]
Pop Educ — Popular Educator
Pop Electr — Popular Electronics
Pop Gard — Popular Gardening
Pop Govt — Popular Government
PopI — Population Index
Pop Index — Population Index
Pop Mech — Popular Mechanics
Pop Mech — Popular Mechanics Magazine
Pop Med (Tokyo) — Popular Medicine (Tokyo)
Pop Music S — Popular Music and Society
Pop Mus Per Ind — Popular Music Periodicals Index
Pop Mus & Soc — Popular Music and Society
POPO — Polar Post. Polar Postal History Society of Great Britain
POPOA — Phosphorus and Potassium
POPPD — Plant/Operations Progress
Pop Per Ind — Popular Periodical Index
Pop Phot — Popular Photography
Pop Photog — Popular Photography
Pop Plast — Popular Plastics
Pop Plast Annu — Popular Plastics Annual
Pop Sci — Popular Science Monthly
Pop Sci (Peking) — Popular Science (Peking)
Pop Sci R — Popular Science Review
Pop Stud — Population Studies [*London*]
Pop Stud (Lo) — Population Studies (London)
Pop Stud (NY) — Population Studies (New York)
Pop Tech Tous — Popular Technique pour Tous
Popular Govt — Popular Government
Popular M Soc — Popular Music and Society
Population Bul — Population Bulletin
Population Bul UN — Population Bulletin. United Nations
Population R — Population Review
Population Research and Policy R — Population Research and Policy Review
Popul et Avenir — Population et Avenir
Popul Bull — Population Bulletin
Popul Bull UN Econ Comm West Asia — Population Bulletin. United Nations Economic Commission for Western Asia
Popul B UN Econ Com West Asia — Population Bulletin. United Nations Economic Commission for Western Asia
Popul Counc Annu Rep — Population Council. Annual Report
Popul et Famille — Population et Famille
Popul et Famille/Bevolk en Gezin — Population et Famille/Bevolking en Gezin

Popul Forum — Population Forum
Popul Ind — Population Index
Popul Newsl — Population Newsletter
Popul Rep (A) — Population Reports. Series A. Oral Contraceptives
Popul Rep (B) — Population Reports. Series B. Intrauterine Devices
Popul Rep (D) — Population Reports. Series D. Sterilization (Male)
Popul Rep (G) — Population Reports. Series G. Prostaglandins
Popul Rep (H) — Population Reports. Series H. Barrier Methods
Popul Rep (I) — Population Reports. Series I. Periodic Abstinence
Popul Rep (J) — Population Reports. Series J. Family Planning Programs
Popul Rep (K) — Population Reports. Series K. Injectables and Implants
Popul Rep (L) — Population Reports. Series L. Issues in World Health
Popul Rep (M) — Population Reports. Series M. Special Topics
Popul Rep Spec Top Monogr — Population Reports. Special Topics. Monographs
Popul Rev — Population Review
Popul et Societes — Population et Societes
Popul Stud — Population Studies
POPYA — Portugaliae Physica
POQ — Public Opinion Quarterly
POR — Pack Report. Fachzeitschrift fuer Verpackungs Marketing und Verpackungs (Technik)
PoR — Poetry Review [*London*]
POr — Porta Orientale
Por — Portugale
Poradnik M — Poradnik Muzyczny
PORCD — Population Reports. Series C [*United States*]
PORDB — Ports and Dredging
PORE — Polar Record
Pork Ind Gaz — Pork Industry Gazette
PORLA — Practica Oto-Rhino-Laryngologica
Poroshk Metall — Poroshkovaya Metallurgiya
Poroshk Metall (Kiev) — Poroshkovaya Metallurgiya (Kiev)
Poroshk Metall (Kuibyshev) — Poroshkovaya Metallurgiya (Kuibyshev)
Porosh Met — Poroshkovaya Metallurgiya
PORS — Polar Research
PORS — Publications in Operations Research Series [*Elsevier Book Series*]
Port — Portugale
Port Acta Biol A — Portugaliae Acta Biologica. A. Morfologia, Fisiologia, Genetica, e Biologia Geral
Port Acta Biol Ser A — Portugaliae Acta Biologica. Serie A
Port Acta Biol Ser B — Portugaliae Acta Biologica. Serie B
Portfo — Portfolio
Portfo (Den) — Portfolio (Dennie's)
Port Gazette — Melbourne Harbour Trust Port Gazette
Portia L J — Portia Law Journal
Port Junta Invest Cient Ultramar Estud Ensaios Doc — Portugal. Junta de Investigacoes Cientificas do Ultramar. Estudos, Ensaios, e Documentos
Port Lab Nac Eng Civ Mem — Portugal. Laboratorio Nacional de Engenharia Civil. Memoria
Portland Cem Ass Advanced Eng Bull — Portland Cement Association. Advanced Engineering Bulletin
Portland Cem Ass J PCA Res Develop Lab — Portland Cement Association. Journal of the PCA Research and Development Laboratories
Portland Cem Assoc Fellowship Natl Bur Stand Pap — Portland Cement Association Fellowship at the National Bureau of Standards. Papers
Portland Cem Assoc Res Dev Lab Dev Dep Bull D — Portland Cement Association. Research and Development Laboratories. Development Department. Bulletin D
Portland Soc N H Pr — Portland Society of Natural History. Proceedings
Port Melb — Port of Melbourne
Port of Melbourne Quart — Port of Melbourne Quarterly
Port Melbourne Quart — Port of Melbourne Quarterly
Port of Melb Q — Port of Melbourne Quarterly
Port Melb Q — Port of Melbourne Quarterly
Port of Melb Quart — Port of Melbourne Quarterly
Port Minist Ultramar Junta Invest Ultramar Mem Ser Antropol — Portugal. Ministerio do Ultramar. Junta de Investigacoes do Ultramar. Memorias. Serie Antropologica e Etnologica
Port Minist Ultramar Junta Invest Ultramar Mem Ser Botanica — Portugal. Ministerio do Ultramar. Junta de Investigacoes do Ultramar. Memorias. Serie Botanica
Port Minist Ultramar Junta Invest Ultramar Mem Ser Geol — Portugal. Ministerio do Ultramar. Junta de Investigacoes do Ultramar. Memorias. Serie Geologica
Port Minist Ultramar Mem Junta Invest Ultramar — Portugal. Ministerio do Ultramar. Memorias da Junta de Investigacoes do Ultramar
Port Of Melbourne Q — Port Of Melbourne Quarterly
Port Phillip Gaz — Port Phillip Gazette
Port Phy — Portugaliae Physica
Port Phys — Portugaliae Physica
Port R — Portland Review
Ports Dredging Oil Rep — Ports and Dredging and Oil Report
Port Serv Fom Min Estud Notas Trab — Portugal. Servico de Fomento Mineiro. Estudos, Notas, e Trabalhos
Port Serv Geol Mem — Portugal. Servicos Geologicos. Memoria

Port Syd — Port of Sydney
Port of Syd — Port of Sydney
Port of Sydney J — Port of Sydney Journal
Portug Acta Biol — Portugaliae Acta Biologica
Portugal Math — Portugaliae Mathematica
Portugal Phys — Portugaliae Physica
POS — Population Studies
POS — Pretoria Oriental Series
POSB — Polish Sociological Bulletin
POSEA — Peredovoi Opyt v Stroitel'stve i Ekspluatatsii Shakht
Posebna Izdan — Posebna Izdanja
Posebna Izd Biol Inst N R Srb Beograd — Posebna Izdanja Bioloski Institut N R Srbije Beograd
Posebna Izd Geol Glas (Sarajevo) — Posebna Izdanja Geoloskog Glasnika (Sarajevo)
POSID — Polyarnye Siyaniya
PosLuth — Positions Lutheriennes [*Paris*]
POSPB — Problemy Osvoeniya Pustyn
Posselt's Text J — Posselt's Textile Journal
POST — Polymer Science and Technology
POST-A — Population Studies
Postal Bull — Postal Bulletin. Weekly
Postal Bull US Postal Serv — Postal Bulletin. United States Postal Service
Postal Spvr — Postal Supervisor
PostB — Postilla Bohemica
Post Bioch — Postepy Biochemii
Postdiplom Sem Fiz — Postdiplomski Seminar iz Fizike
Postdiplom Sem Mat — Postdiplomski Seminar iz Matematike
Post Dir — Post's Paper Mill Directory
Postepy Astron — Postepy Astronomii
Postepy Astronaut — Postepy Astronautyki
Postepy Biochem — Postepy Biochemii
Postepy Biol Komorki — Postepy Biologii Komorki
Postepy Cybernet — Postepy Cybernetyki
Postepy Fiz — Postepy Fizyki
Postepy Fizjol — Postepy Fizjologii
Postepy Fiz Med — Postepy Fizyki Medycznej
Postepy Hig Med Dosw — Postepy Higieny i Medycyny Doswiadczalnej
Postepy Mikrobiol — Postepy Mikrobiologii
Postepy Nauk Roln — Postepy Nauk Rolniczych
Postepy Tech Jad — Postepy Techniki Jadroweki
Postepy Technol Masz Urzadz — Postepy Technologii Maszyn i Urzadzen
Postepy Wiedzy Med — Postepy Wiedzy Medycznej
Postepy Wiedzy Roln — Postepy Wiedzy Rolniczej
Poste Telecommun — Poste e Telecommunicazioni
Postg Med J — Postgraduate Medical Journal
Postgrad Courses Pediatr — Postgraduate Courses in Pediatrics
Postgrad Med — Postgraduate Medicine
Postgrad Med J — Postgraduate Medical Journal
Postgrad Med J Suppl — Postgraduate Medical Journal. Supplement
Postgrad Med Ser — Postgraduate Medicine Series
Postgr Med — Postgraduate Medicine
Post Harvest Technol Cassava — Post Harvest Technology of Cassava
POST-J — Polymer Science and Technology - Journals
Postmasters Adv — Postmasters Advocate
Post-Medieval Arch — Post-Medieval Archaeology
Post-Medieval Archaeol — Post-Medieval Archaeology
Post O E E J — Post Office Electrical Engineers. Journal
Post Off Electr Eng J — Post Office Electrical Engineers. Journal
Post Off (GB) Res Dep Rep — Post Office (Great Britain). Research Department Report
Post Office Hist Soc Trans — Post Office Historical Society. Transactions [*Queensland*]
Post Off Telecommun J — Post Office Telecommunications Journal
POST-P — Polymer Science and Technology - Patents
Post S — Post Script
Post Scr — Post Script
POSWa — Pozprawy Komisji Orientalistycznej Towarzystwa Naukowego Warszawskiego
Po T — Poetics Today
Potash J — Potash Journal
Potash Rev — Potash Review
Potash Trop Agric — Potash and Tropical Agriculture
Potassium Potasio Kalium Symp — Potassium Potasio Kalium Symposium
Potassium Symp — Potassium. Symposium
Potato Grow — Potato Grower
Potato Handb — Potato Handbook
Potato M — Potato Magazine
Potato Res — Potato Research
Pot Aust — Pottery in Australia
P O Telecommun J — Post Office Telecommunications Journal
Potfuzetek Termeszettud Kozl — Potfuzetek a Termeszettudomanyi Kozlonyhoz
POTN — Problems of the North
Potomac Appalachian Trail Club Bull — Potomac Appalachian Trail Club. Bulletin

Potomac L Rev — Potomac Law Review
Potomac R — Potomac Review
Potosi Univ Autonoma Inst Geologia y Metalurgia Fol Tec — Universidad Autonoma Potosina Folletos Tecnicos Publicados por el Instituto de Geologia y Metalurgia
Potravin Chladici Tech — Potravinarska a Chladici Technika
Potter Am Mo — Potter's American Monthly
Pottery — Pottery in Australia
Pottery Aust — Pottery in Australia
Pottery in Aust — Pottery in Australia
Pottery Gaz Glass Trade Rev — Pottery Gazette and Glass Trade Review
Pottery Glass Rec — Pottery and Glass Record
Pottery Glass Trades J — Pottery and Glass Trades Journal
Potvrda Valjanosti Broj Inst Meh Poljopr — Potvrda o Valjanosti Broj-Institut za Mehanizaciju Poljoprivrede
POTWA — Polimery Tworzywa
Poughkeepsie Soc N Sc Pr — Poughkeepsie Society of Natural Science. Proceedings
Poult — Poultry Forum
Poult Advis — Poultry Adviser
Poult Bull — Poultry Bulletin
Poult Egg Situat PES US Dep Agric Econ Res Serv — Poultry and Egg Situation. PES. United States Department of Agriculture. Economic Research Service
Poult Health Symp — Poultry Health Symposium
Poult Ind — Poultry Industry
Poultry Dig — Poultry Digest
Poultry Livestock Comment — Poultry and Livestock Comment
Poultry Process — Poultry Processing and Marketing
Poultry Sci — Poultry Science
Poult Sci — Poultry Science
Poult Trib — Poultry Tribune
Poult World — Poultry World
Pour Sci (Paris) — Pour la Science (Paris) (Edition Francaise de Scientific American)
Poverkhn Yavleniya Polim — Poverkhnostnye Yavleniya v Polimerakh
Poverkhn Yavleniya Zhidk Zhidk Rastvorakh — Poverkhnostnye Yavleniya v Zhidkostyakh i Zhidkikh Rastvorakh
Pov & Human Resour Abstr — Poverty and Human Resources Abstracts
Povolzh Lesotekh Inst Sb Tr — Povolzhskii Lesotekhnicheskii Institut Sbornik Trudov
Povysh Plodorodiya Pochv Nechernozemn Polosy — Povyshenie Plodorodiya Pochv Nechernozemnoi Polosy
Powder Coat — Powder Coatings
Powder Eng — Powder Engineering [*USSR*]
Powder Ind Res — Powder Industry Research
Powder Met — Powder Metallurgy
Powder Metall — Powder Metallurgy
Powder Metall Def Technol — Powder Metallurgy in Defense Technology
Powder Metall Int — Powder Metallurgy International
Powder Technol — Powder Technology
Powder Technol (Lausanne) — Powder Technology (Lausanne)
Powder Technol (Tokyo) — Powder Technology (Tokyo)
Powd Metall — Powder Metallurgy
Powd Tech — Powder Technology
PowerConvers Int — PowerConversion International
Power Eng — Power Engineering
Power Eng (India) — Power Engineer (India)
Power Eng J Acad Sci (USSR) — Power Engineering Journal. Academy of Sciences [*USSR*]
Power Eng (NY Eng Transl) — Power Engineering (New York, English Translation)
Power F — Power Farming
Power Farming Aust — Power Farming in Australia
Power Farming Better Farming Dig Aust NZ — Power Farming and Better Farming Digest in Australia and New Zealand [*Later, Power Farming*]
Power Farming Mag — Power Farming Magazine
Power Fuel Bull — Power and Fuel Bulletin
Power Gener — Power Generation
Power Ind — Power Industry, Including Industrial Power and Industry Power
Power Ind Res — Power Industry Research [*England*]
Power Plant Eng S Afr — Power and Plant Engineering in South Africa
Power Plant S Afr — Power and Plant in Southern Africa
Power Plant South Afr — Power and Plant in Southern Africa
Power Plant Sthn Afr — Power and Plant in Southern Africa
Power Pl Eng — Power Plant Engineering
Power Reactor Technol — Power Reactor Technology [*Japan*]
Power Reactor Technol Reactor Fuel Process — Power Reactor Technology and Reactor Fuel Processing [*United States*]
Power Reactor Technol (Tokyo) — Power Reactor Technology (Tokyo)
Power React Technol — Power Reactor Technology
Power Sources Symp Proc — Power Sources Symposium. Proceedings [*United States*]
Power Trans Des — Power Transmission Design
Power Transm Des — Power Transmission Design
Power Works Eng — Power and Works Engineering

Power & Works Engng — Power and Works Engineering
Powloki Ochr — Powloki Ochronne
Powys N — Powys Newsletter
Powys Rev — Powys Review
POxy — Oxyrhynchus Papyri
POZBDM — Folia Venatoria
Pozharnaya Okhr — Pozharnaya Okhrana
Poznan Rocz Med — Poznanskie Roczniki Medyczne [Poland]
Poznan Stud — Poznan Studies
Poznan Tow Przyj Nauk Pr Kom Biol — Poznanskie Towarzystwo Przyjaciol Nauk. Prace Komisji Biologicznej
Poznan Tow Przyj Nauk Pr Kom Farm — Poznanskie Towarzystwo Przyjaciol Nauk. Prace Komisji Farmaceutycznej
Poznan Tow Przyj Nauk Pr Kom Lek — Poznanskie Towarzystwo Przyjaciol Nauk. Prace Komisji Lekarskiej
Poznan Tow Przyj Nauk Pr Kom Mat Przyr — Poznanskie Towarzystwo Przyjaciol Nauk. Prace Komisji Matematyczno-Przyrodniczej
Poznan Tow Przyj Nauk Pr Kom Mat Przyr Pr Chem — Poznanskie Towarzystwo Przyjaciol Nauk. Prace Komisji Matematyczno-Przyrodniczej. Prace Chemiczne
Poznan Tow Przyj Nauk Pr Kom Mat Przyr Ser B — Poznanskie Towarzystwo Przyjaciol Nauk. Prace Komisji Matematyczno-Przyrodniczej. Seria B
Poznan Tow Przyj Nauk Pr Kom Med Dosw — Poznanskie Towarzystwo Przyjaciol Nauk. Prace Komisji Medycyny Doswiadzalnej
Poznan Tow Przyj Nauk Pr Kom Nauk Podstawowych Stosow — Poznanskie Towarzystwo Przyjaciol Nauk. Prace Komisji Nauk Podstawowych Stosowanych
Poznan Tow Przyj Nauk Pr Kom Nauk Roln Kom Nauk Lesn — Poznanskie Towarzystwo Przyjaciol Nauk. Prace Komisji Nauk Rolniczych i Komisji Nauk Lesnych
Poznan Tow Przyj Nauk Wydz Lek Pr Kom Farm — Poznanskie Towarzystwo Przyjaciol Nauk. Wydzial Lekarski. Prace Komisji Farmaceutycznej
Poznan Tow Przyj Nauk Wydz Lek Pr Kom Med Doswi — Poznanskie Towarzystwo Przyjaciol Nauk. Wydzial Lekarski. Prace Komisji Medycyny Doswiadczalnej [Poland]
Poznan Tow Przyj Nauk Wydz Mat-Przyr Kom Biol Pr — Poznanskie Towarzystwo Przyjaciol Nauk. Wydzial Matematyczno-Przyrodniczy. Komisja Biologiczna Prace [Poland]
PP — Die Palmyrenischen Personennamen
PP — Palestine Post
PP — Pan Pipes
PP — Papyrusfunde und Papyrusforschung
PP — Parliamentary Paper
PP — Parola del Passato
P & P — Past and Present
PP — Patriarchs and Prophets
P and P — Perception and Psychophysics
PP — Philologica Pragensia
PP — Philosophia Patrum
PP — Pinepointer
PP — Population (Paris)
PP — Prace Polonistyczne [Warsaw]
PP — Przeglad Powszechny [Revue Universelle]
PPa — Parola del Passato
PPA Univ KY Coop Ext Serv — PPA. University of Kentucky. Cooperative Extension Service
PPB — Polybiblion. Partie Litteraire
PPBUA — Personnel Practice Bulletin
PPC Jrl — Polymers, Paint, and Colour Journal
PPD — Polish Perspectives
PPDR — Population and Development Review
PPeda — Problemi di Pedagogia
PPENA — Plant and Power Services Engineer
PPERB — Progress in Pediatric Radiology
PPG — Phoenizisch-Punische Grammatik
PPGS — Publications. Pennsylvania German Society
PP Guide — Prescription Proprietaries Guide
PPHID — Plasma Physics Index
P Ph L — Papers in Philippine Linguistics
PPHPB — Problemy Projektowe Hutnictwa i Przemyslu Maszynowego
PPHR — Planned Parenthood Review
PPHRA — Philosophy and Phenomenological Research
PPHRD — Photochemical and Photobiological Reviews
PPHYA — Plant Physiology [English Translation]
PPI — Planen-Pruefen-Investieren
PPI — Popular Periodical Index
PPJ — Prilozi Proucavanju Jezika
PPKCB — Prace Komisji Ceramicznej. Polskiej Akademii Nauk. Ceramica
PPKGA — Ponpu Kogaku
PPL — Journal of Pension Planning and Compliance
PPL — Polybiblion. Partie Litteraire
PPL — Prace Polonistyczne (Lodz)
PPM — Public Personnel Management
PPM — Pulp and Paper Magazine of Canada
PPMMA — Problemy Prochnosti v Mashinostroenii
PPMMB — Periodica Polytechnica. Mechanical Engineering

PPMNA — Polski Przeglad Radiologii i Medycyny Nuklearnej
PPMRC — Proceedings. PMR Conference. Annual Publication of the International Patristic, Mediaeval, and Renaissance Conference
PPMVA — Pishchevaya Promyshlennost [Kiev, 1965]
PPNCFL — Proceedings. Pacific Northwest Conference on Foreign Languages
PPNPD — Progress in Particle and Nuclear Physics
PPol — Pensiero Politico
PPol — Przeglad Polski
PPOTA — Prumysl Potravin
PPow — Przeglad Powszechny
PPP — Pipelines, Politics, and People. Capital Communications Ltd.
PPP — Pulp and Paper International
PPPBDD — Iran. Departement de Botanique. Ministere de l'Agriculture et du Developpement Rural
PPPBDD — Iran. Plant Pests and Diseases Research Institute. Department of Botany. Publication
PPPE — People, Plans, and the Peace. Peace River Planning Commission
PPPMD — Pishchevaya Promyshlennost. Seriya 12. Spirtavya i Likero-Vodochnaya Promyshlennost
P & P Qtly — Pulp and Paper Quarterly Statistics
PPr — Paedagogische Provinz
PPR — Philosophy and Phenomenological Research
P & PR — Psychoanalysis and the Psychoanalytic Review
PPR — Public Productivity Review
PPRAA — Polski Przeglad Radiologiczny
P Prehist S — Proceedings. Prehistoric Society
PPRFA — Poliplasti e Plastici Rinforzati
P Proc Hampshire Field Club — Papers and Proceedings. Hampshire Field Club and Archaeological Society
PProv — Padova e la Sua Provincia
PPRPA — Produits et Problemes Pharmaceutiques
PPrStBrt — Perspectives in Probability and Statistics: in Honor of M. S. Bartlett
PPS — Pension and Profit-Sharing Tax Journal
PPS — Personnel Psychology
PPS — Proceedings. Prehistoric Society
PPS — Publications. Philological Society
PPSE — Petroleum Economist
PPSED3 — Annual Research Reviews. Physiological and Pathological Aspects of Prolactin Secretion
PPSSA — Proceedings. Nuclear Physics and Solid State Physics Symposium
PPSYA — Personnel Psychology
PPTA J — PPTA [Post-Primary Teachers Association] Journal
PPTEC — Polymer-Plastics Technology and Engineering
PPUAES — Publications. Princeton University Archaeological Expedition to Syria in 1904-5 and 1909
PPW — Prace Polonistyczne (Wroclaw)
PPWMA — Progress in Powder Metallurgy
PPYSA — Plant Physiology. Supplement
PPZI — Przeglad Pismiennictwa Zagadnien Informacji
PQ — Pakistan Quarterly
PQ — Philological Quarterly
PQ — Philosophical Quarterly
PQ — Piano Quarterly
PQ — Psychiatric Quarterly
PQCS — Philippine Quarterly of Culture and Society
PQCSD6 — Commissione Internazionale per la Protezione delle Acque Italo-Svizzere. Rapporti
PQM — Pacific Quarterly (Moana): An International Review of Arts and Ideas
PQR — Peruvian Quarterly Report
PQS — Palestine Exploration Fund. Quarterly Statement
P Qu — Philippines Quarterly
PQUEA — Progress in Quantum Electronics
PR — Paris Review
P & R — Parks and Recreation
PR — Partisan Review
PR — Peking Review
PR — Petroleum Review
PR — Pharmaceutical Record [New York]
PR — Philosophical Review
P & R — Philosophy and Rhetoric
PR — Pioneer [Kumasi]
PR — Podravska Revija
PR — Poetry Review
Pr — Practitioner
Pr — Press [Christchurch, New Zealand]
PR — Press Releases [United Kingdom]
Pr — Prevention
Pr — Probe
PR — Proceedings. American Society of University Composers
Pr — Prohemio
Pr — Prometheus
Pr — Prostor [Moscow]
PR — Psychoanalytic Review
PR — Psychological Review

PR — Public Roads
PRA — Parool (Amsterdam)
PrA — Primer Acto [*Madrid*]
Pra Bhar — Prabuddha Bharata [*Calcutta*]
PRACA — Practitioner
Prac Acc — Practical Accountant
Prac Accnt — Practical Accountant
Prac Anth — Practical Anthropology
Prac Appr Pat TM and Copyright — Practical Approach to Patents, Trademarks, and Copyrights
Praca Zabezp Spolecz — Praca i Zabezpieczenie Spoleczne
Prace Brnenske Zakl Ceskoslov Akad Ved — Prace Brnenske Zakladny Ceskoslovenske Akademie Ved
Prace Inst Bad Lesn — Prace Instytut Badawezy Lesnictwa
Prace Inst Fiz — Prace Instytutu Fizyki
Prace Inst Maszyn Przeplywowych — Prace Instytutu Maszyn Przeplywowych
Prace Inst Tech Drewna — Prace Instytut Technologii Drewna
Prace Inst Technol Drewna — Prace Instytut Technologii Drewna
Prace Nauk Akad Ekon Poznan — Prace Naukowe Akademii Ekonomicznej w Poznaniu
Prace Nauk Akad Ekon Wroclaw — Prace Naukowe Akademii Ekonomicznej we Wroclawiw
Prace Nauk Inst Cybernet Techn Politech Wroclaw Ser Konfer — Wroclaw. Politechnika. Instytut Cybernetyki Technicznej. Prace Naukowe. Seria Konferencje
Prace Nauk Inst Cybernet Techn Politech Wroclaw Ser Monograf — Wroclaw. Politechnika. Instytut Cybernetyki Technicznej. Prace Naukowe. Seria Monografie
Prace Nauk Inst Cybernet Techn Wroclaw Ser Stud i Materialy — Wroclaw. Politechnika. Instytut Cybernetyki Technicznej. Prace Naukowe. Seria Studia i Materialy
Prace Nauk Inst Mat Politech Wroclaw Ser Konfer — Wroclaw Politechnika Wroclawska. Instytutu Matematyki. Prace Naukowe. Seria Konferencje
Prace Nauk Inst Mat Politech Wroclaw Ser Monograf — Prace Naukowe Instytutu Matematyki Politechniki Wroclawskiej. Seria Monografie
Prace Nauk Inst Mat Politech Wroclaw Ser Stud Materialy — Politechniki Wroclawskiej. Instytutu Matematyki. Prace Naukowe. Seria Studia i Materialy
Prace Nauk Inst Mat Politech Wroclaw Ser Stud i Materialy — Politechniki Wroclawskiej. Instytutu Matematyki. Prace Naukowe. Seria Studia i Materialy
Prace Nauk Inst Ochr Rosl — Prace Naukowe Instytutu Ochrony Roslin
Prace Nauk Uniw Slask Katowic — Prace Naukowe Uniwersytetu Slaskiego w Katowicach
Prace Stud Vysokej Skoly Doprav Spojov Ziline Ser Mat-Fyz — Prace a Studie Vysokej Skoly Dopravy a Spojov v Ziline. Seria Matematicko-Fyzikalna
Prace Stud Vysokej Skoly Doprav Ziline Ser Mat-Fyz — Prace a Studie Vysokej Skoly Dopravnej v Ziline. Seria Matematicko-Fyzikalna
Prace Vyzkum Ust Lesn Hosp Mysl — Prace Vyzkumneho Ustavu Lesneho Hospodarstvi a Myslivosti
Prace Wroclaw Towarz Nauk Ser A — Prace Wroclawskiego Towarzytstwa Naukowego. Seria A
Prace Zakr Nauk Roln Lesn (Poznan) — Prace z Zakresu Nauk Rolniczych i Lesnych (Poznan)
Prac F — Practical Farmer
Prac Forecast — Practical Forecast for Home Economics
Prac Home Econ — Practical Home Economics
Prac Law — Practical Lawyer
Prac Lawyer — Practical Lawyer
Prac Lek — Pracovni Lekarstvi
Pract Account — Practical Accountant
Pract Adm — Practising Administrator
Pract Colloid Chem — Practical Colloid Chemistry
Pract Comput — Practical Computing
Pract Dig — Practice Digest
Pract Electron — Practical Electronics
Pract Electronics — Practical Electronics
Pract Energy — Practical Energy
Pract Eng (Chicago) — Practical Engineer (Chicago)
Pract Eng (London) — Practical Engineering (London)
Pract House — Practical Householder [*England*]
Practical Comput — Practical Computing
Practition — Practitioner
Pract M — Practical Magazine
Pract Metallogr Spec Issues — Practical Metallography. Special Issues
Pract Methods Electron Microsc — Practical Methods in Electron Microscopy
Pract Mot — Practical Motorist
Pract Otol (Kyoto) — Practica Otologica (Kyoto)
Pract Oto-Rhino-Laryngol — Practica Oto-Rhino-Laryngologica
Pract Pharm (Tokyo) — Practical Pharmacy (Tokyo)
Pract Plast — Practical Plastics
Pract Plast Aust NZ — Practical Plastics in Australia and New Zealand
Pract Power Farming — Practical Power Farming
Pract Spectrosc — Practical Spectroscopy
Pract Spectrosc Ser — Practical Spectroscopy Series
Pract Surf Technol — Practical Surface Technology [*Japan*]

Pract Welder — Practical Welder
Pract Wireless — Practical Wireless
Pract Woodworking — Practical Woodworking [*England*]
Prac Wel — Practical Welder
PRAED — Practical Energy
PrAeg — Probleme der Aegyptologie [*Leiden*]
Praehist Z — Praehistorische Zeitschrift
Praep Pharmazie — Praeparative Pharmazie
PRAGA — Probleme Agricole [*Romania*]
Prager Med Wochenschr — Prager Medizinische Wochenschrift
Prag Micro — Pragmatics Microfiche
PR Agric Exp Stn Bull — Puerto Rico. Agricultural Experiment Station. Bulletin
PR Agric Exp Stn Tech Pap — Puerto Rico. Agricultural Experiment Station. Technical Paper
Prague Bull Math Linguist — Prague Bulletin of Mathematical Linguistics
Prague St — Studies in English by Members of the English Seminar of the Charles University, Prague
Prague Stud Math Linguist — Prague Studies in Mathematical Linguistics
Prairie Gard — Prairie Garden
Prairie Inst Environ Health PIEH — Prairie Institute of Environmental Health. Report PIEH
Prairie Nat — Prairie Naturalist
Prairie Sch — Prairie Schooner
Prairie Schoon — Prairie Schooner
Prairie Sch R — Prairie School Review
PRAJ — Peace Research Abstracts Journal
Prakla-Seismos Rep — Prakla-Seismos Report [*West Germany*]
Prakruti Utkal Univ J Sci — Prakruti Utkal University Journal of Science
Prakt Akad Athenon — Praktika tes Akademias Athenon
Prakt Ak Ath — Praktika tes Akademias Athenon
Prakt Anaesth — Praktische Anaesthesie, Wiederbelebung, und Intensivtherapie
Prakt Arzt — Praktische Arzt
Prakt Bl Pflanzenbau Pflanzenschutz — Praktische Blaetter fuer Pflanzenbau und Pflanzenschutz
Prakt Chem — Praktische Chemie
Prakt Desinfekt — Praktische Desinfektor
Prakt Energiek — Praktische Energiekunde
Prakt Hell Hydrobiol Inst — Praktika. Hellenic Hydrobiological Institute
Praktika — Praktika tes en Athenais Arkhaiologikes Hetairias
Prakt Landtech — Praktische Landtechnik
Prakt Lek — Prakticky Lekar
Prakt Metallogr — Praktische Metallographie
Prakt Metallogr Sonderb — Praktische Metallographie. Sonderbaende
Prakt Schadlingsbekampf — Praktische Schadlingsbekampfer
Prakt Sudebnopsikhiatr Ekspert — Praktika Sudebnopsikhiatricheskoi Ekspertizy
Prakt Tier — Praktische Tieraerzt
Prakt Tierarzt — Praktische Tieraerzt [*German Federal Republic*]
Prakt Tuberk Bl — Praktische Tuberkulose Blaetter
Prakt Vet (Moskva) — Prakticheskaia Veterinariia (Moskva)
Prakt Wegw Bienenz — Praktischer Wegweiser fuer Bienenzuechter
Prakt Yad Fiz — Praktikum po Yadernoi Fizike
PRAMC — Pramana
PRAN — Proust Research Association. Newsletter
PRAODP — Agricultural Research Organization. Preliminary Report (Bet-Dagan)
PraPol — Prace Polonistyczne [*Warsaw*]
Pra S — Prairie Schooner
PRASD3 — Alabama. Agricultural Experiment Station. Progress Report Series (Auburn University)
Pratica Med — Pratica del Medico
Prat Ind Mec — Pratique des Industries Mecanique
Prat Soudage — Pratique du Soudage
Prat Vet Equine — Pratique Veterinaire Equine
PRAUD9 — Agricultural Research Institute Ukiriguru. Progress Report
PRAVA — Pravda
PRAXA — Praxis
Prax Forsch — Praxis und Forschung
Praxis — Praxis des Neusprachlichen Unterrichts
Praxis Int — Praxis International
Praxis Math — Praxis der Mathematik
Prax Kinder — Praxis der Kinderpsychologie und Kinderpsychiatrie
Prax Kinderpsychol Kinderpsychiatr — Praxis der Kinderpsychologie und Kinderpsychiatrie
Prax Klin Pneumol — Praxis und Klinik der Pneumologie
Prax Naturw — Praxis der Naturwissenschaften
Prax Naturwiss Phy — Praxis der Naturwissenschaften. Physik
Prax Naturwiss Phys Unterr Sch — Praxis der Naturwissenschaften. Physik im Unterricht der Schulen
Prax Naturwiss Teil 3 — Praxis der Naturwissenschaften. Teil 3. Chemie [*West Germany*]
Prax Pneumol — Praxis der Pneumologie
Prax Psychother — Praxis der Psychotherapie
Prax Schriftenr Phys — Praxis Schriftenreihe Physik

Prax Vet — Praxis Veterinaria
Prazsky Sbor Hist — Prazsky Sbornik Historicky
PRBCA — Process Biochemistry
PRBCB — Preparative Biochemistry
PRBMD — Physical Review. Section B. Condensed Matter
Pr Bot Sadu Kiiv Derzh Univ — Pratsi Botanichnogo Sadu Kiivs'kii Derzhavnii Universitet
PrC — Proster in Cas
PRCAD — Primary Care
PRCAFL — Publications. Research Center in Anthropology, Folklore, and Linguistics
Pr Cent Inst Ochr Pr — Prace Centralnege Instytutu Ochrony Pracy
Pr Cesk Vyzk Slevarenskeho — Prace Ceskoslovenskeho Vyzkumu Slevarenskeho
Pr Chem — Prace Chemiczne
Pr Chem Pr Nauk Uniw Slask Katowic — Prace Chemiczne. Prace Naukowe Uniwersytetu Slaskiego w Katowicach
PRCMC — Percussionist
PRCMC — Protective Coatings on Metals [*English Translation*]
PR Commonw Water Resour Bull — Puerto Rico Commonwealth. Water Resources Bulletin
PRDE — Preliminary Determination of Epicenters [*National Oceanic and Atmospheric Administration*]
Pr Dzialu Zywenia Rosl Nawoz — Prace Dzialu Zywenia Roslin i Nawozenia [*Poland*]
PRE — Realencyclopaedie fuer Protestantische Theologie und Kirche
PREBD — Population Reports. Series B [*United States*]
PRECA — Pauly-Wissowas Realencyclopaedie der Classischen Altertumswissenschaft
Precamb Res — Precambrian Research
Precambrian Res — Precambrian Research
Precast Concr — Precast Concrete
Precis Eng — Precision Engineering
Precis Engng — Precision Engineering
Precis Met — Precision Metal
Precis Met Molding — Precision Metal Molding
Predel no Dopustimye Konts Atmos Zagryaz — Predel no Dopustimye Kontsentratsii Atmosfernykh Zagryaznenii
Predi 161 — Predicasts. Recreational Vehicles Industry Study 161
Predi 162 — Predicasts. World Rubber and Tire Markets Industry Study 162
Predi 163 — Predicasts. Glass and Advanced Fibers Industry Study 163
Predi 165 — Predicasts. Water Treatment Chemicals Industry Study 165
Predi 168 — Predicasts. World Housing Industry Study 168
PredicadorEv — El Predicador Evangelico [*Buenos Aires*]
Predi P55 — Predicasts. Industrial Packaging Paper Trends P-55
PREEB — Presence
PREGA — Promyshlennaya Energetika
Pregled Naucnoteh Rad Inform Zavod Tehn Drveta — Pregled Naucnotehnickih Radova i Informacija. Zavod za Tehnologiiu Drveta
Pregl Probl Ment Retard Osoba — Pregled Problema Mentalno Retardiranih Osoba
Preh — Prehistoire
Prehist Arieg — Prehistoire Ariegeoise
Prehlad Lesnickej Lit — Prehl'ad Lesnickej. Drevarskej. Celulozovej a Papierenskej Literatury
Prehl Lesn Mysliv Lit — Prehled Lesnicke a Myslivecke Literatury
Prehl Zahr Zemed Lit — Prehled Zahranicni Zemedelske Literatury
Prehl Zemed Lit — Prehled Zemedelske Literatury
Prehl Zemed Lit Zahr Domaci — Prehled Zemedelske Literatury Zahranicni i Domaci
Prehrambeno Tehnol Rev — Prehrambeno Tehnoloska Revija
PRELA — Przeglad Elektroniki [*Poland*]
Prelim Rep Dir Gen Mines (Queb) — Preliminary Report. Direction Generale des Mines (Quebec)
Prelim Rep Rehovot Nat Univ Inst Agr — Preliminary Report. Rehovot. National and University Institute of Agriculture
PRENA — Product Engineering [*New York*]
PR Enferm — Puerto Rico y Su Enferma
Prensa Med Argent — Prensa Medica Argentina
Prensa Med Mex — Prensa Medica Mexicana
PREPA — Przeglad Epidemiologiczny
Prep Bioch — Preparative Biochemistry
Prep Biochem — Preparative Biochemistry
Prep Inorg React — Preparative Inorganic Reactions
Prepr Am Chem Soc Div Fuel Chem — Preprints. American Chemical Society. Division of Fuel Chemistry
Prepr Amer Wood Pres Ass — Preprint. American Wood Preservers' Association
Prepr Am Soc Lubr Eng — Preprints. American Society of Lubrication Engineers
Prepr Annu Sci Meet Aerosp Med Assoc — Preprints. Annual Scientific Meeting. Aerospace Medical Association
Prepr Daresbury Lab — Preprint. Daresbury Laboratory
Prepr Div Pet Chem Am Chem Soc — Preprints. American Chemical Society. Division of Petroleum Chemistry

Preprint Inst Eng Aust Conf — Preprint. Institution of Engineers of Australia. Conference
Prepr Pap Annu Conf Australas Corros Assoc — Australasian Corrosion Association. Preprinted Papers of the Annual Conference
Prepr Pap Natl Meet Div Environ Chem Am Chem Soc — Preprints of Papers Presented at National Meeting. Division of Environmental Chemistry. American Chemical Society
Prepr Pap Natl Meet Div Water Air Waste Chem Am Chem Soc — Preprints of Papers Presented at National Meeting. Division of Water, Air, and Waste Chemistry. American Chemical Society
Prepr Pap Oilseed Process Clin — Preprints of Papers. Oilseed Processing Clinic
Prepr Sci Program Aerosp Med Assoc — Preprints. Scientific Program. Aerospace Medical Association
Prepr Ser — Preprint Series. University of Oslo. Institute of Mathematics
Prepr Ser Inst Math Univ Oslo — Preprint Series. Institute of Mathematics. University of Oslo [*Norway*]
PRER — Prevention Resources
Pres — Presbyterian
PresAfr — Presence Africaine
Presb Q — Presbyterian Quarterly Review
Presb R — Presbyterian Review
Presb & Ref R — Presbyterian and Reformed Review
Presbyt-St. Luke's Hosp Med Bull — Presbyterian-St. Luke's Hospital. Medical Bulletin
Presbyt-St. Luke's Hosp Res Rep — Presbyterian-St. Luke's Hospital. Research Report
Pre-Sch Years — Pre-School Years
Pres Coll Physiol Inst J — Presidency College. Physiological Institute Journal
Presence Afr — Presence Africaine
Preserv Madeiras — Preservacao de Madeiras
Preserv Madeiras Bol Tec — Preservacao de Madeiras. Boletim Tecnico
Pres His S — Presbyterian Historical Society. Journal
Pres His SJ — Presbyterian Historical Society. Journal
Pres J — Presbyterian Journal
Pres Life — Presbyterian Life
Presse Actual — Presse Actualite
Pressedienst Bundesminist Bild Wiss — Pressedienst. Bundesministerium fuer Bildung und Wissenschaft
Presse Med — Presse Medicale
Presse Med Belge — Presse Medicale Belge
Pressemitt Nordrh-Westfalen — Pressemitteilung Nordrhein-Westfalen
Presse Therm Clim — Presse Thermale et Climatique
Presse-Umsch — Presse-Umschau
Pressluft Ind — Pressluft Industrie
Pres Studies Q — Presidential Studies Quarterly
Pres Stud Q — Presidential Studies Quarterly
Pressure Eng — Pressure Engineering [*Japan*]
Prestige de la Photogr — Prestige de la Photographie
Preuss Jahrb — Preussische Jahrbuecher
Preuss Sitzb — Preussische Akademie der Wissenschaften. Sitzungsbericht
Prev Fract Conf Aust Fract Group — Prevention of Fracture. Conference of the Australian Fracture Group
Previd Soc — Previdenza Sociale
Prev Med — Preventive Medicine
Prev Stomatol — Prevenzione Stomatologica
PREXA — Personal Report for the Executive
PREXD — Propellants and Explosives
PRF — Publications Romanes et Francaises
PRFCA — Products Finishing (Cincinnati)
PRFIA — Product Finishing [*London*]
Pr Fiz Pr Nauk Uniw Slaskiego Katowic — Prace Fizyczne. Prace Naukowe Uniwersytetu Slaskiego w Katowicach [*Poland*]
Pr Fiz Pr Nauk Uniw Slask Katowic — Prace Fizyczne. Prace Naukowe Uniwersytetu Slaskiego w Katowicach
PRFO — Prairie Forum. Journal. Canadian Plains Research Centre
PRG — Progresso. Driemaandelijks Tijdschrift van de Nederlands Italiaanse Kamer van Koophandel
PRGEA — Przeglad Geofizyczny
Pr Geol-Mineral Acta Univ Wratislav — Prace Geologiczno-Mineralogiczne. Acta Universitatis Wratislaviensis
PRGLB — Prostaglandins
Pr Gl Inst Gorn — Prace Glownego Instytutu Gornictwa [*Poland*]
Pr Gl Inst Gorn Komun — Prace Glownego Instytutu Gornictwa. Komunikat
Pr Gl Inst Przem Rolnego Spozyw — Prace Glownego Instytutu Przemyslu Rolnego i Spozywczego
Pr Gory Goretskaga Navuk Tav — Pratsy Gory Goretskaga Navukov aga Tavarystva
PRGVB — Progressive
PR Health Bull — Puerto Rico Health Bulletin
PrHlit — Prace Historycznoliterackie
Pri — Priroda
PRIA — Proceedings. Royal Irish Academy
PRIAA — Proceedings. Royal Irish Academy. Section A. Mathematical and Physical Sciences

PRIBA — Proceedings. Royal Irish Academy. Section B. Biological, Geological, and Chemical Science
Pribliz Metod Resen Differencial Uravnen — Priblizennye Metody Resenija Differencial nyh Uravnenii
Prib Metody Anal Izluch — Pribory i Metody Analiza Izluchenii
Pribory i Sistemy Avtomat — Pribory i Sistemy Avtomatiki
Prib Sist Avtom — Pribory i Sistemy Avtomatiki
Prib Sist Upr — Pribory i Sistemy Upravleniya
Prib i Tekh Eksp — Pribory i Tekhnika Eksperimenta
Prib Tekhn — Pribory i Tekhnika Eksperimenta
Prib Ustroistva Sredstv Avtom Telemekh — Pribory i Ustroistva Sredstv Avtomatiki i Telemekhaniki
Price Waterhouse R — Price Waterhouse Review
Price Waterhouse Rev — Price Waterhouse Review
PRIGA — Prace Instytutu Geologii
Prikladnaya Geofiz — Prikladnaya Geofizika
Prikl Biokhim Mikrobiol — Prikladnaya Biokhimiya i Mikrobiologiya
Prikl Geofiz — Prikladnaya Geofizika
Prikl Geom i Inzener Grafika — Prikladnaja Geometrija i Inzenernaja Grafika
Prikl Mat — Prikladnaya Matematika i Mekhanika
Prikl Mat Mekh — Prikladnaya Matematika i Mekhanika
Prikl Mat i Mekh — Prikladnaya Matematika i Mekhanika
Prikl Mat i Programmirovanie — Prikladnaja Matematika i Programmirovanie
Prikl Meh — Akademija Nauk Ukrainskoi SSR. Otdelenie Matematiki. Mehaniki i Kibernetiki. Prikladnaja Mehanika
Prikl Mekh — Akademiya Nauk Ukrainskoi SSR. Otdelenie Matematiki. Mekhaniki i Kibernetiki. Prikladnaya Mekhanika
Prikl Mekh — Prikladnaya Mekhanika
Prikl Mekh Priborostr — Prikladnaya Mekhanika v Priborostroenii
Prikl Problemy Proc i Plast — Gor'kovskii Gosudarstvennyi Universitet Imeni N. I. Lobacevskogo. Prikladnye Problemy Procnosti i Plasticnosti
Prikl Yad Fiz — Prikladnaya Yadernaya Fizika
Prikl Yad Spektrosk — Prikladnaya Yadernaya Spektroskopiya
PrilKJIF — Prilozi za Knjizevnost, Jezik, Istoriju, i Folklor
Prilozi — Prilozi za Knjizevnost, Jezik, Istoriju, i Folklor
PrilPJ — Prilozi Proucavanju Jezika
Primary Educ — Primary Education
Primary J — Primary Journal
Primary Maths — Primary Mathematics
Primary Sci Bull — Primary Science Bulletin
Primates Med — Primates in Medicine
Primatolog — Primatologia
Prim Ed-Pop Ed — Primary Education - Popular Educator
Prim Educ — Primary Education
Primenen Mat Ekonom — Primenenie Matematiki v Ekonomike
Primen Mat Metodov Biol — Primenenie Matematicheskikh Metodov v Biologii
Primen Mikroelem Sel-khoz Akad Nauk UkrSSR — Primenenie Mikroelementov Sel'skom Khozyaistve Akademiya Nauk Ukrainskoi SSR
Primen Polim Mater Nar Khoz — Primenenie Polimernykh Materialov v Narodnom Khozyaistve
Primen Tsifrovykh Analogovykh Vychisl Mash Yad Fiz Tekh — Primenenie Tsifrovykh i Analogovykh Vychislitel'nykh Mashin v Yadernoi Fizike i Tekhnike
Primen Ul'traakust Issled Veshchestva — Primenenie Ul'traakustiki k Issledovaniyu Veshchestva
Princ — Princeton Review
Princ in Counc — Principals in Council
Prince S B — Princeton Seminary Bulletin
Princeton Coll B — Princeton College. Bulletin
Princeton Conf Cerebrovasc Dis — Princeton Conference on Cerebrovascular Diseases
Princeton Conf Cereb Vasc Dis — Princeton Conference on Cerebral Vascular Diseases [*Later, Princeton Conference on Cerebrovascular Diseases*]
Princeton Math Ser — Princeton Mathematical Series
Princeton Mus Rec — Princeton University. Museum of Historic Art. Record
Princeton Stud Math Econom — Princeton Studies in Mathematical Economics
Princeton Univ Lib Chron — Princeton University Library Chronicle
Princ Food Rice — Principal Food. Rice
Principia Cardiol — Principia Cardiologica
Princ ns — Princeton Review (New Series)
PrincSB — Princeton Seminary Bulletin
PrincSemB — Princeton Seminary Bulletin [*Princeton, NJ*]
Princ Theol R — Princeton Theological Review
Princ Univ Bull — Princeton University Bulletin
Pr Inst Badaw Lesn — Prace Instytutu Badawczego Lesnictwa
Pr Inst Celul Papier — Prace Instytutu Celulozowo-Papierniczego
Pr Inst Elektrotech — Prace Instytutu Elektrotechniki
Pr Inst Elektrotech (Warsaw) — Prace Instytutu Elektrotechniki (Warsaw)
Pr Inst Geol Korisnikh Kopalin Akad Nauk Ukr — Pratsi Institut Geologii Korisnikh Kopalin Akademiya Nauk Ukrains'koi
Pr Inst Gidrobiol Akad Nauk Ukr RSR — Pratsi Instytutu Gidrobiologii Akademiya Nauk Ukrains'koi RSR
Pr Inst Gospod Wodnej — Prace Instytutu Gospodarki Wodnej
Pr Inst Hutn — Prace Instytutow Hutniczych

Pr Inst Inz Chem Politech Warsz — Prace Instytutu Inzynierii Chemicznej Politechniki Warszawskiej
Pr Inst Jedwabiu Nat — Prace Instytutu Jedwabiu Naturalnego
Pr Inst Lab Badaw Przem Spozyw — Prace Instytutow i Laboratoriow Badawczych Przemyslu Spozywczego
Pr Inst Lacznosci — Prace Instytutu Lacznosci
Pr Inst Masz Mat — Prace Instytutu Maszyn Matematycznych
Pr Inst Masz Przeplyw — Prace Instytutu Maszyn Przeplywowych
Pr Inst Masz Przeplyw Pol Akad Nauk — Prace Instytutu Maszyn Przeplywowych. Polska Akademia Nauk [*Poland*]
Pr Inst Mech — Prace Instytutow Mechaniki
Pr Inst Mech Precyz — Prace Instytutu Mechaniki Precyzyjnej [*Poland*]
Pr Inst Met — Prace Instytutu Metalurgie
Pr Inst Metal Gliwice (Pol) — Prace Instytutu Metalurgii. Gliwice (Poland)
Pr Inst Metal Zelaza — Prace Instytutu Metalurgii Zelaza
Pr Inst Meteorol Gospod Wodnej — Prace Instytutu Meteorologii i Gospodarki Wodnej
Pr Inst Met Niezelaz — Prace Instytutu Metali Niezelaznych
Pr Inst Minist Hutn (Pol) — Prace Instytutu Ministerstwa Hutnictwa (Poland)
Pr Inst Naft (Krakow) — Prace Instytutu Naftowego (Krakow) [*Poland*]
Pr Inst Obrobki Skrawaniem — Prace Instytutu Obrobki Skrawaniem [*Poland*]
Pr Inst Odlew — Prace Instytutu Odlewnictwa
Pr Inst Odlew Zesz Spec — Prace Instytutu Odlewnictwa. Zeszyty Specjalne
Pr Inst Odlew Zesz Specjalne — Prace Instytutu Odlewnictwa. Zeszyty Specjalne [*Poland*]
Pr Inst Przem Cukrow — Prace Instytutu Przemyslu Cukrowniczego
Pr Inst Przem Miecz — Prace Instytutu Przemyslu Mieczarskiego
Pr Inst Przem Org — Prace Instytutu Przemyslu Organicznego
Pr Inst Przem Skorzanego — Prace Instytutu Przemyslu Skorzanego
Pr Inst Przem Szkla Ceram — Prace Instytutu Przemyslu Szkla i Ceramiki
Pr Inst Przem Wlok Lykowych — Prace Instytutu Przemyslu Wlokien Lykowych
Pr Inst Sadow Ser E Mater Zjazdow Konf — Prace Instytutu Sadownictwa. Seria E. Materialy Zjazdow i Konferencji
Pr Inst Sadow Skierniew — Prace Instytutu Sadownictwa w Skierniewicach
Pr Inst Sadow Skierniewicach — Prace Instytutu Sadownictwa w Skierniewicach
Pr Inst Tech Budow Ser 1 — Prace Instytutu Techniki Budowlanej. Seria 1. Materialy Budowlane i Ich Zastosowanie
Pr Inst Tech Budow Ser 2 — Prace Instytutu Techniki Budowlanej. Seria 2. Konstrukeje Budowlane i Inzynierskie
Pr Inst Tech Ciepl — Prace Instytutu Techniki Cieplnej [*Poland*]
Pr Inst Technol Drewna — Prace Instytut Technologii Drewna
Pr Inst Technol Elektron — Prace Instytutu Technologii Elektronowej
Pr Inst Tele- & Radiotech — Prace Instytutu Tele- i Radiotechnicznego
Pr Inst Wlok — Prace Instytutu Wlokiennictwa
Pr Inst Wlok (Lodz) — Prace Instytutu Wlokiennictwa (Lodz)
Print Art — Printing Art [*Massachusetts*]
Print Art Q — Printing Art Quarterly
Print Bookbind Trade Rev — Printing and Bookbinding Trade Review
Print Coll Q — Print Collector's Quarterly
Print Equip Eng — Printing Equipment Engineer
Print Graph Arts — Printing and Graphic Arts
Printing — Printing Impressions
Printing Abs — Printing Abstracts
Printing Abstr — Printing Abstracts
Printing Impr — Printing Impressions
Printing and Pub — Printing and Publishing
Printing Trades J — Printing Trades Journal
Print Mag — Printing Magazine
Print Mag Natl Lithogr — Printing Magazine National Lithographer
Print Manag — Printing Management
Print Prod — Printing Production
Print & Pub — Printing and Publishing
Print R — Print Review
Print Rev — Print Review
Print Sales — Printed Salesmanship
Print Technol — Printing Technology
Print Trades J — Printing Trades Journal
Pr IPO — Prace IPO [*Instytutu Przemyslu Organicznego*]
PRIRA — Priroda [*Moscow*]
P R Ir Ac A — Proceedings. Royal Irish Academy. Section A. Mathematical, Astronomical, and Physical Science
P R Ir Ac B — Proceedings. Royal Irish Academy. Section B. Biological, Geological, and Chemical Science
P R Ir Ac C — Proceedings. Royal Irish Academy. Section C. Archaeology, Celtic Studies, History, Linguistics, Literature
PRIRB — Priroda (Sofia, Bulgaria)
Prir Gaz Sib — Prirodnyi Gaz Sibiri
Prir-Mat Fak Univ Kiril Metodij-Skopje God Zb Biol — Prirodno-Matematicka Fakultet na Univerzitetot Kiril i Metodij-Skopje. Godisen Zbornik. Biologija
Prir Mat Fak Univ Kiril Metodij-Skopje God Zb Sek A — Prirodno-Matematicka Fakultet na Univerzitetot Kiril i Metodij-Skopje. Godisen Zbornik. Sekcja A. Matematika, Fizika, i Hemija
Prir (Moscow) — Priroda (Moscow)

Prirod-Mat Fak Univ Kiril Metodij Skopje Godisen Zb — Prirodno-Matematicka Fakultet na Univerzitetot Kiril i Metodij Skopje. Godisen Zbornik

Prirod-Mat Fak Univ Kiril i Metodij Skopje Godisen Zb — Prirodno-Matematicka Fakultet na Univerzitetot Kiril i Metodij Skopje. Godisen Zbornik

Prirodonauc Muz Skopje Posebno Izd — Prirodonaucen Muzej Skopje Posebno Izdanie

Prirodosl Istraz Acta Biol — Prirodoslovna Istrazivanja Acta Biologica

Prirodosl Istraz Acta Geol — Prirodoslovna Istrazivanja Acta Geologica

Prirodoved Cas Slezsky — Prirodovedny Casopis Slezsky

Prirodoved Pr Ustavu Cesk Akad Ved Brne — Prirodovedne Prace Ustavu Ceskoslovenske Akademie Ved v Brne

Prir (Sofia) — Priroda (Sofia)

Prir Tr Resur Levoberezhnoi Ukr Ikh Ispolz — Prirodnye i Trudot ye Resursy Levoberezhnoi Ukrainy i Ikh Ispolzovanie

Prir Usloviya Zapadn Sib — Prirodnye Usloviya Zapadnoi Sibiri

Prisadki Smaz Maslam — Prisadki i Smazochnym Maslam

PRISD — Proceedings. Indian Academy of Sciences. Series. Engineering Sciences

Pris Jrnl — Prisoners Journal

Prism Int — Prism International

PrisrAcSci & Hum — Proceedings. Israel Academy of Sciences and Humanities [*Jerusalem*]

PRITA — Problems of Information Transmission

Pr ITME — Prace ITME [*Instytut Technologii Materialow Elektronicznych*]

Privacy Rept — Privacy Report

Private Pract — Private Practice

Priv Lib — Private Library

Priv Libr — Private Library

PrJ — Preussische Jahrbuecher

PRJ — Public Relations Journal

PR J Public Health Trop Med — Puerto Rico Journal of Public Health and Tropical Medicine

PRK — Praktijkgids

PRKNA — Progress in Reaction Kinetics

Pr Kom Biol (Poznan) — Prace Komisji Biologicznej (Poznan)

Pr Kom Biol Poznan Tow Przyj Nauk — Prace Komisji Biologicznej. Poznanskie Towarzystwo Przyjaciol Nauk [*Poland*]

Pr Kom Ceram Pol Akad Nauk Ceram — Prace Komisji Ceramicznej. Polskiej Akademii Nauk. Ceramica

Pr Kom Krystalogr Pol Akad Nauk Inst Nisk Temp Badan Strukt — Prace Komitetu Krystalografii. Polska Akademia Nauk. Instytut Niskich Temperatur i Badan Strukturalnych

Pr Kom Mat-Przyr Poznan Tow Przyj Nauk — Prace Komisji Matematyczno-Przyrodniczej. Poznanskie Towarzystwo Przyjaciol Nauk [*Poland*]

Pr Kom Nauk Roln Kom Nauk Lesn Poznan Tow Przyj Nauk — Prace Komisji Nauk Rolniczych i Komisji Nauk Lesnych. Poznanskiej Towarzystwo Przyjaciol

Pr Kom Roln Lesn (Poznan) — Prace Komisji Nauk Rolniczych i Lesnych. Poznanskie Towarzystwo Przyjaciol Nauk (Poznan)

Pr Kom Nauk Tech Pol Akad Nauk Ser Ceram — Prace Komisji Nauk Technicznych. Polska Akademia Nauk. Serja Ceramika

Pr Kom Technol Drewna Poznan Tow Przyj Nauk — Prace Komisji Technologii Drewna. Poznanskie Towarzystwo Przyjaciol Nauk [*Poland*]

PRKPA — Probleme der Kosmichen Physik

PRKRA — Parks and Recreation

PRLASR — Population Research Laboratory. University of Alberta. Department of Sociology. Alberta Series Report

PRLEA — Pracovni Lekarstvi

PrLit — Prace Literackie

PRLKA — Przeglad Lekarski

PRLTA — Physical Review. Letters

PRLWCSR — Population Research Laboratory. University of Alberta. Department of Sociology. Western Canada Series Report

PRM — Polski Rocznik Muzykologiczny

PRM — PR Magazin. Public Relations und Informationspolitik in Medien und Gesellschaft

PrM — Pravna Misul

PrM — Protestantische Monatshefte

PRMA — Proceedings. Royal Musical Association

Pr Mater Nauk Inst Matki Dziecka — Prace i Materialy Naukowe. Instytut Matki i Dziecka

Pr Mater Pershogo Khark Derzh Med Inst — Pratsi i Materiali Pershogo Kharkivs'kogo Derzhavnogo Medichnogo Institutu

Pr Mater Zootech — Prace i Materialy Zootechniczne

PRMCL — Periodica de Re Morali Canonica Liturgica

PRMCLS — Papers. Regional Meeting. Chicago Linguistics Society

PRMEA — Presse Medicale

Pr Med Opolskie Tow Przyj Nauk Wyd Nauk Med — Prace Medyczne. Opolskie Towarzystwo Przyjaciol Nauk. Wydzial 5. Nauk Medycznych

Pr Molodikh Uch Ukr Akad Sil's'kogospod Nauk — Pratsi Molodikh Uchenikh Ukrains'ka Akademiya Sil's'kogospodars'kikh Nauk

Pr Moravskoslezske Akad Ved Prir — Prace Moravskoslezske Akademie Ved Prirodnich

Pr Morsk Inst Rybackiego Ser A — Prace Morskiego Instytutu Rybackiego. Seria A. Oceanografia i Biologia Rybacka

Pr Morsk Inst Rybackiego Ser B — Prace Morskiego Instytutu Rybackiego. Seria B. Technika Rybacka i Technologia Ryb

Pr Morsk Inst Rybacki Gdyni — Prace Morski Instytut Rybacki w Gdyni [*Poland*]

PRMSA — Progress in Materials Science

PRMSB — Proceedings. Royal Microscopical Society

PRMSC — Proceedings. Annual Reliability and Maintainability Symposium

PRMSD — Problemy Mashinostroeniya

Pr Muz Ziemi — Prace Muzeum Ziemi

PRN — Playfulness, Revelry, Nonsense [*Quarterly Newsletter of Nurses for Laughter*] [*Title is derived from the pharmaceutical term PRN (Pro Re Nata)*]

Pr Naturwiss Teil 3 — Praxis der Naturwissenschaften. Teil 3. Chemie

Pr Nauk Akad Ekon Oskara Langego Wroclaw Chem — Prace Naukowe Akademii Ekonomicznej Imienia Oskara Langego we Wroclawiu. Chemia

Pr Nauk Inst Chem Org Fiz Politech Wroclaw — Prace Naukowe Instytutu Chemii Organicznej i Fizycznej Politechniki Wroclawskiej

Pr Nauk Inst Chem Org Fiz Politech Wroclaw Ser K — Prace Naukowe Instytutu Chemii Organicznej i Fizycznej Politechniki Wroclawskiej. Seria. Konferencje

Pr Nauk Inst Chem Org Fiz Politech Wroclaw Ser Konf — Prace Naukowe Instytutu Chemii Organicznej i Fizycznej Politechniki Wroclawskiej. Seria Konferencje

Pr Nauk Inst Chem Org Fiz Politech Wroclaw Ser S — Prace Naukowe Instytutu Chemii Organicznej i Fizycznej Politechniki Wroclawskiej. Seria Studia i Materialy

Pr Nauk Inst Chem Technol Nafty Wegla Politech Wroclaw — Prace Naukowe Instytutu Chemii i Technologii Nafty i Wegla Politechniki Wroclawskiej [*Poland*]

Pr Nauk Inst Cybern Tech Politech Wroclaw Ser K — Prace Naukowe Instytutu Cybernetyki Technicznej Politechniki Wroclawskiej. Seria Konferencje

Pr Nauk Inst Cybern Tech Politech Wroclaw Ser M — Prace Naukowe Instytutu Cybernetyki Technicznej Politechniki Wroclawskiej. Seria Monografie

Pr Nauk Inst Cybern Tech Politech Wroclaw Ser S — Prace Naukowe Instytutu Cybernetyki Technicznej Politechniki Wroclawskiej. Seria Studia i Materialy

Pr Nauk Inst Fiz Politech Wroclaw — Prace Naukowe Instytutu Fizyki Politechniki Wroclawskiej

Pr Nauk Inst Fiz Politech Wroclaw Ser M — Prace Naukowe Instytutu Fizyki Politechniki Wroclawskiej. Seria Monografie

Pr Nauk Inst Fiz Politech Wroclaw Ser Monogr — Prace Naukowe Instytutu Fizyki Politechniki Wroclawskiej. Seria Monografie

Pr Nauk Inst Fiz Politech Wroclaw Ser S — Prace Naukowe Instytutu Fizyki Politechniki Wroclawskiej. Seria Studia i Materialy

Pr Nauk Inst Fiz Tech Politech Wroclaw — Prace Naukowe Instytutu Fizyki Technicznej Politechniki Wroclawskiej

Pr Nauk Inst Geotech Politech Wroclaw — Prace Naukowe Instytutu Geotechniki Politechniki Wroclawskiej [*Poland*]

Pr Nauk Inst Gorn Politech Wroclaw — Prace Naukowe Instytutu Gornictwa Politechniki Wroclawskiej [*Poland*]

Pr Nauk Inst Gorn Wroclaw — Prace Naukowe Instytutu Gornictwa Politechniki Wroclawskiej

Pr Nauk Inst Inz Chem Urzadz Ciepl Politech Wroclaw Ser M — Prace Naukowe Instytutu Inzynierii Chemicznej i Urzadzen Cieplnych Politechniki Wroclawskiej. Seria. Monografie

Pr Nauk Inst Inz Chem Urzadzen Cieplnych Politech Wroclaw — Prace Naukowe Instytutu Inzynierii Chemicznej i Urzadzen Cieplnych Politechniki Wroclawskiej [*Poland*]

Pr Nauk Inst Inz Ladowej Politech Wroclaw — Prace Naukowe Instytutu Inzynierii Ladowej Politechniki Wroclawskiej

Pr Nauk Inst Inz Ochr Srodowiska Politech Wroclaw — Prace Naukowe Instytutu Inzynierii Ochrony Srodowiska Politechniki Wroclawskiej [*Poland*]

Pr Nauk Inst Inz Ochr Sr Politech Wroclaw — Prace Naukowe Instytutu Inzynierii Ochrony Srodowiska Politechniki Wroclawskiej

Pr Nauk Inst Inz Sanit Wodnej Politech Wroclaw — Prace Naukowe Instytutu Inzynierii Sanitarnej i Wodnej Politechniki Wroclawskiej

Pr Nauk Inst Materialozn Mech Tech Politech Wroclaw — Prace Naukowe Instytutu Materialoznawstwa i Technicznej Politechniki Wroclawskiej

Pr Nauk Inst Materialozn Mech Tech Politech Wroclaw Ser M — Prace Naukowe Instytutu Materialoznawstwa i Mechaniki Technicznej Politechniki Wroclawskiej. Seria. Monografie

Pr Nauk Inst Materialozn Mech Tech Politech Wroclaw Ser S — Prace Naukowe Instytutu Materialoznawstwa i Mechaniki Technicznej Politechniki Wroclawskiej. Seria. Studia i Materialy

Pr Nauk Inst Mat Politech Wroclaw Ser M — Prace Naukowe Instytutu Matematyki Politechniki Wroclawskiej. Seria Monografie

Pr Nauk Inst Mat Politech Wroclaw Ser S — Prace Naukowe Instytutu Matematyki Politechniki Wroclawskiej. Seria Studia i Materialy

Pr Nauk Inst Metrol Elektr Politech Wroclaw Ser K — Prace Naukowe Instytutu Metrologii Elektrycznej Politechniki Wroclawskiej. Seria. Konferencje
Pr Nauk Inst Metrol Elektr Politech Wroclaw Ser Konf — Prace Naukowe Instytutu Metrologii Elektrycznej Politechniki Wroclawskiej. Seria Konferencje
Pr Nauk Inst Metrol Elektr Politech Wroclaw Ser M — Prace Naukowe Instytutu Metrologii Elektrycznej Politechniki Wroclawskiej. Seria. Monografie
Pr Nauk Inst Metrol Elektr Politech Wroclaw Ser S — Prace Naukowe Instytutu Metrologii Elektrycznej Politechniki Wroclawskiej. Seria. Studia i Materialy
Pr Nauk Inst Ochr Rosl — Prace Naukowe Instytutu Ochrony Roslin
Pr Nauk Inst Ochr Rosl (Warsz) — Prace Naukowe Instytutu Ochrony Roslin (Warszawa)
Pr Nauk Inst Przem Org (Warsaw) — Prace Naukowe Instytutu Przemyslu Organicznego (Warsaw)
Pr Nauk Inst Tech Ciepl Mech Plynow Politech Wroclaw — Prace Naukowe Instytutu Techniki Cieplnej i Mechaniki Plynow Politechniki Wroclawskiej
Pr Nauk Inst Tech Ciepl Mech Plynow Politech Wroclaw Ser M — Prace Naukowe Instytutu Techniki Cieplnej i Mechaniki Plynow Politechniki Wroclawskiej. Seria. Monografie
Pr Nauk Inst Tech Ciepl Mech Plynow Politech Wroclaw Ser S — Prace Naukowe Instytutu Techniki Cieplnej i Mechaniki Plynow Politechniki Wroclawskiej. Seria. Studia i Materialy
Pr Nauk Inst Technol Elektron Politech Wroclaw — Prace Naukowe Instytutu Technologii Elektronowej Politechniki Wroclawskiej
Pr Nauk Inst Technol Elektron Politech Wroclaw Ser Monogr — Prace Naukowe Instytutu Technologii Elektronowej Politechniki Wroclawskiej. Seria Monografie
Pr Nauk Inst Technol Elektron Politech Wroclaw Ser S — Prace Naukowe Instytutu Technologii Elektronowej Politechniki Wroclawskiej. Seria. Studia i Materialy
Pr Nauk Inst Technol Nieorg Nawozow Miner Politech Wroclaw — Prace Naukowe Instytutu Technologii Nieorganicznej i Nawozow Mineralnych Politechniki Wroclawskiej
Pr Nauk Inst Technol Org Tworz Sztucz Politech Wroclaw Ser S — Prace Naukowe Instytutu Technologii Organicznej i Tworzyw Sztucznych Politechniki Wroclawskiej. Seria. Studia i Materialy
Pr Nauk Inst Technol Org Tworzyw Sztucznych Politech Wroclaw — Prace Naukowe Instytutu Technologii Organicznej i Tworzyw Sztucznych Politechniki Wroclawskiej
Pr Nauk Inst Telekomun Akust Politech Wroclaw Ser K — Prace Naukowe Instytutu Telekomunikacji i Akustyki Politechniki Wroclawskiej. Seria. Konferencje
Pr Nauk Inst Telekomun Akust Politech Wroclaw Ser M — Prace Naukowe Instytutu Telekomunikacji i Akustyki Politechniki Wroclawskiej. Seria. Monografie
Pr Nauk Inst Telekomun Akust Politech Wroclaw Ser S — Prace Naukowe Instytutu Telekomunikacji i Akustyki Politechniki Wroclawskiej. Seria. Studia i Materialy
Pr Nauk Inst Ukladow Elektromasz Politech Wroclaw Ser S — Prace Naukowe Instytutu Ukladow Elektromaszynowych Politechniki Wroclawskiej. Seria. Studia i Materialy
Pr Nauk Politech Szczecin — Prace Naukowe Politechniki Szczecinskiej [*Poland*]
Pr Nauk Politech Warsz Elektron — Prace Naukowe Politechnika Warszawska Elektronika
Pr Nauk Politech Wroclaw Ser Konf — Prace Naukowe Politechniki Wroclawskiej. Seria Konferencje
Pr Nauk Politech Wroclaw Ser Monogr — Prace Naukowe Politechniki Wroclawskiej. Seria Monografie
Pr Nauk Politech Wroclaw Ser Stud Mater — Prace Naukowe Politechniki Wroclawskiej. Seria Studia i Materialy
Pr Nauk Politech Wroclaw Ser Wspolpraca — Prace Naukowe Politechniki Wroclawskiej. Seria Wspolpraca
Pr Nauk Uniw Slask Katowicach — Prace Naukowe Uniwersytetu Slaskiego w Katowicach
Pr Nauk Uniw Slask Katowic Pr Fiz — Prace Naukowe Uniwersytetu Slaskiego w Katowicach. Prace Fizyczne
Pr Nauk Wyzsz Szk Ekon Wroclawiu — Prace Naukowe Wyzszej Szkoly Ekonomicznej we Wroclawiu
PRNBA — Proceedings. Research Institute for Nuclear Medicine and Biology
PRNHA — Professional Nursing Home
PRNJ — Project North Journal
PRNN — Project North Newsletter
PRO — Pro Musica
PRO — Produktnieuws voor Kantoor en Bedrijf. Investeringsinformatie voor Managers
PRO — Professional Report
Pro Am Gas Inst — Proceedings. American Gas Institute
ProAOS — Proceedings. American Oriental Society [*Baltimore, MD*]
Probab Math Stat — Probability and Mathematical Statistics
Probab Math Statist — Probability and Mathematical Statistics
Prob Actuels ORL — Problemes Actuels d'Oto-Rhino-Laryngologie

Prob Agric Ind Mex — Problemas Agricolas e Industriales de Mexico
Prob Com — Problems of Communism
Prob Commun — Problems of Communism
Prob Econ — Problems of Economics
Prob Khig — Problemi na Khigienata
Probl Actuels Biochim Appl — Problemes Actuels de Biochimie Appliquee
Probl Actuels Endocrinol Nutr — Problemes Actuels d'Endocrinologie et de Nutrition
Probl Actuels Ophthal — Problemes Actuels d'Ophthalmologie
Probl Actuels Otorhinolaryngol — Problems Actuels d'Otorhinolaryngologie
Probl Actuels Paediatr — Problemes Actuels de Paediatrie
Probl Actuels Phoniatr Logop — Problemes Actuels de Phoniatrie et Logopedie
Probl Actuels Psychotherap — Problemes Actuels de Psychotherapie
Probl Agr (Bucharest) — Probleme Agricole (Bucharest)
Probl Agric — Probleme Agricole
Probl Agrofiz — Problemy Agrofizyki
Probl Anal Khim — Problemy Analiticheskoi Khimii
Probl Arkt Antarkt — Problemy Arktiki i Antarktiki
Probl Arktiki Antarkt — Problemy Arktiki i Antarktiki
Probl Arktiki Antarktiki — Problemy Arktiki i Antarktiki [*USSR*]
Probl Attuali Sci Cult — Problemi Attuali di Scienza e di Cultura
Prob Law — Probate Lawyer
Probl Biocybern Biomed Eng — Problems of Biocybernetics and Biomedical Engineering
Probl Biol — Problems in Biology
Probl Biol Krajiny — Problemy Biologie Krajiny
Probl Bioniki — Problemy Bioniki
Probl Bioniki Resp Mezhved Nauchno-Tekh Sb — Problemy Bioniki Respublikanskii Mezhvedomstvennyi Nauchno-Tekhnicheskii Sbornik
Probl Bor'by Protiv Burz Ideol — Problemy Bor'by Protiv Burzuaznoj Ideologii
Probl Bot — Problemy Botaniki
Probl Commu — Problems of Communism
Probl Control Inf Theor — Problems of Control and Information Theory
Probl Control and Inf Theory — Problems of Control and Information Theory
Probl Control and Inf Theory (Engl Transl Pap Rus) — Problems of Control and Information Theory (English Translation of the Papers in Russian)
Probl Cybern — Problems of Cybernetics
Probl Cybern (USSR) — Problems of Cybernetics (USSR)
Probl Dal'nego Vost — Problemy Dal'nego Vostok
Probl Desarr — Problemas del Desarrollo
Probl Dialektiki — Problemy Dialektiki
Probl Drug Depend — Problems of Drug Dependence
Probl Ecol Biocenol — Problems of Ecology and Biocenology
Probl Econ — Problems of Economics
Probl Econ (Bucharest) — Probleme Economice (Bucharest)
Probl Ekol — Problemy Ekologii
Probl Ekon Morja — Problemy Ekonomiki Morja
Probl Ekon (Warszawa) — Problemy Ekonomiczne (Warszawa)
Problemas Bras — Problemas Brasileiros
Probleme de Automat — Probleme de Automatizare
Probleme Prot Plantelor — Probleme de Protectia Plantelor
Problemes Eur — Problemes de l'Europe
Problemi Sicurezza Soc — Problemi della Sicurezza Sociale
Problemi Tehn Kibernet — Problemi na Tehniceskata Kibernetika [*Problems of Engineering Cybernetics*]
Problemi Tekhn Kibernet Robot — Problemi na Tekhnicheskata Kibernetika i Robotika [*Problems of Engineering Cybernetics and Robotics*]
Problems Control Inform Theory/Problemy Upravlen Teor Inform — Problems of Control and Information Theory. Problemy Upravlenija i Teorii Informacii [*Budapest*]
Problems Econ — Problems of Economics
Problems in Geometry — Problems in Geometry in the Key Word Index [*Moscow*]
Problems Inform Transmission — Problems of Information Transmission
Problemy Jadern Fiz i Kosm Lucei — Problemy Jadernoi Fiziki i Kosmiceskih Lucei
Problemy Kibernet — Problemy Kibernetiki
Problemy Kosmich Biol Akad Nauk SSSR — Problemy Kosmicheskoi Biologii Akademiya Nauk SSSR
Problemy Mat — Bydgoszcz. Whzsza Szkola Pedagogiczna. Zeszyty Naukowe. Problemy Matematyczne
Problemy Mat Anal Sloz Sistem — Problemy Matematiceskogo Analiza Sloznyh Sistem
Problemy Matematiceskogo Analiza — Problemy Matematiceskogo Analiza [*Leningrad*]
Problemy Pered Inf — Problemy Peredachi Informatsii
Problemy Slucain Poiska — Akademija Nauk Latviiskoi SSR. Institut Elektroniki i Vyceslitel'noi Tehniki. Problemy Slucainogo Poiska
Problemy Teor Gravitacii i Element Castic — Problemy Teorii Gravitacii i Elementarnyh Castic
Problemy Yadern Fiz i Kosm Luchei — Problemy Yadernoi Fiziki i Kosmicheskikh Luchei
Probl Endokrinol — Problemy Endokrinologii
Probl Endokrinol Gormonoter — Problemy Endokrinologii i Gormonoterapii [*Later, Problemy Endokrinologii*]
Probl Endokrinol (Mosk) — Problemy Endokrinologii (Moskva)

robl Entrep Agric — Problemes de l'Enterprise Agricole
robl Evol — Problemy Evolyutsii
robl Farine — Problemes de Farine
robl Farm — Problemy na Farmatsiyata
robl Festkoerperelektron — Probleme der Festkoerperelektronik
robl Filos Nauc Kommunizma — Problemy Filosofii i Naucnogo Kommunizma
robl Fiz Atmos — Problemy Fiziki Atmosfery
robl Fiz Elem Chastits At Yadra — Problemy Fiziki Elementarnykh Chastits i Atomnogo Yadra
robl Fiziol Gipotal — Problemy Fiziologii Gipotalamusa
robl Fiziol Opt — Problemy Fiziologicheskoj Optiki
robl Fiziol Patol Vyssh Nervn Deyat — Problemy Fiziologii i Patologii Vysshei Nervnoi Deyatel'nosti
robl Fiz Khim — Problemy Fizicheskoi Khimii
robl Funkts Morfol — Problemy Funktsional'noi Morfologii
robl Gastroenterol — Problemy Gastroenterologii
robl Gematol Pereliv Krovi — Problemy Gematologii i Perelivaniya Krovi
robl Geokhim — Problemy Geokhimii
robl Geol Nefti — Problemy Geologii Nefti [USSR]
robl Gestione — Problemi di Gestione
robl Gidroenerg Vod Khoz — Problemy Gidroenergetiki i Vodnogo Khozyaistva
robl Glubokikh Mikozov — Problemy Glubokikh Mikozov
robl Gos Prava — Problemy Gosudarstva i Prava
robl Grippa Ostrykh Respir Zabol — Problemy Grippa i Ostrykh Respiratornykh Zabolevanii
robl Hematol Blood Transfus — Problems of Hematology and Blood Transfusion
robl Hematol Blood Transfus (USSR) — Problems of Hematology and Blood Transfusion (USSR)
robl Inf & Doc — Probleme de Informare si Documentare
robl Inf Docum — Probleme de Informare si Documentare
robl Influenza Acute Respir Dis — Problems of Influenza and Acute Respiratory Diseases
robl Inf Transm — Problems of Information Transmission
robl Inf Transm (USSR) — Problems of Information Transmission (USSR)
robl Inzh Geol Sev Kavk — Problemy Inzhenernoi Geologii Severnogo Kavkaza
robl Kamen Litya — Problemy Kamennogo Lit'ya
robl Khig — Problemi na Khigienata
robl Kibern — Problemy Kibernetiki
robl Kinet Katal — Problemy Kinetiki i Kataliza
robl Kontrolya Zashch Atmos Zagryaz — Problemy Kontrolya i Zashchita Atmosfery ot Zagryazneniya
robl Kosm Biol — Problemy Kosmicheskoi Biologii
robl Kosm Fiz — Problemy Kosmicheskoj Fiziki
robl Kosm Phys — Probleme der Kosmichen Physik [West Germany]
robl Kriolitologii — Problemy Kriolitologii
robl Low Temp Phys Thermodyn — Problems of Low Temperature Physics and Thermodynamics
robl Mashinostr — Problemy Mashinostroeniya [Ukrainian SSR]
robl Mat Fiz — Problemy Matematicheskoj Fiziki
robl Med Wieku Rozwoj — Problemy Medycyny Wieku Rozwojowego
robl Metalloved Fiz Met — Problemy Metallovedeniya i Fiziki Metallov [USSR]
robl Metalloved Term Obrab — Problemy Metallovedeniya i Termicheskoi Obrabotki
robl Metodol Ist-Filos Issled — Problemy Metodologii Istoriko-Filosofskogo Issledovanija
robl Morfopatol — Probleme de Morfopatologie
robl Narodonas Trud Resursov — Problemy Narodonaselenija i Trudovyh Resursov
robl Nauc Kommunizma (Leningrad) — Problemy Naucnogo Kommunizma (Leningrad)
robl Nauc Kommunizma (Moskva) — Problemy Naucnogo Kommunizma (Moskva)
robl Nauc Uprav Soc Processami — Problemy Naucnogo Upravlenija Social'nymi Processami
robl Neftegazonosn Tadzh — Problemy Neftegazonosnosti Tadzhikistana
robl Nefti Gaza Tyumeni — Problemy Nefti i Gaza Tyumeni
robl Neirokhim — Problemy Neirokhimii
robl Neirokhir — Problemy Neirokhirurgii
robl Neirokhir (1955-1963) — Problemy Neirokhirurgii (1955-1963)
robl Neirokhir Resp Mezhved Sb — Problemy Neirokhirurgii Respublikanskii Mezhvedomstvenhyi Sbornik
robl Neirokibern — Problemy Neirokibernetiki
robl Nevrol Resp Mezhved Sb — Problemy Nevrologii Respublikanskii Mezhvedomstvennyi Sbornik
robl North — Problems of the North
robl Obshch Mol Biol — Problemy Obshchei i Molekulyarnoi Biologii
robl Okh Vod — Problemy Okhrany Vod
robl Oncol (Engl Transl Vopr Onkol) — Problems of Oncology (English Translation of Voprosy Onkologii)
robl Onkol (Sofia) — Problemi na Onkologiyata (Sofia)
robl Organ — Problemy Organizacji

Probl Ortop Stomatol — Problemy Ortopedicheskoi Stomatologii
Probl Osad Geol Dokembr — Problemy Osadochnoy Geologii Dokembriya
Probl Osobo Opasnykh Infekts — Problemy Osobo Opasnykh Infektsii
Probl Osoveniya Pustyn — Problemy Osvoeniya Pustyn
Probl Osvo Pustyn — Problemy Osvoeniya Pustyn
Probl Parazitol — Problemy Parazitologii
Probl Patol Comp — Probleme de Patologie Comparata
Probl Peredachi Inf — Problemy Peredachi Informatsii
Probl Pereda Inf — Problemy Peredachi Informatsii
Probl Pnevmol Ftiziatr — Problemi na Pnevmologiyata i Ftiziatriyata
Probl Polesya — Problemy Poles'ya
Probl Polit Soc — Problemes Politiques et Sociaux
Probl Proch Mashinostr — Problemy Prochnosti v Mashinostroenii [USSR]
Probl Prochn — Problemy Prochnosti
Probl Prochn Mashinostr — Problemy Prochnosti v Mashinostroenii
Probl Proj — Problemy Projectowa
Probl Prot Plant — Probleme de Protectia Plantelor
Probl Psychol (Engl Transl Vopr Psikhol) — Problems of Psychology (English Translation of Voprosy Psikhologii)
Probl Razrab Polezn Iskop — Problemy Razrabotki Poleznykh Iskopaemykh
Probl Rentgenol Radiobiol — Problemy na Rentgenologiyata i Radiobiologiyata
Probl Selsk Khoz Priamurya — Problemy Sel'skogo Khozyaistva Priamur'ya
Probl Ser — Problemy Severa
Probl Sicur Soc — Problemi della Sicurezza Sociale
Probl Soc Aktivnosti — Problemy Social'noj Aktivnosti
Probl Social (Milano) — Problemi del Socialismo (Milano)
Probl Soc Prognoz — Problemy Social'nogo Prognozirovanija
Probl Soc Zair — Problemes Sociaux Zairois
Probl Soc Zairois — Problemes Sociaux Zairois
Probl Sov Geol — Problemy Sovetskoi Geologii [USSR]
Probl Sovrem Khim Koord Soedin — Problemy Sovremennoi Khimii Koordinatsionnykh Soedinenii [USSR]
Probl Sovrem Khim Koord Soedin Leningr Gos Univ — Problemy Sovremennoj Khimii Koordinatsionnykh Soedinenij Leningradskij Gosudarstvennyj Universitet
Probl Sovrem Teor Elem Chastits — Problemy Sovremennmoi Teorii Elementarnykh Chastits
Probl Tech Med — Problemy Techniki w Medycynie
Probl Tekh Elektrodin — Problemy Tekhnicheskoi Elektrodinamiki
Probl Tekh Kibern — Problemy na Tekhnicheskata Kibernetika
Probl Tekh Kibern na Robotikata — Problemy na Tekhnicheskata Kibernetika i Robotikata
Probl Teor Gravitatsii Elem Chastits — Problemy Teorii Gravitatsii i Elementarnykh Chastits [USSR]
Probl Teploenerg Prikl Teplofiz — Problemy Teploenergetiki i Prikladnoi Teplofiziki [USSR]
Probl Ter — Probleme de Terapeutica
Probl Ter Stomatol — Problemy Terapeuticheskoi Stomatologii
Probl Treniya Iznashivaniya — Problemy Treniya i Iznashivaniya
Probl Tuberk — Problemy Tuberkuleza
Probl Virol (Engl Transl Vopr Virusol) — Problems of Virology (English Translation of Voprosy Virusologii)
Probl Yad Fiz Kosm Luchej — Problemy Yadernoj Fiziki i Kosmicheskikh Luchej
Probl Zaraznite Parazit Bolesti — Problemi na Zaraznite i Parazitnite Bolesti
Probl Zhivotnovod — Problemy Zhivotnovodstva
Probl Zooteh Vet — Probleme Zootehnice si Veterinare
Prob and Prop — Probate and Property
Prob Vostok — Problemy Vostokovedeniia
PROC — Problems of Communism
Proc — Procellaria
ProcAAAS — Proceedings. American Association for the Advancement of Science
Proc A Biol Colloq — Proceedings. Annual Biology Colloquium
Proc 31 A Blueberry Open House — Proceedings. 31st Annual Blueberry Open House
Proc Abstr Soc Biol Chem (Bangalore) — Proceedings and Abstracts. Society of Biological Chemists (Bangalore)
Proc Acad Nat Sci Phila — Proceedings. Academy of Natural Sciences of Philadelphia
Proc Acad Pol Sci — Proceedings. Academy of Political Science
Proc Acad Sci Armenian SSR — Proceedings. Academy of Sciences of the Armenian SSR
Proc Acad Sci United Prov Agra Oudh India — Proceedings. Academy of Sciences. United Provinces of Agra and Oudh India
Proc Acad Sci USSR Geochem Sect — Proceedings. Academy of Sciences of the USSR. Geochemistry Section
Proc Acad Sci USSR Sect Agrochem — Proceedings. Academy of Sciences of the USSR. Section Agrochemistry
Proc Acad Sci USSR Sect Appl Phys — Proceedings. Academy of Sciences of the USSR. Section Applied Physics
Proc A Conv Am Cranberry Growers' Ass — Proceedings. Annual Convention. American Cranberry Growers' Association
Proc Afr Classical Assoc — Proceedings. African Classical Association
Proc Agric Soc (Trinidad Tobago) — Proceedings. Agricultural Society (Trinidad and Tobago)

Proc Agron Soc NZ — Proceedings. Agronomy Society of New Zealand
Proc Agr Outlook Conf — Proceedings. Agricultural Outlook Conference
Proc Agr Pestic Tech Soc — Proceedings. Agricultural Pesticide Technical Society
Proc Air Pollut Contr Ass — Proceedings. Air Pollution Control Association
Proc Air Pollut Control Assoc — Proceedings. Air Pollution Control Association
Proc Alaska Sci Conf — Proceedings. Alaska Science Conference
Proc Alberta Sulphur Gas Res Workshop — Proceedings. Alberta Sulphur Gas Research Workshop
Proc Alfred Benzon Symp — Proceedings. Alfred Benzon Symposium
Proc All Pak Sci Conf — Proceedings. All Pakistan Science Conference
Proc Alumni Assoc (Malaya) — Proceedings. Alumni Association (Malaya)
Proc Am Acad Arts Sci — Proceedings. American Academy of Arts and Sciences
ProcAmAcAS — Proceedings. American Academy of Arts and Sciences
Proc Am Ant Soc — Proceedings. American Antiquarian Society
Proc Am Assoc Cancer Res — Proceedings. American Association for Cancer Research
Proc Am Assoc Econ Entomol North Cent States Branch — Proceedings. American Association of Economic Entomologists. North Central States Branch
Proc Am Assoc State Highw Off — Proceedings. American Association of State Highway Officials
Proc Am Chem Soc Symp Anal Calorim — Proceedings. American Chemical Society Symposium on Analytical Calorimetry
Proc Am Concr Inst — Proceedings. American Concrete Institute
Proc Am Congr Surv Mapp — Proceedings. American Congress on Surveying and Mapping
Proc Am Cranberry Grow Assoc — Proceedings. American Cranberry Growers' Association
Proc Am Cranberry Growers' Ass — Proceedings. American Cranberry Growers' Association
Proc Am Diabetes Assoc — Proceedings. American Diabetes Association
Proc Am Doc Inst — Proceedings. American Documentation Institute
Proc Am Drug Manuf Assoc Annu Meet — Proceedings. American Drug Manufacturers Association. Annual Meeting
Proc A Meet Coun Fertil Applic — Proceedings. Annual Meeting. Council on Fertilizer Application
Proc A Meeting Sugar Ind Technicians — Proceedings. Annual Meeting of Sugar Industry Technicians
Proc A Meet Pl Physiol Univ MD — Proceedings. Annual Meeting. American Society of Plant Physiologists at the University of Maryland
Proc Amer Acad Arts Sci — Proceedings. American Academy of Arts and Sciences
Proc Amer Ass State Highw Offic — Proceedings. American Association of State Highway Officials
Proc Amer Math Soc — Proceedings. American Mathematical Society
Proc Amer Phil Ass — Proceedings and Addresses. American Philosophical Association
Proc Amer Philosophical Soc — Proceedings. American Philosophical Society
Proc Amer Philos Soc — Proceedings. American Philosophical Society
Proc Amer Phil Soc — Proceedings. American Philosophical Society
Proc Amer Power Conf — Proceedings. American Power Conference
Proc Amer Soc Anim Pro W Sect — Proceedings. American Society of Animal Production. Western Section
Proc Amer Soc Anim Sci W Sect — Proceedings. American Society of Animal Science. Western Section
Proc Amer Soc Bakery Eng — Proceedings. American Society of Bakery Engineers
Proc Amer Soc Brew Chem — Proceedings. American Society of Brewing Chemists
Proc Amer Soc Hort Sci — Proceedings. American Society for Horticultural Science
Proc Amer Soc Testing Materials — Proceedings. American Society for Testing and Materials
Proc Amer Soc U Composers — Proceedings. American Society of University Composers
Proc Amer Wood-Preserv Ass — Proceedings. American Wood-Preservers' Association
Proc Am Hortic Congr — Proceedings. American Horticultural Congress
Proc Am Inst Electr Eng — Proceedings. American Institute of Electrical Engineers
Proc Am Math Soc — Proceedings. American Mathematical Society
Proc Am Peanut Res Educ Assoc — Proceedings. American Peanut Research and Education Association
Proc Am Pet Inst Div Refining — Proceedings. American Petroleum Institute. Division of Refining
Proc Am Pet Inst Refin Dep — Proceedings. American Petroleum Institute. Refining Department
Proc Am Pet Inst Sect 1 — Proceedings. American Petroleum Institute. Section 1
Proc Am Pet Inst Sect 2 — Proceedings. American Petroleum Institute. Section 2. Marketing
Proc Am Pet Inst Sect 3 — Proceedings. American Petroleum Institute. Section 3. Refining

Proc Am Pet Inst Sect 4 — Proceedings. American Petroleum Institute. Section 4. Production
Proc Am Pet Inst Sect 5 — Proceedings. American Petroleum Institute. Section 5. Transportation
Proc Am Pet Inst Sect 6 — Proceedings. American Petroleum Institute. Section 6. Interdivisional
Proc Am Pet Inst Sect 8 — Proceedings. American Petroleum Institute. Section 8. Science and Technology
Proc Am Pet Inst Sect III Refining — Proceedings. American Petroleum Institute. Section III. Refining
Proc Am Pharm Manuf Assoc Annu Meet — Proceedings. American Pharmaceutical Manufacturers' Association. Annual Meeting
Proc Am Pharm Manuf Assoc Midyear East Sect Meet — Proceedings. American Pharmaceutical Manufacturers' Association. Midyear Eastern Section Meeting
Proc Am Philos Soc — Proceedings. American Philosophical Society
Proc Am Phil Soc — Proceedings. American Philosophical Society
Proc Am Phytopathol Soc — Proceedings. American Phytopathological Society
Proc Am Power Conf — Proceedings. American Power Conference
Proc Am Soc Civ Eng — Proceedings. American Society of Civil Engineers
Proc Am Soc Civ Eng Transp Eng J — Proceedings. American Society of Civil Engineers. Transportation Engineering Journal
Proc Am Soc Enol — Proceedings. American Society of Enologists
Proc Am Soc Hortic Sci — Proceedings. American Society for Horticultural Science
Proc Am Soc Hort Sci — Proceedings. American Society for Horticultural Science
Proc Am Soc Inf Sci — Proceedings. American Society for Information Science
Proc Am Soc Test & Mater — Proceedings. American Society for Testing and Materials
Proc Am Vet Med Assoc — Proceedings. American Veterinary Medical Association
Proc Am Water Works Assoc — Proceedings. American Water Works Association
Proc Am Wood-Preserv Assoc — Proceedings. American Wood-Preservers' Association
Proc Anal Div Chem Soc — Proceedings. Analytical Division of the Chemical Society
Proc Anim Care Panel — Proceedings. Animal Care Panel
Proc Annu AIChE Southwest Ohio Conf Energy Environ — Proceedings. Annual AIChE [*American Institute of Chemical Engineers*] Southwestern Ohio Conference on Energy and the Environment
Proc Annu Allerton Conf Circuit Syst Theory — Proceedings. Annual Allerton Conference on Circuit and System Theory [*Later, Proceedings. Annual Allerton Conference on Communication, Control, and Computing*]
Proc Annu Allerton Conf Commun Control Comput — Proceedings. Annual Allerton Conference on Communication, Control, and Computing [*Formerly, Annual Allerton Conference on Circuit and System Theory*] [*United States*]
Proc Annu Arkansas Water Works Pollut Control Conf Short Sch — Proceedings. Annual Arkansas Water Works and Pollution Control Conference and Short School
Proc Annu Battery Res Dev Conf — Proceedings. Annual Battery Research and Development Conference
Proc Annu Biochem Eng Symp — Proceedings. Annual Biochemical Engineering Symposium [*United States*]
Proc Annu Biol Colloq (Oreg State Univ) — Proceedings. Annual Biology Colloquium (Oregon State University)
Proc Annu Biomed Sci Instrum Symp — Proceedings. Annual Biomedical Sciences Instrumentation Symposium
Proc Annu Blueberry Open House — Proceedings. Annual Blueberry Open House
Proc Annu Calif Weed Conf — Proceedings. Annual California Weed Conference
Proc Annu Conf Agron Soc NZ — Proceedings. Annual Conference. Agronomy Society of New Zealand
Proc Annu Conf Autom Control Pet Chem Ind — Proceedings. Annual Conference on Automatic Control in the Petroleum and Chemical Industries
Proc Annu Conf Biol Sonar Diving Mamm — Proceedings. Annual Conference on Biological Sonar and Diving Mammals
Proc Annu Conf Biol Sonar Diving Mammals — Proceedings. Annual Conference on Biological Sonar and Diving Mammals
Proc Annu Conf Can Nucl Assoc — Proceedings. Annual Conference. Canadian Nuclear Association
Proc Annu Conf Energy Convers Storage — Proceedings. Annual Conference on Energy Conversion and Storage
Proc Annu Conf Environ Chem Hum Anim Health — Proceedings. Annual Conference on Environmental Chemicals. Human and Animal Health
Proc Annu Conf Ind Appl X Ray Anal — Proceedings. Annual Conference on Industrial Applications of X-Ray Analysis
Proc Annu Conf Kidney — Proceedings. Annual Conference on the Kidney
Proc Annu Conf Manitoba Agron — Proceedings. Annual Conference of Manitoba Agronomists
Proc Annu Conf MD Del Water Sewage Assoc — Proceedings. Annual Conference. Maryland-Delaware Water and Sewage Association

Proc Annu Conf Microbeam Anal Soc — Proceedings. Annual Conference. Microbeam Analysis Society

Proc Annu Conf Reinf Plast Compos Inst Soc Plast Ind — Proceedings. Annual Conference. Reinforced Plastics/Composites Institute. Society of the Plastics Industry

Proc Annu Conf Southeast Assoc Game Fish Comm — Proceedings. Annual Conference. Southeastern Association of Game and Fish Commissioners

Proc Annu Congr S Afr Sugar Technol Assoc — Proceedings. Annual Congress. South African Sugar Technologists Association

Proc Annu Connector Symp — Proceedings. Annual Connector Symposium

Proc Annu Conv Assoc Am Pestic Control Off — Proceedings. Annual Convention Association. American Pesticide Control Officials

Proc Annu Conv Flavoring Ext Manuf Assoc US — Proceedings. Annual Convention. Flavoring Extract Manufacturers' Association of the United States

Proc Annu Conv Gas Process Assoc Meet Pap — Proceedings. Annual Convention. Gas Processors Association. Meeting Papers

Proc Annu Conv Gas Process Assoc Tech Pap — Proceedings. Annual Convention. Gas Processors Association. Technical Papers

Proc Annu Conv Milk Ind Found — Proceedings. Annual Convention. Milk Industry Foundation

Proc Annu Conv Nat Gasoline Assoc Am Tech Pap — Proceedings. Annual Convention. Natural Gasoline Association of America. Technical Papers

Proc Annu Conv Nat Gas Process Assoc Tech Pap — Proceedings. Annual Convention. Natural Gas Processors Association. Technical Papers [*United States*]

Proc Annu Conv Natur Gas Process Ass Tech Pap — Proceedings. Annual Convention. Natural Gas Processors Association. Technical Papers

Proc Annu Conv Oil Technol Assoc — Proceedings. Annual Convention. Oil Technologists Association

Proc Annu Conv Philipp Sugar Assoc — Proceedings. Annual Convention. Philippine Sugar Association

Proc Annu Conv Sugar Technol Assoc India — Proceedings. Annual Convention. Sugar Technologists' Association of India

Proc Annu Conv West Can Water Sewage Conf — Proceedings. Annual Convention. Western Canada Water and Sewage Conference (1960-1975)

Proc Annu East Theor Phys Conf — Proceedings. Annual Eastern Theoretical Physics Conference

Proc Annu Eng Geol Soils Eng Symp — Proceedings. Annual Engineering Geology and Soils Engineering Symposium

Proc Annu Eng Geol Symp — Proceedings. Annual Engineering Geology Symposium

Proc Annu Environ Water Resour Eng Conf — Proceedings. Annual Environmental and Water Resources Engineering Conference

Proc Annu Fall Meet Calif Nat Gasoline Assoc — Proceedings. Annual Fall Meeting. California Natural Gasoline Association

Proc Annu Fall Meet West Gas Process Oil Refin Assoc — Proceedings. Annual Fall Meeting. Western Gas Processors and Oil Refiners Association

Proc Annu Fall Meet West Gas Process Oil Refiners Assoc — Proceedings. Annual Fall Meeting. Western Gas Processors and Oil Refiners Association

Proc Annu Freq Control Symp — Proceedings. Annual Frequency Control Symposium

Proc Annu Hardwood Symp Hardwood Res Counc — Proceedings. Annual Hardwood Symposium. Hardwood Research Council

Proc Annu Holm Semin Electr Contacts — Proceedings. Annual Holm Seminar on Electrical Contacts

Proc Annu Ind Pollut Conf — Proceedings. Annual Industrial Pollution Conference [*United States*]

Proc Annu Instrum Conf — Proceedings. Annual Instrumentation Conference

Proc Annu Int Conf Can Nucl Assoc — Proceedings. Annual International Conference. Canadian Nuclear Association

Proc Annu Int Conf Fault Tolerant Comput — Proceedings. Annual International Conference on Fault-Tolerant Computing

Proc Annu Int Conf High Energy Phys — Proceedings. Annual International Conference on High Energy Physics

Proc Annu Int Conf Plasma Chem Technol — Proceedings. Annual International Conference of Plasma Chemistry and Technology

Proc Annu Int Game Fish Res Conf — Proceedings. Annual International Game Fish Research Conference

Proc Annu Mar Coat Conf — Proceedings. Annual Marine Coatings Conference

Proc Annu Meat Sci Inst — Proceedings. Annual Meat Science Institute

Proc Annu Meet Agric Res Inst — Proceedings. Annual Meeting. Agricultural Research Institute

Proc Annu Meet Air Pollut Control Assoc — Proceedings. Annual Meeting. Air Pollution Control Association

Proc Annu Meet Am Assoc Vet Lab Diagn — Proceedings. Annual Meeting. American Association of Veterinary Laboratory Diagnosticians

Proc Annu Meet Amer Soc Hort Sci Caribbean Reg — Proceedings. Annual Meeting. American Society for Horticultural Science. Caribbean Region

Proc Annu Meet Am Pet Inst — Proceedings. Annual Meeting. American Petroleum Institute

Proc Annu Meet Am Psychopathol Assoc — Proceedings. Annual Meeting. American Psychopathological Association

Proc Annu Meet Am Sect Int Sol Energy Soc — Proceedings. Annual Meeting. American Section. International Solar Energy Society

Proc Annu Meet Am Soc Anim Sci West Sect — Proceedings. Annual Meeting. American Society of Animal Science. Western Section

Proc Annu Meet Am Soc Bak Eng — Proceedings. Annual Meeting. American Society of Bakery Engineers

Proc Annu Meet Am Soc Inf Sci — Proceedings. Annual Meeting. American Society for Information Science

Proc Annu Meet Am Soybean Assoc — Proceedings. Annual Meeting. American Soybean Association

Proc Annu Meet Biochem (Hung) — Proceedings. Annual Meeting of Biochemistry (Hungary)

Proc Annu Meet Can Nucl Assoc — Proceedings. Annual Meeting. Canadian Nuclear Association

Proc Annu Meet Can Soc Agron — Proceedings. Annual Meeting. Canadian Society of Agronomy

Proc Annu Meet Chem Spec Manuf Assoc — Proceedings. Annual Meeting. Chemical Specialties Manufacturers Association

Proc Annu Meet Compressed Gas Assoc — Proceedings. Annual Meeting. Compressed Gas Association

Proc Annu Meet Conn Pomol Soc — Proceedings. Annual Meeting. Connecticut Pomological Society

Proc Annu Meet Electron Microsc Soc Am — Proceedings. Annual Meeting. Electron Microscopy Society of America

Proc Annu Meet Fert Ind Round Table — Proceedings. Annual Meeting. Fertilizer Industry Round Table

Proc Annu Meet Fla State Hortic Soc — Proceedings. Annual Meeting. Florida State Horticultural Society

Proc Annu Meet Hawaii Sugar Plant Assoc — Proceedings. Annual Meeting. Hawaiian Sugar Planters Association

Proc Annu Meeting Amer Soc Int Law — Proceedings. Annual Meeting. American Society of International Law

Proc Annu Meet Int Magnesium Assoc — Proceedings. Annual Meeting. International Magnesium Association

Proc Annu Meet Jpn Endocrinol Soc — Proceedings. Annual Meeting. Japan Endocrinological Society

Proc Annu Meet Lightwood Res Conf — Proceedings. Annual Meeting. Lightwood Research Conference

Proc Annu Meet Med Sect Am Counc Life Insur — Proceedings. Annual Meeting. Medical Section. American Council of Life Insurance

Proc Annu Meet Met Powder Assoc — Proceedings. Annual Meeting. Metal Powder Association

Proc Annu Meet Nat Assoc Corros Eng — Proceedings. Annual Meeting. National Association of Corrosion Engineers

Proc Annu Meet Nat Ass Wheat Growers — Proceedings. Annual Meeting. National Association of Wheat Growers

Proc Annu Meet Natl Counc Radiat Prot Meas — Proceedings. Annual Meeting. National Council on Radiation Protection and Measurements [*United States*]

Proc Annu Meet Natl Jt Comm Fert Appl — Proceedings. Annual Meeting. National Joint Committee on Fertilizer Application

Proc Annu Meet Nat Res Counc Agr Res Inst — Proceedings. Annual Meeting. National Research Council. Agricultural Research Institute

Proc Annu Meet N Cent Weed Contr Conf — Proceedings. Annual Meeting. North Central Weed Control Conference

Proc Annu Meet NJ — Proceedings. Annual Meeting. New Jersey Mosquito Extermination Association

Proc Annu Meet Northeast Weed Sci Soc — Proceedings. Annual Meeting. Northeastern Weed Science Society

Proc Annu Meet NY State Hort Soc — Proceedings. Annual Meeting. New York State Horticultural Society

Proc Annu Meet Pac Coast Fertil Soc — Proceedings. Annual Meeting. Pacific Coast Fertility Society

Proc Annu Meet Soc Promot Agric Sci — Proceedings. Annual Meeting. Society for the Promotion of Agricultural Science

Proc Annu Meet US Anim Health Assoc — Proceedings. Annual Meeting. United States Animal Health Association

Proc Annu Meet Utah Mosq Abatement Assoc — Proceedings. Annual Meeting. Utah Mosquito Abatement Association

Proc Annu Meet West Div Am Dairy Sci Assoc — Proceedings. Annual Meeting. Western Division. American Dairy Science Association

Proc Annu Meet West Soc Fr Hist — Proceedings. Annual Meeting. Western Society for French History

Proc Annu Meet W Farm Econ Ass — Proceedings. Annual Meeting. Western Farm Economics Association

Proc Annu Mid-Am Spectrosc Symp — Proceedings. Annual Mid-America Spectroscopy Symposium

Proc Annu Midwest Fert Conf — Proceedings. Annual Midwest Fertilizer Conference

Proc Annu Nat Dairy Eng Conf — Proceedings. Annual National Dairy Engineering Conference

Proc Annu Nat Dairy Food Eng Conf — Proceedings. Annual National Dairy and Food Engineering Conference

Proc Annu Northwest Wood Prod Clin — Proceedings. Annual Northwest Wood Products Clinic

Proc Annu Power Sources Conf — Proceedings. Annual Power Sources Conference

Proc Annu Purdue Air Qual Conf — Proceedings. Annual Purdue Air Quality Conference

Proc Annu Recipro Meat Conf Am Meat Sci Assoc — Proceedings. Annual Reciprocal Meat Conference. American Meat Science Association

Proc Annu Reliab Maintainability Symp — Proceedings. Annual Reliability and Maintainability Symposium

Proc Annu Reliab Maintain Symp — Proceedings. Annual Reliability and Maintainability Symposium

Proc Annu Rochester Conf High Energy Nucl Phys — Proceedings. Annual Rochester Conference on High Energy Nuclear Physics

Proc Annu Rocky Mount Bioeng Symp — Proceedings. Annual Rocky Mountain Bioengineering Symposium

Proc Annu Rocky Mt Bioeng Symp — Proceedings. Annual Rocky Mountain Bioengineering Symposium

Proc Annu San Franc Cancer Symp — Proceedings. Annual San Francisco Cancer Symposium

Proc Annu Sci Meet Comm Probl Drug Depend US Nat Res Counc — Proceedings. Annual Scientific Meeting. Committee on Problems of Drug Dependence. United States National Research Council

Proc Annu Senior Staff Conf USARS — Proceedings. Annual Senior Staff Conference. United States Agricultural Research Service

Proc Annu Sess Ceylon Assoc Adv Sci — Proceedings. Annual Session. Ceylon Association for the Advancement of Science

Proc Annu Southwest Pet Short Course — Proceedings. Annual Southwestern Petroleum Short Course [*United States*]

Proc Annu Symp Eng Geol Soils Eng — Proceedings. Annual Symposium on Engineering Geology and Soils Engineering

Proc Annu Symp Eugen Soc — Proceedings. Annual Symposium of the Eugenics Society

Proc Annu Symp Freq Control — Proceedings. Annual Symposium on Frequency Control

Proc Annu Symp Incremental Motion Control Syst Devices — Proceedings. Annual Symposium. Incremental Motion Control Systems and Devices

Proc Annu Tall Timbers Fire Ecol Conf — Proceedings. Annual Tall Timbers Fire Ecology Conference

Proc Annu Tech Conf Soc Vac Coaters — Proceedings. Annual Technical Conference. Society of Vacuum Coaters

Proc Annu Tech Meet Inst Environ Sci — Proceedings. Annual Technical Meeting. Institute of Environmental Sciences

Proc Annu Tech Meet Int Metallogr Soc Inc — Proceedings. Annual Technical Meeting. International Metallographic Society, Inc.

Proc Annu Tech Meet Tech Assoc Graphic Arts — Proceedings. Annual Technical Meeting. Technical Association. Graphic Arts

Proc Annu Tex Nutr Conf — Proceedings. Annual Texas Nutrition Conference

Proc Annu Tung Ind Conv — Proceedings. Annual Tung Industry Convention

Proc Annu UMR-MEC Conf Energy — Proceedings. Annual UMR-MEC [*University of Missouri at Rolla - Missouri Energy Council*] Conference on Energy

Proc Annu West Tex Oil Lifting Short Course — Proceedings. Annual West Texas Oil Lifting Short Course

Proc Annu WWEMA Ind Pollut Conf — Proceedings. Annual WWEMA [*Water and Wastewater Equipment Manufacturers Association*] Industrial Pollution Conference [*United States*]

Proc APCA Annu Meet — Proceedings. APCA [*Air Pollution Control Association*] Annual Meeting

Proc APREA — Proceedings. APREA [*American Peanut Research and Education Association*]

Proc Aris Soc — Proceedings. Aristotelian Society

Proc Ark Acad Sci — Proceedings. Arkansas Academy of Science

Proc Arkansas Acad Sci — Proceedings. Arkansas Academy of Science

Proc Arkansas Water Works Pollut Control Conf Short Sch — Proceedings. Arkansas Water Works and Pollution Control Conference and Short School

Proc Asian-Pac Congr Cardiol — Proceedings. Asian-Pacific Congress of Cardiology

Proc Asiat Soc (Bengal) — Proceedings. Asiatic Society (Bengal)

Proc ASIS Annu Meet — Proceedings. ASIS [*American Society for Information Science*] Annual Meeting

Proc Ass Asphalt Paving Technol — Proceedings. Association of Asphalt Paving Technologists

Proc Ass Econ Biol — Proceedings. Association of Economic Biologists

Proc Assoc Asphalt Paving Technol — Proceedings. Association of Asphalt Paving Technologists

Proc Assoc Clin Biochem — Proceedings. Association of Clinical Biochemists

Proc Assoc Off Seed Anal — Proceedings. Association of Official Seed Analysts

Proc Assoc Off Seed Anal (North Am) — Proceedings. Association of Official Seed Analysts (North America)

Proc Assoc Plant Prot Kyushu — Proceedings. Association for Plant Protection of Kyushu

Proc Assoc South Agric Work — Proceedings. Association of Southern Agricultural Workers

Proc Ass Offic Seed Anal — Proceedings. Association of Official Seed Analysts

Proc Ass Plant Prot Hokuriku — Proceedings. Association of Plant Protection of Hokuriku

Proc Ass Plant Prot Kyushu — Proceedings. Association for Plant Protection of Kyushu

Proc Ass S Agr Workers — Proceedings. Association of Southern Agricultural Workers

Proc Ass Sth Agric Wkrs — Proceedings. Association of Southern Agricultural Workers

Proc ASTM — Proceedings. American Society for Testing and Materials

Proc Astron Soc Aust — Proceedings. Astronomical Society of Australia

Proc Astr Soc Aust — Proceedings. Astronomical Society of Australia

Proc Aust Ass Clin Biochem — Proceedings. Australian Association of Clinical Biochemists

Proc Aust Assoc Neurol — Proceedings. Australian Association of Neurologists

Proc Aust Biochem Soc — Proceedings. Australian Biochemical Society

Proc Aust Bldg Res Congr — Australian Building Research Congress. Proceedings

Proc Aust Build Res Congr — Australian Building Research Congress. Proceedings

Proc Aust Ceram Conf — Australian Ceramic Conference. Proceedings

Proc Aust Ceramic Conf — Australian Ceramic Conference. Proceedings

Proc Aust Clay Miner Conf — Australian Clay Minerals Conference. Proceedings

Proc Aust Comput Conf — Proceedings. Australian Computer Conference

Proc Aust Conf Nucl Tech Anal — Australian Conference on Nuclear Techniques of Analysis. Proceedings

Proc Aust Grasslds Conf — Proceedings. Australian Grasslands Conference

Proc Aust Inst Min and Metall — Australasian Institute of Mining and Metallurgy. Proceedings

Proc Aust Inst Min Metall — Proceedings. Australasian Institute of Mining and Metallurgy

Proc Aust Physiol Pharmacol Soc — Proceedings. Australian Physiological and Pharmacological Society

Proc Aust Pulp Pap Ind Tech Assoc — Proceedings. Australian Pulp and Paper Industry Technical Association

Proc Australasian Poultry Sci Conv — Proceedings. Australasian Poultry Science Convention

Proc Australas Inst Min Eng — Proceedings. Australasian Institute of Mining Engineers

Proc Australas Inst Min and Metall — Australasian Institute of Mining and Metallurgy. Proceedings

Proc Australas Inst Min Metall — Proceedings. Australasian Institute of Mining and Metallurgy

Proc Aust Road Res Bd — Australian Road Research Board. Proceedings

Proc Aust Road Research Board — Australian Road Research Board. Proceedings

Proc Aust Soc Anim Prod — Proceedings. Australian Society of Animal Production

Proc Aust Soc Med Res — Proceedings. Australian Society for Medical Research

Proc Aust Weed Conf — Proceedings. Australian Weed Conference

Proc Auto Div Instn Mech Engrs — Proceedings. Institution of Mechanical Engineers. Auto Division

Proc Bakish Mater Corp Publ — Proceedings. Bakish Materials Corporation Publication

Proc Beltwide Cotton Prod Res Conf — Proceedings. Beltwide Cotton Production Research Conferences

Proc Berkeley Symp Math Stat Probab — Proceedings. Berkeley Symposium on Mathematical Statistics and Probability

Proc Bienn Conf Inst Briquet Agglom — Proceedings. Biennial Conference. Institute for Briquetting and Agglomeration

Proc Bienn Conf Int Briquet Assoc — Proceedings. Biennial Conference. International Briqueting Association

Proc Bienn Gas Dyn Symp — Proceedings. Biennial Gas Dynamics Symposium

Proc Bihar Acad Agric Sci — Proceedings. Bihar Academy of Agricultural Sciences

Proc Bihar Acad Agr Sci — Proceedings. Bihar Academy of Agricultural Sciences

Proc Biol Soc Wash — Proceedings. Biological Society of Washington

Proc Bird Control Semin — Proceedings. Bird Control Seminar

Proc Bos Soc — Proceedings. Bostonian Society

Proc Bot Soc Br Isles — Proceedings. Botanical Society of the British Isles

Proc Br Acad — Proceedings. British Academy

Proc Br Acoust Soc — Proceedings. British Acoustical Society

Proc Br Assoc Refrig — Proceedings. British Association for Refrigeration

Proc Br Ceram Soc — Proceedings. British Ceramic Society

Proc Br Crop Prot Conf — Proceedings. 1980 British Crop Protection Conference. Weeds

Proc Bristol Nat Soc — Proceedings. Bristol Naturalists Society

Proc Brit Ac — Proceedings. British Academy

Proc Brit Acad — Proceedings. British Academy for the Promotion of Historical, Philosophical, and Philological Studies

Proc Brit Ceram Soc — Proceedings. British Ceramic Society

Proc Brit Weed Contr Conf — Proceedings. British Weed Control Conference

Proc Brown Univ Symp Biol Skin — Proceedings. Brown University Symposium on the Biology of Skin

Proc Br Soc Anim Prod — Proceedings. British Society of Animal Production

Proc Br Weed Control Conf — Proceedings. British Weed Control Conference

Proc Buffalo Milan Symp Mol Pharmacol — Proceedings. Buffalo-Milan Symposium on Molecular Pharmacology

Proc Calif Acad Sci — Proceedings. California Academy of Sciences

Proc Calif Ann Weed Conf — Proceedings. California Annual Weed Conference

Proc Calif Zool Club — Proceedings. California Zoological Club

Proc Camb Philos Soc — Proceedings. Cambridge Philosophical Society

Proc Camb Phil Soc Math Phys Sci — Proceedings. Cambridge Philosophical Society. Mathematical and Physical Sciences

Proc Cambridge Antiq Soc — Proceedings. Cambridge Antiquarian Society

Proc Cambridge Ant Soc — Proceedings. Cambridge Antiquarian Society

Proc Cambridge Philos Soc — Proceedings. Cambridge Philosophical Society

Proc Cambridge Phil Soc — Proceedings. Cambridge Philological Society

Proc Can Cancer Res Conf — Proceedings. Canadian Cancer Research Conference

Proc Can Centen Wheat Symp — Proceedings. Canadian Centennial Wheat Symposium

Proc Can Fed Biol Soc — Proceedings. Canadian Federation of Biological Societies

Proc Can Nat Weed Comm E Sect — Proceedings. Canadian National Weed Committee. Eastern Section

Proc Can Nat Weed Comm W Sect — Proceedings. Canadian National Weed Committee. Western Section

Proc Can Nucl Assoc Annu Int Conf — Proceedings. Canadian Nuclear Association Annual International Conference

Proc Can Phytopathol Soc — Proceedings. Canadian Phytopathological Society

Proc Can Rock Mech Symp — Proceedings. Canadian Rock Mechanics Symposium

Proc Can Soc Forensic Sci — Proceedings. Canadian Society of Forensic Science

Proc Caribb Reg Am Soc Hort Sci — Proceedings. Caribbean Region. American Society for Horticultural Science

Proc Cath — Proceedings. Catholic Theological Society of America

Proc Cath Phil Ass — Proceedings. American Catholic Philosophical Association

Proc Cellul Conf — Proceedings. Cellulose Conference

Proc Chem Soc — Proceedings. Chemical Society

Proc Chem Soc (London) — Proceedings. Chemical Society (London)

Proc Chin Physiol Soc Chengtu Branch — Proceedings. Chinese Physiological Society. Chengtu Branch

Proc Clin Dial Transplant Forum — Proceedings. Clinical Dialysis and Transplant Forum

Proc Coal Mining Inst Amer — Proceedings. Coal Mining Institute of America

Proc Coll Med Univ Philipp — Proceedings. College of Medicine. University of the Philippines

Proc Coll Nat Sci Sect 4 Biol Sci Seoul Natl Univ — Proceedings. College of Natural Sciences. Section 4. Biological Sciences. Seoul National University

Proc Coll Nat Sci Sect 2 Seoul Nat Univ — Proceedings. College of Natural Sciences. Section 2. Physics, Astronomy. Seoul National University

Proc Coll Nat Sci Sect 3 Seoul Nat Univ — Proceedings. College of Natural Sciences. Section 3. Chemistry. Seoul National University

Proc Coll Nat Sci Sect 4 Seoul Nat Univ — Proceedings. College of Natural Sciences. Section 4. Life Sciences. Seoul National University

Proc Coll Nat Sci Sect 5 Seoul Nat Univ — Proceedings. College of Natural Sciences. Section 5. Geology, Meteorology, and Oceanography. Seoul National University

Proc Coll Nat Sci Seoul Natl Univ — Proceedings. College of Natural Sciences. Seoul National University

Proc Colloq Int Potash Inst — Proceedings. Colloquium of the International Potash Institute

Proc Commonw Min Metall Congr — Proceedings. Commonwealth Mining and Metallurgical Congress

Proc Conf Aust Road Res Board — Proceedings. Conference of the Australian Road Research Board

Proc Conf Aust Soc Sugar Cane Technol — Australian Society of Sugar Cane Technologists. Proceedings of the Conference

Proc Conf Eng Med Biol — Proceedings. Conference of Engineering in Medicine and Biology

Proc Conf Great Lakes Res — Proceedings. Conference on Great Lakes Research

Proc Conf Hot Lab Equip — Proceedings. Conference on Hot Laboratories and Equipment

Proc Conf (Int) Solid State Devices — Proceedings. Conference (International) on Solid State Devices

Proc Conf Remote Syst Technol — Proceedings. Conference on Remote Systems Technology

Proc Conf Silic Ind — Proceedings. Conference on the Silicate Industry

Proc Conf Solid State Devices — Proceedings. Conference on Solid State Devices

Proc Congenital Anomalies Res Assoc Annu Rep — Proceedings. Congenital Anomalies. Research Association. Annual Report

Proc Cong Mediterr Phytopathol Union — Proceedings. Congress. Mediterranean Phytopathological Union

Proc Congr Ann Corp Ingen For (Quebec) — Proceedings. Congres Annuel. Corporation des Ingenieurs Forestiers (Quebec)

Proc Congr Eur Soc Haematol — Proceedings. Congress of the European Society of Haematology

Proc Congr Hung Assoc Microbiol — Proceedings. Congress of the Hungarian Association of Microbiologists

Proc Congr Int Assoc Sci Study Ment Defic — Proceedings. Congress. International Association for the Scientific Study of Mental Deficiency

Proc Congr Int Potash Inst — Proceedings. Congress of the International Potash Institute

Proc Congr Int Soc Blood Transfus — Proceedings. Congress of the International Society of Blood Transfusion

Proc Congr Int Soc Sugar Cane Technol — Proceedings. Congress. International Society of Sugar Cane Technologists

Proc Congr Int Union For Res Organ — Proceedings. Congress. International Union of Forest Research Organizations

Proc Congr Jpn Soc Cancer Ther — Proceedings. Congress. Japan Society for Cancer Therapy

Proc Congr S Afr Genet Soc — Proceedings. Congress. South African Genetic Society

Proc Congr S Afr Sug Technol Ass — Proceedings. Congress. South African Sugar Technologists' Association

Proc Conv Int Assoc Fish Wildl Agencies — Proceedings. Convention. International Association of Fish and Wildlife Agencies

Proc Cornell Nutr Conf Feed Mfr — Proceedings. Cornell Nutrition Conference for Feed Manufacturers

Proc Cosmic-Ray Res Lab Nagoya Univ — Proceedings. Cosmic-Ray Research Laboratory. Nagoya University

Proc Cotteswold Natur Fld Club — Proceedings. Cotteswold Naturalists' Field Club

Proc Coventry Dist Natur Hist Sci Soc — Proceedings. Coventry District Natural History and Scientific Society

Proc Crayford Manor House Hist Archaeol Soc — Proceedings. Crayford Manor House Historical and Archaeological Society

Proc Crop Sci Chugoku Br Crop Sci Soc — Proceedings. Crop Science. Chugoku Branch of the Crop Science Society

Proc Crop Sci Soc Jap — Proceedings. Crop Science Society of Japan

Proc Crop Sci Soc Jpn — Proceedings. Crop Science Society of Japan

Proc Croydon Nat Hist Sci Soc — Proceedings. Croydon Natural History Science Society

ProcCTS — Proceedings. College Theology Society

ProcCTSA — Proceedings. Catholic Theological Society of America

PROCD — Processing [*Johannesburg*]

Proc Dep Hortic Plant Health Massey Univ — Proceedings. Department of Horticulture and Plant Health. Massey University

Proc Devon Archaeol Soc — Proceedings. Devon Archaeological Society

Proc Devon Arch Soc — Proceedings. Devon Archaeological Society

Proc Distill Feed Conf — Proceedings. Distillers Feed Conference

Proc Distill Feed Res Counc Conf — Proceedings. Distillers Feed Research Council Conference

Proc Divers' Gas Purity Symp — Proceedings. Divers' Gas Purity Symposium

Proc Div Refin Am Pet Inst — Proceedings. Division of Refining. American Petroleum Institute

Proc Dorset Natur Hist Archaeol Soc — Proceedings. Dorset Natural History and Archaeological Society

Proc Dorset Natur Hist Arch Soc — Proceedings. Dorset Natural History and Archaeological Society

Proc East Afr Acad — Proceedings. East African Academy

Proc Easter Sch Agric Sci Univ Nottingham — Proceedings. Easter School in Agricultural Science. University of Nottingham [*England*]

Proc Ecol Soc Aust — Proceedings. Ecological Society of Australia

Proc Edinburgh Math Soc — Proceedings. Edinburgh Mathematical Society

Proc Edinburgh Math Soc 2 — Proceedings. Edinburgh Mathematical Society. Series 2

Proc Edinburgh Math Soc Edinburgh Math Notes — Proceedings. Edinburgh Mathematical Society. Edinburgh Mathematical Notes

Proceedings of the IEEE — Proceedings. Institute of Electrical and Electronics Engineers

Proc Egypt Acad Sci — Proceedings. Egyptian Academy of Sciences

Proc Eighth Br Weed Control Conf — Proceedings. Eighth British Weed Control Conference

Proc Electron Components Conf — Proceedings. Electronic Components Conference

Proc Electron Microsc Soc Am — Proceedings. Electron Microscopy Society of America

Proc Electron Microsc Soc South Afr — Proceedings. Electron Microscopy Society of Southern Africa

Proc Endoc Soc Aust — Proceedings. Endocrine Society of Australia

Proc Eng Soc Hong Kong — Proceedings. Engineering Society of Hong Kong

Proc Eng Soc West PA — Proceedings. Engineers' Society of Western Pennsylvania

Proc Entomol Soc Amer N Cent Br — Proceedings. Entomological Society of America. North Central Branch

Proc Entomol Soc BC — Proceedings. Entomological Society of British Columbia

Proc Entomol Soc Brit Columbia — Proceedings. Entomological Society of British Columbia

Proc Entomol Soc Manit — Proceedings. Entomological Society of Manitoba

Proc Entomol Soc Manitoba — Proceedings. Entomological Society of Manitoba

Proc Entomol Soc Ont — Proceedings. Entomological Society of Ontario

Proc Entomol Soc Ontario — Proceedings. Entomological Society of Ontario

Proc Entomol Soc Wash — Proceedings. Entomological Society of Washington

Proc Entomol Soc Wash DC — Proceedings. Entomological Society of Washington, DC

Proc Ent Soc Br Columb — Proceedings. Entomological Society of British Columbia

Proc Ent Soc Manitoba — Proceedings. Entomological Society of Manitoba

Proc Ent Soc Ont — Proceedings. Entomological Society of Ontario

Proc Ent Soc Wash — Proceedings. Entomological Society of Washington

Proc Environ Eng Sci Conf — Proceedings. Environmental Engineering and Science Conference

Process Autom — Process Automation

Process Bio — Process Biochemistry

Process Biochem — Process Biochemistry

Process Chem Eng — Process and Chemical Engineering

Process Control Autom — Process Control and Automation

Process Des Dev — Process Design and Development

Process Econ Int — Process Economics International

Process Eng — Process Engineering

Process Eng Mag — Process Engineering Magazine

Process Engng — Process Engineering

Process Eng Plant and Control — Process Engineering. Plant and Control

Process Instrum — Process Instrumentation

Process Metall — Process Metallurgy

Process Ser Okla State Univ Agr Exp Sta — Processed Series. Oklahoma State University. Agricultural Experimental Station

Process Stud — Process Studies

Process Technol Int — Process Technology International

Proces-Verb Seances Soc Sci Phys Nat Bordeaux — Proces-Verbaux des Seances. Societe des Sciences Physiques et Naturelles de Bordeaux [*France*]

Proc Eur Conf Mixing — Proceedings. European Conference on Mixing

Proc Eur Dial Transplant Assoc — Proceedings. European Dialysis and Transplant Association

Proc Eur Dial Transplant Assoc Eur Renal Assoc — Proceedings. European Dialysis and Transplant Association - European Renal Association

Proc Eur Soc Toxicol — Proceedings. European Society of Toxicology

Proc Fac Eng Tokai Univ — Proceedings. Faculty of Engineering. Tokai University [*Japan*]

Proc Fac Sci Tokai Univ — Proceedings. Faculty of Science. Tokai University [*Japan*]

Proc Farm Seed Conf — Proceedings. Farm Seed Conference

Proc FEBS Meet — Proceedings. FEBS [*Federation of European Biochemical Societies*] Meeting

Proc Fertil Soc — Proceedings. Fertilizer Society

Proc Finn Dent Soc — Proceedings. Finnish Dental Society of Washington

Proc Fla Acad Sci — Proceedings. Florida Academy of Sciences

Proc Fla Anti-Mosq — Proceedings. Florida Anti-Mosquito Association

Proc Fla Lychee Grow Ass — Proceedings. Florida Lychee Growers Association

Proc Fla State Hortic Soc — Proceedings. Florida State Horticultural Society

Proc Fla State Hort Soc — Proceedings. Florida State Horticultural Society

Proc Fla St Hort Soc — Proceedings. Florida State Horticultural Society

Proc Florida State Hortic Soc — Florida. State Horticultural Society. Proceedings

Proc Food — Processed Prepared Food

Proc For Microclim Symp Can Dep Fish For — Proceedings. Forest Microclimate Symposium. Canada Department of Fisheries and Forestry

Proc For Prod Res Soc — Proceedings. Forest Products Research Society

Proc For Symp LA Sch For — Proceedings. Annual Forestry Symposium. Louisiana State University. School of Forestry and Wildlife Management

Proc Forum Fundam Surg Probl Clin Congr Am Coll Surg — Proceedings. Forum on Fundamental Surgical Problems. Clinical Congress of the American College of Surgeons

Proc (Fourth) NZ Geogr Conf — Proceedings. (Fourth) New Zealand Geographical Conference

Proc FRI Symp For Res Inst NZ For Serv — Proceedings. FRI Symposium. Forest Research Institute. New Zealand Forest Service

Proc Front Educ Conf — Proceedings. Frontiers in Education Conference

Proc Fujihara Mem Fac Eng Keio Univ — Proceedings. Fujihara Memorial Faculty of Engineering. Keio University

Proc Fujihara Mem Fac Eng Keio Univ (Tokyo) — Proceedings. Fujihara Memorial Faculty of Engineering. Keio University (Tokyo)

Proc Gas Cond Conf — Proceedings. Gas Conditioning Conference [*United States*]

Proc Genet Soc Can — Proceedings. Genetics Society of Canada

Proc Gen Meet Soc Ind Microbiol — Proceedings. General Meeting of the Society for Industrial Microbiology

Proc Geoinst — Proceedings. Geoinstitut

Proc Geol Ass Can — Proceedings. Geological Association of Canada

Proc Geol Assoc — Proceedings. Geologists' Association

Proc Geol Soc China — Proceedings. Geological Society of China [*Taipei*]

Proc Geol Soc Lond — Proceedings. Geological Society of London

Proc Geol Soc S Afr — Proceedings. Geological Society of South Africa

Proc Geophys Soc Tulsa — Proceedings. Geophysical Society of Tulsa

Proc Ger Soc Neurosurg — Proceedings. German Society of Neurosurgery

Proc Ghana Acad Arts Sci — Proceedings. Ghana Academy of Arts and Sciences

Proc Grassl Soc South Afr — Proceedings. Grassland Society of Southern Africa

Proc Great Plains Agr Conf — Proceedings. Great Plains Agriculture Conference

Proc Gulf Caribb Fish Inst — Proceedings. Gulf and Caribbean Fisheries Institute

Proc Hampshire Field Club — Proceedings. Hampshire Field Club and Archaeological Society

Proc Hampshire Fld Club Archaeol Soc — Proceedings. Hampshire Field Club and Archaeological Society

Proc Hawaii Acad Sci — Proceedings. Hawaiian Academy of Science

Proc Hawaii Entomol Soc — Proceedings. Hawaiian Entomological Society

Proc Hawaii Ent Soc — Proceedings. Hawaiian Entomological Society

Proc Hawaii Int Conf Syst Sci — Proceedings. Hawaii International Conference on System Science

Proc Hawaii Top Conf Part Phys — Proceedings. Hawaii Topical Conference in Particle Physics

Proc Heat Transfer Fluid Mech Inst — Proceedings. Heat Transfer and Fluid Mechanics Institute

Proc Helminthol Soc Wash — Proceedings. Helminthological Society of Washington

Proc Helminthol Soc (Wash DC) — Proceedings. Helminthological Society (Washington, DC)

Proc Helminth Soc Wash — Proceedings. Helminthological Society of Washington

Proc High Lysine Corn Conf — Proceedings. High Lysine Corn Conference

Prochn Deform Mater Neravnomernykh Fiz Polyakh — Prochnost i Deformatsiya Materialov v Neravnomernykh Fizicheskikh Polyakh

Prochnost Din Aviats Dvigatelei — Prochnost i Dinamika Aviatsionnykh Dvigatelei [*USSR*]

Proc Hokkaido Symp Plant Breed Crop Sci Soc — Proceedings. Hokkaido Symposium of Plant Breeding and Crop Science Society

Proc Hokuriku Br Crop Sci Soc (Jap) — Proceedings. Hokuriku Branch of Crop Science Society (Japan)

Proc Huguenot Soc Lond — Proceedings. Huguenot Society of London

Proc Hung Annu Meet Biochem — Proceedings. Hungarian Annual Meeting for Biochemistry

Proc Hydrol Symp — Proceedings. Hydrology Symposium

Proc IEE-A — Institution of Electrical Engineers. Proceedings. A

Proc IEE-B — Institution of Electrical Engineers. Proceedings. B

Proc IEE-C — Institution of Electrical Engineers. Proceedings. C

Proc IEE D — Institution of Electrical Engineers. Proceedings. D

Proc IEEE — Proceedings. IEEE

Proc IEEE — Proceedings. Institute of Electrical and Electronics Engineers

Proc IEEE Conf Decis Control — Proceedings. IEEE Conference on Decision and Control

Proc IEEE Conf Decis Control Incl Symp Adapt Processes — Proceedings. IEEE Conference on Decision and Control Including the Symposium on Adaptive Processes

Proc IEEE Int Symp Circuits Syst — Proceedings. IEEE International Symposium on Circuits and Systems

Proc IEE F — Institution of Electrical Engineers. Proceedings. F

Proc IEE G — Institution of Electrical Engineers. Proceedings. G

Proc IEE H — Proceedings. Institution of Electrical Engineers. H

Proc IEE I — Proceedings. Institution of Electrical Engineers. I

Proc III Natn Peanut Res Conf — Proceedings. Third National Peanut Research Conference

Proc III Mining Inst — Proceedings. Illinois Mining Institute

Proc Imp Acad Japan — Proceedings. Imperial Academy of Japan

Proc Imp Acad (Tokyo) — Proceedings. Imperial Academy (Tokyo)

Proc Indiana Acad Sci — Proceedings. Indiana Academy of Science

Proc Indian Acad Sci — Proceedings. Indian Academy of Sciences

Proc Indian Acad Sci A — Proceedings. Indian Academy of Sciences. Section A

Proc Indian Acad Sci Anim Sci — Proceedings. Indian Academy of Sciences. Animal Sciences

Proc Indian Acad Sci B — Proceedings. Indian Academy of Sciences. B

Proc Indian Acad Sci Chem Sci — Proceedings. Indian Academy of Sciences. Chemical Sciences

Proc Indian Acad Sci Earth Planetary Sci — Proceedings. Indian Academy of Sciences. Earth and Planetary Sciences

Proc Indian Acad Sci Earth and Planet Sci — Proceedings. Indian Academy of Sciences. Earth and Planetary Sciences

Proc Indian Acad Sci Earth Planet Sci — Proceedings. Indian Academy of Sciences. Earth and Planetary Sciences

Proc Indian Acad Sci Eng Sci — Proceedings. Indian Academy of Sciences. Engineering Sciences

Proc Indian Acad Sci Math Sci — Proceedings. Indian Academy of Sciences. Mathematical Sciences

Proc Indian Acad Sci Plant Sci — Proceedings. Indian Academy of Sciences. Plant Sciences

Proc Indian Acad Sci Sect A — Proceedings. Indian Academy of Sciences. Section A

Proc Indian Acad Sci Sect A Chem Sci — Proceedings. Indian Academy of Sciences. Section A. Chemical Sciences

Proc Indian Acad Sci Sect A Earth Planetary Sci — Indian Academy of Sciences. Proceedings. Section A. Earth and Planetary Sciences

Proc Indian Acad Sci Sect A Math Sci — Proceedings. Indian Academy of Sciences. Section A. Mathematical Sciences

Proc Indian Acad Sci Sect B — Proceedings. Indian Academy of Sciences. Section B

Proc Indian Acad Sci Sect C — Proceedings. Indian Academy of Sciences. Section C. Engineering Sciences [India]

Proc Indian Assoc Cultiv Sci — Proceedings. Indian Association for Cultivation of Sciences

Proc Indian Natl Sci Acad A — Proceedings. Indian National Science Academy. Part A. Physical Sciences

Proc Indian Natl Sci Acad Part A — Proceedings. Indian National Science Academy. Part A

Proc Indian Natl Sci Acad Part A Phys Sci — Proceedings. Indian National Science Academy. Part A. Physical Sciences

Proc Indian Natl Sci Acad Part B — Proceedings. Indian National Science Academy. Part B. Biological Sciences

Proc Indian Natl Sci Acad Part B Biol Sci — Proceedings. Indian National Science Academy. Part B. Biological Sciences

Proc Indian Nat Sci Acad Part A — Proceedings. Indian National Science Academy. Part A. Physical Sciences

Proc Indian Roads Congr — Proceedings. Indian Roads Congress

Proc Indian Sci Congr — Proceedings. Indian Science Congress

Proc Ind Waste Conf — Proceedings. Industrial Waste Conference

Proc Ind Waste Conf Purdue Univ — Proceedings. Industrial Waste Conference. Purdue University

Proc Ind Waste Util Conf — Proceedings. Industrial Waste Utilization Conference

Proc Inst Automob Eng (London) — Proceedings. Institution of Automobile Engineers (London)

Proc Inst Br Foundrymen — Proceedings. Institute of British Foundrymen

Proc Inst Chem (Calcutta) — Proceedings. Institution of Chemists (Calcutta)

Proc Inst Civ Eng — Proceedings. Institution of Civil Engineers [London]

Proc Inst Civ Eng — Proceedings. Institution of Civil Engineers. Part 2. Research and Theory [United Kingdom]

Proc Inst Civ Eng (London) Suppl — Proceedings. Institution of Civil Engineers (London). Supplement

Proc Inst Civ Eng Part 1 — Proceedings. Institution of Civil Engineers. Part 1. Design and Construction

Proc Inst Civ Eng Part 2 — Proceedings. Institution of Civil Engineers. Part 2. Research and Theory [United Kingdom]

Proc Inst Elec Eng (London) — Proceedings. Institution of Electrical Engineers (London)

Proc Inst Elec Eng Pt B Elec Power Appl — Proceedings. Institution of Electrical Engineers. Part B. Electric Power Applications

Proc Inst Elec Eng Pt E Computers Digital Tech — Proceedings. Institution of Electrical Engineers. Part E. Computers and Digital Techniques

Proc Inst Elec Eng Pt F Commun Radar Signal Process — Proceedings. Institution of Electrical Engineers. Part F. Communications, Radar, and Signal Processing

Proc Inst Elec Eng Pt G Electron Circuits Syst — Proceedings. Institution of Electrical Engineers. Part G. Electronics Circuits and Systems

Proc Inst Elec Eng Pt H Microwaves Opt Antennas — Proceedings. Institution of Electrical Engineers. Part H. Microwaves, Optics, and Antennas

Proc Inst Elec Engrs — Proceedings. Institution of Electrical Engineers

Proc Inst Elect — Proceedings. Institution of Electrical Engineers

Proc Inst Electr Eng — Proceedings. Institution of Electrical Engineers

Proc Inst Electr Eng (London) — Proceedings. Institution of Electrical Engineers (London)

Proc Inst Electr Eng Part 1 — Proceedings. Institution of Electrical Engineers. Part 1. General

Proc Inst Electr Eng Part 2 — Proceedings. Institution of Electrical Engineers. Part 2. Power Engineering

Proc Inst Electr Eng Part 3 — Proceedings. Institution of Electrical Engineers. Part 3. Radio and Communication Engineering

Proc Inst Electr Eng Part 4 — Proceedings. Institution of Electrical Engineers. Part 4. Monographs

Proc Inst Electr Eng Part A — Proceedings. Institution of Electrical Engineers. Part A. Power Engineering

Proc Inst Electr Eng Part A Suppl — Proceedings. Institution of Electrical Engineers. Part A. Supplement

Proc Inst Electr Eng Part B — Proceedings. Institution of Electrical Engineers. Part B. Electronic and Communication Engineering Including Radio Engineering

Proc Inst Electr Eng Part B Suppl — Proceedings. Institution of Electrical Engineers. Part B. Supplement

Proc Inst Electr Eng Part C — Proceedings. Institution of Electrical Engineers. Part C. Monographs

Proc Inst Environ Sci — Proceedings. Institute of Environmental Sciences

Proc Inst Fd Sci Technol — Proceedings. Institute of Food Science and Technology

Proc Inst Food Sci Technol UK — Proceedings. Institute of Food Science and Technology of the United Kingdom

Proc Institute Med Chicago — Proceedings. Institute of Medicine of Chicago

Proc Inst Mech Eng — Proceedings. Institution of Mechanical Engineers

Proc Inst Mech Eng (London) — Proceedings. Institution of Mechanical Engineers (London)

Proc Inst Mech Eng Part A — Proceedings. Institution of Mechanical Engineers. Part A. Power and Process Engineering

Proc Inst Mech Eng Part B — Proceedings. Institution of Mechanical Engineers. Part B. Management and Engineering Manufacture

Proc Inst Mech Eng Part C — Proceedings. Institution of Mechanical Engineers. Part C. Mechanical Engineering Science

Proc Inst Mech Engrs — Proceedings. Institution of Mechanical Engineers

Proc Inst Med Chic — Proceedings. Institute of Medicine of Chicago

Proc Inst Med Chicago — Proceedings. Institute of Medicine of Chicago

Proc Inst Nat Sci Nihon Univ — Proceedings. Institute of Natural Sciences. Nihon University

Proc Instn CE — Proceedings. Institution of Civil Engineers

Proc Instn Civ Engrs — Proceedings. Institution of Civil Engineers

Proc Instn Civ Engrs I II — Proceedings. Institution of Civil Engineers. Parts I and II

Proc Instn Elect Engrs — Proceedings. Institution of Electrical Engineers

Proc Instn Mech Engrs — Proceedings. Institution of Mechanical Engineers

Proc Instn Mech Engrs Pt B Mgmt Engng Mf — Proceedings. Institution of Mechanical Engineers. Part B. Management and Engineering Manufacture

Proc Instn Mech Engrs Pt C Mech Engng Sci — Proceedings. Institution of Mechanical Engineers. Part C. Mechanical Engineering Science

Proc Instn Mech Engrs Pt D Transp Engng — Proceedings. Institution of Mechanical Engineers. Part D. Transport Engineering

Proc Instn Radio Electron Engrs Aust — Proceedings. Institution of Radio and Electronics Engineers of Australia

Proc Instn Radio Engrs Aust — Proceedings. Institution of Radio Engineers of Australia

Proc Inst Oceanogr Fish Bulg Acad Sci — Proceedings. Institute of Oceanography and Fisheries. Bulgarian Academy of Sciences

Proc Inst Pomol (Skierniewice Pol) Ser E Conf Symp — Proceedings. Research Institute of Pomology (Skierniewice, Poland). Series E. Conferences and Symposia

Proc Inst Radio Electron Eng Aust — Proceedings. Institution of Radio and Electronics Engineers of Australia

Proc Inst Railw Signal Eng — Proceedings. Institution of Railway Signal Engineers

Proc Inst Refrig — Proceedings. Institute of Refrigeration

Proc Inst Rubber Ind — Proceedings. Institution of the Rubber Industry

Proc Instrum Soc Am — Proceedings. Instrument Society of America

Proc Inst Sewage Purif — Proceedings. Institute of Sewage Purification

Proc Inst Statist Math — Proceedings. Institute of Statistical Mathematics

Proc Inst Teknol Bandung — Proceedings. Institut Teknologi Bandung [Indonesia]

Proc Inst Teknol Bandung Suppl — Proceedings. Institut Teknologi Bandung. Supplement [Indonesia]

Proc Inst Vitreous Enamellers — Proceedings. Institute of Vitreous Enamellers

Proc Int Acad Oral Pathol — Proceedings. International Academy of Oral Pathology

Proc Int Assoc Milk Dealers — Proceedings. International Association of Milk Dealers

Proc Int Assoc Test Mater — Proceedings. International Association for Testing Materials

Proc Int Assoc Theor Appl Limnol — Proceedings. International Association of Theoretical and Applied Limnology

Proc Int Assoc Vet Food Hyg — Proceedings. International Association of Veterinary Food Hygienists

Proc Int Astronaut Congr — Proceedings. International Astronautical Congress

Proc Int Barley Genet Symp — Proceedings. International Barley Genetics Symposium

Proc Int Bedding Plant Conf — Proceedings. International Bedding Plant Conference

Proc Int Bot Congr — Proceedings. International Botanical Congress

Proc Int Clean Air Congr — Proceedings. International Clean Air Congress

Proc Int Colloq Plant Anal Fert Probl — Proceedings. International Colloquium on Plant Analysis and Fertilizer Problems

Proc Int Comm Glass — Proceedings. International Commission on Glass

Proc Int Conf Biochem Probl Lipids — Proceedings. International Conference on Biochemical Problems of Lipids

Proc Int Conf Cent High Energy Form — Proceedings. International Conference. Center for High Energy Forming

Proc Int Conf Cybern Soc — Proceedings. International Conference on Cybernetics and Society

Proc Int Conf Fire Saf — Proceedings. International Conference on Fire Safety

Proc Int Conf Fluid Sealing — Proceedings. International Conference on Fluid Sealing

Proc Int Conf High Energy Phys — Proceedings. International Conference on High Energy Physics

Proc Int Conf High Energy Rate Fabr — Proceedings. International Conference on High Energy Rate Fabrication

Proc Int Conf Int Assoc Water Pollut Res — Proceedings. International Conference of the International Association on Water Pollution Research

Proc Int Conf Lasers — Proceedings. International Conference on Lasers

Proc Int Conf Noise Control Eng — Proceedings. International Conference on Noise Control Engineering

Proc Int Conf Org Coat Sci Technol Technomic Publ — Proceedings. International Conference in Organic Coatings Science and Technology. Technomic Publication

Proc Int Conf Peaceful Uses Atomic Energy — Proceedings. International Conference on the Peaceful Uses of Atomic Energy

Proc Int Conf Plant Growth Regulat — Proceedings. International Conference on Plant Growth Regulation

Proc Int Conf Plant Pathog Bact — Proceedings. International Conference on Plant Pathogenic Bacteria

Proc Int Conf Sci Aspects Mushroom Grow — Proceedings. International Conference on Scientific Aspects of Mushroom Growing

Proc Int Conf Wildl Dis — Proceedings. International Conference on Wildlife Disease

Proc Int Cong Phot — Proceedings. International Congress of Photography

Proc Int Congr Anim Reprod Artif Insemin — Proceedings. International Congress on Animal Reproduction and Artificial Insemination

Proc Int Congr Biochem — Proceedings. International Congress of Biochemistry

Proc Int Congr Crop Prot — Proceedings. International Congress on Crop Protection

Proc Int Congr Ent — Proceedings. International Congress of Entomology

Proc Int Congr Entomol — Proceedings. International Congress of Entomology

Proc Int Congr Food Sci Technol — Proceedings. International Congress of Food Science and Technology

Proc Int Congr Genet — Proceedings. International Congress of Genetics

Proc Int Congr Geront — Proceedings. International Congress on Gerontology

Proc Int Congr Gerontol — Proceedings. International Congress of Gerontology

Proc Int Congr Hist Sci — Proceedings. International Congress of the History of Science

Proc Int Congr Hum Genet — Proceedings. International Congress of Human Genetics

Proc Int Congr Ment Retard — Proceedings. International Congress on Mental Retardation

Proc Int Congr Microbiol Stand — Proceedings. International Congress for Microbiological Standardization

Proc Int Congr Mushroom Sci — Proceedings. International Congress on Mushroom Science

Proc Int Congr Nephrol — Proceedings. International Congress of Nephrology

Proc Int Congr Nutr (Hamburg) — Proceedings. International Congress of Nutrition (Hamburg)

Proc Int Congr Pharmacol — Proceedings. International Congress on Pharmacology

Proc Int Congr Photosynth Res — Proceedings. International Congress on Photosynthesis Research

Proc Int Congr Primatol — Proceedings. International Congress of Primatology

Proc Int Congr Protozool — Proceedings. International Congress on Protozoology

Proc Int Congr Psychother — Proceedings. International Congress of Psychotherapy

Proc Int Congr Pure Appl Chem — Proceedings. International Congress of Pure and Applied Chemistry

Proc Int Congr Radiat Prot — Proceedings. International Congress of Radiation Protection

Proc Int Congr Refrig — Proceedings. International Congress of Refrigeration

Proc Int Congr Virol — Proceedings. International Congress for Virology

Proc Int Congr Zool — Proceedings. International Congress of Zoology

Proc Int Dist Heat Assoc — Proceedings. International District Heating Association

Proc Internat School of Phys Enrico Fermi — Proceedings. International School of Physics "Enrico Fermi"

Proc Intersoc Energy Conver Eng Conf — Proceedings. Intersociety Energy Conversion Engineering Conference

Proc Intersoc Energy Convers Eng Conf — Proceedings. Intersociety Energy Conversion Engineering Conference

Proc Interuniv Fac Work Conf — Proceedings. Interuniversity Faculty Work Conference

Proc Int Grassland Congr — Proceedings. International Grassland Congress

Proc Int Gstaad Symp — Proceedings. International Gstaad Symposium

Proc Int Hort Congr — Proceedings. International Horticultural Congress

Proc Int Hortic Congr — Proceedings. International Horticultural Congress

Proc Int ISA Biomed Sci Instrum Symp — Proceedings. International ISA [*Instrument Society of America*] Biomedical Sciences Instrumentation Symposium

Proc Int Meet Biol Stand — Proceedings. International Meeting of Biological Standardization

Proc Int Microelectron Symp — Proceedings. International Microelectronics Symposium

Proc Int Ornithol Congr — Proceedings. International Ornithological Congress

Proc Int Pharmacol Meet — Proceedings. International Pharmacological Meeting

Proc Int Pl Propag Soc — Proceedings. International Plant Propagators' Society

Proc Int Sch Phys Enrico Fermi — Proceedings. International School of Physics "Enrico Fermi"

Proc Int Sci Congr Cultiv Edible Fungi — Proceedings. International Scientific Congress on the Cultivation of Edible Fungi

Proc Int Seaweed Symp — Proceedings. International Seaweed Symposium

Proc Int Seed Test Ass — Proceedings. International Seed Testing Association

Proc Int Seed Test Assoc — Proceedings. International Seed Testing Association

Proc Int Shade Tree Conf — Proceedings. Annual Meetings. International Shade Tree Conference

Proc Int Soc Soil Sci — Proceedings. International Society of Soil Science

Proc Int Soc Sugar Cane Technol — Proceedings. International Society of Sugar Cane Technologists

Proc Int Symp Enzyme Chem — Proceedings. International Symposium on Enzyme Chemistry

Proc Int Symp Food Irradiation — Proceedings. International Symposium on Food Irradiation

Proc Int Symp Fresh Water Sea — Proceedings. International Symposium on Fresh Water from the Sea

Proc Int Symp Inst Biomed Res Am Med Assoc Educ Res Found — Proceedings. International Symposium of the Institute for Biomedical Research. American Medical Association Education and Research Foundation

Proc Int Symp Med Mycol — Proceedings. International Symposium on Medical Mycology

Proc Int Symp Mult Valued Logic — Proceedings. International Symposium on Multiple-Valued Logic

Proc Int Symp Poll — Proceedings. International Symposium on Pollination

Proc Int Symp Princess Takamatsu Cancer Res Fund — Proceedings. International Symposium of the Princess Takamatsu Cancer Research Fund

Proc Int Symp Remote Sens Environ — Proceedings. International Symposium on Remote Sensing of Environment

Proc Int Symp Remote Sensing Environ — Proceedings. International Symposium on Remote Sensing of Environment

Proc Int Tech Conf APICS — Proceedings. International Technical Conference. American Production and Inventory Control Society

Proc Int Union Biol Sci Ser B — Proceedings. International Union of Biological Sciences. Series B

Proc Int Union Forest Res Organ — Proceedings. International Union of Forest Research Organizations

Proc Int Vet Congr — Proceedings. International Veterinary Congress

Proc Int Water Qual Symp — Proceedings. International Water Quality Symposium

Proc Int Wheat Genet Symp — Proceedings. International Wheat Genetics Symposium

Proc Int Wheat Surplus Util Conf — Proceedings. International Wheat Surplus Utilization Conference

Proc Int Wire Cable Symp — Proceedings. International Wire and Cable Symposium

Proc Int Workshop Nude Mice — Proceedings. International Workshop on Nude Mice

Proc Iowa Acad Sci — Proceedings. Iowa Academy of Science

Proc IPI Congr — Proceedings. IPI [*International Potash Institute*] Congress

Proc Iraqi Sci Soc — Proceedings. Iraqi Scientific Societies

Proc IRE — Proceedings. IRE [*Institute of Radio Engineers*] [*United States*]

Proc ISA — Proceedings. Instrument Society of America

Proc Isle Man Natur Hist Antiq Soc — Proceedings. Isle of Man Natural History and Antiquarian Society

Proc Isle Wight Natur Hist Archaeol Soc — Proceedings. Isle of Wight Natural History and Archaeological Society

Proc Jap Acad — Proceedings. Japan Academy

Proc Japan Acad — Proceedings. Japan Academy

Proc Japan Acad Ser A Math Sci — Proceedings. Japan Academy. Series A. Mathematical Sciences

Proc Japan Acad Ser B Phys Biol Sci — Proceedings. Japan Academy. Series B. Physical and Biological Sciences

Proc Jap Soc Civ Eng — Proceedings. Japan Society of Civil Engineers

ProcJPES — Proceedings. Jewish Palestine Exploration Society

Proc Jpn Acad — Proceedings. Japan Academy

Proc Jpn Acad Ser A — Proceedings. Japan Academy. Series A. Mathematical Sciences

Proc Jpn Acad Ser B — Proceedings. Japan Academy. Series B. Physical and Biological Sciences

Proc Jpn At Ind Forum Inc — Proceedings. Japan Atomic Industrial Forum, Incorporated

Proc Jpn Cem Eng Assoc — Proceedings. Japan Cement Engineering Association

Proc Jpn Conf Radioisot — Proceedings. Japan Conference on Radioisotopes

Proc Jpn Congr Mater Res — Proceedings. Japan Congress on Materials Research

Proc Jpn Congr Test Mater — Proceedings. Japanese Congress for Testing Materials

Proc Jpn Pharmacol Soc — Proceedings. Japanese Pharmacology Society

Proc Jpn Soc Civ Eng — Proceedings. Japan Society of Civil Engineers

Proc Jpn Soc Clin Biochem Metab — Proceedings. Japan Society of Clinical Biochemistry and Metabolism

Proc Jpn Soc Med Mass Spectrom — Proceedings. Japanese Society for Medical Mass Spectrometry

Proc Jpn Soc Reticuloendothel Syst — Proceedings. Japan Society of the Reticuloendothelial System

Proc Kansai Plant Prot Soc — Proceedings. Kansai Plant Protection Society

Proc Kanto-Tosan Plant Prot Soc — Proceedings. Kanto-Tosan Plant Protection Society

Proc Kinki Symp Crop Sci Plant Breed Soc — Proceedings. Kinki Symposium of Crop Science and Plant Breeding Society

Proc K Ned Akad Wet — Proceedings. Koninklijke Nederlandse Akademie van Wetenschappen

Proc K Ned Akad Wet B — Proceedings. Koninklijke Nederlandse Akademie van Wetenschappen. Series B. Physical Sciences

Proc K Ned Akad Wet Ser A — Proceedings. Koninklijke Nederlandse Akademie van Wetenschappen. Series A. Mathematical Sciences

Proc K Ned Akad Wet Ser B — Proceedings. Koninklijke Nederlandse Akademie van Wetenschappen. Series B. Physical Sciences

Proc K Ned Akad Wet Ser B Palaeontol Geol Phys Chem — Proceedings. Koninklijke Nederlandse Akademie van Wetenschappen. Series B. Palaeontology, Geology, Physics, and Chemistry [*Later, Proceedings. Koninklijke Nederlandse Akademie van Wetenschappen. Series B. Palaeontology, Geology, Physics, Chemistry, Anthropology*]

Proc K Ned Akad Wet Ser B Phys Sci — Proceedings. Koninklijke Nederlandse Akademie van Wetenschappen. Series B. Physical Sciences

Proc K Ned Akad Wet Ser C — Proceedings. Koninklijke Nederlandse Akademie van Wetenschappen. Series C. Biological and Medical Sciences

Proc K Ned Akad Wet Ser C Biol Med Sci — Proceedings. Koninklijke Nederlandse Akademie van Wetenschappen. Series C. Biological and Medical Sciences

Proc LA Acad Sci — Proceedings. Louisiana Academy of Sciences

Proc LA Ass Agron — Proceedings. Louisiana Association of Agronomists

Proc Leatherhead Dist Local Hist Soc — Proceedings. Leatherhead and District Local History Society

Proc Lebedev Phys Inst — Proceedings (Trudy). P. N. Lebedev Physics Institute

Proc Leeds Phil Lit Soc Sci Sect — Proceedings. Leeds Philosophical and Literary Society. Scientific Section

Proc Leeds Philos & Lit Soc — Proceedings. Leeds Philosophical and Literary Society

Proc Leeds Philos Lit Soc Lit Hist Sect — Proceedings. Leeds Philosophical and Literary Society. Literary and Historical Section

Proc Leucocyte Cult Conf — Proceedings. Leucocyte Culture Conference

Proc Lincoln Coll Farmers Conf — Proceedings. Lincoln College. Farmer's Conference

Proc Linnean Soc NSW — Proceedings. Linnean Society of New South Wales

Proc Linn Soc Lond — Proceedings. Linnean Society of London

Proc Linn Soc London — Proceedings. Linnean Society of London

Proc Linn Soc NSW — Proceedings. Linnean Society of New South Wales

Proc Linn Soc NY — Proceedings. Linnean Society of New York

Proc Liverpool Geol Soc — Proceedings. Liverpool Geological Society

Proc London Math Soc — Proceedings. London Mathematical Society

Proc London Math Soc 3 — Proceedings. London Mathematical Society. Third Series

Proc Lunar Sci Conf — Proceedings. Lunar Science Conference [*United States*]

Proc Malacol Soc Lond — Proceedings. Malacological Society of London

Proc Mark Milk Conf — Proceedings. Market Milk Conference

Proc Mar Safety Council USCG — Proceedings. Marine Safety Council. United States Coast Guard

Proc Mass Hist Soc — Proceedings. Massachusetts Historical Society

Proc Math Phys Soc (Egypt) — Proceedings. Mathematical and Physical Society (Egypt)

Proc Mayo Clin — Proceedings. Staff Meetings of the Mayo Clinic

Proc Mayo Clin Staff Meet — Proceedings. Mayo Clinic Staff Meeting

Proc MD Del Water Pollut Control Assoc — Proceedings. Maryland-Delaware Water and Pollution Control Association

Proc MD Nutr Conf Feed Manuf — Proceedings. Maryland Nutrition Conference for Feed Manufacturers

Proc Meat Ind Res Conf — Proceedings. Meat Industry Research Conference

Proc Medico-Legal Soc Vict — Proceedings. Medico-Legal Society of Victoria

Proc Meet Anim Husb Wing Board Agric Anim Husb India — Proceedings. Meeting of the Animal Husbandry Wing. Board of Agriculture and Animal Husbandry in India

Proc Meet Jpn Soc Med Mass Spectrom — Proceedings. Meeting of the Japanese Society for Medical Mass Spectrometry

Proc Meet West Indies Sugar Technol — Proceedings. Meeting of West Indies Sugar Technologists

Proc Microbiol Res Group Hung Acad Sci — Proceedings. Microbiological Research Group. Hungarian Academy of Science

Proc Microsc Soc Can — Proceedings. Microscopical Society of Canada

Proc Mid-Atl Ind Waste Conf — Proceedings. Mid-Atlantic Industrial Waste Conference [*United States*]

Proc Midwest Fert Conf — Proceedings. Midwestern Fertilizer Conference

Proc Mid Year Meet Am Pet Inst — Proceedings. Mid-Year Meeting. American Petroleum Institute

Proc Mine Med Off Assoc — Proceedings. Mine Medical Officers Association

Proc Minn Acad Sci — Proceedings. Minnesota Academy of Sciences

Proc Minutes Ann Meet Agric Res Inst — Proceedings and Minutes. Annual Meeting of the Agricultural Research Institute

Proc Mont Acad Sci — Proceedings. Montana Academy of Sciences

Proc Mont Nutr Conf — Proceedings. Montana Nutrition Conference

Proc Montpellier Symp — Proceedings. Montpellier Symposium

Proc Mtg Comm For Tree Breeding Can — Proceedings. Meeting Committee on Forest Tree Breeding in Canada

Proc Mtg Sect Int Union For Res Organ — Proceedings. Meeting of Section. International Union of Forest Research Organizations

Proc Nagano Pref Agr Exp Sta — Proceedings. Nagano Prefectural Agricultural Experiment Station

Proc NA Sci — Proceedings. National Academy of Sciences

Proc Nat Acad Sci — Proceedings. National Academy of Sciences. United States of America

Proc Nat Acad Sci (India) Sect A — Proceedings. National Academy of Sciences (India). Section A

Proc Nat Acad Sci USA — Proceedings. National Academy of Sciences. United States of America

Proc Nat Acad Sci USA Biol Sci — Proceedings. National Academy of Sciences. United States of America. Biological Sciences

Proc Nat Acad Sci USA Phys Sci — Proceedings. National Academy of Sciences. United States of America. Physical Sciences

Proc Nat Ass Wheat Growers — Proceedings. National Association of Wheat Growers

Proc Nat Conf AIAS — Proceedings. National Conference. Australian Institute of Agricultural Science

Proc Nat Conf Fluid Power Annu Meet — Proceedings. National Conference on Fluid Power. Annual Meeting

Proc Nat Electron Conf — Proceedings. National Electronics Conference

Proc Nat Food Eng Conf — Proceedings. National Food Engineering Conference

Proc Nat Gas Process Assoc Tech Pap — Proceedings. Natural Gas Processors Association. Technical Papers

Proc Nat Gas Processors Assoc Annu Conv — Proceedings. Natural Gas Processors Association. Annual Convention

Proc Natl Acad Sci — Proceedings. National Academy of Sciences. United States of America

Proc Natl Acad Sci (India) — Proceedings. National Academy of Sciences (India)

Proc Natl Acad Sci (India) Sect A — Proceedings. National Academy of Sciences (India). Section A. Physical Sciences

Proc Natl Acad Sci (India) Sect A (Phys Sci) — Proceedings. National Academy of Sciences (India). Section A (Physical Sciences)

Proc Natl Acad Sci (India) Sect B — Proceedings. National Academy of Sciences (India). Section B. Biological Sciences

Proc Natl Acad Sci (India) Sect B (Biol Sci) — Proceedings. National Academy of Sciences (India). Section B (Biological Sciences)

Proc Natl Acad Sci USA — Proceedings. National Academy of Sciences. United States of America

Proc Natl Biomed Sci Instrum Symp — Proceedings. National Biomedical Sciences Instrumentation Symposium

Proc Natl Cancer Conf — Proceedings. National Cancer Conference

Proc Natl Conf Adm Res — Proceedings. National Conference on the Administration of Research

Proc Natl Conf Fluid Power — Proceedings. National Conference on Fluid Power [*United States*]

Proc Natl Conf Fluid Power Annu Meet — Proceedings. National Conference on Fluid Power. Annual Meeting

Proc Natl Conf Individ Onsite Wastewater Syst — Proceedings. National Conference for Individual Onsite Wastewater Systems

Proc Natl Conf Methadone Treat — Proceedings. National Conference on Methadone Treatment

Proc Natl Conv Study Inf Doc — Proceedings. National Convention for the Study of Information and Documentation [*Japan*]

Proc Natl Counc Radiat Prot Meas — Proceedings. National Council on Radiation Protection and Measurements

Proc Natl Counc Sci Dev (Repub China) — Proceedings. National Council on Science Development (Republic of China)

Proc Natl Electron Conf — Proceedings. National Electronics Conference

Proc Natl Food Eng Conf — Proceedings. National Food Engineering Conference

Proc Natl Incinerator Conf — Proceedings. National Incinerator Conference

Proc Natl Inst Sci (India) — Proceedings. National Institute of Sciences (India)

Proc Natl Inst Sci (India) A — Proceedings. National Institute of Sciences (India). Part A. Physical Sciences

Proc Natl Inst Sci (India) Part A — Proceedings. National Institute of Sciences (India). Part A. Physical Sciences

Proc Natl Inst Sci (India) Part A Phys Sci — Proceedings. National Institute of Sciences (India). Part A. Physical Sciences

Proc Natl Inst Sci (India) Part A Suppl — Proceedings. National Institute of Sciences (India). Part A. Supplement

Proc Natl Inst Sci (India) Part B — Proceedings. National Institute of Sciences (India). Part B. Biological Sciences

Proc Natl Inst Sci (India) Part B Biol Sci — Proceedings. National Institute of Sciences (India). Part B. Biological Sciences

Proc Natl Meet Biophys Biotechnol Finl — Proceedings. National Meeting on Biophysics and Biotechnology in Finland

Proc Natl Open Hearth Basic Oxygen Steel Conf — Proceedings. National Open Hearth and Basic Oxygen Steel Conference

Proc Natl Sci Counc — Proceedings. National Science Council

Proc Natl Sci Counc (Repub China) — Proceedings. National Science Council (Republic of China)

Proc Natl Shellfish Assoc — Proceedings. National Shellfisheries Association

Proc Natl Symp Radioecol — Proceedings. National Symposium on Radioecology

Proc Natl Telecommun Conf — Proceedings. National Telecommunications Conference

Proc Natn Acad Sci (India) — Proceedings. National Academy of Sciences (India)

Proc Natn Acad Sci USA — Proceedings. National Academy of Sciences. United States of America

Proc Natn Ent Soc (USA) — Proceedings. National Entomological Society (United States of America)

Proc Natn Inst Sci (India) — Proceedings. National Institute of Sciences (India)

Proc Nat Silo Ass — Proceedings. National Silo Association

Proc Nat Telemetering Conf — Proceedings. National Telemetering Conference

Proc Natur Gas Processors Ass — Proceedings. Natural Gas Processors Association

Proc N Cent Brch Am Ass Econ Ent — Proceedings. North Central Branch. American Association of Economic Entomologists

Proc N Cent Brch Ent Soc Am — Proceedings. North Central Branch. Entomological Society of America

Proc ND Acad Sci — Proceedings. North Dakota Academy of Sciences

Proc Near E S Afr Irrig Pract Semin — Proceedings. Near East South Africa Irrigation Practices Seminar

Proc Nebr Acad Sci Affil Soc — Proceedings. Nebraska Academy of Sciences and Affiliated Societies

Proc Ned Akad Wet — Proceedings. Koninklijke Nederlandse Akademie van Wetenschappen

Proc News Aust Oil Colour Chem Assoc — Proceedings and News. Australian Oil and Colour Chemists Association

Proc News Aust Oil Colour Chemists Assoc — Proceedings and News. Australian Oil and Colour Chemists Association

Proc NH Acad Sci — Proceedings. New Hampshire Academy of Science

Proc Ninth Int Grassld Congr — Proceedings. Ninth International Grassland Congress

Proc NJ Hist Soc — Proceedings. New Jersey Historical Society

Proc NJ Mosq Control Assoc — Proceedings. New Jersey Mosquito Control Association

Proc N Mex W Tex Phil Soc — Proceedings. New Mexico-West Texas Philosophical Society

Proc NMFA — Procedure. National Microfilm Association

Proc Nord Aroma Symp — Proceedings. Nordic Aroma Symposium

Proc North Cent Branch Entomol Soc Am — Proceedings. North Central Branch. Entomological Society of America

Proc North Cent Weed Control Conf — Proceedings. North Central Weed Control Conference

Proc Northeast Weed Contr Conf — Proceedings. Northeastern Weed Control Conference

Proc Northeast Weed Sci Soc — Proceedings. Northeastern Weed Science Society

Proc Northwest Conf Struct Eng — Proceedings. Northwest Conference of Structural Engineers

Proc Northwest Wood Prod Clin — Proceedings. Northwest Wood Products Clinic

Proc NS Inst Sci — Proceedings. Nova Scotian Institute of Science

Proc Ntheast For Tree Impr Conf — Proceedings. Northeastern Forest Tree Improvement Conference

Proc Nucl Phys Solid State Phys Symp — Proceedings. Nuclear Physics and Solid State Physics Symposium [*India*]

Proc Nutr Soc — Proceedings. Nutrition Society

Proc Nutr Soc Aust — Proceedings. Nutrition Society of Australia

Proc Nutr Soc South Afr — Proceedings. Nutrition Society of Southern Africa

Proc NY St Hist Assn — Proceedings. New York State Historical Association

Proc NY St Hort Soc — Proceedings. New York State Horticultural Society

Proc NZ Ecol Soc — Proceedings. New Zealand Ecological Society

Proc NZ Grassl Assoc — Proceedings. New Zealand Grassland Association

Proc NZ Grassl Assoc Conf — Proceedings. New Zealand Grassland Association. Conference

Proc NZ Grassld Ass — Proceedings. New Zealand Grassland Association

Proc NZ Inst Agr Sci — Proceedings. New Zealand Institute of Agricultural Science

Proc NZ Soc Anim Prod — Proceedings. New Zealand Society of Animal Production

Proc NZ Weed Conf — Proceedings. New Zealand Weed and Pest Control Conference

Proc NZ Weed Control Conf — Proceedings. New Zealand Weed Control Conference

Proc NZ Weed Pest Contr Conf — Proceedings. New Zealand Weed and Pest Control Conference

Proc NZ Weed & Pest Control Conf — Proceedings. New Zealand Weed and Pest Control Conference

Proc Ohio State Hortic Soc — Proceedings. Ohio State Horticultural Society

Proc Ohio State Hort Soc — Proceedings. Ohio State Horticultural Society

Proc Oil Recovery Conf Tex Petrol Res Comm — Proceedings. Oil Recovery Conference. Texas Petroleum Research Committee

Proc Okla Acad Sci — Proceedings. Oklahoma Academy of Science

Proc Ont Ind Waste Conf — Proceedings. Ontario Industrial Waste Conference

Proc Oreg Acad Sci — Proceedings. Oregon Academy of Science

Proc Oreg Weed Conf — Proceedings. Oregon Weed Conference

Proc Organ Inst NSW — Proceedings. Organ Institute of New South Wales

Proc Osaka Prefect Inst Public Health Ed Ind Health — Proceedings. Osaka Prefectural Institute of Public Health. Edition of Industrial Health

Proc Osaka Public Health Inst — Proceedings. Osaka Public Health Institute [*Japan*]

Proc PA Acad Sci — Proceedings. Pennsylvania Academy of Science

Proc Pac Chem Eng Congr — Proceedings. Pacific Chemical Engineering Congress

Proc Pac Coast Gas Ass — Proceedings. Pacific Coast Gas Association, Inc. [*California*]

Proc Pac Northwest Fert Conf — Proceedings. Pacific Northwest Fertilizer Conference

Proc Pac Northwest Ind Waste Conf — Proceedings. Pacific Northwest Industrial Waste Conference

Proc Pac Sci Congr — Proceedings. Pacific Science Congress

Proc PA Ger Soc — Proceedings and Addresses. Pennsylvania-German Society

Proc Pak Acad Sci — Proceedings. Pakistan Academy of Sciences

Proc Pakistan Statist Assoc — Proceedings. Pakistan Statistical Association

Proc Pakist Sci Conf — Proceedings. Pakistan Science Conference

Proc Pak Sci Conf — Proceedings. Pakistan Science Conference

Proc Pap Annu Conf Calif Mosq Control Assoc — Proceedings and Papers. Annual Conference. California Mosquito Control Association

Proc Pap Annu Conf Calif Mosq Vector Control Assoc — Proceedings and Papers. Annual Conference. California Mosquito and Vector Control Association

Proc Pap Graphic Arts Conf — Proceedings and Papers. Graphic Arts Conference

Proc Pap Int Union Conserv Nature Nat Resour — Proceedings and Papers. International Union for the Conservation of Nature and Natural Resources

Proc Path Soc Phila — Proceedings. Pathological Society of Philadelphia

Proc Paving Conf — Proceedings. Paving Conference

Proc Penn Acad Sci — Proceedings. Pennsylvania Academy of Science

Proc Peoria Acad Sci — Proceedings. Peoria Academy of Science

Proc Pharm Soc Egypt — Proceedings. Pharmaceutical Society of Egypt

Proc Phil As — Proceedings. American Philological Association

Proc Phil Educ Soc Austl — Proceedings. Philosophy of Education Society of Australasia

Proc Phil Educ Soc GB — Proceedings. Philosophy of Education Society of Great Britain

Proc Phil Soc — Proceedings. American Philosophical Society

Proc Phys Math Soc Jpn — Proceedings. Physico-Mathematical Society of Japan

Proc Phys Semin Trondheim — Proceedings. Physics Seminar in Trondheim [*Norway*]

Proc Phys Soc Jpn — Proceedings. Physical Society of Japan

Proc Phys Soc (London) — Proceedings. Physical Society (London)

Proc Phys Soc (London) Sect A — Proceedings. Physical Society (London). Section A

Proc Phys Soc (London) Sect B — Proceedings. Physical Society (London). Section B

Proc Phytochem Soc — Proceedings. Phytochemical Society

Proc Plant Growth Regul Work Group — Proceedings. Plant Growth Regulator Working Group

Proc Plant Propagators' Soc — Proceedings. Plant Propagators' Society [*United States*]

Proc PN Lebedev Phys Inst — Proceedings. P. N. Lebedev Physics Institute

Proc PN Lebedev Phys Inst Acad Sci USSR — Proceedings. P. N. Lebedev Physics Institute. Academy of Sciences of the USSR

Proc Porcelain Enamel Inst Tech Forum — Proceedings. Porcelain Enamel Institute. Technical Forum

Proc Power Plant Dyn Control Test Symp — Proceedings. Power Plant Dynamics. Control and Testing Symposium

Proc Prehist Soc — Proceedings. Prehistoric Society
Proc Prod Liability Prev Conf — Proceedings. Product Liability Prevention Conference
Proc PS — Proceedings. Prehistoric Society
Proc Public Health Eng Conf — Proceedings. Public Health Engineering Conference [*Loughborough University of Technology*]
Proc QD Soc Sug Cane Tech — Queensland Society of Sugar Cane Technologists. Proceedings
Proc QD Soc Sug Cane Technol — Proceedings. Queensland Society of Sugar Cane Technologists
Proc Queensl Soc Sugar Cane Technol — Proceedings. Queensland Society of Sugar Cane Technologists
Proc Queensl Soc Sug Cane Technol — Queensland Society of Sugar Cane Technologists. Proceedings
Proc Queens Soc Sugar Cane Technol — Queensland Society of Sugar Cane Technologists. Proceedings
Proc Radio Club Am — Proceedings. Radio Club of America
Proc Radioisot Soc Philipp — Proceedings. Radioisotope Society of the Philippines
Proc R Agric Hort Soc S Aust — Royal Agricultural and Horticultural Society of South Australia. Proceedings
Proc Rajasthan Acad Sci — Proceedings. Rajasthan Academy of Sciences
Proc R Aust Chem Inst — Proceedings. Royal Australian Chemical Institute
Proc R Can Inst — Proceedings. Royal Canadian Institute
Proc Reg Conf Int Potash Inst — Proceedings. Regional Conference. International Potash Institute
Proc Relay Conf — Proceedings. Relay Conference
Proc Reliab Maint Conf — Proceedings. Reliability and Maintainability Conference
Proc Remote Syst Technol Div ANS — Proceedings. Remote Systems Technology Division of the American Nuclear Society
Proc Rencontre Moriond — Proceedings. Rencontre de Moriond
Proc R Entomol Soc Lond Ser A Gen Entomol — Proceedings. Royal Entomological Society of London. Series A. General Entomology
Proc R Entomol Soc Lond Ser B Taxon — Proceedings. Royal Entomological Society of London. Series B. Taxonomy
Proc Rep Belfast Nat Hist Philos Soc — Proceedings and Reports. Belfast Natural History and Philosophical Society
Proc Rep S Seedmen's Ass — Proceedings and Reports. Southern Seedmen's Association
Proc Res Conf Res Counc Am Meat Inst Found Univ Chicago — Proceedings. Research Conference Sponsored by the Research Council of the American Meat Institute Foundation. University of Chicago
Proc Res Inst Atmos Nagoya Univ — Proceedings. Research Institute of Atmospherics. Nagoya University
Proc Res Inst Nucl Med Biol — Proceedings. Research Institute for Nuclear Medicine and Biology
Proc Res Inst Nucl Med Biol Hiroshima Univ — Proceedings. Research Institute for Nuclear Medicine and Biology. Hiroshima University [*Japan*]
Proc Res Inst Oceanogr Fish (Varna) — Proceedings. Research Institute of Oceanography and Fisheries (Varna)
Proc Res Soc Jpn Sugar Refineries' Technol — Proceedings. Research Society of Japan. Sugar Refineries' Technologists
Proc R Geogr Soc Australas S Aust Br — Proceedings. Royal Geographical Society of Australasia. South Australian Branch
Proc R Geogr Soc Australas South Aust Branch — Proceedings. Royal Geographical Society of Australasia. South Australian Branch
Proc R Geog Soc Aust S Aust Br — Proceedings. Royal Geographical Society of Australasia. South Australian Branch
Proc R Inst GB — Proceedings. Royal Institution of Great Britain
Proc R Instn Gt Br — Proceedings. Royal Institution of Great Britain
Proc R Ir Acad — Proceedings. Royal Irish Academy
Proc R Ir Acad A — Proceedings. Royal Irish Academy. Section A. Mathematical, Astronomical, and Physical Science
Proc R Ir Acad Sect B — Proceedings. Royal Irish Academy. Section B. Biological, Geological, and Chemical Science
Proc R Irish Acad Sect A — Proceedings. Royal Irish Academy. Section A. Mathematical, Astronomical, and Physical Science
Proc R Irish Acad Sect B — Proceedings. Royal Irish Academy. Section B. Biological, Geological, and Chemical Science
Proc R Microsc Soc — Proceedings. Royal Microscopical Society [*England*]
Proc RNS — Proceedings. Royal Numismatic Society
Proc Robert A Welch Found Conf Chem Res — Proceedings. Robert A. Welch Foundation. Conferences on Chemical Research
Proc Rochester Acad Sci — Proceedings. Rochester Academy of Science
Proc Rocky Mt Coal Min Inst — Proceedings. Rocky Mountain Coal Mining Institute
Proc Royal Aust Chem Inst — Proceedings. Royal Australian Chemical Institute
Proc Royal Irish Acad — Proceedings. Royal Irish Academy
Proc Royal Soc Canad — Proceedings. Royal Society of Canada
Proc Royal Soc London Ser A — Proceedings. Royal Society of London. Series A. Mathematical and Physical Sciences
Proc Roy Anthropol Inst — Proceedings. Royal Anthropological Institute

Proc Roy Anthropol Inst Gr Brit Ir — Proceedings. Royal Anthropological Institute of Great Britain and Ireland
Proc Roy Aust Chem Inst — Proceedings. Royal Australian Chemical Institute
Proc Roy Entomol Soc Lond — Proceedings. Royal Entomological Society of London
Proc Roy Entomol Soc Lond C — Proceedings. Royal Entomological Society of London. Series C. Journal of Meetings
Proc Roy Entomol Soc London Ser A — Proceedings. Royal Entomological Society of London. Series A
Proc Roy Geog Soc Austral — Proceedings. Royal Geographical Society of Australia. South Australian Branch
Proc Roy Inst Gr Brit — Proceedings. Royal Institution of Great Britain
Proc Roy Ir Acad B C — Proceedings. Royal Irish Academy. Series B and C
Proc Roy Irish Acad — Proceedings. Royal Irish Academy
Proc Roy Irish Acad Sect A — Proceedings. Royal Irish Academy. Section A. Mathematical, Astronomical, and Physical Science
Proc Roy Phys Soc Edinb — Proceedings. Royal Physical Society of Edinburgh
Proc Roy Soc B — Proceedings. Royal Society of London. Series B. Biological Sciences
Proc Roy Soc Can — Proceedings. Royal Society of Canada
Proc Roy Soc Canada — Proceedings. Royal Society of Canada
Proc Roy Soc Edinb — Proceedings. Royal Society of Edinburgh
Proc Roy Soc Edinb B — Proceedings. Royal Society of Edinburgh. Section B. Biological Sciences
Proc Roy Soc Edinburgh Sect A — Proceedings. Royal Society of Edinburgh. Section A
Proc Roy Soc London — Proceedings. Royal Society of London
Proc Roy Soc London Ser A — Proceedings. Royal Society of London. Series A
Proc Roy Soc Med — Proceedings. Royal Society of Medicine
Proc Roy Soc QD — Royal Society of Queensland. Proceedings
Proc Roy Soc Ser A — Proceedings. Royal Society. Series A
Proc Roy Soc Vict — Royal Society of Victoria. Proceedings
Proc Roy Zool Soc NSW — Royal Zoological Society of New South Wales. Proceedings
Proc R Philos Soc Glasgow — Proceedings. Royal Philosophical Society of Glasgow
Proc R Physiogr Soc Lund — Proceedings. Royal Physiograph Society at Lund
Proc R Phys Soc Edinb — Proceedings. Royal Physical Society of Edinburgh
Proc R Soc A — Proceedings. Royal Society of London. Series A
Proc R Soc B — Proceedings. Royal Society of London. Series B. Biological Sciences
Proc R Soc Can — Proceedings. Royal Society of Canada
Proc R Soc Edinb Nat Environ — Proceedings. Royal Society of Edinburgh. Section B. Natural Environment
Proc R Soc Edinb Sect A — Proceedings. Royal Society of Edinburgh. Section A. Mathematical and Physical Sciences [*Later, Proceedings. Royal Society of Edinburgh. Mathematics*]
Proc R Soc Edinb Sect A Math Phys Sci — Proceedings. Royal Society of Edinburgh. Section A. Mathematical and Physical Sciences [*Later, Proceedings. Royal Society of Edinburgh. Mathematics*]
Proc R Soc Edinb Sect B — Proceedings. Royal Society of Edinburgh. Section B. Biological Sciences
Proc R Soc Edinb Sect B Nat Environ — Proceedings. Royal Society of Edinburgh. Section B. Natural Environment
Proc R Soc Edinburgh — Proceedings. Royal Society of Edinburgh
Proc R Soc Edinburgh B — Proceedings. Royal Society of Edinburgh. Section B. Biological Sciences
Proc R Soc Edinburgh Biol Sci — Proceedings. Royal Society of Edinburgh. Section B. Biological Sciences
Proc R Soc Edinburgh Sect A — Proceedings. Royal Society of Edinburgh. Section A. Mathematical and Physical Sciences
Proc R Soc Edinburgh Sect A — Proceedings. Royal Society of Edinburgh. Section A. Mathematics
Proc R Soc Lond — Proceedings. Royal Society of London. Series B. Biological Sciences
Proc R Soc Lond B Biol Sci — Proceedings. Royal Society of London. Series B. Biological Sciences
Proc R Soc Lond Biol — Proceedings. Royal Society of London. Series B. Biological Sciences
Proc R Soc London A — Proceedings. Royal Society of London. Series A. Mathematical and Physical Sciences
Proc R Soc London Ser A — Proceedings. Royal Society of London. Series A. Mathematical and Physical Sciences
Proc R Soc Med — Proceedings. Royal Society of Medicine
Proc R Soc Med Suppl — Proceedings. Royal Society of Medicine. Supplement [*England*]
Proc R Soc NZ — Proceedings. Royal Society of New Zealand
Proc R Soc QD — Proceedings. Royal Society of Queensland
Proc R Soc Queensl — Proceedings. Royal Society of Queensland
Proc R Soc VIC — Royal Society of Victoria. Proceedings
Proc R Soc Vict — Proceedings. Royal Society of Victoria
Proc R Soc Victoria — Proceedings. Royal Society of Victoria
Proc Ruakura Farmers Conf — Proceedings. Ruakura Farmers' Conference
Proc Ruakura Farmers Conf Week — Proceedings. Ruakura Farmers' Conference Week

Proc Rudolf Virchow Med Soc City NY — Proceedings. Rudolf Virchow Medical Society in the City of New York

Proc R Zool Soc NSW — Proceedings. Royal Zoological Society of New South Wales

Proc S Afr Soc Anim Prod — Proceedings. South African Society of Animal Production

Proc S Afr Sugar Technol Assoc Annu Congr — Proceedings. South African Sugar Technologists Association. Annual Congress

Proc San Diego Biomed Symp — Proceedings. San Diego Biomedical Symposium

Proc SA Scot — Proceedings. Society of Antiquaries of Scotland

Proc S Aust Brch R Geogr Soc Australas — Royal Geographical Society of Australasia. South Australian Branch. Proceedings

Proc SC Hist Assn — Proceedings. South Carolina Historical Association

Proc Sci Assoc Nigeria — Proceedings. Science Association of Nigeria

Proc Sci Inst Kinki Univ — Proceedings. Science Institution. Kinki University

Proc Sci Sect Toilet Goods Assoc — Proceedings. Scientific Section of the Toilet Goods Association

Proc Scotts Turfgrass Res Conf — Proceedings. Scotts Turfgrass Research Conference

Proc SD Acad Sci — Proceedings. South Dakota Academy of Science

Proc S Dak Acad Sci — Proceedings. South Dakota Academy of Science

Proc Sea Grant Conf — Proceedings. Sea Grant Conference

Proc Sec Int Symp Vet Epidemiol Econ — Proceedings. Second International Symposium on Veterinary Epidemiology and Economics

Proc (Second) Malays Soil Conf (Kuala Lumpur) — Proceedings. (Second) Malaysian Soil Conference (Kuala Lumpur)

Proc Sect Sci Is Acad Sci Humanit — Proceedings. Section of Sciences. Israel Academy of Sciences and Humanities

Proc Sect Sci K Ned Akad Wet — Proceedings. Section of Sciences K. Nederlandse Akademie van Wetenschappen

Proc Seed Protein Conf — Proceedings. Seed Protein Conference

Proc Semin Biomass Energy City Farm Ind — Proceedings. Seminar on Biomass Energy for City, Farm, and Industry

Proc Ser Am Water Resour Assoc — Proceedings Series. American Water Resources Association

Proc Serono Symp — Proceedings. Serono Symposia

Proc SESA — Proceedings. Society for Experimental Stress Analysis

Proc Shikoku Br Crop Sci Soc (Jap) — Proceedings. Shikoku Branch of Crop Science Society (Japan)

Proc SID — Proceedings. SID [*Society for Information Display*]

Proc Sigatoka Workshop — Proceedings. Sigatoka Workshop

Proc Silvic Conf — Proceedings. Silviculture Conference

Proc Soc Agric Bacteriol — Proceedings. Society of Agricultural Bacteriologists

Proc Soc Am For — Proceedings. Society of American Foresters

Proc Soc Anal Chem — Proceedings. Society for Analytical Chemistry

Proc Soc Antiq Scot — Proceedings. Society of Antiquaries of Scotland

Proc Soc Antiq Scotland — Proceedings. Society of Antiquaries of Scotland

Proc Soc Appl Bact — Proceedings. Society for Applied Bacteriology

Proc Soc Appl Bacteriol — Proceedings. Society for Applied Bacteriology

Proc Soc Biol Chem India — Proceedings. Society of Biological Chemists of India

Proc Soc Chem Ind (Victoria) — Proceedings. Society of Chemical Industry (Victoria)

Proc Soc Exp Biol Med — Proceedings. Society for Experimental Biology and Medicine

Proc Soc Exp Biol (NY) — Proceedings. Society for Experimental Biology and Medicine (New York)

Proc Soc Exp Stress Anal — Proceedings. Society for Experimental Stress Analysis

Proc Soc Exp Stress Analysis — Proceedings. Society for Experimental Stress Analysis

Proc Soc Ind Microbiol — Proceedings. Society for Industrial Microbiology

Proc Soc Inf Disp — Proceedings. Society for Information Display

Proc Soc Photo Opt Instrum Eng — Proceedings. Society of Photo-Optical Instrumentation Engineers

Proc Soc Promot Agric Sci — Proceedings. Society for the Promotion of Agricultural Science

Proc Soc Protozool — Proceedings. Society of Protozoologists

Proc Soc Relay Eng — Proceedings. Society of Relay Engineers

Proc Soc Study Fertil — Proceedings. Society for the Study of Fertility

Proc Soc Water Treat Exam — Proceedings. Society for Water Treatment and Examination

Proc Soil Crop Sci Soc Fla — Proceedings. Soil and Crop Science Society of Florida

Proc Soil Sci Soc Am — Proceedings. Soil Science Society of America

Proc Soil Sci Soc Amer — Proceedings. Soil Science Society of America

Proc Somerset Arch Natur Hist Soc — Proceedings. Somerset Archaeology and Natural History Society

Proc South Afr Electron Microsc Soc Verrigtings — Proceedings. Southern African Electron Microscopy Society-Verrigtings

Proc Southeast Asian Reg Semin Trop Med Public Health — Proceedings. Southeast Asian Regional Seminar on Tropical Medicine and Public Health

Proc Southeastcon Reg 3 (Three) Conf — Proceedings. Southeastcon Region 3 (Three) Conference [*United States*]

Proc South For Tree Improv Conf — Proceedings. Southern Forest Tree Improvement Conference

Proc South Lond Entom and Nat Hist Soc — Proceedings. South London Entomological and Natural History Society

Proc South Wales Inst Eng — Proceedings. South Wales Institute of Engineers

Proc South Weed Conf — Proceedings. Southern Weed Conference

Proc South Weed Sci Soc — Proceedings. Southern Weed Science Society

Proc Southwest Agr Trade Farm Policy Conf — Proceedings. Southwestern Agricultural Trade Farm Policy Conference

Proc SPE Symp Form Damage Control — Proceedings. Society of Petroleum Engineers. American Institute of Mining, Metallurgical, and Petroleum Engineers. Symposium on Formation Damage Control

Proc SPE Symp Improv Oil Recovery — Proceedings. Society of Petroleum Engineers. American Institute of Mining, Metallurgical, and Petroleum Engineers. Symposium on Improved Oil Recovery

Proc SPI Annu Struct Foam Conf — Proceedings. SPI [*Society of the Plastics Industry*] Annual Structural Foam Conference

Proc SPI Struct Foam Conf — Proceedings. SPI [*Society of the Plastics Industry*] Structural Foam Conference

Proc Sprinkler Irrig Assoc Tech Conf — Proceedings. Sprinkler Irrigation Association. Technical Conference

Proc St — Process Studies

Proc Staff Meetings Mayo Clin — Proceedings. Staff Meetings of the Mayo Clinic

Proc Staffs Iron Steel Inst — Proceedings. Staffordshire Iron and Steel Institute

Proc State Coll Wash Inst Dairy — Proceedings. State College of Washington. Institute of Dairying

Proc State Horti Assoc PA — Proceedings. State Horticultural Association of Pennsylvania

Proc Steel Treat Res Soc — Proceedings. Steel Treating Research Society

Proc Steklov Inst Math — Proceedings. Steklov Institute of Mathematics

Proc Sth Conf For Tree Impr — Proceedings. Southern Conference on Forest Tree Improvement

Proc Sth Weed Control Conf — Proceedings. Southern Weed Control Conference

Proc Sth Weed Sci Soc — Proceedings. Southern Weed Science Society

Proc Stream Workshop — Proceedings. Streams Workshop

Proc Study Fauna Flora USSR Sect Bot — Proceedings on the Study of the Fauna and Flora of the USSR. Section of Botany

Proc 1st Vic Weed Conf — Proceedings. First Victorian Weed Conference

Proc Suffolk Inst Arch — Proceedings. Suffolk Institute of Archaeology

Proc Suffolk Inst Archaeol Hist — Proceedings. Suffolk Institute of Archaeology and History

Proc Sugar Beet Res Assoc — Proceedings. Sugar Beet Research Association

Proc Summer Comput Simul Conf — Proceedings. Summer Computer Simulation Conference

Proc Summer Conf Spectrosc Its Appl — Proceedings. Summer Conference on Spectroscopy and Its Application

Proc Summer Inst Part Phys — Proceedings. Summer Institute on Particle Physics

Proc S Wales Inst Eng — Proceedings. South Wales Institute of Engineers

Proc Symp Appl Math — Proceedings. Symposia in Applied Mathematics

Proc Symp Biol Skin — Proceedings. Symposium on the Biology of Skin

Proc Symp Chem Data Append R Aust Chem Inst — Proceedings. Symposium on Chemical Data. Royal Australian Chemical Institute

Proc Symp Chem Physiol Pathol — Proceedings. Symposium on Chemical Physiology and Pathology

Proc Symp Effects Ionizing Radiat Seed Signific Crop Impr — Proceedings. Symposium on the Effects of Ionizing Radiation on Seeds and Their Significance for Crop Improvement

Proc Symp Eng Probl Fusion Res — Proceedings. Symposium on Engineering Problems of Fusion Research

Proc Symp Explos Pyrotech — Proceedings. Symposium on Explosives and Pyrotechnics

Proc Symp Fertil Indian Soils — Proceedings. Symposium on Fertility of Indian Soils

Proc Symp Isotop Plant Nutr Physiol (Vienna Austria) — Proceedings. Symposium on Isotopes in Plant Nutrition and Physiology (Vienna, Austria)

Proc Sympos Appl Math — Proceedings. Symposia in Applied Mathematics

Proc Sympos Pure Math — Proceedings. Symposia in Pure Mathematics

Proc Symp Particleboard — Proceedings. Symposium on Particleboard

Proc Symp Photogr Sensitivity — Proceedings. Symposium on Photographic Sensitivity

Proc Symp Rock Mech — Proceedings. Symposium on Rock Mechanics

Proc Symp Turbul Liq — Proceedings. Symposium on Turbulence in Liquids

Proc Symp Use Isotop Weed Res — Proceedings. Symposium on the Use of Isotopes in Weed Research [*Vienna, Austria*]

Proc Symp Use Radioisotop Soil Plant Nutr Stud — Proceedings. Symposium on the Use of Radioisotopes in Soil-Plant Nutrition Studies

Proc Symp Waste Manage — Proceedings. Symposium on Waste Management

Proc Synth Pipeline Gas Symp — Proceedings. Synthetic Pipeline Gas Symposium

Proc Tall Timbers Conf Ecol Anim Control Habitat Manage — Proceedings. Tall Timbers Conference on Ecological Animal Control by Habitat Management

Proc Tall Timbers Fire Ecol Conf — Proceedings. Tall Timbers Fire Ecology Conference

Proc Tech Conf Soc Vac Coaters — Proceedings. Technical Conference. Society of Vacuum Coaters

Proc Tech Groups NZ Inst Eng — Proceedings of Technical Groups. New Zealand Institution of Engineers

Proc Tech Mtg Int Union Conserv Nature — Proceedings. Technical Meeting. International Union for Conservation of Nature and Natural Resources

Proc Tech Program Electro-Opt Laser Conf Exp — Proceedings. Technical Program. Electro-Optics/Laser Conference and Exposition

Proc Tech Program Natl Electron Packag Prod Conf — Proceedings. Technical Program. National Electronic Packaging and Production Conference

Proc Tex Nutr Conf — Proceedings. Texas Nutrition Conference

Proc Tex Water Sewage Works Short Sch — Proceedings. Texas Water and Sewage Works Short School

Proc Tex Water Util Short Sch — Proceedings. Texas Water Utilities Short School

Proc Therm Power Conf — Proceedings. Thermal Power Conference

Proc Trans Br Entomol Nat Hist Soc — Proceedings and Transactions. British Entomological and Natural History Society

Proc Trans Croydon Natur Hist Sci Soc — Proceedings and Transactions. Croydon Natural History and Scientific Society

Proc Trans Rhod Sci Assoc — Proceedings and Transactions. Rhodesia Scientific Association

Proc and Trans Rhod Sci Assoc — Proceedings and Transactions. Rhodesia Scientific Association

Proc Trans R Soc Can — Proceedings and Transactions. Royal Society of Canada

Proc Tree Wardens Arborists Util Conf — Proceedings. Tree Wardens, Arborists, and Utilities Conference

Proc and Tr Liverpool Biol Soc — Proceedings and Transactions. Liverpool Biological Society

Proc Tr PN Lebedev Phys Inst — Proceedings (Trudy). P. N. Lebedev Physics Institute

Proc (Trudy) P N Lebedev Phys Inst — Proceedings (Trudy). P. N. Lebedev Physics Institute

ProCTS — Proceedings. College Theology Society

Proc Turbomachinery Symp — Proceedings. Turbomachinery Symposium

Proc Turfgrass Sprinkler Irrig Conf — Proceedings. Turfgrass Sprinkler Irrigation Conference

Proc UNESCO Conf Radioisot Sci Res — Proceedings. UNESCO Conference on Radioisotopes in Scientific Research

Proc Univ Bristol Spelaeol Soc — Proceedings. University of Bristol Spelaeological Society

Proc Univ Durham Phil Soc — Proceedings. University of Durham. Philosophical Society

Proc Univ MD Nutr Conf Feed Mfr — Proceedings. University of Maryland. Nutrition Conference for Feed Manufacturers

Proc Univ MO Annu Conf Trace Subst Environ Health — Proceedings. University of Missouri. Annual Conference on Trace Substances in Environmental Health

Proc Univ Newcastle Upon Tyne Philos Soc — Proceedings. University of Newcastle-Upon-Tyne Philosophical Society

Proc Univ Otago Med Sch — Proceedings. University of Otago Medical School

Proc USAID Ghana Agr Conf — Proceedings. USAID [*United States Agency for International Development*]. Ghana Agriculture Conference

Proc US Natl Mus — Proceedings. United States National Museum

Proc Ussher Soc — Proceedings. Ussher Society

Proc Utah Acad Sci — Proceedings. Utah Academy of Sciences, Arts, and Letters

Proc Utah Acad Sci Arts Lett — Proceedings. Utah Academy of Sciences, Arts, and Letters

Proc Vertebr Pest Conf — Proceedings. Vertebrate Pest Conference

Proc Veterans Adm Spinal Cord Inj Conf — Proceedings. Veterans Administration Spinal Cord Injury Conference

Proc Vib Probl — Proceedings of Vibration Problems

Proc VIC Weeds Conf — Proceedings. Victorian Weeds Science Society

Proc Virchow-Pirquet Med Soc — Proceedings. Virchow-Pirquet Medical Society

Proc Vol Bakish Mater Corp Publ — Proceedings Volume. Bakish Materials Corporation. Publication

Proc Wash Anim Nutr Conf — Proceedings. Washington Animal Nutrition Conference

Proc Wash State Entomol Soc — Proceedings. Washington State Entomological Society

Proc Wash State Univ Int Particleboard/Compos Mater Ser — Proceedings. Washington State University International Particleboard/Composite Materials Series

Proc Wash State Univ Int Symp Particleboard — Proceedings. Washington State University International Symposium on Particleboard

Proc Wash State Univ Symp Particleboard — Proceedings. Washington State University Symposium on Particleboard

Proc Wash St Ent Soc — Proceedings. Washington State Entomological Society

Proc Wash St Hort Ass — Proceedings. Washington State Horticultural Association

Proc Weed Soc NSW — Proceedings. Weed Society of New South Wales

Proc West Can Weed Control Conf — Proceedings. Western Canadian Weed Control Conference

Proc West Chapter Int Shade Tree Conf — Proceedings. Western Chapter. International Shade Tree Conference

Proc West Eur Conf Photosyn — Proceedings. Western Europe Conference on Photosynthesis

Proc West For Conserv Ass — Proceedings. Western Forestry Conference. Western Forestry and Conservation Association

Proc West Found Vertebr Zool — Proceedings. Western Foundation of Vertebrate Zoology

Proc West Pharmacol Soc — Proceedings. Western Pharmacology Society

Proc West Poult Dis Conf — Proceedings. Western Poultry Disease Conference

Proc West Poult Dis Conf Poult Health Symp — Proceedings. Western Poultry Disease Conference and Poultry Health Symposia [*United States*]

Proc West Snow Conf — Proceedings. Western Snow Conference

Proc West Soc Weed Sci — Proceedings. Western Society of Weed Science

Proc West Virginia Acad Sci — Proceedings. West Virginia Academy of Science

Proc Wis Hist Soc — Proceedings. Wisconsin State Historical Society

Proc Wld For Congr — Proceedings. World Forestry Congress

Proc Wld Orchid Conf — Proceedings. World Orchid Conference

Proc Wood Pole Inst Colo State Univ — Proceedings. Wood Pole Institute. Colorado State University

Proc World Congr Agr Res — Proceedings. World Congress of Agricultural Research

Proc World Congr Fertil Steril — Proceedings. World Congress on Fertility and Sterility

Proc World Congr Gastroenterol — Proceedings. World Congress of Gastroenterology

Proc World For Congr — Proceedings. World Forestry Congress

Proc World Pet Congr — Proceedings. World Petroleum Congress

Proc World Poultry Congr — Proceedings. World Poultry Congress

Proc W Va Acad Sci — Proceedings. West Virginia Academy of Science

Proc Yorks Geol Soc — Proceedings. Yorkshire Geological Society [*England*]

Proc Yorkshire Geol Soc — Proceedings. Yorkshire Geological Society

Proc Zool Soc (Calcutta) — Proceedings. Zoological Society (Calcutta)

Proc Zool Soc Lond — Proceedings. Zoological Society of London

PROD — Prisoner Rehabilitation on Discharge

Prod Agric Fr — Producteur Agricole Francais

Prod Anim — Produzione Animale

Prod Eng — Product Engineering

Prod Eng (Cleveland) — Production Engineering (Cleveland)

Prod Eng (Lond) — Production Engineer (London)

Prod Engng — Production Engineering

Prod Engr — Production Engineer [*London*]

Pr Odes Gidrometeorol Inst — Pratsi Odes'kogo Gidrometeorologichnogo Institutu

Prod Finish — Product Finishing [*Cincinnati*]

Prod Finish (Cinci) — Product Finishing (Cincinnati)

Prod Finish (Cincinnati) — Products Finishing (Cincinnati)

Prod Finish (Lond) — Product Finishing (London)

Prod G Am J — Producers Guild of America. Journal

Prod Invent Manage — Production and Inventory Management

Prod and Inventory Manage — Production and Inventory Management

Prod Lait Mod — Production Laitiere Moderne

Prod Liability Int — Product Liability International

Prod Liab Int — Product Liability International

Prod Manage — Production Management

Prod Market — Product Marketing

Prod Marketing — Produce Marketing

Prod Miner Serv Fom Prod Miner Avulso — Producao Mineral Servico de Fomento da Producao Mineral. Avulso

Prod Miner Serv Fom Prod Miner Bol — Producao Mineral Servico de Fomento da Producao Mineral. Boletim

Prod Mkt — Product Marketing

Prod Mktg — Product Marketing

Prod Mon — Producers Monthly [*United States*]

Prodn J — Production Journal

Prod Pharm — Produits Pharmaceutiques [*France*]

Prod Probl Pharm — Produits et Problemes Pharmaceutiques

Prod Proj Trends Bldg — Products, Projects, and Trends in Building

Prod Publ Assoc Off Seed Certifying Agencies — Production Publication. Association of Official Seed Certifying Agencies

Prod Publ Int Crop Impr Ass — Production Publication. International Crop Improvement Association

Prod Res Rep US Dep Agric — Production Research Report. United States Department of Agriculture

Prod Res Rep US Dep Agric Sci Educ Adm — Production Research Report. United States Department of Agriculture. Science and Education Administration

Prod Rev — Producers' Review

Prod with Safety — Production with Safety
Prod Tech (Osaka) — Production and Technique (Osaka) [*Japan*]
Prod Tech (Suita) — Production and Technique (Suita) [*Japan*]
Produccion Anim — Produccion Animal
Producers R — Producers' Review
Producers' Rev — Producers' Review
Product Eng — Product Engineering
Product et Gestion — Production et Gestion
Production — Production Engineering
Produits Pharm — Produits et Problemes Pharmaceutiques
Prod Veg Cereale Plante Teh — Productia Vegetala. Cereale si Plante Tehnice
Prod Veg Mec Agric — Productia Vegetala. Mecanizarea Agriculturii
Prod Yb FAO — Production Yearbook FAO [*Food and Agriculture Organization*]
Proefstn Akkerbouw Lelystad Versl Interprov Proeven — Proefstation voor de Akkerbouw Lelystad. Verslagen van Interprovinciale Proeven
Proefstn Akkerbouw (Wageningen) Versl Interprov Proeven — Proefstation voor de Akkerbouw (Wageningen). Verslagen van Interprovinciale Proeven
Proektn Nauchno-Issled Inst Ural Promstroiniiproekt Tr — Proektnyi i Nauchno-Issledovatel'skii Institut "Ural'skii Promstroiniiproekt." Trudy
Pro Engr — Professional Engineer
Prof Admin — Professional Administration
Prof Build — Professional Builder
Prof Build Apartm Bus — Professional Builder and Apartment Business
Prof Builder & Apt Bus — Professional Builder and Apartment Business
Prof Builder/Apt Bus — Professional Builder and Apartment Business
Prof Camera — Professional Camera
Prof Eng (Pretoria) — Professional Engineer (Pretoria)
Prof Eng (Wash DC) — Professional Engineer (Washington, DC)
Professional Eng — Professional Engineer
Profession Med — Profession Medicale
Professions et Entr — Professions et Entreprises
Prof Geog — Professional Geographer
Prof Geogr — Professional Geographer
Prof Geologist — Professional Geologist
Profile — Profiles
Profils Econ Nord-Pas-De-Calais — Profils de l'Economie Nord-Pas-De-Calais
Prof Inferm — Professioni Infermieristiche
Prof Med Assist — Professional Medical Assistant
Prof Nutr — Professional Nutritionist
Prof Pap Geol Surv — Professional Papers. United States Geological Survey
Prof Pap Ser Fla Dep Nat Resour Mar Res Lab — Professional Papers Series. Florida Department of Natural Resources. Marine Research Laboratory
Prof Pap US Geol Surv — Professional Papers. United States Geological Survey
Prof Photogr — Professional Photographer
Prof Print — Professional Printer
Prof Psycho — Professional Psychology
Prof Regulation N — Professional Regulation News
Prof Rpt — Professional Report
Prof Saf — Professional Safety
Prof Safety — Professional Safety
Prof Sanit Manage — Professional Sanitation Management
Prog — Progressive
Prog Aeronaut Sci — Progress in Aeronautical Science
Prog Aerosp Sci — Progress in Aerospace Sciences
Prog Agric — Progresso Agricolo
Prog Agric Ariz — Progressive Agriculture in Arizona
Prog Agric Vitic — Progres Agricole et Viticole [*France*]
Prog Agri Fr — Progres Agricole de France
Prog Allerg — Progress in Allergy
Prog Allergol Jpn — Progress of Allergology in Japan
Prog Allergy — Progress in Allergy
Prog Anal At Spectrosc — Progress in Analytical Atomic Spectroscopy
Prog Anal Chem — Progress in Analytical Chemistry
Prog Androl — Progres en Andrologie
Prog Anim Biometeorol — Progress in Animal Biometeorology
Prog Appl Mater Res — Progress in Applied Materials Research
Prog Arch — Progressive Architecture
Prog Archit — Progressive Architecture
Prog Astronaut Aeronaut — Progress in Astronautics and Aeronautics
Prog Astronaut Rocketry — Progress in Astronautics and Rocketry
Prog Astronaut Sci — Progress in the Astronautical Sciences
Prog At Med — Progress in Atomic Medicine
Prog Batteries Sol Cell — Progress in Batteries and Solar Cells
Prog Biochem Biophys — Progress in Biochemistry and Biophysics [*People's Republic of China*]
Prog Biochem Pharmacol — Progress in Biochemical Pharmacology
Prog Biochim — Progressi in Biochimica
Prog Biol Sci Relat Dermatol — Progress in the Biological Sciences in Relation to Dermatology
Prog Biomass Convers — Progress in Biomass Conversion
Prog Biometeorol — Progress in Biometeorology
Prog Biometeorol Div A — Progress in Biometeorology. Division A. Progress in Human Biometeorology [*Netherlands*]

Prog Biometeorol Div B — Progress in Biometeorology. Division B. Progress in Animal Biometeorology
Prog Bioorg Chem — Progress in Bioorganic Chemistry
Prog Biophys Biophys Chem — Progress in Biophysics and Biophysical Chemistry
Prog Biophys and Mol Biol — Progress in Biophysics and Molecular Biology
Prog Biophys Mol Biol — Progress in Biophysics and Molecular Biology
Prog Boron Chem — Progress in Boron Chemistry
Prog Bot — Progress in Botany
Prog Bot Fortschr Bot — Progress in Botany-Fortschritt der Botanik
Prog Brain Res — Progress in Brain Research
Prog Cancer Res Ther — Progress in Cancer Research and Therapy
Prog Cardiol — Progress in Cardiology
Prog Cardiovasc Dis — Progress in Cardiovascular Diseases
Prog Ceram Sci — Progress in Ceramic Science
Prog Chem Fats — Progress in the Chemistry of Fats and Other Lipids
Prog Chem Fats Other Lipids — Progress in the Chemistry of Fats and Other Lipids
Prog Chem Fibrinolysis Thrombolysis — Progress in Chemical Fibrinolysis and Thrombolysis
Prog Chem Toxicol — Progress in Chemical Toxicology
Prog Clin Biol Res — Progress in Clinical and Biological Research
Prog Clin Cancer — Progress in Clinical Cancer
Prog Clin Immunol — Progress in Clinical Immunology
Prog Clin Neurophysiol — Progress in Clinical Neurophysiology
Prog Clin Pathol — Progress in Clinical Pathology
Prog Colloid Polym Sci — Progress in Colloid and Polymer Science
Prog Coll & Polym Sci — Progress in Colloid and Polymer Science
Prog Combus Sci Technol — Progress in Combustion Science and Technology
Prog Concept Control — Progress in Conception Control
Prog Contracept Delivery Syst — Progress in Contraceptive Delivery Systems
Prog Cosmic Ray Phys — Progress in Cosmic Ray Physics
Prog Cryog — Progress in Cryogenics
Prog Cryst Growth Charact — Progress in Crystal Growth and Characterization
Prog Cryst Phys — Progress in Crystal Physics
Prog Dielectr — Progress in Dielectrics
Prog Drug Metab — Progress in Drug Metabolism
Prog Drug Res — Progress in Drug Research
Prog Educ — Progress in Education
Prog Educ — Progressive Education
Prog Educ (Poona) — Progress of Education (Poona) [*India*]
Prog Elem Part Cosmic Ray Phys — Progress in Elementary Particle and Cosmic Ray Physics
Prog Energy Combust Sci — Progress in Energy and Combustion Science
Prog Explor Tuberc — Progres de l'Exploration de la Tuberculose
Prog Exp Pers Res — Progress in Experimental Personality Research
Prog Exp Tumor Res — Progress in Experimental Tumor Research
Prog Extr Metall — Progress in Extractive Metallurgy
Prog Ex Tum — Progress in Experimental Tumor Research
Prog F — Progressive Farmer and Farm Woman
Prog Farmer West — Progressive Farmer for the West
Prog Farming — Progressive Farming
Prog Farming/Farmer — Progressive Farming/Farmer
Prog Fire Retard Ser — Progress in Fire Retardancy Series
Prog Fish-C — Progressive Fish-Culturist
Prog Fish-Cult — Progressive Fish-Culturist
Prog Food Nutr Sci — Progress in Food and Nutrition Science
Prog Fotogr (Barcelona) — Progresso Fotografico (Barcelona)
Prog Fotogr (Milan) — Progresso Fotografico (Milan)
Prog Gastroenterol — Progress in Gastroenterology
Prog Geogr — Progress in Geography
Prog Groc — Progressive Grocer
Prog Grocer — Progressive Grocer
Prog Gynecol — Progress in Gynecology
Prog Heat Mass Transf — Progress in Heat and Mass Transfer
Prog Heat Mass Transfer — Progress in Heat and Mass Transfer
Prog Hematol — Progress in Hematology
Prog Hemostasis Thromb — Progress in Hemostasis and Thrombosis
Prog Hemost Thromb — Progress in Hemostasis and Thrombosis
Prog High Polym — Progress in High Polymers
Prog High Temp Phys Chem — Progress in High Temperature Physics and Chemistry
Prog Histochem Cytochem — Progress in Histochemistry and Cytochemistry
Prog Hort — Progressive Horticulture [*India*]
Prog Hortic — Progressive Horticulture
Prog Hum Biometeorol — Progress in Human Biometeorology
Prog Hum Nutr — Progress in Human Nutrition
Prog Immunobiol Stand — Progress in Immunobiological Standardization
Prog Ind Microbiol — Progress in Industrial Microbiology
Prog Infrared Spectrosc — Progress in Infrared Spectroscopy
Prog Inorg Chem — Progress in Inorganic Chemistry
Prog Instr Bul — Programmed Instruction Bulletin
Prog Instr & Ed Tech — Programmed Instruction and Educational Technology
Prog Learn — Programmed Learning and Educational Technology
Prog Learn Disabil — Progress in Learning Disabilities

Prog Lipid Res — Progress in Lipid Research
Prog Liver Dis — Progress in Liver Diseases
Prog Low Temp Phys — Progress in Low Temperature Physics
Prog Mater Sci — Progress in Materials Science
Prog Mat Sc — Progress in Materials Science
Prog Med — Progres Medical
Prog Med Chem — Progress in Medicinal Chemistry
Prog Med Ge — Progress in Medical Genetics
Prog Med Genet — Progress in Medical Genetics
Prog Med (Istanbul) — Progressus Medicinae (Istanbul)
Prog Med Parasitol Jpn — Progress in Medical Parasitology in Japan
Prog Med Psychosom — Progres en Medecine Psychosomatique
Prog Med (Rome) — Progresso Medico (Rome)
Prog Med (Tokyo) — Progress in Medicine (Tokyo)
Prog Med Vi — Progress in Medical Virology
Prog Med Virol — Progress in Medical Virology
Prog Mol Subcell Biol — Progress in Molecular and Subcellular Biology
Prog Neurobiol — Progress in Neurobiology
Prog Neurol Psychiatry — Progress in Neurology and Psychiatry
Prog Neurol Surg — Progress in Neurological Surgery
Prog Neuropathol — Progress in Neuropathology
Prog Neuro-Psychopharmacol — Progress in Neuro-Psychopharmacology
Prog Notes Walter Reed Army Med Cent — Progress Notes. Walter Reed Army Medical Center
Prog Nucleic Acid Res — Progress in Nucleic Acid Research
Prog Nucleic Acid Res Mol Biol — Progress in Nucleic Acid Research and Molecular Biology
Prog Nucl Energy — Progress in Nuclear Energy [*England*]
Prog Nucl Energy Anal Chem — Progress in Nuclear Energy. Analytical Chemistry
Prog Nucl Energy Ser 1 — Progress in Nuclear Energy. Series 1. Physics and Mathematics
Prog Nucl Energy Ser 2 — Progress in Nuclear Energy. Series 2. Reactors
Prog Nucl Energy Ser 3 — Progress in Nuclear Energy. Series 3. Process Chemistry
Prog Nucl Energy Ser 4 — Progress in Nuclear Energy. Series 4. Technology, Engineering, and Safety
Prog Nucl Energy Ser 5 — Progress in Nuclear Energy. Series 5. Metallurgy and Fuels
Prog Nucl Energy Ser 6 — Progress in Nuclear Energy. Series 6 [*England*]
Prog Nucl Energy Ser 8 — Progress in Nuclear Energy. Series 8. The Economics of Nuclear Power Including Administration and Law
Prog Nucl Energy Ser 9 — Progress in Nuclear Energy. Series 9 [*England*]
Prog Nucl Energy Ser 10 — Progress in Nuclear Energy. Series 10. Law and Administration
Prog Nucl Energy Ser 11 — Progress in Nuclear Energy. Series 11. Plasma Physics and Thermonuclear Research
Prog Nucl Energy Ser 12 — Progress in Nuclear Energy. Series 12. Health Physics
Prog Nucl Energy Ser VII Med Sci — Progress in Nuclear Energy. Series VII. Medical Sciences
Prog Nucl Magn Reson Spectrosc — Progress in Nuclear Magnetic Resonance Spectroscopy
Prog Nucl Med — Progress in Nuclear Medicine
Prog Nucl Phys — Progress in Nuclear Physics
Prog Nucl Tech Instrum — Progress in Nuclear Techniques and Instrumentation [*Netherlands*]
Prog Obstet Gynecol — Progres en Obstetrique et Gynecologie
Prog Oceanogr — Progress in Oceanography
Prog Ophtalmol — Progres en Ophtalmologie
Prog Opt — Progress in Optics
Prog Org Chem — Progress in Organic Chemistry
Prog Org Coat — Progress in Organic Coatings
Prog Org Coatings — Progress in Organic Coatings
Prog Oto-Rhino-Laryngol — Progres en Oto-Rhino-Laryngologie
Prog Part Nucl Phys — Progress in Particle and Nuclear Physics [*England*]
Prog Pediatr Hematol/Oncol — Progress in Pediatric Hematology/Oncology
Prog Pediatr Pueric — Progresos de Pediatria y Puericultura
Prog Pediatr Radiol — Progress in Pediatric Radiology [*Switzerland*]
Prog Pediatr Surg — Progress in Pediatric Surgery
Prog Perfum Cosmet — Progressive Perfumery and Cosmetics
Prog Photogr — Progress in Photography
Prog Phys — Progress of Physics [*East Germany*]
Prog Physiol Psychol — Progress in Physiological Psychology
Prog Physiol Sci (Engl Transl Usp Fiziol Nauk) — Progress in Physiological Sciences (English Translation of Uspekhi Fiziologicheskikh Nauk)
Prog Phytochem — Progress in Phytochemistry
Prog Plast — Progressive Plastics
Prog Polym Sci — Progress in Polymer Science
Prog Powder Metall — Progress in Powder Metallurgy
Prog Protozool Proc Int Congr Protozool — Progress in Protozoology. Proceedings. International Congress on Protozoology
Prog Psychiatr Drug Treat — Progress in Psychiatric Drug Treatment
Prog Psychobiol Physiol Psychol — Progress in Psychobiology and Physiological Psychology
Prog Quantum Electron — Progress in Quantum Electronics

Prog Radiat Ther — Progress in Radiation Therapy
Prog Radiopharmacol — Progress in Radiopharmacology
Progr Agr — Progresso Agricolo
Progr Agr Ariz — Progressive Agriculture in Arizona
Progr Agr Vitic — Progres Agricole et Viticole
Program Aid US Dep Agric — Program Aid. United States Department of Agriculture
Program Am Dairy Sci Assoc Annu Meet Branch Abstr — Program. American Dairy Science Association. Annual Meeting and Branch Abstracts
Program Autom Libr Inf Syst — Program. Automated Library and Information Systems [*England*]
Program and Comput Software — Programming and Computer Software
Program Learn and Educ Technol — Programmed Learning and Educational Technology
Programmed Learning — Programmed Learning and Educational Technology
Programming and Comput Software — Programming and Computer Software
Program News Comput Libr — Program. News of Computers in Libraries
Program Notes Assoc Univ Programs Health Adm — Program Notes. Association of University Programs in Health Administration
Progr Bull Alberta Univ Ext Dept — Progress Bulletin. Alberta University Extension Department
Progr Card — Progress in Cardiovascular Diseases
Progr Contr Eng — Progress in Control Engineering
Progr Coop Centroamer Mejor Maiz — Programa Cooperativo Centroamericano para el Mejoramiento del Maiz
Prog React Kinet — Progress in Reaction Kinetics
Prog Rech Cancer — Progres dans les Recherches sur le Cancer
Prog Rech Exp Tumeurs — Progres de la Recherche Experimentale des Tumeurs
Prog Rech Pharm — Progres des Recherches Pharmaceutiques
Prog Rep Ariz Exp Stn — Progress Report. Arizona Experiment Station
Prog Rep Clovers Spec Purpose Legumes Res — Progress Report. Clovers and Special Legumes Research
Prog Rep Colo Exp Stn — Progress Report. Colorado Experiment Station
Prog Rep Exp Stns (Tanzania) — Progress Reports. Experiment Stations (Tanzania)
Prog Rep Minist Agric Fish Fd Exp Husb Fms Exp Hort Stns — Progress Report. Ministry of Agriculture, Fisheries, and Food. Experimental Husbandry Farms and Experimental Horticulture Stations
Prog Rep NM Bur Mines Miner Resour — Progress Report. New Mexico Bureau of Mines and Mineral Resources
Prog Rep Nucl Energy Res Jpn — Progress Report. Nuclear Energy Research in Japan
Prog Reprod Biol — Progress in Reproductive Biology
Prog Rep Texas Agric Exp Stn — Progress Report. Texas Agricultural Experiment Station
Prog Res — Progress thru Research
Progres Arch — Progressive Architecture
Progres Ed — Progressive Education
Prog Res Emphysema Chronic Bronchitis — Progress in Research in Emphysema and Chronic Bronchitis
Progres Med (Paris) — Progres Medical (Paris)
Progreso Med (Habana) — Progreso Medico (Habana)
Prog Respir Res — Progress in Respiration Research
Progres Scientif — Progres Scientifique
Progressive Archit — Progressive Architecture
Progress in Math — Progress in Mathematics
Progress Organic Coatings — Progress in Organic Coatings
Progress Phytochem — Progress in Phytochemistry
Progressv — Progressive
Progres Techn — Progres Technique
Progres Vet — Progres Veterinaire
Progr Hum Geogr — Progress in Human Geography. International Review of Current Research
Progr Mater Sci — Progress in Materials Science
Progr Math (Allahabad) — Progress of Mathematics (Allahabad)
Progr Nucl Energy Ser III Process Chem — Progress in Nuclear Energy. Series III. Process Chemistry
Progr Nucl Energy Ser II Reactors — Progress in Nuclear Energy. Series II. Reactors
Progr Nucl Energy Ser I Phys Math — Progress in Nuclear Energy. Series I. Physics and Mathematics
Progr Nucl Energy Ser IV Technol Eng — Progress in Nuclear Energy. Series IV. Technology and Engineering
Progr Nucl Energy Ser VI — Progress in Nuclear Energy. Series VI. Biological Sciences
Progr Nucl Energy Ser VIII Econ — Progress in Nuclear Energy. Series VIII. Economics
Progr Nucl Energy Ser V Met Fuels — Progress in Nuclear Energy. Series V. Metallurgy and Fuels
Progr Nucl Energy Ser XI Plasma Phys Thermonucl Res — Progress in Nuclear Energy. Series XI. Plasma Physics and Thermonuclear Research
Progr Nucl Energy Ser X Law Admin — Progress in Nuclear Energy. Series X. Law and Administration
Progr Offic Journee Interreg Recolte Mec Mais-Grain — Programme Officiel. Journee Interregionale de Recolte Mechanique du Mais-Grain

Progr Plast — Progressive Plastics
Progr Polymer Sci — Progress in Polymer Science
Progr Powder Met — Progress in Powder Metallurgy
Progr Prob Statist — Progress in Probability and Statistics
Progr Rep Cereal Breed Lab — Progress Report. Cereal Breeding Laboratory
Progr Rep Colo State Univ Agr Exp Sta — Progress Report. Colorado State University. Agricultural Experiment Station
Progr Rep Conn Agr Exp Sta — Progress Report. Connecticut Agricultural Experiment Station
Progr Rep Idaho Agr Res — Progress Report. Idaho Agricultural Research
Progr Rep KY Agr Exp Sta — Progress Report. Kentucky Agricultural Experiment Station
Progr Rep PA Agric Exp Sta — Progress Report. Pennsylvania State University. Agricultural Experiment Station
Progr Rep PA State Univ Agr Exp Sta — Progress Report. Pennsylvania State University. Agricultural Experiment Station
Progr Rep Ser Ala Agr Exp Sta — Progress Report Series. Alabama Agricultural Experiment Station
Progr Rep Tex Agr Exp Sta — Progress Report. Texas Agricultural Experiment Station
Progr Rep Tohoku Agr Exp Sta — Progress Report. Tohoku Agricultural Experiment Station
Progr Rep Univ Nebr Coll Agr Dept Agr Econ — Progress Report. University of Nebraska. College of Agriculture. Department of Agricultural Economics
Progr Rev For Prod Lab (Ottawa) — Program Review. Forest Products Laboratory (Ottawa)
Progr Rev For Prod Lab (Vancouver) — Program Review. Forest Products Laboratory (Vancouver) [*British Columbia, Canada*]
Progr Rubber Technol — Progress of Rubber Technology
Progr Sci Comput — Progress in Scientific Computing
Progr Stiintei — Progresele Stiintei
Progr Theoret Phys — Progress of Theoretical Physics
Progr Theoret Phys Suppl — Progress of Theoretical Physics. Supplement
Prog Sci — Progres Scientifique [*France*]
Prog Sci Technol Rare Earths — Progress in the Science and Technology of the Rare Earths
Prog Semicond — Progress in Semiconductors
Prog Sep Purif — Progress in Separation and Purification
Prog Solid State Chem — Progress in Solid State Chemistry [*England*]
Prog Stereochem — Progress in Stereochemistry
Prog Surf Membr Sci — Progress in Surface and Membrane Science
Prog Surf Sci — Progress in Surface Science
Prog Surg — Progress in Surgery
Prog Tech — Progres Technique
Prog Technol — Progress in Technology [*United States*]
Prog Tekhnol Mashinostr — Progressivnaya Tekhnologiya Mashinostroeniya
Prog Ter — Progresso Terapeutico
Prog Theor Biol — Progress in Theoretical Biology
Prog Theor Org Chem — Progress in Theoretical Organic Chemistry
Prog Theor Phys — Progress of Theoretical Physics
Prog Theor Phys Suppl — Progress of Theoretical Physics. Supplement
Prog Thin-Layer Chromatogr Relat Methods — Progress in Thin-Layer Chromatography and Related Methods
Prog T Phys — Progress of Theoretical Physics
Prog Vac Microbalance Tech — Progress in Vacuum Microbalance Techniques
Progve Agric Ariz — Progressive Agriculture in Arizona
Progve Fmg — Progressive Farming
Prog Vet — Progresso Veterinario
Prog Virol Med — Progres en Virologie Medicale
Prog Water Technol — Progress in Water Technology
PROH — Promoting Health
Proizvod Elektrostali — Proizvodstvo Elektrostali
Proizvod Issled Stalei Splavov — Proizvodstvo i Issledovanie Stalei i Splavov
Proizvod Koksa — Proizvodstvo Koksa
Proizvod Krupnykh Mash — Proizvodstvo Krupnykh Mashin
Proizvod Nauchno-Issled Inst Inzh Izyskaniyam Stroit Tr — Proizvodstvennyi i Nauchno-Issledovatel'skii Institut po Inzhenernym Izyskaniyam v Stroitel'stve Trudy
Proizvod Smaz Mater — Proizvodstvo Smazochnykh Materialov
Proizvod Stochnye Vody — Proizvodstvennye Stochnye Vody
Proizvod Svarnykh Besshovnykh Trub — Proizvodstvo Svarnykh i Besshovnykh Trub
Proizvod Trub — Proizvodstvo Trub
Proizvod Vysokokach Prokata — Proizvodstvo Vysokokachestvennogo Prokata
Proizv Shin RTI i ATI — Proizvodstvo Shin Rezinotekhnicheskikh i Asbestotekhnicheskikh Izdelii
Proj Civ Trav Econ — Projet. Civilisation, Travail, Economie [*France*]
Project Hist Biobibliog — Project for Historical Biobibliography
Project IUCN/Wld Wildl Fund — Project. International Union for Conservation of Nature. World Wildlife Fund. Joint Project Operations
Projektrapp Grafiska Forskningslab — Projektrapport. Grafiska Forskningslaboratoriet
Proj Rep Victoria Minist Conserv Environ Stud Program — Victoria. Ministry for Conservation. Environmental Studies Program. Project Report
PROLDI — Annual Research Reviews. Prolactin

Pro LR — Professional Liability Reporter
P Rom — Papers in Romance
Prom Aerod — Promyshlennaya Aerodinamika [*USSR*]
Pro Med — Pro Medico
Prom Ekon Byull Sov Nar Khoz Ivanov Ekon Adm Raiona — Promyshlenno-Ekonomicheskii Byulleten Sovet Narodnogo Khozyaistva Ivanovskogo Ekonomicheskogo Administrativnogo Raiona
Prom Energ — Promyshlennaya Energetika
Pro Met — Pro Metal
Promet-Meteorol Fortbild — Promet-Meteorologische Fortbildung [*West Germany*]
Promoclim A Actual Equip Tech — Promoclim A. Actualites, Equipement, Technique [*France*]
Promoclim E — Promoclim E. Etudes Thermiques et Aerauliques
Promoclim Ind Therm Aerauliques — Promoclim. Industries Thermiques et Aerauliques
Promot Dent — Promotion Dentaire
Promot Health — Promoting Health
Promozione Soc — Promozione Sociale
Prom Sint Kauch — Promyshlennost Sinteticheskogo Kauchuka
Promst Arm — Promyshlennost Armenii
Prom-st Arm Sov Nar Khoz Arm SSR Tekh-Ekon Byull — Promyshlennost Armenii Sovet Narodnogo Khozyajstva Armyanskoj SSR Tekhniko-Ekonomicheskij Byulleten
Promst Beloruss — Promyshlennost Belorussii
Prom-st Khim Reaktivov Osobo Chist Veshchestv — Promyshlennost Khimicheskikh Reaktivov i Osobo Chistykh Veshchestv [*USSR*]
Promst Khim Reakt Osobo Chist Veshchestv — Promyshlennost Khimicheskikh Reaktivov i Osobo Chistykh Veshchestv
Promst Lub Volokon — Promyshlennost Lubyanykh Volokon
Prom-st Org Khim — Promyshlennost Organicheskoi Khimii [*USSR*]
Prom Stroit — Promyshlennoe Stroitel'stvo
Prom Stroit Inzh Sooruzh — Promyshlennoe Stroitel'stvo i Inzhenernye Sooruzheniya
Promst Stroit Mater — Promyshlennost Stroitel'nykh Materialov
Prom Teplotekh — Promyshlennaya Teplotekhnika [*Ukrainian SSR*]
Pro Mundi Vita — Pro Mundi Vita Bulletin
Pro Mundi Vita Africa Dossier — Pro Mundi Vita Dossiers. Africa
Pro Mundi Vita Asia-Australasia Dossier — Pro Mundi Vita Dossiers. Asia and Australasia
Pro Mundi Vita Europe N Am Dossier — Pro Mundi Vita Dossiers. Europe/North America
Prom Zagryaz Vodoemov — Promyshlennye Zagryazneniya Vodoemov
Pro Nat — Pro Natura
Pr ONPMP — Prace ONPMP [*Osrodek Naukowo-Produkcyjny Materialow Polprzewodnikowych*]
Prop — Property
Propane Can — Propane Canada
Propellants Explos — Propellants and Explosives
Property Mthly Rev — Property Monthly Review
Property Tax J — Property Tax Journal
Proposte Soc — Proposte Sociali
Propr Agric — Propriete Agricole
PrOrChr — Proche-Orient Chretien [*Jerusalem*]
Pr O S — Princeton Oriental Series
Pros — Prospetti
Pros J Natl Dist Att'y A — Prosecutor. Journal of the National District Attorneys Association
Pro Soc Water Treat Exam — Proceedings. Society for Water Treatment and Examination
Prosp R — Prospective Review
Pr Osr Badaw-Rozwoj Elektron Prozniowej — Prace Osrodka Badawczo-Rozwojowego Elektroniki Prozniowej
Pr Osr Nauk Prod Mater Polprzewodn — Prace Osrodek Naukowo-Produkcyjny Materialow Polprzewodnikowych
Pr Osrodka Badawczo-Rozwojowego Przetwornikow Obrazu — Prace Osrodka Badawczo-Rozwojowego Przetwornikow Obrazu
Pr Osrodka Badaw Rozwojowego Elektron Prozniowej — Prace Osrodka Badawczo-Rozwojowego Elektroniki Prozniowej
Prostagland — Prostaglandins
Prostaglandins Med — Prostaglandins and Medicine
Prosthet and Orthotics Int — Prosthetics and Orthotics International
Prosthet Orthot Int — Prosthetics and Orthotics International
Prot — Protestantismo [*Rome*]
PROTA — Protoplasma [*Austria*]
Prot Aer — Protection Aerienne
Prot Civ Secur Ind — Protection Civile et Securite Industrielle
Prot Coat Met — Protective Coatings on Metals
Prot Ecol — Protection Ecology
Protein Nucl Acid Enzyme — Protein Nucleic Acid Enzyme
Protein Synth — Protein Synthesis
Protein Synth Ser Adv — Protein Syntheses: A Series of Advances
Prot Epis His M — Protestant Episcopal Church. Historical Magazine
Protes Dent — Protesista Dental
Protet Stomatol — Protetyka Stomatologiczna

Protides Biol Fluids Proc Colloq — Protides of the Biological Fluids. Proceedings of the Colloquium [*Belgium*]
Protides Biol Fluids Proc Colloq (Bruges) — Protides of the Biological Fluids. Proceedings of the Colloquium (Bruges)
Prot Met — Protection of Metals
Prot Metals — Protection of Metals
Prot Met (USSR) — Protection of Metals (Union of Soviet Socialist Republics)
Protok Fischereitech — Protokolle zur Fischereitechnik
Prot Vitae — Protectio Vitae
Prouchvaniya Mikroelem Mikrotorovete Bulg — Prouchvaniya vurkhu Mikroelementite i Mikrotorovete v Bulgariya
Prov — Provincia
Prov — Provincial
Prov Buenos Aires Com Invest Cient Inf — Provincia de Buenos Aires. Comision de Investigaciones Cientificas. Informes
Prov Buenos Aires Com Invest Cient Mem — Provincia de Buenos Aires. Comision de Investigaciones Cientificas. Memoria
Provebruksmeld Nor Landbruksokonomiske Inst — Provebruksmelding-Norges Landbruksokonomiske Institutt
Provence Hist — Provence Historique
Provence Univ Ann Geol Mediterr — Provence Universite. Annales. Geologie Mediterraneenne
Provence Univ Lab Paleontol Hum Prehist Etud Quat Mem — Provence Universite. Laboratoire de Paleontologie Humaine et de Prehistoire. Etudes Quaternaires. Memoire
Providence Hosp Detroit Med Bull — Providence Hospital of Detroit. Medical Bulletin
Providence Hosp (Southfield Mich) Med Bull — Providence Hospital (Southfield, Michigan). Medical Bulletin
Provincial Bank Can Econ R — Provincial Bank of Canada. Economic Review
Prov Judges J — Provincial Judges Journal
Proyecto Desarrollo Pesq Publ — Proyecto de Desarrollo Pesquero. Publicacion
P Roy Music — Proceedings. Royal Musical Association
P Roy S Med — Proceedings. Royal Society of Medicine
P Roy Soc A — Proceedings. Royal Society of London. Series A. Mathematical and Physical Sciences
P Roy Soc B — Proceedings. Royal Society of London. Series B. Biological Sciences
PRP — Progress in Radiopharmacology [*Elsevier Book Series*]
PrPol — Prace Polonistyczne [*Warsaw*]
Pr Poznan Tow Przyj Nauk Wydz Nauk Roln Lesn — Prace-Poznanskie Towarzystwo Przyjaciol Nauk. Wydzial Nauk Rolniczych i Lesnych
Pr Primer — Prairie Primer
Pr Przem Inst Elektron — Prace Przemyslowego Instytutu Elektroniki
Pr Przem Inst Elektron (Warsaw) — Prace Przemyslowego Instytutu Elektroniki (Warsaw)
Pr Przem Inst Telekomun — Prace Przemyslowego Instytutu Telekomunikacji
PRPSA — Petroleum Press Service
PRPSB — Progress in Polymer Science
PRPT — Probe Post
PRPTA — Proceedings. Association of Asphalt Paving Technologists
PRPYA — Praxis der Psychotherapie
PRQ — Problems of Communism
PRR — Pre-Raphaelite Review
PRR — Presbyterian and Reformed Review
PRR — Public Relations Review
Pr Rady Nauk-Tech Huty Lenina — Prace Rady Naukowo-Technicznej Huty Imienia Lenina
PRRB — Physics Reports. Reprints Book Series [*Elsevier Book Series*]
PRREA — Philips Research Reports
PRS — Perspectives in Religious Studies
PrS — Prairie Schooner
PRS — Press Summary
Prsb Q — Presbyterian Quarterly Review
PRSE — Proceedings. Royal Society of Edinburgh
P RS Edin A — Proceedings. Royal Society of Edinburgh. Section A. Mathematics
P RS Edin B — Proceedings. Royal Society of Edinburgh. Section B. Natural Environment
PRSM — Proceedings. Royal Society of Medicine
PRSMA — Proceedings. Royal Society of Medicine
Prsnrs — Prisoners
PRSSA — Philips Research Reports. Supplements
PRSTA — Progress in Stereochemistry
Pr Statneho Geol Ustavu (Bratisl) — Prace Statneho Geologickeho Ustavu (Bratislava)
Pr Statneho Geol Ustavu (Bratislava) — Prace Statneho Geologickeho Ustavu (Bratislava)
PRSTB — Progresele Stiintei
Pr Stud Vyzk Ustav Vodohospod — Prace a Studie. Vyzkumny Ustav Vodohospodarsky
Pr Stud Zakl Badan Nauk Gorn Okregu Przem Pol Akad Nauk — Prace i Studia Zakladu Badan Naukowych Gornoslaskiego Okregu Przemyslowego Polskiej Akademii Nauk [*Poland*]
PRSUA — Plastic and Reconstructive Surgery
PRSUB — Pribory i Sistemy Upravleniya

PR Sugar Man — Puerto Rico Sugar Manual
PRTCD — Progres Technique
PRTEA — Pribory i Tekhnika Eksperimenta
PR Tex Agric Exp Stn — PR. Texas Agricultural Experiment Station
PRTHA — Progress in Radiation Therapy
PrThR — Princeton Theological Review
PRT Polym Age — PRT Polymer Age
PRTS — Politisch-Religioese Texte aus der Sargonidenzeit
PRTUA — Problemy Tuberkuleza
PRu — Paedagogische Rundschau
Prum Potravin — Prumysl Potravin
PRUND — Plastics and Rubber News
Pr Ustavu Geol Inz — Prace Ustavu Geologickeho Inzenyrstva
Pr Ustavu Naft Vyzk — Prace Ustavu pro Naftovy Vyzkum
Pr Ustavu Vyzk Paliv — Prace Ustavu pro Vyzkum Paliv [*Czechoslovakia*]
Pr Ustavu Vyzk Vyuziti Paliv — Prace Ustavu pro Vyzkum a Vyuziti Paliv
PRv — Philosophical Review
Pr Vinnits'k Derzh Med Inst — Pratsi Vinnits'kogo Derzhavnogo Medichnogo Institutu
PRVOA — Pravda Vostoka
PRVYD — Polyteknisk Revy
Pr Vyzk Ustavu CS Naft Dolu — Prace Vyzkumneho Ustavu CS Naftovych Dolu
Pr Vyzk Ustavu Lesn Hospod Myslivosti (Strnady) — Prace Vyzkumneho Ustavu Lesneho Hospodarstvi a Myslivosti (Strnady)
PRW — Purchasing World
PR Water Resour Bull — Puerto Rico. Water Resources Bulletin
PrWCJewSt — Proceedings. World Congress of Jewish Studies [*Jerusalem*]
Pr Winter — Probability Winter School. Proceedings of the Fourth Winter School on Probability
Pr Wroclaw Tow Nauk Ser B — Prace Wroclawskiego Towarzystwa Naukowego. Seria B
Pr Wydz Nauk Tech Bydgoskie Tow Nauk Ser A — Prace Wydzialu Nauk Technicznych. Bydgoskie Towarzystwo Naukowe. Seria A. Technologia Chemiczna
Pr Wydz Nauk Tech Bydgoskie Tow Nauk Ser C — Prace Wydzialu Nauk Technicznych. Bydgoskie Towarzystwo Naukowe. Seria C. Elektronika, Elektrotechnika
PrZ — Praehistorische Zeitschrift
Pr Zakresu Lesn — Prace z Zakresu Lesnictwa [*Poland*]
Pr Zakresu Nauk Roln — Prace z Zakresu Nauk Rolniczych
Prz Arch — Przeglad Archeologiczny
Przegd St — Przeglad Statystyczny
Przeglad Bibliot — Przeglad Biblioteczny
Przeglad Geog — Przeglad Geograficzny
Przeglad Hist — Przeglad Historyczny
Przeglad Mech — Przeglad Mechaniczny
Przeglad Papier — Przeglad Papierniczy
Przeglad Statyst — Przeglad Statystyczny
Przeglad Statyst — Przeglad Statystyczny. Polska Akademia Nauk. Komitet Statystyki i Ekonometrii
Przeglad Wlok — Przeglad Wlokienniczy
Przegl Antropol — Przeglad Antropologiczny
Przegl Bibl — Przeglad Biblioteczny
Przegl Budow — Przeglad Budowlany
Przegl Dermatol — Przeglad Dermatologiczny
Przegl Dermatol Wenerol — Przeglad Dermatologii i Wenerologii
Przegl Dok Ceram Szlachetnej Szkla — Przeglad Dokumentacyjny Ceramiki Szlachetnej i Szkla
Przegl Dok Nafty — Przeglad Dokumentacyjny Nafty
Przegl Dosw Roln — Przeglad Doswiadczalnictwa Rolniczego
Przegl Elektr — Przeglad Elektroniki
Przegl Elektron — Przeglad Elektroniki
Przegl Elektrotech — Przeglad Elektrotechniczny
Przegl Epidemiol — Przeglad Epidemiologiczny
Przegl Geofiz — Przeglad Geofizyczny
Przegl Geogr — Przeglad Geograficzny
Przegl Geogr Pol Geogr Rev — Przeglad Geograficzny-Polish Geographical Review
Przegl Geol — Przeglad Geologiczny
Przegl Gorn — Przeglad Gorniczy
Przegl Gorn Hutn — Przeglad Gorniczo Hutniczy
Przegl Hist — Przeglad Historycyzny
Przegl Hodowlany — Przeglad Hodowlany
Przegl Komunik — Przeglad Komunikacyjny
Przegl Lek — Przeglad Lekarski
Przegl Mech — Przeglad Mechaniczny
Przegl Morski — Przeglad Morski
Przegl Nauk Lit Zootech — Przeglad Naukowej Literatury Zootechnicznej
Przegl Nauk Tech Akad Gorn Hutn Krakowie Ser G — Przeglad Naukowo Techniczny. Akademia Gorniczo Hutnicza w Krakowie. Seria G. Gornictwo
Przegl Nauk Tech Akad Gorn Hutn Krakowie Ser H — Przeglad Naukowo Techniczny. Akademia Gorniczo Hutnicza w Krakowie. Seria H. Hutnictwo
Przegl Odlew — Przeglad Odlewnictwa

Przegl Organ — Przeglad Organizacji
Przegl Papiern — Przeglad Papierniczy
Przegl Przem Olejowego — Przeglad Przemyslu Olejowego
Przegl Skorzany — Przeglad Skorzany
Przegl Socjol — Przeglad Socjologiczny
Przegl Spawalnictwa — Przeglad Spawalnictwa
Przegl Telekomun — Przeglad Telekomunikacyjny
Przegl Wlok — Przeglad Wlokienniczy
Przegl Wojsk Ladowych — Przeglad Wojsk Ladowych [*Poland*]
Przegl Zachod — Przeglad Zachodni
Przegl Zboz Mlyn — Przeglad Zbozowo Mlynarski
Przegl Zbozowo Mlyn — Przeglad Zbozowo Mlynarski
Przegl Zool — Przeglad Zoologiczny
Przekazy — Przekazy/Opinie
Przem Chem — Przemysl Chemiczny
Przem Drzew — Przemysl Drzewny
Przem Drzewny — Przemysl Drzewny
Przem Ferment — Przemysl Fermentacyjny
Przem Ferment Rolny — Przemysl Fermentacyjny i Rolny
Przem Naft — Przemysl Naftowy
Przem Roln Spozyw — Przemysl Rolny i Spozywczy
Przem Spozyw — Przemysl Spozywczy
Przem Spozywczy — Przemysl Spozywczy
Przem Wlok — Przemysl Wlokienniczy
Przemy Chem — Przemysl Chemiczny
PRZGA — Przeglad Geologiczny
PrzH — Przeglad Humanistyczny
PrzK — Przeglad Kulturalny
PrzKl — Przeglad Klasyczny
PrzOr — Przeglad Orientalistyczny [*Cracow/Warsaw*]
PRZPB — Przeglad Psychologiczny
Prz Stat — Przeglad Statystyczny
PrzZ — Przeglad Zachodni
PS — Pacific Spectator
PS — Palestinskii Sbornik
PS — Pamietnik Slowianski
PS — Pedagogical Seminary and Journal of Genetic Psychology
PS — Pensiero e Scuola
PS — Philippine Studies
PS — Planet Stories
PS — Political Studies
PS — Post Script
PS — Prairie Schooner
PS — Pravoslavnyi Sobesiednik
PS — Process Studies
PS — Prose Studies 1800-1900
PSA — Papeles de Son Armadans
PSa — Philippiniana Sacra
PSA — Police Science Abstracts
PSA — Psychopharmacology Abstracts
PSAC TD — Publications. Societe d'Archeologie Copte. Textes et Documents
Ps Af — Psychopathologie Africaine
PSA Jl — Photographic Society of America. Journal
PSA Journal — Photographic Society of America. Journal
PSAM — Publications. Service des Antiquites du Maroc
PsaQ — Psychoanalytic Quarterly
PsaR — Psychoanalytic Review
PSAS — Papers in International Studies. Africa Series. Ohio University
PSAS — Proceedings. Society of Antiquaries of Scotland
PSAVA — Pribory i Sistemy Avtomatiki
PSb — Palestinskii Sbornik
PSB — Personeelbeleid
PsB — Psychological Bulletin
PSBA — Proceedings. Society of Biblical Archaeology
PSBRA9 — International Committee for Bird Preservation. Pan American Section. Research Report
PSBS — Policy Sciences Book Series [*Elsevier Book Series*]
PSBU — Psychopharmacology Bulletin
PSBUA — Psychological Bulletin
P Sch — Prairie Schooner
PSCHO — Psychopharmacology
PSCL — Papers and Studies in Contrastive Linguistics
PSCOB — Psychiatric Communications
P S Conf Co — Proceedings. Southern Conference on Corrections
PScQ — Political Science Quarterly
P Scribe — Portland Scribe
PSD — Physical Sciences Data [*Elsevier Book Series*]
PS and E — Photographic Science and Engineering
PSE — Prague Studies in English
PSE — Princeton Studies in English
PSEAL — Papers in South East Asian Linguistics
PSEKUT — Paar Sammukest Eesti Kirjanduse Uurimise Teed
PSEL — Publications. Societe Egyptologique a l'Universite d'Etat de Leningrad
PSENA — Photographic Science and Engineering
PSEPB — Progress in Separation and Purification

PSHADL — Publications. Societe Historique et Archeologique dans le Duche de Limbourg
PSHAL — Publications. Societe Historique et Archeologique dans le Duche de Limbourg
PSHED — Psychologie Heute
PSHIGDL — Publications. Section Historique. Institut Grand-Ducal de Luxembourg
PSHIL — Publications. Section Historique. Institut Grand-Ducal de Luxembourg
PSHL — Publications. Societe Historique et Archeologique dans le Duche de Limbourg
PSHP — Pennsylvania Journal for Health, Physical Education, and Recreation
PSI — Piccole Storie Illustrate
PSI — Pubblicazioni. Societa Italiana per la Ricerca dei Papiri Greci e Latini in Egitto [*Florence*]
PSICD — Proceedings. IEEE Computer Society's International Computer Software and Applications Conference
PSIR Bull Monogr — PSIR [*Pakistan Council of Scientific and Industrial Research*] Bulletin Monograph
PSJ — Philosophical Studies of Japan
PSKAD — Promyshlennost Sinteticheskogo Kauchuka
PSKJ — Pitanja Savremenog Knjizevnog Jezika
Pskov Gos Pedagog Inst Uch Zap — Pskovskii Gosudarstvennyi Pedagogicheskii Institut. Uchenye Zapiski
Pskov Ped Inst Fiz-Mat Fak Ucen Zap — Pskovskii Pedagogiceskii Institut. Fiziko-Matematiceskii Fakul'tet. Ucenye Zapiski
PSL — Polymer Science Library [*Elsevier Book Series*]
Psl Admr — Personnel Administrator
PSLC — Pawathy Stare Literatury Ceske
Psl Exec — Personnel Executive
Psl & Guid J — Personnel and Guidance Journal
PSM — Pagine di Storia della Medicina
PSM — Philippine Studies (Manila)
PSM — Public School Magazine
PSM — Pytannja Slov'jans'koho Movoznavstva
PSMDC — Psychological Medicine
PSMEA — Psychosomatic Medicine
PSML — Prague Studies in Mathematical Linguistics
PSMSC — Psychotherapie und Medizinische Psychologie
PSMUD — Psychology of Music
PSNEB — Psychiatric Annals
PSNT — Pismo Swiete Nowego Testamentu [*Posen*]
PSNTA — Progres Scientifique
PSoc — Przeglad Socjologiczny
P Soc Exp M — Proceedings. Society for Experimental Biology and Medicine
PSp — Pacific Spectator
PSP — Provincia de Sao Pedro [*Brazil*]
PSPCD — Proceedings. Annual Southwestern Petroleum Short Course
PSPHA — Psychophysiology
PSPOB — Psychiatria Polska
PSPOS — Philological Society. Publications. Occasional Studies
PSPSB — Psychotherapy and Psychosomatics
PSQ — Philologische Studien und Quellen
PSQ — Political Science Quarterly
PSQAA — Psychoanalytic Quarterly
PSQSA — Psychiatric Quarterly. Supplement
PSQUA — Psychiatric Quarterly
PSR — Pacific Sociological Review
PSR — Petty Sessions Review
PSR — Philippine Sociological Review
PSR — Political Science Review
PsR — Psychoanalytic Review
PsR — Psychological Review
PSRAA — Progress in the Science and Technology of the Rare Earths
PSREA — Psychoanalytic Review
PSRED — Psychological Research
PSRIA — Papers. Ship Research Institute
PSRPD — Prakla-Seismos Report
PSRVA — Psychological Review
PSRWD — Policy Studies Review
PSS — Pubblicazioni del Seminario di Semitistica. Instituto Orientale de Napoli
PSSAB — Physica Status Solidi. Sectio A. Applied Research
PSSEAS — Papers in International Studies. Southeast Asia Series. Ohio University
PSSFB — Progress in Surface Science
PSSGL — Penn State Series in German Literature
PSSHR — Philippine Social Sciences and Humanities Review
PSSR — Philippine Social Science Review
PSSS — Proceedings. Shevchenko Scientific Society. Philological Section
PSSSP — Proceedings. Shevchenko Scientific Society. Philological Section
PSSTA — Progress in Solid State Chemistry
PST — Philological Society. Transactions
PST — Policy Studies Journal. Policy Studies Institute [*London*]
PST — Pontifical Institute of Mediaeval Studies. Studies and Texts
PSt — Prose Studies

PSta — Philippine Statistican
PSTOA — Psychology Today
PStu — Philippine Studies
PSU-ADA — Pennsylvania State University-Abstracts of Doctoral Dissertations
PSUPB — Pribory i Sistemy Upravleniya
PSuQ — Philologische Studien und Quellen
PSURA — Progress in Surgery
PSWEA — Proceedings. South Wales Institute of Engineers
PSWYA — Psychologia Wychowawcza
PsyAb — Psychological Abstracts
Psy B — Psychological Bulletin
PSYBB — Psychopharmacology Bulletin
PSYCA — Psychiatry
PSYCD — Psychendocrinology
Psych Bull — Psychological Bulletin
Psychiat — Psychiatry
Psychiat Cl — Psychiatria Clinica
Psychiat Digest — Psychiatry Digest
Psychiat Fo — Psychiatric Forum
Psychiat Me — Psychiatry in Medicine
Psychiat Opin — Psychiatric Opinion
Psychiat Q — Psychiatric Quarterly
Psychiatr Ann — Psychiatric Annals
Psychiatr Annals — Psychiatric Annals
Psychiatr Clin — Psychiatria Clinica
Psychiatr Clin (Basel) — Psychiatria Clinica (Basel)
Psychiatr Enfant — Psychiatrie de l'Enfant
Psychiatr Fenn — Psychiatria Fennica
Psychiatr Forum — Psychiatric Forum
Psychiatr Hosp — Psychiatric Hospital
Psychiatr J Univ Ottawa — Psychiatric Journal. University of Ottawa
Psychiatr Neurol — Psychiatria et Neurologia
Psychiatr Neurol Jpn — Psychiatria et Neurologia Japonica
Psychiatr Neurol Med Psychol — Psychiatrie, Neurologie, und Medizinische Psychologie
Psychiatr Neurol Med Psychol (Leipz) — Psychiatrie, Neurologie, und Medizinische Psychologie (Leipzig)
Psychiatr Neurol Neurochir — Psychiatria, Neurologia, Neurochirurgia
Psychiatr Neurol Wochenschr — Psychiatrisch Neurologische Wochenschrift
Psychiatr News — Psychiatric News
Psychiatr Opinion — Psychiatric Opinion
Psychiatr Pol — Psychiatria Polska
Psychiatr Prax — Psychiatrische Praxis
Psychiatr Res Rep — Psychiatric Research Reports
Psychiatr Soc — Psychiatrie Sociale
Psychiatry Dig — Psychiatry Digest
Psychiatry Med — Psychiatry in Medicine
Psychiatry Res — Psychiatry Research
Psychic R — Psychical Review
Psych of Music — Psychology of Music
Psychoanal Q — Psychoanalytic Quarterly
Psychoanal R — Psychoanalytic Review
Psychoanal Rev — Psychoanalytic Review
Psychoanal Stud Child — Psychoanalytic Study of the Child
Psychoanal Study Child — Psychoanalytic Study of the Child
Psychoanal Study Child Monogr Ser — Psychoanalytic Study of the Child. Monograph Series
Psychoan Q — Psychoanalytic Quarterly
Psychoan Re — Psychoanalytic Review
Psychocultural R — Psychocultural Review
Psychohist Rev — Psychohistory Review
Psychol Absts — Psychological Abstracts
Psychol Afr — Psychologia Africana
Psychol Africana — Psychologia Africana
Psychol Afr Monogr Suppl — Psychologie Africana. Monograph and Supplement
Psychol B — Psychological Bulletin
Psychol Be — Psychologische Beitraege
Psychol Beitr — Psychologische Beitraege
Psychol Bel — Psychologica Belgica
Psychol Belg — Psychologica Belgica
Psychol Bul — Psychological Bulletin
Psychol Bull — Psychological Bulletin
Psychol Can — Psychologie Canadienne
Psychol Clinic — Psychological Clinic
Psychol Erz — Psychologie in Erziehung und Unterricht
Psychol Forsch — Psychologische Forschung
Psychol Fr — Psychologie Francaise
Psychol Iss — Psychological Issues
Psychol Issues — Psychological Issues
Psychol Issues Monogr — Psychological Issues. Monographs
Psychol Learn & Motiv — Psychology of Learning and Motivation
Psychol Med — Psychological Medicine
Psychol Med — Psychologie Medicale

Psychol Monogr (Gen Appl) — Psychological Monographs (General and Applied)
Psychology M — Psychology of Music
Psychol Prax — Psychologische Praxis
Psychol R — Psychological Review
Psychol Rec — Psychological Record
Psychol Rep — Psychological Reports
Psychol Res — Psychological Research
Psychol Rev — Psychological Review
Psychol Rundsch — Psychologische Rundschau
Psychol Sch — Psychology in the Schools
Psychol in the Schs — Psychology in the Schools
Psychol Stu — Psychological Studies
Psychol Tod — Psychology Today
Psychol Today — Psychology Today
Psychol Women Q — Psychology of Women Quarterly
Psychometri — Psychometrika
Psycho Mycol Stud — Psycho-Mycological Studies
Psychon Sci — Psychonomic Science
Psychon Sci Sect Anim Physiol Psychol — Psychonomic Science. Section on Animal and Physiological Psychology
Psychon Sci Sect Hum Exp Psychol — Psychonomic Science. Section on Human Experimental Psychology
Psychop Afr — Psychopathologie Africaine
Psychopathol Afr — Psychopathologie Africaine
Psychopathol Expression Suppl Encephale — Psychopathologie de l'Expression. Supplement de l'Encephale
Psychopathol Pict Expression — Psychopathology and Pictorial Expression
Psychopharm — Psychopharmacologia
Psychopharmacol Abstr — Psychopharmacology Abstracts
Psychopharmacol Bull — Psychopharmacology Bulletin
Psychopharmacol Commun — Psychopharmacology Communications
Psychopharmacol Suppl — Psychopharmacology. Supplementum
Psychopharmacol Serv Cent Bull — Psychopharmacology Service Center. Bulletin
Psychopharmacol Suppl Encephale — Psychopharmacologie. Supplement de l'Encephale
Psychoph C — Psychopharmacology Communications
Psychophysl — Psychophysiology
Psychos Med — Psychosomatic Medicine
Psychosocial Rehabil J — Psychosocial Rehabilitation Journal
Psychosoc Proc Iss Child Ment Health — Psychosocial Process. Issues in Child Mental Health
Psychosoc Rehabil J — Psychosocial Rehabilitation Journal
Psychosomat — Psychosomatics
Psychosom Med — Psychosomatic Medicine
Psychother Med Psychol — Psychotherapie und Medizinische Psychologie
Psychother Psychosom — Psychotherapy and Psychosomatics
Psychother Psychosom Med Psychol — Psychotherapie, Psychosomatik, Medizinische Psychologie
Psychother Theory Res Pract — Psychotherapy: Theory, Research, and Practice
Psychoth MP — Psychotherapie und Medizinische Psychologie
Psychoth Ps — Psychotherapy and Psychosomatics
Psychoth/TR — Psychotherapy: Theory, Research, and Practice
Psych Prax — Psychologische Praxis
Psych Soc — Psychology and Social Theory
Psych Stud — Psychological Studies [Mysore]
Psych Teaching — Psychology Teaching
Psycul R — Psychocultural Review
Psy R — Proceedings. Society for Psychical Research
PsyR — Psychoanalytic Review
Psy Rund — Psychologische Rundschau
PsyS — Psychonomic Science
PSYSA — Psyche
P Sy St Carletn — Proceedings. Symposium on Statistics and Related Topics. Carleton University
Psy T — Psychology Today
PSZBA — Prace i Studia Zakladu Badan Naukowych Gornoslaskiego Okregu Przemyslowego Polskiej Akademii Nauk
Pszczelnicze Zesz Nauk — Pszczelnicze Zeszyty Naukowe
Pszczel Zesz Nauk — Pszczelnicze Zeszyty Naukowe
PSzL — Polska Sztuka Ludowa
PT — Pamietnik Teatralny
PT — Petroleum Times
PT — Polar Times
PT — Przeglad Teologiczny
PT — Psychology Today
PT — Pytannja Tekstolohiji
PTA — Kunststof en Rubber
PTA — Personnel and Training Abstracts
PTA — Practical Accountant
PTAIOC — Proceedings and Transactions. All-India Oriental Conferences
PTA Mag — PTA [Parent-Teacher Association] Magazine
PTASB — Photographic Applications in Science, Technology, and Medicine

PTB Mitt — PTB [*Physikalisch-Technische Bundesanstalt*] Mitteilungen. Amts- und Mitteilungsblatt der Physikalisch- Technische Bundesanstalt [*Braunschweig-Berlin*]
PTB Mitt Forsch Pruefen — PTB [*Physikalisch-Technische Bundesanstalt*] Mitteilungen. Forschen und Pruefen
PTC — Packung und Transport in der Chemischen Industrie
PTC J — Patent, Trademark, and Copyright Journal
PTCJB — Postepy Techniki Jadrowej
PTCLA — Presse Thermale et Climatique
Ptd Salesmanship — Printed Salesmanship
Ptero — Pterodactyl
PText — Papiere zur Textlinguistik [*Papers in Textlinguistics*]
PTFS — Publications. Texas Folklore Society
PTG — Portugal, Belgique, Luxembourg. Informations Economiques
Ptg Art — Printing Art
PTGMA — Photogrammetria
PTHEA — Physical Therapy
PThR — Princeton Theological Review
PTI — Petroleum Times
PTIND — Paper Technology and Industry
PTJ — Piano Technician's Journal
PTM — Practising Manager
PTMRA — Platinum Metals Review
PTMUD — Postepy Technologii Maszyn i Urzadzen
PTNMA — Protection of Metals [*English Translation*]
PTOC — Progress in Theoretical Organic Chemistry [*Elsevier Book Series*]
PTP — Phase Transition Phenomena [*Elsevier Book Series*]
PTPFA — Poznanskie Towarzystwo Przyjaciol Nauk. Wydzial Lekarski. Prace Komisji Farmaceutycznej
Pt Phil Gaz — Port Phillip Gazette
PTPKA — Progress of Theoretical Physics (Kyoto)
PTPMA — Poznanskie Towarzystwo Przyjaciol Nauk. Wydzial Lekarski. Prace Komisji Medycyny Doswiadczalnej
PTPN — Poznanskie Towarzystwo Przyjaciol Nauk
PT/Procestech — PT/Procestechniek
PTR — Personality Tests and Reviews
PTR — Princeton Theological Review
PTRC — PTRC. Planning and Transport Research and Computation
PTREA — Philips Technical Review
Ptr Ink — Printers' Ink
Ptr Ink Mo — Printers' Ink Monthly
PTRS — Philosophical Transactions. Royal Society of London
PTRSC — Proceedings and Transactions. Royal Society of Canada
PTSLA — Plant Science Letters
PTTDA — Petroleum Today
PTTI Stud — PTTI [*Postal, Telegraph, and Telephone International*] Studies
PTTPD — Bandaoti Xuebao
PU — Problemi di Ulisse
PUA — Public Administration
PUAHC — Proceedings. Union of American Hebrew Congregations
PUASAL — Proceedings. Utah Academy of Sciences, Arts, and Letters
PUB — Pacific University Bulletin
Pub — Publisher
Pub Adm — Public Administration
Pub Admin — Public Administration
Pub Admin Abstr — Public Administration Abstracts and Index of Articles
Pub Admin Survey — Public Administration Survey
Pub Adm R — Public Administration Review
Pub Adm Rev — Public Administration Review
Pub Ad Rev — Public Administration Review
Pub Am Stat Assn — Publications. American Statistical Association
Pub Archives Can Report — Public Archives of Canada. Report
Pub Ast S J — Publications. Astronomical Society of Japan
Pub Ast S P — Publications. Astronomical Society of the Pacific
Pubbl (Bergamo) Sta Sper Maiscoltura — Pubblicazioni (Bergamo) Stazione Sperimentale di Maiscoltura
Pubbl Centro Sper Agr Forest ENCC — Pubblicazioni. Centro di Sperimentazione Agricola e Forestale. Ente Nazionale per la Cellulosa e per la Carta
Pubbl Cent Sper Agric For — Pubblicazioni. Centro di Sperimentazione Agricola e Forestale
Pubbl Cent Sper Agric For (Rome) — Pubblicazioni. Centro di Sperimentazione Agricola e Forestale (Rome)
Pubbl Chim Biol Med Ist "Carlo Erba" Ric Ter — Pubblicazioni Chimiche, Biologiche, e Mediche. Istituto "Carlo Erba" per Ricerche Terapeutiche
Pubbl Ente Naz Cellulosa Carta — Pubblicazioni. Ente Nazionale per la Cellulosa e per la Carta
Pubbl Fac Sci Ing Univ Trieste Ser A — Pubblicazioni. Facolta di Scienze e d'Ingegneria. Universita di Trieste. Serie A
Pubbl Fac Sci Ing Univ Trieste Ser B — Pubblicazioni. Facolta di Scienze e d'Ingegneria. Universita di Trieste. Serie B
Pubbl IAC — Pubblicazioni. Istituto per le Applicazioni del Calcolo. Consiglio Nazionale delle Ricerche

Pubbl Ist Chim Agrar Sper Gorizia Nuovi Ann — Pubblicazione. Istituto Chimico Agrario Sperimentale di Gorizia. Nuovi Annali
Pubbl Ist Geol Mineral Univ Ferrara — Pubblicazioni. Istituto di Geologia e Mineralogia. Universita di Ferrara
Pubbl Ist Mat Appl Fac Ingegneria Univ Stud Roma — Pubblicazioni. Istituto di Matematica Applicata. Facolta di Ingegneria. Universita degli Studi di Roma
Pubbl Oss Geofis Trieste — Pubblicazioni. Osservatorio Geofisico di Trieste
Pubbl Ser III — Pubblicazione Serie III
Pubbl Stn Zool Napoli — Pubblicazioni. Stazione Zoologica di Napoli
Pubbl Univ Studi Firenze Fac Sci Mat Fis Nat — Pubblicazioni. Universita degli Studi di Firenze. Facolta di Scienze Matematiche, Fisiche, e Naturali
Pubbl Univ Stud Perugia Fac Med Vet — Pubblicazioni. Universita degli Studi di Perugia. Facolta di Medicina Veterinaria
Pub Circ — Publishers' Circular and Booksellers' Record
Pub Col Soc Mass — Publications. Colonial Society of Massachusetts
Pub Cont LJ — Public Contract Law Journal
Pub Cont Newsl — Public Contract Newsletter
Pub Contract L J — Public Contract Law Journal
Pub Dom Ast — Publications. Dominion Astrophysical Observatory
Pub Emp — Public Employee
Pub Ent Adv LQ — Publishing, Entertainment, Advertising, and Allied Fields Law Quarterly
Pub Health Nurs — Public Health Nursing
Pub Health Rep — Public Health Reports
Pub Health Rept — Public Health Reports
Pub Health Rep US Pub Health and Mar Hosp Serv — Public Health Reports. United States Surgeon-General. Public Health and Marine Hospital Service
Pub Health Rep US Pub Health Serv — Public Health Reports. United States Public Health Service
Pub Health Soc B — Public Health Society. Bulletin [*Kuala Lumpur*]
Pub Hist Inst Luxembourg — Publications. Section Historique. Institut Grand-Ducal de Luxembourg
Pub Interest — Public Interest
Pub L — Public Law
Publ Adm — Public Administration
Publ Adm R — Public Administration Review
Publ Adm Re — Public Administration Review
Publ Aff B — Public Affairs Bulletin
Publ Agric (Can) — Publication. Agriculture (Canada)
Publ Agric Ext Serv N Carol St Univ — Publication. Agricultural Extension Service. North Carolina State University
Publ Agric Res Serv US Dep Agric — Publication. Agricultural Research Service. United States Department of Agriculture
Publ Alberta Dept Agr — Publication. Alberta Department of Agriculture
Publ Allegheny Obs Univ Pittsburgh — Publications. Allegheny Observatory. University of Pittsburgh
Publ Amakusa Mar Biol Lab Kyushu Univ — Publications. Amakusa Marine Biological Laboratory. Kyushu University
Publ Am Assoc Adv Sci — Publication. American Association for the Advancement of Science
Publ Amer Ass Advan Sci — Publication. American Association for the Advancement of Science
Publ Amer Univ Beirut Fac Agr Sci — Publication. American University of Beirut. Faculty of Agricultural Sciences
Publ Am Inst Biol Sci — Publication. American Institute of Biological Sciences
Publ Am Univ Beirut Fac Agric Sci — Publication. American University of Beirut. Faculty of Agricultural Sciences
Publ ANARE Data Rep Ser — Publications. ANARE [*Australian National Antarctic Research Expedition*] Data Reports Series
Publ Land & Res L Dig — Public Land and Resources Law Digest
Publ Ass For-Cell — Publication. Association Foret-Cellulose
Publ Assoc Etude Paleontol Stratigr Houilleres — Publication. Association pour l'Etude de la Paleontologie et de la Stratigraphie Houilleres
Publ Assoc Ing Fac Polytech Mons — Publications. Association des Ingenieurs. Faculte Polytechnique de Mons
Publ Astron Soc Jpn — Publications. Astronomical Society of Japan
Publ Astron Soc Pac — Publications. Astronomical Society of the Pacific
Publ Aust Natl Univ Res Sch Phys Sci Dep Eng Phys — Australian National University. Research School of Physical Sciences. Department of Engineering Physics. Publication
Publ Avulsa FZB Fund Zoobot Rio Grande Sul — Publicacao Avulsa FZB. Fundacao Zoobotanica do Rio Grande Do Sul
Publ Avulsas Cent Pesqui Aggeu Magalhaes (Recife Braz) — Publicacoes Avulsas. Centro de Pesquisas Aggeu Magalhaes (Recife, Brazil)
Publ Avulsas Inst Aggeu Magalhaes (Recife Braz) — Publicacoes Avulsas. Instituto Aggeu Magalhaes (Recife, Brazil)
Publ Avulsas Mus Nac (Rio De J) — Publicacoes Avulsas. Museu Nacional (Rio De Janeiro)
Publ Avuls Rev Bras Malariol — Publicacoes Avulsas. Revista Brasileira de Malariologia
Publ BC Minist Agric — Publications. British Columbia Ministry of Agriculture

Publ BC Minist Agric Food — Publications. British Columbia Ministry of Agriculture and Food
Publ Beaverlodge Res Stn — Publication. Beaverlodge Research Station
Publ Biol Dir Gen Invest Cient UANL (Univ Auton Nuevo Leon) — Publicaciones Biologicas. Direccion General de la Investigacion Cientifica UANL (Universidad Autonoma de Nuevo Leon)
Publ Brit Columbia Dept Agr — Publication. British Columbia Department of Agriculture
Publ Bur Etud Geol Minieres Colon (Paris) — Publications. Bureau d'Etudes Geologiques et Minieres Coloniales (Paris)
Publ Bur Rech Geol Geophys Minieres (Fr) — Publications. Bureau de Recherches Geologiques, Geophysiques, et Minieres (France)
Publ Cairo Univ Herb — Publications. Cairo University Herbarium
Publ Calif Dep Agric — Publication. California Department of Agriculture
Publ Canada Dep Agric — Publication. Canada Department of Agriculture
Publ Canada Dep For — Publication. Canada Department of Forestry
Publ Can Dep Agric — Publication. Canada Department of Agriculture
Publ Can Dept Agr — Publication. Canada Department of Agriculture
Publ Can For Serv — Publication. Canadian Forestry Service
Publ Center Medieval Ren Stud UCLA — Publications. Center for Medieval and Renaissance Studies. UCLA [*University of California at Los Angeles*]
Publ Cent Estud Entomol Univ Chile — Publicaciones. Centro de Estudios Entomologicos. Universidad de Chile
Publ Cent Estud Leprol — Publicacoes. Centro de Estudos Leprologicos
Publ Cent Etude Util Sciures de Bois — Publication. Centre d'Etude pour l'Utilisation des Sciures de Bois
Publ Cent Natl Exploit Oceans Ser Rapp Sci Tech (Fr) — Publications. Centre National pour l'Exploitation des Oceans. Serie. Rapport Scientifique et Technique (France)
Publ Cent Natl Geol Houillere — Publication. Centre National de Geologie Houillere
Publ Cent Quim Ind (Buenos Aires) — Publicacion. Centro de Quimicos Industriales (Buenos Aires)
Publ Cent Rech Zootech Univ Louvain — Publication. Centre de Recherches Zootechniques. Universite de Louvain
Publ Centre Recherches Math Pures Ser 3 — Publications. Centre de Recherches en Mathematiques Pures. Serie 3
Publ Centre Rech Math Pures — Publications. Centre de Recherches en Mathematiques Pures
Publ Centre Rech Math Pures 1 — Publications. Centre de Recherches en Mathematiques Pures. Serie 1
Publ Centre Rech Math Pures Ser 3 — Publications. Centre de Recherches en Mathematiques Pures. Serie 3
Publ Centre Tech For Trop — Publication. Centre Technique Forestier Tropical
Publ Cent Stud Citogenet Veg CNR — Pubblicazioni. Centro di Studi per la Citogenetica Vegetale. Consiglio Nazionale delle Ricerche
Publ Cent Tech For Trop (Nogent-Sur-Marne Fr) — Publication. Centre Technique Forestier Tropical (Nogent-Sur-Marne, France)
Publ Chile Univ Cent Estud Entomol — Publicaciones. Chile Universidad. Centro de Estudios Entomologicos
Publ Choice — Public Choice
Publ Cient Univ Austral Chile (Fac Ingen For) — Publicaciones Cientificas. Universidad Austral de Chile (Facultad de Ingenieria Forestal)
Publ Clark — Publications. Clark Library Professorship. University of California at Los Angeles
Publ Cleans — Public Cleansing
Publcoes Avuls Mus Parana — Publicacoes Avulsas. Museu Paranaense
Publcoes Cult Co Diam Angola — Publicacoes Culturais. Companhia de Diamantes de Angola
Publcoes Dir Ger Servs Flor Aquic — Publicacoes. Direccao Geral dos Servicos Florestais e Aqueicolas
Publ Coffee Brew Inst — Publication. Coffee Brewing Institute
Publ Com Nac Energ At (Argent) Misc — Publicaciones. Comision Nacional de Energia Atomica (Argentina). Miscelanea
Publ Com Nac Energ At (Argent) Ser Fis — Publicaciones. Comision Nacional de Energia Atomica (Argentina). Serie Fisica
Publ Com Nac Energ At (Argent) Ser Geol — Publicaciones. Comision Nacional de Energia Atomica (Argentina). Serie Geologia
Publ Com Nac Energ At (Argent) Ser Mat — Publicaciones. Comision Nacional de Energia Atomica (Argentina). Serie Matematica
Publ Com Nac Energ At (Argent) Ser Quim — Publicaciones. Comision Nacional de Energia Atomica (Argentina). Serie Quimica
Publ Cons Recur Nat No Renov (Mex) — Publicacion. Consejo de Recursos Naturales No Renovables (Mexico)
Publ Contr LJ — Public Contract Law Journal
Publ Coop Ext Serv Miss State Univ — Publication. Cooperative Extension Service. Mississippi State University
Publ Coop Ext Serv Wash St Univ — Publication. Cooperative Extension Service. Washington State University
Publ Co-Op Ext Univ Calif — Publication. Cooperative Extension. University of California
Publ Cult Cia Diamantes Angola — Publicacoes Culturais. Companhia de Diamantes de Angola
Publ Dep Agric (Can) — Publication. Department of Agriculture (Ottawa, Canada)

Publ Dep Cristalogr Miner CSIC (Spain) — Publicaciones. Departamento de Cristalografia y Mineralogia. Consejo Superior de Investigaciones Cientificas (Spain)
Publ Dep Math Lyon — Publications. Departement de Mathematiques. Faculte des Sciences de Lyon
Publ Dept Agr (Can) — Publications. Department of Agriculture (Canada)
Publ Dept Agr Conserv (Manitoba) — Publications. Department of Agriculture and Conservation (Manitoba)
Publ Dir Gen Geol Minas Repub Ecuador — Publicacion. Direccion General de Geologia y Minas. Republica del Ecuador
Publ Dir Gen Invent Nac For (Mex) — Publicacion. Direccion General del Inventario Nacional Forestal (Coyoacan, Mexico)
Publ Diverses Mus Natl Hist Nat — Publications Diverses. Museum National d'Histoire Naturelle
Publ Dom Astrophys Obs — Publications. Dominion Astrophysical Observatory [*Victoria, British Columbia*]
Publ Dom Astrophys Obs (Victoria BC) — Publications. Dominion Astrophysical Observatory (Victoria, British Columbia)
Publ Dom Obs (Ottawa) — Publications. Dominion Observatory (Ottawa)
Publ Dushanb Inst Epidemiol Gig — Publikatsiya Dushanbinskogo Instituta Epidemiologii i Gigieny
Publ Earth Phys Branch (Can) — Publication. Earth Physics Branch (Canada)
Publ Earth Phys Branch Dep Energy Mines & Resour — Publications. Earth Physics Branch. Department of Energy, Mines, and Resources
Publ Econometriques — Publications Econometriques
Publ Elektrote Fak Univ Beogradu Ser Mat Fiz — Publikacije Elektrotehnickog Fakulteta Univerziteta u Beogradu. Serija Matematika i Fizika
Publ Elektroteh Fak Ser Elektroenerg — Publikacije Elektrotehnickog Fakulteta. Serija Elektroenergetika
Publ Elektroteh Fak Ser Elektron Telekommun Autom — Publikacije Elektrotehnickog Fakulteta. Serija Elektronika Telekommunikacije. Automatika
Publ Elektroteh Fak Ser Mat & Fiz — Publikacije Elektrotehnickog Fakulteta. Serija Matematika i Fizika
Publ Elektroteh Fak Univ Beogr Ser Mat Fiz — Publikacije Elektrotehnickog Fakulteta Univerziteta u Beogradu. Serija Matematika i Fizika
Publ Energ — Publicacion sobre Energia
Publ Ent Adv A — Publishing, Entertainment, Advertising, and Allied Fields Law Quarterly
Publ E Purdue Univ Coop Ext Serv — Publication E. Purdue University. Cooperative Extension Service
Publ Espec Inst Nac Invest Forest (Mex) — Publicacion Especial. Instituto Nacional de Investigaciones Forestal (Mexico)
Publ Espec Inst Oceanogr (San Paulo) — Publicacao Especial. Instituto Oceanografico (San Paulo)
Publ Espec Serv Nac Trigo Min Agr (Madrid) — Publicaciones Especiales. Servicio Nacional del Trigo. Ministerio de Agricultura (Madrid)
Publ Ethnol — Publications in Ethnology
Publ Ext Serv Israel Min Agric — Israel. Ministry of Agriculture. Extension Service Publication
Publ Fac Agron Univ Teheran — Publications. Faculte d'Agronomie. Universite de Teheran
Publ Fac Agr Sci Amer Univ (Beirut) — Publications. Faculty of Agricultural Sciences. American University (Beirut)
Publ Fac Cienc Fisicomat Univ Nac La Plata Ser 2 — Publicaciones. Facultad de Ciencias Fisicomatematicas. Universidad Nacional de La Plata. Serie 2. Revista
Publ Fac Dr Econ Amiens — Publications. Faculte de Droit et d'Economie d'Amiens
Publ Fac Dr Sci Polit Soc Amiens — Publications. Faculte de Droit et des Sciences Politiques et Sociales d'Amiens
Publ Fac Sci Univ Clermont Geol Mineral — Publications. Faculte des Sciences. Universite de Clermont. Geologie et Mineralogie
Publ FAO/ECE Jt Comm Working Tech — Publication. FAO [*Food and Agriculture Organization of the United Nations*]/ECE [*Economic Commission for Europe*] Joint Committee on Forest Working Techniques and Training Forest Workers
Publ Farm (Sao Paulo) — Publicacoes Farmaceuticas (Sao Paulo)
Publ Finan — Public Finance
Publ Finance — Public Finance
Publ Fin Q — Public Finance Quarterly
Publ Fond Agathon de Potter — Publications. Foundation Agathon de Potter
Publ For Commn NSW — Publication. Forestry Commission of New South Wales
Publ Foreign Agric Serv US Dep Agric — Publication. Foreign Agricultural Service. United States Department of Agriculture
Publ Forest Res Brch Canada Dep For — Publication. Forest Research Branch. Canada Department of Forestry
Publ For Res Inst Finl — Publications. Forest Research Institute in Finland
Publ For Serv (Can) — Publication. Forestry Service. Department of Fisheries and Forestry (Ottawa, Canada)
Publ Found Sci Res Surinam Neth Antilles — Publications. Foundation for Scientific Research in Surinam and the Netherlands Antilles
Publ Geol Surv Queensl — Publication. Geological Survey of Queensland
Publ Great Plains Agric Coun — Great Plains Agricultural Council. Publication

Publ Group Adv Psychiatry — Publication. Groups for the Advancement of Psychiatry
Publ Group Av Methodes Spectrogr — Publication. Groupement pour l'Avancement des Methodes Spectrographiques
Publ Gulf Coast Res Lab Mus — Publications. Gulf Coast Research Laboratory. Museum
Publ Haewundae Mar Lab Pusan Fish Coll — Publications. Haewundae Marine Laboratory. Pusan Fisheries College
Publ Hannah Inst Hist Med — Publication. Hannah Institute for the History of Medicine
Publ Heal — Public Health: The Journal of the Society of Community Medicine
Publ Heal R — Public Health Reviews
Publ Health Lab — Public Health Laboratory
Publ Hea Re — Public Health Reports
Publ Hlth Rep (Wash) — Public Health Reports (Washington, DC)
Publ Hung Min Res Inst — Publications. Hungarian Mining Research Institute
Publ Hung Res Inst Mining — Publications. Hungarian Research Institute for Mining
Pub Lib — Public Libraries
Pub Lib Op — Public Library Opinion
Pub Lib Trustee — Public Library Trustee
Publicaciones Dept Agric Costa Rica — Publicaciones. Departamento de Agricultura de Costa Rica
Public Adm — Public Administration
Public Adm Bull — Public Administration Bulletin
Public Admin — Public Administration
Public Admin Bull — Public Administration Bulletin
Public Admin and Development — Public Administration and Development
Public Admin J (Kathmandu) — Public Administration Journal (Kathmandu)
Public Admin R — Public Administration Review
Public Admin Survey — Public Administration Survey
Public Adm R — Public Administration Review
Public Adm Rev — Public Administration Review
Public Affairs Rept — Public Affairs Report
Public Aff Rep — Public Affairs Report
Public Anal Assoc J — Public Analysts Association. Journal [*England*]
Public Budgeting and Fin — Public Budgeting and Finance
Public Fin — Public Finance
Public Fin Account — Public Finance and Accountancy
Public Fin (Berlin) — Public Finance (Berlin)
Public Fin Q — Public Finance Quarterly
Public Health Eng — Public Health Engineer [*England*]
Public Health Eng Abstr — Public Health Engineering Abstracts
Public Health J — Public Health Journal
Public Health Lab — Public Health Laboratory [*United States*]
Public Health Monogr — Public Health Monograph
Public Health Pap — Public Health Papers
Public Health Rep — Public Health Reports
Public Health Rev — Public Health Reviews
Public Health Revs — Public Health Reviews
Public Land Resour Law Dig — Public Land and Resources Law Digest [*United States*]
Public Lib — Public Libraries
Public Opin — Public Opinion
Public Opinion Q — Public Opinion Quarterly
Public Opin Q — Public Opinion Quarterly
Public Pers Manage — Public Personnel Management
Public Rel — Public Relations Journal
Public Relations R — Public Relations Review
Public Relat J — Public Relations Journal
Public Relat Q — Public Relations Quarterly
Public Relat Rev — Public Relations Review
Public Sect — Public Sector. New Zealand Institute of Public Administration
Public Serv Action — Public Service Action
Public TC Review — Public Telecommunications Review
Public Util Fortn — Public Utilities Fortnightly
Public Works Eng Yearb — Public Works Engineers' Yearbook
Public Works Local Gov Eng — Public Works and Local Government Engineering
Public Works Rev — Public Works Review [*Japan*]
Public Works Roads Transp — Public Works, Roads, and Transport
Public Works Ser — Public Works and Services
Public Work (Syd) — Public Works and Services (Sydney)
Publ INCAR — Publicacion INCAR [*Instituto Nacional del Carbon y Sus Derivados "Francisco Pintado Fe"*]
Publ Inst Antart Argent (B Aires) — Publicacion. Instituto Antartico Argentino (Buenos Aires)
Publ Inst Biol Apl (Barc) — Publicaciones. Instituto de Biologia Aplicada (Barcelona)
Publ Inst Biol Apl (Barcelona) — Publicaciones. Instituto de Biologia Aplicada (Barcelona)
Publ Inst Bot "Dr Goncalo Sampaio" Fac Cienc Univ Porto — Publicacoes. Instituto de Botanica "Dr. Goncalo Sampaio." Faculdade de Ciencias. Universidade do Porto

Publ Inst Edafol Hidrol Univ Nac Sur (Bahia Blanca) — Publicaciones. Instituto de Edafologia e Hidrologia. Universidad Nacional del Sur (Bahia Blanca)
Publ Inst Fis "Alonso De St Cruz" — Publicaciones. Instituto de Fisica "Alonso De Santa Cruz"
Publ Inst Florestal — Publicacao. Instituto Florestal
Publ Inst Found Engng Soil Mech Rock Mech Waterways Constr — Publications. Institute of Foundation Engineering, Soil Mechanics, Rock Mechanics, and Waterways Construction
Publ Inst Fr Pet Collect Colloq Semin — Publications. Institut Francais du Petrole. Collection Colloques et Seminaires [*France*]
Publ Inst Geogr (Bogota) — Publication. Instituto Geografico Agustin Codazzi (Bogota)
Publ Inst Geol (Barcelona) — Publicaciones. Instituto Geologico (Barcelona)
Publ Inst Geol Topogr — Publicaciones. Instituto Geologico Topografico
Publ Inst Geophys Pol Acad Sci — Publication. Institute of Geophysics. Polish Academy of Sciences
Publ Inst Geophys Pol Acad Sci Ser A — Publications. Institute of Geophysics. Polish Academy of Sciences. Series A. Physics of the Earth Interior
Publ Inst Geophys Pol Acad Sci Ser C — Publications. Institute of Geophysics. Polish Academy of Sciences. Series C. Earth Magnetism
Publ Inst Geophys Pol Acad Sci Ser F — Publications. Institute of Geophysics. Polish Academy of Sciences. Series F. Planetary Geodesy
Publ Inst Geophys Ser D Pol Acad Sci — Publications. Institute of Geophysics. Polish Academy of Sciences. Series D. Atmosphere Physics
Publ Inst Invest Geol Diputacion Barcelona — Publicaciones. Instituto de Investigaciones Geologicas. Diputacion de Barcelona
Publ Inst Invest Geol Diputacion Prov Barcelona — Publicaciones. Instituto de Investigaciones Geologicas. Diputacion Provincial de Barcelona
Publ Inst Invest Microquim Univ Nac Litoral (Rosario Argent) — Publicaciones. Instituto de Investigaciones Microquimicas. Universidad Nacional del Litoral (Rosario, Argentina)
Publ Inst Mar Sci Nat Fish Univ Busan — Publications. Institute of Marine Sciences. National Fisheries. University of Busan
Publ Inst Mar Sci Univ Tex — Publications. Institute of Marine Science. University of Texas
Publ Inst Mar Sci Univ Texas — Publications. Institute of Marine Science. University of Texas
Publ Inst Math (Belgrade) — Publications. Institut Mathematique. Nouvelle Serie (Belgrade)
Publ Inst Math (Belgrad) NS — Institut Mathematique. Publications. Nouvelle Serie (Belgrade)
Publ Inst Math Univ Nancago — Publications. Institut Mathematique. Universite de Nancago [*Paris*]
Publ Inst Math Univ Strasbourg — Publications. Institut de Mathematiques. Universite de Strasbourg
Publ Inst Mex Recursos Nat Renov — Publicacion. Instituto Mexicano de Recursos Naturales Renovables
Publ Inst Mineral Paleontol Quat Geol Univ Lund — Publications. Institutes of Mineralogy, Paleontology, and Quaternary Geology. University of Lund
Publ Inst Nac Carbon Sus Deriv "Francisco Pintado Fe" — Publicacion. Instituto Nacional del Carbon y Sus Derivados "Francisco Pintado Fe"
Publ Inst Nac Nutr (Argent) Publ Cient — Publicaciones. Instituto Nacional de la Nutricion (Argentina). Publicaciones Cientificas
Publ Inst Nat Etude Agron Congo — Publications. Institut National pour l'Etude Agronomique du Congo
Publ Inst Nat Etude Agron Congo (INEAC) Serie Scientifique — Publications. Institut National pour l'Etude Agronomique du Congo (INEAC). Serie Scientifique
Publ Inst Natl Etude Agron Congo Belge Ser Sci — Publications. Institut National pour l'Etude Agronomique du Congo Belge. Serie Scientifique
Publ Inst Natl Etude Agron Congo Ser Sci — Publications. Institut National pour l'Etude Agronomique du Congo. Serie Scientifique
Publ Inst Natl Etude Agron Congo Ser Tech — Publications. Institut National pour l'Etude Agronomique du Congo. Serie Technique
Publ Inst Opt Madrid — Publicaciones. Instituto de Optica Daza de Valdes de Madrid
Publ Inst Pesqui Mar — Publicacao. Instituto de Pesquisas da Marinha
Publ Inst Quim Fis Rocasolano — Publicaciones. Instituto de Quimica Fisica "Rocasolano"
Publ Inst Rech Sider Ser B — Publications. Institut de Recherches de la Siderurgie. Serie B
Publ Inst Rech Siderurg Ser A — Publications. Institut de Recherches de la Siderurgie [*Saint-Germain-En-Laye*]. Serie A
Publ Inst R Meteorol Belg A — Publications. Institut Royal Meteorologique de Belgique. Serie A. Format in-4
Publ Inst R Meteorol Belg B — Publications. Institut Royal Meteorologique de Belgique. Serie B. Format in-8
Publ Inst R Meteorol Belg Ser A — Publications. Institut Royal Meteorologique de Belgique. Serie A. Format in-4
Publ Inst R Meteorol Belg Ser B — Publications. Institut Royal Meteorologique de Belgique. Serie B
Publ Inst Soil Rock Mech Univ Fridericiana (Karlsruhe) — Publications. Institute for Soil and Rock Mechanics. University of Fridericiana (Karlsruhe)

Publ Inst Statist Univ Paris — Publications. Institut de Statistique. Universite de Paris

Publ Inst Suflos Agrotec (B Aires) — Publicacion. Instituto de Suflos y Agrotecnia (Buenos Aires)

Publ Inst Tecnol Estud Super Monterrey Ser Cienc Biol — Publicaciones. Instituto Tecnologico y de Estudios Superiores de Monterrey. Serie Ciencias Biologicas

Publ Inst Zool "Dr Augusto Nobre" Fac Cienc Porto — Publicacoes. Instituto de Zoologia "Dr. Augusto Nobreda." Faculdade de Ciencias. Universidade do Porto

Publ Inst Zootec (Rio De J) — Publicacao. Instituto de Zootecnia (Rio De Janeiro)

Publ Int Ass Scient Hydrol Symp (Budapest) — Publication. International Association of Scientific Hydrology. Symposium (Budapest)

Publ Inter — Public Interest

Publ Intern Postgrado — Publicaciones Internas del Postgrado

Publishers — Publishers' Weekly

Publius J F — Publius. Journal of Federalism

Publ Junta Nac Prod Pecu Ser A Ser Cient Invest — Publicacoes. Junta Nacional dos Produtos Pecuarios. Serie A. Serie Cientifica e de Investigacao

Publ Korean Natl Astron Obs — Publications. Korean National Astronomical Observatory [*Republic of Korea*]

Publ Lab Biochim Nutr Univ Cathol Louvain Fac Sci Agron — Publication. Laboratoire de Biochimie de la Nutrition. Universite Catholique de Louvain. Faculte des Sciences Agronomiques

Publ Lab Cent Ensayo Mater Constr (Madrid) — Publication. Laboratorio Central de Ensayo de Materiales de Construccion (Madrid)

Publ Lab Jefferson Med Coll Hosp — Publications. Laboratories of the Jefferson Medical College Hospital

Publ Lab Photoelasticite Ecole Polytech Fed (Zurich) — Publications. Laboratoire de Photoelasticite. Ecole Polytechnique Federale (Zurich)

Publ Lab Physiol Chem Univ Amsterdam — Publications. Laboratory of Physiological Chemistry. University of Amsterdam

Publ Law (London) — Public Law (London)

Publ Ld Capability Surv Trinidad & Tobago — Publication. Land Capability Survey of Trinidad and Tobago

Publ Ltg — Public Lighting

Publ Manitoba Beekprs Ass — Publication. Manitoba Beekeepers' Association

Publ Mar Biol Stn (Al Ghardaqa) — Publications. Marine Biological Station (Al Ghardaqa)

Publ Mar Biol Stn (Ghardaqa Red Sea) — Publications. Marine Biological Station (Al Ghardaqa, Red Sea)

Publ Mar Lab Pusan Fish Coll — Publications. Marine Laboratory. Pusan Fisheries College [*South Korea*]

Publ Math Debrecen — Publicationes Mathematicae. Universitatis Debreceniensis

Publ Math Orsay 80 — Publications Mathematiques d'Orsay 80

Publ Math Orsay 81 — Publications Mathematiques d'Orsay 81

Publ Math Orsay 82 — Publications Mathematiques d'Orsay 82

Publ Math Res Center Univ Wisconsin — Publications. Mathematics Research Center. University of Wisconsin

Publ Math Res Cent Univ Wis — Publication. Mathematics Research Center. University of Wisconsin

Publ Math Res Inst (Istanbul) — Publications. Mathematical Research Institute (Istanbul)

Publ Math Soc Japan — Publications. Mathematical Society of Japan

Publ Math Univ Bordeaux — Publications Mathematiques. Universite de Bordeaux

Publ Math Univ Paris VII — Publications Mathematiques. Universite de Paris. VII

Publ Math Univ Pierre et Marie Curie — Publications Mathematiques. Universite Pierre et Marie Curie

Publ Med Exp Univ Chile — Publicaciones de Medicina Experimental. Universidad de Chile

Publ Metaalinst TNO — Publikatie. Metaalinstituut TNO [*Nederlands Centrale Organisatie voor Toegepast-Natuurwetenschappelijk Onderzoek*]

Publ Min Agr Ser Premios Nac Invest Agr — Publicaciones. Ministerio de Agricultura. Serie. Premios Nacionales de Investigacion Agraria

Publ Minist Agric (Can) — Publication. Ministry of Agriculture (Canada)

Publ Misc Agric Univ Chile Fac Agron — Publicaciones Miscelaneas Agricolas. Universidad de Chile. Facultad de Agronomia

Publ Misc Estac Exp Agr Tucuman — Publicaciones Miscelaneas. Estacion Experimental Agricola de Tucuman

Publ Miss State Univ Agr Ext Serv — Publication. Mississippi State University. Agricultural Extension Service

Publ Mus Hist Nat "Javier Prado" Ser A Zool — Publicaciones. Museo de Historia Natural "Javier Prado." Series A. Zoologia

Publ Mus Hist Nat "Javier Prado" Ser B Bot — Publicaciones. Museo de Historia Natural "Javier Prado." Series B. Botanica

Publ Mus Hist Nat Javier Prado Ser C Geol — Publicaciones. Museo de Historia Natural "Javier Prado." Series C. Geologia

Publ Mus Lab Mineral Geol Fac Cienc Porto — Publicacoes. Museu e Laboratorio Mineralogico e Geologico. Faculdade de Ciencias do Porto

Publ Mus Mich State Univ Biol Ser — Publications. Museum. Michigan State University. Biological Series

Publ Nat Acad Sci Nat Res Counc — Publication. National Academy of Sciences. National Research Council

Publ Natn Acad Sci Natn Res Coun (Wash) — Publication. National Academy of Sciences. National Research Council (Washington)

Publ Natuurhist Genoot Limburg — Publicaties. Natuurhistorisch Genootschap in Limburg

Publnes Misc Minist Agric Ganad Repub Argent — Publicaciones Miscelaneas. Ministerio de Agricultura y Ganaderia. Republica de Argentina

Publn Inst Nac Tec Agropec (B Aires) — Publicacion. Instituto Nacional de Tecnologia Agropecuaria (Buenos Aires)

Publ Nor Inst Kosm Fys — Publikasjoner. Norske Institutt foer Kosmisk Fysikk

Publ Obs Univ Mich — Publications. Observatory. University of Michigan

Publ Ocas Mus Cienc Nat (Caracas) Zool — Publicaciones Ocasionales. Museo de Ciencias Naturales (Caracas). Zoologia

Publ OECD (Paris) — Publication. OECD [*Organization for Economic Cooperation and Development*] (Paris)

Publ Ont Dep Agric — Publication. Ontario Department of Agriculture and Food

Publ Opin Q — Public Opinion Quarterly

Publ Pacif Nth-West Co-Op Ext Serv — Publication. Pacific Northwest Cooperative Extension Service

Publ Palaeontol Inst Univ Upps Spec Vol — Publications. Palaeontological Institution. University of Uppsala. Special Volume

Publ Pers M — Public Personnel Management

Publ Personnel Manag — Public Personnel Management

Publ Pol — Public Policy

Publ Policy — Public Policy

Publ Purdue Univ Sch Civ Eng — Publication. Purdue University. School of Civil Engineering

Publ Ramanujan Inst — Publications. Ramanujan Institute

Publ R Coll Physicians Edinburgh — Publication. Royal College of Physicians of Edinburgh

Publ Relat Congo Belg Reg Voisines — Publications Relatives au Congo Belge et aux Regions Voisines

Publ Res Inst Math Sci — Publications. Kyoto University. Research Institute for Mathematical Sciences

Publ Res Inst Math Sci Ser A — Publications. Research Institute for Mathematical Sciences. Series A [*Japan*]

Publ Res Inst Math Sci Ser B — Publications. Research Institute for Mathematical Sciences. Series B [*Japan*]

Publ Roads — Public Roads

Publ R Obs (Edinburgh) — Publications. Royal Observatory (Edinburgh)

Publ S Afr Inst Med Res — Publications. South African Institute for Medical Research

Publs ANARE Data Rep Ser — Publications. ANARE [*Australian National Antarctic Research Expeditions*] Data Reports Series

Publs ANARE Interim Rep Ser — Publications. ANARE [*Australian National Antarctic Research Expeditions*] Interim Reports Series

Publs ANARE Sci Rep Ser — Publications. ANARE [*Australian National Antarctic Research Expeditions*] Scientific Reports Series

Publs Aust Soc Soil Sci — Publications. Australian Society of Soil Science

Publs Aust Soc Soil Science — Publications. Australian Society of Soil Science

Publ Scient Univ Alger Ser B — Publications Scientifiques. Universite d'Alger. Serie B. Sciences Physiques

Publ Sci Tech Min Air — Publications Scientifiques et Techniques. Ministere de l'Air [*France*]

Publ Sci Tech Min Air Bull Serv Tech — Publications Scientifiques et Techniques. Ministere de l'Air. Bulletins des Services Techniques [*France*]

Publ Sci Tech Min Air Notes Tech — Publications Scientifiques et Techniques. Ministere de l'Air [*France*]. Notes Techniques

Publ Sci Tech Minist Air (Fr) — Publications Scientifiques et Techniques. Ministere de l'Air (France)

Publ Sci Tech Minist Air (Fr) Bull Serv Tech — Publications Scientifiques et Techniques. Ministere de l'Air (France). Bul letin des Services Techniques

Publs Co-Op Ext Univ Mass Coll Agric — Publications. Co-Operative Extension Service. University of Massachusetts. College of Agriculture

Publs Dep Agric (Alberta) — Publications. Department of Agriculture (Alberta)

Publs Dep Agric (Can) — Publications. Department of Agriculture (Canada)

Publ Sem Geom Univ Neuchatel Ser 2 — Publications. Seminaire de Geometrie. Universite de Neuchatel. Serie 2

Publ Sem Geom Univ Neuchatel Ser 3 — Publications. Seminaire de Geometrie. Universite de Neuchatel. Serie 3

Publ Sem Mat Garcia De Galdeano — Publicaciones. Seminario Matematico Garcia De Galdeano

Publ Serv Flor Aqueic (Portugal) — Publicacoes. Direccao Geral dos Servicos Florestais e Aqueicolas (Lisbon, Portugal)

Publ Serv Geol Alger Bull — Publications. Service Geologique de l'Algerie. Bulletin

Publ Serv Geol Luxemb — Publications. Service Geologique de Luxembourg

Publ Serv Piscic Ser I-C — Publicacao. Servico de Piscicultura. Serie I-C

Publ Serv Plagas For (Madrid) — Publicacion. Servicio de Plagas Forestales (Madrid)
Publ Seto Mar Biol Lab — Publications. Seto Marine Biological Laboratory
Publs Geol Surv QD — Publications. Geological Survey of Queensland
Publs Geol Surv QD Palaeont Pap — Publications. Geological Survey of Queensland. Palaeontological Papers
Publ S Ill Univ Sch Agr — Publication. Southern Illinois University. School of Agriculture
Publs Indiana Dep Conserv — Publications. Indiana Department of Conservation
Publs Inst Natn Etude Agron Congo Ser Sci — Publications. Institut National pour l'Etude Agronomique du Congo. Serie Scientifique
Publs Manitoba Dep Agric — Publications. Manitoba Department of Agriculture
Publs Maria Moors Cabot Fdn Bot Res — Publications. Maria Moors Cabot Foundation for Botanical Research
Publs Met Dep Melb Univ — Publications. Meteorology Department. University of Melbourne
Publ Smithson Inst — Publication. Smithsonian Institution
Publ Soc Geol Nord — Publication. Societe Geologique du Nord
Publ Soc Savante Alsace Reg Est — Publications. Societe Savante d'Alsace et des Regions de l'Est
Publ Soil Bur (NZ) — Publication. Soil Bureau. Department of Scientific and Industrial Research (New Zealand)
Publs Osaka Mus Nat Hist — Publications. Osaka Museum of Natural History
Publ SP Am Concr Inst — Publication SP. American Concrete Institute
Publs Petrol Search Subsidy Acts — Publications. Petroleum Search Subsidy Acts. Bureau of Mineral Resources, Geology, and Geophysics [*Australia*]
Publ Sta Fed Essais Agr (Lausanne) — Publications. Stations Federales d'Essais Agricoles (Lausanne)
Publ State Inst Agric Chem (Finl) — Publications. State Institute of Agricultural Chemistry (Finland)
Publ State Inst Tech Res — Publications. State Institute for Technical Research
Publ Stn Fed Essais Agric (Lausanne) — Publication. Stations Federales d'Essais Agricoles (Lausanne)
Publ Systematics Ass — Publication. Systematics Association
Publ Tartu Astrofiz Obs — Publikatsii Tartuskoi Astrofizicheskoi Observatorii [*Estonian SSR*]
Publ Tec Estac Exp Agropecuar INTA (Pergamino) — Publicaciones Tecnicas. Estacion Experimental Agropecuaria. INTA [*Instituto Nacional de Tecnologia Agropecuaria*] (Pergamino)
Publ Tec Estac Exp Agropecuar Manfredi (Argentina) — Publicaciones Tecnicas. Estacion Experimental Agropecuaria de Manfredi (Argentina)
Publ Tech Charbon Fr Inf Tech — Publications Techniques des Charbonnages de France. Informations Techniques
Publ Tech Inst Belge Amelior Betterave Tirlemont — Publications Techniques. Institut Belge pour l'Amelioration de la Betterave Tirlemont
Publ Technion Israel Inst Technol Agric Eng Fac — Publication-Technion. Israel Institute of Technology. Agricultural Engineering Faculty
Publ Tech Pap Proc Annu Meet Sugar Ind Technol Inc — Publication of Technical Papers and Proceedings. Annual Meeting of Sugar Industry Technologists, Incorporated
Publ Tech Res Cen Finl Mater Process Technol — Publication. Technical Research Centre of Finland. Materials and Processing Technology
Publ Tech Univ Heavy Ind (Miskoic) Ser B Metall — Publications. Technical University for Heavy Industry (Miskoic). Series B. Metallurgy [*Hungary*]
Publ Tec Inst Patol Veg (B Aires) — Publicacion Tecnica. Instituto de Patologia Vegetal (Buenos Aires)
Publ Tec Patronato Invest Cient Tec "Juan De La Cierva" — Publicaciones Tecnicas. Patronato de Investigacion Cientifica y Tecnica "Juan De La Cierva"
Publ Tehn Fak u Sarajevu — Publikacije Tehnickog Fakulteta u Sarajevu
Publ Thoresby Soc — Publications. Thoresby Society
Publ Trimest Univ Pontif Bolivar — Publicacion Trimestral. Universidad Pontificia Bolivariana
Publ UER Math Pures Appl IRMA — Publications. Unites d'Enseignement et de Recherche de Mathematiques Pures et Appliquees. Institut de Recherche de Mathematiques Avancees
Publ Univ Auton St Domingo — Publicaciones. Universidad Autonoma de Santo Domingo
Publ Univ Calif Agric Ext Serv — Publication. University of California. Agricultural Extension Service
Publ Univ Costa Rica Ser Cienc Nat — Publicaciones. Universidad de Costa Rica. Serie Ciencias Naturales
Publ Univ Europ — Publications Universitaires Europeennes [*Frankfurt Am Main*]
Publ Univ Joensuu Ser B — Publications. University of Joensuu. Series B [*Finland*]
Publ Univ Joensuu Ser B-I — Publications. University of Joensuu. Series B-I
Publ Univ Joensuu Ser B-II — Publications. University of Joensuu. Series B-II
Publ Univ Kuopio Community Health Ser Orig Rep — Publications. University of Kuopio. Community Health Series. Original Reports

Publ Univ Nac Litoral Inst Fisiogr Geol — Publicaciones. Universidad Nacional del Litoral. Instituto de Fisiografia y Geologia
Publ Univ Nac Tucuman Fac Agron Zootec — Publicacion. Universidad Nacional de Tucuman. Facultad de Agronomia y Zootecnia
Publ Univ Off Congo Elisabethville — Publications. Universite Officielle du Congo a Elisabethville
Publ Univ Off Congo Lubumbashi — Publications. Universite Officielle du Congo a Lubumbashi
Publ Univ Pretoria — Publikasies. Universiteit van Pretoria
Publ Univ Sevilla Ser Med — Publicaciones. Universidad de Sevilla. Serie Medicina
Publ Univ Toronto Dep Civ Eng — Publication. University of Toronto. Department of Civil Engineering
Publ Univ Toulouse-Le Mirail Ser A — Publications. Universite de Toulouse-Le Mirail. Serie A.
Publ Univ Wis Ext — Publication. University of Wisconsin Extension
Publ US Agric Res Serv — Publication. United States Agricultural Research Service
Publ US Int Trade Commn — Publication. United States International Trade Commission
Publ US Natl Tech Inf Serv — United States. National Technical Information Service. Publication
Publ Utah Geol Assoc — Publication. Utah Geological Association
Publ Vulkaninst Immanuel Friedlaender — Publikationen Herausgegeben von der Stiftung Vulkaninstitut Immanuel Friedlaender
Publ W — Publishers' Weekly
Publ Wagner Free Inst Sci Philadelphia — Publications. Wagner Free Institute of Science of Philadelphia
Publ Welfar — Public Welfare
Publ Wiss Filmen Sekt Tech Wiss Naturwiss — Publikationen zu Wissenschaftlichen Filmen. Sektion Technische Wissenschaften. Naturwissenschaften
Publ W J Barrow Res Lab — Publication. W. J. Barrow Research Laboratory
Publ Wkly — Publishers' Weekly
Publ Wks — Public Works
Publ Wks Local Govt Engng — Public Works and Local Government Engineering
Pub Manag — Public Management
Pub Mgt — Public Management
Pub Opin — Public Opinion
Pub Opinion Q — Public Opinion Quarterly
Pub Op Q — Public Opinion Quarterly
Pub Pers Mgt — Public Personnel Management
Pub Pol — Public Policy
Pub Rel J — Public Relations Journal
Pub Rel Q — Public Relations Quarterly
Pub Roads — Public Roads
Pub Roch Hist Soc — Publication Fund Series. Rochester Historical Society
Pubs Ceramicas — Publicaciones Ceramicas
Pub Service J Vic — Public Service Journal of Victoria
Pub Serv Management — Public Service Management
Pub Soc Bras Nematol — Publicacao. Sociedade Brasileira de Nematologia
Pubs Petrol Search Subsidy Acts — Publications. Petroleum Search Subsidy Acts. Bureau of Mineral Resources, Geology, and Geophysics [*Australia*]
Pub Util — Public Utilities Fortnightly
Pub Util Fort — Public Utilities Fortnightly
Pub W — Publishers' Weekly
Pub Wel — Public Welfare
PUCaILL — Publications. University of California. Languages and Literature
PUCODM — Conseil Scientifique International de Recherches sur les Trypanosomiases et leur Controle
PUDCPAHM — Poona University and Deccan College Publications in Archaeology and History of Maharashtra
PUDOC Annu Rep — PUDOC [*Centre for Agricultural Publishing and Documentation*] Annual Report
PUDOC (Cent Landbouwpubl Landbouwdoc) Literatuuroverz — PUDOC (Centrum voor Landbouwpublikaties en Landbouwdocumentatie) Literatuuroverzicht
PUEE — Publications. Universite de l'Etat a Elisabethville
Puer Rico — Puerto Rico Libre
Puerto Rico Bus R — Puerto Rico Business Review
Puerto Rico Dept Indus Research Bull — Puerto Rico. Department of Industrial Research. Bulletin
Puerto Rico Univ Agr Expt Sta Tech Paper — Puerto Rico University. Agricultural Experiment Station. Technical Paper
Puerto Rico Water Resources Authority Water Resources Bull — Puerto Rico. Water Resources Authority. Water Resources Bulletin
PUF — Pluimveehouderij
PUF — Presses Universitaires de France
PUF — Public Utilities Fortnightly
PUG — Porzellan und Glas
PUG — Universite de Grenoble
Puglia Chir — Puglia Chirurgica
PUH — Purchasing
PUHS — Proceedings. Unitarian Historical Society

PUKOD — Puresutoresuto Konkurito
PUL — Public Ledger
PULC — Princeton University Library Chronicle
Pull Groupe Etud Rythmes Biol — Bulletin. Groupe d'Etude des Rythmes Biologiques
Pulp & Pa — Pulp and Paper
Pulp & Pa Can — Pulp and Paper Magazine of Canada [*Later, Pulp and Paper (Canada)*]
Pulp Pap — Pulp and Paper
Pulp Pap & Board — Pulp, Paper, and Board
Pulp Pap (Can) — Pulp and Paper (Canada)
Pulp and Pap (Can) — Pulp and Paper (Canada)
Pulp & Pap Eng — Pulp and Paper Engineering
Pulp Paper Mag Can — Pulp and Paper Magazine of Canada [*Later, Pulp and Paper (Canada)*]
Pulp Paper Manual Can — Pulp and Paper Manual of Canada
Pulp Pap Int — Pulp and Paper International
Pulpwood Annu — Pulpwood Annual [*United States*]
Pulpwood Prodn — Pulpwood Production and Sawmill Logging
PUM — PW. Maandblad voor Personeelswerk en Arbeidsverhoudingen
PUM — Pytannja Ukrajins'koho Movoznavstva
Pump Eng (Tokyo) — Pump Engineering (Tokyo)
Pumpen & Verdichter Inf — Pumpen und Verdichter Information
Pumps — Pumps-Pompes-Pumpen [*England*]
Pumps Their Appl — Pumps and Their Applications [*England*]
PUMTA — Trace Substances in Environmental Health
Punjab Med J — Punjab Medical Journal
Punjabrao Krishi Vidyapeeth Coll Agric (Nagpur) Mag — Punjabrao Krishi Vidyapeeth. College of Agriculture (Nagpur). Magazine
Punjabrao Krishi Vidyapeeth Res J — Punjabrao Krishi Vidyapeeth. Research Journal
Punjab Univ J Math (Lahore) — Punjab University. Journal of Mathematics (Lahore)
P U Otago M — Proceedings. University of Otago Medical School
Pur A Chem — Pure and Applied Chemistry
Pur A Geoph — Pure and Applied Geophysics
PURBA — Panjab University. Research Bulletin (Arts)
Purch Adm — Purchasing Administration
Purchasing — Purchasing World
Purch (S Afr) — Purchasing (South Africa)
Purdue Ag — Purdue Agriculturist
Purdue Air Qual Conf Proc — Purdue Air Quality Conference. Proceedings
Purdue Univ Agric Exp Stn Res Bull — Purdue University. Agricultural Experiment Station. Research Bulletin
Purdue Univ Agric Exp Stn Stn Bull — Purdue University. Agricultural Experiment Station. Station Bulletin
Purdue Univ Dept Agr Ext Mimeo AY — Purdue University. Department of Agricultural Extension. Mimeo AY
Purdue Univ Eng Bull Eng Ext Ser — Purdue University. Engineering Bulletin. Engineering Extension Series
Purdue Univ Eng Exp Sta Res Bull — Purdue University. Engineering Experiment Station. Research Bulletin
Purdue Univ Ext Publ — Purdue University. Extension Publications
Purdue Univ Sch Aeronaut Astronaut Eng Sci Res Proj — Purdue University. School of Aeronautics, Astronautics, and Engineering Sciences. Research Project
Purdue Univ Water Resources Research Center Tech Rept — Purdue University. Water Resources Research Center. Technical Report
Purdue Univ Water Resour Res Cent Tech Rep — Purdue University. Water Resources Research Center. Technical Report
Pure Appl Chem — Pure and Applied Chemistry
Pure and Appl Chem — Pure and Applied Chemistry
Pure Appl Cryog — Pure and Applied Cryogenics
Pure and Appl Geophys — Pure and Applied Geophysics
Pure Appl Geophys — Pure and Applied Geophysics
Pure and Appl Math — Pure and Applied Mathematics
Pure Appl Math — Pure and Applied Mathematics
Pure Appl Phys — Pure and Applied Physics
Pure Prod — Pure Products
PURMA — Purasuchikku Materiaru
PUSA — Perspectives USA
PUSC — Pubblicazioni. Universita Cattolica del Sacro Cuore
Puti Povysh Intensivn Prod Fotosint — Puti Povysheniya Intensivnosti i Produktivnosti Fotosinteza
Puti Povysh Intensivn Prod Fotosint Resp Mezhved Sb — Puti Povysheniya Intensivnosti i Produktivnosti Fotosinteza Respublikanskii Mezhvedomstvennyi Sbornik
Puti Sint Izyskaniya Protivoopukholevykh Prep — Puti Sinteza i Izyskaniya Protivoopukholevykh Preparatov
Putnam — Putnam's Monthly Magazine
PUV — Pulp and Paper
PuW — Poesie und Wissenschaft
PV — Pacific Viewpoint
PV — Poesia e Verita
PV — Principe de Viana
PV — Problemy Vostokovedenija

PVAGA — Pochvoznanie i Agrokhimiya
PVBPA — Proceedings of Vibration Problems [*Poland*]
PVBRDX — Brazilian Journal of Veterinary Research
PVC — Points de Vente. Le Magazine des Magasins
PVP — Modern Paint and Coatings
P & V Prod — Paint and Varnish Production
PVR — Platte Valley Review
PVS — Proceedings. Virgil Society
PVSCA — Proceedings. Veterans Administration Spinal Cord Injury Conference
P-V Seances Com Int Poids Mes — Proces-Verbaux des Seances. Comite International des Poids et Mesures
P-V Seances Soc Sci Phys Nat Bord — Proces-Verbaux des Seances. Societe des Sciences Physiques et Naturelles de Bordeaux
P-V Seances Soc Sci Phys Nat Bordeaux — Proces-Verbaux des Seances. Societe des Sciences Physiques et Naturelles de Bordeaux
P V Soc Linn Bordeaux — Proces Verbaux. Societe Linneenne de Bordeaux
PVTMA — Preventive Medicine
PVU — PR Revue. Schweizerische Zeitschrift fuer Public Relations
PVZTA — Plyn
PW — Pension World
PW — Philologische Wochenschrift
PW — Poetry Wales
PW — Protestant World
PW — Publishers' Weekly
PWCJS — Proceedings. Fifth World Congress of Jewish Studies [*1969*]
P West Ph S — Proceedings. Western Pharmacology Society
PWFND — Publikationen zu Wissenschaftlichen Filmen. Sektion Technische Wissenschaften. Naturwissenschaften
PWMIB — Powder Metallurgy International
PWN — Polskie Wydawnictwe Naukowe
PWOQD — Psychology of Women Quarterly
PWPMA — Politechnika Warszawska, Prace Naukowe. Mechanika
P W Rev — Price Waterhouse Review
Pwr Fmg — Power Farming
Pwr Fmg Aust NZ — Power Farming in Australia and New Zealand and Better Farming Digest
Pwr Fmg Mag — Power Farming Magazine
Pwr Frmg — Power Farming in Australia and New Zealand
Pwr Frmg Aust NZ — Power Farming in Australia and New Zealand
Pwr Wks Engng — Power and Works Engineering
PWsp — Przeglad Wspotczesny
PWT — Panstwowe Wydawnictwo Techniczne
PWTCA — Powder Technology
PWTN-A — Prace Wroclawskiego Towarzystwa Naukowego. A
PYACA — Psychoanalytic Study of the Child
PYAFB — Psychologia Africana
PYAIA — Postepy Astronomii
PYB — Problems of Economics. A Journal of Translations
PYCHB — Psychology
PYCOA — Phycologia
PYMOA — Psychological Monographs [*General and Applied*]
PYNNA — Psychiatria, Neurologia, Neurochirurgia
PYPYB — Psychophysiology (Baltimore)
PYRCA — Psychological Record
PYRTA — Psychological Reports
PYSCB — Psychology in the Schools
PYSOA — Physiologist
PYSSB — Psychoanalytic Study of Society
PYTCA — Phytochemistry
PZ — Praehistorische Zeitschrift
PZ — Przeglad Zachodni
PZBUA — Przeglad Budowlany [*Poland*]
PZELA — Przeglad Elektrotechniczny
PZKA — Philologus. Zeitschrift fuer Klassische Altertum
PZLSA — Prace z Zakresu Lesnictwa
PZM — Pod Znamenem Marksizma
PZMEA — Przeglad Mechaniczny
PZTFD — Pis'ma v Zhurnal Tekhnicheskoi Fiziki
PZWS — Panstwowe Zaklady Wydawnictwo Szkolnych

Q

Qd Univ Fac Vet Sci Pap — University of Queensland. Faculty of Veterinary Science. Papers
Qd Univ Geol Dep Pap — University of Queensland. Geology Department. Papers
Qd Univ Pap Zool Dep — University of Queensland. Zoology Department. Papers
Qd Univ Zool Dep Pap — University of Queensland. Zoology Department. Papers
Qd Vet Proc — Queensland Veterinary Proceedings
QeA — Questo e Alto
QEBG — Quellen und Eroerterungen zur Bayerischen Geschichte
Q Econ Comment — Quarterly Economic Commentary
Q Econ R — Quarterly Economic Review [*Seoul*]
Q Ed Off Gaz — Education Office Gazette (Queensland Department of Education)
Q Elec Contractor — Queensland Electrical Contractor
QER — Quarterly Economic Review
QF — Quellen und Forschungen aus Italienischen Archiven und Bibliotheken
QF — Quellen und Forschungen zur Sprach- und Kulturgeschichte der Germanischen Voelker
QFAB — Quellen und Forschungen aus Italienischen Archiven und Bibliotheken
QFI — Quellen und Forschungen aus Italienischen Archiven und Bibliotheken
QFIAB — Quellen und Forschungen aus Italienischen Archiven und Bibliotheken
Q Film Radio TV — Quarterly of Film, Radio, and Television
QFINBL — Queensland. Department of Harbours and Marine. Fisheries Notes
QFR — Quarterly Financial Report for Manufacturing Corporations
QFRNAV — Queensland. Department of Forestry. Research Note
QFRT — Quarterly of Film, Radio, and Television
Q Fruit & Veg News — Queensland Fruit and Vegetable News
QFSK — Quellen und Forschungen zur Sprach- und Kulturgeschichte der Germanischen Voelker
Q Fuel Energy Summ — Quarterly Fuel and Energy Summary [*United States*]
Q Geog J — Queensland Geographical Journal
Q Geol Notes Geol Surv South Aust — South Australia. Geological Survey. Quarterly Geological Notes
QGG — Queensland Government Gazette
QGHR — Quellen zur Geschichte des Humanismus und der Reformation in Facsimile-Ausgaben
QGIG — Queensland Government Industrial Gazette
QGJD — Quellen zur Geschichte der Juden in Deutschland
QGM — Quellen und Studien zur Geschichte der Mathematik
QGMath — Quellen und Studien zur Geschichte der Mathematik
QGMJA — Queensland Government Mining Journal
Q Gov Indus Gaz — Queensland Government Industrial Gazette
Q Govt Min J — Queensland Government Mining Journal
Q Govt PRB News Bul — Queensland Government. Public Relations Bureau. News Bulletin
QGP — Queensland Government Publications
Q Graingrower — Queensland Graingrower
QH — Quaker History
QH — Queensland Heritage
Q Health — Queensland's Health
QHR — Queensland Historical Review
QHTA Bull — QHTA [*Queensland History Teachers Association*] Bulletin
QI — Quaderni Ibero-Americani
QI — Quarterly Index
QIA — Quaderni Ibero-Americani
QIBA — Quaderni Italiani di Buenos Aires
QIER J — QIER [*Queensland Institute for Educational Research*] Journal
QIFL — Quaderni. Istituto di Filologia Latina. Universita di Padova
QIG — Quaderni. Istituto di Glottologia [*Bologna*]
QIGB — Quaderni. Istituto di Glottologia (Bologna)
Q Illust — Quarterly Illustrator
QIMA — QIMA. Institute of Municipal Administration, Queensland Division
Q Ind — Queensland Industry
Q Industry — Queensland Industry
QIP Rep Natl Asphalt Pavement Assoc — QIP Report. National Asphalt Pavement Association
QJ — Quarterly Journal. University of North Dakota
QJAAA — Queensland Journal of Agricultural and Animal Sciences
QJ Agric Econ — Quarterly Journal of Agricultural Economy
QJCA — Quarterly Journal of Current Acquisitions
Q J Crude Drug Res — Quarterly Journal of Crude Drug Research
QJE — Quarterly Journal of Economics
Q J Econ — Quarterly Journal of Economics
QJ Eng Geol — Quarterly Journal of Engineering Geology
QJEPs — Quarterly Journal of Experimental Psychology
QJewR — Quarterly Jewish Review
QJewSt — Quarterly of Jewish Studies. Jewish Chronicle
Q J Exp Physiol — Quarterly Journal of Experimental Physiology and Cognate Medical Sciences
Q J Exp Physiol Cogn Med Sci — Quarterly Journal of Experimental Physiology and Cognate Medical Sciences
Q J Exp Psy — Quarterly Journal of Experimental Psychology

Q J Exp Psychol — Quarterly Journal of Experimental Psychology
Q J Exp Psychol B — Quarterly Journal of Experimental Psychology. B. Comparative and Physiological Psychology
Q J Fla Acad Sci — Quarterly Journal. Florida Academy of Sciences
Q J For — Quarterly Journal of Forestry
Q J Forestry — Quarterly Journal of Forestry
Q J Geol Min Metall Soc (India) — Quarterly Journal. Geological, Mining, and Metallurgical Society (India)
Q J Geol Soc Lond — Quarterly Journal. Geological Society of London
Q J Geol Soc London — Quarterly Journal. Geological Society of London
Q J Indian Chem Soc — Quarterly Journal. Indian Chemical Society
Q J Indian Inst Sci — Quarterly Journal. Indian Institute of Science
QJ Int Agric — Quarterly Journal of International Agriculture
QJLC — Quarterly Journal. Library of Congress
Q J Lib Con — Quarterly Journal. Library of Congress
Q J Liverpool Univer Inst Commer Res Trop — Quarterly Journal. Liverpool University Institute of Commercial Research in the Tropics
Q Jl Microsc Sci — Quarterly Journal of Microscopical Science
Q J Local Self Govt Inst — Quarterly Journal. Local Self-Government Institute [*Bombay*]
Q Jl R Met Soc — Quarterly Journal. Royal Meteorological Society
Q Jl Rubb Res Inst Ceylon — Quarterly Journal. Rubber Research Institute of Ceylon [*later, Sri Lanka*]
QJLSGI — Quarterly Journal. Local Self-Government Institute [*Bombay*]
QJLSI — Quarterly Journal. Local Self-Government Institute [*Bombay*]
Q J Math — Quarterly Journal of Mathematics
Q J Mech Ap — Quarterly Journal of Mechanics and Applied Mathematics
QJ Mech Appl Math — Quarterly Journal of Mechanics and Applied Mathematics
QJ Mech and Appl Math — Quarterly Journal of Mechanics and Applied Mathematics
Q J Med — Quarterly Journal of Medicine
Q J Micro Sc — Quarterly Journal of Microscopical Science
Q J Microsc Sci — Quarterly Journal of Microscopical Science
QJMS — Quarterly Journal. Mythic Society
Q Jnl Speech — Quarterly Journal of Speech
Q J Pakistan Lib Assn — Quarterly Journal. Pakistan Library Association [*Karachi*]
QJ Pharm Allied Sci — Quarterly Journal of Pharmacy and Allied Sciences
Q J Pharm Pharmacol — Quarterly Journal of Pharmacy and Pharmacology
QJP (Mag Cas) — Queensland Justice of the Peace (Magisterial Cases)
QJPR — Queensland Justice of the Peace. Reports
Q J Pub Speak — Quarterly Journal of Public Speaking
QJRAA — Quarterly Journal. Royal Astronomical Society
Q J R Astro — Quarterly Journal. Royal Astronomical Society
QJR Astron Soc — Quarterly Journal. Royal Astronomical Society
QJRMA — Quarterly Journal. Royal Meteorological Society
Q J R Meteo — Quarterly Journal. Royal Meteorological Society
Q J R Meteorol Soc — Quarterly Journal. Royal Meteorological Society
Q J Rubber Res Inst Sri Lanka — Quarterly Journal. Rubber Research Institute of Sri Lanka [*formerly, Ceylon*]
QJS — Quarterly Journal of Speech
Q J Sc — Quarterly Journal of Science
Q J Sc — Quarterly Journal of Science, Literature, and the Arts
QJ Sci Lit Arts — Quarterly Journal of Science, Literature, and the Arts
QJ Seismol — Quarterly Journal of Seismology
QJSp — Quarterly Journal of Speech
QJSPA — Quarterly Journal of Speech
Q J Speech — Quarterly Journal of Speech
Q J Stud Al — Quarterly Journal of Studies on Alcohol
Q J Stud Alcohol — Quarterly Journal of Studies on Alcohol
Q J Stud Alcohol Part A — Quarterly Journal of Studies on Alcohol. Part A
QJ Stud Alcohol Suppl — Quarterly Journal of Studies on Alcohol. Supplement
QJ Surg Sci — Quarterly Journal of Surgical Sciences
Q J Taiwan Mus (Taipei) — Quarterly Journal. Taiwan Museum (Taipei)
QJXPA — Quarterly Journal of Experimental Psychology
Qk Froz Fd — Quick Frozen Foods
QL — Quaderni Linguistici
QL — Queensland Lawyer
QL — Quinzaine Litteraire
Q Law Soc J — Queensland Law Society. Journal
QL Beor — Beor's Queensland Law Reports
QLCR — Queensland Land Court Reports
Qld Geog J — Queensland Geographical Journal
Qld Govt Indust Gaz — Queensland Government Industrial Gazette
Qld Health — Queensland's Health
Qld Heritage — Queensland Heritage
Qld Mus Mem — Queensland Museum. Memoirs
Qld Nat — Queensland Naturalist
Qld Parl Deb — Queensland Parliamentary Debates
Qld Sci Teach — Queensland Science Teacher
Qld Teach J — Queensland Teachers' Journal
Qld Univ Law J — University of Queensland. Law Journal
QLFCAE — Fonds de Recherches Forestieres. Universite Laval. Contribution
Q Liberal — Queensland Liberal
QLing — Quantitative Linguistics

QLit — Quebec. Litteraire
Q LJ — Queen's Law Journal
QLJ — Queensland Law Journal
QLJ (NC) — Queensland Law Journal (Notes of Cases)
QLL — Quaderni di Lingue e Letterature
QLP — Questions Liturgiques et Paroissiales
QLR — Queensland Law Reporter
QLR — Queensland Law Reports
QLR (Beor) — Queensland Law Reports (Beor)
QLSJ — Queensland Law Society. Journal
Q Master Plumber — Queensland Master Plumber
QME — Quarber Merkur
Q Med Rev — Quarterly Medical Review
QMGPA — Quarry Management and Products [*Later, Quarry Management*]
QMP — Quarry, Mine, and Pit
QMS — Quarterly Journal. Mythic Society [*Bangalore*]
Q Museum Memoirs — Memoirs. Queensland Museum
Q Natl Fire Prot Assoc — Quarterly. National Fire Protection Association
QNCCR — Quarterly Notes on Christianity and Chinese Religion
QNL — Quarterly News Letter [*Book Club of California*]
Q Oil Stat — Quarterly Oil Statistics [*France*]
QP — Quaderni Portoghesi
QPD — Queensland Parliamentary Debates
Q Pediatr Bull — Quarterly Pediatric Bulletin
Q Philipp Sugar Inst — Quarterly. Philippine Sugar Institute
QPLR — Queensland Planning Law Reports
Q Police J — Queensland Police Journal
Q Population Bul NZ — Quarterly Population Bulletin (New Zealand)
Q Poul Bull — Quarterly Poultry Bulletin
QPP — Queensland Parliamentary Papers
QPR — Quality Progress
QPR — Queensland Practice Reports
Q Predict — Quarterly Predictions of National Income and Expenditure [*New Zealand*]
QQ — Queen's Quarterly
Q and Q — Quill and Quire
QR — Quarterly Review
QR — Quaternary Research
QRADA — Quaderni di Radiologia
QR Ag Econ — Quarterly Review of Agricultural Economics
Q R Agric Econ — Quarterly Review of Agricultural Economics
Q Rass Mus — Quaderni della Rassegna Musicale
QR Aust Educ — Quarterly Review of Australian Education
QRB — Quality Review Bulletin
QRB — Quarterly Review of Biology
QRBIA — Quarterly Review of Biology
Q R Biol — Quarterly Review of Biology
Q R Biophys — Quarterly Review of Biophysics
QRE — Quarterly Review of Economics and Business
QREB — Quarterly Review of Economics and Business
QREBA — Quarterly Review of Economics and Business
Q R Econ Bu — Quarterly Review of Economics and Business
Q R Econ & Bus — Quarterly Review of Economics and Business
Q Rep Railw Tech Res Inst (Tokyo) — Quarterly Report. Railway Technical Research Institute (Tokyo)
Q Rep Univ W Indies Sch Agric — Quarterly Report. University of the West Indies. School of Agriculture
QRESA — Quaternary Research [*New York*]
Q Rev — Quarterly Review
Q Rev Ag Economics — Quarterly Review of Agricultural Economics
Q Rev Agric Econ — Quarterly Review of Agricultural Economics
Q Rev Am Electroplat Soc — Quarterly Review. American Electroplaters' Society
Q Rev Aust Ed — Quarterly Review of Australian Education
Q Rev Biol — Quarterly Review of Biology
Q Rev Bioph — Quarterly Reviews of Biophysics
Q Rev Biophys — Quarterly Reviews of Biophysics
Q Rev Chem Soc — Quarterly Reviews. Chemical Society
Q Rev Chem Soc (Lond) — Quarterly Reviews. Chemical Society (London)
Q Rev Drill Stat US — Quarterly Review. Drilling Statistics for the United States
Q Rev Econ Bus — Quarterly Review of Economics and Business
Q Rev Environ — Quarterly Review on Environment [*Japan*]
Q Rev Evan Luth Ch — Quarterly Review. Evangelical Lutheran Church
Q Rev Film — Quarterly Review of Film Studies
Q Rev F Studies — Quarterly Review of Film Studies
Q Rev Harefuah — Quarterly Review of the Harefuah
Q Rev Hist S — Quarterly Review of Historical Studies
Q Review of F Studies — Quarterly Review of Film Studies
Q Rev Lit — Quarterly Review of Literature
Q Rev Med — Quarterly Review of Medicine
Q Rev Obstet Gynecol — Quarterly Review of Obstetrics and Gynecology
Q Rev Pediatr — Quarterly Review of Pediatrics
Q Rev Soil Assoc — Quarterly Review. The Soil Association
Q Rev Surg — Quarterly Review of Surgery

Q Rev Surg Obstet Gynecol — Quarterly Review of Surgery. Obstetrics and Gynecology
Q Rev Surg Surg Spec — Quarterly Review of Surgery and Surgical Specialities
Q Rev Urol — Quarterly Review of Urology
Q R Film S — Quarterly Review of Film Studies
Q R Higher Ed Among Negroes — Quarterly Review of Higher Education among Negroes
QR Higher Ed Negroes — Quarterly Review of Higher Education among Negroes
Q R Hist Stud — Quarterly Review of Historical Studies
QR J — QR Journal. Indian Association for Quality and Reliability
QRJOD — QR [*Quality and Reliability*] Journal
QRL — Quarterly Review of Literature
QR of Lit — Quarterly Review of Literature
QRM — Quarterly Review of Marketing
Q R Rural Economy — Quarterly Review of the Rural Economy
QRTIA — Quarterly Report. Railway Technical Research Institute
QS — Quaderni di Semitistica [*Florence*]
QS — Quaderni di Storia
QSCR — Queensland. Supreme Court. Reports
QSCR — Supreme Court Reports (Queensland)
QSem — Quaderni di Semantica
QSGLL — Queensland Studies in German Language and Literature
QSR — State Reports (Queensland)
QST — Quarterly Statements. Palestine Exploration Fund
QS Wkly — Quantity Surveyor Weekly
Qt — Quartet
QTDM — Qazaq Tili Tarychy Men Dyalektology Jasinin Moseleleri
Q Teachers J — Queensland Teachers' Journal
Q Tic Num Ant Clas — Quaderni Ticinesi. Numismatica e Antichita Classiche
QTTA — Quaderni Triestini sul Teatro Antico
QU — Quaderni dell'Umanesimo
Quad — Quadrivium
Quad Acta Neurol — Quaderni di Acta Neurologica
Quad Anat Prat — Quaderni di Anatomia Pratica
Quad Azione Soc — Quaderni di Azione Sociale
Quad Chim CNR (Italy) — Quaderni di Chimica. Consiglio Nazionale delle Ricerche (Italy)
Quad Clin Ostet — Quaderni di Clinica Ostetrica e Ginecologica
Quad Coagulazione Argomenti Connessi — Quaderni della Coagulazione e Argomenti Connessi
Quad Criminol Clin — Quaderni di Criminologia Clinica
Quad Econ (Sarda) — Quaderni dell'Economia (Sarda)
Quad Emiliani — Quaderni Emiliani
Quad Ente Naz Semen Elette — Quaderno. Ente Nazionale Sementi Elette
Quaderni della Ra M — Quaderni della Rassegna Musicale
Quad Formaz — Quaderni di Formazione
Quad Geofis Appl — Quaderni di Geofisica Applicata
Quad G Fis — Quaderni del Giornale di Fisica [*Italy*]
Quad Ing Chim Ital — Quaderni dell'Ingegnere Chimico Italiano
Quad Ist Bot Univ Lab Crittogam (Pavia) — Quaderni. Istituto Botanico. Universita Laboratorio Crittogamico (Pavia)
Quad Mathesis Cosenza — Mathesis di Cosenza. Quaderni
Quad Merceol Ist Merceol Univ Bari — Quaderni di Merceologia. Istituto di Merceologia. Universita Bari
Quad Nutr — Quaderni della Nutrizione
Quad Nutr (Bologna) — Quaderni della Nutrizione (Bologna)
Quad Pignone — Quaderni Pignone
Quad Radiol — Quaderni di Radiologia
Quad Ricerca Sci — Quaderni de la Ricerca Scientifica
Quad Ric Progettazione — Quaderni di Ricerca e Progettazione
Quad Ric Sci — Quaderni de la Ricerca Scientifica
Quad Sardi Econ — Quaderni Sardi di Economia
Quad Sclavo Diagn — Quaderni Sclavo di Diagnostica Clinica e di Laboratorio
Quad Sclavo Diagn Clin Lab — Quaderni Sclavo di Diagnostica Clinica e di Laboratorio
Quad Ser III — Quaderni. Serie III
Quad Sez Perugia Soc Ital Biol Sper — Quaderni. Sezione Perugina. Societa Italiana di Biologia Sperimentale
Quad Sociol — Quaderni di Sociologia
Quad Stor — Quaderni Storici
Quad Storia Sci Med Univ Studi Ferrara — Quaderni di Storia della Scienza e della Medicina. Universita degli Studi di Ferrara
Quad Stor Univ Padova — Quaderni per la Storia. Universita di Padova
Quad Tec Sint Spec Org — Quaderni di Tecniche e Sintesi Speciali Organiche
Quad Urb C — Quaderni Urbinati di Cultura Classica
Quaest Ent — Quaestiones Entomologicae
Quaest Entomol — Quaestiones Entomologicae
Quaest Geobiol — Quaestiones Geobiologicae
Quaest Inf — Quaestiones Informaticae
Quaestiones Math — Quaestiones Mathematicae
QuakerH — Quaker History
Qual Assur — Quality Assurance
Qual Contr Appl Stat — Quality Control and Applied Statistics
Qual Eng — Quality Engineer
Qual Eval — Quality Evaluation

Qualitas Pl Pl Fds Human Nutr — Qualitas Plantarum/Plant Foods for Human Nutrition
Qualite Rev Prat Controle Ind — Qualite. Revue Pratique de Controle Industriel
Quality — Quality of Sheffield and South Yorkshire
Quality Prog — Quality Progress
Qual Plant — Qualitas Plantarum/Plant Foods for Human Nutrition
Qual Plant Mater Veg — Qualitas Plantarum et Materiae Vegetables [*Later, Qualitas Plantarum/Plant Foods for Human Nutrition*]
Qual Plant Plant Foods Hum Nutr — Qualitas Plantarum/Plant Foods for Human Nutrition
Qual Prog — Quality Progress
Qual Quant — Quality and Quantity
Qual Reliab J — Quality and Reliability Journal [*India*]
Qual Rev Prat Controle Ind — Qualite. Revue Pratique de Controle Industriel
Qual Today — Quality Today
Qual Zuverlaessigk — Qualitaet und Zuverlaessigkeit
Qual & Zuverlaessigkeit — Qualitaet und Zuverlaessigkeit
Qual und Zuverlassigkeit — Qualitat und Zuverlassigkeit
Quan Sociol — Quantitative Sociology
Quant Chem Symp — Quantum Chemistry Symposia
Quantitative Appl in the Social Sciences — Quantitative Applications in the Social Sciences
Quantitative Meth Unternehmungsplanung — Quantitative Methoden der Unternehmungsplanung
Quantity Surv — Quantity Surveyor
Quantum Electron (New York) — Quantum Electronics (New York)
Quar — Quarterly Review
Quar Jour Econ — Quarterly Journal of Economics
Quar R Biol — Quarterly Review of Biology
Quar Rev — Quarterly Review
Quarry Manage Prod — Quarry Management and Products [*Later, Quarry Management*]
Quarry Mgmt — Quarry Management
Quarry Mgmt Products — Quarry Management and Products [*Later, Quarry Management*]
Quart Appl Math — Quarterly of Applied Mathematics
Quart Bul Ass Food Drug Offic US — Quarterly Bulletin. Association of Food and Drug Officials of the United States [*Later, Quarterly Bulletin. Association of Food and Drug Officials*]
Quart Bull Int Ass Agric Libr Docum — Quarterly Bulletin. International Association of Agricultural Librarians and Documentalists
Quart Bull Mich Agric Exp Sta — Quarterly Bulletin. Michigan State University. Agricultural Experiment Station
Quart Bull Mich State Univ Agr Exp Sta — Quarterly Bulletin. Michigan State University. Agricultural Experiment Station
Quart Colo Sch Mines — Quarterly. Colorado School of Mines
Quarter Horse Dig — Quarter Horse Digest
Quarterly Appl Math — Quarterly of Applied Mathematics
Quarterly of F R TV — Quarterly of Film, Radio, and Television
Quartermaster Food Container Inst Armed Forces Act Rep — Quartermaster Food and Container Institute for the Armed Forces. Activities Report
Quart J Adm — Quarterly Journal of Administration
Quart J Agr Econ — Quarterly Journal of Agricultural Economy
Quart J Chin For (Taipei) — Quarterly Journal of Chinese Forestry (Taipei)
Quart J Crude Drug Res — Quarterly Journal of Crude Drug Research
Quart J Econ — Quarterly Journal of Economics
Quart J Econom — Quarterly Journal of Economics
Quart J Exp Physiol — Quarterly Journal of Experimental Physiology
Quart J Exp Psychol — Quarterly Journal of Experimental Psychology
Quart J For — Quarterly Journal of Forestry
Quart J Indian Inst Sci — Quarterly Journal. Indian Institute of Science
Quart J Libr Congress — Quarterly Journal. Library of Congress
Quart J Math Oxford Ser 2 — Quarterly Journal of Mathematics. Oxford. Second Series
Quart J Mech Appl Math — Quarterly Journal of Mechanics and Applied Mathematics
Quart J Microsc Sci — Quarterly Journal of Microscopical Science
Quart J Micr Sc — Quarterly Journal of Microscopical Science
Quart J Roy Meteorol Soc — Quarterly Journal. Royal Meteorological Society
Quart J Taiwan Mus — Quarterly Journal. Taiwan Museum
Quart J Vet Sc India — Quarterly Journal of Veterinary Science in India and Army Animal Management
Quart Nebr Agr Exp Sta — Quarterly. Nebraska Agricultural Experiment Station
Quart Newsl (Dehra Dun) — Quarterly News Letter. Forest Research Institute and Colleges (Dehra Dun)
Quart Philippine Sugar Inst — Quarterly. Philippine Sugar Institute
Quart R Agric — Quarterly Review of Agricultural Economics
Quart R Agric Econ — Quarterly Review of Agricultural Economics
Quart R Centr Bank Ireland — Quarterly Review. Central Bank of Ireland
Quart R Econ Busin — Quarterly Review of Economics and Business
Quart Rep Ry Tech Res Inst — Quarterly Report. Railway Technical Research Institute [*Tokyo*]
Quart Rev Agr Econ — Quarterly Review of Agricultural Economics
Quart Rev Agric Econ — Quarterly Review of Agricultural Economics

Quart Rev Biol — Quarterly Review of Biology
Quart Rev Guernsey Soc — Quarterly Review. Guernsey Society
Quart Univ Nebr Coll Agr Home Econ Agr Exp Sta — Quarterly. University of Nebraska. College of Agriculture and Home Economics. Agricultural Experiment Station
QUASD — Quality Assurance
Quaternary Res — Quaternary Research
Quatern Res — Quaternary Research
Quat Res (Jap Assoc Quat Res) — Quaternary Research (Japan Association of Quaternary Research)
Quat Res (NY) — Quaternary Research (New York)
Quat Res (Tokyo) — Quaternary Research (Tokyo)
QUCC — Quaderni Urbinati di Cultura Classica
Quebec Dept Nat Resources Prelim Rept — Quebec. Department of Natural Resources. Preliminary Report
Quebec Dept Nat Resources Spec Paper — Quebec. Department of Natural Resources. Special Paper
Quebec Dept Trade and Commerce Geog Service Pub — Quebec. Department of Trade and Commerce. Geographical Service. Publication
Que Cons Rech Dev For Rapp — Quebec. Conseil de la Recherche et du Developpement Forestiers. Rapport
Que Cons Rech Dev For Rapp Annu — Quebec. Conseil de la Recherche et du Developpement Forestiers. Rapport Annuel
Que Dep Ind Commer Annu Rep — Quebec. Department of Industry and Commerce. Annual Report
Que Dep Lands For Res Serv Res Pap — Quebec. Department of Lands and Forest Research Service. Research Paper
Que Dep Natur Resour Geol Rep — Quebec. Department of Natural Resources. Geological Report
Que Dep Natur Resour Prelim Rep — Quebec. Department of Natural Resources. Preliminary Report
Que Dir Geol Trav Terrain — Quebec. Direction de la Geologie. Travaux sur le Terrain
Que Dp Col Mines Br Rp — Quebec. Department of Colonization, Mines, and Fisheries. Mines Branch. Report on Mining Operations
Queen Q — Queen's Quarterly
Queensl — Queensland Reports
Queensl Agric J — Queensland Agricultural Journal
Queensland Ag J — Queensland Agricultural Journal
Queensland Agr J — Queensland Agricultural Journal
Queensland Dent Mag — Queensland Dental Magazine
Queensland Gov Min J — Queensland Government Mining Journal
Queensland Govt Min Jour — Queensland Government Mining Journal
Queensland Hist R — Queensland Historical Review
Queensland J Agr Anim Sci — Queensland Journal of Agricultural and Animal Sciences
Queensland J Ag Sci — Queensland Journal of Agricultural Science [*Later, Queensland Journal of Agricultural and Animal Sciences*]
Queensland Land Court Rep — Queensland Land Court Reports
Queensland L Soc'y J — Queensland Law Society. Journal
Queensland Pap in Econ Policy — Queensland Papers in Economic Policy
Queensl Dent J — Queensland Dental Journal
Queensl Dep Agric Stock — Queensland. Department of Agriculture and Stock. Annual Report
Queensl Dep Mines Geol Surv Queensl Publ — Queensland. Department of Mines. Geological Survey of Queensland. Publication
Queensl Dep Mines Geol Surv Queensl Rep — Queensland. Department of Mines. Geological Survey of Queensland. Report
Queensl Dep Primary Ind Agric Chem Branch Tech Rep — Queensland. Department of Primary Industries. Agricultural Chemistry Branch. Technical Report
Queensl Dep Primary Ind Div Anim Ind Bull — Queensland. Department of Primary Industries. Division of Animal Industry. Bulletin
Queensl Dep Primary Ind Div Dairy Bull — Queensland. Department of Primary Industries. Division of Dairying. Bulletin
Queensl Dep Primary Ind Div Plant Ind Bull — Queensland. Department of Primary Industries. Division of Plant Industry. Bulletin
Queensl Geogr J — Queensland Geographical Journal
Queensl Geol — Queensland Geology
Queensl Geol Surv 1:250000 Geol Ser — Queensland. Geological Survey. 1:250,000 Geological Series
Queensl Geol Surv Publ — Queensland. Geological Survey. Publication
Queensl Geol Surv Rep — Queensland. Geological Survey. Report
Queensl Gov Min J — Queensland Government Mining Journal
Queensl Herit — Queensland Heritage
Queen's L J — Queen's Law Journal
Queens LJ — Queensland Law Journal and Reports
Queensl J Agric Anim Sci — Queensland Journal of Agricultural and Animal Sciences
Queensl J Agric & Anim Sci — Queensland Journal of Agricultural and Animal Sciences
Queensl J Agric Sci — Queensland Journal of Agricultural Science [*Later, Queensland Journal of Agricultural and Animal Sciences*]
Queensl LJ (Austr) — Queensland Law Journal (Australia)
Queensl LJ & R — Queensland Law Journal and Reports
Queensl LR — Queensland Law Reports

Queensl L Soc'y J — Queensland Law Society. Journal
Queensl Nat — Queensland Naturalist
Queensl Nurses J — Queensland Nurses Journal
Queens LR — Queensland Law Reports (Beor)
Queensl SC (Austr) — Queensland. Supreme Court. Reports (Australia)
Queensl S Ct R — Queensland. Supreme Court. Reports
Queensl Soc Sugar Cane Technol Proc — Queensland Society of Sugar Cane Technologists. Proceedings
Queensl Univ Dep Civ Eng Bull — Queensland University. Department of Civil Engineering. Bulletin
Queensl Univ Dep Civ Eng Bull — University of Queensland. Department of Civil Engineering. Bulletin
Queensl Univ Dep Geol Pap — Queensland University. Department of Geology. Papers
Queensl Vet Proc — Queensland Veterinary Proceedings (Australian Veterinary Association, Queensland Division)
Queen's Nurs J — Queen's Nursing Journal
Queen's Papers in Pure and Appl Math — Queen's Papers in Pure and Applied Mathematics
Queen's Q — Queen's Quarterly
Queen's Quart — Queen's Quarterly
Queens Univ Therm Fluid Sci Group Rep — Queen's University. Thermal and Fluid Science Group. Report
Quellen Stud Philos — Quellen und Studien zur Philosophie
Que Minist Chasse Pech Contrib — Quebec. Ministere de la Chasse et des Pecheries. Contributions
Que Minist Ind Commer Dir Rech Cah Inf — Quebec. Ministere de l'Industrie et du Commerce. Direction de la Recherches Cahiers d'Information
Que Minist Ind Commer Rapp Pech — Quebec. Ministere de l'Industrie et du Commerce. Rapport sur les Pecheries
Que Minist Ind Commer Serv Biol Rapp Annu — Quebec. Ministere de l'Industrie et du Commerce. Service de Biologie. Rapport Annuel
Que Minist Richesses Nat Etude Spec — Quebec. Ministere des Richesses Naturelles. Etude Speciale
Que (Prov) Dep Mines Gen Rep Minist Mines — Quebec (Province). Department of Mines. General Report of the Minister of Mines
Que (Prov) Minist Richesses Nat Rapp Prelim — Quebec (Province). Ministere des Richesses Naturelles. Rapport Preliminaire
Query File Commonw Bur Hortic Plant Crops — Query File. Commonwealth Bureau of Horticulture and Plantation Crops
Que Sci — Quebec Science
Que Soc Prot Plants Rep — Quebec Society for the Protection of Plants. Report
Quest Act Socialisme — Questions Actuelles du Socialisme
Quest For — Questions of Forestry
Quetico-Super Wilderness Res Cent Annu Rep — Quetico-Superior Wilderness Research Center. Annual Report
Quetico-Super Wilderness Res Cent Tech Note — Quetico-Superior Wilderness Research Center. Technical Note
QUF — National Bank of Yugoslavia. Quarterly Bulletin
QU Gazette — Queensland University. Gazette
QUIBA — Quimica e Industria [*Madrid*]
QUIJA — Quintessence International
QUILL — QUILL: Queensland Inter-Library Liaison
Quill & Q — Quill and Quire
Quim Anal — Quimica Analitica
Quim Farm — Quimica y Farmica
Quim Ind (Barcelona) — Quimica e Industria (Barcelona)
Quim Ind (Madrid) — Quimica e Industria (Madrid)
Quim Ind (Montevideo) — Quimica Industrial (Montevideo)
Quim Nova — Quimica Nova
Quintessence Dent Technol — Quintessence of Dental Technology
Quintessence Int — Quintessence International
Quintessencia Protese Lab — Quintessencia de Protese de Laboratorio
Quintessenz J — Quintessenz Journal
Quintessenz Zahntech — Quintessenz der Zahntechnik
Quinz Lit — Quinzaine Litteraire
Quix — Quixote
QU Law J — University of Queensland. Law Journal
QULJ — Queensland University. Law Journal
Qu Minist Ind Commer Serv Rech Cah Inf — Quebec. Ministere de l'Industrie et du Commerce. Service de la Recherche. Cahiers d'Information
Qu Minist Terres For Serv Rech Note — Quebec. Ministere des Terres et Forets. Service de la Recherche. Note
Q Univ Gaz — University of Queensland. Gazette
QUNJA — Queensland Nurses Journal
QUODD — Quodlibet [*Newsletter of the Southeastern Region*]
Qu (Prov) Dep Mines Prelim Rep — Quebec (Province). Department of Mines. Preliminary Report
QURBA — Quarterly Reviews of Biophysics
QUREA — Quarterly Reviews. Chemical Society
Qu Serv Faune Bull — Quebec. Service de la Faune. Bulletin
QUSZA — Quintessenz Journal
QV — Quatro Ventos
QV — Quo Vadis
Q Vit — Quaderni del Vittoriale
Q W — Quarterly West

QWN — Weekly Notes. Queensland

R

R — Radio (BBC Monitoring)
R — Realites
R — Republika [*Zagreb*]
R — Rio De Janeiro
R — Romania
R — Rydge's
Ra — Raduga [*Moscow*]
Ra — Rassegna
Ra — Repertorio Americano
RA — Research Abstracts [*University Microfilms International*]
RA — Reviews in Anthropology
RA — Revue Africaine. Bulletin de la Societe Historique Algerienne
RA — Revue Anglo-Americaine
RA — Revue Archeologique
RA — Revue des Arts
RA — Revue d'Assyriologie
RA — Revue d'Assyriologie et d'Archeologie Orientale [*Paris*]
RA — Rheinisches Archiv
RA — Romanistische Arbeitshefte
RAA — Rendiconti. Accademia di Archeologia, Lettere, e Belle Arti [*Napoli*]
RAA — Revue. Academie Arabe
RAA — Revue Anglo-Americaine
RAA — Revue de l'Art Ancien et Moderne
RAA — Revue des Arts Asiatiques
RAA — Revue d'Assyriologie et d'Archeologie Orientale
RAACA — Radiochimica Acta
RAAD — Revue. Academie Arabe de Damas
RAAEC Nletter — Royal Australian Army. Educational Corps. Newsletter
RAAF Reserve — Royal Australian Air Force Reserve. Magazine
RAAGA — Railway Age [*New York*]
RAAG Res Notes — Research Notes and Memoranda of Applied Geometry for Prevenient Natural Philosophy [*Tokyo*]
RAAM — Revue de l'Art Ancien et Moderne
RAAN — Rendiconti. Accademia di Archeologia, Lettere, e Belle Arti (Napoli)
RAAO — Revue d'Assyriologie et d'Archeologie Orientale
RAAQ — Recherches Amerindiennes au Quebec. Bulletin d'Information
Rab Azovsko-Chernomorsk Nauchn Rybokhoz Stn — Raboty Azovsko-Chernomorskoi Nauchnoi Rybokhozyaistvennoi Stantsii
Rab Fiz Tverd Tela — Raboty po Fizike Tverdogo Tela
Rab Issled Inst Meteorol Gidrol Chast 2 — Raboty i Issledovaniya. Institut Meteorologii i Gidrologii. Chast 2. Gidrologiya
Rab Khim Rastvorov Kompleksn Soedin — Raboty po Khimii Rastvorov i Kompleksnykh Soedinenii
RABM — Revista de Archivos, Bibliotecas, y Museos
RABMA — Radiobiologia si Biologia Moleculara
Rab Molodykh Uch Vses Akad Skh Nauk — Raboty Molodykh Uchenykh Vsesoyuznaya Akademiya Sel'skokhozyaistvennykh Nauk
Rab Neft — Rabochii Neftyanik
RABOA — Radiation Botany
Rabocij Klass Sovrem Mir — Rabocij Klass i Sovremennyj Mir
RABol — Rendiconto. Accademia delle Scienze. Istituto di Bologna
R Abolit — Revue Abolitionniste
RAbr — Rivista Abruzzese

Rab Tyan-Shan Fiz-Geogr Sta — Raboty Tyan-Shan'skoi Fiziko-Geograficheskoi Stantsii. Akademiya Nauk Kirgizskoi SSR
Rab Tyan Shan'skoi Fiz Geogr Stn Akad Nauk Kirg SSR — Raboty Tyan-Shan'skoi Fiziko-Geograficheskoi Stantsii. Akademiya Nauk Kirgizskoi SSR
RAC — Revue de l'Art Chretien
RAC — Rivista di Archeologia Cristiana
RACAA — Radiocarbon
R Acad Cienc y Artes Barcelona Mem — Real Academia de Ciencias y Artes de Barcelona. Memorias
R Acad Farm Barcelona Discursos Recepcion — Real Academia de Farmacia de Barcelona. Discursos de Recepcion
R Acad Farm Barcelona Ses Inaug — Real Academia de Farmacia de Barcelona. Sesion Inaugural
RACathHS — Records. American Catholic Historical Society of Philadelphia
Racc Fis-Chim Ital — Raccolta Fisico-Chimica Italiana
R Ac Cienc Habana An — Real Academia de Ciencias Medicas, Fisicas, y Naturales de la Habana. Anales
Raccoglitore Med Forli — Raccoglitore Medico Fano Forli
Raccolta Mem Turin Univ Fac Sci Agr — Raccolta di Memorie. Turin. Universita. Facolta di Scienze Agrarie
Racc Opuscoli Sci Filol — Raccolta d'Opuscoli Scientifici e Filologici
Race — Race and Class
Race Clas — Race and Class
Race Hyg — Race Hygiene [*Japan*]
Race Rela L R — Race Relations Law Reporter
Race Rela L Sur — Race Relations Law Survey
RACF — Revue Archeologique du Centre de la France
RACHA — Rassegna Chimica
RACHS — Records. American Catholic Historical Society of Philadelphia
RACHSP — Records. American Catholic Historical Society of Philadelphia
RACND3 — Annual Research Reviews. Rheumatoid Arthritis and Related Conditions
RACrist — Rivista di Archeologia Cristiana
R Action Soc — Revue d'Action Sociale
RACYA — Reviews in Analytical Chemistry
RACZA — Revista. Academia de Ciencias Exactas, Fisico-Quimicas, y Naturales de Zaragoza
Rad — Rad Jugoslavenski Akademija Znanosti i Umjetnosti
Rad — Radical Teacher
Rad Am — Radical America
Rad Amer — Radical America
RADAR — Repertoire Analytique d'Articles de Revues de Quebec [*Database*]
RADBA — Radiobiology [*English Translation*]
Rad Clinica — Radiologia Clinica
Rad Clin NA — Radiologic Clinics of North America
Rad Diagn — Radiologia Diagnostica
Rad Eng (London) — Radio Engineering (London)
Radex Rundsch — Radex Rundschau
Radex Runsch — Radex Rundschau
Rad Geoinst — Radovi - Geoinstitut
Rad Hist — Radical History Review
Rad Humanist — Radical Humanist
RADIA — Radiography

Radiata Pine Tech Bull — Radiata Pine Technical Bulletin (Radiata Pine Association of Australia)
Radiat Biol — Radiation Biology [*England*]
Radiat Bot — Radiation Botany
Radiat Data Rep — Radiation Data and Reports
Radiat Eff — Radiation Effects
Radiat Effects — Radiation Effects
Radiat Eff Lett — Radiation Effects. Letters Section
Radiat Eff Lett Sect — Radiation Effects. Letters Section
Radiat Env — Radiation and Environmental Biophysics
Radiat and Environ Biophys — Radiation and Environmental Biophysics
Radiat Environ Biophys — Radiation and Environmental Biophysics
Radiat Phys and Chem — Radiation Physics and Chemistry
Radiat Phys Chem — Radiation Physics and Chemistry
Radiat Prot — Radiation Protection [*Republic of Korea*]
Radiat Prot Aust — Radiation Protection in Australia
Radiat Prot Dosim — Radiation Protection Dosimetry
Radiat Prot ICRP Publ — Radiation Protection. ICRP [*International Commission on Radiological Protection*] Publication
Radiat Prot (Seoul) — Radiation Protection (Seoul)
Radiat Prot (Taiyuan People's Repub China) — Radiation Protection (Taiyuan, People's Republic of China)
Radiat Res — Radiation Research
Radiat Res Polym — Radiation Research on Polymers [*Japan*]
Radiat Res Rev — Radiation Research Reviews
Radiat Res Suppl — Radiation Research. Supplement
Radiats Bezop Zashch AEhS — Radiatsionnaya Bezopasnost' i Zashchita AEhS. Sbornik Statej
Radiats Fiz — Radiatsionnaya Fizika
Radiats Fiz Akad Nauk Latv SSR Inst Fiz — Radiatsionnaya Fizika. Akademiya Nauk Latviiskoi SSR. Institut Fiziki [*Latvian SSR*]
Radiats Fiz Nemet Krist — Radiatsionnaya Fizika Nemetallicheskikh Kristallov
Radiats Fiz Tverd Tela Radiats Materialoved — Radiatsionnaya Fizika Tverdogo Tela i Radiatsionnoe Materialovedenie
Radiats Gig — Radiatsionnaya Gigiena [*USSR*]
Radiat Shielding Inf Cent Rep — Radiation Shielding Information Center. Report
Radiats Tekh — Radiatsionnaya Tekhnika
Radiaz Alta Energ — Radiazioni di Alta Energia
Radiaz Radioisot — Radiazioni e Radioisotopi
Radical Am — Radical America
Radical Commun Med — Radical Community Medicine
Radical Educ Dossier — Radical Education Dossier
Radical His — Radical History Review
Radical Scot — Radical Scotland
Rad Imunol Zavoda (Zagreb) — Radovi Imunoloskog Zavoda (Zagreb)
Rad Inst Geol-Rud Istraz Ispit Nukl Drugih Miner Sirovina — Radovi Instituta za Geolosko-Rudarska Istrazivanja i Ispitivanja Nuklearnih i Drugih Mineralnih Sirovina [*Yugoslavia*]
Rad Inst Proucavanje Suzbijanje Alkohol Drugih Narkomanija — Radovi Instituta za Proucavanje i Suzbijanje Alkoholizma i Drugih Narkomanija u Zagrebu
Rad Inst Sum Istraz — Radovi Institut za Sumarska Istrazivanja. Sumarskog Fakulteta. Sveucilista u Zagrebu
Radioact Sea — Radioactivity in the Sea [*Austria*]
Radioact Surv Data Jap — Radioactivity Survey Data in Japan
Radioact Waste Manage — Radioactive Waste Management
Radioact Waste Manage Nucl Fuel Cycle — Radioactive Waste Management and the Nuclear Fuel Cycle
Radioact Waste Manage and Nucl Fuel Cycle — Radioactive Waste Management and the Nuclear Fuel Cycle
Radioact Waste Manage (Oak Ridge Tenn) — Radioactive Waste Management (Oak Ridge, Tennessee)
Radioact Waste Technol — Radioactive Waste Technology
Radioaktiv Zivotn Prostr — Radioaktivita a Zivotne Prostredie
Radiobiol — Radiobiologiya
Radiobiol Biol Mol — Radiobiologia si Biologia Moleculara [*Romania*]
Radiobiol Inf Byull — Radiobiologiya Informatsionnyi Byulleten'
Radiobiol Lat — Radiobiologica Latina [*Italy*]
Radiobiol Radioter Fis Med — Radiobiologia, Radioterapia, e Fisica Medica
Radiobiol-Radiother — Radiobiologia-Radiotherapia
Radiobiol-Radiother (Berl) — Radiobiologia-Radiotherapia (Berlin)
Radiobiol-Radiother (Berlin) — Radiobiologia-Radiotherapia (Berlin)
Radioch Act — Radiochimica Acta
Radiochem and Radioanal Lett — Radiochemical and Radioanalytical Letters
Radiochem Radioanal Lett — Radiochemical and Radioanalytical Letters
Radiochim Acta — Radiochimica Acta
Radioch Rad — Radiochemical and Radioanalytical Letters
Radio Commun — Radio Communication
Radioekol Vodn Org — Radioekologiya Vodnykh Organizmov
Radio-Electr — Radio-Electronics
Radio Electron — Radio Electronica [*Netherlands*]
Radio-Electron — Radio-Electronics
Radio Electron Commun Syst — Radio Electronics and Communications Systems

Radioelectron and Commun Syst — Radioelectronics and Communication Systems
Radio & Electron Constructor — Radio and Electronics Constructor
Radio and Electron Eng — Radio and Electronic Engineer
Radio Electron Eng — Radio and Electronic Engineer
Radio Electron Eng (London) — Radio and Electronic Engineer (London)
Radio & Electronic Eng — Radio and Electronic Engineer
Radio and Electronics World — Radio and Electronics World
Radio Elec W — Radio Electrical Weekly
Radio Elektron — Radio Elektronica
Radio Elektroniikkalab Tek Korkeakoulu Kertomus — Radio- ja Elektroniikkalaboratoriot. Teknillinen Korkeakoulu. Kertomus
Radio Elektron Schau — Radio Elektronik Schau
Radio El En — Radio and Electronic Engineer
Radio Eng — Radio Engineering
Radio Eng and Electron Phys — Radio Engineering and Electronic Physics
Radio Eng Electron Phys — Radio Engineering and Electronic Physics
Radio Eng Electron (USSR) — Radio Engineering and Electronic Physics (USSR)
Radio Engrg Electron Phys — Radio Engineering and Electronic Physics
Radio Eng (USSR) — Radio Engineering (USSR)
Radio Fernsehen Elektron — Radio Fernsehen Elektronik
Radiogr — Radiographer
Radio Ind — Radio Industria
Radioind Elettron-Telev — Radioindustria Elettronica-Televisione
Radioisot (Praha) — Radioisotopy (Praha)
Radioisot (Tokyo) — Radioisotopes (Tokyo)
Radio Lab Tech Univ Helsinki Intern Rep — Radio Laboratory. Technical University of Helsinki. Internal Report
Radiol Austriaca — Radiologia Austriaca
Radiol Bras — Radiologia Brasileira
Radiol Clin — Radiologia Clinica
Radiol Clin (Basel) — Radiologia Clinica (Basel)
Radiol Clin Biol — Radiologia Clinica et Biologica
Radiol Clin N Am — Radiologic Clinics of North America
Radiol Clin North Am — Radiologic Clinics of North America
Radiol Diagn — Radiologia Diagnostica
Radiol Diagn (Berlin) — Radiologia Diagnostica (Berlin)
Radiol Health Data — Radiological Health Data
Radiol Health Data Rep — Radiological Health Data and Reports
Radiol Iugosl (Ljubljana) — Radiologia Iugoslavica (Ljubljana)
Radiol Kozl — Radiologiai Kozlemenyek
Radiol Manage — Radiology Management
Radiol Med — Radiologia Medica
Radiol Med (Torino) — Radiologia Medica (Torino)
Radiological Protect Bull — Radiological Protection Bulletin
Radiol Prat — Radiologia Pratica [*Italy*]
Radiol Prot Bull — Radiological Protection Bulletin
Radiol Rev Miss Val Med J — Radiological Review and Mississippi Valley Medical Journal
Radiol Technol — Radiologic Technology
Radio Mentor Electron — Radio Mentor Electronic
Radio Mntr — Radio Mentor Electronic
Radiom Polarogr — Radiometer Polarographics
Radio N — Radio News
Radiophysiol Radiother — Radiophysiologie et Radiotherapie
Radiophys Quantum Electron — Radiophysics and Quantum Electronics
Radiophys & Quantum Electron — Radiophysics and Quantum Electronics
Radio Sci — Radio Science
Radio Serv Bul — Radio Service Bulletin
Radio T — Radio Times [*United Kingdom*]
Radiotehn i Elektron — Akademia Nauk SSSR. Radiotehnika i Elektronika
Radiotehn (Kharkov) — Radiotehnika (Kharkov)
Radiotek El — Radiotekhnika i Elektronika
Radiotekh — Radiotekhnika
Radiotekh i Elektron — Radiotekhnika i Elektronika
Radiotekh Elektron — Radiotekhnika i Elektronika
Radiotekhn — Khar'kovski Ordena Trudovogo Krasnogo Znameni Gosudarstvennyi Universitet Imeni A.M. Gor'kogo Radiotekhnika
Radiotekhn i Elektron — Radiotekhnika i Elektronika. Akademiya Nauk SSSR
Radiotekh Proizvod — Radiotekhnicheskoe Proizvodstvo
Radio Telev — Radio Television
Radio Telev Int Rev — Radio - Television International Review
Radio Tel & Hobbies — Radio, Television, and Hobbies
Radioter Radiobiol Fis Med — Radioterapia, Radiobiologia, e Fisica Medica
Radio-TV-Electron — Radio-TV-Electronic [*Later, RTE. Radio-TV-Electronic*]
Radio-TV-Electron Serv — Radio-TV-Electronic Service [*Later, RTE. Radio-TV-Electronic*] [*Switzerland*]
Radio TVH — Radio, Television, and Hobbies
Radio & TV N — Radio and Television News
Radio es TV Szle — Radio es TV Szemle
RadJA — Radovi Jugoslavenske Akademije Znanosti i Umjetnosti
Rad Jugosl Akad Znan Umjet — Radovi Jugoslavenske Akademije Znanosti i Umjetnosti

Rad Jugoslav Akad Znan Umjet — Radovi Jugoslavenske Akademije Znanosti i Umjetnosti
Rad Jugoslav Akad Znan Umjet Odjel Prir Nauke — Radovi Jugoslavenske Akademije Znanosti i Umjetnosti. Odjel za Prirodne Nauke
RADKA — Radiokhimiya
RadL — Radyans'ske Literaturoznavstvo [*Kiev*]
RADLA — Radiology
R Adm — Revue Administrative
Rad Med Fak Rijeka — Radovi Medicinskogo Fakulteta. Rijeka
Rad Med Fak Zagrebu — Radovi Medicinskogo Fakulteta u Zagrebu
R Adm Empresas — Revista. Administracao de Empresas
R Admin Empresas — Revista de Administracao de Empresas
R Admin (Paris) — Revue Administrative (Paris)
R Admin Publica — Revista. Administracion Publica
R Adm Municip (Rio De Janeiro) — Revista. Administracao Municipal (Rio De Janeiro)
R Adm Publ (Madrid) — Revista. Administracion Publica (Madrid)
R Adm Publ (Rio De Janeiro) — Revista. Administracao Publica (Rio De Janeiro)
RADOA — Radiobiologiya
Rad Phil — Radical Philosophy
Rad Phil News — Radical Philosopher's Newsjournal
Rad Poljopriv Fak Univ Saraj — Radovi Poljoprivrednog Fakulteta Univerziteta u Sarajevo
Rad Poljopriv Fak Univ Sarajevu — Radovi Poljoprivrednog Fakulteta Univerziteta u Sarajevu
Rad Rel — Radical Religion
Rad Relig — Radical Religion
Rad Sarajevo Univ Poljopr Fak — Radovi Sarajevo Univerzitet. Poljoprivredni Fakultet
Rad Scien — Radical Science Journal
Rad Sumar Fak Inst Sumar Sarajevo — Radovi Sumarskog Fakulteta i Instituta za Sumarstvo u Sarajevo
Rad Sum Fak i Inst Sum — Radovi Sumarski Fakultet i Institut za Sumarstvo
Rad Teach — Radical Teacher
Rad Ther — Issues in Radical Therapy
Rad Thera — Issues in Radical Therapy
Rad Zavoda Fiz — Radovi Zavoda za Fiziku
RadZSF — Radovi Zavoda za Slavensku Filologiju
RAE — Real Academia Espanola. Boletin
RAE — Revista Augustiniana de Espiritualidad
RAE — Revue Archeologique de l'Est et du Centre-Est
RAE — Revue d'Art et d'Esthetique
RAEFB — Radiation Effects
RAELA — Radiotekhnika i Elektronika
RAf — Revue Africaine
RAFIA — Radiatsionnaya Fizika. Akademiya Nauk Latviiskoi SSR. Institut Fiziki
RAfr — Revue Africaine
R African Pol Economy — Review of African Political Economy
R Afr Manag — Revue Africaine de Management
RAG — Raina un Aspazijas Gadagramata
R de Ag (Cuba) — Revista de Agricultura (Cuba)
R Ag (Cuba) — Revista de Agricultura (Cuba)
RAGEA — Razvedochnaya Geofizika
R Ag France — Revue des Agriculteurs de France
RagL — Raguaglio Librario
RAGOA — Rivista di Agronomia
R Agr Econ Mal — Review of Agricultural Economics of Malaysia
R Agric — Revue de l'Agriculture
R Agric Soc (Cairo) Bull Tech Sect — Royal Agricultural Society (Cairo). Bulletin. Technical Section
R Agric Soc Kenya QJ — Royal Agricultural Society of Kenya. Quarterly Journal
RAH — Reviews in American History
RAHBol — Real Academia de la Historia. Boletin
RAHE — Review of Allied Health Education
RAHS — Royal Australian Historical Society. Journal
RAHSJ — Royal Australian Historical Society. Journal and Proceedings
RAI — Rencontre Assyriologique Internationale
RAI — Rendiconti. Classe di Scienze Morali e Storiche. Accademia d'Italia
RAIAA — Asociacion de Ingenieros Agronomos. Revista
RAIB — Rendiconti. Accademia delle Scienze. Istituto di Bologna
Raiffeisen-Rundsch — Raiffeisen-Rundschau
Rail Clerk — Railway Clerk Interchange
Rail Eng — Railway Engineer [*Later, Railway Engineer International*]
Rail Eng Int — Rail Engineering International
Rail Int — Rail International
Rail M — Railway Magazine
Railroad Gaz — Railroad Gazette
Rail Syst Contr — Railway Systems Control
Railw Age — Railway Age
Railway R — Railway Review
Railways in Aust — Railways in Australia
Railways Union Gaz — Railways Union Gazette
Railway Trans — Railway Transportation

Railw Dev News — Railway Development News
Railw Eng — Railway Engineer [*Later, Railway Engineer International*]
Railw Eng Int — Railway Engineer International
Railw Eng J — Railway Engineering Journal [*Incorporated in Railway Engineer International*]
Railw Eng Maint — Railway Engineering and Maintenance
Railw Engr — Railway Engineer [*Later, Railway Engineer International*]
Railw Gaz — Railway Gazette [*England*] [*Later, Railway Gazette International*]
Railw Gaz Int — Railway Gazette International
Railw Locomot Cars — Railway Locomotives and Cars
Railw Manage Rev — Railway Management Review
Railw Mech Eng — Railway Mechanical Engineer [*United States*]
Railw Rev — Railway Review
Railw Signal Commun — Railway Signalling and Communications [*United States*]
Railw South Afr — Railways Southern Africa
Railw Syst Control — Railway Systems Control
Railw Track Struct — Railway Track and Structures
RAIN — Royal Anthropological Institute. Newsletter
RAINB — Radio Industria
RAIP — Rapport d'Activites. Institut de Phonetique
R Aircr Establ List Reports — Royal Aircraft Establishment. List of Reports
RAIRO Anal Num — RAIRO [*Revue Francaise d'Automatique, d'Informatique, et de Recherche Operationnelle*] Analyse Numerique
RAIRO Anal Numer — RAIRO [*Revue Francaise d'Automatique, d'Informatique, et de Recherche Operationnelle*] Analyse Numerique
RAIRO Anal Numer Numer Anal — RAIRO [*Revue Francaise d'Automatique, d'Informatique, et de Recherche Operationnelle*] Analyse Numerique/ Numerical Analysis
RAIRO Automat — RAIRO [*Revue Francaise d'Automatique, d'Informatique, et de Recherche Operationnelle*] Automatique
RAIRO Autom/Syst Anal and Control — RAIRO [*Revue Francaise d'Automatique, d'Informatique, et de Recherche Operationnelle*] Automatique/Systems Analysis and Control
RAIRO Autom Syst Anal Control — RAIRO [*Revue Francaise d'Automatique, d'Informatique, et de Recherche Operationnelle*] Automatique/Systems Analysis and Control
RAIRO Inf/Comput Sci — RAIRO [*Revue Francaise d'Automatique, d'Informatique, et de Recherche Operationnelle*] Informatique/ Computer Science
RAIRO Inform — RAIRO [*Revue Francaise d'Automatique, d'Informatique, et de Recherche Operationnelle*] Informatique
RAIRO Informat — RAIRO [*Revue Francaise d'Automatique, d'Informatique, et de Recherche Operationnelle*] Informatique
RAIRO Informat Theor — RAIRO [*Revue Francaise d'Automatique, d'Informatique, et de Recherche Operationnelle*] Informatique Theorique
RAIRO Inform Theor — RAIRO [*Revue Francaise d'Automatique, d'Informatique, et de Recherche Operationnelle*] Informatique Theorique/Theoretical Informatics
RAIRO Inf Theor Theor Inf — RAIRO [*Revue Francaise d'Automatique, d'Informatique, et de Recherche Operationnelle*] Informatique Theorique/Theoretical Informatics
RAIRO Operations Research — RAIRO [*Revue Francaise d'Automatique, d'Informatique, et de Recherche Operationnelle*] Recherche Operationnelle/Operations Research
RAIRO Rech Oper Oper Res — RAIRO [*Revue Francaise d'Automatique, d'Informatique, et de Recherche Operationnelle*] Recherche Operationnelle/Operations Research
RAISA — Radioisotopes [*Tokyo*]
RAIT — Rendiconti. Reale Accademia d'Italia
RAIU — Revista de la Alliance Israelite Universelle
Ra JAH — Rackham Journal of the Arts and Humanities
Rajasthan Agric — Rajasthan Agriculturist
Rajasthan J Agric Sci — Rajasthan Journal of Agricultural Sciences
Rajasthan Med J — Rajasthan Medical Journal
Rajasthan Univ Studies Statist — Rajasthan University. Studies in Statistics. Science Series
Rajasthan Univ Stud Statist — Rajasthan University. Studies in Statistics. Science Series
RAJ Tech Bull — RAJ [*Rhodesia Agricultural Journal*] Technical Bulletin
RaKet — Rahnema-Ye Ketab
Raketentech Raumfahrtforsch — Raketentechnik und Raumfahrtforschung
Rakstu Krajums Daugavpils Pedagog Inst — Rakstu Krajums. Daugavpils Pedagogiskais Instituts
RAL — Rendiconti. Classe di Scienze Morali e Storiche. Accademia dei Lincei
RAL — Research in African Literatures
RAL — Revista. Academias de Letras
RALAB — Revue de l'Aluminum et de Ses Applications
RAlb — Rivista d'Albania
RALF — Repertoire Analytique de Litterature Francaise [*Bordeaux*]
R Algerienne Sciences Juridiques Econs et Pols — Revue Algerienne des Sciences Juridiques, Economiques, et Politiques
R Alger Trav — Revue Algerienne du Travail

RALinc — Rendiconti. Classe di Scienze Morali e Storiche. Accademia dei Lincei
RALincei — Rendiconti. Classe di Scienze Morali e Storiche. Accademia dei Lincei
R Allem — Revue d'Allemagne
R Allemagne — Revue d'Allemagne
RALRend — Rendiconti. Classe di Scienze Morali e Storiche. Accademia dei Lincei
RALS — Resources for American Literary Study
RAls — Revue d'Alsace
RAL Scav — Reale Accademia dei Lincei. Atti. Notizie degli Scavi
RALSH — Revue Algerienne des Lettres et des Sciences Humaines
RAM — Radio-Active Magazine
Ra M — Rassegna Musicale
RAM — Revue de l'Ameublement
RAM — Revue d'Ascetique et de Mystique
RAM — Rock Australia Magazine
Raman Res Inst Mem — Raman Research Institute. Memoirs
RAMC — Rassegna di Asetica e Mistica S. Caterina da Siena
RAMEA — Radiologia Medica
RAMED — Reine und Angewandte Metallkunde in Einzeldarstellungen
R Am Hist — Reviews in American History
RaMIsr — Rassegna Mensile di Israel [*Rome*]
Ramp — Ramparts Magazine
Ramp Mag — Ramparts Magazine
RAMSP — Revista do Arquivo Municipal (Sao Paulo)
RAMTB — Revue ATB [*Assistance Technique Belge*] Metallurgie [*Belgium*]
RAN — Rangifer. Nordisk Organ foer Reinforskning
RAN — Rendiconti. Accademia di Archeologia, Lettere, e Belle Arti (Napoli)
RANAM — Recherches Anglaises et Americaines
RANBDM — Institut des Sciences Agronomiques du Burundi [*ISABU*]. Rapport Annuel et Notes Annexes
Ranchi Univ J Agric Res — Ranchi University. Journal of Agricultural Research
Ranchi Univ Math J — Ranchi University. Mathematical Journal
Ranch Mag — Ranch Magazine
Rand — Selected Rand Abstracts
Rand Corp Pap — Rand Corporation. Papers
Rand Corp Rep — Rand Corporation. Report
R ANDI — Revista ANDI [*Asociacion Nacional de Industriales*]
RANF Rev — RANF [*Royal Australian Nursing Federation*] Review
Range Improv Notes US For Serv Intermt Reg — Range Improvement Notes. United States Forest Service. Intermountain Region
Range Improv Studies Calif Dep Conserv Div For — Range Improvement Studies. California Department of Conservation. Division of Forestry
Range Impr Stud Calif Div For — Range Improvement Studies. California Division of Forestry
RANL — Rendiconti. Reale Accademia Nazionale dei Lincei
Rannsoknastofnun Fiskidnadarins Arsskyrs — Rannsoknastofnun Fiskidnadarins Arsskyrsla
RANS — Report. Australian Numismatic Society
R Anthrop — Reviews in Anthropology
R Antropol (Sao Paulo) — Revista de Antropologia (Sao Paulo)
RAO — Recueil d'Archeologie Orientale
RAOU Newsl — RAOU [*Royal Australasian Ornithologists Union*] Newsletter
RAP — Revolutionary Action Power
RAP — Revue de l'Action Populaire [*Later, Projet*]
RAp — Revue Apologetique
RAP — Revue d'Archeologie Polonaise
Rap Bur Nutr Anim Elev — Rapport. Bureau de la Nutrition Animale et de l'Elevage
RAPH — Recherches d'Archeologie, de Philologie,et d'Histoire [*Cairo*]
Rap Inst Fiz Tech Jad AGH — Raport. Instytut Fizyki i Techniki Jadrowej AGH [*Akademia Gorniczo-Hutnicza*]
Rap Inst Nat Etude Agron Congo (INEAC) — Rapport. Institut National pour l'Etude Agronomique du Congo (INEAC)
Rap Inst Tech Jad AGH — Raport. Instytut Techniki Jadrowej AGH [*Akademia Gorniczo-Hutnicza*]
Rapp — Rapport
Rapp Act Serv Geol (Madagascar) — Rapport d'Activite. Service Geologique (Madagascar)
Rapp Act Serv Geol (Malagasy) — Rapport d'Activite. Service Geologique (Malagasy)
Rapp Act Stn Amelior Plant Maraicheres — Rapport d'Activite. Station d'Amelioration des Plants Maraicheres
Rapp Anal Phys Chim Eau Rhin — Rapport sur les Analyses Physico-Chimiques de l'Eau du Rhin
Rapp Annu AFOCEL (Assoc For Cellul) — Rapport Annuel. AFOCEL (Association Foret-Cellulose)
Rapp Annu Serv Geol (Malagasy) — Rapport Annuel. Service Geologique (Malagasy)
Rapp Assoc Int Chim Cerealiere — Rapports. Association Internationale de Chimie Cerealiere
Rapp BIPM — Rapport. BIPM [*Bureau International des Poids et Mesures*]

Rapp Comm Int Mer Mediter — Rapport. Commission Internationale pour la Mer Mediterranee [*France*]
Rapp Commissar Energie Atom — Rapport. Commissariat a l'Energie Atomique [*France*]
Rapp Cons Exp Rech Agron Insp Gen Agric (Algeria) — Rapport. Conseil de l'Experimentation et des Recherches Agronomiques. Inspection Generale de l'Agriculture (Algeria)
Rapp Final Conf Tech OCEAC — Rapport Final. Conference Technique. OCEAC [*Organisation de Coordination pour la Lutte Contre les Endemies en Afrique Centrale*]
Rapp Fonct Tech Inst Pasteur Dakar — Rapport sur le Fonctionnement Technique. Institut Pasteur de Dakar
Rapp Inst Bodemvruchtbaar — Rapport. Instituut voor Bodemvruchtbaarheid
Rapp Instn Virkeslara Skogshogsk — Rapporter. Institutionen for Virkeslara. Skogshogskolan
Rapp Inter Etude Lab J Dedek Raffinerie Tirlemontoise — Rapport Interieur d'une Etude Effectuee au Laboratoire J. Dedek Raffinerie Tirlemontoise
Rapp Korrosionsinst — Rapport. Korrosionsinstitutet
Rapp Lab Prod For Est (Can) — Rapport. Laboratoire des Produits Forestiers de l'Est (Canada)
Rapp Off Int Epizoot — Rapport. Office International des Epizooties
Rapport Conjonct — Rapport de Conjoncture
Rapp Prelim Minist Richesses Nat (Que) — Rapport Preliminaire. Ministere des Richesses Naturelles (Quebec)
Rapp Proefstn Groenteteelt Vollegrond Ned — Rapport. Proefstation voor de Groenteteelt in de Vollegrond in Nederland
Rapp P-V Reun Cons Int Explor Mer — Rapports et Proces-Verbaux des Reunions. Conseil International pour l'Exploration de la Mer
Rapp Rech Lab Cent Ponts Chaussees — Rapport de Recherche. Laboratoire Central des Ponts et Chaussees
Rapp Sci Tech CNEXO (Fr) — Rapports Scientifiques et Techniques. CNEXO [*Centre National pour l'Exploitation des Oceans*] (France)
Rapp Sven Livsmedel-Sinstitutet — Rapport. Svenska Livsmedelsinstitutet
Rapp Uppsats Avd Skogsekol Skogshogsk — Rapporter och Uppsatser. Avdelningen foer Skogsekologi. Skogshogskolan
Rapp Uppsats Instn Skoglig Mat Statist Skogshogsk — Rapporter och Uppsatser. Institutionen foer Skoglig Matematisk Statistik. Skogshogskolan
Rapp Uppsats Instn Skogsforyngr Skogshogsk — Rapporter och Uppsatser. Institutionen foer Skogsforyngring. Skogshogskolan
Rapp Uppsats Instn Skogsgenet Skogshogsk — Rapporter och Uppsatser. Institutionen foer Skogsgenetik. Skogshogskolan
Rapp Uppsats Instn Skogsprod Skogshogsk — Rapporter och Uppsatser. Institutionen foer Skogsproduktion. Skogshogskolan
Rapp Uppsats Instn Skogstax Skogshogsk — Rapporter och Uppsatser. Institutionen foer Skogstaxering. Skogshogskolan
Rapp Uppsats Instn Skogstek Skogshogsk — Rapporter och Uppsatser. Institutionen foer Skogsteknik. Skogshogskolan
RAPRA Abst — RAPRA [*Rubber and Plastics Research Association*] Abstract
RAPRA Members J — RAPRA [*Rubber and Plastics Research Association*] Members Journal [*England*]
RAPRB — Radioprotection
Raptor Res — Raptor Research
RAQ — Wirtschaft und Produktivitaet
RAR — Renaissance and Reformation
R Ar — Revue Archeologique
RArchCr — Rivista di Archeologia Cristiana [*Rome*]
R Archeol — Revue Archeologique
R Arch Hist Art Louvain — Revue des Archeologues et Historiens d'Art de Louvain
RAREA — Radiation Research
Rarefied Gas Dyn Proc Int Symp — Rarefied Gas Dynamics. Proceedings of the International Symposium
RARMB — Razrabotka Rudnykh Mestorozhdenii
RARPC — Roczniki Akademii Rolniczej w Poznaniu
RArq — Revista di Arqueologia
RArqueol — Revista de Arqueologia
RARSA — Radiation Research. Supplement
RArt — Revue de l'Art
RArte — Rivista d'Arte
R des Arts — Revue des Arts
R Arts — Revue des Arts
RAS — Radio Science
RAS — Rassegna. Archivi di Stato
RAS — Rassegna della Letteratura Italiana
RAS — Readers Advisory Service
RAS — Revue Archeologique Syrienne
RASA — Rassegna Abruzzese di Storia ed Arte
RASCA — Radio Science
R Ascetique & Mystique — Revue d'Ascetique et de Mystique
Raschet Konstr Issled Oborud Proizvod Istochnikov Toka — Raschet. Konstruirovanie i Issledovanie Oborudovaniya Proizvodstva Istochnikov Toka
Raschet Konstr Neftezavod Oborud — Raschet i Konstruirovanie Neftezavodskogo Oborudovaniya

Raschet Konstr Neftezvod Oborudovaniya — Raschet i Konstruirovanie Neftezavodskogo Oborudovaniya
Raschety Prochn — Raschety na Prochnost
RasF — Rassegna di Filosofia
RASHA — RAS. Rohr-Armatur-Sanitaer-Heizung
RasI — Rassegna Italiana
RASIB — Rendiconto. Accademia delle Scienze. Istituto di Bologna
RASMA — Revue Agricole et Sucriere de l'Ile Maurice
RAsMyst — Revue d'Ascetique et de Mystique [*Paris*]
RAss — Revue d'Assyriologie et d'Archeologie Orientale
Rass Agr Ital — Rassegna dell'Agricoltura Italiana
Rass Arch Chir — Rassegna ed Archivio di Chirurgia
Rass Chim — Rassegna Chimica
Rass Clin Ter Sci Affini — Rassegna di Clinica Terapia e Scienze Affini
RassCult — Rassegna di Cultura
Rass Econ Afr Ital — Rassegna Economica dell'Africa Italiana
Rass Econ Cam Commer Ind Agr Alessandria — Rassegna Economica. Camera di Commercio, Industria, e Agricoltura di Alessandria
Rass Econ Colon — Rassegna Economica delle Colonie
Rass Econ (Napoli) — Rassegna Economica (Napoli)
Rassegna Ital Sociol — Rassegna Italiana di Sociologia
RassFilos — Rassegna di Filosofia
Rass Fisiopatol Clin Ter — Rassegna di Fisiopatologia Clinica e Terapeutica
Rass Giuliana Med — Rassegna Giuliana di Medicina
Rass IGI — Rassegna Indo-Greco-Italica
Rass Int Stomatol Prat — Rassegna Internazionale di Stomatologia Pratica
Rass d'It — Rassegna d'Italia
Rass Ital Gastro-Enterol — Rassegna Italiana di Gastro-Enterologia
Rass Ital Gastro-Enterol Suppl — Rassegna Italiana di Gastro-Enterologia. Supplemento
Rass Ital Ottalmol — Rassegna Italiana d'Ottalmologia
Rass Ital Sociol — Rassegna Italiana di Sociologia
Rass Let It — Rassegna della Letteratura Italiana
Rass Med — Rassegna Medica
Rass Med Appl Lav Ind — Rassegna di Medicina Applicata al Lavoro Industriale
Rass Med Convivium Sanit — Rassegna Medica - Convivium Sanitatis
Rass Med Cult — Rassegna Medica e Culturale
Rass Med Ind — Rassegna di Medicina Industriale
Rass Med Ind Ig Lav — Rassegna di Medicina Industriale e di Igiene del Lavoro
Rass Med Sarda — Rassegna Medica Sarda
Rass Med Sarda Suppl — Rassegna Medica Sarda. Supplemento
Rass Med Sper — Rassegna di Medicina Sperimentale
Rass Med Sper Suppl — Rassegna di Medicina Sperimentale. Supplemento
Rass Mens Clin Patol Ter Vita Prof Med Condotto Med Prat — Rassegna Mensile di Clinica, di Patologia, di Terapia, e di Vita Professionale del Medico Condotto e del Medico Pratico
Rass Min Metall Ital — Rassegna Mineraria e Metallurgica Italiana
Rass Mus — Rassegna Musicale
Rass Mus Curci — Rassegna Musicale Curci
Rass Neuropsichiatr Sci Affini — Rassegna di Neuropsichiatria e Scienze Affini
R Assoc Canad Educ Langue Franc — Revue. Association Canadienne d'Education de Langue Francaise
Rass Odontotec — Rassegna Odontotecnica
Rass Patol Appar Respir — Rassegna di Patologia dell'Apparato Respiratorio
Rass Psicol Gen Clin — Rassegna di Psicologia Generale e Clinica
Rass Serv Soc — Rassegna di Servizio Sociale
Rass Sind Quad — Rassegna Sindacale. Quaderni
Rass Stor R — Rassegna Storica del Risorgimento
Rass Studi Psichiatr — Rassegna di Studi Psichiatrici
Rass Ter Patol Clin — Rassegna di Terapia e Patologia Clinica
Rass Trimest Odontoiatr — Rassegna Trimestrale di Odontoiatria
RAssyr — Revue d'Assyriologie
Rasteniev'd Nauki — Rasteniev'dni Nauki
Rastenievud Nauk — Rastenievudni Nauki
Rastenievud Nauki — Rastenievudni Nauki
RaStEt — Rassegna di Studi Etiopici [*Rome*]
Rastit Belki — Rastitel'nye Belki
Rastit Krainego Sev Ee Osvoenie — Rastitel'nost Krainego Severa i Ee Osvoenie
Rastit Krainego Sev SSSR Ee Osvoenie — Rastitel'nost Krainego Severa SSSR i Ee Osvoenie
Rastit Latv SSR — Rastitel'nost Latviiskoi SSR
Rastit Resur — Rastitel'nye Resursy
Rastit Zasht — Rastitelna Zashtita
Rastit Zasht Plant Prot — Rastitelna Zashtita/Plant Protection
Rast Nauki — Rastenievudni Nauki
Rast Resursy — Rastitel'nye Resursy
R Astron Soc Can Pr — Royal Astronomical Society of Canada. Selected Papers and Proceedings
Rast Zashch — Rastitelna Zashchita
RASyr — Revue Archeologique Syrienne
RAT — Revue. Academie Internationale du Tourisme
RATEA — Radiotekhnika [*Moscow*]
RATIB — Radiologic Technology

Rationalisierung — Monatsschrift des Rationalisierungs
Ration Drug Ther — Rational Drug Therapy
Rat News Lett — Rat News Letter
RAug — Revue Augustinienne
Raumforsch u-Ordnung — Raumforschung und Raumordnung
Raumforsch und Raumordnung — Raumforschung und Raumordnung
R Aust Chem Inst J Proc — Royal Australian Chemical Institute. Journal and Proceedings
R Aust Chem Inst J Proc Suppl — Royal Australian Chemical Institute. Journal and Proceedings. Supplement
R Aust Chem Inst J Proc — Royal Australian Chemical Institute. Proceedings
R Aust Plann Inst J — RAPIJ: Royal Australian Planning Institute. Journal
RAut & L — Revue des Auteurs et des Livres
RAuv — Revue d'Auvergne
RAW — Raad van Advies voor het Wetenschapsbeleid. Informatiebank. Tweekbericht
RAW — Record of the Arab World [*Beirut*]
Raw Materials Survey Res Rept — Raw Materials Survey. Resource Report
Raw Mater Rep — Raw Materials Report [*Sweden*]
RAXRA — Radex Rundschau (Austria)
Raymond W Brink Selected Math Papers — Raymond W. Brink Selected Mathematical Papers
Rayon — Rayon and Synthetic Textiles
Rayon J — Rayon Journal
Rayon J Cellul Fibers — Rayon Journal and Cellulose Fibers
Rayonnem Ionis — Rayonnements Ionisants
Rayonnem Ionis Tech Mes Prot — Rayonnements Ionisants. Techniques de Mesures et de Protection
Rayon Rev — Rayon Revue
Rayon Synth Text — Rayon and Synthetic Textiles
Rayon Synth Yarn J — Rayon and Synthetic Yarn Journal
Rayon Text Mon — Rayon Textile Monthly
RazFe — Razon y Fe [*Madrid*]
Raziskave Stud Kmetijski Inst Slov — Raziskave in Studije-Kmetijski Institut Slovenije
Razpr Slov Akad Znan Umet IV — Razprave. Slovenska Akademija Znanosti in Umetnosti. IV
Razpr Slov Akad Znan Umet Razred Mat Fiz Teh Vede Ser A — Razprave. Slovenska Akademija Znanosti in Umetnosti. Razred za Matematicne, Fizikalne, in Tehnicne Vede. Serija A. Matematicne, Fizikalne, in Kemicne Vede
Razrab Ehkspl Gazov Gazokondens Mestorozhd — Razrabotka i Ehksplutatsiya Gazovykh i Gazokondensatnykh Mestorozhdenij
Razrab Mestorozhd Polezn Iskop (Kiev) — Razrabotka Mestorozhdenii Poleznykh Iskopaemykh (Kiev)
Razrab Mestorozhd Polezn Iskop (Tiflis) — Razrabotka Mestorozhdenii Poleznykh Iskopaemykh (Tiflis)
Razrab Neft Gazov Mestorozhd — Razrabotka Neftyanykh i Gazovykh Mestorozhdenii
Razrab Rudn Mestorozhd — Razrabotka Rudnykh Mestorozhdenii [*Ukrainian SSR*]
Razred Mat Fiz Teh Vede Dela — Razred za Matematicne, Fizikalne in Tehnicne Vede Dela [*Ljubljana*]
Raz SAZU — Razprave Razreda za Filoloske in Literarne vede Slovenske Akademije Znanoste in Umetnosti
Razved Geofiz — Razvedochnaya Geofizika
Razved Geofiz (Leningrad) — Razvedochnaya Geofizika (Leningrad)
Razved Nedr — Razvedka Nedr [*USSR*]
Razved Okhr Nedr — Razvedka i Okhrana Nedr
Razved i Okhr Nedr — Razvedka i Okhrana Nedr
Razved Promysl Geofiz — Razvedochnaya i Promyslovaya Geofizika
Razved Razrab Neft Gazov Mestorozhd — Razvedka i Razrabotka Neftyanykh i Gazovykh Mestorozhdenii
RB — Recherches Bibliques
RB — Religious Broadcasting
RB — Retail Business
RB — Revista Bibliotecilor [*Bucharest*]
R du B — Revue du Barreau
RB — Revue Benedictine
RB — Revue Biblique
RB — Revue Bossuet
RB — Rivista Biblica [*Rome*]
RBA — Revista de Bellas Artes
RBA — Revue Belge d'Archeologie et d'Histoire de l'Art
RBAA — Revue Belge d'Art et d'Archeologie
RBAADT — Ain Shams University. Faculty of Agriculture. Research Bulletin
RBAB — Revue des Bibliotheques et des Archives de la Belgique
RBACB — Revista Brasileira de Analises Clinicas
RBAHA — Revue Belge d'Archeologie et d'Histoire de l'Art
RBAM — Revista. Biblioteca, Archivo, y Museo del Ayuntamiento de Madrid
RBAMM — Revista. Biblioteca, Archivo, y Museo del Ayuntamiento de Madrid
R Bancaria — Revista Bancaria
R Bancaria Bras — Revista Bancaria Brasileira
R Banco Republ — Revista. Banco de la Republica
RBAPA — Revue du Bois et de Ses Applications

RBArch — Revue Belge d'Archeologie et d'Histoire de l'Art
RBArg — Revista Biblica con Seccion Liturgica [*Buenos Aires*]
RBB — Reference Books Bulletin
RBB — Revue Bibliographique Belge
RBBRD — Revista de Biblioteconomia de Brasilia
RBC — Revista Bimestre Cubana
RBCalb — Revista Biblica. Villa Calbada [*Argentina*]
RBD — Reserve Bank of India. Bulletin
RBD — Revista Bibliografica y Documental [*Madrid*]
RBdeF — Revista Brasileira de Filosofia
RBE — Review of Business and Economic Research
R Belge Archeol — Revue Belge d'Archeologie et d'Histoire de l'Art
R Belge Dr Int — Revue Belge de Droit International
R Belge Droit Internat — Revue Belge de Droit International
R Belge Mus — Revue Belge de Musicologie
R Belge Musicol — Belgisch Tijdschrift voor Muziek-Wetenschap/Revue Belge de Musicologie
R Belge Philol & Hist — Revue Belge de Philologie et d'Histoire
R Belge Securite Soc — Revue Belge de Securite Sociale
R Belge Secur Soc — Revue Belge de Securite Sociale
RBelPhH — Revue Belge de Philogogie et d'Histoire [*Brussels*]
RBen — Revue Benedictine
RBF — Revista Brasileira de Filosofia
RBF — Revista Brasileira de Folclore
RBFl — Revista Brasileira de Filologia
RBFilol — Revista Brasileira de Filologia
RBFSA — Revista Brasileira de Fisica
RBGCA — Revista Brasileira de Geociencias
RBGd — Rocznik Biblioteki Gdanskiej Pan
RBGED3 — Brazilian Journal of Genetics
RBHGPV — Rheinische Beitraege und Hilfsbuecher zur Germanischen Philologie und Volkskunde
RBI — Recherches Bibliques
RBi — Revue Biblique
RBI — Revue Biblique Internationale
RBI — Rivista Biblica Italiana [*Rome*]
RBIB — Reserve Bank of India. Bulletin [*Bombay*]
RBib — Revue Biblique
RBibIT — Rivista Biblica Italiana [*Rome*]
RBibl — Revue des Bibliotheques
R Bible — Revue Biblique
R Biblio Brasilia — Revista de Biblioteconomia de Brasilia
R Bibl Nac (Cuba) — Revista. Biblioteca Nacional de Cuba
RBiIt — Rivista Biblica Italiana [*Rome*]
RBILA — Rivista di Biologia
R Bimestr Inform Banque Maroc Com Ext — Revue Bimestrielle d'Informations. Banque Marocaine du Commerce Exterieur
RBKr — Rocznik Biblioteki Pan w Krakowie
R Bk Rel — Review of Books and Religion
RBL — Revista Brasileira de Linguistica
RBL — Revue Bleue
R Black Pol Econ — Review of Black Political Economy
R Black Pol Economy — Review of Black Political Economy
RBLI — Rassegna Bibliografica della Letteratura Italiana
RBLL — Revista Brasileira de Lingua e Literatura
RBM — Revue Belge de Musicologie
RBML — Repertorium fuer Biblische und Morgenlaendische Litteratur [*Leipzig*]
RBM (Rev Eur Biotechnol Med) — RBM (Revue Europeenne de Biotechnologie Medicale)
RBMus — Revue Belge de Musicologie
RBN — Revista de Bibliografia Nacional [*Madrid*]
RBN — Revue Belge de Numismatique
RBNC — Revista. Biblioteca Nacional de Cuba
RBNH — Revista. Biblioteca Nacional de Cuba
RBNS — Revue Belge de Numismatique et de Sigillographie
R Bolsa Comer Rosario — Revista. Bolsa de Comercio de Rosario
R Bot Garden Edinb Notes — Royal Botanical Garden of Edinburgh. Notes
RBPh — Revue Belge de Philologie et d'Histoire
RBPhil — Revue Belge de Philologie et d'Histoire
RBPMA — Revue Belge de Pathologie et de Medecine Experimentale
RBQ — Revue de la Banque [*Bruxelles*]
RBQSA — Revista Brasileira de Quimica (Sao Paulo)
RBques — Revue des Bibliotheques
RBr — Revista Brasiliense
R Bras Econ — Revista Brasileira de Economia
R Bras Estatistica — Revista Brasileira de Estatistica
R Bras Estud Pol — Revista Brasileira de Estudos Politicos
R Brasil Econ — Revista Brasileira de Economia
R Brasil Estatist — Revista Brasileira de Estatistica
R Brasil Estud Polit — Revista Brasileira de Estudos Politicos
R Brasil Geogr — Revista Brasileira de Geografia
R Brasil Polit Int — Revista Brasileira de Politica Internacional
R Bras Mercado Capitais — Revista Brasileira de Mercado de Capitais
RBRI — Reference Book Review Index
RBRJ — Revista Brasileira (Rio De Janeiro)

RBRLA — Revue Bryologique et Lichenologique
R Bryol & Lichenol — Revue Bryologique et Lichenologique
RBS — Regulae Benedicti Studia
RBSL — Regensburger Beitrage zur Deutschen Sprach- und Literaturwissenschaft
RBSTARO — Revue Belge de Statistique, d'Informatique, et de Recherche Operationnelle
RBT — Reviews in Biochemical Toxicology [*Elsevier Book Series*]
RBTNA — Revista Brasileira de Tecnologia
RBU — Buro und EDV. Zeitschrift fuer Buroorganisation und Datentechnik
R Bus & Econ Res — Review of Business and Economic Research
R Bus and Econ Research — Review of Business and Economic Research
R Bus St John's Univ — Review of Business. St. John's University
RBY — Rotterdam Europoort Delta
RBYOA — Rinsho Byori
RBZ — Rotterdam
RC — La Revue du Caire [*Cairo*]
RC — Rekishi Chiri
R & C — Religion y Cultura
R & C — Religioni e Civitta
RC — Respiratory Care
RC — Review of the Churches
RC — Revista Contemporanea
RC — Revista Cubana
RC — Revue Celtique
RC — Revue Charlemagne
RC — Revue Critique
RC — Rivista delle Colonie
RC — Ruperto-Carola
RCA — Alimentation Moderne. Revue de la Conserve
RCA — Revista Colombiana de Antropologia
RCA — Rozpravy Ceskoslovenske Akademie Ved
Rc Accad Lincei Cl di Sci Mor Stor Fil — Rendiconti. Accademia Nazionale dei Lincei. Classe di Scienze Morali. Storiche e Filologiche
RCAEB — RCA [*Radio Corporation of America*] Engineer
RCA Eng — RCA [*Radio Corporation of America*] Engineer
RCAFA — Revista Cafetalera [*Spain*]
RCAJ — Royal Central Asian Society. Journal
RCal — Revista Calasancia
RCAls — Revue Catholique d'Alsace
RCam — Revista Camoniana [*Sao Paulo*]
RCan — Revue Canonique
R Canad-Amer Et Slaves — Revue Canadienne-Americaine d'Etudes Slaves
R Canad Et Afr — Revue Canadienne des Etudes Africaines
R Can Etud Nationalisme — Revue Canadienne des Etudes sur le Nationalisme
R Can Sciences Info — Revue Canadienne des Sciences de l'Information
RCAPA — Revista de Ciencia Aplicada
RCA R — RCA [*Radio Corporation of America*] Review
RCARC — RCA [*Radio Corporation of America*] Review
RCA Rev — RCA [*Radio Corporation of America*] Review
RCat — Revista de Catalunya
RCA Tech Not — RCA [*Radio Corporation of America*] Technical Notes
RCA Tech Notes — RCA [*Radio Corporation of America*] Technical Notes
Rc Atti Accad Naz Lincei — Rendiconti e Atti. Accademia Nazionale dei Lincei
RCAV — Rozpravy Ceskoslovenske Akademie Ved
RCAVA — Rozpravy Ceskoslovenske Akademie Ved. Rada Matematickych a Prirodnich Ved
RCB — Revista de Cultura Biblica [*Rio De Janeiro/Sao Paulo, Brazil*]
RCB — Revista de Cultura Brasilena
RCBIA — Revue Canadienne de Biologie
RCBOA — Radiologia Clinica et Biologica
RCC — Revue des Cours et Conferences
RCCFB — Revista CENIC [*Centro Nacional de Investigaciones Cientificas*]. Ciencias Fisicas [*Cuba*]
RCCM — Rivista di Cultura Classica e Medioevale
RCCMA — Rivista Critica di Clinica Medica
RCCS — Revista Catolica de las Cuestiones Sociales
RCDIP — Revue Critique de Droit International Prive
RCE — Repertoire Canadien sur l'Education [*See also CEI*]
RCE — Reviews in Cancer Epidemiology [*Elsevier Book Series*]
RCE — Revue Catholique des Eglises
RCEE — Revista. Centro de Estudios Extemoenos
RCEH — Revista Canadiense de Estudios Hispanicos
RCEI — Revista Canaria de Estudios Ingleses
RCel — Revue Celtique
R Centroam Econ — Revista Centroamericana de Economia
RCERB — Ricerche di Termotecnica
RCF — Review of Contemporary Fiction
RCF — Revista Colombiana de Folclor
RCF — Revue du Clerge Francais
RCFNA — Revista. Real Academia de Ciencias Exactas, Fisicas, y Naturales de Madrid
RCG — Revue du Chant Gregorien
RCGJA — Royal College of General Practitioners. Journal

RCh — Revue Charlemagne
R Ch Com Franc Canada — Revue. Chambre de Commerce Francaise au Canada
RCHE — Recherche
RCHG — Revista Chilena de Historia y Geografia
R Ch J — Rencontre. Chretiens et Juifs
RChL — Revista Chilena de Literatura
RCHL — Revue Critique d'Histoire et de Litterature
RChr — Revue Chretienne
RCHRA — Revue de Chimie. Academie de la Republique Populaire Roumaine
RchScR — Recherches de Science Religieuse
RCI — Revista delle Colonie Italiane
RCID — Revue Catholique des Institutions et de Droit
R Ciencia Pol — Revista de Ciencia Politica
R Ciencias Econs — Revista de Ciencias Economicas
R Ciencias Juridicas — Revista de Ciencias Juridicas
R Ciencias Socs (Costa Rica) — Revista de Ciencias Sociales (Costa Rica)
R Ciencias Socs (Puerto Rico) — Revista de Ciencias Sociales (Puerto Rico)
R Cienc Polit — Revista de Ciencia Politica
R Cienc Soc (Ceara) — Revista de Ciencias Sociales (Ceara)
R Cienc Soc (Puerto Rico) — Revista de Ciencias Sociales (Puerto Rico)
R Cin — Revue du Cinema
R Cin — Revue du Cinema/Image et Son
RCINA — Revista Chilena de Ingenieria
R Cinematografo — Rivista del Cinematografo
Rc Ist Lomb Sci Lett — Rendiconti. Istituto Lombardo di Scienze e Lettere
Rc Ist Sup Sanita — Rendiconti. Istituto Superiore di Sanita
RCivB — Revista Civilizacao Brasileira [Rio De Janeiro]
RCJS — Revista de Ciencias Juridicas y Sociales
RCL — Reading-Canada-Lecture
RCL — Review of Contemporary Law
RCl — Rivista Clasica
RCLAD — Ricerca in Clinica e in Laboratorio
RCLADN — Investigacion en la Clinica y en el Laboratorio
RClFr — Revue du Clerge Francais
RCLI — Rassegna Critica della Letteratura Italiana
RCLL — Revista de Critica Literaria Latinoamericana
RCM — Royal College of Music. Magazine
RCMP — RCMP [Royal Canadian Mounted Police] Quarterly
RCMTA — Ricerche di Matematica
RCMUH — Ruperto-Carola. Mitteilungen der Vereinigung der Freunde der Studentenschaft der Universitaet Heidelberg
RCN — Energiespectrum
RCNAA — Radiologic Clinics of North America
RCN Bull — RCN [Reactor Centrum Nederland] Bulletin
RCN Meded — Reactor Centrum Nederland. Mededeling
RCNMR — Royal Canadian Navy. Monthly Review
RCN Rep — Reactor Centrum Nederland. Report
RCOBA — Revista Chilena de Obstetricia y Ginecologia
RCOCB — Research Communications in Chemical Pathology and Pharmacology
RCOGB — Revista Cubana de Obstetricia y Ginecologia
RCol — Rassegna di Coltura
R Collect Loc — Revue des Collectivites Locales
R Coll For Dep Refor Res Notes — Royal College of Forestry. Department of Reforestation. Research Notes
R Coll Sci Technol (Glasg) Res Rep — Royal College of Science and Technology (Glasgow). Research Report
RColt — Rassegna di Coltura
R Comitato G Italia B — Reale Comitato Geologico d'Italia. Bolletino
R Commer — Revue Commerce
RCOND — Resources and Conservation
RCong — Revue Congolaise
RConsAlim — Revue Conserve Alimentation
R Contemp Sociol — Review of Contemporary Sociology
R Coop Int — Revue de la Cooperation Internationale
R Coree — Revue de Coree
RCP — Recrea Plus
RCPBO — Research Communications in Psychology, Psychiatry, and Behavior
RCPEA — Revista Chilena de Pediatria
RCPJA — Royal College of Physicians of London. Journal
RCPRA — Record of Chemical Progress
RCQUD — Revista de Ciencias Quimicas
RCR — Rabbinical Council Record [New York]
RC-R — Revista Chicano-Riquena
RCr — Revue Critique
RCr — Revue Critique d'Histoire et de Litterature
RCRF — Rei Cretariae Romanae Fautorum Acta
RCrit — Ragioni Critiche. Rivista di Studi Linguistici e Letterari
R Crit Dr Int Prive — Revue Critique de Droit International Prive
RcRt — Romantic Reassessment
RCRUA — Revista. Consejo de Rectores. Universidades Chilenas
RCRVA — Russian Chemical Reviews [English Translation]
RCS — Conditionnement Embouteillage. Revue Mensuelle de l'Embouteillage et des Industries du Conditionnement, Traitement, Distribution, Transport

RCSAV — Rozpravy Ceskoslovenske Akademie Ved
RCSCSPL — Russian, Croatian and Serbian, Czech and Slovak, Polish Literature
RCSF — Rivista Critica di Storia della Filosofia
RCSH — Revue Congolaise des Sciences Humaines
RCSMC — Recent Advances in Studies on Cardiac Structure and Metabolism
RCT — Revista Catalana de Teologia
RCTCA — Recherche Technique
RCTEA — Rubber Chemistry and Technology
RCTPA — Russian Castings Production [English Translation]
RCuBib — Revista de Cultura Biblica [Rio De Janeiro/Sao Paulo, Brazil]
R Current Activities Tech Ed — Review of Current Activities in Technical Education
RCuTeol — Revista de Cultura Teologica [Sao Paulo, Brazil]
RCV — Recreatievoorzieningen. Maandblad voor Recreatie, Milieu, en Landschap
RCVRB — Royal Military College of Canada. Civil Engineering Research Report
RCVS — Rassegna di Cultura e Vita Scolastica
RCVTA — Rozpravy Ceskoslovenske Akademie Ved. Rada Technickych Ved
RCVTB — Recherches Veterinaires
RD — Renaissance Drama
RD — Revista de Dialectologia y Tradiciones Populares
R de D — Revue de Droit. Universite de Sherbrooke
RD — Revue Historique de Droit Francais et Etranger
RD — Rivista Dalmatica
RD & A — Research, Development, and Acquisition
RDAC — Report. Department of Antiquities of Cyprus
RDB — Revue du Bois et de Ses Applications
RDBGA — Radiobiologia-Radioterapia
RDBMD — Review on the Deformation Behavior of Materials
RdC — Resto del Carlino
RDC — Revue de Droit Canonique
RDC — Revue de Droit Compare. Association Quebecoise pour l'Etude Comparative du Droit
RDC — Rochester Diocesan Chronicle
RDCTD8 — Australia. Commonwealth Scientific and Industrial Research Organisation. Division of Chemical Technology. Research Review
RdDM — Revue des Deux Mondes
RdDxM — Revue des Deux Mondes
RdE — Revista de las Espanas
Rd'E — Revue d'Egyptologie [Publiee par la Societe Francaise d'Egyptologie] [Cairo]
RDE — Revue d'Esthetique
RdE — Rivista di Estetica
RDEEA — Radio and Electronic Engineer
RdeIE — Revista de Ideas Esteticas
RdeInd — Revista de las Indias
R Der Cienc Polit — Revista de Derecho y Ciencias Politicas. Universidad de San Marcos
R Der (Concepcion) — Revista de Derecho (Concepcion)
R Derechos Humanos — Revista de Derechos Humanos
R Der Int Cienc Diplom — Revista de Derecho Internacional y Ciencias Diplomaticas
RdEt — Revista de Etnografia
R Deux Mondes — Revue des Deux Mondes
R Developpement Internat — Revue du Developpement International
RDF — Revue de France
RdF — Rivista di Filosofia
RDGNA — Radiologia Diagnostica
RDGRA — Radiographer
RDGTA — Rational Drug Therapy
RdH — Revista de Historia
R Dialect & Tradic Popul — Revista de Dialectologia y Tradiciones Populares
RdiE — Rivista di Estetica
RdiF — Rivista di Filosofia
RDIGA — Reader's Digest
RDIn — Rivista di Diritto Internazionale
R Dir Adm — Revista de Direito Administrativo
RdL — Revista de Letras
RdL — Revista do Livro
RdLet — Revista de Letras. Serie Literatura
RDLGB — Radiologe
RDM — Nouvelle Revue des Deux Mondes
RDM — Retail and Distribution Management
RDM — Revue des Deux Mondes
RdM — Revue de la Mediterranee
RdM — Revue de Musicologie [Paris]
RDMAA — R and D [Research and Development] Management
R and D Manage — R and D [Research and Development] Management
RDN — Revue du Nord
RDNamur — Revue Diocesaine de Namur
RDNGB — Ryukyu Daigaku Nogakubu Gakujutsu Hokoku
RdP — Revue de Paris
RdPac — Revista del Pacifico
RDR — Ryukoku Daigaku Ronshu

R/D Res/Develop — R/D. Research/Development
R Dr Homme — Revue des Droits de l'Homme
RDRIA — Radiazioni e Radioisotopi
R Dr Int Dr Comp — Revue de Droit International et de Droit Compare
RDRKB — Ritsumeikan Daigaku Rikogaku Kenkyusho Kiyo
R Droit Int Sci Dipl Pol — Revue de Droit International de Sciences Diplomatiques et Politiques
R Droit Public — Revue du Droit Public et de la Science Politique en France et a l'Etranger
R Droits Homme — Revue des Droits de l'Homme
R Droit Soc — Revue de Droit Social
R Dr Publ Sci Polit — Revue du Droit Public et de la Science Politique en France et a l'Etranger
R Dr Rur — Revue de Droit Rural
RdS — Responsabilita del Sapere
RdS — Revue de Synthese
RdSO — Rivista degli Studi Orientali
Rds Rd Constn — Roads and Road Construction
RDT — Recreatie-Documentatie. Literatuuroverzicht Inzake Dagrecreatie, Verblijfsrecreatie, en Toerisme
RdT — Revista de Teatro
RDTournai — Revue Diocesaine de Tournai
RDTP — Revista de Dialectologia y Tradiciones Populares
R Dublin Soc J Sc Pr — Royal Dublin Society. Journal. Scientific Proceedings
R Dublin Soc Rep — Royal Dublin Society. Report
R D U S — Revue de Droit. Universite de Sherbrooke
RDyTP — Revista de Dialectologia y Tradiciones Populares
RE — Real-Encyclopaedie der Klassischen Altertumswissenschaft
Re — Realidad
Re — Reinsurance
RE — Religious Education
Re — Republic [*Quezon City*]
Re — Response
RE — Review and Expositor
RE — Revista Eclesiastica
RE — Revue d'Egyptologie
RE — Revue Egyptologique
RE — Revue d'Esthetique
REA — Revue de l'Egypte Ancienne [*Paris*]
REA — Revue des Etudes Anciennes
REA — Revue des Etudes Armeniennes
REA — Revue des Etudes Augustiniennes
React Cent Ned Rep — Reactor Centrum Nederland. Report
React Fuel Process — Reactor Fuel Processing
React Fuel-Process Technol — Reactor and Fuel-Processing Technology
React Kin C — Reaction Kinetics and Catalysis Letters
React Kinet — Reaction Kinetics [*Later, Gas Kinetics and Energy Transfer*]
React Kinet Catal Lett — Reaction Kinetics and Catalysis Letters
Reactor Fuel Process — Reactor Fuel Processing
Reactor Mater — Reactor Materials
React Polym — Reactive Polymers [*The Netherlands*]
React Res Soc News — Reaction Research Society. News
React Res Soc Rep — Reaction Research Society. Report
React Technol — Reactor Technology
Read Dig — Reader's Digest
Read Digest — Reader's Digest
Read Educ — Reading Education
Reader — Reader Magazine
Readers D — Reader's Digest
Reader's Dig — Reader's Digest
Read Glass Hist — Readings in Glass History
Read Improv — Reading Improvement
Reading Educ — Reading Education
Reading Univ Geol Rep — Reading University. Geological Reports
Read Man — Reading Manitoba
Read Res Q — Reading Research Quarterly
Read Teach — Reading Teacher
Read Time — Reading Time
Read World — Reading World
R E Ag — Revue des Etudes Augustiniennes
REAIU — Revue des Ecoles de l'Alliance Israelite Universelle
Reakt Bull — Reaktor Bulletin
Reaktortag (Fachvortr) — Reaktortagung (Fachvortraege) [*West Germany*]
Reakt Osobo Chist Veshchestva — Reaktivy i Osobo Chistye Veshchestva
Reakts Metody Issled Org Soedin — Reaktsii i Metody Issledovaniya Organicheskikh Soedinenii [*USSR*]
Reakts Sposobn Koord Soedin — Reaktsionnaya Sposobnost' Koordinatsionnykh Soedinenii
Reakts Sposobn Mekh Reakts Org Soedin — Reaktsionnaya Sposobnost' i Mekhanizmy Reaktsii Organicheskikh Soedinenii
Reakts Sposobn Org Soedin — Reaktsionnaya Sposobnost' Organicheskikh Soedinenii
Reakts Sposobnost' Org Soedin Tartu Gos Univ — Reaktsionnaya Sposobnost' Organicheskikh Soedinenij. Tartuskij Gosudarstvennyj Universitet
REAL — Re: Arts and Letters
Real Anal Exchange — Real Analysis Exchange

REALB — REAL. The Yearbook of Research in English and American Literature
Real Econ — Realta Economica
Real Estate Appraiser & Anal — Real Estate Appraiser and Analyst
Real Estate J — Real Estate Journal
Real Estate L J — Real Estate Law Journal
Real Estate R — Real Estate Review
Real Estate Rev — Real Estate Review
Real Estate & Stock J — Real Estate and Stock Journal
Real Est L — Real Estate Law Journal
Real Est LJ — Real Estate Law Journal
Real Est Re — Real Estate Review
Real Est Rev — Real Estate Review
Realidad Econ — Realidad Economica
Real Ist Veneto Mem — Reale Istituto Veneto di Scienze, Lettere, ed Arti. Memorie
Real M — Realta del Mezzogiorno. Mensile di Politica, Economia, Cultura
RealN — Realta Nuova
Real Prop P — Real Property, Probate, and Trust Journal
Real Prop Probate & Trust J — Real Property, Probate, and Trust Journal
Real Prop Prob and Tr J — Real Property, Probate, and Trust Journal
Real Prop Rep — Real Property Reports
Realta Econ — Realta Economica
Realta Mezzogiorno — Realta del Mezzogiorno
Real Wr — Realist Writer
REAnc — Revue des Etudes Anciennes
Reanim Med Urgence — Reanimation et Medecine d'Urgence
Reanim Organes Artif — Reanimation et Organes Artificiels
REARA — Recherche Aerospatiale
REArm — Revue des Etudes Armeniennes
REArmen — Revue des Etudes Armeniennes
REArmNS — Revue des Etudes Armeniennes. Nouvelle Serie
REA (Rural Electr Adm) Bull (US) — REA (Rural Electrification Administration) Bulletin (United States)
REAug — Revue des Etudes Augustiniennes
REB — Resultaten van de Conjunctuurenquete bij het Bedrijfsleven in de Gemeenschap
ReB — Revista Biblica
REB — Revista Eclesiastica Brasileira
ReB — Revue Biblique
REB — Revue des Etudes Byzantines
REB — Revue Internationale des Etudes Balkaniques
REBras — Revista Eclesiastica Brasileira
REBUD — Renewable Energy Bulletin
REByz — Revue des Etudes Byzantines
Rec — Recurrence
REC — Revista de Estudios Clasicos
Rec Agric Res (Belfast) — Record of Agricultural Research (Belfast)
Rec Agric Res Minist Agric (Nth Ire) — Record of Agricultural Research. Ministry of Agriculture (Northern Ireland)
Rec Agr Res (N Ireland) — Record of Agricultural Research (Northern Ireland)
Rec Ak Inst Mus — Records. Auckland Institute and Museum [*New Zealand*]
Rec Am Cath Hist Soc — Records. American Catholic Historical Society of Philadelphia
Rec Annu Conv Br Wood Preserv Assoc — Record of the Annual Convention. British Wood Preserving Association
Rec Asilomar Conf Circuits Syst Comput — Record. Asilomar Conference on Circuits, Systems, and Computers
Rec Ass'n Bar City of NY — Record. Association of the Bar of the City of New York
Rec Auckland Inst — Records. Auckland Institute and Museum
Rec Auckl Inst Mus — Records. Auckland Institute and Museum
RecAug — Recherches Augustiniennes
Rec Aust Acad Sci — Records. Australian Academy of Science
Rec Aust Mus — Records. Australian Museum
Rec Aust Museum — Records. Australian Museum
Rec Bot Surv India — Records. Botanical Survey of India
Rec Buckinghamshire — Records of Buckinghamshire
Rec Canterbury Mus — Records. Canterbury Museum [*Christchurch, New Zealand*]
Rec Changer — Record Changer
Rec Chem Prog — Record of Chemical Progress
Rec Coll — Record Collector
Rec Conv Brit Wood Pres Ass — Record of the Annual Convention. British Wood Preserving Association
Rec Dom Mus (Wellington) — Records. Dominion Museum (Wellington, New Zealand)
Recd Res Fac Agr Univ Tokyo — Records of Researches. Faculty of Agriculture. University of Tokyo
Rec Electr Commun Eng Conversat Tohoku Univ — Record of Electrical and Communication Engineering Conversation. Tohoku University [*Japan*]
Rec Eng N — Recovery Engineering News
Recent Adv Aerosp Med — Recent Advances in Aerospace Medicine
Recent Advanc Bot — Recent Advances in Botany
Recent Adv Biol Psychiatry — Recent Advances in Biological Psychiatry

Recent Adv Clin Nucl Med — Recent Advances in Clinical Nuclear Medicine
Recent Adv Food Sci — Recent Advances in Food Science
Recent Adv Gastroenterol — Recent Advances in Gastroenterology
Recent Adv Gut Horm Res — Recent Advances in Gut Hormone Research
Recent Adv Phytochem — Recent Advances in Phytochemistry
Recent Adv Renal Dis — Recent Advances in Renal Disease
Recent Adv RES Res — Recent Advances in RES [Reticuloendothelial System] Research
Recent Adv Stud Card Struct Metab — Recent Advances in Studies on Cardiac Structure and Metabolism
Recent Dev Alcohol — Recent Developments in Alcoholism
Recent Dev Chem Nat Carbon Compd — Recent Developments in the Chemistry of Natural Carbon Compounds
Recent Dev Neurobiol Hung — Recent Developments of Neurobiology in Hungary
Recenti Prog Med — Recenti Progressi in Medicina
Recent Lit Hazard Environ Ind — Recent Literature on Hazardous Environments in Industry
Recent Prog Horm Res — Recent Progress in Hormone Research
Recent Prog Med (Roma) — Recenti Progressi in Medicina (Roma)
Recent Prog Microbiol — Recent Progress in Microbiology
Recent Prog Surf Sci — Recent Progress in Surface Science
Recent Publ Gov Probl — Recent Publications on Governmental Problems [United States]
Recent Pubns Governmental Problems — Recent Publications on Governmental Problems
Recent Results Cancer Res — Recent Results in Cancer Research
Recept Ligands Intercell Commun — Receptors and Ligands in Intercellular Communication
RECFD — Revista Cubana de Fisica
Rec Geol Surv Br Guiana — Records. Geological Survey of British Guiana
Rec Geol Surv Dep North Rhod — Records. Geological Survey Department. Northern Rhodesia
Rec Geol Surv Guyana — Records. Geological Survey of Guyana
Rec Geol Surv India — Records. Geological Survey of India
Rec Geol Surv Malawi — Records. Geological Survey of Malawi
Rec Geol Surv New South Wales — Records. Geological Survey of New South Wales
Rec Geol Surv Niger — Records. Geological Survey of Nigeria
Rec Geol Surv NSW — New South Wales. Geological Survey. Records
Rec Geol Surv NSW — Records. Geological Survey of New South Wales
Rec Geol Surv Pak — Records. Geological Survey of Pakistan
Rec Geol Surv Tanganyika — Records. Geological Survey of Tanganyika
Rec Geol Surv Tasm — Tasmania. Geological Survey. Record
Rech — Recherche
RecH — Recusant History
RechA — Recherches Augustiniennes
Rech Aerosp — Recherche Aerospatiale
Rech Aerospat — Recherche Aerospatiale
Rech Aerospat English — La Recherche Aerospatiale. English Edition
Rech Agron — Recherches Agronomiques
Rech Agron (Quebec) — Recherches Agronomiques (Quebec)
Rech Amerind — Recherches Amerindiennes
RechBib — Recherches Bibliques (Journees du Colloque Biblique de Louvain)
RechBibl — Recherches Bibliques (Journees du Colloque Biblique de Louvain)
Rech Chir Eur — Recherches Chirurgicales Europeennes
Rech Clin Lab — Recherche dans la Clinique et le Laboratoire
Rech Econ Louvain — Recherches Economiques de Louvain
Rechentech Datenverarb — Rechentechnik Datenverarbeitung
Recherche Aerospat — La Recherche Aerospatiale
Recherches — Recherches sur la Musique Francaise Classique
Recherche Soc (Paris) — Recherche Sociale (Paris)
Recher Sc Rel — Recherches de Science Religieuses
Rech Geol Afr — Recherches Geologiques en Afrique
Rech Graphique — Recherche Graphique
Rech Graphique Commun — Recherche Graphique. Communications
Rech Hydrobiol Cont — Recherches d'Hydrobiologie Continentale
Rech Int — Recherches Internationales a la Lumiere du Marxism
Rech Invent — Recherches et Inventions
Rechn Transp — Rechnoi Transport
Rech Prod Foret — Recherches sur les Produits de la Foret
Rech Sci Rel — Recherches de Science Religieuse
Rech Sci Relig — Recherches de Science Religieuse
RechScR — Recherches de Science Religieuse
Rech Soc Anonyme Etabl Roure Bertrand Fils Justin Dupont — Recherches. Societe Anonyme des Etablissments Roure Bertrand Fils et Justin Dupont
Rech Sociogr — Recherches Sociographiques
Rech Sociographiques — Recherches Sociographiques
Rech Sociol — Recherches Sociologiques
Rech Soc (Paris) — Recherche Sociale (Paris)
Rech Spat — Recherche Spatiale
Rech Spatiale — Recherche Spatiale
RechSR — Recherches de Science Religieuse
Rech Tech — Recherche Technique

Recht Elektrizitaetswirtsch — Recht der Elektrizitaetswirtschaft [West Germany]
RechTh — Recherches de Theologie Ancienne et Medievale
Recht Landwirtsch — Recht der Landwirtschaft
Recht Steuern Gas-Wasserfach — Recht und Steuern im Gas- und Wasserfach [West Germany]
Rec Hung Agric Exp Stn A — Records. Hungarian Agricultural Experiment Stations. A. Plant Production
Rec Hung Agric Exp Stn C — Records. Hungarian Agricultural Experiment Stations. C. Horticulture
Rec Huntingdonshire — Records of Huntingdonshire
Rech Vet — Recherches Veterinaires
Rech Vet (Paris) — Recherches Veterinaires (Paris)
RECIFS — Recherches et Etudes Comparatistes Ibero-Francaises de la Sorbonne Nouvelle
Rec Indian Mus — Records. Indian Museum
Rec Indian Mus (Calcutta) — Records. Indian Museum (Calcutta)
Rec L — Recovering Literature
REcL — Revue Ecclesiastique de Liege
Reclam Era — Reclamation Era
Reclam Rev — Reclamation Review
Recl Med Vet — Recueil de Medecine Veterinaire
Recl Med Vet Ec Alfort — Recueil de Medecine Veterinaire. Ecole d'Alfort
Recl Trav Bot Neerl — Recueil des Travaux Botaniques Neerlandais
Recl Trav Chim Pays Bas — Recueil des Travaux Chimiques des Pays-Bas
Recl Trav Chim Pays-Bas Belg — Recueil des Travaux Chimiques des Pays-Bas et de la Belgique
Recl Trav Inst Biol (Beogr) — Recueil des Travaux. Institut Biologique (Beograd)
Recl Trav Inst Ecol Biogeogr Acad Serbe Sci — Recueil des Travaux. Institut d'Ecologie et de Biogeographie. Academie Serbe des Sciences
Recl Trav Inst Rech Struct Matiere (Belgrade) — Recueil de Travaux. Institut de Recherches sur la Structure de la Matiere (Belgrade)
Recl Trav Stn Mar Endoume Fac Sci Mars — Recueil des Travaux. Station Marine d'Endoume. Faculte des Sciences de Marseille
Recl Trav Stn Mar Endoume Marseille Fasc Hors Ser Suppl — Recueil des Travaux. Station Marine d'Endoume-Marseille. Fascicule Hors Serie. Supplement
Recl Trav Stn Mar Endoume-Mars Fasc Hors Ser Suppl — Recueil des Travaux. Station Marine d'Endoume-Marseille. Fascicule Hors Serie. Supplement
Rec Malar Surv India — Records of the Malaria Survey of India
Rec Med Vet — Recueil de Medecine Veterinaire
Rec Med Vet Ecole Alfort — Recueil de Medecine Veterinaire. Ecole d'Alfort
Rec Med Vet Exot — Recueil de Medecine Veterinaire Exotique
Rec Mem Med Mil — Recueil des Memoires de Medecine, de Chirurgie, et de Pharmacie Militaires
Rec Mem et Obs Hyg et Med Vet Mil — Recueil des Memoires et Observations sur l'Hygiene et la Medecine Veterinaires Militaires
Rec Obs Med Hop Mil — Recueil des Observations de Medecine des Hopitaux Militaires
Rec Obs Scripps Inst Oceanogr — Records of Observations. Scripps Institution of Oceanography
Rec Oceanogr Works Jpn — Records of Oceanographic Works in Japan
Rec Oceanogr Works Jpn Sp Number — Records of Oceanographic Works in Japan. Special Number
Recomb DNA Tech Bull — Recombinant DNA Technical Bulletin
Recomb DNA Tech Bull Suppl — Recombinant DNA Technical Bulletin. Supplement
R Econ Agr — Rivista di Economia Agraria
R Econ Banque Nat Paris — Revue Economique. Banque Nationale de Paris
R Econ Centre-Est — Revue de l'Economie du Centre-Est
Reconciliation Quart — Reconciliation Quarterly
R Econ Conditions Italy — Review of the Economic Conditions in Italy
R Econ Condit Italy — Review of the Economic Conditions in Italy
R Econ (Cordoba) — Revista de Economia (Cordoba)
R Econ Dr Immob — Revue d'Economie et de Droit Immobilier
R Econ Estadist — Revista de Economia y Estadistica
R Econ y Estadistica — Revista de Economia y Estadistica
R Econ et Fin — Revue Economique et Financiere Ivoirienne
R Econ Fr — Revue Economique Francaise
R Econ Franc — Revue Economique Francaise
R Econ Franc-Comtoise — Revue de l'Economie Franc-Comtoise
R Econ Franco-Suisse — Revue Economique Franco-Suisse
R Econ Fr-Suisse — Revue Economique Franco-Suisse
R Econ Gestion — Revue d'Economie et de Gestion
R Econ Latinoam — Revista de Economia Latinoamericana
R Econ Latinoamer — Revista de Economia Latinoamericana
R Econ Merid — Revue de l'Economie Meridionale
R Econ Nordeste — Revista Economica do Nordeste
R Econ (Paris) — Revue Economique (Paris)
R Econ e Pol Ind — Rivista di Economia e Politica Industriale
R Econ Polit (Madrid) — Revista de Economia Politica (Madrid)
R Econ Polit (Paris) — Revue d'Economie Politique (Paris)
R Econ Pol (Madrid) — Revista de Economia Politica (Madrid)
R Econ Pol (Paris) — Revue d'Economie Politique (Paris)

R Econ Pol (Sao Paulo) — Revista de Economia Politica (Sao Paulo)
R Econ Soc — Revue Economique et Sociale
R Econ et Soc — Revue Economique et Sociale
Recons Surg — Reconstruction Surgery and Traumatology
R Econ & Stat — Review of Economics and Statistics
R Econ Statist — Review of Economics and Statistics
R Econ Statistics — Review of Economics and Statistics
Reconstr Surg Traumatol — Reconstruction Surgery and Traumatology
R Econ Stud — Review of Economic Studies
R Econ Sud-Ouest — Revue Economique du Sud-Ouest
Recontr Surg Traumatol — Reconstruction Surgery and Traumatology
Record — Record. Association of the Bar of the City of New York
Record Broward County Med Assoc — Record. Broward County Medical Association [*Florida*]
Recorder Columbia Med Soc — Recorder. Columbia Medical Society of Richland County [*South Carolina*]
Recorder M Magazine — Recorder and Music Magazine
Recorder and Mus — Recorder and Music
Recorder & Mus Mag — Recorder and Music Magazine
Record of NYCBA — Record. Association of the Bar of the City of New York
Records Queen Museum — Records. Queen Victoria Museum
Records SA Museum — Records. South Australian Museum
RECorses — Revue des Etudes Corses
Recovery Eng News — Recovery Engineering News
RecPap — Recherches de Papyrologie
Rec Papua New Guinea Mus — Records. Papua New Guinea Museum
Rec Past — Records of the Past
RecPh — Recherches Philosophiques
RecPhL — Recherches de Philologie et de Linguistique [*Louvain*]
Rec Queen Vic Mus — Records. Queen Victoria Museum
Rec Queen Vict Mus — Records. Queen Victoria Museum
Rec Queen Victoria Mus — Records. Queen Victoria Museum
Rec Queen Victoria Mus Launceston — Records. Queen Victoria Museum of Launceston
Rec Q Vict Mus — Records. Queen Victoria Museum
RECR — Reclamation Review
Rec R — Record Review
Rec Res — Record Research
Rec Res Fac Agric Univ Tokyo — Records of Researches. Faculty of Agriculture. University of Tokyo
Recr Sci — Recreative Science
RecS — Recorded Sound
Rec S Aust Mus — Records. South Australian Museum
Rec S Aust Mus (Adelaide) — Records. South Australian Museum (Adelaide)
Rec Sci Rel — Recherches de Science Religieuse
Rec Scott Church Hist Soc — Records. Scottish Church History Society
Rec Sound — Recorded Sound
Rec South Aust Mus — Records. South Australian Museum
Rec South Aust Mus (Adelaide) — Records. South Australian Museum (Adelaide)
RecSR — Recherches de Science Religieuse
RecTh — Recherches de Theologie Ancienne et Medievale
RECTR — Restoration and Eighteenth Century Theatre Research
Rec Trav — Recueil des Travaux Relatifs a la Philologie et a l'Archeologie Egyptiennes et Assyriennes
Rec Trav Bot Neerl — Recueil des Travaux Botaniques Neerlandais [*Netherlands*]
Rec Trav Chim — Recueil des Travaux Chimiques des Pays-Bas
Rec Trav Chim Pays-Bas — Recueil des Travaux Chimiques des Pays-Bas
Rec Trav Lab Physiol Veg Fac Sci Bordeaux — Recueil des Travaux. Laboratoire de Physiologie Vegetale. Faculte des Sciences de Bordeaux
Rec Tr Chim — Recueil des Travaux Chimiques des Pays-Bas
Recur Hidraul — Recursos Hidraulicos
Recursos Hidraul — Recursos Hidraulicos [*Mexico*]
Recursos Min — Recursos Minerales
Rec US Dep State — Record. United States Department of State
RECYA — Revue Roumaine d'Embryologie et de Cytologie. Serie d'Embryologie
Recycling Waste Disposal — Recycling and Waste Disposal
Recycl Weltkongr Konf Niederschr — Recycling Weltkongress. Konferenz-Niederschriften
Recycl World Congr Congr Proc — Recycling World Congress. Congress Proceedings
Rec Zool Surv India — Records. Zoological Survey of India
Rec Zool Surv Pak — Records. Zoological Survey of Pakistan
RED — A'Beckett's Reserved Judgements [*New South Wales*]
RED — R & D (Research and Development) Management
R Ed — Religious Education
REDBA — Redbook
REDC — Revista Espanola de Derecho Canonico
Red Cross M — Red Cross Magazine
REDEA — Research/Development
REDI — Revue Egyptienne de Droit International
Redia G Zool — Redia Giornale di Zoologia
Redk Elem — Redkie Elementy
Redk Met — Redkie Metally

Red Menac — Red Menace
Redog ForsknStift Skogsarb — Redogorelse. Forskningsstiftelsen Skogsarbeten
R Ed Res — Review of Educational Research
R Educ — Review of Education
R Educ (Madrid) — Revista de Educacion (Madrid)
R Educ Res — Review of Educational Research
REDV — Resource Development. Incorporating Northern Development and Oceanic Industries
REE — Revista de Estudios Extremenos
REEDN — Records of Early English Drama. Newsletter
Reed's Mar Equip News Mar Dig — Reed's Marine and Equipment News and Marine Digest
Reeduc Orthophon — Reeducation Orthophonique
REELB — Revista Electricidade
REENA — Refrigerating Engineering
REEP — Revista. Escuela de Estudios Penitenciarios
Reeves J — Reeves Journal
Ref — Reformatio
REF — Revista de Etnografie si Folclor
REFA Nachr — REFA [*Reichsausschuss fuer Arbeitsstudien*] Nachrichten
Ref Ch R — Reformed Church Review
Ref Dokl Nauchno-Issled Rab Aspir Ukr Skh Akad — Referaty Dokladov o Nauchno-Issledovatel'skoi Rabote Aspirantov. Ukrainskaya Sel'skokhozyaistvennaya Akademiya
Ref Dok Mosk Skh Akad — Referaty Dokladov Moskovskaya Sel'skokhozyaistvennaya Akademiya Imeni K. A. Timiryazeva
Ref Dopov Nauk Dosl Rob Aspir Ukr Akad Sil's'kogospod Nauk — Referati Dopovidei pro Naukovo-Doslidnu Robotu Aspirantiv. Ukrains'ka Akademiya Sil's'kogospodars'kikh Nauk
RefEgyhaz — Reformatus Egyhaz [*Budapest*]
Referatebl zur Raumentwicklung — Referateblatt zur Raumentwicklung
Referatebl zur Raumordnung — Referateblatt zur Raumordnung
Referat Z — Referativnyi Zhurnal
Referat Zh Biol — Referativnyi Zhurnal. Biologiya
Referat Zh Fotokinotekh — Referat Zhurnal Fotokinotekhnika
Referat Zh Zhivot Vet — Referativnyi Zhurnal. Zhivotnovodstvo i Veterinariya
Refin Eng — Refining Engineer
Refiner Nat Gasoline Manuf — Refiner and Natural Gasoline Manufacturer
Ref J — National Association of Referees in Bankruptcy. Journal
Ref J — Reformed Journal
REFL — Reference Librarian
Reflets Econ Franc-Comtoise — Reflets de l'Economie Franc-Comtoise
Reflets et Perspectives — Reflets et Perspectives de la Vie Economique
Reflets Perspect Vie Econ — Reflets et Perspectives de la Vie Economique
Ref Libr — Reference Librarian
Ref Lit Music — Reformed Liturgy and Music
REFM — Revista de Estudios Franceses (Madrid)
Ref Mag — Referee Magazine
REFNA — REFA [*Reichsausschuss fuer Arbeitsstudien*] Nachrichten
Refor Mon — Reforestation Monthly
Ref Pres W — Reformed and Presbyterian World
Ref Q — Reformed Quarterly Review
Ref R — Reformed Review
REFRA — Refractories [*English Translation*]
Refract Inst Tech Bull — Refractories Institute. Technical Bulletin
Refract J — Refractories Journal
Refract Mater — Refractory Materials
Refractor J — Refractories Journal
Refrig — Refrigeration
Refrig A — Refrigeration Annual
Refrig Air — Refrigeration and Air Conditioning
Refrig Air Cond & Heat — Refrigeration Journal, Incorporating Air Conditioning and Heating
Refrig Air Condit — Refrigeration and Air Conditioning
Refrig Air Condit Heat Recovery — Refrigeration, Air Conditioning, and Heat Recovery
Refrig Ann — Refrigeration Annual
Refrig Annual — Refrigeration Annual
Refrig Cold Stor — Refrigeration, Cold Storage, and Air-Conditioning
Refrig Cold Storage Air Cond — Refrigeration, Cold Storage, and Air-Conditioning
Refrig Eng — Refrigerating Engineering
Refrigeration J — Refrigeration Journal
Refrig J — Refrigeration Journal
Refrig Sci Technol — Refrigeration Science and Technology
Refrig W — Refrigerating World
Ref Serv R — Reference Services Review
Ref Shelf — Reference Shelf
Ref Th R — Reformed Theological Review
RefTR — Reformed Theological Review [*Australia*]
Refu Vet — Refuah Veterinarith
Ref W — Reformed World
Ref Zh — Referativnyi Zhurnal
Ref Zh Astron — Referativnyi Zhurnal. Astronomiya
Ref Zh Astron Geod — Referativnyi Zhurnal. Astronomiya. Geodeziya
Ref Zh Biol — Referativnyi Zhurnal. Biologiya

Ref Zh Biol Khim — Referativnyi Zhurnal. Biologicheskaya Khimiya
Ref Zh Farmakol Khimioter Sredstva Toksikol — Referativnyi Zhurnal. Farmakologiya. Khimioterapeuticheskie Sredstva. Toksikologiya
Ref Zh Fiz — Referativnyi Zhurnal. Fizika
Ref Zh Fiz-Khim Biol Biotekhnol — Referativnyi Zhurnal. Fiziko-Khimicheskaya Biologiya i Biotekhnologiya
Ref Zh Fotokinotekh — Referativnyi Zhurnal. Fotokinotekhnika
Ref Zh Geod — Referativnyi Zhurnal. Geodeziya
Ref Zh Geod Aerosemka — Referativnyi Zhurnal. Geodeziya i Aeros'emka
Ref Zh Geof — Referativnyi Zhurnal. Geofizika
Ref Zh Geol — Referativnyi Zhurnal. Geologiya
Ref Zh Inf — Referativnyi Zhurnal. Informatika
Ref Zh Khim — Referativnyi Zhurnal. Khimiya
Ref Zh Khim Biol Khim — Referativnyi Zhurnal. Khimiya. Biologicheskaya Khimiya
Ref Zh Korroz — Referativnyi Zhurnal. Korroziya
Ref Zh Legk Promst — Referativnyi Zhurnal. Legkaya Promyshlennost
Ref Zh Mekh — Referativnyi Zhurnal. Mekhanika
Ref Zh Metall — Referativnyi Zhurnal. Metallurgiya [*USSR*]
Ref Zh Metrol Izmer Tekh — Referativnyi Zhurnal. Metrologiya i Izmeritel'naya Tekhnika
Ref Zh Nasosostr Kompressorostr Kholod Mashinostr — Referativnyi Zhurnal. Nasosostroenie i Kompressorostroenie. Kholodil'noe Mashinostroenie
Ref Zh Obshch Vop Patol Onkol — Referativnyi Zhurnal. Obshchie Voprosy Patologii. Onkologiya
Ref Zh Okhr Prir Vosproizvod Prir Resur — Referativnyi Zhurnal. Okhrana Prirody i Vosproizvodstvo Prirodnykh Resursov [*USSR*]
Ref Zh Pochvoved Agrokhim — Referativnyi Zhurnal. Pochvovedenie i Agrokhimiya
Ref Zh Radiats Biol — Referativnyi Zhurnal. Radiatsionnaya Biologiya [*USSR*]
Ref Zh Rastenievod — Referativnyi Zhurnal. Rastenievodstvo
Ref Zh Teploenerg — Referativnyi Zhurnal. Teploenergetika
Ref Zh Yad Reakt — Referativnyi Zhurnal. Yadernye Reaktory
Ref Zh Zhivotnovod Vet — Referativnyi Zhurnal. Zhivotnovodstvo i Veterinariya
RefZtg — Reform Zeitung [*Berlin*]
REG — Regional Science and Urban Economics
REg — Revue Egyptologique
REG — Revue des Etudes Grecques
REgA — Revue de l'Egypte Ancienne
Regan Rep Nurs Law — Regan Report on Nursing Law
Reg Cat Earthquakes — Regional Catalogue of Earthquakes
Reg Conf Ser Appl Math — Regional Conference Series in Applied Mathematics
Regelungstech — Regelungstechnik
Regelungstech Prax — Regelungstechnische Praxis
Regelungstech Prax und Prozess-Rechentech — Regelungstechnische Praxis und Prozess-Rechentechnik
Regelungstech Prax Prozess-Rechentech — Regelungstechnische Praxis und Prozess-Rechentechnik
Regelungstech und Prozess-Datenverarb — Regelungstechnik und Prozess-Datenverarbeitung
Regelungstech Prozess-Datenverarb — Regelungstechnik und Prozess-Datenverarbeitung
Regelungstech Prozess-Datenverarbeitung — Regelungstechnik und Prozess-Datenverarbeitung
Regelungstech RT — Regelungstechnik. RT [*West Germany*]
Regensb Univ-Ztg — Regensburger Universitaets-Zeitung
Reger — Mitteilungen. Max Reger Institut [*Bonn*]
Reg Genet Mineral — Regional'naya i Geneticheskaya Mineralogiya
Reg Geol Ser NC Div Resour Plann Eval Miner Resour Sect — Regional Geology Series. North Carolina Division of Resource Planning and Evaluation. Mineral Resources Section
Reg Geol Ser NC Miner Resour Sect — Regional Geology Series. North Carolina Mineral Resources Section
Regia Soc Sci Upsal Nova Acta — Regia Societas Scientiarum Upsaliensis. Nova Acta
Regia Stn Sper Seta Boll Uffic (Italy) — Regia Stazione Sperimentale per la Seta. Bollettino Ufficiale (Italy)
Regional Development J — Regional Development Journal
Regional Stud — Regional Studies [*Oxford*]
Region Develop J — Regional Development Journal
Region Urb Econ — Regional and Urban Economics Operational Methods
Register of Kentucky Hist Soc — Register. Kentucky Historical Society
Reg J Energy Heat Mass Transfer — Regional Journal of Energy, Heat, and Mass Transfer [*India*]
Regnum Veg — Regnum Vegetabile
REGR — Resources Group Review. Suncor, Inc.
REGr — Revue des Etudes Greques
Reg Rep New Hebrides Geol Surv — Regional Report. New Hebrides Geological Survey
REGS-A — Regional Studies
Reg Soc Sci Upsal Nova Acta — Regia Societas Scientiarum Upsaliensis. Nova Acta
Reg Stud — Regional Studies

Reg Stud Assoc Newsl — Regional Studies Association. Newsletter
Reg Tech Meet Am Iron Steel Inst — Regional Technical Meetings. American Iron and Steel Institute
Regul Bull KY Agr Exp Sta — Regulatory Bulletin. Kentucky Agricultural Experiment Station
Regul Pept — Regulatory Peptides
Reg Urban Econ — Regional and Urban Economics [*Netherlands*]
Reg Urb Econ — Regional Science and Urban Economics
Reg Veg — Regnum Vegetabile
R Egypt Dr Int — Revue Egyptienne de Droit International
REH — Revista de Estudios Hispanicos
REH — Revue des Etudes Historiques
REH — Revue des Etudes Hongroises
Rehab — Rehabilitation
Rehab Couns — Rehabilitation Counseling Bulletin
Rehabil Aust — Rehabilitation in Australia
Rehabil Lit — Rehabilitation Literature
Rehabil Nurs — Rehabilitation Nursing
Rehabil SA — Rehabilitation in South Africa
Rehabil S Afr — Rehabilitation in South Africa
Rehabil Suppl (Bratisl) — Rehabilitacia Supplementum (Bratislava)
Rehab Lit — Rehabilitation Literature
REHID — Recursos Hidraulicos
Re Hist De — Revue d'Histoire de la Deuxieme Guerre Mondiale
REHom — Revue des Etudes Homeriques
REH-PR — Revista de Estudios Hispanicos (Rio Piedras, Puerto Rico)
REI — Recycling [*Den Haag*]
REI — Revue des Etudes Indo-Europeennes
REI — Revue des Etudes Islamiques
REI — Revue des Etudes Italiennes
Reichhold-Albert-Nachr — Reichhold-Albert-Nachrichten
Reichsber Phys — Reichsberichte fuer Physik
Reichstoff Ind Kosmet — Reichstoff Industrie und Kosmetik
REIC (Radiat Eff Inf Cent) Rep — REIC (Radiation Effects Information Center) Report
REIE — Revue des Etudes Indo-Europeennes
Reihe Informat — Reihe Informatik
REIMD — Revista da Imagem
Reine Angew Metallkd Einzeldarst — Reine und Angewandte Metallkunde in Einzeldarstellungen
Rein Foie Mal Nutr — Rein et Foie. Maladies de la Nutrition [*France*]
Reinf Plast — Reinforced Plastics
Reinf Plast (London) — Reinforced Plastics (London)
REIsl — Revue des Etudes Islamiques
Reiss-Davis Clin Bull — Reiss-Davis Clinic. Bulletin
REJ — Revue des Etudes Juives
REJOD — Reeves Journal
REJuiv — Revue des Etudes Juives
REJuivHJud — Revue des Etudes Juives et Historia Judaica [*Paris*]
Rel — Religion
REL — Review of English Literature
REL — Revue Ecclesiastique de Liege
REL — Revue des Etudes Latines
RELAA — Recht der Landwirtschaft
RelAb — Religious and Theological Abstracts
Relac Int — Relaciones Internacionales
Relais — Relais Statistiques de l'Economie Picarde
Relais Econ Picarde — Relais Statistiques de l'Economie Picarde
RELat — Revue des Etudes Latines
Relat Annu Inst Geol Publ Hung — Relationes Annuae. Instituti Geologici Publicii Hungarici
Relata Tech Chim Biol Appl — Relata Technica di Chimica e Biologia Applicata
Relat Cient Esc Super Agric Luiz Queiroz Dep Inst Genet — Relatorio Cientifico. Escola Superior de Agricultura Luiz de Queiroz. Departamento e Instituto de Genetica
Relat DNOCS — Relatoria. DNOCS [*Departamento Nacional de Obras Contra as Secas*]
Relat Ind — Relations Industrielles/Industrial Relations
Relat Industr — Relations Industrielles
Relat Int — Relations Internationales
Relat Int (Geneve) — Relations Internationales (Geneve)
Relazione Comm Dirett Ist Zootec Laziale (Roma) — Relazione. Commissione Direttiva. Istituto Zootecnico Laziale (Roma)
Relaz Soc — Relazioni Sociali
RelB — Religion och Bibel [*Uppsala*]
RelBib — Religion och Bibel [*Uppsala*]
RELC — RELC [*Regional English Language Centre*] Journal [*Singapore*]
Rel Cab — Religious Cabinet
Rel Ed — Religious Education
Relevance Logic Newslett — Relevance Logic Newsletter
Relev Log News — Relevance Logic Newsletter
RELHA — Revista Espanola de Literatura, Historia, y Arte
RELIA — Rehabilitation Literature
Reliab Eng — Reliability Engineering
Reliability Eng — Reliability Engineering

Reliable P J — Reliable Poultry Journal
RELiege — Revue Ecclesiastique de Liege [*Belgium*]
Relig Ed — Religious Education
Relig Educ — Religious Education
Relig Hum — Religious Humanism
Relig in Life — Religion in Life
Relig Soc — Religion and Society
Relig Stud — Religious Studies
Relig T J — Religion Teacher's Journal
Rel Ind — Relations Industrielles/Industrial Relations
Rel Ind One — Religion Index One
RELing — Revista Espanola de Linguistica
Rel Life — Religion in Life
RELO — Revue. Organisation Internationale pour l'Etude des Langues Anciennes par Ordinateur
RelPerI — Religious Periodicals Index
RELSA — Radio Elektronik Schau
Rel Soc — Religion and Society
Rel St — Religious Studies
Rel St Rev — Religious Studies Review
Rel Stud — Religious Studies [*London*]
RelTAbstr — Religious and Theological Abstracts [*Myerstown, PA*]
Rel & Theol Abstr — Religious and Theological Abstracts
RELV — Revue de l'Enseignement des Langues Vivantes
REM — Repertoire d'Epigraphie Meroitique
REM — Revue Ecclesiastique de Metz
Re M — Revue Musicale
Remarques Afr — Remarques Africaines
REMC — Revista de Estudios Musicales. Departamento de Musicologia. Universidad Nacional de Cuyo
Remedial Ed — Remedial Education
Remedial Educ — Remedial Education
REMOA — Revista. Escola de Minas [*Brazil*]
Remote Sens Environ — Remote Sensing of Environment
Remote Sensing Earth Resour — Remote Sensing of Earth Resources
Remote Sensing Environ — Remote Sensing of Environment
Rem R — Remington Review
ReMS — Renaissance and Modern Studies
Ren — Renaissance
Ren — Renascence
REN — Revue des Etudes Napoleoniennes
REN — Rural Equipment News
Renais News — Renaissance News
Renaissance Q — Renaissance Quarterly
Renaiss Dr — Renaissance Drama
Renaiss Q — Renaissance Quarterly
Renaiss Ref — Renaissance and Reformation
Renal Physiol — Renal Physiology
Ren B — Renaissance Bulletin
RenBib — Rencontres Biblique
RencAssyrInt — Recontre Assyriologique Internationale. Compte Rendu
RENCB — Revue d'Electroencephalographie et de Neurophysiologie Clinique
Rencontre Biol — Rencontre Biologique
RenD — Renaissance Drama
Rend — Rendezvous
Rend — Rendiconti [*Bologna*]
Rend Accad Naz 40 (Quaranta) — Rendiconti. Accademia Nazionale dei 40 (Quaranta)
Rend Accad Naz XL — Rendiconti. Accademia Nazionale dei XL
Rend Accad Naz XL 4 — Accademia Nazionale dei XL. Rendiconti. Serie 4
Rend Accad Naz XL 5 — Accademia Nazionale dei XL. Rendiconti. Serie 5
Rend Accad Sci Fis Mat (Napoli) — Rendiconto. Accademia delle Scienze Fisiche e Matematiche (Napoli)
Rend Accad Sci Fis Mat Napoli 4 — Societa Nazionale di Scienze, Lettere, ed Arti in Napoli. Rendiconto dell'Accademia delle Scienze Fisiche e Matematiche. Serie 4
Rend Acc It — Atti. Reale Accademia d'Italia. Rendiconti. Classe di Scienze Morali
Rend Atti Accad Sci Med Chir — Rendiconti e Atti. Accademia di Scienze Mediche e Chirurgiche
Rend Circ Mat Palermo — Rendiconti. Circolo Matematico di Palermo
Rend Circ Mat Palermo 2 — Rendiconti. Circolo Matematico di Palermo. Serie II
Rend Gastro — Rendiconti di Gastro-Enterologia
Rendic Accad Sc Fis e Mat (Napoli) — Rendiconto. Accademia delle Scienze Fisiche e Matematiche (Napoli)
Rendic R Accad Sc Ist Bologna — Rendiconto. Reale Accademia delle Scienze. Istituto di Bologna
Rend Istit Mat Univ Trieste — Rendiconti. Istituto di Matematica. Universita di Trieste
Rend Ist Lomb — Reale Istituto Lombardo di Scienze e Lettere. Rendiconti
Rend Ist Lomb Accad Sci Lett A — Rendiconti. Istituto Lombardo. Accademia di Scienze e Lettere. Sezione A. Scienze Matematiche, Fisiche, e Geologiche [*Italy*]

Rend Ist Lomb Accad Sci Lett A Sci Mat Fis Chim Geol — Rendiconti. Istituto Lombardo. Accademia di Scienze e Lettere. Sezione A. Scienze Matematiche, Fisiche, Chimiche, e Geologiche
Rend Ist Lomb Accad Sci Lett B — Rendiconti. Istituto Lombardo. Accademia di Scienze e Lettere. Sezione B. Scienze Biologiche e Mediche [*Italy*]
Rend Ist Lomb Sci Lett A — Rendiconti. Istituto Lombardo di Scienze e Lettere. Sezione A. Scienze Matematiche, Fisiche, Chimiche, e Geologiche
Rend Ist Lomb Sci Lett A Sci Mat Fis Chim Geol — Rendiconti. Istituto Lombardo di Scienze e Lettere. Sezione A. Scienze Matematiche, Fisiche, Chimiche, e Geologiche
Rend Ist Mat Univ Trieste — Rendiconti. Istituto di Matematica. Universita di Trieste
Rend Ist Sci Univ Camerino — Rendiconti. Istituti Scientifici. Universita di Camerino
Rend Ist Super Sanita — Rendiconti. Istituto Superiore di Sanita
Rend Linc — Rendiconti. Reale Accademia dei Lincei
Rend Mat — Rendiconti di Matematica
Rend Mat 6 — Rendiconti di Matematica. Serie VI
Rend Mat 7 — Rendiconti di Matematica. Serie VII
Rend (Nap) — Rendiconti. Reale Accademia di Archeologia, Lettere, ed Arti (Naples)
Rend Pont — Rendiconti. Pontificia Accademia Romana di Archeologia
Rend Pont Acc — Rendiconti. Pontificia Accademia Romana di Archeologia
Rend R Ist Lomb Sci Lett — Rendiconti. Reale Istituto Lombardo di Scienze e Lettere
Rend Riun Annu Assoc Elettrotec Ital — Rendiconti. Riunione Annuale. Associazione Elettrotecnica Italiana [*Italy*]
Rend Riunione Assoc Elettrotec Ital — Rendiconti. Riunione Annuale. Associazione Elettrotecnica Italiana
Rend Rom Gastroenterol — Rendiconti Romani di Gastroenterologia [*Italy*]
Rend Sc Int Fis Enrico Fermi — Rendiconti. Scuola Internazionale di Fisica "Enrico Fermi"
Rend Sc Int Fis Fermi — Rendiconti. Scuola Internazionale di Fisica "Enrico Fermi"
Rend Scu Int Fis Enrico Fermi — Rendiconti. Scuola Internazionale di Fisica "Enrico Fermi" [*Italy*]
Rend Semin Fac Sci Univ Cagliari — Rendiconti del Seminario. Facolta di Scienze. Universita di Cagliari
Rend Semin Mat Fis Milano — Rendiconti. Seminario Matematico e Fisico di Milano
Rend Sem Mat Brescia — Rendiconti. Seminario Matematico di Brescia
Rend Sem Mat Fis Milano — Rendiconti. Seminario Matematico e Fisico di Milano
Rend Sem Mat Univ Padova — Rendiconti. Seminario Matematico. Universita di Padova
Rend Sem Mat Univ Politec Torino — Rendiconti. Seminario Matematico gia Conferenze di Fisica e di Matematica. Universita e Politecnico di Torino
Rend Sem Mat Univ e Politec Torino — Rendiconti. Seminario Matematico. Universita e Politecnico di Torino
Rend Soc Chim Ital — Rendiconti. Societa Chimica Italiana
Rend Soc Ital Mineral Petrol — Rendiconti. Societa Italiana di Mineralogia e Petrologia
RenE — Reinare en Espana
RENEA — Revue Neurologique
R Energie — Revue de l'Energie
Renew — Renewal
Renew Energy Bull — Renewable Energy Bulletin [*England*]
R Eng J — Royal Engineers Journal
R Engl Lit — Review of English Literature
R Engl Stud — Review of English Studies
REngS — Review of English Studies
R Eng Stud — Review of English Studies
R Eng Stud ns — Review of English Studies. New Series
RENH — Revue des Etudes Neo-Helleniques
RENID3 — Annual Research Reviews. Renin
RENJA — Russian Engineering Journal
RENLO — Revue. Ecole Nationale des Langues Orientales
RenN — Renaissance News
Ren News — Renaissance News
RENO — Research on Norway
RenP — Renaissance Papers
RENPA — Radio Engineering and Electronic Physics [*English Translation*]
RenQ — Renaissance Quarterly
Ren & R — Renaissance and Reformation
RENRA — Rentgenologiya i Radiologiya
Ren & Ref — Renaissance and Reformation
Rent Equip — Rental Equipment Register
Rentgenogr Miner Syr'ya — Rentgenografiya Mineral'nogo Syr'ya
Rentgenol Radiol — Rentgenologiya i Radiologiya
R Entomol Soc London Symp — Royal Entomological Society of London. Symposia
Reo — Te Reo. Linguistic Society of New Zealand
Rep — Republika [*Zagreb*]
REP — Revista de Estudios Politicos
REP — Revue d'Economie Politique

Rep AAS (Austral) — Report. Meeting. Association for the Advancement of Science (Australia)

Rep Acad Sci Ukr SSR — Reports. Academy of Sciences of the Ukrainian SSR

Rep Activ Dan Atom Energy Commn — Report. Activities of the Danish Atomic Energy Commission

Rep Aeromed Lab — Reports. Aeromedical Laboratory

Rep Aeronaut Res Inst Univ Tokyo — Report. Aeronautical Research Institute. University of Tokyo

Rep AFL Univ Cincinnati Dep Aerosp Eng — Report AFL. University of Cincinnati. Department of Aerospace Engineering

Rep Agric Coll Swed Ser A — Reports. Agricultural College of Sweden. Series A

Rep Agric Hort Res Stn Univ Bristol — Report. Agricultural and Horticultural Research Station. University of Bristol

Rep Agric Res Coun Radiobiol Lab — Report. Agricultural Research Council. Radiobiological Laboratory

Rep Agron Branch Dep Agric South Aust — Report. Agronomy Branch. Department of Agriculture and Fisheries. South Australia

Rep Aichi Inst Public Health — Report. Aichi Institute of Public Health [*Japan*]

Rep Akita Prefect Inst Public Health — Report. Akita Prefecture. Institute of Public Health [*Japan*]

Rep Alfalfa Improv Conf — Report. Alfalfa Improvement Conference

Rep Am Univ Field Staff — Reports. American Universities Field Staff

Rep Anim Breed Res Organ — Report. Animal Breeding Research Organisation

Rep Anim Res Div (NZ) — Report. Animal Research Division. Department of Agriculture (New Zealand)

Rep Annu Conf Hawaii Sugar Technol — Reports. Annual Conference. Hawaiian Sugar Technologists

Rep Annu Conf Ontario Dept Agr Ext Br — Report. Annual Conference. Ontario Department of Agriculture. Extension Branch

Rep Annu Date Grow Inst — Report. Annual Date Growers Institute

Rep Annu Gen Meet Scott Soc Res Plant Breed — Report. Annual General Meeting. Scottish Society for Research in Plant Breeding

Rep Archit Sci Unit Univ Queensl — Report. Architectural Science Unit. University of Queensland

Rep Ariz Agr Exp Sta — Report. Arizona Agricultural Experiment Station

Rep Ariz Agric Exp Stn — Report. Arizona Agricultural Experiment Station

Rep Ark Agric Exp Stn — Report. Arkansas Agricultural Experiment Station

Rep Army Res Test Lab — Report. Army Research and Testing Laboratory [*South Korea*]

Rep Assoc Hawaii Sugar Technol — Reports. Association of Hawaiian Sugar Technologists

Rep Aust Acad Sci — Report. Australian Academy of Science

Rep Aust Acad Sci — Reports. Australian Academy of Science

Rep Aust At Energy Comm — Report. Australian Atomic Energy Commission

Rep Aust CSIRO Div Text Ind — Australia. Commonwealth Scientific and Industrial Research Organisation. Division of Textile Industry. Report

Rep Aust Def Stand Lab — Australia. Defence Standards Laboratories. Report

Rep Aust Def Stand Lab — Report. Australia Defence Standards Laboratories

Rep BC-X Can For Serv Pac For Res Cent — Report BC-X. Canadian Forestry Service. Pacific Forest Research Centre

Rep Bd Health Calif — Reports. State Board of Health of California

Rep Bd Health Ohio — Reports. State Board of Health of Ohio

RepBibPhil — Repertoire Bibliographique de la Philosophie

Rep Biochem Res Found Franklin Inst — Reports. Biochemical Research Foundation. Franklin Institute

Rep Biomed — Repertoire Biomed

Rep Bot Surv India — Report. Botanical Survey of India

Rep Br Beekprs Ass — Report. British Beekeepers Association

Rep Brit Ass Adv Sc — Report. British Association for the Advancement of Science

Rep Brit Assoc Adv Sci — Report. British Association for the Advancement of Science

Rep Brit Mus Natur Hist — Report. British Museum. Natural History

Rep Bull Agr Exp Sta S Manchuria Ry Co — Research Bulletin. Agricultural Experiment Station. South Manchuria Railway Company

Rep Bur Miner Resour Geol Geophys — Report. (Australia) Bureau of Mineral Resources. Geology and Geophysics

Rep Bur Miner Resour Geol Geophys (Aust) — Report. Bureau of Mineral Resources, Geology, and Geophysics (Australia)

Rep Cacao Res Reg Cent Br Caribb — Report on Cacao Research. Regional Research Centre of the British Caribbean

Rep Cast Res Lab — Report. Castings Research Laboratory

Rep Cast Res Lab Waseda Univ — Report. Castings Research Laboratory. Waseda University

Rep Cent Res Inst Electr Power Ind Agric Lab — Report. Central Research Institute. Electric Power Industry Agricultural Laboratory

Rep Cent Res Inst Electr Power Ind Tech Lab — Report. Central Research Institute. Electric Power Industry Technical Laboratory

Rep Cent Res Lab Nippon Suisan Co — Reports. Central Research Laboratory. Nippon Suisan Company

Rep CE Technion-Isr Inst Technol Dep Chem Eng — Report CE. Technion-Israel Institute of Technology. Department of Chemical Engineering

Rep Chem Branch Mines Dep (West Aust) — Report. Chemical Branch. Mines Department (Western Australia)

Rep Chem Lab Am Med Assoc — Reports. Chemical Laboratory. American Medical Association

Rep Chem Lab (West Aust) — Report. Chemical Laboratory (Western Australia)

Rep Chiba Inst Technol — Report. Chiba Institute of Technology

Rep Chiba Inst Technol Sci Ser — Report. Chiba Institute of Technology. Scientific Series

Rep Chief US Forest Serv — Report of the Chief. United States Forest Service

Rep Class Research — Reporting Classroom Research

Rep Comm Accredit Rehabil Facil — Report. Commission on Accreditation of Rehabilitation Facilities

Rep Commonw Conf Plant Pathol — Report. Commonwealth Conference on Plant Pathology

Rep Commonwealth Entomol Conf — Report. Commonwealth Entomological Conference

Rep Commonwealth Mycol Conf — Report. Commonwealth Mycological Conference

Rep Commonw Mycol Conf — Report. Commonwealth Mycological Conference

Rep Comput Centre Univ Tokyo — Report. Computer Centre. University of Tokyo

Rep Conf Role Wheat World Food Supply — Report. Conference on the Role of Wheat in the World's Food Supply

Rep Congr Eur Ass Res Plant Breed — Report. Congress of the European Association for Research on Plant Breeding

Rep Constr Eng Res Inst Found (Kobe) — Reports. Construction Engineering Research Institute Foundation (Kobe) [*Japan*]

Rep Coop Res Chugoku Reg — Report of the Cooperative Research in Chugoku Region

Rep Crop Res Lesotho — Report on Crop Research in Lesotho

Rep CSIRO Div Fish Oceanogr — Australia. Commonwealth Scientific and Industrial Research Organisation. Division of Fisheries and Oceanography. Report

Rep CSIRO Div Text Ind Aust — Australia. Commonwealth Scientific and Industrial Research Organisation. Division of Textile Industry. Report

Rep CSIRO Sol Energy Stud — Report. Commonwealth Scientific and Industrial Research Organisation. Solar Energy Studies

Rep Def Stand Lab Aust — Australia. Defence Standards Laboratories. Report

Rep Deir-Alla Res Sta — Report. Deir-Alla Research Station [*Jordan*]

Rep Dep Agric Econ Univ Nebr Agric Exp Stn — Report. Department of Agricultural Economics. University of Nebraska. Agricultural Experiment Station

Rep Dep Agric NSW — Report. Department of Agriculture of New South Wales

Rep Dep Fish Fauna West Aust — Report. Department of Fisheries and Fauna. Western Australia

Rep Dep Fish Wildl West Aust — Report. Department of Fisheries and Wildlife. Western Australia

Rep Dep Nucl Tech Univ Oulu (Finl) — Reports. Department of Nuclear Technics. University of Oulu (Finland)

Rep Dep Phys Univ Oulu — Report. Department of Physics. University of Oulu

Rep Dept Agric (Brit East Africa) — Report. Department of Agriculture (British East Africa)

Rep Dept Antiquities Cyprus — Report. Department of Antiquities of Cyprus

Rep Director Vet Serv Dept Agric (Union South Africa) — Report. Director of Veterinary Services and Animal Industry. Department of Agriculture (Union of South Africa)

Rep Dir Gov Chem Lab (West Aust) — Report. Director of Government Chemical Laboratories (Western Australia)

Rep Dir Vet Serv Anim Ind (Onderstepoort) — Report. Director of Veterinary Services and Animal Industry (Onderstepoort)

Rep Div Bldg Res CSIRO — Report. Division of Building Research. Commonwealth Scientific and Industrial Research Organisation

Rep Div Build Res CSIRO — Report. Division of Building Research. Commonwealth Scientific and Industrial Research Organisation

Rep Div Chem Eng CSIRO — Report. Division of Chemical Engineering. Commonwealth Scientific and Industrial Research Organisation

Rep Div Chem Engng CSIRO — Report. Division of Chemical Engineering. Commonwealth Scientific and Industrial Research Organisation

Rep Div Fish Oceanogr CSIRO — Report. Division of Fisheries and Oceanography. Commonwealth Scientific and Industrial Research Organisation

Rep Div Hort Res CSIRO — Report. Division of Horticultural Research. Commonwealth Scientific and Industrial Research Organisation

Rep Div Mech Engng CSIRO — Report. Division of Mechanical Engineering. Commonwealth Scientific and Industrial Research Organisation

Rep Div Miner CSIRO — Report. Division of Mineralogy. Commonwealth Scientific and Industrial Research Organisation

Rep Div Text Ind CSIRO — Report. Division of Textile Industry. Commonwealth Scientific and Industrial Research Organisation

Rep Earth Sci Coll Gen Educ Kyushu Univ — Reports on Earth Science. College of General Education. Kyushu University

Rep Earth Sci Dep Gen Educ Kyushu Univ — Reports on Earth Science. Department of General Education. Kyushu University

Rep East For Prod Lab (Can) — Report. Eastern Forest Products Laboratory (Canada)

Rep ED Eng Sect CSIRO — Report ED. Engineering Section. Commonwealth Scientific and Industrial Research Organisation

Rep E Malling Res Stn — Annual Report. East Malling Research Station

Rep Eng Inst Fac Eng Tokyo Univ — Report. Engineering Institute. Faculty of Engineering. Tokyo University [*Japan*]

Rep Eng Res Lab Obayashi-Gumi Ltd — Report. Engineering Research Laboratory. Obayashi-Gumi Limited [*Japan*]

Rep Ent Soc Ont — Report. Entomological Society of Ontario

Rep Environ Sci Inst Hyogo Prefect — Report. Environmental Science Institute of Hyogo Prefecture

Rep Environ Sci Mie Univ — Report of Environmental Science. Mie University

Rep Environ Sci Res Cent Shiga Prefect — Report. Environmental Science Research Center of Shiga Prefecture

Rep Environ Sci Technol Lab Nippon Bunri Univ — Reports. Environmental Science and Technology Laboratory. Nippon Bunri University

Reperes-Econ Languedoc-Roussillon — Reperes-Economie du Languedoc-Roussillon

Repertoire Anal Litt Francaise — Repertoire Analytique de Litterature Francaise [*Bordeaux*]

Repertorium der Phot — Repertorium der Photographie

Repert Pharm — Repertoire de Pharmacie

Repert Plant Succulentarum — Repertorium Plantarum Succulentarum

Rep Europe — Report from Europe

Rep Evol Comm Roy Soc Lond — Report to the Evolution Committee. Royal Society of London

Rep Exp Res Stn (Cheshunt) — Report. Experimental and Research Station. Nursery and Market Garden Industries Development Society, Ltd. (Cheshunt)

Rep Fac Agr Shizuoka Univ — Reports. Faculty of Agriculture. Shizuoka University

Rep Fac Eng Nagasaki Univ — Reports. Faculty of Engineering. Nagasaki University

Rep Fac Eng Shizuoka Univ — Reports. Faculty of Engineering. Shizuoka University

Rep Fac Fish Prefect Univ Mie — Report. Faculty of Fisheries. Prefectural University of Mie

Rep Fac Sci Engrg Saga Univ Math — Reports. Faculty of Science and Engineering. Saga University. Mathematics

Rep Fac Sci Kagoshima Univ — Reports. Faculty of Science. Kagoshima University

Rep Fac Sci Kagoshima Univ (Earth Sci Biol) — Reports. Faculty of Science. Kagoshima University. Earth Sciences and Biology

Rep Fac Sci Shizuoka Univ — Reports. Faculty of Science. Shizuoka University

Rep Fac Sci Technol Meijyo Univ — Reports. Faculty of Science and Technology. Meijyo University

Rep Fam L — Reports of Family Law

Rep FAO/IAEA Tech Meet (Brunswick-Volkenrode) — Report. FAO [*Food and Agriculture Organization of the United Nations*]/IAEA [*International Atomic Energy Agency*] Technical Meeting (Brunswick-Volkenrode)

Rep Fd Res Inst (Tokyo) — Report. Food Research Institute (Tokyo)

Rep Fed Railroad Adm — Report. Federal Railroad Administration [*United States*]

Rep Ferment Ind — Report on the Fermentation Industries

Rep Ferment Res Inst — Report. Fermentation Research Institute

Rep Ferment Res Inst (Chiba) — Report. Fermentation Research Institute (Chiba)

Rep Fire Res Inst Jpn — Report. Fire Research Institute of Japan

Rep Fish Board Swed Inst Mar Res — Report. Fishery Board of Sweden. Institute of Marine Research

Rep Fish Res Lab Kyushu Univ — Report. Fishery Research Laboratory. Kyushu University

Rep Fla Agric Exp Stn — Report. Florida Agricultural Experiment Station

Rep Food Ind Exp Stn Hiroshima Prefect — Report. Food Industrial Experiment Station. Hiroshima Prefecture

Rep Food Res Inst (Tokyo) — Report. Food Research Institute (Tokyo)

Rep Forest Dep (Tanganyika) — Report. Forest Department (Tanganyika Territory)

Rep Forest Exp Stn Hokkaido — Annual Report. Hokkaido Branch. Government Forest Experiment Station

Rep For Game Manage Res Inst — Reports. Forestry and Game Management Research Institute

Rep For Prod Res Inst (Hokkaido) — Report. Hokkaido Forest Products Research Institute (Asahikawa, Hokkaido)

Rep For Res — Report on Forest Research

Rep For Resour Reconn Surv Malaya — Report. Forest Resources Reconnaissance Survey of Malaya

Rep Forsknstift Skogsarb — Report. Redogorelse. Forskningsstiftelsen Skogsarbeten

Rep FPM-X For Pest Manage Inst — Report FPM-X. Forest Pest Management Institute

Rep Freedom Hunger Campaign — Report. Freedom from Hunger Campaign. FAO [*Food and Agriculture Organization of the United Nations*]

Rep Fukushima Prefect Public Health Inst — Report. Fukushima Prefectural Public Health Institute [*Japan*]

Rep Fys Lab I Tek Hoejsk (Lyngby) — Report. Fysisk Laboratorium I. Danmarks Tekniske Hoejskole (Lyngby)

REPGA — Reprographics

Rep GA For Res Coun — Report. Georgia Forest Research Council

Rep Gen Fish Counc Mediterr — Report. General Fisheries Council for the Mediterranean

Rep Geol Min Explor — Report of Geological and Mineral Exploration [*South Korea*]

Rep Geol Surv Dep (Guyana) — Report. Geological Survey Department (Guyana)

Rep Geol Surv Dep (Zambia) — Report. Geological Survey Department (Zambia)

Rep Geol Surv Hokkaido — Report. Geological Survey of Hokkaido [*Japan*]

Rep Geol Surv Jpn — Report. Geological Survey of Japan

Rep Geol Surv Malays — Report. Geological Survey of Malaysia

Rep Geol Surv Mines Dep (Uganda) — Report. Geological Survey and Mines Department (Uganda)

Rep Geol Surv NSW — Report. Geological Survey of New South Wales

Rep Geol Surv Qd — Report. Geological Survey of Queensland

Rep Geol Surv Queensl — Report. Geological Survey of Queensland

Rep Geol Surv Tasm — Report. Geological Survey of Tasmania

Rep Geol Surv Uganda — Report. Geological Survey of Uganda

Rep Geol Surv Vic — Report. Geological Survey of Victoria

Rep Geol Surv Vict — Report. Geological Survey of Victoria

Rep Geol Surv West Aust — Western Australia. Geological Survey. Report

Rep Geophys Geochem Explor Geol Surv Korea — Report of Geophysical and Geochemical Exploration. Geological Survey of Korea

Rep Geophys Res Stn Kyoto Univ — Reports. Geophysical Research Station. Kyoto University

Rep Geosci Miner Resour — Report on Geoscience and Mineral Resources [*Republic of Korea*]

Rep Glasshouse Crops Res Inst — Report. Glasshouse Crops Research Institute

Rep Gov Chem Ind Res Inst (Tokyo) — Reports. Government Chemical Industrial Research Institute (Tokyo)

Rep Gov Chem Lab (West Aust) — Report. Government Chemical Laboratories (Western Australia)

Rep Gov For Exp Stn — Report. Government Forest Experiment Station

Rep Gov Ind Res Inst (Kyushu) — Reports. Government Industrial Research Institute (Kyushu) [*Japan*]

Rep Gov Ind Res Inst (Nagoya) — Reports. Government Industrial Research Institute (Nagoya)

Rep Gov Ind Res Inst (Osaka) — Reports. Government Industrial Research Institute (Osaka)

Rep Gov Ind Res Inst (Shikoku) — Reports. Government Industrial Research Institute (Shikoku)

Rep Gov Ind Res Inst (Tohoku) — Reports. Government Industrial Research Institute (Tohoku)

Rep Gov Mineral Anal Chem (West Aust) — Report. Government Mineralogist, Analyst, and Chemist (Western Australia)

Rep Govt Inst Vet Research (Fusan Chosen) — Report. Government Institute for Veterinary Research (Fusan, Chosen)

Rep Govt Mech Lab (Tokyo) — Report. Government Mechanical Laboratory (Tokyo)

Rep Gr Brit Agr Res Counc — Report. Great Britain Agricultural Research Council

Rep Gr Brit Colon Pestic Res Unit CPRU/Porton — Report. Great Britain Colonial Pesticides Research Unit. CPRU/Porton

Rep Gt Brit Trop Pestic Res Unit TPRU/Porton — Report. Great Britain Tropical Pesticides Research Unit. TPRU/Porton

REPh — Revue de l'Enseignement Philosophique

Rep Health Soc Subj (Lond) — Reports. Health and Social Subjects (London)

Rep Himeji Inst Technol — Reports. Himeji Institute of Technology

Rep Hokkaido For Prod Res Inst — Report. Hokkaido Forest Products Research Institute [*Japan*]

Rep Hokkaido Inst Public Health — Report. Hokkaido Institute of Public Health

Rep Hokkaido Nat Agr Exp Sta — Report. Hokkaido National Agricultural Experiment Station

Rep Hokkaido Natn Agric Exp Stn — Report. Hokkaido National Agricultural Experiment Station

Rep Hokkaido Pref Agr Exp Sta — Report. Hokkaido Prefectural Agricultural Experiment Station

Rep Horace Lamb Inst Oceanogr — Report. Horace Lamb Institute of Oceanography

Rep Hort Exp Sta (Ontario) — Report. Horticultural Experiment Station (Ontario)

Rep Hort Exp Stn Prod Lab (Vineland) — Report. Horticultural Experiment Station and Products Laboratory (Vineland Station) [*Ontario*]

Rep Hung Acad Sci Cent Res Inst Phys — Report. Hungarian Academy of Sciences. Central Research Institute for Physics. Koezponti Fizikai Kutato Intezet

Rep Hybrid Corn Ind Res Conf — Report. Hybrid Corn Industry. Research Conference

Rep Hyogo Prefect For Exp Stn — Report. Hyogo Prefectural Forest Experiment Station

Rep IA St Apiar — Report of Iowa State Apiarist

REpigr — Revue Epigraphique
Rep Ill Beekeep Ass — Report. Illinois Beekeeping Association
Rep Imp Mycol Conf — Report. Imperial Mycological Conference
Rep Ind Educ Res Cent Chungnam Natl Univ — Report. Industrial Education Research Center. Chungnam National University [*Republic of Korea*]
Rep Ind Res Inst Hyogo Prefect — Reports. Industrial Research Institute. Hyogo Prefecture
Rep Ind Res Inst Ishikawa — Report. Industrial Research Institute of Ishikawa
Rep Ind Res Inst Osaka Prefect — Reports. Industrial Research Institute. Osaka Prefecture [*Japan*]
Rep Inf Cent Jt Inst Lab Astrophys — Report. Information Center. Joint Institute for Laboratory Astrophysics
Rep Inst Agric Res Tohoku Univ — Reports. Institute for Agricultural Research. Tohoku University
Rep Inst Agr Res (Korea) — Report. Institute of Agricultural Research (Korea)
Rep Inst Appl Microbiol Univ Tokyo — Reports. Institute of Applied Microbiology. University of Tokyo
Rep Inst Chem Res Kyoto Univ — Reports. Institute for Chemical Research. Kyoto University
Rep Inst Fish Biol Minist Econ Aff Natl Taiwan Univ — Report. Institute of Fishery Biology. Ministry of Economic Affairs. National Taiwan University
Rep Inst Freshwater Res (Drottningholm) — Report. Institute of Freshwater Research (Drottningholm)
Rep Inst Geol Sci — Report. Institute of Geological Sciences
Rep Inst High Speed Mech Tohoku Univ — Reports. Institute of High Speed Mechanics. Tohoku University
Rep Inst Ind Sci Univ Tokyo — Report. Institute of Industrial Science. University of Tokyo
Rep Inst Ld Wat Mgmt Res — Report. Institute for Land and Water Management Research
Rep Inst Mar Res Fish Board Swed — Report. Institute of Marine Research. Fishery Board of Sweden
Rep Inst Min Res Univ Rhod — Report. Institute of Mining Research. University of Rhodesia
Rep Inst Phys Chem Res — Reports. Institute of Physical and Chemical Research
Rep Inst Sci Labour (Tokyo) — Reports. Institute for Science of Labour (Tokyo)
Rep Inst Sci Technol — Report. Institute of Science and Technology [*Republic of Korea*]
Rep Inst Sci Technol Sung Kyun Kwan Univ — Report. Institute of Science and Technology. Sung Kyun Kwan University
Rep Inst Syst Des Optim Kans State Univ — Report. Institute for Systems Design and Optimization. Kansas State University
Rep Int Assoc Cereal Chem — Reports. International Association of Cereal Chemistry
Rep Int Pac Halibut Comm — Report. International Pacific Halibut Commission
Rep Invest Aust Gov Anal Lab — Australian Government Analytical Laboratories. Report of Investigations
Rep Invest Bur Mines Philipp — Report of Investigations. Bureau of Mines of the Philippines
Rep Invest Div Miner Resour (VA) — Report of Investigations. Division of Mineral Resources (Virginia)
Rep Invest Fla Bur Geol — Report of Investigations. Florida Bureau of Geology
Rep Invest Geol Surv MO — Report of Investigations. Geological Survey of Missouri
Rep Invest Geol Surv S Aust — Report of Investigations. Geological Survey of South Australia
Rep Invest Geol Surv South Aust — Report of Investigations. Geological Survey of South Australia
Rep Invest Gov Chem Labs West Aust — Report of Investigations. Government Chemical Laboratories. Western Australia
Rep Invest Ill State Geol Surv — Report of Investigations. Illinois State Geological Survey
Rep Invest ND Geol Surv — Report of Investigations. North Dakota Geological Survey
Rep Invest US Bur Mines — Report of Investigations. United States Bureau of Mines
Rep Invest WA Govt Chem Labs — Report of Investigations. Government Chemical Laboratories. Western Australia
Rep Ionos Res Jpn — Report of Ionosphere Research in Japan [*Later, Report of Ionosphere and Space Research in Japan*]
Rep Ionos & Space Res Jap — Report of Ionosphere and Space Research in Japan
Rep Ionos and Space Res Jpn — Report of Ionosphere and Space Research in Japan
Rep Ion Spa — Report of Ionosphere and Space Research in Japan
Rep Iowa St Hort Soc — Report. Iowa State Horticultural Society
Rep Kansas Agric Exper Station — Report. Kansas Agricultural Experiment Station
Rep Kans State Board Agr — Report. Kansas State Board of Agriculture
Rep Kevo Subarct Res Stn — Reports. Kevo Subarctic Research Station
Rep Kihara Inst Biol Res — Reports. Kihara Institute for Biological Research [*Japan*]

Rep Kunst W — Repertorium fuer Kunstwissenschaft
Rep Kyushu Br Crop Sci Soc Jap — Report. Kyushu Branch. Crop Science Society of Japan
Rep Kyushu Univ For — Reports. Kyushu University Forests
Rep Lab Soils Fert Fac Agric Okayama Univ — Reports. Laboratory of Soils and Fertilizers. Faculty of Agriculture. Okayama University
Rep Lawrence Livermore Lab — Report. Lawrence Livermore Laboratory. University of California [*Livermore*]
Rep Lib Arts Sci Fac Shizuoka Univ — Report. Liberal Arts of Science Faculty. Shizuoka University
Rep Lib Arts Sci Fac Shizuoka Univ Nat Sci — Reports. Liberal Arts and Science Faculty. Shizuoka University. Natural Science
Rep Liberal Arts Sci Fac Shizuoka Univ Nat Sci — Reports. Liberal Arts and Science Faculty. Shizuoka University. Natural Science [*Japan*]
Rep Local Govt Bd (London) — Reports. Local Government Board (London)
Rep Long Ashton Res Stn — Report. Long Ashton Research Station. University of Bristol
Rep Mater Res Lab Aust — Australia. Materials Research Laboratories. Report
Rep Mathematical Phys — Reports on Mathematical Physics
Rep Math Log — Reports on Mathematical Logic
Rep Math Logic — Reports on Mathematical Logic [*Warsaw/Krakow*]
Rep Math Phys — Reports on Mathematical Physics
Rep Maurit Sug Ind Res Inst — Report. Mauritius Sugar Industry Research Institute
Rep MD Agr Soc — Report. Maryland Agricultural Society
Rep MD Beekprs Ass — Report. Maryland Beekeepers' Association
Rep Mech Developm Comm For Comm (Lond) — Report. Mechanical Development Committee. Forestry Commission (London)
Rep Med and Health Dept (Mauritius) — Report. Medical and Health Department (Mauritius)
Rep Med and Health Work Sudan — Report on Medical and Health Work in the Sudan
Rep Med Res Probl Jpn Anti-Tuberc Assoc — Reports on Medical Research Problems of the Japan Anti-Tuberculosis Association
Rep Meet Aust NZ Assoc Adv Sci — Report. Meeting. Australian and New Zealand Association for the Advancement of Science
Rep Melb Metrop Board Works — Report. Melbourne and Metropolitan Board of Works
Rep Mich Dept Conserv Game Div — Report. Michigan Department of Conservation. Game Division
Rep Miner Bur (S Afr) — Report. Minerals Bureau. Department of Mines (South Africa)
Rep Miner Dev Div (Newfoundland) — Report. Mineral Development Division. Department of Mines (Newfoundland)
Rep Miner Res Lab CSIRO — Report. Division of Mineralogy. Minerals Research Laboratory. Commonwealth Scientific and Industrial Research Organisation
Rep Miss Agr Exp Sta — Report. Mississippi Agricultural Experiment Station
Rep MRL NC State Univ Miner Res Lab — Report MRL. North Carolina State University. Minerals Research Laboratory
Rep Nat Inst Nutr — Report. National Institute of Nutrition
Rep Natl Food Res Inst (Tokyo) — Report. National Food Research Institute (Tokyo)
Rep Natl Ind Res Inst (Korea) — Report. National Industrial Research Institute (Korea)
Rep Natl Ind Stand Res Inst (Korea) — Report. National Industrial Standards Research Institute (Korea)
Rep Natl Inst Metall — Report. National Institute for Metallurgy
Rep Natl Radiol Prot Board — Report. National Radiological Protection Board
Rep Natl Res Inst Met — Report. National Research Institute for Metals [*Tokyo*]
Rep Natl Res Inst Police Sci (Jpn) Res Forensic Sci — Reports. National Research Institute of Police Science (Japan). Research on Forensic Science
Rep Natl Res Inst Pollut Resour (Kawaguchi Jpn) — Report. National Research Institute for Pollution and Resources (Kawaguchi, Japan)
Rep Natl Res Lab Metrol — Report. National Research Laboratory of Metrology
Rep Natl Water Resour Counc Repub Philipp — Report. National Water Resources Council. Republic of the Philippines
Rep Natn Fd Res Inst (Jap) — Report. National Food Research Institute (Japan)
Rep Natn Inst Genet (Misima) — Report. National Institute of Genetics (Misima)
Rep Natn Inst Metall (S Afr) — Report. National Institute of Metallurgy (South Africa)
Rep Nat Res Inst Police Sci — Reports. National Research Institute of Police Science
Rep N Engl Assoc Chem Teach — Report. New England Association of Chemistry Teachers
Rep New Hebrides Geol Surv — Report. New Hebrides Geological Survey
Rep Northeast Corn Impr Conf — Report. Northeastern Corn Improvement Conference
Rep Norw Fish Mar Invest Rep Technol Res — Reports on Norwegian Fishery and Marine Investigation. Reports on Technological Research

Rep Norw For Res Inst — Reports. Norwegian Forest Research Institute

Rep Nottingham Univ Sch Agr — Report. Nottingham University. School of Agriculture

Rep NRL Prog — Report of NRL [*Naval Research Laboratory*] Progress

Rep NY State Vet Coll Cornell Univ — Report. New York State Veterinary College at Cornell University

Rep NZ Sci Cong — Report. New Zealand Science Congress

Rep Ohara Inst Agr Biol — Report. Ohara Institute of Agricultural Biology

Rep Ohara Inst Agric Biol — Report. Ohara Institute of Agricultural Biology

Rep Ont Dep Mines — Reports. Ontario Department of Mines

Rep Ont Vet Coll — Report. Ontario Veterinary College

Rep Ore For Res Lab — Report. Oregon State University. Forest Research Laboratory

Rep Oreg Wheat Comm — Report. Oregon Wheat Commission

Reporter Aust Inst of Crim Qrtly — Reporter. Australian Institute of Criminology. Quarterly

Reports Inst High Speed Mech Tohoku Univ — Reports. Institute of High Speed Mechanics. Tohoku University

Reports Res Inst Appl Mech Kyushu Univ — Reports. Research Institute for Applied Mechanics. Kyushu University

Rep Osaka Prefect Ind Res Inst — Reports. Osaka Prefectural Industrial Research Institute [*Japan*]

Repos Trab LNIV Port Lab Nac Inves Vet — Repositorio de Trabalhos do LNIV-Portugal. Laboratorio Nacional de Investigacao Veterinaria

Rep Pap Northamptonshire Antiq Soc — Reports and Papers. Northamptonshire Antiquarian Society

Rep Phil — Reports on Philosophy

Rep Plann Conf Strategy Virus Manage Potato II — Report. Planning Conference on the Strategy for Virus Management in Potatoes. II

Rep Popul-Fam Plann — Reports on Population-Family Planning

Rep Prefect Ind Res Inst (Shizuoka) — Reports. Prefectural Industrial Research Institute (Shizuoka) [*Japan*]

Rep Proc Int Assoc Ice Cream Manuf — Report of Proceedings. International Association of Ice Cream Manufacturers

Rep Prog Phys — Reports on Progress in Physics

Rep Prog Polym Phys (Jpn) — Reports on Progress in Polymer Physics (Japan)

Rep Progr Appl Chem — Reports on the Progress of Applied Chemistry

Rep Progr Kans Agr Exp Sta — Report of Progress. Kansas Agricultural Experiment Station

Rep Progr Kansas Agric Exp Stn — Report of Progress. Kansas Agricultural Experiment Station

Rep Progr Phys — Reports on Progress in Physics

Rep Proj LA Agr Exp Sta Dept Agron — Report of Projects. Louisiana Agricultural Experiment Station. Department of Agronomy

Rep Pr Phys — Reports on Progress in Physics

Rep Quebec Soc Prot Plant — Report. Quebec Society for the Protection of Plants

REPR — Reports on Polar Research. Berichte zur Polarforschung

Rep Rain Making Jpn — Report of Rain-Making in Japan

Repr BRA — Reprint. Bee Research Association

Repr Bull Bk R — Reprint Bulletin. Book Reviews

Rep Rd Res Lab Minist Transp — Report. Road Research Laboratory. Ministry of Transport

Rep React Cent (Ned) — Report. Reactor Centrum (Nederlandse)

Rep Reelfoot Lake Biol Stn Tenn Acad Sci — Report. Reelfoot Lake Biological Station. Tennessee Academy of Science

Rep Reg Res Cent ICTA (Trinidad) — Report. Regional Research Centre of the British Caribbean. Imperial College of Tropical Agriculture (Trinidad)

Rep Res Cent Assoc Am Railroads — Report. Research Center. Association of American Railroads

Rep Res Dept Kyushu Electr Power Co Inc — Report. Research Department. Kyushu Electric Power Company, Incorporated [*Japan*]

Rep Res Grantees Minist Educ (Jpn) — Reports on Researches by Grantees. Ministry of Education (Japan)

Rep Res Inst Appl Mech — Reports. Research Institute for Applied Mechanics

Rep Res Inst Appl Mech Kyushu Univ — Reports. Research Institute for Applied Mechanics. Kyushu University

Rep Res Inst Brew — Report. Research Institute of Brewing

Rep Res Inst Electr Commun Tohoku Univ — Reports. Research Institute of Electrical Communication. Tohoku University

Rep Res Inst Ind Saf — Reports. Research Institute of Industrial Safety [*Japan*]

Rep Res Inst Ind Sci Kyushu Univ — Reports. Research Institute of Industrial Science. Kyushu University

Rep Res Inst Nat Sci — Report. Research Institute of Natural Sciences [*Republic of Korea*]

Rep Res Inst Nat Sci Chungnam Natl Univ — Reports. Research Institute of Natural Sciences. Chungnam National University

Rep Res Inst Sci Ind Kyushu Univ — Reports. Research Institute of Science and Industry. Kyushu University [*Japan*]

Rep Res Inst Sci Technol Nihon Univ — Report. Research Institute of Science and Technology. Nihon University

Rep Res Inst Strength and Fract Mater — Reports. Research Institute for Strength and Fracture of Materials

Rep Res Inst Strength Fract Mater Tohoku Univ — Reports. Research Institute for Strength and Fracture of Materials. Tohoku University

Rep Res Inst Strength Fracture Mater Tohoku Univ (Sendai) — Reports. Research Institute for Strength and Fracture of Materials. Tohoku University (Sendai) [*Japan*]

Rep Res Inst Underground Resour Min Coll Akita Univ — Report. Research Institute of Underground Resources. Mining College. Akita University [*Japan*]

Rep Res Lab Asahi Glass Co Ltd — Report. Research Laboratory. Asahi Glass Company Limited

Rep Res Lab Eng Mater Tokyo Inst Technol — Report. Research Laboratory of Engineering Materials. Tokyo Institute of Technology

Rep Res Lab Kirin Brew Co — Report. Research Laboratories of Kirin Brewery Company

Rep Res Lab Kirin Brewery Co Ltd — Report. Research Laboratories of Kirin Brewery Company Limited [*Japan*]

Rep Res Lab Shimizu Constr Co Ltd — Reports. Research Laboratory of Shimizu Construction Company Limited [*Japan*]

Rep Res Lab Snow Brand Milk Prod Co — Reports. Research Laboratory. Snow Brand Milk Products Company

Rep Res Lab Surf Sci Okayama Univ — Reports. Research Laboratory for Surface Science. Okayama University

Rep Res Lab Tohoku Electr Power Co Ltd — Report. Research Laboratory. Tohoku Electric Power Company Limited [*Japan*]

Rep Res Nippon Inst Technol — Report of Researches. Nippon Institute of Technology

Rep Resour Res Inst (Kawaguchi) — Report. Resource Research Institute (Kawaguchi) [*Japan*]

Rep Res Progr Ill Agr Exp Sta — Report. Research Progress at the Illinois Agricultural Experiment Station

Rep Res Proj Dis Ornam Pl — Report. Research Project for Diseases of Ornamental Plants (Victorian Plant Research Institute)

Repr For Prod (Aust) — Reprint. Division of Forest Products (Melbourne, Australia)

Rep Rheum Dis — Reports on Rheumatic Diseases

Reprint Bull Bk R — Reprint Bulletin. Book Reviews

Repr NZ For Serv — Reprint. New Zealand Forest Service

Reprocess Newsl — Reprocessing Newsletter

Reprodn Paper News Bull — Reproduction Paper News. Bulletin

Reprodn Rev — Reproductions Review and Methods

Reprod Nutr Dev — Reproduction, Nutrition, Developpement

Reprod Rev — Reproductions Review

Reproduccio — Reproduccion

Reproduction Eng — Reproduction Engineering

Reprographics Q — Reprographics Quarterly

Reprography Newsl — Reprography Newsletter

Reprogr Q — Reprographics Quarterly

Rep Ross Conf Pediatr Res — Report. Ross Conference on Pediatric Research

Rep Rothamsted Exp Sta — Report. Rothamsted Experimental Station

Rep Rothamsted Exp Stn — Report. Rothamsted Experimental Station

Rep Rowett Inst — Report. Rowett Institute

Repr Res SP — Representative Research in Social Psychology

Rep RRL GB Dep Sci Ind Res Road Res Lab — Report RRL. Great Britain Department of Scientific and Industrial Research. Rooad Research Laboratory

REPSA — Revista de Psicoanalisis

Rep S Afr Assoc Adv Sci — Report. South African Association for the Advancement of Science

Rep Sask Dep Miner Resour — Report. Saskatchewan Department of Mineral Resources

Rep Sch Agric Univ Nottingham — Report. School of Agriculture. University of Nottingham

Rep Sci Ind Forum — Report. Science and Industry Forum. Australian Academy of Science

Rep Sci Indust Forum — Report. Science and Industry Forum. Australian Academy of Science

Rep Sci Indust Forum Aust Acad Sci — Report. Science and Industry Forum. Australian Academy of Science

Rep Sci Living — Reports of the Science of Living

Rep Scott Beekprs Ass — Report. Scottish Beekeepers Association

Rep Sea Fish Inst Ser B (Gdynia Pol) — Reports. Sea Fisheries Institute. Series B. Fishing Technique and Fishery Technology (Gdynia, Poland)

Rep Ser Ark Agr Exp Sta — Report Series. Arkansas Agricultural Experiment Station

Rep Ser Ark Agric Exp Stn — Report Series. Arkansas Agricultural Experiment Station

Rep Ser Phys Univ Helsinki — Report Series in Physics. University of Helsinki

Rep Shizuoka Prefect Ind Res Inst — Reports. Shizuoka Prefectural Industrial Research Institute

Rep Silk Sci Res Inst — Reports. Silk Science Research Institute [*Japan*]

Rep (Sixth) Conf Int Ass Quatern Res — Report. Sixth Conference. International Association on Quaternary Research

Rep Smithson Instn — Report. Smithsonian Institution

Rep Soc Res City Futu — Report of the Social Research on the City of Futu

Rep Sol Energy Stud CSIRO — Report. Solar Energy Studies. Commonwealth Scientific and Industrial Research Organisation

Rep South Corn Impr Conf — Report. Southern Corn Improvement Conference

Rep Stanford Univ John A Blume Earthquake Eng Cent — Report. Stanford University. John A. Blume Earthquake Engineering Center

Rep Stat Appl Res UJSE — Reports of Statistical Application Research. Union of Japanese Scientists and Engineers

Rep Stat Appl Res Union Jpn Sci Eng — Reports of Statistical Application Research. Union of Japanese Scientists and Engineers

Rep State Bd Health Iowa — Report. State Board of Health of Iowa

Rep State Energy Comm WA — Report. State Energy Commission of Western Australia

Rep Statist Appl Res Un Japan Sci Engrs — Reports of Statistical Application Research. Union of Japanese Scientists and Engineers

Rep Steno Mem Hosp Nord Insulinlab — Reports. Steno Memorial Hospital and the Nordisk Insulinlaboratorium

Rep Stud Tokyo Coll Domest Sci — Reports of Studies. Tokyo College of Domestic Science

Rep Stud Upland Farming Kawatabi Farm Tohoku Univ — Report of the Studies on Upland Farming in Kawatabi Farm. Tohoku University

Rep Sugar Exp Sta (Taiwan) — Report. Sugar Experimental Station (Taiwan)

Rep Surg Gen US Navy — Report. Surgeon General. United States Navy

Rep Surv Thirty-Two NSW River Valleys — Report. Survey of Thirty-Two New South Wales River Valleys

Rep Swed Deep Sea Exped 1947-1948 — Reports. Swedish Deep-Sea Expedition, 1947-1948

Rep Swed Univ Agric Sci Dep Agric Eng — Report. Swedish University of Agricultural Sciences. Department of Agricultural Engineering

Rep Swed Univ Agric Sci Dep Farm Build — Report. Swedish University of Agricultural Sciences. Department of Farm Buildings

Rep Swed Univ Agric Sci Dep For Prod — Report. Swedish University of Agricultural Sciences. Department of Forest Products

Rep Taiwan Sugar Exp Stn — Report. Taiwan Sugar Experiment Station

Rep Taiwan Sugar Res Inst — Report. Taiwan Sugar Research Institute

Rep Tech Coll Hosei Univ (Tokyo) — Report. Technical College. Hosei University (Tokyo)

Rep Technol Iwate Univ — Report on Technology. Iwate University [*Japan*]

Rep Technol Res Norw Fish Ind — Reports on Technological Research Concerning Norwegian Fish Industry

Rep Tech Res Inst Taisei Corp — Reports. Technical Research Institute. Taisei Corporation

Rep Teleph Eng — Reports on Telephone Engineering

Rep Tex Agric Exp Stn — Report. Texas Agricultural Experiment Station

Rep Tex Water Dev Board — Report. Texas Water Development Board

Rep Tob Res Inst (Taiwan) — Annual Report. Tobacco Research Institute (Taiwan)

Rep Tob Res Inst Taiwan Tob Wine Monop Bur — Report. Tobacco Research Institute. Taiwan Tobacco and Wine Monopoly Bureau

Rep Tohoku Br Crop Sci Soc Jap — Report. Tohoku Branch. Crop Science Society of Japan

Rep Tokai Br Crop Sci Soc Jap — Report. Tokai Branch. Crop Science Society of Japan

Rep Tokushima Agr Exp Sta — Report. Tokushima Agricultural Experiment Station

Rep Tokyo Industr Res Inst — Report. Tokyo Industrial Research Institute

Rep Tokyo-to-Lab Med Sci — Report. Tokyo-to-Lab for Medical Sciences

Rep Tokyo Metrop Ind Res Inst — Reports. Tokyo Metropolitan Industrial Research Institute

Rep Tokyo Metrop Ind Tech Inst — Report. Tokyo Metropolitan Industrial Technic Institute

Rep Tokyo Univ Fish — Report. Tokyo University. Fisheries

Rep Tottori Mycol Inst — Reports. Tottori Mycological Institute

Rept Progr Appl — Reports on the Progress of Applied Chemistry

Rept Progr Phys — Reports on Progress in Physics

Rept Progr Polymer Phys (Japan) — Reports on Progress in Polymer Physics (Japan)

Rep Train Inst Eng Teach Kyoto Univ — Report. Training Institute for Engineering Teachers. Kyoto University [*Japan*]

Rep Trans (Devonshire) — Report and Transactions (Devonshire)

Rep Trans Devonshire Ass — Reports and Transactions. Devonshire Association for the Advancement of Science, Literature, and Art

Rep Transp Tech Res Inst (Tokyo) — Report. Transportation Technical Research Institute (Tokyo)

Rep Trans Soc Guernesiaise — Report and Transactions. Societe Guernesiaise

Rept Statist Appl Res — Report on Statistical Applications Research

Repubb Ital Minist Agri For Collana Verde — Repubblica Italiana Ministero dell'Agricoltura e delle Foreste Collana Verde

Repub Malagasy Ann Geol Madagascar — Republique Malagasy. Annales Geologiques de Madagascar

Repub Malgache Doc Bur Geol — Republique Malgache. Documentation du Bureau Geologique

Repub Malgache Rapp Annu Serv Geol — Republique Malgache. Rapport Annuel du Service Geologique

Repub Philipp Dep Agric Nat Resour Bur Mines Inf Circ — Republic of the Philippines. Department of Agriculture and Natural Resources. Bureau of Mines. Information Circular

Repub Rwandaise Bull Serv Geol — Republique Rwandaise. Bulletin du Service Geologique

Repub S Afr Dep Agric Tech Serv Entomol Mem — Republic of South Africa. Department of Agricultural Technical Services. Entomology Memoirs

Repub S Afr Dep Agric Tech Serv Sci Bull — Republic of South Africa. Department of Agricultural Technical Services. Science Bulletin

Repub S Afr Dep Agric Tech Serv Tech Commun — Republic of South Africa. Department of Agricultural Technical Services. Technical Communication

Repub S Afr Geol Opname Bull — Republiek van Suid-Afrika. Geologiese Opname. Bulletin

Repub S Afr Geol Opname Handb — Republiek van Suid-Afrika. Geologiese Opname. Handboek

Repub S Afr Geol Surv Mem — Republic of South Africa. Geological Survey. Memoir

Repub Venezuela Bol Acad Cienc Fis Mat Natur — Republica de Venezuela. Boletin. Academia de Ciencias Fisicas, Matematicas, y Naturales

Repub Venezuela Bol Acad Ci Fis Mat Natur — Republica de Venezuela. Boletin. Academia de Ciencias Fisicas, Matematicas, y Naturales

Rep Univ Alaska Inst Mar Sci — Report. University of Alaska. Institute of Marine Science

Rep Univ Calif Berkeley Sanit Eng Res Lab — Report. University of California, Berkeley. Sanitary Engineering Research Laboratory

Rep Univ Calif Davis Calif Water Resour Cent — Report. University of California, Davis. California Water Resources Center

Rep Univ Electro-Comm — Reports. University of Electro-Communications

Rep Univ Electro-Commun — Reports. University of Electro-Communications

Rep USA Mar Biol Stn — Reports. USA Marine Biological Station

Rep US Dep Agric For Serv North Reg State Priv For — Report. United States Department of Agriculture Forest Service. Northern Region. State and Private Forestry

Rep VT Wood Prod Conf — Report. Vermont Wood Products Conference

Rep Waite Agric Res Inst — Report. Waite Agricultural Research Institute

Rep Water Res Found Aust — Report. Water Research Foundation of Australia

Rep Water Res Found Aust Ltd — Report. Water Research Foundation of Australia Limited

Rep Water Res Lab NSW Univ — Report. Water Research Laboratory. University of New South Wales

Rep Water Resour Res Inst Univ NC — Report. Water Resources Research Institute. University of North Carolina

Rep Water Resour Surv — Report. Water Resources Survey. Tasmania

Rep Wat Res Fdn — Report. Water Research Foundation of Australia

Rep Wat Res Fdn Aust — Report. Water Research Foundation of Australia

Rep Wat Res Lab NSW Univ — Report. Water Research Laboratory. University of New South Wales

Rep Wellcome Research Lab — Report. Wellcome Research Laboratories

Rep Welsh Pl Breed Stn — Report. Welsh Plant Breeding Station

Rep Welsh Soils Discuss Grp — Report. Welsh Soils Discussion Group

Rep Wheat Qual Conf — Report. Wheat Quality Conference

Rep World Aff — Report on World Affairs

Rep World Congr Agr Res — Report. World Congress on Agricultural Research

Rep W Scot Agr Coll Econ Dept — Report. West of Scotland Agricultural College. Economics Department

Rep Wye Agric Coll — Report. Wye Agricultural College

Rep Wye Coll Dep Hop Res — Report. Wye College. Department of Hop Research

REPYB — Research Policy [*Netherlands*]

Rep Yeungnam Univ Inst Ind Technol — Report. Yeungnam University. Institute of Industrial Technology

Rep Yeungnam Univ Inst Nat Prod — Report. Yeungnam University. Institute of Natural Products

Rep Yr Dublin Univ Coll Agr Dept — Report of the Year. Dublin University College. Agricultural Department

RER — Real Estate Review

RER — Review of Educational Research

RER — Revue des Etudes Rabelaisiennes

RER — Revue des Etudes Roumaines

RERA — Reclamation Era

RERA — RERA: Official Monthly Journal. Radio and Electrical Retailers' Association of New South Wales

RERAA — Reclamation Era

RERo — Revue des Etudes Roumaines

RERTD — Regelungstechnik. RT

RES — Recent Economic Developments [*Jerusalem*]

ReS — Reinare en Espana

ReS — Religion et Societes

RES — Repertoire d'Epigraphie Semitique [*Paris*]

Res — Researcher [*Samar*]

RES — Review of Economics and Statistics

RES — Review of English Studies

RES — Revue de l'Enseignement Superieur

RES — Revue des Etudes Semitiques

RES — Revue des Etudes Slaves

Res/Accel — Research/Accelerators

Res Act Fac Sci Engrg Tokyo Denki Univ — Research Activities. Faculty of Science and Engineering of Tokyo Denki University

Res Act For Comm (Victoria Aust) — Research Activity. Forests Commission (Victoria, Australia)

RESAD — Revista Saude

Res Adv Alcohol Drug Probl — Research Advances in Alcohol and Drug Problems

Res African Lit — Research in African Literatures

Res Afric Lit — Research in African Literatures

Res Afr Lit — Research in African Literatures

Res Annu Nihon Nosan Kogyo — Research Annual. Nihon Nosan Kogyo

Res Appl Ind — Research Applied in Industry

Res Appl Natl Needs Rep NSF/RA (US) — Research Applied to National Needs. Report. NSF/RA [*National Science Foundation/Research Applied*] (United States)

Res Appl Technol Symp Mined-Land Reclam Pap — Research and Applied Technology Symposium on Mined-Land Reclamation. Papers

Res Assoc Br Paint Colour Varn Manuf Bull — Research Association of British Paint, Colour, and Varnish Manufacturers. Bulletin

Res Bib — Research Service Bibliographies

Res Bk — Reserve Bank Bulletin [*New Zealand*]

Res Bk NZ — Reserve Bank of New Zealand. Bulletin

Res Brch Rep Can Dep Agric — Research Branch Report. Canada Department of Agriculture

Res Briefs — Research Briefs

Res Briefs Sch For Resour PA St Univ — Research Briefs. School of Forest Resources. Pennsylvania State University

Res Bull Agr Home Econ Exp Sta Iowa State Coll — Research Bulletin. Agricultural and Home Economics Experiment Station. Iowa State College

Res Bull Agric Exp Stn Univ Idaho — Research Bulletin. Agricultural Experiment Station. University of Idaho

Res Bull Agric Exp Stn Univ Nebr — Research Bulletin. Agricultural Experiment Station. University of Nebraska

Res Bull Agric Exp Stn Univ Wis — Research Bulletin. Agricultural Experiment Station. College of Agriculture. University of Wisconsin

Res Bull Aichi-Ken Agric Res Cent Ser B Hortic — Research Bulletin. Aichi-Ken Agricultural Research Center. Series B. Horticulture [*Japan*]

Res Bull Birla Archaeol Cult Res Inst — Research Bulletin. Birla Archaeological and Cultural Research Institute

Res Bull CIMMYT — Research Bulletin. Centro Internacional de Mejoramiento de Maiz y Trigo

Res Bull Coll Exp For Hokkaido Univ — Research Bulletins. College Experiment Forests. Hokkaido University

Res Bull Coll Expt Forest Hokkaido Univ — Research Bulletins. College Experiment Forests. Hokkaido University

Res Bull Coll Gen Educ Nagoya Univ Nat Sci Psychol — Research Bulletin. College of General Education. Nagoya University. Natural Sciences and Psychology

Res Bull East Panjab Univ — Research Bulletin. East Panjab University

Res Bull Electr Power Dev Co Ltd — Research Bulletin. Electric Power Development Company Limited [*Japan*]

Res Bull Exp For Hokkaido Univ — Research Bulletin. College Experiment Forests. Hokkaido University

Res Bull Fac Agr Gifu Univ — Research Bulletin. Faculty of Agriculture. Gifu University

Res Bull Fac Agric Ain Shams Univ — Research Bulletin. Faculty of Agriculture. Ain Shams University

Res Bull Fac Agric Gifu-Ken Prefect Univ — Research Bulletin. Faculty of Agriculture. Gifu-Ken Prefectural University

Res Bull Fac Agric Gifu Univ — Research Bulletin. Faculty of Agriculture. Gifu University

Res Bull Fac Ed Oita Univ — Research Bulletin. Faculty of Education. Oita University

Res Bull Fac Educ Oita Univ Nat Sci — Research Bulletin. Faculty of Education. Oita University. Natural Science

Res Bull Fac Lib Arts Oita Univ — Research Bulletin. Faculty of Liberal Arts. Oita University

Res Bull For Res Lab Oreg State Univ — Research Bulletin. Forest Research Laboratory. Oregon State University

Res Bull Gifu Imp Coll Agr — Research Bulletin. Gifu Imperial College of Agriculture

Res Bull Hiroshima Inst Technol — Research Bulletin. Hiroshima Institute of Technology

Res Bull Hokkaido Nat Agr Exp Sta — Research Bulletin. Hokkaido National Agricultural Experiment Station

Res Bull Hokkaido Natl Agric Exp Stn — Research Bulletin. Hokkaido National Agricultural Experiment Station

Res Bull Hokkaido Natn Agric Exp Stn — Research Bulletin. Hokkaido National Agricultural Experiment Station

Res Bull Iida Women's Jr Coll — Research Bulletin. Iida Women's Junior College

Res Bull Indiana Agr Exp Sta — Research Bulletin. Indiana Agricultural Experiment Station

Res Bull Int Cent Impr Maize Wheat — Research Bulletin. International Center for the Improvement of Maize and Wheat

Res Bull Iowa Agric Exp Stn — Research Bulletin. Iowa Agricultural Experiment Station

Res Bull Iowa Agric Home Econ Exp Stn — Research Bulletin. Iowa Agricultural and Home Economics Experiment Station

Res Bull Iowa St Univ Agric Home Econ Exp Stn — Research Bulletin. Iowa State University Agricultural and Home Economics Experiment Station

Res Bull Kangweon Natl Univ — Research Bulletin. Kangweon National University [*Republic of Korea*]

Res Bull Mass Agric Exp Stn — Research Bulletin. Massachusetts Agricultural Experiment Station

Res Bull Meguro Parasitol Mus — Research Bulletin. Meguro Parasitological Museum

Res Bull Meisei Univ — Research Bulletin. Meisei University

Res Bull Meisei Univ Phys Sci Eng — Research Bulletin. Meisei University. Physical Sciences and Engineering

Res Bull Missouri Agric Exp Stn — Research Bulletin. Missouri Agricultural Experiment Station

Res Bull MO Agric Exp Sta — Research Bulletin. Missouri Agricultural Experiment Station

Res Bull Nat Hist Parks Site Branch — Research Bulletin. National Historic Parks and Site Branch

Res Bull Neb Agric Exp Stn — Research Bulletin. Nebraska Agricultural Experiment Station

Res Bull Obihiro Univ Ser I — Research Bulletin. Obihiro University. Series I

Res Bull Obihiro Zootech Univ — Research Bulletin. Obihiro Zootechnical University. Series I

Res Bull Obihiro Zootech Univ Ser I — Research Bulletin. Obihiro Zootechnical University. Series I

Res Bull Ohio Agric Res Dev Center — Research Bulletin. Ohio Agricultural Research and Development Center

Res Bull Ohio Agric Res Developm Cent — Research Bulletin. Ohio Agricultural Research and Development Center

Res Bull Ore For Res Lab — Research Bulletin. Oregon State University. Forest Research Laboratory

Res Bull Panjab Univ — Research Bulletin. Panjab University

Res Bull Panjab Univ NS — Research Bulletin. Panjab University. New Series

Res Bull Panjab Univ Sci — Research Bulletin. Panjab University. Science

Res Bull PCSIR Lab — Research Bulletin. PCSIR [*Pakistan Council of Scientific and Industrial Research*] Laboratories

Res Bull Plant Prot Serv (Jap) — Research Bulletin. Plant Protection Service (Japan)

Res Bull Plant Prot Serv (Jpn) — Research Bulletin. Plant Protection Service (Japan)

Res Bull Printing Bur (Tokyo) — Research Bulletin. Printing Bureau. Ministry of Finance (Tokyo)

Res Bull Purdue Univ Agr Exp Sta — Research Bulletin. Purdue University Agricultural Experiment Station

Res Bull Reg Eng Coll (Warangal) — Research Bulletin. Regional Engineering College (Warangal)

Res Bull Saitama Agr Exp Sta — Research Bulletin. Saitama Agricultural Experiment Station

Res Bull Univ Calcutta — Research Bulletin. University of Calcutta

Res Bull Univ Farm Hokkaido Univ — Research Bulletin. University Farm. Hokkaido University

Res Bull Univ GA Exp Stn — Research Bulletin. University of Georgia. Experiment Stations

Res Bull Univ MO Coll Agr Exp Sta — Research Bulletin. University of Missouri. College of Agriculture. Experiment Station

Res Bull Univ Nebr Coll Agr Home Econ Agr Exp Sta — Research Bulletin. University of Nebraska. College of Agriculture and Home Economics. Agricultural Experiment Station

Res Bull West Scotl Agric Coll — Research Bulletin. West of Scotland Agricultural College

Res Bull Wis Agr Exp Sta — Research Bulletin. Wisconsin Agricultural Experiment Station

Res Bull W Scotl Coll Agric — Research Bulletin. West of Scotland College of Agriculture

Res Circ Ohio Agric Exp Stn — Research Circular. Ohio Agricultural Experiment Station

Res Circ Ohio Agr Res Develop Cent — Research Circular. Ohio Agricultural Research and Development Center

Res Clin Lab — Research in Clinic and Laboratory

Res Clin Stud Headache — Research and Clinical Studies in Headache

Res Comm C P — Research Communications in Chemical Pathology and Pharmacology

Res Commun Chem Pathol Pharmacol — Research Communications in Chemical Pathology and Pharmacology

Res Commun Inst Ferment (Osaka) — Research Communications. Institute for Fermentation (Osaka)

Res Commun Psychol Psychiatry Behav — Research Communications in Psychology, Psychiatry, and Behavior

Res Communs Chem Path Pharmac — Research Communications in Chemical Pathology and Pharmacology

Res Constructs Peaceful Uses Nucl Energy — Research Constructs on Peaceful Uses of Nuclear Energy [*Japan*]

Res Corresp — Research Correspondence

Res Counc Alberta Bull — Research Council of Alberta. Bulletin

Res Counc Alberta (Can) Inform Ser — Research Council of Alberta (Canada) Information Series

Res Counc Alberta Econ Geol Rep — Research Council of Alberta. Economic Geology Report

Res Counc Alberta Geol Div Bull — Research Council of Alberta. Geological Division. Bulletin

Res Counc Alberta Geol Div Mem — Research Council of Alberta. Geological Division. Memoir

Res Counc Alberta Mimeogr Circ — Research Council of Alberta. Mimeographed Circular

Res Counc Alberta Rep — Research Council of Alberta. Report

Res Counc Isr Annu Rep — Research Council of Israel. Annual Report

Rescue Archaeol Hampshire — Rescue Archaeology in Hampshire

R Escuela Def Nac — Revista. Escuela de Defensa Nacional

Res Dep Rep Post Off Res Cent (UK) — Research Department Report. Post Office Research Centre (United Kingdom)

Res Des — Research and Design

Res Dev — Research/Development

Res Dev Bull Portland Cem Assoc — Research and Development Bulletin. Portland Cement Association

Res/Develop — Research/Development

Res Developm Pap For Comm (Lond) — Research and Development Paper. Forestry Commission (London)

Res Dev Lab Portland Cem Assoc Res Dep Bull — Research and Development Laboratories. Portland Cement Association. Research Department Bulletin

Res Disclosure — Research Disclosure

Research Bul — Liberal Party of Australia. New South Wales Division. Research Bulletin

Research Council Alberta Bull — Research Council of Alberta. Bulletin

Research Council Alberta Rept — Research Council of Alberta. Report

Research in Ed — Research in Education

Researches Popul Ecol Kyoto Univ — Researches on Population Ecology. Kyoto University

Research F — Research Film

Research Mgt — Research Management

RESEB — Resources in Education

Res Econ Hist — Research in Economic History

Res Educ — Research in Education [*England*]

ResEduc — Resources in Education

RESEE — Revue des Etudes Sud-Est Europeennes

Res Electrotech Lab — Researches. Electrotechnical Laboratory [*Japan*]

Res Electrotech Lab (Tokyo) — Researches. Electrotechnical Laboratory (Tokyo)

RESem — Revue des Etudes Semitiques

Res Eng — Research Engineer

Res Eng Jeonbug Natl Univ — Research of Engineering. Jeonbug National University [*Republic of Korea*]

Res Eng Res Inst Ind Technol Jeonbug Natl Univ — Research of Engineering. Research Institute of Industrial Technology. Jeonbug National University [*Republic of Korea*]

Res Environ Disruption Interdiscip Coop — Research on Environmental Disruption toward Interdisciplinary Cooperation [*Japan*]

Res & Eq J — A'Beckett's Reserved Judgments, New South Wales [*1845*] [*Australia*]

Res & Eq J — Reserved and Equity Judgements [*New South Wales*]

Res & Eq Jud — Reserved and Equity Judgments [*New South Wales*]

Res & Eq Judg — A'Beckett's Reserved Judgments, New South Wales [*1845*] [*Australia*]

Res & Eq Judgm — Reserved and Equity Judgments [*New South Wales*]

Reserve Bank Australia Statis Bul — Reserve Bank of Australia. Statistical Bulletin

Reserve Bank India B — Reserve Bank of India. Bulletin

Reserve Bank NZ Bul — Reserve Bank of New Zealand. Bulletin

Res Esst Oils Aust Flora — Researches on Essential Oils of the Australian Flora

Res Establ Risoe Rep Risoe-M (Den) — Research Establishment Risoe. Report. Risoe-M (Denmark)

Res Establ Risoe Risoe Rep (Den) — Research Establishment Risoe. Risoe Report (Denmark)

Res Exp Econ — Research in Experimental Economics

Res Exp Med — Research in Experimental Medicine

Res Exp Med (Berlin) — Research in Experimental Medicine (Berlin)

Res Exp Rec Minist Agric (Nth Ire) — Research and Experimental Record. Ministry of Agriculture (Northern Ireland)

Res & Farm — Research and Farming [*North Carolina Agricultural Experiment Station*]

Res Farmers — Research for Farmers

Res Farming — Research and Farming [*North Carolina Agricultural Experiment Station*]

Res Farming (NC Agric Exp Stn) — Research and Farming (North Carolina Agricultural Experiment Station)

Res Film — Research Film

Res Fish Annu Rep Coll Fish Univ Wash — Research in Fisheries. Annual Report of the College of Fisheries. University of Washington

Res Futures — Research Futures

RESFV — Renaissance Editions. San Fernando Valley State College

Res High Educ Abstr — Research into Higher Education. Abstracts

Res Higher Educ — Research in Higher Education

Resid Staff Physician — Resident and Staff Physician

Residue Rev — Residue Reviews

Res Immunochem Immunobiol — Research in Immunochemistry and Immunobiology

Res Ind — Research and Industry

Res Indicat Petrol — Resumos Indicativos do Petroleo

Res Ind (New Delhi) — Research and Industry (New Delhi)

Resin Rev — Resin Review

Res Inst Appl Mech Kyushu Univ Report — Research Institute for Applied Mechanics. Kyushu University. Reports

Res Inst Fund Information Sci Res Rep — Research Institute of Fundamental Information Science. Research Report

Res Inst Fund Inform Sci Res Rep — Kyushu University. Research Institute of Fundamental Information Science. Research Report

Res Inst Nedri As (Hveragerdi Icel) Rep — Research Institute Nedri As (Hveragerdi, Iceland). Report

Res Int — Residential Interiors

Res Intell News — Research and Intelligence News

Res & Invt — Research and Invention

Resistencia (Ser Econ e Gestao) — Resistencia (Serie de Economia e Gestao)

RESJA — RES. Journal of the Reticuloendothelial Society

Res J Dir Higher Educ (Indones) — Research Journal. Directorate of Higher Education (Indonesia)

Res J Fac Sci Kashmir Univ — Research Journal. Faculty of Science. Kashmir University

Res J Kanpur Agr Coll — Research Journal. Kanpur Agricultural College

Res J Mahatma Phule Agric Univ — Research Journal. Mahatma Phule Agricultural University

Res J Philo Soc Sci — Research Journal of Philosophy and Social Sciences [*Meerut Cantt, India*]

RES J Reticuloendothel Soc — RES. Journal of the Reticuloendothelial Society

Res Jud — Res Judicatae

Res J Univ Wyo Agric Exp Stn — Research Journal. University of Wyoming. Agricultural Experiment Station

RESL — Revue des Etudes Slaves

Res Lab Commun Sci Univ Electro-Commun Annu Rep — Research Laboratory of Communication Science. University of Electro-Communications. Annual Report

Res Lab Precis Mach Electron — Research Laboratory Precision Machinery and Electronics

Res Lab Rec — Research Laboratory Record

RESlaves — Revue des Etudes Slaves

Res Leafl For Res Inst NZ For Serv — Research Leaflet. Forest Research Institute. New Zealand Forest Service

Res Leafl Sav For Res Sta — Research Leaflet. Savanna Forestry Research Station

Res L & Econ — Research in Law and Economics

Res Libnship — Research in Librarianship

Res Librarianship — Research in Librarianship

Res Life Sci — Research in Life Sciences

Res Lit — Respublica Literaria

RESMA — Research Management

Res Manag — Research Management

Res Mech — Res Mechanica

Res Mech Lett — Res Mechanica Letters

Res Memo Int Inst Appl Syst Anal — Research Memorandum. International Institute for Applied Systems Analysis

Res Meth Neurochem — Research Methods in Neurochemistry

Res Mgt — Research Management

Res Mol Biol — Research in Molecular Biology

Res Monogr Cell Tissue Physiol — Research Monographs in Cell and Tissue Physiology

Res Monogr Ser Natl Inst Drug Abuse (US) — Research Monograph Series. National Institute on Drug Abuse (United States)

Res Natl Mus (Bloemfontein) — Researches. National Museum (Bloemfontein)

RESND — Resources and Energy

Res News Off Res Adm Univ Mich (Ann Arbor) — Research News. Office of Research Administration. University of Michigan (Ann Arbor)

Res Norw Agric — Research in Norwegian Agriculture

Res Note BC For Serv — Research Notes. British Columbia Forest Service

Res Note Bur For (Philippines) — Research Note. Bureau of Forestry (Philippines)

Res Note Colo Coll For Nat Resour — Research Note. Colorado State University. College of Forestry and Natural Resources

Res Note Div For Res (Zambia) — Research Note. Division of Forest Research (Zambia)

Res Note Fac For Univ BC — Research Note. Faculty of Forestry. University of British Columbia

Res Note For Comm NSW — Research Note. Forestry Commission of New South Wales

Res Note For Mgmt Res Ore For Res Lab — Research Note. Forest Management Research. Oregon State University. Forest Research Laboratory

Res Note FPL For Prod Lab — Research Note FPL. Forest Products Laboratory [*United States*]
Res Note N Cent Forest Exp Stn US Dep Agric — Research Note. North Central Forest Experiment Station. US Department of Agriculture
Res Note Pacif SW For Exp Stn — Research Note. Pacific Southwest Forest and Range Experiment Station. US Department of Agriculture
Res Note Prov BC Minist For — Research Note. Province of British Columbia. Ministry of Forests
Res Note QD For Serv — Research Notes. Queensland Forest Service
Res Note Res Prod Counc (NB) — Research Note. Research and Productivity Council (New Brunswick)
Res Notes in Math — Research Notes in Mathematics
Res Notes Memoranda Appl Geom Post-RAAG — Research Notes and Memoranda of Applied Geometry in Post-RAAG [*Research Association of Applied Geometry*]
Res Notes NSW For Comm — New South Wales. Forestry Commission. Research Notes
Res Notes QD Dep For — Research Notes. Queensland Department of Forestry
Res Note Tex For Serv — Research Note. Texas Forest Service
Res Note UBC For Club — Research Notes. University of British Columbia. Forest Club
Res Note Univ Tex Austin Bur Econ Geol — Research Note. University of Texas at Austin. Bureau of Economic Geology
Res Not Ford For Cent — Research Note. Ford Forestry Center
RESNS — Review of English Studies. New Series
Res Nurs Health — Research in Nursing and Health
Res Nurs Hlth — Research in Nursing and Health
RESO — Resources Bulletin. Man and Resources Conference Program
Resoconti Assoc Min Sarda — Resoconti. Associazione Mineraria Sarda
Resour Am L — Resources for American Literary Study
Resour Biosphere (USSR) — Resources of the Biosphere (USSR)
Resour Book Publ — Resources for Book Publishers [*United States*]
Resources Conserv — Resources and Conservation [*Netherlands*]
Resources Pol — Resources Policy
Resour Energy — Resources and Energy [*Netherlands*]
Resour and Energy — Resources and Energy
Resour Manage Optim — Resource Management and Optimization [*United States*]
Resour Policy — Resources Policy
Resour Recovery Conserv — Resource Recovery and Conservation [*Netherlands*]
Resour Recovery Energy Rev — Resource Recovery and Energy Review
Resour Rep Coop Ext Univ Wis — Resource Report. Cooperative Extension. University of Wisconsin
Resour Sharing and Libr Networks — Resource Sharing and Library Networks
Res Outlook — Research Outlook
ResP — Research and Progress
Res Pam (Div For Res Zambia) — Research Pamphlet (Division of Forest Research, Zambia)
Res Pam For Res Inst (Kepong) — Research Pamphlet. Forest Research Institute (Kepong)
Res Pamphl For Res Inst (Malaya) — Research Pamphlet. Forest Research Institute (Malaya)
Res Pap Dep For (QD) — Research Paper. Department of Forestry (Queensland)
Res Pap Dep For (Queensl) — Research Paper. Department of Forestry (Queensland)
Res Paper Horace Lamb Centre Oceanogr Res — Research Paper. Horace Lamb Centre for Oceanographical Research. Flinders University [*South Australia*]
Res Pap Fac For Univ BC — Research Paper. Faculty of Forestry. University of British Columbia
Res Pap For Dep West Aust — Research Paper. Forests Department. Western Australia
Res Pap Forests Dep West Aust — Research Paper. Forests Department. Western Australia
Res Pap (Forest Ser) Fed Dep Forest Res (Niger) — Research Paper (Forest Series). Federal Department of Forest Research (Nigeria)
Res Pap GA For Res Coun — Research Paper. Georgia Forest Research Council
Res Pap Geogr Univ Newcastle — Research Papers in Geography. University of Newcastle
Res Pap Horace Lamb Centre Oceanogrl Res — Research Paper. Horace Lamb Centre for Oceanographical Research. Flinders University [*South Australia*]
Res Pap Ore For Res Lab — Research Paper. Oregon State University. Forest Research Laboratory
Res Pap Phys Educ — Research Papers in Physical Education
Res Pap PNW (Pac Northwest For Range Exp Stn) — Research Paper PNW (Pacific Northwest Forest and Range Experiment Station)
Res Pap Sav For Res Sta — Research Paper. Savanna Forestry Research Station
Res Pap Sch For Resour PA St Univ — Research Paper. School of Forest Resources. Pennsylvania State University
Res Pap Ser Int Rice Res Inst — Research Paper Series. International Rice Research Institute

Res Pap US Forest Serv Lake St Forest Exp Stn — Research Paper. United States Forest Service. Lake States Forest Experiment Station
Res Pap (West Aust) For Dep — Research Paper (Western Australia). Forests Department
Resp C — Respiratory Care
Resp Care — Respiratory Care
RESPD — Revue d'Epidemiologie et de Sante Publique
R Esp Der Int — Revista Espanola de Derecho Internacional
Res Phenomenol — Research in Phenomenology
REspir — Revista de Espiritualidad
Respiration Suppl — Respiration. Supplement [*Switzerland*]
Respir Circ — Respiration and Circulation
Respir Physiol — Respiration Physiology
Respir Technol — Respiratory Technology
Respir Ther — Respiratory Therapy
REspL — Revista Espanola de Linguistica
Res Pol — Research Policy
R Esp Opinion Publica — Revista Espanola de la Opinion Publica
R Esp Opin Publ — Revista Espanola de la Opinion Publica
Res Popul Ecol — Researches on Population Ecology
Res Popul Ecol (Kyoto) — Researches on Population Ecology (Kyoto)
Resp Physl — Respiration Physiology
Res Preview — Research Previews
Res Prog Lithogr Tech Found — Research Progress. Lithographic Technical Foundation
Res Prog Org-Biol Med Chem — Research Progress in Organic-Biological and Medicinal Chemistry
Res Prog Rep Purdue Univ Agric Exp Stn — Research Progress Report. Purdue University. Agricultural Experiment Station [*Indiana*]
Res Prog Rep Tokai-Kinki Natn Agric Exp Stn — Research Progress Report. Tokai-Kinki National Agricultural Experiment Station
Res Prog Rep UK At Energy Res Establ Health Phys Med Div — Research Progress Report. United Kingdom Atomic Energy Research Establishment. Health Physics and Medical Division
Res Progr Rep Indiana Agr Exp Sta — Research Progress Report. Indiana Agricultural Experiment Station
Res Progr Rep Purdue Agric Exp Sta — Research Progress Report. Purdue University. Agricultural Experiment Station [*Indiana*]
Res Progr Rep Purdue Univ Agr Exp Sta — Research Progress Report. Purdue University. Agricultural Experiment Station [*Indiana*]
Res Progr Rep Tokai-Kinki Nat Agr Exp Sta — Research Progress Report. Tokai-Kinki National Agricultural Experiment Station
Res Progr Rep West Weed Control Conf — Research Progress Report. Western Weed Control Conference
Res Proj Ser Victoria Dep Agric — Victoria. Department of Agriculture. Research Project Series
Res Prostaglandins — Research in Prostaglandins
REspT — Revista Espanola de Teologia [*Madrid*]
Resp Technol — Respiratory Technology
Resp Ther — Respiratory Therapy
Res Publ — Res Publica
Res Publ Assoc Res Nerv Ment Dis — Research Publications Association for Research in Nervous and Mental Disease
Res Publ Gen Mot Corp Res Lab — Research Publication. General Motors Corporation. Research Laboratories
Res Publ Kan Agric Exp Stn — Research Publication. Kansas Agricultural Experiment Station
Res Q — Research Quarterly
Res Q (AAHPER) — Research Quarterly. American Association for Health, Physical Education, and Recreation
Res Q Am Alliance Health Phys Educ Recreat — Research Quarterly. American Alliance for Health, Physical Education, and Recreation
Res Q Am Assoc Health Phys Educ Recreation — Research Quarterly. American Association for Health, Physical Education, and Recreation
Res Q Exerc Sport — Research Quarterly for Exercise and Sport
Res Q Ont Hydro — Research Quarterly. Ontario Hydro
Res Quart — Research Quarterly
ReSR — Recherches de Science Religieuse
Res R — Research in Review
Resrce Recv — Resource Recovery Update
Res Rec Malawi For Res Inst — Research Record. Malawi Forest Research Institute
Res Relat Child — Research Relating to Children
Res Rep Agric Exp Stn Mich St Univ — Research Report. Agricultural Experiment Station. Michigan State University
Res Rep Agric Exp Stn Univ Wisc — Research Report. Agricultural Experiment Station. University of Wisconsin
Res Rep Agric Exp Stn Utah St Univ — Research Report. Agricultural Experiment Station. Utah State University
Res Rep Anan Tech College — Research Reports. Anan Technical College
Res Rep Autom Control Lab Fac Eng Nagoya Univ — Research Reports. Automatic Control Laboratory. Faculty of Engineering. Nagoya University
Res Rep Biotech Fac Univ Ljublj Agric Issue — Research Reports. Biotechnical Faculty. University of Ljubljana. Agricultural Issue

Res Rep Can Dept Agr Nat Weed Comm West Sect — Research Report. Canada Department of Agriculture. National Weed Committee. Western Section

Res Rep Cent Highw Res Univ Tex Austin — Research Report. Center for Highway Research. University of Texas at Austin

Res Rep Coll Agric Korea Univ — Research Reports. College of Agriculture. Korea University

Res Rep Coll Agric Univ Wis — Research Report. Experiment Station. College of Agriculture. University of Wisconsin

Res Rep Coll Agric Vet Med Nihon Univ — Research Reports. College of Agriculture and Veterinary Medicine. Nihon University [*Japan*]

Res Rep Coll Eng Busan Natl Univ — Research Report. College of Engineering. Busan National University

Res Rep DAE LA St Univ Agric Exp Stn — Research Report. Department of Agricultural Economics and Agri-Business. Louisiana State University and Agricultural Experiment Station

Res Rep Dep Crop Sci NC State Univ — Research Report. Department of Crop Science. North Carolina State University. Agricultural Experiment Station

Res Rep Dep Electl Engng Melb Univ — Research Report. Department of Electrical Engineering. University of Melbourne

Res Rep Dep Electr Eng Melb Univ — Research Report. Department of Electrical Engineering. University of Melbourne

Res Rep Div Appl Org Chem CSIRO — Research Report. Division of Applied Organic Chemistry. Commonwealth Scientific and Industrial Research Organisation

Res Rep East Sect Nat Weed Comm Can — Research Report. Eastern Section. National Weed Committee of Canada

Res Rep Electron Gen Res Inst — Research Report. Electronics General Research Institute [*Japan*]

Res Rep Fac Biotech Univ Ljublj Vet Issue — Research Reports. Faculty of Biotechnics. University of Ljubljana. Veterinary Issue

Res Rep Fac Eng Kagoshima Univ — Research Reports. Faculty of Engineering. Kagoshima University [*Japan*]

Res Rep Fac Eng Meiji Univ — Research Reports. Faculty of Engineering. Meiji University

Res Rep Fac Eng Nagoya Univ — Research Reports. Faculty of Engineering. Nagoya University

Res Rep Fac Eng Niigata Univ — Research Report. Faculty of Engineering. Niigata University

Res Rep Fac Eng Engrg Tokyo Denki Univ — Research Reports. Faculty of Engineering. Tokyo Denki University

Res Rep Fac Eng Tokyo Denki Univ — Research Reports. Faculty of Engineering. Tokyo Denki University

Res Rep Fac Eng Toyo Univ — Research Report. Faculty of Engineering. Toyo University

Res Rep Fac Sci and Technol Meijyo Univ — Research Reports. Faculty of Science and Technology. Meijyo University

Res Rep Fac Text Seric Shinshu Univ — Research Reports. Faculty of Textiles and Sericulture. Shinshu University

Res Rep Fish Comm Oreg — Research Reports. Fish Commission of Oregon

Res Rep Fish Wildl Serv (US) — Research Report. Fish and Wildlife Service (United States)

Res Rep Fla Agric Exp Stn — Research Report. Florida Agricultural Experiment Station

Res Rep Fla Sch For — Research Report. University of Florida. School of Forestry

Res Rep Flinders Inst Atmos Mar Sci — Research Report. Flinders Institute of Atmospheric and Marine Sciences. Flinders University

Res Rep For Prod Util Lab Miss St Univ — Research Report. Forest Products Utilization Laboratory. Mississippi State University

Res Rep For Res Inst — Research Report. Forest Research Institute

Res Rep Fukui Tech Coll Nat Sci Eng — Research Reports. Fukui Technical College. Natural Science and Engineering [*Japan*]

Res Rep Fukuoka Agr Exp Sta — Research Report. Fukuoka Agricultural Experiment Station

Res Rep Fukuoka Agric Exp Stn — Research Report. Fukuoka Agricultural Experiment Station

Res Rep GA Agr Exp Sta — Research Report. Georgia Agricultural Experiment Stations

Res Rep Hawaii Agric Exp Stn — Research Report. Hawaii Agricultural Experiment Station

Res Rep Helsinki Univ Technol Lab Phys — Research Report. Helsinki University of Technology. Laboratory of Physics

Res Rep Hokkaido Natl Agric Exp Stn — Research Report. Hokkaido National Agricultural Experiment Station

Res Rep Hunter Valley Res Fdn — Research Report. Hunter Valley Research Foundation

Res Rep Hunter Valley Res Found — Research Report. Hunter Valley Research Foundation

Res Rep Inst For Genet — Research Report. Institute of Forest Genetics

Res Rep Inst For Genet (Korea) — Research Report. Institute of Forest Genetics (Suwon, Korea)

Res Rep Inst For Genet (Suwon) Imop Sihomjang — Research Report. Institution of Forest Genetics (Suwon). Imop Sihomjang

Res Rep Inst Industr Res (Nigeria) — Research Report. Federal Institute of Industrial Research (Lagos, Nigeria)

Res Rep Inst Inform Sci Tech Tokyo Denki Univ — Tokyo Denki University. Institute of Information Science and Technology. Research Reports

Res Rep Inst Inf Sci and Technol Tokyo Denki Univ — Research Reports. Institute of Information Science and Technology. Tokyo Denki University

Res Rep Inst Plasma Phys Nagoya Univ — Research Report. Institute of Plasma Physics. Nagoya University

Res Rep Int Food Policy Res Inst — Research Report. International Food Policy Research Institute

Res Rep Kasetsart Univ — Research Reports. Kasetsart University

Res Rep Kitakyushu Tech Coll — Research Report. Kitakyushu Technical College

Res Rep Kochi Univ Agric Sci — Research Reports. Kochi University. Agricultural Science

Res Rep Kogakuin Univ — Research Reports. Kogakuin University [*Japan*]

Res Rep Kurume Tech Coll — Research Reports. Kurume Technical College

Res Rep Kushiro Tech College — Research Reports. Kushiro Technical College

Res Rep Lab Nucl Sci Tohoku Univ — Research Report. Laboratory of Nuclear Science. Tohoku University

Res Rep Lab Nucl Sci Tohoku Univ Suppl — Research Report. Laboratory of Nuclear Science. Tohoku University. Supplement [*Japan*]

Res Rep MAFES — Research Report. MAFES [*Mississippi Agricultural and Forestry Experiment Station*]

Res Rep Maizuru Tech Coll — Research Reports. Maizuru Technical College

Res Rep Mich State Univ Agric Exp Stn — Research Report. Michigan State University. Agricultural Experiment Station

Res Rep Miss Agric For Exp Stn — Research Report. Mississippi Agricultural and Forestry Experiment Station

Res Rep Miyagi Tech College — Research Reports. Miyagi Technical College

Res Rep Miyakonojo Tech Coll — Research Report. Miyakonojo Technical College

Res Rep Mont Agric Exp Stn — Research Report. Montana Agricultural Experiment Station

Res Rep Nagano Tech Coll — Research Report. Nagano Technical College [*Japan*]

Res Rep Nagaoka Tech Coll — Research Reports. Nagaoka Technical College

Res Rep Nagoya Ind Sci Res Inst — Research Reports. Nagoya Industrial Science Research Institute [*Japan*]

Res Rep Nara Tech Coll — Research Reports. Nara Technical College [*Japan*]

Res Rep Natl Geogr Soc — Research Reports. National Geographic Society

Res Rep Natl Inst Nutr — Research Report. National Institute of Nutrition [*Japan*]

Res Rep Nat Sci Council Math Res Center — Research Reports. National Science Council. Mathematics Research Center

Res Rep NC Agr Exp Sta Dept Field Crops — Research Report. North Carolina Agricultural Experiment Station. Department of Field Crops

Res Rep N Cent Weed Contr Conf — Research Report. North Central Weed Control Conference

Res Rep N Dak Agr Exp Sta — Research Report. North Dakota Agricultural Experiment Station

Res Rep NH Agric Exp Stn — Research Report. New Hampshire Agricultural Experiment Station

Res Rep N Mex Agr Exp Sta — Research Report. New Mexico Agricultural Experiment Station

Res Rep Norfolk Agr Exp Sta — Research Report. Norfolk Agricultural Experiment Station

Res Rep North Cent Weed Control Conf — Research Report. North Central Weed Control Conference

Res Rep Nth Cent Weed Control Conf — Research Report. North Central Weed Control Conference

Res Rep Office Rur Dev Minist Agric For (Korea) — Research Reports. Office of Rural Development. Ministry of Agriculture and Forestry (Suwon, South Korea)

Res Rep Off Rural Dev Crop (Suwon) — Research Reports. Office of Rural Development. Crop (Suwon, South Korea)

Res Rep Off Rural Dev Hortic Agric Eng (Korea Repub) — Research Reports. Office of Rural Development. Horticulture and Agricultural Engineering (Korea Republic)

Res Rep Off Rural Dev Hortic (Suwon) — Research Reports. Office of Rural Development. Horticulture (Suwon, South Korea)

Res Rep Off Rural Dev Livest (Korea Republic) — Research Reports. Office of Rural Development. Livestock (Korea Republic)

Res Rep Off Rural Dev Livest Seric (Suwon) — Research Reports. Office of Rural Development. Livestock Sericulture (Suwon, South Korea)

Res Rep Off Rural Dev Livest (Suwon) — Research Reports. Office of Rural Development. Livestock (Suwon, South Korea)

Res Rep Off Rural Dev Plant Environ (Suwon) — Research Reports. Office of Rural Development. Plant Environment (Suwon, South Korea)

Res Rep Off Rural Dev Seric-Vet (Suwon) — Research Reports. Office of Rural Development. Sericulture-Veterinary (Suwon, South Korea)

Res Rep Off Rural Dev (Suwon) — Research Reports. Office of Rural Development (Suwon, South Korea)

Res Rep Off Rural Dev (Suwon) Livestock — Research Reports. Office of Rural Development (Suwon, South Korea). Livestock

Res Rep Off Rural Dev Vet Seric (Korea Republic) — Research Reports. Office of Rural Development. Veterinary and Sericulture (Korea Republic)

Res Rep Off Rural Dev Vet (Suwon) — Research Reports. Office of Rural Development. Veterinary (Suwon, South Korea)

Res Rep Oklahoma Agric Exp St — Oklahoma. Agricultural Experiment Station. Research Report

Res Rep Ore St Univ Forest Res Lab — Research Report. Oregon State University. Forest Research Laboratory

Res Reports Fac Engng Meiji Univ — Research Reports. Faculty of Engineering. Meiji University

Res Rep Oyama Natl Coll Technol — Research Reports. Oyama National College of Technology

Res Rep Oyama Tech Coll — Research Reports. Oyama Technical College

Res Rep P Agric Exp Stn Okla State Univ — Research Report P. Agricultural Experiment Station. Oklahoma State University

Res Reprod — Research in Reproduction

Res Rep Sasebo Tech Coll — Research Reports. Sasebo Technical College

Res Rep Sch Civ Engng Syd Univ — Research Report. School of Civil Engineering. University of Sydney

Res Rep Shibaura Inst Technol — Research Reports. Shibaura Institute of Technology [*Japan*]

Res Rep Taiwan Sugar Exp Stn — Research Report. Taiwan Sugar Experiment Station

Res Rep Timber Dev Assoc (London) — Research Report. Timber Development Association (London)

Res Rep Timb Res Developm Ass — Research Report. Timber Research and Development Association

Res Rep Tokyo Denki Univ — Research Reports. Tokyo Denki University

Res Rep Tokyo Electr Engrg College — Research Reports. Tokyo Electrical Engineering College

Res Rep Tokyo Electrical Engrg College — Research Reports. Tokyo Electrical Engineering College

Res Rep Tokyo Natl Tech Coll — Research Reports. Tokyo National Technical College

Res Rep Univ Arkansas Eng Exp Stn — Research Report. University of Arkansas. Engineering Experiment Station

Res Rep Univ Fla Sch For Resour Conserv — Research Report. University of Florida. School of Forest Resources and Conservation

Res Rep Univ GA Coll Agric Exp Stn — Research Report. University of Georgia. College of Agriculture. Experiment Stations

Res Rep Univ Tex Austin Cent Highw Res — Research Report. University of Texas at Austin. Center for Highway Research

Res Rep US Army Mater Command Cold Reg Res Engng Lab — Research Report. United States Army Material Command. Cold Regions Research and Engineering Laboratory

Res Rep US Fish Wildl Serv — Research Report. United States Fish and Wildlife Service

Res Rep VA Agr Exp Sta — Research Report. Virginia Agricultural Experiment Station

Res Rep Vet Issue — Research Reports. Veterinary Issue

Res Rep West Sect Nat Weed Comm Can — Research Report. Western Section. National Weed Committee of Canada

Res Rep Wis Agr Exp Sta — Research Report. Wisconsin Agricultural Experiment Station

Res Results Dig — Research Results Digest

ResRev — Research Review

Res Rev Can Res Stn (Agassiz BC) — Research Review. Canada Research Station. (Agassiz, British Columbia)

Res Rev CSIRO Div Chem Technol — Australia. Commonwealth Scientific and Industrial Research Organisation. Division of Chemical Technology. Research Review

Res Rev Div Chem Technol CSIRO — Research Review. Division of Chemical Technology. Commonwealth Scientific and Industrial Research Organisation

Res Rev Florida State Univ Bull — Research in Review. Florida State University. Bulletin

Res Rev (Off Aerosp Res) — Research Review (Office of Aerospace Research)

Res Ser Appl Geogr New Engl Univ — Research Series in Applied Geography. University of New England

Res Ser Fowlers Gap Arid Zone Res Stn — Research Series. Fowlers Gap Arid Zone Research Station. University of New England

Res Ser ICAR — Research Series ICAR. Indian Council of Agricultural Research

Res Stat Note — Research and Statistics Note. Social Security Administration. Office of Research and Statistics

Res Stat Note Health Care Financ Adm Off Policy Plann Res — Research and Statistics Note. Health Care Financing Administration. Office of Policy, Planning, and Research

Res Steroids — Research on Steroids

Res Stud — Research Studies

Res Stud Udaipur Univ Coll Agr — Research Studies. Udaipur University. College of Agriculture

Res Stud Wash State Univ — Research Studies. Washington State University [*Pullman*]

Res Sum Ohio Agr Res Develop Cent — Research Summary. Ohio Agricultural Research and Development Center

RESt — Review of English Studies

R Est — Revue de l'Est

RESTA — Revue de Stomatologie [*Later, Revue de Stomatologie et de Chirurgie Maxillo-Faciale*]

RESTAT — Review of Economics and Statistics

Restau Bus — Restaurant Business

Restau & Inst — Restaurants and Institutions

RESTD — Real Estate Today

Res Teach Engl — Research in the Teaching of English

Res Tech Instrum — Research Techniques and Instrumentation

R Esthet — Revue d'Esthetique

R d'Esthetique — Revue d'Esthetique

R Est LJ — Real Estate Law Journal

Res Today — Research Today

Restoration Q — Restoration Quarterly

Restor Eigh — Restoration and Eighteenth Century Theatre Research

Res Trends — Research Trends

Restr Mgt — Restaurant Management

R E Stud — Review of Economic Studies

R Estud Agro-Soc — Revista de Estudios Agro-Sociales

R Estud Penitenciarios — Revista de Estudios Penitenciarios

R Estud Pol — Revista de Estudios Politicos

R Estud Sindic — Revista de Estudios Sindicales

R Estud Soc — Revista de Estudios Sociales

R Estud Vida Loc — Revista de Estudios de la Vida Local

R Estud Vida Local — Revista de Estudios de la Vida Local

RESUB — Resources

Resultate Math — Resultate der Mathematik

Resultats — Resultats Statistiques du Poitou-Charentes

Result Exped Cient Buque Oceanogr "Cornide de Saavedra" — Resultados Expediciones Cientificas del Buque Oceanografico "Cornide de Saavedra"

Results Norw Sci Exped Tristan Da Cunha 1937-1938 — Results of the Norwegian Scientific Expedition to Tristan Da Cunha 1937-1938

Results Probl Cell Differ — Results and Problems in Cell Differentiation

Results Res Annu Rep Univ KY Agr Exp Sta — Results of Research. Annual Report. University of Kentucky. Agricultural Experiment Station

Resumenes Invest INP-CIP — Resumenes de Investigacion. INP-CIP [*Instituto Nacional de la Pesca-Centro de Investigaciones Pesqueras*]

Resur Biosfery — Resursy Biosfery

Res Vet Sci — Research in Veterinary Science [*United Kingdom*]

Res Vol Surrey Archaeol Soc — Research Volumes. Surrey Archaeological Society

Res Wks Georgian Beekeep Res Stn (Tbilisi) — Research Works. Georgian Beekeeping Research Station (Tbilisi)

Res Works Grad Sch Dong A Univ — Research Works of the Graduate School. Dong-A University

RET — Revista Espanola de Teologia [*Madrid*]

Retail Dist Mgmt — Retail and Distribution Management

Retailer of Q — Retailer of Queensland

Retail Packag — Retail Packaging

R Et Comp Est-Ouest — Revue d'Etudes Comparatives Est-Ouest

R Et Coop — Revue des Etudes Cooperatives

RETD — Recueil d'Etudes Theologiques et Dogmatiques

R Ethnol — Review of Ethnology

Retina Found Inst Biol Med Sci Monogr Conf — Retina Foundation. Institute of Biological and Medical Sciences. Monographs and Conferences

Ret Liv — Retirement Living

RETNA — Reactor Technology

Ret News — Retail News

R Etnografie Folclor — Revista de Etnografie si Folclor

Retros — Retrospective Review

R Et Sud-Est Europ — Revue des Etudes Sud-Est Europeennes

RETUA — Revue de Tuberculose

R Etud Byzantines — Revue des Etudes Byzantines

R Etud Coops — Revue des Etudes Cooperatives

R Etud Grecques — Revue des Etudes Grecques

R Etud Islamiques — Revue des Etudes Islamiques

R Etud Juives — Revue des Etudes Juives

REU — AREUEA [*American Real Estate and Urban Economics Association*] Journal

REUMA — Reumatismo

Reun Annu Sci Terre (Programme Resumes) — Reunion Annuelle des Sciences de la Terre (Programme et Resumes)

Reun A Soc Bras Genet — Reuniao Anual. Sociedade Brasileira de Genetica

Reunion Latinoam Prod Anim — Reunion Latinoamericana de Produccion Animal

Reun Latinoamer Fitotec Actas — Reunion Latinoamericana de Fitotecnia. Actas

REURD — Reuse/Recycle

R Europ Sci Soc — Revue Europeenne des Sciences Sociales. Cahiers Vilfredo Pareto

Rev A — Revue A [*Revue Trimestrielle d'Automatique*] [*Belgium*]

RevA — Revue d'Allemagne

Rev ABIA/SAPRO — Revista. ABIA/SAPRO [*Associacao Brasileira das Industrias da Alimentacao/Setor de Alimentos Calorico-Proteicos*]

RevAC — Revue de l'Art Chretien
Rev Acad Cienc Exactas Fis-Quim Nat Zaragoza — Revista. Academia de Ciencias Exactas, Fisico-Quimicas, y Naturales de Zaragoza
Rev Acad Cienc (Zaragoza) — Revista. Academia de Ciencias (Zaragoza)
Rev Acad Cienc Zaragoza 2 — Revista. Academia de Ciencias Exactas, Fisico-Quimicas, y Naturales de Zaragoza. Serie 2
Rev Acad Ci Zaragoza — Revista. Academia de Ciencias Exactas, Fisico-Quimicas, y Naturales de Zaragoza
Rev Acad Colomb Cienc Exactas Fis Nat — Revista. Academia Colombiana de Ciencias Exactas Fisicas y Naturales
Rev Acoust — Revue d'Acoustique
Rev d'Acoustique — Revue d'Acoustique
Act-Metallges AG — Review of Activities - Metallgesellschaft AG
Rev Adm Nac Agua (Argent) — Revista. Administracion Nacional del Agua (Argentina)
Rev Aeronaut — Revista de Aeronautica
Rev Agr — Revue de l'Agriculture
Rev Agr France — Revue Agricole de France
Rev Agri — Revista de Agricultura [*Brazil*]
Rev Agric (Bogota) — Revista Agricola (Bogota)
Rev Agric (Bruss) — Revue de l'Agriculture (Brussels)
Rev Agric Econ Hokkaido Univ — Review of Agricultural Economics. Hokkaido University
Rev Agric Fr — Revue des Agriculteurs de France
Rev Agric Ile Maurice — Revue Agricole de l'Ile Maurice
Rev Agricola (Chicago) — Revista Agricola (Chicago)
Rev Agric (Piracicaba) — Revista de Agricultura (Piracicaba)
Rev Agric (Piracicaba) S Paulo — Revista de Agricultura (Piracicaba). Estado de Sao Paulo
Rev Agric (PR) — Revista de Agricultura (Puerto Rico)
Rev Agric (Recife) — Revista de Agricultura (Recife)
Rev Agric Sucr Ile Maurice — Revue Agricole et Sucriere de l'Ile Maurice
Rev Agricultura — Revista de Agricultura
Rev Agr (Mocambique) — Revista Agricola (Mocambique)
Rev Agron — Revista Agronomica
Rev Agron (Lisb) — Revista Agronomica (Lisbon)
Rev Agron Noroeste Argent — Revista Agronomica del Noroeste Argentino
Rev Agroquim Tecnol Aliment — Revista de Agroquimica y Tecnologia de Alimentos
Rev Agr (Piracicaba) — Revista de Agricultura (Piracicaba)
Rev Alcool — Revue de l'Alcoolisme
Rev Algol — Revue Algologique
Rev Alteneo Paraguayo — Revista del Alteneo Paraguayo
Rev Alum — Revue de l'Aluminum
Rev Alum Ses Appl — Revue d'Aluminium et de Ses Applications [*France*]
Rev Am Hist — Reviews in American History
Rev AMRIGS — Revista. AMRIGS [*Associacao Medica do Rio Grande Do Sul*]
Rev Anal Chem — Reviews in Analytical Chemistry
Rev Anal Numer Teoria Aproximatiei — Revista de Analiza Numerica si Teoria Aproximatiei
Rev Anal Numer Theor Approx — Revue d'Analyse Numerique et de la Theorie de l'Approximation
Rev Anal Numer Theorie Approximation — Revue d'Analyse Numerique et de la Theorie de l'Approximation
Rev Anat Morphol Exp — Revues d'Anatomie et de Morphologie Experimentale
Rev Ang-Am — Revue Anglo-Americaine
Rev Annu Chimiother Physiatr Cancer — Revue Annuelle de Chimiotherapie et de Physiatrie du Cancer
Rev Annu Chimiother Prophyl Cancer — Revue Annuelle de Chimiotherapie et de Prophylaxie du Cancer
Rev Annu Physiatr Prophyl Cancer — Revue Annuelle de Physiatrie et de Prophylaxie du Cancer
Rev Anthropol (Paris) — Revue Anthropologique (Paris)
Rev Antropol (Sao Paulo) — Revista de Antropologia (Sao Paulo)
Rev Appl Elect — Revue des Applications de l'Electricite
Rev Appl Ent — Review of Applied Entomology
Rev Appl Mycol — Review of Applied Mycology
Rev Arch — Revue Archeologique
Rev Arch Bibl Mus — Revista de Archivos, Bibliotecas, y Museos
Rev Arch ECE — Revue Archeologique de l'Est et du Centre-Est
Rev Archeol — Revue Archeologique
Rev Archit Sci Unit Univ Queensl — Review. Architectural Science Unit. University of Queensland
Rev Arch Narbonn — Revue Archeologique de Narbonnaise
Rev Argent Agron — Revista Argentina de Agronomia
Rev Argent Angiol — Revista Argentina de Angiologia
Rev Argent Cancerol — Revista Argentina de Cancerologia
Rev Argent Cardiol — Revista Argentina de Cardiologia
Rev Argent Endocrinol Metab — Revista Argentina de Endocrinologia y Metabolismo
Rev Argent Implantol Estomatol — Revista Argentina de Implantologia Estomatologica
Rev Argent Microbiol — Revista Argentina de Microbiologia

Rev Argent Neurol Psiquiat y Med Leg — Revista Argentina de Neurologia, Psiquiatria, y Medicina Legal
Rev Argent Pueric Neonatol — Revista Argentina de Puericultura y Neonatologia
Rev Argent Radiol — Revista Argentina de Radiologia
Rev Argent Reumatol — Revista Argentina de Reumatologia
Rev Argent Tuberc Enferm Pulm — Revista Argentina de Tuberculosis y Enfermedades Pulmonares
Rev Argent Urol Nefrol — Revista Argentina de Urologia y Nefrologia
Rev Arhiv — Revista Arhivelor
Rev Art — Revue de l'Art
Rev Art Anc — Revue de l'Art Ancien et Moderne
Rev Asoc Argent Criad Cerdos — Revista. Asociacion Argentina Criadores de Cerdos
Rev Asoc Argent Dietol — Revista. Asociacion Argentina de Dietologia
Rev Asoc Argent Microbiol — Revista. Asociacion Argentina de Microbiologia
Rev Asoc Bioquim Argent — Revista. Asociacion Bioquimica Argentina
Rev Asoc Cienc Nat Litoral — Revista. Asociacion de Ciencias Naturales del Litoral
Rev Asoc Geol Argent — Revista. Asociacion Geologica Argentina
Rev Asoc Med Argent — Revista. Asociacion Medica Argentina
Rev Asoc Odontol Argent — Revista. Asociacion Odontologica Argentina
Rev Asoc Prof Hosp Nac Odontol — Revista. Asociacion de Profesionales. Hospital Nacional de Odontologia
Rev Asoc Rural Urug — Revista. Asociacion Rural del Uruguay
Rev Assoc Fr Tech Pet — Revue. Association Francaise des Techniciens du Petrole
Rev Assoc Med Bras — Revista. Associacao Medica Brasileira
Rev Assoc Med Minas Gerais — Revista. Associacao Medica de Minas Gerais
Rev Assoc Med Rio Grande Do Sul — Revista. Associacao Medica do Rio Grande Do Sul
Rev Assoc Paul Cir Dent — Revista. Associacao Paulista de Cirurgioes Dentistas
Rev Assyriol — Revue d'Assyriologie et d'Archeologie Orientale
Rev Astron — Revista Astronomica
Rev Asturiana Cien Med — Revista Asturiana de Ciencias Medicas
Rev Ateneo Catedra Tec Oper Dent — Revista. Ateneo de la Catedra de Tecnica de Operatoria Dental
Rev Atheroscler — Revue de l'Atherosclerose [*France*]
Rev Atheroscler Arteriopathies Peripheriques — Revue de l'Atherosclerose et des Arteriopathies Peripheriques
Rev At Ind — Review of Atomic Industries [*Japan*]
Rev Autom — Revista de Automatica
Rev Auvergne — Revue d'Auvergne
RevB — Revista (Barcelona)
Rev du B — Revue. Barreau de la Province de Quebec
RevBAM — Revista. Biblioteca, Archivo, y Museo del Ayuntamiento de Madrid
Rev Bank NSW — Review. Bank of New South Wales
Rev Banque — Revue de la Banque
Rev Bar — Revue du Barreau
Rev Barreau Que — Revue. Barreau de Quebec
Rev Belge — Revue Belge de Philologie et d'Histoire
Rev Belge du C — Revue Belge du Cinema
Rev Belge Dr Int'l — Revue Belge de Droit International
Rev Belge de Droit Internat — Revue Belge de Droit International
Rev Belge Hist Mil — Revue Belge d'Histoire Militaire
Rev Belge Hist Milit — Revue Belge d'Histoire Militaire
Rev Belge Homoeopath — Revue Belge d'Homoeopathie
Rev Belge Matieres Plast — Revue Belge des Matieres Plastiques
Rev Belge Med Dent — Revue Belge de Medecine Dentaire
Rev Belge Phil Hist — Revue Belge de Philologie et d'Histoire
Rev Belge Philol Hist — Revue Belge de Philologie et d'Histoire
Rev Belge Stat Inf et Rech Oper — Revue Belge de Statistique, d'Informatique, et de Recherche Operationnelle/Belgisch Tijdschrift voor Statistiek, Informatiek, en Operationeel Onderzoek
Rev Belge Transp — Revue Belge des Transports [*Belgium*]
Rev Belg Pathol Med Exp — Revue Belge de Pathologie et de Medecine Experimentale
Rev Bel Ph — Revue Belge de Philologie et d'Histoire
Rev Bened — Revue Benedictine
Rev Bib — Revista Bibliotecilor [*Bucharest*]
Rev Bibl — Revue Biblique
Rev Biochem Toxicol — Reviews in Biochemical Toxicology
Rev Biol Acad Rep Pop Roumaine — Revue de Biologie. Academie de la Republique Populaire Roumaine
Rev Biol (Buchar) — Revue de Biologie (Bucharest)
Rev Biol (Lisb) — Revista de Biologia (Lisbon)
Rev Biol Mar — Revista de Biologia Marina
Rev Biol Med Nucl — Revista de Biologia y Medicina Nuclear
Rev Biol Oral — Revista de Biologia Oral
Rev Biol Trop — Revista de Biologia Tropical
Rev Biol Urug — Revista de Biologia del Uruguay
Rev Bio-Math — Revue de Bio-Mathematique
Rev Bl Pol — Review of Black Political Economy
RevBN — Revista de Bibliografia Nacional [*Madrid*]

Rev Bois Appl — Revue du Bois et de Ses Applications
Rev Bolsa Cereal — Revista. Bolsa de Cereales
Rev Bolsa Comer Rosario — Revista. Bolsa de Comercio de Rosario
Rev Bot Appl Agric Trop — Revue de Botanique Appliquee et d'Agriculture Tropicale
Rev Bra Ec — Revista Brasileira de Economia
Rev Bras Anestesiol — Revista Brasileira de Anestesiologia
Rev Bras Biol — Revista Brasileira de Biologia
Rev Bras Cardiovasc — Revista Brasileira Cardiovascular
Rev Bras Cir — Revista Brasileira de Cirurgia
Rev Bras Clin Ter — Revista Brasileira de Clinica e Terapeutica
Rev Bras Defic Ment — Revista Brasileira de Deficiencia Mental
Rev Bras Enferm — Revista Brasileira de Enfermagem
Rev Bras Eng Quim — Revista Brasileira de Engenharia Quimica
Rev Bras Entomol — Revista Brasileira de Entomologia
Rev Bras Fis — Revista Brasileira de Fisica
Rev Bras Gastroenterol — Revista Brasileira de Gastroenterologia
Rev Bras Geocienc — Revista Brasileira de Geociencias
Rev Bras Geogr — Revista Brasileira de Geografia
Rev Brasil Geogr — Revista Brasileira de Geografia
Rev Brasil Quim — Revista Brasileira de Quimica
Rev Bras Leprol — Revista Brasileira de Leprologia
Rev Bras Malariol Doencas Trop — Revista Brasileira de Malariologia e Doencas Tropicais
Rev Bras Malariol Doencas Trop Publ Avulsas — Revista Brasileira de Malariologia e Doencas Tropicais. Publicacoes Avulsas
Rev Bras Med — Revista Brasileira de Medicina
Rev Bras Odontol — Revista Brasileira de Odontologia
Rev Bras Oftalmol — Revista Brasileira de Oftalmologia
Rev Bras Patol Clin — Revista Brasileira de Patologia Clinica
Rev Bras Pesqui Med Biol — Revista Brasileira de Pesquisas Medicas e Biologicas
Rev Bras Psiquiatr — Revista Brasileira de Psiquiatria
Rev Bras Quim (Sao Paulo) — Revista Brasileira de Quimica (Sao Paulo)
Rev Bras Tecnol — Revista Brasileira de Tecnologia
Rev Bras Tuberc Doencas Torac — Revista Brasileira de Tuberculose e Doencas Toracicas
Rev Bryol Lichenol — Revue Bryologique et Lichenologique
Rev Bulg Geol Soc — Review. Bulgarian Geological Society
Rev Bus Econ Res — Review of Business and Economic Research
RevC — Revista Camoniana [*Sao Paulo*]
Rev C Abo PR — Revista. Colegio de Abogados de Puerto Rico
Rev Cafetalera (Guatem) — Revista Cafetalera (Guatemala)
Rev Cafetera Colomb — Revista Cafetera de Colombia
Rev Canadienne Geographie — Revue Canadienne de Geographie
Rev Can Bio — Revue Canadienne de Biologie
Rev Can Biol — Revue Canadienne de Biologie
Rev Can Econ Publique Coop Can J Public Coop Econ — Revue Canadienne d'Economie Publique et Cooperative. Canadian Journal of Public and Cooperative Economy
Rev Can Gen Electr — Revue Canadienne de Genie Electrique [*Canada*]
Rev Can Med Comp — Revue Canadienne de Medecine Comparee
Rev Can Psychol — Revue Canadienne de Psychologie
Rev Can Sante Publique — Revue Canadienne de Sante Publique
Rev Can Sci Comportement — Revue Canadienne des Sciences du Comportement
Rev Catarinense Odontol — Revista Catarinense de Odontologie
Rev d Caucho — Revista del Caucho
Rev CENIC Cienc Biol — Revista CENIC [*Centro Nacional de Investigaciones Cientificas*]. Ciencias Biologicas
Rev CENIC Cienc Fis — Revista CENIC [*Centro Nacional de Investigaciones Cientificas*]. Ciencias Fisicas [*Cuba*]
Rev Cent Cienc Biomed Univ Fed Santa Maria — Revista. Centro de Ciencias Biomedicas. Universidade Federal de Santa Maria
Rev Cent Cienc Rurais — Revista. Centro de Ciencias Rurais
Rev Cent Ed — Revista. Centro de Estudios Educativos
Rev Cent Estud Cabo Verde Ser Cienc Biol — Revista. Centro de Estudos de Cabo Verde. Serie de Ciencias Biologicas
Rev Cent Nac Patol Anim — Revista. Centro Nacional de Patologia Animal
Rev Centroam Nutr Cienc Aliment — Revista Centroamericana de Nutricion y Ciencias de Alimentos
Rev Centro Estud Agronom y Vet Univ Buenos Aires — Revista. Centro de Estudiantes de Agronomia y Veterinaria. Universidad de Buenos Aires
Rev Ceres — Revista Ceres
Rev CETHEDEC — Revue. Centre d'Etudes Theoriques de la Detection et des Communications
Rev CETHEDEC Cahier — Revue. Centre d'Etudes Theoriques de la Detection et des Communications. Cahier [*Paris*]
Rev C Genie Civil Constr — Revue C. Genie Civil. Construction
Rev Chilena Ing — Revista Chilena de Ingenieria
Rev Chil Entomol — Revista Chilena de Entomologia
Rev Chil Hist Nat — Revista Chilena de Historia Natural
Rev Chil Obstet Ginecol — Revista Chilena de Obstetricia y Ginecologia
Rev Chil Pediatr — Revista Chilena de Pediatria
Rev Chim — Revista de Chimie

Rev Chim Acad Repub Pop Roum — Revue de Chimie. Academie de la Republique Populaire Roumaine [*Romania*]
Rev Chim (Bucharest) — Revista de Chimie (Bucharest)
Rev Chim Mi — Revue de Chimie Minerale
Rev Chim Miner — Revue de Chimie Minerale [*France*]
Rev Chir — Revista de Chirurgie. Stomatologie
Rev Chir Oncol Radiol ORL Oftalmol Stomatol — Revista de Chirurgie Oncologie Radiologie ORL Oftalmologie Stomatologie
Rev Chir Or — Revue de Chirurgie Orthopedique et Reparatrice de l'Appareil Moteur
Rev Cie Gen Electr — Review of Compagnie Generale d'Electricite [*France*]
Rev Cienc — Revista de Ciencias [*Lima*]
Rev Cienc Agron — Revista de Ciencias Agronomicas
Rev Cienc Agron Ser A — Revista de Ciencias Agronomicas. Serie A
Rev Cienc Agron Ser B — Revista de Ciencias Agronomicas. Serie B
Rev Cienc Apl — Revista de Ciencia Aplicada
Rev Cienc Apl (Madrid) — Revista de Ciencias Aplicadas (Madrid)
Rev Cienc Biol (Belem) — Revista de Ciencias Biologicas (Belem)
Rev Cienc Biol (Havana) — Revista de Ciencias Biologicas (Havana)
Rev Cienc Biol Ser A (Lourenco Marques) — Revista de Ciencias Biologicas. Serie A (Lourenco Marques)
Rev Cienc Biol Ser B (Lourenco Marques) — Revista de Ciencias Biologicas. Serie B (Lourenco Marques)
Rev Cienc Mat Univ Lourenco Marques — Revista de Ciencias Matematicas. Universidade de Lourenco Marques
Rev Cienc Med (Lourenco Marques) — Revista de Ciencias Medicas. Serie A (Lourenco Marques)
Rev Cienc Med Ser A (Lourenco Marques) — Revista de Ciencias Medicas. Serie A (Lourenco Marques)
Rev Cienc Med Ser B (Lourenco Marques) — Revista de Ciencias Medicas. Serie B (Lourenco Marques)
Rev Cienc Psicol Neurol (Lima) — Revista de Ciencias Psicologicas y Neurologicas (Lima)
Rev Cienc Quim — Revista de Ciencias Quimicas
Rev Cienc Univ Nac Mayor San Marcos — Revista de Ciencias. Universidad Nacional Mayor de San Marcos
Rev Cienc Vet — Revista de Ciencias Veterinarias
Rev Cien Econ — Revista de Ciencias Economicas
Rev Cient CASL — Revista Cientifica. CASL [*Centro Academico Sarmento Leite*]
Rev Cient Invest Mus Hist Nat San Rafael (Mendoza) — Revista Cientifica de Investigaciones del Museo de Historia Natural de San Rafael (Mendoza)
Rev Cien Vet — Revista de Ciencias Veterinarias
Rev Ci Mat Univ Lourenco Marques — Revista de Ciencias Matematicas. Universidade de Lourenco Marques
Rev Ci Mat Univ Lourenco Marques Ser A — Revista de Ciencias Matematicas. Universidade de Lourenco Marques. Serie A
Rev Cinema — Revue du Cinema/Image et Son. Ecran
Rev Cir — Revista de Cirugia
Rev Circ Argent Odontol — Revista. Circulo Argentino de Odontologia
Rev Circ Odontol Sur — Revista. Circulo Odontologico del Sur
Rev Cir (Mex) — Revista de Cirugia (Mexico)
Rev Clin Esp — Revista Clinica Espanola [*Spain*]
Rev Clin Esp Eur Med — Revista Clinica Espanola. Europa Medica
Rev Clin Med — Revista de Clinica Medica
Rev Clin Sao Paulo — Revista Clinica de Sao Paulo
Rev Coat Corros — Reviews on Coating and Corrosion
Rev Col Med Guatem — Revista. Colegio Medico de Guatemala
Rev Col Nac Enferm — Revista. Colegio Nacional de Enfermeras
Rev Colomb Fis — Revista Colombiana de Fisica
Rev Colombiana Mat — Revista Colombiana de Matematicas
Rev Colomb Obstet Ginecol — Revista Colombiana de Obstetricia y Ginecologia
Rev Col Quim Ing Quim Costa Rica — Revista. Colegio de Quimicos e Ingenieros Quimicos de Costa Rica
Rev Commer — Revue Commerce
Rev Confed Med Panam — Revista. Confederacion Medica Panamericana
Rev Conserve — Revue de la Conserve [*France*]
Rev Conserve Aliment Mod — Revue de la Conserve. Alimentation Moderne
Rev Conserve Fr Outre-Mer — Revue de la Conserve de France et d'Outre-Mer
Rev Conserve Fr Union Fr — Revue de la Conserve de France et de l'Union Francaise
Rev Consor Cent Agr Manabi — Revista. Consorcio de Centros Agricolas de Manabi
Rev Cons Rectores Univ Chilenas — Revista. Consejo de Rectores. Universidades Chilenas
Rev Cont L — Review of Contemporary Law
Rev Coroz — Revista de Coroziune [*Romania*]
Rev Corps Sante Armees — Revue des Corps de Sante des Armees
Rev Corros Prot Mater — Revista de Corrosao e Proteccao de Materiais
Rev CREA (Asoc Argent Consorcios Reg Exp Agric) — Revista. CREA (Asociacion Argentina de Consorcios Regionales de Experimentacion Agricola)
Rev Cresterea Anim — Revista de Cresterea Animalelor
Rev Criad — Revista dos Criadores

Rev Criadores — Revista dos Criadores
Rev Crit de Droit Internat Prive — Revue Critique de Droit International Prive
Rev Crit de Jurispr Belge — Revue Critique de Jurisprudence Belge
Rev Crit L — Revista de Critica Literaria Latinoamericana
Rev C Tijdschr Civ Tech Genie Civ — Revue C. Tijdschrift Civiele Techniek. Genie Civil
Rev Cubana Cardiol — Revista Cubana de Cardiologia
Rev Cubana Cienc Agric — Revista Cubana de Ciencia Agricola
Rev Cubana Cienc Vet — Revista Cubana de Ciencias Veterinarias
Rev Cubana Cir — Revista Cubana de Cirugia
Rev Cubana Estomatol — Revista Cubana de Estomatologia
Rev Cubana Fis — Revista Cubana de Fisica
Rev Cubana Hig Epidemiol — Revista Cubana de Higiene y Epidemiologia
Rev Cubana Invest Biomed — Revista Cubana de Investigaciones Biomedicas
Rev Cubana Lab Clin — Revista Cubana de Laboratorio Clinico
Rev Cubana Med — Revista Cubana de Medicina
Rev Cubana Med Trop — Revista Cubana de Medicina Tropical
Rev Cubana Oftal — Revista Cubana de Oftalmologia
Rev Cubana Pediatr — Revista Cubana de Pediatria
Rev Cub Cienc Vet — Revista Cubana de Ciencias Veterinarias
Rev Current Activities Tech Ed — Review of Current Activities in Technical Education
Rev Cytol Biol Veg — Revue de Cytologie et de Biologie Vegetales [France]
Rev Czech Med — Review of Czechoslovak Medicine
Rev Data Sci Resour — Reviews of Data on Science Resources [United States]
Rev Data Sci Resour Natl Sci Found — Reviews of Data on Science Resources. National Sciences Foundation
Rev Def Natl — Revue de Defense Nationale [France]
Rev Deform Behav Mater — Reviews on the Deformation Behavior of Materials
Rev Dent Liban — Revue Dentaire Libanaise
Rev Dent (St Domingo) — Revista Dental (Santo Domingo)
Rev de Derecho y Cienc Polit — Revista de Derecho y Ciencias Politicas. Organo de la Facultad de Derecho. Universidad Nacional Mayor de San Marcos
Rev de Derecho Internac y Cienc Diplom — Revista de Derecho Internacional y Ciencias Diplomaticas
Rev de Derecho Publ — Revista de Derecho Publico. Universidad de Chile. Escuela de Derecho
Rev Deux Mondes — Revue des Deux Mondes
Rev Diagn Biol — Revista de Diagnostico Biologico
Rev de Direito Adm (Coimbra) — Revista de Direito Administrativo Coimbra
Rev de Direito Adm (Rio De Janeiro) — Revista de Direito Administrativo (Rio De Janeiro)
Rev Dir Gen Geol Minas (Ecuador) — Revista. Direccion General de Geologia y Minas (Ecuador)
Rev Doc — Revue de la Documentation
Rev D P — Revista de Derecho Puertorriqueno
Rev DPR — Revista de Derecho Puertorriqueno
Rev de Dr Int'l de Sci Dip et Pol — Revue de Droit International de Sciences Diplomatiques et Politiques
Rev de Droit — Revue de Droit. Universite de Sherbrooke
Rev de Droit Canonique — Revue de Droit Canonique
Rev de Droit Compare — Revue de Droit International et de Droit Compare
Rev de Droit Internat et de Droit Compare — Revue de Droit International et de Droit Compare
Rev de Droit Internat de Sci Diplom — Revue de Droit International de Sciences Diplomatiques et Politiques
Rev de Droit Penal et de Criminologie — Revue de Droit Penal et de Criminologie
Rev Droit Public Sci Polit — Revue du Droit Public et de la Science Politique en France et a l'Etranger
Rev du Droit Publ et de la Sci Polit en France — Revue du Droit Public et de la Science Politique en France et a l'Etranger
Rev des Droits de l'Homme — Revue des Droits de l'Homme. Droit International et Droit Compare
Rev Droit U Sher — Revue de Droit. Universite de Sherbrooke
Rev E — Revue E. Electricite, Electrotechnique Generale, Courants Forts, et Applications [Belgium]
Rev Ecol Biol Sol — Revue d'Ecologie et de Biologie du Sol
Rev Ecol BS — Revue d'Ecologie et de Biologie du Sol
Rev Econ — Revue Economique
Rev Econ Co — Review of the Economic Conditions in Italy
Rev Econom Statist — Review of Economics and Statistics
Rev Econom Stud — Review of Economic Studies
Rev Economy Emplyment — Review of the Economy and Employment
Rev Econ Polit — Revue d'Economie Politique
Rev Econ S — Review of Economic Studies
Rev Econ St — Review of Economics and Statistics
Rev Econ Stat — Review of Economic Statistics
Rev Econ Stat — Review of Economics and Statistics
Rev Econ Stud — Review of Economic Studies
Rev Ecuat Entomol Parasitol — Revista Ecuatoriana de Entomologia y Parasitologia
Rev Ecuat Hig Med — Revista Ecuatoriana de Higiene y Medicina Tropical
Rev Ecuat Hig Med Trop — Revista Ecuatoriana de Higiene y Medicina Tropical

Rev Ecuat Med Cienc Biol — Revista Ecuatoriana de Medicina y Ciencias Biologicas
Rev Ecuat Pediatr — Revista Ecuatoriana de Pediatria
Rev Educ Re — Review of Educational Research
Rev E Elec Electrotech Gen — Revue E. Electricite, Electrotechnique Generale, Courants Forts, et Applications
Rev Eg — Revue d'Egyptologie
Rev Egypt de Droit Internat — Revue Egyptienne de Droit International
Rev Egyptol — Revue Egyptologique
Rev El Comm — Review. Electrical Communication Laboratory [Tokyo]
Rev Elec Commun Lab (Tokyo) — Review. Electrical Communication Laboratory (Tokyo)
Rev Electr — Revista Electricidade [Portugal]
Rev Electr Commun Lab — Review. Electrical Communication Laboratory
Rev Electr Commun Lab (Tokyo) — Review. Electrical Communication Laboratory (Tokyo)
Rev Electr & Mec — Revue d'Electricite et de Mecanique
Rev Electr Mecan — Revue d'Electricite et de Mecanique [France]
Rev Electroencephalogr Neurophysiol Clin — Revue d'Electroencephalographie et de Neurophysiologie Clinique
Rev Electrotec — Revista Electrotecnica
Rev Electrotec (Buenos Aires) — Revista Electrotecnica (Buenos Aires)
Rev Electrotech Energ Acad Repub Pop Roum — Revue Electrotechnique et Energetique. Academie de la Republique Populaire Roumaine [Romania]
Rev Elevage — Revue de l'Elevage. Betail et Basse Cour
Rev Elev Med Vet Pays Trop — Revue d'Elevage et de Medecine Veterinaire des Pays Tropicaux
Rev Empresas Publicas Medellin — Revista Empresas Publicas de Medellin [Columbia]
Rev Energ — Revue de l'Energie
Rev Energie — Revue de l'Energie
Rev Energ Primaire — Revue de l'Energie Primaire [Belgium]
Rev Enferm (Lisboa) — Revista de Enfermagem (Lisboa)
Rev Enferm Nov Dimens — Revista Enfermagem em Novas Dimensoes
Rev Eng Geol — Reviews in Engineering Geology [United States]
Rev Engl St — Review of English Studies
Rev Engl Stu — Review of English Studies
Rev Engl Stud — Review of English Studies
Rev Entomol Mocambique — Revista de Entomologia de Mocambique
Rev Entomol Mocambique Supl — Revista de Entomologia de Mocambique. Suplemento
Rev Entomol (Rio De J) — Revista de Entomologia (Rio De Janeiro)
Rev Environ Health — Reviews on Environmental Health
Rev Environ Toxicol — Reviews in Environmental Toxicology
Rev Epidem — Revue d'Epidemiologie, Medecine Sociale, et Sante Publique [Later, Revue d'Epidemiologie et de Sante Publique]
Rev Epidemiol Med Soc Sante Publique — Revue d'Epidemiologie, Medecine Sociale, et Sante Publique [Later, Revue d'Epidemiologie et de Sante Publique]
Rev Epidemiol Sante Publique — Revue d'Epidemiologie et de Sante Publique
RevEpigr — Revue Epigraphique
RevER — Revue des Etudes Roumaines
Rev Esc Agron Vet Univ Rio Grande Do Sul (Porto Alegre) — Revista. Escola de Agronomia e Veterinaria da Universidade do Rio Grande Do Sul (Porto Alegre)
Rev Esc Enferm USP — Revista. Escola de Enfermagem. Universidade de Sao Paulo
Rev Esc Odontol Tucuman — Revista. Escuela de Odontologia. Universidad Nacional de Tucuman. Faculdad de Medicina
Rev Esp Anestesiol Reanim — Revista Espanola de Anestesiologia y Reanimacion
Rev Espan Fisiol — Revista Espanola de Fisiologia
Rev Esp Antropol Amer — Revista Espanola de Antropologia Americana
Rev Esp Cardiol — Revista Espanola de Cardiologia
Rev Esp de Derecho Canonico — Revista Espanola de Derecho Canonico
Rev Esp de Derecho Internac — Revista Espanola de Derecho Internacional
Rev Esp de Derecho Mil — Revista Espanola de Derecho Militar
Rev Esp Doc Cient — Revista Espanola de Documentacion Cientifica
Rev Espec — Revista de Especialidades
Rev Esp Electron — Revista Espanola de Electronica
Rev Esp Enferm Apar Dig — Revista Espanola de las Enfermedades del Aparato Digestivo
Rev Esp Enferm Apar Dig Nutr — Revista Espanola de las Enfermedades del Aparato Digestivo y de la Nutricion
Rev Esp Estomatol — Revista Espanola de Estomatologia
Rev Esp Fis — Revista Espanola de Fisiologia
Rev Esp Fisiol — Revista Espanola de Fisiologia
Rev Esp Obstet Ginecol — Revista Espanola de Obstetricia y Ginecologia
Rev Esp Obstet Ginecol Supl — Revista Espanola de Obstetricia y Ginecologia. Suplemento
Rev Esp Oncol — Revista Espanola de Oncologia
Rev Esp Oto-Neuro-Oftalmol Neurocir — Revista Espanola de Oto-Neuro-Oftalmologia y Neurocirugia
Rev Esp Pediatr — Revista Espanola de Pediatria

Rev Esp Reum Enferm Osteoartic — Revista Espanola de Reumatismo y Enfermedades Osteoarticulares

Rev Est — Revue de l'Est

Rev Esth — Revue d'Esthetique

Rev Est His — Revista de Estudios Hispanicos

Rev Estud Extremenos — Revista de Estudios Extremenos

Rev Estud Gerais Univ Mocambique Ser 3 Cienc Med — Revista. Estudos Gerais Universitarios de Mocambique. Serie 3. Ciencias Medicas

Rev Et Armen — Revue des Etudes Armeniennes

Rev Et SE Eur — Revue des Etudes Sud-Est Europeennes

Rev Etud Augustin — Revue des Etudes Augustiniennes

Rev Etud Byz — Revue des Etudes Byzantines

Rev Etud Comp Est Ouest — Revue d'Etudes Comparatives Est-Ouest

Rev Etud Grec — Revue des Etudes Grecques

Rev Etud It — Revue des Etudes Italiennes

Rev Etud Juives — Revue des Etudes Juives et Historia Judaica

Rev Etud Sud Est Eur — Revue des Etudes Sud-Est Europeennes

Rev Eur Endocrinol — Revue Europeenne d'Endocrinologie

Rev Eur Etud Clin Biol — Revue Europeenne d'Etudes Cliniques et Biologiques [*France*]

Rev Europ Papiers Cartons Complexes — Revue Europeenne des Papiers Cartons-Complexes

Rev Eur Pomme Terre — Revue Europeenne de la Pomme de Terre

Rev Exist Psychol Psychiat — Review of Existential Psychology and Psychiatry

Rev Exist Psych Psychiat — Review of Existential Psychology and Psychiatry

RevExp — Review and Expositor

Rev Exp Agrar — Revista de Extension Agraria

Rev and Expositor — Review and Expositor

Rev Fac Agrar Minist Educ Univ Nac Cuyo (Mendoza) — Revista. Facultad de Ciencias Agrarias. Ministerio de Educacion. Universidad Nacional de Cuyo (Mendoza) [*Argentina*]

Rev Fac Agron Alcance (Maracay) — Revista. Facultad de Agronomia Alcance (Maracay)

Rev Fac Agron (Maracay) — Revista. Facultad de Agronomia (Maracay)

Rev Fac Agron Univ Cent Venezuela — Revista. Facultad de Agronomia. Universidad Central de Venezuela

Rev Fac Agron Univ Fed Rio Grande Sul — Revista. Faculdade de Agronomia. Universidade Federal do Rio Grande Do Sul

Rev Fac Agron Univ Nac La Plata — Revista. Facultad de Agronomia. Universidad Nacional de La Plata

Rev Fac Agron Univ Repub Montevideo — Revista. Facultad de Agronomia. Universidad de la Republica Montevideo

Rev Fac Agron Vet (Buenos Aires) — Revista. Facultad de Agronomia y Veterinaria (Buenos Aires)

Rev Fac Agron Vet Univ B Aires — Revista. Facultad de Agronomia y Veterinaria. Universidad de Buenos Aires

Rev Fac Agron Vet Univ Rio Grande Do Sul — Revista. Faculdade de Agronomia e Veterinaria. Universidade do Rio Grande Do Sul

Rev Fac Agron Vet Univ Rio Grande Do Sul — Revista. Faculdade de Agronomia e Veterinaria. Universidade do Rio Grande Do Sul

Rev Fac Agron (Zulia Venez) Univ — Revista. Facultad de Agronomia (Zulia, Venezuela). Universidad

Rev Fac Cienc Agrar Minist Educ Univ Nac Cuyo (Mendoza) — Revista. Facultad de Ciencias Agrarias. Ministerio de Educacion. Universidad Nacional de Cuyo (Mendoza)

Rev Fac Cienc Agrar Univ Nac Cuyo — Revista. Facultad de Ciencias Agrarias. Universidad Nacional de Cuyo

Rev Fac Cienc Agr Univ Nac Cuyo — Revista. Facultad de Ciencias Agrarias. Universidad Nacional de Cuyo

Rev Fac Cienc 2a Ser A Cienc Mat — Revista. Faculdade de Ciencias. Universidade de Lisboa. 2a Serie A. Ciencias Matematicas [*Portugal*]

Rev Fac Cienc Med Buenos Aires — Revista. Facultad de Ciencias Medicas de Buenos Aires

Rev Fac Cienc Med Cordoba — Revista. Facultad de Ciencias Medicas de Cordoba

Rev Fac Cienc Med Univ Catol Parana — Revista. Faculdade de Ciencias Medicas. Universidade Catolica do Parana

Rev Fac Cienc Med Univ Cent Ecuador — Revista. Facultad de Ciencias Medicas. Universidad Central del Ecuador

Rev Fac Cienc Med Univ Nac Cordoba — Revista. Facultad de Ciencias Medicas. Universidad Nacional de Cordoba

Rev Fac Cienc Med Univ Nac Rosario — Revista. Facultad de Ciencias Medicas. Universidad Nacional de Rosario

Rev Fac Cienc Nat Salta Univ Nac Tucuman — Revista. Facultad de Ciencias Naturales de Salta. Universidad Nacional de Tucuman

Rev Fac Cienc Quim Univ Nac La Plata — Revista. Facultad de Ciencias Quimicas. Universidad Nacional de La Plata

Rev Fac Cienc Univ Coimbra — Revista. Faculdade de Ciencias. Universidade de Coimbra

Rev Fac Cienc Univ Lisboa B — Revista. Faculdade de Ciencias. Universidade de Lisboa. Serie B. Ciencias Fisico-Quimicas

Rev Fac Cienc Univ Lisboa Ser B — Revista. Faculdade de Ciencias. Universidade de Lisboa. Serie B. Ciencias Fisico Quimicas

Rev Fac Cienc Univ Lisboa Ser C — Revista. Faculdade de Ciencias. Universidade de Lisboa. Serie C. Ciencias Naturais

Rev Fac Cienc Univ Lisb Ser C Cienc Nat — Revista. Faculdade de Ciencias. Universidade de Lisboa. Serie C. Ciencias Naturais

Rev Fac Cienc Univ Oviedo — Revista. Facultad de Ciencias. Universidad de Oviedo

Rev Fac Cienc Vet La Plata — Revista. Facultad de Ciencias Veterinarias de La Plata

Rev de la Fac de Derecho de Mex — Revista. Facultad de Derecho de Mexico

Rev Fac Eng Univ Porto — Revista. Faculdade de Engenharia. Universidade do Porto

Rev Fac Farm Bioquim Univ Cent Ecuador — Revista. Facultad de Farmacia y Bioquimica. Universidad Central del Ecuador

Rev Fac Farm Bioquim Univ Fed St Maria — Revista. Faculdade de Farmacia e Bioquimica. Universidade Federal de Santa Maria

Rev Fac Farm Bioquim Univ Nac Mayor San Marcos — Revista. Facultad de Farmacia y Bioquimica. Universidad Nacional Mayor de San Marcos

Rev Fac Farm Bioquim Univ Nac Mayor San Marcos (Lima) — Revista. Facultad de Farmacia y Bioquimica. Universidad Nacional Mayor de San Marcos (Lima)

Rev Fac Farm Bioquim Univ Sao Paulo — Revista. Faculdade de Farmacia e Bioquimica. Universidade de Sao Paulo

Rev Fac Farm Odontol Araraquara — Revista. Faculdade de Farmacia e Odontologia de Araraquara

Rev Fac Farm Univ Cent Venez — Revista. Facultad de Farmacia. Universidad Central de Venezuela

Rev Fac Ing Quim Univ Nac Litoral — Revista. Facultad de Ingenieria Quimica. Universidad Nacional del Litoral [*Argentina*]

Rev Fac Med (Maracaibo) — Revista. Facultad de Medicina (Maracaibo)

Rev Fac Med (Mex) — Revista. Facultad de Medicina (Mexico)

Rev Fac Med (Tucuman) — Revista. Facultad de Medicina (Tucuman)

Rev Fac Med Univ Fed Ceara — Revista. Faculdade de Medicina. Universidade Federal do Ceara

Rev Fac Med Univ Fed Santa Maria — Revista. Faculdade de Medicina. Universidade Federal de Santa Maria

Rev Fac Med Univ Nac Colomb (Bogota) — Revista. Facultad de Medicina. Universidad Nacional de Colombia (Bogota)

Rev Fac Med Vet Univ Nac Mayor San Marcos — Revista. Facultad de Medicina Veterinaria. Universidad Nacional Mayor de San Marcos

Rev Fac Med Vet Univ Sao Paulo — Revista. Faculdade de Medicina Veterinaria. Universidade de Sao Paulo

Rev Fac Med Vet Zootec (Bogota) — Revista. Facultad de Medicina, Veterinaria, y Zootecnia (Bogota)

Rev Fac Med Vet Zootec Univ San Carlos — Revista. Facultad de Medicina, Veterinaria, y Zootecnia. Universidad de San Carlos

Rev Fac Med Vet Zootec Univ Sao Paulo — Revista. Faculdade de Medicina Veterinaria e Zootecnia. Universidade de Sao Paulo

Rev Fac Med Vet Zoot Univ Nac Colomb — Revista. Facultad de Medicina, Veterinaria, y Zootecnia. Universidad Nacional de Colombia

Rev Fac Nac Agron (Medellin) — Revista. Facultad Nacional de Agronomia (Medellin)

Rev Fac Nac Agron Univ Antioquia — Revista. Facultad Nacional de Agronomia. Universidad de Antioquia

Rev Fac Nac Agron Univ Nac (Colombia) — Revista. Facultad Nacional de Agronomia. Universidad Nacional (Colombia)

Rev Fac Odontol Aracatuba — Revista. Faculdade de Odontologia de Aracatuba

Rev Fac Odontol Pernambuco — Revista. Faculdade de Odontologia de Pernambuco

Rev Fac Odontol Port Alegre — Revista. Faculdade de Odontologia de Port Alegre

Rev Fac Odontol Sao Jose Dos Campos — Revista. Faculdade de Odontologia de Sao Jose Dos Campos

Rev Fac Odontol Sao Paulo — Revista. Faculdade de Odontologia. Universidade de Sao Paulo

Rev Fac Odontol Tucuman — Revista. Facultad de Odontologia. Universidad Nacional de Tucuman

Rev Fac Odontol Univ Sao Paulo — Revista. Faculdade de Odontologia. Universidade de Sao Paulo

Rev Fac Quim Farm Univ Cent Ecuador — Revista. Facultad de Quimica y Farmacia. Universidad Central del Ecuador

Rev Fac Quim Ind Agric Univ Nac Litoral — Revista. Facultad de Quimica Industrial y Agricola. Universidad Nacional del Litoral

Rev Fac Quim Univ Nac Mayor San Marcos — Revista. Facultad de Quimica. Universidad Nacional Mayor de San Marcos

Rev Fac Sci Univ Istanbul C — Revue. Faculte des Sciences. Universite d'Istanbul [*Istanbul Universitesi fen Fakultesi Mecmuasi*]. Serie C

Rev Fac Sci Univ Istanbul Ser B Sci Nat — Revue. Faculte des Sciences. Universite d'Istanbul. Serie B. Sciences Naturelles

Rev Fac Sci Univ Istanbul Ser C — Review. Faculty of Science. University of Istanbul. Series C [*Istanbul Universitesi fen Fakultesi Mecmuasi. Serie C*]

Rev Farm Bahia — Revista Farmaceutica da Bahia

Rev Farm (B Aires) — Revista Farmaceutica (Buenos Aires)

Rev Farm Bioquim — Revista de Farmacia e Bioquimica

Rev Farm Bioquim Amazonia — Revista de Farmacia e Bioquimica da Amazonia

Rev Farm Bioquim Univ Sao Paulo — Revista de Farmacia e Bioquimica. Universidade de Sao Paulo

Rev Farm (Bucharest) — Revista Farmaciei (Bucharest)

Rev Farm Cuba — Revista Farmaceutica de Cuba

Rev Farm Odontol — Revista de Farmacia e Odontologia

Rev Farm Peru — Revista Farmaceutica Peruana

Rev Farm Quim — Revista de Farmacia y Quimica

Rev Fed Am Hosp — Review. Federation of American Hospitals

Rev Fed Doct Cienc Filos Let (Havana) — Revista. Federacion de Doctors en Ciencias y en Filosofia y Letras (Havana)

Rev Fed Fr Soc Sci Nat — Revue. Federation Francaise des Societes de Sciences Naturelles

Rev Ferment Ind Aliment — Revue des Fermentations et des Industries Alimentaires

Rev F Gy Ob — Revue Francaise de Gynecologie et d'Obstetrique

Rev Filip Med Farm — Revista Filipina de Medicina y Farmacia

Rev Filol Istr Cl — Revista di Filologia e di Isturzione Classica

Rev Filosof (Argentina) — Revista de Filosofia (Argentina)

Rev Filosof Costa Rica — Revista de Filosofia. Universidad de Costa Rica

Rev Filosof (Mexico) — Revista de Filosofia (Mexico)

Rev Filosof (Spain) — Revista de Filosofia (Spain)

Rev Filoz — Revista de Filozofie

Rev Fis — Revista de Fisica

Rev Fis Quim Eng — Revista de Fisica, Quimica, e Engenharia

Rev Fis Quim Eng Ser A — Revista de Fisica, Quimica, e Engenharia. Serie A

Rev FITCE — Revue FITCE [*Federation des Ingenieurs des Telecommunications de la Communaute Europeenne*]

Rev Fiz Chim Ser A — Revista de Fizica si Chimie. Seria A

Rev Fiz Chim Ser B — Revista de Fizica si Chimie. Seria B

Rev Fiziol Norm Patol — Revista de Fiziologie Normala si Patologica

Rev Flora Med — Revista da Flora Medicinai

Rev Foie — Revue du Foie

Rev Fonderie Mod — Revue de Fonderie Moderne

Rev Food Sci Technol (Mysore) — Reviews in Food Sciences and Technology (Mysore)

Rev Food Technol (Mysore) — Reviews in Food Technology (Mysore)

Rev Forest Venezolana — Revista Forestal Venezolana

Rev For Franc — Revue Forestiere Francaise

Rev For Fr (Nancy) — Revue Forestiere Francaise (Nancy)

Rev For Peru — Revista Forestal del Peru

Rev Fort Argent — Revista Forestal Argentina

Rev For Venez — Revista Forestal Venezolana

Rev Fr Alle — Revue Francaise d'Allergologie [*Later, Revue Francaise d'Allergologie et d'Immunologie Clinique*]

Rev Fr Allerg — Revue Francaise d'Allergie

Rev Fr Allergol — Revue Francaise d'Allergologie [*Later, Revue Francaise d'Allergologie et d'Immunologie Clinique*]

Rev Fr Allergol Immunol Clin — Revue Francaise d'Allergologie et d'Immunologie Clinique

Rev Franc Agr — Revue Francais de l'Agriculture

Rev Francaise Automat Inform Rech Oper Ser Bleue — Revue Francaise d'Automatique, d'Informatique, et de Recherche Operationnelle. Serie Bleue

Rev Francaise Automat Inform Rech Oper Ser Jaune — Revue Francaise d'Automatique, d'Informatique, et de Recherche Operationnelle. Serie Jaune

Rev Francaise Automat Inform Rech Oper Ser Rouge Anal Numer — Revue Francaise d'Automatique, d'Informatique, et de Recherche Operationnelle. Serie Rouge. Analyse Numerique

Rev Francaise Automat Inform Rech Oper Ser Verte — Revue Francaise d'Automatique, d'Informatique, et de Recherche Operationnelle. Serie Verte

Rev Franc de Droit Aer — Revue Francaise de Droit Aerien

Rev Franc Phot — Revue Francaise de Photographie

Rev Fr Astronaut — Revue Francaise d'Astronautique [*France*]

Rev Fr Aut Inf Rech Oper Anal Num — Revue Francaise d'Automatique, d'Informatique, et de Recherche Operationnelle. Serie Analyse Numerique

Rev Fr Autom Inf Rech Oper — Revue Francaise d'Automatique, d'Informatique, et de Recherche Operationnelle

Rev Fr de C — Revue Francaise de Communication

Rev Fr Corps Gras — Revue Francaise des Corps Gras

Rev Fr Electr — Revue Francaise de l'Electricite

Rev Fr Endocrinol — Revue Francaise d'Endocrinologie

Rev Fr Endocrinol Clin Nutr Metab — Revue Francaise d'Endocrinologie Clinique, Nutrition, et Metabolisme

Rev Fr Energ — Revue Francaise de l'Energie

Rev Fr Entomol — Revue Francaise d'Entomologie

Rev Fr Etud Clin Biol — Revue Francaise d'Etudes Cliniques et Biologiques

Rev Fr Geotech — Revue Francaise de Geotechnique

Rev Fr Gerontol — Revue Francaise de Gerontologie

Rev Fr Gynecol Obstet — Revue Francaise de Gynecologie et d'Obstetrique

Rev Fr Hist — Revue Francaise d'Histoire d'Outre-Mer

Rev Fr Hist Outre Mer — Revue Francaise d'Histoire d'Outre-Mer

Rev Fr Inf and Rech Oper — Revue Francaise d'Informatique et de Recherche Operationnelle

Rev Frio — Revista del Frio

Rev Fr Mal Respir — Revue Francaise des Maladies Respiratoires

Rev Fr Mec — Revue Francaise de Mecanique

Rev Fr Mkt — Revue Francaise du Marketing

Rev Fr Odonto Stomatol (Paris) — Revue Francaise d'Odonto-Stomatologie (Paris)

Rev Fr Pediatr — Revue Francaise de Pediatrie

Rev Fr Photogr Cinematogr — Revue Francaise de Photographie et de Cinematographie

Rev Fr Sci Polit — Revue Francaise de Science Politique

Rev Fr Sc P — Revue Francaise de Science Politique

Rev Fr Soc — Revue Francaise de Sociologie

Rev Fr Trait Inf — Revue Francaise de Traitement de l'Information

Rev Fr Tran — Revue Francaise de Transfusion [*Later, Revue Francaise de Transfusion et Immuno-Hematologie*]

Rev Fr Transfus — Revue Francaise de Transfusion [*Later, Revue Francaise de Transfusion et Immuno-Hematologie*]

Rev Fr Transfus Immuno-Hematol — Revue Francaise de Transfusion et Immuno-Hematologie

Rev Fuerzas Armadas Venez — Revista de las Fuerzas Armadas de Venezuela

Rev Fund Serv Saude Publica (Braz) — Revista. Fundacao Servicos de Saude Publica (Brazil)

Rev Fund SESP — Revista. Fundacao Servicos de Saude Publica [*Brazil*]

Rev Fund SESP (Braz) — Revista. Fundacao Servicos de Saude Publica (Brazil)

Rev Gastroenterol — Review of Gastroenterology

Rev Gastroenterol Mex — Revista de Gastroenterologia de Mexico

Rev Gaucha Odontol — Revista Gaucha de Odontologia

Rev Gemmol AFG — Revue de Gemmologie. Association Francaise de Gemmologie

Rev Gen Agron — Revue Generale Agronomique

Rev Gen Assur Terr — Revue Generale des Assurances Terrestres

Rev Gen Bot — Revue Generale de Botanique

Rev Gen Caoutch — Revue Generale du Caoutchouc

Rev Gen Caoutch Plast — Revue Generale des Caoutchoucs et Plastiques

Rev Gen Caoutch Plast Ed Plast — Revue Generale des Caoutchoucs et Plastiques. Edition Plastiques

Rev Gen Chem Fer — Revue Generale des Chemins de Fer

Rev Gen Chemins de Fer — Revue Generale des Chemins de Fer

Rev Gen Chemins Fer — Revue Generale des Chemins de Fer

Rev Gen Chim Pure Appl — Revue Generale de Chimie Pure et Appliquee

Rev Gen Clin et Therap — Revue Generale de Clinique et de Therapeutique

Rev Gen Colloides — Revue Generale des Colloides

Rev Gen de Droit — Revue Generale de Droit

Rev Gen Droit — Revue Generale de Droit

Rev Gen Elec — Revue Generale de l'Electricite

Rev Gen Electr — Revue Generale de l'Electricite

Rev Generale de Droit — Revue Generale de Droit

Rev Geneve — Revue de Geneve

Rev Gen Mar — Revista General de Marina

Rev Gen Matieres Color Blanchiment Teint Impress Apprets — Revue Generale des Matieres Colorantes du Blanchiment de la Teinture de l'Impression et des Apprets

Rev Gen Matieres Plast — Revue Generale des Matieres Plastiques

Rev Gen Mec — Revue Generale de Mecanique

Rev Gen Med Vet (Toulouse) — Revue Generale de Medecine Veterinaire (Toulouse)

Rev Gen Nucl — Revue Generale Nucleaire

Rev Gen Sci Pures Appl — Revue Generale des Sciences Pures et Appliquees

Rev Gen Sci Pures Appl Bull Assoc Fr Av Sci — Revue Generale des Sciences Pures et Appliquees et Bulletin. Association Francaise pour l'Avancement des Sciences

Rev Gen Sci Pures Appl Bull Soc Philomath — Revue Generale des Sciences Pures et Appliquees et Bulletin. Societe Philomathique

Rev Gen Sc Pures et Appliq — Revue Generale des Sciences Pures et Appliquees

Rev Gen Tech — Revue Generale des Techniques [*France*]

Rev Gen Therm — Revue Generale de Thermique

Rev Geofis — Revista de Geofisica

Rev Geog — Revista Geografica

Rev Geog Ph — Revue de Geographie Physique et de Geologie Dynamique

Rev Geogr Alpine — Revue de Geographie Alpine

Rev Geographie Alpine — Revue de Geographie Alpine

Rev Geographie Montreal — Revue de Geographie de Montreal

Rev Geogr Maroc — Revue de Geographie du Maroc

Rev Geogr Phys Geol Dyn — Revue de Geographie Physique et de Geologie Dynamique

Rev Geogr Pyrenees Sud-Ouest — Revue Geographique des Pyrenees et du Sud-Ouest

Rev Geol Chile — Revista Geologica de Chile

Rev Geol Dyn Geogr Phys — Revue de Geologie Dynamique et de Geographie Physique

Rev Geol Minas Ecuador Dir Gen Geol Minas — Revista de Geologia y Minas. Ecuador. Direccion General de Geologia y Minas

Rev Geologia — Revista de Geologia

Rev Geomorphol Dyn — Revue de Geomorphologie Dynamique

Rev Geophys — Reviews of Geophysics [*Later, Reviews of Geophysics and Space Physics*]
Rev Geophys — Reviews of Geophysics and Space Physics
Rev Geophysics — Reviews of Geophysics [*Later, Reviews of Geophysics and Space Physics*]
Rev Geophys Space Phys — Reviews of Geophysics and Space Physics
Rev Geophys and Space Phys — Reviews of Geophysics and Space Physics
Rev Geriatr — Revue de Geriatrie
Rev Germ — Revue Germanique
Rev Gerontol Expression Fr — Revue de Gerontologie d'Expression Francaise
Rev of Ghana L — Review of Ghana Law
Rev Ginecol Obstet — Revista de Ginecologia e d'Obstetricia
Rev Goiana Med — Revista Goiana de Medicina
Rev Gospod Agr Stat (Bucharest) — Revista Gospodariilor Agricole de Stat (Bucharest)
Rev G Therm — Revue Generale de Thermique
Rev Guatem Estomatol — Revista Guatemalteca de Estomatologia
Rev Gynae et Chir Abd — Revue de Gynaecologie et de Chirurgie Abdominale
Rev Gynecol Obstet — Revista de Gynecologia e d'Obstetricia
RevH — Revista de Historia [*Lisbon*]
REVHA — Reviews on Environmental Health
Rev Haute Auvergne — Revue de la Haute Auvergne. Societe des Sciences et Arts
Rev Hautes Temp Refract — Revue des Hautes Temperatures et des Refractaires
Rev Hebd Laryngol Otol Rhinol — Revue Hebdomadaire de Laryngologie, d'Otologie, et de Rhinologie
Rev Hellen de Droit Internat — Revue Hellenique de Droit International
Rev Hellenique de Dr Int'l — Revue Hellenique de Droit International
Rev Hematol — Revue d'Hematologie
Rev HF Electron Telecommun — Revue HF, Electronique, Telecommunications
Rev High-Temp Mater — Reviews on High-Temperature Materials
Rev Hig Med Esc — Revista de Higiene y Medicina Escolares
Rev Hig y San Pecuarias — Revista de Higiene y Sanidad Pecuarias
Rev Hig y San Vet (Madrid) — Revista de Higiene y Sanidad Veterinaria (Madrid)
Rev His A F — Revue d'Histoire de l'Amerique Francaise
Rev Hispan — Revista Hispanica Moderna
RevHist — Revista de Historia [*Sao Paulo*]
Rev Hist — Revue Historique
Rev Hist Am — Revista de Historia de America
Rev Hist Am — Revue d'Histoire de l'Amerique Francaise
Rev Hist Am Fr — Revue d'Histoire de l'Amerique Francaise
Rev Hist Armees — Revue Historique des Armees
Rev Hist Bordeaux Dep Gironde — Revue Historique de Bordeaux et du Departement de la Gironde
Rev Hist Canaria — Revista de Historia Canaria
Rev Hist Di — Revue d'Histoire Diplomatique
Rev Hist Econ Soc — Revue d'Histoire Economique et Sociale
Rev Hist L — Revue d'Histoire Litteraire de la France
Rev Hist M — Revue d'Histoire Moderne et Contemporaine
Rev Hist Maghrebine — Revue d'Histoire Maghrebine
Rev Hist Mil — Revista de Historia Militar
Rev Hist Mod Contemp — Revue d'Histoire Moderne et Contemporaine
Rev Hist Nat Appliq — Revue d'Histoire Naturelle Appliquee
Rev Histoire Sci Appl — Revue d'Histoire des Sciences et de Leurs Applications
Rev Hist Ph — Revue d'Histoire et de Philosophie Religieuses
Rev Hist Pharm — Revue d'Histoire de la Pharmacie
Rev Hist R — Revue de l'Histoire des Religions
Rev Hist Relig — Revue de l'Histoire des Religions
Rev Hist Sci — Revue d'Histoire des Sciences
Rev Hist Sci Applic — Revue d'Histoire des Sciences et de Leurs Applications
Rev Hist Sci Leurs Appl — Revue d'Histoire des Sciences et de Leurs Applications
Rev Hist Textes — Revue d'Histoire des Textes
Rev Hist Th — Revue d'Histoire du Theatre
RevHL — Revista de Historia. La Laguna de Tenerife
RevHL — Revista de Historia (Lisbon)
Rev Hong Mines Metall Mines — Revue Hongroise de Mines et Metallurgie. Mines
Rev Hortic — Revue Horticole
Rev Hortic (Paris) — Revue Horticole (Paris)
Rev Hortic Suisse — Revue Horticole Suisse
Rev Hortic Vitic — Revista de Horticultura si Viticultura
Rev Hort Viticult — Revista de Horticultura si Viticultura [*Romania*]
Rev Hosp Clin Fac Med Univ Sao Paulo — Revista. Hospital das Clinicas. Faculdade de Medicina. Universidade de Sao Paulo
Rev Hosp Clin Fac Med Univ Sao Paulo Supl — Revista. Hospital das Clinicas. Faculdade de Medicina. Universidade de Sao Paulo. Suplemento
Rev Hosp Nino (Lima) — Revista. Hospital del Nino (Lima)
Rev Hosp Ninos (B Aires) — Revista. Hospital de Ninos (Buenos Aires)
Rev Hosp Psiquiatr Habana — Revista. Hospital Psiquiatrico de la Habana
Rev Hosp San Juan De Dios (Bogota) — Revista. Hospital de San Juan De Dios (Bogota)
RevHS — Revista de Historia (Sao Paulo)
Rev Hyg — Revue d'Hygiene

Rev Hyg Med Infant Ann Polyclin H de Rothschild — Revue d'Hygiene et de Medecine Infantiles et Annales de la Polyclinique H. de Rothschild
Rev Hyg et Med Prevent — Revue d'Hygiene et de Medecine Preventive
Rev Hyg Med Sc Univ — Revue d'Hygiene et Medecine Scolaire et Universitaire
Rev Hyg Med Soc — Revue d'Hygiene et de Medecine Sociale
Rev Hyg Prof — Revue de l'Hygiene Professionnelle
Rev Hyg Trav — Revue d'Hygiene du Travail
Rev/I — Revista/Review Interamericana
RevIb — Revista Iberoamericana
Rev Iber Endocrinol — Revista Iberica de Endocrinologia
Rev Iberoam — Revista Iberoamericana
Rev Iberoam Educ Quim — Revista Iberoamericana de Educacion Quimica
Rev Iber Parasitol — Revista Iberica de Parasitologia
Rev IBYS — Revista. IBYS [*Instituto de Biologia y Sueroterapia*]
Rev ICIDCA — Revista. ICIDCA [*Instituto Cubano de Investigaciones de los Derivados de la Cana de Azucar*]
Rev IDIEM — Revista. IDIEM [*Instituto de Investigaciones de Engoyes de Materiales*]
RevIE — Revista de Ideas Esteticas
Review — Weekly Review
Review Inst Nucl Power Oper — Review. Institute of Nuclear Power Operations
Rev I F Pet — Revue. Institut Francais du Petrole
Rev Ig — Revista. Igiena, Bacteriologie, Virusologie, Parazitologie, Epidemiologie, Pneumoftiziologie
Rev Ig Bacteriol Virusol Parazitol Epidemiol Pneumoftiziol — Revista. Igiena, Bacteriologie, Virusologie, Parazitologie, Epidemiologie, Pneumoftiziologie
Rev Ig Soc — Revista de Igiena Sociala
RevIMA — Review of Indonesian and Malayan Affairs
Rev Imagem — Revista da Imagem
Rev Immunol — Revue d'Immunologie
Rev Immunol Ther Antimicrob — Revue d'Immunologie et de Therapie Antimicrobienne
Rev Ind — Revue Industrielle
Rev Ind Agric (Tucuman) — Revista Industrial y Agricola (Tucuman)
Rev Ind Aliment Prod Anim — Revista Industriei Alimentare. Produse Animale
Rev Ind Aliment Prod Veg — Revista Industriei Alimentare. Produse Vegetale
Rev Ind Anim — Revista de Industria Animal
Rev Ind Chim — Revue Hebdomadaire des Industries Chimiques
Rev Ind Elec — Revue Hebdomadaire de l'Industrie Electrique et Electronique
Rev Ind Fabril — Revista Industrial y Fabril [*France*]
Rev Indias — Revista de las Indias
Rev Ind Miner — Revue de l'Industrie Minerale
Rev Ind Miner Mines — Revue de l'Industrie Minerale. Mines
Rev Indon & Malayan Affairs — Review of Indonesian and Malayan Affairs
Rev Ind S Paulo — Revista Industrial de Sao Paulo
Rev Industr Agric (Tucuman) — Revista Industrial y Agricola (Tucuman)
Rev Inf & Autom — Revista de Informatica y Automatica
Rev Infect Dis — Review of Infectious Diseases
Rev Infirm — Revue de l'Infirmiere
Rev Inf Med — Revue d'Informatique Medicale
Rev Ing — Revue des Ingenieurs des Ecoles Nationales Superieures des Mines
Rev Ing (Buenos Aires) — Revista de Ingenieria (Buenos Aires)
Rev Ing Ind — Revista de Ingenieria Industrial
Rev Ing (Montevideo) — Revista de Ingenieria (Montevideo)
Rev Ing (Montreal) — Revue de l'Ingenierie (Montreal)
Rev Ing Quim — Revista de Ingenieria Quimica
Rev Ingr — Universidad Catolica Argentina. Facultad de Ciencias Fisicomatematicas e Ingenieria. Revista da Ingenieria
Rev In Haut — Revue Internationale des Hautes Temperatures et des Refractaires
Rev Inst Adolfo Lutz — Revista. Instituto Adolfo Lutz
Rev Inst Agr Catalan San Isidro — Revista. Instituto Agricola Catalan de San Isidro
Rev Inst Antibiot (Recife) — Revista. Instituto de Antibioticos. Universidade Federal de Pernambuco (Recife)
Rev Inst Antibiot Univ Fed Pernambuco — Revista. Instituto de Antibioticos. Universidade Federal de Pernambuco
Rev Inst Antibiot Univ Recife — Revista. Instituto de Antibioticos. Universidade do Recife
Rev Inst Antropol Univ Cordoba — Revista. Instituto de Antropologia. Universidad Nacional de Cordoba
Rev Inst Bacteriol Dep Nac Hig (Argent) — Revista. Instituto Bacteriologico. Departamento Nacional de Higiene (Argentina)
Rev Inst Bacteriol Malbran — Revista del Instituto Bacteriologico Malbran
Rev Inst Colomb Agropecu — Revista. Instituto Colombiano Agropecuario
Rev Inst Franc Petrol — Revue. Institut Francais du Petrole
Rev Inst Fr Pet — Revue. Institut Francais du Petrole
Rev Inst Fr Pet — Revue. Institut Francais du Petrole et Annales des Combustibles Liquides [*Later, Revue. Institut Francais du Petrole*]
Rev Inst Fr Pet Ann Combust Liq — Revue. Institut Francais du Petrole et Annales des Combustibles Liquides [*Later, Revue. Institut Francais du Petrole*]
Rev Inst Geogr Geol (Sao Paulo) — Revista. Instituto Geografico e Geologico (Sao Paulo)

Rev Inst Geol Min Univ Nac Tucuman — Revista. Instituto de Geologia y Mineria. Universidad Nacional de Tucuman

Rev Inst Geol Univ Nac Auton Mex — Revista. Instituto de Geologia. Universidad Nacional Autonoma de Mexico

Rev Inst Hist Geogr Bras — Revista. Instituto Historico e Geografico Brasileiro

Rev Inst Hyg Mines — Revue. Institut d'Hygiene des Mines

Rev Inst Hyg Mines (Hasselt) — Revue. Institut d'Hygiene des Mines (Hasselt)

Rev Inst Invest Tecnol (Bogota) — Revista. Instituto de Investigaciones Tecnologicas (Bogota)

Rev Inst Malbran — Revista. Instituto Malbran

Rev Inst Med Leg Estado Guanabara — Revista. Instituto Medico-Legal do Estado da Guanabara

Rev Inst Med Trop Sao Paulo — Revista. Instituto de Medicina Tropical de Sao Paulo

Rev Inst Mex Pet — Revista. Instituto Mexicano del Petroleo

Rev Inst Mex Petrol — Revista. Instituto Mexicano del Petroleo

Rev Inst Munic Bot (B Aires) — Revista. Instituto Municipal de Botanica (Buenos Aires)

Rev Inst Nac Geol Min (Argent) — Revista. Instituto Nacional de Geologia y Mineria (Argentina)

Rev Inst Nac Hig — Revista. Instituto Nacional de Higiene

Rev Inst Nacl Cancerol (Mex) — Revista. Instituto Nacional de Cancerologia (Mexico)

Rev Inst Nac Med Leg Colombia — Revista. Instituto Nacional de Medicina Legal de Colombia

Rev Inst Napoleon — Revue de l'Institut Napoleon

Rev Inst Pasteur Lyon — Revue. Institut Pasteur de Lyon

Rev Inst Salubr Enferm Trop — Revista. Instituto de Salubridad y Enfermedades Tropicales

Rev Int Bois — Revue Internationale du Bois

Rev Int Bois Matieres Premieres Prod Ind Origine Veg — Revue Internationale du Bois et des Matieres Premieres et Produits Industriels d'Origine Vegetale

Rev Int Bot Appl Agric Trop — Revue Internationale de Botanique Appliquee et d'Agriculture Tropicale

Rev Int Brass Malt — Revue Internationale de Brasserie et de Malterie

Rev Int Choc — Revue Internationale de la Chocolaterie

Rev Int Crim — Revue Internationale du Criminalistique

Rev Int Criminol Police Tech — Revue Internationale de Criminologie et de Police Technique

Rev Int Doc — Revue Internationale de la Documentation

Rev Interamer Cienc Soc — Revista Interamericana de Ciencias Sociales

Rev Interam Radiol — Revista Interamericana de Radiologia

Rev Inter B — Revista Interamericana de Bibliografia [Inter-American Review of Bibliography]

Rev Internat de Droit Compare — Revue Internationale de Droit Compare. Continuation du Bulletin de la Societe de Legislation Comparee

Rev Internat de Droit Penal — Revue Internationale de Droit Penal. Bulletin de l'Association Internationale de Droit Penal

Rev Internat Philos — Revue Internationale de Philosophie

Rev Int Falsif — Revue Internationale des Falsifications

Rev Int Falsif Anal Matieres Aliment — Revue Internationale des Falsifications et d'Analyse des Matieres Alimentaires

Rev Int Hautes Temp Refract — Revue Internationale des Hautes Temperatures et des Refractaires

Rev Int Hautes Temp et Refract — Revue Internationale des Hautes Temperatures et des Refractaires

Rev Int Heliotech — Revue Internationale d'Heliotechnique [France]

Rev Int Hepatol — Revue Internationale d'Hepatologie

Rev Int Hist Banque — Revue Internationale d'Histoire de la Banque

Rev Int Ind Agric — Revue Internationale des Industries Agricoles

Rev Int'l Comm Jurists — Review. International Commission of Jurists

Rev Int Mus — Revue Internationale de Musique

Rev Int Oceanogr Med — Revue Internationale d'Oceanographie Medicale

Rev Int Pediatr — Revue Internationale de Pediatrie

Rev Int Ph — Revue Internationale de Philosophie

Rev Int Pharm — Revue Internationale de Pharmacie

Rev Int Phil — Revue Internationale de Philosophie

Rev Int Prod Trop Mater Trop — Revue Internationale des Produits Tropicaux et du Materiel Tropical

Rev Int Psy — Revue Internationale de Psychologie Appliquee

Rev Int Sc — Revista Internazionale di Scienze Economiche e Commerciali

Rev Int Serv Sante Armees Terre Mer Air — Revue Internationale des Services de Sante des Armees de Terre, de Mer, et de l'Air

Rev Int Soja — Revue Internationale du Soja

Rev Int Tab — Revue Internationale des Tabacs

Rev Int Trach — Revue Internationale du Trachome

Rev Int Trach Pathol Ocul Trop Subtrop — Revue Internationale du Trachome et de Pathologie Oculaire Tropicale et Subtropicale

Rev Inv Cli — Revista de Investigacion Clinica

Rev Invest — Revista de Investigacion

Rev Invest Agr — Revista de Investigaciones Agricolas

Rev Invest Agric — Revista de Investigaciones Agricolas

Rev Invest Agropec Ser — Revista de Investigaciones Agropecuarias. Serie

Rev Invest Agropecuar Ser 2 — Revista de Investigaciones Agropecuarias. Serie 2. Biologia y Produccion Vegetal

Rev Invest Agropecuar Ser 5 — Revista de Investigaciones Agropecuarias. Serie 5. Patologia Vegetal

Rev Invest Agropecu Ser 1 — Revista de Investigaciones Agropecuarias. Serie 1. Biologia y Produccion Animal

Rev Invest Agropecu Ser 3 — Revista de Investigaciones Agropecuarias. Serie 3. Clima y Suelo

Rev Invest Agropecu Ser 4 — Revista de Investigaciones Agropecuarias. Serie 4. Patologia Animal

Rev Invest Agropecu Ser 6 — Revista de Investigaciones Agropecuarias. Serie 6. Economia y Administracion Rural

Rev Invest Agropecu Ser 1 Biol Prod Anim — Revista de Investigaciones Agropecuarias. Serie 1. Biologia y Produccion Animal

Rev Invest Agropecu Ser 2 Biol Prod Veg — Revista de Investigaciones Agropecuarias. Serie 2. Biologia y Produccion Vegetal

Rev Invest Agropecu Ser 3 Clima Suelo — Revista de Investigaciones Agropecuarias. Serie 3. Clima y Suelo

Rev Invest Agropecu Ser 4 Patol Anim — Revista de Investigaciones Agropecuarias. Serie 4. Patologia Animal

Rev Invest Agropecu Ser 5 Patol Veg — Revista de Investigaciones Agropecuarias. Serie 5. Patologia Vegetal

Rev Invest Clin — Revista de Investigacion Clinica

Rev Invest For — Revista de Investigaciones Forestales

Rev Invest Ganad — Revista de Investigaciones Ganaderas

Rev Invest Inst Nac Pesca — Revista de Investigaciones. Instituto Nacional de la Pesca

Rev Invest Salud Publica — Revista de Investigacion en Salud Publica

Rev Invest Univ Guadalajara (Mex) — Revista de Investigacion. Universidad de Guadalajara (Mexico)

Rev Ion — Revista Ion

Rev I Psych — Revue Internationale de Psychologie Appliquee

Rev IRE — Revue. IRE [Institut National des Radioelements]

Rev I Soc — Revue. Institut de Sociologie

Revista CF — Revista Colombiana de Folclor

Rev Jeumont-Schneider — Revue Jeumont-Schneider

Rev J Phil Soc Sci — Review Journal of Philosophy and Social Science

Rev Jur — Revista Juridica

Rev Jur del Peru — Revista Juridica del Peru

Rev Jur Themis — Revue Juridique Themis

Rev Jur de la Univ de Puerto Rico — Revista Juridica. Universidad de Puerto Rico

Rev Jur UPR — Revista Juridica. Universidad de Puerto Rico

Rev Kobe Univ Merc Mar Part 2 — Review. Kobe University of Mercantile Marine. Part 2 [Japan]

Rev Kobe Univ Merc Mar Part 2 Marit Stud Sci Eng — Review. Kobe University of Mercantile Marine. Part 2. Maritime Studies, and Science and Engineering

Rev Kuba Med Trop Parasitol — Revista Kuba de Medicina Tropical y Parasitologia

RevL — Revista de Letras

RevLA — Revista de Letras (Assis)

Rev Lang R — Revue des Langues Romanes

Rev Lang V — Revue des Langues Vivantes/Tijdschrift voor Levende Talen

Rev Lang Viv — Revue des Langues Vivantes

Rev Laryngol Otol Rhinol — Revue de Laryngologie, Otologie, Rhinologie

Rev Laryngol Otol Rhinol (Bord) — Revue de Laryngologie, Otologie, Rhinologie (Bordeaux)

Rev Laryngol Otol Rhino Suppl — Revue de Laryngologie, Otologie, Rhinologie. Supplement [France]

Rev Laser Eng — Review of Laser Engineering [Japan]

Rev Latam Microbiol — Revista Latinoamericana de Microbiologia

Rev Latam P — Revista Latinoamericana de Psicologia

Rev Latam Patol — Revista Latinoamericana de Patologia

Rev Latin de Filosof — Revista Latinoamericana de Filosofia

Rev Latinoam Anat Patol — Revista Latinoamericana de Anatomia Patologica

Rev Latinoam Cir Plast — Revista Latinoamericana de Cirurgia Plastica

Rev Latinoam Ing Quim Quim Apl — Revista Latinoamericana de Ingenieria Quimica y Quimica Aplicada

Rev Latinoam Microbiol — Revista Latinoamericana de Microbiologia

Rev Latinoam Microbiol Parasitol — Revista Latinoamericana de Microbiologia y Parasitologia [Later, Revista Latinoamericana de Microbiologia]

Rev Latinoam Microbiol Supl — Revista Latinoamericana de Microbiologia. Suplemento

Rev Latinoam Patol — Revista Latinoamericana de Patologia

Rev Latinoam Psicol — Revista Latinoamericana de Psicologia

Rev Latinoam Quim — Revista Latinoamericana de Quimica

Rev Latinoam Sider — Revista Latinoamericana de Siderurgia

Rev Leprol Dermatol Sifilogr — Revista de Leprologia, Dermatologia, y Sifilografia

Rev Leprol Sao Paulo — Revista de Leprologia de Sao Paulo

Rev Liberale — Revue Liberale

Rev Ling Rom — Revue de Linguistique Romane

Rev Lit — Revue de Litterature Comparee

Rev Lit Comp — Revue de Litterature Comparee

Rev de Lit Comp — Revue de Litterature Comparee

Rev Louvre — Revue du Louvre et des Musees de France

RevLR — Revista do Livro (Rio)
Rev Lyon Med — Revue Lyonnaise de Medecine
RevM — Revista (Madrid)
Rev M — Revue M [*Belgium*]
Rev Macromol Chem — Reviews in Macromolecular Chemistry
Rev Madeira (Sao Paulo) — Revista da Madeira (Sao Paulo)
Rev Mal Respir — Revue des Maladies Respiratoires
Rev du Marche Commun — Revue du Marche Commun
Rev Market & Ag Econ — Review of Marketing and Agricultural Economics
Rev Market Agric Econ — Review of Marketing and Agricultural Economics
Rev Market Agric Econ (Sydney) — Review of Marketing and Agricultural Economics (Sydney)
Rev Marketing Agr Econ — Review of Marketing and Agricultural Economics
Rev Mat Hisp-Amer — Revista Matematica Hispano-Americana
Rev Math Pures Appl — Revue de Mathematiques Pures et Appliquees
Rev MBLE — Revue MBLE [*Manufacture Belge de Lampes et de Materiel*] [*Belgium*]
Rev Mec Appl — Revue de Mecanique Appliquee
Rev Mec Tijdsch — Revue Mecanique Tijdschrift [*Belgium*]
Rev Med — Revista Medicala
Rev Med Accidents Mal Prof — Revue de Medecine des Accidents et des Maladies Professionnelles
Rev Med Aeronaut — Revista Medica da Aeronautica
Rev Med Aeronaut (Paris) — Revue de Medecine Aeronautique (Paris) [*Later, Medecine Aeronautique et Spatial - Medecine Subaquatique et Hyperbare*]
Rev Med Aeronaut Spat — Revue de Medecine Aeronautique et Spatiale [*Later, Medecine Aeronautique et Spatial - Medecine Subaquatique et Hyperbare*]
Rev Med Aeronaut Spat Med Subaquat Hyperbare — Revue de Medecine Aeronautique et Spatiale - Medecine Subaquatique et Hyperbare
Rev Med Aliment — Revista de Medicina y Alimentacion
Rev Med Angola — Revista Medica de Angola
Rev Med ATM — Revista de Medicina. ATM [*Associacao da Turma Medica*]
Rev Med Bogota — Revista Medica de Bogota
Rev Med Brux — Revue Medicale de Bruxelles
Rev Med Bruxelles — Revue Medicale de Bruxelles
Rev Med Chi — Revista Medica de Chile
Rev Med Chil — Revista Medica de Chile
Rev Med Chile — Revista Medica de Chile
Rev Med Chir — Revista Medico-Chirurgicala
Rev Med-Chir (Iasi) — Revue Medico-Chirurgicale (Iasi)
Rev Med-Chir Mal Foie — Revue Medico-Chirurgicale des Maladies du Foie
Rev Med-Chir Mal Foie Rate Pancreas — Revue Medico-Chirurgicale des Maladies du Foie, de la Rate, et du Pancreas [*France*]
Rev Med-Chir Soc Med Nat din Iasi — Revista Medico-Chirurgicala. Societatii de Medici si Naturalisti din Iasi
Rev Med-Chir Soc Med Nat Iasi — Revista Medico-Chirurgicala. Societatii de Medici si Naturalisti din Iasi
Rev Med Cienc Afines — Revista de Medicina y Ciencias Afines
Rev Med Cir Habana — Revista de Medicina y Cirugia de La Habana
Rev Med Cir Sao Paulo — Revista de Medicina e Cirurgia de Sao Paulo
Rev Med y Cirug (Caracas) — Revista de Medicina y Cirugia (Caracas)
Rev Med y Cirug Habana — Revista de Medicina y Cirugia de La Habana
Rev Med Cordoba — Revista Medica de Cordoba
Rev Med Costa Rica — Revista Medica de Costa Rica
Rev Med Cubana — Revista Medica Cubana
Rev Med Dijon — Revue Medicale de Dijon
Rev Med Est — Revue Medicale de l'Est
Rev Med Estado Guanabara — Revista Medica do Estado da Guanabara
Rev Med Estado Rio De J — Revista Medica do Estado do Rio De Janeiro
Rev Med Estud Gen Navarro — Revista de Medicina del Estudio General de Navarro
Rev Med Exp — Revista de Medicina Experimental
Rev Med Exp (Lima) — Revista de Medicina Experimental (Lima)
Rev Med Fr — Revue Medicale Francaise
Rev Med Galicia — Revista Medica de Galicia
Rev Med (Hanoi) — Revue Medicale (Hanoi)
Rev Med Hondur — Revista Medica Hondurena
Rev Med Hosp Cent Empl (Lima) — Revista Medica. Hospital Central del Empleado (Lima)
Rev Med Hosp Colon — Revista Medica. Hospital Colonia
Rev Med Hosp Colon (Mex) — Revista Medica. Hospital Colonia (Mexico)
Rev Med Hosp Ernesto Dornelles — Revista de Medicina. Hospital Ernesto Dornelles
Rev Med Hosp Esp — Revista Medica. Hospital Espanol
Rev Med Hosp Gen (Mex) — Revista Medica. Hospital General (Mexico)
Rev Med Hosp Gen (Mexico City) — Revista Medica. Hospital General (Mexico City)
Rev Med Hosp Obrero — Revista Medica del Hospital Obrero
Rev Med Hosp Servidores Estado — Revista Medica. Hospital dos Servidores do Estado
Rev Med HSE — Revista Medica. Hospital dos Servidores do Estado

Rev Med Inst Mex Seguro Soc — Revista Medica. Instituto Mexicano del Seguro Social
Rev Med Inst Previdencia Serv Estado Minas Gerais — Revista Medica. Instituto de Previdencia dos Servidores do Estado de Minas Gerais
Rev Med Inst Previdencia Servidores Estado Minas Gerais — Revista Medica. Instituto de Previdencia dos Servidores do Estado de Minas Gerais
Rev Med Interna Med Interna — Revista de Medicina Interna, Neurologie, Psihiatrie, Neurochirurgie, Dermato-Venerologie. Seria Medicina Interna
Rev Med Interna Neurol Psihiatr — Revista de Medicina Interna, Neurologie, Psihiatrie, Neurochirurgie, Dermato-Venerologie. Neurologie, Psihiatrie, Neurochirurgie
Rev Med Interna Neurol Psihiatr Neurochir Dermato-Venerol — Revista de Medicina Interna, Neurologie, Psihiatrie, Neurochirurgie, Dermato-Venerologie
Rev Med Interne — Revue de Medecine Interne
Rev Mediterr Sci Med — Revue Mediterraneenne des Sciences Medicales
Rev Med Juiz de Fora — Revista Medica de Juiz de Fora
Rev Med Leg Colomb — Revista de Medicina Legal de Colombia
Rev Med Liege — Revue Medicale de Liege
Rev Med Liege Suppl — Revue Medicale de Liege. Supplement
Rev Med Limoges — Revue de Medecine de Limoges
Rev Med Louvain — Revue Medicale de Louvain
Rev Med Mil — Revista de Medicina Militar
Rev Med Miniere — Revue Medicale Miniere
Rev Med Moyen-Orient — Revue Medicale du Moyen-Orient
Rev Med Nancy — Revue Medicale de Nancy
Rev Med Nav — Revue de Medecine Navale (Metropole et Outre-Mer)
Rev Med Normandes — Revues Medicales Normandes
Rev Med Panama — Revista Medica de Panama
Rev Med Parag — Revista Medica del Paraguay
Rev Med (Paris) — Revue de Medecine (Paris)
Rev Med Prev — Revue de Medecine Preventive
Rev Med Psychosomat Psychol Med — Revue de Medecine Psychosomatique et de Psychologie Medicale [*France*]
Rev Med-Quir (Buenos Aires) — Revista Medico-Quirurgica (Buenos Aires)
Rev Med Quir Patol Femenina — Revista Medico-Quirurgica de Patologia Femenina
Rev Med Rio Grande do Sul — Revista de Medicina do Rio Grande do Sul
Rev Med d Rosario — Revista Medica del Rosario
Rev Med Rosario — Revista Medica del Rosario
Rev de Med (Rosario) — Revista de Medicina (Rosario)
Rev Med (Sao Paulo) — Revista de Medicina (Sao Paulo)
Rev Med Sevilla — Revista Medica de Sevilla
Rev Med de S Paulo — Revista Medica de Sao Paulo
Rev de Med (S Paulo) — Revista de Medicina (Sao Paulo)
Rev Med Suisse Romande — Revue Medicale de la Suisse Romande
Rev Med (Tirgu-Mures) — Revista Medicala (Tirgu-Mures) [*Romania*]
Rev Med Toulouse — Revue de Medecine de Toulouse
Rev Med Toulouse Suppl — Revue de Medecine de Toulouse. Supplement
Rev Med Tours — Revue de Medecine de Tours
Rev Med Trav — Revue de Medecine du Travail [*France*]
Rev Med Trop — Revista de Medicina Tropical
Rev Med Univ Fed Ceara — Revista de Medicina. Universidade Federal do Ceara
Rev Med Univ Navarra — Revista de Medicina. Universidade de Navarra
Rev Med Uruguay — Revista Medica del Uruguay
Rev Med (Valparaiso) — Revista de Medicina (Valparaiso)
Rev Med Veracruz — Revista Medica Veracruzana
Rev Med Vet — Revista de Medicina Veterinaria
Rev Med Vet (B Aires) — Revista de Medicina Veterinaria (Buenos Aires)
Rev Med Vet (Bogota) — Revista de Medicina Veterinaria (Bogota)
Rev Med Vet Escuela Montevideo — Revista de Medicina Veterinaria. Escuela de Montevideo
Rev Med Vet (Montev) — Revista de Medicina Veterinaria (Montevideo)
Rev Med Vet Mycol — Review of Medical and Veterinary Mycology
Rev Med Vet Parasitol (Maracay) — Revista de Medicina Veterinaria y Parasitologia (Maracay)
Rev Med Vet (Santiago) — Revista de Medicina Veterinaria (Santiago)
Rev Med Vet (Sao Paulo) — Revista de Medicina Veterinaria (Sao Paulo)
Rev Med Vet (Toulouse) — Revue de Medecine Veterinaire (Toulouse)
Rev Med Yucatan — Revista Medica de Yucatan
Rev Mens Asoc Rural Urug — Revista Mensual. Asociacion Rural del Uruguay
Rev Mens Blanchissage Blanchiment Apprets — Revue Mensuelle de Blanchissage, du Blanchiment, et des Apprets
Rev Mens Mal Enf — Revue Mensuelle des Maladies de l'Enfance
Rev Mens Suisse Odonto-Stomatol — Revue Mensuelle Suisse d'Odonto-Stomatologie
Rev Metal — Revista de Metalurgia
Rev Metall — Revue de Metallurgie [*Paris*]
Rev Metall Cah Inf Tech — Revue de Metallurgie. Cahiers d'Informations Techniques
Rev Metall (Paris) — Revue de Metallurgie (Paris)
Rev Metall (Paris) Part 1 — Revue de Metallurgie (Paris) Part 1. Memoires
Rev Metall (Paris) Part 2 — Revue de Metallurgie (Paris) Part 2. Extraits
Rev Metal (Madrid) — Revista de Metalurgia (Madrid)

Rev Metaph — Review of Metaphysics
Rev Metaph Morale — Revue de Metaphysique et de Morale
Rev Metaphy — Review of Metaphysics
Rev Metaphys Morale — Revue de Metaphysique et de Morale
Rev Meteorol — Revista Meteorologica
Rev Met Lit — Review of Metal Literature
Rev Met (Madrid) — Revista de Metalurgia (Madrid)
Rev Met Mor — Revue de Metaphysique et de Morale
Rev Met (Paris) — Revue de Metallurgie (Paris)
Rev Metrol Prat Leg — Revue de Metrologie Pratique et Legale
Rev Met Technol — Review of Metals Technology
Rev Mex Anestesiol — Revista Mexicana de Anestesiologia
Rev Mex Astron Astrof — Revista Mexicana de Astronomia y Astrofisica
Rev Mex Astron Astrofis — Revista Mexicana de Astronomia y Astrofisica
Rev Mex Astron y Astrofis — Revista Mexicana de Astronomia y Astrofisica
Rev Mex Cienc Med Biol — Revista Mexicana de Ciencias Medicas y
    Biologicas
Rev Mex Cir Ginecol Cancer — Revista Mexicana de Cirugia, Ginecologia, y
    Cancer
Rev Mex Constr — Revista Mexicana de la Construccion
Rev Mex Electr — Revista Mexicana de Electricidad
Rev Mex Fis — Revista Mexicana de Fisica
Rev Mex Fis Supl Ensenanza — Revista Mexicana de Fisica. Suplemento de
    Ensenanza
Rev Mex Fis Supl Fis Apl — Revista Mexicana de Fisica. Suplemento de Fisica
    Aplicada
Rev Mex Fis Supl Reactor — Revista Mexicana de Fisica. Suplemento del
    Reactor
Rev Mexicana Astronom Astrofis — Revista Mexicana de Astronomia y
    Astrofisica
Rev Mexicana Fis — Revista Mexicana de Fisica
Rev Mex Lab Clin — Revista Mexicana de Laboratorio Clinico
Rev Mex Pediatr — Revista Mexicana de Pediatria
Rev Mex Radiol — Revista Mexicana de Radiologia
Rev Mex Sociol — Revista Mexicana de Sociologia
Rev Mex Tuberc Apar Respir — Revista Mexicana de Tuberculosis y Aparto
    Respiratorio
Rev Mex Tuber Enferm Apar Respir — Revista Mexicana de Tuberculosis y
    Enfermedades del Aparato Respiratorio
Rev Mex Urol — Revista Mexicana de Urologia
Rev Micr El — Revista de Microscopia Electronica
Rev Microbiol — Revista de Microbiologia
Rev Microbiol Appl Agric Hyg Ind — Revue de Microbiologie Appliquee a
    l'Agriculture, a l'Hygiene, a l'Industrie
Rev Micropaleontol — Revue de Micropaleontologie
Rev Mil — Revista Militar
Rev Mil Med Vet — Revista Militar de Medicina Veterinaria
Rev Mil Remonta Vet — Revista Militar de Remonta e Veterinaria
Rev Mil Vet — Revista Militar de Veterinaria
Rev Mil Vet (Rio De Janeiro) — Revista Militar de Veterinaria (Rio De
    Janeiro)
Rev Min — Revista Mineria
Rev Minas — Revista de Minas
Rev Minas Hidrocarburos — Revista de Minas e Hidrocarburos
Rev Minelor — Revista Minelor
Rev Minelor (Bucharest) — Revista Minelor (Bucharest)
Rev Min Eng — Revista Mineira de Engenharia
Rev Minera Geol Mineral — Revista Minera, Geologia, y Mineralogia
Rev Mineral — Reviews in Mineralogy
Rev Minera y Petrolera — Revista Minera y Petrolera
Rev Min Geol Mineral — Revista Minera, Geologia, y Mineralogia
Rev Mktg Agric Econ (Sydney) — Review of Marketing and Agricultural
    Economics (Sydney)
Rev M Mec — Revue M - Mecanique
Rev Modern Phys — Reviews of Modern Physics
Rev Mod Phys — Reviews of Modern Physics
Rev Moyen A — Revue du Moyen-Age Latin
Rev du Moyen-Age Latin — Revue du Moyen-Age Latin
Rev M Phys — Reviews of Modern Physics
Rev Munic Eng — Revista Municipal de Engenharia
Rev Mus — Revue Musicale
Rev Mus Chilena — Revista Musical Chilena
Rev Mus Hist Nat Mendoza — Revista. Museo de Historia Natural de
    Mendoza
Rev Music — Revue de Musicologie
Rev Musical — Revue Musicale
Rev Music Chilena — Revista Musical Chilena
Rev Mus La Plata — Revista. Museo de La Plata
Rev Mus La Plata Secc Antropol — Revista. Museo de La Plata. Seccion
    Antropologia
Rev Mus La Plata Secc Bot — Revista. Museo de La Plata. Seccion Botanica
Rev Mus La Plata Secc Geol — Revista. Museo de La Plata. Seccion Geologia
Rev Mus La Plata Secc Paleontol — Revista. Museo de La Plata. Seccion
    Paleontologia
Rev Mus La Plata Secc Zool — Revista. Museo de La Plata. Seccion Zoologia
Rev Muz — Revista Muzeelor

Rev Muz M Mon — Revista Muzeelor si Monumentelor. Seria Monumente
    Istorice si Arta
Rev Muz M Muz — Revista Muzeelor si Monumentelor. Seria Muzee
Rev Muz Monum Muz — Revista Muzeelor si Monumentelor. Seria Muzee
Rev Mycol — Revue de Mycologie
Rev Mycol (Paris) — Revue de Mycologie (Paris)
Rev Mycol (Paris) Suppl Colon — Revue de Mycologie. Supplement Colonial
    (Paris)
RevN — Revue Nouvelle [Paris]
Rev Nac Agr — Revista Nacional de Agricultura
Rev Nac Agric (Bogota) — Revista Nacional de Agricultura (Bogota)
Rev Nat Lit — Review of National Literatures
Rev Neurol — Revue Neurologique
Rev Neurol B Aires — Revista Neurologica de Buenos Aires
Rev Neurol Buenos Aires — Revista Neurologica de Buenos Aires
Rev Neurol Clin (Madrid) — Revista de Neurologia Clinica (Madrid)
Rev Neurol (Paris) — Revue Neurologique (Paris)
Rev Neurops — Revue de Neuropsychiatrie Infantile et d'Hygiene Mentale de
    l'Enfance
Rev Neuro-Psiquiatr — Revista de Neuro-Psiquiatria
Rev Neuropsychiatr Infant — Revue de Neuropsychiatrie Infantile et d'Hygiene
    Mentale de l'Enfance
Rev Neuropsychiatr Infant Hyg Ment Enfance — Revue de Neuropsychiatrie
    Infantile et d'Hygiene Mentale de l'Enfance
Rev Neurosci — Reviews of Neuroscience
Rev Nickel — Revue du Nickel
Rev Nord — Revue du Nord
Rev du Not — Revue du Notariat
Rev Not — Revue du Notariat
Rev Notariat — Revue du Notariat
Rev du Notariat — Revue du Notariat
Rev Nouv — Revue Nouvelle [Belgium]
RevNum — Revue Numismatique
Rev Num Arg — Revista Numismatica Argentina
Rev Nutr Anim — Revista de Nutricion Animal
Rev Oak Ridge Natl Lab (US) — Review. Oak Ridge National Laboratory
    (United States)
Rev Obras Pub — Revista de Obras Publicas
Rev Obras Publicas — Revista de Obras Publicas
Rev Obras Sanit Nac (Argent) — Revista de Obras Sanitarias de la Nacion
    (Argentina)
Rev Obras Sanit Nac (B Aires) — Revista de Obras Sanitarias de la Nacion
    (Buenos Aires)
Rev Obstet Ginecol Venez — Revista de Obstetricia y Ginecologia de Venezuela
Rev Oc — Revista de Occidente
Rev Occidente — Revista de Occidente
Rev O Chr — Revue de l'Orient Chretien
Rev Ocrotirea Mediului Inconjurator Nat Terr Nat — Revista Ocrotirea
    Mediului Inconjurator Natura. Terra Natura
Rev Odontoestomatol — Revista Odonto-Estomatologica
Rev Odontoimplantol — Revue Odonto-Implantologique
Rev Odontol Circ Odontol Parag — Revista Odontologica. Circulo de
    Odontologos del Paraguay
Rev Odontol (Cordoba) — Revista Odontologica (Cordoba)
Rev Odontol Costa Rica — Revista Odontologica de Costa Rica
Rev Odontol Ecuat — Revista Odontologica Ecuatoriana
Rev Odontol Parana — Revista Odontologica do Parana
Rev Odonto Stomatol — Revue d'Odonto-Stomatologie
Rev Odonto-Stomatol (Bord) — Revue d'Odonto-Stomatologie (Bordeaux)
Rev Odonto-Stomatol Midi Fr — Revue d'Odonto-Stomatologie du Midi de la
    France
Rev Odonto-Stomatol (Paris) — Revue d'Odonto-Stomatologie (Paris)
Rev Of Fed Med Ecuador — Revista Oficial. Federacion Medica del Ecuador
Rev Oka — Revue d'Oka
Revol Wld — Revolutionary World
Revol World — Revolutionary World
Rev Opt — Revue d'Optique Theorique et Instrumentale
Rev d'Optique — Revue d'Optique
Rev Opt Theor Instrum — Revue d'Optique Theorique et Instrumentale
    [France]
Rev Orl — Revista de Otorrinolaringologia
Rev Orthop Dento-Faciale — Revue d'Orthopedie Dento-Faciale
Rev Ortop Traumatol Latinoam — Revista de Ortopedia y Traumatologia
    Latinoamericana
Rev Oto-Neuro-Oftalmol Cir Neurol Sud-Am — Revista de Oto-Neuro-
    Oftalmologica y de Cirugia Neurologica Sud-Americana
Rev Oto-Neuro-Ophtalmol — Revue d'Oto-Neuro-Ophtalmologie
Rev Oto-Neuro-Ophtalmol (Paris) — Revue d'Oto-Neuro-Ophtalmologie
    (Paris)
Rev Otorrinolaringol — Revista de Otorrinolaringologia
Rev Padurilor — Revista Padurilor
Rev Padurilor-Ind Lemnului Ser Ind Lemnului — Revista Padurilor-Industria
    Lemnului. Seria Industria Lemnului [Hungary]
Rev Padurilor-Ind Lemnului Ser Silvic Exploatarea Padurilor — Revista
    Padurilor-Industria Lemnului. Seria Silvicultura si Exploatarea
    Padurilor

Rev Palaeobot Palynol — Review of Palaeobotany and Palynology
Rev Palaeobot Palynology — Review of Palaeobotany and Palynology
Rev Palae P — Review of Palaeobotany and Palynology
Rev Palais Decouv — Revue du Palais de la Decouverte [*France*]
Rev Palud Med Trop — Revue du Paludisme et de Medecine Tropicale
Rev Path Comp — Revue de Pathologie Comparee
Rev Pathol Comp — Revue de Pathologie Comparee
Rev Pathol Comp Hyg Gen — Revue de Pathologie Comparee et Hygiene Generale
Rev Pathol Comp Med Exp — Revue de Pathologie Comparee et de Medecine Experimentale [*France*]
Rev Pathol Veg Entomol Agr France — Revue de Pathologie Vegetale et d'Entomologie Agricole de France
Rev Pathol Veg Entomol Agric Fr — Revue de Pathologie Vegetale et d'Entomologie Agricole de France
Rev Path Veg et Entom Agric — Revue de Pathologie Vegetale et d'Entomologie Agricole
Rev Patronato Biol Anim — Revista del Patronato de Biologia Animal
Rev Paul Med — Revista Paulista de Medicina
Rev Pediatr — Revue de Pediatrie
Rev Pediatr Obstet Ginecol — Revista de Pediatrie, Obstetrica, si Ginecologie
Rev Pediatr Obstet Ginecol Ser Obstet Ginecol — Revista de Pediatrie, Obstetrica, si Ginecologie. Seria Obstetrica si Ginecologie
Rev Pediatr Obstet Ginecol Ser Pediatr — Revista de Pediatrie, Obstetrica, si Ginecologie. Seria Pediatria
Rev Perinat Med — Reviews in Perinatal Medicine
Rev Peru Entomol — Revista Peruana de Entomologia
Rev Peru Entomol Agr — Revista Peruana de Entomologia Agricola
Rev Peru Entomol Agric — Revista Peruana de Entomologia Agricola
Rev Peru Salud Publica — Revista Peruana de Salud Publica
Rev Peru Tuberc Enferm Respir — Revista Peruana de Tuberculosis y Enfermedades Respiratorias
Rev Petrolifere — Revue Petrolifere
Rev Pet Technol (London) — Reviews of Petroleum Technology (London)
RevPF — Revista Portuguesa de Filosofia
Rev Pharm — Revue Pharmaceutique
Rev Pharmacol Ter Exp — Revue de Pharmacologie et de Therapeutique Experimentale
Rev Pharm Liban — Revue Pharmaceutique Libanaise
Rev Ph Ch J — Review of Physical Chemistry of Japan
Rev Phil — Revue de Philologie, de Litterature, et d'Histoire Anciennes
Rev Phil Fr — Revue Philosophique de la France et de l'Etranger
Rev Phil Louvain — Revue Philosophique de Louvain
Rev Philol — Revue de Philologie
Rev Philos — Revue Philosophique de Louvain
Rev Philos Fr Etrang — Revue Philosophique de la France et de l'Etranger
Rev Philos Louv — Revue Philosophique de Louvain
Rev Phonet Appl — Revue de Phonetique Appliquee
Rev Phys Acad Repub Pop Roum — Revue de Physique. Academie de la Republique Populaire Roumaine [*Romania*]
Rev Phys Ap — Revue de Physique Appliquee
Rev Phys Appl — Revue de Physique Appliquee
Rev Phys Appl (Suppl J Phys) — Revue de Physique Appliquee (Supplement to Journal de Physique)
Rev Phys B — Reviews of Physiology, Biochemistry, and Pharmacology
Rev Phys Chem Jpn — Review of Physical Chemistry of Japan
Rev Physiol Biochem Exp Pharmacol — Reviews of Physiology, Biochemistry, and Experimental Pharmacology
Rev Physiol Biochem Pharmacol — Reviews of Physiology, Biochemistry, and Pharmacology
Rev Phys Technol — Review of Physics in Technology [*United Kingdom*]
Rev Phytother — Revue de Phytotherapie
Rev Planeacion Desarrollo — Revista de Planeacion y Desarrollo
Rev Plant Pathol — Review of Plant Pathology
Rev Plant Prot Res — Review of Plant Protection Research
Rev Plasma Phys — Reviews of Plasma Physics
Rev Plast (Madrid) — Revista de Plasticos (Madrid)
Rev Plast Mod — Revista de Plasticos Modernos
Rev Pol — Review of Politics
Rev Pol Acad Sci — Review. Polish Academy of Sciences
Rev Polarogr — Review of Polarography
Rev Polarogr (Jpn) — Review of Polarography (Japan)
Rev Policlin (Caracas) — Revista de la Policlinica (Caracas)
Rev Polit — Review of Politics
Rev Politec — Revista Politecnica
Rev Polym Technol — Reviews in Polymer Technology
Rev Polytech — Revue Polytechnique [*Switzerland*]
Rev Po Quim — Revista Portuguesa de Quimica
Rev Port Cienc Vet — Revista Portuguesa de Ciencias Veterinarias
Rev Port Estomatol Cir Maxilofac — Revista Portuguesa de Estomatologia e Cirurgia Maxilofacial
Rev Port Farm — Revista Portuguesa de Farmacia
Rev Port Filosof — Revista Portuguesa de Filosofia
Rev Port Pediatr — Revista Portuguesa de Pediatria
Rev Port Quim — Revista Portuguesa de Quimica
Rev Port Quim (Lisbon) — Revista Portuguesa de Quimica (Lisbon)

Rev Port Zool Biol Geral — Revista Portuguesa de Zoologia e Biologia Geral
Rev Powder Metall Phys Ceram — Reviews on Powder Metallurgy and Physical Ceramics
Rev PR — Revista de Derecho Puertorriqueno
Rev Prat — Revue du Praticien
Rev Prat Biol Appl Clin Ther — Revue Pratique de Biologie Appliquee a la Clinique et a la Therapeutique
Rev Prat Controle Ind — Revue Pratique du Controle Industriel [*France*]
Rev Prat Froid — Revue Pratique du Froid [*France*] [*Later, Journal RPF*]
Rev Prat Froid Cond Air — Revue Pratique du Froid et du Conditionnement de l'Air [*Later, Journal RPF*]
Rev Prat Mal Pays Chands — Revue Pratique des Maladies des Pays Chands
Rev Prod Chim — Revue des Produits Chimiques
Rev Prod Chim Actual Sci Reunis — Revue des Produits Chimiques et l'Actualite Scientifique Reunis
Rev Prog Color Relat Top — Review of Progress in Coloration and Related Topics
Rev Prot — Revue de la Protection [*France*]
Rev Prum Obchodu — Revue Prumyslu a Obchodu [*Czechoslovakia*]
Rev Psicol — Revista de Psicologia
Rev Psicol Gen Apl — Revista de Psicologia General y Aplicada
Rev Psiquiatr — Revista de Psiquiatria
Rev Psiquiatr Peru — Revista Psiquiatrica Peruana
Rev Psy App — Revue de Psychologie Appliquee
Rev Pub Dat — Review of Public Data Use
Rev Pub Data Use — Review of Public Data Use
Rev Pure Appl Chem — Reviews of Pure and Applied Chemistry
Rev Pure Appl Pharmacol Sci — Reviews in Pure and Applied Pharmacological Sciences
Rev Questions Sci — Revue des Questions Scientifiques
Rev Quest Sci — Revue des Questions Scientifiques
Rev Quim — Revista Quimica
Rev Quim Farm (Rio De Janeiro) — Revista de Quimica e Farmacia (Rio De Janeiro)
Rev Quim Farm (Santiago) — Revista Quimico-Farmaceutica (Santiago)
Rev Quim Farm (Tegucigalpa) — Revista de Quimica y Farmacia (Tegucigalpa)
Rev Quim Ind (Buenos Aires) — Revista de Quimica Industrial (Buenos Aires)
Rev Quim Ind (Rio De Janeiro) — Revista de Quimica Industrial (Rio De Janeiro)
Rev Quim Ing Quim — Revista de Quimica e Ingenieria Quimica
Rev Quim Pura Apl — Revista de Quimica Pura e Aplicada
Rev Quim Text — Revista de Quimica Textil
RevQum — Revue de Qumran
RevR — Revue Romane
Rev R Acad Cienc Exactas Fis Nat Madr — Revista. Real Academia de Ciencias Exactas, Fisicas, y Naturales de Madrid
Rev R Acad Farm Barcelona — Revista. Real Academia de Farmacia de Barcelona
Rev Radic Polit Econ — Review of Radical Political Economics
Rev Radio Res Lab — Review. Radio Research Laboratories
Rev React Species Chem React — Reviews on Reactive Species in Chemical Reactions
Rev Real Acad Cienc Exact Fis Natur Madrid — Real Academia de Ciencias Exactas, Fisicas, y Naturales de Madrid. Revista
Rev Real Acad Ci Exact Fis Natur Madrid — Revista. Real Academia de Ciencias Exactas, Fisicas, y Naturales de Madrid
Rev Relig — Review for Religious
Rev Rel Res — Review of Religious Research
Rev Rep Inf Cent Pol AEC — Review Report Information Center. Polish Atomic Energy Commission
Revs Revs Australas Ed — Review of Reviews. Australasian Edition
Rev Rhum — Revue du Rhumatisme et des Maladies Osteo-Articulaires
Rev Rhum Mal Osteo-Artic — Revue du Rhumatisme et des Maladies Osteo-Articulaires
Rev River Plate — Review of the River Plate
Rev Ro Bioc — Revue Roumaine de Biochimie
Rev "Roche" Farm — Revista "Roche" de Farmacia
Rev Ro Chim — Revue Roumaine de Chimie
Rev Roman — Revue Romane
Rev Romande Agric Vitic Arboric — Revue Romande d'Agriculture, de Viticulture, et d'Arboriculture
Rev Romande Agr Viticult Arboricult — Revue Romande d'Agriculture, de Viticulture, et d'Arboriculture
Rev Ro Phys — Revue Roumaine de Physique
Rev Roumaine Linguist — Revue Roumaine de Linguistique
Rev Roumaine Math Pures Appl — Revue Roumaine de Mathematiques Pures et Appliquees
Rev Roumaine Phys — Revue Roumaine de Physique
Rev Roumaine Sci Soc — Revue Roumaine des Sciences Sociales. Serie de Sciences Juridiques
Rev Roumaine Sci Tech Ser Electrotech Energet — Revue Roumaine des Sciences Techniques. Serie Electrotechnique et Energetique
Rev Roumaine Sci Tech Ser Mec Appl — Revue Roumaine des Sciences Techniques. Serie de Mecanique Appliquee
Rev Roum Biochim — Revue Roumaine de Biochimie
Rev Roum Biol — Revue Roumaine de Biologie

Rev Roum Biol Ser Biol Veg — Revue Roumaine de Biologie. Serie Biologie Vegetale [Romania]
Rev Roum Biol Ser Bot — Revue Roumaine de Biologie. Serie Botanique
Rev Roum Biol Ser Zool — Revue Roumaine de Biologie. Serie Zoologie
Rev Roum Chim — Revue Roumaine de Chimie
Rev Roum Embryol — Revue Roumaine d'Embryologie
Rev Roum Embryol Cytol Ser Embryol — Revue Roumaine d'Embryologie et de Cytologie. Serie d'Embryologie
Rev Roum Endocrinol — Revue Roumaine d'Endocrinologie
Rev Roum Geol Geophys Geogr Ser Geogr — Revue Roumaine de Geologie, Geophysique, et Geographie. Serie de Geographie
Rev Roum Geol Geophys Geogr Ser Geol — Revue Roumaine de Geologie, Geophysique, et Geographie. Serie de Geologie
Rev Roum Geol Geophys Geogr Ser Geophys — Revue Roumaine de Geologie, Geophysique, et Geographie. Serie de Geophysique
Rev Roum H — Revue Roumaine d'Histoire
Rev Roum Hist — Revue Roumaine d'Histoire
Rev Roum Inframicrobiol — Revue Roumaine d'Inframicrobiologie
Rev Roum Math Pures Appl — Revue Roumaine de Mathematiques Pures et Appliquees
Rev Roum Med — Revue Roumaine de Medecine
Rev Roum Med Endocrinol — Revue Roumaine de Medecine. Endocrinologie
Rev Roum Med Interne — Revue Roumaine de Medecine Interne [Later, Revue Roumaine de Medecine. Medecine Interne]
Rev Roum Med Med Interne — Revue Roumaine de Medecine. Medecine Interne
Rev Roum Med Neurol Psychiatr — Revue Roumaine de Medecine. Neurologie et Psychiatrie
Rev Roum Med Virol — Revue Roumaine de Medecine. Virologie
Rev Roum Metall — Revue Roumaine de Metallurgie
Rev Roum Morphol Embryol — Revue Roumaine de Morphologie et d'Embryologie
Rev Roum Morphol Embryol Physiol Morphol Embryol — Revue Roumaine de Morphologie, d'Embryologie, et de Physiologie. Morphologie et Embryologie
Rev Roum Morphol Embryol Physiol Physiol — Revue Roumaine de Morphologie, d'Embryologie, et de Physiologie. Physiologie
Rev Roum Neurol — Revue Roumaine de Neurologie [Later, Revue Roumaine de Medecine. Serie Neurologie et Psychiatrie]
Rev Roum Neurol Psychiatr — Revue Roumaine de Neurologie et de Psychiatrie [Later, Revue Roumaine de Medecine. Serie Neurologie et Psychiatrie]
Rev Roum Phys — Revue Roumaine de Physique
Rev Roum Physiol — Revue Roumaine de Physiologie [Later, Revue Roumaine de Morphologie, d'Embryologie, et de Physiologie]
Rev Roum Sci Soc Philos Logique — Revue Roumaine des Sciences Sociales. Serie de Philosophie et de Logique
Rev Roum Sci Tech Mec Appl — Revue Roumaine des Sciences Techniques. Serie de Mecanique Applique [Romania]
Rev Roum Sci Tech Ser Electrotech Energ — Revue Roumaine des Sciences Techniques. Serie Electrotechnique et Energetique
Rev Roum Sci Tech Ser Mec Appl — Revue Roumaine des Sciences Techniques. Serie de Mecanique Appliquee
Rev Roum Sci Tech Ser Met — Revue Roumaine des Sciences Techniques. Serie de Metallurgie
Rev Roum Virol — Revue Roumaine de Virologie
Rev Sanid Aeronaut — Revista de Sanidad de Aeronautica
Rev Sanid Fuerzas Policiales — Revista de la Sanidad de las Fuerzas Policiales
Rev Sanid Hig Publica — Revista de Sanidad e Higiene Publica
Rev Sanid Hig Publica (Madr) — Revista de Sanidad e Higiene Publica (Madrid)
Rev Sanid Mil (Argent) — Revista de la Sanidad Militar (Argentina)
Rev Sanid Polic — Revista de la Sanidad de Policia
Rev Sanit Mil — Revista Sanitara Militara
Rev San Mil (Buenos Aires) — Revista de la Sanidad Militar (Buenos Aires)
Rev Sao Paulo Braz Univ Fac Med Vet Zootec — Revista. Sao Paulo Universidade. Faculdade de Medicina Veterinaria e Zootecnia
Rev Saude — Revista Saude
Rev Saude Publica — Revista de Saude Publica
Rev Sci — Revue Scientifique
Rev Sci Bourbonnais Cent Fr — Revue Scientifique du Bourbonnais et du Centre de la France
Rev Sci Ed — Revue des Sciences de l'Education
Rev Scient (Paris) — Revue Scientifique (Paris)
Rev Sci Hum — Revue des Sciences Humaines
Rev Sci Ins — Review of Scientific Instruments
Rev Sci Instr — Review of Scientific Instruments
Rev Sci Instrum — Review of Scientific Instruments
Rev Sci Med — Revue des Sciences Medicales
Rev Sci Nat Auvergne — Revue des Sciences Naturelles d'Auvergne
Rev Sci Natur Auvergne — Revue des Sciences Naturelles d'Auvergne
Rev Sci Ph — Revue des Sciences Philosophiques et Theologiques
Rev Sci Phil Theol — Revue des Sciences Philosophiques et Theologiques
Rev Sci Rel — Revue des Sciences Religieuses
RevScPhTh — Revue des Sciences Philosophiques et Theologiques
RevScR — Regue des Sciences Religieuses [Strasbourg/Paris]

RevScRel — Revue des Sciences Religieuses [Strasbourg/Paris]
Rev Sec Reg — Review of Securities Regulation
Rev Ser IAEA — Review Series. International Atomic Energy Agency
Rev Serv Espec Saude Publica — Revista. Servicio Especial de Saude Publica
Rev Serv Nac Min Geol (Argent) — Revista. Servicio Nacional Minero Geologico (Argentina)
Rev Serv Nac Salud — Revista. Servicio Nacional de Salud
Rev SESDA — Revue du SESDA [Secretariat de Sante Dentaire de l'Afrique]
Rev SESP — Revista. Servicio Especial de Saude Publica
Revs Geophys Space Phys — Reviews of Geophysics and Space Physics
Rev Shorthorn — Revista Shorthorn
Rev Sifilogr Leprol Dermatol — Revista de Sifilografia, Leprologia, y Dermatologia
Rev Silicon Germanium Tin Lead Compd — Reviews on Silicon, Germanium, Tin, and Lead Compounds
Rev Sind Estad — Revista Sindical de Estadistica
Rev Soc Argent Biol — Revista. Sociedad Argentina de Biologia
Rev Soc Argent Neurol y Psiquiat — Revista. Sociedad Argentina de Neurologia y Psiquiatria
Rev Soc Biom Hum — Revue. Societe de Biometre Humaine
Rev Soc Boliv Hist Nat — Revista. Sociedad Boliviana de Historia Natural
Rev Soc Bras Agron — Revista. Sociedade Brasileira de Agronomia
Rev Soc Bras Med Trop — Revista. Sociedade Brasileira de Medicina Tropical
Rev Soc Bras Quim — Revista. Sociedade Brasileira de Quimica
Rev Soc Bras Zootec — Revista. Sociedade Brasileira de Zootecnia
Rev Soc Cient Parag — Revista. Sociedad Cientifica del Paraguay
Rev Soc Colomb Endocrinol — Revista. Sociedad Colombiana de Endocrinologia
Rev Soc Cubana Bot — Revista. Sociedad Cubana de Botanica
Rev Soc Cubana Ing — Revista. Sociedad Cubana de Ingenieros
Rev Soc Ec — Review of Social Economy
Rev Soc Entomol Argent — Revista. Sociedad Entomologica Argentina
Rev Soc Geol Argent — Revista. Sociedad Geologica Argentina
Rev Soc L — Review of Socialist Law
Rev Soc Med Argent — Revista. Sociedad Medica Argentina
Rev Soc Med Cir Sao Jose Rio Preto — Revista. Sociedade de Medicina e Cirurgia de Sao Jose Do Rio Preto
Rev Soc Med Int — Revista. Sociedad de Medicina Interna
Rev Soc Med Vet (Buenos Aires) — Revista. Sociedad de Medicina Veterinaria (Buenos Aires)
Rev Soc Med Vet Chile — Revista. Sociedad de Medicina Veterinaria de Chile
Rev Soc Mex Hig — Revista. Sociedad Mexicana de Higiene
Rev Soc Mex Hist Nat — Revista. Sociedad Mexicana de Historia Natural
Rev Soc Mex Hist Natur — Revista. Sociedad Mexicana de Historia Natural
Rev Soc Mex Lepid AC — Revista. Sociedad Mexicana de Lepidopterologia. AC
Rev Soc Mex Lepidopterol AC — Revista. Sociedad Mexicana de Lepidopterologia. AC
Rev Soc Pediatr Litoral — Revista. Sociedad de Pediatria del Litoral
Rev Soc Quim Mex — Revista. Sociedad Quimica de Mexico
Rev Soc R Belge Ing Ind — Revue. Societe Royale Belge des Ingenieurs et des Industriels
Rev Soc Rural Rosario — Revista. Sociedad Rural de Rosario
Rev Soc Savantes Haute Normandie — Revue des Societes Savantes de Haute-Normandie
Rev Soc Sci Hyg Aliment Aliment Ration Homme — Revue. Societe Scientifique d'Hygiene Alimentaire et de l'Alimentation Rationnelle de l'Homme
Rev Soc Venez Cardiol — Revista. Sociedad Venezolana de Cardiologia
Rev Soc Venez Hist Med — Revista. Sociedad Venezolana de Historia de la Medicina
Rev Soc Venez Quim — Revista. Sociedad Venezolana de Quimica
Rev Soldadura — Revista de Soldadura
Rev Soudre Lastijdschrift — Revue de la Soudure/Lastijdschrift
Rev Soudure — Revue de la Soudure/Lastijdschrift [Brussels]
Rev Soudure Autogene — Revue de la Soudure Autogene
Rev Soudure/Lastijdschrift — Revue de la Soudure/Lastijdschrift
Rev Sov Med Sci — Review of Soviet Medical Sciences
Rev Sport Leisure — Review of Sport and Leisure
RevSR — Revue des Sciences Religieuses [Strasbourg/Paris]
Rev Stat Ap — Revue de Statistique Applique
Rev Statist Appl — Revue de Statistique Appliquee
Rev Stiint "V Adamachi" — Revista Stiintifica "V. Adamachi"
Rev Stomatol — Revue de Stomatologie [France] [Later, Revue de Stomatologie et de Chirurgie Maxillo-Faciale]
Rev Stomatol Chir Maxillo-Fac — Revue de Stomatologie et de Chirurgie Maxillo-Faciale
Rev Stomato-Odontol Nord Fr — Revue Stomato-Odontologique du Nord de la France
Rev Sudam Bot — Revista Sudamericana de Botanica
Rev Sud-Am Cien Med — Revista Sud-Americana de Ciencias Medicas
Rev Sud-Am Endocrin — Revista Sud-Americana de Endocrinologia
Rev Sud-Am Endocrinol Immunol Quimioter — Revista Sud-Americana de Endocrinologia, Immunologia, y Quimioterapia
Rev Sudam Morfol — Revista Sudamericana de Morfologia
Rev Suisse Agric — Revue Suisse d'Agriculture

Rev Suisse Gynecol Obstet — Revue Suisse de Gynecologie et d'Obstetrique
Rev Suisse Gynecol Obstet Suppl — Revue Suisse de Gynecologie et d'Obstetrique. Supplementum
Rev Suisse Hydrol — Revue Suisse d'Hydrologie
Rev Suisse Med Sports — Revue Suisse de Medecine des Sports
Rev Suisse Psychol Pure Appl — Revue Suisse de Psychologie Pure et Appliquee
Rev Suisse Vitic Arboric — Revue Suisse de Viticulture et Arboriculture
Rev Suisse Vitic Arboric Hortic — Revue Suisse de Viticulture et Arboriculture. Horticulture
Rev Suisse Zool — Revue Suisse de Zoologie
Rev Surg — Review of Surgery
Rev Syniatrica — Revista Syniatrica
Revta Agric (Habana) — Revista de Agricultura (Habana)
Revta Agric (Piracicaba) — Revista de Agricultura (Piracicaba)
Revta Agron NE Argent — Revista Agronomica del Noroeste Argentino
Revta Biol — Revista de Biologia
Revta Biol Trop — Revista de Biologia Tropical
Revta Bras Biol — Revista Brasileira de Biologia
Revta Bras Ent — Revista Brasileira de Entomologia
Revta Bras Pesquisas Med Biol — Revista Brasileira de Pesquisas Medicas e Biologicas
Revta Ent (Rio De J) — Revista de Entomologia (Rio De Janeiro)
Revta Esp Fisiol — Revista Espanola de Fisiologia
Revta Fac Agron Univ Cent Venez — Revista. Facultad de Agronomia. Universidad Central de Venezuela
Revta Fac Agron Univ Nac La Plata — Revista. Facultad de Agronomia y Veterinaria. Universidad Nacional de La Plata
Revta Fac Agron Univ Repub (Urug) — Revista. Facultad de Agronomia. Universidad de la Republica (Uruguay)
Revta Fac Agron Vet Univ B Aires — Revista. Facultad de Agronomia y Veterinaria. Universidad de Buenos Aires
Revta Fac Cienc Agrar Univ Nac Cuyo — Revista. Facultad de Ciencias Agrarias. Universidad Nacional de Cuyo
Revta Fac Farm Bioquim S Paulo — Revista. Faculdade de Farmacia e Bioquimica. Universidade de Sao Paulo
Revta Floresta — Revista Floresta
Revta Hort Vitic — Revista de Horticultura si Viticultura
Revta Ind Agric (Tucuman) — Revista Industrial y Agricola (Tucuman)
Revta Interam Psicologia — Revista Interamericana de Psicologia
Revta Invest Agropec (B Aires) — Revista de Investigaciones Agropecuarias (Buenos Aires)
Revta Med Vet Parasit (Caracas) — Revista de Medicina Veterinaria y Parasitologia (Caracas)
Revta Mus Argent Cienc Nat Bernardina Rivadavia Zool — Revista. Museo Argentino de Ciencias Naturales Bernardina Rivadavia. Zoologia
Revta Padur — Revista Padurilor
Revta Peru Ent Agric — Revista Peruana de Entomologia Agricola
Revta Psicol Norm Patol — Revista de Psicologia Normal e Patologica
Revta Stiint Vet — Revista Stiintelor Veterinare
Revta Univ Auton G R Moreno — Revista. Universidad Autonoma Gabriel Rene Moreno
Revta Univ Univ Catol Chile — Revista Universitaria. Universidad Catolica de Chile
Rev Tax Indiv — Review of Taxation of Individuals
Rev Tec — Revista Tecnica
Rev Tec Col Ing Agron Mex — Revista Tecnica. Colegio de Ingenieros Agronomos de Mexico
Rev Tech Batim Constr Ind — Revue Technique du Batiment et des Constructions Industrielles [*France*]
Rev Tech Ind Aliment — Revue Technique de l'Industrie Alimentaire
Rev Tech Ind Cuir — Revue Technique des Industries du Cuir
Rev Tech Luxemb — Revue Technique Luxembourgeoise
Rev Tech Thomson CSF — Revue Technique Thomson - CSF
Rev Tec Inst Nac Electron — Revista Tecnica. Instituto Nacional de Electronica
Rev Tec Intevep — Revista Tecnica INTEVEP [*Instituto de Tecnologia Venezolana del Petroleo*]
Rev Tecn Fac Ingr Univ Zulia — Revista Tecnica. Facultad de Ingenieria. Universidad del Zulia
Rev Tecnol Med — Revista de Tecnologia Medica
Rev Tec Sulzer — Revista Tecnica Sulzer [*Switzerland*]
Rev Tec Text Vestido — Revista Tecnica Textil-Vestido
Rev Tec Yacimientos Pet Fiscales Boliv — Revista Tecnica. Yacimientos Petroliferos Fiscales Bolivianos
Rev Tec Zulia Univ — Revista Tecnica. Zulia University
Rev Teilhard de Chardin — Revue Teilhard de Chardin
Rev Telecommun — Revue des Telecommunications [*France*]
Rev Telecomun (Madrid) — Revista de Telecomunicacion (Madrid)
Rev Telegr Electron — Revista Telegrafica Electronica
Rev Text (Ghent) — Revue Textilis (Ghent)
Rev Textile Progr — Review of Textile Progress
Rev Text (Paris) — Revue Textile (Paris)
Rev Text Tiba — Revue Textile Tiba
Rev Theobroma — Revista Theobroma
Rev Theol Phil — Revue de Theologie et de Philosophie

Rev Ther — Revue Therapeutique
Rev Therap Med-Chir — Revue de Therapeutique Medico-Chirurgicale
Rev Thomiste — Revue Thomiste
Rev Tisiol Neumonol — Revista de Tisiologia y Neumonologia
Rev Trab — Revista de Trabajo
Rev Trach — Revue du Trachome
Rev Transp Telecomun — Revista Transporturilor si Telecomunicatiilor [*Romania*]
Rev Trav Inst Peches Marit — Revue des Travaux. Institut des Peches Maritimes
Rev Trimest Can — Revue Trimestrielle Canadienne
Rev Trimestr de Droit Eur — Revue Trimestrielle de Droit Europeen
Rev Trimestrielle Canadienne — Revue Trimestrielle Canadienne
Rev Tuberc — Revue de Tuberculose
Rev Tuberc Pneumol — Revue de Tuberculose et de Pneumologie [*Later, Revue Francaise des Maladies Respiratoires*]
Rev Turq Hyg Biol Exp — Revue Turque d'Hygiene et de Biologie Experimentale
Rev Tussock Grassl Mt Lands Inst — Review. Tussock Grasslands and Mountain Lands Institute
Revue Agric (Brux) — Revue de l'Agriculture (Bruxelles)
Revue Agric Nouv Caled — Revue Agricole de la Nouvelle-Caledonie et Dependances
Revue Can Biol — Revue Canadienne de Biologie
Revue Comp Anim — Revue du Comportement Animal
Revue Ferment Ind Aliment — Revue des Fermentations et des Industries Alimentaires
Revue For Fr — Revue Forestiere Francaise
Revue Fr Allergol — Revue Francaise d'Allergologie [*Later, Revue Francaise d'Allergologie et d'Immunologie Clinique*]
Revue Fr Allergol Immunol Clin — Revue Francaise d'Allergologie et d'Immunologie Clinique
Revue Fr Apic — Revue Francaise d'Apiculture
Revue Fr Geront — Revue Francaise de Gerontologie
Revue Gen Bot — Revue Generale de Botanique
Revue Gen Gaz — Revue Generale du Gaz [*Belgium*]
Revue Geogr Phys Geol Dyn — Revue de Geographie Physique et de Geologie Dynamique
Revue Geol Dyn Geogr Phys — Revue de Geologie Dynamique et de Geographie Physique [*France*]
Revue Int Apic — Revue Internationale d'Apiculture
Revue Lux — Revue Trimestrielle d'Etudes Linguistiques, Folkloriques, et Toponymiques (Luxembourg)
Revue Med Liege — Revue Medicale de Liege
Revue Med Vet — Revue Medicale et Veterinaire
Revue Oka — Revue d'Oka. Agronomie. Medicine. Veterinaire
Revue Path Comp — Revue de Pathologie Comparee
Revue Path Comp Hyg Gen — Revue de Pathologie Comparee et Hygiene Generale
Revue Path Gen Physiol Clin — Revue de Pathologie Generale et de Physiologie Clinique
Revue Path Veg Ent Agric Fr — Revue de Pathologie Vegetale et d'Entomologie Agricole de France
Revue Quest Scient — Revue des Questions Scientifiques
Revue Romande Agric Vitic Arboric — Revue Romande d'Agriculture, de Viticulture, et d'Arboriculture
Revue Roum Biochim — Revue Roumaine de Biochimie
Revue Roum Biol Ser Bot — Revue Roumaine de Biologie. Serie Botanique
Revue Suisse Zool — Revue Suisse de Zoologie
Revue Zool Afr — Revue de Zoologie Africaine
Revue Zool Agric Appl — Revue de Zoologie Agricole et Appliquee
Revue Zool Bot Afr — Revue de Zoologie et de Botanique Africaines
Rev Un B — Revue. Universite de Bruxelles
Rev Uniao Pharm (Sao Paulo) — Revista Uniao Pharmaceutica (Sao Paulo)
Rev Union Mat Argent — Revista. Union Matematica Argentina
Rev Union Mat Argent Asoc Fis Argent — Revista. Union Matematica Argentina y Asociacion Fisica Argentina
Rev Univ Al I Cuza Inst Politeh Iasi — Revista Universitati "Al. I. Cuza" si a Institutului Politehnic din Iasi
Rev Univ Burundi — Revue. Universite du Burundi
Rev Univ Cauca — Revista. Universidad del Cauca
Rev Univ C I Parhon Politeh Bucuresti Ser Stiint Nat — Revista Universitatii "C. I. Parhon" si a Politehnicii Bucuresti. Seria Stiintelor Naturii
Rev Univers Mines Metall Mec — Revue Universelle des Mines, de la Metallurgie, de la Mecanique, des Travaux Publics, des Sciences, et des Arts Appliques a l'Industrie
Rev Univ Fed Para Ser II — Revista. Universidade Federal do Para. Serie II
Rev Univ Ind Santander — Revista. Universidad Industrial de Santander
Rev Univ Ind Santander Invest — Revista. Universidad Industrial de Santander. Investigaciones
Rev Univ Ind Santander Tecnolo — Revista. Universidad Industrial de Santander. Tecnologia
Rev Univ Los Andes (Bogota) — Revista. Universidad de Los Andes (Bogota)
Rev Univ Madrid — Revista. Universidad de Madrid [*Spain*]
Rev Univ Nac Cordoba — Revista. Universidad Nacional de Cordoba

Rev Univ Nac Tucuman Ser A — Revista. Universidad Nacional de Tucuman. Serie A. Matematica y Fisica Teorica [*Argentina*]
Rev Univ Natl Zaire Campus Lubumbashi Ser B — Revue. Universite Nationale du Zaire. Campus de Lubumbashi. Serie B. Sciences
Rev Univ Norte (Chile) — Revista. Universidad del Norte (Chile)
Rev Univ Ottawa — Revue. Universite d'Ottawa
Rev Univ Univ Nac Cuzco — Revista Universitaria. Universidad Nacional del Cuzco
Rev Univ Zulia — Revista. Universidad del Zulia
Rev Univ Zulia (Maracaibo) — Revista. Universidad del Zulia (Maracaibo)
Rev Un Mat Argentina — Revista. Union Matematica Argentina
Rev Urol (Caracas) — Revista de Urologia (Caracas)
Rev Usem — Revista Usem
Rev Venez Cir — Revista Venezolana de Cirugia
Rev Venez Sanid Asist Soc — Revista Venezolana de Sanidad y Asistencia Social
Rev Venez Urol — Revista Venezolana de Urologia
Rev Ven Filosof — Revista Venezolana de Filosofia
Rev Ver Soie — Revue du Ver a Soie
Rev Vervietoise Hist Nat — Revue Vervietoise d'Histoire Naturelle
Rev Vet Can — Revue Veterinaire Canadienne
Rev Vet Venez — Revista Veterinaria Venezolana
Rev Vet Zootec (Manizales) — Revista de Veterinaria y Zootecnia (Manizales)
Rev Vitic — Revue de Viticulture
Rev Vivarais — Revue du Vivarais
Rev Warren Spring Lab (UK) — Review. Warren Spring Laboratory (United Kingdom)
Rev World — Revolutionary World
Rev X — Revue X [*Belgium*]
Rev Zair Sci Nucl — Revue Zairoise des Sciences Nucleaires [*Zaire*]
Rev Zoo Agr — Revue de Zoologie Agricole et de Pathologie Vegetale
Rev Zooiatr — Revista Zooiatria
Rev Zool Afr — Revue de Zoologie Africaine
Rev Zool Agric Appl — Revue de Zoologie Agricole et Appliquee
Rev Zool Agric Pathol Veg — Revue de Zoologie Agricole et de Pathologie Vegetale
Rev Zool Bot Afr — Revue de Zoologie et de Botanique Africaines
Rev Zootec (B Aires) — Revista Zootecnica (Buenos Aires)
Rev Zooteh Med Vet — Revista de Zootehnie si Medicina Veterinara
R EX — Review and Expositor
R Exist Psych Psych — Review of Existential Psychology and Psychiatry
Rexroth Inf — Rexroth Informationen
Reyon Synth Zellwolle — Reyon, Synthetica, Zellwolle
Reyon Zellwolle Andere Chem Fasern — Reyon, Zellwolle, und Andere Chemie Fasern
Reyrolle Parsons Rev — Reyrolle Parsons Review
Rezanie Instrum — Rezanie i Instrument
Re Zh Khim Neftepererab Polim Mashinostr — Referativnyi Zhurnal. Khimicheskoe. Neftepererabatyuayushchee i Polimerjnoe Mashinostroenie
Rezul't Issled Mezhdunar Geofiz Proektam — Rezul'taty Issledovanyi po Mezhdunarodny Geofizicheskim Proektam [*USSR*]
RF — Rapports des Fouilles
RF — Razon y Fe
RF — Republique Francaise
RF — Revista de Filologie
RF — Revue de France
RF — Rivista di Filologia e di Istruzione Classica
RF — Rivista di Filosofia
RF — Romanische Forschungen
RF — Ruch Filozoficzny
RFA — Revue de l'Energie [*Paris*]
RFA — Revue de la Franco-Ancienne
RFAAD — Revue Francaise d'Automatique, d'Informatique, et de Recherche Operationnelle. Serie Automatique
RFACA — Revista. Facultad de Ciencias Agrarias. Universidad Nacional de Cuyo
R Fac Cienc Ec Com — Revista. Facultad de Ciencias Economicas y Comerciales
R Fac Der (Caracas) — Revista. Facultad de Derecho (Caracas)
R Fac Der Mexico — Revista. Facultad de Derecho de Mexico
RFAGB — Riforma Agraria
RFALA — Revue Francaise d'Allergie
RFAND — Revue Francaise d'Automatique, d'Informatique, et de Recherche Operationnelle. Serie Analyse Numerique
RFAPA — Revista. Facultad de Agronomia. Universidad Nacional de La Plata
RFB — Rabobank
RFBUB — Revista de Farmacia e Bioquimica. Universidade de Sao Paulo (Brazil)
RFC — Revista de Folklore (Colombia)
RFC — Rivista di Filologia Classica
RFC — Rivista di Filologia e di Istruzione Classica
RFCC — Revista de Folklore. Organo de la Comision Nacional de Folklore (Colombia)
RF (Cern) — Revista de Filologie (Cernauti)
RFCO — Revue des Facultes Catholiques de l'Ouest

RFCTA — Rassegna di Fisiopatologia Clinica e Terapeutica
RFE — Radio Free Europe
R Fe — Razon y Fe
RFE — Revista de Filologia Espanola
RFEA — Revue Francaise d'Etudes Americaines
RFECA — Revue Francaise d'Etudes Cliniques et Biologiques
RFELB — Radio Fernsehen Elektronik
RFERB — Radio Free Europe. Research Bulletin
RFFH — Revista. Facultad de Filosofia y Humanidades
RFFLUP — Revista. Faculdade de Filosofia e Letras. Universidade do Parana
RFG — Rhodesian Financial Gazette
RFGND — RoeFo. Fortschritte auf dem Gebiete der Roentgenstrahlen und der Nuklearmedizin
RFH — Revista de Filologia Hispanica
RFHC — Revista. Facultad de Humanidades y Ciencias
RFHL — Revue Francaise d'Histoire du Livre
RFHOM — Revue Francaise d'Histoire d'Outre-Mer
RFHSP — Revista de Filologia e Historia (Sao Paulo)
RFI — Regionalism and the Female Imagination
RFi — Revista de Filosofia
RFIC — Rivista di Filologia e di Istruzione Classica
R Fil — Revista de Filosofia
RFil — Russkaja Filologija
RF Illus — RF [*Rockefeller Foundation*] Illustrated
R Filol Esp — Revista de Filologia Espanola
RFilos — Rivista di Filosofia
R Filoz — Revista de Filozofie
R Fins Publicas — Revista de Financas Publicas
RFIOA — Revue Francaise d'Informatique et de Recherche Operationnelle
RFISA — Revista de Fisica
RFJ — Radio Free Jazz
RFK — Reflets et Perspectives de la Vie Economique
RFKUL — Roczniki Filozoficzne. Towarzystwo Naukowe Katolickiego Uniwersytetu Lubelskiego
RFL — Reports of Family Law
RFL — Revista. Faculdade de Letras. Universidade de Lisboa
RFL 2d — Reports of Family Law. Second Series
RFLHGA — Revue. Faculte de Langues, d'Histoire, et de Geographie. Universite d'Ankara
RFLL — Revista. Faculdade de Letras. Universidade de Lisboa
RFLUL — Revista. Faculdade de Letras. Universidade de Lisboa
RFM — Revista de Filosofia (Madrid)
RFMNB — Rein et Foie. Maladies de la Nutrition
RFM Rev Fr Mec — RFM. Revue Francaise de Mecanique
RFN — Rivista di Filosofia Neo-Scolastica
RFNS — Rivista di Filosofia Neo-Scolastica
RFolc — Revista de Folclor
R Fomento Soc — Revista de Fomento Social
R Fom Soc — Revista de Fomento Social
R For Franc — Revue Forestiere Francaise
R Format Perm — Revue de la Formation Permanente
RForsch — Romanische Forschungen
RFOSA — Revue Francaise d'Odonto-Stomatologie
RFP — Reviews for Physicians [*Elsevier Book Series*]
RFP — Revista de Filologia Portuguesa
RFPRA — Reactor Fuel Processing
RFr — Revolution Francaise
RFr — Revue Francaise
R Fr Affaires Socs — Revue Francaise des Affaires Sociales
R Franc Aff Soc — Revue Francaise des Affaires Sociales
R Francaise Hist Livre — Revue Francaise d'Histoire du Livre
R Francaise Hist Outre-Mer — Revue Francaise d'Histoire d'Outre-Mer
R Francaise Sci Pol — Revue Francaise de Science Politique
R Francaise Sociol — Revue Francaise de Sociologie
R Franc Comptab — Revue Francaise de Comptabilite
R Franc Dr Aer — Revue Francaise de Droit Aerien
R Franc En — Revue Francaise de l'Energie
R Franc Et Amer — Revue Francaise d'Etudes Americaines
R Franc Et Polit Afr — Revue Francaise d'Etudes Politiques Africaines
R Franc Et Polit Medit — Revue Francaise d'Etudes Politiques Mediterraneennes
R Franc Gestion — Revue Francaise de Gestion
R Franc Hist O Mer — Revue Francaise d'Histoire d'Outre-Mer
R Franc Hist Outre-Mer — Revue Francaise d'Histoire d'Outre-Mer
R Franc Mkting — Revue Francaise du Marketing
R Franc Pedag — Revue Francaise de Pedagogie
R Franc Psych — Revue Francaise de Psychoanalyse
R Franc Sci Polit — Revue Francaise de Science Politique
R Franc Soc — Revue Francaise de Sociologie
R Franc Sociol — Revue Francaise de Sociologie
R Fr Energ — Revue Francaise de l'Energie
R Fr Etud Pol Afr — Revue Francaise d'Etudes Politiques Africaines
R Fr Etud Pol Mediterraneennes — Revue Francaise d'Etudes Politiques Mediterraneennes
RFRG — Revista de Filologie Romanica si Germanica [*Bucarest*]
R Fr Gestion — Revue Francaise de Gestion

RFrign — Rassegna Frignanese
R Fr Marketing — Revue Francaise du Marketing
RFRO — Raumforschung und Raumordnung
RFRR-A — Raumforschung und Raumordnung
R Fr Science Pol — Revue Francaise de Science Politique
R Fr Sociol — Revue Francaise de Sociologie
RFS — Revue Francaise de Sociologie
RFSHA — Reports. Liberal Arts and Science Faculty. Shizuoka University. Natural Science
RFSO-A — Revue Francaise de Sociologie
RFSP — Revue Francaise de Science Politique
RFTRA — Revue Francaise de Traitement de l'Information
RG — Readers' Guide to Periodical Literature
RG — Recherches Germaniques
RG — Revista de Guimaraes
RG — Revue Generale
RG — Revue Germanique
RG — Romana Gens
R Gabonaise Etud Pols Econs et Juridiques — Revue Gabonaise d'Etudes Politiques. Economiques et Juridiques
R Gad — Raina Gadagramata
RGand — Romanica Gandensia
RGB — Revue Generale Belge
RGCT — Residential Group Care and Treatment
RGD — Revue Generale de Droit
RGD — Revue de Geomorphologie Dynamique
RGDIP — Revue Generale de Droit International Public
RGDPD — Revue de Geologie Dynamique et de Geographie Physique
RGEFA — Revue Generale du Froid
R Gen — Revue Generale
R Gen — Revue Generale de Droit
R Gen Air Espace — Revue Generale de l'Air et de l'Espace
R Gen Assur Terr — Revue Generale des Assurances Terrestres
R Gen Chem de Fer — Revue Generale des Chemins de Fer
R Gen Dr Int Publ — Revue Generale de Droit International Public
R Gen Sci — Revue Generale des Sciences Pures et Appliquees
R Gen Sci Pures et Ap — Revue Generale des Sciences Pures et Appliquees
R Geog — Revista Geografica
R de Geog de Mtl — Revue de Geographie de Montreal
R Geogr Alpine — Revue de Geographie Alpine
R Geogr Est — Revue Geographique de l'Est
RGeogrH — Revue de Geographie Humaine et d'Ethnologie
R Geogr Lyon — Revue de Geographie de Lyon
R Geogr Maroc — Revue de Geographie du Maroc
R Geogr Pyrenees — Revue Geographique des Pyrenees et du Sud-Ouest
R Geogr (Rio De Janeiro) — Revista Geografica (Rio De Janeiro)
R Geog Soc Pr — Royal Geographical Society. Proceedings
RGer — Recherches Germaniques
RGF — Roemisch-Germanische Forschungen
RGFil — Romano-Germanskaja Filologija
RGFRD4 — Ghana. Fishery Research Unit. Information Report
RGG — Religion in Geschichte und Gegenwart
R Ghana Law — Review of Ghana Law
RGHE — Revue de Geographie Humaine et d'Ethnologie
RGHSDH — Annual Research Reviews. Regulation of Growth Hormone Secretion
RGI — Rivista Geografica Italiana
RGKAI — Roemisch-Germanische Kommission des Archaeologischen Instituts
RGKNA — Rikagaku Kenkyusho Kenkyu Nempo
RGL — Reihe Germanistische Linguistik
RGL — Resources Policy
RGL — Review of Ghana Law
RGL — Revue de Geographie de Lyon
RGMNA — Chijil Kwangmul Chosa Yongu Pokoso
RGNEB — Review of Compagnie Generale d'Electricite
RGNUD — Revue Generale Nucleaire
RGO — Regulation
RGo — Romanica Gothoburgensia
RGPGD — Revue de Geographie Physique et de Geologie Dynamique
RGr — Rassegna Gregoriana
RGR — Revista Germanistilor Romani
RGr — Revue Gregorienne
RGRCD — Geothermal Resources Council. Special Report
R Greenwich Obs Bull — Royal Greenwich Observatory. Bulletins
R Gregor — Revue Gregorienne
RGS Austsia SA Br Proc — Royal Geographical Society of Australasia. South Australian Branch. Proceedings
RGSIA — Records. Geological Survey of India
R G Soc Cornwall Tr — Royal Geological Society of Cornwall. Transactions
R G Soc Ireland J — Royal Geological Society of Ireland. Journal
RGSWA — Records. Geological Survey of New South Wales
RGTHA — Revue Generale de Thermique
R Guardia Fin — Rivista della Guardia di Finanza
RGuim — Revista de Guimaraes
RGUMD — Argument
RGVV — Religionsgeschichtliche Versuche und Vorarbeiten

RGZM — Roemisch-Germanische Zentralmuseum (Mainz)
RGZTA — Railway Gazette [*Later, Railway Gazette International*]
RH — Religious Humanism
RH — Restaurant Hospitality
RH — Revue Hebdomadaire
RH — Revue Hispanique
RH — Revue Historique
RH — Rochester History
RH — Roczniki Humanistyczne
RHA — Revista de Historia de America
RHA — Revue Hittite et Asiatique
R Hacienda — Revista de Hacienda
RHAF — Revue d'Histoire de l'Amerique Francaise
R Hanazono Coll — Review of Hanazono College
RhB — Rheinische Blaetter
RHB — Rheinische Heimatblaetter
RHBNA — Rehabilitation
RHC — Revue d'Histoire Comparee
RHCFA — Revista. Hospital das Clinicas. Faculdade de Medicina. Universidade de Sao Paulo
RHCM — Revue d'Histoire et de Civilisation du Maghreb
RHComp — Revue d'Histoire Comparee
RHCS — Rocznik Historii Czasopismiennictwa Polskiego
RHD — Revue d'Histoire Diplomatique
RHD — Revue d'Histoire du Droit
RHD — Revue Historique de Droit Francais et Etranger
RHDFE — Revue Historique de Droit Francais et Etranger
RHDGM — Revue d'Histoire de la Deuxieme Guerre Mondiale
RHDip — Revue d'Histoire Diplomatique
RHDRA — Radiological Health Data and Reports
RHE — Revue d'Histoire Ecclesiastique
RHEA — Research into Higher Education. Abstracts
RHEAA — Rheologica Acta
RHeb — Revue Hebdomadaire
RHEF — Revue d'Histoire de l'Eglise de France
Rhein Bienenztg — Rheinische Bienenzeitung
Rheinisches Mus Philol — Rheinisches Museum fuer Philologie
Rheinisch-Westfael Akad Wiss Nat- Ing- Wirtschaftswiss Vort — Rheinisch-Westfaelische Akademie der Wissenschaften Natur-, Ingenieur-, und Wirtschaftswissenschaften. Vortraege
Rheinisch Westfael Z Volkskd — Rheinisch-Westfaelische Zeitschrift fuer Volkskunde
Rheinstahl Tech — Rheinstahl Technik
Rhein Vb — Rheinische Vierteljahresblaetter
Rhein-Westfael Akad Wiss Vortr N — Rheinisch-Westfaelische Akademie der Wissenschaften Natur-, Ingenieur-, und Wirtschaftswissenschaften. Vortraege
RHel — Romanica Helvetica
R Hell Dr Int — Revue Hellenique de Droit International
Rheol Abstr — Rheology Abstracts
Rheol Act — Rheologica Acta
Rheol Acta — Rheologica Acta
Rheol Bull — Rheology Bulletin
Rheol Leafl — Rheology Leaflet
Rheol Mem — Rheological Memoirs
Rheol Texture Food Qual — Rheology and Texture in Food Quality
RHES — Revue d'Histoire Economique et Sociale
Rheumatol Balneo Allergol — Rheumatologia, Balneologia, Allergologia
Rheumatol Phys Med — Rheumatology and Physical Medicine
Rheumatol Rehabil — Rheumatology and Rehabilitation
RHF — Revue d'Histoire Franciscaine
RHi — Revue Hispanique
RHiM — Revista Hispanica Moderna
RHis — Revue Historique
RHisp — Revue Hispanique
R Hispan Mod — Revista Hispanica Moderna
R Hist — Revista de Historia
R d'Hist — Revue d'Histoire de l'Amerique Francaise
R Hist — Revue Historique
RHist — Rocczniki Historyczne
R Hist Am — Revista de Historia de America
R Hist Bul — Revue Historique. Bulletins Critiques
R Hist Deuxieme Geurre Mondiale — Revue d'Histoire de la Deuxieme Guerre Mondiale
R Hist Diplom — Revue d'Histoire Diplomatique
R Hist Eccl — Revue Historique de Droit Francais et Etranger
R Hist Eccl — Revue d'Histoire Ecclesiastique
R Hist Fascisme — Revue d'Histoire du Fascisme
R Hist Litt France — Revue d'Histoire Litteraire de la France
RHistM — Roemische Historische Mitteilungen
R Hist Mem — Revue Historique. Memoires et Etudes
R Hist Mod & Contemp — Revue d'Histoire Moderne et Contemporaine
RHistorique — Revue Historique [*Paris*]
R Hist & Philos Rel — Revue d'Histoire et de Philosophie Religieuses
R Hist Ph Rel — Revue d'Histoire et de Philosophie Religieuses
R Hist Rel — Revue de l'Histoire des Religions

R Hist Sci & Ap — Revue d'Histoire des Sciences et de Leurs Applications
R Hist Spiritualite — Revue d'Histoire de la Spiritualite
RhJbV — Rheinisches Jahrbuch fuer Volkskunde
RHJE — Revue de l'Histoire Juive en Egypte
RHKUL — Roczniki Humanistyczne. Towarzystwo Naukowe Katolickiego Uniwersytetu Lubelskiego
RHL — Revista de Historia. La Laguna de Tenerife
RHL — Revue d'Histoire Litteraire de la France
RHLB — Revue d'Histoire Litteraire (Bucharest)
RHLE — Revista Critica de Historia y Literatura Espanolas
RHLF — Revue d'Histoire Litteraire de la France
RHLK — Reihe Hanser Literatur-Kommentare
RHLP — Revista de Historia Literaria de Portugal
RHLR — Revue d'Histoire et de Litterature Religieuse
RHM — Revista Hispanica Moderna
RHM — Revue d'Histoire Moderne
RhM — Rheinische Merkur
RhM — Rheinisches Museum fuer Philologie
RHM — Roemische Historische Mitteilungen
RHMC — Revue d'Histoire Moderne et Contemporaine
RHMH — Revue d'Histoire de la Medicine Hebraique [Paris]
RHMis — Revue d'Histoire des Missions
RhMP — Rheinisches Museum fuer Philologie
Rh M Ph — Rheinisches Museum fuer Philologie
RHMSA — Revue d'Hygiene et de Medecine Sociale
RHMTA — Rhumatologie [Paris]
RHNL — Reindeer Herders Newsletter. Institute of Arctic Biology. University of Alaska
RHODA — Rhodora
Rhod Agric J — Rhodesia Agricultural Journal
Rhod Beekeeping — Rhodesian Beekeeping
Rhod Bee News — Rhodesian Bee News
Rhod Bull For Res — Rhodesia. Bulletin of Forestry Research
Rhod Cotton Res Inst Annu Rep — Rhodesia Cotton Research Institute. Annual Report
Rhod Div Livest Pastures Annu Rep — Rhodesia. Division of Livestock and Pastures. Annual Report
Rhode Isl Agric — Rhode Island Agriculture
Rhod Eng — Rhodesian Engineer
Rhodesia Ag J — Rhodesia Agricultural Journal
Rhodesia Agric J — Rhodesia Agricultural Journal
Rhodesia Agr J — Rhodesia Agricultural Journal
Rhodesian J Agr Res — Rhodesian Journal of Agricultural Research
Rhodesian J Econ — Rhodesian Journal of Economics
Rhodesian Min Jour — Rhodesian Mining Journal
Rhodesian Tob J — Rhodesian Tobacco Journal
Rhodesia Zambia Malawi J Agr Res — Rhodesia, Zambia, and Malawi Journal of Agricultural Research
Rhodes Univ Dep Ichthyol Ichthyol Bull — Rhodes University. Department of Ichthyology. Ichthyological Bulletin
Rhodes Univ Dep Ichthyol Occas Pap — Rhodes University. Department of Ichthyology. Occasional Paper
Rhodes Univ J L B Smith Inst Ichthyol Spec Publ — Rhodes University. J. L. B. Smith Institute of Ichthyology. Special Publication
Rhod Fmr — Rhodesian Farmer
Rhod Geol Surv Bull — Rhodesia. Geological Survey. Bulletin
Rhod Geol Surv Miner Resour Ser — Rhodesia. Geological Survey. Mineral Resources Series
Rhod Geol Surv Short Rep — Rhodesia. Geological Survey. Short Report
Rhod Grassl Res Stn Annu Rep — Rhodesia Grasslands Research Station. Annual Report
Rhod Hist — Rhodesian History
Rhod J Agric Res — Rhodesia Journal of Agricultural Research
Rhod Jl Agric Res — Rhodesian Journal of Agricultural Research
Rhod Librn — Rhodesian Librarian
Rhod Lowveld Res Stn Annu Rep — Rhodesia. Lowveld Research Station. Annual Report
Rhod Minist Agric Dep Res Spec Serv Seed Serv Annu Rep — Rhodesia. Ministry of Agriculture. Department of Research and Specialist Services. Seed Services. Annual Report
Rhod Minist Agric Gatooma Res Stn Annu Rep — Rhodesia. Ministry of Agriculture. Gatooma Research Station. Annual Report
Rhod Minist Agric Grassl Res Stn Annu Rep — Rhodesia. Ministry of Agriculture. Grasslands Research Station. Annual Report
Rhod Nurse — Rhodesian Nurse
Rhod Sci News — Rhodesia Science News
Rhod Tob — Rhodesian Tobacco
Rhod Zambia Malawi J Agric Res — Rhodesia, Zambia, and Malawi Journal of Agricultural Research
RHOSA — Rinsho Hoshasen
R Hospital France — Revue Hospitaliere de France
RHP — Revue d'Histoire de la Philosophie et d'Histoire Generale de la Civilisation
RHPH — Revue d'Histoire de la Philosophie et d'Histoire Generale de la Civilisation

RHPhC — Revue d'Histoire de la Philosophie et d'Histoire Generale de la Civilisation
RHPhR — Revue d'Histoire et de Philosophie Religieuses
RHPhRel — Revue d'Histoire et de Philosophie Religieuses
RHPR — Revue d'Histoire et de Philosophie Religieuses
RHR — Revue de l'Histoire des Religions
RHRCA — Rehabilitation Record
RHS — Revue d'Histoire des Sciences et de Leurs Applications
RHS — Revue d'Histoire de la Spiritualite
RHS — Royal Historical Society. Transactions
RHSA — Revue d'Histoire des Sciences et de Leurs Applications
RHSE — Revue Historique du Sud-Est Europeen
RHSEE — Revue Historique du Sud-Est Europeen
RHSQ — Royal Historical Society of Queensland. Journal
RHSTr — Royal Historical Society. Transactions
RHT — Revue d'Histoire des Textes
RHT — Revue d'Histoire du Theatre
RHTe — Revue d'Histoire des Textes
RHTKA — Rheinstahl Technik
RHTMA — Reviews on High-Temperature Materials
RHTRB — Revue des Hautes Temperatures et des Refractaires
RHUEA — Rheumatism [England]
RHUL — Revista de Historia. Universidad de La Laguna
RHUL — Roczniki Humanistyczne Uniwersitetu Lubelskiego
RHUMA — Rhumatologie
RHV — Revue Historique Vaudoise
RhV — Rheinische Vierteljahresblaetter
RhV — Rheinische Vorzeit in Wort und Bild
RhVJ — Rheinische Vierteljahresblaetter
Rhythmes Monde — Rhythmes du Monde
RI — Rassegna Italiana
R & I — Restaurants and Institutions
RI — Revista Iberoamericana
RI — Revista de las Indias
RI — Rhode Island Music Educators Review
RI — Rice Institute Pamphlet
RI — Risorgimento Italiano
RI — Rivista Israelitica
RI — Rivista d'Italia
RIA — Revista Iberoamericana
RIA — Rivista. Istituto di Archeologia
RIAB — Revista Interamericana de Bibliografia
RI Ag — Rhode Island Agriculture
RI Ag Exp — Rhode Island. Agricultural Experiment Station. Publications
RI Agr — Rhode Island Agriculture. Rhode Island Agricultural Experiment Station
RI Agric — Rhode Island Agriculture
RI Agric Exp Stn Bull — Rhode Island. Agricultural Experiment Station. Bulletin
RI Agric Exp Stn Res Q Rev — Rhode Island. Agricultural Experiment Station. Research Quarterly Review
RIAND — Risk Analysis
RIASB — Richerche Astronomiche
RIB — Review of International Affairs. Politics, Economics, Law, Science, Culture
RIB — Review of International Broadcasting
RIB — Revista Iberoamericana de Bibliografia
RIB — Revue de l'Instruction Publique en Belgique
Ri B — Rivista Biblica
RIBA J — Royal Institute of British Architects. Journal
R Iberoamer Segur Soc — Revista Iberoamericana de Seguridad Social
RIBIB — Revista Interamericana de Bibliotecologia
RIBJ — Rhode Island Bar Journal
RIBJD — RIBA [Royal Institute of British Architects] Journal
RI Bur Industrial Statistics An Rp Nat Res S B — Rhode Island Bureau of Industrial Statistics. Annual Report. Natural Resources Survey. Bulletin
RIC — Review of International Cooperation
Ric Autom — Ricerche di Automatica
RicBibRel — Ricerche Bibliche e Religiose [Milan]
Ric Biol Selvaggina — Ricerche di Biologia della Selvaggina
Ric Clin Lab — Ricerca in Clinica e in Laboratorio
Ric Demos — Ricerche Demoscopiche
Ric Doc Tess — Ricerca e Documentazione Tessile
Ric Econ — Ricerche Economiche
Rice Inst P — Rice Institute Pamphlet
Rice Inst Pam — Rice Institute Pamphlet
Rice J — Rice Journal
Ricerca Scient — Ricerca Scientifica
Ricerca Scient Rc — Ricerca Scientifica. Rendiconti
Ricerche Automat — Ricerche di Automatica
Ricerche Mat — Ricerche di Matematica
Rice Univ Aero-Astronaut Rep — Rice University. Aero-Astronautic Report
Rice Univ Stud — Rice University. Studies
RiceUS — Rice University. Studies
RicF — Ricerche Filosofiche

RICHD — Reviews in Inorganic Chemistry
RICJA — Rice Journal
Rickia Arq Bot Estado Sao Paulo Ser Criptogam Supl — Rickia. Arquivos de Botanica do Estado de Sao Paulo. Serie Criptogamica
Rickia Supl — Rickia. Supplemento
Rickmansworth Hist — Rickmansworth Historian
RicLing — Ricerche Linguistiche
RicM — Ricerche Musicali
Ric Mat — Ricerche di Matematica
Ric Morfol — Ricerche di Morfologia
RICOA — Rivista dei Combustibili
RICP — Revista. Instituto de Cultura Puertorriquena
RicR — Ricerche Religiose
RicRel — Ricerche Religiose
RICS Abs Rev — RICS [*Royal Institution of Chartered Surveyors*] Abstracts and Review
Ric Sci — Ricerca Scientifica
Ric Sci Parte 1 — Ricerca Scientifica. Parte 1. Rivista
Ric Sci Parte 2 Sez A — Ricerca Scientifica. Parte 2. Rendiconti. Sezione A. Biologica
Ric Sci Parte 2 Sez B — Ricerca Scientifica. Parte 2. Rendiconti. Sezione B. Biologica
Ric Sci Prog Tec — Ricerca Scientifica ed il Progresso Tecnico
Ric Sci Quad — Ricerca Scientifica. Quaderni
Ric Sci Rend Sez B — Ricerca Scientifica. Serie Seconda. Parte II. Rendiconti. Sezione B. Biologica
Ric Sci Ricostr — Ricerca Scientifica e Ricostruzione
Ric Sci Suppl — Ricerca Scientifica. Supplemento
RicSL — Ricerche Slavistiche
Ric Spettrosc — Ricerche Spettroscopiche
Ric Spettros Lab Astrofis Specola — Ricerche Spettroscopiche. Laboratorio Astrofisico della Specola Vaticana
RicSRel — Ricerche di Storia Religiosa
RicStRel — Ricerche di Storia Religiosa [*Rome*]
Ric Studi Med Sper — Ricerche e Studi di Medicina Sperimentale
Ric Termotecnica — Ricerche di Termotecnica [*Italy*]
Ric Zool Appl Caccia — Ricerche di Zoologia Applicata alla Caccia
Ric Zool Appl Caccia Suppl — Ricerche di Zoologia Applicata alla Caccia. Supplemento
Rid — Ridotto
RID — Rivista Italiana di Dialettologia
RID — Rivista Italiana del Drama
RIDA — Revue Internationale des Droits de l'Antiquite
RIDC — Revue Internationale de Droit Compare
RIdeP — Revue Internationale de Philosophie
RIDEQ — Revista Iberoamericana de Educacion Quimica
RI Dev Counc Geol Bull — Rhode Island Development Council. Geological Bulletin
RI Devel Council Geol Bull Sci Contr — Rhode Island Development Council. Geological Bulletin. Scientific Contribution
RIE — Revista de Ideas Esteticas
RIE — Revue Internationale de l'Enseignement
RIEAA — Rivista di Economia Agraria
RIEB — Revista. Instituto de Estudos Brasileiros
Riech Aromen Kosmet — Riechstoffe, Aromen, Kosmetica
Riechst Aromen — Riechstoffe und Aromen
Riechst Aromen Koerperpflegem — Riechstoffe, Aromen, Koerperpflegemittel [*Later, Riechstoffe, Aromen, Kosmetica*]
RIEEC — Research Institute for the Education of Exceptional Children
RIEMA — Rapports et Proces-Verbaux des Reunions. Conseil International pour l'Exploration de la Mer
RIEtnN — Revista. Instituto Etnologico Nacional
RIEV — Revista Internacional de Estudios Vascos
RIFAA — Revista Industrial y Fabril
RIFBAZ — Ching Chi Pu Kuo Li Taiwan Ta Hsueh Ho Pan Yu Yeh Sheng Wu Shih Yen So Yen Chiu Pao Kao
RIFD — Rivista Internazionale di Filosofia del Diritto
Riforma Agrar — Riforma Agraria [*Italy*]
Riforma Med — Riforma Medica
RIFPA — Revue. Institut Francais du Petrole et Annales des Combustibles Liquides [*Later, Revue. Institut Francais du Petrole*]
RIG — Bouwadviseur Opinievormend Beroepstijdschrift voor Adviseurs
RIGAA — Rinsho Ganka
Rigasche Ind Ztg — Rigasche Industrie Zeitung
Rigas Med Inst Zinat Rakstu Krajums — Rigas Medicinas Instituta Zinatnisko Rakstu Krajums
Rigas Politeh Inst Zinat Raksti — Rigas Politehniskais Instituts. Zinatniskie Raksti
RIGI — Rivista Indo-Greco-Italico
RIGIB — Radovi Instituta za Geolosko-Rudarska Istrazivanja i Ispitivanja Nuklearnih i Drugih Mineralnih Sirovina
RIGPA — Rezul'taty Issledovanyi po Mezhdunarodny Geofizicheskim Proektam
RI Grad Sch Oceanogr Occas Publ — Rhode Island Graduate School of Oceanography. Occasional Publication
RIH — Rhode Island History

RIHAA — Rivers and Harbors
RIHGSP — Revista. Instituto Historico e Geografico de Sao Paulo
RI Hist — Rhode Island History
RI Hist Soc Coll — Rhode Island Historical Society. Collections
RIHPC — Revue Internationale d'Histoire Politique et Constitutionnelle
RIHTA — Revue Internationale des Hautes Temperatures et des Refractaires
RIHYA — Rinsho Hinyokika
RII — Rivista Inguana et Intemelia
RIIGA — Rivista Italiana d'Igiene
RIISA — Report. Institute of Industrial Science. University of Tokyo
Riista-Kalataloudes Tutkimuslaitos Kalantutkimusosasto Tied — Riista- ja Kalataloudes Tutkimuslaitos Kalantutkimusosasto Tiedonantoja
Riistatiet Julkaisuja — Riistatieteellisia Julkaisuja
RIJAZ — Radovi Instituta Jugoslavenske Akademije Znanosti i Umjetnosti u Zadru
RIJAZUZ — Radovi Instituta Jugoslavenske Akademije Znanosti i Umjetnosti u Zadru
RI Jew Hist Note — Rhode Island Jewish Historical Notes
RI Jewish Historical Notes — Rhode Island Jewish Historical Notes
RIJHN — Rhode Island Jewish Historical Notes
Rijks Geol Dienst Meded Nieuwe Ser (Neth) — Rijks Geologische Dienst. Mededelingen. Nieuwe Serie (Netherlands)
Rijksuniv Utrecht Jaarversl Wet Deel — Rijksuniversiteit Utrecht. Jaarverslag Wetenschappelijk Deel
Rijksw Commun — Rijkswaterstaat Communications
RIJU — Riistatieteellisia Julkaisuja. Finnish Game Research
RIKAA — Rinsho Kagaku
RIKEB — Rinsho Ketsueki
RIL — Rendiconti. Istituto Lombardo di Scienze e Lettere
RILA — Rassegna Italiana di Linguistica Applicata
RILA — Repertoire International de la Litterature de l'Art [*International Repertory of the Literature of Art*]
RILD — Rivista Italiana di Letteratura Dialettale
RILM — RILM [*Repertoire International de la Litterature Musicale*] Abstracts of Music Literature [*City University of New York*] [*Database*]
RiLM — Rivista di Letteratura Moderne
RILOB — Recherches Publiees sous la Direction de l'Institut de Lettres Orientales de Beyrouth
RILSL — Rendiconti. Istituto Lombardo. Classe di Lettere, Scienze Morali, e Storiche
Rimba Indones — Rimba Indonesia
RI Med J — Rhode Island Medical Journal
Rimini Stor Art Cult — Rimini Storia Arte e Cultura
RIMJA — Rhode Island Medical Journal
RIMPA — Rivista degli Infortuni e delle Malattie Professionali
RIn — Revista de las Indias
Rin — Rinascimento
Rin — Rinascita
RIN — Rivista Italiana di Numismatica e Scienze Affini
RINAB — Research Institute Nedri As (Hveragerdi, Iceland). Bulletin
RINASA — Rivista. Istituto Nazionale d'Archeologia e Storia dell'Arte
Rinascenza Med — Rinascenza Medica
R Income Wealth — Review of Income and Wealth
R Ind — Revista de las Indias
RINDA — Revue Industrielle
Rindertuberk Brucell — Rindertuberkulose und Brucellose
R Indias — Revista de las Indias
RIndM — Revista de las Indias (Madrid)
R Indones Malay Aff — Review of Indonesian and Malayan Affairs
R Indones Malayan Aff — Review of Indonesian and Malayan Affairs
Ringing Migr — Ringing and Migration
Ring Int Ornithol Bull — Ring. International Ornithological Bulletin
RINPA — Rivista di Istochimica Normale e Patologica
Rin S — Rinascenza Salentina
R Inst Antropol Cordoba — Revista. Instituto de Antropologia. Universidad de Cordoba
R Inst Chem Lect Monogr Rep — Royal Institute of Chemistry. Lectures, Monographs, and Reports
R Inst Chem Lect Ser — Royal Institute of Chemistry. Lecture Series
R Inst Cienc Soc — Revista. Instituto de Ciencias Sociales
R Instit Europ — Revista de Instituciones Europeas
R Inst Nav Archit (London) Suppl Pap — Royal Institution of Naval Architects (London). Supplementary Papers
R Inst Nav Archit Q Trans — Royal Institution of Naval Architects [*London*]. Quarterly Transactions
R Inst Nav Archit Suppl Pap — Royal Institution of Naval Architects [*London*]. Supplementary Papers
R Inst Pr — Royal Institution of Great Britain. Proceedings
R Inst Public Health Hyg J — Royal Institute of Public Health and Hygiene. Journal
R Inst Sociol — Revue. Institut de Sociologie
RINT — Revista. Instituto Nacional de la Tradicion
R Int Commiss Jurists — Review. International Commission of Jurists
R Int Coop — Review of International Cooperation
R Int Croix Rouge — Revue Internationale de la Croix Rouge

R Int Cr Rouge — Revue Internationale de la Croix Rouge
R Int Dr Comp — Revue Internationale de Droit Compare
R Int Dr Penal — Revue Internationale de Droit Penal
R Integr — Revista de la Integracion
R Integracion y Desarrollo Centroam — Revista de la Integracion y el Desarrollo de Centroamerica
R Interam Bibl — Revista Interamericana de Bibliografia
R Interam Bibliog — Revista Interamericana de Bibliografia
R Interam Cienc Soc — Revista Interamericana de Ciencias Sociales
R Interam Sociol — Revista Interamericana de Sociologia
R Internac Sociol — Revista Internacional de Sociologia
R Internat Affairs — Review of International Affairs
R Internat Hist Banque — Revue Internationale d'Histoire de la Banque
R Internat Rech Urbaine et Reg — Revue Internationale de Recherche Urbaine et Regionale
R Internaz Econ Trasporti — Revista Internazionale del Trasporti
R Internaz Scienze Econ e Commer — Rivista Internazionale di Scienze Economiche e Commerciali
R Internaz Scienze Soc — Rivista Internazionale di Scienze Sociali
RIntMS — Rivista Internazionale di Musica Sacra
R Int Pol Crim — Revue Internationale de Police Criminelle
R Int Politcrim — Revue Internationale de Politicriminelle
R Int Sci Adm — Revue Internationale des Sciences Administratives
R Int Sci Soc — Revue Internationale des Sciences Sociales
R Int Secur Soc — Revue Internationale de la Securite Sociale
R Int Sociol — Revue Internationale de Sociologie [International Review of Sociology] [Rome]
R Int Sociol (Madrid) — Revista Internacional de Sociologia (Madrid)
R Int Stat — Revue Internationale de Statistique
R Int Trav — Revue Internationale du Travail
RINUA — Rivista di Ingegneria Nucleare
RIO — Revue Internationale d'Onomastique
RIO — Russkoe Istoriceskoe Obscestvo
Rio De Janeiro Univ Federal Inst Geociencias Bol Geologia — Universidade Federal do Rio De Janeiro. Instituto de Geociencias. Boletim Geologia
RIOE — Research in Ocean Engineering. University Sources and Resources
Rio Grande Do Sul Inst Geocien Mapa Geol — Universidade Federal do Rio Grande Do Sul. Instituto de Geociencias. Mapa Geologico da Folha de Morretes
Rio Grande Do Sul Inst Pesqui Zootec Bol Tec — Rio Grande Do Sul. Instituto de Pesquisas Zootecnicas. Boletim Tecnico
RIOno — Revue Internationale d'Onomastique
RIP — Revue Internationale de Philosophie
RIP — Rice Institute Pamphlet
RIPB — Revue de l'Instruction Publique en Belgique
RIPC — Rassegna Italiana di Politica e di Cultura
RIPEH — Review of Iranian Political Economy and History
RIPh — Revue Internationale de Philosophie
RIPMA — Revue des Travaux. Institut des Peches Maritimes
RI Port Indus Devel Comm Geol Bull Sci Contr — Rhode Island. Port and Industrial Development Commission. Geological Bulletin. Scientific Contribution
RIPSD3 — Annual Report. Institute of Physics. Academia Sinica
RIPSD3 — Chung Yang Yen Chiu Yuan Wu Li Yen Chiu So Chi K'an
RIR — Revista Istorica Romana
RIRAB — Rivista di Radiologia
R Ir Acad Proc Sect B — Royal Irish Academy. Proceedings. Section B
R Iranienne Relations Internat — Revue Iranienne des Relations Internationales
R Iran Relat Int — Revue Iranienne des Relations Internationales
RIRED — Revue. IRE [Institut National des Radioelements] [Belgium]
RI Resour — Rhode Island Resources
R Irish Ac Pr — Royal Irish Academy. Proceedings
RIS — Rassegna Italiana di Sociologia
RIS — Revista Internacional de Sociologia
RIS — Revue. Institut de Sociologie
RIS — Revue Internationale du Socialisme
Ris — Risorgimento
RIS — Rivista Italiana di Sociologia
RISAA — Rivista Italiana della Saldatura
RISCA — Ricerca Scientifica
RI Sch Des Bul — Rhode Island School of Design. Bulletin
RISE — Rivista Internazionale di Scienze Economiche e Commerciali
RISG — Rivista Italiana di Scienze Giuridiche
RISHB — Rinsho Shinkeigaku
RISI — Review. International Statistical Institute
RISID — Revista Padurilor-Industria Lemnului. Seria Industria Lemnului
Rising Up — Rising Up Angry
Risk Anal — Risk Analysis
Risk Bk Ser — Risk. Book Series
Risk Manage — Risk Management
Risk Mgmt — Risk Management
Risk Mgt — Risk Management
RiSL — Rossija i Slavjanstvo
RISM — Repertoire International des Sources Musicales
RISO — Revista Internacional de Sociologia

RISoc — Revue. Institut de Sociologie [Solvay]
Risoe Inf — Risoe Information [Denmark]
Risoe Natl Lab Rep Risoe-M (Den) — Risoe National Laboratory. Report Risoe-M (Denmark)
Risoe Rep (Den) Res Establ Risoe — Risoe Report. (Denmark) Research Establishment Risoe
Riso Rep — Risoe Report
Risorgiment — Risorgimento
RISPT — Ross Ice Shelf Project. Technical Reports
RISR — Rassegna d'Informazioni. Istituto di Studi Romani
RiSR — Ricerche di Storia Religiosa
RISRA — Report of Ionosphere and Space Research in Japan
RISS — Revue Internationale des Sciences Sociales
RISS — Rivista Internazionale di Scienze Sociali e Discipline Ausiliari
RISTA — Rivista Italiana di Stomatologia
R Istituto Veneto Memorie — Reale Istituto Veneto di Scienze, Lettere, ed Arti. Memorie
R Ist Lomb — Rendiconti. Istituto Lombardo di Scienze e Lettere
Ri St V — Richtlinien fuer das Strafverfahren
RISULB — Revue. Institut de Sociologie. Universite Libre de Bruxelles
RIT — International Labour Review [Geneva]
RIT — Revue Internationale du Travail
RIT — Rivista Italiana del Teatro
RITAA — Revue d'Immunologie et de Therapie Antimicrobienne
R Ital Diritto Lav — Rivista Italiana di Diritto del Lavoro
R Ital Econ Demografia e Statis — Rivista Italiana di Economia. Demografia e Statistica
R Italiana Musicol — Rivista Italiana di Musicologia
R Ital Mus — Nuova Rivista Musicale Italiana
R Ital Mus — Rivista Italiana di Musicologia
RiTh — Revue Internationale de Theologie
RITL — Revista de Istorie si Theori Literara
RITMB — Rayonnements Ionisants
Riun Annu Assoc Elettrot Elettron Ital Rend — Riunione Annuale della Associazione Elettrotecnica ed Elettronica Italiana. Rendiconti
RI Univ Agric Exp Stn Bull — Rhode Island University. Agricultural Experiment Station. Bulletin
RI Univ Div Eng Res Dev Eng Repr — Rhode Island University. Division of Engineering. Research and Development Engineering Reprint
RI Univ Div Eng Res Dev Leafl — Rhode Island University. Division of Engineering. Research and Development Leaflet
RI Univ Eng Exp Stn Bull — Rhode Island University. Engineering Experiment Station. Bulletin
RI Univ Eng Exp Stn Eng Repr — Rhode Island University. Engineering Experiment Station. Engineering Reprint
RI Univ Mar Tech Rep — Rhode Island University. Marine Technical Report
Riv A — Rivista d'Arte
Riv AC — Rivista di Archeologia Cristiana
Riv Aeronaut — Rivista Aeronautica
Riv Aeronaut-Astronaut-Missil — Rivista Aeronautica-Astronautica-Missilistica [Italy]
Riv Aeronaut Astronaut Missil Suppl Tec — Rivista Aeronautica-Astronautica-Missilistica. Supplemento Tecnico
Riv Agric — Rivista di Agricoltura
Riv Agric Subtrop Trop — Rivista di Agricoltura Subtropicale e Tropicale
Riv Agron — Rivista di Agronomia
Riv Agr Subtrop Trop — Rivista di Agricoltura Subtropicale e Tropicale
Riv d'Alb — Rivista d'Albania
Riv Anat Patol Oncol — Rivista di Anatomia Patologica e di Oncologia
Riv Antrop — Rivista di Antropologia
Riv Antropol — Rivista di Antropologia
Riv Arch Crist — Rivista di Archeologia Cristiana
Riv Arte — Rivista d'Arte
Riv B — Rivista Biblica
RivB — Rivista Bibliografica
RivBA — Rivista delle Biblioteche e degli Archivi
RivBibl — Rivista Biblica
Riv Bibl — Rivista delle Biblioteche e degli Archivi
Riv Biol — Rivista di Biologia
Riv Biol Colon — Rivista di Biologia Coloniale
Riv Biol Norm Patol — Rivista di Biologia Normale e Patologica
Riv Biol (Perugia) — Rivista di Biologia (Perugia)
Riv Chim Sci Ind — Rivista di Chimica Scientifica e Industriale
Riv Chir (Como) — Rivista di Chirurgia (Como)
Riv Chir Med — Rivista di Chirurgia e Medicina
Riv Chir Pediat — Rivista di Chirurgia Pediatrica
Riv Civ — Rivista di Diritto Civile
Riv Clin Bologna — Rivista Clinica di Bologna
Riv Clin Med — Rivista di Clinica Medica
Riv Clin Pediat — Rivista di Clinica Pediatrica
Riv Clin Pediatr — Rivista di Clinica Pediatrica
Riv Clin Tossicol — Rivista di Clinica Tossicologia
Riv Clin Univ Napoli — Rivista Clinica. Universita di Napoli
Riv Colore Verniciatura Ind — Rivista del Colore-Verniciatura Industriale
Riv Combust — Rivista dei Combustibili

Riv Comm — Rivista del Diritto Commerciale e del Diritto Generale delle Obbligazioni
Riv Coniglicolt — Rivista di Coniglicoltura
Riv Crit Clin Med — Rivista Critica di Clinica Medica
Riv Crit St — Rivista Critica di Storia della Filosofia
Riv Crit Stor Filos — Rivista Critica di Storia della Filosofia
Riv Cult Class Med — Rivista di Cultura Classica e Medioevale
Riv Cult Mar — Rivista di Cultura Marinara
RivDal — Rivista Dalmatica
Riv Dif Soc — Rivista di Difesa Sociale
Riv Dir Agr — Rivista di Diritto Agrario
Riv Dir Civ — Rivista di Diritto Civile
Riv Dir Comm — Rivista del Diritto Commerciale e del Diritto Generale delle Obbligazioni
Riv Dir Europ — Rivista di Diritto Europeo
Riv Dir Finanz — Rivista di Diritto Finanziario e Scienza delle Finanze
Riv Dir Ind — Rivista del Diritto Industriale
Riv Dir Int — Rivista di Diritto Internazionale
Riv Dir Int'le — Rivista di Diritto Internazionale
Riv di Diritto Internaz — Rivista di Diritto Internazionale
Riv Dir Proc Civ — Rivista di Diritto e Procedura Civile
Riv Dir Sport — Rivista di Diritto Sportivo
Riv Ecol — Rivista di Ecologia
Riv Econ Agr — Rivista di Economia Agraria
Riv Emoter Immunoematol — Rivista di Emoterapia ed Immunoematologia
River Plat — Review of the River Plate
Riv Et — Rivista di Etnografia
Riv Etnogr — Rivista di Etnografia
Riv Farmacol Ter — Rivista di Farmacologia e Terapia
RivFC — Rivista di Filologia e di Istruzione Classica
Riv Fil — Rivista di Filologia e di Istruzione Classica
Riv Fil — Rivista di Filosofia
Riv Fil Class — Rivista di Filologia e di Istruzione Classica
Riv Filol Istruz Classica — Rivista di Filologia e di Istruzione Classica
Riv Filos — Rivista di Filosofia
Riv Filos Neo Scolast — Rivista di Filosofia Neo-Scolastica
Riv Filosof — Rivista di Filosofia
Riv Filosof Neo-Scolas — Rivista di Filosofia Neo-Scolastica
Riv Fin Loc — Rivista della Finanza Locale
Riv Fis Mat Sci Nat — Rivista di Fisica, Matematica, e Scienze Naturali
Riv Fitosanit — Rivista Fitosanitaria
Riv Fotogr Ital — Rivista Fotografica Italiana
Riv Freddo — Rivista del Freddo
Riv Frutti — Rivista di Frutticoltura
Riv Fruttic — Rivista di Frutticoltura
Riv Gastro Enterol — Rivista di Gastro-Enterologia
Riv Geofis Appl — Rivista di Geofisica Applicata
Riv Geogr Ital — Rivista Geografica Italiana
Riv Gerontol Geriatr — Rivista di Gerontologia e Geriatria
Riv Idrobiol — Rivista di Idrobiologia
RivIGI — Rivista Indo-Greco-Italico di Filologia, Lingua, Antichita
Riv Ig e San Pubb — Rivista d'Igiene e Sanita Pubblica
Riv Inf — Rivista di Informatica
Riv Inf — Rivista dell'Informazione
Riv Infort Mal Prof — Rivista degli Infortuni e delle Malattie Professionali
Riv Ing — Rivista di Ingegneria
Riv Ing Int — Rivista Inguana et Intemelia
Riv Ing Nucl — Rivista di Ingegneria Nucleare
Riv Int Agric — Rivista Internazionale di Agricoltura
Riv Int Ec — Rivista Internazionale di Scienze Economiche e Commerciali
Riv Internaz di Filos del Diritto — Rivista Internazionale di Filosofia del Diritto
Riv Int Filosof Diritto — Rivista Internazionale di Filosofia del Diritto
Riv Int Filos Polit Soc Dir Comp — Rivista Internazionale di Filosofia Politica e Sociale e di Diritto Comparato
Riv Int Sci Econ Com — Rivista Internazionale di Scienze Economiche e Commerciali
Riv Int Sci Soc — Rivista Internazionale di Scienze Sociali
Riv Ist Arch — Rivista. Reale Istituto d'Archeologia e Storia dell'Arte
Riv Istochim Norm Patol — Rivista di Istochimica Normale e Patologica
Riv Ist Sieroter Ital — Rivista. Istituto Sieroterapico Italiano
Riv Ist Vaccinogeno Consorzi Prov Antituberc — Rivista. Istituto Vaccinogeno e Consorzi Provinciali Antitubercolari
Riv Ital Essenze — Rivista Italiana delle Essenze
Riv Ital Essenze Profumi — Rivista Italiana delle Essenze e Profumi
Riv Ital Essenze Profumi Piante Off — Rivista Italiana delle Essenze dei Profumi e delle Piante Officinali
Riv Ital Essenze Profumi Piante Off Aromi Saponi Cosmet — Rivista Italiana delle Essenze dei Profumi e delle Piante Officinali Aromi Saponi Cosmetici
Riv Ital Essenze Profumi Piante Offic Aromi Saponi Cosmet — Rivista Italiana delle Essenze dei Profumi e delle Piante Officinali Aromi Saponi Cosmetici
Riv Ital Essenze Profumi Piante Offic Olii Veg Saponi — Rivista Italiana delle Essenze dei Profumi e delle Piante Officinali Olii Vegetali Saponi
Riv Ital Ge — Rivista Italiana di Geofisica e Scienze Affini
Riv Ital Geofis — Rivista Italiana di Geofisica [*Italy*]

Riv Ital Geotec — Rivista Italiana di Geotecnica
Riv Ital Ginecol — Rivista Italiana di Ginecologia
Riv Italiana Paleontologia e Stratigrafia — Rivista Italiana di Paleontologia e Stratigrafia
Riv Ital Ig — Rivista Italiana d'Igiene
Riv Ital Ornitol — Rivista Italiana di Ornitologia
Riv Ital Paleontol Stratigr — Rivista Italiana di Paleontologia e Stratigrafia
Riv Ital Saldatura — Rivista Italiana della Saldatura
Riv Ital Sci Polit — Rivista Italiana di Scienza Politica
Riv Ital Sostanze Grasse — Rivista Italiana delle Sostanze Grasse
Riv Ital Sost Grasse — Rivista Italiana delle Sostanze Grasse
Riv Ital Stomatol — Rivista Italiana di Stomatologia
Riv Ital Trac Patol Ocul Virale Esotica — Rivista Italiana del Tracoma e di Patologia Oculare, Virale, ed Esotica
RivL — Rivista Letteraria. Licei Classico, Scientifico, Artistico, e Istituto Magistrale
Riv Let Mod — Rivista di Letteratura Moderne e Comparate
Riv Lett Mod — Rivista di Letteratura Moderne
Riv Lig — Rivista di Studi Liguri
Riv Malariol — Rivista Malariologia
Riv Maritt — Rivista Marittima
Riv Mat Sci Econom Social — Rivista di Matematica per le Scienze Economiche e Sociali
Riv Mat Univ Parma — Rivista di Matematica. Universita di Parma
Riv Mat Univ Parma 4 — Rivista di Matematica. Universita di Parma. Serie 4
Riv Mecc — Rivista di Meccanica
Riv Med Aer — Rivista di Medicina Aeronautica e Spaziale
Riv Med Aeronaut — Rivista di Medicina Aeronautica e Spaziale
Riv Med Aeronaut Spaz — Rivista di Medicina Aeronautica e Spaziale
Riv Mens Svizz Odontol Stomatol — Rivista Mensile Svizzera di Odontologia e Stomatologia
Riv Meteo A — Rivista di Meteorologia Aeronautica
Riv Meteorol Aeronaut — Rivista di Meteorologia Aeronautica
Riv Mineral Cristallogr Ital — Rivista di Mineralogia e Cristallografia Italiana
Riv Mineraria Sicil — Rivista Mineraria Siciliana [*Italy*]
Riv Min Sicil — Rivista Mineraria Siciliana
Riv Mus Italiana — Rivista Musicale Italiana
Riv Neurobiol — Rivista di Neurobiologia
Riv Neurol — Rivista di Neurologia
Riv Neuropsichiatr Sci Affini — Rivista di Neuropsichiatria e Scienze Affini
Riv Nuovo Cim — Rivista del Nuovo Cimento
Riv Nuovo Cimento Ser I — Rivista del Nuovo Cimento. Serie I
Riv Nuovo Cimento Soc Ital Fis — Rivista del Nuovo Cimento. Societa Italiana di Fisica [*Italy*]
Rivoluzione Ind — Rivoluzione Industriale [*Italy*]
Riv Ortoflorofruttic Ital — Rivista della Ortoflorofrutticoltura Italiana
Riv Osp Roma — Rivista Ospedaliera Roma
Riv Ostet Ginecol (Flor) — Rivista di Ostetricia e Ginecologia (Florence)
Riv Ostet Ginecol Prat — Rivista di Ostetricia e Ginecologia Pratica
Riv Ostet Ginecol Prat Med Perinat — Rivista di Ostetricia e Ginecologia Pratica e di Medicina Perinatale
Riv Oto-Neuro-Oftalmol — Rivista Oto-Neuro-Oftalmologica
Riv Oto-Neuro-Oftalmol Radio-Neuro-Chir — Rivista Oto-Neuro-Oftalmologica e Radio-Neuro-Chirurgica
Riv Parassit — Rivista di Parassitologia
Riv Parassitol — Rivista di Parassitologia
Riv Patol Appar Respir — Rivista Patologia dell'Apparato Respiratorio
Riv Patol Clin — Rivista di Patologia e Clinica
Riv Patol Clin Sper — Rivista di Patologia Clinica e Sperimentale
Riv Patol Clin Tuberc — Rivista di Patologia e Clinica della Tubercolosi
Riv Patol Clin Tuberc Pneumol — Rivista di Patologia e Clinica della Tubercolosi e di Pneumologia
Riv Patol Nerv Ment — Rivista di Patologia Nervosa e Mentale
Riv Patol Sper — Rivista di Patologia Sperimentale
Riv Patol Veg — Rivista di Patologia Vegetale
RivPed — Rivista Pedagogica
Riv Pediatr Sicil — Rivista Pediatrica Siciliana
Riv Per Lav Accad Sc Lett ed Arti Padova — Rivista Periodica del Lavori. Accademia di Scienze, Lettere, ed Arti di Padova
Riv Polit Agr — Rivista di Politica Agraria
Riv Polit Econ — Rivista di Politica Economica
RivR — Rivista delle Religioni
Riv Radiol — Rivista di Radiologia
Riv Rosmin Filos Cult — Rivista Rosminiana di Filosofia e di Cultura
Riv Sci Tecnol Alimenti Nutr Um — Rivista di Scienza e Tecnologia degli Alimenti e di Nutrizione Umana
Riv Sci Tecnol Aliment Nutr Umana — Rivista di Scienza e Tecnologia degli Alimenti e di Nutrizione Umana
Riv Sicil Tuberc Mal Respir — Rivista Siciliana della Tubercolosi e delle Malattie Respiratorie
Riv Sociol — Rivista di Sociologia
Riv Sper Freniatr Med Leg Alienazioni Ment — Rivista Sperimentale di Freniatria e Medicina Legale delle Alienazioni Mentali
Riv Stor — Rivista Storica Italiana
Riv Stor Ital — Rivista Storica Italiana
Riv Stud Croci — Rivista di Studi Crociani

Riv Studi Polit Int — Rivista di Studi Politici Internazionali
RivStudOr — Rivista degli Studi Orientali
Riv Stud Orient — Rivista degli Studi Orientali
Riv Suinicolt — Rivista di Suinicoltura
Riv Svizz Apic — Rivista Svizzera di Apicoltura
Riv Svizz Med Sport — Rivista Svizzera di Medicina dello Sport
Riv Tec Elettr — Rivista Tecnica d'Elettricita
Riv Tec Ferrovie Ital — Rivista Tecnica delle Ferrovie Italiane
Riv Tess — Rivista Tessile
Riv Tossicol Sper Clin — Rivista di Tossicologia Sperimentale e Clinica
Riv Trim Dir Pubbl — Rivista Trimestrale di Diritto Pubblico
Riv Trimest di Diritto Pubbl — Rivista Trimestrale di Diritto Pubblico
Riv Tuberc Mal Appar Respir — Rivista della Tubercolosi e delle Malattie dell'Apparato Respiratorio
Riv Tuberc Mal App Resp — Rivista della Tubercolosi e delle Malattie dell'Apparato Respiratorio
Riv Veneta Sc Med — Rivista Veneta di Scienze Mediche
Riv Vet — Rivista di Veterinaria
Riv Vitic Enol — Rivista di Viticoltura e di Enologia
Riv World — River World
Riv Zootec — Rivista di Zootecnia
Riv Zootec — Rivista di Zootecnia e Veterinaria
Riv Zootec Vet — Rivista di Zootecnia e Veterinaria
RIW — Review of Income and Wealth
RI Water Res Coordinating Board Geol Bull Hydrol Bull — Rhode Island. Water Resources Coordinating Board. Geological Bulletin. Hydrologic Bulletin
RI Water Resour Cent Annu Rep — Rhode Island Water Resources Center. Annual Report
Rizh Med Inst Sb Nauchn Rab — Rizhskii Meditsinskii Institut. Sbornik Nauchnykh Rabot
Riz Rizicult Cult Vivr Trop — Riz et Riziculture et Cultures Vivrieres Tropicales
Rizsk Inst Inz Grazdan Aviacii — Rizskii Institut Inzenerov Grazdanskoi Aviacii Imeni Leninskogo Komsomola
RJ — Revista Javeriana
RJ — Romanistisches Jahrbuch
RJ — Rusky Jazyk
RJaS — Russkij Jazyk v Skole
RJav — Revista Javeriana
RJaz — Rusky Jazyk
Rjazansk Gos Ped Inst Ucen Zap — Rjazanskii Gosudarstvennyi Pedagogiceskii Institut. Ucenye Zapiski
RJb — Romanistisches Jahrbuch
RJICA — Russian Journal of Inorganic Chemistry [*English Translation*]
RJL — Revue Juive de la Lorraine
RJMBA — Roczniki Akademii Medycznej Imienia Juliana Marchlewskiego w Bialymstoku
RJN — Robinson Jeffers Newsletter
RJPCA — Russian Journal of Physical Chemistry [*English Translation*]
RJPIC — Revue Juridique et Politique. Independance et Cooperation
RJR — Russkij Jazyk za Rubezom
RJS — Russkij Jazyk v Skole
RJSCA — Revue Jeumont-Schneider
RJSHDQ — Jugoslovanski Simpozij za Hmeljarstvo Referati
RJT — Revue Juridique Themis
R Jur — Revue Juridique
R Juridique — Revue Juridique
R Juridique et Econ Sud-Ouest Ser Econ — Revue Juridique et Economique du Sud-Ouest. Serie Economique
R Juridique et Pol — Revue Juridique et Politique
R Jur Polit — Revue Juridique et Politique. Independance et Cooperation
RJV — Rheinisches Jahrbuch fuer Volkskunde
RKANA — Rost Kristallov
RKCLA — Reaction Kinetics and Catalysis Letters
RKCSN — Rospravy Kralovske Ceske Spolecnosti Nauk
RKFJ — Rad Kongresa Folklorista Jugoslavije
RKHLit — Rocznik Komisji Historycznoliterackiej Pan
RKHS — Register. Kentucky Historical Society
RKJ — Rozprawy Komisji Jezykowej Lodzkiego Towarzystwa Naukowego
RKJL — Rozprawy Komisji Jezykowej Lodzkiego Towarzystwa Naukowego
RKJW — Rozprawy Komisji Jezykowej Wroclawskiego Towarzystwa Naukowego
RKKHA — Rikagaku Kenkyusho Hokoku
RKM — Risk Management
RKNKA — Rakuno Kagaku No Kenkyu
RKr — Rakstu Krajums
RKS — Rocket Stories
RKTEA — Rakennusteknikka
RKW — Repertorium fuer Kunstwissenschaft
RKZ — Reformierte Kirchenzeitung
RL — Radio Liberty
RL — Religion in Life
RL — Revista de Letras
RL — Revista de Literatura
RL — Revista Lusitana

RL — Revue de Lille
RL — Ricerche Linguistiche
RL — Rivista Letteraria
RL — Ruch Literacki [*Krakow*]
RL — Russian Literature
RLA — Revista de Letras. Faculdade de Filosofia, Ciencias, e Letras (Assis)
RLA — Revista Liturgica Argentina
RLAC — Reallexikon fuer Antike und Christentum
R Lang Rom — Revue des Langues Romanes
RLAQA — Revista Latinoamericana de Quimica
RLaR — Revue des Langues Romanes
R Latinoamer Psicol — Revista Latinoamericana de Psicologia
R Latinoamer Sociol — Revista Latinoamericana de Sociologia
R Latinoam Estud Urbano Reg — Revista Latinoamericana de Estudios Urbano Regionales
RLaV — Revue des Langues Vivantes
RLC — Rassegna Italiana di Lingue e Letteratura Classiche
RLC — Revue de Litterature Comparee
RLCAA — Railway Locomotives and Cars
RLCAD — Revista Latinoamericana de Ciencias Agricolas
RLeIt — Rassegna della Letteratura Italiana
R Let — Revista de Letras
R Lett Mod — Revue des Lettres Modernes
RLFE — Revista. Laboratorio de Fonetica Experimental
RLHAS — Revue de Litterature, Histoire, Arts, et Sciences
RLI — Rassegna della Letteratura Italiana
RLI — Revista de las Indias
RLi — Revue de Linguistique
RLing — Revue de Linguistique
RLing — Ricerche Linguistiche
RLing — Russian Linguistics
RLir — Realismo Lirico
RLiR — Revue de Linguistique Romane
RLit — Revista de Literatura
RLit — Russkaja Literatura
RLitC — Readings in Literary Criticism
R Litt Comp — Revue de Litterature Comparee
RLiv — Rivista di Livorno
RLJ — Rhodes-Livingstone Journal
RLJ — Russian Language Journal
RLL — Reviews in Leukemia and Lymphoma [*Elsevier Book Series*]
RLLO — Revue de Langue et Litterature d'Oc
RLLP — Revue de Langue et Litterature Provencales
RLLProv — Revue de Langue et Litterature Provencales
RLLR — Revue de Louisiane/Louisiana Review
RLM — Revista di Letterature Moderne e Comparate
RLM — Revue des Langues Modernes
RLM — Revue des Lettres Modernes
RLM — Rivista di Letterature Moderne e Comparate
RLMBA — Rendiconti. Istituto Lombardo. Accademia di Scienze e Lettere. Sezione B. Scienze Biologiche e Mediche
RLMC — Rivista di Letteratura Moderne e Comparate
RLMF — Revue du Louvre et des Musees de France
RLMod — Revue des Lettres Modernes
RLMPA — Revista Latinoamericana de Microbiologia y Parasitologia [*Later, Revista Latinoamericana de Microbiologia*]
RLMPB — Proceedings. Reliability and Maintainability Conference
RLOE — Roemische Limes in Oesterreich
RLORA — Revue de Laryngologie, Otologie, Rhinologie
RLOSA — Revue de Laryngologie, Otologie, Rhinologie. Supplement
R Louvre — Revue du Louvre et des Musees de France
R du Louvre — Revue du Louvre et des Musees de France
RLR — Revue des Langues Romanes
RLR — Revue de Linguistique Romane
RLR — Rutgers Law Review
RLRB — Radio Liberty Research Bulletin
RLS — Regional Language Studies [*Newfoundland*]
RLSCA — Research in Life Sciences
R L St — Rackham Literary Studies
RLSTA — Regelungstechnik
RLT — Russian Literature Triquarterly
RLu — Rassegna Lucchese
RLub — Rocznik Lubelski
RLuc — Rassegna Lucchese
RLux — Revue Trimestrielle d'Etudes Linguistiques, Folkloriques, et Toponymiques (Luxembourg)
RLV — Revue des Langues Vivantes
Rly Engng — Railway Engineering Journal [*Incorporated in Railway Engineer International*]
Rly Gaz — Railway Gazette [*Later, Railway Gazette International*]
RLz — Radjans'ke Literaturoznavstvo [*Kiev*]
R Lz — Radjans'ke Literaturoznavstvo. Naukovo-Teoretycnyj Zurnal
RM — Journal of Recreational Mathematics
RM — Rassegna Monetaria
RM — Rassegna Musicale
RM — Religionen der Menschheit

RM — Review of Metaphysics
RM — Revue de Metaphysique et de Morale
RM — Revue Mondiale
RM — Risk Management
RM — Rowohlts Monographien
RM — Russkaja Mysl'
RMA — Royal Musical Association. Proceedings
RMAAD — Revista Mexicana de Astronomia y Astrofisica
RMab — Revue Mabillon
RMAFA — Revista. Union Matematica Argentina y Asociacion Fisica Argentina
RMAL — Revue du Moyen-Age Latin [*Strasbourg*]
RMA Proc — Royal Musical Association. Proceedings
RMARC — Royal Musical Association. Research Chronicle
R Marche Commun — Revue du Marche Commun
RMA Res Chron — RMA [*Royal Musical Association*] Research Chronicle
RMA Research — Royal Musical Association. Research Chronicle
R Marketing & Ag Econ — Review of Marketing and Agricultural Economics
R Marketing and Agric Econ — Review of Marketing and Agricultural Economics
RMBI — Canadian Risk Management and Business Insurance
RMC — Revista Musical Chilena
R & McG — Income Tax Decisions of Australasia (Ratcliffe and McGrath)
R & McG Ct of Rev — Court of Review Decisions (Ratcliffe and McGrath)
R M Ch — Revista Musical Chilena
RMCLB — Revue Medico-Chirurgicale
RMCT — Research Monographs in Cell and Tissue Physiology [*Elsevier Book Series*]
RMD — Revue du Marche Commun
RMDAB — Revue de Medecine Aeronautique
RMDSA — Rivista di Medicina Aeronautica e Spaziale
RME — Railway Age
RMEA — Revista Mexicana de Estudios Antropologicos y Historicos
RMed — Revue de la Mediterranee
RMELB — Radio Mentor Electronic
R Melbourne Hosp Clin Rep — Royal Melbourne Hospital. Clinical Reports
RMEMD — Revue Roumaine de Morphologie, d'Embryologie, et de Physiologie. Serie Morphologie et Embryologie
RMEPD — Revue Roumaine de Morphologie, d'Embryologie, et de Physiologie. Serie Physiologie
RMERA — Rumanian Medical Review
R Mercados — Revista dos Mercados
R Metaphys — Review of Metaphysics
R Mex Agr — Revista del Mexico Agrario
R Mexic Sociol — Revista Mexicana de Sociologia
R Mexic Trab — Revista Mexicana del Trabajo
RMF — Research Management. The International Journal of Research Management
R M F C — Recherches sur la Musique Francaise Classique
RMFEB — Revista Mexicana de Fisica. Suplemento de Ensenanza
RMFFA — Raumfahrtforschung
RMFMA — Rock Mechanics
RMFSA — Revista Mexicana de Fisica. Suplemento del Reactor
RMFZA — Radovi Medicinskogo Fakulteta u Zagrebu
RMG — Russkaja Muzikal'naya Gazeta
RMGCA — Rocky Mountain Association of Geologists. Field Conference
RMGQA — Records Management Quarterly
RMH — Reserve Bank of Malawi. Financial and Economic Review
RMHPB — Reports on Mathematical Physics
RMI — Rassegna Mensile di Israel
RMI — Research Monographs in Immunology [*Elsevier Book Series*]
RMI — Rivista Mensile di Israel
RMI — Rivista Musicale Italiana
RMIIA — Rassegna di Medicina Industriale e di Igiene del Lavoro
R Mil Coll Can Civ Eng Res Rep — Royal Military College of Canada. Civil Engineering Research Report
RMIND — Reviews in Mineralogy
RMIs — Rassegna Mensile di Israel
RMJMA — Rocky Mountain Journal of Mathematics
RMJSA — Roczniki Akademii Medycznej Imienia Juliana Marchlewskiego w Bialymstoku. Suplement
R Mkting Agric Econ — Review of Marketing and Agricultural Economics
RMKUA — Report. Research Institute for Applied Mechanics (Kyushu University)
RML — Review of Metal Literature [*American Society for Metals*]
RML — Revista Mexicana de Literatura
RMLMA — Revue MBLE [*Manufacture Belge de Lampes et de Materiel*]
RMLR — Rocky Mountain Law Review
RMM — Revue de Metaphysique et de Morale
RMM — Revue du Monde Musulman
RMMFA — Revue Medico-Chirurgicale des Maladies du Foie, de la Rate, et du Pancreas
RMMID — Revue Roumaine de Medecine. Serie Medecine Interne
RMMJA — Rocky Mountain Medical Journal
RMMND — Rocky Mountain Mineral Law Newsletter

RMNac — Revista. Museo Nacional
RMNZA — Rudy i Metale Niezelazne
RMod — Revue Moderne
RMP — International Migration
RMP — Rheinisches Museum fuer Philologie
RMPaul — Revista. Museu Paulista
RMPIA — Razrabotka Mestorozhdenii Poleznykh Iskopaemykh
RMPPA — Revue de Medecine Psychosomatique et de Psychologie Medicale
RMQ — Records Management Quarterly
RMR — Rocky Mountain Law Review
RMR — Rocky Mountain Review
RMRHB — Rheumatology and Rehabilitation
RMRMA — Revue M - Mecanique [*Belgium*]
RMS — Renaissance and Modern Studies
RMS — Revista Mexicana de Sociologia
RMSCA — Rivista Mineraria Siciliana
RMSFA — Revista Mexicana de Fisica. Suplemento de Fisica Aplicada
RMSRA — Revue Medicale de la Suisse Romande
RMSSJ — Rocky Mountain Social Science Journal
RMSt — Reading Medieval Studies
RMTAA — Rivista di Meteorologia Aeronautica
RMTRD — Revue de Medicine du Travail
RMTSA — Revista. Instituto de Medicina Tropical de Sao Paulo
RMu — Revue Musicale
R de MU — Revue de Musicologie [*Paris*]
R Mus — Revue Musicale
R de Mus — Revue de Musicologie
R Mus Art Archeol — Revue du Musee d'Art et d'Archeologie
R Mus Chile — Revista Musical Chilena
R Mus Ital — Nuova Rivista Musicale Italiana. Trimestrale di Cultura e Informazione Musicale
R Mus Ital — Rivista Musicale Italiana
R Mus La Plata Antropol — Revista. Museo de La Plata. Seccion Antropologia
R Mus Nac — Revista. Museo Nacional
R Mus de Suisse Romande — Revue Musicale de Suisse Romande
RMZBA — Rudarsko-Metalurski Zbornik
RN — Renaissance News
RN — Revue du Nord
R du N — Revue du Notariat
RN — Revue Nouvelle
RN — Revue Numismatique
RN — Rough Notes
RNAO News — RNAO (Registered Nurses Association of Ontario) News
RNap — Revue Napoleonienne
RNar — Ragioni Narrative
R Navig Fluv Europ — Revue de la Navigation Fluviale Europeenne
RNaz — Rassegna Nazionale
RNBLA — Rivista di Neurobiologia
RNCT — Reports of the Working Committees. Northeast Conference on the Teaching of Foreign Languages
RND — Rocznik Naukowo-Dydaktyczny
RNDPD — Roundup [*United States*]
RNeosc — Revue Neo-Scolastique de Philosophie
RNGMA — Refiner and Natural Gasoline Manufacturer
RNGYA — Rhinology
RNI — Research Notes (Ibadan)
RNI — Research Policy. A Journal Devoted to Research Policy, Research Management, and Planning
RN ID — RN Idaho
RNKID — Rikuyo Nainen Kikan
RNL — Retail Newsletter
RNL — Review of National Literatures
RNM — Revista Nacional (Montevideo)
RN Mag — RN Magazine
RNMTA — Rendiconti di Matematica
RN and O — Raleigh News and Observer
R Nord — Revue du Nord
R du Not — Revue du Notariat
RNOUD — Revue Nouvelle
R Nouv — Revue Nouvelle
RNRLA — Report of Naval Research Laboratory Progress [*United States*]
RNS — Revue Neo-Scolastique de Philosophie
RNSJA — Rinsho Seijinbyo
RNSP — Revue Neo-Scolastique de Philosophie
RNUCA — Rivista del Nuovo Cimento. Societa Italiana di Fisica
RNum — Rassegna Numismatica
RNum — Revue Numismatique
RNVSDY — Kongelige Norske Videnskabers Selskabs. Museet Botanisk Avdeling Rapport
RNWSD — Research News
RNZ — Reserve Bank of New Zealand. Bulletin
RO — Revista de Occidente
RO — Revue Orientale
RO — Rocznik Orientalistyczny
RO — Roemisches Oesterreich. Jahresschrift der Oesterreichischen Gesellschaft fuer Archaeologie

R & O — Roma e l'Oriente
Ro — Romania
ROA — RAS. Rohr-Armatur-Sanitaer-Heizung Informationsblatt fuer den Fachhandel und das Sanitaerfach und Heizungsfach
ROA — Report on the ORT Activities [*Paris/Geneva*]
Road Abstr — Road Abstracts
Road A R — Road Apple Review
Road Maps — Economic Road Maps
Road Note Road Res Lab (UK) — Road Note. Road Research Laboratory (United Kingdom)
Road Res Bull — Road Research Bulletin
Road Res Lab (UK) RRL Rep — Road Research Laboratory (United Kingdom). RRL Report
Road Res Monogr — Road Research Monographs
Road Res Notes — Road Research Notes
Road Res Pap — Road Research Papers
Road Saf — Road Safety
Roads & Bridges — Roads and Bridges
Roads & Constr — Roads and Construction
Roads & Eng Constr — Roads and Engineering Construction
Roads Road Constr — Roads and Road Construction
Roads St — Roads and Streets
Road Transp Aust — Road Transporter of Australia
Road Transp of Aust — Road Transporter of Australia
ROB — Review of Business
ROB — Rijksdienst voor het Oudheidkundig Bodemonderzoek
ROB — Robotics Age
Robert A Taft Sanit Eng Cent Tech Rep — Robert A. Taft Sanitary Engineering Center. Technical Report
Robert A Welch Found Res Bull — Robert A. Welch Foundation. Research Bulletin
Robert Morris Associates Bull — Robert Morris Associates. Bulletin
Robotics T — Robotics Today
Robotron Tech Commun — Robotron Technical Communications
R Obs Ann — Royal Observatory. Annals
R Obs Bull — Royal Observatory. Bulletins
ROC — Revue de l'Orient Chretien
Rocas Miner — Rocas y Minerales
R Occid Musul Mediterr — Revue de l'Occident Musulman et de la Mediterranee
ROCHA — Roczniki Chemii
Roche Image Med Res — Roche Image of Medicine and Research
Roche Med Image Comment — Roche Medical Image and Commentary
Rochester Acad Sci Proc — Rochester Academy of Science. Proceedings
Rochester Conf Data Acquis Processing Biol Med Proc — Rochester Conference on Data Acquisition and Processing in Biology and Medicine. Proceedings
Rochester Hist — Rochester History
Rochester Hist Soc Publ Fund Ser — Rochester Historical Society. Publication Fund Series
Rochester Univ Lib Bul — University of Rochester. Library Bulletin
Roch Patr — Rochester Patriot
Roch Phil — Rochester Philharmonic Orchestra. Program Notes
ROCIA — Rozhledy v Chirurgii
Rocket News Lett — Rocket News Letter
Rocket Propul Technol — Rocket Propulsion Technology
Rock Magn Paleogeophys — Rock Magnetism and Paleogeophysics
Rock Mech — Rock Mechanics
Rock Mech Felsmech Mec Roches — Rock Mechanics/Felsmechanik/ Mecanique des Roches
Rock Prod — Rock Products
Rocks Miner — Rocks and Minerals
Rocky Mountain J Math — Rocky Mountain Journal of Mathematics
Rocky Mount Med J — Rocky Mountain Medical Journal
Rocky Mt Bioeng Symp Proc — Rocky Mountain Bioengineering Symposium. Proceedings
Rocky Mt J Math — Rocky Mountain Journal of Mathematics
Rocky Mt L Rev — Rocky Mountain Law Review
Rocky Mt Med J — Rocky Mountain Medical Journal
Rocky Mt Miner Law Inst Annu Inst Proc — Rocky Mountain Mineral Law Institute. Annual Institute Proceedings
Rocky Mt Min L Inst Proc — Rocky Mountain Mineral Law Institute. Proceedings
Rocky Mtn L Rev — Rocky Mountain Law Review
Rocky Mtn Oil Reporter — Rocky Mountain Oil Reporter
Rocky Mt So — Rocky Mountain Social Science Journal
Rocky Mt Soc Sci J — Rocky Mountain Social Science Journal
Rocky Mt Spectrosc Conf (Program Abstr) — Rocky Mountain Spectroscopy Conference (Program and Abstracts)
Rocla Pipes Ltd Tech J — Rocla Pipes Limited. Technical Journal
RocO — Rocznik Orientalistyczny [*Warszawa*]
Rocz Akad Med Bialostoku — Roczniki Akademii Medycznej Imienia Juliana Marchlewskiego w Bialymstoku
Rocz Akad Med Bialymstoku Supl — Roczniki Akademii Medycznej Imienia Juliana Marchlewskiego w Bialymstoku. Suplement

Rocz Akad Med Juliana Marchlewskiego Bialymstoku — Roczniki Medycznej Imienia Juliana Marchlewskiego w Bialymstoku
Rocz Akad Med Juliana Marchlewskiego Bialymstoku Supl — Roczniki Akademii Medycznej Imienia Juliana Marchlewskiego w Bialymstoku. Suplement
Rocz Akad Roln Poznaniu — Roczniki Akademii Rolniczej w Poznaniu [*Poland*]
Rocz Akad Roln Poznaniu Pr Habilitacyjne — Roczniki Akademii Rolniczej w Poznaniu. Prace Habilitacyjne
Rocz Bialostocki — Rocznik Bialostocki
Rocz Chem — Roczniki Chemii
Rocz Glebozn — Roczniki Gleboznawcze
RoczH — Roczniki Humanistyczne Katolickiego Uniwersytetu
Rocz Hist — Roczniki Historyczne
Rocz Inst Przem Mlecz — Roczniki Instytutu Przemyslu Mleczarskiego [*Poland*]
Rocz Jeleniogorski — Rocznik Jeleniogorski
Rocz Krakowski — Rocznik Krakowski
Rocz Muz Etnogr — Rocznik Muzeum Etnograficznego w Krakowie
Rocz Muz Narod Warszawie — Rocznik Muzeum Narodowego w Warszawie
Rocz Muz Swiet — Rocznik Muzeum Swietokrzyskiego
Rocz Muz Toruniu — Rocznik Muzeum w Toruniu
Roczn Akad Roln Poznan — Roczniki Akademii Rolniczej w Poznaniu
Rocz Nauk Roln — Roczniki Nauk Rolniczych
Rocz Nauk Roln Les — Roczniki Nauk Rolniczych i Lesnych
Rocz Nauk Roln Lesn — Roczniki Nauk Rolniczych i Lesnych
Rocz Nauk Roln Ser A — Roczniki Nauk Rolniczych. Seria A
Rocz Nauk Roln Ser A Prod Rosl — Roczniki Nauk Rolniczych. Seria A. Produkcja Roslinna
Rocz Nauk Roln Ser B — Roczniki Nauk Rolniczych. Seria B. Zootechniczna
Rocz Nauk Roln Ser B Zootech — Roczniki Nauk Rolniczych. Seria B. Zootechniczna
Rocz Nauk Roln Ser C Mech Roln — Roczniki Nauk Rolniczych. Seria C. Mechznizacja Rolnictwa
Rocz Nauk Roln Ser C Tech Roln — Roczniki Nauk Rolniczych. Seria C. Technika Rolnicza [*Continues Seria C. Mechznizacja Rolnictwa*]
Rocz Nauk Roln Ser D — Roczniki Nauk Rolniczych. Seria D. Monografie
Rocz Nauk Roln Ser D Monogr — Roczniki Nauk Rolniczych. Seria D. Monografie
Rocz Nauk Roln Ser E 1953-60 — Roczniki Nauk Rolniczych. Seria E. Weterynarii 1953-60
Rocz Nauk Roln Ser E Ochr Rosl — Roczniki Nauk Rolniczych. Seria E. Ochrona Roslin
Rocz Nauk Roln Ser F — Roczniki Nauk Rolniczych. Seria F. Melioracji i Vzytkow Zielonych
Rocz Nauk Roln Ser F Melio Vzytkow Zielonych — Roczniki Nauk Rolniczych. Seria F. Melioracji i Vzytkow Zielonych
Rocz Nauk Roln Ser H Rybactwo — Roczniki Nauk Rolniczych. Seria H. Rybactwo
Rocz Nauk Zootech — Roczniki Naukowe Zootechniki
Rocz Nauk Zootech Monogr Rozpr — Roczniki Naukowe Zootechniki. Monografie i Rozprawy
Rocz Nauk Zootech Pol J Anim Sci Technol — Rocznik Naukowe Zootechniki. Polish Journal of Animal Science and Technology
Roczn Chem — Roczniki Chemii
Roczni Glebozn — Roczniki Gleboznawcze
Roczn Inst Handlu Wewn — Rocznik Instytutu Handlu Wewnetrznego
Roczn Nauk Roln A — Roczniki Nauk Rolniczych. A. Produkcja Roslinna
Roczn Panst Zakl Hig — Roczniki Panstwowego Zakladu Higieny
Roczn Wyz Szk Roln Poznan — Rocznik Wyzszej Szkoly Rolniczej Poznaniu
RoczOr — Rocznik Orientalistyczny [*Warsaw*]
Rocz Panstw Zakl Hig — Roczniki Panstwowego Zakladu Higieny
Rocz Panst Zakl Hig (Warszawa) — Roczniki Panstwowego Zakladu Higieny (Warszawa)
Rocz Pol Tow Geol — Rocznik Polskiego Towarzystwa Geologicznego
Rocz Pomor Akad Med Im Gen Karola Swierczewskiego Szczecin — Roczniki Pomorska Akademia Medyczna Imeni Generala Karola Swierczewskiego w Szczecinia
Rocz Pomor Akad Med Szczecinie — Rocznik Pomorskiej Akademii Medycznej Imienia Generala Karola Swierczewskiego w Szczecinie [*Poland*]
Rocz Pomor Akad Med Szczecinie — Roczniki Pomorskiej Akademii Medycznej w Szczecinie
Rocz Pomor Akad Med Szczecinie Supl — Roczniki Pomorskiej Akademii Medycznej w Szczecinie. Suplement
Rocz Sekc Dendrol Pol Tow Bot — Rocznik Sekcji Dendrologicznej Polskiego Towarzystwa Botanicznego
RoczSl — Rocznik Slawistyczny
Rocz Technol Chem Zywn — Roczniki Technologii Chemii Zywnosci
Rocz Wojsk Inst Hig Epidemiol — Rocznik Wojskowego Instytutu Higieny i Epidemiologii [*Poland*]
Rocz Wyzs Szkoly Roln Poznaniu — Roczniki Wyzszej Szkoly Rolniczej w Poznaniu
Rocz Wyzsz Roln Poznaniu — Roczniki Wyzszej Szkoly Rolniczej w Poznaniu
Rocz Wyzsz Szk Roln Poznaniu Pr Habilitacyjne — Roczniki Wyzszej Szkoly Rolniczej w Poznaniu. Prace Habilitacyjne

Rod and Gun and Canad Silver Fox News — Rod and Gun and Canadian Silver Fox News
Rodopskii Zbor — Rodopskii Zbornik
RODSB — Revue d'Odonto-Stomatologie
ROE — Review of Economics and Statistics
ROE — Roemisches Oesterreich
RoeFo Fortschr Geb Roentgenstr Nuklearmed — RoeFo. Fortschritte auf dem Gebiete der Roentgenstrahlen und der Nuklearmedizin [*West Germany*]
Roem Jahr Kunstges — Roemisches Jahrbuch fuer Kunstgeschichte
Roem Mitt — Mitteilungen. Deutsches Archaeologische Institut. Abteilung Rome
Roem Q — Roemische Quartalschrift
Roem Q — Roemische Quartalschrift fuer Christliche Altertumskunde und fuer Kirchengeschichte
ROEND — Roentgenstrahlen
Roentgen Ber — Roentgen Berichte
Roentgen-Bl — Roentgen-Blaetter
Roentgen Laboratoriumsprax — Roentgen Laboratoriumspraxis
Roentgenprax — Roentgenpraxis
Roentgen Technol — Roentgen Technology. Official Journal of the Indian Association of Radiological Technologists
ROF — Romanische Forschungen
RofThPh — Review of Theology and Philosophy
ROGLA — Roczniki Gleboznawcze
ROGNA — Rivista di Ostetricia e Ginecologia
RoH — Roumeliotiko Hemerologio
Rohm Haas Rep — Rohm and Haas Reporter
ROHRA — Rohre, Rohrleitungsbau, Rohrleitungstransport
Rohre Rohrleitungsbau Rohrleitungstransp — Rohre, Rohrleitungsbau, Rohrleitungstransport [*West Germany*]
RoHum — Roczniki Humanistyczne
ROJ — Romanistisches Jahrbuch
ROKAA — Rodo Kagaku
ROKOA5 — Folia Entomologica Hungarica
ROL — Revue de l'Orient Latin
RoLit — Romania Literara
Roll Stone — Rolling Stone
Rom — Romania
Roma Econ — Roma Economica
Romagna Med — Romagna Medica
Romance Philol — Romance Philology
Roman Forsc — Romanische Forschungen
Roman Forsch — Romanische Forschungen
Romanian F — Romanian Film
Romanian R — Romanian Review
Roman Note — Romance Notes
Roman Phil — Romance Philology
Roman Philol — Romance Philology
Roman R — Romanic Review
Roman Rev — Romanic Review
Roman Z Lit — Romanistische Zeitschrift fuer Literaturgeschichte [*Cahiers d'Histoire des Litteratures Romanes*]
Rom Com Geol Dari Seama Sedin — Romania Comitetul de Stat al Geologiei. Institutul Geologic. Dari de Seama ale Sedintelor
RomF — Romanische Forschungen
Rom Fgn Tr — Romanian Foreign Trade
Rom G — Romanica Gandensia
Rom Inst Geol Dari Seama Sedin — Romania Institutul Geologic. Dari de Seama ale Sedintelor
Rom Inst Geol Mem — Romania Institutul Geologic. Memorii
Rom Inst Geol Stud Teh Econ Ser B — Romania Institutul Geologic. Studii Tehnice si Economice. Seria B. Prepararea Minereurilor
Rom Inst Geol Stud Teh Econ Ser D — Romania Institutul Geologic. Studii Tehnice si Economice. Seria D. Prospectiuni Geofizice
Rom Inst Geol Stud Teh Econ Ser E — Romania. Institutul Geologic. Studii Tehnice si Economice. Seria E
Rom Inst Geol Stud Teh Econ Ser I — Romania Comitetul de Stat al Geologiei. Institutul Geologic. Studii Tehnice si Economice. Seria I. Mineralogie-Petrografie
Rom Inst Meteorol Hidrol Stud Hidrogeol — Romania Institutul de Meteorologie si Hidrologie. Studii de Hidrogeologie
RomJ — Romanistisches Jahrbuch
Rom J Chem — Romanian Journal of Chemistry
Rom J Med Endocrinol — Romanian Journal of Medicine. Endocrinology
Rom J Med Intern Med — Romanian Journal of Medicine. Internal Medicine
Rom J Med Neurol Psychiatry — Romanian Journal of Medicine. Neurology and Psychiatry
Rom J Med Virol — Romanian Journal of Medicine. Virology
RomLit — Romania Literara [*Bucharest*]
ROMM — Revue de l'Occident Musulman et de la Mediterranee
Rom Med Rev — Romanian Medical Review
RomN — Romance Notes
RomPh — Romance Philology
R⌐nR — Romanic Review

RomSl — Romanoslavica
Rom Today — Romania Today
RoN — Romance Notes
RONOA — Revue d'Oto-Neuro-Ophtalmologie
R Ont Mus J — Royal Ontario Museum. Journal
R Ont Mus Life Sci Contrib — Royal Ontario Museum. Life Sciences. Contributions
R Ont Mus Life Sci Misc Publ — Royal Ontario Museum. Life Sciences. Miscellaneous Publications
R Ont Mus Life Sci Occas Pap — Royal Ontario Museum. Life Sciences. Occasional Paper
R Ont Mus Zool Paleontol Contrib — Royal Ontario Museum of Zoology and Paleontology. Contributions
Roorkee Univ Res J — Roorkee University. Research Journal
Roosevelt Wild Life Bull — Roosevelt Wild Life Bulletin
ROP — Romance Philology
ROPM — Revue. Ordre de Premontre et de Ses Missions
ROPRA — Rock Products
ROPXA — Roentgenpraxis
RoR — Review of Religion
RoR — Romanian Review
ROR — Romanic Review
RORD — Research Opportunities in Renaissance Drama
Rose Annu R Natl Rose Soc — Rose Annual. Royal National Rose Society
RoSlaw — Rocznik Slawistyczny
Ross Conf Med Res Rep — Ross Conference on Medical Research. Report
ROSTA — Roads and Streets
ROSTA Bull — ROSTA [*Victoria. Road Safety and Traffic Authority*] Bulletin
Rost Krist — Rost Kristallov
Rostl Vyroba — Rostlinna Vyroba
Rostl Vyroba Cesk Akad Zemed Ustav Vedeckotech Inf Zemed — Rostlinna Vyroba-Ceskoslovenska Akademie Zemedelska. Ustav Vedeckotechnickych Informaci pro Zemedelstvi
Rostocker Phys Manuskr — Rostocker Physikalische Manuskripte
Rostock Math Kolloq — Rostocker Mathematisches Kolloquium
Rostov Gidrometeorol Obs Sb Rab — Rostovskaya Gidrometeorologicheskaya Observatoriya. Sbornik Rabot
Rostov-na Donu Gos Ped Inst Fiz Mat Fak Ucen Zap — Rostovskii-Na-Donu Gosudarstvennyi Pedagogiceskii Institut. Fiziko-Matematiceskii Fakultet Ucenye Zapiski
Rostov-na-Donu Gos Univ Ucen Zap — Rostovskii-Na-Donu Gosudarstvennyi Universitet. Ucenyi Zapiski
Rost Ustoich Rast — Rost i Ustoichivost Rastenii
Rost Ustoich Rast Respub Mezhved Sb — Rost i Ustoichivost Rastenii Respublikanskii Mezhvedomstvennyi Sbornik
ROT — Rechtsinformation. Berichte und Dokumente zum Auslaendischen Wirtschafts- und Steuerrecht
ROTAA — Road Tar
ROTAD — Round Table
Rotation Method Crystallogr — Rotation Method in Crystallography
Rotenburg Schr — Rotenburger Schriften
Rothamsted Exp Stn Rep — Rothamsted Experimental Station. Report
Rothamsted Exp Stn Rep Part 1 — Rothamsted Experimental Station. Report. Part 1
Rothamsted Exp Stn Rep Part 2 — Rothamsted Experimental Station. Report. Part 2
Rothmill Q — Rothmill Quarterly
RoTKan — Roczniki Teologiczno-Kanoniczne [*Lubin*]
ROTOB — Romania Today
ROUHA — Ropa a Uhlie
Round Tab — Round Table
Roux Archiv EntwMech Organ — Roux Archiv fuer Entwicklungsmechanik der Organismen
Rov Koezlem — Rovartani Koezlemenyek
ROVYA — Rostlinna Vyroba
ROW — Romanian Engineering
Rowett Res Inst Annu Rep Stud Anim Nutr Allied Sci — Rowett Research Institute. Annual Report. Studies in Animal Nutrition and Allied Sciences
ROWJ — Records of Oceanographic Works in Japan
ROWJA — Records of Oceanographic Works in Japan
Roy Aeronaut Soc J — Royal Aeronautical Society. Journal
Royal — [*The*] Royal Magazine
Royal Agric Soc England J — Journal. Royal Agricultural Society of England
Royal Astron Soc Canada Jour — Royal Astronomical Society of Canada. Journal
Royal Astron Soc Geophys Jour — Royal Astronomical Society. Geophysical Journal
Royal Astron Soc Monthly Notices Geophys Supp — Royal Astronomical Society. Monthly Notices. Geophysical Supplements
Royal Astron Soc Quart Jour — Royal Astronomical Society. Quarterly Journal
Royal Aust Army Ed Corps News — Royal Australian Army. Educational Corps. Newsletter

Royal Aust Chem Inst J & Proc — Royal Australian Chemical Institute. Journal and Proceedings

Royal Aust Chem Inst Proc — Royal Australian Chemical Institute. Proceedings

Royal Aust Hist Soc J — Royal Australian Historical Society. Journal and Proceedings

Royal Aust Hist Soc J & Proc — Royal Australian Historical Society. Journal and Proceedings

Royal Australian Planning Inst Jnl — Royal Australian Planning Institute. Journal

Royalauto — Royalauto [*Royal Automobile Club of Victoria*] Journal

Royal Bank Can Mo Letter — Royal Bank of Canada. Monthly Letter

Royal Empire Soc News — Royal Empire Society. News

Royal Geog Soc Asia SA Branch Proc — Royal Geographical Society of Australasia. South Australian Branch. Proceedings

Royal Hist Soc Q Hist Misc — Royal Historical Society of Queensland. Historical Miscellanea

Royal Hist Soc QJ — Royal Historical Society of Queensland. Journal

Royal Hist Soc Trans — Royal Historical Society. Transactions

Royal Hort Soc J — Royal Horticultural Society. Journal

Royal Inst of British Archts Trans — Royal Institute of British Architects. Transactions

Royal Microscopical Soc Proc — Royal Microscopical Society. Proceedings

Royal Ontario Mus Div Zoology and Palaeontology Contr — Royal Ontario Museum. Division of Zoology and Palaeontology. Contributions

Royal Perth Hospital J — Royal Perth Hospital. Journal

Royal Prince Alfred Hospital J — Royal Prince Alfred Hospital. Journal

Royal Soc Arts Jnl — Royal Society of Arts. Journal

Royal Soc Canada Proc — Royal Society of Canada. Proceedings

Royal Soc of Health Jnl — Royal Society of Health. Journal

Royal Soc Hlth J — Royal Society of Health. Journal

Royal Soc NSW J & Proc — Royal Society of New South Wales. Journal and Proceedings

Royal Soc Q Proc — Royal Society of Queensland. Proceedings

Royal Soc SA Trans — Royal Society of South Australia. Transactions

Royal Soc Tasmania Papers and Proc — Royal Society of Tasmania. Papers and Proceedings

Royal Soc Tas Papers & Proc — Royal Society of Tasmania. Papers and Proceedings

Royal Soc Vic Proc — Royal Society of Victoria. Proceedings

Royal Soc Victoria Proc — Royal Society of Victoria. Proceedings

Royal Statis Soc J Ser A Gen — Journal. Royal Statistical Society. Series A. General

Royalton R — Royalton Review

Royal Zoological Soc NSW Proc — Royal Zoological Society of New South Wales. Proceedings

Roy Arch Inst Can J — Royal Architectural Institute of Canada. Journal

Roy Astron Soc Mem — Royal Astronomical Society. Memoirs

Roy Aust Hist J — Royal Australian Historical Society. Journal

Roy Aust Hist Soc J Proc — Royal Australian Historical Society. Journal and Proceedings

Roy Can Inst Trans — Royal Canadian Institute. Transactions

Roy Eng J — Royal Engineers Journal

Roy His S — Royal Historical Society. Transactions

Roy Hist Soc Qld Hist Misc — Royal Historical Society of Queensland. Historical Miscellanea

Roy Hist Soc Qld J — Royal Historical Society of Queensland. Journal

Roy Hist Soc Trans — Royal Historical Society. Transactions

Roy Hist Soc Vic News — Royal Historical Society of Victoria. Newsletter

Roy Hort Soc J — Royal Horticultural Society. Journal

Roy Inst Brit Arch J — Royal Institute of British Architects. Journal

Roy Inst Nav Architects Quart Trans — Royal Institution of Naval Architects [*London*]. Quarterly Transactions

Roy Inst Ph — Royal Institute of Philosophy. Lectures

Roy Meteorol Soc Q J — Royal Meteorological Society. Quarterly Journal

Roy Microscop Soc Proc — Royal Microscopical Society. Proceedings

Roy Micros Soc J — Royal Microscopical Society. Journal

Roy Soc Arts J — Royal Society of Arts. Journal

Roy Soc Can — Royal Society of Canada. Proceedings and Transactions

Roy Soc of Canada Trans — Royal Society of Canada. Proceedings and Transactions

Roy Soc Edinb Trans — Royal Society of Edinburgh. Transactions

Roy Soc of Edinburgh Trans — Royal Society of Edinburgh. Transactions

Roy Soc Hea — Royal Society of Health. Journal

Roy Soc of London Philos Trans — Royal Society of London. Philosophical Transactions

Roy Soc Lond Philos Trans — Royal Society of London. Philosophical Transactions

Roy Soc of New South Wales Jour and Proc — Royal Society of New South Wales. Journal and Proceedings

Roy Soc NSW J — Royal Society of New South Wales. Journal

Roy Soc NSW J & Proc — Royal Society of New South Wales. Journal and Proceedings

Roy Soc NZ J — Royal Society of New Zealand. Journal

Roy Soc NZ Proc — Royal Society of New Zealand. Proceedings

Roy Soc NZ Trans — Royal Society of New Zealand. Transactions

Roy Soc NZ Trans Bot — Royal Society of New Zealand. Transactions. Botany

Roy Soc NZ Trans Earth Sci — Royal Society of New Zealand. Transactions. Earth Sciences

Roy Soc NZ Trans Gen — Royal Society of New Zealand. Transactions. General

Roy Soc NZ Trans Geol — Royal Society of New Zealand. Transactions. Geology

Roy Soc NZ Trans Zool — Royal Society of New Zealand. Transactions. Zoology

Roy Soc Proc — Proceedings. Royal Society

Roy Soc Qld Proc — Royal Society of Queensland. Proceedings

Roy Soc SA Trans — Royal Society of South Australia. Transactions

Roy Soc Tas Papers — Royal Society of Tasmania. Papers and Proceedings

Roy Soc Vic Proc — Royal Society of Victoria. Proceedings

Roy Soc WA J — Royal Society of Western Australia. Journal

Roy Stat Soc J — Royal Statistical Society. Journal

Roy Telev Soc J — Royal Television Society. Journal

Roy Town Plan Inst — Royal Town Planning Institute. Journal

Roy West Aust Hist Soc J Proc — Royal Western Australian Historical Society. Journal and Proceedings

Roy Zool Soc NSW Proc — Royal Zoological Society of New South Wales. Proceedings

Roz Cesk Akad — Rozpravy Ceskoslovenske Akademie Ved

Rozhl Chir — Rozhledy v Chirurgii

Rozhl Tuberk Nemocech Plicn — Rozhledy v Tuberkulose a v Nemocech Plicnich

Roz Narod Tech Muz Praze — Rozpravy Narodniho Technickeho Muzea v Praze

Rozpr Akad Roln Szczecinie — Rozprawy. Akademia Rolnicza w Szczecinie

Rozpravy CSAV — Rozpravy Ceskoslovenske Akademie Ved

Rozprawy Elektrotech — Rozprawy Elektrotechniczne. Polska Akademia Nauk. Instytut Technologii Elektronowej.

Rozprawy Politech Poznan — Rozprawy. Politechnika Poznanska

Rozpr Cesk Akad Rada Tech Ved — Rozpravy Ceskoslovenske Akademie Ved. Rada Technickych Ved [*Czechoslovakia*]

Rozpr Cesk Akad Ved Rada Mat Prir Ved — Rozpravy Ceskoslovenske Akademie Ved. Rada Matematickych a Prirodnich Ved

Rozpr Cesk Akad Ved Rada Tech Ved — Rozpravy Ceskoslovenske Akademie Ved. Rada Technickych Ved

Rozpr Elektrotech — Rozprawy Elektrotechniczne

Rozpr Hydrotech — Rozprawy Hydrotechniczne

Rozpr Inz — Rozprawy Inzynierskie

Rozpr Politech Poznan — Rozprawy. Politechnika Poznanska

Rozpr Politech Rzeszowska Im Ignacego Lukasiewicza — Rozprawy. Politechnika Rzeszowska Imienia Ignacego Lukasiewicza

Rozpr Ustred Ustavu Geol — Rozpravy Ustredniho Ustavu Geologickeho

Rozpr Wydz 3 Nauk Mat Przyr Gdansk Tow Nauk — Rozprawy Wydzialu 3. Nauk Matematyczno-Przyrodniczych. Gdanskie Towarzystwo Naukowe

Rozpr Wydz Nauk Med Pol Akad Nauk — Rozprawy Wydzialu Nauk Medyczynch Polska Akademia Nauk

RP — Regulatory Peptides

RP — Renaissance Papers

RP — Review of Politics

RP — Revista de Portugal

RP — Revue de Paris

RP — Revue de Philologie, de Litterature, et d'Histoire Anciennes

RP — Revue Philosophique

RP — Revue de Phonetique [*Paris*]

RP — Romance Philology

RPA — British Plastics and Rubber

RPa — Revue de Paris

RPA — Revue de Phonetique Appliquee [*Paris*]

RPA — Revue Pratique d'Apologetique

RPA — RPA [*Royal Prince Alfred Hospital*] Magazine

RPAA — Rendiconti. Pontificia Accademia di Archeologia

R Pac — Revue du Pacifique. Etudes de Litterature Francaise

RPACA — Reports on the Progress of Applied Chemistry

RPACDV — Australia. Commonwealth Scientific and Industrial Research Organisation. Division of Applied Organic Chemistry. Research Report

R Palaeobot & Palynol — Review of Palaeobotany and Palynology

RPall — Revue Palladienne

R Paraguaya Sociol — Revista Paraguaya de Sociologia

R de Paris — Revue de Paris

RPAS — Review. Polish Academy of Sciences

R Pays Est — Revue des Pays de l'Est

Rp B Bk R — Reprint Bulletin. Book Reviews

RPCSB — Rivista di Patologia Clinica e Sperimentale

RPD — Radiation Protection Dosimetry

RPD — Review of Public Data Use

RPDED — Revue du Palais de la Deouverte

RPDQDK — Queensland. Department of Forestry. Research Paper

RPE — Revue d'Etudes Comparatives Est-Ouest

RPed — Revue Pedagogique

R Pernambucana Desenvolvimento — Revista Pernambucana de Desenvolvimento

R Peruana Derecho Internac — Revista Peruana de Derecho Internacional

RPF — Revista Portuguesa de Filologia
RPF — Revue de la Pensee Francaise
RPFADG — Forests Department of Western Australia. Research Paper
RPFCA — Revue Pratique du Froid et du Conditionnement de l'Air [*Later, Journal RPF*]
RPFE — Revue Philosophique de la France et de l'Etranger
RPFilos — Revista Portuguesa de Filosofia
RPFL — Revue de Philologie Francaise et de Litterature
RPFUB — Radovi Poljoprivrednog Fakulteta Univerziteta u Sarajevu
RPGPA — Recent Publications on Governmental Problems
RPH — Revista Portuguesa de Historia
RPh — Revue de Philologie
RPh — Revue de Philologie, de Litterature, et d'Histoire Anciennes
RPh — Revue de Philosophie
RPh — Romance Philology
R Ph F E — Revue Philosophique de la France et de l'Etranger
RPhil — Revue de Philosophie
R Phil Louvain — Revue Philosophique de Louvain
R Philos — Revue Philosophique
RPhL — Revue Philosophique de Louvain
RphLH — Revue de Philologie, de Litterature, et d'Histoire Anciennes
RPHRA — Recent Progress in Hormone Research
RPJ — Revue de la Pensee Juive
RPL — Review of the River Plate
RPL — Revue Philosophique de Louvain
RPLAA — Reinforced Plastics
R Plan Desarr (Bogota) — Revista de Planeacion y Desarrollo (Bogota)
R Planeacion y Desarrollo — Revista de Planeacion y Desarrollo
R Plastiq — Revue Generale des Caoutchoucs et Plastiques
RPLHA — Revue de Philologie, de Litterature, et d'Histoire Anciennes. Troisieme Serie
RPLHD — Revista Padurilor-Industria Lemnului. Celuloza si Hirtie. Seria Celuloza si Hirtie
RPLit — Res Publica Litterarum
RPLLD — Revista Padurilor-Industria Lemnului. Celuloza si Hirtie. Seria Industria Lemnului
RPLPA — Reviews of Plasma Physics [*English Translation*]
RPMDA — Recenti Progressi in Medicina
RPMDDQ — Malaysia. Ministry of Agriculture and Rural Development. Risalah Penerangan
RPMKA — Rocznik Pomorskiej Akademii Medycznej Imienia Generala Karola Swierczewskiego w Szczecinie
R & P News — Rubber and Plastics News
R & P News 2 — Rubber and Plastics News. 2
R Pol — Review of Politics
R Pol Econ Terza Ser — Revista di Politica Economica. Terza Serie
R Pol Internac — Revista de Politica Internacional
R Polit — Review of Politics
R Politics — Review of Politics
R Polit Int — Revue de Politique Internationale
R Polit Int (Madrid) — Revista de Politica Internacional (Madrid)
R Polit et Litt — Revue Politique et Litteraire
R Polit Parl — Revue Politique et Parlementaire
R Polit Soc — Revista de Politica Social
R Pol et Litt — Revue Politique et Litteraire
R Pol et Parlementaire — Revue Politique et Parlementaire
RPP — Real Property Practice
RPP — Revue des Pays de l'Est
RPP — Revue Politique et Parlementaire
RPPA — Revue Politique et Parlementaire
RPPHA — Reports on Progress in Physics
RPPJA — Reports on Progress in Polymer Physics (Japan)
RPQEA — Radiophysics and Quantum Electronics [*English Translation*]
RPrag — Romanistica Pragensia
RPrat — Revue Pratique d'Apologetique
R Prat Dr Soc — Revue Pratique de Droit Social
RPRFA — Revue Pratique du Froid [*Later, Journal RPF*]
RPRODG — Annual Research Reviews. Renal Prostaglandins
RPRRA — Revue de Physique. Academie de la Republique Populaire Roumaine
R Psicol Gen Apl — Revista de Psicologia General y Aplicada
RPsP — Revue de Psychologie des Peuples
RPSTA — Rivista di Parassitologia
RPTEA — Reviews of Petroleum Technology
RPTGA — Rocznik Polskiego Towarzystwa Geologicznego
RPTOW — Rocznik Polskiego Towarzystwa
RPu — Rassegna Pugliese
RPUSSR — Research Program of the USSR. New York Series
RPZ — Rada Pomocy Zydom
RPZDA — Regelungstechnik und Prozess-Datenverarbeitung
RPZHA — Roczniki Panstwowego Zakladu Higieny
RQ — Renaissance Quarterly
RQ — Restoration Quarterly
RQ — Revue des Questions Historiques
RQ — Revue de Qumran
RQ — Riverside Quarterly

RQ — Roemische Quartalschrift fuer Christliche Altertumskunde und fuer Kirchengeschichte
RQ — RQ. Reference Quarterly [*American Library Association. Reference Services Division*]
RQA — Roemische Quartalschrift fuer Christliche Altertumskunde und fuer Kirchengeschichte
RQAHA — Research Quarterly. American Association for Health, Physical Education, and Recreation
RQAK — Roemische Quartalschrift fuer Christliche Altertumskunde und fuer Kirchengeschichte
RQCAK — Roemische Quartalschrift fuer Christliche Altertumskunde und fuer Kirchengeschichte
RQCAKG — Roemische Quartalschrift fuer Christliche Altertumskunde und fuer Kirchengeschichte
R Q Ch A K — Roemische Quartalschrift fuer Christliche Altertumskunde und fuer Kirchengeschichte
RQH — Revue des Questions Historiques
RQHist — Revue des Questions Historiques
RQIRA — Revista de Quimica Industrial (Rio De Janeiro)
RQK — Roemische Quartalschrift fuer Kirchengeschichte
RQPAA — Revista de Investigaciones Agropecuarias. Serie 4. Patologia Animal
RQS — Revue des Questions Scientifiques
RQS — Roemische Quartalschrift fuer Christliche Altertumskunde und fuer Kirchengeschichte
RQu — Revue de Qumran
R QUM — Revue de Qumran
RR — Naval Research Reviews
RR — Record Review
RR — Records and Recording
RR — Reformed Review
RR — Review of Religion
RR — Review for Religious
RR — Review of Reviews [*London*]
RR — Ricerche Religiose
RR — Romanic Review
R of R's — Review of Reviews
RRA — Review of Reviews [*United States*]
RRACD — Ciencia e Cultura (Sao Paulo). Suplemento
R Radical Pol Econ — Review of Radical Political Economics
R Radic Polit Econ — Review of Radical Political Economics
RRAEA — Rendiconti. Riunione Annuale. Associazione Elettrotecnica Italiana
RRALA — Radiochemical and Radioanalytical Letters
RRBBA — Revue Roumaine de Biologie. Serie Botanique
RRBODI — Brazilian Journal of Botany
RRB Q Rev — RRB [*Railroad Retirement Board*] Quarterly Review
RRB (Railroad Retirement Bd) Q R — RRB (Railroad Retirement Board) Quarterly Review
RRBVD — Revue Roumaine de Biologie. Serie Biologie Vegetale
RRBZA — Revue Roumaine de Biologie. Serie Zoologie
RRCGDX — Australia. Commonwealth Scientific and Industrial Research Organisation. Division of Animal Genetics. Research Report
RRCHA — Revue Roumaine de Chimie
RRCOD — Resource Recovery and Conservation
RRCRB — Recent Results in Cancer Research
RRDS — Regents Renaissance Drama Series
RRE — Review of Regional Economics and Business
R Regional Econ and Bus — Review of Regional Economics and Business
RRel — Review of Religion
R Rel — Review for Religious
R of Religion — Review of Religion
R Relig Res — Review of Religious Research
R Rel Res — Review of Religious Research
RRENA — Revue Roumaine d'Endocrinologie
RRERD — Resource Recovery and Energy Review
RRESA — Rastitel'nye Resursy
R Rest DS — Regents Restoration Drama Series
RRETA — Reports. Research Institute of Electrical Communication. Tohoku University
RRev — Rijecka Revija
RREVA — Residue Reviews
RRFC — Rivista Rosminiana di Filosofia e di Cultura
RRFIA — Radiobiologia, Radioterapia, e Fisica Medica
RRGA — Revue Roumaine de Geologie, Geophysique, et Geographie. Serie de Geographie [*Rumania*]
RRGAB — Rendiconti Romani di Gastroenterologia
RRIC (Rubber Res Inst Ceylon) Bull — RRIC (Rubber Research Institute of Ceylon) Bulletin
RRIL — Rendiconti. Reale Istituto Lombardo di Scienze e Lettere [*Milan*]
RRIMA — Revue Roumaine d'Inframicrobiologie
RRISL Bull — RRISL [*Rubber Research Institute of Sri Lanka*] Bulletin
RRI Sri Lanka Bull — RRISL (Rubber Research Institute of Sri Lanka) Bulletin
RRITA — Report. Research Institute of Science and Technology. Nihon University
R River Plate — Review of the River Plate

RRJaNS — Rodnoj i Russkij Jazyki v Nacional'noj Skole
RRL — Revue Roumaine de Linguistique
RRLTD — Report. Research Laboratory of Engineering Materials. Tokyo Institute of Technology
RRMIA — Revue Roumaine de Medecine Interne [*Later, Revue Roumaine de Medecine. Medecine Interne*]
RRMPB — Revue Roumaine de Mathematiques Pures et Appliquees
RRMTA — Reactor Materials
RRNGA — Razvedka i Razrabotka Neftyanykh i Gazovykh Mestorozhdenii
RRNUA — Revue Roumaine de Neurologie [*Later, Revue Roumaine de Medecine. Serie Neurologie et Psychiatrie*]
RRo — Rivista Rosminiana
R Roumaine — Revue Roumaine d'Histoire de l'Art
R Roumaine Hist — Revue Roumaine d'Histoire
R Roumaine Hist Art — Revue Roumaine d'Histoire de l'Art
R Roum Et Int — Revue Roumaine d'Etudes Internationales
R Roum Sci Soc — Revue Roumaine des Sciences Sociales
R Roum Sci Soc Ser Philos Logique — Revue Roumaine des Sciences Sociales. Serie de Philosophie et de Logique
R Roum Sci Soc Ser Sci Econ — Revue Roumaine des Sciences Sociales. Serie de Sciences Economiques
R Roum Sci Soc Ser Sci Jur — Revue Roumaine des Sciences Sociales. Serie de Sciences Juridiques
R Roum Sci Soc Ser Sociol — Revue Roumaine des Sciences Sociales. Serie de Sociologie
RRP — Reviews of Research and Practice. Institute for Research into Mental and Multiple Handicap [*Elsevier Book Series*]
RRPHA — Revue Roumaine de Physiologie
RRPQA — Revue Roumaine de Physique
RRPRD — RTP. Regelungstechnische Praxis
RRQ — Romanic Review Quarterly
RRR — Review of Religious Research
RRREA — Radiation Research Reviews
RRRED — Reclamation and Revegetation Research
RRTCD — Tokyo Denki Daigaku Kenkyu Hokoku
RRVRA — Revue Roumaine de Virologie
RS — Realites Secretes
RS — Religious Studies
RS — Research on Steroids [*Elsevier Book Series*]
RS — Research Studies [*Pullman*]
RS — Revue Suisse
RS — Revue de Synthese
RS — Ricerche Slavistiche
RS — Rocznik Slawistyczny
RS — Rolling Stone
RS — Romanische Studien
RS — Rural Sociology
RSA — Rivista di Storia Antica
RSAA — Revue Suisse d'Art et d'Archeologie
RSABA — Revista. Sociedad Argentina de Biologia
RSAC — Recueil des Notices et Memoires. Societe Archeologique de Constantine
R Sanit Inst J — Royal Sanitary Institute. Journal
RSAP — Regional Science Association. Papers and Proceedings
RSAT — Recueil. Societe de Prehistoire et d'Archeologie de Tebessa
RSav — Revue de Savoie
RSB — Revista. Sociedad Bolivariana
RSB — Rivista Storica Benedettina
R Sb Ekonom Promysl D — Referativnyi Sbornik. Ekonomika Promyslennosti. D. Primenenie Matematiceskih Metodov v Ekonomiceskih Issledovanijah i Planirovanii
RSBN — Rivista di Studi Bizantini e Neoellenici
RSC — Railway Systems Control
RSC — Rivista di Studi Classici
RSC — Rivista di Studi Crociani
R Sch Mines J — Royal School of Mines. Journal [*England*]
R Sci — Revue Scientifique
RSCI — Rivista di Storia della Chiesa in Italia
R Sci Financ — Revue de Science Financiere
R Sci Hum — Revue des Sciences Humaines
R Sci Instr — Review of Scientific Instruments
R Sci Philos & Theol — Revue des Sciences Philosophiques et Theologiques
R Sci Ph Th — Revue des Sciences Philosophiques et Theologiques
R Sci Pol — Revue des Sciences Politiques
R Sci Rel — Revue des Sciences Religieuses
R Sci Soc France Est — Revue des Sciences Sociales de la France de l'Est
RSCL — Rivista di Studi Classici
R Scott Mus Inf Ser Geol — Royal Scottish Museum. Information Series. Geology
RScPhilT — Revue des Sciences Philosophiques et Theologiques [*Paris*]
RscPhTh — Revue des Sciences Philosophiques et Theologiques [*Paris*]
RScR — Revue des Sciences Religieuses
RScRel — Revue des Sciences Religieuses
RSCST — Rivista Storico-Critica delle Scienze Teologiche
RSCT — Royal Society of Canada. Transactions
RSDI — Rivista di Storia del Diritto Italiano

RSE — Rassegna di Studi Etiopici
RSE — Renewable Sources of Energy
RSE — Review of Social Economy
RSE — Revue des Sciences Ecclesiastiques
RSE — Rivista di Storia Economica
RSEA — Revue de Sud-Est Asiatique
R Se As Stud — Review of Southeast Asian Studies [*Singapore*]
RSEEA — Remote Sensing of Environment
R Seneg Dr — Revue Senegalaise de Droit
R Servizio Soc — Rivista di Servizio Sociale
RSEt — Rassegna di Studi Etiopici
RSF — Rassegna di Scienze Filosofiche
RSF — Rassegna di Studi Francesi
RSF — Rivista di Storia della Filosofia
RSFFA — Rendiconti. Scuola Internazionale di Fisica "Enrico Fermi"
RSFMA — Rivista Sperimentale di Freniatria e Medicina Legale delle Alienazioni Mentali
RSFPA — Revista de la Sanidad de las Fuerzas Policiales del Peru
RSFR — Rivista di Studi Filosofici e Religiosi
RSFSA — Rendiconti del Seminario. Facolta di Scienze. Universita di Cagliari
RSGPB — Rinsan Shikenjo Geppo
RSh — Revista Shell
RSH — Revue des Sciences Humaines
RSH — Revue de Synthese Historique
RSHC — Research in the Sociology of Health Care
RSHEA — Royal Society of Health. Journal
RSHG — Revue. Societe Haitienne d'Histoire, de Geographie, et de Geologie
RSHNDI — Annual Report. Hokkaido Branch. Forestry and Forest Products Research Institute
RSHum — Revue des Sciences Humaines
RSI — Rivista Storica Italiana
RSI — Roofing/Siding/Insulation
RSIDA — Research and Industry
RSIJA — Journal. Royal College of Surgeons in Ireland
R Sind Estadist — Revista Sindical de Estadistica
R Sindical Estadistica — Revista Sindical de Estadistica
RSIR — International Statistical Institute. Review
RSITD — Revue Francaise d'Automatique, d'Informatique, et de Recherche Operationnelle. Serie Informatique Theorique
RS KY Agric Exp Stn — RS. Kentucky Agricultural Experiment Station
RSl — Revue des Etudes Slaves
RSL — Ricerche Slavistiche
RSL — Rivista di Sintesi Litteraria
RSL — Rivista di Studi Liguri
RSl — Rocznik Slawistyczny
RSlav — Ricerche Slavistiche
RSlav — Romanoslavica
RSII — Radovi Slavenskog Instituta
RSLig — Rivista di Studi Liguri
RSLit — Riverside Studies in Literature
RSLR — Rivista di Storia e Letteratura Religiosa
RSIU — Rocenka Slovanskeho Ustavu v Praze
RSM — Rivista Storico-Critica delle Scienze Mediche e Naturali
RSMFA — Rendiconti. Seminario Matematico e Fisico di Milano
RSMJA — Royal School of Mines. Journal
Rs Mod Physics — Reviews of Modern Physics
RSN — Revue Suisse de Numismatique
RSO — Resonans
RSO — Rivista degli Studi Orientali
RSoc — Revue Socialiste
R Soc — Revue des Societes
R Soc Can — Royal Society of Canada. Transactions
R Soc Can Proc — Royal Society of Canada. Proceedings
R Soc Econ — Review of Social Economy
R Soc Edinb Proc Sect B — Royal Society of Edinburgh. Proceedings. Section B. Biology
R Soc Esp Fis Quim Reun Bienal — Real Sociedad Espanola de Fisica y Quimica. Reunion Bienal
R Soc Et Expans — Revue. Societe d'Etudes et d'Expansion
R Soc Health J — Royal Society of Health. Journal
R Social Economy — Review of Social Economy
R Sociol — Revija za Sociologiju
R Soc Lond Philos Trans — Royal Society of London. Philosophical Transactions
R Soc Lond Philos Trans Ser A — Royal Society of London. Philosophical Transactions. Series A
R Soc Lond Philos Trans Ser B — Royal Society of London. Philosophical Transactions. Series B
R Soc Lond Proc Ser B — Royal Society of London. Proceedings. Series B. Biological Sciences
R Soc NZ Bull — Royal Society of New Zealand. Bulletin
R Soc NZJ — Royal Society of New Zealand. Journal
R Soc Queensl Proc — Royal Society of Queensland. Proceedings
R Soc S Aust Trans — Royal Society of South Australia. Transactions
R Soc Tasmania Pap Proc — Royal Society of Tasmania. Papers and Proceedings

R Soc Theory — Review of Social Theory
R Soc Victoria Proc — Royal Society of Victoria. Proceedings
R Soc West Aust J — Royal Society of Western Australia. Journal
RSOLB — Research Outlook
RSONA — Revue Stomato-Odontologique du Nord de la France
RSov — Rassegna Sovietica
RSP — Revue des Sciences Politiques
RSP — Rivista di Studi Pompeiani
RSPh — Revue des Sciences Philosophiques et Theologiques
RSPhTh — Revue des Sciences Philosophiques et Theologiques
RSPMB — Research in the Psychology of Music
RSPT — Revue des Sciences Philosophiques et Theologiques
RSPTA — Recherche Spatiale
RSQ — Rhetoric Society. Quarterly
RSR — Rassegna Storica del Risorgimento
RSR — Recherches de Science Religieuse
RSR — Reference Services Review
RSR — Revue des Sciences Religieuses. Universite de Strasbourg
RSR — Rivista di Studi Religiosi
RSRel — Revue des Sciences Religieuses. Universite de Strasbourg
RSRis — Rassegna Storica del Risorgimento
RSROD — Revue Francaise d'Automatique, d'Informatique, et de Recherche Operationnelle. Serie Recherche Operationnelle
RSRPB — Research and the Retarded
RSRUS — Revue des Sciences Religieuses. Universite de Strasbourg
RSS — Rassegna Storica Salernitana
RSS — Revue du Seizieme Siecle
RSS — Rivista di Scienze Storiche
RSSAA — Revue Internationale des Services de Sante des Armees de Terre, de Mer, et de l'Air
RSSal — Rassegna Storica Salernitana
RSSCW — Research Studies. State College of Washington [*Pullman*]
RSSJ — Researches in the Social Sciences on Japan. East Asian Institute. Columbia University
RSSJA — Journal. Royal Statistical Society. Series C. Applied Statistics
RSSLI — Radovi Staroslavenskog Instituta
RSSMN — Rivista di Storia delle Scienze Mediche e Naturali
RSSND — Roessing
RSt — Research Studies
RST — Rivista Storica Ticinese
RST — Rivista di Studi Teatrali
RStA — Rivista di Storia Antica
R Statis Quebec — Revue Statistique du Quebec
R Statist (Bucuresti) — Revista de Statistica (Bucuresti)
RStCr — Rivista Storico-Critica delle Scienze Teologiche
R St Lig — Rivista di Studi Liguri
RSTN — Resource Technology
R St O — Rivista degli Studi Orientali
R Storia Contemporanea — Rivista di Storia Contemporanea
R St Pomp — Rivista di Studi Pompeiani
R Stuart Pap — Royal Stuart Papers
RSTUD — Rivista di Scienza e Tecnologia degli Alimenti e di Nutrizione Umana
R Studi Eur — Rivista di Studi Europei
R Stud Liguri — Rivista di Studi Liguri
R Stud Or — Revista degli Studi Orientali [*Rome*]
RSU — Rocenka Slovanskeho Ustavu
RSUED — Regional Science and Urban Economics
R Suisse Zool — Revue Suisse de Zoologie
RSUSEV — Arkansas. Agricultural Experiment Station. Research Series
RSUTA — Reconstruction Surgery and Traumatology
RSV — Revista Signos de Valparaiso
RSVP — Research Society for Victorian Periodicals
RSVR — Roma. Rivista di Studi e di Vita Romana
RSWSU — Research Studies. Washington State University [*Pullman*]
RSYCA — Railway Systems Control
RSyn — Revue de Synthese
R Synd Suisse — Revue Syndicale Suisse
RSZOA — Revue Suisse de Zoologie
RT — Radio Times
RT — Reading Teacher
R & T — Recherches et Travaux
RT — Recueil de Travaux
RT — Recueil des Travaux Relatifs a la Philologie et a l'Archeologie Egyptiennes et Assyriennes
RT — Religious Theatre
RT — Revue Theatrale
RT — Revue Thomiste [*Brussels*]
RT — Revue Tunisienne
R & T — Road and Track
RT — Rough Times [*Formerly, Radical Therapist*]
RTAM — Recherches de Theologie Ancienne et Medievale
RTASM — Revue des Travaux. Academie des Sciences Morales et Politiques
RTATD8 — Annual Report. Tokyo University of Agriculture and Technology
R Taxation Individuals — Review of Taxation of Individuals
RTBCA — Revue Technique du Batiment et des Constructions Industrielles

RTBNA — Recueil des Travaux Botaniques Neerlandais
RTC — Recueil Tablettes Chaldeennes
RTC — Revue Trimestrielle Canadienne
RTCPA — Recueil des Travaux Chimiques des Pays-Bas
RTDE — Revue Trimestrielle de Droit Europeen
RTDVA — Rechentechnik/Datenverarbeitung
RTE — RTE. Radio-TV-Electronics
RTECS — RTECS. Registry of Toxic Effects of Chemical Substances
RTEEA — Revue Roumaine des Sciences Techniques. Serie Electrotechnique et Energetique
RTEID — Revista Tecnica INTEVEP [*Instituto de Tecnologia Venezolana del Petroleo*]
R Telev Soc J — Royal Television Society. Journal
RTESB — Radio-TV-Electronic Service [*Later, RTE. Radio-TV-Electronic*]
RTF — Revue Theologique Francaise
RTH — Retail Business. A Monthly Journal Concerned with Consumer Goods Markets, Marketing and Management, and Distribution in the United Kingdom
RTh — Revue de Theologie et de Philosophie
RTh — Revue Thomiste
RThAbstr — Religious and Theological Abstracts
RThAM — Recherches de Theologie Ancienne et Medievale
R Theol Louvain — Revue Theologique de Louvain
RThL — Revue Theologique de Louvain
RThom — Revue Thomiste
RThPh — Revue de Theologie et de Philosophie
R Th R — Reformed Theological Review
RTI — Review of Taxation of Individuals
RTICBT — Communication. Department of Agricultural Research. Royal Tropical Institute [*Amsterdam*]
R Tiers-Monde — Revue Tiers-Monde
RTK — Roczniki Teologiczno-Kanoniczne
RTKHA — Radiotekhnika (Kharkov)
RTKKUL — Roczniki Teologiczno-Kanoniczne. Katolickiego Uniwersytetu Lubelskiego
RTKL — Roczniki Teologiczno-Kanoniczne. Katolickiego Uniwersytetu Lubelskiego
RTLXA — Revue Technique Luxembourgeoise
RTMAA — Revue Roumaine des Sciences Techniques. Serie de Mecanique Appliquee
RTMTA — Revue Roumaine des Sciences Techniques. Serie de Metallurgie
RTN — RTN: Radio Television News
RTNLB — Rationalisierung [*Munich*]
RTO — Revue de Tourisme [*Berne*]
RTODA — Rassegna Trimestrale di Odontoiatria
RTor — Rocznik Torunski
RTOSA — Revue de Medecine de Toulouse. Supplement
R Tourisme — Revue de Tourisme
RTP — Revue de Theologie et de Philosophie
RTPh — Revue de Theologie et de Philosophie
RTPhil — Revue de Theologie et de Philosophie
RTPI J — Royal Town Planning Institute. Journal
RTPM — Revista de Tradiciones Populares (Madrid)
RTR — Reading Test and Reviews
RTR — Reformed Theological Review
RTR — Restoration and Eighteenth Century Theatre Research
RTr — Rivista della Scuola
R Trab (Madrid) — Revista de Trabajo (Madrid)
R Trav Acad Sci Mor Polit — Revue des Travaux. Academie des Sciences Morales et Politiques
R Trav (Bruxelles) — Revue du Travail (Bruxelles)
RT Regelungstech — RT. Regelungstechnik [*West Germany*]
R Tresor — Revue du Tresor
R Trim Dr Com — Revue Trimestrielle de Droit Commercial
R Trim Dr Europ — Revue Trimestrielle de Droit Europeen
R Trim Droit Eur — Revue Trimestrielle de Droit Europeen
R Trim Dr Sanit Soc — Revue Trimestrielle de Droit Sanitaire et Social
RTRPAEA — Receuil de Travaux Relatifs a la Philologie et a l'Archeologie Egyptiennes et Assyriennes [*Paris*]
RTRPhAEA — Receuil de Travaux Relatifs a la Philologie et a l'Archeologie Egyptiennes et Assyriennes [*Paris*]
RTSD LRTS — RTSD [*Resources and Technical Services Division*] Library Resources and Technical Services
RTSFR — Rivista Trimestrale di Studi Filosofici e Religiosi
RTSS — Revue Tunisienne de Sciences Sociales
RTSTA — Railway Track and Structures
RTSZA — Revista Tecnica Sulzer
RTT — Research in Text Theory/Untersuchungen zur Text-Theorie
RTTCB — Revue Technique Thomson - CSF
RTTLA — Revista Transporturilor si Telecomunicatiilor
R Tunisienne Sciences Socs — Revue Tunisienne de Sciences Sociales
R Tunis Sci Soc — Revue Tunisienne de Sciences Sociales
RU — Revista Universitaria. Universidad Catolica de Chile
RUAGA — Rubber Age
Ruakura Farm Conf Proc — Ruakura Farmers' Conference. Proceedings [*New Zealand*]

Ruakura Farmers Conf Proc — Ruakura Farmers' Conference. Proceedings
RUB — Revue. Universite de Bruxelles
RuB — Russkoe Bogatstvo
RUBA — Revista. Universidad de Buenos Aires
Rubb Board Bull — Rubber Board. Bulletin [*India*]
Rubb Dev — Rubber Developments
Rubber Age Synth — Rubber Age and Synthetics
Rubber Bul — Rubber Statistical Bulletin
Rubber Chem & Tech — Rubber Chemistry and Technology
Rubber Chem Technol — Rubber Chemistry and Technology
Rubber Dev — Rubber Developments
Rubber Devs — Rubber Developments
Rubber Devts — Rubber Developments
Rubber Ind — Rubber Industry
Rubber Ind (London) — Rubber Industry (London)
Rubber J — Rubber Journal
Rubber J Int Plast — Rubber Journal and International Plastics
Rubber Plast Age — Rubber and Plastics Age
Rubber Plast Wkly — Rubber and Plastics Weekly
Rubber Res Inst Ceylon Advis Circ — Rubber Research Institute of Ceylon. Advisory Circular
Rubber Res Inst Ceylon Annu Rep — Rubber Research Institute of Ceylon. Annual Report
Rubber Res Inst Ceylon Annu Rev — Rubber Research Institute of Ceylon. Annual Review
Rubber Res Inst Ceylon Bull — Rubber Research Institute of Ceylon. Bulletin
Rubber Res Inst Ceylon Q Circ — Rubber Research Institute of Ceylon. Quarterly Circular
Rubber Res Inst Ceylon Q J — Rubber Research Institute of Ceylon. Quarterly Journal
Rubber Res Inst Malaya Annu Rep — Rubber Research Institute of Malaya. Annual Report
Rubber Res Inst Malaya Plant Bull — Rubber Research Institute of Malaya. Planters' Bulletin
Rubber Res Inst Malaya Plant Man — Rubber Research Institute of Malaya. Planting Manual
Rubber Res Inst Malaya Q J — Rubber Research Institute of Malaya. Quarterly Journal
Rubber Res Inst Malaya Rep — Rubber Research Institute of Malaya. Report
Rubber Res Inst Malays Annu Rep — Rubber Research Institute of Malaysia. Annual Report
Rubber Res Inst Malays Plant Bull — Rubber Research Institute of Malaysia. Planters' Bulletin
Rubber Res Inst (Sri Lanka) Advis Circ — Rubber Research Institute (Sri Lanka). Advisory Circular
Rubber Res Inst (Sri Lanka) Annu Rev — Rubber Research Institute (Sri Lanka). Annual Review
Rubber Res Inst (Sri Lanka) Q J — Rubber Research Institute (Sri Lanka). Quarterly Journal
Rubber Wld — Rubber World
Rubb (India) — Rubber (India)
Rubb News — Rubber News
Rubb Plast Age — Rubber and Plastics Age
Rubb Plast Fire Flamm Bull — Rubber and Plastics Fire and Flammability Bulletin
Rubb Plast News — Rubber and Plastics News
Rubb Plast News 2 — Rubber and Plastics News. 2
Rubb Statist Bull — Rubber Statistical Bulletin
Rubb Trends — Rubber Trends
Rubb World — Rubber World
Rubey Vol — Rubey Volume
RuBi — Ruch Biblijny i Liturgiczny [*Cracow*]
RUBruxelles — Revue. Universite de Bruxelles [*Brussels*]
Rub Trends — Rubber Trends
RUBWA — Rubber World
RUC — Revista. Universidad de Cordoba
RuC — Ruperto-Carola
RuchBL — Ruch Biblijny i Liturgiczny [*Cracow*]
Ruch L — Ruch Literacki
RuchM — Ruch Muzyczny
Ruch Muz — Ruch Muzyczny
Ruch Prawn Ekon Socjol — Ruch Prawniczy Ekonomiczny i Socjologiczny
RUCP — Revista. Universidad Catolica del Peru
Rud Glas — Rudarski Glasnik
Rud-Metal Zb — Rudarsko-Metalurski Zbornik
Rud-Met Zb — Rudarsko-Metalurski Zbornik
Rudodobiv Metal — Rudodobiv i Metalurgiya
Rudodobiv Metal (Sofia) — Rudodobiv i Metalurgiya (Sofia) [*Bulgaria*]
Rudodob Metal — Rudodobiv i Metalurgiya [*Bulgaria*]
Rudolstaedter Heimath — Rudolstaedter Heimathefte Beitraege zur Heimatkunde des Kreises Rudolstaedt
RUDVA — Rubber Developments
Rudy Met Niezelaz — Rudy i Metale Niezelazne
RUGED — Rural Georgia
RUGLA — Rudarski Glasnik
RUIMB — Ruimtevaart

RUISA — Revista. Universidad Industrial de Santander
RuJ — Rusky Jazyk
RUL — Revue. Universite Laval [*Quebec*]
RUL — Revue. Universite de Lyon
RULet — Revista Universitaria de Letras
RuLit — Ruch Literacki [*Krakow*]
RULP — Revista. Universidad de La Plata
Ru L T — Russian Literature Triquarterly
RUM — Revista. Universidad de Madrid
RUMEA — Rudodobiv i Metalurgiya
RUMG — Revista. Universidade de Minas Gerais
RUMIA — Rundfunktechnische Mitteilungen
RUMMA — Russian Metallurgy [*English Translation*]
Rum Med Rev — Rumanian Medical Review
RUMRA — Revue Universelle des Mines, de la Metallurgie, de la Mecanique, des Travaux Publics, des Sciences, et des Arts Appliques a l'Industrie
RUM Rev Univers Mines — RUM. Revue Universelle des Mines, de la Metallurgie, de la Mechanique, des Travaux Publics, des Sciences
Rum Sci Abstr — Rumanian Scientific Abstracts
RUNAA — Revista. Universidad Nacional de Tucuman. Serie A. Matematica y Fisica Teorica
RUnBrux — Revue. Universite de Bruxelles
RUNC — Revista. Universidad Nacional de Cordoba
Rundfunk & F — Rundfunk und Fernsehen
Rundfunktech Mitt — Rundfunktechnische Mitteilungen
R Union Ind — Revista de la Union Industrial
RUniv — Revue Universelle
R Univ — Revue Universitaire
R de l'Univ Laval — Revue. Universite Laval
R de l'Univ d'Ott — Revue. Universite d'Ottawa
R Univ Ottawa — Revue. Universite d'Ottawa
R de l'Univ de Sherbrooke — Revue. Universite de Sherbrooke
RUnLav — Revue. Universite Laval
Runn Times — Running Times
Runn World — Runner's World
RUnOtt — Revue. Universite d'Ottawa
RUO — Revista. Universidad de Oviedo
RUO — Revue. Universite d'Ottawa
RUOt — Revue. Universite d'Ottawa
RU Ottawa — Revue. Universite d'Ottawa
RUPAA — Rubber and Plastics Age
RUR — Russkaja Rech'
Rur Advis Leafl Edinb Sch Agric — Rural Advisory Leaflet. Edinburgh School of Agriculture
Rur Afr — Rural Africana
Rural Am — Rural America
Rural Develop — Rural Development
Rural Dev Res Educ — Rural Development. Research and Education
Rural Dev Res Rep US Dep Agric Econ Stat Coop Serv — Rural Development Research Report. United States Department of Agriculture. Economics, Statistics, and Cooperatives Service
Rural Elec N — Rural Electrification News
Rural GA — Rural Georgia [*United States*]
Rural Life Res — Rural Life Research
Rural Newsl — Rural Newsletter. Central Coast Agricultural Research and Extension Committee
Rural N Y — Rural New Yorker
Rural Res — Rural Research [*Australia*]
Rural Res — Rural Research. Commonwealth Scientific and Industrial Research Organisation
Rural Res CSIRO — Rural Research. Commonwealth Scientific and Industrial Research Organisation
Rural Socio — Rural Sociology
Rural Sociol — Rural Sociology
RURCA — Rural Research
Rur Newsl — Rural Newsletter
Rur Res — Rural Research
Rur Res CSIRO — Rural Research. Commonwealth Scientific and Industrial Research Organisation
Rur Sociol — Rural Sociology
R Uruguaya Ciencias Socs — Revista Uruguaya de Ciencias Sociales
RUS — Rice University. Studies
RUSCA — Rural Sociology
RUSE — Rutgers University. Studies in English
RUSEng — Rajasthan University. Studies in English
RusF — Russkij Fol'klor
Rush-Presbyt-St Luke's Med Bull — Rush-Presbyterian-St. Luke's Medical Center. Bulletin
Rush-Presbyt-St Luke's Med Cent Res Rep — Rush-Presbyterian-St. Luke's Medical Center. Research Report
Rusk N — Ruskin Newsletter
RusL — Russkaja Literatura
Rus Ling — Russian Linguistics
RusR — Russian Review
RusR — Russkaja Rech'
Rus Re — Russkaja Rech'

Russ Cast Prod — Russian Castings Production
Russ Chem Pharm J — Russian Chemico-Pharmaceutical Journal
Russ Chem Rev — Russian Chemical Reviews
Russell-Cotes Mus Bul — Russell-Cotes Art Gallery and Museum. Bulletin
Russ Eng J — Russian Engineering Journal
Russ En J — Russian Engineering Journal
Russ Hist — Russian History [*Histoire Russe*]
Russian Math Surveys — Russian Mathematical Surveys
Russian R — Russian Review
Russian Rev — Russian Review
Russ J Inorg Chem — Russian Journal of Inorganic Chemistry
Russ J Phys Chem — Russian Journal of Physical Chemistry
Russkaia L — Russkaia Literatura
Russk Med — Russkaia Meditsina
Russ-K Min Ges St Petersburg Verh — Russisch-Kaiserliche Mineralogische Gesellschaft zu St. Petersburg. Verhandlungen
Russk Zhurnal Trop Med — Russkii Zhurnal Tropicheskoi Meditsiny
Russk Zool Zhurnal — Russkii Zoologicheskii Zhurnal
Russ Lit — Russkaja Literatura
Russ Lit Tr — Russian Literature Triquarterly
Russ Math Surv — Russian Mathematical Surveys
Russ Metall — Russian Metallurgy
Russ Met R — Russian Metallurgy-USSR
Russ Pharmacol Toxicol — Russian Pharmacology and Toxicology
Russ R — Russian Review
Russ Rev — Russian Review
Russ Rev Biol — Russian Review of Biology
RUSTA — Rustica
RUT — Rubber Trends
Rut-Cam LJ — Rutgers-Camden Law Journal
Rutgers Camden L J — Rutgers-Camden Law Journal
Rutgers Comput and Technol Law J — Rutgers Computer and Technology Law Journal
Rutgers J Comp & L — Rutgers Journal of Computers and the Law
Rutgers J Computers & Law — Rutgers Journal of Computers and the Law
Rutgers J Computer Tech and L — Rutgers Journal of Computers, Technology, and the Law
Rutgers J Comput & Law — Rutgers Journal of Computers and the Law
Rutgers J Comput Technol and Law — Rutgers Journal of Computers, Technology, and the Law
Rutgers Jrnl — Rutgers Computer and Technology Law Journal
Rutgers LJ — Rutgers Law Journal
Rutgers L Rev — Rutgers Law Review
Rutgers State Univ Coll Eng Eng Res Bull — Rutgers State University. College of Engineering. Engineering Research Bulletin
Rutgers Univ Bur Biol Res Serol Mus Bull — Rutgers University. Bureau of Biological Research. Serological Museum. Bulletin
Rutgers Univ Bur Eng Res Eng Res Publ — Rutgers University. Bureau of Engineering Research. Engineering Research Publication
Rutgers Univ Bur Miner Res Bull — Rutgers University. Bureau of Mineral Research. Bulletin
Rutgers Univ Coll Eng Eng Res Bull — Rutgers University. College of Engineering. Engineering Research Bulletin
Rutg L Rev — Rutgers Law Review
Rutherford Lab Rep — Rutherford Laboratory. Report
Rut J Comp L — Rutgers Journal of Computers, Technology, and the Law
Rut LJ — Rutgers Law Journal
Rut LR — Rutgers Law Review
RUY — Revista. Universidad de Yucatan
RV — Rassegna Volterrana
RV — Raven
RV — Rheinische Vierteljahresblaetter
RV — RV: Recreational Vehicles
RVAEA — Rivista Aeronautica
RVAHA — Revue d'Acoustique
RVAS — Records. Victorian Archaeological Survey
RVASA — Revue de l'Atherosclerose
RVB — Rheinische Vierteljahresblaetter
RVBTA — Revue Belge des Transports
RVC — Review of Economic Studies [*Edinburgh*]
RVCCB — Reviews on Coatings and Corrosion
RVCZA — Revista de Coroziune
RVDSB — Revue Medicale de Liege. Supplement (Belgium)
RVELA — Revista Electrotecnica
RVENA — Rivista di Viticoltura e di Enologia
R Venez Folk — Revista Venezolana de Folklore
R Venezolana Estud Municipales — Revista Venezolana de Estudios Municipales
R Venezolana Folklore — Revista Venezolana de Folklore
R Venezolana Sanidad y Asistencia Soc — Revista Venezolana de Sanidad y Asistencia Social
RvEx — Review and Expositor
RVF — Revista Valenciana de Filologia
RVF — Revista Venezolana de Folklore
RVFO — Revista Venezolana de Folklore
RVGA-A — Revue de Geographie Alpine [*France*]

Rv Gen Sciences — Revue Generale des Sciences Pures et Appliquees
RVGPA — Reviews of Geophysics [*Later, Reviews of Geophysics and Space Physics*]
RVL — Revue Economique et Sociale (Lausanne)
RVLI — Raksti. Latvijas PSR Zinatnu Akademija. Valodas und Literaturas Instituta
RVMCA — Rivista di Meccanica
RVOMA — Revue Internationale d'Oceanographie Medicale
RVOOA — Rivista Oto-Neuro-Oftalmologica
RVPMB — Review of Psychology of Music
RVPTB — Revue Polytechnique
Rv Scient — Revue Scientifique
RVSMB — Revista Sanitara Militara
Rv Trim Can — Revue Trimestrielle Canadienne
RVTSA — Research in Veterinary Science
RVU — Revue Economique [*Paris*]
RVUHA — Revue HF, Electronique, Telecommunications [*Brussels*]
RVUXA — Revue X [*Belgium*]
RVV — Religionsgeschichtliche Versuche und Vorarbeiten
RVV — Romanistische Versuche und Vorarbeiten
RW — Reformed World
RW — Rough Weather
RWAMD — Radioactive Waste Management
RWAVA — Rheinisch-Westfaelische Akademie der Wissenschaften Natur-, Ingenieur-, und Wirtschaftswissenschaften. Vortraege
RWCNEC — Reports of the Working Committees. Northeast Conference
RWE — Review of World Economics
RWE — REWE Echo. Fachzeitschrift fuer Modernen Handel
RWF — Rozprawy Wydzialu Filologicznego Polskiej Akademyi Umiejetnosci
RWMEB — Railway Mechanical Engineer
RWP — Reformacja w Polsce
RWS — Religionswissenschaftliche Studien
R du XVIe S — Revue du Seizieme Siecle
RYa — Russkii Yazyk v Shkole [*Moscow*]
Ry Age — Railway Age
Ryan Advis Health Serv Gov Boards — Ryan Advisory for Health Services Governing Boards
Rybn Khoz — Rybnoe Khozyaistvo
Rybn Khoz Resp Mezhved Temat Nauchn Sb — Rybnoe Khozyaistvo Respublikanskii Mezhvedomstvennyi Tematicheskii Nauchnyi Sbornik
Rybn Prom-st Dal'n Vost — Rybnaya Promyshlennost' Dal'nego Vostoka
RyC — Religion y Cultura
Rydge's — Rydge's Business Journal
Rydge's Constr Civ Eng & Min Rev — Rydge's Construction, Civil Engineering, and Mining Review
RYEJA — Royal Engineers Journal
RyF — Razon y Fe
RyFab — Razon y Fabula
Ry Gaz Int — Railway Gazette International
RYKHA — Rybnoe Khozyaistvo
RYKOD — Ryutai Kogaku
Ry Loco & Cars — Railway Locomotives and Cars
Ry Mech & Elec Eng — Railway Mechanical and Electrical Engineer
Ry Mech Eng — Railway Mechanical Engineer
Ry Mo — Rythmes du Monde
Ryojun Coll Eng Publ — Ryojun College of Engineering. Publications
RYPFA — Revista YPF [*Yacimientos Petroliferos Fiscales*] (Argentina)
Ry R — Railway Review
Ry Track Struct — Railway Track and Structures
RYUSA — Ryusan To Kogyo
RZ — Rada Żydowska
RZ — Radostna Zeme
RZ — Radovi (Filozofski Fakultet-Zadar)
RZ — Referativnyi Zhurnal. Informatika
RZ — Revista Zurita Saragosse
R Z Avtomat Telemeh i Vycisl Tehn — Referativnyi Zhurnal. Avtomatika. Telemehanika i Vycislitelnaja Tehnika
RZBLA — Referativnyi Zhurnal. Biologiya
RZE — Chemiefasern/Textil-Industrie. Zeitschrift fuer die Gesamte Textil Industrie
RZETA — Rozprawy Elektrotechniczne
R Z Fiz — Referativnyi Zhurnal. Fizika
RZFZA — Referativnyi Zhurnal. Fizika
RZh Avtomat Telemekh i Vychisl Tekhn — Akademiya Nauk SSSR. Institut Nauchnoi Informatsii. Referativnyi Zhurnal. Avtomatika. Telemekhanika i Vychislitel'naya Tekhnika
RZh Mat — Akademiya Nauk SSSR. Institut Nauchnoi Informatsii. Referativnyi Zhurnal. Matematika
RZINA — Rozprawy Inzynierskie
RZInformat — Referativnyi Zhurnal. Informatika
RZKibernet — Referativnyi Zhurnal. Kibernetika
RZMat — Referativnyi Zhurnal. Matematika
RZMeh — Referativnyi Zhurnal. Mehanika
RZMTA — Referativnyi Zhurnal. Metallurgiya
RZMVA — Revista de Zootecnic si Medicina Veterinara
RZNDA — Razvedka Nedr

RZONA — Razvedka i Okhrana Nedr
RZOOA — Rivista di Zootecnia
RZSF — Radovi Zavoda za Slavensku Filologiju
RZSND — Revue Zairoise des Sciences Nucleaires

S

S — September
S — Slavia
S — Spectator
S — Speculum
S — Studio
S — Symposium
Sa — Samtiden
SA — Science Abstracts
SA — Scientific American
SA — Sociological Abstracts [*Sociological Abstracts, Inc.*] [*San Diego, CA*]
SA — Sociological Analysis
SA — Sols Africains
SA — South African Law Reports
SA — South Australiana
SA — Sovietskaia Archeologiia
SA — Speech Activities
SA — Studi Americani [*Roma*]
SA — Studies in Astronautics [*Elsevier Book Series*]
SA — Symbolae Arctoae
SAA — Schweizer Anglistische Arbeiten
SAAB — South African Archaeological Bulletin
SAAD Dig — SAAD [*Society for the Advancement of Anaesthesia in Dentistry*] Digest
SA Advertiser (Newspr) — South Australian Advertiser Reports (Newspaper)
SAAFA — Astrometriya i Astrofizika
SAAJA — Soviet Astronomy [*English Translation*]
SAANAn — Societe Archeologique de l'Arrondissement de Nivelles. Annales
SA Arch J — SA [*South African*] Archives Journal
Saatgut-Wirt — Saatgut-Wirtschaft
Saatgut-Wirtsch — Saatgut-Wirtschaft
SAAWA — Schweizer Archiv fuer Angewandte Wissenschaft und Technik
SAB — Shakespeare Association. Bulletin
SAB — Sitzungsberichte. Deutsche (Preussische) Akademie der Wissenschaften zu Berlin. Philosophisch-Historische Klasse [*Berlin*]
SAB — South Atlantic Bulletin
SABA — Societe Archeologique de Bruxelles. Annales
Sabah For Rec — Sabah Forest Record
Sabah Soc J — Sabah Society. Journal
SA Bank Officials J — South Australian Bank Officials' Journal
Sabchota Med — Sabchota Meditsina
SABNWTR — Science Advisory Board of the Northwest Territories. Report [*Canada*]
SABNWTRP — Science Advisory Board of the Northwest Territories. Research Paper [*Canada*]
SABNWTWP — Science Advisory Board of the Northwest Territories. Working Paper
SABOA — Sabouraudia
SABOJ — South Australian Bank Officials' Journal
Sabrao Newslett — Sabrao Newsletter
SABRB — Siemens-Albis Berichte
SABS Bull — SABS [*South African Bureau of Standards*] Bulletin
Sac — Sacris Erudiri. Jaarboek voor Godsdienstwetenschappen
SAC — Studies in the Age of Chaucer
SAC — Studies in Ancient Civilization [*Elsevier Book Series*]
SAC — Sussex Archaeological Collections

SACCD — Saccharum
SacE — Sacris Erudiri. Jaarboek voor Godsdienstwetenschappen
SACED — South African Journal of Continuing Medical Education
SA Census & Statistics Bul — Australia. Commonwealth Bureau of Census and Statistics. South Australian Office. Bulletin
SA Cereb Palsy J — SA [*South African*] Cerebral Palsy Journal
SACh — Studies in Analytical Chemistry [*Elsevier Book Series*]
Sachs Akad d Wiss Philol-Hist Kl Ber u d Verhandl — Saechsische Akademie der Wissenschaften. Philologisch-Historische Klasse. Berichte ueber die Verhandlungen
SACLA — Srpski Arhiv za Celokupno Lekarstvo
Sac M — Sacred Music
SACPB — South African Chemical Processing
Sacred Mus — Sacred Music
SA Dep Agric Tech Bull — South Australia. Department of Agriculture. Technical Bulletin
SADID4 — Annual Research Reviews. Sphingolipidoses and Allied Disorders
Sadivn Resp Mizhvid Nauk-Temat Zb — Sadivnytstvo Respublikanskyi Mizhvidomchyi Naukovo-Tematychnyi Zbirnik
SaDo — Sacra Doctrina
Sadovod — Sadovodstvo
Sadovod Vinograd Vinodel Mold — Sadovodstvo Vinogradarstvo i Vinodelia Moldavii
Sadtler Commer Spectra — Sadtler Commercial Spectra [*United States*]
SAE Australas — SAE [*Society of Automotive Engineers*] Australasia
SAEBA — Soviet Antarctic Expedition. Information Bulletin [*English Translation*]
Saechs Heimatbl — Saechsische Heimatblaetter
Saeculum — Saeculum. Jahrbuch fuer Universalgeschichte
SA Ed — South Australian Education
SA Ed Gaz — Education Gazette (South Australia. Department of Education)
SAED Info — SAED [*Societe Africaine d'Etudes et de Developpement*] Information
SAE J — SAE [*Society of Automotive Engineers*] Journal
SAEJA — SAE [*Society of Automotive Engineers*] Journal
SAE J Automot Eng — SAE [*Society of Automotive Engineers*] Journal of Automotive Engineering
SAE Meet Pap — Society of Automotive Engineers. Meeting. Papers
SAEND — Save Energy
Saenger Musikanten Z — Saenger- und Musikantenzeitung
SAE Prepr — SAE [*Society of Automotive Engineers*] Preprints
SAE Proc — Society of Automotive Engineers. Proceedings
SAE Prog Technol — SAE [*Society of Automotive Engineers*] Progress in Technology [*United States*]
SAERB — South African Electrical Review
SAESA — SAE [*Society of Automotive Engineers*] Special Publications
SAE (Soc Automot Eng) Tech Pap — SAE (Society of Automotive Engineers) Technical Papers
SAE Spec Publ — SAE [*Society of Automotive Engineers*] Special Publications
SAETB — SAE [*Society of Automotive Engineers*] Technical Progress Series
SAE Tech Lit Abstr — SAE [*Society of Automotive Engineers*] Technical Literature Abstracts
SAE Tech Prog Ser — SAE [*Society of Automotive Engineers*] Technical Progress Series

SAE Trans — SAE [*Society of Automotive Engineers*] Transactions
SAF — Studies in American Fiction
Saf Air Ammonia Plants — Safety in Air and Ammonia Plants
SAFD — Plastics (Southern Africa)
Saf Dig — Safety Digest [*Japan*]
SAFEA — Safety
Safe Manag — Safety Management
Safety Ed — Safety Education
Safety Educ — Safety Education
Safety Eng — Safety Engineering
Safety Maint — Safety Maintenance
Safety Maint & Prod — Safety Maintenance and Production
Safety Surv — Safety Surveyor
Saf Health Welfare — Safety, Health, and Welfare
Saf Hlth Bull — Safety and Health Bulletin
Saf Hyg (Osaka) — Safety and Hygiene (Osaka) [*Japan*]
SAFJB — South African Forestry Journal
S Af J Econ — South African Journal of Economics [*Suid-Afrikaanse Tydskrif vir Ekonomie*]
Saf Manage — Safety Management
SAFMem — Societe Nationale des Antiquaires de France. Memoires
Saf Mines — Safety in Mines
Saf News Bull — Safety News Bulletin
Saf Newsl — Safety Newsletter
SAFPD — Safety Practitioner
Saf Pract — Safety Practitioner
S Afr Annu Insur Rev — South African Annual Insurance Review
S Afr Archaeol Bull — South African Archaeological Bulletin
S Afr Archaeol Soc Goodwin Ser — South African Archaeological Society. Goodwin Series
S Afr Arch Ophthalmol — South African Archives of Ophthalmology
S-Afr Argief Oftalmol — Suid-Afrikaanse Argief vir Oftalmologie
S Afr Assoc Adv Sci Spec Publ — South African Association for the Advancement of Science. Special Publication
S Afr Assoc Mar Biol Res Bull — South African Association for Marine Biological Research. Bulletin
S Afr Bank — South African Reserve Bank. Quarterly Bulletin
S Afr Bee J — South African Bee Journal
S-Afr Bosbou Tydskr — Suid-Afrikaanse Bosbou Tydskrif
S Afr Build — South African Builder
S Afr Bur Stand Bull — South African Bureau of Standards. Bulletin
S Afr Cancer Bull — South African Cancer Bulletin
S Afr (Cape Good Hope) Dep Nat Conserv Rep — South Africa (Cape Of Good Hope) Department of Nature. Conservation Report
S Afr Chart Account — South African Chartered Accountant
S Afr Chem Process — South African Chemical Processing
S Afr Constr World — South African Construction World
S Afr Corros J — South African Corrosion Journal
S Afr Counc Sci Ind Res Nat Bldg Res Inst Bull — South Africa. Council for Scientific and Industrial Research. National Building Research Institute. Bulletin
S Afr CSIR Air Pollut Group Annu Rep — South Africa CSIR [*Council for Scientific and Industrial Research*] Air Pollution Group. Annual Report
S Afr CSIR Air Pollut Res Group Annu Rep — South Africa CSIR [*Council for Scientific and Industrial Research*] Air Pollution Research Group. Annual Report
S Afr CSIR Air Pollut Res Group Rep APRG — South African Council for Scientific and Industrial Research. Air Pollution Research Group. Report APRG
S Afr CSIR Annu Rep — South Africa CSIR [*Council for Scientific and Industrial Research*] Annual Report
S Afr CSIR Res Rep — South Africa CSIR [*Council for Scientific and Industrial Research*] Research Report
S Afr CSIR Spec Rep — South Africa CSIR [*Council for Scientific and Industrial Research*] Special Report
SAFRD — South African Food Review
S Afr Dent J — South African Dental Journal
S Afr Dep Agric Fish Tech Commun — South Africa. Department of Agriculture and Fisheries. Technical Communication
S Afr Dep Agric Tech Serv Bot Surv Mem — South Africa Department of Agricultural Technical Services. Botanical Survey Memoir
S Afr Dep Agric Tech Serv Bull — South Africa Department of Agricultural Technical Services. Bulletin
S Afr Dep Agric Tech Serv Entomol Mem — South Africa Department of Agricultural Technical Services. Entomology Memoirs
S Afr Dep Agric Tech Serv Sci Bull — South Africa Department of Agricultural Technical Services. Scientific Bulletin
S Afr Dep Agric Tech Serv Tech Commun — South Africa Department of Agricultural Technical Services. Technical Communication
S-Afr Dep Bosbou Jaarversl — Suid-Afrika. Departement van Bosbou Jaarverslag
S Afr Dep For Annu Rep — South Africa. Department of Forestry. Annual Report
S Afr Dep For Bull — South Africa. Department of Forestry. Bulletin
S-Afr Dep Landbou-Teg Dienste Teg Meded — Suid-Afrika. Departement van Landbou-Tegniese Dienste Tegniese Mededeling

S Afr Dep Landbou Viss Teg Meded — Suid-Afrika. Departement van Landbou en Visserye. Tegniese Mededeling
S Afr Dep Mines Quart Inform Circ Miner — South Africa. Department of Mines. Quarterly Information Circular. Minerals
S Afr Div Sea Fish Annu Rep — South Africa Division of Sea Fisheries. Annual Report
S Afr Div Sea Fish Fish Bull — South Africa Division of Sea Fisheries. Fisheries Bulletin
S Afr Div Sea Fish Invest Rep — South Africa Division of Sea Fisheries. Investigational Report
S Afr Electr Rev — South African Electrical Review
S Afr Eng Electr Rev — South African Engineer and Electrical Review
S Afr Food Rev — South African Food Review
S Afr For J — South African Forestry Journal
S Afr Friesland J — South African Friesland Journal
S Afr Geogr — South African Geographer
S Afr Geogr J — South African Geographical Journal
S Afr Geol Surv Bibliogr Subj Index S Afr Geol — South Africa. Geological Survey. Bibliography and Subject Index of South African Geology
S Afr Geol Surv Bull — South Africa. Department of Mines. Geological Survey. Bulletin
S Afr Geol Surv Mem — South Africa. Department of Mines. Geological Survey. Memoir
S Afr Geol Surv Seismol Ser — South Africa. Geological Survey. Seismologic Series
S Afr Geol Surv South-West Afr Ser — South Africa. Geological Survey. South-West Africa Series
S Afr Hist J — South African Historical Journal
S African J Commun Disorders — South African Journal of Communication Disorders
S African J Psychol — South African Journal of Psychology
S African Lib — South African Libraries
S African Lib Q Bull — South African Library Quarterly Bulletin
S Afr Ind Chem — South African Industrial Chemist
S Afr Inst Mech Eng J — South African Institution of Mechanical Engineers. Journal
S Afr Inst Med Res Annu Rep — South African Institute for Medical Research. Annual Report
S Afr Inst Min Metall J — South African Institute of Mining and Metallurgy. Journal
S Afr Insur Mag — South African Insurance Magazine
S Afr Int — South Africa International
S Afr J Agric Ext — South African Journal of Agricultural Extension
S Afr J Agric Sci — South African Journal of Agricultural Science
S Afr J Agr Sci — South African Journal of Agricultural Science
S Afr J Anim Sci — South African Journal of Animal Science
S Afr J Antarct Res — South African Journal of Antarctic Research
S Afr J Bot — South African Journal of Botany
S Afr J Bus Manage — South African Journal of Business Management
S Afr J Chem — South African Journal of Chemistry
S Afr J Chem/S Afr Tydskr Chem — South African Journal of Chemistry/ Suid-Afrikaanse Tydskrif vir Chemie
S Afr J Clin Sci — South African Journal of Clinical Science
S Afr J Comm Disorders — South African Journal of Communication Disorders
S Afr J Commun Disord — South African Journal of Communication Disorders
S Afr J Contin Med Educ — South African Journal of Continuing Medical Education
S Afr J Crim L — South African Journal of Criminal Law and Criminology
S Afr J Crim Law Criminol — South African Journal of Criminal Law and Criminology
S Afr J Dairy Technol — South African Journal of Dairy Technology
S Afr J Ec — South African Journal of Economics [*Suid-Afrikaanse Tydskrif vir Ekonomie*]
S Afr J Econ — South African Journal of Economics [*Suid-Afrikaanse Tydskrif vir Ekonomie*]
S Afr J Educ — South African Journal of Education
S Afr J Enol Vitic — South African Journal for Enology and Viticulture
S Afr Jersey — South African Jersey
S Afr J Ethnol — South African Journal of Ethnology
S Afr J Hosp Med — South African Journal of Hospital Medicine
S Afr J Ind — South African Journal of Industries
S Afr J Lab Clin Med — South African Journal of Laboratory and Clinical Medicine
S Afr J Labour Relat — South African Journal of Labour Relations
S Afr J Libr Inf Sci — South African Journal for Librarianship and Information Science
S Afr J Med Lab Technol — South African Journal of Medical Laboratory Technology
S Afr J Med Sci — South African Journal of Medical Sciences
S Afr J Musicology — South African Journal of Musicology
S Afr J Music Therap — South African Journal of Music Therapy
S Afr J Nutr — South African Journal of Nutrition
S Afr J Nutr/S Afr Tydskr Voeding — South African Journal of Nutrition/ Suid-Afrikaanse Tydskrif vir Voeding

S Afr J Obstet Gynaecol — South African Journal of Obstetrics and Gynaecology
S Afr J Phys — South African Journal of Physics
S Afr J Physiother — South African Journal of Physiotherapy
S Afr J Plant Soil — South African Journal of Plant and Soil
S Afr J Radiol — South African Journal of Radiology
S Afr J Sci — South African Journal of Science
S Afr J Surg — South African Journal of Surgery
S Afr J Surg/S Afr Tydskr Chir — South African Journal of Surgery/Suid-Afrikaanse Tydskrif vir Chirurgie
S Afr J Wildl Res — South African Journal of Wildlife Research
S Afr J Wild Res — South African Journal of Wildlife Research
S Afr J Zool — South African Journal of Zoology
SAfrL — Studies in African Literature
S Afr Labour Bull — South African Labour Bulletin
S Afr Lapid Mag — South African Lapidary Magazine
S Afr Law J — South African Law Journal
S Afr Libr — South African Libraries
S Afr LJ — South African Law Journal
S Afr LR — South African Law Reports
S Afr Mach Tool Rev — South African Machine Tool Review
S Afr Mater Handl News — South African Materials Handling News
S Afr Mech Eng — South African Mechanical Engineer
S Afr Mech Engr — South African Mechanical Engineer
S Afr Med Equip News — South African Medical Equipment News
S Afr Med J — South African Medical Journal
S-Afr Med Tydskr — Suid-Afrikaanse Mediese Tydskrif
S Afr Min Eng J — South African Mining and Engineering Journal
S Afr Min J — South African Mining Journal
S Afr Min Rev — South African Mining Review
S Afr Min World — South African Mining World
S Afr Music Teach — South African Music Teacher
S Afr Mus Rep — South African Museum Report
S Afr Numis J — South African Numismatic Journal
S Afr Nurs J — South African Nursing Journal
S Afr Optom — South African Optometrist
S Afr Outlook — South African Outlook
S Afr Panorama — South African Panorama
S Afr Pat Trade Marks Off Pat J Incl Trade Marks Des — South Africa. Patent and Trade Marks Office. Patent Journal, Including Trade Marks and Designs
S Afr Pharm J — South African Pharmaceutical Journal
S Afr Pneumoconiosis Rev — South African Pneumoconiosis Review
S Afr Poult Bull — South African Poultry Bulletin
S Afr Radiogr — South African Radiographer
S Afr Railw — South African Railways
S Afr Rep Secr Water Affairs — South Africa. Report of the Secretary for Water Affairs
S Afr Sci — South African Science
S Afr Sea Fish Branch Invest Rep — South Africa Sea Fisheries Branch. Investigational Report
S Afr Shipp News Fish Ind Rev — South African Shipping News and Fishing Industry Review
S-Afr Spoorwee — Suid-Afrikaanse Spoorwee [South Africa]
S Afr Stat — South African Statistical Journal
S Afr Stat J — South African Statistical Journal
S Afr Sugar Assoc Exp Stn Annu Rep — South African Sugar Association Experiment Station. Annual Report
S Afr Sugar Assoc Exp Stn Bull — South African Sugar Association Experiment Station. Bulletin
S Afr Sugar J — South African Sugar Journal
S Afr Sug J — South African Sugar Journal
S Afr Surv J — South African Survey Journal
S Afr Text — South African Textiles
S Afr Transp — South African Transport
S Afr Treas — South African Treasurer
S Afr Tunnel — South African Tunnelling
S Afr Tunnelling — South African Tunnelling
S-Afr Tydsk Natuurwet Tegnol — Suid-Afrikaanse Tydskrif vir Natuurwetenskap en Tegnologie
S-Afr Tydskr Antarkt Navors — Suid-Afrikaanse Tydskrif vir Antarktiese Navorsing
S Afr Tydskr Chem — Suid-Afrikaanse Tydskrif vir Chemie
S-Afr Tydskr Chir — Suid-Afrikaanse Tydskrif vir Chirurgie
S-Afr Tydskr Geneeskd — Suid-Afrikaanse Tydskrif vir Geneeskunde
S-Afr Tydskr Lab Kliniekwerk — Suid-Afrikaanse Tydskrif vir Laboratorium en Kliniekwerk
S-Afr Tydskr Landbouwet — Suid-Afrikaanse Tydskrif vir Landbouwetenskap
S Afr Tydskr Med Lab Tegnol — Suid-Afrikaanse Tydskrif vir Mediese Laboratorium-Tegnologie
S-Afr Tydskr Obstet Ginekol — Suid-Afrikaanse Tydskrif vir Obstetrie en Ginekologie
S Afr Tydskr Plant Grond — Suid-Afrikaanse Tydskrif vir Plant en Grond
S-Afr Tydskr Radiol — Suid-Afrikaanse Tydskrif vir Radiologie
S-Afr Tydskr Suiweltegnol — Suid-Afrikaanse Tydskrif vir Suiweltegnologie
S-Afr Tydskr Veekd — Suid-Afrikaanse Tydskrif vir Veekunde

S-Afr Tydskr Voeding — Suid-Afrikaanse Tydskrif vir Voeding
S-Afr Tydskr Wet — Suid-Afrikaanse Tydskrif vir Wetenskap
S-Afr Wet Nywerheid-Navorsingsraad Navorsingsversl — Suid-Afrikaanse Wetenskaplike en Nywerheidnavorskingsraad. Navorsingsverslag
S-Afr Wet Nywerheid-Navorsingsraad Spes Versl — Suid-Afrikaanse Wetenskaplike en Nywerheidnavorskingsraad. Spesiale Verslag
S Afr Wool Text Res Inst Annu Rep — South African Wool Textile Research Institute. Annual Report
S Afr Wool Text Res Inst Tech Rep — South African Wool Textile Research Institute. Technical Report
S Afr Yearb Int Law — South African Yearbook of International Law
S Afr YIL — South African Yearbook of International Law
Saf Sci Abstr — Safety Science Abstracts Journal
Saf Ser IAEA — Safety Series. IAEA [International Atomic Energy Agency]
Saf Surv — Safety Surveyor [United Kingdom]
Safugetierkd Mitt — Safugetierkundliche Mitteilungen
Sag — Saggiatore
SAG — Stuttgarter Arbeiten zur Germanistik
Saga-Book — Saga-Book. Viking Society for Northern Research
Saga S — Saga och Sed
Sage Annu R Communic Res — Sage Annual Reviews of Communication Research
Sage Elect Stud Yb — Sage Electoral Studies Yearbook
Sage Int Yb For Pol Stud — Sage International Yearbook of Foreign Policy Studies
SA Geol Atlas Ser — South Australia. Geological Survey. Atlas Series
SA Geol Surv Bull — South Australia. Geological Survey. Bulletin
SA Geol Surv Geol Atlas 1 Mile Ser — South Australia. Geological Survey. Geological Atlas. 1 Mile Series
SA Geol Surv Rep Invest — South Australia. Geological Survey. Report of Investigations
Sage Pap CP — Sage Professional Papers in Comparative Politics
Sage Pub Admin Abstr — Sage Public Administration Abstracts
Sage Urban Abs — Sage Urban Abstracts
Sage Urb Stud Abstr — Sage Urban Studies Abstracts
Sage Yb Polit Publ Pol — Sage Yearbooks in Politics and Public Policy
Sage Yb Women's Pol — Sage Yearbook in Women's Policy Studies
Saggi — Saggi e Ricerche di Letteratura Francese
SAGJ — South African Geographical Journal
SAGMN — Sudhoffs Archiv fuer Geschichte der Medizin und der Naturwissenschaften
SAGN — Sagkeeng News [Fort Alexander, MB]
SAH — Sitzungsberichte. Heidelberg Akademie der Wissenschaften. Philosophisch-Historische Klasse
SAH — Stratford-On-Avon Herald
SAH — Svenska Akademiens Handlingar
SAHEA — Sanitaer- und Heizungstechnik
SAHG — Die Sumerischen und Akkadischen Hymnen und Gebete [Zurich/Stuttgart]
SAHLBull — Societe d'Art et d'Histoire du le Diocese de Liege. Bulletin
SAHOA — Saiko To Hoan
SA Homes & Gardens — South Australian Homes and Gardens
SAHS — Swiss American Historical Society. Newsletter
SAI — Seltene Assyrische Ideogramme
SAI — Statistical Abstracts of Israel
SAIBB — Soil Association. Information Bulletin and Advisory Service
SAICDB — Israel. Institute of Field and Garden Crops. Scientific Activities
SAIEDH — Israel. Institute of Agricultural Engineering. Scientific Activities
SAIG — South Australian Industrial Gazette
SAIGA — Saishin Igaku
SAIGB — Sangyo Igaku
SAIHDO — Israel. Institute of Horticulture. Scientific Activities
Sains Malays — Sains Malaysiana [Malaysia]
SA Inst J — South Australian Institutes. Journal
Saint Lawrence Univ Geol Inf and Referral Service Bull — Saint Lawrence University. Geological Information and Referral Service. Bulletin
Saint Louis Univ LJ — Saint Louis University. Law Journal
SAIR — South Australian Industrial Reports
Sairaanh Vuosik — Sairaanhoidon Vuosikirja
SAISDP — Israel. Institute of Animal Science. Scientific Activities
SAIS Rev — SAIS [School of Advanced International Studies] Review
SAIT News — SAIT [South Australian Institute of Teachers] Newsletter
Saito Ho-On Kai Mus Res Bull — Saito Ho-On Kai Museum Research Bulletin
SAJ — South African Journal of Economics
SAJAA — South African Journal of African Affairs
SAJAC — South African Journal of Animal Science
SAJAR — South African Journal of Antarctic Research
SAJCD — South African Journal of Chemistry
SAJE — South African Journal of Economics [Suid-Afrikaanse Tydskrif vir Ekonomie]
SA J Educ Res — South Australian Journal of Education Research
SAJER — South Australian Journal of Education Research
SAJL — Studies in American Jewish Literature
SAJMA — South African Journal of Medical Sciences
SAJPA — South African Journal of Physiotherapy
SAJRA — South African Journal of Radiology

SAJ Res Sport Phys Educ Recreat — SA [*South African*] Journal for Research in Sport. Physical Education and Recreation
SAJS — South African Journal of Science
SAJSA — South African Journal of Science
SAJSB — South African Journal of Surgery
SAJTA — South African Journal of Medical Laboratory Technology
SAJZD — South African Journal of Zoology
SAKAD — Sangyo To Kankyo
Sakharth SSR Mecn Akad Gamothvl Centr Srom — Sakharthvelos SSR Mecnierebatha Akademia Gamothvlithi Centris Sromebi
Sakharth SSR Mecn Akad Marthw Sistem Inst Srom — Sakharthvelos SSR Mecnierebatha Akademia Marthwis Sistemebis Instituti Sromebi
Sakharth SSR Mecn Akad Math Inst Srom — Sakharthvelos SSR Mecnierebatha Akademia A. Razmadzis Sahelobis Thbilsis Mathematikis Institutis Sromebi
Sakharth SSR Mecn Akad Moambe — Sakharthvelos SSR Mecnierebatha Akademia Moambe
SAKHB — Sangyo Anzen Kenkyusho Hokoku
Sakh Prom — Sakharnaya Promyshlennost
Sakh Promst — Sakharnaya Promyshlennost
Sakh Svekla — Sakharnaya Svekla
SAKOD — Sangyo Kogai
Sakura X-Ray Photogr Rev — Sakura X-Ray Photographic Review [*Japan*]
SAL — Sales and Marketing Management
Sal — Salesianum
SAL — Solar Age. A Magazine of the Sun
SAL — Southwestern American Literature
SAL — Studies in African Linguistics
SA Law Soc Bull — South Australian Law Society. Bulletin
SALB — Studia Albanica
SALCR — South Australian Licensing Court. Reports
Saldat Auto — Saldatura Autogena
SALEA — Sanshi Kenkyu
Sales Mgt — Sales Management [*Later, Sales and Marketing Management*]
Sales & Mkt Mgt — Sales and Marketing Management
Sales TC — Sales Tax Cases
Salisbury Med Bull — Salisbury Medical Bulletin
Salisbury Rev — Salisbury Review
SALit — Chu-Shikoku Studies in American Literature
SALit — Studies in American Literature
SA L J — South African Law Journal
Salm — Salmagundi
Salm — Salmanticensis
Salmon Trou Mag — Salmon and Trout Magazine
SALR — South African Law Reports
SALR — South Australian Law Reports
SALRA — Schweizer Aluminium Rundschau
SALSSAH — Serials in Australian Libraries: Social Sciences and Humanities
SALSSAH/NRT — Serials in Australian Libraries: Social Sciences and Humanities/Newly Reported Titles
Salt C R — New Salt Creek Reader
Salt Lake Min Rev — Salt Lake Mining Review
Salt Lake M Rv — Salt Lake Mining Review
Salt Res Ind — Salt Research and Industry
Salt Res Ind J — Salt Research and Industry Journal
Salud Ocup — Salud Ocupacional
Salud Publica Mex — Salud Publica de Mexico
Salute Italia Med — Salute Italia Medica
Salzburger Beitr Paracelsusforsch — Salzburger Beitraege zur Paracelsusforschung
Salzburger Jrbh Phil — Salzburger Jahrbuch fuer Philosophie
Salzburg Haus Nat Ber Abt B Geol-Mineral Samml — Salzburg Haus der Natur. Berichte. Abteilung B. Geologisch-Mineralogische Sammlungen
Salz St Ang — Salzburger Studien zur Anglistik und Amerikanistik
Sam — Samisdat
Sam — Sammlung
S Am — Scientific American
Sam — Serving Advertising in the Midwest [*Later, Adweek*]
SAM — Sitzungsberichte. Bayerische Akademie der Wissenschaften [*Munich*]
SAM Advanced Mgt J — SAM [*Society for Advancement of Management*] Advanced Management Journal
SAM Adv Man — SAM [*Society for Advancement of Management*] Advanced Management Journal
Samaru Agric Newsl — Samaru Agricultural Newsletter
Samaru Agr Newslett — Samaru Agricultural Newsletter
Samaru Inst Agric Res Soil Surv Bull — Samaru Institute for Agricultural Research. Soil Survey Bulletin
Samaru Misc Pap — Samaru Miscellaneous Paper
Samaru Res Bull — Samaru Research Bulletin
SAMBHist — Societe des Antiquaires de la Morinie. Bulletin Historique
SAMEA — South African Mechanical Engineer
SAMEB — SA [*South African*] Mining and Engineering Journal
Same Day Surg — Same-Day Surgery
SA Methodist — South Australian Methodist
SA Min Eng J — SA [*South African*] Mining and Engineering Journal
SAMJA — South African Medical Journal

Saml — Samlaren
SAML — Studies in American Literature [*The Hague*]
Samml Geol Fuehrer — Sammlung Geologischer Fuehrer
Samml Goeschen — Sammlung Goeschen
Sammlung Wichmann NF — Sammlung Wichmann. Neue Folge
Samml Vergiftungsfaellen — Sammlung von Vergiftungsfaellen
Samml Zwangl Abh Geb Psychiatr Neurol — Sammlung Zwangloser Abhandlungen aus dem Gebiete der Psychiatrie und Neurologie
Samoan Pac LJ — Samoan Pacific Law Journal
Samoletostr Tekh Vozdushn Flota — Samoletostroenie i Tekhnika Vozdushnogo Flota
SA Motor — South Australian Motor
SAMPE J — SAMPE [*Society for the Advancement of Material and Process Engineering*] Journal
SAMPE Q — SAMPE [*Society for the Advancement of Material and Process Engineering*] Quarterly
SAMPE Qtly — SAMPE [*Society for the Advancement of Material and Process Engineering*] Quarterly
SAMQA — SAMPE [*Society for the Advancement of Material and Process Engineering*] Quarterly
SAMRD — South African Machine Tool Review
SA Museum Rec — South Australian Museum. Records
SA Mus Tcr — South Africa Music Teacher
SAN — SAN: Journal of the Society for Ancient Numismatics
SANAn — Societe Archeologique de Namur. Annales
SA Nat — South Australian Naturalist
SA Naturalist — South Australian Naturalist
SANBB — Sankhya. Series B
San Bernardino County Med Soc Bull — San Bernardino County Medical Society. Bulletin [*California*]
Sand Dune Res — Sand Dune Research
Sandia SN — Sandia Science News
San Diego L Rev — San Diego Law Review
San Diego Soc Nat Hist Mem — San Diego Society of Natural History. Memoirs
San Diego Soc Nat History Occasional Paper Trans — San Diego Society of Natural History. Occasional Papers. Transactions
San Diego Soc Nat History Trans — San Diego Society of Natural History. Transactions
San Diego Soc N H Tr — San Diego Society of Natural History. Transactions
San DLR — San Diego Law Review
Sandoz Bull — Sandoz Bulletin
SANET — Supplement to Ancient Near Eastern Texts
SanF — San Francisco Magazine
San Fern VL Rev — San Fernando Valley Law Review
San Francisco Bus — San Francisco Business
San Francisco Micro Soc Tr — San Francisco Microscopical Society. Transactions
Sang Natak — Sangeet Natak [*New Delhi*]
SANGruz — Soobscenija Akademiji Nauk Gruzinskoj SSR
SANH — Somerset Archaeology and Natural History
Sanid Aeronaut — Sanidad Aeronautica
Sanid Benef Munic — Sanidad y Beneficiencia Municipal
Sanitary & Heat Eng — Sanitary and Heating Engineering
Sanit Eng Pap Colo State Univ — Sanitary Engineering Papers. Colorado State University
Sanit Heiz Tech — Sanitaer- und Heizungstechnik
Sanit Heizungstech (Duesseldorf) — Sanitaer- und Heizungstechnik (Duesseldorf)
Sanit Heizungstechnik — Sanitaer- und Heizungstechnik [*West Germany*]
Sanit Nytt — Sanitets Nytt Utgitt av Forsvarets Sanitet
Sanit Okh Vodoemov Zagryaz Prom Stochnymi Vodami — Sanitarnaya Okhrana Vodoemov ot Zagryazneniya Promyshlennymi Stochnymi Vodami
Sanit Tekh — Sanitarnaya Tekhnika
SANJA — South African Nursing Journal
San Jose Stud — San Jose Studies
Sankhya A — Sankhya. Series A. Indian Journal of Statistics
Sankhya B — Sankhya. Series B. Indian Journal of Statistics
Sankhya C — Sankhya. Series C. Indian Journal of Statistics
Sankhya Indian J Stat Ser B — Sankhya. Series B. Indian Journal of Statistics
Sankhya Ser A — Sankhya. Series A. Indian Journal of Statistics
Sankhya Ser B — Sankhya. Series B. Indian Journal of Statistics
SANNA — Schweizer Archiv fuer Neurologie, und Psychiatrie
SANNAW — Archives Suisses de Neurologie, Neurochirurgie, et de Psychiatrie/Archivio Svizzero di Neurologia, Neurochirurgia, e Psichiatria
SAns — Studia Anselmiana
SANT — Studien zum Alten und Neuen Testament
S Ant — Suomen Antropologi/Antropologi i Finland
Santa Barbara Mus Nat History Dept Geology Bull — Santa Barbara Museum of Natural History. Department of Geology. Bulletin
Santa Barbara Soc N H B — Santa Barbara Society of Natural History. Bulletin
Santa Clara L — Santa Clara Lawyer
Santa Clara Law — Santa Clara Lawyer

Santa Clara L Rev — Santa Clara Law Review
Sante Publique (Bucur) — Sante Publique. Revue Internationale (Bucuresti)
Sante Secur Soc — Sante Securite Sociale
Santo Domingo Univ Anales Pub — Santo Domingo Universidad. Anales. Publicaciones
Santo Tomas J Med — Santo Tomas Journal of Medicine
SA Nurs J — South African Nursing Journal
SANYD — Sanitets Nytt
SAO — Studia et Acta Orientalia
SAOABX — Archivos. Sociedad Americana de Oftalmologia y Optometria
SAOB — Svenska Akademiens Ordbok
SAOC — Studies in Ancient Oriental Civilization. The Oriental Institute of the University of Chicago
Sao Paulo Brazil Inst Pesqui Tecnol Bol — Sao Paulo, Brazil. Instituto de Pesquisas Tecnologicas. Boletin
Sao Paulo Inst Agron (Campinas) Bol — Sao Paulo. Instituto Agronomico (Campinas). Boletim
Sao Paulo Inst Agron (Campinas) Bol Tec — Sao Paulo. Instituto Agronomico (Campinas). Boletim Tecnico
Sao Paulo Inst Agron (Campinas) Circ — Sao Paulo. Instituto Agronomico (Campinas). Circular
Sao Paulo Inst Geogr Geol Bol — Sao Paulo. Instituto Geografico e Geologico. Boletim
Sao Paulo Inst Geogr Geol Relat — Sao Paulo. Instituto Geografico e Geologico. Relatorio
Sao Paulo Univ Inst Geocienc Bol — Sao Paulo. Universidade. Instituto de Geociencias. Boletim
Sao Paulo Univ Inst Geogr Geogr Planejamento — Sao Paulo. Universidade. Instituto de Geografia. Geografia e Planejamento
Sao Paulo Univ Inst Geogr Geomorfol — Sao Paulo. Universidade. Instituto de Geografia. Geomorfologia
Sao Paulo Univ Inst Geogr Ser Teses Monogr — Sao Paulo. Universidade. Instituto de Geografia. Serie Teses e Monografias
SA Ornithol — South Australian Ornithologist
SA Ornithologist — South Australian Ornithologist
SAP — Studia Anglica Posnaniensia
SA Parl Deb — South Australia. Parliamentary Debates
SA Parl Parl Deb — South Australia. Parliament. Parliamentary Debates
SAPEA — Sapere
SAPED — Salt 'N' Pepper
SAPHD — South African Journal of Physics
SAPNA — South African Panorama
SAPOA — Savremena Poljoprivreda
SAPOAB — Contemporary Agriculture
Sapporo Med J — Sapporo Medical Journal
SAPR — South Australian Planning Reports
SAPRA — Sakharnaya Promyshlennost
SAPTA — SAE [Society of Automotive Engineers] Progress in Technology
SA Pub Serv R — South Australian Public Service Review
SAQ — South Atlantic Quarterly
SAR — South Asian Review
SAR — South Australian Industrial Reports
SAR — Studies in the American Renaissance
Sarabhai M Chem Tech News Serv — Sarabhai M. Chemicals. Technical News Service
SA Railways — South Australian Railways Institute. Magazine
SA Railways Institute Mag — South Australian Railways Institute. Magazine
Saratov Gos-Ped Inst Ucen Zap — Saratovskii Gosudarstvennyi-Pedagogiceskii Institut. Ucenye Zapiski
SarawakMJ — Sarawak Museum. Journal
Sarawak Mus J — Sarawak Museum. Journal
Sarawak Res Branch Dep Agric Annu Rep — Sarawak. Research Branch. Department of Agriculture. Annual Report
SARE — Southeast Asian Review of English
SARE-A — Saturday Review
SA Regr — South Australian Register
SA Regr (Newspr) — South Australian Register Reports (Newspaper)
SA Res Service Bibliog — South Australia. Public Library. Research Service. Bibliographies
SARev — South Asian Review
Sar Gaz — Sarawak Gazette [Kuching]
Sargetia Ser Sci Nat — Sargetia [Acta Devensis]. Series Scientia Naturae
Sar Mus J — Sarawak Museum. Journal [Kuching]
Sarot Otd Gos Nauchno-Issled Inst Ozern Rechn Rybn Khoz Tr — Sarotovskoe Otdelenie Gosudarstvennogo Nauchno-Issledovatel'skogo Instituta Ozernogo i Rechnogo Rybnogo Khozyaistva. Trudy
SaS — Slovo a Slovesnost
SAS — Studia Academica Slovaca
SASAE — Supplements. Annales. Service des Antiquites de l'Egypt [Cairo]
SA Sch Post — South Australian School Post
SASHA — Sanfujinka No Shimpo
SA Shipp News — South African Shipping News and Fishing Industry Review
S Asia R — South Asian Review
SASILO — Schriftenreihe. A. Stifer-Institut des Landes Oberoesterreich

Saskatchewan Dept Nat Res Ann Rept Mineral Res Br Misc Paper — Saskatchewan. Department of Natural Resources. Annual Report. Mineral Resources Branch. Miscellaneous Paper
Saskatchewan Geol Survey Rept — Saskatchewan. Geological Survey. Report
Saskatchewan L Rev — Saskatchewan Law Review
Sask Bar Rev — Saskatchewan Bar Review
Sask BR — Saskatchewan Bar Review
Sask B Rev — Saskatchewan Bar Review
Sask Bul — Saskatchewan Bulletin
Sask Dep Miner Resour Geol Sci Br Precambrian Geol Div Rep — Saskatchewan. Department of Mineral Resources. Geological Sciences Branch. Precambrian Geology Division. Report
Sask Dep Miner Resour Pet Natural Gas Reservoir Ann — Saskatchewan. Department of Mineral Resources. Petroleum and Natural Gas Reservoir. Annual
Sask Dep Miner Resour Rep — Saskatchewan. Department of Mineral Resources. Report
Sask Dep Nat Resour Fish Branch Fish Rep — Saskatchewan. Department of Natural Resources. Fisheries Branch. Fisheries Report
Sask Dep Nat Resour Fish Wildl Branch Fish Rep — Saskatchewan. Department of Natural Resources. Fisheries and Wildlife Branch. Fisheries Report
Sask Ed Admin — Saskatchewan Education Administrator
Sask Gaz — Saskatchewan Gazette
Sask Geol Soc Spec Publ — Saskatchewan Geological Society. Special Publication
Sask Hist — Saskatchewan History
Sask Law Rev — Saskatchewan Law Review
Sask Libr — Saskatchewan Library
Sask LR — Saskatchewan Law Review
Sask L Rev — Saskatchewan Law Review
Sask (Prov) Dep Miner Resour Rep — Saskatchewan (Province). Department of Mineral Resources. Report
Sask Res Counc Eng Div Rep — Saskatchewan Research Council. Engineering Division. Report
Sask Res Counc Geol Div Rep — Saskatchewan Research Council. Geology Division. Report
Sask Res Counc Geol Div Rep G — Saskatchewan Research Council. Geology Division. Report G
SASNA — South African Shipping News and Fishing Industry Review
SASOP — Sudan. Antiquities Service. Occasional Papers
SASR — South Australian State Reports
SASR — State Reports (South Australia)
SASS — South Australian Secrets Summary
SASS — South Australian Social Science
SASSAR — Suid-Afrikaanse Spoorwee/South African Railways
SASTAJ — SASTA [South Australian Science Teachers Association] Journal
SA Storekeepers J — South Australian Storekeepers and Grocers Journal
SAT — Die Schriften des Alten Testaments in Auswahl Neu Uebersetzt und fuer die Gegenwart Erklaert [Goettingen]
Sat — Satellite Science Fiction
SATA — Die Schriften des Alten Testaments in Auswahl Neu Uebersetzt und fuer die Gegenwart Erklaert [Goettingen]
SATDB — Sangyo To Denki
SATEA — Soviet Atomic Energy [English Translation]
SA Teachers J — SA [South Australia] Teachers' Journal
SA Teach J — South Australian Teachers' Journal
Satell Commun — Satellite Communications
Satellite — Satellite Communications
Satel News — Satellite News
Sat E P — Saturday Evening Post
Sat Eve Post — Saturday Evening Post
SATF — Societe des Anciens Textes Francais
SATHA — Schweizer Archiv fuer Tierheilkunde
SatireNL — Satire Newsletter
SATKB — Sanitarnaya Tekhnika
S Atlan Bull — South Atlantic Bulletin
S Atlantic Q — South Atlantic Quarterly
S Atl Q — South Atlantic Quarterly
S Atl Quart — South Atlantic Quarterly
S Atl Rev — South Atlantic Review
Sat N — Saturday Night
Sat R — Saturday Review
SATRA Bull — SATRA [Shoe and Allied Trades Research Association] Bulletin
Sat R Arts — Saturday Review of the Arts
Sat R Ed — Saturday Review of Education
Sat Rev — Saturday Review
Sat R Lit — Saturday Review of Literature
Sat R Sci — Saturday Review of the Sciences
Sat R Soc — Saturday Review of Society
Sat R/World — Saturday Review/World
SATUD — South African Tunnelling
Saturday Rev — Saturday Review
SAU — Sprawozdania Akademii Umiejetnosci
SAUCB — Soviet Automatic Control [English Translation]

Saudi Arabia Dir Gen Miner Resour Bull — Saudi Arabia. Directorate General of Mineral Resources. Bulletin
Saudi Arabia Dir Gen Miner Resour Geol Map — Saudi Arabia. Directorate General of Mineral Resources. Geologic Map
Saudi Arabia Dir Gen Miner Resour Miner Resour Rep Invest — Saudi Arabia. Directorate General of Mineral Resources. Mineral Resources Report of Investigations
Saudi Arabia Dir Gen Miner Resour Miner Resour Res — Saudi Arabia. Directorate General of Mineral Resources. Mineral Resources Research
Saugar Univ J Part 2 — Saugar University. Journal. Part 2. Science
Saugertierkd Mitt — Saugetierkundliche Mitteilungen
Saugertierkundliche Mitt — Saugetierkundliche Mitteilungen
S Aus Nat Gal Bul — South Australia National Gallery. Bulletin
S Aust — South Australiana
S Aust Clinics — South Australian Clinics
S Aust Coal Abstr Bull — South Australian Coal Abstract Bulletin
S Aust Dir Mines Gov Geol Annu Rep — South Australia. Director of Mines and Government Geologist. Annual Report
S Aust Geol Atlas Ser — South Australia. Geological Survey. Atlas Series
S Aust Geol Surv Bull — South Australia. Geological Survey. Bulletin
S Aust Geol Surv 1:250000 Geol Ser — South Australia. Geological Survey. 1:250,000 Geological Series
S Aust Geol Surv Rep Invest — South Australia. Geological Survey. Report of Investigations
S Austl LR — South Australian Law Reports
S Aust LR — South Australian Law Reports
S Aust Miner Resour Rev — South Australia Mineral Resources Review
S Aust Nat — South Australian Naturalist
S Aust Orn — South Australian Ornithologist
S Aust Ornithol — South Australian Ornithologist
S Australia Geol Surv Rep Invest — South Australia. Geological Survey. Report of Investigations
S Australiana — South Australiana
S Aust Rep Mus Board — South Australia Report of the Museum Board
SAUZA — Stroitel'stvo i Arkhitektura Uzbekistana
Sav — Savremenik
SAV — Schweizerisches Archiv fuer Volkskunde
SAV — Slovenska Akademia Vied
Sav Bank J — Savings Bank Journal
Savings Bank J — Savings Bank Journal
Savings Banks Internat — Savings Banks International
SAVL — Studien zur Allgemeinen und Vergleichenden Literaturwissenschaft
Sav & Loan N — Savings and Loan News
Sav Loan News — Savings and Loan News
Savremena Poljopr — Savremena Poljoprivreda
Savrem Med (Sofia) — Savremenna Meditsina (Sofia)
Savrem Poljoprivreda — Savremena Poljoprivreda
SAW — Sitzungsberichte. Akademie der Wissenschaft in Wien
SA Waterabstr — SA [*South African*] Waterabstracts
SAWB — Sitzungsberichte. Akademie der Wissenschaften zu Berlin
SAWM — Sitzungsberichte. Akademie der Wissenschaften zu Muenchen
SAWPHK — Saechsische Akademie der Wissenschaften zu Leipzig. Philologisch-Historische Klasse
Sawtri Bull — Sawtri Bulletin
SAWW — Sitzungsberichte. Akademie der Wissenschaft in Wien
Sawyer's Gas Turbine Int — Sawyer's Gas Turbine International
SAY — Science Fiction Adventures Yearbook
SAYKA — Sovistva Atomnykh Yader
SB — Schweizer Buch
SB — Science Books
SB — Science Books and Films
SB — Selmer Bandwagon
SB — Skandinaviska Banken. Quarterly Review [*Later, Skandinaviska Enskilda Banken. Quarterly Review*]
SB — Sociologisch Bulletin
SB — Soncino Blaetter
SB — Sources Bibliques [*Paris*]
SB — Sovetskaya Bibliografia
SB — Studi Baltici
SB — Studi Bizantini
SB — Studies in Bibliography
SBA — Sitzungsberichte. Bayerische Akademie der Wissenschaften
SBA — Standard Chartered Review
SBA — Studies in Biblical Archaeology
SBAG — Schweizer Beitraege zur Allgemeinen Geschichte
SbAk — Sbornik na Balgarskata Akademija na Naukite
Sb Akad Nauk SSSR — Sbornik Rabot Akademiya Nauk SSSR
SBARMO Bull — SBARMO [*Scientific Ballooning and Radiations Monitoring Organization*] Bulletin
Sb Aspir Rab Kazan Gos Univ Estest Nauki — Sbornik Aspirantskikh Rabot Kazanskii Gosudarstvennyi Universitet Estestvennye Nauki
Sb Aspir Rab Kazan Gos Univ Estest Nauki Biol — Sbornik Aspirantskikh Rabot Kazanskii Gosudarstvennyi Universitet Estestvennye Nauki Biologiya

Sb Aspir Rab Kazan Gos Univ Tochn Nauki Mekh Fiz — Sbornik Aspirantskikh Rabot Kazanskii Gosudarstvennyi Universitet Tochnye Nauki Mekhanika Fizika
Sb Aspir Rab Kazan Khim Tekhnol Inst — Sbornik Aspirantskikh Rabot Kazanskii Khimiko Tekhnologicheskii Institut
Sb Aspir Rab Kazan Univ Estestv Nauk — Sbornik Aspirantskikh Rabot Kazanskogo Universiteta Estestvennykh Nauk
Sb Aspir Rab Ufim Neft Nauchno-Issled Inst — Sbornik Aspirantskikh Rabot Ufimskii Neftyanoi Nauchno-Issledovatel'skii Institut
Sb Aspir Rab Voronezh Lesotekh Inst — Sbornik Aspirantskikh Rabot Voronezhskii Lesotekhnicheskii Institut
Sb Aspir Rab Vses Nauchno Issled Inst Zhivotnovod — Sbornik Aspirantskikh Rabot Vsesoyuznyi Nauchno-Issledovatel'skii Institut Zhivotnovodstva
SBAW — Sitzungsberichte. Bayerische Akademie der Wissenschaften
SBAWW — Sitzungsberichte. Akademie der Wissenschaft in Wien
SBB — Studies in Bibliography and Booklore
Sb Bakteriofagiya — Sbornik Bakteriofagiya
SBBAW — Sitzungsberichte. Bayerische Akademie der Wissenschaften
SBBGA — Studia Universitatis Babes-Bolyai. Series Geologia-Geographia
Sb Biokhim Zerna Akad Nauk SSSR Inst Biokhim A N Bakha — Sbornik. Biokhimiya Zerna. Akademiya Nauk SSSR. Institut Biokhimii Imeni A. N. Bakha
SBBKA — Seibutsu Butsuri Kagaku
Sb Bot Rab Beloruss Otd Vses Bot Ova — Sbornik Botanicheskikh Rabot Belorusskoe Otdelenie Vsesoyuznogo Botanicheskogo Obshchestva
Sb Bot Rabot Vses Bot Obshch Beloruss Otd — Sbornik Botanicheskikh Rabot Vsesoyuznogo Botanicheskogo Obshchestva. Belorusskoe Otdelenie
SBBPA — Studia Universitatis Babes-Bolyai. Series Physica
SBBUD — SBARMO [*Scientific Ballooning and Radiations Monitoring Organization*] Bulletin
SBC — Studies in Browning and His Circle
SBCABE — Annual Symposium on Biomathematics and Computer Science in the Life Sciences. Abstracts
SBCBA — Sounding Brass and the Conductor
SBCED — Scientific Bulletin. Canada Centre for Mineral and Energy Technology
Sb Cesk Akad Zemed — Sbornik Ceskoslovenske Akademie Zemedelske
Sb Cesk Akad Zemed Ved — Sbornik Ceskoslovenske Akademie Zemedelskych Ved
Sb Cesk Akad Zemed Ved Lesn — Sbornik Ceskoslovenske Akademie Zemedelskych Ved. Lesnictvi
Sb Cesk Akad Zemed Ved Rada A — Sbornik Ceskoslovenske Akademie Zemedelskych Ved. Rada A
Sb Cesk Akad Zemed Ved Rada B — Sbornik Ceskoslovenske Akademie Zemedelskych Ved. Rada B
Sb Cesk Akad Zemed Ved Rostl Vyr — Sbornik Ceskoslovenske Akademie Zemedelskych Ved. Rostlinna Vyroba
Sb Cesk Akad Zemed Ved Rostl Vyroba — Sbornik Ceskoslovenske Akademie Zemedelskych Ved. Rostlinna Vyroba
Sb Cesk Akad Zemed Ved Vet Med — Sbornik Ceskoslovenske Akademie Zemedelskych Ved. Veterinarni Medicina
Sb Cesk Akad Zemed Ved Zivocisna Vyroba — Sbornik Ceskoslovenske Akademie Zemedelskych Ved. Zivocisna Vyroba
Sb Csl Akad Zemed Ved Rostlinna Vyroba — Sbornik Ceskoslovenske Akademie Zemedelskych Ved. Rada C. Rostlinna Vyroba
Sb Csl Akad Zemed Ved Zemed Ekon — Sbornik Ceskoslovenske Akademie Zemedelskych Ved. Rada B. Zemedelska Ekonomika
Sb Csl Akad Zemed Ved Ziv Vyroba — Sbornik Ceskoslovenske Akademie Zemedelskych Ved. Rada E. Zivocisna Vyroba
SBD — Schoolbestuur
SBD — Space Business Daily
SBDAW — Sitzungsberichte. Deutsche Akademie der Wissenschaften zu Berlin. Klasse fuer Sprachen, Literatur, und Kunst
SBDAWB — Sitzungsberichte. Deutsche Akademie der Wissenschaften zu Berlin. Klasse fuer Sprachen, Literatur, und Kunst
Sb Dokl Gidrotekh Vses Nauchno Issled Inst Gidrotekh — Sbornik Dokladov po Gidrotekhnike. Vsesoyuznyi Nauchno-Issledovatel'skii Institut Gidrotekhniki
Sb Dokl Nauchn Stud Ova Kalinin Gos Pedagog Inst — Sbornik Dokladov Nauchnogo Studencheskogo Obshchestva Kalininskii Gosudarstvennyi Pedagogicheskii Institut
Sb Donetsk Nauchno Issled Ugoln Inst — Sbornik Donetskii Nauchno-Issledovatel'skii Ugol'nyi Institut
SBE — Semana Biblica Espanola
Sb Ent Odd Nar Mus Praze — Sbornik Entomologickeho Oddeleni Narodniho Musea v Praze
Sber Bayer Akad Wiss — Sitzungsberichte. Bayerische Akademie der Wissenschaften zu Muenchen
Sber Dt Akad Landwiss Berl — Sitzungsberichte. Deutsche Akademie der Landwirtschaftswissenschaften zu Berlin
Sber Ges Morph Physiol Muench — Sitzungsberichte. Gesellschaft fuer Morphologie und Physiologie in Muenchen
Sber Ges Naturf Freunde Berl — Sitzungsberichte. Gesellschaft Naturforschender Freunde zu Berlin
SB & F — Science Books and Films
SBF — Studii Biblici Franciscani. Liber Annuus

Sb Faun Praci Ent Odd Nar Mus Praze — Sbornik Faunistickych Praci Entomologickeho Oddeleni Narodniho Musea v Praze

SBFAW — Sitzungsberichte. Finnische Akademie der Wissenschaften

SBFRA — Schriftenreihe. Bundesminister fuer Wissenschaftliche Forschung (Germany). Radionuklide

SBG — School Board Gazette

SBGDA — Spisanie na Bulgarskoto Geologichesko Druzhestvo

Sb Geol Ved Geol — Sbornik Geologickych Ved. Geologie

Sb Geol Ved Hydrogeol Inz Geol — Sbornik Geologickych Ved. Hydrogeologie, Inzenyrska, Geologie

Sb Geol Ved Loziskova Geol — Sbornik Geologickych Ved. Loziskova Geologie [*Czechoslovakia*]

Sb Geol Ved Paleontol — Sbornik Geologickych Ved. Paleontologie

Sb Geol Ved Rada Loziskova Geol — Sbornik Geologickych Ved. Rada Loziskova Geologie

Sb Geol Ved Rada P Paleontol — Sbornik Geologickych Ved. Rada P: Paleontologie

Sb Geol Ved Rada Uzita Geofyz — Sbornik Geologickych Ved. Rada Uzita Geofyzika

Sb Geol Ved Technol Geochem — Sbornik Geologickych Ved. Technologie, Geochemie

Sb Geol Ved Uzita Geofyz — Sbornik Geologickych Ved. Uzita Geofyzika [*Czechoslovakia*]

SBGGAKOPR — Sitzungsberichte. Gesellschaft fuer Geschichte und Altertumskunde der Ostseeprovinzen Russlands

SBGGAKR — Sitzungsberichte. Gesellschaft fuer Geschichte und Altertumskunde der Ostseeprovinzen Russlands

SBGKAT — Godishnik na Sofiiskiya Universitet. Biologicheski Fakultet. Kniga 2. Botanika, Mikrobiologiya, Fiziologiya, i Biokhimiya Rasteniyata

SBGMA — Sitzungsberichte. Gesellschaft zur Befoerderung der Gesamten Naturwissenschaften zu Marburg

Sb Grozn Neft Inst — Sbornik Groznenskii Neftyanoi Institut

SBHAW — Sitzungsberichte. Heidelberg Akademie der Wissenschaft

SBHC — Studies in Browning and His Circle

SBHLA — Schweizerische Blaetter fuer Heizung und Lueftung

SBHT — Studies in Burke and His Time

Sb Inf Obogashch Briket Uglei — Sbornik Informatsii po Obogashcheniyu i Briketirovaniyu Uglei [*USSR*]

Sb Inst Neorg Khim Elektrokhim Akad Nauk Gruz SSR — Sbornik Institut Neorganicheskoi Khimii i Elektrokhimii Akademiya Nauk Gruzinskoi SSR

SBiz — Studi Bizantini

Sb "Izme Pochv Okul'turiv Klassifik Diagnostika" — Sbornik "Izmenenie Pochv pri Okul'turivanii, Ikh Klassifikatsiya i Diagnostika"

SBJ — Savings Bank Journal

Sb Jihoceskeho Muz Cesk Budejovicich Prir Vedy — Sbornik Jihoceskeho Muzea v Ceskych Budejovicich Prirodni Vedy

Sb Karantinu Rast — Sbornik po Karantinu Rastenii

SBKAW — Sitzungsberichte. Kaiserliche Akademie der Wissenschaften in Wien

SBKAWW — Sitzungsberichte. Kaiserliche Akademie der Wissenschaften in Wien

Sb Klubu Prirodoved Brno — Sbornik Klubu Prirodovedeckeho v Brno

Sb Kratk Soobshch Fiz AN SSSR Fiz Inst PN Lebedeva — Sbornik Kratkie Soobshcheniya po Fizike. Akademiya Nauk SSSR. Fizicheskii Institut Imeni P. N. Lebedeva

Sb Kratk Soobshch Kazan Univ Bot Pochvoved — Sbornik Kratkikh Soobshchenii Kazanskogo Universiteta Botanika i Pochvovedenie

Sb Kratk Soobshch Kazan Univ Zool — Sbornik Kratkikh Soobshchenii Kazanskogo Universiteta po Zoologii

SBL — Schildersblad. Algemeen Vakblad voor het Schildersbedrijf en Afwerkingsbedrijf

SBL — Studies in Black Literature

SBLEA — Sbornik Lekarsky

Sb Lek — Sbornik Lekarsky

Sb Lekar — Sbornik Lekarsky

Sb Leningr Elektro Mekh Inst — Sbornik Leningradskogo Elektro-Mekhanicheskogo Instituta

Sb Leningr Inst Inzh Zheleznodorozhn Transp — Sbornik Leningradskogo Instituta Inzhenerov Zheleznodorozhnogo Transporta

SBL Sem Pap — Society of Biblical Literature. Seminar Papers

SBM — Stuttgarter Biblische Monographien [*Stuttgart*]

Sb Mater Anapskoi Opytn Stn Nauchno Proizvodstvennoi Konf — Sbornik Materialov Anapskoi Opytnoi Stantsii k Nauchno Proizvodstvennoi Konferentsii

Sb Mater Avtom Proizvod Protsessov Dispetcher — Sbornik Materialov po Avtomatizatsii Proizvodstvennykh Protsessov i Dispetcherizatsii

Sb Mater Gorn Delu Obogashch Metall — Sbornik Materialov po Gornomu Delu Obogashcheniyu i Metallurgii

Sb Mater Vak Tekh — Sbornik Materialov po Vakuumnoi Tekhnike

SBMEA — Space Biology and Medicine [*English Translation*]

Sb Mikroelementy i Produktivn Rast — Sbornik Mikroelementy i Produktivnost Rastenii

SBMMB — Studia Universitatis Babes-Bolyai. Series Mathematica-Mechanica

Sb Mosk Inst Stali Splavov — Sbornik Moskovskii Institut Stali Splavov [*USSR*]

Sb Muz Antropol Etnogr — Sbornik Muzeja Antropologii i Etnografii

SBN — Scrip. Leader in World Pharmaceutical News

SBN — Studi Bizantini e Neoellenici

Sb Nar Mus Praze Rada B Prir Vedy — Sbornik Narodniho Muzea v Praze. Rada B: Prirodni Vedy

Sb Nauchni Tr — Sbornik Nauchni Trudove

Sb Nauchno Issled Inst Gidrometeorol Priborostr — Sbornik Nauchno-Issledovatel'skii Institut Gidrometeorologicheskogo Priborostroeniya

Sb Nauchno Issled Inst Osn Podzemn Sooruzh — Sbornik Nauchno-Issledovatel'skii Institut Osnovanii i Podzemnykh Sooruzhenii

Sb Nauchno-Issled Rab Adygeisk Oblast Opyt Sta — Sbornik Nauchno-Issledovatel'skikh Rabot Adygeikaya Oblast Opytnaya Stantsiya

Sb Nauchno Issled Rab Aspir Altai Skh Inst — Sbornik Nauchno-Issledovatel'skikh Rabot Aspirantov. Altaiskii Sel'skokhozyaistvennyi Institut

Sb Nauchno-Issled Rab Aspir Molodykh Uch Altai Skh Inst — Sbornik Nauchno-Issledovatel'skikh Rabot Aspirantov i Molodykh Uchenykh. Altaiskii Sel'skokhozyaistvennyi Institut

Sb Nauchno-Issled Rab Azovo-Chernomorsk S-Kh Inst — Sbornik Nauchno-Issledovatel'skikh Rabot Azovo-Chernomorskogo Sel'skokhozyaistvennogo Instituta

Sb Nauchno-Issled Rab Gor'k Obl Opytn Stn Zhivotnovod — Sbornik Nauchno-Issledovatel'skikh Rabot Gor'kovskoi Oblastnoi Opytnoi Stantsii Zhivotnovodstva

Sb Nauchno-Issled Rab Orlov Gos Sel'-khoz Opyt Sta — Sbornik Nauchno-Issledovatel'skikh Rabot Orlovskoi Gosudarstvennoi Sel'skokhozyaistvennoi Opytnoi Stantsii

Sb Nauchno Issled Rab Tashk Tekst Inst — Sbornik Nauchno-Issledovatel'skikh Rabot Tashkentskogo Tekstil'nogo Instituta

Sb Nauchno-Issled Rab Vses Nauchno-Issled Inst Tab Makhorki — Sbornik Nauchno-Issledovatel'skikh Rabot Vsesoyuznogo Nauchno-Issledovatel'skogo Instituta Tabaka i Makhorki

Sb Nauchno Issled Tr Mosk Tekst Inst — Sbornik Nauchno-Issledovatel'skikh Trudov Moskovskii Tekstil'nyi Institut

Sb Nauchn Rab Angar Nauchno-Issled Inst Gig Tr Prof Zabol — Sbornik Nauchnykh Rabot Angarskogo Nauchno-Issledovatel'skogo Instituta Gigieny Truda i Professional'nykh Zabolevanii

Sb Nauchn Rab Aspir Kabard Balkar Gos Univ — Sbornik Nauchnykh Rabot Aspirantov Kabardino-Balkarskii Gosudarstvennyi Universitet

Sb Nauchn Rab Aspir Voronezh Gos Univ — Sbornik Nauchnykh Rabot Aspirantov Voronezhskogo Gosudarstvennogo Universiteta

Sb Nauchn Rab Aspir Vses Nauchno Issled Inst Khlopkovod — Sbornik Nauchnykh Rabot Aspirantov Vsesoyuznyi Nauchno-Issledovatel'skii Institut Khlopkovodstva

Sb Nauchn Rab Beloruss Nauchno-Issled Kozhnovenerol Inst — Sbornik Nauchnykh Rabot Belorusskogo Nauchno-Issledovatel'skogo Kozhnovenerologicheskogo Instituta

Sb Nauchn Rab Beloruss Tekhnol Inst — Sbornik Nauchnykh Rabot Belorusskii Tekhnologicheskii Institut

Sb Nauchn Rab Checheno Ingush Nauchno Issled Vet Stn — Sbornik Nauchnykh Rabot Checheno-Ingushskoi Nauchno-Issledovatel'skoi Veterinarnoi Stantsii

Sb Nauchn Rab Dal'nevost Nauchno Issled Inst Stroit — Sbornik Nauchnykh Rabot Dal'nevostochnyi Nauchno-Issledovatel'skii Institut po Stroitel'stvu

Sb Nauchn Rab Dnepropetr Gos Med Inst — Sbornik Nauchnykh Rabot Dnepropetrovskii Gosudarstvennyi Meditsinskii Institut

Sb Nauchn Rab Inst Melior Vodn Bolotnogo Khoz Akad Nauk BSSR — Sbornik Nauchnykh Rabot Instituta Melioratsii. Vodnogo i Bolotnogo Khozyaistva. Akademiya Nauk Belorusskoi SSR

Sb Nauchn Rab Izhevsk Med Inst — Sbornik Nauchnykh Rabot Izhevskii Meditsinskii Institut

Sb Nauchn Rab Kazan Gos Med Inst — Sbornik Nauchnykh Rabot Kazanskogo Gosudarstvennogo Meditsinskogo Instituta

Sb Nauchn Rab Khar'k Gos Med Inst — Sbornik Nauchnykh Rabot Khar'kovskii Gosudarstvennyi Meditsinskii Institut

Sb Nauchn Rab Khar'k Gos Med Inst — Sbornik Nauchnykh Rabot Khar'kovskogo Gosudarstvennogo Meditsinskogo Instituta

Sb Nauchn Rab Khar'k Inst Mekh Sots Sel'sk Khoz — Sbornik Nauchnykh Rabot Khar'kovskii Institut Mekhanizatsii Sotsialisticheskogo Sel'skogo Khozyaistva

Sb Nauchn Rab Khar'k Nauchno-Issled Inst Vaktsin Syvorot — Sbornik Nauchnykh Rabot Khar'kovskogo Nauchno-Issledovatel'skogo Instituta Vaktsin i Syvorotok

Sb Nauchn Rab Kiev Voen Gosp — Sbornik Nauchnykh Rabot Kievskii Voennyi Gospital

Sb Nauchn Rab Kirg Med Inst — Sbornik Nauchnykh Rabot Kirgizskii Meditsinskii Institut

Sb Nauchn Rab Kirg Nauchno-Issled Inst Okhr Materin Det — Sbornik Nauchnykh Rabot Kirgizskii Nauchno-Issledovatel'skii Institut Okhrany Materinstva Detstva

Sb Nauchn Rab Kirg Nauchno Issled Inst Okhr Materin Det — Sbornik Nauchnykh Rabot Kirgizskogo Nauchno-Issledovatel'skogo Instituta Okhrany Materinstva i Detstva

Sb Nauchn Rab Kirg Nauchno-Issled Inst Tuberk — Sbornik Nauchnykh Rabot Kirgizskogo Nauchno-Issledovatel'skogo Instituta Tuberkuleza

Sb Nauchn Rab Krasnoyarsk Gos Med Inst — Sbornik Nauchnykh Rabot Krasnoyarskogo Gosudarstvennogo Meditsinskogo Instituta

Sb Nauchn Rab Kurgan Gos S-kh Inst — Sbornik Nauchnykh Rabot Kurganskii Gosudarstvennyi Sel'skokhozyaistvennyi Institut

Sb Nauchn Rab Leningr Gos Inst Usoversh Vrachei — Sbornik Nauchnykh Rabot Leningradskii Gosudarstvennyi Institut Usovershenstvovaniya Vrachei

Sb Nauchn Rab Leningr Inst Sov Torg — Sbornik Nauchnykh Rabot Leningradskii Institut Sovetskoi Torgovli

Sb Nauchn Rab Leningr Khim-Farm Inst — Sbornik Nauchnykh Rabot Leningradskogo Khimiko-Farmatsevticheskogo Instituta

Sb Nauchn Rab Leningr Nauchno Issled Inst Antibiot — Sbornik Nauchnykh Rabot Leningradskii Nauchno-Issledovatel'skii Institut Antibiotikov

Sb Nauchn Rab Minsk Gos Med Inst — Sbornik Nauchnykh Rabot Minskogo Gosudarstvennogo Meditsinskogo Instituta

Sb Nauchn Rab Murm Olenevodcheskaya Opytn Stn — Sbornik Nauchnykh Rabot Murmanskaya Olenevodcheskaya Opytnaya Stantsiya

Sb Nauchn Rab Nauchno-Issled Inst Sadov Im I V Michurina — Sbornik Nauchnykh Rabot Nauchno-Issledovatel'skogo Instituta Sadov Imeni I. V. Michurina

Sb Nauchn Rab Novosib Nauchno Issled Vet Stn — Sbornik Nauchnykh Rabot Novosibirskoi Nauchno-Issledovatel'skoi Veterinarnoi Stantsii

Sb Nauchn Rab Rizh Med Inst — Sbornik Nauchnykh Rabot Rizhskogo Meditsinskogo Instituta

Sb Nauchn Rab Rostov Med Inst — Sbornik Nauchnykh Rabot Rostovskogo Meditsinskogo Instituta

Sb Nauchn Rab Ryazan S-kh Inst — Sbornik Nauchnykh Rabot Ryazanskii Sel'skokhozyaistvennyi Institut

Sb Nauchn Rab Sarat Med Inst — Sbornik Nauchnykh Rabot Saratovskii Meditsinskii Institut

Sb Nauchn Rab Sib Zon Nauchno-Issled Vet Inst — Sbornik Nauchnykh Rabot Sibirskogo Zonal'nogo Nauchno-Issledovatel'skogo Veterinarnogo Instituta

Sb Nauchn Rab Stud Erevan Gos Univ — Sbornik Nauchnykh Rabot Studentov Erevanskii Gosudarstvennyi Universitet

Sb Nauchn Rab Stud Ivanov Gos Med Inst — Sbornik Nauchnyk Rabot Studentov Ivanovskogo Gosudarstvennogo Meditsinskogo Instituta

Sb Nauchn Rab Stud Karelo Fin Gos Univ — Sbornik Nauchnykh Rabot Studentov Karelo-Finskogo Gosudarstvennogo Universiteta

Sb Nauchn Rab Stud Kirg Gos Univ — Sbornik Nauchnykh Rabot Studentov Kirgizskii Gosudarstvennyi Universitet

Sb Nauchn Rab Stud Leningr Gorn Inst — Sbornik Nauchnykh Rabot Studentov Leningradskogo Gornogo Instituta

Sb Nauchn Rab Stud Petrozavodsk Gos Univ — Sbornik Nauchnykh Rabot Studentov Petrozavodskogo Gosudarstvennogo Universiteta

Sb Nauchn Rab Stud Sarat Zootekh Vet Inst — Sbornik Nauchnykh Rabot Studentov Saratovskii Zootekhnichesko-Veterinarnyi Institut

Sb Nauchn Rab Stud Stalingr S-Kh Inst — Sbornik Nauchnykh Rabot Studentov Stalingradskogo Sel'skokhozyaistvennogo Instituta

Sb Nauchn Rab Sverdl Med Inst — Sbornik Nauchnykh Rabot Sverdlovskogo Meditsinskogo Instituta

Sb Nauchn Rab Sverdl Otd Vses O-va Anat Gistol Embriol — Sbornik Nauchnykh Rabot Sverdlovskogo Otdeleniya Vsesoyuznogo Obshchestva Anatomov, Gistologov, i Embriologov

Sb Nauchn Rab Tsentr Nauchno-Issled Lab Rostov Med Inst — Sbornik Nauchnykh Rabot Tsentral'naya Nauchno-Issledovatel'skaya Laboratoriya Rostov'skogo Meditsinskogo Instituta

Sb Nauchn Rab Ukr Nauchno Issled Inst Sadovod — Sbornik Nauchnykh Rabot Ukrainskii Nauchno-Issledovatel'skii Institut Sadovodstva

Sb Nauchn Rab Voen-Med Fak Kuibyshev Med Inst — Sbornik Nauchnykh Rabot Voenno-Meditsinskogo Fakul'teta Kuibyshevskogo Meditsinskogo Instituta

Sb Nauchn Rab Volgogr Gos Med Inst — Sbornik Nauchnykh Rabot Volgogradskoi Gosudarstvennyi Meditsinskii Institut

Sb Nauchn Rab Volgogr Med Inst — Sbornik Nauchnykh Rabot Volgogradskogo Meditsinskogo Instituta

Sb Nauchn Rab Volgogr Obl Klin Boln — Sbornik Nauchnykh Rabot Volgogradskoi Oblastnoi Klinicheskoi Bol'nitsy

Sb Nauchn Rab Volgogr Pedagog Inst — Sbornik Nauchnykh Rabot Volgogradskogo Pedagogicheskogo Instituta

Sb Nauchn Rab Vses Nauchno-Issled Inst Lek Rast — Sbornik Nauchnykh Rabot Vsesoyuznyi Nauchno-Issledovatel'skii Institut Lekarstvennykh Rastenii

Sb Nauchn Rab Vses Nauchno-Issled Inst Sadovod — Sbornik Nauchnykh Rabot Vsesoyuznyi Nauchno-Issledovatel'skii Institut Sadovodstva

Sb Nauchn Rab Vses Nauchno-Issled Inst Zhivotnovod — Sbornik Nauchnykh Rabot Vsesoyuznyi Nauchno-Issledovatel'skii Institut Zhivotnovodstva

Sb Nauchn Rab Yarosl Gorzdravotdela — Sbornik Nauchnykh Rabot Yaroslavskogo Gorzdravotdela

Sb Nauchn Rab Yarosl Med Inst — Sbornik Nauchnykh Rabot Yaroslavskogo Meditsinskogo Instituta

Sb Nauchn Rab Zaochn Inst Sov Torg — Sbornik Nauchnykh Rabot Zaochnyi Institut Sovetskoi Torgovli

Sb Nauchn Soobshch Dagest Gos Univ Kafedra Khim — Sbornik Nauchnykh Soobshchenii Dagestanskii Gosudarstvennyi Universitet Kafedra Khimii

Sb Nauchn Soobshch Kafedry Org Fizk Khim Dagest Gos Univ — Sbornik Nauchnykh Soobshchenii Kafedry Organicheskoi i Fizkolloidnoi Khimii Dagestanskii Gosudarstvennyi Universitet

Sb Nauchn Soobshch Kafedry Zool Biol Khim Dagest Univ — Sbornik Nauchnykh Soobshchenii Kafedry Zoologii Biologii Khimii Dagestanskogo Universiteta

Sb Nauchn Soobshch Sarat Avtomob Dorozhn Inst — Sbornik Nauchnykh Soobshchenii Saratovskii Avtomobil'no Dorozhnyi Institut

Sb Nauchn Statei Vinnitsk Gos Med Inst — Sbornik Nauchnykh Statei Vinnitskogo Gosudarstvennogo Meditsinskogo Instituta

Sb Nauchn Stud Ova Geol Fak Mosk Gos Univ — Sbornik Nauchnogo Studencheskogo Obshchestva Geologicheskii Fakul'tet Moskovskii Gosudarstvennyi Universitet

Sb Nauchn Stud Rab Omsk Gos Pedagog Inst — Sbornik Nauchnykh Studencheskikh Rabot Omskii Gosudarstvennyi Pedagogicheskii Institut

Sb Nauchn Stud Rab Sarat Zoovetinst — Sbornik Nauchnykh Studencheskikh Rabot Saratovskogo Zoovetinstituta

Sb Nauchn Tr Andizh Gos Med Inst — Sbornik Nauchnykh Trudov Andizhanskii Gosudarstvennyi Meditsinskii Institut

Sb Nauchn Tr Andizh Med Inst — Sbornik Nauchnykh Trudov Andizhanskogo Meditsitskogo Instituta

Sb Nauchn Tr Arm Gos Pedagog Inst Ser Fiz Mat — Sbornik Nauchnykh Trudov Armyanskii Gosudarstvennyi Pedagogicheskii Institut. Seriya Fiziko-Matematicheskaya

Sb Nauchn Tr Arm Gos Zaochn Pedagog Inst — Sbornik Nauchnykh Trudov Gosudarstvennogo Zaochnogo Pedagogicheskogo Instituta

Sb Nauchn Tr Arm Otd Vses Bot Ova — Sbornik Nauchnykh Trudov Armyanskogo Otdelnykh Vsesoyuznogo Botanicheskoi Obshchestva

Sb Nauchn Tr Arm S-kh Inst — Sbornik Nauchnykh Trudov Armyanskogo Sel'skokhozyaistvennogo Instituta

Sb Nauchn Tr Azerb Nauchno Issled Inst Gematol Pereliv Krovi — Sbornik Nauchnykh Trudov Azerbaidzhanskogo Nauchno-Issledovatel'skogo Instituta Gematologii i Perelivaniya Krovi

Sb Nauchn Tr Azerb Nauchno-Issled Inst Pereliv Krovi — Sbornik Nauchnykh Trudov Azerbaidzhanskogo Nauchno-Issledovatel'skogo Instituta Perelivanya Krovi

Sb Nauchn Tr Azerb Nauchno Issled Inst Perel Krovi — Sbornik Nauchnykh Trudov Azerbaidzhanskogo Nauchno-Issledovatel'skogo Instituta Perelivaniya Krovi

Sb Nauchn Tr Bashk Gos Med Inst — Sbornik Nauchnykh Trudov Bashkirskogo Gosudarstvennogo Meditsinskogo Instituta

Sb Nauchn Tr Bashk Med Inst — Sbornik Nauchnykh Trudov Bashkirskogo Meditsinskogo Instituta

Sb Nauchn Tr Bashk Nauchno-Issled Trakhomatoznogo Inst — Sbornik Nauchnykh Trudov Bashkirskogo Nauchno-Issledovatel'skogo Trakhomatoznogo Instituta

Sb Nauchn Tr Beloruss Inst Mekh Selsk Khoz — Sbornik Nauchnykh Trudov Beloruss Institut Mekhanizatsii Sel'skogo Khozyaistva

Sb Nauchn Tr Beloruss Lesotekh Inst — Sbornik Nauchnykh Trudov Belorusskogo Lesotekhnicheskogo Instituta

Sb Nauchn Tr Beloruss Nauchno-Issled Inst Pochvoved Agrokhim — Sbornik Nauchnykh Trudov Belorusskii Nauchno-Issledovatel'skii Institut Pochvovedeniya i Agrokhimii

Sb Nauchn Tr Beloruss Nauchno-Issled Inst Zemled — Sbornik Nauchnykh Trudov Belorusskii Nauchno-Issledovatel'skii Institut Zemledeliya

Sb Nauchn Tr Beloruss Nauchno Issled Kozhno Venerol Inst — Sbornik Nauchnykh Trudov Belorusskii Nauchno-Issledovatel'skii Kozhno-Venerologicheskii Institut

Sb Nauchn Tr Beloruss Politekh Inst — Sbornik Nauchnykh Trudov Belorusskii Politekhnicheskii Institut

Sb Nauchn Tr Beloruss S-kh Akad — Sbornik Nauchnykh Trudov Belorusskoi Sel'skokhozyaistvennoi Akademii

Sb Nauchn Tr Chelyab Nauchno Issled Inst Gorn Dela — Sbornik Nauchnykh Trudov Chelyabinskii Nauchno-Issledovatel'skii Institut Gornogo Dela

Sb Nauchn Tr Chelyab Politekh Inst — Sbornik Nauchnykh Trudov Chelyabinskii Politekhnicheskii Institut [USSR]

Sb Nauchn Tr Chit Gos Med Inst — Sbornik Nauchnykh Trudov Chitinskii Gosudarstvennyi Meditsinskii Institut

Sb Nauchn Tr Chuv Nauchno-Issled Trakhomatoznogo Inst — Sbornik Nauchnykh Trudov Chuvashskogo Nauchno-Issledovatel'skogo Trakhomatoznogo Instituta

Sb Nauchn Tr Dagest Gos Med Inst — Sbornik Nauchnykh Trudov Dagestanskii Gosudarstvennyi Meditsinskii Institut

Sb Nauchn Tr Dnepropetr Gos Med Inst — Sbornik Nauchnykh Trudov Dnepropetrovskii Gosudarstvennyi Meditsinskii Institut

Sb Nauchn Tr Dnepropetr Inzh Stroit Inst — Sbornik Nauchnykh Trudov Dnepropetrovskii Inzhenerno-Stroitel'nyi Institut

Sb Nauchn Tr Donskogo S-kh Inst — Sbornik Nauchnykh Trudov Donskogo Sel'skokhozyaistvennogo Instituta

Sb Nauchn Tr Erevan Arm Gos Pedagog Inst Khim — Sbornik Nauchnykh Trudov Erevanskii Armyanskii Gosudarstvennyi Pedagogicheskii Institut. Khimiya

Sb Nauchn Tr Erevan Politekh Inst — Sbornik Nauchnykh Trudov Erevanskii Politekhnicheskii Institut [*Armenian SSR*]

Sb Nauchn Tr Est Nauchno-Issled Inst Zemled Melior — Sbornik Nauchnykh Trudov Estonskogo Nauchno-Issledovatel'skogo Instituta Zemledeliya i Melioratsii

Sb Nauchn Tr Est S-kh Akad — Sbornik Nauchnykh Trudov Estonskaya Sel'skokhozyaistvennaya Akademiya

Sb Nauchn Tr Fiz Tekh Inst Akad Nauk B SSR — Sbornik Nauchnykh Trudov Fiziko-Tekhnicheskii Institut Akademiya Nauk Belorusskoi SSR

Sb Nauchn Tr Fiz Tekh Inst Nizk Temp Akad Nauk Ukr SSR — Sbornik Nauchnykh Trudov Fiziko-Tekhnicheskii Institut Nizkikh Temperatur Akademiya Nauk Ukrainskoi SSR [*Ukrainian SSR*]

Sb Nauchn Tr Gazov Khromatogr — Sbornik Nauchnykh Trudov po Gazovoi Khromatografii

Sb Nauchn Tr Glavgeologii Uzb SSR Tashk Politekh Inst — Sbornik Nauchnykh Trudov Glavgeologii Uzbekskoi SSR i Tashkentskogo Politekhnicheskogo Instituta

Sb Nauchn Tr Gos Nauchno Issled Inst Elektrodnoi Promsti — Sbornik Nauchnykh Trudov Gosudarstvennyi Nauchno-Issledovatel'skii Institut Elektrodnoi Promyshlennosti

Sb Nauchn Tr Gos Nauchno Issled Inst Keram Promsti — Sbornik Nauchnykh Trudov Gosudarstvennyi Nauchno-Issledovatel'skii Institut Keramicheskoi Promyshlennosti

Sb Nauchn Tr Gos Nauchno Issled Inst Keramzitu — Sbornik Nauchnykh Trudov Gosudarstvennyi Nauchno-Issledovatel'skii Institut po Keramzitu

Sb Nauchn Tr Gos Nauchno-Issled Inst Tsvetn Met — Sbornik Nauchnykh Trudov Gosudarstvennogo Nauchno-Issledovatel'skogo Instituta Tsvetnykh Metallov

Sb Nauchn Tr Gos Nauchno Issled Proektn Inst Metall Promsti — Sbornik Nauchnykh Trudov Gosudarstvennyi Nauchno-Issledovatel'skii i Proektnyi Institut Metallurgicheskoi Promyshlennosti

Sb Nauchn Tr Grodn Skh Inst — Sbornik Nauchnykh Trudov Grodnenskii Sel'skokhozyaistvennyi Institut

Sb Nauchn Tr Inst Biol Akad Nauk B SSR — Sbornik Nauchnykh Trudov Institut Biologii Akademiya Nauk Belorusskoi SSR

Sb Nauchn Tr Inst Geol Geofiz Akad Nauk Uzb SSR — Sbornik Nauchnykh Trudov Instituta Geologii i Geofiziki Akademii Nauk Uzbekskoi SSR

Sb Nauchn Tr Inst Melior Vodn Bolotnogo Khoz Akad Nauk BSSR — Sbornik Nauchnykh Trudov Instituta Melioratsii Vodnogo i Bolotnogo Khozyaistva Akademiya Nauk Belorusskoi SSR

Sb Nauchn Tr Inst Metallofiz Akad Ukr SSR — Sbornik Nauchnykh Trudov Instituta Metallofiziki Akademiya Nauk Ukrainskoi SSR [*Ukrainian SSR*]

Sb Nauchn Tr Inst Tsvetn Met — Sbornik Nauchnykh Trudov Institut Tsvetnykh Metallov

Sb Nauchn Tr Irkutsk Gos Nauchno-Issled Inst Redk Met — Sbornik Nauchnykh Trudov Irkutskii Gosudarstvennyi Nauchno-Issledovatel'skii Institut Redkikh Metallov

Sb Nauchn Tr Ivanov Energ Inst — Sbornik Nauchnykh Trudov Ivanovskogo Energeticheskogo Instituta

Sb Nauchn Tr Ivanov Gos Med Inst — Sbornik Nauchnykh Trudov Ivanovskogo Gosudarstvennogo Meditsinskogo Instituta

Sb Nauchn Tr Ivanov Med Inst — Sbornik Nauchnykh Trudov Ivanovskogo Meditsinskogo Instituta

Sb Nauchn Tr Ivanov S-kh Inst — Sbornik Nauchnykh Trudov Ivanovskogo Sel'skokhozyaistvennogo Instituta

Sb Nauchn Tr Kalinin Gos Skh Opytn Stant — Sbornik Nauchnykh Trudov Kalininskaya Gosudarstvennaya Sel'skokhozyaistvennaya Opytnaya Stantisiya

Sb Nauchn Tr Kalinin Gos Skh Opytn Stn — Sbornik Nauchnykh Trudov Kalininskaya Gosudarstvennaya Sel'skokhozyaistvennaya Opytnaya Stantsiya

Sb Nauchn Tr Kamenets Podolsk Skh Inst — Sbornik Nauchnykh Trudov Kamenets-Podol'skogo Sel'skokhozyaistvennogo Instituta

Sb Nauchn Tr Kar'k Gos Med Inst — Sbornik Nauchnykh Trudov Khar'kovskogo Gosudarstvennogo Meditsinskogo Instituta

Sb Nauchn Tr Kaz Gorno-Metall Inst — Sbornik Nauchnykh Trudov Kazakhskii Gorno-Metallurgicheskii Institut

Sb Nauchn Tr Kaz Politekh Inst — Sbornik Nauchnykh Trudov Kazakhskii Politekhnicheskii Institut

Sb Nauchn Tr Khar'k Med Inst — Sbornik Nauchnykh Trudov Khar'kovskogo Meditsinskogo Instituta

Sb Nauchn Tr Khar'k Skh Inst Im V V Dokuchaeva — Sbornik Nauchnykh Trudov Khar'kovskii Sel'skokhozyaistvennyi Institut Imeni V. V. Dokuchaeva

Sb Nauchn Tr Kiev Inst Inzh Grazhd Aviats — Sbornik Nauchnykh Trudov Kievskogo Instituta Inzhenerov Grazhdanskoi Aviatsii [*Ukrainian SSR*]

Sb Nauchn Tr Kiev Inzh Stroit Inst — Sbornik Nauchnykh Trudov Kievskogo Inzhenerno-Stroitel'nogo Instituta

Sb Nauchn Tr Kirg Med Inst — Sbornik Nauchnykh Trudov Kirkizskogo Meditsinskogo Instituta

Sb Nauchn Tr Krasnoyarsk Gos Med Inst — Sbornik Nauchnykh Trudov Krasnoyarskogo Gosudarstvennogo Meditsinskogo Instituta

Sb Nauchn Tr Krivorozh Fil Inst Gorn Dela Akad Nauk Ukr SSR — Sbornik Nauchnykh Trudov Krivorozhskii Filial Instituta Gornogo Dela Akademiya Nauk Ukrainskoi SSR

Sb Nauchn Tr Krivorozh Gornorudn Inst — Sbornik Nauchnykh Trudov Krivorozhskii Gornorudnyi Institut

Sb Nauchn Tr Krym Gos Med Inst — Sbornik Nauchnykh Trudov Krymskogo Gosudarstvennogo Meditsinskogo Instituta

Sb Nauchn Tr Kuibyshev Ind Inst — Sbornik Nauchnykh Trudov Kuibyshevskii Industrial'nyi Institut

Sb Nauchn Tr Kuibyshev Inzh Stroit Inst — Sbornik Nauchnykh Trudov Kuibyshevskii Inzhenerno-Stroitel'nyi Institut

Sb Nauchn Tr Kuibyshev Nauchno Issled Inst Epidemiol Gig — Sbornik Nauchnykh Trudov Kuibyshevskogo Nauchno-Issledovatel'skogo Instituta Epidemiologii i Gigieny

Sb Nauchn Tr Kuibyshev Nauchno Issled Inst Gig — Sbornik Nauchnykh Trudov Kuibyshevskii Nauchno-Issledovatel'skii Institut Gigeny

Sb Nauchn Tr Kuibyshev Nauchno Issled Vet Stn — Sbornik Nauchnykh Trudov Kuibyshevskoi Nauchno-Issledovatel'noi Veterinarnoi Stantsii

Sb Nauchn Tr Kuzbasskii Politekh Inst — Sbornik Nauchnykh Trudov Kuzbasskii Politekhnicheskii Institut

Sb Nauchn Tr Leningr Farm Inst — Sbornik Nauchnykh Trudov Leningradskii Farmatsevticheskii Institut

Sb Nauchn Tr Leningr Inst Sov Torg — Sbornik Nauchnykh Trudov Leningradskii Institut Sovetskoi Torgovli

Sb Nauchn Tr Leningr Inst Tochn Mekh Opt — Sbornik Nauchnykh Trudov Leningradskii Institut Tochnoi Mekhaniki i Optiki

Sb Nauchn Tr Leningr Inst Usoversh Vet Vrachei — Sbornik Nauchnykh Trudov Leningradskii Institut Usovershenstvovaniya Veterinarnykh Vrachei

Sb Nauchn Tr Leningr Inst Usoversh Vet Vrachei — Sbornik Nauchnykh Trudov Leningradskogo Instituta Usovershenstvovaniya Veterinarnykh Vrachei

Sb Nauchn Tr Leningr Inst Usoversh Vrachei — Sbornik Nauchnykh Trudov Leningradskogo Instituta Usovershenstvovaniya Vrachei

Sb Nauchn Tr Leningr Inzh-Stroit Inst — Sbornik Nauchnykh Trudov Leningradskii Inzhenerno-Stroitel'nyi Institut

Sb Nauchn Tr Leningr Khim Farm Inst — Sbornik Nauchnykh Trudov Leningradskii Khimiko-Farmatsevticheskii Institut

Sb Nauchn Tr Leningr Nauchno Issled Inst Antibiot — Sbornik Nauchnykh Trudov Leningradskii Nauchno-Issledovatel'skii Institut Antibiotikov

Sb Nauchn Tr Leningr Nauchno Issled Inst Lesn Khoz — Sbornik Nauchnykh Trudov Leningradskii Nauchno-Issledovatel'skii Institut Lesnogo Khozyaistva

Sb Nauchn Tr Leningr Nauchno Issled Inst Pereliv Krovi — Sbornik Nauchnykh Trudov Leningradskii Nauchno-Issledovatel'skii Institut Perelivaniya Krovi

Sb Nauchn Tr Leningr Nauchno-Issled Inst Pereliv Krovi — Sbornik Nauchnykh Trudov Leningradskogo Nauchno-Issledovatel'skogo Instituta Perelivanya Krovi

Sb Nauchn Tr Leningr Voen Mekh Inst — Sbornik Nauchnykh Trudov Leningradskii Voenno-Mekhanicheskii Institut

Sb Nauchn Tr Lugansk S-kh Inst — Sbornik Nauchnykh Trudov Luganskogo Sel'skokhozyaistvennogo Instituta

Sb Nauchn Tr L'vov Nauchn Ovo Derm Venerol — Sbornik Nauchnykh Trudov L'vovskoe Nauchnoe Obshchestvo Dermato-Venerologov

Sb Nauchn Tr Magnitogorsk Gornometall Inst — Sbornik Nauchnykh Trudov Magnitogorskii Gornometallurgicheskii Institut [*USSR*]

Sb Nauchn Tr Minsk Gos Med Inst — Sbornik Nauchnykh Trudov Minskii Gosudarstvennyi Meditsinskii Institut

Sb Nauchn Tr Mogilev Obl Gos Skh Opytn Stn — Sbornik Nauchnykh Trudov Mogilevskaya Oblastnaya Gosudarstvennaya Sel'skokhozyaistvennaya Opytnaya Stantsiya

Sb Nauchn Tr Morfol Kafedry Bashk Med Inst — Sbornik Nauchnykh Trudov Morfologicheskoi Kafedry Bashkirskogo Meditsinskogo Instituta

Sb Nauchn Tr Mosk Gorn Inst — Sbornik Nauchnykh Trudov Moskovskogo Gornogo Instituta

Sb Nauchn Tr Mosk Inst Tsvetn Met Zolota — Sbornik Nauchnykh Trudov Moskovskii Institut Tsvetnykh Metallov i Zolota

Sb Nauchn Tr Mosk Nauchno Issled Inst Gig Im F F Erismana — Sbornik Nauchnykh Trudov Moskovskii Nauchno-Issledovatel'skii Institut Gigieny Imeni F. F. Erismana

Sb Nauchn Tr Mosk Poligr Inst — Sbornik Nauchnykh Trudov Moskovskii Poligraficheskii Institut

Sb Nauchn Tr Mosk Tekhnol Inst Pishch Promsti — Sbornik Nauchnykh Trudov Moskovskii Tekhnologicheskii Institut Pishchevoi Promyshlennosti

Sb Nauchn Tr Nauchno-Issled Inst Pereliv Krovi Arm SSR — Sbornik Nauchnykh Trudov Nauchno-Issledovatel'skogo Instituta Gematologii i Perelivaniya Krovi Armyanskoi SSR

Sb Nauchn Tr Nauchno-Issled Inst Zemled Echmiadzin (Arm SSR) — Sbornik Nauchnykh Trudov Nauchno-Issledovatel'skii Institut Zemledeliya Echmiadzin (Armenian SSR)

Sb Nauchn Tr Nauchno Issled Kozhno Venerol Inst (Minsk) — Sbornik Nauchnykh Trudov Nauchno-Issledovatel'skii Kozhno-Venerologicheskii Institut (Minsk)

Sb Nauchn Tr Permsk Gorn Inst — Sbornik Nauchnykh Trudov Permskii Gornyi Institut

Sb Nauchn Tr Permsk Gos Med Inst — Sbornik Nauchnykh Trudov Permskii Gosudarstvennyi Meditsinskii Institut

Sb Nauchn Tr Permsk Gos Skh Opytn Stn — Sbornik Nauchnykh Trudov Permskaya Gosudarstvennaya Sel'skokhozyaistvennaya Opytnaya Stantsiya

Sb Nauchn Tr Permsk Med Inst — Sbornik Nauchnykh Trudov Permskogo Meditsinskogo Instituta

Sb Nauchn Tr Permsk Politekh Inst — Sbornik Nauchnykh Trudov Permskij Politekhnicheskij Institut

Sb Nauchn Tr Primorsk S-kh Inst — Sbornik Nauchnykh Trudov Primorskogo Sel'skokhozyaistvennogo Instituta

Sb Nauchn Tr Rostov Donu Gos Med Inst — Sbornik Nauchnykh Trudov Rostovskogo-Na-Donu Gosudarstvennogo Meditsinskogo Instituta

Sb Nauchn Tr Rostov Nauchno-Issled Inst Akad Kommunaln Khoz — Sbornik Nauchnykh Trudov Rostovskii Nauchno-Issledovatel'skii Institut Akademii Kommunal'nogo Khozyaistva

Sb Nauchn Tr Ryazan Med Inst — Sbornik Nauchnykh Trudov Ryazanskogo Meditsinskogo Instituta

Sb Nauchn Tr Ryazan S-kh Inst — Sbornik Nauchnykh Trudov Ryazanskogo Sel'skokhozyaistvennogo Instituta

Sb Nauchn Tr Samark Gos Med Inst — Sbornik Nauchnykh Trudov Samarkandskii Gosudarstvennyi Meditsinskii Institut

Sb Nauchn Tr Samark Gos Med Inst — Sbornik Nauchnykh Trudov Samarkandskogo Gosudarstvennogo Meditsinskogo Instituta

Sb Nauchn Tr Sanit Tekh — Sbornik Nauchnykh Trudov po Sanitarnoi Tekhnike

Sb Nauchn Tr Sev-Oset Gos Med Inst — Sbornik Nauchnykh Trudov Severo-Osetinskii Gosudarstvennyi Meditsinskii Institut

Sb Nauchn Tr Stalinskii Gos Med Inst — Sbornik Nauchnykh Trudov Stalinskii Gosudarstvennyi Meditsinskii Institut

Sb Nauchn Tr Sverdl Fil Mosk Inst Nar Khoz — Sbornik Nauchnykh Trudov Sverdlovskii Filial Moskovskogo Instituta Narodnogo Khozyaistva

Sb Nauchn Tr Tashk Gos Med Inst — Sbornik Nauchnykh Trudov Tashkentskogo Gosudarstvennogo Meditsinskogo Instituta

Sb Nauchn Tr Tashk Gos Univ — Sbornik Nauchnykh Trudov Tashkentskiy Gosudarstvennyy Universitet

Sb Nauchn Tr Teploobmenu Gidrodin — Sbornik Nauchnykh Trudov po Teploobmenu i Gidrodinamike

Sb Nauchn Tr Tomsk Inzh Stroit Inst — Sbornik Nauchnykh Trudov Tomski Inzhenerno-Stroitel'nyi Institut [USSR]

Sb Nauchn Tr Tsentr Aptechn Nauchno-Issled Inst — Sbornik Nauchnykh Trudov Tsentral'nogo Aptechnogo Nauchno-Issledovatel'skogo Instituta

Sb Nauchn Tr Tsentr Aptechn Nauchno-Issled Inst — Sbornik Nauchnykh Trudov Tsentral'nyi Aptechnyi Nauchno-Issledovatel'skii Institut

Sb Nauchn Tr Ukr Inst Usoversh Vrachei — Sbornik Nauchnykh Trudov Ukrainskogo Instituta Usovershenstvovaniy Vrachei

Sb Nauchn Tr Ukr Nauchno-Issled Inst Ogneuporov — Sbornik Nauchnykh Trudov Ukrainskii Nauchno-Issledovatel'skii Institut Ogneuporov [Ukrainian SSR]

Sb Nauchn Tr Ukr Nauchno Issled Inst Solyanoi Promsti — Sbornik Nauchnykh Trudov Ukrainskii Nauchno-Issledovatel'skii Institut Solyanoi Promyshlennosti

Sb Nauchn Tr Ukr Nauchno-Issled Uglekhim Inst — Sbornik Nauchnykh Trudov Ukrainskii Nauchno-Issledovatel'skii Uglekhimcheskii I nstitut [Ukrainian SSR]

Sb Nauchn Tr Vinnitsk Gos Med Inst — Sbornik Nauchnykh Trudov Vinnitskogo Gosudarstvennogo Meditsinskogo Instituta

Sb Nauchn Tr Vitebsk Gos Med Inst — Sbornik Nauchnykh Trudov Vitebskogo Gosudarstvennogo Meditsinskogo Instituta

Sb Nauchn Tr Vitebsk Med Inst — Sbornik Nauchnykh Trudov Vitebskogo Meditsinskogo Instituta

Sb Nauchn Tr Vladimir Vech Politekh Inst — Sbornik Nauchnykh Trudov Vladimirskii Vechernii Politekhnicheskii Institut

Sb Nauchn Tr Vladivost Med Inst — Sbornik Nauchnykh Trudov Vladivostokskii Meditsinskii Institut

Sb Nauchn Tr VNII Monokrist — Sbornik Nauchnykh Trudov VNII [Vsesoyuznyi Nauchno-Issledovatel'skii Institut] Monokristallov

Sb Nauchn Tr Voen Med Fak Sarat Medinst — Sbornik Nauchnykh Trudov Voenno-Meditsinskii Fakul'tet Saratovskom Medinstitut

Sb Nauchn Tr Voronezh Inzh Stroit Inst — Sbornik Nauchnykh Trudov Voronezhskii Inzhenerno-Stroitel'nyi Institut

Sb Nauchn Tr Vses Nauchno-Issled Gorno-Metall Inst Tsvet Met — Sbornik Nauchnykh Trudov Vsesoyuznogo Nauchno-Issledovatel'skogo Gorno-Metallurgiceskogo Instituta Tsvetnykh Metallov [USSR]

Sb Nauchn Tr Vses Nauchno Issled Gornometall Inst Tsvetn Met — Sbornik Nauchnykh Trudov Vsesoyuznyi Nauchno-Issledovatel'skii Gornometallurgicheskii Institut Tsvetnykh Metallov

Sb Nauchn Tr Vses Nauchno Issled Inst Gidrogeol Inzh Geol — Sbornik Nauchnykh Trudov Vsesoyuznyi Nauchno-Issledovatel'skii Institut Gidrogeologii i Inzhenernoi Geologii

Sb Nauchn Tr Vses Nauchno Issled Inst Metall Teplotekh — Sbornik Nauchnykh Trudov Vsesoyuznyi Nauchno-Issledovatel'skii Institut Metallurgicheskoi Teplotekhniki

Sb Nauchn Tr Vses Neftegazov Nauchno Issled Inst — Sbornik Nauchnykh Trudov Vsesoyuznyi Neftegazovyi Nauchno-Issledovatel'skii Institut

Sb Nauchn Tr Vses Sel Genet Inst — Sbornik Nauchnykh Trudov Vsesoyuznogo Selektsionno-Geneticheskogo Instituta

Sb Nauchn Tr Zaochn Inst Sov Torg — Sbornik Nauchnykh Trudov Zaochnyi Institut Sovetskoi Torgovli

Sb Nauchn Tr Zhdan Metall Inst — Sbornik Nauchnykh Trudov Zhdanovskogo Metallurgicheskogo Instituta

Sb Nauchn Tr Zootekh Fak Belotserk Skh Inst — Sbornik Nauchnykh Trudov Zootekhnicheskogo Fakul'teta Belotserkovskii Sel'skokhozyaistvennyi Institut

Sb Nauchn Voen-Med Fak Kuibyshev Med Inst — Sbornik Nauchnykh Rabot Voenno-Meditsinskogo Fakul'teta Kuibyshevskogo Meditsinskogo Instituta [USSR]

Sb Nauchn Vrachei Kabard Balkarii — Sbornik Nauchnykh Vrachei Kabardino Balkarii

Sb Nauch Tr Beloruss Nauch-Issled Inst Zemled — Sbornik Nauchnykh Trudov Belorusskii Nauchno-Issledovatel'skii Institut Zemledeliya

Sb Nauch Tr Eston Sel'skokhoz Akad — Sbornik Nauchnykh Trudov Estonskoi Sel'skokhozyaistvennoi Akademii

Sb Nauch Trud Eston Nauch Inst Zeml Melior — Sbornik Nauchnykh Trudov Estonskogo Nauchnogo Instituta Zemledeliya i Melioratsii

Sb Nauch Trud Eston Sel'khoz Akad — Sbornik Nauchnykh Trudov Estonskoi Sel'skokhozyaistvennoi Akademii

Sb Nauch Trud Leningr Inst Usoversh Vet Vrach — Sbornik Nauchnykh Leningradskogo Instituta Usovershenstvovaniya Veterinarnykh Vrachei

Sb Naucn Soobsc Dagestan Gos Univ — Sbornik Naucnyh Soobscenii Dagestanskii Gosudarstvennyi Universitet Imeni V. I. Lenina

Sb Nauc Trud Jaroslav Pedag Inst — Sbornik Naucnyh Trudov Jaroslavskogo Pedagogiceskij Instituta

SbNU — Sbornik za Narodni Umotvorenija i Narodopis

SBOAA — Sooshcheniya Byurakanskoi Observatorii Akademiya Nauk Armyanskoi SSR

SbOAW — Sitzungsberichte. Oesterreichische Akademie der Wissenschaften in Wien. Philosophisch-Historische Klasse

SBoc — Studi sul Boccaccio

SBol — Strenna Bolognese

Sbor Arch Praci — Sbornik Archivnich Praci

Sbor Narod Muz Praze — Sbornik Narodniho Muzea v Praze [Acta Musei Nationalis Pragae]. Series A: Historia

Sbornik Praci Brnenske U Rada Hud — Sbornik Praci Filosoficke Fakulty Brnenske University. Rada Hudebnevedna

Sborn Rabot v Pam I M Sadovskago (S Peterburg) — Sbornik Rabot v Pamiat Professora Ivana Mikhailovicha Sadovskago (S Peterburg)

Sborn Ved Lesn Ust Vysoke Skoly Zemed — Sbornik Vedeckeho Lesnickeho Ustavu Vysoke Skoly Zemedelske v Praze

Sbor Praci Filos Fak — Sbornik Praci Filosoficke Fakulty Brnenske University

Sbor Vlast Prac Podblanicka — Sbornik Vlastivednych Praci z Podblanicka

SBP — Etudes et Expansion

Sb Pathofysiol Traveni Vyz — Sbornik pro Pathofysiologii Traveni a Vyzivy

SBPAW — Sitzungsberichte. Kaiserliche Preussische Akademie der Wissenschaften [Berlin]

SBPAWB — Sitzungsberichte. Kaiserliche Preussische Akademie der Wissenschaften (Berlin)

Sb Pedagog Fak Plzni Ser Chem — Sbornik Pedagogicke Fakulty v Plzni. Serie Chemie

SBPI — Southern Baptist Periodical Index

Sb Prac Chem Fak SVST — Sbornik Prac Chemickej Fakulty Slovenskej Vysokej Skoly Technickej

Sb Praci Ped Fak v Ostrave Ser A — Sbornik Praci Pedagogicke Fakulty v Ostrave. Seria A

Sb Praci Prirodoved Fak Univ Palackeho v Olomouci — Sbornik Praci Prirodovedecke Fakulty University Palackeho v Olomouci

Sb Praci Prirodoved Fak Univ Palackeho v Olomouci Chem — Sbornik Praci Prirodovedecke Fakulty University Palackeho v Olomouci. Obor Chemica

Sb Praci Prirodoved Fak Univ Palackeho v Olomouci Fyz — Sbornik Praci Prirodovedecke Fakulty University Palackeho v Olomouci. Obor Fyzika

Sb Praci Prirodoved Fak Univ Palackeho v Olomouci Mat — Sbornik Praci Prirodovedecke Fakulty University Palackeho v Olomouci. Obor Matematika

Sb Prazhskogo Khim Tekhnol Inst Sekts Protsessy Appar — Sbornik Prazhskogo Khimiko Tekhnologicheskogo Instituta Sektsiya. Protsessy i Apparaty

SBPR Bol — SBPR Boletin

Sb Prednasek Prac Vyzk Ustavu Tepelne Tech — Sbornik Prednasek Pracovniku Vyzkumneho Ustavu Tepelne Techniky

Sb Pr Pedagog Fak Ostrave Rada A — Sbornik Praci Pedagogicke Fakulty v Ostrave. Rada A. Matematika Fizika

Sb Pr Pedagog Fak Ostrave Rada E — Sbornik Praci Pedagogicke Fakulty v Ostrave. Rada E [Czechoslovakia]

Sb Pr Pedagog Inst Ostrave Prir Vedy Mat — Sbornik Praci Pedagogickeho Instituta i Ostrave Prirodni Vedy a Matematika

Sb Pr Ustavu Vyzk Rud (Prague) — Sbornik Praci Ustavu pro Vyzkum Rud (Prague)

Sb Pr UVP — Sbornik Praci UVP

Sb Pr Vyzk Chem Vyuziti Uhli Dehtu Ropy — Sborník Praci z Vyzkumu Chemickeho Vyuziti Uhli. Dehtu a Ropy [*Czechoslovakia*]

Sb Pr Vyzk Ustavu Zelezorudn Dolu Hrudkoven — Sborník Praci Vyzkumneho Ustavu Zelezorudnych Dolu a Hrudkoven

SBR — Small Business Report

Sb Rab Agron Fiz — Sborník Rabot po Agronomicheskoi Fizike

Sb Rab Ashkhab Gidrometeorol Obs — Sborník Rabot Ashkhabadskoi Gidrometeorologicheskoi Observatorii

Sb Rab Aspir Krasnodar Gos Pedagog Inst — Sborník Rabot Aspirantov Krasnodarskogo Gosudarstvennogo Pedagogicheskogo Instituta

Sb Rab Aspir Tadzh Gos Univ — Sborník Rabot Aspirantov Tadzhikskii Gosudarstvennyi Universitet

Sb Rab Aspir Ukr Nauchno Issled Inst Fiziol Rast — Sborník Rabot Aspirantov Ukrainskii Nauchno-Issledovatel'skii Institut Fiziologii Rastenii

Sb Rab Aspir Voronezh Gos Univ — Sborník Rabot Aspirantov Voronezhskogo Gosudarstvennogo Universiteta

Sb Rab Basseinovoi Gidrometeorol Obs Chern Azovskogo Morei — Sborník Rabot Basseinovoi Gidrometeorologicheskoi Chernogo i Azovskogo Morei

Sb Rab Beloruss Gos Med Inst — Sborník Rabot Belorusskii Gosudarstvennyi Meditsinskii Institut

Sb Rab Biol Tekh Rybolov Tekhnol — Sborník Rabot po Biologii. Tekhnike Rybolovstva i Tekhnologii

Sb Rab Buryat Otd Vses Nauchn Ova Anat Gistol Embriol — Sborník Rabot Buryatskogo Otdel'nogo Vsesoyuznogo Nauchnogo Obshchestva Anatomii, Gistologii, i Embriologii

Sb Rab Chist Prikl Khim — Sborník Rabot po Chistoi i Prikladnoi Khimii

Sb Rab Chuv Resp Vet Lab — Sborník Rabot Chuvashskoi Respublikanskoi Veterinarnoi Laboratorii

Sb Rab Gidrol — Sborník Rabot po Gidrologii

Sb Rab Gidrol Leningr Gos Gidrol Inst — Sborník Rabot po Gidrologii Leningradskogo Gosudarstvennogo Gidrologicheskogo Instituta

Sb Rab Gor'k Volzh Rybinsk Gidrometeorol Obs — Sborník Rabot Gor'kovskoi Volzhskoi i Rybinskoi Gidrometeorologicheskikh Observatorii

Sb Rab Gos Inst Prikl Khim — Sborník Rabot Gosudarstvennyi Institut Prikladnoi Khimii

Sb Rab Ikhtiol Gidrobiol — Sborník Rabot po Ikhtiologii i Gidrobiologii

Sb Rab Inst Prikl Zol Fitopatol — Sborník Rabot Instituta Prikladnoi Zoologii i Fitopatologii

Sb Rab Inst Prikl Zool Fitopatol — Sborník Rabot Instituta Prikladnoi Zoologii i Fitopatologii

Sb Rab Inst Tsitol Akad Nauk SSSR — Sborník Rabot Instituta Tsitologii Akademii Nauk SSSR

Sb Rab Kafedry Fak Khir Sverdl Med — Sborník Rabot Kafedry i Fakul'tete Khirurgii Sverdlovskogo Meditsinskogo

Sb Rab Kaz Resp Nauchn Ova Anat Gistol Embriol — Sborník Rabot Kazakhskogo Respublikanskogo Nauchnogo Obshchestva Anatomov, Gistologov, i Embriologov

Sb Rab Khim Istochnikam Toka — Sborník Rabot po Khimicheskim Istochnikam Toka

Sb Rab Kursk Gidrometeorol Obs — Sborník Rabot Kurskoi Gidrometeorologicheskoi Observatorii

Sb Rab Lab Yuzhn Morei Gos Okeanogr Inst — Sborník Rabot Laboratoriya Yuzhnykh Morei Gosudarstvennyi Okeanograficheskii Institut

Sb Rab Leningr Inst Sov Torg — Sborník Rabot Leningradskii Institut Sovetskoi Torgovli

Sb Rab Leningr Vet Inst — Sborník Rabot Leningradskii Veterinarnyi Institut

Sb Rab Lesn Khoz Mold Mold Lesn Opytn Stn — Sborník Rabot po Lesnomu Khozyaistva Moldavii Moldavskaya Lesnaya Opytnaya Stantsiya

Sb Rab Maslichn Efiromaslichn Kul't — Sborník Rabot po Maslichnym i Efiromaslichnym Kul'turam

Sb Rab Maslichn Kult — Sborník Rabot po Maslichnym Kul'turam

Sb Rab Mezhdunar Geofiz Godu — Sborník Rabot po Mezhdunarodnomu Geofizicheskom Godu

Sb Rab Mikol Algol Akad Kirg SSR — Sborník Rabot po Mikologii i Al'gologii Akademii Kirgizskoi SSR

Sb Rab Mikol Al'gol Kirg SSR — Sborník Rabot po Mikologii i Al'gologii Akademii Kirgiszkoi SSR

Sb Rab Minsk Med Inst — Sborník Rabot Minskogo Meditsinskogo Instituta

Sb Rab Molodykh Uch Akad Nauk Mold SSR — Sborník Rabot Molodykh Uchenykh Akademii Nauk Moldavskoi SSR

Sb Rab Molodykh Uch Gorskogo Skh Inst — Sborník Rabot Molodykh Uchenykh Gorskogo Sel'skokhozyaistvennogo Instituta

Sb Rab Molodykh Vses Sel Genet Inst — Sborník Rabot Molodykh Vsesoyuznogo Selektsii Genetiki Instituta

Sb Rabot Nauch Inst Udobr Insektofungits (Moscow) — Sborník Rabot Nauchnyi Institut po Udobreniyam i Insektofungitsidam (Moscow)

Sb Rab Rostov Gidrometeorol Obs — Sborník Rabot Rostovskoi Gidrometeorologicheskoi Observatorii

Sb Rab Rybinsk Gidrometeorol Obs — Sborník Rabot Rybinskoi Gidrometeorologicheskoi Observatorii

Sb Rab Silikozu — Sborník Rabot po Silikozu

Sb Rab Silikozu Ural Fil Akad Nauk SSSR — Sborník Rabot po Silikozu Ural'skii Filial Akademii Nauk SSSR

Sb Rab Stud Nauchn Ova Leningr Inst Tochn Mekh Opt — Sborník Rabot Studencheskogo Nauchnogo Obshchestva. Leningradskii Institut Tochnoi Mekhaniki i Optiki

Sb Rab Sverdl Gos Med Inst — Sborník Rabot Sverdlovskii Gosudarstvennyi Meditsinskii Institut

Sb Rab Sverdl Med Inst — Sborník Rabot Sverdlovskogo Meditsinskogo Instituta

Sb Rab Sverdl Nauchno Issled Kozhno Venerol Inst — Sborník Rabot Sverdlovskii Nauchno Issledovatel'skii Kozhno Venerologicheskii Institut

Sb Rab Tsentr Muz Pochvoved Im V — Sborník Rabot Tsentral'nogo Muzeya Pochvovedeniya Imeni V. V. Dokuchaeva

Sb Rab Tsentr Muz Pochvoved Im V V Dokuchaeva — Sborník Rabot Tsentral'nogo Muzeya Pochvovedeniya Imeni V. V. Dokuchaeva

Sb Rab Tsentr Nauchno Issled Inst Kozh Obuvn Promsti — Sborník Rabot Tsentral'nyi Nauchno Issledovatel'skii Institut Kozhevenno Obuvnoi Promyshlennosti

Sb Rab Ukr Nauchno Issled Inst Ogneuporov — Sborník Rabot Ukrainskii Nauchno Issledovatel'skii Institut Ogneuporov

Sb Rab Vologod Nauchno-Issled Vet Opytn Stn — Sborník Rabot Vologodskoi Nauchno-Issledovat' Skoi Veterinarnoi Opytnoi Stantsii

Sb Rab Vopr Proizvod Primen Biol Prep — Sborník Rabot Voprosov Proizvodstva i Primeneniya Biologicheskikh Preparatov

Sb Rab Vses Nauchno Issled Inst Okhr Tr — Sborník Rabot Vsesoyuznyi Nauchno Issledovatel'skii Institut Okhrany Truda

Sb Rab Vses Zaochn Inst Pishch Promsti — Sborník Rabot Vsesoyuznyi Zaochnyi Institut Pishchevoi Promyshlennosti

Sb Rab Vychisl Tsentra Mosk Gos Univ — Sborník Rabot Vychislitel'nogo Tsentral'nogo Moskovskogo Gosudarstvennogo Universiteta

Sb Rost Ustoichivost Rast Akad Nauk Ukr SSR Respub Mezhved — Sborník Rost i Ustoichivost' Rastenii Akademiya Nauk Ukrainskoi SSR Respublikanskii Mezhvedomstvennyi

SBSAW — Sitzungsberichte. Saechsische Akademie der Wissenschaften zu Leipzig. Philologisch-Historische Klasse

SBSAWL — Sitzungsberichte. Saechsische Akademie der Wissenschaften (Leipzig). Philologisch-Historische Klasse

Sb Severocesk Mus Prir Vedy Sci Nat — Sborník Severoceskeho Musea Prirodni Vedy Scientiae Naturales

Sb Statei Aspir Kirg Gos Univ — Sborník Statei Aspirantov Kirgizskogo Gosudarstvennogo Universiteta

Sb Statei Aspir Kirg Univ Fiz-Mat Estestv Nauk — Sborník Statei Aspirantov Kirgizskogo Universiteta Fiziko-Matematicheskikh Estestvennykh Nauk

Sb Statei Erevan Gos Univ — Sborník Statei Erevanskii Gosudarstvennyi Universitet

Sb Statei Geol Gidrogeol — Sborník Statei po Geologii i Gidrogeologii

Sb Statei Gidrogeol Geoterm — Sborník Statei po Gidrogeologii i Geotermii

Sb Statei Leningr Inst Tochn Mekh Opt — Sborník Statei Leningradskii Institut Tochnoi Mekhaniki i Optiki

Sb Statei Leningr Tekhnol Inst Tsellyul Bum Promsti — Sborník Statei Leningradskogo Tekhnologicheskogo Instituta Tsellyulozno-Bumazhnoi Promyshlennosti

Sb Statei Makeev Nauchno Issled Inst Bezop Rab Gorn Promsti — Sborník Statei Makeevskii Nauchno Issledovatel'skii Institut Bezopasnykh Rabot Gornoi Promyshlennosti

Sb Statei Molodykh Nauchn Rab Leningr Inst Vodn Transp — Sborník Statei Molodykh Nauchnykh Rabotnikov Leningradskii Institut Vodnogo Transporta

Sb Statei Mosk Inzh-Fiz Inst — Sborník Statei Moskovskii Inzhenerno-Fizicheskii Institut [*USSR*]

Sb Statei Nauchno Issled Inst Org Poluprod Krasitelei — Sborník Statei Nauchno-Issledovatel'skii Institut Organicheskikh Poluproduktov i Krasitelei

Sb Statei Vses Nauchno Issled Inst Khim Reakt — Sborník Statei Vsesoyuznyi Nauchno-Issledovatel'skii Institut Khimicheskikh Reaktivov

Sb Statniho Geol Ustavu Cesk Repub — Sborník Statniho Geologickeho Ustavu Ceskoslovenski Republiky

Sb Statniho Vyzk Ustavu Tepelne Tech — Sborník Statniho Vyzkumneho Ustavu Tepelne Techniky

Sb Stud Nauchn Issled Rab Arkhang Lesotekh Inst — Sborník Studencheskikh Nauchno Issledovatel'skikh Rabot Arkhangel'skii Lesotekhnicheskii Institut

Sb Stud Nauchn Issled Rab Mosk Vet Akad — Sborník Studencheskikh Nauchno Issledovatel'skikh Rabot Moskovskaya Veterinarnaya Akademiya

Sb Stud Nauchno-Issled Rab Kirg S-kh Inst — Sborník Studencheskikh Nauchno-Issledovatel'skikh Rabot Kirgizskogo Sel'skokhozyaistvennogo Instituta

Sb Stud Nauchn Rab Alma-At Zoovet Inst — Sborník Studencheskikh Nauchnykh Rabot Alma-Atinskogo Zooveterinarnogo Instituta

Sb Stud Nauchn Rab Kabard Balkar Gos Univ — Sborník Studencheskikh Nauchnykh Rabot Kabardino Balkarskii Gosudarstvennyi Universitet

Sb Stud Nauchn Tr Erevan Gos Univ — Sborník Studencheskikh Nauchnykh Trudov Erevanskii Gosudarstvennyi Universitet

Sb Stud Rab Krasnodar Gos Pedagog Inst — Sbornik Studencheskikh Rabot Krasnodarskogo Gosudarstvennogo Pedagogicheskogo Instituta

Sb Stud Rab Mosk Tekhnol Inst Myasn Molochn Promsti — Sbornik Studencheskikh Rabot Moskovskogo Tekhnologicheskogo Instituta Myasnoi i Molochnoi Promyshlennosti

Sb Stud Rab Rostov Gos Univ — Sbornik Studencheskikh Rabot Rostovskogo Gosudarstvennogo Universiteta

Sb Stud Rab Sredneaziat Gos Univ — Sbornik Studencheskikh Rabot Sredneaziatskogo Gosudarstvennogo Universiteta

SBT — Studies in Biblical Theology

SBTDA — Sbornik Trudov Vsesoyuznogo Zaochnogo Politekhnicheskogo Instituta

Sb Tr Agrofiz Nauchno Issled Inst — Sbornik Trudov Agrofizicheskii Nauchno-Issledovatel'skii Institut

Sb Tr Agron Fiz — Sbornik Trudov po Agronomicheskoi Fizike

Sb Tr Andizh Gos Med Inst — Sbornik Trudov Andizhanskii Gosudarstvennyi Meditsinskii Institut

Sb Tr Arkhang Gos Med Inst — Sbornik Trudov Arkhangel'skii Gosudarstvennyi Meditsinskii Institut

Sb Tr Arm Nauchno-Issled Lesn Opytn Stn — Sbornik Trudov Armyanskoi Nauchno-Issledovatel'skoi Lesnoi Opytnoi Stantsii

Sb Tr Aspir Molodykh Nauchn Sotr Vses Inst Rastenievod — Sbornik Trudov Aspirantov i Molodykh Nauchnykh Sotrudnikov Vsesoyuznyi Institut Rastenievodstva

Sb Tr Aspir Tadzh Univ Estest Nauk — Sbornik Trudov Aspirantov Tadzhikskogo Universiteta Estestvennykh Nauk

Sb Tr Astrakh Gos S-kh Opytn Stn — Sbornik Trudov Astrakhanskoi Gosudarstvennoi Sel'skokhozyaistvennoi Opytnoi Stantsii

Sb Tr Astrakh Protivochumn Stn — Sbornik Trudov Astrakhanskoi Protivochumnoi Stantsii

Sb Tr Azerb Gos Inst Usoversh Vrachei — Sbornik Trudov Azerbaidzhanskii Gosudarstvennyi Institut Usovershenstvovaniya Vrachei

Sb Tr Azerb Gos Med Inst — Sbornik Trudov Azerbaidzhanskogo Gosudarstvennogo Meditsinskogo Instituta

Sb Tr Azerb Nauchno-Issled Inst Kurortol Fiz Metod Lech — Sbornik Trudov Azerbaidzhanskogo Nauchno-Issledovatel'skogo Instituta Kurortologii i Fizicheskikh Metodov Lecheniya

Sb Tr Bashk Gos Zapov — Sbornik Trudov Bashkirskogo Zapovednika

Sb Tr Beloruss Gos Med Inst — Sbornik Trudov Belorusskii Gosudarstvennyi Meditsinskii Institut

Sb Tr Bryansk Inst Transp Mashinostr — Sbornik Trudov Bryanskii Institut Transportnogo Mashinostroeniya

Sb Tr Chelyab Elektrometall Komb — Sbornik Trudov Chelyabinskogo Elektrometallurgicheskogo Kombinata

Sb Tr Chelyabinsk Elektrometal Komb — Sbornik Trudov Chelyabinsk Elektrometallurgicheskogo Kombinata [*USSR*]

Sb Tr Dal'nevost Nauchno-Issled Inst Lesn Khoz — Sbornik Trudov Dal'nevostochnyi Nauchno-Issledovatel'skii Institut Lesnogo Khozyaistva

Sb Tr Donetsk Nauchno-Issled Inst Cher Metall — Sbornik Trudov Donetskii Nauchno-Issledovatel'skii Institut Chernoi Metallurgii

Sb Tr Donets Nauchno-Issled Inst Chern Metall — Sbornik Trudov Donetskii Nauchno-Issledovatel'skii Institut Chernoi Metallurgii [*USSR*]

Sb Tr Geobot Eksped L'vov Univ — Sbornik Trudov Geobotanicheskoi Ekspeditsii L'vovskogo Universiteta

Sb Tr Glavniiproekt Energ Inst (USSR) — Sbornik Trudov Glavniiproekt Energeticheskii Institut (USSR)

Sb Tr Gor'k Skh Inst — Sbornik Trudov Gor'kovskogo Sel'skokhozyaistvennogo Instituta

Sb Tr Gos Inst Prikl Khim — Sbornik Trudov Gosudarstvennogo Instituta Prikladnoi Khimii

Sb Tr Gos Inst Proekt Zavodov Sanit Tekh Oborudovaniya — Sbornik Trudov Gosudarstvennyi Institut po Proektirovaniyu Zavodov Sanitarno Tekhnicheskogo Oborudovaniya

Sb Tr Gos Nauchno-Issled Energ Inst Im G M Krzhizhanovskogo — Sbornik Trudov Gosudarstvennyi Nauchno-Issledovatel'skii Energeticheskii Institut Imeni G. M. Krzhizhanovskogo

Sb Tr Gos Nauchno Issled Inst Rentgenol Radiol — Sbornik Trudov Gosudarstvennyi Nauchno-Issledovatel'skii Institut Rentgenologii i Radiologii

Sb Tr Gos Vses Nauchno-Issled Inst Stroit Mater Konstr — Sbornik Trudov Gosudarstvennyi Vsesoyuznyi Nauchno-Issledovatel'skii Institut Stroitel'nykh Materialov i Konstruktsii

Sb Tr Gruz Zootekh Vet Inst — Sbornik Trudov Gruzinskii Zootekhnichesko Veterinarnyi Institut

Sb Tr Gruz Zootekh-Vet Uchebn-Issled Inst — Sbornik Trudov Gruzinskogo Zootekhnichesko-Veterinarnogo Uchebno-Issledovatel'skogo Instituta

Sb Tr Inst Eksp Patol Ter Akad Med Nauk SSSR — Sbornik Trudov Instituta Eksperimental'noi Patologii i Terapii Akademii Meditsinskikh Nauk SSSR

Sb Tr Inst Elektrotekh Akad Nauk Ukr SSR — Sbornik Trudov Instituta Elektrotekhniki Akademiya Nauk Ukrainskoi SSR

Sb Tr Inst Epidemiol Gig Arm SSR — Sbornik Trudov Instituta Epidemiologii i Gigieny Armyanskoi SSR

Sb Tr Inst Gorn Dela Akad Nauk Ukr SSR — Sbornik Trudov Instituta Gornogo Dela Akademiya Nauk Ukrainskoi SSR

Sb Tr Inst Kurortol Fizioter Yerevan — Sbornik Trudov Instituta Kurortologii i Fizioterapii Yerevan

Sb Tr Inst Mashinoved Avtom Akad Nauk B SSR — Sbornik Trudov Institut Mashinovedeniya i Avtomatizats Akademii Nauk Belorusskoi SSR

Sb Tr Inst Neftekhim Protsessov Akad Nauk Az SSR — Sbornik Trudov Institut Neftekhimicheskikh Protsessov Akademiya Nauk Azerbaidzhanskoi SSR

Sb Tr Inst Stroit Mekh Seismostoikosti Akad Nauk Gruz SSR — Sbornik Trudov Institut Stroitel'noi Mekhaniki i Seismostoikosti Akademiya Nauk Gruzinskoi SSR

Sb Tr Inst Urol Akad Med Nauk SSSR — Sbornik Trudov Instituta Urologii Akademii Meditsinskikh Nauk SSSR

Sb Tr Inst Urol Gruz SSR — Sbornik Trudov Instituta Urologii Gruzinskoi SSR

Sb Tr Ivanov Med Inst — Sbornik Trudov Ivanovskogo Meditsinskogo Instituta

Sb Tr Izhevsk Med Inst — Sbornik Trudov Izhevskogo Meditsinskogo Instituta

Sb Tr Kafedry Mikrobiol Orenb Med Inst — Sbornik Trudov Kafedry Mikrobiologii Orenburgskogo Meditsinskogo Instituta

Sb Tr Kazan Gos Med Inst — Sbornik Trudov Kazanskii Gosudarstvennyi Meditsinskii Institut

Sb Tr Khar'k Avtomob Dorozhn Inst — Sbornik Trudov Khar'kovskogo Avtomobil'no Dorozhnogo Instituta

Sb Tr Khar'k Gidrometeorol Inst — Sbornik Trudov Khar'kovskii Gidrometeorologicheskii Institut

Sb Tr Khark Vet Inst — Sbornik Trudov Khar'kovskogo Veterinarnogo Instituta

Sb Tr Kiev Inzh Stroit Inst — Sbornik Trudov Kievskii Inzhenerno-Stroitel'nyi Institut

Sb Tr Kiev Stroit Inst — Sbornik Trudov Kievskii Stroitel'nyi Institut

Sb Tr Kirg Nauchno-Issled Inst Epidemiol Mikrobiol Gig — Sbornik Trudov Kirgizskii Nauchno-Issledovatel'skii Institut Epidemiologii, Mikrobiologii, i Gigieny

Sb Tr Klyuchevskogo Zavoda Ferrosplavov — Sbornik Trudov Klyuchevskogo Zavoda Ferrosplavov

Sb Tr Klyuchevsk Zavoda Ferrosplavov — Sbornik Trudov Klyuchevskogo Zavoda Ferrosplavov [*USSR*]

Sb Tr Krym Gos Med Inst — Sbornik Trudov Krymskogo Gosudarstvennogo Meditsinskogo Instituta

Sb Tr Krym Med Inst — Sbornik Trudov Krymskogo Meditsinskogo Instituta

Sb Tr Kursk Gos Med Inst — Sbornik Trudov Kurskii Gosudarstvennyi Meditsinskii Institut

Sb Tr Kursk Med Inst — Sbornik Trudov Kurskogo Meditsinskogo Instituta

Sb Tr Latv Fil Vses Ova Pochvovedov — Sbornik Trudov Latviiskii Filial Vsesoyuznogo Obshchestva Pochvovedov

Sb Tr Leningr Gos Inst Usoversh Vrachei — Sbornik Trudov Leningradskii Gosudarstvennyi Institut Usovershenstvaniya Vrachei

Sb Tr Leningr Inst Inzh Zheleznodorozhn Transp — Sbornik Trudov Leningradskii Institut Inzhenerov Zheleznodorozhnogo Transporta

Sb Tr Leningr Inst Sov Torg — Sbornik Trudov Leningradskii Institut Sovetskoi Torgovli

Sb Tr Leningr Inst Usoversh Vrachei Im S M Kirova — Sbornik Trudov Leningradskii Institut Usovershenstvovaniya Vrachei Imeni S. M. Kirova

Sb Tr Leningr Inzh-Stroit Inst — Sbornik Trudov Leningradskii Inzhenerno-Stroitel'nyi Institut

Sb Tr Leningr Mekh Inst — Sbornik Trudov Leningradskii Mekhanicheskii Institut

Sb Tr Leningr Nauchno Issled Inst Gematol Pereliv Krovi — Sbornik Trudov Leningradskii Nauchno-Issledovatel'skii Institut Gematologii i Perelivaniya Krovi

Sb Tr Leningr Nauchno-Issled Inst Gematol Pereliv Krovi — Sbornik Trudov Leningradskogo Nauchno-Issledovatel'skogo Instituta Gematologii i Perelivaniya Krovi

Sb Tr Leningr Nauchno Issled Inst Vaktsin Syvorotok — Sbornik Trudov Leningradskii Nauchno-Issledovatel'skii Institut Vaktsin i Syvorotok

Sb Tr Leningr Nauchn O-va Nevropatol Psikhiatr — Sbornik Trudov Leningradskogo Nauchnogo Obshchestva Nevropatologov i Psikhiatrov

Sb Tr Leningr Nauchn Ova Nevropatol Psikhiatrov — Sbornik Trudov Leningradskogo Nauchnogo Obshchestva Nevropatologov i Psikhiatrov

Sb Tr Lesn Khoz (Kazan) — Sbornik Trudov po Lesnomu Khozyaistvu (Kazan)

Sb Tr Med Uchrezhd Mosk Oksko Volzh Vozdravotdela — Sbornik Trudov Meditsinskikh Uchrezhdenii Moskovsko-Oksko-Volzhskogo Vozdravotdela

Sb Tr Mold Nauchno Issled Inst Epidemiol Mikrobiol Gig — Sbornik Trudov Moldavskogo Nauchno-Issledovatel'skii Institut Epidemiologii, Mikrobiologii, i Gigieny

Sb Tr Mold Stn Vses Inst Zashch Rast — Sbornik Trudov Moldavskoi Stantsii Vsesoyuznogo Instituta Zashchity Rastenii

Sb Tr Molodykh Nauchn Rab Inst Bot Akad Nauk Gruz SSR — Sbornik Trudov Molodykh Nauchnykh Rabotnikov Institut Botaniki Akademii Nauk Gruzinskoi SSR

Sb Tr Molodykh Uch Kirg Nauchno Issled Inst Zemled — Sbornik Trudov Molodykh Uchenykh Kirgizskii Nauchno-Issledovatel'skii Institut Zemledeliya

Sb Tr Molodykh Uch Tselinogr Med Inst — Sbornik Trudov Molodykh Uchenykh Tselinogradskogo Meditsinskogo Instituta

Sb Tr Mosk Inzh-Stroitel Inst Im V V Kuibysheva — Sbornik Trudov Moskovskii Inzhenerno-Stroitel'nyi Institut Imeni V. V. Kuibysheva [*USSR*]

Sb Tr Mosk Inzh Stroit Inst — Sbornik Trudov Moskovskii Inzhenerno-Stroitel'nyi Institut

Sb Tr Mosk Nauchno Issled Inst Kosmetol — Sbornik Trudov Moskovskogo Nauchno-Issledovatel'skogo Instituta Kosmetologii

Sb Tr Mosk Poligr Inst — Sbornik Trudov Moskovskii Poligraficheskii Institut

Sb Tr Mosk Tekhnol Inst — Sbornik Trudov Moskovski Tekhnologicheskii Institut

Sb Tr Mosk Vech Metall Inst — Sbornik Trudov Moskovskii Vechernii Metallurgicheskii Institut [*USSR*]

Sb Tr Mosk Zaochn Poligr Inst — Sbornik Trudov Moskovskii Zaochnyi Poligraficheskii Institut

Sb Tr MVTU — Sbornik Trudov MVTU

Sb Tr Nauchn Issled Inst Kurortol Fizioter (Tiflis) — Sbornik Trudov Nauchno-Issledovatel'skii Institut Kurortologii i Fizioterapii (Tiflis)

Sb Tr Nauchn Issled Inst Probl Kursk Magn Anomalii — Sbornik Trudov Nauchno-Issledovatel'skii Institut po Problemen Kurskoi Magnitnoi Anomalii

Sb Tr Nauchno Issled Inst Akush Ginekol (Tbilisi) — Sbornik Trudov Nauchno-Issledovatel'skii Institut Akusherstva i Ginekologii (Tbilisi)

Sb Tr Nauchno-Issled Inst Eksp Klin Ter — Sbornik Trudov Nauchno-Issledovatel'skii Institut Eksperimental'noi i Klinicheskoi Terapii

Sb Tr Nauchno-Issled Inst Eksp Klin Ter Gruz SSR — Sbornik Trudov Nauchno-Issledovatel'skii Instituta Eksperimental'noi Klinicheskoi Terapii Gruzinskoi SSR

Sb Tr Nauchno Issled Inst Epidemiol Mikrobiol Gig — Sbornik Trudov Nauchno-Issledovatel'skii Institut Epidemiologii, Mikrobiologii, i Gigieny

Sb Tr Nauchno-Issled Inst Gematol Pereliv Krovi Gruz SSR — Sbornik Trudov Nauchno-Issledovatel'skogo Instituta Gematologii i Perelivaniya Krovi Gruzinskoi SSR

Sb Tr Nauchno Issled Inst Gematol Pereliv Krovi (Tiflis) — Sbornik Trudov Nauchno-Issledovatel'skii Institut Gematologii i Perelivaniya Krovi (Tiflis)

Sb Tr Nauchno-Issled Inst Gig Tr Profzabol Gruz SSR — Sbornik Trudov Nauchno-Issledovatel'skii Institut Gigieny Truda i Profzabolevanii Gruzinskoi SSR

Sb Tr Nauchno Issled Inst Gig Tr Profzabol (Tiflis) — Sbornik Trudov Nauchno-Issledovatel'skii Institut Gigieny Truda i Profzabolevanii (Tiflis)

Sb Tr Nauchno Issled Inst Kurortol Fizioter Abkhazskii Fil — Sbornik Trudov Nauchno-Issledovatel'skii Institut Kurortologii i Fizioterapii Abkhazskii Filial

Sb Tr Nauchno Issled Inst Med Parazitol Trop Med Gruz SSR — Sbornik Trudov Nauchno-Issledovatel'skogo Instituta Meditsinskoi Parazitologii i Tropicheskoi Meditsiny Gruzinskoi SSR

Sb Tr Nauchno-Issled Inst Prom Stroit Ufa — Sbornik Trudov Nauchno-Issledovatel'skii Institut Promyshlennogo Stroitel'stva Ufa

Sb Tr Nauchno-Issled Inst Rentgenol Med Radiol Gruz SSR — Sbornik Trudov Nauchno-Issledovatel'skogo Instituta Rentgenologii i Meditsinskoi Radiologii Gruzinskoi SSR

Sb Tr Nauchno-Issled Inst Rentgenol Med Radiol (Tiflis) — Sbornik Trudov Nauchno-Issledovatel'skii Institut Rentgenologii i Meditsinskoi Radiologii (Tiflis)

Sb Tr Nauchno-Issled Inst Sanit Gig Gruz SSR — Sbornik Trudov Nauchno-Issledovatel'skogo Instituta Sanitarii i Gigieny Gruzinskoi SSR

Sb Tr Nauchno Issled Inst Sanit Tekh — Sbornik Trudov Nauchno-Issledovatel'skii Institut Sanitarnoi Tekhniki

Sb Tr Nauchno-Issled Inst Travmatol Ortoped Gruz SSR — Sbornik Trudov Nauchno-Issledovatel'skogo Instituta Travmatologii i Ortopedii Gruzinskoi SSR

Sb Tr Nauchno Issled Inst Travmatol Ortop Gruz SSR — Sbornik Trudov Nauchno-Issledovatel'skogo Instituta Travmatologii i Ortopedii Gruzinskoi SSR

Sb Tr Nauchno Issled Inst Zashch Rast Arm SSR — Sbornik Trudov Nauchno-Issledovatel'skogo Institut Zashchity Rastenii Armyanskoi SSR

Sb Tr Nauchno Issled Khozhno Venerol Inst Gruz SSR — Sbornik Trudov Nauchno-Issledovatel'skogo Khozhno-Venerologicheskogo Instituta Gruzinskoi SSR

Sb Tr Nauchnoizsled Inst Tr Khig Prof Bol — Sbornik Trudov na Nauchnoizsledovatelskiya Instituta po Trudova-Khigienna i Professionalni Bolesti

Sb Tr Nauchno Izsled Onkol Inst (Sofia) — Sbornik Trudov Nauchno-Izsledovatelski Onkologichen Institut (Sofia)

Sb Tr Nauchnoizsled Proekt Inst Rudodobiv Obogat Obogat — Sbornik ot Trudov na Nauchnoizsledovatelskiya i Proektantski Institut za Rudodobiv i Obogatyavane. Obogatyavane

Sb Tr Novosb Vseross O-va Otolaringol — Sbornik Trudov Novosibirskogo Otdeleniya Vserossiiskogo Obshchestva Otolaringologov

Sb Tr Novosib Otd Vseross Ova Otolaringol — Sbornik Trudov Novosibirskogo Otdeleniya Vserossiiskogo Obshchestva Otolaringologov

Sb Tr Obshchetekh Kafedr Leningr Tekhnol Inst Kholod Promsti — Sbornik Trudov Obshchetekhnicheskikh Kafedr Leningradskii Tekhnologicheskii Institut Kholodil'noi Promyshlennosti

Sb Tr Odess Inzh Stroit Inst — Sbornik Trudov Odesskii Inzhenerno-Stroitel'nyi Institut

Sb Tr Odess Med Inst — Sbornik Trudov Odesskii Meditsinskii Institut

Sb Tr Osvo Terskokumskikh Peskov — Sbornik Trudov Osvoeniyu Terskokumskikh Peskov

Sb Tr Permsk Gor Psikhiatr Boln — Sbornik Trudov Permskoi Gorodskoi Psikhiatricheskoi Bol'nitsy

Sb Tr Povolzh Lesotekh Inst — Sbornik Trudov Povolzhskogo Lesotekhnicheskogo Instituta

Sb Tr Proektn Nauchno-Issled Inst Ural Promstroiniiproekt — Sbornik Trudov Proektnyi i Nauchno-Issledovatel'skii Institut "Ural'skii Promstroiniiproekt"

Sb Tr Rentgenol — Sbornik Trudov po Rentgenologii

Sb Tr Resp Kostno Tuberk Bol'n Im Lenina — Sbornik Trudov Respubliki Kostno Tuberkuleznaya Bol'nitsa Imeni Lenina

Sb Tr Resp Nauchno-Issled Inst Mestnykh Stroit Mater — Sbornik Trudov Respublikanskii Nauchno-Issledovatel'skii Institut Mestnykh Stroitel'nykh Materialov

Sb Tr Resp Nauchno-Issled Inst Okhr Materin Det — Sbornik Trudov Respublikanskii Nauchno-Issledovatel'skii Institut Okhrany Materinstva Detstva

Sb Tr Samark Med Inst — Sbornik Trudov Samarkandskogo Meditsinskogo Instituta

Sb Tr Sekt Radiobiol Akad Nauk Arm SSR — Sbornik Trudov Sektor Radiobiologii Akademiya Nauk Armyanskoi SSR

Sb Tr Sev Nauchno-Issled Inst Promsti — Sbornik Trudov Severnyi Nauchno-Issledovatel'skii Institut Promyshlennosti

Sb Tr Stalingr Inst Inzh Gor Khoz — Sbornik Trudov Stalingradskii Institut Inzhenerov Gorodskogo Khozyaistva

Sb Tr Stalingr Opytno Melior Stn — Sbornik Trudov Stalingradskaya Opytno-Meliorativnaya Stantsiya

Sb Tr Stavrop Gos Pedagog Inst — Sbornik Trudov Stavropol'skii Gosudarstvennyi Pedagogicheskii Institut

Sb Tr Sud Med Sud Khim — Sbornik Trudov po Sudebnoi Meditsine i Sudebnoi Khimii

Sb Tr Sverdl Gor Klin Bol'n No 1 — Sbornik Trudov Sverdlovskoi Gorodskoi Klinicheskoi Bol'nitsy No. 1

Sb Tr Sverdl Nauchno Issled Inst Pererab Drev — Sbornik Trudov Sverdlovskii Nauchno-Issledovatel'skii Institut Pererabotki Drevesiny

Sb Tr Sverdl Nauchno-Issled Inst Stroit — Sbornik Trudov Sverdlovski Nauchno-Issledovatel'skii Institut po Stroitel'stvu

Sb Tr Tadzh Nauchno-Issled Inst Zemled — Sbornik Trudov Tadzhikskogo Nauchno-Issledovatel'skogo Instituta Zemledeliya

Sb Tr Tbilis Gos Nauchno Issled Inst Stroit Mater — Sbornik Trudov Tbilisskii Gosudarstvennyi Nauchno-Issledovatel'skii Institut Stroitel'nykh Materialov

Sb Tr Tbilis Inst Usoversh Vrachei — Sbornik Trudov Tbilisskogo Instituta Usovershenstvovaniya Vrachei

Sb Tr Tsent Nauchno-Issled Inst Chern Metall — Sbornik Trudov Tsentral'nogo Nauchno-Issledovatel'skogo Instituta Chernoj Metallurgii [*USSR*]

Sb Tr Tsentr Muz Pochvoved — Sbornik Trudov Tsentral'nyi Muzei Pochvovedeniya

Sb Tr Tsentr Nauchno Issled Inst Bum — Sbornik Trudov Tsentral'nogo Nauchno-Issledovatel'skogo Instituta Bumagi

Sb Tr Tsentr Nauchno-Issled Inst Chern Metall — Sbornik Trudov Tsentral'nogo Nauchno-Issledovatel'skogo Instituta Chernoj Metallurgii

Sb Tr Tsentr Nauchno-Issled Inst Olovyannoi Promsti — Sbornik Trudov Tsentral'nyi Nauchno-Issledovatel'skii Institut Olovyannoi Promyshlennosti

Sb Tr Tsentr Nauchno Issled Proektn Inst Lesokhim Promsti — Sbornik Trudov Tsentral'nyi Nauchno-Issledovatel'skii Proektnyi Institut Lesokhiimicheskoi Promyshlennosti

Sb Tr Tskhaltub Fil Nauchno Issled Inst Kurortol Fizioter — Sbornik Trudov Tskhaltubskii Filial Nauchno-Issledovatel'skii Institut Kurortoloogii i Fizioterapii

Sb Trud Agron Fiz — Sbornik Trudov po Agronomicheskoi Fizike

Sb Trud Moskov Obl Pedag Inst — Sbornik Trudov Moskovskogo Oblastskogo Pedagogiceskij Institut

Sb Trud Nauc-Issled Inst Hudoz Promys — Sbornik Trudov Nauchno-Issledovatel'skogo Instituta Hudozestvennoj Promyshlennosti

Sb Trudov Inst Problem Upravlen — Sbornik Trudov Institut Problem Upravlenina

Sb Trudov Odess Elektrotehn Inst Svjazi — Sbornik Trudov Odesskogo Elektrotehniceskogo Instituta Svjazi Imeni A. S. Popova

Sb Trudov Vsesojuz Zaocn Politehn Inst — Sbornik Trudov Vsesojuznogo Zaocnogo Politehniceskogo Instituta

Sb Trud Vopros Zool Kazansk Gos Pedagog Inst — Sbornik Trudov Vopros Zool Kazanskii Gosudarstvennyi Pedagogiceskogo Institut

Sb Trud Zool Muz — Sbornik Trudov Zoologicheskogo Muzeya

Sb Tr Ufim Neft Inst — Sbornik Trudov Ufimskogo Neftyanogo Instituta

Sb Tr Ukr Nauchno-Issled Inst Met — Sbornik Trudov Ukrainskij Nauchno-Issledovatel'skij Institut Metallov

Sb Tr Ukr Nauchno Issled Inst Pishch Promsti — Sbornik Trudov Ukrainskii Nauchno-Issledovatel'skii Institut Pishchevoi Promyshlennosti

Sb Tr Ukr Nauchno Issled Inst Poligr Promsti — Sbornik Trudov Ukrainskogo Nauchno-Issledovatel'skogo Instituta Poligraficheskoi Promyshlennosti

Sb Tr Ukr Nauchno Issled Inst Tsellyul Bum Promsti — Sbornik Trudov Ukrainskogo Nauchno-Issledovatel'skogo Instituta Tsellyulozno-Bumazhnoi Promyshlennosti

Sb Tr Ukr Tsentr Nauchno-Issled Inst Ortop Travmatol — Sbornik Trudov Ukrainskogo Tsentral'nogo Nauchno-Issledovatel'skogo Instituta Ortopedii i Travmatologii

Sb Tr Ural Lesotekh Inst — Sbornik Trudov Ural'skii Lesotekhnicheskii Institut

Sb Tr Vil'nyus Gos Nauchno Issled Inst Stroit Mater — Sbornik Trudov Vil'nyusskogo Gosudarstvennogo Nauchno-Issledovatel'skogo Instituta Stroitel'nykh Materialov

Sb Tr Vladivost Nauchno Issled Inst Epidemiol Mikrobiol Gig — Sbornik Trudov Vladivostokskogo Nauchno-Issledovatel'skogo Instituta Epidemiologii, Mikrobiologii, i Gigieny

Sb Tr VNIIB — Sbornik Trudov VNIIB

Sb Tr Voronezh Inzh Stroit Inst — Sbornik Trudov Voronezhskogo Inzhenerno-Stroitel'nogo Instituta

Sb Tr Voronezh Otd Vses Khim Ova — Sbornik Trudov Voronezhskogo Otdeleniya Vsesoyuznogo Khimicheskogo Obshchestva

Sb Tr Voronezh S-kh — Sbornik Trudov Voronezhskogo Sel'skokhozyaistvennogo Instituta

Sb Tr Voronezh S-Kh Inst — Sbornik Trudov Voronezhskogo Sel'skokhozyaistvennogo Instituta

Sb Tr Vrachei Dorogi — Sbornik Trudov Vrachei Dorogi

Sb Tr Vrachei Pribalt Zhelezn — Sbornik Trudov Vrachei Pribaltiiskogo Zheleznodorozhiya

Sb Tr Vses Inst Rastenievod — Sbornik Trudov Vsesoyuznyi Institut Rastenievodstva

Sb Tr Vses Nauchno-Issled Eksp-Konstr Inst Tary Upakovki — Sbornik Trudov Vsesoyuznyi Nauchno-Issledovatel'skii i Eksperimental'no-Konstruktorskii Institut Tary i Upakovki

Sb Tr Vses Nauchno-Issled Inst Bolezn Ptits — Sbornik Trudov Vsesoyuznogo Nauchno-Issledovatel'skogo Instituta po Boleznyam Ptits

Sb Tr Vses Nauchno Issled Inst Derevoobrab Promsti — Sbornik Trudov Vsesoyuznyi Nauchno-Issledovatel'skii Institut Derevoobrabatyvayuushchei Promyshlennosti

Sb Tr Vses Nauchno-Issled Inst Gidroliza Rastit Mater — Sbornik Trudov Vsesoyuznyi Nauchno-Issledovatel'skii Institut Gidroliza Rastitel'nykh Materialov [*USSR*]

Sb Tr Vses Nauchno Issled Inst "Goznaka" — Sbornik Trudov Vsesoyuznyi Nauchno-Issledovatel'skii Institut "Goznaka"

Sb Tr Vses Nauchno-Issled Inst Nov Stroit Mater — Sbornik Trudov Vsesoyuznyi Nauchno-Issledovatel'skii Institut Novykh Stroitel'nykh Materialov [*USSR*]

Sb Tr Vses Nauchno-Issled Inst Stroit Mater Konstr — Sbornik Trudov Vsesoyuznyi Nauchno-Issledovatel'skii Institut Stroitel'nykh Materialov i Konstruktsii

Sb Tr Vses Nauchno-Issled Inst Tsellyul Bum Promsti — Sbornik Trudov Vsesoyuznyi Nauchno-Issledovatel'skogo Instituta Tsellyulozno-Bumazhnoi Promyshlennosti

Sb Tr Vses Nauchno Issled Inst Tverd Splavov — Sbornik Trudov Vsesoyuznyi Nauchno-Issledovatel'skii Institut Tverdykh Splavov

Sb Tr Vses Nauchno Issled Khim Farm Inst — Sbornik Trudov Vsesoyuznogo Nauchno-Issledovatel'skogo Khimiko-Farmatsevticheskogo Instituta

Sb Tr Vses Nauchno-Issled Proekt Inst Titana — Sbornik Trudov Vsesoyuznyi Nauchno-Issledovatel'skii i Proektnyi Institut Titana [*USSR*]

Sb Tr Vses Nauchno-Issled Proektn Inst Teplotekh Sooruzh — Sbornik Trudov Vsesoyuznyi Nauchno-Issledovatel'skii i Proektnyi Institut po Teplotekhnicheskim Sooruzheniyam

Sb Tr Vses Nauchno Issled Proektn Inst Titana — Sbornik Trudov Vsesoyuznyi Nauchno-Issledovatel'skii i Proektnyi Institut Titana

Sb Tr Vses Zaochn Inzh Stroit Inst — Sbornik Trudov Vsesoyuznyi Zaochnyi Inzhenerno-Stroitel'nyi Institut

Sb Tr Vses Zaochn Politekh Inst — Sbornik Trudov Vsesoyuznogo Zaochnogo Politekhnicheskogo Instituta

Sb Tr Yuzhn Nauchno Issled Inst Prom Stroit — Sbornik Trudov Yuzknyi Nauchno-Issledovatel'skii Institut Promyshlennogo Stroitel'stva

Sb Tr Zool Muz Mosk Univ — Sbornik Trudov Zoologicheskogo Muzeya Moskovskogo Universiteta

Sb Tsentr Nauchno Issled Inst Tekhnol Mashinostr — Sbornik Tsentral'nyi Nauchno-Issledovatel'skii Institut Tekhnologii i Mashinostroeniya

SBU — Mois Economique et Financier

SBU — Symbolae Biblicae Upsalienses

Sb Uch Zap Aspir Latv Nauchno Issled Inst Zemled — Sbornik Uchenykh Zapisok Aspirantov. Latviiskii Nauchno-Issledovatel'skii Institut Zemledeliya

Sb Ustavu Nerostych Surovin Kutne Hore — Sbornik Ustavu Nerostych Surovin v Kutne Hore

Sb Ustav Vedeckotech Inf Genet Slechteni — Sbornik Ustav Vedeckotechnickych Informaci Genetika a Slechteni

Sb Ustav Vedeckotech Inf Melior — Sbornik Ustav Vedeckotechnickych Informaci. Rada Meliorace

Sb Ustav Vedeckotech Inf Zemed Genet Slechteni — Sbornik Ustav Vedeckotechnickych Informaci pro Zemedelstvi, Genetika, a Slechteni

Sb Ustav Vedeckotech Inf Zemed Melior — Sbornik Ustav Vedeckotechnickych Informaci pro Zemedelstvi Rada Meliorace

Sb Ustred Ustavu Geol — Sbornik Ustredniho Ustavu Geologickeho

Sb UVTI Genet Slechteni — Sbornik UVTI [*Ustav Vedeckotechnickych Informaci*] Genetika a Slechteni

Sb UVTI Melior — Sbornik UVTI [*Ustav Vedeckotechnickych Informaci*] Meliorace

Sb UVTI Ochr Rostl — Sbornik UVTI [*Ustav Vedeckotechnickych Informaci*] Ochrana Rostlin

Sb UVTI Ustav Vedeckotech Inf Zahradnictvi — Sbornik UVTI-Ustav Vedeckotechnickych Informaci Zahradnictvi

Sb Ved Lesn Ustav Vys Sk Zemed Praze — Sbornik Vedeckeho Lesnickeho Ustavu Vysoke Skoly Zemedelske v Praze

Sb Ved Praci Ustred Statniho Ust Praze — Sbornik Vedeckych Praci Ustredniho Statniho Ustavu v Praze

Sb Ved Praci Vyzk Ustav Vyz Zvirat — Sbornik Vedeckych Praci-Vyzkumny Ustav Vyzivy Zvirat

Sb Ved Pr Lek Fak Karlovy Univ Hradci Kralove — Sbornik Vedeckych Praci. Lekarske Fakulty Karlovy University v Hradci Kralove

Sb Ved Pr Lek Fak Karlovy Univ Hradci Kralove Suppl — Sbornik Vedeckych Praci Lekarske Fakulty Karlovy University v Hradci Kralove. Supplementum

Sb Ved Pr Lek Fak Univ Karlovy Hradci Kralove — Sbornik Vedeckych Praci Lekarske Fakulty. Karlovy University v Hradci Kralove

Sb Ved Pr VLVDU Hradci Kralove — Sbornik Vedeckych Praci VLVDU [*Vojenskeho Lekarskeho Vyzkumneho a Doskolovaciho Ustavu*] v Hradci Kralove

Sb Ved Pr Vys Sk Banske Ostrave Rada Horn-Geol — Sbornik Vedeckych Praci Vysoke Skoly Banske v Ostrave. Rada Hornicko-Geologicka[*Czechoslovakia*]

Sb Ved Pr Vys Sk Bransk Ostrave — Sbornik Vedeckych Praci Vysoke Skoly Banske v Ostrave

Sb Ved Pr Vys Sk Chem-Technol (Pardubice) — Sbornik Vedeckych Praci. Vysoka Skola Chemickotechnologicka (Pardubice)

Sb "Vop Issled Izpol'z Pochv Moldavii" — Sbornik "Voprosy Issledovaniya i Izpol'zovaniya Pochv Moldavii"

SBVS — Saga-Book. Viking Society for Northern Research

Sb Vses Inst Zashch Rast — Sbornik Vsesoyuznogo Instituta Zashchity Rastenii

Sb Vses Sov Nauchno-Tekh Obshchestv Kom Korroz Zashch Met — Sbornik Vsesoyuznyi Sovet Nauchno-Tekhnickeskikh Obshchestv. Komitet po Korrozi i Zashchite Metallov

Sb Vynalezu — Sbirka Vynalezu

Sb Vys Chem Technol Praze Ekon Rizeni Chem Prum — Sbornik Vysoke Skoly Chemicko-Technologicke v Praze. Ekonomika a Rizeni Chemickeho Prumyslu

Sb Vysk Pr Odboru Celul Pap — Sbornik Vyskumnych Prac z Odboru Celulozy a Papiera

Sb Vysk Sk Chem-Technol Praze (Oddil) Chem Inz — Sbornik Vysoke Skoly Chemicko-Technologicke v Praze (Oddil). Chemicke Inzenyrstvi

Sb Vysk Sk Chem-Technol Praze (Oddil) Chem Inz Autom — Sbornik Vysoke Skoly Chemicko-Technologicke v Praze (Oddil). Chemicke Inzenyrstvi a Automatizace

Sb Vys Sk Chem Technol Praze (Oddil) K — Sbornik Vysoke Skoly Chemicko-Technologicke v Praze (Oddil). K

Sb Vysoke Uceni Tech v Brne — Sbornik Vysokeho Uceni Technickeho v Brne

Sb Vys Sk Chem-Technol Praze — Sbornik Vysoke Skoly Chemicko-Technologicke v Praze

Sb Vys Sk Chem Technol Praze Anal Chem — Sbornik Vysoke Skoly Chemicko-Technologicke v Praze. Analyticka Chemie

Sb Vys Sk Chem Technol Praze Anorg Chem Technol — Sbornik Vysoke Skoly Chemicko-Technologicke v Praze. Anorganicka Chemie a Technologie

Sb Vys Sk Chem Technol Praze Anorg Org Technol — Sbornik Vysoke Skoly Chemicko-Technologicke v Praze. Anorganicka a Organicka Technologie

Sb Vys Sk Chem Technol Praze Anorg Technol — Sbornik Vysoke Skoly Chemicko-Technologicke v Praze. Anorganicka Technologie

Sb Vys Sk Chem Technol Praze Chem Inz Autom — Sbornik Vysoke Skoly Chemicko-Technologicke v Praze. Chemicke Inzenyrstvi a Automatizace

Sb Vys Sk Chem Technol Praze Chem Technol Silik — Sbornik Vysoke Skoly Chemicko-Technologicke v Praze. Chemie a Technologie Silikatu

Sb Vys Sk Chem Technol Praze Mineral — Sbornik Vysoke Skoly Chemicko-Technologicke v Praze. Mineralogie

Sb Vys Sk Chem Technol Praze Oddil Fak Anorg Technol — Sbornik Vysoke Skoly Chemicko-Technologicke v Praze. Oddil Fakult Anorganicke a Organicke Technologie

Sb Vys Sk Chem Technol Praze Oddil Fak Potravin Technol — Sbornik Vysoke Skoly Chemicko-Technologicke v Praze. Oddil Fakulty Poetravinarske Technologie

Sb Vys Sk Chem-Technol Praze (Oddil) Fak Technol Paliv Vody — Sbornik Vysoke Skoly Chemicko-Technologicke v Praze (Oddil). Fakulty Technologie Paliv a Vody

Sb Vys Sk Chem Technol Praze Org Chem Technol — Sbornik Vysoke Skoly Chemicko-Technologicke v Praze. Organicka Chemie a Technologie

Sb Vys Sk Chem-Technol Praze Rada B — Sbornik Vysoke Skoly Chemicko-Technologicke v Praze. Rada B. Anorganicka Chemie a Technologie

Sb Vys Sk Chem Technol Praze Technol Paliv — Sbornik Vysoke Skoly Chemicko-Technologicke v Praze. Technologie Paliv [*Czechoslovakia*]

Sb Vys Sk Chem-Technol Praze Technol Vody — Sbornik Vysoke Skoly Chemicko-Technologicke v Praze. Technologie Vody

Sb Vys Sk Chem-Technol Pr Potraviny — Sbornik Vysoke Skoly Chemicko-Technologicke v Praze. Potraviny

Sb Vys Skola Chem-Technol Fak Potrav Technol — Sbornik Vysoka Skola Chemicko-Technologicka. Fakulta Potravinarske Technologie

Sb Vys Skoly Polnohospod Nitre Prevadzkovo-Ekon Fak — Sbornik Vysokej Skoly Polnohospodarskej v Nitre Prevadzkovo-Ekonomicka Fakulta

Sb Vys Skoly Zemed Brne Rada A — Sbornik Vysoke Skoly Zemedelske v Brne. Rada A

Sb Vys Skoly Zemed Brne Rada B — Sbornik Vysoke Skoly Zemedelske v Brne. Rada B

Sb Vys Skoly Zemed Praze — Sbornik Vysoke Skoly Zemedelske v Praze

Sb Vys Sk Zemed Brne — Sbornik Vysoke Skoly Zemedelske v Brne

Sb Vys Sk Zemed v Brne A — Sbornik Vysoke Skoly Zemedelske v Brne. A

Sb Vys Sk Zemed Brne Rada C Spisy Fak Lesn — Sbornik Vysoke Skoly Zemedelske v Brne. Rada C. Spisy Fakulty Lesnicke

Sb Vys Sk Zemed Lesn Fak Brne Rada C Spisy — Sbornik Vysoke Skoly Zemedelske a Lesnicke Fakulty v Brne. Rada C. Spisy Fakulty Lesnicke

Sb Vys Sk Zemed Praze — Sbornik Vysoke Skoly Zemedelske v Praze

Sb Vys Sk Zemed Praze Fak Agron Rada A — Sbornik Vysoke Skoly Zemedelske v Praze. Fakulta Agronomicka. Rada A. Rostlinna Vyroba

Sb Vys Uceni Tech Brne — Sbornik Vysokeho Uceni Technickeho v Brne

Sb Vys Zemed Lesn Fak Brne B Spisy Fak Vet — Sbornik Vysoke Skoly Zemedelske a Lesnicke Fakulty v Brne. Rada B. Spisy Fakulty Veterinarni

SbWAk — Sitzungsberichte. Wiener Akademie

SBWFA — Schriftenreihe. Bundesminister fuer Wissenschaftliche Forschung (Germany). Strahlenschutz

SBZ Sanit Heiz Klimatech — SBZ Sanitaer-, Heizungs-, und Klimatechnik [*West Germany*]

SC — Science and Culture

Sc — Scientia. Organo Internazionale di Sintesi Scientifica

Sc — Scriptorium

SC — Scuola Cattolica

SC — Social Casework

SC — Social Compass

SC — Socialist Commentary

SC — Soil Conservation

SC — Sources Chretiennes [*Paris*]

SC — South Carolina Musician

SC — Stendhal Club

SC — Studi Colombiani

SC — Studia Catholica

SC — Studia Celtica

SC — Suisse Contemporaine

Sca — Scandinavica

SCA — Science Fiction Classics Annual

SCA — Smithsonian Contributions to Anthropology

SCA — Survey of Current Business [*Washington, DC*]

SC Acad Sci Bull — South Carolina Academy of Science. Bulletin

Sc Advocate — Science Advocate

SC Ag Dept — South Carolina. Department of Agriculture, Commerce, and Industries. Publications

SC Ag Exp — South Carolina. Agricultural Experiment Station. Publications

SC Agric Exp Stn Bull — South Carolina. Agricultural Experiment Station. Bulletin

SC Agric Exp Stn Circ — South Carolina. Agricultural Experiment Station. Circular

SC Agric Exp Stn Tech Bull — South Carolina. Agricultural Experiment Station. Technical Bulletin

SC Agr Res — South Carolina Agricultural Research

S Cal Ac Sc B — Southern California Academy of Sciences. Bulletin

S Calif Law Rev — Southern California Law Review

S Cal Law R — Southern California Law Review

S Cal L Rev — Southern California Law Review

S CA LR — Southern California Law Review

Sc Am — Scientific American

SCAMA — Scientific American

Sc Am Sup — Scientific American. Supplement

Scan — Scandinavian Studies

Scan — Scandinavica

Scand — Scandinavica

Scand Actuar J — Scandinavian Actuarial Journal

Scand Audiol — Scandinavian Audiology

Scand Audiol Suppl — Scandinavian Audiology. Supplement

Scand Ec Hist Rev — Scandinavian Economic History Review

Scand Econ Hist Rev — Scandinavian Economic History Review

Scandinavian Publ Libr Q — Scandinavian Public Library Quarterly

Scandinav J Econ — Scandinavian Journal of Economics

Scand J Clin Lab Invest — Scandinavian Journal of Clinical and Laboratory Investigation

Scand J Clin Lab Invest Suppl — Scandinavian Journal of Clinical and Laboratory Investigation. Supplement

Scand J Dent Res — Scandinavian Journal of Dental Research

Scand J Econ — Scandinavian Journal of Economics

Scand J Gastroenterol — Scandinavian Journal of Gastroenterology

Scand J Gastroenterol Suppl — Scandinavian Journal of Gastroenterology. Supplement

Scand J Haematol — Scandinavian Journal of Haematology

Scand J Haematol Suppl — Scandinavian Journal of Haematology. Supplement

Scand J Haematol Suppl Ser Haematol — Scandinavian Journal of Haematology. Supplement. Series Haematological

Scand J Immunol — Scandinavian Journal of Immunology

Scand J Immunol Suppl — Scandinavian Journal of Immunology. Supplement

Scand J Infect Dis — Scandinavian Journal of Infectious Diseases

Scand J Infect Dis Suppl — Scandinavian Journal of Infectious Diseases. Supplement

Scand J Metall — Scandinavian Journal of Metallurgy

Scand J Plast Reconstr Surg — Scandinavian Journal of Plastic and Reconstructive Surgery

Scand J Plast Reconstr Surg Suppl — Scandinavian Journal of Plastic and Reconstructive Surgery. Supplement

Scand J Plast Recon Surg — Scandinavian Journal of Plastic and Reconstructive Surgery

Scand J Psychol — Scandinavian Journal of Psychology

Scand J Rehabil Med — Scandinavian Journal of Rehabilitation Medicine

Scand J Rehabil Med Suppl — Scandinavian Journal of Rehabilitation Medicine. Supplement

Scand J Respir Dis — Scandinavian Journal of Respiratory Diseases

Scand J Respir Dis Suppl — Scandinavian Journal of Respiratory Diseases. Supplement

Scand J Rheumatol — Scandinavian Journal of Rheumatology

Scand J Rheumatol Suppl — Scandinavian Journal of Rheumatology. Supplement

Scand J Soc Med — Scandinavian Journal of Social Medicine

Scand J Soc Med Suppl — Scandinavian Journal of Social Medicine. Supplement

Scand J St — Scandinavian Journal of Statistics

Scand J Statist — Scandinavian Journal of Statistics. Theory and Applications

Scand J Stat Theory and Appl — Scandinavian Journal of Statistics. Theory and Applications

Scand J Thorac Cardiovasc Surg — Scandinavian Journal of Thoracic and Cardiovascular Surgery

Scand J Thorac Cardiovasc Surg Suppl — Scandinavian Journal of Thoracic and Cardiovascular Surgery. Supplement

Scand J Urol Nephrol — Scandinavian Journal of Urology and Nephrology

Scand J Urol Nephrol Suppl — Scandinavian Journal of Urology and Nephrology. Supplement

Scand J Work Envir Hlth — Scandinavian Journal of Work Environment and Health

Scand J Work Environ Health — Scandinavian Journal of Work Environment and Health

Scand Oil-Gas Mag — Scandinavian Oil-Gas Magazine

Scand Paint Printing Ink Res Inst Rept — Scandinavian Paint and Printing Ink Research Institute. Reports

Scand Pol Stud — Scandinavian Political Studies

Scand Public Lib Q — Scandinavian Public Library Quarterly

Scand R — Scandinavian Review

Scand Refrig — Scandinavian Refrigeration [*Norway*]

Scand Stud — Scandinavian Studies

Scand Stud in L — Scandinavian Studies in Law

Scand Stud Law — Scandinavian Studies in Law

Scand Yb — Scandinavian Yearbook

Scan Electron Microsc — Scanning Electron Microscopy

Scanning Electron Microsc — Scanning Electron Microscopy

Scan R — Scandinavian Review

SCAR — Scandinavian Review

Scarborough Dist Archaeol Soc Res Rep — Scarborough District Archaeological Society. Research Reports

Sc As Trinidad Pr — Scientific Association of Trinidad. Proceedings

SCathol — Studia Catholica

SCAUA — Scientific Australian

SCauc — Studia Caucasica

Sc Azione — Scuola in Azione

SCB — South Central Bulletin

SCB — Studii si Cercetari de Bibliologie

S & C Bank — Standard and Chartered Review [*Formerly, Standard Bank Review*] [*Later, Standard Chartered Review*]

SCBOA — Studii si Cercetari de Biologie. Seria Botanica

SCBUB — Sierra Club. Bulletin

SCBZA — Studii si Cercetari de Biologie. Seria Zoologie

SCC — Science Fiction Chronicle

ScCatt — Scuola Cattolica

SCCBS — Science Council of Canada. Background Study

Sc Conspectus — Science Conspectus

SCCR — Science Council of Canada. Report

SCC Spec — Soap/Cosmetics/Chemical Specialties

SCCSS — Science Council of Canada. Special Study

SCCWRP TR — SCCWRP (Southern California Coastal Water Research Project). TR
SC Dent J — South Carolina Dental Journal
SCDI — Science Dimension
SCDIA — Science Digest [*Chicago*]
SC Div Geol Geol Notes — South Carolina. Division of Geology. Geologic Notes
SC Div Geol Miner Resour Ser — South Carolina. Division of Geology. Mineral Resources Series
SC Div Geol Misc Rep — South Carolina. Division of Geology. Miscellaneous Report
SC Div Geology Mineral Industries Lab Monthly Bull — South Carolina. Division of Geology. Mineral Industries Laboratory. Monthly Bulletin
ScE — Sciences Ecclesiastiques [*Montreal-Brussels*]
SCEAB — Studii si Cercetari de Astronomie
SCECA — Studii si Cercetari de Chimie
ScEccl — Sciences Ecclesiastiques
SCEDA — Studii si Cercetari de Endocrinologie
SCEEA — Studii si Cercetari de Energetica si Electrotehnica
SCEFA — Studii si Cercetari de Fizica
Scen — Scenario
SCENA — Science and Engineering
Scenic Trips Geol Past — Scenic Trips to the Geologic Past
ScEs — Science et Esprit
SCF — Science Fantasy
SCFO — Science Forum
SCFOA — Schiffbauforschung
SCFOB — Science Forum
SCFZA — Studii si Cercetari de Fiziologie
Sc G — Science Gossip
SCGGA — Studii si Cercetari de Geologie, Geofizica, si Geografie. Seria Geologie
SCH — Scherl and Roth Orchestra News
Sch — Scholastik
Sch — School [*Toronto*]
SCh — Sources Chretiennes
Sch Activities — School Activities
Sch Arts — School Arts Magazine
Sch Arts M — School Arts Magazine
Schatzkammer — Schatzkammer der Deutschen Sprachlehre. Dichtung und Geschichte
Sch Bell — School Bell
Sch Coach — Scholastic Coach
Sch & Com — School and Community
Sch Community News — School and Community News
Sch Counsel — School Counselor
Sch Days — School Days
Sch Ed — School and Home Education [*Illinois*]
Sched Discounts Differentials Serv Charges Applying Wheat — Schedule of Discounts, Differentials, and Service Charges Applying to Wheat
Sch (El Ed) — School (Toronto) (Elementary Edition)
Sch Eng Bull NC State Univ — School of Engineering. Bulletin. North Carolina State University
Sch Exec — School Executive
Sch Executives M — School Executives Magazine
SchF — Schultexte aus Fara
SCHGM — South Carolina Historical and Genealogical Magazine
SChH — Studies in Church History
SCHHA — Schiff und Hafen
Sch Health Rev — School Health Review
Sch and Home — School and Home
Schiffstechnik — Schiffstechnik. Forschungshefte fuer Schiffbau und Schiffsmaschinenbau
Schild Steier — Schild von Steier. Beitraege zur Steierischen Vor- und Fruehgeschichte und Muenzkunde
SC His M — South Carolina Historical and Genealogical Magazine
SC Hist Assn Proc — South Carolina Historical Association. Proceedings
SC Hist Mag — South Carolina Historical Magazine
Schizophr Bull — Schizophrenia Bulletin
Schizophr Syndr — Schizophrenic Syndrome
Schizophr Syndr Annu Rev — Schizophrenic Syndrome: An Annual Review
Schlachtofwes Lebensmittelueberwach — Schlachtofwesen Lebensmittelueberwachung
Sch L Bull — School Law Bulletin
Schleif Polier Oberflaechentech — Schleif-, Polier-, und Oberflaechentechnik
Schleif Poliertech (Hoya Weser Ger) — Schleif- und Poliertechnik (Hoya-Weser, Germany)
Schles Ges Jber — Schlesische Gesellschaft fuer Vaterlaendische Kultur. Jahres-Bericht
Schlesw-Holst Bienenztg — Schleswig-Holsteinisches Bienenzeitung
Schleswig Holsteinisches Aerztebl — Schleswig-Holsteinisches Aerzteblatt
Sch Lib — School Librarian
Sch Lib — School Libraries
Sch Lib Assn Calif Bul — School Library Association of California. Bulletin
Sch Lib Can — School Libraries in Canada
Sch Lib J — School Library Journal

Sch Lib Med N — School Library-Media News
Sch Libn — School Librarian
Sch Libr — School Libraries
Sch Lib R — School Library Review and Educational Record
Sch Libr Bull — School Library Bulletin
Sch Librn — School Librarian and School Library Review [*Later, School Librarian*]
Schlief-Poliertech — Schlief- und Poliertechnik [*West Germany*]
Sch Life — School Life
Sch M — Schweizer Monatshefte
SCHM — South Carolina Historical and Genealogical Magazine
Sch Manag — School Management
Sch Manage — School Management Bulletin
Sch Management — School Management
Sch Management Bul — School Management Bulletin
Sch Media Q — School Media Quarterly
Schmerz Narkose Anaesth — Schmerz. Narkose-Anaesthesie
Sch Mgt — School Management
Schmierstoffe Schmierungstech — Schmierstoffe und Schmierungstechnik [*East Germany*]
Schmierst Schmierungstech — Schmierstoffe und Schmierungstechnik
Schmiertech Tribol — Schmiertechnik und Tribologie
Sch Mines Q — School of Mines Quarterly
Schmollers Jahrb — Schmollers Jahrbuch fuer Gesetzgebung, Verwaltung und Volkswirtschaft im Deutschen Reiche
Sch Mus — School Music
Sch MZ — Schweizerische Musikzeitung
SCHND — Soon Chun Hyang Taehak Nonmunjip
Schneeberger Hb — Schneeberger Heimatbuechlein
Schnell Inf Hydraul & Pneum — Schnell Informationen Hydraulik und Pneumatik
Schnurpfeils Rev Glass Works — Schnurpfeil's Review for Glass Works
Schoenberg Inst — Arnold Schoenberg Institute. Journal
Schol — Scholastik. Vierteljahresschrift fuer Theologie und Philosophie
Scholarly Pub — Scholarly Publishing
Scholar Pub — Scholarly Publishing
Scholastic — Senior Scholastic [*Teacher Edition*]
Scholastic D — Scholastic Debater
Schol Coach — Scholastic Coach
Schol S — Scholia Satyrica
Schol Teach — Scholastic Teacher
Schol Teach JH/SH Ed — Scholastic Teacher. Junior/Senior High Teacher's Edition
School Arts M — School Arts Magazine
School & Col — School and College
School Fam — School Family
School Law Bul (Univ NC) — School Law Bulletin (University of North Carolina)
School Lib — School Libraries
Schoolmens W Univ PA Proc — Schoolmen's Week. University of Pennsylvania. Proceedings
School Mus — School Musician
School Rev — School Review. A Journal of Secondary Education
School and Soc — School and Society
Schopenhauer-Jahr — Schopenhauer-Jahrbuch
Schopenhauer-Jahrb — Schopenhauer-Jahrbuch
Schott Inf — Schott Information
SchP — Scholarly Publishing
Sch & Parent — School and Parent
SCHPB — Bulletin et Memoires. Societe des Chirurgiens de Paris
Sch Pharm Bull Univ Wis Ext Div — School of Pharmacy. Bulletin. University of Wisconsin. Extension Division
Sch R — School Review
SchR — Schweizer Rundschau
Sch Rev — School Review
Schr Geb Brennst Geol — Schriften aus dem Gebiet der Brennstoff-Geologie
Schriftenr Aerztl Fortbild — Schriftenreihe der Aerztlichen Fortbildung
Schriftenr Agrarwiss Fak Univ Kiel — Schriftenreihe. Agrarwissenschaftliche Fakultaet. Universitaet Kiel
Schriften Bayer Landesamt Wasserwirt — Schriftenreihe. Bayerisches Landesamt fuer Wasserwirtschaft
Schriftenr Bundesminist Wiss Forsch Forsch Bild — Schriftenreihe. Bundesminister fuer Wissenschaftliche Forschung. Forschung und Bildung [*West Germany*]
Schriftenr Bundesminist Wiss Forsch (Ger) Radionuklide — Schriftenreihe. Bundesminister fuer Wissenschaftliche Forschung (West Germany). Radionuklide
Schriftenr Bundesminist Wiss Forsch (Ger) Strahlenschutz — Schriftenreihe. Bundesminister fuer Wissenschaftliche Forschung (West Germany). Strahlenschutz
Schriftenr Bundesminist Wiss Forsch Kernenergierecht — Schriftenreihe. Bundesminister fuer Wissenschaftliche Forschung. Kernenergierecht [*West Germany*]
Schriftenr Bundesminist Wiss Forsch Strahlenschutz — Schriftenreihe. Bundesminister fuer Wissenschaftliche Forschung. Strahlenschutz

Schriftenr Bundesverb Dtsch Kalkind — Schriftenreihe. Bundesverband der Deutschen Kalkindustrie

Schriften Dtsch Atomforums — Schriftenreihe des Deutschen Atomforums

Schriftenreihe Didaktik Math — Schriftenreihe Didaktik der Mathematik

Schriftenreihe Math — Schriftenreihe fuer Mathematik

Schriftenreihe Math Inst Univ Muenster — Schriftenreihe. Mathematisches Institut. Universitaet Muenster

Schriftenreihe Rechenzentrum Univ Koeln — Schriftenreihe des Rechenzentrums. Universitaet zu Koeln

Schriftenreihe Zentralinst Math Mech — Schriftenreihe. Zentralinstitut fuer Mathematik und Mechanik

Schriften Forschungsgem Schweiz Lackfabr — Schriftenreihe. Forschungsgemeinschaft Schweizerischer Lackfabrikanten

Schriftenr Forstl Fak Univ Goettingen — Schriftenreihe. Forstliche Fakultaet. Universitaet Goettingen und Mitteilungen. Niedersaechsische Forstliche Versuchsanstalt

Schriften Intensivmed Notfallmed Anaesthesiol — Schriftenreihe Intensivmedizin, Notfallmedizin, Anaesthesiologie

Schriften Int Ges Nahr Vitalst Forsch eV — Schriftenreihe. Internationale Gesellschaft fuer Nahrungs- und Vitalstoff-Forschung eV

Schriftenr Landesanst Immissionischutz — Schriftenreihe. Landesanstalt fuer Immissionisschutz [West Germany]

Schriftenr Landschaftspflege Naturschutz — Schriftenreihe fuer Landschaftspflege und Naturschutz

Schriftenr Lebensmittelchem Lebensmittelqual — Schriftenreihe. Lebensmittelchemie, Lebensmittelqualitaet

Schriftenr Neurol — Schriftenreihe Neurologie

Schriftenr Neurol-Neurol Ser — Schriftenreihe Neurologie-Neurology Series

Schriftenr Oesterr Wasserwirtschaftsverb — Schriftenreihe. Oesterreichischer Wasserwirtschaftsverband

Schriftenr Schweissen Schneiden Ber — Schriftenreihe Schweissen Schneiden. Bericht

Schriftenr Theor Prax Med Psychol — Schriftenreihe zur Theorie und Praxis der Medizinischen Psychologie

Schriftenr Vegetationskd — Schriftenreihe fuer Vegetationskunde

Schriftenr Versuchstierkd — Schriftenreihe Versuchstierkunde

Schriftenr Ver Wasser Boden Lufthyg — Schriftenreihe. Verein fuer Wasser, Boden, und Lufthygiene

Schriftenr Zementind — Schriftenreihe der Zementindustrie

Schriften Wirtschaftwiss Forsch — Schriften zur Wirtschaftwissenschaftlichen Forschung

Schrift Naturf Gesellsch Kopenhagen — Schriften. Naturforschende Gesellschaft zu Kopenhagen

Schrifttum Agrarwirt — Schrifttum der Agrarwirtschaft

Schr Math Inst Univ Muenster 2 — Schriftenreihe. Mathematisches Institut der Universitaet Muenster. 2 Serie

Schr Math Inst Univ Munster — Schriftenreihe. Mathematisches Institut. Universitaet Muenster

Schr Naturwiss Ver Schleswig-Holstein — Schriften. Naturwissenschaftlicher Verein fuer Schleswig-Holstein

Schrreihe Forstl Fak Univ Goettingen — Schriftenreihe. Forstliche Fakultaet. Universitaet Goettingen

Schr Ver Verbr Naturwiss Kennt Wien — Schriften. Verein zur Verbreitung Naturwissenschaftlicher Kenntnisse in Wien

SCHSA — Soap and Chemical Specialties [Later, Soap/Cosmetics/Chemical Specialties]

Sch Sci & Math — School Science and Mathematics

Sch Sci Rev — School Science Review [England]

Sch (Sec Ed) — School (Toronto) (Secondary Edition)

Sch Shop — School Shop

Sch & Soc — School and Society

Sch Trust — School Trustee

SCHVD — Sachverhalte

SCHWA — Schweisstechnik Soudure

Schwaeb Imkerkal — Schwaebischer Imkerkalender

Schw A Neur — Schweizer Archiv fuer Neurologie, Neurochirurgie, und Psychiatrie

SchwArchV — Schweizerisches Archiv fuer Volkskunde

Schweiz Aerzteztg — Schweizerische Aerztezeitung

Schweiz Alum Rundsch — Schweizer Aluminium Rundschau

Schweiz Anst Forstl Versuchswes Mitt — Schweizerische Anstalt fuer das Forstliche Versuchswesen. Mitteilungen

Schweiz Apoth Ztg — Schweizerische Apotheker-Zeitung

Schweiz Arch — Schweizer Archiv

Schweiz Arch Angew Wiss Tech — Schweizer Archiv fuer Angewandte Wissenschaft und Technik

Schweiz Archiv f Volksk — Schweizerisches Archiv fuer Volkskunde

Schweiz Arch Neurol Neurochir Psychiatr — Schweizer Archiv fuer Neurologie, Neurochirurgie, und Psychiatrie

Schweiz Arch Neurol Psychiatr — Schweizer Archiv fuer Neurologie und Psychiatrie

Schweiz Arch Tierh — Schweizer Archiv fuer Tierheilkunde

Schweiz Arch Tierh (Bern) — Schweizerisches Archiv fuer Tierheilkunde und Tierzucht (Bern)

Schweiz Arch Tierheilkd — Schweizer Archiv fuer Tierheilkunde

Schweiz Arch Verkehrswiss und Verkehrspol — Schweizerisches Archiv fuer Verkehrswissenschaft und Verkehrspolitik

Schweiz Bauztg — Schweizerische Bauzeitung

Schweiz Beitr Dendrol — Schweizerische Beitrage zur Dendrologie

Schweiz Bienen-Ztg — Schweizerische Bienen-Zeitung

Schweiz Bl Heiz Lueft — Schweizerische Blaetter fuer Heizung und Lueftung [Switzerland]

Schweiz Brau-Rundsch — Schweizerische Brauerei-Rundschau

Schweiz Chem Ztg — Schweizerische Chemiker-Zeitung

Schweiz Chem Ztg Tech Ind — Schweizer Chemiker-Zeitung Technik-Industrie

Schweiz Elektrotech Z — Schweizerische Elektrotechnische Zeitschrift

Schweizer Archiv Verkehrswiss u -Polit — Schweizerisches Archiv fuer Verkehrswissenschaft und Verkehrspolitik

Schweizer Arch Tierheilk — Schweizer Archiv fuer Tierheilkunde

Schweizer Arch Volksk — Schweizer Archiv fuer Volkskunde

Schweizer Mineralog u Petrog Mitt — Schweizerische Mineralogische und Petrographische Mitteilungen

Schweizer Natschutz — Schweizer Naturschutz

Schweizer Palaeont Abh Mem Suisses Paleontologie — Schweizerische Palaeontologische Abhandlungen. Memoires Suisses de Palaeontologie

Schweizer Z Soziol — Schweizerische Zeitschrift fuer Soziologie

Schweizer Z Volkswirtsch u Statist — Schweizerische Zeitschrift fuer Volkswirtschaft und Statistik

Schweiz Gaertnerztg — Schweizerische Gaertnerzeitung

Schweiz Ing & Archit — Schweizer Ingenieur und Architekt

Schweiz Landtech — Schweizer Landtechnik

Schweiz Landw Forsch — Schweizerische Landwirtschaftliche Forschung

Schweiz Landwirtsch Forsch Rech Agron Suisse — Schweizerische Landwirtschaftliche Forschung/La Recherche Agronomique en Suisse

Schweiz Landwirtsch Monatsh — Schweizerische Landwirtschaftliche Monatshefte

Schweiz Landw Mh — Schweizerische Landwirtschaftliche Monatshefte

Schweiz Med Wochenschr — Schweizerische Medizinische Wochenschrift

Schweiz Med Wochenschr Suppl — Schweizerische Medizinische Wochenschrift. Supplementum

Schweiz Med Wschr — Schweizerische Medizinische Wochenschrift

Schweiz Mh — Schweizer Monatshefte

Schweiz Mhefte Pol Wirt Kultur — Schweizer Monatshefte. Zeitschrift fuer Politik, Wirtschaft, Kultur

Schweiz Milchwirtsch Forsch — Schweizerische Milchwirtschaftliche Forschung

Schweiz Milchztg — Schweizerische Milchzeitung

Schweiz Mineral Petrogr Mitt — Schweizerische Mineralogische und Petrographische Mitteilungen

Schweiz Monatsschr Zahnheilkd — Schweizerische Monatsschrift fuer Zahnheilkunde

Schweiz Monatsschr Zahnmed — Schweizerische Monatsschrift fuer Zahnmedizin

Schweiz Muenzbl — Schweizer Muenzblaetter [Switzerland]

Schweiz Mus — Schweizerische Musikzeitung

Schweiz Naturf Ges Verh — Schweizerische Naturforschende Gesellschaft. Verhandlungen

Schweiz Naturschutz Prot Nat — Schweizer Naturschutz. Protection de la Nature

Schweiz Palaeontol Abh — Schweizerische Palaeontologische Abhandlungen

Schweiz Palaeontol Abh-Mem Suisse Palaeontol — Schweizerische Palaeontologische Abhandlungen. Memoires Suisses de Palaeontologie

Schweiz Photorundsch — Schweizerische Photorundschau

Schweiz Photo Ztg — Schweizerische Photo-Zeitung

Schweiz Rdsch — Schweizer Rundschau

Schweiz Strahler — Schweizer Strahler

Schweiz Tech — Schweizerische Technikerzeitung [Switzerland]

Schweiz Tech Z — Schweizerische Technische Zeitschrift [Switzerland]

Schweiz Ver Atomenerg Bull — Schweizerische Vereinigung fuer Atomenergie. Bulletin [Switzerland]

Schweiz Ver Gas-Wasserfachmaennern Monatsbull — Schweizerische Verein von Gas- und Wasserfachmaennern. Monatsbulletin [Switzerland]

Schweiz Ver Lack Farbenchem Bull — Schweizerische Vereinigung der Lack- und Farbenchemiker. Bulletin

Schweiz Volkskd — Schweizer Volkskunde

Schweiz Wochenschr Chem Pharm — Schweizerische Wochenschrift fuer Chemie und Pharmacie

Schweiz Wochenschr Pharm — Schweizerische Wochenschrift fuer Pharmacie

Schweiz Wohnschr Chem u Pharm — Schweizerische Wochenschrift fuer Chemie und Pharmacie

Schweiz Z Allg Path Bakt — Schweizerische Zeitschrift fuer Allgemeine Pathologie und Bakteriologie

Schweiz Z Allg Pathol Bakterol — Schweizerische Zeitschrift fuer Allgemeine Pathologie und Bakteriologie

Schweiz Z Biochem — Schweizerische Zeitschrift fuer Biochemie

Schweiz Z Forstwes — Schweizerische Zeitschrift fuer Forstwesen

Schweiz Z Gesch — Schweizerische Zeitschrift fuer Geschichte

Schweiz Z Gynaekol Geburtshilfe — Schweizerische Zeitschrift fuer Gynaekologie und Geburtshilfe

Schweiz Z Gynaekol Geburtshilfe Suppl — Schweizerische Zeitschrift fuer Gynaekologie und Geburtshilfe. Supplementum

Schweiz Z Hydrol — Schweizerische Zeitschrift fuer Hydrologie
Schweiz Z Obst-u Weinb — Schweizerische Zeitschrift fuer Obst- und Weinbau
Schweiz Z Obst-Weinbau — Schweizerische Zeitschrift fuer Obst- und Weinbau
Schweiz Z Pathol Bakteriol — Schweizerische Zeitschrift fuer Pathologie und Bakteriologie
Schweiz Z Pharm — Schweizerische Zeitschrift fuer Pharmacie
Schweiz Z Pilzkd — Schweizerische Zeitschrift fuer Pilzkunde
Schweiz Z Pilzkd Bull Suisse Mycol — Schweizerische Zeitschrift fuer Pilzkunde. Bulletin Suisse de Mycologie
Schweiz Z Psychol Anwend — Schweizerische Zeitschrift fuer Psychologie und Ihre Anwendungen
Schweiz Z Sozialversicherung — Schweizerische Zeitschrift fuer Sozialversicherung
Schweiz Z Sportmed — Schweizerische Zeitschrift fuer Sportmedizin
Schweiz Z Tuberk Pneumonol — Schweizerische Zeitschrift fuer Tuberkulose und Pneumonologie
Schweiz Z Verkehrswirt — Schweizerische Zeitschrift fuer Verkehrswirtschaft
Schweiz Z Vermess Photogramm Kulturtech — Schweizerische Zeitschrift fuer Vermessung, Photogrammetrie, und Kulturtechnik
Schweiz Z Volkswirt und Statis — Schweizerische Zeitschrift fuer Volkswirtschaft und Statistik
Schwenk — Schwenckfeldiana
Schwest Rev — Schwestern Revue
Schwiez Z Path Bakt — Schweizerische Zeitschrift fuer Pathologie und Bakteriologie
SchwKiZ — Schweizerische Kirchenzeitung [*Lucerne*]
SchwKZ — Schweizerische Kirchenzeitung [*Lucerne*]
SchwM — Schweizer Monatshefte
Schw Med Wo — Schweizerische Medizinische Wochenschrift
SchwMH — Schweizer Monatshefte [*Zurich*]
Schw Musikz — Schweizerische Musikzeitung/Revue Musicale Suisse
SchwRundschau — Schweizer Rundschau
SchwV — Schweizer Volkskunde
Schw Z Gesc — Schweizerische Zeitschrift fuer Geschichte
Schw Z Psyc — Schweizerische Zeitschrift fuer Psychologie und Ihre Anwendungen
Schw Z Soz — Schweizerische Zeitschrift fuer Sozialversicherung
SCI — Science
SCI — Science Citation Index
SCI — Scripta Classica Israelica
ScI — Scripta Islandica
SciA — Scientific American
SCIA — Studii si Cercetari de Istoria Artei. Seria Arta Plastica
SciAb — Science Abstracts
Sci Abstr China Biol Sci — Science Abstracts of China. Biological Sciences
Sci Abstr China Chem Chem Technol — Science Abstracts of China. Chemistry and Chemical Technology
Sci Abstr China Math Phys Sci — Science Abstracts of China. Mathematical and Physical Sciences
Sci Abstr China Med — Science Abstracts of China. Medicine
Sci Abstr China Tech Sci — Science Abstracts of China. Technical Sciences
SCIADJ — Centro Internacional de Agricultura Tropical [*CIAT*]. Series Seminars
Sci Adv Mater Process Eng Proc — Science of Advanced Materials and Process Engineering. Proceedings
Sci Adv Mater Process Eng Q — Science of Advanced Materials and Process Engineering. Quarterly [*United States*]
Sci Aer Aerotech — Science Aerienne et l'Aerotechnique
Sci Ag — Scientific Agriculture
Sci Agr — Scientific Agriculture
Sci Agric — Science in Agriculture
Sci Agric Bohemoslov — Scientia Agriculturae Bohemoslovaca
Sci Agric PA State Univ Agric Exp Stn — Science in Agriculture. Pennsylvania State University. Agricultural Experiment Station
Sci Agron Rennes — Sciences Agronomiques Rennes
Sci Alaska Proc Alaskan Sci Conf — Science in Alaska. Proceedings. Alaskan Science Conference
Sci Aliment — Scienza dell'Alimentazione
Sci Am — Scientific American
Sci Amer — Scientific American
Sci Am Monthly — Scientific American Monthly
Sci Am S — Scientific American. Supplement
Sci Appliance — Science and Appliance
SciArch — Science and Archaeology
Sci & Archaeol — Science and Archaeology
Sci Atmos Sin — Scientia Atmospherica Sinica
Sci Aust — Scientific Australian
Sci & Aust Technol — Science and Australian Technology
Sci Aust Technol — Science and Australian Technology
Sci Avenir — Sciences et Avenir [*France*]
SCIBA — Studii si Cercetari de Inframicrobiologie
Sci Basis Med — Scientific Basis of Medicine
Sci Basis Med Annu Rev — Scientific Basis of Medical Annual Reviews
Sci Biol J — Science of Biology Journal

Sci Biol Ser — Science of Biology Series
Sci Bk — Science Books and Films
Sci Bks — Science Books
Sci Bks & Films — Science Books and Films
Sci Bul — Science Bulletin for Teachers in Secondary Schools
Sci Bull Academ Min Metall (Krakow) Geol — Scientific Bulletins. Academy of Mining and Metallurgy (Krakow). Geology
Sci Bull Acad Min Metall (Krakow) Ceram — Scientific Bulletins. Academy of Mining and Metallurgy (Krakow). Ceramics
Sci Bull Acad Min Metall (Krakow) Electrif Mech Min Metall — Scientific Bulletins. Academy of Mining and Metallurgy (Krakow). Electrification and Mechanization in Mining and Metallurgy
Sci Bull Acad Min Metall (Krakow) Math Phys Chem — Scientific Bulletins. Academy of Mining and Metallurgy (Krakow). Mathematics, Physics, Chemistry
Sci Bull Acad Min Metall (Krakow) Metall Foundry Pract — Scientific Bulletins. Academy of Mining and Metallurgy (Krakow). Metallurgy and Foundry Practice
Sci Bull Acad Min Metall (Krakow) Min — Scientific Bulletins. Academy of Mining and Metallurgy (Krakow). Mining
Sci Bull Acad Min Metall (Krakow) Spec Ser — Scientific Bulletins. Academy of Mining and Metallurgy (Krakow). Special Series
Sci Bull At Energy New Energ Organ — Scientific Bulletin. Atomic Energy and New Energies Organization
Sci Bull Can Cent Miner Energy Technol — Scientific Bulletin. Canada Centre for Mineral and Energy Technology
Sci Bull Coll Agric Univ Ryukyus Okinawa — Science Bulletin. College of Agriculture. University of Ryukyus. Okinawa
Sci Bull Cotton Res Inst Sindos — Science Bulletin. Cotton Research Institute. Sindos
Sci Bull Dep Agric For Un S Afr — Science Bulletin. Department of Agriculture and Forestry. Union of South Africa
Sci Bull Dep Agric NSW — Science Bulletin. Department of Agriculture. New South Wales
Sci Bull Dept Agr NSW — Science Bulletin. Department of Agriculture. New South Wales
Sci Bull Dept Agr S Afr — Science Bulletin. Department of Agriculture. South Africa
Sci Bull Fac Agric Kyushu Univ — Science Bulletin. Faculty of Agriculture. Kyushu University
Sci Bull Fac Agr Kyushu Univ — Science Bulletin. Faculty of Agriculture. Kyushu University
Sci Bull Fac Ed Nagasaki Univ — Science Bulletin. Faculty of Education. Nagasaki University
Sci Bull Fac Educ Nagasaki Univ — Science Bulletin. Faculty of Education. Nagasaki University
Sci Bull Repub S Afr Dept Agr Tech Serv — Science Bulletin. Republic of South Africa. Department of Agricultural Technical Services
Sci Bull Sci Found Philipp — Science Bulletin. Science Foundation of the Philippines
Sci Bull Stanislaw Staszic Univ Min Metall Ceram — Scientific Bulletins. Stanislaw Staszic University of Mining and Metallurgy. Ceramics
Sci Bull Stanislaw Staszic Univ Min Metall Geol — Scientific Bulletins. Stanislaw Staszic University of Mining and Metallurgy. Geology
Sci Bull Stanislaw Staszic Univ Min Metall Math Phys Chem — Scientific Bulletins. Stanislaw Staszic University of Mining and Metallurgy. Mathematics, Physics, Chemistry
Sci Bull Stanislaw Staszic Univ Min Metall Min — Scientific Bulletins. Stanislaw Staszic University of Mining and Metallurgy. Mining
Sci Bull Stanislaw Staszic Univ Min Metall Sozol Sozotech — Scientific Bulletins. Stanislaw Staszic University of Mining and Metallurgy. Sozology and Sozotechnics
Sci Bull Stanislaw Staszic Univ Min Metall Spec Ser — Scientific Bulletins. Stanislaw Staszic University of Mining and Metallurgy. Special Series
Sci Bull Univ Kans — Science Bulletin. University of Kansas
Sci Bull Univ Kansas — Science Bulletin. Kansas University
Sci Ceram — Science of Ceramics [*England*]
Sci & Child — Science and Children
Sci Chron (Karachi) — Science Chronicle (Karachi)
Sci Cit Ind — Science Citation Index
Sci Comput Program — Science of Computer Programming
Sci Comput Programming — Science of Computer Programming
Sci Conf Ges Dtsch Naturforsch Aerzte — Scientific Conference. Gesellschaft Deutscher Naturforscher und Aerzte
Sci Counc Afr South Sahara Publ — Scientific Council for Africa South of the Sahara. Publication
Sci Counc Jap Annu Rep — Science Council of Japan. Annual Report
Sci Couns — Science Counselor
Sci and Cult — Science and Culture
Sci Cult — Science and Culture
Sci Cult (New Delhi) — Science and Culture (New Delhi)
SCID-A — Studies in Comparative International Development
Sci Dep Bull United Plant Assoc South India — Scientific Department Bulletin. United Planters' Association of Southern India
Sci Dig — Science Digest
Sci Digest — Science Digest

Sci Diliman — Science Diliman
Sci Dimens — Science Dimension
Sci Dimension — Science Dimension
SCIEA — Science
Sci Ed — Science Education
Sci Ed News — Science Education Newsletter
Sci Educ — Science Education
Sci 80 (Eighty) — Science 80 (Eighty)
Sci Elec — Scientia Electrica
Sci Electr — Scientia Electrica
Science — Science for People
Science Ed — Science Education
Science et Industrie Phot — Science et Industries Photographiques
Science N L — Science News Letter
Science Prog — Science Progress
Sciences Assoc Fr Av Sci — Sciences. Association Francaise pour l'Avancement des Sciences
Sciences NY Acad Sci — Sciences. New York Academy of Sciences
Sciences Pol — Sciences Politiques
Science and Tech Libs — Science and Technology Libraries
Sciencia Med — Sciencia Medica
Sci Eng — Science and Engineering
Sci and Eng Rep Def Acad — Scientific and Engineering Reports. Defense Academy
Sci and Eng Rep Natl Def Acad (Jpn) — Scientific and Engineering Reports. National Defense Academy (Japanese)
Sci & Eng Rep Saitama Univ C — Science and Engineering Reports. Saitama University. Series C
Sci and Eng Rep Saitama Univ Ser C — Science and Engineering Reports. Saitama University. Series C
Sci Eng Rev Doshisha Univ — Science and Engineering Review. Doshisha University
Sci Enseign Sci — Sciences et l'Enseignement des Sciences
Scient Agric — Scientific Agriculture
Scient Am — Scientific American
Scient Amer — Scientific American
Scient Am Suppl — Scientific American. Supplement
Scient Hort — Scientific Horticulture
Scientia Genet — Scientia Genetica
Scientiarum Hist — Scientiarum Historia
Scient Instrum — Scientific Instruments
Scient Mon — Scientific Monthly
Scient Month — Scientific Monthly
Scient Pap Coll Gen Educ Tokyo — Scientific Papers. College of General Education. University of Tokyo
Scient Papers Civil Vet Dept (Madras) — Scientific Papers. Civil Veterinary Department (Madras)
Scient Proc R Dubl Soc — Scientific Proceedings. Royal Dublin Society
Scient Rep Fac Agric Okayama Univ — Scientific Reports. Faculty of Agriculture. Okayama University
Scient Rep Govt Inst Infect Dis Tokyo Imp Univ — Scientific Reports. Government Institute for Infectious Diseases. Tokyo Imperial University
Scient Rep Kyoto Prefect Univ Agric — Scientific Reports. Kyoto Prefectural University. Agriculture
Scient Res (Bangladesh) — Scientific Researches (Bangladesh)
Sci Environ — Science and Environment
Scienza Aliment — Scienza dell'Alimentazione
Scienza Tecnol Aliment — Scienza e Tecnologia degli Alimenti
Sci Esprit — Science et Esprit
Sci Exploration — Science Exploration [*Changsha*]
SCIF — Science Forum
Sci Farm — Scienza del Farmaco
Sci Farmer — Science for the Farmer
Sci Fiction Bk Rev Ind — Science Fiction Book Review Index
Sci Fict St — Science Fiction Studies
Sci Forum — Science Forum
SCIGA — Society of Chemical Industry (London). Monograph
SCIGB — Sicherheitsingenieur
Sci Geol Bull — Sciences Geologiques. Bulletin
Sci Geol Bull Inst Geol Univ Louis Pasteur Strasbourg — Sciences Geologiques. Bulletin. Institut de Geologie. Universite Louis Pasteur de Strasbourg [*France*]
Sci Geol S — Scientia Geologica Sinica
Sci Geol Sin — Scientia Geologica Sinica
Sci Gov Rep — Science and Government Report [*United States*]
Sci Govt Rep — Science and Government Report
Sci Hist — Scientiarum Historia
Sci Hort — Scientific Horticulture
Sci Hortic — Scientia Horticulturae
Sci Hum Life — Science of Human Life
SCII — Science in Iceland
Sci Icel — Science in Iceland
Sci Ilus — Science Illustrated
Sci Ind — Science and Industry
Sci Ind Equip Bull — Scientific and Industrial Equipment Bulletin
Sci Ind (Karachi) — Science and Industry (Karachi)

Sci in Ind (Lond) — Science in Industry (London)
Sci Ind (Philips) — Science and Industry (Philips) [*The Netherlands*]
Sci Ind Photogr — Science et Industries Photographiques
Sci Ind Spat — Sciences et Industries Spatiales [*Switzerland*]
Sci Ind Spatiales Space Res Eng Weltraumforsch Ind — Sciences et Industries Spatiales, Space Research and Engineering, Weltraumforschung und Industrie
Sci Inf Notes — Scientific Information Notes
Sci Info N — Scientific Information Notes
Sci Insect Control (Kyoto) — Scientific Insect Control (Kyoto)
Sci Instr — Scientific Instruments
Sci Instrum — Journal of Physics. E: Scientific Instruments
Sci Invest Freshw Salmon Fish Res Scott Home Dep — Scientific Investigations. Freshwater and Salmon Fisheries Research. Scottish Home Department
Sci J — Science Journal
Sci Jour — Science Journal
Sci J Shivaji Univ — Science Journal. Shivaji University
SCIL — Small Computers in Libraries
Sciland — Scienceland
Sci Leafl — Science Leaflet
SCILF — Studii si Cercetari de Istorie Literara si Folclor
Sci Life — Science and Life
Sci Light — Science of Light
Sci Lubr — Scientific Lubrication
Sci Lubr Liq Fuel — Scientific Lubrication and Liquid Fuel
Sci Mac — Science of Machine [*Japan*]
Sci March — Science on the March
Sci Mat — Scienze Matematiche
Sci Mech — Science and Mechanics
Sci Med — Sciences Medicales
Sci Med Ital — Scientia Medica Italica
Sci Med Ital (Engl Ed) — Scientia Medica Italica (English Edition)
Sci Meet — Scientific Meetings
Sci Mo — Scientific Monthly
Sci Monogr Univ Wyo Agric Exp Stn — Science Monograph. University of Wyoming. Agricultural Experiment Station
Sci Monogr Wyo Expl Stn — Science Monograph. Wyoming Experimental Station
Sci N — Science News
SCINA — Science and Culture
Sci Nat — Science et Nature
Sci New Guinea — Science in New Guinea
Sci News — Science News
Sci News (Harmondsworth) — Science News (Harmondsworth)
Sci News Lett — Science News Letter [*United States*]
Sci Nourishment — Science of Nourishment
Sci Nuncius Radiophonicus — Scientiarum Nuncius Radiophonicus
Sci Opin — Scientific Opinion
Sci Orient — Scientia Orientalis
Sci Paed Ex — Scientia Paedagogica Experimentalis
Sci Pap Coll Gen Educ Univ Tokyo — Scientific Papers. College of General Education. University of Tokyo
Sci Pap Coll Gen Educ Univ Tokyo (Biol Part) — Scientific Papers. College of General Education. University of Tokyo (Biological Part)
Sci Paperbacks — Science Paperbacks
Sci Papers College Gen Ed Univ Tokyo — Scientific Papers. College of General Education. University of Tokyo
Sci Papers Prague ICT C — Scientific Papers. Prague Institute of Chemical Technology. Part C. Organic Chemistry and Technology
Sci Pap Fac Eng Tokushima Univ — Scientific Papers. Faculty of Engineering. Tokushima University
Sci Pap Imp Fuel Res Inst (Jpn) — Scientific Papers. Imperial Fuel Research Institute (Japan)
Sci Pap Inst Algol Res Fac Sci Hokkaido Univ — Scientific Papers. Institute of Algological Research. Faculty of Science. Hokkaido University
Sci Pap Inst Chem Technol (Prague) Chem Eng Autom — Scientific Papers. Institute of Chemical Technology (Prague). Chemical Engineering and Automation
Sci Pap Inst Phys and Chem Res — Scientific Papers. Institute of Physical and Chemical Research
Sci Pap Inst Phys Chem Res (Jpn) — Scientific Papers. Institute of Physical and Chemical Research (Japan)
Sci Pap Inst Phys Chem Res (Tokyo) — Scientific Papers. Institute of Physical and Chemical Research (Tokyo)
Sci Pap Osaka Univ — Scientific Papers. Osaka University
Sci Pap Prague Inst Chem Technol Sect Chem Eng — Scientific Papers. Prague Institute of Chemical Technology. Section: Chemical Engineering
Sci Peche — Science et Peche
Sci Peo — Science for People
Sci Peopl — Science for People
Sci Pest Contr — Scientific Pest Control
Sci Pest Control — Scientific Pest Control
Sci Pharm — Scientia Pharmaceutica
Sci Pharm Biol Lorraine — Sciences Pharmaceutiques et Biologiques de Lorraine
Sci Pict — Science Pictorial [*People's Republic of China*]

Sci Pro — Science Progress
Sci Pro — Scientific Progress [*London*]
Sci Proc Cardiff Med Soc — Scientific Proceedings. Cardiff Medical Society
Sci Proc R Dublin Soc — Scientific Proceedings. Royal Dublin Society
Sci Proc R Dublin Soc A — Scientific Proceedings. Royal Dublin Society. Series A
Sci Proc R Dublin Soc Ser A — Scientific Proceedings. Royal Dublin Society. Series A
Sci Proc R Dublin Soc Ser B — Scientific Proceedings. Royal Dublin Society. Series B
Sci Proc Roy Dublin Soc Ser B — Scientific Proceedings. Royal Dublin Society. Series B
Sci Prog — Science Progress
Sci Prog Decouverte — Science Progres Decouverte
Sci Prog (Lond) — Science Progress (London)
Sci Prog (London) — Science Progress (London)
Sci Prog Nat — Science Progres la Nature
Sci Prog (New Haven) — Science in Progress (New Haven)
Sci Prog (Oxf) — Science Progress (Oxford)
Sci Progr — Science Progress
Sci Progr Decouverte — Science Progres Decouverte
Sci Psychoanal — Science and Psychoanalysis
Sci Publ Af — Science and Public Affairs. Bulletin of the Atomic Scientists
Sci Publ Fuji Photo Film C — Scientific Publications. Fuji Photo Film Company Ltd.
Sci Publ Fuji Photo Film Co Ltd — Scientific Publications. Fuji Photo Film Company Limited [*Japan*]
Sci Public Aff Bull At Sci — Science and Public Affairs. Bulletin of the Atomic Scientists
Sci Public Policy — Science and Public Policy
Sci Publ Pol — Science and Public Policy
Sci Publ Sci Mus Minn — Scientific Publications. Science Museum of Minnesota
Sci Publ Sci Mus (St Paul) — Scientific Publications. Science Museum of Minnesota (St. Paul)
Sci Q Natl Univ Peking — Science Quarterly. National University of Peking
SCIRA — Science Review [*Manila*]
S Circular — South Circular
Sci Rec — Science Record
Sci Rec (Chin Ed) — Science Record (Chinese Edition) [*People's Republic of China*]
Sci Rec (Peking) — Science Record (Peking)
Sci Rec S M Kirov Kaz State Univ — Scientific Records. S. M. Kirov Kazakh State University
Sci Rep Agric Coll Norway — Scientific Reports. Agricultural College of Norway
Sci Rep Cent Res Inst Kasauli — Scientific Report. Central Research Institute. Kasauli
Sci Rep College Gen Ed Osaka Univ — Science Reports. College of General Education. Osaka University
Sci Rep Coll Gen Educ Osaka Univ — Science Reports. College of General Education. Osaka University [*Japan*]
Sci Rep Ehime Agric Coll — Scientific Reports. Ehime Agricultural College
Sci Rep Fac Agr Ibaraki Univ — Scientific Report. Faculty of Agriculture. Ibaraki University
Sci Rep Fac Agric Ibaraki Univ — Scientific Report. Faculty of Agriculture. Ibaraki University
Sci Rep Fac Agric Kobe Univ — Science Reports. Faculty of Agriculture. Kobe University
Sci Rep Fac Agric Meijo Univ — Scientific Reports. Faculty of Agriculture. Meijo University
Sci Rep Fac Agr Okayama Univ — Scientific Report. Faculty of Agriculture. Okayama University
Sci Rep Fac Ed Gifu Univ Natur Sci — Science Reports. Faculty of Education. Gifu University. Natural Science
Sci Rep Fac Educ Fukushima Univ — Science Reports. Faculty of Education. Fukushima University [*Japan*]
Sci Rep Fac Educ Gunma Univ — Science Reports. Faculty of Education. Gunma University
Sci Rep Fac Liberal Art Educ Gifu Univ Natur Sci — Science Report. Faculty of Liberal Arts and Education. Gifu University. Natural Science
Sci Rep Fac Sci Ege Univ — Scientific Reports. Faculty of Science. Ege University
Sci Rep Fac Sci Kyushu Univ Geol — Science Reports. Faculty of Science. Kyushu University. Geology [*Japan*]
Sci Rep Gov Inst Infect Dis Tokyo Imp Univ — Scientific Reports. Government Institute for Infectious Diseases. Tokyo Imperial University
Sci Rep Hirosaki Univ — Science Reports. Hirosaki University
Sci Rep Hokkaido Fish Exp Stn — Scientific Reports. Hokkaido Fisheries Experimental Station
Sci Rep Hokkaido Salmon Hatchery — Scientific Reports. Hokkaido Salmon Hatchery
Sci Rep Hoyo Univ Agr — Scientific Report. Hoyo University of Agriculture
Sci Rep Hyogo Univ Agr Fac Agr Kobe Univ — Science Reports. Hyogo University of Agriculture and Faculty of Agriculture. Kobe University
Sci Rep Hyogo Univ Agric — Science Reports. Hyogo University of Agriculture

Sci Rep Hyogo Univ Agric Ser Agric — Science Reports. Hyogo University of Agriculture. Series Agriculture
Sci Rep Hyogo Univ Agric Ser Agric Chem — Science Reports. Hyogo University of Agriculture. Series Agricultural Chemistry
Sci Rep Hyogo Univ Agric Ser Agric Hortic — Science Reports. Hyogo University of Agriculture. Series Agriculture and Horticulture
Sci Rep Hyogo Univ Agric Ser Agric Technol — Science Reports. Hyogo University of Agriculture. Series Agriculture Technology
Sci Rep Hyogo Univ Agric Ser Nat Sci — Science Reports. Hyogo University of Agriculture. Series Natural Science
Sci Rep Hyogo Univ Agric Ser Plant Prot — Science Reports. Hyogo University of Agriculture. Series Plant Protection
Sci Rep Hyogo Univ Agric Ser Zootech Sci — Science Reports. Hyogo University of Agriculture. Series Zootechnical Science
Sci Rep (India) — Science Reporter (India)
Sci Rep Indian Agric Res Inst — Scientific Reports. Indian Agricultural Research Institute
Sci Rep Inter-Union Comm Geodyn — Scientific Report. Inter-Union Commission on Geodynamics
Sci Rep Ist Super Sanita — Scientific Reports. Istituto Superiore di Sanita
Sci Rep Kagawa Prefect Fish Exp Stn — Scientific Reports. Kagawa Prefectural Fisheries Experimental Station
Sci Rep Kagoshima Univ — Science Reports. Kagoshima University
Sci Rep Kanazawa Univ — Science Reports. Kanazawa University
Sci Rep Kanazawa Univ Part II Biol Geol — Science Reports. Kanazawa University. Part II. Biology and Geology
Sci Rep Kyoto Prefect Univ Agric — Scientific Reports. Kyoto Prefectural University. Agriculture
Sci Rep Kyoto Prefect Univ Nat Sci Life Sci — Scientific Reports. Kyoto Prefectural University. Natural Science and Life Science [*Japan*]
Sci Rep Kyoto Prefect Univ Nat Sci Living Sci Welfare Sci — Scientific Reports. Kyoto Prefectural University. Natural Science, Living Science, and Welfare Science [*Japan*]
Sci Rep Kyoto Prefect Univ Natur Sci Living Sci — Kyoto Prefectural University. Scientific Reports. Natural Science and Living Science
Sci Rep Kyoto Pref Univ — Scientific Report. Kyoto Prefectural University
Sci Rep Kyoto Pref Univ Natur Sci Living Sci — Kyoto Prefectural University. Scientific Reports. Natural Science and Living Science
Sci Rep Matsuyama Agric Coll — Scientific Reports. Matsuyama Agricultural College
Sci Rep Meiji Seika Kaisha — Scientific Reports. Meiji Seika Kaisha
Sci Rep Miyagi Agr Coll — Scientific Report. Miyagi Agricultural College
Sci Rep Natl Tsing Hua Univ Ser A — Science Reports. National Tsing Hua University. Series A. Mathematical, Physical, and Engineering Sciences
Sci Rep Natl Tsing Hua Univ Ser C — Science Reports. National Tsing Hua University. Series C. Geological, Geographical, and Meteorological Sciences
Sci Rep Natl Univ Peking — Science Reports. National University of Peking
Sci Rep Niigata Univ Ser A — Science Reports. Niigata University. Series A. Mathematics
Sci Rep Niigata Univ Ser B — Science Reports. Niigata University. Series B. Physics
Sci Rep Niigata Univ Ser C — Science Reports. Niigata University. Series C. Chemistry
Sci Rep Niigata Univ Ser D Biol — Science Reports. Niigata University. Series D. Biology
Sci Rep Niigata Univ Ser E — Science Reports. Niigata University. Series E. Geology and Mineralogy
Sci Rep Niigata Univ Ser F Geol Mineral — Science Reports. Niigata University. Series F. Geology and Mineralogy
Sci Rep Osaka Univ — Science Reports. Osaka University
Sci Rep Res Inst Engrg Kanagawa Univ — Science Reports. Kanagawa University. Research Institute for Engineering
Sci Rep Res Inst Theor Phys Hiroshima Univ — Scientific Reports. Research Institute for Theoretical Physics. Hiroshima University [*Japan*]
Sci Rep Res Inst Tohoku Univ — Science Reports. Research Institutes. Tohoku University
Sci Rep Res Inst Tohoku Univ A — Science Reports. Research Institutes. Tohoku University. Series A. Physics, Chemistry, and Metallurgy
Sci Rep Res Inst Tohoku Univ Med — Science Reports. Research Institutes. Tohoku University. Series C. Medicine
Sci Rep Res Inst Tohoku Univ Ser A — Science Reports. Research Institutes. Tohoku University. Series A. Physics, Chemistry, and Metallurgy
Sci Rep Res Inst Tohoku Univ Ser B — Science Reports. Research Institutes. Tohoku University. Series B. Technology
Sci Rep Res Inst Tohoku Univ Ser C — Science Reports. Research Institutes. Tohoku University. Series C. Medicine
Sci Rep Res Inst Tohoku Univ Ser C Med — Science Reports. Research Institutes. Tohoku University. Series C. Medicine
Sci Rep Res Inst Tohoku Univ Ser D — Science Reports. Research Institutes. Tohoku University. Series D
Sci Rep Res Inst Tohoku Univ Ser D Agric — Science Reports. Research Institutes. Tohoku University. Series D. Agriculture
Sci Rep Saitama Univ Ser A — Science Reports. Saitama University. Series A. Mathematics, Physics, and Chemistry

Sci Rep Saitama Univ Ser B Biol Earth Sci — Science Reports. Saitama University. Series B. Biology and Earth Sciences

Sci Rep Shiga Pref Jr Coll — Scientific Report. Shiga Prefectural Junior College

Sci Rep Shima Marinel — Science Report. Shima Marineland

Sci Rep Soc Res Phys Chem — Science Reports. Society for the Research of Physics Chemistry

Sci Rep Tohoku Imp Univ Ser 1 — Science Reports. Tohoku Imperial University. Series 1. Mathematics, Physics, Chemistry

Sci Rep Tohoku Imp Univ Ser 3 — Science Reports. Tohoku Imperial University. Series 3. Mineralogy, Petrology, Economic Geology

Sci Rep Tohoku Imp Univ Ser 4 — Science Reports. Tohoku Imperial University. Series 4. Biology

Sci Rep Tohoku Univ — Science Reports. Tohoku University

Sci Rep Tohoku Univ Eighth Ser Phys and Astron — Science Reports. Tohoku University. Eighth Series. Physics and Astronomy

Sci Rep Tohoku Univ Fifth Ser Geophys — Science Reports. Tohoku University. Fifth Series. Geophysics

Sci Rep Tohoku Univ First Ser — Science Reports. Tohoku University. First Series [*Japan*]

Sci Rep Tohoku Univ Fourth Ser (Biol) — Science Reports. Tohoku University. Fourth Series. Biology

Sci Rep Tohoku Univ I — Science Reports. Tohoku University. First Series

Sci Rep Tohoku Univ Second Ser (Geol) — Science Reports. Tohoku University. Second Series. Geology

Sci Rep Tohoku Univ Ser 5 — Science Reports. Tohoku University. Fifth Series. Geophysics [*Japan*]

Sci Rep Tohoku Univ Ser IV — Scientific Report. Tohoku University. Series IV. Biology

Sci Rep Tohoku Univ Seventh Ser — Science Reports. Tohoku University. Seventh Series [*Japan*]

Sci Rep Tohoku Univ Third Ser — Science Reports. Tohoku University. Third Series. Mineralogy, Petrology, and Economic Geology [*Japan*]

Sci Rep Tohoku Univ 8th Series — Science Reports. Tohoku University. 8th Series

Sci Rep Tokyo Bunrika Daigaku Sect A — Science Reports. Tokyo Bunrika Daigaku. Section A. Mathematics, Physics, Chemistry

Sci Rep Tokyo Bunrika Daigaku Sect B — Science Reports. Tokyo Bunrika Daigaku. Section B

Sci Rep Tokyo Bunrika Daigaku Sect C — Science Reports. Tokyo Bunrika Daigaku. Section C

Sci Rep Tokyo Kyoiku Daigaku Sect A — Science Reports. Tokyo Kyoiku Daigaku. Section A

Sci Rep Tokyo Kyoiku Daigaku Sect B — Science Reports. Tokyo Kyoiku Daigaku. Section B

Sci Rep Tokyo Kyoiku Daigaku Sect C — Science Reports. Tokyo Kyoiku Daigaku. Section C

Sci Rep Tokyo Woman's Christian College — Science Reports. Tokyo Woman's Christian College

Sci Rep Tokyo Woman's Christian Univ — Tokyo Woman's Christian University. Science Reports

Sci Rep Univ Chekiang — Science Reports. University of Chekiang

Sci Rep Whales Res Inst (Tokyo) — Scientific Reports. Whales Research Institute (Tokyo)

Sci Rep Yamaguchi Univ — Science Reports. Yamaguchi University

Sci Rep Yokohama Natl Univ I — Science Reports. Yokohama National University. Section I. Mathematics, Physics, and Chemistry

Sci Rep Yokohama Natl Univ Ser I — Science Reports. Yokohama National University. Section I. Mathematics, Physics, and Chemistry

Sci Rep Yokohama Natl Univ Sect II Biol Geol Sci — Science Reports. Yokohama National University. Section II. Biological and Geological Sciences

Sci Rep Yokohama Nat Univ Sect 2 — Science Reports. Yokohama National University. Section 2. Biological and Geological Sciences

Sci Rep Yokohama Nat Univ Sect I — Science Reports. Yokohama National University. Section I. Mathematics and Physics

Sci Rep Yokosuka City Mus — Science Report. Yokosuka City Museum

Sci Rep Yokosuka Cy Mus — Science Report. Yokosuka City Museum

Sci Res — Scientific Researches

Sci Res Abstr — Science Research Abstracts

Sci Res Br Univ Coll — Scientific Research in British Universities and Colleges

Sci Res Counc Jam J — Scientific Research Council of Jamaica. Journal

Sci Res (Dacca) — Scientific Research (Dacca) [*Pakistan*]

Sci Res (Dacca, Bangladesh) — Scientific Researches (Dacca, Bangladesh)

Sci Res Natl Sci Ed — Scientific Research. Natural Science Edition [*People's Republic of China*]

Sci Res News — Science Research News

Sci Res (NY) — Scientific Research (New York)

Sci Resour Lett — Science Resource Letter

Sci Rev — Scienca Revuo

Sci Rev — Science Review

Sci Rev (Belgrade) — Scienca Revuo (Belgrade)

Sci Rev Int Sci Asoc Esperantista — Scienca Revuo. Internacia Scienca Asocio Esperantista

Sci Rev (Neth) — Scienca Revuo (Netherlands)

Sci Rondo — Scienca Rondo

Sci R Toh A — Science Reports. Research Institutes. Tohoku University. Series A. Physics, Chemistry, and Metallurgy

SCIS — Social Change in Sweden

Sci S Afr — Scientific South Africa

Sci & Scty — Science and Society

Sci Serves Farm — Science Serves Your Farm

Sci Silvae — Scientia Silvae

Sci Sin — Scientia Sinica

Sci Sinica — Scientia Sinica

Sci Sinica Ser A — Scientia Sinica. Series A. Mathematical, Physical, Astronomical, and Technical Sciences

Sci Sinica Ser B — Scientia Sinica. Series B. Chemical, Biological, Agricultural, Medical, and Earth Sciences

Sci Sinica Suppl — Scientia Sinica. Supplement

Sci Sinter — Science of Sintering

Sci Sintering — Science of Sintering

Sci & Soc — Science and Society

Sci Soc — Science and Society

Sci Soc — Sciences Sociales

Sci Sol — Science du Sol

Sci Stud — Science Studies

Sci Stud St Bonaventure Univ — Science Studies. St. Bonaventure University

SCIT — Science Teacher

Sci Teach — Science Teacher

Sci Teach (New Delhi) — Science Teacher (New Delhi)

Sci Teach News — Science Teachers News

Sci Tec — Scienza e Tecnica

Sci Tech — Science and Australian Technology

Sci & Tech — Science and Technology

Sci Tech — Science and Technology

Sci Tech Aerosp Rep — Scientific and Technical Aerospace Reports [*NASA*]

Sci & Tech Aerosp Reports — Scientific and Technical Aerospace Reports

Sci Tech Armement — Sciences et Techniques de l'Armement

Sci Tech Human Values — Science, Technology, and Human Values

Sci Tech Inf Process — Scientific and Technical Information Processing

Sci Tech Inf Process (Engl Transl) — Scientific and Technical Information Processing (English Translation)

Sci Tech Inf Process (Eng Transl Nauchno-Tekh Inf Ser I) — Scientific and Technical Information Processing (English Translation of Nauchno-Tekhnicheskaya Informatsiya Seriya I)

Sci Techn Aerospace Rep — Scientific and Technical Aerospace Reports

Sci Tech News — Science and Technology News

Sci Technol — Science and Technology

Sci Technol — Sciences and Technologies. Korea University [*Republic of Korea*]

Sci Technol Aliment — Science et Technologie Alimentaire [*People's Republic of China*]

Sci Technol China — Science and Technology in China

Sci Technol Jpn — Science and Technology of Japan

Sci Technol Korea Univ — Sciences and Technologies. Korea University

Sci Technol Ser — Science Technology Series [*United States*]

Sci Technol (Surrey Hills Aust) — Science and Technology (Surrey Hills, Australia)

Sci Tech (Paris) — Sciences et Techniques (Paris)

Sci Tech Pharm — Sciences et Techniques Pharmaceutiques

Sci Tec Latt-Casearia — Scienza e Tecnica Lattiero-Casearia

Sci Tecnol Alimenti — Scienza e Tecnologia degli Alimenti

Sci Terre — Sciences de la Terre

Sci Terre Inf Geol — Sciences de la Terre. Informatique Geologique

Sci Terre Mem — Sciences de la Terre. Memoires

Sci Today (Bombay) — Science Today (Bombay)

Sci Tools — Science Tools

Sci Total Environ — Science of the Total Environment

Sci Tree Top — Scientific Tree Topics

SCIV — Studii si Cercetari de Istorie Veche [*Later, Studii si Cercetari de Istorie Veche si Arheologie*]

SCIVA — Studii si Cercetari de Istorie Veche si Arheologie

Sci Vie — Science et Vie

Sci Works High Med Inst Pleven — Scientific Works. Higher Medical Institute of Pleven

Sci Works Res Inst Epidemiol Microbiol (Sofia) — Scientific Works. Research Institute of Epidemiology and Microbiology (Sofia)

Sci World — Scholastic Science World

Sci World — Scientific World [*England*]

Sci Yearb Vet Fac (Thessalonica) — Scientific Yearbook. Veterinary Faculty (Thessalonica)

SCJ — Siberian Chemistry Journal

SCJ — Sixteenth Century Journal

SCJ — Sydney Cinema Journal

S C Jap — Studia Celtica Japonica

Sc J Cl Inv — Scandinavian Journal of Clinical and Laboratory Investigation

Sc J Dent R — Scandinavian Journal of Dental Research

Sc J Gastr — Scandinavian Journal of Gastroenterology

Sc J Haemat — Scandinavian Journal of Haematology

Sc J Hist — Scandinavian Journal of History

Sc J Immun — Scandinavian Journal of Immunology

Sc J In Dis — Scandinavian Journal of Infectious Diseases
Sc J Plast — Scandinavian Journal of Plastic and Reconstructive Surgery
Sc J Psycho — Scandinavian Journal of Psychology
Sc J Re Med — Scandinavian Journal of Rehabilitation Medicine
Sc J Resp D — Scandinavian Journal of Respiratory Diseases
Sc J Rheum — Scandinavian Journal of Rheumatology
Sc J S Med — Scandinavian Journal of Social Medicine
ScJTh — Scottish Journal of Theology [*Edinburgh*]
Sc J Thor C — Scandinavian Journal of Thoracic and Cardiovascular Surgery
SCJUA — Science Journal Incorporating Discovery
Sc J Urol N — Scandinavian Journal of Urology and Nephrology
SCL — Santa Clara Lawyer
SCL — Southern California Law Review
SCL — Stendhal Club
SCL — Studies in Canadian Literature
SCL — Studii si Cercetari Lingvistice
SClas — Studii Clasice
SCLE — Society and Leisure [*Czechoslovakia*]
SC Libn — South Carolina Librarian
SCLing — Siouan and Caddoan Linguistics
Sc L J — Scottish Literary Journal
Scl & Lbr Bul — Social and Labour Bulletin
Scl Problems — Social Problems
SC L Q — South Carolina Law Quarterly
SC LR — South Carolina Law Review
SCLRA — School Review
SC L Rev — South Carolina Law Review
SCLSA — Scandinavian Journal of Clinical and Laboratory Investigation.
     Supplement
Scl Sci Q — Social Science Quarterly
Scl Sec Bul — Social Security Bulletin
SCM — School Musician. Director and Teacher
SCM — Sussex County Magazine
SCMAA — Studii si Cercetari de Mecanica Aplicata
SCMB — Seaby's Coin and Medal Bulletin
SCMP — South China Morning Post
SCMPBN — South China Morning Post (Business News)
SCN — Seventeenth-Century News
SCN — Studii si Cercetari de Numismatica
SCNCA — Sciences [*New York*]
SCNEB — Science News [*Washington, DC*]
SC Nurs — South Carolina Nursing
SCO — Studi Classici e Orientali
ScoGaelS — Scottish Gaelic Studies
ScoGS — Scottish Gaelic Studies
Scone & Upper Hunter Hist Soc J — Scone and Upper Hunter Historical
     Society. Journal
ScoS — Scottish Studies
SCOSA — Sadtler Commercial Spectra
Scot Agr — Scottish Agriculture
Scot AL — Scottish Art and Letters
Scot Archaeol Forum — Scottish Archaeological Forum
Scot Art R — Scottish Art Review
Scot Art Rev — Scottish Art Review
Scot Edu St — Scottish Educational Studies
Scot Geog M — Scottish Geographical Magazine
Scot Geogr Mag — Scottish Geographical Magazine
Scot GM — Scottish Geographical Magazine
Scot Hist R — Scottish Historical Review
Scot Hist Riv — Scottish Historical Review
Scot J Geol — Scottish Journal of Geology
Scot J Pol Econ — Scottish Journal of Political Economy
Scot J Poli — Scottish Journal of Political Economy
Scot J Rel — Scottish Journal of Religious Studies
Scot J Rel St — Scottish Journal of Religious Studies
ScotJt — Scottish Journal of Theology
Scot J Th — Scottish Journal of Theology
Scot J Theo — Scottish Journal of Theology
ScotL — Scottish Language
Scotl Dep Agric Fish Mar Res — Scotland Department of Agriculture and
     Fisheries. Marine Research
Scotl Dep Agric Fish Tech Bull — Scotland Department of Agriculture and
     Fisheries. Technical Bulletin
Scot Lit J — Scottish Literary Journal
Scot LR — Scottish Law Review
Scot L Rev — Scottish Law Review
Scot Med J — Scottish Medical Journal
Scot R — Scottish Review
Scots Mag — Scots Magazine
Scotsman Mag — Scotsman Magazine
Scot Stud — Scottish Studies
Scott Agric — Scottish Agriculture
Scott Art Rev — Scottish Art Review
Scott Australas — Scottish Australasian
Scott Bankers Mag — Scottish Bankers Magazine
Scott Bee J — Scottish Bee Journal

Scott Beekeep — Scottish Beekeeper
Scott Beekpr — Scottish Beekeeper
Scott Birds — Scottish Birds
Scott Birds J Scott Ornithol Club — Scottish Birds. Journal. Scottish
     Ornithologists' Club
Scott Econ Bull — Scottish Economic Bulletin
Scott Econ Soc Hist — Scottish Economic and Social History
Scott Educ Rev — Scottish Educational Review
Scott Elect Engr — Scottish Electrical Engineer
Scott Field — Scottish Field
Scott Fish Bull — Scottish Fisheries Bulletin
Scott Fish Res Rep — Scottish Fisheries Research Report
Scott Fmr — Scottish Farmer and Farming World
Scott For — Scottish Forestry
Scott For J — Scottish Forestry Journal
Scott Genealog — Scottish Genealogist
Scott Geogr Mag — Scottish Geographical Magazine
Scott Hist Rev — Scottish Historical Review
Scott Ind Hist — Scottish Industrial History
Scottish Art R — Scottish Art Review
Scottish Bankers M — Scottish Bankers Magazine
Scottish Econ Bul — Scottish Economic Bulletin
Scottish Ednl J — Scottish Educational Journal
Scottish Ednl Studies — Scottish Educational Studies
Scottish Geog Mag — Scottish Geographical Magazine
Scottish Georgian Soc Bull — Scottish Georgian Society. Bulletin
Scottish J Pol Economy — Scottish Journal of Political Economy
Scottish Mus — Scottish Music and Drama
Scott J Adult Educ — Scottish Journal of Adult Education
Scott J Agric — Scottish Journal of Agriculture
Scott J Geol — Scottish Journal of Geology
Scott J Polit Econ — Scottish Journal of Political Economy
Scott J Theology — Scottish Journal of Theology
Scott Labour Hist Soc J — Scottish Labour History Society Journal
Scott Lang — Scottish Language
Scott Life-Boat — Scottish Life-Boat
Scott Lit J — Scottish Literary Journal
Scott Mar Biol Assoc Annu Rep — Scottish Marine Biological Association.
     Annual Report
Scott Marxist — Scottish Marxist
Scott Med J — Scottish Medical Journal
Scott Nat — Scottish Naturalist
Scott Rep — Scott Report
Scotts Turfgrass Res Conf Proc — Scotts Turfgrass Research Conference.
     Proceedings
Scott Trade Union Rev — Scottish Trade Union Review
Scott Tradit — Scottish Tradition
Scouting in NSW — Scouting in New South Wales
SCP — Scoops
Sc Parliament — Science in Parliament
Sc for People — Science for People
SCPGB — Revista. Sociedad Cientifica del Paraguay
SCPRA — Science Progress [*Oxford*]
SCPYB — Social Policy
Scr — Scrinium
SCR — Scrutiny
SCR — South Carolina Review
SCR — Soviet Cybernetics Review
S Cr — Strumenti Critici
SCR — Studies in Comparative Religion
SCraneN — Stephen Crane Newsletter
Scr Demolinguist — Scritti Demolinguistici
SCRE — Scandinavian Review
SCREB — Scientific Research
Screen Ed — Screen Education
Screen Ed Notes — Screen Education Notes
SC Research Plan Devel Board Bull — South Carolina Research Planning and
     Development Board. Bulletin
SC Resour Cent Tech Rep — South Carolina Marine Resources Center.
     Technical Report
Scr Fac Sci Nat Univ Purkynianae Bru Biol — Scripta Facultatis Scientiarum
     Naturalium Universita J. E. Purkyne Brunensis. Biiologia
Scr Geobot — Scripta Geobotanica
Scr Geogr — Scripta Geographica
Scr Geol (Leiden) — Scripta Geologica (Leiden)
ScrH — Scripta Hierosolymitana
ScrHier — Scripta Hierosolymitana [*Jerusalem*]
ScrHierosol — Scripta Hierosolymitana [*Jerusalem*]
Scr Hierosolymitana — Scripta Hierosolymitana
Scr Hierosolymitana Publ Heb Univ (Jerus) — Scripta Hierosolymitana.
     Publications of the Hebrew University (Jerusalem)
Scrib — Scribner's Monthly
Scrib Com — Scribner's Commentator
Scrib M — Scribner's Magazine
Scri Geol — Scripta Geologica

Scri Med Fac Med Univ Brun Purkynianae — Scripta Medica. Facultatis Medicae. Universitatis Brunensis Purkynianae
Scrip — Scriptorium
Scrip Metal — Scripta Metallurgica
Scripps Inst Oceanogr Contrib — Scripps Institution of Oceanography. Contributions
Script — Scriptorium
Scripta Fac Sci Natur UJEP Brunensis Biol — Scripta Facultatis Scientiarum Naturalium Universita J. E. Purkyne Brunensis. Biologia
Scripta Fac Sci Natur UJEP Brunensis Chem — Scripta Facultatis Scientiarum Naturalium Universita J. E. Purkyne Brunensis. Chemia
Scripta Fac Sci Natur UJEP Brunensis Geol — Scripta Facultatis Scientiarum Naturalium Universita J. E. Purkyne Brunensis. Geologia
Scripta Fac Sci Natur UJEP Brunensis Math — Scripta Facultatis Scientiarum Naturalium Universita J. E. Purkyne Brunensis. Mathematica
Scripta Fac Sci Natur UJEP Brunensis Phys — Scripta Facultatis Scientiarum Naturalium Universita J. E. Purkyne Brunensis. Physica
Scripta Math — Scripta Mathematica
ScriptB — Scripture Bulletin [*London*]
ScrJud — Scripta Judaica [*Oxford*]
SCR (L) — Supreme Court Reports (Law) [*New South Wales*]
Scr Med (Brno) — Scripta Medica (Brno)
Scr Med Fac Med Univ Brun Olomuc — Scripta Medica. Facultatum Medicinae. Universitatum Brunensis et Olomucencis [*Czechoslovakia*]
Scr Met — Scripta Metallurgica
Scr Metall — Scripta Metallurgica
Scr Minora — Scripta Minora-Regiae Societatis Humaniorum Litterarum Lundensis
SCR (NS) (NSW) — Supreme Court Reports (New Series) (New South Wales)
SCR (NSW) — Supreme Court Reports (New South Wales)
SCR (NSW) Eq — Supreme Court Reports (Equity) (New South Wales)
SCRPA — Science Reporter [*New Delhi*]
SCR (Q) — Queensland. Supreme Court. Reports
Scr Sci Med Annu Sci Pap — Scripta Scientifica Medica. Annual Scientific Papers
ScrTheol — Scripta Theologica [*Pamplona*]
ScS — Scandinavian Studies and Notes
ScS — Scottish Studies
SCSCA — Schweissen und Schneiden
SCSFI — Studii si Cercetari Stiintifice. Filologie (Iasi)
ScSl — Scandoslavica
SCSLA — Science du Sol
ScSo — Science and Society
S & C Spec — Soap/Cosmetics/Chemical Specialties
ScSt — Scandinavian Studies
SC State Devel Board Div Geology Bull Geol Notes — South Carolina State Development Board. Division of Geology. Bulletin. Geologic Notes
Sc Stud — Scandinavian Studies
Sc Stud Law — Scandinavian Studies in Law
SCSZ — Sbornik Ceskoslovenske Spolecnosti Zemepisne
SCTCA — Schweisstechnik [*Berlin*]
SCTE — Science of the Total Environment
SCTHA — Ssu Ch'uan Ta Hsueh Hsueh Pao - Tzu Jan K'o Hsueh
SCTOA — Science Tools
Sc Total Env — Science of the Total Environment
S Ct Rev — Supreme Court Review
SCTTB — Schmiertechnik und Tribologie
SCTYB — Science Today (Bombay)
SCU — Schweizer Buchhandel
ScUB — Scandinavian University Books
SCUL — Soundings. University of California. Library [*Santa Barbara*]
Sculp Int — Sculpture International
Sculpt R — Sculpture Review
SC Univ Pubs Phys Sci Bull — South Carolina University. Publications. Physical Sciences Bulletin
SCVIA — Science et Vie
SCW — Schoenwereld. Vakblad voor de Schoenlederbranche
SC Water Resour Comm Rep — South Carolina. Water Resources Commission. Report
SCWFA — Schip en Werf
SCWIA — South Carolina Wildlife
SC Wildl — South Carolina Wildlife
SCZFA — Schweizerische Zeitschrift fuer Forstwesen
SD — Sammlung Dieterich
SD — Scientific Detective Monthly
SD — South Dakota Musician
SD — Space Digest
Sd — Sprachdienst
SD — Sprache und Dichtung
SD — Storm Data
SD — Studi Danteschi
SD — Studia Delitschiana
SD Ag Exp — South Dakota. Agricultural Experiment Station. Publications
SD Agric Exp Stn Bull — South Dakota. Agricultural Experiment Station. Bulletin

S Dak Agr Expt Sta Tech Bull — South Dakota. Agricultural Experiment Station. Technical Bulletin
S Dak Farm Home Res — South Dakota Farm and Home Research
S Dak Geol Surv Bull — South Dakota. Geological Survey. Bulletin
S Dak Geol Surv Circ — South Dakota. Geological Survey. Circular
S Dak His R — South Dakota Historical Review
S Dak His S — South Dakota State Historical Society. Collections
S Dak J Med — South Dakota Journal of Medicine
S Dak Lib Bull — South Dakota Library Bulletin
S Dak Rev — South Dakota Review
S Dak State Geologist Bienn Rept — South Dakota State Geologist. Biennial Report
S Dak State Univ Coop Ext Serv — South Dakota State University. Cooperative Extension Service
SDAW — Sitzungsberichte. Deutsche Akademie der Wissenschaften zu Berlin
SDAWB — Sitzungsberichte. Deutsche Akademie der Wissenschaften zu Berlin
SDB — Supplement au Dictionnaire de la Bible
SD Bird Notes — South Dakota Bird Notes
SDD-NU — Summaries of Doctoral Dissertations. Northwestern University
SDDRA — Showa Densen Denran Rebyu
SDDUW — Summaries of Doctoral Dissertations. University of Wisconsin
Sdelovaci Tech — Sdelovaci Technika
SD Farm Home Res — South Dakota Farm and Home Research
SDFRA — Reports. Faculty of Science. Shizuoka University
SDG — Schriften. Droste-Gesellschaft
SdG — Studii de Gramatica
SD Geol Surv Bull — South Dakota. Geological Survey. Bulletin
SD Geol Surv Misc Invest — South Dakota. Geological Survey. Miscellaneous Investigations
SD Geol Surv Rep Invest — South Dakota. Geological Survey. Report of Investigations
SD Geol Surv Spec Rep — South Dakota. Geological Survey. Special Report
SDGRA — Report of Investigations. South Dakota Geological Survey
SDH — Slavistische Drukken en Herdrukken
SDHI — Studia et Documenta Historiae et Iuris
SDi — Slovenske. Revue Dramatickych Umeni
SDIOA — Studia et Documenta ad Iura Orientis Antiqui Pertinenta
SDIOAP — Studia et Documenta ad Iura Orientis Antiqui Pertinenta
SD J Med — South Dakota Journal of Medicine
SD J Med Pharm — South Dakota Journal of Medicine and Pharmacy
SDKK — Studia z Dziejow Kosciola Katolickiego
SDKOD — Saitama Daigaku Kiyo. Kogakubu
SDKSB — Saitama Daigaku Kiyo. Shizenkagaku-Hen
SD LR — South Dakota Law Review
SD L Rev — South Dakota Law Review
SdM — Siglo de las Misiones
SDMAA — Stroitel'nye i Dorozhnye Mashiny
SDMEA — South Dakota Journal of Medicine
SDNIA — Saga Daigaku Nogaku Iho
SD Nurse — South Dakota Nurse
SDO — Serra Dor
SDOG — Sendschrift. Deutsche Orient-Gesellschaft [*Leipzig*]
SDR — Sezione Demografia e Razza
SDR — South Dakota Review
SDRSA — Shimane Daigaku Ronshu: Shizen Kagaku
SDS — Sydsvenska Dagbladet Snaellposten
SD Sch Mines Bull — South Dakota. School of Mines. Bulletin
SDSD — Studi e Documenti di Storia e Diritto
SDTGA — Staedtetag
S Dv — Sprache und Datenverarbeitung
SD Water Resour Comm Rep Invest — South Dakota. Water Resources Commission. Report of Investigations
SE — Sciences Ecclesiastiques
Se — Semeia
Se — Semiotica
SE — Slovenski Etnograf
SE — Social Education
SE — Studi Etruschi
SE — Studia Estetyczne
SE — Studies in English
SE — Sunday Express [*United Kingdom*]
Sea — Sankt Eriks Arsbok
SEA — Studies in Economic Analysis
SEA — Studies in Educational Administration
SEA — Studies in English and American
SEA — Svensk Exegetisk Arsbok
Sea Fish Res Stn (Haifa) Bull — Sea Fisheries Research Station (Haifa). Bulletin
Seafood Bus — Seafood Business
Seafood Export J — Seafood Export Journal
Seafood Merch — Seafood Merchandising
Sea Front — Sea Frontiers
Sea Grant Coll Tech Rep Univ Wis — Sea Grant College Technical Report. University of Wisconsin
SEAJS — Southeast Asian Journal of Sociology [*Singapore*]

SEAJT — South East Asia Journal of Theology
Seamens J — Seamen's Journal
Seance Pub Ann Acad Pharm — Seance Publique Annuelle. Academie de Pharmacie
Sean O Cas — Sean O'Casey Review
SEAPA — Society of Petroleum Engineers. American Institute of Mining, Metallurgical, and Petroleum Engineers. Papers
SeAQ — Southeast Asia Quarterly
Seara Med — Seara Medica
Seara Med Neurocir — Seara Medica Neurocirurgica
Search Agric Ent (Ithaca NY) — Search Agriculture. Entomology (Ithaca, New York)
Search Agric (Geneva NY) — Search Agriculture (Geneva, New York)
Search Agric NY State Agric Exp Stn (Ithaca) — Search Agriculture. New York State Agricultural Experiment Station (Ithaca)
Search and Seizure L Rep — Search and Seizure Law Report
Sears Found Marine Research Mem — Sears Foundation for Marine Research. Memoir
SEAS — Seasons. Federation of Ontario Naturalists
Se As Aff — Southeast Asian Affairs [*Singapore*]
Se As Chron — Southeast Asia Chronicle
SE Asia — Southeast Asia Chronicle
SE Asia J Th — Southeast Asia Journal of Theology
Se As Iron Steel Inst Q — Southeast Asia Iron and Steel Institute Quarterly [*Singapore*]
Se As J Soc Sci — Southeast Asian Journal of Social Science [*Singapore*]
Se As J Theo — South East Asia Journal of Theology [*Singapore*]
S E As R — South East Asia Review [*India*]
S E As Stud — South East Asian Studies [*Kyoto*]
SEATA — Sea Technology
Sea Technol — Sea Technology
SEATO Med Res Monogr — Southeast Asia Treaty Organization. Medical Research Monograph
Seattle Sym — Seattle Symphony Orchestra. Program Notes
Sea View Hosp Bull — Sea View Hospital. Bulletin
Seaway Rev — Seaway Review
SEB — Statistische Studien (Brussels)
SEBAn — Societe d'Emulation de Bruges. Annales
SEBUA — Seibutsu Butsuri
SeC — Scuola e Cultura del Mondo
SEC — SEC: Bi-Monthly Magazine for Employees of the State Electricity Commission of Victoria
Se C — Second Coming
SEC — Secretary
SEC — Societe de l'Ecole des Chartes
SECC — Studies in Eighteenth-Century Culture
Sec City — Second City
Sec D & M — Security Distributing and Marketing
Sec Ed — Secondary Education
Sec and Fed Corp L Rep — Securities and Federal Corporate Law Report
Sechenov Physiol J USSR — Sechenov. Physiological Journal of the USSR
Sec Ind Digest — Secondary Industries Digest
SECJA — Southern Economic Journal [*United States*]
Sec L Rev — Securities Law Review
SEC Mag — SEC Magazine: Journal of the State Electricity Commission of Victoria
SECMem — Societe d'Emulation de Cambrai. Memoires
Sec Mgmt — Security Management
Sec Mgt — Security Management
SECN — Sex Education Coalition News
SEC News — SEC [*US Securities and Exchange Commission*] News Digest
Secondary Teach — Secondary Teacher
Second Cent — Second Century
S Econ J — Southern Economic Journal
Sec Reg LJ — Securities Regulation Law Journal
Sec Reg & L Rep — Securities Regulation and Law Reports [*Bureau of National Affairs*]
Sec Reg & Trans — Securities Regulations and Transfer Report
Secr Pap Int Wheat Counc — Secretariat Papers. International Wheat Council
SECTDQ — Centro Internacional de Agricultura Tropical [*CIAT*]. Series EE
Sec Teach — Secondary Teacher
Sec Teacher — Secondary Teacher
Security Surv — Security Surveyor
Secur Manage — Security Management
Secur Med Trav — Securite et Medecine du Travail
Secur R Law — Securities Regulation Law Journal
Sec Wave — Second Wave
Sec World — Security World
SED — Survey of English Dialects
SEDA — Side Effects of Drugs. Annual [*Elsevier Book Series*]
Sedalia N H Soc B — Sedalia Natural History Society. Bulletin
SEDES — Societe d'Editions d'Enseignement Superieur
Sed Geol — Sedimentary Geology
Sediment Ge — Sedimentary Geology
Sediment Geol — Sedimentary Geology
Seed Bull — Seed Bulletin

Seed Gard Merch — Seed and Garden Merchandising
Seed and Nursery Tr — Seed and Nursery Trader
Seed Res (New Delhi) — Seed Research (New Delhi)
Seed Sci Technol — Seed Science and Technology
Seed Trade Rev — Seed Trade Review
SEEE — Studies in Electrical and Electronic Engineering [*Elsevier Book Series*]
SEEJ — Slavic and East European Journal
SEER — Slavonic and East European Review
SEERB — South African Engineer and Electrical Review
SEES — Slavic and East European Studies
SE Eur — Southeastern Europe
Sef — Sefarad
SEF — Supermarketing
SE & FBR — Science Fiction and Fantasy Book Review
Seg — Segismundo
SEG — Supplementum Epigraphicum Graecum
SEGEA — Orthopaedic Surgery
Seguranca Desenvolv — Seguranca e Desenvolvimento. ADESG [*Revista da Associacao dos Diplomados da Escola Superior de Guerra*] [*Brazil*]
SEH — Southern Economic Journal
SEHR — Scandinavian Economic History Review
SEIE — Solvent Extraction and Ion Exchange
Seifen Fachbl — Seifen Fachblatt
Seifen Ole — Seifen, Oele, Fette, Waesche
Seifensieder Ztg — Seifensieder Zeitung
Seifensieder Ztg Allg Oel Fett Ztg — Seifensieder-Zeitung in Gemeinschaft auf Kriegsdauer mit Allgemeine Oel- und Fett-Zeitung
SEIGA — Seishin Igaku
Sei-I-Kai Med J — Sei-I-Kai Medical Journal
SEIJAN — Congenital Anomalies
SEIJD — Seijinbyo
Seism Instrum — Seismic Instruments
Seismol Bull — Seismological Bulletin
Seismol and Geol — Seismology and Geology
Seismolog Soc Am Bull — Seismology Society of America. Bulletin
Seismol Ser Earth Phys Branch — Seismological Series of the Earth Physics Branch
Seismol Ser Geol Surv (S Afr) — Seismologic Series. Geological Survey (South Africa)
Seismol Serv Can Seismol Ser — Seismological Service of Canada. Seismological Series
Seismol Soc Am Bul — Seismological Society of America. Bulletin
Seismostoikost Sooruzh — Seismostoikost Sooruzhenii [*USSR*]
Seism Prib Instrum Sredstva Seism Nabl — Seismichiskie Pribory. Instrumental'naye Sredstva Seismicheskikh Nablyudenii
SEITA Ann Dir Etud Equip Sect 2 — SEITA [*Service d'Exploitation Industrielle des Tabacs et des Allumettes*] Annales de la Direction des Etudes de l'Equipement. Section 2
SEITA Annls — Service d'Exploitation Industrielle des Tabacs et des Allumettes. Annales de la Direction des Etudes et de l'Equipement
SEJ — Australian Stock Exchange Journal
SEJ — Security Pacific National Bank. Quarterly Economic Report
SEJ — Southern Economic Journal
SEJG — Sacris Erudiri. Jaarboek voor Godsdienstwetenschappen
SEL — Studies in English Literature
Sel Annu Rev Anal Sci — Selected Annual Reviews of the Analytical Sciences
Sel Bibliogr Algae — Selected Bibliography on Algae
Sel Bibliogr Middle East Geol — Selected Bibliography of Middle East Geology
Selec Ed R — Selections from the Edinburgh Review
Selecta Math Soviet — Selecta Mathematica Sovietica
Selecta Statist Canadiana — Selecta Statistica Canadiana
Selected Reports — Selected Reports in Ethnomusicology
Selected Water Resources Abstr — Selected Water Resources Abstracts
Select J — Select Journal
Selec Water Resources Abstr — Selected Water Resources Abstracts
Selek Semenovod — Selektsiya i Semenovodstvo
Selekts Semenov — Selektsiya i Semenovodstvo
SelEnv — Selected References on Environmental Quality
Selez Tec Molit — Selezione di Tecnica Molitoria
Self Rel — Self-Reliance
SE Libn — Southeastern Librarian
SELID — Serials Librarian
SELit — Studies in English Literature [*Japan*]
SELJ — Studies in English Literature (Japan)
Sel'Khoz Beloruss — Sel'skoe Khozyaisto Belorussii
Sel'-khoz Biol — Sel'skokhozyaistvennaya Biologiya
Sel'Khoz Kirgizii — Sel'skoe Khozyaistvo Kirgizii
Sel'Khoz Povol — Sel'skoe Khozyaistvo Povolzh'ya
Sel'Khoz Sev Kavkaz — Sel'skoe Khozyaistvo Severnogo Kavkaza
Sel'Khoz Sev-Zapad Zony — Sel'skoe Khozyaistvo Severo-Zapadnoi Zony
Sel Khoz Sev Zap Zony — Sel'skoe Khozyaistvo Severo-Zapadnoi Zony
Sel'Khoz Sib — Sel'skoe Khozyaistvo Sibiri
Sel'Khoz Tadzhikistana — Sel'skoe Khozyaistvo Tadzhikistana
Sel Khoz Turkmen — Sel'skoe Khozyaistvo Turkmenistana
SELL — Studies in English Literature and Language [*Japan*]

Sel Math Sov — Selecta Mathematica Sovietica
Sel Org Transform — Selective Organic Transformations
Sel Pap Environ Isr — Selected Papers on the Environment in Israel
Sel PRC Mag — Selections from People's Republic of China Magazines [*Hong Kong*]
Sel Rand Abstr — Selected Rand Abstracts
Sel Sci Pap Ist Super Sanita — Selected Scientific Papers. Istituto Superiore di Sanita .
Sel Semenovod (Mosc) — Selektsiya i Semenovodstvo (Moscow)
Sel Semenovod Resp Mezhved Temat Sb — Selektsiya i Semenovodstvo Respublikanskii Mezhvedomstvennyi Tematicheskii Sborrnik
Sel'sk Khoz — Sel'skoe Khozyaistvo
Sel'sk Khoz Kaz — Sel'skoe Khozyaistvo Kazakhstana
Sel'sk Khoz Kirg — Sel'skoe Khozyaistvo Kirgizii
Sel'sk Khoz Mold — Sel'skoe Khozyaistvo Moldavii
Sel'sk Khoz Povolzh'ya — Sel'skoe Khozyaistvo Povolzh'ya
Sel'sk Khoz Rubezhom Rastenievod — Sel'skoe Khozyaistvo za Rubezhom. Rastenievodstvo
Sel'sk Khoz Sev Zapadn Zony — Sel'skoe Khozyaistvo Severo-Zapadnoi Zony
Sel'sk Khoz Tadzh — Sel'skoe Khozyaistvo Tadzhikistana
Sel'sk Khoz Tatar — Sel'skoe Khozyaistvo Tatarii
Sel'sk Khoz Tatarii — Sel'skoe Khozyaistvo Tatarii
Sel'sk Khoz Turkm — Sel'skoe Khozyaistvo Turkmenistana
Sel'skokhoz Biol — Sel'skokhozyaistvennaya Biologiya
Sel'skokhoz Proizv Nechernozem Zony — Sel'skokhozyaistvennoe Proizvodstvo Nechernozemnoi Zony
Sel'skokhoz Proizv Povol — Sel'skokhozyaistvennoe Proizvodstvo Povolzh'ya
Sel'skokhoz Proizv Sev Kavkaza TSCHO — Sel'skokhozyaistvennoe Proizvodstvo Severnogo Kavkaza i TSCHO
Sel'skokhoz Proizv Sib Dal'nego Vostoka — Sel'skokhozyaistvennoe Proizvodstvo Sibiri i Dal'nego Vostoka
Sel'skokhoz Proizv Urala — Sel'skokhozyaistvennoe Proizvodstvo Urala
Selskostop Misal — Selskostopanska Misal
Selskostop Misul — Selskostopanska Misul
Selskostop Nauka — Selskostopanska Nauka
Selskostop Tekh — Selskostopanska Tekhnika
Sel Sortoizuch Agrotekh Plodovykh Yagodnykh Kul't — Selektsiya, Sortoizuchenie, Agrotekhnika Plodovykh i Yagodnykh Kul'tur
Sel Top Solid State Phys — Selected Topics in Solid State Physics
Sel Vet Ist Zooprofil Sper Lomb Emilia — Selezione Veterinaria-Istituto Zooprofilattico Sperimentale della Lombardia e dell'Emilia
Sel Water Res Abstr — Selected Water Resources Abstracts
SEM — Security Management
Sem — Semana
Sem — Seminar
Sem — Semitica [*Paris*]
S-EM — Suck-Egg Mule
Semaine Med — Semaine Medicale
Semaine Vet — Semaine Veterinaire
Sem Anal — Seminaire d'Analyse
Sem Anal Moderne — Seminaire d'Analyse Moderne
Semana Med — Semana Medica
SemBEsp — Semana Biblica Espanola [*Madrid*]
Semen Elette — Sementi Elette
Sem Hematol — Seminars in Hematology
Sem Hop — Semaine des Hopitaux
Sem Hop Inf — Semaine des Hopitaux. Informations
Sem Hop Paris — Semaine des Hopitaux de Paris
Sem Hop Paris Suppl Sem Med Prof Med Soc — Semaine des Hopitaux de Paris. Supplement: Semaine Medicale Professionnelle et Medico-Sociale
Sem Hop-The — Semaine des Hopitaux-Therapeutique
Semicond and Insul — Semiconductors and Insulators
Semicond Insul — Semiconductors and Insulators
Semicond Int — Semiconductor International
Semicond Prod — Semiconductor Products
Semicond Prod and Solid State Technol — Semiconductor Products and Solid State Technology [*Later, Solid State Technology*]
Semicond Semimet — Semiconductors and Semimetals
Semin Arthritis Rheum — Seminars in Arthritis and Rheumatism
Semin Biomass Energy City Farm Ind — Seminar on Biomass Energy for City, Farm, and Industry
Semin Chim Etat Solide — Seminaires de Chimie de l'Etat Solide
Semin Drug Treat — Seminars in Drug Treatment
Semin Estratigrafia — Seminarios de Estratigrafia [*Madrid*]
Semin Hematol — Seminars in Hematology
Semin Nucl Med — Seminars in Nuclear Medicine
Semin Oncol — Seminars in Oncology
Semin Perinatol — Seminars in Perinatology
Semin Psychiatry — Seminars in Psychiatry
Semin Roentgenol — Seminars in Roentgenology
Sem Inst Prikl Mat Annotac Dokladov — Seminar Instituta Prikladnoi Matematiki. Annotacii Dokladov
Semin Thromb Hemostas — Seminars in Thrombosis and Hemostasis
Semin Thromb Hemostasis — Seminars in Thrombosis and Hemostasis
SEMKA — Semento Kogyo
Sem Kond — Seminarium Kondakovianum

Sem Math Sci — Seminar on Mathematical Sciences [*Yokohama*]
Sem Math Sup — Seminaire de Mathematiques Superieures
Sem Math Superieures — Seminaire de Mathematiques Superieures [*Montreal*]
Sem Math V A Steklov — Seminars in Mathematics. V. A. Steklov Mathematical Institute [*Leningrad*]
Sem Med — Semana Medica
Sem Med Prof Med Soc — Semaine Medicale Professionnelle et Medico-Sociale
Sem Nota — Seminaro Nota
Sem Roentg — Seminars in Roentgenology
Sem S — Semiotic Scene
Sem Ther — Semaine Therapeutique [*France*]
Se Mulli (New Phys) — Se Mulli (New Physics)
Sem Vitivinic — Semana Vitivinicola [*Spain*]
SeN — Seara Nova
SENAAL — Agricultural Science [*Sofia*]
Senckenb Biol — Senckenbergiana Biologica
Senckenberg Biol — Senckenbergiana Biologica
Senckenbergische Nat Ges Frankfurt Ber — Senckenbergische Naturforschende Gesellschaft in Frankfurt Am Main. Bericht
Senckenberg Marit — Senckenbergiana Maritima
Senckenb Lethaea — Senckenbergiana Lethaea
Senckenb Marit — Senckenbergiana Maritima
Senckenb Naturforsch Ges Abh — Senckenbergische Naturforschende Gesellschaft. Abhandlungen
Sendai Astron Rap — Sendai Astronomiaj Raportoj
Senegal Cent Rech Oceanogr Dakar-Thiaroye Arch — Senegal. Centre de Recherches Oceanographiques de Dakar-Thiaroye. Archive
Senegal Cent Rech Oceanogr Dakar-Thiaroye Doc Sci — Senegal. Centre de Recherches Oceanographiques de Dakar-Thiaroye. Document Scientifique
Senegal Dir Mines Geol Bull — Senegal. Direction des Mines et de la Geologie. Bulletin
S in Eng — Studies in English
SEngL — Studies in English Literature [*The Hague*]
SENPD — Senpaku
Sen R — Seneca Review
Sens and Actuators — Sensors and Actuators
SENSB — Sense Processes
Sen Schol — Senior Scholastic
SENSD — Studies in Environmental Science
Sensibilizirovannaya Fluorests Smesej Parov Met — Sensibilizirovannaya Fluorestsentsiya Smesej Parov Metallov
Sensing — Remote Sensing
Sensor Rev — Sensor Review
Sens Process — Sensory Processes
Seoul J Med — Seoul Journal of Medicine
Seoul Natl Univ Eng Rep — Seoul National University. Engineering Reports
Seoul Nat Univ Econ R — Seoul National University. Economic Review
Seoul Nat Univ Fac Pap Bio Agric Ser — Seoul National University. Faculty Papers. Biology and Agriculture Series
Seoul Nat Univ Fac Pap Med Pharm Ser — Seoul National University. Faculty Papers. Medicine and Pharmacy Series
Seoul Nat Univ Fac Pap Sci Technol Ser — Seoul National University. Faculty Papers. Science and Technology Series
Seoul University J Pharm Sci — Seoul University. Journal of Pharmaceutical Sciences
Seoul Univ Fac Pap Ser C — Seoul University Faculty Papers. Series C. Science and Technology
Seoul Univ Fac Pap Ser D — Seoul University Faculty Papers. Series D. Medicine and Pharmacy
Seoul Univ Fac Pap Ser E — Seoul University. Faculty Papers. Series E. Biology and Agriculture
Seoul Univ J Biol Agric Ser B — Seoul University. Journal. Series B. Biology and Agriculture
Seoul Univ J Biol Agr Ser B — Seoul University. Journal. Series B. Biology and Agriculture
Seoul Univ J Med Pharm Ser C — Seoul University. Journal. Series C. Medicine and Pharmacy
Seoul Univ J Nat Sci Ser A — Seoul University. Journal. Series A. Natural Science
Seoul Univ J Nat Sci Ser B — Seoul University. Journal. Series B. Natural Science
Seoul Univ J Nat Sci Ser C — Seoul University. Journal. Series C. Natural Science
Seoul Univ J Sci Technol Ser A — Seoul University. Journal. Series A. Science and Technology
SEP — Saturday Evening Post
SEP — Secretaria de Educacion Publica [*Mexico*]
Separ Sci — Separation Science [*Later, Separation Science and Technology*]
SEPM Core Workshop — Society of Economic Paleontologists and Mineralogists. Core Workshop
SEPP — Seppyo. Journal. Japanese Society of Snow and Ice
Sep Purif M — Separation and Purification Methods
Sep Purif Methods — Separation and Purification Methods

SEPRD — Sensory Processes
SEPS — Socio-Economic Planning Sciences
SEPS-B — Socio-Economic Planning Sciences
Sep Sci — Separation Science [*Later, Separation Science and Technology*]
Sep Sci Technol — Separation Science and Technology
SEQ — String Education Quarterly
Ser — Service
SeR — Sewanee Review
SeR — Studi e Ricerche
SERAA — Seramikkusu
Ser Astron Uniw Adama Mickiewicza Poznaniu — Seria Astronomia. Uniwersytet Imeni Adama Mickiewicza w Poznaniu
Serb Acad Sci Arts Bull — Serbian Academy of Sciences and Arts. Bulletin
Serb Acad Sci Arts Glas — Serbian Academy of Sciences and Arts. Glas
Serbian Acad Sci and Arts Monogr Dep Tech Sci — Serbian Academy of Sciences and Arts. Monographs. Department of Technical Sciences
Ser Bibliogr INTA (Pergamino) — Serie Bibliografica. Instituto Nacional de Tecnologia Agropecuaria (Pergamino, Argentina)
Ser Biol Uniw Adama Mickiewicza Poznaniu — Seria Biologia. Uniwersytet Imeni Adama Mickiewicza w Poznaniu
Ser Cana Azucar — Serie Cana de Azucar
Ser Chem Uniw Adama Mickiewicza Poznaniu — Seria Chemia. Uniwersytet Imeni Adama Mickiewicza w Poznaniu
Ser Conf Union Math Internat — Serie des Conferences. Union Mathematique Internationale
Ser Defects Cryst Solids — Series Defects in Crystalline Solids
Ser Didact Univ Nac Tucuman Fac Agronom Zooteh — Serie Didactica. Universidad Nacional de Tucuman. Facultad de Agronomia y Zootecnia
Ser Div Ind Chem CSIRO — Serial. Division of Industrial Chemistry. Commonwealth Scientific and Industrial Research Oganisation
Ser Divulg Agron Angolana — Serie Divulgacao. Agronomia Angolana
Ser Divulg Projeto Desenvolvimento Pesqui Florestal — Serie Divulgacao. Projeto de Desenvolvimento e Pesquisa Florestal
Ser Emp — Service Employee
Serengeti Res Inst Annu Rep — Serengeti Research Institute. Annual Report
Ser Entomol (The Hague) — Series Entomologica (The Hague)
Ser Geol Econ (Braz) Sup Desenvolvimento Nordeste Div Geol — Serie Geologia Economica (Brazil). Superintendencia do Desenvolvimento do Nordeste. Divisao de Geologia
Ser Haematol — Series Haematologica
Serials BLL — Serials in the British Lending Library
Serials Libn — Serials Librarian
Serials R — Serials Review
Sericult Res — Sericultural Research [*Japan*]
Ser Inf Conf Cursos Reun Interam Inst Agric Sci — Serie Informes de Conferencias. Cursos y Reuniones-Inter-American Institute of Agricultural Sciences
Ser L — Serie Linguistica
Ser Lib — Serials Librarian
Ser Libr — Serials Librarian
SERM — Syncrude Environmental Research Monograph
Ser Mat Fis — Serie di Matematica e Fisica
Ser Monogr Inst Zootec — Serie Monografias. Instituto de Zootecnia
Serol Mus Bull — Serological Museum Bulletin
Serono Symp Proc — Serono Symposia. Proceedings
Ser Paedopsychiatr — Series Paedopsychiatrica
Ser Piper — Serie Piper
Ser Poeyana Inst Biol Acad Cienc Cuba — Serie Poeyana. Instituto de Biologia. Academia de Ciencias de Cuba
Ser Poeyana Inst Zool Acad Cienc Cuba — Serie Poeyana. Instituto de Zoologia. Academia de Ciencias de Cuba
Ser Publ US Northeast Reg Plant Introd Stn — Serial Publication. United States Northeast Regional Plant Introduction Station
Ser R — Serials Review
SerrC — Serraika Chronika
Ser Sl — Serial Slants
SERT J — SERT [*Society of Electronic and Radio Technicians*] Journal
Ser Universitaria — Serie Universitaria
Serv — Service: A Review of Agricultural and Chemical Progress
Serv Can Faune Cah Biol — Service Canadien de la Faune. Cahiers de Biologie
Serv Cent Prot Rayonnem Ionis (Fr) Rapp Act — Service Central de Protection Contre les Rayonnements Ionisants (France). Rapport d'Activite
Serv Esp Saude Publica Rev (Brazil) — Servico Especial de Saude Publica. Revista (Brazil)
Serv Farm Ranch Home — Serving Farm, Ranch, and Home. Quarterly. University of Nebraska. College of Agriculture and Home Economics. Agricultural Experiment Station
Serv Geol Bolivia Bol — Servicio Geologico de Bolivia. Boletin
Serv Geol Ital Mem Descr Carta Geol Ital — Servizio Geologico d'Italia. Memorie Descrittive della Carta Geologica d'Italia
Serv Geol Port Mem — Servicos Geologics de Portugal. Memoria
Service Soc — Service Social
Servico Soc de Comer Bol Bibl — Servico Social de Comercio. Boletim Bibliografico
Servico Soc e Soc — Servico Social e Sociedade

Serv Nac Min Geol (Argent) Rev — Servicio Nacional Minero Geologico (Argentina). Revista
Serv Shell Agric Ser A — Servicio Shell para el Agricultor. Serie A
Serv Shell Agr Ser A — Servicio Shell para el Agricultor. Serie A. Informe
Serv Soc (Bruxelles) — Service Social (Bruxelles)
Serv Soc Monde — Service Social dans le Monde
Serv Soc (Quebec) — Service Social (Quebec)
Serv World — Service World International
SES — Schriften far Ekonomik un Statistik
SES — Social and Economic Studies
SES — Sophia English Studies
SES — Studies in Environmental Science [*Elsevier Book Series*]
SESA Pap — SESA [*Society for Experimental Stress Analysis*] Papers
SeSL — Studi e Saggi Linguistici
SES Rep CSIRO Sol Energy Stud — SES Report. Solar Energy Studies Unit. Commonwealth Scientific and Industrial Research Organisation
SeT — Studi e Testi [*Rome*]
SET — Studies in English (University of Texas)
Seta Artif — Seta Artificiale
Set Hall Leg J — Seton Hall Legislative Journal
Set H LR — Seton Hall Law Review
SET Manpower Comments — Scientific Engineering. Technical Manpower Comments
Seto Mar Biol Lab Publ — Seto Marine Biological Laboratory. Publications
Seton Hall Leg J — Seton Hall Legislative Journal
Seton Hall L Rev — Seton Hall Law Review
Settim Med — Settimana Medica [*Italy*]
Settim Osp — Settimana Ospitaliera
SEU — Dynamik im Handel
Sev Cent N — Seventeenth-Century News
Seven Ct N — Seventeenth-Century News
Severni Morava — Severni Morava Vastivedny Sbornik
Sev-Oset Gos Pedagog Inst Uch Zap — Severo-Osetinskii Gosudarstvennyi Pedagogicheskii Institut. Uchenye Zapiski
SEVPEN — Service d'Edition et de Vente des Publications de l'Education Nationale
Sev-Vost Kompleks Nauch-Issled Inst Akad Nauk SSSR Sib Otd — Severo-Vostochnyy Kompleksnyy Nauchno-Issledovatel'skiy Institut Akademiya Nauk SSSR Sibirskoye Otdeleniye
Sev Zapad Evr Chasti SSSR — Severo-Zapad Evropeiskoi Chasti SSSR
Sev Zapadn Zaochn Politekh Inst Tr — Severo-Zapadnyi Zaochnyi Politekhnicheskii Institut Trudy
Sew — Sewanee Review
Sewage Ind Waste Eng — Sewage and Industrial Waste Engineering
Sewage Ind Wastes — Sewage and Industrial Wastes
Sewage Purif Land Drain Water River Eng — Sewage Purification. Land Drainage. Water and River Engineering
Sewage Works Eng Munic Sanit — Sewage Works Engineering and Municipal Sanitation
Sewage Works J — Sewage Works Journal
Sewanee R — Sewanee Review
Sewanee Rev — Sewanee Review
Sewan R — Sewanee Review
Sew R — Sewanee Review
Sew Rev — Sewanee Review
Sex Disabil — Sexuality and Disability
Sex Scien — Working Papers on Sex, Science, and Culture
Sex Transm Dis — Sexually-Transmitted Diseases
Seybold Rep Off Systems — Seybold Report on Office Systems
Seychelles Dep Agric Annu Rep — Seychelles Department of Agriculture. Annual Report
SEZ — Seifen, Oele, Fette, Waechse. Die Internationale Fachzeitschrift
SEzik — Sapostavitelno Ezikoznanie
SF — Sbornik Filologicky
SF — Science Fiction
SF — Social Forces
SF — Socialisticki Front
SF — Soils and Fertilizers
Sf — Sprachforum
SF — Studi Francesi
SF — Studia Fennica
SF — Studia Filozoficzne
SFA — Science Fiction Adventures [*1952-1954*]
SFAB — Science Fiction Adventures [*1958-1963*]
SFAC — Science Fiction Adventure Classics
SFAD — Science Fiction Adventures [*1956-1958*]
SFB — Sbornik Filosoficke Fakulty v Bratislave
SFB — Science Fantasy
SFB — Sugarcane Farmers Bulletin [*Quezon City*]
SF Bay — San Francisco Bay Guardian
SF Bay Gdn — San Francisco Bay Guardian
SFC — San Francisco Examiner and Chronicle [*This World Section*]
SFC — Science Fiction Adventure Classics
SFC — SF Commentary
SFC — Sweden Now
SFCHD — Solid Fuel Chemistry [*English translation*]

SFCTDX — Centro Internacional de Agricultura Tropical [*CIAT*]. Series FE

SFD — Science Fiction Digest

SFD — Sound and Vibration

SFDH — Schriften des Freien Deutschen Hochstifts

SFE — Studies in Financial Economics [*Elsevier Book Series*]

SFELT — Societe Francaise d'Editions Litteraires et Techniques

SFen — Studia Fennica

SFFBU — Sbornik Praci Filosoficke Fakulty Brnenske University

SFFF — Societas pro Fauna et Flora Fennica

SFFFM — Societas pro Fauna et Flora Fennica. Memoranda

SFFUK — Sbornik Filozofickej Fakulty Univerzity Komenskeho. Philologica

SFFUP — Sbornik Filozofickej Fakulty Univerzity P. J. Safarika v Presove

SFG — SF Greats

SFG — Spanische Forschungen. Gorresgesellschaft

SFH — SF Horizons

SFI — SF Impulse

SFI — Statistiques Financieres Internationales

SFI — Studi di Filogia Italiana

SFIB — SFI [*Sport Fishing Institute*] Bulletin

S Fict R — Science Fiction Review

SFil — Studime Filologjike

SFIQ — Science Fiction Quarterly [*1951-1958*]

SFIS — Stanford French and Italian Studies

SFK — Periodiekenparade

SFKGA — Sprechsaal fuer Keramik, Glas, Email, Silikate

SFL — Studies in French Literature

SFLR — University of San Francisco. Law Review

SFM — Science Fiction Monthly

SFM — Symposia. Fondation Merieux [*Elsevier Book Series*]

S 8 Fmkr — Super 8 Filmaker

SFN — SFRA Newsletter

SFNL — Shakespeare on Film Newsletter

SFNYA — Southern Florist and Nurseryman [*United States*]

SFORD — Sozialistische Forstwirtschaft

SFP — Science Fiction Plus

SFPE Technol Rep — SFPE [*Society of Fire Protection Engineers*] Technology Report

SFPS — Studia z Filologii Polskiej i Slowianskiej

SFQ — Science Fiction Quarterly [*1940-1943*]

SFQ — Southern Folklore Quarterly

SFR — San Francisco Review

SF & R — Scholars' Facsimiles and Reprints

SFR — Science Fiction Review

SFR — Stanford French Review

S Fr — Studi Francesi

SFran — Studi Francescani

SFRB — San Francisco Review of Books

SF Rev Bks — San Francisco Review of Books

SFrL — Studies in French Literature

SFRM — Science Fiction Review. Monthly

SFrQ — San Francisco Quarterly

SFRSAY — Food Research Institute. Studies [*Stanford*]

SFS — Science Fiction Stories

SFS — Science Fiction Studies

SFS — Science for Schools [*Manila*]

SFSL — Science Fiction. Review of Speculative Literature

SFSLA — Sbornik Trudov po Agronomicheskoi Fizike

SFSS — Svenska Fornskriftssaellskapets Skrifter

SFST — Science Fiction Studies

SFSt — Swiss-French Studies [*Etudes Romandes*]

SFSUA — Studia Forestalia Suecica

SFSV — Svenska Forfattare Utgivna av Svenska Vitterhetssamfundet

SF Sym — San Francisco Symphony. Program Notes

SFT — Sheffield Morning Telegraph

SFT — Soviet and Eastern European Foreign Trade

SFT — Studi di Filogia Todeska

SFTB — Science Fiction Times

SFUJA — Steam and Fuel Users' Journal

SFUK — Sbornik Filozofickej Fakulty Univerzity Komenskeho

SFUPD — Synthetic Fuels Update

SFUS — Sbornik Filozofickej Fakulty Univerzity P. J. Safarika

SFUS — Sovetskoe Finno-Ugrovedenie/Soviet Fenno-Ugric Studies

SFVK — Svenska Folkskolans Vaenner. Kalender

SFY — Science Fiction Yearbook

SG — Siculorum Gymnasium

SG — Sinte Geertruydtsbronne

SG — Sprach der Gegenwart

SG — Studi Genuesi

SG — Studi Germanici

SG — Studi Goriziani

SG — Studium Generale

SG — Sydney Gazette

SGA J — SGA [*Society of Gastrointestinal Assistants*] Journal

SGAK — Studien zur Germanistik, Anglistik und Komparatistik

SGAOR — Sitzungsberichte. Gesellschaft fuer Geschichte und Altertumskunde der Ostseeprovinzen Russlands

SGB — Schlesische Geschichtsblaetter (Breslau)

SGB — Studien und Mitteilungen zur Geschichte des Benediktiner-Ordens

SGBIA — Symposia Genetica et Biologica Italica

SGCL — Studies in General and Comparative Literature

SGD — Solar-Geophysical Data

SGEGA — Studia Geophysica et Geodaetica

SGen — Studium Generale

SGer — Studia Germanica

S Ger S — Stanford German Studies

SGF — Stockholmer Germanistische Forschungen

SGFMV — Sammendrag af Groenlands Fangstilister MV

SGF Publ — SGF [*Sveriges Gummitekniska Foerening*] Publicerande

SGG — Studia Germanica Gandensia

SGGAOPR — Sitzungsberichte. Gesellschaft fuer Geschichte und Altertumskunde der Ostseeprovinzen Russlands

SGH — Generale Maatschappij van Belgie. Informatieblad

SGh — Studia Ghisleriana [*Pavia*]

SGHLA — Stadt- und Gebaeudetechnik

SGI — Studi di Grammatica Italiana

SGL — Spiegel [*Hamburg*]

SGL — Studies in German Literature

SGLF — Symposia. Giovanni Lorenzini Foundation [*Elsevier Book Series*]

SGLI — Societe Geographique de Liege. Bulletin [*Belgium*]

SGLL — Studies in the Germanic Languages and Literatures

SGLSA — Stomatoloski Glasnik Srbije

SGM — Scottish Geographical Magazine

SGMH — Study Group. Institute for Research into Mental and Multiple Handicap [*Elsevier Book Series*]

SGN — Simulation Gaming News

SGNAD — Shoni Geka Naika

SGNRA — Surgical Neurology [*Tryon, NC*]

SGo — Studi Goriziani

SGOBA — Surgery, Gynecology, and Obstetrics

SGoldoniani — Studi Goldoniani

SGor — Studi Goriziani

SGR — Science and Government Report

SGr — Studii de Gramatica

SGram — Studii de Gramatica

SGRT — Soviet Geography. Review and Translations

SGS — Scottish Gaelic Studies

SGSHA — Shigen Gijutsu Shikenjo Hokoku

SGSYB — Stadler Genetics Symposia

SGT — Schriften. Gesellschaft fuer Theatergeschichte

SGTID — Sawyer's Gas Turbine International

Sgtl — Sightlines

SGTPA — Sbornik Trudov Nauchno-Issledovatel'skii Institut Gigieny Truda i Profzabolevanii Imeni N. I. Makhviladze

SGU — Studia Germanistica Upsaliensia

SGV — Summlung Gemeinverstaendlicher Vortraege und Schriften aus dem Gebiet der Theologie und Religionsgeschichte [*Tuebingen*]

SGVGA — Sbornik Geologickych Ved. Geologie

SGVLA — Sbornik Geologickych Ved. Loziskova Geologie

SGVS — Summlung Gemeinverstaendlicher Vortraege und Schriften aus dem Gebiet der Theologie und Religionsgeschichte [*Tuebingen*]

SGVUA — Sbornik Geologickych Ved, Uzita Geofyzika

SGym — Siculorum Gymnasium

SGZAB — Sanyo Gijutsu Zasshi

Sh — Shadforth's Reserved Judgements

S H — Slovenska Hudba

SH — Speighel Historiael van de Bond van Gentse Germanisten

SH — Studia Hellenistica

SH — Studia Hibernica [*Dublin*]

SH — Sun-Herald

SH — Sydney Herald

SHA — Sitzungsberichte. Heidelberg Akademie der Wissenschaft

SHAGAn — Societe d'Histoire et d'Archeologie de Gand. Annales

SHAGBull — Societe d'Histoire et d'Archeologie de Gand. Bulletin

Shakes Jah — Shakespeare-Jahrbuch

Shakespeare-Jahrb — Shakespeare-Jahrbuch

Shakespeare Q — Shakespeare Quarterly

Shakespeare S — Shakespeare Survey

Shakes Q — Shakespeare Quarterly

Shakes Surv — Shakespeare Survey

Shakhtnoe Stroit — Shakhtnoe Stroitel'stvo [*USSR*]

Shak-Jahrb — Shakespeare-Jahrbuch

ShakS — Shakespeare Studies

Shale Ctry — Shale Country

Shale Rev — Shale Review

SHALPub — Societe Historique et Archeologique dans le Duche de Limbourg. Publications

Shanghai Iron Steel Res Inst Tech Rep — Shanghai Iron and Steel Research Institute. Technical Report [*China*]

Shantung Med J — Shantung Medical Journal [*People's Republic of China*]

Sharpe — Sharpe's London Magazine

SHATAn — Societe Historique et Archeologique de Tournai. Annales

SHAW — Sitzungsberichte. Heidelberg Akademie der Wissenschaft

ShawB — Shaw Bulletin
Shaw R — Shaw Review
Shaw Rev — Shaw Review
S and H Bull — Smoking and Health Bulletin
Shchorichnyk Ukrayins'ke Bot Tov — Shchorichnyk Ukrayins'ke Botanichne
     Tovarystvo
SHCS — Springer Series on Health Care and Society
SHCSR — Spicilegium Historicum Congregationis Smi Redemptoris
SHECD — Solar Heating and Cooling
Sheepfarming Annu — Sheepfarming Annual
Sheepfarming Annu Massey Agr Coll — Sheepfarming Annual. Massey
     Agricultural College
Sheet Met Ind — Sheet Metal Industries
Sheet Met Platework News — Sheet Metal and Plateworking News
Sheffield Univ Geol Soc J — Sheffield University. Geological Society. Journal
SHEH — Stanford Honors Essays in the Humanities
Shell Agric — Shell in Agriculture
Shell Aviat News — Shell Aviation News
Shell Bitum Rev — Shell Bitumin Review
Shell Devel Co Explor and Production Research Div Pub — Shell Development
     Company. Exploration and Production Research Division. Publication
Shellfish — Shellfish. Market Review and Outlook
Shell House J — Shell House Journal
Shell J — Shell Journal
Shell Mag — Shell Magazine [*England*]
Shell Polym — Shell Polymers
Shelter — Shelterforce
Shen — Shenandoah
Sherst Delo — Sherstyanoe Delo
SHF — Societe de l'Histoire de France
SHFABull — Societe de l'Histoire de France. Annuaire Bulletin
SHGED — Shoni Geka
SHGNA — Shigen
SHHPB — Shu-Hsueh Hsueh-Pao
SHib — Studia Hibernica
SHIGD4 — Japanese Journal of Psychosomatic Medicine
Shikoku Acta Med — Shikoku Acta Medica
Shikoku Agr Res — Shikoku Agricultural Research
Shimadzu Rev — Shimadzu Review
Shinagawa Tech Rep — Shinagawa Technical Report
Shinko Electr J — Shinko Electric Journal
Shinshu Med J — Shinshu Medical Journal [*Japan*]
Shinshu Univ Fac Sci J — Shinshu University. Faculty of Science. Journal
Shipbldg Mar Engng Int — Shipbuilding and Marine Engineering International
Shipbldg Shipp Rec — Shipbuilding and Shipping Record
Ship Boat — Ship and Boat
Ship and Boat — Ship and Boat International
Ship & Boat Int — Ship and Boat International
Shipbuild Mar Engine Build — Shipbuilder and Marine Engine Builder
     [*England*]
Shipbuild Mar Eng Int — Shipbuilding and Marine Engineering International
Shipbuild & Mar Engng Int — Shipbuilding and Marine Engineering
     International
Shipcare Marit Manage — Shipcare and Maritime Management
Ship Com Aviation — Shipping, Commerce, and Aviation of Australia
Shipping Statis — Shipping Statistics
Shipping Statis and Econ — Shipping Statistics and Economics
Shipp Weekly — Shipping Weekly
Shipp Wld Shipbldr — Shipping World and Shipbuilder
Shipp World & Shipbuild — Shipping World and Shipbuilder
Shire & Munic R — Shire and Municipal Record
Shire Munic Rec — Shire and Municipal Record
Shire & Munic Rec — Shire and Municipal Record
Shirley Inst Bull — Shirley Institute. Bulletin
Shirley Inst Mem — Shirley Institute. Memoirs
Shivaji Univ J — Shivaji University. Journal
Shivaji Univ Sci J — Shivaji University. Science Journal
Shizenshi-Kenkyu Occas Pap Osaka Mus Nat Hist — Shizenshi-Kenkyu
     Occasional Papers. Osaka Museum of Natural History
Sh-J — Shakespeare-Jahrbuch
Sh-Jb — Shakespeare-Jahrbuch
SHJMD — Soon Chun Hyang Journal of Medicine
SHK — Shock
SHKEA5 — Japanese Journal of Psychology
SHKKA — Shika Kiso Igakkai Zasshi
Sh Metal Inds — Sheet Metal Industries
SHMRD — Shire and Municipal Record
ShN — Shakespeare Newsletter
SHNAD — Shoni Naika
Shock Cir Homeostasis Trans Conf — Shock and Circulatory Homeostasis.
     Transactions of the Conference
Shock Vib Bull — Shock and Vibration Bulletin
Shock Vib Dig — Shock and Vibration Digest
Shoe Leather Rep — Shoe and Leather Reporter
Shokubai Suppl — Shokubai. Supplement [*Japan*]
Shokubutsu Boeki Plant Prot — Shokubutsu Boeki/Plant Protection

SHOND — Shoni No Noshinkei
Short Rep Rhod Geol Surv — Short Report. Rhodesia Geological Survey
Showa Wire Cable Rev — Showa Wire and Cable Review [*Japan*]
Show-Me — Show-Me News and Views [*Missouri*]
Show Me Lib — Show-Me Libraries
ShP — Shakespeare Pictorial
Shp — Starship. The Magazine about Science Fiction
SHPA — Shelf Paper. Alaska Outer Continental Shelf Office
SHPHUJ — Scripta Hierosolymitana. Publications of the Hebrew University
     (Jerusalem)
Sh Q — Shakespeare Quarterly
SHQ — Southwestern Historical Quarterly
SHR — Hotel Revue. Wochenzeitung fuer Hotellerie und Tourismus
SHR — Scottish Historical Review
ShR — Shakespeare Review
SHR — Southern Humanities Review
SHRTA — Scientia Horticulturae (Amsterdam)
ShS — Shakespeare Survey
SHSPB — Soviet Hydrology. Selected Papers
ShStud — Shakespeare Studies [*Tokyo*]
SHT — Recycling [*Dusseldorf*]
SHT — Svensk Humanistisk Tidskrift
SHUJA — Shujutsu
SHum — Studies in the Humanities
S Hum Rev — Southern Humanities Review
Shuttle — Shuttle, Spindle, and Dyepot
SHVE — Sammelblatt der Historischer Verein Eichstatt
SHVF — Sammelblatt der Historischer Verein Freising
SHVI — Sammelblatt der Historischer Verein Ingolstadt
SHWPA — Sheng Wu Hua Hsueh Yu Sheng Wu Wu Li Hsueh Pao
SHZAA — Shoyakugaku Zasshi
SHZAAY — Japanese Journal of Pharmacognosy
SI — Scuola Italiana
SI — Sing Out
Si — Sistema
SI — Spettatore Italiano
SI — Sports Illustrated
SI — Studia Islamica
SI — Studii Italiene
SI — Svizzera Italiana
SIAC — Studies in Automation and Control [*Elsevier Book Series*]
SIA J — SIA [*Société des Ingenieurs de l'Automobile*] Journal [*France*]
SIAJ — SIAJ: Singapore Institute of Architects. Journal
SIAM J Algebraic Discrete Methods — SIAM [*Society for Industrial and
     Applied Mathematics*] Journal on Algebraic and Discrete Methods
SIAM J Algebraic and Discrete Methods — SIAM [*Society for Industrial and
     Applied Mathematics*] Journal on Algebraic and Discrete Methods
SIAM J A Ma — SIAM [*Society for Industrial and Applied Mathematics*]
     Journal on Applied Mathematics
SIAM J Appl Math — SIAM [*Society for Industrial and Applied
     Mathematics*] Journal on Applied Mathematics
SIAM J App Math — SIAM [*Society for Industrial and Applied Mathematics*]
     Journal on Applied Mathematics
SIAM J Comput — SIAM [*Society for Industrial and Applied Mathematics*]
     Journal on Computing
SIAM J Cont — SIAM [*Society for Industrial and Applied Mathematics*]
     Journal on Control
SIAM J Control — SIAM [*Society for Industrial and Applied Mathematics*]
     Journal on Control
SIAM J Control Optim — SIAM [*Society for Industrial and Applied
     Mathematics*] Journal on Control and Optimization
SIAM J Control and Optimiz — SIAM [*Society for Industrial and Applied
     Mathematics*] Journal on Control and Optimization
SIAM J Control Optimization — SIAM [*Society for Industrial and Applied
     Mathematics*] Journal on Control and Optimization
SIAM J Math — SIAM [*Society for Industrial and Applied Mathematics*]
     Journal on Mathematical Analysis
SIAM J Math Anal — SIAM [*Society for Industrial and Applied
     Mathematics*] Journal on Mathematical Analysis
SIAM J Num — SIAM [*Society for Industrial and Applied Mathematics*]
     Journal on Numerical Analysis
SIAM J Numer Anal — SIAM [*Society for Industrial and Applied
     Mathematics*] Journal on Numerical Analysis
SIAM J Sci and Stat Comput — SIAM [*Society for Industrial and Applied
     Mathematics*] Journal on Scientific and Statistical Computing
SIAM J Sci Stat Comput — SIAM [*Society for Industrial and Applied
     Mathematics*] Journal on Scientific and Statistical Computing
SIAM J Sci Statist Comput — SIAM [*Society for Industrial and Applied
     Mathematics*] Journal on Scientific and Statistical Computing
SIAM R — SIAM [*Society for Industrial and Applied Mathematics*] Review
SIAM Rev — SIAM [*Society for Industrial and Applied Mathematics*] Review
SIAM Stud Appl Math — SIAM [*Society for Industrial and Applied
     Mathematics*] Studies in Applied Mathematics
SIAM Studies in Appl Math — SIAM [*Society for Industrial and Applied
     Mathematics*] Studies in Applied Mathematics
Sibelius — Sibelius-Mitteilungen

Siberian Math J — Siberian Mathematical Journal
Sib Geogr Sb — Sibirskii Geograficheskii Sbornik
Sibirsk Mat Z — Sibirskii Matematiceskii Zurnal
Sibirsk Mat Zh — Akademiya Nauk SSSR. Sibirskoe Otdelenie. Sibirskii Matematicheskii Zhurnal
Sibirsk Vrach Viedom — Sibirskiia Vrachebnyia Viedomosti
Sib Mat Zh — Sibirskij Matematiceskij Zhurnal
Sib Vest Sel'Khoz Nauki — Siberskii Vestnik Sel'skokhozyaistvennoi Nauki
SICAB — Sichere Arbeit
SicG — Siculorum Gymnasium
SICHD — Sicherheit
Sicherheit Chem Umwelt — Sicherheit in Chemie und Umwelt
Sicherheitspol Heute — Sicherheitspolitik Heute
Sicilia Arch — Sicilia Archaeologica. Rassegna Periodica di Studi, Notizie e Documentazione
SICJA — Siberian Chemistry Journal [English Translation]
SICMAU — International Congress for Microbiology. Symposia
S Icon — Studies in Iconography
SICSA — Sicher Ist Sicher
Sida Contrib Bot — Sida Contributions to Botany
Side Eff Drugs Annu — Side Effects of Drugs. Annual
Sider Latinoam — Siderurgia Latinoamericana
SID J — SID [Society for Information Display] Journal
Sid Mess — Sidereal Messenger
SIDZD — Saitama Ika Daigaku Zasshi
SIE — Studies in International Economics [Elsevier Book Series]
Siemens-Albis Ber — Siemens-Albis Berichte
Siemens Components (Engl Ed) — Siemens Components (English Edition)
Siemens Electron Components Bull — Siemens Electronic Components Bulletin
Siemens Energietech — Siemens Energietechnik [West Germany]
Siemens Forsch Entwickl — Siemens Forschungs- und Entwicklungsberichte. Research and Development Reports
Siemens Forsch- und Entwicklungsber — Siemens Forschungs- und Entwicklungsberichte
Siemens Forsch Entwicklungsber — Siemens Forschungs- und Entwicklungsberichte
Siemens Forsch Entwicklungsber Res Dev Rep — Siemens Forschungs- und Entwicklungsberichte. Research and Development Reports
Siemens Power Eng — Siemens Power Engineering [West Germany]
Siemens Rev — Siemens Review
Siemens-Z — Siemens-Zeitschrift
SIEND — Saiensu
Sierra — Sierra Club. Bulletin
Sierra Club B — Sierra Club. Bulletin
Sierra Ed News — Sierra Educational News
Sierra Leone Agric Div Minist Agric Nat Resour Rep — Sierra Leone Agricultural Division. Ministry of Agriculture and Natural Resources. Report
Sierra Leone Fish Div Tech Pap — Sierra Leone Fisheries Division. Technical Paper
Sierra Leone Rep Geol Surv Div — Sierra Leone. Report on the Geological Survey Division
SIF — Studi Internazionali di Filosofia
SIFC — Studi Italiani di Filologia Classica
SIFEA — Silva Fennica
Sig — Sigma. Revue du Centre d'Etudes Linguistiques d'Aix Montpellier
SIG — Sylloge Inscriptionum Graecarum
SIGAB — Saigai Igaku
SIGEA — Silvae Genetica
Sight & S — Sight and Sound
Sight-Sav R — Sight-Saving Review
Sight-Sav Rev — Sight-Saving Review
Siglo Med — Siglo Medico
Sigma Ser Pure Math — Sigma Series in Pure Mathematics
Signalmans J — Signalman's Journal
Signal Process — Signal Processing
Sign Lang Stud — Sign Language Studies
Sigurnost Rudn — Sigurnost u Rudnicima
SIGZA — Showa Igakkai Zasshi
SIHED — Sanitaer-Installateur und Heizungsbauer
SIINA — Silicates Industriels [Belgium]
SIJ — Small Industry Journal [Quezon City]
SIK — Studi Italici (Kyoto)
SiK — Sztuka i Krytyka
Sikh R — Sikh Review [Calcutta]
SIKTA — Silikaty
SIL — Studies in Linguistics
SILAD — Siderurgia Latinoamericana
Silent Pic — Silent Picture
Silicates Indus — Silicates Industriels
Silik — Silikaty
Silk Rayon Ind India — Silk and Rayon Industries of India
Silkworm Inf Bull — Silkworm Information Bulletin
Silliman J — Silliman Journal
S Ill ULJ — Southern Illinois University. Law Journal
SILOP — Studies in Linguistics. Occasional Papers

SILTA — Studi Italiani di Linguistica Teorica ed Applicata
Silvaecult Trop Subtrop — Silvaecultura Tropica et Subtropica
Silvae Genet — Silvae Genetica
Silva Fenn — Silva Fennica
Silvic Sao Paulo — Silvicultura em Sao Paulo
Silv Notes Ont Dep Lds For — Silvicultural Notes. Ontario Department of Lands and Forests
Silv Res Note (Tanz) — Silviculture Research Note (Tanzania)
SIMA — Studies in Mediterranean Archaeology
SIMArsbok — Svenska Israels-Missionens Arsbok [Stockholm]
SIME — Studies in Mechanical Engineering [Elsevier Book Series]
SIMG — Sammelbaende. Internationale Musik Gesellschaft
SIMJA — Singapore Medical Journal
SIMM — Studies in Indo-Muslim Mysticism
Simon's Town Hist Soc — Simon's Town Historical Society
SIMPA — Rendiconti. Societa Italiana di Mineralogia e Petrologia
Simp Otlalennoi Gibrid Rast — Simpozium po Otlalennoi Gibridizatsii Rastenii
SiMS — Studier i Modern Sprakvetenskap
SIMUA — Simulation
Simulat Gam — Simulation and Games
Simulat & Games — Simulation and Games
Simulations Councils Proc — Simulations Councils. Proceedings
Simul Counc Proc Ser — Simulation Councils. Proceedings Series
Simul and Games — Simulation and Games
SIN — Scientific Information Notes
SiN — Sin Nombre
SIND — Saskatchewan Indian
SINDB — Science and Industry [Karachi]
S Ind Stud — Southern Indian Studies
Sind Univ Res J Sci Ser — Sind University Research Journal. Science Series
Sinema — Andere Sinema
Sinet Ethiop J Sci — Sinet: An Ethiopian Journal of Science
SINFUB — Skrifter Utgitt. Instituttet foer Nordisk Filologi. Universitetet i Bergen
Singapore Bus — Singapore Business
Singapore J Primary Ind — Singapore Journal of Primary Industries
Singapore Lib — Singapore Libraries
Singapore L Rev — Singapore Law Review
Singapore Med J — Singapore Medical Journal
Singapore Natl Inst Chem Bull — Singapore National Institute of Chemistry. Bulletin
Singapore Statist Bull — Singapore Statistical Bulletin
Sing Kir — Singende Kirche
Sing LR — Singapore Law Review
Sing Pub Health B — Singapore Public Health Bulletin
Sing Stat B — Singapore Statistical Bulletin
Sinister — Sinister Wisdom
Sin N — Sin Nombre
SIN Newsl — SIN [Schweizerisches Institut fuer Nuklearforschung] Newsletter
Sino-Am Rels — Sino-American Relations [Taiwan]
Sinop Odontol — Sinopse de Odontologia
SINSU — Skrifter Utgivna. Institutionen foer Nordiska Sprak Vid. Uppsala Universitet
SINSUU — Skrifter Utgivna. Institutionen foer Nordiska Sprak Vid. Uppsala Universitet
Sint Almazy — Sinteticheskie Almazy
Sint Anal Strukt Org Soedin — Sintez, Analiz, i Struktura Organicheskikh Soedinenii [USSR]
Sintesi Econ — Sintesi Economica
Sint Fiz-Khim Polim — Sintez i Fiziko-Khimiya Polimerov
Sint Org Soedin — Sintezy Organicheskikh Soedinenij
SIOBA — Sbornik Informatsii po Obogashcheniyu i Briketirovaniyu Uglei
Sip — Sipario
SIP — Subject Index to Periodicals
SIPL — Studies in Philippine Linguistics
SIPN — Security Industry and Product News
SIPO — Soobshcheniia Imperatorskovo Pravoslavnovo Palestinskovo Obshchestva
SIQR — Studies: An Irish Quarterly Review of Letters, Philosophy, and Science
SIR — Studies in Romanticism
Sirag — Sirag. Amsagir Grakanut ean ew Aruesdi
SIREA — SIAM [Society for Industrial and Applied Mathematics] Review
SIRRBJ — Institutionen foer Skogsforyngring Rapporter och Uppsatser
SIs — Scripta Islandica
SIS — Sino-Indian Studies
SISIMS — Say It So It Makes Sense
SIsl — Studia Islamica
Si & So — Sight and Sound
SISRBO — Institutionen foer Skogszoologi Rapporter och Uppsatser
Sist e Autom — Sistemi e Automazione
Sist Avtom Nauchn Issled — Sistemy Avtomatisatsii Nauchnykh Issledovanii
Sistema — Sistema Revista de Ciencias Sociales
Sistem Metod Sovrem Nauka — Sistemnyj Metod i Sovremennaja Nauka
Sisters — Sisters Today

Sist Nerv — Sistema Nervoso
Sistole Rev Urug Cardiol — Sistole. Revista Uruguaya de Cardiologia
Site Sel Hdbk — Site Selection Handbook
SITKA — Silikattechnik [*East Germany*]
Sitzungsber d Akadem d Wiss — Sitzungsberichte. Akademie der Wissenschaften
Sitzungsber Akad Wiss DDR Math-Naturwiss-Tech Jahrgang 1977 — Sitzungsberichte. Akademie der Wissenschaften der DDR. Mathematik-Naturwissenschaften-Technik. Jahrgang 1977
Sitzungsber Akad Wiss DDR Math-Naturwiss Tech Jahrgang 1979 — Sitzungsberichte. Akademie der Wissenschaften der DDR. Mathematik-Naturwissenschaften-Technik. Jahrgang 1979
Sitzungsber Berl Ges Naturforsch Freunde — Sitzungsberichte. Berlinische Gesellschaft Naturforschender Freunde
Sitzungsber Deut Akad Landwirt Wiss Berlin — Sitzungsberichte. Deutsche Akademie der Landwirtschaftswissenschaften zu Berlin
Sitzungsber Deut Akad Wiss Berlin Kl Math Phys Tech — Sitzungsberichte. Deutsche Akademie der Wissenschaften zu Berlin. Klasse fuer Mathematik, Physik, und Technik
Sitzungsber Finn Akad Wiss — Sitzungsberichte. Finnische Akademie der Wissenschaften
Sitzungsber Ges Befoerd Ges Naturwiss Marburg — Sitzungsberichte. Gesellschaft zur Befoerderung der Gesamten Naturwissenschaften zu Marburg [*West Germany*]
Sitzungsber Ges Naturforsch Freunde Berlin — Sitzungsberichte. Gesellschaft Naturforschender Freunde zu Berlin
Sitzungsber Heidelb Akad Wiss Math-Naturwiss Kl — Sitzungsberichte. Heidelberg Akademie der Wissenschaften. Mathematisch-Naturwissenschaftliche Klasse
SIV — Vierteljahrshefte zur Wirtschaftsforschung
SIX — Sigma
Six — Sixties
Six Ct J — Sixteenth Century Journal
Sixteen Cent J — Sixteenth Century Journal
SIZSA — Sapporo Igaku Zasshi
SJ — Saalburg-Jahrbuch
SJ — Shakespeare-Jahrbuch
SJ — Silliman Journal
SJ — Simulation Journal
SJ — Slovensky Jazyk
SJA — Southwestern Journal of Anthropology
SJAEA — Soviet Journal of Atomic Energy
SJAnth — Southwestern Journal of Anthropology
SJB — Zeitschrift fuer Wirtschaftswissenschaften und Sozialwissenschaften
SJCCA — Stroke
SJCLA — Scandinavian Journal of Clinical and Laboratory Investigation
SJCOA — SIAM [*Society for Industrial and Applied Mathematics*] Journal on Control
SJCOD — SIAM [*Society for Industrial and Applied Mathematics*] Journal on Control and Optimization
SJCT — SJC Today. Sheldon Jackson College [*Sitka, AK*]
SJDBA — Soviet Journal of Developmental Biology
SJE — Swedish Journal of Economics
SJECA — Soviet Journal of Ecology [*English Translation*]
SJER — Scandinavian Journal of Educational Research
SJF — Japanese Finance and Industry
SJFMA — Soviet Journal of Non-Ferrous Metals [*English Translation*]
SJFT — Svenska Jerusalems-Foereningens Tidskrift
SJGHA — Sumitomo Jukikai Giho
SJGRA — Scandinavian Journal of Gastroenterology
SJH — Shakespeare-Jahrbuch (Heidelberg)
SJHAA — Scandinavian Journal of Haematology
SJL — Semitic Journal of Linguistics
SJL — Slovensky Jazyk a Literatura v Skole
SJLA — Studies in Judaism in Late Antiquity
SJLR — St. John's Law Review
SJMAA — SIAM [*Society for Industrial and Applied Mathematics*] Journal on Mathematical Analysis
SJMED — South African Journal of Hospital Medicine
SJMS — Speculum
SJNAA — SIAM [*Society for Industrial and Applied Mathematics*] Journal on Numerical Analysis
SJNCA — Soviet Journal of Nuclear Physics [*English Translation*]
SJNTA — Soviet Journal of Nondestructive Testing [*English Translation*]
SJO — Jahrbuch. Deutsche Shakespeare-Gesellschaft Ost
SJOTB — Soviet Journal of Optical Technology [*English Translation*]
SJP — Scottish Journal of Political Economy
SJP — Southern Journal of Philosophy
SJPE — Scottish Journal of Political Economy
S J Phil — Southern Journal of Philosophy
SJPNA — Soviet Journal of Particles and Nuclei
SJPRB — Scandinavian Journal of Plastic and Reconstructive Surgery
SJPYA — Scandinavian Journal of Psychology
SJR — Social Justice Review
SJR — Textile Month
SJRDA — Scandinavian Journal of Respiratory Diseases

SJS — San Jose Studies
SJSUD — Science Journal. Shivaji University
SJT — Scottish Journal of Theology
SJT — Southwestern Journal of Theology
SJTCA — Scandinavian Journal of Thoracic and Cardiovascular Surgery
SJUNA — Scandinavian Journal of Urology and Nephrology
SJV — Kyoto University. Jimbun Kagaku Kenkyu-sho. Silver Jubilee Volume
SjV — Sirp ja Vasar
SJW — Shakespeare-Jahrbuch (Weimar)
SJ(Weimar) — Shakespeare-Jahrbuch (Weimar)
SJZ — Schweizerische Juristen-Zeitung
SK — Seminarium Kondakovianum
SK — Sovetskii Kollektsioner
SKA — Skandinaviska Enskilda Banken. Quarterly Review
Skand — Skandinavistik
Skand Ensk Bank Quart R — Skandinaviska Enskilda Banken. Quarterly Review
Skandia Int Symp — Skandia International Symposia
Skandinavis — Skandinavistik
Skandinaviska Enskilda Banken Q R — Skandinaviska Enskilda Banken. Quarterly Review
Skand Numis — Skandinavisk Numismatik
Skat Mag — Skating Magazine
SKAWW — Sitzungsberichte. Kaiserliche Akademie der Wissenschaften in Wien
SKBGD — Sangyo Kogai Boshi Gijutsu
SKD — Svenska Dagbladet
SKDGQ — Sammlung Ausgewaehlter Kirchen- und Dogmengeschichtlichen Quellenschriften
SKEIA — Sanshi Kagaku Kenkyusho Iho
Skeletal Radiol — Skeletal Radiology
SkFi — Skandinavskaga Filologija
SKF Psychiatr Rep — SK and F [*Smith, Kline, and French*] Psychiatric Reporter
SKG — Srpski Knjizevni Glasnik
SKGG — Schriften. Koenigsberger Gelehrten-Gesellschaft
SKGGD — Sammlung Kurzer Grammatiken Germanischer Dialekte
SKGND — Sanup Kwahak Gisul Yeonguso Nonmunjip [*Inha University*]
SKGSA — Sekiyu Gakkaishi
SKH — Staatsblad van het Koninkrijk der Nederlanden
S-kh Biol — Sel'skokhozyaistvennaya Biologiya
S-kh Proizvod Urala — Sel'skokhozyaistvennoe Proizvodstvo Urala
S-kh Rub Rastenievod — Sel'skokhozyaistvo za Rubezhom Rastenievodstvo
SKHVL — Skrifter Utgivna av Kungliga Humanistiska Vetenskapssamfundet i Lund
SkHVSU — Skrifter Utgivna. Humanistiska Vetenskapssamfundet i Uppsala
Skillings' Min Rev — Skillings' Mining Review
Skil Mining — Skillings' Mining Review
Skin Diver Mag — Skin Diver Magazine
Skin Res — Skin Research
SKKEA — Sklar a Keramik
SKKNAJ — Annual Report. Sankyo Research Laboratories
SKKOA — Shin Kinzoku Kogyo
SKM — Schweizerische Kreditanstalt. Bulletin
SKMRA — Skillings' Mining Review
SKNEA7 — Annual Report. Shionogi Research Laboratory
SKNSB — Shokuhin Shosha
Skoda Rev — Skoda Review
Skogshoegsk Inst Skogstek Rapp Uppsats Res Notes — Skogshoegskolan, Institutionen foer Skogsteknik, Rapporter och Uppsatser. Research Notes [*Sweden*]
Skogs-Lantbruksakad Tidskr — Skogs- och Lantbruksakademiens Tidskrift
SKPanKr — Sprawozdania z Posiedzen Komisji Pan. Oddzial w Krakowie
SKRAD — Skeletal Radiology
Skriftser Roskilde Universitetsbibl — Skriftserie. Roskilde Universitetsbibliotek
Skr Lund — Skrifter Utgivna. Vetenskaps-Societeten i Lund
Skr Mineral Paleontol Geol Inst — Skrifter fran Mineralogisk och Paleontologisk-Geologiska Institutionerna
Skr Norske Vid-Akad Oslo I — Skrifter Utgitt. Norske Videnskaps-Akademi i Oslo. I. Matematisk-Naturvidenskapelig Klasse
Skr Nor Vidensk-Akad Oslo I Mat-Naturvidensk Kl — Skrifter. Norske Videnskaps-Akademi i Oslo. I. Matematisk-Naturvidenskapelig Klasse
Skr Szk Gl Gospod Wiejsk-Akad Roln Warszawie Ogrod — Skrypty Szkoly Glownej Gospodarstwa Wiejskiego-Akademii Rolniczej w Warszawie. Ogrodnictwo
Skr Udgivet Univ Zool Mus (Kbh) — Skrifter Udgivet. Universitetets Zoologiske Museum (Kobenhavn)
Skr Uppsala — Skrifter Utgivna av Kungliga Humanist. Vetenskaps-Samfundet i Uppsala
SKS — Suomalainen Kirjallisuuden Seura
SkSb — Skandinavskij Sbornik
SKTEA — Sky and Telescope
SKWKA — Sanop Kwa Kisul
Sky — Skywriting
SKYOA — Shikizai Kyokaishi

Sky & Tel — Sky and Telescope
Sky Telesc — Sky and Telescope
SKZ — Schweizerische Kirchenzeitung
Sl — Slavia
SL — Soviet Life
SL — Soviet Literature
SL — Special Libraries
SL — Studia Linguistica [*Lund*]
SL — Studies in Linguistics
SL — Sumarski List
SL — Sumerisches Lexikon [*Rome*]
SL — Svenska Landsmal och Svenskt Folkliv
Sla — Slavia
SLA — Studies in Linguistic Analysis [*Elsevier Book Series*]
SLA Adv & Mkt Div Bul — Special Libraries Association. Advertising and
    Marketing Division. Bulletin
SLA Alabama Chap Bul — Special Libraries Association. Alabama Chapter.
    Bulletin
SLA Biol Sci Div Reminder — Special Libraries Association. Biological
    Sciences Division. Reminder
Slaboproudy Obz — Slaboproudy Obzor [*Czechoslovakia*]
SLA Bus & Fin Div Bul — Special Libraries Association. Business and
    Financial Division. Bulletin
SLA Fin Div Bul — Special Libraries Association. Financial Division. Bulletin
SLA GA Chap Bul — Special Libraries Association. Georgia Chapter. Bulletin
SLA Geog & Map Div Bul — Special Libraries Association. Geography and
    Map Division. Bulletin
SLA Geog and Map Div Bull — Special Libraries Association. Geography and
    Map Division. Bulletin
SLA Ind Chap Slant — Special Libraries Association. Indiana Chapter. Slant
SLA Metals Div News — Special Libraries Association. Metals Division. News
SLA Mich Chap Bul — Special Libraries Association. Michigan Chapter.
    Bulletin
SLA Montreal Chap Bul — Special Libraries Association. Montreal Chapter.
    Bulletin
SLA Museum Div Bul — Special Libraries Association. Museum Division.
    Bulletin
SLA News — SLA [*Scottish Library Association*] News
S Lang — Studies in Language
SlAnt — Slavia Antiqua
Slants Khim Prom-st — Slantsevaya i Khimicheskaya Promyshlennost
    [*Estonian SSR*]
SLAPC — Studies in Latin American Popular Culture
SLA Picture Div Picturescope — Special Libraries Association. Picture
    Division. Picturescope
SLA Pittsburgh Chap Bul — Special Libraries Association. Pittsburgh Chapter.
    Bulletin
SLARD — Saskatchewan Law Review
SLA Sci-Tech News — Special Libraries Association. Science-Technology
    Division. News
Slaski Kwar Hist Sobotka — Slaski Kwartalnik Historyczny Sobotka
SLATA — Secondary Learning Assistance Teachers' Association. Newsletter
SLA Texas Chap Bul — Special Libraries Association. Texas Chapter. Bulletin
SLA Toronto Chap Bul — Special Libraries Association. Toronto Chapter.
    Bulletin
Slav — Slavia
SlavA — Slavia Antiqua
Slav E Eur — Slavic and East European Journal
SlavF — Slavjanskaja Filologija
Slavia Ant — Slavia Antiqua
Slavic E Eu — Slavic and East European Journal
Slavic & E Eur J — Slavic and East European Journal
Slavic R — Slavic Review
Slavic Rev — Slavic Review
SlavO — Slavica Othiniensia
Slavon E Eu — Slavonic and East European Review
Slavon & E Eur R — Slavonic and East European Review
Slavonic & E Eur R — Slavonic and East European Review
Slavonic R — Slavonic Review
SlavP — Slavica Pragensia
SlavR — Slavic Review
Slav R — Slavische Rundschau
SlavR — Slavisticna Revija
SLAVR — Slavonic Review
SlavRev — Slavisticna Revija
SlavS — Slavica Slovaca
Slav S — Slavisticki Studii
SLA Western NY Chap Bul — Special Libraries Association. Western New
    York Chapter. Bulletin
SLB — Schaulade. Unabhaengiges Internationales Fachblatt fuer Porzellan,
    Keramik, Glas, Geschenkartikel, und Hausrat
SLB — Studia ad Tabulas Cuneiformes Collectas a de Liagre Boehl Pertinentia
SL Council Phila & Vicinity Bul — Special Libraries Council of Philadelphia
    and Vicinity. Bulletin
SLCS — Studies in Language. Companion Series
SLD — Studia Litteraria (University of Debrecen)

Sleep Sick Bureau Bull — Sleeping Sickness Bureau. Bulletin
SLESP — Suplemento Literario do Estado de Sao Paulo
Sleszky Num — Sleszky Numismatik
SLet — Sestante Letterario
SLEVA — Slevarenstvi
SLF — Svenska Litteratursaellskapet i Finland
SLFA — Svensklaerarfoereningens Arsskrift
SLFU — Skrifter Utgivna. Genom Landsmals-och Folk-Minnesarkivet i
    Uppsala
SLG — Scottish Law Gazette
SLG — Studia Linguistica Germanica
SLI — Special Libraries
SLI — Studi Linguistici Italiani
SLI — Studies in the Literary Imagination
SLIC — School Libraries in Canada
SLif — Slovjans'ke Literaturoznavstvo i Fol'klorystyka
S Lincolnshire Archaeol — South Lincolnshire Archaeology
SLit — Slovenska Literatura
SLit — Studies in Literature
SLitI — Studies in the Literary Imagination
S Lit J — Southern Literary Journal
S Liv — Southern Living
SLJ — School Library Journal
SLJ — Southern Literary Journal
SLJ — Southwestern Law Journal
SLK — Schwerpunkte Linguistik und Kommunikationswissenschaft
SLKW — Schwerpunkte Linguistik und Kommunikationswissenschaft
SLL — Skrifter Utgivna. Genom Landsmalsarkivet i Lund
SLL — Studies in Language Learning
SLLR — Sierra Leone Language Review
SLM — Sales and Marketing Management
SLM — Sealift Magazine
SLM — Southern Literary Messenger
SlMov — Sloc'jans'ke Movoznavstvo
SLN — Sinclair Lewis Newsletter
SLO — Slavia Orientalis
Sloan — Sloan Management Review
Sloan Manag — Sloan Management Review
Sloan Manage Rev — Sloan Management Review
Sloan Mgmt Rev — Sloan Management Review
Sloan Mgt R — Sloan Management Review
SLOc — Slavia Occidentalis
SLOcc — Slavia Occidentalis
Slo L — Slovo Lektora
SLoP — Slovansky Prehled
SLOR — Slavia Orientalis
Slov Akad Znan Umet Razred Prirodosl Vede Dela — Slovenska Akademija
    Znanosti in Umetnosti. Razred za Prirodoslovne Vede. Dela
Slovak Mus — Slovak Musik
Slov Arch — Slovenska Archeologia
Slov Archeol — Slovenska Archeologia
Slov Ceb — Slovenski Cebelar
Slov Etnogr — Slovenski Etnografi
Slov Hud — Slovenska Hudba
Slov Lit — Slovenska Literatura
SlovN — Slovensky Narodopis
Slov Numiz — Slovenske Numizmatika
SlovP — Slovensky Pohl'ady
Slov Preh — Slovansky Prehled
SlovS — Slovene Studies
Slow Learn — Slow Learning Child
Slow Learn Child — Slow Learning Child
SLOZA — Slaboproudy Obzor
SLP — Serie Linguistica Peruana
SLP — Slovansky Prehled
SLP — Slovensky Pohl'ady
SLP — Slovensky Porocevalec
SLPo — Slovensky Pohl'ady
SLPoh — Slovensky Pohl'ady
SLPr — Slavica Pragensia
SLPR — Slavistic Printings and Reprintings
SLPRB — Steroids and Lipids Research
SLQ — Saint Louis Quarterly [*Baguio City*]
SLR — Slager. Vakblad voor de Vleesspecialist
SLR — Slavische Rundschau
SLR — Slavisticna Revija
SLR — Slavonic and East European Review
SLR — Stanford Law Review
SLR — Sydney Law Review
SLRAAA — Sprache und Literatur. Regensburger Arbeiten zur Anglistik und
    Amerikanistik
SLRec — Slovenska Rec
SLRev — Slavonic and East European Review
SLRev — Slavonic Review
SLRJ — St. Louis University. Research Journal. Graduate School of Arts and
    Sciences

SlRund — Slavische Rundschau
SLS — Sign Language Studies
SLSA — Svenska Linne-Sallsapet Arsskrift [*Uppsala*]
SlSb — Slezsky Sbornik
SLSc — Studies in the Linguistic Sciences
SLSF — Svenska Landsmal och Svenskt Folkliv [*Uppsala*]
SLSp — Slovensky Spisovatel
SLT — Scots Law Times
SLT — Svensk Litteraturtidskrift
SLTerm — Slavjanska Lingvisticna Terminologija
SLTM — Storia delle Letterature di Tutto il Mondo
SLU — Spil. Een Progressief Onafhankelijk Maandblad voor Zelfstandigen en Werknemers in het Middenbedrijf en Kleinbedrijf
SLU — Studii de Literatura Universala [*Bucharest*]
SLU — Svenska Litteratursaellskapet i Uppsala
Sludge Mag — Sludge Magazine
SLULJ — St. Louis University. Law Journal
SLUMA — Southern Lumberman [*United States*]
SLURJ — Saint Louis University. Research Journal [*Baguio City*]
Sl UVAN — Slavistica. Praci Institutu Slov'janoznavstva Ukrajins'koji Vil'noji Akademiji Nauk
SLWFA — Schweizerische Landwirtschaftliche Forschung
SLY — Slijtersvakblad. Vakblad voor de Drankenbranche
SM — Sacred Music
SM — Sales Management [*Later, Sales and Marketing Management*]
SM — Sales and Marketing Management
SM — Sammlung Metzler
SM — Schweizer Muenzblaetter [*Gazette Numismatique Suisse*]
SM — Scientific Monthly
Sm — Smena [*Moscow*]
Sm — Smithsonian
SM — Speech Monographs
SM — Sports Medicine
SM — Studi Medievali
S M — Studia Musicologica. Academiae Scientiarum Hungaricae
SM — Summer
S & M — Sun and Moon
SM — Sydney Mail
S M (A) — Studies in Music (Australia)
SMA — Syrie et Monde Arabe [*Damascus*]
SMAGD — Solaire 1 Magazine
Small Bus — Small Business Reporter
Small Bus Comput — Small Business Computers
Small Bus Comput News — Small Business Computer News
Small Business — Small Business Report
Small Gr B — Small Group Behavior
Small Group Behav — Small Group Behavior
Small Mamm Newsl — Small Mammal Newsletters
Small Pr — Small Press Review
Small Stock Mag — Small Stock Magazine
Small Sys — Small Systems World
Small Sys Soft — Small Systems Software
Small Syst Software — Small Systems Software
Small Syst World — Small Systems World
SM Arch — Solid Mechanics Archives
Smaskrift Landbruksdep Opplysningstjenesten — Smaskrift-Norway. Landbruksdepartementet. Opplysningstjenesten
SMATA — Studia Mathematica
SMBC — Studien und Mitteilungen aus dem Benediktiner- und dem Cistercienser-Orden
SMBCO — Studien und Mitteilungen aus dem Benediktiner- und dem Cistercienser-Orden
SMBCOZ — Studien und Mitteilungen aus dem Benediktiner- und dem Cistercienser-Orden
SMBD — Stat'i Materialy po Bolgarskoj Dialektologii
SMC — Smithsonian Miscellaneous Collections
SMC — Studies in Medieval Culture
SMCPA — Simulation Councils. Proceedings Series
SMDL — Stoff- und Motivgeschichte der Deutschen Literatur
SMDTB — School Musician. Director and Teacher
SMe — Studi Medievali
SMEA — Studi Micenei ed Egeo-Anatolici
SMEC Mag — SMEC [*Snowy Mountains Engineering Corporation*] Magazine
SME Collect Pap — Society of Manufacturing Engineers. Collective Papers
SME Creative Mfg Semin Tech Pap — Society of Manufacturing Engineers. Creative Manufacturing Seminars. Technical Papers
SMed — Studi Medievali
SME Tech Pap — Society of Manufacturing Engineers. Technical Paper
SME Tech Pap Ser EE — Society of Manufacturing Engineers. Technical Paper. Series EE (Electrical Engineering)
SME Tech Pap Ser EM — Society of Manufacturing Engineers. Technical Paper. Series EM (Engineering Materials)
SME Tech Pap Ser FC — Society of Manufacturing Engineers. Technical Paper. Series FC (Finishing and Coating)

SME Tech Pap Ser MF — Society of Manufacturing Engineers. Technical Paper. Series MF (Material Forming)
SME Tech Pap Ser MR — Society of Manufacturing Engineers. Technical Paper. Series MR (Material Removal)
SME West Metal Tool Expos Conf Tech Pap — Society of Manufacturing Engineers. Western Metal and Tool Exposition and Conference. Technical Papers
SMF — Skrifter Utgivna. Modernsmalslararnas Forening
SMG — Schweizerische Musikforschende Gesellschaft. Mitteilungsblatt
SMGB — Studien und Mitteilungen zur Geschichte des Benediktiner-Ordens und Seiner Zweige
SMGBOZ — Studien und Mitteilungen zur Geschichte des Benediktiner-Ordens und Seiner Zweige (Salzburg)
SMH — Speelgoed en Hobby. Vakblad voor de Speelgoedbranche
SMH — Sydney Morning Herald
SMH (Newspr) (NSW) — Sydney Morning Herald Reports (Newspaper) (New South Wales)
SMHR — Smoking and Health Reporter
SMIJA — South African Mining and Engineering Journal
SMIL — Statistical Methods in Linguistics
SMiss — Studia Missionalia
Smith — Smithsonian
Smith Coll — Smith College. Studies in Social Work
Smith Coll Mus Bul — Smith College. Museum of Art. Bulletin
Smith Coll Stud Social Work — Smith College. Studies in Social Work
Smiths Inst — Smithsonian Institution
Smithson Ann Flight — Smithsonian Annals of Flight
Smithson Contr Bot — Smithsonian Contributions to Botany
Smithson Contrib Anthropol — Smithsonian Contributions to Anthropology
Smithson Contrib Astrophys — Smithsonian Contributions to Astrophysics
Smithson Contrib Bot — Smithsonian Contributions to Botany
Smithson Contrib Earth Sciences — Smithsonian Contributions to Earth Sciences
Smithson Contrib Paleobiol — Smithsonian Contributions to Paleobiology
Smithson Contrib Zool — Smithsonian Contributions to Zoology
Smithson Contr Zool — Smithsonian Contributions to Zoology
Smithson Inst Annu Rep — Smithsonian Institution. Annual Report
Smithson Inst Cent Short-Lived Phenom Annu Rep Rev Events — Smithsonian Institution. Center for Short-Lived Phenomena. Annual Report and Review of Events
Smithson Misc Colins — Smithsonian Miscellaneous Collections
Smithson Misc Collect — Smithsonian Miscellaneous Collections
Smithson Rep — Smithsonian Institution. Annual Report
Smithson Rept — Smithsonian Institution. Reports
SMIU — Studies by Members of the Istanbul University English Department
SMIZD — Sei Marianna Ika Daigaku Zasshi
SMJ — Sarawak Museum. Journal
SMJ — Siberian Mathematical Journal
SMJ — Society of Malawi. Journal
SMJMA — SIAM [*Society for Industrial and Applied Mathematics*] Journal on Applied Mathematics
SMJOA — Southern Medical Journal [*United States*]
SMKRA — Stroitel'naya Mekhanika i Raschet Sooruzheniy
SML — Statistical Methods in Linguistics [*Stockholm*]
SML — Stimmen aus Maria-Laach
SMLAA — Smokeless Air [*England*]
SMLF — Skrifter Utgivna. Modernsmalslararnas Forening
SMLJ — St. Mary's Law Journal
SMLV — Studi Mediolatini e Volgari
SMMART — Society for Mass Media and Resource Technology. Journal
SMMRT Journal — Society for Mass Media and Resource Technology. Journal
SMN — Studia Musicologica Norvegica
SMNSA — Soviet Mining Science [*English Translation*]
Smolensk Gos Ped Inst Ucen Zap — Smolenskii Gosudarstvennyi Pedagogiceskii Institut. Ucenye Zapiski
SMon — Studia Monastica
SMPKA — Sempaku
Sm Pr R — Small Press Review
SMPTA — Schweizerische Mineralogische und Petrographische Mitteilungen
SMPTE J — Society of Motion Picture and Television Engineers. Journal
SMQ — School Media Quarterly
S & MR — Shire and Municipal Record
S & M Record — Shire and Municipal Record
SMRRA — Report. Saskatchewan Department of Mineral Resources
SMRVA — Sloan Management Review
SMS — Startling Mystery Stories
SMS — Studier i Modern Sprakvetenskap
SMSNA — Smithsonian
SMSpr — Studier i Modern Sprakvetenskap
SMSR — Studi e Materiali di Storia della Religioni
SMSRAH — Institutionen foer Skoglig Matematisk Statistik Rapporter och Uppsatser
SMS Report — Socioeconomic Monitoring System Report
SMSS — Studies in Management Science and Systems [*Elsevier Book Series*]
SMT — Studies in Modern Thermodynamics [*Elsevier Book Series*]

SMTLB — Strength of Materials [*English Translation*]
SMTSDS — Annual Research Reviews. Somatostatin
SMus — Studia Musicologica [*Budapest*]
SMV — Studi Mediolatini e Volgari
SMVMA — Sbornik Trudov Moskovskii Vechernii Metallurgicheskii Institut
S Mw — Studien zur Musikwissenschaft
SMWOA — Schweizerische Medizinische Wochenschrift
S Mz — Schweizerische Musikzeitung/Revue Musicale Suisse
SMZHA — Sibirskii Matematiceskii Zurnal
SN — Saturday Night
SN — Science News
SN — Shakespeare Newsletter
SN — Slovensky Narodopis
SN — Sovetskaja Nauka
SN — Sporting News
S & N — Statesman and Nation
SN — Studia Neophilologica
SN — Sunday Nation
SNA — Shakespeariana
SNa — Sot la Nape
SNAG — Short Notes on Alaskan Geology. Alaska Department of Natural Resources. Geologic Report
SNDL — Studienausgaben zur Neueren Deutschen Literatur
SNDR — Shimane Daigaku Ronshu: Jinbun Kagaku [*Journal of the Shimane University: Humanistic Sciences*]
SNDSB — Sonderschule
SNEIA — Sbornik Nauchnykh Trudov Ivanovskogo Energeticheskogo Instituta
SNERA — Statistica Neerlandica
SNF — Selskab foer Nordisk Filologi Arsberetning
SNGRA — Sangre
SNIC Bull — SNIC [*Singapore National Institute of Chemistry*] Bulletin
SNL — Satire Newsletter
SNL — Shakespeare Newsletter
SNLN — Saskatchewan Native Library Services Newsletter
SNM — Sbornik Narodniho Muzea
SNMAD — Southwest Bulletin
SNNG — Schakels Nederlands Nieuw Guinea
SNNSB3 — Food Irradiation [*Japan*]
SNNTS — Studies in the Novel. North Texas State University
SNoF — Studier i Nordisk Filologi
SNov — Seara Nova
Snow Revel — Snow Revelry
SNP — Studia Neophilologica
SNPh — Studia Neophilologica
SNQ — Scottish Notes and Queries
SNQ — Sussex Notes and Queries
SNR — Schweizerische Numismatische Rundschau
SNR — Sudan Notes and Records
SNS — Slovo na Storozi
SNS — Spanish Economic News Service
SNSS — Skrifter Utgivna. Namnden foer Svensk Sprakvard
SNT — Supplements. Novum Testamentum [*Leiden*]
SNTSB — Studiorum Novi Testamenti Societas. Bulletin
SNTSMS — Studiorum Novi Testamenti Societas. Monograph Series
SNUCD — Software Newsletter
SNVAO — Skrifter Utgitt. Det Norske Videnskaps-Akademi i Oslo
SNVKB — Sbornik Nauchnykh Rabot Voenno-Meditsinskogo Fakul'teta Kuibyshevskogo Meditsinskogo Instituta
SNVO — Skrifter. Norske Videnskaps-Akademi i Oslo
SNW — Schip en Werf. Tijdschrift Gewijd aan Scheepsbouw en Werktuigbouw, Elektrotechniek, Scheepvaart, en Aanverwante Vakken
SNWTH — Sources for NWT [*Northwest Territory*] History. Prince of Wales Northern Heritage Centre [*Canada*]
SO — Sibirskie Ogni
SO — Slavia Occidentalis
So — Societa
So — Sojourner
So — Sokrates
So — Sophia: Studies in Western Civilization and the Cultural Interaction of East and West [*Tokyo*]
So — Soundings
SO — Studia Oliveriana
SO — Studia Orientalia
SO — Symbolae Osloenses
SOA — Sydsvenska Ortnamns-Saellskapets Arsskrift
SoAB — South Atlantic Bulletin
So Africa — Southern Africa
So African L — South African Law Reports
So African LJ — South African Law Journal
So Afr LJ — South African Law Journal
So Afr LR — South African Law Reports
SoAfrStJ — South African Statistical Journal
SOAGD — Solar Age
SOAMB — Soviet Applied Mechanics [*English Translation*]
SoANGr — Soobscenija Akademiji Nauk Gruzinskoj SSR

Soap Chem Spec — Soap and Chemical Specialties [*Later, Soap/Cosmetics/Chemical Specialties*]
Soap & Chem Spec — Soap and Chemical Specialties [*Later, Soap/Cosmetics/Chemical Specialties*]
Soap Cosmet — Soap/Cosmetics/Chemical Specialties
Soap/Cosmet/Chem Spec — Soap/Cosmetics/Chemical Specialities
Soap Perfum Cosmet — Soap, Perfumery, and Cosmetics
Soap Prf Cos — Soap, Perfumery, and Cosmetics
Soap & San Chem — Soap and Sanitary Chemicals
So AS — Somersetshire Archaeological and Natural History Society. Proceedings [*Later, Somerset Archaeology and Natural History*]
SOAS JLCR — School of Oriental and African Studies. Jordan Lectures in Comparative Religion
So Assn Q — Southern Association Quarterly
SOAS ULLOS — School of Oriental and African Studies. University of London. London. Oriental Series
So Atlan Bul — South Atlantic Bulletin
So Atlan Q — South Atlantic Quarterly
So Atl Quar — South Atlantic Quarterly
So Aus Bul — National Gallery of South Australia. Bulletin
So Aus LR — South Australian Law Reports
So Aust LR — South Australian Law Reports
So Austr L — South Australian Law Reports
So Austr St — South Australian State Reports
SOAW — Sitzungsberichte. Oesterreichische Akademie der Wissenschaften in Wien. Philosophisch-Historische Klasse
SOBIA — Social Biology
So Biv — Southern Bivouac
So Bod — Sounding Board
Sobre Deriv Cana Azucar — Sobre los Derivados de la Cana de Azucar [*Cuba*]
SOC — Soap, Perfumery, and Cosmetics
Soc — Societas
Soc — Society
SOC — Studies in Organic Chemistry [*Elsevier Book Series*]
Soc A — Sociological Abstracts
SocAb — Sociological Abstracts
Soc Act — Social Action
Soc Act & L — Social Action and the Law
Soc Actuar Trans — Society of Actuaries. Transactions
Soc Adv Electrochem Sci Technol Trans — Society for the Advancement of Electrochemical Science and Technology. Transactions
Soc African J — Societe des Africanistes. Journal
Soc Agric Alger Bull — Societe des Agricultures d'Algerie. Bulletin [*Algeria*]
So Calif L Rev — Southern California Law Review
So Calif Q — Southern California Quarterly
So Calif Quar — Southern California Quarterly
So Cal LR — Southern California Law Review
Soc Alp Giulie Comm Grotte Eugenio Boegan Atti Mem — Societa Alpina delle Giulie. Club Alpino Italiano. Sezione di Trieste. Commissione Grotte "Eugenio Boegan." Atti e Memorie
Soc Altern — Social Alternatives
Soc Alternatives — Social Alternatives [*Australia*]
Soc d Americanistes J — Societe des Americanistes de Paris. Journal
Soc Amer J — Societe des Americanistes de Paris. Journal
Soc Am For — Society of American Foresters. Proceedings
Soc Anal — Sociological Analysis
Soc Anarc — Social Anarchism
Soc Anthropol Paris Bull Mem — Societe d'Anthropologie de Paris. Bulletins et Memoires
Soc Appl Bacteriol Symp Ser — Society for Applied Bacteriology. Symposium Series
Soc Appl Bacteriol Tech Ser — Society for Applied Bacteriology. Technical Series
So Ca R — South Carolina Review
Soc Archeol & Hist Limousin Bul — Societe Archeologique et Historique du Limousin. Bulletin
Soc Arch Hist J — Society of Architectural Historians. Journal
Soc Arch Hist Poitou Arch — Societe des Archives Historiques du Poitou. Archives
Soc Archit Hist J — Society of Architectural Historians. Journal
Soc Archtl Historians Jnl — Society of Architectural Historians. Journal
Soc of Archtl Historians Newsletter — Society of Architectural Historians. Newsletter
Soc Argent Cancerol Bol Trab — Sociedad Argentina de Cancerologia. Boletines y Trabajos
Soc Argent Cir Jornadas Quir — Sociedad Argentina de Cirujanos Jornadas Quirurgicas
So Car Hist Assoc Proc — South Carolina Historical Association. Proceedings
So Car Hist Mag — South Carolina Historical and Genealogical Magazine
So Car LQ — South Carolina Law Quarterly
So Car L Rev — South Carolina Law Review
Soc Army Hist Research Jour — Society for Army Historical Research. Journal [*London*]
Soc Arts J — Society of Arts. Journal
Soc Astron Ital Mem — Societa Astronomica Italiana. Memorie
Soc Auto Eng J — Society of Automotive Engineers. Journal

SoCB — South Central Bulletin
Soc Banque Suisse Bul — Societe de Banque Suisse. Bulletin
Soc Behav Pers — Social Behavior and Personality
Soc Beh Per — Social Behavior and Personality
Soc Belge d'Etudes Geog Bull — Societe Belge d'Etudes Geographiques. Bulletin
Soc Belge G B — Societe Belge de Geologie. Bulletin
Soc Belge Geol Bull — Societe Belge de Geologie. Bulletin
Soc Biol — Social Biology
Soc Bot France B — Societe Botanique de France. Bulletin
Soc Brotheriana Bol — Sociedade Brotheriana. Boletim
Soc Casework — Social Casework
Soccer J — Soccer Journal
Soc Chem Ind J — Society of Chemical Industry. Journal
Soc Chem Ind (Lond) Monogr — Society of Chemical Industry (London). Monograph
Soc Chem Ind Victoria Proc — Society of Chemical Industry of Victoria. Proceedings
Soc Cient Ant Alz Mem — Sociedad Cientifica "Antonio Alzate." Memorias y Revista
Soc Cient Parag Rev — Sociedad Cientifica del Paraguay. Revista
SOC Coll — Studia Orientalia Christiana. Collectanea
Soc Comp — Social Compass
Soc Compass — Social Compass
Soc Con — Social Concept
Soc Cubana Historia Nat Mem — Sociedad Cubana de Historia Natural. Memorias
Soc Cubana Ingenieros Rev — Sociedad Cubana de Ingenieros. Revista
Soc Cubana Ing Rv — Sociedad Cubana de Ingenieros. Revista
Soc Def — Social Defence [*New Delhi*]
Soc Dyers & Col J — Society of Dyers and Colourists. Journal
Soc Dyn — Social Dynamics
Soc Econ — Social Economist
Soc Econ Admin — Social and Economic Administration
Soc Econ Paleontol Mineral Pac Sect Guideb — Society of Economic Paleontologists and Mineralogists. Pacific Section. Guidebooks
Soc Econ Paleontol Mineral Permian Basin Sect Publ — Society of Economic Paleontologists and Mineralogists. Permian Basin Section. Publication
Soc Econ Paleontol Mineral Repr Ser — Society of Economic Paleontologists and Mineralogists. Reprint Series
Soc Econ Paleontol Mineral Spec Publ — Society of Economic Paleontologists and Mineralogists. Special Publication
Soc Econ Paleontologists and Mineralogists Special Pub — Society of Economic Paleontologists and Mineralogists. Special Publication
Soc Econ Paleontologists and Mineralogists Spec Pub — Society of Economic Paleontologists and Mineralogists. Special Publication
Soc-Econ Plan Sci — Socio-Economic Planning Sciences
Soc & Econ Stud — Social and Economic Studies
Soc Econ Stud — Social and Economic Studies
Soc Ed — Social Education
Soc Educ — Social Education
Soc Eng (London) J — Society of Engineers (London). Journal
Soc Espan Hist Nat Bol Secc Geol — Sociedad Espanola de Historia Natural. Boletin. Seccion Geologica
Soc Espanola H N An — Sociedad Espanola de Historia Natural. Anales
Soc d'Etudes Sc d'Angers B — Societe d'Etudes Scientifiques d'Angers. Bulletin
Soc Etud et Expansion R — Societe d'Etudes et d'Expansion. Revue
Soc Etud Indochinoises Bul — Societe des Etudes Indochinoises. Bulletin
Soc Exp Biol Semin Ser — Society for Experimental Biology. Seminar Series
Soc Explor Geophys Annu Int Meet Abstr — Society of Exploration Geophysics. Annual International Meeting. Abstracts
Soc Exp Stress Anal Pap — Society for Experimental Stress Analysis. Papers
Soc Fauna Flora Fenn Flora Fenn — Societas pro Fauna et Flora Fennica. Flora Fennica
Soc Fauna Flora Fenn Memo — Societatis pro Fauna et Flora Fennica. Memoranda
Soc Forces — Social Forces
Soc Francaise Mineralogie et Cristallographie Bull — Societe Francaise de Mineralogie et de Cristallographie. Bulletin
Soc Franc Miner B — Societe Francaise de Mineralogie. Bulletin
Soc Fr Dermatol Syphiligr Bull — Societe Francaise de Dermatologie et de Syphiligraphie. Bulletin
Soc Fr Gynecol C R — Societe Francaise de Gynecologie. Comptes Rendus
Soc Fribourgeoise Sc Nat B Mem — Societe Fribourgeoise des Sciences Naturelles. Bulletin. Memoires
Soc Fr Mineral Cristallogr Bull — Societe Francaise de Mineralogie et de Cristallographie. Bulletin
Soc F TV Arts J — Society of Film and Television Arts. Journal
Soc G Belgique An — Societe Geologique de Belgique. Annales
Soc Gen Physiol Ser — Society of General Physiologists. Series
Soc Geog Fenniae Acta Geog — Societas Geographica Fenniae. Acta Geographica
Soc Geog Liege Bul — Societe Geographique de Liege. Bulletin
Soc Geog Lima Bol — Sociedad Geografica de Lima. Boletin

Soc Geog Mex B — Sociedad de Geografia y Estadistica de la Republica Mexicana. Boletin
Soc Geog (Paris) B — Societe de Geographie (Paris). Bulletin
Soc Geog Que B — Societe de Geographie de Quebec. Bulletin
Soc Geogr Bol (Madrid) — Sociedad Geografica. Boletin (Madrid)
Soc Geol Belg Ann — Societe Geologique de Belgique. Annales
Soc Geol Belgique Annales — Societe Geologique de Belgique. Annales
Soc Geol France Bull — Societe Geologique de France. Bulletin
Soc Geol Fr Bull — Societe Geologique de France. Bulletin
Soc Geol Fr Mem — Societe Geologique de France. Memoires
Soc Geol Fr Mem Hors Ser — Societe Geologique de France. Memoire Hors Serie
Soc Geol Mex Bol — Sociedad Geologica Mexicana. Boletin
Soc Geol Mexicana Bol — Sociedad Geologica Mexicana. Boletin
Soc Geol Mineral Bretagne Bull — Societe Geologique et Mineralogique de Bretagne. Bulletin
Soc Geol et Mineralog Bretagne Bull — Societe Geologique et Mineralogique de Bretagne. Bulletin
Soc Geol Nord Ann — Societe Geologique du Nord. Annales
Soc Geol Normandie Bull — Societe Geologique de Normandie. Bulletin
Soc Geol Peru Bol — Sociedad Geologica del Peru. Boletin
Soc Geol Port Bol — Sociedade Geologica de Portugal. Boletim
Soc G France B Mem — Societe Geologique de France. Bulletin. Memoires
Soc G Italiana B — Societa Geologica Italiana. Bollettino
Soc Glass Technology Jour — Society of Glass Technology. Journal
Soc G Mex B — Sociedad Geologica Mexicana. Boletin
Soc G Nord An Mem — Societe Geologique du Nord. Annales. Memoires
Soc G Normandie B — Societe Geologique de Normandie. Bulletin
Soc Haitienne Histoire Geographie Geologie Revue — Societe Haitienne d'Histoire de Geographie et de Geologie. Revue
Soc Hist — Social History
Soc Hist/Hist Soc — Social History/Histoire Sociale
So C Hist Mag — South Carolina Historical Magazine
Soc Hist Nat Toulouse Bull — Societe d'Histoire Naturelle de Toulouse. Bulletin
Soc Hongroise Geog Abrege B — Societe Hongroise de Geographie. Abrege du Bulletin
Soc Hygiene — Social Hygiene
Social Biol — Social Biology
Social Case — Social Casework
Social Comp — Social Compass
Social en Democr — Socialisme en Democratie
Social Ec A — Social and Economic Administration
Social Econ — Social and Economic Studies
Social and Econ Admin — Social and Economic Administration
Social & Econ Stud — Social and Economic Studies
Social Educ — Social Education
Social Forc — Social Forces
Social Ind — Social Indicators Research
Social Indicators Res — Social Indicators Research
Socialist Wkr — Socialist Worker
Social Pol — Social Policy
Social Policy Admin — Social Policy and Administration
Social Prax — Social Praxis
Social Prob — Social Problems
Social Psy — Social Psychiatry
Social Psychol Q — Social Psychology Quarterly
Social Res — Social Research
Social Revol — Socialist Revolution
Social Sci — Social Science Quarterly
Social Scie — Social Science
Social Science J (Fort Collins) — Social Science Journal (Fort Collins)
Social Science Q — Social Science Quarterly
Social Sci Inf — Social Science Information
Social Sci Q — Social Science Quarterly
Social Sc M — Social Science and Medicine
Social Sec — Social Security Bulletin [*US*]
Social Security Bul — Social Security Bulletin
Social Se R — Social Service Review
Social Service R — Social Service Review
Social Services Abs — Social Services Abstracts
Social Services J — Social Services Journal
Social St S — Social Studies of Science
Social Stud — Social Studies
Social Theor Pract — Social Theory and Practice
Social Trud — Socialisticeskij Trud
Societe d'Etudes et d'Expansion Revue — Societe d'Etudes et d'Expansion. Revue
Soc Imp Nat Moscou B — Societe Imperiale des Naturalistes de Moscou. Bulletin
Soc Indep Prof Earth Sci Bull — Society of Independent Professional Earth Scientists. Bulletin
Soc Indicators Res — Social Indicators Research
Soc Indic Res — Social Indicators Research
Soc Ind Min B C R Men — Societe de l'Industrie Minerale. Bulletin. Comptes Rendus Mensuels des Reunions

Soc Ind Res — Social Indicators Research

Soc l'Industrie Minerale Cong Cent — Societe de l'Industrie Minerale. Congres du Centenaire

Soc Ing Civils France Mem — Societe des Ingenieurs Civils de France. Memoires

Socio-Econ — Socio-Economic Planning Sciences

Socioecon Newsletter — Socioeconomic Newsletter

Socio-Econ Plann Sci — Socio-Economic Planning Sciences

Socioecon Rep — Socioeconomic Report. California Medical Association

Sociol Anal — Sociological Analysis

Sociol Anal Theory — Sociological Analysis and Theory

Sociol B (Bombay) — Sociological Bulletin (Bombay)

Sociol Bull — Sociological Bulletin

Sociol Cas — Sociologicky Casopis

Sociol Contemp — Sociologie Contemporaine

Sociol of Ed — Sociology of Education

Sociol Educ — Sociology of Education

Sociol Educ Abstr — Sociology of Education Abstracts

Sociol Focu — Sociological Focus

Sociol Fors — Sociologisk Forskning

Sociol Gids — Sociologische Gids

Sociol Health Illness — Sociology of Health and Illness

Sociol Inq — Sociological Inquiry

Sociol Inquiry — Sociological Inquiry

Sociol Int (Berlin) — Sociologia Internationalis (Berlin)

Sociol Issled (Moskva) — Sociologiceskie Issledovanija (Moskva)

Sociol Issled (Sverdlovsk) — Sociologiceskie Issledovanija (Sverdlovsk)

Sociol Law — Sociology of Law

Sociol Meddel — Sociologiske Meddelelser

Sociol Meth — Sociological Methods and Research

Sociol Methods & Res — Sociological Methods and Research

Sociol Neer — Sociologia Neerlandica

Sociological R — Sociological Review

Sociologus — Sociologus Zeitschrift fuer Empirische Soziologie, Sozialpsychologische, und Ethnologische Forschung

Sociol Org — Sociologia dell'Organizzazione

Sociol Q — Sociological Quarterly

Sociol Quart — Sociological Quarterly

Sociol R — Sociological Review

Sociol Rev — Sociological Review

Sociol Rev Monogr — Sociological Review. Monograph

Sociol R Mg — Sociological Review. Monograph

Sociol R NS — Sociological Review. New Series

Sociol Rur — Sociologia Ruralis

Sociol Ruralis — Sociologia Ruralis

Sociol Rural Life Minn Univ Agric Ext Serv — Sociology of Rural Life. Minnesota University. Agricultural Extension Service

Sociol Sela — Sociologija Sela

Sociol et Soc — Sociologie et Societes

Sociol Soc — Sociology and Social Research

Sociol Soci — Sociologie et Societes

Sociol & Social Res — Sociology and Social Research

Sociol & Soc Res — Sociology and Social Research

Sociol Symp — Sociological Symposium

Sociol Trav — Sociologie du Travail

Sociol Wk Occupat — Sociology of Work and Occupations

Sociol W Oc — Sociology of Work and Occupations

Sociol Yb Relig Britain — Sociological Yearbook of Religion in Britain

Sociom — Sociometry

Socio Meth — Sociological Methodology

Socio R — Sociological Review

Socio-Tech B — Social-Technological Bulletin [Quezon City]

Soc Italiana Sc Nat Milano Atti — Societa Italiana di Scienze Naturali in Milano. Atti

Soc Ital Sci Farm Doc — Societa Italiana di Scienze Farmaceutiche Documento

Soc Ital Sci Nat Mus Civ Stor Nat Milano Atti — Societa Italiana di Scienze Naturali e Museo Civico di Storia Naturale di Milano. Atti

Soc Jus R — Social Justice Review

SocJust — Social Justice Review

Socker Handli — Socker Handlingar

Soc Languedoc Geogr — Societe Languedocienne de Geographie

Soc Languedocienne Geogr Bull — Societe Languedocienne de Geographie. Bulletin

SOCLD — Solar Cells

Soc and Leisure — Society and Leisure

Soc Ligustica Sc Nat Geog Atti — Societa Ligustica di Scienze Naturali e Geografiche. Atti

Soc Linn Bord Bull — Societe Linneenne de Bordeaux. Bulletin

Soc Linneenne Normandie Bull — Societe Linneenne de Normandie. Bulletin

Soc Linn Lyon Bull — Societe Linneenne de Lyon. Bulletin Mensuel

Soc Maandbl Arb — Sociaal Maandblad Arbeid

Soc Malac Belgique An — Societe Malacologique de Belgique. Annales

Soc Malacologica Rev — Sociedad Malacologica. Revista

Soc Malawi J — Society of Malawi. Journal

Soc Manuf Eng Tech Pap Ser AD — Society of Manufacturing Engineers. Technical Paper. Series AD (Assembly Division)

Soc Manuf Eng Tech Pap Ser EE — Society of Manufacturing Engineers. Technical Paper. Series EE (Electrical Engineering)

Soc Manuf Eng Tech Pap Ser EM — Society of Manufacturing Engineers. Technical Paper. Series EM (Engineering Materials)

Soc Manuf Eng Tech Pap Ser FC — Society of Manufacturing Engineers. Technical Paper. Series FC (Finishing and Coating)

Soc Manuf Eng Tech Pap Ser IQ — Society of Manufacturing Engineers. Technical Paper. Series IQ (Inspection and Quality)

Soc Manuf Eng Tech Pap Ser MF — Society of Manufacturing Engineers. Technical Paper. Series MF (Material Forming)

Soc Manuf Eng Tech Pap Ser MR — Society of Manufacturing Engineers. Technical Paper. Series MR (Material Removal)

Soc Manuf Eng Tech Pap Ser MS — Society of Manufacturing Engineers. Technical Paper. Series MS

Soc Mass Media Resour Technol J — Society for Mass Media and Resource Technology. Journal

Soc Med-Chir Hop Form Sanit Armees — Societe Medico-Chirurgicale des Hopitaux et Formations Sanitaires des Armees

Soc Med Mil Franc Bull — Societe de Medecine Militaire Francaise. Bulletin

Soc Mex Geog Estadistica B — Sociedad Mexicana de Geografia y Estadistica. Boletin

Soc Mexicana Geografia y Estadistica Bol — Sociedad Mexicana de Geografia y Estadistica. Boletin

Soc Mexicana Historia Nat Rev — Sociedad Mexicana de Historia Natural. Revista

Soc Micros Can Bull — Societe de Microscopie du Canada. Bulletin

Soc Miner France — Societe Mineralogique de France. Bulletin

SocN — Sociolinguistics Newsletter

Soc Nat Luxemb Bull — Societe des Naturalistes Luxembourgeois. Bulletin

Soc Nat Pet Aquitaine Bull Cent Rech Pau — Societe Nationale des Petroles d'Aquitaine. Bulletin de Centres de Recherches de Pau

Soc Nav Architects Mar Eng Tech Res Bull — Society of Naval Architects and Marine Engineers. Technical and Research Bulletin [New York]

Soc Nav Architects Mar Eng Trans — Society of Naval Architects and Marine Engineers of New York. Transactions

Soc Nav Archit Mar Eng Trans — Society of Naval Architects and Marine Engineers. Transactions [United States]

Soc Nematol Spec Publ — Society of Nematologists. Special Publication

Soc Neuchatel Geogr Bull — Societe Neuchateloise de Geographie. Bulletin

Soc Neurosci Symp — Society for Neuroscience. Symposia

Soc Nucl Med Southeast Chapter Contin Educ Lect — Society of Nuclear Medicine. Southeastern Chapter. Continuing Education Lectures

Soc Num Mexico Bol — Sociedad Numismatica de Mexico. Boletin

Soc Nurs Hist Gaz — Society for Nursing History. Gazette

Soc Occup Medicine J — Society of Occupational Medicine. Journal

Soc Ocean J — Societe des Oceanistes. Journal

Soc Paleontol Ital Boll — Societa Paleontologica Italiana. Bollettino

Soc Pet E J — Society of Petroleum Engineers. American Institute of Mining, Metallurgical, and Petroleum Engineers. Journal

Soc Pet Eng AIME Improv Oil Recovery Field Rep — Society of Petroleum Engineers. American Institute of Mining, Metallurgical, and Petroleum Engineers. Improved Oil Recovery Field Reports

Soc Pet Eng AIME J — Society of Petroleum Engineers. American Institute of Mining, Metallurgical, and Petroleum Engineers. Journal

Soc Pet Eng AIME Pap — Society of Petroleum Engineers. American Institute of Mining, Metallurgical, and Petroleum Engineers. Papers

Soc Pet Eng AIME Trans — Society of Petroleum Engineers. American Institute of Mining, Metallurgical, and Petroleum Engineers. Transactions

Soc Pet Eng J — Society of Petroleum Engineers. American Institute of Mining, Metallurgical, and Petroleum Engineers. Journal

Soc Pet Engr J — Society of Petroleum Engineers. American Institute of Mining, Metallurgical, and Petroleum Engineers. Journal

Soc Pet Engrs J — Society of Petroleum Engineers. American Institute of Mining, Metallurgical, and Petroleum Engineers. Journal

Soc Petrol Eng J — Society of Petroleum Engineers. American Institute of Mining, Metallurgical, and Petroleum Engineers. Journal

Soc Petrol Eng Trans — Society of Petroleum Engineers. American Institute of Mining, Metallurgical, and Petroleum Engineers. Transactions

Soc Petroleum Engineers AIME Trans — Society of Petroleum Engineers. American Institute of Mining, Metallurgical, and Petroleum Engineers. Transactions

Soc Petroleum Engineers Jour — Society of Petroleum Engineers. American Institute of Mining, Metallurgical, and Petroleum Engineers. Journal

Soc Phot Instr Eng Newsletter — Society of Photographic Instrumentation Engineers. Newsletter

Soc Photo-Opt Instrum Eng Proc — Society of Photo-Optical Instrumentation Engineers. Proceedings [United States]

Soc Plant Prot North Jpn Spec Rep — Society of Plant Protection of North Japan. Special Report

Soc Plast Eng Div Tech Conf Tech Pap — Society of Plastics Engineers. Divisional Technical Conference. Technical Papers

Soc Plast Ind Struct Foam Conf Proc — Society of the Plastics Industry. Structural Foam Conference. Proceedings

Soc Pol — Social Policy
Soc Policy — Social Policy
Soc-Polit Soc-Ekon Probl Razvit Social Obsc — Social'no-Politiceskie i Social'no-Ekonomiceskie Problemy Razvitogo Socialisticeskogo Obscestva
Soc Pr — Social Progress
Soc Prax — Social Praxis
Soc Prehist Francais Bull — Societe Prehistorique Francaise. Bulletin
Soc Prehist Francaise Bul — Societe Prehistorique Francaise. Bulletin
Soc Prehist Fr Bull — Societe Prehistorique Francaise. Bulletin
Soc Prob — Social Problems
Soc Probl — Social Problems
Soc Probl Nauc-Tehn Revol — Social'nye Problemy Naucno-Tehniceskogo Revoljucii
Soc Promotion Agr Sc Pr — Society for the Promotion of Agricultural Science. Proceedings of the Annual Meeting
Soc Psichol Filos — Social'naja Psichologija i Filosofija
Soc Psychiatry — Social Psychiatry
Soc Psychol — Social Psychology
Soc Psychol Q — Social Psychology Quarterly
Soc Psych Res Proc — Society for Psychical Research. Proceedings
Soc Que Prot Plant Rapp — Societe de Quebec pour la Protection des Plantes. Rapport
Soc Quim Mexico Rev — Sociedad Quimica de Mexico. Revista
Soc R — Social Research
Soc R — Socialist Review
Soc R — Sociological Review
SoCR — South Carolina Review
Soc Regis — Socialist Register
Soc Rehabil Rec — Social and Rehabilitation Record
Soc Res — Social Research
Soc Res — Social Reserve
Soc Res Child Devel Monogr — Society for Research in Child Development. Monographs
Soc Research Administrators J — Journal. Society of Research Administrators
Soc Resp — Social Responsibility
Soc Rev — Socialist Review
Soc Revol — Socialist Revolution
Soc R di Nap Accad di Archeol Atti — Societa Reale di Napoli. Accademia di Archeologia, Lettere, e Belle Arti. Atti
Soc R di Nap Accad di Sci Mor e Pol Atti — Societa Reale di Napoli. Accademia di Scienze Morali e Politiche. Atti
Soc R di Napoli Accad di Archeol Atti — Societa Reale di Napoli. Accademia di Archeologia, Lettere, e Belle Arti. Atti
Soc R di Napoli Accad d Sci Fis e Mat Atti — Societa Reale di Napoli. Accademia delle Scienze, Fisiche, e Matematiche. Atti
Soc Royale Econ Pol Belgique Seance — Societe Royale d'Economie Politique de Belgique Seances
Soc Roy Belge de Geog B — Societe Royale Belge de Geographie. Bulletin
Soc Roy Econ Polit Belgique — Societe Royale d'Economie Politique de Belgique
Soc Sci — Social Sciences
Soc Scientist — Social Scientist
Soc Sci Fenn Arsb-Vuosik — Societas Scientiarum Fennicae. Arsbok-Vuosikirja
Soc Sci Fenn Commentat Biol — Societas Scientiarum Fennica. Commentationes Biologicae
Soc Sci Fenn Commentat Phys-Math — Societas Scientiarum Fennica. Commentationes Physico-Mathematicae
Soc Sci Fenn Comment Phys-Math — Societas Scientiarum Fennica. Commentationes Physico-Mathematicae
Soc Sci Fennica Arsb — Societas Scientiarum Fennica. Arsbok
Soc Sci Fennica Commentations Phys-Math — Societas Scientiarum Fennica. Commentationes Physico-Mathematicae
Soc Sci Ind — Social Sciences Index
Soc Sci Inf — Social Science Information
Soc Sci Inform — Social Science Information
Soc Sci Inf Stud — Social Science Information Studies
Soc Sci J — Social Science Journal
Soc Sci Lettres & Arts Pau Bul — Societe des Sciences, Lettres, et Arts. Pau Bulletin
Soc Sci Lodz Acta Chim — Societatis Scientiarum Lodziensis. Acta Chimica
Soc Sci and Med — Social Science and Medicine
Soc Sci Med — Social Science and Medicine
Soc Sci Med A — Social Science and Medicine. Part A. Medical Sociology
Soc Sci Med B — Social Science and Medicine. Part B. Medical Anthropology
Soc Sci Med C — Social Science and Medicine. Part C. Medical Economics
Soc Sci Med D — Social Science and Medicine. Part D. Medical Geography
Soc Sci Medic — Social Science and Medicine
Soc Sci Med (Med Anthropol) — Social Science and Medicine (Medical Anthropology)
Soc Sci Med (Med Geogr) — Social Science and Medicine (Medical Geography)
Soc Sci Med (Med Psychol Med Sociol) — Social Science and Medicine (Medical Psychology and Medical Sociology)
Soc Sci Monographs — Social Science Monographs

Soc Sci Nat Ouest Fr Bull — Societe des Sciences Naturelles de l'Ouest de la France. Bulletin
Soc Sci Nat Phys Maroc C R Seances Mens — Societe des Sciences Naturelles et Physiques du Maroc. Comptes Rendus des Seances Mensuelles
Soc Sci Q — Social Science Quarterly
Soc Sci R — Social Science Review [*Bangkok*]
Soc Sci Res — Social Science Research
Soc Sci Res Council Bull — Social Science Research Council. Bulletin
Soc Sci (Winfield) — Social Science (Winfield)
Soc & Scl Res — Sociology and Social Research
Soc Sc Nat Neuchatel B — Societe des Sciences Naturelles de Neuchatel. Bulletin
Soc Sec Bull — Social Security Bulletin [*US*]
Soc Sec Rep — Social Security Reporter
Soc Secur Bull — Social Security Bulletin
Soc Serbe Geographie Mem — Societe Serbe de Geographie. Memoires
Soc Ser Rev — Social Service Review
Soc Serv — Social Service
Soc Serv J — Social Services Journal
Soc Serv Q — Social Service Quarterly
Soc Serv R — Social Service Review
Soc Serv Rev — Social Service Review
Soc Soc Hist Med Bull — Society for the Social History of Medicine. Bulletin
Soc Statist Paris J — Societe de Statistique de Paris. Journal
Soc de Statist de Paris J — Societe de Statistique de Paris. Journal
Soc Stud — Social Studies
Soc Studies — Social Studies
Soc Stud Sci — Social Studies of Science [*United Kingdom*]
Soc Sur — Social Survey
Soc Surv — Social Survey
Soc Survey — Social Survey
Soc Theory & Pract — Social Theory and Practice
Soc Thought — Social Thought
Soc Thr — Socialist Theory and Practice
Soc Toscana Sci Nat Atti Mem Ser A — Societa Toscana di Scienze Naturali. Atti. Memorie. Serie A
Soc Travail — Sociologie du Travail
Soc Trends — Social Trends
Soc Tss — Socialt Tidsskrift
Soc Vac Coaters Proc Annu Conf — Society of Vacuum Coaters. Proceedings. Annual Conference
Soc Vaudoise Sci Nat Bull — Societe Vaudoise des Sciences Naturelles. Bulletin
Soc Venez Cienc Nat Bol — Sociedad Venezolana de Ciencias Naturales. Boletin
Soc Venezolana Ciencias Natur Bol — Sociedad Venezolana de Ciencias Naturales. Boletin
Soc Ven Sci Nat Lav — Societa Veneziana di Scienze Naturali Lavori
Soc W — Social Work
Soc Welfare — Social Welfare
Soc Wetensch — Sociale Wetenschappen
Soc Wk (Albany) — Social Work (Albany)
Soc Work — Social Work
Soc Work Health Care — Social Work in Health Care
Soc Work Lect — Social Work Lectures [*New Zealand*]
Soc Workr — Socialist Worker
Soc Work Res Abstr — Social Work Research and Abstracts
Soc Work Today — Social Work Today
SOCYA — Society
Soc Zemed — Socialisticke Zemedelstvi
Soc Zemes Ukis — Socialistinis Zemes Ukis
Soc Zemjod — Socijalisticko Zemjodelstvo
Soc Zool France B — Societe Zoologique de France. Bulletin
Soc Zool Fr Bull — Societe Zoologique de France. Bulletin
SOD — Socialisme en Democratie
SODAA — Solnechnye Dannye
So Dak Hist — South Dakota History
So Dak Hist Coll — South Dakota Historical Collections
So Dak L Rev — South Dakota Law Review
So Dakota Lib Bul — South Dakota Library Bulletin
So Dak R — South Dakota Review
SOE — Socio-Economic Planning Sciences
SOE — Soft Drinks Trade Journal
SOECA — Soviet Electrochemistry [*English Translation*]
So Econ J — Southern Economic Journal
So Educ Report — Southern Education Report
SOEEA — Soviet Electrical Engineering [*English Translation*]
SOEMD — Solar Energy Materials
SOEND — Solar Engineering
Soester Z — Soester Zeitschrift
So Expose — Southern Exposure
SoF — Samtid och Framtid
SOF — Suedost-Forschungen
Sofia Univ Geol-Geogr Fak God Kn 2 Geogr — Sofia Universitet. Geologo-Geografski Fakultet. Godishnik. Kniga 2. Geografiya

ofia Univ Geol-Geogr Fak God Kniga 1 Geol — Sofia Universitet. Geologo-Geografski Fakultet. Godishnik. Kniga 1. Geologiya

ofia Vissh Minno Geol Inst God — Sofia Vissh Minno-Geolozhki Institut. Godishnik

OFMA — Soviet Fluid Mechanics [*English Translation*]

OFOA — Social Forces

o Folklore Q — Southern Folklore Quarterly

oft Eng — IEEE. Transactions on Software Engineering

oft Eng Notes — Software Engineering Notes

oft News — Software News

oftware — Software: Practice and Experience

oftware N — Software News

oftware Pract Exper — Software: Practice and Experience

oftware Pract and Exper — Software: Practice and Experience

oftware Rev — Software Review

oftware Tools Commun — Software Tools Communications

oftw Newsl — Software Newsletter

oft World — Software World

OGEA — Southeastern Geology [*United States*]

OGEB — Soviet Genetics [*English Translation*]

OHED — Sowjetunion Heute

OHID — Sohioan

o His S — Southern Historical Society

o Hist Pap — Southern Historical Society. Papers

oHR — Southern Humanities Review

OIFA — Soils and Fertilizers

oil Assoc Inf Bull Advis Serv — Soil Association. Information Bulletin and Advisory Service [*England*]

oil Biochem — Soil Biochemistry

oil Biol B — Soil Biology and Biochemistry

oil Biol and Biochem — Soil Biology and Biochemistry

oil Biol Biochem — Soil Biology and Biochemistry

oil Biol Microbiol — Soil Biology and Microbiologie

oil Cons — Soil Conservation

oil Conser — Soil Conservation

oil Conserv — Soil Conservation

oil Conserv US Soil Conserv Serv — Soil Conservation. United States Soil Conservation Service

oil Cons Serv NSW J — Soil Conservation Service of New South Wales. Journal

oil Crop Sci Soc Fla Proc — Soil and Crop Science Society of Florida. Proceedings

oil Fert — Soils and Fertilizers

oil Fert Taiwan — Soils and Fertilizers in Taiwan

oil Ld-Use Surv Br Caribb — Soil and Land-Use Surveys of the British Caribbean

o Ill LJ — Southern Illinois University. Law Journal

o Ill ULJ — Southern Illinois University. Law Journal

oil Mech Found Eng — Soil Mechanics and Foundations Engineering

oil Mech Found Engng — Soil Mechanics and Foundation Engineering

oil Mech Found Eng Reg Conf Afr Proc — Soil Mechanics and Foundation Engineering. Regional Conference for Africa. Proceedings

oil Publ — Soil Publication. Commonwealth Scientific and Industrial Research Organisation [*Australia*]

oil Publ CSIRO — Soil Publication. Commonwealth Scientific and Industrial Research Organisation [*Australia*]

oils Bull FAO — Soils Bulletin. Food and Agriculture Organization

oil Sci — Soil Science

oil Sci Agrochem — Soil Science and Agrochemistry

oil Sci Agron — Soil Science and Agronomy

oil Sci Plant Nutr — Soil Science and Plant Nutrition

oil Sci Plant Nutr (Tokyo) — Soil Science and Plant Nutrition (Tokyo)

oil Sci Pl Nutr — Soil Science and Plant Nutrition

oil Sci So — Soil Science Society of America. Proceedings

oil Sci Soc America Proc — Soil Science Society of America. Proceedings

oil Sci Soc Am J — Soil Science Society of America. Journal

oil Sci Soc Am Proc — Soil Science Society of America. Proceedings

oil Sci Soc Fla Proc — Soil Science Society of Florida. Proceedings

oil Ser Dep Soil Sci Minnesota Univ — Minnesota University. Department of Soil Science. Soil Series

oil Ser Minn Univ Agr Ext Serv — Soil Series. Minnesota University. Agriculture Extension Service

oils Fert — Soils and Fertilizers [*England*]

oils Fertil — Soils and Fertilizers

oils Fertil Taiwan — Soils and Fertilizers in Taiwan

oils Found — Soils and Foundations

oils Land Use Ser Div Soils CSIRO — Soils and Land Use Series. Division of Soils. Commonwealth Scientific and Industrial Research Organisation

oils Ld Use Ser Div Soils CSIRO — Soils and Land Use Series. Division of Soils. Commonwealth Scientific and Industrial Research Organisation

oils Rep Manitoba Soil Surv — Soils Report. Manitoba Soil Survey

oil Surv Invest Rep — Soil Survey Investigations. Report

oil Surv Pap Neth Soil Surv Inst — Soil Survey Papers. Netherlands Soil Survey Institute

oil Tillage Res — Soil and Tillage Research

oil and Water Conser News — Soil and Water Conservation News

Soil and Water Conserv Jour — Soil and Water Conservation Journal

SoJA — Soviet Jewish Affairs

Sojuzot Zdruzenijata Farm Farm Teh SR Maked Bilt — Sojuzot na Zdruzenijata na Farmacevtite i Farmacevtskite Tehnicari na SR Makedonija. Bilten

Sok — Sokrates

SOK — Sprog og Kultur

SOKAB — Sosei To Kako

Sol — Solicitor

Sol — Solidarity [*Manila*]

Sol Act — Solar Activity

Sol Age — Solar Age

Solaire 1 Mag — Solaire 1 Magazine [*France*]

Solar E D — Solar Energy Digest

Solar En D — Solar Energy Digest

Solar Energ — Solar Energy

Solar Intel — Solar Energy Intelligence Report

Solar L Rep — Solar Law Reporter

Solar Phys — Solar Physics

Solar Syst Res — Solar System Research

Sol Cells — Solar Cells

Sol Energy — Solar Energy

Sol Energy Intell Rep — Solar Energy Intelligence Report

Sol Energy Mater — Solar Energy Materials [*Netherlands*]

Sol Energy Prog Aust NZ — Solar Energy Progress in Australia and New Zealand

Sol Energy Res Dev Rep — Solar Energy Research and Development Report

Sol Energy Res Rep Univ Queensl — Solar Energy Research Report. University of Queensland

Sol Energy Update — Solar Energy Update

Sol Eng — Solar Engineering

Sol Eng Mag — Solar Engineering Magazine

Sol Heat Cool — Solar Heating and Cooling

SOLI — Soviet Life

Solicitors' J — Solicitors' Journal

SOLID — Solar Life

Solid Fuel Chem — Solid Fuel Chemistry [*English translation of Khimiya Tverdogo Topliva*]

Solid Fuel Chem (Engl Transl) — Solid Fuel Chemistry (English Translation)

Solid Mech Arch — Solid Mechanics Archives

Solid St Abstr — Solid State Abstracts

Solid Stat — Solid State Technology

Solid State Commun — Solid State Communications

Solid-State Electron — Solid-State Electronics

Solid State J — Solid State Journal

Solid State Phys — Solid State Physics

Solid State Phys Chem — Solid State Physics and Chemistry [*Japan*]

Solid State Phys (New York) — Solid State Physics. Advances in Research and Applications (New York)

Solid State Technol — Solid State Technology

Solid St Commun — Solid State Communications

Solid Waste Bull — Solid Waste Bulletin

Solid Wastes Manage — Solid Wastes Management [*Later, World Wastes*] [*England*]

Solid Wastes Manage Refuse Removal J — Solid Wastes Management/Refuse Removal Journal [*Later, World Wastes*]

Solid Wastes Mgmt — Solid Wastes Management [*Later, World Wastes*]

Solid Waste Syst — Solid Waste Systems

Solid WM — Solid Wastes Management [*Later, World Wastes*]

SOLINEWS — Southeastern Library Network. Newsletter

So Lit J — Southern Literary Journal

SOliv — Studia Oliveriana

Sol J — Solicitors' Journal

SoLJ — Southern Literary Journal

Sol Jo (Eng) — Solicitors' Journal (England)

Sol Law Rep — Solar Law Reporter

Sol Life — Solar Life

SOLMD — Solar Magazine

Soln Akt — Solnechnaya Aktivnost

Soln Dannye — Solnechnye Dannye [*USSR*]

Sol News Int — Solar News International [*West Germany*]

Solo Cent Acad "Luiz De Queiroz" Univ Sao Paulo — Solo Centro Academico "Luiz De Queiroz." Universidade de Sao Paulo

Sol Phys — Solar Physics

SOLQA — Sociological Quarterly

Sols Afr — Sols Africains

Sol St Comm — Solid State Communications

Sol-St Elec — Solid-State Electronics

Sol St Tech — Solid State Technology

Sol Syst Res — Solar System Research

SOLTA — Sotsialisticheskiy Trud

Sol Terr Environ Res Jpn — Solar Terrestrial Environmental Research in Japan

Sol Therm Components — Solar Thermal Components

Sol Therm Energy Util — Solar Thermal Energy Utilization

Sol Therm Heat Cool — Solar Thermal Heating and Cooling

Sol Therm Power Gener — Solar Thermal Power Generation

Sol Therm Rep — Solar Thermal Report
Sol Times — Solar Times
Solvent Extr Ion Exch — Solvent Extraction and Ion Exchange
Solvent Extr Rev — Solvent Extraction Reviews
SOM — Sociaal Maandblad Arbeid. Tijdschrift voor Sociaal Recht en Sociaal Geleid
So M — Southern Magazine
SOMA — Soobscenija Otdela Machanizacii i Avtomatizacii Informacionnych Rabot
Somatic Cell Genet — Somatic Cell Genetics
Somatic Cell Mol Genet — Somatic Cell and Molecular Genetics
SOMBA — Southern Medical Bulletin [*United States*]
Som Cell G — Somatic Cell Genetics
SOMDA — Southwestern Medicine [*United States*]
SOMEA — Sovetskaya Meditsina
Somerset Archaeol Natur Hist — Somerset Archaeology and Natural History
Somerset Arch Nat Hist — Somerset Archaeology and Natural History
Somerset Industrial Archaeology Soc Jnl — Somerset Industrial Archaeology Society. Journal
Somerset Levels Pap — Somerset Levels Papers
Somogyi Muesz Sz — Somogyi Mueszaki Szemle [*Hungary*]
SOMSA — Soviet Materials Science [*English Translation*]
SON — Slovenske Odborne Nazvoslovie
Sonderdr Internist Welt — Sonderdruck aus Internistische Welt [*West Germany*]
Sonderh Bayer Landw Jb — Sonderhefte. Bayerisches Landwirtschaftliches Jahrbuch
Sonderhefte zum Allgemein Statist Arch — Sonderhefte zum Allgemeinen Statistischen Archiv
Sonderh Landw Forsch — Sonderheft zur Zeitschrift "Landwirtschaftliche Forschung"
Sonderh Z PflKrankh PflPath PflSchutz — Sonderheft. Zeitschrift fuer Pflanzenkrankheiten, Pflanzenpathologie, und Pflanzenschutz
Sonderjydsk M-skr — Sonderjydsk Manedsskrift
Song Hits Mag — Song Hits Magazine
Songklanakarin J Sci Technol — Songklanakarin Journal of Science and Technology
Songwriter — Songwriter Magazine
Songwriters R — Songwriter's Review
SONKA — Shonika
Sonnenenerg — Sonnenenergie
Sonnenenerg Waermepumpe — Sonnenenergie und Waermepumpe
SOnoM — Studia Ononmastica Monacensia
So NQ — Somerset Notes and Queries
Son Spec — Sonorum Speculum
SONWD — Sonnenenergie und Waermepumpe
Soob A N Gruz SSR — Soobshcheniia Akademii Nauk Gruzinskoi SSR
Soob G Ermitazh — Soobshcheniia Gosudarstvennogo Ermitazha
Soob G Muz Izob Isk Pushkin — Soobshcheniia Gosudarstvennyi Muzei Izobrazitel'nykh Iskusstv Imeni A. S. Pushkina
Soob Kherson Muz — Soobshcheniia Khersonnesskogo Muzeia [*Sebastopol*]
SoobMP — Soobscenija du Musee d'Art Pouchkine
Soobscenija Akad Nauk Gruz SSR — Soobscenija Akademiji Nauk Gruzinskoj SSR
Soobsc Gosud Russk Muz — Soobscenija Gosudarstvennogo Russkogo Muzeja
Soobsc Muz Isk Nar Vostoka — Soobscenija Muzeja Iskusstva Narodov Vostoka
Soobsc Vycisl Mat — Soobscenija po Vychislitel noi Matematike
Soobshch Akad Nauk Gruzin SSR — Soobshcheniya Akademiya Nauk Gruzinskoi SSR
Soobshch Akad Nauk Gruz SSSR — Soobshcheniya Akademiya Nauk Gruzinskoi SSSR
Soobshch Byurakan Obs Akad Nauk Arm SSR — Soobshcheniya Byurakanskoj Observatorii Akademii Nauk Armyanskoj SSR
Soobshch Chuv Zon Agrokhim Lab — Soobshcheniya Chuvashskoi Zonal'noi Agrokhimicheskoi Laboratorii
Soobshch Dal'Nevost Fil Sib Otd Aka Nauk SSSR — Soobshcheniya Dal'Nevostochnogo Filiala Sibirskogo Otdla Akademii Nauk SSSR
Soobshch Inst Agrokhim Probl Gidroponiki Akad Nauk Arm SSR — Soobshcheniya Instituta Agrokhimicheskikh Problem i Gidroponiki Akademii Nauk Armyanskoi SSR [*Armenian SSR*]
Soobshch Inst Lesa Akad Nauk SSSR — Soobshcheniya Instituta Lesa Akademii Nauk SSSR
SoobshchIPPO — Soobshcheniia Imperialnovo Pravoslavnovo Palestinskavo Obshchestva
Soobshch Mosk Otd Vses Bot Ova — Soobshcheniya Moskovskogo Otdeleniya Vsesoyuznogo Botanicheskogo Obshchestva
Soobshch Nauchno Issled Rab Kiev Politekh Inst — Soobshcheniya o Nauchno-Issledovatel'skoi Rabote Kievskii Politekhnicheskii Institut
Soobshch Ob'edin Inst Yad Issled (Dubna) — Soobshcheniya Ob'edinennogo Instituta Yadernykh Issledovanii (Dubna)
Soobshch Obshch Lab Agrokhim Akad Nauk Armyan SSR — Soobshcheniya Obshchestvoi Laboratorii Agrokhimii Akademii Nauk Armyanskoi SSR
Soobshch Sakhalin Fil Akad Nauk SSSR — Soobshcheniya Sakhalinskogo Filiala Akademii Nauk SSSR

Soobshch Shemakhinskoi Astrofiz Obs Akad Nauk Azerb SSR — Soobshcheskoi Shemakhinskoi Astrofizicheskoi Observatorii Akademyi Nauk Azerbaidzhan SSR [*Azerbaidzhan SSR*]
Soochow J Hum — Soochow Journal of Humanities [*Taipei*]
Soochow J Lit Soc Stud — Soochow Journal of Literature and Social Studies [*Taipei*]
Soochow J Math — Soochow Journal of Mathematics [*Taipei*]
Soochow J Math Natur Sci — Soochow Journal of Mathematical and Natural Sciences [*Later, Soochow Journal of Mathematics*]
Soon Chun Hyang J Med — Soon Chun Hyang Journal of Medicine [*Republic of Korea*]
SOPAA — Soviet Physics. Acoustics [*English Translation*]
Sophia Econ R — Sophia Economic Review [*Tokyo*]
Sophia:T — Sophia: Studies in Western Civilization and the Cultural Interaction of East and West (Tokyo)
SOPJA — Soviet Physics Journal [*English Translation*]
SOPLA — Soviet Plastics [*English Translation*]
SOPPA — Soviet Plant Physiology [*English Translation*]
SOPUA — Soviet Physics. Uspekhi [*English Translation*]
So Q — Southern Quarterly Review
SOR — Serie Orientale Roma
So R — Southern Review [*US*]
SoR — Southern Review: An Australian Journal of Literary Studies
So R A — Southern Review: An Australian Journal of Literary Studies
S O Rev — Sean O'Casey Review
So R ns — Southern Review: New Series [*US*]
SoS — Saga och Sed
SoS — Syn og Segn
SOS — Systems, Objectives, Solutions
Sos Aikakausk — Sosiaalinen Aikakauskirja
So School News — Southern School News
So St — Southern Studies
SoT — Sloejd och Ton
SOTCA — Soudage et Techniques Connexes
SOTIB — Sotsialisticheskaya Industriya
SOTID — Solar Times
Sotilaslaak Aikak — Sotilaslaaketieteellinen Aikakauslehti
Sots Pollum — Sotsialistik Pollumajandus
Sots Sel'Khoz Azerb — Sotsialisticheskoe Sel'skoe Khozyaistvo Azerbaidzhana
Sots Sel'Khoz Uzbek — Sotsialisticheskoe Sel'skoe Khozyaistvo Uzbekistana
Sots Sel'sk Khoz Azerb — Sotsialisticheskoe Sel'skoe Khozyaistvo Azerbaidzhana
Sots Sel'sk Khoz Uz — Sotsialisticheskoe Sel'skoe Khozyaistvo Uzbekistana
Sots Trud — Sotsialisticheskiy Trud [*USSR*]
Sots Tvarinnit — Sotsialistichne Tvarinnitstvo
Sots Tvarynnytstvo — Sotsialistychne Tvarynnytstvo
SOU — South. The Third World Magazine
Sou Aus LR — South Australian Law Reports
Soudage Tech Connexes — Soudage et Techniques Connexes
Soud Lek — Soudni Lekarstvi
Soul Il — Soul Illustrated
So U LR — Southern University Law Review
So U L Rev — Southern University Law Review
Soun — Soundings
Sound — Soundings
Sound Brass — Sounding Brass and the Conductor
Sound (Can) — Sound (Canada)
Sound Vib — Sound and Vibration
Sound & Vib — Sound and Vibration
Sound Vis Broadc — Sound and Vision Broadcasting
So Univ L Rev — Southern University Law Review
SOUR — Sourdough Journal. Alaska Library Association
SouR — Southern Review [*US*]
Sources Hist Math Phys Sci — Sources in the History of Mathematics and Physical Sciences
Sources in Hist of Math and Phys Sci — Sources in the History of Mathematics and Physical Sciences
Sources Sci — Sources of Science
Sources and Stud Hist Arabic-Islamic Sci Hist of Math Ser — Sources and Studies in the History of Arabic-Islamic Science. History of Mathematics Series
Sources Stud Hist Arabic-Islamic Sci Hist of Tech Ser — Sources and Studies in the History of Arabic-Islamic Science. History of Technology Series
Sources Stud Hist Arabic Math — Sources and Studies in the History of Arabic Mathematics
SOUTB — Statens Offentliga Utredningar
South Afr Archaeol B — South African Archaeological Bulletin
South Afr Geogr J — South African Geographical Journal
South African J African Affairs — South African Journal of African Affairs
South African J Econ — South African Journal of Economics [*Suid-Afrikaanse Tydskrif vir Ekonomie*]
South African Labour Bul — South African Labour Bulletin
South African Med J — South African Medical Journal
South African Med Rec — South African Medical Record
South African Min Eng Jour — South African Mining and Engineering Journal
South African Statist J — South African Statistical Journal

South Afr Int Quart — South Africa International Quarterly

South Afr J Afr Aff — South African Journal of African Affairs

South Afr J Econ — South African Journal of Economics [*Suid-Afrikaanse Tydskrif vir Ekonomie*]

South Afr J Sci — South African Journal of Science

South Afr LJ — South African Law Journal

South Afr Text — Southern Africa Textiles

South Ariz Guideb — Southern Arizona Guidebook

South As Dig Reg Writ — South Asian Digest of Regional Writing [*Heidelberg*]

South Asian R — South Asian Review

South Asian Stud — South Asian Studies

South As Stud — South Asian Studies [*Jaipur*]

South As Surv — South Asian Survey [*New Delhi*]

South Atlan Q — South Atlantic Quarterly

South Aus LR — South Australian Law Reports

South Aust Dep Agric Fish Agron Branch Rep — South Australia. Department of Agriculture and Fisheries. Agronomy Branch. Report

South Aust Dep Agric Fish Agron Bran Rep — South Australia. Department of Agriculture and Fisheries. Agronomy Branch. Report

South Aust Dep Mines Miner Resour Rev — South Australia. Department of Mines. Mineral Resources Review

South Aust Geol Surv Bull — South Australia. Geological Survey. Bulletin

South Aust Geol Surv 1:250000 Geol Ser — South Australia. Geological Survey. 1:250,000 Geological Series

South Aust Geol Surv Q Geol Notes — South Australia. Geological Survey. Quarterly Geological Notes

South Aust Geol Surv Rep Invest — South Australia. Geological Survey. Report of Investigations

South Aust Mot — South Australian Motor

South Aust Nat — South Australian Naturalist

South Aust Orn — South Australian Ornithologist

South Aust Rep Mus Board — South Australia Report of the Museum Board

South Bus — South Business

South Calif Coastal Water Res Proj Annu Rep — Southern California Coastal Water Research Project. Annual Report

South Calif L Rev — Southern California Law Review

South Calif Q — Southern California Quarterly

South Canner Packer — Southern Canner and Packer

South Cant J — South Canterbury Journal

South Carolina Acad Sci Bull — South Carolina Academy of Science. Bulletin

South Carolina Div Geology Geol Notes — South Carolina. Division of Geology. Geologic Notes

South Carolina Div Geology Misc Rept — South Carolina. Division of Geology. Miscellaneous Report

South Carolina L Rev — South Carolina Law Review

South Car R — South Carolina Review

South Chem — Southern Chemist

South Chem Ind — Southern Chemical Industry

South Conf Gerontol Rep — Southern Conference on Gerontology. Report

South Coop Ser Bull — Southern Cooperative Series Bulletin

South Corn Impr Conf Rep — Southern Corn Improvement Conference. Report

South Dairy Prod J — Southern Dairy Products Journal

South Dakota Geol Survey Guidebook — South Dakota. Geological Survey. Guidebook

South Dakota Geol Survey Rept Inv — South Dakota. Geological Survey. Report of Investigations

South Dakota Geol Survey Spec Rept — South Dakota. Geological Survey. Special Report

South Dakota Geol Survey Water Resources Rept — South Dakota Geological Survey and South Dakota Water Resources Commission. Water Resources Report

South Dakota L Rev — South Dakota Law Review

Southeast Asia Bldg Materials & Equipment — Southeast Asia Building Materials and Equipment

Southeast Asia J Theol — Southeast Asia Journal of Theology

Southeast Asian Conf Soil Eng Proc — Southeast Asian Conference on Soil Engineering. Proceedings

Southeast Asian J Soc Sci — Southeast Asian Journal of Social Science

Southeast Asian J Trop Med Public Health — Southeast Asian Journal of Tropical Medicine and Public Health

South East Asian Stud — South East Asian Studies

Southeast Asia Pet Explor Soc Proc — Southeast Asia Petroleum Exploration Society. Proceedings

Southeastcon Reg 3 (Three) Conf Proc — Southeastcon Region 3 (Three) Conference Proceedings [*United States*]

Southeastern Geology Spec Pub — Southeastern Geology. Special Publication

Southeast Geol — Southeastern Geology

Southeast Geol Soc Field Conf Guideb — Southeastern Geological Society. Field Conference Guidebook

Southeast Geol Spec Publ — Southeastern Geology. Special Publication

South Econ — Southern Economist [*Bangalore*]

South Econ J — Southern Economic Journal

South Econ Jour — Southern Economic Journal

Southern Calif Acad Sci Bull — Southern California Academy of Sciences. Bulletin

Southern Econ J — Southern Economic Journal

Southern Folklore Q — Southern Folklore Quarterly

Southern H R — Southern Humanities Review

Southern Hum R — Southern Humanities Review

Southern J Med Phys Sc — Southern Journal of the Medical and Physical Sciences

Southern Lit J — Southern Literary Journal

Southern P R — Southern Poetry Review

Southern Pulp Paper Mfr — Southern Pulp and Paper Manufacturer

Southern R — Southern Review

Southern Rev — Southern Review

South Exposure — Southern Exposure [*United States*]

South Fisherman — Southern Fisherman

South Florist Nurseryman — Southern Florist and Nurseryman [*United States*]

South Folkl Q — Southern Folklore Quarterly

South Folkl Quart — Southern Folklore Quarterly

South Folk Q — Southern Folklore Quarterly

South Food Process — Southern Food Processor

South Hist Assoc Publ — Southern Historical Association. Publications

South Hist Soc Papers — Southern Historical Society. Papers

South Hort — Southern Horticulture [*New Zealand*]

South Hortic — Southern Horticulture

South Hosp — Southern Hospitals

South Ill ULJ — Southern Illinois University. Law Journal

South Indian Hortic — Southern Indian Horticulture

South J Agric Econ — Southern Journal of Agricultural Economics

South J Appl For — Southern Journal of Applied Forestry

South Liv — Southern Living

South Lumberman — Southern Lumberman

South M — South Magazine

South Med — Southern Medicine

South Med Bull — Southern Medical Bulletin

South Med J — Southern Medical Journal

South Med Surg — Southern Medicine and Surgery

South Methodist Univ Inst Stud Earth Man Rep — Southern Methodist University. Institute for the Study of Earth and Man. Reports of Investigations

South Pac Bull — South Pacific Bulletin

South Pac Comm Tech Pap — Southern Pacific Commission. Technical Paper

South Pacific B — South Pacific Bulletin

South Pacific Bul — South Pacific Bulletin

South Pacific J Ed — South Pacific Journal of Education

South Pac J Teach Educ — South Pacific Journal of Teacher Education

South Pharm J — Southern Pharmaceutical Journal

South Plast Chem — Southern Plastics and Chemicals

South Power Ind — Southern Power and Industry

South Power J — Southern Power Journal

South Pract — Southern Practitioner

South Pulp Pap J — Southern Pulp and Paper Journal

South Pulp Pap Manuf — Southern Pulp and Paper Manufacturer

South Q — Southern Quarterly

South Quar — Southern Quarterly Review

South Quart — Southern Quarterly

South R — South Carolina Review

South R — Southern Review

South Rag — Southern Rag

South Res Inst Bull — Southern Research Institute. Bulletin [*United States*]

South Rhod Geol Surv Bull — Southern Rhodesia. Geological Survey. Bulletin

South Seedsman — Southern Seedsman

South Speech Comm J — Southern Speech Communication Journal

South Stars — Southern Stars

South Stud — Southern Studies

South Texas Geol Soc Bull — South Texas Geological Society. Bulletin

South Texas LJ — South Texas Law Journal

South Text Bull — Southern Textile Bulletin

South UL Rev — Southern University Law Review

Southwest Afr Ann — Southwest Africa Annual

Southwest Bull — Southwest Bulletin [*United States*]

Southwest Entomol — Southwestern Entomologist

Southwestern As Petroleum G B — Southwestern Association of Petroleum Geologists. Bulletin

Southwestern LA Jour — Southwestern Louisiana Journal

Southwestern LJ — Southwestern Law Journal

Southwestern UL Rev — Southwestern University. Law Review

Southwestern Univ L Rev — Southwestern University. Law Review

Southwest Hist Q — Southwestern Historical Quarterly

Southwest J — Southwest Journal

Southwest J Anthropol — Southwestern Journal of Anthropology

Southwest Med — Southwestern Medicine [*United States*]

Southwest Miller — Southwestern Miller

Southwest Mus Paper — Southwest Museum. Papers

Southwest Nat — Southwestern Naturalist

Southwest Pet Short Course Proc Annu Meet — Southwestern Petroleum Short Course. Proceedings of the Annual Meeting [*United States*]

Southwest UL Rev — Southwestern University. Law Review

Southwest Vet — Southwestern Veterinarian [*United States*]
Southwest Water Works J — Southwest Water Works Journal
Southw His Q — Southwestern Historical Quarterly
Southw Hist Quar — Southwestern Historical Quarterly
SouthWJTh — Southwestern Journal of Theology [*Fort Worth, TX*]
Southw Lore — Southwestern Lore
Southw Pol Sci Quar — Southwestern Political Science Quarterly
Southw Pol and Soc Sci Q — Southwestern Political and Social Science
　　Quarterly
Southw Rev — Southwest Review
Southw Soc Sci Quar — Southwestern Social Science Quarterly
Sov Aeronaut — Soviet Aeronautics [*English Translation of Izvestiya VUZ.
　　Aviatsionnaya Teknika*]
Sov Antarct Exped Inform Bull — Soviet Antarctic Expedition. Information
　　Bulletin
Sov Antarkt Eksped Inform Byull — Sovetskaya Antarkticheskaya Ekspeditsiya
　　Informatsionnyy Byulleten
Sov Anthr A — Soviet Anthropology and Archeology
Sov Anthro Arch — Soviet Anthropology and Archeology [*New York*]
Sov Appl Mech — Soviet Applied Mechanics
Sov Arh — Sovetskie Arhivi
Sov Arkh — Sovetskie Arkhivy
Sov Arkheol — Sovetskaya Arkheologiya
Sov Astron — Soviet Astronomy
Sov Astron Lett — Soviet Astronomy. Letters
Sov Astron Lett (Engl Transl) — Soviet Astronomy. Letters (English
　　Translation)
Sov At Energy — Soviet Atomic Energy
Sov At En R — Soviet Atomic Energy (USSR)
Sov Atom Energy — Soviet Atomic Energy
Sov Automat Contr — Soviet Automatic Control
Sov Autom Control — Soviet Automatic Control
Sov Bibliog — Sovetskaya Bibliografia
Sov Bibliotekov — Sovetskaia Bibliotekovedenie
Sov Chem Ind — Soviet Chemical Industry
Sov Cybern Rev — Soviet Cybernetics Review
SOVEA — Southwestern Veterinarian [*United States*]
Sov East Europ For Trade — Soviet and Eastern European Foreign Trade
Sov Educ — Soviet Education
Sov E E For — Soviet and Eastern European Foreign Trade
Sov Elec Eng — Soviet Electrical Engineering
Sov Electr Eng — Soviet Electrical Engineering [*English Translation of
　　Elektrotekhnika*]
Sov Electrochem — Soviet Electrochemistry
Sov Eng J — Soviet Engineering Journal
Sov Engng Res — Soviet Engineering Research
Sov Eng Res — Soviet Engineering Research
SovEt — Sovetskaya Etnografija
Sovet Geol — Sovetskaya Geologiya
Sovet Geologiya — Sovetskaya Geologiya
Sovet Muz — Sovetskaya Muzyka
SovEtn — Sovetskaya Etnografija
Sov Etnogr — Sovetskaja Etnografija
Sovetskoe Bibl — Sovetskoe Bibliotekovedenie
Sov Export — Soviet Export
Sov Farm — Sovetskaya Farmatsiya
Sov Film — Soviet Film
Sov Finno-Ugroved — Sovetskoje Finno-Ugrovedenie
Sov Fluid Mech (Engl Transl) — Soviet Fluid Mechanics (English Translation)
Sov Foto — Sovetskoe Foto
SovFU — Sovetskoje Finno-Ugrovedenie
Sov Genet — Soviet Genetics
Sov Genet (Engl Transl Genetika) — Soviet Genetics (English Translation of
　　Genetika)
Sov Geogr — Soviet Geography. Review and Translations
Sov Geogr R — Soviet Geography. Review and Translations
Sov Geol — Sovetskaya Geologiya
Sov Geol Geophys — Soviet Geology and Geophysics
Sov Geol and Geophys — Soviet Geology and Geophysics
Sov Geol Geophys (Engl Transl) — Soviet Geology and Geophysics (English
　　Translation)
Sov Gos Pravo — Sovetskoe Gosudarstvo i Pravo
SovH — Sovetish Heymland
Sov Hydrol — Soviet Hydrology. Selected Papers
Sov Hydrol Sel Pap — Soviet Hydrology. Selected Papers
SOVIA — Sound and Vibration
Soviet Aeronaut — Soviet Aeronautics
Soviet Agric Sci — Soviet Agricultural Science
Soviet Appl Mech — Soviet Applied Mechanics
Soviet Astronom — Soviet Astronomy
Soviet Automat Control — Soviet Automatic Control
Soviet Ed — Soviet Education
Soviet F — Soviet Film
Soviet J Ecol — Soviet Journal of Ecology
Soviet J Nuclear Phys — American Institute of Physics. Soviet Journal of
　　Nuclear Physics

Soviet J Particles and Nuclei — Soviet Journal of Particles and Nuclei
Soviet Law and Govt — Soviet Law and Government
Soviet L & Govt — Soviet Law and Government
Soviet Lit — Soviet Literature
Soviet Math Dokl — Soviet Mathematics. Doklady
Soviet Math (Iz VUZ) — Soviet Mathematics (Izvestija Vyssih Ucebnyh
　　Zavedenii. Matematika)
Soviet Phys Acoust — Soviet Physics. Acoustics
Soviet Phys Cryst — Soviet Physics. Crystallography
Soviet Physics Acoust — Soviet Physics. Acoustics
Soviet Physics Dokl — Soviet Physics. Doklady
Soviet Physics J — Soviet Physics Journal
Soviet Phys J — Soviet Physics Journal
Soviet Phys JETP — Soviet Physics. JETP [*Journal of Experimental and
　　Theoretical Physics of the Academy of Sciences of the USSR*]
Soviet Phys Uspekhi — Soviet Physics. Uspekhi
Soviet Plant Physiol — Soviet Plant Physiology
Soviet Pl Physiol — Soviet Plant Physiology
Soviet Soil Sci — Soviet Soil Science
Soviet Stud — Soviet Studies
Soviet Stud Phil — Soviet Studies in Philosophy
Sov Instrum & Control J — Soviet Journal of Instrumentation and Control
Sovistva At Yader — Sovistva Atomnykh Yader [*USSR*]
SovJa — Sovetska Jazykoveda
Sov J At — Soviet Journal of Atomic Energy
Sov J Coord Chem (Engl Transl) — Soviet Journal of Coordination Chemistry
　　(English Translation)
Sov J Dev Biol (Engl Transl Ontogenez) — Soviet Journal of Developmental
　　Biology (English Translation of Ontogenez)
Sov J Ecol — Soviet Journal of Ecology
Sov J Ecol (Engl Transl Ekologiya) — Soviet Journal of Ecology (English
　　Translation of Ekologiya)
Sov Jew Aff — Soviet Jewish Affairs
Sov J Glass Phys and Chem — Soviet Journal of Glass Physics and Chemistry
Sov J Glass Phys Chem — Soviet Journal of Glass Physics and Chemistry
Sov J Glass Phys Chem (Engl Transl) — Soviet Journal of Glass Physics and
　　Chemistry (English Translation)
Sov J Instrum Control — Soviet Journal of Instrumentation and Control
Sov J Low Temp Phys — Soviet Journal of Low Temperature Physics
Sov J Low Temp Phys (Engl Transl) — Soviet Journal of Low Temperature
　　Physics (English Translation)
Sov J Mar Biol — Soviet Journal of Marine Biology
Sov J Mar Biol (Engl Transl) — Soviet Journal of Marine Biology (English
　　Translation)
Sov J Nondestr Test — Soviet Journal of Nondestructive Testing
Sov J Nondestruct Test — Soviet Journal of Nondestructive Testing
Sov J Non-Ferrous Met — Soviet Journal of Non-Ferrous Metals
Sov J Nucl Phys — Soviet Journal of Nuclear Physics
Sov J Nuc R — Soviet Journal of Nuclear Physics (USSR)
Sov J Opt Technol — Soviet Journal of Optical Technology
Sov J Part Nucl — Soviet Journal of Particles and Nuclei
Sov J Plasma Phys — Soviet Journal of Plasma Physics
Sov J Quant Electron — Soviet Journal of Quantum Electronics
Sov J Quantum Electron — Soviet Journal of Quantum Electronics
Sov Khlopok — Sovetskii Khlopok
Sov Kino Fotopromst — Sovetskaya Kino-Fotopromyshlennost
SovKniga — Sovetskaya Kniga
Sov Krasnyi Krest — Soveti Krasnyi Krest [*USSR*]
SovL — Soviet Literature
SOVLA — Sovetskaya Latviya
Sov Law Gov — Soviet Law and Government
Sov Lit — Soviet Literature
Sov M — Sovetskaya Muzyka
Sov Mater Sci — Soviet Materials Science
Sov Mater Sci (Engl Transl) — Soviet Materials Science (English Translation of
　　Fiziko-Khimicheskaya Mekhanika Materialov)
Sov Math — Soviet Mathematics
Sov Med — Sovetskaya Meditsina
Sovmestnaya Sov-Mong Nauchno-Issled Geol Eksped — Sovmestnaya Sovetsko-
　　Mongol'skaya Nauchno-Issledovatel'skaya Geologicheskaya
　　Ekspeditsiya
Sovmestnaya Sov-Mong Nauchno-Issled Geol Eksped Tr — Sovmestnaya
　　Sovetsko-Mongol'skaya Nauchno-Issledovatel'skaya Geologicheskaya
　　Ekspeditsiya Trudy
Sov Metall — Sovetskaya Metallurgiya
Sov Meteorol Hydrol — Soviet Meteorology and Hydrology [*English
　　translation of Meteorologiya i Gidrologiya*]
Sov Meteorol and Hydrol — Soviet Meteorology and Hydrology [*English
　　translation of Meteorologiya i Gidrologiya*]
Sov Meteorol Hydrol (Engl Transl) — Soviet Meteorology and Hydrology
　　(English Translation)
Sov Microelectron — Soviet Microelectronics
Sov Min Sci — Soviet Mining Science
Sov Nauka — Sovetskaya Nauka
Sov Neurol Psychiatry — Soviet Neurology and Psychiatry
Sov Neur R — Soviet Neurology and Psychiatry (USSR)

Sov Non-Ferrous Met Res — Soviet Non-Ferrous Metals Research
Sov Non-Ferrous Met Res (Engl Transl) — Soviet Non-Ferrous Metals
   Research (English Translation)
Sov Oceanogr — Soviet Oceanography
Sov Pedag — Soviet Pedagogy
Sov Ph Ac R — Soviet Physics. Acoustics (USSR)
Sov Ph Se R — Soviet Physics. Semiconductors (USSR)
Sov Phys Acoust — Soviet Physics. Acoustics
Sov Phys Collect — Soviet Physics. Collection
Sov Phys Coll (Engl Transl) — Soviet Physics. Collection (English Translation)
Sov Phys Cryst — Soviet Physics. Crystallography
Sov Phys Crystallogr — Soviet Physics. Crystallography
Sov Phys Dokl — Soviet Physics. Doklady
Sov Phys J — Soviet Physics Journal
Sov Phys JETP — Soviet Physics. JETP [Journal of Experimental and
   Theoretical Physics of the Academy of Sciences of the USSR]
Sov Phys Lebedev Inst Rep — Soviet Physics. Lebedev Institute Reports
   [English Translation of Sbornik Kratkie Soobshcheniya po Fizike]
Sov Phys Lebedev Inst Rep (Engl Transl) — Soviet Physics. Lebedev Institute
   Reports (English Translation)
Sov Phys Semicond — Soviet Physics. Semiconductors
Sov Phys Solid State — Soviet Physics. Solid State [English translation of
   Fizika Tverdogo Tela]
Sov Phys Sol St — Soviet Physics. Solid State Physics
Sov Phys Tech Phys — Soviet Physics. Technical Physics
Sov Phys Tech Phys Lett — Soviet Physics. Technical Physics. Letters
Sov Phys T P — Soviet Physics. Technical Physics
Sov Phys Usp — Soviet Physics. Uspekhi
Sov Phys Uspekhi — Soviet Physics. Uspekhi
Sov Plant Physiol — Soviet Plant Physiology
Sov Plant Physiol (Engl Transl Fiziol Rast) — Soviet Plant Physiology (English
   Translation of Fiziologiya Rastenii)
Sov Plast — Soviet Plastics
Sov Powder Metall and Met Ceram — Soviet Powder Metallurgy and Metal
   Ceramics
Sov Powder Metall Met Ceram — Soviet Powder Metallurgy and Metal
   Ceramics
Sov Powder Met Metal Ceram — Soviet Powder Metallurgy and Metal
   Ceramics
Sov Power Eng — Soviet Power Engineering
Sov Power Eng (Engl Transl) — Soviet Power Engineering (English Translation
   of Elektricheskie Stantsii)
Sov Prog Chem — Soviet Progress in Chemistry
Sov Psikhonevrol — Sovetskaya Psikhonevrologiya
Sov Psychol — Soviet Psychology
Sov Psyco R — Soviet Psychology (USSR)
Sov Public Health — Soviet Public Health
Sov Public Health (Engl Transl) — Soviet Public Health (English Translation)
SovR — Soviet Review
Sov Radiochem — Soviet Radiochemistry
Sov Radio Eng — Soviet Radio Engineering
Sov Radiophys — Soviet Radiophysics
Sov Radiophys (Engl Transl) — Soviet Radiophysics (English Translation of
   Izvestiya Vysshikh Uchebnykh Zavedenii Radiofizika)
Sovrem Metody Issled — Sovremennye Metody Issledovaniya
Sovrem Probl Deyat Str Tsentr Nervn Sist — Sovremennye Problemy
   Deyatel'nosti i Stroeniya Tsentral'noe Nervnoi Sistemy
Sovrem Probl Fiz Khim — Sovremennye Problemy Fizicheskoi Khimii
Sovrem Probl Gastroenterol — Sovremennye Problemy Gastroenterologii
Sovrem Probl Gastroenterol Resp Mezhved Sb — Sovremennye Problemy
   Gastroenterologii Respublikanskii Mezhvedomstvennyi-Sbornik
Sovrem Probl Gematol Pereliv Krovi — Sovremennye Problemy Gematologii i
   Perelivaniya Krovi
Sovrem Probl Onkol — Sovremennye Problemy Onkologii
Sovrem Probl Org Khim — Sovremennye Problemy Organicheskoi Khimii
Sovrem Probl Otolaringol Resp Mezhved Sb — Sovremennye Problemy
   Otolaringologii Respublikanskoi Mezhvedomstvennyi Sbornik
Sovrem Probl Radiobiol — Sovremennye Problemy Radiobiologii [USSR]
Sovrem Psikhotropnye Sredstva — Sovremennye Psikhotropnye Sredstva
Sovrem Vopr Endokrinol — Sovremennye Voprosy Endokrinologii
Sovrem Vopr Sud Med Ekspertnoi Prak — Sovremennye Voprosy Sudebnoi
   Meditsiny i Ekspertnoi Praktiki
Sovrem Zadachi Tochn Naukakh — Sovremennye Zadachi v Tochnykh
   Naukakh
Sov Res Phys — Soviet Research in Physics
Sov Rubber Technol — Soviet Rubber Technology
SovS — Soviet Studies
SovS — Soviet Survey
Sov Sakhar — Sovetskii Sakhar
Sov Sci — Soviet Science
Sov Sci (Engl Transl) — Soviet Science (English Translation)
Sov Sci Rev — Soviet Science Review [England]
Sov Shakhtior — Sovetskii Shakhtior [USSR]
SovSlav — Sovetskoe Slavjanovedenie
Sov Soc — Soviet Sociology
Sov Sociol — Soviet Sociology

Sov Soil Sci — Soviet Soil Science
Sov Soil Sci Suppl — Soviet Soil Science. Supplement
Sov Stat & Dec — Soviet Statutes and Decisions
Sov St Hist — Soviet Studies in History
Sov St Lit — Soviet Studies in Literature
Sov St Phil — Soviet Studies in Philosophy
Sov Stud — Soviet Studies
Sov Stud Hist — Soviet Studies in History
Sov Subtrop (Moscow) — Sovetskie Subtropiki (Moscow)
Sov Subtrop (Sukhumi USSR) — Sovetskie Subtropiki (Sukhumi, USSR)
SovT — Sovetskaja Tjurkologija
Sov Tech Phys Lett — Soviet Technical Physics. Letters
Sov Tech Phys Lett (Engl Transl) — Soviet Technical Physics. Letters (English
   Translation)
Sov Tjurkolog — Sovetskaja Tjurkologija
Sov T P Lett — Soviet Technical Physics. Letters
Sov Union — Soviet Union
Sov Veda Chem — Sovetska Veda. Chemie
SovVo — Sovetskoje Vostokovedenije
Sov Vrach Zh — Sovetskii Vrachebnyi Zhurnal
Sov Zdravookhr — Sovetskoe Zdravookhranenie
Sov Zdravookhr Kirg — Sovetskoe Zdravookhranenie Kirgizii
Sov Zdravookhr Turkm — Sovetskoe Zdravookhranenie Turkmenii
Sov Zootekh — Sovetskaya Zootekhniya
So West LJ — Southwestern Law Journal
Sowjetw Ges — Sowjetwissenschaft Gesellschaft
Sowjetwiss — Sowjetwissenschaft
So Workm — Southern Workman
SoWS — Southern Writers Series
Soybean Dig — Soybean Digest
SoZ — Sovremennye Zapiski
Soz Arbeit — Soziale Arbeit
SOZDA — Sovetskoe Zdravookhranenie
Soz Forstwirtsch — Sozialistische Forstwirtschaft
Soz Fortschritt — Sozialer Fortschritt
Sozialdemokr Pressedienst — Sozialdemokratische Pressedienst
Sozial Forstw — Sozialistische Forstwirtschaft
Sozialistische Arbeitswiss — Sozialistische Arbeitswissenschaft
Sozialistische Finwirt — Sozialistische Finanzwirtschaft
Sozialmed Paedagog Jugendkd — Sozialmedizinische und Paedagogische
   Jugendkunde
Sozial Polit — Sozialistische Politik
Soz Kommun — Sozialisation und Kommunikation
Soz- Praeventivmed — Sozial- und Praeventivmedizin
Soz Sicherheit — Soziale Sicherheit
Soz Welt — Soziale Welt
Soz und Wirtpol MSpiegel — Sozial- und Wirtschaftspolitischer Monatsspiegel
   aus Zeitungen und Zeitschriften
Soz Wiss Jb Polit — Sozialwissenschaftliches Jahrbuch fuer Politik
SP — Scholarly Publishing
SP — Slovansky Prehled
SP — Space Propulsion
Sp — Spectator
Sp — Speculum
SP — Spring
Sp — Sputnik [Moscow]
SP — Studia Papyrologica
SP — Studia Patristica
SP — Studies in Philology
SP — Suisse Primitive
SPA — Dagblad Scheepvaart
SPA — Science and Public Affairs. Bulletin of the Atomic Scientists
SPA — Sitzungsberichte. Preussische Akademie der Wissenschaften
SPAA — Sage Public Administration Abstracts
S Pac — South Pacific
SPACA — Spectrochimica Acta
SPACD8 — Israel. Agricultural Research Organization. Special Publication
SPACDocRap — Societe Paleontologique et Archeologique de
   l'Arrondissement Judiciaire de Charleroi. Documents et Rapports
Space/Aeronaut — Space/Aeronautics
Space Biol Med (Engl Transl) — Space Biology and Medicine (English
   Translation)
Space Cit — Space City News
Space Congr Proc — Space Congress. Proceedings [United States]
Space Life Sci — Space Life Sciences
Space Res — Space Research
Space Res Bulg — Space Research in Bulgaria
Space Sci Instrum — Space Science Instrumentation
Space Sci R — Space Science Reviews
Space Sci Rev — Space Science Reviews
Space Sol Power Rev — Space Solar Power Review
S Pacific — South Pacific
S Pacific Bull — South Pacific Bulletin
SPAEA — Space/Aeronautics
SPAFA — Sports Afield
Spain Estac Cent Ecol Bol — Spain. Estacion Centro de Ecologia. Boletin

Spain Inst Geol Min Bol Geol Min — Spain. Instituto Geologico y Minero. Boletin Geologico y Minero

Spain Inst Geol Min Mem — Spain. Instituto Geologico y Minero. Memorias

Spain Junta Energ Nucl Rep — Spain. Junta de Energia Nuclear. Report

SPA Jnl — School of Planning and Architecture. Journal

SpAk — Spisanie na Bulgarskata Akademiya na Naukite

SPAN — South Pacific Association for Commonwealth Literature and Language Studies. Newsletter

SPAN — SPAN. Shell Public Health and Agricultural News

SPAN — SPAN: State Planning Authority News

SPap — Studia Papyrologica

SPARD — Sparkasse

Sparkasse — Zeitschrift des Deutschen Sparkassen

Spark's Am Biog — Spark's Library of American Biography

SPARMO Bull — SPARMO [*Solar Particles and Radiation Monitoring Organization*] Bulletin

SPat — Studia Patavina

S Patriot — Southern Patriot

SPAW — Sitzungsberichte. Preussische Akademie der Wissenschaften

Spawanie Ciecie Met — Spawanie i Ciecie Metali

SPAZD9 — Agronomy Society of New Zealand. Special Publication

SpB — Sprakliga Bidrag [*Lund*]

SPB — Studia Post-Biblica [*Leiden*]

SpBA — Spisanie na Bulgarskata Akademiya na Naukite

SPBAA — Spisanie na Bulgarskata Akademiya na Naukite

SpBAkN — Spisanie na Bulgarskata Akademiya na Naukite

SpBAN — Spisanie na Bulgarskata Akademiya na Naukite

SPBUA — SPARMO [*Solid Particles and Radiation Monitoring Organization*] Bulletin

Sp na Bulg Akad na Naukite — Spisanie na Bulgarskata Akademiya na Naukite

Sp na Bulg Geol D-vo — Spisanie na Bulgarskoto Geologichesko Druzhestvo

Sp Bulg Geol D-vo — Spisanie na Bulgarskoto Geologichesko Druzhestvo

SPC — IEEE. Spectrum

SPCHB — Soviet Progress in Chemistry [*English Translation*]

SPCHDX — Carnegie Museum of Natural History. Special Publication

SPCPB — Space Congress. Proceedings

SPCQB — SPC [*South Pacific Commission*] Quarterly Bulletin

SPC Quart Bull — SPC [*South Pacific Commission*] Quarterly Bulletin

SPCSDW — Commonwealth Bureau of Soils. Special Publication

SPCT — Studi e Problemi di Critica Testuale

SPDVB — Science Progres Decouverte

SPe — Spettatore Italiano

SPE — Studies in Public Economics [*Elsevier Book Series*]

SPE — Suriname Post

Spec — Spectator

Spec — Spectrum

Spec — Speculation

Spec — Speculum

SPECA — Spectrum [*Oxford*]

Spec Bull Coll Agric Utsunomiya Univ — Special Bulletin. College of Agriculture. Utsunomiya University

Spec Bull Coll Agr Utsunomiya Univ — Special Bulletin. College of Agriculture. Utsunomiya University

Spec Bull Dep Agric S Aust — Special Bulletin. Department of Agriculture. South Australia

Spec Bull Dep Agric South Aust — Special Bulletin. Department of Agriculture. South Australia

Spec Bull First Agron Div Tokai-Kinki Natl Agric Exp Stn — Special Bulletin. First Agronomy Division. Tokai-Kinki National Agricultural Experiment Station

Spec Bull Mich Agric Exp Stn — Special Bulletin. Michigan Agricultural Experiment Station

Spec Bull Mich State Univ Agr Exp Sta — Special Bulletin. Michigan State University. Agricultural Experiment Station

Spec Bull Okayama Agr Exp Sta — Special Bulletin. Okayama Agricultural Experiment Station

Spec Bull Rehovot Nat Univ Inst Agr — Special Bulletin. Rehovot. National and University Institute of Agriculture

Spec Bull Taiwan For Res Inst — Special Bulletin. Taiwan Forestry Research Institute

Spec Bull Tottori Agric Exp Stn — Special Bulletin. Tottori Agricultural Experiment Station

Spec Care Dentist — Special Care in Dentistry

Spec Ceram — Special Ceramics

Spec Circ Mass Ext Serv — Special Circular. Massachusetts Extension Service

Spec Circ Ohio Agr Exp Sta — Special Circular. Ohio Agricultural Experiment Station

Spec Circ Ohio Agric Res Dev Cent — Special Circular. Ohio Agricultural Research and Development Center

Spec Circ PA State Univ Coll-Agric Ext Serv — Special Circular. Pennsylvania State University. College of Agriculture. Extension Service

Spec Circ Univ Wis Coll Agr Ext Serv — Special Circular. University of Wisconsin. College of Agriculture. Extension Service

Spec Collect — Special Collections

Spec Conf Atmos Deposition Proc — Specialty Conference on Atmospheric Deposition. Proceedings

Spec Contrib Geophys Inst Kyoto Univ — Special Contributions. Geophysical Institute. Kyoto University [*Japan*]

Spec Contrib Inst Geophys Natl Cent Univ (Miaoli Taiwan) — Special Contributions. Institute of Geophysics. National Central University (Miaoli, Taiwan)

Spec Courses Fd Ind — Specialist Courses for the Food Industry

Spec Courses Food Ind — Specialist Courses for the Food Industry [*Food Industry News*]

SPECD — Spectrum [*Berlin*]

Spec Discuss Faraday Soc — Special Discussions. Faraday Society

Spec Ed Counc News — Special Education Council. Newsletter

Spec Educ — Special Education. Forward Trends

Spec Educ Bull — Special Education Bulletin

Spec Educ Forward Trends — Special Education. Forward Trends

Spec Eng — Specifying Engineer

Special Bull Univ Minnesota Agric Exten Div — Special Bulletin. University of Minnesota. Agricultural Extension Division

Special Ed — Special Education

Special Ed — Special Education in Canada

Specialised Nat Councils' M (Egypt) — Specialised National Councils' Magazine (Egypt)

Speciality Chem — Speciality Chemicals

Special Lib — Special Libraries

Special Rep Ser Med Research Com (London) — Special Report Series. Medical Research Committee (London)

Special Sch Bul (NT) — Special Schools Bulletin (Northern Territory)

Special Sch Bul (Qld) — Special Schools Bulletin (Queensland Department of Education)

Specif Eng — Specifying Engineer

Specif Engr — Specifying Engineer

Spec Int — Specialties International

Spec Issue Plant Cell Physiol — Special Issue of Plant and Cell Physiology

Spec Libr — Special Libraries

Spec Libr Ass Toronto Chapter Bull — Special Libraries Association. Toronto Chapter. Bulletin

Spec Pap Cent Precambrian Res Univ Adelaide — Special Paper. Centre for Precambrian Research. University of Adelaide

Spec Pap Dep Nat Resour (Qd) — Special Papers. Department of Natural Resources (Queensland)

Spec Pap Palaeontol — Special Papers in Palaeontology

Spec Pap Univ Adelaide Cent Precambrian Res — Special Paper. University of Adelaide. Centre for Precambrian Research

Spec Period Rep Alicyclic Chem — Specialist Periodical Reports. Alicyclic Chemistry

Spec Period Rep Aliphatic Chem — Specialist Periodical Reports. Aliphatic Chemistry

Spec Period Rep Aliphatic Relat Nat Prod Chem — Specialist Periodical Reports. Aliphatic and Related Natural Product Chemistry

Spec Period Rep Alkaloids — Specialist Periodical Reports. Alkaloids

Spec Period Rep Amino-Acids Peptides Proteins — Specialist Periodical Reports. Amino-Acids, Peptides, and Proteins

Spec Period Rep Biosynth — Specialist Periodical Reports. Biosynthesis

Spec Period Rep Carbohydr Chem — Specialist Periodical Reports. Carbohydrate Chemistry

Spec Period Rep Catal — Specialist Periodical Reports. Catalysis

Spec Period Rep Foreign Compd Metab Mamm — Specialist Periodical Reports. Foreign Compound Metabolism in Mammals

Spec Period Rep Gas Kinet Energy Transfer — Specialist Periodical Reports. Gas Kinetics and Energy Transfer

Spec Period Rep Gen Synth Methods — Specialist Periodical Reports. General and Synthetic Methods

Spec Period Rep Mol Struct Diffr Methods — Specialist Periodical Reports. Molecular Structure by Diffraction Methods

Spec Period Rep React Kinet — Specialist Periodical Reports. Reaction Kinetics

Spec Period Rep Terpenoids Steroids — Specialist Periodical Reports. Terpenoids and Steroids

Spec Prog News — Special Programmes News

Spec Pub Agric Res Org — Special Publication. Agricultural Research Organization

Spec Publ Acad Nat Sci Phila — Special Publication. Academy of Natural Sciences. Philadelphia

Spec Publ Am Littoral Soc — Special Publication. American Littoral Society

Spec Publ Am Soc Agron — Special Publication. American Society of Agronomy

Spec Publ Am Soc Mammal — Special Publication. American Society of Mammalogists

Spec Publ Aust Conserv Fdn — Special Publication. Australian Conservation Foundation

Spec Publ Aust Conserv Found — Special Publication. Australian Conservation Foundation

Spec Publ Br Ceram Res Assoc — Special Publication. British Ceramics Research Association

Spec Publ Chicago Acad Sci — Special Publications. Chicago Academy of Science

Spec Publ Coll Agric Natl Taiwan Univ — Special Publication. College of Agriculture. National Taiwan University

Spec Publ Coll Agr Nat Taiwan U — Special Publications. College of Agriculture. National Taiwan University

Spec Publ Commonw Bur Soils — Special Publication. Commonwealth Bureau of Soils

Spec Publ Entomol Soc Am — Special Publication. Entomological Society of America

Spec Publ Geol Soc Aust — Special Publication. Geological Society of Australia

Spec Publ Geol Soc London — Special Publication. Geological Society of London

Spec Publ Geol Soc Zimbabwe — Special Publication. Geological Society of Zimbabwe

Spec Publ Geol Surv S Afr — Special Publications. Geological Survey of South Africa

Spec Publ (Isr) Agric Res Org — Special Publication (Israel). Agricultural Research Organization

Spec Publ KY Geol Surv — Special Publication. Kentucky Geological Survey

Spec Publ NM Geol Soc — Special Publication. New Mexico Geological Society

Spec Publ S Afr Assoc Adv Sci — Special Publication. South African Association for the Advancement of Science

Spec Publs Am Ass Econ Ent — Special Publications. American Association of Economic Entomology

Spec Publ Ser Int Atl Salmon Found — Special Publication Series. International Atlantic Salmon Foundation

Spec Publ Ser Soil Sci Soc Amer — Special Publication Series. Soil Science Society of America

Spec Publ US Bur Mines — Special Publications. United States Bureau of Mines

Spec Publ US Natn Bur Stand — Special Publications. United States National Bureau of Standards

Spec Publ West Aust Mus — Special Publication. Western Australian Museum

Spec Pub R Soc Tasm — Royal Society of Tasmania. Special Publications

Spec Rep Agric Exp Stn Coop Ext Serv Univ Arkansas — Special Report. Agricultural Experiment Station. Cooperative Extension Service. University of Arkansas

Spec Rep Agric Exp Stn Oreg State Univ — Special Report. Agricultural Experiment Station. Oregon State University

Spec Rep Arctic Inst N Am — Special Report. Arctic Institute of North America

Spec Rep Ark Agr Exp Sta — Special Report. Arkansas Agricultural Experiment Station

Spec Rep Ark Agric Exp Stn — Special Report. Arkansas Agricultural Experiment Station

Spec Rep Colo Dep Game Fish Parks — Special Report. Colorado Department of Game, Fish, and Parks

Spec Rep Colo Div Game Fish Parks — Special Report. Colorado Division of Game, Fish, and Parks

Spec Rep Colo Div Wildl — Special Report. Colorado Division of Wildlife

Spec Rep Commonw Exp Bldg Stn — Special Report. Commonwealth Experimental Building Station

Spec Rep Electr Power Res Inst EPRI ER (Palo Alto, Calif) — Special Report. Electric Power Research Institute. EPRI ER (Palo Alto, California)

Spec Rep Electr Power Res Inst EPRI FP (Palo Alto, Calif) — Special Report. Electric Power Research Institute. EPRI FP (Palo Alto, California)

Spec Rep EPRI SR Electr Power Res Inst (Palo Alto Calif) — Special Report. Electric Power Research Institute. EPRI SR (Palo Alto, Califor nia)

Spec Rep GB For Prod Res — Special Report. Great Britain Forest Products Research

Spec Rep Geol Soc Lond — Special Reports. Geological Society of London

Spec Rep ICSU Comm Data Sci Technol — Special Report. International Council of Scientific Unions. Committee on Data for Science and Technology

Spec Rep Indiana Geol Surv — Special Report. Indiana Geological Survey

Spec Rep Iowa State Univ Coop Ext Serv — Special Report. Iowa State University. Cooperative Extension Service

Spec Rep Johns Hopkins Univ Appl Phys Lab — Special Report. Johns Hopkins University. Applied Physics Laboratory

Spec Rep Nebr Agr Exp Sta — Special Report. Nebraska Agricultural Experiment Station

Spec Rep NY State Agric Exp Stn (Geneva) — Special Report. New York State Agricultural Experiment Station (Geneva)

Spec Rep (Oregon) Agric Exp Stn — Special Report (Oregon). Agricultural Experiment Station

Spec Rep Oreg State Coll Agr Exp Sta — Special Report. Oregon State College Agricultural Experiment Station

Spec Rep Robert Wood Johnson Foundation — Special Report. Robert Wood Johnson Foundation

Spec Rep Ser Indian Counc Med Res — Special Report Series. Indian Council of Medical Research

Spec Rep Ser Med Res Counc (UK) — Special Report Series. Medical Research Council (United Kingdom)

Spec Rep Soc Plant Prot North Jpn — Special Report. Society of Plant Protection of North Japan

Spec Rep Univ Ill Urbana Champaign Water Resour Cent — Special Report. University of Illinois at Urbana-Champaign. Water Resources Center

Spec Rep Univ Minn Agr Ext Serv — Special Report. University of Minnesota. Agricultural Extension Service

Spec Rep Univ MO Coll Agr Exp Sta — Special Report. University of Missouri. College of Agriculture. Experiment Station

Spec Rep Univ MO Columbia Agric Exp Stn — Special Report. University of Missouri, Columbia. Agricultural Experiment Station

Spec Rep Wood Res Lab VA Polyt Inst — Special Report. Wood Research Laboratory. Virginia Polytechnic Institute

Spec Sci Rep FL Dep Nat Resour Mar Res Lab — Special Scientific Report. Florida Department of Natural Resources. Marine Research Laboratory

Spec Sci Rep Wildlife US Fish Wildlife Serv — Special Scientific Report. Wildlife. United States Fish and Wildlife Service

Spec Ser Fla Dep Agric — Special Series. Florida Department of Agriculture

Spec Steel — Special Steel [*Japan*]

Spec Steels Rev — Special Steels Review

Spec Steels Tech Rev (Sheffield) — Special Steels Technical Review (Sheffield)

Spect — Spectator

Spect Act A — Spectrochimica Acta. Part A. Molecular Spectroscopy

Spect Act B — Spectrochimica Acta. Part B. Atomic Spectroscopy

Spec Tech Assoc Publ — Special Technical Association. Publication

Spec Tech Publs Am Soc Test Mater — Special Technical Publications. American Society for Testing Materials

Spect Lett — Spectroscopy Letters

Spec Transp Plann Practice — Specialized Transportation Planning and Practice

Spectrochim Acta — Spectrochimica Acta

Spectrochim Acta A — Spectrochimica Acta. Part A. Molecular Spectroscopy

Spectrochim Acta B — Spectrochimica Acta. Part B. Atomic Spectroscopy

Spectrochim Acta Part A — Spectrochimica Acta. Part A. Molecular Spectroscopy

Spectrochim Acta Part A Mol Spectrosc — Spectrochimica Acta. Part A. Molecular Spectroscopy

Spectrochim Acta Part B — Spectrochimica Acta. Part B. Atomic Spectroscopy

Spectrochim Acta Part B At Spectrosc — Spectrochimica Acta. Part B. Atomic Spectroscopy

Spectrosc Lett — Spectroscopy Letters

Spectrosc Mol — Spectroscopia Molecular

Spectros Prop Inorg Organomet Compd — Spectroscopic Properties of Inorganic and Organometallic Compounds

Spectrum Int — Spectrum International

Specu — Speculum

Speculations Sci and Technol — Speculations in Science and Technology

Specul Sci Technol — Speculations in Science and Technology [*Switzerland*]

SPEDA — Special Education

SPEE — Studies in Production and Engineering Economics [*Elsevier Book Series*]

Speech Commun — Speech Communication

Speech Mon — Speech Monographs

Speech Monogr — Speech Monographs

Speech Teac — Speech Teacher

Speech Technol — Speech Technology

SPEJ — Society of Petroleum Engineers. American Institute of Mining, Metallurgical, and Petroleum Engineers. Journal

SPE J — SPE [*Society of Plastics Engineers*] Journal

SPEJA — SPE [*Society of Plastics Engineers*] Journal

SPEJ Soc Pet Eng J — SPEJ. Society of Petroleum Engineers [*of AIME*] Journal [*United States*]

Spektrum Wiss — Spektrum der Wissenschaft [*German Federal Republic*]

SPELD Info — SPELD [*Societe de Promotion a l'Etranger du Livre de Droit*] Information

Speleol Abstr — Speleological Abstracts

Speleol Biul Speleoklubu Warsz — Speleologia Biuletyn Speleoklubu Warszawskiego

SPEND — Specifying Engineer

Spenser St — Spenser Studies

SPERA — Sperimentale

Sper Arch Biol Norm Patol — Sperimentale. Archivio di Biologia Normale e Patologica

SPE Reg Tech Conf Tech Pap — SPE [*Society of Plastics Engineers*] Regional Technical Conference. Technical Papers

SPE Repr Ser — Society of Petroleum Engineers. American Institute of Mining, Metallurgical, and Petroleum Engineers. Reprint Series [*United States*]

Spe Rep Ser Ohio Agr Exp Sta — Special Report Series. Ohio Agricultural Experiment Station

Sperimentale Arch Biol Norm e Patol — Sperimentale. Archivio di Biologia Normale e Patologica

Sperimentale Sez Chim Biol — Sperimentale. Sezione di Chimica Biologica

Sperry Technol — Sperry Technology

SPE Soc Pet Eng AIME Publ — SPE. Society of Petroleum Engineers of AIME [*American Institute of Mining, Metallurgical, and Petroleum Engineers*] Publications
SPetr — Studi Petrarcheschi
Spets Stali Splavy — Spetsial'nye Stali Splavy [*USSR*]
Spettatore Int — Spettatore Internazionale
Spettatore M — Spettatore Musicale
SPF — Space Science Fiction
SPF — Space Science Fiction Magazine
Spf — Sprachforum
SPFB — Sbornik Pedagogicke Fakulty v Brne
SPFB — Sbornik Praci Filosoficke Fakulty Brnenske University
Spfdr — Springfielder
SPFFBU — Sbornik Praci Filosoficke Fakulty Brnenske University
SPFLA — Spaceflight
SPFO — Sbornik Pedagogicke Fakulty (Ostrava)
SPFOL — Sbornik Pedagogicke Fakulty (Olomouci)
SPGCA — Survey of Progress in Chemistry
SPGKA — Senpaku Gijutsu Kenkyujo Hokoku
SPGL — Studien zur Poetik und Geschichte der Literatur
SPH — Social Process in Hawaii
SPh — Studiea Phonetica
S in Ph — Studies in Philology
SPh — Studies in Philology
SPHCA — Soviet Physics. Crystallography [*English Translation*]
SPHDA — Soviet Physics. Doklady [*English Translation*]
SPHJA — Soviet Physics. JETP [*Journal of Experimental and Theoretical Physics of the Academy of Sciences of the USSR*] [*English translation*]
SPhNC — Studies in Philology. University of North Carolina
SPhon — Studia Phonologica [*Kyoto*]
SPhP — Symbolae Philologorum Posnaniensium
SPHQ — Swedish Pioneer Historical Quarterly
SPIBB — Sbornik Pedagogickeho Institutu v Banskej Bystrici
SPIEC — Proceedings. Society of Photo-Optical Instrumentation Engineers
Spiegel Hist — Spiegel Historical
Spiegel Let — Spiegel der Letteren
SPIE J — SPIE [*Society of Photo-Optical Instrumentation Engineers*] Journal [*Later, Optical Engineering*]
SPIE Journal — Society of Photographic Instrumentation Engineers. Journal
SPIE Semin Proc — SPIE [*Society of Photo-Optical Instrumentation Engineers*] Seminar Proceedings
SPIE Vol — SPIE [*Society of Photo-Optical Instrumentation Engineers*] Volume [*United States*]
SPIFDN — International Commission for the Northwest Atlantic Fisheries. Selected Papers
SPIG — Sbornik Praci Pedagogickeho Institutu v Gottwaldove
SPILA — Sports Illustrated
SPILB — Spiegel
SPIMD — Siauliu Pedagoginio Instituto Mokslo Darbai
SPIN — Sbornik Pedagogickeho Institutu v Nitre
Spinner Weber Textilveredl — Spinner, Weber, Textilveredlung
SPIO — Sbornik Praci Pedagogickeho Institutu v Ostrave
SPIOL — Sbornik Pedagogickeho Institutu v Olomouci
SPIP — Sbornik Pedagogickeho Institutu v Plzni
SPIPA — Scientific Papers. Institute of Physical and Chemical Research
SPIPL — Sbornik Pedagogickeho Institutu v Plzni
Spirit — Spirit That Moves Us
Spirit Mis — Spirit of Missions
Spirit Pilg — Spirit of the Pilgrims
Spirit Verkauf — Spirituosen-Verkauf
Spir Life — Spiritual Life
Spir Tod — Spirituality Today
Spirto Vodochn Promst — Spirto-Vodochnaya Promyshlennost
Spirt Prom-st' — Spirtovaya Promyshlennost'
Spis Bulg Akad Nauk — Spisanie na Bulgarskata Akademiya na Naukite [*Bulgaria*]
Spis Bulg Akad Nauk — Spisanie na Bulgarskata Akademiya na Naukite
Spis Bulg Geol Druzh — Spisanie na Bulgarskoto Geolichesko Druzhestvo
Spis Bulg Geol Druzhu — Spisania na Bulgarsoto Geolichesko Druzhestvo
Spis Nauchno-Issled Inst Minist Zemed Gorite — Spisanie na Nauchno-Issledovatelskite Instituti pri Ministrvstvata na Zemedelete i Gorite
Spis Nauchnoizsled Inst Minist Zemed (Bulg) — Spisanie na Nauchnoizsledovatelskite Instituti pri Ministerstvoto na Zemedelieto (Bulgaria)
SPI Struct Foam Conf Proc — SPI [*Society of the Plastics Industry*] Structural Foam Conference. Proceedings
Spisy Lek Fak Masaryk Univ (Brno) — Spisy Lekarske Fakulty Mesarykovy University (Brno)
Spisy Pedagog Fak Ostrave — Spisy Pedagogicke Fakulty v Ostrave
Spisy Prir Fak Univ Brne — Spisy Prirodovedecke Fakulty Universita v Brne [*Czechoslovakia*]
Spisy Priroved Fak Univ J E Purkyne Brne — Spisy Prirodovedecke Fakulty University J. E. Purkyne v Brne
Spisy Vydavane Prirodoved Fak Massarykovy Univ — Spisy Vydavane Prirodovedeckou Fakultou Massarykovy University
SPIU — Sbornik Praci Pedagogickeho Institutu, Usti Nad Labem

SPKYB — Shih P'in Kung Yeh
SpL — Spiegel der Letteren
SPL — Studie a Prace Linguisticke
SPLEB — Spectroscopy Letters
Sp Lib — Special Libraries
SPLID — SpeciaList
SPLK — Studie Prazskeho Linguistickeho Krouzku
SPLSA — Space Life Sciences
SPM — Salud Publica de Mexico
SPM — South Pacific Mail
Sp M — Spicilegio Moderno
SPMCA — Soviet Powder Metallurgy and Metal Ceramics [*English Translation*]
SPMGA — Speech Monographs
Sp Mon — Speech Monographs
SPMXA — Salud Publica de Mexico
SPN — School Product News
SPo — Sao Paulo. Revista do Arquivo Municipal
SPO — Spotlight
SPOA — Soviet Panorama
SPol — Storia e Politica
Spold Kwartal Nauk — Spoldzielczy Kwartalnik Naukomy
Spolia Zeylan — Spolia Zeylanica
Spolia Zool Mus Haun — Spolia Zoologica Musei Hauniensis
SpomSAN — Spomenik Srpske Akademije Nauka
Sportarzt Sportmed — Sportarzt Sportmedizin
Sport Leis — Sport and Leisure
Sport Rec — Sport and Recreation
Sports Ill — Sports Illustrated
Sports Illus — Sports Illustrated
Sports Med (Auckland) — Sports Medicine (Auckland)
Sports Turf Bull — Sports Turf Bulletin
Sport es Testn — Sport es Testneveles
Sposoby Zap Inf Besserebr Nositelyakh — Sposoby Zapisi Informatsii na Besserebryanykh Nositelyakh
SPPGA — Society of Economic Paleontologists and Mineralogists. Pacific Section. Guidebooks
SPPLB — Science and Public Policy
SPPMA — Southern Pulp and Paper Manufacturer [*United States*]
SPR — Slavistic Printings and Reprintings
SPR — Southern Poetry Review
Spr — Sprache
Sprache Tech Zeit — Sprache im Technischen Zeitalter
Sprague's J ME His — Sprague's Journal of Maine History
Sprakvetensk Sallsk i Uppsala Forhandl — Sprakvetenskapliga Sallskapets i Uppsala Foerhandlingar
SPRAM — Sao Paulo. Revista do Arquivo Municipal
Spraw — Sprawozdania
Spraw Opolskie Tow Przyj Nauk Wydz Nauk Med — Sprawozdania Opolskie Towarzystwo Przyjaciol Nauk. Wydzial Nauk Medycznych
Sprawozdania Kom Nauk PAN — Sprawozdania z Posiedzen Komisji Naukowych. Polskiej Akademii Nauk
Spraw Poznan Tow Przyj Nauk — Sprawozdania Poznanskiego Towarzystwa Przyjaciol Nauk
Spraw Pr Pol Tow Fiz — Sprawozdania i Prace Polskiego Towarzystwa Fizycznego
Spraw Tow Nauk Lwowie — Sprawozdania Towarzystwa Naukowego we Lwowie
Spraw Tow Nauk Toruniu — Sprawozdania Towarzystwa Naukowego w Toruniu
Spraw Wroclaw Tow Nauk — Sprawozdania Wroclawskiego Towarzystwa Naukowego
Spraw Wroclaw Tow Nauk Ser A — Sprawozdania Wroclawskiego Towarzystwa Naukowego. Seria A
Spraw Wroclaw Tow Nauk Ser B — Sprawozdania Wroclawskiego Towarzystwa Naukowego. Seria B
SprB — Sprakliga Bidrag
Sprechsaal Keram Glas Silik — Sprechsaal fuer Keramik, Glas, Email, Silikate
SPRF — Societe de Publications Romanes et Francaises
Springer Semin Immunopathol — Springer Seminars in Immunopathology
Springer Ser Chem Phys — Springer Series in Chemical Physics
Springer Ser Electrophys — Springer Series in Electrophysics
Springer Ser Inform Sci — Springer Series in Information Sciences
Springer Ser Optical Sci — Springer Series in Optical Sciences
Springer Ser Opt Sci — Springer Series in Optical Sciences
Springer Ser Solid-State Sci — Springer Series in Solid-State Sciences
Springer Ser Statist — Springer Series in Statistics
Springer Ser Synergetics — Springer Series in Synergetics
Springer Tracts Modern Phys — Springer Tracts in Modern Physics
Springer Tracts Mod Phys — Springer Tracts in Modern Physics
Springer Tracts Nat Philos — Springer Tracts in Natural Philosophy
SprKJ — Sprawozdania z Posiedzen Komisji Jezykowej Towarzystwa Naukowego Warszawskiego
SprKUL — Sprawozdania z Czynnosci Wydawniczej i Posiedzen Naukowych Oraz Kronika Towarzystwa Naukowego Katolockiego Uniwersytetu Lubelskiego

SprLTN — Sprawozdania z Czynnosci i Posiedzen Lodzkiego Towarzystwa Naukowego
Spr Miedzyn — Sprawy Miedzynarodowe
SPROE — Software Protection
SprPAUm — Sprawozdania z Czynnosci i Posiedzen Polskiej Akademii Umiejetnosci
SprPTPN — Sprawozdania Poznanskiego Towarzystwa Przyjaciol Nauk
SprSUF — Sprakvetenskapliga Sallskapets i Uppsala Foerhandlingar
SprTNW — Sprawozdania z Posiedzen Towarzystwa Naukowego Warszawskiego
SprTT — Sprawozdania Towarzystwa Naukowego w Toruniu
SprV — Sprachkunst (Vienna)
SPS — Space Stories
SPS — Specimina Philologiae Slavicae
SpSAN — Spomenik Srpske Akademije Nauka
SPSDC — Surface and Defect Properties of Solids
SPSEA — Soviet Physics. Semiconductors [*English translation*]
SPsp — Sprachspiegel. Schweizerische Zeitschrift fuer die Deutsche Muttersprache
SPSRA — Space Science Reviews
SPSU — Studia Philologiae Scandinavicae Upsaliensia
SPT — Openbaar Vervoer
SPT — Space Travel
SpT — Speech Teacher
SPTC — Studies in Physical and Theoretical Chemistry [*Elsevier Book Series*]
SPTN — Spill Technology Newsletter
SPTPA — Soviet Physics. Technical Physics [*English Translation*]
SPTPN — Sprawozdania Poznanskiego Towarzystwa Przyjaciol Nauk
SPU — Statutes of Practical Utility
SPUTA — Scientific Papers. College of General Education. University of Tokyo
SPUVB — Sbornik Praci UVP
SPV — Space Adventures
Spvry Mgt — Supervisory Management
SPW — Shipping World and Shipbuilder
SPW — Spaceway Science Fiction
SQ — Shakespeare Quarterly
SQ — Southern Quarterly
SQF — Socialist Thought and Practice
SQR — State Reports (Queensland)
S Quart — Southern Quarterly
Squibb Abstr Bull — Squibb Abstract Bulletin
SR — New South Wales State Reports
SR — Saturday Review
SR — Schweizer Rundschau
SR — Sciences Religieuses
SR — Sewanee Review
SR — Slave River Journal [*Fort Smith, Northwest Territory*]
SR — Slavisticna Revija
SR — Slavonic Review
SR — Slovenska Rec
SR — Social Research
SR — Sociologia Religiosa
SR — Southern Review [*US*]
SR — Southwest Review
SR — Statistical Reporter [*Manila*]
SR — Stereo Review
SR — Studia Rosenthaliana [*Assen*]
SR — Studies in Religion
SR — Studies and Reports. Ben-Zvi Institute [*Jerusalem*]
SR — Studies in Romanticism
SRA — Saturday Review of the Arts
SRA — Seatrade
SRA — Syria. Revue d'Art Oriental et d'Archeologie
SRA-J Soc R — SRA - Journal of the Society of Research Administrators
SR Arts — Saturday Review of the Arts
Sr Autobahn — Strasse und Autobahn
SRAZ — Studia Romanica et Anglica Zagrabiensia
SRBUD — Space Research in Bulgaria
SRC — Studies in Religion: A Canadian Journal
SRCS — Sustancia. Revista de Cultura Superior
SRDDD — Solar Energy R and D in the European Community. Series D
SRDRD — Solar Energy Research and Development Report
SRE — Saturday Review of Education
SRe — Science Review [*Manila*]
SRE — Statistical Reporter
S Rel Sc Rel — Studies in Religion/Sciences Religieuses
SRen — Studies in the Renaissance
SRev — Sayers Review
SRev — School Review
SRev — Slavic Review
SRev — Southwest Review
S Rev (Adel) — Southern Review (Adelaide)
S Rev (Baton) — Southern Review (Baton Rouge)
SRG — Schriften. Raabe-Gesellschaft
S Rhodesia Geol Surv Bull — Southern Rhodesia. Geological Survey Bulletin

SRI — British Steel
SRI — Sveriges Runinskrifter
SRICDS — Inter-American Tropical Tuna Commission. Special Report
SRIELA — Selected Reports: Publication of the Institute of Ethnomusicology of the University of California at Los Angeles
SRIIA — Silk and Rayon Industries of India
SRI J — SRI [*Stanford Research Institute*] Journal
Sri Lan J Hum — Sri Lanka Journal of Humanities [*Peradeniya*]
Sri Lanka Assoc Adv Sci Proc Annu Sess — Sri Lanka Association for the Advancement of Science. Proceedings of the Annual Session
Sri Lanka Geol Surv Dep Econ Bull — Sri Lanka. Geological Survey Department. Economic Bulletin
Sri Lanka Lab Gaz — Sri Lanka Labour Gazette
SRI Pestic Res Bull — SRI [*Stanford Research Institute*] Pesticide Research Bulletin
SRISS — Scientia: Revista Internazionale di Sintesi Scientifica
SRJKAK — Annual Report. Sado Marine Biological Station. Niigata University
SRL — Saturday Review of Literature
SRL — Securities Regulation Law Journal
SRL — Studies in Romance Languages
SRLF — Saggi e Ricerche di Letteratura Francese
SRLing — Studia Romanica et Linguistica
SRLR — Securities Regulation and Law Reports
SRMBDB — Marine Sciences Research Center [*Stony Brook*]. Special Report
SRMSDS — Montana. Forest and Conservation Experiment Station. Study Report
SRN — Saturn Science Fiction and Fantasy
SRN — Souvenir Nieuws
SRNB — Sociology. Reviews of New Books
SRNSW — New South Wales State Reports
SR (NSW) — State Reports (New South Wales)
SR (NSW) B & P — State Reports (New South Wales). Bankruptcy and Probate
SR (NSW) Eq — State Reports (New South Wales). Equity
SRO — Shakespearean Research Opportunities
SRo — Studi Romani [*Rome*]
SRom — Studi Romani [*Rome*]
SRP — Studia Rossica Posnaniensia
Srp Akad Nauka Umet Od Prir-Mat Nauka Glas — Srpska Akademija Nauka i Umetnosti Odeljenje Prirodno-Matematickikh Nauka Glas
Srp Akad Nauka Umet Posebna Izdan Od Prir Mat Nauka — Srpska Akademija Nauka i Umetnosti Posebna Izdanja Odeljenje Prirodno-Matematickikh Nauka
Srp Arh Celok Lek — Srpski Arhiv za Celokupno Lekarstvo
Srp Arkh Tselok Lek — Srpski Arkhiv za Tselokupno Lekarstvo
SRPO — Soobchtcheniia Russkago Palestinskago Obchtshestva
SRPR — Surtsey Research Progress Report
Srpsko Hem Drus Bull — Srpsko Hemiskog Drustvo. Bulletin
SRQ — State Reports (Queensland)
SRR — Schuh Kurier. Das Wirtschaftmagazin der Schuhbranche
SRRA — Sage Race Relations Abstracts
SRREEC — Institute of Soil Science. Academia Sinica. Soil Research Report
SRS — Salzburg Renaissance Studies
SRS — Social and Rehabilitation Service. Publications
SRS — Strange Stories
SRSC — Saturday Review of the Sciences
Sr Schol — Senior Scholastic
SR-Sci — Saturday Review of the Sciences
Sr Sci — Senior Science
SRSD — Saturday Review of Society
SRSI — Sikh Religious Studies Information
SRSIB — Salt Research and Industry
SRSO — Saturday Review of Society
SR-Soc — Saturday Review of Society
SRSS — Scientia: Revista Sintesi di Scientifica
SRSUE — Studies in Regional Science and Urban Economics [*Elsevier Book Series*]
SRTGA — Science Reports. Tohoku University. Seventh Series
SRTG-A — Science Reports. Tohoku University. Seventh Series. Geography [*Japan*]
SRu — Studi Rumeni [*Rome*]
SRUEA — Structural Engineer
SRUTA — Soviet Rubber Technology [*English translation*]
SRv — Southwest Review
SRVSB — Saturday Review of the Sciences
SRW — Saturday Review/World
SR (WA) — State Reports (Western Australia)
SRWA — Swiss Review of World Affairs
SRW Nachr — SRW [*Siemens-Reiniger-Werke*] Nachricht [*West Germany*]
SR/World — Saturday Review/World
SRZ — Studia Romanica Zagrabiensia
SS — Scandinavian Studies
S & S — School and Society
SS — School and Society
S & S — Science and Society

SS — Senior Scholastic
SS — Shakespeare Survey
SS — Sight and Sound
S & S — Sight and Sound
SS — Slovo a Slovesnost
SS — Smokeshop
SS — Social Studies
SS — Sociological Studies
SS — Sound and Sense [*Baguio City*]
S & S — Stars & Stripes
SS — Startling Stories
SS — Studi Sardi
SS — Studi Semitici
SS — Studi Storici
SS — Studia Serdicensia
SS — Sugar Series [*Elsevier Book Series*]
SS — Syn og Segn
S & S — Syntax and Semantics
SSA — Social Science Abstracts
SSA — Social Security Administration. Publications
SSAA — Salzburger Studien zur Anglistik und Amerikanistik
SSAEA — Safety Series. IAEA [*International Atomic Energy Agency*]
SSAL — Scientific Serials in Australian Libraries
SSAL Suppt — SSAL [*Scientific Serials in Australian Libraries*] Supplement
SSAOA — Soobshcheniya Shemakhinskoi Astrofizicheskoi Observatorii, Akademiya Nauk Azerbaidzhanskoi SSR
SSAPD — Symposium on Salt. Proceedings
SSar — Studi Sardi
SSARB — Sassar
SSASH — Studia Slavica. Academiae Scientiarum Hungaricae
SSAWL — Sitzungsberichte. Saechsische Akademie der Wissenschaften (Leipzig). Philologisch-Historische Klasse
SSB — Reserve Bank of Australia. Statistical Bulletin
SSb — Skandinavskij Sbornik
SSB — Social Security Bulletin [*US*]
SSBLA — Sel'skokhozyaistvennaya Biologiya
SSCA — Stockholm Studies in Classical Archaeology
SSCES — Stanford Studies in the Civilizations of Eastern Asia
SSCI — Social Sciences Citation Index [*Institute for Scientific Information*] [*Database*]
SSCISAM — Settimane di Studio del Centro Italiano di Studi sull'Alto Medioevo
SSCJ — Southern Speech Communication Journal
SSCRA — School Science Review
SSE — North-Holland Series in Systems Science and Engineering [*Elsevier Book Series*]
SSE — Strangest Stories Ever Told
SSe — Studi Secenteschi
SSEL — Stockholm Studies in English Literature
SSELER — Salzburg Studies in English Literature. Elizabethan and Renaissance
SSELRR — Salzburg Studies in English Literature. Romantic Reassessment
SSEng — Sydney Studies in English
SSept — Studia Septentrionalia
SSF — Studies in Short Fiction
SSF — Super Science Fiction
SSF CHL — Societas Scientiarum Fennicae. Commentationes Humanarum Litterarum
SSFS — Samlingar Utgivna av Svenska Fornskriftssallskapet (Stockholm)
SSG — Schriften. Theodor-Storm-Gesellschaft
SSGED — Seikei-Saigai Geka
SSGMB — Sbornik Nauchnogo Studencheskogo Obshchestva Geologicheskii Fakul'tet Moskovskii Gosudarstvenyi Universitet
SSGS — Stanford Studies in Germanics and Slavics
SSGW — Sitzungsberichte. Saechsische Gesellschaft der Wissenschaften (Leipzig)
SSH — Site Selection Handbook
SSH — Skytteanska Samfundets Handlinger
SSH — Social Sciences and Humanities Index
SSH — Studia Slavica. Academiae Scientiarum Hungaricae
SSH — Studies in Society and History
SSHum — Social Sciences and Humanities Index
SSI — Short Story International
SSI — Social Science Information
SSI/ISS — Social Science Information/Information sur les Sciences Sociales
SSINA — Scientia Sinica [*English Edition*]
SSIOD — Solid State Ionics
SSIP — Secondary Students Information Press
SSJ — Southern Speech Journal
SSJM — United States Embassy. Summary of Selected Japanese Magazines
SSL — Scandoslavica [*Copenhagen*]
SSL — Studi e Saggi Linguistici
SSL — Studies in Scottish Literature
SSL — Studies in Semitic Languages and Linguistics
SSlav — Studia Slavica. Academiae Scientiarum Hungaricae
SSlav — Symbolae Slavicae

SSLF — Skrifter Utgivna. Svenska Litteratursallskapet i Finland
SSLI — Studies in Semitic Languages and Linguistics
SS Lit — Soviet Studies in Literature
SSLL — Stanford Studies in Language and Literature
SSLSN — Skrifter Utgivna. Svenska Litteratursallskapet Studier i Nordisk Filologi
SSM — Space Science Fiction Magazine
SSM — Studies in Statistical Mechanics [*Elsevier Book Series*]
SSMHA — Studia Scientiarum Mathematicarum Hungarica
SSMLN — Society for the Study of Midwestern Literature. Newsletter
SSMP — Stockholm Studies in Modern Philology
SSN — Scandinavian Studies and Notes
SSN — Studia Semitica Neerlandica [*Assen*]
SSO — Schweizerische Monatsschrift fuer Zahnheilkunde
SSO — Srednee Spetsial'noe Obrazovanie [*Moscow*]
SSO — Studier fra Sprog- og Oldtidsforskning
SSORD — Software Review
SSOSM — Studi Storici dell'Ordine dei Servi de Maria
SSP — Selected Topics in Solid State Physics [*Elsevier Book Series*]
SSPDPT — Salzburg Studies. Poetic Drama and Poetic Theory
S Speech Commun J — Southern Speech Communication Journal
SSPHA — Solid State Physics
SSpJ — Southern Speech Journal
SSQ — Social Science Quarterly
SSQTA — Social Science Quarterly
SSR — Social Security Rulings [*on Old Age, Survivors, and Disability Insurance*] [*US*]
SSR — Sociology and Social Research
SSR — Studi e Materiali di Storia della Religioni
SSRC Newsl — SSRC [*Social Science Research Council*] Newsletter
SSREA — Sight-Saving Review
SSRL — Stockholm Studies in Russian Literature
SSRWA — Soviet Science Review
SSS — Super Science Stories
SSSA Spec Publ — SSSA [*Soil Science Society of America*] Special Publication
SSSA Spec Publ Ser — SSSA [*Soil Science Society of America*] Special Publication Series
SSSC — Studies in Surface Science and Catalysis [*Elsevier Book Series*]
SSSCA — Soviet Soil Science [*English translation*]
SSSCD — Social Studies of Science
SSSJD — Soil Science Society of America. Journal
SSS Journal — State Shipping Service of Western Australia. Journal
SSSP — Stockholm Studies in Scandinavian Philology
SSSQ — Southwestern Social Science Quarterly
SSSR — Southwestern Social Science Review
SST — Science Stories
SST — Shakespeare Studies (Tokyo)
SSt — Sowjet Studien
SSt — Spenser Studies
SSTJA — Solid State Journal
SSTRD — Special Steels Technical Review
SST Sver Skogsvaardsfoerb Tidskr — SST. Sveriges Skogsvaardsfoerbunds Tidskrift
SStud — Shakespeare Studies
SSUF — Sprakvetenskapliga Sallskapets i Uppsala Foerhandlingar
SSUR — Springfield Sunday Union and Republican
SsvOA — Sydsvenska Ortnamns-Saellskapets Arsskrift
SSZBA — Sbornik Vysoke Skoly Zemedelski v Brne. Rada B
ST — Journal of Structural Engineering
ST — Signes du Temps
S & T — Sky and Telescope
ST — Slovo a Tvar
ST — Speech Teacher
St — Star [*Johannesburg*]
ST — Statsoekonomisk Tidsskrift
ST — Stereo
St — Stereo Review
ST — Strad
St — Strannik: Dukhovnyi, Ucheno-Literaturnyi Zhurnal
S & T — Strategy and Tactics
ST — Studi Tassiani
ST — Studia Taiwanica
ST — Studia Theologica
St — Studies
St — Studium
ST — Sunday Telegraph
ST — Sunday Times [*United Kingdom*]
ST — Svensk Tidskrift
STA — Strange Adventures
StA — Studi Anselmiana
STA — Syrie et Monde Arabe. Etude Mensuelle Economique, Politique, et Statistique
STAACT J — STAACT [*Science Teachers Association of the Australian Capital Territory*] Journal
Staat u Recht — Staat und Recht

Staatsanz Baden-Wuerttemb — Staatsanzeiger fuer Baden-Wuerttemberg
Staatsanz Rheinl-Pfalz — Staatsanzeiger fuer Rheinland-Pfalz [*German Federal Republic*]
Staatsblad K Ned — Staatsblad van het Koninkrijk der Nederlanden
Staatsbl Koninkrijk Ned — Staatsblad van het Koninkrijk der Nederlanden
Staatsbuerger-Beil Bayer Staatsztg — Staatsbuerger-Beilage der Bayerischen Staatszeitung
Staat und Wirt in Hessen — Staat und Wirtschaft in Hessen
Sta Bull Oreg State Coll Agr Exp Sta — Station Bulletin. Oregon State College. Agricultural Experiment Station
Sta Bull Univ Minn Agr Exp Sta — Station Bulletin. University of Minnesota. Agricultural Experiment Station
Sta Circ Wash Agr Exp Sta — Station Circular. Washington Agricultural Experiment Station
Staden-Jb — Staden-Jahrbuch
Stadler Genet Symp — Stadler Genetics Symposia
Stadt- Gebaeudetech — Stadt- und Gebaeudetechnik [*German Democratic Republic*]
Stadt (Wien) — Informationsdienst der Stadt (Wien)
Staff J (University of Reading) — Staff Journal (University of Reading)
Staffordshire Archaeol — Staffordshire Archaeology
Staff Pap — Staff Papers
Staff Pap P Minn Univ Dep Agric Appl Econ — Staff Paper P. Minnesota University. Department of Agricultural and Applied Economics
Staff Pap Univ Florida Food Resour Econ Dep — Staff Paper. University of Florida. Food and Resources Economics Department
St A H — Studies in American Humor
STAHA — Stahlbau
Stahlbau Rundsch — Stahlbau Rundschau [*Austria*]
Stahlbau Tech — Stahlbau-Technik
Stahlia Misc Pap — Stahlia Miscellaneous Papers
Stainless Steel Ind — Stainless Steel Industry
Stainl Steel — Stainless Steel [*South Africa*]
Stain Tech — Stain Technology
Stain Technol — Stain Technology
Staleplavil'n Proizvod — Staleplavil'noe Proizvodstvo
Staleplavil'n Proizvod (Moscow) — Staleplavil'noe Proizvodstvo (Moscow)
Stal Nemet Vklyucheniya — Stal'e Nemetallicheskie Vklyucheniya
STAL Sci Tech Anim Lab — STAL. Sciences et Techniques de l'Animal de Laboratoire
STAM — Statistics in Medicine
St Am Renaissance — Studies in the American Renaissance
Standard Chartered R — Standard Chartered Review
Stand Ass Aust Aust Stand — Standards Association of Australia. Australian Standard
Stand Ass Aust Commercial Stand — Standards Association of Australia. Commercial Standard
Stand Ass Aust Miscell Pub — Standards Association of Australia. Miscellaneous Publication
Stand Bank — Standard Bank Review
Stand Kach — Standarty i Kachestvo
Stand Methods Clin Chem — Standard Methods of Clinical Chemistry
Stand News — Standardization News
Stand Philip Per Ind — Standard Philippine Periodicals Index
Stand Qual — Standardisierung und Qualitaet [*German Democratic Republic*]
St Andrew Univ Sociol R — St. Andrew's University. Sociological Review
Stan Env't Ann — Stanford Environmental Annual
Stan Env't Ann — Stanford Environmental Law Annual
Stanf J Int — Stanford Journal of International Studies
Stanford Fr — Stanford French Review
Stanford Ichthyol Bull — Stanford Ichthyological Bulletin
Stanford J Internat Law — Stanford Journal of International Law
Stanford J Internat Studies — Stanford Journal of International Studies
Stanford J Int'l Stud — Stanford Journal of International Studies
Stanford J Int Stud — Stanford Journal of International Studies
Stanford La — Stanford Law Review
Stanford Law R — Stanford Law Review
Stanford Law Rev — Stanford Law Review
Stanford L Rev — Stanford Law Review
Stanford Med Bull — Stanford Medical Bulletin
Stanford Research Inst Jour — Stanford Research Institute. Journal
Stanford Stud Med Sci — Stanford Studies in Medical Sciences
Stanford Stud Psychol — Stanford Studies in Psychology
Stanford Univ Dep Civ Eng Tech Rep — Stanford University. Department of Civil Engineering. Technical Report
Stanford Univ Dep Mech Eng Tech Rep — Stanford University. Department of Mechanical Engineering. Technical Report
Stanford Univ Publ Geol — Stanford University Publications in the Geological Sciences
Stanford Univ Publ Univ Ser Biol Sci — Stanford University. Publications. University Series. Biological Sciences
Stanford Univ Publ Univ Ser Eng — Stanford University. Publications. University Series. Engineering
Stanford Univ Publ Univ Ser Math Astron — Stanford University. Publications. University Series. Mathematics and Astronomy

Stanford Univ Publ Univ Ser Med Sci — Stanford University. Publications. University Series. Medical Sciences
Stan J Intl L — Stanford Journal of International Law
Stan J Intl St — Stanford Journal of International Studies
Stan J Int'l Stud — Stanford Journal of International Studies
Stanki i Instrum — Stanki i Instrument
Stanki Rezhushchie Instrum — Stanki i Rezhushchie Instrumenty
Stan Law — Stanford Lawyer
Stan LR — Stanford Law Review
Stan L Rev — Stanford Law Review
Sta Note For Exp Sta (Idaho) — Station Note. Forest, Wildlife, and Range Experiment Station (Moscow, Idaho)
StANT — Studien zum Alten und Neuen Testament [*Munich*]
St Anth — St. Anthony Messenger
Sta Pap For Exp Sta (Idaho) — Station Paper. Forest, Wildlife, and Range Experiment Station (Moscow, Idaho)
Stapp Car Crash Conf Proc — Stapp Car Crash Conference. Proceedings
St A R — St. Andrews Review
STAR — Scientific and Technical Aerospace Reports [*NASA*]
Star — Starship
Star — Starship. The Magazine about Science Fiction
Starchroom Laundry J — Starchroom Laundry Journal
STARD — Starch/Staerke
STA Rept Abstr — Scientific and Technical Aerospace Reports Abstract
STASD — Stainless Steel
Sta Sper Maiscolt (Bergamo) — Stazione Sperimentale di Maiscoltura (Bergamo)
Stat — Stat. Bulletin of the Wisconsin Nurses' Association
Stat Ab (NZ) — Monthly Abstract of Statistics (New Zealand)
Stat Bull Metrop Life Insur Co — Statistical Bulletin. Metropolitan Life Insurance Company
Stat Bull Metropol Life Ins Co — Statistical Bulletin. Metropolitan Life Insurance Company
State Agric Coll Oreg Eng Exp Stn Circ — State Agricultural College of Oregon. Engineering Experiment Station. Circular
State Court J — State Court Journal
State Fish Chief Secr Dep NSW Res Bull — State Fisheries Chief. Secretary's Department. New South Wales. Research Bulletin
State Geologists Jour — State Geologists Journal
State Gov — State Government
State Govt — State Government
State Govt News — State Government News
State Hortic Assoc PA Proc — State Horticultural Association of Pennsylvania. Proceedings
State Ill Div State Geol Surv Bull — State of Illinois. Division of the State Geological Survey. Bulletin
State Legis — State Legislatures
State Libn — State Librarian
State Libr — State Librarian
State and Local Govt R — State and Local Government Review
State Locl & Urb L Newsl — State, Local, and Urban Law Newsletter
State Loc and Urb L Newsl — State, Local, and Urban Law Newsletter
Staten Island As Pr — Staten Island Association of Arts and Sciences. Proceedings
Staten Island Inst Arts Sci Proc — Staten Island Institute of Arts and Sciences. Proceedings
Statens Inst Byggnadsforsk Handl (Trans) — Statens Institut foer Byggnadsforskning. Handlingar (Translations)
Statens Inst Byggnadsforsk Natl Swedish Bldg Res Doc — Statens Institut foer Byggnadsforskning. National Swedish Building Research Document
Statens Lantbrukskem Kontrollanst Medd — Statens Lantbrukskemiska Kontrollanstalt. Meddelande
Statens Lantbrukskem Lab Medd — Statens Lantbrukskemiska Laboratorium. Meddelande
Statens Naturvetensk Forskningsrad Ekologikomm Bull — Statens Naturvetenskapliga Forskningsrad Ekologikommitter Bulletin
Statens Offentliga Utredn — Statens Offentliga Utredningar
Statens Skadedyrlab Arsberet — Statens Skadedyrlaboratorium Arsberetning
Statens Vaeginst (Swed) Medd — Statens Baeginstitut (Sweden). Meddelande
Statens Vaeginst (Swed) Rapp — Statens Vaeginstitut (Sweden). Rapport
Statens Vaxtskyddsanst Medd — Statens Vaxtskyddsanstalt Meddelanden
State Plann and Environ Comm Tech Bull — State Planning and Environment Commission. Technical Bulletin
State Wash Dep Fish Res Div Inf Bkl — State of Washington. Department of Fisheries. Research Division. Information Booklet
State Wash Dep Fish Res Div Inf Booklet — State of Washington. Department of Fisheries. Research Division. Information Booklet
Stat Instrum (Lond) — Statutory Instrument (London)
Statis et Etud Fins (Ser Bleue) — Statistiques et Etudes Financieres (Serie Bleue)
Statis et Etud Fins (Ser Orange) — Statistiques et Etudes Financieres (Serie Orange)
Statis et Etud Fins (Ser Rouge) — Statistiques et Etudes Financieres (Serie Rouge)
Statis et Etud Midi Pyrenees — Statistiques et Etudes Midi-Pyrenees
Statis Judiciaires — Statistiques Judiciaires

Statis Mhefte Rheinland-Pfalz — Statistische Monatshefte Rheinland-Pfalz
Statis Nachr (Austria) NF — Statistische Nachrichten (Austria). Neue Folge
Statis Neerl — Statistica Neerlandica [*Netherlands*]
Statis Reporter — Statistical Reporter
Statist Abstr US — Statistical Abstract. United States
Statist Anal Donnees — Statistique et Analyse des Donnees. Bulletin de l'Association des Statisticiens Universitaires
Statist Bull USDA — Statistical Bulletin. United States Department of Agriculture
Statist Canad Consumpt Prodn Invent Rubb — Statistics Canada. Consumption. Production Inventories of Rubber and Other Selected Sections
Statist Decisions Econom — Statistique et Decisions Economiques [*Paris*]
Statist et Develop Loire — Statistique et Developpement Pays de la Loire
Statist Distributions Sci Work — Statistical Distributions in Scientific Work
Statist Econ Normande — Statistiques pour l'Economie Normande
Statist i Elektron-Vycisl Tehn v Ekonom — Statistika i Elektronno-Vycislitel'naja Tehnika v Ekonomike Naucno-Issledovatel'skii Institut po Proektirovanija Vycislitel'nyh Centrov i Sistem Ekonomiceskoi Informacii CSU SSSR
Statist Et Finance Et Econ (Ser Orange) — Statistiques et Etudes Financieres. Etudes Economiques (Serie Orange)
Statist Et Financ (Ser Bleue) — Statistiques et Etudes Financieres (Serie Bleue)
Statist Et Financ (Ser Rouge) — Statistiques et Etudes Financieres (Serie Rouge)
Statist Et Midi-Pyrenees — Statistiques et Etudes Midi-Pyrenees
Statist Foreign Trade B — Statistics of Foreign Trade. Series B. Annual. Tables by Reporting Countries
Statist Hefte — Statistische Hefte
Statistical Register of SA — Statistical Register of South Australia
Statistical Register of WA — Statistical Register of Western Australia
Statist M L — Statistical Methods in Linguistics
Statist Neerlandica — Statistica Neerlandica
Statist Newslett Abstr — Statistical Newsletter and Abstracts. Indian Council of Agricultural Research
Statist Paper — Statistics of Paper
Statist Probab Lett — Statistics and Probability Letters
Statist R (Beograd) — Statisticka Revija (Beograd)
Statist Sect Pap For Comm (Lond) — Statistics Section Paper. Forestry Commission (London)
Statist Theory Method Abstracts — Statistical Theory and Method Abstracts
Statist Trav Suppl B Mens — Statistiques du Travail. Supplement au Bulletin Mensuel
Statiszt Szle — Statisztikai Szemle
Stat LR — Statute Law Review
Stat Mech — Statistical Mechanics
STAT News — Science Teachers Association of Tasmania. Newsletter
Stat News Lett (New Delhi) — Statistical News Letter (New Delhi)
Statni Tech Knih Praze Vymena Zkusenosti — Statni Technicka Knihovna v Praze. Vymena Zkusenosti
Statni Vyzk Ustav Sklarsky Kradec Kralove Inf Prehl — Statni Vyzkumny Ustav Sklarsky. Kradec Kralove. Informativni Prehled
Stat Notes Health Plann — Statistical Notes for Health Planners
Stato Soc — Stato Sociale
Stat Rep — Statistical Reporter
Stat Rptr — Statistical Reporter
Statsokon Tss — Statsoekonomisk Tidsskrift
Statsvet Ts — Statsvetenskaplig Tidskrift
Stat Textb Monogr — Statistics Textbooks and Monographs
Stat Theor Meth Abstr — Statistical Theory and Method Abstracts
Stat Tidskr — Statistisk Tidskrift
Stat Tidskrift — Statistick Tidskrift
Stat Use Radiat Jpn — Statistics on the Use of Radiation in Japan
Statute L Rev — Statute Law Review
Staub J — Staub Journal
Staub-Reinhalt Luft — Staub, Reinhaltung der Luft
St Autobahn — Strasse und Autobahn
STAVA — Stavivo [*Czechoslovakia*]
Stavby Jadrovej Energ — Stavby Jadrovej Energetiky [*Supplement to Inzenyrske Stavby*] [*Czechoslovakia*]
Stavebnicky Cas — Stavebnicky Casopis
StB — Stenografische Berichte. Fuenf Hauptversammlungen. Verband der Deutschen Juden
StB — Studi sul Boccaccio
St Barbara Mus Nat Hist Contrib Sci — Santa Barbara Museum of Natural History. Contributions in Science
StBFranc — Studii Biblici Franciscani [*Jerusalem*]
StBFranc LA — Studii Biblici Franciscani. Liber Annuus [*Jerusalem*]
STBGA — Structure and Bonding [*Berlin*]
STBIB — Studia Biophysica
StBiz — Studi Bizantini e Neoellenici
StBM — Stuttgarter Biblische Monographien
St Bonaventure Sci Stud — St. Bonaventure Science Studies
StBoT — Studien zu den Bogazkoey-Texten [*Wiesbaden*]
StBSt — Stuttgarter Bibelstudien [*Stuttgart*]
STBT — Straits Times. Business Times
STC — Sales Tax Cases

STC — Short-Title Catalogue
StC — Studia Catholica
StC — Studia Celtica
St Can Lit — Studies in Canadian Literature
StCau — Studia Caucasica
StCILF — Studii si Cercetari de Istorie Literara si Folclor
StCL — Studii si Cercetari Lingvistice
StClOr — Studi Classici e Orientali
StCrN — Stephen Crane Newsletter
St CS — Studies in Contemporary Satire
StCSF — Studii si Cercetari Stiintifice. Filologie
St Ct J — State Court Journal
STD — Standaard. Dagblad voor Staatkundige, Matschappelijke, en Economische Belangen
StD — Studi Danteschi
StD — Studies and Documents
STDHA — Staedtehygiene
STDJ — Studies on the Texts of the Desert of Judah
STDNA — ASTM [*American Society for Testing and Materials*] Standardization News
Std Obraztsy Chern Metall — Standartnye Obraztsy v Chernoi Metallurgii
STE — Stahl und Eisen. Zeitschrift fuer Technik und Wissenschaft der Herstellung und Verarbeitung von Eisen und Stahl
Ste — Steaua
St E — Studienreihe Englisch
Steam Eng — Steam Engineer
Steam Fuel Users J — Steam and Fuel Users' Journal
Steam and Heat Eng — Steam and Heating Engineer
Steam Heat Eng — Steam and Heating Engineer
Steam Heat Engr — Steam and Heating Engineer
Steam Plant Eng — Steam Plant Engineering
Steam Pwr — Steam Power
Steamusers Fuel Users J — Steamusers' and Fuel Users' Journal
Stechert-Hafner Bk News — Stechert-Hafner Book News
STEDA — Steroids
Steel Const — Steel Construction
Steel Constr — Steel Construction
Steel Fabric J — Steel Fabrication Journal
Steel Fabr J — Steel Fabrication Journal
Steel Founders' Res J — Steel Founders' Research Journal
Steel Furn Mon — Steel Furnace Monthly
Steel Horiz — Steel Horizons
Steel Ind Jpn Annu — Steel Industry of Japan Annual
Steel Int — Steel International
Steel Met Int — Steels and Metals International
Steel Process — Steel Processing
Steel Process Convers — Steel Processing and Conversion
Steel Rev — Steel Review
Steel Times Int — Steel Times International [*England*]
STEIA — Stahl und Eisen
Steinbeck M — Steinbeck Monograph Series
Steinbeck Q — Steinbeck Quarterly
Steinind Steinstrassenbau — Steinindustrie und Steinstrassenbau
Stein-Ind Strassenbau — Stein-Industrie und -Strassenbau
Steinkohlenbergbauver Kurznachr — Steinkohlenbergbauverein Kurznachrichten
SteiQ — Steinbeck Quarterly
Steirische Beitr Hydrogeol — Steirische Beitraege zur Hydrogeologie
Steirisch Imkerbote — Steirischer Imkerbote
Steklo i Keram — Steklo i Keramika
Steklo Keram — Steklo i Keramika
Steklo Sitally Silik Mater — Steklo, Sitally, i Silikatnye Materialy [*Belorussian SSR*]
Stekolnaya Keram Promst — Stekol'naya i Keramicheskaya Promyshlennost
Stekol'naya Prom-st — Stekol'naya Promyshlennost [*USSR*]
STEL — Sunday Telegraph [*United Kingdom*]
STELB — Stereo Review
Stellenbosse Stud — Stellenbosse Student
Stendhal Cl — Stendhal Club
STeol — Studii Teologice
Stephen F Austin State Coll Sch For Bull — Stephen F. Austin State College. School of Forestry. Bulletin
STER — Sterna
Stereo — Stereo Review
Stereochem Fundam Methods — Stereochemistry. Fundamentals and Methods
Stereo R — Stereo Review
Steroids Lipids Res — Steroids and Lipids Research
Steroids Suppl — Steroids. Supplement
STES Newsl — STES [*Seasonal Thermal Energy Storage*] Newsletter [*United States*]
StEtr — Studi Etruschi
Stetson L Rev — Stetson Law Review
Stettin Ent Ztg — Stettiner Entomologische Zeitung
STEUA — Steuerungstechnik
StEv — Studia Evangelica [*Berlin*]
Stevens Ind — Stevens Indicator

Stevens Inst Technol (Hoboken NJ) Davidson Lab Rep — Stevens Institute of Technology (Hoboken, New Jersey). Davidson Laboratory. Report
S Texas LJ — South Texas Law Journal
S Tex LJ — South Texas Law Journal
STF — Soviet Studies. A Quarterly Journal on the USSR and Eastern Europe
STF — Strange Fantasy
StFil — Studia Filozoficzne
STFM — Societe des Textes Francais Modernes
St Form Sp — Studies in Formative Spirituality
St For Note Calif Div For — State Forest Notes. California Division of Forestry
STFPA — Strahlenschutz in Forschung und Praxis
StFr — Studi Francescani
STG — State Government
StG — Studi Germanici
StG — Studium Generale [*Heidelberg*]
STG — Sydney Tourist Guide
StGAK — Studien zur Germanistik, Anglistik und Komparatistik
STGEA — Studium Generale
StGKA — Studien zur Geschichte und Kultur des Altertums
Stgr — Studia Grammatica
St Gr I — Studi di Grammatica Italiana
StGThK — Studien zur Geschichte der Theologie und der Kirche
STh — Studia Theologica
STHEA — Steam and Heating Engineer
StHefte — Statistische Hefte
Sthn Afr Fam Pract — Southern African Family Practice
Sthn Afr Text — Southern Africa Textiles
Sthn Birds — Southern Birds
STHP — Shih-Ta Hsueh-Pao [*Bulletin of Taiwan Normal University*]
STHPD — Shih-Ta Hsueh-Pao
STHRD — Solar Thermal Report
SThU — Schweizerische Theologische Umschau
St Hum — Studies in the Humanities
STHV — Science, Technology, and Human Values
SThZ — Schweizerische Theologische Zeitschrift [*Zurich*]
StI — Studi Ispanici
StI — Studi Italiani
StI — Studia Islandica
StI — Studies: An Irish Quarterly Review of Letters, Philosophy, and Science
Sticht Bosbouwproefsta "Dorschkamp" Ber — Stichting Bosbouwproefstation "De Dorschkamp." Berichten
Sticht Bosbouwproefsta "Dorschkamp" Korte Meded — Stichting Bosbouwproefstation "De Dorschkamp." Korte Mededelingen
Sticht Bosbouwproefsta "Dorschkamp" Uitv Versl — Stichting Bosbouwproefstation "De Dorschkamp." Uitvoerige Verslagen
Sticht Bosbouwproefstn De Dorschkamp Korte Meded — Stichting Bosbouwproefstation "De Dorschkamp." Korte Mededeling
Sticht Coord Cult Onderz Broodgraan Jaarb — Stichting voor Coordinate van Cultuur en Onderzoek van Broodgraan Jaarboekje
Sticht Energieonderz Cent Ned Rep — Stichting Energieonderzoek Centrum Nederland. Report
Sticht Fundam Onderz Mater Jaarb — Stichting voor Fundamenteel Onderzoek der Materie. Jaarboek
Sticht Inst Kernphys Onderz Jaarb — Stichting Instituut voor Kernphysisch Onderzoek. Jaarboek
Sticht Inst Pluimveeonderz "Het Spelderholt" Jaarversl — Stichting Instituut voor Pluimveeonderzoek "Het Spelderholt" Jaarverslag
Sticht Inst Pluimveeonderz Spelderholt Jaarversl — Stichting Instituut voor Pluimveeonderzoek "Het Spelderholt" Jaarverslag
St I I — Studien zur Indologie und Iranistik
Stiinta Sol — Stiinta Solului
StIL — Studi. Istituto Linguistico
Stimm Zeit — Stimmen der Zeit
Stimul Newsl — Stimulation Newsletter
STINA — Stanki i Instrument
StIR — Stanford Italian Review
Stirling E N — Stirling Engine Newsletter
STISA — Sbornik Nauchnykh Trudov Tomskii Inzhenerno-Stroitel'nyi Institut
StIsl — Studia Islandica
StIslam — Studia Islamica [*Paris*]
Sti Solului — Stiinta Solului
StIsp — Studi Ispanici
StIt — Studi Italici [*Kyoto*]
St Ital — Studi Italiani di Filologia Classica
STJ — Steel Today and Tomorrow
StJb — Stifter-Jahrbuch
STJCA — Strojnicky Casopis
St J LR — St. John's Law Review
St John's L Rev — St. John's Law Review
StJud — Studia Judaica. Forschungen zur Wissenschaft des Judentums [*Berlin*]
STJVA — Strojniski Vestnik
STK — Svensk Teologisk Kvartalskrift
STKAB — Standarty i Kachestvo
STKMBC — Mammalogical Informations
STKRA — Steklo i Keramika

STKv — Svensk Teologisk Kvartalskrift
STL — Startling Stories
St L — Student Lawyer
StL — Studentski List
StL — Studia Linguistica
StL — Studies on the Left
STL — Studies in Logic and the Foundations of Mathematics [*Elsevier Book Series*]
STL — Sunday Times (London)
StLF — Studi di Letteratura Francese
StLI — Studi di Letteratura Ispano-Americana
StLing — Studies in Linguistics
St Lit — Studia Liturgica
S T L J — South Texas Law Journal
STLJD — South Texas Law Journal
St L J Th — St. Luke's Journal of Theology
St L M — Studien zur Literatur der Moderne
St Lngst — Statistical Methods in Linguistics
StLo — Studia Logica
StLog — Studia Logica
St Louis Commer — Saint Louis Commerce
St Louis Metropol Med — St. Louis Metropolitan Medicine
St Louis Mus Bul — St. Louis City Art Museum. Bulletin
St Louis U L J — St. Louis University. Law Journal
St Louis Univ B — St. Louis University. Bulletin
St Louis Univ Public Law Forum — Saint Louis University. Public Law Forum
St Louis U Res J — Saint Louis University. Research Journal [*Baguio City*]
St Lou ULJ — St. Louis University. Law Journal
St L P — Studia Linguistica et Philologica
STL-QPSR — Speech Transmission Laboratory. Royal Institute of Technology. Stockholm. Quarterly Progress and Status Reports
STLTA — Steel Times
St Luke J — St. Luke's Journal of Theology
St Luke's Hosp Gaz — St. Luke's Hospital Gazette
St LU LJ — St. Louis University. Law Journal
StM — Studi e Materiali di Storia delle Religioni
StM — Studia Monastica
STMA — Statistical Theory and Method Abstracts
St Marianna Med J — St. Marianna Medical Journal [*Japan*]
St Mark R — St. Mark's Review
St Mark Rev — St. Mark's Review
St Marks R — St. Mark's Review
St Marks Rev — St. Mark's Review
St Mary's L J — St. Mary's Law Journal
StMBC — Studien und Mitteilungen aus dem Benediktiner- und dem Cistercienser-Orden
St Med — Studi Medievali
StMed — Studia Mediewistyczne
S T Mf — Svensk Tidskrift foer Musikforskning
STMGA — Salmon and Trout Magazine
StMGB — Studien und Mitteilungen zur Geschichte des Benediktiner-Ordens
St Mis — Studia Missionalia
St Misc — Studi Miscellanei, Seminario di Archeologia e Storia dell'Arte Greca e Romana dell'Universita di Roma
STMLA — Stomatologia [*Bucharest*]
St M LJ — St. Mary's Law Journal
StMon — Studia Monastica
St MS — Steinbeck Monograph Series
StMSR — Studi e Materiali di Storia delle Religioni [*Rome/Bologna*]
STMTA — Stomatologica [*Genoa*]
STMYA — Stomatologiya
St Myst — Studia Mystica
St N — St. Nicholas
STN — Staff Papers
StN — Studia Neotestamentica [*Paris/Bruges*]
Stn Biol Mar Grande Riviere Que Rapp Annu — Station de Biologie Marine. Grande Riviere, Quebec. Rapport Annuel
Stn Bull Agric Exp Stn Univ Minn — Station Bulletin. Minnesota Agricultural Experiment Station
Stn Bull Dep Agri Econ Agric Exp Stn Purdue Univ — Station Bulletin. Department of Agricultural Economics. Agricultural Experiment Station. Purdue University
Stn Bull New Hamps Agric Exp Stn — Station Bulletin. Agricultural Experiment Station. University of New Hampshire
Stn Bull Ore Agric Exp Stn — Station Bulletin. Oregon Agricultural Experiment Station
Stn Chim Agrar Sper Torino Annu — Stazione Chimico-Agraria Sperimentale di Torino. Annuario
Stn Circ Ore Agric Exp Stn — Station Circular. Oregon Agricultural Experiment Station
STNEA — Sterne
StNeerla — Statistica Neerlandica
St Neophil — Studia Neophilologica
StNF — Studier i Nordisk Filologi
Stn Fed Essais Agric (Lausanne) Publ — Stations Federales d'Essais Agricoles (Lausanne). Publication

Stn L — Stanford Law Review
STNLB — Stimulation Newsletter
Stn Rep Hort Res Stn (Tatura) — Station Report. Horticultural Research Station (Tatura)
Stns Circ Wash Agric Exp Stns — Stations Circular. Washington Agricultural Experiment Stations
Stn Sper Agrar Ital — Stazione Sperimentali Agrarie Italiane
Stn Sper Vitic Enol (Conegliano Italy) Annu — Stazione Sperimentale di Viticoltura e di Enologia (Conegliano, Italy). Annuario
STNT — Sprawozdania Towarzystwa Naukowego w Toruniu
StNT — Studien zum Neuen Testament
Stn Tech Bull Ore Agric Exp Stn — Station Technical Bulletin. Oregon Agricultural Experiment Station
STNWA — Sci-Tech News
STNYA — Science and Technology [*New York*]
StO — Stimmen des Orients
StO — Studia Oliveriana
STOAA — Stomatologiya [*Moscow*]
STOCD — Software Tools Communications
Stochastic Processes Appl — Stochastic Processes and Their Applications
Stoch Processes Appl — Stochastic Processes and Their Applications
Stockh Contrib Geol — Stockholm Contributions in Geology
Stockholm Contrib Geol — Stockholm Contributions in Geology
Stockholm Tek Hogsk Avh — Stockholm. Tekniska Hogskolan. Avhandling
Stockholm Tek Hogsk Handl — Stockholm. Tekniska Hogskolan. Handlingar [*Transactions*]
StocProc — Stochastic Processes and Their Applications
Stomach Intest — Stomach and Intestine [*Japan*]
S Tomas Nurs J — Santo Tomas Nursing Journal
Stomatol DDR — Stomatologie der DDR [*East Germany*]
Stomatol Glas Srb — Stomatoloski Glasnik Srbije
Stomatol Zpr — Stomatologicke Zpracy
Stone C — Stone Country
Stone D — Stone Drum
Stony — Stony Hills
Stop Pregl — Stopanski Pregled
StOr — Studia Orientalia. Edidit Societas Orientalis Fennica [*Helsinki*]
Storage Handl Distrib — Storage Handling Distribution
Stor Art — Storia dell'Arte
StOrChrColl — Studia Orientalia Christiana. Collectanea [*Cairo*]
Stor Ebr It — Storia dell'Ebraismo in Italia. Sezione Toscana
Storefront — Storefront Classroom
Storia e Polit — Storia e Politica
Stotz-Kontakt-Roemmler Nachr — Stotz-Kontakt-Roemmler Nachrichten
STP — NAVAS [*Nederlandse Aannemersvereniging van Afbouwen Stukadoorswerken*] 77
STP — North-Holland Studies in Theoretical Poetics [*Elsevier Book Series*]
StP — Studi Petrarcheschi
StP — Studia Palmyrenskie [*Warsaw*]
StP — Studia Patristica
StPa — Studia Patristica
StPapyr — Studia Papyrologica [*Barcelona*]
StPatrist — Studia Patristica [*Berlin-Ost*]
St Paul Med J — St. Paul Medical Journal
StPB — Studia Post-Biblica
St P Brook — Staff Papers. Brookings Institution
St Petersb Med Wchnschr — St. Petersburger Medizinische Wochenschrift
STPGA — Steel Processing
STPHB — Springer Tracts in Modern Physics
St Philon — Studia Philonica
STPSA — Studia Psychologica
STR — Soul-Taehakkyo Ronmunjip. Inmun-Sahoe-Kwahak [*Seoul University Journal. Humanities and Social Sciences*]
STR — Star Science Fiction
STR — Stereo Review
StR — Studi Religiosi
StR — Studi Romagnoli
STr — Studi Trentini
STr — Studi Trentini di Scienze Storiche
StR — Studia Romanica
StR — Studie o Rukopisech
STRAA — Strahlentherapie
STRAB — Strain
Strahlenschutz Forsch Prax — Strahlenschutz in Forschung und Praxis [*West Germany*]
Strahlenthe — Strahlentherapie
Strahlenther Sonderb — Strahlentherapie. Sonderbaende
Straits Times A — Straits Times Annual [*Singapore*]
Strand — Strand Magazine
Strand (Lond) — Strand Magazine (London)
Strand (NY) — Strand Magazine (New York)
Strasb Med — Strasbourg Medical
Strateg Anal — Strategic Analysis [*India*]
Strategic Dig — Strategic Digest
Strategic R — Strategic Review
Strateg Manage J — Strategic Management Journal

Strathclyde Bioeng Semin — Strathclyde Bioengineering Seminars
Strat R — Strategic Review [*Washington, DC*]
Strauss — Internationale Richard-Strauss-Gesellschaft. Mitteilungen
Str Autobahn — Strasse und Autobahn
STRC — Scientific and Technical Research Centres in Australia
StRel/ScRel — Studies in Religion/Sciences Religieuses
Strem Chem — Strem Chemiker
St Ren — Studies in the Renaissance
Strength Mater — Strength of Materials
Strenna Stor Bolognese — Strenna Storica Bolognese
St Rep (NSW) — State Reports (New South Wales)
STRHA — Staub, Reinhaltung der Luft
St Riv Wat Supply Comm Tech Bull — Victoria. State Rivers and Water Supply Commission. Technical Bulletin
STRJA — Strojirenstvi
STRKA — Staerke
STR M — Strand Magazine
STRND — Sternenbote
StRo — Studi Romani [*Rome*]
Stroemungsmech Stroemungsmasch — Stroemungsmechanik und Stroemungsmaschinen
Stroezh Funkts Mozuka — Stroezh i Funktsii na Mozuka
Stroit Alyum Konstr — Stroitel'nye Alyuminievye Konstruktsii
Stroit Arkhit Leningrada — Stroitel'stvo i Arkhitektura Leningrada
Stroit Arkhit Uzb — Stroitel'stvo i Arkhitektura Uzbekistana
Stroit Dorog — Stroitel'stvo Dorog
Stroit Dorozhn Mash — Stroitel'nye i Dorozhnye Mashiny
Stroit Keram — Stroitel'naya Keramika
Stroit Konstr — Stroitel'nye Konstruktsii
Stroit Konstr Alyum Splavov — Stroitel'nye Konstruktsii iz Alyuminievkh Splavov
Stroit Mater — Stroitel'nye Materialy
Stroit Mater (1929-32) — Stroitel'nye Materialy (1929-32)
Stroit Mater (1933-38) — Stroitel'nye Materialy (1932-38)
Stroit Mater Betony — Stroitel'nye Materialy i Betony
Stroit Mater Detali Izdeliya — Stroitel'nye Materialy. Detali i Izdeliya
Stroit Mater Izdeliya Konstr — Stroitel'nye Materialy. Izdeliya i Konstruktsii
Stroit Mater Konstr — Stroitel'nye Materialy i Konstruktsii
Stroit Mater Silik Prom-st — Stroitelni Materiali i Silikatna Promishlnost [*Bulgaria*]
Stroit Mekh Raschet Sooruz — Stroitel'naya Mekhanika i Raschet Sooruzheniy [*USSR*]
Stroit Predpr Neft Promsti — Stroitel'stvo Predpriyatii Neftyanoi Promyshlennosti
Stroit Promst — Stroitel'naya Promyshlennost
Stroit Truboprovodov — Stroitel'stvo Truboprovodov [*USSR*]
Strojir Vyroba — Strojirenska Vyroba
Strojnicky Cas — Strojnicky Casopis [*Czechoslovakia*]
Strojniski Vestn — Strojniski Vestnik
Stroj Vest — Strojniski Vestnik
StRom — Studia Romanica
StRom — Studies in Romanticism
Strompraxis — Strompraxis
St R (Q) — State Reports (Queensland)
St R (Qd) — State Reports (Queensland)
St R (Queensl) — State Reports (Queensland)
Str Tiefbau — Strassen- und Tiefbau
Struc Rev — Structuralist Review
Struct Bonding — Structure and Bonding
Struct Concr — Structural Concrete
Struct Eng — Structural Engineer
Struct Engr — Structural Engineer
Struct Foam Conf Proc — Structural Foam Conference. Proceedings
Struct Funct Brain — Structure and Functions of the Brain
Struct Glass — Structure of Glass
Struct Mater Note Aust Aeronaut Res Lab — Australia. Department of Supply. Aeronautical Research Laboratories. Structures and Materials Note
Struct Mater Rep Aust Aeronaut Res Lab — Australia. Aeronautical Research Laboratories. Structures and Materials Report
Struct Note Aust Aeronaut Res Lab — Australia. Aeronautical Research Laboratories. Structures Note
Struct Rep — Structure Reports
Struct Rep Aust Aeronaut Res Lab — Australia. Aeronautical Research Laboratories. Structures Report
Struct Rep Dep Archit Sci Syd Univ — Structures Report. Department of Architectural Science. University of Sydney
Struct Saf — Structural Safety
Struct Surv — Structural Survey
Strukt Funkts Fermentov — Struktura i Funktsiya Fermentov
Strukt Modif Khlopk Tsellyul — Struktura i Modifikatsiya Khlopkovoi Tsellyulozy
Strukt Rol Vody Zhivom Org — Struktura i Rol Vody v Zhivom Organizme
Strukt Svoistva Krist — Struktura i Svoistva Kristallov
Strukt Svoistva Litykh Splavov — Struktura i Svoistva Litykh Splavov
Strukturn i Mat Lingvistika — Strukturnaja i Matematiceskaja Lingvistika
Strum Crit — Strumenti Critici

Strum una Nuova Cultur Guida e Manual — Strumenti per una Nuova Cultura. Guida e Manuali

Str Verkehr — Strasse und Verkehr

STS — Scottish Text Society

STS — Stirring Science Stories

StS — Studia Slavica

StSa — Studi Salentini

StSec — Studi Secenteschi

StSem — Studi Semitici

StSemNeerl — Studia Semitica Neerlandica [Assen]

StSl — Studia Slavica

StSLL — Studies in Semitic Languages and Linguistics

STSODQ — Annual Report. Natural Products Research Institute. Seoul National University

STSS — Studi Trentini di Scienze Storiche

Ststcian — Statistician

STT — Science Stories

STT — Strange Tales of Mystery and Terror

StT — Studi Tassiani

STT — Svensk Traevaru- och Pappersmassetidning

STTBA — Strassen- und Tiefbau

StTCL — Studies in Twentieth-Century Literature

STTEA — Stain Technology

StTeol — Studii Teologice [Bucharest]

StTEstmatn — Statistical Theory of Estimation

STTF — Sanskrittexte aus den Turfanfunden

StTh — Studia Theologica

StTheol — Studia Teologica

StThL — Studia Theologica Lundensia. Skrifter Utgivna av Teologiska Fakulteten i Lund

StThVars — Studia Theologica Varsaviensia [Warsaw]

St Tomas J Med — Santo Tomas Journal of Medicine

STTRA — Stroitel'stvo Truboprovodov

St Twen Ct — Studies in Twentieth-Century Literature

STU — Schweizerische Theologische Umschau

Stu — Studia

STU — Studies on International Relations [Warsaw]

Stu — Studium

Stu Cer Fiz — Studii si Cercetari de Fizica

Stud — Studien

Stud — Studies

Stud — Studies: An Irish Quarterly Review of Letters, Philosophy, and Science

Stud Acta Orient — Studia et Acta Orientalia

StudActOr — Studia et Acta Orientalia

StudAeg — Studia Aegyptiaca [Rome]

Stud Afr Linguist — Studies in African Linguistics

Stud Age Chaucer — Studies in the Age of Chaucer

Stud Ag Econ — Stanford University Food Research Institute Studies in Agricultural Economics, Trade, and Development

Stud Alb — Studia Albanica

Stud Algebra Anwendungen — Studien zur Algebra und Ihre Anwendungen

Stud Aliment Apa — Studii de Alimentari cu Apa

Stud Am Fic — Studies in American Fiction

Stud Angew Wirtschaftsforsch Statist — Studien zur Angewandten Wirtschaftsforschung und Statistik

Stud Appl M — Studies in Applied Mathematics

Stud Appl Math — Studies in Applied Mathematics

Stud Appl Mech — Studies in Applied Mechanics

Stud Art Ed — Studies in Art Education

Stud Art Educ — Studies in Art Education

Stud Automat Control — Studies in Automation and Control

Stud Bayesian Econometrics — Studies in Bayesian Econometrics

Stud Bibliog — Virginia University. Bibliographical Society. Studies in Bibliography

Stud Bibliog & Bklore — Studies in Bibliography and Booklore

Stud Biol — Studies in Biology

Stud Biol Acad Sci Hung — Studia Biologica. Academiae Scientiarum Hungaricae

Stud Biol Hung — Studia Biologica Hungarica

Stud Biophy — Studia Biophysica

Stud Biophys — Studia Biophysica

Stud Black Lit — Studies in Black Literature

Stud Bot Cech — Studia Botanica Cechoslavaca

Stud Bot Hung — Studia Botanica Hungarica

Stud Br His — Studies in British History and Culture

Stud Broadcast — Studies of Broadcasting

Stud Brown — Studies in Browning and His Circle

StudBT — Studia Biblica et Theologica [New Haven, CT]

Stud Burke Time — Studies in Burke and His Time

Stud Can — Studia Canonica

StudCath — Studia Catholica

Stud Cerc Buzan — Studii si Cercetari de Istorie Buzoiana

Stud Cerc Docum — Studii si Cercetari de Documentare

Stud Cerc Econom — Studii si Cercetari Economice

Stud Cercet Agron Acad Rep Pop Romine Fil (Cluj) — Studii si Cercetari de Agronomie. Academia Republicii Populare Romine Filiala (Cluj)

Stud Cercet Antropol — Studii si Cercetari de Antropologie

Stud Cercetari Istoria Artei — Studii si Cercetari de Istoria Artei

Stud Cercet Astron — Studii si Cercetari de Astronomie

Stud Cercet Biochim — Studii si Cercetari de Biochimie

Stud Cercet Biol — Studii si Cercetari de Biologie

Stud Cercet Biol Acad Rep Pop Romine Fil (Cluj) — Studii si Cercetari de Biologie. Academia Republicii Populare Romine Filiala (Cluj)

Stud Cercet Biol Acad Rep Pop Romine Ser Biol Veg — Studii si Cercetari de Biologie. Academia Republicii Populare Romine. Seria Biologi Vegetala

Stud Cercet Biol Ser Bot — Studii si Cercetari de Biologie. Seria Botanica

Stud Cercet Biol Ser Zool — Studii si Cercetari de Biologie. Seria Zoologie

Stud & Cercet Calcul Econ & Cibern Econ — Studii si Cercetari de Calcul Economic si Cibernetica Economica

Stud Cercet Chim — Studii si Cercetari de Chimie

Stud & Cercet Doc — Studii si Cercetari de Documentare

Stud Cercet Embriol Citol Ser Embriol — Studii si Cercetari de Embriologie si Citologie. Seria Embriologie [Romania]

Stud Cercet Endocrinol — Studii si Cercetari de Endocrinologie

Stud Cercet Energ — Studii si Cercetari de Energetica

Stud Cercet Energ Electroteh — Studii si Cercetari de Energetica si Electrotehnica

Stud Cercet Energ Ser A — Studii si Cercetari de Energetica. Seria A. Energetica Generala si Electroenergetica

Stud Cercet Energ Ser B — Studii si Cercetari de Energetica. Seria B. Termoenergetica si Utilizarea Energetica a Combustibililor

Stud Cercet Fiz — Studii si Cercetari de Fizica

Stud Cercet Fiziol — Studii si Cercetari de Fiziologie [Romania]

Stud Cercet Geol Geofiz Geogr Ser Geofiz — Studii si Cercetari de Geologie, Geofizica, si Geografie. Seria Geofizica

Stud Cercet Geol Geofiz Geogr Ser Geogr — Studii si Cercetari de Geologie, Geofizica, si Geografie. Seria Geografie

Stud Cercet Geol Geofiz Geogr Ser Geol — Studii si Cercetari de Geologie, Geofizica, si Geografie. Seria Geologie

Stud Cercet Ig Sanat Publica — Studii si Cercetari de Igiena si Sanatate Publica

Stud Cercet Inframicrobiol — Studii si Cercetari de Inframicrobiologie

Stud Cercet Inframicrobiol Microbiol Parazitol — Studii si Cercetari de Inframicrobiologie, Microbiologie, si Parazitologie

Stud Cercet Inst Cercet Piscic — Studii si Cercetari. Institutul de Cercetari Piscicole

Stud Cercet Inst Cercet Proiect Piscic — Studii si Cercetari. Institutul de Cercetari si Proiectari Piscicole

Stud Cercet Inst Meteorol Hidrol Partea 1 — Studii si Cercetari. Institutul de Meteorologie si Hidrologie. Partea 1. Meteorologie

Stud Cercet Inst Meteorol Hidrol Partea 2 — Studii si Cercetari. Institutul de Meteorologie si Hidrologie. Partea 2. Hidrologie

Stud Cercet Mec Apl — Studii si Cercetari de Mecanica Aplicata

Stud Cercet Med (Cluj) — Studii si Cercetari de Medicina (Cluj)

Stud Cercet Med Interna — Studii si Cercetari de Medicina Interna

Stud Cercet Metal — Studii si Cercetari de Metalurgie [Romania]

Stud Cercet Metal Comun Stiint — Studii si Cercetari de Metalurgie. Comunicari Stiintifice

Stud Cercet Neurol — Studii si Cercetari de Neurologie

Stud Cercet Piscic Inst Cercet Proiect Aliment — Studii si Cercetari Piscicole. Institutul de Cercetari si Proiectari Alimentare

Stud Cercet Silvic — Studii si Cercetari de Silvicultura

Stud Cercet Silvic Inst Cercet Amenajari Silvice — Studii si Cercetari de Silvicultura. Institutul de Cercetari si Amenajari Silvice

Stud Cercet Virusol — Studii si Cercetari de Virusologie

Stud Cerc Fiz — Studii si Cercetari de Fizica

Stud Cerc Inst Cerc For (Industr Lemn) — Studii si Cercetari. Institutul de Cercetari Forestiere (Industrializarea Lemnului)

Stud Cerc Inst Cerc For (Mec Lucr For) — Studii si Cercetari. Institutul de Cercetari Forestiere (Mecanizarea Lucrarilor Forestiere)

Stud Cerc Inst Cerc For (Silv) — Studii si Cercetari. Institutul de Cercetari Forestiere (Silvicultura)

Stud Cerc Mat — Studii si Cercetari Matematice

Stud Cerc Mec Apl — Studii si Cercetari de Mecanica Aplicata

Stud Chemother Inst Med Res — Studies. Chemotherapeutic Institute for Medical Research [Japan]

Stud Ch G P — Studies in Chinese Government and Politics

Stud Church Hist — Studies in Church History. American Society of Church History

Stud Cl — Studii Clasice

StudClas — Studii Clasice

Stud Class — Studies of Classical India

Stud Com Co — Studies in Comparative Communism

Stud Com I D — Studies in Comparative International Development

Stud Com L G — Studies in Comparative Local Government

Stud Comm R — Studies in Communism, Revisionism, and Revolution

Stud Comp Com — Studies in Comparative Communism [Los Angeles]

Stud Comp Commun — Studies in Comparative Communism

Stud Comp Communism — Studies in Comparative Communism

Stud Comp Int Dev — Studies in Comparative International Development [New Jersey]

Stud Comp Int Develop — Studies in Comparative International Development

Stud in Comp Local Govt — Studies in Comparative Local Government
Stud Comp R — Studies in Comparative Religion
Stud Comp Relig — Studies in Comparative Religion
Stud Comun (Brukenthal) — Studii si Comunicari (Brukenthal)
Stud Comun (Pitesti) — Studii si Comunicari (Pitesti)
Stud Comun (Satu Mare) — Studii si Comunicari (Satu Mare)
Stud Conserv — Studies in Conservation
Stud in Contin Educ — Studies in Continuing Education
Stud Cosmic Ray — Studies of Cosmic Ray [*Japan*]
Stud Demogr — Studia Demograficzne
Stud Develop — Middle East Technical University. Studies in Development
Stud Develop Special Issue — Studies in Development. Special Issue. Middle East Technical University
Stud Dipl — Studia Diplomatica [*Brussels*]
Stud Diplom — Studia Diplomatica
Stud & Doc His Jur — Studia et Documenta Historiae et Juris
Stud Docum Asian Docum — Studies and Documents. Asian Documentation and Research Center
Stud Econ — Studi Economici
Stud Ed — Studies in Education
Stud Eight — Studies in Eighteenth-Century Culture
Stud Eighteenth-Century Cult — Studies in Eighteenth-Century Culture
Stud Engl L — Studies in English Literature, 1500-1900
Stud Engl Lit — Studies in English Literature
Stud Engl Phil — Studien zur Englischen Philologie
Stud Engl (T) — Studies in English Literature (Tokyo)
Student Adv — Student Advocate
Studente Vet — Studente Veterinario
Student Law — Student Lawyer
Student Musicol — Student Musicologists at Minnesota
Stud Entomol — Studia Entomologica
Student Q J Instn Elec Engrs — Institution of Electrical Engineers. Student Quarterly Journal
Students'ky Nauk Pratsi Kyyv Derzh Unyv — Students'ky Naukovi Pratsi Kyyivs'kyyi Derzhavnyyi Unyversytet
Stud Epurarea Apelor — Studii de Epurarea Apelor
Stud Europ Soc — Studies in European Society
Stud Fam Pl — Studies in Family Planning
Stud Fam Plann — Studies in Family Planning
Stud Fauna Curacao Other Caribb Isl — Studies on the Fauna of Curacao and Other Caribbean Islands
Stud Fauna Suriname Other Guyanas — Studies of the Fauna of Suriname and Other Guyanas
Stud Fenn — Studia Fennica
Stud Filol — Studime Filologjike
Stud Finans — Studia Finansowe
Stud Form Spir — Studies in Formative Spirituality
Stud For Suec — Studia Forestalia Suecica
Stud For Suec (Skogshogsk) — Studia Forestalia Suecica (Skogshogskolan)
Stud Found Methodol Philos Sci — Studies in the Foundations, Methodology, and Philosophy of Science
Stud Fran — Studi Francesi
Stud Gen — Studium Generale
Stud Genet — Studies in Genetics
Stud Geogr Cesk Akad Ved Geogr Ustav (Brno) — Studia Geographica. Ceskoslovenska Akademie Ved. Geograficky Ustav (Brno)
Stud Geol Mineral Inst Tokyo Univ Educ — Studies from the Geological and Mineralogical Institute. Tokyo University of Education
Stud Geol Pol — Studia Geologica Polonica
Stud Geol Salamanca — Studia Geologica. Universidad de Salamanca
Stud Geol (Tulsa Okla) — Studies in Geology (Tulsa, Oklahoma)
Stud Geol Univ Salamanca — Studia Geologica. Universidad de Salamanca
Stud Geomorphol Carpatho-Balcanica — Studia Geomorphologica Carpatho-Balcanica
Stud Geoph — Studia Geophysica et Geodaetica
Stud Geophys Geod — Studia Geophysica et Geodaetica
Stud Geophys Geod (Cesk Akad Ved) — Studia Geophysica et Geodaetica (Ceskosloven-Akademie Ved)
Stud Geotech — Studia Geotechnica. Politechnika Wroclawaka
Stud Geotech Mech — Studia Geotechnica et Mechanica
Stud Geoteh Fund Constr Hidroteh — Studii de Geotekhnica. Fundatii si Constructii Hidrotehnice
Stud Gesch Akad Wiss DDR — Studien zur Geschichte der Akademie der Wissenschaften der Deutsche Demokratische Republik
Stud H Art — Studies in the History of Art
Stud Helminthol — Studia Helminthologica
Stud Hist — Studime Historike
Stud Hist Art — Studies in the History of Art
Stud Hist Biol — Studies in History of Biology
Stud Hist Math Phys Sci — Studies in the History of Mathematics and Physical Sciences
Stud Hist Med — Studies in History of Medicine
Stud Hist Modern Sci — Studies in the History of Modern Science
Stud Hist P — Studies in History and Philosophy of Science
Stud Hist Philos Sci — Studies in History and Philosophy of Science
Stud Hist & Soc — Studies in History and Society

Studia Alban — Studia Albanica
Studia Automat — Studia z Automatiki
Studia Can — Studia Canonica
Studia Ent — Studia Entomologica
Studia Forest Suecica — Studia Forestalia Suecica
Studia For Suec — Studia Forestalia Suecica
Studia Geotech Mech — Studia Geotechnica et Mechanica
Studia I — Studia Iranica
Studia Leibnitiana Suppl — Studia Leibnitiana. Supplementa
Studia M — Studia Missionalia
Studia Math — Studia Mathematica
Studia Math/Math Lehrbuecher — Studia Mathematica/Mathematische Lehrbuecher
Studia Math/Math Lehrbuecher Taschenbuch — Studia Mathematica/Mathematische Lehrbuecher. Taschenbuch
Studia Mus — Studia Musicologica
Studia Mus Nor — Studia Musicologica Norvegica
Studia Neophil — Studia Neophilologica
Studia Sci Math Hungar — Studia Scientiarum Mathematicarum Hungarica
Studia Ser Math — Studia. Series Mathematica
Studia Univ Babes-Bolyai Math — Universitatis Babes-Bolyai. Studia. Series Mathematica
Studia Univ Babes-Bolyai Ser Math-Mech — Studia Universitatis Babes-Bolyai. Series Mathematica-Mechanica
Studia Univ Babes-Bolyai Ser Phys — Studia Universitatis Babes-Bolyai. Series Physica
Studia Zool R Scient Univ Hung Budapest — Studia Zoologica Regiae Scientiarum Universitatis Hungaricae Budapestensis
Studi Cl Orient — Studi Classici e Orientali
Studiecent TNO Scheepsbouw Navig Commun — Studiecentrum TNO [*Toegepast Natuurwetenschappelijk Onderzoek*] voor Scheepsbouw en Navigatie. Communication
Studiecent TNO Scheepsbouw Navig Rep — Studiecentrum TNO [*Toegepast Natuurwetenschappelijk Onderzoek*] voor Scheepsbouw en Navigatie. Report
Studi Econ (Cagliari) — Studi di Economia (Cagliari)
Studi Econ (Naples) — Studi Economici (Naples)
Studi Emigr — Studi Emigrazione
Studienb Naturwiss Tech — Studienbuecher Naturwissenschaft und Technik
Studienskripten zur Soziol — Studienskripten zur Soziologie
Studies — Studies in Political Economy
Studies Appl Math — Studies in Applied Mathematics
Studies App Math — Studies in Applied Mathematics
Studies in Art Ed — Studies in Art Education
Studies in Aust Bibliog — Studies in Australian Bibliography
Studies in Can Lit — Studies in Canadian Literature
Studies Conserv — Studies in Conservation
Studies Econ Analysis — Studies in Economic Analysis
Studies in Hum — Studies in the Humanities
Studies L & Econ Develop — Studies in Law and Economic Development
Studies Mus — Studies in Music
Studies Parasitol and Gen Zool — Studies in Parasitology and General Zoology
Studies Philol — Studies in Philology
Studies Pol Economy — Studies in Political Economy
Studies Zool Lab Univ Nebr — Studies. Zoological Laboratory. University of Nebraska
Studii Cerc Biol — Studii si Cercetari de Biologie
Studii Cerc Biol Biol Anim — Studii si Cercetari de Biologie. Seria Biologie Animala
Studii Cerc Biol Zool — Studii si Cercetari de Biologie. Seria Zoologie
Studii Cercet Chim — Studii si Cercetari de Chimie
Studii Cercet Econ — Studii si Cercetari Economice
Studii Cerc Stiint Iasi Biol Stiint Agric — Studii si Cercetari Stiintifice. Filiala Iasi. Academia RPR. [*Republicii Populare Romine*]. Biologice si Stiinte Agricole
StudiItalFilol Class — Studi Italiani di Filologia Classica [*Florence*]
Studii Teh Econ Inst Geol Rom — Studii Tehnice si Economice. Institutului Geologic al Romaniei. Stiinta Solului
Studijni Inform Lesnictyi — Studijni Informace. Lesnictyi
Studi M — Studi Musicali
Stud Indo-As Art Cult — Studies in Indo-Asian Art and Culture [*New Delhi*]
Stud In Relat — Studies on International Relations
Stud Inst Divi Thomae — Studies. Institutum Divi Thomae
Stud Inst Med Res (Malaya) — Studies. Institute for Medical Research (Malaya)
Stud Int — Studio International
Stud Intellectual Precocity — Studies of Intellectual Precocity
Stud & Intel Obs — Student and Intellectual Observer
Studio — Studio International
Studio Int — Studio International
Studio Intl — Studio International
Studi Sassaresi Sez II Arch Bimest Sci Med Nat — Studi Sassaresi. Sezione II. Archivio Bimestrale di Scienze Mediche e Naturali
Studi Sassar Sez 2 — Studi Sassaresi. Sezione 2. Archivio Bimestrale di Scienze Mediche e Naturali
Stud Islam — Studia Islamica

Studi Stor — Studi Storici Instituto Gramisci Editor
Studi Teh Econ Inst Geol Rom — Studii Tehnice si Economice. Institutului Geologic al Romaniei
Studi Trentini Sci Nat Sez B Biol — Studi Trentini di Scienze Naturali. Sezione B. Biologica
Studi Urbinati Fac Farm — Studi Urbinati. Facolta di Farmacia
Stud J Inst Electron Telecommun Eng — Students' Journal. Institution of Electronics and Telecommunication Engineers
Stud J Inst Electron and Telecommun Eng — Students' Journal. Institution of Electronics and Telecommunication Engineers
Stud Kulturkunde — Studien zur Kulturkunde
Stud Lang C — Studies in Language. Companion Series
Stud Leibn — Studia Leibnitiana
Stud Leibnit — Studia Leibnitiana
Stud Leibnitiana — Studia Leibnitiana
Stud Ling — Studies in Linguistics
Stud Ling Sci — Studies in the Linguistic Sciences [Urbana]
Stud Lit — Studia Liturgica
Stud Lit Im — Studies in the Literary Imagination
Stud Log — Studia Logica
Stud Magr — Studi Magrebini
Stud Mater Weiterbild Med Tech Laborassistenten — Studien-Material zur Weiterbildung Medizinisch-Technischer Laborassistenten
Stud Math — Studia Mathematica
Stud Math Appl — Studies in Mathematics and Its Applications
Stud Math Managerial Econom — Studies in Mathematical and Managerial Economics
Stud Mat Ist Medie — Studii si Materiale de Istorie Medie
Stud Mat Muz Ist Mil — Studii si Materiale de Muzeografie si Istorie Militara
Stud Mat (Suceava) — Studii si Materiale Muzeul Judetean (Suceava, Romania)
Stud Med Geogr — Studies in Medical Geography
Stud Mediev — Studies in Medieval Culture
Stud Med Szeged — Studia Medica Szegedinensia
Stud Med Szegedinensia — Studia Medica Szegedinensia
Stud Microbiol — Studia Microbiologica
Stud Mitt Gesch Benediktinerorden — Studien und Mitteilungen zur Geschichte des Benediktiner-Ordens und Seiner Zweige
Stud Modern Thermodynamics — Studies in Modern Thermodynamics
StudMon — Studia Monastica
Stud Mycol — Studies in Mycology
Stud Myst — Studia Mystica
Stud Nakamura Gakuin Univ — Studies. Nakamura Gakuin University
Stud Nat Sci — Studies in the Natural Sciences
Stud Nat Sci (Portales NM) — Studies in Natural Sciences (Portales, New Mexico)
Stud Nauchno Issled Rab Sib Tekhnol Inst — Studencheskie Nauchno-Issledovatel'skie Raboty. Sibirskii Tekhnologicheskii Institut
Stud Nauchn Rab Univ Druzhby Nar — Studencheskie Nauchnye Raboty. Universitet Druzhby Narodov
Stud Nauk Polit — Studia Nauk Politycznych
Stud Nauk Pr Kiiv Derzh Univ — Students'ki Naukovi Pratsi Kiivs'kii Derzhavnii Universitet
Stud Neoph — Studia Neophilologica
Stud Neophilol — Studia Neophilologica
StudNeot — Studia Neotestamentica [Paris/Bruges]
Stud Neotrop Fauna — Studies on the Neotropical Fauna [Later, Studies on the Neotropical Fauna and Environment]
Stud Neotrop Fauna Environ — Studies on the Neotropical Fauna and Environment
Stud Neuro Anat — Studies in Neuro-Anatomy
Stud Niger Lang — Studies in Nigerian Languages
Stud Novel — Studies in the Novel
StudNT — Studien zum Neuen Testament [Guetersloh]
StudOr — Studia Orientalia [Helsinki]
Stud Orient — Studia Orientalia [Helsinki]
Stud Ov — Studium Ovetense
Stud Pac Lang Cult — Studies in Pacific Languages and Cultures in Honour of Bruce Biggs
Stud Paint (Osaka) — Studies in Paint (Osaka) [Japan]
StudPal — Studien zur Palaeographie und Papyruskunde [Leipzig]
StudPap — Studia Papyrologica
Stud Papyrol — Studia Papyrologica
Stud Patr — Studia Patristica
Stud Person Psychol — Studies in Personnel Psychology
Stud Pers P — Studies in Personnel Psychology
Stud Phil Christ — Studia Philosophiae Christiane
Stud Phil E — Studies in Philosophy and Education
Stud Phil & Ed — Studies in Philosophy and Education
Stud Phil H — Studies in Philosophy and the History of Philosophy
Stud Phil Hist Phil — Studies in Philosophy and the History of Philosophy
Stud Phil Ling — Studies in Philippine Linguistics [Manila]
Stud Philol — Studies in Philology
Stud Philos — Studies in Philosophy [The Hague]
Stud Philos & Educ — Studies in Philosophy and Education
Stud Philos Med — Studies in Philosophy of Medicine

Stud Phil (Switzerland) — Studia Philosophica (Switzerland)
Stud Phonol — Studia Phonologica
Stud Phys Anthropol — Studies in Physical Anthropology
Stud Picena — Studia Picena
Stud Pneumol Phtiseol Cech — Studia Pneumologica et Phtiseologica Cechoslovaca
Stud Prawno-Ekon — Studia Prawno-Ekonomiczne
Stud Pr Cr — Studi e Problemi di Critica Testuale
Stud Prot Epurarea Apelor — Studii de Protectia si Epurarea Apelor
Stud Psycho — Studia Psychologica [Bratislava]
Stud Psychol — Studia Psychologiczne
Stud Psychol (Bratisl) — Studia Psychologica (Bratislava)
Stud Q J Inst Electr Eng — Students Quarterly Journal. Institution of Electrical Engineers [England]
Stud Radiat Eff Solids — Studies in Radiation Effects in Solids
Stud Regional Sci Urban Econom — Studies in Regional Science and Urban Economics
Stud Rel — Studies in Religion [Ontario]
Stud Relig — Studies in Religion
Stud Rep Hydrol IAHS - UNESCO — Studies and Reports in Hydrology. International Association of Hydrological Sciences - United Nations Educational, Scientific, and Cultural Organization
Stud Res Inst Meteorol Hydrol Part 2 — Studies and Research. Institute of Meteorology and Hydrology. Part 2. Hydrology
Stud Ric Div Geomineraria Com Naz Ric Nucl — Studi e Ricerche. Divisione Geomineraria. Comitato Nazionale per le Ricerche Nucleari
Stud Ric Ist Mineral Petrogr Univ Pavia — Studi e Ricerche. Istituto di Mineralogia e Petrografia. Universita di Pavia
StudRom — Studi Romani [Rome]
StudRom — Studi Romanzi [Padua]
Stud Romagn — Studi Romagnoli
Stud Roman — Studies in Romanticism
Stud Romant — Studies in Romanticism
Stud Romanticism — Studies in Romanticism
StudSal — Studi Salentini
StudSard — Studi Sardi
Stud Sassar Sez 1 — Studi Sassaresi. Sezione 1
Stud Sci Math Hung — Studia Scientiarum Mathematicarum Hungarica [Hungary]
Stud Sc Lit — Studies in Scottish Literature
StudSemNeerl — Studia Semitica Neerlandica [Assen]
Stud Sh Fic — Studies in Short Fiction
Stud Short Fict — Studies in Short Fiction
Stud Short Fiction — Studies in Short Fiction
Stud Sociol — Studi di Sociologia
Stud Socjol — Studia Socjologiczne
Stud Soc Li — Studies in Social Life
Stud Soc Sci Torun Sect A — Studia Societatis Scientiarum Torunensis. Sectio A. Mathematica-Physica
Stud Soc Sci Torun Sect B — Studia Societatis Scientiarum Torunensis. Sectio B (Chemie)
Stud Soc Sci Torun Sect C (Geogr Geol) — Studia Societatis Scientiarum Torunensis. Sectio C (Geographia et Geologia)
Stud Soc Sci Torun Sect D (Bot) — Studia Societatis Scientiarum Torunensis. Sectio D (Botanica)
Stud Soc Sci Torun Sect E (Zool) — Studia Societatis Scientiarum Torunensis. Sectio E (Zoologia)
Stud Soc Sci Torun Sect F — Studia Societatis Scientiarum Torunensis. Sectio F (Astronomia) [Poland]
Stud Soc Sci Torun Sect G (Physiol) — Studia Societatis Scientiarum Torunensis. Sectio G (Physiologia)
Stud Soc Wk — Studies on Social Work
Stud Solid Phys Chem — Studies on Solid State Physics and Chemistry [Japan]
Stud Sov Th — Studies in Soviet Thought
Stud Sov Thought — Studies in Soviet Thought
Stud Spelaeol — Studies in Spelaeology
Stud Speleol — Studies in Speleology
Stud Statist Mech — Studies in Statistical Mechanics
Stud Stat Mech — Studies in Statistical Mechanics
Stud Stn Fish Res Board Can — Studies. Stations of the Fisheries Research Board of Canada
Stud Storic — Studi Storici
Stud Surf Sci Catal — Studies in Surface Science and Catalysis [Netherlands] [Elsevier Book Series]
Stud Teh Econ Inst Geol (Rom) Ser A — Studii Tehnice si Economice. Institutul Geologic (Romania). Seria A. Prospectiuni si Explorari Geologice
Stud Teh Econ Inst Geol (Rom) Ser B — Studii Tehnice si Economice. Institutul Geologic (Romania). Seria B. Chimie
Stud Teh Econ Inst Geol (Rom) Ser C — Studii Tehnice si Economice. Institutul Geologic (Romania). Seria C. Pedologie
Stud Teh Econ Inst Geol (Rom) Ser D — Studii Tehnice si Economice. Institutul Geologic (Romania). Seria D. Prospectiuni Geofizice
Stud Teh Econ Inst Geol (Rom) Ser E — Studii Tehnice si Economice. Institutul Geologic (Romania). Seria E. Hidrogeologie
Stud Teh Econ Inst Geol (Rom) Ser F — Studii Tehnice si Economice. Institutul Geologic (Romania). Seria F. Geologie Tehnice

Stud Teh Econ Inst Geol Ser E — Studii Tehnice si Economice. Institutul Geologic (Romania). Seria E. Hidrogeologie
Stud Teh Econ Inst Geol Ser I — Studii Tehnice si Economice. Institutul Geologic (Romania). Seria I. Mineralogie-Petrografie
Stud Teh Econ Ser D Inst Geol Geofiz (Bucharest) — Studii Tehnice si Economice. Seria D. Prospectiuni Geofizice. Institutul de Geologie si Geofizica (Bucharest) [*Romania*]
Stud Teh Econ Ser E Inst Geol Geofiz — Studii Tehnice si Economice. Seria E. Hidrogeologie. Institutul de Geologie si Geofizica
Stud Th — Studia Theologica
Stud Theol — Studia Theologica
Stud Third World Soc — Studies in Third World Societies [*Williamsburg*]
Stud Tokugawa Inst — Studies. Tokugawa Institute
Stud Tour Rep Dep Prim Ind (Queensl) — Study Tour Report. Department of Primary Industries (Queensland)
Stud Trade Unionists — Studies for Trade Unionists
Stud Trop Oceanogr Inst Mar Sci Univ Miami — Studies in Tropical Oceanography. Institute of Marine Science. University of Miami
Stud Trop Oceanogr (Miami) — Studies in Tropical Oceanography (Miami)
Stud Uch Zap Erevan Gos Univ — Studencheskie Uchenye Zapiski. Erevanskii Gosudarstvennyi Universitet
Stud Univ Babes-Bolyai Biol — Studia Universitatis Babes-Bolyai. Series Biologia
Stud Univ Babes-Bolyai Chem — Studia Universitatis Babes-Bolyai. Series Chemia
Stud Univ Babes-Bolyai Geol-Geogr — Studia Universitatis Babes-Bolyai. Series Geologia-Geographia
Stud Univ Babes-Bolyai Math — Studia Universitatis Babes-Bolyai. Series Mathematica
Stud Univ Babes-Bolyai Phys — Studia Universitatis Babes-Bolyai. Series Physica
Stud Univ Babes-Bolyai Ser Biol — Studia Universitatis Babes-Bolyai. Series Biologia
Stud Univ Babes-Bolyai Ser Chem — Studia Universitatis Babes-Bolyai. Series Chemia
Stud Univ Babes-Bolyai Ser Geol-Minerol — Studia Universitatis Babes-Bolyai. Series Geologia-Mineralogia
Stud Univ Babes-Bolyai Ser Math-Phys — Studia Universitatis Babes-Bolyai. Series Mathematica-Physica
Stud Univ Babes-Bolyai Ser Phys — Studia Universitatis Babes-Bolyai. Series Physica
Stud Urb — Studi Urbinati di Storia, Filosofia, e Letteratura
Stud Urb (Ser A) — Studi Urbinati di Scienze Giuridiche ed Economiche (Ser. A)
Stud Urb St — Studi Urbinati di Storia, Filosofia, e Letteratura
Stud Venez — Studi Veneziani
Stud Voltaire Eighteenth Century — Studies on Voltaire and the Eighteenth Century
Stud VT Geol — Studies in Vermont Geology
Stud W — Student World
Study Elem Particles — Study of Elementary Particles [*Japan*]
Study of Soc — Study of Society
Study Tea — Study of Tea
Stud Zrodloznawcze — Studia Zrodloznawcze. Commentationes
StudzumAuNT — Studien zum Alten und Neuen Testament [*Munich*]
Stu Mon — Studia Monastica
StUmwNT — Studien zur Umwelt des Neuen Testament [*Goettingen*]
StUNT — Studien zur Umwelt des Neuen Testament [*Goettingen*]
STUOA — Sbornik Nauchnykh Trudov Ukrainskii Nauchno-Issledovatel'skii Institut Ogneuporov
Stu Pat — Studia Patavina
Stu Prob & St — Studies in Probability and Statistics
Stu Ros — Studia Rosenthaliana
StuSta — Studia Staropolskie
StuTC — Studies in the Twentieth Century
Stutt Beitr Naturk — Stuttgarter Beitraege zur Naturkunde
Stuttg Beitr Naturkd — Stuttgarter Beitraege zur Naturkunde
Stuttg Beitr Naturkd Ser A (Biol) — Stuttgarter Beitraege zur Naturkunde. Serie A (Biologie)
Stuttg Beitr Naturkd Ser B (Geol Palaeontol) — Stuttgarter Beitraege zur Naturkunde. Serie B (Geologie und Palaeontologie)
Stuttg Beitr Naturk Ser C Allg Aufsaetze — Stuttgarter Beitraege zur Naturkunde. Serie C. Allgemeinverstaendliche Aufsaetze
Stuttg Geogr Stud — Stuttgarter Geographische Studien
STUWA — Sterne und Weltraum
StV — Studies on Voltaire and the Eighteenth Century
Stva — Stvaranje
STVCA — Stavebnicky Casopis
STVFB — Samoletostroenie i Tekhnika Vozdushnogo Flota
StVladSemQ — St. Vladimir's Seminary. Quarterly [*New York*]
Styr Tek Utveckling Inf Energitek — Styrelsen foer Teknisk Utveckling Informerar om Energiteknik [*Sweden*]
STZ — Sprache im Technischen Zeitalter
STZED — Stimmen der Zeit
SU — Samostijna Ukraina [*Independent Ukraine*]
SU — Studi Urbinati

Suara Ekon — Suara Ekonomi [*Singapore*]
SUB — Scandinavian University Books
SUBB — Studia Universitatis Babes-Bolyai. Series Philologia
SUBBA — Studia Universitatis Babes-Bolyai. Series Biologia
SUBBP — Studia Universitatis Babes-Bolyai. Series Philologia
SUBCA — Studia Universitatis Babes-Bolyai. Series Chemia
Sub-Cell Bi — Sub-Cellular Biochemistry
Sub-Cell Biochem — Sub-Cellular Biochemistry
Subj of Day — Subject of the Day
Sub Life — Suburban Life
SUBMD — Studia Universitatis Babes-Bolyai. Series Mathematica
Subnucl Ser — Subnuclear Series
SUBPA — Studia Universitatis Babes-Bolyai. Series Mathematica-Physica
SUBPDJ — Annual Research Reviews. Substance P
Subser Optical Sci Engrg — Subseries on Optical Science and Engineering
Subsidia Med — Subsidia Medica
Subst Alcohol Actions Misuse — Substance and Alcohol Actions/Misuse
Sub Torg — Sovetskaya Torgovlya
Subtrop Kul't — Subtropicheskie Kul'tury
Subtrop Kul't Min Sel'Khoz SSSR — Subtropicheskie Kul'tury. Ministerstvo Sel'skogo Khozyaistva SSSR
SUC — Saggi di Umanismo Cristiano
Success Farming — Successful Farming
Success Farm South — Successful Farming in the South
Successful F — Successful Farming
Success Mtg — Successful Meetings
Suc Farm — Successful Farming
Sucr Belg Sugar Ind Abstr — Sucrerie Belge and Sugar Industry Abstracts
SuD — Sprache und Dichtung
SUD — Sudestasie. Magazine d'Information
SUDAM — Editorial Sudamericana, BA
Sudan Eng Soc J — Sudan Engineering Society. Journal
Sudan Geol Surv Dep Bull — Sudan. Geological Survey Department. Bulletin
Sudan J Econ and Social Studies — Sudan Journal of Economic and Social Studies
Sudan J Vet Sci Anim Husb — Sudan Journal of Veterinary Science and Animal Husbandry
Sudan Notes — Sudan Notes and Records
Sudan Notes Rec — Sudan Notes and Records
Sudan Soc — Sudan Society
Sudebno-Med Ekspert — Sudebno-Meditsinskaya Ekspertiza
SUDENE Bol Recur Nat — SUDENE [*Superintendencia do Desenvolvimento do Nordeste*] Boletim do Recursos Naturais
Sudhoffs Arch — Sudhoffs Archiv fuer Geschichte der Medizin und der Naturwissenschaften
Sudhoffs Arch — Sudhoffs Archiv. Zeitschrift fuer Wissenschaftsgeschichte
Sud Inform Econ Provence-Cote D'Azur-Corse — Sud. Information Economique Provence-Cote D'Azur-Corse
Sud-Med Ekspert — Sudebno-Meditsinskaya Ekspertiza
Sud Med Ekspert Krim Sluzhbe Sledstviya — Sudebno-Meditsinskaya Ekspertiza i Kriminalistika na Sluzhbe Sledstviya
SuedA — Suedostdeutsches Archiv
Sueddt Mh — Sueddeutsche Monatshefte
Sueddtsch Ztg — Sueddeutsche Zeitung
SuedoA — Suedostdeutsches Archiv
Suedosteur Mitt — Suedosteuropa Mitteilungen
Suedost-Forsch — Suedost-Forschungen. Internationale Zeitschrift fuer Geschichte, Kultur, und Landeskunde Sued-Osteuropas
Suedwestdt Imker — Suedwestdeutscher Imker
Suelos Ecuat — Suelos Ecuatoriales
SuF — Sinn und Form
Suffolk Transnatl LJ — Suffolk Transnational Law Journal
Suffolk U L Rev — Suffolk University. Law Review
Suffolk Univ L Rev — Suffolk University. Law Review
Suff Trans LJ — Suffolk Transnational Law Journal
Suff U LR — Suffolk University. Law Review
SuG — Sprache und Gemeinschaft
Sugaku — Sugaku. Mathematical Society of Japan
Sugar — Sugar y Azucar
Sugarbeet Grow — Sugarbeet Grower
Sugar Beet J — Sugar Beet Journal
Sugar Bul — Sugar Bulletin
Sugar Bull — Sugar Bulletin [*United States*]
Sugarcane Breed Newsl — Sugarcane Breeders' Newsletter
Sugar Ind Abstr — Sugar Industry Abstracts
Sugar J — Sugar Journal
Sugar Mol — Sugar Molecule
Sugar Technol Rev — Sugar Technology Reviews
Sug Azuc — Sugar y Azucar
SUGMAW — Glas Srpska Akademija Nauka i Umetnosti Odeljenje Medicinskih Nauka
SUHS — Susitna Hydro Studies
SUICA — Soul Uitae Chapchi
Suicide Life Threat Behav — Suicide and Life-Threatening Behavior
Suid-Afrikaanse Tydskr Natuurwetenskap Tegnol — Suid-Afrikaanse Tydskrif vir Natuurwetenskap en Tegnologie

Suid-Afr Tydskr Geneesk — Suid-Afrikaanse Tydskrif vir Geneeskunde
Suid-Afr Tydskr Landbouwetenskap — Suid-Afrikaanse Tydskrif vir Landbouwetenskap
SUK — Sumitomo Bank Review
SUKGA — Sumitomo Kikai Giho
SUKUA — Subtropicheskie Kul'tury
SUL — Per lo Studio e l'Uso del Latino
SuL — Sprache und Literatur
Sulfuric Acid Ind — Sulfuric Acid and Industry [*Japan*]
SULI — Skrifter Utgivna av Litteraturvetenskapliga Institutionen Vid. Uppsala Universitet
Sulphur Inst J — Sulphur Institute. Journal
Su LR — Suffolk University. Law Review
SUL Rev — Southern University Law Review
Sulzer Tech Rev — Sulzer Technical Review
Sulz Tech Rev — Sulzer Technical Review
Sumatra Res B — Sumatra Research Bulletin
Sumitomo — Sumitomo Bank Review
Sumitomo Bank R — Sumitomo Bank Review
Sumitomo Bull Ind Health — Sumitomo Bulletin of Industrial Health
Sumitomo Elec Tech Rev — Sumitomo Electric Technical Review
Sumitomo Electr Rev — Sumitomo Electric Review [*Japan*]
Sumitomo Electr Tech Rev — Sumitomo Electric Technical Review
Sumitomo Light Metal Tech Rep — Sumitomo Light Metal Technical Reports
Sumitomo Light Met Tech Rep — Sumitomo Light Metal Technical Reports
Sumitomo Mach — Sumitomo Machinery [*Japan*]
Sumitomo Met — Sumitomo Metals
Sumitomo Q — Sumitomo Quarterly
Sum List — Sumarski List
Summa Phytopathol — Summa Phytopathologica
Summer Comput Simul Conf Proc — Summer Computer Simulation Conference. Proceedings
Summer Inst Part Phys Proc — Summer Institute on Particle Physics. Proceedings
Summit Mag — Summit Magazine
Summ Proc Aust Conf Nucl Tech Anal — Australian Conference on Nuclear Techniques of Analysis. Summary of Proceedings
Summ Proc West Cotton Prod Conf — Summary of Proceedings. Western Cotton Production Conference
Summ Rep Electrotech Lab — Summary Reports. Electrotechnical Laboratory [*Japan*]
Sum Proc Soil Sci Soc NC — Summary of Proceedings. Soil Science Society of North Carolina
Sum Rep Electrotech Lab (Tokyo Japan) — Summaries of Reports. Electrotechnical Laboratory (Tokyo, Japan)
Sunday M — Sunday Magazine
Sund M — Sunday Magazine
Sung Kyun Kwan Univ J — Sung Kyun Kwan University. Journal
Sung Stud Newsl — Sung Studies Newsletter
Sun M — Sun and Moon
Sunset Mag — Sunset Magazine
Sunshine State Agric Res Rep — Sunshine State Agricultural Research Report
Sunshine State Agr Res Rep — Sunshine State Agricultural Research Report. Florida University Agricultural Experiment Station
SUNT — Studien zur Umwelt des Neuen Testament [*Goettingen*]
SunT — Sunday Times
Sun Times — Sunday Times
Sun Wld — Sun World
Sun Work Br — Sun at Work in Britain
Suom Elainlaakaril — Suomen Elainlaakarilehti
Suomen Elainlaakril Fin Veterinartidskr — Suomen Elainlaakarilehti. Finsk Veterinartidskrift
Suomen Kem A B — Suomen Kemistilehti A, B
Suomen Kemistil A — Suomen Kemistilehti A
Suomen Maataloust Seura Maataloust Aikakausk — Suomen Maataloustieteellinen Seura. Maataloustieteellinen Aikakauskirj
Suomen Maataloust Seuran Julk — Suomen Maataloustieteellisen Seuran Julkaisuja
Suom Hammaslaak Toim — Suomen Hammaslaakariseuran Toimituksia
Suom Hammaslaak Toimi — Suomen Hammaslaakariseuran Toimituksia
Suom Hyonteistiet Aikak — Suomen Hyonteistieteellinen Aikakauskirja
Suom Kalatalous — Suomen Kalatalous
Suom Kemistil A — Suomen Kemistilehti A
Suom Kemistil B — Suomen Kemistilehti B
Suom Kemistiseuran Tied — Suomen Kemistiseuran Tiedonantoja
Suom Maataloustiet Seuran Julk — Suomen Maataloustieteellisen Seuran Julkaisuja
Suom Maatal Seur Julk — Suomen Maataloustieteellinen Seuran Julkaisuja
Suom Psykiatr — Suomalaista Psykiatriaa
SUP — Spisy University J. E. Purkyne
Sup Ct Rev — Supreme Court Review
Super Mgt — Supervisory Management
Supermkt Bus — Supermarket Business
Super News — Supermarket News
Superphosphat-Mitt — Superphosphat-Mitteilungen
Superv Manage — Supervisory Management

Superv Nurse — Supervisor Nurse
Supl Antropol — Suplemento Antropologico
Suppl Acta Agric Scand — Acta Agriculturae Scandinavica. Supplementum
Suppl Acta Univ Carol Biol — Supplementum. Acta Universitatis Carolinae. Biologica
Suppl Agrokem Talajt — Supplementum. Agrokemia es Talajtan
Suppl Annls Agric Fenn — Annales Agriculturae Fenniae. Supplementum
Suppl Annls Gembloux — Supplement. Annales de Gembloux
Suppl Annls Inst Pasteur (Paris) — Supplement. Annales de l'Institut Pasteur (Paris)
Suppl Certif Eng — Supplement. Certificated Engineer
Suppl Collect Sci Works Charles Univ Fac Med Hradec Kralove — Supplement to Collection of Scientific Works. Charles University Faculty of Medicine. Hradec Kralove
Suppl For Rep (Sixth) Discuss Meet (Edinb) — Supplement to Forestry. Report of the Sixth Discussion Meeting (Edinburgh)
Suppl Geophys — Supplement. Geophysics
Suppl Israel J Bot — Supplement. Israel Journal of Botany
Suppl J Phys Soc Jap — Supplement. Journal of the Physical Society of Japan
Suppl LC Subj Head — Supplement. LC [*United States Library of Congress*] Subject Headings
Suppl Nord Jordbrforsk — Nordisk Jordbrugsforskning. Supplement
Suppl Prog Theor Phys — Supplement. Progress of Theoretical Physics
Suppl Ric Biol Selvaggina — Supplemento alle Ricerche di Biologia della Selvaggina
Suppl Ric Sci — Supplemento a la Ricerca Scientifica
Suppl Sb Ved Pr Lek Fak Univ Karlovy (Hradci Kralove) — Supplementum. Sborniku Vedeckych Praci Lekarske Fakulty University Karlovy (Hradci Kralove)
Supplta Ent — Supplementa Entomologica
Sup Pop Sci Mo — Supplement. Popular Science Monthly
Supp Pr T P — Supplement. Progress of Theoretical Physics
Supr Court — Supreme Court Review
Supreme Court Rev — Supreme Court Review
Sup Stud — Superior Student
SUPUSLL — Stanford University. Publications. University Series. Languages and Literatures
Supvry Mgmt — Supervisory Management
Sur — Revista Sur
SUR — Survey of Current Affairs
SURAB — Surgery Annual
Surface Sci — Surface Science
Surface Techn — Surface Technology
Surfacing J — Surfacing Journal [*United Kingdom*]
Surfactant Sci Ser — Surfactant Science Series
Surf Coat — Surface Coatings
Surf Coat Aust — Surface Coatings Australia
Surf Colloid Sci — Surface and Colloid Science
Surf Defect Prop Solids — Surface and Defect Properties of Solids
Surf Interface Anal — Surface and Interface Analysis
Surf J — Surfacing Journal
Surf Min Reclam Symp — Surface Mining and Reclamation Symposia
Surf Sci — Surface Science
Surf Tech — Surface Technology
Surf Technol — Surface Technology
Surg Annu — Surgery Annual
Surg Bus — Surgical Business
Surg Clin N Am — Surgical Clinics of North America
Surg Clin North Am — Surgical Clinics of North America
Surg Cl NA — Surgical Clinics of North America
Surg Forum — Surgical Forum
Surg Gastroenterol — Surgical Gastroenterology
Surg Gynec and Obst — Surgery, Gynecology, and Obstetrics
Surg Gynecol Obstet — Surgery, Gynecology, and Obstetrics
Surg Gyn Ob — Surgery, Gynecology, and Obstetrics
Surgical — Surgical Business
Surg Ital — Surgery in Italy
Surg Neurol — Surgical Neurology
Surg Technol — Surgical Technologist
Surg Ther — Surgical Therapy [*Japan*]
Surinaam — Surinaamse Landbouw
Surrey Archaeol Collect — Surrey Archaeological Collections
Surrey Arch Coll — Surrey Archaeological Collections
Surtsey Res Prog Rep — Surtsey Research Progress Report
Surv Anesthesiol — Survey of Anesthesiology
Surv Biol Prog — Survey of Biological Progress
Surv Bus — Survey of Business [*United States*]
Surv Cur Bus — Survey of Current Business
Surv Curr Bus — Survey of Current Business
Surv Curr Busin — Survey of Current Business
Survey Bus (Univ Tenn) — Survey of Business (University of Tennessee)
Survey Cur Bus — Survey of Current Business
Survey Current Bus — Survey of Current Business
Survey G — Survey Graphic
Surveying Tech — Surveying Technician
Survey Progr Chem — Survey of Progress in Chemistry

Surveys Reference Works Math — Surveys and Reference Works in Mathematics
Surv High Energy Phys — Surveys in High Energy Physics [*Switzerland*]
Surv-Local Gov Technol — Surveyor-Local Government Technology
Surv & Map — Surveying and Mapping
Surv Mapp — Surveying and Mapping
Surv Munic Cty Eng — Surveyor and Municipal and County Engineer
Surv Ophthalmol — Survey of Ophthalmology
Surv Pap Horace Lamb Centre Oceanogr Res — Survey Paper. Horace Lamb Centre for Oceanographical Research. Flinders University of South Australia
Surv Prog Chem — Survey of Progress in Chemistry
SUS — Studi Urbinati di Storia, Filosofia, e Letteratura
SUS — Suesswaren. Die Fachzeitschrift der Suesswaren Industrie. Produktion, Verpackung, Verkauf
SUS — Suspense
SUS — Susquehanna University. Studies
Sus — Susreti
SUSA — Sage Urban Studies Abstracts
SUSF — Samlingar Utgivna av Svenska Fornskriftssallskapet
SUSFL — Studi Urbinati di Storia, Filosofia, e Letteratura
SUSRA — Steel in the USSR
Sussex Arch Coll — Sussex Archaeological Collections Relating to the Antiquities of the County
SuSu — Suomalainen Suomi
SuSuomi — Suomalainen Suomi
SuSuV — Suomalainen Suomi. Kulttuuripolittinen Aikakauskirja/Valvoja
SUTD — Soviet Union Today
SUUG — Sbornik Ustredniho Ustavu Geologickeho
Suvrem Med — Suvremenna Meditsina [*Bulgaria*]
Suvrem Probl Endokrinol — Suvremenni Problemi na Endokrinologiyata
SUVSL — Skrifter Utgivna. Vetenskaps-Societeten i Lund
SV — Schweizer Volkskunde
SV — Scuola e Vita
SV — Slovesna Veda
SV — Sovetskaia Vostokovedenie
SV — Suvaguq. Pond Inlet
SVABB — Schweizerische Vereinigung fuer Atomenergie. Bulletin
SVACB — Sbornik Vysoke Skoly Chemicko-Technologicke v Praze. Anorganicka Chemie a Technologie
Sv Aeroplan Ab SAAB Tech Notes — Svenska Aeroplan Aktiebolaget [*Linkoping, Sweden*]. SAAB Technical Notes
SVAPA — Svarochnoe Proizvodstvo
Svarka Vzryvom Svoistva Svarnykh Soedin — Svarka Vzryvom i Svoistva Svarnykh Soedinenii
Svar Proizvod — Svarochnoe Proizvodstvo
SVBSA — Sivilt Beredskap
SVBUA — Shock and Vibration Bulletin
SVCIA — Soviet Chemical Industry [*English Translation*]
SVD — Soviet Export. Soviet Foreign Trade Bimonthly
SvD — Svenska Dagbladet
SVDI — Serie de Vocabularios y Diccionarios Indigenas
SvEA — Svensk Exegetisk Arsbok
SVEC — Studies on Voltaire and the Eighteenth Century
Sved Zemed — Svedeniya po Zemedelieto
Sven Bot Tidskr — Svensk Botanisk Tidskrift
Sven Bryggarefoeren Manadsbl — Svenska Bryggarefoereningens Manadsblad
Sven Bryggeritidskr — Svensk Bryggeritidskrift
Sven Faerg Tek Tidskr — Svensk Faerg-Teknisk Tidskrift
Sven Farm Tidskr — Svensk Farmaceutisk Tidskrift
Sven Farm Tidskr Sci Ed — Svensk Farmaceutisk Tidskrift. Scientific Edition
Sven Forfattningssaml — Svensk Foerfattningssamling
Sven Forskningsinst Cem Betong K Tek Hoegsk Stockholm Handl — Svenska Forskningsinstitutet foer Cement och Betong vid Kungliga Tekniska Hoegskolan i Stockholm. Handlingar
Sven Forskningsinst Cem Betong K Tek Hoegsk Stockholm Medd — Svenska Forskningsinstitutet foer Cement och Betong vid Kungliga Tekniska Hoegskolan i Stockholm. Meddelanden
Sven Forskningsinst Cem Betong K Tek Hoegsk Stockholm Saertr — Svenska Forskningsinstitutet foer Cement och Betong vid Kungliga Tekniska Hoegskolan i Stockholm. Saertryck
Sven Forskningsinst Cem Betong K Tek Hoegsk Stockholm Utredn — Svenska Forskningsinstitutet foer Cement och Betong vid Kungliga Tekniska Hoegskolan i Stockholm. Utredningar
Sven Forskningsinst Cem Betong K Tek Hogsk — Svenska Forskningsinstitutet foer Cement och Betong vid Kungliga i Stockholm. Meddelanden Tekniska Hoegskolan [*Sweden*]
Sven Fotogr Tidskr — Svensk Fotografisk Tidskrift
Sven Frotidn — Svensk Froetidning
Sven Gasfoeren Manadsbl — Svenska Gasfoereningens Manadsblad
Sven Gasverksfoeren Aarsb — Svenska Gasverksfoereningens Aarsbok
Sven Hydrogr Biol Komm Skr Ny Ser Biol — Svenska Hydrografisk-Biologiska Kommissionens Skrifter. Ny Serie. Biologi
Sven Inst Konserveringsforsk Publ — Svenska Institutet foer Konserveringsforskning. Publikation
Sven Kem Tidskr — Svensk Kemisk Tidskrift

Sven Kraftverksfoeren Publ — Svenska Kraftverksfoereningens Publikationer
Sven Kraftverksfoeren Publ Medd — Svenska Kraftverksfoereningens Publikationer Meddelande
Sven Laekaresaellsk Foerh — Svenska Laekaresaellskapets Foerhandlingar
Sven Laekartidn — Svenska Laekartidningen
Sven Linne-SallskArsskr — Svenska Linne-Sallskapet Arsskrift
Sven Mejeriernas Riksfoeren Produkttek Avd Medd — Svenska Mejeriernas Riksfoerening. Produkttekniska Avdelningen. Meddelande
Sven Mejeritidn — Svenska Mejeritidningen
Sven Mosskulturfoeren Tidskr — Svenska Mosskulturfoereningens Tidskrift
Sven Naturvetensk — Svensk Naturvetenskap
Sven Papperfoeraedlingstidskr — Svensk Pappersfoeraedlingstidskrift
Sven Pappersmassetidn — Svensk Pappersmassetidning
Sven Papperstidn — Svensk Papperstidning
Svensk Bot Tidskr — Svensk Botanisk Tidskrift
Svensk Froetidn — Svensk Froetidning
Svensk Geog Arsbok — Svensk Geografisk Arsbok
Svensk Kem Tidskr — Svensk Kemisk Tidskrift
Svensk Litt — Svensk Litteraturtidskrift
Sven Skogsvardsforen Tidskr — Svenska Skogsvardsfoereningens Tidskrift
SvenskPapr — Svensk Papperstidning
Svensk Teol Kvartalskr — Svensk Teologisk Kvartalskrift
Svensk Tid — Svensk Tidskrift foer Musikforskning
Svenskt MHistoriskt — Svenskt Musikhistoriskt Arkiv. Bulletin
Svensk Travarutidn — Svensk Traevaru- och Pappersmassetidning
Svensk Vet-tidskr — Svensk Veterinaertidskrift
Svens Pap T — Svensk Papperstidning Tidskrift
Sven Tandlaek Tidskr — Svensk Tandlaekare Tidskrift
Sven Tandlakareforb Tidn — Svensk Tandlaekareforbunds Tidning [*Sweden*]
Sven Tandlak Tidskr — Svensk Tandlaekare Tidskrift
Sven Tids M — Svensk Tidskrift foer Musikforskning
Sven Traevaru-Tidn — Svensk Traevaru-Tidning
Sven Vall Mosskulturfoeren Medd — Svenska Vall- och Mosskulturfoereningens Meddelanden
Sven Vattenkraftfoeren Publ — Svenska Vattenkraftfoereningens Publikationer
Sven Veterinartidn — Svensk Veterinaertidning
Sverdlovsk Gos Ped Inst Naucn Trudy — Sverdlovskii Gosudarstvennyi Pedagogiceskii Institut. Naucnyi Trudy
Sverdlovsk Gos Ped Inst Ucen Zap — Sverdlovskii Gosudarstvennyi Pedagogiceskii Institut. Ucenye Zapiski
Sver Geol Unders Arsb — Sveriges Geologiska Undersoekning. Arsbok
Sver Geol Unders Arsb Ser C Avh Uppsatser — Sveriges Geologiska Undersoekning. Arsbok. Serie C. Avhandlingar och Uppsatser
Sver Gummitek Foren Publ — Sveriges Gummitekniska Foerening. Publicerande
Sveriges Geol Unders Ser C — Sveriges Geologiska Undersoekning. Arsbok. Serie C. Avhandlingar och Uppsatser
Sveriges Riksbank Q R — Sveriges Riksbank. Quarterly Review
Sveriges Skogsvforb Tidskr — Sveriges Skogsvardsfoerbunds Tidskrift
Sveriges Utsaedesfoer Tidskr — Sveriges Utsaedesfoerenings Tidskrift
Sver Mekanforb Mekanresult — Sveriges Mekanforbund, Mekanresultat
Sver Nat — Sveriges Natur
Sver Nat Arsb — Sveriges Natur Arsbok
Sver Off Stat Bergshantering — Sveriges Officiella Statistik Bergshantering. Statistika Centralbyran [*Stockholm*]
Sver Pomol Foeren Arsskr — Sveriges Pomologiska Foerening Arsskrift
Sver Skogsvardsfoerbunds Tidskr — Sveriges Skogsvardsfoerbunds Tidskrift
Sver Skogsvardsforb Tidskr — Sveriges Skogsvardsfoerbunds Tidskrift
Svertyvayushchaya Sist Krovi Akush Ginekol — Svertyvayushchaya Sistema Krovi v Akusherstve i Ginekologii
Sver Utsadesforen Tidskr — Sveriges Utsaedesfoerenings Tidskrift
Sver Utsadesforen Tidskr — Sveriges Utsaedesfoerenings Tidskrift
Svetotekh — Svetotekhnika
Svetotekhnika Svetotekh Kom Akad Nauk SSSR — Svetotekhnika. Svetotekhnicheskaya Komissiya Akademii Nauk SSSR
Svetsaren Dtsch Ausg — Svetsaren. Deutsche Ausgabe
Svetsaren Ed Fr — Svetsaren. Edition Francaise
Svetsaren Weld Rev — Svetsaren: A Welding Review
SvExAb — Svensk Exegetisk Arsbok
SvExArsb — Svensk Exegetisk Arsbok
Sv Farm Tid — Svensk Farmaceutisk Tidskrift
SVF Fachorgan Textilveredl — SVF [*Svetstekniska Foereningen*] Fachorgan fuer Textilveredlung
SVG — Gids voor Personeelsbeleid. Arbeidsvraagstukken en Sociale Verzekering
SVGLA — Sovetskaya Geologiya
SVGU — Sveriges Geologiska Undersoekning
SVI — Sveriges Riksbank. Quarterly Review
SvI — Svizzera Italiana
Svinovod — Svinovodstvo
SVJ — Sovetska Veda. Jazykoveda
SvJerTs — Svenska Jerusalems-Foereningens Tidskrift [*Uppsala*]
Sv Kraftverksfoeren Publ — Svenska Kraftverksfoereningens Publikationer
SVKTA — Strassenverkehrstechnik
SVL — Studien zur Vergleichenden Literaturgeschichte
SVLAA — Svenska Laekartidningen

SVLKAO — Collection of Scientific Works. Faculty of Medicine. Charles University (Hradec Kralove)

SvLm — Svenska Landsmal och Svenskt Folkliv

SvM — Svensk Missionstidskrift

SVNAB — Svensk Naturvetenskap

Svoista Veshchestv Str Mol — Svoistva Veshchestv i Stroenie Molekul

Svojstva At Yader — Svojstva Atomnykh Yader

SVPIA — Surface and Vacuum Physics Index

SVPVA — Sbornik Vedeckych Praci. Vysoka Skola Chemickotechnologicka (Pardubice)

SVRDA — Soviet Radiochemistry [English Translation]

SVS — Saga-Book. Viking Society for Northern Research

SVS — Statistica Neerlandica

SVSHA — Sovetskii Shakhtior

SVSHKG — Schriften. Verein fuer Schleswig-Holsteinische Kirchengeschichte

SVSL — Skrifter Utgivna. Vetenskaps-Societeten i Lund

S V Sound Vib — S V. Sound and Vibration

SVSPO — Sbornik Vysoke Skoly Pedagogicke v Olomouci

SVSPO(JL) — Sbornik Vysoke Skoly Pedagogicke v Olomouci. Jazyka a Literatura

SVSPP — Sbornik Vysoke Skoly Pedagogicke v Praze. Jazyka a Literatura

SVSThR — Sammlung Gemeinverstaendlicher Vortraege und Schriften aus dem Gebiet der Theologie und der Religionsgeschichte

SVT — Supplements. Vetus Testamentum [Leiden]

SvT — Svenska Texter

SvTK — Svensk Teologisk Kvartalskrift

SvTKv — Svensk Teologisk Kvartalskrift

SVTP — Studia in Veteris Testamenti Pseudepigrapha

SVTQ — St. Vladimir's Theological Quarterly

Sv Trav Pap — Svensk Traevaru- och Pappersmassetidning

SvTs — Svensk Tidskrift

SVUOJ — Sri Venkateswara University. Oriental Journal

SW — Science Wonder Stories

SW — Slavic Word

SW — Socialist Worker

SW — South and West

S & W — South and West

SW — Southwestern Musician - Texas Music Educator

SWA — Sitzungsberichte. Wiener Akademie

SwAL — Southwestern American Literature

SWANS — State Wildlife Advisory News Service

Swansea Coll Fac Ed J — University College of Swansea. Collegiate Faculty of Education. Journal

Swarajya A — Swarajya. Annual Number [Madras]

SWAW — Sitzungsberichte. Wiener Akademie der Wissenschaften

Swaziland Annu Rep Geol Surv Mines Dep — Swaziland. Annual Report. Geological Survey and Mines Department

Swaziland Geol Surv Mines Dep Annu Rep — Swaziland. Geological Survey and Mines Department. Annual Report

SWB — Stichting Weg. Bulletin

SWBAA — Schweizerische Bauzeitung

SWBRD — Sun at Work in Britain

SWC — Social Work and Christianity

Swed Dent J — Swedish Dental Journal

Swed Dent J (Suppl) — Swedish Dental Journal (Supplement)

Swed Foersvarets Forskningsanst FOA Rep — Sweden. Foersvarets Forskningsanstalt. FOA Report

Swed Geol Unders Ser Ae Geol Kartbl 1:50000 — Sweden. Geologiska Undersoekning. Serie Ae. Geologiska Kartblad i Skala 1:50,000

Swed Geol Unders Ser C — Sweden. Geologiska Undersoekning. Serie C

Swed Geol Unders Ser Ca Avh Uppsatser — Sweden. Geologiska Undersoekning. Serie Ca. Avhandlingar och Uppsatser

Swed Geotech Inst Proc — Swedish Geotechnical Institute. Proceedings

Swed Geotech Inst Rep — Swedish Geotechnical Institute. Report

Swed Inst Agric Eng Circ — Swedish Institute of Agricultural Engineering. Circular

Swedish Aust & Swedish NZ Trade J — Swedish-Australian and Swedish-New Zealand Trade Journal

Swedish Deep-Sea Expedition Repts — Swedish Deep-Sea Expedition. Reports

Swedish Econ — Swedish Economy

Swedish Hist Soc Yearbook — Swedish Historical Society. Yearbook

Swedish J Econ — Swedish Journal of Economics

Swed J Agric Res — Swedish Journal of Agricultural Research

Swed J Econ — Swedish Journal of Economics

Swed Pap J — Swedish Paper Journal

Swed State Shipbuild Exp Tank Report — Swedish State Shipbuilding Experiment Tank. Report

Swed Weed Conf Rep — Swedish Weed Conference. Reports

SWEHO — Scandinavian Journal of Work Environment and Health

SWEIA — Studies in Wind Engineering and Industrial Aerodynamics [Elsevier Book Series]

SWF — Southwest Folklore

SWGH — Schriften. Strassburger Wissenschaftliche Gesellschaft in Heidelberg

SWH — Sociale Wetenschappen

SWHC — Social Work in Health Care

SW Hist Q — Southwestern Historical Quarterly

SWHQ — Southwestern Historical Quarterly

SWI — Service World International

Swimm Tech — Swimming Technique

Swimm World Jun Swimm — Swimming World and Junior Swimmer

Swine Day Univ Calif — Swine Day. University of California

Swine Rep Univ Hawaii Coop Ext Serv — Swine Report. University of Hawaii. Cooperative Extension Service

Swiss Credit Bank Bul — Swiss Credit Banking Bulletin

Swiss J Hydrol — Swiss Journal of Hydrology

Swiss News — Swiss Economic News

Swiss R Wld Aff — Swiss Review of World Affairs

SW J Anthrop — Southwestern Journal of Anthropology

SW J Phil — Southwestern Journal of Philosophy

Sw J T — Southwestern Journal of Theology

SW J Th — Southwestern Journal of Theology

SW Law J — Southwestern Law Journal

Sw Legal Found Inst on Oil and Gas L and Tax — Southwestern Legal Foundation. Institution on Oil and Gas Law and Taxation [United States]

SW L J — Southwestern Law Journal

SWMCA — Schweizer Maschinenmarkt

SWMGA — Solid Wastes Management

SW Musician — Southwestern Musician

SWNAA — Southwestern Naturalist [United States]

SWNS — Sprawozdanie z Prac Naukowych Wydzialu Nauk Spolecznych Pan

SW Pacific — South West Pacific

SW Phil Stud — Southwest Philosophical Studies [United States]

SWPR — Swedish Polar Research

SwR — Sewanee Review

SWR — Southwest Review

SWRA — Social Work Research and Abstracts

SWS — Southwest Writers Series

SWS — Southwestern Studies [University of Texas, El Paso]

SWSJ — Son of WSFA Journal

SW Social Sci Q — Southwestern Social Science Quarterly

SW St (UTEP) — Southwestern Studies (University of Texas, El Paso)

SWTED — Solar Waerme Technik

SWTN — Sprawozdania Wroclawskiego Towarzystwa Naukowego

Sw U LR — Southwestern University. Law Review

Sw U L Rev — Southwestern University. Law Review

SWW — Hotels and Restaurants International

SWWG — Social Work with Groups

SWY — Swedish Economy

SWZBA — Schweizer Buch

SXD — Notes et Etudes Documentaires

SXI — Singapore Business

SXSKA — Sakura X-Rei Shashin Kenkyu

SXX — Secolul XX

SY — Symposium

SY — Synthesis

Sy — Syria. Revue d'Art Oriental et d'Archeologie

SyBU — Symbolae Biblicae Upsalienses

Syd Jaycee — Sydney Jaycee

Syd Jewish News — Sydney Jewish News

Syd Law R — Sydney Law Review

Syd LR — Sydney Law Review

Syd L Rev — Sydney Law Review

Syd Morning Her — Sydney Morning Herald

Syd Morning Herald — Sydney Morning Herald

Sydney GCN — Sydney Gay Community News

Sydney Law R — Sydney Law Review

Sydney Law Rev — Sydney Law Review

Sydney L Rev — Sydney Law Review

Sydney Q Mag — Sydney Quarterly Magazine

Sydney Univ Med J — Sydney University. Medical Journal

Sydney Univ Sch Civ Eng Res Rep — Sydney University. School of Civil Engineering. Research Report

Sydney Water Bd J — Sydney Water Board. Journal

Sydowia Ann Mycol — Sydowia. Annales Mycologici

Sydowia Ann Mycolog Beih — Sydowia. Annales Mycologici. Beihefte

Syd Stud — Sydney Studies in English

Sydsven Medicinhist — Sydsvenska Medicinhistoriska Saellskapets Arsskrift

Sydsvenska Ortnamns-Sallsk Arsskr — Sydsvenska Ortnamns-Saellskapets Arsskrift

Syd Univ Ag Economics Res Bul — University of Sydney. Department of Agricultural Economics. Research Bulletin

Syd Univ Civ Engng Schl Res Rep — University of Sydney. School of Civil Engineering. Research Report

Syd Univ Dep Agric Econ Mimeo Rep — University of Sydney. Department of Agricultural Economics. Mimeographed Report

Syd Univ Gaz — Sydney University. Gazette

Syd Univ Med J — Sydney University. Medical Journal

Syd Univ Post Grad Comm Med Bul — University of Sydney. Postgraduate Committee in Medicine. Bulletin

Syd Univ Post Grad Comm Med Oration — University of Sydney. Postgraduate Committee in Medicine. Annual Postgraduate Oration
Syd Univ Sch Agric Rep — University of Sydney. School of Agriculture. Report
Syd Wat Bd J — Sydney Water Board. Journal
Syd Water Bd J — Sydney Water Board. Journal
Syd Water Board J — Sydney Water Board. Journal
SYES — Syesis
Sy J Int L — Syracuse Journal of International Law and Commerce
Syl — Syllogos. Journal de la Societe Philologique Grecque de Constantinople
SYLL — Syllogeus
Sy LR — Syracuse Law Review
Sylvatrop Philipp For Res J — Sylvatrop. The Philippine Forest Research Journal
Sym — Symposium
SYMBA — Symbioses
SymbOsl — Symbolae Osloenses
Symb Oslo — Symbolae Osloenses
SYMCA — Symposium (International) on Combustion. Proceedings
SYMED — Synthetic Metals
Sym Mag — Symphony Magazine
Sym News — Symphony News
SYMPA — Symposia on Theoretical Physics and Mathematics
Symp Abnorm Subsurf Pressure Proc — Symposium on Abnormal Subsurface Pressure. Proceedings
Symp Angiol Sanitoriana — Symposia Angiologica Sanitoriana
Symp Biol Hung — Symposia Biologica Hungarica
Symp Br Soc Parasitol — Symposia. British Society for Parasitology
Symp Cell Biol — Symposia for Cell Biology [*Japan*]
Symp Chem Nat Prod Symp Pap — Symposium on the Chemistry of Natural Products. Symposium Papers
Symp Coal Manag Tech Pap — Symposium on Coal Management Techniques. Papers
Symp Coal Mine Drain Res Pap — Symposium on Coal Mine Drainage Research. Papers
Symp Coal Prep Pap — Symposium on Coal Preparation. Papers
Symp Coal Util Pap — Symposium on Coal Utilization. Papers
Symp Ecol Res Humid Trop Vegtn — Symposium on Ecological Research in Humid Tropics Vegetation
Symp Eng Geol Soils Eng Proc — Symposium on Engineering Geology and Soils Engineering. Proceedings
Symp Faraday Soc — Symposia. Faraday Society
Symp Foods — Symposium of Foods
Symp Freq Control Proc — Symposium on Frequency Control. Proceedings
Symp Fundam Cancer Res Collect Pap — Symposium on Fundamental Cancer Research. Collections of Papers
Symp Genet Biol Ital — Symposia Genetica et Biologica Italica
Symp Genet Breed Wheat Proc — Symposium on Genetics and Breeding of Wheat. Proceedings
Symp (Int) Combust Proc — Symposium (International) on Combustion. Proceedings
Symp Int Soc Cell Biol — Symposia. International Society for Cell Biology
Symp Int Union Biol Sci Proc — Symposium. International Union of Biological Sciences. Proceedings
Symp Maize Prod Southeast Asia — Symposium on Maize Production in Southeast Asia
Symp Med Hoechst — Symposia Medica Hoechst
Symp Microb Drug Resist — Symposium on Microbial Drug Resistance
Symp Mine Prep Plant Refuse Disposal Pap — Symposium on Mine and Preparation Plant Refuse Disposal. Papers
Symp Moessbauer Eff Methodol Proc — Symposium on Moessbauer Effect Methodology. Proceedings
Symp Natl Phys Lab (UK) — Symposium. National Physical Laboratory (United Kingdom)
Symp Ocul Ther — Symposium on Ocular Therapy
Symp Oral Sens Percept — Symposium on Oral Sensation and Perception
Symposium — Symposium: A Quarterly Journal in Modern Foreign Literatures
Sympos Math — Symposia Mathematica
Sympos Univ Upsaliensis Annum Quingentesimum Celebrantis — Symposia Universitatis Upsaliensis Annum Quingentesimum Celebrantis
Symp Pap Symp Chem Nat Prod — Symposium Papers. Symposium on the Chemistry of Natural Products
Symp Particleboard Proc — Symposium on Particleboard. Proceedings
Symp Pharmacol Ther Toxicol Group — Symposium. Pharmacology, Therapeutics, and Toxicology Group. International Association for Dental Research
Symp Regul Enzyme Act Synth Norm Neoplast Tissues Proc — Symposium on Regulation of Enzyme Activity and Syntheses in Normal and Neoplastic Tissues. Proceedings
Symp R Entomol Soc Lond — Symposia. Royal Entomological Society of London
Symp R Entomol Soc London — Symposia. Royal Entomological Society of London
Symp Ser Australas Inst Min Metall — Australasian Institute of Mining and Metallurgy. Symposia Series

Symp Ser Immunobiol Stand — Symposia Series in Immunobiological Standardization
Symp Ser Inst Fuel (London) — Symposium Series. Institute of Fuel (London)
Symp Soc Dev Biol — Symposia. Society for Developmental Biology
Symp Soc Exp Biol — Symposia. Society for Experimental Biology
Symp Soc Gen Microbiol — Symposium. Society for General Microbiology
Symp Soc Study Dev Growth — Symposium. Society for the Study of Development and Growth
Symp Soc Study Hum Biol — Symposia. Society for the Study of Human Biology
Symp Soc Study Inborn Errors Metab — Symposium. Society for the Study of Inborn Errors of Metabolism
Symp Surf Min Reclam Pap — Symposium on Surface Mining and Reclamation. Papers
Symp Swed Nutr Found — Symposia. Swedish Nutrition Foundation
Symp Theor Phys Math — Symposia on Theoretical Physics and Mathematics [*United States*]
Symp Turbul Liq Proc — Symposium on Turbulence in Liquids. Proceedings
Symp Underground Min Pap — Symposium on Underground Mining. Papers
Symp Zool Soc Lond — Symposia. Zoological Society of London
Syn — Syntheses
Syn Commun — Synthetic Communications
SYNED — Synerjy
SYNG — Synergy. Syncrude Canada
Syn Hist L — Synthese Historical Library
Syn Inorg Met-Org Chem — Synthesis in Inorganic and Metal-Organic Chemistry [*Later, Synthesis and Reactivity in Inorganic and Metalorganic Chemistry*]
Synopsis R — Synopsis Revue
Syn Reac In — Synthesis and Reactivity in Inorganic and Metalorganic Chemistry
Syn Reactiv Inorg Metal Org C — Synthesis and Reactivity in Inorganic and Metalorganic Chemistry
Synth Commun — Synthetic Communications
Synth Fuels — Synthetic Fuels
Synth Fuels Update — Synthetic Fuels Update
Synth Libr — Synthese Library
Synth Met — Synthetic Metals [*Switzerland*]
Synth Methods Org Chem Yearb — Synthetic Methods of Organic Chemistry Yearbook
Synth Pipeline Gas Symp Proc — Synthetic Pipeline Gas Symposium. Proceedings
Synth React Inorg Metorg Chem — Synthesis and Reactivity in Inorganic and Metalorganic Chemistry
Synth Rubber — Synthetic Rubber
Synth Rubber Ind (Lanzhou People's Repub China) — Synthetic Rubber Industry (Lanzhou, People's Republic of China)
Syr — Syria. Revue d'Art Oriental et d'Archeologie
Syrac Law R — Syracuse Law Review
Syracuse Int'l L & Com — Syracuse Journal of International Law and Commerce
Syracuse L Rev — Syracuse Law Review
Syrian J Stomatol — Syrian Journal of Stomatology
Syr J Int'l L & Com — Syracuse Journal of International Law and Commerce
Sys Proced — Systems and Procedures
Sys and Soft — Systems and Software
Syst — Systems
Syst Assoc Publ — Systematics Association. Publication
Syst Assoc Spec Vol — Systematics Association. Special Volume
Syst Ass Spec Vol — Systematics Association. Special Volume
Syst Bot — Systematic Botany
Syst-Comput-Controls — Systems-Computers-Controls
Syst & Control — Systems and Control
Syst and Control Lett — Systems and Control Letters
Systematics Assoc Pub — Systematics Association. Publication
Systems & Proc J — Systems and Procedures Journal
Systems Sci — Systems Science
Syst Entomol — Systematic Entomology
Syst Int — Systems International
Syst Logiques — Systemes Logiques
Syst Objectives Solutions — Systems, Objectives, Solutions
Syst Sci — Systems Science
Syst Technol — Systems Technology
Syst Theory Res — Systems Theory Research
Syst Zool — Systematic Zoology
Syvrem Med — Syvremenna Meditsina
SZ — Schweizerische Zeitschrift fuer Volkswirtschaft und Statistik
SZ — Sekspirovskij Zbornik
SZ — Shigaku Zasshi
SZ — Sovremennye Zapiski
SZ — Stimmen der Zeit
Szakszerv Szle — Szakszervezeti Szemle
Szamki Koezlem — Szamki Kozlemenyek
SZC — Studia Zrodloznawcze. Commentationes
SZCSAV — Annual Review of the Schizophrenic Syndrome
SZDKA — Sovetskoe Zdravookhranenie Kirgizii

SzDL — Studien zur Deutschen Literatur
SzEP — Studien zur Englischen Philologie
SZG — Schweizerische Zeitschrift fuer Geschichte
SZHYA — Schweizerische Zeitschrift fuer Hydrologie
Szigma Mat-Koezgazdasagi Folyoirat — Szigma. Matematikai-Koezgazdasagi
    Folyoirat
Szk Gl Gospod Wiejsk Akad Roln Warszawie Zesz Nauk Ogrod — Szkola
    Glowna Gospodarstwa Wiejskiego - Akademia Rolnicza w Warszawie.
    Zeszyty Naukowe. Ogrodnictwo
Szk Gl Gospod Wiejsk Akad Roln Warszawie Zesz Nauk Roln — Szkola
    Glowna Gospodarstwa Wiejskiego - Akademia Rolnicza w Warszawie.
    Zeszyty Naukowe. Rolnictwo
Szk Gl Gospod Wiejsk Akad Roln Warszawie Zesz Nauk Zootech — Szkola
    Glowna Gospodarstwa Wiejskiego - Akademia Rolnicza w Warszawie.
    Zeszyty Naukowe. Zootechnika
Szk Gl Gospod Wiejsk Akd Roln Warszawie Zesz Nauk Weter — Szkola
    Glowna Gospodarstwa Wiejskiego - Akademia Rolnicza w Warszawie.
    Zeszyty Naukowe. Weterynaria
SZKKB — Shimizu Kensetsu Kenkyusho-Ho
Szklo Ceram — Szklo i Ceramika
SzL — Schriften zur Literatur
SZL — Spielzeug. Internationales Fachblatt fuer Spielmittel, Hobby- und
    Modellbau-Artikel, Christbaumschmuck, Fest- und Scherzartikel,
    Rohstoffe, Halbteile, Werkzeuge, Maschinen, und Verpackung
SZLGD — Sozialgerichtsbarkeit
SzNU — Sbornik za Narodni Umotvorenija
Szolesz Boraszat — Szoleszet es Boraszat
SZPAA — Schweizerische Zeitschrift fuer Psychologie und Ihre Anwendungen
SZPMA — Sozial- und Praeventivmedizin
SzT — Schriften zur Theaterwissenschaft
SZTZA — Schweizerische Technische Zeitschrift [*Switzerland*]

T

T — Teatar [*Sofia*]
T — Teatr
T — Teuthonista
T — Texana
T — Time
T — Traditio
T — Turin
TA — Theatre Annual
TA — Traduction Automatique
TA — Trierisches Archiv
TAAGA — Transactions. American Association of Genito-Urinary Surgeons
TAAOA — Transactions. American Academy of Ophthalmology and Oto-Laryngology
TAAPA — Transactions. Association of American Physicians
TAB — Tabaktueel Magazine
TableR — La Table Ronde [*Paris*]
TabR — La Table Ronde [*Paris*]
Tabulae Biol — Tabulae Biologicae
TAC — [*The*] Alien Critic
TACC — [*The*] Australian Comic Collector
TAD — [*The*] Armchair Detective
T Ad — Tax Advisor
TAD — Turk Arkeoloji Dergisi [*Ankara*]
TAD J — Technical Aid to the Disabled Journal
Tadzik Gos Univ Trudy Meh-Mat Fak — Tadzikskii Gosudarstvennyi Universitet Imeni V. I. Lenina. Trudy Mehaniko-Matematiceskogo Fakulteta
Tadzik Gos Univ Ucen Zap — Tadzikskii Gosudarstvennyi Universitet Imeni V. I. Lenina. Ucenye Zapiski. Trudy Fiziko-Matematiceskogo Fakulteta. Serija Matematiceskaja
Tadzik S-h Inst Trudy — Tadzikskii Sel'skohozjaistvennyi Institut i Tadzikskii Gosudarstvennyi Universitet. Trudy
TAeB — Tuebinger Aegyptologische Beitraege
TAEDA Newsl — TAEDA [*Technology Assessment of Energy Development in Appalachia*] Newsletter [*United States*]
TAFEQ — TAFE [*New South Wales Department of Technical and Further Education*] Quarterly
TAFSA — Transactions. American Fisheries Society
TAFSD — Technical Report. AFWAL-TR. United States Air Force Wright Aeronautical Laboratories
Tag — Tagoro
TAG — Tijdschrift Aardrijkskundig Genootschap
Tagber Dt Akad Landw-Wiss Berl — Tagungsberichte. Deutsche Akademie der Landwirtschaftswissenschaften zu Berlin
TAGLA — Tropical Agriculture
Tag Muellerei-Technol Ber — Tagung ueber die Muellerei-Technologie. Bericht
TAGUA — Transactions. American Geophysical Union
Tagungsber Akad Landwirtschaftswiss Dtsch Demokr Repub — Tagungsbericht. Akademie der Landwirtschaftswissenschaften der Deutschen Demokratischen Republik
Tagungsber Deut Akad Landwirt Wiss Berlin — Tagungsberichte. Deutsche Akademie der Landwirtschaftswissenschaften zu Berlin
Tagungsber Ges Inn Med DDR — Tagungsbericht. Gesellschaft fuer Innere Medizin der DDR

TAH — [*The*] American Hispanist
TAHCD — Taehan Ankwa Hakhoe Chapchi
TAI — T. A. Informations [*Formerly, Traduction Automatique*]
TAI — Tax Management International Journal
TAik — Teologinen Aikakauskirja. Teologisk Tidskrift [*Helsinki*]
Taikomoji Branduoline Fiz — Taikomoji Branduoline Fizika
TA Inf — Traduction Automatique Informations
Tait — Tait's Edinburgh Magazine
Taiwan Agric Bimon — Taiwan Agriculture Bimonthly
Taiwan Agr Res J — Taiwan Agricultural Research Journal
Taiwan Environ Sanit — Taiwan Environmental Sanitation
Taiwan Fish Res Inst Fish Cult Rep — Taiwan. Fisheries Research Institute. Fish Culture. Report
Taiwan Fish Res Inst Lab Biol Rep — Taiwan. Fisheries Research Institute. Laboratory of Biology. Report
Taiwan Fish Res Inst Lab Fish Biol Rep — Taiwan. Fisheries Research Institute. Laboratory of Fishery Biology. Report
Taiwan J Th — Taiwan Journal of Theology
Taiwan J Vet Med Anim Husb — Taiwan Journal of Veterinary Medicine and Animal Husbandry
Taiwan Sugar Exp Stn Annu Rep — Taiwan. Sugar Experiment Station. Annual Report
Taiwan Sugar Exp Stn Res Rep — Taiwan. Sugar Experiment Station. Research Report
Taiwan Sugar Res Inst Annu Rep — Taiwan. Sugar Research Institute. Annual Report
Taiwan Trade Mo — Taiwan Trade Monthly
Taiw Ind — Taiwan Industrial Panorama
Taiw Svy — Monthly Economic Survey. Taiwan
TAK — Tonan Ajia Kenkyu [*Southeast Asia Studies*]
TAKAAN — Japanese Journal of Physical Fitness and Sports Medicine
TAKC — Taking Care. Newsletter of the Center for Consumer Health Education
TAKEAZ — Japanese Journal of Physical Education
Takenaka Tech Res Rep — Takenaka Technical Research Report
TAL — Taiwan Industrial Panorama
Tal — Taliesin [*England*]
Tal — Talisman
TAL — Taxation for Lawyers
TALIA — Transactions. Association of Life Insurance Medical Directors of America
Tallin Polueteh Inst Toim — Tallinna Poluetehnilise Instituudi Toimetised
Tall Timbers Res Stn Misc Publ — Tall Timbers Research Station. Miscellaneous Publication
TAm — [*The*] Americas: A Quarterly Review of Inter-American Cultural History
TaM — Tarybine Mokykla
TAM — Taxes. The Tax Magazine
TAM — Theatre Arts Magazine
TAM — Theatre Arts Monthly
Tamarack R — Tamarack Review
TamC — Tamil Culture
T Am Fish S — Transactions. American Fisheries Society
T Am Geophy — Transactions. American Geophysical Union
Tamil Nadu J Coop — Tamil Nadu Journal of Co-operation

Tamkang J Math — Tamkang Journal of Mathematics [*Taipei*]
Tamkang R — Tamkang Review
Tamkang Rev — Tamkang Review
TamkR — Tamkang Review
T Am Math S — Transactions. American Mathematical Society
T Am Micros — Transactions. American Microscopical Society
T Am Nucl S — Transactions. American Nuclear Society
TAMPD — TAPPI [*Technical Association of the Pulp and Paper Industry*] Annual Meeting. Proceedings [*United States*]
T Am Phil S — Transactions. American Philosophical Society
TamR — Tamarack Review [*Toronto*]
TAMSA — Transactions. American Microscopical Society
T Am S Art — Transactions. American Society for Artificial Internal Organs
TAMSJ — TAMS [*Token and Medal Society*] Journal
Tamsui Oxford Coll Lecture Notes Ser — Tamsui Oxford College. Lecture Notes Series
TAMTA — Transactions. American Mathematical Society
TANAA — Transactions. American Neurological Association
T Anc Monum — Ancient Monuments Society. Transactions
Tank Bulk Marit Manage — Tanker and Bulker Maritime Management [*England*]
Tanker Bulk Carr — Tanker and Bulk Carrier
Tanker Bulker Int — Tanker and Bulker International [*England*]
Tan Lect HV — Tanner Lectures on Human Values
TANN — Taqrimiut Nipingat News [*Salluit, Quebec*]
TANSA — Transactions. American Nuclear Society
Tanulmanyok Magy Tud Akad Szamitastech es Autom Kut Intez — Tanulmanyok Magyar Tudomanyos Akademia Szamitastechnikai es Automatizalasi Kutato Intezet
Tanulmanyok MTA Szamitastechn Automat Kutato Int (Budapest) — Tanulmanyok. MTA [*Magyar Tudomanyos Akademia*] Szamitastechnikai es Automatizalasi Kutato Intezet (Budapest)
Tanzania Miner Resour Power Annu Rep Geol Surv Div — Tanzania. Ministry of Industries. Mineral Resources and Power. Annual Report of the Geological Survey Division
Tanzania Rec Geol Surv Tanganyika — Tanzania. Records of the Geological Survey of Tanganyika
Tanzania Silvic Res Note — Tanzania Silviculture Research Note
Tanzania Silvic Res Stn Tech Note (New Ser) — Tanzania. Silviculture Research Station. Technical Note (New Series)
TAP — Tabaksplant. Maandblad voor de Sigaren, Sigaretten, en Tabakshandel en Industrie
TAPA — Transactions and Proceedings. American Philological Association
Tap Chi Toan Hoc — Tap Chi Toan Hoc. Progress of Mathematical Sciences
TAPhA — Transactions and Proceedings. American Philological Association
TAPPI Alkaline Pulping Conf Prepr — TAPPI [*Technical Association of the Pulp and Paper Industry*] Alkaline Pulping Conference Preprint
TAPPI Annu Meet Prepr — TAPPI [*Technical Association of the Pulp and Paper Industry*] Annual Meeting. Preprint
TAPPI Annu Meet Proc — TAPPI [*Technical Association of the Pulp and Paper Industry*] Annual Meeting. Proceedings
TAPPI Bibl — TAPPI [*Technical Association of the Pulp and Paper Industry*] Bibliography of Pulp and Paper Manufacture
TAPPI Coat Conf Prepr — TAPPI [*Technical Association of the Pulp and Paper Industry*] Coating Conference. Preprint
TAPPI Environ Conf Proc — TAPPI [*Technical Association of the Pulp and Paper Industry*] Environmental Conference. Proceedings
TAPPI For Biol Wood Chem Conf Conf Pap — TAPPI [*Technical Association of the Pulp and Paper Industry*] Forest Biology - Wood Chemistry Conference. Conference Papers
TAPPI J Tech Assoc Pulp Paper Ind — TAPPI. Journal of the Technical Association of the Pulp and Paper Industry
TAPPI Monogr Ser — TAPPI [*Technical Association of the Pulp and Paper Industry*] Monograph Series
TAPPI Papermakers Conf Pap — TAPPI [*Technical Association of the Pulp and Paper Industry*] Papermakers Conference. Papers
TAPPI Papermakers Conf Proc — TAPPI [*Technical Association of the Pulp and Paper Industry*] Papermakers Conference. Proceedings
TAPPI Special Rept — TAPPI [*Technical Association of the Pulp and Paper Industry*] Special Reports
TAPPI Spec Tech Assoc Publ — TAPPI [*Technical Association of the Pulp and Paper Industry*] Special Technical Association. Publication
TAPS — Transactions. American Philosophical Society
TAQK — Taqralik
TAQO — Tawow. Canadian Indian Cultural Magazine
TAR — Tara. Schweizerische Fachzeitschrift fuer Moderne Verpackung
TAr — Theater Arts
Tar Bak Orm Gen Mud Yay — Tarim Bakanligi. Orman Genel Mudurlugu Yayinlarindan
Tarl — Tarleton Term Reports
Tarl Term R — Tarleton Term Reports
Tarsad Szle — Tarsadalmi Szemle
Tarsadtud Kozl — Tarsadalomtudomanyi Kozlemenyek
TARSD — Tropical Agriculture Research Series
TArts — Theater Arts
Tartu Riikl Ul Toimetised — Tartu Riikliku Uelikooli Toimetised

TARU Research Note — New South Wales. Traffic Accident Research Unit. TARU Research Note
TASA — Teaching Atypical Students in Alberta
T ASAE — Transactions. ASAE [*American Society of Agricultural Engineers*]
Tas Arch — Tasmanian Architect
Tas Architect — Tasmanian Architect
TASB — Texas Archaeological Society. Bulletin
Tas Bldg App R — Tasmanian Building Appeal Reports
Tas Dep Agric Bull — Bulletin. Department of Agriculture (Tasmania)
Tas Div Bul — Institution of Engineers of Australia. Tasmania Division. Bulletin
Tas Ed — Tasmanian Education
Tas Ed Gaz — Tasmanian Education Gazette
Tas Ed Rec — Educational Record. Tasmania Education Department
Tas Educ — Tasmanian Education
Tas Fish — Tasmanian Fisheries Research
Tas Fruitgrower and Farmer — Tasmanian Fruitgrower and Farmer
Tas Geol Surv Geol Atlas 1 Mile Ser — Tasmanian Geological Survey. Geological Atlas. 1 Mile Series
Tas Govt Gaz — Tasmanian Government Gazette
Tas Hist Research Assoc Papers & Proc — Tasmanian Historical Research Association. Papers and Proceedings
Tas Hotel R — Tasmanian Hotel Review
Tas Ind — Tasmanian Industry
TASJ — Transactions. Asiatic Society of Japan
Tas J Ag — Tasmanian Journal of Agriculture
Tas J Agric — Tasmanian Journal of Agriculture
Tas J Ed — Tasmanian Journal of Education
Taskent Gos Ped Inst Ucen Zap — Taskentskii Gosudarstvennyi Pedagogiceskii Institut Imeni Nizami Ucenye Zapiski
Taskent Gos Univ Buharsk Ped Inst Naucn Trudy — Taskentskii Gosudarstvennyi Universitet Buharskii Pedagogiceskii Institut Naucnye Trudy
Taskent Gos Univ Naucn Trudy — Taskentskii Gosudarstvennyi Universitet Imeni V. I. Lenina Naucnye Trudy
Taskent Gos Univ Sb Naucn Trudov — Taskentskii Gosudarstvennyi Universitet Sbornik Naucnyh Trudov
Taskent Inst Inz Zeleznodoroz Transporta Trudy — Taskentskii Institut Inzenerov Zeleznodoroznogo Transporta Trudy
Taskent Inst Narod Hoz Naucn Zap — Taskentskii Institut Narodnogo Hozjaistva Naucnye Zapiski
Taskent Inst Narod Hoz Naucn Zap Mat v Prilozen — Taskentskii Institut Narodnogo Hozjaistva Naucnye Zapiski. Matematika v Prilozenijah
Taskent Politehn Inst Naucn Trudy — Taskentskii Politehniceskii Institut Naucnye Trudy. Novaja Serija
Taskent Politehn Inst Naucn Trudy NS — Taskentskii Politehniceskii Institut Naucnye Trudy. Novaja Serija
Tas Lab & Ind Bul — Tasmania. Department of Labour and Industry. Bulletin
Tas LR — Tasmanian Law Reports
Tas L Rev — University of Tasmania. Law Review
Tasm — Tasmanian State Reports
Tasmania Build J — Tasmanian Building Journal
Tasmania Dep Agric Annu Rep — Tasmania. Department of Agriculture. Annual Report
Tasmania Dep Mines Geol Atlas 1:250000 Ser SK — Tasmania. Department of Mines. Geological Atlas. 1:250,000 Series SK
Tasmania Dep Mines Geol Surv Bull — Tasmania. Department of Mines. Geological Survey. Bulletin
Tasmania Dep Mines Geol Surv Rec — Tasmania. Department of Mines. Geological Survey. Record
Tasmania Dep Mines Geol Surv Rep — Tasmania. Department of Mines. Geological Survey. Report
Tasmania Dep Mines Tech Rep — Tasmania. Department of Mines. Technical Report
Tasmania Dep Mines Underground Water Supply Pap — Tasmania. Department of Mines. Underground Water Supply Paper
Tasmania For Comm Bull — Tasmania. Forestry Commission. Bulletin
Tasmania Geol Surv Bull — Tasmania. Geological Survey. Bulletin
Tasmania Geol Surv Explanatory Rep — Tasmania. Geological Survey. Explanatory Report
Tasmania Geol Surv Explan Rep Geol Atlas 1 Mile Ser — Tasmania. Geological Survey. Explanatory Report. Geological Atlas. 1 Mile Series
Tasmania Geol Surv Rec — Tasmania. Geological Survey. Record
Tasmania Geol Surv Rep — Tasmania. Geological Survey. Report
Tasmania Geol Surv Underground Water Supply Pap — Tasmania. Geological Survey. Underground Water Supply Paper
Tasmania Inland Fish Comm Rep — Tasmania. Inland Fisheries Commission. Report
Tasmania Mines Dep Bull — Tasmania. Department of Mines. Bulletin
Tasmanian Dep Agric Insect Pest Surv — Tasmanian Department of Agriculture. Insect Pest Survey
Tasmanian Fis Res — Tasmanian Fisheries Research
Tasmanian J Agr — Tasmanian Journal of Agriculture
Tasmanian J Agric — Tasmanian Journal of Agriculture
Tasmanian U L Rev — Tasmanian University. Law Review
Tasmanian Univ L Rev — Tasmanian University. Law Review

Tasmania Parl Dir Mines Annu Rep — Tasmania. Parliament. Director of Mines. Annual Report
Tasm Dep Agric Bull — Tasmania. Department of Agriculture. Bulletin
Tasm Dep Agric Res Bull — Tasmania. Department of Agriculture. Research Bulletin
Tasm Fmr — Tasmanian Farmer
Tasm Fruitgr Fmr — Tasmanian Fruitgrower and Farmer
Tasm Fruitgrow Fmr — Tasmanian Fruitgrower and Farmer
Tasm Geol Surv Bull — Tasmania. Geological Survey. Bulletin
Tasm Geol Surv Geol Atlas 1 Mile Ser — Tasmania. Geological Survey. Geological Atlas. 1 Mile Series
Tasm Geol Surv Undergr Wat Supply Pap — Tasmania. Geological Survey. Underground Water Supply Paper
Tasm Hist Res Ass Pap Proc — Tasmanian Historical Research Association. Papers and Proceedings
Tasm J Agr — Tasmanian Journal of Agriculture
Tasm J Agric — Tasmanian Journal of Agriculture
Tasm Nat — Tasmanian Naturalist
Tas Motor Trade & Transport J — Tasmanian Motor Trade and Transport Journal
Tasm SR — Tasmanian State Reports
Tasm St R — Tasmanian State Reports
Tasm UL Rev — Tasmanian University. Law Review
Tasm Univ Law Rev — University of Tasmania. Law Review
Tas Nat — Tasmanian Naturalist
Tas News — Tasmanian Motor News
Tas News — Tasmanian News Reports
Tas Nurse — Tasmanian Nurse
TASP — Texas Archaeological Society. Papers
Tas R — Tasmanian Reports
Tas R — Tasmanian State Reports
Tas S R — Tasmanian State Reports
Tas Teach — Tasmanian Teacher
Tas Teacher — Tasmanian Teacher
Tas Trader — Tasmanian Trader and Successful Independent
Tas Tramp — Tasmanian Tramp
Tas Univ Gaz — University of Tasmania. Gazette
Tas Univ Law R — University of Tasmania. Law Review
Tas Univ Law Rev — University of Tasmania. Law Review
Tas Univ L Rev — Tasmanian University. Law Review
Tas Univ L Rev — University of Tasmania. Law Review
Tatabanyai Szenbanyak Musz Kozgazdasagi Kozl — Tatabanyai Szenbanyak Muszaki Kozgazdasagi Kozlemenyei [*Hungary*]
Tata Inst Fund Res Lectures on Math and Phys — Tata Institute of Fundamental Research. Lectures on Mathematics and Physics
Tata Inst Fund Res Studies in Math — Tata Institute of Fundamental Research. Studies in Mathematics
Tatar Neft — Tatarskaya Neft
TATEJ — Tasmanian Association for the Teaching of English. Journal
Tatslil — Tatslil [*The Chord*]. Forum for Music Research and Bibliography
Tatsuta Tech Rev — Tatsuta Technical Review
Tax — Taxandria
Tax — Taxation
TAX — Taxation for Accountants
Tax Ad — Tax Advisor
Tax Adv — Tax Advisor
Tax in Aust — Taxation in Australia
Tax Conf — Tax Conference
Tax Coun Q — Tax Counselor's Quarterly
Tax Exec — Tax Executive
Tax Fin and Est Pl — Tax, Financial, and Estate Planning for the Owner of a Closely Held Corporation
Tax Law — Tax Lawyer
Tax for Law — Taxation for Lawyers
Tax Law R — Tax Law Review
Tax LR — Tax Law Review
Tax L Rev — Tax Law Review
Tax Management Int'l — Tax Management International Journal
Tax Mo (Manila) — Tax Monthly (Manila)
Taxn in Aust — Taxation in Australia
Taxpayers Bul — Taxpayers' Bulletin
Tax R — Tax Review
Tax Rev — Tax Review
Taylor Soc Bul — Taylor Society. Bulletin
TAZ — Tabak Zeitung. Fachorgan der Tabakwirtschaft
TAzerbPI — Trudy Azerbaidzhanskogo Gosudarstvennogo Pedagogicheskogo Instituta
TB — Tempo Brasileiro
TB — Theologische Blaetter [*Leipzig*]
TB — Thrill Book
TB — Tvorba
TB — Tyndale Bulletin
TBBFA — Trudy Buryatskogo Instituta Estestvennykh Nauk Buryatskii Filial Sibirskoe Otdelenie Akademiya Nauk SSSR
TBBSA — Transactions. British Bryological Society
TBE — Trade Opportunities in Taiwan

TBGU — Trudy Belorusskogo Gosudarstvennogo Universiteta
TBI — Ink and Print
Tbilis Gos Univ Inst Prikl Mat Tr — Tbilisskii Gosudarstvennyi Universitet Institut Prikladnoi Matematiki Trudy
Tbilisis Univ Sromebi — Stalinis Sacheolobis Tbilisis Universitatis Sromebi
Tbiliss Gos Univ Inst Prikl Mat Trudy — Tbilisskii Gosudarstvennyi Universitet Institut Prikladnoi Matematiki Trudy
TBK — Toyo Bungaku Kenkyu [*Studies on Oriental Literature*]
TBKZA — Trudy Instituta Botaniki Akademiya Nauk Kazakhskoi SSR
TBM — Tijdschrift voor Milieu en Recht
TBN — Thailand Business
TBNNA — Trudy Bashkirskii Nauchno-Issledovatel'skii Institut po Pererabotke Nefti
TBR — New York Times Book Review
TBR — Three Banks Review
TBRD — Taxation Board of Review Decisions
TBRD (NS) — Taxation Board of Review Decisions (New Series)
T Br Mycol — Transactions. British Mycological Society
TBT — Trends in Biotechnology
TBU — Hong Kong Enterprise
TBurNII — Trudy Burjatskogo Komplesnogo Naucno-Issledovatel'skogo Instituta
TC — Chronicle (Toowoomba)
TC — Journal of Technical Topics in Civil Engineering
TC — Tamil Culture
T & C — Technology and Culture
TC — Theory of Computation Series [*Elsevier Book Series*]
TC — Trierische Chronik
TC — Twentieth Century
TC — Tworczosc
TCA — Thermochimica Acta
TCAAS — Transactions. Connecticut Academy of Arts and Sciences
TCA Man — TCA [*Tissue Culture Association*] Manual
TCANAQ — Commonwealth Bureau of Animal Nutrition. Technical Communication
TCAus — Twentieth Century (Australia)
TCBAAQ — Commonwealth Bureau of Animal Breeding and Genetics. Technical Communication
TCBS — Transactions. Cambridge Bibliographical Society
TCCND5 — Commonwealth Bureau of Nutrition. Technical Communication
TCCOB — Textile Chemist and Colorist
TCEA — Theoretical Chemical Engineering Abstracts
TCEBA — Tribune. CEBEDEAU [*Centre Belge d'Etude et de Documentation des Eaux et de l'Air*]
TCF — Twentieth Century Fiction
TCGCB — Transactions. Caribbean Geological Conference
TCGE-G — Technika Hronika (Greece)
TCh — Temoignage Chretien
TCH — Trade Channel
TCHHC — Ti Ch'iu Hua Hsueh
TCHMA — Technika v Chemii
T Christ Wet — Tydskrif vir Christelike Wetenskap
TCI — Twentieth Century Interpretations
TCITA — Transactions. Chalmers University of Technology [*Gothenburg, Sweden*]
T & CJ — Town and Country Journal
TCJ — Town and Country Journal
TCJAA — Telecommunication Journal of Australia
TCJOA — Telecommunication Journal
TCKHA — Ti Chih Ko Hsueh
TCL — Twentieth Century Literature
TCLC — Travaux. Cercle Linguistique de Copenhague
TCLP — Travaux. Cercle Linguistique de Prague
TCM — Teratogenesis, Carcinogenesis, and Mutagenesis
TCM — Textil-Mitteilungen. Unabhangige Textil Zeitung fuer Handel und Industrie
TCM — Trade and Commerce
TCM — Twentieth Century Monthly
TCMTA — Technometrics
TCMUA — Telecommunications [*English Translation*]
TCNOA — Technology [*Sindri, India*]
TCNRS — Transactions. Canadian Numismatic Research Society
TCNSB — Technos
TCORA — Teacher's College Record
T C Peirce — Transactions. Charles S. Peirce Society
TCPLA — Town and Country Planning
TCQ — Tax Counselor's Quarterly
TCR — Teacher's College Record
TCR — Technology Review
TCREA — Telecommunications and Radio Engineering [*English Translation*]
T Crit — Texto Critico
TCRUA — Technische Rundschau
TCS — Temperature Controlled Storage and Distribution
T C Ser Soil Conserv Auth (Vic) — T C Series. Soil Conservation Authority (Victoria)

T C Ser Soil Conserv Auth (Vict) — T C Series. Soil Conservation Authority (Victoria)
TCSM — Transactions. Colonial Society of Massachusetts
TCTOA — Tectonophysics
TCV — Twentieth Century Views
TCW — Today's Christian Woman
TCWA — Transactions. Cumberland and Westmorland Antiquarian and Archaeological Society
TCWSA — T'ai-Wan Huan Ching Wei Sheng
TD — Theatre Documentation
TD — Theology Digest [*St. Mary's, KS*]
TD — Tundra Drums
TDA Bull — Timber Development Association. Bulletin
TDAZA — Tautsaimnieciba Derigie Augi
TDC — [*The*] Developing Child
TDED — Istanbul Universitesi Edegiyat Fakultesi Turk Dili ve Edebiyati Dergisi
TDHYA — Tohoku Daigaku Hisuiyoeki Kagaku Kenkyusho Hokoku
TDJKA — Tokyo Daigaku Jishin Kenkyusho Iho
TDK — Toyo Daigaku Kiyo [*Bulletin. Department of Liberal Arts. Tokyo University*]
TDKIB — Tokai Daigaku Kiyo Kogakubu
TDKNAF — Annual Report. Takeda Research Laboratories
TDMOD — Therapeutic Drug Monitoring
TDN — Tendances de la Conjoncture. Graphiques Mensuels
TDNLA — Trudy Universiteta Druzhby Narodov
TDOD — Training and Development Organizations Directory
TDR — Drama Review [*Formerly, Tulane Drama Review*]
TDR — Technology Review
TDR — Thailand Development Report [*Bangkok*]
TDSKB — Reports. Research Institute for Strength and Fracture of Materials. Tohoku University
TDUKA — Tokyo Daigaku Uchu Koku Kenkyusho Hokoku
TDYKA — Tokushima Daigaku Yakugaku Kenkyu Nempo
TDYKA8 — Annual Reports. Faculty of Pharmaceutical Sciences. Tokushima University
TE — Journal of Transportation Engineering
TE — Teacher Education
Te — Teatr [*Moscow*]
Te — Tempo
TE — Teologia Espiritual
TE — Tetlit Tribune [*Fort McPherson*]
TE — Tiger's Eye
TE — Today's Education
TE — Travaux. Musee d'Etat de l'Ermitage
Tea — Tea Boards of Kenya, Uganda, and Tanganyika. Journal
TEA — Tea and Coffee Trade Journal
Teach Aids News — Teaching Aids News
Teach Coll Rec — Teacher's College Record
Teach Col R — Teacher's College Record
Teach Deaf — Teacher of the Deaf
Teach Educ — Teacher Education
Teach Eng — Teaching of English
Teach Engl — Teaching of English
Teach Engl Deaf — Teaching English to the Deaf
Teacher Ed — Teacher Education in New Countries
Teacher Librn — Teacher-Librarian
Teachers J — Teachers' Journal
Teach Excep Child — Teaching Exceptional Children
Teach Feedback — Teacher Feedback
Teach Guild NSW Proc — Teachers Guild of New South Wales. Proceedings
Teach Hist — Teaching History
Teaching Polit Sci — Teaching Political Science
Teach J — Teachers' Journal
Teach J and Abst — Teachers' Journal and Abstract
Teach J Spec Educ — Teachers' Journal of Special Education
Teach J Vic — Teachers' Journal (Victorian Teachers Union)
Teach Lib — Teacher-Librarian
Teach Math — Teaching Mathematics
Teach Phil — Teaching Philosophy
Teach Pol S — Teaching Political Science
Teach Pol Sci — Teaching Political Science
Teach Socio — Teaching Sociology
Teach Sociol — Teaching Sociology
Tea & Coff — Tea and Coffee Trade Journal
Tea East Afr — Tea in East Africa
Tea Lib — Teacher-Librarian
TEAPA — Technikas Apskats
Tea Q — Tea Quarterly
TEARA — Terapevticheskii Arkhiv
Tea Res Assoc Annu Sci Rep — Tea Research Association. Annual Scientific Report
Tea Res Inst Ceylon Annu Rep — Tea Research Institute of Ceylon. Annual Report
Tea Res Inst Sri Lanka Tech Rep — Tea Research Institute of Sri Lanka. Technical Report

Tea Res J — Tea Research Journal
TEAS — Twayne's English Author Series
TEC — Telecommunications Policy
TEC — Transport Environment Circulation
Tec Agr — Tecnica Agricola
Tec Agric (Catania) — Tecnica Agricola (Catania)
Tec Autom — Tecniche dell'Automazione
TECED — Techniques de l'Energie
Tech — Technology
Tech Abstr Bull — Technical Abstract Bulletin
Tech Adv Shikoku Agric — Technical Advances in Shikoku Agriculture
Tech Agri — Technique Agricole [*France*]
Tech Appl Pet — Techniques et Applications du Petrole [*France*]
Tech Apskats — Technikas Apskats [*United States*]
Tech Assn Pa — Technical Association Papers
Tech Bau — Technik am Bau [*West Germany*]
Tech Ber Heinrich-Hertz Inst (Berlin-Charlottenburg) — Technischer Bericht. Heinrich-Hertz Institut (Berlin-Charlottenburg)
Tech Ber Sticht Nederl Graan-Cent — Technisch Bericht. Stichting Nederlands Graan-Centrum
Tech Bibliogr Birmingham Public Lib — Technical Bibliographies. Birmingham Public Libraries
Tech Bibliogr Ser Birmingham Cent Lib — Technical Bibliographies Series. Birmingham Central Libraries
Tech Biochem Biophys Morphol — Techniques of Biochemical and Biophysical Morphology
Tech Bull Agric Res Inst (Cyprus) — Technical Bulletin. Agricultural Research Institute (Cyprus)
Tech Bull Amersham Buchler — Technisches Bulletin - Amerisham Buchler
Tech Bull Anim Ind Agric Branch NT — Technical Bulletin. Animal Industry and Agricultural Branch. Department of the Northern Territory
Tech Bull Anim Ind Agric Br NT — Technical Bulletin. Animal Industry and Agriculture Branch. Northern Territory
Tech Bull Ariz Agr Exp Sta — Technical Bulletin. Arizona Agricultural Experiment Station
Tech Bull Ariz Agric Exp Stn — Technical Bulletin. Arizona Agricultural Experiment Station
Tech Bull At Energy Organ Iran — Technical Bulletin. Atomic Energy Organization of Iran
Tech Bull Banana Res Adv Comm — Technical Bulletin. Banana Research Advisory Committee
Tech Bull Can Inland Waters Dir — Technical Bulletin. Canada Inland Waters Directorate
Tech Bull Colo Agric Exp Stn — Technical Bulletin. Colorado Agricultural Experiment Station
Tech Bull Colo State Univ Agr Exp Sta — Technical Bulletin. Colorado State University. Agricultural Experiment Station
Tech Bull Commonwealth Inst Biol Contr — Technical Bulletin. Commonwealth Institute of Biological Control
Tech Bull Commonw Inst Biol Control — Technical Bulletin. Commonwealth Institute of Biological Control
Tech Bull Cyprus Agr Res Inst — Technical Bulletin. Cyprus Agricultural Research Institute
Tech Bull Dep Agric NSW — New South Wales. Department of Agriculture. Technical Bulletin
Tech Bull Dep Agric Vict — Technical Bulletin. Department of Agriculture. Victoria
Tech Bull Dep Agric West Aust — Technical Bulletin. Department of Agriculture. Western Australia
Tech Bull Exp For Taiwan Univ — Technical Bulletin. Experimental Forest. National Taiwan University
Tech Bull Fac Agric Kagawa Univ — Technical Bulletin. Faculty of Agriculture. Kagawa University
Tech Bull Fac Agr Kagawa Univ — Technical Bulletin. Faculty of Agriculture. Kagawa University
Tech Bull Fac Hort Chiba Univ — Technical Bulletin. Faculty of Horticulture. Chiba University
Tech Bull Fac Hortic Chiba Univ — Technical Bulletin. Faculty of Horticulture. Chiba University
Tech Bull Fla Agric Exp Stn — Technical Bulletin. Florida Agricultural Experiment Station
Tech Bull GA Agr Exp Sta — Technical Bulletin. Georgia Agricultural Experiment Stations. University of Georgia. College of Agriculture
Tech Bull Gt Brit Min Agr Fish Food — Technical Bulletin. Great Britain Ministry of Agiculture, Fisheries, and Food
Tech Bull Harper Adams Agr Coll — Technical Bulletin. Harper Adams Agricultural College
Tech Bull Hawaii Agric Exp Stn — Technical Bulletin. Hawaii Agricultural Experiment Station
Tech Bull Inst Ld Wat Mgmt Res — Technical Bulletin. Institute for Land and Water Management Research
Tech Bull Kagawa Agr Coll — Technical Bulletin. Kagawa Agricultural College
Tech Bull Kans Agr Exp Sta — Technical Bulletin. Kansas Agricultural Experiment Station

Tech Bull Kans Agric Exp Stn — Technical Bulletin. Kansas Agricultural Experiment Station

Tech Bull Land Resour Div Dir Overseas Surv — Technical Bulletin. Land Resources Division. Directorate of Overseas Surveys

Tech Bull Life Sci Agric Exp Stn (Maine) — Technical Bulletin. Life Sciences and Agriculture Experiment Station (Maine)

Tech Bull Mich State Univ Agr Exp Sta — Technical Bulletin. Michigan State University. Agricultural Experiment Station

Tech Bull Minist Agric E Niger — Technical Bulletin. Ministry of Agriculture of Eastern Nigeria

Tech Bull Minist Agric Fish Fd — Technical Bulletin. Ministry of Agriculture, Fisheries, and Food

Tech Bull Minist Agric Fish Food (GB) — Technical Bulletin. Ministry of Agriculture, Fisheries, and Food (Great Britain)

Tech Bull Minn Agric Exp Sta — Technical Bulletin. University of Minnesota. Agricultural Experiment Station

Tech Bull Miss Agr Exp Sta — Technical Bulletin. Mississippi Agricultural Experiment Station

Tech Bull Miss Agric For Exp Stn — Technical Bulletin. Mississippi Agricultural and Forestry Experiment Station

Tech Bull Miyagi Prefect Agr Exp Sta — Technical Bulletin. Miyagi Prefectural Agricultural Experiment Station

Tech Bull Mont Agr Exp Sta — Technical Bulletin. Montana Agricultural Experiment Station

Tech Bull NC Agr Exp Sta — Technical Bulletin. North Carolina Agricultural Experiment Station

Tech Bull NC Agric Exp Sta — Technical Bulletin. North Carolina Agricultural Experiment Station

Tech Bull N Carol Agric Exp Stn — Technical Bulletin. North Carolina Agricultural Experiment Station

Tech Bull N Carol St Coll Agric Exp Stn — Technical Bulletin. North Carolina State College. Agricultural Experiment Station

Tech Bull Okla State Univ Agr Exp Sta — Technical Bulletin. Oklahoma State University. Agricultural Experiment Station

Tech Bull Ore Agric Exp Stn — Technical Bulletin. Oregon Agricultural Experiment Station

Tech Bull Oreg State Coll Agr Exp Sta — Technical Bulletin. Oregon State College. Agricultural Experiment Station

Tech Bull Regist Med Technol — Technical Bulletin. Registry of Medical Technologists

Tech Bull Rhodesia Agric J — Technical Bulletin. Rhodesia Agricultural Journal

Tech Bull S Dak Agr Exp Sta — Technical Bulletin. South Dakota Agricultural Experiment Station

Tech Bull Sulphur Inst — Technical Bulletin. Sulphur Institute

Tech Bull Taiwan Agric Res Inst — Technical Bulletin. Taiwan Agricultural Research Institute

Tech Bull Taiwan Fertil Co — Technical Bulletin. Taiwan Fertilizer Company

Tech Bull Tex Eng Exp Stn — Technical Bulletin. Texas Engineering Experiment Station

Tech Bull Tokushima Bunri Univ — Technical Bulletin. Tokushima Bunri University

Tech Bull UAR Minist Agric Agrar Reform — Technical Bulletin. United Arab Republic Ministry of Agriculture and Agrarian Reform

Tech Bull Univ Maine Life Sci Agric Exp Stn — Technical Bulletin. University of Maine. Life Sciences and Agriculture Experiment Station

Tech Bull Univ Minn Agr Exp Sta — Technical Bulletin. University of Minnesota. Agricultural Experiment Station

Tech Bull Univ Nev Agr Exp Sta — Technical Bulletin. University of Nevada. Agricultural Experiment Station

Tech Bull Univ Philippines Coll Agr — Technical Bulletin. University of the Philippines. College of Agriculture

Tech Bull USDA — Technical Bulletin. United States Department of Agriculture

Tech Bull US Dep Agric — Technical Bulletin. United States Department of Agriculture

Tech Bull US Dep Agric Agric Res Serv — Technical Bulletin. United States Department of Agriculture. Agricultural Research Service

Tech Bull US For Serv — Technical Bulletin. United States Forest Service

Tech Bull VA Agr Exp Sta — Technical Bulletin. Virginia Agricultural Experiment Station

Tech Bull Vic Ctry Rd Bd — Technical Bulletin. Victoria Country Roads Board

Tech Bull Wash Agr Exp Sta — Technical Bulletin. Washington Agricultural Experiment Station

Tech Bull Wash Agric Exp Stn — Technical Bulletin. Washington Agricultural Experiment Station

Tech Bull Wash State Univ Coll Agric Res Cent — Technical Bulletin. Washington State University. College of Agriculture. Research Center

Tech CEM — Techniques CEM [*Compagnie Electro-Mecanique*]

Tech Chem (Prague) — Technika v Chemii (Prague)

Tech Chron — Technika Chronika

Tech Circ Maurit Sug Ind Res Inst — Technical Circular. Mauritius Sugar Industry Research Institute

Tech Commun — Technical Communications

Tech Commun Bur Sugar Exp Stn (Queensl) — Technical Communication. Bureau of Sugar Experiment Stations (Queensland)

Tech Commun Bur Sug Exp Stns (Qd) — Technical Communication. Bureau of Sugar Experiment Stations (Queensland)

Tech Commun Central Inform Libr Edit Sect CSIRO — Technical Communication. Central Information, Library, and Editorial Section. Commonwealth Scientific and Industrial Research Organisation

Tech Commun CILES CSIRO — Technical Communication. Central Information, Library, and Editorial Section. Commonwealth Scientific and Industrial Research Organisation

Tech Commun CSIRO (Aust) — Technical Communication. Minerals Research Laboratories. Commonwealth Scientific and Industrial Research Organisation (Australia)

Tech Commun CSIRO Div Mineral — Australia. Commonwealth Scientific and Industrial Research Organisation. Division of Mineralogy. Technical Communication

Tech Commun CSIRO Div Miner Chem — Australia. Commonwealth Scientific and Industrial Research Organisation. Division of Mineral Chemistry. Technical Communication

Tech Commun CSIRO Inst Earth Resour — CSIRO [*Commonwealth Scientific and Industrial Research Organisation*] Institute of Earth Resources. Technical Communication

Tech Commun CSIRO Miner Res Lab — CSIRO [*Commonwealth Scientific and Industrial Research Organisation*] Minerals Research Laboratories. Technical Communication

Tech Commun Dept Agr Tech Serv Repub S Afr — Technical Communication. Department of Agricultural Technical Services. Republic of South Africa

Tech Commun Div Miner Chem CSIRO — Technical Communication. Division of Mineral Chemistry. Commonwealth Scientific and Industrial Research Organisation

Tech Commun Div Miner CSIRO — Technical Communication. Division of Mineralogy. Commonwealth Scientific and Industrial Research Organisation

Tech Commun For Bur (Oxf) — Technical Communication. Commonwealth Forestry Bureau (Oxford)

Tech Commun Miner Res Lab CSIRO — Technical Communication. Minerals Research Laboratories. Commonwealth Scientific and Industrial Research Organisation

Tech Commun R Sch Mines — Technical Communications. Royal School of Mines

Tech Commun S Afr Dep Agric Fish — Technical Communication. South Africa Department of Agriculture and Fisheries

Tech Commun S Afr Dep Agric Tech Serv — Technical Communications. South Africa Department of Agricultural Technical Services

Tech Commun Woodld Ecol Unit CSIRO — Technical Communication. Woodland Ecology Unit. Commonwealth Scientific and Industrial Research Organisation

Tech & Cult — Technology and Culture

Tech & Culture — Technology and Culture

Tech Cybern USSR — Technical Cybernetics USSR

Tech Data Digest — Technical Data Digest [*United States*]

Tech Dig — Technical Digest

Tech Doc FAO Plant Prot Comm Southeast Asia Pac Reg — Technical Document. Food and Agriculture Organization of the United Nations. Plant Protection Committee for the South East Asia and Pacific Region

Tech Eau — Technique de l'Eau et de l'Assainissement

Tech Econ Publ Tatabanyai Szenbanyak — Technical-Economical Publication. Tatabanyai Szenbanyak

Tech Econ Stud Inst Geol Geophys Ser I — Technical and Economical Studies. Institute of Geology and Geophysics. Series I. Mineralogy-Petrology

Tech Educ — Technical Education

Tech Educ Abstr — Technical Education Abstracts

Tech Educ Yrbk — Technician Education Yearbook

Tech Electrochem — Techniques of Electrochemistry

Tech Electron Son Telev — Techniques Electroniques - Son - Television

Tech Energ — Techniques de l'Energie [*France*]

Tech Energie — Techniques de l'Energie

Tech Energ (Paris) — Techniques de l'Energie (Paris)

Tech Environ — Technology and Environment

Tech Fore — Technology Forecasts and Technology Surveys

Tech Forum Soc Vac Coaters — Technical Forum. Society of Vacuum Coaters

Tech Gem — Technische Gemeinschaft

Tech Gemeindebl — Technisches Gemeindeblatt [*West Germany*]

Tech Gids Ziekenhuis Instelling — Technische Gids voor Ziekenhuis en Instelling

Tech Gospod Morsk — Technika i Gospodarka Morska [*Poland*]

Tech Heute — Technik Heute [*German Federal Republic*]

Tech Hochsch Leipzig Wiss Z — Technische Hochschule Leipzig. Wissenschaftliche Zeitschrift

Tech Hogesch Delft Afd Werktuigbouwkd (Rep) WTHD — Technische Hogeschool Delft. Afdeling der Werktuigbouwkunde (Report) WTHD

Tech-Index Plasmaphys Forsch Fusionreakt — Technik-Index ueber Plasmaphysikalische Forschung und Fusionsreaktoren [*West Germany*]

Tech Inf GRW — Technische Information GRW [*Geraete- und Regler Werke*] [*East Germany*]

Tech Info Service — Technical Information Service

Tech Ing Genie Chim — Techniques de l'Ingenieur. Genie Chimique

Tech Jahrb — Technica Jahrbuch
Tech J Ankara Nucl Res Cent — Technical Journal. Ankara Nuclear Research Center
Tech J Ankara Nucl Res Train Cent — Technical Journal. Ankara Nuclear Research and Training Center
Tech J Jap Broadcast Corp — Technical Journal. Japan Broadcasting Corporation
Tech J Jpn Broadcast Corp — Technical Journal. Japan Broadcasting Corporation
Tech Knih — Technicka Knihovna
Tech Knihovna — Technicka Knihovna
Tech Kurir — Technikai Kurir [*Hungary*]
Tech Lab Cent Res Inst Electr Power Ind Rep — Technical Laboratory. Central Research Institute of the Electrical Power Industry. Report [*Japan*]
Tech Landwirt — Technik und Landwirtschaft. Landtechnischer Ratgeber
Tech Lotnicza Astronaut — Technika Lotnicza i Astronautyczna [*Poland*]
Tech Manpower — Technical Manpower
Tech Mem Calif Inst Technol Jet Propul Lab — Technical Memorandum. California Institute of Technology. Jet Propulsion Laboratory
Tech Memo Daresbury Lab — Technical Memorandum. Daresbury Laboratory
Tech Memo Daresbury Nucl Phys Lab — Technical Memorandum. Daresbury Nuclear Physics Laboratory
Tech Memo Div Appl Geomech CSIRO — Technical Memorandum. Division of Applied Geomechanics. Commonwealth Scientific and Industrial Research Organisation
Tech Memo Div Land Use Res CSIRO — Technical Memorandum. Division of Land Use Research. Commonwealth Scientific and Industrial Research Organisation
Tech Memo Div Wildl Res CSIRO — Technical Memorandum. Division of Wildlife Research. Commonwealth Scientific and Industrial Research Organisation
Tech Memo Jet Propul Lab Calif Inst Technol — Technical Memorandum. Jet Propulsion Laboratory. California Institute of Technology
Tech Mess ATM — Technisches Messen ATM [*Archiv fuer Technisches Messen*]
Tech Methods Polym Eval — Techniques and Methods of Polymer Evaluation
Tech Meun — Technique Meuniere
Tech Mitt — Technische Mitteilungen
Tech Mitt AEG-Telefunken — Technische Mitteilungen AEG- [*Allgemeine Elektrizitaets-Gesellschaft*] Telefunken
Tech Mitteil Krupp Forschungsber — Technische Mitteilungen Krupp. Forschungsberichte
Tech Mitteil Krupp Werksber — Technische Mitteilungen Krupp. Werksberichte
Tech Mitt (Essen) — Technische Mitteilungen (Essen)
Tech Mitt Krupp — Technische Mitteilungen Krupp [*West Germany*]
Tech Mitt Krupp Forschungsber — Technische Mitteilungen Krupp. Forschungsberichte
Tech Mitt Krupp Werksber — Technische Mitteilungen Krupp. Werksberichte
Tech Mitt PTT — Technische Mitteilungen PTT
Tech Mitt RFZ — Technische Mitteilungen. RFZ [*Rundfunk- und Fernsehtechnisches Zentralamt*]
Tech Mod — Technique Moderne
Tech Motoryzacyjna — Technika Motoryzacyjna
Tech Newslett For Prod Res Inst (Ghana) — Technical Newsletter. Forest Products Research Institute (Kumasi, Ghana)
Tech News Serv Sarabhai M Chem — Technical News Service. Sarabhai M. Chemicals
Technical J — Technical Journal
Technic Int — Technic International [*West Germany*]
Technion Isr Inst Technol Dep Chem Eng Rep CE — Technion-Israel Institute of Technology. Department of Chemical Engineering. Report CE
Technmcs — Technometrics
Technol — Technology
Technol Conserv — Technology and Conservation
Technol Cul — Technology and Culture
Technol Dev Rep EPS (Can Environ Prot Serv) — Technology Development Report EPS (Canada Environmental Protection Service)
Technol For — Technological Forecasting and Social Change
Technol Forecast — Technological Forecasting [*Later, Technological Forecasting and Social Change*]
Technol Forecasting — Technological Forecasting [*Later, Technological Forecasting and Social Change*] [*United States*]
Technol Forecasting Soc Change — Technological Forecasting and Social Change
Technol Index Plasmaphys Res Fusion React — Technology Index for Plasmaphysics Research and Fusion Reactors [*West Germany*]
Technol Inf (Sapporo) — Technology and Information (Sapporo)
Technol Ireland — Technology Ireland
Technol J Natl Sci Dev Board (Philip) — Technology Journal. National Science Development Board (Philippines)
Technol-Nachr Manage Inf — Technologie-Nachrichten. Management-Informationen [*West Germany*]
Technol-Nachr Programm-Inf — Technologie-Nachrichten Programm-Informationen

Technol-Nachr Sonderdienst-Programme — Technologie-Nachrichten Sonderdienst-Programme [*German Federal Republic*]
Technol News — Technology News. Bureau of Mines [*United States*]
Technol News Bur Mines — Technology News. Bureau of Mines [*United States*]
Technolog Pap Div Forest Prod CSIRO — Technological Paper. Division of Forest Products. Commonwealth Scientific and Industrial Research Organisation
Technol Pap Div Forest Prod CSIRO — Technological Paper. Division of Forest Products. Commonwealth Scientific and Industrial Research Organisation
Technol Pap Forest Prod Lab Div Appl Chem CSIRO — Technological Paper. Forest Products Laboratory. Division of Applied Chemistry. Commonwealth Scientific and Industrial Research Organisation
Technol Pap Forest Prod Lab Div Bldg Res CSIRO — Technological Paper. Forest Products Laboratory. Division of Building Research. Commonwealth Scientific and Industrial Research Organisation
Technol Pap For Prod Lab Div Appl Chem CSIRO — Technological Paper. Forest Products Laboratory. Division of Applied Chemistry. Commonwealth Scientific and Industrial Research Organisation
Technol Pap For Prod Lab Div Build Res CSIRO — Technological Paper. Forest Products Laboratory. Division of Building Research. Commonwealth Scientific and Industrial Research Organisation
Technol R — Technology Review [*Boston*]
Technol Rep Iwate Univ — Technology Reports. Iwate University
Technol Rep Kansai Univ — Technology Reports. Kansai University
Technol Rep Kyushu Univ — Technology Reports. Kyushu University
Technol Rep Osaka Univ — Technology Reports. Osaka University
Technol Rep Seikei Univ — Technology Reports. Seikei University
Technol Rep Tohoku Univ — Technology Reports. Tohoku University [*Sendaik, Japan*]
Technol Rep Tohoku Univ (Jpn) — Technology Reports. Tohoku University (Japan)
Technol Rep Yamaguchi Univ — Technology Reports. Yamaguchi University
Technol Respir — Technologie Respiratoire
Technol Rev — Technology Review
Technol Rev Chonnam Natl Univ — Technological Review. Chonnam National University [*Republic of Korea*]
Technol Soc — Technology and Society
Technol (Syd) — Technology (Sydney)
Technomet — Technometrics
Tech Note Aust Def Stand Lab — Technical Note. Australia Defence Standards Laboratories
Tech Note Brick Manuf Assoc NSW — Technical Note. Brick Manufacturers Association of New South Wales
Tech Note Brick Mf Assoc NSW — Technical Note. Brick Manufacturers Association of New South Wales
Tech Note Charles Kolling Res Lab — Technical Note. Charles Kolling Research Laboratory. Department of Mechanical Engineering. University of Sydney
Tech Note Def Stand Lab Aust — Australia. Defence Standards Laboratories. Technical Note
Tech Note Dep For Res (Nigeria) — Technical Note. Department of Forest Research (Nigeria)
Tech Note E Afr Agric For Res Organ — Technical Note. East African Agriculture and Forestry Research Organization
Tech Note For Dep (Brit Solomon Islands Protect) — Technical Note. Forestry Department (British Solomon Islands Protectorate)
Tech Note For Dep (Kenya) — Technical Note. Forest Department (Nairobi, Kenya)
Tech Note For Dep (Uganda) — Technical Note. Forest Department (Uganda)
Tech Note For Prod Res Ind Dev Comm (Philipp) — Technical Note. Forest Products Research and Industries Development Commission (Philippines)
Tech Note For Prod Res Inst (Ghana) — Technical Note. Forest Products Research Institute (Ghana)
Tech Note For Timb Bur — Technical Note. Bureau of Forestry and Timber
Tech Note Harbour Tech Res Inst Minist Transp (Jpn) — Technical Note. Port and Harbour Technical Research Institute. Ministry of Transportation (Japan)
Tech Note Mater Res Lab Aust — Australia. Materials Research Laboratories. Technical Note
Tech Note Oji Inst For Tree Impr — Technical Note. Oji Institute for Forest Tree Improvement
Tech Note Quetico-Sup Wild Res Cent — Technical Note. Quetico-Superior Wilderness Research Center
Tech Note Res Inst Ind Saf — Technical Note. Research Institute of Industrial Safety
Tech Notes Clay Prod — Technical Notes on Clay Products [*Brick Development Research Institute*]
Tech Notes For Comm NSW — Technical Notes. Forestry Commission of New South Wales
Tech Notes NSW For Comm Div Wood Technol — New South Wales. Forestry Commission. Division of Wood Technology. Technical Notes
Tech Note Sol Energy Stud CSIRO — Technical Note. Solar Energy Studies. Commonwealth Scientific and Industrial Research Organisation

Tech Notes Rubber Ind — Technical Notes for the Rubber Industry

Tech Pap Agric Exp Stn (P Rico) — Technical Paper. Agricultural Experiment Station (Puerto Rico)

Tech Pap Amer Pulpw Ass — Technical Papers. American Pulpwood Association

Tech Pap Anim Res Lab CSIRO — Technical Paper. Animal Research Laboratories. Commonwealth Scientific and Industrial Research Organisation

Tech Pap (Aust) CSIRO Div Appl Geomech — Technical Paper. (Australia) Commonwealth Scientific and Industrial Research Organisation. Division of Applied Geomechanics

Tech Pap (Aust) CSIRO Div Mineragraphic Invest — Technical Paper. (Australia) Commonwealth Scientific and Industrial Research Organisation. Division of Mineragraphic Investigation

Tech Pap Aust Water Resour Coun — Technical Paper. Australian Water Resources Council

Tech Pap Aust Wat Resour Coun — Technical Paper. Australian Water Resources Council

Tech Pap Calif Dep Agric — Technical Papers. California Department of Agriculture

Tech Pap Canad Pulp Pap Ass — Technical Paper. Canadian Pulp and Paper Association

Tech Pap Dep For (Qd) — Technical Paper. Department of Forestry (Queensland)

Tech Pap Dep For (Queensl) — Technical Paper. Department of Forestry (Queensland)

Tech Pap Div Appl Chem CSIRO — Technical Paper. Division of Applied Chemistry. Commonwealth Scientific and Industrial Research Organisation

Tech Pap Div Appl Geomech CSIRO — Technical Paper. Division of Applied Geomechanics. Commonwealth Scientific and Industrial Research Organisation

Tech Pap Div Appl Miner CSIRO — Technical Paper. Division of Applied Mineralogy. Commonwealth Scientific and Industrial Research Organisation

Tech Pap Div Appl Org Chem CSIRO — Technical Paper. Division of Applied Organic Chemistry. Commonwealth Scientific and Industrial Research Organisation

Tech Pap Div Atmosph Phys CSIRO — Technical Paper. Division of Atmospheric Physics. Commonwealth Scientific and Industrial Research Organisation

Tech Pap Div Atmos Phys CSIRO — Technical Paper. Division of Atmospheric Physics. Commonwealth Scientific and Industrial Research Organisation

Tech Pap Div Bldg Res CSIRO — Technical Paper. Division of Building Research. Commonwealth Scientific and Industrial Research Organisation

Tech Pap Div Build Res CSIRO — Technical Paper. Division of Building Research. Commonwealth Scientific and Industrial Research Organisation

Tech Pap Div Chem Technol CSIRO — Technical Paper. Division of Chemical Technology. Commonwealth Scientific and Industrial Research Organisation

Tech Pap Div Ent CSIRO — Technical Paper. Division of Entomology. Commonwealth Scientific and Industrial Research Organisation

Tech Pap Div Fd Preserv CSIRO — Technical Paper. Division of Food Preservation. Commonwealth Scientific and Industrial Research Organisation

Tech Pap Div Fd Res CSIRO — Technical Paper. Division of Food Research. Commonwealth Scientific and Industrial Research Organisation

Tech Pap Div Fd Res CSIRO (Aust) — Technical Paper. Division of Food Research. Commonwealth Scientific and Industrial Research Organisation (Australia)

Tech Pap Div Fish Oceanogr CSIRO — Technical Paper. Division of Fisheries and Oceanography. Commonwealth Scientific and Industrial Research Organisation

Tech Pap Div Food Res CSIRO — Technical Paper. Division of Food Research. Commonwealth Scientific and Industrial Research Organisation

Tech Pap Div Land Resour Manage CSIRO — Technical Paper. Division of Land Resources Management. Commonwealth Scientific and Industrial Research Organisation

Tech Pap Div Land Use Res CSIRO — Technical Paper. Division of Land Use Research. Commonwealth Scientific and Industrial Research Organisation

Tech Pap Div Ld Res CSIRO — Technical Paper. Division of Land Research. Commonwealth Scientific and Industrial Research Organisation

Tech Pap Div Ld Res Reg Surv CSIRO (Aust) — Technical Papers. Division of Land Research and Regional Survey. Commonwealth Scientific and Industrial Research Organisation (Australia)

Tech Pap Div Ld Use Res CSIRO — Technical Paper. Division of Land Use Research. Commonwealth Scientific and Industrial Research Organisation

Tech Pap Div Math Stat CSIRO — Technical Paper. Division of Mathematics and Statistics. Commonwealth Scientific and Industrial Research Organisation

Tech Pap Div Math Statist CSIRO — Technical Paper. Division of Mathematical Statistics. Commonwealth Scientific and Industrial Research Organisation

Tech Pap Div Mat Statist CSIRO — Technical Paper. Division of Mathematical Statistics. Commonwealth Scientific and Industrial Research Organisation

Tech Pap Div Meteorol Phys CSIRO — Technical Paper. Division of Meteorological Physics. Commonwealth Scientific and Industrial Research Organisation

Tech Pap Div Met Phys CSIRO — Technical Paper. Division of Meteorological Physics. Commonwealth Scientific and Industrial Research Organisation

Tech Pap Div Plant Ind CSIRO — Technical Paper. Division of Plant Industry. Commonwealth Scientific and Industrial Research Organisation

Tech Pap Div Pl Ind CSIRO — Technical Paper. Division of Plant Industry. Commonwealth Scientific and Industrial Research Organisation

Tech Pap Div Pl Ind CSIRO (Aust) — Technical Papers. Division of Plant Industry. Commonwealth Scientific and Industrial Research Organisation (Australia)

Tech Pap Div Soil Mechanics CSIRO — Technical Paper. Division of Soil Mechanics. Commonwealth Scientific and Industrial Research Organisation

Tech Pap Div Soils CSIRO — Technical Paper. Division of Soils. Commonwealth Scientific and Industrial Research Organisation

Tech Pap Div Tech Conf Soc Plast Eng — Technical Papers. Divisional Technical Conference. Society of Plastics Engineers

Tech Pap Div Trop Agron CSIRO — Technical Paper. Division of Tropical Agronomy. Commonwealth Scientific and Industrial Research Organisation

Tech Pap Div Trop Crops Pastures CSIRO — Technical Paper. Division of Tropical Crops and Pastures. Commonwealth Scientific and Industrial Research Organisation

Tech Pap Div Trop Pastures CSIRO — Technical Paper. Division of Tropical Pastures. Commonwealth Scientific and Industrial Research Organisation

Tech Pap Div Wildl Res CSIRO — Technical Paper. Division of Wildlife Research. Commonwealth Scientific and Industrial Research Organisation

Tech Pap For Comm NSW — Technical Paper. Forestry Commission of New South Wales

Tech Pap For Res Inst NZ For Serv — Technical Paper. Forest Research Institute. New Zealand Forest Service

Tech Pap Hydrol — Technical Papers in Hydrology

Tech Pap Intersoc Energy Convers Eng Conf — Technical Papers. Intersociety Energy Conversion Engineering Conference

Tech Pap Natl Meas Lab CSIRO — Technical Paper. National Measurement Laboratory. Commonwealth Scientific and Industrial Research Organisation

Tech Pap Natn Stand Lab CSIRO — Technical Paper. National Standards Laboratory. Commonwealth Scientific and Industrial Research Organisation

Tech Pap NY State Dep Environ Conserv — Technical Paper. New York State Department of Environmental Conservation

Tech Pap SME Ser EE — Technical Paper. Society of Manufacturing Engineers. Series EE (Electrical Engineering)

Tech Pap Soc Manuf Eng Ser AD — Technical Paper. Society of Manufacturing Engineers. Series AD (Assembly Division)

Tech Pap Soc Manuf Eng Ser EE — Technical Paper. Society of Manufacturing Engineers. Series EE (Electrical Engineering)

Tech Pap Soc Manuf Eng Ser EM — Technical Paper. Society of Manufacturing Engineers. Series EM (Engineering Materials)

Tech Pap Soc Manuf Eng Ser FC — Technical Paper. Society of Manufacturing Engineers. Series FC (Finishing and Coating)

Tech Pap Soc Manuf Eng Ser IQ — Technical Paper. Society of Manufacturing Engineers. Series IQ (Inspection and Quality)

Tech Pap Soc Manuf Eng Ser MF — Technical Paper. Society of Manufacturing Engineers. Series MF (Material Forming)

Tech Pap Soc Manuf Eng Ser MR — Technical Paper. Society of Manufacturing Engineers. Series MR (Material Removal)

Tech Pap Univ PR Agr Exp Sta — Technical Paper. University of Puerto Rico. Agricultural Experiment Station

Tech Pet — Techniques du Petrole [*France*]

Tech Phot — Technical Photography

Tech-Phys Monogr — Technisch-Physikalische Monographien

Tech Phys Ser — Techniques of Physics Series

Tech Poszukiwan — Technika Poszukiwan

Tech Poszukiwan Geol — Technika Poszukiwan Geologicznych

Tech Pr — Technika Prace [*Czechoslovakia*]

Tech Prat Agr — Technique et Pratique Agricoles

Tech Prepr Am Soc Lubr Eng — Technical Preprints. American Society of Lubrication Engineers

Tech Prog Rep US Bur Mines — Technical Progress Report. United States Bureau of Mines

Tech Progr Rep Hawaii Agr Exp Sta — Technical Progress Report. Hawaii Agricultural Experiment Station. University of Hawaii

Tech Publ Aust Soc Dairy Technol — Australian Society of Dairy Technology. Technical Publication

Tech Publ Div Wood Technol For Comm NSW — Technical Publication. Division of Wood Technology. Forestry Commission of New South Wales

Tech Publ NY St Coll For — Technical Publication. New York State University. College of Forestry

Tech Publs — Technical Publications

Tech Publs Aust Soc Dairy Technol — Technical Publications. Australian Society of Dairy Technology

Tech Publs Dep Agric (Vict) — Technical Publications. Department of Agriculture (Victoria)

Tech Publs Div Wood Technol NSW For Comm — Technical Publications. Division of Wood Technology. New South Wales Forestry Commission

Tech Publs NSW For Comm Div Wood Technol — Technical Publications. New South Wales Forestry Commission. Division of Wood Technology

Tech Publ State Univ Coll For Syracuse Univ — Technical Publication. State University College of Forestry. Syracuse University

Tech Q — Technology Quarterly and Proceedings. Society of Arts

Tech Quart Master Brew Ass Amer — Technical Quarterly. Master Brewers Association of America

Tech R — Technology Review

Tech Radia & Telew — Technika Radia i Telewizji

Tech Rdsch (Bern) — Technische Rundschau (Bern) [*Switzerland*]

Tech Refrig Air Cond — Technics of Refrigeration and Air Conditioning

Tech Release Amer Pulpw Ass — Technical Release. American Pulpwood Association

Tech Rep AFAPL TR Air Force Aero Propul Lab (US) — Technical Report. AFAPL-TR. Air Force Aero Propulsion Laboratory (United States)

Tech Rep AFFDL TR Air Force Flight Dyn Lab (US) — Technical Report. AFFDL-TR. Air Force Flight Dynamics Laboratory (United States)

Tech Rep AFML TR Air Force Mater Lab (US) — Technical Report. AFML-TR. Air Force Materials Laboratory (United States)

Tech Rep AFWAL-TR US Air Force Wright Aeronaut Lab — Technical Report. AFWAL-TR. United States Air Force Wright Aeronautical Laboratories

Tech Rep Agric Chem Branch (Queensl) — Technical Report. Agricultural Chemistry Branch (Queensland)

Tech Rep Agric Eng Res Stn Min Agric For Ser F — Technical Report. Agricultural Engineering Research Station. Ministry of Agriculture and Forestry. Series F. General [*Japan*]

Tech Rep Agric Ld Serv Minist Agric Fish Fd — Technical Report. Agricultural Land Service. Ministry of Agriculture, Fisheries, and Food

Tech Rep Air Pollut Yokohama-Kawasaki Ind Area — Technical Report on Air Pollution in Yokohama-Kawasaki Industrial Area [*Japan*]

Tech Rep Aust Weapons Res Establ — Australia. Weapons Research Establishment. Technical Report

Tech Rep Aust Weapons Res Establ — Technical Report. Australia Weapons Research Establishment

Tech Rep Bur Met — Technical Report. Bureau of Meteorology

Tech Rep Bur Meteorol — Technical Report. Bureau of Meteorology

Tech Rep Cent Res Inst Electr Power Ind — Technical Report. Central Research Institute of the Electrical Power Industry [*Japan*]

Tech Rep Cent Res Water Resour Univ Tex Austin — Technical Report. Center for Research in Water Resources. University of Texas at Austin

Tech Rep Constr Eng Res Lab — Technical Report. Construction Engineering Research Laboratory [*United States*]

Tech Rep Dep Mines Tas — Technical Report. Department of Mines. Tasmania

Tech Rep Desert Locust Control Organ East Afr — Technical Report. Desert Locust Control Organization for Eastern Africa

Tech Rep Div Appl Geomech CSIRO — Technical Report. Division of Applied Geomechanics. Commonwealth Scientific and Industrial Research Organisation

Tech Rep Div Mech Eng CSIRO — Technical Report. Division of Mechanical Engineering. Commonwealth Scientific and Industrial Research Organisation

Tech Rep Div Mech Engng CSIRO — Technical Report. Division of Mechanical Engineering. Commonwealth Scientific and Industrial Research Organisation

Tech Rep Div Soil Mech CSIRO — Technical Report. Division of Soil Mechanics. Commonwealth Scientific and Industrial Research Organisation

Tech Rep Eng Res Inst Kyoto Univ — Technical Reports. Engineering Research Institute. Kyoto University

Tech Rep Fac For Univ Toronto — Technical Report. Faculty of Forestry. University of Toronto

Tech Rep Grassld Res Inst — Technical Report. Grassland Research Institute

Tech Rep Inst At Energy Kyoto Univ — Technical Reports. Institute of Atomic Energy. Kyoto University

Tech Rep Inst Atom Energy Kyoto Univ — Technical Reports. Institute of Atomic Energy. Kyoto University

Tech Rep Inst Printed Circuits — Technical Report. Institute of Printed Circuits

Tech Rep ISSP (Inst Solid State Phys) Ser A — Technical Report. ISSP (Institute for Solid State Physics). Series A

Tech Rep Jet Propul Lab Calif Inst Technol — Technical Report. Jet Propulsion Laboratory. California Institute of Technology

Tech Rep Kansai Univ — Technology Reports. Kansai University

Tech Rep Nanyang Univ Coll Grad Stud Inst Nat Sci — Technical Report. Nanyang University. College of Graduate Studies. Institute of Natural Sciences

Tech Rep Natl Space Dev Agency Jpn — Technical Report. National Space Development Agency of Japan

Tech Rep Nisshin Steel Co Ltd — Technical Report. Nisshin Steel Company Limited [*Japan*]

Tech Reports Osaka Univ — Technology Reports. Osaka University

Tech Rep Reg Res Sta (Samaru) — Technical Report. Regional Research Station (Samaru)

Tech Repr Graver Water Cond Co — Technical Reprint. Graver Water Conditioning Company

Tech Rep Sch For Resour NC St Univ — Technical Report. School of Forest Resources. North Carolina State University

Tech Rep Ser ARL/TR Aust Radiat Lab — Australia. Australian Radiation Laboratory. Technical Report Series ARL/TR

Tech Rep Ser Carcinog Nat Cancer Inst (US) — Technical Report Series: Carcinogenesis. National Cancer Institute (United States)

Tech Rep Ser Int Atom Energy Ag — Technical Reports Series. International Atomic Energy Agency

Tech Rep Ser Victoria Dep Agric — Victoria. Department of Agriculture. Technical Report Series

Tech Rep Soil Res Inst Ghana Acad Sci — Technical Report. Soil Research Institute. Ghana Academy of Sciences

Tech Rep Syst Am Soc Met — Technical Report System. American Society for Metals

Tech Rep Syst ASM — Technical Report System. American Society for Metals

Tech Rep Tasmania Dep Mines — Tasmania. Department of Mines. Technical Report

Tech Rep Tasm Dep Mines — Technical Report. Tasmania Department of Mines

Tech Rep Tex For Serv — Technical Report. Texas Forest Service

Tech Rep Toyo Kohan Co Ltd — Technical Reports. Toyo Kohan Company Limited [*Japan*]

Tech Rep Univ Tex Austin Cent Res Water Resour — Technical Report. University of Texas at Austin. Center for Research in Water Resources

Tech Rep US Army Eng Waterw Exp Stn — Technical Report. United States Army Engineers. Waterways Experiment Station

Tech Rep Water Resour Res Cent Hawaii Univ — Technical Report. Hawaii University. Water Resource Research Center

Tech Rep Yale Sch For — Technical Report. Yale University. School of Forestry

Tech Res Cent Finland Electr and Nucl Technol Publ — Technical Research Centre of Finland. Electrical and Nuclear Technology Publication

Tech Res Cent Finland Mater and Process Technol Publ — Technical Research Centre of Finland. Materials and Processing Technology Publication

Tech Res Cent Finl Build Technol Community Dev Publ — Technical Research Centre of Finland. Building Technology and Community Development Publication

Tech Res Cent Finl Electr Nucl Technol Publ — Technical Research Centre of Finland. Electrical and Nuclear Technology Publication

Tech Res Cent Finl Gen Div Publ — Technical Research Centre of Finland. General Division Publication

Tech Res Cent Finl Mater Process Technol Publ — Technical Research Centre of Finland. Materials and Processing Technology Publication

Tech Rev Mitsubishi Heavy-Ind (Jpn Ed) — Technical Review. Mitsubishi Heavy-Industries (Japanese Edition)

Tech Rev Sumitomo Heavy Ind Ltd — Technical Review. Sumitomo Heavy Industries Limited

Tech Routiere — Technique Routiere [*Belgium*]

Tech Rundsch — Technische Rundschau

Tech Rundsch Sulzer — Technische Rundschau Sulzer [*Switzerland*]

Tech Sci Aeronaut Spat — Technique et Science Aeronautiques et Spatiales [*France*]

Tech Sci Munic — Techniques et Sciences Municipales [*France*]

Tech Sci Munic Eau — Techniques et Sciences Municipales/l'Eau

Tech Ser Fla Dep Nat Resour Mar Res Lab — Technical Series. Florida Department of Natural Resources. Marine Research Laboratory

Tech Skoda — Technika Skoda

Tech Smarownicza — Technika Smarownicza

Tech Smarownicza Trybol — Technika Smarownicza. Trybologia

Tech Soc Pacific Coast Tr — Technical Society of the Pacific Coast. Transactions

Tech Stud Common Exp Bldg Stn — Technical Studies. Commonwealth Experimental Building Station

Tech Stud Commonw Exp Bldg Stn — Technical Studies. Commonwealth Experimental Building Station

Tech Teach — Technical Teacher

Tech Timber Guide — Technical Timber Guide

Tech Timb Guide — Technical Timber Guide

Tech Times — Technology Transfer Times

Tech Trav — Techniques des Travaux [*Belgium*]

Tech Trav (Liege) — Technique des Travaux (Liege)

Tech Ueberwach — Technische Ueberwachung [*Technological Supervising*]

Tech Umweltschutz — Technik und Umweltschutz [*East Germany*]

Tech Univ Muenchen Jahrb — Technische Universitaet Muenchen. Jahrbuch

Tech W — Technical World [*Chicago*]

Tech W — Technology Week

Tech-Wiss Abh Osram-Ges — Technisch-Wissenschaftliche Abhandlungen der Osram-Gesellschaft

Tech Wk — Technology Week

Tech Wlok — Technik Wlokienniczy

Tech World — Technical World Magazine

Tech Zentralbl — Technisches Zentralblatt

Tech Zukunft — Techniken der Zukunft

TECIB — Technic International

Tec Ind (Madrid) — Tecnica Industrial (Madrid)

Tec Ital — Tecnica Italiana

TECLA — Tecnica (Lisbon)

Tec Metal — Tecnica Metalurgica [*Spain*]

Tec Met (Barcelona) — Tecnica Metalurgica (Barcelona)

Tec Mit K F — Technische Mitteilungen Krupp. Forschungsberichte

Tec Mit K W — Technische Mitteilungen Krupp. Werksberichte

Tec Molit — Tecnica Molitoria

Tecnica Lisb — Tecnica. Rivista de Engenharia (Lisboa)

Tecn Ital — Tecnica Italiana

Tecnol Aliment — Tecnologia Alimentaria

Tecnopolim Resine — Tecnopolimeri e Resine

TECPD — TAPPI [*Technical Association of the Pulp and Paper Industry*] Environmental Conference. Proceedings

Tec Pecuar Mex — Tecnica Pecuaria en Mexico

Tec Pecu Mex — Tecnica Pecuaria en Mexico

Tec R — Technology Review

Tec Regul & Mando Autom — Tecnica de la Regulacion y Mando Automatico

Tec Sint Spec Org — Tecniche e Sintesi Speciali Organiche

Tectonophys — Tectonophysics

T Ed — Theological Educator

TEDGA — Technical Digest

TEE — Tex-Textilis. Technisch Wetenschappelijk Maandblad voor de Benelux Textielindustrie

TEES Tech Bull — TEES [*Texas Engineering Experiment Station*] Technical Bulletin

TEF — Telex Africa

TEFL/TESL Newsl — TEFL [*Teaching English as a Foreign Language*]/ TESL [*Teaching English as a Second Language*] Newsletter

TEFO — Technological Forecasting and Social Change

TEG — Tijdschrift voor Economische en Sociale Geografie

Teg Meded S Afr Dep Landbou Viss — Tegniese Mededeling. Suid Afrika Departement van Landbou en Visserye

TEGNA — Tegnikon

TEGTA — Technische Gemeinschaft

TEH — Topics in Environmental Health [*Elsevier Book Series*]

TEHBA — Tehnika (Belgrade)

Teh Fiz — Tehnicka Fizika

Teh Hronika — Tehnika Hronika

Teh Tootmine — Tehnika ja Tootmine [*Estonian SSR*]

TEICA — Transactions. Engineering Institute of Canada

TEIGA — Teishin Igaku

Teilhard Rev — Teilhard Review [*London*]

Teint Apprets — Teinture et Apprets

TEIRD — Technology Ireland

TEJIA — Transport Engineer

TEJPA — Tejipar

TeK — Text und Kontext

Tek Aikak — Teknillinen Aikakauslehti

Tek Bul Petkim Petrokimya A S Arastirma Mudurlugu — Teknik Bulten. Petkim Petrokimya A. S. Arastirma Mudurlugu

Tek Forum — Tekniskt Forum [*Finland*]

TEKHA — Teoreticheskaya i Eksperimental'naya Khimiya

Tekh Dokl Gidrol — Tekhnicheskie Doklady po Gidrologii

Tekh Ekon Izv Tatabanyai Szenbanyak — Tekhnichesko Ekonomicheskie Izvestiya Tatabanyai Szenbanyak

Tekh Estetika — Tekhnicheskaya Estetika [*USSR*]

Tekh Inf Sov Nar Khoz Kuibyshev Ekon Adm Raiona — Tekhnicheskaya Informatsiya. Sovet Narodnogo Khozyaistva Kuibyshevskogo Ekonomicheskogo Administrativnogo Raiona

Tekh Kibern — Tekhnicheskaya Kibernetika

Tekh Kino Telev — Tekhnika Kino i Televideniya

Tekh Kino i Telev — Tekhnika Kino i Televideniya

Tekh Mis'l — Tekhnicheska Mis'l

Tekh Misul — Tekhnicheska Misul [*Bulgaria*]

Tekh Molodezhi — Tekhnika Molodezhi

Tekhnol Legk Splavov — Tekhnologiya Legkikh Splavov

Tekhnol Mashinostr (Moscow) — Tekhnologiya Mashinostroeniya (Moscow)

Tekhnol Mater — Tekhnologiya Materialov

Tekhnol Neorg Veshchestv — Tekhnologiya Neorganicheskikh Veshchestv

Tekhnol Organ Mekh Liteinogo Proizvod — Tekhnologiya, Organizatsiya, i Mekhanizatsiya Liteinogo Proizvodstva

Tekhnol Organ Proizvod — Tekhnologiya i Organizatsiya Proizvodstva

Tekhnol Proizvod Sukhikh Diagn Pitatel'nykh Sred — Tekhnologiya Proizvodstva Sukhikh Diagnosticheskikh Pitatel'nykh Sred

Tekhnol Stroit Proizvod — Tekhnologiya Stroitel'nogo Proizvodstva

Tek Hoegsk Handl — Tekniska Hoegskolan Handlingar

Tek Hogsk Helsingfors Vetensk Publ — Tekniska Hoegskolan i Helsingfors Vetenskapliga Publikationer

Tekh Sel'Khoz — Tekhnika v Sel'skom Khozyaistve

Tekh Usloviya Metody Opred Vrednykh Veshchestv Vozdukhe — Tekhnicheskie Usloviya na Metody Opredeleniya Vrednykh Veshchestv v Vozdukhe

Tekh Vooruzhenie — Tekhnika i Vooruzhenie [*USSR*]

Tekh Vozdushn Flota — Tekhnika Vozdushnogo Flota

Tekh Zhelezn Dorog — Tekhnika Zheleznykh Dorog

Tek Inf — Teknisk Information [*Sweden*]

TEKKA — Tekkokai

Tek Kem Aikak — Teknillisen Kemian Aikakauslehti [*Finland*]

Tek Medd — Tekniska Meddelanden [*Sweden*]

Tekn Forsknstift Skogsarb — Teknik Forskningsstiftelsen Skogsarbeten

Tekn Kino Televid — Tekhnika Kino i Televideniya

Teknol Avtom Mashinostr — Tekhnologiya i Avtomatizatsiya Mashinostroeniya

TEKSA — Tekhnika (Sofia)

Tek Samf Hand — Tekniska Samfundets Handlingar

Tekstil Prom — Tekstil'naya Promyshlennost

Tekst Ind — Tekstilna Industrija

Tekst Prom (Sofia) — Tekstilna Promishlennost (Sofia)

Tekst Prom-st — Tekstil'naya Promyshlennost

TEKTA — Tekstil

Tek Tidskr — Teknisk Tidskrift

Tek Tidskr Text Beklaedning — Teknisk Tidsskrift for Textil og Beklaedning

Tektonika Sib — Tektonika Sibiri

Tek Ukebl — Teknisk Ukeblad

Tek Vetensk Forsk — Teknisk Vetenskaplig Forskning [*Sweden*]

Tek Yay Kavak Arast Enst (Izmit) — Teknik Yayinlar. Kavakcihk Arastirma Enstitusu (Izmit, Turkey)

TEL — Telegraaf

Telcom Rep — Telcom Report

TELEA — Tetrahedron Letters

Telecom — Telecommunications

Telecom Aust Res Q — Telecom Australia Research Quarterly

Telecom J — Telecommunication Journal of Australia

Telecom J Aust — Telecommunication Journal of Australia

Telecomm — Telecommunications

Telecomm J — Telecommunication Journal

Telecomm J Aust — Telecommunication Journal of Australia

Telecomm Prod — Telecommunication Products and Technology

Telecomms — Telecommunications [*International Edition*]

Telecommun J — Telecommunication Journal

Telecommun J Aust — Telecommunication Journal of Australia

Telecommun J (Engl Ed) — Telecommunication Journal (English Edition)

Telecommun Policy — Telecommunications Policy

Telecommun Radio Eng — Telecommunications and Radio Engineering

Telecommun and Radio Eng Part 1 — Telecommunications and Radio Engineering. Part 1. Telecommunications

Telecommun and Radio Eng Part 2 — Telecommunications and Radio Engineering. Part 2. Radio Engineering

Telecommun Radio Eng (USSR) Part 2 — Telecommunications and Radio Engineering (USSR). Part 2. Radio Engineering

Tele (Engl Ed) — Tele (English Edition)

Telefon Rep — Telefon Report

Telef Rep — Telefon Report

Telefunken-Ztg — Telefunken-Zeitung [*West Germany*]

Telegr & Telef — Telegraaf en Telefoon

Teleph Eng & Manage — Telephone Engineer and Management

Telephone — Telephone Engineer and Management

Tele (Swed Ed) — Tele (Swedish Edition)

Tele-Tech & Electronic Ind — Tele-Tech and Electronic Industries

Television (JR Telev Soc) — Television (Journal of the Royal Television Society)

Telhan Patrica Oilseeds J — Telhan Patrica/Oilseeds Journal

TELLA — Tellus [*Sweden*]

Tellus Ser A — Tellus. Series A. Dynamic Meteorology and Oceanography

TelQ — Tel Quel

Tel Rad E R — Telecommunications and Radio Engineering (USSR)

Tel Vaani — Telugu Vaani [*Hyderabad*]

TEM — Exporter. Malta's Monthly Export Journal

TeM — O Tempo e o Modo

TE & M — Telephone Engineer and Management [*Harcourt Brace Jovanovich Publications, Inc.*] [*Geneva, IL*] [*Information service*]

Temas Odontol — Temas Odontologicos

Temas Socs — Temas Sociales

Temat Sb Inst Fiziol Biofiz Rast Akad Nauk Tadzh SSR — Tematicheskii Sbornik Institut Fiziologii i Biofiziki Rastenii. Akademiya Nauk Tadzhikskoi SSR

Temat Sb Nauc Trud Alma-Atin Semipalatin Zoovet Inst — Tematicheskii Sbornik Nauchnykh Trudov Alma-Atinskogo i Semipalatinskogo Zooveterinarnykh Institutov

Temat Sb Otd Fiziol Biofiz Rast Akad Nauk Tadzh SSR — Tematicheskii Sbornik Otdel Fiziologii i Biofiziki Rastenii Akademiya Nauk Tadzhikskoi SSR

Temat Sb Rab Gel'mintol Skh Zhivotn — Tematicheskii Sbornik Rabot po Gel'mintologii Sel'skokhozyaistvennykh Zhivotnykh

Temat Sb Vses Nauchno Issled Inst Gidrogeol Inzh Geol — Tematicheskii Sbornik Vsesoyuznogo Nauchno-Issledovatel'skogo Instituta Gidrogeologii Inzhenerskoi Geologii

Temat Sb Vses Neftegazov Nauchno Issled Inst — Tematicheskii Sbornik Vsesoyuznyi Neftegazovyi Nauchno-Issledovatel'skii Institut

TEMIA — Technische Mitteilungen

TEMOA — Tecnica Molitoria [*Italy*]

Temp Bar — Temple Bar

Temple Dent Rev — Temple Dental Review

Temple Law — Temple Law Quarterly

Temple L Quart — Temple Law Quarterly

Temp L Q — Temple Law Quarterly

Temps Mod — Temps Modernes

TENCA — Traffic Engineering and Control [*England*]

Tendances Conjonct — Tendances de la Conjoncture

Tendances Polit Act Dom — Tendances et Politiques Actuelles dans le Domaine de l'Habitation de la Construction et de la Planification

TEng — Teaching English

Tenn Ag Exp — Tennessee. Agricultural Experiment Station. Publications

Tenn Agric Exp Stn Annu Rep — Tennessee. Agricultural Experiment Station. Annual Report

Tenn Agric Exp Stn Bull — Tennessee. Agricultural Experiment Station. Bulletin

Tenn Agric Exp Stn Farm Econ Bull — Tennessee. Agricultural Experiment Station. Farm Economics Bulletin

Tenn Apiculture — Tennessee Apiculture

Tenn Bar J — Tennessee Bar Journal

Tenn BJ — Tennessee Bar Journal

Tenn Conservationist — Tennessee Conservationist

Tenn Dep Conserv Div Geol Bull — Tennessee. Department of Conservation. Division of Geology. Bulletin

Tenn Dep Conserv Div Geol Inf Circ — Tennessee. Department of Conservation. Division of Geology. Information Circular

Tenn Dept Labor Ann Rept — Tennessee. Department of Labor. Annual Report

Tenn Div Geol Bull — Tennessee. Division of Geology. Bulletin

Tenn Div Geol Environ Geol Ser — Tennessee. Division of Geology. Environmental Geology Series

Tenn Div Geol Inf Circ — Tennessee. Division of Geology. Information Circular

Tenn Div Geol Inform Circ — Tennessee. Division of Geology. Information Circular

Tenn Div Geol Rep Invest — Tennessee. Division of Geology. Report of Investigations

Tenn Div Water Resour Water Resour Ser — Tennessee. Division of Water Resources. Water Resources Series

Tenn Eng — Tennessee Engineer

Tennessee Acad Sci Jour — Tennessee Academy of Science. Journal

Tennessee Div Geology Geol Map — Tennessee. Division of Geology. Geologic Map

Tennessee Div Geology Rept Inv — Tennessee. Division of Geology. Report of Investigations

Tennessees Bus — Tennessee's Business

Tenn Farm & Home Sci — Tennessee Farm and Home Science

Tenn Farm Home Sci Progr Rep — Tennessee Farm and Home Science. Progress Report. University of Tennessee. Agricultural Experiment Station

Tenn Fm Home Sci Prog Rep — Tennessee Farm and Home Science. Progress Report

Tenn Folk S — Tennessee Folklore Society. Bulletin

Tenn G S Res Tenn B — Tennessee State Geological Survey. Resources of Tennessee. Bulletin

Tenn His M — Tennessee Historical Magazine

Tenn Hist Mag — Tennessee Magazine of History

Tenn Hist Q — Tennessee Historical Quarterly

Tenn Law Rev — Tennessee Law Review

Tenn Libn — Tennessee Librarian

Tenn Librn — Tennessee Librarian

Tenn L R — Tennessee Law Review

Tenn L Rev — Tennessee Law Review

Tenn Mag — Tennessee Magazine

Tenn St Bd Health B Rp — Tennessee State Board of Health. Bulletin. Report

Tenn Surv Bus — Tennessee Survey of Business

Tenn Univ Eng Exp Sta Bull — Tennessee University. Engineering Experiment Station. Bulletin

Tenn Univ Water Resour Res Cent Res Rep — Tennessee University. Water Resources Research Center. Research Report

Tenn Val Auth Chem Eng Bul — Tennessee Valley Authority. Chemical Engineering Bulletin

Tenn Val Auth Natl Fert Dev Cent Bull Y — Tennessee Valley Authority. National Fertilizer Development Center. Bulletin Y

Tenn Valley Perspect — Tennessee Valley Perspective

Tenn Wildl — Tennessee Wildlife

Tensai Kenkyu Hokoku Suppl — Tensai Kenkyu Hokoku. Supplement [*Japan*]

Tenside — Tenside-Detergents

Tenside-Deterg — Tenside-Detergents

Teolisuuden Keskuslab Tied — Teolisuuden Keskuslaboratorion Tiedonantoja

Teollis Tiedottaa — Teollisuuslitto Tiedottaa

Teol Vida — Teologia y Vida

Teor Ehlektrotekh — Teoreticheskaya Ehlektrotekhnika

Teor Eksp Biofiz — Teoreticheskaya i Eksperimental'naya Biofizica

Teor & Eksp Khim — Teoreticheskaya i Eksperimental'naya Khimiya

Teoret Elektrotekhn — L'vovskii Gosudarstvennyi Universitet. Teoreticheskaya Elektrotekhnika

Teoret Mat Fiz — Teoreticeskaja i Matematiceskaja Fizika

Teoret i Prikladna Meh — Teoreticna i Prikladna Mehanika

Teoret i Prikladna Meh — Teoreticna i Prikladna Mehanika Harkivs'kii Derzavnii Universitet Imeni O. M. Gor'kogo

Teoret Prikl Mat — Teoreticna i Prikladna Matematika

Teoret i Prikl Meh — Belorusskii Politehniceskii Institut. Teoreticeskaja i Prikladnaja Mehanika

Teoret i Prikl Mekh — Belorusskii Politekhnicheski Institut. Teoreticheskaya i Prikladnaya Mekhanika

Teoret Priloz Meh — B'lgarska Akademija na Naukite. Teoreticna i Prilozna Mehanika

Teoret i Priloz Meh — Teoreticna i Prilozna Mehanika

Teor Funkcii Funkcional Anal i Prilozen — Har'kovskii Ordena Trudovogo Krasnogo Znameni Gosudarstvennyi Universitet Imeni A. M. Gor'kogo. Teorija Funkcii. Funkcional'nyi Analiz i Ih Prilozenija

Teor Funkcii Funkcional Anal i Prilozen — Teorija Funkcii. Funkcional'nyi Analiz i Ih Prilozenija

Teor Funktsii Funktsional Anal i Prilozhen — Khar'kovskii Ordena Trudovogo Krasnogo Znameni Gosudarstvennyi Universitet Imeni A. M. Gor'kogo Teoriya Funktsii Funktsional'nyi Analiz i Ikh Prilozheniya

Teor Konecn Avtomatov i Prilozen — Institut Elektroniki i Vycislitel'noi Tehniki. Akademija Nauk Latviiskoi SSR. Teorija Konecnyh. Avtomatov i Ee Prilozenija

Teor i Mat Fiz — Teoreticheskaya i Matematicheskaya Fizika

Teor Mat Fiz — Teoreticheskaya i Matematicheskaya Fizika

Teor Metod — Teorie a Metoda

Teor Osn Khim Tekhnol — Teoreticheskie Osnovy Khimicheskoi Tekhnologii

Teor Prakt — Teoriya Praktika

Teor Prakt Fiz Kul't — Teoriya i Praktika Fizicheskoi Kul'tury

Teor Prakt Metall — Teoriya i Praktika Metallurgii (Chelyabinsk) [*USSR*]

Teor Prakt Metall (Chelyabinsk) — Teoriya i Praktika Metallurgii (Chelyabinsk)

Teor Prakt Metall (Dnepropetrovsk) — Teoriya i Praktika Metallurgii (Dnepropetrovsk)

Teor Prakt Podgot Koksovaniya Uglei — Teoriya i Praktika Podgotovki i Koksovaniya Uglei

Teor Prakt Stomatol — Teoriya i Praktika Stomatologii

Teor Prakt Szhiganiya Gaza — Teoriya i Praktika Szhiganiya Gaza [*USSR*]

Teor Prakt Vopr Mikrobiol Epidemiol — Teoreticheskie i Prakticheskie Voprosy Mikrobiologii i Epidemiologii

Teor Prakt Vopr Mikrobiol Epidemiol Resp Mezhved Sb — Teoreticheskie i Prakticheskie Voprosy Mikrobiologii i Epidemiologii Respublikanskii Mezhvedomstvennyi Sbornik

Teor Prakt Vopr Vaktsinno Syvorot Dela — Teoreticheskie i Prakticheskie Voprosy Vaktsinno Syvorotochnogo Dela

Teor Prilozh Mekh — Teoreticna i Prilozhna Mekhanika

Teor Primen Meh — Jugoslovensko Drustvo za Mehaniku. Teorijska i Primenjena Mehanika

Teor Verojatn Mat Stat — Teoriya Verojatnostej i Matematicheskaya Statistika

Teor Verojatnost i Mat Statist — Teorija Verojatnostei i Matematiceskaja Statistika

Teor Veroya — Teoriya Veroyatnostei i Ee Primeneniya

Teor Veroyatn i Primen — Teoriya Veroyatnostei i Ee Primeneniya

Teor Veroyatn Primen — Teoriya Veroyatnostei i Ee Primeneniya

Teor Veroyat Primen — Teoriya Veroyatnostei i Ee Primeneniya [*USSR*]

Teor Vopr Obrab Pochv — Teoreticheskie Voprosy Obrabotki Pochv

Tepl Naprazh Elem Konstr — Teplovye Napryazheniya v Elementakh Konstruktsii

Teploehnerg — Teploehnergetika

Teploenergetika Akad Nauk SSSR Energ Inst — Teploenergetika Akademiya Nauk SSSR. Energeticheskii Institut

Teplofiz Kharakt Veshchestv — Teplofizicheskie Kharakteristiki Veshchestv [*USSR*]

Teplofiz Optim Tepl Protsessov — Teplofizika i Optimizatsiya Teplovykh Protsessov

Teplofiz Svoistva Veshchestv — Teplofizicheskie Svoistva Veshchestv

Teplofiz Svoistva Veshchestv Mater — Teplofizicheskie Svoistva Veshchestv i Materialov

Teplofiz Teplotekh — Teplofizika i Teplotekhnika

Teplofiz Vys Temp — Teplofizika Vysokikh Temperatur

Teploprovodnost Diffuz — Teploprovodnost i Diffuziya

Teplotekh Probl Pryamogo Preobraz Energ — Teplotekhnicheskie Problemy Pryamogo Preobrazovaniya Energii [*Ukrainian SSR*]

TeR — Te Reo

TERAA — Terapia
Ter Arkh — Terapevticheskii Arkhiv
Teratogenesis Carcinog Mutagen — Teratogenesis, Carcinogenesis, and Mutagenesis
TEREA — Technology Review
TERMA — Termotecnica
Termeloeszoevet Tanacsadoja — Termeloeszoevetkezetek Tanacsadoja
Termeszettud Koezloeny — Termeszettudomanyi Koezloeny
Term Obrab Fiz Met — Termicheskaya Obrabotka i Fizika Metallov
Termodin Fiz Kinet Strukturoobraz Stali Chugune — Termodinamika i Fizicheskaya Kinetika Strukturoobrazovaniya v Stali i Chugune
Termodin Fiz Kinet Strukturoobraz Svoistva Chuguna Stali — Termodinamika i Fizicheskaya Kinetika Strukturoobrazovaniya, i Svoistva Chuguna i Stali
Termoprochn Mater Konstr Elem — Termoprochnost Materialov i Konstruktivnykh Elementov [USSR]
Termotecnica Suppl — Termotecnica. Supplemento [Italy]
Ter Ortop Stomatol — Terapevticheskaya i Ortopedicheskaya Stomatologiva
Terra Amer — Terra America
Terra Trent — Terra Trentina
Terre Maroc — Terre Marocaine
Terre Vie Rev Ecol Appl — Terre et la Vie. Revue d'Ecologie Appliquee
Ter Rev Med — Terapeutica. Revista de Medicina
Territ — Territorian
Terr LJ — Territory Law Journal
Terr Magn — Terrestrial Magnetism and Atmospheric Electricity
Ter Stomatol — Terapevticheskaya Stomatologiya
Tertiary Res Spec Pap — Tertiary Research Special Papers
TERU — Teruletrendezes [Hungary]
Tes — Tesaur
TES — Textiles Suisses. Revue de l'Industrie Suisse des Textiles d'Habillement
TES — Times Educational Supplement
TESDA — Tenside [Later, Tenside-Detergents]
TESG — Tijdschrift voor Economische en Sociale Geografie
TESG-A — Tijdschrift voor Economische en Sociale Geografie [Netherlands]
Tesla Electron — Tesla Electronics
Tesla Electron Q Rev Czech Electron Telecommun — Tesla Electronics. Quarterly Review of Czechoslovak Electronics and Telecommunications
TESOB — Terra e Sole
TESOLQ — TESOL [Teachers of English to Speakers of Other Languages] Quarterly
TESOL Quart — TESOL [Teachers of English to Speakers of Other Languages] Quarterly
Test Eng Manage — Test Engineering and Management
Test Instrum Controls — Testing, Instruments, and Controls [Australia]
Test Memor Timb Res Developm Ass — Test Memorandum. Timber Research and Development Association
Test Polym — Testing of Polymers
Test Rec Timb Res Developm Ass — Test Record. Timber Research and Development Association
TeT — Taal en Tongval [Antwerpen]
TETHB — Tethys
Tethys Suppl — Tethys. Supplement
TETRA — Tetrahedron
Tetrahedr L — Tetrahedron Letters
Tetrahedron Lett — Tetrahedron Letters
Tetrahedron Suppl — Tetrahedron. Supplement
Teubner Studienskr — Teubner Studienskripten
Teut — Teuthonista
TEW Tech Ber — TEW [Technische Edelstahlwerke] Technische Berichte [Later, Thyssen Edelstahl Technische Berichte]
TEX — Revue Francaise des Telecommunications
Tex Ag Exp — Texas. Agricultural Experiment Station. Publications
Tex Agric Exp Stn Bull — Texas. Agricultural Experiment Station. Bulletin
Tex Agric Exp Stn Leafl — Texas. Agricultural Experiment Station. Leaflet
Tex Agric Exp Stn Misc Publ — Texas. Agricultural Experiment Station. Miscellaneous Publication
Tex Agric Exp Stn Prog Rep — Texas. Agricultural Experiment Station. Progress Report
Tex Agric Exp Stn Tech Monogr — Texas. Agricultural Experiment Station. Technical Monograph
Tex Agric Ext Serv Fish Dis Diagn Lab — Texas. Agricultural Extension Service. Fish Disease Diagnostic Laboratory
Tex Agric Prog — Texas Agricultural Progress
Tex Agr Progr — Texas Agricultural Progress
Tex A & M Univ Dep Civ Eng Rep — Texas A & M University. Department of Civil Engineering. Report
Tex A M Univ Oceanogr Stud — Texas A & M University. Oceanographic Studies
Tex A & M Univ Syst Tex Agric Ext Serv Fish Dis Diagn Lab — Texas A & M University System. Texas Agricultural Extension Service. Fish Disease Diagnostic Laboratory
Tex A M Univ Syst Tex Agric Ext Serv Fish Dis Diagn Lab FDDL — Texas A & M University System. Texas Agricultural Extension Service. Fish Disease Diagnostic Laboratory. FDDL

Tex A & M Univ Tex Eng Exp Stn Tech Bull — Texas A & M University. Texas Engineering Experiment Station. Technical Bulletin
Texas Acad of Sci Trans — Texas Academy of Sciences. Transactions
Texas Archeol Paleont Soc Bull — Texas Archeological and Paleontological Society. Bulletin
Texas BJ — Texas Bar Journal
Texas Board of Water Engineers Bull — Texas. Board of Water Engineers. Bulletin
Texas Bus Rev — Texas Business Review
Texas Cour Rec Med — Texas Courier Record of Medicine
Texas Eng Expt Sta Research Rept — Texas. Engineering Experiment Station. Research Report
Texas Internat L Forum — Texas International Law Forum
Texas Internat LJ — Texas International Law Journal
Texas Int'l LF — Texas International Law Forum
Texas Int'l LJ — Texas International Law Journal
Texas Jour Sci — Texas Journal of Science
Texas L Rev — Texas Law Review
Texas Memorial Mus Pearce-Sellards Ser — Texas Memorial Museum. Pearce-Sellards Series
Texas Mo — Texas Monthly
Texas Nurs — Texas Nursing
Texas Oil Jour — Texas Oil Journal
Texas Petroleum Research Comm Bull — Texas Petroleum Research Committee. Bulletin
Texas South UL Rev — Texas Southern University. Law Review
Texas Tech L Rev — Texas Tech Law Review
Texas Univ Austin Bur Econ Geology Geol Circ — Texas University at Austin. Bureau of Economic Geology. Geological Circular
Texas Univ Austin Bur Econ Geology Geol Quad Map — University of Texas at Austin. Bureau of Economic Geology. Geologic Quadrangle Map
Texas Univ Austin Bur Econ Geology Guidebook — Texas University at Austin. Bureau of Economic Geology. Guidebook
Texas Univ Austin Bur Econ Geology Rept Inv — University of Texas at Austin. Bureau of Economic Geology. Report of Investigations
Texas Univ Pub Bur Econ Geology Mineral Res Circ Rept Inv — Texas University. Publication. Bureau of Economic Geology. Mineral Resource Circular. Report of Investigations
Texas Water Devel Board Rept — Texas. Water Development Board. Report
Tex B J — Texas Bar Journal
Tex Board Water Eng Bull — Texas. Board of Water Engineers. Bulletin
Tex Board Water Eng Chem Compos Tex Surf Waters — Texas. Board of Water Engineers. Chemical Composition of Texas Surface Waters
Tex Bus Exec — Texas Business Executive
Tex Busin Rev — Texas Business Review
Tex Bus R — Texas Business Review
Tex Bus Rev — Texas Business Review
Tex Dent J — Texas Dental Journal
Tex Energy — Texas Energy
Tex Energy Miner Resour — Texas Energy and Mineral Resources
Tex Eng Exp Stn Bull — Texas. Engineering Experiment Station. Bulletin
Tex Eng Exp Stn News — Texas. Engineering Experiment Station. News
Tex Eng Exp Stn Res Rep — Texas. Engineering Experiment Station. Research Report
Tex For Pap — Texas Forestry Paper
Tex Geogr Mag — Texas Geographic Magazine
Tex G S Rp Prog — Texas. Geological Survey. Report of Progress
Tex His Q — Texas State Historical Association. Quarterly
Tex Hist Assoc Q — Texas State Historical Association. Quarterly
Tex Hosp — Texas Hospitals
Tex Hospitals — Texas Hospitals
Tex Inst — Texas Institutes
Tex Int L Forum — Texas International Law Forum
Tex Int L J — Texas International Law Journal
Tex Intl LJ — Texas International Law Journal
Tex J — Texas Journal
Tex J Pharm — Texas Journal of Pharmacy
Tex J Sci — Texas Journal of Science
Tex J Sci Spec Publ — Texas Journal of Science. Special Publication
Tex Law Rev — Texas Law Review
Tex Lib — Texas Libraries
Tex Lib J — Texas Library Journal
Tex Libr — Texas Libraries
Tex L R — Texas Law Review
Tex L Rev — Texas Law Review
Tex Med — Texas Medicine
Tex Mem Mus Misc Pap — Texas Memorial Museum. Miscellaneous Papers
Tex Mo — Texas Monthly
Tex Nurs — Texas Nursing
Tex Nutr Conf Proc — Texas Nutrition Conference. Proceedings
Tex Outl — Texas Outlook
Tex Parks Wildl — Texas Parks Wildlife
Tex Pharm — Texas Pharmacy
Tex Q — Texas Quarterly
Tex Rep Bio — Texas Reports on Biology and Medicine
Tex Rep Biol Med — Texas Reports on Biology and Medicine

Tex Res — Textile Research
Tex Res J — Textile Research Journal
Tex Rev — Texas Review
Tex So LR — Texas Southern Law Review
Tex So U L Rev — Texas Southern University. Law Review
Tex State Hist Assoc Quar — Texas State Historical Association. Quarterly
Tex State J Med — Texas State Journal of Medicine
Tex St Lit — Texas Studies in Literature and Language
Tex Stud Lit & Lang — Texas Studies in Literature and Language
Tex SUL Rev — Texas Southern University. Law Review
TEXTA — Technical Extracts of Traffic [*National Security Agency*]
Text Abstr — Textile Abstracts
Text Age — Textile Age
Text Am — Textile American
Text Argus — Textile Argus
Text Asia — Textile Asia
Text Beklaedning — Textil og Beklaedning
Text Betr (Poessneck Ger) — Textil-Betrich (Poessneck, Germany)
Text Bull — Textile Bulletin
Text Chem Color — Textile Chemist and Colorist
Text Chim — Textiles Chimiques
Text Color — Textile Colorist
Text Color Converter — Textile Colorist and Converter
Text Cordage Q — Textile and Cordage Quarterly
Text Dyer Printer — Textile Dyer and Printer
Tex Tech LR — Texas Tech Law Review
Tex Tech L Rev — Texas Tech Law Review
Texte Kritisch Psych — Texte zur Kritischen Psychologie
TexteM — Texte Metzler
Textes et Doc (Bruxelles) — Textes et Documents (Bruxelles)
Textes Math — Textes Mathematiques
Tex-Text — Tex-Textilis
Text Faerberei Ztg — Textil und Faerberei-Zeitung
Text Faserstofftech — Textil und Faserstofftechnik
Text Forsch — Textil-Forschung
Text Hist — Textile History
Text Horizons — Textile Horizons
Text I Ind — Textile Institute and Industry
Textilchem Color — Textilchemiker und Colorist
Textile Ind — Textile Industries
Textile Inst Ind — Textile Institute and Industry
Textile J Aust — Textile Journal of Australia
Textile Progr — Textile Progress
Textile Res J — Textile Research Journal
Textile Technol Dig — Textile Technology Digest
Textil Rep — America's Textiles Reporter Bulletin
Textilvered — Textilveredelung
Textil-W — Textil-Wirtschaft
Textil Wld — Textile World Buyer's Guide/Fact File
Text Ind — Textile Industries
Text Ind Exporter — Textile Industry and Exporter
Text Ind (Moenchen Gladbach Ger) — Textil-Industrie (Moenchen Gladbach, Germany)
Text Ind (Munich) — Textil-Industrie (Munich)
Text Ind Sthn Afr — Textile Industries Southern Africa
Text Ind (Zurich) — Textil-Industrie (Zurich)
Text Inst Ind — Textile Institute and Industry
Text J Aust — Textile Journal of Australia
Text Konfekt — Textil och Konfektion
Text Krit — Text und Kritik
Text Mag — Textile Magazine
Text Manuf J — Textile Manufacturer's Journal
Text Mercury Int — Textile Mercury International
Text Mfr — Textile Manufacturer
Text Mon — Textile Month
Text-Prax — Textil-Praxis [*Later, Textil Praxis International*]
Text Prax Int — Textil Praxis International
Text Prog — Textile Progress
Text Q — Textile Quarterly
Tex Transp Res — Texas Transportation Researcher
Text Rec — Textile Recorder
Text Rent — Textile Rental
Text Res J — Textile Research Journal
Text Tech Dig — Textile Technology Digest
Texture Cryst Solids — Texture of Crystalline Solids
Textures and Microstruct — Textures and Microstructures
Text Wkly — Textile Weekly
Text World — Textile World
Text World J — Textile World Journal
Text World R — Textile World Record
Tex Univ B Min S B — Texas University. Bulletin. Mineral Survey Bulletin
Tex Univ Bur Econ Geol Geol Circ — Texas University. Bureau of Economic Geology. Geological Circular
Tex Univ Bur Econ Geol Miner Resour Circ — Texas University. Bureau of Economic Geology. Mineral Resource Circular

Tex Univ Bur Econ Geol Publ — Texas University. Bureau of Economic Geology. Publication
Tex Unlv Bur Econ Geol Rep Invest — Texas University. Bureau of Economic Geology. Report of Investigations
Tex Univ Bur Econ Geol Res Note — Texas University. Bureau of Economic Geology. Research Note
Tex Univ Cent Res Water Resour Tech Rep — Texas University. Center for Research in Water Resources. Technical Report
TE (XVIII) — Textos y Estudios del Siglo XVIII
Tex Water Comm Circ — Texas. Water Commission. Circular
Tex Water Comm Mem Rep — Texas. Water Commission. Memorandum Report
Tex Water Dev Board Rep — Texas. Water Development Board. Report
TeZ — Texte und Zeichen
Tez Doklad Nauch Konf Zootech Sek — Tezisy Dokladov Nauchnoi Konferentsii. Zootekhnicheskaya Sektsiya
Tezhka Prom — Tezhka Promishlenost
Tezisy Dokl Vses Nauchno Metod Konf Vet Patoloanat — Tezisy Dokladov Vsesoyuznoi Nauchno-Metodicheskoi Konferentsii Veterinarnykh Patologoanatomov
TF — Transformation
TFHSA — Tennessee Farm and Home Science
TfK — Tidskrift foer Konstvetinskap
TFKVA — Teplofizicheskie Kharakteristiki Veshchestv
TFM — Textes Francais Modernes
TFORA — Tekniskt Forum
TFR — Technological Forecasting and Social Change. An International Journal
TFS — Technological Forecasting and Social Change
TFSB — Tennessee Folklore Society. Bulletin
TFSCB — Technological Forecasting and Social Change
TFSOA — Transactions. Faraday Society
TFSP — Texas Folklore Society. Publications
TFST — Thin Films Science and Technology [*Elsevier Book Series*]
TFTTA — Teplofizika i Teplotekhnika
TFWBKEL — Theologische Forschung Wissenschaftliche Beitraege zur Kirchlichevangelischen Lehre
TG — Theologie und Glaube
TG — Therapeutic Gazette [*Philadelphia*]
TG — Tijdschrift voor Geschiedenis. Land en Volkenkunde
TG — Toho Gakuho
TG — TV Guide
TGA — Trade with Greece (Athens)
TGA — Tuebinger Germanistische Arbeiten
TGANA — Tsitologiya i Genetika
TGCGA — Transactions. Gulf Coast Association of Geologic Societies
TGDR — Tokyo Gailkokugo Daigaku Ronshu [*Area and Cultural Studies*]
T Geesteswet — Tydskrif vir Geesteswetenskappe
TGegw — Theologie der Gegenwart
TGEOD — Technika Poszukiwan Geologicznych
TGF — Tijdschrift voor Geschiedenis en Folklore
TGGL-B — Travaux Geographique de Liege (Belgium)
TGI — Instellingen
TGKHA — Takenaka Gijutsu Kenkyu Hokoku
TGKZA — Trudy Instituta Geologicheskikh Nauk Akademiya Nauk Kazakhskoi SSR
TGLV — Tijdschrift voor Geschiedenis. Land en Volkenkunde
TGM — Theatre Guild Magazine
TGMEA — Tropical and Geographical Medicine
TGorPI — Trudy Goriiskogo Gosudarstvennogo Pedagogicheskogo Instituta
TGO Tijdschr Ther Geneesmiddel Onder — TGO. Tijdschrift voor Therapie, Geneesmiddel, en Onderzoek
TGP — Tasmanian Government Publications
TGPIA — Trudy Gruzinskii Politekhnicheskii Institut Imeni V. I. Lenina
TGR — Tohoku Gakuin Daigaku Ronshu [*North Japan College Review: Essays and Studies in English Language and Literature*]
TGSDA — Tulsa Geological Society. Digest
TGSG — Transactions. Gaelic Society of Glasgow
TGSI — Transactions. Gaelic Society of Inverness
TGSSA — Transactions. Geological Society of South Africa
TGT — German Tribune
TGUBA — Bulletin. Tokyo Gakugei University
TGUOS — Transactions. Glasgow University Oriental Society
TGW — Theologie der Gegenwart
TGZIA — Technische Gids voor Ziekenhuis en Instelling
TH — Teaching History
TH — Teki Historyczne
Th — Theologia
Th — Theology
Th — Things
Th — Thought
TH — Today's Health
ThA — Theatre Annual
Thai J Agric Sci — Thai Journal of Agricultural Science
Thai J Dev Adm — Thai Journal of Development Administration [*Bangkok*]
Thai J Nurs — Thai Journal of Nursing

Thailand Dep Miner Resour Ground Water Bull — Thailand. Department of Mineral Resources. Ground Water Bulletin

Thailand Dep Miner Resour Rep Invest — Thailand. Department of Mineral Resources. Report of Investigation

Thail Plant Prot Serv Tech Bull — Thailand Plant Protection Service. Technical Bulletin

Thai Natl Sci Pap Fauna Ser — Thai National Scientific Papers. Fauna Series

Thai Nurses Assoc J — Thai Nurses Association Journal

Thai Sci Bull — Thai Science Bulletin

Thalassia Jugosl — Thalassia Jugoslavica

Tharandter Forstl Jahrb — Tharandter Forstliches Jahrbuch

ThArts — Theatre Arts

Th Aust — Theatre Australia

ThB — Theologische Blaetter

THB — Today's Housing Briefs

THB — Trierer Heimatbuch

Thbilis Sahelmc Univ Gamoqeneb Math Inst Srom — Thbilisis Sahelmcipho Universiteti Gamoqenebithi Mathematikis Instituti. Sromebi

Thbilis Univ Srom — Thbilisis Universitetis. Phizika-Mathematikisa de Sabunebismetqvelo Mecnierebani. Sromebi

Thbilis Univ Srom A — Thbilisis Universitetis Sromebi. A. Phizika-Mathematikisa de Sabunebismetqvelo Mecnierebani

THbl — Trierische Heimatblaetter

THC — Topics in Health Care Financing

THCF — Topics in Health Care Financing

ThD — Theology Digest [*St. Mary's, KS*]

ThDig — Theology Digest [*St. Mary's, KS*]

THEA — Theata

Theat Ann — Theatre Annual

Theat C — Theatre Crafts

Theat Craft — Theatre Crafts

Theat Heute — Theater Heute

Theat J — Theatre Journal

Theat Note — Theatre Notebook

Theat Q — Theatre Quarterly

Theat Quart — Theatre Quarterly

Theatre Arts M — Theatre Arts Magazine

Theatre J — Theatre Journal

Theatre M — Theatre Magazine

Theatre Notebk — Theatre Notebook

Theatre Pol — Theatre en Pologne - Theatre in Poland

Theatre Q — Theatre Quarterly

Theatre Res Int — Theatre Research International

Theatre S — Theatre Studies

Theatre S — Theatre Survey

Theat Res I — Theatre Research International

Theat Stud — Theatre Studies

Theat Surv — Theatre Survey

Theat Zeit — Theater der Zeit

Th Ed — Theological Education

T Heden Rom-Holl Reg — Tydskrif vir Hedendaagse Romeins-Hollandse Reg

THE J — THE [*Technological Horizons in Education*] Journal

THE Jrnl — THE [*Technological Horizons in Education*] Journal

Them — Themelios

Themis — Revue Juridique Themis

Theo Ecl — Theological Eclectic

Theokr — Theokratia [*Leiden/Cologne*]

Theol — Theology [*London*]

Theol Dgst — Theology Digest

Theol Evang — Theologia Evangelica

Theo & Lit J — Theological and Literary Journal

Theol Phil — Theologie und Philosophie

Theol Quart-schrift — Theologische Quartalschrift

Theol R — Theologische Revue

Theol & Rel Ind — Theological and Religious Index

Theol Stds — Theological Studies

Theol Stud — Theological Studies

Theol Today — Theology Today

Theol Via — Theologia Viatorum

Theo Mo — Theological Monthly

Theo R — Theological Review

Theor A Gen — Theoretical and Applied Genetics

Theor Appl Genet — Theoretical and Applied Genetics

Theor Appl Mech (Sofia) — Theoretical and Applied Mechanics (Sofia)

Theor Chem — Theoretical Chemistry

Theor Chem Adv Perspect — Theoretical Chemistry. Advances and Perspectives

Theor Chem Engng Abstr — Theoretical Chemical Engineering Abstracts

Theor Chem (NY) — Theoretical Chemistry (New York)

Theor Chem Period Chem Biol — Theoretical Chemistry. Periodicities in Chemistry and Biology

Theor Chim — Theoretica Chimica Acta

Theor Chim Acta — Theoretica Chimica Acta

Theor Comput Sci — Theoretical Computer Science

Theor Decis — Theory and Decision

Theo Repos — Theological Repository

Theoret Appl Genet — Theoretical and Applied Genetics

Theoret Chim Acta — Theoretica Chimica Acta

Theoret Comput Sci — Theoretical Computer Science

Theoret Linguist — Theoretical Linguistics

Theoret and Math Phys — Theoretical and Mathematical Physics

Theoret Population Biol — Theoretical Population Biology

Theoret Population Biology — Theoretical Population Biology

Theor Exp Biol — Theoretical and Experimental Biology

Theor Exp Biophys — Theoretical and Experimental Biophysics

Theor Exp Chem — Theoretical and Experimental Chemistry

Theor Exp Methoden Regelunstech — Theoretische und Experimentelle Methoden der Regelungstechnik

Theor Found Chem Eng — Theoretical Foundations of Chemical Engineering

Theorie et Polit — Theorie et Politique

Theor Klin Med Einzeldarst — Theoretische und Klinische Medizin in Einzeldarstellungen

Theor Klin Med Einzeldarstell — Theoretische und Klinische Medizin in Einzeldarstellungen [*West Germany*]

Theor Math — Theoretical and Mathematical Physics

Theor Math Phys — Theoretical and Mathematical Physics

Theor and Math Phys — Theoretical and Mathematical Physics

Theor Pop B — Theoretical Population Biology

Theor Popul Biol — Theoretical Population Biology

Theor Probability Appl — Theory of Probability and Its Applications

Theor Theor — Theoria to Theory

Theory Exp Exobiol — Theory and Experiment in Exobiology

Theory Probab Appl — Theory of Probability and Its Applications

Theory Probab and Appl — Theory of Probability and Its Applications

Theory Probability and Math Statist — Theory of Probability and Mathematical Statistics

Theory Probab Math Statist — Theory of Probability and Mathematical Statistics

Theory and Soc — Theory and Society

Theory Soc — Theory and Society

Theosophy in Aust — Theosophy in Australia

Theos Q — Theosophical Quarterly

Theo Today — Theology Today

Therapeutic Ed — Therapeutic Education

Therap Gegenw — Therapie der Gegenwart

Therap Halbmonatsh — Therapeutische Halbmonatshefte

Therapie Gegenw — Therapie der Gegenwart

Therap Monatsh Vet-Med — Therapeutische Monatshefte fuer Veterinaermedizin

Ther Ber — Therapeutische Berichte

Ther Drug Monit — Therapeutic Drug Monitoring

Ther Gaz — Therapeutic Gazette

Ther Ggw — Therapie der Gegenwart

Ther Halbmonatsh — Therapeutische Halbmonatshefte

Ther Hung — Therapia Hungarica

Therm Abstr — Thermal Abstracts

Therm Eng — Thermal Engineering

Therm Engng — Thermal Engineering

Therm Engr — Thermal Engineering

Therm Eng (USSR) — Thermal Engineering (USSR)

Therm Nucl Power — Thermal and Nuclear Power [*Japan*]

Thermoc Act — Thermochimica Acta

Thermochim Acta — Thermochimica Acta

Ther Monatsh — Therapeutische Monatshefte

Therm Power Conf Proc — Thermal Power Conference. Proceedings [*United States*]

Therm Power Gener — Thermal Power Generation

Ther Nervensys — Therapie ueber das Nervensystem

Ther Nervensyst — Therapie ueber das Nervensystem

Ther Probl Today — Therapeutic Problems of Today

Ther Recreation J — Therapeutic Recreation Journal

Ther Recr J — Therapeutic Recreation Journal

Ther Sem Hop — Therapeutique. Semaine des Hopitaux

Ther Umsch — Therapeutische Umschau

Thes — Thesaurus

THES — Times Higher Education Supplement

THESA N — Teachers of Home Economics Specialist Association. Newsletter

Theses Cathol Med Coll — Theses. Catholic Medical College

Theses Cathol Med Coll (Seoul) — Theses. Catholic Medical College (Seoul)

Theses Collect Chonnam Univ Chonnam Univ — Theses Collection of Chonnam University. Chonnam University

Theses Collect Incheon Jr Coll — Theses Collection. Incheon Junior College

Theses Collect Kyungnam Ind Jr Coll — Theses Collection. Kyungnam Industrial Junior College [*Republic of Korea*]

Theses Collect Kyungnam Univ — Theses Collection. Kyungnam University [*Republic of Korea*]

Theses Collect Sookmyung Women's Univ — Theses Collection. Sookmyung Women's University

Theses Collect Yeungnam Univ — Theses Collection. Yeungnam University [*Republic of Korea*]

Theses Collect Yeungnam Univ Nat Sci — Theses Collection. Yeungnam University. Natural Sciences [*Republic of Korea*]

Theses Doct Ing Univ Dakar Ser Sci Nat — Theses de Docteur-Ingenieur. Universite de Dakar. Serie Sciences Naturelles
Thesis — Thesis Eleven
Thesis Theo Cassettes — Thesis Theological Cassettes
T Heth — Text der Hethiter
ThF — Theologische Forschung [*Hamburg*]
ThG — Theologie der Gegenwart
ThG — Theologie und Glaube
THGEA — Therapie der Gegenwart
THHP — Tung-Hai Hsueh-Pao [*Tunghai Journal*]
Thiemig-Taschenb — Thiemig-Taschenbuecher
Thieraerzt Mitth (Carlsruhe) — Thieraerztliche Mittheilungen (Carlsruhe)
Thiermed Rundschau — Thiermedicinische Rundschau
Thin Sol Fi — Thin Solid Films
Third Wld — Third World Forum
Third Wld Agric — Third World Agriculture
Third World Planning R — Third World Planning Review
Third World Q — Third World Quarterly
Third World Soc — Third World Socialists
Thirties Soc Jnl — Thirties Society. Journal
Thirty-3 — 33 Magazine
Thirty-Three/33 Mag Met Prod Ind — Thirty-Three/33. Magazine of the Metals Producing Industry
ThisMag — This Magazine
This Mag — This Magazine Is about Schools [*Later, This Magazine: Education, Culture, Politics*]
ThJ — Theologische Jahrbuecher
THJCS — Tsing Hua Journal of Chinese Studies
THJUA — Thalassia Jugoslavica
THKSA — Taiki Hoshano Kansoku Seiseki
ThL — Theologisches Literaturblatt [*Leipzig*]
ThLB — Theologisches Literaturblatt
ThLBl — Theologisches Literaturblatt [*Leipzig*]
Th Life — Theology and Life
Th Lit — Theologische Literaturzeitung
ThLL — Thesaurus Linguae Latinae
ThLZ — Theologische Literaturzeitung
THM — Textos Hispanicos Modernos
Thm — Thomist
THM — Tien Hsia Monthly
THM — Topics in Health Care Materials Management
Th Markings — Theological Markings
Th M S — Thomas Mann-Studien
Thol Ed — Theological Educator
Thom — Thomist
Thompson Yates and Johnston Lab Rep — Thompson, Yates, and Johnston Laboratories Reports
Thompson Yates Lab Rep — Thompson-Yates Laboratories Reports
Thomson's Process Chem Eng — Thomson's Process and Chemical Engineering [*Australia*]
Thorac Cardiovasc Surg — Thoracic and Cardiovascular Surgeon
Thoraxchir Vask Chir — Thoraxchirurgie - Vaskulaere Chirurgie
Thoroton Soc Rec Ser — Thoroton Society. Record Series
Thoth Res — Thoth Research Journal
Th & Ph — Theologie und Philosophie
Th P Q — Theologisch-Praktische Quartalschrift
Th Pr Ma St — Theory of Probability and Mathematical Statistics
Th Prob Ap — Theory of Probability and Its Applications
ThPrQSchr — Theologisch-Praktische Quartalschrift [*Linz, Austria*]
THQ — Tennessee Historical Quarterly
ThQ — Theatre Quarterly
ThQ — Theologische Quartalschrift
ThQ — Tuebinger Theologische Quartalschrift
ThQR — Theological Quarterly Review
ThR — Theatre Research
ThR — Theological Review [*Princeton, NJ*]
ThR — Theologische Revue
ThR — Theologische Rundschau
THR — Thrust. Journal for Employment and Training Professionals
THR — Travaux d'Humanisme et Renaissance
Th Rdschau — Theologische Rundschau
Three Bank — Three Banks Review
Three Banks R — Three Banks Review
Three Banks Rev — Three Banks Review
Three Forks — Three Forks of Muddy Creek
Three R Int — Three R International [*West Germany*]
TH Rep Eindhoven Univ Technol Dep Electr Eng — TH-Report-Eindhoven University of Technology. Department of Electrical Engineering
ThRev — Theologische Revue
Th RI — Theatre Research International
Th Ri Po — Three Rivers Poetry Journal
ThRNF — Theologische Rundschau. Neue Folge [*Tuebingen*]
Thromb Diat — Thrombosis et Diathesis Haemorrhagica
Thromb Diath Haemorrh — Thrombosis et Diathesis Haemorrhagica
Thromb Diath Haemorrh Suppl — Thrombosis et Diathesis Haemorrhagica. Supplementum

Thromb Haemost — Thrombosis and Haemostasis
Thromb Haemostas — Thrombosis and Haemostasis
Thromb Res — Thrombosis Research
Th Rsch — Theologische Rundschau
ThRu — Theologische Rundschau
THRU — Thrust
Th Rv — Theologische Revue
THS — Textes pour l'Histoire Sacree
ThS — Theatre Survey
ThS — Theological Studies
ThS — Theologische Studien und Kritiken
THS — Times Health Supplement [*London*]
THSC — Transactions. Honourable Society of Cymmrodorion
THSG — Transactions. Historical Society of Ghana
ThSK — Theologische Studien und Kritiken [*Hamburg/Berlin*]
THSRB — Tufts Health Science Review
ThSt — Theological Studies
ThStKr — Theologische Studien und Kritiken [*Hamburg/Berlin*]
ThT — Theologisch Tijdschrift
Th T — Theology Today
THTAD — Thiemig-Taschenbuecher
Th Today — Theology Today
ThuGl — Theologie und Glaube
Thule Int Symp — Thule International Symposia
Thur Marsh LJ — Thurgood Marshall Law Journal
ThV — Theologia Viatorum. Jahrbuch der Kirchlichen Hochschule [*Berlin*]
ThViat — Theologia Viatorum. Jahrbuch der Kirchlichen Hochschule [*Berlin*]
THY — Thomas Hardy Yearbook
THYMD — Thymus
Thyssen Edelstahl Tech Ber — Thyssen Edelstahl Technische Berichte
Thyssen Forsch Ber Forsch Betr — Thyssen Forschung. Berichte aus Forschung und Betrieb
Thyssen Tech Ber — Thyssen Technische Berichte
ThZ — Theologische Zeitschrift
TI — Technical Information for Industry
TI — Timarit Pjooreknisfelags Islendinga 1957
TI — Tobacco Intelligence
TI — Tobacco International
TIA — Taxation in Australia
TIA — Tin International [*London*]
TIAC — Techniques and Instrumentation in Analytical Chemistry [*Elsevier Book Series*]
Tianjin J Oncol — Tianjin Journal of Oncology
Tibetan R — Tibetan Review [*New Delhi*]
Tibet J — Tibet Journal [*Dharmasala*]
Tibet Soc B — Tibet Society Bulletin [*United States*]
T I Br Geog — Transactions. Institute of British Geographers
TIBS — Trends in Biochemical Sciences
TIC — International Financial Law Review
T I Chem En — Transactions. Institution of Chemical Engineers and the Chemical Engineer
TICL — Topics in Culture Learning
TICOA — Testing, Instruments, and Controls
TICOJ — Transactions. International Conference of Orientalists in Japan
Tid Dok — Tidskrift foer Dokumentation
Tidn Byggnadskonst — Tidning foer Byggnadskonst
Tidsk Dokum — Tidskrift foer Dokumentation
Tidskr Dok — Tidskrift foer Dokumentation
Tidskr Hushallningssaellsk Skogsvardsstyr Gaevleborgs Laen — Tidskrift foer Hushallningssaellskapet och Skogsvardsstyrelsen i Gaevleborgs Laen
Tidskr Lantmaen Andelsfolk — Tidskrift foer Lantmaen och Andelsfolk
Tidskr Lantm Andelsfolk — Tidskrift foer Lantmaen och Andelsfolk
Tidskr Mil Halsov — Tidskrift i Militar Halsovard [*Sweden*]
Tidskr Sjukvardspedagog — Tidskrift foer Sjukvardspedagoger
Tidskr Skogbruk — Tidskrift foer Skogbruk
Tidskr Skog Lantbruksakad — Tidskrift. Skogs- och Lantbruksakademien
Tidskr Sver Sjukskot — Tidskrift foer Sveriges Sjukskoterskor
Tidskr Sver Skogvardsforb — Tidskrift Sveriges Skogsvardsforbund
Tidskr Sver Utsadesforen — Tidskrift. Sveriges Utsaedesfoereningen
Tidskr Varme- Vent- Sanitetstek — Tidskrift foer Varme-, Ventilations-, och Sanitetsteknik [*Sweden*]
Tids Samfun — Tidsskrift foer Samfunnsforskning
Tidssk Kjemi Bergves Metall — Tidsskrift foer Kjemi. Bergvesen og Metallurgi
Tidsskr Biavl — Tidsskrift foer Biavl
Tidsskr Froavl — Tidsskrift foer Froavl
Tidsskr Hermetikind — Tidsskrift foer Hermetikindustri
Tidsskr Kemi — Tidsskrift foer Kemi
Tidsskr Kemi Farm Ter — Tidsskrift foer Kemi. Farmaci og Terapi
Tidsskr Kjemi Bergves — Tidsskrift foer Kjemi og Bergvesen
Tidsskr Kjemi Bergvesen Met — Tidsskrift foer Kjemi. Bergvesen og Metallurgi
Tidsskr Landokon — Tidsskrift foer Landokonomi
Tidsskr Nor Laegeforen — Tidsskrift foer den Norske Laegeforening
Tidsskr Nor Landbruk — Tidsskrift foer det Norske Landbruk
Tidsskr Norske Landbruk — Tidsskrift foer det Norske Landbruk
Tidsskr Papirind — Tidsskrift foer Papirindustri
Tidsskr Plant — Tidsskrift foer Planteavl

Tidsskr Planteavl — Tidsskrift foer Planteavl
Tidsskr Plavl — Tidsskrift foer Planteavl
Tidsskr Samfunnsforskning — Tidsskrift foer Samfunnsforskning
Tidsskr Skogbr — Tidsskrift foer Skogbruk
Tidsskr Skogbruk — Tidsskrift foer Skogbruk
Tidsskr Textiltek — Tidsskrift foer Textilteknik
Tied Metsateho — Tiedotus Metsateho
Tied Valt Tekn Tutkimusl — Tiedotus. Valtion Teknillinen Tutkimuslaitos
Tied Valt Tek Tutkimuskeskus Poltto Voiteluainelab — Tiedonanto-Valtion Teknillinen Tutkimuskeskus, Poltto-, ja Voiteluainelaboratorio [*Finland*]
TIEED — Transactions. Institute of Electronics and Communication Engineers of Japan. Section E (English)
Tieraerztl Prax — Tieraerztliche Praxis
Tieraerztl Rundsch — Tieraerztliche Rundschau
Tieraerztl Rundschau — Tieraerztliche Rundschau
Tieraerztl Umsch — Tieraerztliche Umschau
Tieraerztl Z — Tieraerztliche Zeitschrift
Tierernaehr Fuetter — Tierernaehrung und Fuetterung
Tierphysiol Tierernaehr Futtermittelk — Tierphysiologie, Tierernaehrung, und Futtermittelkunde
Tierra y Soc — Tierra y Sociedad
Tiet Julk Helsingin Tek Korkeakoulu — Tieteellisia Julkaisuja. Helsingin Teknillinen Korkeakoulu
TIEtn — Trudy Instituta Etnografii Imeni N. N. Miklucho Maklaja Akademija Nauk SSSR
TIGC — Topics in Inorganic and General Chemistry [*Elsevier Book Series*]
TIGRB — Technische Information GRW [*Geraete- und Regler Werke*]
TIGS — Transactions. Inverness Gaelic Society
TIGZD — Teikyo Igaku Zasshi
Tihanyi Biol Kutatointezetenek Evkoen — Tihanyi Biologiai Kutatointezetenek Evkoenyve
TIJa — Trudy Instituta Jazykoznanija
Tijd — Onze Tijd
Tijd Ec Soc — Tijdschrift voor Economische en Sociale Geografie
Tijd Filos — Tijdschrift voor Filosofie
Tijd Gesch — Tijdschrift voor Geschiedenis
Tijd Kindergeneeskd — Tijdschrift voor Kindergeneeskunde
Tijd Logop Audiol — Tijdschrift voor Logopedie en Audiologie
Tijd Ned T — Tijdschrift voor Nederlandsche Taal- en Letterkunde
Tijd Psych — Tijdschrift voor Psychiatrie
Tijdschr Diergeneeskd — Tijdschrift voor Diergeneeskunde
Tijdschr Diergeneeskd Q Engl Issue — Tijdschrift voor Diergeneeskunde. Quarterly English Issue
Tijdschr Econ Soc Geogr — Tijdschrift voor Economische en Sociale Geografie
Tijdschr Ent — Tijdschrift voor Entomologie
Tijdschr Entomol — Tijdschrift voor Entomologie
Tijdschr Filosof — Tijdschrift voor Filosofie
Tijdschr Gastro-Enterol — Tijdschrift voor Gastro-Enterologie
Tijdschr Geneeskd — Tijdschrift voor Geneeskunde
Tijdschr Geschied Natuurwet Wiskd Tec — Tijdschrift voor Geschiedenis Natuurwetenschap Wiskundig. Techniek
Tijdschrift voor Econ en Soc Geog — Tijdschrift voor Economische en Sociale Geografie
Tijdschrift Taal & Lett — Tijdschrift voor Taal en Letteren
Tijdschr Ind Taal- Land- en Volkenkunde — Tijdschrift voor Indische Taal-, Land-, en Volkenkunde
Tijdschr Kindergeneeskd — Tijdschrift voor Kindergeneeskunde
Tijdschr K Ned Heidemaatsch — Tijdschrift der Koninklijke Nederlandsche Heidemaatschappij
Tijdschr Lev Talen — Tijdschrift voor Levende Talen
Tijdschr Ned Dierkd Ver — Tijdschrift der Nederlandsche Dierkundige Vereniging
Tijdschr Ned Elektron- & Radiogenoot — Tijdschrift van het Nederlands Elektronica- en Radiogenootschap
Tijdschr Ned Heidemaatsch — Tijdschrift der Nederlandsche Heidemaatschappij
Tijdschr Ned TL — Tijdschrift voor Nederlandsche Taal- en Letterkunde
Tijdschr Ned Ver Klin Chem — Tijdschrift van de Nederlandse Vereniging voor Klinische Chemie
Tijdschr Oppervlakte Tech Metal — Tijdschrift voor Oppervlakte Technieken van Metalen
Tijdschr Plantenz — Tijdschrift voor Plantenziekten
Tijdschr Plantenziekten — Tijdschrift voor Plantenziekten
Tijdschr Polit — Tijdschrift voor Politicologie [*Netherlands*]
Tijdschr Primaire Energ — Tijdschrift Primaire Energie [*Belgium*]
Tijdschr Soc Geneeskd — Tijdschrift voor Sociale Geneeskunde
Tijdschr Stud Verlichting — Tijdschrift voor Studie. Verlichting
Tijdschr Ther Geneesmiddel Onderz — Tijdschrift voor Therapie, Geneesmiddel, en Onderzoek
Tijdschr Veeartsenijk — Tijdschrift voor Veeartsenijkunde
Tijdschr Veeartsenijk en Veeteelt — Tijdschrift voor Veeartsenijkunde en Veeteelt
Tijdschr Ziekenverpl — Tijdschrift voor Ziekenverpleging
Tijds Econ — Tijdschrift voor Economie
Tijds Soc Wetensch — Tijdschrift voor Sociale Wetenschappen

Til — Tilskueren
TIL — Travaux. Institut de Linguistique
TILAS — Travaux. Institut d'Etudes Latino-Americaines. Universite de Strasbourg
TIM — Time
Timarit Verkfraedingafelags Is — Timarit Verkfraedingafelags Islands
Timb Bull Europe FAO — Timber Bulletin for Europe. Food and Agricultural Organization
Timber Dev Assoc Inf Bull A/IB — Timber Development Association. Information Bulletin A/IB
Timber Dev Assoc Inf Bull B/IB — Timber Development Association. Information Bulletin B/IB
Timber Dev Assoc Inf Bull G/IB — Timber Development Association. Information Bulletin G/IB
Timber Dev Assoc Res Rep C/RR — Timber Development Association. Research Report C/RR
Timber Res Dev Assoc Res Rep C/RR — Timber Research and Development Association. Research Report C/RR
Timber Supp Rev — Timber Supply Review
Timber Technol — Timber Technology
Timber Trades J — Timber Trades Journal and Woodworking Machinery [*Later, Timber Trades Journal and Wood Processing*]
Timb Grower — Timber Grower
Timb Leafl For Dep (Brit Solomon Islands Protect) — Timber Leaflet. Forestry Department (British Solomon Islands Protectorate)
Timb Leafl For Dep (Kenya) — Timber Leaflet. Forest Department (Nairobi, Kenya)
Timb Leafl For Dep (Uganda) — Timber Leaflet. Forest Department (Uganda)
Timb & Plyw Ann — Timber and Plywood Annual
Timb Pres Assoc Aust — Timber Preservers' Association of Australia. Pamphlet
Timb Trades J Wood Process — Timber Trades Journal and Wood Processing
Timb Tr J — Timber Trades Journal
TIMEA — Transactions. Institute of Marine Engineers
Time (Can) — Time (Canada)
Timely Turf Top — Timely Turf Topics
Times Ednl Supp — Times Educational Supplement
Times Educ Supp — Times Educational Supplement
Times Higher Ed Supp — Times Higher Education Supplement
Times Higher Educ Supp — Times Higher Education Supplement
Times Higher Educ Suppl — Times Higher Education Supplement
Times Ind A — Times of India Annual [*Bombay*]
Times L — Times Literary Supplement
Times Lit Supp — Times Literary Supplement
Times Lit Suppl — Times Literary Supplement
Times Rev Ind — Times Review of Industry
Times R Ind & Tech — Times Review of Industry and Technology
Times Sci Rev — Times Science Review
TIMFA — Transactions. Institute of Metal Finishing
Timisoara Inst Politeh Traian Vuia Bul Stiint Teh Ser Chim — Timisoara. Institutul Politehnic "Traian Vuia." Buletinul Stiintific si Tehnic. Seria Chimie
Timisoara Med — Timisoara Medicala [*Romania*]
TIN — Ebanewsletter. Daily Economic and Political News Indicators from Turkey
Tingo Maria Peru Est Exp Agric Bol — Tingo Maria, Peru. Estacion Experimental Agricola. Boletin
Tin Int — Tin International
Tin Intern — Tin International
Tin Print Box Mkr — Tin-Printer and Box Maker
Tin Res Inst (Greenford Engl) Publ — Tin Research Institute (Greenford, England). Publication
TINS — Trends in Neurosciences
Tinsley — Tinsley's Magazine
Tin Uses — Tin and Its Uses
TIOKA — Trudy Instituta Okeanologii Akademiya Nauk SSSR
TIOOA — Transactions. Indiana Academy of Ophthalmology and Otolaryngology
TIP — Tests in Print
TIP — Theory into Practice
TIPGA — Trudy Instituta Prikladnoi Geofiziki
TIPRO Rep — TIPRO [*Texas Independent Producers and Royalty Owners Association*] Reporter
Tiraspol Gos Ped Inst Ucen Zap — Tiraspol'skii Gosudarstvennyi Pedagogiceskii Institut Imeni T. G. Sevcenko. Ucenyi Zapiski
Tire Dealr — Modern Tire Dealer
Tire Rev — Tire Review
Tire Sci Technol — Tire Science and Technology
TIRJa — Trudy Instituto Russkogo Jazyka
T Iron St I — Transactions. Iron and Steel Institute of Japan
TIRS — Travaux. Institut de Recherches Sahariennes
TIRVB — Toronto University. Institute for Aerospace Studies. UTIAS Review
TIS — Times [*London*]
TIS — Tops in Science Fiction
TISCO — TISCO [*Tata Iron & Steel Company*] Technical Journal
TISCO Rev — TISCO [*Tata Iron & Steel Company*] Review

Tissue Anti — Tissue Antigens
TI Tech Inf Ind — TI. Technical Information for Industry [*South Africa*]
TIT J Lif — TIT [*Tower International Technomedical*] Journal of Life Sciences
TIT J Life Sci — TIT [*Tower International Technomedical*] Journal of Life Sciences
TITL — Tijdschrift van het Institut voor Toegepaste Linguistiek Leuven
TITLA — Tecnica Italiana
TITLV — Tijdschrift voor Indische Taal-, Land-, en Volkenkunde
TIZ — Tonindustrie-Zeitung und Keramische Rundschau. Zentralblatt fuer das Gesamtgebiet der Steine und Erden
TJ — Theatre Journal
TJ — Today's Japan
TJ — Tolkien Journal
TJ — Trinity Journal
TJA — Focus Japan (Tokyo)
TJA — Telecommunication Journal of Australia
TJADA — Teratology
TJak — Trudy Instituta Jazyka, Literatury, i Istorii
T Jap I Met — Transactions. Japan Institute of Metals
TJASA — Transactions. Japan Society for Aeronautical and Space Sciences
TJB — Theologischer Jahresbericht
T J Br Cer — Transactions and Journal. British Ceramic Society
TJEMA — Tohoku Journal of Experimental Medicine
TJEMD — Tokai Journal of Experimental and Clinical Medicine
TJHC — Theology. Journal of Historic Christianity
TJHPA — T'u Jang Hsueh Pao
TJI — Tabak Journal International
TJIDA — Tokyo Jikeikai Ika Daigaku Zasshi
TJIZA — Tokyo Joshi Ika Daigaku Zasshi
TJL — [*The*] Jonxis Lectures [*Elsevier Book Series*]
TJPDA — Turkish Journal of Pediatrics
TJQ — Thoreau Journal Quarterly
TJR — Tenri Journal of Religion
TJS — Timber Trades Journal and Woodworking Machinery [*Later, Timber Trades Journal and Wood Processing*] [*London*]
TJSCA — Texas Journal of Science
Tjumen Gos Ped Inst Ucen Zap — Ministerstvo Prosvescenija RSFSR Tjumenskii Gosudarstvennyi Pedagogiceskii Institut. Ucenye Zapiski
TK — Tekawennake. Six Nations. New Credit Reporter
TK — Tetzugaku-Kenkyu [*Tokyo*]
T und K — Text und Kontext
TK — Text und Kritik
TKA — Trudy Kierskoi Dukhovnoi Akademii
TKar — Trudy Karel'skogo Filiala Akademii Nauk SSSR
TKBRAS — Transactions. Korean Branch. Royal Asiatic Society
TKESB — Tekhnicheskaya Estetika
TKFN — Telkwa Foundation. Newsletter [*Telkwa, British Columbia*]
TKGJA — Taisei Kensetsu Gijutsu Kenkyusho-Ho
Tk J — Tamkang Journal
TKKSA — Trudy Khar'kovskogo Sel'skokhozyaistvennogo Instituta
TKKTA — Trudy po Khimii i Khimicheskoi Tekhnologii
TKMEB — Theoretische und Klinische Medizin in Einzeldarstellungen
TKMSB — Tekhnicheska Misul
TKN — Tractatenblad van het Koninkrijk der Nederlanden
TKNGMP — Tijdschrift. Koninklijk Nederlandsch Genootschap voor Munt en Penningkunde
TKNKB — Tekniikka
TKO — Technieuws Tokio. Korte Berichten op Technisch Wetenschappelijk Gebied
TkR — Tamkang Review
TKRAS — Transactions. Korean Branch. Royal Asiatic Society
TKrasPI — Trudy Krasnodarskogo Gosudarstvennogo Pedagogicheskogo Instituta
TKSBB — Tektonika Sibiri
TKSGA — Trudy Koordinatsionnykh Soveshchanyi po Gidrotekhnike
TKSGB — Tektonika i Stratigrafiya
TKST — Tukisiviksat
TKTEA — Tekhnika Kino i Televideniya
TKUAA — Trudy Kuibyshevskii Aviatsionnyi Institut
TKutPI — Trudy Kutaisskogo Gosudarstvennogo Pedagogiceskogo Instituta
TKZRA — Taika Zairyo
TL — Theologisches Literaturblatt [*Leipzig*]
TL — Theoretical Linguistics [*Berlin*]
TL — Trybuna Literacka
TLA — Tax Lawyer
TLAP — Prace Komisji Jezykowej Polskiej Akademii Umiejetnosci. Travaux de la Commission Linguistique de l'Academie Polonaise des Sciences et des Lettres
TLB — Theologisches Literaturblatt
TLBl — Theologisches Literaturblatt
TLCOA — Telecommunications [*Dedham, MA*]
TLD — [*The*] Living Daylights
TLEPA — Trudy Laboratorii Elektromagnitnykh Polei Radiochastot Instituta Gigieny Truda i Professional'nykh Zabolevanii Akademii Meditsinskikh Nauk SSSR

T Letterkd — Tydskrif vir Letterkunde
TLF — Textes Litteraires Francais
T Lg — Travaux de Linguistique
TLIG — Tasmanian Legal Information Guide
TLJ — Transportation Law Journal
TLL — Travaux de Linguistique et de Litterature [*Strasbourg*]
TLLS — Travaux de Linguistique et de Litterature (Strasbourg)
TLMMDD — Malaysia. Ministry of Agriculture. Technical Leaflet
TLNDA — Telonde [*France*]
TLOP — [*The*] Language of Poetry
TLP — Travaux Linguistiques de Prague
TLQ — Temple Law Quarterly
TLQ — Travaux de Linguistique Quantitative
TLQue — Travaux de Linguistique Quebecoise
TLR — Tasmanian Law Reports
TLR — Tax Law Review
TLR — Tulane Law Review
TLS — Times Literary Supplement [*London*]
TLSAP — Wydawnictwa Slaskie Polskiej Akademii Umiejetnosci. Prace Jezykowe. Publications Silesiennes. Academie Polonaise des Sciences et des Lettres. Travaux Linguistiques
TLSM — Talouselama
TLTC — Ta-Lu Tsa-Chih [*Continent Magazine*] [*Taiwan*]
TLTL — Teaching Language through Literature
T Lwyr — Tax Lawyer
TLZ — Theologische Literaturzeitung
TM — Temps Modernes
TM — Tennessee Musician
TM — Textus Minores
TM — Theatre Magazine
Tm — Time
TM — Tlalocan: A Journal of Source Materials on the Native Cultures of Mexico
TM — Tourism Management
TM — Turkiyat Mecmuasi
TM — Tygodnik Morski
TMA — [*The*] Money Advocate
TMA — Top Management Abstracts
TMA — Traffic Management
TMAGD — Tennessee Magazine
TMATB — Technische Mitteilungen AEG- [*Allgemeine Elektrizitaets-Gesellschaft*] Telefunken
TMB — Iemootsies
TMC — Revue Tiers-Monde
TMC — Transition Metal Chemistry
TMCHD — Transition Metal Chemistry
TMCIA — Temperature. Its Measurement and Control in Science and Industry
TMFZA — Teoreticheskaya i Matematicheskaya Fizika
TMH — Texas Military History
TMIEB — Trudy Moskovskii Institut Elektronnogo Mashinostroeniya
TMIG — [*The*] Marketing Information Guide
TMJ — Trade Marks Journal
TMKFA — Technische Mitteilungen Krupp. Forschungsberichte
TMKWA — Technische Mitteilungen Krupp. Werksberichte
TMM — Technocrat. A Monthly Review of Japanese Technology and Industry
TMNP — [*The*] Mystery Readers Newsletter
TMo — O Tempo e o Modo
TMorNII — Trudy Mordovskogo Nauchno-Issledovatel'skogo Instituta Jazyka, Literatury, Istorii, i Ekonomiki
TMPTA — Technische Mitteilungen PTT
TMR — Trade-Mark Reporter
TM Rep — Trade-Mark Reporter
TMRKH — Tromura. Tromsoe Museum Rapportserie. Kulturhistorie
TMRN — [*The*] Mystery Readers Newsletter
TMRNV — Tromura. Tromsoe Museum Rapportserie. Naturvitenskap
TMS — Tlalocan: A Journal of Source Materials on the Native Cultures of Mexico
TMSAA — Transactions. Metallurgical Society of AIME [*American Institute of Mining, Metallurgical, and Petroleum Engineers*]
TMT — Tudomanyos es Muszaki Tajekoztatas
TMV — Todd Memorial Volumes
TMW — Welzijnsweekblad
TMZ — Textile Magazine. Vakblad voor de Handel in Textiel, Kleding, en Woningtextiel
TN — Theatre Notebook
TN — Title News
TN — Top of the News
TN — Travel News
TNA — Tidsskrift foer Norron Arkeologi
TNAEA — Teplovye Napryazheniya v Elementakh Konstruktsii
TNAN — Texas Numismatic Association. News
TNBMD — Bureau of Mines. Technology News [*United States*]
TND — Transnational Data Report. Information Politics and Regulation
TNDNA — Tokyo Nogyo Daigaku Nogaku Shuho
TNDNAG — Journal of Agricultural Science. Tokyo Nogyo Daigaku

TNDSA — Trends
TNHCA — Taehan Naekwa Hakhoe Chapchi
TNI — Tin News. Accurate Information on World Tin Production, Prices, Marketing Developments, and New Uses and Applications
TNizam — Trudy Instituta Literatury i Jazyka Imeni Nizami
TNKPB — Trudy Nauchno-Issledovatel'skogo Instituta Kraevoi Patologii [*Alma-Ata*]
TNKUL — Towarzystwo Naukowe Katolickiego Uniwersytet Lubelskiego
TNKULWP — Towarzystwo Naukowe Katolickiego Uniwersytet Lubelskiego. Wyklady i Przemowienia [*Lublin*]
TN L — Tennessee Law Review
TN LR — Tennessee Law Review
TNLRA — Tennessee Law Review
TNN — TermNet News
TNNIA — Trudy Groznenskogo Neftyanogo Nauchno-Issledovatel'skogo Instituta
TNO Div Nutr Food Res TNO Rep — TNO [*Nederlands Centrale Organisatie voor Toegepast-Natuurwetenschappelijk Onderzoek*] Division for Nutrition and Food Research TNO. Report
TNO Proj — TNO [*Toegepast-Natuurwetenschappelijk Onderzoek*] Project
TNOSA — Tunnels et Ouvrages Souterrains
Tn Plann Rev — Town Planning Review
TNR — [*The*] New Republic
TNR — Tanganyika Notes and Records
TNR — Tanzania Notes and Records
TNS — Timber Trade Review [*Kuala Lumpur*]
TNSKA — Tohoku Nogyo Shikenjo Kenkyu Hokoku
TNSRA — Tensor
TN Stud Lit — Tennessee Studies in Literature
TNSX — Taniisix. Aleutian Regional School District
TNT — Towarzystwo Naukowe w Toruniu
TNT-FF — Towarzystwo Naukowe w Toruniu. Prace Wydziau Filologiczno-Filosoficznego
TNTL — Tijdschrift voor Nederlandsche Taal- en Letterkunde [*Leiden*]
TNW — Towarzystwo Naukowe Warszawskie
T NY Ac Sci — Transactions. New York Academy of Sciences
TO — Take One
TO — Tobacco Observer
TOA — Tijdschrift voor Openbaar Bestuur
TOAP — Prace Komisji Orientalistycznej Polskiej Akademii Umiejetnosci. Travaux de la Commission Orientaliste de l'Academie Polonaise des Sciences et des Lettres
Tob — Tobacco
Tob Abstracts — Tobacco Abstracts
Tobacco J — Tobacco Journal
Tob Int (NY) — Tobacco International (New York)
Tob Leaf — Tobacco Leaf
Tob Res — Tobacco Research
Tob Res Board Rhod Bull — Tobacco Research Board of Rhodesia. Bulletin
Tob Res Counc Res Pap — Tobacco Research Council. Research Paper [*England*]
Tob Sci — Tobacco Science
Tocklai Exp Stn Advis Bull — Tocklai Experimental Station. Advisory Bulletin
Tocklai Exp Stn Advis Leafl — Tocklai Experimental Station. Advisory Leaflet
Tocn i Nadezn Kibernet Sistem — Tocnost i Nadeznost Kiberneticeskih Sistem
TOCS — Oriental Ceramic Society. Transactions
Toda Educ — Today's Education
Today — Today for Tomorrow
Todays Chiro — Today's Chiropractic
Today's Ed — Today's Education
Todays Educ — Today's Education
Todays Exec — Today's Executive
Today's Fmkr — Today's Filmmaker
Today's Sec — Today's Secretary
Todays VD Vener Dis Control Probl — Today's VD. Venereal Disease Control Problem
Today Technol — Today Technology
Today & Tomorrow Educ — Today and Tomorrow in Education
Tod Cath Teach — Today's Catholic Teacher
Tod Parish — Today's Parish
TODrL — Trudy Otdela Drevnerusskoj Literatury
TOELA — Toute l'Electronique
TOF — Tales of the Frightened
Toh J Ex Me — Tohoku Journal of Experimental Medicine
Tohoku Agr Res — Tohoku Agricultural Research
Tohoku Geophys J Sci Rep Tohoku Univ Fifth Ser — Tohoku Geophysical Journal. Science Reports of the Tohoku University. Fifth Series
Tohoku Imp Univ Technol Rep — Tohoku Imperial University Technology Reports [*Japan*]
Tohoku J Agric Res — Tohoku Journal of Agricultural Research
Tohoku J Agr Res — Tohoku Journal of Agricultural Research
Tohoku J Exp Med — Tohoku Journal of Experimental Medicine
Tohoku Math J — Tohoku Mathematical Journal
Tohoku Med J — Tohoku Medical Journal
Tohoku Psychol Folia — Tohoku Psychologica Folia

Tohoku Univ Inst Agric Res Rep — Tohoku University. Institute for Agricultural Research. Reports
Tohoku Univ Sci Rep Ser 2 — Tohoku University. Science Reports. Series 2. Geology
Tohoku Univ Sci Rep Ser 3 — Tohoku University. Science Reports. Series 3. Mineralogy, Petrology, and Economic Geology
Tohoku Univ Sci Rep Ser 5 — Tohoku University. Science Reports. Series 5
Tohoku Univ Sci Repts Geology — Tohoku University. Science Reports. Geology
Toim Eesti NSV Tead Akad Fuus Mat — Toimetised. Eesti NSV Teaduste Akadeemia. Fuusika. Matemaatika
TOK — Toeristenkampioen
Tokai J Exp Clin Med — Tokai Journal of Experimental and Clinical Medicine [*Japan*]
Tokai-Kinki Natl Agric Exp Stn Res Prog Rep — Tokai-Kinki National Agricultural Experiment Station. Research Progress Report
Tokai Technol J — Tokai Technological Journal [*Japan*]
Tokoginecol Prac — Toko-Ginecologia Practica
Toko-Ginecol Pract — Toko-Ginecologia Practica
TOKSA — Tokushuko
TOKTA — Teoreticheskie Osnovy Khimicheskoi Tekhnologii
Tokushima J Exp Med — Tokushima Journal of Experimental Medicine
Tokyo Astron Bull — Tokyo Astronomical Bulletin
Tokyo Astron Bull Ser II — Tokyo Astronomical Bulletin. Series II
Tokyo Astron Obs Rep — Tokyo Astronomical Observatory. Report
Tokyo Bk Dev Centre Newsl — Tokyo Book Development Centre. Newsletter
Tokyo Inst Technol Bull — Tokyo Institute of Technology. Bulletin
Tokyo Jikeika Med J — Tokyo Jikeika Medical Journal
Tokyo J Math — Tokyo Journal of Mathematics
Tokyo J Med Sci — Tokyo Journal of Medical Sciences
Tokyo Kyoiku Daigaku Sci Rep Sec C — Tokyo Kyoiku Daigaku. Science Reports. Section C. Geology, Mineralogy, and Geography
Tokyo Metrop Isot Cent Annu Rep — Tokyo Metropolitan Isotope Centre. Annual Report
Tokyo Metrop Res Inst Environ Prot Annu Rep Engl Transl — Tokyo Metropolitan Research Institute for Environmental Protection. Annual Report. English Translation
Tokyo Metrop Univ Geogr Rep — Tokyo Metropolitan University. Geographical Reports
Tokyo Natl Sci Mus Bull — Tokyo National Science Museum. Bulletin
Tokyo Tanabe Q — Tokyo Tanabe Quarterly
Tokyo Univ Coll Gen Educ Sci Pap — Tokyo University. College of General Education. Scientific Papers
Tokyo Univ Earthquake Research Inst Bull — Tokyo University. Earthquake Research Institute. Bulletin
Tokyo Univ Faculty Sci Jour — Tokyo University. Faculty of Science. Journal
Toledo L Rev — University of Toledo. Law Review
Toledo Mus N — Toledo. Museum of Art. Museum News
Toledo Univ Inst Silicate Research Inf Circ — Toledo University. Institute of Silicate Research. Information Circular
Tol LR — University of Toledo. Law Review
To LR — University of Toledo. Law Review
Tolva — Tolva. Revista del Trigo. Harina y del Pan
Tolvmandsbl — Tolvmandsbladet
Tomsk Gos Pedagog Inst Uch Zap — Tomskii Gosudarstvennyi Pedagogicheskii Institut. Uchenye Zapiski
Tomsk Gos Univ Ucen Zap — Tomskii Gosudarstvennyi Universitet Imeni V. V. Kuibyseva. Ucenye Zapiski
TONGA — Trudy Nauchno-Issledovatel'skogo Instituta Onkologii Gruzinskoi SSR
Tonind-Ztg Keram Rundsch — Tonindustrie-Zeitung und Keramische Rundschau
TONT — Toronto Native Times
TOO — La Tour de l'Orle d'Or
TOOIS — Transactions on Office Information Systems
Tool Die J — Tool and Die Journal
Tool Eng — Tool Engineer
Tool & Mfg Eng — Tool and Manufacturing Engineer
Tool Mfg Eng — Tool and Manufacturing Engineer
Tool Prod — Tooling and Production
Tool and Prod — Tooling and Production
Top Antibiot Chem — Topics in Antibiotic Chemistry
Top Appl Phys — Topics in Applied Physics
Top Astrophys Space Phys — Topics in Astrophysics and Space Physics
Top Autom Chem Anal — Topics in Automatic Chemical Analysis
Top Bioelectrochem Bioenerg — Topics in Bioelectrochemistry and Bioenergetics
Top Chem Mutagen — Topics in Chemical Mutagenesis
Top Clin Nurs — Topics in Clinical Nursing
Top Curr Chem — Topics in Current Chemistry
Top Curr Phys — Topics in Current Physics
Top Emerg Med — Topics in Emergency Medicine
Top Enzyme Ferment Biotechnol — Topics in Enzyme and Fermentation Biotechnology
Top Health Care Financ — Topics in Health Care Financing
Top Horm Chem — Topics in Hormone Chemistry

T Ophth Soc — Transactions. Ophthalmological Societies of the United Kingdom
Top Hum Genet — Topics in Human Genetics
TOPICS — Transcripts of Parlibs Information Classification System [*Queensland Parliamentary Library*]
Topics Clin Nurs — Topics in Clinical Nursing
Topics Current Phys — Topics in Current Physics
Top Infect Dis — Topics in Infectious Diseases
Top Lipid Chem — Topics in Lipid Chemistry
Top Manage Abstr — Top Management Abstracts
Top Math Phys — Topics in Mathematical Physics
Top Med Chem — Topics in Medicinal Chemistry
Top Mol Struct Biol — Topics in Molecular and Structural Biology
Top News — Top of the News
Topology Proc — Topology Proceedings
Top Paediatr — Topics in Paediatrics
Top Phosphorus Chem — Topics in Phosphorus Chemistry
Top Photosynth — Topics in Photosynthesis
Top Probl Psychiatry Neurol — Topical Problems in Psychiatry and Neurology
Top Probl Psychother — Topical Problems of Psychotherapy
TOPRA — Tooling and Production
Top Rep NB Miner Resour Branch — Topical Report. New Brunswick Mineral Resources Branch
Top Stereochem — Topics in Stereochemistry
Top Sulfur Chem — Topics in Sulfur Chemistry
Tor — Torre
TOREA — Toshiba Review
Torfnachrichten Forsch Werbestelle Torf — Torfnachrichten der Forschungs- und Werbestelle fuer Torf
Torf Promst — Torfyanaya Promyshlennost
Tori Bull Ornithol Soc Jpn — Tori. Bulletin of the Ornithological Society of Japan
Torino Univ Ist Geol Pub — Torino Universita. Istituto Geologico. Pubblicazioni
Toronto Univ Dep Mech Eng Tech Publ Ser — Toronto University. Department of Mechanical Engineering. Technical Publication Series
Toronto Univ Inst Aerosp Stud UTIAS Rep — Toronto University. Institute for Aerospace Studies. UTIAS Report
Toronto Univ Inst Aerosp Stud UTIAS Rev — Toronto University. Institute for Aerospace Studies. UTIAS Review
Toronto Univ Inst Aerosp Stud UTIAS Tech Note — Toronto University. Institute for Aerospace Studies. UTIAS Technical Note
Toronto Univ Studies G S — Toronto University Studies. Geological Series
TORPA — Torfyanaya Promyshlennost
Torreia Nueva Ser — Torreia Nueva Serie
Torrey Bot Club Bull — Torrey Botanical Club Bulletin
Torry Res — Torry Research
Torry Res Stn Aberdeen Scotl Annu Rep — Torry Research Station. Aberdeen, Scotland. Annual Report
Torry Res Stn Annu Rep Handl Preserv Fish Fish Prod — Torry Research Station. Annual Report on the Handling and Preservation of Fish and Fish Products
TOS — Texas Ornithological Society. Bulletin
TOSCA — Tobacco Science
Toshiba Rev — Toshiba Review [*Japan*]
Toshiba Rev (Int Ed) — Toshiba Review (International Edition)
Tosh-Kai — Toshokan-Kai
Tosh Kenk — Toshokan Kenkyu
Tosh Zass — Toshokan Zasshi
TOT — Tales of Tomorrow
Toulouse Med — Toulouse Medical
Tourbe Philos — Tourbe Philosophique
Tourism Aust — Tourism Australia
Tourism Engl — Tourism in England
Tourism Intell Q — Tourism Intelligence Quarterly
Toute Electron — Toute l'Electronique
Tov — Tovaris
Tovar Poshir Polit Nauk Znan Ukr SSR — Tovaristvo dlya Poshirennya Politichnikh i Naukovikh Znan Ukrains'koi SSR
TOW — Tales of Wonder
Tower Hamlets Local Trade Dev — Tower Hamlets Local Trade Development
Town & Country Plan — Town and Country Planning
Town Plan Inst J — Town Planning Institute Journal
Town Planning R — Town Planning Review [*United Kingdom*]
Town Plann Inst J — Town Planning Institute Journal
Town Plann Q — Town Planning Quarterly [*New Zealand*]
Town Plann Rev — Town Planning Review
Town Plan R — Town Planning Review
Townsville Nat — Townsville Naturalist
Tox Appl Ph — Toxicology and Applied Pharmacology
TOXIA — Toxicon
Toxic Hazard Waste Disposal — Toxic and Hazardous Waste Disposal
Toxicol Annu — Toxicology Annual
Toxicol Appl Pharmacol — Toxicology and Applied Pharmacology
Toxicol Appl Pharmacol Suppl — Toxicology and Applied Pharmacology. Supplement

Toxicol Environ Chem Rev — Toxicological and Environmental Chemistry Reviews
Toxicol Eur Res — Toxicological European Research
Toxicol Lett — Toxicology Letters
Toxic Subst J — Toxic Substances Journal
Toyo Bunka Kenkyu Kiyo — Toyo Bunka Kenkyusho Kiyo
Toyo Junior Coll Food Technol Toyo Inst Food Technol Res Rep — Toyo Junior College of Food Technology and Toyo Institute of Food Technology. Research Report [*Japan*]
Toyota Eng — Toyota Engineering [*Japan*]
TP — Tempo Presente
TP — Terzo Programma [*Roma*]
TP — Thought Patterns
TP — Tijdschrift voor Philosophie
TP — Topics in Photosynthesis [*Elsevier Book Series*]
TP — T'oung Pao
TPA — T'oung Pao. Archives
TPAPA — Transactions and Proceedings. American Philological Association
TPB — Tennessee Philological Bulletin
TPC — Trade Practices Cases
TPCCA — Topics in Current Chemistry
TPCD — Trade Practices Commission. Decisions and Determinations
TPCDD — Trade Practices Commission. Decisions and Determinations
TPCWDL — Colorado. Division of Wildlife. Technical Publication
TPEMA — Telephone Engineer and Management
TPer — Tetradi Perevodcika
TPETA — Techniques du Petrole
TPG — Town Planning and Local Government Guide
TPh — Tijdschrift voor Philosophie
TPhS — Transactions. Philological Society
TPhS — Transactions. Philosophical Society [*London and Strassburg*]
TPIRA — Trudy Gosudarstvennyi Institut po Proektirovaniyu i Issledovatel'skim Rabotam v Neftedobyvayushchei Promyshlennosti
TPI Rep Trop Prod Inst — TPI Report. Tropical Products Institute
TPJ — Tennessee Poetry Journal
TPJSL — Transactions and Proceedings. Japan Society (London)
TPLGG — Town Planning and Local Government Guide
TP & LGG — Town Planning and Local Government Guide
TPLOA — Teploenergetika [*Moscow*]
TPLQ-A — Town Planning Quarterly [*New Zealand*]
TPLR-A — Town Planning Review [*United Kingdom*]
TPMGA — Teoriya i Praktika Metallurgii
TPMXA — Tecnica Pecuaria en Mexico
TPNO — Tree Planters' Notes
TPO — Nederlands Transport
TPow — Tygodnik Powszechny
TPPYA — Topical Problems of Psychotherapy
TPPYAL — Aktuelle Fragen der Psychotherapie
T P Q — Theologisch-Praktische Quartalschrift
TPQS — Theologisch-Praktische Quartalschrift
TPr — Tempo Presente
TPR — Three Penny Review
TPRRD — Technik-Index ueber Plasmaphysikalische Forschung und Fusionsreaktoren
TPRS — Trade Practices Reporting Service
TPRSL — Transactions and Proceedings. Royal Society of Literature
TPrzPI — Trudy Przeval'skogo Pedagogiceskogo Instituta
TPS — [*The*] Pope Speaks
TPS — Theologie Pastorale et Spiritualite
TPS — Transactions. Philological Society [*London*]
TPSFA — Tohoku Psychologica Folia
TPSM — Tepatshimuwin. Journal d'Information des Attikamekes et des Montagnais
TPSRS — Theologie Pastorale et Spiritualite. Recherches et Syntheses
TQ — Texas Quarterly
TQ — Theatre Quarterly
TQ — Theologische Quartalschrift [*Tuebingen*]
TQ — Toronto Quarterly
TQ — Tri-Quarterly
TQAGA — Technique Agricole
TQE — Technique de l'Eau et de l'Assainissement
TQS — Theologische Quartalschrift
TR — Table Ronde
TR — Technology Review
TR — Theatre Research
TR — Theologische Revue [*Muenster*]
TR — Theologische Rundschau
TR — Tobacco Reporter
TR — Transatlantic Review
Tr — Trivium
Tr — Y Traethodydd
TRA — Television/Radio Age
TrA — Traduction Automatique [*The Hague*]
Trabajos Estadist — Trabajos de Estadistica
Trabajos Estadist Investigacion Oper — Trabajos de Estadistica y de Investigacion Operativa

Trab Antropol Etnol — Trabalhos de Antropologia e Etnologia

Trab Cent Bot Junta Invest Ultramar — Trabalhos. Centro de Botanica. Junta de Investigacoes do Ultramar

Trab Compostelanos Biol — Trabajos Compostelanos de Biologia

Trab 5 Cong Med Latino-Am — Trabajos Presentados al Quinto Congreso Medico Latino-Americano

Trab Dep Bot Fisiol Veg Univ Madrid — Trabajos. Departamento de Botanica y Fisiologia Vegetal. Universidad de Madrid

TrabEsta — Trabajos de Estadistica

Trab Estac Agric Exp Leon — Trabajos. Estacion Agricola Experimental de Leon

Trab Estadistica — Trabajos de Estadistica y de Investigacion

Trab Geol — Trabajos de Geologia

Trab Geol (Oviedo Univ Fac Cienc) — Trabajos de Geologia (Oviedo Universidad. Facultad de Ciencias)

Trab Inst Cajal Invest Biol — Trabajos. Instituto Cajal de Investigaciones Biologicas

Trab Inst Econ Prod Ganad Ebro — Trabajos. Instituto de Economia y Producciones Ganaderas del Ebro

Trab Inst Esp Entomol — Trabajos. Instituto Espanol de Entomologia

Trab Inst Esp Oceanogr — Trabajos. Instituto Espanol de Oceanografia

Trab Inst Fisiol Fac Med Univ Lisboa — Trabajos. Instituto de Fisiologia. Faculdade de Medicina. Universidade do Lisboa

Trab Inst Nac Cienc Med (Madrid) — Trabajos. Instituto Nacional de Ciencias Medicas (Madrid)

Trab Inst Oceanogr Univ Recife — Trabalhos. Instituto Oceanografico. Universidade do Recife

Trab Investigacao 79 — Trabalhos de Investigacao 79

Trab Investigacao 80 — Trabalhos de Investigacao 80

Trab Lab Bioquim Quim Apl Inst Alonso Barba — Trabajo. Laboratorio de Bioquimica y Quimica Aplicada. Instituto "Alonso Barba"

Trab Oceanogr Univ Fed Pernambuco — Trabalhos Oceanograficos. Universidade Federal de Pernambuco

Trab Pesqui Inst Nutr Univ Bras — Trabalhos e Pesquisas. Instituto de Nutricao. Universidade do Brasil

TrAC — Trends in Analytical Chemistry

Trace Subst Environ Health — Trace Substances in Environmental Health

Trace Subst Environ Health Proc Univ Mo Annu Conf — Trace Substances in Environmental Health. Proceedings. University of Missouri. Annual Conference

Track Field Q Rev — Track and Field Quarterly Review

Tracts Math Nat Sci — Tracts in Mathematics and Natural Science

Trad — Traditio

Trad Dep Exploit Util Bois Univ Laval — Traduction. Departement d'Exploitation et Utilisation des Bois. Universite Laval

Trade and Commer — Trade and Commerce

Trade D — Trade Digest

Trade Dig — Trade Digest

Trade Ind — Trade and Industry

Trade-Mark Rep — Trade-Mark Reporter

Trademark Rptr — Trademark Reporter

Trade Mks J — Trade Marks Journal

Trade News N — Trade News North

Trade R — Trade Review. Swedish Chamber of Commerce for Australia

Trades Union D — Trades Union Digest

Traditional Kent Bldgs — Traditional Kent Buildings

Trad Mus — Traditional Music

TRAEA — Technical Report Series. IAEA [*International Atomic Energy Agency*]

Traff Engng Control — Traffic Engineering and Control

Traffic Dig Rev — Traffic Digest and Review

Traffic Eng — Traffic Engineering

Traffic Eng Contr — Traffic Engineering and Control

Traffic Eng & Control — Traffic Engineering and Control

Traffic Manage — Traffic Management

Traffic Q — Traffic Quarterly

Traffic Qly — Traffic Quarterly

Traffic Saf — Traffic Safety

Traffic Saf Res Rev — Traffic Safety Research Review

TRAGB — Trudy po Radiatsionnoi Gigiene Leningradskii Nauchno-Issledovatel'skii Institut Radiatsionnoi Gigieny

TRAIB — Trudy Astrofizicheskogo Instituta Akademiya Nauk Kazakhskoi SSR

Train Agric Rural Dev — Training for Agriculture and Rural Development

Train Dev Aust — Training and Development in Australia

Train & Devel J — Training and Development Journal

Train Dev J — Training and Development Journal

Train Sch B — Training School Bulletin

Trait Surf — Traitements de Surface

Trait Therm — Traitement Thermique

Tr Akad Nauk Gruz SSR Inst Sist Upr — Trudy Akademii Nauk Gruzinskoi SSR Institut Sistem Upravleniya

Tr Akad Nauk Kaz SSR Inst Mikrobiol Virusol — Trudy Akademiia Nauk Kazakhskoi SSR Institut Mikrobiologii i Virusologii

Tr Akad Nauk Latv SSR Inst Mikrobiol — Trudy Akademii Nauk Latviiskoi SSR Institut Mikrobiologii

Tr Akad Nauk Litov SSR Inst Biol — Trudy Akademii Nauk Litovskoi SSR Institut Biologii

Tr Akad Nauk Lit SSR Ser V — Trudy Akademii Nauk Litovskoi SSR. Seriya V

Tr Akad Nauk Lit SSR Ser V Biol Nauki — Trudy Akademii Nauk Litovskoi SSR. Seriya V. Biologicheskie Nauki

Tr Akad Nauk SSSR Inst Biol Vnutr Vod — Trudy Akademiia Nauk SSSR Institut Biologii Vnutrennikh Vod

Tr Akad Nauk SSSR Karel Fil — Trudy Akademii Nauk SSSR Karel'skii Filial

Tr Akad Nauk Tadzh SSR — Trudy Akademii Nauk Tadzhikskoi SSR

Tr Akad Nauk Turkm SSR — Trudy Akademii Nauk Turkmenskoi SSR

Tr Akad Stroit Arkhit SSSR Zapadno Sib Fil — Trudy Akademiya Stroitel'stva i Arkhitektury SSSR Zapadno-Sibirskii Filial

Trak Sel'khozmashiny — Traktory i Sel'khozmashiny [*USSR*]

Trakt Landmasch — Traktor und die Landmaschine

Trakt Sel'khozmash — Traktory i Sel'khozmashiny

Tr Alma-At Med Inst — Trudy Alma-Atinskogo Meditsinskogo Instituta

Tr Alma At Nauchno Issled Proektn Inst Stroit Mater — Trudy Alma-Atinskogo Nauchno-Issledovatel'skogo i Proektnogo Instituta Stroitel'nykh Materialov

Tr Alma-At Zoovet Inst — Trudy Alma-Atinskogo Zooveterinarnogo Instituta

Tr Altai Gorno Metall Nauchno Issled Inst Akad Nauk Kaz SSR — Trudy Altaiskogo Gorno-Metallurgicheskogo Nauchno-Issledovatel'skogo Instituta Akademiya Nauk Kazakhskoi SSR

Tr Am Ass Genito-Urin Surg — Transactions. American Association of Genito-Urinary Surgeons

Tr Am Fish Soc — Transactions. American Fisheries Society

Tr Am Soc Trop Med — Transactions. American Society of Tropical Medicine

Tr Amur Skh Opytn Stn — Trudy Amurskoi Sel'skokhozyaistvennoi Opytnoi Stantsii

TRANA — Transfusion [*Philadelphia*]

Tr Angarsk Fil Irkutsk Politekh Inst — Trudy Angarskogo Filiala Irkutskogo Politekhnicheskogo Instituta

Trans AACE — Transactions. American Association of Cost Engineers

Trans Acad Sci St Louis — Transactions. Academy of Science of St. Louis

Transact Roy Soc Canada — Transactions. Royal Society of Canada

Trans Act Soc Aust & NZ — Transactions. Actuarial Society of Australia and New Zealand

Trans AIChE — Transactions. AIChE [*American Institute of Chemical Engineers*]

Trans All-India Inst Ment Health — Transactions. All-India Institute of Mental Health

Trans All Union Sci Res Inst Confect Ind — Transactions. All-Union Scientific Research Institute of the Confectionery Industry

Trans All Union Sci Res Inst Veg Oils Margarine — Transactions. All-Union Scientific Research Institute for Vegetable Oils and Margarine

Trans Am Acad Ophthalmol Oto-Laryngol — Transactions. American Academy of Ophthalmology and Oto-Laryngology

Trans Am Assoc Genito-Urin Surg — Transactions. American Association of Genito-Urinary Surgeons

Trans Am Assoc Obstet Gynecol — Transactions. American Association of Obstetricians and Gynecologists

Trans Am Assoc Obstet Gynecol Abdom Surg — Transactions. American Association of Obstetricians, Gynecologists, and Abdominal Surgeons

Trans Am Brew Inst — Transactions. American Brewing Institute

Trans Am Broncho-Esophagol Assoc — Transactions. American Broncho-Esophagological Association

Trans Am Ceram Soc — Transactions. American Ceramic Society

Trans Am Clin Climatol Assoc — Transactions. American Clinical and Climatological Association

Trans Am Coll Cardiol — Transactions. American College of Cardiology

Trans Am Crystallogr Assoc — Transactions. American Crystallographic Association

Trans Am Electroch Soc — Transactions. American Electrochemical Society

Trans Am Entomol Soc (Phila) — Transactions. American Entomological Society (Philadelphia)

Trans Am Ent Soc — Transactions. American Entomological Society

Trans Amer Ass Cereal Chem — Transactions. American Association of Cereal Chemists

Trans Amer Foundrymen's Soc — Transactions. American Foundrymen's Society

Trans Amer Geophys Union — Transactions. American Geophysical Union

Trans Amer Math Soc — Transactions. American Mathematical Society

Trans Amer Microscop Soc — Transactions. American Microscopical Society

Trans Amer Nucl Soc — Transactions. American Nuclear Society

Trans Am Fisheries Soc — Transactions. American Fisheries Society

Trans Am Fish Soc — Transactions. American Fisheries Society

Trans Am Geophys Union — Transactions. American Geophysical Union

Trans Am Gynecol Soc — Transactions. American Gynecological Society

Trans Am Inst Chem Eng — Transactions. American Institute of Chemical Engineers

Trans Am Inst Electr Eng — Transactions. American Institute of Electrical Engineers

Trans Am Inst Electr Eng Part 1 — Transactions. American Institute of Electrical Engineers. Part 1. Communication and Electronics

Trans Am Inst Electr Eng Part 2 — Transactions. American Institute of Electrical Engineers. Part 2. Applications and Industry

Trans Am Inst Electr Eng Part 3 — Transactions. American Institute of Electrical Engineers. Part 3. Power Apparatus and Systems

Trans Am Inst Min Eng — Transactions. American Institute of Mining Engineers

Trans Am Inst Min Metall Eng — Transactions. American Institute of Mining and Metallurgical Engineers

Trans Am Inst Min Metall Pet Eng — Transactions. American Institute of Mining, Metallurgical, and Petroleum Engineers

Trans Am Math Soc — Transactions. American Mathematical Society

Trans Am Microsc Soc — Transactions. American Microscopical Society

Trans Am Neurol Assoc — Transactions. American Neurological Association

Trans Am Nucl Soc — Transactions. American Nuclear Society

Trans Am Nucl Soc Suppl — Transactions. American Nuclear Society. Supplement

Trans Am Ophthalmol Soc — Transactions. American Ophthalmological Society

Trans Am Otol Soc — Transactions. American Otological Society

Trans Am Philos Soc — Transactions. American Philosophical Society

Trans Am Soc Agric Eng (Gen Ed) — Transactions. American Society of Agricultural Engineers (General Edition)

Trans Am Soc Agric Engrs Gen Edn — Transactions. American Society of Agricultural Engineers. General Edition

Trans Am Soc Artif Intern Organs — Transactions. American Society for Artificial Internal Organs

Trans Am Soc Heat Air-Cond Eng — Transactions. American Society of Heating and Air-Conditioning Engineers

Trans Am Soc Met — Transactions. American Society for Metals

Trans Am Soc Ophthalmol Otolaryngol Allergy — Transactions. American Society of Ophthalmologic and Otolaryngologic Allergy

Trans Am Soc Steel Treat — Transactions. American Society for Steel Treating

Trans Am Ther Soc — Transactions. American Therapeutic Society

Trans Ann Anthracite Conf Lehigh Univ — Transactions. Annual Anthracite Conference of Lehigh University

Trans Annu Conf Can Nucl Soc — Transactions. Annual Conference. Canadian Nuclear Society

Trans Annu Meet Allen O Whipple Surg Soc — Transactions. Annual Meeting. Allen O. Whipple Surgical Society

Trans Annu Tech Conf Am Soc Qual Control — Transactions. Annual Technical Conference. American Society for Quality Control

Trans Annu Tech Conf ASQC — Transactions. Annual Technical Conference. American Society for Quality Control

Trans Annu Tech Conf Soc Vac Coaters — Transactions. Annual Technical Conference. Society of Vacuum Coaters

Trans Architect Inst Jpn — Transactions. Architectural Institute of Japan

Trans ASAE — Transactions. ASAE [*American Society of Agricultural Engineers*]

Trans ASME J Appl Mech — Transactions. American Society of Mechanical Engineers. Journal of Applied Mechanics

Trans ASME J Biomech Eng — Transactions. ASME [*American Society of Mechanical Engineers*] Journal of Biomechanical Engineering

Trans ASME J Biomech Engng — Transactions. American Society of Mechanical Engineers. Journal of Biomechanical Engineering

Trans ASME J Dyn Syst Meas & Control — Transactions. American Society of Mechanical Engineers. Journal of Dynamic Systems Measurement and Control

Trans ASME J Energy Resour Technol — Transactions. American Society of Mechanical Engineers. Journal of Energy Resources Technology

Trans ASME J Eng Gas Turbines Power — Transactions. ASME [*American Society of Mechanical Engineers*] Journal of Engineering for Gas Turbines and Power

Trans ASME J Eng Ind — Transactions. ASME [*American Society of Mechanical Engineers*] Journal of Engineering for Industry

Trans ASME J Engng Ind — Transactions. American Society of Mechanical Engineers. Journal of Engineering for Industry

Trans ASME J Engng Mater & Technol — Transactions. American Society of Mechanical Engineers. Journal of Engineering Materials and Technology

Trans ASME J Engng Power — Transactions. American Society of Mechanical Engineers. Journal of Engineering for Power

Trans ASME J Eng Power — Transactions. ASME [*American Society of Mechanical Engineers*] Journal of Engineering for Power

Trans ASME J Fluids Engng — Transactions. American Society of Mechanical Engineers. Journal of Fluids Engineering

Trans ASME J Heat Transfer — Transactions. American Society of Mechanical Engineers. Journal of Heat Transfer

Trans ASME J Lubr Technol — Transactions. American Society of Mechanical Engineers. Journal of Lubrication Technology

Trans ASME J Mech Des — Transactions. American Society of Mechanical Engineers. Journal of Mechanical Design

Trans ASME J Pressure Vessel Technol — Transactions. American Society of Mechanical Engineers. Journal of Pressure Vessel Technology

Trans ASME J Sol Energy Engng — Transactions. American Society of Mechanical Engineers. Journal of Solar Energy Engineering

Trans ASME J Tribol — Transactions. ASME [*American Society of Mechanical Engineers*] Journal of Tribology

Trans ASME Ser A — Transactions. ASME [*American Society of Mechanical Engineers*] Series A. Journal of Engineering for Power

Trans ASME Ser A J Eng Power — Transactions. ASME [*American Society of Mechanical Engineers*] Series A. Journal of Engineering for Power

Trans ASME Ser B — Transactions. ASME [*American Society of Mechanical Engineers*] Series B. Journal of Engineering for Industry

Trans ASME Ser C — Transactions. ASME [*American Society of Mechanical Engineers*] Series C. Journal of Heat Transfer

Trans ASME Ser E — Transactions. ASME [*American Society of Mechanical Engineers*] Series E. Journal of Applied Mechanics

Trans ASME Ser E J Appl Mech — Transactions. ASME [*American Society of Mechanical Engineers*] Series E. Journal of Applied Mechanics

Trans ASME Ser F — Transactions. ASME [*American Society of Mechanical Engineers*] Series F. Journal of Lubrication Technology

Trans ASME Ser F J Lubr Technol — Transactions. ASME [*American Society of Mechanical Engineers*] Series F. Journal of Lubrication Technology

Trans ASME Ser G — Transactions. ASME [*American Society of Mechanical Engineers*] Series G. Journal of Dynamic Systems Measurement and Control

Trans ASME Ser GJ Dynamic Systems — Transactions. ASME [*American Society of Mechanical Engineers*] Series G. Journal of Dynamic Systems. Measurement and Control

Trans ASME Ser H — Transactions. ASME [*American Society of Mechanical Engineers*] Series H. Journal of Engineering Materials and Technology

Trans ASME Ser I — Transactions. ASME [*American Society of Mechanical Engineers*] Series I. Journal of Fluids Engineering

Trans ASME Ser J J Pressure Vessel Technol — Transactions. ASME [*American Society of Mechanical Engineers*] Series J. Journal of Pressure Vessel Technology

Trans ASME Ser K J Biomech Eng — Transactions. ASME [*American Society of Mechanical Engineers*] Series K. Journal of Biomechanical Engineering

Trans Assoc Am Physicians — Transactions. Association of American Physicians

Trans Assoc Ind Med Off — Transactions. Association of Industrial Medical Officers

Trans Assoc Life Ins Med Dir Am — Transactions. Association of Life Insurance Medical Directors of America

Transatl R — Transatlantic Review

Trans B'ham Warwks Arch Soc — Transactions. Birmingham and Warwickshire Archaeological Society

Trans Biochem Soc — Transactions. Biochemical Society

Trans Birmingham Warwickshire Archaeol Soc — Transactions. Birmingham and Warwickshire Archaeological Society

Trans Bose Res Inst (Calcutta) — Transactions. Bose Research Institute (Calcutta)

Trans Bot Soc Edinb — Transactions and Proceedings. Botanical Society of Edinburgh

Trans Br Bryol Soc — Transactions. British Bryological Society

Trans Br Ceram Soc — Transactions. British Ceramic Society

Trans Bristol Gloucestershire Archaeol Soc — Transactions. Bristol and Gloucestershire Archaeological Society

Trans Bristol Gloucestershire Arch Soc — Transactions. Bristol and Gloucestershire Archaeological Society

Trans Br Mycol Soc — Transactions. British Mycological Society

Trans Br Soc Hist Pharm — Transactions. British Society for the History of Pharmacy

Trans Caernarvonshire Hist Soc — Transactions. Caernarvonshire Historical Society

Trans Cambridge Philos Soc — Transactions. Cambridge Philosophical Society

Trans Can Inst Mining Soc NS — Transactions. Canadian Institute of Mining and Metallurgy and Mining Society of Nova Scotia

Trans Can Inst Min Metall — Transactions. Canadian Institute of Mining and Metallurgy and Mining Society of Nova Scotia

Trans Can Inst Min Metall Min Soc NS — Transactions. Canadian Institute of Mining and Metallurgy and Mining Society of Nova Scotia

Trans Can Min Inst — Transactions. Canadian Mining Institute

Trans Can Nucl Soc — Transactions. Canadian Nuclear Society

Trans Can Soc Mech Eng — Transactions. Canadian Society for Mechanical Engineers

Trans Can Soc Mech Engrs — Transactions. Canadian Society of Mechanical Engineers

Trans Cardiff Nat Soc — Transactions. Cardiff Naturalists Society

Trans Cardiff Natur Soc — Transactions. Cardiff Naturalists Society

Trans Cave Res Group GB — Transactions. Cave Research Group of Great Britain

Trans Cent Sci Res Inst Confect Ind — Transactions. Central Scientific Research Institute of the Confectionery Industry

Trans Ceylon Coll — Transactions. Ceylon College of Physicians

Trans Chalmers Univ Technol (Gothenburg) — Transactions. Chalmers University of Technology (Gothenburg) [*Sweden*]

Trans Chem Div Am Soc Qual Control — Transactions. Chemical Division. American Society for Quality Control

Trans Chin Assoc Adv Sci — Transactions. Chinese Association for the Advancement of Science

Trans Citrus Eng Conf — Transactions. Citrus Engineering Conference

Trans Coll Med S Afr — Transactions. College of Medicine of South Africa

Trans Coll Physicians Philadelphia — Transactions. College of Physicians of Philadelphia

Trans Conf Cold Inj — Transactions. Conference on Cold Injury

Trans Conf Glaucoma — Transactions. Conference on Glaucoma

Trans Conf Group Processes — Transactions. Conference on Group Processes

Trans Conf Group Soc Adm Hist — Transactions. Conference Group for Social and Administrative History

Trans Conf Neuropharmacol — Transactions. Conference on Neuropharmacology

Trans Conf Physiol Prematurity — Transactions. Conference on Physiology of Prematurity

Trans Conf Polysaccharides Biol — Transactions. Conference on Polysaccharides in Biology

Trans Conn Acad Arts Sci — Transactions. Connecticut Academy of Arts and Sciences

Trans Corn Inst Eng — Transactions. Cornish Institute of Engineers

Trans C S Peirce Soc — Transactions. C. S. Peirce Society

Transcult Psychiat Res — Transcultural Psychiatric Research Review

Trans Cumberland Westmorland Antiq Archaeol Soc N Ser — Transactions. Cumberland and Westmorland Antiquarian and Archaeological Society. New Series

Trans Denbighshire Hist Soc — Transactions. Denbighshire Historical Society

Trans Desert Bighorn Counc — Transactions. Desert Bighorn Council

Transducer Technol — Transducer Technology

Trans Dumfries Galloway Nat Hist Antiq Soc — Transactions. Dumfriesshire and Galloway Natural History and Antiquarian Society

Trans Dumfriesshire Galloway Natur Hist Antiq Soc — Transactions. Dumfriesshire and Galloway Natural History and Antiquarian Society

Trans Dumfriesshire Galloway Natur Hist Ant Soc — Transactions. Dumfriesshire and Galloway Natural History and Antiquarian Society

Trans Dynam Dev — Transactions. Dynamics of Development

Trans East Lothian Antiq Field Nat Soc — Transactions. East Lothian Antiquarian and Field Naturalists' Society

Trans Econ & Oper Anal — Transport Economics and Operational Analysis

Trans Edinburgh Geol Soc — Transactions. Edinburgh Geological Society

Trans Electrochem Soc — Transactions. Electrochemical Society

Trans Electr Supply Auth Eng Inst NZ — Transactions. Electric Supply Authority Engineers' Institute of New Zealand, Inc.

Trans Electr Supply Eng Inst — Transactions. Annual Conference. Electric Supply Authority Engineers' Institute of New Zealand, Inc.

Trans E Lothian Antiq Fld Natur Soc — Transactions. East Lothian Antiquarian and Field Naturalists' Society

Trans Eng Inst Can — Transactions. Engineering Institute of Canada

Trans Engl Ceram Circle — Transactions. English Ceramic Circle

Trans Engl Ceram Soc — Transactions. English Ceramic Society

Trans Essex Arch Soc — Transactions. Essex Archaeological Society

Trans Est Agric Acad — Transactions. Estonian Agricultural Academy

Trans Eur Orthod Soc — Transactions. European Orthodontic Society

Trans Fac Hortic Chiba Univ — Transactions. Faculty of Horticulture. Chiba University

Trans Farady Soc — Transactions. Faraday Society

Trans Fed-Prov Wildl Conf — Transactions. Federal-Provincial Wildlife Conference

Transform (Papeterie) — Transformation (Supplement to La Papeterie)

Trans Geol Soc Glasg — Transactions. Geological Society of Glasgow

Trans Geol Soc S Afr — Transactions. Geological Society of South Africa

Trans Geotherm Resour Counc — Transactions. Geothermal Resources Council [*United States*]

Trans Glasgow Univ Orient Soc — Transactions. Glasgow University Oriental Society

Trans Greenwich Lewisham Antiq Soc — Transactions. Greenwich and Lewisham Antiquarian Society

Trans Gulf Coast Ass Geol Soc — Transactions. Gulf Coast Association of Geological Societies

Trans Gulf Coast Assoc Geol Soc — Transactions. Gulf Coast Association of Geological Societies

Trans Halifax Antiq Society — Transactions. Halifax Antiquarian Society

Trans Hawick Archaeol Soc — Transactions. Hawick Archaeological Society

Trans Hertfordshire Nat Hist Field Club — Transactions. Hertfordshire Natural History Society and Field Club

Trans Hertfordshire Nat Hist Soc Field Club — Transactions. Hertfordshire Natural History Society and Field Club

Trans Highl Agric Soc Scotl — Transactions. Highland and Agricultural Society of Scotland

Trans Hist Soc Ghana — Transactions. Historical Society of Ghana

Trans Hist Soc Lancashire Cheshire — Transactions. Historic Society of Lancashire and Cheshire

Trans Hunter Archaeol Soc — Transactions. Hunter Archaeological Society

Trans Hunter Soc — Transactions. Hunterian Society

Trans Illinois State Acad Sci — Illinois State Academy of Science. Transactions

Trans Ill St Acad Sci — Transactions. Illinois State Academy of Science

Trans Ill State Acad Sci — Transactions. Illinois State Academy of Science

Trans Ill State Hortic Soc — Transactions. Illinois State Horticultural Society

Trans Ill State Hortic Soc Ill Fruit Counc — Transactions. Illinois State Horticultural Society and the Illinois Fruit Council

Trans Ill St Hort Soc — Transactions. Illinois State Horticultural Society

Trans Illum Eng Soc — Transactions. Illuminating Engineering Society

Trans I Mar E — Transactions. Institute of Marine Engineers

Trans Indiana Acad Ophthalmol Otolaryngol — Transactions. Indiana Academy of Ophthalmology and Otolaryngology

Trans Indian Ceram Soc — Transactions. Indian Ceramic Society

Trans Indian Inst Chem Eng — Transactions. Indian Institute of Chemical Engineers

Trans Indian Inst Met — Transactions. Indian Institute of Metals

Trans Indian Inst Metals — Transactions. Indian Institute of Metals

Trans Indian Soc Desert Technol Univ Cent Desert Stud — Transactions. Indian Society of Desert Technology and University Centre of Desert Studies

Trans Ind Inst Chem Eng — Transactions. Indian Institute of Chemical Engineers

Trans Inf Process Soc Jpn — Transactions. Information Processing Society of Japan

Trans Inst Act Aust & NZ — Transactions. Institute of Actuaries of Australia and New Zealand

Trans Inst Brit Geogr — Transactions. Institute of British Geographers

Trans Inst Chem Eng — Transactions. Institution of Chemical Engineers

Trans Inst Chem Engrs — Transactions. Institution of Chemical Engineers

Trans Inst Civ Eng Ir — Transactions. Institution of Civil Engineers of Ireland

Trans Inst Electr Eng Jap — Transactions. Institute of Electrical Engineers of Japan

Trans Inst Electr Eng Jpn — Transactions. Institute of Electrical Engineers of Japan

Trans Inst Electr Eng Jpn B — Transactions. Institute of Electrical Engineers of Japan. Part B

Trans Inst Electr Eng Jpn C — Transactions. Institute of Electrical Engineers of Japan. Part C

Trans Inst Electr Eng Jpn Part A — Transactions. Institute of Electrical Engineers of Japan. Part A

Trans Inst Electr Eng Jpn Part B — Transactions. Institute of Electrical Engineers of Japan. Part B

Trans Inst Electr Eng Jpn Part C — Transactions. Institute of Electrical Engineers of Japan. Part C

Trans Inst Electr Eng Jpn Sect E — Transactions. Institute of Electrical Engineers of Japan. Section E

Trans Inst Electron & Commun Eng Jap A — Transactions. Institute of Electronics and Communication Engineers of Japan. Part A

Trans Inst Electron & Commun Eng Jap C — Transactions. Institute of Electronics and Communication Engineers of Japan. Part C

Trans Inst Electron Commun Eng Jap Sect J Part D — Transactions. Institute of Electronics and Communication Engineers of Japan. Section J [*Japanese*] Part D

Trans Inst Electron and Commun Eng Jpn Part A — Transactions. Institute of Electronics and Communication Engineers of Japan. Part A

Trans Inst Electron and Commun Eng Jpn Part B — Transactions. Institute of Electronics and Communication Engineers of Japan. Part B

Trans Inst Electron Commun Eng Jpn Part B — Transactions. Institute of Electronics and Communication Engineers of Japan. Part B

Trans Inst Electron and Commun Eng Jpn Part C — Transactions. Institute of Electronics and Communication Engineers of Japan. Part C

Trans Inst Electron and Commun Eng Jpn Part D — Transactions. Institute of Electronics and Communication Engineers of Japan. Part D

Trans Inst Electron and Commun Eng Jpn Sect E — Transactions. Institute of Electronics and Communication Engineers of Japan. Section E

Trans Inst Electron Commun Eng Jpn Sect E (Engl) — Transactions. Institute of Electronics and Communication Engineers of Japan. Section E (English)

Trans Inst Eng Aust — Transactions. Institute of Engineers of Australia

Trans Inst Eng Aust Civ Eng — Transactions. Institute of Engineers of Australia. Civil Engineering

Trans Inst Eng Aust Electr Eng — Transactions. Institute of Engineers of Australia. Electrical Engineering

Trans Inst Eng Aust Mech Eng — Transactions. Institute of Engineers of Australia. Mechanical Engineering

Trans Inst Engrs (Aust) Civ Engng — Transactions. Institution of Engineers (Australia). Civil Engineering

Trans Inst Engrs (Aust) Mech Engng — Transactions. Institution of Engineers (Australia). Mechanical Engineering

Trans Inst Eng Shipbuilders Scot — Transactions. Institution of Engineers and Shipbuilders in Scotland

Trans Inst Gas Eng — Transactions. Institution of Gas Engineers [*England*]

Trans Inst Mar Eng — Transactions. Institute of Marine Engineers

Trans Inst Mar Eng Conf Pap — Transactions. Institute of Marine Engineers. Conference Papers

Trans Inst Mar Engrs — Transactions. Institute of Marine Engineers

Trans Inst Mar Eng Ser C — Transactions. Institute of Marine Engineers. Series C

Trans Inst Mar Eng Tech Meet Pap — Transactions. Institute of Marine Engineers. Technical Meeting Papers

Trans Inst Marine Eng — Transactions. Institute of Marine Engineers
Trans Inst Meas & Control — Transactions. Institute of Measurement and Control
Trans Inst Meas Control — Transactions. Institute of Measurement and Control
Trans Inst Measmt Control — Transactions. Institute of Measurement and Control
Trans Inst Met Finish — Transactions. Institute of Metal Finishing
Trans Inst Min Eng — Transactions. Institution of Mining Engineers
Trans Inst Mining Met Sect A — Transactions. Institution of Mining and Metallurgy. Section A
Trans Inst Mining Met Sect B — Transactions. Institution of Mining and Metallurgy. Section B
Trans Inst Mining Met Sect C — Transactions. Institution of Mining and Metallurgy. Section C
Trans Inst Min Metall — Transactions. Institution of Mining and Metallurgy
Trans Inst Min Metall Sec A — Transactions. Institution of Mining and Metallurgy. Section A. Mining Industry
Trans Inst Min Metall Sec B — Transactions. Institution of Mining and Metallurgy. Section B
Trans Inst Min Metall Sec C — Transactions. Institution of Mining and Metallurgy. Section C [*United Kingdom*]
Trans Inst Min Metall Sect A Min Ind — Transactions. Institution of Mining and Metallurgy. Section A. Mining Industry
Trans Inst Min Metall Sect B Appl Earth Sci — Transactions. Institution of Mining and Metallurgy. Section B. Applied Earth Science [*United Kingdom*]
Trans Instn Chem Engrs — Transactions. Institution of Chemical Engineers
Trans Instn E Shipb Scot — Transactions. Institution of Engineers and Shipbuilders in Scotland
Trans Instn Min Metall — Transactions. Institution of Mining and Metallurgy
Trans Inst Plast Ind — Transactions. Institute of the Plastics Industry
Trans Inst Prof Eng — Transactions. Institution of Professional Engineers [*New Zealand*]
Trans Inst Prof Eng (NZ) Civ Eng Sect — Transactions. Institution of Professional Engineers (New Zealand). Civil Engineering Section
Trans Inst Prof Eng (NZ) Electr Mech Chem Eng Sect — Transactions. Institution of Professional Engineers (New Zealand). Electrical/Mechanical/Chemical Engineering Section
Trans Inst Prof Eng (NZ) EMCh — Transactions. Institution of Professional Engineers (New Zealand). Electrical/Mechanical/Chemical Engineering Section
Trans Inst Pure Chem Reagents (Moscow) — Transactions. Institute of Pure Chemical Reagents (Moscow)
Trans Inst Rubber Ind — Transactions. Institution of the Rubber Industry
Trans Inst Water Eng — Transactions. Institution of Water Engineers
Trans Inst Weld (London) — Transactions. Institute of Welding (London)
Trans Int Assoc Math and Comput Simulation — Transactions. International Association for Mathematics and Computers in Simulation
Trans Int Conf Oral Surg — Transactions. International Conference on Oral Surgery
Trans Int Conf Or Ja — Transactions. International Conference of Orientalists in Japan
Trans Int Conf Soil Sci — Transactions. International Conference of Soil Science
Trans Int Congr Agric Engng — Transactions. International Congress for Agricultural Engineering
Trans Int Congr Soil Sci — Transactions. International Congress of Soil Science
Trans Int Soc Geotherm Eng — Transactions. International Society for Geothermal Engineering
Trans Iowa State Hortic Soc — Transactions. Iowa State Horticultural Society
Trans Iron Steel Inst Jap — Transactions. Iron and Steel Institute of Japan
Trans Iron Steel Inst Jpn — Transactions. Iron and Steel Institute of Japan
Transition Met Chem — Transition Metal Chemistry
Transit J — Transit Journal
Transit Met Chem (Weinheim Ger) — Transition Metal Chemistry (Weinheim, Germany)
Trans Japan Soc Civ Engrs — Transactions. Japan Society of Civil Engineers
Trans Japan Soc Compos Mater — Transactions. Japan Society for Composite Materials
Trans Japan Soc Mech Engrs Ser B — Transactions. Japan Society of Mechanical Engineers. Series B
Trans Japan Soc Mech Engrs Ser C — Transactions. Japan Society of Mechanical Engineers. Series C
Trans Jap Inst Met — Transactions. Japan Institute of Metals
Trans Jap Inst Metals — Transactions. Japan Institute of Metals
Trans Jap Soc Aeronaut Space Sci — Transactions. Japan Society for Aeronautical and Space Sciences
Trans Jap Soc Mech Eng — Transactions. Japan Society of Mechanical Engineers
Trans Jap Weld Soc — Transactions. Japan Welding Society
Trans J Br Ceram Soc — Transactions and Journal. British Ceramic Society
Trans and J Br Ceram Soc — Transactions and Journal. British Ceramic Society
Trans J Brit Ceram Soc — Transactions and Journal. British Ceramic Society

Trans J Plast Inst — Transactions and Journal. Plastics Institute [*England*]
Trans Jpn Inst Met — Transactions. Japan Institute of Metals
Trans Jpn Inst Met Suppl — Transactions. Japan Institute of Metals. Supplement
Trans Jpn Pathol Soc — Transactions. Japanese Pathological Society
Trans Jpn Soc Civ Eng — Transactions. Japan Society of Civil Engineers
Trans Jpn Soc Irrig Drain Reclam Eng — Transactions. Japanese Society of Irrigation Drainage and Reclamation Engineering
Trans Jpn Soc Mech Eng Ser B — Transactions. Japan Society of Mechanical Engineers. Series B
Trans Jt Mtg Comm Int Soc Soil Sci — Transactions. Joint Meeting of Commissions. International Society of Soil Science
Trans JWRI — Transactions. JWRI [*Japanese Welding Research Institute*]
Trans K Acad Sci — Transactions. Kentucky Academy of Science
Trans Kans Acad Sci — Transactions. Kansas Academy of Science
Trans Kansai Ent Soc — Transactions. Kansai Entomological Society
Transkei Dev Rev — Transkei Development Review
Trans Koll Geneeskd S-Afr — Transaksies. Kollege van Geneeskunde van Suid-Afrika
Trans Korean Soc Mech Eng — Transactions. Korean Society of Mechanical Engineers [*Republic of Korea*]
Trans KY Acad Sci — Transactions. Kentucky Academy of Science
Trans Latv Branch All Union Soc Soil Sci — Transactions. Latvian Branch. All-Union Society of Soil Science
Transl Beltone Inst Hear Res — Translations. Beltone Institute for Hearing Research
Transl Commonw Sci Industr Res Organ (Aust) — Translation. Commonwealth Scientific and Industrial Research Organisation (CSIRO) (Australia)
Transl Dep Fish For (Can) — Translation. Department of Fisheries and Forestry (Ottawa, Canada)
Trans Leeds Geol Assoc — Transactions. Leeds Geological Association
Trans Leicestershire Archaeol Hist Soc — Transactions. Leicestershire Archaeological and Historical Society
Transl Fac For Univ BC — Translation. Faculty of Forestry. University of British Columbia
Transl For Comm (Lond) — Translation. Forestry Commission (London)
Trans Lich S Staffs Arch Hist Soc — Transactions. Lichfield and South Staffordshire Archaeological and Historical Society
Trans Linn Soc Lond — Transactions. Linnean Society of London
Trans Linn Soc NY — Transactions. Linnaean Society of New York
Trans Liverpool Eng Soc — Transactions. Liverpool Engineering Society
Transl London M'sex Arch — Transactions. London and Middlesex Archaeological Society
Transl Reg-Index — Translations Register-Index
Transl Russ Game Rep — Translations of Russian Game Reports
Transl Soviet Agr US Joint Publ Res Serv — Translations on Soviet Agriculture. United States Joint Publications Research Service
Transl US For Prod Lab (Madison) — Translation. United States Forest Products Laboratory (Madison)
Trans Manchester Assoc Eng — Transactions. Manchester Association of Engineers
Trans Mass Hort Soc — Transactions. Massachusetts Horticultural Society
Trans Math Monographs — Translations of Mathematical Monographs. American Mathematical Society
Transm & Distrib — Transmission and Distribution
Transm Distrib — Transmission and Distribution
Trans Med Soc Lond — Transactions. Medical Society of London
Trans Med Soc London — Transactions. Medical Society of London
Trans Meet Commns II & IV Int Soc Soil Sci — Transactions. Meeting of Commissions II and IV. International Society of Soil Science
Trans Metall Soc AIME (Am Inst Min Metall Pet Eng) — Transactions. Metallurgical Society of AIME (American Institute of Mining, Metallurgical, and Petroleum Engineers)
Trans Mining Geol Met Inst India — Transactions. Mining, Geological, and Metallurgical Institute of India
Trans Min Metall Alumni Assoc — Transactions. Mining and Metallurgical Alumni Association [*Japan*]
Trans Min Metall Assoc (Kyoto) — Transactions. Mining and Metallurgical Association (Kyoto)
Trans MO Acad Sci — Transactions. Missouri Academy of Science
Trans MO Acad Scie — Transactions. Missouri Academy of Science
Trans Morris C Res Counc — Transactions. Morris County Research Council
Trans Moscow Math Soc — Transactions. Moscow Mathematical Society
Trans Mycol Soc Jap — Transactions. Mycological Society of Japan
Trans Mycol Soc Japan — Transactions. Mycological Society of Japan
Trans Mycol Soc Jpn — Transactions. Mycological Society of Japan
Trans N Amer Wildlife Conf — Transactions. North American Wildlife and Natural Resources Conference
Trans N Am Wildl Nat Resour Conf — Transactions. North American Wildlife and Natural Resources Conference
Trans Nat Hist Northumberl Durham Newcastle Upon Tyne — Transactions. Natural History Society of Northumberland Durham and Newcastle Upon Tyne

Trans Nat Hist Soc Northumberl Durham Newcastle-Upon-Tyne — Transactions. Natural History Society of Northumberland, Durham, and Newcastle-Upon-Tyne [*Later, Natural History Society of Northumbria. Transactions*]

Trans Nat Hist Soc Northumbria — Transactions. Natural History Society of Northumbria

Trans Natl Inst Sci India — Transactions. National Institute of Sciences. India

Trans Natl Res Inst Met (Tokyo) — Transactions. National Research Institute for Metals (Tokyo)

Trans Natl Saf Congr — Transactions. National Safety Congress [*United States*]

Trans Nat Res Inst Metals (Tokyo) — Transactions. National Research Institute for Metals (Tokyo)

Trans Nat Vac Symp — Transactions. National Vacuum Symposium

Trans Nebr Acad Sci — Transactions. Nebraska Academy of Sciences

Trans N E Cst Instn Engrs Shipbldrs — Transactions. North East Coast Institution of Engineers and Shipbuilders

Trans Newbury Dist Fld Club — Transactions. Newbury District Field Club

Trans Newcomen Soc Study His Eng Technol — Transactions. Newcomen Society for the Study of the History of Engineering and Technology

Trans New Engl Obstet Gynecol Soc — Transactions. New England Obstetrical and Gynecological Society [*United States*]

Trans New Orleans Acad Ophthalmol — Transactions. New Orleans Academy of Ophthalmology

Trans New York Acad Sci Ser II — Transactions. New York Academy of Sciences. Series II

Trans NJ Obstet Gynecol Soc — Transactions. New Jersey Obstetrical and Gynecological Society

Trans North Am Wildl Conf — Transactions. North American Wildlife Conference

Trans Northeast Sect Wildl Soc — Transactions of the Northeast Section. Wildlife Society

Trans NY Acad Sci — Transactions. New York Academy of Sciences

Trans NZ Inst Eng — Transactions. New Zealand Institution of Engineers

Trans Ophthalmol Soc Aust — Transactions. Ophthalmological Society of Australia

Trans Ophthalmol Soc NZ — Transactions. Ophthalmological Society of New Zealand

Trans Ophthalmol Soc UK — Transactions. Ophthalmological Societies of the United Kingdom

Trans Ophthal Soc Aust — Transactions. Ophthalmological Society of Australia

Transp — Transporter

Trans PA Acad Ophthalmol Otolaryngol — Transactions. Pennsylvania Academy of Ophthalmology and Otolaryngology

Trans-Pac — Trans-Pacific

Trans Pac Coast Obstet Gynecol Soc — Transactions. Pacific Coast Obstetrical and Gynecological Society [*United States*]

Trans Pac Coast Oto-Ophthalmol Soc — Transactions. Pacific Coast Oto-Ophthalmological Society

Trans Pac Coast Oto-Ophthalmol Soc Annu Meet — Transactions. Pacific Coast Oto-Ophthalmological Society. Annual Meeting [*United States*]

Trans Papers L Brit G — Institute of British Geographers. Liverpool. Transactions and Papers

Transp Aust — Transport Australia

Trans Peirce Soc — Transactions. Charles S. Peirce Society

Transp Eng — Transportation Engineering

Transp Eng J ASCE — Transportation Engineering Journal. ASCE [*American Society of Civil Engineers*]

Transp Engng — Transportation Engineering [*Formerly, Traffic Engineering*]

Transp Engng J Proc ASCE — Transportation Engineering Journal. Proceedings of the American Society of Civil Engineers

Transp Engr — Transport Engineer

Trans Peninsula Hortic Soc — Transactions. Peninsula Horticultural Society

Transp En J — Transportation Engineering Journal. ASCE [*American Society of Civil Engineers*]

Trans Philol Soc — Transactions. Philological Society

Trans Phil Soc — Transactions. Philological Society

Transp His — Transportation History

Transp Hist — Transport History

Transp J — Transport Journal

Transp J — Transportation Journal

Transp J of Aust — Transport Journal of Australia

Transp Khranenie Nefti Nefteprod — Transport i Khranenie Nefti i Nefteproduktov [*USSR*]

Transplan P — Transplantation Proceedings

Transplan R — Transplantation Reviews

Transplant — Transplantation

Transplant Bull — Transplantation Bulletin

Transplant Clin Immunol — Transplantation and Clinical Immunology

Transplant Immunol Clin — Transplantation et Immunologie Clinique

Transplantn Proc — Transplantation Proceedings

Transplant Proc — Transplantation Proceedings

Transplant Proc Suppl — Transplantation Proceedings. Supplement

Transplant Rev — Transplantation Reviews

Transplant Soc Int Cong Proc — Transplantation Society. International Congress. Proceedings

Transp L J — Transportation Law Journal

Transp Manage — Transport Management

Transp-Med Vesti — Transportno-Meditsinski Vesti

Transportat — Transportation

Transportation Plann Tech — Transportation Planning and Technology [*London*]

Transportation Q — Transportation Quarterly

Transportation Res — Transportation Research

Transportation Res Part A — Transportation Research. Part A. General

Transportation Res Part B — Transportation Research. Part B. Methodological

Transport D — Transport Digest

Transport Theory Statist Phys — Transport Theory and Statistical Physics

Trans Powder Metall Assoc India — Transactions. Powder Metallurgy Association of India

Transp Plann Technol — Transportation Planning and Technology

Transp Policy Decision Making — Transport Policy and Decision Making

Transp Q — Transportation Quarterly

Transp Res — Transportation Research

Transp Res Board Spec Rep — Transportation Research Board. Special Report

Transp Res Board Transp Res Rec — Transportation Research Board. Transportation Research Record

Transp Res News — Transportation Research News

Transp Res Part A — Transportation Research. Part A. General

Transp Res Part A Gen — Transportation Research. Part A. General [*England*]

Transp Res Part B — Transportation Research. Part B. Methodological

Transp Res Rec — Transportation Research Record [*United States*]

Trans Princeton Conf Cerebrovasc Dis — Transactions. Princeton Conference on Cerebrovascular Diseases

Transp Road Res Lab (GB) TRRL Rep — Transport and Road Research Laboratory (Great Britain). TRRL Report

Trans Proc Birmingham Arch Soc — Transactions and Proceedings. Birmingham Archaeological Society

Trans Proc Bot Soc Edinb — Transactions and Proceedings. Botanical Society of Edinburgh

Trans Proc Geol Soc S Afr — Transactions and Proceedings. Geological Society of South Africa

Trans Proc Palaeontol Soc Jap — Transactions and Proceedings. Palaeontological Society of Japan

Trans Proc Palaeontol Soc Japan New Ser — Transactions and Proceedings. Palaeontological Society of Japan. New Series

Trans Proc Palaeontol Soc Jpn New Ser — Transactions and Proceedings. Palaeontological Society of Japan. New Series

Trans Proc Perthshire Soc Natur Sci — Transactions and Proceedings. Perthshire Society of Natural Science

Transp Sci — Transportation Science

Transp Stroit — Transportnoe Stroitel'stvo [*USSR*]

Transp Theo — Transport Theory and Statistical Physics

Transp Theory Stat Phys — Transport Theory and Statistical Physics

Transp Th St P — Transport Theory and Statistical Physics

Transp Traffic — Transport and Traffic

Trans Q Am Soc Met — Transactions Quarterly. American Society for Metals

Trans R — Transatlantic Review

Trans Radnorshire Soc — Transactions. Radnorshire Society

Trans R Can Inst — Transactions. Royal Canadian Institute

Trans R Entomol Soc Lond — Transactions. Royal Entomological Society of London

Trans R Ent Soc Lond — Transactions. Royal Entomological Society of London

Trans Res A — Transportation Research. Part A. General

Trans Res Abstr — Transportation Research Abstracts

Trans Res B — Transportation Research. Part B. Methodological

Trans R Geol Soc (Corn) — Transactions. Royal Geological Society (Cornwall)

Trans R Highl Agric Soc Scotl — Transactions. Royal Highland and Agricultural Society of Scotland

Trans Rhod Sci Assoc — Transactions. Rhodesia Scientific Association

Trans RINA — Transactions. Royal Institutions of Naval Architects [*London*]

Trans R Instn Naval Archit — Quarterly Transactions. Royal Institution of Naval Architects [*London*]

Trans Roy Inst Technol (Stockholm) — Transactions. Royal Institute of Technology (Stockholm)

Trans Roy Inst Tech (Stockholm) — Transactions. Royal Institute of Technology (Stockholm)

Trans Roy Soc Canada — Transactions. Royal Society of Canada

Trans Roy Soc Canada 4 — Transactions. Royal Society of Canada. Chemical, Mathematical, and Physical Sciences. Fourth Series

Trans Roy Soc NZ Bot — Transactions. Royal Society of New Zealand. Botany

Trans Roy Soc S Aust — Royal Society of South Australia. Transactions

Trans Roy Soc South Africa — Transactions. Royal Society of South Africa

Trans R Sch Dent (Stockh Umea) — Transactions. Royal Schools of Dentistry (Stockholm and Umea)

Trans R Soc Arts — Transactions. Royal Society of Arts

Trans R Soc Can — Transactions. Royal Society of Canada

Trans R Soc Can Sect 3 — Transactions. Royal Society of Canada. Section 3. Chemical, Mathematical, and Physical Sciences

Trans R Soc Can Sect 4 — Transaction. Royal Society of Canada. Section 4. Geological Sciences Including Mineralogy

Trans R Soc Can Sect 5 — Transactions. Royal Society of Canada. Section 5. Biological Sciences

Trans R Soc Can Sect 1 2 3 — Transactions. Royal Society of Canada. Sections 1, 2, and 3

Trans R Soc Edinb — Transactions. Royal Society of Edinburgh

Trans R Soc Edinburgh — Transactions. Royal Society of Edinburgh

Trans R Soc NZ — Transactions. Royal Society of New Zealand

Trans R Soc NZ Biol Sci — Transactions. Royal Society of New Zealand. Biological Science

Trans R Soc NZ Bot — Transactions. Royal Society of New Zealand. Botany

Trans R Soc NZ Earth Sci — Transactions. Royal Society of New Zealand. Earth Science

Trans R Soc NZ Gen — Transactions. Royal Society of New Zealand. General

Trans R Soc NZ Geol — Transactions. Royal Society of New Zealand. Geology

Trans R Soc NZ Zool — Transactions. Royal Society of New Zealand. Zoology

Trans R Soc S Afr — Transactions. Royal Society of South Africa

Trans R Soc S Aust — Transactions. Royal Society of South Australia

Trans R Soc South Aust — Transactions. Royal Society of South Australia

Trans R Soc Trop Med Hyg — Transactions. Royal Society of Tropical Medicine and Hygiene

Trans Russ Inst Appl Chem — Transactions. Russian Institute of Applied Chemistry

Trans SAEST — Transactions. SAEST [*Society for Advancement of Electrochemical Science and Technology*]

Trans S Afr Inst Civ Eng — Transactions. South African Institution of Civil Engineers

Trans S Afr Inst Elec Eng — Transactions. South African Institute of Electrical Engineers

Trans S Afr Inst Electr Eng — Transactions. South African Institute of Electrical Engineers

Trans San Diego Soc Nat Hist — Transactions. San Diego Society of Natural History

Trans Sci — Transportation Science

Trans Sci Soc China — Transactions. Science Society of China

Trans SHASE — Transactions. Society of Heating, Air Conditioning, and Sanitary Engineers [*Japan*]

Trans SHASE Japan — Transactions. SHASE [*Society of Heating, Air Conditioning, and Sanitary Engineers*] (Japan)

Trans Shikoku Entomol Soc — Transactions. Shikoku Entomological Society

Trans Shikoku Ent Soc — Transactions. Shikoku Entomological Society

Trans Shropshire Archaeol Soc — Transactions. Shropshire Archaeological Society

Trans SMPE — Transactions. Society of Motion Picture Engineers

Trans Soc Adv Electrochem Sci Technol — Transactions. Society for Advancement of Electrochemical Science and Technology

Trans Soc Br Ent — Transactions. Society for British Entomology

Trans Soc Br Entomol — Transactions. Society for British Entomology

Trans Soc Heat Air Cond Sanit Eng Jpn — Transactions. Society of Heating, Air Conditioning, and Sanitary Engineers of Japan

Trans Soc Ill Eng — Transactions. Illuminating Engineering Society

Trans Soc Instr Control Eng — Transactions. Society of Instrument and Control Engineers [*Japan*]

Trans Soc Instrum Control Eng — Transactions. Society of Instrument and Control Engineers

Trans Soc Instrum and Control Eng — Transactions. Society of Instrument and Control Engineers

Trans Soc Instrum & Control Engrs (Japan) — Transactions. Society of Instrument and Control Engineers (Japan)

Trans Soc Instrum Technol — Transactions. Society of Instrument Technology [*England*]

Trans Soc Min Eng AIME — Transactions. Society of Mining Engineers. AIME [*American Institute of Mining, Metallurgical, and Petroleum Engineers*]

Trans Soc Min Engrs AIME — Transactions. Society of Mining Engineers. AIME [*American Institute of Mining, Metallurgical, and Petroleum Engineers*]

Trans Soc Motion Pict Eng — Transactions. Society of Motion Picture Engineers

Trans Soc Mot Pict Eng — Transactions. Society of Motion Picture Engineers

Trans Soc NAME — Transactions. Society of Naval Architects and Marine Engineers

Trans Soc Naval Architects Mar Eng — Transactions. Society of Naval Architects and Marine Engineers

Trans Soc Occup Med — Transactions. Society of Occupational Medicine

Trans Soc Pathol Jpn — Transactiones Societatis Pathologicae Japonicae [*Japan*]

Trans Soc Pet Eng AIME — Transactions. Society of Petroleum Engineers of AIME [*American Institute of Mining, Metallurgical, and Petroleum Engineers*]

Trans Soc Rheol — Transactions. Society of Rheology

Trans Southwest Fed Geol Soc — Transactions. Southwestern Federation of Geological Societies

Trans SPWLA Annu Log Symp — Transactions. SPWLA [*Society of Professional Well Log Analysts*] Annual Logging Symposium

Trans S Staffordshire Archaeol Hist Soc — Transactions. South Staffordshire Archaeological and Historical Society

Trans S Staffs Archaeol Hist Soc — Transactions. South Staffordshire Archaeological and Historical Society

Trans S Staffs Arch Hist Soc — Transactions. South Staffordshire Archaeological and Historical Society

Trans State Inst Appl Chem — Transactions. State Institute of Applied Chemistry

Trans St John's Hosp Dermatol Soc — Transactions. St. John's Hospital Dermatological Society

Trans Stud Coll Physicians Phila — Transactions and Studies. College of Physicians of Philadelphia

Trans Suffolk Natur Soc — Transactions. Suffolk Naturalists' Society

Trans Tech Sect Can Pulp Pap Assoc — Transactions. Technical Section. Canadian Pulp and Paper Association

Trans Tech Sect Can Pulp and Pap Assoc — Transactions. Technical Section. Canadian Pulp and Paper Association

Trans Thoroton Soc Nottinghamshire — Transaction. Thoroton Society of Nottinghamshire

Trans Thoroton Soc Notts — Transactions. Thoroton Society of Nottinghamshire

Trans Tottori Soc Agric Sci — Transactions. Tottori Society of Agricultural Sciences

Trans Tottori Soc Agr Sci — Transactions. Tottori Society of Agricultural Science

Trans Udgivet Dan Ing — Transactions. Udgivet af Dansk Ingenioeren [*Denmark*]

Trans Univ Cent Desert Stud (Jodhpur India) — Transactions. University Centre of Desert Studies (Jodhpur, India)

Trans Utah Acad Sci — Transactions. Utah Academy of Sciences

Transvaal Agric J — Transvaal Agricultural Journal

Transvaal Mus Bull — Transvaal Museum. Bulletin

Transvaal Mus Mem — Transvaal Museum. Memoirs

Transvaal Mus Rep — Transvaal Museum. Report

Transvaal Nat Conserv Div Annu Rep — Transvaal Nature Conservation Division. Annual Report

Trans Wagner Free Inst Sci Philadelphia — Transactions. Wagner Free Institute of Science of Philadelphia

Trans West Sect Am Urol Assoc — Transactions. Western Section of the American Urological Association

Trans Wis Acad Sci — Transactions. Wisconsin Academy of Sciences, Arts, and Letters

Trans Wis Acad Sci Arts Lett — Transactions. Wisconsin Academy of Sciences, Arts, and Letters

Trans Woolhope Naturalists — Transactions. Woolhope Naturalists' Field Club

Trans Woolhope Natur Fld Club — Transactions. Woolhope Naturalists' Field Club [*Herefordshire*]

Trans Worcestershire Archaeol Soc 3 Ser — Transactions. Worcestershire Archaeological Society. Series 3

Trans Worcs Arch Soc — Transaction. Worcestershire Archaeological Society

Trans Worcs Arc Soc — Transactions. Worcestershire Archaeological Society

Trans World Energy Conf — Transactions. World Energy Conference

Transylvania J Med — Transylvania Journal of Medicine

Trans Zimbabwe Sci Assoc — Transactions. Zimbabwe Scientific Association

Trans Zimb Sci Assoc — Transactions. Zimbabwe Scientific Association

Trans Zool Soc Lond — Transactions. Zoological Society of London

Tran USA — Transportation USA

TRAQA — Traffic Quarterly

Tr Arkhang Lesotekh Inst — Trudy Arkhangel'skogo Lesotekhnicheskogo Instituta

Tr Arkt Antarkt Nauchno-Issled Inst — Trudy Arkticheskogo i Antarkticheskogo Nauchno-Issledovatel'skogo Instituta

Tr Arm Geol Upr — Trudy Armyanskogo Geologicheskogo Upravleniya

Tr Arm Inst Stroim Sooruzh — Trudy Armyanskogo Instituta Stroimaterialov i Sooruzhenii

Tr Arm Nauchno Issled Inst Gidrotekh Melior — Trudy Armyanskogo Nauchno-Issledovatel'skogo Instituta Gidrotekhniki i Melioratsii

Tr Arm Nauchno Issled Inst Vinograd Vinodel Plodovod — Trudy Armyanskogo Nauchno-Isseldovatel'skogo Instituta Vinogradarstva Vinodeliya i Plodovodstva

Tr Arm Nauchno-Issled Inst Zhivotnovod Vet — Trudy Armyanskogo Nauchno-Issledovatel'skogo Instituta Zhivotnovodstva i Veterinarii

Tr Arm Nauchno-Issled Vet Inst — Trudy Armyanskogo Nauchno-Issledovatel'skogo Veterinarnogo Instituta

Tr Arm Protivochumn Stn — Trudy Armyanskoi Protivochumnoi Stantsii

TRASA — Traktory i Sel'khozmashiny

Trasfus Sangue — Trasfusione del Sangue

Tr Ashkhab Nauchno Issled Inst Epidemiol Gig — Trudy Ashkhabadskogo Nauchno-Issledovatel'skogo Instituta Epidemiologii i Gigieny

Tr Astrakh Gos Med Inst — Trudy Astrakhanskogo Gosudarstvennogo Meditinskogo Instituta

Tr Astrakh Gos Zapov — Trudy Astrakhanskogo Gosudarstvennogo Zapovednika

Tr Astrakh Tekh Inst Rybn Promsti Khoz — Trudy Astrakhanskogo Tekhnicheskogo Instituta Rybnoi Promyshlennosti i Khozyaistva

Tr Astrofiz Inst Akad Nauk Kaz SSR — Trudy Astrofizicheskogo Instituta Akademiya Nauk Kazakhskoi SSR [*Kazakh SSR*]
Tr Atl Nauchno-Issled Inst Ryb Khoz Okeanogr — Trudy Atlanticheskii Nauchno-Issledovatel'skii Institut Rybnogo Khozyaistva i Okeanografii [*USSR*]
Tratt Met — Trattamenti dei Metalli
Tr At Zoovet Inst — Trudy Alma-Atinskogo Instituta
Trav — Travel
Trav — Travel Holiday
Trav — Travelling
TRAVA — Travaux
Travailleur Can — Travailleur Canadien
Trav Alphabet — Travail de l'Alphabetisation
Trav Assoc H Capitant — Travaux. Association Henri Capitant
Travaux Sem Anal Convexe — Travaux. Seminaire d'Analyse Convexe
Trav Cent Rech Etudes Oceanogr — Travaux. Centre de Recherches et d'Etudes Oceanographiques
Trav Chim Aliment Hyg — Travaux de Chimie Alimentaire et d'Hygiene
Trav Com Int Etude Bauxites Oxydes Hydroxydes Alum — Travaux. Comite International pour l'Etude des Bauxites, des Oxydes, et des Hydroxydes d'Aluminium
Trav Communaux — Travaux Communaux [*France*]
Trav Doc Geogr Trop — Travaux et Documents de Geographie Tropicale
Trav Doc ORSTOM — Travaux et Documents. ORSTOM [*Office de la Recherche Scientifique et Technique d'Outre-Mer*]
Trav Geophys (Prague) — Travaux Geophysiques (Prague)
Trav/Holiday — Travel/Holiday
Trav Hum — Travail Humain
Trav Humain — Travail Humain
Trav Inst Franc Et Andines — Travaux. Institut Francais d'Etudes Andines
Trav Inst Geol Anthropol Prehist Fac Sci Poitiers — Travaux. Institut de Geologie et d'Anthropologie Prehistorique. Faculte des Sciences de Poitiers
Trav Inst L — Travaux. Institut de Linguistique de Lund
Trav Inst Rech Sahar — Travaux. Institut de Recherches Sahariennes
Trav Inst Sci Cherifien Fac Sci Rabat Ser Gen — Travaux. Institut Scientifique Cherifien et Faculte des Sciences de Rabat. Serie Generale
Trav Inst Sci Cherifien Fac Sci Ser Sci Phys — Travaux. Institut Scientifique Cherifien et Faculte des Sciences. Serie: Sciences Physiques
Trav Inst Sci Cherifien Fac Sci Ser Zool — Travaux. Institut Scientifique Cherifien et Faculte des Sciences. Serie Zoologie
Trav Inst Sci Cherifien Ser Bot — Travaux. Institut Scientifique Cherifien. Serie Botanique
Trav Inst Sci Cherifien Ser Bot Biol Veg — Travaux. Institut Scientifique Cherifien. Serie Botanique et Biologique Vegetale
Trav Inst Sci Cherifien Ser Geol Geogr Phys — Travaux. Institut Scientifique Cherifien. Serie Geologie et Geographie Physique
Trav Inst Sci Cherifien Ser Sci Phys — Travaux. Institut Scientifique Cherifien. Serie Sciences Physiques
Trav Inst Sci Cherifien Ser Zool — Travaux. Institut Scientifique Cherifien. Serie Zoologique
Trav Inst Speleo "Emile Racovitza" — Travaux. Institut de Speleologie "Emile Racovitza"
Trav IRS — Travaux. Institut de Recherches Sahariennes
Trav Jeunes Sci — Travaux des Jeunes Scientifiques
Trav et Jours — Travaux et Jours
Trav Lab Anthropol Prehist Ethnol Pays Mediterr Occid — Travaux. Laboratoire d'Anthropologie de Prehistoire et d'Ethnologie des Pays de la Mediterranee Occidentale
Trav Lab For Toulouse — Travaux. Laboratoire Forestier de Toulouse
Trav Lab For Toulouse Tome I Artic Divers — Travaux. Laboratoire Forestier de Toulouse. Tome I. Articles Divers
Trav Lab For Toulouse Tome II Etud Dendrol — Travaux. Laboratoire Forestier de Toulouse. Tome II. Etudes Dendrologiques
Trav Lab For Toulouse Tome V Geogr For Monde — Travaux. Laboratoire Forestier de Toulouse. Tome V. Geographie Forestier du Monde
Trav Lab For Univ Toulouse — Travaux. Laboratoire Forestier. Universite de Toulouse
Trav Lab Geol Ec Norm Super (Paris) — Travaux. Laboratoire de Geologie. Ecole Normale Superieure (Paris)
Trav Lab Geol Fac Sci Grenoble — Travaux. Laboratoire de Geologie. Faculte des Sciences de Grenoble
Trav Lab Geol Fac Sci Grenoble Mem — Travaux. Laboratoire de Geologie. Faculte des Sciences de Grenoble. Memoires
Trav Lab Geol Fac Sci Lyon — Travaux. Laboratoire de Geologie. Faculte des Sciences de Lyon
Trav Lab Geol Fac Sci Univ Bordeaux — Travaux. Laboratoire de Geologie. Faculte des Sciences. Universite de Bordeaux
Trav Lab Geol Hist Paleontol Cent St Charles Univ Provence — Travaux. Laboratoire de Geologie Historique et de Paleontologie. Centre Saint Charles. Universite de Provence
Trav Lab Hydrogeol Geochim Fac Sci Univ Bordeaux — Travaux. Laboratoire d'Hydrogeologie Geochimie. Faculte des Sciences Universite de Bordeaux

Trav Lab Matiere Med Pharm Galenique Fac Pharm (Paris) — Travaux. Laboratoires de Matiere Medicale et de Pharmacie Galenique. Faculte de Pharmacie (Paris)
Trav Lab Microbiol Fac Pharm Nancy — Travaux. Laboratoire de Microbiologie. Faculte de Pharmacie de Nancy
Trav Mem Bur Int Poids Mes — Travaux et Memoires. Bureau International des Poids et Mesures
Trav Met Deform — Travail des Metaux par Deformation
Trav et Meth — Travail et Methodes
Trav Mus Hist Nat Gr Antipa — Travaux. Museum d'Histoire Naturelle "Grigore Antipa"
Trav Mus Hist Nat "Grigore Antipa" — Travaux. Museum d'Histoire Naturelle "Grigore Antipa"
Trav Pech Que — Travaux sur les Pecheries du Quebec
Trav Peint — Travaux de Peinture
Trav Quebec — Travail Quebec
Trav et Rech — Travaux et Recherches
Trav Rech Haut Comite Et Inform Alcool — Travaux et Recherches. Haut Comite d'Etude et d'Information sur l'Alcoolisme
Trav Sci Cent Rech Sci Proj Ind Vini (Sofia) — Travaux Scientifiques. Centre de Recherches Scientifiques et de Projections de l'Industrie Vinicole (Sofia)
Trav Sect Scient Tech Inst Fr Pondichery — Travaux. Section Scientifique et Technique. Institut Francais de Pondichery
Trav Sect Sci Tech Inst Franc Pondichery — Travaux. Section Scientifique et Technique. Institut Francais de Pondichery
Trav Sect Sci Tech Inst Fr Pondichery — Travaux. Section Scientifique et Technique. Institut Francais de Pondichery
Trav Secur — Travail et Securite
Trav et Soc — Travail et Societe
Trav Soc Bot Geneve — Travaux. Societe Botanique de Geneve
Trav Soc Pharm Montp — Travaux. Societe de Pharmacie de Montpellier
Trav Soc Pharm Montpellier — Travaux. Societe de Pharmacie de Montpellier [*France*]
Trav Soc Sci Lettres Wroclaw — Travaux. Societe des Sciences et des Lettres de Wroclaw
Trav Sta Rech Groenendaal — Travaux. Station de Recherches des Eaux et Forets. Groenendaal-Hoeilaart
Tr Avtom Svarke Flyusom — Trudy po Avtomaticheskoi Svarke pod Flyusom
Tr Azerb Gos Nauchno Issled Proektn Inst Neft Promsti — Trudy Azerbaidzhanskii Gosudarstvennyi Nauchno-Issledovatel'skii i Proektnyi Institut Neftyanoi Promyshlennosti
Tr Azerb Gos Pedagog Inst — Trudy Azerbaidzhanskogo Gosudarstvennogo Pedagogicheskogo Instituta
Tr Azerb Inst Nefti Khim — Trudy Azerbaidzhanskogo Instituta Nefti i Khimii
Tr Azerb Nauchno Issled Inst Buren Neft Gazov Skvazhin — Trudy Azerbaidzhanskogo Nauchno-Issledovatel'skogo Instituta po Bureniyu Neftyanykh i Gazovykh Skvazhin
Tr Azerb Nauchno Issled Inst Energ — Trudy Azerbaidzhanskogo Nauchno-Issledovatel'skogo Instituta Energetiki
Tr Azerb Nauchno-Issled Inst Gig Tr Prof Zabol — Trudy Azerbaidzhanskogo Nauchno-Issledovatel'skogo Instituta Gigieny Truda i Professional'nykh Zabolevaniya
Tr Azerb Nauchno-Issled Inst Lesn Khoz Agrolesomelior — Trudy Azerbaidzhanskogo Nauchno-Issledovatel'skogo Instituta Lesnogo Khozyaistva i Agrolesomelioratsii
Tr Azerb Nauchno-Issled Inst Med Parazitol Trop Med — Trudy Azerbaidzhanskogo Nauchno-Issledovatel'skogo Instituta Meditsinskoi Parazitologii i Trophicheskoi Meditsiny
Tr Azerb Nauchno Issled Vet Inst — Trudy Azerbaidzhanskogo Nauchno-Issledovatel'skogo Veterinarnogo Instituta
Tr Azerb Nauchno Issled Vet Opytn Stn — Trudy Azerbaidzhanskoi Nauchno-Issledovatel'skoi Veterinarnoi Opytnoi Stantsii
Tr Azerb Neft Nauchno Issled Inst — Trudy Azerbaidzhanskogo Neftyanogo Nauchno-Issledovatel'skogo Instituta
Tr Azerb Vet Nauchno Issled Inst — Trudy Azerbaidzhanskogo Veterinarnogo Nauchno-Issledovatel'skogo Instituta
Tr Azovsko Chernomorsk Nauchn Rybokhoz Stn — Trudy Azovsko-Chernomorskoi Nauchnoi Rybokhozyaistvennoi Stantsii
TRB — Tennyson Research Bulletin
Tr Baik Limnol Stn Akad Nauk SSSR Vost Sib Fil — Trudy Baikal'skoi Limnologicheskoi Stantsii Akademiya Nauk SSSR Vostochno-Sibirskii Filial
Tr Bakinsk Nauchno-Issled Inst Travmatol Ortop — Trudy Bakinskogo Nauchno-Issledovatel'skogo Instituta Travmatologii Ortopedii
Tr Bakinskogo Nauchno Issled Inst Travmatol Ortop — Trudy Bakinskogo Nauchno-Issledovatel'skogo Instituta Travmatologii Ortopedii
Tr Balt Nauchno Issled Inst Rybn Khoz — Trudy Baltiiskogo Nauchno-Issledovatel'skogo Instituta Rybnogo Khozyaistva
Tr Bashk Gos Zapov — Trudy Bashkirskogo Gosudarstvennogo Zapovednika
Tr Bashk Nauchno-Issled Inst Pererab Nefti — Trudy Bashkirskii Nauchno-Issledovatel'skii Institut po Pererabotke Nefti [*USSR*]
Tr Bashk S-kh Inst — Trudy Bashkirskogo Sel'skohozyaistvennogo Instituta
Tr Batum Bot Sada Akad Nauk Gruz SSR — Trudy Batumskogo Botanicheskogo Sada Akademii Nauk Gruzinskoi SSR

Tr Belgorod Gos Skh Opytn Stn — Trudy Belgorodskoi Gosudarstvennoi Sel'skohozyaistvennoi Opytnoi Stantsii
Tr Belgorod Tekhnol Inst Stroit — Trudy Belgorodskogo Tekhnologicheskogo Instituta Stroitel'nyhmaterialov
Tr Belomorsk Biol Stn Mosk Gos Univ — Trudy Belomorskoi Biologicheskoi Stantsii Moskovskogo Gosudarstvennogo Universiteta
Tr Beloruss Nauchno-Issled Inst Melior Vodn Khoz — Trudy Belorusskogo Nauchno-Issledovatel'skogo Instituta Melioratsii i Vodnogo Khozyaistva
Tr Beloruss Nauchno Issled Inst Pochvoved — Trudy Belorusskii Nauchno-Issledovatel'skii Institut Pochvovedenii
Tr Beloruss Nauchno Issled Inst Promsti Prodovol Tovarov — Trudy Belorusskii Nauchno-Issledovatel'skii Institut Promyshlennosti Prodovol'stvennykh Tovarov
Tr Beloruss Nauchno Issled Inst Rybn Khoz — Trudy Belorusskogo Nauchno-Issledovatel'skogo Instituta Rybnogo Khozyaistva
Tr Beloruss Nauchno Issled Inst Zhivotnovod — Trudy Belorusskii Nauchno-Issledovatel'skii Institut Zhivotnovodstva
Tr Beloruss Naucno-Issled Inst Pishch Prom-Sti — Trudy Belorusskogo Nauchno-Issledovatel'skogo Instituta Pishchevoi Promyshlennosti
Tr Beloruss Sel'skokhoz Akad — Trudy Belorusskoi Sel'skokhozyaistvennoi Akademii
Tr Beloruss Skh Akad — Trudy Belorusskoi Sel'skohozyaistvennoi Akademii
Tr Berdyanskii Opytn Neftemaslozavod — Trudy Berdyanskii Opytnyi Neftemaslozavod
Tr Biogeokhim Lab Akad Nauk SSSR — Trudy Biogeokhimicheskoi Laboratorii Akademiya Nauk SSSR
Tr Biol Inst Akad Nauk SSSR Sib Otd — Trudy Biologicheskogo Instituta Akademiya Nauk SSSR Sibirskoe Otdelenie
Tr Biol Inst Zapadno-Sib Fil Akad Nauk SSSR — Trudy Biologicheskogo Instituta Zapadno-Sibirskogo Filiala Akademii Nauk SSSR
Tr Biol Nauchno Issled Inst Biol Stn Permsk Gos Univ — Trudy Biologicheskogo Nauchno-Issledovatel'skogo Instituta i Biologicheskoi Stantsii pri Permskom Gosudarstvennom Universitete
Tr Biol Nauchno Issled Inst Molotov Gos Univ — Trudy Biologicheskogo Nauchno-Issledovatel'skogo Instituta pri Molotovskom Gosudarstvennom Universitete
Tr Biol Pochv Inst Dalnevost Nauchn Tsentr Akad Nauk SSSR — Trudy Biologo-Pochvennogo Instituta Dal'nevostochnyi Nauchnyi Tsentr Akademiya Nauk SSSR
Tr Biol Stn Borok Akad Nauk SSSR — Trudy Biologicheskoi Stantsii "Borok" Akademiya Nauk SSSR
Tr Blagoveshch Gos Med Inst — Trudy Blagoveshchenskogo Gosudarstvennogo Meditsinskogo Instituta
Tr Blagoveshch Skh Inst — Trudy Blagoveshchenskogo Sel'skokhozyaistvennogo Instituta
TRBMA — Texas Reports on Biology and Medicine
Tr Bot Inst Akad Nauk SSSR — Trudy Botanicheskogo Instituta Akademii Nauk SSSR
Tr Bot Inst Akad Nauk SSSR Ser 4 — Trudy Botanicheskogo Instituta Akademii Nauk SSSR. Seriya 4
Tr Bot Inst Akad Nauk SSSR Ser 5 — Trudy Botanicheskogo Instituta Akademii Nauk SSSR. Seriya 5. Rastitel'noe Syr'ye
Tr Bot Inst Akad Nauk SSSR Ser 6 — Trudy Botanicheskogo Instituta Akademii Nauk SSSR. Seriya 6. Introduktsiya Rastenii i Zelenoe
Tr Bot Inst Akad Nauk Tadzhikskoi SSR — Trudy Botanicheskogo Instituta Akademiya Nauk Tadzhikskoi SSR
Tr Bot Inst Akad Nauk Tadzh SSR — Trudy Botanicheskogo Instituta Akademiya Nauk Tadzhikskoi SSR
Tr Bot Inst Azerb Fil Akad Nauk SSSR — Trudy Botanicheskogo Instituta Azerbaidzhanskii Filial Akademii Nauk SSSR
Tr Bot Inst V L Komarova Akad Nauk SSSR Ser VII — Trudy Botanicheskogo Instituta Imeni V. L. Komarova Akademiya Nauk SSSR. Seriya VII
Tr Bot Sada Akad Nauk Ukr SSR — Trudy Botanicheskogo Sada Akademii Nauk Ukrainskoi SSR
Tr Bot Sada Tashk Akad Nauk Uzb SSR — Trudy Botanicheskogo Sada v Tashkente Akademii Nauk Uzbekskoi SSR
Tr Bot Sada Tashkente Akad Nauk Uzb SSR — Trudy Botanicheskogo Sada v Tashkente Akademii Nauk Uzbekskoi SSR
Tr Bot Sada Zapadn-Sib Fil Akad Nauk SSSR — Trudy Botanicheskogo Sada Zapadno-Sibirskogo Filiala Akademii Nauk SSSR
Tr Bot Sadov Akad Nauk Kaz SSR — Trudy Botanicheskikh Sadov Akademii Nauk Kazakhskoi SSR
Tr Briansk Lesokhoz Inst — Trudy Brianskogo Lesokhozyaistvennogo Instituta
Tr Bukhar Obl Opytn Skh Stn — Trudy Bukharskoi Oblastnoi Opytnoi Sel'skokhozyaistvennoi Stantsii
Tr Buryat-Mong Nauchno-Issled Vet Opytn Stn — Trudy Buryat-Mongol'skoi Nauchno-Issledovatel'skoi Veterinarnoi Opytnoi Stantsii
Tr Buryat Mong Zoovet Inst — Trudy Buryat-Mongol'skogo Zooveterinarnogo Instituta
Tr Buryat S-kh Inst — Trudy Buryatskogo Sel'skokhozyaistvennogo Instituta
Tr Buryat Zoovet Inst — Trudy Buryatskogo Zooveterinarnogo Instituta
Tr Chelyab Gos Pedagog Inst — Trudy Chelyabinskii Gosudarstvennyi Pedagogicheskii Institut
Tr Chelyab Inst Mekh Elektrif Selsk Khoz — Trudy Chelyabinskogo Instituta Mekhanizatsii i Elektrifikatsii Sel'skogo Khozyaistva

Tr Chelyab Politekh Inst — Trudy Chelyabinskii Politekhnicheskii Institut [*USSR*]
Tr Chernomorsk Biol Stan Varna — Trudove na Chernomorskata Biologichna Stantsiya v Varna
TRCO — Trade and Commerce
TRCRA — Tobacco Research Council. Research Paper
Tr Dagest Gos Pedagog Inst Estestv-Geogr Fak — Trudy Dagestanskogo Gosudarstvennogo Pedagogicheskogo Instituta Estestvenno-Geograficheskii Fakul'tet
Tr Dagest S-kh Inst — Trudy Dagestanskogo Sel'skokhozyaistvennogo Instituta
Tr Dalnevost Fil Akad Nauk SSSR Ser Geol — Trudy Dal'nevostochnogo Filiala Akademii Nauk SSSR. Seriya Geologicheskaya
Tr Dalnevost Fil Akad Nauk SSSR Ser Khim — Trudy Dal'nevostochnogo Filiala Akademii Nauk SSSR. Seriya Khimicheskaya
Tr Dalnevost Geol Razved Tresta — Trudy Dal'nevostochnogo Geologo-Razvedochnogo Tresta
Tr Dal'nevost Gos Med Inst — Trudy Dal'nevostochnogo Gosudarstvennogo Meditsinskogo Instituta
Tr Dalnevost Gos Univ — Trudy Dal'nevostochnogo Gosudarstvennogo Universiteta
Tr Dalnevost Gos Univ Ser 4 — Trudy Dal'nevostochnogo Gosudarstvennogo Universiteta. Seriya 4. Lesnye Nauki
Tr Dalnevost Gos Univ Ser 5 — Trudy Dal'nevostochnogo Gosudarstvennogo Universiteta. Seriya 5. Sel'skoe Khozyaistvo
Tr Dalnevost Gos Univ Ser 7 — Trudy Dal'nevostochnogo Gosudarstvennogo Universiteta. Seriya 7. Fizika i Khimiya
Tr Dalnevost Gos Univ Ser 8 — Trudy Dal'nevostochnogo Gosudarstvennogo Universiteta. Seriya 8. Biologiya
Tr Dalnevost Gos Univ Ser 11 — Trudy Dal'nevostochnogo Gosudarstvennogo Universiteta. Seriya 11. Geologiya
Tr Dalnevost Gos Univ Ser 12 — Trudy Dal'nevostochnogo Gosudarstvennogo Universiteta. Seriya 12. Gornoe Delo
Tr Dalnevost Gos Univ Ser 13 — Trudy Dal'nevostochnogo Gosudarstvennogo Universiteta. Seriya 13. Tekhnika
Tr Dalnevost Gos Univ Ser 15 — Trudy Dal'nevostochnogo Gosudarstvennogo Universiteta. Seriya 15. Matematika
Tr Dalnevost Kraev Nauchno Issled Inst — Trudy Dal'nevostochnogo Kraevogo Nauchno-Issledovatel'skogo Instituta
Tr Dalnevost Nauchno Issled Gidrometeorol Inst — Trudy Dal'nevostochnogo Nauchno-Issledovatel'skogo Gidrometeorologicheskogo Instituta
Tr Dalnevost Nauchno Issled Vet Inst — Trudy Dal'nevostochnogo Nauchno-Issledovatel'skogo Veterinarnogo Instituta
Tr Dalnevost Politekh Inst — Trudy Dal'nevostochnogo Politekhnicheskogo Instituta
Tr Dalnevost Tekh Inst Rybn Promsti Khoz — Trudy Dal'nevostochnogo Tekhnicheskogo Instituta Rybnoi Promyshlennosti i Khozyaistva
Tr Darvinsk Gos Zapov — Trudy Darvinskogo Gosudarstvennogo Zapovednika
TRDCBC — Datum Collection. Tokai Regional Fisheries Research Laboratory
TRDIA — Transmission and Distribution
Tr Din Raz — Trudy po Dinamike Razvitiya
Tr Dnepropetr Inst Inzh Zheleznodorozhn Transp — Trudy Dnepropetrovskogo Instituta Inzhenerov Zheleznodorozhnogo Transporta
Tr Dnepropetr Khim Tekhnol Inst — Trudy Dnepropetrovskogo Khimiko-Tekhnologicheskogo Instituta
Tr Dnepropetr S-kh Inst — Trudy Dnepropetrovskogo Sel'skokhozyaistvennogo Instituta
Tr Donbasskaya Nauchno Issled Lab — Trudy Donbasskaya Nauchno-Issledovatel'skaya Laboratoriya
Tr Donetsk Gos Med Inst — Trudy Donetskogo Gosudarstvennogo Meditsinskogo Instituta
Tr Donetsk Ind Inst — Trudy Donetskogo Industrial'nogo Instituta [*Ukrainian SSR*]
Tr Donetsk Politekh Inst Ser Fiz Mat — Trudy Donetskogo Politekhnicheskogo Instituta. Seriya Fiziko-Matematicheskaya
Tr Donetsk Politekh Inst Ser Khim Tekhnol — Trudy Donetskogo Politekhnicheskogo Instituta. Seriya Khimiko-Tekhnologicheskaya
Tr Donetsk Politekh Inst Ser Metall — Trudy Donetskogo Politekhnicheskogo Instituta. Seriya Metallurgicheskaya
Treatise Mater Sci Technol — Treatise on Materials Science and Technology
Treatises Sect Med Sci Pol Acad Sci — Treatises of the Section of Medical Sciences. Polish Academy of Sciences
Tree Plant Notes — Tree Planters' Notes
Tree Plant Notes US For Serv — Tree Planter's Notes. United States Forest Service
Tree-Ring Bull — Tree-Ring Bulletin
Trees Mag — Trees Magazine
Trees S Afr — Trees in South Africa
T Regswet — Tydskrif vir Regswetenskap
TREKA — Technical Reports. Engineering Research Institute. Kyoto University
TRENA — Tokyo Toritsu Eisei Kenkyusho Kenkyu Nempo
TREND — Transportation Research News
Trend Eng — Trends in Engineering
Trend Eng Univ Wash — Trends in Engineering. University of Washington
Trend Prognosticke Inf — Trend Prognosticke Informace

Trends Biochem Sci — Trends in Biochemical Sciences

Trends Biochem Sci (Pers Ed) — Trends in Biochemical Sciences (Personal Edition) [*Netherlands*]

Trends Biochem Sci (Ref Ed) — Trends in Biochemical Sciences (Reference Edition) [*Netherlands*]

Trends in Ed — Trends in Education

Trends Ed — Trends in Education

Trends Educ — Trends in Education

Trends Fluoresc — Trends in Fluorescence

Trends Haematol — Trends in Haematology

Trends Neurosci — Trends in Neurosciences [*Netherlands*]

Tr Energ Inst Akad Nauk Az SSR — Trudy Energeticheskogo Instituta Akademiya Nauk Azerbaidzhanskoi SSR

Tr Energ Inst Az SSR — Trudy Energeticheskogo Instituta Azerbaidzhanskoi SSR

Tr Energ Inst Im I G Es'mana Akad Nauk Azerb SSR — Trudy Energeticheskogo Instituta Imeni I. G. Es'mana Akademiya Nauk Azerbaidzhanskoi SSR [*Azerbaidzhan SSR*]

Tr Entom Soc London — Transactions. Entomological Society of London

Tr Erevan Med Inst — Trudy Erevanskogo Meditsinskogo Instituta

Tr Erevan Zootekh Vet Inst — Trudy Erevanskogo Zootekhnichesko-Veterinarnogo Instituta

Tr Erevan Zoovet Inst — Trudy Erevanskogo Zooveterinarnogo Instituta

Tr and Est — Trusts and Estates

Tr Estestvennonauchn Inst Molotov Gos Univ — Trudy Estestvennonauchnogo Instituta pri Molotovskom Gosudarstvennom Universitete

Tr Estestvennonauchn Inst Permsk Gos Univ — Trudy Estestvennonauchnogo Instituta pri Permskom Gosudarstvennom Universitete

Tr Estestv Inst Permsk Gos Univ Radiospektrosk — Trudy Estestvennonauchnogo Instituta pri Permskom Gosudarstvennom Universitete Imeni A. M. Gor'kogo Radiospektroskopiy

TRev — Theologische Revue

TRFA — Trustees for Alaska. Newsletter

Tr Ferg Politekh Inst — Trudy Ferganskogo Politekhnicheskogo Instituta

Tr (Fifteenth) Internat Cong Hyg and Demog — Transactions. Fifteenth International Congress on Hygiene and Demography

Tr Fiz Inst Akad Nauk SSSR — Trudy Fizicheskogo Instituta Imeni P. N. Lebedeva Akademiya Nauk SSSR

Tr Fiz Inst Im Lebedeva — Trudy Ordena Lenina Fizicheskogo Instituta Imeni P. N. Lebedeva

Tr Fiz Inst Im P N Lebedeva Akad Nauk SSSR — Trudy Fizicheskogo Instituta Imeni P. N. Lebedeva Akademiya Nauk SSSR [*USSR*]

Tr Fiziol Biokhim Rast — Trudy po Fiziologii i Biokhimii Rastenii [*Estonian SSR*]

Tr Fiziol Lab Akad Nauk SSSR — Trudy Fiziologicheskoi Laboratorii Akademii Nauk SSSR

Tr Fiziol Patol Zhen — Trudy Fiziologicheskoi Patologii Zhenshchiny

Tr Fiz Mosk Gorn Inst — Trudy po Fizike Moskovskii Gornyi Institut

Tr Fiz Poluprovodn — Trudy po Fizike Poluprovodnikov

Tr Fiz Tekh Inst Akad Nauk Turkm SSR — Trudy Fiziko-Tekhnicheskogo Instituta Akademiya Nauk Turkmenskoi SSR

Tr Frunz Politekh Inst — Trudy Frunzenskogo Politekhnicheskogo Instituta

TRG — Tijdschrift voor Rechtsgeschiedenis

TRG — Travail et Methodes. Revue des Nouvelles au Service de l'Entreprise

Tr Gelmintol Lab — Trudy Gel'mintologicheskoi Laboratorii

Tr Gel'mintol Lab Akad Nauk SSSR — Trudy Gel'mintologicheskaya Laboratoriya Akademiya Nauk SSSR

Tr Geofiz Inst Akad Nauk SSSR — Trudy Geofizicheskogo Instituta Akademiya Nauk SSSR

Tr Geol Bulg Ser Geokhm Mineral Petrogr — Trudove Vurkhu Geologiyata na Bulgariya. Seriya Geokhimaya Mineralogiya i Petrografiya

Tr Geol Bulg Ser Inzh Geol Khidrogeol — Trudove Vurkhu Geologiyata na Bulgariya. Seriya Inzhenerna Geologiya i Khidrogeologiya

Tr Geol Bulg Ser Paleonto — Trudove Vurkhu Geologiyata na Bulgariya. Seriya Paleontologiya

Tr Geol Inst Akad Nauk Gruz SSR — Trudy Geologicheskogo Instituta Akademiya Nauk Gruzinskoi SSR

Tr Geol Inst Akad Nauk Gruz SSR Geol Ser — Trudy Geologicheskogo Instituta Akademiya Nauk Gruzinskoi SSR. Geologicheskaya Seriya

Tr Geol Inst Akad Nauk Gruz SSR Mineral Petrogr Ser — Trudy Geologicheskogo Instituta Akademiya Nauk Gruzinskoi SSR. Mineralogo-Petrograficheskaya Seriya

Tr Geom Semin — Trudy Geometricheskogo Seminara

Tr GIAP — Trudy GIAP

Tr Gidrometeorol Nauchno-Issled Tsentr SSSR — Trudy Gidrometeorologicheskii Nauchno-Issledovatel'skii Tsentral'nogo SSSR

Tr "Giprotsement" — Trudy "Giprotsement"

TRGLA — Triangle [*English Edition*]

TrGlasgUOrS — Transactions. Glasgow University Oriental Society [*Hertford, England*]

Tr Glav Bot Sada — Trudy Glavnogo Botanicheskogo Sada

Tr Glavgeologii (Gl Upr Geol Okhr Nedr) Uzb SSR — Trudy Glavgeologii (Glavnoe Upravlenie Geologii i Okhrany Nedr) Uzbekskoi SSR

TRGLB — Triangle

Tr Gl Bot Sada — Trudy Glavnogo Botanicheskogo Sada

Tr Gl Bot Sada Akad Nauk SSSR — Trudy Glavnogo Botanicheskogo Sada Akademiya Nauk SSSR

Tr Gl Geofiz Obs — Trudy Glavnoi Geofizicheskoi Observatorii [*USSR*]

Tr Golovn Nauchno-Issled Inst Tsem Mashinostr — Trudy Golovnoi Nauchno-Issledovatel'skii Institut Tsementnogo Mashinostroeniya

Tr Goriiskogo Gos Pedagog Inst — Trudy Goriiskogo Gosudarstvennogo Pedagogicheskogo Instituta

Tr Gor'k Golovn Skh Inst — Trudy Gor'kovskii Golovnoi Sel'skokhozyaistvennyi Institut

Tr Gor'k Gos Med Inst — Trudy Gor'kovskogo Gosudarstvennogo Meditsinskogo Instituta

Tr Gor'k Gos Nauchno Issled Inst Gig Tr Profbolezn — Trudy Gor'kovskii Gosudarstvennyi Nauchno-Issledovatel'skii Institut Gigieny Truda i Profboleznei

Tr Gork Gos Pedagog Inst — Trudy Gor'kovskogo Gosudarstvennogo Pedagogicheskogo Instituta

Tr Gork Inst Inzh Vodn Transp — Trudy Gor'kovskogo Instituta Inzhenerov Vodnogo Transporta

Tr Gork Inzh Stroit Inst — Trudy Gor'kovskogo Inzhenero-Stroitel'nogo Instituta

Tr Gork Nauchno Issled Pediatr Inst — Trudy Gor'kovskogo Nauchno-Issledovatel'skogo Pediatricheskogo Instituta

Tr Gor'k Nauchno-Issled Vet Opytn Stn — Trudy Gor'kovskoi Nauchno-Issledovatel'skoi Veterinarnoi Opytnoi Stantsii

Tr Gork Politekh Inst — Trudy Gor'kovskogo Politekhnicheskogo Instituta

Tr Gor'k S-kh Inst — Trudy Gor'kovskogo Sel'skokhozyaistvennogo Instituta

Tr Gorno Geol Inst Akad Nauk SSSR Ural Fil — Trudy Gorno-Geologicheskogo Instituta Akademiya Nauk SSSR Ural'skii Filial

Tr Gorno Geol Inst Akad Nauk SSSR Zapadno Sib Fil — Trudy Gorno-Geologicheskogo Instituta Akademiya Nauk SSSR Zapadno-Sibirskii Filial

Tr Gos Astron Inst Im Shternberga — Trudy Gosudarstvennogo Astronomicheskogo Instituta Imeni P. K. Shternberga

Tr Gos Astron Inst Mosk Gos Univ — Trudy Gosudarstvennogo Astronomicheskogo Instituta Moskovskii Gosudarstvennyi Universitet

Tr Gos Dorozhn Proektno Izyskatel'skii Nauchno Issled Inst — Trudy Gosudarstvennyi Dorozhnyi Proektno-Izyskatel'skii i Nauchno-Issledovatel'skii Institut

Tr Gos Gidrol Inst — Trudy Gosudarstvennogo Gidrologicheskogo Instituta

Tr Gos Inst Prikl Khim — Trudy Gosudarstvennyi Institut Prikladnoi Khimii

Tr Gos Inst Proekt Issled Rab Neftedobyvayushchei Prom-sti — Trudy Gosudarstvennyi Institut po Proektirovaniyu i Issledovatel'skim Rabotam v Neftedobyvayushchei Promyshlennosti [*USSR*]

Tr Gos Inst Usoversh Vrachei I M Lenina — Trudy Gosudarstvennogo Instituta Usovershenstvovaniya Vrachei I. M. Lenina

Tr Gos Issled Elektrokeram Inst — Trudy Gosudarstvennogo Issledovatel'skogo Elektrokeramicheskogo Instituta [*USSR*]

Tr Gos Issled Keram Inst — Trudy Gosudarstvennogo Issledovatel'skogo Keramicheskogo Instituta

Tr Gos Makeev Nauchno-Issled Inst Bezop Rab Gorn Prom-sti — Trudy Gosudarstvennyi Makeevski Nauchno-Issledovatel'skii Institut po Bezopasnosti Rabot v Gornoi Promyshlennosti [*Ukrainian SSR*]

Tr Gos Nauchno Eksp Inst Grazhdanskikh Prom Inzh Sooruzh — Trudy Gosudarstvennogo Nauchno-Eksperimental'nogo Instituta Grazhdanskikh Promyshlennykh i Inzhenernykh Sooruzhenii

Tr Gos Nauchno Issled Elektrokeram Inst — Trudy Gosudarstvennogo Nauchno-Issledovatel'skogo Elektrokeramicheskogo Instituta

Tr Gos Nauchno-Issled Inst Gornokhim Syr — Trudy Gosudarstvennogo Nauchno-Issledovatel'skogo Instituta Gornokhimicheskogo Syr'ya

Tr Gos Nauchno-Issled Inst Gornokhim Syr'ya — Trudy Gosudarstvennogo Nauchno-Issledovatel'skogo Instituta Gornokhimicheskogo Syr'ya [*USSR*]

Tr Gos Nauchno Issled Inst Keram Promsti — Trudy Gosudarstvennogo Nauchno-Issledovatel'skogo Instituta Keramicheskoi Promyshlennosti

Tr Gos Nauchno Issled Inst Khim Promsti — Trudy Gosudarstvennogo Nauchno-Issledovatel'skogo Instituta Khimicheskoi Promyshlennosti

Tr Gos Nauchno-Issled Inst Prom Sanit Ochistke Gazov — Trudy Gosudarstvennogo Nauchno-Issledovatel'skogo Instituta po Promyshlennoi i Sanitarnoi Ochistke Gazov [*USSR*]

Tr Gos Nauchno Issled Inst Psikhiatrii — Trudy Gosudarstvennogo Nauchno-Issledovatel'skogo Instituta Psikhiatrii

Tr Gos Nauchno-Issled Inst Stroit Keram — Trudy Gosudarstvennyi Nauchno-Issledovatel'skii Institut Stroitel'noi Keramiki [*USSR*]

Tr Gos Nauchno-Issled Inst Ukha Gorla Nosa — Trudy Gosudarstvennogo Nauchno-Issledovatel'skogo Instituta Ukha Gorla i Nosa

Tr Gos Nauchno-Issled Keram Inst — Trudy Gosudarstvennogo Nauchno-Issledovatel'skogo Keramicheskogo Instituta

Tr Gos Nauchno-Issled Proekt Inst Splavov Obrab Tsvet Met — Trudy Gosudarstvennyi Nauchno-Issledovatel'skii i Proektnyi Institut Splavov i Obrabotki Tsvetnykh Metallov [*USSR*]

Tr Gos Nauchno Issled Proektn Inst "Gipromorneft" — Trudy Gosudarstvennogo Nauchno-Issledovatel'skogo i Proektnogo Instituta "Gipromorneft"

Tr Gos Nauchno-Issled Proektn Inst Splavov Obrab Tsvetn Met — Trudy Gosudarstvennyj Nauchno-Issledovatel'skij i Proektnyj Institut Splavov i Obrabotki Tsvetnykh Metallov

Tr Gos Nauchno Issled Rentgeno Radiol Inst — Trudy Gosudarstvennyi Nauchno-Issledovatel'skii Rentgeno-Radiologicheskii Institut

Tr Gos Nauchno-Kontrol'n Inst Vet Prep — Trudy Gosudarstvennogo Nauchno-Kontrol'nogo Instituta Veterinarnykh Preparatov

Tr Gos Nikitskii Bot Sad — Trudy Gosudarstvennyi Nikitskii Botanicheskii Sad

Tr Gos Okeanogr Inst — Trudy Gosudarstvennogo Okeanograficheskogo Instituta

Tr Gos Opt Inst — Trudy Gosudarstvennogo Opticheskogo Instituta [*USSR*]

Tr Gos Proektno Issled Inst Vostokgiprogaz — Trudy Gosudarstvennyi Proektno-Issledovatel'skii Institut "Vostokgiprogaz"

Tr Gos Proektno Konstr Nauchno Issled Inst Morsk Transp — Trudy Gosudarstvennyi Proektno-Konstruktorskii i Nauchno-Issledovatel'skii Institut Morskogo Transporta

Tr Gos Soyuzn Nauchno Issled Trakt Inst — Trudy Gosudarstvennyi Soyuznyi-Nauchno-Issledovatel'skii Traktornyi Institut

Tr Gos Tsentr Nauchno Issled Inst Tekhnol Organ Proizvod — Trudy Gosudarstvennyi Tsentral'yni Nauchno-Issledovatel'skii Institut Tekhnologii i Organizatsii Proizvodstva

Tr Gos Vses Dorozhn Nauchno Issled Inst — Trudy Gosudarstvennyi Vsesoyuznyi Dorozhnyi Nauchno-Issledovatel'skii Institut

Tr Gos Vses Inst Proekt Nauchno-Issled Rab Giprotsement — Trudy Gosudarstvennogo Vsesoyuznogo Instituta po Proektirovaniyu i Nauchno-Issledovatel'skim Rabotam "Giprotsement"

Tr Gos Vses Inst Proekt Nauchno-Issled Rab Tsem Promsti — Trudy Gosudarstvennogo Vsesoyuznyi Instituta po Proektirovaniyu i Nauchno-Issledovatel'skim Rabotam v Tsementnoi Promyshlennosti

Tr Gos Vses Proektn Nauchno-Issled Inst Tsem Prom-sti — Trudy Gosudarstvennyi Vsesoyuznyi Proektnyi i Nauchno-Issledovatel'skii Institut Tsementnoi Promyshlennosti [*USSR*]

Tr Grozn Neft Inst — Trudy Groznenskii Neftyanoi Institut

Tr Gruz Nauchno-Issled Inst Energ — Trudy Gruzinskogo Nauchno-Issledovatel'skogo Instituta Energetiki [*Georgian SSR*]

Tr Gruz Nauchno-Issled Inst Gidrotekh Melior — Trudy Gruzinskogo Nauchno-Issledovatel'skogo Instituta Gidrotekhniki i Melioratsii

Tr Gruz Politekh Inst — Trudy Gruzinskogo Politekhnicheskogo Instituta [*Georgian SSR*]

Tr Gruz S-kh Inst — Trudy Gruzinskogo Sel'skokhozyaistvennogo Instituta

TRHS — Transactions. Royal Historical Society

TRHUA — Travail Humain

Tri — Tribuna

Trial Diplomacy J — Trial Diplomacy Journal

Trial Dpl J — Trial Diplomacy Journal

Trial Law G — Trial Lawyer's Guide

Trial Law Guide — Trial Lawyer's Guide

Trial Law Q — Trial Lawyers Quarterly

Trib CEBEDEAU — Tribune. CEBEDEAU [*Centre Belge d'Etude et de Documentation des Eaux et de l'Air*]

Trib Farm (Curitiba) — Tribuna Farmaceutica (Curitiba)

Trib Mus — Tribune Musical

Trib Odontol — Tribuna Odontologica

Tribol Int — Tribology International

Tribol Lubrificazione — Tribologia e Lubrificazione

Tribologia & Lubr — Tribologia e Lubrificazione

Tribology Int — Tribology International

Tribuna Postale — Tribuna Postale e delle Telecomunicazioni

Trier Archiv — Trierisches Archiv

TriererThZ — Trierer Theologische Zeitschrift [*Trier*]

TriererZ — Trierer Zeitschrift fuer Geschichte und Kunst des Trierer Landes und Seiner Nachbargebiete

Trierer Z Gesch Kunst — Trierer Zeitschrift fuer Geschichte und Kunst des Trierer Landes und Seiner Nachbargebiete

TrierThZ — Trierer Theologische Zeitschrift [*Trier*]

Trim Econ — Trimestre Economico

Trimes Econ — Trimestre Economico

Trim Pol — Trimestre Politico

Tr Indiana Med Soc — Transactions. Indiana State Medical Society

TRI Newsl — Textile Research Institute. Newletter

Trinidad Tobago Min Petrol Mines Mon Bull — Trinidad and Tobago. Ministry of Petroleum and Mines. Monthly Bulletin

Trinity J — Trinity Journal

Trinity Sem R — Trinity Seminary Review

Trinkwasser-Verord — Trinkwasser-Verordnung

Tr Inst Biol Akad Nauk Latv SSR — Trudy Institut Biologii Akademiya Nauk Latviiskoi SSR

Tr Inst Biol Akad Nauk SSSR Ural Fil — Trudy Instituta Biologii Akademiya Nauk SSSR Ural'skii Filial [*USSR*]

Tr Inst Biol Bashk Univ — Trudy Instituta Biologii Bashkirskogo Universiteta

Tr Inst Biol Ural Fil Akad Nauk SSSR — Trudy Instituta Biologii Ural'skogo Filiala Akademii Nauk SSSR

Tr Inst Biol Vnutr Vod Akad Nauk SSSR — Trudy Instituta Biologii Vnutrennikh Vod Akademii Nauk SSSR

Tr Inst Biol Yakutsk Fil Sib Otd Akad Nauk SSSR — Trudy Instituta Biologii Yakutskii Filial Sibirskogo Otdeleniya Akademii Nauk SSSR

Tr Inst Bot Akad Nauk Azerb SSR — Trudy Instituta Botaniki Akademiya Nauk Azerbaidzhanskoi SSR

Tr Inst Bot Akad Nauk Kazakh SSR — Trudy Instituta Botaniki Akademiya Nauk Kazakhskoi SSR

Tr Inst Chist Khim Reakt — Trudy Instituta Chistykh Khimicheskikh Reaktivov

Tr Inst Ehkol Rast Zhivotn — Trudy Instituta Ehkologii Rastenii i Zhivotnykh

Tr Inst Ehlektrokhim Akad Nauk SSSR Ural Fil — Trudy Instituta Ehlektrokhimii Akademiya Nauk SSSR Ural'skij Filial

Tr Inst Ehlektrokhim Ural Nauch Tsentr Akad Nauk SSSR — Trudy Instituta Ehlektrokhimii Ural'skij Nauchnyj Tsentr Akademiya Nauk SSSR

Tr Inst Ekol Rast Zhivotn — Trudy Instituta Ekologii Rastenii i Zhivotnykh [*USSR*]

Tr Inst Ekol Rast Zhivotn Ural Fil Akad Nauk SSSR — Trudy Instituta Ekologii Rastenii i Zhivotnykh Ural'skogo Filiala Akademii Nauk SSSR

Tr Inst Ekol Rast Zhivotn Ural Nauchn Tsentr Akad Nauk SSSR — Trudy Instituta Ekologii Rastenii i Zhivotnykh Ural'skii Nauchnyi Tsentr Akademii Nauk SSSR [*USSR*]

Tr Inst Eksp Biol Akad Nauk Kaz SSR — Trudy Instituta Eksperimental'noi Biologii Akademiya Nauk Kazakhskoi SSR

Tr Inst Eksper Biol Akad Nauk Eston SSR — Trudy Instituta Eksperimental'noi Biologii Akademiya Nauk Estonskoi SSR

Tr Inst Eksp Klin Khir Gematol — Trudy Instituta Eksperimental'noi i Klinicheskoi Khirurgii i Gematologii

Tr Inst Eksp Klin Med Akad Nauk Latv SSR — Trudy Instituta Eksperimental'noi i Klinicheskoi Meditsiny Akademii Nauk Latviiskoi SSR

Tr Inst Eksp Klin Onkol Akad Med Nauk SSSR — Trudy Instituta Eksperimental'noi Klinicheskoi Onkologii Akademiya Meditsinskikh Nauk SSSR [*USSR*]

Tr Inst Eksp Med Akad Med Nauk SSR — Trudy Instituta Eksperimental'noi Meditsiny Akademii Meditsinskikh Nauk SSR

Tr Inst Eksp Med Akad Nauk Latv SSR — Trudy Instituta Eksperimental'noi Meditsiny Akademii Nauk Latviiskoi SSR

Tr Inst Eksp Med Akad Nauk Lit SSR — Trudy Instituta Eksperimental'noi Meditsiny Akademii Nauk Litovskoi SSR

Tr Inst Eksp Meteorol — Trudy Institut Eksperimental'noi Meteorologii [*USSR*]

Tr Inst Elektrokhim Ural Nauchn Tsentr Akad Nauk SSSR — Trudy Instituta Elektrokhimii Ural'skii Nauchnyi Tsentr Akademiya Nauk SSSR [*USSR*]

Tr Inst Energ Akad Nauk BSSR — Trudy Instituta Energetiki Akademiya Nauk Belorusskoi SSR [*Belorussian SSR*]

Tr Inst Epidemiol Mikrobiol (Frunze) — Trudy Instituta Epidemiologii i Mikrobiologii (Frunze)

Tr Inst Fiz Akad Nauk Azerb SSR — Trudy Instituta Fiziki Akademiya Nauk Azerbaidzhanskoi SSR [*Azerbaidzhan SSR*]

Tr Inst Fiz Akad Nauk Est SSR — Trudy Instituta Fiziki Akademii Nauk Estonskoi SSR

Tr Inst Fiz Akad Nauk Gruz SSR — Trudy Instituta Fiziki Akademiya Nauk Gruzinskoi SSR [*Georgian SSR*]

Tr Inst Fiz Astron Akad Nauk Ehst SSR — Trudy Instituta Fiziki i Astronomii Akademiya Nauk Ehstonskoj SSR

Tr Inst Fiziol Akad Nauk Gruz SSR — Trudy Instituta Fiziologii Akademiya Nauk Gruzinskoi SSR [*Georgian SSR*]

Tr Inst Fiziol Akad Nauk Kaz SSR — Trudy Instituta Fiziologii Akademiya Nauk Kazakhskoi SSR

Tr Inst Fiziol Akad Nauk SSSR — Trudy Instituta Fiziologii Akademii Nauk SSSR

Tr Inst Fiziol Im I P Pavlova Akad Nauk SSSR — Trudy Instituta Fiziologii Imeni I. P. Pavlova Akademii Nauk SSSR

Tr Inst Fiziol Im I P Pavlova Akad SSSR — Trudy Instituta Fiziologii Imeni I. P. Pavlova. Akademii Nauk SSSR

Tr Inst Fiziol Rast Im K A Timiryazeva — Trudy Instituta Fiziologii Rastenii Imeni K. A. Timiryazeva

Tr Inst Fiz Met Ural Nauchn Tsent Akad SSSR — Trudy Instituta Fiziki Metallov Ural'skogo Nauchnogo Tsentra Akademiya Nauk SSSR [*USSR*]

Tr Inst Fiz Vys Ehnerg — Trudy Instituta Fiziki Vysokikh Ehnergij

Tr Inst Fiz Vys Energ Akad Nauk Kaz SSR — Trudy Instituta Fiziki Vysokikh Energii Akademiya Nauk Kazakhskoi SSR [*Kazakh SSR*]

Tr Inst Fiz Zemli Akad Nauk SSSR — Trudy Instituta Fiziki Zemli Akademiya Nauk SSSR [*USSR*]

Tr Inst Genet Akad Nauk SSSR — Trudy Instituta Genetiki Akademiya Nauk SSSR

Tr Inst Genet Sel Akad Nauk Az SSR — Trudy Instituta Genetiki i Selektsii Akademii Nauk Azerbaidzhanskoi SSR

Tr Inst Geofiz Akad Nauk Gruz SSR — Trudy Instituta Geofiziki Akademiya Nauk Gruzinskoi SSR [*Georgian SSR*]

Tr Inst Geogr Akad Nauk SSSR — Trudy Instituta Geografii Akademiya Nauk SSSR

Tr Inst Geol Akad Nauk Est SSR — Trudy Instituta Geologii Akademiya Nauk Estonskoi SSR [*Estonian SSR*]

Tr Inst Geol Akad Nauk Tadzh SSR — Trudy Instituta Geologii Akademiya Nauk Tadzhikskoi SSR

Tr Inst Geol Geofiz Akad Nauk SSSR Sib Otd — Trudy Instituta Geologii i Geofiziki Akademiya Nauk SSSR Sibirskoe Otdelenie [*USSR*]

Tr Inst Geol Korisnikh Koplain Akad Nauk Ukr RSR — Trudy Institut Geologii Kori Korisnikh Koplain Akademiya Nauk Ukrains'koi RSR [*Ukrainian SSR*]

Tr Inst Geol Nauk Akad Nauk Kaz SSR — Trudy Instituta Geologicheskikh Nauk Akademiya Nauk Kazakhskoi SSR [*Kazakh SSR*]

Tr Inst "Giproninemetallorud" — Trudy Instituta "Giproninemetallorud"

Tr Inst Goryuch Iskop (Moscow) — Trudy Instituta Goryuchikh Iskopaemykh (Moscow)

Tr Inst Istor Estestvozn Tekh Akad Nauk SSSR — Trudy Instituta Istorii Estestvoznaniya i Tekhniki Akademiya Nauk SSSR [*USSR*]

Tr Inst Khig Okhr Tr Prof Zabol — Trudove na Instituta po Khigiena. Okhrana na Truda i Profesionalni Zabolyavaniya

Tr Inst Khim Akad Nauk Kirg SSR — Trudy Instituta Khimii Akademiya Nauk Kirgizskoi SSR

Tr Inst Khim Akad Nauk SSSR Ural Fil — Trudy Instituta Khimii Akademiya Nauk SSSR Ural'skii Filial [*USSR*]

Tr Inst Khim Akad Nauk Tadzh SSR — Trudy Instituta Khimii Akademiya Nauk Tadzhikskoi SSR

Tr Inst Khim Akad Nauk Turkm SSR — Trudy Instituta Khimii Akademiya Nauk Turkmenskoi SSR

Tr Inst Khim Akad Nauk Uzb SSR — Trudy Instituta Khimii Akademiya Nauk Uzbekskoi SSR

Tr Inst Khim Metall Akad Nauk SSSR Ural Fil — Trudy Instituta Khimii i Metallurgii Akademiya Nauk SSSR Ural'skii Filial

Tr Inst Khim Nauk Akad Nauk Kaz SSR — Trudy Instituta Khimicheskikh Nauk Akademiya Nauk Kazakhskoi SSR

Tr Inst Khim Nefti Prir Solei Akad Nauk Kaz SSR — Trudy Instituta Khimii Nefti i Prirodnykh Solei Akademiya Nauk Kazakhskoi SSSR

Tr Inst Khim Ural Nauchn Tsentr Akad Nauk SSSR — Trudy Instituta Khimii Ural'skii Nauchnyi Tsentr Akademiya Nauk SSSR

Tr Inst Klin Eksp Kardiol — Trudy Instituta Klinicheskoi i Eksperimental'noi Kardiologii

Tr Inst Klin Eksp Kardiol Akad Nauk Gruz SSR — Trudy Instituta Klinicheskoi i Eksperimental'noi Kardiologii Akademiya Nauk Gruzinskoi SSR

Tr Inst Klin Eksp Khir Akad Nauk Kaz SSR — Trudy Instituta Klinicheskoi i Eksperimental'noi Khirurgii Akademii Nauk Kazakhskoi SSR

Tr Inst Klin Eksp Nevrol Gruz SSR — Trudy Instituta Klinicheskoi i Eksperimental'noi Nevrologii Gruzinskoi SSR

Tr Inst Kom Stand Mer Izmer Prib Sov Minist SSSR — Trudy Institutov Komiteta Standartov Mer i Izmeritel'nykh Priborov pri Sovete Ministrov SSSR

Tr Inst Kraev Eksp Med Akad Nauk Uzb SSR — Trudy Instituta Kraevoi Eksperimental'noi Meditsiny Akademiya Nauk Uzbekskoi SSR

Tr Inst Kraev Med Akad Nauk Kirg SSR — Trudy Instituta Kraevoi Meditsiny Akademii Nauk Kirgizskoi SSR

Tr Inst Kraev Patol Akad Nauk Kaz SSR — Trudy Instituta Kraevoi Patologii Akademii Nauk Kazakhskoi SSR

Tr Inst Kristallogr Akad Nauk SSSR — Trudy Instituta Kristallografii Akademiya Nauk SSSR

Tr Inst Lesa Akad Nauk Gruzin SSR — Trudy Instituta Lesa Akademiya Nauk Gruzinskoi SSR

Tr Inst Lesa Akad Nauk Gruz SSR — Trudy Instituta Lesa Akademii Nauk Gruzinskoi SSR

Tr Inst Lesa Akad Nauk SSSR — Trudy Instituta Lesa Akademii Nauk SSSR

Tr Inst Lesa Drev Akad Nauk SSSR Sib Otd — Trudy Instituta Lesa i Drevesiny Akademiya Nauk SSSR Sibirskoe Otdelenie

Tr Inst Lesokhoz Probl Khim Drev Akad Nauk Latv SSR — Trudy Instituta Lesokhozyaistvennykh Problem i Khimii Drevesiny Akademiya Nauk Latviiskoi SSR [*Latvian SSR*]

Tr Inst Malyarii Med Parazitol — Trudy Instituta Malyarii i Meditsinskoi Parazitologii

Tr Inst Mat Mekh Akad Nauk Az SSR — Trudy Instituta Matematiki i Mekhaniki Akademii Nauk Azerbajdzhanskoj SSR

Tr Inst Mekh Obrab Polezn Iskop — Trudy Instituta Mekhanicheskoi Obrabotki Poleznykh Iskopaemykh

Tr Inst Melior Vodn Bolotnogo Khoz Akad Nauk B SSR — Trudy Instituta Melioratsii Vodnogo i Bolotnogo Khozyaistva Akademiya Nauk Belorusskoi SSR

Tr Inst Merzlotoved Akad Nauk SSSR — Trudy Instituta Merzlotovedeniya Akademiya Nauk SSSR

Tr Inst Metall Akad Nauk SSSR — Trudy Instituta Metallurgii Akademiya Nauk SSSR

Tr Inst Metall Akad Nauk SSSR Ural Nauchn Tsentr — Trudy Instituta Metallurgii Akademiya Nauk SSSR Ural'skii Nauchnyi Tsentr

Tr Inst Metall Im A A Baikova Akad Nauk SSSR — Trudy Instituta Metallurgii Imeni A. A. Baikova Akademiya Nauk SSSR [*USSR*]

Tr Inst Metall Obogashch Akad Nauk Kaz SSR — Trudy Instituta Metallurgii i Obogashcheniya Akademiya Nauk Kazakhskoi SSR

Tr Inst Metallofiz Metall Akad Nauk SSSR Ural Fil — Trudy Instituta Metallofiziki Metallurgii Akademiya Nauk SSSR Ural'skii Filial

Tr Inst Metall (Sverdlovsk) — Trudy Instituta Metallurgii (Sverdlovsk)

Tr Inst Met (Leningrad) — Trudy Instituta Metallov (Leningrad)

Tr Inst Mikrobiol Akad Nauk Latv SSR — Trudy Instituta Mikrobiologii Akademii Nauk Latviiskoi SSR

Tr Inst Mikrobiol Akad Nauk SSSR — Trudy Instituta Mikrobiologii Akademii Nauk SSSR

Tr Inst Mikrobiol Virusol Akad Nauk Kaz SSR — Trudy Instituta Mikrobiologii i Virusologii Akademii Nauk Kazakhskoi SSR

Tr Inst Morfol Zhivotn Akad Nauk SSSR — Trudy Instituta Morfologii Zhivotnykh Akademii Nauk SSSR

Tr Inst Mosk Inst Tonkoi Khim Tekhnol — Trudy Instituta Moskovskii Institut Tonkoi Khimicheskoi Tekhnologii

Tr Inst Nefti Akad Nauk Az SSR — Trudy Instituta Nefti Akademiya Nauk Azerbaidzhanskoi SSR

Tr Inst Nefti Akad Nauk Kaz SSR — Trudy Instituta Nefti Akademiya Nauk Kazakhoskoi SSR

Tr Inst Nefti Akad Nauk SSSR — Trudy Instituta Nefti Akademiya Nauk SSSR

Tr Inst Norm Patol Fiziol Akad Med Nauk SSSR — Trudy Instituta Normal'noi i Patologicheskoi Fiziologii Akademii Meditsinskikh Nauk SSSR

Tr Inst Nov Lub Syrya — Trudy Instituta Novogo Lubyanogo Syr'ya

Tr Inst Obogashch Tverd Goryuch Iskop — Trudy Instituta Obogashcheniya Tverdykh Goryuchikh Iskopaemykh [*USSR*]

Tr Inst Okeanol Akad Nauk SSSR — Trudy Instituta Okeanologii Akademii Nauk SSSR

Tr Inst Onkol Akad Med Nauk SSSR — Trudy Instituta Onkologii Akademiya Meditsinskikh Nauk SSSR

Tr Inst Org Katal Elektrokhim Akad Nauk Kaz SSR — Trudy Instituta Organicheskogo Kataliza i Elektrokhimii Akademiya Nauk Kazakhskoi SSR [*Kazakh SSR*]

Tr Inst Pastera — Trudy Instituta Imeni Pastera

Tr Inst Pochvoved Agrokhim Akad Nauk Az SSR — Trudy Instituta Pochvovedeniya i Agrokhimii Akademii Nauk Azerbaidzhanskoi SSR

Tr Inst Pochvoved Agrokhim AN UzSSR — Trudy Instituta Pochvovedeniya i Agrokhimii Akademiya Nauk UzSSR

Tr Inst Pochvoved Akad Nauk Gruz SSR — Trudy Instituta Pochvovedeniya Akademii Nauk Gruzinskoi SSR

Tr Inst Pochvoved Akad Nauk Kaz SSR — Trudy Instituta Pochvovedeniya Akademii Nauk Kazakhskoi SSR

Tr Inst Pochvoved (Tashkent) — Trudy Instituta Pochvovedeniya (Tashkent)

Tr Inst Polevod Akad Nauk Gruz SSR — Trudy Instituta Polevodstva Akademii Nauk Gruzinskoi SSR

Tr Inst Polio Virusn Entsefalitov Akad Med Nauk SSSR — Trudy Instituta Poliomielita i Virusnykh Entsefalitov Akademii Meditsinskikh Nauk SSSR

Tr Inst Prikl Geofiz — Trudy Instituta Prikladnoi Geofiziki [*USSR*]

Tr Inst Prikl Khim Elektrokhim Akad Nauk Gruz SSR — Trudy Instituta Prikladnoi Khimii i Elektrokhimii Akademiya Nauk Gruzinskoi SSR

Tr Inst Proektn Nauchno-Issled Inst Ural Promstroiniiproekt — Trudy Instituta Proektnyi i Nauchno-Issledovatel'skii Institut Ural'skii Promstroiniiproekt

Tr Inst Razrab Neft Gazov Mestorozhd Akad Nauk Az SSR — Trudy Instituta Razrabotki Neftyanykh i Gazovykh Mestorozhdenii Akademiya Nauk Azerbaidzhanskoi SSR

Tr Inst Sadovod Vinograd Vinodel Gruz SSR — Trudy Instituta Sadovodstva Vinogradarstva i Vinodeliya Gruzinskoi SSR

Tr Inst Sadovod Vinograd Vinodel (Tiflis) — Trudy Instituta Sadovodstva Vinogradarstva i Vinodeliya (Tiflis)

Tr Inst Sel Semenovod Khlop (Tashkent) — Trudy Instituta Selektsii i Semenovodstva Khlopchatnika (Tashkent)

Tr Inst Sist Upr Akad Nauk Gruz SSR — Trudy Institut Sistem Upravleniya Akademiya Nauk Gruzinskoj SSR

Tr Inst Stroit Dela Akad Nauk Gruz SSR — Trudy Instituta Stroitel'nogo Dela Akademiya Nauk Gruzinskoi SSR

Tr Inst Stroit Mater Miner Proiskhozhd Stekla — Trudy Instituta Stroitel'nykh Materialov Mineral'nogo Proiskhozhdeniya i Stekla

Tr Inst Stroit Mekh Seismostoikosti Akad Nauk Gruz SSR — Trudy Instituta Stroitel'noi Mekhaniki i Seismostoikosti Akademiya Nauk Gruzinskoi SSR

Tr Inst Teor Astron — Trudy Instituta Teoreticeskoi Astronomii [*USSR*]

Tr Inst Teor Geofiz Akad Nauk SSSR — Trudy Instituta Teoreticheskoi Geofiziki Akademiya Nauk SSSR

Tr Inst Torfa Akad Nauk B SSR — Trudy Instituta Torfa Akademiya Nauk Belorusskoi SSR

Tr Inst Vinograd Vinodel Akad Nauk Arm SSR — Trudy Instituta Vinogradarstva i Vinodeliya Akademii Nauk Armyanskoi SSR

Tr Inst Vinograd Vinodel Akad Nauk Gruz SSR — Trudy Instituta Vinogradarstva i Vinodeliya Akademii Nauk Gruzinskoi SSR

Tr Inst Vses Nauchno-Issled Inst Tsellyul Bum Prom-sti — Trudy Instituta. Vsesoyuznyi Nauchno-Issledovatel'skii Institut Tsellyulozno-Bumazhnoi Promyshlennosti [*USSR*]

Tr Inst Vulkanol Akad Nauk SSSR Sib Otd — Trudy Instituta Vulkanologii Akademiya Nauk SSSR Sibirskoe Otdelenie

Tr Inst Vyssh Nervn Deya Akad Nauk SSSR Fiziol — Trudy Instituta Vysshei Nervnoi Deyatel'nosti Akademii Nauk SSSR. Seriya Fiziologicheskaya

Tr Inst Vyssh Nervn Deyat Akad Nauk SSSR Ser Fiziol — Trudy Instituta Vysshei Nervnoi Deyatel'nosti Akademii Nauk SSSR. Seriya Fiziologicheskaya

Tr Inst Vyssh Nervn Deyat Ser Fiziol — Trudy Instituta Vysshei Nervnoi Deyatel'nosti. Seriya Fiziologicheskaya

Tr Inst Vyssh Nervn Deyat Ser Patofiziol — Trudy Instituta Vysshei Nervnoi Deyatel'nosti. Seriya Patofiziologicheskaya

Tr Inst Yad Fiz Akad Nauk Kaz SSR — Trudy Instituta Yadernoi Fiziki Akademiya Nauk Kazakhskoi SSR

Tr Inst Zasch Rast (Tiflis) — Trudy Instituta Zashchity Rastenii (Tiflis) [*Georgian SSR*]

Tr Inst Zashch Rast Akad Nauk Gruz SSR — Trudy Instituta Zashchity Rastenii Akademii Nauk Gruzinskoi SSR

Tr Inst Zashch Rast (Tiflis) — Trudy Instituta Zashchity Rastenii (Tiflis)

Tr Inst Zemled Akad Nauk Azerb SSR — Trudy Instituta Zemledeliya Akademiya Nauk Azerbaidzhanskoi SSR

Tr Inst Zemled Kaz Fil Akad Nauk SSSR — Trudy Instituta Zemledeliya Kazakhskogo Filiala Akademii Nauk SSSR

Tr Inst Zemled (Leningrad) Razdel 3 — Trudy Instituta Zemledeliya (Leningrad). Razdel 3. Pochvovedenie

Tr Inst Zhivotnovod Akad Nauk Turkm SSR — Trudy Instituta Zhivotnovodstva Akademii Nauk Turkmenskoi SSR

Tr Inst Zhivotnovod Dagest Fili Akad Nauk SSSR — Trudy Instituta Zhivotnovodstva Dagestanskogo Filiala Akademii Nauk SSSR

Tr Inst Zhivotnovod Minist Skh Uzb SSR — Trudy Instituta Zhivotnovodstva Ministerstvo Sel'skokhozyaistva Uzbekistanskoi SSR

Tr Inst Zhivotnovod (Tashkent) — Trudy Instituta Zhivotnovodstva (Tashkent)

Tr Inst Zool Akad Nauk Az SSR — Trudy Instituta Zoologii Akademii Nauk Azerbaidzhanskoi SSR

Tr Inst Zool Akad Nauk Gruz SSR — Trudy Instituta Zoologii Akademii Nauk Gruzinskoi SSR

Tr Inst Zool Akad Nauk Kazakh SSR — Trudy Instituta Zoologii Akademiya Nauk Kazakhskoi SSR

Tr Inst Zool Akad Nauk Kaz SSR — Trudy Instituta Zoologii Akademii Nauk Kazakhskoi SSR

Tr Inst Zool Akad Nauk Ukr SSR — Trudy Instituta Zoologii Akademii Nauk Ukrainskoi SSR

Tr Inst Zool Biol (Kiev) — Trudy Instytutu Zoolohiyi ta Biolohiyi (Kiev)

Tr Inst Zool Parazitol Akad Nauk Tadzh SSR — Trudy Instituta Zoologii i Parazitologii Akademiya Nauk Tadzhikskoi SSR

Tr Inst Zool Parazitol Akad Nauk Uzb SSR — Trudy Instituta Zoologii i Parazitologii Akademii Nauk Uzbekskoi SSR

Tr Inst Zool Parazitol Akad Tadzh SSR — Trudy Instituta Zoologii i Parazitologii Akademiya Nauk Tadzhikskoi SSR

Tr Inst Zool Parazitol Kirg Fil Akad Nauk SSR — Trudy Instituta Zoologii i Parazitologii Kirgizskogo Filiala Akademii Nauk SSR

Trin Tob For — Trinidad and Tobago Forester

TriQ — Tri-Quarterly

Tri-Quar — Tri-Quarterly

Tr IREA — Trudy IREA

Tr Irkutsk Inst Nar Khoz — Trudy Irkutskogo Instituta Narodnogo Khozyaistva

Tr Irkutsk Nauchno Issled Inst Epidemiol Mikrobiol — Trudy Irkutsk Nauchno-Issledovatel'skogo Instituta Epidemiologii i Mikrobiologii

Tr Irkutsk Politekh Inst — Trudy Irkutskogo Politekhnicheskogo Instituta [*USSR*]

Tri State Med J (Greensburo NC) — Tri-State Medical Journal (Greensburo, North Carolina)

Tri State Med J (Shreveport LA) — Tri-State Medical Journal (Shreveport, Louisiana)

Tr Ivanov Med Inst — Trudy Ivanovskogo Meditsinskogo Instituta

Tr Ivanov Skh Inst — Trudy Ivanovskogo Sel'skokhozyaistvennogo Instituta

TRIYA — Trade and Industry

Tr Izhevsk Med Inst — Trudy Izhevskogo Meditsinskogo Instituta

Tr Japan Path Soc — Transactions. Japanese Pathological Society

TRJaVUZ — Trudy Kafedry Russkogo Jazyka Vuzov Vostocnoj Sibiri i Dal'nego Vostoka

TRJWD — Transactions. JWRI [*Japanese Welding Research Institute*]

Tr Kafedry Avtomob Trakt Vses Zaochn Mashinostroit Inst — Trudy Kafedry Avtomobili i Traktory Vsesoyuznyi Zaochnyi Mashinostroitel'nyi Institut

Tr Kafedry Gosp Khir Lech Fak Sarat Med Inst — Trudy Kafedry Gospital'noi Khirurgii i Lechebnogo Fakul'teta Saratovskogo Meditsinskogo Instituta

Tr Kafedry Kozhnykh Vener Bolezn Tashk — Trudy Kafedry Kozhnykh i Venericheskikh Boleznei Tashkentskii Meditsinskii Institut

Tr Kafedry Kozhnykh Vener Bolezn Tashk Med Inst — Trudy Kafedry Kozhnykh i Venericheskikh Boleznei Tashkentskii Meditsinskii Institut

Tr Kafedry Norm Anat Sarat Gos Med Inst — Trudy Kafedry Normal'noi Anatomii Saratovskogo Gosudarstvennogo Meditsinskogo Instituta

Tr Kafedry Oper Khir Topogr Anat Tbilis Gos Med Inst — Trudy Kafedry Operativnoi Khirurgii i Topograficheskoi Anatomii Tbilisskogo Gosudarstvennogo Meditsinskogo Instituta

Tr Kafedry Pochvoved Biol Pochv Fak Kaz Gos Univ — Trudy Kafedry Pochvovedeniya Biologo-Pochvennogo Fakul'teta Kazakhskii Gosudarstvennyi Universitet

Tr Kafedry Teor Eksp Fiz Kaliningr Gos Univ — Trudy Kafedry Teoreticheskoi i Eksperimental'noi Fiziki Kaliningradskii Gosudarstvennyi Universitet

Tr Kalinin Gos Med Inst — Trudy Kalininskogo Gosudarstvennogo Meditsinskogo Instituta

Tr Kaliningr Nauchno Issled Vet Stn — Trudy Kaliningradskoi Nauchno-Issledovatel'skoi Veterinarnoi Stantsii

Tr Kaliningr Tekh Inst Rybn Promsti Khoz — Trudy Kaliningradskogo Tekhnicheskogo Instituta Rybnoi Promyshlennosti i Khozyaistva

Tr Kalinin Politekh Inst — Trudy Kalininskii Politekhnicheskii Institut [*USSR*]

Tr Kalinin Torf Inst — Trudy Kalininskogo Torfyanogo Instituta

Tr Kaluzhskoi Gos Obl Skh Opytn Stn — Trudy Kaluzhskoi Gosudarstvennoi Oblastnoi Sel'skokhozyaistvennoi Opytnoi Stantsii

Tr Kamenetsk Podolsk Skh Inst — Trudy Kamenetsk-Podolskogo Sel'skokhozyaistvennogo Instituta

Tr Kamenets Podol'sk Skh Inst — Trudy Kamenets-Podol'skogo Sel'skokhozyaistvennogo Instituta

Tr Kandalakshshkogo Gos Zapov — Trudy Kandalakshskogo Gosudarstvennogo Zapovednika

Tr Kansas Acad Sc — Transactions. Kansas Academy of Science

Tr Karagandin Bot Sada — Trudy Karagandinskogo Botanicheskogo Sada

Tr Karel Fil Akad Nauk SSSR — Trudy Karel'skogo Filiala Akademii Nauk SSSR

Tr Karelo-Fin Uchit Inst — Trudy Karelo-Finskogo Uchitel'skogo Instituta

Tr Karel Otd Gos Nauchno Issled Inst Ozern Rechn Rybn Khoz — Trudy Karel'skogo Otdeleniya Gosudarstvennogo Nauchno-Issledovatel'skogo Instituta Ozernogo i Rechnogo Rybnogo Khozyaistva

Tr Kasp Nauchno Issled Inst Rybn Khoz — Trudy Kaspiiskii Nauchno-Issledovatel'skii Institut Rybnogo Khozyaistva

Tr Kaunas Gos Med Inst — Trudy Kaunasskogo Gosudarstvennogo Meditsinskogo Instituta

Tr Kavk Inst Miner Syrya — Trudy Kavkazskogo Instituta Mineral'nogo Syr'ya

Tr Kazan Aviats Inst — Trudy KAI. Kazanskij Ordena Trudovogo Krasnogo Znameni Aviatsionnyj Institut Imeni A. N. Tupoleva

Tr Kazan Aviats Inst Ser Khim — Trudy Kazanskogo Aviatsionogo Instituta. Seriya Khimicheskaya

Tr Kazan Fil Akad Nauk SSSR Ser Geol Nauk — Trudy Kazanskogo Filiala Akademii Nauk SSSR. Seriya Geologicheskikh Nauk

Tr Kazan Fil Akad Nauk SSSR Ser Khim Nauk — Trudy Kazanskogo Filiala Akademii Nauk SSSR. Seriya Khimicheskikh Nauk

Tr Kazan Gor Astron Obs — Trudy Kazanskoi Gorodskoi Astronomicheskoi Observatorii

Tr Kazan Gos Inst Usoversh Vrachei — Trudy Kazanskogo Gosudarstvennogo Instituta Usovershenstvovaniya Vrachei

Tr Kazan Inst Usoversh Vrachei Im V I Lenina — Trudy Kazanskogo Instituta Usovershenstvovaniya Vrachei Imeni V. I. Lenina

Tr Kazan Inzh Stroit Inst — Trudy Kazanskogo Inzhenerno-Stroitel'nogo Instituta

Tr Kazan Med Inst — Trudy Kazanskogo Meditsinskogo Instituta

Tr Kazan Nauchno-Inst Onkol Radiol — Trudy Kazanskogo Nauchno-Issledovatel'skogo Instituta Onkologii i Radiologii

Tr Kazan Nauchno-Issled Inst Onkol Radiol — Trudy Kazanskogo Nauchno-Issledovatel'skogo Instituta Onkologii i Radiologii

Tr Kazan Nauchno-Issled Inst Travmatol Ortop — Trudy Kazanskogo Nauchno-Issledovatel'skogo Instituta Travmatologii i Ortopedii

Tr Kazan Nauchno Issled Vet Inst — Trudy Kazanskogo Nauchno-Issledovatel'skogo Veterinarnogo Instituta

Tr Kazan S-kh Inst — Trudy Kazanskogo Sel'skokhozyaistvennogo Instituta

Tr Kaz Fil Akad Stroit Arkhit SSSR — Trudy Kazakhskogo Filiala Akademiya Stroitel'stva i Arkhitektury SSSR

Tr Kaz Gos Pedagog Inst — Trudy Kazanskii Gosudarstvennyi Pedagogicheskii Institut

Tr Kaz Gos Skh Inst — Trudy Kazakhskogo Gosudarstvennogo Sel'skokhozyaistvennogo Instituta

Tr Kaz Nauchno-Issled Gidrometeorol Inst — Trudy Kazakhskogo Nauchno-Issledovatel'skogo Gidrometeorologicheskogo Instituta

Tr Kaz Nauchno-Issled Inst Lesn Khoz — Trudy Kazakhskogo Nauchno-Issledovatel'skogo Instituta Lesnogo Khozyaistva

Tr Kaz Nauchno-Issled Inst Lesn Khoz Agrolesomelior — Trudy Kazakhskogo Nauchno-Issledovatel'skogo Instituta Lesnogo Khozyaistva i Agrolesomelioratsii

Tr Kaz Nauchno Issled Inst Miner Syrya — Trudy Kazakhskogo Nauchno-Issledovatel'skogo Instituta Mineral'nogo Syr'ya

Tr Kaz Nauchno-Issled Inst Onkol Radiol — Trudy Kazakhskogo Nauchno-Issledovatel'skogo Instituta Onkologii i Radiologii

Tr Kaz Nauchno-Issled Inst Tuberk — Trudy Kazakhskogo Nauchno-Issledovatel'skogo Instituta Tuberkuleza

Tr Kaz Nauchno Issled Inst Vodn Khoz — Trudy Kazakhskogo Nauchno-Issledovatel'skogo Instituta Vodnogo Khozyaistva

Tr Kaz Nauchno-Issled Inst Zashch Rast — Trudy Kazakhskogo Nauchno-Issledovatel'skogo Instituta Zashchity Rastenii

Tr Kaz Nauchno-Issled Vet Inst — Trudy Kazakhskogo Nauchno-Issledovatel'skogo Veterinarnogo Instituta

Tr Kaz Opytn Stn Pchelovod — Trudy Kazakhskoi Opytnoi Stantsii Pchelovodstva

Tr Kaz Politekh Inst — Trudy Kazakhskogo Politekhnicheskogo Instituta [*Kazakh SSR*]

Tr Kaz S-kh Inst — Trudy Kazakhskogo Sel'skokhozyaistvennogo Instituta

Tr Kaz S-kh Inst Ser Agron — Trudy Kazakhskogo Sel'skokhozyaistvennogo Instituta. Seriya Agronomii

Tr Kemer Obl Gos S-kh Opytn Stn — Trudy Kemerovskoi Oblastnoi Gosudarstvennoi Sel'skokhozyaistvennoi Opytnoi Stantsii

Tr Kerch Ikhtiol Lab — Trudy Kerchenskoi Ikhtiologicheskoi Laboratorii

Tr Kerch Nauchn Rybokhoz Stn — Trudy Kerchenskoi Nauchnoi Rybokhozyaistvennoi Stantsii

Tr Khabar Inst Inzh Zheleznodorozhn Transp — Trudy Khabarovskogo Instituta Inzhenerov Zheleznodorozhnogo Transporta

Tr Khabar Med Inst — Trudy Khabarovskogo Meditsinskogo Instituta

Tr Khabar Politekh Inst — Trudy Khabarobskogo Politekhnicheskogo Instituta

Tr Khar'k Aviats Inst — Trudy Khar'kovskogo Aviatsionnogo Instituta

Tr Khar'k Avtodorozhn Inst — Trudy Khar'kovskogo Avtodorozhnogo Instituta

Tr Khar'k Avtomob Dorozhn Inst — Trudy Khar'kovskogo Avtomobil'no-Dorozhnogo Instituta

Tr Khark Avtomob Dorozhnogo Instituta — Trudy Khar'kovskogo Avtomobil'no-Dorozhnogo Instituta

Tr Khar'k Farm Inst — Trudy Khar'kovskogo Farmatsevticheskogo Instituta

Tr Khark Gos Farm Inst — Trudy Khar'kovskogo Gosudarstvennogo Farmatsevticheskogo Instituta

Tr Khar'k Gos Med Inst — Trudy Khar'kovskii Gosudarstvennyi Meditsinskii Institut

Tr Khark Inst Gorn Mashinostr Avtom Vychisl Tekh — Trudy Khar'kovskogo Instituta Gornogo Mashinostroeniya. Avtomatiki i Vychislitel'noi Tekhniki

Tr Khark Inst Inzh Zheleznodorozhn Transp — Trudy Khar'kovskogo Instituta Inzhenerov Zheleznodorozhnogo Transporta

Tr Khark Inzh Ekon Inst — Trudy Khar'kovskogo Inzhenerno-Ekonomicheskogo Instituta

Tr Khark Khim Tekhnol Inst — Trudy Khar'kovskogo Khimiko-Tekhnologicheskogo Instituta

Tr Khar'k Med Inst — Trudy Khar'kovskogo Meditsinskogo Instituta

Tr Khark Nauchno Issled Khim Farm Inst — Trudy Khar'kovskogo Nauchno-Issledovatel'skogo Khimiko-Farmatsevticheskogo Instituta

Tr Khar'kov Med Inst — Trudy Khar'kovskogo Meditsinskogo Instituta

Tr Khark Politekh Inst — Trudy Khar'kovskogo Politekhnicheskogo Instituta

Tr Khar'k S-kh Inst — Trudy Khar'kovskogo Sel'skokhozyaistvennogo Instituta

Tr Khar'k Skh Inst Im V V Dokuchaeva — Trudy Khar'kovskii Sel'skokhozyaistvennyi Institut Imeni V. V. Dokuchaeva

Tr Khim Inst Im L Ya Karpova — Trudy Khimicheskogo Instituta Imeni L. Ya. Karpova

Tr Khim Khim Tekhnol — Trudy po Khimii i Khimicheskoi Tekhnologii

Tr Khim-Metall Inst Akad Nauk Kaz SSR — Trudy Khimiko-Metallurgicheskogo Instituta Akademiya Nauk Kazakhskoj SSR

Tr Khim Metall Inst Akad Nauk SSSR Sib Otd — Trudy Khimiko-Metallurgicheskogo Instituta Akademiya Nauk SSSR Sibirskoe Otdelenie

Tr Khim Prir Soedin — Trudy po Khimii Prirodnykh Soedinenii

Tr Kiev Politekh Inst — Trudy Kievskogo Politekhnicheskogo Instituta

Tr Kiev Tekhnol Inst Pishch Promsti — Trudy Kievskogo Tekhnologicheskogo Instituta Pishchevoi Promyshlennosti

Tr Kiev Vet Inst — Trudy Kievskogo Veterinarnogo Instituta

Tr Kirg Gos Med Inst — Trudy Kirgizskogo Gosudarstvennogo Meditsinskogo Instituta

Tr Kirg Gos Univ Ser Fiz Nauk — Trudy Kirgizskogo Gosudarstvennogo Universiteta. Seriya Fizicheskikh Nauk

Tr Kirg Inst Epidemiol Mikrobiol Gig — Trudy Kirgizskogo Instituta Epidemiologii, Mikrobiologii, i Gigieny

Tr Kirgiz Nauch Issled Inst Zemled — Trudy Kirgizskogo Nauchno-Issledovatel'skogo Instituta Zemledeliya

Tr Kirg Lesn Opytn Stn — Trudy Kirgizskoi Lesnoi Opytnoi Stantsii

Tr Kirg Nauchno-Issled Inst Onkol Radiol — Trudy Kirgizskogo Nauchno-Issledovatel'skoi Onkologii i Radiologii

Tr Kirg Nauchno-Issled Inst Pochvoved — Trudy Kirgizskogo Nauchno-Issledovatel'skogo Instituta Pochvovedeniya

Tr Kirg Nauchno Issled Inst Zemled — Trudy Kirgizskogo Nauchno-Issledovatel'skogo Instituta Zemledeliya

Tr Kirg Nauchno-Issled Inst Zhivotnovod — Trudy Kirgizskogo Nauchno-Issledovatel'skogo Instituta Zhivotnovodstva

Tr Kirg Nauchno-Issled Inst Zhivotnovod Vet — Trudy Kirgizskogo Nauchno-Issledovatel'skogo Instituta Zhivotnovodstva i Veterinarii

Tr Kirg Opytno-Sel Stn Sakh Svekle — Trudy Kirgizskoi Opytno-Selektsionnoi Stantsii po Sakharnoi Svekle

Tr Kirg Opytn Stn Khlopkovod — Trudy Kirgizskoi Opytnoi Stantsii Khlopkovodstva

Tr Kirg S-kh Inst — Trudy Kirgizskogo Sel'skokhozyaistvennogo Instituta

Tr Kirg Skh Inst Ser Agron — Trudy Kirgizskogo Sel'skokhozyaistvennogo Seriya Agronomii

Tr Kirg Univ Ser Biol Nauk — Trudy Kirgizskogo Universiteta Seriya Biologicheskikh Nauk

Tr Kirov Obl Nauchno Issled Inst Kraeved — Trudy Kirovskogo Oblastnogo Nauchno-Issledovatel'skogo Instituta Kraevedeniya

Tr Kirov Otd Vses Fiziol Ova — Trudy Kirovskogo Otdeleniya Vsesoyuznogo Fiziologicheskogo Obshchestva

Tr Kirov S-kh Inst — Trudy Kirovskogo Sel'skokhozyaistvennogo Instituta

Tr Kishinev Gos Med Inst — Trudy Kishinevskogo Gosudarstvennogo Meditsinskogo Instituta

Tr Kishinev Politekh Inst — Trudy Kishinevskii Politekhnicheskii Institut

Tr Kishinev S-kh Inst — Trudy Kishinevskogo Sel'skokhozyaistvennogo Instituta

Tr Kishinev S-kh Inst Im M V Frunze — Trudy Kishinevskii Sel'skokhozyaistvennyi Institut Imeni M. V. Frunze [*USSR*]

Tr Klin Nervn Bolezn Mosk Obl Nauchno-Issled Klin Inst — Trudy Kliniki Nervnykh Boleznei Moskovskogo Oblastnogo Nauchno-Issledovatel'skogo Klinicheskogo Instituta

Tr Klin Otd Nauchno Issled Inst Gig Tr Profzabol — Trudy Klinicheskogo Otdeleniya Nauchno-Issledovatel'skogo Instituta Gigieny Truda i Profzabolevanii

Tr Kolomenskogo Fil Vses Zaochn Politekh Inst — Trudy Kolomenskogo Filiala Vsesoyuznogo Zaochnogo Politekhnicheskogo Instituta

Tr Kom Anal Khim Akad Nauk SSSR — Trudy Komissii po Analiticheskoi Khimii Akademiya Nauk SSSR [*USSR*]

Tr Kom Borbe s Korroz Met Akad Nauk SSSR — Trudy Komissii po Bor'be s Korroziei Metallov Akademiya Nauk SSSR

Tr Komi Fil Akad Nauk SSSR — Trudy Komi Filiala Akademii Nauk SSSR

Tr Kom Irrig Akad Nauk SSSR — Trudy Komissii po Irrigatsii Akademiya Nauk SSSR

Tr Kom Okhr Prir Ural Fil Akad Nauk SSSR — Trudy Komissii po Okhrane Prirody Ural'skogo Filiala Akademii Nauk SSSR

Tr Kom Pirom Vses Nauchno Issled Inst Metrol — Trudy Komissii po Pirometrii Vsesoyuznyi Nauchno-Issledovatel'skii Institut Metrologii

Tr Kompleksn Eksped Dnepropetr Univ — Trudy Kompleksnoi Ekspeditsii Dnepropetrovskogo Universiteta

Tr Kom Spektros Akad Nauk SSSR — Trudy Komissii po Spektroskopii Akademiya Nauk SSSR [*USSR*]

Tr Koord Soveshch Gidrotekh — Trudy Koordinatsionnykh Soveshchanyi po Gidrotekhnike

Tr Kostrom Skh Inst — Trudy Kostromskogo Sel'skokhozyaistvennogo Instituta "Karavaevo"

Tr Krasnodar Fil Vses Neftegazov Nauchno Issled Inst — Trudy Krasnodarskii Filial Vsesoyuznogo Neftegazovogo Nauchno-Issledovatel'skogo Instituta

Tr Krasnodar Gos Pedagog Inst — Trudy Krasnodarskogo Gosudarstvennogo Pedagogicheskogo Instituta

Tr Krasnodar Inst Pishch Promsti — Trudy Krasnodarskogo Instituta Pishchevoi Promyshlennosti

Tr Krasnodar Nauchno-Issled Inst Pishch Promsti — Trudy Krasnodarskogo Nauchno-Issledovatel'skogo Instituta Pishchevoi Promyshlennosti

Tr Krasnodar Nauchno-Issled Inst Selsk Khoz — Trudy Krasnodarskogo Nauchno-Issledovatel'skogo Instituta Sel'skogog Khozyaistva

Tr Krasnoyarsk Gos Med Inst — Trudy Krasnoyarskogo Gosudarstvennogo Meditsinskogo Instituta

Tr Krasnoyarsk Med Inst — Trudy Krasnoyarskogo Meditsinskogo Instituta

Tr Krasnoyarsk Nauchno Issled Inst Sel'sk Khoz — Trudy Krasnoyarskogo Nauchno-Issledovatel'skogo Instituta Sel'skogo Khozyaistva

Tr Krasnoyarsk S-kh Inst — Trudy Krasnoyarskogo Sel'skokhozyaistvennogo Instituta

Tr Krym Gos Med Inst — Trudy Krymskogo Gosudarstvennogo Meditsinskogo Instituta

Tr Krym Gos Med Inst Im I V Stalina — Trudy Krymskogo Gosudarstvennogo Meditsinskogo Instituta Imeni I. V. Stalina

Tr Krym Gos Skh Opytn Stn — Trudy Krymskoi Gosudarstvennoi Sel'skokhozyaistvennoi Opytnoi Stantsii

Tr Krym Gosud Sel'skokhoz Opyt Sta — Trudy Krymskoi Gosudarstvennoi Sel'skokhozyaistvennoi Opytnoi Stantsii

Tr Krym Med Inst — Trudy Krymskogo Meditsinskogo Instituta

Tr Krym Obl Gos Skh Opytn Stn — Trudy Krymskoi Oblastnoi Gosudarstvennoi Sel'skokhozyaistvennoi Opytnoi Stantsii

Tr Krym Skh Inst — Trudy Krymskogo Sel'skokhozyaistvennogo Instituta

Tr Krym S-kh Inst Im M I Kalinina — Trudy Krymskogo Sel'skokhozyaistvennogo Instituta Imeni M. I. Kalinina

TRKUA — Technology Reports. Kansai University

Tr Kuban Otd Vses Ova Genet Sel — Trudy Kubanskoe Otdelenie Vsesoyuznogo Obshchestva Genetikovi Selektsionerov

Tr Kuban S-kh Inst — Trudy Kubanskogo Sel'skokhozyaistvennogo Instituta

Tr Kuibyshev Aviats Inst — Trudy Kuibyshevskii Aviatsionnyi Institut [*USSR*]

Tr Kuibyshev Gos Nauchno-Issled Inst Neft Prom-sti — Trudy Kuibyshevskii Gosudarstvennyi Nauchno-Issledovatel'skii Institut Neftyanoi Promyshlennosti [*USSR*]

Tr Kuibyshev Inzh-Stroit Inst — Trudy Kuibyshevskii Inzhenerno-Stroitel'nyi Institut

Tr Kuibyshev Med Inst — Trudy Kuibyshevskii Meditsinskii Instituta

Tr Kuibyshev Nauchno-Issled Inst Neft Promsti — Trudy Kuibyshevskii Nauchno-Issledovatel'skii Institut Neftyanoi Promyshlennosti

Tr Kuibyshev S-kh Inst — Trudy Kuibyshevskogo Sel'skokhozyaistvennogo Instituta

Tr Kurgan Mashinostroit Inst — Trudy Kurganskogo Mashinostroitel'nogo Instituta

Tr Kurortol — Trudy po Kurortologii
Tr Kursk Med Inst — Trudy Kurskogo Meditsinskogo Instituta
Tr Kutais Skh Inst — Trudy Kutaisskogo Sel'skokhozyaistvennogo Instituta
Tr Lab Biokhim Fiziol Zhivotn Inst Biol Akad Nauk Latv SSR — Trudy Laboratorii Biokhimii i Fiziologii Zhivotnykh Instituta Biologii Akademiya Nauk Latviiskoi SSR
Tr Lab Eksp Biol Mosk Zooparka — Trudy Laboratorii Eksperimental'noi Biologii Moskovskogo Zooparka
Tr Lab Evol Ekol Fiziol Akad Nauk SSSR Inst Fiziol Rast — Trudy Laboratorii Evolyutsionnoi i Ekologicheskoi Fiziologii Akademiya Nauk SSSR Institut Fiziologii Rastenii
Tr Lab Fiziol Zhivotn Inst Biol Akad Nauk Lit SSR — Trudy Laboratorii Fiziologii Zhivotnykh Instituta Biologii Akademii Nauk Litovskoi SSR
Tr Lab Geol Dokembr Akad Nauk SSSR — Trudy Laboratorii Geologii Dokembriya Akademiya Nauk SSSR
Tr Lab Geol Uglya Akad Nauk SSSR — Trudy Laboratorii Geologii Uglya Akademiya Nauk SSSR
Tr Lab Gidrogeol Probl Akad Nauk SSSR — Trudy Laboratorii Gidrogeologicheskikh Problem Akademiya Nauk SSSR [*USSR*]
Tr Lab Izuch Belka Akad Nauk SSSR — Trudy Laboratorii po Izucheniyu Belka Akademiya Nauk SSSR
Tr Lab Lesoved Akad Nauk SSSR — Trudy Laboratorii Lesovedeniya Akademiya Nauk SSSR
Tr Lab Ozeroved Leningr Gos Univ — Trudy Laboratorii Ozerovedeniya Leningradskii Gosudarstvennyi Universitet
Tr Latviiskogo Nauchno-Issled Inst Zhivotnovod Vet — Trudy Latviiskogo Nauchno-Issledovatel'skogo Instituta Zhivotnovodstva i Veterinarii
Tr Latv Inst Eksp Klin Med Akad Med Nauk SSSR — Trudy Latviiskogo Instituta Eksperimental'noi i Klinicheskoi Meditsiny Akademii Meditsinskikh Nauk SSSR
Tr Latv Nauchno Issled Inst Gidrotekh Melior — Trudy Latviiskogo Nauchno-Issledovatel'skogo Instituta Gidrotekhniki i Melioratsii
Tr Latv Sel'kh Akad — Trudy Latviiskaia Sel'skokhoziaistvennaia Akademiia
Tr Latv S-kh Akad — Trudy Latviiskoi Sel'skokhozyaistvennoi Akademii
Tr Law Guide — Trial Lawyer's Guide
Tr Law Q — Trial Lawyers Quarterly
Tr Legochn Patol Inst Eksp Klin Med Est SSR — Trudy po Legochnoi Patologii Institut Eksperimental'noi i Klinicheskoi Meditsiny Estonskoi SSR
Tr Leningrad Tekhnol Inst Tsellyul-Bumazh Prom — Trudy Leningradskogo Tekhnologicheskogo Instituta Tsellyulozno-Bumazhnoi Promyshlennosti
Tr Leningr Elektrotekh Inst Svyazi — Trudy Leningradskii Elektrotekhnicheskii Institut Svyazi
Tr Leningr Geol Upr — Trudy Leningradskogo Geologicheskogo Upravleniya
Tr Leningr Gidrometeorol Inst — Trudy Leningradskii Gidrometeorologicheskii Institut
Tr Leningr Gos Nauchno Issled Inst Travmatol Ortop — Trudy Leningradskogo Gosudarstvennogo Nauchno-Issledovatel'skogo Instituta Travmatologii i Ortopedii
Tr Leningr Ind Inst — Trudy Leningradskii Industrial'nogo Instituta
Tr Leningr Inst Epidemiol Mikrobiol — Trudy Leningradskogo Instituta Epidemiologii i Mikrobiologii
Tr Leningr Inst Inzh Kommunal'n Stroit — Trudy Leningradskii Institut Inzhenerov Kommunal'nogo Stroitel'stva
Tr Leningr Inst Inzh Zheleznodorozhn Transp — Trudy Leningradskii Institut Inzhenerov Zheleznodorozhnogo Transporta
Tr Leningr Inst Kinoinzh — Trudy Leningradskogo Instituta Kinoinzhenerov
Tr Leningr Inst Sov Torg — Trudy Leningradskii Institut Sovetskoi Torgovli
Tr Leningr Inst Tochn Mekh Opt — Trudy Leningradskii Institut Tochnoi Mekhaniki i Optiki
Tr Leningr Inst Usoversh Vrachei — Trudy Leningradskogo Instituta Usovershenstvovaniya Vrachei
Tr Leningr Inst Vaktsin Syvorotok — Trudy Leningradskogo Instituta Vaktsin i Syvorotok
Tr Leningr Inst Vodn Transp — Trudy Leningradskogo Instituta Vodnogo Transporta
Tr Leningr Inzh Ekon Inst — Trudy Leningradskogo Inzhenerno-Ekonomicheskogo Instituta
Tr Leningr Inzh Ekon Inst Im Pal'miro Tol'yatti — Trudy Leningradskii Inzhenerno-Ekonomicheskii Institut Imeni Pal'miro Tol'yatti
Tr Leningr Khim-Farm Inst — Trudy Leningradskogo Khimiko-Farmatsevticheskogo Instituta
Tr Leningr Khim Tekhnol Inst — Trudy Leningradskogo Khimiko-Tekhnologicheskogo Instituta
Tr Leningr Korablestroit Inst — Trudy Leningradskogo Korablestroitel'nogo Instituta
Tr Leningr Korablestroit'nogo Inst — Trudy Leningradskogo Korablestroitel'nogo Instituta [*USSR*]
Tr Leningr Lesotekh Akad — Trudy Leningradskoi Lesotekhnicheskoi Akademii
Tr Leningr Med Inst — Trudy Leningradskogo Meditsinskogo Instituta
Tr Leningr Mekh Tekhnol Inst Kholod Promsti — Trudy Leningradskogo Mekhaniko-Tekhnologicheskogo Instituta Kholodil'noi Promyshlennosti
Tr Leningr Met Zavod — Trudy Leningradskii Metallicheskii Zavod
Tr Leningr Nauchno-Issled Inst Antibiot — Trudy Leningradskogo Nauchno-Issledovatel'skogo Instituta Antibiotiki

Tr Leningr Nauchno-Issled Inst Epidemiol Mikrobiol — Trudy Leningradskogo Nauchno-Issledovatel'skogo Instituta Epidemiologii i Mikrobiologii
Tr Leningr Nauchno Issled Inst Neirokhir — Trudy Leningradskogo Nauchno-Issledovatel'skogo Instituta Neirokhirurgii
Tr Leningr Nauchno Issled Inst Radiats Gig — Trudy Leningradskogo Nauchno-Issledovatel'skogo Instituta Radiatsii i Gigieny
Tr Leningr Nauchno Issled Inst Tuberk — Trudy Leningradskogo Nauchno-Issledovatel'skogo Instituta Tuberkuleza
Tr Leningr Nauchno-Issled Inst Vaktsin Syvorotok — Trudy Leningradskii Nauchno-Issledovatel'skii Institut Vaktsin i Syvorotok
Tr Leningr Nauchno-Issled Konstr Inst Khim Mashinostr — Trudy Leningradskii Nauchno-Issledovatel'skii i Konstruktorskii Institut Khimicheskogo Mashinostroeniya [*USSR*]
Tr Leningr Nauchno Issled Psikhonevrol Inst — Trudy Leningradskogo Nauchno-Issledovatel'skogo Psikhonevrologisheskogo Instituta
Tr Leningr Nauchno Ova Patologoanat — Trudy Leningradskogo Nauchnogo Obshchestva Patologoanatomov
Tr Leningr Ova Anat Gistol Embriol — Trudy Leningradskogo Obshchestva Anatomov, Gistologov, i Embriologov
Tr Leningr O-va Estestvoispyt — Trudy Leningradskogo Obshchestva Estestvoispytatelei
Tr Leningr Pediatr Med Inst — Trudy Leningradskogo Pediatricheskogo Meditsinskogo Instituta
Tr Leningr Politekh Inst — Trudy Leningradskogo Politekhnicheskogo Instituta Imeni M. I. Kalinina
Tr Leningr Politekh Inst Im M I Kalinina — Trudy Leningradskogo Politekhnicheskogo Instituta Imeni M. I. Kalinina [*USSR*]
Tr Leningr Sanit-Gig Med Inst — Trudy Leningradskogo Sanitarno-Gigienicheskogo Meditsinskogo Instituta
Tr Leningr Tekhnol Inst Im Lensoveta — Trudy Leningradskogo Tekhnologicheskogo Instituta Imeni Lensoveta
Tr Leningr Tekhnol Inst Kholod Prom-St' — Trudy Leningradskogo Tekhnologicheskogo Instituta Kholodil'noi Promyshlennosti
Tr Leningr Tekhnol Inst Pishch Prom-sti — Trudy Leningradskogo Tekhnologicheskogo Instituta Pishchevoi Promyshlennosti
Tr Leningr Tekhnol Inst Tsellyul Bum Promsti — Trudy Leningradskogo Tekhnologicheskogo Instituta Tsellyulozno-Bumazhnoi Promyshlennosti
Tr Leningr Teknol Inst — Trudy Leningradskogo Teknologicheskogo Instituta [*USSR*]
Tr Leningr Tekst Inst — Trudy Leningradskogo Tekstil'nogo Instituta
Tr Leningr Tsentr Gos Travmatol Inst — Trudy Leningradskogo Tsentral'nogo Gosudarstvennogo Travmatologicheskogo Instituta
Tr Leningr Voen Mekh Inst — Trudy Leningradskii Voenno-Mekhanicheskii Institut
Tr Lesotekh Akad — Trudy Lesotekhnicheskoi Akademii
TRLGA — Translog
Tr Limnol Inst Sib Otd Akad Nauk SSSR — Trudy Limnologicheskogo Instituta Siberskogo Otdeleniya. Akademii Nauk SSSR
Tr Litov Inst Eksp Klin Med Akad Med Nauk SSSR — Trudy Litovskogo Instituta Eksperimental'noi i Klinicheskoi Meditsiny Akademii Meditsinskikh Nauk SSSR
Tr Litov Inst Eksp Med Akad Med Nauk SSSR — Trudy Litovskogo Instituta Eksperimental'noi Meditsiny Akademii Meditsinskikh Nauk SSSR
Tr Litov Nauchno Issled Geologorazves Inst — Trudy Litovskogo Nauchno-Issledovatel'skogo Geologorazvedochnogo Instituta
Tr Litov Nauchno Issled Inst Lesn Khoz — Trudy Litovskogo Nauchno-Issledovatel'skogo Instituta Lesnogo Khozyaistva
Tr Litov Nauchno Issled Inst Vet — Trudy Litovskogo Nauchno-Issledovatel'skogo Instituta Veterinarii
Tr LNIIA — Trudy LNIIA [*Leningrad Nauchno-Issledovatel'skii Institut Antibiotikov*]
Tr Lugansk S-kh Inst — Trudy Luganskogo Sel'skokhozyaistvennoi Instituta
TRM — Topics in Health Records Management
Tr M — Traditional Music
Tr Magadan Zon Nauchno Issled Inst Selsk Khoz Sev Vostoka — Trudy Magadanskogo Zonal'nogo Nauchno-Issledovatel'skogo Instituta Sel'skogo Khozyaistva Severo-Vostoka
Tr Marii Gos Pedagog Inst — Trudy Mariiskii Gosudarstvennyi Pedagogicheskii Institut
Tr Mater Donetsk Med Inst — Trudy i Materialy Donetskii Meditsinskii Institut
Tr Mater Donetsk Nauchno Issled Inst Fiziol Tr — Trudy i Materialy Donetskii Nauchno-Issledovatel'skii Institut Fiziologii Truda
Tr Mater Leningr Inst Organ Okhr Tr — Trudy i Materialy Leningradskii Institut Organizatsii i Okhrany Truda
Tr Mater Nauchno Issled Inst Fiziol Tr (Stalino) — Trudy i Materialy Nauchno-Issledovatel'skii Institut Fiziologii Truda (Stalino)
Tr Mater Pervogo Ukr Inst Rab Med — Trudy i Materialy Pervogo Ukrainskogo Instituta Rabochei Meditsiny
Tr Mater Ukr Gos Inst Patol Gig Tr — Trudy i Materialy Ukrainskogo Gosudarstvennogo Instituta Patologii i Gigieny Truda
Tr Mater Ukr Gos Inst Rab Med — Trudy i Materialy Ukrainskogo Gosudarstvennogo Instituta Rabochei Meditsiny
Tr Mater Ukr Tsentr Inst Gig Tr Profzabol — Trudy i Materialy Ukrainskii Tsentral'nyi Institut Gigieny Truda i Profzabolevanii

Tr Mat Inst Akad Nauk SSSR — Trudy Matematicheskogo Instituta Akademiya Nauk SSSR

TRMCA — Transition Metal Chemistry [*New York*]

TRMEA — Trattamenti dei Metalli

Tr Med and Phys Soc Bombay — Transactions. Medical and Physical Society of Bombay

Tr Metrol Inst SSSR — Trudy Metrologicheskih Institutov SSSR

Tr Mezhdunar Konf Fiz Vys Energ — Trudy Mezhdunarodnaya Konferentsiya po Fizike Vysokikh Energii

Tr Mezhdunar Simp Geterog Katal — Trudy Mezhdunarodnogo Simpoziuma po Geterogennomu Katalizu

Tr Mezhdunar Simp Tsitoekol — Trudy Mezhdunarodnogo Simpoziuma po Tsitoekologii

Tr MFTI Ser "Obshch Mol Fiz" — Trudy Moskovskogo Fiziko-Tekhnicheskogo Instituta. Seriya "Obshchaya i Molekulyarnaya Fizika"

Tr Mineral Inst Akad Nauk SSSR — Trudy Mineralogicheskogo Instituta Akademiya Nauk SSSR

Tr Mineral Muz Akad Nauk SSSR — Trudy Mineralogicheskogo Muzeya Akademiya Nauk SSSR [*USSR*]

Tr Minniya Nauchnoizsled Proekto Konstr Inst — Trudove na Minniya Nauchnoizsledovatelski i Proektno Konstruktorski Institut

Tr Minsk Gos Med Inst — Trudy Minskogo Gosudarstvennogo Meditsinskogo Instituta

Tr Moldav Nauch Issled Inst Orosh Zemled Ovoshchev — Trudy Moldavskogo Nauchno-Issledovatel'skogo Instituta Oroshaemogo Zemledeliya i Ovoshchevodstva

Tr Mold Nauchno Issled Inst Epidemiol Mikrobiol Gig — Trudy Moldavskii Nauchno-Issledovatel'skii Institut Epidemiologii, Mikrobiologii, i Gigieny

Tr Mold Nauchno Issled Inst Gig Epidemiol — Trudy Moldavskii Nauchno-Issledovatel'skii Institut Gigieny i Epidemiologii

Tr Mold Nauchno Issled Inst Oroshaemogo Zemled Ovoshchevod — Trudy Moldavskogo Nauchno-Issledovatel'skogo Instituta Oroshaemogo Zemledeliya i Ovoshchevodstva

Tr Mold Nauchno-Issled Inst Orosh Zemled Ovoshchevod — Trudy Moldavskogo Nauchno-Issledovatel'skogo Instituta Oroshaemogo Zemledeliya i Ovoshchevodstva

Tr Mold Nauchno Issled Inst Pishch Promsti — Trudy Moldavskogo Nauchno-Issledovatel'skogo Instituta Pishchevoi Promyshlennosti

Tr Mold Nauchno Issled Inst Tuberk — Trudy Moldavskogo Nauchno-Issledovatel'nogo Instituta Tuberkuleza

Tr Mold Nauchno Issled Inst Zhivotnovod Vet — Trudy Moldavskii Nauchno-Issledovatel'skii Institut Zhivotnovodstva i Veterinarii

Tr Molodykh Uch Dagest Nauchno Issled Inst Selsk Khoz — Trudy Molodykh Uchenykh Dagestanskii Nauchno-Issledovatel'skii Institut Sel'skogo Khozyaistva

Tr Molodykh Uch Spets Chuv Skh Inst — Trudy Molodykh Uchenykh Spetsial'nogo Chuvashskogo Sel'skokhozyaistvennogo Instituta

Tr Molodykh Uch Ukr Skh Akad — Trudy Molodykh Uchenykh Ukrainskoi Sel'skokhozyaistvennoi Akademii

Tr Molodykh Uch Yakutsk Univ — Trudy Molodykh Uchenykh Yakutskogo Universiteta

Tr Molotov Gos Med Inst — Trudy Molotovskogo Gosudarstvennogo Meditsinskogo Instituta

Tr Mord Gos Zapovednika Im PG Smirovicha — Trudy Mordovskogo Gosudarstvennogo Zapovednika Imeni P. G. Smirovicha

Tr Morsk Biol Stn Stalin — Trudove na Morskata Biologichna Stantsiya v Stalin

Tr Morsk Gidrofiz Inst Akad Nauk Ukr SSR — Trudy Morskogo Gidrofizicheskogo Instituta Akademiya Nauk Ukrainskoj SSR

Tr Morsk Rybn Inst Ser A (Gdynia Pol) — Trudy Morskogo Rybnogo Instituta. Seriya A. Okeanografiya i Promyslovaya Ikhtiologiya (Gdynia, Poland)

Tr Morsk Rybn Inst Ser B (Gdynia Pol) — Trudy Morskogo Rybnogo Instituta. Seriya B (Gdynia, Poland)

Tr Mosk Aviats Inst Im S Ordzhonikidze Sb Statei — Trudy Moskovskij Aviatsionnyj Institut Imeni S. Ordzhonikidze Sbornik Statei [*USSR*]

Tr Mosk Aviats Tekhnol Inst — Trudy Moskovskij Aviatsionnyj Tekhnologicheskij Institut

Tr Mosk Avtomob Dorozhn Inst — Trudy Moskovskogo Avtomobil'no Dorozhnogo Instituta

Tr Mosk Ehnerg Inst — Trudy Moskovskogo Ordena Lenina Ehnergiticheskogo Instituta

Tr Mosk Energ Inst — Trudy Moskovskogo Energeticheskogo Instituta [*USSR*]

Tr Mosk Energ Inst Fiz — Trudy Moskovskogo Energeticheskogo Instituta Fizika [*USSR*]

Tr Mosk Fiz Tekh Inst — Trudy Moskovskii Fiziko-Tekhnicheskii Institut

Tr Mosk Fiz Tekh Inst Ser "Obshch Mol Fiz" — Trudy Moskovskogo Fiziko-Tekhnicheskogo Instituta. Seriya "Obshchaya i Molekulyarnaya Fizika"

Tr Mosk Geol Razved Inst — Trudy Moskovskogo Geologo-Razvedochnogo Instituta

Tr Mosk Geol Upr — Trudy Moskovskogo Geologicheskogo Upravlenie

Tr Mosk Gor Bakteriol Inst — Trudy Moskovskii Gorodskoi Bakteriologicheskii Institut

Tr Mosk Gor Inst Epidemiol Bakteriol — Trudy Moskovskii Gorodskoi Institut Epidemiologii i Bakteriologii

Tr Mosk Gor Nauchno Issled Inst Epidemiol Bakteriol — Trudy Moskovskii Gorodskoi Nauchno-Issledovatel'skii Institut Epidemiologii i Bakteriologii

Tr Mosk Gor Nauchno Issled Inst Skoroi Pomoshchi — Trudy Moskovskogo Gorodskogo Nauchno-Issledovatel'skogo Instituta Skoroi Promoshchi

Tr Mosk Gorn Inst — Trudy Moskovskogo Gornogo Instituta

Tr Mosk Inst Elektron Mashinostr — Trudy Moskovskii Institut Elektronnogo Mashinostroeniya [*USSR*]

Tr Mosk Inst Epidemiol Mikrobiol Gig — Trudy Moskovskii Institut Epidemiologii, Mikrobiologii, i Gigieny

Tr Mosk Inst Inzh Gor Stroit — Trudy Moskovskogo Instituta Inzhenerov Gorodskogo Stroitel'stva

Tr Mosk Inst Inzh Zheleznodorozhn Transp — Trudy Moskovskogo Instituta Inzhenerov Zheleznodorozhnogo Transporta

Tr Mosk Inst Khim Mashinostr — Trudy Moskovskogo Instituta Khimicheskogo Mashinostroeniya

Tr Mosk Inst Nar Khoz — Trudy Moskovskogo Instituta Narodnogo Khozyaistva

Tr Mosk Inst Neftekhim Gazov Prom-sti Im I M Gubkina — Trudy Moskovskii Institut Neftekhimicheskoi i Gazovoi Promyshlennosti Imeni I. M. Gubkina [*USSR*]

Tr Mosk Inst Neftekhim Gaz Promsti — Trudy Moskovskii Institut Neftekhimicheskoi i Gazovoi Promyshlennosti

Tr Mosk Inst Radiotekh Elektron Avtom — Trudy Moskovskogo Instituta Radiotekhniki, Elektroniki, i Avtomatiki

Tr Mosk Inst Tonkoi Khim Tekhnol — Trudy Moskovskogo Instituta Tonkoi Khimicheskoi Tekhnologii

Tr Mosk Inzh Ekon Inst — Trudy Moskovskogo Inzhenerno-Ekonomicheskogo Instituta

Tr Mosk Khim-Tekhnol Inst — Trudy Moskovskogo Khimiko-Tekhnologicheskogo Instituta Imeni D. I. Mendeleeva

Tr Mosk Mat O-va — Trudy Moskovskogo Matematicheskogo Obshchestva

Tr Mosk Med Stomatol Inst — Trudy Moskovskogo Meditsinskogo Stomatologichesko Instituta

Tr Mosk Nauchno-Issled Inst Epidemiol Mikrobiol — Trudy Moskovskogo Nauchno-Issledovatel'skogo Instituta Epidemiologii i Mikrobiologii

Tr Mosk Nauchno Issled Inst Epidemiol Mikrobiol Gig — Trudy Moskovskii Nauchno-Issledovatel'skii Institut Epidemiologii, Mikrobiologii, i Gigieny

Tr Mosk Nauchno-Issled Inst Psikhiatr — Trudy Moskovskogo Nauchno-Issledovatel'skogo Instituta Psikhiatrii

Tr Mosk Nauchno-Issled Inst Ukha Gorla Nosa — Trudy Moskovskogo Nauchno-Issledovatel'skogo Instituta Ukha Gorla i Nosa

Tr Mosk Nauchno Issled Inst Virusn Prep — Trudy Moskovskii Nauchno-Issledovatel'skii Institut Virusnykh Preparatov

Tr Mosk Neft Inst — Trudy Moskovskii Neftyanoi Institut

Tr Mosk Obl Nauchno Issled Klin Inst Prakt Nevropatol — Trudy Moskovskogo Oblastnogo Nauchno-Issledovatel'skogo Klinicheskogo Instituta Prakticheskoi Nevropatologii

Tr Mosk Obshch Ispyt Prir Otedel Biol — Trudy Moskovskoe Obshchestvo Ispytatelei Prirody Otedel Biologicheskii

Tr Mosk O-va Ispyt Prir — Trudy Moskovskogo Obshchestva Ispytatelei Prirody [*USSR*]

Tr Mosk O-va Ispyt Prir Otd Biol — Trudy Moskovskogo Obshchestva Ispytatelei Prirody Otdel Biologicheskii [*USSR*]

Tr Mosk Radiotekh Elektron Avtomat — Trudy Moskovskogo Instituta Radiotekhniki, Elektroniki, i Avtomatiki [*USSR*]

Tr Mosk Tekh Inst Rybn Prom-sti Khoz — Trudy Moskovskogo Tekhnologicheskogo Instituta Rybnoi Promyshlennosti i Khozyaistva [*USSR*]

Tr Mosk Tekhnol Inst Myasn Molochn Promsti — Trudy. Moskovskii Tekhnologicheskii Institut Myasnoi i Molochnoi Promyshlennosti

Tr Mosk Tekhnol Inst Myasn Molochn Prom-sti — Trudy Moskovskogo Tekhnologicheskogo Instituta Myasnoi Molochnoi Promyshlennosti

Tr Mosk Tekhnol Inst Pishch Promsti — Trudy. Moskovskii Tekhnologicheskii Institut Pishchevoi Promyshlennosti

Tr Mosk Torf Inst — Trudy Moskovskogo Torfyanogo Instituta

Tr Mosk Vet Akad — Trudy Moskovskoi Veterinarnoi Akademii

Tr Mosk Vyssh Tekh Uchil — Trudy Moskovskogo Vysshego Tekhnicheskogo Uchilishcha [*USSR*]

Tr Murm Biol Stn — Trudy Murmanskoi Biologicheskoi Stantsii

Tr Murm Morsk Biol Inst — Trudy Murmanskogo Morskogo Biologicheskogo Instituta

Tr Nakhich Kompleksn Zon Opytn Stn — Trudy Nakhichevanskoi Kompleksnoi Zonal'noi Opytnoi Stantsii

Tr Nakhich Kompleksn Zon Stn — Trudy Nakhichevanskaya Kompleksnaya Zonal'naya Stantsiya

Tr Nauch Issled Inst Klopkovod (Tashkent) — Trudy Nauchno-Issledovatel'skii Institut po Khlopkovodstvu (Tashkent)

Tr Nauchn Konf Stalinskogo Gos Pedagog Inst — Trudy Nauchnoi Konferentsii Stalinskogo Gosudarstvennogo Pedagogicheskogo Instituta

Tr Nauchn Korresp Inst Stroit Dela Akad Nauk Gruz SSR — Trudy Nauchnykh Korrespondentov Instituta Stroitel'nogo Dela Akademiya Nauk Gruzinskoi SSR

Tr Nauchno-Issled Gidrometerol Inst (Alma-Ata) — Trudy Nauchno-Issledovatel'skogo Gidrometeorologicheskogo Instituta (Alma-Ata) [*Kazakh SSR*]

Tr Nauchno-Issled Inst Betona Zhelezobetona — Trudy Nauchno-Issledovatel'skogo Instituta Betona i Zhelezobetona [*USSR*]

Tr Nauchno-Issled Inst Biol Khar'k Gos Univ — Trudy Nauchno-Issledovatel'skogo Instituta Biologii Khar'kovskogo Gosudarstvennogo Universiteta

Tr Nauchno-Issled Inst Dobyche Pererab Slantsev — Trudy Nauchno-Issledovatel'skogo Instituta po Dobyche i Pererabotke Slantsev [*USSR*]

Tr Nauchno-Issled Inst Eksp Klin Ter Gruz SSR — Trudy Nauchno-Issledovatel'skogo Instituta Eksperimental'noi i Klinicheskoi Terapii Gruzinskoi SSR

Tr Nauchno-Issled Inst Epidemiol Mikrobiol — Trudy Nauchno-Issledovatel'skogo Instituta Epidemiologii i Mikrobiologii

Tr Nauchno Issled Inst Fiziol — Trudy Nauchno-Issledovatel'skogo Instituta Fiziologii

Tr Nauchno Issled Inst Fiziol Patol Zhen — Trudy Nauchno-Issledovatel'skogo Instituta Fiziologii i Patologii Zhenshchiny

Tr Nauchno-Issled Inst Geol Arktiki — Trudy Nauchno-Issledovatel'skogo Instituta Geologii Arktiki [*USSR*]

Tr Nauchno Issled Inst Geol Mineral — Trudy Nauchno-Issledovatel'skogo Instituta Geologii i Mineralogii

Tr Nauchno Issled Inst Gidrometeorol Priborostr — Trudy Nauchno-Issledovatel'skii Institut Gidrometeorologicheskogo Priborostroeniya

Tr Nauchno Issled Inst Gig Vodn Transp — Trudy Nauchno-Issledovatel'skogo Instituta Gigieny Vodnoi Transportatsii

Tr Nauchno Issled Inst Kabeln Prom — Trudy Nauchno-Issledovatel'skogo Instituta Kabel'noi Promyshlennosti

Tr Nauchno Issled Inst Kamnya Silik — Trudy Nauchno-Issledovatel'skogo Instituta Kamnya i Silikatov

Tr Nauchno-Issled Inst Kartofel'nogo Khoz — Trudy Nauchno-Issledovatel'skogo Instituta Kartofel'nogo Khozyaistva

Tr Nauchno Issled Inst Klin Eksp Khir — Trudy Nauchno-Issledovatel'skogo Instituta Klinicheskoi i Eksperimental'noi Khirurgii

Tr Nauchno-Issled Inst Kraev Patol (Alma-Ata) — Trudy Nauchno-Issledovatel'skogo Instituta Kraevoi Patologii (Alma-Ata)

Tr Nauchno-Issled Inst Legk Met — Trudy Nauchno-Issledovatel'skogo Instituta Legkikh Metallov

Tr Nauchno-Issled Inst Med Parazitol Trop Med Gruz SSR — Trudy Nauchno-Issledovatel'skogo Instituta Meditsinskoi Parazitologii i Tropicheskoi Meditsiny Gruzinskoi SSR

Tr Nauchno Issled Inst Mekh Rybn Promsti — Trudy Nauchno-Issledovatel'skogo Instituta Mekhanizatsii Rybnoi Promyshlennosti

Tr Nauchno Issled Inst Mestnoi Topl Promsti — Trudy Nauchno-Issledovatel'skogo Instituta Mestnoi i Toplivnoi Promyshlennosti

Tr Nauchno Issled Inst Minist Radiotekh Promsti SSSR — Trudy Nauchno-Issledovatel'skogo Instituta Ministerstvo Radiotekhnicheskoi Promyshlennosti SSSR

Tr Nauchno Issled Inst Neftekhim Proizvod — Trudy Nauchno-Issledovatel'skii Institut Neftekhimicheskikh Proizvodstv

Tr Nauchno Issled Inst Okhr Tr Prof Zabol — Trudy Nauchno-Issledovatel'skogo Instituta Okhrany Truda i Professional'nykh Zabolevanii

Tr Nauchno-Issled Inst Onkol Gruz SSR — Trudy Nauchno-Issledovatel'skogo Instituta Onkologii Gruzinskoi SSR

Tr Nauchno Issled Inst Onkol (Tiflis) — Trudy Nauchno-Issledovatel'skii Institut Onkologii (Tiflis)

Tr Nauchno Issled Inst Osnovnoi Khim — Trudy Nauchno-Issledovatel'skogo Instituta Osnovnoi Khimii

Tr Nauchno Issled Inst Pishch Promsti — Trudy Nauchno-Issledovatel'skogo Instituta Pishchevoi Promyshlennosti

Tr Nauchno Issled Inst Pochvoved Agrokhim Melior (Tiflis) — Trudy Nauchno-Issledovatel'skogo Instituta Pochvovedeniya Agrokhimii i Melioratsii (Tiflis)

Tr Nauchno Issled Inst Pochvoved Agrokhim Yerevan — Trudy Nauchno-Issledovatel'skogo Instituta Pochvovedeniya i Agrokhimii Yerevan

Tr Nauchno-Issled Inst Profil Pnevmokoniozov — Trudy Nauchno-Issledovatel'skogo Instituta Profilaktiki i Pnevmokoniozov

Tr Nauchno-Issled Inst Rentgenol Radiol Onkol Az SSR — Trudy Nauchno-Issledovatel'skogo Instituta Rentgenologii Radiologii i Onkologii Azerbaidzhanskoi SSR

Tr Nauchno-Issled Inst Sel'sk Khoz Krainego Sev — Trudy Nauchno-Issledovatel'skogo Instituta Sel'skogo Khozyaistva Krainego Severa

Tr Nauchno Issled Inst Sin Spirtov Org Prod — Trudy Nauchno-Issledovatel'skii Institut Sinteticheskikh Spirtov i Organicheskikh Produktov

Tr Nauchno-Issled Inst Slantsev — Trudy Nauchno-Issledovatel'skogo Instituta Slantsev [*USSR*]

Tr Nauchno Issled Inst Teploenerg Priborostr — Trudy Nauchno-Issledovatel'skii Institut Teploenergeticheskogo Priborostroeniya

Tr Nauchno Issled Inst Transp Khraneniyu Nefti Nefteprod — Trudy Nauchno-Issledovatel'skogo Institut po Transportu i Khraneniyu Nefti i Nefteproduktov

Tr Nauchno Issled Inst Tuberk — Trudy Nauchno-Issledovatel'skogo Instituta Tuberkuleza

Tr Nauchno-Issled Inst Udobr Insektofungits — Trudy Nauchno-Issledovatel'skii Institut po Udobreniyam i Insektofungitsidam [*USSR*]

Tr Nauchno Issled Inst Virusol Mikrobiol Gig — Trudy Nauchno-Issledovatel'skogo Instituta Virusologii Mikrobiologii Gigieny

Tr Nauchno Issled Inst Zashch Rast Uzb SSR — Trudy Nauchno-Issledovatel'skogo Instituta Zashchity Rastenii Uzbekskoi SSR

Tr Nauchno Issled Inst Zhivotnovod (Tashkent) — Trudy Nauchno-Issledovatel'skogo Instituta Zhivotnovodstva (Tashkent)

Tr Nauchno Issled Inst Zhivotnovod Uzb Akad Skh Nauk — Trudy Nauchno-Issledovatel'skogo Instituta Zhivotnovodstva. Uzbekskaya Akademiya Sel'skokhozyaistvennykh Nauk

Tr Nauchno Issled Khim Inst Mosk Univ — Trudy Nauchno-Issledovatel'skogo Khimicheskogo Instituta Moskovskii Universitet

Tr Nauchno Issled Konstr Inst Mekh Rybn Prom-sti — Trudy Nauchno-Issledovatel'skogo i Konstruktorskogo Instituta Mekhanizatsii Rybnoi Promyshlennosti

Tr Nauchno Issled Lab Geol Zarub Stran — Trudy Nauchno-Issledovatel'skaya Laboratoriya Geologii Zarubezhnykh Stran

Tr Nauchno Issled Proektn Inst Mekh Obrab Polezn Iskop — Trudy Nauchno-Issledovatel'skii i Proektnyi Institut Mekhanicheskoi Obrabotki Poleznykh Iskopaemykh

Tr Nauchno Issled Protivochumn Inst Kavk Zakavk — Trudy Nauchno-Issledovatel'skogo Protivochumnogo Instituta Kavkaza i Zakavkaz'ya

Tr Nauchno Issled Sekt Mosk Fil Inst "Orgenergostroi" — Trudy Nauchno-Issledovatel'skogo Sektora Moskovskogo Filiala Instituta "Orgenergostroi"

Tr Nauchno Issled Sel'sk Khoz Krainego Sev — Trudy Nauchno-Issledovatel'skogo Instituta Sel'skogo Khozyaistva Krainego Severa

Tr Nauchno Issled Tekhnokhim Inst Bytovogo Obsluzhivaniya — Trudy Nauchno-Issledovatel'skogo Tekhnokhimicheskogo Instituta Bytovogo Obsluzhivaniya

Tr Nauchno Issled Vet Inst Tadzh SSR — Trudy Nauchno-Issledovatel'skogo Veterinarnogo Instituta Tadzhikskoi SSR

Tr Nauchnoizsled Inst Cherna Metal — Trudove na Nauchnoizsledovatelskiya Institut po Cherna Metallurgiya

Tr Nauchnoizsled Inst Epidemio Mikrobiol — Trudove na Nauchnoizsledovatelskiya Instituta po Epidemiologiya i Mikrobiologiya

Tr Nauchnoizsled Inst Okhr Tr Prof Zabol — Trudove na Nauchnoizsledovatelskiya Instituta po Okhrana na Truda i Profesionalnite Zabolyavaniya

Tr Nauchnoizsled Inst Stroit Mater (Sofia) — Trudove na Nauchnoizsledovatelskiya Instituta po Stroitelni Materiali (Sofia)

Tr Nauchnoizsled Inst Vodosnabdyavane Kanaliz Sanit Tekh — Trudove na Nauchnoizsledovatelskiya Institut po Vodosnabdyavane. Kanalizatsiya i Sanitarna Tekhnika [*Bulgaria*]

Tr Nauchnoizsled Inst Vodosnabyavane Kanaliz Sanit Tekh — Trudove na Nauchnoizsledovatelskiya Institut po Vodosnabyavane Kanalizatsiya i Sanitarna Tekhnika

Tr Nauchnoizsled Khim Farm Inst — Trudove na Nauchnoizsledovatelskiya Khimiko-Farmatsevtichen Institut

Tr Nauchnoizsled Proektokonstr Tekhnol Inst Tekst Promst — Trudove na Nauchnoizsledovatelskiya. Proektokonstruktorski i Tekhnologicheski Institut po Tekstilna Promishlenost

Tr Nauchno Khim Farm Inst — Trudy Nauchnogo Khimiko Farmatsevtcheskogo Instituta

Tr Nauchno Proizvod Konf Agron Buryat Zoovet Inst — Trudy Nauchno-Proizvodstvennoi Konferentsii po Agronomii Buryatskii Zooveterinarnyi Institut

Tr Nauchno-Tekh Konf Leningr Elek-Tekh Inst Svyazi — Trudy Nauchno-Tekhnicheskoi Konferentsii Leningradskogo Elektro-Tekhnicheskogo Instituta Svyazi [*USSR*]

Tr Nauchno Tekh Konf Leningr Elektrotekh Inst Svyazi — Trudy Nauchno-Tekhnicheskoi Konferentsii Leningradskogo Elektrotekhnicheskogo Instituta Svyazi

Tr Nauchno Tekh Ova Chern Metall — Trudy Nauchno-Tekhnicheskogo Obshchestva Chernoi Metallurgii

Tr Nauchn Ova Stud Erevan Gos Univ — Trudy Nauchnogo Obshchestva Studentov Erevanskii Gosudarstvennyi Universitet

TRNF — Theologische Rundschau. Neue Folge

TRNGA — Traffic Engineering [*United States*]

Tr NII Metrol Vyssh Uchebn Zaved — Trudy NII [*Nauchno-Issledovatel'skogo Instituta*] Metrologii Vysshikh Uchebnykh Zavedeniy [*USSR*]

Tr Nikitsk Bot Sada — Trudy Nikitskogo Botanicheskogo Sada

Tr Nikolaev Korablestroit Inst — Trudy Nikolaevskogo Korablestroitel'nogo Instituta

Tr NIRMMI — Trudy NIRMMI

Tr Nizhnednepr Nauchno-Issled Stn Obleseniyu Peskov — Trudy Nizhnedneprovskoi Nauchno-Issledovatel'skoi Stantsii po Obleseniyu Peskov

Tr Nizhnevolzh Nauchno Issled Inst Geol Geofiz — Trudy Nizhnevolzhskogo Nauchno-Issledovatel'skogo Instituta Geologii i Geofiziki

TRNJA — Transportation Journal

Tr Norilsk Vech Ind Inst — Trudy Noril'skogo Vechernego Industrial'nogo Instituta

Tr Nov Appar Metod — Trudy po Novoi Apparature i Metodikam

Tr Novocherkassk Politekh Inst — Trudy Novocherkasskogo Politekhnicheskogo Instituta [*USSR*]

Tr Novocherk Inzh Melior Inst — Trudy Novocherkasskogo Inzhenerno-Meliorativnogo Instituta

Tr Novocherk Politekh Inst — Trudy Novocherkasskogo Politekhnicheskogo Instituta

Tr Novocherk Vet Inst — Trudy Novocherkasskogo Veterinarnogo Instituta

Tr Novocherk Zootekh Vet Inst — Trudy Novocherkasskogo Zootekhnichesko-Veterinarnogo Instituta

Tr Novokuz Gos Inst Usoversh Vrachei — Trudy Novokuznetskogo Gosudarstvennogo Instituta Usovershenstvovaniya Vrachei

Tr Novokuz Gos Pedagog Inst — Trudy Novokuznetskogo Gosudarstvennogo Pedagogicheskogo Instituta

Tr Novosib Gos Med Inst — Trudy Novosibirskogo Gosudarstvennogo Meditsinskogo Instituta

Tr Novosib Inst Inzh Zheleznodorozhn Transp — Trudy Novosibirskogo Instituta Inzhenerov Zheleznodorozhnogo Transporta

Tr Novosib Inzh Stroit Inst — Trudy Novosibirskogo Inzhenerno-Stroitel'nogo Instituta

Tr Odess Gidrometeorol Inst — Trudy Odesskogo Gidrometeorologicheskogo Instituta

Tr Odess Nauchno-Issled Inst Epidemiol Mikrobiol — Trudy Odesskogo Nauchno-Issledovatel'skogo Instituta Epidemiologii i Mikrobiologii

Tr Odess S-kh Inst — Trudy Odesskogo Sel'skokhozyaistvennogo Instituta

Tr Odess Tekhnol Inst — Trudy Odesskogo Tekhnologicheskogo Instituta

Tr Odess Tekhnol Inst Konservn Promsti — Trudy Odesskogo Tekhnologicheskogo Instituta Konservnoi Promyshlennosti

Tr Odess Tekhnol Inst Pishch Kholod Promsti — Trudy Odesskogo Tekhnologicheskogo Instituta Pishchevoi i Kholodil'noi Promyshlennosti

TROEA — Tekko Rodo Eisei [*Japan*]

T Rom — Trubuna Romaniei

Tr Omsk Gos Nauchno-Issled Inst Epidemiol Mikrobiol Gig — Trudy Omskogo Gosudarstvennogo Nauchno-Issledovatel'skogo Instituta Epidemiologii Mikrobiologii i Gigieny

Tr Omsk Inst Molochn Khoz Omsk Zon Stn Molochn Khoz — Trudy Omskogo Instituta Molochnogo Khozyaistva i Omskoi Zonal'noi Stantsii po Molochnomu Khozyaistvu

Tr Omsk Med Inst Im M I Kalinina — Trudy Omskogo Meditsinskogo Instituta Imeni M. I. Kalinina

Tromso Mus Skr — Tromsoe Museum. Skrifter

Trop — Tropical Agriculture

Trop Abstr — Tropical Abstracts

Trop Agr — Tropical Agriculture

Trop Agr (Ceylon) — Tropical Agriculturist (Ceylon)

Trop Agric — Tropical Agriculture

Trop Agric (Colombo) — Tropical Agriculturist (Colombo)

Trop Agri (Ceylon) — Tropical Agriculturist (Ceylon)

Trop Agric Res Ser — Tropical Agriculture Research Series

Trop Agric Res Ser (Japan) — Tropical Agriculture Research Series (Japan)

Trop Agricst Mag Ceylon Agric Soc — Tropical Agriculturist and Magazine. Ceylon Agricultural Society

Trop Agron Tech Memo Aust CSIRO Div Trop Crops Pastures — Australia. Commonwealth Scientific and Industrial Research Organisation. Division of Tropical Crops and Pastures. Tropical Agronomy. Technical Memorandum

Trop Anim Health Prod — Tropical Animal Health and Production

Trop Anim Prod — Tropical Animal Production [*Dominican Republic*]

TROPB — Tropenlandwirt

Trop Build Res Notes Div Build Res CSIRO — Tropical Building Research Notes. Division of Building Research. Commonwealth Scientific and Industrial Research Organisation

Trop Dis Bull — Tropical Diseases Bulletin

Trop Doct — Tropical Doctor

Trop Ecol — Tropical Ecology

Tropenlandwirt (Germany FR) — Tropenlandwirtschaft (Germany, Federal Republic)

Tropenmed P — Tropenmedizin und Parasitologie

Tropenmed Parasitol — Tropenmedizin und Parasitologie

Trop For Notes — Tropical Forest Notes

Trop Geogr Med — Tropical and Geographical Medicine

Trop Geo Me — Tropical and Geographical Medicine

Trop Grain Legume Bull — Tropical Grain Legume Bulletin

Trop Grassl — Tropical Grasslands

Trop Grasslands — Tropical Grasslands

Trop Grasslds — Tropical Grasslands

Trophoblast Res — Trophoblast Research

Tropical Ag — Tropical Agriculturist

TROPM — Tropical Man [*Leiden*]

Trop Man — Tropical Man [*Leiden*]

Trop Med — Tropical Medicine

Trop Med Hyg News — Tropical Medicine and Hygiene News

Trop Pest Bull — Tropical Pest Bulletin

Trop Pestic Res Inst Annu Rep — Tropical Pesticides Research Institute. Annual Report

Trop Pestic Res Inst Misc Rep — Tropical Pesticides Research Institute. Miscellaneous Report

Trop Pest Manage — Tropical Pest Management

Trop Prod Inst Crop Prod Dig — Tropical Products Institute. Crop and Product Digest

Trop Prod Inst Rep — Tropical Products Institute. Report

Trop Sci — Tropical Science

Trop Sci Cent Occas Pap (San Jose Costa Rica) — Tropical Science Center. Occasional Paper (San Jose, Costa Rica)

Trop Stored Prod Inf — Tropical Stored Products Information

Trop Stored Prod Inform — Tropical Stored Products Information

Trop Subtrop Pflwelt — Tropische und Subtropische Pflanzenwelt

Trop Vet Bull — Tropical Veterinary Bulletin

Trop Woods — Tropical Woods

Trop Woods Yale Univ Sch For — Tropical Woods. Yale University School of Forestry

Tr Opytn Stn Plodovod Akad Nauk Gruz SSR — Trudy Opytnoi Stantsii Plodovodstva Akademii Nauk Gruzinskoi SSR

Tr Orenb Gos Med Inst — Trudy Orenburgskogo Gosudarstvennogo Meditsinskogo Instituta

Tr Orenb Nauchno Issled Inst Molochno Myasn Skotovod — Trudy Orenburgskii Nauchno-Issledovatel'skii Instituta Molochno-Myasnogo Skotovodstva

Tr Orenb Obl Otd Vseross-Nauchn O-va Ter — Trudy Orenburgskogo Oblastnogo Otdeleniya Vserossiiskogonauchnogo Obshchestva Terapevtov

Tr Orenb Otd Vses Fiziol Ova — Trudy Orenburgskogo Otdeleniya Vsesoyuznogo Fiziologicheskogo Obshchestva

Tr Orenb Otd Vses Ova Fiziol — Trudy Orenburgskogo Otdeleniya Vsesoyuznogo Obshchestva Fiziologov

Tr Orenb Otd Vses Ova Fiziol Biokhim Farmakol — Trudy Orenburgskogo Otdeleniya Vsesoyuznogo Obshchestva Fiziologov, Biokhimikov, i Farmakologov

Tr Orenb Skh Inst — Trudy Orenburgskogo Sel'skokhozyaistvennogo Instituta

TROSA — Tropical Science

Tr Otd Fiziol Biofiz Rast Akad Nauk Tadzh SSR — Trudy Otdel Fiziologii i Biofiziki Rastenii Akademiya Nauk Tadzhikskoi SSR

Tr Otd Geol Buryat Fil Sib Otd Akad Nauk SSSR — Trudy Otdela Geologii Buryatskii Filial Sibirskoe Otdelenie Akademiya Nauk SSSR

Tr Otd Gorn Dela Metall Akad Nauk Kirg SSR — Trudy Otdela Gornogo Dela i Metallurgii Akademii Nauk Kirgizskoi SSR

Tr Otd Pochvoved Akad Nauk Kirg SSR — Trudy Otdela Pochvovedeniya Akademii Nauk Kirgizskoi SSR

Tr Otd Pochvoved Dagest Fil Akad Nauk SSSR — Trudy Otdela Pochvovedeniya Dagestanskogo Filiala. Akademii Nauk SSSR

Trouser — Trouser Press

Tr O-va Fiziol Azerb — Trudy Obshchestva Fiziologov Azerbaidzhana

T Roy Ent S — Transactions. Royal Entomological Society of London

T Roy Soc C — Transactions. Royal Society of Canada

TRP — Transportation Proceedings

TRP — Trefpunt

Tr Paleontol Inst Akad Nauk SSSR — Trudy Paleontologicheskogo Instituta Akademiya Nauk SSSR

Tr Path Soc London — Transactions. Pathological Society of London

TRPC — Tradicion. Revista Peruana de Cultura

Tr Pechoro Ilychskogo Gos Zapov — Trudy Pechoro-Ilychskogo Gosudarstvennogo Zapovednika

Tr Permsk Farm Inst — Trudy Permskogo Farmatseuticheskogo Instituta

Tr Permsk Gos Med Inst — Trudy Permskii Gosudarstvennyi Meditsinskii Institut

Tr Permsk Gos Nauchno-Issled Proektn Inst Neft Prom-sti — Trudy Permskij Gosudarstvennyj Nauchno-Issledovatel'skij i Proektnyj Institut Neftyanoj Promyshlennosti

Tr Permsk Gos Skh Inst — Trudy Permskogo Gosudarstvennogo Sel'skokhozyaistvennogo Instituta

Tr Permsk Nauchno Issled Inst Vaktsin Syvorotok — Trudy Permskogo Nauchno-Issledovatel'skogo Instituta Vaktsin i Syvorotok

Tr Permsk S-kh Inst — Trudy Permskogo Sel'skokhozyaistvennogo Instituta

Tr Perv Mosk Med Inst Im I M Sechenova — Trudy Pervogo Moskovskogo Meditsinskogo Instituta Imeni I. M. Sechenova

Tr 1 Pervogo Mosk Med Inst — Trudy 1 Pervogo Moskovskogo Meditsinskogo Instituta [*USSR*]

Tr Pervogo Mosk Pedagog Inst — Trudy Pervogo Moskovskogo Pedagogicheskogo Instituta

Tr Petergof Estest Nauchn Inst — Trudy Petergofskogo Estestvenno-Nauchnogo Instituta

Tr Petrogr Inst Akad Nauk SSSR — Trudy Petrograficheskogo Instituta. Akademiya Nauk SSSR

TRPLA — Transplantation

Tr Plodoovoshchn Inst — Trudy Plodoovoshchnogo Instituta

Tr Plodovoshchn Inst Im I V Michurina — Trudy Plodovoshchnogo Instituta Imeni I. V. Michurina

Tr Plodovo-Yagodnogo Inst Im Akad R R Shredera — Trudy Plodovo-Yagodnogo Instituta Imeni Akademika R. R. Shredera

Tr Poch Inst V V Dokuchaeva Akad Nauk SSSR — Trudy Pochvennogo Instituta Imeni V. V. Dokuchaeva Akademiya Nauk SSSR

Tr Pochv Inst Im V V Dokuchaeva Akad Nauk SSSR — Trudy Pochvennogo Instituta Imeni V. V. Dokuchaeva Akademii Nauk SSSR

Tr Polyar Nauchno-Issled Proekt Inst Morsk Ryb Khoz Okeanogr — Trudy Polyarnyi Nauchno-Issledovatel'skii i Proektnyi Institut Morskogo Rybnogo Khozyaistva i Okeanografii [*USSR*]

TRPPA — Transplantation Proceedings

TRPRB — Transplantation Reviews

Tr Prik Bot Genet Sel Ser 10 — Trudy po Prikladnoi Botanike. Genetike i Selektsii. Seriya 10. Dendrologiya i Dekorativnoe Sadovodstvo

Tr Prikl Bot Genet Sel — Trudy po Prikladnoi Botanike Genetike i Selektsii [*USSR*]

Tr Prikl Bot Genet Selek — Trudy po Prikladnoi Botanike Genetike i Selektsii

Tr Prikl Bot Genet Sel Ser 1 — Trudy po Prikladnoi Botanike. Genetike i Selektsii. Seriya 1. Sistematika, Geografia, i Ekologia Rastenii

Tr Prikl Bot Genet Sel Ser 2 — Trudy po Prikladnoi Botanike. Genetike i Selektsii. Seriya 2. Genetika, Selektsiya, i Tsitologiya Rastenii

Tr Prikl Bot Genet Sel Ser 3 — Trudy po Prikladnoi Botanike. Genetike i Selektsii. Seriya 3. Fiziologiya, Biokhimiya, i Anatomiya Rastenii

Tr Prikl Bot Genet Sel Ser 4 — Trudy po Prikladnoi Botanike. Genetike i Selektsii. Seriya 4. Semenovedenie i Semennoi Kontrol

Tr Prikl Bot Genet Sel Ser 5 — Trudy po Prikladnoi Botanike. Genetike i Selektsii. Seriya 5. Zernovye Kul'tury

Tr Prikl Bot Genet Sel Ser 13 — Trudy po Prikladnoi Botanike. Genetike i Selektsii. Seriya 13. Regeraty i Bibliografia

Tr Prikl Bot Genet Sel Ser 14 — Trudy po Prikladnoi Botanike. Genetike i Selektsii. Seriya 14. Osvoenie Pustyn

Tr Prikl Bot Genet Sel Ser 15 — Trudy po Prikladnoi Botanike. Genetike i Selektsii. Seriya 15. Severnoe (Pripolyarnoe) Zemledelie

Tr Prikl Bot Genet Sel Ser A — Trudy po Prikladnoi Botanike. Genetike i Selektsii. Seriya A. Sotsialisticheskoe

Tr Primorsk S-kh Inst — Trudy Primorskogo Sel'skokhozyaistvennogo Instituta

Tr Probl Lab Osad Form Osad Rud Tashk Gos Univ — Trudy Problemnoi Laboratorii Osadochnykh Formatsii i Osadochnykh Rud Tashkentskii Gosudarstvennyi Universitet

Tr Probl Temat Soveshch Akad Nauk SSSR Zool Inst — Trudy Problemnykh i Tematicheskikh Soveshchanii Akademiya Nauk SSSR Zoologicheskii Institut

Tr Proizvod Nauchno-Issled Inst Inzh Izyskaniyam Stroit — Trudy Proizvodstvennyi i Nauchno-Issledovatel'skii Institut po Inzhenernym Izyskaniyam v Stroitel'stve

Tr Pskov Obl Gos Skh Opytn Stn — Trudy Pskovskoi Oblastnoi Gosudarstvennoi Sel'skohzyaistvennoi Opytnoi Stantsii

Tr Pushkin Nauchno-Issled Lab Razvedeniya S-kh Zhivotn — Trudy Pushkinskoi Nauchno-Issledovatel'skoi Laboratorii Razvedeniya Sel'skohzyaistvennykh Zhivotnykh

TRQUD — Transportation Quarterly

TRR — [*The*] Rohmer Review

Tr Radiat Gig Leningr Nauchno-Issled Inst Radiats Gig — Trudy po Radiatsionnoi Gigiene Leningradskii Nauchno-Issledovatel'skii Institut Radiatsionnoi Gigieny [*USSR*]

Tr Radiats Gig — Trudy po Radiatsionnoi Gigiene

Tr Radiats Gig Leningr Nauchno-Issled Inst Radiats Gig — Trudy po Radiatsionnoj Gigiene Leningradskij Nauchno-Issledovatel'skij Institut Radiatsionnoj Gigieny

Tr Radievogo Inst Akad Nauk SSSR — Trudy Radievogo Instituta Akademiya Nauk SSSR

Tr Radiotekh Inst — Trudy Radiotekhnicheskogo Instituta [*USSR*]

Tr Radiotekh Inst Akad Nauk SSSR — Trudy Radiotekhnicheskogo Instituta Akademiya Nauk SSSR

TRRB — Transportation Research Board. Special Report [*United States*]

TRRE — Transportation Research Record

TRREB — Transportation Research

TRRED — Transportation Research Record

Tr Resp Inst Epidemiol Mikrobiol — Trudove na Respublikanskiya Instituta po Epidemiologiya i Mikrobiologiya

Tr Resp Opytn Stn Kartofeln Ovoshchn Khoz Kaz SSR — Trudy Respublikanskoi Opytnoi Stantsii Kartofel'nogo i Ovoshchnogo Khozyaistva Kazakhskaya SSR

Tr Resp Ova Ftiziatrov Nauchno Issled Inst Tuberk Kaz SSR — Trudy Respublikanskogo Obshchestva Ftiziatrov Nauchno-Issledovatel'skogo Instituta Tuberkuleza Kazakhskoi SSR

Tr Resp Stn Zashch Rast — Trudy Respublikanskoi Stantsii Zashchity Rastenii

TRRFDP — Israel. Agricultural Research Organization. Division of Forestry. Triennial Report of Research

TRRIA — Translations Register-Index

Tr Rizh Inst Inzh Grazhdanskoi Aviats — Trudy Rizhskogo Instituta Inzhenerov Grazhdanskoi Aviatsii

Tr Rizh Nauchno Issled Inst Travmatol Ortop — Trudy Rizhskii Nauchno-Issledovatel'skii Institut Travmatologii i Ortopedii

TRRL Lab Rep — TRRL [*Transport and Road Research Laboratory*] Laboratory Report

TRRL Rep — TRRL [*Transport and Road Research Laboratory*] Report

TRRL Suppl Rep — TRRL [*Transport and Road Research Laboratory*] Supplementary Report

Tr Ross Inst Prikl Khim — Trudy Rossiiskogo Instituta Prikladnoi Khimii

Tr Rostov na Donu Inst Inzh Zheleznodorozhn Transp — Trudy Rostovskogo-na-Donu Instituta Inzhenerov Zheleznodorozhnogo Transporta

Tr Rostov-Na-Donu Inzh Stroit Inst — Trudy Rostovskii-Na-Donu Inzhenerno Stroitel'nyi Institut

Tr Roy Soc Edinb — Transactions. Royal Society of Edinburgh

Tr Ryazan Med Inst — Trudy Ryazanskogo Meditsinskogo Instituta

Tr Ryazan Radiotekh Inst — Trudy Ryazanskogo Radiotekhnicheskogo Instituta [*USSR*]

TRS — Theologische Rundschau

TRSAA — Transaction. Royal Society of South Africa

Tr Sakhalin Obl Stn Zashch Rast — Trudy Sakhalinskaya Oblastnaya Stantsiya Zashchity Rastenii

Tr Samark Gos Univ — Trudy Samarkandskogo Gosudarstvennogo Universiteta

Tr Samar Skh Inst — Trudy Samarskogo Sel'skokhozyaistvennogo Instituta

Tr Sarat Med Inst — Trudy Saratovskogo Meditsinskogo Instituta

Tr Sarat Otd Vses Nauchno Issled Inst Ozern Rechn Rybn Khoz — Trudy Saratovskogo Otdeleniya Vsesoyuznogo Nauchno-Issledovatel'skogo Instituta Ozernogo i Rechnogo Rybn Khoz

Tr Sarat Ova Estestvoispyt Lyubit Estestvozn — Trudy Saratovskogo Obshchestva Estestvoispytatelei i Lyubitelei Estestvoznaniya

Tr Sarat S-kh Inst — Trudy Saratovskogo Sel'skokhozyaistvennogo Instituta

Tr Sarat Zootekh Vet Inst — Trudy Saratovskogo Zootekhnicheskogo Veterinarnogo Instituta

Tr Sary Chelekskogo Gos Zap — Trudy Sary Chelekskogo Gosudarstvennogo Zapovednikia

TRSC — Transactions. Royal Society of Canada

TRSCA — Transactions. Royal Society of Canada

TRSCB — Transportation Science

Tr Sekt Astrobot Akad Nauk Kazakh SSR — Trudy Sektora Astrobotaniki Akademiya Nauk Kazakhskoi SSR

Tr Sekt Astrobot Akad Nauk Kaz SSR — Trudy Sektora Astrobotaniki Akademiya Nauk Kazakhskoi SSR

Tr Sekt Energ Azerb Fil Akad Nauk SSSR — Trudy Sektora Energetiki Azerbaidzhanskogo Filiala Akademii Nauk SSSR

Tr Sekt Fiziol Akad Nauk Az SSR — Trudy Sektora Fiziologii Akademiya Nauk Azerbaidzhanskoi SSR

Tr Sekt Fiziol Zhivotn Inst Biol Akad Nauk Latv SSR — Trudy Sektora Fiziologii Zhivotnykh Instituta Biologii Akademiya Nauk Latviiskoi SSR

Tr Sel Agrotekh Zashch Rast — Trudy po Selektsii Agrotekhnike i Zashchite Rastenii

Tr Semin "Bionika Mat Model Biol" — Trudy Seminara "Bionika i Matematicheskoe Modelirovanie v Biologii"

Tr Semin Zharostoikim Mater — Trudy Seminara po Zharostoikim Materialam

Tr Semipalat Med Inst — Trudy Semipalatinskogo Meditsinskogo Instituta

Tr Semipalat Zoovet Inst — Trudy Semipalatinskogo Zooveterinarnogo Instituta

Tr Sess Kom Opred Absol Vozrasta Geol Form Akad Nauk SSSR — Trudy Sessii Komissii po Opredeleniyu Absolyutnogo Vozrasta Geologicheskikh Formatsii Akademiya Nauk SSSR

Tr Sevansk Gidrobiol Stn — Trudy Sevanskoi Gidrobiologicheskoi Stantsii

Tr Sevastop Biol Stn Akad Nauk Ukr SSR — Trudy Sevastopol'skoi Biologicheskoi Stantsii Akademiya Nauk Ukrainskoi SSR

Tr Sevastop Biol Stn Im A D Kovalenskogo Akad Nauk Ukr SSR — Trudy Sevastopol'skoi Biologicheskoi Stantsii Imeni A. D. Kovalenskogo Akademii Nauk Ukrainskoi SSR

Tr Severokavkazskogo Gornometall Inst — Trudy Severokavkazskogo Gornometallurgicheskogo Instituta [*USSR*]

Tr Sev Kavk Gornometall Inst — Trudy Severo-Kavkazskogo Gornometallurgicheskogo Instituta

Tr Sev Nauchno Issled Inst Gidrotekh Melior — Trudy Severnyi Nauchno-Issledovatel'skii Institut Gidrotekhniki i Melioratsii

Tr Sev-Oset Med Inst — Trudy Severo-Osetinskogo Meditsinskogo Instituta

Tr Sev-Oset S-kh Inst — Trudy Severo-Osetinskogo Sel'skokhozyaistvennogo Instituta

Tr Sev Vost Kompleksn Inst Dalnevost Tsentr Akad Nauk SSSR — Trudy Severo-Vostochnogo Kompleksnogo Instituta Dal'nevostochnyi Tsentr Akademii Nauk SSSR

Tr Sev Zapadn Nauchno Issled Inst Sel'sk Khoz — Trudy Severo. Zapadnogo Nauchno-Issledovatel'skogo Instituta Sel'skogo Khozyaistva

Tr Sev Zapadn Zaochn Politekh Inst — Trudy. Severo-Zapadnyi Zaochnyi Politekhnicheskii Institut

Tr Sib Fiz Tekh Inst Tomsk Gos Univ — Trudy Sibirskogo Fiziko-Tekhnicheskogo Instituta pri Tomskom Gosudarstvennom Universitete [*USSR*]

Tr Sib Lesotekh Inst — Trudy Sibirskogo Lesotekhnicheskogo Instituta

Tr Sib Nauch-Issled Inst Zhivotn — Trudy Sibirskogo Nauchno-Issledovatel'skogo Instituta Zhivotnovodstva

Tr Sib Nauchno-Issled Inst Energ — Trudy Sibirskogo Nauchno-Issledovatel'skogo Instituta Energetiki [*USSR*]

Tr Sib Nauchno-Issled Inst Geol Geofiz Miner Syr'ya — Trudy Sibirskogo Nauchno-Issledovatel'skogo Instituta Geologii, Geofiziki, i Mineral'nogo Syr'ya

Tr Sib Otd Gos Nauchno-Issled Inst Ozern Rechn Rybn Khoz — Trudy Sibirskogo Otdela Gosudarstvennogo Nauchno-Issledovatel'skogo Instituta Ozernogo i Rechnogo Rybnogo Khozyaistva

Tr Sib Tekhnol Inst — Trudy Sibirskogo Teknhnologicheskogo Instituta
Tr Sikhote-Alinsk Gos Zapov — Trudy Sikhote-Alinskogo Gosudarstvennogo Zapovednika
Tr Skh Samarkanskogo Inst — Trudy Sel'skokhozyaistvennogo Samarkanskogo Instituta
TRSL — Transactions. Royal Society of Literature
TRSLA — TRW Space Log
Tr Smolensk Gos Med Inst — Trudy Smolenskogo Gosudarstvennogo Meditsinskogo Instituta
Tr Smolensk Nauchno Issled Vet Stn — Trudy Smolenskoi Nauchno-Issledovatel'skoi Veterinarnoi Stantsii
Tr Soc Trop Med and Hyg (London) — Transactions. Society of Tropical Medicine and Hygiene (London)
Tr Solyanoi Lab Vses Inst Galurgii Akad Nauk SSSR — Trudy Solyanoi Laboratorii Vsesoyuznyi Institut Galurgii Akademiya Nauk SSSR
Tr Sov Antarkt Eksped — Trudy Sovetskoi Antarkticheskoi Ekspeditsii [*USSR*]
Tr Soveshch Ikhtiol Kom Akad Nauk SSSR — Trudy Soveshchanii Ikhtiologicheskoi Komissii Akademii Nauk SSSR
Tr Soveshch Morfogen Rast — Trudy Soveshchanii po Morfogenezu Rastenii
Tr Soveshch Poliploidiya Selek Akad Nauk SSSR — Trudy Soveshchaniya Poliploidiya i Selektsiya Akademii Nauk SSSR
Tr Sovmestnaya Sov Mong Nauchno Issled Geol Eksped — Trudy Sovmestnaya Sovetsko-Mongol'skaya Nauchno-Issledovatel'skaya Geologicheskaya Ekspeditsiya
Tr Sov Sekts Mezhdunar Assots Pochvovedov — Trudy Sovetskoi Sektsii Mezhdunarodnoi Assotsiatsii Pochvovedov
Tr Soyuzn Geologopoisk Kontora — Trudy Soyuznaya Geologopoiskovaya Kontora
Tr Soyuznogo Nauchno-Issled Inst Priborostr — Trudy Soyuznogo Nauchno-Issledovatel'skogo Instituta Priborostroeniya [*USSR*]
Tr Soyuzn Trest Razved Burovykh Rab — Trudy Soyuznyi Trest Razvedochno-Burovykh Rabot
Tr Sredneaziat Gos Univ — Trudy Sredneaziatskogo Gosudarstvennogo Universiteta
Tr Sredneaziat Gos Univ Ser 6 — Trudy Sredneaziatskogo Gosudarstvennogo Universiteta. Seriya 6. Khimiya
Tr Sredneaziat Gos Univ Ser 11 — Trudy Sredneaziatskogo Gosudarstvennogo Universiteta. Seriya 11. Tekhnika
Tr Sredneaziat Gos Univ Ser 13 — Trudy Sredneaziatskogo Gosudarstvennogo Universiteta. Seriya 13. Varia
Tr Sredneaziat Gos Univ Ser 7a — Trudy Sredneaziatskogo Gosudarstvennogo Universiteta. Seriya 7a. Geologiya
Tr Sredneaziat Gos Univ Ser 7d — Trudy Sredneaziatskogo Gosudarstvennogo Universiteta. Seriya 7d. Pochvovedenie
Tr Sredneaziat Nauchno Issled Gidrometeorol Institut — Trudy Sredneaziat Nauchno-Issledovatel'skii Gidrometeorologicheskii Institut
Tr Sredneaziat Nauchno Issled Inst Geol Miner Syr'ya — Trudy Sredneaziatskii Nauchno-Issledovatel'skii Institut Geologii i Mineral'nogo Syr'ya
Tr Sredne-Aziat Nauchno-Issled Protivochumn Inst — Trudy Sredne-Aziatskogo Nauchno-Issledovatel'skogo Protivochumnogo Instituta
Tr Sredne Volzh Skh Inst — Trudy Sredne-Volzhskogo Sel'skokhozyaistvennogo Instituta
T Rs S Afr — Transactions. Royal Society of South Africa
TRSTA — Transactions. Royal Society of Tropical Medicine and Hygiene
Tr Stalinab Astron Obs — Trudy Stalinabadskoi Astronomicheskoi Observatorii
Tr Stalinab Gos Med Inst — Trudy Stalinabadskogo Gosudarstvennogo Meditsinskogo Instituta
Tr Stalingr S-kh Inst — Trudy Stalingradskogo Sel'skokhozyaistvennogo Instituta
Tr Stalinskogo Gos Med Inst — Trudy Stalinskogo Gosudarstvennogo Meditsinskogo Instituta
Tr Stalinskogo Gos Pedagog Inst — Trudy Stalinskogo Gosudarstvennogo Pedagogicheskogo Instituta
Tr Stavrop Kraev Nauchno-Issled Vet Stn — Trudy Stavropol'skoi Kraevoi Nauchno-Issledovatel'skoi Veterinarnoi Stantsii
Tr Stavrop Nauchno Issled Inst Selsk Khoz — Trudy Stavropol'skogo Nauchno-Issledovatel'skogo Instituta Sel'skogo Khozyaistva
Tr Stavropol Sel'skokhoz Inst — Trudy Stavropol'skogo Sel'skokhozyaistvennogo Instituta
Tr Stavrop S-kh Inst — Trudy Stavropol'skogo Sel'skokhozyaistvennogo Instituta
Tr Stomatol Lit SSR — Trudy Stomatologov Litovskoi SSR
T Rs Trop M — Transactions. Royal Society of Tropical Medicine and Hygiene
Tr Stud Nauchno Tekh Ova Mosk Vyssh Tekh Uchil — Trudy Studencheskogo Nauchno-Tekhnicheskogo Obshchestva Moskovskoe Vysshe Tekhnicheskoe Uchilishche
Tr Stud Nauchn Ova Azerb Gos Med Inst — Trudy Studencheskogo Nauchnogo Obshchestva Azerbaidzhanskii Gosudarstvennyi Meditsinskii Institut
Tr Stud Nauchn Ova Khark Politekh Inst — Trudy Studencheskogo Nauchnogo Obshchestva Khar'kovskii Politekhnicheskii Institut
Tr Sukhum Bot Sada — Trudy Sukhumskogo Botanicheskogo Sada
Tr Sukhum Opytn Stn Efiromaslichn Kult — Trudy Sukhumskoi Opytnoi Stantsii Efiromaslichnykh Kultur
Tr Sverdl Gorn Inst — Trudy Sverdlovskogo Gornogo Instituta

Tr Sverdl Med Inst — Trudy Sverdlovskogo Meditsinskogo Instituta
Tr Sverdl Nauchno Issled Inst Lesn Promsti — Trudy Sverdlovskii Nauchno-Issledovatel'skii Institut Lesnoi Promyshlennosti
Tr Sverdl Nauchno Issled Vet Stn — Trudy Sverdlovskoi Nauchno-Issledovatel'skoi Veterinarnoi Stantsii
Tr Sverdl Skh Inst — Trudy Sverdlovskogo Sel'skokhozyaistvennogo Instituta
Tr SZPI — Trudy SZPI [*Severo-Zapadnyi Zaochnyi Politekhnicheskii Institut*]
Tr Tadzh Astron Obs — Trudy Tadzhikskoi Astronomicheskoi Observatorii
Tr Tadzh Gos Med Inst — Trudy Tadzhikskogo Gosudarstvennogo Meditsinskogo Instituta
Tr Tadzh Med Inst — Trudy Tadzhikskogo Meditsinskogo Instituta
Tr Tadzh Nauchno-Issled Inst Zemled — Trudy Tadzhikskogo Nauchno-Issledovatel'skogo Instituta Zemledeliya
Tr Tallin Pedagog Inst — Trudy Tallinskogo Pedagogicheskogo Instituta [*Estonian SSR*]
Tr Tallin Politekh Inst — Trudy Tallinskogo Politekhnicheskogo Instituta [*Estonian SSR*]
Tr Tallin Politekh Inst Ser A — Trudy Tallinskogo Politekhnicheskogo Instituta. Seriya A [*Estonian SSR*]
Tr Tambov Inst Khim Mashinostr — Trudy Tambovskogo Instituta Khimicheskogo Mashinostroeniya [*USSR*]
Tr Tashk Farm Inst — Trudy Tashkentskogo Farmatsevticheskogo Instituta
Tr Tashk Gos Univ — Trudy Tashkentskogo Gosudarstvennogo Universiteta Imeni V. I. Lenina
Tr Tashk Gos Univ Im V I Lenina — Trudy Tashkentskogo Gosudarstvennogo Universiteta Imeni V. I. Lenina [*USSR*]
Tr Tashk Inst Inzh Irrig Mekh Selsk Khoz — Trudy Tashkentskogo Instituta Inzhenerov Irrigatsii i Mekhanizatsii Sel'skogo Khozyaistva
Tr Tashk Inst Inzh Zh Zheleznodorozhn Transp — Trudy Tashkentskogo Instituta Inzhenerov Zheleznodorozhnogo Transporta
Tr Tashk Nauchno Issled Inst Vaktsin Syvorotok — Trudy Tashkentskogo Nauchno-Issledovatel'skogo Instituta Vaktsin i Syvorotok
Tr Tashk Politekh Inst — Trudy Tashkentskogo Politekhnicheskogo Instituta
Tr Tashk S-kh Inst — Trudy Tashkentskogo Sel'skokhozyaistvennogo Instituta
Tr Tatar Gos Nauchno Issled Proektn Inst Neft Promsti — Trudy Tatarskii Gosudarstvennyi Nauchno-Issledovatel'skii i Proektnyi Institut Neftyanoi Promyshlennosti
Tr Tatar Nauchno Issled Inst Selsk Khoz — Trudy Tatarskii Nauchno-Issledovatel'skii Institut Sel'skogo Khozyaistva
Tr Tatar Neft Nauchno Issled Inst — Trudy Tatarskii Neftyanoi Nauchno-Issledovatel'skii Institut
Tr Tatar Otd Gos Nauchno Issled Inst Ozern Rechn Rybn Khoz — Trudy Tatarskogo Otdeleniya Gosudarstvennogo Nauchno-Issledovatel'skogo Instituta Ozernogo i Rechnogo Rybnogo Khozyaistva
Tr Tatar Resp Mezhved Sb — Trudy Tatarskii Respublikanskii Mezhvedomstvennyi Sbornik
Tr Tatar Resp Skh Opytn Stn — Trudy Tatarskoi Respublikanskoi Sel'skokhozyaistvennoi Opytnoi Stantsii
Tr Tatar Respub Gosud Sel'skokhoz Opyt Sta — Trudy Tatarskoi Respublikanskoi Gosudarstvennoi Sel'skokhozyaistvennoi Opytnoi Stantsii
Tr Tbilis Bot Inst Akad Nauk Gruz SSR — Trudy Tbilisskogo Botanicheskogo Instituta Akademiya Nauk Gruzinskoi SSR
Tr Tbilis Gos Med Inst — Trudy Tbilisskogo Gosudarstvennogo Meditsinskogo Instituta
Tr Tbilis Gos Pedagog Inst — Trudy Tbilisskogo Gosudarstvennogo Pedagogiceskogo Instituta Imeni A. S. Pushkina
Tr Tbilis Gos Univ — Trudy Tbilisskogo Gosudarstvennogo Universiteta
Tr Tbilis Gos Univ Im Stalina — Trudy Tbilisskogo Gosudarstvennogo Universiteta Imeni Stalina
Tr Tbilis Gos Univ Inst Prikl Mat — Trudy Tbilisskii Gosudarstvennyi Universitet Institut Prikladnoi Matematiki
Tr Tbilis Inst Lesa — Trudy Tbilisskogo Instituta Lesa
Tr Tbilis Inst Poliklin Funkts Nervn Zabol — Trudy Tbilisskogo Instituta i Polikliniki Funktsional'nykh Nervnykh Zabolevanii
Tr Tbilis Inst Usoversh Vrachei — Trudy Tbilisskogo Instituta Usovershenstvovaniya Vrachei
Tr Tbilis Mat Inst — Trudy Tbilisskogo Ordena Trudovogo Krasnogo Znameni Matematicheskogo Instituta
Tr Tbilis Nauchno-Issled Gidrometeorol Inst — Trudy Tbilisskogo Nauchno-Issledovatel'skogo Gidrometeorologicheskogo Instituta
Tr Tbilis Nauchno Issled Inst Priborostr Sredstv Avtom — Trudy Tbilisskogo Nauchno-Issledovatel'skogo Instituta Priborostroeniya i Sredstv Avtomatizatsii
Tr Tbilissk Bot Inst — Trudy Tbilisskogo Botanicheskogo Instituta
Tr Tekhnol Inst Pishch Promsti (Kiev) — Trudy Tekhnologicheskogo Instituta Pishchevoi Promyshlennosti (Kiev)
Tr Teor Polya — Trudy po Teorii Polya [*USSR*]
Tr Ternop Gos Med Inst — Trudy Ternopol'skii Gosudarstvennyi Meditsinskii Institut
TRTHB — Traitement Thermique
Tr Tom Nauchno Issled Inst Kabeln Promsti — Trudy Tomskogo Nauchno-Issledovatel'skogo Instituta Kabel'noi Promyshlennosti
Tr Tomsk Gos Univ — Trudy Tomskogo Gosudarstvennogo Universiteta [*USSR*]

Tr Tomsk Gos Univ Im V V Kuibysheva — Trudy Tomskogo Gosudarstvennogo Universiteta Imeni V. V. Kuibysheva

Tr Tomsk Gos Univ Ser Khim — Trudy Tomskogo Gosudarstvennogo Universiteta Imeni V. V. Kuibysheva. Seriya Khimicheskaya [*USSR*]

Tr Tomsk Inst Radioehlektron Ehlektron Tekh — Trudy Tomskogo Instituta Radioehlektroniki i Ehlektronnoj Tekhniki

Tr Tomsk Med Inst — Trudy Tomskogo Meditsinskogo Instituta

Tr Tomsk Nauchno-Issled Inst Kabel'n Promsti — Trudy Tomskogo Nauchno-Issledovatel'skogo Instituta Kabel'noi Promyshlennosti

Tr Tomsk Nauchno-Issled Inst Vaksiny Syvorotok — Trudy Tomskogo Nauchno-Issledovatel'skogo Instituta Vaktsiny i Syvorotok

Tr Transp Energ Inst Akad Nauk SSSR Sib Otd — Trudy Transportno-Energeticheskogo Instituta Akademiya Nauk SSSR Sibirskoe Otdelenie

Tr Troitsk Vet Inst — Trudy Troitskogo Veterinarnogo Instituta

Tr Tselinograd Sel'skokhoz Inst — Trudy Tselinogradskogo Sel'skokhozyaistvennogo Instituta

Tr Tselinogr Gos Med Inst — Trudy Tselinogradskii Gosudarstvennyi Meditsinskii Institut

Tr Tselinogr Med Inst — Trudy Tselinogradskogo Meditsinskogo Instituta

Tr Tselinogr S-kh Inst — Trudy Tselinogradskogo Sel'skokhozyaistvennogo Instituta

Tr Tsent Aerol Obs — Trudy Tsentral'noi Aerologicheskoi Observatorii [*USSR*]

Tr Tsent Nauchno-Issled Gornorazved Inst — Trudy Tsentral'nyi Nauchno-Issledovatel'skii Gornorazvedochnyi Institut [*USSR*]

Tr Tsent Nauchno-Issled Inst Tekhnol Mashinostr — Trudy Tsentral'nyi Nauchno-Issledovatel'skii Institut Tekhnologii i Mashinostroeniya [*USSR*]

Tr Tsent Nauchno-Issled Proekt-Konst Kotloturbinnogo Inst — Trudy Tsentral'nogo Nauchno-Issledovatel'skogo i Proektno-Konstruktorskogo Kotloturbinnogo Instituta [*USSR*]

Tr Tsentr Aerol Obs — Trudy Tsentral'noi Aerologicheskoi Observatorii

Tr Tsentr Aptechn Nauchno-Issled Inst — Trudy Tsentral'nogo Aptechnogo Nauchno-Issledovatel'skogo Instituta

Tr Tsentr Chernozemn Gos Zapov — Trudy Tsentral'nogo Chernozemnogo Gosudarstvennogo Zapovednika

Tr Tsentr Genet Lab I V Michurina — Trudy Tsentral'noi Genetiki Laboratorii I. V. Michurina

Tr Tsentr Genet Lab Vses Akad Skh Nauk — Trudy Tsentral'noi Geneticheskoi Laboratorii Vsesoyuznaya Akademiya Sel'skokhozyaistvennykh Nauk

Tr Tsentr Inst Prognozov — Trudy Tsentral'nogo Instituta Prognozov

Tr Tsentr Inst Travmatol Ortop — Trudy Tsentral'nogo Instituta Travmatologii i Ortopedii

Tr Tsentr Inst Usoversh Vrachei — Trudy Tsentral'nogo Instituta Usovershenstvovaniya Vrachei

Tr Tsentr Kaz Geol Upr — Trudy Tsentral'no-Kazakhstanskogo Geologicheskogo Upravleniya

Tr Tsentr Kom Vodookhr — Trudy Tsentral'nogo Komiteta Vodookhraneniya

Tr Tsentr Nauchno Issled Avtomob Avtomot Inst — Trudy Tsentral'nyi Nauchno-Issledovatel'skii Avtomobil'nyi i Avtomotornyi Institut

Tr Tsentr Nauchno-Issled Dezinfekts Inst — Trudy Tsentral'nogo Nauchno-Issledovatel'skogo Dezinfektsionnogo Instituta

Tr Tsentr Nauchno Issled Dizeln Inst — Trudy Tsentral'nogo Nauchno-Issledovatel'skogo Dizel'nogo Instituta

Tr Tsentr Nauchno-Issled Gornorazved Inst — Trudy Tsentral'nyj Nauchno-Issledovatel'skij Gornorazvedochnyj Institut

Tr Tsentr Nauchno Issled Inst Faner Mebeli — Trudy Tsentral'nogo Nauchno-Issledovatel'skogo Instituta Fanery i Mebeli

Tr Tsentr Nauchno Issled Inst Khim Pishch Sredstv — Trudy Tsentral'nogo Nauchno-Issledovatel'skogo Instituta Khimii Pishchevykh Sredstv

Tr Tsentr Nauchno Issled Inst Konditer Promsti — Trudy Tsentral'nogo Nauchno-Issledovatel'skogo Instituta Konditerskoi Promyshlennosti

Tr Tsentr Nauchno Issled Inst Krakhmalo Patochn Promsti — Trudy Tsentral'nyi Nauchno-Issledovatel'skii Institut Krakhmalo-Patochnoi Promyshlennosti

Tr Tsentr Nauchno Issled Inst Kurortol Fizioter — Trudy Tsentral'nogo Nauchno-Issledovatel'skogo Instituta Kurortologii i Fizioterapii

Tr Tsentr Nauchno Issled Inst Osetr Khoz Nauk SSR — Trudy Tsentral'nogo Nauchno-Issledovatel'skogo Instituta Osetrovogo Khozyaistva Nauk SSR

Tr Tsentr Nauchno Issled Inst Rentgenol Radiol — Trudy Tsentral'nogo Nauchno-Issledovatel'skogo Instituta Rentgenologii i Radiologii

Tr Tsentr Nauchno-Issled Inst Sakh Promsti Moscow — Trudy Tsentral'nogo Nauchno-Issledovatel'skogo Instituta Sakharnoi Promyshlennosti Moscow

Tr Tsentr Nauchno-Issled Inst Spirt Likero-Vodochn Prom-sti — Trudy Tsentral'nogo Nauchno-Issledovatel'skogo Instituta Spirtovoi i Likero-Vodochnoi Promyshlennosti [*USSR*]

Tr Tsentr Nauchno Issled Inst Stroit Konstr — Trudy Tsentral'nyi Nauchno-Issledovatel'skii Institut Stroitel'nykh Konstruktsii

Tr Tsentr Nauchno Issled Inst Tekhnol Sudostr — Trudy Tsentral'nyi Nauchno-Issledovatel'skii Institut Tekhnologii Sudostroeniya

Tr Tsentr Nauchno Issled Inst Tuberk — Trudy Tsentral'nogo Nauchno-Issledovatel'skogo Instituta Tuberkuleza

Tr Tsentr Nauchno Issled Lab Novosib Med Inst — Trudy Tsentral'noi Nauchno-Issledovatel'skoi Laboratorii Novosibirskogo Meditsinskogo Instituta

Tr Tsentr Nauchno Issled Morsk Flota — Trudy Tsentral'nyi Nauchno-Issledovatel'skii Institut Morskogo Flota

Tr Tsentr Nauchno Issled Proektno Konstr Kotloturbinnyi Inst — Trudy Tsentral'nyi Nauchno-Issledovatel'skii i Proektno-Konstruktorskii Kotloturbinnyi Institut

Tr Tsentr Nauchno-Issled Rentgeno-Radiol Inst — Trudy Tsentral'nogo Nauchno-Issledovatel'skogo Rentgeno-Radiologicheskogo Instituta

Tr Tsentr Nauchno Issled Stn Skh Ispol'z Stochnykh Vod — Trudy Tsentral'noi Nauchno-Issledovatel'skoi Stantsii po Sel'skokhozyaistvennomu Ispol'zovaniyu Stochnykh Vod

Tr Tsentr Nauchnoizsled Inst Ribovud Varna Bulg Akad Nauk — Trudove na Tsentralniya Nauchnoizsledovatelski Institut po Ribovudstvo i Ribolov. Varna. Bulgarska Akademiya na Naukite

Tr Tsentr Sib Bot Sada — Trudy Tsentral'nogo Sibirskogo Botanicheskogo Sada

Tr Tul Gos Skh Opytn Stn — Trudy Tul'skoi Gosudarstvennoi Sel'skokhozyaistvennoi Opytnoi Stantsii

Tr Tul Mekh Inst — Trudy Tul'skogo Mekhanicheskogo Instituta

Tr Turkm Bot Sada Akad Nauk Turkm SSR — Trudy Turkmenskogo Botanicheskogo Sada Akademii Nauk Turkmenskoi SSR

Tr Turkm Fil Vses Neft Nauchno Issled Inst — Trudy Turkmenskogo Filiala Vsesoyuznogo Neftyanogo Nauchno-Issledovatel'skogo Instituta

Tr Turkm Gos Med Inst — Trudy Turkmenskogo Gosudarstvennogo Meditsinskogo Instituta

Tr Turkm Nauchno-Issled Inst Kozhynykh Bolezn — Trudy Turkmenskogo Nauchno-Issledovatel'skogo Instituta Kozhynykh Boleznei

Tr Turkm Nauchno Issled Trakhomatoznogo Inst — Trudy Turkmenskogo Nauchno-Issledovatel'skogo Trakhomatoznogo Instituta

Tr Turkm Politekh Inst — Trudy Turkmenskogo Politekhnicheskogo Instituta

Tr Turkm Skh Inst — Trudy Turkmenskogo Sel'skokhozyaistvennogo Instituta

Tr Turkm S-Kh Inst Im M Kalinina — Trudy Turkmenskogo Sel'skokhozyaistvennogo Instituta Imeni M. I. Kalinina

Tr Turk Nauchno Issled Inst Kozhynykh Bolezn — Trudy Turkmenskogo Nauchno-Issledovatel'skogo Instituta Kozhynykh Boleznei

Tr Tuvinskoi Gos Skh Opytn Stn — Trudy Tuvinskoi Gosudarstvennoi Sel'skokhozyaistvennoi Opytnoi Stantsii

Tr Tyazan Radiotekh Inst — Trudy Tyazanskogo Radiotekhnicheskogo Instituta

Tr Tyumen Ind Inst — Trudy Tyumenskogo Industrial'nogo Instituta

Tr Tyumen Otd Vses Nauchn Ova Anat Gistol Embriol — Trudy Tyumenskogo Otdeleniya Vsesoyuznogo Nauchnogo Obshchestva Anatomov, Gistologov, i Embriologov

Tr Tyumenskogo Ind Inst — Trudy Tyumenskogo Industrial'nogo Instituta [*USSR*]

TRu — Theologische Rundschau [*Tuebingen*]

TRU — Trouw

Trubn Proizvod Urala — Trubnoe Proizvodstvo Urala

Truck & Bus Trans — Truck and Bus Transportation

Truck & Bus Transp — Truck and Bus Transportation

Truck Bus Transpn — Truck and Bus Transportation

Truck Off-Highw Ind — Truck and Off-Highway Industries [*United States*]

Trud Viss Ikonom Inst Karl Marks-Sofia — Trudove. Vissija Ikonomiceski Institut Karl Marks-Sofija

Trudy Akad Nauk Litov SSR — Trudy Akademii Nauk Litovskoi SSR

Trudy Akad Nauk Litov SSR Ser A Obsc Nauki — Trudy Akademii Nauk Litovskoj SSR. Serija A. Obscestvennye Nauki

Trudy Akad Nauk Litov SSR Ser B — Trudy Akademii Nauk Litovskoi SSR. Serija B

Trudy Altai Politehn Inst — Trudy Altaiskii Politehniceskii Institut Imeni I. I. Polizunova

Trudy Altaisk Politehn Inst — Trudy Altaiskii Politehniceskii Institut Imeni I. I. Polizunova

Trudy Altaisk Sel'khoz Inst — Trudy Altaiskogo Sel'skokhozyaistvennogo Instituta

Trudy Altajsk Politehn Inst — Trudy Altajskogo Politehniceskogo Instituta

Trudy Andizhan Ped Inst — Trudy Andizhanskii Gosudarstvennyi Pedagogicheskii Institut

Trudy A N Tadzh — Trudy Akademiia Nauk Tadzhikskoi SSR [*Stalinabad, USSR*]

Trudy Arhangel Lesotehn Inst — Trudy Arhangel'skogo Lesotehniceskogo Instituta Imeni V. V. Kuibysheva

Trudy Arkhangel Lesotekh Inst Im V V Kuibysheva — Trudy Arkhangel'skogo Ordena Trudovogo Kraskogo Znameni Lesotekhnicheskogo Instituta Imeni V. V. Kuibysheva

Trudy Armyansk Nauchno-Issled Inst Vinograd Vinodel Plodov — Trudy Armyanskogo Nauchno-Issledovatel'skogo Instituta Vinogradarstva Vinodeliya i Plodovodstva

Trudy Armyansk Nauchno-Issled Inst Zhivot Vet — Trudy Armyanskogo Nauchno-Issledovatel'skogo Instituta Zhivotnovodstva i Veterinarii

Trudy Aspirantov Gruzin Sel'-khoz Inst — Trudy Aspirantov Gruzinskogo Sel'skokhozyaistvennogo Instituta

Trudy Azerbajdzansk Opytn Sta — Trudy Azerbajdzanskogo Opytnoj Stancii

Trudy Azerb Nauchno-Issled Inst Gidrotekh Melior — Trudy Azerbaidzhanskogo Nauchno-Issledovatel'skogo Instituta Gidrotekhniki i Melioratsii

Trudy Azerb Nauchno-Issled Inst Zhivot — Trudy Azerbaidzhanskogo Nauchno-Issledovatel'skogo Instituta Zhivotnovodstva

Trudy Azerb Vet Inst — Trudy Azerbaidzhanskogo Nauchno-Issledovatel'skogo Veterinarnogo Instituta

Trudy Bashkir Nauch Inst Sel Khoz — Trudy Bashkirskogo Nauchnogo Instituta Sel'skogo Khozyaista

Trudy Baskir S-h Inst — Trudy Bashkirskogo Sel'skokhozjaistvennogo Instituta

Trudy Belorussk Nauchno-Issled Inst Pochv — Trudy Belorusskogo Nauchno-Issledovatel'skogo Instituta Pochvovedeniya

Trudy Belorussk Sel'-khoz Akad — Trudy Belorusskoi Sel'skokhozyaistvennoi Akademii

Trudy Biol Inst Sib Otd Akad Nauk SSSR — Trudy Biologicheskogo Instituta Sibirskoe Otdelenie Akademii Nauk SSSR

Trudy Bot Inst Akad Nauk SSSR Ser VI — Trudy Botaniceskij Institut Akademiya Nauk SSSR. Serija VI

Trudy Burjat Inst Obsc Nauk — Trudy Burjatskogo Instituta Obscestvennyh Nauk

Trudy Buryat Mongol Nauchno-Issled Vet Opyt Sta — Trudy Buryat-Mongol'skoi Nauchno-Issledovatel'skoi Veterinarnoi Opytnoi Stantsii

Trudy Buryatsk Sel'khoz Inst — Trudy Buryatskogo Sel'skokhozyaistvennogo Instituta

Trudy CNIIKA — Trudy Gosudarstvennyi Vsesojuznyi Central'nyi Naucno-Issledovatel'skii Institut Kompleksnoi Avtomatizacii

Trudy Dagest Nauchno-Issled Inst Sel Khoz — Trudy Dagestanskogo Nauchno-Issledovatel'skogo Instituta Sel'skogo Khozyaista

Trudy Doneck Politehn Inst — Trudy Doneckogo Politehniceskogo Instituta

Trudy Don Zonal'Inst Sel'Khoz — Trudy Donskogo Zonal'nogo Instituta Sel'skogo Khozyaista

Trudy Fiz Inst Lebedev — Trudy Fiziceskogo Instituta Imeni P. N. Lebedeva

Trudy Frunze Politehn Inst — Trudy Frunzenskogo Politehniceskogo Instituta

Trudy Geogr Fak Kirgiz Univ — Trudy Geograficheskogo Fakul'teta Kirgizskogo Universiteta

Trudy Geometr Sem — Trudy Geometriceskogo Seminara

Trudy Geom Sem Kazan Univ — Trudy Geometriceskogo Seminara Kazanskii Universitet

Trudy G Ermitazh — Trudy Gosudarstvennogo Ermitazha

Trudy Glav Geofiz Obs — Trudy Glavnoi Geofizicheskoi Observatorii Imeni A. I. Voeikova

Trudy Gor'kov Politehn Inst — Trudy Gor'kovskogo Politehniceskii Institut

Trudy Gor'kov Sel'-khoz Inst — Trudy Gor'kovskogo Sel'skokhozyaistvennogo Instituta

Trudy Gorsk Sel'-khoz Inst — Trudy Gorskogo Sel'skokhozyaistvennogo Instituta

Trudy Gos Gidrol Inst — Trudy Gosudarstvennogo Gidrologicheskogo Instituta

Trudy Gruz Nauchno-Issled Pishch Prom — Trudy Gruzinskii Nauchno-Issledovatel'skii Institut Pishchevoi Promyshlennosti

Trudy Gruz Sel'-khoz Inst — Trudy Gruzinskogo Sel'skokhozyaistvennogo Instituta Imeni L. P. Beriya

Trudy Inst Biol Ural Fil (Sverdlovsk) — Trudy Instituta Biologii Ural'skii Filial Akademiya Nauk SSSR (Sverdlovsk)

Trudy Inst Bot (Alma-Ata) — Trudy Instituta Botaniki Akademiya Nauk Kazakhskoi SSR (Alma-Ata)

Trudy Inst Etnogr — Trudy Instituta Etnografii

Trudy Inst Fiziol (Baku) — Trudy Instituta Fiziologii Akademiya Nauk Azerbaidzhanskoi SSR (Baku)

Trudy Inst Fiziol I P Pavlova — Trudy Instituta Fiziologii Imeni I. P. Pavlova Akademiya Nauk SSSR

Trudy Inst Genet — Trudy Instituta Genetiki Akademiya Nauk SSR

Trudy Inst Istor Estestvoznan Tehn — Trudy Instituta Istorii Estestvoznanija i Tehniki

Trudy Inst Jaz Lit Ist Komi Fil Akad Nauk SSSR — Trudy Instituta Jazyka, Literatury, i Istorii Komi Filiala Akademii Nauk SSSR

Trudy Inst Mat i Meh Ural Naucn Centr Akad Nauk SSSR — Trudy Instituta Matematiki i Mehaniki Ural'skii Naucnyi Centr Akademija Nauk SSSR

Trudy Inst Mat i Mekh Ural Nauchn Tsentr Akad Nauk SSSR — Trudy Instituta Matematiki i Mekhaniki Ural'skii Nauchnyi Tsentr Akademiya Nauk SSSR

Trudy Inst Pochv Agrokhim (Baku) — Trudy Instituta Pochvovedeniya i Agrokhimii Akademiya Nauk Azerbaidzhanskoi SSR (Baku)

Trudy Inst Sistem Upravlenija Akad Nauk Gruzin SSR — Trudy Instituta Sistem Upravlenija Akademija Nauk Gruzinskoi SSR

Trudy Inst Sistem Upravleniya Akad Nauk Gruzin SSR — Trudy Instituta Sistem Upravleniya Akademiya Nauk Gruzinskoi SSR

Trudy Inst Teoret Astronom — Trudy Instituta Teoreticeskoi Astronomii

Trudy Inst Zool Parazit (Tashkent) — Trudy Instituta Zoologii i Parazitologii Akademiya Nauk Uzbekskoi SSR (Tashkent)

Trudy Irkutsk Gos Univ — Trudy Irkutskogo Gosudarstvennogo Universiteta

Trudy Ist-Kraev Muz Mold — Trudy Istoriko-Kraevedcheskogo Muzeia Moldavskoi SSR

Trudy Izevsk Sel'skohozjaistv Inst — Trudy Izevskii Sel'skohozjaistvennyi Institut

Trudy Kabardino-Balkarsk Gos Sel'khoz Opyt Sta — Trudy Kabardino-Balkarskoi Gosudarstvennoi Sel'skokhozyaistvennoi Opytnoi Stantsii

Trudy Kaf Teorii Funkcii i Funkcional Anal Moskov Gos Univ — Moskovskii Gosudarstvennyi Universitet. Mehaniko-Matematiceskii Fakul'tet. Kafedra Teorii Funkcii i Funkcional'nogo Analiza. Trudy

Trudy Karagand Gos Med Inst — Trudy Karagandinskii Gosudarstvennyi Meditsinskii Institut

Trudy Karel' Fil Akad Nauk SSSR — Trudy Karel'skogo Filiala Akademii Nauk SSSR

Trudy Kavkaz Gos Zapov — Trudy Kavkazskogo Gosudarstvennogo Zapovednika

Trudy Kazakh Opyt Sta Pchelov — Trudy Kazakhskoi Opytnoi Stantsii Pchelovodstva

Trudy Kazakh Sel'-khoz Inst — Trudy Kazakhskogo Sel'skokhozyaistvennogo Instituta

Trudy Kazan Aviacion Inst — Trudy Kazanskogo Aviacionnogo Instituta. Matematika i Mehanika

Trudy Kazan Gorod Astronom Observator — Trudy Kazanskoi Gorodskoi Astronomiceskoi Observatorii

Trudy Kazan Gos Pedagog Inst — Trudy Kazanskogo Gosudarstvennogo Pedagogicheskogo Instituta

Trudy Kazan Sel'-khoz Inst — Trudy Kazanskogo Sel'skokhozyaistvennogo Instituta

Trudy Kazan S-h Inst — Trudy Kazanskogo Sel'skokhozyaistvennogo Instituta

Trudy Kemerov Gos Sel Khoz Opyt Sta — Trudy Kemerovskoi Gosudarstvennoi Sel'skokhozyaistvennoi Opytnoi Stantsii

Trudy Kharkov Opyt Sta Pchelov — Trudy Khar'kovskaya Opytnaya Stantsiya Pchelovodstva

Trudy Kharkov Sel'-khoz Inst — Trudy Khar'kovskogo Sel'skokhozyaistvennogo Instituta

Trudy Kirgiz Gos Univ Ser Biol Nauk — Trudy Kirgizskogo Gosudarstvennogo Universiteta. Seriya Biologicheskikh Nauk Zoologiya-Fiziologiya

Trudy Kirgiz Gos Univ Ser Mat Nauk — Trudy Kirgizskogo Gosudarstvennogo Universiteta. Serija Matematiceskih Nauk

Trudy Kirgiz Nauchno-Issled Inst Zeml — Trudy Kirgizskogo Nauchno-Issledovatel'skogo Instituta Zemledeliya

Trudy Kirgiz Sel'-khoz Inst — Trudy Kirgizskogo Sel'skokhozyaistvennogo Instituta

Trudy Kishinev Sel'-khoz Inst — Trudy Kishinevskogo Sel'skokhozyaistvennogo Instituta

Trudy Kolomen Filiala Vsesojuz Zaocn Politehn Inst — Trudy Kolomenskogo Filiala Vsesojuznyi Zaocnyi Politehniceskii Institut

Trudy Kom Analit Khim — Trudy Komissii po Analiticheskoi Khimii Akademiya Nauk SSSR

Trudy Komi Fil Akad Nauk SSSR — Trudy Komi Filiala Akademii Nauk SSSR

Trudy Komi Filiala Akad Nauk SSSR — Trudy Komi Filiala Akademii Nauk SSSR

Trudy Konf Pochv Sib Dal'n Vostoka Akad Nauk SSSR — Trudy Konferentsiya Pochvovedov Sibiri i Dal'nego Vostoka Akademiya Nauk SSSR

Trudy Kuban Sel'-khoz Inst — Trudy Kubanskogo Sel'skokhozyaistvennogo Instituta

Trudy (Kujbys Aviac) Inst — Trudy (Kujbysevskij Aviacionnyj) Institut

Trudy Latv Sel'-khoz Inst — Trudy Latviiskogo Sel'skokhozyaistvennogo Instituta

Trudy Leningrad Tehnolog Inst Holod Promysl — Trudy Leningradskogo Tehnologicheskogo Instituta Holodil'noi Promyslennosti

Trudy Leningr Gidromet Inst — Trudy Leningradskogo Gidrometeorologicheskogo Instituta

Trudy Leningr Inst Kul't — Trudy Leningradskii Institut Kul'tury

Trudy Leningr Obshch Estest — Trudy Leningradskogo Obshchestva Estest-voispytatelei

Trudy Litov Nauchno-Issled Inst Zeml — Trudy Litovskogo Nauchno-Issledovatel'skogo Instituta Zemledeliya

Trudy Mat Inst Steklov — Trudy Matematiceskogo Instituta Imeni V. A. Steklova

Trudy Metrolog Inst SSSR — Trudy Metrologiceskih Institutov SSSR

Trudy Mold Akad Nauk — Trudy Ob'edinennoi Nauchnoi Sessii Moldavskii Filial Akademii Nauk SSR

Trudy Mol Ucen Kirigiz Univ — Trudy Molodyh Ucenyh Kirigizskogo Universiteta

Trudy Mosk Ordena Lenina Sel'Khoz Akad — Trudy Moskovskoi Ordena Lenina Sel'sko-Khozyaistvennoi Akademii Imeni K. A. Timiryazeva

Trudy Moskov Elektrotehn Inst Svjazi — Trudy Moskovskogo Elektrotehniceskogo Instituta Svjazi

Trudy Moskov Inst Inzen Zelezno-doroz Transporta — Trudy Moskovskogo Instituta Inzenernov Zeleznodoroznogo Transporta

Trudy Moskov Inst Istoriji — Trudy Moskovskogo Instituta Istoriji, Filosofiji, i Literatury

Trudy Moskov Inst Radiotehn Elektron i Avtomat — Trudy Moskovskogo Instituta Radiotekhniki, Elektroniki, i Avtomatiki

Trudy Moskov Mat Obsc — Trudy Moskovskogo Matematiceskogo Obscestva

Trudy Moskov Mat Obshch — Trudy Moskovskogo Matematicheskogo Obshchestva

Trudy Moskov Orden Lenin Energet Inst — Trudy Moskovskogo Ordena Lenina Energeticeskogo Instituta

Trudy Nakhich Kompleks Zonal Opyt Sta — Trudy Nakhichevanskoi Kompleksnoi Zonal'noi Opytnoi Stantsii

Trudy Nauch Inst Udobr Insektofung — Trudy Nauchnogo Instituta po Udobreniyam i Insektofungitsidam Imeni Ya. V. Satoilova

Trudy Nauchno-Issled Inst Pchelov — Trudy Nauchno-Issledovatel'skogo Instituta Pchelovodstva

Trudy Nauchno-Issled Inst Prud Rybn Khoz — Trudy Nauchno-Issledovatel'skogo Instituta Prudovogo Rybnogo Khozyaistva

Trudy Nauchno-Issled Inst Sel'Khoz Severn Zaural'ya — Trudy Nauchno-Issledovatel'skogo Instituta Sel'skogo Khozyaistva Severnogo Zaural'ya

Trudy Nauc-Issled Inst Sociol Kul't — Trudy Nauchno-Issledovatel'skogo Instituta Sociologiceskoj Kul'tury

Trudy Novocherk Inzh-Melior Inst — Trudy Novocherkasskogo Inzherno-Meliorativnogo Instituta

Trudy Obshch Estest Imp Kazan Univ — Trudy Obshchestva Estestvoispytatelei pri Imperatordkom Kazanskom Universitete Kazan

Trudy Obsh Dietsk Vrach Moskve — Trudy Obshchestva Dietskikh Vrachei v Moskve

Trudy Omsk Vet Inst — Trudy Omskogo Veterinarnogo Instituta

Trudy Omsk Vyss Skoly Milicii — Trudy Omskogo Vyssej Skoly Milicii

Trudy Ped Inst Gruzin SSR Ser Fiz i Mat — Trudy Pedagogiceskih Institutov Gruzinskoi SSR. Serija Fiziki i Matematiki

Trudy Plodov Inst — Trudy Plodovoshchnogo Instituta Imeni I. V. Michurina

Trudy Prikl Bot Genet Selek — Trudy po Prikladnoi Botanike Genetike i Selektsii

Trudy Przeval'sk Gos Ped Inst — Trudy Przeval'skogo Gosudarstvennogo Pedagogiceskogo Instituta

Trudy Radiats Gig Leningr Nauchno-Issled Inst Radiats Gig — Trudy Radiatsii i Gigieny Leningradskogo Nauchno-Issledovatel'skogo Instituta Radiatsii Gigieny

Trudy Rjazan Radiotehn Inst — Trudy Rjazanskogo Radiotehniceskogo Instituta

Trudy Russk Ent Obshch — Trudy Russkogo Entomologicheskogo Obshchestva

Trudy Samarkand Gos Univ — Trudy Samarkandskogo Gosudarstvennogo Universiteta Imeni Alisera Navoi

Trudy Samarkand Gos Univ NS — Ministerstvo Vyssego i Srednigo Obrazovanija UzSSR Trudy Samarkandskogo Gosuda rstvennogo Universiteta Imeni A. Navoi Novaja Serija

Trudy Samarkand Univ — Trudy Samarkandskogo Universiteta

Trudy Saratov Inst Meh S-H — Trudy Saratovskogo Instituta Mehanizacii Sel'skogo-Hozjaistva

Trudy Saratov Nauchno-Issled Vet Sta — Trudy Saratovskoi Nauchno-Issledovatel'skoi Veterinarnoi Stantsii

Trudy Saratov Sel'-khoz Inst — Trudy Saratovskogo Sel'skokhozyaistvennogo Instituta

Trudy Saratov Zootekh Vet Inst — Trudy Saratovskogo Zootekhnicheskogo Veterinarnogo Institut

Trudy Sem Kraev Zadacam — Trudy Seminara po Kraevym Zadacam

Trudy Sem Kraev Zadacham — Trudy Seminara po Kraevym Zadacham

Trudy Sem Mat Fiz Nelinien Koleban — Trudy Seminara po Matematiceskoi Fizike i Nelinienym Kolebanijam

Trudy Sem Petrovsk — Trudy Seminara Imeni I. G. Petrovskogo

Trudy Sem Vektor Tenzor Anal — Trudy Seminara po Vektornomu i Tenzornomu Analizu s ih Prilozenijami k Geometrii. Mehanike i Fizike

Trudy Sibirsk Fiz-Tehn Inst — Trudy Sibirskogo Fiziko-Tehniceskogo Instituta Imeni Akademika V. D. Kuznecova

Trudy SibNIIE — Trudy Sibirskii Naucno-Issledovatel'skii Institut Energetiki

Trudy Solikam Sel'-khoz Opyt Sta — Trudy Solikamskoi Sel'skokhozyaistvennoi Opytnoi Stantsii

Trudy Stavropol' Sel'-khoz Inst — Trudy Stavropol'skogo Sel'skokhozyaistvennogo Instituta

Trudy Sverdlovsk Sel'-khoz Inst — Trudy Sverdlovskogo Sel'skokhozyaistvennogo Instituta

Trudy Tadzhik Nauchno-Issled Inst Sel Khoz — Trudy Tadzhikskogo Nauchno-Issledovatel'skogo Instituta Sel'skogo Khozyaistva

Trudy Tadzik Politehn Inst — Trudy Tadzikskogo Politehniceskogo Instituta

Trudy Tallinsk Politehn Inst — Trudy Tallinskogo Politekhnicheskogo Instituta

Trudy Taskent Gos Univ — Trudy Taskentskogo Gosudarstvennogo Universiteta Imeni V. I. Lenina. Matematika

Trudy Tatar Nauchno-Issled Inst Sel'Khoz — Trudy Tatarskii Nauchno-Issledovatel'skii Institut Sel'skogo Khozyaistva

Trudy Tatar Respub Gos Sel-khoz Opyt Sta — Trudy Tatarskoi Respublikanskoi Gosudarstvennoi Sel'skokhozyaistvennoi Opytnoi Stantsii

Trudy Tbilisk Univ Fiz-Mat Estestv Nauki — Trudy Tbilisskogo Universiteta Fiziko-Matematiceskie i Estestvennyi Nauki

Trudy Tbiliss Mat Inst Razmadze Akad Nauk Gruzin SSR — Trudy Tbilisskogo Matematiceskogo Instituta Imeni A. M. Razmadze Akademija Nauk Gruzinskoi SSR

Trudy Tbiliss Univ — Trudy Tbilisskogo Universiteta Fiziko-Matematiceskie i Estestvennyi Nauki

Trudy Tomsk Gos Univ — Trudy Tomskogo Gosudarstvennogo Universiteta

Trudy Tomsk Univ — Trudy Tomskogo Universiteta

Trudy Tsent Chernoz Gos Zapov — Trudy Tsentral'nogo Chernozemnogo Gosudarstvennogo Zapovednika

Trudy Tsent Sib Bot Sada — Trudy Tsentral'nogo Sibirskogo Botanicheskogo Sada

Trudy Turkmen Sel'Khoz Inst — Trudy Turkmenskogo Sel'sko-Khozyaistvennogo Instituta

Trudy Ufmsk Aviac Inst — Trudy Ufimskogo Aviacionnogo Instituta

Trudy Ukr Gidromet Inst — Trudy Ukrainskogo Gidrometeorologicheskogo Instituta

Trudy Ul'yanov Sel'khoz Inst — Trudy Ul'yanovskogo Sel'skokhozyaistvennogo Instituta

Trudy Univ Druzby Narod — Trudy Universiteta Druzhby Narodov Imeni Patrisa Lumumby

Trudy Ural Politehn Inst — Trudy Ural'skogo Politehniceskogo Instituta

Trudy Volgogr Opytno-Melior Sta — Trudy Volgogradskoi Opytno-Meliorativnoi Stantsii

Trudy Vologod Sel'khoz Inst — Trudy Vologodskogo Sel'skokhozyaistvennogo Instituta

Trudy Voronezh Zoovetinst — Trudy Voronezhskogo Zooveterinarnogo Instituta

Trudy Vost Kazakh Gos Opyt Sta — Trudy Vostochno-Kazakhstanskaya Gosudarstvennaya Sel'skokhozyaistvennaya Opytnaya Stantsiya

Trudy Vost-Sibir Tehnol Inst — Trudy Vostochno-Sibirskogo Tehnologiceskogo Instituta

Trudy Vses Aerogeol Tresta — Trudy Vsesoyuznogo Aerogeologicheskogo Tresta

Trudy Vses Ent Obshch — Trudy Vsesoyuznogo Entomologicheskogo Obshchestva

Trudy Vses Nauchno-Issled Geol Inst — Trudy Vsesoyuznogo Nauchno-Issledovatel'skogo Geologicheskogo Instituta

Trudy Vses Nauchno-Issled Inst Sakharn Svekly Sakhara — Trudy Vsesoyuznogo Nauchno-Issledovatel'skogo Instituta Sakharnoi Svekly i Sakhara

Trudy Vses Nauchno-Issled Inst Torf Prom — Trudy Vsesoyuznogo Nauchno-Issledovatel'skogo Instituta Torfyanoi Promyshlennosti

Trudy Vses Nauchno-Issled Inst Udobr Agrotekh Agropochv — Trudy Vsesoyuznogo Nauchno-Issledovatel'skogo Instituta Udobrenii. Agrotekhniki i Agropochvovedeniya

Trudy Vses Nauchno-Issled Inst Vet Sanit Ektoparazit — Trudy Vsesoyuznogo Nauchno-Issledovatel'skogo Instituta Veterinarnoi Sanitarii i Ektoparazitologii

Trudy Vses Nauchno-Issled Inst Zashch Rast — Trudy Vsesoyuznogo Nauchno-Issledovatel'skogo Instituta Zashchity Rastenii

Trudy Vsesojuz Nauc-Issled Inst Sov Zakon — Trudy Vsesoyuznogo Nauchno-Issledovatel'skogo Instituta Sovetskogo Zakonodatel'stva

Trudy Vsesojuz Nauc-Issled Inst Zascity Rast — Trudy Vsesojuznogo Naucno-Issledovatel'skogo Instituta Zascity Rastenij

Trudy Vsesojuz Naucno-Issled Inst Elektromeh — Trudy Vsesojuznogo Naucno-Issledovatel'skogo Instituta Elektromehaniki

Trudy Vsesojuz Zaocn Energet Inst — Trudy Vsesojuznogo Zaocnogo Energeticeskogo Instituta

Trudy Vses Ordena Lenina Inst Eksp Vet — Trudy Vsesoyuznogo Ordena Lenina Instituta Eksperimental'noi Veterinarii

Trudy VTI — Trudy Vsesojuznogo Teplotehniceskogo Instituta

Trudy Vychisl Tsentra Tartu Gos Univ — Trudy Vychislitel'nogo Tsentra Tartuskii Gosudarstvennyi Universiteta

Trudy Vycisl Centra Akad Nauk Gruzin SSR — Trudy Vycislitel'nogo Centra Akademija Nauk Gruzinskoi SSR

Trudy Vycisl Centra Tartu Gos Univ — Trudy Vycislitel'nogo Centra Tartuskii Gosudarstvennyi Universitet

Trudy Zool Inst (Leningr) — Trudy Zoologicheskogo Instituta Akademiya Nauk SSSR (Leningrad)

Tr Ufim Aviats Inst — Trudy Ufimskogo Aviatsionnogo Instituta

Tr Ufim Nauchno-Issled Inst Gig Profzabol — Trudy Ufimskogo Nauchno-Issledovatel'skogo Instituta Gigieny i Profzabolevanii

Tr Ufim Neft Naucho-Issled Inst — Trudy Ufimskii Neftyanoi Nauchno-Issledovatel'skii Institut

TRUGA — Trudy Ukrainskii Nauchno-Issledovatel'skii Geologo-Razvedochnyi Institut

Tr Ukr Gos Nauchno-Issled Inst Prikl Khim — Trudy Ukrainskogo Gosudarstvennogo Nauchno-Issledovatel'skogo Instituta Prikladnoi Khimii

Tr Ukr Inst Eksp Endokrinol — Trudy Ukrainskogo Instituta Eksperimental'noi Endokrinologii

Tr Ukr Nauch-Issled Gidrometeorol Inst — Trudy Ukrainskogo Nauchno-Issledovatel'skogo Gidrometeorologicheskogo Instituta

Tr Ukr Nauchno Issled Geol Razved Inst — Trudy Ukrainskii Nauchno-Issledovatel'skii Geologo-Razvedochnyi Institut

Tr Ukr Nauchno-Issled Gidrometeorol Inst — Trudy Ukrainskogo Nauchno-Issledovatel'skogo Gidrometeorologicheskogo Instituta [*Ukrainian SSR*]

Tr Ukr Nauchno Issled Inst Klin Med — Trudy Ukrainskogo Nauchno-Issledovatel'skogo Instituta Klinicheskoi Meditsiny

Tr Ukr Nauchno Issled Inst Konservn Promsti — Trudy Ukrainskogo Nauchno-Issledovatel'skogo Instituta Konservnoi Promyshlennosti

r Ukr Nauchno-Issled Inst Lesn Khoz Agrolesomelior — Trudy Ukrainskogo Nauchno-Issledovatel'skogo Instituta Lesnogo Khozyaistva i Agrolesomelioratsii

r Ukr Nauchno Issled Inst Pishch Promsti — Trudy Ukrainskii Nauchno-Issledovatel'skii Institut Pishchevoi Promyshlennosti

r Ukr Nauchno-Issled Inst Prir Gazov — Trudy Ukrainskii Nauchno-Issledovatel'skii Institut Prirodnykh Gazov

r Ukr Nauchno-Issled Inst Rastenievod Sel Genet — Trudy Ukrainskogo Nauchno-Issledovatel'skogo Instituta Rastenievodstva Selektsii i Genetiki

Tr Ukr Nauchno-Issled Inst Spirt Likero Vodochn Promsti — Trudy Ukrainskii Nauchno-Issledovatel'skii Institut Spirtovoi i Likero-Vodochnoi Promyshlennosti

Tr Ukr Nauchno-Issled Inst Zernovogo Khoz — Trudy Ukrainskogo Nauchno-Issledovatel'skogo Instituta Zernovogo Khozyaistva

r Ul'vanovsk Gos Opytn Stn Zhivotnovod — Trudy Ul'yanovskaya Gosudarstvennaya Opytnaya Stantsiya Zhivotnovodstva

Tr Ulyanovsk Politekh Inst — Trudy Ul'yanovskii Politekhnicheskii Institut

Tr Ul'yanovsk S-kh Inst — Trudy Ul'yanovskogo Sel'skokhozyaistvennogo Instituta

r Ul'yanovsk Skh Opytn Stn — Trudy Ul'yanovskoi Sel'skokhozyaistvennoi Opytnoi Stantsii

Tr Univ Druzhby Nar — Trudy Universiteta Druzhby Narodov [*USSR*]

Tr Univ Druzhby Nar Fiz — Trudy Universiteta Druzhby Narodov. Fizika [*USSR*]

Tr Univ Druzhby Nar Im Patrisa Lumumby — Trudy Universiteta Druzhby Narodov Imeni Patrisa Lumumby

Tr Univ Druzhby Nar Ser Fiz — Trudy Universiteta Druzhby Narodov Imeni Patrisa Lumumby. Seriya Fizika

Tr Upr Geol Okhr Nedr Sov Minist Kirg SSR — Trudy Upravleniya Geologii i Okhrany Nedr pri Sovete Ministrov Kirgizskoi SSR

Tr Ural Lesotekh Inst — Trudy Ural'skogo Lesotekhnicheskogo Instituta

Tr Ural Nauchno-Issled Inst Chern Met — Trudy Ural'skogo Nauchno-Issledovatel'skogo Instituta Chernykh Metallov

Tr Ural Nauchno-Issled Inst Sel'sk Khoz — Trudy Ural'skogo Nauchno-Issledovatel'skogo Instituta Sel'skogo Khozyaistva

Tr Ural Nauchno-Issled Khim Inst — Trudy Ural'skogo Nauchno-Issledovatel'skogo Khimicheskogo Instituta

Tr Ural Nauchno-Issled Proekt Inst Mednoi Prom-sti — Trudy Ural'skii Nauchno-Issledovatel'skii i Proektnyi Institut Mednoi Promyshlennosti [*USSR*]

Tr Ural Nauchno-Issled Proektn Inst Mednoi Promsti — Trudy Ural'skii Nauchno-Issledovatel'skii i Proektnyi Institut Mednoi Promyshlennosti

Tr Ural Otd Gos Nauchno-Issled Inst Ozern Rechn Rybn Khoz — Trudy Ural'skogo Otdeleniya Gosudarstvennyi Nauchno-Issledovatel'skii Institut Ozernogo i Rechnogo Rybnogo Khozyaistva

Tr Ural Otd Mosk Ova Ispyt Prir — Trudy Ural'skogo Otdeleniya Moskovskogo Obshchestva Ispytatelei Prirody

Tr Ural Otd Sib Nauchno-Issled Inst Rybn Khoz — Trudy Ural'skogo Otdeleniya Sibirskogo Nauchno-Issledovatel'skogo Instituta Rybnogo Khozyaistva

Tr Ural Politekh Inst — Trudy Ural'skogo Politekhnicheskogo Instituta Imeni S. M. Kirova

Tr Ural Politekh Inst Im S M Kirova — Trudy Ural'skogo Politekhnicheskogo Instituta Imeni S. M. Kirova [*USSR*]

Trust Bull — Trust Bulletin

Trust Newsl — Trust Newsletter [*National Trust of Australia*]

Trust Nletter — Trust Newsletter [*National Trust of Australia*]

Trusts & Es — Trusts and Estates

Trusts & Est — Trusts and Estates

Tr Uzb Geol Upr — Trudy Uzbekskogo Geologicheskogo Upravlenie

Tr Uzb Gos Nauchno-Issled Inst Kurortol Fizioter — Trudy Uzbekskogo Gosudarstvennogo Nauchno-Issledovatel'skogo i Instituta Kurortologii i Fizioterapii

Tr Uzb Inst Malyarii Med Parazitol — Trudy Uzbekistanskogo Instituta Malyarii i Meditsinskoi Parazitologii

Tr Uzb Nauchno-Issled Inst Fizioter Kurortol — Trudy Uzbekistanskogo Nauchno-Issledovatel'skogo Instituta Fizioterapii i Kurortologii

Tr Uzb Nauchno-Issled Inst Ortop Travmatol Prot — Trudy Uzbekistanskogo Nauchno-Issledovatel'skogo Instituta Ortopedii Travmatologii i Protezirovaniya

Tr Uzb Nauchno-Issled Inst Ortop Travmatol Protez — Trudy Uzbekistanskogo Nauchno-Issledovatel'skogo Instituta Ortopedii Travmatologii i Protezirovaniya

Tr Uzb Nauchno-Issled Inst Vet — Trudy Uzbekskogo Nauchno-Issledovatel'skogo Instituta Veterinarii

Tr VAMI — Trudy VAMI

Tr Velikoluk S-kh Inst — Trudy Velikolukskogo Sel'skokhozyaistvennogo Instituta

Tr Vinnitsk Gos Med Inst — Trudy Vinnitskogo Gosudarstvennogo Meditsinskogo Instituta

Tr Vissh Inst Nar Stop (Varna Bulg) — Trudove na Visshiya Institut za Narodno Stopanstvo "D. Blagoev" (Varna Bulgaria)

Tr Vissh Pedagog Inst (Plovdiv) Mat Fiz Khim Biol — Trudove na Visshiya Pedagogicheski Institut (Plovdiv). Matematika, Fizika, Khimiya, Biologiya

Tr Vladivost Nauchno Issled Inst Epidemiol Mikrobiol Gig — Trudy Vladivostokskogo Nauchno-Issledovatel'skogo Instituta Epidemiologii, Mikrobiologii, i Gigieny

Tr VNIGRI — Trudy VNIGRI [*Vsesoyuznogo Neftyanogo Nauchno-Issledovatel'skogo Geologorazvedochnogo Instituta*]

Tr VNIIEI — Trudy VNIIEI [*Vsesoyuznogo Nauchno-Issledovatel'skogo i Proektno-Tekhnologicheskogo Instituta Elektrougol'nykh Izdelii*]

Tr VNII Fiz-Tekh Radiotekh Izmer — Trudy Vsesoyuznyj Nauchno-Issledovatel'skij Institut Fiziko-Tekhnicheskikh i Radiotekhnicheskikh Izmerenij

Tr Volgor Gos Nauchno-Issled Proektn Inst Neft Promsti — Trudy Volgogradskii Gosudarstvennyi Nauchno-Issledovatel'skii i Proektnyi Institut Neftyanoi Promyshlennosti

Tr Volgogr Med Inst — Trudy Volgogradskogo Meditsinskogo Instituta

Tr Volgogr Nauchno-Issled Inst Neft Gazov Promsti — Trudy Volgogradskii Nauchno-Issledovatel'skii Institut Neftyanoi i Gazovoi Promyshlennosti

Tr Volgogr Opytno Melior Stn — Trudy Volgogradskaya Opytno-Meliorativnaya Stantsiya

Tr Volgogr Otd Gos Nauchno-Issled Inst Ozern Rechn Rybn Khoz — Trudy Volgogradskogo Otdeleniya Gosudarstvennogo Nauchno-Issledovatel'skogo Instituta Ozernogo i Rechnogo Rybnogo Khozyaistva

Tr Volgogr S-kh Inst — Trudy Volgogradskogo Sel'skokhozyaistvennogo Instituta

Tr Vologod Molochn Inst — Trudy Vologodskogo Molochnogo Instituta

Tr Vologod Molochno Khoz Inst — Trudy Vologodskogo Molochno-Khozyaistvennogo Instituta

Tr Volzh Kamskogo Gos Zapov — Trudy Volzhsko-Kamskogo Gosudarstvennogo Zapovednika

Tr Voronezh Gos Med Inst — Trudy Voronezhskii Gosudarstvennyi Meditsinskii Institut

Tr Voronezh Gos Univ — Trudy Voronezhskogo Gosudarstvennogo Universiteta

Tr Voronezh Gos Zapov — Trudy Voronezhskogo Gosudarstvennogo Zapovednika

Tr Voronezh Inzh Stroit Inst — Trudy Voronezhskogo Inzhenerno-Stroitel'nogo Instituta

Tr Voronezh Khim Tekhnol Inst — Trudy Voronezhskogo Khimiko-Tekhnologicheskogo Instituta

Tr Voronezh Med Inst — Trudy Voronezhskogo Meditsinskogo Instituta

Tr Voronezh Nauchno Issled Vet Stn — Trudy Voronezhskoi Nauchno-Issledovatel'skoi Veterinarnoi Stantsii

Tr Voronezh Stn Zashch Rast — Trudy Voronezhskogo Stantsii Zashchity Rastenii

Tr Voronezh Tekhnol Inst — Trudy Voronezhskogo Tekhnologicheskogo Instituta

Tr Voronezh Zoovet Inst — Trudy Voronezhskogo Zooveterinarnogo Instituta

Tr Voroshilovgr S-kh Inst — Trudy Voroshilovgradskogo Sel'skokhozyaistvennogo Instituta

Tr Vost Inst Ogneuporov — Trudy Vostochnogo Instituta Ogneuporov [*USSR*]

Tr Vost-Sib Fil Akad Nauk SSSR — Trudy Vostochno-Sibirskogo Filiala Akademii Nauk SSSR

Tr Vost Sib Geol Inst Akad Nauk SSSR Sib Otd — Trudy Vostochno-Sibirskogo Geologicheskogo Instituta Akademiya Nauk SSSR Sibirskoe Otdelenie

Tr Vost Sib Geol Upr — Trudy Vostochno-Sibirskogo Geologicheskogo Upravleniya

Tr Vost Sib Tekhnol Inst — Trudy Vostochno-Sibirskogo Tekhnologicheskogo Instituta

TRVSA — Travail et Securite

Tr Vseross Konf Khir Flebol — Trudy Vserossiiskoi Konferentsii Khirurgov po Flebologii

Tr Vseross Nauchno Issled Inst Sakh Svekly Sakhara — Trudy Vserossiiskogo Nauchno-Issledovatel'skogo Instituta Sakharnoi Svekly i Sakhara

Tr Vses Aerogeol Tresta — Trudy Vsesoyuznogo Aerogeologicheskogo Tresta

Tr Vses Alyum Magnievyi Inst — Trudy Vsesoyuznyi Alyuminievo-Magnievyi Institut

Tr Vses Elektrotekh Inst — Trudy Vsesoyuznogo Elektrotekhnicheskogo i Instituta

Tr Vses Entomol Obshch — Trudy Vsesoyuznogo Entomologicheskogo Obshchestva

Tr Vses Entomol O-va — Trudy Vsesoyuznogo Entomologicheskogo Obshchestva

Tr Vses Geol Razved Obedin — Trudy Vsesoyuznogo Geologo-Razvedochnogo Ob'edineniya

Tr Vses Gidrobiol O-va — Trudy Vsesoyuznogo Gidrobiologicheskogo Obshchestva

Tr Vses Inst Eksp Vet — Trudy Vsesoyuznogo Instituta Eksperimental'noi Veterinarii [*USSR*]

Tr Vses Inst Gel'mintol — Trudy Vsesyuznogo Instituta Gel'mintologii

Tr Vses Inst Rastenievod — Trudy Vsesoyuznogo Instituta Rastenievodstva

Tr Vses Inst Rast Prob Pop Vyssh Rast — Trudy Vsesoyuznyi Institut Rastenievodstva Problema Populatsii u Vysshikh Rastenii

Tr Vses Inst Zashch Rast — Trudy Vsesoyuznogo Instituta Zashchity Rastenii

Tr Vses Mekh Tekhnol Inst Konserv Promsti — Trudy Vsesoyuznogo Mekhaniko-Tekhnologicheskogo Instituta Konservnoi Promyshlennosti

Tr Vses Nauch-Isled Inst Zashch Rast — Trudy Vsesoyuznogo Nauchno-Issledovatel'skogo Instituta Zashchity Rastenii

Tr Vses Nauch-Issled Inst Lub Kul't — Trudy Vsesoyuznyi Nauchno-Issledovatel'skii Institut Lubyanykh Kul'ture

Tr Vses Nauch-Issled Inst Ptitsevod — Trudy Vsesoyuznogo Nauchno-Issledovatel'skogo Instituta Ptitsevodstva

Tr Vses Nauch-Issled Inst Zerna Prod Ego Pererab — Trudy Vsesoyuznyi Nauchno-Issledovatel'skii Institut Zerna i Produktov Ego Pererabotki

Tr Vses Nauch-Issled Inst Zhivotnovod — Trudy Vsesoyuznyi Nauchno-Issledovatel'skii Institut Zhivotnovodstva

Tr Vses Nauchn Inzh Tekh Ova Metall — Trudy Vsesoyuznogo Nauchnogo Inzhenerno-Tekhnicheskogo Obshchestva Metallurgov

Tr Vses Nauchn-Issled Inst Spirt Likero-Vodoch Prom — Trudy Vsesoyuznogo Nauchno-Issledovatel'skogo Instituta Spirtovoi i Likero-Vodochnoi Promyshlennosti [USSR]

Tr Vses Nauchno Issled Alyum Magnievyi Inst — Trudy Vsesoyuznyi Nauchno-Issledovatel'skii Alyuminievo-Magnievyi Institut

Tr Vses Nauchno-Issled Galurgii — Trudy Vsesoyuznogo Nauchno-Issledovatel'skogo Instituta Galurgii

Tr Vses Nauchno-Issled Geol Inst — Trudy Vsesoyuznogo Nauchno-Issledovatel'skogo Geologicheskogo Instituta

Tr Vses Nauchno Issled Geologorazved Inst — Trudy Vsesoyuznogo Nauchno-Issledovatel'skogo Geologorazvedochnogo Instituta

Tr Vses Nauchno-Issled Geologorazved Neft Inst — Trudy Vsesoyuznyi Nauchno-Issledovatel'skii Geologorazvedochnyi Neftyanoi Instituta

Tr Vses Nauchno-Issled Inst Abrazivov Shlifovaniya — Trudy Vsesoyuznyi Nauchno-Issledovatel'skii Institut Abrazivov i Shlifovaniya

Tr Vses Nauchno-Issled Inst Antibiot — Trudy Vsesoyuznogo Nauchno-Issledovatel'skogo Instituta Antibiotikov

Tr Vses Nauchno-Issled Inst Aviats Mater — Trudy Vsesoyuznogo Nauchno-Issledovatel'skogo Instituta Aviatsionnykh Materialov

Tr Vses Nauchno-Issled Inst Burovoi Tekh — Trudy Vsesoyuznyi Nauchno-Issledovatel'skii Institut Burovoi Tekhniki

Tr Vses Nauchno-Issled Inst Efirnomaslichn Kult — Trudy Vsesoyuznogo Nauchno-Issledovatel'skogo Instituta Efirnomaslichnykh Kul'tur

Tr Vses Nauchno-Issled Inst Elektromekh — Trudy Vsesoyuznogo Nauchno-Issledovatel'skogo Instituta Elektromekhaniki

Tr Vses Nauchno-Issled Inst Elektroterm Oborudovaniya — Trudy Vsesoyuznogo Nauchno-Issledovatel'skogo Instituta Elektrotermicheskogo Oborudovaniya

Tr Vses Nauchno-Issled Inst Fermentn Spirt Promsti — Trudy Vsesoyuznyi Nauchno-Issledovatel'skii Institut Fermentnoi i Spirtovoi Promyshlennosti

Tr Vses Nauchno-Issled Inst Fiziol Biokhim Pitan Skh Zhivotn — Trudy Vsesoyuznogo Nauchno-Issledovatel'skogo Instituta Fiziologii, Biokhimii, i Pitaniya Sel'skokhozyaistvennykh Zhivotnykh

Tr Vses Nauchno-Issled Inst Fiziol Biokhim Skh Zhivotn — Trudy Vsesoyuznogo Nauchno-Issledovatel'skogo Instituta Fiziologii i Biokhimii Sel'skokhozyaistvennykh Zhivotnykh

Tr Vses Nauchno-Issled Inst Galurgii — Trudy Vsesoyuznogo Nauchno-Issledovatel'skogo Instituta Galurgii

Tr Vses Nauchno Issled Inst Geofiz Metodov Razved — Trudy Vsesoyuznyi Nauchno-Issledovatel'skii Institut Geofizicheskikh Metodov Razvedki

Tr Vses Nauchno-Issled Inst G Gidrotekh Melior — Trudy Vsesoyuznogo Nauchno-Issledovatel'skogo Instituta Gidrotekhniki i Melioratsii

Tr Vses Nauchno Issled Inst Gidrogeol Inzh Geol — Trudy Vsesoyuznogo Nauchno-Issledovatel'skogo Instituta Gidrogeologii i Inzhenernoi Geologii

Tr Vses Nauchno-Issled Inst Gidrotekh Melior — Trudy Vsesoyuznogo Nauchno-Issledovatel'skogo Instituta Gidrotekhniki i Melioratsii

Tr Vses Nauchno-Issled Inst Ikusstv Zhidk Topl Gaza — Trudy Vsesoiuznogo Nauchno-Issledovatel'skogo Instituta Iskusstvennogo Zhidkogo Topliva i Gaza [USSR]

Tr Vses Nauchno-Issled Inst Khim Pererab Gazov — Trudy Vsesoyuznogo Nauchno-Issledovatel'skogo Instituta Khimicheskoi Pererabotki Gazov

Tr Vses Nauchno-Issled Inst Khim Reakt — Trudy Vsesoyuznogo Nauchno-Issledovatel'skogo Instituta Khimicheskikh Reaktivov

Tr Vses Nauchno-Issled Inst Khlebopek Promsti — Trudy Vsesoyuznyi Nauchno-Issledovatel'skii Institut Khlebopekarnoi Promyshlennosti

Tr Vses Nauchno-Issled Inst Khlopkovod — Trudy Vsesoyuznogo Nauchno-Issledovatel'skogo Instituta Khlopkovodstva

Tr Vses Nauchno-Issled Inst Khlopkovod Nov Raionov — Trudy Vsesoyuznogo Nauchno-Issledovatel'skii Institut Khlopkovodstva Novykh Raionov

Tr Vses Nauchno Issled Inst Konditer Promsti — Trudy Vsesoyuznogo Nauchno-Issledovatel'skogo Instituta Konditerskoi Promyshlennosti

Tr Vses Nauchno-Issled Inst Konservn Ovoshchesush Prom-sti — Trudy Vsesoyuznogo Nauchno-Issledovatel'skogo Instituta Konservnoi i Ovoshchesushyl'noi Promyshlennosti

Tr Vses Nauchno-Issled Inst Korml S-Kh Zhivotn — Trudy Vsesoyuznogo Nauchno-Issledovatel'skogo Instituta Kormleniya Sel'skokhozyaistvennykh Zhivotnykh

Tr Vses Nauchno Issled Inst Krakhmaloprod — Trudy Vsesoyuznyi Nauchno-Issledovatel'skii Institut Krakhmaloproduktov

Tr Vses Nauchno-Issled Inst L'na — Trudy Vsesoyuznogo Nauchno-Issledovatel'skogo Instituta L'na

Tr Vses Nauchno-Issled Inst Med Instrum Oborudovaniya — Trudy Vsesoyuznogo Nauchno-Issledovatel'skogo Instituta Meditsinskikh Instrumentov Oborudovaniya

Tr Vses Nauchno-Issled Inst Med Priborostr — Trudy Vsesoyuznogo Nauchno-Issledovatel'skogo Instituta Meditsinskikh Priborostroenii

Tr Vses Nauchno Issled Inst Metod Tekh Razved — Trudy Vsesoyuznogo Nauchno-Issledovatel'skogo Instituta Metodiki i Tekhniki Razvedki

Tr Vses Nauchno-Issled Inst Molochn Prom-St — Trudy Vsesoyuznogo Nauchno-Issledovatel'skogo Instituta Molochnoi Promyshlennost

Tr Vses Nauchno-Issled Inst Morsk Ryb Khoz Okeanogr — Trudy Vsesoyuznogo Nauchno-Issledovatel'skogo Instituta Morskogo Rybnogo Khozaistva i Okeanografii [USSR]

Tr Vses Nauchno-Issled Inst Morsk Rybn Khoz Okeanogr — Trudy Vsesoyuznogo Nauchno-Issledovatel'skogo Instituta Morskogo Rybnogo Khozyaistva i Okeanografii

Tr Vses Nauchno-Issled Inst Myasn Prom-St — Trudy Vsesoyuznogo Nauchno-Issledovatel'skogo Instituta Myasnoi Promyshlennost

Tr Vses Nauchno-Issled Inst Pererab Ispol'z Topl — Trudy Vsesoyuznogo Nauchno-Issledovatel'skogo Instituta Pererabotki i Ispol'zovaniya Topliva [USSR]

Tr Vses Nauchno-Issled Inst Pererab Nefti — Trudy Vsesoyuznyj Nauchno-Issledovatel'skij Institut po Pererabotke Nefti

Tr Vses Nauchno-Issled Inst Pererab Slantsev — Trudy Vsesoyuznogo Nauchno-Issledovatel'skogo Instituta po Pererabotke Slantsev [USSR]

Tr Vses Nauchno Issled Inst Pivo Bezalkogol'n Promsti — Trudy Vsesoyuznogo Nauchno-Issledovatel'skogo Instituta Pivo-Bezalkogol'noi Promyshlennosti

Tr Vses Nauchno-Issled Inst Pivovar Promsti — Trudy. Vsesoyuznyi Nauchno-Issledovatel'skii Institut Pivovarennoi Promyshlennosti

Tr Vses Nauchno-Issled Inst Podzemn Gazif Uglei — Trudy Vsesoyuznyi Nauchno-Issledovatel'skii Institut Podzemnoi Gazifikatsii Uglei [USSR]

Tr Vses Nauchno-Issled Inst Prir Gazov — Trudy Vsesoyuznyi Nauchno-Issledovatel'skii Institut Prirodnykh Gazov [USSR]

Tr Vses Nauchno-Issled Inst Prod Brozheniya — Trudy Vsesoyuznyi Nauchno-Issledovatel'skii Institut Produktov Brozheniya [USSR]

Tr Vses Nauchno Issled Inst Proizvod Pishch Prod Kartofelya — Trudy Vsesoyuznyi Nauchno-Issledovatel'skii Institut po Proizvodstvu Pishchevykh Produktov iz Kartofelya

Tr Vses Nauchno-Issled Inst Prud Rybn Khoz — Trudy Vsesoyuznogo Nauchno-Issledovatel'skogo Instituta Prudovogo Rybnogo Khozaistva

Tr Vses Nauchno-Issled Inst Radiat Tekh — Trudy Vsesoyuznyj Nauchno-Issledovatel'skij Institut Radiatsionnoj Tekhniki

Tr Vses Nauchno-Issled Inst Rastit Masel Margarina — Trudy Vsesoyuznogo Nauchno-Issledovatel'skogo Instituta Rastitel'nykh Masel i Margarina

Tr Vses Nauchno-Issled Inst Sint Nat Dushistykh Veshchestv — Trudy Vsesoyuznogo Nauchno-Issledovatel'skogo Instituta Sinteticheskikh i Natural'nykh Dushistykh Veshchestv

Tr Vses Nauchno Issled Inst Solvanoi Promsti — Trudy Vsesoyuznyi Nauchno-Issledovatel'skii Institut Solvanoi Promyshlennosti

Tr Vses Nauchno-Issled Inst Spirt Prom-sti — Trudy Vsesoyuznogo Nauchno-Issledovatel'skogo Instituta Spirtovoi Promyshlennosti [USSR]

Tr Vses Nauchno-Issled Inst Stand Obraztsov Spektr Etalonov — Trudy Vsesoyuznogo Nauchno-Issledovatel'skogo Instituta Standartnykh Obraztsov i Spektral'nykh Etalonov [USSR]

Tr Vses Nauchno Issled Inst Steklyannogo Volokna — Trudy Vsesoyuznogo Nauchno-Issledovatel'skogo Instituta Steklyannogo Volokna

Tr Vses Nauchno-Issled Inst Torf Prom-sti — Trudy Vsesoyuznogo Nauchno-Issledovatel'skogo Instituta Torfyanoi Promyshlennosti [USSR]

Tr Vses Nauchno-Issled Inst Udobr Agropochvoved — Trudy Vsesoyuznogo Nauchno-Issledovatel'skogo Instituta Udobreniya i Agropochvovedeniya

Tr Vses Nauchno-Issled Inst Vet Sanit — Trudy Vsesoyuznogo Nauchno-Issledovatel'skogo Instituta Veterinarnoi Sanitarii

Tr Vses Nauchno-Issled Inst Vet Sanit Ektoparazitol — Trudy Vsesoyuznogo Nauchno-Issledovatel'skogo Instituta Veterinarnoi Sanitarii i Ektoparazitologii

Tr Vses Nauchno-Issled Inst Yad Geofiz Geokhim — Trudy Vsesoyuznyi Nauchno-Issledovatel'skii Institut Yadernoi Geofiziki i Geokhimii [USSR]

Tr Vses Nauchno-Issled Inst Zashch Rast — Trudy Vsesoyuznogo Nauchno-Issledovatel'skogo Instituta Zashchity Rastenii

Tr Vses Nauchno-Issled Inst Zerna Prod Pererab — Trudy Vsesoyuznogo Nauchno-Issledovatel'skogo Instituta Zerna i Produktov Ego Pererabotki

Tr Vses Nauchno-Issled Inst Zheleznodorozhn Transp — Trudy Vsesoyuznogo Nauchno-Issledovatel'skogo Instituta Zheleznodorozhnogo Transporta

Tr Vses Nauchno-Issled Inst Zheleznodorzhn — Trudy Vsesoyuznogo Nauchno-Issledovatel'skogo Instituta Zheleznodorozhnogo Transporta

Tr Vses Nauchno Issled Inst Zhirov — Trudy Vsesoyuznyi Nauchno-Issledovatel'skii Institut Zhirov

Tr Vses Nauchno-Issled Inst Zhivotn Syr'ya Pushn — Trudy Vsesoyuznogo Nauchno-Issledovatel'skogo Instituta Zhivotnogo Syr'ya Pushniny

Tr Vses Nauchno-Issled Inst Zolota Redk Met — Trudy Vsesoyuznogo Nauchno-Issledovatel'skogo Instituta Zolota i Redkikh Metallov [USSR]

Tr Vses Nauchno-Issled Konstr Inst Avtog Mashinostr — Trudy Vsesoyuznogo Nauchno-Issledovatel'skogo i Konstruktorskogo Instituta Avtogennogo Mashinostroeniya [*USSR*]

Tr Vses Nauchno Issled Konstr Inst Nauchn Priborostr — Trudy Vsesoyuznyi Nauchno-Issledovatel'skii i Konstruktorskii Institut Nauchnogo Priborostroeniya

Tr Vses Nauchno Issled Proektn Inst Galurgii — Trudy Vsesoyuznogo Nauchno-Issledovatel'skogo i Proektnogo Instituta Galurgii

Tr Vses Nauchno Issled Proektn Inst Mekh Obrab Polezn Iskop — Trudy Vsesoyuznyi Nauchno-Issledovatel'skii i Proektnyi Institut Mekhanicheskoi Obrabotki Poleznykh Iskopaemykh

Tr Vses Neftegazov Nauchno-Issled Inst — Trudy Vsesoyuznyi Neftegazovyi Nauchno-Issledovatel'skii Institut

Tr Vses Neft Nauchno-Issled Geologorazved Inst — Trudy Vsesoyuznogo Neftyanogo Nauchno-Issledovatel'skogo Geologorazvedochnogo Instituta [*USSR*]

Tr Vses Neft Nauchno-Issled Inst Tekh Bezop — Trudy Vsesoyuznyi Neftyanoi Nauchno-Issledovatel'skii Institut po Tekhnike Bezopasnosti

Tr Vses O Genet Sel Kuban Otd — Trudy Vsesoyuznoe Obshchestvo Genetikov i Selektsionerov Kubanskoe Otdelenie

Tr Vses O-va Fiziol Biokhim Farmakol — Trudy Vsesoyuznogo Obshchestva Fiziologov Biokhimikov i Farmakologov

Tr Vses S-kh Inst Zaochn Obraz — Trudy Vsesoyuznogo Sel'skokhozyaistvennogo Instituta Zaochnogo Obrazovaniva

Tr Vses Teplotekh Nauchno-Issled Inst — Trudy Vsesoyuznyi Teplotekhnikii Nauchno-Issledovatel'skii Institut [*USSR*]

Tr Vses Tsentr Nauchno Issled Inst Zhirov — Trudy Vsesoyuznogo Tsentral'nogo Nauchno-Issledovatel'skogo Instituta Zhirov

Tr VTI — Trudy VTI [*USSR*]

Tr Vysokogorn Geofiz Inst — Trudy Vysokogornyj Geofizicheskij Institut

TRWOA — Traffic World

Tr Yakutsk Fil Akad Nauk SSSR Ser Fiz — Trudy Yakutskogo Filiala Akademiya Nauk SSSR Seriya Fizicheskaya

Tr Yakutsk Fil Akad Nauk SSSR Ser Geol — Trudy Yakutskogo Filiala Akademii Nauk SSSR Seriya Geologicheskaya

Tr Yakutsk Nauchno-Issled Inst Selsk Khoz — Trudy Yakutskogo Nauchno-Issledovatel'skogo Instituta Sel'skogo Khozyaistva

Tr Yakutsk Nauchno-Issled Inst Tuberk — Trudy Yakutskogo Nauchno-Issledovatel'skii Instituta Tuberkuleza

Tr Yakutsk Otd Sib Nauchno-Issled Inst Rybn Khoz — Trudy Yakutskogo Otdeleniya Sibirskogo Nauchno-Issledovatel'skogo Instituta Rybnogo Khozyaistva

Tr Yalt Nauchno-Issled Inst Fiz Metodov Lech Med Klimatol — Trudy Yaltinskogo Nauchno-Issledovatel'nogo Instituta Fizicheskikh Metodov Lecheniya i Meditsinskoi Klimatologii

Tr Yarosl Med Inst — Trudy Yaroslavskogo Meditsinskogo Instituta

Tr Yarosl Skh Inst — Trudy Yaroslavskogo Sel'skokhozyaistvennogo Instituta

Tryb Spold — Trybuna Spoldzielcza

TrZ — Trierer Zeitschrift

Tr Zakavk Nauchno-Issled Gidrometeorol Inst — Trudy Zakavkazskogo Nauchno-Issledovatel'skogo Gidrometeorologicheskogo Instituta

Tr Zapadno Sib Fil Akad Stroit Arkhit SSSR — Trudy Zapadno-Sibirskii Filial Akademiya Stroitel'stva i Arkhitektury SSSR

Tr Zool Inst Akad Nauk SSSR — Trudy Zoologicheskogo Instituta Akademiya Nauk SSSR

TS — Theatre Studies

TS — Theatre Survey

TS — Theological Studies

TS — Today's Speech

TSA — Teater SA. Quarterly for South African Theater

TSACA — Transactions. South African Institution of Civil Engineers

TSAEA — Transactions. South African Institute of Electrical Engineers

TSAFA — Traffic Safety

TSamU — Trudy Samarkandskogo Gosudarstvennogo Universiteta Imeni Alisera Navoi

TSB — Theological Studies (Baltimore)

TSB — Thoreau Society Bulletin

TSb — Tjurkologiceskij Sbornik

TSB — Two Complete Science Adventure Books

TS-3 Bibliograf Informacija — TS-3 Bibliografija Informacija

TSBMD — Tellus. Series B. Chemical and Physical Meteorology

T S Booklet — Thoreau Society Booklet

TSBUD — Tennessee Survey of Business

TSCGD — GRS [*Gesellschaft fuer Reaktorsicherheit*] Translations. Safety Codes and Guides

Tschermaks Mineralog u Petrog Mitt — Tschermaks Mineralogische und Petrographische Mitteilungen

Tschermaks Mineral Petrogr Mitt — Tschermaks Mineralogische und Petrographische Mitteilungen

Tsch Min Pe — Tschermaks Mineralogische und Petrographische Mitteilungen

TSCPA — Transactions and Studies. College of Physicians of Philadelphia

TSDTA — Tenside-Detergents

TSE — Texas Studies in English

TSE — Tulane Studies in English

Tselliul Bum Karton — Tselliuloza, Bumaga, i Karton [*USSR*]

Tsem Rastvory Krepleniya Glubokikh Skvazhin — Tsementnye Rastvory dlya Krepleniya Glubokikh Skvazhin

Tsentr Nauchno Issled Dizel'n Inst Tr — Tsentral'nyi Nauchno-Issledovatel'skii Dizel'nyi Institut Trudy

Tsentr Nauchno-Issled Inst Bum Sbor Tr — Tsentral'nyi Nauchno-Issledovatel'skii Institut Bumagi Sbornik Trudov

Tsentr Nauchno-Issled Inst Olovyannoi Promsti Nauchny Tr — Tsentral'nyi Nauchno-Issledovatel'skii Institut Olovyannoi Promyshlennosti Nauchnye Trudy

Tsentr Nauchno-Issled Inst Tekhnol Mashinostr Sb — Tsentral'nyi Nauchno-Issledovatel'skii Institut Tekhnologii i Mashinostroeniya Sbornik

Tsentr Ref Med Zh Ser A — Tsentral'nyi Referativnyi Meditsinskii Zhurnal. Seriya A. Biologiya, Teoreticheskie Problemy Meditsiny

Tsentr Ref Med Zh Ser B — Tsentral'nyi Referativnyi Meditsinskii Zhurnal. Seriya B. Vnutrennye Bolezni

Tsentr Ref Med Zh Ser G — Tsentral'nyi Referativnyi Meditsinskii Zhurnal. Seriya G. Mikrobiologiya, Gigiena, i Sanitariya

Tsentr Ref Med Zh Ser V — Tsentral'nyi Referativnyi Meditsinskii Zhurnal. Seriya V. Khirurgiya

TSF — Ten Story Fantasy

TSF — Test Aankoop

TSF — Theological Student Fellowship. Bulletin

TSFTA — Trudy Sibirskogo Fiziko-Tekhnicheskogo Instituta pri Tomskom Gosudarstvennom Universitete

TsGw — Tydskrif vir Geesteswetenskappe

TSI — Technology and Science of Informatics

TSIGA — Trudy Sibirskogo Nauchno-Issledovatel'skogo Instituta Geologii, Geofiziki, i Mineral'nogo Syr'ya

Tsirk Shemakh Astrofiz Obs — Tsirkulyar Shemakhinskoi Astrofizicheskoi Observatorii [*Azerbaidzhan SSR*]

TsIT — Tijdschrift voor Indische Taal-, Land-, en Volkenkunde

TSITA — Tsitologiya

Tsititiksiny Sovrem Med — Tsititiksiny e Sovremennoi Meditsine

Tsitol — Tsitologiya

Tsitol Genet — Tsitologiya i Genetika

Tsitol Genet Akad Nauk Ukr SSR — Tsitologiya i Genetika Akademiya Nauk Ukrainsoi SSR

Tsitologiya Genet — Tsitologiya i Genetika

TSJSNW — Transactions. Samuel Johnson Society of the Northwest

Ts Jur Foer Finland — Tidskrift Utgiven av Juridiska Foereningen i Finland

TSK — Theologische Studien und Kritiken

TSKTA — Toyo Shokuhin Kogyo Tanki Daigaku. Toyo Shokuhin Kenkyusho Kenkyu Hokokusho

TSKZA — Tekhnika v Sel'skom Khozyaistve

TSL — Tennessee Studies in Literature

TSL — Travaux. Classe I de Linguistique, de Litterature, et de Philosophie. Societe des Sciences et des Lettres de Lodz

Ts LJ — Tulsa Law Journal

TSLL — Texas Studies in Literature and Language

TSM — Tesoro Sacro-Musical

TSM — Texte des Spaeten Mittelalters

TSM — Trends. Financieel Economisch Magazine

TsNAG — Tijdschrift. Koninklijk Nederlandsch Aardrijkskundig Genootschap

TSNGA — Trudy. Sredneaziatskii Nauchno-Issledovatel'skii Institut Geologii i Mineral'nogo Syr'ya

TSNL Index Series — Texas System of Natural Laboratories. Index Series

TsNTL — Tijdschrift voor Nederlandsche Taal- en Letterkunde

TSO — Information Society

T Soc Rheol — Transactions. Society of Rheology

TSP — Tulane Studies in Philosophy

TsPhil — Tijdschrift voor Philosophie

TSPMA — Travaux. Societe de Pharmacie de Montpellier

TSR — [*The*] Shopper Report

TS-3 Referativnyi Sb — TS-3 Referativnyi Sbornik

TSRLD — TRRL [*Transport and Road Research Laboratory*] Supplementary Report

TSRLL — Tulane Studies in Romance Languages and Literature

TSRVA — Times Science Review

TSSD — Telecommunications Systems and Services Directory

TsSV — Tijdschrift voor de Studie van de Verlichting

TST — Textile Science and Technology [*Elsevier Book Series*]

TSTIA — Trudy Sibirskogo Tekhnologicheskogo Instituta

TsTK — Tidsskrift for Teologi og Kirke [*Oslo*]

TSTKA — Tsuchi To Kiso

Tsukuba-Daigaku Shakaigaku J — Tsukuba-Daigaku Shakaigaku Journal

Tsukuba J Math — Tsukuba Journal of Mathematics

Tsukuba Univ Inst Geosci Annu Rep — Tsukuba University. Institute of Geoscience. Annual Report

Tsukumo Earth Sci — Tsukumo Earth Science

Tsvet Metal — Tsvetnye Metally

Tsvetn Met — Tsvetnye Metally

Tsvetn Metall — Tsvetnaya Metallurgiya

Tsvetn Metall Nauchno Tekh Sb — Tsvetnaya Metallurgiya-Nauchno-Tekhnicheskii Sbornik

Tsvetn Metall (Ordzhonikidze, USSR) — Tsvetnaya Metallurgiya (Ordzhonikidze, USSR)

Tsvtn Metall Nauchno Tekh Byull — Tsvetnaya Metallurgiya-Nauchno-Tekhnicheskii Byulleten
TsVUB — Tijdschrift van de Vrige Universiteit van Brussel
TsVV — Tydskrif vir Volkskunde en Volkstaal
TSW — Prace Wroclawskiego Towarzystwa Naukowego
TSW — Three Banks Review
TsWK — Tydskrif vir Wetenskap en Kuns
TSYKDE — Annual Report. Tobacco Research Institute. Taiwan Tobacco and Wine Monopoly Bureau
TSZGK — Thueringisch-Saechsische Zeitschrift fuer Geschichte und Kunst
TT — Taal en Tongval [*Antwerpen*]
TT — Taiga Times '71
TT — Teologisk Tidsskrift
TT — Theologisch Tijdschrift
TT — Theology Today
TT — Time and Tide
T & T — Time and Tide
T & T — Tools and Tillage
TTAE — Turk Tarih. Arkeologya ve Etnografya Dergisi
TTagPI — Trudy Taganrogskogo Gosudarstvennogo Pedagogiceskogo Instituta
TTAV — TTAV [*Technical Teachers Association of Victoria*] News
TTb — Trudy Tbilisskogo Pedagogiceskogo Instituta
TTCMA — Turk Tip Cemiyeti Mecmuasi
TTD — Textile Technology Digest
TTE — Talks to Teachers of English
TTE — Texpress. Economisch en Technisch Weekblad voor de Textiel en Kledingindustrie en Handel in de Benelux
TTEKA — Tokyo Toritsu Eisei Kenkyusho Kenkyu Hokoku
TTele — Tatar Tele Hem Adebijaty
TTG — Travel Trade Gazette UK
TTh — Tijdschrift voor Theologie [*Wageningen*]
T Th Z — Trierer Theologische Zeitschrift
TTI — Tulane Tax Institute
TTIDA — Teknisk Tidskrift [*Sweden*]
TTIIA — Trudy Tashkentskogo Instituta Inzhenerov Irrigatsii i Mekhanizatsii Sel'skogo Khozyaistva
T Times — These Times
TTIS Publ — TTIS [*Translation and Technical Information Service*] Publication
TTJ — Timber Trades Journal and Wood Processing
TTK — Turk Tarih Kurumu
TTK "Belleten" — Turk Tarih Kurumu "Belleten"
TTKi — Tidsskrift for Teologi og Kirke [*Oslo*]
TTKMA — Trudy Tambovskogo Instituta Khimicheskogo Mashinostroeniya
TTKSA — Tokyo-Toritsu Kogyo Shoreikan Hokoku
TTLPA — Tekstil'naya Promyshlennost
TTMTA — Tungsram Technische Mitteilungen
T Today — Theology Today
TTomU — Trudy Tomskogo Gosudarstvennogo Universiteta
TTP — Tamarind Technical Papers
TTP — Trudy Tallinskogo Politekhnicheskogo Instituta. Seriya B, XX
TTPI — Trudy Tbilisskogo Gosudarstvennogo Pedagogiceskogo Instituta
TTQ — Tuebinger Theologische Quartalschrift
TTQS — Tuebinger Theologische Quartalschrift. Stuttgart
TTrA — Textes et Traitement Automatique
TTS — Transactions. Thoroton Society
TTSPB — Transport Theory and Statistical Physics
TTT — Teylers Theologisch Tijdschrift
TTT — Trade Token Topics
TTW — Test
TTZ — Trierer Theologische Zeitschrift
TTZED — TIZ. Tonindustrie-Zeitung
TU — Technische Ueberwachung [*Technological Supervising*]
TU — Texte und Untersuchungen zur Geschichte der Altchristlichen Literatur [*Berlin*]
TU — Tundra Times
TUB — Tulane University. Bulletin
TUBEA — Tubercle
Tuberc Respir Dis — Tuberculosis and Respiratory Diseases
Tuberk Forschungsinst Borstel Jahresber — Tuberkulose Forschungsinstitut Borstel. Jahresbericht
Tuberk Grenzgeb Einzeldarst — Tuberkulose und Ihre Grenzgebiete in Einzeldarstellungen
Tuberk Ihre Grenzgeb Einzeldarst — Tuberkulose und Ihre Grenzgebiete in Einzeldarstellungen
Tubular Struct — Tubular Structures
TUBWPL — Technische Universitaet Berlin. Arbeitspapiere zur Linguistik/Working Papers in Linguistics
TUD — Trudy Universiteta Druzhby Narodov Imeni Patrisa Lumumby
Tud & Musz Tajek — Tudomanyos es Muszaki Tajekoztatas
TUDNL — Trudy Universiteta Druzhby Narodov Imeni Patrisa Lumumby [*Moscow*]
Tudom Musz Tajek — Tudomanyos es Muszaki Tajekoztatas
Tud-szerv Tajekoz — Tudomanyszervezesi Tajekoztato
Tuerk Ark Derg — Tuerk Arkeoloji Dergisi
Tuerk Bitki Koruma Derg — Tuerkiye Bitki Koruma Dergisi

Tuerk Ljiyen Tecruebi Biyol Dergisi — Tuerk Ljiyen ve Tecruebi Biyoloji Dergisi
Tuerk Tar Derg — Tuerk Tarih, Arkeologya ve Etnografya Dergisi
Tuerk Z Hyg Exp Biol — Tuerkische Zeitschrift fuer Hygiene und Experimentelle Biologie
TUeV Mitt Mitglieder Tech Ueberwach-Ver Bayern — TUeV [*Technischer Ueberwachungs-Verein*] Mitteilungen fuer die Mitglieder. Technischer Ueberwachungs-Verein Bayern [*German Federal Republic*]
TUF — Umweltmagazin. Fachzeitschrift fuer Umwelttechnik in Industrie und Kommune
TUFPB — Proceedings. Faculty of Science. Tokai University
Tufs Folia Med — Tufs Folia Medica
Tufts Coll Studies — Tufts College Studies
Tufts Dent Outlook — Tufts Dental Outlook
Tufts Health Sci Rev — Tufts Health Science Review
TUGAL — Texte und Untersuchungen zur Geschichte der Altchristlichen Literatur
TU Gazette — University of Tasmania. Gazette
TUGEA — Teknisk Ukeblad
TUGRA — Report of Investigations. University of Texas at Austin. Bureau of Economic Geology
TUH — Review of Economic Conditions [*Ankara*]
TUI — Tuinderij. Vakblad voor de Intensieve Groenteteelt
TuK — Text und Kritik
Tu L — Tulane Law Review
Tulane Law R — Tulane Law Review
Tulane L Rev — Tulane Law Review
Tulane St — Tulane Studies in English
Tulane Stud Eng — Tulane Studies in English
Tulane Stud Geol — Tulane Studies in Geology
Tulane Stud Geol Paleontol — Tulane Studies in Geology and Paleontology
Tulane Stud Phil — Tulane Studies in Philosophy
Tulane Stud Zool — Tulane Studies in Zoology
Tulane Stud Zool Bot — Tulane Studies in Zoology and Botany
Tulane U Stud Eng — Tulane University. Studies in English
TU Law R — University of Tasmania. Law Review
Tul Gorn Inst Nauchn Tr — Tul'skii Gornyi Institut Nauchnye Trudy
Tul Gos Pedagog Inst Uch Zap Fiz Tekh Nauk — Tul'skii Gosudarstvennyi Pedagogicheskii Institut Uchenye Zapiski Fiziko-Tekhnicheskie Nauki
Tul Gos Ped Inst Ucen Zap Mat Kaf — Tul'skii Gosudarstvennyi Pedagogiceskii Institut Imeni L. N. Tolstogo Ucenye Zapiski Matematiceskih Kafedr
Tul L Rev — Tulane Law Review
Tu LR — Tulane Law Review
TULSA — Petroleum Abstracts [*Online*]
Tulsa Geol Soc Dig — Tulsa Geological Society. Digest
Tulsa Geol Soc Digest — Tulsa Geological Society. Digest
Tulsa L J — Tulsa Law Journal
Tulsa Med — Tulsa Medicine
Tul Tax Inst — Tulane Tax Institute
Tul Tidelands Inst — Tulane Mineral and Tidelands Law Institute
TUMEA — Tunisie Medicale
Tumor Diagn — Tumor Diagnostik
Tumor Diagn Ther — Tumor Diagnostik und Therapie
Tumor Res — Tumor Research
Tuners JL — Tuners' Journal
Tungsram Tech Mitt — Tungsram Technische Mitteilungen
Tunis Agric — Tunisie Agricole
Tunisie Agr — Tunisie Agricole
Tunisie Agric Rev Mens Illus — Tunisie Agricole Revue Mensuelle Illustree
Tunisie Econ — Tunisie Economique
Tunis Med — Tunisie Medicale
Tunnels Ouvrages Souterr — Tunnels et Ouvrages Souterrains
Tunnels Tunnell — Tunnels and Tunnelling
Tunnlg Technol Newsl — Tunneling Technology Newsletter
Tunn Technol Newsl — Tunneling Technology Newsletter [*United States*]
TUPMA — Trudy Ural'skii Nauchno-Issledovatel'skii i Proektnyi Institut Mednoi Promyshlennosti
TUR — Turkish Economy
Turbomach Int — Turbomachinery International
Turbul Meas Liq Proc Symp — Turbulence Measurements in Liquids. Proceedings of Symposium
Turc — Turcica. Revue d'Etudes Turques
TUREA — Tumor Research
Turf Cult — Turf Culture
Turk AEC Ankara Nucl Res Cent Tech J — Turkish Atomic Energy Commission. Ankara Nuclear Research Center. Technical Journal
Turk Biol Derg — Turk Biologi Dergisi
Turk Bull Hyg Exp Biol — Turkish Bulletin of Hygiene and Experimental Biology
Turkey Prod — Turkey Producer
Turk For Pol Rep — Turkish Foreign Policy Report
Turk Gen Kim Kurumu Derg B — Turkiye Genel Kimyagerler Kurumu Dergisi-B
Turk Hemsire Derg — Turk Hemsireler Dergisi

urk Hifzissihha Tecr Biol Mecm — Turk Hifzissihha ve Tecrubi Biologi
  Mecmuasi
urk Hij Deney Biyol Derg — Turk Hijiyen ve Deneysel Biyoloji Dergisi
urk Hij Deneysel Biyol Derg — Turk Hijiyen ve Deneysel Biyoloji Dergisi
urk Hij Tecr Biyol Derg — Turk Hijiyen ve Tecruby Biyoloji Dergisi
urk J Biol — Turkish Journal of Biology
urk Jeol Kurumu Bul — Turkiye Jeoloji Kurumu Bulteni
urk Jeomorfologlar Dernegi Yayini — Turkiye Jeomorfologlar Dernegi.
  Yayini
urk J Nucl Sci — Turkish Journal of Nuclear Sciences
urk J Pediatr — Turkish Journal of Pediatrics
urkmen Gos Univ Ucen Zap — Turkmenskii Gosudarstvennyi Universitet
  Imeni A. M. Gor'kogo Ucenye Zapiski
urk Mikrobiyol Cemiy Derg — Turk Mikrobiyoloji Cemiyeti Dergisi
urk Miner Res Explor Bull — Turkey. Mineral Research and Exploration
  Institute. Bulletin
urkm Iskra — Turkmenskaya Iskra [USSR]
urk Publ Adm Annu — Turkish Public Administration Annual
urk Tip Akad Mecm — Turkiye Tip Akademisi Mecmuasi
urk Tip Cemiy Mecm — Turkiye Tip Cemiyeti Mecmuasi
urk Tip Cem Mecm — Turkiye Tip Cemiyeti Mecmuasi [Turkey]
urk Tip Dern Derg — Turk Tip Dernegi Dergisi
urk Tip Encumeni Ars — Turkiye Tip Encumeni Arsivi
urnbull Libr Rec — Turnbull Library Records
urn Rec — Turnbull Library Record [New Zealand]
uron Yliopiston Julk Sar A-II — Turon Yliopiston Julkaisuja. Sarja A-II
URRA — Turrialba [Costa Rica]
urrialba — Turrialba. Revista Interamericana de Ciencias Agricolas
USAS — Twayne's United States Authors Series
uskegee Exp — Tuskegee Normal and Industrial Institute. Experiment
  Station. Publications
USLA — Trudy Ukrainskii Nauchno-Issledovatel'skii Institut Spirtovoi i
  Likero-Vodochnoi Promyshlennosti
USQA — Quarterly Bulletin. Faculty of Science. Tehran University
ussock Grassl Mt Lands Inst Annu Rep — Tussock Grasslands and Mountain
  Lands Institute. Annual Report
utkimuksia Res Rep — Tutkimuksia Research Reports
utkimus Tek — Tutkimus ja Tekniikka
UTNB — Tunneling Technology Newsletter
UTUB — Tunnels and Tunnelling
uZ — Texte und Zeichen
V — Television
V — Treji Varti
V — Tzertovnyia Viedomosti
VA — Television Age
VA Chem Eng Rept — Tennessee Valley Authority. Chemical Engineering
  Report
vaett Ind — Tvaett Industrin
varinnictvo Ukr — Tvarinnictvo Ukraini
VA Tech Rept — Tennessee Valley Authority. Technical Report
VBTA — Trudy Vsesoyuznyi Nauchno-Issledovatel'skii Institut Burovoi
  Tekhniki
V Commun — TV Communications
VD — Television Digest
VD — Travaux sur Voltaire et le Dix-Huitieme Siecle
VF — Tidskrift foer Teknisk-Vettenskaplig Forskning
VG — Tijdschrift voor Geschiedenis
VG — TV Guide
vG — Tydskrif vir Geesteswetenskappe
VIIJ — Trudy Vojennogo Instituta Inostrannykh Jazykov
VIIJa — Trudy Vojennogo Instituta Inostrannykh Jazykov
V Int — Television International
VL — Tijdschrift voor Liturgei
vL — Tydskrif vir Letterkunde
vl Educ News — Transvaal Educational News
Volkskd Volkstaal — Tydskrif vir Volkskunde en Volkstaal
VPED — Tennessee Valley Perspective
VPRA — Teoriya Veroyatnostei i Ee Primeneniya
V Q — Television Quarterly
V/Radio Age — Television/Radio Age
V/Radio Age Int — Television/Radio Age International
VRG — Tijdschrift voor Rechtsgeschiedenis
VS — Stedebouw en Volkshuisvesting
VT — Tijdschrift voor Theologie
VUB — Tijdschrift van de Vrige Universiteit van Brussel
VXCA — Travaux Communaux
VVYTA — Teplofizika Vysokikh Temperatur
W — Journal of Technical Writing and Communication
W — Tapwe
W — Terre Wallonne
W — Third World
W — Thrilling Wonder Stories
w — Tworczosc
WA — Tijdschrift voor Sociale Wetenschappen
WA — Transactions. Wisconsin Academy of Sciences, Arts, and Letters
WAS — Twayne's World Authors Series

TwC — Twentieth Century
TWDRA — Report. Texas Water Development Board
Twen Cen — Twentieth Century
Twen Ct Lit — Twentieth Century Literature
Twent Cent — Twentieth Century
Twent Cen V — Twentieth Century Views
T Wisc Ac — Transactions. Wisconsin Academy of Sciences, Arts, and Letters
TWLOA — Technik Wlokienniczy
TWN — Thomas Wolfe Newsletter
T Wolfe New — Thomas Wolfe Newsletter
T Wolfe Rev — Thomas Wolfe Review
Tworzywa Sztuczne Med — Tworzywa Sztuczne'w Medycynie
Two-Year College Math J — Two-Year College Mathematics Journal
Two-Yr Coll Math J — Two-Year College Mathematics Journal
TWP — Trondheim Workingpapers
TWQ — Third World Quarterly
TWS — Thrilling Wonder Stories
TWSUA — Taiwan Sugar
TWT — Ingenieursblad
TWX — Transport en Opslag. Maandblad voor Managers en Medewerkers op
  het Gebied van Intern Transport, Opslag, Magazijntechniek, en
  Distributietechniek
TXAPA — Toxicology and Applied Pharmacology
TXB — TextielVisie. Vakblad voor de Textielbranche
TXBRA — Texas Business Review
TX Bus Rev — Texas Business Review
TXCYA — Toxicology
TXE — Tax Executive
TXECB — Toxicological and Environmental Chemistry Reviews
TXHL — Texas Health Letter
TX L — Texas Law Review
TX LR — Texas Law Review
TXLRA — Texas Law Review
TXMDA — Texas Medicine
TxSE — Texas Studies in English
TXV — Texas Business Review
TXV — Textil Revue. Fachblatt fuer Textilhandel, Konfektionsindustrie, und
  Textilindustrie
TY — Tyler's Quarterly Historical and Genealogical Magazine
Tyazh Mashinostr — Tyazhelie Mashinostroenie
TyD — Trabajos y Dias
TYDNAP — Annual Report. Tokyo College of Pharmacy
TYDS — Transactions. Yorkshire Dialect Society
Tydskr Dieetkd Huishoudkd — Tydskrif vir Dieetkunde en Huishoudkunde
  [South Africa]
Tydskr Natuurwet — Tydskrif vir Natuurwetenskappe
Tydskr Natuurwetenskap — Tydskrif vir Natuurwetenskappe. Suid-Afrikaanse
  Akademie vir Wetenskap en Kuns
Tydskr S-Afr Vet Ver — Tydskrif. Suid-Afrikaanse Veterinere Vereniging
Tydskr Skoon Lug — Tydskrif vir Skoon Lug
Tydskr Tandheelkd Ver S-Afr — Tydskrif. Tandheelkundige Vereniging van
  Suid-Afrika
Tydskr Wet Kuns — Tydskrif vir Wetenskap en Kuns
TygP — Tygodnik Powszechny
TYKNAQ — Annual Report. Tohoku College of Pharmacy
Tyler's — Tyler's Quarterly Historical and Genealogical Magazine
Tyler's Quar — Tyler's Quarterly Historical and Genealogical Magazine
TYNAA — Tydskrif vir Natuurwetenskappe
Tyndale Bul — Tyndale Bulletin
TYO — Tokyo Newsletter
Tyoevaeen Taloudell Tutkimus Katsaus — Tyoevaeen Taloudellinen
  Tutkimuslaitos Katsaus
Typ News — Typewriting News
Typographical J — Typographical Journal
Typogr Monatsbl — Typographische Monatsblaetter
Tyres & Access — Tyres and Accessories
TYS — Overzicht van de Economische Ontwikkeling
TZ — Theologische Zeitschrift
TZ — Times of Zambia
TZ — Trierer Zeitschrift
TZA — Finanzierung, Leasing, Factoring
TZBas — Theologische Zeitschrift (Basel)
TZI — Traditiones. Zbornik Instituta za Slovensko Narodopisje
TZKRA — Tonindustrie-Zeitung und Keramische Rundschau
TZ Prakt Metallbearb — TZ fuer Praktische Metallbearbeitung
TZS — Terzake Subsidies

U

U — Uitgelezen
U — Universitas
UA — United Asia
UA — Universidad de Antioquia [*Colombia*]
UA — Ural-Altaische Jahrbuecher
UAA — Universitet i Bergen. Arbok. Historisk-Antikvarisk Rekke
UAC — Universidad de Antioquia (Colombia)
UAegAl — Urkunden die Aegyptischen Altertums
UAERA — United States. Air Force. School of Aerospace Medicine. Technical Report
UAG — USSR. Academy of Science. Proceedings. Geographical Series
UAJ — Ural-Altaische Jahrbuecher
UAJb — Ural-Altaische Jahrbuecher
UALR LJ — University of Arkansas at Little Rock. Law Journal
UAQUA — Urban Affairs Quarterly
UAR Geol Surv Miner Res Dep Pap — United Arab Republic. Geological Survey and Mineral Research Department. Papers
UAR Inst Oceanogr Fish Bull — United Arab Republic. Institute of Oceanography and Fisheries. Bulletin
UARJ Anim Prod — United Arab Republic. Journal of Animal Production
UARJ Bot — United Arab Republic. Journal of Botany
UARJ Chem — United Arab Republic. Journal of Chemistry
UARJ Geol — United Arab Republic. Journal of Geology
UAR J Microbiol — United Arab Republic. Journal of Microbiology
UARJ Pharm Sci — United Arab Republic. Journal of Pharmaceutical Sciences
UAR J Phys — United Arab Republic. Journal of Physics
UARJ Soil Sci — United Arab Republic. Journal of Soil Science
UARJ Vet Sci — United Arab Republic. Journal of Veterinary Science
U Ark Little Rock LJ — University of Arkansas at Little Rock. Law Journal
UAR Minist Agric Agrar Reform Tech Bull — United Arab Republic. Ministry of Agriculture and Agrarian Reform. Technical Bulletin
UAR Minist Agric Tech Bull — United Arab Republic. Ministry of Agriculture. Technical Bulletin
UAR (South Reg) Minist Agric Hydrobiol Dep Notes Mem — United Arab Republic (Southern Region). Ministry of Agriculture. Hydrobiological Department. Notes and Memoirs
UAS — University of Alabama. Studies
UAS — Uralic and Altaic Series. Indiana University. Publications
UAS (Hebbal) Monogr Ser — UAS (Hebbal) Monograph Series
UAVA — Untersuchungen zur Assyriologie und Vorderasiatischen Archaeologie
UB — Urban Buecher
UB — Uttara Bharati
UBA — Universitet i Bergen. Arbok. Historisk-Antikvarisk Rekke
U Baltimore L Rev — University of Baltimore. Law Review
U Balt LR — University of Baltimore. Law Review
U Balt L Rev — University of Baltimore. Law Review
UBC Alumni Chronicle — Alumni Association. University of British Columbia. Chronicle
UBC Legal N — University of British Columbia. Legal Notes
UBC Legal Notes — University of British Columbia. Legal Notes
UBC LR — University of British Columbia. Law Review
UBC L Rev — University of British Columbia. Law Review

UBCNREP — University of British Columbia. Programme in Natural Resource Economics. Resources Paper
UBEA Forum — United Business Education Association. Forum
UBHJ — University of Birmingham. Historical Journal
U Birmingham Hist J — University of Birmingham. Historical Journal
UBJSA — Union of Burma. Journal of Science and Technology
UBKHA — Uspekhi Biologicheskoi Khimii
UBLR — University of Baltimore. Law Review
U Brdgprt LR — University of Bridgeport. Law Review
U Bridgeport L Rev — University of Bridgeport. Law Review
U Brit Col L Rev — University of British Columbia. Law Review
U Brit Colum L Rev — University of British Columbia. Law Review
UBS — University of Buffalo. Studies
UBSB — [*The*] United Bible Societies. Bulletin [*London*]
UBU — UNESCO [*United Nations Educational, Scientific, and Cultural Organization*] Journal of Information Science, Librarianship, and Archives Administration
UBZHA — Ukrayinski Biokhimichnyi Zhurnal
UC — National Union Catalogue
Uc — Uncanny Stories
UC — UNESCO [*United Nations Educational, Scientific, and Cultural Organization*] Chronicle
UCA — Uniform Companies Act
UCASBJ — Agro Sur
UCC — Uniform Commercial Code Law Journal
UCC — University of California. Chronicle
UCCEW — University of Cape Coast. English Department. Workpapers
UCCLJ — Uniform Commercial Code Law Journal
UCD L Rev — UCD [*University of California, Davis*] Law Review
UCDPE — University of California (Davis). Publications in English
Ucenyje Zapiski Belorusskogo Gosud Univ — Ucenyje Zapiski Belorusskogo Gosudarstvennogo Universiteta
Ucenyje Zapiski Jaroslav — Ucenyje Zapiski Jaroslavskogo Universiteta
Ucenyje Zapiski Leningrad — Ucenyje Zapiski Leningradskogo Gosudarstvennogo Universiteta
Ucenyje Zapiski Leningrad Pedag Inst — Ucenyje Zapiski Leningradskogo Gosudarstvennogo Pedagogiceskogo Instituta
Ucenyje Zapiski Moskov Gosud Pedag Inst — Ucenyje Zapiski Moskovskogo Gosudarstvennogo Pedagogiceskogo Instituta Inostraunych Jazykov
Ucenyje Zapiski Moskva — Ucenyje Zapiski Moskovskogo Gosudarstvennogo Universiteta Imeni Lononosova
Ucenyje Zapiski (Tomsk) — Ucenyje Zapiski Tomskogo Gosudarstvennogo Universiteta Imeni Kujbyseva (Tomsk)
Ucen Zap (Azerb Gosud Univ) Ser Ist Filos Nauk — Ucenye Zapiski (Azerbajdzanskij Gosudarstvennyj Universitet) Serija Istoriceskih i Filosofskih Nauk
Ucen Zap (Azerb Univ) Ser Ist Filos Nauk — Ucenye Zapiski (Azerbajdzanskij Universitet) Serija Istoriceskih i Filosofskih Nauk
Ucen Zap CAGI — Ucenyi Zapiski Central'nogo Aero-Gidrodinamiceskogo Instituta
Ucen Zap Dal'nevost Univ — Ucenye Zapiski Dal'nevostocnogo Universiteta
Ucen Zap Dusan Gos Pedag Inst — Ucenye Zapiski Dusanbinskogo Gosudarstvennogo Pedagogiceskogo Instituta
Ucen Zap Erevan Gos Univ Estestv Nauki — Ucenye Zapiski Erevanskogo Gosudarstvennogo Universiteta Estestvennye Nauki

Ucen Zap Hakas Nauc-Issled Inst Jaz Lit Ist — Ucenye Zapiski Hakasskogo Naucno-Issledovatel'skogo Instituta Jazyka, Literatury, i Istorii
Ucen Zap Ivanov Univ — Ucenye Zapiski Ivanovskogo Universitet
Ucen Zap Kaf Obsc Nauk Leningr Filos — Ucenye Zapiski Kafedr Obscestvennykh Nauk Vuzov Leningrada Filosofija
Ucen Zap Kaf Obsc Nauk Vuzov G Leningr Filos — Ucenye Zapiski Kafedr Obscestvennykh Nauk Vuzov Goroda Leningrada Filosofskih
Ucen Zap Kaf Obsc Nauk Vuzov G Leningr Probl Nauc Kommunizma — Ucenye Zapiski Kafedr Obscestvennykh Nauk Vuzov Goroda Leningrada Problemy Naucnogo Kommunizma
Ucen Zap Kalmyk Nauc-Issled Inst Jaz Lit Ist — Ucenye Zapiski Kalmykskogo Naucno-Issledovatel'skogo Instituta Jazyka, Literatury, i Istorii
Ucen Zap Karel Ped Inst Ser Fiz-Mat Nauk — Ucenye Zapiski Karel'skii Pedagogiceskii Institut. Serija Fiziko-Matematiceskih Nauk
Ucen Zap (Kazan Pedag Inst) — Ucenye Zapiski (Kazanskij Pedagogiceskij Institut)
Ucen Zap (Latv Univ) — Ucenye Zapiski (Latvijskogo Universiteta)
Ucen Zap (Lening Pedag Inst) — Ucenye Zapiski (Leningradskij Pedagogiceskij Institut)
Ucen Zap (Moskov Pedag Inst) — Ucenye Zapiski (Moskovskogo Pedagogiceskogo Instituta)
Ucen Zap Perm Univ — Ucenye Zapiski Permskogo Universiteta
Ucen Zap Statist — Ucenyi Zapiski po Statistike Akademija Nauk SSSR Central'nyi Ekonomiko-Matematiceskii Institut
Ucen Zap (Vyss Part Skola CK KPSS) — Ucenye Zapiski (Vyssaja Partijnaja Skola pri CK KPSS)
UCH — China Business Review
Uchen Zap Azerb Gos Univ Ser Biol Nauk — Uchenye Zapiski Azerbaidzhskogo Gosudarstvennogo Universiteta. Seriya Biologicheskikh Nauk
Uchen Zap Azerb Gos Univ Ser Fiz Mat Nauk — Uchenye Zapiski Azerbaidzhskogo Gosudarstvennogo Universiteta. Seriya Fiziko-Matematicheskikh Nauk
Uchen Zap Dal'nevost Univ — Uchenye Zapiski Dal'nevostochnogo Universiteta
Uchen Zap Gor'kov Gos Pedagog Inst — Uchenye Zapiski Gor'kovskogo Gosudarstvennogo Pedagogicheskogo Instituta
Uchen Zap Gor'kov Gos Univ Ser Biol — Uchenye Zapiski Gor'kovskogo Gosudarstvennogo Universiteta Imeni N. I. Lobachevskogo. Seriya Biologichevskaya
Uchen Zap Gor'k Univ Ser Biol — Uchenye Zapiski Gor'kovskogo Universiteta. Seriya Biologiya
Uchen Zap Kabardino-Balkar Gos Univ — Uchenye Zapiski Kabardino-Balkarskogo Gosudarstvennogo Universiteta
Uchen Zap Kabardino-Balkars Univ — Uchenye Zapiski Kabardino-Balkarskogo Gosudarstvennogo Universiteta
Uchen Zap Kazan Gos Univ — Uchenye Zapiski Kazanskogo Gosudarstvennogo Universiteta
Uchen Zap Kazan Vet Inst — Uchenye Zapiski Kazanskogo Veterinarnogo Instituta
Uchen Zap Kirovabad Ped Inst — Uchenye Zapiski Kirovabadskii Pedagogicheskii Institut
Uchen Zap Kishinev Univ — Uchenye Zapiski Kishinevskii Gosudarstvennyi Universitet
Uchen Zap Kursk Pedagog Inst — Uchenye Zapiski Kurskii Gosudarstvennyi Pedagogicheskii Institut
Uchen Zap Leningr Gos Pedagog Inst Gertsena — Uchenye Zapiski Leningradskogo Gosudarstvennogo Pedagogicheskogo Instituta Gertsena
Uchen Zap Mosk Gos Univ — Uchenye Zapiski Moskovskogo Gosudarstvennogo Universiteta
Uchen Zap Novgorod Golovn Pedagog Inst — Uchenye Zapiski Novgorodskogo Golovnogo Pedagogicheskogo Instituta
Uchen Zap Petrozavodsk Gos Univ — Uchenye Zapiski Petrozavodskogo Gosudarstvennogo Universiteta
Uchen Zap Ryazan Gos Pedagog Inst — Uchenye Zapiski Ryazanskogo Gosudarstvennogo Pedagogicheskii Instituta
Uchen Zap Sel Khoz Dal'n Vost (Vladivostok) — Uchenye Zapiski Sel'skogo Khozyaistva Dal'nogo Vostoka (Vladivostok)
Uchen Zap Tartu Gos Univ — Uchenye Zapiski Tartuskogo Gosudarstvennogo Universiteta
Uchen Zap TSAGI — Uchenye Zapiski Tsentral'nogo Aero-Gidrodinamicheskogo Instituta (TSAGI)
Uchen Zap Ural Univ — Uchenye Zapiski Ural'skogo Gosudarstvennogo Universiteta Imeni A. M. Gor'kogo
Uchen Zap Yaroslav Gos Pedagog Inst — Uchenye Zapiski Yaroslavskii Gosudarstvennyi Pedagogicheskii Institut
Uchet Finan Kolkhoz Sovkhoz — Uchet i Finansy v Kolkhozakh i Sovkhozakh
U Chicago L Rev — University of Chicago. Law Review
U Chi L Rec — University of Chicago. Law School. Record
U Chi L Rev — University of Chicago. Law Review
U Chi L Sch Rec — University of Chicago. Law School. Record
U Chi LS Conf Series — University of Chicago. Law School. Conference Series
U Chi L S Rec — University of Chicago. Law School. Record
Uch Tr Gork Gos Med Inst — Uchenye Trudy Gorkovskogo Gosudarstvennogo Meditsinskogo Instituta

Uch Tr Gor'k Med Inst — Uchenye Trudy Gor'kovskii Meditsinskii Institut
Uch Zap Anat Gistol Embriol Resp Sredn Azii Kaz — Uchenye Zapiski Anatomov Gistologov i Embriologov Respublik Srednei Azii i Kazakhstana
Uch Zap Azerb Gos Inst Usoversh Vrachei — Uchenye Zapiski Azerbaidzhanskii Gosudarstvennyi Institut Usovershenstvovaniya Vrachei
Uch Zap Azerb Gos Uiv Im S M Kirova — Uchenye Zapiski Azerbaidzhan-Gosudarstvennogo Universiteta Imeni S. M. Kirova
Uch Zap Azerb Gos Univ — Uchenye Zapiski Azerbaidzhanskogo Gosudarstvennogo Universiteta
Uch Zap Azerb Gos Univ Im S M Kirova — Uchenye Zapiski Azerbaidzhanskogo Gosudarstvennogo Universiteta Imeni S. M. Kirova
Uch Zap Azerb Gos Univ Ser Biol Nauk — Uchenye Zapiski Azerbaidzhanskogo Gosudarstvennogo Universiteta. Seriya Biologicheskikh Nauk
Uch Zap Azerb Gos Univ Ser Fiz Mat Nauk — Uchenye Zapiski Azerbaidzhanskogo Gosudarstvennogo Universiteta. Seriya Fiziko-Matematicheskikh Nauk
Uch Zap Azerb Gos Univ Ser Geol Geogr Nauk — Uchenye Zapiski Azerbaidzhanskogo Gosudarstvennogo Universiteta. Seriya Geologo-Geograficheskikh Nauk
Uch Zap Azerb Gos Univ Ser Khim Nauk — Uchenye Zapiski Azerbaidzhanskogo Gosudarstvennogo Universiteta Imeni S. M. Kirova. Seriya Khimicheskikh Nauk [*Azerbaidzhan SSR*]
Uch Zap Azerb Inst Nefti Khim Ser 9 — Uchenye Zapiski Azerbajdzhanskij Institut Nefti i Khimii. Seriya 9
Uch Zap Azerb Inst Usoversh Vrachei — Uchenye Zapiski Azerbaidzhanskii Institut Usovershenstvovaniya Vrachei
Uch Zap Azerb Med Inst — Uchenye Zapiski Azerbaidzhanskogo Meditsinskogo Instituta
Uch Zap Azerb Med Inst Klin Med — Uchenye Zapiski Azerbaidzhanskogo Meditsinskogo Instituta Klinicheskoi Meditsiny
Uch Zap Azerb Politekh Inst — Uchenye Zapiski Azerbaidzhanskii Politekhnicheskii Institut
Uch Zap Azerb Skh Inst — Uchenye Zapiski Azerbaidzhanskogo Sel'skokhozyaistvennogo Instituta
Uch Zap Azerb Skh Inst Ser Agron — Uchenye Zapiski Azerbaidzhanskogo Sel'skokhozyaistvennogo Instituta. Seriya Agronomii
Uch Zap Azerb S-kh Inst Ser Vet — Uchenye Zapiski Azerbaidzhanskogo Sel'skokhozyaistvennogo Instituta. Seriya Veterinarii
Uch Zap Azerb Univ Ser Biol Nauk — Uchenye Zapiski Azerbaidzhanskogo Universiteta. Seriya Biologicheskoi Nauki
Uch Zap Bashk Univ — Uchenye Zapiski Bashkirskogo Universiteta
Uch Zap Beloruss Gos Univ — Uchenye Zapiski Belorusskogo Gosudarstvennogo Universiteta
Uch Zap Beloruss Inst Inzh Zheleznodorozhn Transp — Uchenye Zapiski Belorusskii Institut Inzhenerov Zheleznodorozhnogo Transporta
Uch Zap Bel'tskii Pedagog Inst — Uchenye Zapiski Bel'tskii Pedagogicheskii Institut
Uch Zap Biol Fak Kirg Univ — Uchenye Zapiski Biologicheskogo Fakul'teta Kirgizskogo Universiteta
Uch Zap Biol Fak Osnovn Gos Pedagog Inst — Uchenye Zapiski Biologicheskogo Fakul'teta Osnovnogo Gosudarstvennogo Pedagogicheskogo Instituta
Uch Zap Birskogo Gos Pedagog Inst — Uchenye Zapiski Birskogo Gosudarstvennogo Pedagogicheskogo Instituta
Uch Zap Brest Gos Pedagog Inst — Uchenye Zapiski Brestskii Gosudarstvennyi Pedagogicheskii Institut
Uch Zap Brst Gos Pedagog Inst — Uchenye Zapiski Brestskii Gosudarstvennyi Pedagogicheskii Institut
Uch Zap Bukhar Gos Pedagog Inst — Uchenye Zapiski Bukharskii Gosudarstvennyi Pedagogicheskii Institut
Uch Zap Buryat Gos Pedagog Inst — Uchenye Zapiski Buryatskii Gosudarstvennyi Pedagogicheskii Institut
Uch Zap Buryat Mong Pedagog Inst — Uchenye Zapiski Buryat-Mongol'skii Pedagogicheskii Institut
Uch Zap Checheno Ingush Gos Pedagog Inst — Uchenye Zapiski Checheno-Ingushskoi Gosudarstvennyi Pedagogicheskii Institut
Uch Zap Chelyab Gos Pedagog Inst — Uchenye Zapiski Chelyabinskogo Gosudarstvennogo Pedagogicheskogo Instituta
Uch Zap Chit Gos Pedagog Inst — Uchenye Zapiski Chitinskii Gosudarstvennyi Pedagogicheskii Institut
Uch Zap Dagest Gos Pedagog Inst — Uchenye Zapiski Dagestanskii Gosudarstvennyi Pedagogicheskii Institut
Uch Zap Dagest Gos Univ — Uchenye Zapiski Dagestanskogo Gosudarstvennogo Universiteta
Uch Zap Dal'nevost Gos Univ — Uchenye Zapiski Dal'nevostochnyi Gosudarstvennyi Universitet
Uch Zap Dushanb Gos Pedagog Inst — Uchenye Zapiski Dushanbinskii Gosudarstvennyi Pedagogicheskii Institut
Uch Zap Erevan Gos Univ — Uchenye Zapiski Erevanskii Gosudarstvennyi Universitet
Uch Zap Erevan Univ — Uchenye Zapiski Erevanskii Universitet
Uch Zap Erevan Univ Estestv Nauk — Uchenye Zapiski Erevanskogo Universiteta Estestvennykh Nauk

Uch Zap Gomel Gos Pedagog Inst — Uchenye Zapiski Gomel'skii Gosudarstvennyi Pedagogicheskii Institut

Uch Zap Gomel Gos Pedagog Inst Im V P Chkalova — Uchenye Zapiski Gomel'skogo Gosudarstvennogo Pedagogicheskogo Instituta Imeni V. P. Chkalova

Uch Zap Gor'k Gos Med Inst Im S M Kirova — Uchenye Zapiski Gor'kovskogo Gosudarstvennogo Meditsinskogo Instituta Imeni S. M. Kirova

Uch Zap Gor'k Gos Pedagog Inst — Uchenye Zapiski Gor'kovskogo Gosudarstvennogo Pedagogicheskogo Instituta

Uch Zap Gor'k Gos Pedagog Inst Im A M Gor'kogo — Uchenye Zapiski Gor'kovskogo Gosudarstvennogo Pedagogicheskogo Instituta Imeni A. M. Gor'kogo

Uch Zap Gor'k Gos Univ — Uchenye Zapiski Gor'kovskogo Gosudarstvennogo Universiteta

Uch Zap Gor'k Univ — Uchenye Zapiski Gor'kovskogo Universiteta

Uch Zap Gor'k Univ Ser Biol — Uchenye Zapiski Gor'kovskogo Universiteta. Seriya Biologiya

Uch Zap Gorno-Altai Gos Pedagog Inst — Uchenye Zapiski Gorno-Altaiskogo Gosudarstvennogo Pedagogicheskogo Instituta

Uch Zap Gos Inst Fiz Kul't Im P F Lesgafta — Uchenye Zapiski Gosudarstvennogo Instituta Fizicheskoi Kul'tury Imeni P. F. Lesgafta

Uch Zap Gos Nauchno-Issled Inst Glazn Bolezn Im Gel'Mgol'Tsa — Uchenye Zapiski Gosudarstvennogo Nauchno-Issledovatel'skogo Instituta Glaznykh Boleznei Imeni Gel'Mgol'Tsa

Uch Zap Gos Nauchno-Issled Inst Glaznykh Bolezn — Uchenye Zapiski Gosudarstvennogo Nauchno-Issledovatel'skogo Instituta Glaznykh Boleznei

Uch Zap Gos Pedagog Inst — Uchenye Zapiski Gosudarstvennogo Pedagogicheskogo Instituta Imeni T. G. Shevchenko

Uch Zap Gos Pedagog Inst Im T G Shevchenko — Uchenye Zapiski Gosudarstvennogo Pedagogicheskogo Instituta Imeni T. G. Shevchenko

Uch Zap Grozn Gos Pedagog Inst — Uchenye Zapiski Groznenskogo Gosudarstvennogo Pedagogicheskogo Instituta

Uch Zap Imp Yur'ev Univ — Uchenyya Zapiskik Imperatorskogo Yur'evskago Universiteta

Uch Zap Irkutsk Gos Pedagog Inst — Uchenye Zapiski Irkutskii Gosudarstvennyi Pedagogicheskii Institut

Uch Zap Irkutsk Inst Nar Khoz — Uchenye Zapiski Irkutskii Institut Narodnogo Khozyaistva

Uch Zap Ivanov Gos Pedagog Inst — Uchenye Zapiski Ivanovskogo Gosudarstvennogo Pedagogicheskogo Instituta

Uch Zap Kabard Balkar Gos Univ — Uchenye Zapiski Kabardino-Balkarskii Gosudarstvennyi Universitet

Uch Zap Kabard-Balkar Nauchno-Issled Inst — Uchenye Zapiski Kabardino-Balkarskogo Nauchno-Issledovatel'skogo Instituta

Uch Zap Kabard Gos Pedagog Inst — Uchenye Zapiski Kabardinskogo Gosudarstvennogo Pedagogicheskogo Instituta

Uch Zap Kalinin Gos Pedagog Inst — Uchenye Zapiski Kalininskii Gosudarstvennyi Pedagogicheskii Institut

Uch Zap Kaliningr Gos Pedagog Inst — Uchenye Zapiski Kaliningradskogo Gosudarstvennogo Pedagogicheskogo Instituta

Uch Zap Kaliningr Gos Univ — Uchenye Zapiski Kaliningradskii Gosudarstvennyi Universitet

Uch Zap Karagand Gos Med Inst — Uchenye Zapiski Karagandinskii Gosudarstvennyi Meditsinskii Institut

Uch Zap Karagand Med Inst — Uchenye Zapiski Karagandinskogo Meditsinskogo Instituta

Uch Zap Karelo Fin Gos Univ Biol Nauki — Uchenye Zapiski Karelo-Finskogo Gosudarstvennogo Universiteta Biologicheskie Nauki

Uch Zap Karelo Fin Gos Univ Fiz Mat Nauki — Uchenye Zapiski Karelo-Finskogo Gosudarstvennogo Universiteta Fiziko Matematicheskie Nauki

Uch Zap Karelo-Fin Pedagog Inst — Uchenye Zapiski Karelo-Finskogo Pedagogicheskogo Instituta

Uch Zap Karel Pedagog Inst — Uchenye Zapiski Karel'skogo Pedagogicheskogo Instituta

Uch Zap Karsh Gos Pedagog Inst — Uchenye Zapiski Karshinskii Gosudarstvennyi Pedagogicheskii Institut

Uch Zap Kazan Gos Pedagog Inst — Uchenye Zapiski Kazanskii Gosudarstvennyi Pedagogicheskii Institut

Uch Zap Kazan Gos Univ — Uchenye Zapiski Kazanskii Gosudarstvennyi Universitet [USSR]

Uch Zap Kazan Univ — Uchenye Zapiski Kazanskogo Universiteta

Uch Zap Kazan Vet Inst — Uchenye Zapiski Kazanskogo Veterinarnogo Instituta

Uch Zap Kazan Yuridicheskogo Inst — Uchenye Zapiski Kazanskogo Yuridicheskogo Instituta

Uch Zap Kaz Gos Uiv Im S M Kirova — Uchenye Zapiski Kazakhskogo Gosudarstvennogo Universiteta Imeni S. M. Kirova

Uch Zap Kaz Gos Univ — Uchenye Zapiski Kazakhskii Gosudarstvennyi Universitet

Uch Zap Kemer Gos Pedagog Inst — Uchenye Zapiski Kemerovskogo Gosudarstvennogo Pedagogicheskogo Instituta

Uch Zap Khabar Gos Pedagog Inst — Uchenye Zapiski Khabarovskogo Gosudarstvennogo Pedagogicheskogo Instituta

Uch Zap Khabar Gos Pedagog Inst Biol Khim Nauk — Uchenye Zapiski Khabarovskii Gosudarstvennyi Pedagogicheskii Institut Biologii i Khimicheskikh Nauk

Uch Zap Khabar Gos Pedagog Inst Ser Biol — Uchenye Zapiski Khabarovskii Gosudarstvennyi Pedagogicheskii Institut. Seriya Biologiya

Uch Zap Khabar Gos Pedagog Inst Ser Estestv Nauk — Uchenye Zapiski Khabarovskii Gosudarstvennyi Pedagogicheskii Institut. Seriya Estestvennykh Nauk

Uch Zap Khabar Nauchno-Issled Inst Epidemiol Mikrobiol — Uchenye Zapiski Khabarovskogo Nauchno-Issledovatel'skogo Instituta Epidemiologii i Mikrobiologii

Uch Zap Khar'k Univ Tr Biol Fak Genet Zool — Uchenye Zapiski Khar'kovskogo Universiteta Trudy Biologicheskogo Fakul'teta po Genetlike i Zoologii

Uch Zap Khar'k Univ Tr Nauchno-Issled Inst Biol Biol Fak — Uchenye Zapiski Khar'kovskogo Universiteta Trudy Nauchno-Issledovatel'skogo Instituta Biologii i Biologicheskogo Fakul'teta

Uch Zap Kiev Nauchno-Isled Rentgeno Radiol Onkol Inst — Uchenye Zapiski Kievskogo Nauchno-Issledovatel'skogo Rentgeno Radiologicheskogo i Onkologicheskogo Instituta

Uch Zap Kirg Zhen Pedagog Inst — Uchenye Zapiski Kirgizskii Zhenskii Pedagogicheskii Institut

Uch Zap Kirovab Pedagog Inst — Uchenye Zapiski Kirovabadskii Pedagogicheskii Institut

Uch Zap Kiroy Gos Pedagog Inst — Uchenye Zapiski Kiroyskogo Gosudarstvennogo Pedagogicheskogo Instituta

Uch Zap Kishinev Gos Univ — Uchenye Zapiski Kishinevskogo Gosudarstvennogo Universiteta

Uch Zap Komsomol'skogo-Na-Amure Gos Pedagog Inst — Uchenye Zapiski Komsomol'skogo-Na-Amure Gosudarstvennogo Pedagogicheskogo Instituta

Uch Zap Kuibyshev Gos Pedagog Inst — Uchenye Zapiski Kuibyshevskogo Gosudarstvennogo Pedagogicheskogo Instituta

Uch Zap Kursk Gos Pedagog Inst — Uchenye Zapiski Kurskogo Gosudarstvennogo Pedagogicheskogo Instituta

Uch Zap Latv Gos Univ — Uchenye Zapiski Latviiskii Gosudarstvennyi Universitet

Uch Zap Latv Gos Univ — Uchenye Zapiski Latvijskogo Gosudarstvennogo Universiteta Imeni Petra Stuchki

Uch Zap Latv Gos Univ Astron — Uchenye Zapiski Latvijskogo Gosudarstvennogo Universiteta Imeni Petra Stuchki. Astronomiya

Uch Zap Latv Univ — Uchenye Zapiski Latviiskogo Universiteta

Uch Zap Lenigr Gos Univ Ser Fiz Nauk — Uchenye Zapiski Leningradskogo Gosudarstvennogo Universiteta. Seriya Fizicheskikh Nauk

Uch Zap Leninab Gos Pedagog Inst — Uchenye Zapiski Leninabadskogo Gosudarstvennogo Pedagogicheskogo Instituta

Uch Zap Leningr Gos Im A A Zhadanova Ser Fiz Geol Nauk — Uchenye Zapiski Leningradskogo Gosudarstvennogo Universiteta Imeni A. A. Zhdanova. Seriya Fizicheskikh i Geologicheskikh Nauk [USSR]

Uch Zap Leningr Gos Inst — Uchenye Zapiski Leningradskogo Gosudarstvennogo Instituta

Uch Zap Leningr Gos Pedagog Inst Im A I Gertsena — Uchenye Zapiski Leningradskogo Gosudarstvennogo Pedagogicheskogo Instituta Imeni A. I. Gertsena

Uch Zap Leningr Gos Univ Im A A Zhdanova Ser Biol Nauk — Uchenye Zapiski Leningradskogo Gosudarstvennogo Universiteta Imeni A. A. Zhdanova. Seriya Biologicheskikh Nauk [USSR]

Uch Zap Leningr Gos Univ Im A A Zhdanova Ser Fiz Nauk — Uchenye Zapiski Leningradskogo Gosudarstvennogo Universiteta Imeni A. A. Zhdanova. Seriya Fizicheskikh Nauk [USSR]

Uch Zap Leningr Gos Univ Im A A Zhdanova Ser Geogr Nauk — Uchenye Zapiski Leningradskogo Gosudarstvennogo Universiteta Imeni A. A. Zhdanova. Seriya Geograficheskikh Nauk

Uch Zap Leningr Gos Univ Im A A Zhdanova Ser Geol Nauk — Uchenye Zapiski Leningradskogo Gosudarstvennogo Universiteta Imeni A. A. Zhdanova. Seriya Geologicheskikh Nauk

Uch Zap Leningr Gos Univ Ser Biol Nauk — Uchenye Zapiski Leningradskogo Gosudarstvennogo Universiteta. Seriya Biologicheskikh Nauk

Uch Zap Leningr Gos Univ Ser Fiz Geol Nauk — Uchenye Zapiski Leningradskogo Gosudarstvennogo Universiteta. Seriya Fizicheskikh i Geologicheskikh Nauk

Uch Zap Leningr Gos Univ Ser Geogr Nauk — Uchenye Zapiski Leningradskogo Gosudarstvennogo Universiteta. Seriya Geograficheskikh Nauk

Uch Zap Leningr Gos Univ Ser Geol Nauk — Uchenye Zapiski Leningradskogo Gosudarstvennogo Universiteta. Seriya Geologicheskikh Nauk

Uch Zap Leningr Gos Univ Ser Khim Nauk — Uchenye Zapiski Leningradskogo Gosudarstvennogo Universiteta. Seriya Khimicheskikh Nauk

Uch Zap Leningr Gos Univ Ser Mat Nauk — Uchenye Zapiski Leningradskogo Gosudarstvennogo Ordena Lenina Universita Imeni A. A. Zhdanova. Seriya Matematicheskikh Nauk

Uch Zap Leningr Gos Univ Ser Mat Nauk — Uchenye Zapiski Leningradskogo Gosudarstvennogo Universiteta. Seriya Matematicheskikh Nauk

Uch Zap Marii Gos Pedagog Inst — Uchenye Zapiski Mariiskii Gosudarstvennyi Pedagogicheskii Institut

Uch Zap Michurinsk Gos Pedagog Inst — Uchenye Zapiski Michurinskii Gosudarstvennyi Pedagogicheskii Institut
Uch Zap Molotov Gos Univ Im A M Gor'kogo — Uchenye Zapiski Molotovskogo Gosudarstvennogo Universiteta Imeni A. M. Gor'kogo
Uch Zap Mord Gos Univ — Uchenye Zapiski Mordovskii Gosudarstvennyi Universitet
Uch Zap Mord Univ — Uchenye Zapiski Mordovskogo Universiteta
Uch Zap Mosk Gos Pedagog Inst Im Lenina — Uchenye Zapiski Moskovskogo Gosudarstvennogo Pedagogicheskogo Instituta Imeni Lenina
Uch Zap Mosk Gos Univ — Uchenye Zapiski Moskovskii Gosudarstvennyi Universitet [*USSR*]
Uch Zap Mosk Inst Tonkoi Khim Tekhnol — Uchenye Zapiski Moskovskogo Instituta Tonkoi Khimicheskoi Tekhnologii
Uch Zap Mosk Nauchno-Issled Inst Gig — Uchenye Zapiski Moskovskii Nauchno-Issledovatel'skii Institut Gigieny
Uch Zap Mosk Nauchno-Issled Inst Glaznym Bolezn — Uchenye Zapiski Moskovskogo Nauchno-Issledovatel'skogo Instituta po Glaznym Boleznam
Uch Zap Mosk Obl Pedagog Inst — Uchenye Zapiski Moskovskogo Oblastnogo Pedagogicheskogo Instituta
Uch Zap Murom Gos Pedagog Inst — Uchenye Zapiski Muromskii Gosudarstvennyi Pedagogicheskii Institut
Uch Zap Namanganskii Gos Pedagog Inst — Uchenye Zapiski Namanganskii Gosudarstvennyi Pedagogicheskii Institut
Uch Zap Nauchno-Issled Inst Geol Arkt Reg Geol — Uchenye Zapiski Nauchno-Issledovatel'skogo Instituta Geologii Arktiki Regional'naya Geologiya
Uch Zap Nauchno-Issled Inst Izuch Lepry — Uchenye Zapiski Nauchno-Issledovatel'skogo Instituta po Izucheniyu Lepry
Uch Zap Novgorod Golovn Gos Pedagog Inst — Uchenye Zapiski Novgorodskii Golovnoi Gosudarstvennyi Pedagogicheskii Institut
Uch Zap Novgorod Gos Pedagog — Uchenye Zapiski Novgorodskogo Gosudarstvennogo Pedagogicheskogo Instituta
Uch Zap Novgorod Gos Pedagog Inst — Uchenye Zapiski Novgorodskogo Gosudarstvennogo Pedagogicheskogo Instituta
Uch Zap Novosib Inst Sov Koop Torg — Uchenye Zapiski Novosibirskii Institut Sovetskoi Kooperativnoi Torgovli
Uch Zap Novozybkovskii Gos Pedagog Inst — Uchenye Zapiski Novozybkovskii Gosudarstvennyi Pedagogicheskii Institut
Uch Zap Omsk Gos Pedagog Inst — Uchenye Zapiski Omskogo Gosudarstvennogo Pedagogicheskogo Instituta
Uch Zap Orenb Gos Pedagog Inst — Uchenye Zapiski Orenburgskii Gosudarstvennyi Pedagogicheskii Institut
Uch Zap Orenb Otd Vses Nauchn Ova Anat Gistol Embriol — Uchenye Zapiski Orenburgskogo Otdela Vsesoyuznogo Nauchnogo Obshchestva Anatomov, Gistologov, i Embriologov
Uch Zap Orlov Gos Pedagog Inst — Uchenye Zapiski Orlovskogo Gosudarstvennogo Pedagogicheskogo Instituta
Uch Zap Osh Gos Pedagog Inst — Uchenye Zapiski Oshskii Gosudarstvennyi Pedagogicheskii Institut
Uch Zap Penz Gos Pedagog Inst — Uchenye Zapiski Penzenskogo Gosudarstvennogo Pedagogicheskogo Instituta
Uch Zap Penz S-kh Inst — Uchenye Zapiski Penzenskogo Sel'skokhozyaistvennogo Instituta
Uch Zap Perm Gos Pedagog Inst — Uchenye Zapiski Permskogo Gosudarstvennyi Pedagogicheskii Institut
Uch Zap Perm Gos Univ — Uchenye Zapiski Permskij Gosudarstvennyj Universitet Imeni A. M. Gor'kogo
Uch Zap Perm Univ Im A M Gor'kogo — Uchenye Zapiski Permskogo Universiteta Imeni A. M. Gor'kogo
Uch Zap Petropavlovsk Gos Inst — Uchenye Zapiski Petropavlovskogo Gosudarstvennogo Instituta
Uch Zap Petrozavodsk Gos Univ Fiz Mat Nauki — Uchenye Zapiski Petrozavodskogo Gosudarstvennogo Universiteta Fiziko-Matematicheskie Nauki
Uch Zap Petrozavodsk Inst — Uchenye Zapiski Petrozavodskogo Instituta
Uch Zap Petrozavodsk Univ — Uchenye Zapiski Petrozavodskogo Universiteta
Uch Zap Pskov Gos Pedagog Inst — Uchenye Zapiski Pskovskogo Gosudarstvennogo Pedagogicheskogo Instituta
Uch Zap Pskov Pedagog Inst Estestv Nauk — Uchenye Zapiski Pskovskogo Pedagogicheskogo Instituta Estestvennykh Nauk
Uch Zap Pyatigorsk Farm Inst — Uchenye Zapiski Pyatigorskii Farmatsevticheskii Institut
Uch Zap Pyatigorsk Gos Nauchno Issled Balneol Inst — Uchenye Zapiski Pyatigorskii Gosudarstvennyi Nauchno-Issledovatel'skii Bal'neologicheskii Institut
Uch Zap Rizh Politekh Inst — Uchenye Zapiski Rizhskii Politekhnicheskii Institut
Uch Zap Rostov Na Donu Gos Pedagog Inst Fiz Mat Fak — Uchenye Zapiski Rostovskii-Na-Donu Gosudarstvennyi Pedagogicheskii Institut Fiziko-Matematicheskii Fakul'tet
Uch Zap Rostov Na Donu Gos Univ — Uchenye Zapiski Rostovskogo-Na-Donu Gosudarstvennogo Universiteta
Uch Zap Rostov-Na-Donu Univ Im V M Molotova — Uchenye Zapiski Rostovskogo-Na-Donu Universiteta Imeni V. M. Molotova

Uch Zap Rostov Na Donu Univ V M Molotva — Uchenye Zapiski Rostovskogo-Na-Donu Universiteta Imeni V. M. Molotova
Uch Zap Ryazan Gos Pedagog Inst — Uchenye Zapiski Ryazanskogo Gosudarstvennogo Pedagogicheskogo Instituta
Uch Zap Rybinsk Gos Pedagog Inst — Uchenye Zapiski Rybinskii Gosudarstvennyi Pedagogicheskii Institut
Uch Zap Sarat Gos Pedagog Inst — Uchenye Zapiski Saratovskogo Gosudarstvennogo Pedagogicheskogo Instituta
Uch Zap Sarat Gos Univ — Uchenye Zapiski Saratovskogo Gosudarstvennogo Universiteta
Uch Zap Sev Oset Gos Pedagog Inst — Uchenye Zapiski Severo-Osetinskii Gosudarstvennyi Pedagogicheskii Institut
Uch Zap Sev-Oset Gos Pedagog Inst Im K L Khetagurova — Uchenye Zapiski Severo-Osetinskogo Gosudarstvennogo Pedagogicheskogo Instituta Imeni K. L. Khetagurova
Uch Zap Smolensk Gos Pedagog Inst — Uchenye Zapiski Smolenskogo Gosudarstvennogo Pedagogicheskogo Instituta
Uch Zap Sredneaziat Nauchno-Issled Inst Geol Miner Syr'ya — Uchenye Zapiski Sredneaziatskii Nauchno-Issledovatel'skii Institut Geologii i Mineral'nogo Syr'ya
Uch Zap Stavrop Gos Med Inst — Uchenye Zapiski Stavropol'skogo Gosudarstvennogo Meditsinskogo Instituta
Uch Zap Sverdl Gos Pedagog Inst — Uchenye Zapiski Sverdlovskii Gosudarstvennyi Pedagogicheskii Institut
Uch Zap Tadzh Gos Univ — Uchenye Zapiski Tadzhikskogo Gosudarstvennogo Universiteta
Uch Zap Tartu Gos Univ — Uchenye Zapiski Tartuskogo Gosudarstvennogo Universiteta [*Estonian SSR*]
Uch Zap Tashk Gos Pedagog Inst — Uchenye Zapiski Tashkentskogo Gosudarstvennogo Pedagogicheskogo Instituta
Uch Zap Tashk Vech Pedagog Inst — Uchenye Zapiski Tashkentskii Vechernii Pedagogicheskii Institut
Uch Zap Tirasp Gos Pedagog Inst — Uchenye Zapiski Tiraspol'skii Gosudarstvennyi Pedagogicheskii Institut
Uch Zap Tomsk Gos Pedagog Inst — Uchenye Zapiski Tomskii Gosudarstvennyi Pedagogicheskii Institut
Uch Zap Tomsk Gos Pedagog Inst — Uchenye Zapiski Tomskogo Gosudarstvennogo Pedagogicheskogo Instituta
Uch Zap Tomsk Gos Univ — Uchenye Zapiski Tomskogo Gosudarstvennogo Universiteta
Uch Zap TsAGI — Uchenye Zapiski TsAGI [*USSR*]
Uch Zap Tsentr Nauchno-Issled Inst Olovyannoi Promsti — Uchenye Zapiski Tsentral'nyi Nauchno-Issledovatel'skii Institut Olovyannoi Promyshlennosti
Uch Zap Tul Gos Pedagog Inst Fiz Tekh Nauki — Uchenye Zapiski Tul'skii Gosudarstvennyi Pedagogicheskii Institut Fiziko-Tekhnicheskie Nauki [*USSR*]
Uch Zap Turkm Gos Pedagog Inst Ser Estest Nauk — Uchenye Zapiski Turkmenskii Gosudarstvennyi Pedagogicheskii Institut Seriya Estestvennykh Nauk
Uch Zap Turkm Gos Univ — Uchenye Zapiski Turkmenskogo Gosudarstvennogo Universiteta
Uch Zap Tyumen Gos Pedagog Inst — Uchenye Zapiski Tyumenskogo Gosudarstvennogo Pedagogicheskogo Instituta
Uch Zap Udmurt Pedagog Inst — Uchenye Zapiski Udmurtskogo Pedagogicheskogo Instituta
Uch Zap Ukr Inst Eksp Endokrinol — Uchenye Zapiski Ukrainskii Institut Eksperimental'noi Endokrinologii
Uch Zap Ukr Nauchno Issled Inst Gig Tr Profzabol — Uchenye Zapiski Ukrainskii Nauchno-Issledovatel'skii Institut Gigieny Truda i Profzabolevanii
Uch Zap Ukr Tsentr Inst Gig Tr Profzabol — Uchenye Zapiski Ukrainskii Tsentral'nyi Institut Gigieny Truda i Profzabolevanii
Uch Zap Ul'yanovsk Pedagog Inst — Uchenye Zapiski Ul'yanovskii Pedagogicheskii Institut
Uch Zap Ural Gos Univ — Uchenye Zapiski Ural'skogo Gosudarstvennogo Universiteta [*USSR*]
Uch Zap Ural Gos Univ Im A M Gor'kogo — Uchenye Zapiski Ural'skogo Gosudarstvennogo Universiteta Imeni A. M. Gor'kogo
Uch Zap Velikoluk Gos Pedagog Inst — Uchenye Zapiski Velikolukskii Gosudarstvennyi Pedagogicheskii Institut
Uch Zap Vitebsk Gos Pedagog Inst Im S M Kirova — Uchenye Zapiski Vitebskogo Gosudarstvennogo Pedagogicheskogo Instituta Imeni S. M. Kirova
Uch Zap Vitebsk Vet Inst — Uchenye Zapiski Vitebskogo Veterinarnogo Instituta
Uch Zap Vladimir Gos Pedagog Inst Ser Bot — Uchenye Zapiski Vladimirskii Gosudarstvennyi Pedagogicheskii Institut. Seriya Botanika
Uch Zap Vladimir Gos Pedagog Inst Ser Bot — Uchenye Zapiski Vladimirskogo Gosudarstvennogo Pedagogicheskogo Institut. Seriya Botanika
Uch Zap Vladimir Gos Pedagog Inst Ser Fiz — Uchenye Zapiski Vladimirskii Gosudarstvennyi Pedagogicheskii Institut. Seriya Fizika
Uch Zap Vladimir Gos Pedagog Inst Ser Fiziol Rast — Uchenye Zapiski Vladimirskii Gosudarstvennyi Pedagogicheskii Institut. Seriya Fiziologiya Rastenii

Uch Zap Vladimir Gos Pedagog Inst Ser Khim — Uchenye Zapiski Vladimirskii Gosudarstvennyi Pedagogicheskii Institut. Seriya Khimiya
Uch Zap Volgogr Gos Pedagog Inst — Uchenye Zapiski Volgogradskogo Gosudarstvennogo Pedagogicheskogo Instituta
Uch Zap Vologod Gos Pedagog Inst — Uchenye Zapiski Vologodskii Gosudarstvennyi Pedagogicheskii Institut
Uch Zap Vybors Gos Pedagog Inst — Uchenye Zapiski Vyborskii Gosudarstvennyi Pedagogicheskii Institut
Uch Zap Yakutsk Gos Univ — Uchenye Zapiski Yakutskogo Gosudarstvennogo Universiteta
Uch Zap Yakutsk Inst — Uchenye Zapiski Yakutskogo Instituta
Uch Zap Yarosl Gos Pedagog Inst — Uchenye Zapiski Yaroslavskii Gosudarstvennyi Pedagogicheskii Institut
Uch Zap Yarosl Tekhnol Inst — Uchenye Zapiski Yaroslavskogo Tekhnologicheskogo Instituta
U Cin L Rev — University of Cincinnati. Law Review
UCLA Forum Med Sci — UCLA [*University of California, Los Angeles*] Forum in Medical Sciences
UCLA Law R — UCLA [*University of California, Los Angeles*] Law Review
UCLA Symp Mol Cell Biol — UCLA [*University of California, Los Angeles*] Symposia on Molecular and Cellular Biology
UCLA (Univ Cal Los Angeles)-Alaska Law R — UCLA (University of California, Los Angeles)-Alaska Law Review
UCLA (Univ Cal Los Angeles) J Environmental Law and Policy — UCLA (University of California, Los Angeles) Journal of Environmental Law and Policy
UCLA (Univ Cal Los Angeles) Pacific Basin Law J — UCLA (University of California, Los Angeles) Pacific Basin Law Journal
UCLR — University of Chicago. Law Review
UCLR — University of Cincinnati. Law Review
UCLR — University of Colorado. Law Review
UCMP — Union Catalog of Medical Periodicals
UCMSA — UCLA [*University of California, Los Angeles*] Forum in Medical Sciences
UCOIP — University of Chicago. Oriental Institute. Publications
U Colo LR — University of Colorado. Law Review
U Colo L Rev — University of Colorado. Law Review
U Color L Rev — University of Colorado. Law Review
U Colo Stud — University of Colorado. Studies
UCOP — University of Cambridge. Oriental Publications
UCP — University of California. Publications in Classical Philology
UCPA — University of California. Publications in Classical Archaeology
UCPES — University of California. Publications in English Studies
UCPFS — University of California. Publications in Folklore Studies
UCPh — Universitas Carolina: Philologica
UCPL — University of California. Publications in Linguistics
UCPM — University of California. Publications in Music
UCPMP — University of California. Publications in Modern Philology
UCPMPh — University of California. Publications in Modern Philology
UCPPh — University of California. Publications in Classical Philology
UCPSP — University of California. Publications in Semitic Philology
UCPSPh — University of California. Publications in Semitic Philology
UCQ — University College Quarterly
UCR — University of Ceylon. Review
UCR — University of Cincinnati. Law Review
UC Rep FM Univ Calif Berkeley Dep Mech Eng — UC. Report FM. University of California, Berkeley. Department of Mechanical Engineering
UCSGS — University of Colorado. Studies. General Series
UCSL — University of California. Studies in Linguistics
UCSLL — University of Colorado. Studies. Series in Language and Literature
UCSMP — University of California. Studies in Modern Philology
UCSSLL — University of Colorado. Studies. Series in Language and Literature
UCTSE — University of Cape Town. Studies in English
Uc Zap Adygejsoskogo Nauc-Issled Inst Jaz Lit Ist — Ucenye Zapiski Adygejoskogo Naucno-Issledovatel'skogo Instituta Jazyka, Literatury, i Istorii
Uc Zap (Stavropol Gos Pedag Inst) — Ucenye Zapiski (Stavropol'skij Gosudarstvennyj Pedagogiceskij Institut)
UD — Unlisted Drugs
U Day LR — University of Dayton. Law Review
U Dayton L Rev — University of Dayton. Law Review
U Det J Urb L — University of Detroit. Journal of Urban Law
U Det L J — University of Detroit. Law Journal
U of Detroit LJ — University of Detroit. Law Journal
U Detroit LJ — University of Detroit. Law Journal
UDKKB — Utsunomiya Daigaku Kyoikugakubu Kiyo, Dai-2-Bu
UDL — Untersuchungen zur Deutschen Literaturgeschichte
UdLH — Universidad de la Habana
UDNGA — Utsonomiya Daigaku Nogakubu Gakujutsu Hokoku
Udobr Urozhai — Udobrenie i Urozhai
Udobr Urozhai (Kom Khim Nar Khaz SSSR) — Udobrenie i Urozhai (Komitet po Khimaisatsii Narodnogo Khozyaistva SSSR)
UDQ — University of Denver. Quarterly
UDR — University of Dayton. Review
UDSKD — Udenrigspolitiske Skrifter. Serie 15
UDURA — Udobrenie i Urozhai [*Ministerstvo Sel'skogo Khozyaistva SSSR*]

UE — Universale Economica
UE — Use of English
UEA — United Evangelical Action
UEE — US Commercial Newsletter [*The Hague*]
UEEBA — Bulletin. Utah Engineering Experiment Station
UEIES — Uppsala English Institute. Essays and Studies
UEJ — University of Edinburgh. Journal
UEL — Uomini e Libri
UELJ — UE [*University of the East*] Law Journal [*Manila*]
UES — UNISA [*University of South Africa*] English Studies
UF — Ugarit-Forschungen
UF — Ulster Folklife [*Belfast*]
U & F — Unterricht und Forschung
UFAJ — University Film Association. Journal
UFA Rev Union Fed Coop Agric Suisse — UFA Revue. Union des Federations Cooperatives Agricoles de la Suisse
UFEBB — Bulletin. Faculty of Education. Utsunomiya University
Ufim Aviacion Inst Trudy — Ufimskii Aviacionnyi Institut Imeni Ordzonikidze Trudy
UFIZA — Ukrainskii Fizicheskii Zhurnal
UFKT — Universitetsforlagets Kronikktjeneste
U Fla L Rev — University of Florida. Law Review
U Florida L Rev — University of Florida. Law Review
UFMH — University of Florida. Monographs. Humanities Series
UFNAA — Uspekhi Fizicheskikh Nauk
UFT — Finance and Trade Review
Ug — Ugaritica [*Paris*]
UGA — Urgeschichtlicher Anzeiger
Uganda Dep Agric Annu Rep — Uganda. Department of Agriculture. Annual Report
Uganda Dep Agric Mem Res Div Ser II Veg — Uganda. Department of Agriculture. Memoirs of the Research Division. Series II. Vegetation
UgandaJ — Uganda Journal
Uganda Natl Parks Dir Rep — Uganda National Parks Director's Report
UGAPB — Publication. Utah Geological Association
Ugeskr Agron Hortonomer — Ugeskrift foer Agronomer og Hortonomer
Ugeskr Laeg — Ugeskrift foer Laeger
Ugeskr Landmaend — Ugeskrift foer Landmaend
Ug F — Ugarit-Forschungen
UgJ — Uganda Journal
UGL — Uitgelezen. Documentatieoverzicht Bibliotheek en Documentatiedienst Ministerie van Sociale Zaken
UGLAA — Ugeskrift foer Laeger
UGLJ — University of Ghana. Law Journal
UGM — University of Georgia. Monographs
Ugol' Ukr — Ugol' Ukrainy
UGOUA — Ugol' Ukrainy
UH — Ukrainian Herald
UH — Universidad de la Habana
U Hart St L — University of Hartford. Studies in Literature
UHQ — Utah Historical Quarterly
UI — Uj Iras
UICC Monogr Ser — UICC [*Union Internationale Contre le Cancer*] Monograph Series
UICC Tech Rep Ser — UICC [*Union Internationale Contre le Cancer*] Technical Report Series
UIEUA — Upravlenie Yadernymi Energeticheskimi Ustanovkami
UILL — University of Illinois. Studies in Language and Literature
U Ill L F — University of Illinois. Law Forum
U Ill L Forum — University of Illinois. Law Forum
UIR/Res Newsl — UIR [*University-Industry Research Program*]/Research Newsletter
Uitgaben Natuurwet Stud Suriname Ned Antillen — Uitgaben Natuurwetenschappelijke Studichring voor Suriname en de Nederlandse Antillen
Uitg Natuurwet Studiekring Suriname Ned Antillen — Uitgaven Natuurwetenschappelijke Studiekring voor Suriname en de Nederlandse Antillen
Uitg Natuurwet Werkgroep Ned Antillen (Curacao) — Uitgaven. Natuurwetenschappelijke Werkgroep Nederlandse Antillen (Curacao)
UIT Rep — UIT [*Ulsan Institute of Technology*] Report
Uitvoerige Versl Sticht Bosbouwproefstn De Dorschkamp — Uitvoerige Verslagen van de Stichting Bosbouwproefstation "De Dorschkamp"
Uitvoer Versl Bosbouwproefsta — Uitvoerige Verslagen van de Stichting Bosbouwproefstation "De Dorschkamp"
UJ — Uganda Journal
UJ — Ungarische Jahrbuecher
UJ — Uniwersytet Jagielloński
UJCT Rep — UJCT [*Ulsan Junior College of Technology*] Report [*Republic of Korea*]
UJDS — Universitetsjubilaeets Danske Samfund
UJISLAA — UNESCO [*United Nations Educational, Scientific, and Cultural Organization*] Journal of Information Science, Librarianship, and Archives Administration
UK — Unknown
UK — Unknown Worlds

U Kan City L Rev — University of Kansas City. Law Review
U of Kansas City L Rev — University of Kansas City. Law Review
U Kans Publ — University of Kansas. Publications. Library Series
UK At Energy Auth At Weapons Res Establ Lib Bibliogr — United Kingdom. Atomic Energy Authority. Atomic Weapons Research Establishment. Library Bibliography
UK At Energy Auth At Weapons Res Establ Rep Ser NR — United Kingdom. Atomic Energy Authority. Atomic Weapons Research Establishment. Report. Series NR
UK At Energy Auth At Weapons Res Establ Rep Ser O — United Kingdom. Atomic Energy Authority. Atomic Weapons Research Establishment. Report. Series O
UK At Energy Auth At Weapons Res Establ Rep Ser R — United Kingdom. Atomic Energy Authority. Atomic Weapons Research Establishment. Report. Series R
UK At Energy Auth Auth Health Saf Branch Mem — United Kingdom. Atomic Energy Authority. Authority Health and Safety Branch. Memorandum
UK At Energy Auth Auth Health Saf Branch Rep — United Kingdom. Atomic Energy Authority. Authority Health and Safety Branch. Report
UK At Energy Auth Dev Eng Group DEG Rep — United Kingdom. Atomic Energy Authority. Development and Engineering Group. DEG Report
UK At Energy Auth Health Saf Code Auth Code — United Kingdom. Atomic Energy Authority. Health and Safety Code. Authority Code
UK At Energy Auth Ind Group IG Rep — United Kingdom. Atomic Energy Authority. Industrial Group. IG Report
UK At Energy Auth Prod Group PG Rep — United Kingdom. Atomic Energy Authority. Production Group. PG Report
UK At Energy Auth Radiochem Cent Mem — United Kingdom. Atomic Energy Authority. Radiochemical Centre. Memorandum
UK At Energy Auth Radiochem Cent Rep — United Kingdom. Atomic Energy Authority. Radiochemical Centre. Report
UK At Energy Auth React Group Rep — United Kingdom. Atomic Energy Authority. Reactor Group. Report
UK At Energy Auth React Group TRG Rep — United Kingdom. Atomic Energy Authority. Reactor Group. TRG Report
UK At Energy Auth Res Group Culham Lab Rep — United Kingdom. Atomic Energy Authority. Research Group. Culham Laboratory. Report
UK At Energy Auth Res Group Culham Lab Transl — United Kingdom. Atomic Energy Authority. Research Group. Culham Laboratory. Translation
UK At Energy Auth Saf Reliab Dir SRD Rep — United Kingdom. Atomic Energy Authority. Safety and Reliability Directorate. SRD Report
UK At Energy Res Establ Anal Method — United Kingdom. Atomic Energy Research Establishment. Analytical Method
UK At Energy Res Establ Bibliogr — United Kingdom. Atomic Energy Research Establishment. Bibliography
UK At Energy Res Establ Health Phys Med Div Res Prog Rep — United Kingdom. Atomic Energy Research Establishment. Health Physics and Medical Division. Research Progress Report
UK At Energy Res Establ Lect — United Kingdom. Atomic Energy Research Establishment. Lectures
UK At Energy Res Establ Memo — United Kingdom. Atomic Energy Research Establishment. Memorandum
UK At Energy Res Establ Rep — United Kingdom. Atomic Energy Research Establishment. Report
UK At Energy Res Establ Transl — United Kingdom. Atomic Energy Research Establishment. Translation
UKC — University of Kansas City. Review
UKCR — University of Kansas City. Review
UKCRv — University of Kansas City. Review
UK Jt Fire Res Organ Fire Res Tech Pap — United Kingdom Joint Fire Research Organization. Fire Research Technical Paper
UKLA — Ukalaha [Quzinkie High School, Alaska]
UKMJB — Ukrainian Mathematical Journal [English Translation]
UKPHS — University of Kansas. Publications. Humanistic Studies
UKPJA — Ukrainian Physics Journal
Ukrain Fiz Z — Ukrainskii Fizicheskii Zhurnal
Ukrain Fiz Zh — Akademiya Nauk Ukrainskoi SSR. Otdelenie Fiziki. Ukrainskii Fizicheskii Zhurnal
Ukrain Geometr Sb — Ukrainskii Geometriceskii Sbornik
Ukrain Geom Sb — Ukrainskii Geometriceskii Sbornik
Ukrainian Math J — Ukrainian Mathematical Journal
Ukrainian Q — Ukrainian Quarterly
Ukrain Mat Z — Ukrainskii Matematicheskii Zhurnal
Ukrain Mat Zh — Akademiya Nauk Ukrainskoi SSR. Institut Matematiki. Ukrainskii Matematicheskii Zhurnal
Ukrain Phys J — Ukrainian Physics Journal
Ukr Biokhim — Ukrainskii Biokhimicheski Zhurnal
Ukr Biokhim Zh — Ukrainskii Biokhimicheskii Zhurnal
Ukr Biokhim Zh — Ukrayins'kyi Biokhimichnyi Zhurnal
Ukr Biokhim Zh (1946-1977) — Ukrains'kii Biokhimichnii Zhurnal (1946-1977) [Ukrainian SSR]
Ukr Bot Zh — Ukrayins'kyi Botanichnyi Zhurnal
Ukr Fiz Zh — Ukrainskii Fizichnii Zhurnal
Ukr Fiz Zh — Ukrainskij Fizicheskij Zhurnal

Ukr Fiz Zh (Kiev) — Ukrayinskoyi Fizichnij Zhurnal (Ukrainian Edition) (Kiev)
Ukr Geom Sb — Ukrainskij Geometricheskij Sbornik
UkrI — Ukrajins'kyj Istoryk
Ukr Ist Zhurnal — Ukrainskyi Istorichnyi Zhurnal
Ukr J Biochem — Ukrainian Journal of Biochemistry
Ukr J Chem — Ukrainian Journal of Chemistry
UkrK — Ukrajins'ka Knyha
Ukr Khem Zh — Ukrains'kii Khemichnii Zhurnal
Ukr Khim Zh — Ukrainskii Khimicheskii Zhurnal
UkrM — Ukrajins'ka Mova i Literatura v Skoli
Ukr Math J — Ukrainian Mathematical Journal
Ukr Mat Zh — Ukrainskij Matematicheskij Zhurnal
Ukr Mov — Ukrajins'ke Movnoznavstvo
Ukr Nauchno Issled Inst Eksp Vet Nauchn Tr — Ukrainskii Nauchno-Issledovatel'skii Institut Eksperimental'noi Veterinarii Nauchnye Trudy
Ukr Nauchno Issled Inst Fiziol Rast Nauchn Tr — Ukrainskii Nauchno-Issledovatel'skii Institut Fiziologii Rastenii Nauchnye Trudy
Ukr Nauchno Issled Inst Pishch Promsti Sb Tr — Ukrainskii Nauchno-Issledovatel'skii Institut Pishchevoi Promyshlennosti Sbornik Trudov
Ukr Phys J — Ukrainian Physics Journal
Ukr Poligr Inst Nauchn Zap — Ukrainskii Poligraficheskii Institut Nauchnye Zapiski
UkrR — Ukrainian Review
UkrS — Ukrajins'kyj Samostijnyk
UKZHA — Ukrainskii Khimicheskii Zhurnal
UI — Ulisse
U e L — Uomini e Libri
ULA — UCLA [University of California, Los Angeles] Law Review
UlbR — Ulbandus Review
ULB-VUB Inter-Univ High Energ Rep — ULB-VUB [Universite Libre de Bruxelles - Vrije Universiteit Brussel] Inter-University Institute for High Energies. Report
ULH — Universidad de la Habana
ULI Lm Rep — Urban Land Institute. Landmark Report
ULI Res Rep — Urban Land Institute. Research Report
ULI Spe Rep — Urban Land Institute. Special Report
Ul'janovsk Gos Ped Inst Ucen Zap — Ul'janovskii Gosudarstvennyi Pedagogiceskii Institut Imeni I. N. Ul'janova. Ucennyi Zapiski
ULLOS — University of London. London Oriental Series
ULM — Union List of Manuscripts [Canada]
U Lond I Cl — University of London. Institute of Classical Studies. Bulletin
ULPOD — Urban Law and Policy
ULQ — Utah Foreign Language Quarterly
ULR — University of Leeds. Review
ULR — Utah Law Review
ULRED — UCLA [University of California, Los Angeles] Law Review
Ulrich's Q — Ulrich's Quarterly
Ulrich's Qtly — Ulrich's Quarterly
ULS — Union List of Serials
UL Sci Mag — UL [University of Liberia] Science Magazine
ULSPD — Ultrasonics Symposium. Proceedings
ULSSCL — Union List of Scientific Serials in Canadian Libraries
Ulster Folk — Ulster Folklife
Ulster J Arch — Ulster Journal of Archaeology
Ulster J Archaeol 3 Ser — Ulster Journal of Archaeology. Series 3
Ulster Med J — Ulster Medical Journal
Ultim Real Mean — Ultimate Reality and Meaning
ULTRA — Ultrasonics
Ultramicrosc — Ultramicroscopy
Ultrason — Ultrasonics
Ultrason Imaging — Ultrasonic Imaging
Ultrason Symp Proc — Ultrasonics Symposium. Proceedings
Ultrasound Med & Biol — Ultrasound in Medicine and Biology
Ultrasound Med Biol — Ultrasound in Medicine and Biology
Ultrastruct Pathol — Ultrastructural Pathology
ULTRD — Ultramicroscopy
Ult Real — Ultimate Reality and Meaning
Ul'yanovsk Skh Opytn Stn Tr — Ul'yanovskaya Sel'skokhozyaistvennaya Opytnaya Stantsiya Trudy
ULz — Ukrajins'ke Literaturoznavstvo
UM — Universidad de Mexico
UM — University Microfilms
U of Malaya L Rev — University of Malaya. Law Review
UMANA — Uspekhi Matematicheskikh Nauk
UMBC Econ R — UMBC Economic Review [Kuala Lumpur]
UMBP — University Museum. Bulletin (Philadelphia)
UMBS — University of Pennsylvania. University Museum. Publications of the Babylonian Section
UMCAA — Union Medicale du Canada
UMCJA — University of Michigan. Medical Center. Journal
UMCMP — University of Michigan. Contributions in Modern Philology
UMCS — Uniwersytet Marii Curie-Sklodowskiej
UMEA Psychol Rep — UMEA Psychological Reports
UMEA Psychol Reports — UMEA Psychological Reports
Umform Tech — Umform Technik

UMHS — University of Miami. Hispanic Studies
U Miami LR — University of Miami. Law Review
U Miami L Rev — University of Miami. Law Review
U Mich Bus R — University of Michigan. Business Review
U Mich J Law Reform — University of Michigan. Journal of Law Reform
U Mich J L Ref — University of Michigan. Journal of Law Reform
U Missouri at KCL Rev — University of Missouri at Kansas City. Law Review
UMJ — Ukrainian Mathematical Journal
UMJOA — Ulster Medical Journal
UMKC LR — UMKC [*University of Missouri, Kansas City*] Law Review
UMKCLR — University of Missouri at Kansas City. Law Review
UMKC L Rev — University of Missouri at Kansas City. Law Review
UMLR — University of Malaya. Law Review
UMLR — University of Miami. Law Review
UMLRB — University of Miami. Law Review
UMLS — Ukrajins'ka Mova i Literatura v Skoli
UMMJ — University of Manitoba. Medical Journal
U MO-Kansas City L Rev — University of Missouri at Kansas City. Law Review
U MO KCL Rev — University of Missouri at Kansas City. Law Review
UMoS — University of Missouri. Studies
UMPAL — University of Minnesota. Pamphlets on American Literature
UMPAW — University of Minnesota. Pamphlets on American Writers
UMPEAL — University of Miami. Publications in English and American Literature
UMPLL — University of Michigan. Publications in Language and Literature
UMR-MEC Conf Energy Resour Proc — UMR-MEC [*University of Missouri, Rolla - Missouri Energy Council*] Conference on Energy Resources. Proceedings
UMS — Ukrajins'ka Mova v Skoli
UMS — University of Maine. Studies
UMS — University of Michigan. Studies
UMS — University of Missouri. Studies
Umschau — Umschau in Wissenschaft und Technik
Umsch Fortschr Wiss Tech — Umschau ueber die Fortschritte in Wissenschaft und Technik
Umsch Wiss und Tech — Umschau in Wissenschaft und Technik
Umsch Wiss Tech — Umschau in Wissenschaft und Technik
UMSE — University of Mississippi. Studies in English
UMSHS — University of Michigan. Studies. Humanistic Series
UMSOA — Umi To Sora
UMT — United Methodist Today
UMTRI (Univ Mich Transportation Research Inst) — UMTRI (University Michigan Transportation Research Institute) Research Review
UMW — Umwelt
Umwelt (Inf Bundesminist Innern) — Umwelt (Informationen des Bundesministers des Innern zur Umweltplanung und zum Umweltschutz)
Umweltpolit Umweltplanung — Umweltpolitik und Umweltplanung
Umwelt-Rep — Umwelt-Report
Umweltschutz Gesundheitstech — Umweltschutz. Gesundheitstechnik
Umweltschutz - Staedtereinig — Umweltschutz - Staedtereinigung
Umwelt Z Biol Stn Wilhelminenberg — Umwelt Zeitschrift der Biologischen Station. Wilhelminenberg
UMW J — United Mine Workers. Journal
UMWLA — Umwelt Zeitschrift der Biologischen Station. Wilhelminenberg
Umw Planungsrecht — Umwelt- und Planungsrecht
UMWTA — Umwelt
UMx — University of Mexico
UMZHA — Ukrainskii Matematicheskii Zhurnal
Unabashed Libn — Unabashed Librarian
UNA Commun — UNA [*Utah Nurses Association*] Communique
UNAGA — Union Agriculture
UNA Nursing J — UNA Nursing Journal [*Royal Victorian College of Nursing*]
UNA Nurs J — UNA [*Utah Nurses Association*] Nursing Journal
Un Apic — Union Apicole
UNASA — Unasylva
Unauth Prac News — Unauthorized Practice News
UNB Law Journal — University of New Brunswick. Law Journal
UNB L J — University of New Brunswick. Law Journal
UNBT — United Nations "Blue Top"
UN Bul — United Nations Bulletin
UN Bull — United Nations Bulletin
Unc — Uncanny Stories
UN Chron — United Nations Chronicle
UNCOA — UNESCO [*United Nations Educational, Scientific, and Cultural Organization*] Courier
UNCR — University of North Carolina. Record. Research in Progress
UNCSCL — University of North Carolina. Studies in Comparative Literature
UNCSGL — University of North Carolina. Studies in Germanic Languages and Literatures
UNCSGLL — University of North Carolina. Studies in Germanic Languages and Literatures
UNCSRL — University of North Carolina. Studies in the Romance Languages and Literatures

UNCSRLL — University of North Carolina. Studies in the Romance Languages and Literatures
Und Child — Understanding the Child
UNDED — Undercurrents
Undercur — Undercurrents
Underground Eng — Underground Engineering
Underground Min Symp — Underground Mining Symposia
Underground Water Conf Aust Newsl — Underground Water Conference of Australia. Newsletter
Undergr Wat Supply Pap (Tasm) — Underground Water Supply Papers (Tasmania)
Undersea Biomed Res — Undersea Biomedical Research
Undersea Technol — Undersea Technology
Under Sign — Under the Sign of Pisces/Anais Nin and Her Circle
Underwater Inf Bull — Underwater Information Bulletin
Underwater J — Underwater Journal
Underwater J & Inf Bull — Underwater Journal and Information Bulletin
Underwater J Inf Bull — Underwater Journal and Information Bulletin
Underwater Nat — Underwater Naturalist
Underwater Sci Technol J — Underwater Science and Technology Journal
Underw J Inf Bull — Underwater Journal and Information Bulletin
Underwriters Lab Stand — Underwriters Laboratories. Standards
Underwrit Lab Bull Res — Underwriters Laboratories. Bulletin of Research
Und-Oder-Nor & Steuerungstech — Und-Oder-Nor und Steuerungstechnik
Und-Oder-Nor Steuerungstech — Und-Oder-Nor und Steuerungstechnik
UNDP/FAO Pakistan Nat For Res Train Proj Rep — UNDP [*United Nations Development Programme*]/FAO [*Food and Agriculture Organization of the United Nations*] Pakistan National Forestry Research and Training Project Report
UNE — Umweltschutzdienst. Informationsdienst fuer Umweltfragen
UNEA — Unearth
UN Econ Comm Asia Far East Water Resour Ser — United Nations Economic Commission for Asia and the Far East. Water Resources Series
UN Econ Comm Eur Comm Agr Prob Work Party Mech Agr AGRI/WP — United Nations Economic Commission for Europe. Committee on Agricultural Problems. Working Party on Mechanization of Agriculture AGRI/WP
UN Econo Comm Asia Far East Miner Resour Develop Ser — United Nations Economic Commission for Asia and the Far East. Mineral Resources Development Series
UN (Educ Sci Cult Organ) Cour — UNESCO (United Nations Educational, Scientific, and Cultural Organization) Courier
Unemployment Ins Statis — Unemployment Insurance Statistics
Unempl Unit Bull Briefing — Unemployment Unit Bulletin and Briefing
UNESCO B Li — UNESCO [*United Nations Educational, Scientific, and Cultural Organization*] Bulletin for Libraries
UNESCO Bul Lib — UNESCO [*United Nations Educational, Scientific, and Cultural Organization*] Bulletin for Libraries
UNESCO Bull Lib — UNESCO [*United Nations Educational, Scientific, and Cultural Organization*] Bulletin for Libraries
UNESCO Bull Libr — UNESCO [*United Nations Educational, Scientific, and Cultural Organization*] Bulletin for Libraries
UNESCO Cour — UNESCO [*United Nations Educational, Scientific, and Cultural Organization*] Courier
UNESCO Inf Circ — Australian National Advisory Committee for UNESCO [*United Nations Scientific, Educational, and Cultural Organization*]. Information Circular
UNESCO J Inf Sci Librarianship and Arch Adm — UNESCO [*United Nations Educational, Scientific, and Cultural Organization*] Journal of Information Science, Librarianship, and Archives Administration
UNESCO Nat Resour Res — United Nations Educational, Scientific, and Cultural Organization. Natural Resources Research
UNESCO Tech Pap Mar Sci — UNESCO [*United Nations Educational, Scientific, and Cultural Organization*] Technical Papers in Marine Science
U New Brunswick LJ — University of New Brunswick. Law Journal
U New South Wales LJ — University of New South Wales. Law Journal
U New S Wales LJ — University of New South Wales. Law Journal
UNFGA — Unternehmensforschung
UNFKA — Uspekhi Nauchnoi Fotografii
Ungar Fil L — Ungar Film Library
Ungerer's Bull — Ungerer's Bulletin
Ung Forstwiss Rundsch — Ungarische Forstwissenschaftliche Rundschau
Ung Z Berg Huettenwes Bergbau — Ungarische Zeitschrift fuer Berg und Huettenwesen. Bergbau
UNHJ — University of Newcastle. Historical Journal
Uni — Universe Science Fiction
UNICIV Rep — UNICIV [*School of Civil Engineering, University of New South Wales*] Report
Unicorn J — Unicorn Journal
UNIDA — Unidia
Unif C Code — Uniform Commercial Code Law Journal
Unif L Conf — Uniform Law Conference
Uni Ljubljai Teh Fak Acta Tech Ser Chim — Univerza v Ljubljani. Tehniska Fakulteta. Acta Technica. Series Chimica
Union Agric — Union Agriculture

Union Burma J Life Sci — Union of Burma. Journal of Life Sciences

Union Burma J Sci Technol — Union of Burma. Journal of Science and Technology

Union Burma J Sci and Technol — Union of Burma. Journal of Science and Technology

Union Carbide Met Rev — Union Carbide Metals Review

Union Int Sci Biol Ser A Gen — Union Internationale des Sciences Biologiques. Serie A. Generale

Union Int Sci Biol Ser B Colloq — Union Internationale des Sciences Biologiques. Serie B. Colloques

Union Med Can — Union Medicale du Canada

Union Med Mexico — Union Medica de Mexico

Union Med (Paris) — Union Medicale (Paris)

Union Oceanogr Fr — Union des Oceanographes de France [*France*]

Union Pharm — Union Pharmaceutique

Union Rec — Union Recorder

Union S Afr Dep Commer Ind Div Fish Invest Rep — Union of South Africa. Department of Commerce and Industries. Division of Fisheries. Investigational Report

Union Soc Fr Hist Nat Bull Trimest — Union des Societes Francaises d'Histoire Naturelle. Bulletin Trimestriel

Union S Q R — Union Seminary. Quarterly Review

Union Tank Car Co Graver Water Cond Div Tech Repr — Union Tank Car Company. Graver Water Conditioning Division. Technical Reprint

Union Univ Q — Union University Quarterly

Uni of Q LR — University of Queensland. Law Review

UNISA Engl Stud — UNISA [*University of South Africa*] English Studies

UNISA Psychol — UNISA [*University of South Africa*] Psychologia

UNISURV G Rep — UNISURV G Report. School of Surveying. University of New South Wales

UNISURV Rep — UNISURV Report. School of Surveying. University of New South Wales

Unit Aborig Messenger — United Aborigines' Messenger

Unita R — Unitarian Review

UNITAR Prepr or Proc — UNITAR [*United Nations Institute for Training and Research*] Preprints or Proceedings

Uni-Taschenb — Uni-Taschenbuecher

Uni of Tas LR — University of Tasmania. Law Review

United Dent Hosp Syd Inst Dent Res Annu Rep — United Dental Hospital of Sydney. Institute of Dental Research. Annual Report

United Dent Hosp Sydney Inst Dent Res Annu Rep — United Dental Hospital of Sydney. Institute of Dental Research. Annual Report

United Fresh Fruit Veg Assoc Yearb — United Fresh Fruit and Vegetable Association. Yearbook

United Plant Assoc South India Sci Dep Bull — United Planters' Association of Southern India. Scientific Department. Bulletin

United Service Q — United Service Quarterly

United Serv Rev — United Services Review

Univ — Universitas

Univ — Universo

UNIVA — Universitas

Univ Abidjan Dep Geol Ser Doc — Universite d'Abidjan. Departement de Geologie. Serie Documentation

Univ Adelaide Cent Precambrian Res Spec Pap — University of Adelaide. Centre for Precambrian Research. Special Paper

Univ Aff/Aff Univ — University Affairs/Affaires Universitaires

Univ Agric Sci (Bangalore) Curr Res — University of Agricultural Sciences (Bangalore). Current Research

Univ Agric Sci (Bangalore) Misc Ser — University of Agricultural Sciences (Bangalore). Miscellaneous Series

Univ Agric Sci (Bangalore) Res Ser — University of Agricultural Sciences (Bangalore). Research Series

Univ Agric Sci (Hebbal Bangalore) Annu Rep — University of Agricultural Sciences (Hebbal Bangalore). Annual Report

Univ Agric Sci (Hebbal Bangalore) Ext Ser — University of Agricultural Sciences (Hebbal Bangalore). Extension Series

Univ Agric Sci (Hebbal Bangalore) Stn Ser — University of Agricultural Sciences (Hebbal Bangalore). Station Series

Univ Agric Sci (Hebbal Bangalore) Tech Ser — University of Agricultural Sciences (Hebbal Bangalore). Technical Series

Univ Alaska Agric Exp Stn Bull — University of Alaska. Agricultural Experiment Station. Bulletin

Univ Alaska Inst Mar Sci Rep — University of Alaska. Institute of Marine Science. Report

Univ Alberta Agric Bull — University of Alberta. Agriculture Bulletin

Univ Alberta Agric For Bull — University of Alberta. Agriculture and Forestry Bulletin

Univ Alberta Dep Civ Eng Struct Eng Rep — University of Alberta. Department of Civil Engineering. Structural Engineering Report

Univ Alberta Fac Agric Bull — University of Alberta. Faculty of Agriculture. Bulletins

Univ Alexandria Fac Eng Bull Chem Eng — University of Alexandria. Faculty of Engineering. Bulletin. Chemical Engineering

Univ Alger Trav Inst Rech Sahariennes — Universite d'Alger. Travaux. Institut de Recherches Sahariennes

Univ Allahabad Stud — University of Allahabad. Studies

Univ Allahabad Stud Biol Sect — University of Allahabad. Studies. Biology Section

Univ Allahabad Stud Bot Sect — University of Allahabad. Studies. Botany Section

Univ Allahabad Stud Chem Sect — University of Allahabad. Studies. Chemistry Section

Univ Allahabad Stud Math Sect — University of Allahabad. Studies. Mathematics Section

Univ Allahabad Stud New Ser — University of Allahabad. Studies. New Series

Univ Allahabad Stud Phys Sect — University of Allahabad. Studies. Physics Section

Univ Allahabad Stud Zool Sect — University of Allahabad. Studies. Zoology Section

Univ Ankara Fac Agri Publ — Universite d'Ankara. Faculte de l'Agriculture. Publications

Univ Ankara Fac Sci Commun Ser A — Universite d'Ankara. Faculte des Sciences. Communications. Serie A. Mathematiques, Physique, et Astronomie

Univ Ankara Fac Sci Commun Ser A2 — Universite d'Ankara. Faculte des Sciences. Communications. Serie A2. Physique

Univ Ankara Fac Sci Commun Ser C — Universite d'Ankara. Faculte des Sciences. Communications. Serie C. Sciences Naturelles

Univ Ankara Yearb Fac Agric — University of Ankara. Yearbook. Faculty of Agriculture

Univ Antioquia — Universidad de Antioquia [*Colombia*]

Univ Ariz Coop Ext Serv Bull — University of Arizona. Cooperative Extension Service. Bulletin

Univ Ariz Coop Ext Serv Circ — University of Arizona. Cooperative Extension Service. Circular

Univ Ariz Coop Ext Serv Ser P — University of Arizona. Cooperative Extension Service. Series P

Univ Arkansas Eng Exp Stn Res Rep Ser — University of Arkansas. Engineering Experiment Station. Research Report Series

Univ Arkansas Lecture Notes in Math — University of Arkansas. Lecture Notes in Mathematics

Univ Austral Chile Fac Cienc Agrar Agro Sur — Universidad Austral de Chile. Facultad de Ciencias Agrarias. Agro Sur

Univ Auton Barcelona Col Univ Gerona Secc Cienc An — Universidad Autonoma de Barcelona. Colegio Universitario de Gerona. Seccion de Ciencias. Anales

Univ Auton Potosina Inst Geol Metal Foll Tec — Universidad Autonoma Potosina. Instituto de Geologia y Metalurgia. Folleto Tecnico

Univ Baghdad Nat Hist Res Cent Annu Rep — University of Baghdad. Natural History Research Center. Annual Report

Univ Baghdad Nat Hist Res Cent Publ — University of Baghdad. Natural History Research Center. Publication

Univ Bahia Esc Geol Publ Avulsa — Universidade de Bahia. Escola de Geologia. Publicacao Avulsa

Univ B Aires Fac Agron Vet Bol Tec Inf — Universidad de Buenos Aires. Facultad de Agronomia y Veterinaria. Boletin Tecnico Informativo

Univ BC Res For Annu Rep — University of British Columbia. Research Forest. Annual Report

Univ Beograd Publ Elektrotehn Fak Ser Mat Fiz — Univerzitet u Beogradu. Publikacije Elektrotehnickog Fakulteta. Serija Matematika i Fizika

Univ Beograd Tehn Fiz — Univerzitet u Beogradu. Tehnicka Fizika

Univ Beograd Zb Radova Gradevin Fak — Univerzitet u Beogradu. Zbornik Radova Gradevinskog Fakulteta u Beogradu

Univ Bergen Arb (Naturv R) — Universitetet i Bergen Arbok (Naturvitenskapelig Rekke)

Univ Bergen Arbok Med Rekke — Universitetet i Bergen Arbok Medisinsk Rekke

Univ Bergen Arbok Naturvitensk Rekke — Universitetet i Bergen Arbok Naturvitenskapelig Rekke

Univ Bergen Arsmeld — Universitetet i Bergen Arsmelding

Univ Bergen Med Avh — Universitetet i Bergen Medisinske Avhandlinger

Univ Bergen Skr — Universitetet i Bergen Skrifter

Univ Botswana Swaziland Agric Res Div Annu Rep — University of Botswana, Swaziland. Agricultural Research Division. Annual Report

Univ Bras Cent Estud Zool Avulso — Universidade do Brasil. Centro de Estudos Zoologicos Avulso

Univ Brasov Lucrari Stiint — Universitatea din Brasov. Lucrari Stiintifice

Univ of Brit Columbia L Rev — University of British Columbia. Law Review

Univ British Columbia Law R — University of British Columbia. Law Review

Univ Bruxelles Inst Phys Bull — Universite de Bruxelles. Institut de Physique. Bulletin

Univ Buenos Aires Fac Agrom Vet Bol — Universidad de Buenos Aires. Facultad de Agronomia y Veterinaria. Boletin

Univ Buenos Aires Inst Anat Publ — Universidad de Buenos Aires. Instituto de Anatomia. Publicacion

Univ Burundi Rev — Universite du Burundi. Revue

Univ Calicut Zool Monogr — University of Calicut. Zoological Monograph

Univ Calif Agric Ext Serv — University of California. Agricultural Extension Service

Univ Calif (Berkeley) Publ Agric Sci — University of California (Berkeley). Publications in Agricultural Sciences

Univ Calif (Berkeley) Publ Bot — University of California (Berkeley). Publications in Botany

Univ Calif (Berkeley) Publ Eng — University of California (Berkeley). Publications in Engineering

Univ Calif (Berkeley) Publ Entomol — University of California (Berkeley). Publications in Entomology

Univ Calif (Berkeley) Publ Health — University of California (Berkeley). Publications in Public Health

Univ Calif (Berkeley) Publ Pharmacol — University of California (Berkeley). Publications in Pharmacology

Univ Calif (Berkeley) Publ Zool — University of California (Berkeley). Publications in Zoology

Univ Calif (Berkeley) Sanit Eng Res Lab Rep — University of California (Berkeley). Sanitary Engineering Research Laboratory. Report

Univ Calif (Berkely) Publ Pathol — University of California (Berkeley). Publications in Pathology

Univ Calif Bull — University of California. Bulletin

Univ Calif Div Agric Sci Bull — University of California. Division of Agricultural Sciences. Bulletin

Univ Calif Div Agric Sci Leafl — University of California. Division of Agricultural Sciences. Leaflet

Univ Calif Lawrence Livermore Lab Rep — University of California. Lawrence Livermore Laboratory. Report

Univ Calif (Los Angeles) Symp Mol Cell Biol — University of California (Los Angeles). Symposia on Molecular and Cellular Biology

Univ Calif Publ Bot — University of California. Publications in Botany

Univ of Calif Publ in English Ling M Ph — University of California. Publications in English, Linguistics, Modern Philology

Univ Calif Publ Entomol — University of California. Publications in Entomology

Univ Calif Publ Geol Sci — University of California. Publications in Geological Sciences

Univ Calif Publications Zool — University of California. Publications in Zoology

Univ Calif Publs Ent — University of California. Publications in Entomology

Univ Calif Publ Zool — University of California. Publications in Zoology

Univ Calif Sea Water Convers Lab Rep — University of California. Sea Water Conversion Laboratory. Report

Univ Calif Univ Los Angeles Publ Biol Sci — University of California. University at Los Angeles. Publications in Biological Sciences

Univ Calif Univ Los Angeles Publ Math Phys Sci — University of California. University at Los Angeles. Publications in Mathematical and Physical Sciences

Univ Calif Water Resour Cent Contrib — University of California. Water Resources Center. Contribution

Univ Camb Dep Appl Biol Mem Rev Ser — University of Cambridge. Department of Applied Biology. Memoirs. Review Series

Univ Cambridge Dep Eng Rep CUDE/A-Aerodyn — University of Cambridge. Department of Engineering. Report. CUDE [*Cambridge University Department of Engineering*]/A-Aerodynamics

Univ Cambridge Dep Eng Rep CUDE/A-Thermo — University of Cambridge. Department of Engineering. Report. CUDE [*Cambridge University Department of Engineering*]/A-Thermo

Univ Cambridge Dep Eng Rep CUDE/A-Turbo — University of Cambridge. Department of Engineering. Report. CUDE [*Cambridge University Department of Engineering*]/A-Turbo

Univ Cambridge Inst Anim Pathol Rep Dir — University of Cambridge. Institute of Animal Pathology. Report of the Director

Univ Canterbury Publ — University of Canterbury. Publications

Univ Cathol Louvain Fac Sci Agron Lab Biochim Nutr Publ — Universite Catholique de Louvain. Faculte des Sciences Agronomiques. Laboratoire de Biochimie de la Nutrition. Publication

Univ Cathol Louv Inst Agron Mem — Universite Catholique de Louvain. Institut Agronomique. Memoires

Univ Catol Bolivar — Universidad Catolica Bolivariana

Univ Cent Desert Stud Trans (Jodhpur India) — University Centre of Desert Studies. Transactions (Jodhpur, India)

Univ Cent Venez Inst Mater Modelos Estruct Bol Tec — Universidad Central de Venezuela. Instituto de Materiales y Modelos Estructurales. Boletin Tecnico

Univ of Chicago L Rev — University of Chicago. Law Review

Univ Chicago Publ — University of Chicago. Publications

Univ Chicago Rep — University of Chicago. Reports

Univ Chic L — University of Chicago. Law Review

Univ Chic M — University of Chicago. Magazine

Univ Chic Rec — University of Chicago. Record

Univ of Chi Law Rev — University of Chicago. Law Review

Univ Chile Dep Prod Agric Publ Misc Agric — Universidad de Chile. Departamento de Produccion Agricola. Publicaciones Miscelaneas Agricolas

Univ Chile Fac Agron Dep Sanid Veg Bol Tec — Universidad de Chile. Facultad de Agronomia. Departamento Sanidad Vegetal. Boletin Tecnico

Univ Chile Fac Agron Publ Misc Agric — Universidad de Chile. Facultad de Agronomia. Publicaciones Miscelaneas Agricolas

Univ Chile Fac Cienc Fis Mat An — Universidad de Chile. Facultad de Ciencias Fisicas y Matematicas. Anales

Univ Chile Fac Cienc Fis Mat Inst Geol Publ — Universidad de Chile. Facultad de Ciencias Fisicas y Matematicas. Instituto de Geologia. Publicacion

Univ Chile Fac Cienc For Bol Tec — Universidad de Chile. Facultad de Ciencias Forestales. Boletin Tecnico

Univ Chile Fac Quim Farm Tesis Quim Farm — Universidad de Chile. Facultad de Quimica y Farmacia. Tesis de Quimicos Farmaceuticos

Univ Chile Inst Invest Ensayes Mater Inf Tec — Universidad de Chile. Instituto de Chile. Instituto de Investigaciones y Ensayes de Materiales. Informe Tecnico

Univ of Cincinnati L Rev — University of Cincinnati. Law Review

Univ Cincin Stud — University of Cincinnati. Studies

Univ of Cinc Law Rev — University of Cincinnati. Law Review

Univ Col Eng Exp Stn Bull — University of Colorado. Engineering Experiment Station. Bulletin

Univ Coll Dublin Agric Fac Rep — University College of Dublin. Agricultural Faculty. Report

Univ Coll Dublin Fac Gen Agric Res Rep — University College of Dublin. Faculty of General Agriculture. Research Report

Univ Coll Wales (Aberystwyth) Memorandum — University College of Wales (Aberystwyth). Memorandum

Univ of Colorado L Rev — University of Colorado. Law Review

Univ Color Stud Ser A — University of Colorado. Studies. Series A. General Series

Univ Color Stud Ser B — University of Colorado. Studies. Series B. Studies in the Humanities

Univ of Colo Studies — University of Colorado. Studies

Univ Colo Stud Ser Anthropol — University of Colorado. Studies. Series in Anthropology

Univ Colo Stud Ser Biol — University of Colorado. Studies. Series in Biology

Univ Colo Stud Ser Chem Pharm — University of Colorado. Studies. Series in Chemistry and Pharmacy

Univ Colo Stud Ser D — University of Colorado. Studies. Series D. Physical and Biological Sciences

Univ Colo Stud Ser Earth Sci — University of Colorado. Studies. Series in Earth Sciences

Univ Col Stud — University of Colorado. Studies

Univ Col Stud Ser C — University of Colorado. Studies. Series C. Studies in the Social Sciences

Univ Conn Occas Pap Biol Sci Ser — University of Connecticut. Occasional Papers. Biological Science Series

Univ Craiova An Ser 3 — Universitatea din Craiova. Analele. Seria a/3. Stiinte Agricole

Univ Craiova An Ser Biol Med Stiinte Agric — Universitatea din Craiova. Analele. Seria. Biologie, Medicina, Stiinte Agricole

Univ Craiova An Ser Mat Fiz Chim Electroteh — Universitatea din Craiova. Analele. Seria. Matematica, Fizica, Chimie, Electrotehnica

Univ Debaters Annual — University Debaters' Annual

Univ Del Mar Lab Inf Ser Publ — University of Delaware. Marine Laboratories. Information Series Publication

Univ Durham King's Coll Dep Civ Eng Bull — University of Durham. King's College. Department of Civil Engineering. Bulletin

Univ Edinb Pfizer Med Monogr — University of Edinburgh. Pfizer Medical Monographs

Univ Edinburgh J — University of Edinburgh. Journal

Universe Nat Hist Ser — Universe Natural History Series

Univers Farm — Universal Farmacia

Universitas (Bogota) — Universitas Pontificia Universidad Catolica Javeriana (Bogota)

Universities Q — Universities Quarterly

University of Singapore School of Archre Jnl — University of Singapore. School of Architecture. Journal

University of Southern Calif School of Archre Yearbook — University of Southern California. School of Architecture. Yearbook

Univ Fed Pernambuco Esc Quim Dep Technol Publ Avulsa — Universidade Federal de Pernambuco. Escola de Quimica. Departamento de Technologia. Publicacao Avulsa

Univ Fed Pernambuco Inst Biocienc Publ Avulsa — Universidade Federal de Pernambuco. Instituto de Biociencias. Publicacao Avulsa

Univ Fed Pernambuco Inst Micol Publ — Universidade Federal de Pernambuco. Instituto de Micologia. Publicacao

Univ Fed Pernambuco Mem Inst Biocienc — Universidade Federal de Pernambuco. Memorias do Instituto de Biociencias

Univ Fed Rio De Janeiro Inst Geocienc Geol Bol — Universidade Federal do Rio De Janeiro. Instituto de Geociencias. Geologia. Boletim

Univ Fed Rio De J Inst Geocienc Bol Geol — Universidade Federal do Rio De Janeiro. Instituto de Geociencias. Boletim Geologia

Univ Fed Rio De J Inst Geocienc Dep Geol Contrib Dida — Universidade Federal do Rio De Janeiro. Instituto de Geociencias. Departamento de Geologia. Contribuicao Didatica

Univ Fed Rural Rio Grande Do Sul Dep Zootec Bol Tec — Universidade Federal Rural do Rio Grande Do Sul. Departamento do Zootecnia. Boletin Tecnico

Univ Fed Vicosa Bibl Centr Ser Bibliogr Espec — Universidade Federal de Vicosa. Biblioteca Central. Serie Bibliografias Especializadas

Univ Fed Vicosa Ser Tec Bol — Universidade Federal de Vicosa. Serie Tecnica. Boletim

Univ Ferrara Ann Sez 6 — Universita di Ferrara. Annali. Sezione 6. Fisiologia e Chimica Biologica

Univ Ferrara Mem Geopaleontol — Universita di Ferrara. Memorie Geopaleontologiche

Univ Fla Agric Ext Serv Circ — University of Florida. Agricultural Extension Service. Circular

Univ Fla Coastal Oceanogr Eng Lab Rep UFL COEL TR — University of Florida. Coastal and Oceanographic Engineering Laboratory. Report. UFL/COEL/TR

Univ Fla Coop Ext Serv Bull — University of Florida. Cooperative Extension Service. Bulletin

Univ Fla Inst Food Agric Sci Annu Res Rep — University of Florida. Institute of Food and Agricultural Sciences. Annual Research Report

Univ Fla Inst Food Agri Sci Publ — University of Florida. Institute of Food and Agricultural Sciences. Publication

Univ Fla Inst Gerontol Ser — University of Florida. Institute of Gerontology Series

Univ Fla Publ Biol Sci Ser — University of Florida. Publications. Biological Science Series

Univ Fla Water Resour Res Cent Publ — University of Florida. Water Resources Research Center. Publication

Univ of Florida L Rev — University of Florida. Law Review

Univ Fl SSM — University of Florida. Social Sciences Monograph

Univ For Bois (Sopron) Publ Sci — Universite Forestiere et du Bois (Sopron). Publications Scientifiques

Univ Forst Holzwirtsch (Sopron) Wiss Mitt — Universitaet fuer Forst- und Holzwirtschaft (Sopron). Wissenschaftliche Mitteilungen

Univ For Timber Ind (Sopron) Sci Publ — University of Forestry and Timber Industry (Sopron). Scientific Publications

Univ F Study — University Film Study Center. Newsletter

Univ Gaz — University Gazette [*University of Melbourne*]

Univ Genova Pubbl Ist Mat — Universita di Genova. Pubblicazioni dell'Istituto di Matematica

Univ Geograd Radovi Zavoda za Fiz — Univerzitet u Geogradu Radovi. Zavoda za Fiziku

Univ Ghana Agric Irrig Res Stn (Kpong) Annu Rep — University of Ghana. Agricultural Irrigation Research Station (Kpong). Annual Report

Univ Ghana Agric Res Stn (Kpong) Annu Rep — University of Ghana. Agricultural Research Station (Kpong). Annual Report

Univ de Grenoble Annales n s Sci — Universite de Grenoble. Sciences-Medecine. Annales

Univ Hawaii Coll Trop Agric Dep Pap — University of Hawaii. College of Tropical Agriculture. Departmental Paper

Univ Hawaii Coop Ext Ser Misc Publ — University of Hawaii. Cooperative Extension Service. Miscellaneous Publication

Univ Hawaii Hawaii Inst Geophys Bienn Rep — University of Hawaii. Hawaii Institute of Geophysics. Biennial Report

Univ Hawaii Hawaii Inst Geophys Rep HIG — University of Hawaii. Hawaii Institute of Geophysics. Report HIG

Univ Hawaii Occas Pap — University of Hawaii. Occasional Papers

Univ Hawaii Res Publ — University of Hawaii. Research Publications

Univ Hisp An Ser Med — Universidad Hispalense. Anales. Serie Medicina

Univ H Sch J — University High School. Journal

Univ Human Rights — Universal Human Rights

Univ Hum Rts — Universal Human Rights

Univ IL Law — University of Illinois. Law Forum

Univ of Illinois L Forum — University of Illinois. Law Forum

Univ Ill L Forum — University of Illinois. Law Forum

Univ Ill Urbana-Champaign Water Resour Cent Res Rep — University of Illinois at Urbana-Champaign. Water Resources Center. Research Report

Univ Ill Urbana-Champaign Water Resour Cent Spec Rep — University of Illinois at Urbana-Champaign. Water Resources Center. Special Report

Univ Indore Res J Sci — University of Indore. Research Journal. Science

Univ Ind Santander Bol Geol — Universidad Industrial de Santander. Boletin de Geologia

Univ Iowa Monogr Studies in Med — University of Iowa. Monographs. Studies in Medicine

Univ Iowa Stud Nat Hist — University of Iowa. Studies in Natural History

Univ J Busan Natl Univ — University Journal. Busan National University [*South Korea*]

Univ J Busan Sanup Univ — University Journal. Busan Sanup University

Univ J of Business — University Journal of Business

Univ J Nat Sci Ser — University Journal. Natural Sciences Series. Busan National University [*Republic of Korea*]

Univ Kansas Sci Bull — University of Kansas. Science Bulletin

Univ Kans Mus Nat Hist Misc Publ — University of Kansas. Museum of Natural History. Miscellaneous Publication

Univ Kans Mus Nat Hist Monogr — University of Kansas. Museum of Natural History. Monograph

Univ Kans Paleontol Contrib Artic — University of Kansas. Paleontological Contributions. Article

Univ Kans Paleontol Contrib Pap — University of Kansas. Paleontological Contributions. Paper

Univ Kans Primary Rec Psychol Publ — University of Kansas. Primary Records in Psychology. Publication

Univ Kans Publ Mus Nat Hist — University of Kansas. Publications. Museum of Natural History

Univ Kans Sci Bull — University of Kansas. Science Bulletin

Univ Kans Sci Bull Suppl — University of Kansas. Science Bulletin. Supplement

Univ KC R — University of Kansas City. Review

Univ K Inst Min Miner Res Tech Rep — University of Kentucky. Institute for Mining and Minerals Research. Technical Report

Univ Kiril Metodij-Skopje Fac Math — Universite Kiril et Metodij-Skopje. Faculte des Mathematiques

Univ KY Coll Agric Coop Ext Ser Rep — University of Kentucky. College of Agriculture. Cooperative Extension Service. Report

Univ KY Coop Ext Serv Circ — University of Kentucky. Cooperative Extension Service. Circular

Univ KY Coop Ext Serv 4-H — University of Kentucky. Cooperative Extension Service. 4-H

Univ KY Coop Ext Serv Leafl — University of Kentucky. Cooperative Extension Service. Leaflet

Univ KY Coop Ext Serv Misc — University of Kentucky. Cooperative Extension Service. Miscellaneous

Univ KY Eng Exp Stn Bull — University of Kentucky. Engineering Experiment Station. Bulletin

Univ KY Inst Min Miner Res Rep IMMR — University of Kentucky. Institute for Mining and Minerals Research. Report IMMR

Univ KY Inst Min Miner Res Tech Rep IMMR — University of Kentucky. Institute for Mining and Minerals Research. Technical Report. IMMR

Univ KY Off Res Eng Ser Bull — University of Kentucky. Office of Research and Engineering Services. Bulletin

Univ KY Publ Anthropol Archaeol — University of Kentucky. Publications in Anthropology and Archaeology

Univ Laval Dep Exploit Util Bois Note Rech — Universite Laval. Departement d'Exploitation et Utilisation des Bois. Note de Recherches

Univ Laval Dep Exploit Util Bois Note Tech — Universite Laval. Departement d'Exploitation et Utilisation des Bois. Note Technique

Univ Leeds Med J — University of Leeds. Medical Journal

Univ Lesn Khoz Derevoobrab Prom-Sti (Sopron) Nauchn Publ — Universitet Lesnogo Khozyaistva i Derevoobrabatyvaoushchei Promyshlennosti (Sopron) Nauchnye Publikatsii

Univ Libre Bruxelles Inter-Univ Inst High Energ Rep — Universite Libre de Bruxelles. Inter-University Institute for High Energies. Report

Univ Liege Fac Sci Appl Coll Publ — Universite de Liege. Faculte des Sciences Appliques. Collection des Publications [*Belgium*]

Univ Lisboa Fac Farm Bol — Universidade de Lisboa. Faculdade de Farmacia. Boletim

Univ Lisboa Rev Fac Cienc A 2 — Universidade de Lisboa. Revista da Faculdade de Ciencias. 2. Serie A. Ciencias Matematicas

Univ Lisboa Revista Fac Ci A — Universidade de Lisboa. Revista da Faculdade de Ciencas. 2a. Serie A. Ciencias Matematicas

Univ Liverp Rec — University of Liverpool. Recorder

Univ London Galton Lab Univ Coll Eugen Lab Mem — University of London. Galton Laboratory. University College Eugenics Laboratory. Memoirs

Univ Lond Univ Coll Galton Lab Eugen Lab Mem — University of London. University College. Galton Laboratory. Eugenics Laboratory. Memoirs

Univ Lund Dep Anat Commun — University of Lund. Department of Anatomy. Communications

Univ M — University Magazine [*Montreal*]

Univ Madr Fac Vet Publ — Universidad de Madrid. Facultad de Veterinaria. Publicacion

Univ Maine Orono Life Sci Agric Exp Stn Annu Rep — University of Maine at Orono. Life Sciences and Agriculture Experiment Station. Annual Report

Univ Maine Orono Life Sci Agric Exp Stn Tech Bull — University of Maine at Orono. Life Sciences and Agriculture Experiment Station. Technical Bulletin

Univ of Maine Studies — University of Maine. Studies

Univ Maria Curie-Sklodowsk Ann Sect B — Universitas Maria Curie-Sklodowsk. Annales. Sectio B

Univ Mass Dep Geol Contrib — University of Massachusetts. Department of Geology. Contribution

Univ MD Nat Resour Inst Contrib — University of Maryland. Natural Resources Institute. Contribution

Univ MD Water Resour Res Cent Tech Rep — University of Maryland. Water Resources Research Center. Technical Report

Univ MD Water Resour Res Cent WRRC Spec Rep — University of Maryland. Water Resources Research Center. WRRC Special Report

Univ Med Rec (London) — Universal Medical Record (London)

Univ Melb Gaz — University of Melbourne. Gazette

Univ Melb Sch For Bull — University of Melbourne. School of Forestry. Bulletin

Univ Miami Law R — University of Miami. Law Review

Univ Miami Law Rev — University of Miami. Law Review

Univ of Miami L Rev — University of Miami. Law Review

Univ Miami Rosenstiel Sch Mar Atmos Sci Annu Rep — University of Miami. Rosenstiel School of Marine and Atmospheric Science. Annual Report

Univ Miami Sea Grant Program Sea Grant Field Guide Ser — University of Miami. Sea Grant Program. Sea Grant Field Guide Series

Univ Miami Sea Grant Program Sea Grant Tech Bull — University of Miami. Sea Grant Program. Sea Grant Technical Bulletin

Univ Mich (Ann Arbor) Off Res Adm Res News — University of Michigan (Ann Arbor). Office of Research Administration. Research News

Univ Mich Bus R — University of Michigan. Business Review

Univ Mich Bus Rev — University of Michigan. Business Review

Univ Mich Dep Nav Archit Mar Eng Rep — University of Michigan. Department of Naval Architecture and Marine Engineering. Report

Univ of Michigan J of Law Reform — University of Michigan. Journal of Law Reform

Univ Mich Inst Sci Tech Rep — University of Michigan. Institute of Science and Technology. Report

Univ Mich J Law Reform — University of Michigan. Journal of Law Reform

Univ Mich Med Bull — University of Michigan. Medical Bulletin

Univ Mich Med Cent J — University of Michigan. Medical Center. Journal

Univ Mich Mus Anthropol Tech Rep — University of Michigan. Museum of Anthropology. Technical Reports

Univ Mich Mus Zool Circ — University of Michigan. Museum of Zoology. Circular

Univ Minn Agric Ext Serv Ext Bull — University of Minnesota. Agricultural Extension Service. Extension Bulletin

Univ Minn Agric Ext Serv Ext Folder — University of Minnesota. Agricultural Extension Service. Extension Folder

Univ Minn Agric Ext Serv Ext Pam — University of Minnesota. Agricultural Extension Service. Extension Pamphlet

Univ Minn Agric Ext Serv Misc — University of Minnesota. Agricultural Extension Service. Miscellaneous Publications

Univ Minn Agric Ext Serv Misc Publ — University of Minnesota. Agricultural Extension Service. Miscellaneous Publications

Univ Minn Agric Ext Serv Spec Rep — University of Minnesota. Agricultural Extension Service. Special Report

Univ Minn Contin Med Educ — University of Minnesota. Continuing Medical Education

Univ Minn Med Bull — University of Minnesota. Medical Bulletin

Univ Mississippi Stud Engl — University of Mississippi. Studies in English

Univ of Missouri at Kansas City L Rev — University of Missouri at Kansas City. Law Review

Univ Missouri Stud — University of Missouri. Studies

Univ MO Bull Eng Exp Stn Ser — University of Missouri. Bulletin. Engineering Experiment Station Series

Univ MO Eng Exp Sta Eng Ser Bull — University of Missouri. Engineering Experiment Station. Engineering Series. Bulletin

Univ Montreal Chercheurs — Universite de Montreal. Chercheurs

Univ MO Sch Mines Metall Bull Tech Ser — University of Missouri. School of Mines and Metallurgy. Bulletin. Technical Series

Univ MO Stud — University of Missouri. Studies

Univ of MO Studies — University of Missouri. Studies

Univ Mus Bull Univ PA — University Museum. Bulletin. University of Pennsylvania

Univ Nac Auton Mex Inst Geol An — Universidad Nacional Autonoma de Mexico. Instituto de Geologia. Anales

Univ Nac Auton Mex Inst Geol Bol — Universidad Nacional Autonoma de Mexico. Instituto de Geologia. Boletin

Univ Nac Auton Mex Inst Geol Paleontol Mex — Universidad Nacional Autonoma de Mexico. Instituto de Geologia Paleontologicas Mexicanas

Univ Nac Auton Mex Inst Geol Rev — Universidad Nacional Autonoma de Mexico. Instituto de Geologia. Revista

Univ Nac Cordoba Fac Cienc Med Rev — Universidad Nacional de Cordoba. Facultad de Ciencias Medicas. Revista

Univ Nac Cuyo Fac Cien Agrar Bol Tec — Universidad Nacional de Cuyo. Facultad de Ciencias Agrarias. Boletin Tecnico

Univ Nac de Cuyo Fac Cienc Agrar Bol de Ext — Universidad Nacional de Cuyo. Facultad de Ciencias Agrarias. Boletin de Extension

Univ Nac Cuyo Fac Cienc Fis-Quim Mat Ses Quim Argent — Universidad Nacional de Cuyo. Facultad de Ciencias Fisico-Quimico Matematicas. Sesiones Quimicas Argentinas

Univ Nac Cuyo Inst Pet Publ — Universidad Nacional de Cuyo. Instituto del Petroleo. Publicacion

Univ Nac Eva Peron Fac Cienc Fisicomat Publ Ser 2 — Universidad Nacional de Eva Peron. Facultad de Ciencias Fisicomatematicas. Publicaciones. Serie 2. Revista

Univ Nac La Plata Fac Agron Lab Zool Agric Bol — Universidad Nacional de La Plata. Facultad de Agronomia. Laboratorio de Zoologia Agricola. Boletin

Univ Nac La Plata Fac Cienc Nat Mus Ser Tec Didact — Universidad Nacional de La Plata. Facultad de Ciencias Naturales y Museo. Serie Tecnica y Didactica

Univ Nac La Plata Notas Mus Bot — Universidad Nacional de La Plata. Notas del Museo. Botanica

Univ Nac La Plata Notas Mus Geol — Universidad Nacional de La Plata. Notas del Museo. Geologia

Univ Nac La Plata Notas Mus Zool — Universidad Nacional de La Plata. Notas del Museo. Zoologia

Univ Nac La Plata Publ Fac Cienc Fisicomat — Universidad Nacional de La Plata. Publicaciones. Facultad de Ciencias Fisicomatematicas

Univ Nac La Plata Publ Fac Cienc Fisicomat Ser 2 — Universidad Nacional de La Plata. Publicaciones. Facultad de Ciencias Fisicomatematicas. Serie 2. Revista

Univ Nac Tucuman Fac Agron Misc — Universidad Nacional de Tucuman. Facultad de Agronomia. Miscelanea

Univ Nac Tucuman Fac Agron Zootec Misc — Universidad Nacional de Tucuman. Facultad de Agronomia y Zootecnia. Miscelanea

Univ Nac Tucuman Fac Agron Zootec Publ Espec — Universidad Nacional de Tucuman. Facultad de Agronomia y Zootecnia. Publicacion Especial

Univ Nac Tucuman Fac Agron Zootec Ser Didact — Universidad Nacional de Tucuman. Facultad de Agronomia y Zootecnia. Serie Didactica

Univ Nac Tucuman Fund Inst Miguel Lillo Misc — Universidad Nacional de Tucuman. Fundacion e Instituto Miguel Lillo. Miscelanea

Univ Nac Tucuman Inst Fis Publ — Universidad Nacional de Tucuman. Instituto de Fisica. Publicacion

Univ Nac Tucuman Inst Geol Min Rev — Universidad Nacional de Tucuman. Instituto de Geologia y Mineria. Revista

Univ Nac Tucuman Inst Ing Quim Pub — Universidad Nacional de Tucuman. Instituto de Ingenieria Quimica. Publicacion

Univ Nac Tucuman Rev Ser A — Universidad Nacional de Tucuman. Facultad de Ciencias Exactas y Tecnologia. Revista. Serie A. Matematicas y Fisica Teorica

Univ de Nancy Fac d Lettres Annales de l'Est — Universite de Nancy. Faculte des Lettres. Annales de l'Est

Univ Natal Wattle Res Inst Rep — University of Natal. Wattle Research Institute. Report

Univ Nebr Coll Agric Home Econ Q — University of Nebraska. College of Agriculture and Home Economics. Quarterly

Univ NE Bul — University of New England. Bulletin

Univ N Engl Annu Rep — University of New England. Annual Report

Univ N Engl Explor Soc Aust Rep — University of New England. Exploration Society of Australia. Report

Univ Nev Mackay Sch Mines Geol Min Ser Bull — University of Nevada. Mackay School of Mines. Geological and Mining Series. Bulletin

Univ Nev Max C Fleischmann Coll Agric R — University of Nevada. Max C. Fleischmann College of Agriculture. R Series

Univ Nev Max C Fleischmann Coll Agric Rep — University of Nevada. Max C. Fleischmann College of Agriculture. Report

Univ Nev Max C Fleischmann Coll Agric Ser B — University of Nevada. Max C. Fleischmann College of Agriculture. B Series

Univ Nev Max C Fleischmann Coll Agric T Ser — University of Nevada. Max C. Fleischmann College of Agriculture. T Series

Univ of New Brunswick LJ — University of New Brunswick. Law Journal

Univ Newcastle Upon Tyne Rep Dove Mar Lab Third Ser — University of Newcastle Upon Tyne. Report of the Dove Marine Laboratory. Third Series

Univ New Eng Bull — University of New England. Bulletin

Univ New South Wales Occas Pap — University of New South Wales. Occasional Papers [Australia]

Univ NM Bull Biol Ser — University of New Mexico. Bulletin. Biological Series

Univ NM Bull Geol Ser — University of New Mexico. Bulletin. Geological Series

Univ NM Inst Meteorit Spec Publ — University of New Mexico. Institute of Meteoritics. Special Publication

Univ NM Publ Anthropol — University of New Mexico. Publications in Anthropology

Univ NM Publ Biol — University of New Mexico. Publications in Biology

Univ NM Publ Geol — University of New Mexico. Publications in Geology

Univ NM Publ Meteorit — University of New Mexico. Publications in Meteoritics

Univ Nottingham Dep Agric Hortic Misc Publ — University of Nottingham. Department of Agriculture and Horticulture. Miscellaneous Publication

Univ u Novom Sadu Zb Rad Prirod-Mat Fak — Univerzitet u Novom Sadu. Zbornik Radova Prirodno-Matematickog Fakulteta

Univ NSW LJ — University of New South Wales. Law Journal

Univ of NSW LJ — University of New South Wales. Law Journal

Univ NSW Occas Pap — University of New South Wales. Occasional Papers

Univ NSW Q — University of New South Wales. Quarterly

Univ Oriente Inst Oceanogr Bol — Universidad de Oriente. Instituto Oceanografico. Boletin

Univ Oriente Inst Oceanogr Bol Bibliogr — Universidad de Oriente. Instituto Oceanografico. Boletin Bibliografico

Univ Oxford Dept Eng Sci Rep — University of Oxford. Department of Engineering. Science Reports

Univ PA Bull Vet Ext Q — University of Pennsylvania. Bulletin. Veterinary Extension Quarterly

Univ Palermo Ann Fac Econom Commercio — Universita di Palermo. Annali della Facolta di Economia e Commercio

Univ Palermo Ann Fac Econom e Commercio — Universita di Palermo. Annali della Facolta di Economia e Commercio

Univ PA Libr Chron — University of Pennsylvania. Library Chronicle

Univ PA Med Bull — University of Pennsylvania. Medical Bulletin

Univ of PA Pub Pol Econ — University of Pennsylvania. Publications in Political Economy

Univ Paris Conf Palais Decouverte Ser A — Universite de Paris. Conferences du Palais de la Decouverte. Serie A

Univ Penn Law Rev — University of Pennsylvania. Law Review
Univ of Pennsylvania L Rev — University of Pennsylvania. Law Review
Univ Peshawar J — University of Peshawar. Journal
Univ of Pittsburgh L Rev — University of Pittsburgh. Law Review
Univ Pontif Bolivariana Publ Trimest — Universidad Pontificia Bolivariana. Publicacion Trimestral
Univ Pontif Bolivar Publ Trimest — Universidad Pontificia Bolivariana. Publicacion Trimestral
Univ Pretoria Publ Ser 2 — University of Pretoria. Publications. Series 2. Natural Sciences
Univ Q — Universalist Quarterly Review [*Boston*]
Univ Q — Universities Quarterly [*London*]
Univ Qd Agric Dep Pap — University of Queensland. Agriculture Department. Papers
Univ Qd Bot Dep Pap — University of Queensland. Botany Department. Papers
Univ Qd Ent Dep Pap — University of Queensland. Entomology Department. Papers
Univ Q Gaz — University of Queensland. Gazette
Univ Q Law J — University of Queensland. Law Journal
Univ Qld Gaz — University of Queensland. Gazette
Univ Qld Law J — University of Queensland. Law Journal
Univ Q LJ — University of Queensland. Law Journal
Univ Quart — Universities Quarterly
Univ of Queensland LJ — University of Queensland. Law Journal
Univ Queensl Comput Cent Pap — University of Queensland. Computer Centre. Papers
Univ Queensl Great Barrier Reef Comm Heron Isl Res Stn — University of Queensland. Great Barrier Reef Committee. Heron Island Research Station
Univ Queensl Pap Dep Bot — University of Queensland. Papers. Department of Botany
Univ Queensl Pap Dep Chem — University of Queensland. Papers. Department of Chemistry
Univ Queensl Pap Dep Entomol — University of Queensland. Papers. Department of Entomology
Univ Queensl Pap Dep Geol — University of Queensland. Papers. Department of Geology
Univ Queensl Pap Dep Zool — University of Queensland. Papers. Department of Zoology
Univ Queensl Pap Fac Vet Sci — University of Queensland. Papers. Faculty of Veterinary Science
Univ R — Universal Review
Univ R — University Review
Univ Reading Natl Inst Res Dairy Bienn Rev — University of Reading. National Institute for Research in Dairying. Biennial Reviews
Univ Reading Natl Inst Res Dairy Rep — University of Reading. National Institute for Research in Dairying. Report
Univ Rec — University Record
Univ Repub Fac Agron Bol (Montev) — Universidad de la Republica. Facultad de Agronomia. Boletin (Montevideo)
Univ Repub (Montevideo) Fac Agron Bol — Universidad de la Republica (Montevideo). Facultad de Agronomia. Boletin
Univ Rhod Fac Med Res Lect Ser — University of Rhodesia. Faculty of Medicine. Research Lecture Series
Univ of Richmond L Rev — University of Richmond. Law Review
Univ RI Mar Publ Ser — University of Rhode Island. Marine Publication Series
Univ Rio Grande Do Sul Esc Geol Avulso — Universidade do Rio Grande Do Sul. Escola de Geologia. Avulso
Univ Rio Grande Do Sul Esc Geol Bol — Universidade do Rio Grande Do Sul. Escola de Geologia. Boletim
Univ Rochester Lib Bull — University of Rochester. Library Bulletin
Univ Rochester Libr Bull — University of Rochester. Library Bulletin
Univ Roma Ist Autom Not — Universita di Roma. Istituto di Automatica. Notiziario
Univ Roorkee Res J — University of Roorkee. Research Journal
Univ Rural Pernambuco Comun Tec — Universidade Rural de Pernambuco. Comunicado Tecnico
Univ of San Francisco L Rev — University of San Francisco. Law Review
Univ Sao Paulo Esc Politec Geol Metal Bol — Universidade de Sao Paulo. Escola Politecnica, Geologia, e Metalurgia. Boletim
Univ Sao Paulo Fac Filos Cienc Let Bol Bot — Universidade de Sao Paulo. Faculdade de Filosofia, Ciencias, e Letras. Boletim. Botanica
Univ Sao Paulo Fac Filos Cienc Let Bol Geol — Universidade de Sao Paulo. Faculdade de Filosofia, Ciencias, e Letras. Boletim. Geologia
Univ Sao Paulo Fac Filos Cienc Let Bol Mineral — Universidade de Sao Paulo. Faculdade de Filosofia, Ciencias, e Letras. Boletim. Mineralogia
Univ Sao Paulo Fac Filos Cienc Let Bol Quim — Universidade de Sao Paulo. Faculdade de Filosofia, Ciencias, e Letras. Boletim Quimica
Univ Sao Paulo Inst Geocienc Astron Bol — Universidade de Sao Paulo. Instituto de Geociencias e Astronomia. Boletim
Univ Sao Paulo Inst Geocienc Bol IG — Universidade de Sao Paulo. Instituto de Geociencias. Boletim IG [*Instituto de Geociencias*]
Univ Sevilla Publ Ser Med — Universidad de Sevilla. Publicaciones. Serie Medicina

Univ Skopje Sumar Fak God Zb — Univerzitet vo Skopje. Sumarski Fakultet. Godisen Zbornik
Univ South Calif Allan Hancock Found — University of Southern California. Allan Hancock Foundation
Univs Q — Universities Quarterly
Univ Strathclyde Annu Rep — University of Strathclyde. Annual Report
Univ Strathclyde Res Rep — University of Strathclyde. Research Report
Univ Stud — University Studies in History and Economics
Univ Stud Hist — University Studies in History
Univ Stud Hist Ec — University Studies in History and Economics
Univ Studies — University Studies in History and Economics
Univ Studies — University Studies in Western Australian History
Univ Studies Math — University Studies in Mathematics
Univ Studi Trieste Fac Econ Commer Ist Merceol Pubbl — Universita degli Studi di Trieste. Facolta di Economia e Commercio. Istituto di Merceologia. Pubblicazione
Univ Studi Trieste Fac Ing Ist Chim App Pubbl — Universita degli Studi di Trieste. Facolta di Ingegneria. Istituto di Chimica Applicata. Pubblicazioni
Univ Studi Trieste Fac Sci Ist Chim Pubbl — Universita degli Studi di Trieste. Facolta di Scienze. Istituto di Chimica. Pubblicazioni
Univ Studi Trieste Fac Sci Ist Geol Pubbl — Universita degli Studi di Trieste. Facolta di Scienze. Istituto di Geologia. Pubblicazioni
Univ Studi Trieste Ist Chim Farm Tossicol Pubbl — Universita degli Studi di Trieste. Istituto di Chimica Farmaceutica e Tossicologica. Pubblicazioni
Univ Studi Triest Fac di Sci Ist Geol Pubbl — Universita degli Studi di Trieste. Facolta di Scienze. Istituto di Geologia. Pubblicazioni
Univ Stud Trieste Fac Farm Ist Chim Farm Tossicol Pubbl — Universita degli Studi di Trieste. Facolta di Farmacia. Istituto di Chimica, Farmaceutica, e Tossicologica. Pubblicazioni
Univ Stud Trieste Fac Farm Ist Tec Farm Pubbl — Universita degli Studi di Trieste. Facolta di Farmacia. Istituto di Tecnica Farmaceutica. Pubblicazioni
Univ Stud Trieste Ist Tec Farm Pubbl — Universita degli Studi di Trieste. Istituto di Tecnica Farmaceutica. Pubblicazioni
Univ Stud Univ Neb — University Studies. University of Nebraska
Univ Sydney Med J — University of Sydney. Medical Journal
Univ Syd Post Grad Ctee Med Bull — University of Sydney. Postgraduate Committee in Medicine. Bulletin
Univ Tas Gaz — University of Tasmania. Gazette
Univ Tas LR — University of Tasmania. Law Review
Univ of Tasmania L Rev — University of Tasmania. Law Review
Univ Tenn Rec — University of Tennessee. Record
Univ Tenn Surv Bus — University of Tennessee. Survey of Business
Univ Tex Austin Bur Econ Geol Handb — University of Texas at Austin. Bureau of Economic Geology. Handbook
Univ Tex Austin Bur Econ Geol Miner Resour Circ — University of Texas at Austin. Bureau of Economic Geology. Mineral Resource Circular
Univ Tex Austin Bur Econ Geol Res Note — University of Texas at Austin. Bureau of Economic Geology. Research Note
Univ Tex Austin Cent Highw Res Res Rep — University of Texas at Austin. Center for Highway Research. Research Report
Univ Tex Austin Cent Res Water Resour Tech Rep — University of Texas at Austin. Center for Research in Water Resources. Technical Report
Univ Tex Bull — University of Texas. Bulletin
Univ Tex Bur Econ Geol Rep Invest — University of Texas. Bureau of Economic Geology. Report of Investigations
Univ Timisoara An Stiinte Fiz Chim — Universitatea din Timisoara. Analele. Stiinte Fizice-Chimice
Univ TLR — University of Tasmania. Law Review
Univ Toledo Law R — University of Toledo. Law Review
Univ of Toledo L Rev — University of Toledo. Law Review
Univ Toronto Fac For Tech Rep — University of Toronto. Faculty of Forestry. Technical Report
Univ Toronto Inst Environ Sci Eng Publ EH — University of Toronto. Institute of Environmental Sciences and Engineering. Publication EH
Univ Toronto Inst Environ Stud Publ EH — University of Toronto. Institute for Environmental Studies. Publication EH
Univ of Toronto LJ — University of Toronto. Law Journal
Univ Toronto Med J — University of Toronto. Medical Journal
Univ Toronto Q — University of Toronto. Quarterly
Univ Toronto Stud Biol Ser — University of Toronto. Studies. Biological Series
Univ Toronto Stud Geol Ser — University of Toronto. Studies. Geological Series
Univ Toronto Stud Pap Chem Lab — University of Toronto. Studies. Papers from the Chemical Laboratories
Univ Toronto Stud Pathol Ser — University of Toronto. Studies. Pathological Series
Univ Toronto Stud Physiol Ser — University of Toronto. Studies. Physiological Series
Univ Toronto Stud Phys Ser — University of Toronto. Studies. Physics Series
Univ Tor Q — University of Toronto. Quarterly
Univ Tripoli Bull Fac Eng — University of Tripoli. Bulletin. Faculty of Engineering
Univ Udaipur Res J — University of Udaipur. Research Journal
Univ Udaipur Res Stud — University of Udaipur. Research Studies

Univ Umea Commun Res Unit Proj Rep — University of Umea. Communication Research Unit. Project Report
Univ Utah Anthropol Pap — University of Utah. Anthropological Papers
Univ Utah Biol Ser — University of Utah. Biological Series
Univ V — University Vision
Univ WA Ann L Rev — Annual Law Review. University of Western Australia
Univ WA L Rev — University of Western Australia. Annual Law Review
Univ WA Law Rev — University of Western Australia. Law Review
Univ WA L Rev — University of Western Australia. Law Review
Univ Warsaw Dep Radiochem Publ — University of Warsaw. Department of Radiochemistry. Publication
Univ Wash Coll Fish Tech Rep — University of Washington. College of Fisheries. Technical Report
Univ Wash Eng Exp Stn Bull — University of Washington. Engineering Experiment Station. Bulletin
Univ Wash Eng Exp Stn Rep — University of Washington. Engineering Experiment Station. Report
Univ Wash Eng Exp Stn Tech Note — University of Washington. Engineering Experiment Station. Technical Note
Univ Wash Inst For Prod Contrib — University of Washington. Institute of Forest Products. Contributions
Univ Wash Publ Biol — University of Washington. Publications in Biology
Univ Wash Publ Fish — University of Washington. Publications in Fisheries
Univ Wash Publ Oceanogr — University of Washington. Publications in Oceanography
Univ Waterloo Biol Ser — University of Waterloo. Biology Series
Univ Waterloo Fac Environ Stud Occas Pap — University of Waterloo. Faculty of Environmental Studies. Occasional Paper
Univ of West Australia L Rev — University of Western Australia. Law Review
Univ Western Australia Law R — University of Western Australia. Law Review
Univ Western Ontario Series in Philos Sci — University of Western Ontario. Series in Philosophy of Science
Univ West Indies Reg Res Cent Soil Land Use Surv — University of the West Indies. Regional Research Centre. Soil and Land Use Surveys
Univ West Ont Med J — University of Western Ontario. Medical Journal
Univ West Ont Ser Philos Sci — University of Western Ontario. Series in Philosophy in Science
Univ Windsor R — University of Windsor. Review
Univ Wis Coll Agric Life Sci Res Div Bull — University of Wisconsin. College of Agricultural and Life Sciences. Research Division. Bulletin
Univ Wis Coll Agric Life Sci Res Div Res Rep — University of Wisconsin. College of Agricultural and Life Sciences. Research Division. Research Report
Univ Wis Eng Exp Stn Rep — University of Wisconsin. Engineering Experiment Station. Report
Univ Wis-Madison Coll Agric Life Sci Res Div Res Bull — University of Wisconsin-Madison. College of Agricultural and Life Sciences. Research Division. Research Bulletin
Univ Wis Sea Grant Coll Tech Rep — University of Wisconsin. Sea Grant College. Technical Report
Univ Wis Sea Grant Program Tech Rep — University of Wisconsin. Sea Grant Program. Technical Report
Univ Wis Water Resour Cent Eutrophication Inf Prog Lit Rev — University of Wisconsin. Water Resources Center. Eutrophication Information Program. Literature Review
Univ Witwatersrand Dep Geogr Environ Stud Occas Pap — University of the Witwatersrand. Department of Geography and Environmental Studies. Occasional Paper
Univ of Wyoming Publ — University of Wyoming. Publications
Univ Wyo Publ — University of Wyoming. Publications
Univ Yaounde Fac Sci Ann Ser 3 — Universite de Yaounde. Faculte des Sciences. Annales. Serie 3. Biologie-Biochimie
Uniw Adama Mickiewicza Poznaniu Inst Chem Ser Chem — Uniwersytet Imienia Adama Mickiewicza w Poznaniu. Instytut Chemii. Seria Chemia
Uniw Adama Mickiewicza Poznaniu Ser Astron — Uniwersytet Imienia Adama Mickiewicza w Poznaniu. Seria Astronomia
Uniw Adama Mickiewicza Poznaniu Ser Biol — Uniwersytet Imienia Adama Mickiewicza w Poznaniu. Seria Biologia
Uniw Adama Mickiewicza Poznaniu Ser Chem — Uniwersytet Imienia Adama Mickiewicza w Poznaniu. Seria Chemia
Uniw Gdanski Wydz Mat Fiz Chem Zesz Nauk Ser Chem — Uniwersytet Gdanski Wydzial Matematyki, Fizyki, Chemii, Zeszyty Naukowe. Seria Chemia
Uniw Lodz Acta Univ Lodz Ser 2 — Uniwersytet Lodzki. Acta Universitatis Lodziensis. Seria 2
Uniw Marii Curie-Sklodowskiej Ann Sect AA — Uniwersytet Marii Curie-Sklodowskiej. Annales. Sectio AA. Physica et Chemia
Uniw Slaski w Katowicach Prace Nauk — Uniwersytet Slaski w Katowicach. Prace Naukowe
Uniw Slaski w Katowicach Prace Naukowe — Uniwersytet Slaski w Katowicach. Prace Naukowe
Uniw Slaski w Katowicach Prace Naukowe Prace Mat — Uniwersytet Slaski w Katowicach. Prace Naukowe. Prace Matematyczne
Uniw Slaski w Katowicach Prace Nauk-Prace Mat — Uniwersytet Slaski w Katowicach. Prace Naukowe. Prace Matematyczne

Unk — Unknown Worlds
UNK — Zeitschrift fuer Operations Research
UNL — Umwelt. Forschung, Gestaltung, Schutz
Un Med Can — Union Medicale du Canada
UN Mo Chron — UN Monthly Chronicle
Unm Ox — Unmuzzled Ox
UNN — Unternehmung. Schweizerische Zeitschrift fuer Betriebswirtschaft
Unnumbered Rep US Dep Agric Econ Stat Coop Serv Stat Res Div — Unnumbered Report. United States Department of Agriculture. Economics, Statistics, and Cooperatives Service. Statistical Research Division
UNNUS — Uralic News and Notes from the United States
U Notr D St — University of Notre Dame. Studies in the Philosophy of Religion
Unpartizan R — Unpartizan Review
Unpop R — Unpopular Review
Un Prac News — Unauthorized Practice News
UN R — United Nations Review
UN Rev — United Nations Review
UNRP — University of Nottingham. Research Publications
UNS — University of Nebraska. Studies
UN Sec Bur Soc Aff Ser K — United Nations Secretariat. Bureau of Social Affairs. Series K
UnSemQR — Union Seminary. Quarterly Review [*New York*]
Unser Sozial Dorf — Unser Sozialistisches Dorf
Un Serv M — United Service Magazine
Un Serv (Phila) — United Service (Philadelphia)
UNSPD — Underground Space
UNSWLJ — University of New South Wales. Law Journal
UN Symp Dev Use Geotherm Resour Abstr — United Nations Symposium on the Development and Use of Geothermal Resources. Abstracts
UN Symp Dev Use Geotherm Resour Proc — United Nations Symposium on the Development and Use of Geothermal Resources. Proceedings
UnT — Uncanny Tales
UNT — Untersuchungen zum Neuen Testament
UNT — Uppsala Nya Tidning
UNTEA — Undersea Technology
Unternehm — Unternehmung. Schweizerische Zeitschrift fuer Betriebswirtschaft
Unters Angebot Nachfrage Miner Rohst — Untersuchungen ueber Angebot und Nachfrage Mineralischer Rohstoffe
UNTP — Universidad de Tucuman. Publications
UNVS-A — Universo [*Italy*]
UNWAL Rev — University of Western Australia. Law Review
UN W Bul — United Nations Weekly Bulletin
UN World — United Nations World
UNWSA — Unterrichtswissenschaft
UO — Ukrainica Occidentalia [*Winnipeg*]
UO — Ulm-Oberschwaben
UP — Journal of Urban Planning and Development
UP — Uniwersytet Imienia Adama Mickiewicza w Poznaniu
UP — Unterrichtspraxis
UPAL — Utrechtse Publikaties voor Algemene Literatuurwetenschap
U PA Law Rev — University of Pennsylvania. Law Review and American Law Register
U PA L Rev — University of Pennsylvania. Law Review
UPB — Universidad Pontificia Bolivariana
Update — Update on Law-Related Education
UPHR — Up Here
UPHTDE — Annual Research Reviews. Ultrastructural Pathology of Human Tumors
U Pit Law — University of Pittsburgh. Law Review
U Pitt L R — University of Pittsburgh. Law Review
U Pitt L Rev — University of Pittsburgh. Law Review
U of Pitt L Rev — University of Pittsburgh. Law Review
U of PLR — University of Pennsylvania. Law Review
U of PL Rev — University of Pennsylvania. Law Review
UPMB — University of Pennsylvania. Museum Bulletin
UPMFF — University of Pennsylvania. Monographs in Folklore and Folklife
U P News — Unauthorized Practice News
Uppsala Univ G Inst B — Uppsala University. Geological Institution. Bulletin
Upps Arsskr — Uppsala Universitets Arsskrift
Upps Univ Geol Inst Bull — Uppsala University. Geological Institution. Bulletin
UPr — Ucilisten Pregled
Upravlenie Slozn Sistemami — Upravlenie Sloznymi Sistemami. Rizskii Politehniceskii Institut
Upravlyaemye Sistemy — Upravlyaemye Sistemy Institut Matematiki Institut Kataliza Sibirskogo Otdeleniya Akademii Nauk SSSR
Uprawa Rosl Nawozenie — Uprawa Roslin i Nawozenie
UPR Co — Union Pacific Railroad Company
UP Res Dig — UP [*University of the Philippines*] Research Digest
Uprochnyayushchaya Term Termomekh Obrab Prokata — Uprochnyayushchaya Termicheskaya i Termomekhanicheskaya Obrabotka Prokata
Upr Sist Mash — Upravlyayushchie Sistemy i Mashiny [*Ukrainian SSR*]

Upr Yad Energ Ustanovkami — Upravlenie Yadernymi Energeticheskimi Ustanovkami
Upsala J Med Sci — Upsala Journal of Medical Sciences
Upsala J Med Sci Suppl — Upsala Journal of Medical Sciences. Supplement
UPSEELL — University of Pennsylvania. Studies in East European Languages and Literatures
Ups J Med Sci — Upsala Journal of Medical Sciences
Ups J Med Sci Suppl — Upsala Journal of Medical Sciences. Supplement
U Puget Sound L Rev — University of Puget Sound. Law Review
UP Vet — UP [*University of the Philippines*] Veterinarian
UPWBA — Uniwersytet Imienia Adama Mickiewicza w Poznaniu. Wydzial Biologii i Nauk o Ziemi. Prace. Seria Geologia
UQ — Ukrainian Quarterly
UQ — Universities Quarterly
UQLJ — University of Queensland. Law Journal
UQP — University of Queensland. Papers
U Qsld P SS — University of Queensland. Papers. Social Sciences
U Queens L J — University of Queensland. Law Journal
U of Queensl LJ — University of Queensland. Law Journal
U Queensl LJ — University of Queensland. Law Journal
U Queens LR — University of Queensland. Law Review
UR — Ukrainian Review [*London*]
UR — Umjetnost Rijeci
UR — University Review
URAAA — Urania [*Poland*]
Ural Gos Univ Mat Zap — Ural'skii Gosudarstvennyi Universitet Imeni A. M. Gor'kogo Ural'skoe Matematiceskoe Obscestvo Matematiceskie Zapiski
Ural Metall — Ural'skaya Metallurgiya
Ural Politehn Inst Sb — Ural'skii Politehniceskii Institut Imeni S. M. Kirova Sbornik
Uranium Abstr — Uranium Abstracts
Uranium Min Metall — Uranium Mining and Metallurgy
URB — University of Riyad. Bulletin. Faculty of Arts [*Saudi Arabia*]
Urb Aff Abstr — Urban Affairs Abstracts
Urb Aff Ann R — Urban Affairs Annual Review
Urb Aff Q — Urban Affairs Quarterly
Urb Aff Quart — Urban Affairs Quarterly
Urban Abs — Urban Abstracts
Urban Aff Abs — Urban Affairs Abstracts
Urban Affairs Q — Urban Affairs Quarterly
Urban Anthr — Urban Anthropology
Urban Data Service Rept — Urban Data Service Report
Urban Des — Urban Design
Urban Design Intl — Urban Design International
Urban Des Int — Urban Design International
Urban Des Q — Urban Design Quarterly
Urban Ecol — Urban Ecology
Urban Ed — Urban Education
Urban Educ — Urban Education
Urban Hist — Urban History Review [*Revue d'Histoire Urbaine*]
Urban Hist R — Urban History Review
Urban Hist Yearb — Urban History Yearbook
Urban Innov Abroad — Urban Innovation Abroad
Urban Inst Policy Res Rep — Urban Institute. Policy and Research Report
Urban L Ann — Urban Law Annual
Urban Law — Urban Lawyer
Urban Law An — Urban Law Annual
Urban Lif C — Urban Life and Culture [*Later, Urban Life*]
Urban R — Urban Review
Urban Rev — Urban Review
Urban Soc C — Urban and Social Change Review
Urban Stud — Urban Studies
Urban Syst — Urban Systems
Urb Anthrop — Urban Anthropology
Urban Transp Abroad — Urban Transportation Abroad
URBE — Urban Ecology [*Netherlands*]
URBH — Urban Health
Urb L Ann — Urban Law Annual
Urb Law — Urban Lawyer
Urb Law Pol — Urban Law and Policy
Urb Life — Urban Life
Urb Life & Cult — Urban Life and Culture [*Later, Urban Life*]
Urb L and P — Urban Law and Policy
Urb L and Poly — Urban Law and Policy
Urb L Rev — Urban Law Review
URBN-A — Urbanisme [*France*]
URBS-A — Urban Studies [*United Kingdom*]
Urb Soc Change R — Urban and Social Change Review
Urb Stud — Urban Studies
Urdmurt i Glazov Ped Inst Ucen Zap — Urdmurtskogo i Glazovskogo Pedagogiceskogo Instituta Ucenye Zapiski
Urdmurt Ped Inst Ucen Zap — Urdmurtskogo Pedagogiceskogo Instituta Ucenye Zapiski
URECD — Urban Ecology
Uremia Invest — Uremia Investigation
Urethane — Urethane Plastics and Products

Urethane Plast Prod — Urethane Plastics and Products
URev — University Review [*Dublin*]
URGAB — Urologe. Ausgabe A
URGYA — Urology [*Ridgewood, NJ*]
U Rich LR — University of Richmond. Law Review
U Rich L Rev — University of Richmond. Law Review
U Richmond L Rev — University of Richmond. Law Review
URINA — Urologia Internationalis
URLAA — Urban Land
URLB — University of Rochester. Library Bulletin
URLBB — Urologe. Ausgabe B
URLGA — Urologe. Ausgabe A
URLH — Urban Renewal and Low Income Housing
URNEA — Urologiya i Nefrologiya
Urner Miner Freund — Urner Mineralien Freund
Urol Ausg A — Urologe. Ausgabe A
Urol Clin North Am — Urologic Clinics of North America
Urol Cutaneous Rev — Urologic and Cutaneous Review
Urol i Nefrol — Urologiya i Nefrologiya
Urol Int — Urologia Internationalis
Urol Intern — Urologia Internationalis
Urol Nefrol (Mosk) — Urologiia i Nefrologiia (Moskva)
Urol Nephrol Sz — Urologiai es Nephrologiai Szemle [*Hungary*]
Urologe A — Urologe. Ausgabe A
Urologe A — Urologe. Ausgabe A. Zeitschrift fuer Klinische und Praktische Urologie
Urologe B — Urologe. Ausgabe B. Organ des Berufverbandes der Deutschen Urologen
Urol Panam — Urologia Panamericana
Urol Pol — Urologia Polska
Urol Radiol — Urologic Radiology
Urol Res — Urological Research
Urol Suppl (Treviso) — Urologia. Supplemento (Treviso)
Urol Surv — Urological Survey
URP — Untersuchungen zur Romanischen Philologie
URPT-A — Urban and Rural Planning Thought [*India*]
URSUA — Urological Survey
URX — Ubersee Rundschau
US — Universale Studium
US — Uusi Suomi
US1 — United States 1 Worksheets
USAEC Rep CONF — US Atomic Energy Commission. Report. CONF
USAEC Rep GJO — United States. Atomic Energy Commission. Report GJO
USAEC Res Dev Rep AEC-TR — US Atomic Energy Commission. Research and Development Report. AEC-TR
USAEC Res Dev Rep ANL — US Atomic Energy Commission. Research and Development Report. ANL
USAEC Res Dev Rep BNL — US Atomic Energy Commission. Research and Development Report. BNL
USAEC Res Dev Rep COO — US Atomic Energy Commission. Research and Development Report. COO
USAEC Res Dev Rep HASL — US Atomic Energy Commission. Research and Development Report. HASL
USAEC Res Dev Rep HW — US Atomic Energy Commission. Research and Development Report. HW
USAEC Res Dev Rep LAMS (LA) — US Atomic Energy Commission. Research and Development Report. LAMS (LA)
USAEC Res Dev Rep LF — US Atomic Energy Commission. Research and Development Report. LF
USAEC Res Dev Rep NYO — US Atomic Energy Commission. Research and Development Report. NYO
USAEC Res Dev Rep ORINS — US Atomic Energy Commission. Research and Development Report. ORINS
USAEC Res Dev Rep ORNL — US Atomic Energy Commission. Research and Development Report. ORNL
USAEC Res Dev Rep ORO — US Atomic Energy Commission. Research and Development Report. ORO
USAEC Res Dev Rep RLO — US Atomic Energy Commission. Research and Development Report. RLO
USAEC Res Dev Rep SCR — US Atomic Energy Commission. Research and Development Report. SCR
USAEC Res Dev Rep TID — US Atomic Energy Commission. Research and Development Report. TID
USAEC Res Dev Rep UCD — US Atomic Energy Commission. Research and Development Report. UCD
USAEC Res Dev Rep UCLA — US Atomic Energy Commission. Research and Development Report. UCLA
USAEC Res Dev Rep UCRL — US Atomic Energy Commission. Research and Development Report. UCRL
USAEC Res Dev Rep UCSF — US Atomic Energy Commission. Research and Development Report. UCSF
USAEC Res Dev Rep UH — US Atomic Energy Commission. Research and Development Report. UH
USAEC Res Dev Rep UR — US Atomic Energy Commission. Research and Development Report. UR

USAEC Res Dev Rep WT — US Atomic Energy Commission. Research and Development Report. WT

USAEC Symp Ser — US Atomic Energy Commission. Symposium Series

US Aerosp Med Res Lab Tech Rep AMRL-TR — United States. Aerospace Medical Research Laboratory. Technical Report. AMRL-TR

US Aerosp Res Lab Rep — United States. Aerospace Research Laboratories. Reports

USAF AFHRL — United States. Air Force. Human Resources Laboratory

USAF Nucl Saf — USAF [*United States Air Force*] Nuclear Safety

US Agric — United States. Department of Agriculture. Publications

US Agric Mark Serv AMS Series — United States. Agriculture Marketing Service. AMS Series

US Agric Res Serv ARS-NC — US Agricultural Research Service. ARS-NC

US Agric Res Serv ARS-NE — US Agricultural Research Service. ARS-NE

US Agric Res Serv ARS-S — US Agricultural Research Service. ARS-S

US Agric Res Serv ARS-W — US Agricultural Research Service. ARS-W

US Agric Res Serv CA — US Agricultural Research Service. CA

US Agric Res Serv East Reg Res Lab Publ — United States. Agricultural Research Service. Eastern Regional Research Laboratory. Publication

US Agric Res Serv Mark Res Rep — US Agricultural Research Service. Marketing Research Report

US Agric Res Serv North Cent Reg Rep — United States. Agricultural Research Service. North Central Region. Report

US Agric Res Serv Northeast Reg Rep ARS NE — US Agricultural Research Service. Northeastern Region Report. ARS-NE

US Agric Res Serv South Reg Rep — US Agricultural Research Service. Southern Region Report

US Air Force Aeronaut Syst Div Tech Note — United States. Air Force. Aeronautical Systems. Division Technical Note

US Air Force Aeronaut Syst Div Tech Note — US Air Force. Aeronautical Systems Division. Technical Note

US Air Force Aeronaut Syst Div Tech Rep — US Air Force. Aeronautical Systems. Division Technical Report

US Air Force Cambridge Res Lab Instrum Pap — United States. Air Force. Cambridge Research Laboratories. Instrumentation Papers

US Air Force Cambridge Res Lab Phy Sci Res Pap — United States. Air Force. Cambridge Research Laboratories. Physical Sciences Research Papers

US Air Force Hum Resour Lab Tech Rep AFHRL-TR — United States. Air Force. Human Resources Laboratory. Technical Report AFHRL-TR

US Air Force Hum Resour Lab Tech Rep AFHRL-TR — US Air Force. Human Resources Laboratory. Technical Report AFHRL-TR

US Air Force Syst Command Air Force Flight Dyn Lab Tech Rep — United States. Air Force. Systems Command Air Force Flight Dynamics Laboratory. Technical Report

US Air Force Syst Command Air Force Mater Lab Tech Rep AFML — United States. Air Force. Systems Command Air Force Materials Laboratory. Technical Report AFML

US Air Force Syst Command Res Technol Div Tech Doc Rep ASD — United States. Air Force. Systems Command Research and Technology Division. Technical Documentary Report. ASD

US Air Force Tech Doc Rep — United States. Air Force. Technical Documentary Report

US Air Force Tech Doc Rep AFSWC-TDR — US Air Force. Technical Documentary Report. AFSWC-TDR

US Air Force Tech Doc Rep AMRL-TDR — US Air Force. Technical Documentary Report. AMRL-TDR

US Air Force Tech Doc Rep ARL-TDR — US Air Force. Technical Documentary Report. ARL-TDR

US Air Force Tech Doc Rep ASD-TDR — US Air Force. Technical Documentary Report. ASD-TDR

US Air Force Tech Doc Rep RTD-TDR — US Air Force. Technical Documentary Report. RTD-TDR

US Air Force Tech Doc Rep SEG-TDR — US Air Force. Technical Documentary Report. SEG-TDR

US Air Force WADC Tech Rep — United States. Air Force. Wright Air Development Center. Technical Report

US Air Force Weapons Lab Tech Rep AFWL-TR — United States. Air Force. Weapons Laboratory Technical Report AFWL-TR

US Air Force Weapons Lab Tech Rep AFWL-TR — US Air Force. Weapons Laboratory. Technical Report AFWL-TR

US Air Force Wright Air Dev Cent Tech Notes — US Air Force. Wright Air Development Center. Technical Notes

US Air Force Wright Air Dev Cent Tech Rep — US Air Force. Wright Air Development Center. Technical Report

U San Francisco L Rev — University of San Francisco. Law Review

U San Fran LR — University of San Francisco. Law Review

U San Fran L Rev — University of San Francisco. Law Review

US-Arab Commer — US-Arab Commerce

US Argonne Nat Lab Biol Med Res Div Semiannu Rep — United States. Argonne National Laboratory. Biological and Medical Research Division. Semiannual Report

US Argonne Natl Lab Rep — US Argonne National Laboratory. Report

US Armed Forces Food Container Inst Libr Bull — United States. Armed Forces Food and Container Institute. Library Bulletin

US Armed Forces Food Container Inst Libr Bull — US Armed Forces. Food and Container Institute. Library Bulletin

US Armed Forces Med J — US Armed Forces. Medical Journal

US Army Armament Res Dev Command Tech Rep — US Army. Armament Research and Development Command. Technical Report

US Army Behav Sci Res Lab Tech Res Note — US Army. Behavioral Science Research Laboratory. Technical Research Note

US Army Behav Syst Res Lab Tech Res Note — United States. Army. Behavior and Systems Research Laboratory. Technical Research Note

US Army Behav Syst Res Lab Tech Res Rep — United States. Army. Behavior and Systems Research Laboratory. Technical Research Report

US Army Coastal Eng Res Cent Misc Pap — United States. Army. Coastal Engineering Research Center. Miscellaneous Paper

US Army Coastal Eng Res Cent Tech Memo — US Army. Coastal Engineering Research Center. Technical Memorandum

US Army Corps Eng Cold Reg Res Eng Lab Res Rep — United States. Army Corps of Engineers. Cold Regions Research and Engineering Laboratory [*Hanover, New Hampshire*]. Research Report

US Army Corps Eng Cold Reg Res Eng Lab Tech Rep — United States. Army Corps of Engineers. Cold Regions Research and Engineering Laboratory [*Hanover, New Hampshire*]. Technical Report

US Army Corps of Engineers Comm Tidal Hydraulics Rept — United States. Army Corps of Engineers. Committee on Tidal Hydraulics. Report

US Army Corps Engineers Waterways Expt Sta Misc Paper — United States. Army Corps of Engineers. Waterways Experiment Station. Miscellaneous Paper

US Army Corps Engineers Waterways Expt Sta Tech Rept — United States. Army Corps of Engineers. Waterways Experiment Station. Technical Report

US Army Diamond Ordnance Fuze Lab Tech Rep — United States. Army. Diamond Ordnance Fuze Laboratories. Technical Report

US Army Eng Waterw Exp Stn Tech Rep — US Army Engineers. Waterways Experiment Station. Technical Report

US Army Med Res Lab Rep — United States. Army. Medical Research Laboratory. Report

US Army Natick Lab Tech Rep Microbiol Ser — US Army. Natick Laboratories. Technical Report. Microbiology Series

US Atom Energy Commn Pub — US Atomic Energy Commission. Publication

US Atomic Energy Comm Map Prelim Map — United States. Atomic Energy Commission. Map. Preliminary Map

US Atomic Energy Comm Rept — US Atomic Energy Commission. Report

US Banker — United States Banker

US Beach Erosion Board Bull Tech Memo Tech Rept — United States. Beach Erosion Board. Bulletin. Technical Memorandum. Technical Report

USBIA — Uspekhi Sovremennoi Biologii

US Bur Am Ethnology Bull — US Bureau of American Ethnology. Bulletin

US Bur Commer Fish Rep Cal Year — US Bureau of Commercial Fisheries. Report for the Calendar Year

US Bureau Sport Fish Wildl Invest Fish Control — US Bureau of Sport Fisheries and Wildlife. Investigations in Fish Control

USBurEducBul — United States. Bureau of Education. Bulletins

USBurEducCirc — United States. Bureau of Education. Circulars

US Bur Mines Bull — United States. Bureau of Mines. Bulletin

US Bur Mines Inf Circ — US Bureau of Mines. Information Circular

US Bur Mines Inform Circ — United States. Bureau of Mines. Information Circular

US Bur Mines Miner Yearb — United States. Bureau of Mines. Minerals Yearbook

US Bur Mines New Publ — United States. Bureau of Mines. New Publications Monthly List

US Bur Mines Rep Invest — United States. Bureau of Mines. Report of Investigations

US Bur Mines Rept Inv — US Bureau of Mines. Report of Investigations

US Bur Mines Tech Pa — United States. Bureau of Mines. Technical Paper

US Bur Mines Tech Prog Rep — United States. Bureau of Mines. Technical Progress Report

US Bur Reclam Div Des Dams Br Rep — United States. Department of the Interior. Bureau of Reclamation. Division of Design [*Denver, Colorado*]. Dams Branch Report

US Bur Reclam Eng Monogr — United States. Department of the Interior. Bureau of Reclamation [*Denver, Colorado*]. Engineering Monographs

US Bur Reclam Res Rep — United States. Department of the Interior. Bureau of Reclamation. Research Report

US Bur Reclam Tech Rec Des Constr — United States. Department of the Interior. Bureau of Reclamation. Technical Record of Design and Construction (Dams and Powerplants)

US Bur Soils B — US Bureau of Soils. Bulletin

US Bur Sport Fish Wildl Invest Fish Control — United States. Bureau of Sport Fisheries and Wildlife. Investigations in Fish Control

US Bur Sport Fish Wildl Resour Publ — United States. Bureau of Sport Fisheries and Wildlife. Resource Publication

US Bur Sport Fish Wildl Resour Publ — US Bureau of Sport Fisheries and Wildlife. Resource Publication

US Bur Sport Fish Wildl Res Rep — US Bureau of Sport Fisheries and Wildlife. Research Report

US Bur Sport Fish Wildl Tech Pap — US Bureau of Sport Fisheries and Wildlife. Technical Papers

USCAD — University of Southern California. Abstracts of Dissertations

US & Can Av — United States and Canadian Aviation Reports

US Cath — United States Catholic

US Cath Hist Rec — US Catholic Historical Society. Historical Records and Studies

US Cath M — United States Catholic Magazine

US Cath S — United States Catholic Historical Society. Historical Records and Studies

US & C Avi Rep — United States and Canadian Aviation Reports

US & C Av R — United States and Canadian Aviation Reports

USCFSTI AD Rep — United States. Clearinghouse for Federal Scientific and Technical Information. AD Reports

USCFSTI PB Rep — United States. Clearinghouse for Federal Scientific and Technical Information. PB Report

US Chil Bur Pub — United States. Children's Bureau. Publications

US China Bus R — US-China Business Review [*Washington, DC*]

USCM — Usibelli Coal Miner [*Usibelli, AK*]

US Coast and Geod Survey Pub — US Coast and Geodetic Survey. Publication

US Coast Geod Surv Magnetograms Hourly Values MHV — US Department of Commerce. Coast and Geodetic Survey. Magnetograms and Hourly Values MHV

US Cong — United States Congress

US Consum Marketing Serv C & MS — US Consumer and Marketing Service. C & MS

USDA Agr Econ Rep — US Department of Agriculture. Agricultural Economic Report

USDA Agr Handb — United States. Department of Agriculture. Agricultural Handbook

USDA Bur Biol Surv Bull — US Department of Agriculture. Bureau of Biological Survey. Bulletin

USDA Fert — US Department of Agriculture. Fertilizer Supply

USDA For Ser Res Bull PNW US Pac Northwest For Range Exp Stn — USDA [*United States Department of Agriculture*]. Forest Service. Resource Bulletin PNW-United States. Pacific Northwest Forest and Range Experiment Station

USDA For Ser Res Pap PSW US Pac Southwest For Range Exp Stn — USDA [*United States Department of Agriculture*]. Forest Service. Research Paper PSW-United States. Pacific Southwest Forest and Range Experiment Station

USDA For Serv Gen Tech Rep INT Intermt For Range Exp Stn — USDA [*United States Department of Agriculture*]. Forest Service. General Technical Report INT-United States. Intermountain Forest and Range Experiment Station

USDA For Serv Gen Tech Rep NC US North Cent For Exp Stn — USDA [*United States Department of Agriculture*]. Forest Service. General Technical Report NC-United States. North Central Forest Experiment Station

USDA For Serv Gen Tech Rep NE NE For Exp Stn — USDA [*United States Department of Agriculture*]. Forest Service. General Technical Report NE-United States. Northeastern Forest Experiment Station

USDA For Serv Gen Tech Rep PSW US Pac Southwest For Exp Stn — USDA [*United States Department of Agriculture*]. Forest Service. General Technical Report PSW-United States. Pacific Southwest Forest and Range Experiment Station

USDA For Serv Gen Tech Rep SE US Southeast For Exp Stn — USDA [*United States Department of Agriculture*]. Forest Service. General Technical Report SE-United States. Southeastern Forest Experiment Station

USDA For Serv Res Note FPL US For Prod Lab — USDA [*United States Department of Agriculture*]. Forest Service. Research Note FPL-United States. Forest Products Laboratory

USDA For Serv Res Note ITF Inst Trop For — USDA [*United States Department of Agriculture*]. Forest Service. Research Note ITF-United States. Institute of Tropical Forestry

USDA For Serv Res Note (PNW) — USDA [*United States Department of Agriculture*]. Forest Service. Research Note (Pacific Northwest)

USDA For Serv Res Note PSW US Pac Southwest For Range Exp St — USDA [*United States Department of Agriculture*]. Forest Service. Research Note PSW-United States. Pacific Southwest Forest and Range Experiment Station

USDA For Serv Res Note RM US Rocky Mt For Range Exp Stn — USDA [*United States Department of Agriculture*]. Forest Service. Research Note RM-United States. Rocky Mountain Forest and Range Experiment Station

USDA For Serv Res Note SE US Southeast For Exp Stn — USDA [*United States Department of Agriculture*]. Forest Service. Research Note SE-United States. Southeastern Forest Experiment Station

USDA For Serv Resour Bull NC US North Cent For Exp Stn — USDA [*United States Department of Agriculture*]. Forest Service. Resource Bulletin NC-United States. North Central Forest Experiment Station

USDA For Serv Res Pap INT US Intermt For Range Exp Stn — USDA [*United States Department of Agriculture*]. Forest Service. Research Paper INT-United States. Intermountain Forest and Range Experiment Station

USDA For Serv Res Pap NC US North Cent For Exp Stn — USDA [*United States Department of Agriculture*]. Forest Service. Research Paper NC-United States. North Central Forest Experiment Station

USDA For Serv Res Pap NE US Northeast For Exp Stn — USDA [*United States Department of Agriculture*]. Forest Service. Research Paper NE-United States. Northeastern Forest Experiment Station

USDA For Serv Res Pap (PNW) — USDA [*United States Department of Agriculture*]. Forest Service. Research Paper (Pacific Northwest)

USDA For Serv Res Pap RM US Rocky Mt For Range Exp Stn — USDA [*United States Department of Agriculture*]. Forest Service. Research Paper RM-United States. Rocky Mountain Forest and Range Experiment Station

USDA For Serv Res Pap SO — USDA [*United States Department of Agriculture*]. Forest Service. Research Paper SO

USDA PA — United States. Department of Agriculture. PA [*Program Aid*]

USDA Prod Res Rep — United States. Department of Agriculture. Production Research Report

US Dep Agric Agric Handb — US Department of Agriculture. Agriculture Handbook

US Dep Agric Agric Inf Bull — US Department of Agriculture. Agriculture Information Bulletin

US Dep Agric Agric Monogr — United States. Department of Agriculture. Agriculture Monograph

US Dep Agric Agric Res Serv ARS Ser — United States. Department of Agriculture. Agricultural Research Service. ARS Series

US Dep Agric Agric Res Serv Rep — United States. Department of Agriculture. Agricultural Research Service. Report

US Dep Agric Agric Res Serv Stat Bull — United States. Department of Agriculture. Agricultural Research Service. Statistical Bulletin

US Dep Agric Bull — United States. Department of Agriculture. Bulletin

US Dep Agric Circ — US Department of Agriculture. Circular

US Dep Agric Conserv Res Rep — US Department of Agriculture. Conservation Research Report

US Dep Agric Farmers' Bull — US Department of Agriculture. Farmers' Bulletin

US Dep Agric For Serv For Prod Lab Rep — United States. Department of Agriculture. Forest Service. Forest Products Laboratory. Report

US Dep Agric For Serv Res Note (PNW) — United States. Department of Agriculture. Forest Service. Research Note (Pacific Northwest)

US Dep Agric For Serv Res Pap NC — United States. Department of Agriculture. Forest Service. Research Paper NC

US Dep Agric For Serv Res Pap (PNW) — US Department of Agriculture. Forest Service. Research Paper (Pacific Northwest)

US Dep Agric Home Econ Res Rep — United States. Department of Agriculture. Home Economics Research Report

US Dep Agric Home Gard Bull — US Department of Agriculture. Home and Garden Bulletin

US Dep Agric Index-Cat Med Vet Zool Spec Publ — United States. Department of Agriculture. Index-Catalogue of Medical and Veterinary Zoology. Special Publication

US Dep Agric Index-Cat Med Vet Zool Suppl — United States. Department of Agriculture. Index-Catalogue of Medical and Veterinary Zoology. Supplement

US Dep Agric Leafl — US Department of Agriculture. Leaflet

US Dep Agric Mark Res Rep — United States. Department of Agriculture. Marketing Research Report

US Dep Agric Misc Publ — US Department of Agriculture. Miscellaneous Publications

US Dep Agric Northeast For Exp Stn Stn Pap — United States. Department of Agriculture. Northeastern Forest Experiment Station. Station Paper

US Dep Agric Prod Res Rep — US Department of Agriculture. Production Research Report

US Dep Agric Res Serv Mark Res Rep — United States. Department of Agriculture. Agricultural Research Service. Marketing Research Report

US Dep Agric Sci Educ Adm Agric Res Man — US Department of Agriculture. Science and Education Administration. Agricultural Research Manual

US Dep Agric Soil Conserv Ser Soil Surv — United States. Department of Agriculture. Soil Conservation Service. Soil Survey

US Dep Agric Soil Conserv Serv Soil Surv Invest Rep — US Department of Agriculture. Soil Conservation Service. Soil Survey Investigation Report

US Dep Agric Soil Surv — United States. Department of Agriculture. Soil Survey

US Dep Agric Stat Bull — US Department of Agriculture. Statistical Bulletin

US Dep Agric Tech Bull — US Department of Agriculture. Technical Bulletin

US Dep Agric Util Res Rep — United States. Department of Agriculture. Utilization Research Report

US Dep Agric Yearb Agric — US Department of Agriculture. Yearbook of Agriculture

US Dep Commer Natl Bur Stand Tech Note — US Department of Commerce. National Bureau of Standards. Technical Note

US Dep Commer Natl Mar Fish Serv Circ — US Department of Commerce. National Marine Fisheries Service. Circular

US Dep Commer Natl Mar Fish Serv Spec Sci Rep Fish — US Department of Commerce. National Marine Fisheries Service. Special Scientific Report. Fisheries

US Dep Commer Off Tech Serv PB Rep — United States. Department of Commerce. Office of Technical Services. PB Report

US Dep Energy Bartlesville Energy Technol Cent Pet Prod Surv — US Department of Energy. Bartlesville Energy Technology Center. Petroleum Product Surveys

US Dep Energy Bartlesville Energy Technol Cent Publ — US Department of Energy. Bartlesville Energy Technology Center. Publications

US Dep Energy Environ Meas Lab Environ Rep — US Department of Energy. Environmental Measurements Laboratory. Environmental Report

US Dep Health Educ Welfare Annu Rep — US Department of Health, Education, and Welfare [*Later, US Department of Health and Human Services*] Annual Report

US Dep Health Educ Welfare DHEW Publ (FDA) — United States. Department of Health, Education, and Welfare. DHEW [*Department of Health, Education, and Welfare*] Publication. (FDA) [*Food and Drug Administration*]

US Dep Health Educ Welfare DHEW Publ (NIH) — US Department of Health, Education, and Welfare [*Later, US Department of Health and Human Services*] DHEW Publication (NIH)

US Dep Health Educ Welfare Health Serv Adm Publ HSA — United States. Department of Health, Education, and Welfare. Health Services Administration. Publication HSA [*Health Services Administration*]

US Dep Inter Bur Mines New Publ — United States. Department of the Interior. Bureau of Mines. New Publications

US Dep Inter Conserv Yearb — US Department of the Interior. Conservation Yearbook

US Dep Inter Fish Wildl Res Rep — United States. Department of the Interior. Fish and Wildlife Service. Research Report

US Dep Inter MESA Inf Rep — US Department of the Interior. Mining Enforcement and Safety Administration. Informational Report

US Dep Inter Off Libr Serv Bibliogr Ser — United States. Department of the Interior. Office of Library Services. Bibliography Series

US Dep State Bur Public Aff Backgr Notes — United States. Department of State. Bureau of Public Affairs. Background Notes

US Dept Agriculture Tech Bull Yearbook — United States. Department of Agriculture. Technical Bulletin. Yearbook

US Dept HEW Publ — US Department of Health, Education, and Welfare [*Later, US Department of Health and Human Services*] Publications

US Dept HHS Publ — US Department of Health and Human Services. Publications

US Dep Transp (Rep) DOT/TST — US Department of Transportation (Report). DOT/TST

US Dp Agr B — US Department of Agriculture. Bulletin

US Dp Int — US Department of the Interior. Publication

US Econ Res Serv Foreign Agric Econ Rep — US Economic Research Service. Foreign Agricultural Economic Report

US Egg — United States Egg and Poultry Magazine

US Energy Res Dev Adm Rep CONF — United States. Energy Research and Development Administration. Report CONF

US Energy Res Dev Adm (Rep) GJO — US Energy Research and Development Administration (Report) GJO [*Grand Junction Office*]

US Environ Prot Agency Munic Constr Div Rep — United States. Environmental Protection Agency. Municipal Construction Division. Report

US Environ Prot Agency Natl Environ Res Cent Ecol Res Ser — US Environmental Protection Agency. National Environmental Research Center. Ecological Research Series

US Environ Prot Agency Off Air Qual Plann Stand Tech Rep — US Environmental Protection Agency. Office of Air Quality Planning and Standards. Technical Report

US Environ Prot Agency Off Pestic Programs Rep — United States. Environmental Protection Agency. Office of Pesticide Programs. Report

US Environ Prot Agency Off Radiat Programs EPA — US Environmental Protection Agency. Office of Radiation Programs. EPA

US Environ Prot Agency Off Radiat Programs EPA-ORP — US Environmental Protection Agency. Office of Radiation Programs. EPA-ORP

US Environ Prot Agency Off Radiat Programs Tech Rep — United States. Environmental Protection Agency. Office of Radiation Programs. Technical Report

US Environ Prot Agency Off Radiat Programs Tech Rep ORP-SID — US Environmental Protection Agency. Office of Radiation Programs. Technical Reports ORP-SID

US Environ Prot Agency Off Res Dev Rep EPA — United States. Environmental Protection Agency. Office of Research and Development. Report EPA

US Environ Prot Agency Publ AP Ser — US Environmental Protection Agency. Publication. AP Series

US EPA Ecol Res — US Environmental Protection Agency. Ecological Research

US EPA Envir Health Res — US Environmental Protection Agency. Environmental Health Effects Research

US EPA Envir Monit — United States. Environmental Protection Agency. Environmental Monitoring

US EPA Envir Prot Technol — US Environmental Protection Agency. Environmental Protection Technology

US EPA Socioecon Studies — United States. Environmental Protection Agency. Socioeconomic Environmental Studies

U Serv M — United Service Magazine

USF — University of Santa Fe

US Farm — US Farm News

US Fed Railroad Adm Rep — US Federal Railroad Administration. Report

US Fish and Wildlife Service Fishery Bull — US Fish and Wildlife Service. Fishery Bulletin

US Fish Wildl Serv Bur Commer Fish Fish Leafl — US Fish and Wildlife Service. Bureau of Commercial Fisheries. Fishery Leaflet

US Fish Wildl Serv Bur Commer Fish Stat Dig — US Fish and Wildlife Service. Bureau of Commercial Fisheries. Statistical Digest

US Fish Wildl Serv Bur Sport Fish Wildl EGL — US Fish and Wildlife Service. Bureau of Sport Fisheries and Wildlife. EGL

US Fish Wildl Serv Circ — US Fish and Wildlife Service. Circular

US Fish Wildl Serv Fish Distrib Rep — US Fish and Wildlife Service. Fish Distribution Report

US Fish Wildl Serv Invest Fish Control — US Fish and Wildlife Service. Investigations in Fish Control

US Fish Wildl Serv N Am Fauna — US Fish and Wildlife Service. North American Fauna

US Fish Wildl Serv Resour Publ — US Fish and Wildlife Service. Resource Publication

US Fish Wildl Serv Res Rep — US Fish and Wildlife Service. Research Report

US Fish Wildl Serv Spec Sci Rep Fish — US Fish and Wildlife Service. Special Scientific Report. Fisheries

US Fish Wildl Serv Spec Sci Rep Wildl — US Fish and Wildlife Service. Special Scientific Report. Wildlife

US Fish Wildl Serv Tech Pap — US Fish and Wildlife Service. Technical Papers

US Fish Wildl Serv Wildl Res Rep — US Fish and Wildlife Service. Wildlife Research Report

US Fish Wild Serv Fish Bull — US Fish and Wildlife Service. Fishery Bulletin

USFLQ — USF Language Quarterly

USFLR — University of San Francisco. Law Review

USF L Rev — University of San Francisco. Law Review

USFOA — Uspekhi Fotoniki

US Food Drug Adm DHEW Publ — United States. Food and Drug Administration. DHEW [*Department of Health, Education, and Welfare*] Publication

US Forest Serv Agr Hdb — United States. Forest Service. Agriculture Handbooks

US Forest Serv Res Note — US Forest Service. Research Notes

US Forest Serv Res Paper — US Forest Service. Research Papers

US For Prod Lab Res Note FPL — United States. Forest Products Laboratory. Research Note FPL

US For Prod Lab Tech Notes — United States. Forest Products Laboratory. Technical Notes

US For Serv AIB — US Forest Service. AIB

US For Serv Div State Priv For North Reg Rep — US Forest Service. Division of State and Private Forestry. Northern Region Report

US For Serv For Pest Leafl — US Forest Service. Forest Pest Leaflet

US For Serv For Prod Lab Annu Rep — US Forest Service. Forest Products Laboratory. Annual Report

US For Serv For Prod Lab Gen Tech Rep FPL — United States. Forest Service. Forest Products Laboratory. General Technical Report FPL

US For Serv For Resour Rep — United States. Forest Service. Forest Resource Report

US For Serv For Res What's New West — US Forest Service. Forestry Research. What's New in the West

US For Serv Gen Tech Rep INT — US Forest Service. General Technical Report. INT

US For Serv Gen Tech Rep NC — US Forest Service. General Technical Report. NC

US For Serv Gen Tech Rep NE — US Forest Service. General Technical Report. NE

US For Serv Gen Tech Rep PNW — US Forest Service. General Technical Report. PNW

US For Serv Gen Tech Rep PSW — US Forest Service. General Technical Report. PSW

US For Serv Gen Tech Rep RM — US Forest Service. General Technical Report. RM

US For Serv Gen Tech Rep SE — US Forest Service. General Technical Report. SE

US For Serv Gen Tech Rep SO — US Forest Service. General Technical Report. SO

US For Serv Northeast For Exp Stn Ann Rep — United States. Forest Service. Northeastern Forest Experiment Station. Annual Report

US For Serv Northeast For Exp Stn Annu Rep — US Forest Service. Northeastern Forest Experiment Station. Annual Report

US For Serv Northeast For Exp Stn Stn Pap — United States. Forest Service. Northeastern Forest Experiment Station. Station Paper

US For Serv North Reg For Environ Prot — US Forest Service. Northern Region. Forest Environmental Protection

US For Serv Pac Northwest For Range Experiment Stn Res Notes — United States. Forest Service. Pacific Northwest Forest and Range Experiment Station. Research Notes

US For Serv Pac Northwest For Range Exp Stn Ann Rep — United States. Forest Service. Pacific Northwest Forest and Range Experiment Station. Annual Report

US For Serv Pac Northwest For Range Exp Stn Annu Rep — US Forest Service. Pacific Northwest Forest and Range Experiment Station. Annual Report

US For Serv Pac Northwest For Range Exp Stn Res Pap — United States. Forest Service. Pacific Northwest Forest and Range Experiment Station. Research Paper

US For Serv Pac Northwest For Range Exp Stn Res Pap PNW — US Forest Service. Pacific Northwest Forest and Range Experiment Station. Research Paper PNW

US For Serv Pac Northwest For Range Exp Stn Res Prog — US Forest Service. Pacific Northwest Forest and Range Experiment Station. Research Progress

US For Serv Pac Southwest For Range Exp Stn Misc Pap — United States. Forest Service. Pacific Southwest Forest and Range Experiment Station. Miscellaneous Paper

US For Serv Res Note FPL — US Forest Service. Research Note. FPL

US For Serv Res Note Inst Trop For — United States. Forest Service. Research Note. Institute of Tropical Forestry

US For Serv Res Note INT — US Forest Service. Research Note. INT

US For Serv Res Note Intermt For Range Exp Sta — United States. Forest Service. Research Note. Intermountain Forest and Range Experiment Station

US For Serv Res Note ITF — US Forest Service. Research Note. ITF

US For Serv Res Note NC — US Forest Service. Research Note. NC

US For Serv Res Note NE — US Forest Service. Research Note. NE

US For Serv Res Note Nth Cent For Exp Sta — United States. Forest Service. Research Note. North Central Forest Experiment Station

US For Serv Res Note Ntheast For Exp Sta — United States. Forest Service. Research Note. Northeastern Forest Experiment Station

US For Serv Res Note Nth For Exp Sta — United States. Forest Service. Research Note. Northern Forest Experiment Station

US For Serv Res Note Pacif Nthwest For Range Exp Sta — United States. Forest Service. Research Note. Pacific Northwest Forest and Range Experiment Station

US For Serv Res Note Pacif Sthwest For Range Exp Sta — US Forest Service. Research Note. Pacific Southwest Forest and Range Experiment Station

US For Serv Res Note PNW — US Forest Service. Research Note. PNW

US For Serv Res Note PSW — US Forest Service. Research Note. PSW

US For Serv Res Note RM — US Forest Service. Research Note. RM

US For Serv Res Note Rocky Mt For Range Exp Sta — US Forest Service. Research Note. Rocky Mountain Forest and Range Experiment Station

US For Serv Res Note SE — US Forest Service. Research Note. SE

US For Serv Res Note SO — US Forest Service. Research Note. SO

US For Serv Res Note Stheast For Exp Sta — US Forest Service. Research Note. Southeastern Forest Experiment Station

US For Serv Res Note Sth For Exp Sta — United States. Forest Service. Research Note. Southern Forest Experiment Station

US For Serv Res Note US For Prod Lab (Madison) — US Forest Service. Research Note. US Forest Products Laboratory (Madison, Wisconsin)

US For Serv Resour Bull INT — US Forest Service. Resource Bulletin. INT

US For Serv Resour Bull NC — US Forest Service. Resource Bulletin. NC

US For Serv Resour Bull NE — US Forest Service. Resource Bulletin. NE

US For Serv Resour Bull PNW — US Forest Service. Resource Bulletin. PNW

US For Serv Resour Bull PSW — US Forest Service. Resource Bulletin. PSW

US For Serv Resour Bull SE — US Forest Service. Resource Bulletin. SE

US For Serv Resour Bull SO — US Forest Service. Resource Bulletin. SO

US For Serv Resource Bull Intermt For Range Exp Sta — United States. Forest Service. Resource Bulletin. Intermountain Forest and Range Experiment Station

US For Serv Resource Bull Nth Cent For Exp Sta — US Forest Service. Resource Bulletin. North Central Forest Experiment Station

US For Serv Resource Bull Ntheast For Exp Sta — US Forest Service. Resource Bulletin. Northeastern Forest Experiment Station

US For Serv Resource Bull Nth For Exp Sta — US Forest Service. Resource Bulletin. Northern Forest Experiment Station

US For Serv Resource Bull Pacif Nthwest For Range Exp Sta — United States. Forest Service. Pacific Northwest Forest and Range Experiment Station. Resource Bulletin

US For Serv Resource Bull Pacif Sthwest For Range Exp Sta — US Forest Service. Resource Bulletin. Pacific Southwest Forest and Range Experiment Station

US For Serv Resource Bull Stheast For Exp Sta — US Forest Service. Resource Bulletin. Southeastern Forest Experiment Station

US For Serv Resource Bull Sth For Exp Sta — US Forest Service. Resource Bulletin. Southern Forest Experiment Station

US For Serv Res Pap FPL — US Forest Service. Research Paper. FPL

US For Serv Res Pap Inst Trop For — US Forest Service. Research Paper. Institute of Tropical Forestry

US For Serv Res Pap INT — US Forest Service. Research Paper. INT

US For Serv Res Pap Intermt For Range Exp Sta — US Forest Service. Research Paper. Intermountain Forest and Range Experiment Station

US For Serv Res Pap ITF — US Forest Service. Research Paper. ITF

US For Serv Res Pap NC — US Forest Service. Research Paper. NC

US For Serv Res Pap NE — US Forest Service. Research Paper. NE

US For Serv Res Pap Nth Cent For Exp Sta — US Forest Service. Research Paper. North Central Forest Experiment Station

US For Serv Res Pap Ntheast For Exp Sta — US Forest Service. Research Paper. Northeastern Forest Experiment Station

US For Serv Res Pap Nth For Exp Sta — United States. Forest Service. Research Paper. Northern Forest Experiment Station

US For Serv Res Pap Pacif Nthwest For Range Exp Sta — US Forest Service. Research Paper. Pacific Northwest Forest and Range Experiment Station

US For Serv Res Pap Pacif Sthwest For Range Exp Sta — US Forest Service. Research Paper. Pacific Southwest Forest and Range Experiment Station

US For Serv Res Pap PNW — US Forest Service. Research Paper. PNW

US For Serv Res Pap PSW — US Forest Service. Research Paper. PSW

US For Serv Res Pap RM — US Forest Service. Research Paper. RM

US For Serv Res Pap Rocky Mt For Range Exp Sta — United States. Forest Service. Research Paper. Rocky Mountain Forest and Range Experiment Station

US For Serv Res Pap SE — US Forest Service. Research Paper. SE

US For Serv Res Pap SO — US Forest Service. Research Paper. SO

US For Serv Res Pap Stheast For Exp Sta — US Forest Service. Research Paper. Southeastern Forest Experiment Station

US For Serv Res Pap Sth For Exp Sta — US Forest Service. Research Paper. Southern Forest Experiment Station

US For Serv Res Pap US For Prod Lab (Madison) — United States. Forest Service. Research Paper. United States Forest Products Laboratory (Madison, Wisconsin)

US For Serv Res Pap WO — US Forest Service. Research Paper. WO

US For Serv Rocky Mount For Range Exp Stn For Sur Release — United States. Forest Service. Rocky Mountain Forest and Range Experiment Station. Forest Survey Release

US For Serv Rocky Mount For Range Exp Stn Res Notes — United States. Forest Service. Rocky Mountain Forest and Range Experiment Station. Research Notes

US For Serv Southeast For Exp Stn Res Notes — United States. Forest Service. Southeastern Forest Experiment Station. Research Notes

US For Serv Southeast For Exp Stn Stn Pap — United States. Forest Service. Southeastern Forest Experiment Station. Station Paper

US For Serv South For Exp Stn Annu Rep — US Forest Service. Southern Forest Experiment Station. Annual Report

US For Serv South For Exp Stn For Surv Release — United States. Forest Service. Southern Forest Experiment Station. Forest Survey Release

US For Serv Tech Bull — US Forest Service. Technical Bulletin

US For Serv Tree Plant Notes — US Forest Service. Tree Planters' Notes

USFWSWRR — United States. Fish and Wildlife Service. Wildlife Research Report

USGA Green Sect Rec US Golf Assoc — USGA Green Section Record. US Golf Association

US Geog G S Rocky Mtn Reg (Powell) — United States Geographical and Geological Survey of the Rocky Mountain Region (Powell)

US Geol S Bul — United States. Geological Survey. Bulletin

US Geol S Professional Pa — United States. Geological Survey. Professional Paper

US Geol Surv Annu Rep — United States. Geological Survey. Annual Report

US Geol Surv Bull — United States. Geological Survey. Bulletin

US Geol Surv Circ — United States. Geological Survey. Circular

US Geol Surv Coal Invest Map — US Geological Survey. Coal Investigations Map

US Geol Survey Bull — United States. Geological Survey. Bulletin

US Geol Survey Circ — US Geological Survey. Circular

US Geol Survey Coal Inv Map — US Geological Survey. Coal Investigations Map

US Geol Survey Geol Quad Map — United States. Geological Survey. Geological Quadrangle Map

US Geol Survey Geol Quadrangle Map — US Geological Survey. Geologic Quadrangle Map

US Geol Survey Geophys Inv Map — US Geological Survey. Geophysical Investigations Map

US Geol Survey Hydrol Inv Atlas — US Geological Survey. Hydrologic Investigations Atlas

US Geol Survey Index Geol Mapping US — US Geological Survey. Index to Geologic Mapping in the United States

US Geol Survey Mineral Inv Field Studies Map — US Geological Survey. Mineral Investigations Field Studies Map

US Geol Survey Mineral Inv Res Map — US Geological Survey. Mineral Investigations Resource Map

US Geol Survey Misc Geol Inv Map — United States. Geological Survey. Miscellaneous Geologic Investigations Map

US Geol Survey Oil and Gas Inv Chart — US Geological Survey. Oil and Gas Investigations Chart

US Geol Survey Oil and Gas Inv Map — United States. Geological Survey. Oil and Gas Investigations Map

US Geol Survey Prof Paper — US Geological Survey. Professional Paper

US Geol Survey Water-Supply Paper — United States. Geological Survey. Water-Supply Paper

US Geol Surv Geol Quadrangle Map — US Geological Survey. Geologic Quadrangle Map

US Geol Surv Geophys Invest Map — United States. Geological Survey. Geophysical Investigations Map

US Geol Surv Hydrol Invest Atlas — US Geological Survey. Hydrologic Investigations Atlas

US Geol Surv Miner Invest Field Stud Map — United States. Department of the Interior. Geological Survey. Mineral Investigations Field Studies Map

US Geol Surv Misc Field Stud Map — US Geological Survey. Miscellaneous Field Studies Map

US Geol Surv Misc Geol Invest Map — United States. Geological Survey. Miscellaneous Geologic Investigations Map

US Geol Surv Oil Gas Invest Chart — US Geological Survey. Oil and Gas Investigations Chart

US Geol Surv Oil Gas Invest Map — US Geological Survey. Oil and Gas Investigations Map

US Geol Surv Open-File Rep — US Geological Survey. Open-File Report

US Geol Surv Prof Pap — United States. Geological Survey. Professional Paper

US Geol Surv Trace Elem Memo Rep — United States. Geological Survey. Trace Elements Memorandum Report

US Geol Surv Water-Resour Invest — US Geological Survey. Water-Resources Investigations

US Geol Surv Water-Supply Pap — US Geological Survey. Water-Supply Paper

US G Geog S Terr (Hayden) — United States Geological and Geographies Survey of the Territories (Hayden)

US Gov Res Dev Rep — US Government Research and Development Reports

US Gov Res Rep — US Government Research Reports

US Govt Paper Spec Std — US Government Paper. Specification Standards

US Govt Res Develop Rept — United States Government Research and Development Reports

US Govt Res Rept — United States Government Research Report

USGS An Rp PPB W-S P Mon Min Res G Atlas Top Atlas — United States. Geological Survey. Annual Report. Professional Paper. Bulletin. Water-Supply Paper Monograph. Mineral Resources Geology Atlas

USGSB — United States. Geological Survey. Bulletin

USGSC — United States. Geological Survey. Circular

USGSPP — United States. Geological Survey. Professional Paper

USGS Terr — United States Geological Survey of the Territories

US Gym Fed Gym News — United States Gymnastic Federation. Gymnastic News

US Hydrog Office Pub — US Hydrographic Office. Publication

USI — United States Investor

USI — Usine Nouvelle

US-IBP Anal Ecosyst Program Interbiome Abstr — US-IBP [*International Biological Program*] Analyses of Ecosystems Program. Interbiome Abstracts

US-IBP Ecosyst Anal Stud Abstr — US-IBP [*International Biological Program*] Ecosystem Analysis Studies Abstracts

US-IBP Synth Ser — US-IBP [*International Biological Program*] Synthesis Series

Usine Nouv — Usine Nouvelle

Usine Nouv Ed Suppl — Usine Nouvelle. Edition Supplementaire [*France*]

Usine Nouv Suppl — Usine Nouvelle. Edition Supplementaire

US Inst Text Res Bull — United States Institute for Textile Research. Bulletin

US Interdep Comm Atmos Sci Rep — US Interdepartmental Committee for Atmospheric Sciences. Report

US Joint Publ Res Serv Transl E Eur Agr Forest Food Ind — United States. Joint Publication Research Service. Translations on East European Agriculture, Forestry, and Food Industries

USKHA — Uspekhi Khimii

Uskor Mosk Inzh-Fiz Inst Sb Statei — Uskoriteli. Moskovskii Inzherno-Fizicheskii Institut. Sbornik Statei [*USSR*]

US Law R — United States Law Review

US Lit Gaz — United States Literary Gazette

USLL — Utah Studies in Literature and Linguistics

USL Rev — United States Law Review

USM — United Service Magazine

USM — Usine Nouvelle

US Med — US Medicine

USMKA — Uspekhi Mikrobiologii

USNASA Conf Publ — United States. National Aeronautics and Space Administration. Conference Publication

US Natl Aeronaut Space Admin Spec Publ — US National Aeronautics and Space Administration. Special Publication

US Natl Bur Stand Handb — US National Bureau of Standards. Handbook

US Natl Bur Stand J Res — United States. National Bureau of Standards. Journal of Research

US Natl Bur Stand J Res Sec A — US National Bureau of Standards. Journal of Research. Section A

US Natl Cancer Inst Carcinog Tech Rep Ser — US National Cancer Institute. Carcinogenesis Technical Report Series

US Natl Fert Dev Cent Bull Y — United States National Fertilizer Development Center. Bulletin Y

US Natl Ind Pollut Control Counc Publ — US National Industrial Pollution Control Council. Publications

US Natl Inst Health Natl Toxicol Program Tech Rep Ser — US National Institutes of Health. National Toxicology Program Technical Report Series

US Natl Inst Health Publ — US National Institutes of Health. Publication

US Natl Lab (Oak Ridge Tenn) Rev — United States National Laboratory (Oak Ridge, Tennessee). Review

US Natl Mar Fish Serv Curr Fish Stat — US National Marine Fisheries Service. Current Fisheries Statistics

US Natl Mar Fish Serv Fish Bull — US National Marine Fisheries Service. Fishery Bulletin

US Natl Mar Fish Serv Fish Facts — US National Marine Fisheries Service. Fishery Facts

US Natl Mar Fish Serv Mar Fish Rev — US National Marine Fisheries Service. Marine Fisheries Review

US Natl Mar Fish Serv Rep Natl Mar Fish Serv — US National Marine Fisheries Service. Report of the National Marine Fisheries Service

US Natl Mar Fish Serv Stat Dig — US National Marine Fisheries Service. Statistical Digest

US Natl Mus Bull — US National Museum. Bulletin

US Natl Mus Bull Proc — United States National Museum. Bulletin. Proceedings

US Natl Oceanic Atmos Adm Environ Data Serv Tech Memo — United States. National Oceanic and Atmospheric Administration. Environmental Data Service. Technical Memorandum

US Natl Oceanic Atmos Adm Key Oceanogr Rec Doc — US National Oceanic and Atmospheric Administration. Key to Oceanographic Records Documentation

US Natl Oceanog Data Center Pub — US National Oceanographic Data Center. Publication

US Natl Park Serv Ecol Serv Bull — US National Park Service. Ecological Services Bulletin

US Natl Park Serv Fauna Natl Parks US Fauna Ser — US National Park Service. Fauna of the National Parks of the United States. Fauna Series

US Natl Park Service Nat History Handb Ser — US National Park Service. Natural History Handbook Series

US Natl Park Serv Natl Cap Reg Sci Rep — US National Park Service. National Capitol Region Scientific Report

US Natl Park Serv Occas Pap — US National Park Service. Occasional Paper

US Natl Park Serv Sci Monogr Ser — US National Park Service. Scientific Monograph Series

US Natl Sci Found Res Appl Natl Needs Rep — United States. National Science Foundation. Research Applied to National Needs Report

US Nat Mus Bull — United States National Museum. Bulletin

US Nat Mus Rept — United States National Museum. Reports

US Nav Aerosp Med Inst (Pensacola) Monogr — US Naval Aerospace Medical Institute (Pensacola). Monograph

US Nav Aerosp Med Inst (Pensacola) NAMI — US Naval Aerospace Medical Institute (Pensacola). NAMI

US Nav Aerosp Med Res Lab (Pensacola) NAMRL — US Naval Aerospace Medical Research Laboratory (Pensacola). NAMRL

US Nav Aerosp Med Res Lab (Pensacola) Spec Rep — US Naval Aerospace Medical Research Laboratory (Pensacola). Special Report

US Nav Air Dev Cent NADC — US Naval Air Development Center. NADC

US Naval Med Bull — United States Naval Medical Bulletin

US Naval Ordnance Test Sta NAVORD Report — United States. Naval Ordnance Test Station. NAVORD Report

US Naval Res Lab Shock Vib Bull — United States. Naval Research Laboratories. Shock and Vibration Bulletin

US Naval Submar Med Cent Rep — US Naval Submarine Medical Center. Report

US Nav Civ Eng Lab Tech Rep — United States. Department of the Navy. Naval Civil Engineering Laboratory [*Port Hueneme, California*]. Technical Report

US Nav Inst Proc — US Naval Institute. Proceedings

US Nav Med Res Lab Rep — US Naval Medical Research Laboratory. Report

US Nav Oceanogr Off Spec Publ — US Naval Oceanographic Office. Special Publication

US Nav Postgrad Sch Tech Rep/Res Paper — United States. Naval Postgraduate School. Technical Report/Research Paper

US Nav Sch Aviat Med Monogr — US Naval School of Aviation Medicine. Monograph

US Nav Sch Aviat Med Res Rep — US Naval School of Aviation Medicine. Research Report

US Nav Ship Eng Cent Ship Struct Com Rep — United States. Department of the Navy. Naval Ship Engineering Center. Ship Structure Committee. Report

US Nav Ship Res Dev Cent Rep — United States. Naval Ship Research and Development Center. Report

US Nav Submar Med Cent Memo Rep — US Naval Submarine Medical Center. Memorandum Report

US Nav Submar Med Cent Rep — United States. Naval Submarine Medical Center. Report

US Nav Submar Med Res Lab Memo Rep — United States. Naval Submarine Medical Research Laboratory. Memorandum Report

US Nav Submar Med Res Lab Rep — US Naval Submarine Medical Research Laboratory. Report

US Navy Electronics Lab Rept — United States. Navy Electronics Laboratory. Report

US Navy Med — US Navy Medicine

US News — United States News and World Report

US News — US News and World Report

US News World Rep — US News and World Report

USNIP — United States. Naval Institute. Proceedings

US North Cent For Exp Stn Res Pap NC — US North Central Forest Experiment Station. Research Paper NC

US NTIS AD Rep — United States. National Technical Information Service. AD Report

USNWR — US News and World Report

US Oak Ridge Natl Lab Radiat Shield Inf Cent Rep — United States. Oak Ridge National Laboratory. Radiation Shielding Information Center. Report

U So Carol — University of South Carolina. Business and Economic Review

US Office Ed Bul — United States. Office of Education. Bulletin

US Office Ed Circ — United States. Office of Education. Circulars

US Office Ed Pub — United States. Office of Education. Publications

US Office Ed Voc Div Bul — United States. Office of Education. Vocational Division. Bulletin

US Office Saline Water Research and Devel Progress Rept — United States. Office of Saline Water Research and Development. Progress Report

US Off Libr Serv Bibliogr Ser — US Office of Library Service. Bibliography Series

US Off Nav Res Rep ACR — United States. Office of Naval Research. Report ACR

US Off Pub Roads B — US Office of Public Roads. Bulletin

USP — Under the Sign of Pisces

US Pacific RR Expl — US War Department. Pacific Railroad Explorations

US Pac Northwest For Range Exp Stn Res Note PNW — US Pacific Northwest Forest and Range Experiment Station. Research Note PNW

US Pap Maker — United States Paper Maker

US Pat Off Off Gaz US Pat Off Pat — US Patent Office. Official Gazette of the United States Patent Office. Patents

US Pat Trademark Off Off Gaz US Pat Trademark Off Pat — US Patent and Trademark Office. Official Gazette of the United States Patent and Trademark Office. Patents

Usp Biol Khim — Uspekhi Biologicheskoi Khimii [*USSR*]

Uspehi Fiz Nauk — Akademija Nauk SSSR. Uspehi Fiziceskih Nauk

Uspehi Mat Nauk — Akademija Nauk SSSR i Moskovskoe Matematiceskoe Obscestvo. Uspehi Matematiceskih Nauk

Uspekhi Fiz Nauk — Uspekhi Fizicheskih Nauk

Uspekhi Mat Nauk — Uspekhi Matematiceskih Nauk

Usp Fiziol Nauk — Uspekhi Fiziologicheskikh Nauk

Usp Fiz Nau — Uspekhi Fizicheskikh Nauk

Usp Fiz Nauk — Uspekhi Fizicheskii Nauk

Usp Foton — Uspekhi Fotoniki

Usp Fotoniki — Uspekhi Fotoniki

Usp Kh — Uspekhi Khimii

Usp Khim — Uspekhi Khimii

Usp Khim Fosfororg Seraorg Soedin — Uspekhi Khimii Fosfororganicheskikh i Seraorganicheskikh Soedinenii

Usp Khim Tekhnol Polim — Uspekhi Khimii i Tekhnologii Polimerov

Usp Mat Nauk — Uspekhi Matematicheskikh Nauk

Usp Mikrobiol — Uspekhi Mikrobiologii

Usp Mol Biol — Uspekhi na Molekulyarnata Biologiya

Usp Nauchn Fotogr — Uspekhi Nauchnoi Fotografii

Usp Sovrem Biol — Uspekhi Sovremennoi Biologii

Usp Sovrem Genet — Uspekhi Sovremennoi Genetiki

US Public Health Serv Public Health Monogr — United States. Public Health Service. Public Health Monograph

US Public Health Serv Radiol Health Data Rep — US Public Health Service. Radiological Health Data and Reports

USQ — United States Quarterly Book Review

US Q Bk R — United States Quarterly Book Review

USQBL — United States Quarterly Book List

USQBR — United States Quarterly Book Review

USQR — Union Seminary. Quarterly Review

US Quartermaster Food Container Inst Armed Forces Libr Bull — US Quartermaster Food and Container Institute for the Armed Forces. Library Bulletin

USR — Union Seminary. Review

US Res Developm Rep — United States Government Research and Development Reports

US Sci Educ Adm Agric Res Man — US Science and Education Administration. Agricultural Research Manual

US Seed Rep — United States Seed Reporter

US Serv M — United States Service Magazine

USSGA — Uspekhi Sovremennoi Genetiki

US Ship Struct Com Rep — United States. Ship Structure Committee. Report

US Soil Conserv Service Sedimentation Bull (TP) — United States. Soil Conservation Service. Sedimentation Bulletin (Technical Publication)

US Soil Conserv Serv Soil Surv — US Soil Conservation Service. Soil Survey

USSR Comp Info B — USSR. Union of Composers. Information Bulletin

USSR Computational Math and Math Phys — USSR Computational Mathematics and Mathematical Physics

USSR Comput Math Math Phys — USSR Computational Mathematics and Mathematical Physics

USSR Comput Math and Math Phys — USSR Computational Mathematics and Mathematical Physics

USSR Rep Eng Equip — USSR Report. Engineering Equipment

US Steel News — United States Steel News

US Tariff Comm Rep — United States. Tariff Commission. Reports

US Tariff Comm TC Publ — United States. Tariff Commission. TC Publication

Ustav Jad Fyz Cesk Akad Ved Rep — Ustav Jaderne Fyziky Ceskoslovenska Akademia Ved. Report

Ustav Vedeckotech Inf Sb UVTI Genet Slechteni — Ustav Vedeckotechnickych Informaci. Sbornik UVTI. Genetika a Slechteni

Ustav Vedeckotech Inf Sb UVTI Melior — Ustav Vedeckotechnickych Informaci. Sbornik UVTI. Rada. Meliorace

Ustav Vedeckotech Inf Zemed — Ustav Vedeckotechnickych Informaci pro Zemedelstvi

Ustav Vedeckotech Inf Zemed Sb UVTIZ Melior — Ustav Vedeckotechnickych Informaci pro Zemedelstvi. Sbornik UVTIZ. Rada. Meliorace

Ustav Vedeckotech Inf Zemed Stud Inf Ochr Rostl — Ustav Vedeckotechnickych Informaci pro Zemedelstvi Studijni Informace Ochrana Rostlin

Ustav Vyzk Vyuziti Paliv Monogr — Ustav pro Vyzkum a Vyuziti Paliv Monografie

US Tax Rpt — United States Tax Report

USTJ — United States Tobacco Journal

Ust Ved Inf MZLVH Rostl Vyroba — Ustav Vedeckotechnickych Informaci. Ministerstva Zemedelstvi. Lesniho a Vodnlho Hospodarstvi. Rostlinna Vyroba

Ust Ved Inf MZLVH Stud Inf Pudoz — Ustav Vedeckotechnickych Informaci. MZLVH [*Ministerstva Zemedelstvi. Lesniho a Vodnlho Hospodarstvi*] Studijni Informace Pudoznalstvi a Meliorace

Ust Ved Inf MZ Rostl Vyroba — Ustav Vedeckotechnickych Informaci. Ministerstva Zemedelstvi. Rostlinna Vyroba

Ust Ved Inf MZVZ Rostl Vyroba — Ustav Vedeckotechnickych Informaci. Ministerstva Zemedelstvi a Vyzivy. Rostlinna Vyroba

USUMS — Utah State University. Monograph Series

US Veterans Adm (W) Dep Med Surg Bull Prosthet Res — United States. Veterans Administration (Washington, DC). Department of Medicine and Surgery. Bulletin of Prosthetics Research

US Veterans Bureau Med Bull — United States. Veterans Bureau. Medical Bulletin

US War Dp Chief Eng An Rp — United States. War Department. Chief of Engineers. Annual Report

US Waterw Exp Stn Contract Rep — United States. Waterways Experiment Station. Contract Report

US Waterw Exp Stn Misc Pap — United States. Waterways Experiment Station. Miscellaneous Paper

US Waterw Exp Stn Res Rep — United States. Waterways Experiment Station. Research Report

US Waterw Exp Stn Tech Rep — United States. Waterways Experiment Station. Technical Report

US Waterw Exp Stn (Vicksburg Miss) Misc Pap — United States. Waterways Experiment Station (Vicksburg, Mississippi). Miscellaneous Paper

US Waterw Exp Stn (Vicksburg Miss) Res Rep — United States. Waterways Experiment Station (Vicksburg, Mississippi). Research Report

US Waterw Exp Stn (Vicksburg Miss) Tech Rep — United States. Waterways Experiment Station (Vicksburg, Mississippi). Technical Report

US Women's Bur Bul — United States. Women's Bureau. Bulletin

UT — Ugaritic Text

UT — Unser Tsait/Unzer Tsayt

UT — Utah Music Educator

Utah Acad Sci Proc — Utah Academy of Sciences, Arts, and Letters. Proceedings

Utah Ac Sc Tr — Utah Academy of Sciences. Transactions

Utah Ag Exp — Utah. Agricultural Experiment Station. Publications

Utah Agric Exp Stn Bull — Utah. Agricultural Experiment Station. Bulletin

Utah Agric Exp Stn Circ — Utah. Agricultural Experiment Station. Circular

Utah Agric Exp Stn Res Rep — Utah. Agricultural Experiment Station. Research Report

Utah Agric Exp Stn Spec Rep — Utah. Agricultural Experiment Station. Special Report

Utah Agric Exp Stn Utah Resour Ser — Utah. Agricultural Experiment Station. Utah Resources Series

Utah Bar Bull — Utah Bar Bulletin

Utah B Bull — Utah Bar Bulletin

Utah BJ — Utah Bar Journal

Utah Dep Nat Resour Tech Publ — Utah. Department of Natural Resources. Technical Publication

Utah Dep Nat Resour Water Cir — Utah. Department of Natural Resources. Water Circular

Utah Dept Nat Resources Tech Pub — Utah. Department of Natural Resources. Division of Water Rights. Technical Publication

Utah Div Water Resources Coop Inv Rept — Utah. Division of Water Resources. Cooperative Investigations Report

Utah Econ and Bus R — Utah Economic and Business Review

Utah Eng Exp Stn Bull — Utah. Engineering Experiment Station. Bulletin

Utah Farm Home Sci — Utah Farm and Home Science

Utah Geol — Utah Geology

Utah Geol Assoc Publ — Utah Geological Association. Publication

Utah Geol and Mineralog Survey Bull — Utah. Geological and Mineralogical Survey. Bulletin

Utah Geol and Mineralog Survey Circ — Utah. Geological and Mineralogical Survey. Circular

Utah Geol and Mineralog Survey Quart Rev — Utah. Geological and Mineralogical Survey. Quarterly Review

Utah Geol and Mineralog Survey Spec Studies — Utah. Geological and Mineralogical Survey. Special Studies

Utah Geol and Mineralog Survey Water Resources Bull — Utah. Geological and Mineralogical Survey. Water Resources Bulletin

Utah Geol Mineral Surv Bull — Utah. Geological and Mineralogical Survey. Bulletin

Utah Geol Mineral Surv Circ — Utah. Geological and Mineralogical Survey. Circular

Utah Geol Mineral Surv Spec Stud — Utah. Geological and Mineralogical Survey. Special Studies

Utah Geol Mineral Surv Water Resour Bull — Utah. Geological and Mineralogical Survey. Water Resources Bulletin

Utah Geol Miner Surv Circ — Utah. Geological and Mineralogical Survey. Circular

Utah Geol Miner Surv Q Rev — Utah. Geological and Mineralogical Survey. Quarterly Review

Utah Geol Miner Surv Surv Notes — Utah. Geological and Mineralogical Survey. Survey Notes

Utah Geol Soc Guidebook to Geology of Utah — Utah Geological Society. Guidebook to the Geology of Utah

Utah Hist Q — Utah Historical Quarterly

Utah Hist Quar — Utah Historical Quarterly

Utah Hist Quart — Utah Historical Quarterly

Utah Lib — Utah Libraries

Utah Lib Assn Newsl — Utah Library Association. Newsletter

Utah Libr — Utah Libraries

Utah LR — Utah Law Review

Utah L Rev — Utah Law Review

Utah M — Utah Genealogical and Historical Magazine

Utah Med Bull — Utah Medical Bulletin

Utah Resour Ser Utah Agr Exp Sta — Utah Resources Series. Utah Agricultural Experiment Station

Utah Sci — Utah Science

Utah Sci Utah Agric Exp Stn — Utah Science. Utah Agricultural Experiment Station

Utah State Engineer Bienn Rept Tech Pub — Utah State Engineer. Biennial Report. Technical Publications

Utah State Engineer Inf Bull — Utah State Engineer. Information Bulletin

Utah State Eng Off Basic Data Rep — Utah. State Engineer's Office. Basic Data Report

Utah State Eng Tech Publ — Utah State Engineer. Technical Publication

Utah State Med J — Utah State Medical Journal

Utah State Univ Agric Exp Stn Bull — Utah State University. Agricultural Experiment Station. Bulletin

Utah Univ Anthropol Papers Bull — Utah University. Anthropological Papers. Bulletin

Utah Univ Eng Exp Stn Tech Pap — Utah University. Engineering Experiment Station. Technical Paper

Utah Univ Eng Expt Sta Bull — Utah University. Engineering Experiment Station. Bulletin

U Tas LR — University of Tasmania. Law Review

U Tasmania L Rev — University of Tasmania. Law Review

U Tasm L Rev — University of Tasmania. Law Review

UT BJ — Utah Bar Journal

UTCEU — Universidad de Tucuman. Cuadernos de Extension Universitaria

UTD — Kermisgids

UTDEMS — University of Tulsa. Department of English. Monograph Series

U Tech Umweltmag — U das Technische Umweltmagazin [*West Germany*]

U T Fac L Rev — University of Toronto. Faculty of Law. Review

UT Faculty LR — Faculty of Law Review. University of Toronto

UTFS — University of Toronto. French Series

UTHS — University of Texas. Hispanic Studies

Utilitas Math — Utilitas Mathematica

UTLJ — University of Toronto. Law Journal

UT LR — Utah Law Review

U Toledo L Rev — University of Toledo. Law Review

U Tol Law — University of Toledo. Law Review

U Tol LR — University of Toledo. Law Review

U Tol L Rev — University of Toledo. Law Review

Utopian E — Utopian Eyes

U Tor Fac LR — University of Toronto. Faculty of Law. Review

U Tor Law J — University of Toronto. Law Journal

U Tor LJ — University of Toronto. Law Journal

U Toronto Fac L Rev — University of Toronto. Faculty of Law. Review

U Toronto Faculty L Rev — University of Toronto. Faculty of Law. Review

U Toronto L J — University of Toronto. Law Journal

U Toronto Q — University of Toronto. Quarterly

UTPLF — Universita di Torino. Pubblicazioni della Facolta di Lettere e Filosofia

UTQ — University of Toronto. Quarterly

UTQA — Uutuqtwa. Bristol Bay High School

UT R — University of Tampa. Review

Utredn Norsk Tretekn Inst — Utredning. Norsk Treteknisk Institutt

Utr Micropaleontol Bull — Utrecht Micropaleontological Bulletins

Utr Micropaleontol Bull Spec Publ — Utrecht Micropaleontological Bulletins. Special Publication

UTSCB — Utah Science

UTSE — University of Texas. Studies in English

UTSH — University of Tennessee. Studies in the Humanities

Uttar Pradesh Dir Geol Min Monogr — Uttar Pradesh. Directorate of Geology and Mining. Monograph

UTTBA — Bulletin. International Union Against Tuberculosis

UTVS — Ucebni Texty Vysokych Skol

UUA — Uppsala Universitets Arsskrift

UVL — Untersuchungen zur Vergleichenden Literatur [*Hamburg*]

UVM — University of Virginia. Magazine

UVMag — University of Virginia. Magazine

UV Spectrom Group Bull — UV Spectrometry Group. Bulletin

UW — Us Wurk

UWALR — University of Western Australia. Law Review

UWAL Rev — University of Western Australia. Law Review

UW Austl L Rev — University of Western Australia. Law Review

UWCCARG — University of Washington. Contributions. Cloud and Aerosol Research Group

UWCCPGR — University of Washington. Contributions. Cloud Physics Group. Collections from Reprints

UWCETG — University of Washington. Contributions. Energy Transfer Group. Collections from Reprints

UWD — UWD [*Umweltschutz-Dienst*] Informationsdienst fuer Umweltfragen

U West Aust Ann L Rev — University of Western Australia. Annual Law Review

U of West Aust L Rev — University of Western Australia. Law Review

U Western Aust Ann L Rev — University of Western Australia. Annual Law Review

U Western Aust L Rev — University of Western Australia. Law Review

U Western Ont L Rev — University of Western Ontario. Law Review

U West LA L Rev — University of West Los Angeles. Law Review

U West Los Angeles L Rev — University of West Los Angeles. Law Review

UWLA LR — University of West Los Angeles. Law Review

UWLA L Rev — University of West Los Angeles. Law Review

UWOL Rev — University of Western Ontario. Law Review

UWO Med J — UWO [*University of Western Ontario*] Medical Journal

UW Ont L Rev — University of Western Ontario. Law Review

UWOPGS — University of Warwick. Occasional Papers in German Studies

UWO (Univ West Ont) Med J — UWO (University of Western Ontario) Medical Journal

UWPLL — University of Washington. Publications in Language and Literature

UWR — University of Windsor. Review

UWTCA — Umschau in Wissenschaft und Technik

UZ — Ustredna Zidov [*Slovakia*]

UZAstPI — Ucenye Zapiski Astrachanskogo Gosudarstvennogo Pedagogiceskogo Instituta

UZAzPI — Ucenye Zapiski Pedagogiceskogo Instituta Jazykov Imeni M. F. Achundova. Serija Filologiceskaja

UZAzU — Ucenye Zapiski Azerbaidzhanskii Gosudarstvennyi Universitet [*Baku*]

UZAzU — Ucenye Zapiski Azerbajdzanskogo Gosudarstvennogo Universiteta Imeni S. M. Kirova. Jazyk i Literatura

UZBasU — Ucenye Zapiski Baskirskogo Gosudarstvennogo Universiteta. Serija Filologiceskich Nauk

Uzb Biol Zh — Uzbekskii Biologicheskii Zhurnal

Uzbek Biol Zh — Uzbekskii Biologicheskii Zhurnal

Uzbek Geol Zh — Uzbekskiy Geologicheskii Zhurnal

Uzbek Iztim Fanlar — Uzbekiztonda Iztimoii Fanlar

Uzbek Khim Zh — Uzbekskii Khimicheskii Zhurnal

Uzb Khim Zh — Uzbekskii Khimicheskii Zhurnal

UZBurPI — Ucenye Zapiski Burjatskogo Gosudarstvennogo Pedagogiceskogo Instituta Imeni Dorzi Banzarova. Istoriko-Filologiceskaja Serija. Ulan-Ude

UZBZA — Uzbekskii Biologicheskii Zhurnal

UZCerepPI — Ucenye Zapiski Cerepoveckogo Gosudarstvennogo Pedagogiceskogo Instituta

UZChabPI — Ucenye Zapiski Chabarovskogo Gosudarstvennogo Pedagogiceskogo Instituta

UZChakNII — Ucenye Zapiski Chakasskogo Naucno-Issledovatel'skogo Instituta Jazyka, Literatury, i Istorii
UZCharU — Ucenye Zapiski Charkovskogo Universiteta Imeni A. M. Gorkogo Trudy Filologiceskogo Fakul'teta
UZCIngPI — Ucenye Zapiski Ceceno-Ingusskogo Pedagogiceskogo Instituta. Serija Filolo Giceskaja
UZCuvNII — Ucenye Zapiski Naucno-Issledovatel'skogo Instituta Jazyka, Literatury, Istorii, i Ekonomiki Pri Sovete Ministrov Cuvasskoj ASSR
UZDag — Ucenye Zapiski Dagestanskogo Filiala Akademii Nauk SSSR. Serija Filologiceskaja
UZDagU — Ucenye Zapiski Dagestanskogo Gosudarstvennogo Universiteta. Serija Filologiceskaja
UZDalU — Ucenye Zapiski Dal'nevostocnogo Universiteta. Serija Filologiceskaja
UZDusPI — Ucenye Zapiski Dusanbinskogo Gosudarstvennogo Pedagogiceskogo Instituta Imeni T. G. Seveenko Filologiceskaja Serija
UZElPI — Ucenye Zapiski Elabuzskogo Gosudarstvennogo Pedagogiceskogo Instituta. Serija Istorii i Filologii
UZEnPI — Ucenye Zapiski Enisejskogo Gosudarstvennogo Pedagogiceskogo Instituta Kafedra Russkogo Jazyka
UZErevU — Ucenye Zapiski Erevanskogo Gosudarstvennogo Universiteta. Serija Filologiceskich Nauk
UZGIYa — Ucenye Zapiski Gor'kovskii Pedagogicheskii Institut Inostrannykh Yazykov [*Gor'kii*]
UZGorPI — Ucenye Zapiski Gor'kovskogo Gosudarstvennogo Pedagogiceskogo Instituta Imeni M. Gor'kogo. Serija Filologiceskaja
UZGorPIIJa — Ucenye Zapiski Gor'kovskogo Pedagogiceskogo Instituta Inostrannych Jazykov
UZGorU — Ucenye Zapiski Gor'kovskogo Universiteta Imeni N. I. Lobacevskogo. Serija Istoriko-Filologiceskaja
UZGPI — Ucenye Zapiski Gor'kovskii Gosudarstvennyi Pedagogicheskii Institut [*Gor'kii*]
UZGurPI — Ucenye Zapiski Gur'evskogo Gosudarstvennogo Pedagogiceskogo Instituta. Serija Istoriko-Filologiceskaja
UZGZA — Uzbekskii Geologiceskii Zhurnal
UZII — Ucenye Zapiski Instituta Istorii
UZIMach — Ucenye Zapiski Instituta Istorii, Jazyka, i Literatury Imeni G. Cadasy. Serija Filologiceskaja. Machackala
UZIMO — Ucenye Zapiski Institut Mezdunarodnych Otnosenij
UZIPI — Ucenye Zapiski Irkutskii Pedagogiceskii Institut [*Irkutsk*]
UZIrkutPI — Ucenye Zapiski Irkutskogo Gosudarstvennogo Pedagogiceskogo Instituta Inostrannych Jazykov
UZISL — Ucenye Zapiski Instituta Slavjanovedenija
UZIV — Ucenye Zapiski Instituta Vostokovedenija Akademija Nauk SSSR
UZIVAz — Ucenye Zapiski Instituta Vostokovedenija Akademii Nauk Azerbajdzanskoj SSSR
UZKa — Ucenye Zapiski Kalininskii Gosudarstvennyi Pedagogicheskii Institut [*Kalinin*]
UZKalinPI — Ucenye Zapiski Kalininskogo Pedagogiceskogo Instituta Imeni M. I. Kalinina. Serija Filologiceskaja
UZKalPI — Ucenye Zapiski Kaluzskogo Gosudarstvennogo Pedagogiceskogo Instituta
UZKaragPI — Ucenye Zapiski Karagandinskogo Pedagogiceskogo Instituta Filologiceske Nauki
UZKarelPI — Ucenye Zapiski Karel'skogo Pedagogiceskogo Instituta
UZKarPI — Ucenye Zapiski Karsinskogo Gosudarstvennogo Pedagogiceskogo Instituta. Filologiceskaja Serija
UZKazanU — Ucenye Zapiski Kazanskogo Universiteta Imeni V. I. Ul'janova'lenina
UZKBI — Ucenye Zapiski Kabardino-Balkarskij Naucno-Issledovatel'skij Institut pri Sovete Ministrov Kbassr
UZKemPI — Ucenye Zapiski Kemerovskogo Gosudarstvennogo Pedagogiceskogo Instituta
UZKGPI — Ucenye Zapiski Kujbysevskogo Gosudarstvennogo Pedagogiceskogo Instituta Imeni V. V. Kujbyseva
UZKi — Ucenye Zapiski Kishinevskii Universitet [*Kishinev*]
UZKirovPI — Ucenye Zapiski Kirovabadskogo Pedagogiceskogo Instituta
UZKisU — Ucenye Zapiski Kisinevskogo Gosudarstvennogo Universiteta
UZKokPI — Ucenye Zapiski Kokandskogo Pedagogiceskogo Instituta Imeni Mukimi. Serija Filologiceskaja
UZKolPI — Ucenye Zapiski Kolomenskogo Gosudarstvennogo Pedagogiceskogo Instituta Istoriko-Filologiceskij Fakul'tet Kafedry Russkogo Jazyka
UZKomPI — Ucenye Zapiski Komi Gosudarstvennogo Pedagogiceskogo Instituta Kafedra Russkogo Jazyka
UZKr — Ucenye Zapiski Krasnodarskii Pedagogicheskii Institut [*Krasnodar*]
UZKujPI — Ucenye Zapiski Kujbysevskogo Gosudarstvennogo Pedagogiceskogo Instituta Imeni V. V. Kujbyseva
UZKVA — Uchenye Zapiski Kazanskogo Veterinarnogo Instituta
UZKZA — Uzbekskii Khimiceskii Zhurnal
UZLa — Ucenye Zapiski Latviiskii Gosudarstvennyi Universitet [*Riga*]
UZLenPI — Ucenye Zapiski Leningradskogo Pedagogiceskogo Instituta Imeni S. M. Kirova
UZLPedI — Ucenye Zapiski Leningradskogo Pedagogiceskogo Instituta Imeni A. I. Gercena

UZLPI — Ucenye Zapiski Leningradskogo Pedagogiceskogo Instituta Imeni A. I. Gercena
UZLU — Ucenye Zapiski Leningradskogo Gosudarstvennogo Ordena Lenina Universiteta Imeni A. A. Zdanova
UZLU — Ucenye Zapiski Leningradskogo Universiteta
UZLU-FN — Ucenye Zapiski Leningradskogo Universiteta. Serija Filologiceskikh Nauk
UZL'vovU — Ucenye Zapiski l'Vovskogo Gosudarstvennogo Universiteta
UZMagPI — Ucenye Zapiski Magnitorskogo Gosudarstvennogo Pedagogiceskogo Instituta
UZMIK — Ucenye Zapiski Moskovskii Gosudarstvennyi Institut Kul'tury [*Moscow*]
UZMKrup — Ucenye Zapiski Moskovskogo Oblastnogo Pedagogiceskogo Instituta Imeni N. K. Krupskoj
UZMOPI — Ucenye Zapiski Moskovskii Oblastnoi Pedagogicheskii Institut Imeni N. K. Krupskoi [*Moscow*]
UZMorU — Ucenye Zapiski Mordovskogo Universiteta. Serija Filologiceskich Nauk
UZMPedI — Ucenye Zapiski Moskovskogo Gosudarstvennogo Pedagogiceskogo Instituta
UZMPI — Ucenye Zapiski Moskovskii Gosudarstvennyi Pedagogicheskii Institut Imeni Lenina [*Moscow*]
UZMPI — Ucenye Zapiski Moskovskogo Gosudarstvennogo Pedagogiceskogo Instituta Imeni Potemkina
UZMPIIJa — Ucenye Zapiski Moskovskogo Gosudarstvennogo Pedagogiceskogo Instituta Inostrannych Jazykov
UZMPIIYa — Ucenye Zapiski I-I Moskovskii Pedagogicheskii Institut Inostrannych Jazykov [*Moscow*]
UZMU — Ucenye Zapiski Moskovskogo Universiteta
UZNovPI — Ucenye Zapiski Novgorodskogo Gosudarstvennogo Pedagogicesko Instituta Kafedra Russkogo Jazyka
UZOrenPI — Ucenye Zapiski Orenburgskogo Gosudarstvennogo Pedagogiceskogo Instituta Imeni V. P. Ckalova
UZPe — Ucenye Zapiski Penzenskii Pedagogicheskii Institut [*Penza*]
UZPer — Ucenye Zapiski Permskii Universitet [*Perm'*]
UZPerm — Ucenye Zapiski Permskogo Gosudarstvennogo Universiteta Imeni A. M. Gor'kogo
UZPs — Ucenye Zapiski Pskovskii Pedagogicheskii Institut [*Pskov*]
UZPU — Ucenye Zapiski Petrozavodskogo Universiteta Filologiceskie Nauk
UZRjazPI — Ucenye Zapiski Rjazanskogo Gosudarstvennogo Pedagogiceskogo Instituta
UZRovPI — Ucenye Zapiski Rovenskogo Gosudarstvennogo Pedagogiceskogo Instituta Filologiceskij Fakul'tet
UZSachPI — Ucenye Zapiski Sachtinskogo Gosudarstvennogo Pedagogiceskogo Instituta
UZSarPedI — Ucenye Zapiski Saratovskogo Gosudarstvennogo Pedagogiceskogo Instituta
UZSGU — Ucenye Zapiski Saratovskogo Gosudarstvennogo Universiteta
UZSmolPI — Ucenye Zapiski Smolenskogo Gosudarstvennogo Pedagogiceskogo Instituta
UZSterPI — Ucenye Zapiski Sterlitamakskogo Gosudarstvennogo Pedagogiceskogo Instituta. Serija Filologiceskaja
UZTar — Ucenye Zapiski Tartusskii Universitet [*Tartu*]
UZTarU — Ucenye Zapiski Tartuskogo Gosudarstvennogo Universiteta
UZTasPIIn — Ucenye Zapiski Taskentskogo Pedagogiceskogo Instituta Inostrannych Jazykov
UZTasPINiz — Ucenye Zapiski Taskentskogo Pedagogiceskogo Instituta Imeni Nizami
UZTFA — Uchenye Zapiski Tul'skii Gosudarstvennyi Pedagogicheskii Institut Fiziko-Tekhnicheskie Nauki
UZTI — Ucenye Zapiski Tikhookeanskogo Instituta
UZTjPI — Ucenye Zapiski Tjumenskogo Pedagogiceskogo Instituta Kafedra Russkogo Jazyka
UZTomU — Ucenye Zapiski Tomskogo Universiteta Imeni V. V. Kujbyseva
UZToU — Ucenye Zapiski Tomskii Universitet [*Tomsk*]
UZTPI — Ucenye Zapiski Tomskii Gosudarstvennyj Pedagogiceskij Institut
UZTuvNII — Ucenye Zapiski Tuvinskogo Naucno-Issledovatel'skogo Instituta Jazyka, Literatury, i Istorii
UZUlPI — Ucenye Zapiski Ul'janovskogo Gosudarstvennogo Pedagogiceskogo Instituta Imeni I. N. Ul'janova
UZUPI — Ucenye Zapiski Ural'skogo Pedagogiceskogo i Ucitel'skogo Instituta Imeni Puskina
UZUzPI — Ucenye Zapiski Uzbekskogo Respublikanskogo Pedagogiceskogo Instituta Kafedra Russkogo Jazyka i Literatury
UZVinPI — Ucenye Zapiski Vinnickogo Gosudarstvennogo Pedagogiceskogo Instituta Kafedra Russkogo Jazyka i Literatury
UZVolPI — Ucenye Zapiski Vologodskogo Gosudarstvennogo Pedagogiceskogo Instituta

V

V — Valencia
V — Variety
V — Verbo
V — Vision
Va — Vasari
VA — Vorderasiatische Abteilung der Staatlichen Museen zu Berlin
VAA — Verhandelingen. Koninklijke Akademie van Wetenschappen te Amsterdam
VA Ag Dept — Virginia. Department of Agriculture and Immigration. Publications
VA Ag Exp — Virginia Polytechnic Institute. Agricultural Experiment Station. Publications
VA Agric Exp Stn Bull — Virginia. Agricultural Experiment Station. Bulletin
VA Agric Exp Stn Tech Bull — Virginia. Agricultural Experiment Station. Technical Bulletin
VA BAJ — Virginia Bar Association. Journal
VABBA — Vestsi Akademii Navuk BSSR. Seryya Biyalagichnykh Navuk
VABFA — Vestsi Akademii Navuk BSSR. Seryya Fizika-Tekhnichnykh Navuk
VA Cavalcade — Virginia Cavalcade
VACCJ — VACC [Victorian Automobile Chamber of Commerce] Journal
Vac Microbalance Tech — Vacuum Microbalance Techniques
VACUA — Vacuum
Vacuum Chem — Vacuum Chemistry [Japan]
Vacuum R — Vacuum Review
VA Dent J — Virginia Dental Journal
VA Dept Highways Div Tests Geol Yearbook — Virginia. Department of Highways. Division of Tests. Geological Yearbook
VA Dept Labor and Industry Ann Rept — Virginia. Department of Labor and Industry. Annual Report
VA Div Geol Bull — Virginia. Division of Geology. Bulletin
VA Div Geology Bull Reprint Ser — Virginia. Division of Geology. Bulletin. Reprint Series
VA Div Mineral Res Bull Inf Circ Mineral Res Circ — Virginia. Division of Mineral Resources. Bulletin. Information Circular. Mineral Resources Circular
VA Div Miner Resour Bull — Virginia. Division of Mineral Resources. Bulletin
VA Div Miner Resour Inf Cir — Virginia. Division of Mineral Resources. Information Circular
VA Div Miner Resour Miner Resour Rep — Virginia. Division of Mineral Resources. Mineral Resources Report
VA Div Miner Resour Rep Invest — Virginia. Division of Mineral Resources. Report of Investigations
Vaerml Bergsmannafoeren Ann — Vaermlaendska Bergsmannafoereningens Annaler
VAE VA Agric Econ VA Polytech Inst State Univ Coop Ext Serv — VAE. Virginia Agricultural Economics. Virginia Polytechnic Institute and State University. Cooperative Extension Service
Vaextskyddsanst-Notiser — Vaextskyddsanstalt-Notiser
VA Farm Econ VA Polytech Inst Agr Ext Serv — Virginia Farm Economics. Virginia Polytechnic Institute. Agricultural Extension Service
VA Fish Lab Educ Ser — Virginia Fisheries Laboratory. Educational Series
VA Fruit — Virginia Fruit
VAG — Vastgoed
Vaga — Vagabond

VA Geol Surv Circ — Virginia. Geological Survey. Circular
VA Geol Survey Bull — Virginia. Geological Survey. Bulletin
VA Geol Surv Repr Ser — Virginia. Geological Survey. Reprint Series
VA GSB — Virginia. Geological Survey. Bulletin
VA Hist Soc Coll — Virginia Historical Society. Collections
VA Horse Ind Yearb — Virginia Horse Industry Yearbook
VA Inst Mar Sci Spec Sci Rep — Virginia Institute of Marine Science. Special Scientific Report
VA J Ed — Virginia Journal of Education
VA J Educ — Virginia Journal of Education
VA J Int L — Virginia Journal of International Law
VA J Intl L — Virginia Journal of International Law
VA J Nat Resources L — Virginia Journal of Natural Resources Law
VA J Nat Resour Law — Virginia Journal of Natural Resources Law
VA Jour Sci — Virginia Journal of Science
VA J Sci — Virginia Journal of Science
Vakbl Biol — Vakblad voor Biologen
Vak Inf — Vakuum Information
VAKTA — Vakuum-Technik
Vak-Tech — Vakuum-Technik
Vak-Technik — Vakuum-Technik
VAL — Valuation
VA L — Virginia Law Review
Valachica — Acta Valachica. Studii si Materiale de Istorie a Culturii
VA Law R — Virginia Law Review
VA Law Rev — Virginia Law Review
Vale Evesham Hist Soc Res Pap — Vale of Evesham Historical Society. Research Papers
VA Lib Bul — Virginia Library Bulletin
VA Libn — Virginia Librarian
Vallalatvez -szerv — Vallalatvezetes-Vallalatszervezes
VALN — Victorian Adult Literacy News
Valparaiso Univ Law R — Valparaiso University. Law Review
Valparaiso Univ L Rev — Valparaiso University. Law Review
VA LR — Virginia Law Review
VA L Rev — Virginia Law Review
Valsa — Valsalva
Valt Maatalouskoetoiminnan Julk — Valtion Maatalouskoetoiminnan Julkaisuja
Valt Tek Tutkimuskeskus Reaktorilab Tied — Valtion Teknillinen Tutkimuskeskus. Reaktorilaboratorio. Tiedonanto
Valt Tek Tutkimuslaitos Julk — Valtion Teknillinen Tutkimuslaitos. Julkaisu
Valt Tek Tutkimuslaitos Tiedotus Sar 2 — Valtion Teknillinen Tutkimuslaitos. Tiedotus. Sarja 2. Metalli
Valt Tek Tutkimuslaitos Tiedotus Sar 4 — Valtion Teknillinen Tutkimuslaitos. Tiedotus. Sarja 4. Kemia
Valt Tek Tutkimuslaitos Tiedotus Sar 1 Puu — Valtion Teknillinen Tutkimuslaitos. Tiedotus. Sarja 1. Puu
Valt Tek Tutkimuslaitos Tied Sar 2 — Valtion Teknillinen Tutkimuslaitos. Tiedotus. Sarja 2. Metalli
Valt Tek Tutkimuslaitos Tied Sar 3 — Valtion Teknillinen Tutkimuslaitos. Tiedotus. Sarja 3. Rakennus
Value Eng — Value Engineering
Value Line — Value Line Investment Survey
Val U LR — Valparaiso University. Law Review

Val U L Rev — Valparaiso University. Law Review
Valvo Tech Inf Ind — Valvo Technische Informationen fuer die Industrie
VA M — Virginia Magazine of History and Biography
VA Mag Hist — Virginia Magazine of History and Biography
VA Mag Hist Biog — Virginia Magazine of History and Biography
VA Mag Hist Biogr — Virginia Magazine of History and Biography
VA Med — Virginia Medical
VA Med Mon — Virginia Medical Monthly [*Later, Virginia Medical*]
VA Miner — Virginia Minerals
VAN — Vanderbilt Law Review
Van — Vanguard Science Fiction
VAN — Vestnik Akademii Nauk SSSR
VAN — Voluntary Action News
VANB — Vesci Akademii Navuk BSSR
Vancoram Rev — Vancoram Review
Vanderbilt J Transnat'l L — Vanderbilt Journal of Transnational Law
Vanderbilt Univ Abs Theses Bull — Vanderbilt University. Abstracts of Theses. Bulletin
Vander Law — Vanderbilt Law Review
Vand Int — Vanderbilt International
Vand J Trans L — Vanderbilt Journal of Transnational Law
Vand J Transnatl L — Vanderbilt Journal of Transnational Law
Vand LR — Vanderbilt Law Review
Vand L Rev — Vanderbilt Law Review
VAN SSSR — Vestnik Akademii Nauk SSSR
VA Num — Virginia Numismatist
VA Nurse — Virginia Nurse
VA Nurse Q — Virginia Nurse Quarterly [*Later, Virginia Nurse*]
Van Zee Ld — Van Zee tot Land
VAPHD — Virchows Archiv. A. Pathological Anatomy and Histology
VA Polytech Inst Bull Eng Expt Sta Ser — Virginia Polytechnic Institute. Bulletin. Engineering Experiment Station Series
VA Polytech Inst Eng Ext Ser Cir — Virginia Polytechnic Institute. Engineering Extension Series. Circular
VA Polytech Inst Res Div Bull — Virginia Polytechnic Institute. Research Division. Bulletin
VA Polytech Inst Res Div Wood Res Wood Constr Lab Bull — Virginia Polytechnic Institute. Research Division. Wood Research and Wood Construction Laboratory [*Blacksburg*]. Bulletin
VA Polytech Inst State Univ Res Div Bull — Virginia Polytechnic Institute and State University. Research Division. Bulletin
VA Polytech Inst State Univ Res Div Monogr — Virginia Polytechnic Institute and State University. Research Division. Monograph
VA Polytech Inst State Univ Res Div Rep — Virginia Polytechnic Institute and State University. Research Division. Report
VA Polytech Inst State Univ VA Water Resour Res Cent Bull — Virginia Polytechnic Institute and State University. Virginia Water Resources Research Center. Bulletin
VA Polytech Inst State Univ Water Resour Res Cent Bull — Virginia Polytechnic Institute and State University. Water Resources Research Center. Bulletin
VA Q R — Virginia Quarterly Review
VA Q Rev — Virginia Quarterly Review
VAR — Variety
Vara Palsd — Vara Palsdjur
Vari — Variegation
Varian Instrum Appl — Varian Instrument Applications
Varilna Teh — Varilna Tehnika
Various Publ Ser — Various Publications Series [*Aarhus*]
Varme- o Sanit-Tek — Vearme- och Sanitetsteknikern
Var Sci Inst Rebois Tunis — Varietes Scientifiques. Institut de Reboisement de Tunis
VARTA Spez Rep — VARTA Spezial Report [*West Germany*]
VAS — Vorderasiatische Schriftdenkmaeler der Koeniglichen [*or Staatlichen*] Museen zu Berlin
Vasa Suppl — Vasa Supplementum
Vasc Dis — Vascular Diseases
Vasc Surg — Vascular Surgery
VASD — Veroeffentlichungen. Deutsche Akademie fuer Sprache und Dichtung
VaSd — Vorderasiatische Schriftdenkmaeler der Koeniglichen [*or Staatlichen*] Museen zu Berlin
VA Social Science J — Virginia Social Science Journal
Vassar Bros Inst Tr — Vassar Brothers Institute. Transactions
VA State Lib Bull — Virginia State Library. Bulletin
Vasterbotten — Vasterbottens Lans Hambygdsforenings Arsbok
Vastergotlands Fornminnesforen Tidskr — Vastergotlands Fornminnesforenings Tidskrift
Vastmanlands Fornminnesforen Arsskr — Vastmanlands Fornminnesforenings Arsskrift
Vasuti Tud Kut Intez Evk — Vasuti Tudomanyos Kutato Intezet Evkoenyve [*Hungary*]
VA Tax R — Virginia Tax Review
VA Teach — Virginia Teacher
VATEJ — Victorian Association for the Teaching of English. Journal
VATISJ — VATIS [*Victorian Association of Teachers in Independent Schools*] Journal

VA Truck Exp — Virginia Truck Experiment Station. Publications
VA Univ Ph Soc B Sc S — Virginia University. Philosophical Society. Bulletin. Scientific Series
VAV — Veroeffentlichungen zum Archiv fuer Voelkerkunde
VA Water Resour Res Cent Bull — Virginia Water Resources Research Center. Bulletin
VA Wildl — Virginia Wildlife
Vaxt-Nar-Nytt — Vaxt-Narings-Nytt
Vaxtodling Inst Vaxtodlingslara Lantbrukshogsk — Vaextodling. Institutionen foer Vaextodlingslara. Lantbrukshoegskolan
Vaxtskyddsnotiser Sver Lantbruksuniver — Vaxtskyddsnotiser. Sveriges Lantbruksuniversitet
Vazduhoplovni Glas — Vazduhoplovni Glasnik [*Yugoslavia*]
VB — Voks Bulletin
VBA — NIMO [*Nederlands Instituut voor Maatschappelijke Opbouw*] Kroniek. Nieuwsbulletin
VB (B) — Voelkischer Beobachter (Berlin)
VBelGrN — Vesci Akademii Navuk Belaruskaj SSR. Seryja Gramadskich Navuk
VBKTPS — Vierteljahrschrift fuer Bibelkunde, Talmudische, und Patristische Studien
VBL — Vakblad voor de Bloemisterij
VB (Mu) — Voelkischer Beobachter (Muenich)
VBN — Victorian Bar News
VBO — Bouwwereld. Universeel Veertiendaags Vaktijdschrift voor de Bouwnijverheid
VBQ — Visvabharati Quarterly
VBSFA — Vestsi Akademii Navuk BSSR. Seryya Fizika-Matematychnykh Navuk
VBSKA — Vestsi Akademii Navuk BSSR. Seryya Khimichnykh Navuk
VBT — Tabak Plus
VBTPS — Vierteljahrschrift fuer Bibelkunde, Talmudische, und Patristische Studien
VBV — Documentatieblad voor Onderwijs en Wetenschappen
VBW — Vakbondskrant van Nederland
VBW — Vortraege der Bibliothek Warburg
VC — Vigiliae Christianae
VC — Virginia Cavalcade
VCA — Vestnik Ceske Akademie Ved a Umeni
VCA — Vestnik Ceskoslovenske Akademie Ved
Vcela Morav — Vcela Moravska
VChr — Vigiliae Christianae
V Christ — Vetera Christianorum
VCK — Veckans Affarer
VCSAV — Vestnik Ceskoslovenske Akademie Ved
VCS Bul — VCS [*Victorian Computer Society*] Bulletin
VCT — Vector
VCTA General J — Victorian Commercial Teachers' Association. General Journal
VDASD — Veroeffentlichungen. Deutsche Akademie fuer Sprache und Dichtung
VDEFA — VDE [*Verband Deutscher Elektrotechniker*] Fachberichte
VDE Fachber — VDE [*Verband Deutscher Elektrotechniker*] Fachberichte
VDEW (Ver Dtsch Elektrizitaetswerke) Informationsdienst — VDEW (Vereinigung Deutscher Elektrizitaetswerke) Informationsdienst (German Federal Republic)
VDF — Vorkaempfer Deutscher Freiheit. Series [*Munich*]
VDFAN — Vestnik Dal'nevostochnogo Filiala Akademii Nauk SSSR
VDGIA — Verhandlungen. Deutsche Gesellschaft fuer Innere Medizin
VDGKA — Verhandlungen. Deutsche Gesellschaft fuer Kreislaufforschung
VDGPA — Verhandlungen. Deutsche Gesellschaft fuer Pathologie
VDGRA — Verhandlungen. Deutsche Gesellschaft fuer Rheumatologie
VdGSA — Viola da Gamba Society of America. Journal
VDI — Vestnik Drevnei Istorii
VDI Ber — VDI [*Verein Deutscher Ingenieure*] Berichte
VDIFA — VDI [*Verein Deutscher Ingenieure*] Forschungsheft
VDI Forschungsh — VDI [*Verein Deutscher Ingenieure*] Forschungsheft
VDI Nachr — Verein Deutscher Ingenieure. Nachrichten
VDI Z — VDI [*Verein Deutscher Ingenieure*] Zeitschrift
VDI Z Fortschr Ber Reihe 5 — VDI [*Verein Deutscher Ingenieure*] Zeitschriften. Fortschritt-Berichte. Reihe 5. Grund- und Werkstoffe
VDNAA — VDI [*Verein Deutscher Ingenieure*] Nachrichten
VDP — Von Deutscher Poeterey
VDPh — Verhandlung. Versammlung Deutscher Philologen
VDS — Veroeffentlichungen. Deutsche Schillergesellschaft
VDTJ — Voprosy Dialektologii Tjurkskich Jazykov
VE — Vermont Music Educators News
VE — Vestnik Evropy
VE — Vox Evangelica
VEAB Ert — VEAB Ertesitoe [*Hungary*]
VEB — Financieel Ekonomische Tijd
VEB Verlag Tech Mon Tech Rev — VEB [*Volkseigener Betrieb*] Verlag Technik. Monthly Technical Review
VeC — Vertice (Coimbra)
Veda Tech Mladezi — Veda a Technika Mladezi [*Czechoslovakia*]
Veda Tech SSSR — Veda a Technika v SSSR

Veda Vyzk Potravin Prum — Veda a Vyzkum v Potravinarskem Prumyslu
Veda Vyzk Prum Sklarskem — Veda a Vyzkum v Prumyslu Sklarskem
Veda Vyzk Prum Text — Veda a Vyzkum v Prumyslu Textilnim
Vedeckovyzk Uhelny Ustav Sb Vyzk Pr — Vedeckovyzkumny Uhelny Ustav Sbornik Vyzkumnych Praci [*Czechoslovakia*]
Ved Inf CSAV — Vedecke Informace CSAV [*Ceskoslovenska Akademie Ved*]
Ved Kes — Vedanta Kesari [*Madras*]
VeDo — Verbum Domino
Ved Prace Ustr Vyzk Ustavu Rost Vyr (Praha) — Vedecke Prace Ustredniho Vyzkumneho Ustavu Rostlinne Vyroby (Praha)
Ved Prace Vyskum Ust Lesn Hosp Zvolen — Vedecke Prace Vyskumny Ustav Lesneho Hospodarstva v Zvolene
Ved Prace Vysk Ustavu Kukurice Trnave — Vedecke Prace Vyskumneho Ustavu Kukurice v Trnave
Ved Prace Vysk Ustavu Rastlinnej Vyr — Vedecke Prace Vyskumneho Ustavu Rastlinnej Vyroby
Ved Prace Vysk Ustavu Zavlahov Hospod Bratislave — Vedecke Prace Vyskumneho Ustavu Zavlahoveho Hospodarstva v Bratislave
Ved Prace Vysk Ustavu Zivoc Nitre — Vedecke Prace Vyskumneho Ustavu Zivocisnej Vyroby v Nitre
Ved Prace Vyzkum Ust Melior — Vedecke Prace Vyzkumneho Ustavu Zemedelsko-Lesnickych Melioraci CSAZV [*Ceskoslovenska Akademie Zemedelskych Ved*] v Praze
Ved Pr Cesk Zemed Muz — Vedecke Prace Ceskoslovenskeho Zemedelskeho Muzea
Ved Pr Lab Podoznalectva Bratisl — Vedecke Prace Laboratoria Podoznalectva v Bratislave
Ved Pr Ustavu Zelinarskeho Olomouci — Vedecke Prace Ustavu Zelinarskeho v Olomouci
Ved Pr Ustr Vyzk Ust Rostl Vyroby Praze-Ruzyni — Vedecke Prace Ustredniho Vyzkumneho Ustavu Rostlinne Vyroby v Praze-Ruzyni
Ved Pr VSCHK (Slatinany) — Vedecke Prace VSCHK [*Vyzkumna Stanice pro Chov Koni*] (Slatinany)
Ved Pr Vysk Ustav Rastl Vyroby Piestanoch — Vedecke Prace Vyskumnu Ustavu Rastlinnej Vyroby v Piestanoch
Ved Pr Vysk Ustavu Chov Hydiny Ivanka Dunaji — Vedecke Prace Vyskumneho Ustavu pro Chov Hydiny v Ivanka pri Dunaji
Ved Pr Vysk Ustavu Chov Skotu Caz Rapotine — Vedecke Prace Vyskumneho Ustavu pro Chov Skotu Caz v Rapotine
Ved Pr Vysk Ustavu Kukurice Trnave — Vedecke Prace Vyskumneho Ustavu Kukurice v Trnave
Ved Pr Vysk Ustavu Lesn Hospod Zvolene — Vedecke Prace Vyskumneho Ustavu Lesneho Hospodarstva Vo Zvolene
Ved Pr Vysk Ustavu Luk Pasienkov Banskej Bystrici — Vedecke Prace Vyskumneho Ustavu Luk a Pasienkov v Banskej Bystrici
Ved Pr Vysk Ustavu Ovciar Trencine — Vedecke Prace Vyskumneho Ustavu Ovciarskeho v Trencine
Ved Pr Vysk Ustavu Podoznalectva Vyz Rastlin Bratisl — Vedecke Prace Vyskumneho Ustavu Podoznalectva a Vyzivy Rastlin v Bratislave
Ved Pr Vysk Ustavu Rastlinnej Vyroby Piestanoch — Vedecke Prace Vyskumneho Ustavu Rastlinnej Vyroby v Piestanoch
Ved Pr Vysk Ustavu Zavlahoveho Hospod Bratisl — Vedecke Prace Vyskumneho Ustavu Zavlahoveho Hospodarstva v Bratislave
Ved Pr Vysk Ustavu Zivocisnej Vyroby Nitre — Vedecke Prace Vyskumneho Ustavu Zivocisnej Vyroby v Nitre
Ved Pr Vysk Ust Rastl Vyroby Piestanoch — Vedecke Prace Ustredniho Vyskumneho Ustavu Rastlinnej Vyroby Piestanoch
Ved Pr Vysk Ust Rastl Vyroby Praze-Ruzyni — Vedecke Prace Ustredniho Vyskumneho Ustavu Rastlinnej Vyroby CSAZV [*Ceskoslovenska Akademie Zemedelskych Ved*] v Praze-Ruzyni
Ved Pr Vyzk Stanice Chov Koni Slatinany — Vedecke Prace Vyzkumna Stanice pro Chov Koni Slatinany
Ved Pr Vyzk Ustav Melior — Vedecke Prace. Vyzkumny Ustav Melioraci
Ved Pr Vyzk Ustavu Bramborarskeho Havlickove Brode — Vedecke Prace Vyzkumneho Ustavu Bramborarskeho v Havlickove Brode
Ved Pr Vyzk Ustavu Chov Prasat Kostelci Nad Orlice — Vedecke Prace Vyzkumneho Ustavu pro Chov Prasat v Kostelci Nad Orlice
Ved Pr Vyzk Ustavu Chov Skotu Caz Rapotine — Vedecke Prace Vyzkumneho Ustavu pro Chov Skotu Caz v Rapotine
Ved Pr Vyzk Ustavu Krmivarskeho Czaz Brne — Vedecke Prace Vyzkumneho Ustavu Krmivarskeho Czaz v Brne
Ved Pr Vyzk Ustavu Melior Praze Zbraslavi — Vedecke Prace Vyzkumneho Ustavu Melioraci v Praze or Zbraslavi
Ved Pr Vyzk Ustavu Obilnarskeho Kromerizi — Vedecke Prace Vyzkumneho Ustavu Obilnarskeho v Kromerizi
Ved Pr Vyzk Ustavu Okrasneho Zahradnictvi Pruhonicich — Vedecke Prace Vyzkumneho Ustavu Okrasneho Zahradnictvi v Pruhonicich
Ved Pr Vyzk Ustavu Ovilnarskeho Kromerizi — Vedecke Prace Vyzkumneho Ustavu Ovilnarskeho v Kromerizi
Ved Pr Vyzk Ustavu Rostl Vyroby Praze-Ruzyni — Vedecke Prace Vyzkkumnych Ustavu Rostlinne Vyroby v Praze-Ruzyni
Ved Pr Vyzk Ustavu Vet CSAZV Brne — Vedecke Prace Vyzkumneho Ustavu Veterinarni CSAZV [*Ceskoslovenska Akademie Zemedelskych Ved*] v Brne
Ved Pr Vyzk Ustavu Vet Lek Brne — Vedecke Prace Vyzkumneho Ustavu Veterinarniho Lekarstvi v Brne [*Czechoslovakia*]

Ved Pr Vyzk Ustavu Zavlahoveho Hospod Bratislave — Vedecke Prace Vyzkumneho Ustavu Zavlahoveho Hospodarstva v Bratislave
Veeartsenijk Blad Nederl-Indie — Veeartsenijkundige Bladen voor Nederlandsch-Indie
Veeteelt Zuivelber — Veeteelt- en Zuivelberichten
VEF Inf Bul — VEF [*Victorian Employers' Federation*] Information Bulletin
Veg Crops Ser Calif Univ Dept Veg Crops — Vegetable Crops Series. California University. Department of Vegetable Crops
Vegetarian Mo — Vegetarian Monthly
Veg Grower — Vegetable Grower
Veg Grow News — Vegetable Growers News
Veg Situat TVS US Dep Agric Econ Res Serv — Vegetable Situation. United States Department of Agriculture. Economic Research
Veg Times — Vegetarian Times
Vegyip Kut Intez Kozl — Vegyipari Kutato Intezetek Kozlemenyei
Veh Syst Dyn — Vehicle System Dynamics
VEJ — DHZ Markt. Vakblad voor de Doe het Zelf Ondernemer
Vel — Veltro'
Vel Lt Trap — Velvet Light Trap
Vema Res Ser — Vema Research Series
VEN — Venture Science Fiction
Vend — Vending Times International Buyers Guide and Directory
Venez Dir Geol Bol Geol — Venezuela. Direccion de Geologia. Boletin de Geologia
Venez Dir Geol Bol Geol Publ Esp — Venezuela. Direccion de Geologia. Boletin de Geologia. Publicacion Especial
Venez Inst Nac Nutr Publ — Venezuela. Instituto Nacional de Nutricion. Publicacion
Venez Min Minas Hidrocarburos Dir Geol Bol Geol — Venezuela. Ministerio de Minas e Hidrocarburos. Direccion de Geologia. Boletin de Geologia
Venez Univ Cent Esc Geol Minas Lab Petrogr Geoquimica Inf — Venezuela. Universidad Central. Escuela de Geologia y Minas. Laboratorio de Petrografia y Geoquimica. Informe
Vengarskaya Farmakoter — Vengarskaya Farmakoterapiya
Veng Zh Gorn Dela Metall Gorn Delo — Vengerskii Zhurnal Gornogo Dela i Metallurgii. Gornoe Delo
Vent Kond Vozdukha Zdanii — Ventilyatsiya i Konditsionirovanie Vozdukha Zdanii
Vent Kond Vozdukha Zdanii Sooruzh — Ventilyatsiya i Konditsionirovanie Vozdukha Zdanii Sooruzhenii
Vent Ochistka Vozdukha — Ventilyatsiya i Ochistka Vozdukha
Vent Shakht Rudn — Ventilyatsiya Shakht i Rudnikov
Venus Jpn J Malacol — Venus: The Japanese Journal of Malacology
VEOFA — Vestnik Oftal'mologii
VEP — Verpakken. Het Vakblad voor de Verpakkende Industrie en Verpakkingsindustrie
VEP — Vojno-Ekonomski Pregled
VEQUD — Veterinary Quarterly
VeR — Verbum (Rio De Janeiro)
VER — Verfkroniek
Ver — Verri
Ver — Versty
Verb C — Verbum Caro
Ver Bibl Landes NRW Mitt — Verband der Bibliotheken des Landes Nordrhein-Westfalen. Mitteilungsblatt
Ver Destill Ztg — Vereinigte Destillateur-Zeitungen
Ver Dtsch Ing Z — Verein Deutscher Ingenieure. Zeitschrift
Ver Dtsch Ing Z Fortschr Ber Reihe 5 — Verein Deutscher Ingenieure. Zeitschriften. Fortschritt-Berichte. Reihe 5. Grund- und Werkstoffe
Vereinigung Schweizer Petroleum-Geologen u Ingenieure Bull — Vereinigung Schweizerischer Petroleum-Geologen und Ingenieure. Bulletin
Vereinte Nationen — Zeitschrift fuer die Vereinten Nationen und Ihre Sonderorganisationen
Ver Erdk Dresden Mitt — Verein fuer Erdkunde zu Dresden. Mitteilungen
Ver Erdk Leipzig Mitt — Verein fuer Erdkunde zu Leipzig. Mitteilungen
Ver Exploit Proefzuivelboerderij Hoorn Versl — Vereniging tot Exploitatie eener Proefzuivelboerderij te Hoorn. Verslag
Verfahrenstech — Verfahrenstechnik International
Verfass Recht Uebersee — Verfassung und Recht in Uebersee
Verfassung u -Wirklichkeit — Verfassung und Verfassungswirklichkeit
Verfinst TNO Circ — Verfinstituut TNO [*Nederlands Centrale Organisatie voor Toegepast - Natuurwetenschappelijk Onderzoek*] Circulaire
Ver Freunde Naturg Mecklenberg Arch — Verein der Freunde der Naturgeschichte in Mecklenberg. Archiv
Ver Freunden Erdk Leipzig Jber — Verein von Freunden der Erdkunde zu Leipzig. Jahresbericht
Ver f d Gesch Berlins Schr — Verein fuer die Geschichte Berlins. Schriften
Ver f Gesch Dresdens Mitt — Verein fuer Geschichte Dresdens. Mitteilungen
Verh Anat Ges — Verhandlungen. Anatomische Gesellschaft
Verhandl Deutsch Path Gesellsch — Verhandlungen. Deutsche Pathologische Gesellschaft
Verhandl Deutsch Zool Gesellsch — Verhandlungen. Deutsche Zoologische Gesellschaft
Verhandl DPG — Verhandlungen. Deutsche Physikalische Gesellschaft [*Stuttgart*]
Verhandl Geol Bundesanstalt — Verhandlungen. Geologische Bundesanstalt

Verhandl Gesellsch Deutsch Naturf u Aerzte — Verhandlungen. Gesellschaft Deutscher Naturforscher und Aerzte

Verhandl Naturw Ver Hamburg — Verhandlungen. Naturwissenschaftlicher Verein in Hamburg

Verhandl Naturw Ver Karlsruhe — Verhandlungen. Naturwissenschaftlicher Verein in Karlsruhe

Verhandl Schweiz Naturf Gesellsch — Verhandlungen. Schweizerische Naturforschende Gesellschaft

Verhandlungsber Kolloid-Ges — Verhandlungsberichte. Kolloid-Gesellschaft

VerhBer Dt Zool Ges — Verhandlungsbericht. Deutsche Zoologische Gesellschaft

Verh Bot Ver Prov Brandenb — Verhandlungen. Botanischer Verein der Provinz Brandenburg

Verh Dt Ges Angew Ent — Verhandlungen. Deutsche Gesellschaft fuer Angewandte Entomologie

Verh Dtsch Ges Exp Med — Verhandlungen. Deutsche Gesellschaft fuer Experimentelle Medizin

Verh Dtsch Ges Inn Med — Verhandlungen. Deutsche Gesellschaft fuer Innere Medizin

Verh Dtsch Ges Kreislaufforsch — Verhandlungen. Deutsche Gesellschaft fuer Kreislaufforschung

Verh Dtsch Ges Pathol — Verhandlungen. Deutsche Gesellschaft fuer Pathologie

Verh Dtsch Ges Rheumatol — Verhandlungen. Deutsche Gesellschaft fuer Rheumatologie

Verh Dtsch Phys Ges — Verhandlungen. Deutsche Physikalische Gesellschaft

Verh Dtsch Zool Ges — Verhandlungen. Deutsche Zoologische Gesellschaft

Verh Dt Zool Ges Bonn — Verhandlungen. Deutsche Zoologische Gesellschaft in Bonn [*Rhein*]

Verh Dt Zool Ges Erlangen — Verhandlungen. Deutsche Zoologische Gesellschaft in Erlangen

Verh Dt Zool Ges Frankfurt — Verhandlungen. Deutsche Zoologische Gesellschaft in Frankfurt

Verh Dt Zool Ges Jena — Verhandlungen. Deutsche Zoologische Gesellschaft in Jena

Verh Dt Zool Ges (Kiel) — Verhandlungen. Deutsche Zoologische Gesellschaft (Kiel)

Verh Dt Zool Ges (Tuebingen) — Verhandlungen. Deutsche Zoologische Gesellschaft (Tuebingen)

Verh Dt Zool Ges (Wien) — Verhandlungen. Deutsche Zoologische Gesellschaft (Wien)

Verh Dt Zool Ges (Wilhelmshaven) — Verhandlungen. Deutsche Zoologische Gesellschaft (Wilhelmshaven)

Verh Geol Bundesanst — Verhandlungen. Geologische Bundesanstalt

Verh Geol Bundesanst Bundeslaenderser — Verhandlungen. Geologische Bundesanstalt. Bundeslaenderserie

Verh Ges Dsch Naturfrsch Aerzte — Verhandlungen. Gesellschaft Deutscher Naturforscher und Aerzte

Verh Inst Praev Geneeskd — Verhandelingen. Instituut voor Praeventieve Geneeskunde

Verh Int Psychother Kongr — Verhandlungen. Internationaler Psychotherapie Kongress

Verh Int Ver Theor Angew Limnol — Verhandlungen. Internationaler Vereinigung fuer Theoretische und Angewandt e Limnologie

Verh K Acad Geneeskd Belg — Verhandelingen. Koninklijke Academie voor Geneeskunde van Belgie

Verh K Acad Wet Lett & Schone Kunsten Belg — Verhandelingen. Koninklijke Academie voor Wetenschappen. Letteren en Schone Kunsten van Belgie

Verh K Acad Wet Lett Schone Kunsten Belg Kl Wet — Verhandelingen. Koninklijke Academie voor Wetenschappen. Letteren en Schone Kunsten van Belgie. Klasse der Wetenschappen

Verh K Acad Wet Lett en Schone Kunsten Belg Kl Wet — Verhandelingen. Koninklijke Academie voor Wetenschappen. Letteren en Schone Kunsten van Belgie. Klasse der Wetenschappen

Verh K Akad Wet Amsterdam Afd Natuurkd — Verhandelingen. Koninklijke Akademie van Wetenschappen te Amsterdam. Afdeeling Natuurkunde

Verh K Ned Akad Wet Afd Natuurkd Reeks 1 — Verhandelingen. Koninklijke Nederlandse Akademie van Wetenschappen. Afdeling Natuurkunde. Reeks 1

Verh K Ned Akad Wet Afd Natuurkd Reeks 2 — Verhandelingen. Koninklijke Nederlandse Akademie van Wetenschappen. Afdeling Natuurkunde. Reeks 2

Verh K Ned Akad Wet Afd Natuurkd Tweede Reeks — Verhandelingen. Koninklijke Nederlandse Akademie van Wetenschappen. Afdeling Natuurkunde. Tweede Reeks

Verh K Ned Akad Wetensch Afd Natuurk Reeks 1 — Verhandelingen. Koninklijke Nederlandse Akademie van Wetenschappen. Afdeling Natuurkunde. Reeks 1 [*Netherlands*]

Verh K Ned Akad Wetensch Afd Natuurk Reeks 2 — Verhandelingen. Koninklijke Nederlandse Akademie van Wetenschappen. Afdeling Natuurkunde. Reeks 2 [*Netherlands*]

Verh K Ned Geol Mijnbouwkd Genoot — Verhandelingen. Koninklijke Nederlandse Geologisch Mijnbouwkundig Genootschap

Verh K Ned Geol Mijnbouwkd Genoot Geol Ser — Verhandelingen. Koninklijke Nederlandse Geologisch Mijnbouwkundig Genootschap. Geologische Serie

Verh K Ned Geol Mijnbouwkd Genoot Mijnbouwkd Ser — Verhandelingen. Koninklijke Nederlandse Geologisch Mijnbouwkundig Genootschap. Mijnbouwkundige Serie

Verh Konink Acad Wetensch Belgie — Verhandelingen. Koninklijke Academie voor Wetenschappen. Letteren en Schone Kunsten van Belgie

Verh Kon Nederl Ak Wetensch Afd Lett — Verhandelingen. Koninklijke Nederlandse Akademie van Wetenschappen. Afdeling Letterkunde

Verh K Vlaam Acad Geneesk Belg — Verhandelingen. Koninklijke Vlaamse Academie voor Geneeskunde van Belgie [*Belgium*]

Verh K Vlaam Acad Wetensch Belg Kl Wetensch — Verhandelingen. Koninklijke Vlaamse Academie voor Wetenschappen, Letteren, en Schone Kunsten van Belgie. Klasse der Wetenschappen [*Belgium*]

Verh Naturforsch Ges Basel — Verhandlungen. Naturforschende Gesellschaft in Basel

Verh Naturforsch Ver Bruenn — Verhandlungen. Naturforschender Verein in Bruenn

Verh Natur-Med Ver Heidelb — Verhandlungen. Naturhistorisch-Medizinischer Verein zu Heidelberg

Verh Ornithol Ges Bayern — Verhandlungen. Ornithologische Gesellschaft in Bayern

Verh Phys-Med Ges Wuerzburg — Verhandlungen. Physikalisch-Medizinische Gesellschaft in Wuerzburg

Verh Rijksinst Natuurbeheer — Verhandelingen. Rijksinstituut voor Natuurbeheer

Verh Schweiz Naturforsch Ges — Verhandlungen. Schweizerische Naturforschende Gesellschaft

Verh Schweiz Naturforsch Ges Wiss Teil — Verhandlungen. Schweizerische Naturforschende Gesellschaft. Wissenschaftlicher Teil

Verh Ver Schweiz Physiol — Verhandlungen. Verein der Schweizer Physiologen

Verh Zool-Bot Ges Wien — Verhandlungen. Zoologisch-Botanische Gesellschaft in Wien

Verkehrsmed Grenzgeb — Verkehrsmedizin und Ihre Grenzgebiete

Verkehrsmed Ihre Grenzgeb — Verkehrsmedizin und Ihre Grenzgebiete [*German Democratic Republic*]

VerkF — Verkuendigung und Forschung [*Munich*]

Verksamheten Stift Rasforadl Skogstrad — Verksamheten. Stiftelsen foer Rasforadling av Skogstrad

Vermess-Inf — Vermessungs-Informationen

Verm Nox Weeds Destr Board Leafl — Leaflet. Vermin and Noxious Weeds Destruction Board [*Victoria*]

Verm Nox Weeds Destrn Bd (Melb) Surv — Vermin and Noxious Weeds Destruction Board (Melbourne). Survey

Vermont Geol Survey Bull — Vermont. Geological Survey. Bulletin

Vermont Lib — Vermont Libraries

Vermont L Rev — Vermont Law Review

Vernacular Architect — Vernacular Architecture

Vernacular Archre — Vernacular Architecture

Veroeff Bundesanst Alp Landwirtsch Admont — Veroeffentlichungen. Bundesanstalt fuer Alpine Landwirtschaft in Admont

Veroeff Dtsch Geod Komm Reihe A — Veroeffentlichungen. Deutsche Geodaetiske Kommission. Bayerische Akademie der Wissenschaften. Reihe A [*West Germany*]

Veroeffentlich Schweizer Gesellsch Medizin Naturwissensch — Veroeffentlichungen. Schweizerische Gesellschaft fuer Geschichte der Medizin und der Naturwissenschaft

Veroeffentl J-Vet-Ber Beamt Tieraerzte Preuss — Veroeffentlichungen aus den Jahres-Veterinaer-Berichten. Beamtete Tieraerzte Preussen

Veroeffentl Leibniz-Archivs — Veroeffentlichungen. Leibniz-Archiv

Veroeff Geobot Inst Eidg Tech Hochsch Stift Ruebel Zuer — Veroeffentlichungen. Geobotanisches Institut. Eidgenoessische Technische Hochschule Stiftung Ruebel in Zuerich

Veroeff Geobot Inst Eidg Tech Hochsch Stift Ruebel Zuerich — Veroeffentlichungen. Geobotanisches Institut. Eidgenoessische Technische Hochschule Stiftung Ruebel in Zuerich

Veroeff Geobot Inst Ruebel — Veroeffentlichungen. Geobotanisches Institut Ruebel

Veroeff Inst Meeresforsch Bremerhaven — Veroeffentlichungen. Institut fuer Meeresforschung in Bremerhaven

Veroeff Inst Meeresforsch Bremerhaven Suppl — Veroeffentlichungen. Institut fuer Meeresforschung in Bremerhaven. Supplement

Veroeff Kaiser Wilhelm Inst Silikatforsch Berlin Dahlem — Veroeffentlichungen. Kaiser-Wilhelm-Institut fuer Silikatforschung in Berlin-Dahlem

Veroeff Landwirtsch Chem Bundesversuchsanst (Linz) — Veroeffentlichungen. Landwirtschaftlich-Chemische Bundesversuchsanstalt (Linz)

Veroeff Meteorol Dienstes DDR — Veroeffentlichungen. Meteorologischer Dienst. Deutsche Demokratische Republik

Veroeff Meterol Hydrol Dienstes DDR — Veroeffentlichungen. Meteorologischer und Hydrologischer Dienst. Deutsche Demokratische Republik

Veroeff Morphol Pathol — Veroeffentlichungen aus der Morphologischen Pathologie

Veroeff Naturh Mus (Wien) — Veroeffentlichungen. Naturhistorischer Museum (Wien)

Veroeff Naturschutz Landschaftspflege Baden Wuerttemb — Veroeffentlichungen fuer Naturschutz und Landschaftspflege in Baden-Wuerttemberg

Veroeff Naturschutz Landschaftspflege Baden-Wuerttemb Beih — Veroeffentlichungen fuer Naturschutz und Landschaftspflege in Baden-Wuerttemberg. Beihefte

Veroeff Pathol — Veroeffentlichungen aus der Pathologie

Veroeff Reichsgesundheitsamts — Veroeffentlichungen. Reichsgesundheitsamt

Veroeff Ueberseemus (Bremen) Reihe A — Veroeffentlichungen. Uebersseemuseum (Bremen). Reihe A

Veroeff Wiss Photo Lab (Wolfen) — Veroeffentlichungen. Wissenschaftliche Photo-Laboratorien (Wolfen)

Veroeff Wiss Zent Lab Photogr Abt AGFA — Veroeffentlichungen. Wissenschaftliches Zentral Laboratorium. Photographische Abteilung AGFA

Veroeff Zentralinst Phys Erde — Veroeffentlichungen. Zentralinstitut Physik der Erde [*Czechoslovakia*]

Veroeff Zool Staatssamml (Muench) — Veroeffentlichungen. Zoologische Staatssammlung (Muenchen)

Veroeff Zool StSamml (Muench) — Veroeffentlichungen. Zoologische Staatssammlung (Muenchen)

Veroff Inst Agrarmet Univ (Leipzig) — Veroeffentlichungen. Institut fuer Agrarmeteorologie und des Agrarmeteorologischen Observatoriums. Karl Marx-Universitaet (Leipzig)

Veroff Land-Hauswirtsch Auswertungs-Informationsdienst — Veroeffentlichungen. Land- und Hauswirtschaftlicher Auswertungs- und Informationsdienst

Verpack Chemiebetr — Verpackung im Chemiebetrich

Verpack-Rundsch — Verpackungs-Rundschau

Verres Refract — Verres et Refractaires

Verre Text Plast Renf — Verre Textile, Plastiques Renforces [*France*]

Verrigtinge Kongr S-Afr Genet Ver — Verrigtinge van die Kongres van dis Suid-Afrikaanse Genetiese Vereniging

Ver Schweizer Petroleum-Geologen u Ingenieure Bull — Vereinigung Schweizerischer Petroleum-Geologen und Ingenieure. Bulletin

Ver Schweiz Pet-Geol Ing Bull — Vereinigung Schweizerischer Petroleum-Geologen und Ingenieure. Bulletin

Vers Landbouwkd Onderz — Verslagen van Landbouwkundige Onderzoekingen

Versl Interprov Proeven Proefstn Akkerbouw Lelystad (Neth) — Verslagen van Interprovinciale Proeven. Proefstation voor de Akkerbouw Lelystad (Netherlands)

Versl Interprov Proeven Proefstn Akkerbouw (Wageningen) — Verslagen van Interprovinciale Proeven. Proefstation voor de Akkerbouw (Wageningen)

Versl Landbouwkd Onderz A — Verslagen van Landbouwkundige Onderzoekingen A. Rijkslandbouwproefstation en Bodemkundig Instituut te Groningen

Versl Landbouwkd Onderz (Agric Res Rep) — Verslagen van Landbouwkundige Onderzoekingen (Agricultural Research Reports)

Versl Landbouwkd Onderz B — Verslagen van Landbouwkundige Onderzoekingen B. Bodemikundig Instituut te Groningen

Versl Landbouwkd Onderz Rijkslandbouwproefstn — Verslagen van Landbouwkundige Onderzoekingen van de Rijkslandbouwproefstations

Versl Landbouwk Onderz — Verslagen van Landbouwkundige Onderzoekingen

Versl Landbouwk Onderz Cent Lanbouwpubl Landbouwdoc — Verslagen van Landbouwkundige Onderzoekingen. Centrum voor Landbouwpublikatien en Landbouwdocumentatie

Versl Landbouwk Onderz Ned — Verslagen van het Landbouwkundig Onderzoek in Nederland

Versl Meded Kon Vl Ak Taal & Letterk — Verslagen en Mededeelingen. Koninklijke Vlaamse Akademie voor Taal- en Letterkunde

Versl Meded K Vlaam Acad Taal Lett — Verslagen en Mededelingen van de Koninklijke Vlaamse Academie voor Taalen Letterkunde

Versl Meded Rijkslandbouwconsul Westelijk Drenthe — Verslagen en Mededelingen van het Rijkslandbouwconsulentschap Westelijk Drenthe

Versl Tien-Jarenplan Graanonderzoek Sticht Nederl Graan-Cent — Verslagen. Tien-Jarenplan voor Graanonderzoek. Stichting Nederlands Graan-Centrum

Versl Ver Chem Tech Landbouwkd Advis — Verslagen der Vereniging van Chemisch-Technischen. Landbouwkundig Adviseurs

Verstaendliche Wiss — Verstaendliche Wissenschaft

Versuchsergeb Bundesanst Pflanzenbau Samenpruefung Wien — Versuchsergebnisse der Bundesanstalt fuer Pflanzenbau und Samenpruefung in Wien

Versuchsgrubenges Quartalsh — Versuchsgrubengesellschaft Quartalshefte [*West Germany*]

Vertebr Hung — Vertebrata Hungarica

Vertebr Palasiat — Vertebrata Palasiatica

Vertebr Palasiatica — Vertebrata Palasiatica

Vert File Ind — Vertical File Index

Ver f Thuer Gesch u Alt Ztsch — Verein fuer Thueringische Geschichte und Altertumskunde. Zeitschrift

Ver Vaterl Naturk Wuerttemberg Jahresh — Verein fuer Vaterlaendische Naturkunde in Wuerttemberg. Jahreshefte

Ver Verbr Naturwiss Kenntnisse Wien Schr — Verein zur Verbreitung Naturwissenschaftlicher Kenntnisse in Wien. Schriften

Verwaltung — Zeitschrift fuer Verwaltungswissenschaft

Verwarm Vent — Verwarming en Ventilatie

Verzam Overdruk Plantenziektenk Dienst (Wageningen) — Verzamelde Overdrukken. Plantenziektenkundige Dienst (Wageningen)

Verzekerings-Arch — Verzekerings-Archief

VESADE — Electron Microscopy Society of Southern Africa. Proceedings

VESADE — Elektronmikroskopievereniging van Suidelike Afrika. Verrigtings

Ves Akad Nauk Kirg SSR — Vestnik Akademii Nauk Kirgizskoi SSR

Vesci Akad Navuk BSSR Ser Fiz-Mat Navuk — Vesci Akademii Navuk BSSR. Seryja Fizika-Matematycnyh Navuk

Vesn Zavod Geol Geofiz Istraz NR Srb — Vesnik Zavod za Geoloska i Geofizicka Istrazivanja NR Srbije

Vesn Zavod Geol Geofiz Istraz Ser A — Vesnik Zavod za Geoloska i Geofizicka Istrazivanja. Serija A. Geologija

Vesn Zavod Geol Geofiz Istraz Ser C — Vesnik Zavod za Geoloska i Geofizicka Istrazivanja. Serija C. Priminjena Geofizika

Vest Akad Nauk SSSR — Vestnik Akademii Nauk SSSR

Vest Ces Akad Zemed — Vestnik Ceskoslovenske Akademie Zemedelske

Vest Csl Spol Zool — Vestnik Ceskoslovenske Spolecnosti Zoologicke

Vest Dal'nevost Fil Akad Nauk SSSR — Vestnik Dal'nevostochnogo Filiala Akademii Nauk SSSR

Vest Gos Muz Gruz — Vestnik Gosudarstvennogo Muzeja Gruzii Imeni Akademika S. N. Dzhanashia

Vest Inst Pchelovodstva — Vestnik Institut Pchelovodstva

Vest Ist Mirov Kul't — Vestnik Istorii Mirovoi Kul'tury

Vest Khar'k Univ Radiofiz Elektron — Vestnik Khar'kovskogo Universiteta. Radiofizika, Elektronika [*USSR*]

Vest Latv PSR Akad — Vestis Latvijas Pasomju Socialistikas Republikas Zinatu Akademija [*Riga, USSR*]

Vest Leningr Gos Univ Ser Biol — Vestnik Leningradskogo Gosudarstvennogo Universiteta. Seriya Biologii

Vest Leningr Inst — Vestnik Leningradskogo Instituta

Vest Mikrobiol Epidemiol Parazitol — Vestnik Mikrobiologii, Epidemiologii, i Parazitologii

Vest Mosk Gos Univ Ser VI — Vestnik Moskovskogo Gosudarstvennogo Universiteta. Seriya VI

Vest Mosk Inst Biol Pochv — Vestnik Moskovskogo Instituta. Seriya Biologiya, Pochvovedenie

Vest Mosk Inst Geogr — Vestnik Moskovskogo Instituta Geografii

Vest Mosk Univ Ser Biol Pochv Geol Geogr — Vestnik Moskovskogo Universiteta. Seriya Biologii, Pochvovedeniya, Geologii, Geografii

Vest Mosk Univ Ser 15 Vychisl Mat Kibern — Vestnik Moskovskogo Universiteta. Seriya 15. Vychislitel'naya Matematika i Kibernetika [*USSR*]

Vestn Akad Med Nauk SSSR — Vestnik Akademii Meditsinskikh Nauk SSSR

Vestn Akad Nauk Belorussk SSR Ser Obsc Nauk — Vestnik Akademii Nauk Belorusskoj SSR. Serija Obscestvennyh Nauk

Vestn Akad Nauk Kazah SSR — Vestnik Akademii Nauk Kazahskoj SSR

Vestn Akad Nauk Kazakh SSR — Vestnik Akademiya Nauk Kazakhskoi SSR

Vestn Akad Nauk Kaz SSR — Vestnik Akademii Nauk Kazakhskoi SSR

Vestn Akad Nauk SSSR — Vestnik Akademii Nauk SSSR

Vest Nauchno-Issled Inst Pchel — Vestnik Nauchno-Issledovatel'skii Institut Pchelovodstva

Vestn Beloruss Gos Univ Ser 1 — Vestnik Belorusskogo Gosudarstvennogo Universiteta. Seriya 1. Matematika, Fizika, Mekhanika

Vestn Beloruss Gos Univ Ser 2 Biol Khim Geol Geogr — Vestnik Belorusskogo Gosudarstvennogo Universiteta. Seriya 2. Biologiya, Khimiya, Geologiya, Geografiya

Vestn Beloruss Univ — Vestnik Belorusskogo Universiteta

Vestn Cesk Akad Zemed — Vestnik Ceskoslovenske Akademie Zemedelske

Vestn Cesk Akad Zemed Ved — Vestnik Ceskoslovenske Akademie Zemedelskych Ved

Vestn Ceskoslov Akad Zemed Ved — Vestnik Ceskoslovenske Akademie Zemedelskych Ved

Vestn Cesk Spol Zool — Vestnik Ceskoslovenske Spolecnosti Zoologicke

Vestn Chkal Otd Vses Khim O-va Im D I Mendeleeva — Vestnik Chkalovckogo Otdeleniya Vsesoyuznogo Khimicheskogo Obshchestva Imeni D. I. Mendeleeva

Vestn Dermatol Venerol — Vestnik Dermatologii i Venerologii

Vestn Drevnej Istor — Vestnik Drevnej Istorii. Revue d'Histoire Ancienne

Vestn Drevn Ist — Vestnik Drevnei Istorii

Vestn Elektroprom-sti — Vestnik Elektropromyshlennosti [*USSR*]

Vestn Elektrotekh — Vestnik Elektrotekhniki

Vestn Gos Muz Gruz — Vestnik Gosudarstvennogo Muzeja Gruzii

Vestn Gosud Muz Gruzii — Vestnik Gosudarstvennogo Muzeja Gruzii Imeni Akademika S. N. Dzhanashia

Vestn Gruz Bot Ova — Vestnik Gruzinskogo Botanicheskogo Obshchestva

Vestnik Akad Nauk Kazah SSR — Vestnik Akademii Nauk Kazahskoj SSR

Vestnik Akad Nauk Kazakh SSR — Vestnik Akademii Nauk Kazakhskoi SSR

Vestnik Akad Nauk SSSR — Vestnik Akademii Nauk SSSR

Vestnik Beloruss Gos Univ Ser 1 — Vestnik Belorusskogo Gosudarstvennogo Universiteta Imeni V. I. Lenina. Naucnyi Zurnal. Seriya 1. Matematika, Fizika, Mekhanika

Vestnik Har'kov Gos Univ — Vestnik Har'kovskogo Gosudarstvennogo Universiteta

Vestnik Har'kov Politehn Inst — Vestnik Har'kovskogo Politehniceskogo Instituta
Vestnik Karakalpak Fil Akad Nauk UzSSR — Akademija Nauk UzSSR. Karakalpakskii Filial. Vestnik
Vestnik K Ceske Spolec Nauk v Praze Trida Mat Prirod — Vestnik Kralovske Ceske Spolecnosti Nauk v Praze Trida Matematicko Prirodovedecka
Vestnik Leningrad Univ Fiz Him — Vestnik Leningradskogo Universiteta. Fizika i Himija
Vestnik Leningrad Univ Fiz Khim — Vestnik Leningradskogo Universiteta. Fizika i Khimiya
Vestnik Leningrad Univ Math — Vestnik Leningrad University. Mathematics
Vestnik Leningrad Univ Mat Mekh Astronom — Vestnik Leningradskogo Universiteta. Matematika, Mekhanika, Astronomiya
Vestnik Leningrad Univ Ser Fiz Khim — Vestnik Leningradskogo Universiteta. Seriya Fiziki i Khimii
Vestnik Leningr Gosud Univ — Vestnik Leningradskogo Gosudarstvennogo Universiteta
Vestnik L'vov Politehn Inst — Vestnik L'vovskogo Politehniceskogo Instituta
Vestnik Mikrobiol i Epidemiol — Vestnik Mikrobiologii i Epidemiologii
Vestnik Mikrobiol Epidemiol i Parazitol — Vestnik Mikrobiologii, Epidemiologii, i Parazitologii
Vestnik Moskov Univ Ser III Fiz Astronom — Vestnik Moskovskogo Universiteta. Serija III. Fizika, Astronomija
Vestnik Moskov Univ Ser I Mat Meh — Vestnik Moskovskogo Universiteta. Serija I. Matematika, Mehanika
Vestnik Moskov Univ Ser XV Vycisl Mat Kibernet — Vestnik Moskovskogo Universiteta. Serija XV. Vycislitel'naja Matematika i Kibernetika
Vestnik Mosk Univ Ser Khim — Vestnik Moskovskogo Universiteta. Seriya 2. Khimiya
Vestnik Obsh Vet (S Peterburg) — Vestnik Obshchestvennoi Veterinarii (S. Peterburg)
Vestnik Rentg i Radiol — Vestnik Rentgenologii i Radiologii
Vestnik Sovrem Vet — Vestnik Sovremennoi Veterinarii
Vestnik Statist — Vestnik Statistiki
Vestnik Ustredniho Ustavu Geol — Vestnik Ustredniho Ustavu Geologickeho
Vestn Inzh Tekh — Vestnik Inzhenerov i Tekhnikov [*USSR*]
Vestn Jaroslav Univ — Vestnik Jaroslavskogo Universiteta
Vestn Kabard Balkar Nauc-Issled Inst — Vestnik Kabardino-Balkarskogo Naucno-Issledovatel'skogo Instituta
Vestn Karakalp Fil Akad — Vestnik Karakalpakskogo Filiala Akademii Nauk Uzbekskoi SSR
Vestn Karakalp Fil Akad Nauk Uzb SSR — Vestnik Karakalpakskogo Filiala Akademii Nauk Uzbekskoi SSR
Vestn Kaz Fil Akad Nauk SSSR — Vestnik Kazakhskogo Filiala Akademii Nauk SSSR
Vestn Khar'k Politekh Inst — Vestnik Khar'kovskogo Politekhnicheskogo Instituta [*Ukrainian SSR*]
Vestn Khark Univ — Vestnik Khar'kovskogo Universiteta
Vestn Khar'k Univ Astron — Vestnik Khar'kovskogo Universiteta. Astronomiya [*Ukrainian SSR*]
Vestn Khar'k Univ Geol Geogr — Vestnik Khar'kovskogo Universiteta. Geologiya i Geografiya [*Ukrainian SSR*]
Vestn Khar'k Univ Ser Biol — Vestnik Khar'kovskogo Universiteta. Seriya Biologicheskaya
Vestn Khar'k Univ Ser Geol — Vestnik Khar'kovskogo Universiteta. Seriya Geologicheskaya [*Ukrainian SSR*]
Vestn Khar'k Univ Ser Khim — Vestnik Khar'kovskogo Universiteta. Seriya Khimicheskaya
Vestn Khar'k Univ Vopr Ehlektrokhim — Vestnik Khar'kovskogo Universiteta. Voprosy Ehlektrokhimii
Vestn Khir — Vestnik Khirurgii Imeni I. I. Grekova
Vestn Khir Im I I Grekova — Vestnik Khirurgii Imeni I. I. Grekova
Vestn Kiev Politekh Inst Ser Mashinostr — Vestnik Kievskogo Politekhnicheskogo Instituta. Seriya Mashinostroeniya
Vestn Kiev Politekh Inst Ser Priborostr — Vestnik Kievskogo Politekhnicheskogo Instituta. Seriya Priborostroeniya
Vestn Kiev Politekh Inst Ser Teploenerg — Vestnik Kievskogo Politekhnicheskogo Instituta. Seriya Teploenergetiki
Vestn Kral Ceske Spol Nauk Trida Mat Prirodoved — Vestnik Kralovske Ceske Spolecnosti Nauk Trida Matematicko Prirodovedecka
Vestn La Upr Metallopromsti — Vestnik Lavnogo Upravleniya Metallopromyshlennosti
Vestn Leningrad Univ Ser Biol — Vestnik Leningradskogo Universiteta. Seriya Biologii
Vestn Leningr Univ — Vestnik Leningradskogo Universiteta
Vestn Leningr Univ Biol — Vestnik Leningradskogo Universiteta. Biologiya
Vestn Leningr Univ Fiz & Khim — Vestnik Leningradskogo Universiteta. Fizika i Khimiya
Vestn Leningr Univ Geol Geogr — Vestnik Leningradskogo Universiteta. Geologiya, Geografiya
Vestn Leningr Univ Ist Jaz Lit — Vestnik Leningradskogo Universiteta. Istorija, Jazyka, i Literatury
Vestn Leningr Univ Mat Mekh Astron — Vestnik Leningradskogo Universiteta. Matematika, Mekhanika, Astronomiya
Vestn Leningr Univ Ser Ekon Filos Pravo — Vestnik Leningradskogo Universiteta. Serija Ekonomiki, Filosofii, i Pravo

Vestn Leningr Univ Ser Fiz Khim — Vestnik Leningradskogo Universiteta. Seriya Fiziki i Khimi [*USSR*]
Vestn Leningr Univ Ser Geol Geogr — Vestnik Leningradskogo Universiteta. Seriya Geologii i Geografii [*USSR*]
Vestn Leningr Univ Ser Mat Fiz Khim — Vestnik Leningradskogo Universiteta. Seriya Matematiki, Fiziki, i Khimii
Vestn Leningr Univ Ser Mat Mekh & Astron — Vestnik Leningradskogo Universiteta. Seriya Matematika, Mekhanika, i Astronomiya
Vestn Lening Univ Ser Biol Geogr Geol — Vestnik Leningradskogo Universiteta. Seriya Biologii, Geografii, i Geologii
Vestn L'viv Derzh Univ Ser Fiz — Vestnik L'vivs'kogo Derzhavnogo Universitetu. Seriya Fizichna [*Ukrainian SSR*]
Vestn Mashinostr — Vestnik Mashinostroeniya
Vestn Metallopromsti — Vestnik Metallopromyshlennosti
Vestn Minist Zdrav — Vestnik Ministerstva Zdravotnictvi [*Czechoslovakia*]
Vestn Moskovskogo Univ Fiz-Astron — Vestnik Moskovskogo Universiteta. Seriya Fizika-Astronomiya
Vestn Moskovskogo Univ Khim — Vestnik Moskovskogo Universiteta. Seriya Khimiya
Vestn Moskov Univ Ser 6 — Vestnik Moskovskogo Universiteta. Seriya 6
Vestn Moskov Univ Ser Ekon — Vestnik Moskovskogo Universiteta. Seriya Ekonomika
Vestn Moskov Univ Ser Filos — Vestnik Moskovskogo Universiteta. Seriya Filosofija
Vestn Moskov Univ Ser Geogr — Vestnik Moskovskogo Universiteta. Serija Geografija
Vestn Moskov Univ Ser Ist — Vestnik Moskovskogo Universiteta. Serija Istorija
Vestn Moskov Univ Ser Pravo — Vestnik Moskovskogo Universiteta. Serija Pravo
Vestn Moskov Univ Teorija Nauc Kommunizma — Vestnik Moskovskogo Universiteta Teorija Naucnogo Kommunizma
Vestn Mosk Univ — Vestnik Moskovskogo Universiteta
Vestn Mosk Univ Biol Pochvoved — Vestnik Moskovskogo Universiteta. Biologiya, Pochvovedenie
Vestn Mosk Univ Fiz Astron — Vestnik Moskovskogo Universiteta. Fizika, Astronomiya
Vestn Mosk Univ Geogr — Vestnik Moskovskogo Universiteta. Geografiya
Vestn Mosk Univ Geol — Vestnik Moskovskogo Universiteta. Geologiya
Vestn Mosk Univ Khim — Vestnik Moskovskogo Universiteta. Khimiya
Vestn Mosk Univ Mat Mekh — Vestnik Moskovskogo Universiteta. Matematika, Mekhanika
Vestn Mosk Univ Ser 1 — Vestnik Moskovskogo Universiteta. Seriya 1. Matematika, Mekhanika
Vestn Mosk Univ Ser 3 — Vestnik Moskovskogo Universiteta. Seriya 3. Fizika, Astronomiya
Vestn Mosk Univ Ser 15 — Vestnik Moskovskogo Universiteta. Seriya 15. Vychislitel'naya Matematika i Kibernetika
Vestn Mosk Univ Ser 16 Biol — Vestnik Moskovskogo Universiteta. Seriya 16. Biologiya
Vestn Mosk Univ Ser 6 Biol Pochvoved — Vestnik Moskovskogo Universiteta. Seriya 6. Biologiya, Pochvovedenie
Vestn Mosk Univ Ser Biol Pochvoved Geol Geogr — Vestnik Moskovskogo Universiteta. Seriya Biologii, Pochvovedeniya, Geologii, Geografii
Vestn Mosk Univ Ser 3 Fiz Astron — Vestnik Moskovskogo Universiteta. Seriya 3. Fizika, Astronomiya
Vestn Mosk Univ Ser Fiz-Mat Estestv Nauk — Vestnik Moskovskogo Universiteta. Seriya Fiziko-Matematicheskikh i Estestvennykh Nauk [*USSR*]
Vestn Mosk Univ Ser 5 Geogr — Vestnik Moskovskogo Universiteta. Seriya 5. Geografiya
Vestn Mosk Univ Ser 4 Geol — Vestnik Moskovskogo Universiteta. Seriya 4. Geologiya
Vestn Mosk Univ Ser II — Vestnik Moskovskogo Universiteta. Nauchnyj Zhurnal. Seriya II. Khimiya
Vestn Mosk Univ Ser 2 Khim — Vestnik Moskovskogo Universiteta. Seriya 2. Khimiya
Vestn Mosk Univ Ser 1 Mat Mekh — Vestnik Moskovskogo Universiteta. Seriya 1. Matematika, Mekhanika
Vestn Mosk Univ Ser Mat Mekh Astron Fiz Khim — Vestnik Moskovskogo Universiteta. Seriya Matematiki, Mekhaniki, Astronomii, Fiziki, Khimii
Vestn Mosk Univ Ser 17 Pochvved — Vestnik Moskovskogo Universiteta. Seriya 17. Pochvovedenie
Vestn Mosk Univ Ser 16 Ser Biol — Vestnik Moskovskogo Universiteta. Seriya 16. Seriya Biologiia
Vestn Mosk Univ Ser 15 Vychisl Mat Kibern — Vestnik Moskovskogo Universiteta. Seriya 15. Vychislitel'naya Matematika i Kibernetika
Vestn Nauchn Inf Zabaik Fil Geogr Ova SSSR — Vestnik Nauchnoi Informatsii Zabaikal'skogo Filiala Geograficheskogo Obshchestva SSSR
Vestn Nauchno-Issled Inst Gidrobiol (Dnepropetr) — Vestnik Nauchno-Issledovatel'skogo Instituta Gidrobiologii (Dnepropetrovski)
Vestn Obsc Nauk Akad Nauk Arm SSR — Vestnik Obscestvennyh Nauk. Akademija Nauk Armjanskoj SSR
Vestn Oftal'mol — Vestnik Oftal'mologii
Vestn ORL — Vestnik Oto-Rino-Laringologii
Vestn Otorinolaringol — Vestnik Otorinolaringologii

Vestn Protivovozdushnoi Oborony — Vestnik Protivovozdushnoi Oborony
Vestn Rentgenol Radiol — Vestnik Rentgenologii i Radiologii
Vestn Respub Inst Okhr Prir Estestvennonauchn Muz Titograde — Vestnik Respublikanskogo Instituta za Okhranu Prirodyi Estestvennonauchnogo Muzeya v Titograde
Vestn Sel'skokhoz Nauki (Alma-Ata) — Vestnik Sel'skokhozyaistvennoi Nauki (Alma-Ata)
Vestn Sel'skokhoz Nauki (Moscow) — Vestnik Sel'skokhozyaistvennoi Nauki (Moscow)
Vestn S-kh Nauki (Alma-Ata) — Vestnik Sel'skokhozyaistvennoi Nauki (Alma-Ata) [*Kazakh SSR*]
Vestn S-Kh Nauki Kaz — Vestnik Sel'skokhozyaistvennoi Nauki Kazakhstana. Ezhemesiachnyi Nauchnyi Zhurnal
Vestn S-kh Nauki (Mosc) — Vestnik Sel'skokhozyaistvennoi Nauki (Moscow)
Vestn Slov Kem Drus — Vestnik Slovenskega Kemijskega Drustva
Vestn Sots Rastenievod — Vestnik Sotsialisticheskogo Rastenievodstva
Vestn Stand — Vestnik Standartizatsii
Vestn Statis — Vestnik Statistiki
Vestn Statist — Vestnik Statistiki
Vestn Statniho Geol Ustavu Cesk Repub — Vestnik Statniho Geologickiho Ustavu Ceskoslovenske Republiky
Vestn Stud Nauchn Ova Kazan Gos Univ Estestv Nauki — Vestnik Studencheskogo Nauchnogo Obshchestva Kazanskii Gosudarstvennyi Universitet Estestvennye Nauki
Vestn Tbilis Bot Sada Akad Nauk Gruz SSR — Vestnik Tbilisskogo Botanicheskogo Sada Akademii Nauk Gruzinskoi SSR
Vestn Uradu Vynalezy Objevy — Vestnik Uradu pro Vynalezy a Objevy
Vestn Uradu Vynalezy Objevy Cast A Vynalezy — Vestnik Uradu pro Vynalezy a Objevy. Cast A. Vynalezy
Vestn Uradu Vynalezy Objevy Cast B Ochr Znamky Prum Vzory — Vestnik Uradu pro Vynalezy a Objevy. Cast B. Ochranne Znamky. Prumyslovy Vzory
Vestn Uradu Vynalezy Objevy Ochr Znamky Prum Vzory — Vestnik Uradu pro Vynalezy a Objevy. Ochranne Znamky. Prumyslovy Vzory
Vestn Uradu Vynalezy Objevy Vynalezy — Vestnik Uradu pro Vynalezy a Objevy. Vynalezy
Vestn USSR Acad Med Sci — Vestnik. USSR Academy of Medical Science
Vestn Ustred Ustavu Geol — Vestnik Ustredniho Ustavu Geologickeho
Vestn Vyssh Shk — Vestnik Vysshej Shkoly
Vestn Vyzk Ustavu Zemed — Vestnik Vyzkumnych Ustavu Zemedelskych
Vestn Zapadno Sib Geol Upr — Vestnik Zapadno-Sibirskogo Geologicheskogo Upravleniya
Vestn Zapadno Sib i Novosib Geol Upr — Vestnik Zapadno-Sibirskogo i Novosibirskogo Geologicheskikh Upravlenii
Vestn Zashch Rast — Vestnik Zashchity Rastenii
Vestn Zool — Vestnik Zoologii
Vestn Zool Zool Rec — Vestnik Zoologii/Zoological Record
Vest Oftal (Kiev) — Vestnik Oftal'mologii (Kiev)
Vest Oftal (Mosk) — Vestnik Oftal'mologii (Moskva)
Vest Oto-rino-lar — Vestnik Otorinolaringologii
Vest Sel'-khoz Nauki (Alma-Ata) Minist Sel Khoz Kazakh SSR — Vestnik Sel'skokhozyaistvennoi Nauki (Alma-Ata). Ministerstvo Sel'skogo Khozyaistva Kazakhskoi SSR
Vest Sel-Khoz Nauki (Mosk) — Vestnik Sel'skokhozyaistvennoi Nauki (Moskva) [*USSR*]
Vestsi Akad Navuk BSSR Ser Khim Navuk — Vestsi Akademii Navuk Belaruskai SSR. Khimichnykh Navuk
Vestsi Akad Navuk BSSR Ser — Vestsi Akademii Navuk Belaruskai SSR. Seriya
Vestsi Akad Navuk BSSR Ser Biyal Navuk — Vestsi Akademii Navuk Belaruskai SSR. Seryya Biyalagichnykh Navuk
Vestsi Akad Navuk BSSR Ser Fiz-Ehnerg Navuk — Vestsi Akademii Navuk BSSR. Seryya Fizika-Ehnergetychnykh Navuk
Vestsi Akad Navuk BSSR Ser Fiz-Mat — Vestsi Akademii Navuk BSSR. Seriya Fizika-Matematicheskikh
Vestsi Akad Navuk BSSR Ser Fiz-Mat Navuk — Vestsi Akademii Navuk BSSR. Seryya Fizika-Matematychnykh Navuk
Vestsi Akad Navuk BSSR Ser Fiz-Tekh Navuk — Vestsi Akademii Navuk BSSR. Seryya Fizika-Tekhnichnykh Navuk
Vestsi Akad Navuk BSSR Ser Gramadskikh Navuk — Vestsi Akademii Navuk BSSR. Seryya Gramadskikh Navuk [*Belorussian SSR*]
Vestsi Akad Navuk BSSR Ser Khim — Vestsi Akademii Navuk BSSR. Seriya Khimicheskikh [*USSR*]
Vestsi Akad Navuk BSSR Ser Khim Navuk — Vestsi Akademii Navuk Belaruskai SSR. Seryya Khimichnykh Navuk
Vestsi Akad Navuk BSSR Ser Sel'skagas Navuk — Vestsi Akademii Navuk Belaruskai SSR. Seryya Sel'skagaspadar Navuk
Vestsi Belarus Akad Navuk Ser Biyal Navuk — Vestsi Belaruskaya Akademiya Navuk. Seryya Biyalagichnykh Navuk
Vestsyi Akad Navuk BSSR Ser Fyiz-Ehnerg Navuk — Vestsyi Akademhyiyi Navuk BSSR. Seryya Fyizyika-Ehnergetychnykh Navuk
Vestsyi Akad Navuk BSSR Ser Fyiz-Mat Navuk — Vestsyi Akademhyiyi Navuk BSSR. Seryya Fyizyika-Matehmatychnykh Navuk
Vestsyi Akad Navuk BSSR Ser Fyiz-Tehkh Navuk — Vestsyi Akademhyiyi Navuk BSSR. Seryya Fyizyika-Tehkhnyichnykh Navuk

Vestsyi Akad Navuk BSSR Ser Khyim Navuk — Vestsyi Akademhyiyi Navuk BSSR. Seryya Khyimyichnykh Navuk
Vest Ustred Ust Geol — Vestnik Ustredniho Ustavu Geologickeho
Vest Zool — Vestnik Zoologii
Veszpremi Vegyip Egy Tud Ulesszakanak Eloadasai — Veszpremi Vegyipari Egyetem Tudomanyos Ulesszakanak Eloadasai [*Hungary*]
Veszprem Megyei Muz — Veszprem Megyei Muzeumok Koezlemenyei
Veszprem Megyei Muz Koezlem — Veszprem Megyei Muzeumok Koezlemenyei
Veszprmi Vegyip Egy Kozl — Veszpremi Vegyipari Egyetem Kozlemenyei
Vet — Veterinaria
Vet Anesth — Veterinary Anesthesia
Vet Annu — Veterinary Annual
Vet Arh — Veterinarski Arhiv
Vet Bull — Veterinary Bulletin
Vet Bull (London) — Veterinary Bulletin (London)
Vet Bull (Weybridge Eng) — Veterinary Bulletin (Weybridge, England)
Vet Cas (Kosice) — Veterinarsky Casopis (Kosice)
VetChr — Vetera Christianorum
Vet Clin North Am — Veterinary Clinics of North America
Vet Clin North Am (Large Anim Pract) — Veterinary Clinics of North America (Large Animal Practice)
Vet Clin North Am (Small Anim Pract) — Veterinary Clinics of North America (Small Animal Practice)
Vetensk Publ Tek Hoegsk Helsingfors — Vetenskapliga Publikationer. Tekniska Hoegskolan i Helsingfors
Vetensk Soc i Lund Arsbok — Vetenskaps-Societeten i Lund. Aarsbok
Ve Tes — Vetus Testamentum
Vet Espan — Veterinaria Espanola
Vet Glas — Veterinarski Glasnik
Vet Hist — Veterinary History Bulletin. Veterinary History Society
Vet Hum Toxicol — Veterinary and Human Toxicology
Vet Immunol Immunopathol — Veterinary Immunology and Immunopathology
Vet Insp Annu Inst Vet Insp NSW — Veterinary Inspector Annual. Institute of Veterinary Inspectors of New South Wales
Vet Ital — Veterinaria Italiana
Vet J — Veterinary Journal
Vet J and Ann Comp Path — Veterinary Journal and Annals of Comparative Pathology
Vet J (Bratislava) — Veterinary Journal (Bratislava)
Vet Mag — Veterinary Magazine
Vet Med — Veterinarni Medicina
Vet Med — Veterinary Medicine
Vet Med — Veterinary Medicine and Small Animal Clinician
Vet Med Nauki — Veterinarno Meditsinski Nauki
Vet Med Nauki (Sofia) — Veterinarno Meditsinski Nauki (Sofia)
Vet Med (Prague) — Veterinarni Medicina (Prague)
Vet Med (Praha) — Veterinarni Medicina (Praha)
Vet Med/SAC — Veterinary Medicine and Small Animal Clinician
Vet Med Sci — Veterinary Medical Science
Vet Med Small Anim Clin — Veterinary Medicine and Small Animal Clinician
Vet Med & Small Anim Clin — Veterinary Medicine and Small Animal Clinician
Vet Microbiol — Veterinary Microbiology [*Netherlands*]
Vet News — Veterinary News
Vet Obozr — Veterinarnoe Obozrienie
Vet Parasitol — Veterinary Parasitology
Vet Path — Veterinary Pathology
Vet Pathol — Veterinary Pathology
Vet Pathol (Suppl) — Veterinary Pathology. Supplement
Vet QQJ Vet Sci — Veterinary Quarterly. Quarterly Journal of Veterinary Science
Vet Radiol — Veterinary Radiology
Vet Rec — Veterinary Record
Vet Resp Mezhved Temat Nauchn Sb — Veterinariya Respublikanskii Mezhvedomstvennyi Tematicheskii Nauchnyi Sbornik
Vet Resp Mizhvid Temat Nauk Zb — Veterinariya Respublikanskyu Mizhvidomchyi Tematychnyi Naukovyi Zbirnyk
Vet Rev — Veterinary Review
Vetro Silic — Vetro e Silicati
VetSb — Veterinarna Sbirka
Vet Sb (Bratislava) — Veterinarsky Sbornik (Bratislava)
Vet Sbirka — Veterinarna Sbirka
Vet Sbir (Sof) — Veterinarna Sbirka (Sofia)
Vet Sb (Sofia) — Veterinarna Sbirka (Sofia)
Vet Sci Commun — Veterinary Science Communications
Vet Stars — Vets Stars and Stripes for Peace
Vet Surg — Veterinary Surgery
Vet Test — Vetus Testamentum
Vet Toxicol — Veterinary Toxicology
Vet Urug — Veterinaria Uruguay
Vetus Test — Vetus Testamentum
Vet World — Veterinary World
Vet Zh (Bratislava) — Veterinarnyi Zhurnal (Bratislava)
VEV — Verre Oosten. Orgaan van de Landenkamers Verre Oosten

Vezelinst TNO Delft VI Pam — Vezelinstituut TNO [*Nederlands Centrale Organisatie voor Toegepast-Natuurwetenschappelijk Onderzoek*] Delft VI Pamflet
Vezetestud — Vezetestudomany
VF — De Vrije Fries
VF — Verkuendigung und Forschung [*Munich*]
VF — Vilagirodalmi Figyelo
VF — Voprosy Filologii
VF — Voprosy Filosofii
VFB — Vierteljahrschrift fuer Bibelkunde, Talmudische, und Patristische Studien
VFCBA9 — Forests Commission Victoria. Bulletin
VFDBA — VFDB [*Vereinigung zur Foerderung des Deutschen Brandschutzes eV*] Zeitschrift
VFDB (Ver Foerd Dtch Brandschutzes) Z — VFDB (Vereinigung zur Foerderung des Deutschen Brandschutzes eV) Zeitschrift
VFDB Z — Vereinigung zur Foerderung des Deutschen Brandschutzes. Zeitschrift
VFFM — Vestlandets Forstilige Forsoksstasjon. Meddelelse
VFG — Visual Flight Guide
VFHG — Versammlungen der Freunde des Humanistischen Gymnasiums
VFil — Voprosy Filologii
VFR — Victorian Fiction Research Guides
VFSSMCQ — Victorian Federation of State Schools Mothers Clubs. Quarterly Review
VFSW — Vierteljahrsschrift fuer Sozial- und Wirtschaftsgeschichte
V & G — Vergangenheit und Gegenwart
VGEBA — Verhandlungen. Geologische Bundesanstalt (Austria)
VGIEMTP — Veroeffentlichungen. Grabmann Institut zur Erforschung der Mittelalterlichen Theologie und Philosophie
VGJ — Vorgeschichtliches Jahrbuch
VGLKV — Vierteljahrsschrift fuer Geschichte und Landeskunde Vorarlbergs
VGLL — Valstybine Grozines Literaturos Leidykla
VGP — Victorian Government Publications
VGQ — Vocational Guidance Quarterly
VGTSA — Voprosy Gigieny Truda v Slantsevoi Promyshlennosti Estonskoi SSR
VH — Vermont History
VHFS — Videnskabernes Selskabs Historisk-Filologiske Skrifter
VHis — Vida Hispanica
VHJ — Victorian Historical Journal
VHM — Victorian Historical Magazine
VHSKA — Vital and Health Statistics. Series 11 [*United States*]
VHVNB — Verhandlungen. Historischer Verein von Niederbayern
VHVOR — Verhandlungen. Historischer Verein von Oberpfalz und Regensburg
Vi — Viator
VI — Viol
V & I — Voix et Images. Etudes Quebecoises
VI — Voprosy Istorii
Viata Med — Viata Medicala. Revista a Unuinii Societatelor de Stiinte Medicale din Republica Socialista [*Romania*]
Viata Med (Buchar) — Viata Medicala (Bucharest)
Viata Med (Medii Sanit) — Viata Medicala. Revista de Informare Profesionala se Stiintifica a Cadrelor (Medii Sanitare)
Viator Med — Viator. Medieval and Renaissance Studies
VIBJ — Virgin Islands Bar Journal
Vib Spectra Struct — Vibrational Spectra and Structure
Vic Assn Teach Eng J — Victorian Association for the Teaching of English. Journal
Vic Bar News — Victorian Bar News
Vic CC — County Court Reports (Victoria)
Vic Chamber of Manufactures Econ Serv — Victorian Chamber of Manufactures. Economic Service
Vic Chap News — Victorian Chapter Newsletter [*Australian College of Education*]
Vic Comm Teach Assn General J — Victorian Commercial Teachers' Association. General Journal
Vic Comput — Vic Computing
Vic Conf Soc Welfare Proc — Victorian Conference of Social Welfare. Proceedings
Vic Creditman — Victorian Creditman
Vic Dairyfarmer — Victorian Dairyfarmer
Vic Dep Agric Tech Bull — Victoria. Department of Agriculture. Technical Bulletin
Vic Ed Gaz — Education Gazette and Teachers Aid (Victoria)
Vic Elec Contractor — Victorian Electrical Contractor
Vic Employers' Federation AR — Victorian Employers' Federation. Annual Report
Vicenza Econ — Vicenza Economica
Vic For Comm Bull — Victoria. Forests Commission. Bulletin
Vic Geogr J — Victorian Geographical Journal
Vic Govt Gaz — Victorian Government Gazette
Vic Hist Mag — Victorian Historical Magazine
Vic Hortic Dig — Victorian Horticultural Digest
Vic Inst Coll News — Victoria Institute of Colleges. Newsletter

Vic Legal Exec — Victorian Legal Executive
Vic LSAJ — Victorian LSA [*Limbless Soldiers' Association*] Journal
VicN — Victorian Naturalist
Vic Nat — Victorian Naturalist
Vic Naturalist — Victorian Naturalist
VIC News — Victoria Institute of Colleges. Newsletter
Vic Parl Deb — Victorian Parliamentary Debates
Vic Parl Parl Deb — Victoria. Parliament. Parliamentary Debates
Vic Poultry J — Victorian Poultry Journal
Vic Railways Newsletter — Victorian Railways Newsletter
Vic Resour — Victoria's Resources
Vic Resources — Victoria's Resources
Vic Rev — Victorian Review
Vic Stat Pub — Victorian Statistics Publications
Vict — Victorian Reports
Vict Cancer News — Victorian Cancer News
Vict Dairyfmr — Victorian Dairyfarmer
Vic Teachers J — Victorian Teachers Journal
Vic Teach J — Victorian Teachers Journal
Vict For Comm Bull — Victoria. Forests Commission. Bulletin
Vict For Comm For Tech Pap — Victoria. Forests Commission. Forestry Technical Paper
Vict For Comm Misc Publ — Victoria. Forests Commission. Miscellaneous Publication
Vict Geogr J — Victorian Geographical Journal
Vict Geol Surv Bull — Victoria. Geological Survey. Bulletin
Vict Geol Surv Mem — Victoria. Geological Survey. Memoirs
Vict Hist Mag — Victorian Historical Magazine
Vict Hort Dig — Victorian Horticultural Digest
Vict LJ — Victorian Law Journal
Vict LR — Victorian Law Reports
Vict LT — Victorian Law Times
Vict Nat — Victorian Naturalist
Vict Naturalist — Victorian Naturalist
Vict Newsl — Victorian Newsletter
Victoria Country Roads Board Eng Note — Victoria. Country Roads Board. Engineering Note
Victoria Country Roads Board Tech Bull — Victoria. Country Roads Board. Technical Bulletin
Victoria Dep Agric Res Proj Ser — Victoria. Department of Agriculture. Research Project Series
Victoria Dep Agric Tech Bull — Victoria. Department of Agriculture. Technical Bulletin
Victoria Dep Agric Tech Rep Ser — Victoria. Department of Agriculture. Technical Report Series
Victoria Fish Wildl Dep Fish Contrib — Victoria. Fisheries and Wildlife Department. Fisheries Contribution [*Australia*]
Victoria Fish Wildl Dep Wildl Contrib — Victoria. Fisheries and Wildlife Department. Wildlife Contribution
Victoria Geol Bull — Victoria. Geological Survey. Bulletin
Victoria Geol Surv Mem — Victoria. Geological Survey. Memoirs
Victoria Inst Tr — Victoria Institute or Philosophical Society of Great Britain. Journal of the Transactions
Victoria Inst (Trinidad) Pr — Victoria Institute (Trinidad). Proceedings
Victoria Mines Dep Annu Rep — Victoria. Mines Department. Annual Report
Victoria Mines Dep Groundwater Invest Program Rep — Victoria. Mines Department. Groundwater Investigation Program. Report [*Australia*]
Victoria Minist Conserv Environ Stud Program Proj Rep — Victoria. Ministry for Conservation. Environmental Studies Program. Project Report
Victorian Entomol — Victorian Entomologist
Victorian Hist J — Victorian Historical Journal
Victorian Hist Mag — Victorian Historical Magazine
Victorian Nat — Victorian Naturalist
Victorian Natl Parks Assoc J — Victorian National Parks Association. Journal
Victorian Railw — Victorian Railways
Victorian Stud — Victorian Studies
Victoria's Resour — Victoria's Resources
Victoria State Rivers Water Supply Comm Annu Rep — Victoria. State Rivers and Water Supply Commission. Annual Report
Victoria Univ Antarct Data Ser — Victoria University of Wellington. Antarctic Data Series [*New Zealand*]
Vict Poet — Victorian Poetry
Vict Poetry — Victorian Poetry
Vict Rep — Victorian Reports
Vict Rep (Austr) — Victorian Reports (Australian)
Vict Rep (Eq) — Victorian Reports (Equity)
Vict Rep (Law) — Victorian Reports (Law)
Vict Res — Victoria's Resources
Vict Resour — Victoria's Resources
Vict Rev — Victorian Review
Vict Soil Conserv Auth TC — Victoria. Soil Conservation Authority. TC Report
Vict Soil Conserv Auth TC Rep — Victoria. Soil Conservation Authority. TC Report
Vict Stud — Victorian Studies
Vict U C L Rev — Victoria University. College Law Review
Vict U of Wellington L Rev — Victoria University of Wellington. Law Review

Vict U Well L Rev — Victoria University of Wellington. Law Review
Vict Vet Proc — Australian Veterinary Association. Victorian Division. Annual General Meeting. Proceedings
Vict Vet Proc — Australian Veterinary Association. Victorian Division. Victorian Veterinary Proceedings
Vic Veg Grower — Victorian Vegetable Grower
Vic Vet Proc — Victorian Veterinary Proceedings
Vic Yrbk — Victoria Yearbook
VID — Vidipress Nieuwsbrief
VID — Vspomogatel'nye Istoricheskie Distsipliny
Vida Agr — Vida Agricola
VidaL — Vida Literaria
Vida Med — Vida Medica
Videnskabs-Selsk Christiana Forh — Videnskabs-Selskabet i Christiania. Forhandlingar
Vidensk Medd Dan Naturhist Foren — Videnskabelige Meddelelser fra Dansk Naturhistorisk Forening
Vidensk Medd Dan Naturhist Foren Khobenhavn — Videnskabelige Meddelelser fra Dansk Naturhistorisk Forening i Khobenhavn
Video — Video-Tronics
Video Syst — Video Systems
Vide Tech-Appl — Vide. Technique-Applications [France]
VIDSL — Veroeffentlichungen. Institut fuer Deutsche Sprache und Literatur. Deutsche Akademie der Wissenschaften zu Berlin
VIDV — Veroeffentlichungen. Institut fuer Deutsche Volkskunde. Deutsche Akademie der Wissenschaften zu Berlin
Vidya B — Vidya. Section B. Sciences
Vidya Bhar — Vidya Bharati [Bangalore]
Vie Acad Acad Sci (Paris) — Vie Academique. Academie des Sciences (Paris)
Vie Agric et Rurale — Vie Agricole et Rurale
Vie Econ (Berne) — Vie Economique (Berne)
Vie Med — Vie Medicale
Vie Med Can Fr — Vie Medicale au Canada Francais
Vie Milie A — Vie et Milieu. Serie A. Biologie Marine
Vie Milie B — Vie et Milieu. Serie B. Oceanographie
Vie Milie C — Vie et Milieu. Serie C. Biologie Terrestre
Vie Milieu Ser A — Vie et Milieu. Serie A. Biologie Marine [France]
Vie Milieu Ser A Biol Mar — Vie et Milieu. Serie A. Biologie Marine
Vie Milieu Ser B Oceanogr — Vie et Milieu. Serie B. Oceanographie
Vie Milieu Ser C Biol Terr — Vie et Milieu. Serie C. Biologie Terrestre
Vie Mus — Vie Musicale
Vie Mus Belge — Vie Musicale Belge
Vienna Circle Coll — Vienna Circle Collection
VIER Bul — Victorian Institute of Educational Research. Bulletin
VIER Bull — Victorian Institute of Educational Research. Bulletin
Vierteljahreschr Gerichtl Med Oeff Sanitaetswes — Vierteljahrschrift fuer Gerichtliche Medizin und Oeffentliches Sanitaetswesen
Vierteljahrsschr Prakt Pharm — Vierteljahrschrift fuer Praktische Pharmazie
Vierteljahrsschr Naturforsch Ges (Zuer) — Vierteljahrsschrift. Naturforschende Gesellschaft (Zuerich)
Vierteljahrsschr Naturforsch Ges (Zuerich) — Vierteljahrsschrift. Naturforschende Gesellschaft (Zuerich)
Vierteljahrsschr f Wiss Philos — Vierteljahrsschrift fuer Wissenschaftliche Philosophie und Soziologie
Viert Naturf Ges Zuerich — Vierteljahrschrift der Naturforschenden Gesellschaft in Zuerich
Vier Zeitg — Vierteljahrshefte fuer Zeitgeschichte
Vie Sci Econ — Vie et Sciences Economiques
Vie et Sciences Econs — Vie et Sciences Economiques
Vie Soc — Vie Sociale
Viet Stud — Vietnamese Studies [Hanoi]
Vie Wallonne — La Vie Wallonne. Revue Mensuelle Illustree
View Bot — View from the Bottom
Vieweg Tracts Pure Appl Phys — Vieweg Tracts in Pure and Applied Physics
Viewpoints Biol — Viewpoints in Biology
Viewpoint Ser Aust Conserv Fdn — Viewpoint Series. Australian Conservation Foundation
Viewpoints Teach & Learn — Viewpoints in Teaching and Learning
Views & R — Views and Reviews
VIG — Vojnoistoriski Glasnik
Vig C — Vigiliae Christianae
Vig Chr — Vigiliae Christianae
Viitor Soc — Viitorul Social
VIJ — Vishveshvaranand Indological Journal
Vik — Viking. Norsk Arkeologisk Selskap
Viking Fund Publ Anthropol — Viking Fund Publication in Anthropology
VIK Mitt — VIK [Vereinigung Industrielle Kraftwirtschaft] Mitteilungen
Vikram Quart Res J Vikram University — Vikram. Quarterly Research Journal of Vikram University
V I Lenin Sakharth Politekh Inst Samecn Srom — V. I. Leninis Sahelobis Sromis Citheli Drosis Ordenosani Sakharthvelos Politekhnikuri Instituti. Samecniero Sromebi
Villanova L Rev — Villanova Law Review
Vill L Rev — Villanova Law Review
Vil V — Village Voice

VIMBA — Veroeffentlichungen. Institut fuer Meeresforschung in Bremerhaven
Vin — Vinduet
Vina Q — Vina Quarterly
Vinar Obz — Vinarsky Obzor
VIndJ — Vishveshvaranand Indological Journal
Vingt Siecle Feder — Vingtieme Siecle Federaliste
Vinifera Wine Grow J — Vinifera Wine Growers Journal
Vini Ital — Vini d'Italia
Vinodel Vinograd SSSR — Vinodelie i Vinogradarstvo SSSR
Vinograd Plodovod (Budapest) — Vinogradarstvo i Plodovodstvo (Budapest)
Vinograd Vinar (Budapest) — Vinogradarstvo i Vinarstvo (Budapest)
Vinograd Vinorobstvo — Vinogradarstvo i Vinorobstvo
Vinyls Polym — Vinyls and Polymers [Japan]
VIO — Veroeffentlichungen. Institut fuer Orientforschung. Deutsche Akademie der Wissenschaften zu Berlin
VIODAWB — Deutsche Akademie der Wissenschaften zu Berlin. Institut fuer Orientforschung. Veroeffentlichungen
VIP — Voix et Images du Pays [University of Quebec]
ViPe — Vita e Pensiero [Milan]
ViR — Viata Romaneasca [Bucharest]
Vir — Virittaja. Kotikielen Seuran Aikakauslehti [Helsinki]
Vir — Virittaja. Revue de Kotikielen Seura
VIR — Virtuoso
VIRA — Voprosy Istorii Religii i Ateizma. Sbornik Statei [Moscow]
Virc Arch A — Virchows Archiv. A. Pathological Anatomy and Histology
Virc Arch B — Virchows Archiv. B. Cell Pathology
Virchows Arch Abt A — Virchows Archiv. Abteilung A. Pathologische Anatomie
Virchows Arch Abt A Pathol Anat — Virchows Archiv. Abteilung A. Pathologische Anatomie
Virchows Arch Abt B — Virchows Archiv. Abteilung B. Zellpathologie
Virchows Arch Abt B Zellpathol — Virchows Archiv. Abteilung B. Zellpathologie
Virchows Arch A Pathol Anat Histol — Virchows Archiv. A. Pathological Anatomy and Histology
Virchows Arch B Cell Pathol — Virchows Archiv. B. Cell Pathology
Virchows Arch Path Anat — Virchows Archiv fuer Pathologische Anatomie
Virchows Arch Pathol Anat Physiol Klin Med — Virchows Archiv fuer Pathologische Anatomie und Physiologie und fuer Klinische Medizin
Virginia Div Mineral Rsources Rept Inv — Virginia. Division of Mineral Resources. Report of Investigations
Virginia Jour Sci — Virginia Journal of Science
Virginia J Sci — Virginia Journal of Science
Virginia Med Month — Virginia Medical Monthly [Later, Virginia Medical]
Virginia Polytech Inst Research Div Bull — Virginia Polytechnic Institute. Research Division. Bulletin
Virginia Polytech Inst Research Div Mon — Virginia Polytechnic Institute. Research Division. Monograph
Virginia Q R — Virginia Quarterly Review
Virg J Int'l L — Virginia Journal of International Law
Virol — Virology
Virol Abstr — Virology Abstracts
Virol Monogr — Virology Monographs
Vir Q R — Virginia Quarterly Review
VIRS — Veroeffentlichungen. Institut fuer Romanische Sprachwissenschaft. Deutsche Akademie der Wissenschaften zu Berlin
Virus Res — Virus Research
VIS — Veroeffentlichungen. Institut fuer Slawistik. Deutsche Akademie zu Berlin
VIs — Voprosy Istorii [Moscow]
Vis Aids News — Visual Aids News
Vis Aids Rev — Visual Aids Review
Visbl Lang — Visible Language
VISCA Rev Visayas State Coll Agric — VISCA Review. Visayas State College of Agriculture
Vis Educ — Visual Education
Vish Indo J — Vishveshvaranand Indological Journal [Hoshiarpur]
Visible Lang — Visible Language
Vis Ind — Vision Index
Visindafelag Isl Rit — Visindafelag Islendinga Rit
Vision Res — Vision Research
VISl — Veroeffentlichungen. Institut fuer Slawistik. Deutsche Akademie der Wissenschaften zu Berlin
Visn Akad Nauk Ukr RSR — Visnyk Akademiyi Nauk Ukrayins'koyi RSR
Visnik Kiiv Univ Ser Mat Meh — Visnik Kiivs'kogo Universitetu. Serija Matematiki ta Mehaniki
Visnik Kiiv Univ Ser Mat Mekh — Visnik Kiivs'kogo Universitetu. Seriya Matematiki ta Mekhaniki
Visnik L'viv Derz Univ Ser Meh-Mat — Visnik L'vivs'kogo Ordena Lenina Derzavogo Universitetu Imeni Ivana Franka. Serija Mehaniko-Matematicna
Visnik L'viv Politehn Inst — Visnik L'vivs'kogo Politehnicnogo Institutu
Visn Kharkiv Univ Astron — Visnik Kharkivs'kogo Universitetu. Astronomiya [Ukrainian SSR]

Visn Kharkiv Univ Radiofiz — Visnik Kharkivs'kogo Universitetu. Radiofizika [*Ukrainian SSR*]
Visn Kharkiv Univ Radiofiz Elektron — Visnik Kharkivs'kogo Universitetu. Radiofizika i Elektronika [*Ukrainian SSR*]
Visn Kiiv Politekh Inst Ser Khim Mashinobuduv Teknol — Visnik Kiivs'kogo Politekhnichnogo Institutu. Seriya Khimichnogo Mashinobuduvannya ta Tekhnologii [*Ukrainian SSR*]
Visn Kiiv Univ Ser Astron — Visnik Kiivs'kogo Universitetu. Seriya Astronomii [*Ukrainian SSR*]
Visn Kiiv Univ Ser Astron Fiz Khim — Visnik Kiivs'kogo Universitetu. Seriya Astronomii, Fiziki, ta Khimii
Visn Kiiv Univ Ser Biol — Visnik Kiivs'kogo Universitetu. Seriya Biologii [*Ukrainian SSR*]
Visn Kiiv Univ Ser Fiz — Visnik Kiivs'kogo Universitetu. Seriya Fiziki
Visn Kiiv Univ Ser Fiz Khim — Visnik Kiivs'kogo Universitetu. Seriya Fiziki ta Khimii [*Ukrainian SSR*]
Visn Kiiv Univ Ser Geol Geogr — Visnik Kiivs'kogo Universitetu. Seriya Geologii ta Geografii
Visn Kiiv Univ Ser Khim — Visnik Kiivs'kogo Universitetu. Seriya Khimii [*Ukrainian SSR*]
Visn Kiyiv Univ Ser Fiz — Visnik Kiyivs'kogo Universitetu. Seriya Fizika [*Ukrainian SSR*]
Visn Kyyiv Univ Ser Biol — Visnyk Kyyivs'koho Universytetu. Seriya Biolohiyi
Visn L'viv Derzh Univ Ser Biol — Visnik L'vivs'kogo Derzhavnogo Universitetu. Seriya Biologichna
Visn L'viv Derzh Univ Ser Fiz — Visnik L'vivs'kii Derzhavnii Universitet Imeni Ivana Franka. Seriya Fizichna [*Ukrainian SSR*]
Visn L'viv Derzh Univ Ser Fiz — Visnik L'vivs'kogo Derzhavnogo Universitetu. Seriya Fizichna
Visn L'viv Derzh Univ Ser Geol — Visnik L'vivs'kogo Derzhavnogo Universitetu. Seriya Geologichna
Visn L'viv Derzh Univ Ser Khim — Visnik L'vivs'kogo Derzhavnogo Universitetu Imeni Ivana Franka. Seriya Khimichna [*Ukrainian SSR*]
Visn L'viv Derzh Univ Ser Khim — Visnik L'vivs'kogo Derzhavnogo Universitetu. Seriya Khimichna
Visn L'viv Univ Ser Biol Heohr — Visnyk L'vivs'koho Universytetu. Seriya Biolohiyi, Heohrafiyi, ta Heolohiyi
Visn L'viv Univ Ser Biol Heohr Heol — Visnyk L'vivs'koho Universytetu. Seriya Biolohiyi, Heohrafiyi, ta Heolohiyi
Visn Sil-hospod Nauky — Visnyk Sil's'ko-hospodars'koyi Nauky
Visn Sil's'kohospod Nauki — Visnyk Sil's'kohospodars'koy Nauki
Visn Sil's'kohospod Nauky — Visnyk Sil's'kohospodars'koyi Nauky
Visn Tsentr Resp Bot Sad Akad Nauk Ukr RSR — Visnik Tsentral'nii Respublikans'kii Botanichnii Sad Akademiya Nauk Ukrains'koi RSR
Visnyk Akad Nauk Ukr RSR — Visnyk Akademiyi Nauk Ukrayins'koyi RSR
Vissh Inst Arkhit Stroit Sofiya God — Vissh Institut po Arkhitektura i Stroitelstvo-Sofiya. Godishnik
VISSI — Visindafelag Islendinga. Societas Scientiarum Islandica
Vistas Astron — Vistas in Astronomy
Vistas Astronaut — Vistas in Astronautics
Vistas Bot — Vistas in Botany
Vistas Volunt — Vistas for Volunteers
Visti Akad Nauk Ukr RSR — Visti Akademii Nauk Ukrains'koi RSR
Visti Inst Fiz Khim Akad Nauk Ukr RSR — Visti Institutu Fizichnoi Khimii Akademiya Nauk Ukrains'koi RSR
Visti Ukr Nauk Dosl Inst Fiz Khim — Visti Ukrains'kogo Naukovo Doslidchogo Institutu Fizichnoi Khimii
Visual Aids R — Visual Aids Review
Visual Com — Studies in Visual Communication
Visual Ed — Visual Education
Visual Med — Visual Medicine
Visual Sonic Med — Visual Sonic Medicine
VIT — Vital Speeches of the Day
Vita — Vita. Revue Bimensuelle. Confederation de l'Alimentation Belge
Vita Hum — Vita Humana
Vita Int — Vita International
Vita Ital — Vita Italiana
Vital C — Vital Christianity
Vital Health Stat 1 — Vital and Health Statistics. Series 1. Programs and Collection Procedures [*Unied States*]
Vital Health Stat 2 — Vital and Health Statistics. Series 2. Data Evaluation and Methods Research [*United States*]
Vital Health Stat 3 — Vital and Health Statistics. Series 3. Analytical Studies [*United States*]
Vital Health Stat 4 — Vital and Health Statistics. Series 4. Documents and Committee Reports [*United States*]
Vital Health Stat 10 — Vital and Health Statistics. Series 10. Data from the National Health Survey [*United States*]
Vital Health Stat 11 — Vital and Health Statistics. Series 11. Data from the National Health Survey [*United States*]
Vital Health Stat 13 — Vital and Health Statistics. Series 13. Data from the National Health Survey [*United States*]
Vital Health Stat 14 — Vital and Health Statistics. Series 14. Data on National Health Resources [*United States*]
Vital Health Stat 20 — Vital and Health Statistics. Series 20. Data from the National Vital Statistics System [*United States*]

Vital Health Stat 21 — Vital and Health Statistics. Series 21. Data from the National Vital Statistics System [*United States*]
Vital Health Stat 23 — Vital and Health Statistics. Series 23. Data from the National Survey of Family Growth [*United States*]
Vital Health Statist Ser 2 Data Evaluation Methods Res — Vital and Health Statistics. Series 2. Data Evaluation and Methods Research
Vital Speeches — Vital Speeches of the Day
Vital Speeches Day — Vital Speeches of the Day
Vitalstoffe — Vitalstoffe Zivilisationskrankheiten
Vitalst Zivilisationskr — Vitalstoffe Zivilisationskrankheiten
Vitam D Dig — Vitamin D Digest
Vitam Eksp Klin — Vitaminy v Eksperimente i Klinike
Vitam Horm — Vitamins and Hormones
Vita Mon — Vita Monastica
Vitam Resur Ikh Ispol'z — Vitaminnye Resursy i Ikh Ispol'zovanie
Vitams Horm — Vitamins and Hormones
Vitic Arboric — Viticulture, Arboriculture
Vitic Enol (Budapest) — Viticulture and Enology (Budapest)
Viti-Vinic (Budapest) — Viti-Viniculture (Budapest)
Viv — Vivarium
VIVI — Vivienda [*Mexico*]
VIY — Visserij. Voorlichtingsblad voor de Nederlandse Visserij
Vizgazdalkodasi Tud Kut Intez Tanulmanyok Kut Eredmenyek — Vizgazdalkodasi Tudomanyos Kutato Intezet Tanulmanyok es Kutatasi Eredmenyek
Vizugyi Kozl — Vizugyi Kozlemenyek
Vizugyi Kozlem — Vizugyi Kozlemenyek
VizV — Vizantiiskii Vremenik
VJ — Vassar Journal of Undergraduate Studies
VJ — Voprosy Jazykoznanija [*Lvov*]
VJa — Voprosy Jazykoznanija [*Moscow*]
VJaL — Voprosy Jazyka i Literatury
Vjber — Vierteljahresberichte
Vjesn Bibliot Hrv — Vjesnik Bibliotekara Hrvatske
Vjhber Probl Entwickllaend — Vierteljahresberichte Probleme der Entwicklungslaender
Vjhefte Zeitgesch — Vierteljahrshefte fuer Zeitgeschichte
Vjh Wirtsch-Forsch — Vierteljahreshefte zur Wirtschaftsforschung
Vjh Zeitgesch — Vierteljahreshefte fuer Zeitgeschichte
VJLB — Veterans Jewish Legion. Bulletin
Vjschr Naturf Ges (Zuerich) — Vierteljahrsschrift. Naturforschende Gesellschaft (Zuerich)
Vjschr Soz- und Wirtschaftsgesch — Vierteljahrschrift fuer Sozial- und Wirtschaftsgeschichte
VJWPh — Vierteljahrsschrift fuer Wissenschaftliche Philosophie
VK — Vedanta Kesari [*Mylapore*]
VK — Voelkische Kultur
VK — Volkskrant
VKAW — Verhandelingen. Koninklijke Akademie van Wetenschappen
VKC — Tijdschrift voor Vervoerswetenschap
VKCSN — Vestnik Kralovske Ceske Spolecnosti Nauk
VKF — Voprosy Klassicekoj Filologii
VKFLA — Voprosy Kurortologii, Fizioterapii, i Lechebnoi Fizicheskoi Kul'tury
VKL — Verhandelingen. Koninklijke Akademie van Wetenschappen. Letterkunde [*Elsevier Book Series*]
VKN — Verhandelingen. Koninklijke Akademie van Wetenschappen. Natuurkunde [*Elsevier Book Series*]
VKNA — Verhandelingen. Koninklijke Nederlandse Akademie van Wetenschappen. Afdeling Letterkunde
VKNAL — Verhandelingen. Koninklijke Nederlandse Akademie van Wetenschappen. Afdeling Letterkunde
VKNAW — Verhandelingen. Koninklijke Nederlandse Akademie van Wetenschappen
VKR — Volkstum und Kultur der Romanen
VKR — Voprosy Kul'tury Reci
VKS — Vlees en Vleeswaren
VKyjU — Visnyk Kyjivs'koho Universytetu
VL — Deutsche Vierteljahrsschrift fuer Literaturwissenschaft und Geistesgeschichte
VL — Vetenskaps-Societeten i Lund
V & L — Vie et Langage
VL — Voprosy Literatury
VLa — Vie et Langage
Vlaams Diergeneeskd Tijdschr — Vlaams Diergeneeskundig Tijdschrift
Vlaams Diergeneesk Tijdschr — Vlaams Diergeneeskundig Tijdschrift
Vladimir Gos Ped Inst Ucen Zap — Vladimirskii Gosudarstvennyi Pedagogiceskii Institut Imeni P. I. Lebedeva-Poljanskogo. Ucenyi Zapiski
Vladimir Vecer Politehn Inst Sb Naucn Trudov — Vladimirskii Vecernyi Politehniceskii Institut. Sbornik Naucnyh Trudov
Vladivost Med Inst Sb Nauchn Tr — Vladivostokskii Meditsinskii Institut. Sbornik Nauchnykh Trudov
V Lang — Visible Language
VLD — Victorian Licensing Decisions
VLE — Victorian Legal Executive
V Lenin Fiz — Vestnik Leningradskogo Universiteta. Seriya Fiziki i Khimii

V Lenin Mek — Vestnik Leningradskogo Universiteta. Seriya Matematiki i Mekhaniki
VLenU — Vestnik Leningradskogo Gosudarstvennogo Universiteta
VLF — Installatie
VLG — Vlaamse Gids
VLIB — Valodas un Literaturas Instituta Biletens
VLIR — Valodas un Literaturas Instituta Raksti
VLit — Voprosy Literatury
Vliyanie Rab Sred Svoistva Mater — Vliyanie Rabochikh Sred na Svoistva Materialov
VLJaTas — Voprosy Literaturovedenija i Jazykoznanija (Tasent)
VLONAB — Agricultural Research Reports [*Wageningen*]
VLR — Vanderbilt Law Review
VLR — Victorian Law Reports
VLR — Virginia Law Review
VLR (Adm) — Victorian Law Reports (Admiralty)
VLR (E) — Victorian Law Reports (Equity)
VLR (Eq) — Victorian Law Reports (Equity)
VLR (IP & M) — Victorian Law Reports (Insolvency, Probate, and Matrimonial)
VLR (L) — Victorian Law Reports (Law)
VLR (M) — Victorian Law Reports (Mining)
VLR (P & M) — Victorian Law Reports (Probate and Matrimonial)
VLS — Village Voice. Literary Supplement
VLS — Voice Literary Supplement
VLT — Victorian Law Times
VLU — Vestnik Leningradskogo Gosudarstvennogo Universiteta
VLU — Vestnik Leningradskogo Universiteta. Seriya Istorii, Jazyka, i Literatury
VLUist — Vestnik Leningradskogo Gosudarstvennogo Universiteta
VLvivU — Visnyk L'vivs'koho Derzavnoho Universytetu
VLVM — Vlastivedny Vestnik Moravsky
VM — Verslagen en Mededeelingen
VMarJa — Voprosy Marijskogo Jazykoznanija
VMAW — Verslagen en Mededeelingen. Koninklijke Akademie van Wetenschappen
VMB — Vandringar Med Boeker
VMDKA — Voprosy Meditsinskoi Khimii
VMHB — Virginia Magazine of History and Biography
VMI — Meubel. Weekblad voor de Meubelindustrie, Meubelhandel, Woninginrichting, en Toeleveringsbedrijven
VMKA — Verslagen en Mededeelingen. Koninklijke Akademie voor Nederlandse Taal- en Letterkunde
VMKVA — Verslagen en Mededeelingen. Koninklijke Vlaamse Akademie voor Taal- en Letterkunde
VMMMA — Vestnik Moskovskogo Universiteta. Seriya 1. Matematika, Mekhanika
VMMOA — Virginia Medical Monthly [*Later, Virginia Medical*]
VMOGA — Vestnik Moskovskogo Universiteta. Seriya 5. Geografiya
V Mosk Fiz — Vestnik Moskovskogo Universiteta. Seriya Fiziki i Astronomii
V Mosk Mekh — Vestnik Moskovskogo Universiteta. Seriya Matematiki i Mekhaniki
V Mosk U Kh — Vestnik Moskovskogo Universiteta. Seriya Khimiya
VMSDA — Vysokomolekulyarnye Soedineniya
VMU — Vestnik Moskovskogo Gosudarstvennogo Universiteta
VMUBA — Vestnik Moskovskogo Universiteta. Seriya 6. Biologiya, Pochvovedenie
VMUFA — Vestnik Moskovskogo Universiteta. Seriya 3. Fizika, Astronomiya
VMUGA — Vestnik Moskovskogo Universiteta. Seriya 4. Geologiya
VMUist — Vestnik Moskovskogo Gosudarstvennogo Universiteta
VMUKA — Vestnik Moskovskogo Universiteta. Seriya 2. Khimiya
VMUZh — Vestnik Moskovskogo Universiteta Zhurnalistika
VMVBORG — Verslagen en Mededeelingen van de Vereeniging tot Beoefening van Overijsselsch Recht en Geschiedenis
VMVOVR — Verslagen en Mededeelingen van de Vereeniging tot Uitgaaf van der Bronnen van het Oud-Vaderlandsche Recht
V Mw — Vierteljahrsschrift fuer Musikwissenschaft
VN — Victorian Newsletter
VNAWAG — Koninklijke Nederlandse Akademie van Wetenschappen. Verhandelingen. Afdeling Natuurkunde. Tweede Reeks
VND — Vprasanja Nasih Dni
Vnesn Torg — Vnesnjaja Torgovlja
VNFH — Vjesnik Narodnog Fronta Hrvatske
VNGGA — Verhandelingen. Koninklijke Nederlands Geologisch Mijnbouwkundig Genootschap. Geologische Serie
Vnitr Lek — Vnitrni Lekarstvi
VNL — Victorian Newsletter
VNL — Vrij Nederland
VNM — Tijdschrift van de Vereeniging voor Nederlandse Muziekgeschiedenis
VNRN — Vladimir Nabokov Research Newletter
VNS — Bondsspaarbanken
VNZ — Schweizerische Handelskammer in den Niederlanden. Mitteilungen an die Mitglieder
VO — Vesnjani Orbriji [*Kyjiv*]
VO — Voice
Vo — Voices

VOA — Voorlichter
VOC — VM. Voorlichtingsblad van het Ministerie van Volksgezondheid en Milieuhygiene
Voc Aspect Ed — Vocational Aspect of Education
Vocat Guid — Vocational Guidance Quarterly
Vocational Aspect — Vocational Aspect of Education
Vocat Training — Vocational Training
VocEd Insider — VocEd Business and Office Insider. Journal of the American Vocational Association
Voc Educ — Vocational Education
Voc Educ M — Vocational Education Magazine
Voc Guid Q — Vocational Guidance Quarterly
Vodn Hospod — Vodni Hospodarstvi
Vodn Hospod Rada B — Vodni Hospodarstvi. Rada B
Vodni Hospod — Vodni Hospodarstvi
Vodni Hospod A — Vodni Hospodarstvi. Rada A [*Czechoslovakia*]
Vodni Hospod Rada B — Vodni Hospodarstvi. Rada B
Vodn Resur — Vodnye Resursy [*USSR*]
Vodohospod Cas — Vodohospodarsky Casopis
Vodopodgot Ochistka Prom Stokov — Vodopodgotovka i Ochistka Promyshlennykh Stokov
Vodorosli Griby Sib Dal'nego Vostoka — Vodorosli i Griby Sibiri i Dal'nego Vostoka
Vodosnabzh Kanaliz Gidrotekh Sooruzh — Vodosnabzhenie Kanalizatsiya Gidrotekhnicheskie Sooruzheniya
Vodosnabzh Sanit Tekh — Vodosnabzhenie i Sanitarnaya Tekhnika
Vodos Sanit Tekhn — Vodosnabzhenie i Sanitarnaya Tekhnika
Voedingsmiddelen Technol — Voedingsmiddelen Technologie
VOEI — Veroeffentlichungen. Osteuropa-Institut
Voen Khim — Voennaya Khimiya
Voen Med Delo — Voenno Meditsinsko Delo
Voen Med Fak Sarat Medinst Sb Nauchn Tr — Voenno-Meditsinskii Fakul'tet pri Saratovskom Medinstitute. Sbornik Nauchnykh Trudov
Voen-Med Zh — Voenno-Meditsinskii Zhurnal
Voenna Tekh — Voenna Tekhnika [*Bulgaria*]
Voenno-Ist Zhurnal — Voenno-Istoricheskii Zhurnal
Voenno-Med Zh — Voenno-Meditsinskii Zhurnal
Voenno Med Zhurnal (Leningrad) — Voenno-Meditsinskii Zhurnal (Leningrad)
Voenno-Med Zhurnal (S Peterburg) — Voenno-Meditsinskii Zhurnal (S. Peterburg)
Voen Sanit Delo — Voenno-Sanitarnoe Delo
Voen Vest — Voennyi Vestnik [*USSR*]
Voen Znaniya — Voennye Znaniya [*USSR*]
Vog Liv — Vogue Living
VOH — Grootkeuken. Voedingsblad voor Instellingen en Bedrijven
VOIB — Veroeffentlichungen. Abteilung fuer Slavische Sprachen und Literaturen. Osteuropa-Institut [*Slavisches Seminar*]. Freie Universitaet Berlin
Voice — Village Voice
Voith Forsch Konstr — Voith Forschung und Konstruktion
Voith Res & Constr — Voith Research and Construction
VOIZD — Voice of Z-39
Vojen Zdrav Listy — Vojenske Zdravotnicke Listy
Vojnoekon Pregl — Vojnoekonomski Pregled [*Yugoslavia*]
Vojnosanit Pregl — Vojnosanitetski Pregled
VOK — Volkskrant
VOKS — Soviet Union Society for Cultural Relations with Foreign Countries. Weekly News Bulletin
VOLAD — Voice of the Lakes
Volcani Inst Agric Res Div For Ilanot Leafl — Volcani Institute of Agricultural Research. Division of Forestry. Ilanot Leaflet
Volcani Inst Agric Res Div Sci Publ Pam — Volcani Institute of Agricultural Research. Division of Scientific Publications. Pamphlet
Volcanol Bull Jpn Meterol Agency — Volcanological Meteorological Bulletin. Japan Meteorological Agency
Volcanol Soc Jap Bull — Volcanological Society of Japan. Bulletin
Vol Effort Q — Voluntary Effort Quarterly
Vol Feeding Mgt — Volume Feeding Management
Volgograd Gos Ped Inst Ucen Zap — Volgogradskogo Gosudarstvennogo Pedagogiceskogo Instituta Imeni A. S. Serafimovica Ucenye Zapiski
Volksmus — Volksmusik. Zeitschrift fuer das Musikalische Laienschaffen
Volkstum Landschaft — Volkstum und Landschaft. Heimatblaetter der Muensterlaendische Tageszeitung
Volleyball Mag — Volleyball Magazine
Volleyball Tech J — Volleyball Technical Journal
Vologod Gos Ped Inst Ucen Zap — Vologodskii Gosudarstvennyi Pedagogiceskii Institut. Ucenye Zapiski
Vologod I Cerepovec Gos Ped Inst Ucen Zap — Vologodskii Gosudarstvennyi Pedagogiceskii Institut. Cerepoveckii Gosudarstvennyi Pedagogiceskii Institut. Ucenye Zapiski
Vo LR — Villanova Law Review
VOLRA — Volta Review
Volta R — Volta Review
Volt Electr Trade Mon — Volt. Electrical Trade Monthly [*Japan*]
Volunt Action — Voluntary Action
Volunt Action Leadersh — Voluntary Action Leadership

Volunt Adm — Volunteer Administration
Volunt Forum Abs — Voluntary Forum Abstracts
Volunt Housing — Voluntary Housing
Volunt Leader — Volunteer Leader
Volz Mat Sb — Volzskii Matematiceskii Sbornik
VON — Vestnik Otdelenija Obscestvennych Nauk. Akademija Nauk Gruzinskoj SSR
VONEA — Voprosy Neirokhirurgii
Von Roll Mitt — Von Roll Mitteilungen
Voorlichting Onderz — Voorlichting en Onderzoek
Vop Bot Akad Nauk Litov SSR Inst Bot — Voprosy Botaniki. Akademiya Nauk Litovski SSR. Institut Botaniki
Vop Erozii Povysh Prod Sklon Zemel' Moldavii — Voprosy Erozii i Povysheniya Produktivnosti Sklonovykh Zemel' Moldavii
Vop Fil — Voprosy Filosofii
Vop Genez Krypnomashtabn Kartir Pochv Kazan Univ — Voprosy Genezisa i Krypnomashtabnoi Kartirovanii Pochv Kazanskii Universitet
Vop Geogr Mordovsk ASSR — Voprosy Geografii Mordovskoi ASSR
VopIst — Voprosy Istorii
Vop Med Kh — Voprosy Meditsinskoi Khimii
Vop Mikrobiol Akad Nauk Armyan SSR — Voprosy Mikrobiologii. Akademiya Nauk Armyanskoi SSR
Vop Pitan — Voprosy Pitaniya
Vop Psikhol — Voprosy Psikhologii
Vopr Antropol — Voprosy Antropologii
Vopr At Nauki Tekh Ser Fiz Plazmy Probl Upr Termodad Reakts — Voprosy Atomnoi Nauki i Tekhniki. Seriya Fizika Plazmy i Problemy Upravlyaemykh Termodadernykh Reaktsii [*Ukrainian SSR*]
Vopr At Nauki Tekh Ser Fiz Vys Energ At Yadra — Voprosy Atomnoi Nauki i Tekhniki. Seriya Fizika Vysokikh Energii i Atomnogo Yadra [*Ukrainian SSR*]
Vopr At Nauki Tekh Ser Obshch Yad Fiz — Voprosy Atomnoi Nauki i Tekhniki. Seriya Obshchaya i Yadernaya Fizika [*Ukrainian SSR*]
Vopr At Nauki Tekh Ser Radiats Tekh — Voprosy Atomnoi Nauki i Tekhniki. Seriya Radiatsionnaya Tekhnika
Vopr At Nauki Tekh Ser Yad Konstanty — Voprosy Atomnoi Nauki i Tekhniki. Seriya Yadernye Konstanty
Vopr Bezopasn Ugol'n Shakhtakh — Voprosy Bezopasnosti v Ugol'nykh Shakhtakh
Vopr Biokhim — Voprosy Biokhimii
Vopr Biokhim Mozga — Voprosy Biokhimii Mozga
Vopr Biokhim Nervn Myshechnoi Sist — Voprosy Biokhimii Nervnoi i Myshechnoi Sistem [*Georgian SSR*]
Vopr Biokhim Nervn Sist — Voprosy Biokhimii Nervnoi Sistemy
Vopr Biol — Voprosy Biologii
Vopr Biol Kraev Med — Voprosy Biologii i Kraevoi Meditsiny
Vopr Bor'by Silikozom Sib — Voprosy Bor'by s Silikozom v Sibiri
Vopr Cenoobraz — Voprosy Cenoobrazovanija
Vopr Din Prochn — Voprosy Dinamiki i Prochnosti
Vopr Din Teor Rasprostr Seism Voln — Voprosy Dinamicheskoi Teorii Rasprostraneniya Seismicjeskikh Voln [*USSR*]
Vopr Dozim Zasch Izluch Mosk Inzh Fiz Inst Sb Statei — Voprosy Dozimetrii i Zaschity ot Izluchenii. Moskovskii Inzhenerno Fizicheskii Institut Sbornik Statei [*USSR*]
Vopr Dozim Zashch Izluch — Voprosy Dozimetrii i Zashchity ot Izluchenii
Vopr Ekol Biotsenol — Voprosy Ekologii i Biotsenologii
Vopr Ekon — Voprosy Ekonomiki
Vopr Eksp Klin Radiol — Voprosy Eksperimental'noi i Klinicheskoi Radiologii [*Ukrainian SSR*]
Vopr Endokrinol Obmena Veshchestv Resp Mezhved Sb — Voprosy Endokrinologii Obmena Veshchestvennyi Respublikanskoi Mezhvedomstvennyi Sbornik
Vopr Erozii Povysh Prod Sklonovykh Zemel Mold — Voprosy Erozii i Povysheniya Produktivnosti Sklonovykh Zemel' Moldavii
Vopr Etiol Patog Opukholei — Voprosy Etiologii i Patogeneza Opukholei
Vopr Filos — Voprosy Filosofii
Vopr Fiz Gorn Porod — Voprosy Fiziki Gornykh Porod
Vopr Fiziol Akad Nauk Azerb SSR Sekt Fiziol — Voprosy Fiziologii Akademiya Nauk Azerbaidzhanskoi SSR. Sektor Fiziologii [*Azerbaidzhan SSR*]
Vopr Fiziol Biokhim Kul't Rast — Voprosy Fiziologii i Biokhimii Kul'turnykh Rastenii
Vopr Fiziol Biokhim Zool Parazitol — Voprosy Fiziologii, Biokhimii, Zoologii, i Parazitologii
Vopr Fiziol Chel Zhivotn — Voprosy Fiziologii Cheloveka i Zhivotnykh
Vopr Fiziol Rast Mikrobiol — Voprosy Fiziologii Rastenii i Mikrobiologii
Vopr Fiz Tverd Tela — Voprosy Fiziki Tverdogo Tela
Vopr Fiz Zasch Reaktorov — Voprosy Fiziki Zaschity Reaktorov [*USSR*]
Vopr Fiz Zashch Reakt — Voprosy Fiziki Zashchity Reaktorov
Vopr Fotosint — Voprosy Fotosinteza
Vopr Gazotermodin Energoustanovok — Voprosy Gazotermodinamiki Energoustanovok [*Ukrainian SSR*]
Vopr Gematol Pereliv Krovi Krovozamenitelei — Voprosy Gematologii Perelivaniya Krovi i Krovozamenitelei
Vopr Geogr — Voprosy Geografii
Vopr Geogr Dal'nego Vostoka — Voprosy Geografii Dal'nego Vostoka

Vopr Geogr Kaz — Voprosy Geografii Kazakhstana
Vopr Geogr Mordov ASSR — Voprosy Geografii Mordovskoi ASSR
Vopr Geokhim Tipomorfizm Miner — Voprosy Geokhimii i Tipomorfizm Mineralov
Vopr Geol Buren Neft Gazov Skvazhin — Voprosy Geologii i Bureniya Neftyanykh i Gazovykh Skvazhin
Vopr Geol Metallog Kol'sk Poluostrova — Voprosy Geologii i Metallogenii Kol'skogo Poluostrova
Vopr Geol Metod Razved Zolota — Voprosy Geologii i Metodiki Razvedki Zolota
Vopr Geol Mineral Rudn Mestorozhd Ukr — Voprosy Geologii i Mineralogii Rudnykh Mestorozhdenii Ukrainy
Vopr Geol Neftegazonosn Uzb — Voprosy Geologii i Neftegazonosnosti Uzbekistana
Vopr Geol Neftenosn Sredn Povolzh'ya — Voprosy Geologii i Neftenosnosti Srednego Povolzh'ya
Vopr Geol Tadzh — Voprosy Geologii Tadzhikistana
Vopr Geol Uzb — Voprosy Geologii Uzbekistana
Vopr Geol Vost Okrainy Russ Platformy Yuzhn Urala — Voprosy Geologii Vostochnoi Okrainy Russkoi Platformy i Yuzhnogo Urala
Vopr Geol Yuzhn Urala Povolzh'ya — Voprosy Geologii Yuzhnogo Urala i Povolzh'ya
Vopr Geomorfol Geol Bashk — Voprosy Geomorfologii i Geologii Bashkirii
Vopr Gerontol Geriatr — Voprosy Gerontologii i Geriatrii
Vopr Gidrodin Teploobmena Kriog Sist — Voprosy Gidrodinamiki i Teploobmena v Kriogennykh Sistemakh
Vopr Gidrogeol Inzh Geol Ukr — Voprosy Gidrogeologii i Inzhenernoi Geologii Ukrainy
Vopr Gidrol — Voprosy Gidrologii
Vopr Gidrotekh — Voprosy Gidrotekhniki
Vopr Gig Pitan — Voprosy Gigieny Pitaniya
Vopr Gig Tr Profpatol Prom Toksikol — Voprosy Gigieny Truda Profpatologii i Promyshlennoi Toksikologii
Vopr Gig Tr Slants Promsti Est SSR — Voprosy Gigieny Truda v Slantsevoi Promyshlennosti Estonskoi SSR
Vopr Ikhtiol — Voprosy Ikhtiologii
Vopr Immunol — Voprosy Immunologii
Vopr Infekts Patol Immunol — Voprosy Infektsionnoi Patologii i Immunologii
Vopr Inf Teor Prakt — Voprosy Informatsionnoi Teorii i Praktiki
Vopr Introd Rast Zelenogo Stroit — Voprosy Introduktsii Rastenii i Zelenogo Stroitel'stva
Vopr Inzh Geol Gruntoved — Voprosy Inzhenernoi Geologii i Gruntovedeniya
Vopr Inzh Seismol — Voprosy Inzhenernoi Seismologii [*USSR*]
Vopr Issled Ispol'z Pochv Mold — Voprosy Issledovaniya i Ispol'zovaniya Pochvovedeniya Moldavii
Vopr Issled Lessovykh Gruntov Osn Fundam — Voprosy Issledovaniya Lessovykh Gruntov Osnovanii i Fundamentov
Vopr Ist — Voprosy Istorii
Vopr Ist KPSS — Voprosy Istorii KPSS [*Kommunisticheskaya Partiya Sovietskogo Soyuza*]
Vopr Istor — Voprosy Istorii
Vopr Istor Estestvozn Tekh — Voprosy Istorii Estestvoznaniya i Tekhniki
Vopr Ist Udm — Voprosy Istorii Udmurtii
Vopr Karstoved — Voprosy Karstovedeniya
Vopr Khim Biokhim Sist Soderzh Marganets Polifenoly — Voprosy Khimii i Biokhimii Sistem. Soderzhashchikh Marganets i Polifenoly
Vopr Khim Khim Tekhnol — Voprosy Khimii i Khimicheskoj Tekhnologii [*USSR*]
Vopr Kinet Katal — Voprosy Kinetiki i Kataliza
Vopr Klin Eksp Onkol — Voprosy Klinicheskoi i Eksperimental'noi Onkologii
Vopr Klin Eskp Khir — Voprosy Klinicheskoi i Eksperimental'noi Khirurgii
Vopr Klin Lech Zlokach Novoobraz — Voprosy Kliniki i Lecheniya Zlokachestvennykh Novoobrazovanii
Vopr Klin Med — Voprosy Klinicheskoi Meditsiny
Vopr Kommunal'n Gig — Voprosy Kommunal'noi Gigieny
Vopr Kosmog — Voprosy Kosmogonii
Vopr Kraev Patol Akad Nauk Uzb SSR — Voprosy Kraevoi Patologii Akademii Nauk Uzbekskoi SSR
Vopr Kriog Tekh — Voprosy Kriogennoi Tekhniki
Vopr Kurortol Fizioter (Frunze) — Voprosy Kurortologii i Fizioterapii (Frunze)
Vopr Kurortol Fizioter Lech Fiz Kul't — Voprosy Kurortologii, Fizioterapii, i Lechebnoi Fizicheskoi Kul'tury
Vopr Kurortol Revatol — Voprosy Kurortologii i Revmatologii
Vopr Leikozol — Voprosy Leikozologii
Vopr Leprol Dermatol — Voprosy Leprologii i Dermatologii
Vopr Lesoved — Voprosy Lesovedeniya
Vopr Litol Petrogr — Voprosy Litologii i Petrografii
Vopr Magmat Metamorf — Voprosy Magmatizma i Metamorfizma
Vopr Magmat Metamorfiz — Voprosy Magmatizma i Metamorfizma [*USSR*]
Vopr Magn Gidrodin Akad Nauk Latv SSR Inst Fiz — Voprosy Magnitnoi Gidrodinamiki. Akademiya Nauk Latviiskoi SSR. Institut Fiziki [*Latvian SSR*]
Vopr Med Khim — Voprosy Meditsinskoi Khimii
Vopr Med Khim Akad Med Nauk SSR — Voprosy Meditsinskoi Khimii Akademiya Meditsinskikh Nauk SSSR

Vopr Med Teor Klin Prakt Kurortnogo Lech — Voprosy Meditsinskoi Teorii Klinicheskoi Praktiki i Kurortnogo Lecheniya

Vopr Med Virusol — Voprosy Meditsinskoi Virusologii

Vopr Mekh — Voprosy Mekhanika [*USSR*]

Vopr Mekh Real'nogo Tverd Tela — Voprosy Mekhaniki Real'nogo Tverdogo Tela

Vopr Metalloved Korroz Met — Voprosy Metallovedeniya i Korrozii Metallov

Vopr Metod Nauki — Voprosy Metodologii Nauki

Vopr Mikrobiol — Voprosy Mikrobiologii

Vopr Mikrodozim — Voprosy Mikrodozimetrii

Vopr Mikrodozim — Voprosy Mikrodozimetrii Ministerstvo Vysshego i Srednego Spetsial'nogo Obrazovaniya SSSR

Vopr Mineral Osad Obraz — Voprosy Mineralogii Osadochnykh Obrazonanii

Vopr Neftekhim — Voprosy Neftekhimii

Vopr Neirokhir — Voprosy Neirokhirurgii

Vopr Obsc Nauki — Voprosy Obscestvennych Nauk

Vopr Obshch Khim Biokhim — Voprosy Obshchei Khimii i Biokhimii

Vopr Okhr Materin Det — Voprosy Okhrany Materinstva i Detstva

Vopr Onkol — Voprosy Onkologii

Vopr Onkol (Leningr) — Voprosy Onkologii (Leningrad)

Vopr Org Geokhim Gidrogeol Neftegazonosn Basseinov Uzb — Voprosy Organicheskoi Geokhimii i Gidrogeologii Neftegazonosnykh Basseinov Uzbekistana

Voprosy Dinamiki i Procnosti — Rizskii Politehniceskii Institut. Voprosy Dinamiki i Procnosti

Voprosy Filos — Voprosy Filosofii

Voprosy Gidrotekh — Voprosy Gidrotekhniki

Voprosy Informacion Teorii i Praktiki — Voprosy Informacionnoi Teorii i Praktiki

Voprosy Informatsion Teorii i Praktiki — Akademiya Nauk SSSR. Vsesoyuznyi Institut Nauchnoi i Tekhnicheskoi Informatsii. Voprosy Informatsionnoi Teorii i Praktiki

Voprosy Istor Estestvoznan i Tehn — Voprosy Istorii Estestvoznanija i Tehniki

Voprosy Kibernet (Moscow) — Voprosy Kibernetiki (Moscow)

Voprosy Kibernet (Tashkent) — Voprosy Kibernetiki (Tashkent)

Voprosy Teor Sistem Avtomat Upravleniya — Leningradskii Universitet Voprosy Teorii Sistem Avtomaticheskogo Upravleniya

Voprosy Vychisl i Prikl Mat — Akademiya Nauk Uzbekskoi SSR Trudy Ordena Trudovogo Krasnogo Znameni Instituta Kibernetiki s Vychislitel'nym Tsentrom. Voprosy Vychislitel'noi i Prikladnoi Matematiki

Voprosy Vycisl i Prikl Mat — Voprosy Vycislitel'noi i Prikladnoi Matematiki

Vopr Patol Krovi Krovoobrashch — Voprosy Patologii Krovi i Krovoobrashcheniya

Vopr Pediatr Ohkr Materin Det — Voprosy Pediatrii i Ohkrany Materinstva i Detstva

Vopr Peredachi Inf — Voprosy Peredachi Informatsii [*Ukrainian SSR*]

Vopr Pitan — Voprosy Pitaniya

Vopr Prikl Geokhim — Voprosy Prikladnoi Geokhimii

Vopr Proekt Sodovykh Zavodov — Voprosy Proekhitovaniya Sodovykh Zavodov

Vopr Proizvod Stali — Voprosy Proizvodstva Stali

Vopr Proizvod Vaktsin Syvorotok — Voprosy Proizvodstva Vaktsin i Syvorotok

Vopr Psikhiat Nevropatol — Voprosy Psikhiatrii i Nevropatologii [*USSR*]

Vopr Psikhiatr Nevropatol — Voprosy Psikhiatrii i Nevropatologii

Vopr Psikhol — Voprosy Psikhologii

Vopr Radiobiol — Voprosy Radiobiologii

Vopr Radiobiol Akad Nauk Arm SSR — Voprosy Radiobiologii. Akademiya Nauk Armyanskoi SSR

Vopr Radiobiol Biol Deistviya Tsitostatich Prep — Voprosy Radiobiologii i Biologicheskogo Deistviya Tsitostaticheskikh Preparatov

Vopr Radiobiol Biol Dejstv Tsitostatich Prep — Voprosy Radiobiologii i Biologicheskogo Dejstviya Tsitostaticheskikh Preparatov [*USSR*]

Vopr Radiobiol Klin Radiol — Voprosy Radiobiologii i Klinicheskoi Radiologii

Vopr Radiobiol Sb Tr — Voprosy Radiobiologii. Sbornik Trudov [*Armenian SSR*]

Vopr Radiobiol (Yerevan) — Voprosy Radiobiologii (Yerevan)

Vopr Radioelektron — Voprosy Radioelektroniki

Vopr Ratsion Pitan — Voprosy Ratsional'nogo Pitaniya

Vopr Razved Geofiz — Voprosy Razvedochnoi Geofiziki

Vopr Razvit Gazov Promsti Ukr SSR — Voprosy Razvitiya Gazovoi Promyshlennosti Ukrainskoi SSR

Vopr Razvit Licnosti — Voprosy Razvitija Licnosti

Vopr Reg Geol Metallog Zabaikal'ya — Voprosy Regional'noi Geologii i Metallogenii Zabaikal'ya

Vopr Rentgenol Onkol — Voprosy Rentgenologii i Onkologii

Vopr Revm — Voprosy Revmatizma

Vopr Rud Geofiz — Voprosy Rudnoi Geofiziki [*USSR*]

Vopr Rud Geofiz Minist Geol Okhr Nedr SSSR — Voprosy Rudnoi Geofiziki. Ministerstvo Geologii i Okhrany Nedr SSSR [*USSR*]

Vopr Rudn Geofiz — Voprosy Rudnoi Geofiziki

Vopr Rudn Radiom — Voprosy Rudnoi Radiometrii

Vopr Rudn Transp — Voprosy Rudichnogo Transporta

Vopr Sel'sk Lesn Khoz Dal'n Vost — Voprosy Sel'skogo i Lesnogo Khozyaistva Dal'nego Vostoka

Vopr Sov Finno-Ugroved — Voprosy Sovetskogo Finno-Ugrovedenija

Vopr Strat Takt Marks-Lenin Partij — Voprosy Strategii i Taktiki Marksistsko-Leninskih Partij

Vopr Sudebno-Med Ekspert — Voprosy Sudebno-Meditsinskoi Ekspertizy

Vopr Tekhnol Obrab Vody Prom Pit'evogo Vodoshnabzh — Voprosy Tekhnologii Obrabotki Vody Promyshlennogo i Pit'evogo Vodosnabzheniya

Vopr Tekhnol Tovaroved Izdelii Legk Promsti — Voprosy Tekhnologii i Tovarovedeniya Izdelii Legkoi Promyshlennosti

Vopr Tekhnol Ulavlivaniya Pererab Prod Koksovaniya — Voprosy Tekhnologii Ulavlivaniya i Pererabotki Produktov Koksovaniya

Vopr Tekh Teplofiz — Voprosy Tekhnicheskoi Teplofiziki [*Ukrainian SSR*]

Vopr Teor At Stolknovenii — Voprosy Teorii Atomnykh Stolknovenii [*USSR*]

Vopr Teorii Metod Ideol Raboty — Voprosy Teorii i Metodov Ideologiceskoj Raboty

Vopr Teor Plazmy — Voprosy Teorii Plazmy

Vopr Teplofiz Yad Reakt — Voprosy Teplofiziki Yadernykh Reaktorov [*USSR*]

Vopr Tuberk (Riga) — Voprosy Tuberkuleza (Riga)

Vopr Vet Virusol — Voprosy Veterinarnoi Virusologii

Vopr Virusol — Voprosy Virusologii

Vopr Vodn Khoz — Voprosy Vodnogo Khozyaistva

Vopr Vychisl Mat Tekh (Tashkent) — Voprosy Vychislitel'noi Matematiki i Tekhniki (Tashkent)

VOPSA — Voprosy Psikhologii

Vop Virusol — Voprosy Virusologii

VOR — Vortex Science Fiction

VORLA — Vestnik Oto-Rino-Laringologii

Vorlesungen Fachbereich Math Univ Essen — Vorlesungen aus dem Fachbereich Mathematik. Universitaet Essen

Vorlesungen Math Inst Giessen — Vorlesungen. Mathematisches Institut Giessen

Voronez Gos Univ Trudy Mat Fak — Voronezskii Gosudarstvennyi Universitet Imeni Leninskogo Komsomola. Trudy Matematiceskogo Fakul'teta

Voronez Gos Univ Trudy Naucn Issled Inst Mat VGU — Voronezskii Ordena Lenina Gosudarstvennyi Universitet Imeni Leninskogo Komsomola. Trudy Naucno-Issledovatel'skogo Instituta Matematiki

Voronez Gos Univ Trudy Sem Funkcional Anal — Ministerstvo Vyssego Obrazovanija SSSR Voronezskii Gosudarstvennyi Universitet Trudy Seminara po Funkcional'nomu Analizu

Voronez Tehn Inst Trudy — Voronezskii Tehnologiceskii Institut. Trudy

Vortr Gesamtgeb Bot — Vortraege aus dem Gesamtgebiet der Botanik

Vortr Pflanzenz Deut Landwirt Ges Pflanzenzuchtabt — Vortraege fuer Pflanzenzuchter. Deutsche Landwirtschaftliche Gesellschaft Pflanzenzuchtabteilung

VOSAA — Vox Sanguinis

VoSanD — Voenno-Sanitarnoe Delo

V Ost Geschichtsv — Veroeffentlichungen. Verband Oesterreichischer Geschichts- Vereine

Vost Neft — Vostochnaya Neft

VOT — Vision of Tomorrow

Vox Sang — Vox Sanguinis

Vox Sanguin — Vox Sanguinis

VoxTh — Vox Theologica [*Assen*]

VoxTheol — Vox Theologica [*Assen*]

VOYA — Voice of Youth Advocates

Vozes — Vozes Revista Catolica de Cultura

Voz Farm (Lima) — Voz Farmaceutica (Lima)

VOZNA — Voennye Znaniya

Vozr — Vozrozdenie

VP — Victorian Poetry

VP — Vita e Pensiero

V e P — Vita e Pensiero

VP — Voce del Passato

V & P — Votes and Proceedings

VPA — Verpackung. Schweizerische Fachzeitschrift fuer Verpackung, Technologie, Package Design, Marketing

VPA — Victorian Planning Appeal Decisions

VPARD — Veterinary Parasitology

VPC — Verpackungsberater

VPD — Vremennik Puskinskogo Doma

VPen — Vita e Pensiero

VPIMD — Vilniaus Pedagoginio Instituto Mokslo Darbai

VPITA — Voprosy Pitaniya

VPMLL — Valstybine Politines ir Mokslines Literatu

VPN — Victorian Periodicals Newsletter

VPR — Verpackungs-Rundschau

VPW — Vorarbeiten zum Pommerschen Woerterbuch

VQ — Vermont Quarterly

VQ — Visvabharati Quarterly

VQR — Virginia Quarterly Review

VR — Viata Romaneasca [*Bucharest*]

VR — Victorian Reports

VR — Viera i Razum

VR — Villanova Law Review

VR — Volja Rossii

VR — Vox Romanica

VRA — Vraag en Aanbod voor Techniek, Nijverheid, Bouwvak, en Handel
Vrach Delo — Vrachebnoe Delo
Vrach Gaz — Vrachebnaia Gazeta
VRARA — Voprosy Radiobiologii. Sbornik Trudov
Vrashchenie i Prilivnye Deform Zemli — Vrashchenie i Prilivnye Deformatsii Zemli
VRB — Verordeningenblad Bedrijfsorganisatie
VRDEA — Vrachebnoe Delo
VRE — Venezuelan Economic Review
VR (E) — Victorian Reports (Equity)
Vrednaya Polezn Fauna Bespozvon Mold — Vrednaya i Poleznaya Fauna Bespozvonochnykh Moldavii
Vremennik Gl Palaty Mer Vesov — Vremennik Glavnoi Palaty Mer i Vesov
VR (Eq) — Victorian Reports (Equity)
VR (IE & M) — Victorian Reports (Insolvency, Ecclesiastical, and Matrimonial)
Vrije Univ Brussel Inter-Univ Inst High Energ Rep — Vrije Universiteit Brussel. Inter-University Institute for High Energies. Report
VRJa — Voprosy Russkogo Jazykoznanija
VR (L) — Victorian Reports (Law)
VRL — Voprosy Russkoi Literatury. Respublikanskii Mezhvedomstvennyi Nauchnyi Sbornik
VR (Law) — Victorian Law Reports (Law)
VR Newsletter — Victorian Railways Newsletter
VRo — Viata Romaneasca
VROA — Verslagen Omtrent's Rijks Oude Archieven
VRU — Verfassung und Recht in Uebersee
VS — La Vie Spirituelle [*Paris*]
VS — Verbum Salutis [*Paris*]
VS — Victorian Studies
VS — Vida Sobrenatural
VS — Videnskabs Selskapet Skrifter
VS — Videnskapsselskapets Skrifter. Kristiana
VSA — Violin Society of America. Journal
VSAV — Vydavtel'stvo Slovenskej Akademie Vied
VSB — Victorian Studies Bulletin
VSB — Vision. The European Business Magazine
VSD — Vendredi, Samedi, Dimanche
Vse — Vsesvit [*Kiev*]
Vses Geogr O-vo Izv — Vsesoyuznoye Geograficheskoye Obshchestvo. Izvestiia
Vses Nauchno Issled Geol Inst Inf Sb — Vsesoyuznyi Nauchno-Issledovatel'skii Geologicheskii Institut. Informatsionnyi Sbornik
Vses Nauchno-Issled Geol Inst Tr — Vsesoyuznyy Nauchno-Issledovatel'skiy Geologicheskiy Institut. Trudy
Vses Nauchno-Issled Geologorazved Neft Inst Tr — Vsesoyuznyy Nauchno-Issledovatel'skiy Geologorazvedochnyi Neftyanoy Institut. Trudy
Vses Nauchno Issled Inst Eksp Vet Im Ya R Kovalenko Byull — Vsesoyuznyi Nauchno-Issledovatel'skii Institut Eksperimental'noi Veterinarii Imeni Ya. R. Kovalenko. Byulleten
Vses Nauchno Issled Inst Geofiz Metodov Razved Tr — Vsesoyuznyi Nauchno-Issledovatel'skii Institut Geofizicheskikh Metodov Razvedki. Trudy
Vses Nauchno Issled Inst Gidrogeol Inzh Geol Tr — Vsesoyuznyi Nauchno-Issledovatel'skii Institut Gidrogeologii i Inzhenernoi Geologii. Trudy
Vses Nauchno Issled Inst Khlopkovod Sb Nauchn Rab Aspir — Vsesoyuznyi Nauchno-Issledovatel'skii Institut Khlopkovodstva. Sbornik Nauchnykh Rabot Aspirantov
Vses Nauchno Issled Inst Konditer Promsti Tr — Vsesoyuznyi Nauchno-Issledovatel'skii Institut Konditerskoi Promyshlennosti. Trudy
Vses Nauchno Issled Inst Solyanoi Promsti Tr — Vsesoyuznyi Nauchno-Issledovatel'skii Institut Solyanoi Promyshlennosti. Trudy
Vses Nauchno Issled Inst Tsellyul Bum Promsti Sb Tr — Vsesoyuznyi Nauchno-Issledovatel'skii Institut Tsellyulozno-Bumazhnoi Promyshlennosti. Sbornik Trudov
Vses Nauchno Issled Inst Zhirov Tr — Vsesoyuznyi Nauchno-Issledovatel'skii Institut Zhirov. Trudy
Vses Nauchno Issled Khim Farm Inst Khim Med — Vsesoyuznyi Nauchno-Issledovatel'skii Khimiko-Farmasevticheskii Institut. Khimiya i Meditsina
Vses Nauchno Issled Proektn Inst Galurgii Tr — Vsesoyuznyi Nauchno-Issledovatel'skii i Proektnyi Institut Galurgii. Trudy
Vses Nauchno Issled Proektn Inst Mekh Obrab Polezn Iskop Tr — Vsesoyuznyi Nauchno-Issledovatel'skii i Proektnyi Institut Mekhanicheskoi Obrabotki Poleznykh Iskopaemykh. Trudy
Vses Nauchn O-vo Neirokhir — Vsesoyuznoe Nauchnoe Obshchestvo Neirokhirurgii
Vses Neft Nauchno Issled Geologorazved Inst Tr — Vsesoyuznyi Neftyanoi Nauchno-Issledovatel'skii Geologorazvedochnyi Institut. Trudy
Vsesojuz Zaocn Politehn Inst Sb Trudov — Vsesojuznyi Zaocnyi Politehniceskii Institut. Sbornik Trudov
Vsesoyunaya Nauchno Metod Konf Vet Patologoanat — Vsesoyuznaya Nauchno-Metod Konferentsiya Veterinarnykh Patologoanatomov
Vsesoyuznoe Paleont Obshch Ezhegodnik — Vsesoyuznoe Paleontologicheskoe Obshchestvo Ezhegodnik
VSG — Vierteljahrsschrift fuer Sozial- und Wirtschaftsgeschichte
VSH — Vie Economique. Rapports Economics et de Statistique Sociale
VSL — Metaal en Kunststof

VSL — Vetenskaps-Societeten i Lund
VSLA — Vetenskaps-Societeten i Lund. Aarsbok
VSL Bibs — Research Service Bibliographies. State Library of Victoria
VSlJa — Voprosy Slavjanskogo Jazykoznanija
VSlJa (Lvov) — Voprosy Slavjanskogo Jazykoznanija (Lvov)
VSlJa (Moskva) — Voprosy Slavjanskogo Jazykoznanija (Moskva)
VSO — Handel. Zeitschrift fuer Theorie und Praxis des Innenhandels in der Deutschen Demokratischen Republik
VSPP — Vangiya Sahitya Parisat Patrika
VSS — Videnskabs Selskapet Skrifter
VSSF — Videnskabs Selskapet Skrifter. Forhandlingar
VS Suppl — Vie Spirituelle. Supplement
VSTCB — Vuoto, Scienza, e Tecnologia
VStil — Voprosy Stilistiki
VSTKJ — Vesientutkimuslaitoksen Julkaisuja [*Publications. Finnish Water Research Institute*]
VSv — Vokrug Sveta [*Moscow*]
VSW — Vierteljahrsschrift fuer Sozial- und Wirtschaftsgeschichte
VSWG — Vierteljahrsschrift fuer Sozial- und Wirtschaftsgeschichte
VSystems — Video Systems
VT — Vetus Testamentum
VT — Viere i Tzerkov
VTA — Verkeerskunde
VT Ag Exp — Vermont. Agricultural Experiment Station. Publications
VT Agric Exp Stn Bull — Vermont. Agricultural Experiment Station. Bulletin
VtB — Verfahrenstechnische Berichte [*Chemical and Process Engineering Abstracts*] [*Leverkusen, West Germany*]
VTBHA — Vuoriteollisuus/Bergshanteringen
VT Bul — Vermont. Free Public Library Commission and State Library. Bulletin
VT Farm & Home Sci — Vermont Farm and Home Science
VT Farm Home Sci — Vermont Farm and Home Science
VTFDA — Ankara Universitesi. Veteriner Fakultesi. Dergisi
VTG — Vojno-Tehnicki Glasnik
VT Geol Sur Econ Geol — Vermont. Geological Survey. Economic Geology
VT Geol Surv Bull — Vermont. Geological Survey. Bulletin
VT Geol Surv Water Resour Dep Environ Geol — Vermont. Geological Survey. Water Resources Department. Environmental Geology
VT His S — Vermont Historical Society. Proceedings
VT Hist — Vermont History
VtHS — Vermont Historical Society. Proceedings
VT Lib — Vermont Libraries
VT L Rev — Vermont Law Review
VTMDA — Veterinarni Medicina
VTMIDB — Annual Research Reviews. Vitamin-Trace Mineral-Protein Interactions
VTMRJa — Voprosy Teorii i Metodiki Izucenijy Russkogo Jazyka
VTop — Voprosy Toponomastiki
VTPAI — Victorian Town Planning Appeals Tribunal. Index of Appeals Decisions
VtQ — Vermont Quarterly
VT Regist Nurse — Vermont Registered Nurse
VTS — Vetus Testamentum. Supplementum [*Leiden*]
VT St G Rp — Vermont State Geologist. Report
VTSuppl — Vetus Testamentum. Supplementum [*Leiden*]
VTTJA — Valtion Teknillinen Tutkimuslaitos. Julkaisu
VT Verfahrenstech — VT. Verfahrenstechnik
VTX — Vertex
VU — Voice of Uganda
VUCLR — Victoria University. College Law Review
Vues Econ Aquitaine — Vues sur l'Economie d'Aquitaine
VuF — Verkuendigung und Forschung
VuG — Vergangenheit und Gegenwart
Vulkanol Seismol — Vulkanologiya i Seismologiya
VULR — Valparaiso University. Law Review
VULT — Voprosy Uzbekskogo Jazyka i Literatury
VUMD — Vilniaus Valstybinio V. Kapsuko Vardo Universiteto Mokslo Darbai
Vuorit Bergshant — Vuoriteollisuus/Bergshanteringen
Vuoto — Vuoto, Scienza, e Tecnologia
Vuoto Sci Tecnol — Vuoto, Scienza, e Tecnologia
VURB-A — Vie Urbaine [*France*]
VUSH — Vanderbilt University. Studies in the Humanities
Vutr Boles — Vutreshni Bolesti
VUWLR — Victoria University of Wellington. Law Review
VUWL Rev — Victoria University of Wellington. Law Review
VV — Village Voice
VV — Vizantiiskii Vremenik
VV — Volk und Volkstum
VVa — Vida Vasca
VVL — Vee en Vlees. Het Vakblad voor Handelaar en Producent
VVM — Vlastivedny Vestnik Moravsky
VVS Tidsk Energ VVS-Tek — VVS. Tidskrift foer Energi- och VVS [*Vaerme, Ventilation, Sanitet*]-Teknik
VVS Tidskr Vaerme Vent Sanit Kyltetek — VVS. Tidskrift foer Vaerme, Ventilation, Sanitet, och Kyltekenik

VVS Tidskr Varme Vent Sanit — VVS. Tidskrift foer Vaerme, Ventilation, Sanitet [*Sweden*]
VVTBA — Vaeg- och Vattenbyggaren
VVUU Zpr — VVUU [*Vedeckovyzkumny Uhelny Ustav*] Ostrava-Radvanice Zprava
VW — Vie Wallonne
VWM — Virginia Woolf Miscellany
VWN — Virginia Woolf Newsletter
VWQ — Virginia Woolf Quarterly
Vya — Voprosy Yazykoznaniya [*Moscow*]
Vyber Inf Organ Vypocetni Tech — Vyber Informaci z Organizacni a Vypocetni Techniky
Vychisl Metody Progam — Vychislitel'nye Metody i Programmirovanie
Vychisl Metody & Program — Vychislitel'nye Metody i Programmirovanie
Vychisl Metody i Programmirovanie — Moskovskii Universitet. Sbornik Rabot Vychislitelnogo Tsentra Moskovskogo Universiteta. Vychislitel'nye Metody i Programmirovanie
Vychisl Prikl Mat — Kievskii Gosudarstvennyi Universitet Mezhvedomstvennyi Nauchnyi Sbornik Vychislitel'naya i Prikladnaya Matematika
Vychisl Prikl Mat — Vychislitel'naya i Prikladnaya Matematika
Vychisl Seismol — Vychislitel'naya Seismologiya [*USSR*]
Vychisl Sist — Vychislitel'nye Sistemy
Vychisl Tekhn i Voprosy Kibernet — Leningradskii Gosudarstvennyi Universitet Vychislitel'nyi Tsentr Moskovskii Gosudarstvennyi Universitet Vychislitel'nyi Tsentr Vychislitel'naya Tekhnika i Voprosy Kibernetiki
Vychisl Tekh i Vopr Kibern — Vychislitel'naya Tekhnika i Voprosy Kibernetiki
Vycisl Mat i Vycisl Tehn (Kharkov) — Vycislitel'naja Matematika i Vycislitel'naja Tehnika (Kharkov)
Vycisl Metody i Programmirovanie — Vycislitel'nye Metody i Programmirovanie. Moskovskii Universitet. Sbornik Rabot Vycislitel'nogo Centra Moskovskogo Universiteta
Vycisl Prikl Mat (Kiev) — Vycislitel'naja i Prikladnaja Matematika (Kiev)
Vycisl Sistemy — Akademija Nauk SSSR. Sibirskoe Otdelenie. Institut Matematiki. Vycislitel'nye Sistemy. Sbornik Trudov
Vycisl Tehn v Masinostroen — Vycislitel'naja Tehnika v Masinostroenii
Vycisl Tehn i Voprosy Kibernet — Vycislitel'naja Tehnika i Voprosy Kibernetiki
Vyestsi Akad Navuk BSSR Syer Biyal Navuk — Vyestsi Akademii Navuk BSSR. Syeryya Biyalagichnykh Navuk
Vyestsi Akad Navuk BSSR Syer Syel' Skahaspad Navuk — Vyestsi Akademii Navuk BSSR. Syeryya Syel' Skahaspadarchukh Navuk
Vyisn Akad Nauk Ukr RSR — Vyisnik Akademyiyi Nauk Ukrayins'koyi RSR
Vyisn Kiyiv Unyiv Ser Astron — Vyisnik Kiyivs'kogo Unyiversitetu. Seryiya Astronomii
Vyisn Kiyiv Unyiv Ser Fyiz — Vyisnik Kiyivs'kogo Unyiversitetu. Seryiya Fyizika [*USSR*]
Vyisn L'vyiv Derzh Unyiv Ser Fyiz — Vyisnik L'vyivs'kij Derzhavnij Unyiversitet Imeni I. Franka. Seryiya Fyizichna
Vyisn Syil'skogospod Nauki — Vyisnik Syil'skogospodars'koyi Nauki
VYNAA — Vynalezy
Vynohrad Vynorobstvo — Vynohradarstvo i Vynorobstvo
Vysk Pra Odboru Pap Celul — Vyskumne Prace z Odboru Papiera a Celulozy
Vyskum Pr Odboru Papiera Celulozy — Vyskumne Prace z Odboru Papiera a Celulozy
Vysk Ustav Lesn Hospod Zvolene Lesn Stud — Vyskumny Ustav Lesneho Hospodarstvavo Zvolene Lesnicke Studie
Vysk Ustav Ovciar Trencine Ved Pr — Vyskumny Ustav Ovciarsky v Trencine. Vedecke Prace
Vysokomol Soed — Vysokomolekulyarnye Soedineniya
Vysokomol Soedin — Vysokomolekulyarnye Soedineniya
Vysokomol Soedin Geterotsepnye Vysokomol Soedin — Vysokomolekulyarnye Soedineniya Geterotsepnye Vysokomolekulyarnye Soedineniya [*USSR*]
Vysokomol Soedin Ser A — Vysokomolekulyarnye Soedineniya. Seriya A
Vysokomol Soedin Ser B — Vysokomolekulyarnye Soedineniya. Seriya B
Vysokomol Soedin Vses Khim Ovo — Vysokomolekulyarnye Soedineniya Vsesoyuznoe Khimicheskoe Obshchestvo
Vyso Soed A — Vysokomolekulyarnye Soedineniya. Seriya A
Vyso Soed B — Vysokomolekulyarnye Soedineniya. Seriya B
Vyssh Nervn Deyat Norme Patol — Vysshaya Nervnaya Deyatel'nost v Norme i Patologii
Vyssh Uchebn Zaved Izv Geol Razved — Vysshoye Uchebnoye Zavedeniye. Izvestiya Geologiya i Razvedka
Vys Sk Chem-Technol Praze Sb Oddil Chem Inz — Vysoka Skola Chemicko-Technologicka v Praze. Sbornik. Oddil. Chemicke Inzenyrstvi
Vys Soed B — Vysokomolekulyarnye Soedineniya. Seriya B
Vytr Boles — Vytreshni Bolesti
VyV — Verdad y Vida [*Milan*]
VYV — Wegvervoer
Vyzk Ustav Vodohospodar Pr Stud — Vyzkumny Ustav Vodohospodarsky. Prace a Studie
Vyzk Ustav Vodohospod Pr Stud — Vyzkumny Ustav Vodohospodarsky. Prace a Studie
Vyz Lidu — Vyziva Lidu

Vyznach Prisnovod Vodor Ukr RSR — Vyznachnyk Prisnovodnykh Vodorostei Ukrains'koi RSR
Vyz Rodine — Vyziva v Rodine
VyzS — Vyzvol'nyj Sljax
Vyz Zdravie — Vyzica a Zdravie
VZ — Vostocnye Zapiski
Vznik Pocatky Slov — Vznik a Pocatky Slovanu [*Origine et Debuts des Slaves*]
VZP — Verenigde Verzekeringspers. Wekelijks Verschijnend Vakblad voor het Verzekeringswezen in Binnenland en Buitenland
Vzryvnoe Delo Nauchno-Tekh Gorn O-vo Sb — Vzryvnoe Delo. Nauchno-Tekhnicheskoe Gornoe Obshchestvo Sbornik [*USSR*]

W

W — Whitehorse Star
W — Winter
W — Wortkunst
WA — Voice of Washington Music
Wa — Warsaw
WA — Weltwirtschaftliches Archiv
WA — West Africa
WA — Wissenschaftliche Annalen
WA — World Archaeology
WAA — World Aluminum Abstracts
WAAN — West African Archaeological Newsletter
WA Ann LR — University of Western Australia. Annual Law Review
WAAR — Western Australian Arbitration Reports
WA Arb R — Western Australian Arbitration Reports
WA Art Gall Bull — Western Australian Art Gallery. Bulletin
W A'B & W — Webb, A'Beckett, and Williams' Reports
W A'B & W Eq — Webb, A'Beckett, and Williams' Equity Reports
W A'B & W IE & M — Webb, A'Beckett, and Williams' Insolvency,
    Ecclesiastical, and Matrimonial Reports
W A'B & W Min — Webb, A'Beckett, and Williams' Mining Cases
WAC — World Aeronautical Charts [*Air Force*]
WA Craftsman — Western Australian Craftsman
WAD — Warta Ekonomi Maritim. Facts and Analysis in Communications,
    Commerce, and Finance
WAD — World Aviation Directory
WADA — Wissenschaftliche Annalen. Deutsche Akademie
WA Democrat — West Australian Democrat
WADL — Wiener Arbeiten zur Deutschen Literatur
Wadley Med Bull — Wadley Medical Bulletin
Wadsworth Ath Bul — Wadsworth Atheneum. Bulletin
W Adv — Wesleyan Advocate
WAE — Waterkampioen
WA Ed Circ — Education Circular. Education Department. Western Australia
WA Educ News — WA Education News. Education Department of Western
    Australia
WA Egg Marketing Board Nletter — Western Australia. Egg Marketing
    Board. Newsletter
WAELD — Wave Electronics
WA Electr Contract — WA [*Western Australian*] Electrical Contractor
Waerme Kaeltetch — Waerme- und Kaeltetechnik
Waerme- Stoffuebertrag — Waerme- und Stoffuebertragung
Waerme und Stoffuebertrag — Waerme- und Stoffuebertragung
Waerme Stoffuebertrag/Thermo Fluid Dyn — Waerme- und
    Stoffuebertragung/Thermo and Fluid Dynamics
Waermetech — Waermetechnik
WAERSA — World Agricultural Economics and Rural Sociology Abstracts
WAF — West Africa
WAFLT Forum — Washington Association of Foreign Language Teachers.
    Forum
Wa For LR — Wake Forest Law Review
W African Rel — West African Religion
W Afr J Arc — West African Journal of Archaeology
WA Fruitgrower — Western Australian Fruitgrower
WAG — World Agricultural Economics and Rural Sociology Abstracts
WAGEA — Waste Age

Wage-Price Law and Econ R — Wage-Price Law and Economics Review
Wage-Price L & Econ Rev — Wage-Price Law and Economics Review
Wage-Pr L — Wage-Price Law and Economics Review
WAGG — Western Australia Government Gazette
Wagga Hist Soc News — Wagga Wagga and District Historical Society.
    Newsletter
Wagner Free Inst Sci Bull Cards — Wagner Free Institute of Science. Bulletin.
    Cards
Wagner Free I Sc Tr — Wagner Free Institute of Science [*Philadelphia*].
    Transactions
WA Govt Gaz — Western Australia Government Gazette
WAGSO — Wiener Archiv fuer Geschichte des Slawentums und Osteuropas
WAH — Writings on American History
WA Hist Soc J — Western Australian Historical Society. Journal and
    Proceedings
WAI — Wall Street Journal. European Edition
WAIG — Western Australian Industrial Gazette
Waikato Univ Antarct Res Unit Rep — Waikato University. Antarctic
    Research Unit. Reports
WA Ind Gaz — Western Australian Industrial Gazette
WA Indus Gaz — Western Australian Industrial Gazette
WAJA — West African Journal of Archaeology
WAJE — West African Journal of Education
WAJML — West Africa Journal of Modern Language
Wakayama Med Rep — Wakayama Medical Reports
Wake Forest L Rev — Wake Forest Law Review
Wake For L Rev — Wake Forest Law Review
Wake For Univ Dev Nations Monogr Ser Ser II Med Behav Sci — Wake Forest
    University. Developing Nations Monograph Series. Series II. Medical
    Behavioral Science
Wake For Unive Dev Nations Monogr Ser Ser II Med Behav Sci — Wake Forest
    University. Developing Nations Monograph Series. Series II. Medical
    Behavioral Science
Waksman Inst Microbiol Rutgers Univ Annu Rep — Waksman Institute of
    Microbiology. Rutgers University. Annual Report
WAL — Western American Literature
WALA News — West African Library Association. News
Walford's Antiq — Walford's Antiquarian and Bibliographer
Wallaces F — Wallaces Farmer
Walla Walla Coll Publ — Walla Walla College. Publications
Wallerstein Lab Commun — Wallerstein Laboratories. Communications
Wallerstein Lab Commun Sci Pract Brew — Wallerstein Laboratories.
    Communications on the Science and Practice of Brewing
Wallraf-Richartz Jahr — Wallraf-Richartz Jahrbuch
Wall St J — Wall Street Journal
Wall St J East Ed — Wall Street Journal. Eastern Edition
Wall St J Midwest Ed — Wall Street Journal. Midwest Edition
Wall St Jnl — Wall Street Journal
Wall St J Three Star East Ed — Wall Street Journal. Three Star Eastern
    Edition
Wall St R Bk — Wall Street Review of Books
Wall Str J — Wall Street Journal
Wall St T — Wall Street Transcript
WALMS — West African Language Monograph Series
WALR — University of Western Australia. Law Review

Wa LR — Washington Law Review
WALR — Western Australian Law Reports
Walsh's R — Walsh's American Review
Wal Steve J — Wallace Stevens Journal
Walter Reed Army Med Cent Prog Notes — Walter Reed Army Medical Center. Progress Notes
Walter Reed Gen Hosp Dep Med Prog Notes — Walter Reed General Hospital. Department of Medicine. Progress Notes
Walters J — Walters Art Gallery [*Baltimore*]. Journal
Walt Whit R — Walt Whitman Review
WAM — Wiltshire Archaeological Magazine
WA Manuf — West Australian Manufacturer
WA Manufacturer — West Australian Manufacturer
WA Mining & Commercial R — West Australian Mining and Commercial Review
WAMOD — Wave Motion
WA Nat — Western Australian Naturalist
WA Naturalist — Western Australian Naturalist
WA News — West Australian News
WA Parent & Cit — Western Australian Parent and Citizen
WA Parent & Citizen — Western Australian Parent and Citizen
WA Parl Deb — Western Australia. Parliamentary Debates
WAPLA — Water, Air, and Soil Pollution
WAPOA — Water Power [*England*]
WAPRA — Wissenschaftliche Abhandlungen der Physikalische- Technischen Reichsanstalt
WA Primary Princ — WA Primary Principal. West Australian Primary Principals Association
WAR — Western Australian Reports
WAR — Wisconsin Academy. Review
WARBA — Water Resources Bulletin
Warburg & Courtauld Inst Jnl — Warburg and Courtauld Institute. Journal
War C — War Cry
W Arch — Western Architect
Ward AW — Ward's Auto World
Wards Auto — Ward's Automotive Reports
Ward's Bull — Ward's Bulletin
WARE — Water Research
Warehousing Superv Bull — Warehousing Supervisor's Bulletin [*United States*]
War Emerg Proc Inst Mech Eng — War Emergency Proceedings. Institution of Mechanical Engineers
WARMA — Waerme
War Med — War Medicine
WARR — Water Resources Research
Warsaw Agric Univ SGGW-AR Ann Anim Sci — Warsaw Agricultural University. SGGW-AR [*Szkola Glowna Gospodarstwa Wiejskiego - Akademia Rolnicza*] Annals. Animal Science
Warta Geol — Warta Geologi
Warta Geol (Kuala Lumpur) — Warta Geologi (Kuala Lumpur)
WAS — Waste International
WAS — Witchcraft and Sorcery
WAS — Worcester Archaeological Society. Transactions
WAS — World Animal Science [*Elsevier Book Series*]
WASBB — Waerme- und Stoffuebertragung
WascanaR — Wascana Review
Waseda Polit Stud — Waseda Political Studies
Waseda Pol Studies — Waseda Political Studies
Wash Actions Health — Washington Actions on Health
Wash Ag Exp — Washington. Agricultural Experiment Station. Publications
Wash Agric Exp Stn Bull — Washington. Agricultural Experiment Station. Bulletin
Wash Agric Exp Stn Cir — Washington. Agricultural Experiment Station. Circular
Wash Agric Exp Stn Stn Circ — Washington. Agricultural Experiment Station. Station Circular
Wash Agric Exp Stn Tech Bull — Washington. Agricultural Experiment Station. Technical Bulletin
Washburn Coll Lab N H B — Washburn College. Laboratory of Natural History. Bulletin
Washburn L J — Washburn Law Journal
Wash Bus L Rpr — Washington Business Law Reporter
Wash Dep Ecol State Water Program Bienn Rep — Washington. Department of Ecology. State Water Program. Biennial Report
Wash Dep Ecol Tech Rep — Washington. Department of Ecology. Technical Report
Wash Dep Ecol Water Supply Bull — Washington. Department of Ecology. Water Supply Bulletin
Wash Dep Fish Annu Rep — Washington. Department of Fisheries. Annual Report
Wash Dep Fish Fish Res Pap — Washington. Department of Fisheries. Fisheries Research Papers
Wash Dep Fish Res Bull — Washington. Department of Fisheries. Research Bulletin
Wash Dep Fish Tech Rep — Washington. Department of Fisheries. Technical Report

Wash Dep Water Resour Water Supply Bull — Washington. Department of Water Resources. Water Supply Bulletin
Wash Div Geol Earth Resour Geol Map — Washington. Division of Geology and Earth Resources. Geologic Map
Wash Div Geol Earth Resour Inf Circ — Washington. Division of Geology and Earth Resources. Information Circular
Wash Div Mines Geol Bull — Washington. Department of Natural Resources. Division of Mines and Geology. Bulletin
Wash Div Mines Geol Inform Circ — Washington. Department of Conservation. Division of Mines and Geology. Information Circular
Wash Div Mines Geol Inform Circ — Washington. Division of Mines and Geology. Information Circular
Wash Div Mines Geol Rep Invest — Washington. Department of Conservation. Division of Mines and Geology. Report of Investigations
Wash Div Mines Geol Rep Invest — Washington. Division of Mines and Geology. Report of Investigation
Wash Div Mines Min Rep Invest — Washington. Division of Mines and Mining. Report of Investigations
Wash Geol Earth Resour Div Bull — Washington. Department of Natural Resources. Geology and Earth Resources Division. Bulletin
Wash GSB — Washington. Geological Survey. Bulletin
Wash Health Costs Let — Washington Health Costs Letter
Wash His Q — Washington Historical Quarterly
Wash His S — Washington State Historical Society. Publications
Wash Hist Q — Washington Historical Quarterly
Washington Acad Sci Jour — Washington Academy of Sciences. Journal
Washington Dept Water Resources Water Supply Bull — Washington. Department of Water Resources. Water Supply Bulletin
Washington Div Mines and Geology Bull — Washington. Division of Mines and Geology. Bulletin
Washington Div Mines and Geology Geol Map — Washington. Division of Mines and Geology. Geologic Map
Washington Div Mines and Geology Inf Circ — Washington. Division of Mines and Geology. Information Circular
Washington and Lee L Rev — Washington and Lee Law Review
Washington L Rev — Washington Law Review
Washington M — Washington Monthly
Washington Univ L Quart — Washington University. Law Quarterly
Wash Law Re — Washington Law Review
Wash and Lee LR — Washington and Lee Law Review
Wash & Lee L Rev — Washington and Lee Law Review
Wash LR — Washington Law Review
Wash L Rev — Washington Law Review
Wash M — Washington Monthly
Wash Med Ann — Washington Medical Annals
Wash Mon — Washington Monthly
Wash News Beat — Washington News Beat
Wash Nurse — Washington Nurse
Wash Post — Washington Post
Wash Prop L Rpr — Washington Property Law Reporter
Wash Rep — Washington Report
Wash Rep Med Health — Washington Report on Medicine and Health
Wash State Coll Agric Exp Stn Tech Bull — Washington State College. Washington Agricultural Experiment Station. Institute of Agricultural Sciences. Technical Bulletin
Wash State Coll Research Studies — Washington State College. Research Studies
Wash State Council Highway Research Eng Soils Manual — Washington State. Council for Highway Research Engineering. Soils Manual
Wash State Dent J — Washington State Dental Journal
Wash State For Prod Inst Bull New Wood Use Ser — Washington State Forest Products Institute. Bulletins. New Wood-Use Series
Wash State Inst Technology Bull — Washington State Institute of Technology. Bulletin
Wash State Inst Technol Tech Rep — Washington State Institute of Technology. Technical Report
Wash State J Nurs — Washington State Journal of Nursing
Wash State Univ Agric Exp Stn Tech Bull — Washington State University. Agricultural Experiment Station. Institute of Agricultural Sciences. Technical Bulletin
Wash State Univ Coll Agric Res Cent Bull — Washington State University. College of Agriculture. Research Center. Bulletin
Wash State Univ Coll Agric Res Cent Tech Bull — Washington State University. College of Agriculture. Research Center. Technical Bulletin
Wash State Univ Coll Eng Bull — Washington State University. College of Engineering. Bulletin
Wash State Univ Coop Ext Serv Ext Bull — Washington State University. Cooperative Extension Service. Extension Bulletin
Wash State Univ Ext Serv EM — Washington State University. Extension Service. EM
Wash State Univ Int Symp Particleboard Proc — Washington State University. International Symposium on Particleboard. Proceedings
Wash State Univ Publ Geol Sci — Washington State University. Publications in Geological Sciences
Wash State Univ Symp Particleboard Proc — Washington State University. Symposium on Particleboard. Proceedings

Wash St G An Rp — Washington State Geologist. Annual Report
Wash U L Q — Washington University. Law Quarterly
Wash Univ Bull — Washington University. Bulletin
Wash Univ Dep Geol Sci Abstr Res — Washington University. Department of Geological Sciences. Abstracts of Research
Wash Univ Pub G — Washington University. Publications in Geology
Wash Univ St Hum Ser — Washington University. Studies. Humanistic Series
Wash Univ St Sci Ser — Washington University. Studies. Scientific Series
Wash Univ Stud Lang & Lit — Washington University. Studies. Language and Literature
Wash Univ Stud Sci & Tech — Washington University. Studies. Science and Technology
Wash Univ Stud Sci & Tech NS — Washington University. Studies. Science and Technology. New Series
Wash Univ Stud Social & Philos Sci — Washington University. Studies. Social and Philosophical Sciences
Wash Univ Stud Social & Philos Sci NS — Washington University. Studies. Social and Philosophical Sciences. New Series
Wasmann J Biol — Wasmann Journal of Biology
WASP — Water, Air, and Soil Pollution
WASP — Water Spectrum
WASPB — Water Spectrum
Was Polit — Waseda Political Studies
Wasser- Energiewirt — Wasser- und Energiewirtschaft
Wasser Luft Betr — Wasser, Luft, und Betrieb
Wasserwirtsch-Wassertech — Wasserwirtschaft-Wassertechnik
Wasserwirt-Wassertech — Wasserwirtschaft-Wassertechnik
W Assn Map Lib Inf Bull — Western Association of Map Libraries. Information Bulletin
Wasswirt Wasstech — Wasserwirtschaft-Wassertechnik
Waste Disposal & Water Manage in Aust — Waste Disposal and Water Management in Australia
Waste Disposal Water Manage Aust — Waste Disposal and Water Management in Australia
Waste Dispos Water Manage Aust — Waste Disposal and Water Management in Australia
Waste Disp Recyc Bull — Waste Disposal and Recycling Bulletin
Waste Mgmt Inf Bull — Waste Management Information Bulletin
Waste Mgmt Res — Waste Management Research
Wastes Eng — Wastes Engineering
Wastes Mgmt — Wastes Management
WAT — What Acronym's That?
Wat Aust — Water in Australia
WA Teachers J — Western Australian Teachers' Journal
WA Teach J — Western Australian Teachers' Journal
Water Air Soil Pollut — Water, Air, and Soil Pollution
Water Air and Soil Pollut — Water, Air, and Soil Pollution
Water Am Inst Chem Eng — Water. American Institute of Chemical Engineers
Water A S P — Water, Air, and Soil Pollution
Water Biol Syst — Water in Biological Systems
Water Electrolyte Metab Proc Symp — Water and Electrolyte Metabolism. Proceedings of the Symposium
Water Eng — Water and Wastes Engineering
Water Invest Mich Geol Surv Div — Water Investigation. Michigan Geological Survey Division
Water Law Newsl — Water Law Newsletter [*United States*]
Water Manage News — Water Management News
Water Manage Techn Rep Colorado State Univ — Colorado State University. Water Management Technical Report
Water Poll Abstr — Water Pollution Abstracts
Water Poll Cont Fed J — Water Pollution Control Federation. Journal
Water Poll Control Fed J — Water Pollution Control Federation. Journal
Water Pollut Control — Water Pollution Control
Water Pollut Control (Don Mills Can) — Water and Pollution Control (Don Mills, Canada)
Water Pollut Control (London) — Water Pollution Control (London)
Water Pollut Control Res Ser — Water Pollution Control Research Series
Water Pollut Res Can — Water Pollution Research in Canada
Water Pollut Res (Stevenage) — Water Pollution Research (Stevenage)
Water Purif Liquid Wastes Treat — Water Purification and Liquid Wastes Treatment [*Japan*]
Water Qual Instrum — Water Quality Instrumentation
Water Res — Water Research
Water Res Found Aust Annu Rep Balance Sheet — Water Research Foundation of Australia. Annual Report and Balance Sheet
Water Res Found Aust Bull — Water Research Foundation of Australia. Bulletin
Water Res Found of Aust Newsl — Water Research Foundation of Australia. Newsletter
Water Res Found Aust Rep — Water Research Foundation of Australia. Report
Water Res News — Water Research News
Water Resour — Water Resources
Water Resour Bull — Water Resources Bulletin
Water Resour Bull Nev Div Water Resour — Water Resources Bulletin. Nevada Division of Water Resources

Water Resour Bull (PR) — Water Resources Bulletin (Puerto Rico)
Water Resour Res — Water Resources Research
Water Resour Circ Arkansas Geol Comm — Water Resources Circular. Arkansas Geological Commission
Water Resour Invest — Water Resources Investigations
Water Resour Invest US Geol Surv — Water Resources Investigations. United States Geological Survey
Water Resour Manag Ser — Water Resource Management Series
Water Resour Newsl — Water Resources Newsletter
Water Resour Reconnaissance Ser Nev Div Water Resour — Water Resources. Reconnaissance Series. Nevada Division of Water Resources
Water Resour Rep Ariz State Land Dep — Water Resources Report. Arizona State Land Department
Water Resour Rep Ont Minist Environ Water Resour Branch — Water Resources Report. Ontario Ministry of the Environment. Water Resources Branch
Water Resour Res — Water Resources Research
Water Resour Res Cent VA Polytech Inst State Univ Bull — Water Resources Research Center. Virginia Polytechnic Institute and State University. Bulletin
Water Resour Rev Streamflow Ground-Water Cond — Water Resources Review for Streamflow and Ground-Water Conditions [*United States - Canada*]
Water Resour Ser Tenn Div Water Resour — Water Resources Series. Tennessee Division of Water Resources
Water Resour Symp — Water Resources Symposium
Water Res R — Water Resources Research
Water (S Afr) — Water (South Africa)
Water and San — Water and Sanitation
Water Sanit Eng — Water and Sanitary Engineer
Water Sci & Technol — Water Science and Technology
Water Serv — Water Services
Water & Sewage Works — Water and Sewage Works
Water Supply Manage — Water Supply and Management [*England*]
Water Supply Pap Geol Surv GB Hydrogeol Rep — Water Supply Papers. Geological Survey of Great Britain. Hydrogeological Report
Water Supply Pap US Geol Surv — Water Supply Paper. United States Geological Survey
Water Treat Exam — Water Treatment and Examination
Water Waste — Water and Wastes Engineering
Water & Waste Engng — Water and Waste Engineering
Water Wastes Dig — Water and Wastes Digest
Water Wastes Eng — Water and Wastes Engineering
Water Wastes Eng Ind — Water and Wastes Engineering/Industrial
Water Waste Treat — Water and Waste Treatment
Water Wastewater Treat Plants Oper Newsl — Water and Wastewater Treatment Plants Operators' Newsletter
Water Water Eng — Water and Water Engineering
Water (WC and IC Staff Journal) — Water (Water Conservation and Irrigation Commission Staff Journal)
Water Well J — Water Well Journal
Water Well Jour — Water Well Journal
Water Works Eng — Water Works Engineering
WatPolAb — Water Pollution Abstracts
Wat Pollut Control — Water Pollution Control
Wat Pwr — Water Power
WATRA — Water Research
WatResAb — Water Resources Abstracts
Wat Res Fdn Aust Bull — Water Research Foundation of Australia. Bulletin
Wat Res Fdn Rep — Water Research Foundation of Australia. Report
Wat Resour Res — Water Resources Research
Wat Serv — Water Services
Wattle Res Inst Univ Natal (S Afr) Rep — Wattle Research Institute. University of Natal (South Africa). Report
Wat Vict — Water in Victoria
Wat Waste Treat — Water and Waste Treatment
Wat Wat Engng — Water and Water Engineering
WAU Law R — University of Western Australia. Law Review
WAULR — Western Australia University. Law Review
WA Univ Gaz — University of Western Australia. Gazette
WA Univ Geog Lab Res Rept — University of Western Australia. Geography Laboratory. Research Report
W Aust For Dep Bull — Western Australia. Forests Department. Bulletin
W Aust Geol Surv Bull — Western Australia. Geological Survey. Bulletin
W Aust Geol Surv 1:250000 Geol Ser — Western Australia. Geological Survey. 1:250,000 Geological Series
W Aust Nat — Western Australian Naturalist
Wave Electron — Wave Electronics
Wave Part Dualism — Wave. Particle Dualism
Wayne L Rev — Wayne Law Review
Way Suppl — Way. Supplement
WB — Weimarer Beitraege
WB — Wiener Blaetter fuer die Freunde der Antike
WB — Worlds Beyond
WB — Wort und Brauch
WBC — Bloembollencultuur

WBD — Worlds Beyond
WBE — Weekblad voor Fiscaal Recht
WBEP — Wiener Beitraege zur Englischen Philologie
WBKL — Wiener Beitraege zur Kulturgeschichte und Linguistik
Wbl voor Fiscaal Recht — Weekblad voor Fiscaal Recht
WBN — Wolfenbuetteler Barock-Nachrichten
WBNP — Wood Buffalo National Park. Newsletter
WBOLA — Wasser, Boden, Luft
WBP — Woodwind World - Brass and Percussion
WBV — Woningraad. Informatiekrant voor Woningcorporaties
WBW — World Business Weekly
WC — Wordsworth Circle
WC — Wspolczesnosc
W Can J Ant — West Canadian Journal of Anthropology
WCBD (VIC) — Workers Compensation Board Decisions (Victoria)
WCBD (WA) — Workers Compensation Board Decisions (Western Australia)
WCB (VIC) — Workers Compensation Board Decisions (Victoria)
WCC — Workers' Compensation Cases
WCC — Workmen's Circle Call
WCH — Workshop Conferences Hoechst [*Elsevier Book Series*]
Wchnbl K K Gesellsch Aerzte Wien — Wochenblatt. K. K. Gesellschaft der Aerzte in Wien
Wchnschr Ges Heilk — Wochenschrift fuer die Gesamte Heilkunde
Wchnschr Tierh u Viehzucht — Wochenschrift fuer Tierheilkunde und Viehzucht
WCJ — White Cloud Journal of American Indian/Alaska Native Mental Health
WCJA — Western Canadian Journal of Anthropology
WCN — World Coin News
WCOD — Western Canada Outdoors. Combining The Whooper and Defending All Outdoors
WCoins — World Coins
W Comp Pres Docs — Weekly Compilation of Presidential Documents
WCR — West Coast Review
WCR — Workers' Compensation Reports [*New South Wales*]
WCRB — West Coast Review of Books
WCRED — WESCON [*Western Electronics Show and Convention*] Conference Record
WCR (NSW) — Workers' Compensation Reports (New South Wales)
WCR (Q) — Workers' Compensation Reports (Queensland)
WCR (Qld) — Workers' Compensation Reports (Queensland)
WCR (Qn) — Worker's Compensation Reports (Queensland)
WCSMLL — Western Canadian Studies in Modern Languages and Literature
WCWN — William Carlos Williams Newsletter
WD — [*The*] Weekly Dispatch
WD — Winter's Digest
WD — Wittenberg Door
WD — Woman's Day
Wd — Word
Wd — World
W & D — Wort und Dienst
WD — Writers Digest
WDB — Suedosteuropa. Zeitschrift fuer Gegenwartsforschung
WDEFA — Welding Design and Fabrication
WDGB — Wuerzburger Diozesangeschichtsblaetter
Wdl — Wirkung der Literatur
WdO — Welt des Orients. Wissenschaftliche Beitraege zur Kunde des Morgenlandes [*Wuppertal/Stuttgart/Goettingen*]
WDRAA — Welding Research Abroad
WDRKA — Waseda Daigaku Rikogaku Kenkyusho Hokoku
WDRSA — Wood Research
WdSL — Welt der Slaven
WDWRA — Welding in the World
WE — Winesburg Eagle
WEA Bul — WEA [*Workers Educational Association*] Bulletin
Weather and Clim — Weather and Climate
Weather C & M — Weather, Crops, and Markets
Weather Dev Res Bull — Weather Development and Research Bulletin [*Australia, Commonwealth Bureau of Meteorology*]
Weather Research Bull — Weather Research Bulletin
WEB — National Westminster Bank. Quarterly Review
Webb A'B & W — Webb, A'Beckett, and Williams' Reports
Webb A'B & W Eq — Webb, A'Beckett, and Williams' Equity Reports
Webb A'B & W IE & M — Webb, A'Beckett, and Williams' Insolvency, Ecclesiastical, and Matrimonial Reports
Webb A'B & W IP & M — Webb, A'Beckett, and Williams' Insolvency, Probate, and Matrimonial Reports
Webb A'B & W Min — Webb, A'Beckett, and Williams' Mining Cases
Webbia Racc Scr Bot — Webbia; Raccolta di Scritti Botanici
Web R — Webster Review
WEC — Whole Earth Catalog
W Econ J — Western Economic Journal
WEE — Weerberichten. Informatiebulletin over Windenergie en Zonne-Energie
Weed Abstr — Weed Abstracts
Weed Res — Weed Research

Weed Sci — Weed Science
WEEGA — Welding Engineer
Week-End R — Australian Week-End Review of Current Books, the Arts, and Entertainments
Weekly Compilation Presidential Docum — Weekly Compilation of Presidential Documents
Weekly Comp of Pres Doc — Weekly Compilation of Presidential Documents
Weekly N L — Weekly News Letter. United States Department of Agriculture
Weekly Underw — Weekly Underwriter
Week No — New South Wales Weekly Notes
WEESA — Weed Science
WEG — Wegen
WEH — Hungarian News Agency. Weekly Bulletin
Wehrmed Monatsschr — Wehrmedizinische Monatsschrift
Wehrtech — Wehrtechnik
WEHSA — Work-Environment-Health
WEI — World Energy Industry
Weibulls Arsb — Weibulls Arsbok
Weinbau Kellerwirtsch (Budapest) — Weinbau und Kellerwirtschaft (Budapest)
Wein-Wiss — Wein-Wissenschaft
Weiterbildungszentrum Math Kybernet Rechentech — Weiterbildungszentrum fuer Mathematische Kybernetik und Rechentechnik
Weizmann Mem Lect — Weizmann Memorial Lectures
WEJ — Western Economic Journal
WEJUA — Welding Journal [*Miami*]
WEK — Werkgever
WEKLA — Wiadomosci Ekologiczne
WEL — Weltwirtschaftliches Archiv
Weld Des Fabr — Welding Design and Fabrication
Weld Des and Fabr — Welding Design and Fabrication
Weld Eng — Welding Engineer
Weld Fabrication Design — Welding Fabrication and Design
Weld Fabric Design — Welding Fabrication and Design
Welding J — Welding Journal
Weld Int — Welding International [*United Kingdom*]
Weld J (London) — Welding Journal (London)
Weld J (Miami) — Welding Journal (Miami)
Weld J (NY) — Welding Journal (New York)
Weld J Res Suppl — Welding Journal Research. Supplement
Weld Metal Fabr — Welding and Metal Fabrication
Weld Met Fabr — Welding and Metal Fabrication
Weld News — Welding News
Weld Prod — Welding Production
Weld Prod (USSR) — Welding Production (USSR)
Weld Res Abroad — Welding Research Abroad
Weld Res C — Welding Research Council. Bulletin
Weld Res Counc Bull — Welding Research Council. Bulletin
Weld Res Counc Prog Rep — Welding Research Council. Progress Reports
Weld Res Int — Welding Research International
Weld Res (Miami) — Welding Research (Miami)
Weld Res (Miami Fla) — Welding Research (Miami, Florida)
Weld Res News — Welding Research News
Weld Rev — Welding Review
Weld Tech — Welding Technique [*Japan*]
Weld Wld — Welding in the World/Le Soudage dans le Monde
Weld World — Welding in the World
Weld World Soudage Monde — Welding in the World/Le Soudage dans le Monde
Welf Focus — Welfare Focus
Well Inventory Ser (Metric Units) Inst Geol Sci — Well Inventory Series (Metric Units). Institute of Geological Sciences
Well Serv — Well Servicing
Wells Frgo — Wells Fargo Bank. Business Review
Wellworthy Top — Wellworthy Topics
Welsh Bee J — Welsh Bee Journal
Welsh Beekprs' Ass Q Bull — Welsh Beekeepers' Association. Quarterly Bulletin
Welsh Hist Rev — Welsh History Review
Welsh H R — Welsh History Review
Welsh J Agric — Welsh Journal of Agriculture
Welsh Plant Breed Stn (Aberystwyth) Rep — Welsh Plant Breeding Station (Aberystwyth). Report
Welsh Plant Breed Stn (Aberystwyth) Tech Bull — Welsh Plant Breeding Station (Aberystwyth). Technical Bulletin
Welsh Plant Breed Stn Bull Ser — Welsh Plant Breeding Station. Bulletin Series
Welt Isl — Die Welt des Islam
Weltraumfahrt Raketentech — Weltraumfahrt und Raketentechnik
Weltwir Arc — Weltwirtschaftliches Archiv
Weltwirt — Weltwirtschaft
Weltwirtschaft Archiv — Weltwirtschaftliches Archiv [*Kiel*]
Weltwirtsch Archiv — Weltwirtschaftliches Archiv
WEM — Western Miner
WEMOB — Wehrmedizinische Monatsschrift
WENMD — Water Engineering and Management

Wenner-Gren Cent Int Symp Ser — Wenner-Gren Center. International Symposium Series
Wentworth Mag — Wentworth Magazine
WEO — West-Ost-Journal
WEP — Waseda Economic Papers
WEPRA — Welding Production [*English Translation*]
WER — Week End Review
Werk — Werk/Archithese
WERKA — Werkstatttechnik
Werkstatt und Betr — Werkstatt und Betrieb
Werkstatt Betr — Werkstatt und Betrieb
Werkstattstech Z Ind Fertigung — Werkstatttechnik Zeitschrift fuer Industrielle Fertigung
Werkst Korros — Werkstoffe und Korrosion
Werkst u Korrosion — Werkstoffe und Korrossion (Wernheim)
Wernerian N H Soc Mem — Wernerian Natural History Society. Memoirs
WESCON Tech Pap — WESCON [*Western Electronics Show and Convention*] Technical Papers [*United States*]
Wesley Th J — Wesleyan Theological Journal
Wesley W Spink Lect Comp Med — Wesley W. Spink Lectures on Comparative Medicine
West Afr Cocoa Res Inst Tech Bull — West African Cocoa Research Institute. Technical Bulletin
West African J of Ed — West African Journal of Education
West Afr Inst Oil Palm Res Annu Rep — West African Institute for Oil Palm Research. Annual Report
West Afr J Archaeol — West African Journal of Archaeology
West Afr J Biol Appl Chem — West African Journal of Biological and Applied Chemistry
West Afr J Biol Chem — West African Journal of Biological Chemistry
West Afr J Pharmacol Drug Res — West African Journal of Pharmacology and Drug Research
West Afr Med J — West African Medical Journal
West Afr Med J Nigerian Pract — West African Medical Journal and Nigerian Practitioner
West Afr Pharm — West African Pharmacist
West Am Lit — Western American Literature
West Am Sc — West American Scientist
West Assn Map Libs Inf Bul — Western Association of Map Libraries. Information Bulletin
West AULR — Western Australia University. Law Review
West Aust Clin Rep — Western Australian Clinical Reports
West Aust Conf Australas Inst Min Metall — Western Australian Conference. Australasian Institute of Mining and Metallurgy
West Aust Dep Agric Annu Rep — Western Australia. Department of Agriculture. Annual Report
West Aust Dep Fish Fauna Rep — Western Australia. Department of Fisheries and Fauna. Report
West Aust Dep Fish Wildl Rep — Western Australia. Department of Fisheries and Wildlife. Report
West Aust Dep Mines Annu Rep — Western Australia. Department of Mines. Annual Report
West Aust Dep Mines Miner Resour West Aust Bull — Western Australia. Department of Mines. Mineral Resources of Western Australia. Bulletin
West Aust Dep Mines Min Resour West Aust Bull — Western Australia. Department of Mines. Mineral Resources of Western Australia. Bulletin
West Aust Dep Mines Rep Gov Mineral Anal Chem — Western Australia. Department of Mines. Report of the Government Mineralogist, Analyst, and Chemist
West Aust Geol Surv Annu Prog Rep — Western Australia. Geological Survey. Annual Progress Report
West Aust Geol Surv Annu Rep — Western Australia. Geological Survey. Annual Report
West Aust Geol Surv Bull — Western Australia. Geological Survey. Bulletin
West Aust Geol Surv 1:250000 Geol Ser — Western Australia. Geological Survey. 1:250,000 Geological Series
West Aust Geol Surv Geol Ser Explan Notes — Western Australia. Geological Survey. Geological Series. Explanatory Notes
West Aust Geol Surv Miner Resour Bull — Western Australia. Geological Survey. Mineral Resources Bulletin
West Aust Geol Surv Rep — Western Australia. Geological Survey. Report
West Aust Inst Technol Gaz — Western Australian Institute of Technology. Gazette
West Austl — Western Australian Reports
West Aust L Rev — University of Western Australia. Law Review
West Aust Mar Res Lab Fish Res Bull — Western Australian Marine Research Laboratories. Fisheries Research Bulletin
West Aust Mus Spec Publ — Western Australian Museum. Special Publication
West Aust Nat — Western Australian Naturalist
West Aust Naturalist — Western Australian Naturalist
West Aust Rep Gov Chem Lab — Western Australia. Government Chemical Laboratories. Report
West Aust Rep Gov Chem Lab — Western Australia. Report. Government Chemical Laboratories
West Austr L — Western Australian Law Reports
West Aust Sch Mines — Western Australian School of Mines

West Aust SWANS — Western Australia SWANS [*State Wildlife Authority News Service*]
West Aust Wildl Res Cent Wildl Res Bull — Western Australia Wildlife Research Centre. Wildlife Research Bulletin
West Bird Bander — Western Bird Bander
West Build — Western Building [*United States*]
West Bus — Western Business
West Canad J Anthropol — Western Canadian Journal of Anthropology
West Can Beekpr — Western Canada Beekeeper
West Can J Anthropol — Western Canadian Journal of Anthropology
West Canner Packer — Western Canner and Packer
West Can Water Sewage Conf Pap Annu Conv — Western Canada Water and Sewage Conference. Papers Presented at the Annual Convention
West Can Water and Sewage Conf Proc Annu Conv — Western Canada Water and Sewage Conference. Proceedings of the Annual Convention
West Chapter Int Shade Tree Conf Proc — Western Chapter. International Shade Tree Conference. Proceedings
West Chem Metall — Western Chemist and Metallurgist
Westchester Co Hist Soc Publ — Westchester County Historical Society. Publications
Westchester Med Bull — Westchester Medical Bulletin [*New York*]
West City — Western City
West Coast R — West Coast Review
West Constr — Western Construction
West Contract — Western Contractor
West Crop Farm Manage N Ed — Western Crops and Farm Management. Northern Edition
West Crop Farm Manage S Ed — Western Crops and Farm Management. Southern Edition
West Drug — Western Druggist
West Econ Jour — Western Economic Journal
West Elec E — Western Electric Engineer
West Electr Eng — Western Electric Engineer
Westerm M — Westermanns Monatshefte
Westerm Monatsh — Westermanns Monatshefte
Western Am Lit — Western American Literature
Western Australia Geol Survey Rept — Western Australia. Geological Survey. Report. Government Printer
Western Australia Main Roads Dep Tech Bull — Western Australia. Main Roads Department. Technical Bulletin
Western EE — Western Electric Engineer
Western Electric Eng — Western Electric Engineer
Western Eng — Western Engineering
Western Hist Q — Western Historical Quarterly
Western Hum R — Western Humanities Review
Western Hum Rev — Western Humanities Review
Western Law Jour — Western Law Journal (Reprint)
Western Ont L Rev — Western Ontario Law Review
Western Pol Q — Western Political Quarterly
Western Reserve Hist Soc Tracts — Western Reserve Historical Society. Tracts
Western Res L Rev — Western Reserve Law Review
Western Rv Sc — Western Review of Science and Industry
Western Speleol Inst Bull — Western Speleological Institute. Bulletin
Western Wash Ag Exp B — Western Washington Agricultural Experiment Station. Monthly Bulletin
West Europe Ed — Western European Education
West Eur Politics — West European Politics
West-Eur Symp Clin Chem — West-European Symposia on Clinical Chemistry
Westfael Bienenztg — Westfaelische Bienenzeitung
West Farmer — Western Farmer
Westf Bienenztg — Westfaelische Bienenzeitung
West Feed — Western Feed
West Feed Seed — Western Feed and Seed
West Folk — Western Folklore
West Folkl — Western Folklore
West Found Vertebr Zool Occas Pap — Western Foundation of Vertebrate Zoology. Occasional Papers
Westfriesch Jb — Westfriesch Jaarboek
West Frozen Foods — Western Frozen Foods
West Fruit Grow — Western Fruit Grower
West Gas — Western Gas
West Hist Q — Western Historical Quarterly
West Horse — Western Horseman
West HR — Western Humanities Review
West Humanities Rev — Western Humanities Review
West Hum R — Western Humanities Review
West Hum Rev — Western Humanities Review
West Ind Bull — West Indian Bulletin
West Indian Med J — West Indian Medical Journal
Westinghouse Eng — Westinghouse Engineer
Westinghouse Engr — Westinghouse Engineer
West J Agric Econ — Western Journal of Agricultural Economics
West J Med — Western Journal of Medicine
West J Nurs Res — Western Journal of Nursing Research
West J Surg Obstet Gynecol — Western Journal of Surgery. Obstetrics and Gynecology

West Law J — Western Law Journal
West Law Jour — Western Law Journal (Reprint)
West Lit J — Western Literary Journal
West Livestock J — Western Livestock Journal
West LJ — Western Law Journal
West LJ (Ohio) — Western Law Journal (Ohio)
West Locker — Western Locker
West M — Western Monthly Magazine
Westm — Westminster Review
West Mach Steel World — Western Machinery and Steel World
West Malays Geol Surv Dist Mem — West Malaysia. Geological Survey. District Memoir
West Malays Geol Surv Econ Bull — West Malaysia. Geological Survey. Economic Bulletin
West Med — Western Medicine
West Met — Western Metals
West Metalwork — Western Metalworking
West Miner — Western Miner
Westminster Inst Rev — Westminister Institute Review
West Mo R — Western Monthly Review
Westm Th J — Westminster Theological Journal
West Nat — Western Naturalist
West New Engl L Rev — Western New England Law Review
West Oil Refin — Western Oil Refining
West Oil Rep — Western Oil Reporter
West Ont L Rev — Western Ontario Law Review
West PA Hist Mag — Western Pennsylvania Historical Magazine
West Paint Rev — Western Paint Review
West Pak J Agric Res — West Pakistan Journal of Agricultural Research
West Penn Hist Mag — Western Pennsylvania Historical Magazine
West Pet Refiners Assoc Tech Publ — Western Petroleum Refiners Association. Technical Publication
West Plast — Western Plastics
West Polit Q — Western Political Quarterly
West Polit Quart — Western Political Quarterly
West Pol Q — Western Political Quarterly
West Poult Dis Conf — Western Poultry Disease Conference
Westpr Geschichtsv Ztsch — Westpreussischer Geschichtsverein. Zeitschrift
West Pulp Pap — Western Pulp and Paper
West R — Western Review
West Reg Ext Publ Co-op Ext US Dep Ag — Western Region Extension Publication. Cooperative Extension. United States Department of Agriculture
West Reg Pub Colo St Univ Exp Stn — Western Regional Publication. Colorado State University. Experiment Station
West Reserve Law Rev — Western Reserve Law Review
West Res Law Rev — Western Reserve Law Review
West Res L Rev — Western Reserve Law Review
West Resour Conf — Western Resources Conference
West Rev — Westminster Review
West Roads — Western Roads
West Scot Agric Coll Res Bull — West of Scotland Agricultural College. Research Bulletin
West Scot Iron Steel Inst J — West of Scotland Iron and Steel Institute. Journal
West Scotl Agric Coll Res Bull — West of Scotland Agricultural College. Research Bulletin
West Shade Tree Conf Proc Annu Meet — Western Shade Tree Conference. Proceedings of the Annual Meeting
West Soc Eng J — Western Society of Engineers. Journal
West Soc Malacol Annu Rep — Western Society of Malacologists. Annual Report
West Soc Malacol Occas Pap — Western Society of Malacologists. Occasional Paper
West States Jew Hist Q — Western States Jewish Historical Quarterly
West States Sect Combust Inst Pap — Western States Section. Combustion Institute. Paper
West State UL Rev — Western State University. Law Review
West St U LR — Western State University. Law Review
West St U L Rev — Western State University. Law Review
West Teach — Western Teacher
West Tenn Hist Soc Pap — West Tennessee Historical Society. Papers
West Texas Geol Soc Pub — West Texas Geological Society. Publication
West Tex Today — Western Texas Today
West Th J — Westminster Theological Journal
WestTJ — Westminster Theological Journal [*Philadelphia*]
West Union Tech Rev — Western Union Technical Review
West Va Lib — West Virginia Libraries
West Vet — Western Veterinarian
West Virginia Geol and Econ Survey Basic Data Rept — West Virginia. Geological and Economic Survey. Basic Data Report
West Virginia Geol and Econ Survey Circ — West Virginia. Geological and Economic Survey. Circular
West Virginia L Rev — West Virginia Law Review
West Wildlands — Western Wildlands

Wet Bydraes PU CHO Reeks B Natuurwet — Wetenskaplike Bydraes van die PU [*Potchefstroomse Universiteit*] vir CHO [*Christelike Hoere Onderwys*]. Reeks B: Natuurwetenskappe
Wetenskap Studiereeks — Wetenskaplike Studiereeks
Wet Ground Mica Assoc Inc Tech Bull — Wet Ground Mica Association, Incorporated. Technical Bulletin
Wet Meded KNNV — Wetenschappelijke Mededeling KNNV [*Koninklijke Nederlandse Natuurhistorische Vereniging*]
Wet Samenleving — Wetenschap en Samenleving
Wet Tijd — Wetenschappelijke Tijdingen. Vereniging voor Wetenschapp de Gent
Wett Leben — Wetter und Leben
W Europe Educ — Western European Education
W Eur Policies — West European Policies
W Eur Politics — West European Politics
WEV — World Economy
WEVO — Waehrungsergaenzungsverordnung
WEW — Wasser- und Energiewirtschaft
WeW — Welt und Wort
Weyerhauser For Pap — Weyerhauser Forestry Paper
WF — Wege der Forschung, Darmstadt, Wissenschaftliche Buchgesellschaft
WF — Wehrforschung
WF — Western Folklore
WF — Westfaelische Forschungen
WFA — Worlds of Fantasy [*1968-*]
WFI — World Faiths Insight
WFZ — Wirtschaftswoche
WG — Waehrungsgesetz
Wg — Wandlung
WG — Water Resources News-Clipping Service. General Issue. Water Management Service. Department of the Environment [*Ottawa*]
WG — Welt als Geschichte Zeitschrift fuer Universalgeschichtliche Forschung
W & G — Wissen und Glauben
WG — Wissenschaft und Gegenwart
WGCR — West Georgia College. Review
WGI — Nieuwe West-Indische Gids
WGI — Wirtschaftsgeograpnisches Institut
WH — Wald und Holz
Whartn Mag — Wharton Magazine
Wharton — Wharton Magazine
Wharton M — Wharton Magazine
Wharton Mag — Wharton Magazine
Wharton Q — Wharton Quarterly
Whats New Bldg — What's New in Building
What's New Comput — What's New in Computing
Whats New in For Res — What's New in Forest Research
Whats New Home Econ — What's New in Home Economics
Whats New Plant Physiol — What's New in Plant Physiology
WHB — Which?
WHB — Wiener Humanistische Blaetter
WH Bl — Wiener Humanistische Blaetter
Wheat Board Gaz — Wheat Board Gazette
Wheat Inform Serv — Wheat Information Service
Wheat Inf Serv — Wheat Information Service
Wheat Situation Bur Agr Econ (Aust) — Wheat Situation. Bureau of Agricultural Economics (Australia)
Wheat Stud Food Res Inst — Wheat Studies. Food Research Institute
WHEE — Wheel Extended
Wheel Ext — Wheel Extended
Where to Find Out More about Educ — Where to Find Out More about Education
Whet — Whetstone
WHG — Wasserhaushaltsgesetz
WHI — World Trade Information
Which Comput — Which Computer?
Which Word Process — Which Word Processor?
Which Word Process and Off Syst — Which Word Processor and Office System?
WHIMSY — Western Humor and Irony Membership. Serial Yearbook [*Tempe, Arizona*]
W Hist Q — Western Historical Quarterly
White Met News Lett — White Metal News Letter
Whittier L Rev — Whittier Law Review
Whitt L Rev — Whittier Law Review
WHOC-A — WHO [*World Health Organization*] Chronicle [*Switzerland*]
WHOCA — World Health Organization. Chronicle
WHO Chron — WHO [*World Health Organization*] Chronicle
WHO Food Addit Ser — WHO [*World Health Organization*] Food Additives Series
WHO Int Agency Res Cancer Annu Rep — World Health Organization International Agency for Research on Cancer. Annual Report
WHOI Technical Report — Woods Hole Oceanographic Institution. Technical Report
WHO Libr Ne — WHO [*World Health Organization*] Library News
WHO Monogr Ser — World Health Organization. Monograph Series
WHO Offset Publ — WHO [*World Health Organization*] Offset Publication

WHO Pestic Residues Ser — WHO [*World Health Organization*] Pesticide Residues Series
WHO Publ — WHO [*World Health Organization*] Publications
WHO Publ Hlth Pap — WHO [*World Health Organization*] Public Health Papers
WHO Public Health Papers — World Health Organization. Public Health Papers
WHO Tech Rep Ser — World Health Organization. Technical Report Series
WHO Tech Rep Sers — World Health Organization. Technical Report Series
WHQ — Western Historical Quarterly
WHR — Welsh History Review
WHR — Western Humanities Review
WHS — Weekly Hansard - Senate
WHS — Works. Richard Hakluyt Society
WHTCA — Wehrtechnik
WI — Welt des Islams
WI — Wiadomosci
Wi — Wiez
WI — Wisconsin School Musician
WI — Wohnungswirtschaftliche Informationen
WI — Wood Industries
WI — Woprosy Istorii
WIA — Wirtschaftskonjunktur. Analysen, Perspektiven, Indikatoren
Wiad Bot — Wiadomosci Botaniczne
Wiad Chem — Wiadomosci Chemiczne
Wiad Ekol — Wiadomosci Ekologiczne
Wiad Elektrotech — Wiadomosci Elektrotechniczne
Wiad Gorn — Wiadomosci Gornicze [*Poland*]
Wiad Hist — Wiadomosci Historyczne
Wiad Hutn — Wiadomosci Hutnicze
Wiad Inst Melior Uzytkow Zielon (Warsaw) — Wiadomosci. Instytut Melioracji i Uzytkow Zielonych (Warsaw)
Wiad Lek — Wiadomosci Lekarskie
Wiad Mat — Wiadomosci Matematyczne
Wiad Melior Lak — Wiadomosci Melioracyjne i Lakarskie
Wiad Melior Lakarsk — Wiadomosci Melioracyjne i Lakarskie
Wiad Meteorol Gospod Wodnej — Wiadomosci Meteorologii i Gospodarki Wodnej
Wiad Naft — Wiadomosci Naftowe
Wiad Num Arch — Wiadomosci Numizmatyczno-Archeologiczne [*Later, Wiadomosci Numizmatyczne*]
Wiadom Mat — Wiadomosci Matematyczne
Wiadom Mat 2 — Roczniki Polskiego Towarzystwa Matematycznego. Seria II. Wiadomosci Matematyczne
Wiadom Statyst — Wiadomosci Statystyczne
Wiad Parazyt — Wiadomosci Parazytologiczne
Wiad Parazytol — Wiadomosci Parazytologiczne
Wiad Stat — Wiadomosci Statystyczne
Wiad St Hydrol Met — Wiadomosci Sluzby Hydrologicznej i Meteorologicznej
Wiad Telekomun — Wiadomosci Telekomunikacyjne
Wiad Zielarskie — Wiadomosci Zielarskie
WIB — Wetenschapsbeleid
WI Bl — Wirtschaftsrechtliche Informations-Blaetter
Wi Ch — Wirtschaftspolitische Chronik
Wi Di — Wirtschaftsdienst
Wiederbeleb Organersatz Intensivmed — Wiederbelebung. Organersatz. Intensivmedizin
Wiederg G — Gesetz zur Regelung der Wiedergutmachung Nationalsozialistischen Unrechts fuer Angehoerige des Oeffentlichen Dienstes
Wien Arch Innere Med — Wiener Archiv fuer Innere Medizin
Wien Arch Psychol Psychiat Neurol — Wiener Archiv fuer Psychologie, Psychiatrie, und Neurologie
Wien Beitr — Wiener Beitraege zur Englischen Philologie
Wien Beitr Chir — Wiener Beitraege zur Chirurgie
Wien Beitr Gesch Med — Wiener Beitraege zur Geschichte der Medizin
Wien Chem Ztg — Wiener Chemiker Zeitung
Wien Entom Monatschr — Wiener Entomologische Monatsschrift
Wien Ent Rd — Wiener Entomologische Rundschau
Wiener Ethnohist Bl — Wiener Ethnohistorische Blaetter
Wiener Voelkerk Mitt — Wiener Voelkerkundliche Mitteilungen
Wiener Z Kunde Sud — Wiener Zeitschrift fuer die Kunde Suedasiens und Archiv fuer Indische Philosophie [*Vienna*]
Wien Geschichtsbl — Wiener Geschichtsblaetter
Wien Jahrb Kunstgesch — Wiener Jahrbuch fuer Kunstgeschichte
Wien Klin W — Wiener Klinische Wochenschrift
Wien Klin Wochenschr — Wiener Klinische Wochenschrift
Wien Klin Wochenschr Suppl — Wiener Klinische Wochenschrift. Supplementum
Wien Klin Ws — Wiener Klinische Wochenschrift
Wien Landwirtsch Ztg — Wiener Landwirtschaftliche Zeitung
Wien Med Presse — Wiener Medizinische Presse
Wien Med Wochenschr — Wiener Medizinische Wochenschrift
Wien Med Wochenschr (Beih) — Wiener Medizinische Wochenschrift (Beihefte)

Wien Med Wochenschr Suppl — Wiener Medizinische Wochenschrift. Supplementum
Wien Med Ws — Wiener Medizinische Wochenschrift
Wien Med Wschr — Wiener Medizinische Wochenschrift
Wien Mitt Photogr Inhalts — Wiener Mitteilungen Photographischen Inhalts
Wien Mitt Wasser Abwasser Gewaesser — Wiener Mitteilungen. Wasser, Abwaesser, Gewaesser
Wien Naturh Mus Annalen — Wien Naturhistorischer Museum. Annalen
Wien Pharm Wochenschr — Wiener Pharmazeutische Wochenschrift
Wien Praehist Z — Wiener Praehistorische Zeitschrift [*Austria*]
Wien Stud Z Klass Philol — Wiener Studien. Zeitschrift fuer Klassische Philologie
Wien Tieraerztl Monatsschr — Wiener Tieraerztliche Monatsschrift
Wien Tieraerztl Mschr — Wiener Tieraerztliche Monatsschrift
Wien Voelkerk Mitt — Wiener Voelkerkundliche Mitteilungen
Wien Z Inn Med Ihre Grenzgeb — Wiener Zeitschrift fuer Innere Medizin und Ihre Grenzgebiete
Wien Z Kunde Morgenlandes — Wiener Zeitschrift fuer die Kunde des Morgenlandes
Wien Z Kunde Sued Ostasiens — Wiener Zeitschrift fuer die Kunde Sued- und Ostasiens und Archiv fuer Indische Philosophie
Wien Z Nervenheilk Grenzgeb — Wiener Zeitschrift fuer Nervenheilkunde und Deren Grenzgebiete [*Austria*]
Wien Zs Inn Med — Wiener Zeitschrift fuer Innere Medizin und Ihre Grenzgebiete
Wien Zt — Wiener Zeitung
WIERD — Wind Energy Report
WiF — William Faulkner
WIF — Worlds of If
WIFO — Wildfowl
WIG — West-Indische Gids
WIHP — Journal. Wisconsin Association for Health, Physical Education, and Recreation
WIJ — Warburg Institute. Journal
Wijsig Perspect — Wijsgerig Perspectief op Maatschappij en Wetenschap
WIK — Deutsches Institut fuer Wirtschaftsforschung. Wochenbericht
Wiko — Wirtschaftskonjunktur
WIL — Wirtschaftliche Lage in der Bundesrepublik Deutschland
WI Law Rev — Wisconsin Law Review
Wild Barfield Heat-Treat J — Wild Barfield Heat-Treatment Journal
Wild Barfield J — Wild Barfield Journal
Wild Cat — Wild Cat Monthly
Wildenowia Beih — Wildenowia Beiheft
Wildfire Stat US Dep Agric For Serv — Wildfire Statistics. United States Department of Agriculture. Forest Service
Wildl Aust — Wildlife in Australia
Wildl Dis — Wildlife Diseases
Wildl Dis Assoc Bull — Wildlife Disease Association. Bulletin
Wildlife — Wildlife in Australia
Wildlife Aust — Wildlife in Australia
Wild Life Rev — Wild Life Review
Wildl Manage Bull (Ottawa) Ser 1 — Wildlife Management Bulletin (Ottawa). Series 1
Wildl Manage Bull (Ottawa) Ser 2 — Wildlife Management Bulletin (Ottawa). Series 2
Wildl Monogr — Wildlife Monographs
Wildl Rev — Wildlife Review
Wildl Rev NZ Wildl Serv — Wildlife Review. New Zealand Wildlife Service
Wildl Soc Bull — Wildlife Society. Bulletin
Wiley Lib Newsl — Wiley-Interscience Librarian's Newsletter
Wiley Ser Curr Top Reprod Endocrinol — Wiley Series on Current Topics in Reproductive Endocrinology
Wilhelm-Pieck Univ Rostock Wiss Z Math Naturwiss Reihe — Wilhelm-Pieck-Universitaet Rostock. Wissenschaftliche Zeitschrift. Mathematisch-Naturwissenschaftliche Reihe
Wilhelm Roux' Arch — Wilhelm Roux' Archiv fuer Entwicklungsmechanik der Organismen [*Later, Roux' Archives of Developmental Biology*]
Wilhelm Roux' Arch Dev Biol — Wilhelm Roux' Archives of Developmental Biology
Wilhelm Roux' Arch Entwicklungsmech Org — Wilhelm Roux' Archiv fuer Entwicklungsmechanik der Organismen [*Later, Roux' Archives of Developmental Biology*]
Wilhelm Roux Arch EntwMech Org — Wilhelm Roux' Archiv fuer Entwicklungsmechanik der Organismen
Willamette L J — Willamette Law Journal
Willamette L Rev — Willamette Law Review
Willdenowia Beih — Willdenowia Beiheft
William Car — William Carlos Williams Review
William L Hutcheson Mem For Bull — William L. Hutcheson Memorial Forest. Bulletin
William and Mary Law R — William and Mary Law Review
William & Mary L Rev — William and Mary Law Review
William Mitchell L Rev — William Mitchell Law Review
William M Q — William and Mary Quarterly
Williston Basin Oil Rev — Williston Basin Oil Review
Will LJ — Willamette Law Journal

WILM — Wildlife Monographs
WILN — Wildlife News
WILPFNSW Branch Monthly Bulletin — WILPF [*Women's International League for Peace and Freedom*]. New South Wales Branch. Monthly Bulletin
Wil Q — Wilson Quarterly
WI LR — Wisconsin Law Review
Wilson — Wilson Quarterly
Wilson B — Wilson Bulletin
Wilson Bull — Wilson Bulletin
Wilson Lib Bul — Wilson Library Bulletin
Wilson Libr Bull — Wilson Library Bulletin
Wilson Q — Wilson Quarterly
Wilts Beekprs Gaz — Wiltshire Beekeepers' Gazette
Wiltshire Archaeol Natur Hist Mag — Wiltshire Archaeological and Natural History Magazine
Wiltshire Arch Mag — Wiltshire Archaeological Magazine [*Later, Wiltshire Archaeological and Natural History Magazine*]
Wiltshire Arch Natur Hist Mag — Wiltshire Archaeological and Natural History Magazine
Win — Win Magazine
Win — Winter
Wind Energy Rep — Wind Energy Report [*United States*]
Wind Eng — Wind Engineering [*England*]
Wind Engng — Wind Engineering
W Indian Dig — West Indian Digest
W Indian Med J — West Indian Medical Journal
W Indian World — West Indian World
Wind Inst Melior Uzytkow Zielonych — Windomosci Instytutu Melioracji i Uzytkow Zielonych
W Ind Med J — West Indian Medical Journal
Wind O — Windless Orchard
Wind Power Dig — Wind Power Digest
Windsor — Windsor Magazine
Wind Technol J — Wind Technology Journal
Wine Rev — Wine Review
Winnip Clin Q — Winnipeg Clinic. Quarterly
Wintertag — Wintertagung
Winter Tb — Winter's Naturwissenschaftliche Taschenbuecher
Winterthur Jb — Winterthur Jahrbuch
Winthr St M — Winthrop Studies on Major Modern Writers
WIP — Work in Progress
Wi Pr — Wirtschafts-Praxis
WIQUD — Wilson Quarterly
WIR — Western Intelligence Report
Wirbelsacule Forsch Prax — Wirbelsacule in Forschung und Praxis
WIRE — Wildlife Review. British Columbia Ministry of Environment
Wire — Wire [*Draht Fachzeitschrift*]
Wire Ind — Wire Industry
Wire J — Wire Journal
Wireless Eng — Wireless Engineer
Wirel Wld — Wireless World
Wirel World — Wireless World
Wire Prod — Wire and Wire Products
Wire and Wire Prod — Wire and Wire Products
Wire World Int — Wire World International
Wiring Install and Supplies — Wiring Installations and Supplies
Wirkerei Strickerei Tech — Wirkerei und Strickerei Technik
WIRS — Western Illinois Regional Studies
Wirt — Wirtschaftsdienst
WirtBer Lateinam Laender sowie Spanien und Port — Wirtschaftsbericht ueber die Lateinamerikanischen Laender sowie Spanien und Portugal
Wirt Futter — Wirtschaftseigene Futter
Wirt und Ges — Wirtschaft und Gesellschaft
Wirt und Investment — Wirtschaft und Investment
Wirt Pol — Monatsblaetter fuer Freiheitliche Wirtschaftspolitik
Wirt und Recht — Wirtschaft und Recht
Wirtschaft — Wirtschafts-Blaetter
Wirtschaftspol Chron — Wirtschaftspolitische Chronik
Wirtschaftswiss — Wirtschaftswissenschaft
Wirtsch-Dienst — Wirtschaftsdienst
Wirtsch u Recht — Wirtschaft und Recht
Wirtschseig Futter — Wirtschaftseigene Futter
Wirtsch Stat — Wirtschaft und Statistik
Wirtsch Verwalt — Wirtschaft und Verwaltung [*German Federal Republic*]
Wirtsch Wettbewerb — Wirtschaft und Wettbewerb [*West Germany*]
Wirtsch Wiss — Wirtschaft und Wissenschaft
Wirtsch-Wiss — Wirtschaftswissenschaft
Wirt und Sozwiss Inst Mitt — Wirtschafts- und Sozialwissenschaftliches Institut. Mitteilungen
Wirtswoche — Wirtschaftswoche
Wirt u Wiss — Wirtschaft und Wissen
WIS — World of Islam
Wis Acad Sci Arts Lett — Wisconsin Academy of Sciences, Arts, and Letters
Wis Acad Sciences Trans — Wisconsin Academy of Sciences, Arts, and Letters. Transactions

Wis Acad of Sci Trans — Wisconsin Academy of Sciences, Arts, and Letters. Transactions
Wis Ag Dept — Wisconsin. Department of Agriculture. Publications
Wis Ag Exp — Wisconsin. Agricultural Experiment Station. Publications
Wis Agric Exp Stn Bull — Wisconsin. Agricultural Experiment Station. Bulletin
Wis Agric Exp Stn Res Bull — Wisconsin. Agricultural Experiment Station. Research Bulletin
Wis Agric Exp Stn Res Rep — Wisconsin. Agricultural Experiment Station. Research Report
Wis Agric Exp Stn Spec Bull — Wisconsin. Agricultural Experiment Station. Special Bulletin
Wis Alum M — Wisconsin Alumni Magazine
Wis Arch — Wisconsin Archaeologist
WISB — Wildlife Society. Bulletin
Wis Badger Bee — Wisconsin's Badger Bee
Wis B Bulletin — Wisconsin Bar Bulletin
Wis Beekeep — Wisconsin Beekeeping
Wisc LB — Wisconsin Library Bulletin
Wisc Lib Bull — Wisconsin Library Bulletin
Wisc LR — Wisconsin Law Review
Wis Coll Agric Life Sci Res Div Res Rep — Wisconsin College of Agricultural and Life Sciences. Research Division. Research Report
Wis Coll Agric Life Sci Res Div Sci Rep Bull — Wisconsin College of Agricultural and Life Sciences. Research Division. Science Report Bulletin
Wis Conserv Bull — Wisconsin Conservation Bulletin
Wis Conserv Dep Tech Bull — Wisconsin Conservation Department. Technical Bulletin
Wisconsin Acad Sci Arts and Letters Trans — Wisconsin Academy of Sciences, Arts, and Letters. Transactions
Wisconsin Acad Sci Arts Lett Trans — Wisconsin Academy of Sciences, Arts, and Letters. Transactions
Wisconsin Agric Exp Stn Bull — Wisconsin. Agricultural Experiment Station. Bulletin
Wisconsin L Rev — Wisconsin Law Review
Wisconsin Med J — Wisconsin Medical Journal
Wis Dep Nat Resour Publ — Wisconsin. Department of Natural Resources. Publication
Wis Dep Nat Resour Tech Bull — Wisconsin. Department of Natural Resources. Technical Bulletin
Wis Energy Ext Serv Agric-Energy Transp Dig — Wisconsin. Energy Extension Service. Agricultural-Energy Transportation Digest
Wis Eng — Wisconsin Engineer
Wis Eng Exp Stn Repr — Wisconsin. Engineering Experiment Station. Reprint
Wis Engineer — Wisconsin Engineer
WiseR — Wiseman Review
Wis Geol Nat Hist Surv Bull — Wisconsin. Geological and Natural History Survey. Bulletin
Wis Geol Survey Bull Inf Circ — Wisconsin. Geological Survey. Bulletin. Information Circular
Wis G S — Wisconsin. Geological and Natural History Survey
Wis G S G Wis B — Wisconsin. Geological Survey. Geology of Wisconsin. Bulletin [*Later, Wisconsin Geological and Natural History Survey*]
Wis His Col — Wisconsin State Historical Society. Collections
Wis His Proc — Wisconsin Historical Society. Proceedings
Wis His S Domesday Bk — Wisconsin State Historical Society. Domesday Book
Wis Hist Soc Proc — Wisconsin State Historical Society. Proceedings
Wis Hort — Wisconsin Horticulture
Wis J Ed — Wisconsin Journal of Education
Wis Lib Bul — Wisconsin Library Bulletin
Wis L Rev — Wisconsin Law Review
Wis M — Wisconsin Magazine of History
Wis Mag Hist — Wisconsin Magazine of History
Wis Med J — Wisconsin Medical Journal
Wis M Hist — Wisconsin Magazine of History
Wis Nat Resour Bull — Wisconsin Natural Resources Bulletin
Wis N H Soc B — Wisconsin Natural History Society. Bulletin
Wis Paper Ind Newsl — Wisconsin Paper Industry. Information Service Newsletter
Wis Pharm — Wisconsin Pharmacist
Wis Pharm Ext Bull — Wisconsin. Pharmacy Extension Bulletin
Wiss Abh Dtsch Materialpruefungsanst — Wissenschaftliche Abhandlungen der Deutschen Materialpruefungsanstalten
Wiss Abh Phys-Tech Reichsanst — Wissenschaftliche Abhandlungen der Physikalische-Technischen Reichsanstalt [*West Germany*]
Wiss Alpenvereinshefte — Wissenschaftliche Alpenvereinshefte
Wiss Ann — Wissenschaftliche Annalen
Wiss Arch Landwirtsch Abt B — Wissenschaftliches Archiv fuer Landwirtschaft. Abteilung B. Archiv fuer Tierernaehrung und Teirzucht
Wiss Beitr Ingenieurhochsch Zwickau — Wissenschaftliche Beitraege. Ingenieurhochschule Zwickau [*German Democratic Republic*]
Wiss Beitr Martin Luther Univ (Halle Wittenberg) Reihe M — Wissenschaftliche Beitrage. Martin Luther Universitaet (Halle-Wittenberg). Reihe M

Wiss Beitr Univ (Halle) — Wissenschaftliche Beitrage. Martin-Luther-Universitaet (Halle-Wittenberg)
Wiss Ber AEG-Telefunken — Wissenschaftliche Berichte AEG-Telefunken
Wiss Ber HMFA Braunschweig — Wissenschaftliche Berichte aus der Hochmagnetfeldanlage. Physikalische Institute. Technische Universitaet Braunschweig
Wiss Dienst Ostmitteleur — Wissenschaftlicher Dienst fuer Ostmitteleuropa
Wiss Dienst Sudosteuropa — Wissenschaftlicher Dienst Suedosteuropa
Wissenschaftstheorie- Wissenschaft Philos — Wissenschaftstheorie-Wissenschaft und Philosophie
Wissenschaftstheor Wiss Philos — Wissenschaftstheorie- Wissenschaft und Philosophie
Wissensch Meeresuntersuch — Wissenschaftliche Meeresuntersuchungen
Wissensch Sitzungen Stochastik 80 — Wissenschaftliche Sitzungen zur Stochastik 80
Wissensch Taschenbuecher Reihe Math Phys — Wissenschaftliche Taschenbuecher. Reihe Mathematik/Physik
Wissensch Taschenbuecher Reihe Texte Stud — Wissenschaftliche Taschenbuecher. Reihe Texte und Studien
Wiss Forschungsber Naturwiss Reihe — Wissenschaftliche Forschungsberichte. Naturwissenschaftliche Reihe
Wiss Fortschr — Wissenschaft und Fortschritt
Wiss Konf Ges Dtsch Naturforsch Aerzte — Wissenschaftliche Konferenz. Gesellschaft Deutscher Naturforscher und Aerzte
Wiss Kult — Wissenschaft und Kultur
WisSL — Wisconsin Studies in Literature
Wiss Mitt Historiker-Ges DDR — Wissenschaftliche Mitteilungen. Historiker-Gesellschaft der DDR
Wiss Mitt Pharm Forsch Fortbild Inst Oesterr Apoth Ver — Wissenschaftliche Mitteilungen. Pharmazeutisches Forschungs- und Fortbildungs Institut. Oesterreichischer Apotheker-Verein
Wiss Schriftenr Tech Hochsch Karl-Marx-Stadt — Wissenschaftliche Schriftenreihe. Technische Hochschule Karl-Marx-Stadt
Wiss Taschenb — Wissenschaftliche Taschenbuecher
Wis State Cartogr Off Inf Circ — Wisconsin State Cartographer's Office. Information Circular
Wiss-Tech Fortschr Landw — Wissenschaftlich-Technischer Fortschritt fuer die Landwirtschaft
Wiss-Tech Inf VEB Kombinat Automatisierungsanlagenbau — Wissenschaftlich-Technische Informationen des VEB Kombinat Automatisierungsanlagenbau
Wis Stud Contemp Lit — Wisconsin Studies in Contemporary Literature [*Later, Contemporary Literature*]
Wiss Umwelt ISU — Wissenschaft und Umwelt ISU [*Interdisziplinaerer Sonderbereich Umweltschutz*] [*German Federal Republic*]
Wiss Veroeff Siemens-Werken — Wissenschaftliche Veroeffentlichungen aus den Siemens-Werken
Wiss Veroeff Tech Hochsch (Darmstadt) — Wissenschaftliche Veroeffentlichungen. Technische Hochschule (Darmstadt)
Wiss Wb — Wissenschaft und Weltbild
Wiss Weis — Wissenschaft und Weisheit
Wiss Welt — Wissenschaft und Weltbild
Wiss Wirtsch Polit — Wissenschaft, Wirtschaft, Politik
Wiss Z — Wissenschaftliche Zeitschrift
WissZ — Wissenschaftliche Zeitung. Humboldt-Universitaet
Wiss Z Elektrotech — Wissenschaftliche Zeitschrift der Elektrotechnik
Wiss Z Ernst Moritz Arndt Univ (Greifswald) Math Natur Reihe — Wissenschaftliche Zeitschrift. Ernst-Moritz-Arndt-Universitaet (Greifswald). Mathematisch-Naturwissenschaftliche Reihe
Wiss Z Ernst Moritz Arndt Univ Greifswald Math Naturw Reihe — Wissenschaftliche Zeitschrift. Ernst-Moritz-Arndt-Universitaet (Greifswald). Mathematisch-Naturwissenschaftliche Reihe
Wiss Z Ernst-Moritz-Arndt-Univ Greifsw Math Naturwiss Reihe — Wissenschaftliche Zeitschrift. Ernst-Moritz-Arndt-Universitaet (Greifswald). Mathematisch-Naturwissenschaftliche Reihe
Wiss Z Friedrich-Schiller-Univ (Jena) Math Naturwiss Reihe — Wissenschaftliche Zeitschrift. Friedrich-Schiller-Universitaet (Jena). Mathematisch-Naturwissenschaftliche Reihe
Wiss Z Hochsch Bauwes (Cottbus) — Wissenschaftliche Zeitschrift. Hochschule fuer Bauwesen (Cottbus)
Wiss Z Hochsch Bauwes (Leipzig) — Wissenschaftliche Zeitschrift. Hochschule fuer Bauwesen (Leipzig) [*East Germany*]
Wiss Z Hochsch Bauw (Leipzig) — Wissenschaftliche Zeitschrift. Hochschule fuer Bauwesen (Leipzig)
Wiss Z Hochsch Elektrotech (Ilmenau) — Wissenschaftliche Zeitschrift. Hochschule fuer Elektrotechnik (Ilmenau)
Wiss Z Hochsch Landwirtsch Produktionsgenoss (Meissen) — Wissenschaftliche Zeitschrift. Hochschule fuer Landwirtschaftliche Produktionsgenossenschaften (Meissen)
Wiss Z Hochsch Maschinenbau (Karl Marx-Stadt) — Wissenschaftliche Zeitschrift. Hochschule fuer Maschinenbau (Karl Marx-Stadt)
Wiss Z Hochsch Schwermaschinenbau (Magdeburg) — Wissenschaftliche Zeitschrift. Hochschule fuer Schwermaschinenbau (Magdeburg)
Wiss Z Hochschule — Wissenschaftliche Zeitschrift. Hochschule fuer Oekonomie [*Berlin*]

Wiss Z Hochsch Verkehrswesen (Dresden) — Wissenschaftliche Zeitschrift. Hochschule fuer Verkehrswesen (Dresden)
Wiss Z Hochsch Verkehrswesen Friedrich List (Dresden) — Wissenschaftliche Zeitschrift. Hochschule fuer Verkehrswesen "Friedrich List" (Dresden). Die Anwendung Mathematischer Methoden im Transport- und Nachichtenwesen
Wiss Z Humboldt-Univ (Berl) — Wissenschaftliche Zeitschrift. Humboldt-Universitaet (Berlin)
Wiss Z Humboldt-Univ (Berlin) Math-Natur Reihe — Wissenschaftliche Zeitschrift. Humboldt-Universitaet (Berlin). Mathematisch-Naturwissenschaftliche Reihe
Wiss Z Humboldt Univ (Berlin) Math Naturwiss Reihe — Wissenschaftliche Zeitschrift. Humboldt-Universitaet (Berlin). Mathematisch-Naturwissenschaftliche Reihe
Wiss Z Humboldt Univ (Berl) Math Naturwiss — Wissenschaftliche Zeitschrift. Humboldt-Universitaet (Berlin). Mathematisch-Naturwissenschaftliche Reihe
Wiss Z Humboldt-Univ (Berl) Math-Naturwiss Reihe — Wissenschaftliche Zeitschrift. Humboldt-Universitaet (Berlin). Mathematisch-Naturwissenschaftliche Reihe
Wiss Z Karl-Marx Univ — Wissenschaftliche Zeitschrift. Karl-Marx-Universitaet
Wiss Z Karl-Marx-Univ (Leipzig) Math Natur Reihe — Wissenschaftliche Zeitschrift. Karl-Marx-Universitaet (Leipzig). Mathematisch-Naturwissenschaftliche Reihe
Wiss Z Karl-Marx-Univ (Leipzig) Math-Naturwiss Reihe — Wissenschaftliche Zeitschrift. Karl-Marx-Universitaet (Leipzig). Mathematisch-Naturwissenschaftliche Reihe
Wiss Z Karl-Marx-Univ (Leipz) Math-Naturwiss Reihe — Wissenschaftliche Zeitschrift. Karl-Marx-Universitaet (Leipzig). Mathematisch-Naturwissenschaftliche Reihe
Wiss Z Martin Luther Univ — Wissenschaftliche Zeitschrift. Martin-Luther-Universitaet (Halle-Wittenberg). Mathematisch-Naturwissenschaftliche Reihe
Wiss Z Martin-Luther-Univ (Halle-Wittenb) — Wissenschaftliche Zeitschrift. Martin-Luther Universitaet (Halle-Wittenberg)
Wiss Z Martin-Luther-Univ (Halle-Wittenberg) — Wissenschaftliche Zeitschrift. Martin-Luther-Universitaet (Halle-Wittenberg)
Wiss Z Martin-Luther-Univ Halle Wittenberg Math Natur Reihe — Wissenschaftliche Zeitschrift. Martin-Luther-Universitaet (Halle-Wittenberg). Mathematisch-Naturwissenschaftliche Reihe
Wiss Z Math Naturwiss Reihe Halle Univ — Wissenschaftliche Zeitschrift. Mathematisch-Naturwissenschaftliche Reihe. Halle Universitaet
Wiss Z Paedagog Hochsch Karl Liebknecht (Potsdam) — Wissenschaftliche Zeitschrift. Paedagogische Hochschule Karl Liebknecht (Potsdam) [*East Germany*]
Wiss Z Tech Hochsch Chem Carl Schorlemmer (Leuna-Merseburg) — Wissenschaftliche Zeitschrift. Technische Hochschule fuer Chemie "Carl Schorlemmer" (Leuna-Merseburg)
Wiss Z Tech Hochsch Chem (Leuna-Merseburg) — Wissenschaftliche Zeitschrift. Technische Hochschule fuer Chemie (Leuna-Merseburg)
Wiss Z Tech Hochsch (Dresden) — Wissenschaftliche Zeitschrift. Technische Hochschule (Dresden) [*East Germany*]
Wiss Z Tech Hochsch (Ilmenau) — Wissenschaftliche Zeitschrift. Technische Hochschule (Ilmenau)
Wiss Z Tech Hochsch Karl-Marx-Stadt — Wissenschaftliche Zeitschrift. Technische Hochschule Karl-Marx-Stadt
Wiss Z Tech Hochsch Karl-Marx-Stadt Sonderh — Wissenschaftliche Zeitschrift. Technische Hochschule Karl-Marx-Stadt. Sonderheft
Wiss Z Tech Hochsch (Leipzig) — Wissenschaftliche Zeitschrift. Technische Hochschule (Leipzig)
Wiss Z Tech Hochsch (Leuna-Merseburg) — Wissenschaftliche Zeitschrift. Technische Hochschule fuer Chemie "Carl Schorlemmer" (Leuna-Merseburg)
Wiss Z Tech Hochsch (Magdeburg) — Wissenschaftliche Zeitschrift. Technische Hochschule Otto Von Guericke (Magdeburg)
Wiss Z Tech Hochsch Otto von Guericke (Magdeb) — Wissenschaftliche Zeitschrift. Technische Hochschule Otto Von Guericke (Magdeburg)
Wiss Z Tech Hochsch Otto v Guericke (Magdeburg) — Wissenschaftliche Zeitschrift. Technische Hochschule Otto Von Guericke (Magdeburg)
Wiss Z Tech Hochsch Otto Von Guericke — Wissenschaftliche Zeitschrift. Technische Hochschule Otto Von Guericke
Wiss Z Techn Hochsch Chem (Leuna-Merseburg) — Wissenschaftliche Zeitschrift. Technische Hochschule fuer Chemie (Leuna-Merseburg)
Wiss Z Techn Hochsch (Ilmenau) — Wissenschaftliche Zeitschrift. Technische Hochschule (Ilmenau)
Wiss Z Techn Hochsch Karl-Marx-Stadt — Wissenschaftliche Zeitschrift. Technische Hochschule Karl-Marx-Stadt
Wiss Z Techn Hochsch (Leuna-Merseburg) — Wissenschaftliche Zeitschrift. Technische Hochschule (Leuna-Merseburg)
Wiss Z Techn Univ (Dresden) — Wissenschaftliche Zeitschrift. Technische Universitaet (Dresden)
Wiss Z Tech Univ (Dres) — Wissenschaftliche Zeitschrift. Technische Universitaet (Dresden)
Wiss Z Tech Univ (Dresden) — Wissenschaftliche Zeitschrift. Technische Universitaet (Dresden)

Wiss Z Univ (Greifswald) — Wissenschaftliche Zeitschrift. Ernst-Moritz-Arndt-Universitaet (Greifswald)
Wiss Z Univ (Greifswald) Math-Naturwiss Reihe — Wissenschaftliche Zeitschrift. Ernst-Moritz-Arndt-Universitaet (Greifswald). Mathematisch-Naturwissenschaftliche Reihe
Wiss Z Univ (Halle) — Wissenschaftliche Zeitschrift. Martin-Luther-Universitaet (Halle-Wittenberg)
Wiss Z Univ (Halle-Wittenberg) Math-Naturwiss Reihe — Wissenschaftliche Zeitschrift. Martin-Luther-Universitaet (Halle-Wittenberg). Mathematisch-Naturwissenschaftliche Reihe
Wiss Z Univ (Jena) Math-Naturwiss Reihe — Wissenschaftliche Zeitschrift. Friedrich-Schiller-Universitaet (Jena). Mathematisch-Naturwissenschaftliche Reihe
Wiss Z Univ (Leipzig) Ges-u Sprachwiss R — Wissenschaftliche Zeitschrift. Karl-Marx-Universitaet (Leipzig). Gesellschafts- und Sprachwissenschaftliche Reihe
Wiss Z Univ (Leipzig) Math-Naturwiss Reihe — Wissenschaftliche Zeitschrift. Karl-Marx-Universitaet (Leipzig). Mathematisch-Naturwissenschaftliche Reihe
Wiss Z Univ Rostock Ges Sprachwiss Reihe — Wissenschaftliche Zeitschrift. Universitaet Rostock. Gesellschafts- und Sprachwissenschaftliche Reihe
Wiss Z Univ Rostock Ges- & Sprachwiss Reihe — Wissenschaftliche Zeitschrift. Universitaet Rostock. Gesellschafts- und Sprachwissenschaftliche Reihe
Wiss Z Univ Rostock Ges-Wiss — Wissenschaftliche Zeitschrift. Universitaet Rostock. Gesellschafts- und Wissenschaftliche Reihe
Wiss Z Univ Rostock Math-Natur Reihe — Universitaet Rostock. Wissenschaftliche Zeitschrift. Mathematisch-Naturwissenschaftliche Reihe
Wiss Z Univ Rostock Math Naturwiss Reihe — Wissenschaftliche Zeitschrift. Universitaet Rostock. Mathematisch-Naturwissenschaftliche Reihe
Wiss Z Univ Rostock Reihe Math Naturw — Wissenschaftliche Zeitschrift. Universitaet Rostock. Reihe Mathematik und Naturwissenschaften
WIST — WIST. Wirtschaftswissenschaftliches Studium
Wis U Bul Eng S — Bulletin. University of Wisconsin. Engineering Series
Wis Univ Coll Eng Eng Exp Stn Rep — Wisconsin University. College of Engineering. Engineering Experiment Station. Report
Wis Univ Dept Meteorology Rept Lakes and Streams Inv Comm — Wisconsin University. Department of Meteorology. Report to the Lakes and Streams Investigations Committee
Wis Univ Eng Exp Stn Bull — Wisconsin University. Engineering Experiment Station. Bulletin
Wis Univ Geol Nat Hist Surv Spec Rep — Wisconsin University. Geological and Natural History Survey. Special Report
Wis Univ Geol Natur Hist Surv Inform Circ — Wisconsin University. Geological and Natural History Survey. Information Circular
Wittheit Bremen Jahrb — Wittheit zu Bremen. Jahrbuch
WIV — Vakblad voor Textielreiniging
WiZ — Wiedza i Zycie
WiZ — Wort in der Zeit
WJ — Wiener Jahreshefte
WJ — Wolfram-Jahrbuch
WJA — Wuerzburger Jahrbuecher fuer die Altertumswissenschaft
WJCAR — World Jewish Congress Annual Report [*New York*]
WJCIB — World Jewish Congress Information Bulletin [*New York*]
WJh — Wiener Jahreshefte
WJK — Wiener Jahrbuch fuer Kunstgeschichte
WJMDA — Western Journal of Medicine [*United States*]
WJR — Washington Journalism Review
WJSUD — World Journal of Surgery
Wkg Girls Newsl — Working with Girls Newsletter
Wkly Energy Rep — Weekly Energy Report [*United States*]
Wkly Inf Bull — Weekly Information Bulletin
Wkly Rec — Weekly Record [*United States*]
WKMIA — Wakayama Igaku
WKNDDH — Annual Report. Research Institute for Wakan-Yaku Toyama Medical and Pharmaceutical University
WKP — Wochenschrift fuer Klassische Philologie
Wks Engng — Works Engineering
Wks Engng Fact Serv — Works Engineering and Factory Services
Wks Mgmt — Works Management
Wk Study — Work Study
Wk Study Mgmt Serv — Work Study and Management Services [*Later, Management Services*]
WKUBA — Werkstatt und Betrieb
WKWSA — Wiener Klinische Wochenschrift. Supplementum (Austria)
W & L — Washington and Lee Law Review
W & L — Women and Literature
WL — Wydawnictwo Literackie
WL — Wydawnictwo Lodzkie
WLB — Wiener Library Bulletin [*London*]
WLB — Wilson Library Bulletin
Wld Aerospace Syst — World Aerospace System
Wld Aff — World Affairs
Wld Anim Rev — World Animal Review
Wld Cem — World Cement

Wld Crops — World Crops
Wld Develop — World Development
Wld Fishg — World Fishing
Wld For Congr — World Forestry Congress
Wld Hlth Org Techn Rep Ser — World Health Organization. Technical Report Series
Wld Marx R — World Marxist Review
Wld Med — World Medicine
Wld Orchid Conf — World Orchid Conference
Wld Polit — World Politics
Wld Pollen Spore Flora — World Pollen and Spore Flora
Wld P & PDem — World Pulp and Paper Demand, Supply, and Trade
Wld Pumps — World Pumps
WLDRA — Welder [*England*]
Wld Refrig Air Condit — World Refrigeration and Air Conditioning
Wld Rev Pest Control — World Review of Pest Control
Wld's Pap Trade Rev — World's Paper Trade Review
Wld Surv — World Survey
Wld Today — World Today
Wld Work Rep — World of Work Report
W LF — Women's Law Forum
WLFMA — Welding and Metal Fabrication
WLG — Wiener Linguistische Gazette
WLHPA — Wu Li Hsueh Pao
W Lit — World Literature Written in English
WLJ — Washburn Law Journal
WLJ — Western Law Journal
WLJ — Wyoming Law Journal
WL Jour — Washburn Law Journal
WL Jour — Western Law Journal
WL Jour — Willamette Law Journal
WL Jour — Wyoming Law Journal
WLLR — Washington and Lee Law Review
WLN — Wired Librarian's Newsletter
WLNED — Water Law Newsletter
WLQ — Washington University. Law Quarterly
WLR — Washington Law Review
WLR — Wasser, Luft, und Betrieb. Zeitschrift fuer Umwelttechnik
WLR — Wisconsin Law Review
WLSBA — Wildlife Society. Bulletin
WLT — World Literature Today
WLub — Wydawnictwo Lubelskie
WLWE — World Literature Written in English
WM — Washington Monthly
WM — Westermanns Monatshefte
W & M — William and Mary Law Review
WM — Works Management
WM — World Meetings
WM — World of Music [*London*]
W Mail — Western Mail
W Mail Ann — Western Mail Annual
WMB — Women in Business
WMCQ — William and Mary College. Quarterly
WMD — Water Mineral Development
W M Day Studies — Romance Studies Presented to William Morton Day
WMH — Wisconsin Magazine of History
WMHE — Women and Health
WML — Willamette Law Journal
Wm LJ — Willamette Law Journal
W and M LR — William and Mary Law Review
WMLR — William and Mary Law Review
WMLR — William Mitchell Law Review
W & M L Rev — William and Mary Law Review
Wm Mar Q — William and Mary Quarterly
Wm and Mary L Rev — William and Mary Law Review
Wm & Mary Q — William and Mary Quarterly
Wm Mitchell L Rev — William Mitchell Law Review
WMMTA — World Minerals and Metals
WMN — Western Morning News [*United Kingdom*]
Wmn Lib — Women's Liberation
WMOBA — WMO [*World Meteorological Organization*] Bulletin
WMO Bull — WMO [*World Meteorological Organization*] Bulletin
WMO Publ — WMO [*World Meteorological Organization*] Publication
WMO Rep Mar Sci Aff — World Meteorological Organization. Reports on Marine Science Affairs
WMO Spec Environ Rep — World Meteorological Organization. Special Environmental Report
WMO Tech Note — World Meteorological Organization. Technical Note
WMQ — William and Mary Quarterly
W & M Q — William and Mary Quarterly
WMSJ — William Morris Society. Journal
WMT — Auslandmerkte/Marches Etrangers [*Lausanne*]
WMWG — Weichselland, Mitteilungen des Westpreussischen Geschichtsvereins
WMWOA — Wiener Medizinische Wochenschrift
WMY — Weird Mystery

WN — Wake Newsletter
WN — Wawatay News [*Sioux Lookout, Ontario*]
WN — Wiadomosci Numizmatyczne
WNA — Welcome to the North Atlantic
WN Covers (NSW) — Weekly Notes Covers (New South Wales)
W N Eng LR — Western New England Law Review
W New Eng L Rev — Western New England Law Review
WNJ — Whitman Numismatic Journal
Wn L — Wayne Law Review
Wn LR — Washington Law Review
Wn LR — Wayne Law Review
WNNR Spes Versl — WNNR [*Suid-Afrikaanse Wetenskaplike en Nywerheidnavorsingsraad*] Spesiale Verslag
WN (NSW) — Weekly Notes (New South Wales)
WNS — Technieuws Washington. Korte Berichten op Technisch Wetenschappelijk Gebied
WNT — Foreign Trade
Wntr Sldr — Winter Soldier
WO — Welt des Orients
WO — World of Opera
WOC — Work and Occupations
WOC — World Coal
Wochbl Papierfabr — Wochenblatt fuer Papierfabrikation
Wochenschr Brau — Wochenschrift fuer Brauerei
WOCOD — World Coal
WODED — World Development
WOE — World Economy
Woelm Publ — Woelm Publication
Woert Sach — Woerter und Sachen
WOF — Worlds of Fantasy [*1950-1954*]
WOHE — World Health
Wojsk Przegl Tech — Wojskowy Przeglad Techniczny [*Poland*]
WOL — Weird and Occult Library
Wolfen-Buetteler B — Wolfenbuetteler Beitraege
Wolfenbuetteler Forsch — Wolfenbuetteler Forschungen
Wollen- Leinen-Ind — Wollen- und Leinen-Industrie
WOMAA — Works Management
Woman Art J — Woman's Art Journal
Woman Cit — Woman Citizen
Woman Home C — Woman's Home Companion
Woman's H C — Woman's Home Companion
Woman's J — Woman's Journal
Women — Women/Poems
Women Coach Clin — Women's Coaching Clinic
Women of Eur — Women of Europe
Women and Hist — Women and History
Women and L — Women and Law
Women Law J — Women Lawyers Journal
Women Lawyers J — Women Lawyers Journal
Women & Lit — Women and Literature
Women Lit — Women and Literature
Women L Jour — Women Lawyers Journal
Women Rev — Women and Revolution
Women Rights L Rep — Women's Rights Law Reporter
Women's Bur Bull — Women's Bureau Bulletin
Women's Review — Women's Review of Books
Women's Rights L Rep — Women's Rights Law Reporter
Women's Rights L Rptr — Women's Rights Law Reporter
Women's Stud Assoc Conf Pap — Women's Studies Association. Conference Papers [*New Zealand*]
Women's Studies — Women's Studies: An Interdisciplinary Journal
Womens Studs Newsl — Women's Studies Newsletter
Women Stud — Women's Studies: An Interdisciplinary Journal
Women Stud Abstracts — Women Studies Abstracts
Women Wkrs Bull — Women Workers Bulletin
WomHealth — Women and Health
Wom March — Women on the March [*New Delhi*]
Womn Prss — Women's Press
Womn Rgts — Women's Rights Law Reporter
Womn Sprt — Womanspirit
WOMUA — World of Music
W Ont L Rev — Western Ontario Law Review
Wood Brass Perc — Woodwind, Brass, and Percussion
Wood Ind — Wood Industry
Woodlds Res Index — Woodlands Research Index. Pulp and Paper Research Institute of Canada
Woodl Pap Pulp Pap Res Inst Can — Woodlands Papers. Pulp and Paper Research Institute of Canada
Woodl Res Note Union Camp Corp — Woodland Research Notes. Union Camp Corporation
Woodl Sect Index Canad Pulp Pap Ass — Woodlands Section Index. Canadian Pulp and Paper Association
Wood Mag — Woodwind Magazine
Wood Preserv — Wood Preserving
Wood Preserv (Chicago) — Wood Preserving (Chicago)
Wood Preserv N — Wood Preserving News

Wood Preserv News — Wood Preserving News
Wood Pres Rep For Prod Res Ind Developm Comm (Philippines) — Wood Preservation Report. Forest Products Research and Industries Development Commission College (Laguna, Philippines)
Wood Res — Wood Research
Wood Sci — Wood Science
Wood Sci Te — Wood Science and Technology
Wood Sci Technol — Wood Science and Technology
Woods Hole Oceanogr Inst Annu Rep — Woods Hole Oceanographic Institution. Annual Report
Woods Hole Oceanogr Inst Collect Reprints — Woods Hole Oceanographic Institution. Collected Reprints
Wood South Afr — Wood Southern Africa
Wood Sthn Afr — Wood Southern Africa
Woodwkg Ind — Woodworking Industry
Wood & Wood Prod — Wood and Wood Products
Wood Wood Prod — Wood and Wood Products
Wood World — Woodwind World [*Later, Woodwind World - Brass and Percussion*]
Wood World-Brass — Woodwind World - Brass and Percussion
Wool Rec — Wool Record
Wool Rec Text World — Wool Record and Textile World
Wool Sci Rev — Wool Science Review
Wool Tech — Wool Technology
Wool Tech — Wool Technology and Sheep Breeding
Wool Technol — Wool Technology
Wool Technol — Wool Technology and Sheep Breeding
Wool Technol Sheep Breed — Wool Technology and Sheep Breeding
Wool Technol (Syd) — Wool Technology (Sydney)
Wool Tech & Sheep — Wool Technology and Sheep Breeding
Wool Tech & Sheep Breeding — Wool Technology and Sheep Breeding
Woo Sok Univ Med J — Woo Sok University. Medical Journal
WOPHA — Woman Physician
WOPOP — WOPOP: Working Papers on Photography
WOR — Wool Record and Textile World
WoR — World Review
Wor — Worldview
Worcester Med News — Worcester Medical News [*Massachusetts*]
Worcester Mus Ann — Worcester, Massachusetts. Worcester Art Museum. Annual
Worcester Mus N Bul — Worcester, Massachusetts. Worcester Art Museum. News Bulletin and Calendar
Worc M — Worcester Magazine
Word and Inf Process — Word and Information Processing
Word Process Now — Word Processing Now
Word Process World — Word Processing World
WordsC — Wordsworth Circle
Wordsworth — Wordsworth Circle
Word W — Word Watching
WORKD — Worklife
Work-Environ-Health — Work-Environment-Health
Working Papers — Working Papers for a New Society
Work Pap Aust Arid Zone Res Conf — Working Papers. Australian Arid Zone Research Conference
Work Pap Aust Cereal Pasture Plant Breed Conf — Working Papers. Australian Cereal and Pasture Plant Breeding Conference
Work Pap Bur Meteorol — Working Paper. Bureau of Meteorology
Work Papers — Working Papers Magazine
Work Pap Giannini Found Agric Econ Calif Agric Exp Stn — Working Paper. Giannini Foundation of Agricultural Economics. California Agricultural Experiment Station
Work Pap Lang Linguist — Working Papers in Language and Linguistics
Work Pap Ling (H) — Working Papers in Linguistics (Honolulu)
Work Pap New Soc — Working Papers for a New Society
Work Plant Maint — Work and Plant Maintenance
Work Prog — Work in Progress
Work Rel Abstr — Work Related Abstracts
Works Eng — Works Engineering [*England*]
Works Eng Fact Serv — Works Engineering and Factory Services
Workshop Ser Pharmacol Sect Nat Inst Ment Health — Workshop Series. Pharmacology Section. National Institute of Mental Health
Works Inst Higher Nerv Act Acad Sci USSR Pathophysiol Ser — Works. Institute of Higher Nervous Activity. Academy of Sciences of the USSR. Pathophysiological Series
Works Inst Higher Nerv Act Acad Sci USSR Physiol Ser — Works. Institute of Higher Nervous Activity. Academy of Sciences of the USSR. Physiological Series
Works Pavlov Inst Physiol Acad Sci USSR — Works. Pavlov Institute of Physiology. Academy of Sciences of the USSR
Works and Plant Maint — Works and Plant Maintenance
Work Vang — Workers Vanguard
Work Wom — Working Woman
World — National Geographic World
World — World Magazine
World Aff — World Affairs
World Aff Q — World Affairs Quarterly

World Ag — World Agriculture
World Agr — World Agriculture
World Agric — World Agriculture
World Agri Econ & Rural Sociol Abstr — World Agricultural Economics and Rural Sociology Abstracts
World Alum Abstr — World Aluminum Abstracts
World Anim Rev — World Animal Review
World Archa — World Archaeology
World Archaeol — World Archaeology
World Assn for Adult Ed B — World Association for Adult Education. Bulletin
World Bus W — World Business Weekly
World Cem Technol — World Cement Technology [*Later, World Cement*]
World Conf Earthquake Eng Proc — World Conference on Earthquake Engineering. Proceedings
World Constr — World Construction
World Dev — World Development [*Oxford*]
World Devel — World Development
World Dredging & Mar Const — World Dredging and Marine Construction
World Dredging Mar Constr — World Dredging and Marine Construction
World Econ — World Economy [*England*]
World Educ Rep — World Education Reports
World Energy Conf Trans — World Energy Conference. Transactions
World Farm — World Farming
World Fish Abstr — World Fisheries Abstracts
World For Ser Bull — World Forestry Series. Bulletin
World Health Organ Chron — World Health Organization. Chronicle
World Health Organ Tech Rep Ser — World Health Organization. Technical Report Series
World Health Stat Q — World Health Statistics. Quarterly
World Health Stat Rep — World Health Statistics. Report
World Highw — World Highways
World Hosp — World Hospitals
World Ir Nurs — World of Irish Nursing
World Jnl Trib — World Journal Tribune [*Defunct New York City afternoon newspaper*]
World J Surg — World Journal of Surgery
World Jus — World Justice
World List Pub Stds — Worldwide List of Published Standards
World Lit T — World Literature Today
World Lit Today — World Literature Today
World Marxist R — World Marxist Review
World Marx R — World Marxist Review
World Med — World Medicine
World Med Electron — World Medical Electronics [*England*]
World Med Instrum — World Medical Instrumentation [*England*]
World Med J — World Medical Journal
World Meet Outside US Can — World Meetings: Outside United States and Canada
World Meet Outs US Can — World Meetings: Outside United States and Canada
World Meet US Can — World Meetings: United States and Canada
World Meteorol Organ Bull — World Meteorological Organization. Bulletin
World Meteorol Organ Publ — World Meteorological Organization. Publications
World Min — World Mining
World Miner Met — World Minerals and Metals
World Min US Ed — World Mining. United States Edition
World Mus — World of Music
World Neurol — World Neurology
World O — World Order
World Obstet Gynecol — World of Obstetrics and Gynecology [*Japan*]
World Oil — World Oil Forecast. Review Issue
World Outl — World Outlook
World Pet — World Petroleum
World Pet Cong Prepr — World Petroleum Congress. Preprints
World Pet Congr Proc — World Petroleum Congress. Proceedings
World Petrol — World Petroleum
World Pol — World Politics
World Poult — World's Poultry Science Journal
World Poultry Sci J — World's Poultry Science Journal
World Press R — World Press Review
World R — World Review
World Refrig — World Refrigeration [*England*]
World Rep — World Report
World Rev — World Review
World Rev Anim Prod — World Review of Animal Production
World Rev Nutr Diet — World Review of Nutrition and Dietetics
World Rev Pest Contr — World Review of Pest Control
World Rev Pest Control — World Review of Pest Control
World R Pest Control — World Review of Pest Control
World's Butter Rev — World's Butter Review
World Sci News — World Science News [*India*]
World's Pap Trade Rev — World's Paper Trade Review
World's Poultry Cong Conf Papers Sect C — World's Poultry Congress. Conference Papers. Section C
World's Poultry Sci J — World's Poultry Science Journal

World's Poult Sci J — World's Poultry Science Journal
World Steel (Jpn) — World of Steel (Japan)
World Surface Coat Abs — World Surface Coatings Abstracts
World Surf Coat — World Surface Coatings Abstracts
World Surv — World Survey
World Text Abstr — World Textile Abstracts
World Textile Abs — World Textile Abstracts
World Textile Abstr — World Textile Abstracts
Worldwatch Pap — Worldwatch Paper
Worldwide List Published Stand — Worldwide List of Published Standards
World-Wide MinAbs — World-Wide Mining Abstracts
Worldwide Nucl Power — Worldwide Nuclear Power
World Yr Bk Ed — World Year Book of Education
Worm R — Wormwood Review
Worm Runner's Dig — Worm Runner's Digest
Wor R — World Review
Wort Wahr — Wort und Wahrheit
WOS — Wonders of the Spaceways
WOT — Worlds of Tomorrow
WOW — Wereld in Ontwikkeling. Veertiendaags Overzicht van Tijdschriftartikelen en Rapporten over Problemen van de Ontwikkelingsgebieden
Wow — Wort und Wahrheit
WoWa — Wort und Wahrheit
WOWBDG — Instytut Zootechniki w Polsce Wyniki Oceny Wartosci Hodowlanej Buhajow
WP — Waman Puma
WP — Washington Post
WP — Wiedza Powszechna
WP — Woodstock Papers
WP — Work in Progress
WP — World Petroleum
WP — World Politics
W PA Hist Mag — Western Pennsylvania Historical Magazine
W Pakistan J Agr Res — West Pakistan Journal of Agricultural Research
WPCF — Water Pollution Control Federation. Journal
WPCF Highlights — Water Pollution Control Federation. Highlights
WPCFJ — Water Pollution Control Federation. Journal
WPFDM — Working Papers. Fondazione Dalle Molle
WPHM — Western Pennsylvania Historical Magazine
WPHUJ — Working Papers. Hebrew University of Jerusalem
WPL — Working Papers in Linguistics
WPLUH — Working Papers in Linguistics (University of Hawaii)
WPNGL — Workpapers in Papua New Guinea Languages
WPOC — Water and Pollution Control
WPOCA — Water Pollution Control [*Maidstone, England*]
W Pol Q — Western Political Quarterly
WPQ — Western Political Quarterly
WPR — Weekblad voor Privaatrecht, Notariaat, en Registratie
WPRCDZ — International Conference on Water Pollution Research. Proceedings
WPT — Paper. European Journal for the Pulp, Paper, and Board Industries
WPYEEJS — Working Papers in Yiddish and East European Jewish Studies
WPZ — Wiener Praehistorische Zeitschrift
WQ — Science Wonder Quarterly
WQ — Wind Quarterly
WQ — Wonder Stories Quarterly
WQ — Wool Quarterly
WR — Journal of Water Resources Planning and Management
WR — Washington Report. News and World Report Newsletter
WR — Weekly Record
WR — Weekly Review
WR — Western Review
WR — Wiseman Review
WRA — Water Resources Abstracts [*Database*]
WRA — Work Related Abstracts
WRABD — Wilhelm Roux' Archives of Developmental Biology
WRAMC Prog Notes — WRAMC [*Walter Reed Army Medical Center*] Progress Notes
WRC Inf — WRC [*Water Research Centre*] Information
WRC Research Report — Water Resources Center. Research Report
WRD — World's Fair
WRE — Tokyo Financial Review
WRERA — Water Resources Research
W Res L Rev — Western Reserve Law Review
W R Far East — Weekly Review of the Far East
WRI Rep — WRI [*Wattle Research Institute*] Report
WRIS Technical Bulletin — Water Resources Information System. Technical Bulletin
Writ Cent S — Writers of the 21st Century. Series
Writ Ring — Writers' Ring
WRJ — Wallraf-Richartz-Jahrbuch
Wrk Paper — Working Papers for a New Society
Wrk Power — Workers Power
Wrk World — Workers' World
W R LR — Women's Rights Law Reporter

Wrocl Zap Num — Wroclawskie Zapiski Numizmatyczne
W Roux A DB — Wilhelm Roux' Archives of Developmental Biology
WRP — United States News and World Report
WRRC — Women's Research and Resources Centre Newsletter
WRRC Report (Washington) — Water Resources Research Center. Report (Washington)
WRRC Spec Rep Univ MD — WRRC [*Water Resources Research Center*] Special Report. University of Maryland
WRRI Auburn Univ Bull — WRRI [*Water Resources Research Institute*]. Auburn University. Bulletin
WRU — Western Reserve University. Bulletin
WRZAA — Weltraumfahrt und Raketentechnik
WS — Welt der Slaven
WS — Western Speech
WS — Wiener Studien
WS — Woerter und Sachen
W & S — Woerter und Sachen
WS — Women's Studies: An Interdisciplinary Journal
WS — Wonder Stories
WS — Word Study
WS — Wort und Sinn
WSA — Intereconomics. Monthly Review of International Trade and Development
WSA — Wolfenbuetteler Studien zur Aufklarung
WSA — Women Studies Abstracts
WSA — Wonder Story Annual
WSAH — World Smoking and Health
Wsb — Washburn Law Journal
WSBU — Wahlenbergia. Scripta Botanica Umensia
WSC — Ebareport. Weekly Special Survey of Turkish Business, Industrial Investment, and Contracts Markets
WSC — Western Snow Conference. Proceedings
WSC — World Survey of Climatology [*Elsevier Book Series*]
WSCA — World Surface Coatings Abstracts [*Paint Research Association*] [*Database*] [*Teddington, Middlesex, England*]
WSCF Books — World Student Christian Federation Books
WSCHP — Wen Shih Che Hsueh-Pao [*Taiwan University*]
WSCL — Wisconsin Studies in Contemporary Literature [*Later, Contemporary Literature*]
WSCPA — Western States Section. Combustion Institute. Paper [*United States*]
WSCS — Washington State College. Studies
WSD — Wirtschaftsdienst. Wirtschaftspolitische Monatsschrift
WS and H — World Smoking and Health
WSIA J — WSIA [*Water Supply Improvement Association*] Journal [*United States*]
WSI Mitt — WSI [*Wirtschafts- und Sozialwissenschaftliches Institut*] Mitteilungen [*German Federal Republic*]
WSJ — Wall Street Journal
WSJ — Wiener Slawistisches Jahrbuch
WSJ — WSFA [*Washington Science Fiction Association*] Journal
WSJHQ — Western States Jewish Historical Quarterly
W S Jour — Wallace Stevens Journal
WSK — Waste Age
Ws L — Washington Law Review
WSL — Welt der Slaven
W Sl A — Wiener Slawistischer Almanach
WSlav — Welt der Slaven
WSLBA — Wasser, Luft, und Betrieb
WSLJb — Wiener Slawistisches Jahrbuch
WSM — World Solar Markets
WSMYA — Washington Monthly
WSN — Wallace Stevens Newsletter
WSNA Mini J — Washington State Nurses Association. Mini Journal
W Soc E J — Western Society of Engineers. Journal
Wsp — Wspolczesnosc [*Warsaw*]
WSQ — Wonder Stories Quarterly
WSR — Waterschapsbelangen
WSRB — Wall Street Review of Books
WST — Wine and Spirit
WSt — Word Study
WSTED — Water Science and Technology
WSTSA — Wall Street Transcript
W St UL Rev — Western State University. Law Review
WSW — Wirtschaftswissenschaft
WSWOA — Water and Sewage Works
WSWSA — Wasserwirtschaft-Wassertechnik
WSWTA — Wasserwirtschaft
WSZ — Vereniging Surinaams Bedrijfsleven. Weekbericht
WT — Weird Tales
WT — Wetenschappelijke Tijdingen
WT — Wieczory Teatralne
WT — World Tobacco
WTA — World Tax Report [*London*]
WTD — World Today [*London*]
WTF — Welcome to Finland

WTGR — Welcome to Greenland
W Th J — Westminster Theological Journal
WTHRA — Weather [*London*]
WTHWA — Weatherwise
WTI — Welcome to Iceland
WTJ — Westminster Theological Journal
WTKK — Wen-Tzu Kai-Ko
WTN — Journal of World Trade Law
WTN — Wroclawskie Towarzystwo Naukowe
WTR — World Travel
WTS — Watersport. Maandblad voor de Zeilsport. Motorbootsport
WTT — Weird Terror Tales
WTTF — Welcome to the Faeroes
WTW — Materials Reclamation Weekly
WTW — Writers and Their Work
WTW — Wroclawskie Towarzystwo Naukowe
WT (Werkstattstech) Z Ind Fertigung — WT (Werkstattstechnik). Zeitschrift fuer Industrielle Fertigung
WTZ — Weird Tales [*1973-*]
WTZIA — WT [*Werkstattstechnik*]. Zeitschrift fuer Industrielle Fertigung
Wt Z Ind Fe — Werkstattstechnik Zeitschrift fuer Industrielle Fertigung
WT Z Ind Fertigung — WT [*Werkstattstechnik*]. Zeitschrift fuer Industrielle Fertigung
WU — Weekly Underwriter
WUBOA — Wasser und Boden
WuD — Wort und Dienst. Jahrbuch der Theologischen Schule Bethel [*Bethel Bei Bielefeld*]
Wuerttemberg Blaetter Km — Wuerttembergische Blaetter fuer Kirchenmusik
Wuerttemb Wochenbl Landwirt — Wuerttembergisches Wochenblatt fuer Landwirtschaft
Wuerzburg Geogr Arb — Wuerzburger Geographische Arbeiten
Wuerz Jb — Wuerzburger Jahrbuecher fuer die Altertumswissenschaft
WuG — Wissenschaft und Gegenwart
Wuhan Univ J Nat Sci — Wuhan University Journal. Natural Sciences [*People's Republic of China*]
W Underw — Weekly Underwriter
WUR — Wirtschaft und Recht. Zeitschrift fuer Wirtschaftspolitik und Wirtschaftsrecht mit Einschluss des Sozialrechtes und Arbeidsrechtes
WUS — Washington University. Studies
WUS — Wirtschaft und Statistik
WuW — Welt und Wort
WuWahr — Wort und Wahrheit
WuWelt — Wissenschaft und Weltbild
WV — World Vision
WVA — West Vlaanderen Werkt
W Va Acad Sci Proc — West Virginia Academy of Sciences. Proceedings
W Va Ag Dept — West Virginia. Department of Agriculture. Publications
W Va Ag Exp — West Virginia. Agricultural Experiment Station. Publications
W Va Agric Exp Stn Bull — West Virginia. Agricultural Experiment Station. Bulletin
W Va Agric Exp Stn Cir — West Virginia. Agricultural Experiment Station. Circular
W Va Agric Exp Stn Circ — West Virginia. Agricultural Experiment Station. Circular
W Va Agric Exp Stn Curr Rep — West Virginia. Agricultural Experiment Station. Current Report
W Va Agric Exp Stn Misc Publ — West Virginia. Agricultural Experiment Station. Miscellaneous Publication
W Va Agric For — West Virginia Agriculture and Forestry
W Va Agric For Exp Stn Bull — West Virginia. Agricultural and Forestry Experiment Station. Bulletin
W Va Coal Min Inst Proc — West Virginia Coal Mining Institute. Proceedings
W Va Dent J — West Virginia Dental Journal
W Va Dep Mines Annu Rep — West Virginia. Department of Mines. Annual Report
W Va For Notes — West Virginia Forestry Notes
W Va Geol Econ Surv Basic Data Rep — West Virginia. Geological and Economic Survey. Basic Data Report
W Va Geol Econ Surv Bull — West Virginia. Geological and Economic Survey. Bulletin
W Va Geol Econ Surv Circ Ser — West Virginia. Geological and Economic Survey. Circular Series
W Va Geol Econ Surv Cir Ser — West Virginia. Geological and Economic Survey. Circular Series
W Va Geol Econ Surv Coal Geol Bull — West Virginia. Geological and Economic Survey. Coal Geology Bulletin
W Va Geol Econ Surv Environ Geol Bull — West Virginia. Geological and Economic Survey. Environmental Geology Bulletin
W Va Geol Econ Surv Miner Resour Ser — West Virginia. Geological and Economic Survey. Mineral Resources Series
W Va Geol Econ Surv Newsl — West Virginia. Geological and Economic Survey. Newsletter
W Va Geol Econ Surv Rep Archeol Invest — West Virginia. Geological and Economic Survey. Report of Archeological Investigations
W Va Geol Econ Surv Rep Invest — West Virginia. Geological and Economic Survey. Report of Investigations

W Va Geol Econ Surv River Basin Bull — West Virginia. Geological and Economic Survey. River Basin Bulletin
W Va Geol Surv Rep — West Virginia. Geological Survey. Reports
W Va Geol Surv Rep Invest — West Virginia. Geological Survey. Report of Investigations
W Va G S — West Virginia. Geological Survey
WVaH — West Virginia History
W Va His — West Virginia History
W Va Hist — West Virginia History. A Quarterly Magazine
W Va Law Q — West Virginia Law Quarterly and the Bar
W Va Law R — West Virginia Law Review
W Va Lib — West Virginia Libraries
W Va Libr — West Virginia Libraries
W Va LR — West Virginia Law Review
W Va L Rev — West Virginia Law Review
W Va Med J — West Virginia Medical Journal
W Va Univ Agri Exp Stn Bull — West Virginia University. Agricultural Experiment Station. Bulletin
W Va Univ Bull Proc Annu Appalachian Gas Meas Short Course — West Virginia University. Bulletin. Proceedings. Annual Appalachian Gas Measurement Short Course
W Va Univ Coal Res Bur Sch Mines Tech Rep — West Virginia University. Coal Research Bureau. School of Mines. Technical Report [*Morgantown, West Virginia*]
W Va Univ Coal Res Bur Tech Rep — West Virginia University. Coal Research Bureau. Technical Report
W Va Univ Eng Exp Sta Tech Bull — West Virginia University. Engineering Experiment Station. Technical Bulletin
W Va Univ Eng Exp Stn Bull — West Virginia University. Engineering Experiment Station. Bulletin
W Va Univ Eng Exp Stn Res Bull — West Virginia University. Engineering Experiment Station. Research Bulletin
W Va Univ Eng Exp Stn Tech Bull — West Virginia University. Engineering Experiment Station. Technical Bulletin
W Va Univ Rp Bd Reg — West Virginia University. Report of the Board of Regents
W Va U Phil — West Virginia University. Philological Papers
WVDOG — Wissenschaftliche Veroeffentlichungen. Deutsche Orient-Gesellschaft
WVF — West Virginia Folklore
WVH — West Virginia History
WVHP — West Virginia Association for Health, Physical Education, Recreation, and Dance. Journal
WVL — West Virginia Law Review
WVLG — Wuerttembergische Vierteljahresschrift fuer Landesgeschichte
WVLR — West Virginia Law Review
WVM — Wiener Voelkerkundliche Mitteilungen
WVUBPL — West Virginia University. Bulletin. Philological Studies
WVUPP — West Virginia University. Philological Papers
WW — Australian Women's Weekly
WW — Journal of Waterway, Port, Coastal, and Ocean Engineering
WW — Wirkendes Wort
W u W — Wirtschaft und Wettbewerb [*German*]
WW — Wissenschaft und Weisheit
WW — Working Woman
Ww — Wroclaw
W & W — Wyatt and Webb's Victorian Reports
WWA — World Water
W & W & A'B — Wyatt, Webb, and A'Beckett's Reports
WW & A'B — Wyatt, Webb, and A'Beckett's Victorian Reports
WW & A'B (E) — Wyatt, Webb, and A'Beckett's Reports (Equity)
W & W & A'B (Eq) — Wyatt, Webb, and A'Beckett's Reports (Equity)
WW & A'B (IE & M) — Wyatt, Webb, and A'Beckett's Reports (Insolvency, Ecclesiastical, and Matrimonial)
WW & A'B (M) — Wyatt, Webb, and A'Beckett's Reports (Mining)
W & W & A'B (Min) — Wyatt, Webb, and A'Beckett's Reports (Mining)
WWAEA — Water and Wastes Engineering
WWARA — Weltwirtschaftliches Archiv
WWATA — Water and Waste Treatment
W Ways — Word Ways
WW & CB — Weekly Weather and Crop Bulletin
WWD — Weird World
WWD — Women's Wear Daily
WWe — Wissenschaft und Weisheit
W & W (E) — Wyatt and Webb's Reports (Equity)
WWENA — Water and Water Engineering
W & W (Eq) — Wyatt and Webb's Reports (Equity)
WWI — Who's Who in Israel
W & W (IE & M) — Wyatt and Webb's Reports (Insolvency, Ecclesiastical, and Matrimonial)
WWJ — Who's Who in Japan
WWJOA — Water Well Journal
WWK — Continental Iron and Steel Trade Reports. Iron and Steel Trade Market Reports and Special Information
W & W (L) — Wyatt and Webb's Reports (Law)

WWM — Ons Nuis Vakblad voor de Meubelhandel, Meubelmakerij, Meubelindustrie, Interieurarchitecteur, Behangerij, Stoffeerderij, en Detailhandel in Woningtextiel
WWM — Weekly Women's Magazine [*Manila*]
WWM — Working Woman
WWN — Walt Whitman Newsletter
W Work (Lond) — World's Work (London)
WWR — Walt Whitman Review
WWS — Western Writers Series
WWSCA — Wirtschaft und Wissenschaft
WWW — Wirtschaft und Wettbewerb. Zeitschrift fuer Kartellrecht, Wettbewerbsrecht, Marktorganisation
WX — Wawatay News Extra. Special Issues
WY — Wyoming Music Educator News-Letter
Wyatt & W — Wyatt and Webb's Reports
Wyatt W & A'B (Eq) — Wyatt, Webb, and A'Beckett's Reports (Equity)
Wyatt W & A'B IE & M — Wyatt, Webb, and A'Beckett's Reports (Insolvency, Ecclesiastical, and Matrimonial)
Wyatt W & A'B IP & M — Wyatt, Webb, and A'Beckett's Victorian Insolvency, Probate, and Matrimonial Reports
Wyatt W & A'B Min — Wyatt, Webb, and A'Beckett's Reports (Mining)
Wyatt & Webb — Wyatt and Webb's Reports
Wyatt & W (Eq) — Wyatt and Webb's Reports (Equity)
Wyatt & W (IE & M) — Wyatt and Webb's Reports (Insolvency, Ecclesiastical, and Matrimonial)
Wyatt & W (IP & M) — Wyatt and Webb's Reports (Insolvency, Probate, and Matrimonial)
Wychowanie M Szkole — Wychowanie Muzyczne w Szkole
Wydz Mat Fiz Chem Uniw Poznan Ser Fiz — Wydzial Matematyki Fizyki i Chemii Uniwersytet Imeni Adama Mickiewicza w Poznaniu Seria Fizyaka
Wye Coll Dep Hop Res Annu Rep — Wye College. Department of Hop Research. Annual Report
WY Energy Ext Serv Update — Wyoming. Energy Extension Service. Update
Wykeham Eng Technol Ser — Wykeham Engineering and Technology Series
Wykeham Sci Ser — Wykeham Science Series
WY LJ — Wyoming Law Journal
Wyo Ag Exp — Wyoming. Agricultural Experiment Station. Publications
Wyo Agric Exp Stn Bull — Wyoming. Agricultural Experiment Station. Bulletin
Wyo Agric Exp Stn Cir — Wyoming. Agricultural Experiment Station. Circular
Wyo Agric Exp Stn Res J — Wyoming. Agricultural Experiment Station. Research Journal
Wyo Agric Exp Stn Sci Monogr — Wyoming. Agricultural Experiment Station. Science Monograph
Wyo Agric Ext Serv Bull — Wyoming. Agricultural Extension Service. Bulletin
Wyo Game Fish Comm Bull — Wyoming. Game and Fish Commission. Bulletin
Wyo Geol Assoc Earth Sci Bull — Wyoming Geological Association. Earth Science Bulletin
Wyo Geol Assoc Guideb Ann Field Conf — Wyoming Geological Association. Guidebook. Annual Field Conference
Wyo Geol Survey Bull Rept Inv — Wyoming. Geological Survey. Bulletin. Report of Investigations
Wyo Geol Surv Prelim Rep — Wyoming. Geological Survey. Preliminary Report
Wyo Geol Surv Rep Invest — Wyoming. Geological Survey. Report of Investigations
Wyo G Off B Wyo St G — Wyoming. Geologist's Office. Bulletin. Wyoming State Geologist
Wyo His Col — Wyoming State Historical Department. Proceedings and Collections
Wyo Issues — Wyoming Issues
Wyo Lib Roundup — Wyoming Library Roundup
Wyo L J — Wyoming Law Journal
Wyoming Geol Survey Prelim Rept — Wyoming. Geological Survey. Preliminary Report
Wyoming Hist G Soc Pr Pub — Wyoming Historical and Geological Society. Proceedings and Collections. Publications
Wyo Nurse — Wyoming Nurse [*Formerly, Wyoming Nurses Newsletter*]
Wyo Nurses News — Wyoming Nurses Newsletter [*Later, Wyoming Nurse*]
Wyo Range Manage — Wyoming Range Management
Wyo Roundup — Wyoming Roundup
Wyo St G — Wyoming State Geologist
Wyo Univ Dep Geol Contrib Geol — Wyoming University. Department of Geology. Contributions to Geology
Wyo Univ Nat Resour Res Inst Bull — Wyoming University. Natural Resources Research Institute. Bulletin
Wyo Univ Nat Resour Res Inst Inf Cir — Wyoming University. Natural Resources Research Institute. Information Circular
Wyo Univ Natur Resour Inst Inform Circ — Wyoming University. Natural Resources Research Institute. Information Circular
Wyo Univ Sch Mines B — Wyoming University. School of Mines. Bulletin
Wyo Univ Water Resour Res Inst Water Resour Ser — Wyoming University. Water Resources Research Institute. Water Resources Series
Wyo Wild Life — Wyoming Wild Life

Wythe Cty Hist Rev — Wythe County Historical Review
WyTJ — Wesleyan Theological Journal
WYW — Weltwirtschaft
Wyz Szkol Ped Krakow Rocznik Nauk-Dydakt Prace Dydakt Mat — Wyzsza Szkola Pedagogiczna w Krakowie. Rocznik Naukowo-Dydaktyczny. Prace z Dydaktyki Matematyki
Wyz Szkol Ped Krakow Rocznik Nauk-Dydakt Prace Mat — Wyzsza Szkola Pedagogiczna w Krakowie. Rocznik Naukowo-Dydaktyczny. Prace Matematyczne
WZ — Westfaelische Zeitschrift
WZ — Wiedza i Zycie
WZ — Wort in der Zeit
W i d Z — Wort in der Zeit
WZ (Berlin) — Wissenschaftliche Zeitschrift. Humboldt-Universitaet (Berlin)
WzD — Wege zur Dichtung
WZEMAUG — Wissenschaftliche Zeitschrift. Ernst-Moritz-Arndt-Universitaet (Greifswald). Gesellschafts- und Sprachwissenschaftliche Reihe
WZE Wiss Z Elektrotech — WZE. Wissenschaftliche Zeitschrift der Elektrotechnik [*East Germany*]
WZFMA — Wissenschaftliche Zeitschrift. Friedrich-Schiller-Universitaet (Jena). Mathematisch-Naturwissenschaftliche Reihe
WZFSU — Wissenschaftliche Zeitschrift. Friedrich-Schiller-Universitaet (Jena). Gesellschafts- und Sprachwissenschaftliche Reihe
WZFSUJ — Wissenschaftliche Zeitschrift. Friedrich-Schiller-Universitaet (Jena). Gesellschafts- und Sprachwissenschaftliche Reihe
WZFSUJ GSR — Wissenschaftliche Zeitschrift. Friedrich-Schiller-Universitaet (Jena). Gesellschafts- und Sprachwissenschaftliche Reihe
WZGK — Westdeutsche Zeitschrift fuer Geschichte und Kunst
WZ (Griefswald) — Wissenschaftliche Zeitschrift. Ernst-Moritz-Arndt-Universitaet (Greifswald)
WZ (Halle) — Wissenschaftliche Zeitschrift. Martin-Luther-Universitaet (Halle-Wittenberg)
WZHMA — Wissenschaftliche Zeitschrift. Humboldt-Universitaet (Berlin). Mathematisch-Naturwissenschaftliche Reihe
WZHU — Wissenschaftliche Zeitschrift. Humboldt-Universitaet (Berlin). Gesellschafts- und Sprachwissenschaftliche Reihe
WZHUB — Wissenschaftliche Zeitschrift. Humboldt-Universitaet (Berlin). Gesellschafts- und Sprachwissenschaftliche Reihe
WZJ — Wissenschaftliche Zeitschrift. Friedrich-Schiller-Universitaet (Jena)
WZ Jena — Wissenschaftliche Zeitschrift. Friedrich-Schiller-Universitaet (Jena)
WZKM — Wiener Zeitschrift fuer die Kunde des Morgenlandes
WZKMU — Wissenschaftliche Zeitschrift. Karl-Marx-Universitaet [*Leipzig*]
WZKMUL — Wissenschaftliche Zeitschrift. Karl-Marx-Universitaet (Leipzig). Gesellschafts- und Sprachwissenschaftliche Reihe
WZKS — Wiener Zeitschrift fuer die Kunde Suedasiens und Archiv fuer Indische Philosophie
WZKSO — Wiener Zeitschrift fuer die Kunde Sued- und Ostasiens und Archiv fuer Indische Philosophie
WZL — Wissenschaftliche Zeitschrift. Karl-Marx-Universitaet (Leipzig)
WZ (Leipzig) — Wissenschaftliche Zeitschrift. Karl-Marx-Universitaet (Leipzig)
WZMLU — Wissenschaftliche Zeitschrift. Martin-Luther-Universitaet
WZMLUH — Wissenschaftliche Zeitschrift. Martin-Luther-Universitaet (Halle-Wittenberg). Gesellschafts- und Sprachwissenschaftliche Reihe
WZMU — Wissenschaftliche Zeitschrift. Karl-Marx-Universitaet [*Leipzig*]. Gesellschafts- und Sprachwissenschaftliche Reihe
WZNDA — Wiener Zeitschrift fuer Nervenheilkunde und Deren Grenzgebiete
WZPHP — Wissenschaftliche Zeitschrift. Paedagogische Hochschule Potsdam. Gesellschafts- und Sprachwissenschaftliche Reihe
WZ Rostock — Wissenschaftliche Zeitschrift. Universitaet Rostock
WZsl — Wissenschaftliche Zeitschrift. Karl-Marx-Universitaet. Gesellschafts- und Sprachwissenschaftliche Reihe [*Leipzig*]
WZTDA — Wissenschaftliche Zeitschrift. Technische Hochschule (Dresden)
WZTKA — Wissenschaftliche Zeitschrift. Technische Hochschule Karl-Marx-Stadt
WZUB — Wissenschaftliche Zeitschrift. Humboldt-Universitaet (Berlin). Gesellschafts- und Sprachwissenschaftliche Reihe
WZUG — Wissenschaftliche Zeitschrift. Ernst-Moritz-Arndt-Universitaet (Greifswald)
WZUH — Wissenschaftliche Zeitschrift. Martin-Luther-Universitaet (Halle-Wittenberg). Gesellschafts- und Sprachwissenschaftliche Reihe
WZUHW — Wissenschaftliche Zeitschrift. Martin-Luther-Universitaet (Halle-Wittenberg). Gesellschafts- und Sprachwissenschaftliche Reihe
WZUJ — Wissenschaftliche Zeitschrift. Friedrich-Schiller-Universitaet (Jena)
WZUL — Wissenschaftliche Zeitschrift. Karl-Marx-Universitaet (Leipzig)
WZUL — Wissenschaftliche Zeitschrift. Universitaet Leipzig. Gesellschafts- und Sprachwissenschaftliche Reihe
WZULeipzig — Wissenschaftliche Zeitschrift. Karl-Marx Universitaet. Gesellschafts- und Sprachwissenschaftliche Reihe (Leipzig)
WZUR — Wissenschaftliche Zeitschrift. Universitaet Rostock
WZUW — Wissenschaftliche Zeitschrift. Universitaet Wien
WZV — Wiener Zeitschrift fuer Volkskunde

X-Y-Z

Xa — Xanadu
XALNA — Research Note FPL. Forest Products Laboratory [*United States*]
XBMIA — Report of Investigations. United States Bureau of Mines
XCRDA — Research and Development Report. United States Office of Coal Research
XDIGA — US Geological Survey. Bulletin
XF — Xudozestvennyj Fol'klor
XH — Xerogrammata Hochschulschriften
XIMIA — Information Circular. United States Bureau of Mines
XIWSA — US Geological Survey. Water-Supply Paper
XL — Xudozestvennaja Literatura
XMOFA — Bureau of Mines. Open File Report [*United States*]
XMTPB — Technical Progress Report. United States Bureau of Mines
XNBSA — National Bureau of Standards. Special Publication [*United States*]
XNIPA — United States. Naval Institute. Proceedings
XNWRA — US News and World Report
XR — X: A Quarterly Review
X-Ray Spect — X-Ray Spectrometry
X-Ray Spectrom — X-Ray Spectrometry
XUS — Xavier University. Studies
XVII S — XVIIe Siecle
Y — Yukon News
YA — Yeda-'am. Journal. Hebrew Folklore Society [*Tel-Aviv*]
YA — YIVO Annual
YAA — Yugoslav Survey
Yacht — Yachting
Yad Energ — Yadrena Energiya
Yadernaya Fiz — Akademiya Nauk SSSR. Yadernaya Fizika
Yad Fiz — Yadernaya Fizika
Yad Geofiz — Yadernaya Geofizika
Yad-Geofiz Issled Geofiz Sb — Yaderno-Geofizicheskie Issledovaniya, Geofizicheskii Sbornik [*USSR*]
Ya Div Q — Yale Divinity Quarterly [*New Haven, CT*]
Yad Konstanty — Yadernye Konstanty
Yad Magn Rezon — Yadernyi Magnitnyi Rezonans
Yad Magn Rezon Org Khim — Yadernyi Magnitnyi Rezonans v Organicheskoi Khimii
Yad Priborostr — Yadernoe Priborostroenie [*USSR*]
Yad Vashem Stud Eur Jew Catastrophe Resist — Yad Vashem Studies on the European Jewish Catastrophe and Resistance
YAJ — Yeda-'am. Journal. Hebrew Folklore Society [*Tel-Aviv*]
YAJ — Yorkshire Archaeological Journal
YAKUA — Yakuzaigaku
YAKUA2 — Archives of Practical Pharmacy
Yakugaku Zasshi J Pharmaceut Soc Jap — Yakugaku Zasshi/Journal of the Pharmaceutical Society of Japan
Yale Art Gal Bul — Yale University. Art Gallery. Bulletin
Yale Associates Bul — Yale University. Associates in Fine Arts. Bulletin
Yale Bicen Pub Contr Miner — Yale Bicentennial Publications. Contributions to Mineralogy and Petrography
Yale ClSt — Yale Classical Studies
Yale Div Q — Yale Divinity Quarterly
Yale Forestry Bull — Yale University. School of Forestry. Bulletin
Yale French Stud — Yale French Studies
Yale Fr St — Yale French Studies

Yale Fr Stud — Yale French Studies
Yale Ital S — Yale Italian Studies
Yale J Biol — Yale Journal of Biology and Medicine
Yale J Biol Med — Yale Journal of Biology and Medicine
Yale J World Pub Ord — Yale Journal of World Public Order
Yale Law J — Yale Law Journal
Yale Lit Mag — Yale Literary Magazine
Yale L J — Yale Law Journal
Yale Math Monographs — Yale Mathematical Monographs
Yale R — Yale Review
Yale Rev — Yale Review
Yale Sci — Yale Scientific
Yale Scient Mag — Yale Scientific Magazine
Yale Sci Mag — Yale Scientific Magazine
Yale Sc Mo — Yale Scientific Monthly
Yale Stud World PO — Yale Studies in World Public Order
Yale Stud World Pub Ord — Yale Studies in World Public Order
Yale St Wld Pub Ord — Yale Studies in World Public Order
Yale U Lib Gaz — Yale University. Library. Gazette
Yale U Libr — Yale University. Library. Gazette
Yale Univ Art Gal Bull — Yale University. Art Gallery. Bulletin
Yale Univ Lib Gaz — Yale University. Library. Gazette
Yale Univ Peabody Mus Nat Hist Annu Rep — Yale University. Peabody Museum of Natural History. Annual Report
Yale Univ Peabody Mus Nat Hist Bull — Yale University. Peabody Museum of Natural History. Bulletin
Yale Univ Peabody Mus Nat History Bull — Yale University. Peabody Museum of Natural History. Bulletin
Yale Univ Sch For Bull — Yale University. School of Forestry. Bulletin
Yale Univ Sch For Environ Stud Bull — Yale University. School of Forestry and Environmental Studies. Bulletin
Yalkut Le-sivim Tekhnol U-Minhal Shel Tekst — Yalkut Le-sivim Tekhnologyah U-Minhal Shel Tekstil
Y Alm — Yurosholayimer Almanakh
Yamaguchi Med — Yamaguchi Medicine [*Japan*]
YAPRA — Yadernoe Priborostroenie
Yard R — Yardbird Reader
Yarosl Gos Univ Mezhvuz Temat Sb — Yaroslavskii Gosudarstvennyi Universitet. Mezhvuzovskii Tematicheskii Sbornik
Yawata Tech Rep — Yawata Technical Report
Yb — Yearbook of Comparative and General Literature
YB — YIVO Bleter [*Vilna/New York*]
YB — Yorkshire Bulletin of Economic and Social Research
YB — Ysgrifau Beirniadol
Yb Agric Coop — Yearbook of Agricultural Cooperation
Yb Agric US Dep Agric — Yearbook of Agriculture. US Department of Agriculture
Yb Calif Avocado Soc — Yearbook. California Avocado Society
Yb Educ — Yearbook of Education
Yb Gen Med — Yearbook of General Medicine
Yb Gen Surg — Yearbook of General Surgery
Yb Gloucester Beekprs Ass — Yearbook. Gloucestershire Bee-Keepers Association
YBICSU — Yearbook. International Council of Scientific Unions
Yb Ind Orthop Surg — Yearbook of Industrial and Orthopedic Surgery

Yb Inter Amer M Research — Yearbook for Inter-American Musical Research
Yb Int Folk M Council — Yearbook. International Folk Music Council
YbLitgSt — Yearbook of Liturgical Studies [*Notre Dame, IN*]
Yb Med — Yearbook of Medicine
Yb Med Ass Great Cy NY — Yearbook. Medical Association of the Greater City of New York
Yb Neurol Psychiat Endocr — Yearbook of Neurology, Psychiatry, Endocrinology, and Neurosurgery
Yb Ophthal — Yearbook of Ophthalmology
Yb Pediat — Yearbook of Pediatrics
Yb Phys Med Rehabil — Yearbook of Physical Medicine and Rehabilitation
Yb Phys Soc — Yearbook. Physical Society
YBPS — Yearbook. British Pirandello Society
Yb R Hort Soc — Yearbook. Royal Horticulture Society
Yb R Vet Agric Coll — Yearbook. Royal Veterinary and Agricultural College
Yb Soc — Yearbook. Royal Society of London
Yb Soc Pol Britain — Yearbook of Social Policy in Britain
Yb US Dep Agric — Yearbook. United States Department of Agriculture
Yb Wld Aff — Yearbook of World Affairs
Yb World Aff — Yearbook of World Affairs
Yb Yorks Beekprs Ass — Yearbook. Yorkshire Beekeepers Association
YCC — Yearbook of Comparative Criticism
YCGL — Yearbook of Comparative and General Literature
YCHP — Yenching Journal of Chinese Studies
YCLS — Yale Classical Studies
YCOMA — Yearbook. Coke Oven Managers' Association
YCS — Yale Classical Studies
YCS — Yorkshire Celtic Studies
YCSN — Yukon Conservation Society. Newsletter
Y C T — Young Cinema and Theatre
YDKGA — Yamaguchi Daigaku Kogakubu Kenkyu Hokoku
YDQ — Yale Divinity Quarterly
YDS — Yorkshire Dialect Society. Transactions
Yearb Agr Co-op — Yearbook of Agricultural Co-operation
Yearb Agric US Dep Agric — Yearbook of Agriculture. US Department of Agriculture
Yearb Agr USDA — Yearbook of Agriculture. US Department of Agriculture
Yearb Am Pulp Pap Mil Supt Assoc — Yearbook. American Pulp and Paper Mill Superintendents Association
Yearb Anesth — Yearbook of Anesthesia
Yearb Bharat Krishak Samaj — Yearbook. Bharat Krishak Samaj
Yearb Bur Miner Resour Geol Geophys — Yearbook. Bureau of Mineral Resources. Geology and Geophysics
Yearb Calif Macad Soc — Yearbook. California Macadamia Society
Yearb Carnegie Inst Wash — Yearbook. Carnegie Institute of Washington
Yearb Child Lit Assoc — Yearbook. Children's Literature Association
Yearb Coke Oven Managers' Assoc — Yearbook. Coke Oven Managers' Association [*England*]
Yearb Dermatol Syphilol — Yearbook of Dermatology and Syphilology
Yearb Drug Ther — Yearbook of Drug Therapy
Yearb Endocrinol — Yearbook of Endocrinology
Yearb Engl Stud — Yearbook of English Studies
Yearb Est Learned Soc Am — Yearbook. Estonian Learned Society in America
Yearb Fac Agr Univ Ankara — Yearbook. Faculty of Agriculture. University of Ankara
Yearb Gen Surg — Yearbook of General Surgery
Yearb Inst Geochem Sib Div Acad Sci (USSR) — Yearbook. Institute of Geochemistry. Siberian Division. Academy of Sciences (USSR)
Yearb Leo Baeck Inst — Yearbook. Leo Baeck Institute
Yearb Med — Yearbook of Medicine
Yearb Nat Farmers' Ass — Yearbook. National Farmers' Association
Yearb Natl Inst Sci India — Yearbook. National Institute of Sciences of India
Year Book Aust — Year Book Australia
Year Book Carnegie Inst Wash — Year Book. Carnegie Institution of Washington
Yearbook East-Eur Econ — Yearbook of East-European Economics
Year Book Indian Natl Sci Acad — Year Book. Indian National Science Academy
Year Book Indian Nat Sci Acad — Year Book. Indian National Science Academy
Year Book Natl Auricula Primula Soc North Sec — Year Book. National Auricula and Primula Society. Northern Section
Year Book Nucl Med — Year Book of Nuclear Medicine [*United States*]
Yearb Pap Ind Manage Assoc — Yearbook. Paper Industry Management Association
Yearb Pathol Clin Pathol — Yearbook of Pathology and Clinical Pathology
Yearb Pediatr — Yearbook of Pediatrics
Yearb Phys Anthropol — Yearbook of Physical Anthropology
Yearb R Asiat Soc Bengal — Yearbook. Royal Asiatic Society of Bengal
Year Endocrinol — Year in Endocrinology
Year Metab — Year in Metabolism
YEE — Yale Economic Essays
Yellow B R — Yellow Brick Road
Yellowstone-Bighorn Research Proj Contr — Yellowstone-Bighorn Research Project. Contribution

Yellowstone Libr and Mus Assoc Yellowstone Interpretive Ser — Yellowstone Library and Museum Association. Yellowstone Interpretive Series
YER — Yeats Eliot Review
YES — Yearbook of English Studies
Yessis Rev — Yessis Review of Soviet Physical Education and Sports
Yeung Nam Univ Inst Ind Technol Rep — Yeung Nam University. Institute of Industrial Technology. Report
YFS — Yale French Studies
YGKKA — Yuki Gosei Kagaku Kyokaishi
YGKSA — Yogyo Kyokai Shi
YGNR — Yukon Government News Release
YGS — Yale Germanic Studies
YHMAN — Yukon Historical and Museums Association. Newsletter
YI — Yukon Indian News
YIFMC — Yearbook. International Folk Music Council
YIS — Yearbook of Italian Studies
Y It S — Yale Italian Studies
YIVO — YIVO Annual of Jewish Social Science
YJ — Youth Journal
YJCS — Yenching Journal of Chinese Studies
YK — Yiddishe Kultur
YKIGA — Yokohama Igaku
YKKKA — Yakugaku Kenkyu
YKKKA8 — Japanese Journal of Pharmacy and Chemistry
YKKZA — Yakugaku Zasshi
YKYRA — Yakubutsu Ryoho
YLG — Yale University. Library. Gazette
YLG News — Library Association. Youth Libraries Group News
YLJ — Yale Law Journal
YLM — Yale Literary Magazine
YLT — Yu-Yen-Hsueh Lun-Ts'ung [*Essays in Linguistics*]
YM — Young Man
YM — Young Miss Magazine
YMTM — Yikal Maya Than (Mexico)
YN — Yellowknifer
YN — Young Numismatist
YNER — Yale Near Eastern Researches [*New Haver/London*]
Yoga Jnl — Yoga Journal
Yokogawa Tech Rep — Yokogawa Technical Report [*Japan*]
Yokohama Math J — Yokohama Mathematical Journal
Yokohama Med Bull — Yokohama Medical Bulletin
Yokohama Med J — Yokohama Medical Journal [*Japan*]
Yoko Iga — Yokohama Igaku
Yoko Med Bull — Yokohama Medical Bulletin
Yokufukai Geriatr J — Yokufukai Geriatric Journal
Yona Acta Med — Yonago Acta Medica
Yon Act Med — Yonago Acta Medica
Yonago Acta Med — Yonago Acta Medica
Yona Iga Zass — Yonago Igaku Zasshi
Yonsei Eng Rep — Yonsei Engineering Report
Yonsei Eng Rev — Yonsei Engineering Review [*South Korea*]
Yonsei J Med Sci — Yonsei Journal of Medical Science
Yonsei Med J — Yonsei Medical Journal
Yonsei Rep Trop Med — Yonsei Reports on Tropical Medicine
YOR — Bulletin of Economic Research
YorkCoHS — York County Historical Society. Papers
York Papers Ling — York Papers in Linguistics
Yorks Beekpr — Yorkshire Beekeeper
Yorks Geol Soc Occas Publ — Yorkshire Geological Society. Occasional Publication
Yorkshire Archaeol J — Yorkshire Archaeological Journal
Yorkshire Arch J — Yorkshire Archaeological Journal
Yorkshire Archt — Yorkshire Architect
Yorkshire Geol Soc Proc — Yorkshire Geological Society. Proceedings
Yorkshire G Polyt Soc Pr — Yorkshire Geological and Polytechnic Society. Proceedings
YOS — Yale Oriental Series
YoShiR — Yokohama Shiritsu Daigaku Ronso [*Bulletin. Yokohama Municipal University Society*]
YOSR — Yale Oriental Series. Researches
Young Athl — Young Athlete
Young Child — Young Children
Young Cinema — Young Cinema and Theatre/Jeune Cinema et Theatre
Young Lib — Young Liberal
Your Mus Cue — Your Musical Cue
Your Okla Dent Assoc J — Your Oklahoma Dental Association Journal
Your Radiol — Your Radiologist
Youth Aid Bull — Youth Aid Bulletin
Youth Soc — Youth and Society
Youth and Soc — Youth and Society
YOYUA — Yoyuen
YP — Yorkshire Post
Yperm — Yperman. Bulletin de la Societe Belge d'Histoire de la Medecine
YPHJA — Yo-Up Hoeji
YPL — York Papers in Linguistics

YPLA — Your Public Lands. US Department of the Interior. Bureau of Land Mangement
YPR — Yale Poetry Review
YQ — Youth Quarterly
YR — Yale Review
Yr Bk (Charleston SC) — Year Book (Charleston, South Carolina)
Yrbk Compar & Gen Lit — Yearbook of Comparative and General Literature
Yrbk Comp & Gen Lit — Yearbook of Comparative and General Literature
Yrbk Sch Law — Yearbook of School Law
Yrbk Sp Educ — Yearbook of Special Education
Yrbk World Aff — Yearbook of World Affairs [*London*]
YRS — Yale Romanic Studies
YRS — Yearbook of Romanian Studies
YRTMA — Yonsei Reports on Tropical Medicine
YS — Yidishe Shprakh
YSCECP Reports — Yugoslav-Serbo-Croatian-English Contrastive Project. Reports
YSCECP Studies — Yugoslav-Serbo-Croatian-English Contrastive Project. Studies
YSE — Yale Studies in English
YSh — Yidishe Shprakh
YSKOD8 — Japanese Journal of Psychopharmacology
YTELSA — Yearbook. Estonian Learned Society in America
YU — Yukon News
Yu — Yunost' [*Moscow*]
Yuasa Tech Inf — Yuasa Technical Information [*Japan*]
Yugoslav L — Yugoslav Law
Yugosl Chem Pap — Yugoslav Chemical Papers
Yugosl Law — Yugoslav Law
Yugosl Surv — Yugoslav Survey
Yugosl Zavod Geol Geofiz Istrazivanja Raspr — Yugoslavia Zavod za Geoloska i Geofizicka Istrazivanja. Rasprave-Service Geologique et Geophysique. Memoires
Yugosl Zavod Geol Geofiz Istrazivanja Vesn Geol — Yugoslavia Zavod za Geoloska i Geofizicka Istrazivanja-Institut de Recherches Geologiques et Geophysiques. Vesnik. Geologija. Serija A [*Belgrade*]
Yug Soc Soil Sci Publ — Yugoslav Society of Soil Science. Publication
Yug Surv — Yugoslav Survey
YUIN — Yukon Indian News
YULG — Yale University. Library. Gazette
YUTR — Yukon Teacher
YUUD — Yukon Update
YUWM — Yukon Water Management Bulletin. Westwater Research Centre
Y Viewers — Young Viewers
YVS — Yad Vashem Studies
YW — Year's Work in English Studies
YW — Young Woman
YWA — Year's Work in Archaeology
YWC — Year's Work in Classical Studies
YWCS — Year's Work in Classical Studies
YWE — Year's Work in English Studies
YWES — Year's Work in English Studies
YWML — Year's Work in Modern Language Studies
YWMLS — Year's Work in Modern Language Studies
YYYC — Yu-Yen Yen-Chiu [*Linguistic Researches*]
Z — Zagreb
Z — Zivot
Z — Zora
Z — Zven'ya
Z — Zwingliana
Z — Zycie
Z-A — Zaire-Afrique
Z f A — Zeitschrift fuer Agrargeschichte und Agrarsoziologie
Z f A — Zeitschrift fuer Anatomie und Entwicklungsgeschichte
ZA — Zeitschrift fuer Assyriologie und Verwandte Gebiete
ZA — Zeitschrift fuer Assyriologie und Vorderasiatische Archaeologie [*Berlin*]
Z f A — Zeitschrift fuer Astrophysik
ZA — Zionist Archives
ZA — Ziva Antika
ZA — Zunz Archive. Jewish National and University Library [*Jerusalem*]
ZAA — Zeitschrift fuer Anglistik und Amerikanistik
Z Aachener Geschichtsver — Zeitschrift. Aachener Geschichtsverein
ZAAK — Zeitschrift fuer Aesthetik und Allgemeine Kunstwissenschaft
ZABIA — Zastita Bilja
ZACFA — Fresenius' Zeitschrift fuer Analytische Chemie
Z Acker-Pflanzenb — Zeitschrift fuer Acker- und Pflanzenbau
Z Acker Pflanzenbau — Zeitschrift fuer Acker- und Pflanzenbau
Z Acker u Pflbau — Zeitschrift fuer Acker- und Pflanzenbau
ZACMA — Zeitschrift fuer Anorganische Chemie
ZADS — Zeitschrift. Allgemeiner Deutsche Sprachverein
ZAED Phys Daten — ZAED [*Zentralstelle fuer Atomkernenergie-Dokumentation*] Physik Daten
ZAeg — Zeitschrift fuer Aegyptische Sprache und Altertumskunde
Z Aegypt Sprache — Zeitschrift fuer Aegyptische Sprache und Altertumskunde

Z Aegypt Sprache Altertumskd — Zeitschrift fuer Aegyptische Sprache und Altertumskunde
ZAEKD — Zeszyty Naukowe. Akademia Ekonomiczna w Krakowie
Za Ekon Mater — Za Ekonomiyu Materialov
Za Ekon Topl — Za Ekonomiyu Topliva
Z Aerosol Forsch Ther — Zeitschrift fuer Aerosol Forschung und Therapie
Z Aerztl Fortbild — Zeitschrift fuer Aerztliche Fortbildung
Z Aerztl Fortbild (Jena) — Zeitschrift fuer Aerztliche Fortbildung (Jena)
ZAeS — Zeitschrift fuer Aegyptische Sprache und Altertumskunde
Z Aes Allg Kunst — Zeitschrift fuer Aesthetik und Allgemeine Kunstwissenschaft
ZAFBA — Zeitschrift fuer Aerztliche Fortbildung
Zagad Ekon Roln — Zagadnienia Ekonomiki Rolnej
Zagadn Ekon Roln — Zagadnienia Ekonomiki Rolnej
Zagadn Eksploatacji Masz — Zagadnienia Eksploatacji Maszyn [*Poland*]
Zagadnienia Drgan Nieliniowych — Zagadnienia Drgan Nieliniowych [*Nonlinear Vibration Problems*]
Zagadnienie Dyn Rozwoju Czlowieka Zesz Probl Kosmosu — Zagadnienie Dynamiki Rozwoju Czlowieka Zeszyty Problemowe Kosmosu
ZAGGD — Zeszyty Naukowe Akademii Gorniczo-Hutniczej Imienia Stanislawa Staszica. Gornictwo
Z Agrargesch Agrarsoziol — Zeitschrift fuer Agrargeschichte und Agrarsoziologie
Z Agrargesch u -Soziol — Zeitschrift fuer Agrargeschichte und Agrarsoziologie
ZAGV — Zeitschrift. Aachener Geschichtsverein
Zahnaerztebl (Baden-Wuerttemb) — Zahnaerzteblatt (Baden-Wuerttemberg)
Zahnaerztl Gesundheitsdienst — Zahnaerztlicher Gesundheitsdienst
Zahnaerztl Mitt — Zahnaerztliche Mitteilungen
Zahnaerztl Prax — Zahnaerztliche Praxis
Zahnaerztl Praxisfuehr — Zahnaerztliche Praxisfuehrung
Zahnaerztl Rundsch — Zahnaerztliche Rundschau
Zahnaerztl Welt — Zahnaerztliche Welt
Zahnaerztl Welt Zahnaerztl Reform — Zahnaerztliche Welt und Zahnaerztliche Reform
Zahnaerztl Welt Zahnaerztl Rundsch — Zahnaerztliche Welt, Zahnaerztliche Rundschau
Zahn-Mund-Kieferheilkd — Zahn-, Mund-, und Kieferheilkunde
Zahn- Mund- Kieferheilkd Zentralbl — Zahn-, Mund-, und Kieferheilkunde mit Zentralblatt [*German Democratic Republic*]
Zaire-Afr — Zaire-Afrique
ZAK — Zeitschrift fuer Aesthetik und Kunstwissenschaft
Zakhist Rosl — Zakhist Roslin
Zakhyst Rosl Resp Mizhvid Temat Nauk Zb — Zakhyst Roslyn Respublikans 'Kyi Mizhvidomchyi Tematychnyi Naukovyi Zbirnyk
Zakonomern Raspred Promesnykh Tsentrov Ionnykh Krist — Zakonomernosti Raspredeleniya Promesnykh Tsentrov v Ionnykh Kristallakh
Zakonomern Razmeshcheniya Polezn Iskop — Zakonomernosti Razmeshcheniya Poleznykh Iskopaemykh
Zakupki Sel'skokhoz Prod — Zakupki Sel'skohozyaistvennykh Produktov
ZAL — Zeitschrift fuer Arabische Linguistik
ZAL — Zeitschrift fuer Auslaendische Landwirtschaft
Z Allgemeine Wissenschaftstheorie — Zeitschrift fuer Allgemeine Wissenschaftstheorie
Z Allgemeinmed — Zeitschrift fuer Allgemeinmedizin
Z f Allg Med — Zeitschrift fuer Allgemeinmedizin
Z Allg Mikr — Zeitschrift fuer Allgemeine Mikrobiologie
Z Allg Mikrobiol — Zeitschrift fuer Allgemeine Mikrobiologie
Z Allg Mikrobiol — Zeitschrift fuer Allgemeine Mikrobiologie, Morphologie, Physiologie, Genetik, und Oekologie der Mikrorganismen
Z Allg Oesterr Apoth Ver — Zeitschrift. Allgemeiner Oesterreichische Apotheker-Verein
Z Allg Physiol — Zeitschrift fuer Allgemeine Physiologie
Z Allg Wiss — Zeitschrift fuer Allgemeine Wissenschaftstheorie
Z Allg Wissenschaftstheor — Zeitschrift fuer Allgemeine Wissenschaftstheorie
Z Alternsforsch — Zeitschrift fuer Alternsforschung
Z Altt W — Zeitschrift fuer die Alttestamentliche Wissenschaft
Z Alt Wiss — Zeitschrift fuer die Alttestamentliche Wissenschaft
ZAM — Zeitschrift fuer Askese und Mystik
Zambia Dep Game Fish Fish Res Bull — Zambia. Department of Game and Fisheries. Fisheries Research Bulletin
Zambia Dep Wildl Fish Natl Parks Annu Rep — Zambia. Department of Wildlife, Fisheries, and National Parks. Annual Report
Zambia Div For Res Annu Rep — Zambia. Division of Forest Research. Annual Report
Zambia For Res Bull — Zambia Forest Research Bulletin
Zambia Geogr Assoc Mag — Zambia Geographical Association. Magazine
Zambia Geol Surv Annu Rep — Zambia. Geological Survey. Annual Report
Zambia Geol Surv Dep Annu Rep — Zambia. Geological Survey. Department Annual Report
Zambia Geol Surv Dep Econ Rep — Zambia. Ministry of Lands and Mines. Geological Survey Department. Economic Report
Zambia Geol Surv Econ Rep — Zambia. Geological Survey. Economic Report
Zambia Geol Surv Rec — Zambia. Geological Survey. Records
Zambia Geol Surv Tech Rep — Zambia. Geological Survey. Technical Report

Zambia J Sci Technol — Zambia Journal of Science and Technology
Zambia Minist Lands Nat Resour For Res Bull — Zambia. Ministry of Lands and Natural Resources. Forest Research Bulletin
Zambia Minist Rural Dev For Res Bull — Zambia. Ministry of Rural Development. Forest Research Bulletin
Zambia Nurse J — Zambia Nurse Journal
Zambia Rep Geol Surv — Zambia. Ministry of Lands and Mines. Report of the Geological Survey
ZAMNA — ZFA (Zeitschrift fuer Allgemeinmedizin)
ZAMP — Zeitschrift fuer Angewandte Mathematik und Physik
Z Anal Chem — Fresenius' Zeitschrift fuer Analytische Chemie
Z Analyt Chem — Zeitschrift fuer Analytische Chemie
Z Anat Entwicklungsgesch — Zeitschrift fuer Anatomie und Entwicklungsgeschichte
ZANCA — Zeitschrift fuer Analytische Chemie
ZANCO Ser A — ZANCO. Scientific Journal of Sulaimaniyah University. Series A. Pure and Applied Sciences
ZANF — Zeitschrift fuer Assyriologie und Vorderasiatische Altertumskunde. Neue Folge
Z Ang & Amerik — Zeitschrift fuer Anglistik und Amerikanistik
Z Angew Baeder Klimaheilkd — Zeitschrift fuer Angewandte Baeder und Klimaheilkunde
Z Angew Chem — Zeitschrift fuer Angewandte Chemie und Zentralblatt fuer Technische Chemie
Z Angew Entomol — Zeitschrift fuer Angewandte Entomologie
Z Angew Geol — Zeitschrift fuer Angewandte Geologie
Z Angew Math Mech — Zeitschrift fuer Angewandte Mathematik und Mechanik
Z Angew Math und Mech — Zeitschrift fuer Angewandte Mathematik und Mechanik
Z Angew Math Phys — Zeitschrift fuer Angewandte Mathematik und Physik
Z Angew Met — Zeitschrift fuer Angewandte Meteorologie
Z Angew Mikrosk Klin Chem — Zeitschrift fuer Angewandte Mikroskopic und Klinische Chemie
Z Angew Photogr Wiss Tech — Zeitschrift fuer Angewandte Photographie in Wissenschaft und Technik
Z Angew Phys — Zeitschrift fuer Angewandte Physik
Z Angew Psychol — Zeitschrift fuer Angewandte Psychologie und Psychologische Forschung
Z Angew Zool — Zeitschrift fuer Angewandte Zoologie
Z Ang Geol — Zeitschrift fuer Angewandte Geologie
Z Anglis Am — Zeitschrift fuer Anglistik und Amerikanistik
Z Ang Ma Me — Zeitschrift fuer Angewandte Mathematik und Mechanik
Z Ang Math — Zeitschrift fuer Angewandte Mathematik und Physik
Z Anorg A C — Zeitschrift fuer Anorganische und Allgemeine Chemie
Z Anorg Allg Chem — Zeitschrift fuer Anorganische und Allgemeine Chemie
Z Anorg Chem — Zeitschrift fuer Anorganische und Allgemeine Chemie
ZANPA — Zeitschrift fuer Experimentelle und Angewandte Psychologie
ZAnt — Ziva Antika
Z Antimikrob Antineoplast Chemother — Zeitschrift fuer Antimikrobielle und Antineoplastische Chemotherapie
Zanzibar Protect Ann Rep Med Dept — Zanzibar Protectorate. Annual Report on the Medical Department
ZAO RV — Zeitschrift fuer Auslaendisches Oeffentliches Recht und Voelkerrecht
Za Ovladenie Tekh Kamenougol'n Promsti — Za Ovladenie Tekhnikoi v Kamenougol'noi Promyshlennosti
Zapadne Karpaty Ser Geol — Zapadne Karpaty. Seria Geologia
Zapadn Karpaty Ser Paleontol — Zapadne Karpaty. Seria Paleontologia
Zap Arm Otd Vses Mineral Ova — Zapiski Armyanskogo Otdeleniya Vsesoyuznogo Mineralogicheskogo Obshchestva
Zap Beloruss Gos Inst Sel'sk Lesn Khoz — Zapiski Belorusskogo Gosudarstvennogo Instituta Sel'skogo i Lesnogo Khozyaistva
Zap Cukotsk Kraeved Muz — Zapiski Cukotskogo Kraevedcheskogo Muzeja
Zap Inst Khim Akad Nauk Ukr RSR — Zapiski Institutu Khimii Akademiya Nauk Ukrains'koi RSR
Zapisnici Srp Geol Drus — Zapisnici Srpskog Geoloskog Drustva
Zap Khar'k S-kh Inst — Zapiski Khar'kovskogo Sel'skokhozyaistvennogo Instituta
Zap Kiiv Tov Prirodozn — Zapiski Kiivs'kogo Tovaristva Prirodoznavtsiv
Zap Kirg Otd Vses Mineral Ova — Zapiski Kirgizskogo Otdeleniya Vsesoyuznogo Mineralogicheskogo Obshchestva
Zap Leningrad Sel'skokhoz Inst — Zapiski Leningradskogo Sel'skokhozyaistvennogo Instituta
Zap Leningr Gorn Inst — Zapiski Leningradskogo Gornogo Instituta [*USSR*]
Zap Leningr Sel'-khoz Inst — Zapiski Leningradskogo Sel'skokhozyaistvennogo Instituta
Zap Leningr S-kh Inst — Zapiski Leningradskogo Sel'skokhozyaistvennogo Instituta
Zap Nauchn Semin — Zapiski Nauchnykh Seminarov
Zap Nauchn Semin Leningr Otd Mat Inst Akad Nauk SSSR — Zapiski Nauchnykh Seminarov Leningradskogo Otdelenie Matematicheskii Institut Akademia Nauk SSSR [*USSR*]
Zap Nauchn Sem Leningrad Otdel Mat Inst Steklov (LOMI) — Zapiski Nauchnykh Seminarov Leningradskogo Otdeleniya Matematicheskogo Instituta Imeni V. A. Steklova Akademii Nauk SSSR (LOMI)

Zap Naucn Sem Leningrad Otdel Mat Inst Steklov — Zapiski Naucnyh Seminarov Leningradskogo Otdelenija Matematiceskogo Instituta Imeni V. A. Steklova Akademii Nauk SSSR
Zap Odess Ark Obshch — Zapiski Odesskoe Arkheologicheskoe Obshchestvo [*Odessa, USSR*]
Za Prog Proizvod — Za Progress Proizvodstva
Zap Ross Mineral Ova — Zapiski Rossiiskogo Mineralogicheskogo Obshchestva
Zap SKK Gor NII — Zapiski Severo-Kavkazskogo Kraevogo Gorskogo Naucno-Issledovatel'skogo Instituta
Zap Sverdl Otd Vses Bot Ova — Zapiski Sverdlovskogo Otdeleniya Vsesoyuznogo Botanicheskogo Obshchestva
Zap Sverdlov Otd Vsesoyuz Bot Obshch — Zapiski Sverdlovskogo Otdeleniya Vsesoyuznogo Botanicheskogo Obshchestva
Zap Tadzh Otd Vses Mineral Ova — Zapiski Tadzhikskogo Otdeleniya Vsesoyuznogo Mineralogicheskogo Obshchestva
Zap Tsentr Kavk Otd Vses Bot Ova — Zapiski Tsentral'no-Kavkazskogo Otdeleniya Vsesoyuznogo Botanicheskogo Obshchestva
Zap Ukr Otd Vses Mineral Ova — Zapiski Ukrainskogo Otdeleniya Vsesoyuznogo Mineralogicheskogo Obshchestva
Zap Uzb Otd Vses Mineral Ova — Zapiski Uzbekistanskogo Otdeleniya Vsesoyuznogo Mineralogicheskogo Obshchestva
Zap Voronezh Sel'-Khoz Inst — Zapiski Voronezhskogo Sel'sko-Khozyaist-Vennogo Instituta
Zap Voronezh S-kh Inst — Zapiski Voronezhskogo Sel'sko-Khozyaist-Vennogo Instituta
Zap Vost Sib Otd Vses Mineral Ova — Zapiski Vostochno-Sibirskogo Otdeleniya Vsesoyuznogo Mineralogicheskogo Obshchestva
Zap Vses Mineral Obshchest — Zapiski Vsesoyuznogo Mineralogicheskogo Obshchestva
Zap Vses Mineral O-va — Zapiski Vsesoyuznogo Mineralogicheskogo Obshchestva
Zap Zabaik Fil Geogr Ova SSSR — Zapiski Zabaikal'skogo Filiala Geograficheskogo Obshchestva SSSR
Zap Zabaik Otd Vses Geogr O-va — Zapiski Zabaikal'skogo Otdela Vsesoyuznogo Geograficheskogo Obshchestva
Z Arbeitsgem Oesterr Entomol — Zeitschrift. Arbeitsgemeinschaft Oesterreichischer Entomologen
Z Arbeitswiss N F — Zeitschrift fuer Arbeitswissenschaft. Neue Folge
Z Archaeol — Zeitschrift fuer Archaeologie
Za Rekonstr Tekst Promsti — Za Rekonstruktsiyu Tekstil'noi Promyshlennosti
ZARSA — Zeszyty Naukowe. Akademia Rolnicza w Szczecinie
ZarSl — Zaranie Slaskie
ZAS — Zeitschrift fuer Aegyptische Sprache und Altertumskunde
ZASA — Zeitschrift fuer Aegyptische Sprache und Altertumskunde
Zashch Korroz Khim Promsti — Zashchita ot Korrozii v Khimicheskoi Promyshlennosti
Zashch Met — Zashchita Metallov
Zashch Pokrytia Met — Zashchitnye Pokrytiya na Metallakh
Zashch Rast (Kiev) — Zashchita Rastenii (Kiev)
Zashch Rast (Leningrad) — Zashchita Rastenii (Leningrad)
Zashch Rast (Mosc) — Zashchita Rastenii (Moscow)
Zashch Rast (Moscow) — Zashchita Rastenii (Moscow)
Zashch Rast Vred Bolez — Zashchita Rastenii ot Vreditelei i Boleznei
Zashch Rast Vred Bolezn — Zashchita Rastenii ot Vreditelei i Boleznei
Zashch Rast Vredit Bolez — Zashchita Rastenii ot Vreditelei i Boleznei
Zashch Truboprovodov Korroz — Zashchita Truboprovodov ot Korrozii
Z Asiat Studien — Zentralasiatische Studien [*Bonn*]
Za Soc Zemed — Za Socialisticke Zemedelstvi
Za Sots Sel' -khoz Nauku — Za Sotsialisticheskuyu Sel'skokhozyaistvennuyu Nauku
Za Sots Sel'skokhoz Nauku Ser A — Za Sotsialisticheskuyu Sel'skokhozyaistvennuyu Nauku. Seriya A
Z Assyr — Zeitschrift fuer Assyriologie
Zast Bilja — Zastita Bilja
Z Asthet Al — Zeitschrift fuer Asthetik und Allgemeine Kunstwissenschaft
ZastMat — Zastosowania Matematyki
Zast Mater — Zastita Materijala
Zastos Mat — Polska Akademia Nauk. Instytut Matematyczny. Zastosowania Matematyki
Zastosow Mat — Zastosowania Matematyki
Z Astrophys — Zeitschrift fuer Astrophysik [*West Germany*]
ZATB — Zeitschrift fuer die Alttestamentliche Wissenschaft. Beihefte
Za Tekh Prog (Baku) — Za Tekhnicheskii Progress (Baku)
Za Tekh Prog (Gorkly) — Za Tekhnicheskii Progress (Gorkly)
ZATPA — Za Tekhnicheskii Progress
Za Turf Ind — Za Turfyanuyu Industriyu
ZATW — Zeitschrift fuer die Alttestamentliche Wissenschaft
Z Augenheilkd — Zeitschrift fuer Augenheilkunde
Z Auslaend Landwirtsch — Zeitschrift fuer Auslaendische Landwirtschaft
Z Auslaend Oeff Voelkerrecht — Zeitschrift fuer Auslaendisches Oeffentliches Recht und Voelkerrecht
Z Ausland Landwirt — Zeitschrift fuer Auslaendische Landwirtschaft
Z Ausl Oeff R — Zeitschrift fuer Auslaendisches Oeffentliches Recht und Voelkerrecht

Z Ausl Oeff Recht Voelkerrecht — Zeitschrift fuer Auslaendisches Oeffentliches Recht und Voelkerrecht

Z Ausl Oeff RVR — Zeitschrift fuer Auslaendisches Oeffentliches Recht und Voelkerrecht

ZAVA — Zeitschrift fuer Assyriologie und Vorderasiatische Archaeologie

Zav Lab — Zavodskaya Laboratoriya

Zavod Lab — Zavodskaya Laboratoriya

ZAW — Zeitschrift fuer die Alttestamentliche Wissenschaft

ZAWEA — Zahnaerztliche Welt

ZB — Zeitschrift fuer Balkanologie

ZB — Zeitschrift fuer Betriebswirtschaft

ZB — Zeitschrift fuer Botanik

ZB — Zentralblatt fuer Bibliothekswesen

ZBA — Zeitschrift fuer Arbeitswissenschaft

ZBalk — Zeitschrift fuer Balkanologie

Z Bayer Kg — Zeitschrift fuer Bayerische Kirchengeschichte

Z Bayer Ldg — Zeitschrift fuer Bayerische Landesgeschichte

Z Bayer Revisions Ver — Zeitschrift. Bayerischer Revisions Verein

ZBB — Zeitschrift fuer Bibliothekswesen und Bibliographie

ZBB — Zentralblatt fuer Bibliothekswesen

Zb f Bibl — Zentralblatt fuer Bibliothekswesen

Zb Bioteh Fak Univ Ljubljani — Zbornik Biotehniske Fakultete Univerze v Ljubljani

Zb Bioteh Fak Univ Ljublj Kmetijstvo — Zbornik Biotehniske Fakultete Univerze v Ljubljani. Kmetijstvo

Zb Bioteh Fak Univ Ljublj Vet — Zbornik Biotehniske Fakultete Univerze v Ljubljani. Veterinarstvo

Zb Bioteh Fak Univ Ljublj Vet Supl — Zbornik Biotehniske Fakultete Univerze v Ljubljani. Veterinarstvo. Suplement

Zb Biotehn Fak Univ Ljublj — Zbornik Biotehniske Fakultete Univerze v Ljubljani

ZBBW — Zentralblatt fuer Bibliothekswesen

ZBCSA — Zentralblatt fuer Chirurgie. Supplement

ZBDLG — Zuercher Beitraege zur Deutschen Literatur und Geistesgeschichte

ZBDSS — Zuercher Beitraege zur Deutschen Sprach- und Stilgeschichte

Z Beih — Beihefte. Zeitschrift fuer Romanische Philologie

Z Beleuchtungswes Heizungs- Lueftungstech — Zeitschrift fuer Beleuchtungswesen Heizungs- und Lueftungstechnik

Z Berg Gesch V — Zeitschrift. Bergischer Geschichtsverein

Z Berg Huetten Salinenwes Dtsch Reich — Zeitschrift fuer das Berg-, Huetten-, und Salinenwesen im Deutschen Reich

Z Bergrecht — Zeitschrift fuer Bergrecht [*West Germany*]

Z Betriebsw — Zeitschrift fuer Betriebswirtschaft

Z Betriebswirtsch — Zeitschrift fuer Betriebswirtschaft

Z Bevoelkerungswiss — Zeitschrift fuer die Bevoelkerungswissenschaft

Z Bewasserungswirtsch — Zeitschrift fuer Bewaesserungswirtschaft

ZBF — Zeitschrift fuer Betriebswirtschaftliche Forschung

ZBF — Zeitschrift fuer Buecherfreunde

ZbFL — Zbornik za Filologiju i Lingvistiku

ZBG — Zeitschrift. Bergischer Geschichtsverein

Zb Geol Vied Zapadne Karpaty — Zbornik Geologichych Vied Zapadne Karpaty

ZBGR — Schweizerische Zeitschrift fuer Beurkundungs- und Grundbuchrecht

ZBGV — Zeitschrift. Bergischer Geschichtsverein

Z Bibl und Bibliog — Zeitschrift fuer Bibliothekswesen und Bibliographie

Z Bibliot u Bibliog — Zeitschrift fuer Bibliothekswesen und Bibliographie

Z Bibliothekswes Bibliogr — Zeitschrift fuer Bibliothekswesen und Bibliographie

Z Bibliothekswesen und Bibl — Zeitschrift fuer Bibliothekswesen und Bibliographie

Z Bienenforsch — Zeitschrift fuer Bienenforschung

Z Binnenfisch DDR — Zeitschrift fuer die Binnenfischerei der DDR

Zb Inst Khim Tekhnol Akad Nauk Ukr RSR — Zbirnik Instituta Khimichnoi Tekhnologii Akademiya Nauk Ukrains'koi RSR

Z Biochem — Zeitschrift fuer Biochemie

Z Biol — Zeitschrift fuer Biologie

Z Biol Tech Method — Zeitschrift fuer Biologische Technik und Methodik

Zbirka Izbran Poglav Fiz — Zbirka Izbranih Poglavij iz Fizike

Zbirka Izbran Poglav Mat — Zbirka Izbranih Poglavij iz Matematike

ZbirP — Zbirnyk Prac' Naukovoji Sevcenkivs'koji Konferenciji

ZBJV — Zeitschrift. Bernischer Juristen-Verein

ZBK — Zeitschrift fuer Bildende Kunst

ZBK — Zeitschrift fuer Buchkunde

ZBKG — Zeitschrift fuer Bayerische Kirchengeschichte

ZBL — Zeitschrift fuer Bayerische Landesgeschichte

Zbl — Zentralblatt fuer Mathematik und Ihre Grenzgebiete

Zbl Allg Path — Zentralblatt fuer Allgemeine Pathologie und Pathologische Anatomie

Zbl A Med — Zentralblatt fuer Arbeitsmedizin und Arbeitsschutz [*Later, Zentralblatt fuer Arbeitsmedizin, Arbeitsschutz, und Prophylaxe*]

Zbl Bakt A — Zentralblatt fuer Bakteriologie. Reihe A

Zbl Bakt B — Zentralblatt fuer Bakteriologie. Reihe B

Zbl f Bibl — Zentralblatt fuer Bibliothekswesen

ZBLG — Zeitschrift fuer Bayerische Landesgeschichte

Zbl Math — Zentralblatt fuer Mathematik und Ihre Grenzgebiete

Zbl Vet A — Zentralblatt fuer Veterinaermedizin. Reihe A

Zbl Vet B — Zentralblatt fuer Veterinaermedizin. Reihe B

Zb Meteorol Hidrol Rad — Zbornik Meteoroloskih i Hidroloskih Radova [*Yugoslavia*]

ZbMS — Zbornik Matice Srpske

Zb Nauk Pr Aspir Kiiv Inzh Budiv Inst — Zbirnik Naukovikh Prats Aspirantiv Kiivs'kii Inzhenerno-Budivel'nii Institut

Zb Nauk Pr Aspir Kyyiv Univ Pryr Nauky — Zbirnyk Naukovykh Prats' Aspirantiv Kyyivski Universytet Pryrodni Nauky

Zb Nauk Pr Kiiv Budiv Inst — Zbirnik Naukovikh Prats Kiivs'kii Budivel'nii Institut

Zb Nauk Pr L'viv Med Inst — Zbirnyk Naukovykh Prats' L'viv'kyi Medychyni Instytut

Zb Nauk Pr Umans'kyi Sil'skohospod Inst — Zbirnyk Naukovykh Prats' Umans'kyi Sil'skohospodarskyi Instytut

Zb Nauk Rob Khark Derzh Med Inst — Zbirnik Naukovikh Robit Kharkivs'kogo Derzhavnogo Medichnogo Institutu

ZbNPAF — Zbirnyk Naukovych Prac' Aspirantiv z Filolohiji

Zbor Arheol Muz — Zbornik na Arheoloskiot Muzej

Zbor Narod Muz Beogradu — Zbornik Narodnog Muzeja u Beogradu

Zborn Biotehn Fak Univ Ljublj Kmet — Zbornik Biotehniske Fakultete Univerze v Ljubljani. Kmetijstvo

Zbornik Rad Mat Inst (Beograd) — Zbornik Radova. Matematicki Institut (Beograd)

Zborn Rad — Zbornik Radova

Zborn Rad Poljopriv Fak Univ Beogr — Zbornik Radova. Poljoprivrednog Fakulteta. Universitet u Beogradu

Zborn Slov Nar Muz Prir Vedy — Zbornik Slovenskeho Narodneho Muzea Prirodne Vedy

Zbor Slov Narod Muz — Zbornik Slovenskeho Narodneho Muzea

Z Bot — Zeitschrift fuer Botanik

ZBPHA — Zentralblatt fuer Bakteriologie, Parasitenkunde, Infektionskrankheiten, und Hygiene. Abteilung 1. Medizinisch-Hygienische Bakteriologie, Virusforschung, und Parasitologie. Originale

Zb Prac Chem Fak SVST (Bratislava) — Zbornik Prac Chemickotechnologickej Fakulty SVST (Bratislava)

Zb Prav Fak Zagrebu — Zbornik Pravnog Fakulteta u Zagrebu

Zb Pr Belarus Dzyarzh Med Inst — Zbornik Prats. Belaruski Dzyarzhauny Medychny Instytut

Zb Pr Chemickotechnol Fak SVST — Zbornik Prac Chemickotechnologickij Fakulty SVST

Zb Pr Chem-Technol Fak SVST — Zbornik Prac Chemickotechnologickej Fakulty SVST

Zb Pr Inst Teploenerg Akad Nauk Ukr RSR — Zbirnik Prats' Institut Teploenergetiki Akademiya Nauk Ukrains'koi RSR

Zb Prir Nauke Matica Srp — Zbornik za Prirodne Nauke Matica Srpska

Zb Pr Nauk Inst Fiziol Kyyiv Univ — Zbirnyk Prats' Naukovodoslidnyts'koho Instytuta Fiziolohiyi Kyyivs'koho Universytetu

Zb Pr Naukovodosl Inst Fiziol Kyyiv Univ — Zbirnyk Prats' Naukovodoslidnyts'koho Instytuta Fiziolokiyi Kyyivs'koho Universytetu

Zb Pr Ukr Derzh Inst Nauk Prakt Vet — Zbirnyk Prats' Ukrains'kii Derzhavnii Institut Naukovoi ta Praktichnoi Veterin arii

Zb Pr Ukr Inst Eksp Vet — Zbirnik Prats' Ukrains'kogo Institutu Eksperimental'noi Veterinarii

Zb Pr Zool Muz Akad Nauk Ukr RSR — Zbirnyk Prats' Zoolohichnoho Muzeyu Akademiyi Nauk Ukrayinskoyi RSR

ZbR — Zbirnyk Robit Aspirantiv Romano-Germans'koji i Klazycnoji Filolohiji

Zb Rab Belarus Sel'ska-Gaspad Inst — Zbornik Rabot Belaruskaga Sel'ska-Gaspadarchaga Instytuta

Zb Rad Biol Inst (Beograd) — Zbornik Radova. Bioloski Institut (Beograd)

Zb Rad Biol Inst NR Srbye Beogr — Zbornik Radova. Bioloski Institut NR Srbye Beograd

Zb Rad Math Inst Beograd NS — Beograd Matematicki Institut. Zbornik Radova. Nouvelle Serie

Zb Rad Poljopr Inst Osijek — Zbornik Radova. Poljoprivredni Institut Osijek

Zb Rad Poljopriv Fak Univ Beogradu — Zbornik Radova. Poljoprivrednog Fakulteta. Universitet u Beogradu

Zb Rad Prir Mat Fak — Zbornik Radova. Prirodno-Matematichkog Fakulteta [*Yugoslavia*]

Zb Rad Prir-Mat Fak Ser Fiz — Zbornik Radova. Prirodno-Matematickog Fakulteta. Serija za Fiziku

Zb Rad Prir-Mat Fak Univ Novom Sadu — Zbornik Radova. Prirodno-Matematichkog Fakulteta Univerzitet u Novom Sadu

Zb Rad Srp Akad Nauka Geol Inst — Zbornik Radova. Srpska Akademija Nauka Geoloski Institut

Zb Rad Zavod Ratarstvo (Sarajevo) — Zbornik Radova. Zavod za Ratarstvo (Sarajevo)

Zbraslav Res Inst Land Reclam Improv Sci Monogr — Zbraslav Research Institute for Land Reclamation and Improvement. Scientific Monograph

ZbRFFZ — Zbornik Radova. Filozofskog Fakulteta. Svencilista u Zagrebu

ZbRL — Zbirnyk Robit Aspirantiv L'Vivskij Derzavnyj Universitet

Zb Robit Aspir L'Viv Univ Pryr Nauk — Zbirnyk Robit Aspirantiv L'Vivs'kyi Universytet Pryrodnykh Nauk

ZBRS — Z's Briefs. CPSU [*Cooperative Park Studies Unit, University of Alaska*] Newsletter

ZbS — Zbornik za Slavistiku

ZBS — Zeitschrift. Deutscher Verein fuer Buchwesen und Schrifttum

ZbSAN — Zbornik Radova. Srpske Akademije Nauke
Zb Slov Nar Muz Prir Vedy — Zbornik Slovenskeho Narodneho Muzea Prirodne Vedy
Zb Ved Prac Lesn Fak Vys Sk Lesn Drev Zvolene — Zbornik Vedeckych Prac Lesnickej Fakulty Vysokej Skoly Lesnickej a Drevarskej vo Zvolene [*Czechoslovakia*]
Zb Ved Pr Vys Sk Tech Kosiciach — Zbornik Vedeckych Prac. Vysokej Skoly Technickej v Kosiciach
Zb Vojnomed Akad — Zbornik Vojnomedicinske Akademije
Zb Vysk Pr Vysk Ustav Zvaracskeho Bratislave — Zbornik Vyskumnych Prac Vyskumneho Ustavu Zvaracskeho v Bratislave
ZBW — Zeitschrift fuer Betriebswirtschaft
ZBW — Zentralblatt fuer Bibliothekswesen
Zb Zgodovino Naravoslovja Tek — Zbornik za Zgodovino Naravoslovja in Teknike
Z Chem — Zeitschrift fuer Chemie
Z Chemie (Lpz) — Zeitschrift fuer Chemie (Leipzig)
Z Chemother Verw Geb Teil 1 — Zeitschrift fuer Chemotherapie und Verwandte Gebiete. Teil 1. Originale
Z Chemother Verw Geb Teil 2 — Zeitschrift fuer Chemotherapie und Verwandte Gebiete. Teil 2. Referate
ZChK — Zeitschrift fuer Christliche Kunst
ZChrK — Zeitschrift fuer Christliche Kunst
ZCK — Zeitschrift fuer Christliche Kunst
ZCP — Zeitschrift fuer Celtische Philologie
ZCPh — Zeitschrift fuer Celtische Philologie
ZCzest — Ziemia Czestochowska
ZD — Zeitschrift fuer Deutschkunde
ZD — Zielsprache Deutsch
ZDA — Zeitschrift fuer Deutsches Altertum und Deutsche Literatur
ZDADL — Zeitschrift fuer Deutsches Altertum und Deutsche Literatur
Z f D Altert — Zeitschrift fuer Deutsches Altertum und Deutsche Literatur
Z Dampfkessel Maschinenbetr — Zeitschrift fuer Dampfkessel und Maschinenbetrieb
Z Dampfkesselunters Versicher Ges — Zeitschrift. Dampfkesseluntersuchungs- und Versicherungs-Gesellschaft
ZDB — Zeitschrift fuer Deutsche Bildung
ZDemogr — Zeitschrift fuer Demographie und Statistik der Juden
Z Desinfekt Gesundheitswes — Zeitschrift fuer Desinfektions- und Gesundheitswesen
Z Deut Alt — Zeitschrift fuer Deutsches Altertum und Deutsche Literatur
Z Deut Geol Ges — Zeitschrift. Deutsche Geologische Gesellschaft
Z Deuts Morgen G — Zeitschrift. Deutsche Morgenlaendische Gesellschaft [*Wiesbaden*]
ZDFALP — Z Dziejow Form Artystycznych Literaturze Polskiej
ZDG — Zeitschrift fuer Deutsche Geistesgeschichte
ZDG — Zeitschrift fuer Deutsche Geisteswissenschaft
ZDGG — Zeitschrift fuer Deutsche Geistesgeschichte
ZDK — Zeitschrift fuer Deutschkunde
ZDKAA — Zdravookhranenie Kazakhstana
ZDKP — Zeitschrift fuer Deutsche Kulturphilosophie
ZDL — Zeitschrift fuer Dialektologie und Linguistik
ZDM — Zeitschrift fuer Deutsche Mundarten
ZDM — Zentralblatt fuer Didaktik der Mathematik
ZDMG — Zeitschrift. Deutsche Morgenlaendische Gesellschaft
ZD Musik — Zeitschriftendienst Musik
Z Dnipr INO — Zapiski Dnipropetrovs'kogo Institutu Narodnoi Osviti
Zdorov'e Nauch Pop Gig Zhurnal — Zdorov'e Nauchno Populiarnyi Gigienicheskii Zhurnal
ZDP — Zeitschrift fuer Deutsche Philologie
ZDPh — Zeitschrift fuer Deutsche Philologie
Z f D Phil — Zeitschrift fuer Deutsche Philologie
ZDPV — Zeitschrift. Deutscher Palaestinaverein
Zdrav Aktual — Zdravotnicke Aktuality
Zdrav Delo — Zdravno Delo
Zdravookhr Beloruss — Zdravookhranenie Belorussii
Zdravookhr Belorussii — Zdravookhranenie Belorussii
Zdravookhr Kaz — Zdravookhranenie Kazakhstana
Zdravookhr Kirg — Zdravookhranenie Kirgizii
Zdravookhr Ross Fed — Zdravookhranenie Rossiiskoi Federatsii
Zdravookhr Sov Est Sb — Zdravookhranenie Sovetskoi Estonii Sbornik
Zdravookhr Tadzh — Zdravookhranenie Tadzhikistana
Zdravookhr Turkm — Zdravookhranenie Turkmenistana
Zdrav Prac — Zdravotnicka Pracovnice
Zdravst Vest — Zdravstveni Vestnik
Zdrav Techn Vzduchotech — Zdravotni Technika a Vzduchotechnika
Zdrav Tech Vzduchotech — Zdravotni Technika a Vzduchotechnika
Zdrav Vestn — Zdravstveni Vestnik
Zdrow Publiczne — Zdrowie Publiczne
ZDS — Zeitschrift fuer Deutsche Sprache
ZDSJ — Zeitschrift fuer Demographie und Statistik der Juden
ZDStJ — Zeitschrift fuer Demographie und Statistik der Juden
Z Dt Geol Ges — Zeitschrift. Deutsche Geologische Gesellschaft
Z Dt Phil — Zeitschrift fuer Deutsche Philologie
Z Dtschen Morgenlaend Ges — Zeitschrift. Deutsche Morgenlaendische Gesellschaft

Z Dtsch Geol Ges — Zeitschrift. Deutsche Geologische Gesellschaft
Z Dtsch Morgenl Ges — Zeitschrift. Deutsche Morganlaendische Gesellschaft
Z Dt Spr — Zeitschrift fuer Deutsche Sprache
ZDVGMS — Zeitschrift. Deutscher Verein fuer die Geschichte Maehrens und Schlesiens
ZDV f Kw — Zeitschrift. Deutscher Verein fuer Kunstwissenschaft
ZDV Kw — Zeitschrift. Deutscher Verein fuer Kunstwissenschaft
ZDW — Zeitschrift fuer Deutsche Wortforschung
ZDWDSU — Zeitschrift fuer Deutschwissenschaft und Deutschunterricht
ZDWF — Zeitschrift fuer Deutsche Wortforschung
ZE — Zeitschrift fuer Ethnologie
ZEASA — Zeitschrift fuer Astrophysik
ZEBED — Zeitschrift fuer Bergrecht
ZEBFA — Zhurnal Evolyutsionnoi Biokhimii i Fiziologii
ZEBLA — Zeitschrift fuer Biologie
ZED — Zimbabwe Environment and Design
ZED — Zur Erkenntnis der Dichtung
ZEE — Zeitschrift fuer Evangelische Ethik
Z EEG-EMG — Zeitschrift fuer EEG-EMG [*Elektroenzephalographie, Elektromyographie, und Verwandte Gebiete*] [*German Federal Republic*]
ZEELA — Zeitschrift fuer Elektrochemie
Zeews Fruittelersbl — Zeeuws Fruittelersblad
ZEF — Zeitschrift fuer Erziehungswissenschaftliche Forschung
ZEH — Zeit. Wochenzeitung
Zei — Das Zeichen
Zeich Zeit — Zeichen der Zeit
ZEINA — Zeitschrift fuer Instrumentenkunde
Z Eisenbahnwes und Verkehrstech Glasers — Zeitschrift fuer Eisenbahnwesen und Verkehrstechnik. Glasers. Annalen
Z Eisenbahnwes Verkehrstech Glasers Ann — Zeitschrift fuer Eisenbahnwesen und Verkehrstechnik. Glasers. Annalen
Z Eis Kaelte Ind — Zeitschrift fuer Eis-und Kaelte-Industrie
Zeiss Inf — Zeiss Information
Zeiss Mitt — Zeiss Mitteilungen
Zeiss-Mitt Fortschr Tech Opt — Zeiss-Mitteilungen ueber Fortschritte der Technischen Optik
Zeiss-Mitt Fortsch Tech Optik — Zeiss-Mitteilungen ueber Fortschritte der Technischen Optik
Zeit f Deutk — Zeitschrift fuer Deutschkunde
Zeit f Deut Phil — Zeitschrift fuer Deutsche Philologie
Zeitgeschic — Zeitgeschichte
Zeit f Rom Phil — Zeitschrift fuer Romanische Philologie
Zeitschr Angew Geologie — Zeitschrift fuer Angewandte Geologie
Zeitschr Anorg u Allg Chemie — Zeitschrift fuer Anorganische und Allgemeine Chemie
Zeitschr Geomorphologie — Zeitschrift fuer Geomorphologie
Zeitschr Geomorphologie Neue Folge — Zeitschrift fuer Geomorphologie. Neue Folge
Zeitschr Geophysik — Zeitschrift fuer Geophysik
Zeitschr Gletscherkunde u Glazialgeologie — Zeitschrift fuer Gletscherkunde und Glazialgeologie
Zeitschr Kristallographie — Zeitschrift fuer Kristallographie
Zeitschr Physikal Chemie — Zeitschrift fuer Physikalische Chemie
Zeit f Volk — Zeitschrift fuer Volkskunde
Zeitw — Zeitwende
Zeitwahr — Zeitschrift fuer Wahrscheinlichkeitstheorie
ZEIZA — Zeitschrift fuer Elektrische Informations- und Energietechnik
ZEK — Zeitschrift fuer Evangelisches Kirchenrecht
ZEKIA — Zeitschrift fuer Kinderheilkunde
Z Eks Klin Med — Zurnal Eksperimental'noj i Kliniceskoj Mediciny
Z Eksper Teoret Fiz — Zurnal Eksperimental'noi i Teoreticeskoi Fiziki
ZELAD — Zeitschrift fuer Laermbekaempfung
Z El Ch — Zeitschrift fuer Elektrochemie uno Angewandte Physikalische Chemie
Z Elek Informations- und Energietech — Zeitschrift fuer Elektrische Informations- und Energietechnik
Z Elektr Inf & Energietech — Zeitschrift fuer Elektrische Informations- und Energietechnik [*IET*]
Z Elektr Inf Energietech — Zeitschrift fuer Elektrische Informations- und Energietechnik
Z Elektr Informationstech Energietech — Zeitschrift fuer Elektrische Informations- und Energietechnik [*IET*]
Z Elektr Inform Energietech — Zeitschrift fuer Elektrische Informations- und Energietechnik
Z Elektrochem — Zeitschrift fuer Elektrochemie
Z Elektrochem Angew Phy Chem — Zeitschrift fuer Elektrochemie und Angewandte Physikalische Chemie
Z Elektrotech — Zeitschrift fuer Elektrotechnik [*West Germany*]
Zelezarski Zb — Zelezarski Zbornik
Zell Papier — Zellstoff und Papier
Zellstoffchem Abh — Zellstoffchemische Abhandlungen
Zellst Pap (Berlin) — Zellstoff und Papier (Berlin)
Zellst Pap (Leipzig) — Zellstoff und Papier (Leipzig)
Zellwolle Dtsch Kunstseiden Ztg — Zellwolle und Deutsche Kunstseiden-Zeitung

ZELTB — Zeitschrift fuer Elektrotechnik
Z El Techn — Zeitschrift fuer Elektrotechnik
Zem Beton — Zement und Beton
Zemed Arch — Zemedelsky Archiv
Zemed Tech — Zemedelska Technika [*Czechoslovakia*]
Zemed Zahr — Zemedeistvi v Zahranici
Zemep Sb — Zemepisny Sbornik
ZEMGA — Zeszyty Naukowe Akademii Gorniczo-Hutniczej. Elektryfikacja i Mechanizacja Gornictwa i Hutnictwa
ZEMHA — Zeitschrift fuer Erzbergbau und Metallhuettenwesen
Zem-Kalk-Gips — Zement-Kalk-Gips
Zemled — Zemledelie
Zemled Mekh — Zemledel'cheskaya Mekhanika
Zemled Zhivotnovod Mold — Zemledelie i Zhivotnovodstvo Moldavii
Zemlerob Resp Mizhvid Temat Nauk Zb — Zemlerobstvo Respublikans'kyi Mizhvidomchyi Tematychnyi Naukovyi Zbirnyk
Zemleustroistvo Plan Sel'sk Naselennykh Punktov Geod — Zemleustroistvo. Planirovka Sel'skikh Naselennykh Punktov i Geodeziya
Zemlj Biljka — Zemljiste i Biljka
Zem ve Sk — Zemepis ve Skole
Z Energiewirtsch — Zeitschrift fuer Energiewirtschaft [*German Federal Republic*]
Zentbl Bakt ParasitKde — Zentralblatt fuer Bakteriologie, Parasitenkunde, Infektionskrankheiten, und Hygiene
Zentbl Bakt ParasitKed Abt I or II — Zentralblatt fuer Bakteriologie, Parasitenkunde, Infektionskrankheiten, und Hygiene. Abteilung I or II
Zentbl Biblioth — Zentralblatt fuer Bibliothekswesen
Zentbl Vet Med B — Zentralblatt fuer Veterinaermedizin. B
Zent Math — Zentralblatt fuer Mathematik und Ihre Grenzgebiete
Zentralbl Allg Pathol Pathol Anat — Zentralblatt fuer Allgemeine Pathologie und Pathologische Anatomie
Zentralbl Arbeitsmed — Zentralblatt fuer Arbeitsmedizin und Arbeitsschutz
Zentralbl Arbeitsmed Arbeitsschutz — Zentralblatt fuer Arbeitsmedizin und Arbeitsschutz
Zentralbl Arbeitsmed Arbeitsschutz Prophyl — Zentralblatt fuer Arbeitsmedizin, Arbeitsschutz, und Prophylaxe [*West Germany*]
Zentralbl Arbeitsmed Arbeitsschutz Prophylaxe — Zentralblatt fuer Arbeitsmedizin, Arbeitsschutz, und Prophylaxe
Zentralbl Arbeitsmed Arbeitsschutz Prophyl Ergon — Zentralblatt fuer Arbeitsmedizin, Arbeitsschutz, Prophylaxe, und Ergonomie [*German Federal Republic*]
Zentralbl Bakteriol (B) — Zentralblatt fuer Bakteriologie, Parasitenkunde, Infektionskrankheiten, und Hygiene. Erste Abteilung Originale. Reihe B. Hygiene, Betriebshygiene, Praeventive Medizin
Zentralbl Bakteriol Mikrobiol Hyg Abt 1 Orig A — Zentralblatt fuer Bakteriologie, Mikrobiologie, und Hygiene. Abteilung 1. Originale A. Medizinische Mikrobiologie, Infektionskrankheiten, und Parasitologie
Zentralbl Bakteriol Mikrobiol Hyg Ser A — Zentralblatt fuer Bakteriologie, Mikrobiologie, und Hygiene. Series A. Medical Microbiology, Infectious Diseases, Virology, Parasitology
Zentralbl Bakteriol Naturwiss — Zentralblatt fuer Bakteriologie, Parasitenkunde, Infektionskrankheiten, und Hygiene. Zweite Naturwissenschaftliche Abteilung. Mikrobiologie der Landwirtschaft der Technologie und des Umweltschutzes
Zentralbl Bakteriol Orig A — Zentralblatt fuer Bakteriologie, Parasitenkunde, Infektionskrankheiten, und Hygiene. Erste Abteilung. Originale Reihe A. Medizinische, Mikrobiologie, und Parasitologie
Zentralbl Bakteriol (Orig B) — Zentralblatt fuer Bakteriologie, Parasitenkunde, Infektionskrankheiten, und Hygiene. Erste Abteilung Originale. Reihe B. Hygiene, Praeventive Medizin
Zentralbl Bakteriol Parasitenkd Infektionskrankheiten Hyg II — Zentralblatt fuer Bakteriologie, Parasitenkunde, Infektionskrankheiten, und Hygiene. Naturwissenschaftliche Abteilung
Zentralbl Bakteriol Parasitenkd Infektionskr Hyg Abt 1 Ref — Zentralblatt fuer Bakteriologie, Parasitenkunde, Infektionskrankheiten, und Hygiene. Abteilung 1. Medizinisch-Hygienische Bakteriologie, Virusforschung, und Parasitologie. Referate
Zentralbl Bakteriol Parasitenkd Infektionskr Hyg Abt 1 Suppl — Zentralblatt fuer Bakteriologie, Parasitenkunde, Infektionskrankheiten, und Hygiene. Abteilung 1. Supplementheft
Zentralbl Bakteriol Parasitenkd Infektionskr Hyg Abt 2 — Zentralblatt fuer Bakteriologie, Parasitenkunde, Infektionskrankheiten, und Hygiene. Abteilung 2. Allgemeine Landwirtschaftliche und Technische Mikrobiologie
Zentralbl Bakteriol Parasitenkd Infektionskr Hyg Abt I Orig — Zentralblatt fuer Bakteriologie, Parasitenkunde, Infektionskrankheiten, und Hygiene. Abteilung I Originale
Zentralbl Bakteriol Parasitenk Infektionskr Hyg — Zentralblatt fuer Bakteriologie, Parasitenkunde, Infektionskrankheiten, und Hygiene
Zentralbl Bauverwaltung — Zentralblatt der Bauverwaltung
Zentralbl Bibliothekswesen — Zentralblatt fuer Bibliothekswesen
Zentralbl Biochem Biophys — Zentralblatt fuer Biochemie und Biophysik
Zentralbl Biol Aerosol-Forsch — Zentralblatt fuer Biologische Aerosol-Forschung
Zentralbl Chir — Zentralblatt fuer Chirurgie
Zentralbl Chir Suppl — Zentralblatt fuer Chirurgie. Supplement

Zentralbl Exp Med — Zentralblatt der Experimentellen Medizin
Zentralbl Geol Palaeontol Teil 1 — Zentralblatt fuer Geologie und Palaeontologie. Teil 1. Allgemeine, Angewandte, Regionale, und Historische Geologie
Zentralbl Geol Palaeontol Teil 2 — Zentralblatt fuer Geologie und Palaeontologie. Teil 2. Palaeontologie
Zentralbl Gesamte Forstwes — Zentralblatt fuer das Gesamte Forstwesen
Zentralbl Gesamte Hyg Einschluss Bakteriol Immunitaetsl — Zentralblatt fuer die Gesamte Hygiene mit Einschluss der Bakteriologie und Immunitaetslehre
Zentralbl Gesamte Hyg Ihre Grenzgeb — Zentralblatt fuer die Gesamte Hygiene und Ihre Grenzgebiete
Zentralbl Gesamte Physiol Pathol Stoffwechsels — Zentralblatt fuer die Gesamte Physiologie und Pathologie des Stoffwechsels
Zentralbl Gesamte Rechtsmed — Zentralblatt fuer die Gesamte Rechtsmedizin und Ihre Grenzgebiete
Zentralbl Ges Hyg — Zentralblatt fuer die Gesamte Hygiene und Ihre Grenzgebiete
Zentralbl Gewerbehyg Unfallverhuet — Zentralblatt fuer Gewerbehygiene und Unfallverhuetung
Zentralbl Gynaekol — Zentralblatt fuer Gynaekologie
Zentralbl Huetten Walzwerke — Zentralblatt der Huetten- und Walzwerke
Zentralbl Industriebau — Zentralblatt fuer Industriebau
Zentralbl Inn Med — Zentralblatt fuer Innere Medizin
Zentralbl Mineral Geol Palaeontol — Zentralblatt fuer Mineralogie, Geologie, und Palaeontologie
Zentralbl Mineral Geol Palaeontol Teil 1 — Zentralblatt fuer Mineralogie, Geologie, und Palaeontologie. Teil 1. Kristallographie und Mineralogie
Zentralbl Mineral Geol Palaeontol Teil 2 — Zentralblatt fuer Mineralogie, Geologie, und Palaeontologie. Teil 2. Gesteinskunde, Lagerstaettenkunde, Allgemeine, und Angewandte Geologie
Zentralbl Mineral Geol Palaeontol Teil 3 — Zentralblatt fuer Mineralogie, Geologie, und Palaeontologie. Teil 3. Historische und Regionale Geologie, Palaeontologie
Zentralbl Mineral Teil 1 — Zentralblatt fuer Mineralogie. Teil 1. Kristallographie und Mineralogie
Zentralbl Mineral Teil 2 — Zentralblatt fuer Mineralogie. Teil 2. Petrographie, Technische Mineralogie, Geochemie, und Lagerstaettenkunde
Zentralbl Neurochir — Zentralblatt fuer Neurochirurgie
Zentralbl Papierind — Zentralblatt fuer die Papierindustrie
Zentralbl Pharm — Zentralblatt fuer Pharmazie
Zentralbl Pharm Pharmakother Laboratoriumsdiagn — Zentralblatt fuer Pharmazie, Pharmakotherapie, und Laboratoriumsdiagnostik
Zentralbl Phlebol — Zentralblatt fuer Phlebologie
Zentralbl Physiol — Zentralblatt fuer Physiologie
Zentralbl Verkehrs-Med Verkehrs-Psychol Luft- Raumfahrt-Med — Zentralblatt fuer Verkehrs-Medizin, Verkehrs-Psychologie Luft-, und Raumfahrt-Medizin
Zentralbl Veterinaermed — Zentralblatt fuer Veterinaermedizin
Zentralbl Veterinaermed Beih — Zentralblatt fuer Veterinaermedizin. Beiheft
Zentralbl Veterinaermed Reihe A — Zentralblatt fuer Veterinaermedizin. Reihe A
Zentralbl Veterinaermed Reihe B — Zentralblatt fuer Veterinaermedizin. Reihe B
Zentralbl Veterinaermed Reihe C — Zentralblatt fuer Veterinaermedizin. Reihe C
Zentralinst Kernforsch Rossendorf Dresden (Ber) — Zentralinstitut fuer Kernforschung Rossendorf bei Dresden (Bericht)
Zentralinst Versuchstierzucht Annu Rep — Zentralinstitut fuer Versuchstierzucht. Annual Report
Zentr Bibl — Zentralblatt fuer Bibliothekswesen
Zentr Org Ges Chir — Zentralorgan fuer die Gesamte Chirurgie und Ihre Grenzgebiete
Z Entwick P — Zeitschrift fuer Entwicklungspsychologie und Paedagogische Psychologie
Zent Ztg Opt Mech — Zentral-Zeitung fuer Optik und Mechanik
ZEPAD — Zeitschrift fuer Parlamentsfragen
Z Erdkundeunterricht — Zeitschrift fuer den Erdkundeunterricht
Z Erdk Unt — Zeitschrift fuer den Erdkundeunterricht
ZERED — Zeitschrift fuer Rechtspolitik
Z Erkr Atmungsorgane — Zeitschrift fuer Erkrankungen der Atmungsorgane
Z Ernaehrung — Zeitschrift fuer Ernaehrungswissenschaft
Z Ernaehrungsw — Zeitschrift fuer Ernaehrungswissenschaft
Z Ernaehrungswiss — Zeitschrift fuer Ernaehrungswissenschaft
Z Ernaehrungswiss (Suppl) — Zeitschrift fuer Ernaehrungswissenschaft. (Supplementa)
Zernovye Maslichn Kul't — Zernovye i Maslichnye Kul'tury
Zero Popul Growth Natl Rep — Zero Population Growth. National Reporter
Z Erzbergbau Metallhuettenwes — Zeitschrift fuer Erzbergbau und Metallhuettenwesen [*German Federal Republic*]
ZES — Zeitschrift fuer Eingeborenen-Sprachen
ZESIA — Zeitschrift fuer Sinnephysiologie
ZE Spr — Zeitschrift fuer Eingeborenen-Sprachen
ZESTA — Zeitschrift fuer Schweisstechnik
Zesz Muz Etnogr Wrocl — Zeszyty Muzeum Etnograficznego Wroclawie

Zesz Nauk Akad Ekon — Zeszyty Naukowe Akademii Ekonomicznej w Katowicach

Zesz Nauk Akad Ekon Krakow — Zeszyty Naukowe Akademii Ekonomicznej w Krakowie

Zesz Nauk Akad Ekon Poznan — Zeszyty Naukowe Akademii Ekonomicznej w Poznaniu

Zesz Nauk Akad Ekon Poznaniu Ser 2 — Zeszyty Naukowe. Akademia Ekonomiczna w Poznaniu. Seria 2. Prace Habilitacyjne i Doktorskie

Zesz Nauk Akad Ekon Wroclaw — Zeszyty Naukowe Akademii Ekonomicznej w Wroclawiu

Zesz Nauk Akad Gorn Hutn (Cracow) Eletryf Mech Gorn Hutn — Zeszyty Naukowe Akademii Gorniczo-Hutniczej (Cracow). Elektryfikacja i Mechanizacja Gornictwa i Hutnictwa

Zesz Nauk Akad Gorn Hutn Cracow Geol — Zeszyty Naukowe Akademii Gorniczo-Hutniezej Cracow Geologia

Zesz Nauk Akad Gorn-Hutn (Cracow) Mat Fiz Chem — Zeszyty Naukowe Akademii Gorniczo-Hutniczej (Cracow). Matematyka, Fizyka, Chemia

Zesz Nauk Akad Gorn-Hutn (Cracow) Metal Odlew — Zeszyty Naukowe Akademii Gorniczo-Hutniczej (Cracow). Metalurgia i Odlewnictwo

Zesz Nauk Akad Gorn Hutn (Cracow) Rozpr — Zeszyty Naukowe Akademii Gorniczo-Hutniczej (Cracow). Rozprawy

Zesz Nauk Akad Gorn-Hutn Im Stanislawa Staszica Ceram — Zeszyty Naukowe Akademii Gorniczo-Hutniczej Imienia Stanislawa Staszica. Ceramica

Zesz Nauk Akad Gorn-Hutn Im Stanislawa Staszica Geol — Zeszyty Naukowe Akademii Gorniczo-Hutniczej Imienia Stanislawa Staszica. Geologia

Zesz Nauk Akad Gorn-Hutn Im Stanislawa Staszica Gorn — Zeszyty Naukowe Akademii Gorniczo-Hutniczej Imienia Stanislawa Staszica. Gornictwo

Zesz Nauk Akad Gorn-Hutn Im Stanislawa Staszica Mat Fiz Chem — Zeszyty Naukowe Akademii Gorniczo-Hutniczej Imienia Stanislawa Staszica. Matematyka, Fizyka, Chemia

Zesz Nauk Akad Gorn-Hutn Im Stanislawa Staszica Metal Odlew — Zeszyty Naukowe Akademii Gorniczo-Hutniczej Imienia Stanislawa Staszica. Metalurgia i Odlewnictwo

Zesz Nauk Akad Gorn-Hutn Im Stanislawa Staszica Ser Autom — Zeszyty Naukowe Akademii Gorniczo-Hutniczej Imienia Stanislawa Staszica. Seria Automatyka [*Poland*]

Zesz Nauk Akad Gorn-Hutn Im Stanislawa Staszica Zesz Spec — Zeszyty Naukowe Akademii Gorniczo-Hutniczej Imienia Stanislawa Staszica. Zeszyt Specjalny

Zesz Nauk Akad Gorn-Hutn Im Staszica Gorn — Zeszyty Naukowe Akademii Gorniczo-Hutniczej Imienia Stanislawa Staszica. Gornictwo

Zesz Nauk Akad Gorn-Hutn Im Staszica Mat Fiz Chem — Zeszyty Naukowe Akademii Gorniczo-Hutniczej Imienia Stanislawa Staszica. Matematyka, Fizyka, Chemia

Zesz Nauk Akad Gorn-Hutn Im Staszica Zesz Spec — Zeszyty Naukowe Akademii Gorniczo-Hutniczej Imienia Stanislawa Staszica. Zeszyt Specjalny

Zesz Nauk Akad Gorn-Hutn (Krakow) Ceram — Zeszyty Naukowe Akademii Gorniczo-Hutniczej (Krakow). Ceramika

Zesz Nauk Akad Gorn-Hutn (Krakow) Elektryf Mech Gorn Hutn — Zeszyty Naukowe Akademii Gorniczo-Hutniczej (Krakow). Elektryfikacja i Mechanizacja Gornictwa i Hutnictwa

Zesz Nauk Akad Gorn-Hutn (Krakow) Geol — Zeszyty Naukowe Akademii Gorniczo-Hutniczej (Krakow). Geologia

Zesz Nauk Akad Gorn-Hutn (Krakow) Gorn — Zeszyty Naukowe Akademii Gorniczo-Hutniczej (Krakow). Gornictwo

Zesz Nauk Akad Gorn-Hutn Krakowie Rozpr — Zeszyty Naukowe Akademii Gorniczo-Hutniczej w Krakowie. Rozprawy [*Poland*]

Zesz Nauk Akad Gorn-Hutn (Krakow) Mat Fiz Chem — Zeszyty Naukowe Akademii Gorniczo-Hutniczej (Krakow). Matematyka, Fizyka, Chemia

Zesz Nauk Akad Gorn-Hutn (Krakow) Metal Odlew — Zeszyty Naukowe Akademii Gorniczo-Hutniczej (Krakow). Metalurgia i Odlewnictwo

Zesz Nauk Akad Gorn-Hutn (Krakow) Ses Nauk — Zeszyty Naukowe Akademii Gorniczo-Hutniczej (Krakow). Sesja Naukowa

Zesz Nauk Akad Gorn-Hutn (Krakow) Sozologia Sozotechnika — Zeszyty Naukowe Akademii Gorniczo-Hutniczej (Krakow). Sozologia i Sozotechnika [*Poland*]

Zesz Nauk Akad Gorn-Hutn (Krakow) Zesz Spec — Zeszyty Naukowe Akademii Gorniczo-Hutniczej (Krakow). Zeszyty Specjalny

Zesz Nauk Akad Gorn-Hutn Stanislawa Staszica Geol — Zeszyty Naukowe Akademii Gorniczo-Hutniczej Imienia Stanislawa Staszica. Geologia

Zesz Nauk Akad Gorn-Hutn Stanisl Staszica — Zeszyty Naukowe Akademii Gorniczo-Hutniczej Imienia Stanislawa Staszica. Metalurgia i Odlewnictwo

Zesz Nauk Akad Gorn-Hutn Stanisl Staszica Autom — Zeszyty Naukowe Akademii Gorniczo-Hutniczej Imienia Stanislawa Staszica. Automatyka

Zesz Nauk Akad Gorn-Hutn Stanisl Staszica Geol — Zeszyty Naukowe Akademii Gorniczo-Hutniczej Imienia Stanislawa Staszica. Geologia [*Poland*]

Zesz Nauk Akad Gorn-Hutn Stanisl Staszica Mat Fiz Chem — Zeszyty Naukowe Akademii Gorniczo-Hutniczej Imienia Stanislawa Staszica. Matematyka, Fizyka, Chemia

Zesz Nauk Akad Roln Szczecinie — Zeszyty Naukowe. Akademia Rolnicza w Szczecinie [*Poland*]

Zesz Nauk Akad Roln Szczecinie Ser Rybactwo Morsk — Zeszyty Naukowe Akademii Rolniczej w Szczecinie. Seria Rybactwo Morskie [*Poland*]

Zesz Nauk Akad Roln Tech Olsztynie — Zeszyty Naukowe Akademii Rolniczo-Technicznej w Olsztynie

Zesz Nauk Akad Roln Tech Olsztynie Roln — Zeszyty Naukowe Akademii Rolniczo-Technicznej w Olsztynie. Rolnictwo

Zesz Nauk Akad Roln Tech Olsztynie Technol Zywn — Zeszyty Naukowe Akademii Rolniczo-Technicznej w Olsztynie. Technologie Zywnosci

Zesz Nauk Akad Roln Warszawie Melior Rolne — Zeszyty Naukowe Akademii Rolniczej w Warszawie. Melioracje Rolne

Zesz Nauk Akad Roln Warszawie Ogrod — Zeszyty Naukowe Akademii Rolniczej w Warszawie. Ogrodnictwo

Zesz Nauk Akad Roln Warszawie Technol Drewna — Zeszyty Naukowe Akademii Rolniczej w Warszawie. Technologia Drewna

Zesz Nauk Akad Roln Warszawie Zootech — Zeszyty Naukowe Akademii Rolniczej w Warszawie. Zootechnika

Zesz Nauk Akad Roln Wroclawiu Melior — Zeszyty Naukowe Akademii Rolniczej we Wroclawiu. Melioracja

Zesz Nauk Akad Roln Wroclawiu Weter — Zeszyty Naukowe Akademii Rolniczej we Wroclawiu. Weterynaria

Zesz Nauk Akad Roln Wroclawiu Zootech — Zeszyty Naukowe Akademii Rolniczej we Wroclawiu. Zootechnika

Zesz Nauk Akad Roln Wrocl Wet — Zeszyty Naukowe Akademii Rolniczej we Wroclawiu. Weterynaria

Zesz Nauk Inst Ciezkiej Synt Org Blachowni Slask — Zeszyty Naukowe Instytut Ciezkiej Syntezy Organicznej w Blachowni Slaskiej

Zesz Nauk Mat Fiz Chem — Zeszyty Naukowe. Matematyka, Fizyka, Chemia [*Poland*]

Zesz Nauk Mechan Budownictwo Akad Roln-Tech Olsztyn — Zeszyty Naukowe. Mechanika i Budownictwo-Akademia Rolniczo-Techniczna w Olsztynie

Zesz Nauk Ochr Wod Rybactwo Srodladowe — Zeszyty Naukowe. Ochrona Wod i Rybactwo Srodladowe

Zesz Nauk Politech Czestochow — Zeszyty Naukowe Politechniki Czestochowskiej

Zesz Nauk Politech Czestochow Metal — Zeszyty Naukowe Politechniki Czestochowskiej. Metalurgia

Zesz Nauk Politech Czestochow Nauki Tech Hutn — Zeszyty Naukowe Politechniki Czestochowskiej. Nauki Techniczne. Hutnictwo [*Poland*]

Zesz Nauk Politech Gdansk Chem — Zeszyty Naukowe Politechniki Gdanskiej. Chemia

Zesz Nauk Politech Gdansk Elektr — Zeszyty Naukowe Politechniki Gdanskiej. Elektryka

Zesz Nauk Politech Gdansk Fiz — Zeszyty Naukowe Politechniki Gdanskiej. Fizyka

Zesz Nauk Politech Gdansk Mat — Zeszyty Naukowe Politechniki Gdanskiej. Matematyka

Zesz Nauk Politech Gdansk Mech — Zeszyty Naukowe Politechniki Gdanskiej. Mechanika

Zesz Nauk Politech Krakow Chem — Zeszyty Naukowe Politechniki Krakowskiej. Chemia

Zesz Nauk Politech Krakow Mech — Zeszyty Naukowe Politechniki Krakowskiej. Mechanika

Zesz Nauk Politech Lod Budow — Zeszyty Naukowe Politechniki Lodzkiej. Budownictwo

Zesz Nauk Politech Lodz Chem — Zeszyty Naukowe Politechniki Lodzkiej. Chemia

Zesz Nauk Politech Lodz Chem Spozyw — Zeszyty Naukowe Politechniki Lodzkiej. Chemia Spozywcza

Zesz Nauk Politech Lodz Elek — Zeszyty Naukowe Politechniki Lodzkiej. Elektryka

Zesz Nauk Politech Lodz Elektr — Zeszyty Naukowe Politechniki Lodzkiej. Elektryka

Zesz Nauk Politech Lodz Inz Chem — Zeszyty Naukowe Politechniki Lodzkiej. Inzynieria Chemiczna

Zesz Nauk Politech Lodz Mech — Zeszyty Naukowe Politechniki Lodzkiej. Mechanika

Zesz Nauk Politech Lodz Wlok — Zeszyty Naukowe Politechniki Lodzkiej. Wlokiennictwo

Zesz Nauk Politech Poznan Chem Inz Chem — Zeszyty Naukowe Politechniki Poznanskiej. Chemia i Inzynieria Chemiczna

Zesz Nauk Politech Poznan Elektr — Zeszyty Naukowe Politechniki Poznanskiej. Elektryka

Zesz Nauk Politech Rzeszowskiej — Zeszyty Naukowe Politechniki Rzeszowskiej

Zesz Nauk Politech Slask — Zeszyty Naukowe Politechniki Slaskiej

Zesz Nauk Politech Slaska Energ — Zeszyty Naukowe Politechnika Slaska. Energetyka

Zesz Nauk Politech Slask Chem — Zeszyty Naukowe Politechniki Slaskiej. Chemia

Zesz Nauk Politech Slask Energ — Zeszyty Naukowe Politechniki Slaskiej. Energetyka

Zesz Nauk Politech Slask Gorn — Zeszyty Naukowe Politechniki Slaskiej. Gornictwo

Zesz Nauk Politech Slask Hutn — Zeszyty Naukowe Politechniki Slaskiej. Hutnictwo

Zesz Nauk Politech Slask Ser Elektr — Zeszyty Naukowe Politechniki Slaskiej. Seria Elektryka

Zesz Nauk Politech Slask Ser Mat-Fiz — Zeszyty Naukowe Politechniki Slaskiej. Seria Matematyka-Fizyka

Zesz Nauk Politech Swietokrz Probl Nauk Podst — Zeszyty Naukowe Politechniki Swietokrzyska. Problemy Nauk Podstawowych

Zesz Nauk Politech Warsz Chem — Zeszyty Naukowe Politechniki Warszawskiej. Chemia

Zesz Nauk Politech Wroclaw Chem — Zeszyty Naukowe Politechniki Wroclawskiej. Chemia [Poland]

Zesz Nauk Roln Akad Roln Warsz — Zeszyty Naukowe. Rolnictwo Akademia Rolnicza w Warszawie

Zesz Nauk Szk Gl Gospod Wiejsk Akad Roln Warszawie Ogrod — Zeszyty Naukowe Szkoly Glownej Gospodarstwa Wiejskiego. Akademii Rolniczej w Warszawie. Ogrodnictwo

Zesz Nauk Szk Gl Gospod Wiejsk Akad Roln Warszawie Wter — Zeszyty Naukowe Szkoly Glownej Gospodarstwa Wiejskiego. Akademii Rolniczej w Warszawie. Weterynaria

Zesz Nauk Szk Gl Gospod Wiejsk Akad Roln Warszawie Zootech — Zeszyty Naukowe Szkoly Glownej Gospodarstwa Wiejskiego. Akademii Rolniczej w Warszawie. Zootechnika

Zesz Nauk Szk Gl Gospod Wiejsk Warszawie Melior Rolne — Zeszyty Naukowe Szkoly Glownej Gospodarstwa Wiejskiego w Warszawie. Melioracje Rolne

Zesz Nauk Szk Gl Gospod Wiejsk Warszawie Ogrod — Zeszyty Naukowe Szkoly Glownej Gospodarstwa Wiejskiego w Warszawie. Ogrodnictwo

Zesz Nauk Szk Gl Gospod Wiejsk Warszawie Roln — Zeszyty Naukowe Szkoly Glownej Gospodarstwa Wiejskiego w Warszawie. Rolnictwo [Poland]

Zesz Nauk Szk Gl Gospod Wiejsk Warszawie Technol Drewna — Zeszyty Naukowe Szkoly Glownej Gospodarstwa Wiejskiego w Warszawie. Technologia Drewna

Zesz Nauk Szk Glow Gospod Wiejsk Warszawie — Zeszyty Naukowe Szkoly Glownej Gospodarstwa Wiejskiego w Warszawie

Zesz Nauk Szk Glown Plan Statystyki — Zeszyty Naukowe Szkoly Glownej Planowania i Statystyki

Zesz Nauk Szkol Gospod Wiejsk Warsz (Lesn) — Zeszyty Naukowe Szkola Glowna Gospodarstwa Wiejskiego w Warszawie (Lesnictwo)

Zesz Nauk Szkol Gospod Wiejsk Warsz Technol Drewna — Zeszyty Naukowe Szkola Glowna Gospodarstwa Wiejskiego w Warszawie. Technologia Drewna

Zesz Nauk Technol Drewna Akad Roln Warsz — Zeszyty Naukowe. Technologia Drewna-Akademia Rolnicza w Warszawie

Zesz Nauk Tech Wyzsza Szk Inz Lublinie — Zeszyty Naukowo-Techniczny Wyzsza Szkola Inzynierska w Lublinie

ZeszNauKUL — Zeszyty Naukowe Katolickiego Uniwersytetu Lubelskiego [Lublin]

Zesz Nauk Uniw Jagiellon Acta Cosmol — Zeszyty Naukowe Uniwersytetu Jagiellonskiego. Acta Cosmologica

Zesz Nauk Uniw Jagiellon Pr Biol Mol — Zeszyty Naukowe Uniwersytetu Jagiellonskiego. Prace Biologii Molekularnej [Poland]

Zesz Nauk Uniw Jagiellon Pr Chem — Zeszyty Naukowe Uniwersytetu Jagiellonskiego. Prace Chemiczne [Poland]

Zesz Nauk Uniw Jagiellon Pr Etnogr — Zeszyty Naukowe Uniwersytetu Jagiellonskiego. Prace Etnograficzne

Zesz Nauk Uniw Jagiellon Pr Fiz — Zeszyty Naukowe Uniwersytetu Jagiellonskiego. Prace Fizyczne

Zesz Nauk Uniw Jagiellon Ser Nauk Mat Przy — Zeszyty Naukowe Uniwersytetu Jagiellonskiego. Seria Nauk Matematyezno-Prztrodniezych. Matematyka Fizyka Chemia

Zesz Nauk Uniw Jagiellonsk Pr Bot — Zeszyty Naukowe Uniwersytetu Jagiellonskiego. Prace Botaniczne

Zesz Nauk Uniw Lodz — Zeszyty Naukowe Uniwersytetu Lodzkiego

Zesz Nauk Uniw Lodz Fiz — Zeszyty Naukowe Uniwersytetu Lodzkiego. Fizyka

Zesz Nauk Uniw Lodz Nauki Humanist-Spolecz — Zeszyty Naukowe Uniwersytetu Lodzkiego. Nauki Humanistyczno-Spoleczne

Zesz Nauk Uniw Lodz Nauki Mat Przyr — Zeszyty Naukowe Uniwersytetu Lodzkiego. Nauki Matematyczno-Przyrodnicze

Zesz Nauk Uniw Lodz Ser 2 — Zeszyty Naukowe Uniwersytetu Lodzkiego. Seria 2. Nauki Matematyczno-Przyrodnicze [Poland]

Zesz Nauk Uniw Lodz Ser II — Zeszyty Naukowe Uniwersytetu Lodzkiego. Seria II

Zesz Nauk Uniw Lodz Ser III — Zeszyty Naukowe Uniwersytetu Lodzkiego. Seria III

Zesz Nauk Uniw Poznaniu Mat Fiz Chem — Zeszyty Naukowe Uniwersytetu Imienia Adama Mickiewicza w Poznaniu. Matematyka, Fizyka, Chemia

Zesz Nauk Uniw Slaski Katowicach Seke Chem — Zeszyty Naukowe Uniwersytet Slaski w Katowicach Sekeja Chemii

Zesz Nauk Wydz Mat Fiz Chem Uniw Gdanski Chem — Zeszyty Naukowe Wydzialu Matematyki, Fizyki, Chemii. Uniwersytet Gdanski. Seria Chemia

Zesz Nauk Wyzs Szk Ekon Poznaniu — Zeszyty Naukowe Wyzszej Szkoly Ekonomicznej w Poznaniu

Zesz Nauk Wyzs Szk Roln Krakowie — Zeszyty Naukowe Wyzszej Szkoly Rolniczej w Krakowie

Zesz Nauk Wyzs Szk Roln Krakowie Zootech — Zeszyty Naukowe Wyzszej Szkoly Rolniczej w Krakowie. Zootechnika

Zesz Nauk Wyzs Szk Roln Olsztynie — Zeszyty Naukowe Wyzszej Szkoly Rolniczej w Olsztynie

Zesz Nauk Wyzs Szk Roln Szczecinie — Zeszyty Naukowe Wyzsza Szkola Rolnicza w Szczecinie

Zesz Nauk Wyzs Szk Roln Wroclawiu — Zeszyty Naukowe Wyzszej Szkoly Rolniczej we Wroclawiu

Zesz Nauk Wyzs Szk Roln Wroclawiu Wet — Zeszyty Naukowe Wyzszej Szkoly Rolniczej we Wroclawiu. Weterynaria

Zesz Nauk Wyzsza Szk Ekon Poznaniu Ser 2 — Zeszyty Naukowe Wyzsza Szkola Ekonomiczna w Poznaniu. Seria 2. Prace Habilitacyjne i Doktorskie

Zesz Nauk Wyz Szkol Ekon — Zeszyty Naukowe Wyzszej Szkoly Ekonomicznej w Katowicach

Zesz Nauk Wyzsz Szk Inz Bialymstoku Mat Fiz Chem — Zeszyty Naukowe Wyzszej Szkoly Inzynierskiej w Bialymstoku Matematyka, Fizyka, Chemia

Zesz Nauk Wyzsz Szkoly Ekon Katowic — Zeszyty Naukowe Wyzszej Szkoly Ekonomicznej w Katowicach

Zesz Nauk Wyzsz Szkoly Ekon Poznan — Zeszyty Naukowe Wyzszej Szkoly Ekonomicznej w Poznaniu

Zesz Nauk Wyzsz Szk Pedagog Gdansku Mat Fiz Chem — Zeszyty Naukowe Wyzszej Szkoly Pedagogicznej w Gdansku. Matematyka, Fizyka, Chemia

Zesz Nauk Wyzsz Szk Pedagog Katowicach Sekc Fiz — Zeszyty Naukowe Wyzszej Szkoly Pedagogicznej w Katowicach. Sekcja Fizyki

Zesz Nauk Wyzsz Szk Roln Olsztynie — Zeszyty Naukowe Wyzszej Szkoly Rolniczej w Olsztynie

Zesz Nauk Wyzsz Szk Roln Szczecinie — Zeszyty Naukowe Wyzszej Szkoly Rolniczej w Szczecinie

Zesz Nauk Wyzsz Szk Roln Wroclawiu Melior — Zeszyty Naukowe Wyzszej Szkoly Rolniczej we Wroclawiu. Melioracja

Zesz Nauk Wyzsz Szk Roln Wroclawiu Roln — Zeszyty Naukowe Wyzszej Szkoly Rolniczej we Wroclawiu. Rolnictwo

Zesz Nauk Wyzsz Szk Roln Wroclawiu Weter — Zeszyty Naukowe Wyzszej Szkoly Rolniczej we Wroclawiu. Weterynaria

Zesz Nauk Wyzsz Szk Roln Wroclawiu Zootech — Zeszyty Naukowe Wyzszej Szkoly Rolniczej we Wroclawiu. Zootechnika

Zesz Nauk Wyzsz Szk Roln Wrocl Melior — Zeszyty Naukowe Wyzszej Szkoly Rolniczej we Wroclawiu. Melioracja

Zesz Nauk Wyzsz Szk Roln Wrocl Roln — Zeszyty Naukowe Wyzszej Szkoly Rolniczej we Wroclawiu. Rolnictwo

Zesz NWSP — Zeszyty Naukowe Wyzsza Szkola Pedagogiczna w Katowicach

Zesz Probl Gorn — Zeszyty Problemowe Gornictwa

Zesz Probl Kosmosu — Zeszyty Problemowe Kosmosu

Zesz Probl Nauki Pol — Zeszyty Problemowe Nauki Polskiej

Zesz Probl Postep Nauk Roln — Zeszyty Problemowe Postepow Nauk Rolniczych

Zesz Probl Postepow Nauk Roln — Zeszyty Problemowe Postepow Nauk Rolniczych

Zesz Prob Postepow Nauk Roln — Zeszyty Problemowe Postepow Nauk Rolniczych

Zeszty Nauk Uniw Jagiellon Prace Mat — Zeszyty Naukowe Uniwersytetu Jagiellonskiego. Prace Matematyczne

Zesz Wrocl — Zeszyty Wroclawskie

Zeszyty Nauk Akad Gorn-Hutniczej Mat Fiz Chem — Zeszyty Naukowe Akademii Gorniczo-Hutniczej Imienia Stanislawa Staszica. Matematyka, Fizyka, Chemia

Zeszyty Nauk Politech Lodz Mat — Zeszyty Naukowe Politechniki Lodzkiej. Matematyka

Zeszyty Nauk Politech Slask Automat — Zeszyty Naukowe Politechniki Slaskiej. Automatyka

Zeszyty Nauk Politech Slask Mat-Fiz — Zeszyty Naukowe Politechniki Slaskiej. Seria Matematyka-Fizyka

Zeszyty Nauk Politech Szczecin — Zeszyty Naukowe Politechniki Szczecinskiej

Zeszyty Nauk Szkoly Glown Planowania i Statyst — Zeszyty Naukowe Szkoly Glownej Planowania i Statystyki

Zeszyty Nauk Uniw Jagiellon Prace Fiz — Zeszyty Naukowe Uniwersytetu Jagiellonskiego. Prace Fizyczne

Zeszyty Nauk Wyz Szkoly Ped w Opolu Fiz — Zeszyty Naukowe Wyzszej Szkoly Pedagogicznej w Opolu. Fizyka

Zeszyty Nauk Wyz Szkoly Ped w Opolu Mat — Zeszyty Naukowe Wyzszej Szkoly Pedagogicznej w Opolu. Matematyka

ZETF — Zurnal Eksperimental'noi i Teoreticeskoi Fiziki

ZETFA — Zhurnal Eksperimentalnoi i Teoreticheskoi Fiziki

ZEthn — Zeitschrift fuer Ethnologie

Z Ethnolog — Zeitschrift fuer Ethnologie

ZETUA — Zeitschrift fuer Tuberkulose und Erkrankungen der Thoraxorgane

ZEUMD — Zeitschrift fuer Umweltpolitik

Zeumer's Q St — Zeumer's Quellen und Studien zur Verfassungsgeschichte des Deutschen Reichs in Mittelalter und Neuzeit

ZEURA — Zeitschrift fuer Urologie

Z Evan Eth — Zeitschrift fuer Evangelische Ethik

ZEVBA — Zeitschrift fuer Vererbungslehre

Z Ev Ethik — Zeitschrift fuer Evangelische Ethik
ZEV Glasers Ann — ZEV [*Zeitschrift fuer Eisenbahnwesen und Verkehrstechnik*] Glasers. Annalen
Z Ev K — Zeitschrift fuer Evangelisches Kirchenrecht
Z Ev Kr — Zeitschrift fuer Evangelisches Kirchenrecht
Z Exp Angew Psychol — Zeitschrift fuer Experimentelle und Angewandte Psychologie
Z Exp A Psy — Zeitschrift fuer Experimentelle und Angewandte Psychologie
Z Exp Chir — Zeitschrift fuer Experimentelle Chirurgie
Z Exp Chir Chir Forsch — Zeitschrift fuer Experimentelle Chirurgie und Chirurgische Forschung
Z Exp Chir Transplant Kuenstliche Organe — Zeitschrift fuer Experimentelle Chirurgie. Transplantation und Kuenstliche Organe
Z Exper & Angew Psychol — Zeitschrift fuer Experimentelle und Angewandte Psychologie
Z Exp Pathol Ther — Zeitschrift fuer Experimentelle Pathologie und Therapie
ZF — Zentralblatt fuer das Gesamte Forstwesen
ZF — Zona Franca
ZfA — Zeitschrift fuer Archaeologie
ZFA (Dresden) — Zeitschrift fuer Alternsforschung (Dresden)
Z Farben Ind — Zeitschrift fuer Farben Industrie
Z Farben Text Chem — Zeitschrift fuer Farben- und Textil-Chemie
ZFA (Stuttgart) — Zeitschrift fuer Allgemeinmedizin (Stuttgart)
ZFA (Stuttgart) — ZFA (Zeitschrift fuer Allgemeinmedizin) (Stuttgart)
ZfB — Zeitschrift fuer Buecherfreunde
ZFDF — Zeitschrift fuer Freie Deutsche Forschung
ZFDG — Zeitschrift fuer Deutsche Geistesgeschichte
ZFDPh — Zeitschrift fuer Deutsche Philologie
ZfDSdJ — Zeitschrift fuer Demographie und Statistik der Juden
ZfE — Zeitschrift fuer Ethnologie
ZFEU — Zeitschrift fuer Franzoesischen und Englischen Unterricht
ZFFB — Zbornik Filozofskog Fakulteta (Belgrade)
ZFGV — Zeitschrift. Freiburger Geschichtsvereine
ZfHb — Zeitschrift fuer Hebraeische Bibliographie
ZFI-Mitt — ZFI [*Zentralinstitut fuer Isotopen- und Strahlenforschung*]-Mitteilungen [*East Germany*]
Z Fisch Hilfswiss — Zeitschrift fuer Fischerei und Deren Hilfswissenschaften
ZfK — Zeitschrift fuer Kunstgeschichte
ZFKPhil — Zbornik Filozofickej Fakulty Univerzity Komenskeho-Philologica
ZFL — Zbornik za Filologiju i Lingvistiku
Z Fleisch Milchhyg — Zeitschrift fuer Fleisch- und Milchhygiene
Z Flugwiss — Zeitschrift fuer Flugwissenschaften
Z Flugwiss und Weltraumforsch — Zeitschrift fuer Flugwissenschaften und Weltraumforschung
Z Flugwiss Weltraumforsch — Zeitschrift fuer Flugwissenschaften und Weltraumforschung
ZFM — Zeitschrift fuer Musik
Zf Mus Theorie — Zeitschrift fuer Musiktheorie
ZfN — Zeitschrift fuer Numismatik
ZFNU — Zeitschrift fuer Neusprachlichen Unterricht
ZFO — ZFO. Zeitschrift fuer Fuehrung und Organisation
Z Forst Jagdwes — Zeitschrift fuer Forst- und Jagdwesen
ZfPhF — Zeitschrift fuer Philosophische Forschung
Z Franzoesische Spr Lit — Zeitschrift fuer Franzoesische Sprache und Literatur
ZfRG — Zeitschrift fuer Religions- und Geistesgeschichte
ZfRP — Zeitschrift fuer Romanische Philologie
ZFRPH — Zeitschrift fuer Romanische Philologie
ZFRsL — Zeitschrift fuer Franzoesische Sprache und Literatur
ZfRuGg — Zeitschrift fuer Religions- und Geistesgeschichte
ZfS — Zeitschrift fuer Semitistik und Verwandte Gebiete [*Leipzig*]
ZfSchKg — Zeitschrift fuer Schweizerische Kirchengeschichte
ZFSL — Zeitschrift fuer Franzoesische Sprache und Literatur
Zft f Celt Phil — Zeitschrift fuer Celtische Philologie
Zft f D Alt — Zeitschrift fuer Deutsches Altertum und Deutsche Literatur
Zft f Fr Sp u Lit — Zeitschrift fuer Franzoesische Sprache und Literatur
Zft f Rom Phil — Zeitschrift fuer Romanische Philologie
ZFV — Zeitschrift fuer Volkskunde
ZFYZD — Zhonghua Fangshe Yixue Yu Fanghu Zazhi
ZfZ — Zeitschrift fuer Assyriologie [*Leipzig/Berlin*]
ZG — Zeitschrift fuer Germanistik
Z Gaerungsphysiol — Zeitschrift fuer Gaerungsphysiologie
ZGAKE — Zeitschrift fuer Geschichte und Altertumskunde der Ermlands
Z Gastroent — Zeitschrift fuer Gastroenterologie
Z Gastroenterol — Zeitschrift fuer Gastroenterologie
Z Gastroenterol Verh — Zeitschrift fuer Gastroenterologie. Verhandlungsband
ZGDJ — Zeitschrift zur Geschichte des Deutschen Judentums
Z Geburtshilfe Gynaekol — Zeitschrift fuer Geburtshilfe und Gynaekologie [*Later, Zeitschrift fuer Geburtshilfe und Perinatologie*]
Z Geburtshilfe Perinatol — Zeitschrift fuer Geburtshilfe und Perinatologie
ZGEIA — Zhurnal Gigieny, Epidemiologii, Mikrobiologii i Immunologii
ZGEMA — Zeitschrift fuer die Gesamte Experimentelle Medizin
Z Geol Wiss — Zeitschrift fuer Geologische Wissenschaften
Z Geomorph — Zeitschrift fuer Geomorphologie
Z Geomorphol — Zeitschrift fuer Geomorphologie
Z Geomorphol Suppl — Zeitschrift fuer Geomorphologie. Supplementband

Z Geophys — Zeitschrift fuer Geophysik [*German Federal Republic*]
Z Ger Ling — Zeitschrift fuer Germanistische Linguistik
Z Gerontol — Zeitschrift fuer Gerontologie
Z Gesamte Brauwes — Zeitschrift fuer das Gesamte Brauwesen
Z Gesamte Exp Med — Zeitschrift fuer die Gesamte Experimentelle Medizin
Z Gesamte Exp Med Einschl Exp Chir — Zeitschrift fuer die Gesamte Experimentelle Medizin. Einschliesslich Experimenteller Chirurgie
Z Gesamte Forstwes — Zeitschrift fuer das Gesamte Forstwesen
Z Gesamte Genossenschaftswes — Zeitschrift fuer das Gesamte Genossenschaftswesen
Z Gesamte Genossenschaftswesen — Zeitschrift fuer das Gesamte Genossenschaftswesen
Z Gesamte Getreide Muehlen Baeckereiwes — Zeitschrift fuer das Gesamte Getreide Muehlen- und Baeckereiwesen
Z Gesamte Getreidewes — Zeitschrift fuer das Gesamte Getreidewesen
Z Gesamte Giessereiprax — Zeitschrift fuer die Gesamte Giessereipraxis
Z Gesamte Hyg — Zeitschrift fuer die Gesamte Hygiene und Ihre Grenzgebiete
Z Gesamte Hyg Grenzgeb — Zeitschrift fuer die Gesamte Hygiene und Ihre Grenzgebiete
Z Gesamte Hyg Ihre Grenzgeb — Zeitschrift fuer die Gesamte Hygiene und Ihre Grenzgebiete
Z Gesamte Inn Med — Zeitschrift fuer die Gesamte Innere Medizin und Ihre Grenzgebiete
Z Gesamte Inn Med Grenzgeb — Zeitschrift fuer die Gesamte Innere Medizin und Ihre Grenzgebiete
Z Gesamte Inn Med Grenzgeb Klin Pathol Exp — Zeitschrift fuer die Gesamte Innere Medizin und Ihre Grenzgebiete. Klinik, Pathologie, Experiment
Z Gesamte Inn Med Ihre Grenzgeb — Zeitschrift fuer die Gesamte Innere Medizin und Ihre Grenzgebiete
Z Gesamte Inn Med Ihre Grenzgeb Suppl — Zeitschrift fuer die Gesamte Innere Medizin und Ihre Grenzgebiete. Supplementum [*East Germany*]
Z Gesamte Kaelte Ind — Zeitschrift fuer die Gesamte Kaelte-Industrie
Z Gesamte Kaelte Ind Beih Ser 1 — Zeitschrift fuer die Gesamte Kaelte-Industrie. Beihefte. Serie 1
Z Gesamte Kaelte Ind Beih Ser 2 — Zeitschrift fuer die Gesamte Kaelte-Industrie. Beihefte. Serie 2
Z Gesamte Kaelte-Ind Beih Ser 3 — Zeitschrift fuer die Gesamte Kaelte-Industrie. Beihefte. Serie 3
Z Gesamte Kreditwesen — Zeitschrift fuer das Gesamte Kreditwesen
Z Gesamte Muehlenwes — Zeitschrift fuer das Gesamte Muehlenwesen
Z Gesamte Naturwiss — Zeitschrift fuer die Gesamte Naturwissenschaft
Z Gesamte Nervenheilkd Psychother — Zeitschrift fuer die Gesamte Nervenheilkunde und Psychotherapie [*German Democratic Republic*]
Z Gesamte Neurol Psychiatr — Zeitschrift fuer die Gesamte Neurologie und Psychiatrie
Z Gesamte Phys Ther — Zeitschrift fuer die Gesamte Physikalische Therapie
Z Gesamte Schiess-Sprengstoffw — Zeitschrift fuer das Gesamte Schiess- und Sprengstoffwesen mit der Sonderabteilung Gasschutz [*West Germany*]
Z Gesamte Schiess Sprengstoffwes — Zeitschrift fuer das Gesamte Schiess- und Sprengstoffwesen
Z Gesamte Staatswiss — Zeitschrift fuer die Gesamte Staatswissenschaft
Z Gesamte Textilind — Zeitschrift fuer die Gesamte Textilindustrie
Z Gesamte Text-Ind — Zeitschrift fuer die Gesamte Textil-Industrie
Z Gesamte Versicherungswiss — Zeitschrift fuer die Gesamte Versicherungswissenschaft
Z Gesch Erzieh u Unterr — Zeitschrift fuer Geschichte der Erziehung und des Unterrichts
Z Geschichtsw — Zeitschrift fuer Geschichtswissenschaft
ZGeschJud — Zeitschrift fuer die Geschichte der Juden
Z Gesch Oberrhein — Zeitschrift fuer die Geschichte des Oberrheins
Z Gesch Saar — Zeitschrift fuer die Geschichte der Saargegend
Z Geschv (Muelheim) — Zeitschrift. Geschichtsverein Muelheim an der Ruhr (Muelheim, West Germany)
Z Gesch-Wiss — Zeitschrift fuer Geschichtswissenschaft
Z Ges Exp Med — Zeitschrift fuer die Gesamte Experimentelle Medizin
Z Ges Inn Med — Zeitschrift fuer die Gesamte Innere Medizin und Ihre Grenzgebiete
Z Ges Staatswiss — Zeitschrift fuer die Gesamte Staatswissenschaft
Z Gesundheitstech Staedtehyg — Zeitschrift fuer Gesundheitstechnik und Staedtehygiene
ZGEU — Zeitschrift fuer Geschichte der Erziehung und des Unterrichts
ZGG — Zeitschrift fuer das Gesamte Genossenschaftswesen
ZGGJT — Zeitschrift. Gesellschaft fuer die Geschichte der Juden in der Tschechoslowakei
ZGGYA — Zeitschrift fuer Geburtshilfe und Gynaekologie [*Later, Zeitschrift fuer Geburtshilfe und Perinatologie*]
ZGJ — Zeitschrift fuer die Geschichte der Juden
ZGJD — Zeitschrift fuer die Geschichte der Juden in Deutschland [*Braunschwig/Berlin*]
ZGJT — Zeitschrift. Gesellschaft fuer die Geschichte der Juden in der Tschechoslowakei
ZGL — Zeitschrift fuer Germanistische Linguistik
Z Gletscherk Glazialgeol — Zeitschrift fuer Gletscherkunde und Glazialgeologie
ZGMFA — Zeszyty Naukowe Akademii Gorniczo-Hutniczej (Cracow). Matematyka, Fizyka, Chemia

ZGMPA — Zeitschrift fuer Geomorphologie

ZGO — Zeitschrift fuer die Geschichte des Oberrheins

Z Godschmiede Juwelerie Graveure — Zeitschrift fuer Goldschmiede Juwelerie und Graveure

ZGOR — Zeitschrift fuer die Geschichte des Oberrheins

ZGOrh — Zeitschrift fuer die Geschichte des Oberrheins

ZGS — Zeitschrift fuer die Gesamte Staatswissenschaft

ZGSHG — Zeitschrift. Gesellschaft fuer Schleswig-Holsteinische Geschichte

ZGSSA — Zeitschrift fuer das Gesamte Schiess- und Sprengstoffwesen mit der Sonderabteilung Gasschutz

ZGW — Zeitschrift fuer Geschichtswissenschaft

ZGZAE6 — Chinese Journal of Orthopedics

Z Hals Nasen Ohrenheilkd — Zeitschrift fuer Hals Nasen- und Ohrenheilkunde

Zh Analit Khim — Zhurnal Analiticheskoi Khimii

Zh Anal Khim — Zhurnal Analiticheskoi Khimii

Z Haut-Geschlechtskr — Zeitschrift fuer Haut- und Geschlechtskrankheiten

Z Hautkr — Zeitschrift fuer Hautkrankheiten

ZHB — Zeitschrift fuer Hebraeische Bibliographie

Zh Ehksp Teor Fiz Pis'ma Red — Zhurnal Ehksperimental'noj i Teoreticheskoj Fiziki Pis'ma - Redaktsiyu [*USSR*]

Zh Eksp Biol Med — Zhurnal Eksperimental'noi Biologii i Meditsiny

Zh Eksp Klin Med — Zhurnal Eksperimentalnoi i Klinicheskoi Meditsiny

Zh Eksp Teo — Zhurnal Eksperimentalnoi i Teoreticheskoi Fiziki

Zh Eksp i Teor Fiz — Zhurnal Eksperimentalnoi i Teoreticheskoi Fiziki

Zh Eksp Teor Fiz — Zhurnal Eksperimentalnoi i Teoreticheskoi Fiziki

Zh Eksp Teor Fiz Pis — Zhurnal Eksperimentalnoi i Teoreticheskoi Fiziki. Pis'ma

Zh Eksp Teor Fiz Pis'ma — Zhurnal Eksperimental'noi i Teoreticheskoi Fiziki. Pis'ma

Zh Eksp and Teor Fiz Pis'ma v Red — Zhurnal Eksperimental'noi i Teoreticheskoi Fiziki. Pis'ma v Redaktsiyu

Zheleznodorozhn Transp — Zheleznodorozhnyi Transport [*USSR*]

Zhelezn Splavy — Zheleznye Splavy

Zhelezobeton Konstr Chelyabinsk — Zhelezobetonnye Konstruktsii Chelyabinsk

Zh Evol Biokhim Fiziol — Zhurnal Evolyutsionnoi Biokhimii i Fiziologii

ZHF — Schmalenbachs Zeitschrift fuer Betriebswirtschaftliche Forschung

Zh Fiz Khem Tsiklu Vseukr Akad Nauk — Zhurnal Fizichno-Khemichnogo Tsiklu Vseukrains'ka Akademiya Nauk

Zh Fiz Khim — Zhurnal Fizicheskoi Khimii

Zh Geofiz — Zhurnal Geofiziki

Zh Gig Epidemiol Mikrobiol Immunol — Zhurnal Gigieny, Epidemiologii, Mikrobiologii, i Immunologii

Zhidkofazn Okislenie Nepredel'nykh Org Soedin — Zhidkofaznoe Okislenie Nepredel'nykh Organicheskikh Soedinenii

Zhilishchnoe Kommunal'n Khoz — Zhilishchnoe i Kommunal'noe Khozyaistvo

Z Hist Fors — Zeitschrift fuer Historische Forschung

Zhivot Nauki — Zhivotnovudni Nauki

Zhivotnov'd Nauki — Zhivotnov'dni Nauki

Zhivotnovod — Zhivotnovodstvo

Zhivotnovod Vet — Zhivotnovodstvo i Veterinariya

Zhivotnovud — Zhivotnovodstvo

Zhivotnovud Nauki — Zhivotnovudni Nauki

ZHJID — Zhongguo Jiguang

Zh Khim Promsti — Zhurnal Khimicheskoi Promyshlennosti

ZHKPA — Zhurnal Khimicheskoi Promyshlennosti

Zh Mikrob E — Zhurnal Mikrobiologii, Epidemiologii, i Immunobiologi

Zh Mikrobiol Epidemiol Immunobiol — Zhurnal Mikrobiologii, Epidemiologii, i Immunobiologii

Zh Mikrobiol Immunobiol — Zhurnal Mikrobiologii i Immunobiologii

Zh Nauchnoi i Prikl Fotogr i Kinematogr — Zhurnal Nauchnoi i Prikladnoi Fotografii i Kinematografii

Zh Nauchn Prikl Fotogr Kinematogr — Zhurnal Nauchnoi i Prikladnoi Fotografii i Kinematografii

Zh Nauch Prik Foto Kinematog — Zhurnal Nauchnoi i Prikladnoi Fotografii i Kinematografii

Zh Neorg Kh — Zhurnal Neorganicheskoi Khimii

Zh Neorg Khim — Zhurnal Neorganicheskoi Khimii

Zh Nevropatol Psikhiatr — Zhurnal Nevropatologii i Psikhiatrii Imeni S. S. Korsakova

Zh Nevropatol Psikhiatr Im S S Korsakova — Zhurnal Nevropatologii i Psikhiatrii Imeni S. S. Korsakova

ZHNID — Zhongguo Niangzao

Zh NP Fotog — Zhurnal Nauchnoi i Prikladnoi Fotografii i Kinematografii

Zh Obs Biol — Zhurnal Obshchei Biologii

Zh Obshch Biol — Zhurnal Obshchei Biologii

Zh Obshchei Khim — Zhurnal Obshchei Khimii

Zh Obshch Khim — Zhurnal Obshchei Khimii

Zh Obs Kh — Zhurnal Obshchei Khimii

Zh Opytn Agron — Zhurnal Opytnoi Agronomii

Zh Org Kh — Zhurnal Organicheskoi Khimii

Zh Org Khim — Zhurnal Organicheskoj Khimii

ZHPMA — Zentralblatt fuer Bakteriologie, Parasitenkunde, Infektionskrankheiten, und Hygiene. Erste Abteilung. Originale Reihe B. Hygiene, Betriebshygiene, Praeventive Medizin

Zh Priki Mekhan Tekh Fiz — Zhurnal Prikladnoi Mekhaniki i Tekhnicheskoi Fiziki

Zh Prikl Fiz — Zhurnal Prikladnoi Fiziki

Zh Prikl Khim — Zhurnal Prikladnoi Khimii

Zh Prikl Mekh Tekh Fiz — Zhurnal Prikladnoi Mekhaniki i Tekhnicheskoi Fiziki

Zh Prikl Spektrosk — Zhurnal Prikladnoi Spektroskopii

Zh Rezin Promsti — Zhurnal Rezinovoi Promyshlennosti

Zh Russ Fiz-Khim Ova — Zhurnal Russkago Fiziko-Khimicheskago Obshchestva

Zh Russ Fiz-Khim Ova Chast Fiz — Zhurnal Russkogo Fiziko-Khimicheskogo Obshchestva Chast Fizicheskaya

Zh Russ Fiz Khim Ova Chast Khim — Zhurnal Russkogo Fiziko-Khimicheskogo Ovshchestva Chast Khimicheskaya

Zh Russ Khim Ova — Zhurnal Russkago Khimicheskago Obshchestva

Zh Russ Khim Ova Fiz Ova — Zhurnal Russkago Khimicheskago Obshchestva i Fizicheskago Obshchestva

Zh Russ Metall Ova — Zhurnal Russkogo Metallurgicheskogo Obshchestva

Zh Sakh Promsti — Zhurnal Sakharnoi Promyshlennosti

Zh Strukt Khim — Zhurnal Strukturnoi Khimii

ZHT — Zeitschrift fuer Historische Theologie

Zh Tekh Fiz — Zhurnal Tekhnicheskoi Fiziki

ZHUCA — Zpravy Hornickeho Ustavu CSAV [*Ceskoslovenska Akademie Ved*]

Zhurnal Mikrobiol — Zhurnal Mikrobiologii

Zh Ushn Nos Gorl Bolezn — Zhurnal Ushnykh Nosovykh i Gorlovykh Boleznei

Zh Ushn Nosov Gorlov Bolez — Zhurnal Ushnykh Nosovykh i Gorlovykh Boleznei

Zhu Us Nos i Gorl Bol — Zhurnal Ushnykh Nosovykh i Gorlovykh Boleznei

ZHVNS — Zeitschrift. Historischer Verein fuer Niedersachsen

Zh Vopr Neirokhir — Zhurnal Voprosy Neirokhirurgii Imeni N. N. Burdenko

ZHVS — Zeitschrift. Historischer Verein fuer Steiermark

Zh Vses Khi — Zhurnal Vsesoyuznogo Khimicheskogo Obshchestva Imeni D. I. Mendeleeva

Zh Vses Khim O-va Im D I Mendeleeva — Zhurnal Vsesoyuznogo Khimicheskogo Obshchestva Imeni D. I. Mendeleeva

Zh Vychisl Mat and Mat Fiz — Zhurnal Vychislitel'noi Matematiki i Matematicheske Fiziki

Zh Vychisl Mat Mat Fiz — Zhurnal Vychislitelnoi Matematiki i Matematicheskoj Fiziki

Zh Vyssh Nerv Deiatel — Zhurnal Vysshei Nervnoi Deiatel'nosti

Zh Vyssh Nervn Deyat Im I P Pavlova — Zhurnal Vysshei Nervnoi Deyatel'nosti Imeni I. P. Pavlova

Zh Vyss Ner — Zhurnal Vysshei Nervnoi Deyatel'nosti Imeni I. P. Pavlova

ZHW — Ziekenhuis

Z Hyg — Zeitschrift fuer Hygiene

ZHYGA — Zeitschrift fuer die Gesamte Hygiene und Ihre Grenzgebiete

Z Hyg Infektionskr — Zeitschrift fuer Hygiene und Infektionskrankheiten

Z Hyg Infekt Kr — Zeitschrift fuer Hygiene und Infektionskrankheiten

Z Hyg InfektKrankh — Zeitschrift fuer Hygiene und Infektionskrankheiten

Z Hyg Zool Schaedlingsbekaempf — Zeitschrift fuer Hygienische Zoologie und Schaedlingsbekaempfung

Z I — Zeitschrift fuer Instrumentenbau

ZIALA — Zeitschrift fuer Immunitaets- und Allergieforschung

ZIAVA — Zeitschrift fuer Induktive Abstammungs- und Vererbungslehre

ZII — Zeitschrift fuer Indologie und Iranistik [*Leipzig*]

ZI Int — ZI [*Ziegelindustrie*] International [*West Germany*]

ZIK — Zbornik Istorije Knjizevnosti

ZiM — Ziemia i Morze

Zimbabwe Agric J — Zimbabwe Agricultural Journal

Zimbabwe J Econ — Zimbabwe Journal of Economics

Zimb Agric J — Zimbabwe Agricultural Journal

Zimb J Agric Res — Zimbabwe Journal of Agricultural Research

Zimb Libr — Zimbabwe Librarian

ZIMG — Zeitschrift. Internationale Musik Gesellschaft

Z Immun -Allergie-Forsch — Zeitschrift fuer Immunitaets- und Allergieforschung

Z Immun Exp — Zeitschrift fuer Immunitaetsforschung. Experimentelle und Klinische Immunologie

Z ImmunForsch Exp Ther — Zeitschrift fuer Immunitaetsforschung und Experimentelle Therapie

Z Immunitaets-Allergieforsch — Zeitschrift fuer Immunitaets- und Allergieforschung

Z Immunitaetsforsch — Zeitschrift fuer Immunitaetsforschung

Z Immunitaetsforsch Allerg Klin Immunol — Zeitschrift fuer Immunitaetsforschung. Allergie und Klinische Immunologie

Z Immunitaetsforsch Exp Klin Immunol — Zeitschrift fuer Immunitaetsforschung. Experimentelle und Klinische Immunologie

Z Immunitaetsforsch Exp Klin Immunol Suppl — Zeitschrift fuer Immunitaetsforschung. Experimentelle und Klinische Immunologie. Supplemente

Z Immunitaetsforsch Exp Ther — Zeitschrift fuer Immunitaetsforschung und Experimentelle Therapie

Z Immunitaetsforsch Exp Ther 1 — Zeitschrift fuer Immunitaetsforschung und Experimentelle Therapie. 1. Originale

Z Immunitaetsforsch Exp Ther 1 Abt Orig — Zeitschrift fuer Immunitaetsforschung und Experimentelle Therapie. 1. Abteilung Originale

Z Immunitaetsforsch Immunobiol — Zeitschrift fuer Immunitaetsforschung. Immunobiology

Z Immunitaetsforsch Immunobiol Suppl — Zeitschrift fuer Immunitaetsforschung. Immunobiology. Supplemente

Z Immunitaetsforsch Suppl — Zeitschrift fuer Immunitaetsforschung. Supplemente

ZIMordASSR — Zapiski Naucno-Issledovatel'nogo Instituta pri Sovete Ministrov Mordovskoj ASSR

Zinat Raksti Rigas Politeh Inst — Zinatniskie Raksti. Rigas Politehniskais Instituts

Zinc Res Dig — Zinc Research Digest

Z Indukt Abstammungs-Vererbungsl — Zeitschrift fuer Induktive Abstammungs- und Vererbungslehre

Zinn Verwend — Zinn und Seine Verwendung

Z Instrum — Zeitschrift fuer Instrumentenkunde [*West Germany*]

Z Instrumentenk — Zeitschrift fuer Instrumentenkunde

Z Instrumentenkd — Zeitschrift fuer Instrumentenkunde

Z Int Inst Zuckerruebenforsch — Zeitschrift. Internationales Institut fuer Zuckerruebenforschung

Z Int Ver Bohring Bohrtech — Zeitschrift. Internationaler Verein der Bohringenieure und Bohrtechniker

ZiP — Za i Przeciw

Ziraat Derg — Ziraat Dergisi

Ziraat Fak Derg Ege Univ — Ziraat Fakultesi Dergisi Ege Universitesi

Zisin (J Seismol Soc Jpn) — Zisin (Journal of the Seismological Society of Japan)

Zisin (Seismol Soc Jap J) — Zisin (Seismological Society of Japan. Journal)

ZIS Mitt — ZIS [*Zentralinstitut fuer Schweisstechnik*] Mitteilungen

ZIS (Zentralinst Schweisstech DDR) Mitt — ZIS (Zentralinstitut fuer Schweisstechnik der Deutschen Demokratischen Republik) Mitteilungen

Ziv A — Archiv fuer die Zivilistische Praxis

Ziva — Ziva. Casopis pro Biologickou Praci

ZIVAN — Zapiski Instituta Vostokovoden'ia Akademii Nauk SSSR

Zivocisna Vyroba Cesk Akad Zemed Ustav Vedeckotech Inf Zemed — Zivocisna Vyroba-Ceskoslovenska Akademie Zemedelska. Ustav Vedeckotechnickych Informaci pro Zemedelstvi

Zivoc Vyroba — Zivocisna Vyroba

Zivotn Prostr — Zivotne Prostredie

ZIVP — Zivotne Prostredie [*Czechoslovakia*]

ZJ — Zeszyty Jezykoznawcze

ZJ — Zivi Jezici

Z Jagdwiss — Zeitschrift fuer Jagdwissenschaft

ZJKF — Zpravy Jednoty Klasickych Filologu

ZJSTD — Zambia Journal of Science and Technology

ZK — Zeitschrift fuer Keilschriftforschung und Verwandte Gebiete

ZK — Zeitschrift fuer Kunstgeschichte

ZKA — Zeitschrift fuer Kulturaustausch

Z Kardiol — Zeitschrift fuer Kardiologie

Z Kardiol Suppl — Zeitschrift fuer Kardiologie. Supplementum

ZKG — Zeitschrift fuer Kirchengeschichte

Z Kindch G — Zeitschrift fuer Kinderchirurgie und Grenzgebiete

Z Kinderchir Grenzgeb — Zeitschrift fuer Kinderchirurgie und Grenzgebiete

Z Kinderheilkd — Zeitschrift fuer Kinderheilkunde

Z Kinder-Jugendpsychiatr — Zeitschrift fuer Kinder- und Jugendpsychiatrie

Z Kinderpsychiatr — Zeitschrift fuer Kinderpsychiatrie

Z Kind Jug — Zeitschrift fuer Kinder- und Jugendpsychiatrie

Z Kirch G — Zeitschrift fuer Kirchengeschichte

ZKJ — Zbornik za Knjizevnost i Jezik

ZKKOBW — Cancer Research and Clinical Oncology

ZKKODY — Gerontology Extension Lectures

ZKLCA — Zeitschrift fuer Klinische Chemie

Z Klin Chem — Zeitschrift fuer Klinische Chemie und Klinische Biochemie

Z Klin Chem Klin Biochem — Zeitschrift fuer Klinische Chemie und Klinische Biochemie

Z Klin Med — Zeitschrift fuer Klinische Medizin

Z Klin Psychol Psychother — Zeitschrift fuer Klinische Psychologie und Psychotherapie

ZKM — Zeitschrift fuer die Kunde des Morgenlandes

Z Koeln Zoo — Zeitschrift des Koelner Zoo

Z Kompr Fluess Gase Pressluft-Ind — Zeitschrift fuer Komprimierte und Fluessige Gase Sowie fuer die Pressluft-Industrie

ZKPVF — Zeitschrift fuer Keltische Philologie und Volksforschung

ZKR — Zeitschrift fuer das Gesamte Kreditwesen

ZKR — Zeitschrift fuer Kirchenrecht

Z Krankenpfl — Zeitschrift fuer Krankenpflege

Z Krebsf Kl — Zeitschrift fuer Krebsforschung und Klinische Onkologie

Z Krebsforsch — Zeitschrift fuer Krebsforschung

Z Krebsforsch Klin Onkol — Zeitschrift fuer Krebsforschung und Klinische Onkologie

Z Kreislaufforsch — Zeitschrift fuer Kreislaufforschung

Z Krist — Zeitschrift fuer Kristallographie, Kristallgeometrie, Kristallphysik, Kristallchemie

Z Kristall — Zeitschrift fuer Kristallographie. Kristallgeometrie, Kristallphysik, Kristallchemie

Z Kristallogr — Zeitschrift fuer Kristallographie

Z Kristallogr Kristallgeom Kristallphys Kristallchem — Zeitschrift fuer Kristallographie, Kristallgeometrie, Kristallphysik, Kristallchemie

Z Kristallogr Mineral — Zeitschrift fuer Kristallographie und Mineralogie

ZKRU — Zeitschrift fuer Katholischen Religionsunterricht

ZKT — Zeitschrift fuer Katholische Theologie

ZKTh — Zeitschrift fuer Katholische Theologie

ZKuG — Zeitschrift fuer Kunstgeschichte

Z Kult-Tech Flurberein — Zeitschrift fuer Kulturtechnik und Flurbereinigung

Z Kulturaustausch — Zeitschrift fuer Kulturaustausch

Z Kulturtech — Zeitschrift fuer Kulturtechnik

Z Kulturtech Flurbereinig — Zeitschrift fuer Kulturtechnik und Flurbereinigung

ZKunstG — Zeitschrift fuer Kunstgeschichte

Z Kunstges — Zeitschrift fuer Kunstgeschichte

Z Kunstgesc — Zeitschrift fuer Kunstgeschichte

Z Kunstgesch — Zeitschrift fuer Kunstgeschichte

Z Kunstwis — Zeitschrift fuer Kunstwissenschaft

ZKW — Zeitschrift fuer Kunstwissenschaft

ZKWL — Zeitschrift fuer Kirchliche Wissenschaft und Kirchliches Leben [*Leipzig*]

ZL — Zycie Literackie

Z Laboratoriumsdiagn — Zeitschrift fuer Laboratoriumsdiagnostik

Z Landeskult — Zeitschrift fuer Landeskultur

Z Landwirt Vers Untersuchungsw — Zeitschrift fuer Landwirtschaftliches Versuchs- und Untersuchungswesen

Z Landw Ver u Unters Wes — Zeitschrift fuer Landwirtschaftliches Versuchs- und Untersuchungswesen

Z Laryngol Rhinol Otol — Zeitschrift fuer Laryngologie, Rhinologie, Otologie, und Ihre Grenzgebiete

Z Laryngol Rhinol Otol Grenzgeb — Zeitschrift fuer Laryngologie, Rhinologie, Otologie, und Ihre Grenzgebiete

Z Laryngol Rhinol Otol Ihre Grenzgeb — Zeitschrift fuer Laryngologie, Rhinologie, Otologie, und Ihre Grenzgebiete

Z Lebensmit — Zeitschrift fuer Lebensmittel- Untersuchung und Forschung

Z Lebensmittel Untersuch Forsch — Zeitschrift fuer Lebensmittel- Untersuchung und Forschung

Z Lebens-Technol-Verfahrenstech — Zeitschrift fuer Lebensmittel- Technologie und Verfahrenstechnik [*German Federal Republic*]

Z Lebensm-Unters Forsch — Zeitschrift fuer Lebensmittel- Untersuchung und Forschung

ZLGIA — Zapiski Leningradskogo Gornogo Instituta

ZLit — Zycie Literackie [*Krakow*]

ZLROA — Zeitschrift fuer Laryngologie, Rhinologie, Otologie

ZLSIA — Zapiski Leningradskogo Sel'skokhozyaistvennogo Instituta

ZLThK — Zeitschrift fuer die Gesamte Lutherische Theologie und Kirche [*Leipzig*]

Z Luft-Weltraumrecht — Zeitschrift fuer Luft- und Weltraumrecht

Z Lymphol — Zeitschrift fuer Lymphologie

ZM — Zeitschrift fuer Missionskunde

ZM — Zeitschrift fuer Mundartforschung

ZM — Zeitschrift fuer Musik

ZM — Zycie i Mysl

ZMaF — Zeitschrift fuer Mundartforschung

ZMag — Z Magazine [*Zambia*]

Z Math Log — Zeitschrift fuer Mathematische Logik und Grundlagen der Mathematik

Z Math Logik Grundlagen Math — Zeitschrift fuer Mathematische Logik und Grundlagen der Mathematik

Z Math Logik Grundlag Math — Zeitschrift fuer Mathematische Logik und Grundlagen der Mathematik

Z Mat Phys — Zeitschrift fuer Mathematik und Physik [*East Germany*]

ZMBTA — Zement und Beton

Z Med Chem — Zeitschrift fuer Medizinische Chemie

Z Med Lab Diagn — Zeitschrift fuer Medizinische Laboratoriumsdiagnostik

Z Med Laboratoriumsdiagn — Zeitschrift fuer Medizinische Laboratoriumsdiagnostik

Z Med Labortech — Zeitschrift fuer Medizinische Labortechnik

Z Med Mikrobiol Immunol — Zeitschrift fuer Medizinische Mikrobiologie und Immunologie

ZMEIA — Zhurnal Mikrobiologii, Epidemiologii, i Immunobiologii

Z Menschl Vererb-Konstitutionsl — Zeitschrift fuer Menschliche Vererbungs- und Konstitutionslehre

Z Metallk — Zeitschrift fuer Metallkunde

Z Metallkd — Zeitschrift fuer Metallkunde

Z Metallkun — Zeitschrift fuer Metallkunde

Z Meteorol — Zeitschrift fuer Meteorologie

Z Met Schmuckwaren Fabr Verchrom — Zeitschrift fuer Metall- und Schmuckwaren. Fabrikation sowie Verchromung

ZMF — Zeitschrift fuer Mundartforschung

ZMFWA — Zeszyty Naukowe. Matematyka, Fizyka, Chemia

ZMH — Zeitschrift des Museums Hildesheim

Z Mikrosk Anat Forsch — Zeitschrift fuer Mikroskopische-Anatomische Forschung

Z Mikrosk-Anat Forsch (Leipz) — Zeitschrift fuer Mikroskopische-Anatomische Forschung (Leipzig)
Z Militaermed — Zeitschrift fuer Militaermedizin [*East Germany*]
Z Miss-u Relig Wiss — Zeitschrift fuer Missionswissenschaft und Religionswissenschaft
Z Miss W — Zeitschrift fuer Missionswissenschaft und Religionswissenschaft
ZMK — Zeitschrift fuer Missionskunde und Religionswissenschaft
ZMK — Zpravodaj Mistopisne Komise CSAV [*Ceskoslovenske Akademie Ved*]
ZMM — Zeitschrift fuer Marktforschung, Meinungsforschung, und Zukunftsforschung
ZMNP — Zurnal Ministerstva Narodnogo Prosvescenija
Z Morphol Anthropol — Zeitschrift fuer Morphologie und Anthropologie
Z Morphol Oekol Tiere — Zeitschrift fuer Morphologie und Oekologie der Tiere
Z Morphol Tiere — Zeitschrift fuer Morphologie der Tiere
Z Morph Tie — Zeitschrift fuer Morphologie der Tiere
ZMOTA — Zeitschrift fuer Morphologie und Oekologie der Tiere
ZMP — Zurnal Moskovskoi Patriarkhii [*Moscow*]
ZMPHA — Zeitschrift fuer Mathematik und Physik
ZMR — Zeitschrift fuer Missionswissenschaft und Religionswissenschaft
ZMRW — Zeitschrift fuer Missionswissenschaft und Religionswissenschaft
ZMS — Zbornik Matice Srpske
ZMVKA — Zeitschrift fuer Menschliche Vererbungs- und Konstitutionslehre
ZMW — Zeitschrift fuer Missionswissenschaft
Z Mw — Zeitschrift fuer Musikwissenschaft
ZN — Zeitschrift fuer Nationaloekonomie
ZN — Zeitschrift fuer Numismatik
ZN — Zeszyty Naukowe
Zn — Znamya [*Moscow*]
ZN — Zycie Nauki
ZNa — Zycie Nauki
ZNACD — Zeszyty Naukowe Akademii Gorniczo-Hutniczej Imienia Stanislawa Staszica. Matematyka, Fizyka, Chemia
ZNAGA — Zeszyty Naukowe Akademii Gorniczo-Hutniczej w Krakowie. Rozprawy
ZNAGB — Zeszyty Naukowe Akademii Gorniczo-Hutniczej (Krakow). Gornictwo
ZNAGD — Zeszyty Naukowe Akademii Gorniczo-Hutniczej Imienia Stanislawa Staszica. Geologia
ZNAGDF — Akademia Gorniczo-Hutnicza Imjenia Stanislawa Staszica w Krakowie Zeszyty Naukowe Geologia
ZNAHD — Zeszyty Naukowe Akademii Gorniczo-Hutniczej Imienia Stanislawa Staszica. Elektryfikacja i Mechanizacja Gornictwa i Hutnictwa
Z Nahrungsm Unters Hyg Warenkd — Zeitschrift fuer Nahrungsmittel-Untersuchung Hygiene und Warenkunde
ZNAND — Zootecnica e Nutrizione Animale
Z Nationalo — Zeitschrift fuer Nationaloekonomie
Z Nationaloekonom — Zeitschrift fuer Nationaloekonomie
Z Nat-Oekon — Zeitschrift fuer Nationaloekonomie
Z Naturf B — Zeitschrift fuer Naturforschung. Teil B
Z Naturf C — Zeitschrift fuer Naturforschung. Teil C. Biochemie, Biophysik, Biologie, Virologie
Z Naturfo A — Zeitschrift fuer Naturforschung. A
Z Naturfo B — Zeitschrift fuer Naturforschung. B
Z Naturfo C — Zeitschrift fuer Naturforschung. C
Z Naturforsch — Zeitschrift fuer Naturforschung
Z Naturforsch A — Zeitschrift fuer Naturforschung. Teil A. Astrophysik, Physik, und Physikalische Chemie
Z Naturforsch B — Zeitschrift fuer Naturforschung. Teil B
Z Naturforsch B Anorg Chem Org Chem — Zeitschrift fuer Naturforschung. Teil B. Anorganische Chemie, Organische Chemie
Z Naturforsch B Anorg Chem Org Chem Biochem Biophys Biol — Zeitschrift fuer Naturforschung. Teil B. Anorganische Chemie, Organische Chemie, Biochemie, Biophysik, Biologie [*West Germany*]
Z Naturforsch C Biochem Biophys Biol Virol — Zeitschrift fuer Naturforschung. Teil C. Biochemie, Biophysik, Biologie, Virologie [*West Germany*]
Z Naturforsch C Biosci — Zeitschrift fuer Naturforschung. Teil C. Biosciences [*West Germany*]
Z Naturforsch Sect B — Zeitschrift fuer Naturforschung. Section B. Inorganic Chemistry, Organic Chemistry
Z Naturforsch Sect C Biosci — Zeitschrift fuer Naturforschung. Section C. Biosciences
Z Naturforsch Teil A — Zeitschrift fuer Naturforschung. Teil A
Z Naturforsch Teil C — Zeitschrift fuer Naturforschung. Teil C. Biosciences
Z Naturforsch Teil C Biochem Biophys Biol Virol — Zeitschrift fuer Naturforschung. Teil C. Biochemie, Biophysik, Biologie, Virologie
Z Naturheilk — Zeitschrift fuer Naturheilkunde
Z Naturwiss-Med Grundlagenforsch — Zeitschrift fuer Naturwissenschaftlich-Medizinische Grundlagenforschung
Z Naurforsch Teil B — Zeitschrift fuer Naturforschung. Teil B. Anorganische Chemie, Organische Chemie
ZNCAV — Zdenku Nejedlemu Ceskoslovenska Akademie Ved
Z Neurol — Zeitschrift fuer Neurologie

Z Neut W — Zeitschrift fuer die Neutestamentliche Wissenschaft
Z Neut Wiss — Zeitschrift fuer die Neutestamentliche Wissenschaft und die Kunde der Alteren Kirche
ZNF — Zeitschrift fuer Namenforschung
ZNG — Zeszyty Naukowe Wydzialu Humanistycznego, Wyzsza Szkola Pedagogiczna w Gdansku
ZNGGA — Zeszyty Naukowe Akademii Gorniczo-Hutniczej (Krakow). Geologia
ZNIO — Zaklad Narodowy Imeni Ossolinskich
ZNK — Zeszyty Naukowe, Sekcja Jezykoznawcza, Wyzsza Szkola Pedagogiczna w Katowicach
ZNKUL — Zeszyty Naukowe Katolickiego Uniwersytetu Lubelskiego
ZNLSA — Zeszyty Naukowe Politechniki Lodzkiej. Chemia Spozywcza
ZNO — Zeitschrift fuer Nationaloekonomie
ZNPEA — Zeszyty Naukowe Politechniki Lodzkiej. Elektryka
ZNPED — Zeszyty Naukowe Politechniki Poznanskiej. Elektryka
ZNPIA — Zhurnal Nevropatologii i Psikhiatrii Imeni S. S. Korsakova
ZNPPD — Zeszyty Naukowe Politechniki Swietokrzyskiej. Seria P. Problemy Nauk Podstawowych
ZNS — Zeitschrift fuer Neuere Sprachen
ZNSCA — Zeszyty Naukowe Politechniki Slaskiej. Chemia
ZNSGA — Zeszyty Naukowe Politechniki Slaskiej. Gornictwo
ZNSPK — Zeszyty Naukowe Wyzszej Szkoly Pedagogicznej. Katowice
ZNSPO — Zeszyty Naukowe Wyzszej Szkoly Pedagogicznej. Opole
ZNSSA — Zeszyty Naukowe Akademii Gorniczo-Hutniczej (Krakow). Sozologia i Sozotechnika
ZNTFA — Zeitschrift fuer Naturforschung
ZNTHA — Zeszyty Naukowe Politechniki Czestochowskiej. Nauki Techniczne. Hutnictwo
ZNTS — Zapysky Naukovoho Tovarystva Imeny Svecenka (Linguistic Series)
ZNTSL — Zapysky Naukovoho Tovarystva Imeny Svecenka (Literature Series)
ZNTW — Zeitschrift fuer die Neutestamentliche Wissenschaft
ZNTZA — Zeszyty Naukowe Akademii Rolniczo-Technicznej w Olsztynie. Technologia Zywnosci
ZNU — Zeitschrift fuer Neusprachlichen Unterricht
ZNUFA — Zeszyty Naukowe Uniwersytetu Jagiellonskiego. Prace Fizyczne
ZNUG — Zeszyty Naukowe Uniwersytetu Gdanskiego
ZNUIA — Zeszyty Naukowe Uniwersytetu Imienia Adama Mickiewicza w Poznaniu. Matematyka, Fizyka, Chemia
ZNUJ — Zeszyty Naukowe Uniwersytetu Jagiellonskiego
ZNUL — Zeszyty Naukowe Uniwersytetu Lodzkiego
ZNULHist — Zeszyty Naukowe Uniwersytetu Lodzkiego. Nauki Humanistyczno-Spoleczne. Historia
ZNum — Zeitschrift fuer Numismatik
ZNUMD — Zeszyty Naukowe Uniwersytetu Jagiellonskiego. Prace Biologii Molekularnej
ZNUMK — Zeszyty Naukowe Uniwersytetu M. Kopernika
ZNUnWr — Zeszyty Naukowe Uniwersytetu Wroclawskiego
ZNUP — Zeszyty Naukowe Uniwersytetu Imienia Adama Mickiewicza w Poznaniu
ZNUPHSzt — Zeszyty Naukowe Uniwersytetu Imienia Adama Mickiewicza w Poznaniu. Historia Sztuki
ZNUT — Zeszyty Naukowe Uniwersytetu M. Kopernika w Toruniu. Nauki Humanistyczno-Spoleczne
ZNUW — Zeszyty Naukowe Uniwersytetu Wroclawskiego Imeni B. Bieruta
ZNUZA — Zeszyty Naukowe Uniwersytetu Jagiellonskiego. Prace Zoologiczne
ZNW — Zeitschrift fuer die Neutestamentliche Wissenschaft
ZNW — Zeitschrift fuer die Neutestamentliche Wissenschaft und die Kunde des Urchristentums
ZNWFA — Zeszyty Naukowe Wyzszej Szkoly Pedagogicznej w Katowicach. Sekcja Fizyki
ZNWKAK — Zeitschrift fuer die Neutestamentliche Wissenschaft und die Kunde der Aelteren Kirche
ZNWKU — Zeitschrift fuer die Neutestamentliche Wissenschaft und die Kunde des Urchristentums
ZNWSPK — Zeszyty Naukowe Wyzszej Szkoly Pedagogicznej. Katowice
ZNWSPO — Zeszyty Naukowe Wyzszej Szkoly Pedagogicznej. Opole
ZNWSPOp — Zeszyty Naukowe, Jezykoznawstwo, Wyzsza Szkola Pedagogiczna w Opolu
ZNZSA — Zeszyty Naukowe Akademii Gorniczo-Hutniczej (Cracow). Zeszyt Specjalny
ZO — Zeitschrift fuer Ortsnamenforschung
ZO — Zeitschrift fuer Ostforschung
Zobozdrav Vestn — Zobozdravstveni Vestnik
ZOBW — Zeitschrift fuer Oesterreichisches Bibliothekswesen
Z Oeff Gem Wirtsch Unterneh — Zeitschrift fuer Oeffentliche und Gemeinwirtschaftliche Unternehmen
ZOEG — Zeitschrift fuer die Oesterreichischen Gymnasien
ZOEG — Zeitschrift fuer Osteuropaeische Geschichte
ZOEMS — Zeitschrift fuer die Oesterreichischen Mittelschulen
Z Oesterr Entomol Ver — Zeitschrift. Oesterreichischer Entomologe-Verein
Z Oesterr Ver Gas Wasserfachmaennern — Zeitschrift. Oesterreichischer Verein von Gas- und Wasserfachmaennern
ZOest G — Zeitschrift fuer die Oesterreichischen Gymnasien

ZOf — Zeitschrift fuer Ostforschung
ZOfo — Zeitschrift fuer Ostforschung
ZOG — Zeitschrift fuer Osteuropaeische Geschichte
ZOLGA — Zoologica
Zolnierz Pol — Zolnierz Polski [*Poland*]
Zolotaya Promst — Zolotaya Promyshlennost
ZON — Zeitschrift fuer Ortsnamenforschung
Zoning and Plan L Rep — Zoning and Planning Law Report
Zooiatr Rev Med Vet Prod Pecu — Zooiatria Revista de Medicina Veterinaria y Produccion Pecuaria
Zool Abh (Dres) — Zoologische Abhandlungen (Dresden)
Zool Afr — Zoologica Africana
Zool Ann — Zoologische Annalen
Zool Anz — Zoologischer Anzeiger
Zool Anzeiger — Zoologischer Anzeiger
Zool Anz (Leipzig) — Zoologischer Anzeiger (Leipzig)
Zool Anz Suppl — Zoologischer Anzeiger. Supplement
Zool B — Zoological Bulletin
Zool Beitr — Zoologische Beitraege
Zool Ber — Zoologischer Bericht
Zool Bidr Upps — Zoologiska Bidrag fran Uppsala
Zool Bidr Uppsala — Zoologiska Bidrag fran Uppsala
Zool Bijdr — Zoologische Bijdragen
Zool Biol Mar — Zoologia e Biologia Marinha
Zool Biol Mar (Sao Paulo) (Nova Ser) — Zoologia e Biologia Marinha (Sao Paulo) (Nova Serie)
Zool Entomol Listy — Zoologicke a Entomologicke Listy
Zool Gaert — Zoologische Gaerten
Zool Gart — Zoologische Gaerten
Zool Gart (Lpz) — Zoologische Gaerten (Leipzig)
Zool Inst Fac Sci Univ Tokyo Annu Rep — Zoological Institute. Faculty of Science. University of Tokyo. Annual Report
Zool Jahrb Abt Allg Zool Physiol Tiere — Zoologische Jahrbuecher. Abteilung fuer Allgemeine Zoologie und Physiologie der Tiere
Zool Jahrb Abt Anat Ontog Tiere — Zoologische Jahrbuecher. Abteilung fuer Anatomie und Ontogenie der Tiere
Zool Jahrb Abt Syst (Jena) — Zoologische Jahrbuecher. Abteilung fuer Systematik Oekologie und Geographie der Tiere (Jena)
Zool Jahrb Abt Syst Oekol Geogr Tiere — Zoologische Jahrbuecher. Abteilung fuer Systematik Oekologie und Geographie der Tiere
Zool Jb — Zoologische Jahrbuecher
Zool Jb Abt Allg Zool Physiol Tiere — Zoologische Jahrbuecher. Abteilung fuer Allgemeine Zoologie und Physiologie der Tiere
Zool Jb Abt Syst Okol Geog Tiere — Zoologische Jahrbuecher. Abteilung fuer Systematik Oekologie und Geographie der Tiere
Zool Jhrb Abt Allg Zool Physiol Tiere — Zoologische Jahrbuecher. Abteilung fuer Allgemeine Zoologie und Physiologie der Tiere
Zool J Linn — Zoological Journal. Linnean Society
Zool J Linn Soc — Zoological Journal. Linnean Society
Zool Listy — Zoologicke Listy
Zool Mag — Zoological Magazine
Zool Mag (Tokyo) — Zoological Magazine (Tokyo)
Zool Meded (Leiden) — Zoologische Mededelingen (Leiden)
Zool Meded Rijks Mus Nat Hist Leiden — Zoologische Mededelingen. Rijks Museum van Natuurlijke Historie te Leiden
Zool Muz Raksti Invertebrata — Zoologijas Muzeja Raksti. Invertebrata
Zoologica Pol — Zoologica Poloniae
Zoologica Scr — Zoologica Scripta
Zool Pol — Zoologica Poloniae
Zool Publ Victoria Univ Wellington — Zoology Publications. Victoria University of Wellington
Zool Rec — Zoological Record
Zool Revy — Zoologisk Revy
Zool Sci — Zoological Science
Zool Scr — Zoologica Scripta
Zool Scr — Zoologien Scripta
Zool Soc Egypt Bull — Zoological Society of Egypt. Bulletin
Zool Soc London Pr — Zoological Society of London. Proceedings
Zool Soc London Proc — Zoological Society of London. Proceedings
Zool Verh (Leiden) — Zoologische Verhandelingen (Leiden)
Zool Z — Zoologiceskij Zhurnal
Zool Zentralbl — Zoologisches Zentralblatt
Zool Zh — Zoologicheskii Zhurnal
Zoonoses Res — Zoonoses Research
Zoon Suppl — Zoon. Supplement
Zoophysiol Ecol — Zoophysiology and Ecology
Zoo Rec — Zoological Record
Zoo Rev Parque Zool Barc — Zoo Revista del Parque Zoologico de Barcelona
Zootech Experiment Stn Res Bull — Zootechnical Experiment Station. Research Bulletin
Zootec Nutr Anim — Zootecnica e Nutrizione Animale
Zootec Vet — Zootecnica e Veterinaria
Zootec Vet Agric — Zootecnica. Veterinaria e Agricoltura
Zootec Vita — Zootecnia e Vita
Z Operations Res Ser A-B — Zeitschrift fuer Operations Research. Serie A. Serie B

Z Oper Res B — Zeitschrift fuer Operations Research. Serie B. Praxis
Z Oper Res Ser A — Zeitschrift fuer Operations Research. Serie A. Theorie
Z Oper Res Ser B — Zeitschrift fuer Operations Research. Serie B. Praxis
Z Organ — Zeitschrift fuer Organisation
ZORPB — Zeitschrift fuer Operations Research. Serie B. Praxis
Z Orthop — Zeitschrift fuer Orthopaedie und Ihre Grenzgebiete
Z Orthop Grenzgeb — Zeitschrift fuer Orthopaedie und Ihre Grenzgebiete
Z Orthop Ihre Grenzgeb — Zeitschrift fuer Orthopaedie und Ihre Grenzgebiete
ZOSC — Zoologica Scripta
Z Ostforsch — Zeitschrift fuer Ostforschung
ZOVBW — Zeitschrift. Oesterreichischer Verein fuer Bibliothekswesen
ZP — Zeitschrift fuer Phonetik
ZP — Zeitschrift fuer Politik
ZPAAD — Zeitschrift fuer Physik. Sektion A. Atoms and Nuclei
ZPalV — Zeitschrift. Deutscher Palaestinaverein
Z Papyrologie Epigraphik — Zeitschrift fuer Papyrologie und Epigraphik
Z Parapsych — Zeitschrift fuer Parapsychologie und Grenzgebiete der Psychologie
Z Parasiten — Zeitschrift fuer Parasitenkunde
Z Parasitenkd — Zeitschrift fuer Parasitenkunde
Z ParasitKde — Zeitschrift fuer Parasitenkunde
Z Parlamentsfr — Zeitschrift fuer Parlamentsfragen [*German Federal Republic*]
Z Parlamentsfragen — Zeitschrift fuer Parlamentsfragen
ZPAS — Zeitschrift fuer Phonetik und Allgemeine Sprachwissenschaft
ZPBBD — Zeitschrift fuer Physik. Sektion B. Condensed Matter and Quanta
ZPCAA — Zeitschrift fuer Physikalische Chemie. Abteilung A
ZPCBA — Zeitschrift fuer Physikalische Chemie. Abteilung B
ZPCHA — Zeitschrift fuer Physiologische Chemie
ZPCLA — Zeitschrift fuer Physikalische Chemie (Leipzig)
ZPDBA — Zeitschrift fuer Pflanzenernaehrung Duengung Bodenkunde
ZPE — Zeitschrift fuer Papyrologie und Epigraphik
ZPF — Zeitschrift fuer Philosophische Forschung
Z Pflanzenernaehr Bodenkd — Zeitschrift fuer Pflanzenernaehrung und Bodenkunde
Z Pflanzenernaehr Dueng Bodenkd — Zeitschrift fuer Pflanzenernaehrung, Duengung, und Bodenkunde [*Later, Zeitschrift fuer Pflanzenernaehrung und Bodenkunde*]
Z Pflanzenkr — Zeitschrift fuer Pflanzenkrankheiten
Z Pflanzenkr Gallenkd — Zeitschrift fuer Pflanzenkrankheiten und Gallenkunde
Z Pflanzenkr Pflanzenpathol Pflanzenschutz — Zeitschrift fuer Pflanzenkrankheiten, Pflanzenpathologie, und Pflanzenschutz
Z Pflanzenkr Pflanzenpathol Pflanzenschutz Sonderh — Zeitschrift fuer Pflanzenkrankheiten, Pflanzenpathologie, und Pflanzenschutz. Sonderheft
Z Pflanzenkr Pflanzenschutz — Zeitschrift fuer Pflanzenkrankheiten und Pflanzenschutz
Z Pflanzenp — Zeitschrift fuer Pflanzenphysiologie
Z Pflanzenphysiol — Zeitschrift fuer Pflanzenphysiologie
Z Pflanzenz — Zeitschrift fuer Pflanzenzuechtung
Z Pflanzenzuecht — Zeitschrift fuer Pflanzenzuechtung
Z PflErnahr Bodenk — Zeitschrift fuer Pflanzenernaehrung und Bodenkunde
Z PflErnahr Dung Bodenk — Zeitschrift fuer Pflanzenernaehrung, Duengung, und Bodenkunde [*Later, Zeitschrift fuer Pflanzenernaehrung und Bodenkunde*]
Z PflKrankh — Zeitschrift fuer Pflanzenkrankheiten, Pflanzenpathologie, und Pflanzenschutz
Z PflKrankh PflSchutz — Zeitschrift fuer Pflanzenkrankheiten Pflanzenschutz
Z PflPhysiol — Zeitschrift fuer Pflanzenphysiologie
ZPh — Zeitschrift fuer Psychologie
ZPhF — Zeitschrift fuer Philosophische Forschung
Z Phil Forsch — Zeitschrift fuer Philosophische Forschung
Z Philos Forsch — Zeitschrift fuer Philosophische Forschung
ZPhon — Zeitschrift fuer Phonetik und Allgemeine Sprachwissenschaft
Z Phonetik Sprachwiss Komm Forsch — Zeitschrift fuer Phonetik, Sprachwissenschaft, und Kommunikationsforschung
Z Phon Sprachwiss Kommunikationsforsch — Zeitschrift fuer Phonetik, Sprachwissenschaft, und Kommunikationsforschung
Z Phys — Zeitschrift fuer Physik
Z Phys A — Zeitschrift fuer Physik. Sektion A. Atoms and Nuclei
Z Phys B — Zeitschrift fuer Physik. Sektion B. Condensed Matter and Quanta
Z Phys C — Zeitschrift fuer Physik. Sektion C. Particles and Fields [*German Federal Republic*]
Z Phys Chem Abt A — Zeitschrift fuer Physikalische Chemie. Abteilung A. Chemische Thermodynamik, Kinetik, Elektrochemie, Eigenschaftslehre
Z Phys Chem Abt B — Zeitschrift fuer Physikalische Chemie. Abteilung B. Chemie der Elementarprozesse, Aufbau der Materie
Z Phys Chem Frankf Ausg Neue Folge — Zeitschrift fuer Physikalische Chemie. Frankfurter Ausgabe. Neue Folge [*West Germany*]
Z Phys Chem (Frankfurt/Main) — Zeitschrift fuer Physikalische Chemie (Frankfurt/Main)
Z Phys Chemie Stoechiom Verwandschaftsl — Zeitschrift fuer Physikalische Chemie, Stoechiometrie, und Verwandschaftslehre
Z Phys Chem (Leipzig) — Zeitschrift fuer Physikalische Chemie (Leipzig)

Z Phys Chem Materialforsch — Zeitschrift fuer Physikalisch-Chemische Materialforschung

Z Phys Chem Neue Folge — Zeitschrift fuer Physikalische Chemie. Neue Folge

Z Phys Chem Neue Fo (Wiesbaden) — Zeitschrift fuer Physikalische Chemie. Neue Folge (Wiesbaden)

Z Phys Chem (Wiesbaden) — Zeitschrift fuer Physikalische Chemie (Wiesbaden)

Z Phys Ch F — Zeitschrift fuer Physikalische Chemie (Frankfurt)

Z Phys Ch (L) — Zeitschrift fuer Physikalische Chemie (Leipzig)

Z Phys Diaet Ther — Zeitschrift fuer Physikalische und Diaetetische Therapie

Z Physik — Zeitschrift fuer Physik

Z Physiol Chem — Zeitschrift fuer Physiologische Chemie

Z Physiol Chem Hoppe-Seylers — Zeitschrift fuer Physiologische Chemie. Hoppe-Seylers [*German Federal Republic*]

Z Physiother — Zeitschrift fuer Physiotherapie

Z Pilzkd — Zeitschrift fuer Pilzkunde

ZPJIAK — Zbirnyk Prat Jewrejskiej Istorychno-Arkheologichnoj Komisji [*Kiev*]

Z Plast Chir — Zeitschrift fuer Plastische Chirurgie

ZPMPA — Zeitschrift fuer Psychotherapie und Medizinische Psychologie

Z Polit — Zeitschrift fuer Politik

Z Politik — Zeitschrift fuer Politik

Z Pol N F — Zeitschrift fuer Politik. Neue Folge

ZPPA — Zeitschrift fuer Wissenschaftliche Photographie, Photophysik, und Photochemie

Z Praeklin Geriatr — Zeitschrift fuer Praeklinische Geriatrie

Z Praeklin Klin Geriatr — Zeitschrift fuer Praeklinische und Klinische Geriatrie

Z Praeventivmed — Zeitschrift fuer Praeventivmedizin

Z Prakt Anaesth — Zeitschrift fuer Praktische Anaesthesie, Wiederbelebung, und- Intensivtherapie

Z Prakt Geol — Zeitschrift fuer Praktische Geologie

Zpravy — Zpravy pro Cestinare

Zpr Cesk Keram Sklarske Spol — Zpravy Ceskoslovenske Keramicke a Sklarske Spolecnosti

Z Prikl Meh i Tehn Fiz — Zurnal Prikladnoi Mehaniki i Tehniceskoi Fiziki

ZprMK — Zpravodaj Mistopisne Komise CSAV [*Ceskoslovenske Akademie Ved*]

ZPs — Zeitschrift fuer Psychologie

ZPSEA — Zeszyty Naukowe Politechnika Slaska. Energetyka

ZPSIA — Zeitschrift fuer Psychologie und Physiologie der Sinnesorgane

ZPSK — Zeitschrift fuer Phonetik, Sprachwissenschaft, und Kommunikationsforschung

ZPSMA — Zeitschrift fuer Psychosomatische Medizin

ZPSS — Z Polskich Studiow Slawistycznych

Z Psych Hyg — Zeitschrift fuer Psychische Hygiene

Z Psychol — Zeitschrift fuer Psychologie

Z Psycholog — Zeitschrift fuer Psychologie

Z Psychol Physiol Sinnesorg — Zeitschrift fuer Psychologie und Physiologie der Sinnesorgane [*East Germany*]

Z Psychol Z Angew Psychol — Zeitschrift fuer Psychologie mit Zeitschrift fuer Angewandte Psychologie

Z Psychol Z Angew Psychol Charakterkd — Zeitschrift fuer Psychologie mit Zeitschrift fuer Angewandte Psychologie und Charakterkunde

Z Psychos M — Zeitschrift fuer Psychosomatische Medizin und Psychoanalyse

Z Psychosom Med — Zeitschrift fuer Psychosomatische Medizin [*Later, Zeitschrift fuer Psychosomatische Medizin und Psychoanalyse*]

Z Psychosom Med Psychoanal — Zeitschrift fuer Psychosomatische Medizin und Psychoanalyse

Z Psychother Med Psychol — Zeitschrift fuer Psychotherapie und Medizinische Psychologie

Z Psychot M — Zeitschrift fuer Psychotherapie und Medizinische Psychologie

ZPWCA — Zeszyty Naukowe Politechniki Wroclawskiej. Chemia

ZPYFA — Zeitschrift fuer Physikalische Chemie. Frankfurter Ausgabe. Neue Folge

ZR — Zadarska Revija

ZR — Zionist Record

ZR — Zionist Review

Z Rechtsmed — Zeitschrift fuer Rechtsmedizin [*Journal of Legal Medicine*]

Z Rechtspolit — Zeitschrift fuer Rechtspolitik

Z Reich Geschmackstoffe — Zeitschrift fuer Reich- und Geschmackstoffe

Z Rel Geistesges — Zeitschrift fuer Religions- und Geistesgeschichte [*Koeln*]

Z Rel Gg — Zeitschrift fuer Religions- und Geistesgeschichte

Z Relig Geistesgesch — Zeitschrift fuer Religions- und Geistesgeschichte

Z Relig- u Geistesgesch — Zeitschrift fuer Religions- und Geistesgeschichte

Z Reproduktionstech — Zeitschrift fuer Reproduktionstechnik

ZRG — Zeitschrift fuer Religions- und Geistesgeschichte

ZRG — Zeitschrift. Savigny-Stiftung fuer Rechtsgeschichte

ZRGA — Zeitschrift. Savigny-Stiftung fuer Rechtsgeschichte. Germanistische Abteilung

ZRGG — Zeitschrift fuer Religions- und Geistesgeschichte

ZRG (GA) — Zeitschrift. Savigny-Stiftung fuer Rechtsgeschichte. Germanistische Abteilung

ZRGGB — Zeitschrift fuer Religions- und Geistesgeschichte. Beihefte

ZRGGS — Zeitschrift fuer Religions- und Geistesgeschichte. Sonderhefte

Z Rheumaforsch — Zeitschrift fuer Rheumaforschung

Z Rheumatol — Zeitschrift fuer Rheumatologie

Z Rheumatol Suppl — Zeitschrift fuer Rheumatologie. Supplement

ZRHMB — Zeitschrift fuer Rheumatologie

ZRI — Zeitschrift fuer die Religioesen Interessen des Judentums [*Berlin*]

ZRI — Zosen

ZRL — Zagadnienia Rodzajow Literackich

ZRNI — Zapiski Russkogo Naucnogo Instituta

Z Roman Ph — Zeitschrift fuer Romanische Philologie

Zroschuvane Zemlerob — Zroshuvane Zemlerobstvo

Zrosh Zemlerob — Zroshuvane Zemlerobstvo

ZRP — Zeitschrift fuer Romanische Philologie

ZRPBA — Zbornik Radova. Poljoprivrednog Fakulteta. Universitet u Beogradu

ZRPH — Zeitschrift fuer Romanische Philologie

ZRSAN — Zbornik Radova. Srpske Akademije Nauke

ZRTLS — Zwolse Reeks van Taal- en Letterkundige Studies

ZRU — Zeitschrift fuer den Russisch-Unterricht

ZRZ — Zbornik Radova. Svenciliste u Zagrebu

ZS — Zeitschrift fuer die Gesamte Staatswissenschaft

ZS — Zeitschrift fuer Semitistik und Verwandte Gebiete [*Leipzig*]

ZS — Zeitschrift fuer Slawistik [*Berlin*]

Z Saeugetierkd — Zeitschrift fuer Saeugetierkunde

ZSAK — Zeitschrift fuer Schweizerische Archaeologie und Kunstgeschichte

ZSAKG — Zeitschrift fuer Schweizerische Archaeologie und Kunstgeschichte

Zs Allg Erdk — Zeitschrift fuer Allgemeine Erdkunde

Zs Anorg Chem — Zeitschrift fuer Anorganische Chemie

ZSav — Zeitschrift. Savigny-Stiftung fuer Rechtsgeschichte. Romanistische Abteilung

Z Savigny-Stift Rechtsgesch Kanon Abt — Zeitschrift. Savigny-Stiftung fuer Rechtsgeschichte. Kanonistische Abteilung

ZSavRG — Zeitschrift. Savigny-Stiftung fuer Rechtsgeschichte. Romanistische Abteilung [*Weimar*]

Zs Berg- Huetten- u Salinen-Wesen — Zeitschrift fuer das Berg-, Huetten-, und Salinenwesen

Zschft Savigny-Germ — Zeitschrift. Savigny-Stiftung fuer Rechtsgeschichte. Germanistische Abteilung

Zschft Savigny-Kanon — Zeitschrift. Savigny-Stiftung fuer Rechtsgeschichte. Kanonistische Abteilung

Zschft Savigny-Rom — Zeitschrift. Savigny-Stiftung fuer Rechtsgeschichte. Romanistische Abteilung

Zschft f Vergl Rechtswissenschaft — Zeitschrift fuer Vergleichende Rechtswissenschaft

Zschift f Ausl Offentl Recht — Zeitschrift fuer Auslaendisches Oeffentliches Recht und Voelkerrecht

Z Schles Holst Gesch — Zeitschrift. Gesellschaft fuer Schleswig-Holsteinische Geschichte (Kiel, West Germany)

Z Schw AKg — Zeitschrift fuer Schweizerische Archaeologie und Kunstgeschichte

Z Schweisstech — Zeitschrift fuer Schweisstechnik

Z Schweiz Archaeol Kunstgesch — Zeitschrift fuer Schweizerische Archaeologie und Kunstgeschichte

Z Schweiz Arch Kunstgesch — Zeitschrift fuer Schweizerische Archaeologie und Kunstgeschichte

ZSchwG — Zeitschrift fuer Schweizerische Geschichte

ZSDG — Zeitschrift fuer Sudetendeutsche Geschichte

ZSEM — Zeitschrift fuer Semitistik und Verwandte Gebiete [*Leipzig*]

ZSF — Zeitschrift fuer Sozialforschung

ZSG — Zeitschrift fuer Schweizerische Geschichte

Zs Ges Naturw — Zeitschrift fuer die Gesamten Naturwissenschaften

Zs Gletscherk — Zeitschrift fuer Gletscherkunde

Z Sinnephysiol — Zeitschrift fuer Sinnephysiologie [*East Germany*]

ZSISA — Zeszyty Naukowe Politechniki Slaskiej. Inzynieria Sanitarna

ZSK — Ze Skarbca Kultury

ZSKG — Zeitschrift fuer Schweizerische Kirchengeschichte

ZSKHA — Zeitschrift fuer Kinderheilkunde. Referate

Zs Kryst — Zeitschrift fuer Krystallographie und Mineralogie

ZSL — Zeitschrift fuer Slawistik

Z Slav Philol — Zeitschrift fuer Slavische Philologie

Z Slawistik — Zeitschrift fuer Slawistik

ZSLPh — Zeitschrift fuer Slavische Philologie

Zs Miner (Leonhard) — Zeitschrift fuer Mineralogie (Leonhard)

ZSNUA — Zeitschrift fuer Neurologie

Z Soz — Zeitschrift fuer Sozialpsychologie

Z Sozialpsy — Zeitschrift fuer Sozialpsychologie

Z Sozialreform — Zeitschrift fuer Sozialreform [*German Federal Republic*]

Z Soziol — Zeitschrift fuer Soziologie

Z Soziolog — Zeitschrift fuer Soziologie

Z Soz Psychol — Zeitschrift fuer Sozialpsychologie

ZSP — Zeitschrift fuer Slavische Philologie

Z Spiritusind — Zeitschrift fuer Spiritusindustrie

Zs Prak G — Zeitschrift fuer Praktische Geologie

ZSRK — Zeitschrift. Savigny-Stiftung fuer Rechtsgeschichte. Kanonistische Abteilung

ZSSGerm — Zeitschrift. Savigny-Stiftung fuer Rechtsgeschichte. Germanistische Abteilung

ZSSKanon — Zeitschrift. Savigny-Stiftung fuer Rechtsgeschichte. Kanonistische Abteilung [*Weimar*]

ZSSRGGerm — Zeitschrift. Savigny-Stiftung fuer Rechtsgeschichte. Germanistische Abteilung

ZSSRGKan — Zeitschrift. Savigny-Stiftung fuer Rechtsgeschichte. Kanonistische Abteilung

ZSSRGRom — Zeitschrift. Savigny-Stiftung fuer Rechtsgeschichte. Romanistische Abteilung

ZSSRom — Zeitschrift. Savigny-Stiftung fuer Rechtsgeschichte. Romanistische Abteilung

ZST — Zeitschrift fuer Systematische Theologie

ZSTh — Zeitschrift fuer Systematische Theologie [*Guetersloh/Berlin*]

Z Strukturn Him — Zurnal Strukturnoi Himii. Akademija Nauk SSR. Sibirskoe Otdelenie

ZSV — Schweizerische Zeitschrift fuer Volkswirtschaft und Statistik

Zs Vulkan — Zeitschrift fuer Vulkanologie

ZSW — Zeitschrift fuer Sozialwissenschaft

ZSWRA — Zeszyty Naukowe Szkoly Glownej Gospodarstwa Wiejskiego w Warszawie. Rolnictwo

ZSysTh — Zeitschrift fuer Systematische Theologie [*Guetersloh/Berlin*]

ZT — Zeitschrift fuer Tierpsychologie

Ztbl — Zentralblatt

Z Tech Biol — Zeitschrift fuer Technische Biologie

Z Tech Phys — Zeitschrift fuer Technische Physik

Z Tech Ueberwach — Zeitschrift fuer die Technische Ueberwachung

Z Tech Univ (Berlin) — Zeitschrift. Technische Universitaet (Berlin)

Z Tech Univ (Hannover) — Zeitschrift. Technische Universitaet (Hannover) [*German Federal Republic*]

ZTGAK — Zeitschrift fuer Thueringische Geschichte und Altertumskunde

Ztg Gesunde — Zeitung fuer Gesunde

Z Theol Kir — Zeitschrift fuer Theologie und Kirche

Z Th K — Zeitschrift fuer Theologie und Kirche

Z Th Kirche — Zeitschrift fuer Theologie und Kirche

Z Tierernaehr Futtermittelkd — Zeitschrift fuer Tierernaehrung und Futtermittelkunde

Z Tierphysiol — Zeitschrift fuer Tierphysiologie, Tierernaehrung, und Futtermittelkunde

Z Tierphysiol Tierernaehr Futtermittelk — Zeitschrift fuer Tierphysiologie, Tierernaehrung, und Futtermittelkunde

Z Tierphysiol Tiernaehr Futtermittelkd — Zeitschrift fuer Tierphysiologie, Tierernaehrung, und Futtermittelkunde

Z Tierpsychol — Zeitschrift fuer Tierpsychologie

Z Tierpsychol Beih — Zeitschrift fuer Tierpsychologie. Beiheft

Z Tierz Zuechtungsbiol — Zeitschrift fuer Tierzuechtung und Zuechtungsbiologie

ZTK — Zeitschrift fuer Theologie und Kirche

ZTOS — Zydowskie Towarzystwo Ochrony Sierot

ZTOS — Zydowskie Towarzystwo Opieki Spolecznej

ZTP — Zydowskie Towarzystwo Prezeciwgruzliczego

ZTPHA — Zeitschrift fuer Technische Physik

ZTPSA — Zeitschrift fuer Psychologie

Ztrbl — Zentralblatt

Z Tropenmed Parasitol — Zeitschrift fuer Tropenmedizin und Parasitologie

Ztsch f Angew Psychol — Zeitschrift fuer Angewandte Psychologie und Psychologische Forschung

Ztsch f Angew Psychol Sammelforsch — Zeitschrift fuer Angewandte Psychologie und Psychologische Sammelforschung

Ztsch Gesch Erzieh u Unterr — Zeitschrift fuer Geschichte der Erziehung und des Unterrichts

Ztsch Mikr Fleischschau — Zeitschrift fuer Mikroskopische Fleischschau und Populaere Mikroskopie

Ztsch Militaeraerzte (Tokyo) — Zeitschrift fuer Militaeraerzte (Tokyo)

Ztschr Aerztli Fortbild — Zeitschrift fuer Aerztliche Fortbildung

Ztschr Augenh — Zeitschrift fuer Augenheilkunde

Ztschr Fleisch u Milchhyg — Zeitschrift fuer Fleisch- und Milchhygiene

Ztschr Genossensch Tierversich — Zeitschrift fuer Genossenschaftlichen Tierversicherung

Ztschr Gewerbe Hyg — Zeitschrift fuer Gewerbe Hygiene

Ztschr Hyg — Zeitschrift fuer Hygiene

Ztschr Hyg u Infektionskr — Zeitschrift fuer Hygiene und Infektionskrankheiten

Ztschr Immunitaetsforsch u Exper Therap — Zeitschrift fuer Immunitaetsforschung und Experimentelle Therapie

Ztschr Infektionskr Haustiere — Zeitschrift fuer Infektionskrankheiten, Parasitaere Krankheiten, und Hygiene der Haustiere

Ztschr Klin Med (Berlin) — Zeitschrift fuer Klinische Medizin (Berlin)

Ztschr Krebsforsch — Zeitschrift fuer Krebsforschung

Ztschr Morphol u Oekol Tiere — Zeitschrift fuer Morphologie und Oekologie der Tiere

Ztschr Ophth — Zeitschrift fuer die Ophthalmologie

Ztschr Parasitenk (Berlin) — Zeitschrift fuer Parasitenkunde (Berlin)

Ztschr Parasitenk (Jena) — Zeitschrift fuer Parasitenkunde (Jena)

Ztschr Physiol Chem — Zeitschrift fuer Physiologische Chemie

Ztschr Tokio Med Gesellsch — Zeitschrift. Tokio Medizinischen Gesellschaft

Ztschr Vergleich Physiol — Zeitschrift fuer Vergleichende Physiologie

Ztschr Veterinaerk — Zeitschrift fuer Veterinaerkunde

Ztschr Wissensch Mikr — Zeitschrift fuer Wissenschaftliche Mikroskopie

Ztschr Wissensch Zool — Zeitschrift fuer Wissenschaftliche Zoologie

Z Tuberk — Zeitschrift fuer Tuberkulose

Z Tuberkulose Erkr Thoraxogane — Zeitschrift fuer Tuberkulose und Erkrankungen der Thoraxorgane

ZTUWA — Zeitschrift Technische Ueberwachung

ZuB — Zuercher Bibelkommentare

Zucker Beih — Zucker Beihefte

Zucker Frucht Gemueseverwert — Zucker- Frucht- und Gemueseverwertung

Zucker Sonderbeil — Zucker Sonderbeilage

Zucker Suesswaren Wirtsch — Zucker- und Suesswaren Wirtschaft

Zuck u SuesswarWirt — Zucker- und Suesswaren Wirtschaft

Zuer Univ Geol Inst-Eidgenoss Tech Hochsch Geol Inst Mitt — Zuerich Universitaet. Geologisches Institut - Eidgenoessische Technische Hochschule. Geologisches Institut. Mitteilungen

ZugerNjb — Zuger Neujahrsblatt

ZUJCA — Zeszyty Naukowe Uniwersytetu Jagiellonskiego. Prace Chemiczne

Z Umweltpolit — Zeitschrift fuer Umweltpolitik

ZUNBA — Zhurnal Ushnykh Nosovykh i Gorlovykh Boleznei

Z Unfallmed Berufskr — Zeitschrift fuer Unfallmedizin und Berufskrankheiten

Z Unter Lebensm — Zeitschrift fuer Untersuchung der Lebensmittel

Z Unters Lebensmittel — Zeitschrift fuer Untersuchung der Lebensmittel

Z Unters Nahr Genussm Gebrauchsgegenstaende — Zeitschrift fuer Untersuchung der Nahrungs- und Genussmittel Sowie der Gebrauchsgegenstaende

Z Unters Nahr-u Genussmittel — Zeitschrift fuer Untersuchung der Nahrungs- und Genussmittel

Zur Didak Phys Chem — Zur Didaktik der Physik und Chemie

Z Urol — Zeitschrift fuer Urologie [*German Democratic Republic*]

Z Urol Nephrol — Zeitschrift fuer Urologie und Nephrologie

Z & V — Zeiten und Voelker

ZV — Zeitschrift fuer Volkskunde

Zv — Zvezda

Zvaracsky Sb — Zvaracsky Sbornik

Z Verbraucherpol — Zeitschrift fuer Verbraucherpolitik

Z Verbungsl — Zeitschrift fuer Vererbungslehre

Z Ver Dtsch Ing — Zeitschrift. Verein Deutscher Ingenieure

Z Ver Dtsch Zucker Ind — Zeitschrift. Verein der Deutschen Zucker-Industrie

Z Ver Dtsch Zucker Ind Allg Teil — Zeitschrift. Verein der Deutschen Zucker-Industrie. Allgemeiner Teil

Z Ver Dtsch Zucker Ind Tech Teil — Zeitschrift. Verein der Deutschen Zucker-Industrie. Technischer Teil

Z Vererbungsl — Zeitschrift fuer Vererbungslehre

Z Vergl Physiol — Zeitschrift fuer Vergleichende Physiologie

Z Ver Hessische Gesch — Zeitschrift. Verein fuer Hessische Geschichte und Landeskunde

Z Verkehrssicherheit — Zeitschrift fuer Verkehrssicherheit

Z Verkehrswiss — Zeitschrift fuer Verkehrswissenschaft

Z Vermessungswes — Zeitschrift fuer Vermessungswesen

Zverolek Obz — Zverolekarsky Obzor

Z Vers Kund — Zeitschrift fuer Versuchstierkunde

Z Versuchstierkd — Zeitschrift fuer Versuchstierkunde

ZVGAK — Zeitschrift fuer Vaterlaendische Geschichte und Altertumskunde

Z Vgl Physiol — Zeitschrift fuer Vergleichende Physiologie

ZVGMS — Zeitschrift. Deutscher Verein fuer die Geschichte Maehrens und Schlesiens

ZVHFA — Zeitschrift fuer Vitamin-, Hormon-, und Fermentforschung

ZVHG — Zeitschrift. Verein fuer Hamburgische Geschichte

ZVHGLK — Zeitschrift. Verein fuer Hessische Geschichte und Landeskunde

Z VitamForsch — Zeitschrift fuer Vitaminforschung

Z Vitam-Horm- u Fermentforsch — Zeitschrift fuer Vitamin-, Hormon-, und Fermentforschung

Z Vitam-Horm-Fermentforsch — Zeitschrift fuer Vitamin-, Hormon-, und Fermentforschung

Z Vitaminforsch — Zeitschrift fuer Vitaminforschung

ZVK — Zeitschrift fuer Volkskunde

ZVKOA — Zhurnal Vsesoyuznogo Khimicheskogo Obshchestva Imeni D. I. Mendeleeva

ZVKPS — Zeitschrift. Verein fuer Kirchengeschichte in der Provinz Sachsen und Anhalt

ZVL — Zeitschrift fuer Vergleichende Literaturgeschichte

ZVNDA — Zhurnal Vysshei Nervnoi Deyatel'nosti Imeni I. P. Pavlova

ZVO — Zapiski Vostochnovo Otdelenia

Z Volksernaehr — Zeitschrift fuer Volksernaehrung

Z Volkskund — Zeitschrift fuer Volkskunde

Z Volkskunde — Zeitschrift fuer Volkskunde

ZVORAO — Zapiski Vostochnovo Otdeleniia Imperatorskovo Ruskavo Arkheologicheskavo Obshchestva

ZVRW — Zeitschrift fuer Vergleichende Rechtswissenschaft

ZVS — Zeitschrift fuer Vergleichende Sprachforschung

ZVT — Zeitschrift fuer Verkehrswissenschaft

ZVTGA — Zeitschrift. Verein fuer Thueringische Geschichte und Altertumskunde

ZVTGAK — Zeitschrift. Verein fuer Thueringische Geschichte und Altertumskunde

ZVV — Zeitschrift. Verein fuer Volkskunde

ZvV — Zvezda Vostoka
Z Vycisl Mat i Mat Fiz — Zurnal Vycislitel'noi Matematiki i Matematiceskoi
  Fiziki
ZW — Zeitwende Monatsschrift
Z Wahrscheinlichkeitstheorie und Verw Gebiete — Zeitschrift fuer
  Wahrscheinlichkeitstheorie und Verwandte Gebiete
Z Wahrsch V — Zeitschrift fuer Wahrscheinlichkeitstheorie und Verwandte
  Gebiete
Z Wahrsch Verw Gebiete — Zeitschrift fuer Wahrscheinlichkeitstheorie und
  Verwandte Gebiete
Z Wasser Abwasser Forsch — Zeitschrift fuer Wasser- und Abwasserforschung
Z Wasser u Abwasserforsch — Zeitschrift fuer Wasser- und
  Abwasserforschung
Z Wasserrecht — Zeitschrift fuer Wasserrecht
Z Wasser Versorg Abwasserkunde — Zeitschrift fuer Wasser-Versorgung und
  Abwasserkunde
ZWBAA — Zeitschrift fuer Wissenschaftliche Biologie. Abteilung A
Z Weltforstwirtsch — Zeitschrift fuer Weltforstwirtschaft
Z Werkstofftech — Zeitschrift fuer Werkstofftechnik
Z Werkstofftech J Mater Technol — Zeitschrift fuer Werkstofftechnik/Journal
  of Materials Technology
ZWF Z Wirtsch Fertigung — ZWF. Zeitschrift fuer Wirtschaftliche Fertigung
ZWG — Sudhoffs Archiv. Zeitschrift fuer Wissenschaftsgeschichte
ZWIBA — Zeitschrift fuer Wissenschaftliche Insektenbiologie
Z Wien Ent Ges — Zeitschrift. Wiener Entomologische Gesellschaft
Z Wien Entomol Ges — Zeitschrift. Wiener Entomologische Gesellschaft
Z Wien Entomol Ver — Zeitschrift. Wiener Entomologe-Verein
Zwierzeta Lab — Zwierzeta Laboratoryjne
Z Wirtschaftsgeographie — Zeitschrift fuer Wirtschaftsgeographie [*West
  Germany*]
Z Wirtschaftsgruppe Zuckerind — Zeitschrift. Wirtschaftsgruppe
  Zuckerindustrie
Z Wirtschaftsgruppe Zuckerind Allg Teil — Zeitschrift. Wirtschaftsgruppe
  Zuckerindustrie. Allgemeiner Teil
Z Wirtschaftsgruppe Zuckerind Tech Teil — Zeitschrift. Wirtschaftsgruppe
  Zuckerindustrie. Technischer Teil
Z Wirtschaftspol — Zeitschrift fuer Wirtschaftspolitik
Z Wirtsch Fertigung — Zeitschrift fuer Wirtschaftliche Fertigung
Z Wirtsch -u Soz -Wiss — Zeitschrift fuer Wirtschafts- und
  Sozialwissenschaften
Z Wiss Biol Abt A — Zeitschrift fuer Wissenschaftliche Biologie. Abteilung A
  [*West Germany*]
Z Wiss InsektBiol — Zeitschrift fuer Wissenschaftliche Insektenbiologie
Z Wiss Insektenbiol — Zeitschrift fuer Wissenschaftliche Insektenbiologie
  [*West Germany*]
Z Wiss Mikrosk — Zeitschrift fuer Wissenschaftliche Mikroskopie und fuer
  Mikroskopische Technik
Z Wiss Mikrosk Mikrosk Tech — Zeitschrift fuer Wissenschaftliche
  Mikroskopie und Mikroskopische Technik
Z Wiss Photogr Photophys Photchem — Zeitschrift fuer Wissenschaftliche
  Photographie, Photophysik, und Photochemie
Z Wiss Photogr Photophys Photochem — Zeitschrift fuer Wissenschaftliche
  Photographie, Photophysik, und Photochemie [*East Germany*]
Z Wiss Zool — Zeitschrift fuer Wissenschaftliche Zoologie
Z Wiss Zool Abt A — Zeitschrift fuer Wissenschaftliche Zoologie. Abteilung A
ZWL — Zeitschrift fuer Wuerttembergische Landesgeschichte
ZWLG — Zeitschrift fuer Wuerttembergische Landesgeschichte
ZWMIA — Zeitschrift fuer Wissenschaftliche Mikroskopie und fuer
  Mikroskopische Technik
ZWMZDP — Chinese Journal of Microbiology and Immunology [*Beijing*]
ZWPGV — Zeitschrift. Westpreussischer Geschichtsverein
ZWR — ZWR. Zahnaerztliche Welt, Zahnaerztliche Rundschau,
  Zahnaerztliche Reform
ZWT — Zeitschrift fuer Wissenschaftliche Theologie
ZWTh — Zeitschrift fuer Wissenschaftliche Theologie
Zy — Zygon
Zycie Weteryn — Zycie Weterynaryjne
Zymol Chem Colloidi — Zymologica e Chemica dei Colloidi
ZYWE — Zeszyty Wroclawskie
Z d Z — Zeichen der Zeit
ZZACA — Zeitschrift fuer Zellforschung und Mikroskopische Anatomie
Z Zellforsch Mikrosk Anat — Zeitschrift fuer Zellforschung und
  Mikroskopische Anatomie
Z Zellforsch Mikrosk Anat Abt Histochem — Zeitschrift fuer Zellforschung
  und Mikroskopische Anatomie. Abteilung Histochemie
Z Zool Syst Evolutionsforsch — Zeitschrift fuer Zoologische Systematik und
  Evolutionsforschung
ZzS — Zbornik za Slavistiku
Z Zuckerind — Zeitschrift fuer die Zuckerindustrie
Z Zuckerind Boehm — Zeitschrift fuer die Zuckerindustrie in Boehmen
Z Zuckerind Boehm Machren — Zeitschrift fuer die Zuckerindustrie in
  Boehmen-Machren
Z Zuckerind Cech Repub — Zeitschrift fuer die Zuckerindustrie der
  Cechoslovakoschen Republik
Z Zuckind — Zeitschrift fuer die Zuckerindustrie
Z Zuecht A — Zeitschrift fuer Zuechtung. A